Dedication

The Foundation for American Christian Education dedicates this facsimile edition of Noah Webster's 1828 Dictionary to the Christian students of America, who, under the guidance of their parents and teachers, are developing a character of obedience to God's Biblical principles of life and liberty.

J. De Mare
From a Miniature in Ivory

George Washington at the Age of Twenty-five

After eight long years as Commander-in-Chief of the army of the Republic, Washington was ready to resign his commission. He wrote from his Head Quarters at Newburgh, June 14, 1783, in his circular letter to the States, "I now make it my earnest prayer, that God would have you, and the State over which you preside, in his holy protection, that he would incline the hearts of the Citizens to cultivate a spirit of subordination and obedience to Government, to entertain a brotherly affection and love for one another, for their fellow Citizens of the United States at large, and particularly for their brethren who have served in the Field, and finally, that he would most graciously be pleased to dispose us all, to do Justice, to love mercy, and to demean ourselves with that Charity, humility and pacific temper of mind, which were the Characteristicks of the Divine Author of our blessed Religion, and without an humble imitation of whose example in these things, we can never hope to be a happy Nation."

"America has furnished to the world the character of Washington! And if our American institutions had done nothing else, that alone would have entitled them to the respect of mankind." – Daniel Webster, Bunker Hill Monument Address, 1843

AMERICAN

CHRISTIAN

HISTORY

EDUCATION

SERIES

Sequoia gigantea, or Big Tree, grows only on the western slopes of the Sierra Nevada Mountains in California at elevations varying from 5,000 to 8,500 feet above sea level. Individuals of this species are the largest living things on the face of the globe. Ranging from 250 to 330 feet high their diameters at the base vary approximately from 20 to 35 feet.

The Sequoia gigantea seems to go on living indefinitely and may stand as long as one hundred generations. The cells of its cambrium layer and of the growing tips appear never to lose the ability to grow and reproduce. The tannin content of bark and wood discourages insects and fungi and retards fire. Even when fallen, the heartwood may stay sound for hundreds of years.

Giant Sequoias seldom produce cones until they are at least one hundred years of age. Each cone, from one to three inches long, contains 100 to 300 seeds, but these are so small that it takes 3,000 to weigh one ounce. Without the industrious pine squirrel very few sequoia cones would be dropped by the sequoias. Scampering in the treetops the squirrels cut off cones which sometimes fall as fast as seven or eight per minute. Later the squirrels hide the cones in holes and logs, and other likely niches — provision for the winter ahead. Cones stored in damp places usually remain closed, but those that can dry soon open and shed their seeds.

The age of living sequoias is difficult to determine but the annual ring count of cut trees has indicated that many are from 3,000 to 4,000 years old. Some of these trees in California were already majestic giants when the star of Bethlehem rose in the heavens. Here they reremained while the Chain of Christianity moved westward with "signs following" — the liberty of the individual, and of nations. Just yesterday, in a sequoia's life, came the flowering of these Bethlehem principles in government — "We hold these Truths to be self-evident, that all Men are created equal, that they are endowed by their Creator with certain unalienable Rights, that among these are Life, Liberty, and the Pursuit of Happiness — That to secure these Rights, Governments are instituted among Men. . . ."

"WHERE THE SPIRIT OF THE LORD IS,
THERE IS LIBERTY." II CORINTHIANS 3:17

NOAH WEBSTER'S FIRST EDITION OF AN AMERICAN DICTIONARY OF THE ENGLISH LANGUAGE

REPUBLISHED IN FACSIMILE EDITION BY

FOUNDATION FOR AMERICAN CHRISTIAN EDUCATION

TO DOCUMENT AND DEMONSTRATE:

I. THE UNIQUE NATURE OF OUR FORM OF GOVERNMENT AND OF OUR CIVIL INSTITUTIONS WHICH "REQUIRES AN APPROPRIATE LANGUAGE OF THE DEFINITION OF WORDS."

II. "TO THE YOUTH OF THE UNITED STATES" THE BEST AMERICAN AND ENGLISH AUTHORS AS AUTHORITIES IN THE USE AND DEFINITION OF LANGUAGE.

III. TO ALL AMERICANS "THAT THE PRINCIPLES OF REPUBLICAN GOVERNMENT HAVE THEIR ORIGIN IN THE SCRIPTURES."

PREFACED BY AN ARTICLE:

NOAH WEBSTER, FOUNDING FATHER OF AMERICAN SCHOLARSHIP AND EDUCATION

BY ROSALIE J. SLATER, M.A.

"IF THE FOUNDATIONS BE DESTROYED, WHAT CAN THE RIGHTEOUS DO?" PSALM XI:3

FOUNDATION FOR AMERICAN CHRISTIAN EDUCATION

SAN FRANCISCO, CALIFORNIA

Permission to reprint the 1828 edition
granted by G. & C. Merriam Company

Published by the Foundation for American Christian Education
P.O. Box 9588, Chesapeake, Virginia 23321-9588

Thirtieth Printing, 2023

Printed by Core Publishing Solutions

Designed by John Grossman
Woodacre, California

Library of Congress Catalog Card Number: 91-179826
ISBN 978-0-912498-03-4

This edition is printed facsimile from an original 1828 copy, which had some uneven inking, smears, etc. An effort has been made to clean up and clarify unreadable distortions, but some imperfections remain.

Cover Embossed Eagle:
Original cast in iron, gilded, by Paul Revere (1735–1818),
32" high x 66" wide, weighing 200 pounds
One of four commissioned in 1789 by General Henry Knox
Private Collection, Plymouth, Massachusetts

NOAH WEBSTER'S 1828 DICTIONARY
NEEDED TO RESTORE
AN AMERICAN CHRISTIAN EDUCATION
IN THE HOME, THE CHURCH
AND THE SCHOOL

"If the foundations be destroyed, what can the righteous do?" Psalms 11:3

BIBLICAL DEFINITIONS RESTORED

Noah Webster's 1828 *American Dictionary of the English Language* was produced during the years when the American home, church and school were established upon a Biblical and a patriotic basis. Webster, descended on his mother's side from Pilgrim Governor, William Bradford of Plymouth Plantation, made important contributions to an American educational system which kept the nation upon a Christian Constitutional course for many years. The famous "blue-backed Speller," his "Grammars," and "Readers," all contained Biblical and patriotic themes and Webster spearheaded the flood of educational volumes emphasizing Christian, Constitutional values for more than a century. It is not surprising, therefore, that the 1828 *American Dictionary* should contain the greatest number of Biblical definitions given in any secular volume. Webster considered "education useless without the Bible" and while he cautioned against too extensive use of the Bible in the schools as "tending to irreverence" he reiterated "In my view, the Christian religion is the *most important and one of the first things* in which *all* children, under a free government, ought to be instructed. . . . No truth is more evident to my mind than that the Christian religion must be the basis of any government intended to secure the rights and privileges of a free people. . . ."

Today when the Biblical basis of education is under systematic attack we need to capitalize upon the availability of our first American dictionary — the only dictionary in the world to *"draw water out of the wells of salvation"* — to utilize God's written word as a key to the meaning of words. Historically, it documents the degree to which the Bible was America's basic text book in all fields.

CHRISTIAN CONSTITUTIONAL MEANINGS RESTORED

Upon Horace Mann rests the blame for removing from the curriculum the study of an American philosophy of government. Opposed to the fundamental conceptions of our American Constitution namely, property, self-government and voluntary union, Horace Mann, "the father of progressive education," removed the *spirit* of Constitutionalism and allowed only the *letter* to remain. The Bible, which Noah Webster indicated as the source of "the principles of republican government" was closed to its primary function — namely to testify of God's redeeming grace for mankind through Jesus Christ. Actually, it was Horace Mann in the 1840's who removed the Bible and its sacred purpose from the schools, not the United States Supreme Court in the 1960's.

Through the European pilgrimages of Horace Mann and his contemporaries the alien seeds of foreign ideologies and philosophies of education were implanted in American soil. The independence from European "maxims of government" which Noah Webster had worked so diligently to achieve was subverted during the early years when American education was made the ward of the state. *A Federal Catechism,* part of *The American Spelling Book,* had introduced civics into the curriculum in 1794. It gave a short explanation of the principles of the American Constitutional form of government and defined America as "a representative republic." The "defects of democracy" were discussed and students learned distinctly why a "federal representative republic" is "a better form of government." Shortly after schools became organized under state systems the substitution of *democracy* for *republic* was made.

Today the necessity for restoring the clarity and identity of Constitutional meanings is obvious if we are to make substantial progress in rebuilding the foundations upon which this nation was established. Without a standard of reference for America's history and philosophy of government students can not be expected to make the distinctions and discriminations between similar terms used in history texts today.

A STANDARD FOR AMERICAN LANGUAGE RESTORED

Noah Webster, the lexicographer, claimed to have coined only one word — *demoralize,* which he defined: *"To corrupt or undermine the morals of; to destroy or lessen the effect of moral principles on; to render corrupt in morals."*

Today the field of lexicography has been *demoralized* by those who would make *"contemporary usage"* and *"slang"* a standard of reference for students in our schools. Pornographic terminology has come to have educational significance in state schools where *Dictionary of American Slang* has received academic acceptance.

Noah Webster recognized that each age is subject to the demoralization of its language by the *"literary"* or *"modish"* segment of society. Thus he put, as a check and balance upon each other, *universal undisputed practice* and the *common law of language,* or established principles of analogy. Change for the sake of change, vulgarity, cant, slang for its own sake, was to Webster like the principle of motion in physics — if not controlled it became the principle of destruction. Thus "expressions peculiar to, and generally understood only by, members of a particular sect, class, or occupation; as (a) the secret jargon of thieves, tramps, etc., (b) the special idiom of a profession or trade, or, (c) a mode of talking used merely out of convention; esp., the insincere use of pious phraseology" found no place in Noah Webster's dictionaries.

The responsibility to establish a standard of reference which will enable students to study the history and literature of our founding period in its original context is critical today. We need the "primary" Biblical, Christian and Constitutional meanings of words. Noah Webster spent a lifetime endeavoring to liberate America from European ties of "folly, corruption and tyranny." He sought to build an educational system in the school, the church and the home embodying "a love of virtue, patriotism and religion." In the Preface to his History of the United States he wrote:

"Republican government loses half its value, where the moral and social duties are imperfectly understood, or negligently practiced. To exterminate our popular vices is a work of far more importance to the character and happiness of our citizens, than any other improvements in our system of education."

NOAH WEBSTER

FOUNDING FATHER OF AMERICAN SCHOLARSHIP AND EDUCATION

"An immense effect may be produced by small powers wisely and steadily directed." Noah Webster, 1821

The Declaration of Independence, July 4, 1776, served to announce to the world the separation of the American colonies from Great Britain, their establishment as "free and independent states," and their "firm reliance on the Protection of divine Providence." To this ringing declaration of faith in God was affixed the signatures of the 56 men who mutually pledged to "each other" the *property* of their "Lives" their "Fortunes" and their "sacred Honor." It took the seven long years of the American Revolution to "dissolve the Political Bands" which connected them to England, and six more years until the document detailing the Christian philosophy of American government took shape and form. But political separation alone would not suffice to keep the young republic on her Christian Constitutional course. If American liberty was to be complete all moorings with the old world must be cast off — especially those which might bind her to alien philosophies of government and hence to educational systems lending them support:

"This country must in some future time, be as distinguished by the superiority of her literary improvements, as she is already by the liberality of her civil and ecclesiastical constitutions. Europe is grown old in folly, corruption and tyranny — in that country laws are perverted, manners are licentious, literature is declining and human nature debased. For America in her infancy to adopt the present maxims of the old world, would be to stamp the wrinkles of decrepid age upon the bloom of youth and to plant the seeds of decay in a vigorous constitution. American glory begins to dawn at a favourable period, and under flattering circumstances. We have the experience of the whole world before our eyes; but to receive indiscriminately the maxims of government, the manners and the literary taste of Europe and make them the ground on which to build our systems in America, must soon convince us that a durable and stately edifice can never be erected upon the mouldering pillars of antiquity. It is the business of Americans to select the wisdom of all nations, as the basis of her constitutions, — to avoid their errours, — to prevent the introduction of foreign vices and corruptions and check the career of her own, — to promote virtue and patriotism, — to embellish and improve the sciences, — to diffuse an uniformity and purity of language, — to add superior dignity to this infant Empire and to human nature."

American Independence from European Manners

This statement was made by the young Noah Webster whose Master's thesis from Yale College was entitled, *Dissertation . . . upon the Universal diffusion of Literature, as introductory to the universal diffusion of Christianity.* "Literature" here has reference to education or, as Samuel Johnson defines it in his *A Dictionary of the English Language,* 1755, "learning, skill in letters." Noah

Webster's statement appears in the preface to that slender volume which, along with the Holy Bible, was to establish the uniqueness of American Education. For more than 100 years the American speller, known more familiarly as the *"blue-backed speller"* was to teach Americans *"skill in letters"* and the fundamentals concerning our Constitutional republic.

A great concern for "posterity" and for the youth of the country is evident among our founders. They recognized that the nature of our American Christian form of government demanded a quality of individual responsibility and a capacity for self-government never before required in any nation. An American education was, therefore, greatly needed to extend the new independence into every field of activity. Noah Webster, as did most Americans of his day, *"affirmed that the principles of republican government have their origin in the Scriptures,"* and he sought to build an educational system embodying *"a love of virtue, patriotism, and religion":*

"In my view, the Christian religion is the *most important and one of the first things* in which *all* children, under a free government, ought to be instructed. . . . No truth is more evident to my mind than that the Christian religion must be the basis of any government intended to secure the rights and privileges of a free people. . . . When I speak of the Christian religion as the basis of government, I do not mean an ecclesiastical establishment, a creed, or rites, forms, and ceremonies, or any compulsion of conscience. I mean primitive Christianity in its simplicity as taught by Christ and His apostles, consisting in a belief in the being, perfections, and moral government of God; in the revelation of His will to men, as their supreme rule of action; in man's accountability to God for his conduct in this life; and in the indispensable obligation of all men to yield entire obedience to God's commands in the moral law and in the Gospel. This belief and this practice may consist with different forms of church government, which, not being essential to Christianity, need not enter into any system of education."

Christian Religion Basis of American Government

The relationship of American government to Christianity is evident in the writings of the founding fathers of our republic and in the sermons preached by the American clergy. Thus, it is not surprising that men like Noah Webster were desirous of establishing an American system of education which would support the American Christian philosophy of government and extend the blessings of liberty to every individual. But Noah Webster's system of education included rather than excluded the influence of the American home:

"All government originates in families, and if neglected there, it will hardly exist in society. . . . The foundation of all free government and of all social order must be laid in families and in the discipline of youth. . . . The Education of youth, an employment of more consequence than making laws and preaching the gospel, because it lays the foundation on which both law and gospel rest for success. . . ."

Noah Webster's own childhood had been blessed with a Christian home. His Pilgrim heritage through Governor Bradford provided him with the ingredients of Christian self-government, responsibility and work habits which would serve him well throughout a long, active life. When the family farm was mortgaged to send him to Yale College he took this parental benediction with him:

"We wish to have you serve your generation and do good in the world and be useful and may so behave as to gain the esteem of all virtuous people that are acquainted with you and gain a comfortable subsistence, but especially that you may so live as to obtain the favor of Almighty God and His grace in this world and a saving interest in the merits of Jesus Christ, without which no man be happy."

From the first the public life of Noah Webster had a bearing on the course of the young republic. Supplementing his law practice through teaching, Noah Webster observed our dependence upon the maternal country for direction in education:

"However detestable personal pride may be, yet there is a national pride and a provincial, that are the noblest passions of the republican patriot. . . . For my own part, I frankly acknowledge, I have too much pride not to wish to see America assume a national character. I have too much pride to stand indebted to Great Britain for books to learn (sic) our children the letters of the alphabet. . . . America must be as independent in *literature* as she is in *politics,* as famous for *arts* as for *arms;* and it is not impossible but a person of my youth may have some influence in exciting a spirit of literary industry."

An Independent American Character

The youthful Noah Webster, then 25 years of age, continued to supply America for the next 60 years with this independence in literature. By dint of his own unflagging industry he produced a repository of school texts unequalled for its consistency in teaching the precepts of American spelling, pronunciation and grammar, American history, civics, geography and literature. Throughout the innumerable revisions and republications the theme of American Christian morality and patriotism never wavered. Though Webster believed that the Bible should not be used extensively in the schools, as this tended to irreverence, he sprinkled its admonitions profusely throughout all his works. In his *Moral Catechism* he indicated clearly that there is no other basis upon which to base moral conduct: *"God's word, contained in the Bible, has furnished all necessary rules to direct our conduct."*

The publication of Noah Webster's *"Speller"* in 1783 was followed with a *"Grammar"* in 1784, and a *"Reader"* in 1785. These were Parts I, II, and III of *A Grammatical Institute of the English Language,* whose title was suggested by President Ezra Stiles of Yale College. These volumes republished again and again became the basis of an American system of education and their influence grew with the history of the young republic. Indeed, Noah Webster's *The American Spelling Book,* the famous *"blue-backed speller,"* set a publishing record unlikely to be equalled by any school text in America. Over a period of one hundred years more than *one hundred million* copies were worn out by Americans as they learned their letters, their morality and their patriotism, from north to south, from east to west. Noah Webster's *"Speller"* was compatible with the hearthside of a log cabin in the wilderness, it travelled on the flatboats of the Ohio, churned down the Mississippi and creaked across the prairies of the far west as pioneer mothers taught their children from covered wagons. Wherever an individual wished to challenge his own ignorance or quench his thirst for knowledge, there, along with the Holy Bible and Shakespeare, were Noah Webster's slim and inexpensive Spellers, Grammars, Readers, and his *Elements of Useful Knowledge* containing the history and geography of the United States. Indeed if his Biblical name should have any significance to America it might be said that Noah's books were an *ark* in which the American Christian spirit rode the deluge of rising anti-Christian and anti-republican waters which threatened so often to inundate the nation.

Noah Webster's American System of Education

The first such tide came during the 1790's when apostles of the French Revolution, at home and abroad, imported a subversive doctrine to these shores. In a series of historical and political articles published in his *American Minerva Magazine,* Noah Webster endeavored to educate the American public to the dangers inherent in Jacobinism:

"I consider as a matter of infinite consequence the cautious admission of foreigners to the rights of citizenship. Numbers of them who have within the past year arrived and settled in this city come with violent prejudices against arbitrary government, and they seem to make no great distinction between arbitrary government and a government of laws founded on free elections. Many of them are warm democrats; and the Emigration Society here is headed by Democrats of our own — in short the opposers of our government are literally wriggling themselves into all sorts of company to carry their points. One main article of their policy is to attach foreigners to their principles the moment of their landing. If that system of creating a popular interest extraneous from the legislature to influence their proceedings — that system of raising a multitude of isolated private clubs over the nation as its guardian — should spread thro the country, we may bid adieu to our Constitution. Our safety is in the country people, who more scattered and more independent, are out of the reach of demagogues."

Secret Influence of Jacobinism

An exchange of letters with Joseph Priestley in 1800 takes that eminent British scientist severely to task for living in the United States and deliberately propagating a subversive doctrine:

"Sir, In your second letter, pages 8 and 9, you define *democracy* with a view to explain away the odious sense annexed to the word *Democrat.* You call the Constitution of this country a *democracy,* and every man who is not a *Democrat,* an enemy to this Constitution. But whatever you may call the true meaning of these words, the practice of our country has annexed to them and established a different signification. By *democracy* is intended a government where the legislative powers are exercised directly by all the citizens, as formerly in Athens and Rome. In our country this power is not in the hands of the people but of their representatives. The powers of the people are principally restricted to the direct exercise of the rights of suffrage. Hence a material distinction between our form of government and those of the ancient democracies. Our form of government has acquired the appellation of a *Republic,*

Distinction Between a Democracy and a Republic

by way of distinction, or rather of a *representative Republic.*

"Hence the word *Democrat* has been used as synonymous with the word *Jacobin* in France; and by an additional idea, which arose from the attempt to control our government by private popular associations, the word has come to signify a person who attempts an undue opposition to or influence over our government by means of private clubs, secret intrigues, or by public popular meetings which are extraneous to the constitution. By *Republicans* we understand the friends of our Representative Governments, who believe that no influence whatever should be exercised in a state which is not directly authorized by the Constitution and laws."

It is significant that many of the founding fathers recognized the relationship between education and the success of the American philosophy of government. Republican principles under the new Constitution received tremendous support from Noah Webster's *A Federal Catechism.* It was the first introduction of civics into the curriculum appearing in a 1794 edition of *The American Spelling Book. A Federal Catechism* contained "a short explanation of the Constitution of the United States of America, and the Principles of Government." Among those subjects specifically taught was a discussion of the "defects of democracy" and a definition of a "better form of government," namely, that of a "representative republic." Students learned distinctly that the United States is "a federal representative republic," and that the "states are all governed by constitutions that fall under the name of representative republics."

George Washington's School of Political Philosophy

Noah Webster, who once stated that his political philosophy had been learned *"in the school of Washington and of the great and worthy men who assisted in obtaining Independence, and in the formation and organization of the government,"* was eminently qualified to teach the principles of the American Constitution. It was he who had first publically promoted the idea of a constitutional convention as he travelled from New Hampshire to North Carolina during the years 1785–1787. His 48-page pamphlet entitled *Sketches of American Policy,* was carried to Mount Vernon in 1785 for George Washington's perusal. During the Constitutional Convention in Philadelphia the 29-year old school master was visited by many of the most outstanding delegates. Webster's Diary records visits with George Washington, Benjamin Franklin, James Madison, Rufus King, Abraham Baldwin, Edmund Randolph, William Samuel Johnson, Oliver Ellsworth, Roger Sherman, William Livingston and John Marshall. Two days before the Convention adjourned Thomas Fitzsimmons, a delegate from Pennsylvania, wrote Noah Webster requesting him to prepare an essay in support of the now completed document. The request came on September 1st, it was written on October 9th and published October 17th. Containing 55 pages it was dedicated to Benjamin Franklin. Dr. David Ramsay wrote from Charlestown: *"I have read it with pleasure, and it is now in brisk circulation among my friends. I have heard every person who has read it express his high approbation of its contents. It will doubtless be of singular service in recommending the adoption of the new Constitution."*

Although admittedly by Webster "a hasty production," nevertheless, *An examination into the leading principles of the Federal Constitution proposed by the late Convention held at Philadelphia, with Answers to the principal objections that have been raised against the system. By a citizen of America*, served to crystallize many of the major arguments. In his discussion of principles Webster touched upon that of *property* and its relationship to the "whole basis of national freedom":

Property the Basis of American Liberty

"The liberty of the press, trial by jury, the Habeas Corpus writ, even Magna Charta itself, although justly deemed the palladia of freedom, are all inferior considerations, when compared with a general distribution of real property among every class of people. The power of entailing estates is more dangerous to liberty and republican government than all the constitutions that can be written on paper, or even than a standing army. Let the people have property and they will have power — a power that will forever be exerted to prevent a restriction of the press, and abolition of trial by jury, or the abridgement of any other privilege. The liberties of America, therefore, and her forms of government, stand on the broadest basis. . . ."

John Locke on the Preservation of Property

The American clergy had for one hundred years prior to the American Revolution preached on the subject of property — its Biblical basis and responsibility. They often quoted John Locke's writings on "civil government." In his discussion of property he identifies man, in Paul's words, as the property of God and the earth, as indicated in Genesis, as God's capital gift to man for the investment of his labors in response to Scriptural admonition. Locke's most oft repeated phrase in Colonial Constitutional literature was "The great and chief End therefore, of Mens uniting into Commonwealths, and putting themselves under Government, is the *Preservation of their Property.*"

James Madison, known as "the Father of the Constitution" in reiterating the purpose of government as instituted to "protect property of every sort" indicates its Christian base when he states that "Conscience is the most sacred of all property." Noah Webster, also, considered the "preservation of property" a key to individual liberty under the American Constitutional system. His first efforts to preserve the fruits of his labors came during those years when he travelled to each of the colonial legislatures to secure copyright protection for his blue-backed speller. For more than fifty years Noah Webster worked to achieve the protection of *"authors of useful inventions"* for he considered that *"the production of genius and the imagination are if possible more really and exclusively property than houses and lands, and are equally entitled to legal security."* His untiring efforts were instrumental in bringing about the passage of copyright legislation first at the state level and finally at the national level. Noah Webster's foresight in securing his *"literary property"* stood him in good stead during the long lean years of labor on the monumental *American Dictionary.* It was the slim speller which constituted the main support of the Webster family while its founder explored, studied and compared language from a Scriptural position. The importance of land ownership meant much to him and he regarded it as the foundation of a republican government:

Webster Secures his Literary Property through Copyright

"I am a farmer's son, & have collected all the small portion of property which I possess, by untiring efforts & labor to promote the literary improvement of my fellow citizens, & to establish the freedom & tranquillity of my country."

Property and productivity are related to character, and Christian character was the basis of Noah Webster's educational system. His famous *Grammatical Institute* contained the Scriptural admonition: *"Train up a child in the way he should go, and when he is old he will not depart from it."* His Spellers, Grammars, Readers, Histories and Dictionaries all implemented this thesis. The examples, illustrations and definitions used in his volumes were replete with ideals of virtue and industry, of piety and patriotism. But it was Noah Webster, himself, who best exemplified the character of the young republic and who illustrated the *"immense effect"* produced by one individual *"wisely and steadily directed."* The discipline of work learned during the early years on his father's farm, coupled with his tremendous capacity to complete the many projects initiated, enabled Noah Webster to work effectively in many fields. He was always productive with his time and talents, whether recording scientific data on weather and temperature, collecting statistics on disease and epidemics, counting the houses in the cities and towns visited in his travels, studying population trends and voting records, or writing informatively on many questions of concern. Like most of the founding father generation, Noah Webster was interested in everything. His writings cover an unbelievable range of topics: religious, political, educational, musical, economic, commercial, medical, social and scientific. Rarely was Noah Webster afforded a platform from which to voice his convictions. He created his own forums for stating his positions, not only through his books, addresses, articles, and letters, but through the establishment of publications such as *The American Magazine* in 1787, and the *American Minerva* in 1793. From the vantage point of his periodicals and newspapers, Noah Webster challenged the political opponents of constitutionalism and constructed a visible structure of Americanism furnishing an historical interpretation of current events and advocating many measures of civic betterment to improve the quality of living.

The Private Enterprise of Noah Webster

While never occupying an elective position above the state level the influence of his published opinions can be calculated by the quality and quantity of his opposition and the untiring efforts to discredit and to silence him. Throughout the years he supplied consistent support to the administration of George Washington. In 1793 the *Address from the Inhabitants of Hartford to the President of the United States* written with John Trumbull and Chauncey Goodrich, afforded President Washington with a public statement of calm and fearless support rising above the popular hysteria:

Webster Supports Washington's Administration

"Warmly attached to our government, both by interest and affection, we take the liberty to assure you, that we shall ever stand ready by our utmost exertions, in every legal and constitutional way, to support the just measures of your administration; and to lend our assistance in maintaining the peace and harmony of the States, and in opposing the insidious designs of those persons, if there be any so deluded, who may wish to subject the country to foreign influence, and involve it in the horrors of war."

Again, in 1795 when the proposed Jay Treaty was being used by Jefferson's Democratic Clubs as an attack upon Washington, Noah Webster joined his efforts to those of James Kent and Alexander Hamilton. Under the name of "Curtius" Noah Webster's twelve essays *"operated more powerfully than any other publication in calming the public mind and restoring confidence in the administration."*

Noah Webster was notable for his challenges and he was often labelled controversial and contentious. But if he demolished a structure by his attacks he labored diligently to raise another and a better one in its place. He *"chearfully"* threw his mite into *"the common treasure of patriotic exertions."* Despite his active participation in the educational, political and scientific life of the nation his own family life exemplified what love and discipline centered in Christ could accomplish in forming the character of the next generation. His six daughters and one son enjoyed both his tender solicitude for their intellectual development as well as his superintending guidance of their spiritual growth. Concerning the education of women he valued an American education — fitting them for their decisive role in a republic in the discipline and education of youth in the family. *"Their own education should therefore enable them to implant in the tender mind, such sentiments of virtue, propriety and dignity, as are suited to the freedom of our governments."*

Noah Webster's Christian Family

A unique feature of America has been the position of womanhood brought to her full flowering through Christianity. As understood by the founding generations the American woman was to stand beside her husband with a role equally important to the republic though not identical with that of a man. This American Christian concept of womanhood Noah Webster continued to teach through his educational system and *The American Spelling Book* of 1843 contained a section entitled *Precepts Concerning Social Relations* in which are described qualities which a young man should identify in his future life partner:

"But when thou findest sensibility of heart joined with softness of manners; an accomplished mind and religion, united with sweetness of temper, modest deportment, and a love of domestic life — Such is the woman who will divide the sorrows, and double the joys of thy life. Take her to thyself; she is worthy to be thy nearest friend, thy companion, the wife of thy bosom."

Noah Webster's marriage to Rebecca Greenleaf of French Huguenot descent provided him with a domestic center of power from which to sally forth in his encounters with a world of conflicting ideas and ideals. Noah Webster's *Diary* records in 1790 the first year of a happy, successful marriage, one which was to ripen to more than a golden half century. Noah and Rebecca had gently wagered *"one flitch of bacon"* to be paid to her if their first year of marriage should contain any untoward words of quarrelling. *"Anniversary of our marriage, one year past & no quarreling, of course the Flitch of bacon is won. . . ."*

Marriage and "a Flitch of Bacon"

The greatest test of family support of Noah Webster's long career of establishing American scholarship and education came during that period when he was devoting the major portion of his talents to producing the first truly American dictionary of the English language. Noah Webster's recognition of the importance of the American language to American government dated from his early declarations of the need for American literary independence from England. His challenge to English grammarians in the *Grammatical Institute* of 1783, 1784, 1785, brought him into confrontation with the many theories of orthography, pronunciation, definition and grammar. In an effort to interest others in the need for more scholarly research into the etymology of language, Noah Webster was instrumental in establishing the Philological Society in 1788, *"founded for the particular purpose of ascertaining and improving the American tongue."* It was the first society of its kind on the continent. When, in the same year, the title of *The Institute* was changed to *The American Spelling Book,* he stated that future editions *"must be copied from the last edition, which is corrected by the Philological Society & recommended as the elements of a* federal *language. . . ."*

On June 4, 1800, the following announcement appeared in the New Haven newspapers:

"Mr. Webster of this city, we understand, is engaged in completing the system for the instruction of youth, which he began in the year 1783. He has in hand a Dictionary of the American Language, a work long since projected, but which other occupations have delayed till this time.

The plan contemplated extends to a small Dictionary for schools, one for the counting-house, and a large one for men of science. The first is nearly ready for the press — the second and third will require the labor of some years.

"It is found that a work of this kind is absolutely necessary on account of considerable differences between the American and English language. New circumstances, new modes of life, new laws, new ideas of various kinds give rise to new words, and have already made many material differences between the language of England and America. Some new words are introduced in America, and many more new significations are annexed to words, which it is necessary to explain. It is probable that the alternations in the tenures of land and the ecclesiastical polity, will dismiss from the language in America several hundred words which belong in the English. The differences in the language of the two countries will continue to multiply, and render it necessary that we should have *Dictionaries* of the *American* language."

Once again the keynote of Webster's plan began with the identification of an *American* language as distinct from that of England. With the publication in 1806 of *A Compendious Dictionary of the English Language* Noah Webster began to lay the foundation of his own American Dictionary. The *Compendious Dictionary* built upon and expanded the work of an English schoolmaster, John Entick, who had published *The New Spelling Dictionary* in 1784. It was not, however, just the addition of 5,000 new words to Entick's original 32,000 which represented Noah Webster's significant contributions to the field of lexicography. His twenty years of philological studies, his mastery of more than ten languages by 1806, his conviction that earlier students had *"mistaken many of the fundamentals of language,"* provided him with the ammunition for a cannonade levelled chiefly at the most respected name in English language — Dr. Samuel Johnson. The effrontery of such an attack by an American caused Harvard College to reject the plan of Yalesman, Noah Webster. But the faculties of Yale, Princeton, Dartmouth, Williams and Middlebury Colleges gave *"unqualified approbation of the design."*

Webster's *Compendious Dictionary*

Noah Webster's thesis had first been articulated in 1785 as he toured the colonies lecturing on the English language. Later, with some additions, he published in 1789 his *Dissertations on the English Language* which led him into his profound study of etymology and philology and caused him ultimately to master more than 26 languages. Essentially Noah Webster never deviated from his original premise:

"As an independent nation, our honor requires us to have a system of our own, in language as well as government. Great Britain, whose children we are, and whose language we speak, should no longer be our standard; for the taste of her writers is already corrupted, and her language on the decline. But if it were not so, she is at too great a distance to be our model, and to instruct us in the principles of our own tongue.

Dissertations on the English Language

"It must be considered further, that English is the common root or stock from which our national language will be derived. All others will gradually waste away — and within a century and a half, North America will be peopled with a hundred millions of men, *all speaking the same language*. . . .

"Whether the inhabitants of America can be brought to a perfect uniformity in the pronunciation of words, it is not easy to predict; but it is certain that no attempt of the kind has been made, and an experiment, begun and pursued on the right principles, is the only way to decide the question. . . .

"The two points therefore, which I conceive to be the basis of a standard in speaking, are these; *universal undisputed practice,* and the *principle of analogy. Universal practice* is generally, perhaps always, a rule of propriety; and in disputed points where people differ in opinion and practice, *analogy,* should always decide the controversy.

"These are authorities to which all men will submit — they are superior to the opinions and caprices of the great, and to the negligence and ignorance of the multitude. The authority of individuals is always liable to be called in question — but the unanimous consent of a nation, and a fixed principle interwoven with the very construction of a language, coeval and co-extensive with it, are like the common laws of a land, or the immutable rules of morality, the propriety of which every man, however refractory, is forced to acknowledge, and to which most men will readily submit. Fashion is usually the child of caprice and the being of a day, principles of propriety are founded in the very nature of things, and remain unmoved and unchanged, amidst all the fluctuations of human affairs and the revolutions of time. . . ."

Noah Webster set forth in the 18th century a structure containing the balance of two forces in language — forces with which many scholars have struggled: *change* and *changelessness.* While admitting that *"standard usage"* was the outgrowth of *"current speech,"* and that *"languages are changing, from age to age, in proportion to improvements in science,"* Noah Webster recognized that language contained both the *centrifugal* and the *centripetal* forces *working together. "These changes are the necessary consequences of changes in customs, the introduction of new arts, and new ideas in the sciences. Still the body of a language and its general rules remain for ages the same, and the new words usually conform to these rules; otherwise they stand as exceptions, which are not to overthrow the principle of analogy already established."* Change and innovation were sources of enrichment and vitalization of a language — but not its chief impetus. "It is nearly the same here as in physics, where motion, the source of life, becomes the principle of destruction." Change for the sake of change was not countenanced by Noah Webster:

The Two Forces in Language in Check and Balance

"The language is composed of a variety of materials, and it requires some labor to adjust the parts and reduce them to order.

"To accomplish this purpose, we must search for such principles of analogy as still exist in its construction, and make them the pillars of a regular system. Where such principles cannot be found, let us examine the opinions of the learned, and the practice c the nations which speak the pure English, that we may determine by weight of authority, the *common law* of language, those questions which do not come within any established rules."

In his preface to the *Compendious Dictionary,* Noah Webster set forth his proposals for a gradual reform of spelling, and an Americanization of pronunciation, including the addition of some words unique to Americans. He was also concerned with the re-definition of words to rescue them from a purely literary or pedantic meaning.

In spelling the changes proposed by Noah Webster in 1807, with few exceptions, have been retained and preferred by Americans. These include the rejection of the final *k* in works like *musick,* the dropping of the *u* in *honour* and similar words, the use of *er* in the endings for all words whether *re* or *er* in the original language such as *theater, luster* and others.

Noah Webster believed that *"the New England style"* of pronunciation was preferred by Americans rather than the affected elegance of the English theater. His main criticism of the Johnsonian school of pronunciation was that it was not drawn from *"standard usage"* but that it favored *"the practice of the gay and fashionable world."* He set himself in opposition to *"authors and writers pretending to purify and refine the language."* It was not the people who corrupted the language but, rather, the literary and *"modish"* segment of society who attempted to put into permanent circulation *"temporary," "capricious,"* and *"gross improprieties."* Noah Webster was convinced that the perversion of language by the *literati* would be offset by the *"yeomanry"* in daily usage. The *"yeomanry,"* or common man of America to whom Noah Webster referred, reflected a fundamental distinction based upon the American form of government. On this continent the *"common man"* was the *"uncommon man":*

The Corruption of Language by Authors and Writers

"Let Englishmen notice that when I speak of American yeomanry, the latter are not to be compared to the illiterate peasantry of their own country. The Yeomanry of this country consists of substantial independent freeholders, masters of their own persons and Lords of their own soil. These men have considerable education. They not only learn to read, write and keep accounts; but a vast proportion of them read newspapers every week, and besides the Bible, which is found in all families, they read the best English sermons and treatises upon religion, ethics, geography and history. . . . The people of distant counties in England can hardly understand one another, so various are their dialects; but in the exent of twelve hundred miles in America, there are very few, I question whether a hundred words, except such as are used in employments wholly local, which are not universally intelligible."

While Webster believed that *"general custom"* and *"standard usage"* contributed to producing a national uniformity in language, the *"higher tribunal"* was to be found in the best of written language:

"Hence from the practice of the gay and fashionable world, there is always an appeal to a higher tribunal, the great body of literary and well informed men in a nation, whose opinion of propriety is not to be seduced, nor their judgement perverted by the influence of names and fashion."

In the first reader he produced for use in the schools, *An American Selection of Lessons in Reading and Speaking,* Noah Webster included many patriotic selections taken from the speeches, addresses and writings of Washington,

Hancock, and others, as well as the Declaration of Independence, Addresses from Congress, and poems and epics written to celebrate American events. These were *Calculated to improve the Minds and refine the Taste of Youth. And also to instruct them in Geography, History, and Politics of the United States. To Which is prefixed, Rules in Elocution, and Directions for expressing the principal Passions of the Mind.*

The *Compendious Dictionary* had one Websterian touch which was to have a definite influence on the construction of future dictionaries. For the first time material of an encyclopedic nature was included: tables of moneys, of weights and measures, the divisions of times among all nations, an official list of post-offices in the United States and the values of exports as well as *"new and interesting chronological tables of remarkable events and discoveries."* Webster characterized the American trait of being interested in everything, a feature which is reflected in the great variety of almanacs, digests and encyclopedia published every year in the United States.

Encyclopedic Information in Webster's Dictionary

The *Compendious Dictionary* was modestly priced for $1.50 and the following year, 1807, Noah Webster produced an abridgment for $1.00 *"compiled for the use of common schools in the United States."* Neither of these dictionaries yielded the income which he hoped to derive while at work on the larger *American Dictionary.* It was not until 1817 that a new edition of this work could find a market. But the important point had been established — Noah Webster had demonstrated that a volume of such authority and importance as a dictionary could be priced so that the average American could own his own copy.

In 1807 Noah Webster endeavored to gain some financial support for his projected *American Dictionary.* He addressed a circular entitled *To the Friends of Literature in the United States* to men in various towns and cities, requesting that they give the circulars wide circulation. Not much encouragement was forthcoming and a sum of barely one thousand dollars obtained, some of which Webster paid back as he could. He had long deplored the lack of interest in the study of the American language and had hoped that his circulars discussing his work and plans might attract scholars with whom he could exchange his findings. As his old classmate, Oliver Wolcott expressed it *"we have able, generous & learned Men, but they want wealth. The Men of wealth are in various ways taxed for very considerable sums, but they have not the faculty of discriminating the most suitable objects of encouragement."*

Men of Wealth Lacking Discrimination

Among those men of generosity and discrimination was John Jay who gave both support and encouragement to Noah Webster:

"It is not improbable that doubts prevail respecting the design and tendency of the work you have on hand. The literary productions of Great Britain and America being interesting to each other, many are of opinion (and I concur in it) that the English language and its orthography should be the same in both countries.

"Apprehensions have been entertained that your dictionary would tend to impair that sameness, and those apprehensions may to an uncertain degree, have had an unfavorable influence.

"The progress of the subscription having been so long suspended, I think it better to enclose what I intended to subscribe than trouble your agents at New York with it.

"If any plan to render your prospects more promising, and in my power to promote should be adopted, be pleased to communicate it to me."

But, as is so often the case in the lives of dedicated men and women, just at the moment when human help seems to be exhausted God moves into the picture. During the winter of 1807 an event occurred which would forever after provide Noah Webster with that peace and security which the world can neither give nor take away. His own words written to Judge Thomas Dawes, brother-in-law, best describe the significance of that winter:

"For a number of years just past I have been more and more impressed with the importance of regulating my conduct by the precepts of Christianity. Of the being and attributes of God I have never entertained a doubt, and my studies as well as frequent contemplations on the works of nature have led my mind to most sublime views of His character and perfections. . . .

"Still I had doubts respecting some of the doctrines of the Christian faith, such as regeneration, election, salvation by free grace, the atonement, and the divinity of Christ; these doubts served as an apology for my forebearing to make a profession of religion; for though I could never read or hear that solemn declaration of our Savior, *'Whosoever shall confess me before men, him will I confess*

Noah Webster's Confession of Jesus Christ as Saviour

before my Father who is in heaven,' without some compunction and alarm; yet I endeavored to justify my neglect by a persuasion that I could not conscientiously assent to the usual confession required in Calvinistic churches as the condition of admission to their communion. That is, in plain terms, I sheltered myself as well as I could from the attacks of conscience for neglect of duty under a species of scepticism, and endeavored to satisfy my mind that a profession of religion is not absolutely necessary to salvation. In this state of mind I placed great reliance on good works or the performance of moral duties as the means of salvation, although I cannot affirm that I wholly abandoned all dependence on the merits of a Redeemer. You may easily suppose that in this state of distraction and indecision of opinions I neglected many duties of piety.

"About a year ago an unusual revival of religion took place in New Haven, and frequent conferences of private meetings for religious purposes were held by pious and well disposed persons in the Congregational societies. I felt some opposition to these meetings, being apprehensive that they would, by affecting the passions too strongly, introduce an enthusiasm or fanaticism which might be considered as real religion. I expressed these fears to some friends and particularly to my family, inculcating on them the importance of a *rational religion* and the danger of being misled by the passions.

"My wife, however, was friendly to these meetings and she was joined by two eldest daughters who were among the first subjects of serious impressions. I did not forbid but rather discouraged their attendance on conferences. . . .

"These impressions I attempted to remove by reasoning with myself and endeavoring to quiet my mind by a persuasion that my opposition to my family and the awakening was not a real opposition to *rational religion* but to enthusiasm or *false religion*. I continued some weeks in this situation, utterly unable to quiet my own mind and without resorting to the only source of peace and consolation. The impressions, however, grew stronger till at length I could not pursue my studies without frequent interruptions. My mind was suddenly arrested, without any previous circumstance of the time to draw it to this subject and, as it were, fastened to the awakening and upon my own conduct. I closed my books, yielded to the influence which could not be resisted or mistaken, and was led by a spontaneous impulse to repentence, prayer, and entire submission and surrender of myself to my Maker and Redeemer. My submission appeared to be cheerful, and was soon followed by that peace of mind which the world can neither give nor take away.

Noah Webster Accepts Salvation by Redemption

"This, my dear friend, is a short but faithful narration of facts. That these impressions were not the effect of any of my own passions nor of enthusiasm is to me evident, for I was in complete possession of all my rational powers, and that the influence was supernatural is evident from this circumstance; it was not only independent of all volition but opposed to it. You will readily suppose that after such evidence of the direct operation of the divine spirit upon the human heart, I could no longer question or have a doubt respecting the Calvinistic and Christian doctrines of regeneration, of free grace, and of the sovereignty of God. I now began to understand and relish many parts of the scriptures, which before appeared mysterious and unintelligible or repugnant to my natural pride. For instance, I was remarkably struck with the 26th verse of John 14th: *'But the Comforter, which is the Holy Ghost, whom the Father will send in my name, he shall teach you all things, and bring all things to your remembrance, whatsoever I have said to you'* — a passage which I had often read without realizing its import. In short, my view of the scriptures, of religion, of the whole Christian scheme of salvation, and of God's moral government are very much changed, and my heart yields with delight and confidence to whatever appears to be the divine will.

"Permit me here to remark, in allusion to a passage in your letter, that I had for almost fifty years exercised my talents such as they are, to obtain knowledge and to abide by its dictates, but without arriving at the truth, or what now appears to me to be the truth, of the gospel. I am taught now the utter insufficiency of our own powers to effect a change of the heart, and am persuaded that a reliance on our own talents or powers is a fatal error, springing from natural pride and opposition to God, by which multitudes of men, especially of the more intelligent and moral part of society are deluded into ruin. I now look, my dear friend, with regret on the largest portion of the ordinary life of man, spent *'without hope and without God in the world.'* I am particularly affected by a sense of my ingratitude to that Being who made me and without whose constant agency I cannot draw a breath, who has showered upon me a profusion of temporal blessings and provided a Savior for my immortal soul. . . .

Former Pride and Opposition to God

"In the month of April last I made a profession of faith; in this most solemn and affecting of all transactions of my life I was accompanied with my two eldest daughters; while I felt a degree of compunction that I had not sooner dedicated myself to God, it was with heartfelt delight I could present myself before my Maker and say, 'Here am I, with the children which thou hast given me.'

"Mrs. Webster was confined at the time and could not be a witness of this scene, so interesting to her as well as to us who were personally concerned, but you may easily conceive how much she was affected the first time she met her husband and children at the Communion. . . ."

Noah Webster's confession of faith became the basis of an evangelistic tract entitled *The Peculiar Doctrines of the Gospel, Explained and Defended.* It was well received by the Trinitarian clergy, among whom was Abiel Holmes, father of Oliver Wendell Holmes:

"We have been much gratified in the perusal of your Letter in explanation and defence of the 'Peculiar Doctrines of the Gospel.' I hope the publication of it will promote the interests of pure Christianity. Arguments used by *us,* who are *set for the defence of the gospel,* are often inefficacious, because we are considered as merely 'labouring in our vocation.' When men of learning and talents, in other professions, voluntarily engage in the defence of our holy religion, the world is less apt to suppose them *interested,* and therefore more ready to listen to their arguments. I rejoice to find you defending, not the outworks merely, but the citadel; not the truth of Christianity in general, but the peculiar doctrines of it — *the truth as it is in Jesus."*

Noah Webster's Defence of the Gospel

The widespread circulation of Webster's religious convictions brought forth the venom of Unitarian Harvard and Boston who attacked not the Christian but the philologist in the hope of discountenancing the *Compendious Dictionary.* Moses Stuart, now a professor at Andover wrote:

"The *Anthology* is outrageous against you. I believe it will do good, and promote the very cause it is meant to destroy. May the Lord turn their haughty and unfriendly designs into foolishness! Be assured, the object of their vengance is more against your religion than against you."

In 1811 Noah Webster moved his family of six daughters and one son from busy New Haven to Amherst, a rural community outside of Northampton, Massachusetts. Webster needed to conserve his slim resources and he wished to devote more time to the completion of his major work the *American Dictionary.*

"Our new home on one side of the Amherst Green, as it was called, was a very pleasant home and my dear Father seemed to love it" *wrote Julia, who later married the young Chauncey A. Goodrich.* "He went there to lessen the expenses, and to live a more uninterrupted life, while pursuing his great work the Dictionary. His habits were very regular. He rose early in the morning and went to his study, a room in front of the house filled with books, and the view from the front window commanded the hill on which now stand the Buildings of the College, which he helped to found. . . . The view was most enchanting. Mount Tom and Mount Holyoke and the Valley of the Connecticut by their base and Hadley and Northampton. The scene was inspiring and the thought of God as a *real* Father crept into my soul there always. I think Father went to his study for prayer as soon as he was dressed. In about half an hour he would pass the rooms of us children and say, 'Up, up, children!' We never lingered after that call like the youth of more modern days. We assembled for prayer in the common parlor, and Father read the Scriptures, and then from a little book of his own composing he offered prayer."

The Webster Home in Amherst, Massachusetts

Noah Webster, to whom the cultivation of the soil was a delight and a resource, employed the ten acres of meadowland surrounding the house agriculturally. He set out an orchard and grafted the finest kinds of apples and pears he could find, growing peaches and cherries from the stones. His large, sweet white grapes, raised from a fine native vine taken out of his father's farm in West Hartford, were known as *"the Webster vine."* His flowers and the vegetable garden also flourished and prospered and he could say reverently *"for some years past I have rarely cast my eyes to heaven or plucked the fruit of my garden without feeling emotions of gratitude and adoration.*

Webster called the people of Amherst and Old Hampshire County *"as respectable and patriotic republicans as ever trod the soil of a free country."* Despite his best intentions to confine himself to his Dictionary he soon found that with characteristic ardor, interest and sympathy, his considerable talents were called into active community service. His experiments in agriculture were contributed to the *Hampshire Gazette* and here he found a further platform for his 20-year interest in forest conservation. The nine Websters made a considerable impact upon the First Church and soon he and the three eldest daughters had organized a choir and were active in soul winning during revivals. In addition he organized a Sunday School and was often called upon to moderate in church affairs. Naturally, the Webster home was a focal point for visiting ministers.

Political interests had caused him to play a small part in the matter of the Hartford Convention from the sidelines. But, even as he had been in Connecticut for nine sessions a member of the General Assembly (1800–1807), councilman of New Haven (1799–1804), alderman (1806–1809) and Judge of the County Court (1806–1810), now he stood for the Massachusetts Legislature where he served as a Member of the General Court in 1814, 1815, and 1817. In Amherst he also served as selectman of the town. Two more of his local activities were his directorship of the Hampshire Bible Society, and his vice-presidency of the Hampshire and Hampden Agricultural Society.

Elective Offices Held by Noah Webster

While articulate on many subjects Webster's focus lay in education and its importance to the republic. In the Massachusett's House of Representatives he endeavored to secure for Massachusetts a permanent school fund similar to that of Connecticut:

"I should rejoice to see a system adopted that should lay a foundation for a permanent fund for public schools, and to have more pains taken to discipline our youth in early life in sound maxims of moral, political, and religious duties."

Local interest in the schools produced his ardent support of the founding of Amherst Academy. While he could not give financially, it was his tenacity and persistence which secured the Act of Incorporation in 1816. In 1817 Noah Webster was again asked to lend his enthusiasm and influence in obtaining both the funds and the support for a college. Calvinists had become alarmed at the growth of Unitarian doctrines taught at Harvard and they determined to establish a college which should propagate the principles of the Gospel. *"The gospel only can convert swords into plough shares and spears into pruning hooks — the gospel only can supersede the necessity of bolts and bars — the gospel only can dispeople the state prison and the penetentiary."* When the venture was successfully established Webster, with characteristic thoroughness, resigned as President of the Board of Trustees and once more endeavored to seclude himself with the Dictionary.

Noah Webster, Founder of Amherst College, 1821

Although occupied with civic and educational concerns Webster had not neglected his exhaustive philological research. In 1817 his ten-year study of twenty languages was complete in manuscript form ready to challenge both English and German studies in comparative linguistics. A letter to John Jay explains why he felt this necessary:

"When I began the compilation of a large Dictionary of the English Language, I limited my views chiefly to a correction of such errors as had escaped former compilers and the supply of such new terms as have sprung from modern improvements in science. But in searching for the originals of English words, I soon found the field of etymology had been very imperfectly explored: and one discovery succeeding another, my curiosity was excited to persevere in the pursuit. At length finding no safe clue to conduct me through the labyrinth, I adopted a new plan of investigation, that of examining and comparing the primary elements, articulations or consonants of words in 20 different languages or dialects, the vowels having been found so mutable as to be of no use. The result of this examination has been the formation of a synopsis of radical words in more than 20 languages which is complete or nearly so. This will probably form a Quarto, and be an appendix to the Dictionary. This has occupied about ten years, but I do not, and I think the world will not regret the delay which this has occasioned, for if I am not deceived, the discoveries, proceeding from this investigation will be quite important, and as *new* in Europe as in America. This synopsis exhibits a vast number of affinities between the languages examined, which have never before been detected; but what I think of more value, this investigation has developed in a multitude of words, the primary sense of the root, which has not hitherto been known. . ."

Synopsis of Words in Twenty Languages

In 1807 Webster had mastered twelve languages. By 1813 he had learned twenty different languages, these were: Chaldaic, Syriac, Arabic, Samaritan, Hebrew, Ethiopic, Persian, Irish (Hyberne, Celtic), Amoric, Anglo-Saxon, German, Dutch, Swedish, Danish, Greek, Latin, Italian, Spanish, French, Russian, later adding Portuguese, Welsh, Gothic, and the early dialects of English and German. English, of course, was included in this list.

"In the second story of his new home, in a large room,

with windows looking to the south and east, Webster set up anew the large circular table which he had used for some years at New Haven," *so wrote his granddaughter, Emily Ellsworth Fowler Ford.* "This table was about two feet wide, built in the form of a hollow circle. Dictionaries and grammars of all obtainable languages were laid in successive order upon its surface. Webster would take the word under investigation, and standing at the right end of the lexicographer's table, look it up in the first dictionary which lay at that end. He made a note, examined a grammar, considered some kindred word, and then passed to the next dictionary of some other tongue. He took each word through the twenty or thirty dictionaries, making notes of his discoveries, and passing around his table many times in the course of a day's labor of minute and careful study. This was comparative philology which has given such great results to modern philologists."

Webster's Lexicographer's Table

In 1822 the Websters were able to move back to New Haven, closer to the intellectual world and closer to his two married daughters, Mrs. William Wolcott Ellsworth, and Mrs. Chauncey A. Goodrich. In 1823 Yale College recognized her eminent son with an honorary degree of Doctor of Laws. Now approaching the last lap of his extensive work on the *American Dictionary* Noah Webster wished to exhaust one last avenue of research — the libraries of France and England. Refusing to jeopardize or put in hazard the family property he sought once again for funds to underwrite his research. The response came — from within the closeknit family circle:

"If one thousand dollars will assist in affording aid to my dearest Father in his contemplated Journey to England, he is at liberty to draw this sum in the name of his daughter, with the hope that should he succeed in his wishes, he may at some future time be able to repay it. But if otherwise and Providence should see fit that *disappointment* should be the result of the undertaking, then let this sum be considered as the *free* and cheerful gift of an affectionate child. Harriet."

Harriet's Gift to Her Father

Accompanied by his son William, Noah Webster set sail for France where the sight of row upon row of books in the Royal Library, more books than in all the colleges of America, overwhelmed the Pilgrim from Connecticut. His letters to *"My dear Bacca"* and to his daughters were full of bright pertinent detail about French customs and cookery and he impatiently awaited the chatty, newsy letters from home. England, however, was his real goal scholastically and he had written Samuel Lee, Professor of Arabic at Cambridge University:

"Reverend and Dear Sir,

"As I have crossed the Atlantic for the purpose of completing and publishing a dictionary of our language, it would be very gratifying to me and to my countrymen, and I think by no means useless in England, to settle, by the united opinions of learned men, some points in pronunciation, orthography, and construction, in which the practice of good writers and speakers is not uniform, either in England or in the United States; and it is desirable that as far as the people have the same things and the same ideas, the words to express them should remain the same. . . .

"Besides this, the English language is to be the instrument of propagating sciences, arts, and the Christian religion to an extent probably exceeding that of any other language. It is therefore important that its principles should be adjusted, and uniformity of spelling and pronunciation established and preserved, as far as the nature of a living language will admit. In regard to the great body of the language, its principles are now settled by usage, and are uniform in this country and the United States. But there are many points in which respectable men are not agreed, and it is the sincere desire of my fellow citizens that such a diversity may no longer exist. If a delegation of gentlemen from the two universities of Oxford and Cambridge could be induced to meet and consult on this subject, either in Oxford or Cambridge or in London, I would meet them with pleasure and lay before them such points of difference in the practice of the two countries as it is desirable to adjust, and the gentlemen would consider any other points that they might think it expedient to determine. . . ."

Professor Lee supplied Noah Webster with information concerning rooms, rules regulating library use, and mild enthusiasm concerning his remarks. No meeting of scholars was forthcoming although there were some regrets later that the quiet coming and going of the solitary researcher might have been better known.

Noah Webster at Cambridge

"It would have been a great pleasure to many of my brethren here to have had more frequent opportunities of intercourse with you, & we are sorry not to have formed an earlier acquaintance with a gentleman of such attainments and character."

At a meeting of the Cambridge Bible Society Webster was graciously received and he reported *"what our people are doing in America for spreading the gospel, and among other things I told them that my fair countrywomen far outstrip the men in all works of Charity. . . ."*

But it was here at Cambridge, alone, amidst walls of historic and academic splendor that Noah Webster arrived at the last word in his monumental *American Dictionary*:

Webster Completes the Last Word in His Great Dictionary

"I finished writing my Dictionary in January, 1825, at my lodgings in Cambridge, England. When I had come to the last word, I was seized with a trembling which made it somewhat difficult to hold my pen steady for writing. The cause seems to have been the thought that I might not then live to finish the work, or the thought that I was so near the end of my labors. But I summoned strength to finish the last word, and then walking about the room a few minutes I recovered."

The Entire Work Written in His Own Hand

"It is interesting to know," *writes his granddaughter,* "that Webster himself performed the great manual as well as mental labor; for the entire work — with all the authorities, quotations, and passages cited to illustrate the meaning of words — was written out in his own hand. Such was also the fact with the *Synopsis of Words in Twenty Languages,* and indeed with the whole series of his productions from the earliest years of his life. He never had the aid of an amanuensis in any of his literary labors, except in the proof-reading of his *Dictionary* — and later in its revision when his eyes began to fail him, at the age of eighty."

English publishers, engaged in a new edition of Samuel Johnson's Dictionary were indifferent to Webster's scholarly research and refused his manuscript. Like his forebears Noah set sail for America and more hospitable shores. But, despite approval of the project, an American publisher was forthcoming only when Webster endorsed a large share of the cost. An agreement was finally made with Sherman Converse and on May 8, 1827 the printing was begun by Hezekiah Howe in New Haven. In November, 1828, the last pages were completed and bound into two bulky quarto volumes. At long last *An American Dictionary of the English Language* was finally complete!

What made the 1828 *American Dictionary of the English Language* of Noah Webster unique and distinct for its times?

First, in sheer number of words it surpassed every known dictionary adding 12,000 words to the latest Johnson edition and bringing the total number of words defined to 70,000. But it was in the selection of words that the *American Dictionary* completed its independence from the mother country, for it included a new vocabulary directly related to the American philosophy of government. The Christian concept of individual liberty and property established under the United States Constitution had produced, for the first time in human history, unlimited opportunity for every man and woman. An explosion of interest and exploration in every field occurred and invention and the arts flourished. Every man needed to know everything and thus a literary, Johnsonian type of dictionary was not sufficient for an American. New terms in science, industry and commerce were multiplying daily and these were significant in a country where men were independent and *"masters of their own persons and Lords of their own soil."*

Americans Require an American Dictionary

Second, Noah Webster's untiring etymological research had for the first time established the correct principle for arranging the definitions of words. He believed that all of the meanings of a word could be deduced from one fundamental idea:

"There is a primary sense of every word, from which all others have proceeded; and whenever this can be discovered, this sense should stand first in order."

Words could now be arranged with the etymologically primary meanings first. Webster's *Synopsis of Languages* became a useful tool with which he was able to trace the primary meaning of a word from its source, or head-waters, through the various tributaries of its meaning. This exactness in defining the original *idea* of a word freed the lexicographer from dependence on synonyms as substitutes for exact meaning. Changes of meanings in individual words Webster also anticipated and these distinctions were carefully traced and elaborated.

The "Idea" of a Word Defined

Third, Noah Webster set a standard of *purity* when he refused to admit the putrifying streams of *cant* and *vulgarism* into the main flow of American language:

"The authority of individuals is always liable to be called in question — but the unanimous consent of a nation, and a fixed principle interwoven with the very construction of a language, coeval and co-extensive with it, are like the common laws of a land, or the immutable rules of morality, the propriety of which every man, however refractory, is forced to acknowledge, and to which most men will readily submit."

While the vitality of the young nation might contribute many new terms to the English Language yet *deviation* from the norm was not a criterion of legitimate lexicography. Diversity of expression was always to be balanced with the constancy of a fixed principle — liberty with law rather than freedom from control. Webster's prime example was physics *"where motion, the source of life, becomes the principle of destruction."*

In a letter to David Ramsay of Charlestown, who had informed him that the *"prejudices against any American attempt to improve Dr. Johnson are very strong in that city"* Webster questioned Johnson's impropriety in introducing many vulgarisms into his 1755 Dictionary:

Webster Censures Johnson's Vulgarisms

"It is questionable how far vulgar and cant words are to be admitted into a Dictionary; but one thing must be acknowledged by any man who will inspect the several dictionaries in the English language, that if any portion of such words are inadmissable, Johnson has transgressed the rules of lexicography beyond any other compiler; for his work contains more of the lowest of all vulgar words than any other now extant. . . . Let the admirers of Johnson's Dictionary be a little more critical in comparing his vocabulary and mine and blush for their illiberal treatment of me! Instead of *increasing* the list of vulgar terms, I have *reduced* it by expunging *two thirds* of such words inserted by Johnson! Any person who will have the patience and the candor to compare my dictionary with others will find that there is not a vocabulary of the English language extant so free from *local, vulgar,* and *obscene* words as mine! . . ."

Fourth, Noah Webster had the courage of his convictions when he placed the best American authors on a par with British authors. Taking a cue from Johnson, who asserted *"the chief glory of a nation arises from its authors,"* Webster affirmed:

Distinguished American Authors

"I do not indeed expect to add celebrity to the names of *Franklin, Washington, Adams, Jay, Madison, Marshall, Ramsay, Dwight, Smith, Trumbull, Hamilton, Belknap, Ames, Mason, Kent, Hare, Silliman, Cleaveland, Walsh, Irving,* and many other Americans distinguished by their writings or by their science; but it is with pride and satisfaction that I can place them as authorities on the same page with those of *Boyle, Hooker, Milton, Dryden, Addison, Ray, Milner, Cowper, Davy, Thomson,* and *Jameson. . . . Franklin* and *Washington,* whose language is their hereditary mother tongue, unsophisticated by modern grammar, present as pure models of genuine English as *Addison* or *Swift. . . ."*

Webster went farther and specified the fields in which *"our country has produced some of the best models of composition. . . ."* equalling the best of British authors and surpassed by none.

The question might be asked, what makes the 1828 *American Dictionary of the English Language* unique and distinct for *our* times?

Webster and America's Christian History

Noah Webster's 1828 *American Dictionary* remains today the pure repository of three essential ingredients of *America's Christian History.* It reflects our Christian philosophy of life, our Christian philosophy of government, and our Christian philosophy of education. Unmistakably it reveals the degree to which the Bible was America's basic textbook and how it was related to all fields. Noah Webster as a Christian scholar laid his foundation of etymology upon the Scriptures and his research into the origin of language stems from this premise. One cannot read his definitions nor study his discussion of the grammatical construction of our language without encountering at every point a Scriptural Christian philosophy of life.

Noah Webster's words describing the American institutions of government indicate the distinctness of terms required when a nation such as ours has its origin in the Scriptures. Words like "govern," "government," "constitution," "fast-day," "republic," "democracy," and others reflect the uniqueness of America's Christian founding and God's purpose for her.

For more than 60 years Noah Webster devoted a major portion of his talents to defining and establishing an American Christian educational system. He recognized that the only effective defense against the influence of alien philosophies of government or education was to construct permanent foundations based upon the Word of God. Specifically, he provided the fundamental texts for spelling, grammar, reading, history, geography, civics, literature and an American dictionary. Written from a Christian, Biblical position, these texts taught pupils the ingredients of Christian character needed to maintain our American republic.

Thus, today, the 1828 *American Dictionary of the English Language* represents a veritable treasury of America's Christian history and education. It provides us with a primary *source* for the original meaning of Christian Constitutional terms as used in the founding years of this nation.

With the publication of Noah Webster's *American Dictionary* began the *"war of the dictionaries"* taking up where the *"spelling book war"* had left off. Raging for many years after Webster's death the critics of his Biblical American system of language only helped to establish him as the final authority and arbiter in the field. A number of state legislatures voted Webster as the standard over his opponents. The courts and the *"counting house"* adopted him as did our national Congress. Even England finally elevated Noah Webster as supreme over Samuel Johnson. Webster's detractors succeeded in making his position more secure and certainly no author in America has been so plagiarized and imitated. Americans finally came to realize how much one man had contributed to bringing together the infinite diversity of many national origins under one national language. Wrote Southerner, Jefferson Davis in 1859:

Webster Becomes the Supreme Authority

"Above all other people we are one, and above all books which have united us in the bond of common language, I place the good Old Spelling-Book of Noah Webster. We have a unity of language no other people possess, and we owe this unity, above all else, to Noah Webster's Yankee Spelling-Book."

"A national language is a band of national union," wrote New Englander, Noah Webster in 1789, the year in which the Constitution of the United States was ratified:

"Let us then seize the present moment, and establish a *national language,* as well as a national government. Let us remember that there is a certain respect due to the opinions of other nations. As an independent people, our reputation abroad demands that in all things we should be federal; be *national;* for if we do not respect *ourselves,* we may be assured that *other* nations will not respect us. In short, let it be impressed upon the mind of every American that to neglect the means of commanding respect abroad is treason against the character and dignity of a brave independent people."

A National Language for Americans

One more task remained for Noah Webster — the crowning of his labors for his God and his country. This work, which he called *"the most important enterprise of my life,"* was the publication in 1833, in his 75th year, of the first American revised version of the Bible. *The Holy Bible, containing the Old and New Testaments, in the Common Version. With Amendments of the language.* While other works would follow, the translation of the Scriptures from their original tongues represented the completion of his educational system for America.

The First American Revised Version of the Bible, 1833

Writing one hundred years after this event and celebrating the *Centenary of Noah Webster's Bible,* Dr. Harry Warfel states:

"By his *Institute* (speller, grammar, reader) he had supplied the correct standard for language in our schools; given a religious tone to all our textbooks, and had fostered patriotic pride. His *Dictionary* became the undisputed arbiter of spelling and definition. *The Bible,* the greatest popular textbook, needed amendment in language so it might conform to the American idiom. . . . The Bible gave Americans Scriptures for daily reading *correctly* translated into their own language. . . ."

Working in the tradition of earlier English scholars who desired that *"even a boy that driveth a plow"* should have access to the Scriptures in his own tongue, Noah Webster, like Tyndale, Luther, and Coverdale, labored to produce the first American version. He was unwilling to alter without cause the 1611 King James simplicity and beauty of langauge. He did wish, however, to correct those errors which impaired or obscured the message or offended decency. He worked in the original Hebrew and Greek, altering only those passages and words which seemed grammatically incorrect or obscure. He was particularly concerned with words which might offend:

Webster Amends Errors in the Bible

"The language of the Bible has no inconsiderable influence in forming and preserving our national language. On this account, the language of the common version ought to be correct in grammatical construction, and in the use of appropriate words. . . . Language which cannot be uttered in company without a violation of decorum or the rules of good breeding, exposes the scriptures to the scoffs of unbelievers, impairs their authority, and multiplies or confirms the enemies of our holy religion."

Forty years after Noah Webster's first American revision a company of theologians and linguists, both European and American, embarked on a similar venture. Commenting on these two efforts Mrs. Ford states:

"Moreover, the alterations of Webster are not nearly as numerous nor as marked as those of the Committee of Revision. His was the gentle removal from the face of a friend of the accidental smouch or defacement, done with a loving and tender hand. He led in the direction in which the revisers followed, but his love for the strong, simple Anglo-Saxon language made him stop far short of their changes, and in many ways they have gone far beyond him. Doubtless the combined wisdom of many educated minds may arrive at large results, yet there must always be compromise where many work together, and compromises are not convictions. The work of the individual has always more harmony, consistency, and directness than the work of separate minds combined."

Webster Worked Alone on His Revision of the Bible

For two years Noah Webster's edition of the Bible moved slowly amidst criticism until the honorable faculty of Yale recommended it. Thereafter it spread throughout the schools and churches of Connecticut until it was in use in almost every Congregational church. Demands for cheaper editions were forthcoming in 1839 and 1841. Webster, as educator to the republic, wrote a companion piece to his edition of the Bible in 1834 entitled *Value of the Bible, and the excellence of the Christian religion: for the use of families and schools.*

The rich years of fruition from 75 to 85 were vigorous and active, religiously, educationally and politically as Noah Webster continued to register his American Christian Constitutional principles by voice and in print. In 1832 appeared his *History of the United States,* a widely used text in American schools. While Noah Webster had been the first to introduce the study of American History into schoolbooks he had never devoted an entire work to the subject. The importance of this volume was its recording of *America's Christian History* as Webster traced the Hand of God and the relationship of America to Christianity and the Bible. In 1841 he prepared a second edition of the *American Dictionary,* and in 1843 *A Collection of Papers on Political, Literary & Moral Subjects* was published. Even the beloved *American Spelling Book* received one more revision and correction as it appeared in a new edition in 1843.

Webster's Christian United States History, 1832

But it was the family as the foundation of the republic which received Noah Webster's especial attention. Celebrating the Golden Anniversary of his marriage to Rebecca Greenleaf in 1839, Grandfather Noah Webster presented a new Bible to each grandchild, lovingly inscribed. He rejoiced in their growth of Christian character and conviction and as he made his annual journeys throughout the United States each summer he visited the homes of his son and daughters. His passing in 1843 surrounded by a devoted family and pastor is a tender testimonial to the depth of affection which bound this American Christian home to Christ and to each other.

Noah Webster represents the *"immense effect"* of one life — a *"small power wisely and steadily directed."* He worked as ***one individual,*** initiating, challenging and establishing. He was not impelled to action merely by *external* demand or provocation but as, documented by his own words, from within the inspiration of his own internal conviction.

Today, even as the *International Dictionary* which still bears his name is produced by a corps of trained scholars, specialists and editors, it is *startling* and *encouraging* to remember that Noah Webster's work in every field was *an individual production!*

The greatest legacy that Noah Webster leaves to us, his posterity — is the testimony of his own life and effort demonstrating unmistakably the power and influence of one individual — if that individual is consciously dedicated to Christ and country. As he states in the 1828 preface to his *American Dictionary:*

"To that great and benevolent Being, who, during the preparation of this work, has sustained a feeble constitution, amidst obstacles and toils, disappointments, infirmities, and depression; who has borne me and my manuscripts in safety across the Atlantic, and given me strength and resolution to bring this work to a close, I would present the tribute of my most grateful acknowledgements. And if the talent which he intrusted to my care, has not been put to the most profitable use in his service, I hope it has not been *'kept laid up in a napkin,'* and that any misapplication of it may be graciously forgiven."

Webster's Legacy of Individual Christian Character

Rosalie J. Slater

San Francisco, September 17, 1967

Painted by S. F. B. Morse *Eng. by A. B. Durand*

NOAH WEBSTER LL.D.

Printed by J. R. Burton

AN AMERICAN DICTIONARY OF THE ENGLISH LANGUAGE:

INTENDED TO EXHIBIT,

I. The origin, affinities and primary signification of English words, as far as they have been ascertained.
II. The genuine orthography and pronunciation of words, according to general usage, or to just principles of analogy.
III. Accurate and discriminating definitions, with numerous authorities and illustrations.

TO WHICH ARE PREFIXED,

AN INTRODUCTORY DISSERTATION ON THE ORIGIN, HISTORY AND CONNECTION OF THE LANGUAGES OF WESTERN ASIA AND OF EUROPE, AND A CONCISE GRAMMAR OF THE ENGLISH LANGUAGE.

BY NOAH WEBSTER, LL. D.

IN TWO VOLUMES.

VOL. I.

He that wishes to be counted among the benefactors of posterity, must add, by his own toil, to the acquisitions of his ancestors.—*Rambler.*

NEW YORK:
PUBLISHED BY S. CONVERSE.
PRINTED BY HEZEKIAH HOWE—NEW HAVEN.
1828.

DISTRICT OF CONNECTICUT, ss.

L. S. Be it remembered, That on the fourteenth day of April, in the fifty-second year of the Independence of the United States of America, Noah Webster, of the said District, hath deposited in this office the title of a Book, the right whereof he claims as Author, in the words following, to wit:

"An American Dictionary of the English Language; intended to exhibit, I. The origin, affinities, and primary signification of English words, as far as they have been ascertained. II. The genuine orthography and pronunciation of words, according to general usage, or to just principles of analogy. III. Accurate and discriminating definitions, with numerous authorities and illustrations. To which are prefixed, an introductory dissertation on the origin, history and connection of the languages of Western Asia and of Europe, and a concise grammar of the English language. By Noah Webster, LL. D. In two volumes."

In conformity to the act of Congress of the United States, entitled, "An act for the encouragement of learning, by securing the copies of Maps, Charts and Books, to the authors and proprietors of such copies, during the times therein mentioned."—And also to the act, entitled, "An act supplementary to an act, entitled 'An act for the encouragement of learning, by securing the copies of maps, charts, and books, to the authors and proprietors of such copies during the times therein mentioned,' and extending the benefits thereof to the arts of designing, engraving, and etching historical and other prints."

CHAS. A. INGERSOLL, *Clerk of the District of Connecticut.*

A true copy of Record, examined and sealed by me,

CHAS. A. INGERSOLL, *Clerk of the District of Connecticut.*

April 14th, 1828.

PREFACE.

In the year 1783, just at the close of the revolution, I published an elementary book for facilitating the acquisition of our vernacular tongue, and for correcting a vicious pronunciation, which prevailed extensively among the common people of this country. Soon after the publication of that work, I believe in the following year, that learned and respectable scholar, the Rev. Dr. Goodrich of Durham, one of the trustees of Yale College, suggested to me, the propriety and expediency of my compiling a dictionary, which should complete a system for the instruction of the citizens of this country in the language. At that time, I could not indulge the thought, much less the hope, of undertaking such a work; as I was neither qualified by research, nor had I the means of support, during the execution of the work, had I been disposed to undertake it. For many years therefore, though I considered such a work as very desirable, yet it appeared to me impracticable; as I was under the necessity of devoting my time to other occupations for obtaining subsistence.

About twenty seven years ago, I began to think of attempting the compilation of a Dictionary. I was induced to this undertaking, not more by the suggestion of friends, than by my own experience of the want of such a work, while reading modern books of science. In this pursuit, I found almost insuperable difficulties, from the want of a dictionary, for explaining many new words, which recent discoveries in the physical sciences had introduced into use. To remedy this defect in part, I published my Compendious Dictionary in 1806; and soon after made preparations for undertaking a larger work.

My original design did not extend to an investigation of the origin and progress of our language; much less of other languages. I limited my views to the correcting of certain errors in the best English Dictionaries, and to the supplying of words in which they are deficient. But after writing through two letters of the alphabet, I determined to change my plan. I found myself embarrassed, at every step, for want of a knowledge of the origin of words, which Johnson, Bailey, Junius, Skinner and some other authors do not afford the means of obtaining. Then laying aside my manuscripts, and all books treating of language, except lexicons and dictionaries, I endeavored, by a diligent comparison of words, having the same or cognate radical letters, in about twenty languages, to obtain a more correct knowledge of the primary sense of original words, of the affinities between the English and many other languages, and thus to enable myself to trace words to their source.

I had not pursued this course more than three or four years, before I discovered that I had to unlearn a great deal that I had spent years in learning, and that it was necessary for me to go back to the first rudiments of a branch of erudition, which I had before cultivated, as I had supposed, with success.

I spent ten years in this comparison of radical words, and in forming a synopsis of the principal words in twenty languages, arranged in classes, under their primary elements or letters. The result has been to open what are to me new views of language, and to unfold what appear to be the genuine principles on which these languages are constructed.

After completing this synopsis, I proceeded to correct what I had written of the Dictionary, and to complete the remaining part of the work. But before I had finished it, I determined on a voyage to Europe, with the view of obtaining some books and some assistance which I wanted; of learning the real state of the pronunciation of our language in England, as well as the general state of philology in that country; and of attempting to bring about some agreement or coincidence of opinions, in regard to unsettled points in pronunciation and grammatical construction. In some of these objects I failed; in others, my designs were answered.

It is not only important, but, in a degree necessary, that the people of this country, should have an *American Dictionary* of the English Language; for, although the body of the language is the same as in England, and it is desirable to perpetuate that sameness, yet some differences must exist. Language is the expression of ideas; and if the people of one country cannot preserve an identity of ideas, they cannot retain an identity of language. Now an identity of ideas depends materially upon a sameness of things or objects with which the people of the two countries are conversant. But in no two portions of the earth, remote from each other, can such identity be found. Even physical objects must be different. But the principal differences between the people of this country and of all others, arise from different forms of government, different laws, institutions and customs. Thus the practice of hawking and hunting, the institution of heraldry, and the feudal system of England originated terms which formed, and some of which now form, a necessary part of the language of that country; but, in the United States, many of these terms are no part of our present language,—and they cannot be, for the things which they express do not exist in this country. They can be known to us only as obsolete or as foreign words. On the other hand, the institutions in this country which are new and peculiar, give rise to new terms or to new applications of old terms, unknown to the people of England; which cannot be explained by them and which will not be inserted in their dictionaries, unless copied from ours. Thus the terms, *land-office; land-warrant; location of land; consociation* of churches; *regent* of a university; *intendant* of a city; *plantation, selectmen, senate, congress, court, assembly, escheat,* &c. are either words not belonging to the language of England, or they are applied to things in this country which do not exist in that. No person in this country will be satisfied with the English definitions of the words *congress, senate* and *assembly, court,* &c. for although these are words used in England, yet they are applied in this country to express ideas which they do not express in that country. With our present constitutions of government, *escheat* can never have its feudal sense in the United States.

But this is not all. In many cases, the nature of our governments, and of our civil institutions, requires an appropriate language in the definition of words, even when the words express the same thing, as in England. Thus the English Dictionaries inform us that a *Justice* is one deputed by the *King* to do right by way of judgment—he is a *Lord* by his office—Justices of the peace are appointed by the *King's commission*—language which is inaccurate in respect to this officer in the United States. So *constitutionally* is defined by Todd or Chalmers, *legally*, but in this country the distinction between *constitution* and *law* requires a different definition. In the United States, a *plantation* is a very different thing from what it is in England. The word *marshal*, in this country, has one important application unknown in England or in Europe.

A great number of words in our language require to be defined in a phraseology accommodated to the condition and institutions of the people in these states, and the people of England must look to an American Dictionary for a correct understanding of such terms.

The necessity therefore of a Dictionary suited to the people of the United States is obvious; and I should suppose that this fact being admitted, there could be no difference of opinion as to the *time*, when such a work ought to be substituted for English Dictionaries.

There are many other considerations of a public nature, which serve to justify this attempt to furnish an American Work which shall be a guide to the youth of the United States. Most of these are too obvious to require illustration.

One consideration however which is dictated by my own feelings, but which I trust will meet with approbation in correspondent feelings in my fellow citizens, ought not to be passed in silence. It is this. "The chief glory of a nation," says Dr. Johnson, "arises from its authors." With this opinion deeply impressed on my mind, I have the same ambition which actuated that great man when he expressed a wish to give celebrity to Bacon, to Hooker, to Milton and to Boyle.

I do not indeed expect to add celebrity to the names of *Franklin, Washington, Adams, Jay, Madison, Marshall, Ramsay, Dwight, Smith, Trumbull, Hamilton, Belknap, Ames, Mason, Kent, Hare, Silliman, Cleaveland, Walsh, Irving*, and many other Americans distinguished by their writings or by their science; but it is with pride and satisfaction, that I can place them, as authorities, on the same page with those of *Boyle, Hooker, Milton, Dryden, Addison, Ray, Milner, Cowper, Davy, Thomson* and *Jameson.*

A life devoted to reading and to an investigation of the origin and principles of our vernacular language, and especially a particular examination of the best English writers, with a view to a comparison of their style and phraseology, with those of the best American writers, and with our colloquial usage, enables me to affirm with confidence, that the genuine English idiom is as well preserved by the unmixed English of this country, as it is by the best *English* writers. Examples to prove this fact will be found in the Introduction to this work. It is true, that many of our writers have neglected to cultivate taste, and the embellishments of style; but even these have written the language in its genuine *idiom*. In this respect, Franklin and Washington, whose language is their hereditary mother tongue, unsophisticated by modern grammar, present as pure models of genuine English, as Addison or

PREFACE.

Swift. But I may go farther, and affirm, with truth, that our country has produced some of the best models of composition. The style of President Smith; of the authors of the Federalist; of Mr. Ames; of Dr. Mason; of Mr. Harper; of Chancellor Kent; [the prose] of Mr. Barlow; of the legal decisions of the Supreme Court of the United States; of the reports of legal decisions in some of the particular states; and many other writings; in purity, in elegance and in technical precision, is equaled only by that of the best British authors, and surpassed by that of no English compositions of a similar kind.

The United States commenced their existence under circumstances wholly novel and unexampled in the history of nations. They commenced with civilization, with learning, with science, with constitutions of free government, and with that best gift of God to man, the christian religion. Their population is now equal to that of England; in arts and sciences, our citizens are very little behind the most enlightened people on earth; in some respects, they have no superiors; and our language, within two centuries, will be spoken by more people in this country, than any other language on earth, except the Chinese, in Asia, and even that may not be an exception.

It has been my aim in this work, now offered to my fellow citizens, to ascertain the true principles of the language, in its orthography and structure; to purify it from some palpable errors, and reduce the number of its anomalies, thus giving it more regularity and consistency in its forms, both of words and sentences; and in this manner, to furnish a standard of our vernacular tongue, which we shall not be ashamed to bequeath to *three hundred millions of people*, who are destined to occupy, and I hope, to adorn the vast territory within our jurisdiction.

If the language can be improved in regularity, so as to be more easily acquired by our own citizens, and by foreigners, and thus be rendered a more useful instrument for the propagation of science, arts, civilization and christianity; if it can be rescued from the mischievous influence of sciolists and that dabbling spirit of innovation which is perpetually disturbing its settled usages and filling it with anomalies; if, in short, our vernacular language can be redeemed from corruptions, and our philology and literature from degradation; it would be a source of great satisfaction to me to be one among the instruments of promoting these valuable objects. If this object cannot be effected, and my wishes and hopes are to be frustrated, my labor will be lost, and this work must sink into oblivion.

This Dictionary, like all others of the kind, must be left, in some degree, imperfect; for what individual is competent to trace to their source, and define in all their various applications, popular, scientific and technical, *sixty* or *seventy thousand* words! It satisfies my mind that I have done all that my health, my talents and my pecuniary means would enable me to accomplish. I present it to my fellow citizens, not with frigid indifference, but with my ardent wishes for their improvement and their happiness; and for the continued increase of the wealth, the learning, the moral and religious elevation of character, and the glory of my country.

To that great and benevolent Being, who, during the preparation of this work, has sustained a feeble constitution, amidst obstacles and toils, disappointments, infirmities and depression; who has twice borne me and my manuscripts in safety across the Atlantic, and given me strength and resolution to bring the work to a close, I would present the tribute of my most grateful acknowledgments. And if the talent which he entrusted to my care, has not been put to the most profitable use in his service, I hope it has not been "kept laid up in a napkin," and that any misapplication of it may be graciously forgiven.

New Haven, 1828.

N. WEBSTER.

INTRODUCTION.

DEFINITION OF LANGUAGE.

Language or *Speech* is the utterance of articulate sounds or voices, rendered significant by usage, for the expression and communication of thoughts.

According to this definition, language belongs exclusively to intellectual and intelligent beings, and among terrestrial beings, to man only; for no animal on earth, except man, can pronounce words. The word *language* is sometimes used in a more comprehensive sense, and applied to the sounds by which irrational animals express their feelings or affections; as to the neighing of the horse, the lowing of the ox, the barking of the dog, and to the cackling and chirping of fowls; for the sounds uttered by these animals are perfectly understood by the respective species. So also language is figuratively applied to the signs by which deaf and dumb persons manifest their ideas; for these are instruments of communicating thoughts.

But language, in its proper sense, as the medium of intercourse between men, or rational beings, endowed with the faculty of uttering articulate sounds, is the subject now to be considered.

Written language is the representation of significant sounds by letters, or characters, single or combined in words, arranged in due order, according to usage.

ORIGIN OF LANGUAGE.

We read, in the Scriptures, that God, when he had created man, "Blessed them and said to them, Be fruitful and multiply and replenish the earth and subdue it; and have dominion over the fish of the sea, &c." God afterwards planted a garden, and placed in it the man he had made, with a command to keep it, and to dress it; and he gave him a rule of moral conduct, in permitting him to eat the fruit of every tree in the garden, except one, the eating of which was prohibited. We further read, that God brought to Adam the fowls and beasts he had made, and that Adam gave them names; and that when his female companion was made, he gave her a name. After the eating of the forbidden fruit, it is stated that God addressed Adam and Eve, reproving them for their disobedience, and pronouncing the penalties, which they had incurred. In the account of these transactions, it is further related that Adam and Eve both replied to their Maker, and excused their disobedience.

If we admit what is the literal and obvious interpretation of this narrative, that vocal sounds or words were used in these communications between God and the progenitors of the human race, it results that Adam was not only endowed with intellect for understanding his Maker, or the signification of words, but was furnished both with the faculty of speech, and with speech itself, or the knowledge and use of words, as signs of ideas, and this before the formation of the woman. Hence we may infer that language was bestowed on Adam, in the same manner as all his other faculties and knowledge, by supernatural power; or in other words, was of divine origin; for supposing Adam to have had all the intellectual powers of any adult individual of the species, who has since lived, we cannot admit as probable, or even possible, that he should have invented and constructed even a barren language, as soon as he was created, without supernatural aid. It may even be doubted, whether without such aid, men would ever have learnt the use of the organs of speech, so far as to form a language. At any rate, the invention of words, and the construction of a language must have been by a slow process, and must have required a much longer time, than that which passed between the creation of Adam and of Eve. It is therefore probable that *language* as well as the faculty of speech, was the *immediate gift of God.* We are not however to suppose the language of our first parents in paradise to have been copious, like most modern languages; or the identical language they used, to be now in existence. Many of the primitive radical words may and probably do exist in various languages; but observation teaches that languages must improve and undergo great changes as knowledge increases, and be subject to continual alterations, from other causes incident to men in society.

A brief account of the origin and progress of the principal languages, ancient and modern, that have been spoken by nations between the Ganges and the Atlantic ocean.

We learn from the Scriptures that Noah, who, with his family, was preserved from destruction by the deluge, for the purpose of re-peopling the earth, had three sons, Shem, Ham and Japheth. This fact, a little obscured by tradition, was retained by our rude German ancestors, to the age of Tacitus.*

Japheth was the eldest son; but Shem, the ancestor of the Israelites, and of the writers of the Scriptures, is named first in order.

The descendants of Shem and Ham peopled all the great plain, situated north and west of the Persian Gulf, between that Gulf and the Indian ocean on the east and the Arabic Gulf and the Mediterranean Sea on the west, with the northern coast of Africa; comprehending Assyria, Babylonia or Chaldea, Syria, Palestine, Arabia, Egypt, and Lybia. The principal languages or dialects used by these descendants, are known to us under the names of Chaldee, or Chaldaic, which is called also Aramean, Syriac, Hebrew, Arabic, Ethiopic, Samaritan and Coptic. Of these, the Chaldee, and Hebrew are no longer living languages, but they have come down to us in books; the Samaritan is probably extinct or lost in the modern languages of the country, but the language survives in a copy of the Pentateuch; the Coptic is nearly or quite extinct, and little of it remains; the Syriac, Arabic and Ethiopic are yet living languages, but they have suffered and are continually suffering alterations, from which no living language is exempt.

These languages, except the Coptic, being used by the descendants of Shem, I call *Shemitic*, or *Assyrian*, in distinction from the *Japhetic.* As the descendants of Japheth peopled Asia Minor, the northern parts of Asia, about the Euxine and Caspian, and all Europe, their languages, have, in the long period that has elapsed since their dispersion, become very numerous.

All languages having sprung from one source, the original words from which they have been formed, must have been of equal antiquity. That the Celtic and Teutonic languages in Europe are, in this sense, as old as the Chaldee and Hebrew, is a fact not only warranted by history and the common origin of Japheth and Shem, but susceptible of proof from the identity of many words yet existing, in both stocks. But there is a marked difference between the Shemitic and Japhetic languages; for even when the radical words are unquestionably the same, the modifications, or inflections and combinations which form the compounds are, for the most part, different.

As it has been made a question which of the Shemitic languages is the most ancient, and much has been written to prove it to be the Hebrew, I will state briefly my opinion on what appears to me to be one of the plainest questions in the history of nations. We have for our certain guides, in determining this question—1st. The historical narrative of facts in the book of Genesis, and 2d. The known and uniform progress of languages, within the period of authentic profane history.

1. The Scripture informs us that, before the dispersion, the whole earth was of one language and of one or the same speech; and that the descendants of Noah journeyed from the east, and settled on the plain of Shinar, or in Chaldea. The language used at that time, by the inhabitants of that

---

* Celebrant, carminibus antiquis, Tuistonem deum terrâ editum, et filium Mannum, originem gentis conditoresque. Manno tres filios assignant.—*De Mor. Germ.* 2.

In ancient songs they celebrate Tuisto, a god sprung from the earth, and his son Mannus [Man], the origin and founders of their nation. To Mannus they assign *three sons.*

Noah is here called *Man.*

plain, must then have been the oldest or the primitive language of man. This must have been the original Chaldee.

2. The Scripture informs us, that in consequence of the impious attempts of the people to build a city and a tower, whose top might reach to heaven, with a view to make themselves a name and prevent their dispersion, God interposed and confounded their language, so that they could not understand each other; in consequence of which they were dispersed "from thence over the face of all the earth."

3. If the confusion of languages at Babel originated the differences which gave rise to the various languages of the families which separated at the dispersion, then those several languages are all of equal antiquity. Of these the Hebrew, as a distinct language, was not one; for the Hebrew nation was of posterior origin.

4. All the words of the several great races of men, both in Asia and Europe, which are vernacular in their several languages, and unequivocally the same, are of equal antiquity, as they must have been derived from the common Chaldee stock which existed before the dispersion. The words common to the Syrians and Hebrews, could not have been borrowed from the Hebrew, for the Hebrews originated from Heber and Abram, several centuries after Syria and Egypt were populous countries. This fact is attested by the Scripture history, which declares that when Abram migrated from Chaldea, and came into Canaan or Palestine, "The Canaanite was then in the land;" and when he returned from Egypt, "the Perizzite dwelt in the land." These declarations, and the history of Abimelech, and of the war of four kings or chieftains with five; as also of the cities of Sodom and Gomorrah, prove Syria to have been, at that time, well-peopled. The language of the inhabitants then must have been coeval with the nation, and long anterior to the Hebrew as a distinct dialect. It may be added that in the early periods of the world, when no books existed, nations, living remote or distinct, never borrowed words from each other. One nation, living in the midst of another, as the Hebrews did among the Egyptians, may adopt a single word, or a few words; but a family of words thus adopted is an occurrence rarely or never known. The borrowing of words, in modern times, is almost wholly from the use of books.

5. It is probable that some differences of language were produced by the confusion; but neither that event nor any supernatural event is necessary to account for the differences of dialect or of languages, now existing. The different modern languages of the Gothic or Teutonic stock, all originated in the natural course of events; and the differences are as great between them as they are between the languages of the Shemitic stock.

6. Soon after two races of men of a common stock have separated and placed themselves in distant countries, the language of each begins to diverge from that of the other, by various means.—1. One tribe or nation will suffer one word to become obsolete and be forgotten; another, will suffer the loss of another; sometimes a whole family of words will be lost; at other times, a part only; at other times, a single word only of a numerous family will be retained by one nation, while another nation will retain the whole. 2. The same word will be differently applied by two distant races of men, and the difference will be so great as to obscure the original affinity. 3. Words will be compounded by two nations in a different manner, the same radical words taking a different prefix or suffix, in different languages. Thus *wisdom* in English is in German *weisheit*, [wisehead, wisehood] from *wise*, *weis*. In English *mislead* is in Danish *förleder*, from *lead*, *leder*. 4. The pronunciation and orthography of words will often be so much changed, that the same word in two languages, cannot without difficulty, be recognized as identical. No person, without a considerable attention to the changes which letters have suffered, would at once suspect or believe the English *let* and the French *laisser* to be the same word.

7. As Abram migrated from Chaldea, he must have spoken the Chaldee language, and probably, at that time, the Syriac, Arabic and Egyptian, had not become so different, as to render it impracticable for him to converse with the inhabitants of Palestine and Egypt. But the language of Abram's descendants, and that of the land of Shinar or the Chaldee must, in the natural course of things, have begun to diverge, soon after the separation; and the changes in each language being different, would, in the course of a few centuries, form somewhat different languages. So in the days of Hezekiah the Syriac and Hebrew had become, in a degree, distinct languages. 2 Kings xviii. In which of these languages, the greatest number of alterations were produced, we do not know; but from the general observations I have made, in my researches, it appears that the Chaldee dialect, in the use of dental letters instead of sibilants, is much the most general in the Celtic and Teutonic languages of Europe. Thus the German only has a sibilant in *wasser*, when the other Teutonic languages have a dental, *water*. I think also that there are far more words in the European languages which accord with the Chaldee or Arabic, than there are words which accord with the Hebrew. If this observation is well-founded, the Hebrew must have suffered the loss of more primitive words than the other languages of the Shemitic family. This however is true, that all of them have lost some words, and in some cases, the Hebrew retains what the others have lost.

8. The Hebrew Scriptures are, by many centuries, the most ancient writings extant. Hence probably the strange inference, that the Hebrew is the oldest language; as if the inhabitants of Chaldea and Syria had had no language, for ages before the progenitor of the Hebrews was born.

9. The vernacular words in the Celtic and Teutonic languages of modern Europe, which are evidently the same words as still exist in the Shemitic languages, are of the same antiquity; being a part of the common language which was used on the plain of Shinar, before the dispersion.

The descendants of Japheth peopled the northern part of Asia, and all Europe; or if some colonies from Egypt planted themselves in Greece, at an early period, they or their descendants must have been merged in the mass of Japhetic population. Certain it is that the Greek language is chiefly formed on the same radical words, as the Celtic and Teutonic languages.

The Japhetic tribes of men, whose descendants peopled the south and west of Europe, were first established in the country now called Persia, or by the natives themselves, Iran. Of this fact, the evidence now existing is decisive. The numerous words found in the Greek, Latin, Gaelic, English and the kindred tongues, which are still used in Persia, prove, beyond all question, that Persia must have been the residence of the people whose descendants introduced into Europe the languages from which the modern languages are derived. The fact proves further that a great body of the original Persians remained in their own country, and their descendants constitute the mass of the population at this day.

In the early stages of society, men dwelt or migrated in families, tribes or clans. The family of Abraham and Jacob in Asia, and the clans of the Gaels in Scotland, exhibit to us the manner in which societies and nations were originally formed. The descendants of a man settled around him, and formed a clan, or tribe, of which the government was patriarchal. Such families often migrated in a body, and often the personal characteristics of the progenitor might be distinctly traced in his descendants for many generations. In process of time, some of these families became nations; more generally, by means of wars and migrations, different tribes became blended, and the distinction of families was lost.

In rude ages, the families or tribes of men are named from some characteristic of the people; or more generally, from the place of their residence. The Greeks gave the name of *Scythia* to the north of Europe and Asia, but the primitive inhabitants of the west of Europe, they called Κελτοι, *Kelts*, *Celts*, a word signifying *woods men*.* These were descendants from the same ancestors as the Greeks and Romans themselves, but they had pushed their migrations into Gaul, Spain and Britain. The first settlers or occupiers of these countries were driven forward by successive hords, until they were checked by the ocean; there they made their stand, and there we find their descendants at this day. These may be considered as the descendants of the earliest settlers, or first inhabitants of the countries where they are found. Among these are the inhabitants of France, south of the Garonne, and those of the north of Spain, called by the Romans Aquitani and Cantabri, in more modern times Gascoigns, Basques, and Cantabrians, who still retain their native language; and in Great Britain, the Gaels in Scotland, and the natives of the north and west of Ireland, who also retain their primitive language.†

The first inhabitants of the north and west of Europe, known to the Greeks and Romans, to whom we are indebted for our earliest accounts of that region, were the Cimbri, who inhabited the peninsula of Denmark, now called Jutland, and the tribes which belonged to the Teutonic and Gothic races, which were established in Germany and on both sides of the Baltic. Whether tribes of Celtic origin had overspread the latter countries, before the arrival of the Gothic and Teutonic races, and all Europe had been inhabited by

* Welsh *celt*, a cover, or shelter, a *Celt; celtiad*, an inhabitant of the covert or wood; *celu*, to conceal, Lat. *celo*. In Gaelic the word is *coilt* or *ceilt*. The Celts were originally a tribe or nation inhabiting the north of Italy, or the still more northern territory.

† I purposely omit all consideration of the different families, tribes or nations which first peopled Greece and Italy. In Greece, we read of the Γραιοι or Γραικοι, the Hellenes, the Achæans, the Dorians, the Æolians, the Ionians, the Pelasgi, &c. In Italy, of the Illyrians, the Liburni, the Siculi, the Veneti or Heneti, the Iberi, Ligures, Sicani, Etrusci, Insubres, Sabini, Latini, Samnites, and many others. But as these nations or their descendants gave the name of CELTS to the Umbri, or nations that dwelt in the north, in the less cutivated parts of Europe, and to the inhabitants of Gaul; and as all the tribes, under whatever denomination they were known, were branches of the great Japhetic stock, I shall call them by that general name, CELTS; and under the general name of Goths or Teutons, shall comprehend the various tribes that inhabited the north of Germany, and the country north of the Baltic or Scandinavia.

A late writer seems to consider the Teutonic races, as the only ancestors of the Greeks and Romans. But from Celtic words, still found in the Greek and Latin; words not belonging to any of the Gothic or Teutonic languages; it is demonstrably certain that the primitive settlers in Greece and Italy, belonged to the Celtic races. Thus the Greek βραχιων, Lat. *brachium*, the arm, is formed on the Gaelic *braigh*, *raigh*, W. *braiç*, a word not found among the Teutonic nations. So the Welsh *mociaw*, to mock, is found in the Greek μωκαω, and French *moquer*, to mock, and Ir. *mogadh*, a mocking; but not in any of the Gothic or Teutonic languages. Many similar facts prove that the Celtic races were among the earliest inhabitants of Greece.

the Celts, even to the borders of Sarmatia, has been a question much disputed by historians and antiquaries. The German and French writers generally contend that the Celts inhabited all the north of Europe, as far at least as Sarmatia; but some respectable English writers are of a different opinion. Now it is agreed that the Welsh are descendants of the Cimbri, inhabitants of Jutland, and their language bears a strong affinity to the Celtic languages, which still exist; a fact that countenances the opinion of the German and French writers. But the dispute is of little moment: the Celtic, Teutonic and Gothic races being all of the Japhetic stock, migrating from Asia through Asia Minor at different times, and pursuing different courses westward. The first tribes probably sought the warm climates along the north coast of the Mediterranean, and established themselves in Greece and Italy. Others followed the course of the Danube and its subsidiary streams, till they fell upon the rivers that conducted them to the Baltic. The first inhabitants of Greece and Italy were probably of the Celtic race; but if they were, it is very evident that tribes of the Teutonic or Gothic races invaded those countries before they were civilized, and intermingled with the original inhabitants. The Pelasgi may have been among the number. This is an inference which I draw from the affinities of the Greek and Latin languages, with those of Teutonic origin. The Teutonic and Gothic races impressed their language upon all the continent of Europe west of the Vistula, and from that river to the Rhine, or rather to the Seine, anterior to the conquest of Gaul by Julius Cesar. The same races invading and conquering the south of Europe, in the fourth and fifth century, on the downfall of the Roman empire, infused a portion of their language into the Italian and Spanish, which is still distinguishable.

The ancient Sarmatia, including Poland and Russia, was probably peopled originally by races of men who passed into Europe by the country north of the Euxine. Their original residence was along the rivers Kur and Araxes, or on the mountains between the Euxine and Caspian. The name of the *Russ* or Russians is clearly recognized in the *Roxolani* of Pliny and Ptolemy, and possibly the ancestors of this race may have entered Europe by Asia Minor. That the Teutonic races, originally from Persia, inhabited Asia Minor, and migrated westward by that course, is evident from the names which they impressed on mountains, rivers and places—Such are the *Cragus* of Pliny, the Welsh and English *crag*;* *Perga* in Pamphylia, now *burg* or *bergen*; *Thymbreck*, the name of a small stream, near the site of Troy; a word in which we recognize the English *brook*. It was contracted by the Greeks into *Thymbrius*.†

It is admitted by all gentlemen, acquainted with oriental literature, that the Sanscrit, or ancient language of India, the parent of all the dialects of that great peninsula, is radically the same language or from the same stock as the Greek and Latin; the affinities between them being remarkably clear and decisive. If so, the inhabitants of India and the descendants of the Celtic and Teutonic nations are all of one family, and must have all migrated from one country, after the separation of the nations of the Shemitic stock from those of the Japhetic race.‡

Whether that country was Persia, or Cashmir, or a country farther east, is a point not easily determined. One important inference results from this fact, that the white men of Europe and the black or tawny men of India, are direct descendants from a common ancestor.

Of the languages of Europe, the Greek was first improved and refined, and next to that the Latin. The affinity between these languages, and those of the west and north of Europe is very striking, and demonstrates their common origin. It is probable however that there are some words in the Greek derived from Africa, if Egyptian colonies were established in Greece, as historians inform us.

The modern Italian, Spanish, French and Portuguese, are composed chiefly of Latin words, much altered however both in orthography and inflections. Perhaps nine tenths of all the words now found in those languages are of Latin origin; being introduced by the Romans, who held Gaul in subjection, five or six centuries, and Spain much longer; or being borrowed from Latin authors, since the revival of letters. All these languages however retain many words of Celtic origin; the primitive language not having been entirely extirpated. In some instances, the same word has been transmitted through both channels, the Celtic and the Latin, and is yet retained. Thus in French *céder*, and in Italian *cedere*, is directly from the Latin *cedo*; while the French, *congedier*, and Italian, *congedare*, are composed of the same word, with a prefix, derived from the Celtic, and retained in the Welsh *gadaw*, to quit, to leave. [L. *concedo*.] And this same verb probably appears also in *quit*, a word common to the Teutonic and to the Celtic languages. See *Conge*, in the Dictionary.

It must be observed further, that the Spanish language contains some words of African origin, introduced by the Carthaginians, before the Roman conquest of Spain, or afterwards by the Moors, who, for several centuries, were masters of that country. It contains also some words of Gothic origin, introduced by the Goths who conquered that country, at the downfall of the Roman Empire. The French also contains some words of Teutonic origin, either from the Belgic tribes who occupied the country to the Seine, at the time of Cesar's invasion, or from the Franks who established the dynasty of the Merovingian Kings in the fifth century, or from the Normans who obtained possession of the northern part of that kingdom in the tenth century, or from all these sources.

The German, Dutch or Belgic, Anglo-Saxon, Danish and Swedish languages are of Teutonic or Gothic origin.* They are all closely allied; a great part of the words in them all being the same or from the same roots, with different prefixes or affixes. There is however a greater difference between the Danish and Swedish, which are of the Gothic stock, and the German and Dutch, which are of Teutonic origin, than between two languages of the same stock, as between the Danish and Swedish. The Norwegian, Icelandic, and some of the languages or dialects of Switzerland, belong to the same stock; but of these I have no particular knowledge.

The Basque or Cantabrian in Spain; the Gaelic in the north of Scotland, and the Hiberno-Celtic, or native language of Ireland, are the purest remains of the ancient Celtic. From a comparison of a vocabulary of the Gaelic and Hiberno-Celtic, I find little or no difference between them; and from a long and attentive examination of this language, and of the languages of Teutonic origin, I find less difference between them, than most authors have supposed to exist.

The Armoric or language of Brittany in the northwest angle of France, and the Cornish, in the southwest of England, are also of Celtic origin. The Cornish is now extinct; but the Armoric is a living language.

The English as now spoken, is a language composed of words from several others. The basis of the language is Anglo-Saxon, or, as I shall, for the sake of brevity, call it, Saxon, by which it is closely allied to the languages of Teutonic and Gothic origin on the continent. But it retains a great number of words from the ancient languages of Britain, the Belgic, or Lloegrian, and the Cymraeg, or Welsh; particularly from the latter, and some from the Cornish. Cesar informs us, that before he invaded Britain, Belgic colonies had occupied the southern coast of England; and the inhabitants of the interior, northern and western parts, were the ancestors of the present Welsh, who call themselves *Cymry*, and their country *Cymru*, a name which indicates their origin from the Cimbri, inhabitants of the modern Denmark, or Cimbric Chersonese, now Jutland.

The modern Welsh contains many Latin words introduced by the Romans, who had possession of Britain for five hundred years. But the body of the language is probably their vernacular tongue. It is more nearly allied to the languages of Celtic origin, than to those of the Teutonic and Gothic stock; and of this British language, the Cornish and Armoric are dialects.

It has been commonly supposed that the Britons were nearly exterminated by the Saxons, and that the few that survived, escaped into the west of England, now Wales. It is true that many took refuge in Wales, which their descendants still retain; but it cannot be true that the other parts of England were entirely depopulated. On the other hand, great numbers must have escaped slaughter, and been intermixed with their Saxon conquerors. The Welsh words, which now form no unimportant part of the English language, afford decisive evidence of this fact. It is probable however that these words were for a long time used only by the common people, for few of them appear in the early Saxon writers.

The English contains also many words, introduced by the Danes, who were, for some time, masters of England; which words are not found in the Saxon. These words prevail most in the northern counties of England; but many of them are incorporated into the body of the language, and are used in the United States.

After the conquest, the Norman Kings endeavored to extirpate the English language, and substitute the Norman. For this purpose, it was ordained that all law proceedings and records should be in the Norman language; and hence the early records and reports of law cases came to be written in Norman. But neither royal authority, nor the influence of courts, could change the vernacular language. After an experiment of three hundred years, the law was repealed; and since that period, the English has been, for the most part, the official, as well as the common language of the nation. A few Norman words however remain in the English; most of them in law language.

Since the conquest, the English has not suffered any shock from the intermixture of conquerors with the natives of England; but the language has undergone great alterations, by the disuse of a large portion of Saxon words, and the introduction of words from the Latin and Greek languages, with some French, Italian, and Spanish words. These words have, in some instances, been borrowed by authors, directly from the Latin and Greek; but most of the Latin words have been received through the medium of the French and Italian. For terms in the sciences, authors have generally resorted to the Greek; and from this source, as discoveries in science demand new terms, the vocabulary of the English language is receiving continual

*Plin. N. H. Lib. 5, cap. 27. Strabo, Lib. 7. 6, informs us that the Dalmatians had the singular practice of making a division of their fields every eighth year. Hence perhaps the name from *deal*, and *math* or *madh*, country.

† Clarke's Travels.

‡ See the word *chuk* in the Dictionary.

*In strictness, the Swedish and Danish are of Gothic origin, and the German and Saxon, of Teutonic origin.

augmentation. We have also a few words from the German and Swedish, mostly terms in mineralogy, and commerce has introduced new commodities of foreign growth or manufacture, with their foreign names, which now make a part of our language.—Such are *camphor*, *amber*, *arsenic*, and many others.

The English then is composed of,

1st, Saxon and Danish words of Teutonic and Gothic origin.

2d, British or Welsh, Cornish and Armoric, which may be considered as of Celtic origin.

3d, Norman, a mixture of French and Gothic.

4th, Latin, a language formed on the Celtic and Teutonic.

5th, French, chiefly Latin corrupted, but with a mixture of Celtic.

6th, Greek, formed on the Celtic and Teutonic, with some Coptic.

7th, A few words directly from the Italian, Spanish, German, and other languages of the continent.

8th, A few foreign words, introduced by commerce, or by political and literary intercourse.

Of these, the Saxon words constitute our mother tongue; being words which our ancestors brought with them from Asia. The Danish and Welsh also are primitive words, and may be considered as a part of our vernacular language. They are of equal antiquity with the Chaldee and Syriac.

AFFINITY OF LANGUAGES.

On comparing the structure of the different languages of the Shemitic and Japhetic stocks, we cannot but be struck with the fact, that although a great number of words, consisting of the same or of cognate letters, and conveying the same ideas, are found in them all; yet in the inflections, and in the manner of forming compounds and derivatives, there are remarkable differences between the two great families. In the modifications of the verb, for expressing person, time, and mode, very little resemblance is observable between them. If we could prove that the personal terminations of the verb, in the Japhetic languages, were originally pronouns, expressive of the persons, we should prove an affinity between the words of the two races, in a most important particular. Some attempts of this kind have been made; but not with very satisfactory results.*

In the formation of nouns, we recognize a resemblance between the English termination *th*, in *birth*, *truth*, *drouth*, [Saxon *drugothe*] *warmth*, &c., and the Shemitic terminations ית and ות; and the old plural termination *en*, retained in *oxen*, and the Welsh plural ending *ion*, coincide nearly with the Arabic termination of the dual number انِ and the regular masculine plural termination ونَ, as well as with the Chaldee, Hebrew, and Syriac ין. And it is justly remarked by Mitford, that in the variety of plural terminations of nouns, there is a striking resemblance between the Arabic and the Welsh. There is one instance, in the modern languages of Teutonic origin, in which we find the Arabic nunnation:—this is the German and Dutch *binnen*, the Saxon *binnan* or *binnon*, signifying *within*, Hebrew and Chaldee בין, Ar. بَيْنَ without the mark of nunnation, when it signifies *within*; but when it signifies separation, space, interval, the original sense, it is written بَيْنٌ, and pronounced, with the nunnation, like the Teutonic word.

One mode of forming nouns from verbs in the Shemitic languages is by prefixing *m*. I know of no instance of this manner of formation, in the Japhetic languages, except in some names which are of oriental origin. Mars is said to be from αρης, but if so, the word was undoubtedly formed in the east. So we find *Morpheus*, the god of sleep, to be probably formed with the prefix *m*, from the Ethiopic አዐረፈ to rest, to fall asleep; whence we infer that *Morpheus* is sleep deified.†

But as many words in all the languages of Europe and Asia, are formed with prepositions, perhaps it may be found on examination, that some of these prefixes may be common to the families of both stocks, the Japhetic and the Shemitic. We find in German, *gemüth*, in Dutch, *gemoed*, from *muth*, *moed*, mind, *mood*. We find *mad* in Saxon is *gemaad*; *polish*, the Latin *polio*, is in Welsh *caboli*; *mail* in Italian is both *maglia* and *camaglia*; *belief* in Saxon is *geleaf*, and in German, *glaube*. We find that in the Shemitic languages מלא signifies to fill or be full, and we find in the Arabic كَمَلَ has the same signification. In Syriac ܡܠ signifies to remove; and دهل signifies to wander in mind, to be delirious. In Chaldee and Syriac, דמר is to wonder, precisely the Latin *demiror*, which is a compound of *de* and *miror*.

We find also that nations differ in the orthography of some initial sounds, where the words are the same. Thus the Spanish has *llamar*, *llorar*, for the Latin *clamo*, *ploro*, and the Welsh has *llawr*, for the English *floor*, *llabi*, a tall, lank person, coinciding with *flabby*, *llac* for *slack*, and the like.

As the prepositions and prefixes, in all languages, constitute an important class of words, being used in composition to vary the sense of other parts of speech, to an almost unlimited extent, it may be useful to give them a particular consideration.

The simple prepositions are, for the most part, verbs or participles, or derived from them; when verbs, they are the radical or primary word, sometimes varied in orthography by the addition or alteration of a single vowel, or perhaps, in some cases, by the loss of the initial consonant, or aspirate. Such are the Greek παρα, περι, κατα; the Latin *con* and *per*; the English *for*, which retain their original consonants. The following, *of*, *by*, *in*, *on*, *un*; the Latin *ab*, *ad*, *pro*, *præ*, *re*; the Greek απο, επι, προ, may have lost the initial or final consonants; *of* for *hof*; *in* for *hin*; *ab* for *hab*; *pro* for *prod*. In some words, this loss can only be conjectured; in others, it is known or obvious. Thus the English *by* and *be* was originally *big*, as it is in the Saxon; and the Latin *re*, is written also *red*, evidently a derivative of an Arabic verb still existing; the Latin *sub* and *super* are formed probably from the Greek υπο, υπερ, by the change of an aspirate into *s*, or the Greek words have lost that letter. The English *but* in the phrase "They are all here *but* one," is a participle; the Sax. *butan*, or *buton*; Dutch *buiten*, from *buiten*, to rove. *Among* is the Saxon *gemang*, the verb, or the participle of *gemengan*, to *mingle*.

In general, the primary sense of the preposition is moving, or moved. Thus *to* in English and *ad* in Latin, primarily denote advancing towards a place or object; as in the sentence, "We are going *to* town." *From*, *of*, Lat. *ab*, Gr. απο, denote motion from a place or object. The French *près*, is from the Italian *presso*, and this is the Latin participle *pressus*, pressed; hence it denotes *near*, *close*.

In some instances prepositions are compounds, as the English *before*; that is, *be* or *by fore*, by the front, and the Fr. *auprès*, at or at near.

Prepositions, from their frequent use, and from the ease with which their primary signification is modified to express differences of position, motion or relation, as occasions demand, have, in many instances, a great variety of applications; not indeed as many as lexicographers sometimes assign to them, but several different, and sometimes opposite significations; as for examples, the English *for*, *with*; the Latin *con*, and the Greek παρα. *For*, which is from the root of Saxon *faran*, Gr. πορευομαι, to pass, denotes *towards*, as in the phrase "A ship bound *for* Jamaica;" or it denotes *in favor of*, as "This measure is *for* the public benefit;" or "The present is *for* a friend." But it denotes also opposition or negation, as in *forbear*, *forgive*, *forbid*.

With is a verb, but has rather the sense of a participle. It is found in the Gothic with a prefix, *ga-withan*, to join or unite. Its primary sense then is joined, close; hence, in company; as in the sentences—"go *with* him," "come *with* me." It has the sense also of *from*, *against*, *contrariety*, *opposition*, as in *withdraw*, *withstand*, *without*. In Saxon it had also the sense of *towards*, as "*with* eorthan," towards the earth; also of *for*, denoting substitution or equivalent in exchange, as "sylan *with* dæges weorce," to give *for* a day's work; also of *opposite*, *over against*, as "*with* tha sæ," opposite the sea.

Con in Latin generally signifies *with*, *towards* or *to*, denoting closeness or union, approach, joint operation and the like, as in *concurro*, *conjungo*, *congredior*; but it has also the sense of *against* or *opposition*, as in *contendo*.

The Greek παρα, is doubtless from the root of the English *fare*, Saxon *faran*, to go, to pass. It signifies *from*, that is, departure—also *at*, *to*, Lat. *ad*; *near*, *with*, *beyond*, and *against*.

To understand the cause of the different and apparently contrary significations, we are to attend to the primary sense. The effect of passing to a place is nearness, *at*, *presso*, *près*, and this may be expressed by the participle, or in a contracted form, by the verb. The act of passing or moving towards a place readily gives the sense of such prepositions as *to*, and the Latin *ad*, and this advance may be in favor or for the benefit of a person or thing, the primary sense of which may perhaps be best expressed by *towards*; "a present or a measure is *towards* him,"—But when the advance of one thing towards another, is in enmity or opposition, we express the sense by *against*, and this sense is especially expressed when the motion or approach is in front of a person, or intended to meet or counteract another motion. Hence the same word is often used to express both senses; the context determining which signification is intended. Thus *for* in English, in the sentence, "He that is not *for* us is against us," denotes *in favor of*. But in the phrase "*for* all that," it denotes opposition. "It rains, but *for* all that, we will take a ride," that is, in opposition to that, or notwithstanding the rain, we will ride.

The Greek παρα, among other senses, signifies beyond, that is, past, and *over*, Hebrew עבר.

* According to Dr. Edwards, there is a remarkable resemblance between the Shemitic languages, and the Muhhekaneew, or Mohegan, one of the native languages of New England, in the use of the pronouns as prefixes and affixes to verbs.—*Observations*, &c. *p.* 13.

† Ludolf, Col. 446, 447.

The prepositions which are used, as distinct words, are called separable prepositions, or more generally *prepositions* :—those which are used only in composition are called inseparable prepositions. For the sake of brevity, I give to all words or single letters, prefixed to other words in composition, the general name of *prefixes*.

One of the best modes of ascertaining the true sense of a preposition, is, to examine its various uses in composition, and discover what effect it has in modifying the signification of the word to which it is prefixed.

Prepositions, used in compounds, often suffer the loss or change of a letter, for the sake of euphony, or the ease of pronunciation. Thus *ad* in Latin becomes *f* in *affero; con* becomes *col* in *colligo;* the Gr. παρα loses a letter in παρειμι, as does αντι, in many words.

The following sketch of the principal prepositions and prefixes in several languages of Europe will exhibit some of the affinities of these languages, and in a degree, illustrate the uses of this class of words.

SAXON AND GOTHIC.

And, Sax. and Goth, signifies *against*, *opposite*. This is the Gr. αντι, and Latin *ante*, not borrowed from the Greek or Latin, but a native word. Examples, *andstandan*, to stand against, to resist. *Andswarian*, *answarian*, to answer; that is, to speak again, against or in return.

Amb, *emb*, *ymb*, usually *emb*, Saxon, signifying *about*, *around;* coinciding with the Latin *amb*, and Gr. αμφι. Example, *emb-faran*, to go around, to walk about; *embutan*, about; *emb*, about, and *butan*, without. See *But*. *Ambeht*, *embeht*, *ymbeht*, office, duty, whence we have *embassador*. This in Gothic is *andbahtei*, and a bailiff, minister or servant is *andbahts*. The Germans have the word contracted in *amt*, charge, office, Dutch *ampt*, Dan. *ambt*. The Gothic orthography gives rise to the question whether *amb*, *emb*, and αντι, Sax. and Goth. *and*, are not radically the same word; and it is very certain that the Gothic and Saxon *and*, is radically the same word as the Latin *in*, Dan. *ind*. So in Gothic, "*and* wigans," *in* the ways, into the highways. Luke, xiv. 23. "*and* haimos" per vicos, through the towns. Luke, ix. 6.

This preposition, *amb*, is in Dutch *om;* in German *um;* in Swedish and Danish *om*.

At, is a Gothic preposition and prefix, coinciding with Eng. *at*, Lat. *ad*.

Be, in Saxon, as a preposition and prefix, is always written *be*, or *big*, answering to the English *by*, a preposition, and *be* in *beset*. In Gothic, it is written *bi*, *by* and *be*, being contractions of *big*. The primary and principal signification is *near*, *close;* as "stand or sit *by* me." So in the word *bystander*. It is a prefix of extensive use in the Saxon, German, Dutch, Danish and Swedish. Its use in denoting instrumentality, may be from the sense of *nearness*, but more probably it is from *passing*, like *per*, through, or it denotes *proceeding from*, like *of*, as salvation is *of* the Lord.

For, in Saxon, as in English, is a preposition and prefix of extensive use. In Saxon *for* signifies a going, from *faran*, to go, to fare. It is radically the same word as *fore*, in the sense of *in front*, *before*. Its primary sense is *advancing;* hence *moving towards;* hence the sense of *in favor of*, and that of opposition, or negation. See the preceding remarks.

This word in German is *für*, but, with this orthography, the word is little used in composition. Yet the German has *fürbitte*, intercession or praying *for;* *fürwort*, intercession, recommendation, and a pronoun [*for-word;*] and *für-wahr*, forsooth.

In the sense of *fore*, the German has *vor*, a word of extensive use as a prefix. Thus in Saxon *foreseon*, to foresee, is in German *vorsehen*. The identity of these words will not be questioned. But in German as in Dutch the preposition *ver*, which is the English *far*, and Saxon *fyr*, is used in composition, in words in which the Saxon and English have *for*. Thus *forgifan*, to *forgive*, is in German, *vergeben*, and in Dutch, *vergeeven*—Saxon, *forgitan*, to forget; German *vergessen;* Dutch *vergeeten*. Hence we see that the Saxon *for*, *fore*, *fyr*, the English *for*, *fore*, *far*, and the German *für*, *vor* and *ver*, are from the same radix.

In Dutch, *for* and *fore* are represented by *voor*, and *ver* represents *for* and *far*.

The Danish also unites *for* and *fore*, as does the Swedish.

The French has this word in *pour*, and the Spanish and Portuguese in *por*. The latter signifies not only *for*, but *through*, as in Portuguese, "Eu passarei *por* França." "I will pass *through* France. Here we see the sense of moving. In Spanish and Portuguese this word is written also *para*, as if from the Greek. It is evidently the same word, probably received through a different channel from that of *por*. Now *through* is the exact sense of the Latin *per;* and *per* is the Italian preposition answering to *for* and *por*. But what is more to the purpose, the Spanish, Italian and Portuguese word, equivalent to the English *forgive*, is in Spanish *perdonar;* in Italian, *perdonare*, and in Portuguese, *perdoar;* and the French is *pardonner*. Here then we have strong, if not conclusive evidence, that *for*, *pour*, *por*, *per*, *par*, and *para*, in different languages, are all from one stock, the word being varied in dialect, or by the different families; just as we have *far*, *farther*, as well as the Saxon *fyr*, and the English *forth*, *further*, from the same primitive word. We have the same word in *pursue* and *purchase*, from the French *pour*.

The Greek has περαν, and παρα, probably from the same root, as well as πορευομαι, πορος.

Ga, in Gothic, and *ge* in Saxon, is a prefix of very extensive use. In Saxon, it is prefixed to a large portion of all the verbs in the language. According to Lye, it has sometimes the sense of the Latin *cum;* but in most words I cannot discern any effect of this prefix on the signification of the simple verb. It is retained in the Danish and in some German and Dutch words, especially in the participles of verbs, and in nouns formed from them. But it is remarkable that although the Saxon is our mother tongue, we have not remaining in the language a single instance of this prefix, with the original orthography. The only remains of it are in the contraction, *a*, as in *awake*, *adrift*, *ashamed*, &c. from *gewæcan*, *awæcan;* *gedrifan*, *adrifan;* *gesceamian*, *ascamian*. The letter *y* prefixed to verbs and participles used by Chaucer, as *yberied*, *yblent*, *ybore*, *ydight*, and a few others, is the remnant of the *ge*. The words *yclad*, and *ycleped*, are the last English words used, in which this letter appears.

It is possible that the first syllable of *govern*, from Lat. *guberno*, Gr. κυβερναω, may be the same prefix; or it may be the Welsh prefix *go*, which occurs in *goberu*, to work, which the Romans wrote *operor*. But I know not whether the first syllable of *govern* is a prefix or not.

There is another word which retains this prefix corrupted, or its equivalent; this is *common*, which we have received from the Latin *communis*. This word in the Teutonic dialects is, Sax. *gemæne;* Ger. *gemein;* Dutch, *gemeen;* Dan. *gemeen;* Sw. *gemen*. Now if this is the Latin *communis*, and of the identity of the last component part of the word, there can, I think, be no doubt; then the first part of the word is the Teutonic *ge* altered to *com*, or what is more probable, *com* is the equivalent of *ge*, or *ge* may be a contracted and corrupted form of *cum*, *com*. In either case, we arrive at the conclusion that the Teutonic *ge*, and the Latin *cum*, are equivalent in signification.

In, is used in the Saxon and Gothic, as in modern English. It is in German *ein*, Dutch and Swedish *in*, Danish *ind*, Greek εν, Lat. *in*, Fr. *en*. This is radically the same word as *on* and *un*, the German *an*, Dutch *aan*, and Welsh *an*. In its original sense, it implies moving, advancing towards, and hence its use as a particle of negation or contrariety. "Eunt *in* urbem," they are going to the city. "Hæc audio *in* te dici," I hear these things said against you. In modern military usage, *on* is used in the same sense of advancing. "The army is marching *on* Liege."

Mid, in Saxon, signifies *with*. It is the Gothic *mith*, German *mit*, Dutch *mede* or *met*, and the Gr. μετα; but not retained in English. It seems to have the same origin as *mid*, *middle*, *amidst*. In the Gothic it is used as a prefix.

Mis, a prefix, is the verb *miss*, to deviate. It is used in Saxon, German, Dutch, Swedish and Danish, in nearly the same sense, as in English. Its radical sense is to depart or wander.

Of, is a preposition and prefix of extensive use in the Saxon, as in English. It denotes primarily issuing, or proceeding from; hence separation, departure, and distance; in the latter sense, it is written *off*. It is the Latin *ab*, written by the early Romans *af;* the Greek απο, the German *ab*, the Dutch *af;* Dan. and Sw. *af*. The Saxons often prefixed this word, in cases where we use it after the verb as a modifier; as *of-drifan*, to *drive off;* as it is still used by the Germans, Dutch, Swedes and Danes. We retain it as a prefix, in *offset* and *offspring*, Sax. *of-spring*. As it denotes *proceeding from*, it is the proper sign of the genitive case; the case expressing production.

Ofer, Eng. *over*, Goth. *ufar*, G. *über*, D. *over*, Dan. *over*, Sw. *ofver*, is a preposition and prefix, in all the Teutonic and Gothic languages, which I have examined; and in the same or similar senses. This seems to be the Greek υπερ, from which the Latins formed *super*, by converting the aspirate of the Greek vowel into *s*. This is probably the Heb. Ch. Syr. Ar. עבר, to pass, a passing, beyond.

On, is a Saxon preposition and prefix of very extensive use. It is obviously a different orthography of *in*, and it is used for *in*, in the Saxon, as "on onginn," in the beginning. It has also the sense we now give to *on* and *upon*, with other modifications of signification.

In composition, it signifies *into*, or *towards*, as *on-blawan*, to blow in; *onclifian*, to adhere, to *cleave to;* and it is also a particle of negation, like *un*, as *onbindan*, to unbind. This *on* is only a different spelling of *un*, in Dutch *on*, German *un*, used as a word of negation. The Gothic has *un* and *und*, in the like sense, as the Danish has *un;* the D. *ont*. In this sense, *un* answers precisely to the Greek αντι, and as this is sometimes written *und* in Gothic, as *in* is written *ind*, in Danish, there can be little doubt, that *in*, *on*, *un*, αντι, are all from one stock. The original word may have been *han*, *hin*, or *hon;* such loss of the first letter is very common; and *inn*, from the Ch. and Heb. חנה, presents us with an example. See *in* and *inn*.

The German has *an*, and the Dutch *aan*, in the sense of *in* and *on*.

Oth, is a Saxon preposition and prefix, sometimes written *ath* and *ed*, and answering nearly to the Latin *ad* and *re;* as in *oth-witan*, to twit, to throw in the teeth. It has also the sense of *from*, or *away*, or *against*, as in *oth-swerian*, to abjure. This preposition is obsolete, but we have the remains of it in *twit*, and perhaps in a few other words.

Sam, *samod*, a prefix. See the Danish and Swedish *infra*.

To, is a preposition and prefix of extensive use in our mother tongue. It occurs as a prefix, in such words as, *to-bræcan*, to break; *to-beran*, to bring or bear, [*ad-ferre.*] We retain it in *together*, Sax. *togædere;* and in *towards*, Sax. *toward, towardes;* and in *to-morrow, to-day, to-night*. The Dutch write it *toe*, and the Germans *zu*, and both nations use it extensively as a prefix. In Gothic it is written *du*, as in *du-ginnan*, to gin, that is, to begin. It would be gratifying to learn whether the Ethiopic ተ, which is prefixed to many verbs, is not the remains of the same preposition.

Un, is a Saxon prefix of extensive use, as a privative or particle of negation. See *on* and *in*.

Under, is a Saxon preposition and prefix of considerable use, in the present English sense. The Germans write it *unter*, and the Dutch *onder*, and use it in like manner. The Danes and Swedes write it *under*, and use it in the same sense.

Up, uppe, is a Saxon preposition and prefix of considerable use, in the present English sense. The Gothic has *uf*, in the sense of the Latin *sub*. The Germans write it *auf* and the Dutch *op*, the Danes *op* and the Swedes *up*, and all use it as a prefix.

Us, in Gothic, is a preposition and prefix. This is the German *aus*, and equivalent to the Latin *ex*. It is the Saxon *ut*, the English *out*, Dutch *uit*, Swedish *ut*, and Danish *ud*, dialectically varied. To this answers the Welsh *ys*, used in composition, but *ys* seems rather to be a change of the Latin *ex*, for the Latin *expello* is written in Welsh *yspeliaw*, and *extendo* is *estyn*.

Wither, in Saxon, from the root of *with*, denotes *against*, or *opposition*. It is a prefix in Saxon, written in German *wider*, in Dutch, *weder;* Dan. and Swedish *veder*. It is obsolete, but retained in the old law term *withernam*, a counter-taking or distress.

In the German language, there are some prepositions and prefixes not found in the Saxon; as,

Ent, denoting from, out, away.

Er, without, out or to. Dan. *er*.

Nach, properly *nigh*, as in *nachbar*, neighbor; but its most common signification in composition is *after;* as in *nachgehen*, to go after. This sense is easily deducible from its primary sense, which is close, near, from urging, pressing, or following. In Dutch, this word is contracted to *na*, as in *nabuur*, neighbor; *nagaan*, to follow. The Russ has *na* also, a prefix of extensive use, and probably the same word. This fact suggests the question, whether the ancestors of these great families of men had not their residence in the same or an adjoining territory. It deserves also to be considered whether this *na*, is not the Shemitic נ, occurring as a prefix to verbs.

Weg, is a prefix used in the German and Dutch. It is the Saxon, German, and Dutch *weg, way;* in the sense of *away*, or passing from, from the verb, in Saxon, *wægan, wegan*, to carry, to weigh, Eng. to *wag*, the sense of which is to move or pass; as Ger. *wegfallen*, to fall off or away.

Zer, in German, denotes separation.

In the Gothic dialects, Danish and Swedish, *fra* is used as a prefix. This is the Scottish *fra*, Eng. *from*, of which it may be a contraction.

Fram in Swedish, and *frem* in Danish, is also a prefix. The primary sense is to go, or proceed, and hence it denotes moving to or towards, forth, &c., as in Danish *fremförer*, to bring forth; *fremkalder*, to call for. But in Danish, *fremmed* is strange, foreign, and it is probable that the English *from* is from the same root, with a different application. It may be from the same stock as the Gothic *frum*, origin, beginning, Latin *primus*, signifying to shoot forth, to extend, to pass along.

Gien, igien, in Danish, and *igen*, in Swedish, is the English *gain* in *again, against*. This is a prefix in both these Gothic languages. It has the sense of the Latin *re*, as in *igienkommer*, to come back, to return; of *against*, as in *igienkalder*, to countermand, or recall; of *again*, as *gienbinder*, to bind again. This may be the Latin *con*.

Mod, in Danish, and *mot, emot*, in Swedish, is a preposition, signifying *to, towards, against, contrary, for, by, upon, out*, &c.; as "*mod staden*," towards the city; *modstrider*, to resist; *modgift*, an antidote; *modbör*, a contrary wind; *modvind*, the same. This is the English *meet*, in the Gothic orthography, *motyan*, to meet, whence to *moot*.

O, in Swedish, is a negative or privative prefix, as in *otidig*, immature, in English, *not tidy*. It is probably a contracted word.

Paa, in Danish, *på* in Swedish, is a preposition and prefix, signifying *on, in, upon*. Whether this is allied to *be, by*, and the Russ. *po*, I shall not undertake to determine, with confidence; but it probably is the same, or from the same source.

Samman, signifying together, and from the root of *assemble*, is a prefix of considerable use in both languages. It answers to the Saxon *sam, samod*, equivalent to the Latin *con* or *cum*. It seems to be allied to *same* and the Latin *similis*.

Til, both in Danish and Swedish, is a prefix, and in Danish, of very extensive use. It is equivalent to the English *to* or *towards*, and signifies also *at, in, on, by*, and *about*, and in composition often has the sense of *back* or *re*, as in *tilbage*, backwards, that is, *to back;* but generally it retains the sense of *to* or *onward;* as in *tilbyder*, to offer, that is, to speak or order to; *tildriver*, to drive on; *tilgiver*, to allow, to pardon, that is, to give to, and hence to give back, to remit. This is the English *till*, which we use in the same sense as the Danes, but in English it always refers to *time*, whereas in Danish and Swedish, it refers to *place*. Thus we cannot say, "We are going *till* town:" but we say, "wait *till* I come, *till* my arrival;" literally, "wait *to* I come," *to* my arrival; that is, to the time of arrival. The difference is not in the sense of the preposition, but in its application.

The Scotch retain the Danish and Swedish use of this word; no slight evidence of their origin.

U, in Danish, the Swedish *O*, is a prefix, equivalent to *in*, and is used as a privative or negative; as in *uaar*, an unseasonable year; *uartig*, uncivil.

RUSSIAN.

Vo or *ve*, signifies *in, at, by*, and may possibly be from the same root as the Eng. *be, by*. But see *po*.

Za, is a prefix signifying *for, on account of, by reason of, after*, as in *zaviduyu*, to envy, from *vid*, visage; *viju*, to see, Lat. *video; zadirayu*, from *deru*, to *tear; zamirayu*, to be astonished or stupified, from the root of Lat. *miror*, and Russ. *mir*, peace; *miryu*, to pacify, to reconcile; *mirnie*, pacific; *zamirenie*, peace, pacification; *zamiriayu*, to make peace; Arm. *miret*, to hold, to stop; the radical sense of wonder, astonishment, and of peace.

Ko, a preposition signifying *to, towards, for*.

Na, a preposition and prefix, signifying *on, upon, at, for, to*, seems to be the Germ. *nach*, Dutch *na*, as in *nagrada*, recompense; *na*, and the root of Lat. *gratia; nasidayu*, to *sit* down, &c.

Nad, a preposition, signifying *above* or *upon*.

O, a preposition, signifying *of* or *from*, and *for*.

Ob, a preposition and prefix, signifying *to, on, against, about*, as *obnemayu*, to surround, to embrace; *ob* and Sax. *neman*, to take.

Ot, is a preposition, signifying *from*, and it may be the Eng. *out*.

Po, is a preposition and prefix of extensive use, signifying *in, by, after, from*, &c. as *podayu*, to give to; *polagayu*, to *lay*, to expend, employ, *lay* out; to tax or assess; to establish or fix; to believe or suppose; *po* and *lay*. This corresponds with Eng. *by*, and the Latin has it in *possideo*, and a few other words. [Sax. *besittan*.] *Pomen*, remembrance, *po* and *mens, mind*.

Rad, a preposition signifying *for*, or *for the love of*.

So, a preposition and prefix of extensive use, signifying *with, of, from;* and as a mark of comparison, it answers nearly to the Eng. *so* or *as*.

Y, with the sound of *u*, is a preposition and prefix of extensive use. It signifies *near, by, at, with*, as *uberayu*, to put in order, to adjust, to cut, to reap, to mow, to dress, Fr. *parer*, Lat. *paro; ugoda*, satisfaction; *ugodnei*, good, useful, Eng. *good; udol*, a dale, from *dol*.

WELSH.

The prefixes in the Welsh Language are numerous. The following are the principal.

Am, about, encompassing, Sax. *amb*, Gr. *αμφι*.

An. See Sax. *in*.

Cy, cyd, cyv, cym, implying union, and answering to *cum, con* and *co* in Latin. Indeed *cym*, written also *cyv*, seems to be the Latin *cum*, and *cy* may be a contraction of it, like *co* in Latin. *Ca* seems also to be a prefix, as in *caboli*, to polish, Lat. *polio*.

Cyn, cynt, former, first, as if allied to *begin*.

Di, negative and privative.

Dis, negative and precise.

Dy, iterative.

E and *ec*, adversative.

Ed and *eit*, denoting repetition, like *re*, Sax, *ed, oth*.

Es, separating, like Lat. *ex*. See *ys*.

Go, extenuating, inchoative, approaching, going, denotes diminution or a less degree, like the Latin *sub;* as in *gobrid*, somewhat dear. This seems to be from the root of English *go*.

Han, expressive of origination.

Lled, partly, half.

Oll, all.

Rhag, before.

Rhy, over, excessive.

Tra, over, beyond. Lat. *trans*.

Try, through.

Ym, mutual, reflective.

Ys, denoting from, out of, separation, proceeding from, answering to the Latin *ex;* as *yspeliaw*, to expel. So *es*, Welsh *estyn*, to *extend*.

Most of these prepositions, when used as prefixes, are so distinct as to be known to be prefixes.

But in some instances, the original preposition is so obscured by a loss or change of letters, as not to be obvious, nor indeed discoverable, without resorting to an ancient orthography. Thus without the aid of the Saxon orthography, we should probably not be able to detect the component parts of the English *twit*. But in Saxon it is written *edwitan* and *othwitan;* the preposition or prefix *oth*, with *witan*, to disallow, reproach or cast in the teeth.

It has been above suggested to be possible, that in the Shemitic languages, the נ in triliteral roots, may be the same prefix as the Russian *na*, the Dutch *na*, and German *nach*. Let the reader attend to the following words.

INTRODUCTION.

Heb. נבט To look, to behold, to regard. The primary sense of *look*, is, to reach, extend or throw.

Ch. To look; also to *bud* or sprout.

Ar. نبط To spring, or issue as water; to flow out; to devise or strike out; to draw out.

If the first letter is a prefix, the Hebrew word would accord with Lat. *video;* the Chaldee, with *video* and with *bud*, Sp. *botar*, Fr. *bouton*, *bouter*, to *put*, and Eng. to *pout*, and Fr. *bout*, end, from shooting, extending.

Ar. نبت To *bud;* to germinate. See Ch. *supra*.

Heb. נבל To *fall;* to sink down; to wither; to fall off, as leaves and flowers; to act foolishly; to disgrace. Derivative, foolish; a *fool;* נפל Heb. Ch. Syr. Sam. to *fall*.

Ch. נבל To make *foul;* to *defile;* that is, to throw or put on.

Ar. نبل To shoot, as an arrow; to drive as camels; to excel; also to die, that is probably to *fall*.

Can there be any question, that *fall*, *foul* and *fool* are this very word, without the first consonant? The Arabic without the first consonant agrees with Gr. βαλλω, and the sense of *falling* then, is to throw one's self down.

Heb. נטר To keep, guard, preserve, retain, observe.

Ch. To observe; to keep; to lay up.

Syr. and Sam. *id.*

Eth. ነጠረ To shine.

Ar. نطر To keep; to see; to look; to attend.

Remove the first letter, and this coincides with the Greek τηρεω.

No person will doubt whether נמל to circumcise, is formed on מול.

Ch. נסר to cut; to saw. Syr. id. Lat. *serra*, *serro*.

Ar. نفد To *fade*, to vanish, to perish, to be empty, to fail.

Heb. נפח to blow, to breathe. Ch. Syr. Eth. Ar. id. from פוח, to blow.

If the Shemitic נ in these and similar words is a prefix or the remains of a preposition, it coincides very closely with the Russ. and Dutch *na*, and the latter we know to be a contraction of the German *nach*. Now the German *nach* is the English *nigh;* for no person can doubt the identity of the German *nachbar* and the English *neighbor*.

In the course of my investigations, I very early began to suspect that *b*, *f*, *p*, *c*, *g* and *k* before *l* and *r*, are either casual letters, introduced by peculiar modes of pronunciation, or the remains of prepositions; most probably the latter. I had advanced far in my dictionary, with increasing evidence of the truth of this conjecture, before I had received Owen's Dictionary of the Welsh language. An examination of this work has confirmed my suspicions, or rather changed them into certainty.

If we attend to the manner of articulating the letters, and the ease with which *bl*, *br*, *fl*, *fr*, *pl*, *pr*, *cl*, *cr*, *gl*, *gr* are pronounced, without an intervening vowel, even without a sheva, we shall not be surprised that a preposition or prefix, like *be*, *pe*, *pa*, *po*, or *ge* should, in a rapid pronunciation, lose its vowel, and the consonant coalesce closely with the first letter of the principal word. Thus *blank*, *prank*, might naturally be formed from *belank*, *perank*. That these words are thus formed, I do not know; but there is nothing in the composition of the words to render it improbable. Certain it is, that a vast number of words are formed with these prefixes, on other words, or the first consonant is a mere adventitious addition; for they are used with or without the first consonant. Take the following examples.

Hiberno-Celtic, or Irish, *brac* or *brach*, the arm, is written also *raigh*, Welsh *braiç*, whence βραχιων, brachium. *Braigh*, the neck, Sax. *hraca*, Eng. *rack*, Gr. ραχις. *Fraoch*, heath, ling, *brake*, L. *erica*.

Welsh, *llawr*, Basque, *lurra*, Eng. *floor*.

Lat. *floccus*, Eng. *flock* or *lock*.

Sax. *hraccan*, Eng. to *reach*, in vomiting.*

Sax. *hracod*, Eng. *ragged*.

Ger. *rock*, Eng. *frock*.

Dutch, *geluk*, Ger. *gluck*, Eng. *luck*.

Greek, Eolic Dialect, βροδον, for ροδον, a rose.

Latin, *clunis*, Eng. *loin*, G. *lende*, W. *clun*, from *llun*.

Eng. *cream*, Ger. *rahm*, Dutch, *room*.

Sax. *hlaf*, Polish *chlieb*, G. *leib*, Eng. *loaf*.

Sax. *hladan*, Eng. to *lade* or *load*, Russ. *kladu*, to lay.

Greek. κλινω, Lat. *clino*, Sax. *hlinian*, *hleonan*, Russ. *klonyu*, Eng. to *lean*.

Greek, λαγηνος, Lat. *lagena*, Eng. *flagon*.

Sax. *hrysan*, Eng. to *rush*.

---

* *H* before *l* and *r* in Saxon corresponds to the Greek κ, and Latin *c*, before the same letters.

French, *frapper*, Eng. to *rap*.

Sax. *geraedian*, to make ready; in Chaucer, *greith*, to make ready. Sax. *hræd*, quick; *hradian*, to hasten; *hrædnes*, Eng. *readiness*.

Spanish, *frisar*, to curl or frizzle; *rizar*, the same.

Sax. *gerefa*, Eng. *reeve*, G. *graf*, D. *graaf*.

Lat. *glycyrrhiza*, from the Greek; Eng. *liquorice*.

But in no language, have we such decisive evidence of the formation of words, by prefixes, as in the Welsh.

Take the following instances, from a much greater number that might be produced, from Owen's Welsh Dictionary.

Blanc, a colt, from *llanc*.

Blith, milk, from *lith*.

Bliant, fine linen, from *lliant*.

Plad, a flat piece or *plate*, from *llad*.

Pled, a principle of extension, from *lled*.

Pledren, a *bladder*, from *pledyr*, that distends, from *lled*.

Pleth, a braid, from *lleth*, Eng. *plait*.

Plicciaw, to *pluck*, from *llig*.

Ploc, a *block*, from *lloc;* *plociaw*, to *block*, to *plug*.

Plwng, a *plunge*, from *llwng*, our vulgar *lunge*.

Glwth, a *glutton*, from *llwth*.

Glas, a blue color, verdancy, a green plat, whence Eng. *glass*, from *llas*.

Glyd, *gluten*, *glue*, from *llyd*.

Claer, *clear*, from *llaer*.

Clav, sick, from *llav*.

Clwpa, a *club*, a knob, from *llwb*.

Clwt, a piece, a *clout*, from *llwd*, *llwt*.

Clamp, a mass, a *lump*.

Clawd, a thin board, from *llawd*.

Cledyr, a board or shingle, whence *cledrwy*, *lattice*, from *lled*.

Bran, Eng. *bran*, from *rhan;* *rhanu*, to *rend*.

Brid, a breaking out, from *rhid*.

Broç, noise, tumult, a *brock*, from *rhoc*.

Broç, froth, foam, anger, *broçi*, to chafe or fret, from *brwc*, a boiling or ferment, from *rhwc*, something *rough*, a grunt, Gr. βρυχω.

Bryd, what moves, impulse, mind, thought, from *rhyd*.

Brys, quickness, *brisiaw*, to hasten, to shoot along, from *rhys*, Eng. to *rush*, and *crysiaw*, to hasten, from *rhys*, to *rush*. [Here is the same word *rhys*, with different prefixes, forming *brysiaw* and *crysiaw*. Hence W. *brysg*, Eng. *brisk*.]

Graz, [pronounced *grath*,] a step, a degree, from *rhaz*, Lat. *gradus*, *gradior*.

Greg, a cackling, from *rheg*.

Grem, a crashing, gnash, a murmur, *gremiaw*, to crash or gnash, from *rhem*. Hence Lat. *fremo*, Gr. βρεμω.*

We have some instances of similar words in our own language; such *flag* and *lag;* *flap* and *lap;* *clump* and *lump*.

There is another class of words which are probably formed with a prefix of a different kind. I refer to words in which *s* precedes another consonant, as *scalp*, *skull*, *slip*, *slide*, *sluggish*, *smoke*, *smooth*, *speed*, *spire*, *spin*, *stage*, *steep*, *stem*, *swell*, *spout*. We find that *tego*, to cover, in Latin, is in Greek ϛεγω; the Latin *fallo*, is in Greek σφαλλω. We find μαραγδος

---

* I do not follow Owen to the last step of his analysis, as I am of opinion that, in making monosyllabic words to be compound, he often errs. For example, he supposes *broç* a tumult, to be from *rhoç*, a broken or rough utterance; a grunt or groan; and this, to be a compound of *rhy*, excess, what is over or beyond, and *oç*, a forcible utterance, a groan. I believe *rhoç* to be a primitive uncompounded word, coinciding with the English *rough*.

Owen supposes *plad*, a flat thing, a *plate*, to be from *llad*, with *py*. *Llad* he explains, what is given, a gift, good things, and *py*, what is inward or involved. I have no doubt that the first letter is a prefix in *plad*, but beyond all question, *llad* is from the same root as *lled*, breadth, coinciding with Lat. *latus;* both from a common root signifying to extend. But I do not believe *llad* or *lled* to be compound words.

Dug, a duke, Owen supposes to be formed on *ug*, over; which cannot be true, unless the Latin *dux*, *duco*, are compounds. *Dur*, steel, he derives from *ur*, extreme, over, but doubtless it is from the root of the Latin *durus*.

So *par*, signifying what is contiguous, a state of readiness or preparation, a *pair*, fellow, or match, Owen makes a compound of *py*, and *ar;* *py*, as above explained, and *ar*, a word of various significations, *on*, *upon*, *surface*, &c. But there can be no doubt that *par* is from the root of the Latin *paro*, to prepare, being the Latin *par*, equal; the root of a numerous family of words not only in the Japhetic languages of Europe, but in the Shemitic languages of Asia. It certainly is not a Welsh compound, nor is there the least evidence to induce a belief that it is not an uncompounded word. Had the learned author of the Welsh Dictionary extended his researches to a variety of other languages, and compared the monosyllabic roots in them with each other, I think he would have formed a very different opinion as to their origin. I am very well convinced that many of the words which he supposes to be primitive or radical, are contractions, such as *rhy*, *lle*, *lly*, the last consonant being lost.

is written also σμαραγδος; and it may be inquired whether the English *spin*, is not from the same root as πηνη, web or woof, πηνιον, a spindle, πηνιζω, to spin. *Sprout* in English is in Spanish *brota*.

We find the Welsh *ysbrig*, the English *sprig*, is a compound of *ys*, a prefix denoting *issuing* or *proceeding from*, like the Lat. *ex*, and *brig*, top, summit.

Ysgar, a separate part, a *share; ysgar, ysgaru*, to divide; *ysgariaw*, to separate, is composed of *ys* and *car*, according to Owen; but the real root appears distinctly in the Gr. χειρω. This is the English *shear, shire*.

Ysgegiaw, to *shake* by laying hold of the throat, to shake roughly, is a compound of *ys* and *cegiaw*, to choke, from *ceg*, the mouth, an entrance, a choking. This may be the English *shake;* Sax. *sceacan*.

Ysgin, a robe made of *skin; ys* and *cin*, a spread or covering.

Ysgodi, to *shade; ysgawd*, a shade; *ys* and *cawd*.

Ysgrab, what is drawn up or puckered, a *scrip; ys* and *crab*, what shrinks. See Eng. *crab, crabbed*.

Yygravu, to *scrape; ys* and *crav*, claws, from *rhav*.

Ysgreç, a scream, a *shriek*, *ysgreçiaw*, to *shriek*, from *creç*, a shriek, *creçian*, to *shriek*, from *creg, cryg*, hoarse, rough, from *rhyg*, rye, that is *rough;* the grain so named from its *roughness*. This is the English *rough*, Lat. *raucus*. Here we have the whole process of formation, from the root of *rough*. We retain the Welsh *creçian*, to shriek, in our common word, to *creak*, and with a formative prefix, we have *shriek*, and our vulgar *screak*. The Latin *ruga*, a wrinkle, Eng. *rug, shrug*, are probably from the same source.

Ysgrivenu, to write, Lat. *scribo*, from *ysgriv*, a writing, from *criv*, a mark cut, a row of notches; *criviaw*, to cut, to *grave;* from *rhiv*, something that divides. Hence *scrivener*.

Ysgub, a sheaf or besom, *ysgubaw*, to sweep, Lat. *scopæ*, from *cub*, a collection, a heap, a *cube*.

Ysgud, something that whirls; *ysgudaw*, to whisk or *scud;* from *cud*, celerity, flight; *ysguth, ysguthaw*, the same.

Ysgwth, a push; *ysgwthiaw*, to push or thrust; from *gwth, gwthiaw*, the same; probably allied to Eng. *shoot*. The Welsh has *ysgythu*, to jet or spout, from the same root.

Yslac, slack, loose; *yslaciaw*, to *slacken;* from *llac*, loose, *slack, llaciaw*, to slacken, from *llag*, slack, *sluggish;* allied to Eng. *lag* and *slow*.

Yslapiaw, to *slap*, to *flap*, from *yslab*, what is lengthened or distended, from *llab*, a flag, a strip, a stroke. *Llabi*, a tall, lank person, a stripling, a *looby*, a *lubber*, is from the same root; *llabiaw*, to *slap*.

Ysled, a *sled*, from *lled*, says Owen, which denotes breadth, but it is probably from the root of *slide*, a word probably from the same root as *lled*, that is, to extend, to stretch along.

Ysmot, a patch, a spot; *ysmotiaw*, to spot, to dapple, from *mod*, Eng. *mote*.

Ysmwciaw, ysmygu, to dim with *smoke*, from *mwg, smoke*. So *smooth* from Welsh *mwyth*.

Yspail, *spoil*, from *pail*, farina, says Owen. I should say from the root of *palea*, straw, refuse, that is, from the root of *peel*, to strip. *Yspeiliota*, to be *pilfering*.

Yspeliaw, to *expel*, from *pel*, a *ball*, says Owen: but this is the Latin *expello*, from *pello*. *Ball* may be from the same root.

Yspig, a *spike*, a spine; *yspigaw*, to spike; from *pig*, a sharp point, a *pike*. Hence Eng. *spigot*.

Yspin, a spine, from *pin, pen*.

Ysgynu, to *ascend*, Lat. *ascendo*, from *cyn*, first, chief, foremost. The radical sense is to shoot up.

Yslwç, a *slough*, from *llwc*, a collection of water, a *lake*.

Yspar, a *spear*, from *pâr*, a cause or principle of producing, the germ or seed of a thing, a *spear*. This consists of the same elements as *ber*, a spit, and Eng. *bar*, and in Italian *bar* is *sbarra*. The primary sense is to shoot, thrust, drive.

Yspinc, a *finch*, from *pinc*, gay, fine brisk; a sprig, a *finch*.

Ysplan, clear, bright; *ysplana*, to explain; from *plan*, that is parted off, a ray, a shoot, a planting, a *plane;* whence *plant*, a child; Eng. a *plant; planu*, to shoot, as a plant. Hence *splendor*, W. *ysplander*.

Ysporthi, to support, from *porth*, a bearing, a *port*, passage, &c. Lat. *porta, porto*.

Ystàc, a *stack*, a heap; *ystaca*, a standard; from *tag*, a state of being stuffed or clogged.

Ystad, a *state; ystadu*, to *stay;* from *tad*, that spreads, a continuity. The primary sense is to set.

Ystain, that is spread; a *stain; tin*, Lat. *stannum; ystaeniaw*, to spread over, to stain; *ystaenu*, to *tin*, or cover with *tin;* from *taen*, a spread, a layer. Qu. is *tin* from spreading?

Ystawl, a *stool*, from *tawl*, a cast or throw. The sense is to set, to throw down. *Tawl* is the root of *deal*.

Ystor, a *store*, that forms a bulk, from *tor*, a swell, a prominence.

Ystorm, a *storm*, from *torm*, that is stretched, but the sense is a rushing.

Ystrym, a *stream*, from *trym*, compact, *trim*, that is, stretched, straight, from extending.

Ystwmp, a *stump*, from *twmp*, a round mass, a tump.

Yswatiaw, to *squat*, from *yswad*, a throw, or falling down, from *gwad*, a denial; *gwadu*, to deny, or disown. If this deduction is correct, the sense of denial is a throwing or thrusting back, a repelling. It is so in other words.

Yswitiaw, to chirp, twitter, from *yswid*, that makes a quick turn. Qu. *twitter*.

In some of the foregoing words, it appears evident that the Welsh prefix, *ys*, is an alteration of the Latin *ex*, and the words, in which this is the case, were probably borrowed from the Latin, while the Roman armies had possession of England. But there is a vast number of words, with this prefix, which are not of Latin origin; and whether *ys* is a native prefix in the Welsh, may be a question. One thing is certain, that *s* before another consonant, and coalescing with it, is, in a great number of words, a prefix.

The modern Italian affords abundant proof of the extensive use of *s*, as the remains or representative of *ex;* as *sballare*, to unpack, *unbale; sbarbato*, beardless; *sbattere*, to abate; *sbrancare*, to pluck off branches; *scaricare*, to discharge; *scommodare*, to incommode; *sconcordia*, discord; *scornare*, to break the horns; *scrostare*, to pull off the crust; and a great number of others.

Now if the same manner of forming words with this prefix has actually prevailed among the northern nations of Europe, we may rationally suppose that many English words, and perhaps all of this class, are thus formed. Thus *scatter* may be formed from a root in *Cd; shape*, from *Cb, Cf* or *Cp; skill*, from the root of Lat. *calleo; slip*, from the root of Lat. *labor; smart*, from the root of Lat. *amarus*, bitter, Heb. מר; *smite*, from the root of Latin *mitto; span*, from the root of *pan*, to stretch; *spar*, from the root of *bar; speak*, from the root of Lat. *voco: speed*, from a root in *Pd*, perhaps Lat. *peto; steal*, from the root of Lat. *tollo; steep*, from the root of *deep; stretch*, from the root of *reach; sweep*, from the root of *wipe; swan*, from *wan*, white; *swell*, from the root of to *well*, Sax. *wellan*, to boil, &c. That many English and other Teutonic and Gothic words are thus formed, appears to be certain.

These facts being admitted, let us examine a little further. In Russ. *svadiba* is a wedding. Is not this formed on the root of *wed*, with *s* for a prefix? *Svara* is a quarrel. Is not this formed on the root of *vary, variance*, or of *spar? Sverlo* is a borer; qu. *bore* and *veru; svertivayu*, to roll; qu. Lat. *verto; skora*, furs, peltry; qu. Fr. *cuir; skot*, a beast; qu. *cattle; skupayu*, to purchase in gross; qu. *cheap*, Dan. *kioben*, and its root; *slabei*, weak; qu. Lat. *labor, lapsus; slagayu*, to fold; qu. *lay*, and *plico; slivayu*, to pour out liquors; qu. Lat. *libo; slupayu*, to peel off bark or skin; qu. Lat. *liber; snimayu*, to take away; qu. Sax. *neman*, to take; *snova*, new; qu. Lat. *novus; snig, sneig*, snow, Fr. *neige*. The Lat. *nivis* is from this root, with *g* opened to *v*. Russ. *spletayu*, to *plait*, &c.

The Russ. prefix *so* occurs in a great number of words; *sobirayu*, to collect or assemble, precisely the Heb. and Ch. צבר.

It now becomes an interesting question, to determine how far any analogy exists, between the languages of the Japhetic and Shemitic families, in regard to prefixes. For example, in the Shemitic languages, ב is a prefix of extensive use, corresponding almost exactly with the English and Dutch *by*, the Saxon *be*, and German *bei*. This preposition and prefix has several senses in the Saxon which are now obsolete; but its present prevailing sense occurs in all the Shemitic languages. ברוח קדים עזה, *by* a strong east wind. Ex. xiv. 21. Compare the following definitions of this preposition; the Sax. from Lye. and the Shemitic from Castle.

Sax. *de, e, ex, in, secus, ad, juxta, secundum, pro, per, super, propter, circa*.

Heb. Ch. Syr. *in, e, ex, cum, propter, usque ad, adeo ut, ad, super, per, contra, ante*.

Eth. *in, per, pro, propter, cum, secundum, apud*.

Ar. *in, cum, propter, per, ad, erga*.

In Numbers, xiv. 34, it signifies *according to*, or *after;* במספר הימים, according to the number of days. This signification is now perhaps obsolete in English, but was common in the Saxon; as, "*be* his mægnum," according to his strength; pro viribis suis. So "*be* tham mæstan;" *by* the most, is now expressed by, *at* the most.

Now it is remarkable that this word in Hebrew, Arabic and Persic, is the preposition used in oaths, precisely as it is in English. Gen. xxii. 16, בי, *By myself* have I sworn. Arabic, ballah or by Allah; Persic, بخدا, bechoda, or begoda, *by God*, the very words now used in English. The evidence then is decisive that the Shemitic prefix ב is the Teutonic *be, by, bei* contracted, and this Teutonic word is certainly a contraction of *big*, which is used in the Saxon, especially in compound words, as in *bigspell*, [*by-spell*] a fable; *bigstandan*, to stand *by*. This prefix then was in universal use by the original stock of mankind, before the dispersion; and this word alone is demonstrative proof of the common origin of the Shemitic and Teutonic languages. Now it is equally certain that this is the prefix *b*, and probably *p*, before *l* and *r*, in *block, braigh*, and a multitude of words in all the modern languages; and probably, the same letter is a prefix in many Shemitic words.

We know that *be* in the Saxon *bedælan*, and Dutch *bedeelen*, is a prefix, as the simple verb is found in all the Teutonic and Gothic languages. The Hebrew and Chaldee בדל corresponds exactly in elements and in signification, with the Saxon and Dutch. Whether the first letter is a prefix in the latter languages, let the reader judge. See the word *deal*, which when traced, terminates in the Welsh *tawl*, a cast off, a throw; separation; *tawlu*, to cast or throw off, to separate.

In Chaldee, בדר signifies to scatter, to disperse. The word has the same signification in the Syriac and Samaritan.

In Ethiopic, the word with አ prefixed, signifies to wish, love, desire, and with ተ prefixed, to strive, to endeavor, and without a prefix, strife, course, race. Both these significations are from stretching, straining.

In Arabic بَدَرَ signifies generally to hasten, to run to; but بَذَرَ signifies to disperse, to sow or scatter seed.

This verb is written in Hebrew בזר with precisely the same signification. The Arabic also has the verb with this orthography, signifying to sow, and also to beat or strike with a stick.

Now in Syriac ܕܪ, dar, signifies to strive, or struggle. Here we have the simple verb, *without* the prefix, with the sense of the Ethiopic, *with* a prefix. Supra.

We find also the Arabic ذَرَّ tharra, the simple verb, signifies to sprinkle.

We find in Chaldee דרא, דרה and דרר, the simple verb, signifies to disperse; in Syriac, the same. In Arabic ذَرَا signifies to sow, like the foregoing verb, and hence to procreate. Both this and the former verb signify also to whiten, as the hair of the head, as we say, to *sprinkle* with gray hairs. The Arabic دَرَا signifies to drive, to impel, to repel, to contend, to strive; to shine, to sparkle. And here we have the literal signification of this whole class of verbs; to drive, urge, throw, send; hence to scatter, to strive, to shoot as rays of light, procreate, &c.

The Hebrew corresponding verb is זרה or זרע to scatter, to sow; and the word with the like orthography occurs in Ch. Syr. and Ar. This is the Latin *sero*. And who can doubt that ב is a prefix in the verb בדר above mentioned?

In Welsh, *goberu* signifies to work, to operate; *gober*, work, operation; formed by the prefix *go* and *per; go* denoting progress towards, approach, and *per* rendered by Owen, that pervades, a fruit, a pear; but the real sense is to strain, to bring forth, to drive, thrust, urge, &c.

This word, in the Armoric dialect, is written either *gober* or *ober;* in Latin *operor*, whence Eng. *operate*. The same word is in the Ethiopic, ገብረ gaber, to make, to do. አገበረ agabar, to cause to be made; ተገበረ tagabar, to work, operate, negotiate; ገበረ gabar, a maker.

This is the Heb. and Ch. גבר to be strong, to prevail, to establish, and as a noun, a man; Ar. جَبَرَ jabara, to make strong, to heal, as a broken bone; to strengthen.

That this Shemitic word and the Welsh and Ethiopic are all radically one, there cannot be a question; and the Welsh proves indisputably that *go* is a prefix. This then is a word formed on בר or ברא. The Heb. אביר, strong, that is, strained, and אבר, a wing, that is, a shoot, are from the same root, and in Arabic أَبَرَ abara, signifies to prick, to sting, and its derivatives, the extremity of a thing, a point, a needle, corresponding with the Welsh *bar*, a summit, a tuft, a branch, a *bar*, and the Welsh *ber*, a pike, a lance, a spit, a *spear*, Lat. *veru*; in Welsh also, *pâr*, a spear, and *per*, a spit, are all doubtless of the same origin.

In Syriac, ܨܒܪ, *tsabar*, signifies to make, to work or operate. Is this the same root with a different prefix?

The same word in Arabic صَبَرَ signifies to be patient, to *bear*, to sustain.

We observe, that in the Teutonic and Gothic languages, the same word is used with different prefixes. Thus in our mother tongue, *begin* is written *gynnan*, the simple radical word, and *aginnan, beginnan*, and *ongynnan;* and in the Gothic, *duginnan*, which, in English, would be, *togin*.

Should it appear upon investigation, that verbs in the Assyrian languages have the same prefixes which occur in the European languages, the fact will evidence more affinity between the languages of these two stocks than has yet been known to exist.

Let us now attend to the natural causes which may be supposed to have obscured or destroyed the identity or resemblance of languages which had a common origin.

The affinity of words, in two or more different languages, is known by identity of letters and identity of signification; or by letters of the same organ, and a signification obviously deducible from the same sense. Letters of the same organ, as for example, *b, f, p* and *v* are so easily converted, the one into the other, and the change is so frequent, that this circumstance seldom occasions much obscurity. The changes of signification occasion more difficulty, not so much by necessity, as because this branch of philology is less understood.

1. CHANGE OF ARTICULATIONS, OR CONSONANTS.

The articulations, letters which represent the junctions or joinings of the organs, usually called consonants, are the stamina of words. All these are convertible and frequently converted into their cognates. The English word *bear* represents the Latin *fero* and *pario*, and *fero* is the Greek φερω. The Latin *ventus* is *wind* in English; and *habeo* is *have*. The Latin *dens*, in Dutch, Danish and Swedish is *tand;* and *dance* in English is in German *tanz*.

These changes are too familiar to require a multiplication of examples. But there are others less common and obvious, which are yet equally certain. Thus in the Gaelic or Hiberno-Celtic, *m* and *mb* are convertible with *v;* and in Welsh *m* and *v* are changed, even in different cases of the same word. Thus in Irish the name of the hand in written either *lamh* or *lav*, and in Welsh *maen*, a stone, is written also *vaen*. The Greek β is always pronounced *as* the English *v*, as βουλομαι, Lat. *volo*, English *will*, German *wollen;* and the sound of *b* the Greeks express by μβ.

In the Chaldee and Hebrew, one remarkable distinction is the use of a dental letter in the former, where the latter has a sibilant. As כות cuth in Chaldee is כוש cush in Hebrew; דהב, gold, in Chaldaic, is זהב in Hebrew. The like change appears in the modern languages; for *water* which, in most of the northern languages, is written with a dental, is, in German, written *wasser*, and the Latin *dens*, W. *dant*, Dutch *tand*, Swedish and Danish *tand*, is, in German, *zahn*. The like change is frequent in the Greek and Latin. Φραττω, in one dialect, is φρασσω, in another; and the Latins often changed *t* of the indicative present, or infinitive, into *s* in the preterit and participle, as *mitto, mittere, misi, missus*.

L and *R*, though not considered as letters of the same organ, are really such and changed the one into the other. Thus the Spaniards write *blandir* for *brandish*, and *escolta* for *escort*. The Portuguese write *brando* for *bland*, and *branquear*, to whiten, for *blanch*. The Greek has φραγελλιον for the Latin *flagellum*. In Europe however this change seems to be limited chiefly to two or three nations on the coast of the Mediterranean. *L* is sometimes commutable with *D*.

We have a few instances of the change of *g* or *gh* into *f*. Thus *rough* is pronounced *ruf*, and *trough, trauf*.

The Russians often change the *d* of a noun into the sound of *j*, or the compound *g*, in the verb formed from that noun; as *lad*, accord, harmony, *laju*, to accord, or agree; *bred*, damage, loss; *breju*, to injure.

The Italians and French have also changed a dental into a palatal letter, in many words; as Italian *raggio*, a ray, from Lat. *radius;* and *ragione*, reason, from *ratio;* Fr. *manger*, to eat, from Lat. *mando*, or *manduco*.

In the south of Europe, the Greek χ has been changed, in some instances, into the Italian or Spanish *z*, and then by the French into *s*. It seems that the Spanish *z* has, at some former period, been pronounced as a guttural. Thus the Gr. βραχιων, Lat. *brachium*, the arm, is in Spanish *brazo*, and the Spaniards have the word from the Latin, or from the same source as the Latin and Greek, the Celtic *braiç*. This word, *brazo*, the French changed into *bras*, and from that we have *brace* and *embrace*. A similar change occurs in *Durazzo*, from *Dyrrachium*, and in the Spanish *luz*, light.

The Teutonic nations often used *h* to express the power of the Greek κ, and the Latin *c*, as *heart* for καρδια, *horn* for *cornu*. Hence we find that the Saxon *hlinian, hleonian* or *hlynian*, to lean, is the Greek κλινω, Latin *clino*. The letter *h* is now dropped and we write the word *lean*.

In like manner, the Saxon *hlid*, which we now write *lid*, is from the same root as the Latin *claudo, cludo*, the Greek κλειδοω, which is contracted into κλειω. And in this word we may notice another fact, that the word signifies not only to shut, but to praise or celebrate, proving that this word and the Latin *plaudo*, are the same, with different prefixes, the same as *laudo*, and that the primary sense is to *strain*. This in Saxon appears in *hlud*, loud, *hlydan*, to cry out.

In Latin, *f* and *h* have been converted, as *hordeum* for *fordeum;* and the Spaniards now write *h* for *f*, as *hacer* for the Latin *facere; hilo* for *filum; herir* for *ferire*, &c.

2. CHANGE OF VOWELS.

The change of vowels is so common, as to occasion no difficulty in determining the sameness of words; indeed little or no regard is to be had to them, in ascertaining the origin and affinity of languages. In this opinion I accord with almost all writers on this subject; but I have to combat the opinion of that elegant scholar, Sir William Jones, who protests against the licentiousness of etymologists, not only in transposing letters, but in *totally disregarding the vowels*, and seems to admit the common origin of words only when written with the same letters, and used in a sense precisely the same.*

---

* Asiatic Researches, vol. 3, p. 489.

INTRODUCTION.

I am not at all surprised at the common prejudice existing against etymology. As the subject has been treated, it is justly liable to all the objections urged against it. But it is obvious that Sir W. Jones had given very little attention to the subject, and that some of its most common and obvious principles had escaped his observation. His opinion with regard to both articulations and vowels is unequivocally erroneous, as will appear from the following list of words, taken from modern languages, and respecting the identity of which, that gentleman himself, if living, could not have the slightest doubt.

ENGLISH.	SAXON.	DUTCH.	GERMAN.	SWEDISH.	LATIN.
draw, drag,	dragan,	trekken,	tragen,	draga,	traho.
give,	gifan,	geeven,	geben,	gifva,	
foot, feet,	fot, fet,	voet,	fuss,	fot,	pes. Gr. πους.
hook,	hoc,	haak,	haken,	hake,	
day,	dag, dæg,	daag,	tag,	dag,	
have,	habban,	hebben,	haben,	hafva,	habeo.
	[Fr. avoir, ai, as, a, avons, avez, ont.]				
leap,	hleapan,	loopen,	laufen,	löpa.	
burn,	byrnan,	branden,	brennen,	brinna,	
will,	willan,	willen,	wollen,	willja,	volo, velle.
stone,	stan,	steen,	stein,	sten,	
broad,	bred,	breed,	breit,	bred,	
earth,	eorth,	aarde,	erde,	jord, Dan. *iord.*	
who,	hwa,	wie,		ho, Dan. hvo.	
seek,	secan,	zoeken,	suchen,	söka,	sequor.
bean,	bean,	boon,	bohne,	böna, Dan. bönne.	

Here are scarcely two words written with the same letters in two languages; and yet no man ever called in question their identity, on account of the difference of orthography. The diversity is equally great in almost all other words of the same original. So in the same words we often find the vowel changed, as in the Lat. *facio, feci; ago, egi; sto, steti; vello, vulsi.* Nothing is more certain than that the Welsh *gwyz*, and the English *wood*, are the same word, although there is one letter only common to them both. It is pronounced *gooyth*, that is, *g*, and *wyth;* as *guard* for *ward*.

3. CHANGE OR LOSS OF RADICAL LETTERS.

There are some words, which, in certain languages, have suffered a change of a radical letter; while in others it is wholly lost. For example, *word*, in Danish and Swedish is *ord; wort*, a plant, is *urt;* the Saxon *gear*, or *ger*, English *year*, in Danish is *aar*, in Swedish is *år*, in Dutch *jaar*, and in German *jahr*.

In the word, *yoke*, and its affinities, we have a clear and decisive example of changes in orthography. *Yoke*, the Latin *jugum*, is from the Chaldee, Syriac, and Arabic זוג, zug, to join, to couple; a word not found in the Hebrew. The Greeks retained the original letters in ζυγος, ζυγοω; the Latins changed the first letter to *j* in *jugum*, and inserted a casual *n* in *jungo*. From the Latin, the Italians formed *giogo*, a yoke, and *giugnere*, to join; the Spaniards, *yugo*, a yoke, and *juntar*, to join; the French, *joug*, a yoke, and *joindre*, to join. In Saxon, *yoke* is *geoc* or *ioc;* in Dutch, *juk;* G. *joch;* Sw. *ok*.

One of the most general changes that words have undergone is the entire loss of the palatal letter *g*, when it is radical and final in verbs; or the opening of that articulation to a vowel or diphthong. We have examples in the English *bow*, from Saxon *bugan*, to bend; *buy*, from *bycgan; brow*, from *breg; lay*, from *lægan*, or *lecgan; say*, from *sægan; fair*, from *fæger; flail*, from the German *flegel*, Lat. *flagellum;* French *nier*, from Lat. *nego, negare*.

The same or similar changes have taken place in all the modern languages of which I have any knowledge.

The loss and changes of radical letters in many Greek verbs deserve particular notice. We find in the Lexicons, πραγμα, πραγος, πρακτικος, are referred to πρασσω, πραττω, as the theme or root; ταγμα, to τασσω; ρητωρ, to ρεω; and φραγμα, to φρασσω. This reference, so far as it operates as a direction to the student where to find the verb to which the word belongs, and its explanation, is useful and necessary. But if the student supposes that these words are formed from the theme, so called, or the first person of the indicative mode, present tense, he is deceived. I am confident no example can be found, in any language, of the palatals γ and κ, formed from the dentals and sibilants, τ and σ, nor is ρητωρ, or any similar word formed by the addition of the dental to a verb ending in a vowel. The truth is, the last radical in ρεω is lost, in the indicative mode, and in πρασσω, πραττω, it is changed. The radical lost in ρεω is δ or θ; the original word was ρεδω or ρεθω, and the derivatives ρητωρ, ρητορικη, were formed before the radical letter was dropped in the verb. No sooner is the verb restored to its primitive form, than we recognize its connection with the Irish *raidham*, to speak; Saxon *ræd*, speech; *rædan*, to read; German *rath*, Dutch *raad*, &c.

The original root of πρασσω, was πραγω, πραχω, or πρακω, and from this were formed πραγμα, πρακτικος, before the last radical was changed. No sooner is the original orthography restored, than we see this to be the Teutonic verb, German *brauchen*, Dutch *gebruiken*, Danish *bruger*, Sw. *bruka*, Sax. *brucan*, to use, to *practice*, and hence the English *broker*.

The same remarks are applicable to ταγμα and τασσω; φραγμα and φρασσω; αλλαγη and αλλασσω; χαρακτηρ and χαρασσω, and many other words of like formation. In all these cases, the last radical letter is to be sought in the *derivatives* of the verb, and in one of the past tenses, particularly in an aorist. This fact affords no feeble evidence that in Greek, as in the Shemitic languages, the preterit tense or an aorist, was the radix of the verb.*

But it is not in the Greek language only that we are to seek for the primitive radical letters, not in what is now called the root of the verb, but in the derivatives. The fact is the same in the Latin, and in the English. The Latin *fluctus* and *fluxi*, cannot be deduced from *fluo;* but the orthography of these words proves demonstrably that the original root was *flugo*, or *fluco*. So in English *sight* cannot be deduced from *see*, for no example can be found of the letter *g* introduced to form the participles of verbs. *Sight*, in Saxon *gesicht*, D. *zigt*, G. *sicht*, Dan. *sigt*, Sw. *sickt*, is a participle; but the verb in the infinitive, in Saxon is *seon, geseon*, Ger. *sehen*, D. *zien*, Dan. *seer*, Sw. *se;* in which no palatal letter is found, from which *g* or *ch* can be deduced. The truth then is that the original verb was *segan*, or in Dutch *zegen;* the *g* being lost as it is in the French *nier*, from the Lat. *nego*.

In the change of letters in the Greek verbs before mentioned, the process seems to have been from γ or κ to ξ, and then to σ and *t*; πραγω, πραξω, πρασσω, πραττω. This is certainly a process which is natural and common. The Latin *brachium* thus became in Spanish *brazo*, and then in French *bras;* and thus in the Italian, *Alexandria* has become *Alessandria*.

When the last radical of a Greek verb is a dental, it may not be certain whether the original letter was *d*, or *th* or *t*. We find the Greek verb σπαω, to draw, forms its derivatives with σ, σπασμα, σπασις; and this is probably the Armoric *spaza*, from which we have *spay*. So φραζω, φρασις, and φραδη, are evidently of the same family. It is not improbable that the original letter might have a compound sound, or it might correspond nearly to the Arabic ظ or ض, or the English *dh* or *th*, or *ds*, so as easily to pass into *d* or into *s*.

It is equally clear that many Greek words have lost an initial consonant. The letter most generally lost is probably the oriental ח, but obviously the palatals, γ and κ, have, in many instances, been dropped. There seems to be no question that the Greek ολος is the English *whole* and perhaps *all*. This in Welsh is *oll* or *holl*, in Saxon *al* or *geall;* and this is undoubtedly the Shemitic כל. So the Gr. ολλυμι is the Welsh *colli*, to lose; and ειλεω may be the English *coil*, Fr. *cueillir*.

In like manner, the Greek has, in many words, lost a labial initial, answering to the English *b, f* or *v*. The Greek ειδω is undoubtedly the Latin *video;* εργον is from the same root as *work;* ιδιος is from the root of *vid*, in the Latin *divido*, and *individuus*, that is, separate, and from the Arabic, بدّ badda, to separate.

In many instances, the Latin retained or restored the lost letter; thus *hamaxa*, for αμαξα; *harpago* for αρπαγη; *harmonia* for αρμονια; *video* for ειδω.

If the marks of breathing, called spiritus asper and spiritus lenis, now prefixed to Greek words, were intended to represent the letters lost, or to stand in the place of them, they answer this purpose very imperfectly. The spiritus asper may stand for a palatal or guttural letter, but it does not designate which letter, the ח, or the כ; much less does this or the other spiritus justly represent the labials, *b, f, v* or *w*. Whenever the Latins wrote *h* in the place of the Greek spiritus, we may conclude that the original letter was ח or a cognate letter; and we may conclude also that the *v* in *video*, and in *divido, viduus, individuus*, stands for the original labial lost in ειδω, and ιδιος. But there are many words, I apprehend, in which the lost letter is unknown, and in which the loss cannot be recovered, by any marks prefixed to the words. We may well suppose that *hymnus* exhibits the correct written form of υμνος; but what is there in the Greek υφη, to lead us to consider this word as the English *woof*, and υφαω, to be the same as *weave?* Both the Greek words have the spiritus asper.

What proportion of Greek words have been contracted by the loss of an initial or final consonant, cannot, I apprehend, be determined with any precision; at least, not in the present state of philological knowledge. It is probable the number of contracted words amounts to one fourth of all the verbs, and it may be more.

Similar contractions have taken place in all other languages; a circumstance that embarrasses the philologist and lexicographer at every step of his researches; and which has led to innumerable mistakes in Etymology. We know that the Swedish *år*, and Danish *aar*, a year, have lost the articulation *g*, and that the English *y* in *year*, is the representative of *g*, as *j* is in the Dutch *jaar*, and German *jahr:* for the *g* is found in our mother tongue; and in a multitude of words, one language will supply the means of deter-

---

* Κραζω, in Greek, is to cry like a crow or rook; but the last radical is changed from γ, as in the second aorist, it forms κραγεις. Now in Danish, *crow* is *krage*, in Ger. *krähe*, in D. *kraai*, in Sw. *kråka;* a fact that demonstrates the last radical letter to be a palatal, which in English is opened to *o*, in *crow*.

mining the real origin or true orthography which cannot be ascertained by another. But doubtless many changes have taken place of which the evidence is uncertain; the chain which might conduct us to the original orthography being broken, and no means now remaining of repairing the loss.

In no language, has the rejection or change of consonants served so effectually to obscure the original words as in the French. So extensive have been the changes of orthography in that language, that had not the early lexicographers indicated the loss of letters by a mark, it would be impossible now to discover the original orthography, or to trace the connection of words with other languages, in a large portion of them. And it is with regret we observe the influence of the French practice of suppressing consonants, extending itself to other countries. It is owing to the most servile obsequiousness of nations, that *Basil* or *Basilea*, the elegant name of a town in Switzerland, has been corrupted to *Basle*, and pronounced most barbarously *bale*. The Germans are pursuing a like course in suppressing the palatal letters; a most unfortunate circumstance for the strength of the language.

The Italians also have a disposition to reject letters when they interfere with their habits of pronunciation, and hence we see, in their language, *piano*, written for *plano; fiore* for *flore; fiocco* for *flocco;* a change that has removed a radical consonant, and thus obscured or rather destroyed the affinity between the Italian and the Latin words.

Another difference of writing and pronouncing, has been produced by the change of a sibilant letter into an aspirate: or e converso, by the change of an aspirate into a sibilant. No person doubts whether the Latin *super* is the Greek υπερ; or ομαλος is *similis;* or αλς is *sal, salt.* The latter in Welsh is *halen, hal.* So *helyg*, a willow, in Welsh, is in Latin *salix.* The Greek επτα is the Latin *septem*, English *seven.* This in Persic is هفت heft or haft, which approaches the Greek επτα. It has been commonly supposed, that in this case, the aspirate in Greek has been converted into an *s.* There are however strong reasons for believing that the change has been the reverse, and that *s* has been dropped, and its place supplied by an aspirate. The word *seven* is, beyond a question, the Shemitic سبع, שבע, whence שבת, Eng. *sabbath;* and the Gaelic *sean*, old, whence Latin *senex*, in Welsh *hen*, seems clearly to be the Ar. سن sanna, to be old. It is then clear that in these words *s* is radical. It is probable however that the aspirate, in some cases, has been changed into *s.*

It deserves to be noticed that the radix of a word is sometimes obscured, in Greek and Latin, by the loss or change of a radical letter in the nominative case. We find in Latin *nepos*, in the nominative, is *nepotis* in the genitive; *honos, honoris*, &c. In these changes, I suppose the letter restored in the oblique cases to be the true radical letter. Thus *adamant* has been deduced by our etymologists from the Greek *a* negative and δαμαω, to subdue, on the supposition that the stone was named from its hardness. This is a good example of a great part of all etymological deductions; *they are mere conjectures.* It did not occur to the inquirer that *adamas*, in the nominative, becomes in the gentive *adamantis;* that *n* is radical, and that this word cannot be regularly deduced from the Greek verb. Any person, by looking into a Welsh dictionary, may see the original word.

In some words it is not easy to determine whether *n* before *d* is casual or radical. In such words as the Latin *fundo*, to pour, and *tundo*, to beat, there is reason to think the *n* is casual, for the preterit is formed without it, *fudi, tutudi.* But in other words *n* before *d* seems to be radical, and the *d* casual; as in *fundo, fundare*, to found. For this word coincides with the Irish *bun*, foundation, and with the Shemitic בנה, banah, to build. So the English *find* is in Swedish *finna*, and *in* is in Danish *ind.*

Another fact of considerable consequence, is, the casual sound of *n* given to *g*, which produced the effect of doubling the γ in Greek, and of occasioning the insertion of *n* before *g* in the Latin, as also in the Teutonic and Gothic languages. Thus we see the γ is doubled in the Greek αγγελλω, and we know, in this case, how the change originated; for the original word is in the Gaelic and Irish, *agalla.* So γ is prefixed to another palatal or guttural letter in αγχω, ογχος, εγγιζω.

A similar nasal sound of *g* probably introduced the *n* before *g* in *lingo*, to *lick; linquo*, to leave.

We may be confident, in all cases, that *n* is not radical, when it is dropped in the supine and participle, as in *lictum, lictus*, from *linquo.* When *n* is retained in the supine and participle, there may be more reason for doubt; but in this case, the question may often be determined by the corresponding word in another language, or by some other word evidently of the same family. Thus we can have little doubt that *lingo* and the English *lick* are the same word, or that the Lat. *lingua* and *ligula* are of one family.

This casual insertion of *n* in words of this class must be carefully noticed by the etymologist, or he will overlook the affinity of words, which are evidently the same. We have many words in English which are written with *n* before a *g* or a *k*, when the ancient words in the Gothic and Teutonic languages, and some of them in the modern Danish and Swedish, are written without *n.* Thus *sink*, in Gothic is *sigcwan;* to think, is *thagkyan.* It is not improbable that the Gothic word was pronounced with the sound of *n* or *ng* as in English. So also in *sigguah*, to sing; *laggs*, long. In a few instances, we find the Swedes and Danes have the word written in both ways, as *tånka, tænker* and *tycka, tykker*, to think. But in general the Germans, Danes, Swedes and Dutch write words of this sort with *ng.*

To show how important it is to know the true original orthography, I will mention one instance. In our mother tongue, the word to *dye*, or color, is written *deagan;* the elements or radical letters are *dg.* To determine whether this and the Latin *tingo* are the same words, we must first know whether *n* in *tingo* is radical or casual. This we cannot know with certainty, by the form of the word itself, for the *n* is carried through all the tenses and forms of the verb. But by looking into the Greek, we find the word written with γ, τεγγω; and this clearly proves the alliance of the word with *deagan.* See *Dye* in the Dictionary.

We have many English words, in which a *d* has been inserted before *g*, as in *badge, budge, lodge, pledge, wedge.* In all words, I believe, of this class, the *d* is casual, and the *g* following is the radical letter, as *pledge* from the French *pleige; wedge* from the Saxon *wecg.* The practice of inserting *d* in words of this sort seems to have originated in the necessity of some mode of preserving the English sound of *g*, which might otherwise be sounded as the French *g* before *e.* And it is for this reason we still retain, and ought to retain *d* in *alledge, abridge.* In like manner the Teutonic *c* has been changed into the sound of *ch*, as Sax. *wacian, wæcian*, to wake, to *watch;* Sax. *thac*, thatch.

There are some nations which, in many words, pronounce and write *g* before *u* or *w;* as in the French *guerre*, for *war; guede*, for *woad; guetter.* for *wait:* in Welsh, *gwal*, for *wall; gwain*, for *wain; gwared*, for *guard*, which in English is *ward*, Sp. *guarda.* In some instances, the *u* or *w* is dropped in modern writing, as in the French *garenne*, a *warren: garde*, for *guard.* This difference of orthography makes it difficult, in some cases, to ascertain the true radical letters.

CHANGE OF SIGNIFICATION.

Another cause of obscurity in the affinity of languages, and one that seems to have been mostly overlooked, is, the change of the primary sense of the radical verb. In most cases, this change consists in a slight deflection, or difference of application, which has obtained among different families of the same stock. In some cases, the literal sense is lost or obscured, and the figurative only is retained. The first object, in such cases, is to find the primary or literal sense, from which the various particular applications may be easily deduced. Thus, we find in Latin, *libeo, libet*, or *lubeo, lubet*, is rendered, to please, to like; *lubens*, willing, glad, cheerful, pleased; *libenter, lubenter*, willingly, gladly, readily. What is the primary sense, the visible or physical action, from which the idea of *willing* is taken? I find, either by knowing the radical sense of *willing, ready*, in other cases, or by the predominant sense of the elements *lb*, as in Lat. *labor*, to slide, *liber*, free, &c. that the primary sense is to move, incline or advance towards an object, and hence the sense of willing, ready, prompt. Now this Latin word is the English *love*, German *lieben, liebe.* "Lubet me ire." I *love* to go; I am inclined to go; I go with cheerfulness; but the affinity between *love* and *lubeo* has been obscured by a slight difference of application, among the Romans and the Teutonic nations.

Perhaps no person has suspected that the English words *heat, hate* and *hest*, in *behest*, are all radically the same word. But this is the fact. Sax. *hatian*, to heat, or be hot, and to hate; *hætan*, to heat and to call; *hatan*, to call, to order, to command; *ge-hætan* or *gehatan*, to grow warm, to promise, to vow; Gothic, *gahaitan*, to call, to promise; Dutch, *heeten*, to heat, to name, to call, bid or command; German, *heitzen*, to heat; *heissen*, to call; *hitzen*, to heat, to hoist; Swedish, *hetsa*, to inflame, to provoke; Danish, *heder*, to heat, to be called. *Behest*, we have from the German or Swedish dialect. *Heat* coincides with the Latin *æstus* for *hæstus*, which is written with *s*, like the German. *Hate* coincides with the Latin *odi, osus*, so written for *hodi, hosus*, and as the Teutonic *h* often represents the Latin *c*, as in *horn, cornu*, the Danish orthography *heder*, coincides with the Latin *cito*, to call. Now what is the radical sense? Most obviously to stir, agitate, rouse, raise, implying a driving or impulse; and hence in Latin *æstuo*, to be hot, and to rage or storm; hence to *excite*, and hence the sense of the Latin *cito*, quickly, from stirring, rousing to action. In this case *hatred*, as well as *heat*, is violent excitement. We find also in the Saxon and Gothic the sense of vowing, that is, of driving out the voice, uttering, declaring, a sense allied to calling and commanding, and to this is allied the sense of the Latin *recito*, to *recite.*

In English *befall* signifies to fall on, to happen to; in German the same word, *befallen*, has the like signification. But in Saxon *gefeallan* signifies to fall, to rush on, while in German *gefallen* signifies to please, that is, to suit, to come to one's mind, to be agreeable. The Danish *gefalder* has the same signification as the German.

We find by the Saxon, that the English *reck*, to care, and *reckon*, and the Latin *rego*, to rule, are all the same word, varied in orthography and application. To find the primary sense of *reck*, to care, we are then to examine the various derivative senses. And we need go no farther than to the Latin *rectus* and English *right*, the sense of which is *straight*, for this sense is derived from *straining, stretching. Care* then is a *straining of the mind,* a stretching towards an object, coinciding with the primary sense of *attention*. The primary sense of *reckon* is to strain out sounds, to speak, tell, relate; a sense now disused.

The Saxon *carc*, care, *cærcian*, to care, to cark, is connected in origin with the Latin *carcer*, a prison; both from the sense of straining, whence holding or restraint.

To prove how the primary general sense of a word may ramify into different senses, by special appropriation of the word among separate families of men proceeding from the same stock, let us observe the different senses in which *leap* is used by the English, and by the nations on the continent. In English, to *leap* is simply to spring; as, to *leap* a yard; to *leap* over a fence. But on the continent it signifies to *run*. Now it will be seen that this word as used by the Germans cannot always be translated by itself, that is, by the same word, into English. Take for illustration the following passage from Luther's Version of the Scriptures. 1. Sam. xvii. 17. "Nimm für deine brüder diese epha sangen, und diese zehen brod, und *lauf* ins heer zu deinen brüdern." "Take now for thy brethren an ephah of this parched corn, and these ten loaves, and *leap* to the camp to thy brethren." *Leap*, instead of *run*, is good German, but bad English.* There are two other words in this passage, of which a like remark may be made. The German *brod*, loaves, is our *bread*, which admits of no plural; and *sangan* is our *singed*, which we cannot apply to parched corn.

So in some of the Teutonic languages, to *warp* kittens or puppies, to *warp* eggs, is correct language, though to our ears very odd; but this is only a particular application of the primary sense, to *throw*. We say to *lay* eggs, but to *lay* is to *throw* down.

By this comparison of the different uses and applications of a word, we are able, in most cases, to detect its original signification. And it is by this means, I apprehend, that we may arrive at a satisfactory explanation of the manner in which the same word came to have different and even opposite significations.

It is well known, for example, that the Hebrew word ברך, is rendered, in our version of the Scriptures, both to *bless* and to *curse*. The propriety of the latter rendering is controverted by Parkhurst, who labors to prove, that in Kings and in Job, where it is rendered, to *curse*, it ought to be rendered, to *bless;* and he cites, as authorities, the ancient versions. It is true that in 1 Kings xxi. 10. 13; and in Job i. 11, and ii. 5, the seventy have rendered the word by ευλογεω, to bless; and other ancient versions agree with the Septuagint. But let the word be rendered by *bless* in the following passages. "Put forth thy hand now, and touch his bone, and his flesh, and he will *bless* thee to thy face." "*Bless* God and die." How very absurd does such a translation appear. It shows the immense importance of understanding the true theory of language, and the primary sense of radical words. Let us then endeavor to discover, if possible, the source of the difficulty in the case here mentioned. To be enabled to arrive at the primary sense, let us examine the word in the several languages, first, of the Shemitic, and then of the Japhetic stock.

Heb. ברך To bless; to salute, or wish a blessing to.
2. To curse; to blaspheme.
3. To couch or bend the knee, to kneel.
Deriv. A blessing, and the knee.

Chaldee, ברך To bless; to salute at meeting, and to bid farewell at parting.
2. To bend the knee.
3. To dig; to plow; to set slips of a vine or plant for propagation. *Talm.* and *Rabbin.*
Deriv. The knee; a blessing; a cursing; a cion; the young of fowls.

Syriac, ܒܪܟ To fall on the knees; to fall or bow down. Judg. v. 27.
2. To issue or proceed from. Math. xv. 19.
3. To bless.

Samaritan, ࠁࠓࠊ To bless.

Ethiopic, ባረከ To bless. Deriv. the knee.

Arabic, برك To bend the knee; to fall on the breast, as a camel.
2. To be firm, or fixed.
3. To rain violently; to pour forth rain, as the clouds. Gr. βρεχω.
4. To detract from; to traduce; to *reproach* or pursue with reproaches; to revile.
5. To bless; to pray for a blessing on; to prosper; to be blessed.
6. To hasten; to rush, as on an enemy; to assail.
Deriv. The breast; the bason of a fountain; a fish pond, or receptacle of water, as in Heb. and Ch.: also increase; abundance; constancy; splendor; a flash of light.

In the latter sense, usually from برق Heb. and Ch. ברק.

The Arabic word supplies us with the certain means of determining the radical sense; for among other significations, it has the sense of pouring forth rain; and this is precisely the Greek βρεχω. The primary sense then is to send, throw, or drive, in a transitive sense; or in an intransitive sense, to rush, to break forth.

To *bless* and to *curse* have the same radical sense, which is, to send or pour out words, to drive or to strain out the voice, precisely as in the Latin *appello*, from *pello*, whence *peal*, as of thunder or of a bell. The *two* senses spring from the *appropriation* of loud words to express particular acts. This depends on usage, like all other particular applications of one general signification. The sense in Scripture is to utter words either in a good or bad sense; to bless, to salute, or to rail, to scold, to *reproach;* and this very word is probably the root of *reproach*, as it certainly is of the Latin *precor*, used, like the Shemitic word, in both senses, *praying* and *cursing*, or deprecating.* It is also the same word as the English *pray*, It. *pregare*, L. *precor*, the same as *preach*, D. *preeken*, W. *pregethu*. To the same family belong the Gr. βραχω, βρυχω, βρυχαομαι, to *bray*, to roar, to low, Lat. *rugio*. Here we see that *bray* is the same word, applied to the voice of the ass and to breaking in a mortar, and both are radically the same word as *break*.

The sense of kneeling, if radical, is to throw, and if from the noun, the sense of the noun is a throwing, a bending.

The Chaldee sense of digging, if radical, is from thrusting in an instrument, or *breaking* the ground; but perhaps it is a sense derived from the name of a shoot or cion, and in reality, to set a shoot, to plant.

The Syriac use of this word in Matthew xv. 19, is intransitive, to issue, to shoot or break forth. So in Arabic, to rush on, to assault. The sense of firmness in Arabic is from setting, throwing down, as in kneeling; and hence the sense of breast, the fixed, firm part.

That this word has the sense both of blessing and of cursing or reproaching, we have demonstrative evidence in the Welsh language. *Rhêg*, in Welsh, is ברך, without the prefix. It signifies a sending out; utterance; a gift or present; a consigning; a ban, a curse or imprecation. *Rhegu*, to give; to consign; to curse. From *rhêg* is formed *preg*, a greeting, or salutation, [the very Hebrew and Chaldee word,] *pregeth*, a sermon, and *pregethu*, to preach. Here we have not only the origin of *preach*, but another important fact, that *preg*, and of course ברך, is a compound word, composed of a prefix, *p* or *b*, and *rhêg*. But this is not all; the Welsh *greg*, a cackling, *gregar*, to cackle, is formed with the prefix *g* on this same *rhêg*. [Dan. *krage*, a crow.]

In Welsh, *bregu* signifies to *break; brêg*, a breach, a rupture. This Owen deduces from *bar*, but no doubt erroneously. It is from *rhegu*, and there is some reason to think that *break* is from ברך, rather than from פרק, but probably both are from one radix, with different prefixes.

We observe one prominent sense of the Arabic برك baraka, is to rain violently; to pour forth water, as clouds. This is precisely the Greek βρεχω; a word found in all the Teutonic and Gothic languages, but written either with or without its prefix.

Saxon, *rægn* or *regn*, rain; *regnan*, to rain.
Dutch, *regen*, rain; *regenen*, *beregenen*, to rain upon.
German, *regen*, rain; *regnen*, to rain; *beregnen*, to rain on.
Swedish, *regna*, to rain.
Danish, *regn*, rain; *regner*, to rain.
Saxon, *racu*, rain; Cimbric, *rækia*, id.

Here we find that the English *rain*, is from the same root as the Welsh *rhêg*, *rhegu*, and the Shemitic ברך.

Pursuing the inquiry further, we find that the Saxon *recan*, or *reccan*, [W. *rhegu*,] signifies to speak, to tell, to relate, to *reckon*, the primary sense of which last is to speak or tell; also, to rule, which shows this to be the Latin *rego;* also to care, which is the English *reck*. That this is the same word as *rain*, we know from the Danish, in which language, *regner* signifies both to *rain* and to *reckon*, to tell, to count or compute. In the German, the words are written a little differently; *rechnen*, to reckon, and *regnen*, to rain. So in Dutch, *reekenen* and *regenen;* but this is a fact by no means uncommon.

Here we find that the English *reckon* and *reck*, and the Latin *rego*, are the same word. The primary sense is to strain, to *reach*, to *stretch*. Care is a *stretching* of the mind, like *attention*, from the Latin *tendo*, and restraint is the radical sense of governing. Hence *rectus*, *right*, that is, straight, stretched.

Hence we find that *rain* and the Latin *regnum*, *reign*, are radically the same word.

Now in Saxon *racan*, or *ræcan*, is the English *reach*, to stretch or extend, from the same root, and probably *reek*, Saxon *recan*, *reocan*, to fume or smoke; for this is, to send off.

I might have mentioned before, that the Chaldee בריכה, a cion or branch, is precisely the Celtic word for arm; Irish *braic*, or *raigh*; Welsh *braiç;* whence the Greek βραχιων, the Latin *brachium*, whence the Spanish *brazo*, whence the French *bras*, whence the English *brace*. The arm is a shoot, a branch, and *branch* is from this root or one of the family, *n* being casual; *branch* for *brach*.

* He walks, he leaps, he runs.—*Cowper*.

* "Improbus urget *iratis precibus*."—*Horace*.

INTRODUCTION.

On this word, let it be further observed, or on פרק or ברק, if radically different, are formed, with the prefix *s*, the German *sprechen*, to speak, *sprache*, speech; Dutch *spreeken, spraak;* Swedish *språka, språk;* Danish *sprog*, speech; and Swedish *spricka*, to *break;* Danish *sprekker.* The same word with *n* casual is seen in *spring*, the *breaking* or opening of the winter; and here we see the origin of the marine phrase, to *spring* a mast, Danish *springer*, to burst, crack or spring. This in Swedish is written without *n*, *spricka*, to *break*, burst, split; but a noun of this family has *n*, *springa*, a crack, and *spring*, a spring, a running.

Now let us attend to other Shemitic words consisting of cognate elements.

Chaldee, פרך To rub or scrape; to rub out or tread out, as grain from the ear or sheaf; Latin *frico, frio.*

2. To collect and bind, as sheaves; perhaps English, to *rake.*

3. To *break* or *break* down.

4. To question; to doubt. In Saxon and Gothic *frægnan, fragan*, signifies to ask.

Deriv. Froward; perverse. Prov. ii. 12. So in English *refractory.*

This verb is not in the Hebrew; but there are two derivatives, one signifying the inner vail of the temple; so called probably from its use in *breaking*, that is, interrupting access, or separation, like *diaphragm* in English. The other derivative is rendered *rigor*, or cruelty; that which strains, oppresses, breaks down, or *rakes*, harasses.

With this verb coincides the Irish *bracaim*, to *break*, to harrow, that is, to *rake.*

Syr. ܦܪܟ To rub, so rendered, Luke vi. 1. Lat. *frico.* A derivative signifies to comminute.

Deriv. Distortion; winding; twisting. *Let this be noted.*

Ar. فرك To rub, Lat. *frico.*

2. To hate, as a husband or wife; to be languid, or relaxed.

Deriv. Laxity; frangibility; friability.

Heb. פרק To *break*, burst, or rend; to break off; to separate.

Deriv. A *breaking* or parting of a road.

Ch. פרק To *break.*

2. To redeem, that is, to free, separate or deliver.

3. To explain, as a doubtful question.

Deriv. One who ransoms or delivers; a rupture; the neck or its juncture; a joint of the fingers, &c.; the ankle; the joint of a reed; a chapter, or section of a book; explanation; exposition. פרוק, a rupture, coinciding with the English *broke.*

Syr. ܦܪܩ To redeem.

2. To depart; to remove; to separate.

Deriv. A recess, or withdrawing; separation; liberation; redemption; safety; vertebra.

Sam. The same as the Syriac verb.

Ar. فرق to separate; to divide; to withdraw; to disperse, [qu. Lat. *spargo;*] to lay open; to disclose; to cast out; to immerse.

Deriv. Separation; distinction; distance; interval; dispersion; aurora, as we say, the *break* of day; also, a garment reaching to the middle of the thigh, qu. *frock;* also *breech.*

I have placed these two words together, because I am convinced they are both of one family, or formed on the same radical word. The latter coincides exactly with the Latin *frango, fregi, fractum*, for *n* in *frango*, is undoubtedly casual. Now in Welsh *bregu*, to *break*, would seem to be directly connected with ברך, yet doubtless *bregu* is the English *break*, the German *brechen*, the Dutch *breeken*, &c. In truth, the three words ברך, פרך and פרק are probably all from one primitive root, formed with different prefixes, or rather with the same prefix differently written; the different words bearing appropriate senses, among different tribes of men.

We observe in the Chaldee word the sense of questioning. Perhaps this may be the Gothic *fragan*, to ask, and if so, it coincides with the Latin *rogo*, the latter without the prefix. In the sense of *break*, we find, in the Greek, ρηγνυω, without a prefix.

Most of the significations of these verbs are too obvious to need illustration. But we find in the Syriac the sense of distortion, a sense which at first appears to be remote from that of *breaking* or *bursting asunder.* But this is probably the primary sense, to strain, to stretch, a sense we retain in the phrase, to *break* upon the wheel, and by dropping the prefix, we have the precise word in the verb, to *rack.*

Now if this is the genuine sense, we find it gives the English *wreck* and *wrack*, the Danish *vrag*, Sw. *vrak*, a wreck. In Saxon, *wræcan, wrecan*, is the English *wreak*, that is, to drive, or throw on; *wrace*, is an exile, a *wretch.* In Dan. *vrager* signifies to reject; Sw. *vråka*, to throw away; all implying a driving force, and that *wreck* is connected with *break* is probable for another reason, that the Latin *fractus, frango*, forms a constituent part of *naufragium*, the English *shipwreck*, which in Danish is simply *vrag.*

Now if *straining, distortion*, is one of the senses of this root, the English *wring, wrong*, Danish *vrang*, Sw. *vrång*, may be deduced from it, for undoubtedly *n* is not radical in these words. The Dutch have *wringen*, but the German drops the first letter and has *ringen*, both to twist or wind and to *ring* or sound; the latter sense from straining or throwing, as in other cases. Without *n*, *wring* would be *wrig*, and *wrong, wrog; wrang, wrag*, Dan. *vrag.*

In Greek, ρηγος is a blanket or coverlet, and connected with ρηγνυμι; that is, a spread, from stretching, or throwing over.

We find also among the Chaldee derivatives the sense of a neck, and a joint. Now we find this word in Irish, *braigh*, the neck; in Greek, without the prefix, ραχις, the spine of the back, Saxon, *hracca*, English, the *rack*, and from the Greek, the *rickets*, from distortion.

Coinciding with the Greek ρηγνυω, to break, we find in Welsh *rhwgaw*, to rend, and coinciding with ραχια, a *rock*, a *crag*, Welsh, *craig*, and connected with these, the Saxon *hracod*, English *ragged*, that is, broken; evidently the participle of a verb of this family.

Hence we find the senses of *distortion* and *breaking* connected in this root, in a great variety of instances.

The Shemitic ברק, to lighten, to shine or flash, is one of this family. The sense is to shoot or dart, to throw, as in all like cases. And under this root, the Arabic has the sense, to adorn, as a female; to make bright or shining; which gives the English *prank* and *prink*, D. *pragt*, G. *pracht. Prance* is of the same family, from leaping, starting, darting up.

In Greek βραχυς, short, stands in the Lexicons as a primary word or root. But this is from the root of *break*, which is lost in Greek, unless in ρηγνυμι, without the prefix. From βραχυς, or the root of this word, the French language has *abreger*, to *abridge*, and what is less obvious, but equally certain, is, that from the same root the Latin has *brevis*, by sinking the palatal letter, as we do in *bow*, from *bugan*, and in *lay*, from *lecgan;* so that *abridge* and *abbreviate, brief*, are from one root.

It should have been before mentioned that the Latin *refragor*, signifies to resist, to strive against, to deny, whence *refractory;* a sense that demonstrates the primary sense to be to strain, urge, press; and *refraction*, in optics, is a *breaking* of the direct course of rays of light by *turning* them; a sense coinciding with that of *distortion.*

We see then that one predominant sense of *break*, is, to strain, to distort. Let us now examine some of the biliteral roots in *rg* and *rk*, which, if *b* is a prefix, must be the primary elements of all the words above mentioned.

Ch. רגג To desire, to long for. This is the Greek ορεγω, and English to *reach;* for desire is expressed by reaching forward, stretching the mind towards the object. So in Latin *appeto*, and *expeto*, from *peto*, to move towards. This coincides nearly with the Latin *rogo*, to ask, and the Goth. *fragnan*, Sax. *frægnan.*

Syr. ܪܓ To desire; and with olaph prefixed, ܐܪܓ to desire, or long; also to wet or moisten; also ܪܓܐ to moisten—Latin *rigo, irrigo*, to irrigate.

Deriv. Tender, soft, fresh, from moisture or greenness. Qu. Lat. *recens*, a derivative.

Here *desire* and *irrigation* are both from one root; desire is a reaching forward, and irrigation is a spreading of water.

This root, in Hebrew ארג, signifies to weave, or connect as in texture and net work; but the primary sense is to stretch or strain.

In Arabic, the same verb أرج signifies to emit an agreeable smell; to breathe fragrance; radically to throw or send out; to eject; a mere modification of the same sense. This is the Latin *fragro*, whence *fragrant*, with a prefix; but according exactly with the English *reek.*

ארך in Ch. Heb. Syr. and Sam., signifies to prolong, to extend. In Ar. as in Heb. in Hiph. to delay, or retard; that is, to draw out in time.

רגע in Heb. has been differently interpreted; indeed, it has been rendered by words of directly contrary signification. The more modern interpreters, says Castle, render it, to split, divide, separate, or break; the ancient interpreters rendered it, to stiffen, to make rigid or rough, to wrinkle or corrugate. Castle and Parkhurst, however, agree in rendering it, in some passages, to quiet, still, allay. Jer. xlvii. 6. l. 34. In Job vii. 5. our translators have rendered it *broken*, my skin is *broken*, [rough, or rigid.] In Job. xxvi. 12. it is rendered by *divide.* "He divideth the sea by his power." In Vanderhooght's Bible it is in this place rendered by *commovet*—He agitates the sea. The Seventy render it by κατεπαυσε, he stilled; and this is the sense which Parkhurst gives it.

In Isaiah li. 15, and Jer. xxxi. 35, it is rendered in our version by *divide.* "But I am the Lord thy God, that *divided* the sea, whose waves roared."

In Vanderhooght's Bible it is rendered in Isaiah li. 15, "I am Jehovah thy God, *qui commovens mare*, ut perstrepant fluctus ejus." In Jer. xxxi. 35, *commovens mare*, ut tumultuenter fluctus—agitating or moving the sea, that the waves roar, or may roar. The passage in Isaiah is rendered by the seventy, οτι ο Θεος σου, ο ταρασσων την θαλασσαν, και ηχων τα κυματα αυτης, agitating the sea and causing its waves to roar and resound. In the French translation, the passage in Isaiah is "qui fend la mer, et ses flots bruient." [I] who divide the sea and the waves roar. In Jeremiah the passage is "qui agite la mer et les flots en bruient." Who agitates the sea and therefore the waves roar. In Italian, the passage in Isaiah is rendered "che muovo il mare, e le sue onde romoreggiano." In Jeremiah, "che commuove il mare, onde le sue onde romoreggiano." Who moveth the sea, wherefore its waves roar, or become tumultuous.

These different renderings show the importance of understanding the literal or primary sense of words ; for whatever may be the real sense in the passages above mentioned, it cannot be to *divide*. If we are give to vau in the following word, its usual sense of *and*, it is difficult to make sense of the word רגע, by translating it, *he stilleth: he stilleth the sea and its waves are tumultuous*, or he stilleth the sea that the waves may roar or be agitated ! This will not answer. The more rational version would be, he *roughens* the sea, and its waters roar, or he drives, impels it into agitation. In Ethiopic, the same word signifies to coagulate, to freeze, to become rigid ; and this is undoubtedly the Latin *rigeo*, and with a prefix, *frigeo*, and this signification is perhaps allied to Lat. *rugo*, to wrinkle ; for as a general rule, the radical sense of wrinkle is to draw, as in *contract*, *contraho*, and this seems to be the sense of *rigeo*. Both these words are allied to *rough*, which is from breaking or wrinkling. This sense would perhaps well suit the context in these two passages, as it would also that in Job vii. 5 : My skin is *rough*.

Now in Arabic, the general signification of רגע is to return, to repeat, to withdraw, which may be from drawing back ; a different application of the original sense, to strain, stretch, or extend.

The root רוק in Chaldee signifies to spit, and this is probably the Latin *ructo*, somewhat varied in application. The same verb in Arabic راق signifies to drive off, to reject, to shoot or grow long as teeth, to strain, purify or make clear as wine ; precisely the English to *rack ;* also to spread, and to pour out. Hebrew רק, to empty, to draw out, to attenuate or make thin, and as a noun, spittle ; Syriac, to spit, to draw out, to attenuate ; Samaritan, to pour out, to draw out, to extend ; Ethiopic, to be fine, slender, or thin ; Arabic, to be soft, tender, thin. The verb רך has a like signification, and is perhaps from the same original root. רקע Hebrew, to spread, stretch, extend. But, says Castle, all the ancient interpreters rendered the word, to ordain, establish, make firm ; to strike, to beat, as plates of metal. But the sense is to stretch, to spread, and the beating is only the means of extending. Hence רקיע the firmament, which agrees well with Lat. *regio*, an extent ; in Hebrew, properly an expanse. And to reconcile the ancient and modern interpretations of this word, let it be remembered that *strength* and *firmness* are usually or always from *stretching*, *tension*.

Now let us hear Ainsworth on the word *regio*. " Regio a *rego* quod priusquam provinciæ fierent, regiones sub regibus erant atque ab his regebantur." How much more natural is it to deduce *regio* from the primary sense of *rego*, which is to stretch, to strain, to extend ! *Regio* is an extent, a word of indefinite signification.

In Chaldee and Arabic this verb signifies to mend, to repair, to make whole, from extending spreading over or making strong. See the root כל infra.

We observe that רגג and רקע agree in original signification, with the English *reach*, on the root of which or some of its derivatives was formed *stretch*. That ברך, פרך and פרק were formed on any of the foregoing biliteral roots we may not be able to affirm ; but it is certain from the Welsh that the first consonant of the triliteral root is a prefix, and it is certain from the Shemitic languages that the primary sense is the same in the biliteral and triliteral roots, or that all the applications or particular significations may readily be deduced from one general signification.

To illustrate this subject more fully, let us attend to the various applications of some other Shemitic words of extensive use.

ברא.

Heb. ברא To create. This, by most lexicographers, is given as the first signification, in all the Shemitic languages. Parkhurst says, to create ; to produce into being. Gen. i. 1.

2. To form, by accretion or concretion of matter. Gen. i. 21.
3. In Hiph. To make fat ; to fatten or batten. 1 Sam. ii. 29.
4. To do or perform something wonderful. Num. xvi. 30.
5. In Niph. To be renewed. In Kal, to renew, in a spiritual sense. Ps. li. 12.

Castle says,

1. To create from nothing, or to produce something new or excellent from another thing. Gen. i. Is. xlii. 5.
2. In Niph. To be renewed or re-created. Is. xlviii. 7. Ps. cii. 19.
3. To cut off ; to take away ; to *bear* away, or remove ; also to select ; to prepare. Josh. xvii. 15. 18. Ezek. xxiii. 47.

Gesenius says,

1. Strictly, to hew, to hew out. [Ar. to cut, to cut out, to plane.]
2. To form ; to make ; to produce. Ar. برا The order of significations is, as in the Ar. خلق galaka, to be smooth, to make smooth. 2. To plane. 3. To form, make. Gen. i. 1. 21. 27.
1. Niph. passive of Kal. No. 2. Gen. ii. 4.
2. To be born. Ezek. xxi. 30. Ps. cii. 18.

Pi. ברא, the verb differently pointed, to hew, to cut down. Josh. xvii. 15. 18.
2. To cut down with the sword ; to kill. Ez. xxiii. 47.
3. To make fat. 1 Sam. ii. 29.

Thus far the Hebrew.

Chal. ברא To create. Gen. i. 1.
2. To cut off. Is. xl. 20.
3. To make fat ; to grow sound or strong. Talm.
Deriv. Fat ; whole ; sound ; strong. *Castle.*

Syr. ܒܪܐ To create. Gen. i. 1. Mark xiii. 19.
2. To remove to a distance, and Deriv. distance, distant. *Castle.*

Sam. ࠁࠓࠀ To create. Gen. i. 22. Deut. iv. 32. *Castle.*

Ar. برا To create. Job xxxviii. 7. [qu. 4 and 6.]
2. To be free, or guiltless, not obnoxious to punishment. Num. v. 28. 31, and xxxii. 22. Rom. vii. 6.
3. To free ; to absolve, from a crime ; to liberate ; to dismiss ; to justify. Ex. xx. 7. Num. xiv. 18.
4. To escape ; to forsake.
5. To recover from disease ; to be healed ; to restore to health. Lev. xiii. 18. Josh. v. 8. Math. iv. 23.
6. To cleanse ; to free from impurities.
7. To abstain from.
Deriv. Creator ; free ; unobnoxious ; clean ; empty.

Ar. برا To create.
2. To cut off ; to hew or *pare*.
3. To separate ; to distinguish.
4. To make thin.
5. To oppose ; to strive ; to resist.
6. To provoke ; to boast, or make a parade.
7. To distribute ; to disperse. *Castle.*

According to Gesenius, the primary sense of this verb is to *hew*, to *cut out*, and thus to make smooth, and thus to create ; and he deduces these senses in the same order, as he does those of the Arabic verb, which gives the word *like*. But there is no ground for this opinion ; and doubtless the verb originated before the use of edge tools.

The predominant senses of this word, are, to separate, to free, to remove ; as we see by the Arabic and Syriac.

Now *hewing* is indeed separating, and we have the English word *pare* from this root ; but we must seek for a signification which is more general than that of *paring*, or we shall not be able to account for the sense of making fat, sound, entire, and strong, nor for that of being born.

The truth undoubtedly is, this word is of the same family with the English *bear*, the Latin *pario*, and the radical sense is to *throw*, to *thrust*, to *send*, to *drive*, to *extend ;* hence to throw out, to produce, as applied to the birth of children or of the world. To *throw* or *drive*, is the primary sense of separation and division, that is, to drive off. The English word *deal*, when traced to its root, presents the same fact. See *Deal*. To *create*, is to *produce* or *bring forth*, the same sense as that of *birth*, applied to a different object. The sense of *hewing* and *paring* is from driving off, separation. In Syriac, we observe the general application, in *removal*, or *departure* to a distance. The sense of fattening is derivative, and allied to that of healing or making whole, sound, strong, in the Arabic, that is, preparing, bringing to a good state, or from tension, the usual primary sense of strength and power.

To obtain a more full and satisfactory view of this subject, let us attend to the same word in the modern languages of Europe.

LATIN.

Paro, to prepare, make ready, procure, design, &c. The radical sense of *paro* is probably the same as in the Shemitic languages ; to produce, to bring forward. So also *ready* implies an advancing, and so does *promptness*. But the various ways of preparing a thing for use naturally give to the word, in process of time, a variety of particular significations ; each of which results in bringing the thing to the state desired. The compounds of *paro*, are *apparo*, to prepare, to furnish, accouter or set out ; *comparo*, to prepare or procure, to make equal, to compare, to join, to dress or make ready ; *præparo*, to prepare ; *reparo*, to repair, to create anew, to regain, to compensate ; *separo*, to separate. Let the Latin uses of this word be compared with the same Hebrew word in Joshua xvii. 15, where it is rendered *cut down*. " Ascend to the wood country and cut down for thyself ;" Septuagint, εκκαθαρον σεαυτω, clear for thyself. This is one mode of preparation for use. In Ezek. xxi. 19, it is rendered choose. Septuagint, διαταξεις, appoint.

ITALIAN.

Parare, to prepare ; to garnish ; to adorn ; to propose an occasion ; to *parry*, or ward off, as a blow ; to defend ; to cover from or shelter ; to repair, to teach a horse to stop, and in horsemanship, to stop; *parata*, a warding off, a garnishing; *parato*, prepared, ready, prompt, warded off or parried, shielded, defended.

Apparare, to learn; *apparato*, learned, prepared; *apparato*, preparation, garnishment.

Parecchio, a preparation; also equal, even, [L. *par;*] *parecchiare*, to prepare; *pareggiare*, to make equal, to compare; *apparecchiare*, to prepare, to ornament or garnish, to set in order; *appareggiare*, to put in competition, to match, to equal.

Comparare, to compare.

Disparare, to forget; *disparare*, *sparare*, to unfurnish, to disgarnish, to make unready, to disbowel, to separate, disjoin, unpair; to discharge, as artillery.

Imparare, to learn.

Riparare, to repair, to restore to the first state; to repair, or resort to, or have access to; to *parry*, or ward off; *riparo*, reparation, a fort, a bank, fence, mound, remedy, shelter.

SPANISH.

Parar, to prepare; to stop, detain, prevent; to end; to treat or use ill; to stake at cards; to point out the game, as pointers.

Parada, a halt or stopping, end, pause; a fold for cattle; a relay, as of horses; a dam or bank; a stake or bet; a *parade*, or a place where troops are assembled to exercise; *parado*, remiss, careless, unemployed.

Par, a pair; a peer; after-birth; the handle of a bell.

Aparar, to stretch out the hands or skirts of a garment for receiving any thing; to dig and heap earth round plants; to close the upper and hind quarter of a shoe to the sole; to couple male and female animals; to dub as a ship.

Aparador, a sideboard, a dresser in a kitchen, a workshop, a wardrobe; *aparato*, preparation, pomp, show.

Aparear, to match; to suit one thing to another [pair.]

Aparejo, preparation, harness, sizing of a piece of linen or board on which something is to be painted, tackle, rigging employed on board of a ship. [*Apparel, parrel.*]

Comparar, to compare.

Desparejar, to make unequal.

Disparar, to discharge, as fire arms.

Amparar, to shelter; to protect. [Aragon, to sequester, as goods.]

Emparedar, to confine or shut up.

Reparar, to repair; to observe carefully, to consider; to mend or correct; to suspend or detain; to guard, defend, protect; to regain strength or recover from sickness; to right the helm.

Separar, to separate.

PORTUGUESE.

Parar, v. i. to stop, to cease to go forward; to confine upon, to meet at the end, to touch, to be bounded; to tend, to drive at something, to aim at, to come to; to imply, involve, or comprise: "Naõ posso parar com fome," I cannot *bear* hunger. "Ninguem pode aqui parar," nobody can live or stay here. [Eng. *bear.*]

Parar, v. t. to stop, to hinder from proceeding; to *parry* or ward off; to turn or change with regard to inclination or morals; to lay or stake as a wager. *Parada*, a stopping or place of stopping; a bet or wager.

Amparar, to protect, shelter, defend, abet.

Comparar, to compare; *comprar*, to buy, to procure.

Aparar, to *pare*, as an apple; to mend or make a pen; to *parry* a blow.

Aparelhar, to prepare, to fit, to cut out or rough hew; *aparelho*, tackle in a ship for hoisting things, Eng. a *parrel.*

Disparar, to shoot, to discharge, as fire-arms.

Reparar, to repair; to *parry* in fencing; to advert; to observe; to make amends; to retrieve; to recover; to recruit; to shelter; *reparo*, in fortification, defense.

FRENCH.

Parer, to deck, adorn, trim, set off, embellish; to *parry* or ward off. "*Parer* des cuirs," to dress lether; "*parer* le pied d'un cheval," to *pare* a horse's hoof.

Parer, v. i. to stop; *paresse*, idleness.

Pari, a lay, bet or wager; *parier*, to bet or lay a wager.

Appareil, preparation, furniture, train, retinue, [Eng. *apparel.*] *Apparaux*, tackle, sails and rigging, [Eng. *parrel.*]

Pair, a peer, an equal; *paire*, a pair; *apparier*, to pair, to match.

S'emparer, to seize, to invade.

Reparer, to repair.

Separer, to separate.

ARMORIC.

Para, to dress, to trim, to stop, to *parry*, to prepare.

RUSSIAN.

Uberayu, to put in order, to adjust, to mow or reap, to cut, to dress as the hair. This word has the common prefix *u.*

PERSIC.

پريدن poridan, to cut off.

WELSH.

Par, something contiguous, or that is in continuity; a state of readiness or preparedness; a *pair* or couple; a fellow, match.

Pâr, a cause; the essence, germ or seed of a thing; a *spear.*

Para, to continue, to endure, to persevere.

Parad, a causing; *parai*, that causes to be.

Parawd, prepared, ready; *parodi*, to prepare.

That all the foregoing words in the present European languages, [and several others might have been added,] are formed from one stock or radix, coinciding with the Latin *paro*, is a fact that admits of no question. The only doubt respecting the correctness of the whole preceding statement, is, whether the Latin *paro* is radically the same as the oriental ברא; and with regard to this point, I should suppose the evidence to be convincing. Indeed there is good reason to believe that the oriental verbs ברא, ברר, חבר, and עבר, are all formed from one primitive radix. Certain it is that the English *bear* comprehends both the Latin *fero* and *pario*, and the latter corresponds nearly with פרה and Eth. ፈረየ to bear.

But admitting only what is certain, that all the foregoing European words are from one radix, we are then to seek for a primary meaning from which may be deduced the following significations; Lat. to *prepare;* Ital. to adorn, to *parry*, to stop, to defend, to *repair*, to learn; Span. to *prepare*, to stop, to lay or stake as a wager, a *pair* or couple; Port. to stop, to confine upon or be contiguous, to drive or aim at, to *parry*, to *pare;* Fr. to deck, to *parry*, to stop, to *pare;* Arm. to dress, to *prepare*, to *parry;* Russ. to adjust, to dress, to mow or reap; Welsh, *preparedness*, contiguity, a *pair*, a cause, to continue or endure; and several other significations.

The various significations result from throwing, sending, driving. To separate or remove is to drive or force apart; hence to *parry*, and hence to defend. Separation implies extension, a drawing out in length or time; hence the Portuguese senses of confining upon, reaching to the limit. This gives the sense of *par*, equal, that is, of the same extent, and hence coming to, and suiting, as in Latin *convenio.*

Here let it be observed that admitting the word *par*, equal, to belong to this family, as in the Welsh, we have strong reason to believe that the Shemitic חבר, to join, or fit together, to associate, whence as a noun, an associate, is formed from the same root, or ברא; for in the Saxon, we find not only *fera*, but *gefera*, a companion, fellow or *peer*; *gefera*, answering precisely to the oriental word.

The sense of betting is from throwing down, as we say, to *lay* a wager. The sense of stopping is from setting, fixing, or from parrying. The sense of adorning is from putting on, which is from sending, or from extension, enlargement, as we say, to *set off*, and hence it is allied to the sense of show, display, *parade.* Preparation is from producing, bringing forward, or adjusting, making right; and often implies advancing, like *ready*, *prompt*, and the latter word, *prompt*, from *promo*, to bring forth, affords a good illustration of the words derived from *paro.*

The senses of cutting off, *paring*, and the like, require no explanation.

The Italian, *disparare*, and the Spanish and Portuguese, *disparar*, to discharge fire arms, present the original sense of the root, to send or drive. This sense gives that of the Welsh *pâr*, a spear, as well as a cause, or that which impels. A *spear* is a shoot, from the sense of thrusting; and our word *spear* is probably formed from the root of *bar* and Welsh *ber*, a spit, a pike, a lance, a spear, Lat. *veru.* Now in Chaldee, a *bar* is עברא from עבר, to pass, a verb which is probably of the same family with ברא. It is further to be observed that in Italian, *bar* is written both *barra* and *sbarra.*

It is observed above that ברא is the English *bear* and the Latin *pario;* but *pario* would seem to be the Hebrew פרה, parah, to be fruitful, to bear fruit, applied to plants and animals. But this word seems to denote producing in general, rather than the production of children. However this may be, it is certain that *bear* in English, as well as in Saxon, expresses the sense of both *pario* and *fero* in Latin. The Latin *fero*, and the Greek φερω, signify both to carry and to produce, as young or fruit. *Pario*, does not. So in the Gothic, *bairan* is to carry, *gabairan* is to carry and to produce young. In German, *führen* is to carry, and *gebären*, to bring forth, to bear a child. In Dutch, *beuren* is to lift; *voeren*, to carry; and *baaren*, to bring forth, as children, to bear, to beget, to cause. Danish, *bærer*, to carry, to support, and to yield or produce. Sw. *băra*, to carry; *barn*, a son. Irish, *beirim*, to bear or bring forth, and to tell or relate, like the Latin *fero*, whence Fr. *parler*, to speak.

It appears then that the English *bear* and the Saxon from which we have received it, and the Gothic and the Danish corresponding words unite, in the same orthography, the senses of two words of different orthography in other languages. I have found other examples of a similar kind. There is therefore solid ground to believe that all these words are from one primitive root; the different modes of writing the word, and the several appropriations having originated in different families of the great races of men, before languages were reduced to writing; and when they came to be written, each word was written according to its usual pronunciation, and defined according to its use in each family. And by the intermixture of tribes, two or three derivatives of the same stock might have become a part of the same national language. Unquestionably the Greek φερω, and φορεω, are branches of the same stock.

We have, in the modern languages, decisive evidence that different verbs may have, and in fact have a common radix. Thus in English *list* and *lust*, are different modes of writing the same word; both are united in the other Teutonic dialects. So in Latin *libet* and *lubet;* and similar instances I have found in almost every language which I have examined.

The Latin *pareo*, to *appear*, to come to light, if not a compound word, may be of this family. *Paries*, a wall, if primarily a partition wall, is of the same stock. *Per*, belongs to this family, as its signification is *passing*. The Sax. *faran*, to fare, Gr. πορευομαι, seems to be from one branch of this stock, probably עבר. See the word *pass* in the Dictionary, in the derivative senses of which there are some resemblances to those of ברא.

כפר.

This verb, says Lowth, means to *cover*, to cover sin, and so to expiate; and it is never used in the sense of *breaking* or *dissolving* a covenant, though that notion occurs so often in the Scriptures; nor can it be forced into this sense, but by a great deal of far fetched reasoning. See Isaiah xxviii. 18. *Lowth on Isaiah. Prelim. Diss.*

כפר, says Castle, "texuit, operuit, Anglice, to *cover;* per metathesin, κρυπτω, κρυφη, peculiariter bitumine, sive glutinosa aliqua materia obduxit; picavit." Gen. vi. 14.

Parkhurst gives to this verb the sense of *covering* or *overspreading*, as primary; and deduces from it the Greek κρυπτω, and English *cover* and *coffer*. He however admits that in Isaiah xxviii. 18, it signifies, to annul, as a covenant. He also considers the sense of atonement or expiation to be radically that of *covering*.

Gesenius agrees with the English Lexicographers, in assigning to this verb the primary sense of *covering* or *overlaying*, as in Gen. vi. 14. He admits that this word has the sense, in Isaiah xxviii. 18, of *blotting out, obliterating*. But he gives to it the sense of *forgiving*, in some passages, in which our version has that of *purging away*. Ps. lxv. 3, and lxxix. 9. In these passages, Castle renders the word, to be *merciful* or *propitious*.

In all these authors, there is, I conceive, a radical mistake, in supposing the primary sense to be to *cover*, and in the opinion that this Hebrew word is the English verb to *cover*. A still greater mistake is in the supposition of Castle and Parkhurst, that this, by a metathesis, gives the Greek κρυπτω.

The English word *cover* comes to us through the French *couvrir*, from the Italian *coprire*, a contraction of the Latin *co-operio*, whence *co-opertus*, Italian *coperto*, covered, Eng. *covert*.* The Latin *aperio*, is to open, and *operio*, is to cover, both from *pario*, or one of the roots in *Br*, which has just been explained. The root in these words is *per* or *par*, and the sense is varied by prefixes; perhaps *ad-pario* or *ab-pario* and *ob-pario*. Now *cover* can have no connection with כפר, unless this latter word is a compound, with כ for a prefix. This may be the fact, but the connection, even in that case, is very remote.

Let us see if we can gain any light upon the subject of the primary sense of כפר from the cognate languages.

Chaldee, כפר To deny, to reject. Prov. xxx. 9.

2. To wipe; "She eateth and *wipeth* her mouth." Prov. xxx. 20.

3. To wash or cleanse. Matt. xxvii. 24. *Castle.*

Syriac, ܟܦܪ To deny. Gen. xviii. 15. Luke xii. 9.

2. To wipe, to wipe away, to disannul, to abolish. Prov. xxx. 20. Is. xxviii. 18. *Castle.*

Arabic, كَفَرَ To deny; to disbelieve; to be an infidel; to be impious; to blaspheme. Acts iii. 13, 14. 2 Pet. ii. 1. 5. Jude 15.

2. To cover; to conceal.

3. To expiate; to make expiation for one, and free him from crime. *Castle.*

Now the senses of the Chaldee, Syriac and Arabic, to *deny*, to *reject*, to *disannul*, to *wipe*, *wash*, or to *cleanse* by these acts, cannot be deduced from *covering*.

In Hebrew, the word has the sense of *covering*, as the ark, with bitumen or pitch, in Gen. vi. 14; that is, to *smear*, or *pay over*, as our seamen now express it. But it should be considered that the sense of *covering* is rarely or never *primary;* it is usually, from the sense of *putting on*, which is from the sense of *throwing* or *pressing*, or it is from *overspreading*, which is a *spreading, stretching* or *throwing over;* hence the derivative senses of *covering* and *hiding*. These latter senses are sometimes derived from others: but these are the most general. And in this passage of Genesis, the literal sense is probably to put on, or to *rub* or *spread* over, a sense which coincides with that of the Chaldee and Syriac, Prov. xxx. 20, though differently applied.

The real original sense of this Shemitic verb is to remove, to separate, by thrusting away or driving off. Hence its application, in the Chaldee, Syriac and Arabic, to denial, the rejection of God or truth. To *deny* or *reject*, is to thrust away. Hence from the Arabic, *caffer*, an infidel, one who denies and rejects the Mohammedan religion; hence *Caffraria*, the southern part of Africa, the country of infidels; so called by the followers of Mohammed, just as the christians gave the name of *pagans*, to the inhabitants of villages, [*pagus*,] who rejected the christian religion.

This signification explains the Hebrew uses of this word. Its literal sense is applied to the cleansing or purification of sacred things, as the altar. Lev. xvi. 18. In a spiritual sense, to the purification of the soul, a type of the purification by the blood of Christ; hence it is rendered *atonement*, or *expiation*. Hence probably the sense of appeasing, Gen. xxxii. 21. Prov. xvi. 14, though this may be from removing, or smoothing.

The sense of forgiveness is from thrusting away or giving back, precisely as in the modern languages; Lat. *remitto*, to send back or away; *forgive*, to give back or away: *pardon*, in French, Spanish, and Italian, has a like sense, which is more clearly exhibited by the Dutch *vergeeven*, German *vergeben; ver* being the English *far*, to *give far*, to *give away*, hence to reject, and remember no more. The sense of *give* and of the French *donner*, is nearly the same as that of כפר. To *give*, is to send, to cause to pass; and so of *donner*.

Now it is a question of some moment whether the opinion that כפר is the same as the English *cover*, has not inclined lexicographers and commentators to render it by this word, in several passages, where the true sense is to *forgive*, or to purify by cleansing from sin.

However this may be, the interpretation given above will fully disprove Lowth's assertion, that this word is never used in the sense of *breaking* or *disannulling* a covenant. So confident is the learned Bishop on this point that he ventures to call in question the reading, Isaiah xxviii. 18; and to suppose the true word to be תפר from פור to break. With respect to the reading I shall offer no opinion; but if the present reading is correct, I am confident that no word in the Hebrew language is better fitted to express the sense. Your covenant with death shall be *wiped away, abolished*, or as in the version, *disannulled*. And so is the rendering in the Syriac.

If כפר is a compound word and the first letter a prefix, it may be from the same root as the Arabic غَفَرَ gafara, whose signification is to cover. But the primary sense is to throw or put on. It signifies also to *forgive*, but to forgive is to send back or away, *remitto*, and not to cover. And I apprehend that for want of knowing the primary sense of such verbs, the word *cover* has been often substituted for *forgive*, in the translating of this verb.

כל

No. 1. Heb כול, כל To *hold*, to contain; Sw. *hålla*. כלכל To hold, to sustain, to maintain, to comprehend.

Ch. כול To measure, that is, to ascertain the contents, or to stretch, and comprehend the whole.

Pah. To feed, to nourish. See אכל.

Deriv. A measure; also, custom, rite, manner, probably from holding or continued practice.

Syr. In Aph. To measure. Deriv. A measure.

Eth. ሆወለ To follow; to go behind; Gr. ακολουθεω; that is, to hold to, or to press after.

Deriv. The hinder part; the poop of a ship; behind. French, *cul*.

No. 2. Heb. כלל To finish; to complete; to make perfect. Gr. καλος. כל *all;* the whole; Gr. ολος, Eng. *all*, by the loss of the first letter: but in Welsh, *holl*, or *oll;* and in Saxon *al, æl* and *geall*.

Ch. כלל To crown; to adorn

Pih. To perfect; to complete; to comprehend; to embrace.

Deriv. Comprehending; universality; a general rule, &c.

Syr. ܟܠܠ To crown. Deriv. a crown; all; every one.

Sam. ࠊࠋࠋ As the Chaldee.

Eth. ከለለ The same; also, to cover.

Ar. كَلَّ To be weary or dull; to be languid; to tire: also, to crown: to shine.

Deriv. All; dullness; heaviness.

No. 3. Heb. כלא To *hold;* to restrain; to shut or confine; to check: Gr. κωλυω; Sw. *hålla*.

* In this deduction of *cover* from the Latin, I am supported by Lunier, the ablest French etymologist, whose works I have seen.

INTRODUCTION.

Deriv. A place of confinement; Lat. *caula.*

Ch. כלא, כלה, כלי To hold; to restrain; also, to trust; to confide in, or rely on; to hope. (See No. 6.) Also, to finish; to perfect; also, to consume; to cause to fail.

In Aph. To *call;* to cry out; to thunder; Gr. καλεω; Lat. *calo*; W. *galw*; Eng. to *call;* Lat. *gallus,* from crowing.

Syr. ܟܠܐ To hold; to restrain; to forbid; to deny.

Deriv. *all*; a cork, bar or bolt.

Sam. ࠊࠋࠀ To hold, or restrain.

Eth. ከለአ To hold, restrain, or prohibit.

Deriv. Lat. *alius*; a fellow, or companion.

Ar. كلا To keep; to preserve; to turn the face towards a thing and look repeatedly. So in English, to *behold.* Also, to come to the end, as of life; also, to feed, to devour food; also, to abound in pasture; also, to hinder, or detain; also, to look attentively; also, to sprout; also, to take upon a pledge, or upon trust; supra, Chaldee. (See No. 6.)

No. 4. Heb. כלה To finish; to consume; to bring to naught; to waste; to fail. (See No. 8.)

No. 5. Ch. אכל To eat; to consume; also, to take; to hold; to contain. In Aph. to feed; to give food; also, to *call;* to thunder; to roar, or bellow; also, to publish; to accuse; to defame.

Heb. to eat; to consume.

Sam. ࠀࠊࠋ To eat.

Syr. ܐܟܠ To publish; to divulge, as a crime; to accuse.

Eth. ከሀለ To suffice, as we say, it is well, Lat. *valeo;* also, to be or exist; that is, to be *held,* or to be fixed or permanent, to continue.

Ar. to eat; to devour; to corrode; Lat. *helluo.*

No. 6. Ar. وَكَلَ To trust, to commit to another in confidence. (See No. 3.)

Eth. ወከለ with a prefix; to trust, as above.

No. 7. Heb. יכל To be able; to prevail; Lat. *calleo;* W. *gallu*; Eng. *could.*

No. 8. Ch. עכל To digest; to consume. (No. 5.)

Ar. عَقَلَ To collect; to tie; to bind; to unite; also, to divide, impel, or compel. This is the primary sense of the word, or rather of this root; to press; to strain; to urge, or impel; also, to extend. These verbs are different modifications of one radix; and hence the English *hold, call, hollow, heal, hale;* the Latin *calo, caulis, calleo, callus;* Greek, κολλα, χαλος or καλλος; and a multitude of words in all the modern languages of Europe.

The sense of holding, restraining, forbidding, hindering, and keeping, are too obvious to need any explanation. They are from straining. To this sense is nearly allied the sense of measuring, or ascertaining what is held or contained. That which is contained is *all,* the *whole* that is comprehended, from the sense of extension.

The signification of finishing or perfecting, seems, in a good sense, to be from that of soundness; a sense which is from stretching or strength. Or it may be from *coming* to the end, like *finish* and *achieve,* or from *shutting, closing.* And the sense of consuming, wasting, failing, may be from *bringing* to an end. In Latin, to *consume* is to *take all;* and possibly this may be the sense of this verb. But the Arabic sense of failure would seem rather to be from holding, stopping, or coming to an end.

The sense of eating may be from consuming, or taking apart, but from some of the derivatives of No. 5, I am inclined to think the primary sense is to feed, to crowd, to stuff; the primary sense of the root applied to this particular act; for under the Chaldee root we find words which signify the nut of a species of oak, the Gr. αχυλος, and a collection or crowd of people, [Gr. οχλος,] both of which are from collecting or pressing together.

The sense of *seeing* and *looking* is from *reaching* or *casting* and *striking,* or from *holding* or *fixing* the eyes on.

The sense of *trusting* seems also to be that of *holding to* or *resting on.* The English *hold* in *behold* is from this root.

The sense of *calling, roaring,* and *thunder,* is from impelling the voice or sound; a pressing, driving, or straining, applied to sound; like the Latin *appello,* from *pello.* Hence the sense of publishing, accusing and defaming.

The sense of sprouting, in the Arabic, is a shooting or pushing out, as in other cases; Lat. *caulis.*

The sense of ability, power, strength, in No. 7, is from straining, stretching, or holding, as in other words of the like sense. Hence Lat. *calleo,* to be skilled, and to be hard, *callus.*

On this root כל, is probably formed סכל, a word differently pointed in the Hebrew and Chaldee. This word signifies in Hebrew to pervert, to err, to be foolish or infatuated, to act foolishly.

In Chaldee, to understand, know, or consider; to look or behold; to cause to understand; Rabbinic, to be ignorant; whence its derivatives, knowledge, wisdom, ignorance. These different significations may result from the different effects of the prefix on the original verb.

In Syr. ܣܟܠ the same word, signifies to be foolish, or mad; to cause to know, or to give understanding; to observe; to search or know thoroughly; to ask or seek to understand; to discern or distinguish; also to err, to sin, to be foolish, or perverse.

In Sam. the same word signifies to look, and to be accustomed. See Castell. col. 2523.

That שכל is formed on the same root with a different prefix, is obvious and certain, from the correspondence of significations. This word in Hebrew signifies to understand, or know; to cause to understand; to be wise, or to act wisely; corresponding with the Ch. סכל above; and being a mere dialectical orthography of the word. It signifies also to deprive, strip, bereave; and to waste, scatter and destroy; also, to cast, as fruit or offspring; also, to prosper.

Ch. to understand, and Ch. שכלל to complete, to finish; also, to found, to lay the foundation. This is כלל with ש prefixed.

Syr. to found, to finish, to adorn.

Ar. شَكَلَ shakala, to bind under the belly; to gird; to bind the feet; to fetter; to *shackle;* to form, or fashion; to be dubious, obscure, and intricate; to agree, suit or answer to; to be like; to have a beautiful form; to know, perceive, or comprehend; to hesitate; to be ignorant. Derivative, a *shackle.* See Castell. Col. 3750.

To this root Castle refers the English *skill;* and it is certain the words correspond both in elements and in sense. Now in the Gothic and Teutonic languages, the verbs corresponding to these Shemitic verbs, signify in Saxon, *scylan,* to separate, to distinguish; Icelandic and Swedish, *skilia,* to divide, separate, sever; whence *shield,* that which separates, and hence defends; D. *scheelen,* to differ; *schillen,* to peel, or pare; whence *scale* and *shell.* To this root our lexicographers refer *skill.* The prefix in this word would seem to have the force of a negative, like L. *ex.* Now is it possible to suppose that these words can be formed from a common root? The sense of *sin* and *folly* is probably from wandering, deviating, as in delirium; and this is only a modification of the primary sense of כל, to stretch or extend; that is, departure, separation. Or the ש has, in these senses, the force of a negative.

The sense of *knowing, understanding,* is usually or always from *taking, holding,* or *extending to;* as we say, I *take* your meaning. In this application these words would seem to be directly from the Eth. and Ch. כהל to be able; the Latin *calleo,* to be hard, and to know or be well *skilled.* That this word כהל is from the same root as כלה, כלא, כלל, we know by the Samaritan ࠊࠋࠋ which signifies *all,* and which is a mere dialectical spelling of the Heb. and Ch. כל.

The sense of depriving and wasting, in the Hebrew, is from separation, the sense of the Gothic and Teutonic words; but it is to be noticed that this sense seems to imply throwing, as one mode of parting, and this is also the direct act of founding, laying the foundation.

When we turn our attention to the Arabic, new affinities are disclosed. The first definition is to *bind,* to gird, to *shackle,* and hence the English word. The radical sense of *bind* is to strain, the sense of *hold.* And here we arrive at the origin and primary sense of *shall, should*; Saxon *scealan,* to be obliged; that is, to be bound or constrained. Hence we see why the words *scale, shell* and *shall* are all written alike in Saxon, *sceal;* for *scale* and *shell* are from peeling, or covering, binding.

From this verb the Saxon has *scyld,* a crime, or guilt, Lat *scelus,* and *scyld,* a shield. The German has the same word in *schuld,* guilt, culpability, debt; Dutch, *schuld;* Danish *skulde,* should, and *scyld,* a debt, a fault, a crime; Sw. *skuld,* the same. This word *scyld, skuld,* and *schuld,* is the English *should,* the preterit of the verb *shall;* and it is the word used in the Saxon, German, Dutch, Danish, Swedish, Norwegian, Icelandic, and Swiss Lord's prayer, to express what is rendered in English *debts;* forgive us our *debts.* Here we see the primary sense of the word is to be *held,* or bound; hence, liable. The English word *guilt* may be from the same root, without a prefix; but whether it is or not, we observe the word expresses more than the English word debt, trespass or offense; it comprehends the sense of *fault,* or *sin,* with that of being *held,* or *liable* to answer or to punishment. *Debt,* in the modern use of the word, implies the latter, but not the former; *trespass* and *offense* imply the *sin,* but not the liability to answer. We have no English word that includes both senses, except *guilt,* and this seems to be hardly adequate to express the full sense of *scyld.*

To account for the various significations of the same word, in different languages, and often in the same language, it is necessary to find the primary action expressed by the root; and in compound words it is necessary to observe or ascertain the different effects produced on the original word by the prefixes. Thus the verb *inculpo* in Low Latin signifies to *excuse;* but some modern writers use *inculpate* in a directly different sense; that is, to *blame.*

In like manner *impartible* has two different significations; *that may be imparted;* and in law, *not partible,* or divisible. Such is the fact also with *impassionate.* I am persuaded a vast number of instances of similar diversities in the application of prefixes may be found in the Shemitic languages; and this will account for differences which otherwise seem utterly irreconcilable.

We find in our mother tongue, that the same word signifies to *heal*, and to *conceal*, Lat. *celo;* Saxon *hæl*, health; *hælan, helan*, to heal, to conceal; *ge-hælan* and *ge-helan*, to heal and to conceal; Old English *hele*. Hence we see that the English *heal* and the Latin *celo* are the same word differently applied, but from a common signification, which is to make strong or fast, or to hold, from the sense of pressing. Or perhaps the Latin *celo* may have this sense of holding, restraining; and *heal* may rather be from making perfect. No. 2. Supra.

We may now also see the radical sense of *holy;* Saxon *hal* and *ge-hal*, *whole*, sound, safe; *halig*, holy; *halgian*, to hallow. If this word contains the sense of separation, or driving off, like Latin *sacer*, as it may, it is from shutting, confining, or restraining intercourse. But I am inclined to believe the primary sense of *holy* is sound, entire, coinciding with the radical sense of *heal*.

Clod, Laudo, Claudo.

In Welsh *clod* is praise, from *llod*, a forcible utterance. This is the English *loud*, and Lat. *laudo*, which with a prefix becomes *plaudo*. In Welsh, *llodi* signifies to reach out, to crave, from the radical sense of *llod*, to thrust out or extend; but according to Owen, *llodi* is from *llawd*, which signifies a shooting out, or a going onward, productiveness, a *lad*, and as an adjective, tending forward, craving, *lewd; llodig*, craving, brimming; *llodineb*, lewdness. Now, beyond all question, these words are the Chaldee, Syriac, Hebrew, and Samaritan ילד to beget; to bring forth; to cause to be be born; and as a noun, a child of either sex, a *lad*. The Arabians and Ethiopians use *vau* or *waw*, where the Hebrews use *yod*. The Arabic corresponding word is ولد, the Ethiopic ወለደ to beget, to bring forth.

But this is not all. In Greek, the verb κλειω, a contraction of κλειδοω, signifies to praise, to celebrate. Here we have precisely the Welsh *llod*, above, corresponding with the Latin *laudo* and *plaudo*. But the same Greek word κλειω, κλειδοω, signifies to shut or make fast. This is the Latin *cludo, claudo*. The Saxons used *h* for the Greek κ and the Latin *c*; and with these words accords the Saxon *hlid*, a cover; English a *lid*; that which shuts or makes fast. That these words are all from one root, is a fact, apparent beyond any reasonable doubt; nor is there the least difficulty in ascertaining the affinity, for the radical sense, to reach forward, to thrust, to strain, solves the whole mystery. To *thrust*, gives the sense of begetting and producing; to strain or throw out the voice, gives the sense of praise; and to thrust or press together, gives the sense of closing and making fast. In this manner, words, which, at first view, appear to have no connection, will, when pursued through different languages, assimilate and unite, not only without forced analogies, but in defiance of all preconceived opinions; and the reluctant mind is at last compelled to admit their identity.

There is another set of words whose derivation from the same root is very certain, though perhaps less obvious. These are the Danish *slutter*, to shut, close, conclude, finish, determine; *slutter*, a key-keeper, a jailor; Swedish, *sluta*, claudere, obserare, to shut, or shut up, or end; *slott*, a castle; D. *sleutel*, a key; *slot*, a lock, a castle, a conclusion; *sluiten*, to shut, lock, close, stop, conclude; G. *schloss*, a lock; *schliessen*, to close, conclude, finish, fetter, shackle; *schleuse*, a sluice; D. *sluis*, id. Eng. *sluice*, that is, which shuts or fastens; Low Latin, *exclusa*. See *Spelman's Glossary*. These words are unequivocally formed from the root of *claudo, clausi*, by the prefix *s*, just as the Welsh *yslac*, slack, loose, is formed on *llac*, and *yspeiliaw*, on *yspail*, spoil, and this on the root of *peel*. We observe all the Teutonic dialects use the dental *t*, as the final radical, except the German. The Latins use both the dental and a sibilant, *claudo, clausi, clausus*.

If the Danish *lyd*, sound, Sw. *lyda*, to sound, is the same word as English *loud*, these words belong to this family.

Cradle.

Another example. The English word *cradle*, Saxon *cradel*, is in Welsh *cryd*, a rocking, a shaking, a *cradle*. In Welsh, the verbs *crydu, crydiaw, crydian*, signify to shake, to tremble. These correspond to the Irish *creatham*, to shake; Greek κραδαω, to shake, to swing. The Welsh verbs are by Owen, deduced from *rhyd*, which signifies a moving. Now רעד in Hebrew, Chaldee, and Ethiopic, signifies to shake or tremble. The same word in Arabic رعد signifies to thunder; to impress terror; to tremble; to shake. This coincides with the Latin *rudo*, to roar, to bray; and we know from the voice of the ass, that roughness or shaking is an ingredient in the sense of this word. We know it also from *rudis*, one of the affinities of *rudo*. There is also in Arabic راد which is rendered to run hither and thither; to move one way and the other; to tremble; to shake. In Hebrew חרד signifies to tremble or shake, and to palpitate; in Syriac and Eth. to rub or scrape. This connects the word directly with *cradle*, through the Hebrew; and through the Syriac, with the Latin *rado*. Here again we find the sense of roughness or grating. Then turning to the Welsh, we find *grydiaw*, which signifies to utter a rough sound; to shout, hoop or scream; *grydwst*, a murmur, from *gryd*, a shout or hoop, and this from *rhyd*, the word above mentioned; so that *crydu*, to shake, whence *cradle*, is from the same root as *grydiaw*, to shout, and this is the Italian *gridare*; Sp. and Port. *gritar*; Saxon *grædan;* Sw. *gråta*; Dan. *græder;* Dutch *kryten;* German *greiten*. This word in French is contracted, by the omission of the last radical, into *crier* for *crider;* whence, probably, we have *cry*, W. *cri*. Hence we find that the sense of *cry* is to utter a rough sound; and this is connected with the braying of the ass, with shaking, trembling, and with roaring, murmuring, and thunder. The connection in this example, is so marked as to preclude all hesitation as to the identity of the words.

The Shemitic roots גרד, חרט, חרת, and קרד, all, in some of the languages of that stock, coincide in sense and elements with the English *grate*, French *gratter;* and if the first letter is a prefix, they would seem to unite with the Latin *rado*. But this is a point I would not undertake to determine.

One fact more. The Welsh *cri*, above mentioned, signifies a *cry;* and as an adjective, rough, raw. Now this coincides with the Latin *crudus*, in sense; and *crudus* with the Welsh *cryd*, above mentioned.

The Dan. *brygger*, English to *brew*, are probably connected with *break*, with *freckle*, and with *rough*. So under this root, the Welsh *grediaw*, signifies to heat, scorch, parch, whence *greidyll*, a griddle, from *graid*, that shoots in rays, heat, ardency, from *gra*, that shoots, or rises, as the nap or frieze of cloth. The latter is probably a contracted word, of the same family, but not the root, as Owen supposes. But the radical sense implies a shaking, agitation and roughness.

Meet, mete, measure.

Saxon.—*Mætan*, to put, to place; Fr. *mettre*, It. *mettere*, Sp. Port. *meter*, Lat. *mitto*.

Mætan, metan, to find, to *meet*, or meet with; to paint; to dream; to *measure*, to *mete*, Lat. *metior, metor*, Gr. μετρεω, μετρον, Lat. *mensus*, with a casual *n*, that is, *mesus*, Fr. *mesure*.

Ametan, gemetan, to *meet*, to find, to measure.

Gemeting, gemetung, a *meeting*.

Gemet, gemete, fit, suitable, Eng. *meet;* also, painted or portrayed.

Gemetegan, gemetian, to *moderate; gemetlic, moderate, modest*.

Mete, measure, mode, Lat. *modius, modus*.

Meter, measure in verse, meter. [Not *metre*.]

Metere, an inventor, a painter.

Mæte, middling, [mediocris,] modest, moderate.

Mot, gemot, a meeting, a council.

Witena-gemot, a council of wise men.

Motian, to meet, especially for debate. Eng. to *moot*.

Gothic.—*Motyan, gamotyan*, to meet, to find.

Mota, a place for the receipt of toll or customs.

Dutch.—*Ontmoeten*, to *meet*, to encounter.

Meeten, and *toemeeten*, to *measure*.

Meeter, a *measurer*.

Gemoeten, to *meet; gemoet*, a *meeting*.

German.—*Mass, measure, meter; masse*, moderation.

Messen, vermessen, to *measure; messer*, a *measurer*.

Gemäss, measure; also conformable, suitable; Eng. *meet*, suitable; German *gemässigt*, temperate, *moderate*.

Swedish.—*Möta*, to *meet*, to fall on, to come to, to happen. [This is the sense of *finding*.]

Möte, a meeting.

Mot, and *emot*, towards, against; as in *motstå*, to stand against, to resist.

Mäta, to *measure; mätt, measure, meter, mode*.

Mättelig, moderate, middling, frugal, temperate.

Mätta, to be sufficient, to satisfy, to cloy.

Danish.—*Möder*, to *meet*, to convene; *möde* or *mode*, a *meeting; mod*, contrary, opposite, against, to, towards, for, on, by, aside, abreast, as in *modsetter*, to set against, to oppose; *modsiger*, to say against, to contradict; *mod-vind*, a contrary wind.

Moed, moden, ripe, mellow, *mature*. [Qu. Lat. *mitis*.]

Mode, manner, fashion. [Probably from the Latin.]

Maade, measure, form, style of writing, way, mode, manner, fashion. [This is the native Danish word corresponding to the Lat. *modus*.]

Maadelig, moderate, temperate.

Mæt, enough, sufficient; *mætter*, to satisfy, or sate, to glut.

From the same root are the G. *mit*, D. *met, mede*, Sw. and Dan. *med*, Gr. μετα, signifying *with*.

By the first signification of the Saxon *mætan*, or *metan*, we find that this word, which is the English *meet*, is also the French *mettre* and Lat. *mitto*, the sense of which is to throw or send, to put, to lay. *Meet* is only a modification of the same sense, to come to, to fall, to reach, hence to find; as we say, to *fall on*.

The sense of painting or portraying is peculiar to the Saxon. I am not confident that this sense is from finding; but we observe that *metere* is rendered an inventor and a painter. The sense of *paint* then may be to find out, to devise or contrive.

The sense of dreaming is also peculiar to the Saxon. The sense may be to devise or imagine, or it may be to *rove*, as in some other words of like signification. If so, this sense will accord with the Syriac ܡܛ infra.

The other significations present no difficulty. To *meet*, is to come to, to reach in proceeding or in extending; hence to find. The primary sense of *measure* is to extend, to stretch to the full length or size of a thing.

Meet, fit, suitable, like *par*, *peer*, *pair*, is from extending or reaching to. So *suit* is from the Latin *sequor*, through the French, to follow, to press or reach toward. See *par*, under ברא, supra.

The English *meet* and *mete* appear to be from the Saxon dialect, but *moot* from the Gothic.

Let it be remarked that in the Saxon, *meet* and *mete*, are united in the same orthography; and in the Dutch the orthography is not very different; *ontmoeten*, *gemoeten*, to meet, and *meeten*, to measure. Not so in the other languages.

In German, *mass* is measure, and *messen*, to measure; but the sense of *meet*, does not occur. Yet that *mass* is the same word as *meet*, fit, varied only in dialect, appears from this, that *gemass*, with a prefix, is suitable, answering to the English *meet*.

The Swedish and Danish words follow the Gothic orthography; Swedish *möta*, to meet, to fall on, to come to, to happen. These significations give the sense of finding, and are closely allied to the senses of the Arabic verb مدّ infra.

The Danish verb is *möder*, to meet, but in both the Swedish and Danish, the sense of measure is expressed by a different orthography. Sw. *mäta*, to measure; *mått*, measure; Dan. *maade*, measure, mode. In these two languages we find also the sense of sufficiency, and to satisfy. See infra, the Ar. مدّ and Heb. and Ch. מצא.

But in these Gothic dialects, there is one application of *meeting*, which deserves more particular notice. In Swedish, *mot* and *emot* is a preposition of the same signification as the English *against*. It is rendered toward, against. So in Danish, *mod* is contrary, opposite, against, to, toward, by, aside, abreast. This preposition is the simple verb, without any addition of letters, prefix or suffix. We hence learn that the sense of such prepositions is a meeting or coming to, which gives the sense of *to* or *toward;* but when one meets another in front, it gives the sense of opposition, or contrary direction. This coming to or meeting, may be for a friendly purpose, and hence in one's favor, like *for* in English. Thus in Danish, "Guds godhed *mod* os," God's goodness or mercy *towards* us. In other cases, *mod* signifies against and implies counteraction or opposition; as *modgift*, an antidote; *modgang*, adversity. So *for* in English signifies towards, or in favor of; and also opposition and negation, as in *forbid*.

In the Danish we find *moed*, *moden*, ripe, *mature*. We shall see this sense in the Chaldee מטא. The sense is to reach, extend, or come to.

The Latin *modus* is from this root, and by its orthography, it seems to have been received from the Gothic race. The sense is measure, limit, from extending, or comprehending. This then becomes the radix of many words which express limitation or restraint, as *moderate*, *modest*, *modify;* a sense directly contrary to that of the radical verb.

This leads us a step further. In Saxon, Gothic, and other northern languages, *mod*, *moed*, signifies mind, courage, spirit, anger, whence English *moody*. The primary sense is an advancing or rushing forward, which expresses mind or intention, that is, a setting or stretching forward, and also spirit, animation, heat, and lastly, anger. So the Latin *animus*, gives rise to animosity; and the Greek μενος, mind, signifies also, strength, force, vehemence, and anger. *Mania* is from the same radical sense.

Let us now connect this root or these roots, with the Shemitic languages.

In Hebrew and Chaldee, מדד signifies to measure; מד, a measure. This coincides with the Latin *metior*, and Gr. μετρεω, as well as with the Saxon, Dutch, Danish, and Swedish, which all write the word with a dental, but the German is *mass*.

In Syriac ܡܛ signifies to escape, to get free, that is, to depart, a modification of the sense of extending in the Arabic. A derivative in Syriac signifies a duty, toll or tribute; and we have seen in the Gothic, that *mota* is a toll-house. It may be from measuring, that is, a portion, or perhaps income.

This word in Arabic مدّ madda, signifies,

1. To stretch or extend, to draw out, to make or be long, to delay or give time, to forbear, to bring forth. To extend is the radical sense of *measure*.

2. To separate, or throw off or out; to secern, secrete or discharge. Hence to become *matter* or sanies, to produce pus, to *maturate*. Here we have the origin of the word *matter*, in the sense of *pus*. It is an excretion, from throwing out, separating, freeing, discharging. Here we have the sense of the Latin *mitto*, *emitto*.

3. To assist, to supply. This sense is probably from coming to, that is, to approach or visit. "I was sick and ye visited me. I was in prison and ye came to me." Math. xxv.

This application coincides with the English *meet*, but particularly with the Swedish and Danish sense of the word.

4. To make thin, to attenuate; probably from stretching.

Among the Arabic nouns formed under this root, we find a *measure*, or *modius*, showing that this verb is the same as the Chaldee and Hebrew; we find also *matter* or pus, and lenity. Qu. Lat. *mitis*.

In Chaldee, מטא or מטה, signifies to come to, to happen, to reach, [to *meet*,] to be ripe or *mature*, to cause to come, to bring or produce. The first sense gives that of finding, and the latter gives that of maturing, and we observe that *matter*, or pus, is from the Arabic مدّ madda, and the sense of *mature* from the Chaldee מטא mita. Yet in the use of *maturate* from the Latin *maturo*, we connect the words, for to *maturate*, is to ripen, and to generate *matter*.

In Syriac, this verb signifies the same as the Chaldee, to come to; and also to be strong, to prevail, that is, to strain or stretch, the radical sense of power.

In Hebrew, מצא has the sense of the foregoing verb in the Chaldee, to find, to come to, to happen.

In Chaldee, this verb signifies to find, and to be strong, to prevail; hence both in Hebrew and Chaldee, to be sufficient. Here we see the Danish and Swedish, *mætter*, and *måtta*, to be sufficient. This is also *meet*, dialectically varied.

In Syriac also this verb signifies to be strong or powerful; also in Pah. to bring or press out, to defecate, which sense unites this word with the Heb. מצה, to press, to squeeze. In Ethiopic, this verb signifies to come, to happen, to cause to come, to bring in, to bring forth. Now it is evident that מצא, and the Chaldee מטא, are dialectical forms of the same word; the former coinciding with the German *mass*, in orthography, but with the other languages, in signification.

In Chaldee, מצע signifies the *middle*, and as a verb, to set in the middle, to pass the middle, in Syriac, to be divided in the middle. Qu. Is not this a branch of the family of *meet?*

The Chaldee אמד, amad, to measure, is evidently from מד, with a prefix or formative א. This word, in Syriac, signifies like the simple verb, to escape, to be liberated. In Pael, to liberate.

In Arabic, this verb أمد amida, signifies, to be terminated, to end, whence the noun, an end, limit, termination, Latin *meta*, which, Ainsworth informs us, signifies, in a *metaphorical* sense, a limit. The fact is the reverse; this is its primary and literal sense, and that of a pillar and goal are particular appropriations of that sense.

In Hebrew, נמד signifies a cubit, a measure of length.

The same in the Rabbinic, from מד, with a prefix.

In Chaldee, this verb signifies to be contracted, to shrink.

Is not this sense from מד, measure, modus, a limit, or a drawing.

That the Shemitic words, מדד, מטא, מצא and אמד, are words of the same stock with *meet*, *mete*, Lat. *metior*, there can be no doubt, but it is not easy to understand why the different significations of *meeting* and *measuring*, should be united in one word, in the Saxon language, when they are expressed by very different words in the Shemitic, and in most of the Teutonic languages. We know indeed that in German a sibilant letter is often used, in words which are written with a dental in all the other kindred languages. But in this case the German *mass*, measure, must coincide with מד, as must the Swedish *måta*, and Dan. *maade*, and the Saxon *metan*, Dutch *gemoeten*, Goth. *motyan*, Sw. *möta*, Dan. *möder*, with the Chaldee מטא, but not with the word מצא.

It may not be impossible nor improbable that all these words are from one stock or radix, and that the different orthographies and applications are dialectical changes of that root, introduced among different families or races of men, before languages were reduced to writing.

In the Latin *mensus*, from *metior*, the *n* is probably casual, the original being *mesus*, as in the French *mesure*. I have reason to think there are many instances of this insertion of *n* before *d* and *s*.

From this exhibition of words and their significations, we may fairly infer the common origin of the following words. Lat. *mitto*, French *mettre*, English *meet*, to come to, *meet*, fit, and *mete*, to measure, Lat. *metior*, *metor*, Gr. μετρον, μετρεω, Lat. *mensura*, Fr. *mesure*, Eng. *measure*, Lat. *modus*, mode, Sax. and Goth. *mod*, mind, anger, whence *moody*, Eng. *moot*, Lat. *maturus*, mature, and Eng. *matter*.

In Welsh, *madu* signifies, to cause to proceed; to send, [Lat. *mitto*;] to suffer to go off; to render productive; to become beneficial; and *mâd* signifies, what proceeds or goes forward, hence what is good; and *mad*, the adjective, signifies, proceeding, advancing, progressive, good or beneficial. This word then affords a clear proof of the radical sense of *good*. We have like evidence in the English *better*, *best*, and in *prosperity*, which is from the Greek προσφερω, to advance.

In Welsh also we find *madrez*, *matter*, pus; *madru*, to dissolve, to putrefy, to become pus. That these words are from the same root as the Arabic

ܡܕ supra, I think to be very obvious; and here we observe that the Welsh have one important sense derived from the root, that of *good*, which occurs in none of the other languages. But the primary sense is the same as that of the other significations, to go forward, to advance; hence to promote interest or happiness. Here we have undeniable evidence that the sense of good, Welsh *mad*, and the sense of *matter*, pus, proceed from the same radix.

LEGO.

The Greek λεγω is rendered, to speak or say; to tell, count, or number; to gather, collect, or choose; to discourse; and to lie down. This last definition shows that this word is the English *lie* and *lay;* and from this application, doubtless, the Latins had their *lectus*, a bed, that is, a spread, a lay.

The Latin *lego*, the same verb, is rendered, to gather; to choose; to read; to steal, or collect by stealing; and the phrase, *legere oram*, signifies to coast, to sail along a coast; *legere vela*, is to furl the sails; *legere halitum*, to take breath; *legere littus*, to sail close to the shore; *legere milites*, to enlist or muster soldiers; *legere pugno*, to strike, perhaps to *lay on* with the fist.

It would seem, at first view, that such various significations cannot proceed from one radix. But the fact that they do is indubitable. The primary sense of the root must be to throw, strain or extend, which in this, as in almost all cases, gives the sense of *speaking*. The sense of collecting, choosing, gathering, is from throwing, or drawing out, or separating by some such act; or from throwing together. The sense of lying down is, probably, from throwing one's self down. The sense of reading, in Latin, is the same as that of speaking in the Greek, unless it may be from collecting, that is, separating the letters, and uniting them in syllables and words; for in the primitive mode of writing, diacritical points were not used. But probably the sense of *reading* is the same as in *speaking*.

The phrases *legere oram, legere littus*, in Latin, may coincide with that of our seamen, to stretch or *lay* along the shore or coast, or to *hug* the land; especially if this word *lay* in Sanscrit signifies to *cling*, as I have seen it stated in some author, but for which I cannot vouch. If this sense is attached to the word, it proves it closely allied to the L. *ligo*, to bind.

That the sense of throwing, or driving, is contained in this word, is certain from its derivatives. Thus, in Greek, απολεγω signifies to select, to collect; and also to reject, to repudiate, and to forbid; which imply throwing, thrusting away.

Now, if throwing, sending, or driving, is the primary sense, then the Latin *lego*, to read, and *lego, legare*, to send, are radically the same word; the inflections of the verb being varied, arbitrarily, to designate the distinct applications, just as in *pello, appello, appellere*, to drive, and *appello, appellare*, to call.

And here it may be worth a moment's consideration, whether several words with prefixes, such as *slay, flog*, and the Latin *plico*, W. *plygu*, are not formed on the root of *lay*, that is, *lag* or *lak*. The sense of *slay*, Sax. *slagan, slæan*, is properly to strike, to beat; hence in Saxon, "Hig slogon heora wedd," they *slew* their league, or contract; that is, they struck a bargain. It signifies also to throw, as to *slag* one into prison; also to fall; to set or lay. The sense of killing is derivative from that of striking, a striking down.

Flog, Lat. *fligo*, signifies primarily to *rush, drive, strike*, Eng. to *lick;* and if formed on the root of *lay*, is precisely the popular phrase, to *lay on*.

If *plico* is formed with a prefix on *lay* or its root, it must have been originally *pelico*, that is, *belico*, belay. Then to fold, would be to *lay on* or *close;* to lay one part to another. Now this word is the Welsh *plygu*, to fold, which Owen makes to be a compound of *py* and *lly*. The latter word must be a contraction of *llyg*.

We know that the word *reply* is from the French *repliquer*, the Latin *replico*. Now, to *reply*, is not to *fold back*, but to send back, to throw back, as words, or an answer; and this gives the precise sense of *lay*, to throw, to send, which must be the sense of the radical word.

It is no inconsiderable evidence of the truth of my conjecture, that we constantly use the phrase to *lay on*, or *lay to*, as synonymous with *ply*, a word belonging to this family. To *pledge*, another of this family, is to *lay* down, to deposit; and the primary sense of *play*, Sax. *plegan*, Dan. *leger*, Sw. *leka*, is to strike or drive.

In Welsh, *lluçiaw* signifies to throw, fling, cast, or dart; to pelt; to drift; from *lluç*, a darting, a flash, glance, or sudden throw; hence *lluçed*, lightning. *Llug* signifies also, that breaks, or begins to open, a gleam, a breaking out in blotches; the plague. *Llwg* signifies also, that is apt to break out, that is bright, a tumor, eruption. These words coincide with English *light*, Lat. *luceo;* the primary sense of which is to throw, shoot, or dart; and these words all contain the elements of *flog* and *fling*.

In Welsh, *llyçu* signifies to fall flat, to lie extended, or to squat. This is evidently allied to *lay* and *lie*.

These senses agree also with that of *luck*, to fall, or come suddenly; that is, to rush or drive along.

In Russ. *vlagayu* is to lay, or put in; equivalent to the German *einlegen*.

The Latin *fluo* is contracted from *flugo;* and the radical sense of *flow* is the same as that of *light*. So the river *Aar*, in Europe, is doubtless from the same source as the Orienntal אור, to shine, whence *air*. And נהר, which, in Hebrew, signifies to flow as water, as well as to shine, chiefly signifies in Chaldee and Syriac, to shine.

To show the great importance, or rather the absolute necessity, of ascertaining the primary sense of words, in order to obtain clear ideas of the sense of ancient authors, more particularly of difficult passages in dead languages, let the reader attend to the following remarks.

In commenting on certain parts of Isaiah xxviii, Lowth observes in his Preliminary Dissertation, the difficulty of determining the meaning of חזה, in verse 15th. In our version, as in others, it is rendered *agreement;* but, says Lowth, "the word means no such thing in any part of the Bible, except in the 18th verse following; nor can the lexicographers give any satisfactory account of the word in this sense." Yet he agrees with Vitringa, that in these passages it must have this signification. The difficulty, it seems, has arisen from not understanding the primary sense of *seeing*, for the verb generally signifies to *see;* and as a noun the word signifies sight, vision; and so it is rendered in the Latin version annexed to Vanderhooght's Bible. The seventy render it by συνθηκη, a covenant or league; and they are followed by the moderns. "Nous avons *intelligence* avec le sépulchre." *French.* "Noi habbiam fatta *lega* col sepulcro." *Italian of Diodati.*

Parkhurst understands the word to signify, to fasten, to settle, and he cites 2 Sam. xx, 9, תחז, "Joab *took* Amasa by the beard." Here the sense is obvious; and from this and other passages, we may infer with certainty, that the radical sense is to *reach* to, or to *seize, hold*, or *fix*. If the sense is to *reach* to, then it accords with *covenant*, conveniens, coming to; if the sense is to fix, or fasten, then it agrees with *league*, Lat. *ligo*, and with *pact, pactum*, from *pango*, to make fast; all from the sense of extension, stretching, straining. Hence the meaning of חזה, the breast; that is, the firm, fixed, strong part. And if the English *gaze* is the same word, which is not improbable, this determines the appropriate sense of seeing in this word, to be to fix, or to look or reach with the eye fixed.

But we have other and decisive evidence of the primary signification of this word in the obvious, undisputed meaning of אחז, the same word with a prefix, which signifies to catch, or lay hold on; to seize; hence, behind, following, as if attached to; and hence drawing out in time, to delay.

Now it is not improbable that the Arabic حاز hauz, may be a word of the same stock; and this signifies among other senses, to collect, contract or draw together, to accumulate, to have intercourse or commerce with another. The latter sense would give nearly the signification of the Hebrew word.

Lexicographers are often embarrassed to account for the different signification of words that are evidently derived from the same root. Thus, in Hebrew, שור is rendered to sing; to look, behold, or observe; and to rule; and its derivatives, a ruler, a wall, the navel-string, a chain or necklace, &c. How can a word signify to rule, and to sing, and to look? Nothing can be more easy or natural. The sense is in both cases to stretch or strain, to reach. To sing is to strain the voice; to rule is to restrain men; and to see is to reach, or to hold in view.

In Latin *sero*, signifies to sow, to plant, to beget, to spread; *consero*, to sow, and to close or join; *desero*, to leave off, to *desert; assero*, to plant by or near, and to *assert*, affirm, and pronounce; *dissero*, to discourse; *insero*, to *insert*, to implant; *resero*, to unlock, to open, to disclose. *Desero*, to desert, Ainsworth says, is a compound of *de* and *sero*, "ut sit desertum quod non seritur nec colitur." And *dissero* he supposes must be a metaphorical use of the word. Now, on the principles I have unfolded, nothing is easier than an explanation of these words. The sense of *sero* is to throw, to thrust; its literal sense is applied to sowing and planting; *consero* is to thrust or drive together; *desero* is to throw from; *assero* is to throw, in words, or to throw out, as in *appello; dissero* is to throw words or arguments, with the sense of spreading, expatiating; *insero* is to throw or thrust in; *resero* is to throw or drive from, hence to unlock or open.

It is by resorting to the primary idea of words that we are able to explain applications, apparently, or in fact, diverse and even contrary. A very common example of this contrariety occurs in words which signify to guard or defend. For instance, the Latin *arceo* signifies to drive off, and to protect, secure, hold, restrain, or keep from departing or escaping; two senses directly opposite. This is extremely natural; for *arceo* signifies to thrust off, repel, drive back; and this act defends the person or object attacked. Or if we suppose the sense of *straining* to be anterior to that of repulsion, which is not improbable, then the act of straining or holding produces both effects; to repel or stop what advances to assault, and protect what is inclosed or assaulted. The words *guard* and *warren* present a similar application of the primary idea; and all languages which I have examined, furnish a multitude of similar examples.

These examples illustrate the utility of extensive researches in language; as all cognate languages throw light on each other; one language often retaining the radical meaning of a word which the others have lost. Who, for instance, that is acquainted only with the English use of the verb to *have*, would suspect that this word and *happen* are radically one, and that the primary sense is to *fall* or *rush*, hence to fall on and seize? Yet nothing is more certain. In the Spanish language the senses of both verbs are retained in *haber;* and the Welsh *hapiaw* gives us the true original signification.

In like manner the primary sense of *venio* in Latin, cannot be certainly determined without resorting to other words, and to kindred languages. In Latin, the word signifies to *come* or *arrive*; but in Spanish, *venida*, from *venir*, the Latin *venio*, signifies not only a coming or arrival, but an attack in fencing. *Venio* coincides in origin with the English *find;* Saxon *findan;* German and Dutch *finden*, to find, to fall or light on; Danish *finder;* Swedish *finna*, to find, to discover, to meet, to strike against [offendere.] The primary sense of *venio* then is not merely to come or arrive, but to rush or move with a driving force; and this sense is applicable to *coming* or *going*.

That the primary sense is to fall or rush, we have evidence in the Latin *ventus*, and English *wind*, both from the root of this verb. We have still further evidence in the word *venom*, which in Welsh is *gwenwyn; gwen*, white, and *gwyn*, rage, smart, whence *gwynt*, wind. *Venom* is that which frets or excites a raging pain. Hence we may infer that L. *venor*, to hunt, to chase, is of the same family; and so is *venia*, leave, or leave to depart, or a departure, a leaving, coinciding in signification with *leave*.

The latter word, *venia*, proves another fact, that the primary sense of *venio* is, in general, to move in any direction, and that the Latin sense, to *come*, is a particular appropriation of that sense.

In ascertaining the primary sense of words, it is often useful or necessary to recur to the derivatives. Thus the Latin *lædo* is rendered to *hurt;* but, by adverting to *allido*, *elido*, and *collido*, we find that the original signification is to *strike*, *hit*, or *dash* against. *Hurt* then is the secondary sense; the effect of the primary action expressed by the verb.

So the Latin *rapio*, to seize, does not give the sense of *rapidus*, rapid, but the sense of the latter proves the primary sense of *rapio* to be to *rush*, and in its application, to rush on and seize.

These examples will be sufficient to show how little the affinities of language have been understood. Men have been generally satisfied with a knowledge of the *appropriate* sense of words, without examining from what visible or physical action, or *primary* sense, that particular application has been derived. Hence the obscurity that still rests on the theory of language. It has been supposed that each word, particularly each verb, has an original specific sense, or application, distinct from every other verb. We find, however, on a close examination and comparison of the same word in different languages, that the fact is directly the reverse; that a verb expressing some action, in a general sense, gives rise to various appropriate senses, or particular applications. And in the course of my researches, I have been struck with the similarity of manner in which different nations have appropriated derivative and figurative senses. For example, all nations, as far as my researches extend, agree in expressing the sense of *justice* and *right*, by *straightness*, and *sin*, *iniquity*, *wrong*, by a deviation from a straight line or course. Equally remarkable is the simplicity of the analogies in language, and the small number of radical significations; so small indeed, that I am persuaded the primary sense of all the verbs in any language, may be expressed by thirty or forty words.

We cannot, at this period of the world, determine, in all cases, which words are primitive, and which are derivative; nor whether the verb or the noun is the original word. Mon. Gebelin, in his *Monde Primitif*, maintains that the noun is the root of all other words. Never was a greater mistake. That some nouns may have been formed before the verbs with which they are connected, is possible; but as languages are now constructed, it is demonstrably certain, that the verb is the radix or stock from which have sprung most of the nouns, adjectives, and other parts of speech belonging to each family. This is the result of all my researches into the origin of languages. We find, indeed, that many modern verbs are formed on nouns; as to *practice* from *practice;* but the noun is derived from a Greek verb. So we use *wrong* as a verb from the adjective *wrong;* but the latter is primarily a participle of the verb to *wring*. Indeed a large part of all nouns were originally participles or adjectives, and the things which they denote were named from their qualities. So *pard*, *pardus*, is from ברד barad, hail; and the animal so named from his spots as if sprinkled with hail, or rather from the sense of separation. *Crape*, the Fr. *crêpe*, is from *crêper*, to crisp. *Sight* signifies, primarily, seen; it being the participle of *seon* contracted from *sigan*. *Draught* is the participle of *draw*, that which is drawn, or the act of drawing; *thought* is the participle of *think*.

As the verb is the principal radix of other words, and as the proper province of this part of speech is to express *action*, almost all the modifications of the primary sense of the verb may be comprehended in one word, to *move*.

The principal varieties of motion or action may be expressed by the following verbs.

1. To drive, throw, thrust, send, urge, press.
2. To set, fix, lay. But these are usually from thrusting, or throwing down.
3. To strain, stretch, draw, whence holding, binding, strength, power, and often health.
4. To turn, wind, roll, wander.
5. To flow, to blow, to rush.
6. To open, part, split, separate, remove, scatter. See No. 16.
7. To swell, distend, expand, spread.
8. To stir, shake, agitate, rouse, excite.
9. To shoot as a plant; to grow; allied to No. 1.
10. To break, or burst; allied sometimes to No. 3.
11. To lift, raise, elevate; allied to No. 9.
12. To flee, withdraw, escape; to fly; often allied to No. 1.
13. To rage; to burn; allied to No. 7 and 8.
14. To fall; to fail; whence fading, dying, &c.
15. To approach, come, arrive, extend, reach. This is usually the sense of *gaining*. No. 34.
16. To go, walk, pass, advance; allied to No. 6.
17. To seize, take, hold; sometimes allied to No. 31.
18. To strike; to beat; allied to No. 1.
19. To swing; to vibrate. No. 29.
20. To lean; to incline; allied to the sense of wandering, or departing.
21. To rub, scratch, scrape; often connected with driving, and with roughness.
22. To swim; to float.
23. To stop, cease, rest; sometimes at least from straining, holding, fastening.
24. To creep; to crawl; sometimes connected with scraping.
25. To peel, to strip, whence spoiling.
26. To leap, to spring; allied to No. 9 and 1.
27. To bring, bear, carry; in some instances connected with producing, throwing out.
28. To sweep.
29. To hang. No. 19.
30. To shrink, or contract; that is, to draw. See No. 3.
31. To run; to rush forward; allied to No. 1.
32. To put on or together; to unite; allied to No. 1 and 3.
33. To knit, to weave.
34. To gain, to win, to get. See No. 15.

These and a few more verbs express the literal sense of all the primary roots. But it must be remarked that all the foregoing significations are not distinct. So far from it, that the whole may be brought under the signification of a very few words. The English words to *send*, *throw*, *thrust*, *strain*, *stretch*, *draw*, *drive*, *urge*, *press*, embrace the primary sense of a great part of all the verbs in every language which I have examined. Indeed it must be so, for the verb is certainly the root of most words; and the verb expresses *motion*, which always implies the application of force.

Even the verbs which signify to hold or *stop*, in most instances at least, if not in all, denote primarily to strain or restrain by exertion of force; and to *lie* is primarily to throw down, to lay one's self down. So that intransitive verbs are rarely exceptions to the general remark above made, that all verbs primarily express motion or exertion of force. The substantive verb has more claims to be an exception, than any other; for this usually denotes, I think, permanence or continued being; but the primary sense of this verb may perhaps be to *set* or *fix;* and verbs having this sense often express *extension in time* or *duration*. So τεινω in Greek is to stretch, but the same word *teneo* in Latin, is to hold; hence *continuance*.

Let us now attend to the radical sense of some of the most common verbs.

Speaking, *calling*, *crying*, *praying*, *utterance of sounds*, is usually from the sense of *driving* or *straining*. Thus in Latin, *appello* and *compello*, though of a different conjugation from *pello*, *depello*, *impello*, are from the same root; and although the Latin *repello* does not signify to *recall*, yet the corresponding word in Italian *rappellare*, and the French *rappeler*, signify to *recall*, and hence the English *repeal*. Hence also *peal*, either of a bell or of thunder. This is the Greek βαλλω, and probably παλλω is from the same root. The sense of *striking* is found in the Greek verb, and so it is in the Lat. *loquor*, Eng. *clock*. But in general, speaking, in all its modifications, is the straining, driving, or impulse of sounds. Sometimes the sense coincides more exactly with that of *breaking* or *bursting*.

Singing is a driving or straining of the voice; and we apply *strain* to a passage of music, and to a course of speaking.

I am not confident that I can refer the sensation of *hearing* to any visible action. Possibly it may sometimes be from striking, hitting, touching. But we observe that *hear* is connected in origin with *ear*, as the Latin *audio* is with the Greek ους, ωτος, the ear; whence it appears probable that the verb to *hear*, is formed from the name of the ear, and the *ear* is from some verb which signifies to shoot or extend, for it signifies a limb.

The primary sense of *seeing*, is commonly to extend to, to reach; as it were, to reach with the eye. Hence the use of *behold*, for the radical sense of *hold* is to strain; and hence its signification in *beholden*, held, bound, obligated. See the verb *See* in the Dictionary.

The sense of *look* may be somewhat different from that of *see*. It appears in some instances to have for its primary signification to *send*, *throw*, *cast;* that is, to send or cast the eye or sight.

The primary sense of *feeling* is to touch, hit, or strike; and probably this is the sense of *taste*.

Wonder and astonishment are usually expressed by some word that signifies to *stop* or *hold*. Hence the Latin *miror*, to wonder, is the Armoric *miret*, to stop, hold, hinder; coinciding with the English *moor*, and Spanish *amarrar*, to *moor*, as a ship.

INTRODUCTION.

To begin is to come, or fall on; to thrust on. We have a familiar example in the Latin *incipio, in* and *capio;* for *capio* is primarily to fall or rush on and seize. See *Begin* in the Dictionary.

Attempt is expressed by straining, stretching, as in Latin *tento.* See *Assay* and *Essay.*

Power, strength, and the corresponding verb, to *be able,* are usually expressed by *straining, stretching,* and this is the radical sense of *ruling* or *governing.* Of this the Latin *rego* is an example, which gives *rectus, right,* that is, *stretched, straight.*

Care, as has been stated, is usually from *straining,* that is, a *tension* of the mind.

Thinking is expressed by *setting.* To *think* is to set or fix or hold in the mind. It approaches to the sense of *suppose,* Lat. *suppono.*

And under this word, let us consider the various applications of the Latin *puto.* The simple verb *puto* is rendered to prune, lop or dress, as vines, that is, according to Ainsworth, putum, *i. e.* purum reddo, purgo, by which I understand him to mean, that *putum* is either a change of *purum,* or used for it; a most improbable supposition, for the radical letters *t* and *r* are not commutable. *Puto* is rendered also, to make even, clear, adjust, or cast up accounts; also to think or consider; to suppose; to debate. Its compounds are *amputo,* to cut off, prune, amputate, to remove; *computo,* to *compute,* to reckon, to think or deem; *disputo,* to make clear, to adjust or settle, to *dispute* or debate, to reason; *imputo,* to impute, to ascribe or lay to, to place to account; *reputo,* to consider, to revolve, to reckon up, to impute. The Latin *deputo* signifies to think, judge or esteem, to account or reckon, and to prune; but the Italian *deputare,* Spanish *diputar,* and French *deputer,* from the Latin word, all signify, to send. How can the sense of *think,* and that of *lop* or *prune,* be deduced from a common root or radical sense? We find the solution of this question in the verb to *depute.* The primary sense is to throw, thrust or send, or to set or lay, which is from throwing, driving. To prune is to separate, remove, or drive off; to force off; to *think* is a setting in the mind; to *compute* is to throw or put together, either in the mind or in numbers; to *dispute* is to throw against or apart, like *debate,* to beat from; to *impute,* is to throw or *put* to or on; and to *repute,* is to think or throw in the mind, repeatedly. To *amputate,* is to separate by cutting round. *Puto* then in Latin is from the same root probably, as the English *put,* or the same word differently applied; and also the Dutch *pooten,* to plant; *poot,* a paw, a twig or shoot, Gr. φυτον, &c.

In attempting to discover the primary sense of words, we are to carry our reflections back to the primitive state of mankind, and consider how rude men would effect their purposes, before the invention or use of the instruments which the moderns employ. The English verb to *cut,* signifies ordinarily to separate with an edged tool; and we are apt to consider this as the chief and original sense. But if so, how can *cut,* the stroke of a whip, which is a legitimate sense of the word, be deduced from the act of severing by an edged tool? We have, in this popular use of the word, a clew to guide us to the primary sense, which is, to drive, urge, press, and applied to the arm, to strike. But we have better evidence. In the popular practice of speaking in New England, it is not uncommon to hear one person call to another when running, and say, *cut on, cut on;* that is, hurry, run faster, drive, press on; probably from striking a beast which one rides on. This is the original sense of the word. Hence we see, that this verb is the Latin *cædo,* to strike, to cut down, somewhat differently applied, and *cado,* to fall, is only a modified sense of the same root, and the compounds *incido,* to cut, and *incido,* to fall on, are of one family. To *cut,* is therefore primarily to strike, or drive, and to *cut off,* if applied to the severing of bodies, before edged tools were used, was to force off, or to strike off; hence the sense of separating in the phrase to *cut off* a retreat or communication.

So the Latin *carpo* is the English *carve,* originally to separate by plucking, pulling, seizing and tearing, afterwards, by cutting.

Asking is usually expressed by the sense of *pressing, urging.* We have a clear proof of this in the Latin *peto* and its compounds. This verb signifies primarily to rush, to drive at, to assault, and this sense, in Dictionaries, ought to stand first in the order of definitions. We have the force of the original in the words *impetus* and *impetuous.* So the Latin *rogo,* coincides in elements with *reach.*

The act of *understanding* is expressed by *reaching* or *taking, holding, sustaining;* the sense of *comprehend,* and of *understand.* We have a popular phrase which well expresses this sense, "I *take* your meaning or your idea." So in German, *begreifen,* to *begripe,* to apprehend.

Knowing seems to have the same radical sense as *understanding.*

Pain, grief, distress, and the like affections, are usually expressed by *pressure* or *straining.* *Affliction* is from *striking.*

Joy, mirth, and the like affections, are from the sense of *rousing, exciting, lively action.*

Covering, and the like actions are from spreading over or cutting off, interruption.

Hiding, is from covering or from withdrawing, departure; or concealment may be from withholding, restraining, suppressing, or making fast, as in the Latin *celo.*

Heat usually implies excitement; but as the effect of heat as well as of cold is sometimes to contract, I think both are sometimes from the same radix. Thus *cold* and the Lat. *caleo,* to be warm, and *callus* and *calleo,* to be hard, have all the same elementary letters, and I suppose them all to be from one root, the sense of which is, to draw, strain, shrink, contract. I am the more inclined to this opinion, for these words coincide with *calleo,* to be strong or able, to know; a sense that imples straining and holding.

Hope is probably from reaching forward. We express strong desire by *longing,* reaching towards.

Earnestness, boldness, daring, peril, promptness, readiness, willingness, love and favor, are expressed by *advancing* or *inclining.*

Light is often expressed by opening, or the shooting of rays, radiation; and probably in many cases, the original word was applied to the dawn of day in the morning. *Whiteness* is often connected in origin with light. We have an instance of this in the Latin *caneo,* to shine and to be white. And that the primary sense of this word, is to shoot, to radiate, that is, to throw out or off, we have evidence in the verb *cano,* to sing, whence *canto,* the sense of which is retained in our popular use of *cant;* to *cant* a stone; to *cant* over a cask; give the thing a *cant;* for all these words are from one stock.

The Latin *virtus,* the English *worth,* is from the root of *vireo,* to grow, that is, to stretch forward, to shoot; hence the original sense is strength, a sense we retain in its application to the qualities of plants. Hence the Latin sense of *virtus,* is bravery, coinciding with the sense of *boldness,* a projecting forward.

Pride is from swelling or elevation, the primary sense of some other words nearly allied to it.

Fear is usually from *shrinking* or from *shaking, trembling;* or sometimes perhaps from *striking,* a being struck, as with surprise.

Holiness and *sacredness* are sometimes expressed by *separation,* as from common things. The Teutonic word *holy* however seems to be from the sense of *soundness, entireness.*

Faith and *belief* seem to imply a resting on, or a *leaving.* It is certain that the English *belief* is a compound of the prefix *be* and *leaf,* leave, permission. To *believe* one then is to *leave* with him, to rest or suffer to rest with him, and hence not to dispute, contend or deny.

Color may by from spreading over or putting on; but in some instances, the primary sense is to *dip.* See *Dye* and *Tinge.*

Spots are from the sense of *separating* or from *sprinkling, dispersion.*

The radical sense of *making* is to press, drive, or force. We use *make* in its true literal sense, in the phrases, *make* your horse draw, *make* your servant do what you wish.

Feeding is from the sense of *pressing, crowding, stuffing,* that is, from *driving* or *thrusting.* Eating seems to have a somewhat different sense.

Drinking is from *drawing,* or from wetting, plunging. *Drench* and *drink* are radically one word.

Anger, and the like violent passions imply excitement, or violent action. Hence their connection with *burning* or *inflammation,* the usual sense of which is *raging* or *violent commotion.*

Agreement, harmony, are usually from meeting, or union, or from extending, reaching to.

Dwelling, abiding, are from the sense of throwing or setting down, or resting, or from stretching; as we see by the Latin *continuo,* from *teneo,* Gr. τεινω, to extend.

Guarding and *defending,* are from roots that signify to *stop,* or to *cut off;* or more generally, from the sense of *driving off,* a repelling or striking back. In some cases perhaps from holding.

Opposition is usually expressed by meeting, and hence the prepositions which express opposition. Thus the Danish preposition *mod,* Swedish *mot* or *emot,* against, contrary, is the English word to *meet.*

Words which express *spirit* denote primarily *breath, air, wind,* the radical sense of which is to *flow, move* or *rush.* Hence the connection between *spirit* and *courage, animus, animosus;* hence passion, *animosity.* So in Greek φρενιτις, frenzy, is from φρην, the mind, or rather from its primary sense, a moving or rushing.

So in our mother-tongue, *mod* is mind or spirit; whence *mood,* in English, and Sax. *modig,* moody, angry. Hence *mind* in the sense of *purpose,* its primary signification, is a setting forward, as *intention* is from *intendo,* to stretch, to strain, the sense that ought to stand first in a Dictionary.

Reproach, chiding, rebuke, are from the sense of scolding, or throwing out words with violence.

Sin, is generally from the sense of deviating, wandering, as is the practice of lewdness.

Right, justice, equity, are from the sense of stretching, making straight, or from laying, making smooth.

Falsehood is from *falling, failing,* or from *deviation, wandering, drawing aside.*

The primary sense of *strange* and *foreign,* is distant, and from some verb signifying to *depart.* *Wild* and *fierce* are from a like sense.

Vain, vanity, wane, and kindred words, are from *exhausting, drawing out,* or from *departing, withdrawing, falling away.*

Paleness is usually from *failure,* a departure of color.

Glory is from opening, expanding, display, or making clear.

Binding, making fast or close, is from pressure, or straining.

Writing is from scratching, engraving, the sense of all primitive words which express this act.

A *crowd*, a *mass*, a *wood*, &c., are from collecting or pressing, or some allied signification.

Vapor, steam, smoke, are usually from verbs which signify to exhale or throw off.

Stepping seems to be from opening, expanding, stretching. Thus *passus* in Latin is from *pando*, to open, but this agrees in origin with *pateo*, and with the Greek πατεω. *Gradus* in Latin coincides with the Welsh *rhawd*, a way, and this, when traced to its root, terminates in the oriental רדה, רד, Chaldee, to open, stretch or expand: in Syriac ܪܕܐ radah, to go, to pass. Walking may be sometimes from a like source; but the word *walk* signifies primarily to roll, press, work and full, as a hat, whence *walker* signifies a fuller.

Softness and *weakness* are usually named from *yielding, bending, withdrawing*, as is relaxation. Softness however is sometimes connected with smoothness, and perhaps with moisture.

Sweetness seems to have for its primary sense, either softness or smoothness.

Roughness is from sharp points, wrinkling or breaking; and *acidity* is from sharpness or pungency, and nearly allied to roughness.

Death is expressed by falling or departure; *life* by fixedness or continuance, or from animation, excitement.

Selling is primarily, a passing or transfer. *Sellan*, in Saxon, signifies to *give* as well as to *sell*.

A *coast* or *border*, is usually the extreme point, from extending.

Law is from setting, establishing.

The primary sense of son, daughter, offspring, is usually a *shoot*, or as we say, *issue*. Hence in Hebrew בן ben, signifies both a son, a cion, a branch, and the young of other animals. A son, says Parkhurst, is from בנה banah, to build, and hence he infers that a son is so called, because he builds up or continues his father's house or family. But if so, how does the word apply to a branch, or an arrow? What do these build up? The mistake of this author, and of others, proceeds from their not understanding the original meaning of the verb, which is *not to erect*, or *elevate*, but to throw, to set, to found; and this verb is probably retained in our word *found*. A son is that which is thrown or shot out, a cion or branch is the same, an *offset*, one an *offset* of the human body, the other of a plant, and an arrow is that which is shot or thrown. Hence probably the Hebrew אבן eben or even, a stone, W. *maen*, or *vaen*, that which is set, so named from its compactness or hardness. And in Arabic أبن abana, signifies to think, Lat. *opinor*, that is, to set in the mind.

Few and *small* are senses often expressed by the same word. Thus, although *few* in English expresses merely a small number, yet the same word in French, *peu*, and in the Italian, *poco*, signifies *little* in quantity, as well as *few* in number.

Cause is from the sense of *urging, pressing, impelling*. Hence it well expresses that which produces an effect; and hence it is peculiarly expressive of that by which a man seeks to obtain a claim in law. A *cause* in court is properly a *pressing for right*, like *action* from *ago*; and *prosecution* from the Latin *sequor*, which is our word *seek*. Hence the Latin *accuso*, to *accuse*, to throw upon, to press or load with a charge. The Saxon *saca*, contention, suit in law, is synonymous with cause, and from the root of *seek, sequor*. It is the English *sake*.

The word *thing* is nearly synonymous with *cause* and *sake*. See *Thing* in the Dictionary.

The primary sense of *time, luck, chance, fortune*, is to fall, to come, to arrive, to happen. *Tide, time* and *season*, have a like original sense. *Tide* in Saxon is *time*, not a flow of the sea, the latter being a secondary and modern application of the word. This primary signification of time will unfold to us what I formerly could not understand, and what I could find no person to explain, that is, why the Latin *tempora* should signify *times* and the *temples*. It seems that *tempora* are the *falls* of the head. Hence also we understand why *tempest* is naturally deducible from *tempus*, as the primary sense is to fall, to rush. Hence *tempestivus*, seasonable, that comes in good time. *Season* has a like sense.

Hence also we are led to understand, what has seemed inexplicable, how the French *heureux*, lucky, happy, can be regularly deduced from *heure*, an hour. We find that in Greek and Latin, the primary sense of *hour* is *time*, and *time* is a coming, a falling, a happening, like the English *luck*, and hence the sense of lucky; hence fortunate and happy. The word *fortunate* is precisely of the same character.

The primary sense of the Shemitic דבר davar, or thavar, corresponds almost precisely with that of *cause* and *thing* in English, that is, to strain, urge, drive, fall or rush. Hence it signifies, to speak, and in Ch. and Syr. to lead, to direct, to govern. As a noun, it signifies a word, that which is uttered; a thing, cause or matter, that is, that which happens or falls, like *event* from evenio; also a plague, or great calamity, that is, that which falls, or comes on man or beast, like *plague*, a stroke or *affliction*, from striking. And it may be observed, that if the first letter is a prefix answering to the Gothic *du*, Saxon and English *to*, in the Saxon *to-drifan*, to drive, then the root בר coincides exactly with the Welsh *peri*, to command, which is retained in composition in the Lat. *impero*. Indeed if the first syllable of *guberno* is a prefix, the root of this word may be the same. The object however for which this word is here mentioned, is chiefly to show the uniformity which men have observed in expressing their ideas; making use of the same visible physical action to represent the operations of the mind and moral ideas.

Silence, deafness, dumbness, are from *stopping, holding*, or *making fast*.

War is from the sense of *striving, driving, struggling*.

Good is generally from *enlarging*, or *advancing*, like *prosperous*.

Evil is from wandering, departing, or sometimes from softness, weakness, flowing or fluxibility, as is the case with the Latin *malum*, from the Welsh *mall*.

The primary sense of the names of natural and material objects cannot always be ascertained. The reasons are obvious. Some of these names are detached branches of a family of words, which no longer form a part of our language, the verb and all the derivatives, except a single name, being extinct or found only in some remote country. Others of these names have suffered such changes of orthography, that it is difficult or impossible to ascertain the primary or radical letters, and of course the family to which they belong. Numerous examples of such words occur in English, as in every other language.

But from such facts as have occurred to me, in my researches, I may venture to affirm with confidence, that most names of natural objects are taken from some obvious quality or action, or some supposed quality of the thing; or from the particular action or operation by which it is produced. Thus *tumors* are named from *pushing*, or *swelling*; and *redness*, or *red*, seems, in some instances at least, to be named from *eruptions* on the body. The human body is named from *shaping*, that is, *setting, fixing*, or *extending*, and hence sometimes, the general name of the human race. The arm is a *shoot*, a *push*, as is the branch of a tree. A board, a table, a floor, is from *spreading*, or *expanding, extending*. Skin, and bark are from *peeling, stripping*, &c.

The names of particular animals and plants cannot always be traced to their source; but as far as I have been able to discover their origin, I find animals to be generally named from some striking characteristic of external appearance, from the voice, from habits of life, or from their office. There is reason for believing that the Greek στρουθος and Latin *struthio*, or ostrich, is from the same root as the English *strut*, the strutter; the primary sense of which root is, to stretch, which explains all the senses of the Greek and Latin words of this family. It is certain that the *crow* is named from its cry, and the *leopard* from his spots.

Thus plants were named from their qualities: some from their form, others from their color, others from their effects, others from the place of their growth. The English *root*, Lat. *radix*, is only a particular application of *rod* and *ray, radius*; that is, a shoot. *Spurge* is undoubtedly from the root of the Latin *purgo*.

There is reason to think that many names of plants were originally adjectives, expressing their qualities, or the name was a compound used for the same purpose, one part of which has been dropped, and the other remaining as the name of the plant. Thus *pine, pinus*, is from *pin, pinna, penna*; for in Welsh *pin* is a *pin* and a *pen* or style for writing, and *pinbren* is a pine-tree. The tree then was named from its leaf.

Fir has a similar origin and signification.

It is probable or rather certain that some natural objects, as plants and minerals, received their names from their *supposed* qualities; as in ages of ignorance and superstition, men might ascribe effects to them, by mistake. The whole history of magic and enchantment leads us to this conclusion.

Minerals are, in many instances, named from their obvious qualities, as *gold* from its yellowness, and *iron* from its hardness. The names can, in some cases, be traced to their original, as that of *gold* and of the Latin *ferrum*; but many of them, are not easily ascertained. Indeed the greatest part of the specific names of animals, plants and minerals appear to be obscure. Some of them appear to have no connection with any family of words in our language, and many of them are derived to us from Asia, and from roots which can be found only, if found at all, in the Asiatic languages.

These observations and explanations will be sufficient to show the importance of developing, as far as possible, the origin of words, and of comparing the different uses of the same word in different languages, in order to understand either the philosophy of speech, or the real force and signification of words in their practical application.

If it should be found to be true, that many of the Shemitic verbs are formed with prefixes, like those of the European languages, this may lead to new illustrations of the original languages of the scriptures. In order to determine this fact, it will be useful to examine whether the Chaldee and Hebrew ב is not often a prefix answering to *be* in the Teutonic languages; whether ג and כ are not prefixes answering to the *ga* and *ge* of the Gothic and Teutonic; whether ד, ט and ת, and ז, a dialectical form of ט, do not coincide with the Gothic *du*, the Saxon *to*, the Dutch *toe*, and the German *zu*; whether נ does not answer to the Russ. and Dutch *na*, the German *nach*; and whether ס and ש do not answer to *s, sh*, and *sch* in the modern English and German.

If many of the Shemitic triliteral verbs are compound, it follows that the primary radix has not been detected. At any rate, I have no hesitation in affirming that the primary sense of many of the roots in the Shemitic languages, that sense which is almost indispensable to an understanding of many obscure passages in the scriptures, has been hitherto overlooked or mistaken. In order fully to comprehend many uses of the words, it will be necessary to compare them with the uses of the words of the same family in the modern languages, and this comparison must be far more extensive than any hitherto made, and conducted on principles which have not been before duly appreciated and applied.

I have introduced the foregoing comparative view of the several significations of the same word in different languages, not merely to illustrate the general principles of language, but with a special reference to an explanation of the etymologies which occur in this work. Should my synopsis ever be published, the learned enquirer might pursue the subject at his pleasure.

The results of the foregoing remarks and illustrations may be thus recapitulated.

1. The nations which now constitute the distinct families or races of Japhet and Shem, are descendants of the common family which inhabited the plain of Shinar, before the dispersion.

2. The families at the dispersion retained a large proportion of the words which were in common use, before that event, and the same were conveyed to their posterity. In the course of time, some of these words were dropped by one family or tribe, and some by another, till very few of them are retained in their original form and signification by all the nations which have sprung from the main stock. A few of them however are still found in all or nearly all the languages which I have examined, bearing nearly the same signification and easily recognized as identical.

3. Although few of the primitive words can now be recognized, as existing in *all* the languages, yet as we better understand the changes which have been made in the orthography and signification of the same radical words, the more affinities are discovered; and particularly, when we understand the *primary* sense, we find this to unite words whose *appropriate* or *customary* significations appear to have no connection.

4. A great number of the primitive radical words are found in compounds, formed in different languages, with different affixes and prefixes, which obscure the affinity. Thus *veritas* in Latin is *wahrheit* in German; the first syllable in each is the same word, the last, different. In other instances, both difference of orthography, of formation and of application concur to obscure the affinity of words. Thus, the English word *strong* is in Danish *streng*, signifying stern, severe, rigid, strict; and *strenghed* [stronghood] is severity, rigor, strictness. Now, *n* in these words is not radical; remove this letter and we have *strog*, *streg*, which coincide with the Latin *stringo*, *strictus;* and these words are found to be from the same radix, which signifies to draw, to strain, to stretch.

5. It appears that *b*, *p* and *f* are often prefixes, either the remains of prepositions, or casual additions to words, introduced by peculiar modes of pronunciation, which prefixes now precede consonants with which they readily coalesce in pronunciation, as *l* and *r*, forming triliteral words on biliteral roots; as in *block* from *lloc*, or *lock; play*, Saxon *plegan*, from *leg* or *lek*, Swedish *leka*, Dan. *leger; flow*, Lat. *fluo*, from *lug*, or *luc*, which appears in *light*, *lux*, *luceo*, and in *lug*, a river, retained in *Lugdunum*.

6. It appears also that *c* or *k* and *g*, are often prefixes before the same consonants, *l* and *r*, as in Lat. *clunis*, Eng. *loin;* W. *clod*, *praise*, from *llod*, Latin, *laus*, *laudo;* German *gluck*, English *luck;* Lat. *gratia*, W. *rhad.*

7. It appears also that *s* is a prefix in a vast number of words, as in *speed*, *spoil*, *swell*, *sweep;* and it is very evident that *st* are prefixed to many words whose original, radical, initial consonant was *r*, as in *straight*, *strict*, *strong*, *stretch*, from the root of *right*, *rectus*, *reach*, and in *stride*, from the root of the Latin *gradior*, W. *rhaz.*

If these inferences are just, as I am persuaded they are, it follows that there is a more near resemblance and a much closer affinity between the languages of Europe and of Western Asia, than has hitherto been supposed to exist. It follows also that some of the most important principles or rudiments of language have hitherto escaped observation, and that philology is yet in its infancy. Should this prove, on further examination, to be the state of philology, it is reserved for future investigators to examine the original languages of the scriptures on new principles, which may serve to illustrate some obscure and difficult passages, not hitherto explained to the general satisfaction of critics and commentators.

If any persons should be disposed to doubt or contradict these facts, let them first consider that my conclusions are not *hasty* opinions, formed on isolated facts; but that they have been forced upon me, in opposition to all my former habits of thinking, by a series of successive proofs and accumulating evidence, during a long course of investigation, in which I have compared most of the radical words, in more than twenty languages, *twice* and some of them *three times.*

No part of my researches has given me more trouble or solicitude, than that of arriving at the precise radical signification of moral ideas; such for example, as *hope, love, favor, faith.* Nor has it been with much less labor that I have obtained a clear knowledge of some of our physical actions. It is literally true that I have sometimes had a word under consideration for two or three years, before I could satisfy my own mind, as to the primary signification. That I have succeeded at last, in every instance, can hardly be supposed—yet, in most cases, I am perfectly satisfied with the results of my researches.

Progress and Changes of the English Language.

It has been already observed that the mother tongue of the English is the Anglo-Saxon. The following are specimens of that language as it was spoken or written in England before the Norman conquest. The first is from the Saxon Chronicle. The original is in one column, and the literal translation in the other. The English words in italics are Saxon words. The number of these will show how large a proportion of the words is retained in the present English.

An. DCCCXCI. Her for se here east, and Earnulf cyning gefeaht with thæm ræde-here ær tha scipu comon, mid East-Francum, and Seaxum, and Bægerum, and hine geflymde. And thry Scottas cwomon to Ælfrede cyninge on anum bate, butan ælcum gerethum, of Hibernia; and thonon hi hi bestælon, forthon the hi woldon for Godes lufan on eltheodinesse bion, hy ne rohton hwær.	An. 891. *Here* [this year] *fared* the army *east and* Earnulf, the *king*, *fought with* the cavalry [*ride* army] *ere the ships come*, with the *East*-Francs, *and* Saxons *and* Bavarians, *and* put them to flight. *And three* Scots *come to* Ælfred, the *king*, *in a* [*an*] *boat*, without any *rowers*, from Hibernia, *and thence* they privately withdrew [*bestole*] because that they *would*, *for God's love be* [or live] *where* they should not be anxious—[reck, care.]
Se bat wæs geworht of thriddan healfre hyde, the hie on foron, and hi namon mid him that hie hæfdon to seofon nihtum mete, and tha comon hie ymb seofon niht, to londe on Cornwealum, and foran tha sona to Ælfrede cyninge.	The *boat was wrought of two hides and a half* [*third half hide*,] in which they *fared* [came] *and* they took with them *that* they *had* for *seven nights meat*, *and* they *come* about the *seventh night*, *to land* in Cornwall, *and fared* [went] *soon to* Ælfred, the *king*.

The following specimen is from the Anglo-Saxon version of Orosius, supposed to be made by King Alfred.

Ohthere sæde his hlaforde, Ælfrede kyninge, thæt he ealra Northmanna north mest bude. He cwæth that he bude on thæm lande northeweardum with tha west sæ. He sæde theah thæt thæt land sy swythe north thanon; ac hit is eall west buton on feawum stowum sticce mælum wiciath Finnas, on huntathe on wintra, and on sumera on fiscothe be there sæ. He sæde thæt he æt sumum cyrre wolde fandiam hu lange thæt land north right læge.	Octhere told [*said*] *his lord*, *king* Alfred, *that he* lived *north most* of *all* the *north men*. *He quoth that he* dwelt in the [*them*] *land northward*, opposite [with] the *west sea*. *He said though*, *that that land* is due *north* from *thence*, and that *it is all waste* except [*but*] in a *few* places [stows] where the *Finns* for the most part dwell, for *hunting in winter*, *and* in *summer* for *fishing* in that *sea*, [by the sea.] *He said that he*, at *some* time, *would find how long that land* lay *right north*.

Laws of King Æthelbert.

Gif Cyning his leode to him gehatath, and heom mon thær yfel gedo, II bote and cyning L. scillinga.	*If* the *King* shall call [*cite*] *his* people *to him*, *and* any one [*man*] shall there *do evil*, let double compensation be made, *and* fifty *shillings* to the *King*.
Gif in Cyninges tune man mannan *ofsleah*, L. scill. gebete.	*If in* the *King's town* a *man slay* a man, let him compensate [*boot*] with fifty *shillings*.
Gif on Eorles tune man mannan ofsleath, XII Scil. gebete.	*If in* an *Earl's town* one *man slayeth* another *man*, let him pay twelve *shillings* for reparation.
Gif man thone man ofslæhth, XX scil. gebete.	*If man*, [any one] *slayeth* any *man*, let him compensate with twenty *shillings*.
Gif thuman (of a slæhth) XX scil. Gif thuman nægl of weordeth III scil. gebete. Gif man scytefinger (of a slæhth,) VIII scil. gebete. Gif man middle finger (of a slæhth,) IV. scil. gebete. Gif man gold-finger (of a slæhth,) VI scil. gebete. Gif man thon litlan finger (of a slæhth) XI scil. gebete.	*If* the *thumb* shall be cut off, twenty *shillings*. *If* the *thumb nail* shall be cut off, three *shillings* shall be the compensation. *If* any one [*off slayeth*, striketh off,] cutteth off the fore finger [*shoot finger*,] let him compensate with eight *shillings*. *If* one cutteth off the *middle finger*, let him pay four *shillings*. *If* any one cutteth off the *gold finger* [ring finger,] let him pay six *shillings*. *If* any one cutteth off the *little finger*, let pay eleven *shillings*.

INTRODUCTION.

Laws of King Eadgar.

We lærath that ælc cristen man his bearn to cristendome *geornlice* wænige and him pater noster and credon tæce.	We order or instruct *that* each *christian man earnestly* accustom [*wean*] *his* children *to* christianity [*Christendom*] *and teach him* the Pater Noster *and* Creed.
We lærath that preost ne beo hunta ne hafecere ne tæflere ; ac plegge on his bocum swa his hade gebirath.	We direct *that* a *priest be* not a *hunter*, nor *hawker*, nor a gamester ; but that he *apply* to *his books*, as it becomes *his* order.

We observe by these extracts that rather more than half the Saxon words have been lost, and now form no part of our language.

This language, with some words introduced by the Danes, continued to be used by the English, till the Norman conquest. After that event, great numbers of Saxon words went into disuse, not suddenly, but gradually, and French and Latin words, were continually added to the language, till it began to assume its present form, in the fourteenth and fifteenth centuries. Yet the writings of Gower and Chaucer cannot now be fully understood without a glossary.

But it was not in the loss of native Saxon words and the accession of French and Latin words alone that the change of our language consisted. Most important alterations were made in the sounds of the vowels. It is probable, if not certain, that our first vowel *a* had usually or always the broad sound, as we now pronounce it in *fall*, or in some words perhaps the Italian sound, as it is now called, and as we pronounce it in *ask*. The sound of *e* was probably nearly the same as it is in French and Italian, and in the northern languages on the continent of Europe ; which is nearly that of *a* in *favor*. The Saxon sound of *i* was probably the same as it is still on the continent, the sound of *ee* or long *e*. The sound of *u* was that of our present *oo*, French *ou*, the sound it still has in Italian, and in most countries on the European continent. It is probable that the change of the sound of *u* happened in consequence of the prevalence of the French pronunciation after the conquest; for the present sound of *u* may be considered as intermediate, between the full sound of *oo*, or French *ou*, and the French sound of *u*.

These changes, and the various sounds given to the same character, now serve to perplex foreigners, when learning English ; and tend, in no small degree, to retard or limit the extension of our language. This is an unfortunate circumstance, not only in obstructing the progress of science, but of christianity.

The principal changes in the articulations are the *use* of *k* for *c*, as in *look* for *locian ;* the loss of *h* before *l*, as in *loaf* from *hlaf*, *lot* for *hlot*, *lean* for *hlinian ;* and the entire loss of the prefix *ge* or *ga*, as in *deal* for *ge-dælan*, *deem* for *ge-deman ;* and of *to* as a prefix, as in *to-helpan*, to help ; *to-dailan*, to deal. In no instance do we feel more sensibly the change of sounds in the vowels, than in that of *i*, which in French, Spanish and Italian, is *e* long ; for in consequence of this, persons, who are not acquainted with these foreign languages, mispronounce such words as *marino*, *Messina*, *Lima*, giving to *i* its English sound, when in fact the words are to be pronounced *mareeno*, *Messeena*, *Leema*.

In grammatical structure, the language has suffered considerable alterations. In our mother tongue, nouns were varied to form cases, somewhat as in Latin. This declension of nouns has entirely ceased, except in the possessive or genitive case, in which an apostrophe before *s* has been substituted for the regular Saxon termination *es*. Some of our pronouns retain their declensions, somewhat varied. The plural termination in *en* has been dropped, in a number of words, and the regular plural termination been substituted, as *houses* for *housen*.

In most cases, the Saxon termination of the infinitive mode of verbs, has been dropped, and for *gifan*, we now write, *to give*. The variations of the verb, in the several persons, have been materially changed. Thus for the Saxon—

Ic lufige,	We lufiath,
Thu lufast,	Ge lufiath,
He lufath.	Hi lufiath.

we now write—

I love,	We love,
Thou lovest,	Ye love,
He loveth or loves.	They love.

In the Saxon plural however we see the origin of the vulgar practice, still retained in some parts of England and of this country. *We loves, they loves*, which are contractions of *lufiath*.

In the substantive verb, our common people universally, and most persons of better education, unless they have rejected their traditionary language, retain the Gothic dialect, in the past tense.

I was,	We was,
Thou wast,	Ye was,
He was.	They was.

However people may be ridiculed for this language, it is of genuine origin, as old as the Saxon word *were*. In Gothic, the past tense runs thus—

Ik was,	Weis wesum,
Thu wast,	Yus wesuth,
Is was.	Eis wesun.*

In the present tense of the substantive verb, our common people use *ā'nt* as in this phrase : "he *ā'nt* present." This is evidently a contraction of the Swedish and Danish, år, *er*, present, indicative, singular, of the substantive verb, *vara* or *værer*, to be, which we retain in *are* and *were*.

In Swedish, han år, and in Danish, han *er*, he is. Hence he *er not* or *ar not*, contracted into he *a'nt* or *e'nt*.

These facts serve to show how far the Gothic dialect has been infused into the English language.

It would be tedious and to most readers uninteresting, to recite all the changes in the forms of words or the structure of sentences which have taken place, since the Norman conquest. Since the invention of printing, changes in the language have been less rapid, than before ; but no art nor effort can completely arrest alterations in a living language. The distinguished writers in the age of Queen Elizabeth, improved the language, but could not give it stability. Many words then in common use are now obsolete or have suffered a change of signification. In the period between Queen Elizabeth, and the beginning of the eighteenth century, the language was improved in grammar, orthography, and style. The writers in the reign of Queen Ann and of George I, brought the language nearly to perfection ; and if any improvement has since been made, it is in the style or diction, by a better selection of words, and the use of terms in science and philosophy with more precision.

In regard to grammatical construction, the language, for half a century past, has, in my apprehension, been suffering deterioration, at least as far as regards its written form. This change may be attributed chiefly to the influence of the learned Bishop Lowth, whose grammar made its appearance nearly sixty years ago. I refer particularly to his form of the verb, which was adjusted to the practice of writers in the age of Queen Elizabeth, instead of the practice of authors in the age of William and Mary, Queen Ann, and George I. Hence he gives for the form of the verb in the subjunctive mode, after the words which express a condition, *if, though*, &c. *I love, thou love, he love*, observing in a note, that in the subjunctive mode, the event being spoken of under a condition or supposition, or in the form of a wish, and therefore doubtful and contingent, the verb itself in the present, and the auxiliary both of the present and past imperfect times, often carry with them somewhat of a future sense ; as "if he come to-morrow, I may speak to him"—"If he should come, I should speak to him." This is true ; but for that very reason, this form of the verb belongs to the future tense, or should be arranged as such in Grammars. *If he come*, would be in Latin *si venerit*, in the subjunctive future.

But the learned author has entirely overlooked the important distinction between an event or fact, of uncertain existence in the *present* time, and which is mentioned under the condition of *present* existence, and a *future* contingent event. "If the mail that has arrived *contains* a letter for me, I shall soon receive it," is a phrase that refers to the present time, and expresses an uncertainty in my mind, respecting the fact. "If the mail *contain* a letter for me," refers to a future time, that is, "if the mail of to-morrow *contain* [shall or should contain] a letter for me." The first event, conditional or hypothetical, should be expressed by the indicative mode, and the latter by the subjunctive future. The Saxon form of the verb, *if he slay, if he go*, is evidently a contingent future, and is so used in the laws.

This distinction, one of the most important in the language, has been so totally overlooked, that no provision has been made for it in British Grammars ; nor is the distinction expressed by the form of the verb, as used by a great part of the best writers. On the other hand, they continually use one form of the verb to express both senses. The fact is the same in the common version of the scriptures. *If he go, if he speak*, sometimes express a present conditional tense, and sometimes a contingent future. In general this subjunctive form of the verb in scripture, expresses future time. "If he thus *say*, I have no delight in thee," expresses a future contingent event. 2 Sam. xv. 26. "If iniquity *be* in thine hand, put it far away," expresses a fact, under a condition, in the present time. Job xi. 14.

In many instances, the translators have deviated from the original, in using the subjunctive form of the English verb to express what in Greek, is expressed in the indicative. Thus Matthew iv. 6. Ει υιος ει του Θεου, if thou *be* [art] the son of God.

Ch. v. 29 and 30. Ει δε ο οφθαλμος σου ο δεξιος σκανδαλιζει σε ; if thy right eye *offend*, [offendeth] thee ; ει η δεξια σου χειρ σκανδαλιζει σε, if thy right hand *offend*, [offendeth] thee.

So also in Chapter xviii. 8 and 9.

---

* This is probably the Latin *esse*. The Latins dropped the first articulation *v*, which answers to our *w*.

The present tense indicative mode of the Latin verb, with the *v* restored, would be written thus.

Ego vesum,	nos vesumus, [was,]
tu ves,	vos vestis, [was,]
ille vest.	illi vesunt, [was.]

INTRODUCTION.

Ch. xii. 26. *Ει ο σατανας τον σαταναν εκβαλλει*, if Satan *cast* [casteth] out Satan.

Ch. xix. 10. *Ει ουτως εςιν η αιτια του ανθρωπου μετα της γυναικος*, if the case of the man *be* [is] so with his wife.

Ch. xxii. 45. *Ει ουν Δαβιδ καλει αυτον* Κυριον, if David then *call* [calleth] him Lord.

2 Cor. iv. 16. *Ει ο εξω ημων ανθρωπος διαφθειρεται*, though our outward man *perish*, [perishes or is perishing.]

In all these passages, the English verb, in the subjunctive, properly expresses a conditional, contingent or hypothetical future tense, contrary to the sense of the original, except in the last passage cited, where the apostle evidently speaks of the perishing of the outward man as a fact admitted, which renders the translation still more improper.

Let us now attend to the following passages.

Matthew vii. 9. Η *τις εςιν εξ υμων ανθρωπος, ον εαν αιτηση ο υιος αυτου αρτον*, or what man is there of you, whom if his son *ask* [shall ask] bread, *will* he give him a stone.

Και *εαν ιχθυν αιτηση*, if he *ask* [shall ask] a fish, *will* he give him a serpent.

Here the original tense is varied to express a future or hypothetical event, yet the verb in English is in the same tense as in the first class of examples; and what renders the version more objectionable, is, that the verb in the first clause, does not correspond with that in the second clause. There is no possible way of making good English of the translation, but by supposing the verb in the first clause *ask*, to be in the future tense. So it would be in Latin, and so it is, "si petierit." If thy son shall ask (or should ask) a fish, will he give, (or would he give) him a serpent?

This fault runs through the whole English version of the scriptures, and a distinction of tenses clearly marked in the original languages, is generally neglected in the translation.

Now the most unlettered man in this country, would express the sense in English, with the same marked distinction of tenses, which appears in the Greek. If thou *art* the son of God; if thy right eye *offends* thee; if the case of the man *is* such; if David *calls* him Lord; or if the sense is understood to be future and contingent, if thy son *shall ask* bread, or if he *should ask* bread, would be the uniform language of any of the common people of our country. There would not probably be a single exception, unless in the use of the substantive verb, which is often used in the subjunctive form. And the most unlettered man would use the corresponding verbs in the two clauses, if he *shall* ask, *will* he give; or if he *should* ask, *would* he give. The use of the verb in all similar phrases, is perfectly well settled in this country, and perfectly uniform among the higher and lower classes of men; unless when the practice has been varied by the influence of Grammars, in which the conjugation of the verb is according to the antiquated practice of the age of Elizabeth.

1 Tim. v. 4. *Ει δε τις χηρα τεκνα η εκγονα εχει*, if any widow, have [has] children or nephews.

Verse 8. *Ει δε τις των ιδιων και μαλιςα των οικειων ου προνοει*, if any provide [provideth] not for his own, and especially for those of his own house.

This subjunctive form of the verb, *if he be; if he have; if he go; if he say; if thou write; whether thou see; though he fall*, which was generally used by the writers of the sixteenth century, was, in a great measure, discarded before the time of Addison. Whether this change was in consequence of the prevalence of colloquial usage over grammar rules, or because discerning men perceived the impropriety and inconsistency of the language of books, I pretend not to determine. Certain it is, that Locke, Watts, Addison, Pope, and other authors of the first distinction, who adorned the close of the seventeenth and beginning of the eighteenth century, generally used the indicative mode to express condition, uncertainty, and hypothesis in the present and past tenses. Thus Locke writes—"If these two propositions *are* by nature imprinted." "If principles *are* innate." "If any person *hath* never examined this notion." "Whether that substance *thinks* or no." "If the soul *doth* think in sleep." "If one *considers* well these men's way of speaking." "If he *does* not reflect." "Unless that notion *produces* a constant train of successive ideas." "If your Lordship *means*." Such is the language of Locke.

Now what is remarkable, the learned Dr. Lowth, the very author who has, by his grammar, done much to sanction the subjunctive form of the verb, in such cases, often uses the indicative in his own writings. "If he *does* not carefully attend to this—if this pleasure *arises* from the shape of the composition—if this *is* not firmly and well established." These verbs are in contradiction of his own principles. *On Isaiah. Prelim. Diss.*

Addison. "If the reader *has* a mind to see a father of the same stamp." "If exercise *throws* off all superfluities—if it *clears* the vessels—if it *dissipates* a growing distemper." Such is the language of Addison, the most elegant writer of the genuine English idiom in the nation.

"If the thief *is* poor—if it *obliges* me to be conversant with scenes of wretchedness." *Wilberforce.*

"If America *is* not to be conquered. *Lord Chatham.*

"If we *are* to be satisfied with assertions." "If it *gives* blind confidence to any executive government." "If such an opinion *has* gone forth." "If our conduct *has* been marked with vigor and wisdom." *Fox.*

"If my bodily strength *is* equal to the task." "A negro, if he *works* for himself and not a for master, will do double the work." "If there *is* any aggravation of our guilt." If their conduct *displays* no true wisdom." "The honorable gentleman may, if he *chooses*, have the journals read again." "Whether this *is* a sufficient tie to unite them." "If this measure *comes* recommended." "If there *exists* a country which contains the means of protection." *Pitt.*

"If the prudence of reserve and decorum *dictates* silence." "If an assembly *is* viciously or feebly composed." If any persons *are* to make good deficiences." "If the King of the French *has* really deserved these murderous attempts." "If this representation of M. Neckar *was* false." "Whether the system, if it *deserves* the name." "The politician looks for a power that our workmen call a *purchase*, and if he *finds* the power." "If he *feels* as men commonly feel." *Burke.*

"If climate *has* such an effect on mankind." "If the effects of climate *are* casual." *Coxe's Russ.*

"If he *finds* his collection too small." "If he *thinks* his judgment not sufficiently enlightened." "Whether it *leads* to truth." "If he *warns* others against his own failings." This is generally the language of *Johnson.*

In regard to this distinguished author, I would observe that, except the substantive verb, there is in his Rambler but a single instance of the subjunctive form of the verb in conditional sentences. In all other cases the use of the indicative is uniform.

Such also is the language of the most distinguished men in the United States, particularly of those who wrote their native language as they received it from tradition, and before grammars had made any impression on its genuine construction.

"The prince that acquires new territory, if he *finds* it vacant." "If we *are* industrious we shall never starve." "If one *has* more corn than he can consume, and another *has* less." Such is the language of *Franklin.*

"If any persons thus qualified *are* to be found." "If it *is* thought proper." "If the congress *does* not choose to point out the particular regiment." "If I *am* rightly informed." "If the army *has* not removed." "If a proposition *has* not been made." Such is the language of *Washington.*

"If any philosopher *pretends*." "If he *has* food for the present day." "If a revelation *is* not impossible." "If the Christian system *contains* a real communication to mankind." "If the former of these facts *opposes* our reception of the miraculous history of the gospel." "If the preceding reflections *are* just." Such is the language of the late President Smith.*

"*If* any government *deems* the introduction of foreigners or their merchandize injurious." "Unless he *violates* the law of nations." "If a person *has* a settlement in a hostile country." "If he *resides* in a belligerent country." "If a foreign Consul *carries* on trade as a merchant." Such is the language of the ex-Chancellor Kent.

But neither the authors here mentioned, nor most others, even the most distinguished for erudition, are uniform and consistent with themselves in the use of the tenses. In one sentence we find the indicative used, "If it *is* to be discovered only by the experiment." "If other indications *are* to be found." In the next sentence, "If to miscarry in an attempt *be* a proof of having mistaken the direction of genius." *Johnson.*

"If the former *be* refined—if those virtues *are* accompanied with equal abilities." *Gibbon.*

"If love *reward* him, or if vengeance *strike*." *Cowper.*

"Or if it *does* not brand him to the last." *Cowper.*

"If he *is* a pagan—if endeavors *are* used—if the person *hath* a liberal education—if man *be* subject to these miseries. *Milner.*

The following expressions occur in Pope's Preface to Homer's Iliad, in the compass of thirteen lines.

"If he *has* given a regular catalogue of an army."
"If he *has* funeral games for Patroclus."
"If Ulysses *visit* the shades."
"If he *be* detained from his return."
"If Achilles *be* absent."
"If he *gives* his hero a suit of celestial armor."

I recollect one English author only, who has been careful to avoid this inconsistency; this is Gregory, who, in his *Economy of Nature*, has uniformly used the indicative form of the verb in conditional sentences of this kind.

The like inconsistency occurs in almost all American writings. "If moral disposition *lie* here." "If preference necessarily *involves* the knowledge of obligation." "If the proposition *is* true." "If the proposition *be* confirmed." "If he *refutes* any thing."

In a pamphlet now before me, there are no less than *fifty* of these inconsistencies in the compass of *ninety* pages; and *three* of them in *one* sentence.

---

*The substantive verb is often used in the subjunctive form by writers who never use that form in any other verb. The reason doubtless is that *be* is primarily the indicative as well as the subjunctive mode of that verb. *I be, we be*, as used in Scripture. So in German *Ich bin.*

How, in this case, is a foreigner to understand the author? and how can such sentences be translated into another language without a deviation from the original?

The propriety of using the indicative form of the verb to express a present or past event conditionally, does not rest solely on usage; it is most correct upon principle. It is well known, that most of the words which are used to introduce a condition or hypothesis, and called most improperly conjunctions, are *verbs*, having not the least affinity to the class of words used to connect sentences. *If* is the Saxon *gif*, give, having lost its first letter; *if* for the ancient *gif*. *Though* is also a verb now obsolete, except in the imperative mode. Now let us analyze this conditional tense of the verb. "If the man *knows* his true interest, he will avoid a quarrel." Here is an omission of the word *that* after *if*. The true original phrase was "*If that* the man knows his true interest, he will avoid a quarrel"—that is, *give that* [admit the fact which is expressed in the following clause] *the man knows his true interest*, then the consequence follows, he will avoid a quarrel. *That* in this sentence is a relative or demonstrative substitute for the following clause. This will more plainly appear by transposing the clauses. "The man *knows* his true interest; *give that* [admit that;] he will then avoid a quarrel. Now let the subjunctive form be used. "The man *know* his true interest; give that; he will avoid a quarrel."

Here the impropriety of this form of the verb appears in a strong light. It will appear more clearly by the use of other words of equivalent signification. *Grant* the man *know* his true interest, he will avoid a quarrel. *Allow* the man *know* his true interest. *Suppose* the man *know* his true interest. We never use the subjunctive form after the three last verbs which introduce the condition. *Though* is sometimes followed by the indicative; sometimes by the subjunctive; but it ought always to be followed by the indicative, for it supposes the fact to be given; and so does *admit*, when used in hypothetical sentences. Admit that the man *knows* his interest. We have then decisive proof that the use of the indicative form of the verb after *if*, when it expresses a conditional event in present time, is most correct; indeed it is the only correct form. This remark is equally applicable to the past tense, conditional.

The language of Addison, Johnson, and other distinguished writers of the last century, in the use of the indicative, is therefore, more correct than the language of the writers in the age of Elizabeth; and their practice is principally the common usage of our country at this day.

I have, therefore, constructed a grammar on this usage; bringing down the standard of writing a century and a half later than Bishop Lowth. I have done this, *first*, on the authority of strict analogical principles, as above stated; *secondly*, on the authority of the best usage of that cluster of distinguished writers who adorned the beginning of the last century; and *thirdly*, on the authority of universal colloquial practice, which I consider as the *real* and *only genuine language*. I repeat this remark, that *general and respectable* usage in *speaking* is the genuine or legitimate language of a country to which the *written* language ought to be conformed. Language is that which is uttered by the tongue, and if men do not write the language as it is *spoken* by the great body of respectable people, they do not write the *real* language. Now, in colloquial usage, the subjunctive form of the verb, in conditional sentences, is rarely used, and perhaps never, except when the substantive verb is employed. Our students are taught in school the subjunctive form, *if thou have, if he come*, &c. and some of them continue, in after life, to *write* in that manner; but in the course of more than forty years, I have not known three men who have ventured to use that form of the verb in conversation. We toil in school to learn a language which we dare not introduce into conversation, but which the force of custom compels us to abandon. In this respect, the present study of grammar is worse than useless.

This colloquial custom accords with other languages. The French say and write *s' il est*, if he is. The Latins often used the same form, "*si* quid *est* in me ingenii, judices;" but the use of the Latin subjunctive depends on certain other words which precede; as "*cum sit civis*," as he *is* a citizen, or, since he *is* a citizen; and the present tense is often used to express what we express by an auxiliary. That the Greeks used the indicative to express a conditional present tense, we have seen by citations above.

By this arrangement of the verb, the indicative form after *if* and other verbs introducing a condition or hypothesis, may be used uniformly to express a fact or event under a condition or supposition, either in the present or past tenses; the speaker being uncertain respecting the fact, or representing it as doubtful.

If the man *is* honest, he will return what he has borrowed. If the ship *has* arrived, we shall be informed of it tomorrow. If the bill *was* presented, it was doubtless paid. If the law *has* been passed, we are precluded from further opposition.

On the other hand, when it is intended to speak of a future contingent event, I would always use the auxiliaries that are proper for the purpose. "If it *shall* or *should rain* tomorrow, we shall not ride to town." I would never use the subjunctive form *if it rain* in prose; and in poetry, only from necessity, as an abridged phrase for if it *shall* or *should rain*. In this manner, the distinction between the tenses, which are now constantly confounded, may be preserved and made obvious, both to natives and foreigners.

The effect of the study of Lowth's principles, which has been greatly extended by the popularity of Murray's grammar,* has been to introduce, or establish a form of the verb in writing, which is obsolete in colloquial language; to fill our books with a confusion of tenses, and thus to keep the language unsettled. Nothing can be more perplexing to the student than every where to meet with discrepancies between rules and practice.

There is another erroneous manner of writing, common to the best authors in the language, which seems to have escaped notice. This is, to connect a verb in the past tense with a preceding one in the same tense, when the latter verb is intended to express a very different time from the former. Thus, "Then Manasseh *knew* that the Lord, he *was* God." 2 *Chron.* xxxiii. 13.

The Latins, in this case, would probably have used the infinitive; Manasseh novit Jehovam deum esse. In English we ought to write and say, "Manasseh *knew* Jehovah *to be* God," or, Manasseh *knew* that Jehovah he *is* God. In most similar cases, the use of the infinitive in English is as elegant as in Latin. But there are many cases where the infinitive cannot be used. We cannot use it after *say*; "he *said* him *to be* a good man," is not English; though he *declared*, or *affirmed*, or *believed* him *to be* a good man, is elegant.

In order to understand the impropriety of the common mode of using the latter verb, as in the example above cited, it may be remarked, that the present tense is that which is used to express what exists at all times. Thus we say, God *is* or *exists*, whenever we speak of his permanent existence; we say, gold *is* yellow or ductile; iron *is* a most valuable metal; it *is* not convertible into silver; plants and animals *are* very distinct living beings. We do not say, gold *was* yellow; iron *was* a valuable metal; for we mean to express permanent qualities. Hence, in the passage cited from Chronicles, the first verb *knew*, referring to a fact past, is correct; but the last, which is intended to express the permanent being or character of God, should be in the infinitive or the indicative present tense. The following are examples of correct language: "His master had *taught* him that happiness *consists* in virtue." *Anacharsis*, ii. 120.

"Sabellius, who openly *taught* that there *is* but one person in the Godhead." *Encyclopedia.*

"Our Savior *taught* that eternal death *is* the proper punishment of sin." *Emmons.*

But very different is the following: "Having believed for many years, that water *was* [is] an elastic fluid." The following would be still better: "Having believed water to be an elastic fluid."

So the following: "We know not the use of the epidermis of shells. Some authors *have supposed* that it *secured* [secures] the shells from being covered with vermes." *Edin. Encyc.*

"It *was* just *remarked*, that marine fossils *did* not [do not] comprise vegetable remains." *Ib.*

"If my readers will turn their thoughts back on their old friends, they will find it difficult to call a single man to remembrance who *appeared* to know that life *was* short [is short,] till he was about to lose it." *Rambler, No.* 71.

"They considered the body as a hydraulic machine, and the fluids as passing through a series of chemical changes; forgetting that animation *was* [is] its essential characteristic." *Darwin.*

"It was *declared* by Pompey, that if the Commonwealth *was* [should be] violated, he could stamp with his foot and raise an army out of the ground." *Rambler, No.* 10.

In the foregoing sentence, the past tense is used for the future contingent.

"It was affirmed in the last discourse, that much of the honorable practice of the world *rested* [rests] on the substratum of selfishness; that society *was* [is] held together, in the exercise of its relative virtues, mainly by the tie of reciprocal advantage; that a man's own interest *bound* [binds] him to all those average equities which *obtained* [obtain] in the neighborhood around him; and in which if he *proved* [should prove] himself glaringly deficient, he would be abandoned by the respect, and the confidence, and the good will of the people with whom he *had* [might have, or should have] to do." *Chalmer's Com. Dis.* 4.

"In the last discourse, I observed that love *constituted* [constitutes] the whole moral character of God," *Dwight's Theology.*

"And he said, nay, father Abraham; but if one *went* [shall or should go] to them from the dead, they will repent. And he said to him, if they hear not Moses and the prophets, neither will they be persuaded though one *rose* [shall or should rise] from the dead." *Luke*, xvi. 30, 31.

"Independent of parties in the national legislature itself, as often as the period of discussion *arrived*, the state legislatures, who *will* always *be* not

* Lindley Murray, in the introduction to his grammar, "acknowledges, in general terms, that the authors to whom the grammatical part of this compilation is principally indebted for its materials are, Harris, Johnson, Lowth, Priestley, Beattie, Sheridan, Walker, and Coote." But on examination, it appears that the greatest portion of the grammatical part is from Lowth, whose principles form the main structure of Murray's compilation. Some valuable notes and remarks are taken from Priestley's grammar. I studied grammar in the originals long before Murray's compilation appeared, and, in citing authorities, deem it proper to cite the originals.

only vigilant, but suspicious and jealous guardians of the rights of the citizens, against encroachments from the federal government, *will* constantly have their attention awake to the conduct of the national rulers, and will be ready enough, if any thing improper *appears*, to sound the alarm to the people."

Let any man attempt to resolve the foregoing sentence, if he can, or render it into another language.

"Cicero vindicated the truth, and inculcated the value of the precept, that nothing *was* [is] truly useful which *was* [is] not honest."

"He undertook to show that justice *was* [is] of perpetual obligation."

"The author concedes much of his argument, and admits that the sea *was* [is] susceptible of dominion." [Better still; he admits the sea *to be* susceptible of dominion.]

"A nation would be condemned by the impartial voice of mankind, if it voluntarily *went* [should go] to war, on a claim of which it *doubted* [should doubt] the legality."

"The Supreme Court observed that they were not at liberty to depart from the rule, whatever doubt might have been entertained, if the case *was* [had been] entirely new."

"He held that the law of nations *prohibited* [prohibits] the use of poisoned arms."

"He insisted that the laws of war *gave* [give] no other power over a captive than to keep him safely."

"The general principle on the subject is, that, if a commander *makes* a compact with the enemy, and it *be* of such a nature that the power to make it *could be* reasonably implied from the nature of the trust, it *would be* valid and binding, though he *abused* his trust." Let any man translate this sentence into another language, if he can, without reducing the verbs to some consistency.

"Congress have declared by law, that the United States *were* [are] entitled to priority of payment over private creditors, in cases of insolvency."

"The Supreme Court decided, that the acts of Congress, giving that general priority to the United States, *were* [are] constitutional.

"It was admitted that the government of the United States *was* [is] one of enumerated powers."

"From his past designs and administrations we could never argue at all to those which *were future*." [This is an odd combination of words.]

"Jesus knowing that the father had given all things into his hands, and that he was come from God and *went* to God." John xiii. 3.

"Alexander dispatched Eumenes with three hundred horse to two free cities—with assurance that if they *submitted* and *received* him, [should or would submit and receive,] as a friend, no evil *should befall* them."

"The apostle *knew* that the present season *was* [is] the only time allowed for this preparation."

"What would be the real effect of that overpowering evidence, which our adversaries *required*, [should require,] in a revelation, it is difficult to *foretell*."

"It could not otherwise have been known that the word *had* [has] this meaning."

I told him if he *went* [should go] to-morrow, I would go with him.

This fault occurs in our hearing every hour in the day.

A like fault prevails in other languages; indeed the English may have been led into it by reading foreign authors. "Mais on a remarqué avec raison, que l'espace conchoidal *etait* infini." *Lunier*. It has been remarked with reason that the conchoidal space *was* [is] infinite.

But whatever may be the practice of other nations, there would be no difficulty in correcting such improprieties in our own language, if as much attention were given to the study of its true principles, as is given to other subjects of literature and science. But if in this particular, there is a British or American author who writes his vernacular language correctly, his writings have not fallen under my inspection.

There is another fault very common among English writers, though it is less frequent in the United States; this is the conversion of an intransitive verb into a passive one. It is surprising that an error of this kind should have gained such an established use, in some foreign languages, as to be incurable. Barbarous nations may indeed form languages; but it should be the business of civilized men to purify their language from barbarisms.

In the transitive verb, there is an agent that performs some action on an object, or in some way affects it. When this verb becomes passive, the agent and the object change places in the sentence. Thus, *John loves Peter*, is transitive, but *Peter is loved by John*, is passive. In the intransitive verb, the case is different; for the action is limited to the agent; and when it is stated that a thing is done, there is no agent by which it is done. *I perish* is intransitive; *I am perished* is the passive form; but the latter neither expresses nor implies an agent by which I perish.

This fault occurs frequently in the common version of the Scriptures.

"Yea, whereto might the strength of their hands profit me, in whom old age *was* [had] *perished*." Job xxx. 2.

"Their memorial *is* [has] *perished* with them." Ps. ix. 6.

"The heathen *are* [have] *perished* out of this land." Ps. x. 16.

"Israel *is* [has] fled before the Philistines." 1 Sam. iv. 17.

"David *is* [has] fled." 2 Sam. xix. 9.

"The days *were* [had] not *expired*." 1 Sam. xviii. 26.

"And when the year *was* [had] expired." 2 Chron. xxxvi. 10.

"I only *am* [have] escaped alone to tell thee." Job i. 15.

"And it came to pass, when he *was* [had] *returned*." Luke xix. 15.

Return is sometimes a transitive verb, and sometimes intransitive. When a sum of borrowed money *is returned*, the phrase is correct, for this is the passive form of a transitive verb. But when a *man is returned*, we may ask, who has returned him? In this case, the man returns by his own act, and he cannot be said to *be returned*.

"He found the Empress *was* [had] *departed*." *Coxe*.

"They *were* [had] *arrived* within three days journey of the spice country." *Gibbon*, Ch. i. Note.

"Neither Charles nor Diocletian *were* [had] *arrived* at a very advanced period of life." *Ib*. Ch. xiii.

"The posterity of so many gods and heroes *was* [had] *fallen* into the most abject state." *Ib*. Ch. ii.

"Silver *was* [had] *grown* more common." *Ib*.

"He *was* [had] *risen* from the dead, and *was* [had] just *ascended* to heaven." *Milner*, i. 20.

"Hearing that they *were* [had] *arrived*." *Ib*. 211.

"Claudius—vexed because his wife *was* [had] *become* a christian." *Ib*. 274.

"Does not the reader see how much we *are* [have] already *departed* from christian simplicity?" *Ib*. 299.

"My age *is* [has] *departed*." Isaiah xxxviii. 12.

"The man out of whom the demons *were* [had] *departed*." Luke viii. 35.

"Workmen *were* [had] *arrived* to assist them." *Mitford*.

"A body of Athenian horse *was* [had] just *arrived*." *Ib*.

This fault is common in Mitford's History of Greece. In the writings of Roscoe, which are more elegant, it occurs, but less frequently.

"The time limited for the reception of the cardinal *was expired*." *Roscoe*, Leo. X.

"He inquired whether the report was true, that a legate *was arrived*." *Ib*. L. Med.

"The nation *being* [having] once more *got* into a course of borrowing." *Price on Liberty*.

"When he *was* [had] *retired* to his tent." *Coxe's Russ*.

"He *was* [had] not yet *arrived*."* *Ib*.

The intransitive verb *grow* is constantly used by the English as a transitive verb, as to *grow* wheat. This is never used in the northern states, unless by persons who have adopted it recently from the English.

It seems almost incredible that such errors should continue, to this time, to disfigure the language of the most distinguished writers, and that they should escape animadversion. The practice has evidently been borrowed from the French or Italian; but surely no lover of correctness can excuse such violation of the best established principles in our language.

This fault occurs in a few instances, in the writings of the best American authors, as in the writings of Ames and Hamilton. It is however very rare, either in books or in colloquial usage. Even our common people are remarkably accurate in using the auxiliary *have* with the participles of intransitive verbs. They always, I believe, say, a ship *has* arrived, a plant *has* perished, the enemy *had* fled, the price *had* fallen, the corn *has* or *had* grown, the time *has* expired, the man *has* returned, the vessel *had* departed. Such also is the language of our most eminent writers.

"The Generals Gates and Sullivan *have* both arrived." *Washington's Letters*.

"The Indians of the village *had* fled." *B. Trumbull*.

"Our Tom *has* grown a sturdy boy." *Progress of Dullness*.

"Our patriots *have* fallen." *Discourse of D. Webster*, Aug. 1826.

"Our commissary *had* not arrived." *Ellicott*.

The exceptions to this correct practice are chiefly in the use of the participles of *come* and *go*. It is very common to hear the expressions he *is* come or *is* gone, in which case, the participle seems to take the character of an adjective; although in most instances, the regular form of expression, he *has* come or *has* gone, is to be preferred. So *dead*, originally a participle, is used only as an adjective; and *deceased* and *departed* are often used in the like manner. We say, a *deceased*, or *departed* friend; but it should be remarked that the original expression was, our friend *has* deceased, or *has* departed this life; and this phraseology, by an easy but heedless transition, became *is* deceased or *is* departed. In general, however, the conversion of an intransitive verb or form of expression into the passive form, is very rare among the people of New England.

There is a grammatical error running through the writings of so respectable a writer as Mitford, which ought not to be passed unnoticed; as it seems to be borrowed from the French language, whose idioms are different from the English, but which the English are too apt to follow. This fault is, in using the preterit or perfect tense, instead of the past tense indefinite, usu-

---

* On this use of intransitive verbs, as the ship *was departed*, it may be asked, who departed it? The mail *is arrived*, who has arrived it? The tree *is perished*, who has perished it? The enemy *was fled*, who fled them? The time *was expired*, who expired it?

ally called most improperly, the *imperfect*. Take the following sentences for examples. "The conduct of Pelopidas towards Arcadia and its minister at the Persian court—*has* scarcely *been* the result of mere caprice or resentment." The verb here ought to be *was*.

"The oration [of Isocrates] *has been* [was] a favorite of Dionysius of Halicarnassus."

This form of expressing the time would be good in French, but is very bad in English. And it may be here remarked, that the tense *he was, he arrived, he wrote*, is not properly named *imperfect*. These verbs, and all verbs of this form denote actions finished or perfect, as "in six days God *created* the heaven and the earth." Imperfect or unfinished action is expressed in English in this manner, he *was reading*, they *were writing*. The error of calling the former tense *imperfect* has probably proceeded from a servile adoption of the Latin names of the tenses, without considering the difference of application.

There are some errors in all the English Grammars, that have been derived to us from antiquity. Such is the arrangement of *that* among the conjunctions, like the Greek οτι, and the Latin *ut*. Και μακαρια η πιςευσασα οτι εςαι τελειωσις τοις λελαλημενοις αυτη παρα Κυριου. And blessed is she who believed *that* there shall be a performance of the things which were told her from the Lord. Luke i. 45. In our version, οτι is rendered *for*, but most erroneously. The true meaning and character of οτι will best appear, by a transposition of the clauses of the verse. "There shall be a performance of the things told her from the Lord; blessed or happy is she who believed *that*." Here οτι, *that*, appears to be what it really is, a relative or substitute for the whole clause in Greek succeeding it. So in Luke xxii. 18. Λεγω γαρ υμιν οτι ου μη πιω, &c. I say to you *that* I will not drink. I will not drink, I say to you *that*. It is the same in Latin, "Dico enim vobis *quod* non bibam." *Quod* is here a relative governed by *dico*, and referring to the following clause of the sentence.

So also Matthew ix. 28. Πιςευετε οτι δυναμαι τουτο ποιησαι ; Do ye believe *that* I am able to do this? [I am able to do this, do ye believe *that?*]

This error runs through all Grammars, Greek, Latin, French, English, &c. But how such an obvious fact, that the word *that* and its corresponding words in other languages, refer to the clause of a sentence, should escape observation, age after age, it is not easy to explain. How could it be supposed that a word is a conjunction which does *not* join words or sentences? *That* is used, in the passages cited, not to *unite two* sentences, but to *continue the same* sentence, by an additional clause.

The relative, when referring to a sentence or the clause of a sentence, is not varied, for a variation of case is not wanted.

So *notwithstanding* and *provided* in English, and *pourvu que* in French, are called conjunctions: but most improperly; as they are participles, and when called conjunctions, they always form, with a word, clause or sentence, the case absolute or independent. Thus, "it rains, but notwithstanding *that*, [it rains,] I must go to town." That fact, (it rains,) not opposing or preventing me, that is, in opposition to that, I must go to town; hoc non obstante.

"I will ride, *provided* you will accompany me." That is, I will ride, the fact, *you will accompany me*, being provided.

Such is the structure of these sentences. See my Philosophical and Practical Grammar. It is the same in French, *pourvu que*, that being provided, *que* referring to the following clause.

There are other points in grammar equally faulty. Not only in English grammar, but in the grammars of other languages, men stumble at the threshold, and teach their children to stumble. In no language whatever can there be a part of speech properly called an *article*. There is no word or class of words that falls within the signification of *article*, a joint, or that can otherwise than arbitrarily be brought under that denomination. The definitive words called *articles*, are all *adjectives* or *pronouns*. When they are used with nouns, they are *adjectives*, modifying the signification of the nouns, like other adjectives; for this is their proper office. When they stand alone, they are *pronouns*, or *substitutes* for nouns. Thus *hic, ille, ipse* in Latin, when used with nouns expressed, are adjectives; *hic homo*, this man; *ille homo*, that man. When they stand alone, *hic, ille*, they stand in the place of nouns. The fact is the same in other languages.

The English *the* is an adjective, which, for distinction, I call a *definitive adjective*, and for brevity, a *definitive*, as it defines the person or thing to which it refers, or rather designates a particular person or thing. But why this should be selected as the only definitive in our language, is very strange; when obviously *this* and *that* are more exactly definitive, designating more precisely a particular person or thing than *the*. These words answer to the Latin *hic* and *ille*, which were always used by the Romans, when they had occasion to specify definite persons or things.

As to the English *an* or *a*, which is called in grammars, the *indefinite article*, there are two great mistakes. *A* being considered as the original word, it is said to become *an* before a vowel. The fact is directly the reverse. *An* is the original word, and this is contracted to *a* by dropping the *n* before a consonant.

But *an* is merely the Saxon orthography of *one, un, unus*, an adjective found in nearly all the languages of Europe, and expressing a single person or thing. It is merely a word of number, and no more an *article* than *two, three, four*, and every other number in the language. Take the following examples.

Bring me *an* orange from the basket; that is, any *one* of the number.

Bring me *two* oranges from the basket; that is, any *two* of the number.

Bring me *three* oranges from the basket; that is, any *three* of the number; and so on to any number ad infinitum.

When thus used, *an, two, three*, are all indefinite; that is, they are used with nouns which are indefinite, or expressing things not particularly designated. But this is not owing to the essential character of the adjectives, *an, one, two, three*, for any of them may be used with definite nouns; and *an* is continually thus used.

"I will be *an* adversary to thine adversaries."

"The angel stood for *an* adversary against Balaam."

"Make this fellow return, lest in the battle he be *an* adversary to us."

"Rezon—was *an* adversary to Israel all the days of Solomon."

"And he spake *a* parable to them to this end."

"And there was *a* widow in that city."

"And seeing the multitude, he went up into *a* mountain."

"I will be *a* God to thee and thy seed after thee."

"Thou art *a* God ready to pardon."

Now let any of these phrases be tested by the common definition of *an* or *a*, "that it is used in a vague sense, to point out one single thing of the kind; in other respects indeterminate." *Lowth.*

"I will be *an* adversary to thine adversaries;" that is, "I will be *any* adversary, one of the kind, but vague or indeterminate."

"Rezon was *an* adversary to Israel;" that is, in a vague sense *any* adversary, indeterminate.

"And he spake *a* parable to them;" that is, *any* parable, indeterminate.

"Thou art *a* God, ready to pardon;" that is, *any* God, one of the kind, in a vague sense, indeterminate!

If it should be said, the noun is rendered determinate, by other words in the sentence, and not by *an* or *a*, this may be and generally is true; but this shows that *an* does not give to the noun its character of definiteness or indefiniteness; it always retains its proper signification, which is *one*, and nothing more; and it is used indifferently before nouns definite or indefinite.

This mistake of the character of *an* is found in other languages; but I was gratified to find a French Grammar in Paris, recommended by the Institute, the author of which had discarded the indefinite article.

In English, *an* or *a* is, for the most part, entirely useless. Used with a noun in the singular number, it serves no purpose, except that which the form of the word, in the singular number, is intended to answer. It expresses *unity* only, and this is the province of the singular number. Were it not for habit, "give me orange," would express the sense of "give me an orange," with precision and certainty. In this respect the Latin language has the advantage over the English. But the use of such a short word is not very inconvenient, and the usage cannot be changed. Other languages are subject to the same inconvenience; even the definite articles, or definitives, in Greek and in French, are very often useless, and were it not for usage, would be improper.

ORTHOGRAPHY.

From the period of the first Saxon writings, our language has been suffering changes in orthography. The first writers, having no guide but the ear, followed each his own judgment or fancy; and hence a great portion of Saxon words are written with different letters, by different authors; most of them are written two or three different ways, and some of them, fifteen or twenty. To this day, the orthography of some classes of words is not entirely settled; and in others, it is settled in a manner to confound the learner and mislead him into a false pronunciation. Nothing can be more disreputable to the literary characterof a nation, than the history of English orthography, unless it is that of orthoepy.

1. The Saxon dipthong *æ*, which probably had a specific and uniform sound or combination of sounds, has been discarded and *ea* generally substituted in its place, as *bræth*, breath. Now *ea* thus united have not a uniform sound, and of course they are no certain guide to pronunciation. In some instances, where the Saxon spelling was not uniform, the modern orthography follows the most anomalous and difficult, instead of that which is regular. Thus the Saxons wrote *fæther* and *fether*, more generally the latter, and the moderns write *feather*.

2. The letter *g* in Saxon words, has, in many English words, been sunk in pronunciation, and either wholly lost, or it is now represented by *y* or *w*. Thus *dæg*, or *dag*, has become *day; gear* is *year*, *bugan* is *bow*, and *fæger* is *fair*.

3. The Saxons who adopted the Roman alphabet, with a few alterations, used *c* with its hard sound like that of *k*. Thus *lic*, like; *locian*, to look. But after the Norman conquest, *c* before *e, i*, and *y*, took the sound of *s*; hence arose the necessity of changing this letter in words and syllables, where it was necessary to retain the sound of *k* before these vowels. Thus the Saxon *licean*, pronounced originally *likean*, becomes, with our present sound of *c* before *e*, *lisean;* and *locian* becomes *losian*. To remedy this

evil, our ancestors introduced *k* from the Greek, writing it generally after *c*, as in *lick*, *stick*, though in some instances, omitting *c*, as in *like* and *look*. Hence in all monosyllables in which a syllable beginning with *e* or *i* is added to the word, as in the past time and participles of verbs, we use *k* in the place of the Saxon *c*, as in *licked, licking*.

Our early writers attempted to extend this addition to words introduced from the Latin and Greek, in which no such reason exists for the use of *k*. Thus they wrote *publick*, *musick*, *rhetorick*. In these and similar words the Latins used *c* for the Greek κ, as *musicus*, for μουσικος, and the early English writers took both letters, the Roman *c* and Greek κ. This was absurd enough; but they never proceeded so far as to carry the absurdity through the derivatives; never writing *publickation, musickal, rhetorickal*. After a long struggle with the force of authority, good sense has nearly banished this pedantic orthography from use; and all words of this kind now appear, in most of our public acts and elegant writings, in their proper simplicity; *public, publication, music, musical*.

In many words, formerly ending in *ie*, these letters have been discarded from the singular number, and *y* substituted. Thus *remedie, memorie*, are now written *remedy, memory*. But what is very singular, the plural of these words retains the *ie*, with the addition of *s*, as in *remedies*. This anomaly however creates no great inconvenience, except that it has been extended by negligent writers to words ending in *ey*, as in *attornies*. But words ending in *ey* properly make the plural by simply taking *s*, as in *surveys*, *attorneys*. The same rule applies to verbs when an *s* is added, as in *conveys*.

5. In a vast number of words, the vowel *e* has been discarded as useless; as in *eggs* for *egges; certain* for *certaine; empress* for *emprese; goodness* for *goodnesse*. This is an improvement, as the *e* has no sound in modern pronunciation. But here again we meet with a surprising inconsistency; for the same reason which justifies this omission, would justify and require the omission of *e* final in *motive, pensive, juvenile, genuine, sanguine, doctrine, examine, determine*, and a multitude of others. The introduction of *e*, in most words of these classes, was at first wrong, as it could not plead any authority in the originals; but the retaining of it is unjustifiable, as the letter is not merely useless, but, in very numerous classes of words, it leads to a false pronunciation. Many of the most respectable English authors, a century ago or more, omitted *e* in such words as *examin, determin, famin, ductil, fertil, definit*, &c. but these improvements were afterwards rejected to the great injury of orthography. In like manner, a final *e* is inserted in words of modern coinage, as in *alumine, chlorine, chloride, oxyde*, &c. without the least necessity or propriety.

6. A similar fate has attended the attempt to anglicize the orthography of another class of words, which we have received from the French. At a very early period, the words *chambre, desastre, desordre, chartre, monstre, tendre, tigre, entre, fievre, diametre, arbitre, nombre*, and others were reduced to the English form of spelling; *chamber, disaster, disorder, charter, monster, tender, tiger, enter, fever, diameter, arbiter, number*. At a later period, Sir Isaac Newton, Camden, Selden, Milton, Whitaker, Prideaux, Hook, Whiston, Bryant, and other authors of the first character, attempted to carry through this reformation, writing *scepter, center, sepulcher*. But this improvement was arrested, and a few words of this class retain their French orthography; such are *metre, mitre, nitre, spectre, sceptre, theatre, sepulchre*, and sometimes *centre*. It is remarkable that a nation distinguished for erudition, should thus reject improvements, and retain anomalies, in opposition to all the convenience of uniformity. I am glad that so respectable a writer as Mitford has discarded this innovation, and uniformly written *center, scepter, theater, sepulcher*. In the present instance, want of uniformity is not the only evil. The present orthography has introduced an awkward mode of writing the derivatives, for example, *centred, sceptred, sepulchred*; whereas Milton and Pope wrote these words as regular derivations of *center, scepter, sepulcher:* thus, "*Sceptered* King." So Coxe, in his travels, "The principal wealth of the church is *centered* in the monasteries." This is correct.

7. Soon after the revival of letters in Europe, English writers began to borrow words from the French and Italian; and usually with some little alteration of the orthography. Thus they wrote *authour, embassadour, predecessour, ancestour, successour;* using *our* for the Latin termination *or*, and the French *eur*, and writing similar words, in like manner, though not of Latin or French original. What motive could induce them to write these words, and *errour, honour, favour, inferiour*, &c. in this manner, following neither the Latin nor the French, I cannot conceive. But this orthography continued down to the seventeenth century, when the *u* began to be rejected from certain words of this class, and at the beginning of the last century, many of these words were written, *ancestor, author, error*, &c. as they are now written. But *favor, honor, labor, candor, ardor, terror, vigor, inferior, superior*, and a few others, were written with *u*, and Johnson introduced this orthography into his dictionary. Nothing in language is more mischievous than the mistakes of a great man. It is not easy to understand why a man, whose professed object was to reduce the language to some regularity, should write *author* without *u* and *errour* and *honour* with it! That he should write *labour* with *u* and *laborious* without it! *Vigour*, with *u*, and *vigorous, invigorate*, without it! *Inferiour, superiour*, with *u*, but *inferiority*, and *superiority*, without it! Strange as it is, this inconsistency runs through his work, and his authority has been the means of continuing it, among his admirers, to this day.

In this country, many of our best writers have rejected the *u* from all words of this class, and reduced the whole to uniformity.* This is a desirable event; every rejection of an anomaly being a valuable improvement, which sound judgment approves, and the love of regularity will vindicate and maintain. I have therefore followed the orthography of General Washington, and the Congress of the United States, of Ash in his Dictionary, of Mitford in his History of Greece, &c.

8. There is another class of words the orthography of which is not uniform, nor fully settled, such as take the termination *able* to form an adjective. Thus Johnson writes *proveable* with *e*, but *approvable* and *reprovable*, without it. So *moveable*, but *immovable* and *removable; tameable*, but *blamable, censurable, desirable, excusable; saleable*, but *ratable*.

With like inconsistency Walker and Todd write *daub* with *u* and *bedawb* with *w*, deviating in this instance, from Johnson. Todd writes *abridgement* and *judgement* with *e*, but *acknowledgment* without it. Walker writes these words without *e*, but adds it to *lodgement*. I have reduced all words of this kind to uniformity.

9. Johnson writes *octoedrical;* Todd *octoedral;* Sheridan, Walker and Jones follow Johnson; but Jones has *octahedron*, which is not in the other Dictionaries. The Greek, in words of this kind, is inconsistent, for οκτω is changed, in compound words, to οκτα. I have followed the Greek compounds, and have inserted *h* which I consider as almost indispensable in the English orthography, as *octahedron*.

10. Johnson introduced *instructer*, in the place of *instructor*, in opposition to every authority which he has himself adduced to exemplify his definitions; Denham, Milton, Roscommon, Locke, Addison, Rogers, and the common version of the Scriptures. But what is more singular, this orthography, *instructer*, is contrary to his own practice; at least, in *four* editions of his Rambler which I have examined, the word is uniformly written *instructor*. The fact is the same with *visitor*.

This is a point of little importance in itself; but when *instructor* had been from time immemorial, the established orthography, why unsettle the practice? I have in this word and in *visitor* adhered to the old orthography. There is not a particle of reason for altering *instructor* and *visitor*, which would not apply to *collector, cultivator, objector, projector*, and a hundred other words of similar termination.

11. Most of these and some other inconsistencies have been of long continuance. But there are others of more recent date, which admit of no apology, as they are changes from right to wrong. Such is the change of the old and correct orthography of *defense, expense, offense, pretense*, and *recompense*, by substituting *c* for *s* as in *defence*. This change was probably made or encouraged by printers, for the sake of avoiding the use of the old long *s;* but since this has been discarded, that reason no longer exists. The old orthography, *defense*, &c. is justified, not only by the Latin originals, but by the rule of uniformity; for the derivatives are always written with *s, defensive, extensive, offensive, pretension, recompensing*.

12. No less improper was the change of *sceptic* into *skeptic*. In favor of this innovation, it is alledged that the word is from the Greek σκεπτικος. True; but is not *scene* derived from the Greek σκηνη, and *scepter* from σκηπτρον, and *ascetic* from ασκητικος, and *ocean* from ωκεανος? Are not all these words in exact analogy with each other, in their original orthography? Were they not formerly analogous in the English orthography? Why violate this analogy? Why introduce an anomaly? Such innovations, by dividing opinions and introducing discrepancies in practice, in classes of words of like formation, have a mischievous effect, by keeping the language in perpetual fluctuation.

13. In like manner, *dispatch*, which had, from time immemorial, been written with *i*, was changed into *despatch*, on the wonderful discovery, that the word is derived from the French *depêcher*. But why change one vowel and not the other? If we must follow the French, why not write *despech*, or *depech?* And why was this innovation limited to a single word? Why not carry the change through this whole class of words, and give us the benefit of uniformity? Is not *disaster* from the French *desastre?* Is not *discharge* from *decharger?* Is not *disarm* from *desarmer?* Is not *disobey* from *desobeir?* Is not *disoblige* from *desobliger?* Is not *disorder* from *desordre?* The prefix *dis* is more properly English than *de*, though both are used with propriety. But *dispatch* was the established orthography; why then disturb the practice? Why select a single word from the whole class, and introduce a change which creates uncertainty where none had existed for ages, without the smallest benefit to indemnify us for the perplexity and discordance occasioned by the innovation?

It is gratifying to observe the stern good sense of the English nation, presenting a firm resistance to such innovations. Blackstone, Paley, Coxe, Milner, Scott and Mitford, uniformly use the old and genuine orthography of *instructor, visitor, sceptic* and *dispatch*.

14. The omission of one *l* in *befall, install, installment, recall, enthrall*, &c., is by no means to be vindicated; as by custom, the two letters *ll*, serve as a guide to the true pronunciation, that of broad *a* or *aw*. According to the established rules of English pronunciation, the letter *a* in *instal-*

* The reformation commenced or received its most decided support and authority at the revolution. See *Washington's Letters*, in two volumes, 8vo, 1795.

ment would have the sound it has in *balance;* it is therefore expedient to retain both letters in all words of this class.

15. It is an established rule, in the English language, that monosyllabic verbs, ending in a single consonant, not preceded by a long vowel, and other verbs ending in a single accented consonant, and of course not preceded by a long vowel, double the final consonant, in all the derivatives, which are formed by a termination beginning with a vowel. Thus, *fit, blot, bar*, when they take the terminations, *ed, eth, ing*, are written *fitted, fitteth, fitting; blotted, blotteth, blotting; barred, barreth, barring. Abet, compel*, form the like derivatives; *abetted, abetteth, abetting; compelled, compelleth, compelling.* The reason of this rule is, that without this duplication of the last consonant, the vowel of the primitive word would, in the derivative, be naturally pronounced wrong, that is, with its long sound; *fited, bloting, bared, competed.* Hence we see the reason why verbs, having the long sound of a vowel, do not double the last consonant, as *feared, repealed, repeated.*

The converse of this rule is, that verbs, ending in a single consonant, but having the accent on the first syllable, or on a syllable preceding the last, ought *not* to double the final consonant in the derivatives. Thus *limit, labor, charter, clatter, pardon, deliver, hinder*, have for their derivatives, *limited, laboreth, chartered, pardoning, delivering, hinderest.* But strange as it may seem, the rule is wholly neglected and violated, in most of the words of this class in the language. Thus we observe, in all authors, *ballotting, bevelling, levelled, travelled, cancelled, revelling, rivalling, worshipped, worshipper, apparelled, embowelled, libelling*, and many others, in which the last consonant is doubled, in opposition to one of the oldest and best established rules in the language. Perry, in his Dictionary, lays down the rule for guidance, but has not been careful, in all cases, to observe it. I have endeavored to reduce these classes of words to a regular and uniform orthography. In like manner, nouns formed from such verbs are written with a single consonant, as *jeweler, traveler, worshiper*, for the purpose of establishing a general rule, to which there may be no exception. What should we say to a man who should write *audittor, alterrer, barterrer, banterrer, gardenner, laborrer?* Yet no good reason can be assigned why the final consonant should not be doubled in these words as well as in *jeweller, traveller, enameller.* The truth is, the syllable to be added is the usual termination *er* or *or*, and nothing more.

Not less remarkable is the practice of doubling the last consonant in *equalled, equalling*, but not in the verb *equalize.* And to add to the inconsistency, the last consonant is sometimes doubled in *tranquillize*, a word in exact analogy with *equalize.*

With regard to words which recent discoveries have introduced into the sciences, there may be some apology for differences of orthography, as writers have not established usage for a guide. Hence we find *oxyd* is written also *oxide* and *oxyde; oxygen* and *hydrogen*, are written also *oxigene, oxygene* and *hydrogene. Sulphate, nitrate*, &c., are written also *sulphat, nitrat.*

In this case, what course is the Lexicographer to pursue? Shall he adopt the method by which Walker attempts to settle pronunciation, and cite authorities in favor of each mode of spelling? Then the result is, so many names appear on one side, and so many on the other. But who, it may be asked, will undertake to graduate the scale by which the weight of authorities is to be determined? Numbers will not always decide questions of this sort to the satisfaction of the public.

In this case, I have determined to conform the orthography to established English analogies; the only authority from which there can be no legitimate appeal. Now, no rule in orthography is better established, than that which we have adopted from the Latin language, of representing the Greek *upsilon* by the letter *y*. In the orthography of *oxygen* and *hydrogen*, from ὀξυς and ὑδωρ, this rule has been observed; and why should *oxyd* be an exception?

With regard to *sulphate, nitrate*, and other names of that class of compounds, I consider the final *e* as essential to the words, to prevent a false pronunciation; the vowel *a* having its first sound as in *fate*, though slightly pronounced.

The word *chimistry* has undergone two or three changes, according to fancy or to conjectural etymology. Men have blundered about the plainest thing imaginable; for to determine its true orthography, nothing was necessary but to open an Arabic Lexicon. The inhabitants of the South of Europe, who introduced the word, doubtless knew its origin, and wrote it correctly with *i*, not with *y* or *e;* and had the English been contented to take it as they found it, the orthography would have been correct and uniform.

In introducing words from other languages, it is desirable that the orthography should be conformed, as nearly as may be, to established English analogies. For this reason I must approve of the practice of Darwin who drops the Latin termination of *pyrites*, writing *pyrite*, with the accent on the first syllable. *Botanic Garden, Canto* 2. 350.

Stalactite has in like manner, been anglicized; and *barytes*, it is hoped, may suffer the like change. In this manner, the words, in the English form, become susceptible of a regular plural; *barytes* and *pyrites* in two syllables, and *stalactites* in three: and further they admit of regularly formed adjectives, *pyritic, barytic, stalactitic*, which cannot be regularly formed from the Greek terminations.

The word *talc* is also ill-formed. The original word on the continent of Europe is *talk* or *talg;* and the change of *k* into *c* is not merely needless, but worse, for it precludes the use of the regular adjective, *talcy.* Hence we see the adjective used is *talcose*, an awkward compound of a Teutonic word with a Latin termination. This word should be written *talk* or *talck*, which would admit regular derivatives, *talcky, talckiness.* In like manner, *zinc*, if written *zink*, would admit the regular adjective *zinky*, as written by Kirwan.

In botany, as the sexual system of the celebrated Swedish naturalist is now generally received, it seems proper to make the new terms, by which the classes and orders of plants are designated, a part of our language. Hitherto these names have not been anglicized; but from the technical terms, English and American writers have begun to form adjectives which are at variance with the analogies of our language. We see in books such words as *hexandrous, monogamous, polygamous*, and *syngenesious.* The writers who use these words, seem not to be aware of the importance of pursuing settled rules in the coining of words, as uniformity aids both in learning and in recollecting new names. The regular mode of forming adjectives from nouns ending in *a* or *ia*, is to add *n* to the noun, not *ous.* So we form *Italian* from *Italia; American* from *America.* In some cases, the termination *ic* is used, but rarely or never *ous;* or if it is, it is an anomaly.

To arrest, if possible, the progress of these irregularities, and at the same time, to make the more important botanical terms really English, by giving them appropriate English terminations, and further to abridge the language of description, I have ventured to anglicize the names of all the classes and orders, and insert them in this work.

Thus from *monandria*, the name of the class containing plants with flowers having one stamen, I form *monander*, the name of an individual plant of that character. From *monogynia*, the name of the order containing plants with flowers which have one pistil, I form *monogyn*, [pronounced *monojyn*] to express an individual plant of that order. The adjectives are formed from the nouns with regular English terminations; *monandrian, monogynian, syngenesian, diecian, monecian*, &c.

In describing a plant technically, according to this nomenclature, instead of saying, it is of the class monondria and order monogynia, the botanist will call it a *monogynian monander*, a *digynian pentander*, a *trigynian octander*, a *pentandrian diadelph.* These terms designate the class and order, as perfectly as the use of the Latin technical names: and in this manner we unite, in our botanical language, technical precision, with brevity, correctness and elegance.

It is with no small regret, that I see new terms formed, without a due regard to regular English analogies. New terms are often necessary, or at least very useful; but they ought to be coined according to the settled principles of the language. A neglect of these principles is observable in the word *systematize*, which, not being borrowed from the Greek, ought to follow the general rule of English formation, in agreement with *legalize, modernize, civilize, animalize*, and others, and be written *systemize.* This is the more important, as the derivatives *systemizing, systemization*, are of more easy utterance, than those of *systematize*, and particularly the noun *systematization.*

I observe in modern works on Natural History, the words *crustaceology*, and *testaceology;* terms that are intended to designate the science of different kinds of shells, from *crustacea, testacea.* But who can countenance the use of such words? Where do we find another instance of similar terms formed from adjectives? Why should we violate an established principle in coining words of this family? Besides, who can endure the derivatives, *crustaceological, testaceological*, and much less the adverbs, if they should ever be wanted? I have not admitted these anomalous words into this vocabulary; but have inserted the proper words, *crustalogy, testalogy*, which are regularly formed, like *mineralogy.*

On this head I would subjoin a remark or two on the mode of writing Indian names of rivers, mountains and places in America, which we have adopted.

The French were the first Europeans who explored the country between the great lakes and the gulf of Mexico, and of course, the first to commit to writing the Indian names which occurred to them in their travels. In doing this, they attempted to express the sounds in letters, according to the French manner of pronunciation. Hence it happened that they wrote *ch*, where we should have written *sh*, had we first reduced those names to writing. Thus we have *Chenango, Michigan* and *Michillimackinac*,* in the French orthography. And as the French have no *w* in their language, they could not express the proper sound of the first syllable of *Wabash, Wisconsin, Wachita*, otherwise than by writing them *Ouabache, Ouisconsin, Ouachita*, and *Missoori* in French is *Missouri.* All this is very proper for Frenchmen, for the letters used express the true sounds of the words. But in English, the letters used lead to a false pronunciation, and for this reason, should not be used in English compositions. It is to be deeply regretted that our language is thus doomed to be a heterogeneous medley of English and foreign languages; as the same letters representing

* This word is, I believe, customarily pronounced *Mackinaw*, and the original may well be suffered to fall into disuse.

different sounds, in different languages, serve to embarrass the reader who understands only his own.

The irregularities in the English orthography have always been a subject of deep regret, and several attempts have been made to banish them from the language. The first attempt of this kind was made by Sir Thomas Smith, Secretary of State, to Queen Elizabeth; another was made by Dr. Gill, a celebrated master of St. Paul's School in London; another by Charles Butler; several attempts were made in the reign of Charles I.; an attempt was made by Elphinstone, in the last century; and lastly, another effort was made by Dr. Franklin. The latter gentleman compiled a dictionary on his scheme of reform, and procured types to be cast, which he offered to me, with a view to engage me to prosecute his design. This offer I declined to accept; for I was then, and am still convinced, that the scheme of introducing new characters into the language, is neither practicable nor expedient. Any attempt of this kind must certainly fail of success.

But that some scheme for expressing the distinct sounds of our letters by visible marks, ought to be adopted, is a point about which there ought to be, and I trust there can be, but one opinion. That such a scheme is practicable as well as expedient, I should presume to be equally evident. Such is the state of our written language, that our own citizens never become masters of orthography, without great difficulty and labor; and a great part of them never learn to spell words with correctness. In addition to this, the present orthography of some classes of words leads to a false pronunciation.

In regard to the acquisition of our language by foreigners, the evil of our irregular orthography is extensive, beyond what is generally known or conceived. While the French and Italians have had the wisdom and the policy to refine and improve their respective languages, and render them almost the common languages of all well-bred people in Europe; the English language, clothed in a barbarous orthography, is never learned by a foreigner but from necessity; and the most copious language in Europe, embodying an uncommon mass of science and erudition, is thus very limited in its usefulness. And to complete the mischief, the progress of arts, science and christianity among the heathen, and other rude or unevangelized nations, is most sensibly retarded by the difficulties of mastering an irregular orthography.

The mode of ascertaining the proper pronunciation of words by marks, points and trifling alterations of the present characters, seems to be the only one which can be reduced to practice. This mode resembling the use of points in the Hebrew, has been adopted by some of the nations on the continent; and I have pursued it, to a certain extent, in designating distinctions in the sounds of letters, in this work. The scheme I have invented is not considered as perfect; but it will accomplish some important purposes, by removing the most numerous classes of anomalies. With this scheme, the visible characters of the language will present to the eye of a reader the true sounds of words; and the scheme itself is so simple, that it may be learned in a few moments. To complete a scheme of this kind, a few other alterations would be necessary, but such as would not materially change the orthography, or occasion the least difficulty to the learner or reader.

After these alterations, there would remain a few words whose anomalies may be considered as incorrigible, such as *know, gnaw, rough*, &c., which may be collected into tables and easily learned, and all the other irregularities may be so classed under general rules, as to be learned with very little labor.

The adoption of this or any other scheme for removing the obstacles which the English orthography presents to learners of the language, must depend on public opinion. The plan I have adopted for representing the sounds of letters by marks and points, in this work, is intended to answer two purposes. First, to supersede the necessity of writing and printing the words a second time in an orthography adapted to express their pronunciation. The latter method pursued by the English orthoepists, as applicable to most words, is I think not only unnecessary but very inexpedient. The second purpose is, to exhibit to my fellow citizens the outline of a scheme for removing the difficulties of our irregular orthography, without the use of new characters; a scheme simple, easy of acquisition, and sufficient to answer all the more important purposes of a regular orthography.

PRONUNCIATION.

As our language has been derived from various sources, and little or no systematic effort has been made to reduce the orthography to any regularity, the pronunciation of the language is subject to numerous anomalies. Each of our vowels has several different sounds; and some of the consonants represent very different articulations of the organs. That part of the language which we have received from the Latin, is easily subjected to a few general rules of pronunciation. The same is the fact with most of the derivatives from the Greek. Many words of French origin retain their French orthography, which leads to a very erroneous pronunciation in English; and a large portion of our monosyllabic words of Saxon origin are extremely irregular both in orthography and pronunciation.

If we can judge, with tolerable certainty, from the versification of Chaucer, the pronunciation of words must have been, in many respects, different in his age, from that of the present day; particularly in making a distinct syllable of *e* final, and of the termination *ed*. But no effort was probably ever made to settle the pronunciation of words, till the last century. In England, which was settled by various nations, there are numerous dialects or diversities of language, still retained by the great mass of the population.

The first settlers of New England, were almost all of English origin, and coming from different parts of England, they brought with them some diversities of language. But in the infancy of the settlements, the people lived in towns adjacent or near to each other, for mutual aid and protection from the natives: and the male inhabitants of the first generation frequently assembled for the purpose of worship or for government. By the influence of these and other causes, particularly by that of common schools, the differences of language among our citizens have been gradually lost; so that in this part of the United States, there can hardly be said to exist a difference of dialect.

It is to be remarked further, that the first ministers of the gospel, who migrated to this country, had been educated at the English universities, and brought with them all the learning usually acquired in those institutions, and the English language as it was then spoken. The influence of these men, who were greatly venerated, probably had no small effect in extinguishing differences of speech.

Hence it has happened that the traditional pronunciation of the language of well-educated people has been nearly the same in both countries, to this day. Among the common people, whose pronunciation in all countries is more or less corrupt, the diversities in this country are far less numerous than in England.

About fifty or sixty years ago, Thomas Sheridan, an Irish gentleman, who had been the pupil of an intimate friend of Dean Swift, attempted to reduce the pronunciation of English words to some system, and to introduce it into popular use. His analysis of the English vowels is very critical, and in this respect, there has been little improvement by later writers, though I think none of them are perfectly correct. But in the application of his principles, he failed of his object. Either he was not well acquainted with the best English pronunciation, or he had a disposition to introduce into use some peculiarities, which the English did not relish. The principal objection made to his scheme is that he gives to *s* the sound of *sh*, in *sudorific, superb*, and other words where *s* is followed by *u* long. These he pronounces *shooderific, shooperb, shooperfluity*, &c. This pronunciation of *s* corresponding to the Shemitic ש, he probably learnt in Ireland, for in the Irish branch of the Celtic, *s* has often the sound of *sh*. Thus *sean*, old, is pronounced *shean*. This pronunciation was no sooner published, than condemned and rejected by the English.

Another most extraordinary innovation of Sheridan was, his rejection of the Italian sound of *a*, as in *father, calm, ask*, from every word in the language. Thus his notation gives to *a* in *bar*, the same sound as in *barren, barrel, bat;* to *a* in *father, pass, mass, pant*, the same sound as in *fat, passion, massacre, pan, fancy*. Such a gross deviation from established English usage was of course condemned and rejected.

In his pronunciation of *ti* and *ci*, before a vowel, as in *partiality, omniscience*, Sheridan is more correct than Walker, as he is in some other words; such for example as *bench, tench, book, took*, and others of the same classes.

Sheridan also contributed very much to propagate the change of *tu* into *chu*, or *tshu;* as in *natshur, cultshur, virtshue*. This innovation was vindicated on the supposed fact, that the letter *u* has the sound of *yu;* and *natyur, cultyur, virtyue*, in a rapid enunciation, become *natshur*, &c. And to this day, this error respecting the sound of *u* is received in England as truth. But the fact is otherwise, and if not, it does not justify the practice; for in usage, *u* is short in *nature, culture*, as in *tun;* so that on the principles of Sheridan himself, this letter can have no effect on the preceding articulation.

This innovation however has prevailed to a considerable extent, although Sheridan subjected the change of *tu* to no rules. He is consistent in applying this change equally to *tu*, whether the accent follows the *t* or not. If *tu* is to be changed to *tshu*, in *future*, and *perpetual*, it ought to undergo the same change in *futurity*, and *perpetuity;* and Sheridan, in pronouncing *tutor, tutelage, tumult*, as if written *tshootor, tshootelage, tshoomult*, is certainly consistent, though wrong in fact. In other words, however, Sheridan is inconsistent with himself; for he pronounces *multitshood, rectitshood, servitshood*, while *habitude, beatitude, certitude, decrepitude, gratitude*, &c. retain the proper sound of *t*.

Walker's rule for changing *tu* to *chu*, only when the accent precedes, is entirely arbitrary, and evidently made by him to suit his own practice. It has however the good effect of reducing the *chus*, and removing the outrageous anomalies of *tshootor, tshoomult*, &c.

There are many other words which Sheridan has marked for a pronunciation, which is not according to good usage, and which the later orthoepists have corrected. In general, however, it may be asserted that his notation does not warrant a tenth part as many deviations, from the present respectable usage in England, as Walker's; yet as his Dictionary was republished in this country, it had no small effect in corrupting the pronunciation of some classes of words, and the effects of its influence are not yet extinct. What the precise effect of Sheridan's scheme of pronunciation was in England, I am not able to determine. But I have had information from the late venerable Dr. Johnson of Stratford, and from the late Dr. Hubbard of New Haven, who were in England between the year 1765 and the revolution, that about that period, the change of *t* into *chu* had not taken place, to any extent. It began to prevail on the stage and among the younger barristers and members of parliament, before Dr. Johnson left England, just before the war with America, and Sheridan's Dictionary, published soon after, undoubtedly contributed to extend the innovation. This change presents a new obstacle to the acquisition of a language, whose anomalies were before frightfully formidable and perplexing. The favorers of innovation, seem not to reflect on the immense inconvenience of a correct notation of sounds in a language, by its proper characters; the utility of uniformity and permanence in that notation; and the extensive evil of destroying or impairing the use of alphabetical writing. The man who perverts or changes the established sound of a single letter, especially of a consonant, does an injury to that language, and to the community using it, which fifty men of the same talents, can never repair.

In a few years after the publication of Sheridan's Dictionary, appeared Walker's, the author of which introduces the work to the public, with the following remarks, on the labors of his predecessors.

"Among those writers who deserve the first praise on this subject, is Mr. Elphinstone; who, in his principles of the English language, has reduced the chaos to a system, and laid the foundation of a just and regular pronunciation. But this gentleman, by treating his subject with an affected obscurity, and by absurdly endeavoring to alter the whole orthography of the language, has unfortunately lost his credit with the public, for the part of his labors which entitles him to the highest praise."

"After him Dr. Kenrick contributed a portion of improvement, by his Rhetorical Dictionary, but he has rendered his Dictionary extremely imperfect, by entirely omitting a great number of words of doubtful and difficult pronunciation; those very words for which a Dictionary of this kind would naturally be consulted." [Let it be noted, that the same objection lies in full force against Sheridan, Walker, and Jones.]

"To him succeeded Mr. Sheridan, who not only divided the words into syllables, and placed figures over the vowels, as Dr. Kenrick had done, but by spelling these syllables as they are pronounced, seemed to complete the idea of a Pronouncing Dictionary, and to leave but little expectation of improvement. It must be confessed that his Dictionary is generally superior to every thing that preceded it, and his method of conveying the sound of of words by spelling them as they are pronounced, is highly rational and useful. But here sincerity obliges me to stop. The numerous instances I have given of impropriety, inconsistency, and want of acquaintance with the analogies of the language, sufficiently show how imperfect I think his Dictionary is, upon the whole, and what ample room was left for attempting another, that might better answer the purpose of a guide to pronunciation."

"The last writer on this subject is Mr. Nares, who, in his elements of orthoepy, has shown a clearness of method, and an extent of observation, which deserve the highest encomiums. But he seems, *on many occasions*,* to have mistaken the best usage, and to have paid too little attention to the first principles of pronunciation."

Soon after the publication of Walker's Dictionary, appeared the Dictionary of Stephen Jones, who undertakes to correct the errors of Sheridan and Walker. This author objects to Sheridan, that he has not introduced the Italian sound of *a*, [as in *father*,] in a single instance, and that Walker has been too sparing in the use of it. He objects that Sheridan has not, by any peculiar marks, pointed out the sound of *oi* or *oy*, as in *noise* and *cloy;* and that Walker has given distinctive marks of pronunciation to the diphthong *ou*, which are terrific to the learner, and not well calculated to express the exact sound. He considers it as no trivial error in Walker's system, that he uses the long *e* in place of the short *y*, which gives to *asperity*, for example, the ludicrous sound of *aspereetee*. He notices also as a fault in Walker's scheme, that he makes no difference in the sound of *oo* in *tool, tooth*, and in *look, took*.

In all these particulars, except that of *oi* and *oy*, I think every man who understands genuine English, will accord with Jones. From careful observation, while in England, I know that Jones's notation is far more correct than that of Sheridan or Walker, and except in two or three classes of words, his pronunciation is exactly that which I uniformly heard in England, and nearly the same as that of well-educated gentlemen in New England.

A few years after the appearance of Jones's Dictionary, William Perry published a pronouncing dictionary, in which an attempt is made to indicate the sounds of the letters by certain arbitrary marks. In this work, the author has rejected most of the peculiarities of Sheridan, Walker and Jones, and given the language nearly as it was spoken, before those authors undertook to regulate the pronunciation. This author's manner of designating the sounds of the letters is too complex for convenience, but his pronunciation is nearer to the actual usage in England, than that of either of his predecessors before mentioned. His orthography also is more correct, according to present usage, than that of his predecessors.

During the year past, appeared the dictionary of R. S. Jameson, of Lincoln's Inn, intended to combine the merits of the most popular dictionaries, and to correct the false pronunciation of Walker, whose notation in some classes of words, he entirely rejects. He condemns, as a slovenly enunciation, the sound given to *d*, which, before *i* and *u*, Walker directs, in certain words, to be pronounced like *j*. He rejects also his notation of *ch*, or *tsh*, in *congratulation, flatulent, natural*, and all similar words. He rejects also the affected pronunciation of Sheridan and Walker, in such words as *guide* and *kind*. Most of the other errors of Walker, he copies, as he does his antiquated orthography.

The English orthoepists have analyzed, and in general, have well defined or described, the sounds and appropriate uses of the letters of the alphabet. Sheridan's analysis, which appeared a few years before Walker's, is for the most part, correct; but in describing the sounds of what may be called the diphthongal vowel *i*, I think he has erred, in making it to consist of the broad *a* or *aw* and *e*. He admits indeed that the voice does not rest on the sound *aw*, but he contends that the mouth is opened to the same degree of aperture, and is in the same position, as if it were going to sound *aw;* but before the voice can get a passage to the lips, the under jaw is drawn up to the position, for sounding *e*. On this it is justly remarked by Walker, that *aw* and *e* are precisely the component elements of the diphthong *oi* and *oy*. If the *aw* is pronounced, I would add, then *i* and *oy* must be pronounced exactly alike; and if *aw* is *not* pronounced, then it is not a component part of the diphthongal vowal *i*.

Walker contends that this diphthong *i*, is composed of the sound of the Italian *a*, as in *father*, and the sound of *e*. If so, he must have given to *a*, a very different sound from that which we are accustomed to give it. But this is a mistake; that sound of *a* is no more heard in *i*, than the sound of *aw*. The sound of *i* in *fight, mind, time, idle*, is not *faweght, mawend, tawem, awedle;* nor is it *fàeght, màend, tàem, àedle*. Let any man utter the *aw* or the Italian *a* before the *e*, and he will instantly perceive the error, and reject both definitions, as leading to a false pronunciation. The truth is, the mouth, in uttering *i*, is not opened so wide as in uttering *aw* or *à;* the initial sound is *not* that of *aw* or *à;* nor is it possible, by any characters we possess, to express the true sound on paper. The initial sound is not formed so deep in the throat as *aw* or *à;* the position of the organs is nearly, yet not exactly the same. The true sound can be learned only by the ear.

Equally inaccurate is the definition of the diphthongal *u*, or long *u;* which these writers alledge to consist of the sounds of *e* and *oo* or *yu*. It has this sound indeed in certain words, as in *unite, union*, and others; but this is a departure from the proper sound of this character, as heard in *cube, abuse, durable, human, jury*. These words are not pronounced, *keoob, abeoose, deoorable, heooman, jeoory*. The effort to introduce this affected pronunciation is of most mischievous tendency. The sound of *e* is not heard in the proper enunciation of the English *u*, and for that reason, it should not be so stated on paper, nor named *yu;* as the error naturally leads to a corrupt pronunciation. Dr. Kenrick remarks that we might as well prefix *y* to the other vowels, as to *u*, and pronounce them *ya, ye, yi, yo*.

But this is not the whole evil; this analysis of *u* has led orthoepists to give to our first or long *u*, two distinct sounds, or rather to make a diphthong and a vowel of this single letter. Thus they make it a diphthong in almost all situations, except after *r*, where they make it a vowel equivalent to *oo* or the French *ou*. They represent *u* as being equivalent to *ew*, that is, *e* and *oo*, in *cube, tube, duty, confusion, endure*, pronounced, *kewbe, tewbe, dewty, confewsion, endewre*, but in *brute, fruit, rude, intrude, ruby*, they make *u* equivalent to *oo;* thus, *broote, froot, roode, introode, rooby*.

I know not where this affectation originated; it first appeared in Sheridan's Dictionary, but it is a most unfounded distinction, and a most mischievous error. No such distinction was known to Dr. Johnson; he gives the long *u* but one sound, as in *confusion;* and no such distinction is observed among good speakers generally, either in this country or in England. I was particularly attentive to the public speakers in England, in regard to this point, and was happy to find, that very few of them made the distinction here mentioned. In that country as in this, the long *u* has a uniform sound after all the consonants.

The source of the error in this as in another case to be mentioned hereafter, may be an inattention to the manner in which the articulations affect the vowels which follow them. To understand this, it will be necessary or useful to examine the anatomical formation of articulate sounds.

"An *articulate* sound," says Lowth, "is the sound of the human voice, formed by the organs of speech. A vowel is a simple articulate sound."

These definitions seem not to be sufficiently accurate. Articulation, in human speech, is the jointing, juncture or closing of the organs, which precedes and follows the vowels or open sounds, and which partially or totally intercepts the voice. A vowel or vocal sound is formed simply by opening the mouth. Thus in sounding *a* or *o*, the mouth is opened in a particular manner, but without any articulation or closing of the organs. In strictness therefore, a simple vowel is *not* an articulate sound, as Lowth supposes; and it is certain that many irrational animals, without the power of articulation, do utter vowel sounds with great distinctness.

An articulate sound then is properly a sound preceded or followed or both, by an articulation or junction of the organs. Thus *ba, ab*, and *bad*, are articulate sounds; the vowel being begun or closed, with a junction of the lips, interrupting the voice, in *ba* and *ab;* and in *bad* the vocal sound being preceded by one articulation and followed by another. The power of arti-

* *In many instances*, I suppose the writer means.

culation constitutes the great difference between men and brutes; the latter being unable to articulate, can utter only vocal sounds. The imperfect articulations of the parrot and some other animals form no exception that deserves notice.

I give the name articulation, to the act of joining the organs, and to the character or letter which represents the junction. In the latter sense, the word is equivalent to *consonant;* and articulation may be considered the preferable term, as it expresses the fact of closing the organs.

Human speech then consists of vocal sounds separated and modified by articulations of the organs. We open the mouth, in a particular manner, to utter a vowel; we then close the organs, interrupt that sound, and open the organs to utter a second vowel, and continue this opening and closing, to the end of the word. This process is carried on with surprising rapidity.

Now in passing from an articulation or close position, to an open position for uttering a vowel, it happens often that a very slight sound of *e* is uttered so as to be perceptible to the ear, either before or after the utterance of the proper vowel. This is remarkably the case with the long vowels preceding *r*, for such is the nature of that letter, that *bare, mire, more, parent, apparent*, &c., cannot well be pronounced without a slight sound of *e*, between the long vowel and the consonant. Thus the words above named are pronounced nearly *baer, mier, moer, paerent, appaerent*, and *bare, mire*, really form two syllables, though they are considered to be monosyllables.

A like case, though less obvious, occurs in uttering *u*, particularly after the labial and palatal articulations. In passing from the articulations, *eb, eg, em, ep*, or *pe*, to the sound of *u*, as in *mute* and *pure*, we are apt insensibly to utter a slight sound of *e;* and this utterance, which proceeds from the particular situation of the organs, has been mistaken for the first component sound of the diphthongal *u*. The same cause has given rise to the pronunciation of *e* before the vowel in such words as *guide, guard, kind, guise*. This is precisely similar to the vulgar pronunciation of *cow, gown, county, town*, &c., that is, *keow, geown, keounty, teown;* a pronunciation formerly common in New England, and not yet wholly extinct. This vicious pronunciation, in all words of this kind, whether countenanced by men of low life or of fashionable life, ought to be carefully avoided; as the slender sound of *e*, in such cases, gives a feebleness to the words utterly inconsistent with that full, open and manly enunciation which is essential to eloquence.

The genuine sound of *u* long, detached from the influence of consonants, is the same in all the words above specified; and the reason why it has been made a distinct vowel after *r*, as in *rude* [rood,] is, that the organs are open, before the sound commences; whereas when it follows most of our consonants, the sound is commenced immediately after an articulation, or close position of the organs, as in *mutable* and *infusion*. For this reason, *u* has more distinctly its diphthongal sound after labials and palatals, than after *r;* but this accidental circumstance should not be the ground of radical distinctions, equivalent to the sounds of different letters.

There is, in Walker's analysis of the alphabet, an error peculiar to himself. This is, in making a distinction between the short *i* when it is followed by a consonant, and when it is not; as in *ability*. In this case, he calls the first *i*, in *abil*, short; but the second he calls open, and equivalent to *e* in *equal*. See principles 107, 544. He also makes the unaccented *y* at the end of a syllable precisely like the first sound of *e*, in *me, meter*. *Ability* then written according to his principles would be *abileetee*. Never was a grosser mistake. The sound of *i* and *y* in unaccented syllables, whether followed by an articulation or not, is always the short sound of *e* long, that is, *e* shortened; the same sound in quality or kind, but not in quantity. To prove this fact, nothing is necessary but an attention to the manner in which the words *little* and *tiny*, are pronounced, when they are made emphatical by utterance. They are then pronounced *leetle, teeny*—and this we hear every day, not only among children, but often among adults. In this change of pronunciation, there is nothing more than a prolongation of the sound of *i*, which, in the syllables, *lit, tin*, is short, in *leetle, teeny*, is long.

In consequence of this mistake, Walker has uniformly made a different notation of *i* when accented, and followed by a consonant in the same syllable, and when it stands alone in the syllable and unaccented. Thus to the first *i* in *ability* he assigns a different sound from that of the second; and in *article*, he gives to *i* the sound of *e* long, *arteecle;* but in *articular, articulate*, he gives it the short sound, *tik*. It is in consequence of this mistake, that he has throughout his Dictionary assigned to *i* and *y* unaccented and to *y* unaccented terminating words, the sound of *e* long; an error, which it is ascertained by actual enumeration, extends to more than *eleven thousand vowels* or syllables; an error, which, if carried to the full extent of his principles, would subvert all the rules of English versification. Jones and Perry have corrected this error in their notations, throughout the language.

If it should be said, that Walker did not intend to direct *y* in this case, to be pronounced as *e* long, but that his notation is intended only to mark the *quality* of the sound; it may be replied, he either intended the sound to be that of *e* long, according to his express direction, or he did not. If he did, his notation is not according to any good practice, either in England or the U. States, and by changing a short vowel into a long one, his notation would subvert the rules of metrical composition. If he did not, his notation is adapted to mislead the learner, and it does mislead learners, wherever his book is strictly followed. In truth, this notation is generally condemned in England, and universally rejected in practice.*

In the notation of sounds, there is a mistake and inconsistency in all the orthoepists, which deserves notice, not on account of its practical importance, so much, as to expose an error in syllabication or the division of words into syllables, which has been maintained by all writers in Great Britain, from time immemorial. The rule is that "a single consonant between two vowels, must be joined to the latter syllable." According to this rule, habit, baron, tenet, are to be divided thus, ha-bit, ba-ron, te-net.

This rule is wholly arbitrary, and has for ages, retarded and rendered difficult, the acquisition of the language by children. How is it possible that men of discernment should support a rule that, in thousands of words, makes it necessary, to break a syllable, detaching one of the letters essential to it, and giving it a place in the next? In the words above mentioned, *hab, bar, ten*, are distinct syllables, which cannot be divided without violence. In many words, as in these, this syllable is the radix of the word; the other syllable being formative or adventitious. But where this is not the case, convenience requires that syllables should, if possible, be kept entire; and in all cases, the division of syllables should, as far as possible, be such as to lead the learner to a just pronunciation.

As in our language the long and short vowels are not distinguished by differences of character, when we see a single consonant between vowels, we cannot determine, from the preceding vowel character, whether the sound is long or short. A stranger to the language knows not whether to pronounce habit, *ha-bit* or *hab-it*, till he is instructed in the customary pronunciation. It was probably to avoid this inconvenience that our ancestors wrote two consonants instead of one in a great number of words, as in *banner, dinner*. In this respect however there is no uniformity in English; as we have generally retained the orthography of the languages from which we have received the words, as in *tutor, rigor, silent*, and the like.

Now it should be observed that although we often see the consonant doubled, as in *banner*, yet no more than one articulation in these cases is ever used in speaking. We close the organs but once between the first and second syllable, nor is it possible to use both the letters *n*, without pronouncing *ban*, then intermitting the voice entirely, opening the organs and closing them a second time. Hence in all cases, when the same consonant is written twice between vowels, as in *banner, dinner, better*, one of them only is represented by an articulation of the organs, the other is useless, except that it prevents any mistake, as to the sound of the preceding vowel.

In the notation of all the orthoepists, there is inconsistency, at least, if not error. If they intend to express the true pronunciation by using the precise letters necessary for the purpose, they all err. For instance, they write *bar'run* for *bar'on*, when one articulation only is, or possibly can be, used; so also *ballance, biggot, biggamy, mellon, mettaphor, mellody*. This is not only useless, for the use of the accent after the consonant, as *bar'on, bal'ance, big'ot, mel'on*, &c. completely answers the purpose of determining the pronunciation; but it is contradictory to their own practice in a vast number of cases. Thus they write one consonant only in *civil, civic, rivet;* and Walker writes *kollonade*, doubling *l*, but *kolony, kolonise*, with a single *l*. This want of system is observable in all the books which are offered to the public as standards of orthoepy.

A still greater fault, because it may lead to innumerable practical errors, consists in the notation of unaccented syllables. In this particular, there is error and discrepancy in the schemes of the orthoepists, which shows the utter impossibility of carrying them into effect. The final *y* unaccented, Walker makes to be *e* long, as I have before observed; while Sheridan, Jones, and Perry, make it equivalent to short *i*, or at least, give it a short sound, according to universal practice. Walker pronounces the last vowel in *natural* and *national*, as *a* short; Sheridan, as *e* short, *naturel;* Jones, as *u* short, *naturul*. Sheridan's notation may be a mistake, for he gives to *al* in *national*, the sound of *ul*. In the adjective *deliberate*, Walker and Jones give *a* in the last syllable its proper long sound; and Sheridan, the sound of *e* short, *deliberet*. *Dignitary* is pronounced by Sheridan *dignitery*, and Walker and Jones give to *a* its short sound, as in *at*. The terminating syllable *ness* is pronounced by Walker and Jones *nes*, by Sheridan *nis*, as *blessednes, blessednis*. The same difference exists in their notation of *less;* Sheridan, pronouncing it *lis*, as in *blamelis*, and Walker and Jones,

---

* From the fact, which Walker relates of himself, Prin. 246, that he made a distinction between the sound of *ee* in *flee* and in *meet*, until he had consulted good speakers and particularly Mr. Garrick, who could find no difference in the sound, it might be inferred that his ear was not very accurate. But his mistake evidently arose from not attending to the effect of the articulation in the latter word, which stops the sound suddenly, but does not vary it. It is the same mistake which he made in the sound of *i* in the second syllable of *ability*, which he calls short, while the sound of the second *i* and of *y* is that of long *e*. The celebrity of Walker as a teacher of elocution, and his key to the pronunciation of ancient names, which, with a few exceptions, is a good standard work, have led many persons to put more confidence in his English Orthoepy than a close examination of its principles will support.

giving *e* its proper sound. These differences, and many others, run through their works, and appear in a large portion of all the words in the language.

Now it is probable that all these gentlemen pronounced these words alike, or so nearly alike that no difference would be noticed by a bystander. The mischief of these notations is, that attempts are made to express minute distinctions or shades of sounds, so to speak, which cannot be represented to the eye by characters. A great part of the notations must, necessarily, be inaccurate, and for this reason, the notation of the vowels in unaccented syllables should not be attempted. From a careful attention to this subject, I am persuaded that all such notations are useless, and many of them mischievous, as they lead to a wrong pronunciation. In no case can the true pronunciation of words in a language be accurately and completely expressed on paper; it can be caught only by the ear, and by practice. No attempt has ever been made to mark the pronunciation of all the vowels, in any other language; and in our language it is worse than useless.

As Walker's pronunciation has been represented to the people of this country as *the standard*, I shall confine my remarks chiefly to his work, with a view to ascertain its merits, and correct any erroneous impressions which have been received from such representations.

1. The first class of words which I shall mention, is that in which *a* has what is called, its Italian sound, as we pronounce it in *father, psalm, calm.* From a hasty enumeration of words of this class, I find there are two or three hundred in number, in which Walker gives to *a* its short sound, as in *fat, bat, fancy,* when, in fact, the most respectable usage in England, as well as in the United States, gives that letter its Italian sound. This error Jones and Perry have corrected. To be correct in this class of words, we have only to retain the customary pronunciation of the northern States.

2. The notation of the sound of *oo* by Walker is wrong in most or all the words in which *oo* are followed by *k*, and in some others. Notwithstanding the distinction between the long and short sound of *oo* is clear and well established in a great number of words, yet he assigns the short sound to eight words only, viz. *wool, wood, good, hood, foot, stood, understood,* and *withstood.* Principles 307. It seems inconceivable that a man, bred or resident in London, should assign to *oo* in *book, cook, took,* and other like words, the same sound as in *cool, boom, boot, food.* Jones and Perry have corrected this notation, and given the pronunciation according to good usage, and just according to our customary pronunciation. While in England, I did not hear a single word of this class pronounced according to Walker's notation.

3. To the letters *ch* in *bench, bunch, clinch, drench, inch, tench, wrench,* and many other words, Walker gives the French sound, that is, the sound of *sh*, instead of *ch*, as *bensh, insh,* &c. It would seem by this and other examples of wrong notation, that the author had been accustomed to some local peculiarities, either in London where all kinds of dialects are heard, or in some other place. In this instance, he gives to these words a pronunciation different from that of other orthoepists, and one which I have never heard either in England or in this country. His notation is palpably wrong, as our customary pronunciation is universally correct.

4. It has been already remarked, that Walker's notation of the sound of *i* and *y* short, in unaccented syllables, which he directs to be pronounced like *e* long, in *me, mete,* is contrary to all good usage, and is rejected by every other orthoepist, except Jameson. Walker admits *i* to be short when followed by a consonant in the same syllable. Thus the first *i* in *ability* is short, but the second *i* and the *y* are long *e*, abileetee. Now observe the consequence. In the plural, *abilities*, according to his rule, must be pronounced *abileeteez;* but the word is never thus pronounced; universally it is pronounced *abilitiz;* the last vowel sound is in practice immediately followed by a consonant, and by his own rule must be short. Then the result is, *y* in *ability* is long *e*, but *ie* in the plural is short *i*. And for this change of sound no provision is made in Walker's scheme, nor in any other that I have ever seen.

5. In the analysis of the sounds of our letters, Walker alledges the diphthong *ou, ow*, to consist of the broad *a*, or *aw*, and the Italian sound of *u*. According to his scheme, *about, abound, round, now, vow*, are to be pronounced, *abawut, abawund, rawund, nawu, vawu.* But whoever heard this pronunciation? The fact is not so; the broad sound of *a* is *not* the initial sound of this diphthong; it is not commenced as deep in the throat, or with the same aperture as *aw*; it is a sound that can be learned only by the ear. The pronunciation of this diphthong is uniform in both countries.

6. In noting the sound of the unaccented vowels, and those which have the secondary accent, there are mistakes without number, in all the schemes which I have seen, and one continued series of differences between the orthoepists. The following is a specimen.

Sheridan.	*Walker.*	*Jones.*
Deliverense.	Deliveranse.	Deliveranse.
Dignytery.	Dignetare.	Dignytary.
Anser.	Ansur.	Ansur,
Assembledzh.	Assembladje.	Assembladzhe.
Averaje.	Averaje.	Averedzh.
Barrin.	Barren.	Barren.
Penal.	Penal.	Penul.
Pennens.	Pennanse.	Pennunse.
Pennytenshel.	Pennetenshal.	Pennytenshul.
Pennytensherry.	Pennetenshare.	Pennytenshary.
Persunidzh.	Persunidje.	Persunedje.
Proksymet.	Proksemat.	Proksymet.
Proflyget.	Proflegat.	Proflyget.
Pennetrent	Pennetrant.	Pennetrant.
Akkuzaturry.	Akkuzatore.	Akkuzatury.
Akkrymunny.	Akkremone.	Akkrymunny.
Allymunny.	Allemunne.	Allymunny.
Seremunny.	Seremone.	Serymony.

I take no notice of the different letters by which these writers express the same sound, one using *e* where another uses *y*, but of the *different sounds* which they give to the vowels in the second, third, or last syllable. Now, I appeal to any person who has a tolerably correct ear, whether it is the sound of *a* that is uttered by good speakers, or any speakers in *deliverance* and *dignitary?* Is it the sound of *a* that we hear in the last syllable of *penance, penetrant,* and *assemblage?* Do we hear in the last syllable of *profligate,* the short *a*, as in *fat?* So far from it, that a public speaker, who should utter the sound of *a* so that it should be distinctly recognized in any polite audience, would expose himself to ridicule. The sound of the last vowel approaches to that of *e* or *u*, and the notation of Sheridan is nearest the truth. But any notation is worse than useless; for without it, there would be no difference in customary pronunciation.

To show the utter impracticability of expressing the unaccented vowels, in all cases, with precision, let the reader observe Walker's notation of *a* in the word *moderate* and its derivatives. In the adjective and verb, the *a* is long, as in *fate;* in *moderately* and *moderateness*, it is short, as in *fat.* This is certainly incorrect notation; no good speaker ever pronounces these words *moderatly, moderatness.* In addition to this, the *a* in the verb to *moderate* is more distinctly pronounced than it is in the adjective, in which it has rather the sound of *e* short, *moderet;* at least the sound is more nearly that of *e* than of *a*. And this distinction of sound, between letters in the same word, when an adjective, and when a verb, occurs in a multitude of cases; a distinction for which no provision is made in any system of orthoepy that I have seen, and one which must be left to the cognizance of the ear alone.

There is another class of vowel sounds that comprises too many inaccuracies to be overlooked. This is the class in which the first syllable has an unaccented *e*, as in *debate.* In all words of this kind, Walker directs the letter *e* to have its long sound, as in *me, mete.* Then, become, bedeck, begin, debate, debar, declare, elect, legitimate, mechanic, medicinal, memorial, necessity, peculiar, petition, rebuke, recant, relate, secure, select, velocity, &c. are to be pronounced beecome, beedeck, beegin, deebate, deebar, deeclare, eelect, leegitimate, meechanic, meedicinal, meemorial, neecessity, peeculiar, peetition, reebuke, reecant, reelate, seecure, seelect, veelocity, &c.

According to this notation, the first vowel *e* in *evil, even,* and in *event,* is to have the same sound, being all marked with the same figure. Now, let me ask, where a speaker can be found who pronounces these words in this manner? Who ever heard of such a pronunciation? This notation is erroneous and mischievous, as it is inconsistent with the regular accent, which carries the stress of voice forward to the next syllable, and must, necessarily, leave the first vowel with the feeble sound of short *i* or *y*. This short sound is that which we always hear in such words.

The like error occurs in Walker's notation of *i* in *direct, diminish,* and many other words. Walker himself, under *despatch*, calls the sound of *e* the short *i*, but under rule 107, says this sound of *i* cannot be properly said to be *short*, as it is not closed by a consonant; yet it has half its diphthongal sound, the sound of *e!!* This reason that *i* or *e* is not short, because the sound is not closed by a consonant, is entirely groundless, and contradicted by the universal pronunciation of thousands of English words. To direct such words to be pronounced *deerect, deeminish,* is inexcusable. This error corresponds with that specified under No. 4, supra.

Thus, there is neither uniformity nor consistency among the orthoepists in the notation of the unaccented vowels; and it is hardly possible there should be, for many of the sounds are so slight, in ordinary pronunciation, that it is almost impossible for the ear to recognize the distinctions, and absolutely impossible to express them on paper. In truth, as Dr. Ash remarks, in a dissertation prefixed to his Dictionary, the sounds of the five vowels, in unaccented, short, and insignificant syllables, are nearly coincident; and it must be a nice ear that can distinguish the difference of sound in the concluding syllable of *altar, alter, manor, murmur, satyr.* It is for this reason that the notation of such vowels at all savors of hypercritical fastidiousness, and by aiming at too much nicety and exactness, tends only to generate doubts and multiply differences of opinion. If the accent is laid on the proper syllable, and the vowel of that syllable correctly pronounced, the true pronunciation of the word will follow of course; at least, the pronunciation is more likely to be right than wrong, and no mistake will occur, which shall be an object of notice.

Nor can I approve the practice of writing all words, in different characters, to express their pronunciation, as if their proper letters were so many hieroglyphics, requiring interpretation. A great part of English words have an orthography sufficiently regular, and so well adapted to express the true pronunciation, that a few general rules only are wanted as a guide to the learner.

7. Another error of notation, in most of the English books, is that of the vowel in the first syllable of *circle*, *circumstance*, and many other words, the first syllable of which Sheridan first and afterwards Walker and Jones directed to be pronounced *ser*. This pronunciation I have never heard either in England or in this country. Perry's notation makes the syllable *sur*, according to all the usage with which I am acquainted.

8. Another objection to the books offered as standards of pronunciation, particularly to the dictionaries of Sheridan and Walker, is that the rules are inconsistent, or the execution of the work is inconsistent with the rules. Thus Walker lays it down as a rule, No. 357, that *c* after the accent and followed by *ea*, *ia*, *ie*, *io*, or *eous*, takes the sound of *sh*, as in *ocean*, *social*, *Phocion*, *saponaceous*, which are pronounced as if written *oshean*, *sosheal*, *Phosheon*, *saponasheous*. But in the Dictionary, the author departs from the rule, and directs these words to be pronounced as if written *oshun*, *soshal*, *saponashus*. So also in *gracious*, *ancient*, *especial*, *provincial*, *tenacious*, *rapacious*, and I know not how many others, the author departs from his own rule; so that either his rule or his practice must be wrong.

And here it may be proper to notice a mistake of the author which has led to an erroneous notation in a great number of words. The mistake is, that he assigns to *c* and *t* before the vowels *ea*, *ia*, *ie*, *eo*, and *io*, the sound of *sh*. Thus in *ocean*, he considers *c* as pronounced like *sh*; and in *partial* he considers the sound of *sh* as proceeding from *t* only. Now the truth is, that the sound of *sh* in these and in all similar cases, results from the combination of *c*, *t*, or *s* with the following vowel; that is, from the rapid enunciation and blending of the two letters. Then the sound of the first vowel being blended with *c* or *t*, it ought not to be repeated and form a distinct syllable. To make three syllables of *ocean*, is to use the vowel *e* twice. In most cases, all the orthoepists agree in pronouncing these combinations correctly in dissyllables, and primitive words; as *oshun*, *grashus*, *tenashus*, *parshal*, *substanshal*, *nashun*, *relashun*, *preshus*, and the like. But in a number of words that are primitive in our language, Walker and Jones depart from this rule; for although they pronounce *conscience* in two syllables, *conshense*, yet they pronounce *nescience* and *prescience*, in three, *neshyense*, *preshyense*. So also when they make *tial* one syllable in the primitive word, they make two syllables of these letters in the derivatives; *partial* is *parshal*, but *partiality* is *parsheality*. Thus one error has led to another, and a large part of all words of this kind are mispronounced. Sheridan and Perry, in this respect, are consistent and correct; making one syllable only of *cia*, *cie*, *cio*, *tia*, *tio*, both in primitives and derivatives, throughout the language. A single line of poetry ought to settle this point forever.

Expatiate free o'er all this scene of man. *Pope.*

9. A remarkable instance of inconsistency occurs in the following words. *Armature*, *aperture*, *breviature*, *feature*, &c., Walker pronounces *armatshure*, *apertshure*, *breviatshure*, *overtshure*; but *forfeeture* is *forfeetyure*, and *judicature*, *ligature*, *literature*, *miniature*, *nunciature*, *portraiture*, *prefecture*, *quadrature*, *signature*, are pronounced as here written. Can any reason be possibly assigned for such inconsistency?

10. *Obedience* and its family of words, Walker pronounces *obejeence*, *obejeent*, *obejeently*, but *disobedience*, *disobedient*, as here written. *Expedient* is either as here written, or *expejeent*; but *expedience* without the alternative. Why this inconsistency?

11. *Obdurate*, *obduracy*, are marked to be pronounced *obdurate* or *objurate*, *obduracy* or *objuracy*; but *objurately*, *objurateness*, without an alternative. In these last words occurs another error, the *a* in the third syllable is made short, as if pronounced *rat*; a deviation from all good usage.

This notation of *obdurate* is inconsistent also with that of *indurate*, and with that of *obdure*; an inconsistency which appears to have no plausible pretext.

The conversion of *d* into *j* before *i*, is rejected, I believe, in all words, by Jones, Perry and Jameson, and before *u* is rejected by Perry and Jameson, and in many words by Jones. It is a departure from orthography wholly inexcusable.

12. Walker, Principles No. 92, lays it down as a rule, that when *a* is preceded by the gutturals hard *g* or *c*, [he should have said palatals,] it is, in polite pronunciation, softened by the intervention of a sound like *e*, so that *card*, *cart*, *guard*, *regard*, are pronounced like *keard*, *keart*, *gheard*, *regheard*. Now it is remarkable that in the vocabulary or dictionary, the author has departed from his rule, for in not one of the foregoing words, except *guard*, nor in a multitude of other words which fall within the rule, has he directed this sound of *e* before the following vowel. Had he conformed to his own rule, he must have perverted the pronunciation of *car*, *carbuncle*, *care*, *carcass*, *cardinal*, *cargo*, *garden*, *garter*, *discard*, and a long list of other words, too long to be here enumerated. The English orthoepists now confine this prepositive sound of *e* to *guard*, *guaranty*, *guardian*, *guile*, *kind*, and a few others. The probable origin of this fault, has been already assigned, in treating of the letter *u*. It is an affected pronunciation, which Nares calls "a *monster*, peculiar to the stage." Indeed this slender sound of *e* before another vowel, is wholly incompatible with that manly enunciation which is peculiarly suited to the genius of the language. Perry and Jameson have rejected it.

13. In the first edition of Walker's Dictionary, the author, under the word *tripod*, observes, that "all words of two syllables, with the accent on the first, and having one consonant between two vowels, ought to have the vowel in the first syllable long." But this was too rash, for such words as *cem'ent*, *des'ert*, *pref'ace*, *pres'ent*, *prof'it*, *reb'el*, *trop'ic*, and a multitude of others, stand, in the author's book, in direct opposition to his own rule. In a subsequent edition, the author, or some other person, has qualified the rule by an exception in favor of settled usage. This exception destroys the value of the rule; and indeed there is, and there can be no rule applicable to words of this class. The pronunciation of the first vowel can be known only by the usage.

14. The derivatives of *nation* and *ratio*, Walker and Jones pronounce *nash'onal*, *rash'onal*. If this should be defended on the ground of the shortening power of the antepenultimate accent, then let me ask why we have not *nosh'onal* from *notion*, *devosh'onal* from *devotion*, *probash'oner* from *probation*, *stash'onary* from *station*? Why make rules and not apply them? Why indulge such palpable inconsistences and multiply anomalies?

15. *Possess* is, by the English orthoepists, pronounced *pozzess*; but why not then pronounce *assess*, *assist*, *assassin*, *consession*, *obsession*, with the sound of *z*? Can any good reason be assigned for making *possess* an exception to the pronunciation of this class of words? This utterance of sounds through the nose is always disagreeable to the ear, and should be restricted to words in which usage is established. Good taste should rather induce a limitation, than an extension of this practice. This remark applies also to some words beginning with *dis*, in which Walker goes beyond other orthoepists in giving to *s* this nasal sound.

16. Walker lays it down as a fact, that *u* has the sound of *e* and *oo* or *yu*. This is true in many words, as in *union*, *unite*, *unanimity*, &c. Hence according to his principle, *u* in these words is to be pronounced *yunion*, *yunite*, without the letter *y* prefixed. Yet he writes these and similar words with *y*, *yunion*, which upon his principles, would prefix *yu* to the sound of *yu*, and the pronunciation would be *yuyunite*, or *eooyunite*. But his notation of this sound of *u* is not uniform; for he writes *disunion* and *disunite* without *y*, though it must be as proper in the compound as in the simple word. The same inconsistency occurs between *use*, written *yuse*, *yuze*, and *disuse*, *disuze*.

17. There is a fault in Walker's notation of *o*, when it has the sound of *oo*, the French *ou*. In the Key, he marks *o* when it has this sound with the figure 2, and gives *move* as an example. Then according to his Key, *o* alone when thus marked, sounds as *oo*. But in the vocabulary, he thus marks both vowels in *book*, *look*, *boot*, and all similar words. Then according to his notation, each of the vowels has the sound of *oo*, and *book*, *look*, are to be pronounced *boo-ook*, *loo-ook*. He certainly did not intend this; but such is precisely his direction, or the result of his notation; and a foreigner, without counter-direction, must be led into this pronunciation.

The same fault occurs in his notation of *ee*, as in *meet* and *seek*.

18. *Volume*, Walker and Jones pronounce *volyume*; why not then change *column* into *colyum*? Will it be said that in *volume* the *u* is long? This is not the fact; at least I never heard it thus pronounced either in England or America; it is always short in common usage, and so marked by Perry.

19. *Ink*, *uncle*, *concord*, *concourse*, *concubine*, are pronounced by Walker, *ingk*, *ungkl*, *kongkord*, *kongkorse*, *kongkubine*; and these odious vulgarisms are offered for our adoption. There can be no apology for such attempts to corrupt our language.

20. The words *bravery*, *finery*, *knavery*, *nicety*, *scenery*, *slavery*, are, by Walker and the other orthoepists, pronounced in three syllables, and *imagery*, in four; the final *e* of the primitive word being detached from it, and uttered with *r* as a distinct syllable. Why *savagery* has escaped the same fate, I do not know. It is obvious that in negligent practice, these words have often been thus pronounced. But the most correct pronunciation retains the original word entire in the derivative, the slight sound of *e* before *r* no more constituting a syllable, than it does in *more* and *mire*. Take the following examples.

Of marble stone was cut
An altar carv'd with cunning *imagery*. *Spenser.*
When in those oratories might you see
Rich carvings, portraitures, and *imagery*. *Dryden.*
Your gift shall two large goblets be
Of silver, wrought with curious *imagery*. *Dryden.*
What can thy *imagery* of sorrow mean? *Prior.*

Pronounced in four syllables, *imagery*, in these lines, makes a syllable too much, and injures the measure, and in the last example, utterly destroys it. The true pronunciation of Spenser, Dryden and Prior is the same as it always has been in my elementary books.

21. Formerly, the words *puissance*, *puissant*, had the accent on the second syllable; although the poets seem, in some instances, to have blended the four first letters into one syllable. But the modern change of the accent to the first syllable is not in accordance with English analogies, and it impairs the measure of many lines of poetry in which these words occur. In the adverb *puissantly* it has a very bad effect.

The foregoing observations extend to whole classes of words, in which the genuine pronunciation has been changed, unsettled and perverted. It would be inconsistent with the limited nature of this Introduction, to enter into an examination of every particular word of disputable pronunciation. It seems to be inexpedient and useless to bestow, as Walker has done, half a page or a page, on a single word, in attempting to settle some trifling point, or, in many cases, to settle a point that, in this country, has never been disputed.

To give a brief statement of the errors, diversities and contradictions of the principal schemes of orthoepy, which have been offered to the public, within the last half century, two classes of words only will be sufficient, as specimens.

The following lists are not complete, but they comprehend the greatest number of words in their respective classes. The dates at the head of the columns designate the year when the dictionaries in my possession were published, indicating nearly, but not exactly, the origin of each scheme. In the orthography, I have given the letters used by each author, in the syllable which contains the difference of pronunciation; in the others, I have followed the common orthography.

Sheridan, 1784.	*Walker,* 1794.	*Jones,* 1798.	*Perry,* 1805.	*Jameson,* 1827.
Abbrévyature,	Abbréveatshure,	Abbréviature,	Abbrev'iature,	Abbréveature.
Accentuate,	Accentshuate,	Accentuate,	Accentuate,	Accentuate.
Accentuation,	Accentshuation,	Accentuation,	Accentuation,	Accentuation.
Actual,	Actshual,	Actual,	Actual,	Actual.
Actuate, &c.	Actshuate,	Actuate,	Actuate,	Actuate.
Admikstshur,	Admikstshure,	Admixture,	Admixture,	Admixture.
Adventual,	Adventshual,	Adventual,	Adventual,	Adventual.
Adventshur,	Adventshure,	Adventure,	Adventure,	Adventure.
Agriculture,	Agricultshure,	Agriculture,	Agriculture,	Agriculture.
Aperture,	Apertshure,	Aperture,	Aperture,	Aperture.
Arkitektshur,	Architectshure,	Architectshure,	Architecture,	Architecture.
Armature,	Armatshure,	Armature,	Armature,	
Artuate,	Artshuate,	Artuate,		
Attaintshur,	Attaintshure,	Attainture,	Attainture.	
Aventshur,	Aventshure,	Aventure,		Aventure.
Befortune.	Befortshune,	Befortune,	Befortune,	Befortune.
Bountyus,	Bountcheous,	Bounteous,	Bounteous,	Bounteous.
Calenture,	Calentshure,	Calenture,	Calenture,	Calenture.
Capitulate,	Capitulate,	Capitulate,	Capitulate,	Capitulate.
Capsular,	Capshular,	Capshular,	Capsular,	Capsular.
Captshur,	Captshure,	Captshur,	Capture,	Capture.
Cartulary,	Cartshulary,	Cartulary,	Cartulary,	Cartulary.
Celature,	Celatshure,	Celatshure,	Celature,	Celature.
Cinctshur,	Cinctshure,	Cincture,	Cincture,	Cingkture.
Claushur,	Clauzhure,	Clauzhure,	Clauzhure,	Clauzhur.
Commensurate,	Commenshurate,	Commenshurate,	Commensurate,	Commensurate.
Commutual,	Commutshual,	Commutshual,	Commutual,	Commutual.
Compactshur,	Compactshure,	Compacture,	Compacture,	Compacture.
Compostshur,	Compostshure,	Compostshure,	Composture,	
Concretshur,	Concretshure,	Concretshure,	Concreture,	Concreture.
Congratulate,	Congratshulate,	Congratulate,	Congratulate,	Congratulate.
Conjectshur,	Conjectshure,	Conjectur,	Conjecture,	Conjecture.
Conjunctshur,	Conjunctshure,	Conjunctur,	Conjuncture,	Conjunkture.
Connatural,	Connatshural,	Connatshural,	Connatural,	Connatural.
Constituent,	Constitshuent,	Constituent,	Constituent,	Constituent.
Constructshur,	Constructshure,	Constructure,	Constructure,	Constructure.
Contextshur,	Contextshure,	Contextshure,	Contexture,	Contexture
Conventual,	Conventshual,	Conventual,	Conventual,	Conventual.
Counternatural,	Counternatshural,	Counternatural,	Counternatural,	
Courtshus,	Courtsheous,	Courteous,	Curtcheous,	Courteous.
Creatshur,	Cretshure,	Creatshure,	Creature,	Creture.
Cultshur,	Cultshure,	Culture,	Culture,	Culture.
Debentshur,	Debentshure,	Debenture,	Debenture,	Debenture.
Decoctshur,	Decoctshure,	Decocture,	Decocture,	Decocture.
Defeatshur,	Defeatshure,	Defeature,	Defeature,	
Dejectshur,	Dejectshure,	Dejecture,	Dejecture,	Dejecture.
Departshur,	Departshure,	Departshure,	Departure,	Departure.
Dictatshur,	Dictatshure,	Dictature,		Dictature.
Discomfitshur,	Discomfityure,	Discomfityure,	Discomfiture,	Discomfiture.
Discourtshus,	Discourtshus,	Discourteous,	Discurcheous,	Discourteous.
Disnaturalize,	Disnatshuralize,	Disnaturalize,	Disnaturalize,	Disnaturalize.
Disnatshured,	Disnatshured,	Disnatshured,	Disnatured.	
Divestshur,	Divestshure,	Divestshure,	Divesture,	Divesture.
Dutyus,	Duteous or Dutsheous,	Duteous,	Duteous,	Duteous.
Effectual,	Effectshual,	Effectual,	Effectual,	Effectual.
Enraptshur,	Enraptshure,	Enraptshure,	Enrapture,	Enrapture.
Estuary,	Estshuary,	Estuary,	Estuary,	Estuary.
Estuate,	Estshuate,	Estuate,	Estuate,	Estuate.
Eventual,	Eventshual,	Eventual,	Eventual,	Eventual.
Expostulate,	Expostshulate,	Expostulate,	Expostulate,	Expostulate.
Factshur,	Factshure,	Facture,	Facture,	Facture,
Fastuous,	Fastshuous,	Fastshuous,	Fastuous,	
Featshur,	Featshure,	Featshure,	Feature,	Feteyer.
Fistula,	Fistshula,	Fistshula,	Fistula,	Fistula.
Flatulence,	Flatshulence,	Flatulence,	Flatulence,	Flatulence.
Flatuous,	Flatshuous,	Flatuous,	Flatuous.	
Fluctuate,	Fluctshuate,	Fluctuate,	Fluctuate,	Fluctuate.
Fortune,	Fortshune,	Fortshune,	Fortune,	Fortune.
Fractshur,	Fractshure,	Fractshure,	Fracture,	Fracture.
Fructuous,	Fructshuous,	Fructuous,	Fractuous,	Fructuous.
Futshur,	Futshure,	Futshur,	Future,	Futyure.
Garnitshur,	Garnitshure,	Garniture,	Garniture,	Garniture,

INTRODUCTION.

Sheridan, 1784.	*Walker,* 1794.	*Jones,* 1798.	*Perry,* 1805.	*Jameson,* 1827.
Gestshur,	**Gestshure,**	**Gestshure,**	**Gesture,**	**Gesture.**
Gratulate,	**Gratshulate,**	**Gratulate,**	**Gratulate,**	**Gratulate.**
Guttural,	**Guttshural,**	**Guttural,**	**Guttural,**	**Guttural.**
Habitual,	**Habitshual,**	**Habitual,**	**Habitual,**	**Habitual.**
Horticultshur,	**Horticultshure,**	**Horticulture,**	**Horticulture,**	**Horticulture.**
Hortulan,	**Hortshulan,**	**Hortulan,**	**Hortulan,**	**Hortulan.**
Illnatshur,	**Illnatshure,**	**Illnatshure,**	**Illnature,**	**Illnatyur.**
Immenshurable,	**Immenshurable,**	**Immenshurable,**	**Immenshurable,**	**Immensurable.**
Impetuous,	**Impetshuous,**	**Impetshuous,**	**Impetuous,**	**Impetuous.**
Importunate,	**Importshunate,**	**Importshunate,**	**Importunate,**	**Importunate.**
Impostshur,	**Impostshure,**	**Impostshure,**	**Imposture,**	**Impostyur.**
Incestuous,	**Incestshuous,**	**Incestshuous,**	**Incestuous,**	**Incestuous.**
Indentshur,	**Indentshure,**	**Indentshure,**	**Indenture,**	**Indentyur.**
Ineffectual,	**Ineffectshual,**	**Ineffectshual,**	**Ineffectual,**	**Ineffectual.**
Infatuate,	**Infatshuate,**	**Infatuate,**	**Infatuate,**	**Infatuate.**
Insculptshur,	**Insculptshure,**	**Insculptshure,**	**Insculpture,**	**Insculptyur.**
Insular,	**Inshular,**	**Insular,**	**Insular,**	**Insular.**
Insulated,	**Inshulated,**	**Insulated,**	**Insulated,**	**Insulated.**
Intellectual,	**Intellectshual,**	**Intellectshual,**	**Intellectual,**	**Intellectual.**
Jointshur,	**Jointshure,**	**Jointure,**	**Jointure,**	**Jointyur.**
Junctshur,	**Junktshure,**	**Junctshure,**	**Juncture,**	**Junctyur.**
Lectshur,	**Lectshure,**	**Lectshure,**	**Lecture,**	**Lectyur.**
Legislatshur,	**Legislatshure,**	**Legislature,**	**Legislature,**	**Legislatyur.**
Mantua,	**Mantshua,**	**Mantua,**	**Mantua,**	**Mantua.**
Manufactshur,	**Manufactshure,**	**Manufactshure,**	**Manufacture,**	**Manufactyur.**
Maturate,	**Matshurate,**	**Matshurate,**	**Maturate,**	**Maturate.**
Menshurable,	**Menshurable,**	**Menshurable,**	**Mensurable,**	**Mensurable.**
Meteor,	**Meteor or Metsheor,**	**Meteor,**	**Meteor,**	**Meteor.**
Misfortshun,	**Misfortshune,**	**Misfortshune,**	**Misfortune,**	**Misfortune.**
Mixtshur,	**Mixtshure,**	**Mixtshure,**	**Mixture,**	**Mixtyur.**
Moistshur,	**Moistshure,**	**Moistshure,**	**Moisture,**	**Moistyur.**
Morshur,	**Morshure,**	**Morshure,**	**Morshure.**	
Mutshual,	**Mutshual,**	**Mutshual,**	**Mutual,**	**Mutual.**
Natshur,	**Natshure,**	**Natshur,**	**Natchure,**	**Nateyur.**
Natshural,	**Natshural,**	**Nattshural,**	**Natural,**	**Natural.**
Noctshuary,	**Noctshuary,**	**Noctuary,**	**Noctuary,**	**Noctuary.**
Nurtshur,	**Nurtshure,**	**Nurtshure,**	**Nurture,**	**Nurtyur.**
Overtshur,	**Overtshure,**	**Overture,**	**Overture,**	**Overture.**
Paintshur,	**Paintshure,**	**Paintshure,**	**Painture,**	
Pastshur,	**Pastshure,**	**Pastshure,**	**Pasture,**	**Pastyur.**
Peninshula,	**Peninshula,**	**Peninshula,**	**Peninsula,**	**Peninsula.**
Periostshum,	**Periostshum,**	**Periosteum,**	**Periosteum,**	**Periosteum.**
Perpetshual,	**Perpetshual,**	**Perpetshual,**	**Perpetual,**	**Perpetual.**
Perpetshuity,	**Perpetuity,**	**Perpetuity,**	**Perpetuity,**	**Perpetuity.**
Pictshur,	**Pictshure,**	**Pictshur,**	**Picture,**	**Pictyur.**
Piteous,	**Pitcheous,**	**Piteous,**	**Piteous,**	**Piteous.**
Plentshus,	**Plentshus,**	**Plenteous,**	**Plenteous,**	**Plenteous.**
Postshur,	**Postshure,**	**Postshure,**	**Posture,**	**Postyur.**
Postshulate,	**Postshulate,**	**Postshulate,**	**Postulate,**	**Postulate.**
Presumptuous,	**Prezumtshuous,**	**Prezumtshuous,**	**Presumptuous,**	**Presumptuous.**
Projectshur,	**Projectshure,**	**Projectshure,**	**Projecture,**	**Projecture.**
Promptshur,	**Promptshure,**	**Promptshure,**	**Prompture,**	**Promptyur.**
Punctshual,	**Punctshual,**	**Punctual,**	**Punctual,**	**Pungtual.**
Punctshur,	**Punctshure,**	**Punctshure,**	**Puncture,**	**Pungktyur.**
Pustshul,	**Pustshule,**	**Pustshule,**	**Pustule,**	**Pustule.**
Raptshur,	**Raptshure,**	**Raptshur,**	**Rapture,**	**Raptyur.**
Recapittshulate,	**Recapittshulate,**	**Recapittshulate,**	**Recapitulate,**	**Recapitulate.**
Ritshual,	**Ritshual,**	**Ritshual,**	**Ritual,**	**Ritual.**
Ruptshur,	**Ruptshure,**	**Ruptshure,**	**Rupture,**	**Ruptyur.**
Sanctshuary,	**Sanctshuary,**	**Sanctuary,**	**Sanctuary,**	**Sangktuary.**
Satshurate,	**Satshurate,**	**Satshurate,**	**Saturate,**	**Saturate.**
Scriptshur,	**Scriptshure,**	**Scriptshure,**	**Scripture,**	**Scriptyur.**
Sculptshur,	**Sculptshure,**	**Sculptshure,**	**Sculpture,**	**Sculptyur.**
Septshuagint,	**Septshuagint,**	**Septuagint,**	**Septuagint,**	**Septuagint.**
Sittshuate,	**Sittshuate,**	**Situate,**	**Situate,**	**Situate.**
Spirittshual,	**Spirittshual,**	**Spirittshual,**	**Spiritual,**	**Spiritual.**
Sportshul,	**Sportshule,**	**Sportshule.**		
Stattshuary,	**Stattshuary,**	**Stattshuary,**	**Statuary,**	**Statuary.**
Stattshu,	**Stattshu,**	**Stattshu,**	**Statu,**	**Statu.**
Stattshur,	**Stattshure,**	**Stattshure,**	**Stature,**	**Statyur.**
Stattshut,	**Stattshute,**	**Stattshute,**	**Statute,**	**Statute.**
Strictshur,	**Strictshure,**	**Strictshure,**	**Stricture,**	**Strictyur.**
Structshur,	**Structshure,**	**Structshure,**	**Structure,**	**Structyur.**
Sumptshuous,	**Sumptshuous,**	**Sumtshuous,**	**Sumptuous,**	**Sumptuous.**
Shootshur,	**Sutshure,**	**Sutshure,**	**Suture,**	**Suteyur.**
Tarantshula,	**Tarantshula,**	**Tarantshula,**	**Tarantula,**	**Tarantula.**
Tempestuous,	**Tempestshuous,**	**Tempestshuous,**	**Tempestuous,**	**Tempestuous.**
Tenshur,	**Tenshure,**	**Tenshure,**	**Tenshur,**	**Tenshur.**
Textshuary,	**Textshuary,**	**Textshuary,**	**Textuary,**	**Textuary.**
Textshur,	**Textshure,**	**Textshure,**	**Texture,**	**Textyur.**
Tinctshur,	**Tinctshure,**	**Tinctshure,**	**Tincture,**	**Tingktyur.**

INTRODUCTION.

Sheridan, 1784.	*Walker,* 1794.	*Jones,* 1798.	*Perry,* 1805.	*Jameson,* 1827.
Titshular,	Tittshular,	Titshular,	Titular,	Titular.
Tortshur,	Tortshure,	Tortshure,	Torture,	Tortyur.
Tortshuous,	Tortshuous,	Tortshuous,	Tortuous,	Tortuous.
Tritshuration,	Tritshuration,	Tritshuration,	Triturate,	Trituration.
Tshoomultshuous,	Tumultshuous,	Tumultshuous,	Tumultuous,	Tumultuous.
Unctshuous,	Ungktshuous,	Unctuous,	Unctuous,	Ungktuous.
Unstattshutable,	Unstattshutable,	Unstattshutable,	Unstatutable.	
Vestshur,	Vestshure,	Vestshure,	Vesture,	Vestyur.
Ventshur,	Ventshure,	Ventshure,	Venture,	Ventyur.
Veolentchelo,	Veolentshelo,	Veolonchelo,	Violoncello,	Veolontsello.
Vertshu,	Vertshu,	Vertshu,	Virtue,	Virtu.
Vitshuline,	Vitshuline,	Vitshuline,	Vituline.	
Voluptshuous,	Voluptshuous,	Voluptshuous,	Voluptuous,	Voluptuous.
Vultshur,	Vultshure,	Vultshure,	Vulture,	Vultyur.
Waftshur,	Waftshure,	Waftshure,	Wafture.	

This table of words may perhaps be thought a burlesque on English orthoepy. It certainly presents a phenomenon altogether novel in the history of language.

Of these five authorities, the notation of Perry, with the exception of a few words ending in *ure*, is most nearly accordant to the present usage in England, as far as my observations, while in that country, extended. That of Walker is by far the most remote from that usage. From an actual enumeration of the syllables in certain classes of words in which the vowel is erroneously pronounced, in Walker's scheme, I have ascertained that the number amounts to more than *twelve thousand*, without including several classes of unaccented syllables, which would swell the number by some thousands. Of this whole number, I did not, while in England, hear one vowel pronounced according to Walker's notation. The zeal manifested in this country, to make his pronunciation a standard, is absolute infatuation, as if adopted in its full extent, it would introduce many differences in the pronunciation of words in the two countries, where sameness now exists; and even the attempt, should it not be successful, must multiply discordancies and distract opinions, and thus place the desired uniformity at a greater distance than ever. Fortunately, Walker's pronunciation has never been generally received in England, and where it has been received, we see, by Jameson's Dictionary, that it is becoming unpopular and obsolete.

We observe in the following list, that the three first of these orthoepists have no rule by which their pronunciation is regulated. Hence the want of uniformity in words of like orthography. See *bounteous, courteous, duteous* and *plenteous*. Why should *plenteous* be reduced to two syllables, when *bounteous* is pronounced in three? And what reason can be assigned for the different notation of *capitulate* and *recapitulate*?

A remarkable instance of inconsistency in Walker's notation occurs in words of more syllables than two, ending in *ture*. Thus we find *ture* converted into *chure* [tshure] in

Abbreviatshure.	Celatshure.	Contextshure
Admixtshure.	Calentshure.	Debentshure.
Adventshure.	Compactshure.	Decoctshure.
Agricultshure.	Compostshure.	Defeatshure.
Apertshure.	Concretshure.	Dejectshure.
Attaintshure.	Conjectshure.	Departshure.
Aventshure.	Conjunctshure.	Dictatshure.
Impostshure.	Overtshure.	Divestshure.
Indentshure.		Projectshure.

But in the following words the terminating syllable remains unaltered.

Illiterature.	Literature.	Prelature.
Intemperature.	Miniature.	Quadriture.
Investiture.	Nunciature.	Serrature.
Judicature.	Nutriture.	Signature.
Ligature.	Prefecture.	Temperature.
Limature.		

In this class of words, Sheridan and Jones are also inconsistent with themselves, though not to the same extent as Walker. Perry and Jameson retain, in all these words, the true orthography and pronunciation. In these words also, Walker gives to *u*, in the last syllable, its first or long sound; but this is an inaccurate notation; the sound, in actual usage, is that of short *u*, at least so far as my observation extends, either in England or the United States.

In the following classes of words, as pronounced by Walker, there is either error or inconsistency, or both.

Assidjuous,	Individual or individjual,
Commodious or commojeus,	Ingrejent [for ingredient,]
Credjulous,	Insidious or insidjeus,
Dividual or dividjual,	Intermedial or intermejeal,
Fastidious or fastidjeous,	Invidious or invidjeus,
Gradient or grajeent,	Mediocrity or mejeocrity,
Gradual or gradjual,	Medium or mejeum,
Guardian or guarjean,	Melodious or melojeus,
Hideus or hidjeus,	Meridian or meridjean,
Immediacy or immejeasy,	Modulate or modjulate,
Incendiary or incenjeary.	Nidjulation,
Nodjule,	Prelujeus,
Noctidyal or noctidjeal,	Presidjeal,
Obejeence,	Procejure,
Obejeent,	Quotijean,
Obduracy or objuracy,	Radiate or rajeate,
Obdurate or objurate,	Radiant or rajeant,
Occidjuus,	Radius or rajeus,
Odium or ojeum,	Rezidjual,
Ojus or ojeus,	Sardius or sarjeus,
Ordeal or orjeal,	Sedulous or sedjulous,
Penjulous,	Studious or stujeus,
Penjulum,	Tedious or tejeus.
Predial or prejeal,	

It would seem that, in a large part of these words, we may take our choice, either to retain the proper sound of *d*, or to convert it into that of *j*. This choice certainly makes an odd kind of standard. But why *mediate* should retain the sound of *d*, while *immediacy* and *medium* suffer a change; or why *radiate* should be given in the alternative, *radiate* or *rajeate*, while *irradiate* and *irradiance* are not subjected to any change; or why *obedience* should be changed into *obejeence*, and *disobedience* remain unchanged, I am not able to conjecture.

These classes of words exhibit a specimen of the modern ORTHOEPY, so called, of our language; it is indeed a brief and imperfect specimen, for I have ascertained by actual enumeration, that a catalogue of *all* the differences of notation in these authors, would comprehend about *one third* of all the words in their vocabularies. Amidst this mass of errors and contradictions, our consolation is that the good sense of the English nation, a learned and respectable people, is triumphing over the follies and caprices of fashion, and frowning on this most mischievous spirit of innovation.

In proportion as the importance of settled usages and of preserving inviolate the proper sounds of letters, as the true and only safe landmarks of pronunciation, shall be appreciated by an enlightened people, just in that proportion will all attempts of affected speakers to innovate upon such established usages be reprobated and resisted.

The intentions of the men who have undertaken to give a standard of pronunciation, have unquestionably been upright and sincere; but facts have proved that instead of *good* they have, on the whole, done *harm;* for instead of reducing the pronunciation of words to uniformity, they have, to a considerable extent, unsettled it, and multiplied differences. The whole process of these attempts, from Sheridan's first publication, is within my memory, and I am confident, that whatever has been the effect of these attempts in Great Britain, the result of them in the United States, has been to multiply greatly the diversities of pronunciation. And such is the present state of the authorities, offered as standards, that it is impossible from books to gain a correct knowledge of what is the general usage. If I had no other means of knowing this general usage, than the English books, I should be utterly unable to ascertain it and should give up the attempt as hopeless.*

Some of the differences of notation, in the several books, may be rather *apparent* than *real;* but with all due allowance for this imperfection of the schemes, I am persuaded that there are *ten* differences among these orthoepists, where there is *one* in the actual pronunciation of respectable people in England and the United States; and in most of them, the notation, if strictly followed, will lead to *ten* differences of pronunciation, where *one* only now exists in the actual practice of the two countries.

This effect of multiplying doubts and diversities, has resulted from very obvious causes.

1. The limited acquaintance of orthoepists with the general usage, and

---

* The multiplicity of books for instructing us in our vernacular language is an evil of no small magnitude. Every man has some peculiar notions which he wishes to propagate, and there is scarcely any peculiarity or absurdity for which some authority may not be found. The facility of book-making favors this disposition, and while a chief qualification for authorship is a dextrous use of an inverted pen, and a pair of scissors, we are not to expect relief from the evil.

their taking the pronunciation of London, or some dialect or local practice in that city, for the *best usage*. The propagation of such a dialectical or peculiar practice would of course disturb the uniformity of any other practice, in other parts of England or in this country.

2. The difficulty or rather impracticability of representing sounds, and nice distinctions of sound, on paper; especially in unaccented syllables.

3. The partiality of authors for the practice of particular speakers, either stage players or others, which would lead them to denominate that the *best* practice, which had been adopted by their favorites.

4. A spirit of fastidious hypercriticism, which has led writers to make minute distinctions, that are liable to be disputed, and which tend only to perplex the inquirer, and generate uncertainty or diversity, where no essential difference had previously existed in practice. This spirit is continually producing new books and new schemes of orthoepy, and every additional book serves only to increase the difficulty of uniting opinions and establishing uniformity.

This view of the subject is probably the most favorable that can be presented. The real fact seems to be this; these men have taken for the standard, what they were pleased to call the *best usage*, which, in many cases, is a local usage or some favorite peculiarity of particular speakers, at least if they have had any authority at all; or they have given the pronunciation which happened to please their fancy, though not authorised by usage. In this manner, they have attempted to bend the common usage to their particular fancies.

It has been in this manner, by presenting to the public *local* or *particular* practice, or mere innovation, for a standard, instead of general or national usage, that the authors above mentioned have unsettled the pronunciation of many words and multiplied diversities of practice. These attempts to obtrude *local usage* on the public, and bend to it the general or national usage, are the boldest assumptions of authority in language that the history of literature has ever exhibited. In England however these pretensions to direct the pronunciation of the nation have less effect than they have in the United States, for this obvious reason, that in England pronunciation is regulated almost exclusively by the practice of the higher classes of society, and not by books; hence if books do not exhibit the customary pronunciation, the falsity of notation is easily detected, and the work which offers it is neglected. But in this country, where the people resort chiefly to books for rules of pronunciation, a false notation of sounds operates as a deception and misleads the inquirer. How long the citizens of this country will submit to these impositions, time only can determine.

The English language, when pronounced according to the genuine composition of its words, is a nervous, masculine language, well adapted to popular eloquence; and it is not improbable that there may be some connection between this manly character of the language and the freedom of the British and American constitutions. They may perhaps act and react upon each other mutually, as cause and effect, and each contribute to the preservation of the other. At the same time, the language is, by no means, incapable of poetical sweetness and melody. The attempts to refine upon the pronunciation, within the last half century, have, in my opinion, added nothing to its smoothness and sweetness, but have very much impaired its strength of expression as well as its regularity. The attempts to banish the Italian sound of *a* and to introduce the sound of *e* before *i* and *u*, as in *kind, guard, duty*, &c. ought to be resisted, as injurious to the manly character of the genuine English pronunciation.*

In order to produce and preserve a tolerable degree of uniformity, and the genuine purity of our language, two things appear to be indispensable, viz.

1. To reject the practice of noting the sounds of the vowels in the unaccented syllables. Let any man, in genteel society or in public, pronounce the distinct sound of *a* in the last syllable of *important*, or the distinct sound of *e* in the terminations *less* and *ness*, as in *hopeless, happiness*, and he would pass for a most inelegant speaker. Indeed so different is the slight sound of a great part of the unaccented vowels, in elegant pronunciation, from that which is directed in books of orthoepy, that no man can possibly acquire the nicer distinction of sounds, by means of books; distinctions which no characters yet invented can express. Elegant pronunciation can be learned only by the ear. The French and Italians, whose languages are so popular in Europe, have never attempted to teach the sounds of their letters by a system of notation, embracing the finer sounds of the vowels.

2. To preserve purity and uniformity in pronunciation, it is necessary to banish from use all books which change the orthography of words to adapt the pronunciation to the fashion of the day. The scheme now pursued is the most mischievous project for corrupting the language, that human ingenuity ever devised. By removing the landmarks of language, all the fences which can secure the purity and regularity of the language from unlicensed depredations without end are demolished, the chief use and value of alphabetical writing are destroyed, and every thing is given to chance and to caprice.

In determining the pronunciation of words in this work, I have availed myself of the most respectable English authorities, as well as of my own personal observations in both countries, and of the observations of American gentlemen of erudition who have visited England. In selecting from a mass of contradictory authorities, I may not, in all cases, have adopted the best pronunciation; but I have spared no pains to execute this part of the work with fidelity.

In general, the rules I have prescribed to myself are these. 1. The usage of respectable people in England and the United States, when identical in the two countries, settled and undisputed. This rule comprehends most of the words in the language. 2. When usage is unsettled or uncertain, I have adjusted the pronunciation to the regular, established analogies of the language, as far as these can be definitely ascertained; having however, in accentuation, some regard to euphony, or the prosaic melody which proceeds from a due succession of accented and unaccented syllables.

There are some words, differently pronounced by respectable people, in which no decisive reasons appear for preferring one mode of pronouncing them to another; either might be adopted, without any injury to melody or analogy. I see no particular reason, why *pat'ent* should have its first vowel short, and *ma'tron, pa'tron*, and *pa'triot*, the first vowel long. Much less do I approve the reasons assigned for making the *a* short in *mat'ronal*, and not in *ma'tronly*, or short in *pat'ronal*, and not in *pa'troness*. The reasons assigned by Walker appear to me to be absolute trifling. The rule of uniformity is paramount to every other, excepting that of general undisputed custom; and when the practice is unsettled, it seems to be the duty of the lexicographer to be guided by that rule, for his authority may lead to the uniformity desired.

In a few instances, the common usage of a great and respectable portion of the people of this country accords with the analogies of the language, but not with the modern notation of English orthoepists. In such cases, it seems expedient and proper, to retain our own usage. To renounce a practice confessedly regular for one confessedly anomalous, out of respect to foreign usage, would hardly be consistent with the dignity of lexicography. When we have principle on our side, let us adhere to it. The time cannot be distant, when the population of this vast country will throw off their leading strings, and walk in their own strength; and the more we can raise the credit and authority of principle over the caprices of fashion and innovation, the nearer we approach to uniformity and stability in practice.

It is difficult, if not impracticable, to reconcile the opinions of a nation, in regard to every point, either of orthography or pronunciation. Every attempt that has yet been made, in regard to the English language, has served only to increase the difficulty; and as a gentleman remarked to me in London, a convention of learned men could not effect the object, for no two men would think alike on the subject.

The language of a nation is the common property of the people, and no individual has a right to make inroads upon its principles. As it is the medium of communication between men, it is important that the same *written words* and the same *oral sounds* to express the same ideas, should be used by the whole nation. When any man therefore attempts to change the established orthography or pronunciation, except to correct palpable errors and produce uniformity, by recalling wanderers into the pale of regular analogies, he offers an indignity to the nation. No local practice, however respectable, will justify the attempt. There is great dignity, as well as propriety, in respecting the universal and long established usages of a nation.

With these views of the subject, I feel myself bound to reject all modern innovations, which violate the established principles and analogies of the language, and destroy or impair the value of alphabetical writing. I have therefore endeavored to present to my fellow citizens the English language, in its genuine purity, as we have received the inheritance from our ancestors, without removing a landmark. If the language is fatally destined to be corrupted, I will not be an instrument of the mischief.

ETYMOLOGY.

Irregular as is the orthography of the English Language, and unsettled or corrupt as is the pronunciation, there is nothing either in English or in any other language of which I have any knowledge, which exhibits so strikingly the low state of philology as the etymological deductions of words, or the history of their origin, affinities and primary signification. To enable the young inquirer to estimate the erudition, correctness, or negligence of writers on this subject, and to awaken more attention to this branch of learning, I will state briefly the results of my researches and the opinions which I have been compelled to form on the merits of the principal treatises on this subject. And if these opinions or this statement should be charged to egotism, or my over-weening confidence in the success of my own investigations, my apology is, that I have suffered so much myself by a misplaced confidence in the erudition of writers; I have so often embraced errors

*The French language, by the loss or imperfect use of articulations, though rendered easy in utterance, has become so feeble in sound as to be unfit for bold, impressive eloquence. From the specimens which I witnessed in the Chamber of Deputies in Paris, I should suppose the orator must depend almost entirely on his own animation and action for success in popular speaking, with little or no aid from the strength and beauty of language. The language of popular eloquence should be neither the mouthing cant of the stage, nor the mincing affectation of dandies, nor the baby talk of the nursery. Such was not the language of Demosthenes nor of Cicero; and such may never be the language of the British Chatham, and of the American Ames.

INTRODUCTION.

which it has cost me more labor to unlearn than to learn; that if I can prevent my fellow-citizens, who have a taste for this study, from being subjected to the same evils, I shall think the advantage obtained more than a balance for any unmerited imputation.

The first example of etymology which I shall mention, is that of Josephus, the historian of the Jews, who informs his readers, that the first man "was called *Adam*, which in the Hebrew tongue signifies one that is *red*, because he was formed out of *red earth* compounded together; for of that kind is virgin and true earth." Here is a mistake proceeding from a mere resemblance of words; it being certain that *Adam* no more signifies *red earth*, than it does *red cedar*. This mistake is connected with another, that Adam was the proper name of the first man, an individual; whereas the word is the generic name of the human species, and like *man* in English, signifies form, shape, image, expressing distinctively the characteristic eminence or distinction of form of the human race. This fact explains the use of the plural pronoun, in the account of the creation of the species. "And God said, Let us make man in our image, after our likeness; and let *them* have dominion over the fish of the sea, &c." Gen. i. 26. It is evident also that the words used in relation to the species, the *image*, the *likeness* of God, have reference, not only to their intellectual and moral faculties, but also to their external form; and so the Apostle interprets the words, 1 Cor. xi. 7. Not that God has any bodily shape of which man can be the image, but that man has a superior or super-excellent form, corresponding to his intellectual powers, and distinguishing him from all other animals. Now the mistake of Josephus has infected the christian world for eighteen hundred years, and the mistake, with erroneous inferences from it, enters into the most recently published systems of theology.

Among the most celebrated authors of antiquity, who have written on the subject of language, is Varro, who has left a treatise *De Lingua Latina*. On this author's learning, Cicero, Quinctilian and Augustine have bestowed the most unbounded praises. He is pronounced to have been *vir egregius; eruditissimus Romanorum; peritissimus* linguæ Latinæ et omnis antiquitatis, sine ulla dubitatione, *doctissimus*.* He was doubtless a man of uncommon erudition for the age in which he lived, and his etymological treatise may be consulted with advantage by persons who have knowledge enough of this subject to separate the *certain* or *probable* from the *improbable* and *conjectural*. But it is certain from what remains of his treatise, that his knowledge of the origin of words did not extend beyond the most obvious facts and principles. Thus he deduces *initium* from *ineo; exitus* from *exeo; victoria* from *vinco*. All this is well; and we have reason to think him correct, in deducing *vellus*, fleece, from *vellere*, to pluck, as doubtless fleeces were plucked from sheep, before the use of shears. And we have reason to believe him when he informs us that *imber* was originally written *himber;* that *hircus* was written by the Sabines *fircus*, and *hædus*, *fedus*.

Very different must be our opinion of the following etymologies.

Pater, says Varro, is from *patefacio; ager cultus* is so called because in it seeds coalesce or unite with the earth; referring *ager* perhaps to the root of *agger*, or the Greek αγειρω. *Campus*, he says, was so named because fruits were first gathered from the open field, deducing the word from *capio*. Next to this, were the hills, *colles*, so named *colendo*, from *colo*, because these were cultivated next to the open plain. That land or field which appeared to be the *foundation* of cattle and money was called *fundus*, or it was so called because it pours forth [*fundat*] annual crops. He deduces *cogitare* from *cogendo; concilium* from *cogitatione; cura* from burning *cor*, the heart; *volo* from *voluntas*, and *a volatu*, a flying, because the mind flies instantly whither it will. How low must have been the state of philology, when such improbable conjectures as these could attract the encomiums before mentioned from Cicero and Quinctilian!

The reader will find many things in Isidore and Priscian, worthy of his attention, though much of what their works contain is now so familiar to scholars of moderate attainments, as scarcely to repay the labor of perusal. But he who learns that Isidore makes *oratio*, a compound of *oris ratio; nomen*, a contraction of *notamen;* and that he derives *verbum*, from *verberato aere*, will hardly think it worth his labor to pursue his researches into that author's works. Nor will he be disposed to relish Priscian's deduction of *litera* from *legilitera*, because a letter affords the means of reading, or from *lituro*, to obliterate, because the ancients used to write on wax tables, and afterwards to obliterate what they had written.

Vossius wrote a folio on the etymology of Latin words; but from repeated examinations of his book, I am persuaded that most of his deductions are far-fetched, conjectural and fanciful; many of them are certainly erroneous.

Menage and Minshew I have not consulted; chiefly because from such extracts as I have seen, from their writings, I am certain that little reliance can be placed on their opinions, except in cases too plain to be mistaken.

Junius and Skinner, the authorities for most of the etymologies of Bailey and Johnson, are sufficiently correct in referring English words to the language from which they are immediately derived, especially when the orthography is too plain to be mistaken. They inform us that *father* is from the Saxon *fæder*, that *drop* is from Sax. *droppan*, that *picket* is from the French *piquet*, and the like. So Johnson informs us that *accent* is from the Latin *accentus*, and *accept* from the French *accepter*, Latin *accipio*. All this is well, but it can hardly be called etymology, or the deduction of words from their originals.

Whiter, in his Etymologicon Magnum, the first volume only of which I have perused, began his work on a good plan, that of bringing together words of the same or of cognate radical letters, and in pursuance of his plan, he has collected many real affinities. But he has destroyed the value of his work by mistaking the radical sense of many words, and by confounding words of different elements.

Jamieson, in his Etymological Dictionary of the Scottish Language, has collected the affinities of words in that language, particularly words of Gothic and Teutonic origin, with industry and probably with judgment and a good degree of accuracy. In some instances, I think he has departed from correct principles of etymology, and mistaken facts, and he, as well as Whiter, falls very short of truth in a most important particular, a clear understanding of the primary sense of words. Jamieson's Dictionary however contains a valuable addition to our stock of etymological materials.*

To Horne Tooke are we indebted for the first explanation of certain indeclinable words, called conjunctions and prepositions; and for this let him have all merited praise. But his researches were very limited, and he has fallen into most material errors, particularly in his second volume. I have made no use of his writings, in this work.

* Thus far had I written, before I had seen this author's Hermes Scythicus. By this work I find the author agrees with me in regard to the identity and common origin of many of the Gothic and Greek prepositions. Indeed I had supposed that proof of such an obvious fact could hardly be necessary, in the present state of philological knowledge. Some of these prepositions he has illustrated with a good degree of accuracy; although should this work ever fall into his hands, I think he will be convinced that in one or two important points, his explanations are defective. In regard to other prepositions, I am satisfied the author has ventured upon unsafe ground, at least his opinions appear to me not to be well supported.

In respect to his explanations of the names of the mythological deities, it appears to me the author, like all other authors whose works I have seen, wanders in darkness. From all my researches into the origin of words, I have drawn this conclusion, that the pagan deities are mostly the powers or supposed powers of nature, or imaginary beings supposed to preside over the various parts of creation, or the qualities of men, *deified*, that is, exalted and celebrated as supernatural agents. There are few of the names of these deities which I pretend to understand; but there are a few of them that seem to be too obvious to be mistaken. No person, I think, can doubt that the *Dryads* are named from δρυς, an oak or tree. Hence I infer that this name was applied to certain imaginary beings inhabiting the forests.

No person can doubt, that *Nereus*, the deity of the sea, and the *nereids*, nymphs of the sea, are named from the oriental נהר, نهر a river, from the corresponding verb, to flow. No person doubts that *Flora*, the goddess of flowers, is merely a flower deified.

Hence I infer that the true method of discovering the origin of the pagan deities, is to find the meaning of their names.

Now *Diana* is the goddess of hunting. What quality then is most necessary for a hunter? What quality would rude men, destitute of the weapons which we possess, most value as useful in obtaining subsistence? Doubtless courage and swiftness. Thus we have substantial reasons for believing that *Diana* is the Celtic *dan* or *dian*, which signifies bold, strong, vehement, impetuous, the root of *Danube, Don*, and other names of large rivers.

If we examine the name of *Minerva*, we shall find that the first syllable contains the elements of *manus*, the hand, and of *mind;* and the last constituent part of the word corresponds well with the German *arbeit, D. arbeid*, labor, work, the last consonant being lost. Well, what are the characteristics of Minerva? Why, she is the goddess of wisdom and of the arts. The sense of μενος, would give one of her characteristics, and that of *manus* and *arbeit*, the other; but which is the true word, I do not know.

The two circumstances which chiefly distinguish Hercules are his *labors* and his *club*. We never hear of Hercules but with these accompaniments. Now the first syllable of his name is precisely the root of the Greek εργον, εργαω, that is, εργ or ερκ, which would give the sense of work, labor. Whether the last constituent of the name is κλειος or from that root, I shall not pretend to affirm. Indeed, I offer these explanations rather as *probable*, than as clearly proved; but they do appear to be *probably* well founded. *Hercules* then was a name given to any bold, heroic leader of a tribe of rude men, who was distinguished for his achievements as a warrior; and this name must have originated in very early ages, when *clubs* were the principal weapons of war, and instruments of defense. And hence probably the origin of the scepter, as a badge of royalty. Now it is worthy of remark that the war club of rude nations, at this day, especially of the savage nations of the south sea isles, is of the same shape as the ancient scepter.

* Of the full value of these encomiums we can hardly judge, as most of Varro's writings have perished, and some of those which survive appear in a mutilated form. But the greater his erudition, the more striking will appear his ignorance of this subject.

INTRODUCTION.

The Hermes of Harris, according to Dr. Lowth, "is the most beautiful and perfect example of analysis, that has been exhibited since the days of Aristotle." This, in my opinion, is not the character of the work, which, for the most part, consists of passages from the works of Aristotle, Ammonius, Apollonius, Priscian, and other grammarians. It is little more than a collection of the opinions of the ancient writers on philology, whose metaphysical subtilties rather obscure than illustrate the subject. To show how easily men may be misled by metaphysics, when applied to the plainest subject imaginable, take the following example from the Hermes.

"*A* respects our *primary* perception, and denotes individuals as *unknown; the* respects our *secondary* perception, and denotes individuals as known." [This is nearly a literal translation of a passage in Priscian, Lib. 17.]

To illustrate the truth of this observation, the author gives the following example. "There goes *a* beggar with *a* long beard"—indicating that the man had not been seen before; and therefore *a* denotes the primary perception. A week after the man returns and I say, "There goes *the* beggar with *the* long beard;" the article *the* here indicating the secondary perception, that is, that the man had been seen before. All this is very well. But let us try the rule by other examples, and see whether it is universal, or whether it is the peculiar and proper office of *an* or *a* to denote primary perception.

"The article *a*, says Harris, leaves the individual *unascertained.*" Let us examine this position.

"But Peter took him, saying, stand up; I myself also am *a* man." Now, according to Harris, *a* here denotes the *primary* perception, and the individual is *unascertained.* That is, this man is one, I have never seen before.

"He that cometh to God must believe that he is, and that he is *a* rewarder of them that diligently seek him." Whether *a*, in this sentence, denotes first perception, I cannot determine; but sure I am the individual is not left *unascertained.*

A B says to me, "I have lately dismissed *an* old servant, who has lived with me for thirty years." Here *an* may present a primary perception to the hearer, but not so to the speaker. To both, the individual must be well *ascertained.*

It appears then that this definition of *an* or *a* is incorrect, and the pains of these metaphysical writers who form such *perfect analyses* of language, is little better than *learned trifling.* On testing the real character of *an* or *a* by usage and facts, we find it is merely the adjective *one*, in its Saxon orthography, and that its sole use is to denote *one*, whether the individual is known or unknown, definite or indefinite.

Again Harris translates, and adopts the definition which Aristotle has given of a conjunction. "An articulate sound or part of speech devoid of signification by itself, but so formed as to help signification, by making two or more significant sentences to be one significant sentence."

This is so far from being true, that some of the conjunctions are verbs, equivalent to *join, unite* or *add*, in the imperative mode. In like manner, the prepositions called inseparable, and used as prefixes, are all significant *per se*, although by custom, they sometimes lose their appropriate use. For example, *re*, which denotes repetition, has lost its use in *recommend*, which is equivalent to *commend*, without the sense of repetition. But still it has ordinarily an appropriate sense, which is perfectly understood, even when first prefixed to a word. Let any person prefix this word to *pronounce* for the first time, and direct a boy of fourteen years old to *repronounce* his oration, and he would perfectly well understand the direction.

Bryant, the author of "An Analysis of Ancient Mythology," whose works I should love to read, if I could have confidence in his opinions, has given to the public a history of the Cuthites or descendants of Ham, a race of bold adventurers, who, as he supposes, made expeditions by sea and land, introducing arts, founding cities, and corrupting religion by the propagation of Sabianism. For proof of his opinions, he relies very much on etymology and the signification of names. Two or three examples of his deductions will be sufficient to show his manner of proof. *Ham* or *Cham*, signifying heat and the sun, he deduces from חמם to be hot, to heat. So far he may be correct. But he goes on to deduce from this root, also, as Castle had done before him, the Greek καυμα, heat, not considering that this is from καιω, to burn, in which *m* is not radical, but probably *s* is the radical consonant, as this occurs in the derivatives. Καυμα has no connection with *Ham.* From Cam or Cham he then deduces the Latin *Camera*, Gr. καμαρα, an arched roof or vault, whence our *chamber*, though it is not easy to discover the connection between this word and heat, and from the same root, he deduces *Camillus, Camilla*, and many other words, without any support for his opinions, but a mere similarity of orthography in the first syllable. In all this, he is certainly wrong.

The Greek Θεος, God, he supposes most unwarrantably to be formed from the Egyptian *Theuth* or *Thoth*, Mercury.

The sun he supposes to have been styled *El-uc; El* [ηλιος] and *uc* or *och*, a title of honor among the Babylonians. This word, says Bryant, the Greeks changed into λυκος, [a wolf,] and hence the Latin *lux, luceo.* A strange conjecture this, not to call it by a harsher name. Now if Bryant had examined the Teutonic dialects, and the Welsh, he would have seen his mistake; for the Saxon *leoht, liht*, Dutch and German *licht*, are from the common root of the Welsh *llug*, a shooting or gleaming, *lluciaw*, to throw, *lluc*, a darting or flashing, the root of *luceo*; a simple root, that can have no connection with *El-uc.*

Excepting Faber's work on the Cabiri, I have seen scarcely a book in any language, which exhibits so little etymological knowledge, with such a series of erroneous or fanciful deductions, as Bryant's Analysis. Drummond's *Origines* abounds with etymological deductions of a similar character.

Gebelin, a French writer, in his *Monde Primitif*, has bestowed much labor in developing the origin and signification of words; but a large part of his labor has produced no valuable effect. His whole system is founded on a mistake, that the noun is the root of all other words.

Of all the writers on etymology, whose works I have read or consulted, Spelman and Lluyd are almost the only ones, in whose deductions much confidence can be placed. I do not name Camden, Hicks, Selden and Gibson, as their etymological inquiries, though generally judiciously conducted, were very limited. This is true also in some degree of Spelman and Lluyd; but the researches of Spelman into the origin of law terms, and words of the middle ages, have generally produced very satisfactory results. From the limited nature of the designs of Spelman and Lluyd, errors may have occasionally escaped them; but they are few, and very pardonable.

I know of no work in any language in which words have been generally traced to their original signification, with even tolerable correctness. In a few instances, this signification is too obvious to be mistaken, but in most instances, the ablest etymologist is liable to be misled by first appearances, and the want of extensive investigation. I have been often misled myself, by these means, and have been obliged to change my opinions, as I have advanced in my inquiries. Hence the tendency of my researches has been very much to increase my caution in referring words to their originals; and such, I am persuaded, will be the result of all critical and judicious investigations into the history and affinities of language.

A principal source of mistakes on this subject, is a disregard of the identity of the radical consonants, and a licentious blending and confounding of words, whose elementary letters are *not commutable.* Another source of error is an unwarrantable license in prefixing or inserting letters, for the purpose of producing an identity or resemblance of orthography; a fault very justly opposed by Sir William Jones.

The learned Dr. Good, in his *Book of Nature*, Lecture IX, of the second series, suggests it to be probable that both *papa* and *father*, issued from the Hebrew source אב, אבא, אבת. He then fearlessly ventures to affirm, that there is scarcely a language or dialect in the world, polished or barbarous, in which the same idea is not expressed by the radical of one or the other of these terms. True; the letter א is found in most words of this signification; although our knowledge of languages is too limited to warrant such a broad assertion. But the attempt to deduce all words signifying *father* from the Hebrew must certainly fail; for we know from history that a great part of Asia and of Europe was inhabited before the existence of the Hebrew nation. Besides, a large portion of the European population have no word for *father* which can be rationally deduced from אב. The Welsh *tâd*, whence our *daddy*, the Gothic *atta*, Irish *aithair*, Basque *aita*, and Laponnic *atki*, cannot be formed from the Hebrew word, the letter D and T not being commutable with B. One would suppose that a learned physiologist could not fail to assign the true cause of the similarity of words, bearing the sense of *father* and *mother*, among the nations of the earth. The truth is, the sound of *a* is very easy and probably the easiest for children, being formed by simply opening the mouth, without any exertion of the organs to modulate the sound. So also the articulations *b, m*, and *d* or *t*, being natural and easy, will generally enter into the first words formed by children. The labials are formed by simply closing the lips, and the dentals, by placing the tongue against the root of the upper teeth; the position which it naturally occupies in a healthy child. From these circumstances, we may fairly infer, *a priori*, that such words as *ab, aba, papa, tad, mamma*, must be the first words uttered by children. Indeed, were the whole human race to lose their present names for *father, mother*, and *nurse*, similar names would be formed by a great portion of mankind, without any communication between different nations.

The author further observes, that the generic terms for the Deity are chiefly the three following, *Al* or *Allah, Theus* or *Deus*, and *God.* "Besides these, there is scarcely a term of any kind, by which the Deity is designated, in any part of the world, whether among civilized or savage man. Yet these proceed from the same common quarter of the globe." True; men, and of course words, all came from a common quarter of the globe. But it so happens, that these three terms must have originated among different families, or from different sources, for they are all formed with different radicals, and can have had no connection with a common radix. But it happens also, that not one of these terms, as far as I can learn, exists among the Slavonic nations, who compose a large portion of all the population of Europe, and whose name of God is *Bog*, a word radically distinct from all which the author has mentioned.

The author proceeds to say, "that the more common etymon for *death*, among *all* nations, is *mor, mort* or *mut.*" But if either of these terms for *death*, is a native word among the great Gothic, Teutonic, and Slavonic families, which constitute the half or two thirds of all the inhabitants of Europe,

I have not been able to find it. Besides, *mor* and *mut* are words radically distinct, and thus originated in different families.

"Sir," says the author, "is, in our language, the common title of respect; and the same term is employed in the *same sense throughout every quarter of the globe.* In the Sanscrit and Persian, it means the *organ of the head itself.*" He finds the word in Arabia, Turkey, in Greek, among the Peruvians in South America, in Germany, Holland, and the contiguous countries. In some of the languages of these countries, I have found no such word; but if it exists, the author's inference, that the *name* of the *head* gave rise to this term of respect, (for this is what I understand him to mean,) is totally unfounded; and equally fanciful and unfounded is his supposition, that, by the loss of *h* from *sher*, the pronoun *her*, and the German *herr*, lord, are to be deduced from *sir*. In all this, it is demonstrably certain there is no truth or even semblance of reality.

Man, the author deduces from the Hebrew מנה to discern or discriminate, [a sense I do not find in the Lexicons,] and hence he infers that the radical idea of *man* is that of a *thinking* or *reasonable being*. With this word he connects *Menu, Menes, Minos*, and μενος, *mens, mind;* a sweeping inference made at random from a similarity of orthography, without a distant conception of the true primary meaning of either of these words. But what is worse, he appears, if I do not mistake his meaning, to connect with these words, the *tane, tanato*, or *tangi*, of the Sandwich isles; words, which are formed with a radical initial consonant not convertible with *m*, and most certainly unconnected with *man*. See the words *father, man*, and *sir*, in the Dictionary.

The author offers some other etymologies and affinities equally remote from truth, and even from probability.

The governing principles of etymology are, *first*, the identity of radical letters, or a coincidence of cognates, in different languages; no affinity being admissible, except among words whose primary consonants are articulations of the same organs, as B, F, M, P, V and W; or as D, T, Th and S; or as G, C hard, K and Q; R, L and D. Some exceptions to this rule must be admitted, but not without collateral evidence of the change, or some evidence that is too clear to be reasonably rejected.

Second. Words in different languages are not to be considered as proceeding from the same radix, unless they have the same signification, or one closely allied to it, or naturally deducible from it. And on this point, much knowledge of the primary sense of words, and of the manner in which collateral senses have sprung from one radical idea, is necessary to secure the inquirer from mistakes. A competent knowledge of this branch of etymology cannot be obtained from any one, or from two or three languages. It is almost literally true, that in examining more than twenty languages, I have found *each* language to throw some light on *every other.*

That the reader may have more clear and distinct ideas of what is intended by *commutable letters*, and the principles by which etymological deductions are to be regulated, it may be remarked that *commutable* or *interchangeable letters* are letters of the *same organs;* that is, letters or articulations formed by the same parts of the mouth. Thus *b, m* and *p*, are formed immediately by the lips, the position of which is slightly varied to make the distinction between these letters. *F* and *v* are formed by the lips, but with the aid of the upper teeth. Now the difference of the jointings of the organs to utter these letters is so small, that it is easy for men in utterance to slide from one form into another.

The following examples will illustrate this subject.

Labial letters commuted for other labials.

English *bear*, Lat. *fero, pario*, G. φερω, φορεω, D. *voeren*, G. *führen*.

Here is the same word written in different languages, with five different initial letters.

German *wahr*, true, L. *verus.*
Celtic *lamh, lav*, the hand, Goth. *lofa.*
L. *guberno*, Fr. *gouverner*, Eng. *govern.*

Dental letters commuted for other dentals.

Eng. *dew*, G. *thau.*
Eng. *good*, G. *gut.*
Eng. *dare*, Gr. θαρρεω.
Eng. *day*, G. *tag.*
Eng. *thank*, D. *danken.*
Eng. *brother*, D. *broeder.*

Palatal letters commuted for other palatals.

Eng. *call*, W. *galw*, Gr. καλεω.
Eng. *get*, It. *cattare.*
Greek χειμα, L. *hiems*, winter.

Dentals converted into sibilants.

Eng. *water*, G. *wasser.*
Lat. *dens*, a tooth, G. *zahn.*
Eng. *let*, Fr. *laisser.*
Ch. כות, Heb. כוש.
Sax. *tid*, time, G. *zeit.*

Change of linguals.

Eng. *escort*, Sp. Port. *escolta.*
Fr. *blanc*, white, Port. *branco.*

Letters formed by different organs are not commutable; hence we are not to admit a radical word beginning or ending with *b, f* or *v*, to be the same as a word beginning or ending with *g, d, t, r* or *s;* nor a word whose radical letters are *m, n*, to be the same as one whose elements are *r, d*, or *s, t*. If such words are in any case the same, they must have suffered some anomalous changes; changes which are very unusual and which are never to be admitted without the clearest evidence.

When this work was in the press, I first obtained a sight of a "History of the European Languages," by the late Dr. Alexander Murray, Professor of Oriental languages in the University of Edinburgh.

From a hasty perusal of the first volume, I find this learned professor studied the European languages with much attention and profit. He has gone further into the origin and formation of languages, than any author whose works I have read; and his writings unfold many valuable principles and facts. But he formed a theory which he attempted to support, in my opinion with little success: at least, on his principles, all the usual rules of etymology are transgressed, and all distinction between words of different radical letters is abandoned. According to his theory, *nine* words are the foundations of language, viz. *ag, wag, hwag, bag* or *bwag*, [of which *fag* and *pag* are softer varieties,] *dwag, thwag* or *twag, gwag* or *cwag, lag* and *hlag, mag, nag*, and *hnag, rag* and *hrag, swag.* "*By the help of these nine words and their compounds all the European languages have been formed.*" These are the author's words.

To make out his scheme, he joins *ag*, having, to *wag*, move, and forms a diminutive, *wagag*, to move a little or often. With *ba*, bear or bring, and *la*, hold, *wagaba* signifies literally *move-bearing*, and *wagla* is *move-having*. Then *wagaba* contracted into *wabba*, to wave, to weave, and *wagla* into *wala*, to turn. From *dag*, to wet, bedew, comes *damp;* from *ceag*, to chew, comes *champ; fal*, joined, wrought together, from *fag*, to work, to join; *hwal* and *hal*, to hold, and turn, from *hwag; bat* from *bagd* or *bagt*; *bigt*, a bite, from *bigt; bladder* from *blag; modera, mother*, the producer, from *magd*, produced; *bottom* from *bogd*, a stump, root or foundation; *field* from *fagd; earth* from *airtha, acertha*, from *acer, aker, ager; field*, an uncultivated plain, from *fag*, to make to fall.

It seems that in order to maintain his theory, it was necessary to make it appear that *g* formed a part of all original words, and that this letter has, in modern words, been dropped. The author then introduces this letter into words where it never had any place, such as *field, earth, bat*, &c. The author's work presents one of the most singular medleys of truth and error, of sound observation and visionary opinions, that has ever fallen under my notice.

On the same principles, he must have inserted the letter *g* in *bear, fero, pario*, ברא; in *bend, found, tame*, δαμαω, *domo;* in *dream, wander, turn*, &c.; and supposed them to have been originally *beager, fegro, pagrio*, בגרא, *begnd, fougnd, tagme*, δαγμαω, *dogmo, dreagm, wagnder, tugrn*, &c.

Now on such a principle as this we might deduce any word in the language from any other word, or from any root that could be imagined. In short, all such theories are the produce of wild conjecture, and they serve no purpose but to confound the student and bring the study of etymology into contempt.

ACCENTUATION.

Accent is the more forcible utterance of a particular syllable of a word, by which it is distinguished from the others. The accented syllable of a word serves therefore as a kind of resting place or support of the voice, which passes over the unaccented syllables with more rapidity and a less distinct utterance.

Accent is of two kinds, or rather of two degrees of force, *primary* and *secondary*. Words of one syllable can have no accent. Words of two syllables have the primary accent only. Words of three and four syllables may have the primary and secondary accent; but many of them have no secondary accent that deserves notice; such are *dignity, enemy, annuity, fidelity.* In words of four, five or more syllables, a secondary accent is often essential to a clear distinct articulation of the several syllables. Thus *heterogeneous* cannot be well uttered without two accented syllables; the fourth syllable receiving the principal stress of the voice, and the first clearly distinguished by more forcible utterance, than the second, third, fifth, and sixth.

The accent of most English words has been long established; and evidently, it has been determined by the natural ease of speaking, without the aid of rules or instruction. If any man should ask, why we lay the accent of such words as *elocution, meditation, relation, congratulation*, on the last syllable, except one; the answer is, that such accentuation renders the pronunciation more easy to the organs of speech and more agreeable to the ear, than the accentuation of any other syllable. The ease of speaking, and a kind of prosaic melody, resulting from a due proportion of accented and unaccented syllables, which enables the speaker to bound with ease from one accented syllable to another, without omitting those which are unaccented, are the two great principles by which the accentuation of words has been regulated. And it is to be extremely regretted that these principles should, in any instances, be neglected, or forced to yield to arbitrary reasons of derivation, or to a pedantic affectation of foreign pronunciation. When we know that the great mass of a nation naturally fall into a particular manner of pronouncing a word, without any rule or instruction, we may rely upon this tendency as a pretty certain indication that their accentuation is according to the analogies of the language, by which their habits of speaking have been formed; and this tendency cannot be opposed without doing violence to those analogies and to national habits.

Thus formerly, the word *horizon* was universally accented on the first syllable, and this accentuation was according to the settled analogy of the language. But the early poets had a fancy for conforming the English to the Greek pronunciation, and accented the second syllable; the orthoepists followed them; and now we have this forced, unnatural pronunciation of the learned in collision with the regular, analogous popular pronunciation. By this affectation of the Greek accent, the flowing smoothness of the word is entirely lost.

In like manner, an imitation of the French pronunciation of *confesseur*, and *successeur*, led the early poets to accent the English words on the first syllable, in violation of analogy and euphony; and some orthoepists affect to follow them; but public usage frowns on this affectation, and rejects their authority.

There are many words in the English language, indeed a large part of the whole number, which cannot be reduced under any general rule of accentuation, as the exceptions to any rule formed will be nearly as numerous as the words which the rule embraces. And in most instances, we shall find, in the structure of the words, satisfactory reasons for the difference of pronunciation.

DISSYLLABLES.

No general rule can be given for the accentuation of words of two syllables. It is however, worth observing that when the same word is both a noun or an adjective and a verb, it happens, in many instances, that the noun or adjective has the accent on the first syllable, and the verb on the last. Instances of which we have in *ab'sent*, to *absent'*; *con'cert*, to *concert'*; *ex'port*, to *expórt*. The reason is, the preterit and participles of the verbs require to have the same syllable accented, as the verb; but if the first syllable of the preterit and participles were to be accented, it would be difficult to pronounce the words, as may be perceived by attempting to pronounce *ab'senting, con'certed, con'ducted*, with the accent on the first syllable.

In a few instances, the word has a different accent when a noun, from that which it has when an adjective; as *Au'gust, august'*; *gallant', gal'lant*.

TRISSYLLABLES.

Words of three syllables, derived from dissyllables, usually retain the accent of their primitives. Thus

Póet, póetess; pleas'ant, pleas'antly; gra'cious, gráciously; reláte, reláted; poli'te, poli'test.

In like manner, words of four syllables, formed from dissyllables, generally retain the accent of the primitives; as in *collect'ible* from *collect'*, *ser'viceable* from *ser'vice*.

In all cases, the preterit and participles of verbs retain the accent of the verbs.

Words ending in *tion, sion, tian, cious, tious, cial, cian, tial, tiate, tient, cient*, have the accent on the syllable preceding that termination; as *motion, christian, precious, erudition, patient*, &c.

Words of more than two syllables, ending in *ly*, have, for the most part, the accent on the antepenult; as *gratuity, propriety, prosperity, insensibility.*

Trissyllables ending in *ment*, for the most part have the accent on the first syllable, as *compliment, detriment*; but to this rule there are many exceptions, and particularly nouns formed from verbs, as *amendment, commandment.*

Words with the following terminations have the accent on the last syllable except two, or antepenult.

——*fluous*, as *super'fluous, mellif'luous.*
——*ferous*, as *baccif'erous, argentif'erous.*
——*fluent*, as *circum'fluent.*
——*cracy*, as *democ'racy, theoc'racy.*
——*gonal*, as *diag'onal, sexag'onal.*
——*gony*, as *cosmog'ony, theog'ony.*
——*machy*, as *logom'achy, theom'achy.*
——*loquy*, as *ob'loquy, ventril'oquy.*
——*mathy*, as *polym'athy.*
——*meter*, as *barom'eter, hygrom'eter.*
——*nomy*, as *econ'omy, astron'omy.*
——*pathy*, as *ap'athy, antip'athy.*
——*phony*, as *eu'phony, sym'phony.*
——*parous*, as *ovip'arous, vivip'arous.*
——*scopy*, as *deuteros'copy, aeros'copy.*
——*strophe*, as *apos'trophe, catas'trophe.*
——*vomous*, as *igniv'omous.*
——*vorous*, as *carniv'orous, graminiv'orous.*
——*tomy*, as *anat'omy, lithot'omy.*
——*raphy*, as *geog'raphy, orthog'raphy.*

Compound words, as *book-case, ink-stand, pen-knife, note-book*, usually have a slight accent, that is, one syllable is distinguished by some stress of voice; but as the other syllable is significant by itself, it is uttered with more distinctness than the syllables of other words which are wholly unaccented. And in some words, there are two accents, one on each component part of the word, which are barely distinguishable. Thus in *legislative, legislator, legislature*, the accent on the first syllable can hardly be distinguished from that on the third; and if a speaker were to lay the primary accent on the third syllable, his pronunciation would hardly be noticed as a singularity. Indeed there are some compound words, in which there is so little distinction of accent, that it is deemed unnecessary to mark either syllable or part of the word as accented.

As to a great part of English words, their accent must be learned from dictionaries, elementary books, or practice. There is no method of classification, by which they can be brought under a few simple general rules, to be easily retained by the memory; and attempts to effect this object must only burden the memory, and perplex the learner.

The differences in the accentuation of words, either in books or in usage, are not very numerous. In this respect, the language is tolerably well settled, except in a few words. Among these are *acceptable, commendable, confessor, successor, receptacle, receptory, deceptory, refragable, dyspepsy*, which the orthoepists incline to accent on the first syllable. But with regard to most of these words, their accentuation is contrary to common usage, and with regard to all of them, it ought to be rejected. The ease of pronunciation requires the accent to be on the second syllable, and no effort to remove it can ever succeed.

The words *accessory, desultory, exemplary* and *peremptory* would all have the accent on the second syllable, were it not very difficult, with this accent, to articulate the three last syllables of the derivatives, *accessorily, desultorily, exemplarily, peremptorily.* It is for this reason, that the primary accent is laid on the first syllable, and then a secondary accent on the third enables the speaker to articulate distinctly and with tolerable ease the last syllables. If the primary accent is laid on the second syllable, there can be no secondary accent. Yet the natural accent of the primitives being on the second syllable of the three first, and the derivatives little used, we find good speakers often lay the accent on the second syllable; nor is it easy to change the practice.

This circumstance of regarding the pronunciation of derivative words, in settling the accent, has been either wholly overlooked, or not sufficiently observed in practice. Hence the orthoepists accent the second syllable of the verbs *alternate, demonstrate, contemplate, compensate, extirpate, confiscate, expurgate.* Notwithstanding all authorities however, such is the tendency to consult ease and melody in utterance, that many respectable speakers lay the accent of these and similar words on the first syllable. The reason of this is obvious, although perhaps it never occurs to the speakers themselves. It is, that when the accent is laid on the second syllable, the two last syllables of the participles, *altern'ating, demon'strating, compen'sated*, &c. are either pronunced with difficulty, being wholly unaccented, or they are disgustingly feeble. How very difficult it is to utter distinctly the words *alternating, demonstrating*, &c. with the accent on the second syllable; the organs being compelled to change their position and form three, four, five, or six articulations in an instant, to utter the two last syllables! But place the primary accent on the first syllable, and a secondary one on the third, and the voice resting on these, the speaker is enabled to bound with ease from syllable to syllable and utter the whole word distinctly without effort, *al'ternating, dem'onstrating.*

In *extirpate, compensate* and *confiscate*, the accent on the second syllable leaves the last syllables of the participle most miserably weak. What a feeble line is this of Pope:

Each seeming ill *compen'sated* of course.

This evil is remedied by placing the primary accent on the first syllable, and a secondary one on the third; *com'pensated; com'pensating; ex'tirpating; ex'tirpated; con'fiscating; con'fiscated;* the full sound of *a* giving due strength to the last syllables.

It is further to be observed that there are some words which, in poetry and prose, must be differently accented, as the accent has been transferred by usage from one syllable to another within the two last centuries. Nares enumerates more than a hundred words, whose accent has been thus changed since the age of Shakspeare. Of this class of words are *aspect, process, sojourn, convex, contest, retinue, converse*, the noun *horizon*, which Milton accents on the second syllable, and *acceptable*, which he accents on the first, as he does *attribute* and *contribute*. But the accent of all these words has been changed; the seven first have the accent indisputably on the first syllable; the two last, on the second syllable; and although some difference of opinion may exist, as to the accentuation of *horizon* and *acceptable*, yet the common popular practice of accenting *horizon* on the first and *acceptable* on the second, is according to regular analogies and cannot well be altered. Nor ought it to be; the poetic accent, in both, is harsh and unnatural. This difference of accent is a slight inconvenience; but custom is the arbiter in language; and when well settled and general, there is no appeal from its decisions, the inconvenience admits of no remedy.

INTRODUCTION.

Of Johnson's Dictionary, and of the manner in which the following work is executed.

Dr. Johnson was one of the greatest men that the English nation has ever produced; and when the exhibition of truth depended on his own gigantic powers of intellect, he seldom erred. But in the compilation of his dictionary, he manifested a great defect of research, by means of which he often fell into mistakes; and no errors are so dangerous as those of great men. The authority created by the general excellence of their works gives a sanction to their very mistakes, and represses that spirit of inquiry which would investigate the truth, and subvert the errors of inferior men. It seems to be owing to this cause chiefly that the most obvious mistakes of Johnson's Dictionary have remained to this day uncorrected, and still continue to disfigure the improved editions of the work recently published.

In like manner, the opinions of this author, when wrong, have a weight of authority that renders them extremely mischievous. The sentiment contained in this single line

Quid te exempta juvat spinis de pluribus una?

is of this kind; that we are to make no corrections, because we cannot complete the reformation; a sentiment that sets itself in direct opposition to all improvement in science, literature and morals; a sentiment, which, if it had been always an efficacious principle of human conduct, would have condemned not only our language, but our manners and our knowledge to everlasting rudeness. And hence whenever a proposition is made to correct the orthography of our language, it is instantly repelled with the opinion and *ipse dixit* of Johnson. Thus while the nations on the European continent have purified their languages and reduced the orthography to a good degree of regularity, our enemies of reform contend most strenuously for retaining the anomalies of the language, even to the very rags and tatters of barbarism. But what is more extraordinary, the very persons who thus struggle against the smallest improvement of the *orthography* are the most ready to innovate in the *pronunciation*, and will, at any time, adopt a change that fashion may introduce, though it may infringe the regularity of the language, multiply anomalies, and increase the difficulty of learning it. Nay, they will not only innovate themselves, but will use their influence to propagate the change, by deriding those who resist it, and who strive to retain the resemblance between the written and spoken language.

A considerable part of Johnson's Dictionary is however well executed; and when his definitions are correct and his arrangement judicious, it seems to be expedient to follow him. It would be mere affectation or folly to alter what cannot be improved.

The principal faults in Johnson's Dictionary are

1. The want of a great number of well authorized words belonging to the language. This defect has been in part supplied by Mason and Todd; but their supplemental list is still imperfect even in common words, and still more defective from the omission of terms of science.

2. Another great fault, that remains uncorrected, is the manner of noting the accented syllable; the accent being laid uniformly on the vowel, whether it closes the syllable or not. Thus the accent is laid on *e* in *te'nant* as well as in *te'acher*, and the inquirer cannot know from the accent whether the vowel is long or short. It is surprising that such a notation should still be retained in that work.

3. It is considered as a material fault, that in some classes of words, Johnson's orthography is either not correct upon principle or not uniform in the class. Thus he writes *heedlessly*, with *ss*, but *carelesly*, with one *s; defence*, with *c*, but *defensible, defensive*, with *s; rigour, inferiour*, with *u*, but *rigorous, inferiority*, without it; *publick, authentick* with *k*, but *publication, authenticate*, without it; and so of many other words of the same classes.

4. The omission of the participles or most of them, is no small defect, as many of them by use have become proper adjectives, and require distinct definitions. The additions of this kind in this work are very numerous. It is also useful both to natives and foreigners, to be able, by opening a dictionary, to know when the final consonant of a verb is doubled in the participle.

5. The want of due discrimination in the definitions of words that are nearly synonymous, or sometimes really synonymous, at other times not, is a fault in all the dictionaries of our language, which I have seen. *Permeate*, says Johnson, signifies, *to pass through*, and *permeable*, *such as may be passed through*. But we *pass through* a door or gate; although we do not *permeate* it, or say that it is *permeable*. *Obedience*, says Johnson, is *obsequiousness*, but this is rarely the present sense of the word; so far from it that *obedience* is always honorable, and *obsequiousness* usually implies meanness. *Peculation*, says Johnson, is *robbery* of the public, *theft* of public money. But as *robbery* and *theft* are now understood, it is neither. Inaccuracies of this kind are very numerous.

6. There are in Johnson's Dictionary, some palpable mistakes in orthography, such as *comptroller, bridegroom, redoubt*, and some others, there being no such legitimate words in the language. In other instances, the author mistook the true origin of words, and has erred in the orthography, as in *chymistry* and *diocess*.

7. The mistakes in etymology are numerous; and the whole scheme of deducing words from their original is extremely imperfect.

8. The manner of defining words in Johnson, as in all other dictionaries, is susceptible of improvement. In a great part of the more important words, and particularly verbs, lexicographers, either from negligence or want of knowledge, have inverted the true order, or have disregarded all order in the definitions. There is a primary sense of every word, from which all the other have proceeded; and whenever this can be discovered, this sense should stand first in order. Thus the primary sense of *make* is to *force* or *compel;* but this in Johnson's Dictionary is the *fifteenth* definition; and this sense of *facio* in Ainsworth, the *nineteenth.*

9. One of the most objectionable parts of Johnson's Dictionary, in my opinion, is the great number of passages cited from authors, to exemplify his definitions. Most English words are so familiarly and perfectly understood, and the sense of them so little liable to be called in question, that they may be safely left to rest on the authority of the lexicographer, without examples. Who needs extracts from three authors, Knolles, Milton and Berkeley, to prove or illustrate the literal meaning of *hand?* Who needs extracts from Shakspeare, Bacon, South and Dryden, to prove *hammer* to be a legitimate English word, and to signify an instrument for driving nails? So under *household*, we find seven passages and nearly thirty lines employed to exemplify the plain interpretation, *a family living together*.

In most cases, one example is sufficient to illustrate the meaning of a word; and this is not absolutely necessary, except in cases where the signification is a deviation from the plain literal sense, a particular application of the term; or in a case, where the sense of the word may be doubtful, and of questionable authority. Numerous citations serve to swell the size of a Dictionary, without any adequate advantage. But this is not the only objection to Johnson's exemplifications. Many of the passages are taken from authors now little read, or not at all; whose style is now antiquated, and by no means furnishing proper models for students of the present age.

In the execution of this work, I have pursued a course somewhat different; not however without fortifying my own opinion with that of other gentlemen, in whose judgment I have confidence. In many cases, where the sense of a word is plain and indisputable, I have omitted to cite any authority. I have done the same in many instances, where the sense of a word is wholly obsolete, and the definition useful only to the antiquary. In some instances, definitions are given without authority, merely because I had neglected to note the author, or had lost the reference. In such cases, I must stand responsible for the correctness of the definition. In all such cases, however, I have endeavored to be faithful to the duty of a lexicographer; and if in any instance, a mistake has escaped me, I shall be happy to have it suggested, that it may be corrected.

In general, I have illustrated the significations of words, and proved them to be legitimate, by a short passage from some respectable author, often abridged from the whole passage cited by Johnson. In many cases, I have given brief sentences of my own; using the phrases or sentences in which the word most frequently occurs, and often presenting some important maxim or sentiment in religion, morality, law or civil policy. Under words which occur in the scriptures, I have often cited passages from our common version, not only to illustrate the scriptural or theological sense, but even the ordinary significations of the words. These passages are short, plain, appropriate, and familiar to most readers. In a few cases, where the sense of a word is disputed, I have departed from the general plan, and cited a number of authorities.

In the admission of words of recent origin, into a Dictionary, a lexicographer has to encounter many difficulties; as it is not easy, in all cases, to determine whether a word is so far authorized as to be considered legitimate. Some writers indulge a licentiousness in coining words, which good sense would wish to repress. At the same time, it would not be judicious to reject all new terms; as these are often necessary to express new ideas; and the progress of improvement in arts and science would be retarded, by denying a place in dictionaries, to terms given to things newly discovered. But the lexicographer is not answerable for the bad use of the privilege of coining new words. It seems to be his duty to insert and explain all words which are used by respectable writers or speakers, whether the words are destined to be received into general and permanent use or not. The future use must depend on public taste or the utility of the words; circumstances which are not within the lexicographer's control.

Lexicographers are sometimes censured for inserting in their vocabularies, vulgar words, and terms of art known only to particular artisans. That this practice may be carried too far, is admitted; but it is to be remarked that, in general, vulgar words are the oldest and best authorized words in language; and their use is as necessary to the classes of people who use them, as elegant words are to the statesman and the poet. It may be added that such words are often particularly useful to the lexicographer, in furnishing him with the primary sense, which is no where to be found, but in *popular use.* In this work, I have not gone quite so far as Johnson and Todd have done, in admitting vulgar words. Some of them are too low to deserve notice.

The catalogue of *obsolete* words in Johnson has been considerably augmented by Mason and Todd. I have, though somewhat reluctantly, inserted nearly the whole catalogue, which, I presume, amounts to seven or eight, and perhaps, to ten thousand words. Most of these may be useful to the antiquary; but to the great mass of readers, they are useless.*

I have also inserted many words which are local in England; being retained from the different languages that have been spoken in that country, but which are no more a part of our present language in the United States, than so many Lapland words. These however occur in books which treat of agriculture and the arts; books which are occasionally read in this country.

Law-terms, which are no part of the proper language of the U. States, and never can be, as the things they express do not exist in this country, are however retained, as it is necessary that the gentlemen of the bar should understand them; and it will be time to dismiss them from books, when they are obsolete in practice.

As to Americanisms, so called, I have not been able to find many words, in respectable use, which can be so denominated. These I have admitted and noted as peculiar to this country. I have fully ascertained that most of the new words charged to the coinage of this country, were first used in England.

In exhibiting the origin and affinities of English words, I have usually placed *first in order* the corresponding word, in the language from or through which we have received it; then the corresponding words in the languages of the same family or race; then the corresponding word in the languages of other families. Thus, for example, the word *break* we have from our Saxon ancestors; I therefore give the Saxon word first; then the same word in the other Teutonic and Gothic languages; then the Celtic words; then the Latin; and lastly the Hebrew, Chaldaic and Arabic. This order is not followed in every instance, even of vernacular words, but it is the more general course I have pursued. When there can be no rational doubt respecting the radical identity of words, I have inserted them without any expression of uncertainty. When there appears to be any reason to question that identity, I have mentioned the probability only of an affinity, or inserted a query, to invite further investigation. Yet I am aware that many things, which, in my view, are not doubtful, will appear so to persons not versed in this subject, and who do not at once see the chain of evidence which has led me to my inferences. For this there is no remedy but further investigation.

In regard to words, which have been introduced into the language in modern days, I have generally referred them to the language, from which the English immediately received them. A great part of these are from the Latin through the French; sometimes probably through the Italian or Spanish. In some instances however the order is reversed; indeed it cannot always be known from which language the words have been received, nor is it a matter of any consequence.

One circumstance however deserves to be particularly noticed; that when I refer a vernacular word to the corresponding word in one of the Shemitic languages, I would not have it understood that the English word was *derived* or *borrowed* from that oriental word. For example, I have given the Shemitic פרק as the verb corresponding with the English *break*, that is, the same word in those languages; not intending by this that our ancestors borrowed or received that word from the Chaldeans, Hebrews or other Shemitic nation. This is not the fact. It would be just as correct for the compiler of a Chaldee or Hebrew lexicon to derive פרק from the English *break* or German *brechen*. So when I deduce *coin*, through the French, Spanish or Italian, from the Arabic قَانَ, I do not consider the word as borrowed from the Arabic but as proceeding from a common radix. With regard to *vernacular* words, in any European language, such deduction is always incorrect. Yet errors of this kind abound in every book I have seen, which treats of this subject. The truth is, all *vernacular* words in the languages of Europe, are as old as the same words in Asia; and when the same words are found in the Shemitic and Japhetic languages, it is almost demonstrably certain that these words were in use *before the dispersion;* the nations of both families have them from the common stock, and the words, like the families of men, which use them, are to be considered as of the same antiquity.

When therefore I state the words of another language as corresponding with *vernacular* words in the English, they are offered as affinities, or the same word, varied dialectically perhaps, in orthography or signification, but words from the same root as the English. Thus under the word *bright,* I state the Saxon word, and then the corresponding word in the Ethiopic, the participle of a verb; not that our ancestors borrowed the word from the Ethiopians, but that the verb, from which *bright* was derived, though lost in the Saxon, is still retained in the Ethiopic. This fact proves that the ancestors of the Saxons once used the verb, but suffered it to go into disuse, substituting shine, *scinan*, in its place.

It is much to be regretted that British authors and travelers admit into their writings foreign words without conforming them, in orthography, to regular English analogies. It is owing to this disregard of the purity and regular form of orthography in English, that we are perplexed with such words as *burlesque, soup, group, tour, corps, depot, suite, pacha, ennui*, and many others. In this respect, modern writers manifest less taste than the writers of former centuries, who, when they borrowed foreign words, wrote them in conformity to English analogies. This practice of blending with the English many words of an orthography, which in our language is anomalous, is very embarrassing to readers who know only their vernacular tongue, and often introduces an odious difference between the pronunciation of different classes of people; an evil more sensibly felt in this country, than in Great Britain, where differences of rank exist: in short, it multiplies the irregularities of a language, already so deformed by them as to render it nearly impracticable for our own citizens ever to overcome the difficulties of its orthography; irregularities which foreigners deem a reproach to the taste of a literary nation.

Where is the good sense which should dictate a manly firmness in preserving the regular analogies and purity of the language? Where is there a due attachment to UNIFORMITY which constitutes the principal beauty and excellence of a language, and beyond all other means facilitates its acquisition? I would not refuse to admit foreign words into the language, if necessary or useful; but I would treat them as our laws treat aliens; I would compel them to submit to the formalities of naturalization, before they should be admitted to the rights of citizenship; I would convert them into English words, or reject them. Nor would I permit the same word to be written and pronounced in two different ways, one English, the other French. The French *suite* in English is *suit*, whether it signifies a set of clothes, or of apartments, or of armor, or of attendants.

In the orthography of certain classes of words, I have aimed at uniformity; but I have not proceeded so far in this desirable reformation of the common spelling, as my own wishes, and strict propriety might dictate. Thus if *vicious*, from the Latin *vitium*, is written with *c*, the verb *vitiate* should regularly be written with the same letter, and we have precedents in the words *appreciate* and *depreciate*, from the Latin *pretium*. In like manner, *expatiate* should be conformed to the orthography of *spacious; exceed, proceed*, and *succeed*, should follow the analogy of *concede, intercede*, and *recede*. These are points of minor importance, but far from being unimportant.

In writing the termination of such verbs as *civilize, legalize, modernize*, there is a diversity which may be corrected without inconvenience. We indeed have some of the verbs of this class from the French in which language *iser* is the termination; but most of them we have borrowed directly from the Latin or Greek, or perhaps from the Spanish or Italian, or they are of our own coinage. As the termination *ize* is conformable to the Greek original, and as it expresses the true pronunciation in English, it seems expedient to reduce the whole class to a uniformity of orthography.

Enterprise, devise, comprise, revise, compromise, and *surprise*, belong to a different class and retain the orthography of their originals.

There is a fact respecting the pronunciation of *gn*, in *cognizance*, and *recognizance*, which seems to have escaped observation; this is, that *g* was introduced to express a nasal sound, as in the French *gn*, or Spanish *ñ*, but not for the purpose of being pronounced as *g*. It is probable that the Latins changed *con* before *nosco* into *cog* for this reason; and it may be inferred from the modern pronunciation of these words, that the Greeks omitted or softened the sound of γ in γιγνωσκω and γιγνομαι. However this may be, the old pronunciation of the words was undoubtedly *conusance*, or *conizance*, *reconizance*, and hence in the old writers on law, the letter *g* was omitted. Indeed there is a harshness in the pronunciation of *g* in these words, that offends the organs both of the speaker and hearer, and which well justifies the pronunciation of the old lawyers; a pronunciation which we frequently hear, at this day, among gentlemen of the bar.

Whether the Latins pronounced the letter *g* in such words as *benignus, condignus, malignus*, it is of no moment for us to determine. In our mode of writing *benign, condign, malign*, the sound of *g* must be dropped; but it is resumed in the derivatives *benignity, condignity, malignity:* so in *design, designate; resign, resignation.**

In noting the obsolete words which amount to some thousands, I may have committed mistakes; for words obsolete in one part of the British dominions, or in some part of the United States, may be words in common use, in some other part of such dominions, not within my knowledge. The rule I have generally observed has been to note as obsolete such words as I have not heard in colloquial practice, and which I have not found in any writer of the last century. The notation of such words as are disused may be of use to our own youth, and still more to foreigners, who learn our language.

Under the head of etymology, in books, the reader will observe references to another work, for a more full explanation or view of the affinities of the words under which these references occur. These are references to a Synopsis of the principal uncompounded words in twenty languages; a work that is not published, and it is uncertain whether it will ever be published. But if it should be, these references will be useful to the philologist, and I thought it expedient to insert them

*There is, among some poets of the present day, an affectation of reviving the use of obsolete words. Some of these may perhaps be revived to advantage; but when this practice proceeds so far as to make a glossary necessary to the understanding of a poem, it seems to be a violation of good taste. How different is the simple elegance of Dryden, Pope, Gray, Goldsmith and Cowper!

*The Spanish *puño* is the Latin *pugnus;* and our word *puwn*, the D. *pand*, is the Latin *pignus*. So we pronounce *impune*, for *impugn*, French *impugner*, from the Latin *pugno, pugna*. How far these facts tend to show the Latin pronunciation, let the reader judge.

A

PHILOSOPHICAL AND PRACTICAL GRAMMAR

OF THE

ENGLISH LANGUAGE.

ADVERTISEMENT.

In the year 1803, I received a Letter from Lindley Murray, with a copy of his Grammar. The following is a copy of the Letter.

"I take the liberty of requesting that the author of 'Dissertations on the English Language,' will do me the favor to accept a copy of the new edition of my grammar, as a small testimony of my respect for his talents and character. At the same time, I hope he will permit me to thank him for the pleasure and improvement, which I have derived from perusing his ingenious and sensible writings.

"If, on looking over the Grammar, any thing should occur to him, by which he thinks the work may be further improved, I will take the communication of it, as a particular favor; and will give it an attentive and respectful consideration. Should he prepare any remarks, he will be so good as to send his letter to my brother John Murray, jun., Pearl Street, New York, who will carefully forward them to me. I am very respectfully, &c.

LINDLEY MURRAY."

Holdgate, near York, 1803."

Twenty years before the date of this letter, I had prepared and published a Grammar, on the model of Lowth's, with some variations, and on the same principles, as Murray has constructed his. This work passed through many editions, before Murray's book appeared in this country. But before this period, my researches into the structure of language had convinced me that some of Lowth's principles are erroneous, and that my own Grammar wanted material corrections. In consequence of this conviction, believing it to be immoral to publish what appeared to be false rules and principles, I determined to suppress my Grammar, and actually did so; although the public continued to call for it, and my bookseller urged for permission to continue the publication of it. As I had the same objections to Murray's Grammar, as I had to my own, I determined on the publication of a new work, which was executed in 1807; and with a view to answer Lindley Murray's request, but in a different manner, I sent him a polite letter, with a copy of my Grammar. I have understood from his friends in New York, that these never reached him; but he received a copy of my Grammar from his friends, and soon afterward prepared for publication a new edition of his own Grammar, in the octavo form. In the preface to this edition, dated in 1808, he informs his readers, that, "in preparing for the octavo edition, the author examined the most respectable publications on the subject of grammar, that *had recently appeared;* and he has, in consequence, been the better enabled to *extend* and *improve* his work." On carefully comparing this work with my own Grammar, I found most of his *improvements* were selected from my book,

ADVERTISEMENT.

In the first edition of this work, the compiler gave me credit for one passage only, (being nearly three pages of my Grammar,) which he acknowledged to be *chiefly* taken from my work. In the later editions, he says, this is *in part* taken from my book, and he further acknowledges that a *few positions* and *illustrations*, among the syntactical notes and observations, were selected from my Grammar. Now the fact is, the passages borrowed amount to *thirty* or more, and they are so incorporated into his work, that no person except myself would detect the plagiarisms, without a particular view to this object. It may be further observed that these passages are original remarks, some of them illustrating principles overlooked by all British writers on the subject.

This octavo edition of Murray's Grammar, has been repeatedly published in this country, and constantly used in our higher seminaries of learning; while the student probably has no suspicion that he is learning *my* principles in Murray's Grammar.

For the injustice done to me, by this publication, in violation of the *spirit*, if not of the *letter* of the law, for securing to authors the copy-right of their works, I have sought no redress; but while I submit to the injury, it seems to be my duty to bear testimony against this species of immorality. A man's *reputation*, and *character*, and *writings*, are as much his property, as his *land*, and it is to be hoped that correct morality will, in due time, place the protection of the former on as high ground as that of the latter.

Being perfectly satisfied that some principles of Lowth's Grammar, which constitutes the body of Murray's, are entirely erroneous, I have prefixed a brief Grammar to this Dictionary; which is committed to my fellow citizens, as the mature result of all my investigations. It is the last effort I shall make to arrest the progress of error, on this subject. It needs the club of Hercules, wielded by the arm of a giant, to destroy the hydra of educational prejudice. The club and the arm, I pretend not to possess, and my efforts may be fruitless; but it will ever be a satisfaction to reflect that I have discharged a duty demanded by a deep sense of the importance of *truth*. It is not possible for me to think with indifference, that half a million of youth in our schools are daily toiling to learn that which is not true. It has been justly observed that *ignorance* is preferable to *error*.

Some of the more prominent errors of the English Grammars, are,

1. The admission of the *article*, as a distinct part of speech, and an entire mistake respecting what is called the indefinite article. The word article signifies, if any thing, a *joint;* but there is no class of words, unless it may be the conjunctions, which can, with a shadow of propriety, be brought under that denomination. The words called *articles*, are, in all languages, *adjectives;* words limiting or in some way qualifying the sense of names or nouns. In most languages, they are varied like the nouns which they qualify, and attached to them like other adjectives.

2. The arrangement of words in a class to which they do not belong. Thus, *that* is called sometimes a pronoun, and sometimes a conjunction, when in fact it is always a pronoun or substitute, and never a conjunction. So also *if*, *though*, *unless*, *notwithstanding*, are called conjunctions; which is a most palpable mistake. *Notwithstanding*, is placed by Murray among the conjunctions. But after he procured my Grammar, he inserted, under his twenty-first rule of Syntax, the following remark. "It is very frequent, when the word *notwithstanding* agrees with a number of words, or with an entire clause, to omit the whole, except this word; and in this use of *notwithstanding*, we have a striking proof of the value of abbreviations in language," &c. The whole passage, taken from my Grammar, and the two subsequent passages, are too long to be here recited. The remark to be made here is, that the author, by attempting to patch a defective system, falls into the absurdity of making *notwithstanding* a conjunction, in one part of his book, and in another, he makes it a *word agreeing with a number of words*, or *with an entire clause!*

3. There is no correct and complete exhibition of the English verb in any British Grammar which I have seen. The *definite* tenses, which are as important as the *indefinite*, are wholly wanting; and the second future in Murray is imperfect. It seems that he had in his first editions inserted this form, *thou shalt*, or *ye shall have loved*, but in his octavo edition, he informs us that *shall* in the second and third persons is incorrectly applied. To prove this, he gives the following examples. "Thou *shalt* have served thy apprenticeship, before the end of the year." "He *shall* have completed his business, when the messenger arrives." Very true; but the author forgot that by placing *when* or *after*, as an introduction to the sentence, the use of *shall* is not only correct, but in many cases, necessary. When thou *shalt* or you *shall* have served an apprenticeship, after he *shall* have completed his business, are perfectly correct expressions. But in consequence of this oversight, Murray's second future is defective throughout the whole paradigm.

ADVERTISEMENT.

4. The Syntax of every British Grammar that I have seen, is extremely imperfect. There are many English phrases which are perfectly well established and correct, which are not brought within the rules; and of course they cannot be parsed or resolved by the student.

5. There are several false rules of construction which mislead the learner; rules which are in direct opposition to the practice of the best writers.

6. There are some phrases or modes of expression, frequently used by authors, which are not good English, and which it is the business of the Grammarian to correct, but which are not noticed in any British Grammar. Some of these have been considered in the preceding Introduction.

There is a great difficulty in devising a correct classification of the several sorts of words; and probably no classification that shall be simple and at the same time philosophically correct, can be invented. There are some words that do not strictly fall under the description of any class yet devised. Many attempts have been made and are still making to remedy this evil; but such schemes as I have seen, do not, in my apprehension, correct the defects of the old schemes, nor simplify the subject. On the other hand, all that I have seen, serve only to obscure and embarrass the subject, by substituting new arrangements and new terms, which are as incorrect as the old ones, and less intelligible.

On the subject of the tenses of the verbs, for example, we may attempt philosophical accuracy, and say that there are, and there can be *three* tenses only, to express the natural division of time into *past*, *present*, and *future*. But a language which should have words to express these three divisions only, would be miserably imperfect. We want to express not only the *past*, the *present*, and the *future*, with respect to ourselves or the time of speaking and writing, but the *past* with respect to *other* times or events. When we say, *the mail will have arrived before sun-set*, we express not only a *future* event, at the time of speaking, but an event to be *past* before another event, the setting of the sun. Hence I have given to that form of words, the denomination of the *prior-future*. So of the past time. *He had delivered the letter*, *before I arrived*, denotes an event not only *past*, as to the time of speaking, but past *before* another event, my arrival. This tense I call the *prior-past*. These denominations, like the terms of the new chimistry, define themselves. The old names of the latter tense, *pluperfect* or *preterpluperfect*, more than finished or past, or beyond more than finished or past, I have discarded. These small alterations of the old system will, I hope, be well received.

If it should be said, that our verbs have not tenses, because they have not variations of termination to express them; I would reply, that this may be considered as a mistake, proceeding from an early bias, impressed upon us by the Greek and Latin forms of the tenses. A *tense* is a term intended to denote a form of verbs used for expressing time or some division of it, and it is just as properly applied to a *combination of words* for that purpose, as to a *modification* of the simple verb. The use of it is entirely arbitrary. *Locutus sum* are not the less a tense, because two words are employed. It is the *time* and not the form of words used to express it, which stamps propriety on the denomination.

If we attempt to dispense with some of the English tenses, by analyzing them, and resolving them into their primary elements, that is, parsing the words composing them, each distinctly, we shall meet with insuperable difficulties. Let a man attempt to make out the sense of this phrase, *he had been writing*, by analysing it. *Had* alone denotes *held*, *possessed*, as in the phrase, "he *had* an estate in New York." Then in the phrase above, it will signify, *he held or possessed* been writing.

It is alledged that the auxiliary verbs are *not secondary*, but the *most important* verbs in the language. The point of importance must be determined by this fact, that by themselves they do not make complete sense; they leave the sense or affirmation imperfect. *He may*, *he can*, *he will*, *he shall*, are incomplete sentences, without another verb *expressed* or *understood*. They express nothing definite which is intended to be affirmed. When I ask, whether you can lend me a sum of money, and you reply, *I can*, the verb *lend* is understood. Not so with the verbs considered as *principal*. When I say, *I write*, *I walk*, the sense or affirmation is complete without the use of another verb. Hence it is with perfect propriety, that such verbs as can be used only in connection with others, should be considered as of a *secondary* character, and being used to aid in forming the tenses, they may very justly be denominated *auxiliars* or *auxiliaries*.

Some of our verbs are used either as principal or as auxiliary, as *have* and *will*; and *will* takes a different and regular form when principal; I *will*, thou *willest*, he *willeth* or *wills* an estate or a legacy; but when auxiliary, thou *wilt*, he *will* bequeath his estate.

ADVERTISEMENT.

Will, indeed, in its primary use, expresses volition, as when we say, "I *will* walk or ride; but as an auxiliary, it often loses this signification. When it is said, "it *will* rain to-morrow," what relation has *will* to volition?

To show the utter futility of attempting to explain phrases by the primary signification of the auxiliaries, take the following example. *May* and *might* express power, liberty or possibility; *have* and *had* express holding or possession. On this plan of explanation, resolve the following sentence. "He *might have had* more prudence than to engage in speculation;" that is, he was able, or had power, to hold or possess, held or possessed more prudence than to engage in speculation.

So the following. "It *may have rained* on the land." That is, it has power or is possible, to hold or possess, rained on the land.

All attempts to simplify our forms of the tenses by such resolution, must not only fail, but prove to be perfectly ridiculous. It is the *combination of words* only that admits of definition; and these must be exhibited as *tenses;* forms of expression presenting to the hearer or reader the precise time of action. This is necessary for our own citizens; but for foreigners, indispensable, as they want to know the tenses in English which correspond with the tenses in their own languages.

Nor shall we succeed much better in attempting to detect the primary elements of the terminations which form the variations of the simple verb. We may conjecture any thing; we may suppose *loved* to be a contraction of *love-did;* but in opposition to this, we find in our mother tongue, this termination *ed*, was *od*, or *ode*. Ic *lufode*, I loved; we *lufodon*, we loved. Besides, if I mistake not, this termination is the same as that in the early Roman laws, in which *esto* was written *estod;* and I believe we have no evidence that *do* and *did* ever belonged to the Latin language. But what settles this question, is, that *did* itself is formed of *do* and this same termination, *do-ed.* Here the question may rest.

We may conjecture that the personal terminations of the verbs were originally pronouns, and this conjecture is certainly better founded than many others; but we find in our mother tongue, the verb *love*, in the plural number, is written, *we lufiath, ge lufiath, thi lufiath*, all the persons having the same termination; but certainly the same word was never used to express *we*, *you* or *ye*, and *they*.

I have attentively viewed these subjects, in all the lights which my opportunities have afforded, and I am convinced that the distribution of words, most generally received, is the best that can be formed, with some slight alterations adapted to the particular construction of the English language. Our language is rich in tenses, beyond any language in Europe; and I have endeavored to exhibit all the combinations of words forming them, in such a manner that students, natives or foreigners, may readily understand them.

I close with this single remark, that from all the observations I have been able to make, I am convinced the dictionaries and grammars which have been used in our seminaries of learning, for the last forty or fifty years, are so incorrect and imperfect, that they have introduced or sanctioned more errors than they have amended; in other words, had the people of England and of these States been left to learn the pronunciation and construction of their vernacular language solely by tradition, and the reading of good authors, the language would have been spoken and written with more purity than it has been and now is, by those who have learned to adjust their language by the rules which dictionaries and grammars prescribe.

PHILOSOPHICAL AND PRACTICAL GRAMMAR, &c.

THE Grammar of a language is a collection of principles and rules, taken from the established usages of the nation using that language; in other words, an exhibition of the genuine structure of the language. These principles and rules are derived from the natural distinctions of words, or they are arbitrary, and depend for their authority wholly on custom.

A *rule* is an established form of construction in a particular class of words. Thus it is a rule in English that the plural number of nouns is formed by adding *s* or *es* to the singular, as *hand, hands, cage, cages, fish, fishes.*

An *exception* to a rule is, the deviation of a word from the common construction. Thus the regular plural of *man* would be *mans;* but the actual plural is *men.* This word then is an *exception* to the general rule of forming plural nouns.

Grammar is usually divided into four parts—orthography, etymology, syntax, and prosody.

Orthography treats of the letters of a language, their sounds and use, whether simple or in combination; and teaches the true mode of writing words, according to established usage.

Etymology treats of the derivation of words from their radicals or primitives, and of their various inflections and modifications to express person, number, case, sex, time and mode.

Syntax is a system of rules for constructing sentences.

Prosody treats of the quantity or rather of the accent of syllables, of poetic feet, and the laws of versification.

The elements of language are articulate sounds. These are represented on paper by letters or characters, which are the elements of *written* language.

A syllable is a simple sound, or a combination or succession of sounds uttered at one breath or impulse of the voice.

A word consists of one syllable or of a combination of syllables.

A sentence consists of a number of words, at the pleasure of the speaker or writer; but forming complete sense.

ENGLISH ALPHABET.

The English Alphabet consists of twenty six letters or characters, viz.: A a—B b—C c—D d—E e—F f—G g—H h—I i—J j—K k—L l—M m—N n—O o—P p—Q q—R r—S s—T t—U u—V v—W w—X x—Y y—Z z.

Of these, three, *a, e,* and *o,* are always vowels; *i* and *u* are either vowels or diphthongs; and *y* is a vowel, diphthong, or consonant. To these may be added *w,* which is actually a vowel. *H* is an aspirate or mark of breathing, and the rest are consonants, or articulations.

A vowel is a simple sound formed by opening the mouth, in a particular manner. This may be known by the power we have of prolonging the sound, without changing the position of the organs, as in uttering *a, e,* and *o.* When the position of the organs is necessarily varied, during the utterance, the sound is not simple, but diphthongal; as in uttering *i* and *u.*

The vowel characters in English have each several different sounds.

A has four sounds; First or long, as in *fate, ale.*

2. Short, as in *at, bat, ban.* This is nearly the fourth sound shortened.

3. Broad, as in *all, fall,* and shortened, as in *what.*

4. Italian, as in *father, calm, ask.*

E has two sounds; First or long, as in *mete, me, meter.*

2. Short, as in *met, bet, pen.* This is nearly the first sound of *a* shortened.

E has also the sound of *a* long, as in *prey, vein;* but this is an anomaly.

I has two sounds; First or long, and diphthongal, as in *fine, wine, mind.*

2. Short, as in *pit, ability.* This is the short sound of *e* long.

O has three sounds; First or long, as in *note, roll.*

2. Short, as in *not, nominal.* This is the short sound of broad *aw,* as in *what, warrant.*

3. The sound of *oo,* or French *ou,* as in *move, tomb, lose.*

U has three sounds; First or long, as in *cube, rude, enumerate;* a diphthongal sound.

2. Short, as in *cub, but, number.*

3. The Italian *u,* as in *bush, bullet;* the short sound of *oo.*

Y has two sounds; the first and long is the same as that of *i* long, as in *defy, rely, try, chyle.*

2. Short, as in *symptom, pity;* the same as the short sound of *i.*

At the beginning of words, *y* may be considered a consonant, as in *year.*

W is properly a vowel, having the same sound as *oo,* in *wool,* the French *ou,* the Italian, German, and Spanish *u.* It is the same in English as in the Welsh. Thus *dwell* is pronounced *dooell.* When initial, it has been considered to be a consonant, as in *well, will, ooell, ooill;* but although the position of the organs in uttering this letter at the beginning of words may be a little closer, it can hardly be called an articulation. In this combination, the two vowels are rather diphthongal.

Consonants or articulations are characters that represent the junctions, jointings, or closings of the organs, which precede or follow the vocal sounds. Some of them are close articulations, which wholly intercept the voice. Such are *k, p,* and *t,* as in the syllables *ek, ep, et.* These are usually called *mutes,* or *pure mutes.* Others admit a short prolongation of sound, as *b, d,* and *g,* in the syllables *eb, ed, eg.* These are called *impure mutes.*

Others are imperfect articulations, not entirely interrupting the voice, but admitting a kind of hum, a hiss, or a breathing; and for this reason, they are sometimes called semi-vowels. Such are *f, l, m, n, r, s, v,* and *z,* as in the syllables *ef, el, em, en, er, es, ev, ez.*

J and the soft *g* represent a compound sound, or rather a union of sounds, which may be expressed by *edge,* or *dje,* as in *join, general.*

X represents the sounds of *ks,* or *gz.*

Th have an aspirated sound, as in *thing, wreath;* or a vocal sound, as in *thus, thou, breathe.*

Sh may be considered as representing a simple sound, as in *esh, she, shall.* This sound, rendered vocal, becomes *ezh,* for which we have no character. It is heard in *fusion,* pronounced *fuzhun.*

The letters *ng* in combination have two sounds; one as in *sing, singer;* the other as in *finger, longer.* The latter requires a closer articulation of the palatal organs, than the former; but the distinction can be communicated only by the ear. The orthoepists attempt to express it by writing *g* after the *ng,* as *fing-ger.* But the peculiar sound of *ng* is expressed, if expressed at all, solely by the first syllable, as will be obvious to any person, who will write *sing-ger* for *singer;* for let *sing* in this word be pronounced as it is by itself, *sing,* and the additional letter makes no difference, unless the speaker pauses at *sing,* and pronounces *ger* by itself.

The articulations in English may all be thus expressed: *eb, ed, ef, eg, ek, el, em, en, ep, er, es, et, ev, ez, eth,* aspirate and vocal, *esh, ezh, ing.*

These articulations may be named from the organs whose junctions they represent—Thus

Labials, or letters of the lips, *eb, ef, ev, ep, em.*

Dentals, *ed, et, eth, es, esh, ez, ezh, en.*

Palatals, *eg, ek, el, er.*

Nasals, *em, en, ing.*

The letters *s* and *z,* are also called sibilants, or hissing letters—to which may be added, *esh,* and *ezh.*

Q is precisely equivalent to *k;* but it differs from it in being always followed by *u.* It is a useless letter; for *quest* might as well be written *kuest* or *kwest,* in the Dutch manner.

A diphthong is a union of two vowels or simple sounds uttered so rapidly and closely, as to form one syllable only, or what is considered as one syllable; as *oi* and *oy* in *voice* and *joy, ou* in *sound,* and *ow* in *vow.*

A triphthong is a union of three vowels in one syllable; as in *adieu.*

There are many combinations of vowels in English words, in which one vowel only is sounded: as *ai, ea, ie, ei, oa, ui, ay, ey,* &c. These may be called digraphs. They can be reduced to no rule of pronunciation.

The combinations *au* and *aw* have generally the sound of the broad *a,* as in *fraud,* and *law.* The combination *ew* has the sound of *u* long, as in *pew, new, crew;* and sometimes at the beginning of words the sound of *yu,* as in *eucharist, euphony.*

The letters *cl, kl,* at the beginning of a word, are pronounced as *tl,* as in *clear.* *Gl* at the beginning of words are pronounced as *dl,* as in *glory.*

DIVISION OF SYLLABLES.

The first and principal rule in dividing syllables, is not to separate letters that belong to the same syllable, except in cases of anomalous pronunciation.

The best division of syllables is that which leads the learner most easily to a just pronunciation. Thus, *hab-it, ham-let, bat-ter, ho-ly, lo-cal, en-gage, an-i-mal, al-i-ment, pol-i-cy, eb-o-ny, des-ig-nate, lam-ent-a-ble, pref-er-a-ble.*

An exception to this rule occurs in such words as *vicious, ambition,* in which the *ci* and *ti* are pronounced like *sh.* In this case, it seems preferable to divide the words thus, *vi-cious, am-bi-tion.*

In dividing the syllables of derivative words it seems advisable to keep the original entire, unless when this division may lead to a wrong pronunciation. Thus *act-or, help-er, op-press-or,* may be considered as a better division than *ac-tor, hel-per, op-pres-sor.* But it may be eligible in many cases, to deviate from this rule. Thus *op-pres-sion* seems to be more convenient both for children in learning and for printers, than *op-press-ion.*

RULES FOR SPELLING.

1. Verbs of one syllable, ending with a single consonant preceded by a short vowel, and verbs of more syllables than one, ending with an accented consonant preceded by a short vowel, double the final consonant in the participle, and when any syllable is added beginning with a vowel. Thus,

Abet,	Sin,	Permit,
Abetted,	Sinned,	Permitted,
Abetting,	Sinning,	Permitting,
Abettor.	Sinner.	Permitter.

2. When the final consonant is preceded by a long vowel, the consonant is usually not doubled. Thus,

Seal,	Repeal,	Defeat,
Sealed,	Repealed,	Defeated,
Sealing,	Repealing,	Defeating,
Sealer.	Repealer.	Defeater.

3. When the accent falls on any syllable except the last, the final consonant of the verb is not to be doubled in the derivatives. Thus,

Bias,	Quarrel,	Worship,	Equal,
Biased,	Quarreled,	Worshiped,	Equaled,
Biasing,	Quarreling,	Worshiping,	Equaling,
Biaser.	Quarreler.	Worshiper.	Equaler.

The same rule is generally to be observed in nouns, as in *jeweler,* from *jewel.*

These are general rules; though possibly special reasons may, in some instances, justify exceptions.

CLASSIFICATION OF WORDS.

Words are classified according to their uses. Writers on grammar are not perfectly agreed in the distribution of words into classes. But I shall, with one exception, follow the common distribution. Words then may be distributed into eight classes or parts of speech. 1. The *name* or *noun.* 2. The *pronoun* or *substitute.* 3. The *adjective, attribute* or *attributive.* 4. The *verb.* 5. The *adverb.* 6. The *preposition.* 7. The *connective* or *conjunction.* 8. The *exclamation* or *interjection.*

The participle is sometimes treated as a distinct part of speech; it is a derivative from the verb, and partakes of its nature, expressing motion or action. But it sometimes loses its verbal character, and becomes a mere adjective, expressing quality or habit, rather than action.

Names or Nouns.

A name or noun is that by which a thing is called; and it expresses the idea of that which exists, material or immaterial. Of material substances, as man, horse, tree, table—of immaterial things, as faith, hope, love. These and similar words are, by customary use, made the *names* of things which exist, or the symbols of ideas, which they express without the help of any other word.

Division of Names.

Names are of two kinds; *common,* or those which represent the idea of a whole kind or species; and *proper* or *appropriate,* which denote individuals. Thus *animal* is a name common to all beings, having organized bodies and endowed with life, digestion, and spontaneous motion. *Plant* and *vegetable* are names of all beings which have organized bodies and life, *without* the power of spontaneous motion. *Fowl* is the common name of all fethered animals which fly—*fish,* of animals which live wholly in water.

On the other hand, Thomas, John, William, are *proper* or appropriate names, each denoting an individual of which there is no species or kind. London, Paris, Amsterdam, Rhine, Po, Danube, Massachusetts, Hudson, Potomac, are also proper names, being appropriate to individual things.

Proper names however become common when they comprehend two or more individuals; as, the Capets, the Smiths, the Fletchers.

"*Two Roberts* there the pagan force defy'd." *Hoole's Tasso,* b. 20.

Limitation of Names.

Proper names are sufficiently definite without the aid of another word to limit their meaning, as Boston, Baltimore, Savannah. Yet when certain individuals have a common character, or predominant qualities which create a similitude between them, this common character becomes in the mind *a species,* and the proper name of an individual possessing this character, admits of the definitives and of plural number, like a common name. Thus a conspirator is called *a* Cataline; and numbers of them Catalines or *the* Catalines of their country. A distinguished general is called *a* Cesar—an eminent orator *the* Cicero of his age.

But names, which are common to a whole kind or species, require often to be limited to an individual or a certain number of individuals of the kind or species. For this purpose the English language is furnished with a number of words, as *an,* or *a, the, this, that, these, those,* and a few others, which define the extent of the signification of common names, or point to the particular things mentioned. These are all adjectives or *attributes,* having a dependence on some noun expressed or implied.

Rule I.—A noun or name, without a preceding definitive, is used either in an unlimited sense, extending to the whole species, or in an indefinite sense, denoting a number or quantity, but not the whole.

"The proper study of mankind is *man.*" *Pope.*

Here *man* comprehends the whole species.

"In the first place, *woman* has, in general, much stronger propensity than *man* to the perfect discharge of parental duties." *Life of Cowper.*

Here *woman* and *man* comprehend each the whole species of its sex.

Note.—The rule laid down by Lowth, and transcribed implicitly by his followers, is general. "A substantive without any article to limit it, is taken in its *widest sense;* thus *man* means *all mankind.*" The examples already given prove the inaccuracy of the rule. But let it be tried by other examples.

"There are *fishes* that have wings, and are not strangers to the airy regions."—Locke, b. 3. ch. 6. 12. If the rule is just, that *fishes* is to be "taken in its widest sense," then *all fishes* have wings!

Rule II.—The definitive *an* or *a,* being merely *one,* in its *English* orthography, and precisely synonymous with it, limits a common name to an individual of the species. Its sole use is to express *unity,* and with respect to number, it is the most definite word imaginable; as *an* ounce, *a* church, *a* ship, that is, *one* ship, *one* church. It is used before a name which is indefinite, or applicable to any one of a species; as

——————"He bore him in the thickest troop,
As doth *a* lion in *a* herd of neat." *Shakspeare.*

Here *a* limits the sense of the word *lion,* and that of *herd* to *one*—but does not specify the particular one—"As *any* lion does or would do in *any* herd."

This definitive is used also before names which are definite and as specific as possible: as, "Solomon built *a* temple." "The Lord God planted *a* garden eastward in Eden." London is *a* great commercial city. *A* decisive battle was fought at Marengo. The English obtained *a* signal naval victory at the mouth of the Nile.

Note.—When the sense of words is sufficiently certain, by the construction, the definitive may be omitted; as, "*Duty* to your majesty, and *regard* for the preservation of ourselves and our posterity, require us to entreat your royal attention."

It is also omitted before names whose signification is general, and requires no limitation—as "*wisdom* is justified of her children"—"*anger* resteth in the bosom of fools."

The definitive *a* is used before plural names preceded by *few* or *many*—as *a* few days, *a* great many persons. It is also used before any collective word, as *a* dozen, *a* hundred, even when such words are attached to plural nouns; as *a* hundred years.

It is remarkable that *a* never precedes *many* without the intervention of *great* between them—but follows *many,* standing between this word and a name—and what is equally singular, *many,* the very essence of which is to mark plurality, will, with *a* intervening, agree with a name in the singular number; as

"Full *many a gem* of purest ray serene." *Gray.*
"Where *many a rose* bud rears its blushing head." *Beattie.*

Rule. III.—The definitive *the* is employed before names, to limit their signification to one or more specific things of the kind, discriminated from others of the same kind. Hence the person or thing is understood by the reader or hearer, as *the* twelve Apostles, *the* laws of morality, *the* rules of good breeding.

This definitive is also used with names of things which exist alone, or which we consider as single, as the Jews, the Sun, the Globe, the Ocean; and also before words when used by way of distinction, as the Church, the Temple.

Rule IV.—*The* is used rhetorically before a name in the singular number, to denote the whole species, or an indefinite number; as, "*the fig-tree* putteth forth her green figs." *Sol. Song.*

"*The almond tree* shall flourish, and *the grasshopper* shall be a burden."
"Or ever *the silver cord* shall be loosed, or *the golden bowl* be broken," &c. *Ecclesiastes.*

"*The Christian*, who, with pious horror, avoided the abominations of the circus or the theater, found himself encompassed with infernal snares," &c.
Gib. Rom. Emp. ch. 15.

"*The heart* likes naturally to be moved and affected."
Campbell's Rhet. ch. 2.

NOTE 1.—This definitive is also used before names employed figuratively in a general sense; as,

"His mates their safety to *the waves* consign." *Lusiad*, 2.

Here *waves* cannot be understood of any particular *waves;* but the word is a metaphor for a particular thing, the *ocean.*

NOTE 2.—The definitive *the* is used before an attribute, which is selected from others belonging to the same object; as, "The very frame of spirit proper for being diverted with *the laughable* in objects, is so different from that which is necessary for philosophizing on them." *Campbell's Rhet*. 1. 2.

Number.

As men have occasion to speak of a single object, or of two or more individuals of the same kind, it has been found necessary to vary the noun or name, and usually the termination, to distinguish plurality from unity. The different forms of words to express one or more are called in Grammar, *numbers;* of which there are in English, two, the *singular* and the *plural.* The *singular* denotes an individual, or a collection of individuals united in a body; as, a man, a ship, an office, a company, a society, a dozen. The *plural* denotes two or more individuals, not considered as a collective body; as, men, ships, offices, companies, societies. The plural number is formed by the addition of *s* or *es* to the singular.

RULE 1. When the terminating letter of a noun will admit the sound of *s* to coalesce with the name or the last syllable of it, *s* only is added to form the plural; as sea, seas; hand, hands; pen, pens; grape, grapes; vale, vales; vow, vows.

2. When the letter *s* does not combine in sound with the word or last syllable of it, the addition of *s* increases the number of syllables, as, house, houses; grace, graces; page, pages; rose, roses; voice, voices; maze, mazes.

3. When the name ends in *x, ss, sh,* or *ch* with its English sound, the plural is formed by adding *es* to the singular; for a single *s* after those letters cannot be pronounced; as, fox, foxes; glass, glasses; brush, brushes; church, churches. But after *ch* with its Greek sound, like *k*, the plural is formed by *s* only; as monarch, monarchs.

4. When a name ends with *y* after a consonant, the plural is formed by dropping *y* and adding *ies;* as vanity, vanities. *Alkali* has a regular plural, *alkalies.*

But after *ay, ey,* and *oy, s* only is added; as, delay, delays; valley, valleys; joy, joys; money, moneys.

NOTE.—A few English nouns deviate from the foregoing rules in the formation of the plural number:—

CLASS 1.—In some names, *f* in the singular, is for the convenience of utterance, changed into *v;* as,

life,	lives.	self,	selves.	sheaf,	sheaves.
knife,	knives.	half,	halves.	shelf,	shelves.
wife,	wives.	beef,	beeves.	wolf,	wolves.
leaf,	leaves.	staff,	staves.	wharf,	wharves.
calf,	calves.	loaf,	loaves.	thief,	thieves.

CLASS 2.—The second class consists of words which are used in both numbers, with plurals irregularly formed; as,

child,	children.	hypothesis,	hypotheses.
foot,	feet.	brother,	brothers or brethren.
tooth,	teeth.	penny,	pennies or pence.
man,	men.	die,	dies or dice.
woman,	women.	pea,	peas or pease.
ox,	oxen.	criterion,	criterions or criteria.
louse,	lice.	focus,	focuses or foci.
goose,	geese.	radius,	radiuses or radii.
beau,	beaux.	index,	indexes or indices.
thesis,	theses.	calx,	calxes or calces.
emphasis,	emphases.	phenomenon,	phenomena.
antithesis,	antitheses.		

Pennies is used for real coins; *pence* for their value in computation.—*Dies* denotes stamps for coining; *dice*, pieces used in games.—*Peas* denotes the seeds as distinct objects; *pease* the seeds in a mass.—*Brothers* is the plural used in common discourse; *brethren*, in the scripture style, but is not restricted to it.

Cherubim and *Seraphim* are real Hebrew plurals; but such is the propensity in men to form regular inflections in language, that these words are used as in the singular, with regular plurals, cherubims, seraphims. In like manner, the Hebrew singulars, *cherub* and *seraph*, have obtained regular plurals.

The influence of this principle is very obvious in other foreign words, which the sciences have enlisted into our service; as may be observed in the words radius, focus, index, &c. which now begin to be used with regular English plural terminations. This tendency to regularity is, by all means, to be encouraged; for a *prime excellence in language is the uniformity of its inflections.* The facts here stated will be evinced by a few authorities.

"Vesiculated corallines are found adhering to rocks, shells and *fucuses.*"
Encyc. art. Corallines.

"Many *fetuses* are deficient at the extremities."
Dar. Zoon. Sect. 1, 3, 9.

"Five hundred *denariuses*." *Baker's Livy*, 4. 491.

"The radiations of that tree and its fruit, the principal *focuses* of which are in the Maldivia islands." *Hunter's St. Pierre*, vol. 3.

"The reduction of metallic *calxes* into metals."
Ency. art. Metallurgy.

See also *Mediums*, Campbell's Rhetoric, 1, 150—*Calyxes*, Darwin's Zoon. 1, 74—*Caudexes*, Phytologia, 2, 3—*Irises*, Zoon. 1. 444. *Reguluses* and *residuums.* *Ency. art. Metal.*

In authorities equally respectable, we find *stamens, stratums, funguses;* and in pursuance of the principle, we may expect to see *lamens* for lamina; *lamels* for lamellæ; *baryte* for barytes; *pyrite* for pyrites; *strontite* for strontites; *stalactite* for the plural *stalactites.* These reforms are necessary to enable us to distinguish the singular from the plural number.

CLASS 3.—The third class of irregulars consists of such as have no plural termination; some of which represent ideas of things which do not admit of plurality; as rye, barley, flax, hemp, flour, sloth, pride, pitch, and the names of metals, gold, silver, tin, zink, antimony, lead, bismuth, quicksilver. When, in the progress of improvement, any thing, considered as not susceptible of plurality, is found to have varieties, which are distinguishable, this distinction gives rise to a plural of the term. Thus in early ages our ancestors took no notice of different varieties of *wheat*, and the term had no plural. But modern improvements in agriculture have recognized varieties of this grain, which have given the name a plural form. The same remark is applicable to fern, clay, marl, sugar, cotton, &c. which have plurals, formerly unknown. Other words may hereafter undergo a similar change.

Other words of this class denote plurality, without a plural termination; as cattle, sheep, swine, kine, deer, hose, trout, salmon, carp, perch, and many other names of fish. *Fish* has a plural, but it is used in the plural sense without the termination; as,

"We are to blame for eating *these fish.*" *Anacharsis* 6. 272.

"The *fish* reposed in seas and crystal floods,
"The beasts retired in covert of the woods." *Hoole T*. 2. 726.

Cannon, shot and *sail*, are used in a plural sense; as,

"One hundred *cannon were* landed from the fleet."
Burchett, Naval Hist. 732.

"*Several shot* being fired." *Ibm*. 455.

"*Several sail* of ships." *Ibm*. 426.

In the sense in which *sail* is here used, it does not admit of a plural ending.

Under this class may be noticed a number of words, expressing time, distance, measure, weight, and number, which, though admitting a plural termination, are often, not to say generally, used without that termination, even when used with attributes of plurality; such are the names in these expressions, two year, five mile, ten foot, seven pound, three tun, hundred, thousand, or million, five bushel, twenty weight, &c. Yet the most unlettered people never say, two minute, three hour, five day, or week, or month; nor two inch, yard or league; nor three ounce, grain, dram, or peck.

A like singularity is observable in the Latin language. "Tritici quadraginta millia modium." *Liv. lib*. 26. 47. Forty thousand modium of wheat. "Quatuor millia pondo auri," four thousand pound of gold. *Ibm*. 27. 10.

Here we see the origin of our *pound.* Originally it was merely *weight*—four thousand of gold *by weight.* From denoting weight generally, *pondo* became the term for a certain division or quantity; retaining however its signification of unity, and becoming an indeclinable in Latin. *Twenty pound* then, in strictness, is twenty divisions *by weight;* or as we say, with a like abbreviation, *twenty weight.*

The words *horse, foot* and *infantry*, comprehending bodies of soldiers, are used as plural nouns and followed by verbs in the plural. *Cavalry* is sometimes used in like manner.

CLASS 4.—The fourth class of irregular nouns consists of words which have the plural termination only. Some of these denoting plurality, are always joined with verbs in the plural; as the following:

Annals,	drawers,	lees,	customs,
archives,	downs,	lungs,	shears,
ashes,	dregs,	matins,	scissors,
assets,	embers,	mallows,	shambles,
betters,	entrails,	orgies,	tidings,
bowels,	fetters,	nippers,	tongs,
compasses,	filings,	pincers, or	thanks,
clothes,	goods,	pinchers,	vespers,
calends,	hatches,	pleiads,	vitals,
breeches,	ides,	snuffers,	victuals.

Letters, in the sense of *literature*, may be added to the foregoing list. *Manners*, in the sense of *behavior*, is also plural.

Other words of this class, though ending in *s*, are used either wholly in the singular number, or in the one or the other, at the pleasure of the writer.

Amends,	wages,	conics,	economics,
alms,	billiards,	catoprics,	mathematics,
bellows,	fives,	dioptrics,	mechanics,
gallows,	sessions,	acoustics,	hydraulics,
odds,	measles,	pneumatics,	hydrostatics,
means,	hysterics,	statics,	analytics,
pains,	physics,	statistics,	politics.
news,	ethics,	spherics,	
riches,	optics,	tactics,	

Of these, *pains, riches*, and *wages*,* are more usually considered as plural—*news* is always singular—*odds* and *means* are either singular or plural—the others are more strictly singular; for *measles* is the name of a disease, and in strictness, no more plural than gout or fever. Small *pox*, for *pocks*, is sometimes considered as a plural, but it ought to be used as singular. *Billiards* has the sense of *game*, containing unity of idea; and *ethics, physics* and other similar names, comprehending each the whole system of a particular science, do not convey the ideas of parts or particular branches, but of a whole collectively, a unity, and hence seem to be treated as words belonging to the singular number.

AUTHORITIES.

Pre-eminent by so *much odds*. *Milt. P. L.* 4. 474.
With *every odds* thy prowess I defy. *Hoole Tas.* 6. 19. 40.
Where the *odds* is considerable. *Camp. Rhet*, ch. 5.
The *wages* of sin *is* death. *Bible.*
Much pains has been taken. *Enfield Hist. Phil.* ch. 2.
Let *a gallows* be made of fifty cubits high. *Bible.*
Here he erected a fort and *a gallows*. *Lusiad* 1. 134.
The *riches* we had in England *was* the slow result of long industry and wisdom, and *is* to be regained, &c. *Davenant*, 2. 12.
Mathematics informs us. *Encyc. art. strength of Materials.*
Politics is the art of producing individual good by general measures. *Beddoes' Hygeia.* 2. 79.
Politics contains two parts. *Locke*, vol. 2. 408.

Locke however uses a plural verb with ethics. "The ideas that *ethics are* conversant about."—*B.* 4. 12. 8.

Pains, when preceded by *much*, should always have a singular verb.

Means is so generally used in either number, every means, all means, this means, and these means, that authorities in support of the usage are deemed superfluous.

Gender.

GENDER, in grammar, is a difference of termination, to express distinction of sex.

There being two sexes, *male* and *female*, words which denote males are said to be of the *masculine* gender; those which denote females, of the *feminine* gender. Words expressing things without sex, are said to be of *neuter* gender. There are therefore but *two* genders; yet for convenience the neuter is classed with the genders; and we say there are *three*, the masculine, feminine and neuter. The English modes of distinguishing sex are these:

1. The regular termination of the feminine gender, is *ess;* which is added to the name of the masculine; as lion, lioness. But when the word ends in *or*, the feminine is formed by retrenching a vowel, and blending two syllables into one; as actor, actress. In a few words, the feminine gender is represented by *ix*, as testatrix, from testator; and a few others are irregular. The following are most of the words which have a distinct termination for the feminine gender:

Actor,	actress.	deacon,	deaconess.
abbot,	abbess.	duke,	duchess.
adulterer,	adultress.	embassador,	embassadress.
baron,	baroness.	emperor,	empress.
benefactor,	benefactress.	tiger,	tigress.
governor,	governess.	songster,	songstress.
hero,	heroine.	seamster,	seamstress.
heir,	heiress.	viscount,	viscountess.
peer,	peeress.	jew,	jewess.
priest,	priestess.	lion,	lioness.
poet,	poetess.	master,	mistress.
prince,	princess.	marquis,	marchioness.
prophet,	prophetess.	patron,	patroness.
shepherd,	shepherdess.	protector,	protectress.
sorceror,	sorceress.	executor,	executrix.
tutor,	tutoress.	testator,	testatrix.
instructor,	instructress.	elector,	electress.
traitor,	traitress,	administrator,	administratrix.
count,	countess.	widower,	widow.

2. In many instances, animals, with which we have most frequent occasions to be conversant, have different words to express the different sexes; as man and woman; brother and sister; uncle and aunt; son and daughter; boy and girl; father and mother; horse and mare; bull and cow.

Man however is a general term for the whole race of mankind; so also, *horse* comprehends the whole species. A law to restrain *every man* from an offence would comprehend *women* and *boys;* and a law to punish a trespass committed by *any horse*, would comprehend all *mares* and *colts*.

3. When words have no distinct termination for the female sex, the sexes are distinguished by prefixing some word indicating sex; as a male rabbit, a female opossum; a he goat, a she goat; a man servant, a maid servant; a male coquet, a female warrior; a cock-sparrow, a hen-sparrow.

4. In all cases, when the sex is sufficiently indicated by a separate word, names may be used to denote females without a distinct termination. Thus, although females are rarely soldiers, sailors, philosophers, or mathematicians, and we seldom have occasion to say, she is a soldier, or an astronomer, yet there is not the least impropriety in the application of these names to females, when they possess the requisite qualifications; for the sex is clearly marked by the word *she* or *female*, or the appropriate name of the woman; as "Joan of Arc was a warrior." "The Amazons, were a nation of female warriors."* *Encyc. art. Amazons.*

5. Although the English language is philosophically correct in considering things without life as of neither gender, yet by an easy analogy, the imagination conceives of inanimate things as animated and distingnished by sex. On this fiction, called *personification*, depends much of the descriptive force and beauty of poetry. In general, those objects which are remarkable for their strength, influence, and the attribute of imparting, take the masculine gender; those which are remarkable for the more mild and delicate qualities, for beauty and the attribute of producing, become feminine; the sun darts *his* scorching rays; the moon sheds *her* paler light.

"Indus or Ganges rolling *his* broad wave." *Akenside.*
"There does the soul
Consent *her* soaring fancy to restrain." *Ibm.*
"Now morn *her* rosy steps in th' eastern clime
Advancing—" *Milton P. L.* b. 5.
"The north east spends *his* rage." *Thomson.*

Case.

CASE in Grammar denotes a variation of words to express the relation of things to each other. In English, most of the relations are expressed by separate words; but the relation of property, ownership or possession, is expressed by adding *s* to a name, with an apostrophy; thus, John's book; which words are equivalent to "the book of John." This is called the *Possessive Case.* In English therefore names have two cases only, the *nominative* or simple name, and the *possessive.* The *nominative* before a verb and the *objective* after a verb are not distinguished by inflections, and are to be known only by position or the sense of the passage.

When the letter *s*, added as the sign of the possessive, will coalesce with the name, it is pronounced in the same syllable; as *John's.* But if it will not coalesce, it adds a syllable to the word; as Thomas's bravery, pronounced as if written *Thomasis;* the Church's prosperity, *Churchis* prosperity. These examples show the impropriety of retrenching the vowel; but it occasions no inconvenience to natives.

When words end in *es* or *ss*, the apostrophy is added without *e;* as on eagles' wings; for righteousness' sake.

Pronouns or Substitutes.

PRONOUNS or substitutes are of two kinds; those which are used in the place of the names of persons only, and may be called *personal;* and those which represent names, attributes, a sentence or part of a sentence, or a series of propositions.

The pronouns which are appropriate to persons, are, I, thou, you, he, she, we, ye, and who.

I is used by a speaker to denote himself, and is called the *first person* of the singular number.

When a speaker includes others with himself, he uses *we.* This is the *first person* of the plural number.

Thou and *you* represent the person addressed—*thou*, in solemn discourse, and *you*, in common language. These are the *second person.* In the plural, *ye* is used in solemn style, and *you* in familiar language.

He represents the name of a male, and *she*, that of a female, who is the subject of discourse, but not directly addressed. These are called the *third person.*

It is a substitute for the name of any thing of the neuter gender in the third person, and for a sentence.

They is a substitute for the names of persons or things, and forms the third person of the plural number.

*Originally *wagis*, and really singular.

* The termination *or* in Latin, is a contraction of *vir*, a man; as *er* in English is of *wer*, the same word in Saxon. But in common understanding, the idea of gender is hardly attached to these terminations; for we add *er* to words to denote an agent, without life, as grater, heater.

Who is a relative or personal pronoun, used to introduce a new clause or affirmation into a sentence, which clause has an immediate dependence on the preceding one. *Who* is also used to ask questions, and hence it is called an interrogative.

Which is also a relative, but is of neuter gender. It is also interrogative.

These pronouns have two cases; the nominative which precedes a verb, and the objective which follows it. They are inflected in the following manner.

	Sing.	*Plu.*		*Sing.*	*Plu.*
Nominative	I	we	Nom. - - -	she	they
Objective	me	us	Obj. - - -	her	them
Nom. - -	thou	ye	Nom. - - -	it	they
Obj. - -	thee	you	Obj. - - -	it	them
Nom. - -	you	you	Nom. - - -	who	who
Obj. - -	you	you	Obj. - - -	whom	whom
Nom. - -	he	they			
Obj. - -	him	them			

NOTE.—Mine, thine, his, hers, yours and theirs, are usually considered as the *possessive case.* But the three first are either attributes, and used with nouns, or they are substitutes. The three last are always substitutes, used in the place of names which are understood, as may be seen in the note below.*

Its and *whose* have a better claim to be considered as a possessive case; but as they equally well fall under the denomination of attributes, I have, for the sake of uniformity, assigned them a place with that part of speech.

* That *mine, thine, his, yours, hers* and *theirs*, do not constitute a possessive case, is demonstrable; for they are constantly used as the nominatives to verbs and as the objectives after verbs and prepositions, as in the following passages. "Whether it could perform its operations of thinking and memory out of a body organized as *ours is*,"—*Locke*, b. 2. 27. "In referring our ideas to those of other men called by the same name, *ours may be false.*"—"It is for no other reason but that *his* agrees not with *our ideas.*"—*ibm.* ch. 32. 9 and 10.

"You may imagine what kind of faith *theirs was.*"
Bacon, Unity in Religion.

"He ran headlong into his own ruin whilst he endeavoured to precipitate *ours.*"
Bolingbroke, Let. to Windham.

"The reason is that his subject is generally things; *theirs*, on the contrary, *is* persons."
Camp. Rhet. b. 1. ch. 10.

"Yours of the 26th Oct. I have received, as I have always done *yours*, with no little satisfaction."
Wycherley to Pope.

"Therefore leave your forest of beasts for *ours* of brutes, called men." *Ibm.*

"These return so much better out of your hands than they went from *mine.*"
Ibm.

"Your letter of the 20th of this month, like the rest of *yours*—tells me with so much more wit, sense and kindness than *mine* can express," &c.
Ibm.

"Having good works enough of your own besides to ensure *yours* and their immortality."
Ibm.

"The omission of repetitions is but one, and the easiest part of *yours* and of *my design.*"
Pope to Wycherley.

"My *sword* and *yours* are kin."
Shakspeare.

It is needless to multiply proofs. We observe these pretended *possessives* uniformly used as nominatives or objectives. To say that, in these passages, *ours, yours, theirs,* and *mine* form a possessive case, is to make the possessive perform the office of a nominative case to verbs, and an objective case after verbs and prepositions—a manifest solecism.

Should it be said that a noun is understood; I reply, this cannot be true, in regard to the grammatical construction; for supply the noun for which the word is a substitute, and the pronoun must be changed into an adjective. "*Yours* of the 26th of October," becomes *your letter*—"he endeavoured to precipitate *ours*," becomes *our ruin.*" This shows that the words are *real* substitutes, like *others*, where it stands for *other men* or *things.*

Besides in three passages, just quoted, the word *yours* is joined by a connective to a name in the same case; "to ensure *yours* and *their immortality.*" "The easiest part of *yours* and of *my design.*" "My sword and *yours* are kin." Will any person pretend that the connective here joins different cases?

Another consideration is equally decisive of this question. If *yours, ours,* &c. are real possessives, then the same word admits of two different signs of the case; for we say correctly, "an acquaintance of *yours, ours,* or *theirs*" —*of* being the sign of the possessive; but if the words in themselves are possessives, then there must be two signs of the same case, which is absurd.†

Compare these words with a name in the possessive case—"*My* house is on a hill; my father's is on a plain." Here *father's* is a real possessive case; the word *house* being understood; and the addition of the noun makes no alteration in the word *father's*; "my father's is, or my father's house is."

† This case does not compare with that of names. We say, a "soldier of the king's," or a soldier of the king's soldiers; but we cannot say, "an acquaintance of your's acquaintance."

But it must be observed, that although *it* and *who* are real substitutes, never united to names, like attributes—it day—who man; yet *its* and *whose* cannot be detached from a name expressed or implied—as, *its* shape, *its* figure—*whose* face—*whose* works—*whose* are they? that is, *whose* works. These are therefore real adjectives.

In the use of substitutes, it is to be remarked, that *I, thou, you, ye* and *we* are generally employed without an antecedent name. When *I*, and the name of the person are both employed, as they are in formal writings, oaths and the like, the pronouns precede the name; as, "I, Richard Roe, of Boston." In similar language, *you* and *we* also precede the name; as, "You, John Doe, of New-York." "We, Richard Roe and John Doe, of Philadelphia."

You is used by writers very indefinitely, as a substitute for any person who may read the work—the mind of the writer *imagining* a person addressed.

He and *they* are used in the same indefinite manner; as, "*He* seldom lives frugally, *who* lives by chance." "Blessed are *they* that mourn, for *they* shall be comforted."

He and *they*, in such sentences, represent any persons who fall within the subsequent description.

Who and *whom* are always substitutes for *persons*, and never for things or brutes. *Whose* is equally applicable to persons as to things.

Whoever is often employed as the nominative to two verbs; as, "*Whoever expects* to find in the scriptures a specific direction for every moral doubt that arises, *looks* for more than he will meet with." *Paley, Phil. ch.* 4.

Mine, thine and *his* are equally well used as substitutes, or as attributes. "The silver is *mine*, and the gold is *mine.*" *Hag.* ii. 8. "The day is *thine*, the night also is *thine.*" *Ps.* lxxiv, 16. "The lord knoweth them that are *his.*" 2 *Tim.* ii. 19. In these examples the words, *mine, thine, his,* may be considered as substitutes—"The silver is mine," that is, *my silver.*

In this character the words usually follow the verb; but when emphatical, they may precede it; as "*His* will I be." 2. *Sam.* xvi. 18. "*Thine*, O Lord, is the greatness, the power and the glory." "*Thine is the kingdom.*" 1. *Ch.* xxix. 11.

Those words are also used as attributes of possession; as, "Let not *mine* enemies triumph." "So let *thine* enemies perish." "And Abram removed *his* tent." *Mine* and *thine* are however not used in familiar language; but in solemn and elevated style, they are still used as attributes.

"*Mine* eyes beheld the messenger divine." *Lusiad. B.* 2.

There is another class of substitutes, which supply the place of names, attributes, sentences or parts of a sentence.

It.

In the following sentence, *it* is the substitute for a name. "The sun rules the day; *it* illumines the earth." Here *it* is used for *sun,* to prevent a repetition of the word.

In the following passage, *it* has a different use. "The Jews, *it* is well known, were at this time under the dominion of the Romans." *Porteus, Lect.* 8. Here *it* represents the whole of the sentence, except the clause in which it stands. To understand this, let the order of the words be varied. "The Jews were at this time under the dominion of the Romans, *it* [all that] is well known.

"*It* is a testimony as glorious to his memory, as *it* is singular, and almost unexampled in his circumstances, *that he loved the Jewish nation*, and *that* he gave a very decisive proof of *it*, by building them a synagogue." *ibm.*

To discover what is represented by the first *it*, we must inquire, what is a glorious testimony? Why, clearly that he loved the Jewish nation, and gave them a decisive proof of *it*, by building them a synagogue. *It* then is a substitute for those clauses of the sentence. The second *it* refers to the same clauses. In the latter part of the sentence, he gave a magnificent proof of *it*—of what? of what is related in a preceding clause—*He loved the Jewish nation*—of *that* he gave a decisive and magnificent proof. Here *it* represents that member of the sentence.

"As for *the pulling of them down*, if the affairs require *it.*" *Bacon on Ambition.* Require what? "The pulling of them down"—for which part of the sentence, *it* is a substitute.

"And how could he do this so effectually, as by performing works, which *it* utterly exceeded all the strength and ability of men to accomplish." *Porteus, Lect.* 5.

What utterly exceeded? To what does *it* refer? Let us invert the order of the words—"as by performing works *to accomplish* which exceeded all the strength of men." Here we find *to accomplish*, a verb in the infinitive, is the nominative to *exceeded*, and for that verb, *it* is a substitute.

This inceptive use of *it* forms a remarkable idiom of our language, and deserves more particular illustration. It stands as the substitute for a subsequent member or clause of a sentence; and is a sort of pioneer to smooth the way for the verb. Thus, "*It* is remarkable, *that* the philosopher Seneca makes use of the same argument." *Porteus Lect.* 6. If we ask, what is remarkable? The answer must be, the fact stated in the last clause of the sentence. That this is the real construction, appears from a transposition of the clauses. "The philosopher Seneca makes use of the same argument, *that* is remarkable." In this order we observe the true use of *that*, which is also a substitute for the preceding clause of the sentence, and *it* becomes redundant. The use then of the inceptive *it* appears to be to enable us to begin a sentence, without placing a verb as the introductory word; and by the use of *it* and *that* as substitutes for subsequent members of the sentence, the order is inverted without occasioning obscurity.

It is to be noticed also that this neuter substitute, *it*, is equally proper to begin sentences, when the name of a *person* is afterwards used; as, "*It* was John who exhibited such powers of eloquence." But if we transpose the words, and place *who* or *that*, the substitute which begins a new clause, next after the inceptive word, we must use *he* for the inceptive—"*He, who* or *that* exhibited such powers of eloquence, was John."

In interrogative sentences, the order of words is changed, and *it* follows the verb. Who is *it* that has been thus eloquent?

There is a sentence in Locke, in which the inceptive *it* is omitted. "Whereby comes to pass, that, as long as any uneasiness remains in the mind. *B. ch.* 21. In strictness, this is not a defective sentence, for *that* may be considered as the nominative to *comes*. Whereby *that* comes to pass which follows. Or the whole subsequent sentence may be considered as the nominative—for all that comes to pass. But the use of the inceptive *it* is so fully established as the true idiom of the language, that its omission is not to be vindicated.

This and *that*, *these* and *those*.

This and *that* are either definite attributes or substitutes. As attributes, they are used to specify individuals, and distinguish them from others; as, "*This* my son was dead and is alive again." "Certainly *this* was a righteous man." "The end of *that* man is peace." "Wo to *that* man by whom the son of man is betrayed." *This* and *that* have plurals, *these* and *those*.

The general distinction between *this* and *that*, is, *this* denotes an object to be present or near in time or place; *that*, to be absent. But this distinction is not always observed. In correspondence however with this distinction, when, in discourse, two things are mentioned, *this* and *these* refer to the last named, or nearest in the order of construction; *that* and *those* to the most distant; as,

"*Self love* and *reason* to one end aspire,
Pain their aversion, pleasure their desire;
But greedy *that* [self love] its object would devour,
This [reason] taste the honey and not wound the flower." *Pope.*
"Some place the bliss in action, some in ease,
Those call it pleasure, and contentment *these*." *Ibm.*

The poets sometimes contrast these substitutes in a similar manner, to denote individuals acting or existing in detached parties, or to denote the whole acting in various capacities; as,

"'Twas war no more, but carnage through the field,
Those lift their sword, and *these* their bosoms yield."
Hoole's Tasso. b. 20.
"Nor less the rest, the intrepid chief retain'd;
These urged by threats, and *those* by force constrain'd." *Ibm.*

There is a peculiarity in the use of *that*; for when it is an attribute, it is always in the singular number; but as a substitute for persons or things, it is plural as well as singular, and is used for persons as well as things more frequently than any word in the language; as,

"I knew a man *that* had *it* for a by-word, when he saw men hasten to a conclusion, 'Stay a little that we may make an end the sooner.'"
Bacon on Dispatch.

Here *that* is the representative of *man*, and *it* stands for the last clause of the sentence or by-word.

"Let states *that* aim at greatness take heed how their nobility and gentlemen multiply too fast." *Bacon.*

Here *that* is a substitute for a plural name. So also in the following. "They *that* are whole need not a physician, but they *that* are sick." "They *that* had eaten were about four thousand"—"they *that* are in the flesh"—"they *that* weep"—"bless them *that* curse you."

Another very common use of *this* and *that*, is to represent a sentence or part of a sentence; as,

"It is seldom known *that*, authority thus acquired is possessed without insolence, or *that*, the master is not forced to confess *that*, he has enslaved himself by some foolish confidence." *Rambler, No.* 68.

In this sentence, the first *that* represents the next member—"Authority thus acquired is possessed without insolence, *that* is seldom known." *It* represents the same clause. The second *that* represents all which follows, including two clauses or members. The third *that* is the substitute for the last clause. In strictness the comma ought always to be placed after *that*; which punctuation would elucidate the use of the substitute and the true construction; but the practice is otherwise, for *that*, in this and like sentences, is either a nominative or an objective. The first *that* in the foregoing sentence is the nominative, coinciding with *it*, or in apposition to it; and when the clauses are transposed, the inceptive *it*, being redundant, is dropped, and *that* becomes the nominative. The same remark is applicable to the second *that*; the verb and first clause, *it is seldom known*, being understood. The third *that* is the objective after *confess*. "The master has enslaved himself by some foolish confidence—he is forced to confess *that*—all that is seldom known."

Such is the true construction of sentences—the definitive *that*, instead of being a conjunction, is the representative of a sentence or distinct clause, preceding that clause, and pointing the mind to it, as the subject which follows. And it is as definite or demonstrative in this application to sentences, as when it is applied to a name or noun.

The following sentence will exhibit the true use of *that* as a substitute—"He recited his former calamities; to which *was* now to be added *that* he was the destroyer of the man who had expiated him.
Beloe's Herodotus, Clio, 45.

According to our present grammars, *that* is a conjunction; if so, the preceding verb *was*, has no nominative word. But the sense is, "to which was to be added *that*" which is related in the following words.

The use and importance of this substitute are more clearly manifest, when it denotes purpose or effect; as in this passage, "And he came and dwelt in a city called Nazareth; *that* it might be fulfilled *which* was spoken by the prophets, 'He shall be called a Nazarine.'" *Matt.* ii. 23. Here *that* is equivalent to *that purpose or effect*.—He came and dwelt in Nazareth, *for the purpose expressed in what follows. It* and *which* represent the last clause in the sentence—"He shall be called a Nazarene." The excellence and utility of substitutes and abbreviations are strikingly illustrated by this use of *that*.

This substitute has a similar use in this introductory sentence. *That we may proceed—that* here refers to the following words. The true construction is, *But that we may proceed*—but, as will hereafter be shown, denoting *supply* or *something more* or *further*—So that the literal intepretation of the expression is—*More that*—or *further that, we may proceed.* It is the simple mode our ancestors used to express addition to what has preceded, equivalent to the modern phrase, *let us add*, or *we may add* what follows, by way of illustrating or modifying the sense of what has been related.

That, like *who* and *which*, has a connecting power, which has given to these words the name of *relative*; in which character, it involves one member of a sentence within another, by introducing a new verb; as, "He, that keepeth his mouth, keepeth his life." *Prov.* xiii. In this passage, *that keepeth his mouth*, is a new affirmation, interposed between the first nominative and its verb, but dependant on the antecedent nominative.

"The poor of the flock, *that* waited upon me, knew *that, it* was the word of the Lord." *Zech.* xi. 11. In this passage we have *that* in both its characters—the first *that* is a substitute for *poor* of the flock; the second, for the last clause of the sentence, *it was the word of the Lord.*

This exposition of the uses of *that* enables us to understand the propriety of *that that* joined in construction.

"Let me also tell you *that, that* faith, which proceeds from insufficient or bad principles, is but little better than infidelity." In this passage, the first *that* is a substitute for the whole subsequent part of the sentence; the second *that* is an attribute agreeing with *faith*—"That faith which proceeds from bad principles is little better than infidelity—let me tell you *that*." Hence it might be well always to separate the two words by a comma. We now distinguish these words by a stronger emphasis on the last.

"He, whom thou now hast, is not thy husband; in *that* saidst thou truly." *John* iv. 18. That is, in that whole declaration.

From these passages and the explanation, we learn that *that* is a substitute, either for a single word or a sentence; nor has it any other character, except when an attribute.

This is much less frequently a substitute for sentences than *that*, but is used in this character, as well as in that of an attribute; as, "Let no prince measure the danger of discontents by *this, whether they be just or unjust;* for *that* were to imagine people to be reasonable, who do often spurn at their own good; nor yet by *this, whether the griefs whereupon they rise be in fact great or small.*" *Bacon on Kingdoms.*

Here *this*, in each part of the sentence, is the representative of the clause in Italics succeeding.

"Can we suppose that all the united powers of hell are able to work such astonishing miracles, as were wrought for the confirmation of the christian religion? Can we suppose that they can control the laws of nature at pleasure, and that with an air of sovereignty, and professing themselves the lords of the universe, as we know Christ did? If we can believe *this*, then we deny," &c. We observe here, *this* represents a series of sentences.

In some cases, *this* represents a few words only in a preceding sentence, as in the following—"The rule laid down is in general certain, that the king only can *convoke a parliament.* And *this*, by the ancient statutes of the realm, he is bound *to do*, every year or oftener, if need be."
Blacks. Comment. B. 1. *ch.* 2.

If we ask, what is the king bound to do? The answer must be, *convoke a parliament;* for which words alone *this* is the substitute, and governed by *do*.

The plurals, *these* and *those*, are rarely or never used as substitutes for sentences.

Which.

Which is also a substitute for a sentence, or part of a sentence, as well as for a single word; as, "if there can be any other way shown, how men may come to that universal agreement, in the things they do consent in, *which* I presume may be done." *Locke on Und. B.* 1. 2.

Which, in this passage, represents all which precedes—*which* or *all that is above related*, may be done.

"Another reason that makes me doubt of any innate practical principles, is, that I think there cannot any one moral rule be proposed, whereof a man may not justly demand a reason; *which* would be perfectly ridiculous and absurd, if they were innate, or so much as *self-evident*, *which* every innate principle must needs be." *Ibm. Chap.* 3.

In this passage, the first *which* represents the next preceding part of the sentence, *a man may justly demand a reason*—which *power of demanding a reason* would be ridiculous—The second *which* is a substitute for *self-evident; which*, that is, *self-evident*, every principle must be.

"Judas declared him *innocent*, *which* he could not be, had he, in any respect, deceived the disciples." *Porteus, Lect.* 2. Here *which* represents the attribute *innocent*.

That would equally well represent the same word, with a connective. "Judas declared him innocent, and *that* he could not be," &c.

"We shall find the reason of it to be the *end of language*, *which* being to communicate thoughts"—that is, *end of language*, and for those words, is *which* the substitute.

What.

This substitute has several uses. *First*, it has the sense of *that which;* as, "I have heard what has been alledged."

Secondly—What stands for any indefinite idea; as, "He cares not *what* he says or does." "We shall the better know *what* to undertake." *Locke on Und.* 1. 6.

Thirdly—What is an attribute, either in the singular or plural number, and denotes something uncertain or indeterminate; as, "In *what* character, Butler was admitted into that lady's service, is unknown." *Johnson's Life of Butler.*

"It is not material *what* names are assigned to them." *Camp. Rhet.* 1. 1.

"I know not *what* impressions time may have made upon your person." *Life of Cowp. Let.* 27.

"To see *what* are the causes of wrong judgment." *Locke* 2. 21.

Fourthly—What is used by the poets preceding a name, for *the* or *that which*, but its place cannot be supplied by these words, without a name between them; as,

"*What time* the sun withdrew his cheerful light,
And sought the sable caverns of the night." *Hoole's Tasso. b.* 7.

That is, *at the time when* or *in which*.

Fifthly—A principal use of *what* is to ask questions; as, "*What* will be the consequence of the revolution in France?"

This word has the singular property of containing *two cases;* that is, it performs the office of a word in the nominative, and of another in the objective case; as, "I have, in *what goes* before, been engaged in physical inquiries farther than I intended." *Locke* 2. 8. Here *what* contains the object after *in* and the nominative to *goes*.

What is used with a name as an attribute and a substitute; as, "It was agreed that *what goods* were aboard his vessels, should be landed." *Mickle's Discovery of India.* 89. Here *what goods*, are equivalent to the *goods which;* for *what goods* include the nominative to two verbs, *were* and *should be landed*. This use of the word is not deemed elegant.

As.

As, primarily signifies *like, similar;* the primary sense of which is *even*, equal. It is used adverbially in the phrases, *as* good, *as* great, *as* probable; the sense of which is *like* or *equally* good, great or probable. Hence it frequently follows *such*. "Send him such books *as* will please him." But in this and similar phrases, *as* must be considered as the nominative to *will please;* or we must suppose an ellipsis of several words. "Send him such books as *the books which* will please him, or as *those which* will please him." So in the following sentences.

"We have been accustomed to repose on its veracity with such humble confidence *as* suppresses curiosity." *Johnson's Life of Cowley.*

"All the punishment which God is concerned to see inflicted on sin is only such *as answers* the ends of government."

"Many wise men contented themselves with such probable conclusions *as* were sufficient for the practical purposes of life." *Enfield, Hist. Phil.* 2. 11.

"The malcontents made such demands *as* none but a tyrant could refuse." *Bolingbroke on Hist. Let.* 7.

In the last example, if *as* is to be considered as a pronoun, or substitute, it is in the objective case.

These and similar phrases are anomalous; and we can resolve them only by supplying the ellipsis, or by considering *as* in the nature of a pronoun, and the nominative to the verb.

In the following form of expression, we may supply *it* for the nominative. "Do every thing *as* was said about mercury and sulphur." *Encyc.*

"As *it* was said."

In poetry, *as* supplies the place of *such*.

"From whence might contest spring and mutual rage,
As would the camp in civil broils engage." *Hoole's Tasso.*

In prose we would say, "*such* contest and rage *as*."

As sometimes refers to a sentence or member of a sentence, and sometimes its place may be supplied by *which*. "On his return to Egypt, *as* I learned from the same authority, he levied a mighty army." *Beloe, Herod.*

Which I learned. "On his return to Egypt, he levied a mighty army, *which* [fact] I learned from the same authority.

As often begins a sentence. "*As* to the three orders of pronouns already mentioned, they may be called prepositive, *as* may indeed all substantives." *Harris.* That is, *concerning*, *respecting* the three orders, or to explain that which respects the three orders, &c.

Both.

Both is an adjective of number, but it is a substitute also for names, sentences, parts of sentences, and for attributes.

"Abraham took sheep and oxen, and gave them unto Abimelech, and *both* of them made a covenant." *Genesis* xxi. 27.

Here *both* is the representative of *Abraham* and *Abimelech*.

"He will not bear the *loss of his rank*, because he can bear *the loss of his estate;* but he will bear *both*, because he is prepared for *both*." *Boling. on Exile.*

In the last example, *both* represents the parts of the sentences in italics.

When it represents two attributes, it may and usually does precede them; as, "He endeavored to render commerce *both* disadvantageous and infamous." *Mickle, p.* 159.

As an attribute, it has a like position before names; as, "Tousa confessed he had saved *both* his life and his honor." *Ibm.* 160.

"It is *both* more accurate, and proves no inconsiderable aid to the right understanding of things, to discriminate by different signs such as are truly different." *Campbell's Rhet.* 1. 33.

In this passage, *both* represents *more accurate*, and the following member of the sentence; but the construction is harsh.

"The necessity which a speaker is under, of suiting himself to his audience, *both that* he may be understood by them, and *that* his words may have an influence upon them." *Camp. Rhet. ch.* 10.

Here *both* represents the two following clauses of the sentence. The definitive *the* is placed between *both* and its noun; as, "To *both* the preceding kinds, the term *burlesque* is applied." *Camp. Rhet.* 1. 2.

Same.

The attribute *same* is often used as a substitute for persons and sentences or parts of a sentence; as, "Nothing appears so clearly an object of the mind or intellect only, as the *future* does, since we can find no place for its existence any where else. Not but the *same*, if we consider, is equally true of the *past*." *Hermes, p.* 112.

In this ill constructed sentence, *same* has reference to all which is predicated of the future tense—that is, *that it is an object of intellect only, since we can find no place for its existence any where else*—The *same, all this*, is true of the *past* also.

"For *brave* and *generous* ever are the *same*." *Lusiad,* 1.

Many, few, all, any.

These words we often find used as substitutes for names. "For *many* shall come in my name, saying, I am Christ, and shall deceive *many*." *Matt.* xxiv. 5. "*Many* are called, but *few* chosen." xx. 16. "*All* that come into the tent, and *all* that is in the tent shall be unclean seven days." *Num.* xix. 14. "If a soul shall sin against *any* of the commandments." *Lev.* iv. 2. "Neither is there *any*, that can deliver out of my hand." *Deut.* xxxii. 39.

First, last, former, latter, less, least, more, most,

are often used as substitutes.

"The victor's laurel, as the martyr's crown,
The *first* I hope, nor less the *last* I prize." *Hoole's Tasso.* 6. 8.
"The *last* shall be *first*, and the *first last*." *Matt.* xx. 16.

"It will not be amiss to inquire into the cause of this strange phenomenon; *that*, even a man of discernment should write without meaning, and not be sensible that he hath no meaning; and *that* judicious people should read what hath been written in this way, and not discover the defect. *Both* are surprising, but the *first* much more than the *last*." *Camp. Rhet.* 2. 7.

Here *both* represents the two clauses of the sentence, preceded by *that*—*both* of those propositions are surprising. *First* and *last* stand in the place of the same clauses.

"Sublimity and vehemence are often confounded, the *latter* being considered as a species of the *former*. *Camp. Rhet.* 1. 1.

"Leonis refused to go thither with *less* than the appointed equipment." *Mickle*, 1. 181. Here *less* supplies the place of *equipment*, and prevents the necessity of its repetition.

"To the relief of these, Noronha sent some supplies, but while he was preparing to send *more*, an order from Portugal arrived." *Mickle*, 1. 180.

Here *more* is sufficiently intelligible without a repetition of the name—*supplies*.

"And the children of Israel did so, and gathered some *more*, some *less*." *Exod.* xvi. 17.

"I cannot go beyond the word of the Lord, my God, to do *less* or *more*." *Numb.* xxii. 18.

"Then began he to upbraid the cities wherein *most* of his mighty works were done." *Matt.* xi. 20.

"Was not this love indeed?
We men say *more*, swear *more*, but indeed
Our shews are more than will." *Shaks. Twelfth Night.*

Such.

"Jabal was the father of *such* as dwell in tents." *Gen.* iv.

"Thou shalt provide able men *such* as fear God." *Ex.* xviii.

"Objects of importance must be portrayed by objects of importance; *such* as have grace, by things graceful." *Camp. Rhet.* 1. 2.

Such here supplies the place of a name or noun, but it retains its attributive sense and the name may be added.

Self and *own.*

Self is said to have been originally an attribute, but is now used as an intensive word to give emphasis to substitutes and attributes. Sometimes it is used as a noun. In the plural, it forms *selves*. It is added to the attributes *my, your, own*, as myself, yourself,* ourselves; and to *him, her, them*, as himself, herself, themselves. And though annexed to substitutes in the objective case, these words are indifferently in the nominative or objective. *Self* is never added to *his, their, mine*, or *thine*.

The compounds *himself, herself, thyself, ourselves, themselves*, may be placed immediately after the personal substitute, as *he himself* wrote a letter to the minister, or immediately after the following verb or its object, as "He wrote a letter *himself*,"—"he went *himself* to the admiralty." In such phrases *himself* not only gives emphasis to the affirmation; but gives to an implied negative, the force of one expressed. "He went himself to the minister," carries with it a direct negation that another person went. In negative sentences, it has a different effect. "He did not write the letter himself," implies strongly that he wrote it by an agent, or had an agency in procuring it to be written.

These compound substitutes are used after verbs when reciprocal action is expressed; as, "They injure themselves."

Itself is added to names for emphasis; as, "this is the book *itself*."

Own is an attribute denoting property, used with names to render the sense emphatical; as, "this book is my *own*."

Own is sometimes a substitute; as, "He came unto his *own* and his *own* received him not." *John* i. 11.

"This is an invention of his *own*."

One, other, another, none.

The attribute *one* is very often a substitute; *other* is used in the same manner, and often opposed to *one*. "All rational or deductive evidence is derived from *one* or the *other* of these two sources." *Camp. Rhet. ch.* 5.

To render these words more definite, and the specification of the alternative more explicit, the definitive *the* is placed before them; as, "either he will hate *the one* and love *the other*."

Another has sometimes a possessive case; as, "the horse is another's;" but this form of speech is but little used.

Another is the Saxon *an*, one, and *other*—*one other*. It is an attribute, but often used as a substitute. "Let *another* praise thee and not thine own mouth." *Prov.* xxvii. 2.

None [no one] is often a substitute; as, "Ye shall lie down and *none* shall make you afraid." *Lev.* xxvi. 6. It is used in the plural as well as the singular number.

The cardinal numbers are all used as substitutes, when the things to which they refer are understood by the train of discourse, and no ambiguity is created by the omission of the name; as, "The rest of the people also cast lots, to bring *one* of *ten* to dwell in Jerusalem." *Neh.* xi. 1.

One has sometimes the possessive form; as, "One's person is to be protected by law;" and frequently the plural number; as, "I have commanded my sanctified *ones*, and I have called my mighty *ones*." *Isa.* xiii. 3.

---

* In this compound, we have a strong confirmation of what I have alledged respecting the arrangement of *you* in the singular number, when used of a single person. *Self* is invariably in the singular—*selves* in the plural. Now if *you* is to be classed with plurals in *all* cases, we must, to be consistent, apply *yourselves* to a single person. Yet we make the proper distinction—*yourself* is applied to one person—*yourselves* to more. But upon the principle of our grammars, that *you* must *always* be joined to a verb in the plural, we are under the necessity of saying "*You yourself were*," when we address a single person—which is false construction. Whatever verb therefore is used with *you* when applied to an individual, must be considered as a verb in the singular number.

One, when contrasted with *other*, sometimes represents plural names, and is joined with a plural verb, as in this passage, "The reason why *the one are* ordinarily taken for real qualities, and the *other*, only for bare powers, seems to be," &c. *Locke, b.* 2. *ch.* 8. 25.

One and *another*, have a peculiar distributive use in the following and the like expressions; "Brethren, let us love *one another*." The effect of these words seems to be, to separate an act affirmed of a number collectively, and distribute it among the several individuals—"Let us love—let each one love the other." "If ye have love one to another"—"by love serve one another." *One another*, in this phraseology, have the comprehensive sense of *every one*. "By love serve"—every one serve the other. *Each* is used in a like sense—They loved each other—that is—they loved—each loved the other.

Several.

Several is an attribute, denoting originally one thing *severed* from others. But this sense seems to be now confined to technical law language; as a "joint and *several* estate." In common use, it is always plural, expressive of an indefinite number, not very large. It is frequently a substitute; as, "*Several* of my unknown correspondents." *Spectator*, 281.

Some.

The attribute *some* is often used as a substitute; as, "*Some* talk of subjects they do not understand; others praise virtue who do not practice it." *Johnson.*

Each, every, either, neither.

Each is a distributive attribute, used to denote every individual of a number, separately considered; as, "The king of Israel and the king of Judah sat *each* on his throne." "Thou also and Aaron, take *each* of you his censer." "The *four* beasts had *each* of them six wings."

In these passages, *each* is a substitute for the name of the persons or objects, one separate from the other.*

Every denotes all the individuals of a number considered separately. It is therefore a distributive attribute, but sometimes a substitute, chiefly in the law style; as, "*every* of the clauses and conditions." It is generally followed by the name to which it belongs, or by the cardinal number *one*.

We sometimes see *every* separated from its name by the definitive *the* and an attribute of the superlative degree; as, "every the least variation." *Locke.*

Either and *neither* are usually classed with the conjunctions; but in strictness, they are always attributes or substitutes. Their correlatives *or* and *nor*, though considered as conjunctions, belong to the latter class of words; *or* being merely an abbreviation of *other*, and *nor* being the same word with the Saxon negative prefixed, as will be hereafter shown.

Either and *or* denote an alternative; as, "I will take *either* road at your pleasure." That is, I will take one road or the other. In this use, *either* is an attribute.

Either is also a substitute for a name; as, "*Either* of the roads is good." It also represents a sentence or a clause of a sentence; as, "No man can serve two masters, for *either*, he will hate the one and love the other, or else," &c. *Matt.* vi. 24. To understand the true import of *either*, let *or* be also reduced back to its original orthography, "for *either*, he will hate the one and love the other; *other* else he will hold to the one and despise the other." Here we are presented with the sentence as it would have stood in the Saxon; and we see two distinct affirmations, to the first of which is prefixed *either*, and to the last *other*. These words then are substitutes for the following sentences when they are intended to be alternative. *Either* and *or* are therefore signs of an alternative, and may be called *alternatives*.

Either is used also for *each*; as, "Two thieves were crucified—on *either* side one." This use of the word is constantly condemned by critics, and as constantly repeated by good writers; but it was the true original sense of the word, as appears by every Saxon author.

Either is used also to represent an alternative of attributes; as, "the emotion must be *either* not violent *or* not durable." *Camp. Rhet.* 1. 2.

Neither is *not either*, from the Saxon *ne-either*; and *nor* is *ne-other, not other*. As *either* and *or* present an alternative or a choice of two things, so *neither* and *nor* deny both or the whole of any number of particulars; as, "Fight *neither* with small *nor* great." 1 *Kings*, xxii. 31. Which sentence when resolved stands thus; "Fight not either with small, not other with great." Such is the curious machinery of language!

Neither is also used as an attribute and as a substitute for a name; as, "*Neither* office is filled, but *neither* of the offices will suit the candidate."

NOTE.—*Or, either, nor* and *neither* are here explained in their true original character; but when they stand for sentences, it is more natural to consider them as *connectives*, under which head I have arranged them.

In general, any attribute [adjective] which describes persons or things with sufficient clearness, without the name to which it strictly belongs, may

---

* Each is as applicable to a *hundred* or *thousand* as to *two*. "The prince had a body guard of a thousand men, *each* of whom was six feet high."

be used as a substitute; as, "The *rich* have many friends"—"Associate with the *wise* and *good*"—"*The future* will resemble the *past*"—"Such is the opinion of the *learned*."

Attributes or *Adjectives.*

Attributes or Adjectives, in grammar, are words which denote the qualities inherent in, or ascribed to things; as, a *bright* sun; a *splendid* equipage; a *miserable* hut; a *magnificent* house; an *honest* man; an *amiable* woman; *liberal* charity; *false* honor; a *quiet* conscience.

As qualities may exist in different degrees, which may be compared with each other, suitable modes of speech are devised to express these comparative degrees. In English, most attributes admit of *three* degrees of comparison, and a few admit of *four*. There are therefore *four* degrees of comparison.

The *first* denotes a slight degree of the quality, and is expressed by the termination *ish;* as *reddish, brownish, yellowish.* This may be denominated the *imperfect* degree of the attribute.

The *second* denotes such a degree of the attribute as to constitute an absolute or distinct quality; as *red, brown, great, small, brave, wise.* This is called the *positive* degree.

The *third* denotes a greater or less degree of a quality than exists in another object, with which it is compared; as *greater, smaller, braver, wiser.* This is called the *comparative* degree.

The *fourth* denotes the utmost or least degree of a quality; as *bravest, wisest, poorest, smallest.* This is called the *superlative degree.*

The imperfect degree is formed by adding *ish* to an attribute; as *yellow, yellowish.* If the attribute ends in *e*, this vowel is omitted; as *white, whitish.*

The comparative degree is formed by adding *r* to adjectives ending with *e*, as *wise, wiser;* and by adding *er* to words ending with an articulation, as *cold, colder;* or by prefixing *more* or *less*, as *more just, less noble.*

The superlative degree is formed by adding *st* to attributes ending with *e*, as *wise, wisest;* and *est* to those which end with an articulation, as *cold, coldest;* or by prefixing *most* and *least*, as *most brave, least charitable.*

Every attribute, susceptible of comparison, may be compared by *more* and *most, less* and *least.*

All monysyllables admit of *er* and *est*, and dissyllables when the addition may be easily pronounced; as happy, happier, happiest; lofty, loftier, loftiest. But few words of more syllables than one will admit of *er* and *est.* Hence most attributes of more syllables than one are compared by *more* and *most, less* and *least;* as *more fallible, most upright, less generous, least splendid.*

When attributes end in *y* after a consonant, this letter is dropped, and *i* substituted before *er* and *est;* as lofty, loftier, loftiest.

A few attributes have different words or irregular terminations for expressing the degrees of comparison; as *good, better, best; bad* or *evil, worse, worst; fore, former, first; less* or *lesser, least; much, more, most; near, nearer, nearest* or *next; old, older, oldest* or *eldest; late, later, latest* or *last.*

When qualities are incapable of increase or diminution, the words which express them do not admit of comparison. Such are the numerals, *first, second, third,* &c., and attributes of mathematical figures, as square, spherical, rectangular; for it will readily appear, that if a thing is *first* or *square*, it cannot be more or less so.

The sense of attributes however is not restricted to the modification, expressed by the common signs of comparison, but may be varied in an indefinite number of ways, by other words. Thus the attribute *very*, which is the French *vrai*, true, formerly written *veray*, is much used intensively to express a great degree of a quality, but not the greatest; as *very wise* or *learned.* In like manner are used *much, far, extremely, exceedingly*, and most of the modifiers in *ly.*

Some attributes, from particular appropriate uses, have received names, by which they are distinguished. But the usual classification is by no means correct. The following distribution seems to result from the uses of the words named.

An or *a, the, this, that, these, those, other, another, one, none, some,* may be called *definitives*, from their *office*, which is to limit or define the extent of the name to which they are prefixed, or to specify particulars.

My, thy, her, our, your, their, and *mine, thine, his,* when used as attributes, with names, are *possessive attributes*, as they denote possession or ownership. *Its* and *whose*, if ranked with attributes, belong to the same class.

Each and *every* are *distributives*, but they may be classed with the *definitives.*

Either is an *alternative*, as is *or*, which is now considered merely as a connective.

Own is an *intensive* adjective. The words to which *self* is affixed, *himself, myself, themselves, yourself, yourselves, ourselves, thyself, itself,* may be denominated *intensive substitutes*, or for brevity, *intensives.* Or they may be called *compound substitutes.*

Verb.

The verb is a *primary* part of speech, and next to the *name* or noun, is of the most importance. The uses of the verb are,

1st. To affirm, assert, or declare; as, the sun shines; John loves study; God is just; and negatively, avarice is not commendable.

2d. To command, exhort or invite; as go, attend, let us observe.

3d. To pray, request, entreat; as, O may the spirit of grace dwell in us.

4th. To inquire, or question; as, does it rain? Will he come?

From the various uses and significations of verbs, have originated several divisions or classes. The only one in English which seems to be correct and sufficiently comprehensive, is, into *transitive* and *intransitive.* To these may be added a combination of the verb *be*, with certain auxiliaries and participles, which is called a *passive verb.*

1. A *transitive* verb denotes action or energy, which is exerted upon some object, or in producing some effect. In natural construction, the word expressing the object, follows the verb, without the intervention of any other word, though the order may be sometimes varied. Thus, "ridicule provokes anger," is a complete proposition; *ridicule* is the agent or nominative word, which causes the action; *provoke* is the verb, or affirmation of an act; *anger* is the object or effect produced, following the transitive verb *provoke.*

"The wind propels a ship," is the affirmation of an act of the wind exerted on a ship. *Wind* is the agent; *propels*, the verb; and *ship*, the object.

2. An *intransitive* verb denotes simple being or existence in a certain state, as *to be, to rest;* or it denotes action, which is limited to the subject. Thus, "*John sleeps*," is an affirmation, in which *John*, the nominative to *sleeps*, is the subject of the affirmation; *sleeps* is a verb intransitive, affirming a particular thing of *John*, which extends to no other object.

3. The *passive* verb in English is formed by adding certain auxiliaries and participles to the verb *be.* It denotes passion or suffering; that is, that the subject of the affirmation or nominative is affected by the action affirmed; as, "John is convinced;" "Laura is loved and admired."

In this form of the verb, the agent and object change places In the transitive form the agent precedes the verb, and the object follows; as, "John has convinced Moses." In the passive form the order is changed, and the agent follows the verb preceded by a preposition; as, "Moses is convinced by John."

To correspond with their nominatives, verbs are used in both numbers, and with the three persons in each.

As action and being may be mentioned as present, past and future, verbs have modifications to express time, which are called *tenses.* And as action and being may be represented in various ways, verbs have various modifications to answer these purposes, called *modes* or *moods.* Hence to verbs belong person, number, tense and mode.

The persons, which have been already explained, are I, thou or you, he, she, it, in the singular number; in the plural, we, ye or you, they. The numbers have been before explained.

Tenses.

There are *six tenses* or modifications of the verb to express time. Each of these is divided into two forms, for the purpose of distinguishing the *definite* or *precise* time from the *indefinite.* These may be thus explained and exemplified.

Present Tense, indefinite.

This form of the present tense affirms or denies action or being, in present time, without limiting it with exactness to a given point. It expresses also facts which exist generally, at all times, general truths, attributes which are permanent, habits, customary actions, and the like, without reference to a specific time; as, God *is* infinitely great and just; man *is* imperfect and dependent; plants *spring* from the earth; birds *fly*; fishes *swim.*

Present Tense, definite.

This form expresses the present time with precision; usually denoting action or being which corresponds in time with another action; as, *I am writing*, while *you are waiting.*

Past Tense, indefinite.

This form of the past tense represents action which took place at a given time past, however distant and completely past; as, "In six days, God *created* the heavens and the earth." "Alexander *conquered* the Persians." "Scipio *was* as virtuous as brave." "The Earl of Chatham *was* an eloquent statesman."

Past Tense, definite, [imperfect.]

This form represents an action as taking place and unfinished in some specified period of past time; as, "I *was standing* at the door when the procession passed."

---

*The common distribution into *active, neuter* and *passive*, is very objectionable. Many of our neuter verbs imply action in a pre-eminent degree, as to *run*, to *walk*, to *fly;* and the young learner cannot easily conceive why such verbs are not called *active.*

Perfect Tense, indefinite.

This form of the perfect tense represents an action completely past, and often at no great distance, but the time not specified; as, "I *have accomplished* my design." But if a particular time is named, the tense must be the *past;* as, "I accomplished my design last week." "I have seen my friend last week," is not correct English. In this respect, the French idiom is different from the English, for "J'ai vu mon ami hier" is good French, but "I have seen my friend yesterday" is not good English. The words must be translated, "I saw my friend yesterday." No fault is more common than a mistranslation of this tense.

It is to be noted however that this perfect indefinite tense is that in which we express *continued* or *repeated* action; as, "My father *has lived* about eighty years." "The king *has reigned* more than forty years. "He *has been frequently heard* to lament." *Life of Cowper.* We use it also when a specified past time is represented, if that time is expressed as a *part of the present period.* Thus, although we cannot say, "We have been together yesterday," we usually say, "We have been together this morning, or this evening." We even use this tense in mentioning events which happened at a greater distance of time, if we connect that time with the present; as, "His brother has visited him once within two years." "He has not seen his sister, since the year 1800."

Perfect Tense, definite.

This form represents an action as just finished; as, "I *have been reading* a history of the revolution in France."

Prior-past Tense, indefinite, [pluperfect.]

This form of the prior past tense expresses an action which was past at or before some other past time specified; as, "he *had received* the news before the messenger arrived."

Prior-past, definite.

This form denotes an action to be just past, at or before another time specified; as, "I *had been reading* your letter when the messenger arrived."

Future Tense, indefinite.

This form of the future tense gives notice of an event to happen hereafter; as, "Your son *will obtain* a commission in the navy." "We *shall have* a fine season."

Future Tense, definite.

This form expresses an action which is to take place and be unfinished at a specified future time; as, "He *will be preparing* for a visit, at the time you arrive."

Prior-Future, indefinite.

This form of the future tense denotes an action which will be past at a future time specified; as, "They *will have performed* their task, by the appointed hour."

Prior-Future, definite.

This form represents an action which will be just past at a future specified time; as, "We *shall have been making* preparations, a week before our friends arrive."*

In the use of the present tense, the following things are to be noticed.

1. The present tense is customarily used to express future time, when by any mode of expression, the mind is transported forward to the time, so as to conceive it present; as, "I cannot determine, till the mail *arrives.*" "As soon as it *is* light, we shall depart." "When he *has* an opportunity, he will write." The words *till, when, as soon as,* carry the mind to the time of an event to happen, and we speak of it as present.

2. By an easy transition, the imagination passes from an author to his writings; these being in existence and present, though long after his decease, we substitute the writer's name for his works, and speak of him as living, or in the present tense; thus, Milton *resembles* Homer in sublimity and invention, as Pope *resembles* Virgil, in smoothness of versification. Plato *is* fanciful; Aristotle *is* profound.

3. It gives great life and effect to description, in prose or verse, to represent past events as present; to introduce them to the view of the reader or hearer, as having a present existence. Hence the frequent use of the present tense for the future, by the historian, the poet and the orator:

"She spoke; Minerva *burns* to meet the war;
And now heaven's empress *calls* the blazing car;
At her command *rush* forth the steeds divine,
Rich with immortal gold, the trappings shine." *Iliad,* 5.

The definite tenses, it will be observed, are formed by the participle of the present tense, and the substantive verb, *be.* This participle always expresses present time, even when annexed to a past or future tense; for, *I was writing,* denotes that, at the past time mentioned, the action was present; *I shall be writing,* denotes future time, but an action then to be present.

The past tense of every regular verb ends in *ed; d* being added to a verb ending in *e,* and *ed* to a verb with other terminations; as hate, hated; look, looked.

The future tense is formed by the present tense of *shall* and *will;* for, I shall go, he will go, are merely an appropriate use of *I shall to go, I will to go.* See an explanation of these words under the head of auxiliaries.

There are other modes of expressing future time; as, "I am going to write"; "I am about to write." These have been called the *inceptive* future, as they note the commencement of an action, or an intention to commence an action without delay.

We have another mode of expression, which does not strictly and positively foretell an action, yet it implies a necessity of performing an act, and clearly indicates that it will take place. For example, "I *have to pay* a sum of money to morrow." That is, I am under a *present* necessity or obligation to do a *future* act.

The substantive verb followed by a radical verb, forms another idiomatic expression of future time; as, "John *is to command* a regiment." "Eneas went in search of the seat of an empire which *was,* one day, *to command* the world." The latter expression is a future past; that is, *past* to the narator, but *future* as to the event, at the time specified.

Modes.

Mode, in grammar, is the manner of representing action and being, or the wishes and determinations of the mind. This is performed by inflections of the verb, or by combinations of verbs with auxiliaries and participles, and by their various positions.

As there are scarcely two authors who are agreed in the number and denominations of the modes in English, I shall offer a distribution of the verbs, and a display of their inflections and combinations, somewhat different from any which I have seen.

1. The first and most simple form of the verb, is the verb without inflections, and unconnected with persons. This form usually has the prefix *to;* as *to love.*

This form of the verb, not being restricted to person or number, is usually called the *Infinitive Mode.*

2. Another use of the verb is to *affirm, assert* or *declare* some action or existence, either positively, as *he runs,* or negatively, as *you are not in health.* This form is called the *Indicative Mode.*

3. Another office of the verb is to command, direct, ask, or exhort; as *arise, make haste, let us be content.* This is called the *Imperative Mode.*

4. Another form of the verb is used to declare the power, liberty, possibility or necessity of acting or being, by means of certain words called auxiliaries, as may, can, must, &c. This form is called the *Potential Mode;* as, *I may* or *can write; he must wait.**

5. Another use of verbs is to represent actions or events which are uncertain, conditional or contingent; as, *if he shall go; if they would attend.* This is called the *Subjunctive Mode,* but would better be denominated the *Conditional.* The Indicative and Potential become *conditional,* by means of words used to express condition; as *if, though, unless, whether.*

The MODES then are five; the Infinitive, the Indicative, the Imperative, the Potential, and the Subjunctive.

It may also be observed that the combinations and arrangements of our verbs and auxiliaries to express negative and interrogative propositions, are really *modes* of the verb, and a place might be assigned to the verb for each purpose, were it not for the inconvenience of having *modes* of *modes.* For the sake of distinction, I denominate these verbs *interrogative* and *negative,* and have exhibited the conjugation of each.

Participles.

Participles are derivatives from *verbs,* formed by particular terminations, and having the sense of verbs, attributes or names.

There are two species of participles; one denoting present time, and formed by adding *ing* to the verb, as *turn, turning,* or when the verb ends with *e,* by dropping that letter and adding *ing,* as *place, placing.* But *e* is

---

*The common names and distribution of the tenses, are so utterly incorrect and incompetent to give a just idea of their uses, that I have ventured to offer a new division, retaining the old names, as far as truth will warrant. The terms *prior-past,* and *prior-future,* are so perfectly descriptive of the tenses arranged under them, that I cannot but think they will be well received. The distinction of indefinite and definite is not wholly new; but I have never seen the definite forms displayed, though they are as necessary as the indefinite forms. Indeed, I see not how a foreigner can learn our language, as the tenses are commonly distributed and defined.

* This mode is inserted in compliance with the opinions of many Grammarians, but in opposition to my own. It is in fact the indicative mode, affirming the *power,* &c. of acting, instead of the act itself.

retained in *dyeing* from *dye*, to color, to distinguish it from *dying*, the participle of *die;* in which word, *y* is used to prevent the duplication of *i*. In *singeing* from *singe*, *e* is retained to soften *g*, and to distinguish the word from *singing;* so also in *twingeing*.

This participle of the present tense is used, as before observed, to form the definite tenses. But it often loses the sense of the verb, and becomes an attribute; as a *loving* friend, *lasting* friendship. In this use, it admits of comparison by more or less, most and least; as *more lasting, less saving, most promising*.

This participle also becomes an adverb or modifier by receiving the termination *ly*, as *lovingly, laughingly;* and this species of modifiers admits of comparison, as *more lovingly, most charmingly*.

This participle also becomes a name and admits of the definitive; as, "the *burning* of London in 1666." In this capacity, it takes the plural form; as, "the *overflowings* of the Nile;" "he seeth all his *goings*." And sometimes the plural is used when a modifier is attached to the participle; as, "the *goings out*, the *comings in*." *Ezek.* xliii. 11. But this use of the participle is not esteemed elegant, nor is it common.

In a few instances, the participle in *ing* becomes a name by receiving the termination *ness;* as *willingness*, from *willing*.

The other species of participle is formed from the verb, by adding *d* or *ed*, and in regular verbs, it corresponds exactly with the past time; as *loved, preceded*. This may be called the participle of the *perfect* tense.

This participle, when its verb is *transitive*, may be joined with the verb *be*, in all its inflections, to form a passive verb, and the participle, in such combination, is called *passive*.

But this participle, when formed from an *intransitive* verb, cannot, except in a few instances, be joined to the substantive verb, or used in a passive sense; but it unites with the other auxiliaries.

This participle often loses its verbal character, and becomes an attribute; as a *concealed* plot, a *painted* house. In this character it admits of comparison, as "a more admired artist," "a most respected magistrate;" and a few of these verbal attributes receive the termination *ly*, and become modifiers, as *pointedly, more conceitedly, most dejectedly*.

Those verbs, whose past tense and participle end in *ed*, are deemed regular. All which deviate from this rule, are deemed irregular, and their participles of the perfect tense end mostly in *t*, *n* and *g*. A list of them will be found in the sequel.

Auxiliaries.

In English, a few monosyllabic verbs are chiefly employed to form the modes and tenses of other verbs, and from this use, are denominated *auxiliaries* or *helping verbs*. These are followed by other verbs, without the prefix *to*, as "he may go;" though they were originally principal verbs, and some of them still retain that character, as well as that of auxiliaries.

The verbs which are always auxiliary to others, are *may, can, shall, must;* those which are sometimes auxiliaries, and sometimes principal verbs, are *will, have, do* and *be*. To these may be added *need* and *dare*.

May conveys the idea of *liberty* or permission; as, "he may go, if he will." Or it denotes *possibility;* as, "he may have written or not."*

Can has the sense of *to be able*.

Shall, in its primitive sense, denotes *to be obliged*, coinciding nearly with *ought;* which sense it retains in the German. But this signification, though evidently the root of the present uses of this word, is much obscured. The following remarks will illustrate the several uses of *will* and *shall*.

Will has a common origin with the Latin *volo*. Hence the German *wollen*, the old English *woll*, and the present contraction *won't*, that is, *woll-not*.†

This was originally a principal verb, and is still used as such in our language. It denotes the act of the mind in determining, or a determination; for he *wills to go*, and *he will go*, are radically of the same import.

* The primitive idea expressed by *may* was *power;* Sax. *magan*, to be able.

† It is supposed that the Roman *v* was pronounced as our *w*, *wolo*.

When a man expresses his own determination of mind, *I will*, we are accustomed to consider the event, or act willed as certain; for we naturally connect the power to act, with the intention; hence we make the declaration of *will* a ground of confidence, and by an easy association of ideas, we connect the declaration, with an *obligation* to carry the determination into effect. Hence *will* expressed by a person himself, came to denote a *promise*.

But when a person declares the will of another, he is not supposed to possess the power to decide for him, and to carry his will into effect. He merely offers an opinion, grounded on information or probable circumstances, which give him more or less confidence of an event depending on another's will. Hence *will* in the second and third person simply *foretells*, or expresses an opinion of what will take place.

Shall, in some of its inflections, retains its primitive sense—*to be obliged* or *bound in duty;* but in many of its uses, its sense is much varied. In the first person, it merely foretells; as, "I shall go to New-York to-morrow." In this phrase, the word seems to have no reference to *obligation;* nor is it considered by a second person as imposing an obligation on the person uttering it. But when *shall* is used in the *second* and *third* persons, it resumes its primitive sense, or one nearly allied to it, implying obligation; as when a superior commands with authority, *you shall go;* or implying a right in the second and third person to expect, and hence denoting a promise in the speaker; as, "you *shall* receive your wages." This is radically saying, "you *ought* to receive your wages;" but this *right* in the second person to receive, implies an *obligation* in the person speaking to pay. Hence *shall* in the first person *foretells;* in the second, *promises, commands*, or *expresses determination*. When *shall* in the second and third persons, is uttered with emphasis, it expresses *determination* in the speaker, and implies an authority to enforce the act. "You *shall* go."

Must expresses necessity, and has no variation for person, number or tense.

Do is a principal and a transitive verb, signifying *to act* or *make;* but is used in the present or past tenses as an auxiliary to give emphasis to a declaration, to denote contrast, or to supply the place of the principal verb.

"It would have been impossible for Cicero to inflame the minds of the people to so high a pitch against *oppression*, considered in the abstract, as he actually *did* inflame them against Verres the *oppressor*." *Camp. Rhet.* 1. 10. Here *did* expresses emphasis.

"It was hardly possible that he should not distinguish you as he has *done*." *Cowp. Let.* 40. Here *done* stands in the place of *distinguished you*. For it must be observed that when *do* is the substitute for another verb, it supplies the place not only of the *verb*, but of the *object* of the verb.

——"He loves not plays
As thou *dost*, Anthony."

That is, as *thou lovest plays*.

Do is also used in negative and interrogative sentences; the present and past tenses of the Indicative Mode being chiefly formed by this auxiliary; as, "I *do* not reside in Boston." "*Does* John hold a commission?"

Have is also a principal and transitive verb, denoting to *possess;* but much used as an auxiliary, as "He *has* lately been to Hamburg." It is often used to supply the place of a principal verb, or participle, preventing a repetition of it, and the object after it; as, "I have not seen Paris, but my brother has," that is, *has seen Paris*.

Equally common and extensive is the use of *be*, denoting existence, and hence called the *substantive* verb. Either in the character of a principal verb, or an auxiliary, it is found in almost every sentence of the language.

The inflection of a verb, in all the modes, tenses, numbers and persons, is termed *Conjugation*. The English verbs have few inflections, or changes of termination; most of the tenses and modes being formed by means of the auxiliaries.

NOTE.—In the following conjugations, a small *n* in an Italic character, is inserted in the place where *not* should stand in negative sentences. The same place is generally occupied by *never*, but not in every case. It is believed this letter will be very useful, especially to foreigners. The learner may conjugate the verb with or without *not*, at pleasure.

CONJUGATION OF THE AUXILIARIES.

MAY.—Present Tense.

	Singular.	*Plural.*
1st. *Person,*	I may *n*	We may *n*
2d. *Person,*	Thou mayest *n* / You may *n**	Ye may *n* / You may *n*
3d. *Person,*	*mas.* He may *n* / *fem.* She may *n* / *neut.* It may *n*	They may *n*

Past Tense.

Singular.	*Plural.*
I might *n*	We might *n*
Thou mightest *n* / You might *n*	Ye might *n* / You might *n*
He might *n*	They might *n*

CAN.—Present Tense.

I can *n*	We can *n*
Thou canst *n* / You can *n*	Ye can *n* / You can *n*
He can *n*	They can *n*

*It may be remarked once for all, that *thou* and *ye* are the second person used in the sacred style, and sometimes in other grave discourses. In all other cases, *you* is the second person of the singular number, as well as of the plural. It is not one of the most trivial absurdities which the student must now encounter at every step, in the study of English grammar, that he meets with *you* in the plural number only, though he finds it the representative of an individual. Now if *you* is always plural, then *you yourself* is not grammatical, but absurd; the true expression then must be, *you yourselves*, applied to an individual. Then I must say to a friend, who visits me, *please to seat yourselves, Sir.* This is equal to the royal style, *we ourself!*

Past Tense.

Singular.	*Plural.*
I could *n*	We could *n*
Thou couldst *n*	Ye could *n*
You could *n*	You could *n*
He could *n*	They could *n*

SHALL.—Present Tense.

I shall *n*	We shall *n*
Thou shalt *n*	Ye shall *n*
You shall *n*	You shall *n*
He shall *n*	They shall *n*

Past Tense.

I should *n*	We should *n*
Thou shouldst *n*	Ye should *n*
You should *n*	You should *n*
He should *n*	They should *n*

WILL.—Present Tense.

I will *n*	We will *n*
Thou wilt *n*	Ye will *n*
You will *n*	You will *n*
He will *n*	They will *n*

Past Tense.

I would *n*	We would *n*
Thou wouldst *n*	Ye would *n*
You would *n*	You would *n*
He would *n*	They would *n*

NOTE.—*Will*, when a principal verb, is regularly conjugated; I will, thou willest, he wills. Past tense, *I willed.*

MUST.

Must has no change of termination, and is joined with verbs only in the following tenses.

Present Tense.

I must *n* love	We must *n* love
Thou must *n* love	Ye must *n* love
You must *n* love	You must *n* love
He must *n* love	They must *n* love

Perfect Tense.

I must *n* have loved	We must *n* have loved
Thou must *n* have loved	Ye must *n* have loved
You must *n* have loved	You must *n* have loved
He must *n* have loved	They must *n* have loved

DO.—*Indicative Mode*—Present Tense.

I do *n* love	We do *n* love
Thou dost *n* love	Ye do *n* love
You do *n* love	You do *n* love
He does or doth *n* love	They do *n* love

Past Tense.

I did *n* love	We did *n* love
Thou didst *n* love	Ye did *n* love
You did *n* love	You did *n* love
He did *n* love	They did *n* love

Infinitive Mode.	Participles.
To do.	*Doing, done, having done.*

NOTE.—In the third person singular of the present tense, *doth* is used in sacred and solemn language; *does* in common and familiar language. This verb, when principal and transitive, has all the tenses and modes, I have done, I had done, I will do, &c.

HAVE.–Infinitive Mode, Present Tense.–*To have.*

Perfect Tense.—*To have had.*

Participle of the Present Tense.—*Having.*

Of the Perfect Tense.—*Had.*

Compound.—*Having had.*

Indicative Mode.—Present Tense.

I have *n*	We have *n*
Thou hast *n*	Ye have *n*
You have *n*	You have *n*
He has or hath *n**	They have *n*

Past Tense.

I had *n*	We had *n*
Thou hadst *n*	Ye had *n*
You had *n*	You had *n*
He had *n*	They had *n*

NOTE.—In the foregoing tenses, this verb is used either as a principal verb or an auxiliary.

* *Hath* is used in the solemn style; *has* in the familiar.

Perfect Tense.

Singular.	*Plural.*
I have *n* had	We have *n* had
Thou hast *n* had	Ye have *n* had
You have *n* had	You have *n* had
He has or hath *n* had	They have *n* had

Prior-past Tense.

I had *n* had	We had *n* had
Thou hadst *n* had	Ye had *n* had
You had *n* had	You had *n* had
He had *n* had	They had *n* had

NOTE.—In these tenses, the *perfect* and *prior-past*, this verb is always principal and transitive.

Future Tense.

In this tense the verb is principal or auxiliary, with the same form of conjugation.

The following form foretells.

I shall *n* have	We shall *n* have
Thou wilt *n* have	Ye will *n* have
You will *n* have	You will *n* have
He will *n* have	They will *n* have

The following form promises, commands or determines.

I will *n* have	We will *n* have
Thou shalt *n* have	Ye shall *n* have
You shall *n* have	You shall *n* have
He shall *n* have	They shall *n* have

Prior-Future.

This tense foretells, and is used only when the verb is principal.

I shall *n* have had	We shall *n* have had
Thou shalt or wilt *n* have had	Ye shall or will *n* have had
You shall or will *n* have had	You shall or will *n* have had
He shall or will *n* have had	They shall or will *n* have had

NOTE.—*Will* is not used in the first person of this tense; it being incompatible with the nature of a promise. We cannot say, "*I will have had* possession a year, on the first of October next;" but *I shall have had*, is a common expression.

Imperative Mode.

Singular.	*Plural.*
Have *n* or have thou *n*	Have ye *n*, have you *n*
Have you *n* or do *n* you have	Do *n* you have
Let me *n* have	Let us *n* have
Let him *n* have	Let them *n* have

NOTE.—A command, request or exhortation, must, in the nature of things, be addressed to the *second* person; nor can these phrases, *let me have, let us have*, be considered, in strictness, as the first person of this mode, nor *let him have*, as the third; but they answer to the first and third persons of this mode in other languages, and the mere naming of them is wholly immaterial.

The true force and effect of the verb, in this mode, depend on its application to characters, and the manner of utterance. *Come, go, let him go*, if uttered with a respectful address, or in a civil manner, may express entreaty, request or exhortation. On the other hand, such words uttered with a tone of authority, and addressed to inferiors, express command.

Potential Mode.—Present Tense.

In the following tense, this verb is either auxiliary or principal.

I may or can *n* have	We may or can *n* have
Thou mayest or canst *n* have	Ye may or can *n* have
You may or can *n* have	You may or can *n* have
He may or can *n* have	They may or can *n* have

Must is used in the foregoing tense, and in the perfect also.

Past Tense.

In this tense, the verb is principal or auxiliary.

I might *n* have	We might *n* have
I should *n* have	We should *n* have
I could *n* have	We could *n* have
I would *n* have	We would *n* have
Thou mightest *n* have	Ye might *n* have
Thou shouldst *n* have	Ye should *n* have
Thou couldst *n* have	Ye could *n* have
Thou wouldst *n* have	Ye would *n* have
You might *n* have	You might *n* have
You should *n* have	You should *n* have
You could *n* have	You could *n* have
You would *n* have	You would *n* have
He might *n* have	They might *n* have
He should *n* have	They should *n* have
He could *n* have	They could *n* have
He would *n* have	They would *n* have

Perfect Tense.

In this tense, *have* is a principal verb only.

I may *n* have had	We may *n* have had
Thou mayest *n* have had	Ye may *n* have had
You may *n* have had	You may *n* have had
He may *n* have had	They may *n* have had

Prior-past Tense—the principal verb only.

I might *n* have had	We might *n* have had
Thou mightest *n* have had	Ye might *n* have had
You might *n* have had	You might *n* have had
He might *n* have had	They might *n* have had

In the same manner with *should, could* and *would.*

There is no future tense, distinct from that of the indicative mode.

Conditional or Subjunctive Mode.

The Conditional or Subjunctive Mode is the same as the Indicative, with some preceding word expressing condition, supposition or contingency. These words are, *if, though* or *although, unless, except, whether, lest, albeit.*

If is a corruption of *gif*, the imperative of *gifan*, the Saxon orthography of *give. Though*, the Saxon *theah*, signifies permit, allow. *Although* is a compound of *all* and *though*, give or allow all. The old word *thof*, still used in some parts of England, is the imperative of the Saxon *thafian*, to allow. *Unless* is the imperative of the Saxon *onlysan*, to loose or dissolve. *Except* is the imperative of that verb. *Lest* is from *lesan*, to lease or dissolve. *Albeit* is a compound of *all, be* and *it*, let it be so.

These words, *if, though*, answer in signification and use, to the following: *admit, grant, allow, suppose*, as signs of a condition or hypothesis. "If you shall go," is simply, "give, you shall go;" that is, give that condition or fact; allow or suppose it to be so.

It has been, and is still customary for authors to omit the personal terminations of the second and third persons of the verb in the present tense, to form the subjunctive mode; *if thou go, if he write.*

The correct construction of the subjunctive mode is precisely the same as that of the indicative; as it is used in popular practice, which has preserved the true idiom of the language; *if thou hast, if he has or hath;* to denote *present uncertainty.* But a *future contingency* may be expressed by the omission of the personal terminations; *if he go*, that is, *if he shall go.*

Be.

Be is a verb denoting existence, and therefore called the *substantive* verb. It is very irregular, being derived from different radicals, and having undergone many dialectical changes.

Infinitive Mode, Present Tense.—*To be.*

Perfect Tense.—*To have been.*

Participle of the Present Tense.—*Being.*

Of the Perfect.—*Been.*

Compound.—*Having been.*

Indicative Mode.—Present Tense.

I am *n*	We are *n*
Thou art *n*	Ye are *n*
You are *n*	You are *n*
He is *n* She is *n* It is *n*	They are *n*

The foregoing form of the present tense is now generally used by good writers. But the following form is the most ancient, and is still very general in popular practice.

I be *n*	We be *n*
You be *n*	Ye or you be *n*
He is *n*	They be *n*

Thou beest, in the second person, is not in use.

Past Tense.

I was *n*	We were *n*
Thou wast *n* / You was or were *n*	Ye were *n* / You were *n*
He was *n*	They were *n*

Perfect Tense.

I have *n* been	We have been
Thou hast *n* been / You have *n* been	Ye have been / You have *n* been
He hath or has *n* been	They have *n* been

Prior-past Tense.

I had *n* been	We had *n* been
Thou hadst *n* been / You had *n* been	Ye had *n* been / You had *n* been
He had *n* been	They had *n* been

Future Tense.

I shall or will *n* be	We shall or will *n* be
Thou shalt or wilt *n* be / You shall or will *n* be	Ye shall or will *n* be / You shall or will *n* be
He shall or will *n* be	They shall or will *n* be

Prior-future Tense.

I shall *n* have been	We shall *n* have been
Thou shalt or wilt *n* have been / You shall or will *n* have been	Ye shall or will *n* have been / You shall or will *n* have been
He shall or will *n* have been	They shall or will *n* have been

Imperative Mode.

Command { Be *n*; be thou *n*; do *n* thou be, or do *n* be; be ye *n*; do *n* you be, or do you *n* be, or do *n* be.

Exhortation / Entreaty { Let me *n* be, let him *n* be, let us *n* be, let them *n* be.

Potential Mode.

I may or can *n* be	We may or can *n* be
Thou mayst or canst *n* be / You may or can *n* be	Ye may or can *n* be / You may or can *n* be
He may or can *n* be	They may or can *n* be

Must is used in this tense, and in the perfect also.

Past Tense.

I might *n* be	We might *n* be
Thou mightest *n* be / You might *n* be	Ye might *n* be / You might *n* be
He might *n* be	They might *n* be

In the same manner with *could, should* and *would.*

Perfect Tense.

I may or can have *n* been	We may or can *n* have been
Thou mayest or canst *n* have been / You may or can *n* have been	Ye may or can *n* have been / You may or can *n* have been
He may or can *n* have been	They may or can *n* have been

Prior-past Tense.

I might *n* have been	We might *n* have been
Thou mightest *n* have been / You might *n* have been	Ye might *n* have been / You might *n* have been
He might *n* have been	They might *n* have been

In the same manner with *could, would* and *should.* There is no future tense in this mode.

Subjunctive Mode.

This Mode is formed by prefixing any sign of condition, hypothesis or contingency, to the indicative mode in its various tenses.

Present Tense.

If I am	We are
Thou art / You are	Ye are / You are
He is	They are

Past Tense.

If I was	We were
Thou wast / You was or were	Ye were / You were
He was	They were

The foregoing tenses express uncertainty, whether a fact exists or existed; or they admit the fact. The following form is used for the like purposes:

If I be	We be
Thou be / You be	Ye be / You be
He be	They be

But this is more properly the form of the conditional future; that is, the verb without the sign of the future—*if he be*, for *if he shall be.*

The following is the form of expressing supposition or hypothesis, and may be called the

Hypothetical Tense.

If I were	We were
Thou wert / You was or were	Ye were / You were
He were	They were

"If I were," supposes I am *not;* "if I were not," supposes I am.

The other tenses are the same as in the indicative mode.

The Conjugation of a Regular Verb.

Love.—Infinitive Mode, Present Tense.

To love.

Perfect Tense.—*To have loved.*

Participle of the Present Tense.—*Loving.*

Of the Perfect.—*Loved.*

Compound.—*Having loved.*

Indicative Mode. Present Tense, indefinite.

I love *n*	We love *n*
Thou lovest *n* / You love *n*	Ye love *n* / You love *n*
He loveth or loves *n*	They love *n*

With the auxiliary *do.*

I do *n* love	We do *n* love
Thou dost *n* love / You do *n* love	Ye do *n* love / You do *n* love
He doth or does *n* love	They do *n* love

Definite.

I am *n* loving	We are *n* loving
Thou art *n* loving / You are *n* loving	Ye are *n* loving / You are *n* loving
He is *n* loving	They are *n* loving

Past Tense, indefinite.

I loved *n*	We loved *n*
Thou lovedst *n* / You loved *n*	Ye loved *n* / You loved *n*
He loved *n*	They loved *n*

With the auxiliary *did.*

I did *n* love	We did *n* love
Thou didst *n* love / You did *n* love	Ye did *n* love / You did *n* love
He did *n* love	They did *n* love

Definite.

I was *n* loving	We were *n* loving
Thou wast *n* loving / You was *n* loving	Ye were *n* loving / You were *n* loving
He was *n* loving	They were *n* loving

Perfect Tense, indefinite.

I have *n* loved	We have *n* loved
Thou hast *n* loved / You have *n* loved	Ye have *n* loved / You have *n* loved
He has or hath *n* loved	They have *n* loved

Definite.

I have *n* been loving	We have *n* been loving
Thou hast *n* been loving / You have *n* been loving	Ye have *n* been loving / You have *n* been loving
He has or hath *n* been loving	They have *n* been loving

Prior-past, indefinite.

I had *n* loved	We had *n* loved
Thou hadst *n* loved / You had *n* loved	Ye had *n* loved / You had *n* loved
He had *n* loved	They had *n* loved

Definite.

I had *n* been loving	We had *n* been loving
Thou hadst *n* been loving / You had *n* been loving	Ye had *n* been loving / You had *n* been loving
He had *n* been loving	They had *n* been loving

Future Tense, indefinite.

The form of predicting.

I shall *n* love	We shall *n* love
Thou wilt *n* love / You will *n* love	Ye will *n* love / You will *n* love
He will *n* love	They will *n* love

The form of promising, commanding and determining.

I will *n* love	We will *n* love
Thou shalt *n* love / You shall *n* love	Ye shall *n* love / You shall *n* love
He shall *n* love	They shall *n* love

Definite.

I shall or will *n* be loving	We shall or will *n* be loving
Thou shalt or wilt *n* be loving / You shall or will *n* be loving	Ye shall or will *n* be loving / You shall or will *n* be loving
He shall or will *n* be loving	They shall or will *n* be loving

Prior-future, indefinite.

I shall *n* have loved	We shall *n* have loved
Thou shalt or wilt *n* have loved / You shall or will *n* have loved	Ye shall or will *n* loved / You shall or will *n* have loved
He shall or will *n* have loved	They shall or will *n* have loved

Definite.

I shall *n* have been loving	We shall *n* have been loving
Thou shalt or wilt *n* have been loving / You shall or will *n* have been loving	Ye shall or will *n* have been loving / You shall or will *n* have been loving
He shall or will *n* have been loving	They shall or will *n* have been loving

Imperative Mode.

Let me *n* love	Let us *n* love
Love *n*	Love *n*
Do *n* love	Do *n* love
Do thou *n* love	Do ye or you *n* love
Do you *n* love	Let them *n* love
Let him *n* love	

In the place of *let*, the poets employ the verb without the auxiliary.

"*Perish* the lore that deadens young desire."
Beat. Minst.

That is, let the lore perish.

"*Be* ignorance thy choice, where knowledge leads to woe." *Ibm.*

Potential Mode.—Present Tense, indefinite.

I may or can *n* love	We may or can *n* love
Thou mayst or canst *n* love / You may or can *n* love	Ye may or can *n* love / You may or can *n* love
He may or can *n* love	They may or can *n* love

Must is used in this tense and in the perfect.

Definite.

I may or can *n* be loving	We may or can *n* be loving
Thou mayst or canst *n* be loving / You may or can *n* be loving	Ye may or can *n* be loving / You may or can *n* be loving
He may or can *n* be loving	They may or can *n* be loving

Past Tense, indefinite.

I might *n* love	We might *n* love
Thou mightest *n* love / You might *n* love	Ye might *n* love / You might *n* love
He might *n* love	They might *n* love

With *could, would* and *should* in the same manner.

Definite.

I might *n* be loving — We might *n* be loving
Thou mightest *n* be loving — Ye might *n* be loving
You might *n* be loving — You might *n* be loving
He might *n* be loving — They might *n* be loving

With *could, would* and *should* in the same manner.

Perfect Tense, indefinite.

I may or can *n* / Thou mayest or canst *n* / You may can *n* / He may or can *n* — have loved
We / Ye / You / They — may or can *n* have loved

Definite.

I may or can *n* have been loving — We may or can *n* have been loving
Thou mayest or canst *n* have been loving — Ye may or can *n* have been loving
You may or can *n* have been loving — You may or can *n* have been loving
He may or can *n* have been loving — They may or can *n* have been loving

Prior-past Tense, indefinite.

I might *n* have loved — We might *n* have loved
Thou mightest *n* have loved — Ye might *n* have loved
You might *n* have loved — You might *n* have loved
He might *n* have loved — They might *n* have loved

Definite.

I might *n* have been loving — We might *n* have been loving
Thou mightest *n* have been loving — Ye might *n* have been loving
You might *n* have been loving — You might *n* have been loving
He might *n* have been loving — They might *n* have been loving

With *could, would* and *should* in the same manner, in the two last forms.

The potential mode becomes conditional by means of the modifiers, if, though, unless, &c. prefixed to its tenses, without any variation from the foregoing inflections. This may, for distinction, be called the *Conditional Potential.*

Subjunctive Mode.—Present Tense.

If, though, unless, whether, suppose, admit, &c.

I love *n* — We love *n*
Thou lovest *n* — Ye love *n*
You love *n* — You love *n*
He loveth or loves *n* — They love *n*

Some authors omit the personal terminations in the second and third persons—*if thou love, if he love.* With this single variation, which I deem contrary to the principles of our language, the subjunctive mode differs not in the least from the indicative, and to form it the learner has only to prefix a sign of condition, as *if, though, unless,* &c. to the indicative, in its several tenses. With this exception, however, that in the future tense, the auxiliary may be and often is suppressed. Thus instead of

If I shall or will love — We shall or will love
Thou shalt or will love — Ye shall or will love
You shall or will love — You shall or will love
He shall or will love — They shall or will love

Authors write,

If, &c. I love — We love
Thou love — Ye love
You love — You love
He love — They love

This form is properly used, when *shall* or *will* may precede the verb, and when the verb is preceded by a command or admonition; as, "See that none *render* evil for evil to any man."

1 *Thess.* v. 15.

In the subjunctive mode, there is a peculiarity in the tenses which should be noticed. When I say, *if it rains,* it is understood that I am *uncertain* of the fact, at the time of speaking. But when I say, "*If it rained,* we should be obliged to seek shelter," it is not understood that I am uncertain of the fact; on the contrary, it is understood that I am certain, it *does not rain* at the time of speaking. Or if I say, "*if it did not rain,* I would take a walk," I convey the idea that it *does* rain at the moment of speaking. This form of our tenses in the subjunctive mode has never been the subject of much notice, nor ever received its due explanation and arrangement. For this hypothetical verb is actually a present tense, or at least indefinite—it certainly does not belong to past time. It is further to be remarked, that a negative sentence always implies an affirmative—"if it did *not* rain," implies that it *does* rain. On the contrary, an affirmative sentence implies a negative—"if it *did* rain," implies that it does *not.*

In the past time, a similar distinction exists; for "if it rained yesterday," denotes uncertainty in the speaker's mind—but "if it had *not* rained yesterday," implies a certainty, that it *did* rain.

Passive form of the Verb.

Indicative Mode.—Present Tense.

I am *n* loved — We are *n* loved
Thou art *n* loved — Ye are *n* loved
You are *n* loved — You are *n* loved
He is *n* loved — They are *n* loved

Past Tense.

I was *n* loved — We were *n* loved
Thou wast *n* loved — Ye were *n* loved
You was or were *n* loved — You were *n* loved
He was *n* loved — They were *n* loved

Perfect Tense.

I have *n* been loved — We have *n* been loved
Thou hast *n* been loved — Ye have *n* been loved
You have *n* been loved — You have *n* been loved
He has or hath *n* been loved — They have *n* been loved

Prior-past Tense.

I had *n* been loved — We had *n* been loved
Thou hadst *n* been loved — Ye had *n* been loved
You had *n* been loved — You had *n* been loved
He had *n* been loved — They had *n* been loved

Future Tense.

I shall or will *n* be loved — We shall or will *n* be loved
Thou shalt or wilt *n* be loved — Ye shall or will *n* be loved
You shall or will *n* be loved — You shall or will *n* be loved
He shall or will *n* be loved — They shall or will *n* be loved

Prior-future Tense.

I shall *n* have been loved — We shall *n* have been loved
Thou shalt or wilt *n* have been loved — Ye shall or will *n* have been loved
You shall or will *n* have been loved — You shall or will *n* have been loved
He shall or will *n* have been loved — They shall or will *n* have been loved

Imperative Mode.

Let me *n* be loved — Let us *n* be loved
Be *n* loved — Be *n* loved
Be thou or you *n* loved — Be ye or you *n* loved
Do you *n* be loved* — Do you *n* be loved
Let him *n* be loved — Let them *n* be loved

Potential Mode.—Present Tense.

I may, can or must *n* be loved — We may, can or must *n* be loved
Thou mayest, canst or must *n* be loved — Ye may, can or must *n* be loved
You may, can or must *n* be loved — You may, can or must *n* be loved
He may, can or must *n* be loved — They may, can or must *n* be loved

Past Tense.

I might *n* be loved — We might *n* be loved
Thou mightest *n* be loved — Ye might *n* be loved
You might *n* be loved — You might *n* be loved
He might *n* be loved — They might *n* be loved

With *could, should* and *would* in the same manner.

Perfect Tense.

I may, can or must *n* have been loved — We may, can or must *n* have been loved
Thou mayest, canst or must *n* have been loved — Ye may, can or must *n* have been loved
You may, can or must *n* have been loved — You may, can or must *n* have been loved
He may, can or must *n* have been loved — They may, can or must *n* have been loved

Prior-past Tense.

I might *n* / Thou mightest *n* / You might *n* / He might *n* — have been loved
We / Ye / You / They — might *n* have been loved

In the same manner with *could, would* and *should.*

Subjunctive Mode.—Present Tense.

If, &c. I am *n* loved — We are *n* loved
Thou art *n* loved — Ye are *n* loved
You are *n* loved — You are *n* loved
He is *n* loved — They are *n* loved

Or thus:

If, &c. I be *n* loved — We be *n* loved
Thou be *n* loved — Ye be *n* loved
You be *n* loved — You be *n* loved
He be *n* loved — They be *n* loved

Past Tense.

If, &c. I was *n* loved — We were *n* loved
Thou wast *n* loved — Ye were *n* loved
You was or were *n* loved — You were *n* loved
He was *n* loved — They were *n* loved

Or thus:

If, &c. I were *n* loved — We were *n* loved
Thou wert *n* loved — Ye were *n* loved
You were *n* loved — You were *n* loved
He were *n* loved — They were *n* loved

Perfect Tense.

If, &c. I have *n* been loved — We have *n* been loved
Thou hast *n* been loved — Ye have *n* been loved
You have *n* been loved — You have *n* been loved
He has or hath *n* been loved — They have *n* been loved

Prior-past Tense.

If, &c. I had *n* been loved — We had *n* been loved
Thou hadst *n* been loved — Ye had *n* been loved
You had *n* been loved — You had *n* been loved
He had *n* been loved — They had *n* been loved

Future Tense.

If, &c. I shall, will or should *n* be loved — We shall, will or should *n* be loved
Thou shalt, wilt or shouldst *n* be loved — Ye shall, will or should *n* be loved
You shall, will or should *n* be loved — You shall, will or should *n* be loved
He shall, will or should *n* be loved — They shall, will or should *n* be loved

Prior-future Tense.

If, &c. I shall or should *n* have been loved — We shall or should *n* have been loved
Thou shalt or shouldst *n* have been loved — Ye shall or should *n* have been loved
You shall or should *n* have been loved — You shall or should *n* have been loved
He shall or should *n* have been loved — They shall or should *n* have been loved

The future is often elliptical, the auxiliary being omitted. Thus instead of *if I shall be loved,* &c. are used the following forms:

* The *not* is usually placed after *do,* and contracted into *don't.*

ENGLISH LANGUAGE.

If, &c. I be *n* loved	We be *n* loved
Thou be *n* loved	Ye be *n* loved
You be *n* loved	You be *n* loved
He be *n* loved	They be *n* loved

An exhibition of the verb in the interrogative form, with the sign of the negative.

Indicative Mode.—Present Tense, indefinite.

Love I *n*?	Love we *n*?
Lovest thou *n*?	Love ye *n*?
Love you *n*?	Love you *n*?
Loveth or loves he *n*?	Love they *n*?

The foregoing form is but little used. The following is the usual mode of asking questions.

Do I *n* love?	Do we *n* love?
Dost thou *n* love?	Do ye *n* love?
Do you *n* love?	Do you *n* love?
Does or doth he *n* love?	Do they *n* love?

Definite.

Am I *n* loving?	Are we *n* loving?
Art thou *n* loving?	Are ye *n* loving?
Are you *n* loving?	Are you *n* loving?
Is he *n* loving?	Are they *n* loving?

Past Tense, indefinite.

Did I *n* love?	Did we *n* love?
Didst thou *n* love?	Did ye *n* love?
Did you *n* love?	Did you *n* love?
Did he *n* love?	Did they *n* love?

The other form of this tense, loved he? is seldom used.

Definite.

Was I *n* loving?	Were we *n* loving?
Wast thou *n* loving?	Were ye *n* loving?
Was or were you *n* loving?	Were you *n* loving?
Was he *n* loving?	Were they *n* loving?

Perfect Tense, indefinite.

Have I *n* loved?	Have we *n* loved?
Hast thou *n* loved?	Have ye *n* loved?
Have you *n* loved?	Have you *n* loved?
Has or hath he *n* loved?	Have they *n* loved?

Definite.

Have I *n* been loving?	Have we *n* been loving?
Hast thou *n* been loving	Have ye *n* been loving?
Have you *n* been loving	Have you *n* been loving?
Has or hath he *n* been loving?	Have they *n* been loving?

Prior-past, indefinite.

Had I *n* loved?	Had we *n* loved?
Hadst thou *n* loved?	Had ye *n* loved?
Had you *n* loved?	Had you *n* loved?
Had he *n* loved?	Had they *n* loved

Definite.

Had I *n* been loving?	Had we *n* been loving?
Hadst thou *n* been loving?	Had ye *n* been loving?
Had you *n* been loving?	Had you *n* been loving?
Had he *n* been loving?	Had they *n* been loving?

Future Tense, indefinite.

Shall I *n* love?	Shall we *n* love?
Shalt or wilt thou *n* love?	Shall or will ye *n* love?
Shall or will you *n* love?	Shall or will you *n* love?
Shall or will he *n* love?	Shall or will they *n* love?

Definite.

Shall I *n* be loving?	Shall we *n* be loving?
Shalt or wilt thou *n* be loving?	Shall or will ye *n* be loving?
Shall or will you *n* be loving?	Shall or will you *n* be loving?
Shall or will he *n* be loving?	Shall or will they *n* be loving?

Prior-future, indefinite.

Shall I *n* have loved?	Shall we *n* have loved?
Shalt or wilt thou *n* have loved?	Shall or will ye *n* have loved?
Shall or will you *n* have loved?	Shall or will you *n* have loved?
Shall or will he *n* have loved?	Shall or will they *n* have loved?

The definite form of this tense is little used.

Will, in this tense, is not elegantly used in the first person.

The interrogative form is not used in the imperative mode; a command and a question being incompatible.

It is not necessary to exhibit this form of the verb in the potential mode. Let the learner be only instructed that in interrogative sentences, the nominative follows the verb when alone, or the first auxiliary when one or more are used; and the sign of negation *not*, (and generally *never*,) immediately follows the nominative.

IRREGULAR VERBS.

All verbs whose past tense and perfect participle do not end in *ed* are deemed irregular. The number of these is about one hundred and seventy seven. They are of three kinds.

1. Those whose past tense, and participle of the perfect are the same as the present; as, *beat, burst, cast, cost, cut, hit, hurt, let, put, read, rent, rid, set, shed, shred, shut, slit, split, spread, thrust, sweat, wet. Wet* has sometimes *wetted; heat* sometimes *het;* but the practice is not respectable. *Light* and *quit* have *lit* and *quit* in the past time and participle, but they are also regular.

2. Verbs whose past time and participle are alike, but different from the present; as, *meet, met; sell, sold.*

3. Verbs whose present and past tense and participle are all different; as, *know, knew, known.*

A few ending with *ch, ck, x, p, ll, ess,* though regular, suffer a contraction of *ed* into *t;* as, *snatcht* for *snatched, checkt* for *checked, snapt* for *snapped, mixt* for *mixed, dwelt* for *dwelled, past* for *passed.* Others have a digraph shortened; as, *dream, dreamt; feel, felt; mean, meant; sleep, slept; deal, dealt.* In a few, *v* is changed into *f;* as *bereave, bereft; leave, left.*

As some of the past tenses and participles are obsolete or obsolescent, it is deemed proper to set these in separate columns for the information of the student.

IRREGULAR VERBS.

Infin.	*Past tense.*	*Participle.*	*Past tense obs.*	*Part. obs.*
Abide	abode	abode		
Am	was	been		
Arise, rise	arose, rose	arisen, risen		
Awake	awoke, awaked	awaked		
Bear	bore	borne	bare	
Beat	beat	beat, beaten		
Begin	begun, began	begun		
Bend	bended, bent	bended, bent		
Bereave	bereaved, bereft	bereaved, bereft		
Beseech	besought	besought		
Bid	bid	bid	bade	bidden
Bind	bound	bound		bounden
Bite	bit	bit, bitten		
Bleed	bled	bled		
Blow	blew	blown		
Break	broke	broke, broken	brake	
Breed	bred	bred		
Bring	brought	brought		
Build	builded, built	built		
Burst	burst	burst		
Buy	bought	bought		
Cast	cast	cast		
Catch	catched, caught	catched, caught		
Chide	chid	chid		chidden
Chuse, choose	chose	chose, chosen		
Cleave, to stick	cleaved	cleaved	clave	
Cleave, to split	cleft	cleft	clove	cloven
Cling	clung	clung		
Clothe	clothed	clothed		clad
Come	came, come	come		
Cost	cost	cost		
Crow	crowed	crowed	crew	
Creep	crept	crept		
Cut	cut	cut		
Dare	durst, dared*	dared		
Deal	dealt, dealed	dealt, dealed		
Dig	dug, digged	dug, digged		
Do	did	done		
Draw	drew	drawn		
Drive	drove	driven, drove	drave	
Drink	drank	drank		drunken, drunk
Dwell	dwelt, dwelled	dwelt, dwelled		
Eat	eat, ate	eat, eaten		
Engrave	engraved	engraven, engraved		
Fall	fell	fallen		
Feel	felt	felt		
Fight	fought	fought		
Find	found	found		
Flee	fled	fled		
Fling	flung	flung		
Fly	flew	flown		
Forget	forgot	forgot, forgotten	forgat	
Forsake	forsook	forsaken, forsook		
Freeze	froze	frozen, froze		
Get	got	got, gotten	gat	
Gild	gilded, gilt	gilded, gilt		
Gird	girded, girt	girded, girt		
Give	gave	given		
Go	went	gone		
Grave	graved	graved, graven		
Grind	ground	ground		
Grow	grew	grown		
Have	had	had		
Hang	hanged, hung	hanged, hung		
Hear	heard	heard		
Hew	hewed	hewed, hewn		
Hide	hid	hid, hidden		
Hit	hit	hit		
Hold	held	held		holden

* When transitive, this verb is always regular; as, "he dared him."

Infin.	*Past tense.*	*Participle.*	*Past tense obs.*	*Part. obs.*
Hurt	hurt	hurt		
Keep	kept	kept		
Knit	knit	knit		
Know	knew	known		
Lade	laded	laden		
Lay	laid	laid		
Lead	led	led		
Leave	left	left		
Lend	lent	lent		
Let	let	let		
Lie (down)	lay	lain		
Lose	lost	lost		
Make	made	made		
Meet	met	met		
Mow	mowed	mowed, mown		
Pay	paid	paid		
Put	put	put		
Read	read	read		
Rend	rent	rent		
Rid	rid	rid		
Ride	rode, rid	rid		ridden
Ring	rung	rung	rang	
Rise	rose	risen		
Rive	rived	rived, riven		
Run	ran, run	run		
Saw	sawed	sawed, sawn		
Say	said	said		
See	saw	seen		
Seek	sought	sought		
Sell	sold	sold		
Send	sent	sent		
Set	set	set		
Shake	shook	shaken, shook		
Shape	shaped	shaped		shapen
Shave	shaved	shaved		shaven
Shear	sheared	sheared		shorn
Shed	shed	shed		
Shine	shone, shined	shone, shined		
Shew	shewed	shewn		
Show	showed	shown, showed		
Shoe	shod	shod		
Shoot	shot	shot		
Shrink	shrunk	shrunk	shrank	
Shred	shred	shred		
Shut	shut	shut		
Sing	sung	sung	sang	
Sink	sunk	sunk	sank	
Sit	sat	sat		sitten
Slay	slew	slain		
Sleep	slept	slept		
Slide	slid	slid		slidden
Sling	slung	slung		
Slink	slunk	slunk		
Slit	slit, slitted	slit, slitted		
Smite	smote	smitten, smit		
Sow	sowed	sowed, sown		
Speak	spoke	spoke, spoken	spake	
Speed	sped	sped		
Spend	spent	spent		
Spill	spilled, spilt	spilled, spilt		
Spin	spun	spun		
Spit	spit	spit	spat	spitten
Spread	spread	spread		
Spring	sprung	sprung	sprang	
Stand	stood	stood		
Steal	stole	stole, stolen		
Sting	stung	stung		
Stink	stunk	stunk	stank	
Stride	stride, strode	strid		stridden
Strike	struck	struck		stricken
String	strung	strung		
Strive	strove	striven		
Strow	strowed	strowed, strown		
Strew	strewed	strewed		
Swear	swore	sworn	sware	
Sweat	sweat	sweat		
Swell	swelled	swelled		swollen
Swim	swum, swam	swum		
Swing	swung	swung		
Take	took	taken, took		
Teach	taught	taught		
Tear	tore	torn, tore		
Tell	told	told		
Think	thought	thought		
Thrive	thrived	thrived	throve	thriven
Throw	threw	thrown		
Thrust	thrust	thrust		
Tread	trod	trod, trodden		
Wax	waxed	waxed		waxen
Wear	wore	worn, wore		
Weave	wove	woven, wove		
Weep	wept	wept		
Win	won	won		
Wind	wound	wound		
Work	worked, wrought	worked, wrought		
Wring	wrung, wringed	wrung, wringed		
Write	wrote, writ	writ, written		

Note 1.—The old forms of the past tense, *sang, spake, sprang, forgat,* &c. are here placed among the obsolete words. They are entirely obsolete, in ordinary practice, whether popular or polite; and it seems advisable not to attempt to revive them. In addition to this reason for omitting them, there is one which is not generally understood. The sound of *a* in these and all other like cases, was originally the broad *a* or *aw;* which sound, in the Gothic and Saxon, as in the modern Scotch, corresponded nearly with *o* in *spoke, swore. Spoke* is therefore nearer to the original than *spake*, as we now pronounce the vowel *a* with its first or long sound, as in *sake*.

Note 2.—In the use of the past tense and participle of some of these verbs, there is a diversity of practice; some authors retaining those which others have rejected as obsolete. Many words which were in use in the days of Shakspeare and Lord Bacon are now wholly laid aside; others are used only in books; while others are obsolescent, being occasionally used; and a few of the old participles, having lost the verbal character, are used only as adjectives. Of the last mentioned species, are *fraught, drunken, molten, beholden, shorn, clad, bounden, cloven. Holpen* is entirely obsolete. *Holden, swollen, gotten* and *forgotten*, are nearly obsolete in common parlance. *Wrought* is evidently obsolescent. *Stricken* is used only in one phrase, *stricken in age or years*, which we learn from the bible; but in every other case, is inelegant and pedantic.

Bishop Lowth has attempted to revive the use of many of the obsolescent past tenses and participles, for which he has, and I think deservedly, incurred the severe animadversions of eminent critics. "Is it not surprising," says Campbell on Rhetoric, b. 2, ch. 2, "that one of Lowth's penetration should think a single person entitled to revive a form of inflection in a particular word, which had been rejected by all good writers of every denomination, for more than a hundred and fifty years." This writer declares what Lowth has advanced on the use of the past tense and participle, to be inconsistent with the very first principles of grammar. He observes justly that authority is every thing in language, and that this authority consists in reputable, national, present usage.

Independent of authority however, there are substantial reasons in the language itself for laying aside the participles ending with *en*, and for removing the differences between the past time and participle. In opposition to the opinion of Lowth, who regrets that our language has so few inflections, and maintains that we should preserve all we have, I think it capable of demonstration that the differences between the past time and participle of the past tense of our irregular verbs, is one of the greatest inconveniences in the language. If we used personal terminations to form our modes and tenses like the Greeks, it would be desirable that they should be carefully retained. But as we have no more than about half a dozen different terminations, and are therefore obliged to form our modes and tenses by means of auxiliaries, the combination of these forms a part of the business of learning the language, which is extremely difficult and perplexing to foreigners. Even the natives of Scotland and Ireland do not always surmount the difficulty. This difficulty is very much augmented by the difference between the past tense and the participle. To remove this difference, in words in which popular usage has given a lead, is to obviate, in a degree, this inconvenience. This is recommended by another circumstance—it will so far reduce our irregular verbs to an analogy with the regular, whose past tense and participle of the perfect are alike.

In a number of words, the dropping of *n* in the participle, will make a convenient distinction between the participle and the adjective; for in the latter, we always retain *en*—we always say, a *written* treatise, a *spoken* language, a *hidden* mystery—though the best authors write, a "mystery *hid* from ages;" "the language *spoke* in Bengal."

Besides, whenever we observe a tendency in a nation to contract words, we may be assured that the contraction is found to be convenient, and is therefore to be countenanced. Indeed if I mistake not, we are indebted to such contractions for many real improvements; as *write* from *gewrite; slain* from *ofslegen; fastened* from *gefastnode; men* from *mannan; holy* from *haligan*, &c. And as a general remark, we may be assured that no *language ever suffers the loss of a useful word or syllable.* If a word or syllable is ever laid aside in national practice, it must be because it is not wanted, or because it is harsh and inconvenient in use, and a word or syllable more consonant to the general taste of a nation or state of society, is substituted.

Such is the fact with our participles in *en;* the *e* being suppressed in pronunciation, we have the words *spokn, writtn, holdn,* in actual practice. Nothing can be more weak, inefficient and disagreeable than this nasal sound of the half vowel *n;* it is disagreeable in prose, feeble in verse, and in music, intolerable. Were it possible to banish every sound of this kind from the language, the change would be desirable. At any rate, when people in general have laid aside any of these sounds, writers, who value the beauties of language, should be the last to revive them.

Defective Verbs.

Verbs which want the past time or participle, are deemed defective. Of these we have very few. The auxiliaries *may, can, will, shall, must,* having no participle, belong to this class. *Ought* is used in the present and past tenses only, with the regular inflection of the second person only—*I ought, thou oughtest, he ought, We, you, they ought. Quoth* is wholly obsolete, except in poetry and burlesque. It has no inflection, and is used chiefly in the third person, with the nominative following it, *quoth he.*

Wit, to know, is obsolete, except in the infinitive, to introduce an explanation or enumeration of particulars; as, "There are seven persons, *to wit,* four men and three women." *Wot* and *wist* are entirely obsolete.

Adverbs or Modifiers.

Adverbs are a secondary part of speech. Their uses are to enlarge, restrain, limit, define, and in short, to *modify* the sense of other words.

Adverbs may be classed according to their several uses.

1. Those which qualify the actions expressed by verbs and participles; as, "a good man lives *piously;*" "a room is *elegantly* furnished." Here *piously* denotes the *manner of living; elegantly* denotes the *manner of being furnished.*

In this class may be ranked a number of other words, as *when, soon, then, where, whence, hence,* and many others, whose use is to modify verbs.

2. Another class of adverbs are words usually called prepositions, used with verbs to vary their signification; for which purpose they generally follow them in construction, as *to fall on, give out, bear with, cast up;* or they are prefixed and become a part of the word, as *overcome, underlay.* In these uses, these words *modify* or change the sense of the verb, and when prefixed, are united with the verb in orthography.

A few modifiers admit the terminations of comparison; as *soon, sooner, soonest; often, oftener, oftenest.* Most of those which end in *ly,* may be compared by *more* and *most, less* and *least;* as *more justly, more excellently; less honestly, least criminally.*

Prepositions.

Prepositions, so called from their being *put before* other words, serve to connect words and show the relation between them, or to show the condition of things. Thus a man *of* benevolence, denotes a man who possesses benevolence. Christ was crucified *between* two thieves. Receive the book *from* John and give it *to* Thomas.

The prepositions most common, are *to, for, by, of, in, into, on, upon, among, between, betwixt, up, over, under, beneath, against, from, out, with, through, at, towards, before, behind, after, without, across.*

We have a number of particles, which serve to vary or modify the words to which they are prefixed, and which are sometimes called *inseparable prepositions,* because they are never used, but as parts of other words. Such are *a, be, con, mis, pre, re, sub,* in *abide, become, conjoin, mistake, prefix, return, subjoin, &c.* These may be called *prefixes.*

Connectives or Conjunctions.

Connectives are words which unite words and sentences in construction, joining two or more simple sentences into one compound one, and continuing the sentence at the pleasure of the writer or speaker. They also begin sentences after a full period, manifesting some relation between sentences in the general tenor of discourse.

The connectives of most general use, are *and, or, either, nor, neither, but, than.* To which may be added *because.*

And is supposed to denote an *addition;* as, "The book is worth four shillings *and* sixpence." That is, it is worth four shillings, *add* sixpence, or with sixpence *added.* "John resides at New York, and Thomas, at Boston," That is, John resides at New York, *add,* [add this which follows,] Thomas resides at Boston. From the great use of this connective in joining words of which the same thing is affirmed or predicated, it may be justly called the *copulative* by way of eminence.

The distinguishing use of the connective is to save the repetition of words; for this sentence, "John, Thomas and Peter reside at York," contains three simple sentences; "John resides at York,"—"Thomas resides at York,"—"Peter resides at York;" which are all combined into one, with a single verb and predicate, by means of the copulative.

Either and *or* have been already explained under the head of substitutes, for in strictness they are the representatives of sentences or words; but as *or* has totally lost that character, both these words will be here considered as connectives. Their use is to express an alternative, and I shall call them *alternatives.* Thus, "*Either* John *or* Henry will be at the Exchange," is an alternative sentence; the verb or predicate belonging to one or the other, but not to both; and whatever may be the number of names or propositions thus joined by *or,* the verb and predicate belong to one only.

One very common use of *or,* is to join to a word or sentence, something added by way of explanation or definition. Thus, "No disease of the mind can more fatally disable it from benevolence, than ill-humor *or* peevishness." *Rambler, No.* 74. Here *peevishness* is not intended as a distinct thing from *ill-humor,* but as another term for the same idea. In this case, *or* expresses only an *alternative of words,* and not of signification.

As *either* and *or* are affirmative of one or other of the particulars named, so *neither* and *nor* are negative of all the particulars. Thus, "For I am persuaded that *neither* death, *nor* life, *nor* angels, *nor* principalities, *nor* powers, *nor* things present, *nor* things to come, *nor* highth, *nor* depth, *nor* any other creature shall be able to separate us from the love of God." *Rom.* viii. 38, 39. Here *neither* is in fact a substitute for each of the following particulars, all of which it denies to be able to effect a certain purpose—*not either* of these which follow shall separate us from the love of God. It is laid down as a rule in our grammars, that *nor* must always answer to *neither;* but this is a great mistake, for the negation of *neither,* not either, extends to every one of the following alternatives. But *nor* is more generally used, and in many cases, as in the passage just recited, is far the most emphatical.

But is used for two Saxon words, originally by mistake, but now by established custom; *bet* or *bote,* the radical of our modern words *better, boot,* and denoting *sufficiency, compensation, more, further,* or *something additional,* by way of amendment; and *buton* or *butan,* equivalent to *without* or *except.*

In the former sense, we have the word in this sentence; "John resides at York, *but* Thomas resides at Bristol." The primitive sense here is, John resides at York; *more, add* or *supply,* Thomas resides at Bristol. It does not signify *opposition,* as is usually supposed, but some addition to the sense of what goes before.

In the latter sense, or that of *butan,* it is used in this passage, "He hath not grieved me, *but* in part." 2 *Cor.* ii. 5. That is, "He hath not grieved me, *except* in part." The first assertion is a complete negation; the word *but,* (butan,) introduces an exception. "Nothing, *but* true religion, can give us peace in death." Here also is a complete negation, with a saving introduced by *but.* Nothing, except true religion.

These were the only primitive uses of *but,* until by means of a mistake, a third sense was added, which is that of *only.* Not knowing the origin and true meaning of *but,* authors omitted the negation in certain phrases where it was essential to a true construction; as in the following passages, "Our light affliction, which is *but* for a moment." 2 *Cor.* iv. "If they kill us, we shall *but* die." 2 *Kings,* vii.

The *but,* in these passages, is *buton,* be out, except; and according to the true original sense, *not* should precede, to give the sentence a negative turn. "Our light affliction is not, *but* (except) for a moment." "We shall not, *but* die." As they now stand, they would in strictness signify, Our light affliction is *except* for a moment—We can *except* die, which would not be sense. To correct the sense, and repair the breach made in the true English idiom, by this mistake, we must give *but* a new sense, equivalent to *only.* Thus we are obliged to patch and mend, to prevent the mischiefs of innovation.

The history of this word *but* should be, as Johnson expresses the idea, "a guide to reformers, and a terror to innovators." The first blunder or innovation blended two words of distinct meanings into one, in orthography and pronunciation. Then the sense and etymology being obscured, authors proceeded to a further change, and suppressed the negation, which was essential to the *buton.* We have now therefore one word with three different and unallied meanings; and to these may be reduced the whole of Johnson's eighteen definitions of *but.*

Let us however trace the mischief of this change a little further. As the word *but* is now used, a sentence may have the same meaning *with* or *without* the negation. For example: "he hath *not* grieved me, *but* in part," and "he hath grieved me, *but* in part," have, according to our present use of *but,* precisely the same meaning. Or compare different passages of scripture, as they now stand in our bibles.

He hath *not* grieved me, *but* in part.

Our light affliction *is but* for a moment.

This however is not all; for the innovation being directed neither by knowledge nor judgment, is not extended to all cases, and in a large proportion of phrases to which *but* belongs, it is used in its original sense with a preceding negation, especially with *nothing* and *none.* "There is none good, *but* one, that is God." *Matt.* xix. 17. This is correct—there is none good, except one, that is God. "He saw a fig-tree in the way, and found nothing thereon *but* leaves only." *Matt.* xxi. 19. This is also correct—"he found nothing, except leaves;" the *only* is redundant. "It amounts to no more *but* this." *Locke, Und. b.* 1. 2. This is a correct English phrase; "it amounts to no more, *except* this;" but it is nearly obsolete.

Hence the propriety of these phrases. "They could not, *but* be known before." *Locke,* 1. 2. "The reader may be, nay cannot choose *but* be very fallible in the understanding of it." *Locke*, 3. 9. Here *but* is used in its true sense. They could not, except this, be known before. That is, the contrary was not possible. The other phrase is frequently found in Shakspeare and other old writers, but is now obsolete. They *cannot choose but*, that is, they have no choice, power or alternative, *except* to be very fallible.

But is called in our grammars, a *disjunctive conjunction*, connecting sentences, but expressing opposition in the sense. To illustrate the use of this word which *joins* and *disjoins* at the same time, Lowth gives this example; "You and I rode to London, *but* Peter staid at home."—Here the Bishop supposed the *but* to express an opposition in the sense. But let *but* be omitted, and what difference will the omission make in the sense? "You and I rode to London, Peter staid at home." Is the opposition in the sense less clearly marked than when the conjunction is used? By no means. And the truth is, that the opposition in the sense, when there is any, is never expressed by the connective at all, but always by the following sentence or phrase. "They have mouths, *but* they speak not; eyes have they, *but* see not." *Psalm* cxv. 5. Let *but* be omitted. "They have mouths, they speak not; eyes have they, they see not." The omission of the connectives makes not the smallest alteration in the sense, so far as opposition or difference of idea in the members of the sentence is concerned. Indeed the Bishop is most unfortunate in the example selected to illustrate his rule; for the copulative *and* may be used for *but*, without the least alteration in the sense—"You and I rode to London, *and* Peter staid at home." In this sentence the opposition is as completely expressed as if *but* was used; which proves that the opposition in the sense has no dependence on the connective.

Nor is it true that an opposition in the sense always follows *but*. "Man shall not live by bread alone, *but* by every word which proceedeth out of the mouth of God." *Matt.* iv. 4. Here the last clause expresses no opposition, but merely an additional fact. The true sense of *but* when used for *bote*, is *supply, more, further, something additional*, to complete the sense; it may be in opposition to what has preceded or in continuation only. In general, however, the word *but* is appropriately used before a clause of a sentence, intended to introduce a new and somewhat different idea, by way of modifying the sense of the preceding clause. This use is very naturally deduced from the original sense of the word, something further which is to make complete or qualify what has preceded.

Than is a connective of comparison; "John is taller *than* Peter."

Because is a mere compound of *by* and *cause*—by cause. "It is the case of some to contrive some false periods of business, *because* they may seem men of dispatch." *Bacon on Dispatch.* See also *Apoth.* 7. 6. This is a correct English idiom, Dr. Lowth's criticism to the contrary notwithstanding; but it is now obsolete.

Exclamations.

Exclamations are sounds uttered to express passions and emotions; usually those which are violent or sudden. They are called *interjections*, words *thrown in* between the parts of a sentence. But this is not always the fact, and the name is insignificant. The more appropriate name is, *exclamations;* as they are mere irregular sounds, uttered as passion dictates and not subject to rules.

A few of these sounds however become the customary modes of expressing particular passions and feelings in every nation. Thus in English, joy, surprise and grief are expressed by *oh*, uttered with a different tone and countenance. *Alas* expresses grief or great sorrow—*pish, pshaw*, express contempt. Sometimes verbs, names, and attributes are uttered by way of exclamation in a detached manner; as, Hail! Welcome! Bless me! Gracious heavens!

In two or three instances, exclamations are followed by names and substitutes in the nominative and objective; as, *O thou*, in the nominative; *ah me*, in the objective. Sometimes *that* follows *O*, expressing a wish; "O that the Lord would guide my ways." But in such cases, we may consider *wish* or some other verb to be understood.

Derivation.

However numerous may be the words in a language, the number of radical words is small. Most words are formed from others by addition of certain words or syllables, which were originally distinct words, but which have lost their distinct character, and are now used only in combination with other words. Thus *er* in *lover*, is a contraction of *wer*, a Saxon word denoting *man*, [the Latin *vir*;] *ness* denotes state or condition; *ly* is an abbreviation of *like* or *liche; fy* is from *facio*, to make, &c.

Most of the English derivatives fall under the following heads:—

1. Nouns formed from nouns, or more generally from verbs, by the addition of *r, er* or *or*, denoting an agent; as lover, hater, assignor, flatterer, from love, hate, assign, flatter. In a few instances, words thus formed are less regular; as glazier, from glass; courtier, from court; parishioner, from parish.

2. Nouns converted into verbs by the prefix *to;* as from water, cloud, to water, to cloud.

3. Adjectives converted into verbs in the same manner; as to lame, to cool, to warm, from lame, cool, warm.

4. Verbs formed from nouns and adjectives by the termination *ize;* as method, methodize; system, systemize; moral, moralize. When the primitive ends with a vowel, the consonant *t* is prefixed to the termination; as stigma, stigmatize.

5. Verbs formed from nouns and adjectives by the addition of *en* or *n;* as lengthen, widen, from length, wide.

6. Verbs formed by *fy;* as brutify, stratify, from brute, stratum.

7. Nouns formed from adjectives by *ness;* as goodness, from good; graciousness, from gracious.

8. Nouns formed by *dom* and *ric*, denoting jurisdiction; as kingdom, bishopric, from king and bishop. *Dom* and *ric*, are nouns denoting jurisdiction or territory.

9. Nouns formed by *hood* and *ship*, denoting state or condition; as manhood, lordship, from man, lord.

10. Nouns ending in *ment* and *age*, from the French, denoting state or act; as commandment, parentage, from command, parent.

11. Nouns in *er, or* and *ee*, used by way of opposition, the former denoting the agent, the latter the receiver or person to whom an act is performed; as assignor, assignee; indorser, indorsee.

12. Adjectives formed from nouns by the addition of *y*; as healthy, from health; pithy, from pith: or *ly* added to the noun; as stately, from state. *Ly* is a contraction of *like.*

13. Adjectives formed from nouns by the addition of *ful;* as hopeful, from hope.

14. Adjectives formed from nouns or verbs by *ible* or *able;* as payable, from pay; creditable, from credit; compressible, from compress. *Able* denotes power or capacity.

15. Adjectives formed from nouns or adjectives by *ish;* as whitish, from white; blackish, from black; waggish, from wag.

16. Adjectives formed from nouns by *less*, noting destitution; as fatherless, from father.

17. Adjectives formed from nouns by *ous;* as famous, from fame; gracious, from grace.

18. Adjectives formed by adding *some* to nouns; as delightsome, from delight.

19. Adverbs formed from adjectives by *ly;* as sweetly, from sweet.

20. Nouns to express females formed by adding *ess* to the masculine gender; as heiress, from heir.

21. Nouns ending in *ty*, some directly from the Latin, others formed from adjectives; as responsibility, from responsible; contractility, from contractile; probity, from probitas.

22. Adjectives formed by adding *al* to nouns; as national, from nation.

23. Adjectives ending in *ic*, mostly from the Latin or French, but some of them by the addition of *ic* to a noun; as balsamic, from balsam; sulphuric, from sulphur.

24. Nouns formed by *ate*, to denote the union of substances in salts; as carbonate, in the chemical nomenclature, denotes carbonic acid combined with another body.

25. Nouns ending in *ite*, from other nouns, and denoting salts formed by the union of acids with other bodies; as sulphite, from sulphur.

26. Nouns ending in *ret*, formed from other nouns, and denoting a substance combined with an alkaline, earthy or metallic base; as sulphuret, carburet, from sulphur and carbon.

27. Nouns formed from other nouns by adding *cy;* as ensigncy, captaincy, from ensign, captain.

Words are also formed by prefixing certain syllables and words, some of them significant by themselves, others never used but in composition; as *re, pre, con, mis, sub, super:* and great numbers are formed by the union of two words; as bed-room, ink-stand, pen-knife.

Syntax.

Syntax teaches the rules to be observed in the construction of sentences.

A sentence is a number of words arranged in due order, and forming a complete affirmation or proposition. In philosophical language, a sentence consists of a subject and a predicate, connected by an affirmation. Thus, "God is omnipotent," a complete proposition or sentence, composed of *God*, the subject, *omnipotent*, the predicate or thing affirmed, connected by the verb *is*, which forms the affirmation.

The predicate is often included in the verb; as, "the sun shines."

A simple sentence then contains one subject and one personal verb, that is, the *noun* and the *verb;* and without these, no proposition can be formed.

A compound sentence consists of two or more simple sentences, joined by connectives. The divisions of a compound sentence may be called members or clauses.

Sentences are *declaratory*, as, I am writing, the wind blows—*imperative*, as, go, retire, be quiet—*interrogative*, as, where am I? who art thou?—or *conditional*, as, if he should arrive.

The rules for the due construction of sentences fall under three heads: *First*, concord or agreement—*Second*, government—*Third*, arrangement and punctuation.

In agreement, the *name* or noun is the controlling word, as it carries with it the verb, the substitute and the attribute. In government, the verb is the controlling word; but names and prepositions have their share of influence also.

Agreement or Concord.

RULE I.—A verb must agree with its nominative in number and person.

Examples.

In solemn style. "*Thou hast* loved righteousness." *Heb.* i. 9.
"*Thou shalt* not steal." *Commandment.*
"*Art thou* called, being a servant?" 1 *Cor.* vii. 21.
"But *ye are* washed, but *ye are* sanctified." 1 *Cor.* vi. 11.

In familiar language. I *write;* John *reads; Newton was* the first of astronomers.

NOTE 1.—The nominative to a verb is found by young learners, by asking *who* or *what* does what is affirmed. "Eumenes, a young man of great abilities, inherited a large estate from his father. His father harassed with competitions, and perplexed with a multiplicity of business, recommended the quiet of a private station." Let the question be asked, who inherited a large estate? The answer is *Eumenes*, which is the nominative to the verb *inherited*. Who recommended the quiet of a private station? *His father*, which is therefore the nominative to the verb *recommended*.

NOTE 2.—Let the following rules be observed respecting the position of the nominative.

I. The nominative usually precedes the verb in declaratory phrases; as, "God created the world;" "the law is a rule of right." But the nominative may be separated from its verb, by a member of a period; as, "*Liberty*, say the fanatic favorers of popular power, *can* only be found in a democracy." *Anarcharsis, ch.* 62.

II. The nominative often follows an intransitive verb, for such a verb can have no object after it, and that position of the nominative creates no ambiguity; thus, "Above it stood the *Seraphim.*" *Is.* vi. "Gradual sinks the *breeze.*" *Thomson.*

III. When the verb is preceded by *here, there, hence, thence, then, thus, yet, so, nor, neither, such, the same, herein, therein, wherein*, and perhaps by some other words, the nominative may follow the verb, especially *be;* as, "here are five men;" "there was a man sent from God;" "hence arise wars;" "thence proceed our vicious habits;" "then came the scribes and pharisees;" "thus saith the Lord." "Yet required not I bread of the governor." *Neh.* v. 18. "So panteth my soul after thee, O Lord." *Psalm* xlii. "Neither hath this man sinned nor his parents." *John* ix. "Such were the facts;" "the same was the fact." "Herein consists the excellency of the English government." *Blackstone's Comm. b.* 1.

IV. When an emphatical attribute introduces a sentence, the nominative may follow the verb; as, "Great is the Lord, glorious are his works, and happy is the man who has an interest in his favor."

V. In certain phrases, which are conditional or hypothetical, the sign of the condition may be omitted, and the nominative placed after the auxiliary; as, "Did he but know my anxiety," for if he did but know—"Had I known the fact," for if I had known—"Would they consent," for if they would, &c.

VI. When the words *whose, his, their, her, mine, your*, &c. precede the verb with a governing word, the nominative may follow the verb; as, "*Out of whose* modifications have been made most complex modes." *Locke*, 2. 22. 10.

VII. In interrogative sentences, the nominative follows the verb when alone, or the first auxiliary; as, Believest thou? Will he consent? Has he been promoted? The nominative also follows the verb in the imperative mode; as, go thou; "be ye warmed and filled." But after a single verb, the nominative is commonly omitted; as, arise, flee.

NOTE 3.—In poetry, the nominative is often omitted in interrogative sentences, in cases where in prose the omission would be improper; as, "Lives there who loves his pain." *Milton.* That is, lives there a man or person.

NOTE 4.—In the answer to a question, the whole sentence is usually omitted, except the name, which is the principal subject of the interrogation; as, "who made the chief discoveries concerning vapor? Black."

NOTE 5.—In poetry, the verb in certain phrases is omitted, chiefly such verbs as express an address or answer; as, "To whom the monarch"—that is, said or replied.

NOTE 6.—When a verb is placed between two nominatives in different numbers, it may agree with either, but generally is made to agree with the first, and this may be considered as preferable; as, "His *meat was* locusts and wild honey." "*It* [piracy] *is* the remains of the manners of ancient Greece." *Anarch. ch.* 36.

NOTE 7.—Verbs follow the connective *than*, without a nominative expressed; as, "Not that any thing occurs in consequence of our late loss, more afflictive than *was* to be expected." *Life of Cowper, Let.* 62.

"He felt himself addicted to philosophical speculations, with more ardor than *consisted* with the duties of a Roman and a senator." *Murphy's Tacitus*, 4. 57.

"All words that lead the mind to any other ideas, than *are* supposed really to exist in that thing." *Locke*, 2. 25.

These forms of expression seem to be elliptical; "more afflictive than *that which* was to be expected." *That which* or *those which* will generally supply the ellipsis.

NOTE 8.—We sometimes see a nominative introducing a sentence, the sense suddenly interrupted, and the nominative left without its intended verb; as, "The name of a procession; what a great mixture of independent ideas of persons, habits, tapers, orders, motions, sounds, does it contain," &c. *Locke*, 3. 5. 13. This form of expression is often very striking in animated discourse. The first words being the subject of the discourse and important, are made to usher in the sentence, to invite attention; and the mind of the speaker, in the fervor of animation, quitting the trammels of a formal arrangement, rushes forward to a description of the thing mentioned, and presents the more striking ideas in the form of exclamation.

RULE II.—A name, a nominative case, or a sentence, joined with a participle of the present tense, may stand in construction without a verb, forming the *case absolute*, or *clause independent;* as, "Jesus had conveyed himself away, *a multitude being in that place.*" *John* v. 13. Here *multitude*, the noun, joined with *being*, stands without a verb.

"By memory we conceive heat or light, yellow or sweet, *the object being removed.*" *Locke*, 2. 10.

"I have, *notwithstanding this discouragement*, attempted a dictionary of the English language." *Johnson's Preface.*

"Whatever substance begins to exist, it must, *during its existence*, necessarily be the same." *Locke*, 2. 27. 28.

"The penalty shall be fine and imprisonment, *any law or custom to the contrary notwithstanding.*"

The latter phraseology is peculiar to the technical law style. In no other case, does *notwithstanding* follow the sentence. But this position makes no difference in the true construction, which is, "any law or custom to the contrary not opposing"—the real clause independent.

It is very common, when this participle agrees with a number of words, or a whole clause, to omit the whole except the participle; and in this use of *notwithstanding*, we have a striking proof of the value of abbreviations in language. For example: "Moses said, let no man leave of it till the morning. *Notwithstanding*, they hearkened not unto Moses." *Ex.* xvi. 19. 20. Here *notwithstanding* stands without the clause to which it belongs; to complete the sense in words, it would be necessary to repeat the whole preceding clause or the substance of it—"Moses said, let no man leave of it until the morning. *Notwithstanding this command of Moses*, or *notwithstanding Moses said that which has been recited*, they hearkened not unto Moses."

"Folly meets with success in this world; but it is true, *notwithstanding*, that it labors under disadvantages." *Porteus, Lecture* 13. This passage at length would read thus—"Folly meets with success in the world; but it is true, *notwithstanding folly meets with success in the world*, that it labors under disadvantages." By supplying what is really omitted, yet perfectly well understood, we learn the true construction; so that *notwithstanding* is a participle always agreeing with a word or clause, expressed or understood, and forming the independent clause, and by a customary ellipsis, it stands alone in the place of that clause.

Such is its general use in the translation of the Scriptures. In the following passage, the sentence is expressed—"Notwithstanding I have spoken unto you." *Jer.* xxxv. That is, "This fact, *I have spoken unto you*, not opposing or preventing." Or in other words, "In opposition to this fact."

It is also very common to use a substitute, *this, that, which* or *what*, for the whole sentence; as, "Bodies which have no taste, and no power of affecting the skin, may, *notwithstanding this*, [notwithstanding they have no taste, and no power to affect the skin,] act upon organs which are more delicate." *Fourcroy, Translation.*

I have included in hooks, the words for which *this* is a substitute.

"To account for the misery that men bring on themselves, *notwithstanding that, they do all in earnest pursue happiness*, we must consider how things come to be represented to our desires under deceitful appearances." *Locke*, 2. 21. 61.

Here *that*, a substitute, is used, and the sentence also for which it is a substitute. This is correct English, but it is usual to omit the substitute, when the sentence is expressed—"*Notwithstanding they do all in earnest pursue happiness.*"

It is not uncommon to omit the participle of the present tense, when a participle of the perfect tense is employed. "The son of God, while clothed in flesh, was subject to all the frailties and inconveniences of human nature, *sin excepted.*" *Locke*, 3. 9. That is, *sin being excepted*—the clause independent.

This omission is more frequent when the participle *provided* is used, than in any other case. "In the one case, *provided the facts on which it is founded be sufficiently numerous*, the conclusion is said to be morally certain." *Campbell on Rhet.* 1. 114. Here *being* is omitted, and the whole clause in italics is independent—"*The facts on which it is founded are sufficiently numerous*, that *being provided*, the conclusion is morally certain." *Provided*, in such cases, is equivalent to *given, admitted* or *supposed.*

"In mathematical reasoning, *provided you are ascertained of the regular procedure of the mind*, to affirm that the conclusion is false, implies a contradiction." *Ibm.* 134.

In this phrase, *that* may follow *provided—provided that*, you are ascertained, &c., as in the case of *notwithstanding*, before mentioned; *that* being a definitive substitute, pointing to the following sentence—*that which follows being provided*.*

It is not uncommon for authors to carry the practice of abridging discourse so far as to obscure the common regular construction. An instance frequently occurs in the omission both of the nominative and the participle in the case independent. For example: "*Conscious of his own weight and importance*, his conduct in parliament would be directed by nothing but the constitutional duty of a peer." *Junius, Let.* 19. Here is no noun expressed to which *conscious* can be referred. We are therefore to supply the necessary words, to complete the construction—"He being conscious"—forming the clause independent.

Rule III.—A sentence, a number of words, or a clause of a sentence may be the nominative to a verb, in which case the verb is always in the third person of the singular number; as, "*All that is in a man's power in this case, is*, only to observe what the ideas are which take their turns in the understanding." *Locke* 2. 14. Here the whole clause in italics is the nominative to *is*.

"*To attack vices in the abstract, without touching persons, may be* safe fighting indeed, but it is fighting with shadows." *Pope, Let.* 48.

"I deny that *men's coming to the use of reason, is* the time of their discovery." *Locke*, 1. 2.

"*That any thing can exist without existing in space, is* to my mind incomprehensible." *Darwin, Zoon. sect.* 14. Here the definitive substitute may be transferred to a place next before the verb—"Any thing can exist, without existing in space," that [whole proposition] *is* incomprehensible.

Rule IV.—The infinitive mode may be the nominative to a personal verb; as, "*to see* is desirable;" "*to die* is the inevitable lot of men." Sometimes an attribute is joined with the infinitive; as, "*to be blind* is calamitous." In this case the attribute has no name expressed to which it refers. The proposition is abstract, and applicable to any human being, but not applied to any.

Rule V.—In some cases the imperative verb is used without a definite nominative; as, "I will not take any thing that is thine—*save* only that which the young men have eaten." *Gen.* xiv. 23. 24.

"Israel burned none, *save* Hazor only." *Josh.* xi. 13.

"I would that all were such as I am, *except* these bonds. *Acts* xxvi. 29.

"Our ideas are movements of the nerves of sense, as of the optic nerve in recollecting visible ideas, *suppose* of a triangular piece of ivory. *Darwin, Zoon. sect.* 39.

This use of certain verbs in the imperative is very frequent, and there is a peculiar felicity in being thus able to use a verb in its true sense and with its proper object, without specifying a nominative; for the verb is thus left applicable to the first, second or third person. I may save or except, or you may except, or we may suppose. If we examine these sentences, we shall be convinced of the propriety of the idiom; for the ideas require no application to any person whatever.

Rule VI.—When the same thing is affirmed or predicated of two or more subjects, in the singular number, the nominatives are joined by the copulative *and*, with a verb agreeing with them in the plural number; as, "John and Thomas and Peter reside at Oxford." In this sentence, *residence at Oxford* is a predicate common to three persons; and instead of three affirmations—John resides at Oxford, Thomas resides at Oxford, Peter resides at Oxford, the three names are joined by *and*, and one verb in the plural applied to the whole number.

"*Reason* and *truth constitute* intellectual gold, which defies destruction." *Johnson.* "Why *are whiteness* and *coldness* in snow?" *Locke.* "Your *lot* and *mine*, in this respect, *have been* very different." *Cowp. Let.* 38.†

Note 1.—The rule for the use of a plural verb with two or more names in the singular number, connected by *and*, is laid down by critics with too much positiveness and universality. On original principles, all the names, except the first, are in the objective case; for it is probable that *and* contains in it the verb *add*. "John and Thomas and Peter reside at York," on primitive principles must be thus resolved—"John, add Thomas, add Peter reside at York." But without resorting to first principles, which are now lost or obscured, the use of the singular verb may be justified by considering the verb to be *understood* after each name, and that which is expressed, agreeing only with the last; as, "Nor were the young fellows so wholly lost to a sense of right, as *pride* and *conceit has* since made them affect to be." *Rambler, No.* 97. That is, as pride *has* and as conceit *has*. "Their safety and welfare *is* most concerned." *Spectator, No.* 121. In our best authors the singular verb is frequent in such sentences.‡

What will the hypercritic say to this sentence, "Either sex and every age *was* engaged in the pursuits of industry." *Gibbon, Rom. Emp. ch.* 10. Is not the distributive effect of *either* and *every*, such as to demand a singular verb? So in the following: "The judicial and every other power *is* accountable to the legislative." *Paley, Phil.* 6. 8.

Note 2.—When names and substitutes belonging to different persons, are thus joined, the plural substitute must be of the first person in preference to the second and third, and of the second in preference to the third. *I, you* and *he* are represented by *we; you* and *he*, by *you*. Pope in one of his letters makes *you* or *I* to be represented by *we* or *you*. "Either you or I *are* not in love with the other." The sentence is an awkward one, and not to be imitated.

Rule VII.—When an affirmation or predicate refers to one subject only among a number, which are separately named in the singular number, the subjects are joined by the alternative *or*, or *nor*, with a verb, substitute and name in the singular number; as, "Either John or Peter was at the Exchange yesterday; but neither John nor Peter *is* there to day."

Errors.—"A circle *or* square *are* the same in idea." *Locke*, 2. 8.

"But whiteness or redness *are* not in the porphyry." *Ibm.*

"Neither of them [Tillotson and Temple,] *are* remarkable for precision." *Blair.*

Substitutes for sentences, whether they represent a single clause, or the parts of a compound sentence, are always in the singular number; as, "*It* is true indeed *that* many have neglected opportunities of raising themselves to honor and to wealth, and rejected the kindest offers of fortune." *Rambler, No.* 58. Here *it* and *that* refer to the clauses which follow—"*It* is true *that*, many have rejected the kindest offers," &c.

Rule VIII.—Collective or aggregate names, comprehending two or more individuals under a term in the singular number, have a verb or substitute to agree with them in the singular or plural; as, the council *is* or *are* unanimous; the company *was* or *were* collected; *this* people, or *these* people.

No precise rule can be given to direct, in every case, which number is to be used. Much regard is to be had to usage, and to the unity or plurality of idea. In general, modern practice inclines to the use of the plural verb and substitute; as may be seen in the daily use of clergy, nobility, court, council, commonalty, audience, enemy and the like.

"The *clergy* began to withdraw *themselves* from the temporal courts." *Blackstone's Comm. Introduction.*

"Let us take a view of the principal incidents, attending the nobility, exclusive of *their* capacity as hereditary counselors of the crown." *Blackstone's Comm.* 1. 12.

"The commonalty *are* divided into several degrees." *Ibm.*

"The enemy *were* driven from their works." *Portuguese Asia. Mickle.* 163.

"The chorus *prepare* resistance at his first approach—the chorus *sings* of the battle—the chorus *entertains* the stage." *Johnson's Life of Milton.*

"The nobility *are* the pillars to support the throne." *Blackstone's Comm.* 1. 2.

Party and *army*, in customary language, are joined with a verb in the singular number. *Constitution* cannot be plural. *Church* may be singular or plural. *Mankind* is almost always plural.

The most common and palpable mistakes in the application of this rule, occur in the use of *sort* and *kind*, with a plural attribute—*these sort, those kind*. This fault infects the works of our best writers; but these words are strictly singular, and ought so to be used.

When a collective name is preceded by a definitive which clearly limits the sense of the word to an aggregate with an idea of unity, it requires a verb and substitute to agree with it in the singular number; as, *a* company of troops *was* detached; *a* troop of cavalry *was* raised; *this* people *is* become a great nation; *that* assembly *was* numerous; "a government established by *that* people." *Blackstone's Comm.* 1. 2.

Yet our language seems to be averse to the use of *it*, as the substitute for names, even thus limited by *a, this* or *that*. "How long will *this people* provoke me, and how long will it be ere *they* will believe me for all the signs that I have shewed among *them?*" *Num.* xiv. 11. "Liberty should reach every individual of *a people;* as *they* all share one common nature." *Spectator, No.* 287. In these passages, *it* in the place of *they*, would not be relished by an English ear; nor is it ever used in similar cases.*

Rule IX.—When the nominative consists of several words, and the last of the names is in the plural number, the verb is commonly in the plural also; as, "A *part of the exports* consist of raw silk." "The *number of oysters increase.*" *Golds. Anim. Nat. vol.* 4, *ch.* 3. "Of which seeming equality we have no other measure, but such as the *train of our ideas have* lodged in our memories." *Locke*, 2. 14. 21. "The greater *part of philosophers have* acknowledged the excellence of this government." *Anarch. vol.* 5. 272.

Rule X.—Pronouns or substitutes must agree with the names they represent, in number, gender and person; as,

---

* *Provided that*, says Johnson, is an *adverbial expression*, and we sometimes see *provided* numbered among the conjunctions, as its correspondent word is in French. What strange work has been made with Grammar!

† Is this last example an evidence that *mine* is in the possessive case!

‡ This was also a very common practice with the best Greek and Roman writers. *Mens* enim, et *ratio*, et *consilium*, in senibus *est*. *Cicero. de Senec. ca.* 19. "Sed etiam ipsius terræ *vis* ac *natura delectat*. *Ibm.* 15.

* The Romans used a greater latitude in joining plurals with collective names, than we can. "Magna *pars* in villis *repleti* cibo vinoque." *Liv.* 2. 26. Here is an attribute plural of the masculine gender, agreeing with a noun in the singular, of the feminine gender.

"Mine *answer* to them that do examine me is *this*." 1 *Cor*. ix. 13.

"*These* are not the *children* of God." *Rom*. ix. 8.

"Speak to the *children* of Israel and say to *them*, when *ye* come into the land whither I bring *you*." *Numb*. xv. 18.

"This is the heir; come, let us kill *him*, and let us seize on *his* inheritance." *Matt*. xxi. 38.

"*Esther* put on *her* royal apparel—*she* obtained favor in his sight—then the king said unto *her*." *Esth*. v.

"A river went out of Eden to water the garden, and *it* was parted—" *Gen*. ii. 10.

"The *woman whom* thou gavest to be with me." *Gen*. iii. 12.

"*Ignatius, who* was bishop of Antioch, conversed with the apostles." *Paley, Evid. sect*. 3.

"A *letter, which* is just received, gives us the news."

"O *thou who rulest* in the heavens."

Who and *whom* are exclusively the substitutes for persons; *whose* is of all genders, and as correctly applied to things as to persons.

"The question *whose solution* I require." *Dryden*.

"That forbidden *fruit whose* mortal taste." *Milton*.

"A *system whose* imagined suns." *Goldsmith*.

"These are the charming agonies of *love*,
Whose miseries delight." *Thomson*.

It, though neuter, is used as the substitute for *infant* or *child;* the distinction of sex in the first period of life being disregarded.

Formerly *which* was used as a substitute for *persons;* as appears from old authors, and especially in the vulgar version of the scriptures—"mighty *men which* were of old." But this use of the word is entirely discarded. *Which* however represents persons, when a question is asked or discrimination intended; as, *which* of the men was it; I know not *which* person it was.

Who is sometimes used as the substitute for things, but most unwarrantably. "The countries who—." *Davenant on Rev*. 2. 13. "The towns who—." *Hume Contin*. 11. *ch*. 10. "The faction or party who—." Equally faulty is the use of *who* and *whom* for brutes; "the birds who—."

The use of *it* for a sentence, seems to have given rise to a very vague application of the word in phrases like this: How shall I contrive *it* to attend court? How fares *it* with you? But such phrases, whatever may have given rise to them, are used chiefly in familiar colloquial language, and are deemed inelegant in any other style.

A more justifiable use of *it* is seen in this sentence: "But it is not this real essence that distinguishes them into species; *it* is men who range them into sorts," &c. *Locke*, 3. 6. 36.

Here *it* is in the singular, though referring to *men* in the plural. The cause or origin of this, in our language as in others, may perhaps be found in the disposition of the mind to combine the particular agents employed in performing an act, into a single agent. The *unity* of the *act* or *effect* seems to predominate in idea, and control the grammatical construction of the substitute.

RULE XI.—In compound sentences, a single substitute or relative, *who, which* or *that*, employed to introduce a new clause, is the nominative to the verb or verbs belonging to that clause, and to others connected with it; as, "The thirst after curiosities, *which* often draws contempt." *Rambler, No*. 83. "He *who suffers* not his faculties to lie torpid, has a chance of doing good." *Ibm*. "They *that are* after the flesh, do mind the things of the flesh." *Rom*. viii. 5. "Among those *who are* the most richly *endowed* by nature, and [are] *accomplished* by their own industry, how few are there whose virtues are not obscured by the ignorance, prejudice or envy of their beholders." *Spect. No*. 255.

In a few instances, the substitute for a sentence or a clause, is introduced as the nominative to a verb, *before* the sentence or clause, which it represents; as, "There was therefore, *which is* all that we assert, a course of life pursued by them, different from that which they before led." *Paley's Evid. ch*. 1. Here *which* is the representative of the whole of the last part of the sentence, and its natural position is *after* that clause.

The substitute *what* combines in itself the offices of two substitutes, which, if expressed, would be the nominatives to two verbs, each in distinct subsequent clauses; as, "Add to this, *what*, from its antiquity *is* but little known, *has* the recommendation of novelty." *Hermes, pref*. 19. Here *what* stands for *that, which;* and the two following verbs have no other nominative.

This use of *what* is not very common. But *what* is very frequently used as the representative of two cases; one, the objective after a verb or preposition, and the other, the nominative to a subsequent verb. Examples:

"I heard *what* was said." "He related *what* was seen."

"We do not so constantly love *what* has done us good." *Locke*, 2. 20. 14.

"Agreeable to *what* was afterwards directed." *Black. Com. b*. 2. *ch*. 3.

"Agreeable to *what* hath been mentioned." *Prideaux, p*. 2, 6, 3.

"There is something so overruling in *whatever* inspires us with awe." *Burke on the Sublime*, 304. In these sentences *what* includes an object after a verb or preposition, and a nominative to the following verb. "I have heard *that, which* was said."

RULE XII.—When a new clause is introduced into a sentence, with two pronouns, or with one pronoun and a noun, one of them is the nominative to the verb, and the other is governed by the verb or a preposition in the objective case, or by a noun in the possessive; as, "Locke, *whom* there is no *reason* to *suspect* of favoring idleness, has advanced." *Ramb*. 89. Here *reason* is the nominative to *is*, and *whom* is governed by *suspect*.

"Take thy only son Isaac, *whom thou* lovest." *Gen*. xxii. Here are two substitutes, one the nominative to the verb, and the other governed by it in the objective.

"God is the sovereign of the universe, whose majesty ought to fill us with awe, *to whom* we owe all possible reverence, and *whom* we are bound to obey."

It is not unusual to see in periods, a third clause introduced within a second, as a second is within the first, each with a distinct substitute for a nominative; as, "Those modifications of any simple idea, *which, as* has been said, I call simple modes, are distinct ideas." *Locke*, 2. 13.

Involution to this extent may be used with caution, without embarrassing a period; but beyond this, if ever used, it can hardly fail to occasion obscurity. Indeed the third member included in a second, must be very short, or it will perplex the reader.

Substitutes are sometimes made to precede their principals: thus, "When a man declares in autumn, when he is eating *them*, or in spring when there are *none*, that he loves *grapes*—." *Locke*, 2. 20. But this arrangement is usually awkward and seldom allowable.

RULE XIII.—When there are antecedents in different persons, to which a nominative substitute refers, the substitute and verb following may agree with either, though usage may sometimes offer a preference; as, "I am the Lord that make all things; that stretch forth the heavens alone; that spread abroad the earth," &c. *Isa*. xliv. Here *I* and *Lord* are of different persons, and *that* may agree with either. If it agrees with *I*, the verbs must be in the first person: "I am the Lord *that make*." If *that* agrees with *Lord* in the third person, the verb must be in the third person: "I am the Lord that *maketh*." But in all cases, the following verbs should all be of the same person.

RULE XIV.—The definitive adjectives, *this* and *that*, the only attributes which are varied to express number, must agree in number with the names to which they refer; as, this city, that church; these cities, those churches.

This and *that* are often used as substitutes for a name in the singular number, which is omitted, but the same name in the plural immediately follows after a connective; as in this example, "The mortality produced by *this* and other *diseases*." *Life of Washington*, 3. 6. That is, by this disease and other diseases. The sentence may be varied thus, by this disease and others; but the first form is the most common, and it occasions no obscurity.

Other adjectives and participles, used as adjectives, are joined to the names which they qualify without inflection; as, a wise man, wise men; an amiable child, or amiable children; a received truth, or received truths; a shining character, or shining characters.

Adjectives are often used as substitutes for the names of men and things which they describe by their qualities; as, *few* were present; the *wise* are respected; the *bravest* are not always victorious.

In this character, adjectives take the plural form, and are qualified by other adjectives; as the *goods* of fortune, two *finites* or *infinites, universals, generals*, the *chief* good, a *happy few*. "The *extraordinary great*." *Burke on the Sublime*, 304. "The *blue profound*." *Akenside*.

When nouns are joined by a copulative, an adjective preceding the first is applied to the others without being repeated; as, "From *great* luxury and licentiousness, converted to *strict* sobriety and frugality of manners." *Enfield*. Here *great* belongs to licentiousness as well as to luxury.

RULE XV.—Adjectives are usually placed before the nouns to which they belong; as, a *wise* prince; an *obedient* subject; a *pious* clergyman; a *brave* soldier.

Exception 1. When some word or words are dependent on an adjective, it follows the noun; as, knowledge *requisite* for a statesman; furniture *convenient* for a family.

Exception 2. When an adjective becomes a title, or is emphatically applied to a noun, it follows it; as Charles the Great; Henry the First; Lewis the Gross; Wisdom incomprehensible.

Exception 3. Several adjectives belonging to the same noun, may precede or follow the noun to which they belong; as a learned, wise and martial prince, or a prince learned, wise and martial.

Exception 4. The verb *be* often separates the noun from its adjective; as, war *is* expensive; gaming *is* ruinous.

Exception 5. An emphatical adjective is often used to introduce a sentence, in which case it precedes the noun which it qualifies, and sometimes at a considerable distance; as, "*Great* is the Lord;" *auspicious* will be that event; *fortunate* is that young man who escapes the snares of vice.

Exception 6. The adjective *all* may be separated from its noun by *the*, which never precedes it in construction; as, "all the nations of Europe." *Such* and *many* are separated from nouns by *a;* as, "such a character is rare;" "many a time."

All adjectives are separated from nouns by *a*, when preceded by *so* and *as*, as "*so* rich a dress," "*as* splendid a retinue;" and they are separated by *a* or *the*, when preceded by *how* and *however*, as "how distinguished *an* act of bravery," "how brilliant the prize," "however just the complaint."

The word *soever* may be interposed between the adjective and the noun; as, "how clear soever this idea of infinity;" "how remote soever it may seem." *Locke.*

Double is separated from its noun by *the;* as "double the distance"—*the* in such cases, never preceding *double.* But *a* precedes *double*, as well as other adjectives.

All and *singular* or *every* precede *the* before the noun in these phrases—"All and singular the articles, clauses and conditions"—"All and every of the articles"—phrases of the law style.

Rule XVI.—Adjectives belong to verbs in the infinitive mode; as, "to see is pleasant;" "to ride is more agreeable than to walk;" "to calumniate is detestable."

Sometimes the adjective belongs to the infinitive in union with another adjective or a noun; as, "to be blind is unfortunate;" "to be a coward is disgraceful." Here the attribute *unfortunate* is the attributive of the first clause, *to be blind, &c.*

Rule XVII.—Adjectives belong to sentences, or whole propositions. Examples:

"*Agreeable* to this, *we read of names being blotted out of God's Book.*" *Burder's Oriental Customs,* 375.

What is agreeable to this? The answer is found in the whole of the last clause of the sentence.

"Antiochus—to verify the character prophetically given of him by Daniel, *acted the part of a vile and most detestable person, agreeable* to what hath been aforementioned of him." *Prideaux, part* 2. *b.* 3.

"Her majesty signified her pleasure to the admiral, that as soon as *he had left a squadron for Dunkirk, agreeable* to what he had proposed, he should proceed with the fleet." *Burchet's Nav. Hist.* 439.

"*Independent* of his person, *his nobility, his dignity, his relations and friends may be urged,*" &c. *Guthrie's Quintilian.*

"No body can doubt but that *these ideas of mixed modes are made by a voluntary collection of ideas put together in the mind, independent* from any original patterns in nature." *Locke,* 3. 5.

"Whereupon God was provoked to anger, and put them in mind how, *contrary* to his directions, *they had spared the Canaanites.*" *Whiston's Josephus, b.* 5. *ch.* 2.

"Greece, which had submitted to the arms, in her turn, subdued the understandings of the Romans, and *contrary* to that which in these cases commonly happens, *the conquerors adopted the opinions and manners of the conquered.*" *Enfield, Hist. Phil. b.* 3. 1.

"This letter of Pope Innocent enjoined the *payment of tithes to the parsons of the respective parishes, where any man inhabited, agreeable* to what was afterwards directed by the same Pope in other countries." *Blackstone's Comm. b.* 2. *ch.* 3.

"*Agreeable* to this, we find *some of the Anglo-Saxon ladies were admitted into their most august assemblies.*" *Henry, Hist. Brit. b.* 2. *ch.* 7. and *b.* 4. *ch.* 1. *sect.* 4.

"As all language is composed of significant words variously combined, *a knowledge of them is necessary, previous* to our acquiring an adequate idea of language." *Encyc. art. Grammar.*

"*His empire could not be established, previous* to the institution of pretty numerous societies." *Smellie, Phil. Nat. Hist.* 339.

"*Suitable* to this, we find that *men, speaking of mixed modes, seldom imagine,* &c. *Locke,* 3. 5. 11.

"*No such original convention of the people was ever actually held, antecedent* to the existence of civil government in that country." *Paley, Phil. b.* 6. *ch.* 3.

Note.—Writers and critics, misapprehending the true construction of these and similar sentences, have supposed the attribute to belong to the verb, denoting the *manner of action.* But a little attention to the sense of such passages will be sufficient to detect the mistake. For instance, in the example from Enfield, the attribute *contrary* cannot qualify the verb *adopted;* for the conquerors did not adopt the opinions of the conquered in a *manner contrary* to what usually happens—the *manner of the act* is not the thing affirmed, nor does it come into consideration. The sense is this, the fact, that *the conquerors adopted the opinions and manners of the conquered,* was *contrary* to what commonly happens in like cases. The attribute belongs to the whole sentence or proposition. The same explanation is applicable to every similar sentence.

In consequence of not attending to this construction, our hypercritics, who are very apt to distrust popular practice, and substitute their own rules for customary idioms founded on common sense, have condemned this use of the attribute; and authors, suffering themselves to be led astray by these rules, often use an adverb in the place of an adjective.

"The greater part of philosophers have acknowledged the excellence of this government, which they have considered, some *relatively* to society, and others as it has relation to the general system of nature." *Anarch. ch.* 62.

"The perceptions are exalted into a source of exquisite pleasure *independently* of every particular relation of interest." *Studies of Nature,* 12.

In the first of these examples, *relatively* is used very awkwardly for *as relative,* or *as relating,* or as *it relates,* or *in relation;* for the word has a direct reference to *government.*

In the second example, *independently* is used as if it had been intended to modify the verb *exalt*—the perceptions are *independently exalted.* But the *manner of exalting* is not the thing described. It is not that the perceptions are exalted in an independent manner, nor in a manner independent of a relation to interest; but the fact, that the *perceptions are exalted into a source of exquisite pleasure,* is independent of every relation of interest. Equally faulty is the following sentence:—

"*Agreeably* to this law, children are bound to support their parents." *Paley, Phil.*

Rule XVIII.—Adjectives are used to modify the action of verbs, and to express the qualities of things in connection with the action by which they are produced. Examples:

"*Open* thine hand *wide.*" *Deut.* xv. 8.

We observe in this passage, that *wide,* the attribute of hand, has a connection with the verb *open;* for it is not "open thy *wide hand,*" but the attribute is supposed to be the *effect* of the act of opening. Nor can the modifier, *widely,* be used; for it is not simply the *manner* of the act which is intended, but the *effect.*

"Let us write *slow* and *exact.*" *Guthrie's Quintilian,* 2. 375.

We might perhaps substitute *slowly* for *slow,* as describing only the manner of writing; but *exactly* cannot be substituted for *exact,* for this word is intended to denote the *effect* of writing, in the correctness of what is written. The adjective expresses the idea with a happy precision and brevity.

As this is one of the most common, as well as most beautiful idioms of our language, which has hitherto escaped due observation, the following authorities are subjoined to illustrate and justify the rule.

"We could hear distinctly the bells—which sounded sweetly *soft* and *pensive.*" *Chandler's Travels, ch.* 2.

"A southernly wind succeeded blowing *fresh.*" *Ibm. vol.* 2. 3.

"His provisions were grown very *short.*" *Burchet's Nav. Hist.* 357.

"When the caloric exists *ready* combined with the water of solution." *Lavoisier, Trans. ch.* 5.

"The purest clay is that which burns *white.*" *Encyc. art. Chimistry.*

"*Bray,* to pound or grind *small.*" *Johnson's Dict.*

"When death lays *waste* thy house." *Beattie's Minst.*

"All which looks *very little like* the steady hand of nature." *Paley, Phil. ch.* 5.

"Magnesia feels *smooth;* calcarious earths feel *dry;* lithomarga feels very *greasy* or at least *smooth,* yet some feels *dry* and *dusty.*" *Kirwan, vol.* 1. 12. 189.

"By this substance, crystals and glasses are colored *blue.*" *Chaptal, Trans.* 299.

"There is an apple described in Bradley's work, which is said to have one side of it a sweet fruit, which boils *soft,* and the other side a *sour* fruit, which boils *hard.*" *Darwin, Phytol.* 105.

"Drink *deep* or taste not the Pierian spring." *Pope.*

"Heaven opened *wide* her ever during gates." *Milton, P. L.* 7.

"The victory of the ministry cost them *dear.*" *Hume, Contin.* 11. 9.

"And *just* as *short* of reason he must fall." *Pope.*

"*Thick* and more *thick* the steely circle grows." *Hoole's Tasso. b.* 8.

"Ancus marched *strait* to Fidenæ." *Hooke, Rom. Hist.* 1. 6.

"The cakes eat *short* and *crisp.*" *Vicar of Wakefield.*

"A steep ascent of steps which were cut *close* and *deep* into the rock." *Hampton's Polybius,* 2. 265.

"It makes the plow go *deep* or *shallow.*" *Encyc. art. Agriculture.*

"The king's ships were getting *ready.*" *Lusiad,* 1. 91.

"After growing *old* in attendance." *Spect. No.* 282.

"The sun shineth *watery.*" *Bacon. Apoph.*

"*Soft* sighed the flute." *Thomson, Spring.*

"I made him *just* and *right.*" *Milton,* 3. 98.

"He drew not *nigh* unheard." *Ibm.* 645.

"When the vowel of the preceding syllable is pronounced *short.*" *Murray's Grammar.*

"Here grass is cut *close* and gravel rolled *smooth.* Is not that trim?" *Boswell, Johnson,* 3.

"*Slow* tolls the village clock—*deep* mourns the turtle." *Beattie's Minstrel.*

"If you would try to live *independent.*" *Pope, Let.*

"He obliged the Nile to run *bloody* for your sakes."* *Whiston's Josephus,* 3. 5.

"Correct the heart and all will go *right.*" *Porteus, Lect.* 3.

The poets sometimes use adjectives in this manner, when modifiers would express the idea. Sometimes they are induced to it by the measure, and not unfrequently by the obvious superiority of the adjective in expressing the idea with force and precision.

---

* "*Cruentam* etiam fluxisse aquam Albanam, quidam auctores erant." *Liv. lib.* 27. 11. Some authors related that the Alban river ran *bloody.*

When two qualifying words are wanted, the latter may be an adjective, though applied to a verb; as, "He beat time *tolerably exact.*" *Goldsmith, An. Nat. ch.* 12.

"The air will be found diminished in weight *exactly equal* to what the iron has gained." *Lavoisier, ch.* 3.

"Horses are sold *extremely dear.*" *Goldsmith.*

"And *greatly independent* lived." *Thomson, Spring.*

"This was applying a just principle *very ill.*" *Vattel, Trans.* 2. 7.

It will be remarked that we have no adverbial form of the adjective in the comparative and superlative degrees, except that of *more* and *most, less* and *least*, prefixed. But we use the adjectives with the regular terminations, in these degrees, to qualify verbs. Examples:

"To hands that *longer* shall the weapon wield." *Hoole's Tasso.* 7.

——"Then the pleasing force
Of nature and her kind parental care,
Worthier I'd sing." *Akenside, Pleas. of Imag.* 1. 323.

"So while we taste the fragrance of the rose,
Glows not her blush the *fairer?*" *Ibm.* 2. 77.

"When we know our strength, we shall the *better* know what to undertake with hopes of success." *Locke,* 1. 6.

"And he that can *most* inform or *best* understand him, will certainly be welcomed." *Rambler, No.* 99.

"How much *nearer* he approaches to his end."

"I have dwelt the *longer* on the discussion of this point." *Junius, Let.* 17.

"The next contains a spirited command and should be pronounced much *higher.*" *Murray's Grammar.**

"Leviathan, which God of all his works
Created *hugest* that swim th' ocean's stream." *Milton,* 1. 201.

"But mercy first and last shall *brightest* shine." *Ibm.* 3. 134.

"Such opinions as seemed to approach *nearest* [to] the truth." *Enfield, Hist. Phil.* 2. 59.

"Her smiles, amid the blushes, *lovelier* show;
Amid her smiles, her blushes *lovelier* glow." *Hoole's Tasso. b.* 15.

Authors, misguided by Latin rules, and conceiving that every word which is used to qualify a verb, must be an *adverb*, have pronounced many of the passages here recited and similar ones to be incorrect; and in such as are too well established to bear censure, they call the adjective an *adverb.* Were it not for this influence in early education, which impresses a notion that all languages must be formed with the like idioms, we should never have received an idea that the same word may not modify a noun, an adjective and a verb.

So far are the words here used from being adverbs, that they cannot be changed into adverbs, without impairing the beauty, weakening the force, or destroying the meaning of the passages. Let the sentences be put to the test—Magnesia feels smoothly—the cakes eat shortly and crisply—the apples boil softly or hardly—glows not her blush the more fairly. Every English ear rejects this alteration at once; the sentences become nonsense. Nor can the adjective be separated from the verb—"Amid her smiles, her blushes, being lovelier, glow"—this is not the sense; nor will it answer to say, "Her lovelier blushes glow"—this is not the idea. The sense is, that the attribute expressed by *lovelier*, is not only a quality of *blushes*, but a quality derived, in a degree, from the action of the verb, *glow.*

Thus, clay burns *white*—objects may be seen *double*—may rise *high*—fall *low*—grow *strait*, or *thick*, or *thin*, or *fat*, or *lean*—one may speak *loud*—the sun shines *clear*—the *finer* a substance is pulverized—to grow *wiser*, to plunge *deeper*, spread *wider*—and similar expressions without number, constitute a well established idiom, as common as it is elegant.

RULE XIX.—Some adjectives are used to modify the sense of others and of participles; as, a *very clear* day; *red hot* iron; a *more* or *most* excellent character; *more* pressing necessity; *most* grating sound. "Without coming *any* nearer." *Locke.* "A *closer* grained wood." *Lavoisier, Trans.*

"*Full* many a gem of purest ray serene." *Gray.*

"Some deem'd him *wondrous* wise." *Beattie's Minstrel.*

In these expressions the last attribute belongs more immediately to the noun expressing its quality; and the *first* attribute qualifies the *second.*

Not unfrequently two attributes are used to modify a third, or the principal one; as, "The manner in which external force acts upon the body is *very little* subject to the will." *Rambler, No.* 78.

RULE XX.—Adjectives are used to qualify the sense of adverbs; as, a city was *very* bravely defended; the soldiers were *most* amply rewarded; a donation *more* beneficially bestowed; a house *less* elegantly furnished; a man the *least* peaceably disposed.

We have a few other words which are often used to modify adjectives as well as verbs; as, a *little;* a *great deal;* a *trifle.* "Many letters from persons of the best sense—do not a *little* encourage me." *Spectator,* 124. "It is a *great deal* better;" a *trifle* stronger; the last of which expressions is colloquial.

RULE XXI.—The adjectives *each, every, either* and *neither*, have verbs and substitutes agreeing with them in the singular number; as,

"*Each one was* a head of the house of *his* fathers." *Josh.* xxii. 14.

"*Every one* that *findeth* me, shall slay me." *Gen.* iv. 14.

"And take *every* man *his* censer." *Num.* xvi. 17.

"Nadab and Abihu took *either* of them *his* censer." *Lev.* x. 1.

"*Neither* of the ways of separation, real or mental, *is* compatible to pure space." *Locke,* 2. 13.

Errors. "Let *each* esteem others better than *themselves.*" It ought to be *himself.*

"There are bodies, *each* of which *are* so small." *Locke,* 2. 8. It ought to be *is.*

NOTE.—A plural verb, which affirms something of a number of particulars, is often followed by a distributive which assigns the affirmation to the particular objects or individuals. Thus, "If metals have, *each* a peculiar earth." Hence we may consider *each* as the nominative to *has* understood—"If metals have, if each metal has a peculiar earth." There is no other way of resolving the phrase. This manner of expression is common, though quite useless; as the last clause, "if each metal has," is sufficient. It has not the merit of an abbreviation. This phrase, "Let us love one another," is of a similar construction, but it is not easy to find a substitute of equal brevity.

RULE XXII.—Nouns of measure or dimension stand without a governing word, followed by an adjective; as, "a wall seven feet high and two feet thick;" "a carpet six yards wide;" "a line sixty fathoms long;" "a kingdom five hundred miles square;" "water ten feet deep."

"An army forty thousand strong," is a similar phrase.

NOTE.—Double comparatives and superlatives, *most straitest, most highest*, being improper and useless, are not to be used. The few which were formerly used are obsolete. *Worser*, a mistake in spelling *wyrsa*, is obsolete; but *lesser*, a mistake for *lessa*, is still used, as well as its abbreviation, *less.*

The superlative form of certain attributes, which in the positive degree, contain the utmost degree of the quality, as *extremest, chiefest*, is improper and obsolete. But authors indulge in a most unwarrantable license of annexing comparison to attributes whose negative sense precludes increase or diminution; as in these sentences, "These are more formidable and *more impassable* than the mountains." *Goldsmith, An. Nat. ch.* 2. "This difficulty was rendered still *more insurmountable* by the licentious spirit of our young men." *Murphy, Tacit. Orat.* 35. "The contradictions of impiety are still *more incomprehensible.*" *Massillon, Serm. to the Great.*

Similar to these are numerous expressions found in good authors—more impossible, more indispensable, less universal, more uncontrollable; and others, in which the sign of comparison is not only improper, but rather enfeebles the epithet; for the word itself expressing the full extent of the idea, ought to bear some emphasis, which, if a qualifying word is prefixed, will naturally be transferred to that word.*

In a few instances, this usage seems to be too well established to be altered, and particularly in the use of *more* and *most, less* and *least perfect.* In general, it would indicate more precision of thought to apply a term of *diminution* to the *affirmative* attribute *less possible, less surmountable, less controllable*, rather than a term of *increase* to a *negative* attribute.

NOTE 2.—In English, two nouns are frequently united to form a new noun; as earth-worm, drill-plow, ink-stand, book-case. In some cases, these compounds are by custom effectually blended into one term; in other cases, they are separated into their component parts by a hyphen. In other cases, words are united, and the first term forms a sort of occasional adjective to the second; as *family-use*, or *family-consumption.*

NOTE 3.—From a disposition to abridge the number of words in discourse, we find many expressions which are not reducible to any precise rule, formed at first by accident or ellipsis. Such are, *at first, at last, at best, at worst, at most, at least, at farthest, at the utmost.* In these expressions there may have been an ellipsis of some noun; but they are well established, brief and significant, and may be numbered among the *pinions of Mercury.*

NOTE 4.—We have certain adjectives which follow a verb and a noun to which they belong, but never precede the noun. Such are, *adry, afeared, afraid, alone, alike, aware, akin, alive, asleep, awake, athirst, aloft, aghast, afloat, askew, ashamed, pursuant, plenty, worth;* to which may be added, *amiss, aground, ashore, aside*, and a few others which may be used as attributes or modifiers. We say, one is *adry, ashamed, alive* or *awake;* but never an *adry* person, an *ashamed* child, &c. We say, "A proclamation was issued *pursuant* to advice of council." But we can in no case place *pursuant* before a noun.

* In remarking upon such phrases as "The vices which enter *deeper* or *deepest* into the soul," Murray says, *deeper* and *deepest*, should be *more deeply, most deeply.* Change the attribute in the two passages I have cited—"The vowel of the preceding syllable is pronounced *shortly*"—"The next should be pronounced much *more highly!*" This alteration will put his rule to the test.

* This effect may proceed also from another consideration. If the adjective alone is used, its sense precludes the idea of increase or diminution—it expresses all that can be expressed. But admit comparison, and it ceases to express the utmost extent of the quality.

Worth not only follows the noun which it qualifies, but is followed by a noun denoting price or value; as, a book *worth* a *dollar* or a *guinea;* it is well *worth* the money. "It is *worth observation.*" *Beloe's Herodotus, Erato.* 98. If a substitute is used after *worth*, it must be in the objective case. *It is worth them* or *it.*

But *worthy*, the derivative of *worth*, follows the usual construction of adjectives, and may precede the noun it qualifies; as, a worthy man.

Regimen or Government.

Rule XXIII.—One noun signifying the same thing with another, or descriptive of it, may be in apposition to it; that is, may stand in a like character or case, without an intervening verb; as, Paul, the apostle; John, the baptist; Newton, the philosopher; Chatham, the orator and statesman.

Note 1.—In the following sentence, a noun in the plural stands in apposition to two nouns in the singular, joined by an alternative. "The terms of our law will hardly find words that answer them in the *Spanish* or *Italian*, no scanty *languages*." *Locke*, 3. 5. 8.

Note 2.—Nouns are not unfrequently set in apposition to sentences; as, "Whereby if a man had a positive idea of infinite, either duration or space, he could add two infinites together; nay, make one infinite infinitely bigger than another: *absurdities* too gross to be confuted." *Locke*, 2. 17. 20. Here the *absurdities* are the whole preceding propositions.

"You are too *humane* and *considerate; things* few people can be charged with." *Pope Let.* Here *things* is in opposition to *humane* and *considerate.* Such a construction may be justified, when the ideas are correct, but it is not very common.

"The Dutch were formerly in possession of the coasting trade and freight of almost all other trading nations; they were also the bankers for all Europe: *advantages* by which they have gained immense sums." *Zimmerman's Survey*, 170. Here *advantages* is put in apposition to the two first members of the sentence.

Rule XXIV.—When two nouns are used, one denoting the possessor, the other the thing possessed, the name of the possessor precedes the other in the possessive case; as, "In my *Father's house* are many mansions." Men's bravery; England's fleet; a Christian's hope; Washington's prudence.

Note 1.—When the thing possessed is obvious, it is usual to omit the noun; as, "Let us go to St. Paul's," that is, church; "He is at the President's," that is, house.

"Nor think a lover's are but fancied woes." *Cowper.*

That is, a lover's woes. "Whose book is this? William's."

Note 2.—When the possessor is described by two or more nouns, the sign of the possessive is generally annexed to the last; as, "Edward, the second of England's Queen." *Bacon on Empire.*

"In Edward the third's time." *Blackstone's Comm. b.* 1, *ch.* 2.

"John the Baptist's head." *Matt.* xiv.

"*A member of parliament's paying* court to his constituents." *Burke.*

But if the thing possessed is represented as belonging to a number severally specified, the sign of the possessive is repeated with each; as, "He has the surgeon's and the physician's advice." "It was my father's, mother's, and uncle's opinion."*

Note 3.—When *of* is used before the possessive case of nouns, there is a double possessive, the thing possessed not being repeated; as, "Vital air was a discovery *of Priestley's.*" "Combustion, as now understood, was a discovery *of Lavoisier's.*" The sense of which is, that vital air was one of the discoveries of Priestley. This idiom prevents the repetition of the same word.

Note 4.—The possessive may be supplied by *of*, before the name of the possessor; as, "the hope of a christian." But *of* does not always denote possession; it denotes also *consisting of*, or *in, concerning*, &c. and in these cases, its place cannot be supplied by the possessive case. Thus *cloth of wool*, cannot be converted into *wool's cloth;* nor a *cup of water*, into *water's cup;* nor an *idea of an angel*, into an *angel's idea;* nor the *house of Lords*, into the *Lord's house.*

Rule XXV.—Participles are often used for nouns, and have the like effect in governing them in the possessive case; as, "A courier arrived from Madrid, with an account of his Catholic *majesty's having agreed* to the neutrality." "In case of his Catholic *majesty's dying* without issue." "Averse to the *nation's involving* itself in another war." *Hume, Contin. vol.* 7, *b.* 2, *ch.* 1. "Who can have no notion of the same *person's possessing* different accomplishments." *Spectator, No.* 150.

This is the true idiom of the language; yet the omission of the sign of the possessive is a common fault among modern writers, who learn the language by grammar, and neglect usages which are much better authority, and the basis of correct grammar. "Pieces of iron arranged in such a way as seemed most favorable for the *combustion being* communicated to every part." *Lavoisier, Trans.*

"There is no reason for *hydrogen being* an exception." *Ibm.* These expressions are not English.

Rule XXVI.—Transitive verbs and their participles require the objective case or the object of action to follow them; as, "In the beginning, God *created* the *heaven* and the *earth.*"

"If ye love *me*, keep my commandments." "O righteous father, the world hath not known *thee.*"

Sometimes the object and often the objective case of substitutes precedes the governing verb; as, "The spirit of truth, *whom* the world cannot *receive.*" "*Whom* ye ignorantly worship, *him* declare I unto you."

Whom and *which*, when in the objective case, always precede the verb.

In verse, a greater license of transposition is used, than in prose, and nouns are often placed before the governing verb.

"But through the heart
Should jealousy its *venom* once *diffuse.*" *Thomson.*

"She with extended arms his *aid implores.*" *Ibm.*

A noun with *whatever, whatsoever* or *whichever*, preceding, is placed before the governing verb; as, "*whatsoever* positive *ideas* we *have.*" *Locke*, 2. 17.

Note 1.—We have some verbs which govern two words in the objective case; as,

"Did I request thee, maker, from my clay
To mould *me man?*" *Milton*, 10. 744.

"God seems to have made *him what* he was." *Life of Cowper.*

"Ask *him* his *opinion.*" "You have asked *me the news.*"

Will it be said that the latter phrases are elliptical, for "ask *of* him his opinion?" I apprehend this to be a mistake. According to the true idea of the government of a transitive verb, *him* must be the *object* in the phrase under consideration, as much as in this, "Ask *him* for a guinea;" or in this, "ask *him* to go."

This idiom is very ancient, as we often see it in the Latin. "Interrogatus sententiam." *Liv.* 26. 33. "Se id Scipionem orare." *Ibm.* 27. 17. "Auxilia regem orabant." *Ibm. lib.* 28. 5. The idiom in both languages had a common origin.

Note 2.—Some verbs were formerly used as transitive, which are no longer considered as such; as, "he repented *him*"—"flee *thee* away"—"he *was* swerved"—"the sum *was* amounted," &c. which are held improper.

Cease, however, is used as a transitive verb by our best writers. "Cease this impious rage." *Milton.* "Her lips their music cease." *Hoole's Tasso.*

Rule XXVII.—Intransitive verbs are followed by the name of the *act* or *effect*, which the verb expresses in *action;* as, "to *live* a *life* of virtue;" "to *die* the *death* of the righteous;" "to *dream dreams;*" "to *run* a *race;*" "to *sleep* the *sleep* of death."

We observe, in these examples, *life* is the *name of living* supposed to be complete, as *race* is the name of the *act of running* when accomplished.

Note.—Nearly allied to this idiom is that of using, after verbs transitive or intransitive, certain nouns which are not the objects of the verb, nor of precisely the same sense, but which are either the names of the result of the verb's action, or closely connected with it. Examples: "A guinea weighs five penny weight, six grains;" "a crown weighs nineteen penny weight;"* "a piece of cloth measures ten yards."

"And on their hinges grate harsh thunder." "And rivers run potable gold." "The crispid brook ran nectar." "Groves whose rich trees wept odorous gums and balm." "Grin a ghastly smile." *Milton.*

"Her lips blush deeper sweets." *Thomson.*

"To ascend or descend a flight of stairs, a ladder, or a mountain."

"To cost a guinea."

Under this rule or the following may be arranged these expressions. "Let them go *their way.*" "When matters have been brought *this length.*" *Lavoisier, Translation.* "We turn our eyes *this way* or *that way.*" "Reckoning *any way* from ourselves, a yard, a mile, &c." *Locke*, 2. 17.

Similar to this idiom are the phrases, to *go west* or *east—pointing north* or *south, north-west* or *south-east*, and the like, which I find to be Saxon phrases and very ancient.

In some instances verbs of this sort are followed by two objects; as, "a ring cost the *purchaser* an eagle."

Rule XXVIII.—Names of certain portions of time and space, and especially words denoting continuance of time or progression, are used without a governing word; as, "Jacob said, I will serve thee *seven years* for Rachel." "And dust shalt thou eat *all the days of thy life.*" "And he abode with

---

* The contrary rule in Murray is egregiously wrong; as exemplified in this phrase, "This was my father, mother and uncle's advice." This is not English. When we say, "the king of England's throne," the three words, *king of England*, are one noun in effect, and can have but one sign of the possessive. But when two or three distinct nouns are used, the article possessed is described as belonging to each. "It was my father's advice, my mother's advice, and my uncle's advice." We can omit *advice* after the two first, but by no means, the sign of the possessive.

* The radical idea of *weight* is *carry, bear* or *sustain*, from the Saxon *wæg*, a balance. The idiom in question has its originial in that idea—a guinea *weighs* five penny weights, six grains—that is, *carries* or *sustains* that weight in the scales. How much of the propriety, and even of the beauty of language is lost, by neglecting to study its primitive state and principles!

him the *space of a month*." "The tree of life yielded her fruit *every month*." "In those days I Daniel was mourning *three full weeks*." "Whosoever shall urge thee to go a *mile*, go with him *twain*." "To walk a *mile*, or a *league*."

"Effects occurring *every moment* to ourselves."

"You have asked me news *a hundred times*." *Pope.*

Words expressing particular or precise points of time, are usually preceded by a preposition; as, "at that hour;" "on that day." But to both these rules there are exceptions.

RULE XXIX.—The verb *be* has the same case after it as before it; or two substitutes connected with *be* in construction are in the same case. "*It* is *I*, be not afraid." "*Thou* art *she*." "*It* is *he*." "*Who* was *he*?" "*Who* do men say that *I* am?" "*Whom* do they represent *me* to be." But "*Whom* do men say that I am," is incorrect.

RULE XXX.—Transitive verbs and their participles admit of a sentence, a clause or number of words as their object; as, "He is not alarmed so far, as to consider *how much nearer he approaches to his end*." *Rambler, No.* 78.

Consider what? The whole following clause, which is the object of the verb.

"If he escapes *being banished* by others, I fear he will banish himself." *Pope, Let. to Swift.*

Here *being banished* stands in the place of a noun, as the object after *escapes*.

"Add to this, *what, from its antiquity is but little known, has from that very circumstance, the recommendation of novelty*." *Hermes, Preface.* In this sentence the whole of the clauses in italics, is what is to be added, and is the actual object governed by the verb *add*.

"Suppose then *the world we live in to have had a creator*"—"Suppose *the disposition which dictated this council to continue*." *Paley, Ev.* 1.

"For that mortal dint,
Save *he who reigns above*, none can resist." *Milton*, 2. 815.

"I wish I could give you any good reasons for your coming hither, except *that, I earnestly invite you*." *Pope, Let.*

"Lord Bathurst is too great a husbandman to like barren hills, except *they are his own to improve*." *Pope, Let. Sept.* 3, 1726.

In these and similar passages, the object of the verb is a whole proposition or statement, in a sentence or clause of a sentence. In this passage, "Except *ye repent*, ye shall all likewise perish," the fact excepted is affirmed in a single verb. *Take away this fact* "*that you shall repent*," and the consequence must be, you will perish. This is one of the modes of abbreviation in language which I have so frequently mentioned, and which constitutes a principal excellence of the English.

We observe, in some of the passages here cited, the pronoun *that*, after the verb. This is probably the true original construction; the substitute, *that*, pointing to the whole following clause. "He could do no mighty works there, save *that*, [except that single fact which follows,] he laid his hand on a few sick and healed them."

NOTE.—It may be here observed that in some of the passages cited the verb has no definitive nominative; the verbs *save, except, suppose, add, &c.* are in the imperative mode, but the address is not made to any particular person or persons. And this probably has led authors to class *save* and *except* among conjunctions, prepositions or adverbs, or to consider them as used adverbially; for it has been already observed that the class of adverbs has been a sort of common sink to receive all words which authors have not been able to comprehend.

Is it not strange that *suppose, add, admit, allow*, and other verbs, which are constantly used in the same manner, should have hitherto escaped the same doom? In the passages above cited from Paley, *suppose* is used precisely in the same manner, as *except* and *save* in others. Indeed nothing but the most inexcusable negligence could have led critics to this classification of *save* and *except*—for in many passages of scripture, these very words, in the sense in which they are called conjunctions or adverbs, have an object following them, like other transitive verbs; as, "Israel burned none of them, *save Hazor only*." *Josh.* xi. 13. "Ye shall not come into the land, *save Caleb and Joshua*." *Num.* xiv. 30. "I would that all were as I am, *except these bonds*." *Acts*, xxvi.

This use of verbs without a definite nominative occasions no inconvenience; for the address is not made to any particular person, but is equally applicable to any one who will apply it. See the subject further explained under rule 38. The following passage in Locke, 2. 27. 2. contains another verb used in the same manner: "Could two bodies be in the same place at the same time, then those two parcels of matter must be one and the same, *take* them great or little."

The error of considering *save* as an adverb or conjunction, has however produced a multitude of mistakes in construction, as in these passages: "Save *he* who reigns above." *Milton.* "Which no man knoweth, saving *he* that receiveth it." *Rev.* ii. 17. The nominative *he* cannot be reconciled to any principle of true construction. *He* ought to be *him*, the object after the verb. *Except* might have been used, and this word being *called* a preposition, would have required after it the objective case. But both words are verbs, and ought to have the same construction.

RULE XXXI.—The infinitive mode follows, first, another verb or participle; as, "he loves *to cherish* the social affections;" "be persuaded *to abandon* a vicious life;" "he is willing *to encounter* danger;" "he was proceeding *to relate* his adventures."

2dly. The infinitive follows a noun; as, "The next thing natural for the mind *to do*." *Locke.* "He has a task *to perform*."

3dly. It follows an adjective or verbal attribute; as, "a question difficult *to be solved*." "It is delightful *to contemplate* the goodness of Providence." "God is worthy *to be loved and trusted*." "Be prepared *to receive* your friend."

4thly. It follows *as*; thus, "an object so high *as to be* invisible;" "a question so obscure *as to perplex* the understanding."

5thly. It follows *than* after a comparison; as, "Nothing makes a man suspect much, more *than to know* little." *Bacon on Suspicion.*

6thly. It follows the preposition *for*, noting cause or motive; as, "What went ye out *for to see*?" *Matt.* xi.

This is the true original idiom, but it is usual now to omit *for*; as, "he went *to see* a reed shaken with the wind." In every phrase of this sort, *for* is implied in the sense; but the use of the word is vulgar.

The infinitive mode is independent, standing as a substitute for a whole phrase; as, "It is not once in ten attempts that you can find the case you seek, in any law book; *to say* nothing of those numerous points of conduct concerning which the law professes not to prescribe." *Paley, Phil. ch.* 4.

RULE XXXII.—The verbs, *bid, make, see, hear, feel, let*, with the auxiliaries, *may, can, must, shall* and *will*, and *dare* and *need*, when used as auxiliaries, are followed by the infinitive without the prefix *to*; as, "he bids me *come*;" "we cannot make them *understand*;" "let me see you *write*;" "we heard him *relate* the story;" "we felt the earth *tremble*." "Which they let *pass*." *Locke.* "He may *go*, can *go*, must *go*, shall *go*, will *go*." "I dare *engage*; I dare *say*." "He need not *be* anxious."

NOTE 1.—In the uses of *dare* and *need*, there are some peculiarities which deserve remark.

When *dare* signifies to *defy* or *challenge*, it is regular in the tenses and persons, is a transitive verb, and is followed by the infinitive with the usual prefix; as, "he dares me to enter the list." But when it is intransitive, denoting to *have courage*, it more generally drops the personal terminations, has an anomalous past tense, and is followed by the infinitive without *to*; in short it has the form of an auxiliary, and in the German, it is classed with the auxiliaries. Examples: "I dare engage." *Pope's Works, Letter to Gay.* "I dare not confess." *Swift to Gay.* "I dare say." *Locke.* "But my Lord, you dare not do either." *Junius, Let.* 28. "Durst I *venture* to deliver my own sentiments." *Hume, Es.* 7.

The past tense, when regular, is followed by the infinitive with the usual prefix. "You have *dared to throw* more than a suspicion upon mine." *Junius, Let.* 20. The same remark may be extended to the future tense. "He will not *dare to attack* his adversary."

In like manner, *need*, when a transitive verb, is regular in its inflections; as, "A man needs more prudence"—"The army needed provisions." But when intransitive, it drops the personal terminations in the present tense, is formed like an auxiliary, and is followed by a verb, without the prefix *to*; as, "Nobody need *be* afraid he shall not have scope enough." *Locke*, 2. 22. 9. "I need not *go* any farther." *Ibm.* "Nor need we *wonder*." *Ibm.* "The lender need *be* under no fear." *Anarch. ch.* 69. "There need *be* no difficulty." *Beddoes, Hygeia*, 1. 27. "She need *dig* no more." *Spectator, No.* 121. "A man need not *be* uneasy on these grounds." *Boswell*, 3. 41. "He need not *urge* to this honorable court." *Judge Chase.*

In the use of this verb, there is another irregularity, which is peculiar, the verb being without a nominative, expressed or implied. "Whereof here *needs* no account." *Milton, P. L.* 4. 235. "There is no evidence of the fact, and there *needs* none." This is an established use of *need*.

NOTE 2.—The infinitive mode has, in its sense and use, a near affinity to a noun and often has the construction of one. It is much employed to introduce sentences which are the nominatives to verbs, as well as the objects following them; as, "*To will* is present with me, but *to perform* that which is good I find not." Here the first infinitive is the nominative to *is*, and the second begins the sentence which is the object after *find*.

NOTE 3.—A common mistake in the use of the infinitive is, to use the perfect tense after another verb in the past time, when in fact one of the verbs in the past time would correctly express the sense; thus, "It *would have been* no difficult matter *to have compiled* a volume of such amusing precedents." *Cowper to Hill, Let.* 29. Here the first verb states the time past when it was not difficult to compile a volume; at that time the compilation could not be past; the verb therefore should have been *to compile*, which is present and always indefinite.

In the following passage, we have a like use of verbs which is correct. "A free pardon was granted to the son, who *was known to have offered* indignities to the body of Varus." *Murphy's Tacitus*, 6. 1. Here the *offering of indignities* was a fact precedent to the time stated in the verb *was known*; and therefore the verb, *to have offered*, is well employed.

RULE XXXIII.—The infinitive signifying motive or purpose, often introduces a clause or sentence which is not the nominative or objective to any verb; as, "*To see* how far this reaches, and what are the causes of wrong judgment, we must remember that things are judged good or bad in a double sense." *Locke*, 2. 21. 61. "*To prevent* property from being too unequally distributed, no person should be allowed to dispose of his possessions to the prejudice of his lawful heirs." *Anarch. ch.* 62.

NOTE.—This form of sentence seems to be derived from the use of *for* before the verb, *for to see*. The modern practice is to prefix some noun, as *in order to see*, or "With a view to prevent."

RULE XXXIV.—In the use of the passive form, there is often an inversion of the order of the subject and object; thus, "The bishops and abbots were allowed their seats in the house of Lords."

Blackstone, Comm. b. 1, *ch.* 2.

Here the true construction would be, "Seats in the house of Lords were allowed to the bishops and abbots."

"Theresa was forbid the presence of the emperor." *Murphy's Tacitus*, 2. 540. NOTE.—This is a common phrase. It may be resolved thus: The presence of the emperor was forbid to Theresa—or, Theresa was forbid to approach the presence of the emperor.

RULE XXXV.—The participle of the present tense without a definitive *a* or *the*, or with any possessive attribute, usually retains the sense of its verb, and has the objective case after it; as, "The clerk is *engrossing* the bill." "The love we bear our friends is generally caused by *our finding the same dispositions* in them, which we feel in ourselves."

Pope's Letters.

"In return to *your inviting me* to your forest." *Ibm.*

But when the participle is preceded by *a* or *the*, it takes the character and government of a noun, and in most cases, must be followed by *of*; as, "The middle station of life seems to be most advantageously situated for *the gaining of* wisdom. Poverty turns our thoughts too much upon *the supplying of* our wants, and riches, upon *enjoying* our superfluities."

Spectator, No. 464.

In many cases this participle becomes a noun, without *a* or *the*; as, "It is more properly *talking* upon paper, than *writing*." *Pope, Let.*

NOTE.—The foregoing rule is often violated by our best writers, and to make it universal is to assume an authority much too dictatorial. "Some were employed in *blowing of* glass; others in *weaving of* linen."

Gibbon, Rom. Emp. ch. 10.

RULE XXXVI.—Participles of the present tense, either single or in union with the participle of the perfect tense, often perform, at once, the office of a verb and a noun; as, "*The taking* from another what is his, without his knowledge or allowance, is called stealing." *Locke*, 2. 28. 16.

"By the *mind's changing the object* to which it compares any thing."

Locke, 2. 25.

"To save them from other *people's damning them*." *Wycherley to Pope.*

"Such a plan is not capable of *being carried* into execution."

Anarch. ch. 62.

"They could not avoid *submitting* to this influence."

Boling. on Hist. Let. 8.

NOTE 1.—The participle in *ing*, though strictly active in its signification, is not unfrequently used by modern authors in a passive sense; as, "More living particles are produced—than are necessary for nutrition or for the restoration of *decomposing* organs," that is, organs suffering decomposition. *Darwin, Zoon. sect.* 39. 9. "From which caloric is *disengaging*," that is, undergoing the process of separation. *Lavoisier, Translation.* "The number is *augmenting* daily." *Ibm.* "They seemed to think Cesar was *slaying* before their eyes rather than that he was slain." *Guth. Quin.* 2. 18. "The nation had cried out loudly against the crime while it was *committing*." *Boling. on Hist. Let.* 8. "My lives are *re-printing*." *Johnson to Boswell*, 1782.

Many of this kind of participles have become mere attributes; as writing paper; looking glass; spelling or pronouncing dictionary. *Wanting* and *owing* have long had the character of passive participles, with the sense of *wanted, owed.*

NOTE 2.—The use of two participles in the place of a noun is one of the most frequent practices of our best writers; as, "This did not prevent John's *being acknowledged* and *solemnly inaugurated* Duke of Normandy." *Henry, Hist. Brit. b.* 3. The participle *being* with an attribute, supplies the place of a noun also. "As to the difference of *being more general*, that makes this maxim more remote from *being innate*." *Locke*, 1. 2. 20.

RULE XXXVII.—Participles, like attributes, agree with a sentence, a part of a sentence, or a substitute for a sentence; as, "*Concerning* relation in general, *these things may be considered*." *Locke*, 2. 25.

Here *concerning* relates to the whole of the last clause of the sentence—"These things may be considered"—all which is *concerning* relation in general.

"*This criterion will be different, according* to the nature of the object which the mind contemplates." *Enfield, Hist. Phil.* 2. 15.

That is, the difference of criterion will *accord* with the nature of the object.

"*According* to Hierocles, Ammonius was induced to execute the plan of a distinct eclectic school," &c. *Ibm. p.* 63.

Here the whole statement of facts in the last clause was *according to Hierocles*; that is, it accorded with his testimony.

"I have accepted thee, *concerning* this thing also." *Gen.* 19.

"I speak *concerning* Christ and the church." *Eph.* v. 32.

"Thus shalt thou do unto the Levites, *touching* their charge."

Num. viii. 26.

RULE XXXVIII.—Participles often stand without a noun, sentence or substitute, on which they immediately depend, being referable to either of the persons indefinitely; as, "It is not possible to act otherwise, *considering* the weakness of our nature." *Spectator.*

NOTE.—Johnson, in his Dictionary, calls this a *kind of conjunction*, and adds—"It had been more grammatically written *considered; vu*, French; but *considering* is always used."

This criticism indicates an incorrect view of the subject. *Considered*, cannot be used without a change in the structure of the sentence—"The weakness of our nature being considered." But to make this form of expression correspondent to the other clause, that ought also to be varied, and a definite person introduced; thus, "It does not appear (to us) possible to act otherwise, the weakness of our nature being considered." But this amendment would be of no advantage.

To comprehend the use of such expressions, we should consider that men find it useful to deal in abstract propositions and lay down truths without reference to persons. This manner of discoursing is often less invidious than to apply propositions or opinions to persons. To accomplish this purpose, men have devised words and modes of speech which enable them thus to communicate their ideas. In the passage cited, the first clause contains a general abstract proposition, equally applicable to any person—"It is not possible to act otherwise." That is, it is not possible for me, for you, for him, or for her; but it might be invidious to specify persons. It is not possible for John or Thomas to act otherwise, he considering the weakness of his nature. Hence the proposition is left without application; and it follows naturally that the persons who are to consider the cause, the *weakness of our nature*, should be left indefinite, or unascertained. Hence *considering* is left without a direct application to any person.

Whatever foundation there may be for this explanation, the idiom is common and well authorized.

"Generally *speaking*, the heir at law is not bound by the intention of the testator." *Paley, Phil.* 23.

"*Supposing* that electricity is actually a substance, and *taking* it for granted that it is different from caloric, does it not in all probability contain caloric, as well as all other bodies?" *Thomson, Chim. art. Caloric.*

Here is no noun expressed or implied, to which *supposing* and *taking* can be referred; *we* would be most naturally understood.

"*Supposing* the first stratum of particles to remain in their place, after their union with caloric, *we* can conceive an affinity, &c." *Ibm.* Here *supposing* may be referred to *we*, but is this the real construction?

"For *supposing* parliament had a right to meet spontaneously, without being called together, it would be impossible to conceive that all the members would agree," &c. *Blackstone, Comm. B.* 1. 2.

"The articles of this charge, *considering* by whom it was brought, were not of so high a nature as might have been expected."

Henry, Brit. B. 4. *ch.* 1.

"It is most reasonable to conclude that, *excepting* the assistance he may be supposed to have derived from his countrymen, his plan of civilization was the product of his own abilities." *Enfield, Hist. Phil.* 1. *ch.* 9.

"None of us put off our clothes, *saving* that every one put them off for washing." *Neh.* iv. 23.

"And he said unto them, hinder me not, *seeing* the Lord hath prospered my way." *Gen.* xxiv. 56.

"Lie not one to another, *seeing* that ye have put off the old man with his deeds." *Col.* iii. 9.

"*Comparing* two men, in reference to a common parent, it is easy to frame the ideas of brothers." *Locke*, 2. 25.

"*Granting* this to be true, it would help us in the species of things no farther than the tribes of animals and vegetables." *Locke*, 3. 6. 23.

RULE XXXIX.—Adverbs or Modifiers are usually placed near the words whose signification they are intended to affect.

First. They are placed before adjectives: as, *truly* wise; *sincerely* upright; *unaffectedly* polite.

Secondly. They usually follow a verb when single; as, he spoke *eloquently*: and if a verb is transitive with an object following, the adverb follows the object; as, "John received the present *gratefully*."

To this rule, the exceptions are very numerous, and not to be classed under general heads. "So it *frequently* happens." "Men *often* deceive themselves." Indeed, in many cases the position of the modifier makes no difference in the sense, and may be regulated entirely by the preference of sound, in the general structure of the period, provided it is not such as to mislead the reader, in the application of the word.

Thirdly. When one auxiliary and a participle are used, the modifier is usually placed between them or it follows the participle; as, "he was *graciously* received," or "he was received *graciously*." The first is the most elegant.

Fourthly. When two auxiliaries are used, the adverb is usually placed after the second; as, "We have been *kindly* treated." But it may follow the participle, as "We have been treated kindly;" and in some cases it may precede the auxiliaries, as "And *certainly* you must have known."

Junius, Letter 8

Fifthly. When adverbs are emphatical, they may introduce a sentence, and be separated from the word to which they belong; as, "*How completely* this most amiable of human virtues *had taken possession* of his soul!" *Port. Lect.* 8. This position of the modifier is most frequent in interrogative and exclamatory phrases.

The adverb *always* is usually placed before a verb.

Never commonly precedes a single verb, except *be*, which it follows; as, "We are *never absent* from Church on Sunday." It is sometimes placed before an auxiliary, as "He *never* has been at court;" but it is more correctly and elegantly placed after the first auxiliary, as "He has never been at court," "he has never been intoxicated."

This word has a peculiar use in the phrase; "Ask me *never* so much dowry." *Gen.* xxxiv. "The voice of charmers, charming *never* so wisely." *Ps.* lviii. The sense is, "Ask me so much dowry as *never was asked before;*" an abbreviation singularly expressive of the idea of asking to any amount or extent. Authors not understanding it, have substituted *ever* for *never*, which impairs the force, if it does not destroy the sense, of the phrase. The use of both is now common, but *never* is preferable. "Some agreements indeed, though *never* so expressly made, are deemed of so important a nature, that they ought not to rest in verbal promise only."

Blackstone, Comm. B. 3. *ch.* 9.

The use of *here* and *there*, in the introduction of sentences before verbs, forms an authorized idiom of the language; though the words may be considered as redundant. The practice may have originated in the use of the hand in pointing, in the early stage of society.

Here, there, and *where*, originally denoting *place*, are now used in reference to words, subjects and various ideas of which place is not predicable. "It is not so with respect to volitions and actions; *here* the coalesence is intimate." *Hermes, ch.* 8. "We feel pain, in the sensations, *where* we expected pleasure." *Locke*, 2. 7. 4.

Hence, whence, and *thence*, denoting the place from which a departure is stated, are used either *with* or *without* the preposition *from*. In strictness, the idea of *from* is included in the words, and it ought not to be used. These words also are used not only in reference to place, but to any argument, subject, or idea, in a discourse.

Hither, thither, and *whither*, denoting *to* a place, are obsolete in popular practice, and obsolescent in writing; being superseded by *here, there, where.* This change is evidently the effect of the all-controlling disposition of men to abridge speech, by dismissing useless syllables, or by substituting short words of easy pronunciation for those which are more difficult. Against this disposition and its effects, the critic remonstrates in vain; and we may rest assured that common convenience and utility are better guides in whatever respects the use of words, than the opinions of men in their closets. No word or syllable in a language, which is essential, or very useful, is ever lost.

While is a noun denoting *time*, and not a modifier. In this phrase, "I will go *while* you stay," the word is used in its primitive manner, without government, like many other names of portions of time—*a month, a week.*

We are accustomed to use, as modifiers, *a little* and *a great deal.* "The many letters I receive, do not *a little* encourage me." *Spectator, No.* 124. Many names are used in like manner, as modifiers of the sense of verbs. "You don't care *six-pence* whether he was wet or dry." *Johnson.*

Rule XL.—In polite and classical language, two negatives destroy the negation and express an affirmative; as, "*Nor* did he *not* perceive them," that is, he did perceive them. This phraseology is not common nor agreeable to the genius of our tongue.

The following is a common and well authorized use of negatives. "His manners are not inelegant," that is, are elegant. This manner of expression, however, when not accompanied with particular emphasis, denotes a moderate degree of the quality.

Note.—In popular language, two negatives are used for a negation, according to the practice of the ancient Greeks and the modern French. This idiom was primitive, and was retained in the Saxon; as, "Oc se kining Peada *ne* rixade *nane* while." *Sax. Chron.* p. 33. And the king Peada did *not* reign *none* while, that is, not a long time. The learned, with a view to philosophical correctness, have rejected the use of *two* negatives for *one* negation. The consequence is, we have two modes of speaking directly opposite to each other, but expressing the same thing. "He did not owe nothing," in vulgar language, "and he owed nothing," in the style of the learned, mean precisely the same thing.

Rule XLI.—Prepositions are followed by the names of objects and the objective case; as, *from* New York *to* Philadelphia; *across* the Delaware; *over* land; *by* water; *through* the air; *with* us; *for* me; *to* them; *in* you; *among* the people; *toward* us.

The preposition *to* is supposed to be omitted after verbs of *giving, yielding, affording*, and the like; as, "give them bread," instead of give bread *to* them. "Afford him protection;" "furnish her with books." But this idiom seems to be primitive, and not elliptical.

From is sometimes suppressed; as in this phrase, "He was banished the kingdom."

Home, after a verb denoting motion *to*, is always used without *to;* as, "We are going home."

After the attribute *near, to* is often omitted; as, "To bring them nearer the truth." *Massillon.* Also after *adjoining;* as, "a garden adjoining a river."

The preposition is sometimes separated from the word which governs; as, "With a longing for that state *which* he is charmed *with*," instead of *with which* he is charmed.

In many cases, the relative pronoun may be suppressed, as "I did not see the person he came *with*," that is, *with whom* he came; and in other cases, *what* is employed for the word governed, as "I know not what person he gave the present *to*."

This separation of the preposition from the word governed by it, and the suppression of the substitute, are most common and most allowable in colloquial and epistolary language. In the grave and elevated style, they are seldom elegant, and never to be admitted to the prejudice of perspicuity; as in the following passage, "Of a space or number, *which*, in a constant and endless enlarging progression, it can in thought never attain *to*."

Locke, 2. 17. 8.

A separation of the preposition to such a distance from the word with which it is connected in construction, is perplexing and inelegant.

Note.—In the use of *who* as an interrogative, there is an apparent deviation from a regular construction—it being used without distinction of case; as, "Who do you speak to?" "Who is she married to?" "Who is this reserved for?" "Who was it made by?" This idiom is not merely colloquial; it is found in the writings of our best authors. It is the Latin *cui* and *quo.*

Rule XLII.—Prepositions govern sentences and clauses or members of sentences; as, "*Without* seeking any more justifiable reasons of hostility." *Hume*, 1. 5.

"*Besides* making an expedition into Kent." *Hume*, 1. 36.

"*From* what has been said." *Blair, Serm.*

"*To* the general history of these periods will be added, &c." *Enfield, Prelim.*

"*About* the beginning of the eleventh century." *Ibm.*

"*By* observing these rules and precautions." *Ibm.*

"*In* comparing the proofs of questionable facts." *Ibm.*

"*For* want of carefully attending to the preceding distinction." *Enfield, Hist. Phil. b.* 2.

"*After* men became christians." *Paley, Evid. ch.* 1.

"*Before* you were placed at the head of affairs." *Junius, Let.* 8.

"Personal bravery is not enough to constitute the general, *without* he animates the whole army with courage." *Fielding's Socrates, p.* 188.

"Pray, get these verses by heart *against* I see you." *Chesterfield, Let.*

"*After* having made me believe that I possessed a share in your affection." *Pope, Let.*

"Ambition, envy,—will take up our minds, *without* we can possess ourselves with sobriety." *Spectator, No.* 143.

Note.—We observe, in the foregoing passages, the preposition has two uses. One is to precede a word to which other words are annexed as necessary to complete the sense—"about the beginning." Here the sense is not complete; the time is not designated. To define the time which is the object of the preposition *about*, it is necessary to add the words—"of the eleventh century"—*about that time.* So that the whole clause is really the object after the preposition.

The other use of the preposition is to precede nouns, verbs or other words which are not the object of the preposition, but which have a construction independent of it; as, "*after* men became christians." Here *men* is the nominative to *became;* yet the whole proposition is as really the object governed by *after*, as the word *hour*, in the phrase, *after that hour.* "Against I see you," is a phrase of like construction. No single word is an object or in the objective case after *against;* but the whole affirmation is the object. "*Without* we can possess ourselves," has a like construction, and though superseded, in a degree, by *unless*, a word of similar import, is a true English phrase. After [this fact] men became christians—Against [that time when] I see you—Without [this fact] we can possess ourselves.

Rule XLIII.—The modifiers of sentences, *if, though, unless,* and *lest*, may be followed by verbs in the future tense, without the usual auxiliaries, *shall, will* or *should;* as, "If his son *ask* bread, will he give him a stone?" "If he *ask* a fish, will he give him a serpent?" "Though he *slay* me, yet will I trust in him." "He shall not eat of the holy things, unless he *wash* his flesh with water." "Lest thou *say* I have made Abram rich."

Except has a like effect upon the following verb; as, "I will not let thee go, except thou *bless* me." *Whether* has been numbered also among the conjunctions, which require the conditional mode, but by an egregious mistake. It is not a connective, nor does it imply a condition or hypothesis, but an alternative.

Rule XLIV.—Connectives join two or more clauses or members in a compound sentence; as, "Keep thy tongue from evil, *and* thy lips from speaking guile."

Here are two clauses united by *and*, which continues the sense and prevents the repetition of the verb *keep.*

"I sought the Lord, *and* he heard me, *and* delivered me from all my fears." Here are three clauses combined into a sentence or period by the help of *and;* but a new verb is introduced in each, and the second connective prevents the repetition of the substitute *he* only.

"A wise son heareth his father's instruction; *but* a scorner heareth not rebuke." Here *but* joins the two clauses, but a new character is the nominative to a distinct verb, in the second clause, which exhibits a contrast to the first, and no word is omitted.

Rule XLV.—Connectives join single words, which are the nominatives to the same verb, expressed or understood, or words which follow a transitive verb or a preposition in the same case. Connectives also join verbs, adjectives, and adverbs. Example:

"*Peter* and *John* went up into the Temple."

Connectives join attributes and modifiers; as, "He is wise *and* virtuous." "An orator pleads eloquently *and* plausibly."

The connectives perform a very important office in abridging language, by enabling us to omit words which must otherwise be repeated. Thus when I say, "I esteem religion and virtue," two affirmations, "I esteem religion, I esteem virtue," are actually included in the sentence.

When several words or clauses succeed each other, it is not uncommon to omit the connective; as, "We hear nothing of causing the blind to see, the lame to walk, the deaf to hear, the lepers to be cleansed." *Paley, Evid.*

After the connective *than*, there may be and usually is an ellipsis of a verb, a noun, or other words; as, "There is none greater in this house than I." *Gen.* xxxix. 9. That is, than I am.

"Only in the throne will I be greater than thou." *Gen.* xli. That is, than thou shalt be.

"He loves his money more than his honor," that is, more than he loves his honor.

"The king of the north shall return and set forth a multitude greater than the former." *Dan.* xi. 13. That is, than the former multitude.

"I. will pull down my barns and build greater." *Luke* xii. That is, greater barns.

Sometimes other words may be suppressed without obscuring the sense; as, "It is better for me to die than to live." *Jonah* iv. That is, better than *for me* to live.

Precise rules for the ellipsis of words, in all cases, cannot be given. In general, a writer will be governed by a regard to perspicuity, and omit no word, when the want of it leaves the sense obscure or ambiguous, nor when it weakens the strength of expression. But the following remarks and examples may be of use to the student.

1. When a number of words are joined in construction, the definitive may be omitted, except before the first; as *the* sun, moon and stars; a house and garden. So also when two or more attributes agree with the same name; as a great, wise and good prince. But when attributes or names are particularly emphatical, the definitive should be expressed before each; as the sun, the moon and the stars.

2. The repetition of names adds emphasis to ideas; as, "Christ, the power of God and the wisdom of God," is more emphatical than "Christ, the power and the wisdom of God."

3. An adjective belonging to two or more nouns joined by a connective, may be omitted except before the first; as *my* house and garden; *good* qualities and actions. "*Their* interest and solicitation—" *Rambler*, 56. Nor does it make any difference that the nouns are in different numbers, as our adjectives have no distinction of number, the same word may be applied to the singular number and the plural; as a *magnificent* house and gardens; *his* house and lands. But when *a* precedes the first adjective, this construction is not elegant.

4. In compound sentences, a nominative pronoun or noun may be omitted before all the verbs except the first; as, I love, fear and respect the magistrate—instead of, I love, I fear and I respect. The substitute may sometimes be suppressed; as the man I saw, for the man *whom* I saw.

5. An adverb need not be repeated with every word which it qualifies, the connective *and* rendering it unnecessary; as, he spoke and acted *gracefully*. Here *gracefully* belongs to *speaking* as well as to *acting*.

A preposition may be omitted after a connective; as, he walked *over* the hills and the valleys, that is, *over* the valleys.

After *like* and *near*, *to* is usually omitted; as, "Like three distinct powers in mechanics." *Blackstone's Comm.* 1. 2. That is, like *to* three. "Such opinions as seemed to approach nearest the truth." *Enfield*, 2. 59. That is, nearest *to* the truth.

Likewise after *join* and *adjoin*, *to* is sometimes omitted; as, "a garden adjoining the river."

For is omitted by the poets after *mourn*.

"He mourn'd no recreant friend, no mistress coy." *Beattie.*

PUNCTUATION.

Punctuation is the marking of the several pauses which are to be observed, in reading or speaking a sentence or continued discourse. By means of pauses, a discourse is divided into periods or complete sentences, and periods into clauses or simple sentences, and these, into phrases.

A period is a sentence complete, making perfect sense, and not connected in construction with what follows. The pause after the period is marked by a point [.] and in speaking, is distinguished by a cadence or fall of the voice.

The members of a period, or clauses and phrases, are all more or less connected in sense, and according to the nearness of the connection, are marked by a comma [,] a semicolon [;] or a colon [:]

The comma is the shortest pause, and is often used to mark the construction, where very little interruption of voice is allowable.

A simple sentence or clause contains an affirmation, a command or a question, that is, one personal verb, with its nominative and adjuncts. By *adjunct*, is meant any phrase or number of words added by way of modifying or qualifying the primary words. Thus when it is said, "Cicero was an orator *of a diffuse style*," the latter words, *of a diffuse style*, are the *adjunct* of *orator*, and the whole forms a complete simple sentence, with one verb or affirmation.

A phrase contains no assertion, or does not amount to a proposition.

Comma.

Rule I. In general the parts of a simple sentence or clause are not to be separated by any point whatever; as, "Hope is necessary in every condition of life." But when a simple sentence is long, or contains a distinct phrase or phrases, modifying the affirmation, it may be divided by a comma; as, "To be very active in laudable pursuits, is the distinguishing characteristic of a man of merit." "By revenging an injury, a man is but even with his enemy." In most cases, where a short pause will give distinctness to ideas, a comma is well placed after an important word; as, "To mourn without measure, is folly; not to mourn at all, insensibility." The pause after *measure*, in this sentence, is essential to the strength of the expression. "The idea of beauty is vague and undefined, different in different minds, and diversified by time or place." *Rambler.*

Rule II. When a connective is omitted between two or more words, whether names, adjectives, pronouns, verbs or modifiers, the place is supplied by a comma; as, "Love, joy, peace and blessedness are reserved for the good." "The miseries of poverty, of sickness, of captivity, would, without hope, be insupportable." *Rambler.* "We hear nothing of causing the blind to see, the lame to walk, the deaf to hear, the lepers to be cleansed." *Paley.* "He who loves, serves and obeys his maker, is a pious man." "Industry steadily, prudently and vigorously pursued, leads to wealth." "David was a brave, martial, enterprising prince." "The most innocent pleasures are the most rational, the most delightful and the most durable."

Rule III. Two or more simple sentences closely connected in sense, or dependent on each other, are separated by a comma only; as, "When our vices leave us, we flatter ourselves we leave them." "The temperate man's pleasures are durable, because they are regular." "That all the duties of morality ought to be practised, is without difficulty discoverable, because ignorance or uncertainty would immediately involve the world in confusion and distress." *Rambler.*

Rule IV. The sentence independent or case absolute, detached affirmations or phrases involved in sentences, and other important clauses, must be separated from the other parts of a sentence, by a comma; as, "The envoy has returned, his business being accomplished." The envoy, having accomplished his business, has returned." "Providence has, I think, displayed a tenderness for mankind." *Rambler.* "The decision of patronage, who was but half a goddess, has been sometimes erroneous." *Ibm.* "The sciences, after a thousand indignities, retired from the palace of patronage." *Ibm.* "It is, in many cases, apparent." *Ibm.*

Rule V. A comma is often required to mark contrast, antithesis, or remarkable points in a sentence, and sometimes very properly separates words closely dependent in construction; as, "a good man will love himself too well to *lose*, and his neighbor too well to *win*, an estate by gaming." "Prosperity *gains* friends, and adversity *tries* them." "It is harder to avoid censure, than to gain applause."

"Though deep, yet clear; though gentle, yet not dull."

Rule VI. A single name in apposition is not separated by a comma; as, "the Apostle Peter:" but when such name is accompanied with an adjunct, it should be separated; as, "Parmenio, a friend of Alexander's, hearing the great offers that Darius had made, said, "Were I Alexander, I would accept them." "So would I," replied Alexander, "were I Parmenio."

Rule VII. Terms of address, and words of others repeated, but not introduced as a quotation, are separated by a comma; as, "Wherefore, Sirs, be of good cheer." "My son, hear the counsel of thy father." "Thus shalt thou say unto the children of Israel, I AM hath sent me unto you." *Exodus.*

Rule VIII. Modifying words and phrases, as however, nay, hence, besides, in short, finally, formerly, &c. are usually separated by a comma; as, "It is, however, the task of criticism to establish principles." *Rambler.*

Semicolon.

The semicolon is placed between the clauses of a period, which are less closely connected than such as are separated by a comma.

First. When the first division of a sentence completes a proposition, so as to have no dependence on what follows, but the following clause has a dependence on the preceding, the two parts are separated generally by a semicolon; as, "It may be laid down as a maxim, that it is more easy to take away superfluities than to supply defects; and therefore he that is culpable, because he has passed the middle point of virtue, is always accounted a fairer object of hope, than he who fails by falling short." *Rambler.* In this sentence the part of the sentence preceding the semicolon is a perfect period in itself, and might have been closed with a full point; but the author has added another division, by way of inference, and this is dependent on the first division. The author proceeds—"The one has all that perfection requires, and more, but the excess may be easily retrenched; the other wants the qualities requisite to excellence." Here the first division makes a complete proposition; but the antithesis begun by the numeral *one*, is not complete, without the last division.

"Economy is no disgrace; for it is better to live on a little, than to outlive a great deal."

"Be in peace with many; nevertheless, have but one counselor of a thousand."

"A friend cannot be known in prosperity; an enemy cannot be hid in adversity."

In general then, the semicolon separates the divisions of a sentence, when the latter division has a dependence on the former, whether the former has a dependence on the latter or not.

Secondly. When several members of a sentence have a dependence on each other, by means of a substitute for the same principal word, and the clauses, in other respects, constitute distinct propositions, the semicolon may be used; as, "Wisdom hath builded her house; *she* hath hewn out her seven pillars; *she* hath killed her beasts; *she* hath mingled her wine; *she* hath also furnished her table." *Prov.* ix.

Colon.

The Colon is used when the sense of the division of a period is complete, so as to admit of a full point, but something is added by way of illustration; as, "A brute arrives at a point of perfection that he can never pass: in a few years he has all the endowments he is capable of, and were he to live ten thousand more, would be the same thing he is at present."
Spectator, No. 111.

Period.

The Period or full point marks a completion of the sense, a cadence of the voice, and the longest pause used between sentences. It closes a discourse also, or marks a completion of a subject, chapter or section.

The full point is used also after initials when used alone, as after N. S. for New Style; and after abbreviations, as *Croc. Anglic.* for Crocus Anglicanus.

To these may be added,

The dash [—] which marks a break in the sentence or an abrupt turn; as, "If thou art he—but O how fallen!"

The interrogation point [?] that closes a sentence which asks a question; as, "How long, ye simple ones, will ye love simplicity?"

The exclamation point [!] which is used after sudden expressions of surprise, or other emotions; as, "O happiness! Our being's end and aim!"

The parenthesis ( ) and hooks [ ] include a remark or clause not essential to the sentence in construction, but useful in explaining it or introducing an important idea. They mark a moderate pause, and the clause included is read with a depressed tone of voice; as,

"Know then this truth (enough for man to know)
Virtue alone is happiness below." *Pope.*

It will be readily seen that the sentence is not at all dependent on the parenthetical clause; but the converse is not true, for that clause has a dependence more or less remote on the sentence. Thus, *enough for man to know*, is not intelligible without connecting it with the parts of the sentence preceding and following. So in this passage; "If any one pretends to be so sceptical, as to deny his own existence (for really to doubt of *it*, is manifestly impossible) let him enjoy his beloved happiness." *Locke*, 4. 10. 2. The included clause here is connected with the preceding part of the sentence, and *it* is a substitute for *existence*.

With regard to the duration of the pauses, it may be observed that the comma, semicolon, colon and full point, may bear to each other the proportion of one, two, four and six; and the interrogation point and exclamation point may be considered each as equal in time to the colon or period. But no precise rule can be given, which shall extend to every case; the length of the pauses must depend much on the nature of the discourse, and their respective proportions may be often varied to advantage by a judicious speaker.

DIRECTIONS

FOR THE

PRONUNCIATION OF WORDS.

The principal sounds of the vowels are the *first* or *long*, and the *second* or *short*.

Examples of the first or long sound.	*Examples of the second or short sound.*
a in make, fate, grace.	a in mat, ban, grand.
e in me, mete, meter.	e in bet, men, send.
i in pine, bind, strife.	i in bit, pin, miss.
o in note, hold, port.	o in not, boss, bond.
u in true, duty, rude.	u in dun, must, refund.
y in dry, defy, imply.	y in pity, cycle, synonym.

The principal things to be regarded in learning the pronunciation of English words, are the accent and the sound of the vowel of the accented syllable.

RULE I. This mark ′ called an accent, designates the accented syllable.

II. The accent placed immediately after a vowel indicates the vowel to have its first or long sound, either at the end or in the middle of a syllable; as in sa′cred, pre′cept, ri′ot, po′et, mu′sic, cy′press; degra′de, reple′te, divi′de, explo′de, intru′de.

III. A horizontal mark or point over a vowel shows it to be long, and when no accent is found in the word, this mark designates the accented syllable; as in discōurse, encrōach, bestōw, enrōll, cōurser, sūitable.

IV. An accent placed immediately after a consonant, or combination of consonants in the same syllable, indicates that the vowel of that syllable, if unpointed, is short; as in hab′it, ten′et, con′duct, ul′cer, sym′bol; adapt′, intend′, predict′, despond′, abrupt′.

Exceptions.

1. A pointed vowel has the sound designated by the point or points; as in full′ness, al′terable, book′ish, convey′.
2. *a* before *ll*, *ld* and *lk*, in monosyllables or accented syllables, has its broad sound like *aw;* as in befall′, bald′ness, walk′ing.
3. *o* before *ll* is long; as in enrōll′.

V. An accent immediately after a diphthong, or after a syllable containing one, designates the accented syllable, but the diphthong has its proper sound; as in renew′, devour′, avow′, appoint′, annoy′.

VI. This mark ‵ called in Greek the grave accent, placed before a vowel, indicates that vowel to have its Italian sound, as in ‵ask, b‵ar, f‵ather, m‵ask. In words of two or more syllables, when no other accent is used, this designates the accented syllable; as in ‵answerable, b‵argain.

VII. Two accents immediately before *c*, *t* or *s*, indicate that *c*, *t* or *s*, in pronunciation, coalesces with the following vowel, and form the sound of *sh* or *zh*, which closes the syllable, and of course the preceding vowel is short. Thus, vi″cious, ambi″tion, are pronounced vish′us, ambish′on; vi′sion is pronounced *vizh′un*.

VIII. *C* before *a*, *o* and *u*, and in some other situations, is a close articulation, like *k*, and in the vocabulary of this work, whenever it is equivalent to *k*, it is marked thus Ͼ.

Before *e*, *i* and *y*, *c* is precisely equivalent to *s*, in *same, this;* as in cedar, civil, cypress, capacity.

IX. *E* final answers the following purposes.

1. It indicates that the preceding vowel is long; as in hate, mete, sire, robe, lyre; abate, recede, invite, remote, intrude.
2. It indicates that *c* preceding has the sound of *s*, as in lace, lance, and that *g* preceding has the sound of *j*, as in charge, page, challenge.
3. In proper English words, *e* final never forms a syllable, and in most words, in the terminating unaccented syllable, it is silent and useless. Thus, motive, genuine, examine, juvenile, reptile, granite, are pronounced motiv, genuin, examin, juvenil, reptil, granit.

In a few words of foreign origin, *e* final forms a syllable; as in syncope, simile. These are noted in their place.

X. *E* final is silent after *l* in the following terminations, ble, cle, dle, fle, gle, kle, ple, tle, zle; as in able, manacle, cradle, ruffle, mangle, wrinkle, supple, rattle, puzzle, which are pronounced a′bl, man′acl, cra′dl, ruf′fl, man′gl, wrin′kl, sup′pl, puz′zl.

XI. In the termination *en*, *e* is usually silent; as in token, broken, pronounced tokn, brokn.

XII. The termination *ous* in adjectives and their derivatives is pronounced *us;* as in gracious, pious, pompously.

XIII. The combinations *ce*, *ci*, *ti*, before a vowel, have the sound of *sh;* as in cetaceous, gracious, motion, partial, ingratiate, pronounced cetashus, grashus, moshon, parshal, ingrashate.

But *ti* after a consonant have the sound of *ch;* as in christian, bastion, mixtion, pronounced chrischan, baschan, mixchun. So in combustion, digestion.

Si after an accented vowel are pronounced like *zh;* as in Ephesian, confusion, pronounced Ephezhan, confuzhon.

When *ci* or *ti* precede similar combinations, as in pronunciation, negotiation, they may be pronounced *ce*, instead of *she*, to prevent a repetition of the latter syllable; as pronunciashon, instead of pronunshashon.

XIV. *Gh*, both in the middle and at the end of words, are silent; as in caught, bought, fright, nigh, sigh; pronounced caut, baut, frite, ni, si.

Exceptions. In the following words *gh* are pronounced as *f*—cough, chough, clough, enough, hough, laugh, rough, slough, tough, trough.

XV. When *wh* begin a word, the aspirate *h* precedes *w* in pronunciation, as in what, whiff, whale, pronounced hwat, hwif, hwale; *w* having precisely the sound of *oo*, French *ou*.

In the following words, *w* is silent—who, whom, whose, whoop, whole, whore.

XVI. *H* after *r* has no sound nor use; as in rheum, rhyme, pronounced reum, ryme.

XVII. *K* and *g* before *n* are silent; as in know, gnaw, pronounced no, naw.

XVIII. *W* before *r* is silent; as in wring, wreath, pronounced ring, reath.

XIX. *B* after *m* is silent; as in dumb, numb, pronounced dum, num.

XX. *L* before *k* is silent; as in baulk, walk, talk, pronounced bauk, wauk, tauk.

XXI. *Ph* have the sound of *f;* as in philosophy.

XXII. The combination *ng* has two sounds; one, as in sing, singer; the other, as in finger, linger, longer. The latter is the more close palatal sound; but the distinction can only be learned by the ear.

XXIII. The letters *cl*, answering to *kl*, are pronounced as if written *tl;* clear, clean, are pronounced tlear, tlean.

Gl are pronounced as *dl;* glory is pronounced dlory.

XXIV. *N* after *m*, and closing a syllable, is silent; as in hymn, condemn.

XXV. *P* before *s* and *t* is mute; as in psalm, pseudology, ptarmigan, pronounced s‵am, sudology, tarmigan.

The letter *y* unaccented and terminating words of more syllables than one is short, like *i* in pity and ability. This letter, in the plural number of nouns and in the third person singular of the present tense of verbs, is dropped, and *ie* substituted and followed by *s*. The termination thus formed is pronounced *iz;* as from vanity, is formed vanities, pronounced vanitiz; from the verb to *pity* is formed pities, pronounced pitiz.

But when *y* in monosyllabic verbs, and accented *y* in other verbs ends the word, the termination *ies* in the third person is pronounced *ize;* as in flies from fly, defies from defy. So cries, both the verb and noun, is pronounced crize.

S has two sounds; its proper sound as in *see*, and that of *z* as in *his*. It has its proper sound after the following consonants *f, p, t, k,* Ȼ, and *th* aspirate, whether they end the word or are followed by *e* final; as in chiefs, caps, streets, franks, hates, hopes, fates, flakes, breaths, wreaths. It has the sound of *z*, after *b, c* followed by *e* final, *d, g, gh, l, m, n, n, r, s* and *ss, z, v, aw, ay, ew, ey, ow, oy, sh, ng, th* vocal, *ch, oe, ie,* both in nouns and verbs, and whether these letters end the word or are followed by *e* final; as in robs, robes, races, rods, rides, rags, rages, toils, dreams, sighs, rains, bars, waves, roses, passes, mazes, laws, days, news, preys, vows, joys, brushes, sings, breathes, churches, foes, goes, flies.

Sc before *e, i* and *y*, have only the sound of the single letter *s* or *c*. Thus *scene* is pronounced *sene; sciolist, siolist.*

S before *m*, in the terminations, *asm, esm, ism*, has the sound of *z;* as in spasm, telesm, baptism.

The pronunciation of the word which is radical or primitive in English is to be observed in the derivatives. Thus the letter *s* is directed to be pronounced as *z* in *bruise*, and this direction is to be observed in all its derivatives. *Earth* being directed to be pronounced *erth*, all its derivatives and compounds are to follow the same direction. So *freight* is pronounced *frate.*

POINTED LETTERS.

Ạ has the short sound of *aw;* as in *alter, what.*
Ȼ [*ke*] is the same as *k;* as in *cape, access.*
Ẹ whether by itself or followed by *i* or *y*, has the sound of *a* long; as in *where, there, vein, survey.*
Ï has the sound of *e* long, or *ee;* as in *machine.*
Ö has the sound of *oo*, or French *ou;* as in *move.*
Ŏ has the sound of short *u;* as in *come, wonder.*
ỌỌ have the short sound of *oo;* as in *book, look.*
Ụ has the sound of *oo;* as above, as in *full, pull.*
C̄H have the French sound, like *sh;* as in *chaise.*
Ġ has the sound of *j.*
T̄H have their vocal sound; as in *thou, this.*
Ʊ has the sound of *yu;* as in *unite, use,* pronounced *yunite, yuse.*

In digraphs or combinations of vowels, of which one only is pronounced, the mark over one vowel designates the sound, and the other vowel is quiescent; as in beār, bōat, cōurse, sōul, blŏod, bōw, lōw, crōw, bestōw.

The digraphs *ea, ee, ei, ie* have uniformly the sound of long *e;* as in meat, feet, seize, siege.

Before the letter *r*, there is a slight sound of *e* between the vowel and the consonant. Thus bare, parent, apparent, mere, mire, more, pure, pyre, are pronounced nearly baer, paerent, appaerent, me-er, mier, moer, puer, pyer. This pronunciation proceeds from the peculiar articulation *r*, and it occasions a slight change of the sound of *a*, which can be learned only by the ear.

The vowels in unaccented syllables are either short, or they have their first sound slightly pronounced. Thus in the words *produce, domestic, o* has its first sound, but pronounced rapidly and without force. In syllables which have a secondary accent, the vowel is often long, and little distinguishable from that in syllables having the primary accent; as in legislature, in which *a* in the third syllable has its long sound.

In syllables wholly unaccented, the sounds of the vowels are so rapidly uttered, that they cannot be designated by written characters; they are all sounded nearly alike, and any attempt at a proper notation of such evanescent sounds serves only to perplex or mislead the learner.

Words of anomalous pronunciation, not falling under the foregoing rules, are printed in an orthography which expresses their true pronunciation.

The Welsh *z* has the sound of the vocal *th*, in thou.

In the expression of the sounds of foreign words in English characters there is often an insurmountable difficulty, as there are sounds, in some languages, which English characters, according to our use of them, will not express with precision. But in regard to etymology, such exact expression of sounds is not necessary. For example, in regard to the affinity of words, it is wholly immaterial whether the Hebrew ב is expressed by *b, v,* or *bh;* whether ד is expressed by *d, th,* or *dh;* whether ח is expressed by *h* or *ch;* and whether ק is expressed by *k, q,* or *qu*. So in Arabic it is immaterial whether ذ is expressed by *th* or *ds*, and غ by *g* or *kh*.

The Arabic vowel *fatha*, I am informed, is differently pronounced by the Persians and Arabians; the one nation pronouncing it as the English *a* in *mate;* the other, generally, as *a* in *fall*. I have expressed it by *a* or *aw*.

It was desirable that the Russ, Saxon, Swedish, and German words should be printed with the appropriate types; but the utility would have hardly compensated for the expense of suitable fonts, and no essential inconvenience can result from the want of them; the English characters being sufficient to express the sounds of the letters, with all the exactness which etymology requires.

ABBREVIATIONS EXPLAINED.

a.	stands	for adjective.
adv.	,,	for adverb.
con.	,,	for connective or conjunction.
exclam.	,,	for exclamation, or interjection.
n.	,,	for name or noun.
Obs.	,,	for obsolete.
prep.	,,	for preposition.
pp.	,,	for participle passive.
ppr.	,,	for participle of the present tense.
pret.	,,	for preterit tense.
pron.	,,	for pronoun.
v. i.	,,	for verb intransitive.
v. t.	,,	for verb transitive.
Ar.	,,	for Arabic.
Arm.	,,	for Armoric.
Ch.	,,	for Chaldee.
Corn.	,,	for Cornish.
Dan.	,,	for Danish.
D.	,,	for Dutch or Belgic.
Eng.	,,	for England or English.
Eth.	,,	for Ethiopic.
Fr.	,,	for French.
G. or *Ger.*	,,	for German.
Gr.	,,	for Greek.
Goth.	,,	for Gothic.
Heb.	,,	for Hebrew.
Ice.	,,	for Icelandic.
Ir.	,,	for Irish, Hiberno-Celtic, and Gaelic.
It.	,,	for Italian.
Lat. or *L.*	,,	for Latin.
Per.	,,	for Persic or Persian.
Port.	,,	for Portuguese.
Russ.	,,	for the Russ language, or Russian.
Sam.	,,	for Samaritan.
Sans.	,,	for Sanscrit.
Sax.	,,	for Saxon, or Anglo-Saxon.
Sp.	,,	for Spanish.
Sw.	,,	for Swedish.
Syr.	,,	for Syriac.
W.	,,	for Welsh.

ALPHABETS.

Hebrew and Chaldee.		*Samaritan.*
Aleph	א	ࠀ
Beth	ב	ࠁ
Gimel	ג	ࠂ
Daleth	ד	ࠃ
He	ה	ࠄ
Vau	ו	ࠅ
Zain	ז	ࠆ
Cheth	ח	ࠇ
Teth	ט	ࠈ
Yod	י	ࠉ
Caph	כ ך	ࠊ
Lamed	ל	ࠋ
Mem	מ ם	ࠌ
Nun	נ ן	ࠍ
Samech	ס	ࠎ
Ain	ע	ࠏ
Phe	פ ף	ࠐ
Tzaddi	ץ צ	ࠑ
Koph	ק	ࠒ
Resch	ר	ࠓ
Sin Shin	שׂ שׁ	ࠔ
Thau	ת	ࠕ

Arabic. Names.	final.	medial.	initial.
Elif	ا ـا	ـا	ا
Be	ب ـب	ـبـ	بـ
Jim	ج ـج	ـجـ	جـ
Dal	د ـد	ـد	د
Dhal	ذ ـذ	ـذ	ذ
He	ه ـه	ـهـ	هـ
Wau	و ـو	ـو	و
Ze	ز ـز	ـز	ز
Ha	ح ـح	ـحـ	حـ
Kha	خ ـخ	ـخـ	خـ
Ta	ط ـط	ـطـ	طـ
Tha	ظ ـظ	ـظـ	ظـ
Ye	ي ـي	ـيـ	يـ
Kef	ك ـك	ـكـ	كـ
Lam	ل ـل	ـلـ	لـ
Mim	م ـم	ـمـ	مـ
Nun	ن ـن	ـنـ	نـ
wanting	—	—	—
Ain	ع ـع	ـعـ	عـ
Gain	غ ـغ	ـغـ	غـ
Fe	ف ـف	ـفـ	فـ
Tsad	ص ـص	ـصـ	صـ
Dhad	ض ـض	ـضـ	ضـ
Kaf	ق ـق	ـقـ	قـ
Re	ر ـر	ـر	ر
Sin	س ـس	ـسـ	سـ
Shin	ش ـش	ـشـ	شـ
Te	ت ـت	ـتـ	تـ
The	ث ـث	ـثـ	ثـ

Syriac. Names.	final.	medial.	initial.
Olaph	ܐ ܐ	ܐ	ܐ
Beth	ܒ ܒ	ܒ	ܒ
Gomal	ܓ ܓ	ܓ	ܓ
Dolath	ܕ ܕ	ܕ	ܕ
He	ܗ ܗ	ܗ	ܗ
Vau	ܘ ܘ	ܘ	ܘ
Zain	ܙ ܙ	ܙ	ܙ
Heth	ܚ ܚ	ܚ	ܚ
Teth	ܛ ܛ	ܛ	ܛ
Yud	ܝ ܝ	ܝ	ܝ
Coph	ܟ ܟ	ܟ	ܟ
Lomad	ܠ ܠ	ܠ	ܠ
Mim	ܡ ܡ	ܡ	ܡ
Nun	ܢ ܢ	ܢ	ܢ
Semcath	ܣ ܣ	ܣ	ܣ
Ee	ܥ ܥ	ܥ	ܥ
Pe	ܦ ܦ	ܦ	ܦ
Tsode	ܨ ܨ	ܨ	ܨ
Kuph	ܩ ܩ	ܩ	ܩ
Rish	ܪ ܪ	ܪ	ܪ
Shin	ܫ ܫ	ܫ	ܫ
Tau	ܬ ܬ	ܬ	ܬ

The Arabic vowels are only *three*, viz. Fatha َ a, e. Kesra ِ e, i. Dhamma ُ o, u.
The diacritical signs are Jesm ْ or quiescent Sheva. Teshdid ّ or Dagesh forte. Hamza ء placed over Elif when *radical*.
Nunnation or double final vowels, ً ٍ ٌ, showing that they are to be pronounced *an*, *en* or *in*, *on* or *un*.

The Persians use the Arabic alphabet with the addition of Pe پ; Che چ; Ghaf ——; and Zhe ژ.

Ethiopic.

	Short.			Long.					Short.			Long.			
Alph	አ a	ኡ u	ኢ i	ኣ a	ኤ e	እ y	ኦ o	Mai	መ ma	ሙ mu	ሚ mi	ማ ma	ሜ me	ም my	ሞ mo
Bet	በ ba	ቡ bu	ቢ bi	ባ ba	ቤ be	ብ by	ቦ bo	Nahas	ነ na	ኑ nu	ኒ ni	ና na	ኔ ne	ን ny	ኖ no
Gemel	ገ ga	ጉ gu	ጊ gi	ጋ ga	ጌ ge	ግ gy	ጎ go	Saut	ሠ sa	ሡ su	ሢ si	ሣ sa	ሤ se	ሥ sy	ሦ so
Den	ደ da	ዱ du	ዲ di	ዳ da	ዴ de	ድ dy	ዶ do	Ain	ዐ a	ዑ u	ዒ i	ዓ a	ዔ e	ዕ y	ዖ o
Hoi	ሀ ha	ሁ hu	ሂ hi	ሃ ha	ሄ he	ህ hy	ሆ ho	Af	ፈ fa	ፉ fu	ፊ fi	ፋ fa	ፌ fe	ፍ fy	ፎ fo
Waw	ወ wa	ዉ wu	ዊ wi	ዋ wa	ዌ we	ው wy	ዎ wo	Pait	ጰ pa	ጱ pu	ጲ pi	ጳ pa	ጴ pe	ጵ py	ጶ po
Zai	ዘ za	ዙ zu	ዚ zi	ዛ za	ዜ ze	ዝ zy	ዞ zo	Psa	ፐ pa	ፑ pu	ፒ pi	ፓ pa	ፔ pe	ፕ py	ፖ po
Haut	ሐ ha	ሑ hu	ሒ hi	ሓ ha	ሔ he	ሕ hy	ሖ ho	Zadai	ጸ za	ጹ zu	ጺ zi	ጻ za	ጼ ze	ጽ zy	ጾ zo
Hharm	ኀ ha	ኁ hu	ኂ hi	ኃ ha	ኄ he	ኅ hy	ኆ ho	Zappi	ፀ zza	ፁ zzu	ፂ zzi	ፃ zza	ፄ zze	ፅ zzy	ፆ zzo
Tait	ጠ tha	ጡ thu	ጢ thi	ጣ tha	ጤ the	ጥ thy	ጦ tho	Kaf	ቀ ka	ቁ ku	ቂ ki	ቃ ka	ቄ ke	ቅ ky	ቆ ko
Yaman	የ ya	ዩ yu	ዪ yi	ያ ya	ዬ ye	ይ yy	ዮ yo	Rees	ረ ra	ሩ ru	ሪ ri	ራ ra	ሬ re	ር ry	ሮ ro
Quaf	ከ ka	ኩ ku	ኪ ki	ካ ka	ኬ ke	ክ ky	ኮ ko	Saat	ሰ sa	ሱ su	ሲ si	ሳ sa	ሴ se	ስ sy	ሶ so
Lawi	ለ la	ሉ lu	ሊ li	ላ la	ሌ le	ል ly	ሎ lu	Tawi	ተ ta	ቱ tu	ቲ ti	ታ ta	ቴ te	ት ty	ቶ to

Note.—In the foregoing alphabets, the order of the Arabic and Ethiopic letters is conformed to that of the Chaldee and Hebrew. The reader will observe two or three defects, which are owing to the imperfection of the fonts of type.

VOL. I.

AN AMERICAN DICTIONARY OF THE ENGLISH LANGUAGE.

A A A

A is the first letter of the Alphabet in most of the known languages of the earth; in the Ethiopic however it is the *thirteenth*, and in the Runic the *tenth*. It is naturally the first letter, because it represents the first vocal sound naturally formed by the human organs: being the sound uttered with a mere opening of the mouth without constraint, and without any effort to alter the natural position or configuration of the lips. Hence this letter is found in many words first uttered by infants; which words are the names of the objects with which infants are first concerned, as the breast, and the parents. Hence in Hebrew אם am, is mother, and אב ab, is father. In Chaldee and Syriac *abba* is father; in Arabic, *aba*; in Ethiopic, *abi*; in Malayan and Bengalese, *bappa*; in Welsh, *tad*, whence we retain *daddy*; in Old Greek and in Gothic *atta*; in Irish, *aithair*; in Cantabrian, *aita*; in Lapponic, *atki*; in Abyssinian, *abba*; in Amharic, *aba*; in Shilhic and Melindane, African dialects, *baba*; and *papa* is found in many nations. Hence the Latin *mamma*, the breast, which is, in popular use, the name of mother; in Swedish, *amma*, is a nurse. This list might be greatly extended; but these examples prove *A* to be the first natural vocal sound, and entitled to the first place in alphabets. The Hebrew name of this letter, *aleph*, signifies an *ox* or a *leader*.

A has in English, three sounds; the long or slender, as in *place*, *fate*; the broad, as in *wall*, *fall*, which is shortened in *salt*, *what*; and the open, as in *father*, *glass*, which is shortened in *rather*, *fancy*. Its primitive sound was probably *aw*. *A* is also an abbreviation of the Saxon *an* or *ane*, *one*, used before words beginning with an articulation; as *a* table, instead of *an* table, or one table. This is a modern change; for in Saxon *an* was used before articulations, as well as vowels, as, *an tid*, a time, *an gear*, a year [See *An*.]

This letter serves as a prefix to many English words, as in *asleep; awake; afoot; aground; agoing*. In some cases, this is a contraction of the Teutonic *ge*, as in *asleep*, *aware*, from the Saxon *geslapan*, to sleep; *gewarian*, to beware; the Dutch *gewaar*. Sometimes it is a corruption of the Saxon *on*, as *again* from *ongean*, *awake* from *onwacian*, to watch or wake. Before participles, it may be a contraction of the Celtic *ag*, the sign of the participle of the present tense; as, *ag-radh*, saying; *a saying*, *a going*. Or this may be a contraction of *on*, or what is equally probable, it may have proceeded from a mere accidental sound produced by negligent utterance. In some words, *a* may be a contraction of *at*, *of*, *in*, *to*, or *an*. In some words of Greek original, *a* is privative, giving to them a negative sense, as in *anonymous*, from *a* and ονομα name.

Among the ancients, *A* was a numeral denoting 500; and with a dash Ā 5000. In the Hebrew, Syr. Ch. Sam. and Ar. it denotes *one* or unity. In the Julian Calendar, *A* is the first of the seven dominical letters.

Among logicians, *A*, as an abbreviation, stands for a universal affirmative proposition. *A* asserts; *E* denies. Thus in *barbara*, *a* thrice repeated denotes so many of the propositions to be universal.

The Romans used *A* to signify a negative or dissent in giving their votes; *A* standing for *antiquo*, I oppose or object to the proposed law. Opposed to this letter were *U R*, *uti rogas*, be it as you desire—the words used to express assent to a proposition. These letters were marked on wooden ballots, and each voter had an affirmative and a negative put into his hands, one of which at pleasure he gave as his vote.—In criminal trials, *A* stood for *absolvo*, I acquit; *C* for *condemno*, I condemn; and *N L* for *non liquet*, it is not evident; and the judges voted by ballots thus marked.—In inscriptions, *A* stands for *Augustus*; or for *ager*, *aiunt*, *aurum*, *argentum*, &c.

A is also used for *anno*, or *ante*; as in *Anno Domini*, the year of our Lord; *anno mundi*, the year of the world; *ante meridiem*, before noon; and for *arts*, in *artium magister*, master of arts. Among the Romans, *A U C* stood for *anno ab urbe condita*, from the building of the city or Rome.

In *algebra*, *a* and the first letters of the alphabet represent known quantities—the last letters are sometimes used to represent unknown quantities.

In *music*, *A* is the nominal of the sixth note in the natural diatonic scale—called by Guido *la*. It is also the name of one of the two natural moods; and it is the open note of the 2d string of the violin, by which the other strings are tuned and regulated.

In *pharmacy*, *a* or *aa*, abbreviations of the Greek *ana*, signify *of each separately*, or that the things mentioned should be taken in quantities of the same weight or measure.

In *chimistry*, *A A A* stand for *amalgama*, or *amalgamation*.

In *commerce*, *A* stands for *accepted*, as in case of a bill of exchange. Merchants also number their books by the letters—A, B, C, instead of figures. Public officers number their exhibits in the same manner; as the document A, or B.

Alpha and Omega, the first and last letters of the Greek Alphabet, are used in Scripture for the *beginning* and *end*—representative of Christ.

In *mathematics*, letters are used as representatives of numbers, lines, angles and quantities. In *arguments*, letters are substituted for persons, in cases supposed, or stated for illustration, as *A* contracts with *B* to deliver property to *D*.—In the English phraseology "a landlord has a hundred *a* year," "the sum amounted to ten dollars *a* man," *a* is merely the adjective *one*, and this mode of expression is idiomatic; a hundred in *a* [*one*] year; ten dollars to *a* [*one*] man.

AAM, *n.* [Ch. אמה, or אמא a cubit, a measure containing 5 or 6 palms.] A measure of liquids among the Dutch equal to 288 English pints.

AARON'IC, *a.* Pertaining to Aaron, the Jewish High Priest, or to the priesthood of which he was the head. *Doddridge.*

AB, In English names, is an abbreviation of Abbey or Abbot; as *Abbingdon, Abbeytown, Abbeyhill, Abbot-town.*

AB, a prefix to words of Latin origin, and a Latin preposition, as in *abscond*, is the Greek απο, and the Eng. *of*, Ger. *ab*, D. *af*, Sw. Dan. *af*, written in ancient Latin *af*. It denotes *from*, separating or departure.

AB, The Hebrew name of Father. See *Abba.*

AB, The eleventh month of the Jewish civil year, and the fifth of the ecclesiastical year, answering to a part of July, and a part of August. In the Syriac Calendar, *ab* is the name of the last summer month.

AB'ACIST, *n.* [from *abacus.*]
One that casts accounts; a calculator. [*Not much used.*]

ABACK' *adv.* [*a* and *back*, Sax. *on bæc*; at, on or towards the back. See *Back.*]
Towards the back; on the back part; backward. In seamen's language it signifies the situation of the sails, when pressed back against the mast by the wind.
Taken aback, is when the sails are carried back suddenly by the wind.
Laid aback, is when the sails are purposely placed in that situation to give the ship sternway. *Mariner's Dict.*

AB'ACOT, *n.* The cap of State, formerly used by English Kings, wrought into the figure of two crowns.

ABAC'TOR, *n.* [Latin from *abigo*, *ab* and *ago*, to drive.]
In *law*, one that feloniously drives away or steals a herd or numbers of cattle at once, in distinction from one that steals a sheep or two.

AB'ACUS *n.* [L. *abacus*, any thing flat, as a cupboard, a bench, a slate, a table or board for games; Gr. αβαξ. Usually deduced from the Oriental, אבק abak, dust, because the ancients used tables covered with dust for making figures and diagrams.]

1. Among the Romans, a cupboard or buffet.
2. An instrument to facilitate operations in arithmetic; on this are drawn lines; a counter on the lowest line, is *one*; on the next, *ten*; on the third, a *hundred*, &c. On the spaces, counters denote half the number of the line above. Other schemes are called by the same name. The name is also given to a table of numbers cast up, as an *abacus* of addition; and by analogy, to the art of numbering, as in Knighton's Chronicon. *Encyc.*
3. In *architecture*, a table constituting the upper member or crowning of a column and its capital. It is usually square, but sometimes its sides are arched inwards. The name is also given to a concave molding on the capital of the Tuscan pedestal; and to the plinth above the boultin in the Tuscan and Doric orders. *Encyc.*

AB'ACUS PYTHAGORICUS, The multiplication table, invented by Pythagoras.

ABACUS HARMONICUS, The structure and disposition of the keys of a musical instrument.

ABACUS MAJOR, A trough used in mines, to wash ore in. *Encyc.*

AB'ADA, *n.* A wild animal of Africa, of the size of a steer, or half grown colt, having two horns on its forehead and a third on the nape of the neck. Its head and tail resemble those of an ox, but it has cloven feet, like the stag. *Cyc.*

ABAD'DON, *n.* [Heb. Ch. Syr. Sam. אבד, to be lost, or destroyed, to perish.]
1. The destroyer, or angel of the bottomless pit. Rev. ix.
2. The bottomless pit. *Milton.*

AB'AFT, *adv.* or *prep.* [Sax. *eft* or *æft*, again. Hence *efter* or *æfter*, after, subsequent; Sax. *æftan*, behind in place; to which word *be* is prefixed—*beæftan*, behind, and this word is corrupted into *abaft.*]
A sea-term signifying in or at the hinder part of a ship, or the parts which lie towards the stern; opposed to *afore*. Relatively it denotes *further aft* or towards the stern; as *abaft* the mainmast. *Abaft the beam*, is in that arch of the horizon which is between a line drawn at right angles with the keel, and the point to which the stern is directed. It is often contracted into *aft.* *Mar. Dict.*

AB'AGUN, *n.* The name of a fowl in Ethiopia, remarkable for its beauty and for a sort of horn, growing on its head. The word signifies stately Abbot. *Crabbe.*

ABAISANCE, [See *Obeisance.*]

ABA LIENATE *v. t.* [See *Alienate, Aliene.*]
To transfer the title of property from one to another—a term of the civil law—*rarely or never used in common law proceedings.*

ABALIENA'TION, *n.* The transferring of title to property. [See *Alienation.*]

ABAN'DON, *v. t.* [Fr. *abandonner*; Sp. and Port. *abandonar*; It. *abbandonare*; said to be from *ban*, and *donner*, to give over to the ban or proscription; or from *a* or *ab* and *bandum*, a flag or ensign.]
1. To forsake entirely; as to *abandon* a hopeless enterprize.

> Wo to that generation by which the testimony of God shall be *abandoned*. *Dr. Mason.*

2. To renounce and forsake; to leave with a view never to return; to desert as lost or desperate; as to *abandon* a country; to *abandon* a cause or party.
3. To give up or resign without control, as when a person yields himself, without restraint, to a propensity; as to *abandon* one's self *to* intemperance. Abandoned *over* and abandoned *of* are obsolete.
4. To resign; to yield, relinquish, or give over entirely.

> Verus *abandoned* the cares of empire to his wiser colleague. *Gibbon.*

ABAN'DON, *n.* One who totally forsakes or deserts. *Obs.*
2. A relinquishment. [*Not used.*] *Kames.*

ABAN'DONED, *pp.* Wholly forsaken or deserted.
2. Given up, as to a vice; hence, extremely wicked, or sinning without restraint; irreclaimably wicked.

ABAN'DONER, *n.* One who abandons.

ABAN'DONING, *ppr.* Forsaking or deserting wholly; renouncing; yielding one's self without restraint.

ABAN'DONING, *n.* A forsaking; total desertion.

> He hoped his past meritorious actions might outweigh his present *abandoning* the thought of future actions. *Clarendon.*

ABAN'DONMENT, *n.* A total desertion; a state of being forsaken.

ABAN'GA, *n.* The ady; a species of Palmtree. [See *Ady.*]

ABANNI''TION, *n.* [*Low Lat.*]
A banishment for one or two years for manslaughter. [*Not used.*] *Dict.*

ABAPTIS'TON, *n.* The perforating part of the trephine, an instrument used in trepanning. *Coxe.*

ABA'RE, *v. t.* [Sax. *abarian.* See *Bare.*]
To make bare; to uncover. [*Not in use.*]

ABARTICULA'TION, *n.* [See *Articulate.*]
In *anatomy*, that species of articulation or structure of joints, which admits of manifest or extensive motion; called also diarthrosis and dearticulation. *Encyc. Coxe.*

ABAS', *n.* A weight in Persia used in weighing pearls, one eighth less than the European carat. *Encyc.*

ABA'SE, *v. t.* [Fr. *abaisser*, from *bas*, low, or the bottom; W. *bais*; Latin and Gr. *basis*; Eng. *base*; It. *Abbassare*; Sp. *baxo*, low. See *Abash.*]
1. The literal sense of *abase* is to lower or depress, to throw or cast down, as used by Bacon, "to *abase* the eye." But the word is seldom used in reference to material things.
2. To cast down; to reduce low; to depress; to humble; to degrade; applied to the passions, rank, office, and condition in life.

> Those that walk in pride he is able to *abase*. Dan. iv.
>
> Whosoever exalteth himself shall be *abased*. Mat. xxiii. Job, xl. 2 Cor. xi.

ABA'SED, *pp.* Reduced to a low state, humbled, degraded.
In *heraldry*, it is used of the wings of eagles, when the tops are turned downwards towards the point of the shield; or when the wings are shut, the natural way of bearing them being spread, with the top pointing to the chief of the angle. *Bailey. Chambers.*

ABA'SEMENT, *n.* The act of humbling or bringing low; also a state of depression, degradation, or humiliation.

ABASH', *v. t.* [Heb. and Ch. בוש bosh, to be confounded, or ashamed.]
To make the spirits to fail; to cast down the countenance; to make ashamed; to confuse or confound, as by exciting suddenly a consciousness of guilt, error, inferiority, &c.

> They heard and were *abashed*. *Milton.*

ABASH'ED, *pp.* Confused with shame; confounded; put to silence; followed by *at.*

ABASH'ING, *ppr.* Putting to shame or confusion.

ABASH'MENT, *n.* Confusion from shame. [*Little used.*]

ABA'SING, *ppr.* Humbling, depressing, bringing low.

ABAS'SI, or ABAS'SIS, *n.* A silver coin of Persia, of the value of twenty cents, about ten pence sterling. *Encyc.*

ABA'TABLE, *a.* That may or can be abated; as an *abatable* writ or nuisance.

ABA'TE, *v. t.* [Fr. *abattre*, to beat down; *battre*, to beat, to strike; Sp. *batir*, *abatir*; Port. *bater*, *abater*; It. *battere*, *abbattere*; Heb. Ch. חבט, to beat; Syr. ܚܒܛ id. Ar. خبط gabata, to beat, and كبت kabatha, to beat down, to prostrate. The Saxon has the participle *gebatod*, abated. The prefix is sunk to *a* in *abate*, and lost in *beat*. See Class Bd. No. 23, 33.]

1. To beat down; to pull down; to destroy in any manner; as to *abate* a nuisance.
2. To lessen; to diminish; to moderate; as to *abate* zeal; to *abate* pride; to *abate* a demand; to *abate* courage.
3. To lessen; to mitigate; as to *abate* pain or sorrow.
4. To overthrow; to cause to fail; to frustrate by judicial sentence; as to *abate* a writ.
5. To deject; to depress; as to *abate* the soul. *Obs.*
6. To deduct;

   Nothing to add and nothing to *abate*. *Pope.*

7. To cause to fail; to annul. By the English law, a legacy to a charity is *abated* by a deficiency of assets.
8. In *Connecticut*, to remit, as to *abate* a tax.

ABA'TE, *v. i.* To decrease, or become less in strength or violence; as pain *abates*; a storm *abates*.

2. To fail; to be defeated, or come to naught; as a writ *abates*. By the civil law a legacy to a charity does not *abate* by deficiency of assets.
3. In *law*, to enter into a freehold after the death of the last occupant, and before the heir or devisee takes possession. *Blackstone.*
4. In *horsemanship*, to perform well a downward motion. A horse is said to *abate*, or take down his curvets, when, working upon curvets, he puts both his hind legs to the ground at once, and observes the same exactness in all the times. *Encyc.*

ABA'TED, *pp.* Lessened; decreased; destroyed; mitigated; defeated; remitted; overthrown.

ABA'TEMENT, *n.* The act of abating; the state of being abated.

2. A reduction, removing, or pulling down, as of a nuisance. *Blackstone.*
3. Diminution, decrease, or mitigation, as of grief or pain.
4. Deduction, sum withdrawn, as from an account.
5. Overthrow, failure, or defeat, as of a writ. *Blackstone.*
6. The entry of a stranger into a freehold after the death of the tenant, before the heir or devisee. *Blackstone.*
7. In *heraldry*, a mark of dishonor in a coat of arms, by which its dignity is debased for some stain on the character of the wearer.

ABA'TER, *n.* The person or thing that abates.

ABA'TING, *ppr.* Pulling down, diminishing, defeating, remitting.

ABA'TOR, *n.* A person who enters into a freehold on the death of the last possessor, before the heir or devisee. *Blackstone.*

AB'ATTIS, } *n.* [from *beating* or pulling
AB'ATIS, } down. Fr. *abattre.*]
Rubbish. In *fortification*, piles of trees, or branches of trees sharpened, and laid with the points outward, in front of ramparts, to prevent assailants from mounting the walls. *Encyc.*

AB'ATURE, *n.* [from *abate.*] Grass beaten or trampled down by a stag in passing. *Dict.*

ABB, *n.* [Sax. *ab* or *ob.*] Among weavers, yarn for the warp. Hence *abb-wool* is wool for the *abb*. *Encyc.*

AB'BA, *n.* In the Chaldee and Syriac, a father, and figuratively a superior. Sans. *appen.*

In the Syriac, Coptic and Ethiopic churches, it is a title given to the Bishops, and the Bishops bestow the title, by way of distinction, on the Bishop of Alexandria. Hence the title Baba, or Papa, Pope or great father, which the Bishop of Alexandria bore, before the Bishop of Rome.

AB'BACY, *n.* [from *abba*, Low Lat. *abbatia.*] The dignity, rights and privileges of an abbot. It comprehends the government and revenues.

ABBAT'ICAL, } *a.* Belonging to an abbey.
ABBA'TIAL, }

AB'BE, *n.* *Ab'by*, [from *abba.*]
In a monastic sense, the same as an *abbot*; but more generally, a title, in Catholic countries, without any determinate rank, office or rights. The abbes are numerous, and generally have some literary attainments; they dress as academics or scholars, and act as instructors, in colleges and private families; or as tutors to young gentlemen on their travels; and many of them become authors.

AB'BESS, *n.* [from *abba.*]
A female superior or governess of a nunnery, or convent of nuns, having the authority over the nuns which the abbots have over the Monks. [See *Abbey.*]

AB'BEY, *n. plu.* *abbeys*, [from *abba.*]
A monastery or society of persons of either sex, secluded from the world and devoted to religion. The males are called *monks*, and governed by an abbot; the females are called *nuns*, and governed by an *abbess*. These institutions were suppressed in England by Henry VIII.; but they still exist in Catholic countries.

AB'BEY-LUBBER, *n.* A name given to monks, in contempt for their idleness.

AB'BOT, *n.* [formerly abbat, from *abba*, latinized *abbas*, or from Heb. plural אבות.]
The superior or governor of an abbey or monastery. Originally monasteries were founded in retired places, and the religious had no concern with secular affairs, being entirely subject to the prelates. But the abbots possessing most of the learning, in ages of ignorance, were called from their seclusion to aid the churches in opposing heresies; monasteries were founded in the vicinity of cities; the abbots became ambitious and set themselves to acquire wealth and honors; some of them assumed the miter, threw off their dependence on the bishops, and obtained seats in parliament. For many centuries, princes and noblemen bore the title of abbots. At present, in catholic countries, abbots are *regular*, or such as take the vow, and wear the habit of the order; and *commendatory*, such as are seculars, but obliged, when of suitable age, to take orders. The title is borne also by some persons, who have not the government of a monastery; as bishops, whose sees were formerly abbeys. *Encyc.*

AB'BOTSHIP, *n.* The state of an abbot.

ABBREUVOIR, *n.* [Fr. *abreuvoir*, from *abreuver*, to water; Sp. *abrevar*, id.; from Gr. Βρεχω.]
Among *masons*, the joint between stones in a wall, to be filled with mortar. *Dict.*

[*I know not whether it is now used.*]

ABBRE'VIATE, *v. t.* [It. *abbreviare*; Sp. *abreviar*; Port. *abbreviar*; from L. *abbrevio*, *brevio*, from *brevis*, short; contracted from Gr. Βραχυς, from the root of *break*, which see.]

1. To shorten; to make shorter by contracting the parts. [*In this sense, not much used, nor often applied to material substances.*]
2. To shorten; to abridge by the omission or defalcation of a part; to reduce to a smaller compass; as to *abbreviate* a writing.
3. In *mathematics*, to reduce fractions to the lowest terms. *Wallis.*

ABBRE'VIATED, *pp.* Shortened; reduced in length; abridged.

2. In *botany*, an abbreviated perianth is shorter than the tube of the corol. *Martyn.*

ABBRE'VIATING, *ppr.* Shortening; contracting in length or into a smaller compass.

ABBREVIA'TION, *n.* The act of shortening or contracting.

2. A letter or a few letters used for a word; as Gen. for Genesis; U. S. A. for United States of America.
3. The reduction of fractions to the lowest terms.

ABBRE'VIATOR, *n.* One who abridges or reduces to a smaller compass.

ABBRE'VIATORS, a college of seventy-two persons in the chancery of Rome, whose duty is to draw up the Pope's briefs, and reduce petitions, when granted, to a due form for bulls.

ABBRE'VIATORY, *a.* Shortening, contracting.

ABBRE'VIATURE, *n.* A letter or character for shortening; an abridgment, a compend.

A. B. C. The three first letters of the alphabet, used for the whole alphabet. Also a little book for teaching the elements of reading. *Shak.*

AB'DALS, *n.* The name of certain fanatics in Persia, who, in excess of zeal, sometimes run into the streets, and attempt to kill all they meet who are of a different religion; and if they are slain for their madness, they think it meritorious to die, and by the vulgar are deemed martyrs. *Encyc.*

AB'DERITE, *n.* An inhabitant of Abdera, a maritime town in Thrace. Democritus is so called, from being a native of the place. As he was given to laughter, foolish or incessant laughter, is called *abderian*. *Whitaker.*

AB'DICANT, *a.* [See *Abdicate.*] Abdicating; renouncing.

AB'DICATE, *v. t.* [L. *abdico*; *ab* and *dico*, to dedicate, to bestow, but the literal primary sense of *dico* is to send or thrust.]

1. In a *general sense*, to relinquish, renounce, or abandon. *Forster.*
2. To abandon an office or trust, without a formal resignation to those who conferred it, or without their consent; also to abandon a throne, without a formal surrender of the crown. *Case of King James, Blackstone.*
3. To relinquish an office before the expiration of the time of service. *Case of Diocletian, Gibbon; also Case of Paul III. Coxe's Russ.*
4. To reject; to renounce; to abandon as a right. *Burke.*
5. To cast away; to renounce; as to *abdicate* our mental faculties. [*Unusual.*] *J. P. Smith.*
6. In the *civil law*, to disclaim a son and expel him from the family, as a father; to disinherit during the life of the father. *Encyc.*

AB'DICATE, *v. i.* To renounce; to abandon; to cast off; to relinquish, as a right, power, or trust.

Though a King may *abdicate* for his own person, he cannot *abdicate* for the monarchy. *Burke.*

AB'DICATED, *pp.* Renounced; relinquished without a formal resignation; abandoned.

AB'DICATING, *ppr.* Relinquishing without a formal resignation; abandoning.

ABDICA'TION, *n.* The act of abdicating; the abandoning of an office or trust, without a formal surrender, or before the usual or stated time of expiration.

2. A casting off; rejection.

AB'DICATIVE, *a.* Causing or implying abdication. [*Little used.*] *Dict.*

AB'DITIVE, *a.* [L. *abdo*, to hide; *ab* and *do.*] Having the power or quality of hiding. [*Little used.*] *Dict.*

AB'DITORY, *n.* A place for secreting or preserving goods. *Cowel.*

AB'DOMEN, or **ABDO'MEN**, *n.* [L. perhaps *abdo* and *omentum.*]

1. The lower belly, or that part of the body which lies between the thorax and the bottom of the pelvis. It is lined with a membrane called peritoneum, and contains the stomach, liver, spleen, pancreas, kidneys, bladder and guts. It is separated from the breast internally by the diaphragm, and externally, by the extremities of the ribs. On its outer surface it is divided into four regions—the epigastric, the umbilical, the hypogastric and lumbar. *Quincy.*
2. In *insects*, the lower part of the animal, united to the corslet by a thread. In some species, it is covered with wings, and a case. It is divided into segments and rings, on the sides of which are small spiracles by which the insect respires. *D. Nat. Hist.*

ABDOM'INAL, *a.* Pertaining to the lower belly.

ABDOM'INAL, *n. plu.* abdominals. In ichthyology the abdominals are a class of fish whose ventral fins are placed behind the pectoral, and which belong to the division of *bony fish.* The class contains nine genera—the loche, salmon, pike, argentine, atherine, mullet, flying fish, herring and carp. *Encyc.*

ABDOM'INAL RING, or **INGUINAL RING**, an oblong tendinous ring in both groins, through which pass the spermatic cord in men, and the round ligaments of the uterus in women. *Med. Dict.*

ABDOM'INOUS, *a.* Pertaining to the abdomen; having a large belly. *Cowper.*

ABDU'CE, *v. t.* [L. *abduco*, to lead away, of *ab* and *duco*, to lead. See *Duke.*]

To draw from; to withdraw, or draw to a different part; used chiefly in anatomy.

ABDU'CENT, *a.* Drawing from, pulling back; used of those muscles which pull back certain parts of the body, for separating, opening, or bending them. The *abducent* muscles, called *abductors*, are opposed to the *adducent* muscles or *adductors.* *Med. Dict.*

ABDUC'TION, *n.* In a *general sense*, the act of drawing apart, or carrying away.

2. In *surgery*, a species of fracture, in which the broken parts recede from each other.
3. In *logic*, a kind of argumentation, called by the Greeks *apagoge*, in which the major is evident, but the minor is not so clear, as not to require farther proof. As in this syllogism, "all whom God absolves are free from sin; God absolves all who are in Christ; therefore all who are in Christ are free from sin." *Encyc.*
4. In *law*, the taking and carrying away of a child, a ward, a wife, &c. either by fraud, persuasion, or open violence. *Blackstone.*

ABDUC'TOR, *n.* In *anatomy*, a muscle which serves to withdraw, or pull back a certain part of the body; as the *abductor oculi*, which pulls the eye outwards.

ABEA'R, *v. t. abáre*, [Sax. *abæran.*] To bear; to behave. *Obs.* *Spenser.*

ABEA'RANCE, *n.* [from *abear*, now disused; from *bear*, to carry.] Behavior, demeanor. [*Little used.*] *Blackstone.*

ABECEDA'RIAN, *n.* [a word formed from the first four letters of the alphabet.] One who teaches the letters of the alphabet, or a learner of the letters.

ABECE'DARY, *a.* Pertaining to, or formed by the letters of the alphabet.

ABED', *adv.* [See *Bed.*] On or in bed.

ABE'LE, or **ABEL-TREE**, *n.* An obsolete name of the white poplar. [See *Poplar.*]

ABE'LIANS, **ABELO'NIANS** or **A'BELITES**, in Church history, a sect in Africa which arose in the reign of Arcadius; they married, but lived in continence, after the manner, as they pretended, of Abel, and attempted to maintain the sect by adopting the children of others. *Encyc.*

A'BELMOSK, *n.* A trivial name of a species of hibiscus, or Syrian mallow. The plant rises on a herbaceous stalk, three or four feet, sending out two or three side branches. The seeds have a musky odor, (whence its name, μοσχος,) for which reason the Arabians mix them with coffee.

ABER'RANCE, **ABER'RANCY**, } *n.* [L. *aberrans*, *aberro*, to wander from; of *ab* and *erro*, to wander.]

A wandering or deviating from the right way, but rarely used in a literal sense. In a figurative sense, a deviation from truth, error, mistake; and in morals, a fault, a deviation from rectitude. *Brown.*

ABER'RANT, *a.* Wandering, straying from the right way. [*Rarely used.*]

ABERRA'TION, *n.* [L. *aberratio.*] The act of wandering from the right way; deviation from truth or moral rectitude; deviation from a strait line.

2. In *astronomy*, a small apparent motion of the fixed stars, occasioned by the progressive motion of light and the earth's annual motion in its orbit. By this, they sometimes appear twenty seconds distant from their true situation. *Lunier.*
3. In *optics*, a deviation in the rays of light, when inflected by a lens or speculum, by which they are prevented from uniting in the same point. It is occasioned by the figure of the glass, or by the unequal refrangibility of the rays of light. *Encyc.*

Crown of aberration, a luminous circle surrounding the disk of the sun, depending on the aberration of its rays, by which its apparent diameter is enlarged. *Cyc.*

ABER'RING, *part. a.* Wandering; going astray. *Brown.*

ABERRUN'CATE, *v. t.* [L. *averrunco.*] To pull up by the roots; to extirpate utterly. [*Not used.*] *Dict.*

ABET', *v. t.* [Sax. *betan*, *gebetan*; properly to push forward, to advance; hence to amend, to revive, to restore, to make better; and applied to fire, to increase the flame, to excite, to promote. Hence to aid by encouraging or instigating. Hence in Saxon, "Na bete nan man that fyr." Let no man bet, [better, excite] the fire, LL. Ina. 78.]

1. To encourage by aid or countenance, but now used chiefly in a bad sense. "To *abet* an opinion," in the sense of *support*, is used by Bishop Cumberland; but this use is hardly allowable.
2. In *law*, to encourage, counsel, incite or assist in a criminal act.

ABET', *n.* The act of aiding or encouraging in a crime. [*Not used.*]

ABET'MENT, *n.* The act of abetting.

ABET'TED, *pp.* Incited, aided, encouraged to a crime.

ABET'TING, *ppr.* Counselling, aiding or encouraging to a crime.

ABET'TOR, *n.* One who abets, or incites, aids or encourages another to commit a crime. In *treason*, there are no abettors; all persons concerned being principals.

ABEVACUA'TION, *n.* [*ab* and *evacuation.*] In *medicine*, a partial evacuation of morbid humors of the body, either by nature or art. *Cyc.*

ABEY'ANCE, *n.* pron. *abáyance.* [Norm. *abbaiaunce*, or *abaizance*, in expectation; *boyance*, expectation. Qu. Fr. *bayer*, to gape, to look a long time with the mouth open; to stand looking in a silly manner; It. *badare*, to amuse one's self, to stand trifling; "tenere a bada," to keep at bay; "Star a bada," to stand trifling. If B d are the radical letters, it seems to belong to the root of *abide.* See *Bay.*]

In expectation or contemplation of law. The fee simple or inheritance of lands and tenements is in *abeyance*, when there is no person in being in whom it can vest; so that it is in a state of expectancy or waiting until a proper person shall appear.

Thus if land is leased to a man for life, remainder to another for years, the remainder for years is in *abeyance*, till the death of the lessee, for life. *Blackstone.*

ABHOR′, *v. t.* [L. *abhorreo*, of *ab* and *horreo*, to set up bristles, shiver or shake; to look terrible.]

1. To hate extremely, or with contempt; to lothe, detest or abominate. *Shak.*
2. To despise or neglect. Ps. xxii. 24. Amos vi. 8.
3. To cast off or reject. Ps. lxxxix. 38.

ABHOR′RED, *pp.* Hated extremely, detested.

ABHOR′RENCE, } **ABHOR′RENCY**, } *n.* Extreme hatred, detestation, great aversion.

ABHOR′RENT, *a.* Hating, detesting, struck with abhorrence.

2. Contrary, odious, inconsistent with, expressive of extreme opposition, as, "Slander is *abhorrent* to all ideas of justice." In this sense, it should be always followed by *to*—abhorrent *from* is not agreeable to the English idiom.

ABHOR′RENTLY, *adv.* With abhorrence.

ABHOR′RER, *n.* One who abhors.

ABHOR′RING, *ppr.* Having great aversion, detesting. As a noun, it is used in Isaiah lxvi. for the object of hatred—"An *abhorring* to all flesh."

A′BIB, *n.* [Heb. אב, swelling, protuberant. Ch. אבב, to produce the first or early fruit; אביב, a full grown ear of corn.]

The first month of the Jewish ecclesiastical year, called also Nisan. It begins at the spring equinox, and answers to the latter part of March and beginning of April. Its name is derived from the full growth of wheat in Egypt, which took place anciently, as it does now, at that season.

ABI′DE, *v. i.* pret. and part. *abode.* [Ar. ابد abada, to be, or exist, to continue; W. *bod*, to be; Sax. *bidan, abidan*; Sw. *bida*; D. *beiden*; Dan. *bier*; Russ. *vitayu*, to dwell, rest, continue, stand firm, or be stationary for any time indefinitely. Class Bd. No 7.]

1. To rest, or dwell. Gen. xxix. 19.
2. To tarry or stay for a short time. Gen. xxiv. 55.
3. To continue permanently or in the same state; to be firm and immovable. Ps. cxix. 90.
4. To remain, to continue. Acts, xxvii. 31. Eccles. viii. 15.

ABI′DE, *v. t.* To wait for; to be prepared for; to await.

Bonds and afflictions *abide* me. Acts, xx. 23. [*For* is here understood.]

2. To endure or sustain.

To *abide* the indignation of the Lord. Joel x.

3. To bear or endure; to bear patiently. "I cannot *abide* his impertinence."

This verb when intransitive, is followed by *in* or *at* before the place, and *with* before the person. "Abide *with* me—*at* Jerusalem or *in* this land." Sometimes by *on*, the sword shall abide *on* his cities; and in the sense of *wait*, by *for*, abide *for* me. Hosea, iii. 3. Sometimes by *by*, abide *by* the crib. Job, xxxix.

In general, *abide by* signifies to adhere to, maintain, defend, or stand to, as to abide *by* a promise, or *by* a friend; or to suffer the consequences, as to *abide by* the event, that is, to be fixed or permanent in a particular condition.

ABI′DER, *n.* One who dwells or continues.

ABI′DING, *ppr.* Dwelling; remaining; continuing; enduring; awaiting.

ABI′DING, *n.* Continuance; fixed state; residence; an enduring.

ABI′DINGLY, *adv.* In a manner to continue; permanently. *Haweis.*

ABIL′ITY, *n.* [Fr. *habileté*; It. *abilità*; Sp. *habilidad*; L. *habilitas*, ableness, fitness, from *habeo*, to have or hold.]

1. Physical power, whether bodily or mental; natural or acquired; force of understanding; skill in arts or science. *Ability* is active power, or power to perform; as opposed to *capacity*, or power to receive. In the plural, *abilities* is much used in a like sense; and also for faculties of the mind, and acquired qualifications. *Franklin.*
2. Riches, wealth, substance, which are the means, or which furnish the *power*, of doing certain acts.

They gave after their *ability* to the work. Ez. ii.

3. Moral power, depending on the will—a *metaphysical* and *theological sense.*
4. Civil or legal power; the power or right to do certain things, as an *ability* to transfer property or dispose of effects—*ability* to inherit. It is opposed to *disability.* *Cyc.*

ABINTEST′ATE, *a.* [L. *ab* and *intestatus*—dying without a will, from *in* and *testor*, to bear witness; W. *tyst*; Arm. *test*, witness. See *Test* and *Testify.*]

In the *civil law*, inheriting the estate of one dying without a will.

ABJECT′, *v. t.* To throw away; to cast out. *Obs.* *Spenser.*

AB′JECT, *a.* [L. *abjectus*, from *abjicio*, to throw away, from *ab* and *jacio*, to throw.]

1. Sunk to a low condition; *applied to persons or things.* Hence,
2. Worthless, mean, despicable, low in estimation, without hope or regard.

AB′JECT, *n.* A person in the lowest condition and despicable. Ps. xxxv.

ABJECT′EDNESS, *n.* A very low or despicable condition. [*Little used.*]

ABJEC′TION, *n.* A state of being cast away; hence a low state; meanness of spirit; baseness.

AB′JECTLY, *adv.* In a contemptible manner; meanly; servilely.

AB′JECTNESS, *n.* The state of being abject; meanness; servility.

ABJURA′TION, *n.* [See *Abjure.*]

1. The act of abjuring; a renunciation upon oath; as "an *abjuration* of the realm," by which a person swears to leave the country, and never to return. It is used also for the oath of renunciation. Formerly in England, felons, taking refuge in a church, and confessing their guilt, could not be arrested and tried, but might save their lives by *abjuring* the realm; that is, by taking an oath to quit the kingdom forever.
2. A rejection or denial with solemnity; a total abandonment; as "an *abjuration* of heresy."

ABJU′RATORY, *a.* Containing abjuration. *Encyc.*

ABJU′RE, *v. t.* [L. *abjuro*, to deny upon oath, from *ab* and *juro*, to swear.]

1. To renounce upon oath; to abandon; as to *abjure* allegiance to a prince.
2. To renounce or reject with solemnity; to reject; as to *abjure* errors; *abjure* reason.
3. To recant or retract. *Shak.*
4. To banish. [*Not used.*]

ABJU′RED, *pp.* Renounced upon oath; solemnly recanted.

ABJU′RER, *n.* One who abjures.

ABJU′RING, *ppr.* Renouncing upon oath; disclaiming with solemnity.

ABLAC′TATE, *v. t.* [L. *ablacto*; from *ab* and *lac*, milk.] To wean from the breast. [*Little used.*]

ABLACTA′TION, *n.* [L. *ab* and *lac*, milk. *Lacto*, to suckle.]

1. In *medical authors*, the weaning of a child from the breast.
2. Among ancient gardeners, a method of grafting in which the cion was not separated from the parent stock, till it was firmly united to that in which it was inserted. This is now called *grafting by approach* or *inarching*. [See *Graft.*] *Encyc.*

ABLAQUEA′TION, [L. *ablaqueatio*, from *ab* and *laquear*, a roof or covering.]

A laying bare the roots of trees to expose them to the air and water—a practice among gardeners.

ABLA′TION, *n.* [L. *ab* and *latio*, a carrying.]

A carrying away. In *medicine*, the taking from the body whatever is hurtful; evacuations in general. In *chimistry*, the removal of whatever is finished or no longer necessary.

AB′LATIVE, *a.* [F. *ablatif*; It. *ablativo*; L. *ablativus*; L. *ablatus*, from *aufero*, to carry away, of *ab* and *fero.*]

A word applied to the sixth case of nouns in the Latin language, in which case are used words when the actions of *carrying away*, or *taking from*, are signified.

Ablative absolute, is when a word in that case, is independent, in construction, of the rest of the sentence.

ABLE, *a. a′bl.* [L. *habilis*; Norm. *ablez.*]

1. Having physical power sufficient; having competent power or strength, bodily or mental; as a man *able* to perform military service—a child is not *able* to reason on abstract subjects.
2. Having strong or unusual powers of mind, or intellectual qualifications; as an *able* minister.

Provide out of all Israel *able* men. Ex. xviii.

3. Having large or competent property; or simply having property, or means.

Every man shall give as he is *able*. Deut. xvi.

4. Having competent strength or fortitude.

He is not *able* to sustain such pain or affliction.

5. Having sufficient knowledge or skill.

He is *able* to speak French.
She is not *able* to play on the piano.

6. Having competent moral power or qualifications.

An illegitimate son is not *able* to take by inheritance.

A′BLE-BODIED, *a.* Having a sound, strong body, or a body of competent strength for service. In *marine language*, it denotes skill in seamanship. *Mar. Dict.*

AB'LEN, or **AB'LET**, *n.* A small fresh water fish, the bleak.

A'BLENESS, *n.* Ability of body or mind; force; vigor; capability.

AB'LEPSY, *n.* [Gr. αβλεψια.] Want of sight; blindness.

A'BLER, and **A'BLEST**, Comp. and superl. of able.

AB'LOCATE, *v. t.* [L. *abloco*, *ab* and *loco*, to let out.] To let out; to lease. *Calvin.*

ABLOCA'TION, *n.* A letting to hire.

ABLU'DE, *v.t.* [L. *abludo*, *ab* and *ludo*, to play.] To be unlike; to differ. [*Not used.*] *Hall.*

AB'LUENT, *a.* [L. *abluo*, to wash away; *ab* and *luo*, or *lavo*, to wash; Ir. *lo* or *lua*, water.]
Washing clean; cleansing by water or liquids. [*Little used except as a noun.*]

AB'LUENT, *n.* In *medicine*, that which thins, purifies or sweetens the blood. *Quincy.*
[See *Diluent* and *Abstergent.*]

ABLU'TION, *n.* [L. *ablutio*, from *ab* and *luo* or *lavo* to wash.]
1. In a general sense, the act of washing; a cleansing or purification by water.
2. Appropriately, the washing of the body as a preparation for religious duties, enjoined by Moses and still practiced in many countries.
3. In *chimistry*, the purification of bodies by the affusion of a proper liquor, as water to dissolve salts. *Quincy.*
4. In *medicine*, the washing of the body *externally*, as by baths; or *internally*, by diluting fluids.
5. Pope has used *ablution* for the water used in cleansing.
6. The cup given to the laity without consecration, in popish churches. *Johnson.*

A'BLY, *adv.* In an able manner; with great ability.

AB'NEGATE, *v. t.* To deny. [*Not used.*]

ABNEGA'TION, *n.* [L. *abnego*, to deny, from *ab* and *nego*; W. *naca*, *nacau*; Sw. *neka*, to deny; W. *nac*, no; Eng. *nay*; L. *nec*, not; Ir. *nach*, not.] A denial; a renunciation; self-denial. *Hammond.*

AB'NEGATOR, *n.* One who denies, renounces, or opposes any thing. *Sandys.*

ABNODA'TION, *n.* [L. *abnodo*; *ab* and *nodus*, a knot.] The act of cutting away the knots of trees. *Dict.*

ABNORM'ITY, *n.* [L. *abnormis*, irregular; *ab* and *norma*, a rule.] Irregularity; deformity. [*Little used.*] *Dict.*

ABNORM'OUS, *a.* [L. *abnormis*, supra.] Irregular; deformed. [*Little used.*] *Dict.*

ABOARD, *adv.* [*a* and *board.* See *Board.*] Within a ship, vessel, or boat.
To go aboard, to enter a ship, to embark.
To fall aboard, to strike a ship's side.
Aboard main tack, an order to draw a corner of the main-sail down to the chess-tree. *Encyc. Mar. Dict.*

ABO'DANCE, *n.* [from *bode.*] An omen. [*Not used.*] *Johnson.*

ABO'DE, *pret.* of *abide.*

ABO'DE, *n.* [See *Abide.*] Stay; continuance in a place; residence for a longer or shorter time.
2. A place of continuance; a dwelling; a habitation.
3. To *make abode*, to dwell or reside.

ABO'DE, *v.t.* [See *Bode.*] To foreshow. *Shak.*

ABO'DE, *v.i.* To be an omen. *Dryden.*

ABO'DEMENT, *n.* [from *bode.*] A secret anticipation of something future. *Shak.*

ABO'DING, *n.* Presentiment; prognostication. *Hall.*

ABOL'ISH, *v.t.* [Fr. *abolir*; L. *aboleo*; from *ab* and *oleo*, *olesco*, to grow.]
1. To make void; to annul; to abrogate; applied chiefly and appropriately to established laws, contracts, rites, customs and institutions—as to *abolish* laws by a repeal, actual or virtual.
2. To destroy, or put an end to; as to *abolish* idols. Isa. ii. To *abolish* death, 2 Tim. i. This sense is not common. To *abolish* posterity, in the translation of Pausanias, Lib. 3. Ca. 6. is hardly allowable.

ABOL'ISHABLE, *a.* That may be annulled, abrogated, or destroyed, as a law, rite, custom, &c.

ABOL'ISHED, *pp.* Annulled; repealed; abrogated, or destroyed.

ABOL'ISHER, *n.* One who abolishes.

ABOL'ISHING, *ppr.* Making void; annulling; destroying.

ABOL'ISHMENT, *n.* The act of annulling; abrogation; destruction. *Hooker.*

ABOLI''TION, *n. abolishun.* The act of abolishing; or the state of being abolished; an annulling; abrogation; utter destruction; as the *abolition* of laws, decrees, ordinances, rites, customs, debts, &c.
The application of this word to persons and things, is now unusual or obsolete. To abolish persons, canals and senses, the language of good writers formerly, is no longer legitimate.

ABOM'INABLE, *a.* [See *Abominate.*] Very hateful; detestable; lothesome.
2. This word is applicable to whatever is odious to the mind or offensive to the senses. *Milton.*
3. Unclean. Levit. vii.

ABOM'INABLENESS, *n.* The quality or state of being very odious; hatefulness.

ABOM'INABLY, *adv.* Very odiously; detestably; sinfully. 1 Kings xxi.
2. In *vulgar language*, extremely, excessively.

ABOM'INATE, *v. t.* [L. *abomino*, supposed to be formed by *ab* and *omen*; to deprecate as ominous; may the Gods avert the evil.]
To hate extremely; to abhor; to detest. *Southern.*

ABOM'INATED, *pp.* Hated utterly; detested; abhorred.

ABOM'INATING, *ppr.* Abhorring; hating extremely.

ABOMINA'TION, *n.* Extreme hatred; detestation. *Swift.*
2. The object of detestation, a *common signification in scripture.*

The way of the wicked is an *abomination* to the Lord. Prov. xv.

3. Hence, defilement, pollution, in a physical sense, or evil doctrines and practices, which are moral defilements, idols and idolatry, are called *abominations.* The Jews were an *abomination* to the Egyptians; and the sacred animals of the Egyptians were an *abomination* to the Jews. The Roman army is called the *abomination* of *desolation.* Mat. xxiv. 13. In short, whatever is an object of extreme hatred, is called an *abomination.*

ABO'RD, *n.* [Fr. See *Border.*] Literally, arrival, but used for first appearance, manner of accosting, or address, but not an English word. *Chesterfield.*

ABO'RD, *v. t.* To accost. [*Not in use.*]

ABO'REA, *n.* A species of duck, called by Edwards, the black-bellied whistling duck. This fowl is of a reddish brown color, with a sort of crest on its head; the belly is spotted with black and white. It belongs to the genus, *anas.*

ABORIG'INAL, *a.* [L. *ab* and *origo*, origin. See *Origin.*]
First; original; primitive; *aboriginal* people are the first inhabitants of a country.

Aboriginal tribes of America. *President Smith.*

ABORIG'INAL, *n.* An original, or primitive inhabitant. The first settlers in a country are called *aboriginals*; as the Celts in Europe, and Indians in America. *President Smith.*

ABORIG'INES, *n.* plur. Aboriginals—but not an English word.
It may be well to let it pass into disuse. [See *Aboriginal.*]

ABORSEMENT, *n. abors'ment.* [See *Abort.*] Abortion. [*Not in use.*]

ABORT', *v. i.* [L. *aborto*; *ab* and *ortus*, *orior.*] To miscarry in birth. [*Not in use.*] *Herbert.*

ABORT', *n.* An abortion. [*Not in use.*] *Burton.*

ABOR'TION, *n.* [L. *abortio*, a miscarriage; usually deduced from *ab* and *orior.*]
1. The act of miscarrying, or producing young before the natural time, or before the fetus is perfectly formed.
2. In a *figurative sense*, any fruit or produce that does not come to maturity, or any thing which fails in its progress, before it is matured or perfect, as a design or project.
3. The fetus brought forth before it is perfectly formed.

ABOR'TIVE, *a.* Brought forth in an immature state; failing, or coming to naught, before it is complete.
2. Failing in its effect; miscarrying; producing nothing; as an *abortive* scheme.
3. Rendering abortive; as *abortive* gulf, in Milton, but not legitimate.
4. Pertaining to abortion; as *abortive* vellum, made of the skin of an abortive calf. *Encyc.*
5. In *botany*, an abortive flower is one which falls without producing fruit. *Martyn.*

ABOR'TIVE, *n.* That which is brought forth or born prematurely. [*Little used.*]

ABOR'TIVELY, *adv.* Immaturely; in an untimely manner.

ABOR'TIVENESS, *n.* The state of being abortive; a failing in the progress to perfection or maturity; a failure of producing the intended effect.

ABORT'MENT, *n.* An untimely birth. *Bacon.*

ABOUND', *v.i.* [L. *abundo*; Fr. *abonder*; It. *abbondare*; Sp. *abundar*. If this word is from L. *unda*, a wave, the latter has probably lost its first consonant. *Abound* may naturally be deduced from the Celtic. Arm. *fonn*, plenty; *fonna*, to abound; W. *fyniaw*, to produce, to generate, to abound, from *fwn*, a source, the root of *fynon*, L. *fons*, a fountain.]

1. To have or possess in great quantity; to be copiously supplied; followed by *with* or *in;* as to *abound with* provisions; to *abound in* good things.
2. To be in great plenty; to be very prevalent.
   Where sin *abounded*, grace did much more *abound*. Rom. v.

ABOUND'ING, *ppr.* Having in great plenty; being in great plenty; being very prevalent; generally prevailing.

ABOUND'ING, *n.* Increase. *South.*

ABOUT', *prep.* [Sax. *abutan, onbutan, embutan,* about, around; *on* or *emb*, coinciding with Gr. αμφι, and *butan*, without, [see *but,*] literally, *around, on the outside.*]
1. Around; on the exterior part or surface.
   Bind them *about* thy neck. Prov. iii. 3. Isa. l. Hence,
2. Near to in *place*, with the sense of circularity.
   Get you up from *about* the tabernacle. Num. xvi.
3. Near to in *time.*
   He went out *about* the third hour. Mat. xxi. 3.
4. Near to, in *action*, or near to the performance of some act.
   Paul was *about* to open his mouth.
   They were *about* to flee out of the ship. Acts, xviii. 14—xxvii. 30.
5. Near to the *person;* appended to the clothes. Every thing *about* him is in order. Is your snuff box *about* you?
   From *nearness* on all sides, the transition is easy to a concern with. Hence,
6. Concerned in, engaged in, relating to, respecting.
   I must be *about* my father's business. Luke, ii. 49. The painter is not to take so much pains *about* the drapery as *about* the face. *Dryden.*
   What is he *about?*
7. In compass or circumference; two yards *about* the trunk.

ABOUT', *adv.* Near to in number or quantity.
   There fell that day *about* three thousand men. Ex. xxxii.
2. Near to in quality or degree; as *about* as high, or as cold.
3. Here and there; around; in one place and another.
   Wandering *about* from house to house. 1. Tim. v.
4. Round, or the longest way, opposed to *across*, or the shortest way. A mile *about*, and half a mile *across.*

To bring about, to bring to the end; to effect or accomplish a purpose.

To come about, to change or turn; to come to the desired point. In a like sense, seamen say *go about*, when a ship changes her course and goes on the other tack.

Ready about, about ship, are orders for tacking.

To go about, signifies to *enter upon;* also to *prepare;* to *seek the means.*
   Why go ye *about* to kill me. John, vii.

ABÖVE', *prep.* [Sax. *abufan, bufan, bufon;* D. *boven.*]
1. Literally, higher in place.
   The fowls that fly *above* the earth. Gen. i. 20.
2. Figuratively, superior in any respect.
   I saw a light *above* the brightness of the Sun, Acts, xxvi.
   The price of a virtuous woman is *above* rubies, Prov. xxxi.
3. More in number or quantity.
   He was seen by *above* five hundred brethren at once, 1. Cor. xv. 6.
   The weight is *above* a tun.
4. More in degree; in a greater degree.
   Hannaniah feared God *above* many. Neh. vii. 2.
   The serpent is cursed *above* all cattle. Gen. iii.
5. Beyond; in excess.
   In stripes *above* measure. 2 Cor. xi.
   God will not suffer you to be tempted *above* what ye are able, 1. Cor. x. 13.
6. Beyond; in a state to be unattainable; as things *above* comprehension.
7. Too proud for.
   This man is *above* his business.
8. Too elevated in mind or rank; having too much dignity for; as
   This man is *above* mean actions.
9. It is often used elliptically, for heaven, or the celestial regions.
   Let not God regard it from *above,* Job, iii.
   The powers *above.*
10 In a book or writing, it denotes *before* or in a former place, as what has been said *above*; supra. This mode of speaking originated in the ancient manner of writing, on a strip of parchment, beginning at one end and proceeding to the other. The beginning was the *upper* end.

ABÖVE', *adv.* Overhead; in a higher place. *Bacon.*
2. Before. *Dryden.*
3. Chief in rank or power. Deut. xxviii.

Above all is elliptical; above all considerations; chiefly; in preference to other things.

Above board; above the board or table; in open sight; without trick, concealment or deception. This expression is said by Johnson to be borrowed from gamesters, who, when they change their cards, put their hands under the table.

ABOVE-CITED, Cited before, in the preceding part of a book or writing.

ABOVE-GROUND, Alive, not buried.

ABOVE-MENTIONED, Mentioned before.

A. Bp. Abbrev. for Archbishop.

ABRAƐADAB'RA, The name of a deity worshipped by the Syrians: a cabalistic word. The letters of his name, written on paper, in the form of an inverted cone, were recommended by Samonicus as an antidote against certain diseases. *Encyc.*

ABRA'DE, *v. t.* [L. *abrado*, to scrape, from *rado.*]
To rub or wear off; to waste by friction; used especially to express the action of sharp, corrosive medicines, in wearing away or removing the mucus of the membranes.

ABRA'DED, *pp.* Rubbed or worn off; worn; scraped.

ABRA'DING, *ppr.* Rubbing off; wearing.

ABRAHAM'IƐ, *a.* Pertaining to Abraham, the patriarch, as *Abrahamic* Covenant. *Mason.*

ABRA'SION, *n. abra'zhun.* The act of wearing or rubbing off; also substance worn off by attrition. *Quincy.*

ABREAST', *adv. abrest'*, [from *a* and *breast.*]
1. Side by side; with the breasts in a line. Two men rode *abreast.*
2. In marine language, ships are *abreast* when their heads are equally advanced; and they are *abreast* of objects when the objects are on a line with the beam.—Hence,
3. Opposite; against; on a line with—as a ship was *abreast* of Montauk point.—*A seaman's phrase.*

ABRIDĠE', *v. t. abridj'*, [Fr. *abréger*, from Gr. βραχυς, short, or its root, from the root of *break* or a verb of that family.]
1. To make shorter; to epitomize; to contract by using fewer words, yet retaining the sense in substance—used of writings.
   Justin *abridged* the history of Trogus Pompeius.
2. To lessen; to diminish; as to *abridge* labor; to *abridge* power or rights. *Smith.*
3. To deprive; to cut off from; followed by *of;* as to *abridge* one of his rights, or enjoyments. To *abridge from*, is now obsolete or improper.
4. In *algebra*, to reduce a compound quantity or equation to its more simple expression. The equation thus abridged is called a formula.

ABRIDĠ'ED *pp.* Made shorter; epitomized; reduced to a smaller compass; lessened; deprived.

ABRIDĠ'ER, *n.* One who abridges; one who makes a compend.

ABRIDĠ'ING, *ppr.* Shortening; lessening; depriving; debarring.

ABRIDĠ'MENT, *n.* An epitome; a compend, or summary of a book.
2. Diminution; contraction; reduction—as an *abridgment* of expenses.
3. Deprivation; a debarring or restraint—as an *abridgment* of pleasures.

ABROACH, *adv.* [See *Broach.*]
Broached; letting out or yielding liquor, or in a posture for letting out; as a cask is *abroach.* Figuratively used by Shakespeare for setting loose, or in a state of being diffused, "Set mischief *abroach;*" but this sense is unusual.

ABROAD, *adv. abrawd'.* [See *Broad.*]
In a general sense, at large; widely; not confined to narrow limits. Hence,
1. In the open air.
2. Beyond or out of the walls of a house, as to walk *abroad.*
3. Beyond the limits of a camp. Deut. xxiii. 10.
4. Beyond the bounds of a country; in foreign countries—as to go *abroad* for an education.—We have broils at home and enemies *abroad.*
5. Extensively; before the public at large.
   He began to blaze *abroad* the matter. Mark i. 45. Esther i.
6. Widely; with expansion; as a tree spreads its branches *abroad.*

AB'ROGATE, *v. t.* [L. *abrogo*, to repeal. from *ab* and *rogo*, to ask or propose. See the English *reach.* Class Rg.]
To repeal; to annul by an authoritative act; to abolish by the authority of the maker or his successor; applied to the repeal of laws, decrees, ordinances, the abolition of established customs &c.

AB'ROGATED *pp.* Repealed; annulled by an act of authority.

AB'ROGATING, *ppr.* Repealing by authority; making void.

ABROGA'TION, *n.* The act of abrogating; a repeal by authority of the legislative power.

ABROOD' *adv.* [See *Brood.*] In the action of brooding. [*Not in use.*] *Sancroft.*

ABROOD'ING, *n.* A sitting abrood. [*Not in use.*] *Basset.*

ABRỌOK', *v. t.* To brook, to endure. [*Not in use.* See *Brook.*] *Shak.*

ABRO'TANUM, *n.* [Gr. Αβροτονον.] A species of plant arranged under the Genus, Artemisia; called also southern wood.

ABRUPT', *a.* [L. *abruptus*, from *abrumpo*, to *break off*, of *ab* and *rumpo*. See *Rupture*.]

1. *Literally*, broken off, or broken short. Hence,

2. Steep, craggy; applied to rocks, precipices and the like.

3. *Figuratively*, sudden; without notice to prepare the mind for the event; as an *abrupt* entrance and address.

4. Unconnected; having sudden transitions from one subject to another; as an *abrupt* style. *Ben Jonson.*

5. In *botany*, an abrupt pinnate leaf is one which has neither leaflet, nor tendril at the end. *Martyn.*

ABRUPT' *n.* A chasm or gulf with steep sides. "Over the vast abrupt." *Milton.* [*This use of the word is infrequent.*]

ABRUP'TION, *n.* A sudden breaking off; a violent separation of bodies. *Woodward.*

ABRUPT'LY, *adv.* Suddenly; without giving notice, or without the usual forms; as, the Minister left France *abruptly.*

ABRUPT'NESS, *n.* A state of being broken; craggedness; steepness.

2. *Figuratively*, suddenness; unceremonious haste or vehemence.

AB'SCESS, *n.* [L. *abscessus*, from *ab* and *cedo*, to go from.] An imposthume. A collection of morbid matter, or pus in the cellular or adipose membrane; matter generated by the suppuration of an inflammatory tumor. *Quincy. Hooper.*

ABSCIND', *vt.* [L. *abscindo.*] To cut off. [*Little used.*]

AB'SCISS, *n.* [L. *abscissus*, from *ab* and *scindere*, to cut; Gr. σχιζω. See *Scissors*.] In *conics*, a part of the diameter, or transverse axis of a conic section, intercepted between the vertex or some other fixed point, and a semiordinate. *Encyc.*

ABSCIS''SION, *n.* [See *Absciss.*] A cutting off, or a being cut off. In *surgery*, the separation of any corrupted or useless part of the body, by a sharp instrument; applied to the soft parts, as amputation is to the bones and flesh of a limb. *Quincy.*

ABSCOND', *v. i.* [L. *abscondo*, to hide, of *abs* and *condo*, to hide, i. e. to withdraw, or to thrust aside or into a corner or secret place.]

1. To retire from public view, or from the place in which one resides or is ordinarily to be found; to withdraw, or absent one's self in a private manner; to be concealed; appropriately, used of persons who secrete themselves to avoid a legal process.

2. To hide, withdraw or be concealed; as, "the marmot *absconds* in winter. [*Little used.*] *Ray.*

ABSCOND'ER, *n.* One who withdraws from public notice, or conceals himself from public view.

ABSCOND'ING, *ppr.* Withdrawing privately from public view; as, an *absconding debtor*, who confines himself to his apartments, or absents himself to avoid the ministers of justice. In the latter sense, it is properly an adjective.

AB'SENCE, *n.* [L. *absens*, from *absum*, *abesse*, to be away; *ab* and *sum*.]

1. A state of being at a distance in place, or not in company. It is used to denote any distance indefinitely, either in the same town, or country, or in a foreign country; and primarily supposes a prior presence. "Speak well of one in his *absence*."

2. Want; destitution; *implying no previous presence.* "In the *absence* of conventional law." *Ch. Kent.*

3. *In law*, non-appearance; a not being in court to answer.

4. Heedlessness; inattention to things present. *Absence* of mind is the attention of the mind to a subject which does not occupy the rest of the company, and which draws the mind from things or objects which are present, to others distant or foreign.

AB'SENT, *a.* Not present; not in company; at such a distance as to prevent communication. It is used also for being in a foreign country.

A gentleman is *absent* on his travels.

Absent from one another. Gen. xxxi. 49.

2. Heedless; inattentive to persons present, or to subjects of conversation in company.

An *absent* man is uncivil to the company.

3. In *familiar language*, not at home; as, the master of the house is *absent.* In other words, he does not wish to be disturbed by company.

ABSENT', *v. t.* To depart to such a distance as to prevent intercourse; to retire or withdraw; to forbear to appear in presence; used with the reciprocal pronoun. Let a man *absent himself* from the company.

ABSENTEE', *n.* One who withdraws from his country, office or estate; one who removes to a distant place or to another country.

ABSENT'ER, *n.* One who absents himself.

ABSENT'MENT, *n.* A state of being absent. *Barrow.*

ABSINTH'IAN, *a.* [from *absinthium.*] Of the nature of wormwood. *Randolph.*

ABSINTH'IATED, *a.* Impregnated with wormwood. *Dict.*

ABSINTH'IUM, *n.* [Gr. αψινθιον; Per. افسنتين afsinthin; the same in Chaldaic. Budæus in his commentaries on Theophrast, supposes the word composed of α priv. and ψινθος, delight, so named from its bitterness. But it may be an Oriental word.] The common wormwood; a bitter plant, used as a tonic. A species of Artemisia.

AB'SIS, In *astronomy.* [See *Apsis.*]

AB'SOLUTE, *a.* [L. *absolutus.* See *Absolve.*]

1. *Literally, in a general sense*, free, independent of any thing extraneous. Hence,

2. Complete in itself; positive; as an *absolute* declaration.

3. Unconditional, as an *absolute* promise.

4. Existing independent of any other cause, as God is *absolute.*

5. Unlimited by extraneous power or control, as an *absolute* government or prince.

6. Not relative, as *absolute* space. *Stillingfleet.*

In *grammar*, the case *absolute*, is when a word or member of a sentence is not immediately dependent on the other parts of the sentence in government.

Absolute equation, in astronomy, is the aggregate of the optic and eccentric equations. The apparent inequality of a planet's motion in its orbit, arising from its unequal distances from the earth at different times, is called its optic equation: the eccentric inequality is caused by the uniformity of the planet's motion, in an *elliptical* orbit, which, for that reason, appears not to be uniform.

Absolute numbers, in algebra, are such as have no letters annexed, as 2a+36=48. The two latter numbers are *absolute* or pure. *Encyc.*

Absolute space, in physics, is space considered without relation to any other object. *Bailey.*

Absolute gravity, in philosophy, is that property in bodies by which they are said to weigh so much, without regard to circumstances of modification, and this is always as the quantity of matter they contain. *Bailey.*

AB'SOLUTELY, *adv.* Completely, wholly, as a thing is *absolutely* unintelligible.

2. Without dependence or relation; in a state unconnected.

Absolutely we cannot discommend, we cannot *absolutely* approve, either willingness to live, or forwardness to die. *Hooker.*

3. Without restriction or limitation; as God reigns *absolutely.*

4. Without condition, as God does not forgive *absolutely*, but upon condition of faith and repentance.

5. Positively, peremptorily, as command me *absolutely* not to go. *Milton.*

AB'SOLUTENESS, *n.* Independence; completeness in itself.

2. Despotic authority, or that which is subject to no extraneous restriction, or control.

ABSOLU'TION, *n.* In the *civil law*, an acquittal or sentence of a judge declaring an accused person innocent. In the *canon law*, a remission of sins pronounced by a priest in favor of a penitent. Among protestants, a sentence by which an excommunicated person is released from his liability to punishment. *Ayliffe. South.*

AB'SOLUTORY, *a.* Absolving; that absolves.

ABSOLV'ATORY, *a.* [from *absolve.*] Containing absolution, pardon, or release; having power to absolve. *Cotgrave.*

ABSOLVE', *v. t. abzolv'*, [L. *absolvo*, from *ab* and *solvo*, to loose or release; Ch. שלה, to absolve, to finish; Heb. של, to loose or loosen. See *Solve.*] To set free or release from some obligation, debt or responsibility; or from that which subjects a person to a burden or penalty; as to *absolve* a person from a promise; to *absolve* an offender, which amounts to an acquittal and remission of his punishment. Hence, in the civil law, the word was used for *acquit;* and in the canon law, for *forgive*, or a sentence of remission. In ordinary language, its sense is to *set free* or *release* from an engagement. Formerly, good writers used the word in the sense of *finish, accomplish;* as to *absolve* work, in Milton; but in this sense, it seems to be obsolete.

ABSOLV'ED, *pp.* Released; acquitted; remitted; declared innocent.

ABSOLV'ER, *n.* One who absolves: also one that pronounces sin to be remit.

ABSOLV'ING, *ppr.* Setting free from a debt, or charge; acquitting; remitting.

AB'SONANT, *a.* [See *Absonous.*] Wide from the purpose; contrary to reason.

AB'SONOUS, *a.* [L. *absonus; ab* and *sonus*, sound.] Unmusical, or untunable. *Fotherby.*

ABSORB', *v. t.* [L. *absorbeo, ab* and *sorbeo*, to drink in; Ar. شَرَبَ sharaba; Eth. ሰረበ or ሠረበ, id.; Rab. שרף, to draw or drink in; whence *sirup, sherbet, shrub.*]
1. To drink in; to suck up; to imbibe; as a spunge, or as the lacteals of the body.
2. To drink in, swallow up, or overwhelm with water, as a body in a whirlpool.
3. To waste wholly or sink in expenses; to exhaust; as, to *absorb* an estate in luxury.
4. To engross or engage wholly, as, *absorbed* in study or the pursuit of wealth.

ABSORBABIL'ITY, *n.* A state or quality of being absorbable.

ABSORB'ABLE, *a.* That may be imbibed or swallowed. *Kerr's Lavoisier.*

ABSORB'ED, or **ABSORPT'**, *pp.* Imbibed; swallowed; wasted; engaged; lost in study; wholly engrossed.

ABSORB'ENT, *a.* Imbibing; swallowing.

ABSORB'ENT, *n.* In *anatomy*, a vessel which imbibes, as the lacteals, lymphatics, and inhaling arteries. In *medicine*, a testaceous powder, or other substance, which imbibes the humors of the body, as chalk or magnesia. *Encyc.*

ABSORB'ING, *ppr.* Imbibing; engrossing; wasting.

ABSORP'TION, *n.* The act or process of imbibing or swallowing; either by water which overwhelms, or by substances, which drink in and retain liquids; as the *absorption* of a body in a whirlpool, or of water by the earth, or of the humors of the body by dry powders. It is used also to express the swallowing up of substances by the earth in chasms made by earthquakes, and the sinking of large tracts in violent commotions of the earth.
2. In *chimistry*, the conversion of a gaseous fluid into a liquid or solid, by union with another substance. *Ure.*

ABSORP'TIVE, *a.* Having power to imbibe. *Darwin.*

ABSTA'IN, *v. i.* [L. *abstineo*, to keep from; *abs* and *teneo*, to hold. See *Tenant.*]
In *a general sense*, to forbear, or refrain from, voluntarily; but used chiefly to denote a restraint upon the passions or appetites; to refrain from indulgence.

Abstain from meats offered to idols. Acts, xv.

To *abstain* from the use of ardent spirits; to *abstain* from luxuries.

ABSTE'MIOUS, *a.* [L. *abstemius;* from *abs* and *temetum*, an ancient name of strong wine, according to Fabius and Gellius. But Vossius supposes it to be from *abstineo*, by a change of *n* to *m*. It may be from the root of *timeo*, to fear, that is, to withdraw.] Sparing in diet; refraining from a free use of food and strong drinks.

Instances of longevity are chiefly among the *abstemious.* *Arbuthnot.*

2. Sparing in the enjoyment of animal pleasures of any kind. [*This sense is less common, and perhaps not legitimate.*]
3. Sparingly used, or used with temperance; belonging to abstinence; as an *abstemious* diet; an *abstemious* life.

ABSTE'MIOUSLY, *adv.* Temperately; with a sparing use of meat or drink.

ABSTE'MIOUSNESS, *n.* The quality of being temperate or sparing in the use of food and strong drinks.
This word expresses a greater degree of abstinence than *temperance.*

ABSTERĠE', *v. t. absterj'.* [L. *abstergeo*, of *abs* and *tergeo*, to wipe. *Tergeo* may have a common origin with the Sw. *torcka*, G. *trocknen*, D. *droogen*, Sax. *drygan*, to dry; for these Teutonic verbs signify to *wipe*, as well as to dry.]
To wipe or make clean by wiping; to cleanse by resolving obstructions in the body. [*Used chiefly as a medical term.*]

ABSTERĠ'ENT, *a.* Wiping; cleansing.

ABSTERĠ'ENT, *n.* A medicine which frees the body from obstructions, as soap; but the use of the word is nearly superseded by *detergent*, which see.

ABSTER'SION, *n.* [from L. *abstergeo, abstersus.*] The act of wiping clean; or a cleansing by medicines which resolve obstructions. [See *Deterge, Detersion.*] *Bacon.*

ABSTER'SIVE, *a.* Cleansing; having the quality of removing obstructions. [See *Detersive.*]

AB'STINENCE, *n.* [L. *abstinentia.* See *Abstain.*] In general, the act or practice of voluntarily refraining from, or forbearing any action. "*Abstinence* from every thing which can be deemed labor." *Paley's Philos.*

More appropriately,
2. The refraining from an indulgence of appetite, or from customary gratifications of animal propensities. It denotes a total forbearance, as in fasting, or a forbearance of the usual quantity. In the latter sense, it may coincide with *temperance*, but in general, it denotes a more sparing use of enjoyments than *temperance.* Besides, *abstinence* implies previous free indulgence; *temperance* does not.

AB'STINENT, *a.* Refraining from indulgence, especially in the use of food and drink.

AB'STINENTLY, *adv.* With abstinence.

AB'STINENTS, a sect which appeared in France and Spain in the third century, who opposed marriage, condemned the use of flesh meat, and placed the Holy Spirit in the class of created beings.

ABSTRAƇT', *v. t.* [L. *abstraho*, to draw from or separate; from *abs* and *traho*, which is the Eng. *draw.* See *Draw.*]
1. To draw from, or to separate; as to *abstract* an action from its evil effects; to *abstract* spirit from any substance by distillation; but in this sense *extract* is now more generally used.
2. To separate ideas by the operation of the mind; to consider one part of a complex object, or to have a partial idea of it in the mind. *Horne.*
3. To select or separate the substance of a book or writing; to epitomize or reduce to a summary. *Watts.*
4. In *chimistry*, to separate, as the more volatile parts of a substance by repeated distillation, or at least by distillation.

AB'STRAƇT, *a.* [L. *abstractus.*] Separate; distinct from something else. An *abstract* idea, in metaphysics, is an idea separated from a complex object, or from other ideas which naturally accompany it, as the solidity of marble contemplated apart from its color or figure. *Encyc.*
Abstract terms are those which express abstract ideas, as beauty, whiteness, roundness, without regarding any subject in which they exist; or *abstract* terms are the names of orders, genera, or species of things, in which there is a combination of similar qualities. *Stewart.*
Abstract numbers are numbers used without application to things, as, 6, 8, 10: but when applied to any thing, as 6 feet, 10 men, they become concrete.
Abstract or pure mathematics, is that which treats of magnitude or quantity, without restriction to any species of particular magnitude, as arithmetic and geometry; opposed to which is mixed mathematics, which treats of simple properties, and the relations of quantity, as applied to sensible objects, as hydrostatics, navigation, optics, &c. *Encyc.*
2. Separate, existing in the mind only; as an *abstract* subject; an *abstract* question; and hence difficult, abstruse.

AB'STRAƇT, *n.* A summary, or epitome, containing the substance, a general view, or the principal heads of a treatise or writing. *Watts.*
2. Formerly, an extract, or a smaller quantity, containing the essence of a larger.
In *the abstract*, in a state of separation, as a subject considered in the *abstract*, i. e. without reference to particular persons or things.

ABSTRAƇT'ED, *pp.* Separated; refined; exalted; abstruse; absent in mind. *Milton. Donne.*

ABSTRAƇT'EDLY, *adv.* In a separate state, or in contemplation only. *Dryden.*

ABSTRAƇT'EDNESS, *n.* The state of being abstracted. *Baxter.*

ABSTRAƇT'ER, *n.* One who makes an abstract, or summary.

ABSTRAƇT'ING, *ppr.* Separating; making a summary.

ABSTRAƇ'TION, *n.* The act of separating, or state of being separated.
2. The operation of the mind when occupied by abstract ideas; as when we contemplate some particular part, or property of a complex object, as separate from the rest. Thus, when the mind considers the branch of a tree by itself, or the color of the leaves, as separate from their size or figure, the act is called *abstraction.* So also, when it considers *whiteness, softness, virtue, existence*, as separate from any particular objects. *Encyc.*

The power which the understanding has of separating the combinations which are presented to it, is distinguished by logicians, by the name of *abstraction.* *Stewart.*

Abstraction is the ground-work of classification, by which things are arranged in orders, genera, and species. We separate in idea the qualities of certain objects which are of the same kind, from others which are different in each, and arrange the objects having the same properties in a class, or collected body.

3. A separation from worldly objects; a recluse life; as a hermit's *abstraction*.
4. Absence of mind; inattention to present objects.
5. In the process of distillation, the term is used to denote the separation of the volatile parts, which rise, come over, and are condensed in a receiver, from those which are fixed. It is chiefly used, when a fluid is repeatedly poured upon any substance in a retort, and distilled off, to change its state, or the nature of its composition. *Nicholson.*

ABSTRACT'IVE, *a.* Having the power or quality of abstracting.

ABSTRACT'IVE, ABSTRACTI''TIOUS, } *a.* Abstracted, or drawn from other substances, particularly from vegetables, without fermentation. *Cyc.*

AB'STRACTLY, *adv.* Separately; absolutely; in a state or manner unconnected with any thing else; as, matter *abstractly* considered.

AB'STRACTNESS, *n.* A separate state; a state of being in contemplation only, or not connected with any object.

ABSTRU'DE, *v. t.* [*Infra.*] To thrust or pull away. [*Not used.*]

ABSTRU'SE, *a.* [L. *abstrusus*, from *abstrudo*, to thrust away, to conceal; *abs* and *trudo;* Ar. طرد tarada; Ch. טרד, to thrust; Syr. Sam. id.; Eng. to *thrust.*] Hid; concealed; hence, remote from apprehension; difficult to be comprehended or understood; opposed to what is *obvious.* [*Not used of material objects.*]

Metaphysics is an *abstruse* science. *Encyc.*

ABSTRU'SELY, *adv.* In a concealed manner; obscurely; in a manner not to be easily understood.

ABTRU'SENESS, *n.* Obscurity of meaning; the state or quality of being difficult to be understood. *Boyle.*

ABSURD', *a.* [L. *absurdus*, from *ab* and *surdus*, deaf, insensible.] Opposed to manifest truth; inconsistent with reason, or the plain dictates of common sense. An *absurd* man acts contrary to the clear dictates of reason or sound judgment. An *absurd* proposition contradicts obvious truth. An *absurd* practice or opinion is repugnant to the reason or common apprehension of men. It is *absurd* to say six and six make ten, or that plants will take root in stone.

ABSURD'ITY, *n.* The quality of being inconsistent with obvious truth, reason, or sound judgment. Want of judgment, applied to men; want of propriety, applied to things. *Johnson.*
2. That which is absurd; in this sense it has a plural; the *absurdities* of men.

ABSURD'LY, *adv.* In a manner inconsistent with reason, or obvious propriety.

ABSURD'NESS, *n.* The same as *absurdity*, and less used.

ABUND'ANCE, *n.* [F. *abondance.* See *Abound.*] Great plenty; an overflowing quantity; ample sufficiency; in strictness applicable to quantity only; but customarily used of number, as an *abundance* of peasants. *Addison.*

In scripture, the *abundance* of the rich is great wealth. Eccl. v. Mark, xii. Luke, xxi.

The *abundance* of the seas is great plenty of fish. Deut. xxxiii.

It denotes also fullness, overflowing, as the *abundance* of the heart. Mat. xii Luke, vi.

ABUND'ANT, *a.* Plentiful; in great quantity; fully sufficient; as an *abundant* supply. In *scripture*, abounding; having in great quantity; overflowing with.

The Lord God is *abundant* in goodness and truth. Ex. xxxiv.

Abundant number, in arithmetic, is one, the sum of whose aliquot parts exceeds the number itself. Thus 1, 2, 3, 4, 6, the aliquot parts of 12, make the sum of 16. This is opposed to a *deficient* number, as 14, whose aliquot parts are 1, 2, 7, the sum of which is 10; and to a *perfect* number, which is equal to the sum of its aliquot parts, as 6, whose aliquot parts are 1, 2, 3.

ABUND'ANTLY, *adv.* Fully; amply; plentifully; in a sufficient degree.

ABU'SAGE, *n.* Abuse. [*Not used.*]

ABU'SE, *v. t. s* as *z.* [Fr. *abuser;* Sp. *abusar;* It. *abusare;* L. *abutor, abusus*, of *ab* and *utor*, to use; Ir. *idh;* W. *gweth*, use; Gr. εθω, to accustom. See *Use.*]
1. To use ill; to maltreat; to misuse; to use with bad motives or to wrong purposes; as, to *abuse* rights or privileges.

They that use this world as not *abusing* it. 1 Cor. vii.

2. To violate; to defile by improper sexual intercourse. *Spenser.*
3. To deceive; to impose on.

Nor be with all these tempting words *abused.* *Pope.*

4. To treat rudely, or with reproachful language; to revile.

He mocked and *abused* them shamefully. *Mac.*

5. To pervert the meaning of; to misapply; as to *abuse* words.

ABU'SE, *n.* Ill use; improper treatment or employment; application to a wrong purpose; as an *abuse* of our natural powers; an *abuse* of civil rights, or of religious privileges; *abuse* of advantages, &c.

Liberty may be endangered by the *abuses* of liberty, as well as by the *abuses* of power. *Federalist, Madison.*

2. A corrupt practice or custom, as the *abuses* of government.
3. Rude speech; reproachful language addressed to a person; contumely; reviling words. *Milton.*
4. Seduction.

After the *abuse* he forsook me. *Sidney.*

5. Perversion of meaning; improper use or application; as an *abuse* of words.

ABU'SED, *pp. s* as *z.* Ill-used; used to a bad purpose; treated with rude language; misemployed; perverted to bad or wrong ends; deceived; defiled; violated.

ABU'SEFUL, *a.* Using or practicing abuse; abusive. [*Not used.*] *Bp. Barlow.*

ABU'SER, *n. s* as *z.* One who abuses, in speech or behavior; one that deceives; a ravisher; a sodomite. 1 Cor. vi.

ABU'SING, *ppr. s* as *z.* Using ill; employing to bad purposes; deceiving; violating the person; perverting.

ABU'SION, *n. abu'zhon.* Abuse; evil or corrupt usage; reproach. [*Little used.*]

ABU'SIVE, *a.* Practicing abuse; offering harsh words, or ill treatment; as an *abusive* author; an *abusive* fellow.
2. Containing abuse, or that is the instrument of abuse, as *abusive* words; rude; reproachful. In the sense of deceitful, as an *abusive* treaty. [*Little used.*] *Bacon.*

ABU'SIVELY, *adv.* In an abusive manner; rudely; reproachfully.

ABU'SIVENESS, *n.* Ill-usage; the quality of being abusive; rudeness of language, or violence to the person. *Barlow.*

ABUT', *v. i.* [Fr. *aboutir.* See *About.*] To border upon; to be contiguous to; to meet; in strictness, to adjoin to at the end; but this distinction has not always been observed. The word is chiefly used in describing the bounds or situation of land, and in popular language, is contracted into *but*, as *butted* and *bounded.*

ABUT'MENT, *n.* The head or end; that which unites one end of a thing to another; chiefly used to denote the solid pier or mound of earth, stone or timber, which is erected on the bank of a river to support the end of a bridge and connect it with the land.
2. That which abuts or borders on another. *Bryant.*

ABUT'TAL, *n.* The butting or boundary of land at the end; a head-land. *Spelman. Cowel.*

ABY', *v. t.* or *i.* [Probably contracted from *abide.*] To endure; to pay dearly; to remain. *Obs.* *Spenser.*

ABYSM', *n. abyzm'.* [Old Fr., now *abime.* See *Abyss.*] A gulf. *Shak.*

ABYSS', *n.* [Gr. Αβυσσος, bottomless, from α priv. and βυσσος, bottom, Ion. for βυθος. See *Bottom.*] A bottomless gulf; used also for a deep mass of waters, supposed by some to have encompassed the earth before the flood.

Darkness was upon the face of the deep, or abyss, as it is in the Septuagint. Gen. i. 2.

The word is also used for an immense cavern in the earth, in which God is supposed to have collected all the waters on the third day of the creation. It is used also for hell, Erebus.
2. That which is immeasurable; that in which any thing is lost.

Thy throne is darkness, in the *abyss* of light. *Milton.*

The *abyss* of time. *Dryden.*

3. In *antiquity*, the temple of Proserpine, so called from the immense treasures it was supposed to contain.
4. In *heraldry*, the center of an escutcheon.

He bears azure, a fleur de lis, in *abyss.*

ABYSSIN'IAN, *a.* Ar. حبش habashon, Abyssinians, Ethiopians, from حبش habasha, to collect, or congregate. A name denoting a mixed multitude or a black race. *Ludolf. Castle.*

ABYSSIN'IANS, *n.* A sect of christians in Abyssinia, who admit but one nature in Jesus Christ, and reject the council of Chalcedon. They are governed by a bishop, or metropolitan, called *Abuna*, who is appointed by the Coptic patriarch of Cairo. *Encyc.*

AC, in Saxon, oak, the initial syllable of names, as *acton*, oaktown.

ACAC'ALOT, AC'ALOT, } *n.* A Mexican fowl, the Tantalus Mexicanus, or Corvus aquaticus, water raven. See *Acalot.*

ACA'CIA, *n.* [L. *acacia*, a thorn, from Gr. ακη, a point.]

Egyptian thorn, a species of plant ranked by Linne under the genus *mimosa*, and by others, made a distinct genus. Of the flowers of one species, the Chinese make a yellow dye which bears washing in silks, and appears with elegance on paper. *Encyc.*

ACACIA, in *medicine*, is a name given to the inspissated juice of the unripe fruit of the Mimosa Nilotica, which is brought from Egypt in roundish masses, in bladders.

Externally, it is of a deep brown color; internally, of a reddish or yellowish brown; of a firm consistence, but not very dry. It is a mild astringent. But most of the drug which passes under this name, is the inspissated juice of sloes. *Encyc.*

ACACIA, among *antiquaries*, is a name given to something like a roll or bag, seen on medals, as in the hands of emperors and consuls. Some take it to represent a handkerchief rolled up, with which signals were given at the games; others, a roll of petitions; and some, a purple bag of earth, to remind them of their mortality. *Encyc.*

ACA′CIANS, in *Church History*, were certain sects, so denominated from their leaders, Acacius, bishop of Cesarea, and Acacius, patriarch of Constantinople. Some of these maintained that the Son was only a similar, not the same, substance with the Father; others, that he was not only a distinct but a dissimilar substance. *Encyc.*

ACADE′ME; *n.* An academy; a society of persons. [*Not used.*]

ACADE′MIAL, *a.* Pertaining to an academy.

ACADE′MIAN, *n.* A member of an academy; a student in a university or college.

ACADEM′IC, } *a.* Belonging to an
ACADEM′ICAL, } academy, or to a college or university—as *academic* studies; also noting what belongs to the school or philosophy of Plato—as the *academic* sect.

ACADEM′IC, *n.* One who belonged to the school or adhered to the philosophy of Socrates and Plato. The latter is considered as the founder of the academic philosophy in Greece.

He taught, that matter is eternal and infinite, but without form, refractory, and tending to disorder; and that there is an intelligent cause, the author of spiritual being, and of the material world. *Enfield.*

ACADEM′ICALLY, *adv.* In an academical manner.

ACADEMI′′CIAN, *n.* [Fr. *académicien.*]
A member of an academy, or society for promoting arts and sciences; particularly, a member of the French academies.

ACAD′EMISM, *n.* The doctrine of the academic philosophy. *Baxter.*

ACAD′EMIST, *n.* A member of an Academy for promoting arts and sciences; also an academic philosopher.

ACAD′EMY, *n.* [L. *academia*, Gr. Ακαδημια.]
Originally, it is said, a garden, grove, or villa, near Athens, where Plato and his followers held their philosophical conferences.

1. A school, or seminary of learning, holding a rank between a university or college, and a common school; also a school, for teaching a particular art, or particular sciences, as a *military academy.*
2. A house, in which the students or members of an academy meet; a place of education.
3. A society of men united for the promotion of arts and sciences in general, or of some particular art.

AC′ALOT, *n.* [Contracted from *acacalotl.*]
A Mexican fowl, called by some the aquatic crow. It is the ibis, or a fowl that very much resembles it.

ACAMAC′U, *n*, A bird, the Brazilian fly catcher, or *Todus.* *Cyc.*

ACANA′CEOUS, *a.* *acana′shus.* [Gr. ακανος, a prickly shrub.]
Armed with prickles. A class of plants are called *acanaceæ.* *Milne.*

ACANTH′A, *n.* [Gr. ακανθα, a spine or thorn.]
In *botany*, a prickle; in *zoology*, a spine or prickly fin; an acute process of the vertebers. *Encyc.*

ACANTHA′CEOUS, *a.* Armed with prickles, as a plant.

ACAN′THARIS, *n.* In *entomology*, a species of Cimex, with a spinous thorax, and a ciliated abdomen, with spines; found in Jamaica. *Cyc.*

ACANTH′INE, *a.* [See *Acanthus.*]
Pertaining to the plant, *acanthus.* The *acanthine* garments of the ancients were made of the down of thistles, or embroidered in imitation of the *acanthus.* *Encyc.*

ACANTHOPTERYG′IOUS, *a.* [Gr ακανθος, a thorn, and πτερυγιον, a little feather, from πτερον, a feather.]
In *zoology*, having back fins, which are hard, bony and pricky, *a term applied to certain fishes.* *Linne.*

ACANTH′US *n.* [Gr. ακανθος, L. *acanthus*, from ακανθα, a prickle or thorn. See *acantha.*]
1. The plant bear's breech or brank ursine; a genus of several species, receiving their name from their prickles.
2. In *architecture*, an ornament resembling the foliage or leaves of the acanthus, used in capitals of the Corinthian and Composite orders. *Milton. Encyc.*

ACAN′TICONE, *n.* See *Pistacite.*

ACARN′AR, *n.* A bright star, of the first magnitude, in Eridanus. *Bailey.*

ACATALEC′TIC, *n.* [Gr. ακαταληκτος, not defective at the end, of κατα and ληγω to cease; Ir. *lieghim.*] A verse, which has the complete number of syllables without defect or superfluity. *Johnson.*

ACAT′ALEPSY, *n.* [Gr. ακαταληψια; α and καταλαμβανω to comprehend.]
Impossibility of complete discovery or comprehension; incomprehensibility. [*Little used.*] *Whitaker.*

ACAT′ECHILI, *n.* A Mexican bird, a species of Fringilla, of the size of the siskin.

ACATER, ACATES. See *Caterer* and *Cates.*

ACAU′LINE, } *a.* [L. *a.* priv. and *caulis*, Gr.
ACAU′LOUS, } καυλος, a stalk; W. *kaul;* D. *kool*, cabbage. See *Colewort.*]
In *botany*, without a stem, having flowers resting on the ground; as the Carline thistle.

ACCE′DE, *v. i.* [L. *accedo*, of *ad* and *cedo*, to yield or give place, or rather to move.]
1. To agree or assent, as to a proposition, or to terms proposed by another. Hence in a negotiation.
2. To become a party, by agreeing to the terms of a treaty, or convention.

ACCE′DING, *ppr.* Agreeing; assenting: becoming a party to a treaty by agreeing to the terms proposed.

ACCEL′ERATE, *v. t.* [*L. accelero*, of *ad* and *celero*, to hasten, from *celer*, quick: Gr. κελης; Heb. Ch. Syr. and Eth. קלל, קלה or קל, to be light, nimble; Syr. to hasten. In Ch. and Ar. this root signifies also to be small, or minute.]
1. To cause to move faster; to hasten; to quicken motion; to add to the velocity of a moving body. It implies previous motion or progression.
2. To add to natural or ordinary progression; as to *accelerate* the growth of a plant. or the progress of knowledge.
3. To bring nearer in time; to shorten the time between the present time and a future event; as to *accelerate* the ruin of a government; to *accelerate* a battle. *Bacon.*

ACCEL′ERATED, *pp.* Quickened in motion; hastened in progress.

ACCEL′ERATING, *ppr.* Hastening; increasing velocity or progression.

ACCELERA′TION, *n.* The act of increasing velocity or progress; the state of being quickened in motion or action. Accelerated motion in mechanics and physics, is that which continually receives accessions of velocity; as, a falling body moves towards the earth with an *acceleration* of velocity. It is the opposite of retardation.

Acceleration of the moon, is the increase of the moon's mean motion from the sun, compared with the diurnal motion of the earth; the moon moving with more velocity now than in ancient times—a discovery made by Dr. Halley.

The *diurnal acceleration* of the fixed stars, is the time by which they anticipate the mean diurnal revolution of the sun, which is nearly three minutes, fifty-six seconds. *Cyc.*

ACCEL′ERATIVE, *a.* Adding to velocity; quickening progression. *Reid.*

ACCEL′ERATORY, *a.* Accelerating; quickening motion.

ACCEND′, *v. t.* [L. *accendo*, to kindle; *ad* and *candeo*, *caneo*, to be white, *canus*, white; W. *can*, white, bright; also a song. Whence, *canto*, to sing, to chant; *cantus*, a song; Eng. *cant;* W. *canu*, to bleach or whiten, and to sing; *cynnud*, fuel. Hence, *kindle*, L. *candidus*, *candid*, white. The primary sense is, to throw, dart, or thrust; to shoot, as the rays of light. Hence, to *cant*, to throw. See *Chant* and *Cant.*]
To kindle; to set on fire. [*The verb is not used.*]

ACCENDIBIL′ITY, *n.* Capacity of being kindled, or of becoming inflamed.

ACCEND′IBLE, *a.* Capable of being inflamed or kindled. *Ure.*

ACCEN′SION, *n.* The act of kindling or setting on fire; or the state of being kindled; inflammation. *Chimistry.*

AC′CENT, *n.* [L. *accentus*, from *ad* and *cano*, *cantum*, to sing; W. *canu;* Corn. *kana:* Ir. *canaim.* See *Accend.*]

1. The modulation of the voice in reading or speaking, as practiced by the ancient Greeks, which rendered their rehearsal musical. More strictly, in English,
2. A particular stress or force of voice upon certain syllables of words, which distinguishes them from the others. Accent is of two kinds, primary and secondary; as in as'pira'tion. In uttering this word, we observe the *first* and *third* syllables are distinguished; the *third* by a full sound, which constitutes the *primary* accent; the *first*, by a degree of force in the voice which is less than that of the primary accent, but evidently greater than that which falls on the second and fourth syllables.

When the full accent falls on a vowel, that vowel has its long sound, as in *vo'cal;* but when it falls on an articulation or consonant, the preceding vowel is short, as in *hab'it*. Accent alone regulates English verse.

3. A mark or character used in writing to direct the stress of the voice in pronunciation. Our ancestors borrowed from the Greek language three of these characters, the acute (′,) the grave (‵) and the circumflex (˜ or ˆ.) In the Greek, the first shows when the voice is to be raised; the second, when it is to be depressed; and the third, when the vowel is to be uttered with an undulating sound.
4. A modulation of the voice expressive of passions or sentiments.

The tender *accents* of a woman's cry. *Prior.*

5. Manner of speaking.

A man of plain *accent*. *Obs.* *Shak.*

6. Poetically, words, language, or expressions in general.

Words, on your wings, to heaven her *accents* bear,
Such words as heaven alone is fit to hear.
Dryden.

7. In *music*, a swelling of sounds, for the purpose of variety or expression. The principal accent falls on the first note in the bar, but the third place in common time requires also an accent.
8. A peculiar tone or inflection of voice.

AC'CENT, *v. t.* To express accent; to utter a syllable with a particular stress or modulation of the voice. In poetry, to utter or pronounce in general. Also to note accents by marks in writing. *Locke. Wotton.*

AC'CENTED, *pp.* Uttered with accent; marked with accent.

AC'CENTING, *ppr.* Pronouncing or marking with accent.

ACCENT'UAL, *a.* Pertaining to accent.

ACCENT'UATE, *v. t.* To mark or pronounce with an accent or with accents.

ACCENTUA'TION, *n.* The act of placing accents in writing, or of pronouncing them in speaking.

ACCEPT', *v. t.* [L. *accepto*, from *accipio*, *ad* and *capio*, to take; Fr. *accepter;* Sp. *aceptar;* Port. *aceiter;* It. *accettare*. See Lat. *capio*. Class G. b.]

1. To take or receive what is offered, with a consenting mind; to receive with approbation or favor.

Bless, Lord, his substance, and *accept* the work of his hands. Deut. xxxiii.

He made an offer which was *accepted*.

Observe the difference between *receive* and *accept*.

He *received* an appointment or the offer of a commission, but he did not *accept* it.

2. To regard with partiality; to value or esteem.

It is not good to *accept* the person of the wicked. Prov. xviii. 2 Cor. viii.

In *theology*, acceptance with God implies forgiveness of sins and reception into his favor.

3. To consent or agree to; to receive as terms of a contract; as, to *accept* a treaty; often followed by *of*.

Accept *of* the terms.

4. To understand; to have a particular idea of; to receive in a particular sense.

How is this phrase to be *accepted?*

5. In *commerce*, to agree or promise to pay, as a bill of exchange. [See *Acceptance*.]

ACCEPT'ABLE, *a.* That may be received with pleasure; hence pleasing to a receiver; gratifying; as an *acceptable* present.

2. Agreeable or pleasing in person; as, a man makes himself *acceptable* by his services or civilities.

ACCEPT'ABLENESS, } *n.* The quality of
ACCEPTABIL'ITY, } being agreeable to a receiver, or to a person with whom one has intercourse. [*The latter word is little used, or not at all.*]

ACCEPT'ABLY, *adv.* In a manner to please, or give satisfaction.

Let us have grace whereby we may serve God *acceptably*. Heb. xii.

ACCEPT'ANCE, *n.* A receiving with approbation or satisfaction; favorable reception; as work done to *acceptance*.

They shall come up with *acceptance* on my altar. Isa. lx.

2. The receiving of a bill of exchange or order, in such a manner, as to bind the acceptor to make payment. This must be by express words; and to charge the drawer with costs, in case of non payment, the acceptance must be in writing, under, across, or on the back of the bill. *Blackstone.*
3. An agreeing to terms or proposals in commerce, by which a bargain is concluded and the parties bound.
4. An agreeing to the act or contract of another, by some act which binds the person in law; as, a bishop's taking rent reserved on a lease made by his predecessor, is an *acceptance* of the terms of the lease and binds the party. *Law.*
5. In *mercantile language*, a bill of exchange accepted; as a merchant receives another's *acceptance* in payment.
6. Formerly, the sense in which a word is understood. *Obs.* [See *Acceptation*.]

ACCEPTA'TION, *n.* Kind reception; a receiving with favor or approbation.

This is a saying worthy of all *acceptation*. 1 Tim. i.

2. A state of being acceptable; favorable regard.

Some things are of great dignity and *acceptation* with God. *Hooker.*

But in this sense *acceptableness* is more generally used.

3. The meaning or sense in which a word or expression is understood, or generally received; as, a term is to be used according to its usual *acceptation*.
4. Reception in general. *Obs.*

ACCEPT'ED, *pp.* Kindly received; regarded; agreed to; understood; received as a bill of exchange.

ACCEPT'ER, or **ACCEPT'OR**, *n.* A person who accepts; the person who receives a bill of exchange so as to bind himself to pay it. [See *Acceptance*.]

ACCEPT'ING, *ppr.* Receiving favorably; agreeing to; understanding.

ACCEP'TION, *n.* The received sense of a word. [*Not now used.*] *Hammond.*

ACCEPT'IVE, *a.* Ready to accept. [*Not used.*] *B. Jonson.*

ACCESS', *n.* [L. *accessus*, from *accedo*. See *Accede*. Fr. *accès*.]

1. A coming to; near approach; admittance; admission; as to gain *access* to a prince.
2. Approach, or the way by which a thing may be approached; as, the *access* is by a neck of land. *Bacon.*
3. Means of approach; liberty to approach; implying previous obstacles.

By whom also we have *access* by faith. Rom. v.

4. Admission to sexual intercourse.

During coverture, *access* of the husband shall be presumed, unless the contrary be shown. *Blackstone.*

5. Addition; increase by something added; as an *access* of territory; but in this sense *accession* is more generally used.
6. The return of a fit or paroxysm of disease, or fever. In this sense *accession* is generally used.

ACCESSARILY, See **ACCESSORILY**.

ACCESSARINESS, See **ACCESSORINESS**.

ACCESSARY, See **ACCESSORY**.

ACCESSIBIL'ITY, *n.* The quality of being approachable; or of admitting access.

ACCESS'IBLE, *a.* That may be approached or reached; approachable; *applied to things;* as an *accessible* town or mountain.

2. Easy of approach; affable; *used of persons.*

ACCESS'ION, *n.* [L. *accessio*.] A coming to; an acceding to and joining; as a king's *accession* to a confederacy.

2. Increase by something added; that which is added; augmentation; as an *accession* of wealth or territory.
3. In *law*, a mode of acquiring property, by which the owner of a corporeal substance, which receives an addition by growth, or by labor, has a right to the thing added or the improvement; provided the thing is not changed into a different species. Thus the owner of a cow becomes the owner of her calf. *Blackstone.*
4. The act of arriving at a throne, an office, or dignity.
5. That which is added.

The only *accession* which the Roman Empire received, was the province of Britain. *Gibbon.*

6. The invasion of a fit of a periodical disease, or fever. It differs from exacerbation. *Accession* implies a total previous intermission, as of a fever; exacerbation implies only a previous remission or abatement of violence.

ACCESS'IONAL, *a.* Additional.

ACCESSO'RIAL, *a.* Pertaining to an accessory; as *accessorial* agency, *accessorial* guilt. *Burr's Trial.*

AC'CESSORILY, *adv.* [See *Accessory*.] In the manner of an accessory; by subordinate means, or in a secondary character; not as principal, but as a subordinate agent.

AC'CESSORINESS, *n.* The state of being accessory, or of being or acting in a secondary character.

AC'CESSORY, *a.* [L. *Accessorius*, from *accessus, accedo.* See *Accede.* This word is accented on the first syllable on account of the derivatives, which require a secondary accent on the third; but the natural accent of *accessory* is on the second syllable, and thus it is often pronounced by good speakers.]

1. Acceding; contributing; aiding in producing some effect, or acting in subordination to the principal agent. Usually, in a bad sense, as John was *accessory* to the felony.
2. Aiding in certain acts or effects in a secondary manner, as *accessory* sounds in music. *Encyc.*

AC'CESSORY, *n.* In *law*, one who is guilty of a felony, not by committing the offense in person or as principal, but by advising or commanding another to commit the crime, or by concealing the offender. There may be accessories in all felonies, but not in treason. An accessory *before* the fact, is one who counsels or commands another to commit a felony, and is not present when the act is executed; *after* the fact, when one receives and conceals the offender.

2. That which accedes or belongs to something else, as its principal.

Accessory nerves, in anatomy, a pair of nerves, which arising from the medulla in the vertebers of the neck, ascend and enter the skull; then passing out with the par vagum, are distributed into the muscles of the neck and shoulders.

Accessory, among painters, an epithet given to parts of a history-piece which are merely ornamental, as vases, armor, &c.

AC'CIDENCE, *n.* [See *Accident.*] A small book containing the rudiments of grammar.

AC'CIDENT, *n.* [L. *accidens*, falling, from *ad* and *cado*, to fall; W. *codum*, a fall, *cwyzaw*, to fall; Ir. *kudaim;* Corn. *kotha;* Arm. *kuetha*, to fall. See *Case* and *Cadence.* Class G d.]

1. A coming or falling; an event that takes place without one's foresight or expectation; an event which proceeds from an unknown cause, or is an unusual effect of a known cause, and therefore not expected; chance; casualty; contingency.
2. That which takes place or begins to exist without an efficient intelligent cause and without design.

> All of them, in his opinion, owe their being, to fate, *accident*, or the blind action of stupid matter. *Dwight.*

3. In *logic*, a property, or quality of a being which is not essential to it, as *whiteness* in paper. Also all qualities are called *accidents*, in opposition to *substance*, as *sweetness, softness*, and things not essential to a body, as *clothes.* *Encyc.*
4. In *grammar*, something belonging to a word, but not essential to it, as gender, number, inflection. *Encyc.*
5. In *heraldry*, a point or mark, not essential to a coat of arms. *Encyc.*

ACCIDENT'AL, *a.* Happening by chance, or rather unexpectedly; casual; fortuitous; taking place not according to the usual course of things; opposed to that which is constant, regular, or intended; as an *accidental* visit.

2. Non-essential; not necessarily belonging to; as songs are *accidental* to a play.

Accidental colors, are those which depend upon the affections of the eye, in distinction from those which belong to the light itself. *Encyc.*

Accidental point, in perspective, is that point in the horizontal line, where the projections of two lines parallel to each other, meet the perspective plane.

ACCIDENT'ALLY, *adv.* By chance; casually; fortuitously; not essentially.

ACCIDENT'ALNESS, *n.* The quality of being casual. [*Little used.*]

ACCIDEN'TIARY, *a.* Pertaining to the accidence. [*Not used.*] *Morton.*

ACCIP'ITER, *n.* [L. *ad* and *capio*, to seize.]

1. A name given to a fish, the milvus or lucerna, a species of Trigla. *Cyc.*
2. In *ornithology*, the name of the order of rapacious fowls.

The accipiters have a hooked bill, the superior mandible, near the base, being extended on each side beyond the inferior. The genera are the vultur, the falco, or hawk, and the strix, or owl.

ACCIP'ITRINE, *a.* [*Supra.*] Seizing; rapacious; as the *accipitrine* order of fowls. *Ed. Encyc.*

ACCI'TE, *v. t.* [L. *ad* and *cito*, to cite.] To call; to cite; to summon. [*Not used.*]

ACCLA'IM, *v. t.* [L. *acclamo, ad* and *clamo*, to cry out; Sp. *clamar;* Port. *clamar;* It. *clamare;* W. *llevain;* Ir. *liumham.* See *Claim, Clamor.*] To applaud. [*Little used.*] *Hall.*

ACCLA'IM, *n.* A shout of joy; acclamation. *Milton.*

ACCLAMA'TION, *n.* [L. *acclamatio.* See *Acclaim.*]

A shout of applause, uttered by a multitude. Anciently, acclamation was a form of words, uttered with vehemence, somewhat resembling a song, sometimes accompanied with applauses which were given by the hands. Acclamations were ecclesiastical, military, nuptial, senatorial, synodical, theatrical, &c.; they were musical, and rythmical; and bestowed for joy, respect, and even reproach, and often accompanied with words, repeated, five, twenty, and even sixty and eighty times. In the later ages of Rome, acclamations were performed by a chorus of music instructed for the purpose.

In modern times, acclamations are expressed by huzzas; by clapping of hands; and often by repeating *vivat rex, vivat respublica*, long live the king or republic, or other words expressive of joy and good wishes.

ACCLAM'ATORY, *a.* Expressing joy or applause by shouts, or clapping of hands.

ACCLI'MATED, *a.* [*Ac* for *ad* and *climate.*] Habituated to a foreign climate, or a climate not native; so far accustomed to a foreign climate as not to be peculiarly liable to its endemical diseases. *Med. Repository.*

ACCLIV'ITY, *n.* [L. *acclivus, acclivis*, ascending, from *ad* and *clivus*, an ascent; Ir. *clui;* Gr. Eol. κλιτυς; Sax. *clif*, a *cliff*, bank or shore; *clifian, cleofian*, to cleave, or split. See *Cliff.*]

A slope or inclination of the earth, as the side of a hill, considered as *ascending*, in opposition to *declivity*, or a side *descending.* Rising ground; ascent; the talus of a rampart.

ACCLI'VOUS, *a.* Rising, as a hill with a slope.

ACCLOY', *v. t.* To fill; to stuff; to fill to satiety. [*Not used.*] [See *Cloy.*] *Spenser.*

ACCOIL'. [See *Coil.*]

AC'COLA, *n.* A delicate fish eaten at Malta.

ACCOLA'DE, *n.* [L. *ad* and *collum*, neck.] A ceremony formerly used in conferring knighthood; but whether an embrace or a blow, seems not to be settled. *Cyc.*

ACCOM'MODABLE, *a.* [Fr. *accommodable.* See *Accommodate.*]

That may be fitted, made suitable, or made to agree. [*Little used.*]

ACCOM'MODATE, *v. t.* [L. *accommodo*, to apply or suit, from *ad* and *commodo*, to profit or help; of *con*, with, and *modus*, measure, proportion, limit, or manner. See *Mode.*]

1. To fit, adapt, or make suitable; as, to *accommodate* ourselves to circumstances; to *accommodate* the choice of subjects to the occasions. *Paley.*
2. To supply with or furnish; followed by *with;* as, to *accommodate* a man *with* apartments.
3. To supply with conveniences, as to *accommodate* a friend.
4. To reconcile things which are at variance; to adjust; as to *accommodate* differences.
5. To show fitness or agreement; to apply; as, to *accommodate* prophecy to events.
6. To lend—a *commercial sense.*

In an intransitive sense, to agree, to be conformable to, as used by Boyle. *Obs.*

ACCOM'MODATE, *a.* Suitable; fit; adapted; as means *accommodate* to the end. *Ray. Tillotson.*

ACCOM'MODATED, *pp.* Fitted; adjusted; adapted; applied; also furnished with conveniences.

> We are well *accommodated* with lodgings.

ACCOM'MODATELY, *adv.* Suitably; fitly. [*Little used.*] *More.*

ACCOM'MODATENESS, *n.* Fitness. [*Little used.*]

ACCOM'MODATING, *ppr.* Adapting; making suitable; reconciling; furnishing with conveniences; applying.

ACCOM'MODATING, *a.* Adapting one's self to; obliging; yielding to the desires of others; disposed to comply, and to oblige another; as an *accommodating* man.

ACCOMMODA'TION, *n.* Fitness; adaptation; followed by *to.*

> The organization of the body with *accommodation* to its functions. *Hale.*

2. Adjustment of differences; reconciliation; as of parties in dispute.
3. Provision of conveniences.
4. In the *plural;* conveniences; things furnished for use; chiefly applied to *lodgings.*
5. In *mercantile language, accommodation* is used for a loan of money; which is often a great *convenience.* An *accommodation*

note, in the language of bank directors, is one drawn and offered for discount, for the purpose of borrowing its amount, in opposition to a note, which the owner has received in payment for goods.

In England, *accommodation bill*, is one given instead of a loan of money. *Crabbe.*

6. It is also used of a note lent merely to *accommodate* the borrower.

7. In theology, *accommodation* is the application of one thing to another by analogy, as of the words of a prophecy to a future event.

Many of those quotations were probably intended as nothing more than *accommodations*. *Paley.*

8. In marine language, an *accommodation-ladder* is a light ladder hung over the side of a ship at the gangway.

ACCOM'MODATOR, *n.* One that accommodates; one that adjusts. *Warburton.*

ACCŎM'PANABLE, *a.* [See *Accompany.*] Sociable. [*Not used.*]

ACCŎM'PANIED, *pp.* Attended; joined with in society.

ACCŎM'PANIMENT, *n.* [Fr. *Accompagnement.* See *Accompany.*] Something that attends as a circumstance, or which is added by way of ornament to the principal thing, or for the sake of symmetry. Thus instruments of music attending the voice; small objects in painting; dogs, guns and game in a hunting piece; warlike instruments with the portrait of a military character, are *accompaniments.*

ACCŎM'PANIST, *n.* The performer in music who takes the accompanying part. *Busby.*

ACCŎM'PANY, *v. t.* [Fr. *accompagner*; Sp. *acompañar*; Port. *acompanhar.* See *Company.*]

1. To go with or attend as a companion or associate on a journey, walk, &c.; as a man *accompanies* his friend to church, or on a tour.

2. To be with as connected; to attend; as pain *accompanies* disease.

ACCŎM'PANY, *v. i.* To attend; to be an associate; as to *accompany* with others. *Obs.* *Bacon.*

2. To cohabit. *Milton.*

3. In *music*, to perform the accompanying part in a composition. *Busby.*

ACCOM'PANYING, *ppr.* Attending; going with as a companion.

ACCOM'PLICE, *n.* [Fr. *complice*; L. *complicatus*, folded together, of *con*, with, and *plico*, to fold; W. *plegy*, to plait; Arm. *plega.* See *Complex* and *Pledge.*] An associate in a crime; a partner or partaker in guilt. It was formerly used in a good sense for a co-operator, but this sense is wholly obsolete. It is followed by *with* before a person; as, *A* was an accomplice *with B* in the murder of *C.* Dryden uses it with *to* before a thing.

ACCOM'PLISH, *v. t.* [Fr. *accomplir*, to finish, from *ad* and L. *compleo*, to complete. See *Complete.*] To complete; to finish entirely.

That He would *accomplish* seventy years in the desolation of Jerusalem. Dan. ix.

2. To execute; as to *accomplish* a vow, wrath or fury. Lev. xiii. and xx.

3. To gain; to obtain or effect by successful exertions; as to *accomplish* a purpose. Prov. xiii.

4. To fulfil or bring to pass; as, to *accomplish* a prophecy.

This that is written must yet be *accomplished* in me. Luke, xxii.

5. To furnish with qualities which serve to render the mind or body *complete*, as with valuable endowments and elegant manners.

ACCOM'PLISHED, *pp.* Finished; completed; fulfilled; executed; effected.

2. *a.* Well endowed with good qualities and manners; complete in acquirements; having a finished education.

3. Fashionable. *Swift.*

ACCOM'PLISHER, *n.* One who accomplishes.

ACCOM'PLISHING, *ppr.* Finishing; completing; fulfilling; executing; effecting; furnishing with valuable qualities.

ACCOM'PLISHMENT, *n.* Completion; fulfilment; entire performance; as the *accomplishment* of a prophecy.

2. The act of carrying into effect, or obtaining an object designed; attainment; as the *accomplishment* of our desires or ends.

3. Acquirement; that which constitutes excellence of mind, or elegance of manners, acquired by education.

ACCOMPT'. *Obs.* [See *Account.*]

ACCOMPT'ANT. *Obs.* [See *Accountant.*]

ACCORD', *n.* [Fr. *accord*, agreement, consent; *accorder*, to adjust, or reconcile; Sp. *acordar*; Arm. *accord, accordi*; It. *accordo, accordare.* The Lat. has *concors, concordo.* Qu. *cor* and *cordis*, the heart, or from the same root. In some of its applications, it is naturally deduced from *chorda*, It. *corda*, the string of a musical instrument.]

1. Agreement; harmony of minds; consent or concurrence of opinions or wills.

They all continued with one *accord* in prayer. Acts, i.

2. Concert; harmony of sounds; the union of different sounds, which is agreeable to the ear; agreement in pitch and tone; as the *accord* of notes; but in this sense, it is more usual to employ *concord* or *chord.*

3. Agreement; just correspondence of things; as the *accord* of light and shade in painting.

4. Will; voluntary or spontaneous motion; used of the will of persons, or the natural motion of other bodies, and preceded by *own.*

Being more forward of his own *accord.* 2 Cor. viii.

That which groweth of its own *accord* thou shalt not reap. Lev. xxv.

5. Adjustment of a difference; reconciliation.

The mediator of an *accord.*

6. In *law*, an agreement between parties in controversy, by which satisfaction for an injury is stipulated, and which, when executed, bars a suit. *Blackstone.*

7. Permission, leave.

ACCORD', *v. t.* To make to agree, or correspond; to adjust one thing to another.

Her hands *accorded* the lute's music to the voice. *Sidney.*

2. To bring to an agreement; to settle, adjust or compose; as to *accord* suits or controversies. *Hall.*

ACCORD', *v. i.* To agree; to be in correspondence.

My heart *accordeth* with my tongue. *Shak.*

2. To agree in pitch and tone.

ACCORD'ABLE, *a.* Agreeable; consonant. *Gower.*

ACCORD'ANCE, *n.* Agreement *with* a person; conformity *with* a thing.

ACCORD'ANT, *a.* Corresponding; consonant; agreeable.

ACCORD'ED, *pp.* Made to agree; adjusted. *Shak.*

ACCORD'ER, *n.* One that aids, or favors. [*Little used.*]

ACCORD'ING, *ppr.* Agreeing; harmonizing.

Th' *according* music of a well mixt state. *Pope.*

2. Suitable; agreeable; in accordance with. In these senses, the word agrees with or refers to a sentence.

Our zeal should be *according* to knowledge. *Sprat.*

Noble is the fame that is built on candor and ingenuity, *according* to those beautiful lines of Sir John Denham. *Spectator.*

Here the whole preceding parts of the sentence are to *accord*, i. e. agree with, correspond with, or be suitable to, what follows. *According*, here, has its true participial sense, *agreeing*, and is always followed by *to.* It is never a preposition.

ACCORD'INGLY, *adv.* Agreeably; suitably; in a manner conformable to.

Those who live in faith and good works, will be rewarded *accordingly.*

ACCORP'ORATE, *v. t.* To unite; [*Not in use.*] [See *Incorporate.*] *Milton.*

ACCOST' *v. t.* [Fr. *accoster*; *ad* and *côte*, side, border, coast; G. *küste*; D. *kust*; Dan. *kyst.*]

To approach; to draw near; to come side by side, or face to face. [*Not in use.*]

2. To speak first to; to address. *Milton.* *Dryden.*

ACCOST', *v. i.* To adjoin. [*Not in use.*] *Spenser.*

ACCOST'ABLE, *a.* Easy of access; familiar. *Howell.*

ACCOST'ED, *pp.* Addressed; first spoken to. In *heraldry*, being side by side.

ACCOST'ING, *ppr.* Addressing by first speaking to.

ACCOUCHEUR, *n.* *accooshàre.* [Fr.] A man who assists women in childbirth.

ACCOUNT', *n.* [Fr. *conte*; It. *conto*; Sp. *cuenta*; Arm. *count*; an account, reckoning, computation. Formerly writers used *accompt* from the Fr. *compte.* See *Count.*]

1. A sum stated on paper; a registry of a debt or credit; of debts and credits, or charges; an entry in a book or on paper of things bought or sold, of payments, services &c., including the names of the parties to the transaction, date, and price or value of the thing.

Account signifies a single entry or charge, or a statement of a number of particular debts and credits, in a book or on a separate paper; and in the plural, is used for the books containing such entries.

2. A computation of debts and credits, or a general statement of particular sums; as, the *account* stands thus; let him exhibit his *account.*

3. A computation or mode of reckoning; applied to other things, than money or trade; as the Julian *account* of time.

4. Narrative; relation; statement of facts;

recital of particular transactions and events, verbal or written; as an *account* of the revolution in France. Hence,

5. An assignment of reasons; explanation by a recital of particular transactions, given by a person in an employment, or to a superior, often implying responsibility.

Give an *account* of thy stewardship. Luke, xvi.

Without responsibility or obligation.

He giveth not *account* of his matters. Job, xxxiii.

6. Reason or consideration, as a motive; as on all *accounts*, on every *account*.
7. Value; importance; estimation; that is, such a state of persons or things, as renders them worthy of more or less estimation; as men of *account*.

What is the son of man that thou makest *account* of him. Ps. cxliv.

8. Profit; advantage; that is, a result or production worthy of estimation. To find our *account* in a pursuit; to turn to *account*. *Philip.* 4.
9. Regard; behalf; sake; a sense deduced from charges on book; as on *account* of public affairs.

Put that to mine *account*. Philem. xviii.

To *make* account, that is, to have a previous opinion or expectation, is a sense now obsolete.

A *writ of account*, in law, is a writ which the plaintiff brings demanding that the defendant should render his just account, or show good cause to the contrary; called also an *action of account*. *Cowel.*

ACCOUNT′, *v. t.* To deem, judge, consider, think, or hold in opinion.

I and my son Solomon shall be *accounted* offenders. 1. Kings, i.

2. To *account of*, to hold in esteem; to value.

Let a man so *account of* us as of ministers of Christ. 1 Cor. iv.

Silver was not any thing *accounted of* in the days of Solomon. 1 Kings, x.

3. To reckon, or compute; as, the motion of the sun whereby years are *accounted*—also to assign as a debt; as, a project *accounted* to his service; but these uses are antiquated.

ACCOUNT′, *v. i.* To render an account or relation of particulars. An officer must *account with* or *to* the Treasurer *for* money received.

2. To give reasons; to assign the causes; to explain; with *for*; as, idleness *accounts for* poverty.
3. To render reasons; to answer for in a responsible character.

We must *account* for all the talents entrusted to us.

ACCOUNTABIL′ITY, *n.* The state of being liable to answer for one's conduct; liability to give account, and to receive reward or punishment for actions.

The awful idea of *accountability*. *R. Hall.*

2. Liability to the payment of money or of damages; responsibility for a trust.

ACCOUNT′ABLE, *a.* Liable to be called to account; answerable to a superior.

Every man is *accountable* to God *for* his conduct.

2. Subject to pay, or make good, in case of loss. A sheriff is *accountable*, as bailiff and receiver of goods.

Accountable for, that may be explained. [*Not elegant.*]

ACCOUNT′ABLENESS, *n.* Liableness to answer or to give account; the state of being answerable, or liable to the payment of money or damages.

ACCOUNT′ANT, *n.* One skilled in mercantile accounts; more generally, a person who keeps accounts; an officer in a public office who has charge of the accounts. In Great Britain, an officer in the court of chancery, who receives money and pays it to the bank, is called *accountant-general.*

ACCOUNT′-BOOK, *n.* A book in which accounts are kept. *Swift.*

ACCOUNT′ED, *pp.* Esteemed; deemed; considered; regarded; valued.

Accounted for, explained.

ACCOUNT′ING, *ppr.* Deeming; esteeming; reckoning; rendering an account.

Accounting for, rendering an account; assigning the reasons; unfolding the causes.

ACCOUNT′ING, *n.* The act of reckoning or adjusting accounts.

ACCOUPLE, *v. t.* *accup′ple.* To couple; to join or link together. [See *Couple.*]

ACCOUPLEMENT, *n.* *accup′plement.* A coupling; a connecting in pairs; junction. [*Little used.*]

ACCOUR′AGE, *v. t.* *accur′age.* [See *Courage.*] To encourage. [*Not used.*] *Spenser.*

ACCOURT, *v. t.* [See *Court.*] To entertain with courtesy. [*Not used.*] *Spenser.*

ACCOÜTER, *v. t.* *accoot′er.* [Fr. *accoutrer*; contracted from *accoustrer*, from Norm. *coste*, a coat, *coster*, a rich cloth or vestment for festivals. I think this to be the true origin of the word, rather than *coudre*, *couture*, *couturier.*]

In *a general sense*, to dress; to equip; but appropriately, to array in a military dress; to put on, or to furnish with a military dress and arms; to equip the body for military service.

ACCOÜT′ERED, *pp.* Dressed in arms; equipped.

ACCOÜT′ERING, *ppr.* Equipping with military habiliments.

ACCOÜT′ERMENTS, *n.* plu. Dress; equipage; furniture for the body; appropriately, military dress and arms; equipage for military service.

2. In *common usage*, an old or unusual dress.

ACCOY′, *v. t.* [old Fr. *accoisir*. *Todd.*]

To render quiet or diffident; to soothe; to caress. [*Obs.*] *Spenser.*

ACCRED′IT, *v. t.* [Fr. *accrediter*; Sp. *acreditar*; It. *accreditare*; to give authority or reputation; from L. *ad* and *credo*, to believe, or give faith to. See *Credit.*]

To give credit, authority, or reputation; to *accredit* an envoy, is to receive him in his public character, and give him credit and rank accordingly.

ACCREDITA′TION, *n.* That which gives title to credit. [*Little used.*]

ACCRED′ITED, *pp.* Allowed; received with reputation; authorized in a public character. *Christ. Obs.*

ACCRED′ITING, *ppr.* Giving authority or reputation.

ACCRES′CENT, *a.* [See *Accretion.*] Increasing. *Shuckford.*

ACCRE′TION, *n.* [Lat. *accretio*, increase; *accres′co*, to increase, literally, to grow to; *ad* and *cresco*; Eng. *accrue*; Fr. *accroître*. See *Increase*, *Accrue*, *Grow.*]

1. A growing to; an increase by natural growth; applied to the increase of organic bodies by the accession of parts.

Plants have an *accretion*, but no alimentation. *Bacon.*

2. In *the civil law*, the adhering of property to something else, by which the owner of one thing becomes possessed of a right to another; as, when a legacy is left to two persons, and one of them dies before the testator, the legacy devolves to the survivor by right of *accretion*. *Encyc.*

ACCRE′TIVE, *a.* Increasing by growth; growing; adding to by growth; as the *accretive* motion of plants.

ACCROACH, *v. i.* [Fr. *accrocher*, to fix on a hook; from *croc*, *crochet*, a hook, from the same elements as *crook*, which see.]

1. To hook, or draw to, as with a hook; *but in this sense not used.*
2. To encroach; to draw away from another. Hence in old laws to assume the exercise of royal prerogatives. *Blackstone.*

The noun *accroachment*, an encroachment, or attempt to exercise royal power, is rarely or never used. [See *Encroach.*]

ACCRUE, *v. i.* *accru′.* [Fr. *accroître*, *accru*, to increase; L. *accresco*, *cresco*; Sp. *crecer* and *acrecer*; It. *crescere*, *accrescere*; Port. *crecer*; Arm. *crisqi.*]

Literally, to *grow to*; hence to arise, proceed or come; to be added, as increase, profit or damage; as, a profit *accrues* to government from the coinage of copper; a loss *accrues* from the coinage of gold and silver.

ACCRUE, *n.* *accru′.* Something that accedes to, or follows the property of another. *Obs.*

ACCRU′ING, *ppr.* Growing to; arising; coming; being added.

ACCRU′MENT, *n.* Addition; increase. [*Little used.*] *Montagu.*

ACCUBA′TION, *n.* [L. *accubatio*, a reclining, from *ad* and *cubo*, to lie down. See *Cube.*] A lying or reclining on a couch, as the ancients at their meals. The manner was to recline on low beds or couches with the head resting on a pillow or on the elbow. Two or three men lay on one bed, the feet of one extended behind the back of another. This practice was not permitted among soldiers, children, and servants; nor was it known, until luxury had corrupted manners. *Encyc.*

ACCUMB′, *v. i.* [L. *accumbo*; *ad* and *cubo.*] to recline as at table. [*Not used.*]

ACCUM′BENCY, *n.* State of being accumbent or reclining.

ACCUM′BENT, *a.* [L. *accumbens*, *accumbo*, from *cubo*. See *Accubation.*] Leaning or reclining, as the ancients at their meals.

ACCU′MULATE, *v. t.* [L. *accumulo*, *ad* and *cumulo*, to heap; *cumulus*, a heap; Sp. *acumular*; It. *accumulare*; Fr. *accumuler*, *combler.*]

1. To heap up; to pile; to amass; as, to *accumulate* earth or stones.
2. To collect or bring together; as to *accumulate* causes of misery; to *accumulate* wealth.

ACCU′MULATE, *v. i.* To grow to a great

size, number or quantity; to increase greatly; as public evils *accumulate.*

ACCU′MULATE, *a.* Collected into a mass, or quantity. *Bacon.*

ACCU′MULATED, *pp.* Collected into a heap or great quantity.

ACCU′MULATING, *ppr.* Heaping up; amassing; increasing greatly.

ACCUMULA′TION, *n.* The act of accumulating; the state of being *accumulated;* an amassing; a collecting together; as an *accumulation* of earth or of evils.

2. In *law,* the concurrence of several titles to the same thing, or of several circumstances to the same proof. *Encyc.*

3. In *Universities,* an *accumulation of degrees,* is the taking of several together, or at smaller intervals than usual, or than is allowed by the rules. *Encyc.*

ACCU′MULATIVE, *a.* That accumulates; heaping up; accumulating.

ACCU′MULATOR, *n.* One that accumulates, gathers, or amasses.

AC′CURACY, *n.* [L. *accuratio,* from *accurare,* to take care of; *ad* and *curare,* to take care; *cura,* care. See *Care.*]

1. Exactness; exact conformity to truth; or to a rule or model; freedom from mistake; nicety; correctness; precision which results from care. The *accuracy* of ideas or opinions is conformity to truth. The value of testimony depends on its *accuracy;* copies of legal instruments should be taken with *accuracy.*

2. Closeness; tightness; as a tube sealed with *accuracy.*

AC′CURATE, *a.* [L. *accuratus.*] In exact conformity to truth, or to a standard or rule, or to a model; free from failure, error, or defect; as an *accurate* account; *accurate* measure; an *accurate* expression.

2. Determinate; precisely fixed; as, one body may not have a very *accurate* influence on another. *Bacon.*

3. Close; perfectly tight; as an *accurate* sealing or luting.

AC′CURATELY, *adv.* Exactly; in an accurate manner; with precision; without error or defect; as a writing *accurately* copied.

2. Closely; so as to be perfectly tight; as a vial *accurately* stopped. *Comstock.*

AC′CURATENESS, *n.* Accuracy; exactness; nicety; precision.

ACCURSE, *v. t.* *accurs′,* [*Ac* for *ad* and *curse.*] To devote to destruction; to imprecate misery or evil upon. [*This verb is rarely used.* See *Curse.*]

ACCURS′ED, *pp.* or *a.* Doomed to destruction or misery:

> The city shall be *accursed.* John vi.

2. Separated from the faithful; cast out of the church; excommunicated.

> I could wish myself *accursed* from Christ. *St. Paul.*

3. Worthy of the curse; detestable; execrable.

> Keep from the *accursed* thing. Josh. vi.

Hence,

4. Wicked; malignant in the extreme.

ACCU′SABLE, *a.* That may be accused; chargeable with a crime; blamable; liable to censure; followed by *of.*

ACCU′SANT, *n.* One who accuses. *Hall.*

ACCUSA′TION, *n.* The act of charging with a crime or offense; the act of accusing of any wrong or injustice.

2. The charge of an offense or crime; or the declaration containing the charge.

> They set over his head his *accusation.* Mat. xxvii.

ACCU′SATIVE, *a.* A term given to a case of nouns, in Grammars, on which the action of a verb terminates or falls; called in English Grammar the *objective* case.

ACCU′SATIVELY, *adv.* In an accusative manner.

2. In relation to the accusative case in Grammar.

ACCU′SATORY, *a.* Accusing; containing an accusation; as an *accusatory* libel.

ACCU′SE, *v. t.* *s* as z. [L. *accuso,* to blame, or accuse; *ad* and *causor,* to blame, or accuse; *causa,* blame, suit, or process, *cause;* Fr. *accuser;* Sp. *acusar;* Port. *accusar;* It. *accusare;* Arm. *accusi.* The sense is, to attack, to drive against, to charge or to fall upon. See *Cause.*]

1. To charge with, or declare to have committed a crime, either by plaint, or complaint, information, indictment, or impeachment; to charge with an offense against the laws, judicially or by a public process; as, to *accuse* one of a high crime or misdemeanor.

2. To charge with a fault; to blame.

> Their thoughts, in the meanwhile, *accusing* or excusing one another. Rom. ii.

It is followed by *of* before the subject of accusation; the use of *for* after this verb is illegitimate.

ACCU′SED, *pp.* Charged with a crime, by a legal process; charged with an offense; blamed.

ACCU′SER, *n.* One who accuses or blames; an officer who prefers an accusation against another for some offense, in the name of the government, before a tribunal that has cognizance of the offense.

ACCU′SING, *ppr.* Charging with a crime; blaming.

ACCUS′TOM, *v. t.* [Fr. *accoutumer,* from *ad* and *coutume, coustume,* custom. See *Custom.*]

To make familiar by use; to form a habit by practice; to habituate or inure; as to *accustom* one's self to a spare diet.

ACCUS′TOM, *v. i.* To be wont, or habituated to do any thing. [*Little used.*]

2. To cohabit. [*Not used.*] *Milton.*

ACCUS′TOM, *n.* Custom. [*Not used.*] *Milton.*

ACCUS′TOMABLE, *a.* Of long custom; habitual; customary. [*Little used.*]

ACCUS′TOMABLY, *adv.* According to custom or habit. [*Little used.*]

ACCUS′TOMANCE, *n.* Custom; habitual use or practice. [*Not used.*] *Boyle.*

ACCUS′TOMARILY, *adv.* According to custom or common practice. [See *Customarily.*] [*Little used.*]

ACCUS′TOMARY, *a.* Usual; customary [See *Customary.*] [*Little used.*]

ACCUS′TOMED, *pp.* Being familiar by use; habituated; inured.

2. *a.* Usual; often practiced; as in their *accustomed* manner.

ACCUS′TOMING, *ppr.* Making familiar by practice; inuring.

ACE, *n.* [L. *as,* a unit or pound; Fr. *as;* It. *asso;* D. *aas;* G. *ass;* Sp. *as.*]

A unit; a single point on a card or die; or the card or die so marked.

2. A very small quantity; a particle; an atom; a trifle; as a creditor will not abate an *ace* of his demand.

ACEL′DAMA, *n.* [Ch. חקל, a field, and דמא, Ch. Syr. and Sam., blood.]

A field said to have lain south of Jerusalem, the same as the potters field, purchased with the bribe which Judas took for betraying his master, and therefore called the *field of blood.* It was appropriated to the interment of strangers.

ACEPH′ALOUS, *a.* [Gr. α priv. and κεφαλη, a head.]

Without a head, headless. In history, the term Acephali, or Acephalites was given to several sects who refused to follow some noted leader, and to such bishops as were exempt from the jurisdiction and discipline of their patriarch. It was also given to certain levelers who acknowledged no head in the reign of Henry 1st. It was also applied to the Blemmyes, a pretended nation of Africa, and to other tribes in the East, whom ancient naturalists represented as having no head; their eyes and mouth being placed in other parts. Modern discoveries have dissipated these fictions. In English Laws, men who held lands of no particular lord, and clergymen who were under no bishop. *L. L. Hen. I. Cowel.*

ACEPH′ALUS, *n.* An obsolete name of the tænia or tape worm, which was formerly supposed to have no head; an error now exploded. The term is also used to express a verse defective in the beginning.

ACERB′, *a.* [L. *acerbus;* G. *herbe,* harsh, sour, tart, bitter, rough, whence *herbst,* autumn, *herbstzeit,* harvest time; D. *herfst,* harvest. See *Harvest.*]

Sour, bitter, and harsh to the taste; sour, with astringency or roughness; a quality of unripe fruits. *Quincy.*

ACERB′ITY, *n.* A sourness, with roughness, or astringency.

2. *Figuratively,* harshness or severity of temper in man.

ACER′IC, *a.* [L. *acer,* a maple tree.]

Pertaining to the maple; obtained from the maple, as *aceric* acid. *Ure.*

AC′EROUS, *a.* [L. *acerosus,* chaffy, from *acus,* chaff or a point.] In *botany,* chaffy; resembling chaff.

2. An acerous or acerose leaf is one which is linear and permanent, in form of a needle, as in pine. *Martyn.*

ACES′CENCY, *n.* [L. *acescens,* turning sour, from *acesco.* See *Acid.*] A turning sour by spontaneous decomposition; a state of becoming sour, tart, or acid; and hence a being moderately sour.

ACES′CENT, *a.* Turning sour; becoming tart or acid by spontaneous decomposition. Hence slightly sour; but the latter sense is usually expressed by *acidulous* or *subacid.* *Nicholson.*

ACES′TE, *n.* In *entomology,* a species of papilio or butterfly, with subdentated wings, found in India. *Cyc.*

ACES′TIS, *n.* [Gr.] A factitious sort of chrysocolla, made of Cyprian verdigris, urine, and niter. *Cyc.*

ACETAB′ULUM, *n.* [L. from *acetum,* vinegar. See *Acid.*] Among the Romans a vinegar cruse or like vessel, and a measure of about one eighth of a pint.

1. In *anatomy*, the cavity of a bone for receiving the protuberant end of another bone, and therefore forming the articulation called enarthrosis. It is used especially for the cavity of the os innominatum, which receives the head of the thigh bone.
2. In *botany*, the trivial name of a species of peziza, the cup peziza; so called from its resemblance to a cup.
3. A glandular substance found in the placenta of some animals.
4. It is sometimes used in the sense of Cotyledon.
5. A species of lichen. *Cyc.*

AC'ETARY, *n.* [See *Acid.*] An acid pulpy substance in certain fruits, as the pear, inclosed in a congeries of small calculous bodies, towards the base of the fruit. *Grew.*

AC'ETATE, *n.* [See *Acid.*] In *chimistry*, a neutral salt formed by the union of the acetic acid, or radical vinegar, with any salifiable base, as with earths, metals, and alkalies; as the *acetate* of alumine, of lime, or of copper. *Lavoisier.*

AC'ETATED, *a.* [See *Acid.*] Combined with acetic acid, or radical vinegar.

ACE'TIC, *a.* [See *Acid.*] A term used to denote a particular acid, *acetic* acid, the concentrated acid of vinegar, or radical vinegar. It may be obtained by exposing common vinegar to frost—the water freezing leaves the *acetic* acid, in a state of purity.

ACETIFICA'TION, *n.* The act of making acetous or sour; or the operation of making vinegar. *Cyc.*

ACE'TIFY, *v. t.* To convert into acid or vinegar. *Aikin.*

AC'ETITE, *n.* [See *Acid.*] A neutral salt formed by the acetous acid, with a salifiable base; as the *acetite* of copper, aluminous *acetite.* *Lavoisier.*

ACETOM'ETER, *n.* [L. *acetum*, vinegar, and μετρον, measure.]
An instrument for ascertaining the strength of vinegar. *Ure.*

ACE'TOUS, *a.* [See *Acid.*] Sour; like or having the nature of vinegar. *Acetous* acid is the term used by chimists for distilled vinegar. This acid, in union with different bases, forms salts called acetites.

ACE'TUM, *n.* [L. See *Acid.*] Vinegar; a sour liquor, obtained from vegetables dissolved in boiling water, and from fermented and spirituous liquors, by exposing them to heat and air.
This is called the acid or acetous fermentation.

ACHE, *v. i. ake.* [Sax. *ace*, *ece*; Gr. αχεω, to ache or be in pain; αχος, pain. The primary sense is to be pressed. Perhaps the oriental עוק to press.]

1. To suffer pain; to have or be in pain, or in continued pain; as, the head *aches.*
2. To suffer grief, or extreme grief; to be distressed; as, the heart *aches.*

ACHE, *n. ake.* Pain, or continued pain, in opposition to sudden twinges, or spasmodic pain. It denotes a more moderate degree of pain than pang, anguish, and torture.

ACHE'AN, *a.* Pertaining to Achaia in Greece, and a celebrated league or confederacy established there. This State lay on the gulf of Corinth, within Peloponnesus.

ACHERN'ER, *n.* A star of the first magnitude in the southern extremity of the constellation Eridanus.

ACH'ERSET, *n.* An ancient measure of corn, supposed to be about eight bushels. *Encyc.*

ACHIE'VABLE, *a.* [See *Achieve.*] That may be performed. *Barrow.*

ACHIE'VANCE, *n.* Performance. *Elyot.*

ACHIE'VE, *v. t.* [Fr. *achever*, to finish; Arm. *acchui*; old Fr. *chever*, to come to the end, from Fr. *chef*, the head or end; old Eng. *cheve*; Sp. and Port. *acabar*, from *cabo*, end, *cape.* See *Chief.*]

1. To perform, or execute; to accomplish; to finish, or carry on to a final close. It is appropriately used for the effect of efforts made by the hand or bodily exertion, as deeds *achieved* by valor.
2. To gain or obtain, as the result of exertion.

> Show all the spoils by valiant Kings *achieved.* *Prior.*

ACHIE'VED, *pp.* Performed; obtained; accomplished.

ACHIE'VEMENT, *n.* The performance of an action.

2. A great or heroic deed; something accomplished by valor, or boldness.
3. An obtaining by exertion.
4. An escutcheon or ensigns armorial, granted for the performance of a great or honorable action. *Encyc.*

ACHIE'VER, *n.* One who accomplishes a purpose, or obtains an object by his exertions.

ACHIE'VING, *ppr.* Performing; executing; gaining.

A'CHING, *ppr.* Being in pain; suffering distress.

A'CHING, *n.* Pain; continued pain or distress.

A'CHIOTE, *n.* The anotta, a tree, and a drug used for dyeing red. The bark of the tree makes good cordage, and the wood is used to excite fire by friction. [See *Anotta.*] *Clavigero.*

A'CHOR, *n.* [Gr. αχωρ, sordes capitis.]

1. The scald head, a disease forming scaly eruptions, supposed to be a critical evacuation of acrimonious humors; a species of herpes. *Hooper. Quincy.*
2. In *mythology*, the God of flies, said to have been worshipped by the Cyreneans, to avoid being vexed by those insects. *Encyc.*

ACHROMAT'IC, *a.* [Gr. α priv. and χρωμα, color.]
Destitute of color. *Achromatic* telescopes are formed of a combination of lenses, which separate the variously colored rays of light to equal angles of divergence, at different angles of refraction of the mean ray. In this case, the rays being made to refract towards contrary parts, the whole ray is caused to deviate from its course, without being separated into colors, and the optical aberration arising from the various colors of light, is prevented. This telescope is an invention of Dolland. *Nicholson.*

ACIC'ULAR, *a.* [L. *acicula*, Priscian, a needle, from Gr. αχη, L. *acies*, a point. See *Acid.*]
In the shape of a needle; having sharp points like needles. *Kirwan. Martyn.*
An *acicular* prism is when the crystals are slender and straight. *Phillips.*

ACIC'ULARLY, *adv.* In the manner of needles, or prickles.

AC'ID, *a.* [L. *acidus*; Sax. *æced*, vinegar; from the root of *acies*, *edge*; Gr. αχη; W. *awç*, an edge or point. See *Edge.*]
Sour, sharp or biting to the taste, having the taste of vinegar, as *acid* fruits or liquors.

AC'ID, *n.* In *chimistry*, acids are a class of substances, so denominated from their taste, or the sensation of sourness which they produce on the tongue. But the name is now given to several substances, which have not this characteristic in an eminent degree. The properties, by which they are distinguished, are these:

1. When taken into the mouth, they occasion the taste of sourness. They are corrosive, unless diluted with water; and some of them are caustic.
2. They change certain vegetable blue colors to red, and restore blue colors which have been turned green, or red colors which have been turned blue by an alkali.
3. Most of them unite with water in all proportions, with a condensation of volume and evolution of heat; and many of them have so strong an attraction for water, as not to appear in the solid state.
4. They have a stronger affinity for alkalies, than these have for any other substance; and in combining with them, most of them produce effervescence.
5. They unite with earths, alkalies and metallic oxyds, forming interesting compounds, usually called salts.
6. With few exceptions, they are volatilized or decomposed by a moderate heat.

The old chimists divided acids into animal, vegetable, and mineral—a division now deemed inaccurate. They are also divided into oxygen acids, hydrogen acids, and acids destitute of these acidifiers. Another division is into acids with simple radicals, acids with double radicals, acids with triple radicals, acids with unknown radicals, compound acids, dubious acids, and acids destitute of oxygen.
Lavoisier. Thomson. Nicholson. Aikin.

ACIDIF'EROUS, *a.* [*Acid* and L. *fero.*] Containing acids, or an acid.
Acidiferous minerals are such as consist of an earth combined with an acid; as carbonate of lime, aluminite, &c. *Phillips.*

ACID'IFIABLE, *a.* [From *Acidify.*]
Capable of being converted into an acid, by union with an acidifying principle, without decomposition.

ACIDIFICA'TION, *n.* The act or process of acidifying or changing into an acid.

ACID'IFIED, *pp.* Made acid; converted into an acid.

ACID'IFIER, *n.* That which by combination forms an acid, as oxygen and hydrogen.

ACID'IFY, *v. t.* [*Acid* and L. *facio.*]
To make acid; but appropriately to convert into an acid, chimically so called, by combination with any substance.

ACID'IFYING, *ppr.* Making acid; converting into an acid; having power to change into an acid. Oxygen is called the *acidifying* principle or element.

ACIDIM'ETER, *n.* [*Acid* and Gr. μετρον, measure.]
An instrument for ascertaining the strength of acids. *Ure.*

ACID'ITY, *n.* [Fr. *acidité*, from *acid.*]
The quality of being sour; sourness; tartness; sharpness to the taste.

AC'IDNESS, *n.* The quality of being sour; acidity.

ACID'ULATE, *v. t.* [L. *acidulus*, slightly sour; Fr. *aciduler*, to make sour. See *Acid.*]
To tinge with an acid; to made acid in a moderate degree. *Arbuthnot.*

ACID'ULATED, *pp.* Tinged with an acid; made slightly sour.

ACID'ULATING, *ppr.* Tinging with an acid.

AC'IDULE, } *n.* In *chimistry*, a compound
ACID'ULUM, } salt, in which the alkaline base is supersaturated with acid; as, tartareous *acidulum*; oxalic *acidulum*.

ACID'ULOUS, *a.* [L. *acidulus.* See *Acid.*]
Slightly sour; sub-acid, or having an excess of acid; as, *acidulous* sulphate.

ACINAC'IFORM, *a.* [L. *ăcinăces*, a cimeter, Gr. ακιναχης, and L. *forma*, form.]
In *botany*, formed like, or resembling a cimeter. *Martyn.*

AC'INIFORM, *a.* [L. *acinus*, a grape stone, and *forma*, shape.]
Having the form of grapes; being in clusters like grapes. The uvea or posterior lamen of the iris in the eye, is called the *aciniform* tunic. Anatomists apply the term to many glands of a similar formation. *Quincy. Hooper.*

AC'INOSE, } *a.* [From L. *acinus.* See
AC'INOUS, } *Aciniform.*]
Consisting of minute granular concretions; used in *mineralogy.* *Kirwan.*

AC'INUS, *n.* [L.] In *botany*, one of the small grains, which compose the fruit of the blackberry, &c.

AC'IPENSER, *a.* In *ichthyology*, a genus of fishes, of the order of chondropterygii, having an obtuse head; the mouth under the head, retractile and without teeth. To this genus belong the sturgeon, sterlet, huso, &c. *Cyc.*

ACIT'LI, *n.* A name of the water hare, or great crested grebe or diver. *Dict. of Nat. Hist.*

AЄKNOWL'EDĠE, *v. t.* *Aknol'edge*, [*ad* and *knowledge.* See *Know.*]
1. To own, avow or admit to be true, by a declaration of assent; as to *acknowledge* the being of a God.
2. To own or notice with particular regard.
   In all thy ways *acknowledge* God. Prov. iii. Isa. xxxiii.
3. To own or confess, as implying a consciousness of guilt.
   I *acknowledge* my transgressions, and my sin is ever before me. Ps. li. and xxxii.
4. To own with assent; to admit or receive with approbation.
   He that *acknowledgeth* the son, hath the the father also. 1 John ii. 2 Tim. ii.
5. To own with gratitude; to own as a benefit; as, to *acknowledge* a favor, or the receipt of a gift.
   They his gifts *acknowledged* not. *Milton.*
6. To own or admit to belong to; as, to *acknowledge* a son.
7. To receive with respect.
   All that see them shall *acknowledge* that they are the seed which the Lord hath blessed. Isa. vi. 1 Cor. xvi.
8. To own, avow or assent to an act in a legal form, to give it validity; as, to *acknowledge* a deed before competent authority.

AЄKNOWL'EDĠED, *pp.* Owned; confessed; noticed with regard or gratitude; received with approbation; owned before authority.

AЄKNOWL'EDĠING, *ppr.* Owning; confessing; approving; grateful; but the latter sense is a gallicism, not to be used.

AЄKNOWL'EDĠMENT, *n.* The act of owning; confession; as, the *acknowledgment* of a fault.
2. The owning, with approbation, or in the true character; as the *acknowledgment* of a God, or of a public minister.
3. Concession; admission of the truth; as, of a fact, position, or principle.
4. The owning of a benefit received, accompanied with gratitude; and hence it combines the ideas of an *expression of thanks.* Hence, it is used also for something given or done in return for a favor.
5. A declaration or avowal of one's own act, to give it legal validity; as the *acknowledgment* of a deed before a proper officer.

Acknowledgment-money, in some parts of England, is a sum paid by tenants, on the death of their landlord, as an acknowledgment of their new lords. *Encyc.*

AЄ'ME, *n.* *Ac'my.* [Gr. ακμη.]
The top or highest point. It is used to denote the maturity or perfection of an animal. Among *physicians*, the crisis of a disease, or its utmost violence. Old medical writers divided the progress of a disease into four periods, the *arche*, or beginning, the *anabasis*, or increase, the *acme*, or utmost violence, and the *paracme*, or decline. But *acme* can hardly be considered as a legitimate English word.

AЄ'NE, *n.* *Ac'ny.* [Gr.]
A small hard pimple or tubercle on the face. *Quincy.*

AЄNES'TIS, *n.* [Gr. α priv. and κναω, to rub or gnaw.]
That part of the spine in quadrupeds which extends from the metaphrenon, between the shoulder blades, to the loins; which the animal cannot reach to scratch. *Coxe. Quincy.*

AЄ'O, *n.* A Mediterranean fish, called also sarachus.

AЄ'OLIN, *n.* A bird of the partridge kind in Cuba. Its breast and belly are white; its back and tail of a dusky yellow brown. *Dict. of Nat. Hist.*

AЄOL'OTHIST, }
AЄ'OLYTE, } *n.* [Gr. ακολουθεω.]
In *the ancient church*, one of the subordinate officers, who lighted the lamps, prepared the elements of the sacraments, attended the bishops, &c. An officer of the like character is still employed in the Romish Church. *Encyc.*

AЄ'ONITE, *n.* [L. *aconitum*; Gr. ακονιτον.]
The herb wolf's bane, or monks-hood, a poisonous plant; and in poetry, used for poison in general.

AЄON'TIAS, n. [Gr. ακοντιας; ακοντιον, a dart, from ακων.]
1. A species of serpent, called dart-snake, or jaculum, from its manner of darting on its prey. This serpent is about three feet in length; of a light gray color with black spots, resembling eyes; the belly perfectly white. It is a native of Africa and the Mediterranean isles; is the swiftest of its kind, and coils itself upon a tree, from which it darts upon its prey.
2. A comet or meteor resembling the serpent.

AЄOP', *adv.* [*a* and *cope.*]
At the top. *Obs. Jonson.*

A'ЄORN, *n.* [Sax. *æcern*, from *ace* or *ac*, oak, and *corn*, a grain.]
1. The seed or fruit of the oak; an oval nut which grows in a rough permanent cup.
   The first settlers of Boston were reduced to the necessity of feeding on clams, muscles, ground nuts, and *acorns.* *B. Trumbull.*
2. In *marine language*, a small ornamental piece of wood, of a conical shape, fixed on the point of the spindle above the vane, on the mast head, to keep the vane from being blown off. *Mar. Dict.*
3. In *natural history*, the Lepas, a genus of shells of several species found on the British coast. The shell is multivalvular, unequal, and fixed by a stem; the valves are parallel and perpendicular, but they do not open, so that the animal performs its functions by an aperture on the top. These shells are always fixed to some solid body.

A'ЄORNED, *a.* Furnished or loaded with acorns.

A'ЄORUS, *n.* [L. from Gr. ακορον.]
1. Aromatic Calamus, sweet flag, or sweet rush.
2. In *natural history*, blue coral, which grows in the form of a tree, on a rocky bottom, in some parts of the African seas. It is brought from the Camarones and Benin. *Encyc.*
3. In *medicine*, this name is sometimes given to the great galangal. *Encyc.*

AЄOTYL'EDON, *n.* [Gr. α priv. and κοτυληδων from κοτυλη, a hollow.]
In *botany*, a plant whose seeds have no side lobes, or cotyledons. *Martyn.*

AЄOTYLED'ONOUS, *a.* Having no side lobes.

AЄOUS'TIЄ, *a.* [Gr. ακουστικος, from ακουω, to hear.]
Pertaining to the ears, to the sense of hearing, or to the doctrine of sounds.

Acoustic duct, in *anatomy*, the meatus auditorius, or external passage of the ear.

Acoustic vessels, in *ancient theaters*, were brazen tubes or vessels, shaped like a bell, used to propel the voice of the actors, so as to render them audible to a great distance; in some theaters at the distance of 400 feet. *Encyc.*

Acoustic instrument, or auricular tube, called in popular language, a speaking trumpet. *Encyc.*

Acoustics, or *acousmatics*, was a name given to such of the disciples of Pythagoras, as had not completed their five years probation.

AЄOUS'TIЄS, *n.* The science of sounds, teaching their cause, nature, and phenomena. This science is, by some writers, divided into *diacoustics*, which explains the properties of sounds coming directly from the sonorous body to the ear; and *catacoustics*, which treats of reflected sounds. But the distinction is considered of little real utility.
2. In *medicine*, this term is sometimes used

for remedies for deafness, or imperfect hearing. *Quincy.*

ACQUA'INT, *v. t.* [Old Fr. *accointer*, to make known; whence *accointance*, acquaintance. Qu. Per. کُنْدَا kunda, knowing, intelligent; Ger. *kunde*, knowledge; *kund*, known, public; D. *kond* or *kunde*, knowledge; Sw. *kånd*, known; Dan. *kiender*, to know, to be acquainted with. These words seem to have for their primitive root the Goth. and Sax. *kunnan*, to know, the root of *cunning*; Ger. *kennen*; D. *kunnen*, *kan*; Eng. *can*, and *ken*; which see.]

1. To make known; to make fully or intimately known; to make familiar.

A man of sorrows and *acquainted* with grief. Isaiah liii.

2. To inform; to communicate notice to; as, a friend in the country *acquaints* me with his success. *Of* before the object, as to *acquaint* a man *of* this design, has been used, but is obsolete or improper.

3. To *acquaint one's self*, is to gain an intimate or particular knowledge of.

Acquaint now *thyself* with him and be at peace. Job xxii.

ACQUAI'NTANCE, *n.* Familiar knowledge; a state of being acquainted, or of having intimate or more than slight or superficial knowledge; as, I *know* the man, but have no *acquaintance* with him. Sometimes it denotes a more slight knowledge.

2. A person or persons well known; usually persons we have been accustomed to see and converse with; sometimes, persons more slightly known.

Lover and friend hast thou put far from me, and mine *acquaintance* into darkness. Ps. lxxxviii.

My *acquaintance* are estranged from me. Job xix.

Acquaintances, in the plural, is used, as applied to individual persons known; but more generally, *acquaintance* is used for one or more.

Acquaintant, in a like sense, is not used.

ACQUA'INTED, *pp.* Known; familiarly known; informed; having personal knowledge.

ACQUA'INTING, *ppr.* Making known to; giving notice, or information to.

ACQUEST', *n.* [L. *acquisitus*, *acquiro*.]

1. Acquisition; the thing gained. *Bacon.*

2. Conquest; a place acquired by force.

ACQUIESCE, *v. i.* *acquiess'.* [L. *acquiesco*, of *ad* and *quiesco*, to be quiet; *quies*, rest; Fr. *acquiescer*.]

1. To rest satisfied, or apparently satisfied, or to rest without opposition and discontent; usually implying previous opposition, uneasiness, or dislike, but ultimate compliance, or submission; as, to *acquiesce* in the dispensations of providence.

2. To assent to, upon conviction; as, to *acquiesce* in an opinion; that is, to rest satisfied of its correctness, or propriety.

Acquiesced in, in a passive sense, complied with; submitted to, without opposition; as, a measure has been *acquiesced in*.

ACQUIES'CENCE, *n.* A quiet assent; a silent submission, or submission with apparent content; distinguished from avowed consent on the one hand, and on the other, from opposition or open discontent; as, an *acquiescence* in the decisions of a court, or in the allotments of providence.

ACQUIES'CENT, *a.* Resting satisfied; easy; submitting; disposed to submit. *Johnson.*

ACQUIES'CING, *ppr.* Quietly submitting; resting content.

ACQUI'RABLE, *a.* That may be acquired.

ACQUI'RE, *v. t.* [L. *acquiro*, *ad* and *quæro*, to seek, that is to follow, to press. to urge; *acquiro* signifies to pursue to the end or object; Fr. *acquerir*; Sp. *adquirir*; Ar. قَرَا, Heb. חקר to seek, to make towards, to follow. The L. *quæsivi*, unless contracted, is probably from a different root. See class Gr. and Gs.]

To gain, by any means, something which is in a degree permanent, or which becomes vested or inherent in the possessor; as, to *acquire* a title, estate, learning, habits, skill, dominion, &c. Plants *acquire* a green color from the solar rays. A mere temporary possession is not expressed by *acquire*, but by *gain*, *obtain*, *procure*; as, to *obtain* [not *acquire*] a book on loan.

Descent is the title whereby a man, on the death of his ancestor, *acquires* his estate, by right of representation, as his heir at law. *Blackstone.*

ACQUI'RED, *pp.* Gained, obtained, or received from art, labor, or other means, in distinction from those things which are bestowed by nature. Thus we say, abilities, natural and *acquired*. It implies title, or some permanence of possession.

ACQUI'REMENT, *n.* The act of acquiring, or that which is acquired; attainment. It is used in opposition to natural gifts; as, eloquence, and skill in music and painting, are *acquirements*; genius, the gift of nature. It denotes especially *personal* attainments, in opposition to material or external things gained, which are more usually called *acquisitions*; but this distinction is not always observed.

ACQUI'RER, *n.* A person who acquires.

ACQUI'RING, *ppr.* Gaining by labor or other means, something that has a degree of permanence in the possessor.

ACQUI'RY, *n.* Acquirement. [*Not used.*] *Barrow.*

AC'QUISITE, *a.* *s* as *z.* Gained. [*Not used.*] *Burton.*

ACQUISI''TION, *n.* [L. *acquisitio*, from *acquisitus*, *acquæsivi*, which are given as the *part.* and *pret.* of *acquiro*; but *quæsivi* is probably from a different root; W. *ceisiaw*; Eth. ሐሠሠ chasas, chas; Ar. قَسَّ kassa, to seek. Class Gs.]

1. The act of acquiring; as, a man takes pleasure in the *acquisition* of property, as well as in the possession.

2. The thing acquired, or gained; as, learning is an *acquisition*. It is used for intellectual attainments, as well as for external things, property, or dominion; and in a good sense, denoting something estimable.

ACQUIS'ITIVE, *a.* That is acquired; acquired; [*but improper.*] *Walton.*

ACQUIS'ITIVELY, *adv.* Noting acquirement, with *to* or *for* following. *Lilly's Grammar.*

ACQUIST', *n.* See *Acquest.* [*Not used.*] *Milton.*

ACQUIT', *v. t.* [Fr. *acquitter*; W. *gadu*, *gadaw*; L. *cedo*; Arm. *kitat*, or *quytaat*, to leave, or forsake; Fr. *quitter*, to forsake; Sp. *quitar*; Port. *quitar*; It. *quitare*, to remit, forgive, remove; D. *kwyten*; Ger. *quittiren*.]

To set free; to release or discharge from an obligation, accusation, guilt, censure, suspicion, or whatever lies upon a person as a charge or duty; as, the jury *acquitted* the prisoner; we *acquit* a man of evil intentions. It is followed by *of* before the object; to acquit *from* is obsolete. In a reciprocal sense, as, the soldier *acquitted himself* well in battle, the word has a like sense, implying the discharge of a duty or obligation. Hence its use in expressing *excellence in performance*; as the orator *acquitted himself* well, that is, in a manner that his situation and public expectation demanded.

ACQUIT'MENT, *n.* The act of acquitting, or state of being acquitted. *South.*

[This word is superseded by *acquittal*.]

ACQUIT'TAL, *n.* A judicial setting free, or deliverance from the charge of an offense; as, by verdict of a jury, or sentence of a court.

The *acquittal* of a principal operates as an *acquittal* of the accessories.

ACQUIT'TANCE, *n.* A discharge or release from a debt.

2. The writing, which is evidence of a discharge; a receipt in full, which bars a further demand.

ACQUIT'TED, *pp.* Set free, or judicially discharged from an accusation; released from a debt, duty, obligation, charge, or suspicion of guilt.

ACQUIT'TING, *ppr.* Setting free from accusation; releasing from a charge, obligation, or suspicion of guilt.

ACRA'SE, } *v. t.* To make crazy; to in-
ACRA'ZE, } fatuate. [*Not in use.*] [See *Crazy.*]

2. To impair; to destroy. [*Not in use.*]

AC'RASY, *n.* [Gr. ακρασια, from α priv. and κρασις, constitution or temperament.]

In *medical authors*, an excess or predominancy of one quality above another, in mixture, or in the human constitution. *Bailey.*

ACRE, *n.* *a'ker.* [Sax. *acer*, *acera*, or *æcer*; Ger. *acker*; D. *akker*; Sw. *acker*; Dan. *ager*; W. *eg*; Ir. *acra*; Gr. αγρος; Lat. *ager*. In these languages, the word retains its primitive sense, an open, plowed, or sowed field. In Eng. it retained its original signification, that of any open field, until it was limited to a definite quantity by statutes 31. Ed. 35. Ed. 1. 24. H. 8. *Cowel.*]

1. A quantity of land, containing 160 square rods or perches, or 4840 square yards. This is the English statute acre. The acre of Scotland contains 6150 2-5 square yards. The French arpent is nearly equal to the Scottish acre, about a fifth larger than the English. The Roman *juger* was 3200 square yards.

2. In the Mogul's dominions, *acre* is the same as *lack*, or 100,000 rupees, equal to £12,500 sterling, or $55,500.

Acre-fight, a sort of duel in the open field,

formerly fought by English and Scotch combatants on their frontiers.

Acre-tax, a tax on land in England, at a certain sum for each acre, called also *acre-shot*.

A'CRED, *a.* Possessing acres or landed property. *Pope.*

AC'RID, *a.* [Fr. *acre*; L. *acer.*]
Sharp; pungent; bitter; sharp or biting to the taste; acrimonious; as *acrid* salts.

AC'RIDNESS, *n.* A sharp, bitter, pungent quality.

ACRIMO'NIOUS, *a.* Sharp; bitter; corrosive; abounding with acrimony.
2. *Figuratively*, severe; sarcastic; applied to language or temper.

ACRIMO'NIOUSLY, *adv.* With sharpness or bitterness.

AC'RIMONY, *n.* [L. *acrimonia*, from *acer*, sharp. The latter part of the word seems to denote likeness, state, condition, like *head, hood*, in *knighthood*; in which case it may be from the same root as *maneo*, Gr. μενω.]
1. Sharpness; a quality of bodies, which corrodes, dissolves, or destroys others; as, the *acrimony* of the humors. *Bacon.*
2. *Figuratively*, sharpness or severity of temper; bitterness of expression proceeding from anger, ill-nature, or petulance. *South.*

AC'RISY, *n.* [Gr. α priv. and κρισις, judgment.]
A state or condition of which no right judgment can be formed; that of which no choice is made; matter in dispute; injudiciousness. [*Little used.*] *Bailey.*

AC'RITUDE, *n.* [See *Acrid.*]
An acrid quality; bitterness to the taste; biting heat.

ACROAMAT'IC, *a.* [Gr. ακροαματικος, from ακροαομαι, to hear.]
Abstruse; pertaining to deep learning; an epithet applied to the secret doctrines of Aristotle. *Enfield.*

ACROAT'IC, *a.* [Gr. ακροατικος.]
Abstruse; pertaining to deep learning; and opposed to *exoteric.* Aristotle's lectures were of two kinds, *acroatic, acroamatic*, or *esoteric*, which were delivered to a class of select disciples, who had been previously instructed in the elements of learning; and *exoteric*, which were delivered in public. The former respected being, God, and nature; the principal subjects of the latter were logic, rhetoric, and policy. The abstruse lectures were called *acroatics.* *Enfield.*

ACROCERAU'NIAN, *a.* [Gr. ακρα, a summit, and κεραυνος, thunder.]
An epithet applied to certain mountains, between Epirus and Illyricum, in the 41st degree of latitude. They project into the Adriatic, and are so termed from being often struck with lightning. *Encyc.*

ACRO'MION, *n.* [Gr. ακρος, highest, and ωμος, shoulder.]
In *anatomy*, that part of the spine of the scapula, which receives the extreme part of the clavicle. *Quincy.*

ACRON'IC, } *a.* [Gr. ακρος, extreme, and
ACRON'ICAL, } νυξ, night.]
In *astronomy*, a term applied to the rising of a star at sun set, or its setting at sun rise. This rising or setting is called *acronical.* The word is opposed to *cosmical.* *Bailey. Encyc. Johnson.*

ACRON'ICALLY, *adv.* In an acronical manner; at the rising or setting of the sun.

AC'ROSPIRE, *n.* [Gr. ακρος, highest, and σπειρα, a spire, or spiral line.]
A shoot, or sprout of a seed; the plume, or plumule, so called from its spiral form. *Mortimer.*

AC'ROSPIRED, *a.* Having a sprout, or having sprouted at both ends. *Mortimer.*

ACROSS', *prep. akraus'.* [*a* and *cross.* See *Cross.*]
1. From side to side, opposed to *along*, which is in the direction of the length; athwart; quite over; as, a bridge is laid *across* a river.
2. Intersecting; passing over at any angle; as a line passing *across* another.

ACROS'TIC, *n.* [Gr. ακρα, extremity or beginning, and στιχος, order, or verse.]
A composition in verse, in which the first letters of the lines, taken in order, form the name of a person, kingdom, city, &c., which is the subject of the composition, or some title or motto.

ACROS'TIC, *a.* That relates to, or contains an acrostic.

ACROS'TICALLY, *adv.* In the manner of an acrostic.

ACROTELEU'TIC, *n.* [Gr. ακρος, extreme, and τελευτη, end.]
Among *ecclesiastical writers*, an appellation given to any thing added to the end of a psalm, or hymn; as a doxology.

AC'ROTER, *n.* [Gr. ακροτηρ, a summit.]
In *architecture*, a small pedestal, usually without a base, anciently placed at the two extremes, or in the middle of pediments or frontispieces, serving to support the statues, &c. It also signifies the figures placed as ornaments on the tops of churches, and the sharp pinnacles that stand in ranges about flat buildings with rails and balusters. Anciently the word signified the extremities of the body, as the head, hands, and feet. *Encyc.*

ACROTHYM'ION, *n.* [Gr. ακρος, extreme, and θυμος, thyme.]
Among *physicians*, a species of wart, with a narrow basis and broad top, having the color of thyme. It is called *Thymus.* *Celsus.*

ACT, *v. i.* [Gr. αγω, Lat. *ago*, to urge, drive, lead, bring, do, perform, or in general, to move, to exert force; Cantabrian, *eg*, force; W. *egni*; Ir. *eigean*, force; Ir. *aige*, to *act* or carry on; *eachdam*, to do or *act*; *actaim*, to ordain; *eacht, acht*, deed, *act*, condition; F. *agir*; It. *agire*, to do or act.]
1. To exert power; as, the stomach *acts* upon food; the will *acts* upon the body in producing motion.
2. To be in action or motion; to move.

> He hangs between in doubt to *act* or rest. *Pope.*

3. To behave, demean, or conduct, as in morals, private duties, or public offices; as, we know not why a minister has *acted* in this manner. But in this sense, it is most frequent in popular language; as, how the man *acts* or *has acted.*

To *act up to*, is to equal in action; to fulfil, or perform a correspondent action; as, he has *acted up* to his engagement or his advantages.

ACT, *v. t.* To perform; to represent a character on the stage.

> *Act* well your part, there all the honor lies. *Pope.*

2. To feign or counterfeit. *Obs. or improper.*

> With *acted* fear the villain thus pursued. *Dryden.*

3. To put in motion; to actuate; to regulate movements.

> Most people in the world are *acted* by levity. *South. Locke.*

[*In this latter sense, obsolete and superseded by actuate, which see.*]

ACT, *n.* The exertion of power; the effect, of which power exerted is the cause; as, the *act* of giving or receiving. In this sense, it denotes an operation of the mind. Thus, to discern is an *act* of the understanding; to judge is an *act* of the will.
2. That which is done; a deed, exploit, or achievement, whether good or ill.

> And his miracles and his *acts* which he did in the midst of Egypt. Deut. xi.

3. Action; performance; production of effects; as, an *act* of charity. *But this sense is closely allied to the foregoing.*
4. A state of reality or real existence, as opposed to a possibility.

> The seeds of plants are not at first in *act*, but in possibility, what they afterwards grow to be. *Hooker.*

5. In general, *act* denotes *action completed*; but preceded by *in*, it denotes incomplete action.

> She was taken in the very *act*. John viii.

In act is used also to signify incipient action, or a state of preparation to exert power; as, "In act to strike," a *poetical use.*
6. A part or division of a play, to be performed without interruption; after which the action is suspended to give respite to the performers. Acts are divided into smaller portions, called *scenes.*
7. The result of public deliberation, or the decision of a prince, legislative body, council, court of justice, or magistrate; a decree, edict, law, judgment, resolve, award, determination; as an *act* of parliament, or of congress. The term is also transferred to the book, record, or writing, containing the laws and determinations. Also, any instrument in writing to verify facts.

In the sense of *agency*, or power to produce effects, as in the passage cited by Johnson, from Shakespeare, the use is improper.

> To try the vigor of them and apply
> Allayments to their *act.*

Act, in *English Universities*, is a thesis maintained in public, by a candidate for a degree, or to show the proficiency of a student. At Oxford, the time when masters and doctors complete their degrees is also called the *act*, which is held with great solemnity. At Cambridge, as in the United States, it is called *commencement.* *Encyc.*

Act of faith, auto da fe, in Catholic countries, is a solemn day held by the Inquisition, for the punishment of heretics, and the absolution of accused persons found innocent; or it is the sentence of the Inquisition.

Acts of the Apostles, the title of a book in the New Testament, containing a history of the transactions of the Apostles.

Acta Diurna, among the Romans, a sort of

Gazette, containing an authorized account of transactions in Rome, nearly similar to our newspapers.

Acta populi, or *acta publica*, the Roman registers of assemblies, trials, executions, buildings, births, marriages, and deaths of illustrious persons, &c.

Acta Senatus, minutes of what passed in the Roman senate, called also commentarii, commentaries.

ACT'ED, *pp.* Done; performed; represented on the stage.

AC'TIAN, *a.* Relating to Actium, a town and promontory of Epirus, as *Actian* games, which were instituted by Augustus, to celebrate his naval victory over Anthony, near that town, Sep. 2, B. C. 31. They were celebrated every five years. Hence, *Actian* years, reckoned from that era. *Encyc.*

ACT'ING, *ppr.* Doing; performing; behaving; representing the character of another.

ACT'ING, *n.* Action; act of performing a part of a play. *Shak. Churchill.*

AC'TINOLITE, *n.* [Gr. ακτιν, a ray, and λιθος, a stone.]

A mineral, called, by Werner, strahlstein, ray-stone, nearly allied to hornblend. It occurs in prismatic crystals, which are long, and incomplete, and sometimes extremely minute and even fibrous. Its prevailing color is green of different shades, or shaded with yellow or brown. There are several varieties, as the common, the massive, the acicular, the glassy, and the fibrous. *Werner. Kirwan. Cleaveland.*

Actinolite is crystalized, asbestiform, and glassy. *Phillips.*

ACTINOLIT'IC, *a.* Like or pertaining to actinolite.

AC'TION, *n.* [L. *actio*. See *Act*.]

1. *Literally*, a driving; hence, the state of acting or moving; exertion of power or force, as when one body acts on another; or *action* is the effect of power exerted on one body by another; motion produced. Hence, action is opposed to rest. Action, when produced by one body on another, is *mechanical;* when produced by the will of a living being, *spontaneous* or *voluntary.* [See Def. 3.]

2. An act or thing done; a deed.

The Lord is a God of knowledge, and by him are *actions* weighed. 1. Sam. ii.

3. In *mechanics*, agency; operation; driving impulse; effort of one body upon another; as, the *action* of wind upon a ship's sails. Also the effect of such action.

4. In *ethics*, the external signs or expression of the sentiments of a moral agent; conduct; behavior; demeanor; that is, motion or movement, with respect to a rule or propriety.

5. In *poetry*, a series of events, called also the subject or fable; this is of two kinds; the principal action which is more strictly the fable, and the incidental action or episode. *Encyc.*

6. In *oratory*, gesture or gesticulation; the external deportment of the speaker, or the accommodation of his attitude, voice, gestures, and countenance to the subject, or to the thoughts and feelings of the mind. *Encyc.*

7. In *physiology*, the motions or functions of the body, vital, animal, and natural; *vital* and involuntary, as the action of the heart and lungs; *animal*, as muscular, and all voluntary motions; *natural*, as manducation, deglutition, and digestion. *Encyc.*

8. In *law*, literally, an urging for right; a suit or process, by which a demand is made of a right; a claim made before a tribunal. Actions are *real*, *personal* or *mixed*; *real*, or *feudal*, when the demandant claims a title to real estate; *personal*, when a man demands a debt, personal duty, or damages in lieu of it, or satisfaction for an injury to person or property; and *mixed*, when real estate is demanded, with damages for a wrong sustained. Actions are also *civil* or *penal; civil*, when instituted solely in behalf of private persons, to recover debts or damages; *penal*, when instituted to recover a penalty, imposed by way of punishment. The word is also used for a *right of action*; as, the law gives an *action* for every claim. *Blackstone.*

A chose in action, is a right to a thing, in opposition to the possession. A bond or note is a *chose in action* [Fr. *chose*, a thing,] and gives the owner a right to prosecute his claim to the money, as he has an absolute property in a *right*, as well as in a *thing*, in possession.

9. In some countries of Europe, *action* is a share in the capital stock of a company, or in the public funds, equivalent to our term *share;* and consequently, in a more general sense, to stocks. The word is also used for movable effects.

10. In *painting* and *sculpture*, the attitude or position of the several parts of the body, by which they seem to be actuated by passions; as, the arm extended, to represent the act of giving or receiving.

11. Battle; fight; engagement between troops in war, whether on land or water, or by a greater or smaller number of combatants. This and the 8th definition exhibit the literal meaning of *action*—a driving or urging.

Quantity of action, in physics, the product of the mass of a body by the space it runs through and its velocity. *Encyc.*

In many cases *action* and *act* are synonymous: but some distinction between them is observable. *Action* seems to have more relation to the *power* that acts, and its operation and process of acting; and *act*, more relation to the *effect* or operation complete. *Action* is also more generally used for ordinary transactions; and *act*, for such as are remarkable, or dignified; as, all our *actions* should be regulated by prudence; a prince is distinguished by *acts* of heroism or humanity. *Encyc.*

Action taking, in Shakespeare, is used for litigious.

AC'TIONABLE, *a.* That will bear a suit, or for which an action at law may be sustained; as, to call a man a thief is *actionable.*

AC'TIONABLY, *adv.* In a manner that subjects to legal process.

AC'TIONARY or **AC'TIONIST**, *n.* In *Europe*, a proprietor of stock in a trading company; one who owns *actions* or shares of stock.

ACT'IVE, *a.* [L. *activus;* Fr. *actif.*] That has the power or quality of acting; that contains the principle of action, independent of any visible external force; as, attraction is an *active* power: or it may be defined, that communicates action or motion, opposed to *passive*, that receives action; as, the *active* powers of the mind.

2. Having the power of quick motion, or disposition to move with speed; nimble; lively; brisk; agile; as an *active* animal. Hence,

3. Busy; constantly engaged in action; pursuing business with vigor and assiduity; opposed to *dull, slow*, or *indolent;* as an *active* officer. It is also opposed to *sedentary*, as an *active* life.

4. Requiring action or exertion; practical; operative; producing real effects; opposed to *speculative;* as, the *active* duties of life.

5. In *grammar*, *active* verbs are those which not only signify action, but have a noun or name following them, denoting the object of the action or impression; called also *transitive*, as they imply the *passing* of the action expressed by the verb to the object; as, a professor *instructs* his *pupils.*

6. *Active capital*, or *wealth*, is money, or property that may readily be converted into money, and used in commerce or other employment for profit. *Hamilton.*

7. *Active commerce*, the commerce in which a nation carries its own productions and foreign commodities in its own ships, or which is prosecuted by its own citizens; as contradistinguished from *passive* commerce, in which the productions of one country are transported by the people of another country.

The commerce of Great Britain and of the United States is *active;* that of China is *passive.*

It may be the interest of foreign nations to deprive us, as far as possible, of an *active* commerce in our own bottoms. *Federalist, Hamilton.*

ACT'IVELY, *adv.* In an active manner; by action; nimbly; briskly; also in an active signification, as a word is used *actively.*

ACT'IVENESS, *n.* The quality of being active; the faculty of acting; nimbleness; quickness of motion; less used than *activity.*

ACTIV'ITY, *n.* The quality of being active; the active faculty; nimbleness; agility; also the habit of diligent and vigorous pursuit of business; as, a man of *activity.* It is applied to persons or things.

Sphere of activity, is the whole space in which the virtue, power, or influence of any object, is exerted.

To put in activity, a French phrase, for putting in action or employment.

ACT'OR, *n.* He that acts or performs; an active agent.

2. He that represents a character or acts a part in a play; a stage player.

3. Among *civilians*, an advocate or proctor in civil courts or causes.

ACT'RESS, *n.* A female who acts or performs, and especially, on the stage, or in a play.

ACT'UAL, *a.* [Fr. *actuel.* See *Act.*] Real or effective, or that exists truly and absolutely; as, *actual* heat, opposed to that, which is *virtual* or *potential; actual* cautery, or the burning by a red-hot iron, opposed to a cautery or caustic application, that may produce the same effect upon the body by a different process.

2. Existing in act; real; in opposition to speculative, or existing in theory only; as an *actual* crime.

3. In *theology*, *actual* sin is that which is committed by a person himself, opposed to *original* sin, or the corruption of nature supposed to be communicated from Adam.

4. That includes action.

Besides her walking and other *actual* performances. [*Hardly legitimate.*] *Shak.*

ACTUAL'ITY, *n.* Reality. *Haweis.*

AC'TUALLY, *adv.* In fact; really; in truth.

AC'TUARY, *n.* [L. *actuarius.*]

A register or clerk; a term of the civil law, and used originally in courts of civil law jurisdiction; but in Europe used for a clerk or register generally.

AC'TUATE, *a.* Put in action. [*Little used.*]

AC'TUATE, *v. t.* [from *act.*]

To put into action; to move or incite to action; as, men are *actuated* by motives, or passions. It seems to have been used formerly in the sense of *invigorate*, noting increase of action; but the use is not legitimate.

AC'TUATED, *pp.* Put in action; incited to action.

AC'TUATING, *ppr.* Putting in action; inciting to action.

ACTUA'TION, *n.* The state of being put in action; effectual operation. *Glanville.*

AC'TUS, *n.* Among the Romans, a measure in building equal to 120 Roman feet. In *agriculture*, the length of one furrow.

AC'UATE, *v. t.* [L. *acuo*, to sharpen. See *Acid.*]

To sharpen; to make pungent, or corrosive. [*Little used.*] *Harvey.*

ACUBE'NE, *n.* A star of the fourth magnitude in the southern claw of Cancer.

ACUI''TION, *n.* [from L. *acuo*, to sharpen.]

The sharpening of medicines to increase their effect.

ACU'LEATE, *a.* [L. *aculeus*, from *acus*, Gr. ακη, a point, and the diminutive *ul.* See *Acid.*]

In *botany*, having prickles, or sharp points; pointed; used chiefly to denote prickles fixed in the bark, in distinction from thorns, which grow from the wood. *Milne.*

2. In *zoology*, having a sting.

ACU'LEI, *n.* [L.] In *botany* and *zoology*, prickles or spines.

ACU'LON, or **ACU'LOS**, *n.* [Gr. ακυλος, probably from *ac*, an oak.]

The fruit or acorn of the ilex, or scarlet oak.

ACU'MEN, *n.* [L. *acumen*, from *acus* or *acuo.*]

A sharp point; and figuratively, quickness of perception, the faculty of nice discrimination.

ACU'MINATE, *a.* [L. *acuminatus*, from *acumen.*]

Ending in a sharp point; pointed.

ACU'MINATED, *a.* Sharpened to a point.

ACUMINA'TION, *n.* A sharpening; termination in a sharp point.

ACUPUNC'TURE, *n.* [L. *acus*, needle, and *punctura*, or *punctus*, a pricking.]

Among the Chinese, a surgical operation, performed by pricking the part affected with a needle, as in head-aches and lethargies. *Encyc.*

AC'URU, *n.* The name in India of a fragrant aloe-wood. *As. Researches.*

A'CUS, *n.* [L.] The needle-fish, or gar-fish.

2. The ammodyte or sand eel. *Cyc.*

3. The oblong cimex. *Cyc.*

ACU'TE, *a.* [L. *acutus*, sharp-pointed; Qu. from *acuo*, *acus*, or from the Oriental חד had or chad, sharp, Heb. Ch. Ar.]

Sharp at the end; ending in a sharp point; opposed to *blunt* or *obtuse.* An *acute angle* in geometry, is one which is less than a right angle, or which subtends less than ninety degrees. An *acute angled* triangle is one whose three angles are all acute, or less than ninety degrees each.

2. *Figuratively*, applied to mental powers; penetrating; having nice discernment; perceiving or using minute distinctions; opposed to *dull* or *stupid;* as an *acute* reasoner.

3. *Applied to the senses;* having nice or quick sensibility; susceptible of slight impressions; having power to feel or perceive small objects; as, a man of *acute* eyesight, hearing, or feeling.

4. An *acute* disease, is one which is attended with violent symptoms, and comes speedily to a crisis, as a pleurisy; opposed to *chronic.*

5. An *acute* accent, is that which elevates or sharpens the voice.

6. In *music*, *acute* is applied to a tone which is sharp, or high; opposed to *grave.*

7. In *botany*, ending in an acute angle, as a leaf or perianth. *Martyn.*

ACU'TELY, *adv.* Sharply; keenly; with nice discrimination.

ACU'TENESS, *n.* Sharpness; but seldom used in this literal sense, as applied to material things.

2. *Figuratively*, the faculty of nice discernment or perception; applied to the senses, or the understanding. By an *acuteness* of feeling, we perceive small objects or slight impressions; by an *acuteness* of intellect, we discern nice distinctions.

3. Sharpness, or elevation of sound, in rhetoric or music. *Boyle.*

4. Violence of a disease, which brings it speedily to a crisis.

ACUTIA'TOR, *n.* In *the middle ages*, a person whose office was to sharpen instruments. Before the invention of fire-arms, such officers attended armies, to sharpen their instruments. *Encyc.*

AD. A Latin preposition, signifying *to.* It is probably from Heb. Ch. Syr. Sam. Eth. אתה, Ar. أَتَي, to come near, to approach; from which root we may also deduce *at.* In *composition*, the last letter is usually changed into the first letter of the word to which it is prefixed. Thus for *adclamo*, the Romans wrote *acclamo;* for *adgredior*, *aggredior;* for *adfirmo*, *affirmo;* for *adlego*, *allego;* for *adpono*, *appono;* for *adripio*, *arripio;* for *adscribo*, *ascribo;* for *adtineo*, *attineo.* The reason of this change is found in the ease of pronunciation, and agreeableness of the sounds.

Ad hominem, to the man, in logic, an argument, adapted to touch the prejudices of the person addressed.

Ad inquirendum, in law, a judicial writ commanding inquiry to be made.

Ad libitum, [L.] at pleasure.

Ad valorem, according to the value, in commerce and finance, terms used to denote duties or charges laid upon goods, at a certain rate per cent. upon their value, as stated in their invoices; in opposition to a specific sum upon a given quantity or number.

AD'AGE, *n.* [L. *adagium*, or *adagio;* It. *adagio.*]

A proverb; an old saying, which has obtained credit by long use; a wise observation handed down from antiquity.

ADA'GIO, *n.* [It. *adagio*, a compound of *ad* and *agio*, leisure; Sp. and Port. *ocio;* L. *otium;* Fr. *aise;* Eng. *ease.*]

In *music*, a slow movement. As an adverb, slowly, leisurely, and with grace. When repeated, *adagio, adagio*, it directs the movement to be very slow.

AD'AM, *n.* In Heb. Ch. Syr. Eth. Ar., *Man;* primarily, the name of the human species, mankind; appropriately, the first Man, the progenitor of the human race. The word signifies form, shape, or suitable form; hence, species. As a verb, the word signifies, in Ethiopic, to please or be agreeable; in Arabic, to join, unite, or be accordant, to agree. It is evidently connected with דמה damah, Heb. Ch. Syr., to be like or equal, to form an image, to assimilate. Whence the sense of likeness, image, form, shape; Gr. δεμας, a body, like. [See *Man.*]

Adam's apple, a species of citron, [see *Citron;*] also the prominent part of the throat.

Ad'am's needle, the popular name of the yucca, a plant of four species, cultivated in gardens. Of the roots, the Indians make a kind of bread. [See *Yucca.*]

AD'AMANT, *n.* [Gr. αδαμας; L. *adamas;* a word of Celtic origin; W. *ehedvaen*, a load stone, from *ehed*, to fly or move, and *vaen*, or *maen*, a stone. Chaucer uses adamant for the load stone. *Romaunt of the Rose*, *L.* 1182. Ger. *diamant*, is adamant and diamond; Sp. *diamante;* Sw. *damant;* Fr. *aimant*, loadstone. See *Diamond.*]

A very hard or impenetrable stone; a name given to the diamond and other substances of extreme hardness. The name has often been given to the load stone; but in modern mineralogy, it has no technical signification.

ADAMANTE'AN, *a.* Hard as adamant. *Milton.*

ADAMANT'INE, *a.* Made of adamant; having the qualities of adamant; that cannot be broken, dissolved, or penetrated; as *adamantine* bonds, or chains.

Adamantine Spar, a genus of earths, of three varieties. The color of the first is gray, with shades of brown or green; the form when regular, a hexangular prism, two sides large and four small, without a pyramid; its surface striated, and with a thin covering of white mica, interspersed with particles of red felspar; its fracture, foliaceous and sparry. The second variety is whiter, and the texture more foliaceous. The third variety is of a reddish brown color. This stone is very hard, and of difficult fusion. *Encyc.*

A variety of corundum. *Cleaveland.*

AD'AMIC, *a.* Pertaining to Adam. *Adamic earth*, is the term given to common red clay, so called by means of a mistaken opinion that Adam means red earth.

AD'AMITES, in *Church history*, a sect of visionaries, who pretended to establish a state of innocence, and like Adam, went naked. They abhorred marriage, holding it to be the effect of sin. Several attempts have been made to revive this sect; one as late as the 15th century. *Encyc.*

ADAMIT'IC, *a.* Like the Adamites. *Taylor.*

ADANSO'NIA, *n.* Ethiopian sour gourd, monkey's bread, or African calabash-tree. It is a tree of one species, called *baobab*, a native of Africa, and the largest of the vegetable kingdom. The stem rises not above twelve or fifteen feet, but is from sixty-five to seventy-eight feet in circumference. The branches shoot horizontally to the length of sixty feet, the ends bending to the ground. The fruit is oblong, pointed at both ends, ten inches in length, and covered with a greenish down, under which is a hard ligneous rind. It hangs to the tree by a pedicle two feet long, and contains a white spungy substance. The leaves and bark, dried and powdered, are used by the negroes, as pepper, on their food, to promote perspiration. The tree is named from M. Adanson, who has given a description of it.

ADAPT', *v. t.* [Sp. *adaptar;* It. *adattare;* L. *ad.* and *apto*, to fit; Gr. απτω.]

To make suitable; to fit or suit; as, to *adapt* an instrument to its uses; we have provision *adapted* to our wants. It is applied to things material or immaterial.

ADAPT'ABLE, *a.* That may be adapted.

ADAPTA'TION, *n.* The act of making suitable, or the state of being suitable, or fit; fitness.

ADAPT'ED, *pp.* Suited; made suitable; fitted.

ADAPT'ER. See *adopter.*

ADAPT'ING, *ppr.* Suiting; making fit.

ADAP'TION, *n.* Adaptation; the act of fitting. [*Little used, and hardly legitimate.*]

ADAPT'NESS, *n.* A state of being fitted. [*Not used.*] *Newton.*

A'DAR, *n.* A Hebrew month, answering to the latter part of February and the beginning of March, the 12th of the sacred and 6th of the civil year; so named from אדר, to become glorious, from the exuberance of vegetation, in that month, in Egypt and Palestine. *Parkhurst.*

ADAR'CE, *n.* [Gr. αδαρκης.]

A saltish concretion on reeds and grass in marshy grounds in Galatia. It is lax and porous, like bastard spunge, and used to clear the skin in leprosy, tetters, &c. *Quincy. Plot.*

ADAR'CON, *n.* In *Jewish antiquity*, a gold coin worth about three dollars and a third, or about fifteen shillings sterling.

ADAR'ME, *n.* A Spanish weight, the sixteenth of an ounce; Fr. *demi-gros.* The Spanish ounce is seven per cent. lighter than that of Paris. *Encyc. Span. Dict.*

AD'ATIS, *n.* A muslin or species of cotton cloth from India. It is fine and clear; the piece is ten French ells long, and three quarters wide.

AD'AUNT, *v. t.* To subdue. [*Not used.* See *Daunt.*] *Skelton.*

ADAW', *v. t.* To daunt; to subject. [*Not used.*] *Spenser.*

ADA'YS, *adv.* On or in days; as in the phrase, now *adays.*

ADD, *v. t.* [L. *addo*, from *ad* and *do*, to give.]

1. To set or put together, join, or unite, as, one thing or sum to another, in an aggregate; as, *add* three to four, the sum is seven.

2. To unite in idea or consideration; to subjoin.

To what has been alledged, let this argument be *added.*

3. To increase number.

Thou shalt *add* three cities more of refuge. Deut. xix.

4. To augment.

Rehoboam said, I will *add* to your yoke. 1 Kings, xii.

Ye shall not *add* to the word which I command you. Deut. iv.

As here used, the verb is intransitive, but there may be an ellipsis.

To *add to*, is used in scripture, as equivalent to *give*, or *bestow upon.* Gen. xxx. Matt. vi. In Gal. ii. the word is understood to signify instruction. "In conference they *added* nothing to me." In narration, he or they *added*, is elliptical; he *added* words, or what follows, or he continued his discourse.

In general, when used of things, *add* implies a principal thing, to which a smaller is to be annexed, as a part of the whole sum, mass, or number.

ADDEC'IMATE, *v. t.* [L. *ad* and *decimus*, tenth.]

To take, or to ascertain tithes. *Dict.*

ADD'ED, *pp.* Joined in place, in sum, in mass or aggregate, in number, in idea or consideration; united; put together.

ADDEE'M, *v. t.* [See *Deem.*] To award; to sentence. [*Little used.*]

AD'DER, *n.* [Sax. *aetter* or *aettor*, a serpent and poison; D. *adder.* Qu. Sax. *naedre*, a serpent; Goth. *nadr;* G. *natter;* W. *neider;* Corn. *naddyr;* Ir. *nathair;* L. *natrix*, a serpent.]

A venomous serpent or viper, of several species.

AD'DER-FLY, *n.* A name of the dragon-fly or *libellula;* sometimes called *adder-bolt.*

ADDER'S-GRASS, *n.* A plant about which serpents lurk.

ADDER'S-TONGUE, *n.* A plant whose seeds are produced on a spike resembling a serpent's tongue.

ADDER'S-WORT, *n.* Snakeweed, so named from its supposed virtue in curing the bite of serpents.

ADDIBIL'ITY, *n.* The possibility of being added. *Locke.*

AD'DIBLE, *a.* [See *Add.*] That may be added. *Locke.*

AD'DICE, *obs.* [See *Adz.*]

ADDICT', *a.* Addicted. [*Not much used.*]

ADDICT', *v. t.* [L. *addico*, to devote, from *ad* and *dico*, to dedicate.]

To apply one's self habitually; to devote time and attention by customary or constant practice; *sometimes in a good sense.*

They have *addicted* themselves to the ministry of the saints. 1 Cor. xv.

More usually, in a bad sense, to follow customarily, or devote, by habitually practising that which is ill; as, a man is *addicted* to intemperance.

To *addict one's self to a person*, a sense borrowed from the Romans, who used the word for assigning debtors in service to their creditors, is found in Ben Jonson, but is not legitimate in English.

ADDICT'ED, *pp.* Devoted by customary practice.

ADDICT'EDNESS, *n.* The quality or state of being addicted.

ADDICT'ING, *ppr.* Devoting time and attention; practicing customarily.

ADDIC'TION, *n.* The act of devoting or giving up in practice; the state of being devoted.

His *addiction* was to courses vain. *Shak.*

2. Among the Romans, a making over goods to another by sale or legal sentence; also an assignment of debtors in service to their creditors. *Encyc.*

ADD'ING, *ppr.* Joining; putting together; increasing.

ADDIT'AMENT, *n.* [L. *additamentum*, from *additus* and *ment.* See *Add.*]

An addition, or rather the thing added, as furniture in a house; any material mixed with the principal ingredient in a compound. Ancient anatomists gave the name to an epiphysis, or junction of bones without articulation. [*Little used in either sense.*]

ADDI''TION, *n.* [L. *additio*, from *addo.*]

1. The act of adding, opposed to subtraction, or diminution; as, a sum is increased by *addition.*

2. Any thing added, whether material or immaterial.

3. In *arithmetic*, the uniting of two or more numbers in one sum; also the rule or branch of arithmetic which treats of adding numbers. *Simple* addition is the joining of sums of the same denomination, as pounds to pounds, dollars to dollars. *Compound* addition is the joining of sums of different denominations, as dollars and cents.

4. In *law*, a title annexed to a man's name, to show his rank, occupation or place of residence; as, John Doe, *Esq.*; Richard Roe, *Gent*; Robert Dale, *Mason*; Thomas Way, *of New-York.*

5. In *music*, a dot at the side of a note, to lengthen its sound one half.

6. In *heraldry*, something added to a coat of arms, as a mark of honor, opposed to abatements, as bordure, quarter, canton, gyron, pile, &c. See these terms. *Encyc.*

7. In *distilling*, any thing added to the wash or liquor in a state of fermentation.

8. In *popular language*, an advantage, ornament, improvement; that is, an addition by way of eminence.

ADDI''TIONAL, *a.* That is added. It is used by Bacon for *addition;* but improperly.

ADDI''TIONALLY, *adv.* By way of addition.

ADD'ITIVE, *a.* That may be added, or that is to be added.

ADD'ITORY, *a.* That adds, or may add.

AD'DLE, *a.* [W. *hadyl*, corrupt; *hadlu*, to decay, to putrify; Heb. חדל, to fail; Ar. حدل, to decline, and خذل to frustrate, to fail, to cease.]

In a morbid state; putrid; applied to eggs. Hence, barren, producing nothing.

His brains grow *addle.* *Dryden.*

AD'DLED, *a.* Morbid, corrupt, putrid, or barren. *Brown.*

AD'DLE-PATED, *a.* Having empty brains. *Dryden.*

ADDOOM', *v. t.* [See *Doom.*] To adjudge. *Spenser.*

ADDORS'ED, *a.* [L. *ad* and *dorsum*, the back.]

In *heraldry*, having the backs turned to each other, as *beasts.*

ADDRESS', *v. t.* [Fr. *adresser*; Sp. *endetezar*; It. *dirizzare*, to direct, to make straight. This is supposed to be from L. *dirigo*; it also coincides with Ch. תרץ, Ar. ترص, Syr. *id.*, to direct, to rectify, to fit. See *Dress.*]

1. To prepare; to make suitable dispositions for.

> Turnus *addressed* his men *to* single fight. *Dryden.*
>
> The archangel and the evil spirit *addressing* themselves *for* the combat. *Addison.*

[*This sense is, I believe, obsolete or little used.*]

2. To direct words or discourse; to apply to by words; as, to *address* a discourse to an assembly; to *address* the judges.

3. To direct in writing, as a letter; or to direct and transmit; as, he *addressed* a letter to the speaker. Sometimes it is used with the reciprocal pronoun, as, he *addressed himself* to the speaker, instead of, he *addressed* his discourse. The phrase is faulty; but less so than the following. To such I would *address* with this most affectionate petition.

> Young Turnus to the beauteous maid *addrest.* *Dryden.*

The latter is admissible in poetry, as an elliptical phrase.

4. To present an address, as a letter of thanks or congratulation, a petition, or a testimony of respect; as, the legislature *addressed* the president.

5. To court or make suit as a lover.

6. In *commerce*, to consign or entrust to the care of another, as agent or factor; as, the ship was *addressed* to a merchant in Baltimore.

ADDRESS', *n.* A speaking to; verbal application; a formal manner of speech; as, when introduced, the president made a short *address.*

2. A written or formal application; a message of respect, congratulation, thanks, petition, &c.; as, an *address* of thanks; an officer is removable upon the *address* of both houses of assembly.

3. Manner of speaking to another; as, a man of pleasing *address.*

4. Courtship; more generally in the plural, *addresses*; as, he makes or pays his *addresses* to a lady.

5. Skill; dexterity; skillful management; as, the envoy conducted the negotiation with *address.*

6. Direction of a letter, including the name, title, and place of residence of the person for whom it is intended. Hence these particulars are denominated, a man's *address.*

ADDRESS'ED, *pp.* Spoken or applied to; directed; courted; consigned.

ADDRESS'ER, *n.* One who addresses or petitions.

ADDRESS'ING, *ppr.* Speaking or applying to; directing; courting; consigning.

ADDU'CE, *v. t.* [L. *adduco*, to lead or bring to; *ad* and *duco*, to lead. See *Duke.*]

1. To bring forward, present or offer; as, a witness was *adduced* to prove the fact.

2. To cite, name or introduce; as, to *adduce* an authority or an argument.

ADDU'CED, *pp.* Brought forward; cited; alledged in argument.

ADDU'CENT, *a.* Bringing forward, or together; a word applied to those muscles of the body which pull one part towards another. [See *Adductor.*]

ADDU'CIBLE, *a.* That may be adduced.

ADDU'CING, *ppr.* Bringing forward; citing in argument.

ADDUC'TION, *n.* The act of bringing forward.

ADDUC'TIVE, *a.* That brings forward.

ADDUC'TOR, *n.* [L.]

A muscle which draws one part of the body towards another; as the *adductor oculi*, which turns the eye towards the nose; the *adductor pollicis manus*, which draws the thumb towards the fingers.

ADDULCE, *v. t.* *adduls'.* [L. *ad* and *dulcis*, sweet.]

To sweeten. [*Not used.*] *Bacon.*

AD'EB, *n.* An Egyptian weight of 210 okes, each of three rotolos, which is a weight of about two drams less than the English pound. But at Rosetta, the adeb is only 150 okes. *Encyc.*

ADELANTA'DO, *n.* [Spanish.] A governor of a province; a lieutenant governor. *Robertson.*

AD'ELING, *n.* A title of honor, given by our Saxon ancestors to the children of princes, and to young nobles. It is composed of *adel*, or rather *æthel*, the Teutonic term for *noble*, *illustrious*, and *ling*, young, posterity. *Spelman.* Sw. *adelig*; D. *edel*; Ger. *edel* and *adelig*, noble; Sp. *hidalgo*. We observe the term in many Saxon names of princes, as *Ethel-wolf*, noble wolf, or noble help, *Ethel-bald*, noble bold, *Ethel-bert*, noble brightness. Ar. أثل athala, to be well rooted, to be of noble stock or birth. Class Dl.

AD'ELITE, *n.* Adelites or Almoganens, in Spain, were conjurers, who predicted the fortunes of individuals by the flight and singing of birds, and other accidental circumstances. *Ed. Encyc.*

ADEMP'TION, *n.* [L. *adimo*, to take away; of *ad* and *emo*, to take.]

In *the civil law*, the revocation of a grant, donation, or the like.

ADENOG'RAPHY, *n.* [Gr. αδην, a gland, and γραφω, to describe.]

That part of anatomy which treats of the glands.

AD'ENOID, *a.* [Gr. αδην, a gland, and ειδος, form.]

In the form of a gland; glandiform; glandulous; applied to the prostate glands.

ADENOLOG'ICAL, *a.* Pertaining to the doctrine of the glands. *Encyc.*

ADENOL'OGY, *n.* [Gr. αδην, a gland, and λογος, discourse.

In *anatomy*, the doctrine of the glands, their nature, and their uses.

AD'ENOS, *n.* A species of cotton, from Aleppo, called also *marine cotton.*

ADEPT', *n.* [L. *adeptus*, obtained, from *adipiscor.*]

One fully skilled or well versed in any art. The term is borrowed from the Alchimists, who applied it to one who pretended to have found the philosopher's stone, or the panacea. *Encyc.*

ADEPT', *a.* Well skilled; completely versed or acquainted with. *Boyle.*

ADEP'TION, *n.* [L. *adeptio.*]

An obtaining; acquirement. *Obs. Bacon.*

AD'EQUACY, *n.* [L. *adæquatus*, of *ad* and *æquatus*, made equal.]

The state or quality of being equal to, proportionate, or sufficient; a sufficiency for a particular purpose; as, "the *adequacy* of supply *to* the expenditure." *War in Disguise.*

AD'EQUATE, *a.* Equal; proportionate; correspondent to; fully sufficient; as, means *adequate* to the object; we have no *adequate* ideas of infinite power.

Adequate ideas, are such as exactly represent their object.

AD'EQUATE, *v. t.* To resemble exactly. [*Not used.*] *Shelford.*

AD'EQUATELY, *adv.* In an adequate manner; in exact proportion; with just correspondence, representation, or proportion; in a degree equal to the object.

AD'EQUATENESS, *n.* The state of being adequate; justness of proportion or representation; sufficiency.

ADEQUA'TION, *n.* Adequateness. [*Not used.*] *Bp. Barlow.*

ADESSENA'RIANS, *n.* [L. *adesse*, to be present.]

In *church history*, a sect who hold the real presence of Christ's body in the eucharist, but not by transubstantiation. They differ however as to this presence; some holding the body of Christ to be *in* the bread; others, *about* the bread. *Encyc.*

ADFECT'ED, *a.* In *algebra*, compounded; consisting of different powers of the unknown quantity. *Bailey.*

ADFIL'IATED, *a.* Adopted as a son. [See *Affiliate.*]

ADFILIA'TION, *n.* [L. *ad* and *filius*, a son.]

A Gothic custom, by which the children of a former marriage, are put upon the same footing with those of a succeeding one; still retained in some parts of Germany.

ADHE'RE, *v. i.* [L. *adhæreo*, *ad* and *hæreo*, to stick; Ir. *adharadh.*]

1. To stick to, as glutinous substances, or by natural growth; as, the lungs sometimes *adhere* to the pleura.

2. To be joined, or held in contact; to cleave to.

3. *Figuratively*, to hold to, be attached, or remain fixed, either by personal union or conformity of faith, principle, or opinion; as, men *adhere* to a party, a leader, a church, or creed.

4. To be consistent; to hold together as the parts of a system.

> Every thing *adheres* together. *Shak.*

ADHE'RENCE, *n.* The quality or state of sticking or adhering.

2. *Figuratively*, a being fixed in attachment;

fidelity; steady attachment; as, an *adherence* to a party or opinions.

ADHE′RENCY, *n.* The same as adherence. In the sense of *that which adheres*, not legitimate. *Decay of Piety.*

ADHE′RENT, *a.* Sticking, uniting, as glue or wax; united with, as an *adherent* mode in Locke, that is, a mode accidentally joined with an object, as *wetness* in a cloth.

ADHE′RENT, *n.* The person who adheres; one who follows a leader, party or profession; a follower, or partisan; a believer in a particular faith or church.

In the sense of an appendage. *Obs.*

ADHE′RENTLY, *adv.* In an adherent manner.

ADHE′RER, *n.* One that adheres; an adherent.

ADHE′SION, *n.* *adhe′zhun.* [L. *adhæsio.*]

1. The act or state of sticking, or being united and attached to; as the *adhesion* of glue, or of parts united by growth, cement, and the like. *Adhesion* is generally used in a literal; *adherence*, in a metaphorical sense.

2. Sometimes *figuratively*, adherence, union or steady attachment; firmness in opinion; as, an *adhesion* to vice: but in this sense nearly obsolete. The union of bodies by attraction is usually denominated *cohesion*.

ADHE′SIVE, *a.* Sticky; tenacious, as glutinous substances; apt or tending to adhere. Thus gums are *adhesive*.

ADHE′SIVELY, *adv.* In an adhesive manner.

ADHE′SIVENESS, *n.* The quality of sticking or adhering; stickiness; tenacity.

ADHIB′IT, *v. t.* [L. *adhibeo*, *ad* and *habeo*, to have.]

To use, or apply. [*Rarely used.*]

ADHIBI′′TION, *n.* Application; use. *Whitaker.*

AD′HIL, *n.* A star of the sixth magnitude, upon the garment of Andromeda, under the last star in her foot. *Encyc.*

ADHORTA′TION, *n.* [L. *adhortatio.*]

Advice. [*Seldom used.*]

ADHORT′ATORY, *a.* [L. *adhortor*, to advise, *ad* and *hortor.*]

Advisory; containing counsel or warning. *Potter's Antiq.*

ADIAPH′ORISTS, *n.* [Gr. αδιαφορος, indifferent.]

Moderate Lutherans; a name given in the sixteenth century, to certain men that followed Melancthon, who was more pacific than Luther. *Encyc.*

The adiaphorists held some opinions and ceremonies to be indifferent, which Luther condemned as sinful or heretical.

ADIAPH′OROUS, *a.* Indifferent; neutral; a name given by Boyle to a spirit distilled from tartar, and some other vegetable substances, neither acid, nor alkaline, or not possessing the distinct character of any chimical body.

ADIEU′, *Adv′.* [Fr. *à dieu*, to God; a compound word, and an elliptical form of speech, for *I commend you to God.* It is called an adverb, but it has none of the properties of a modifying word.]

Farewell; an expression of kind wishes at the parting of friends.

ADIEU′, *n.* A farewell, or commendation to the care of God; as an everlasting *adieu.*

ADIPOC′ERATE, *v. t.* To convert into adipocere.

ADIPOCERA′TION, *n.* The act or process of being changed into adipocere.

AD′IPOCERE, *n.* [L. *adeps*, fat, and *cera*, Fr. *cire*, wax.]

A soft unctuous or waxy substance, of a light brown color, into which the muscular fibers of dead animal bodies are converted, when protected from atmospheric air, and under certain circumstances of temperature and humidity. This substance was first discovered by Fourcroy, in the burying ground of the Church des Innocens, when it was removed in 1787. It is speedily produced, when the body is immersed in running water. *Lunier. Med. Repos. Ed. Encyc.*

AD′IPOSE, } *a.* [L. *adiposus*, from *adeps*,
AD′IPOUS, } fat. Qu. Ch. טפש, to grow fat; Heb. and Ch., fat, gross, stupid; Ar. طفش, fat, bulky.]

Fat. The *adipose* membrane is the cellular membrane, containing the fat in its cells, and consisting of ductile membranes, connected by a sort of net-work. The *adipose* vein spreads itself on the coat and fat that covers the kidneys. The *adipose* ducts are the bags and ducts which contain the fat. *Quincy. Coxe.*

AD′IT, *n.* [L. *aditus*, from *adeo*, *aditum*, to approach, *ad* and *eo*, to go.]

An entrance or passage; a term in mining, used to denote the opening by which a mine is entered, or by which water and ores are carried away. It is usually made in the side of a hill. The word is sometimes used for *air-shaft*, but not with strict propriety. *Encyc.*

ADJA′CENCY, *n.* [L. *adjaceo*, to lie contiguous, from *ad* and *jaceo*, to lie.]

The state of lying close or contiguous; a bordering upon, or lying next to; as the *adjacency* of lands or buildings. In the sense of *that which is adjacent*, as used by Brown, it is not legitimate.

ADJA′CENT, *a.* Lying near, close, or contiguous; bordering upon; as, a field *adjacent* to the highway.

ADJA′CENT, *n.* That which is next to or contiguous. [*Little used.*] *Locke.*

ADJECT′, *v. t.* [L. *adjicio*, of *ad* and *jacio*, to throw.]

To add or put, as one thing to another. *Macknight.*

ADJEC′TION, *n.* The act of adding, or thing added. [*Little used.*] *Brown.*

ADJECTI′′TIOUS, *a.* Added. *Parkhurst, Gram.*

AD′JECTIVE, *n.* In *grammar*, a word used with a noun, to express a quality of the thing named, or something attributed to it, or to limit or define it, or to specify or describe a thing, as distinct from something else. It is called also an *attributive* or *attribute.* Thus, in the phrase, a *wise ruler*, *wise* is the adjective or attribute, expressing a particular property of *ruler.*

AD′JECTIVELY, *adv.* In the manner of an adjective; as, a word is used *adjectively.*

ADJOIN′, *v. t.* [Fr. *adjoindre;* L. *adjungo*, *ad* and *jungo.* See *Join.*]

To join or unite to; to put to, by placing in contact; to unite, by fastening together with a joint, mortise, or knot. But in these transitive senses, it is rarely used. [See *Join.*]

ADJOIN′, *v. i.* To lie or be next to, or in contact; to be contiguous; as, a farm *adjoining* to the highway. This is the common use of the word, and *to* is often omitted; as, *adjoining* the highway.

ADJOIN′ANT, *a.* Contiguous to. [*Not used.*] *Carew.*

ADJOIN′ED, *pp.* Joined to; united.

ADJOIN′ING, *ppr.* Joining to; adjacent; contiguous.

ADJOURN′, *v. t.* *Adjurn′.* [Fr. *ajourner*, from *journée*, a day, or day's work, or *journey;* It. *giorno.* See *Journal, Journey.*]

Literally, to put off, or defer to another day; but now used to denote a formal intermission of business, a putting off to any future meeting of the same body, and appropriately used of public bodies or private commissioners, entrusted with business; as, the court *adjourned* the consideration of the question.

ADJOURN′, *v. i.* To suspend business for a time; as, from one day to another, or for a longer period, usually public business, as of legislatures and courts, for repose or refreshment; as, congress *adjourned* at four o'clock. It is also used for the act of closing the session of a public body; as, the court *adjourned* without day.

It was moved that parliament should *adjourn* for six weeks. *Select Speeches*, Vol. v. 403.

ADJOURN′ED, *pp.* Put off, delayed, or deferred for a limited time.

2. As an *adjective*, existing or held by adjournment, as an *adjourned* session of a court, opposed to *stated* or *regular.*

ADJOURN′ING, *ppr.* Deferring; suspending for a time; closing a session.

ADJOURN′MENT, *n.* The act of adjourning; as, in legislatures, the *adjournment* of one house is not an *adjournment* of the other.

2. The putting off till another day or time specified, or *without day;* that is, the closing of a session of a public or official body.

3. The time or interval during which a public body defers business; as, during an *adjournment.* But a suspension of business, between the forming of a house and an *adjournment* for refreshment, is called a *recess.* In Great Britain, the close of a *session* of parliament is called a *prorogation;* as the close of a parliament is a *dissolution.* But in Great Britain, as well as in the United States, *adjournment* is now used for an intermission of business, for any indefinite time; as, an *adjournment* of parliament for six weeks. *Select Speeches*, Vol. v. 404.

ADJUDGE′, *v. t.* [Fr. *adjuger*, from *juge*, judge. See *Judge.*]

To decide, or determine, in the case of a controverted question; to decree by a judicial opinion; used appropriately of courts of law and equity.

The case was *adjudged* in Hilary term.

The prize was *adjudged* to the victor; a criminal was *adjudged* to suffer death.

It has been used in the sense of *to judge*; as, he *adjudged* him unworthy of his friendship. But this sense is unusual.

ADJUDǴED, *pp.* Determined by judicial opinion; decreed; sentenced.

ADJUDǴING, *ppr.* Determining by judicial opinion; sentencing.

ADJUDǴMENT, *n.* The act of judging; sentence. *Temple.*

ADJU'DIEATE, *v. t.* [L. *adjudico*, to give sentence. See *Judge.*]

To adjudge; to try and determine, as a court. It has the sense of *adjudge.*

ADJU'DIEATE, *v. i.* To try and determine judicially; as, the court *adjudicated* upon the case.

ADJU'DIEATED, *pp.* Adjudged; tried and decided.

ADJU'DIEATING, *ppr.* Adjudging; trying and determining.

ADJUDIEA'TION, *n.* The act of adjudging; the act or process of trying and determining judicially; as, a ship was taken and sent into port for *adjudication.*

2. A judicial sentence; judgment or decision of a court.

Whose families were parties to some of the former *adjudications.* *Blackstone.*

3. In *Scots law*, an action by which a creditor attaches the heritable estate of his debtor, or his debtor's heir, in payment or security of his debt; or an action by which the holder of an heritable right, laboring under a defect in point of form, may supply that defect. *Encyc.*

AD'JUMENT, *n.* [L. *adjumentum.*]

Help; support. [*Not used.*]

AD'JUNET, *n.* [L. *adjunctus*, joined, from *adjungo.* See *Join.*]

1. Something added to another, but not essentially a part of it; as, *water* absorbed by a cloth or spunge is its *adjunct.* Also a person joined to another.

2. In *metaphysics*, a quality of the body or the mind, whether natural or acquired; as *color*, in the body; *thinking*, in the mind.

3. In *grammar*, words added to illustrate or amplify the force of other words; as, the History of the *American revolution.* The words in Italics are the adjuncts of *History.*

4. In *music*, the word is employed to denominate the relation between the principal mode and the modes of its two fifths. *Encyc.*

The *adjunct* deities, among the Romans, were inferior deities which were added as assistants to the principal gods; as *Bellona*, to Mars; to Vulcan, the *Cabiri;* to the Good Genius, the *Lares;* to the Evil, the *Lemures.*

In the royal academy of sciences at Paris, the *adjuncts* are certain members attached to the study of particular sciences. They are twelve in number, created in 1716. *Encyc.*

Adjunct has been used for a *colleague*, but rarely. *Wotton.*

AD'JUNET, *a.* Added to or united with, as an *adjunct* professor.

ADJUNE'TION, *n.* The act of joining; the thing joined.

ADJUNE'TIVE, *a.* Joining; having the quality of joining.

ADJUNE'TIVE, *n.* That which is joined.

ADJUNE'TIVELY, *adv.* In an adjunctive manner.

ADJUNET'LY, *adv.* In connection with; consequently.

ADJURA'TION, *n.* The act of adjuring; a solemn charging on oath, or under the penalty of a curse.

2. The form of oath. *Addison.*

ADJU'RE, *v. t.* [L. *adjuro*, to swear solemnly, or compel one to swear; from *ad* and *juro*, to swear.]

1. To charge, bind or command on oath, or under the penalty of a curse.

Joshua *adjured* them at that time, saying, cursed be the man before the Lord, that riseth up and buildeth this city of Jericho. Josh. vi.

2. To charge earnestly and solemnly, on pain of God's wrath.

I *adjure* thee by the living God. Mat. xxvi. Acts, xix.

3. To conjure; to charge, urge or summon with solemnity.

The magistrates *adjured* by all the bonds of civil duty. *Milton.*

Ye sacred stars, be all of you *adjured.* *Dryden.*

The Commissioners *adjured* them not to let pass so favorable an opportunity of securing their liberties. *Marshall's Life of Washington.*

ADJU'RED, *pp.* Charged on oath, or with a denunciation of God's wrath; solemnly urged.

ADJU'RER, *n.* One that adjures; one that exacts an oath.

ADJU'RING, *ppr.* Charging on oath, or on the penalty of a curse; beseeching with solemnity.

ADJUST', *v. t.* [Sp. *ajustar;* Port. *id;* It. *aggiustare;* Fr. *ajuster*, to fit or frame; of L. *ad*, and *justus*, just, exact. See *Just.*]

1. To make exact; to fit; to make correspondent, or conformable; as, to *adjust* a garment *to* the body, an event *to* the prediction, or things *to* a standard. *Swift. Locke. Addison.*

2. To put in order; to regulate or reduce to system; as to *adjust* a scheme; to *adjust* affairs.

3. To make accurate; to settle or bring to a satisfactory state, so that parties are agreed in the result; as to *adjust* accounts; the differences are *adjusted.*

ADJUST'ED, *pp.* Made exact or conformable; reduced to a right form or standard; settled.

ADJUST'ER, *n.* A person who adjusts; that which regulates.

ADJUST'ING, *ppr.* Reducing to due form; fitting; making exact or correspondent; settling.

ADJUST'MENT, *n.* The act of adjusting; regulation; a reducing to just form or order; a making fit or conformable; settlement. *Watts. Woodward.*

AD'JUTANCY, *n.* [See *Adjutant.*] The office of an adjutant; skillful arrangement. *Burke.*

AD'JUTANT, *n.* [L. *adjutans*, aiding; from *adjuto*, to assist; of *ad* and *juvo, jutum*, to help.]

In *military affairs*, an officer whose business is to assist the Major by receiving and communicating orders. Each battalion of foot, and each regiment of horse has an adjutant, who receives orders from the Brigade Major, to communicate to the Colonel, and to subalterns. He places guards, receives and distributes ammunition, assigns places of rendezvous, &c.

Adjutant-General, in an army, is the chief adjutant.

Adjutants General, among the Jesuits, were a select number of fathers, who resided with the general of the order, each of whom had a province or country assigned to his care. Their business was to correspond with that province, by their delegates, emissaries or visitors, and give information of occurrences to the father general. *Encyc.*

ADJU'TE, *v. t.* To help. [*Not used.*]

ADJU'TOR, *n.* A helper. [*Little used; its compound* coadjutor *is in common use.*]

ADJU'VANT, *a.* Helping; assisting. *Howell.*

ADLEGA'TION, *n.* [L. *ad* and *legatio*, an embassy, from *lego*, to send. See *Legate.*]

In *the public law of the German Empire*, a right claimed by the states, of joining their own ministers with those of the Emperor, in public treaties and negotiations, relating to the common interest of the Empire. *Encyc.*

ADLOEU'TION, *n.* [See *Allocution.*]

ADMEAS'URE, *v. t. admezh'ur.* [*ad* and *measure.* See *Measure.*]

1. To measure or ascertain dimensions, size or capacity; used for *measure.*

2. To apportion; to assign to each claimant his right; as, to *admeasure* dower or common of pasture. *Blackstone.*

ADMEAS'URED, *pp.* Measured; apportioned.

ADMEAS'UREMENT, *n.* The measuring of dimensions by a rule, as of a ship, cask, and the like.

2. The measure of a thing, or dimensions ascertained.

In these uses the word is equivalent to *measurement, mensuration* and *measure.*

3. The adjustment of proportion, or ascertainment of shares, as of dower or pasture held in common. This is done by writ of *admeasurement*, directed to the sheriff. *Blackstone.*

ADMEAS'URER, *n.* One that admeasures.

ADMEAS'URING, *ppr.* Measuring; apportioning.

ADMENSURA'TION is equivalent to *admeasurement*, but not much used. [See *Mensuration.*]

ADMIN'IELE, *n.* [L. *adminiculum.*]

Help; support. [*Not used.*]

ADMINIE'ULAR, *a.* Supplying help; helpful.

ADMIN'ISTER, *v. t.* [L. *administro*, of *ad* and *ministro*, to serve or manage. See *Minister.*]

1. To act as minister or chief agent, in managing public affairs, under laws or a constitution of government, as a king, president, or other supreme officer. It is used also of absolute monarchs, who rule not in subordination; but is more strictly applicable to limited monarchs and other supreme executive officers, and to governors, vice-roys, judges and the like, who are under the authority of laws. A king or a president *administers* the government or laws, when he executes them, or carries them into effect. A judge *administers* the laws, when he applies them to particular cases or persons. In short, *to administer* is to direct the execution or application of laws.

2. To dispense, as to *administer* justice or the sacrament.
3. To afford, give or furnish; as, to *administer* relief, that is, to act as the agent. To *administer* medicine is to direct and cause it to be taken.
4. To give, as an oath; to cause to swear according to law.

ADMIN'ISTER, *v. i.* To contribute; to bring aid or supplies; to add something; as, a shade *administers* to our comfort.
2. To perform the office of administrator; as, A *administers* upon the estate of B.

ADMIN'ISTERED, *pp.* Executed; managed; governed; afforded; given; dispensed.

ADMINISTE'RIAL, *a.* Pertaining to administration, or to the executive part of government.

ADMIN'ISTERING, *ppr.* Executing; carrying into effect; giving; dispensing.

ADMIN'ISTRATE, in the place of *administer*, has been used, but is not well authorized.

ADMINISTRA'TION, *n.* The act of administering; direction; management; government of public affairs; the conducting of any office or employment.
2. The executive part of government, consisting in the exercise of the constitutional and legal powers, the general superintendence of national affairs, and the enforcement of laws.
3. The persons collectively, who are entrusted with the execution of laws, and the superintendence of public affairs; the chief magistrate and his council; or the council alone, as in Great Britain.
4. Dispensation; distribution; exhibition; as the *administration* of justice, of the sacrament, or of grace. 1 Cor. xii. 2 Cor. ix.
5. The management of the estate of an intestate person, under a commission from the proper authority. This management consists in collecting debts, paying debts and legacies, and distributing the property among the heirs.
6. The power, office or commission of an administrator.

> Surrogates are authorized to grant *administration.* *Laws of New-York.*
>
> It is more usual to say, *letters of administration.* *Blackstone.*

7. This name is given by the Spaniards, to the staple magazine or warehouse, at Callao, in Peru, where foreign ships must unload. *Encyc.*

ADMIN'ISTRATIVE, *a.* That administers, or by which one administers.

ADMINISTRA'TOR, *n.* A man who, by virtue of a commission from the Ordinary, Surrogate, Court of Probate, or other proper authority, has the charge of the goods and estate of one dying without a will.
2. One who administers, or who directs, manages, distributes, or dispenses laws and rites, either in civil, judicial, political, or ecclesiastical affairs.
3. In *Scots law*, a tutor, curator or guardian, having the care of one who is incapable of acting for himself. The term is usually applied to a father who has power over his children and their estate, during their minority. *Encyc.*

ADMINISTRA'TORSHIP, *n.* The office of an administrator.

ADMINISTRA'TRIX, *n.* A female who administers upon the estate of an intestate; also a female who administers government.

AD'MIRABLE, *a.* [L. *admirabilis.*]
To be admired; worthy of admiration; having qualities to excite wonder, with approbation, esteem or reverence; used of persons or things; as, the *admirable* structure of the body, or of the universe.

AD'MIRABLENESS, *n.* The quality of being admirable; the power of exciting admiration.

AD'MIRABLY, *adv.* In a manner to excite wonder, mingled with approbation, esteem or veneration.

AD'MIRAL, *n.* [In the Latin of the middle ages, *Amira, Amiras, Admiralis*, an Emir; Sp. *almirante;* Port. *id.*; It. *ammiraglio;* Fr. *amiral;* from Ar. أمر amara, to command, أمير, a commander; Sans. *amara;* Heb. Ch. Syr. Sam. אמר, to speak. The terminating syllable of *admiral* may be from ἁλς, the sea. This word is said to have been introduced into Europe by the Turks, Genoese or Venetians, in the 12th or 13th century.]
A marine commander in chief; the commander of a fleet or navy.
1. The *Lord High Admiral*, in Great Britain, is an officer who superintends all maritime affairs, and has the government of the navy. He has also jurisdiction over all maritime causes, and commissions the naval officers.
2. The *Admiral of the fleet*, the highest officer under the admiralty. When he embarks on an expedition, the union flag is displayed at the main top gallant mast head.
3. The *Vice Admiral*, an officer next in rank and command to the Admiral, has command of the second squadron. He carries his flag at the fore top gallant mast head. This name is given also to certain officers who have power to hold courts of vice-admiralty, in various parts of the British dominions.
4. The *Rear Admiral*, next in rank to the Vice Admiral, has command of the third squadron, and carries his flag at the mizen top gallant mast head.
5. The commander of any single fleet, or in general any flag officer.
6. The ship which carries the admiral; also the most considerable ship of a fleet of merchantmen, or of fishing vessels. *Encyc.*
7. In *zoology*, a species of shell-fish. [See *Voluta.*]
2. Also a butterfly, which lays her eggs on the great stinging nettle, and delights in brambles. *Encyc.*

AD'MIRALSHIP, *n.* The office or power of an admiral. [*Little used.*]

AD'MIRALTY, *n.* In Great Britain, the office of Lord High Admiral. This office is discharged by one person, or by Commissioners, called *Lords of the Admiralty;* usually seven in number.
The *admiralty court*, or *court of admiralty*, is the supreme court for the trial of maritime causes, held before the Lord High Admiral, or Lords of the admiralty.
In general, a *court of admiralty* is a court for the trial of causes arising on the high seas, as prize causes and the like. In the United States, there is no admiralty court, distinct from others; but the district courts, established in the several states by Congress, are invested with admiralty powers.

ADMIRA'TION, *n.* Wonder mingled with pleasing emotions, as approbation, esteem, love or veneration; a compound emotion excited by something novel, rare, great, or excellent; applied to persons and their works. It often includes a slight degree of surprise. Thus, we view the solar system with *admiration.*

> Very near to *admiration* is the wish to admire. *Anon.*

It has been sometimes used in an ill sense, denoting wonder with disapprobation.

> Your boldness I with *admiration* see. *Dryden.*
>
> When I saw her I wondered with great *admiration.* Luke xvii.

ADMI'RATIVE, *n.* A note of admiration, thus! [*Not used.*] *Cotgrave.*

ADMI'RE, *v. t.* [L. *admiror, ad* and *miror*, to wonder; Sp. and Port. *admirar;* Fr. *admirer;* It. *ammirare*; Fr. *mirer*, to look, to take aim; Corn. *miras*, to look, see or face; Arm. *miret*, to stop, hold, keep; W. *mir*, visage; also fair, comely; and *maer*, one that looks after, keeps or guards, a *mayor*, or bailiff; Russ. *zamirayu*, to be astonished or stupified; *za*, a prefix, and *mir*, peace; *miryu*, to pacify; *zamiriayu*, to make peace. The primary sense is to hold, to stop, or strain. Ch. and Syr. דמר; L. *demiror.* See *Moor* and *Mar.*]
1. To regard with wonder or surprise, mingled with approbation, esteem, reverence or affection.

> When he shall come to be glorified in his saints and be *admired* in all them that love him. 2 Thes. i.

This word has been used in an ill sense, but seems now correctly restricted to the sense here given, and implying something great, rare or excellent, in the object admired.
2. To regard with affection; a familiar term for *to love greatly.*

ADMI'RE, *v. i.* To wonder; to be affected with slight surprise; sometimes with *at;* as, to *admire at* his own contrivance. *Ray.*
To *admire at* sometimes implies disapprobation.

ADMI'RED, *pp.* Regarded with wonder, mingled with pleasurable sensations, as esteem, love or reverence.

ADMI'RER, *n.* One who admires; one who esteems or loves greatly.

ADMI'RING, *ppr.* Regarding with wonder united with love or esteem.

ADMI'RINGLY, *adv.* With admiration; in the manner of an admirer.

ADMISSIBIL'ITY, *n.* The quality of being admissible. *Chase.*

ADMISS'IBLE, *a.* [See *admit.*] That may be admitted, allowed or conceded; as, the testimony is *admissible.*

ADMISS'ION, *n.* [L. *admissio.*]
1. The act or practice of admitting, as the

admission of aliens into our country; also the state of being admitted.

2. Admittance; power or permission to enter; entrance; access; power to approach; as, our laws give to foreigners easy *admission* to the rights of citizens; the *admission* of a clerk to a benefice.

3. Allowance; grant of an argument or position not fully proved.

ADMIT′, *v. t.* [L. *admitto*, from *ad* and *mitto*, to send, Fr. *mettre*.]

1. To suffer to enter; to grant entrance; whether into a place, or an office, or into the mind, or consideration; as to *admit* a student into college; to *admit* a serious thought into the mind.

2. To give right of entrance; as, a ticket *admits* one into a play house.

3. To allow; to receive as true; as, the argument or fact is *admitted*.

4. To permit, grant or allow, or to be capable of; as, the words do not *admit* of such a construction. In this sense, *of* may be used after the verb, or omitted.

ADMIT′TABLE, *a.* That may be admitted or allowed.

ADMIT′TANCE, *n.* The act of admitting; allowance. More usually,

2. Permission to enter; the power or right of entrance; and hence, actual entrance; as, he gained *admittance* into the church.

3. Concession; admission; allowance; as the *admittance* of an argument. [*Not used.*]

4. Skakespeare uses the word for the custom or prerogative of being admitted; "Sir John, you are a gentleman of excellent breeding, of great *admittance*": but the license is unwarrantable.

ADMIT′TED, *pp.* Permitted to enter or approach; allowed; granted; conceded.

ADMIT′TER, *n.* He that admits.

ADMIT′TING, *ppr.* Permitting to enter or approach; allowing; conceding.

ADMIX′, *v. t.* To mingle with something else. [See *Mix*.]

ADMIX′TION, *n.* admix′chun, [L. *admixtio*, or *admistio*; of *ad* and *misceo*, to mix. See *Mix*.]

A mingling of bodies; a union by mixing different substances together. It differs from *composition* or chimical combination; for *admixtion* does not alter the nature of the substances mixed, but merely blends them together; whereas in *composition*, the particles unite by affinity, lose their former properties, and form new compounds, with different properties.

ADMIX′TURE, *n.* [From *admix*.]

The substance mingled with another; sometimes the act of mixture. We say, an *admixture* of sulphur with alum, or the *admixture* of different bodies.

ADMON′ISH, *v. t.* [L. *admoneo*, *ad* and *moneo*, to teach, warn, admonish; Fr. *admonéter*; Norm. *amonester*; Sp. *amonestar*; Port. *amoestar*, or *admoestar*; It. *ammonire*; G. *mahnen*, *ermahnen*; D. *maanen*, to dun, *vermaanen*, to admonish; Sw. *mana*, *formana*; Dan. *maner*, *formaner*; Sax. *mœnan*, to mean.]

1. To warn or notify of a fault; to reprove with mildness.

Count him not as an enemy, but *admonish* him as a brother. 2 Thess. iii.

2. To counsel against wrong practices; to caution or advise.

Admonish one another in psalms and hymns. Col. iii.

3. To instruct or direct.

Moses was *admonished* of God, when he was about to make the tabernacle. Heb. viii.

4. In *ecclesiastical affairs*, to reprove a member of the church for a fault, either publicly or privately; the first step of church discipline. It is followed by *of*, or *against*; as, to admonish *of* a fault committed, or *against* committing a fault. It has a like use in colleges.

ADMON′ISHED, *pp.* Reproved; advised; warned; instructed.

ADMON′ISHER, *n.* One who reproves or counsels.

ADMON′ISHING, *ppr.* Reproving; warning; counseling; directing.

ADMON′ISHMENT, *n.* Admonition. *Shak.*

ADMONI″TION, *n.* Gentle reproof; counseling against a fault; instruction in duties; caution; direction. Tit. iii. 1 Cor. x. In *church discipline*, public or private reproof to reclaim an offender; a step preliminary to excommunication.

ADMONI″TIONER, *n.* A dispenser of admonitions. *Hooker.*

ADMON′ITIVE, *a.* Containing admonition. *Barrow.*

ADMON′ITOR, *n.* An admonisher, a monitor.

ADMON′ITORY, *a.* Containing admonition; that admonishes.

ADMORTIZA′TION, *n.* The reducing of lands or tenements to mortmain. [See *Mortmain.*] *Encyc.*

ADMÖVE′, *v. t.* [L. *admoveo.*]

To move to; to bring one thing to another. [*Little used.*] *Brown.*

ADNAS′CENT, *a.* [L. *ad* and *nascens*, growing.]

Growing on something else. *Evelyn.*

ADNA′TA, *n.* [L. *ad* and *natus*, grown, from *nascor*, to grow.]

1. In *anatomy*, one of the coats of the eye, which is also called *albuginea*, and is sometimes confounded with the *conjunctiva*. It lies between the sclerotica, and conjunctiva.

2. Such parts of animal or vegetable bodies, as are usual and natural, as the hair, wool, horns; or accidental, as fungus, misletoe, and excrescences.

3. Offsets of plants, germinating under ground, as from the lily, narcissus, and hyacinth. *Quincy. Encyc.*

AD′NATE, *a.* [L. *ad* and *natus*, grown.]

In *botany*, pressing close to the stem, or growing to it. *Martyn.*

AD′NOUN, *n.* [*ad* and *noun*.]

In *grammar*, an adjective, or attribute. [*Little used.*]

ADÖ′, *n.* [Qu. *a* and *do*.]

Bustle; trouble; labor; difficulty; as, to make a great *ado* about trifles; to persuade one with much *ado*.

ADOLES′CENCE, *n.* [L. *adolescens*, growing, of *ad* and *olesco*, to grow, from *oleo*. Heb. עלה, to ascend; Ar. علا, to be high.]

The state of growing, applied to the young of the human race; youth, or the period of life between *childhood* and *manhood*.

ADOLES′CENT, *a.* Growing; advancing from childhood to manhood.

ADONE′AN, *a.* Pertaining to Adonis.

Fair *Adonean* Venus. *Faber*

ADO′NIA, *n.* Festivals celebrated anciently in honor of Adonis, by females, who spent two days in lamentations and infamous pleasures. *Encyc.*

ADO′NIC, *a.* *Adonic Verse*, a short verse, in which the death of Adonis was bewailed. It consists of a dactyl and spondee or trochee. *Bailey. Cyc.*

ADO′NIC, *n.* An Adonic verse.

ADO′NIS, *n.* In *mythology*, the favorite of Venus, said to be the son of Cinyras, king of Cyprus. He was fond of hunting, and received a mortal wound from the tusk of a wild boar. Venus lamented his death, and changed him into the flower, anemony.

ADO′NIS, in *botany*, bird's eye or pheasant's eye.

ADO′NISTS, *n.* [Heb. Ch. and Syr. ארון *adon*, Lord, a scriptural title of the Supreme Being.]

Among *critics*, a sect or party who maintain that the Hebrew points ordinarily annexed to the consonants of the word *Jehovah*, are not the natural points belonging to that word, and that they do not express the true pronunciation of it; but that they are vowel points belonging to the words, *Adonai* and *Elohim*, applied to the ineffable name *Jehovah*, which the Jews were forbid to utter, and the true pronunciation of which was lost; they were therefore always to pronounce the word *Adonai*, instead of *Jehovah*. *Encyc.*

ADOPT′, *v. t.* [L. *adopto*, of *ad* and *opto*, to desire or choose. See *Option.*]

1. To take a stranger into one's family, as son and heir; to take one who is not a child, and treat him as one, giving him a title to the privileges and rights of a child.

2. In *a spiritual sense*, to receive the sinful children of men into the invisible church, and into God's favor and protection, by which they become heirs of salvation by Christ. *Brown.*

3. To take or receive as one's own, that which is not naturally so; as, to *adopt* the opinions of another; or to receive that which is new; as, to *adopt* a particular mode of husbandry.

4. To select and take; as, which mode will you *adopt*?

ADOPT′ED, *pp.* Taken as one's own; received as son and heir; selected for use.

ADOPT′EDLY, *adv.* In the manner of something adopted.

ADOPT′ER, *n.* One who adopts.

2. In *chimistry*, a large round receiver, with two necks, diametrically opposite to each other, one of which admits the neck of a retort, and the other is joined to another receiver. It is used in distillations, to give more space to elastic vapors, or to increase the length of the neck of a retort.

ADOPT′ING, *ppr.* Taking a stranger as a son; taking as one's own.

ADOP′TION, *n.* [L. *adoptio.*]

1. The act of adopting, or the state of being adopted; the taking and treating of a stranger as one's own child.

2. The receiving as one's own, what is new or not natural.

3. God's taking the sinful children of men into his favor and protection. Eph. iv.

Adoption by arms, an ancient ceremony of presenting arms to one for his merit or valor, which laid the person under an obligation to defend the giver.

Adoption by baptism is the spiritual affinity which is contracted by god-fathers and god-children, in the ceremony of baptism. It was introduced into the Greek church, and afterwards among the ancient Franks. This affinity was supposed to entitle the god-child to a share of the god-father's estate. *Encyc.*

Adoption by hair was performed by cutting off the hair of a person and giving it to the adoptive father. Thus Pope John VIII adopted Boson, king of Arles.

Adoption by matrimony is the taking the children of a wife or husband, by a former marriage, into the condition of natural children. This is a practice peculiar to the Germans; but is not so properly *adoption* as *adfiliation*. *Encyc.*

Adoption by testament is the appointing of a person to be heir, by will, on condition of his taking the name, arms, &c. of the adopter. *Encyc.*

In Europe, *adoption* is used for many kinds of admission to a more intimate relation, and is nearly equivalent to *reception*; as, the admission of persons into hospitals, or monasteries, or of one society into another. *Encyc.*

ADOPT'IVE, *a.* [L. *adoptivus.*]

That adopts, as an *adoptive* father; or that is adopted, as an *adoptive* son.

ADOPT'IVE, *n.* A person or thing adopted.

ADO'RABLE, *a.* That ought to be adored; worthy of divine honors. In popular use, worthy of the utmost love or respect.

ADO'RABLENESS, *n.* The quality of being adorable, or worthy of adoration.

ADO'RABLY, *adv.* In a manner worthy of adoration.

ADORA'TION, *n.* The act of paying honors to a divine being; the worship paid to God; the act of addressing as a God. *Adoration* consists in external homage, accompanied with the highest reverence. It is used for the act of praying, or preferring requests or thanksgiving, to the Supreme Being.

2. Homage paid to one in high esteem; profound reverence.

Adoration, among the Jews, was performed by bowing, kneeling and prostration. Among the Romans, the devotee, with his head uncovered, applied his right hand to his lips, bowing and turning himself from left to right. The Persians fell on the face, striking the forehead against the earth, and kissing the ground. The adoration paid to the Grecian and Roman emperors, consisted in bowing and kneeling at the feet of the prince, laying hold of his robe, then withdrawing the hand and clapping it to the lips. In modern times, adoration is paid to the pope by kissing his feet, and to princes, by kneeling and kissing the hand. This word was used by the Romans for acclamation or great applause, given to public performers; and the election of a pope is sometimes by adoration, that is, by sudden acclamation without scrutiny. *Encyc.*

ADO'RE, *v. t.* [L. *adoro.* In Ch. and Heb. הדר, to honor, reverence or glorify, to adorn; Heb. אדר, to be magnificent or glorious, to magnify, to glorify. This word is usually referred to the Latin *ad orare*, to carry to one's mouth; *ad* and *os, oris*; as, in order to kiss one's hand, the hand is carried to one's mouth. See *Calmet, ad verbum*, who cites, in confirmation of this opinion, the ancient practice of kissing the hand. See Job. xxxi. 1 Kings, xix. Ps. ii. Gen. xli. Ainsworth supposes the word to be a compound of *ad* and *oro*, to pray; and if the word is compound, as I suspect, this opinion is most probably correct.]

1. To worship with profound reverence; to address with exalted thoughts, by prayer and thanksgiving; to pay divine honors to; to honor as a god or as divine. *Dryden.*

2. To love in the highest degree; to regard with the utmost esteem, affection and respect; as, the people *adore* their prince. *Tatler.*

ADO'RED, *pp.* Worshipped as divine; highly reverenced; greatly beloved.

ADO'RER, *n.* One who worships, or honors as divine; in *popular language*, an admiring lover.

ADO'RING, *ppr.* or *a.* Honoring or addressing as divine; regarding with great love or reverence.

ADORN', *v. t.* [L. *adorno, ad* and *orno*, to deck, or beautify, to dress, set off, extol, furnish; Fr. *orner;* Sp. Port. *ornar;* It. *ornare;* Arm. *aourna.* *Orno* is probably the Saxon *hrinan, gerenian, gerinan, gehrinan*, to touch, to strike, to adorn, that is, to put on.]

1. To deck or decorate; to make beautiful; to add to beauty by dress; to deck with external ornaments.

A bride *adorneth* herself with jewels. Isa. vi.

2. To set off to advantage; to add ornaments to; to embellish by any thing external or adventitious; as, to *adorn* a speech by appropriate action, sentiments with elegance of language, or a gallery with pictures.

3. To make pleasing, or more pleasing; as, great abilities *adorned* by virtue or affability.

4. To display the beauty or excellence of; as, to *adorn* the doctrine of God. Titus ii.

ADORN', *n.* Ornament. *Obs.* *Spenser.*

ADORN', *a.* Adorned; decorated. *Obs.* *Milton.*

ADORN'ED, *pp.* Decked; decorated; embellished.

ADORN'ING, *ppr.* Ornamenting; decorating; displaying beauty.

ADORN'ING, *n.* Ornament; decoration. 1 Pet. iii.

ADOSCULA'TION, *n.* [L. *ad* and *osculatio*, a kissing, from *osculum*, a kiss, or mouth.]

The impregnation of plants by the falling of the farina on the pistils. *Encyc.*

Adosculation is also defined to be the inserting of one part of a plant into another. *Crabbe.*

ADOS'SED, *a.* [Fr. *adossée*, part. of *adosser*, to set back to back; *dos*, the back.]

In *heraldry*, denoting two figures or bearings placed back to back. *Encyc.*

ADOWN', *prep.* [*a* and *down.*] From a higher to a lower situation; downwards; implying descent.

ADOWN', *adv.* Down; on the ground; at the bottom.

ADREAD', *a.* *Adred'.* [See *Dread.*] Affected by dread. *Obs.*

ADRIAT'IC, *a.* [L. *Adria*, or *Hadria*, the gulf of Venice.]

Pertaining to the Gulf, called, from Venice, the Venetian Gulf.

ADRIAT'IC, *n.* The Venetian Gulf; a Gulf that washes the eastern side of Italy.

ADRIFT', *a.* or *adv.* [Sax. *adrifan, gedrifan*, and *drifan*, to drive. See *Drive.* *Adrift* is the participle of the verb.]

Literally, driven; floating; floating at random; impelled or moving without direction. *As an adjective, it always follows its noun;* as, the boat was *adrift.*

ADROGA'TION, *n.* [L. *ad* and *rogo*, to ask. See *Interrogate* and *Rogation.*]

A species of adoption in ancient Rome, by which a person, capable of choosing for himself, was admitted into the relation of a son. So called from the questions put to the parties. *Encyc.*

ADROIT', *a.* [Fr. from *droit*, right, straight, *direct;* whence *droite*, the right hand; It. *diritto*, right, straight, contracted from the L. *directus, dirigo;* Arm. *dret.* See *Right.*]

Dextrous; skilful; active in the use of the hands, and *figuratively*, in the exercise of the mental faculties; ingenious; ready in invention or execution.

ADROIT'LY, *adv.* With dexterity; in a ready skilful manner. *Chesterfield.*

ADROIT'NESS, *n.* Dexterity; readiness in the use of the limbs, or of the mental faculties. *Horne.*

ADRY', *a.* [Sax. *adrigan*, to dry.]

Thirsty, in want of drink. [*This adjective always follows the noun.*] *Spectator.*

ADSCITI''TIOUS, *a.* [L. *ascititius*, from *adscisco, ascisco*, to add or join.]

Added; taken as supplemental; additional; not requisite. *Warton.*

ADSTRIC'TION, *n.* [L. *adstrictio, astrictio*, of *ad* and *stringo*, to *strain* or bind fast. See *Strict.*]

A binding fast. Among *physicians*, the rigidity of a part of the body, occasioning a retention of usual evacuations; costiveness; a closeness of the emunctories; also the styptic effects of medicines. *Encyc.* *Quincy.*

ADSTRIC'TORY, ADSTRING'ENT. [See *Astringent.*]

ADULA'RIA, *n.* [From *Adula*, the summit of a Swiss mountain.]

A mineral deemed the most perfect variety of felspar; its color white, or with a tinge of green, yellow, or red. *Cleaveland.*

ADULA'TION, *n.* [L. *adulatio.*]

Servile flattery; praise in excess, or beyond what is merited; high compliment. *Shak.*

AD'ULATOR, *n.* A flatterer; one who offers praise servilely.

AD'ULATORY, *a.* Flattering; containing excessive praise or compliments; servilely praising; as, an *adulatory* address.

AD'ULATRESS, *n.* A female that flatters with servility.

ADULT′, *n.* [L. *adultus*, grown to maturity, from *oleo*, to grow; Heb. עלה, to ascend.] Having arrived at mature years, or to full size and strength; as an *adult* person or plant.

ADULT′, *n.* A person grown to full size and strength, or to the years of manhood. It is also applied to full grown plants. Among *civilians*, a person between fourteen and twenty-five years of age. *Encyc.*

ADUL′TERANT, *n.* The person or thing that adulterates.

ADUL′TERATE, *v. t.* [L. *adultero*, from *adulter*, mixed, or an adulterer; *ad* and *alter*, other.]

To corrupt, debase, or make impure by an admixture of baser materials; as, to *adulterate* liquors, or the coin of a country. *Boyle.*

ADUL′TERATE, *v. i.* To commit adultery. *Obs.*

ADUL′TERATE, *a.* Tainted with adultery; debased by foreign mixture.

ADUL′TERATED, *pp.* Corrupted; debased by a mixture with something of less value.

ADUL′TERATENESS, *n.* The quality or state of being debased or counterfeit.

ADUL′TERATING, *ppr.* Debasing; corrupting; counterfeiting.

ADULTERA′TION, *n.* The act of adulterating, or the state of being adulterated, corrupted or debased by foreign mixture.

The *adulteration* of liquors, of drugs, and even of bread and beer, is common, but a scandalous crime.

ADUL′TERER, *n.* [L. *adulter.*]

1. A man guilty of adultery; a man who has sexual commerce with any married woman, except his wife. [See *Adultery.*]
2. In *scripture*, an idolater. Ezek. xxiii.
3. An apostate from the true faith, or one who violates his covenant engagements; a very wicked person. Jer. ix. and xxiii.
4. One devoted to earthly things. James, iv.

ADUL′TERESS, *n.* A married woman guilty of incontinence.

ADUL′TERINE, *a.* Proceeding from adulterous commerce; spurious. *Hall.*

ADUL′TERINE, *n.* In the *civil law*, a child issuing from an adulterous connection.

ADUL′TEROUS, *a.* Guilty of adultery; pertaining to adultery.

2. In *scripture*, idolatrous, very wicked. Mat. xii. and xvi. Mark, viii.

ADUL′TERY, *n.* [L. *adulterium.* See *Adulterate.*]

1. Violation of the marriage bed; a crime, or a civil injury, which introduces, or may introduce, into a family, a spurious offspring.

By the *laws of Connecticut*, the sexual intercourse of any man, with a married woman, is the *crime* of adultery in both: such intercourse of a married man, with an unmarried woman, is fornication in both, and adultery of the man, within the meaning of the law respecting divorce; but not a felonious adultery in either, or the crime of adultery at common law, or by statute. This latter offense is, in England, proceeded with only in the ecclesiastical courts.

In *common usage*, adultery means the unfaithfulness of any married person to the marriage bed. In *England*, Parliament grant absolute divorces, for infidelity to the marriage bed in either party; and the spiritual courts divorce *a mensa et thoro.*

2. In a *scriptural sense*, all manner of lewdness or unchastity, as in the seventh commandment.
3. In *scripture*, idolatry, or apostasy from the true God. Jer. iii.
4. In *old laws*, the fine and penalty imposed for the offense of adultery.
5. In *ecclesiastical affairs*, the intrusion of a person into a bishopric, during the life of the bishop. *Encyc.*
6. Among *ancient naturalists*, the grafting of trees was called adultery, being considered as an unnatural union. *Pliny.*

ADULT′NESS, *n.* The state of being adult.

ADUM′BRANT, *a.* [See *Adumbrate.*] Giving a faint shadow, or slight resemblance.

ADUM′BRATE, *v. t.* [L. *adumbro*, to shade, from *umbra*, a shade; Fr. *ombre;* Sp. *sombra;* It. *ombra.*]

To give a faint shadow, or slight likeness; to exhibit a faint resemblance, like a shadow.

ADUMBRA′TION, *n.* The act of making a shadow or faint resemblance.

2. A faint sketch; an imperfect representation of a thing. *Bacon.*
3. In *heraldry*, the shadow only of a figure, outlined, and painted of a color darker than the field. *Dict.*

ADUNA′TION, *n.* [L. *ad* and *unus*, *unio.*] The state of being united; union. [*Not used.*] *Cranmer.*

ADUN′CITY, *n.* [L. *aduncitas*, hookedness, of *ad* and *uncus*, a hook.]

Hookedness; a bending in form of a hook. *Arbuthnot.*

ADUN′COUS, *a.* [L. *aduncus.*]

Hooked; bent or made in the form of a hook. *Bacon.*

ADUNQUE, *a.* *Adunk′.* Hooked. [*Not used.*] *Bacon.*

ADU′RE, *v. t.* [L. *aduro*, *ad* and *uro*, to burn.]

To burn up. [*Not used.*] *Bacon.*

ADUST′, *a.* [L. *adustus*, burnt, the participle of *aduro*, to burn.]

Burnt; scorched; become dry by heat; hot and fiery.

ADUST′ED, *a.* Become hot and dry; burnt; scorched.

ADUS′TION, *n.* The act of burning, scorching, or heating to dryness; a state of being thus heated or dried.

ADV′ANCE, *v. t.* *adv′ans.* [Fr. *avancer;* Sp. *avanzar*, to move forward; It. *avanzare*, to get or increase; Arm. *avans*, to advance. This word is formed on *van*, the front, which seems to be the Ch. and Heb. פנה, פנים, surface, face; whence, Fr. *avant*, It. *avanti*, before.]

1. To bring forward; to move further in front. Hence,
2. To promote; to raise to a higher rank; as, to *advance* one from the bar to the bench.
3. To improve or make better, which is considered as a *progression* or moving forward; as, to *advance* one's true interests.
4. To forward; to accelerate growth; as, to *advance* the growth of plants.
5. To offer or propose; to bring to view or notice; as, to *advance* an opinion or an argument.
6. In *commerce*, to supply beforehand; to furnish on credit, or before goods are delivered, or work done; or to furnish as a part of a stock or fund; as, to *advance* money on loan or contract, or towards a purchase or establishment.
7. To furnish for others; to supply or pay for others, in expectation of reimbursement.

They *advanced* the money out of their own funds, and took the sheriff's deeds in their own name. *Kent, Johnson's Rep.*

8. To raise; to enhance; as, to *advance* the price of goods.

ADV′ANCE, *v. i.* To move or go forward; to proceed; as, the troops *advanced.*

2. To improve, or make progress; to grow better, greater, wiser or older; as, to *advance* in knowledge, in stature, in wisdom, or in years.
3. To rise in rank, office, or consequence; to be preferred, or promoted; as, to *advance* in political standing.

ADV′ANCE, *n.* A moving forward, or towards the front. *Clarendon.*

2. Gradual progression; improvement; as, an *advance* in religion or knowledge. *Atterbury.*
3. Advancement; promotion; preferment; as, an *advance* in rank or office.
4. First hint by way of invitation; first step towards an agreement; as, *A* made an *advance* towards a reconciliation with *B.* In this sense, it is very frequently used in the plural.

The amours of an empress require the plainest *advances.* *Gibbon.*

5. In *trade*, additional price; profit; as, an *advance* on the prime cost of goods.
6. A giving beforehand; a furnishing of something, on contract, before an equivalent is received, as money or goods, towards a capital or stock, or on loan; or the money or goods thus furnished; as, *A* made large *advances* to *B.*
7. A furnishing of money or goods for others, in expectation of reimbursement; or the property so furnished.

I shall, with great pleasure, make the necessary *advances.* *Jay.*

The account was made up with intent to show what *advances* had been made. *Kent.*

In *advance*, in front; before; also beforehand; before an equivalent is received, or when one partner in trade has furnished more than his proportion; as, *A* is in *advance* to *B* a thousand dollars or pounds.

ADV′ANCED, *pp.* Moved forward; promoted; improved; furnished beforehand; situated in front, or before the rest; also old, having reached the decline of life; as, *advanced* in years; an *advanced* age.

ADV′ANCEMENT, *n.* The act of moving forward or proceeding.

2. The state of being advanced; preferment; promotion, in rank or excellence; the act of promoting.
3. Settlement on a wife, or jointure.
4. Provision made by a parent for a child, by gift of property, during his, the parent's life, to which the child would be entitled as heir, after his parent's death. *R. M. Sherman.*

ADV'ANCER, *n.* One who advances; a promoter.

Among *sportsmen*, a start or branch of a buck's attire, between the back antler and the palm. *Encyc.*

ADV'ANCING, *ppr.* Moving forward; proceeding; promoting; raising to higher rank or excellence; improving; supplying beforehand, as on loan, or as stock in trade.

ADV'ANCIVE, *a.* Tending to advance, or promote.

ADV'ANTAGE, *n.* [Fr. *avantage*, from *avant*, before; It. *vantaggio*; Sp. *ventaja.*]

1. Any state, condition, or circumstance, favorable to success, prosperity, interest, or reputation.

   The enemy had the *advantage* of elevated ground.

2. Benefit; gain; profit.

   What *advantage* will it be to thee? Job xxxv.

   There exists, in the economy and course of nature, an indissoluble union between virtue and happiness; between duty and *advantage*. *Washington.*

3. Means to an end; opportunity; convenience for obtaining benefit; as, students enjoy great *advantages* for improvement.

   The General took *advantage* of his enemy's negligence.

4. Favorable state or circumstances; as, jewels set to *advantage*.

5. Superiority, or prevalence over; with *of* or *over*.

   Lest Satan should get an *advantage of* us, (or *over* us.) 2 Cor. ii.

6. Superiority, or that which gives it; as, the *advantage* of a good constitution.

7. Interest; increase; overplus.

   And with *advantage* means to pay thy love. *Obs.* *Shak.*

8. Additional circumstance to give preponderation.

ADV'ANTAGE, *v. t.* To benefit; to yield profit or gain.

   What is a man *advantaged*, if he gain the whole world, and lose himself, or be cast away? Luke ix.

2. To promote; to advance the interest of.

ADV'ANTAGEABLE, *a.* Profitable; convenient; gainful. [*Little used.*]

ADV'ANTAGED, *pp.* Benefitted; promoted.

ADV'ANTAGE-GROUND, *n.* Ground that gives advantage or superiority; a state that gives superior advantages for annoyance or resistance. *Clarendon.*

ADVANTA'GEOUS, *a.* Being of advantage; furnishing convenience, or opportunity to gain benefit; gainful; profitable; useful; beneficial; as, an *advantageous* position of the troops; trade is *advantageous* to a nation.

ADVANTA'GEOUSLY, *adv.* In an advantageous manner; profitably; usefully; conveniently. *Arbuthnot.*

ADVANTA'GEOUSNESS, *n.* The quality or state of being advantageous; profitableness; usefulness; convenience. *Boyle.*

ADV'ANTAGING, *ppr.* Profiting; benefiting.

ADVE'NE. *v. i.* [L. *advenio*, to come to, *ad* and *venio.*]

To accede, or come to; to be added to, or become a part of, though not essential. [*Little used.*]

ADVE'NIENT, *a.* Advening; coming from outward causes.

AD'VENT, *n.* [L. *adventus*, from *advenio*, of *ad* and *venio*, to come. See *Find.*]

A coming; appropriately the coming of our Savior, and in the calendar, it includes four sabbaths before Christmas, beginning on St. Andrew's Day, or on the sabbath next before or after it. It is intended as a season of devotion, with reference to the coming of Christ in the flesh, and his second coming to judge the world. *Encyc.*

ADVENT'INE, *a.* Adventitious. [*Not used.*] *Bacon.*

ADVENTI''TIOUS, *a.* [L. *adventitius*, from *advenio*. See *Advent.*]

Added extrinsically; accidental; not essentially inherent; casual; foreign.

   Diseases of continuance get an *adventitious* strength from custom. *Bacon.*

ADVENTI''TIOUSLY, *adv.* Accidentally.

ADVENT'IVE, *a.* Accidental; adventitious. [*Little used.*] *Bacon.*

ADVENT'IVE, *n.* The thing or person that comes from without. [*Little used.*] *Bacon.*

ADVENT'UAL, *a.* Relating to the season of advent. *Saunderson.*

ADVENT'URE, *n.* [Fr. *aventure*, from *advenio*. See *Advent.*]

1. Hazard; risk; chance; that of which one has no direction; as, at all *adventures*, that is, at all hazards. [See *Venture.*]

2. An enterprize of hazard; a bold undertaking, in which hazards are to be encountered, and the issue is staked upon unforeseen events. *Dryden.*

3. That which is put to hazard; a sense in popular use with seamen, and usually pronounced *venture*. Something which a seaman is permitted to carry abroad, with a view to sell for profit.

A *bill of adventure*, is a writing signed by a person, who takes goods on board of his ship, wholly at the risk of the owner. *Encyc.*

ADVENT'URE, *v. t.* To risk, or hazard; to put in the power of unforeseen events; as, to *adventure* one's life. [See *Venture.*]

ADVENT'URE, *v. i.* To dare; to try the chance; as, to *adventure* on "the tempestuous sea of liberty."

ADVENT'URED, *pp.* Put to hazard; ventured; risked.

ADVENT'URER, *n.* One who hazards, or puts something at risk, as merchant-*adventurers*.

2. One who seeks occasions of chance, or attempts bold, novel, or extraordinary enterprizes.

ADVENT'URESOME, *a.* Bold; daring; incurring hazard. [See *Venturesome.*]

ADVENT'URESOMENESS, *n.* The quality of being bold and venturesome.

ADVENT'URING, *ppr.* Putting to risk; hazarding.

ADVENT'UROUS, *a.* [Fr. *aventureux.*]

1. Inclined or willing to incur hazard; bold to encounter danger; daring; courageous; enterprizing: *applied to persons.*

2. Full of hazard; attended with risk; exposing to danger; requiring courage: *applied to things;* as, an *adventurous* undertaking.

   And followed freedom on the *adventurous* tide. *Trumbull.*

ADVENT'UROUSLY, *adv.* Boldly; daringly; in a manner to incur hazard.

ADVENT'UROUSNESS, *n.* The act or quality of being adventurous.

AD'VERB, *n.* [L. *adverbium*, of *ad* and *verbum*, to a verb.]

In *grammar*, a word used to modify the sense of a verb, participle, adjective or attribute, and usually placed near it; as, he writes *well;* paper *extremely* white. This part of speech might be more significantly named a *modifier*, as its use is to *modify*, that is, to vary or qualify the sense of another word, by enlarging or restraining it, or by expressing form, quality or manner, which the word itself does not express. The term *adverb*, denoting position merely, is often improper.

ADVERB'IAL, *a.* Pertaining to an adverb.

ADVERB'IALLY, *adv.* In the manner of an adverb.

ADVERSA'RIA, *n.* [L. from *adversus*. See *Adverse.*]

Among *the ancients*, a book of accounts, so named from the placing of debt and credit in opposition to each other. A common-place book. *Encyc.*

AD'VERSARY, *n.* [See *Adverse.*]

1. An enemy or foe; one who has enmity at heart.

   The Lord shall take vengeance on his *adversaries*. Nah. i.

   In *scripture*, Satan is called THE ADVERSARY, by way of eminence. 1 Pet. v.

2. An opponent or antagonist, as in a suit at law, or in single combat; an opposing litigant.

AD'VERSARY, *a.* Opposed; opposite to; adverse. In *law*, having an opposing party, as an *adversary* suit; in distinction from an application, in law or equity, to which no opposition is made.

ADVERS'ATIVE, *a.* Noting some difference, contrariety, or opposition; as, John is an honest man, *but* a fanatic. Here *but* is called an *adversative* conjunction. This denomination however is not always correct; for *but* does not always denote opposition, but something additional.

ADVERS'ATIVE, *n.* A word denoting contrariety or opposition.

AD'VERSE, *a.* [L. *adversus*, opposite; of *ad* and *versus*, turned; from *verto*, to turn. See *Advert.* This word was formerly accented, by some authors, on the last syllable; but the accent is now settled on the first.]

1. Opposite; opposing; acting in a contrary direction; conflicting; counteracting; as, *adverse* winds; an *adverse* party.

2. *Figuratively*, opposing desire; contrary to the wishes, or to supposed good; hence, unfortunate; calamitous; afflictive; pernicious; unprosperous; as, *adverse* fate or circumstances.

ADVERSE, *v. t. advers'.* To oppose. [*Not used.*] *Gower.*

AD'VERSELY, *adv.* In an adverse manner; oppositely; unfortunately; unprosperously; in a manner contrary to desire or success.

AD'VERSENESS, *n.* Opposition; unprosperousness.

ADVERS'ITY, *n.* An event, or series of events, which oppose success or desire;

misfortune; calamity; affliction; distress; state of unhappiness.

In the day of *adversity*, consider. Eccl. vii.

Ye have rejected God, who saved you out of all your *adversities*. 1 Sam. x.

ADVERT', *v. i.* [L. *adverto*, of *ad* and *verto*, to turn.]

To turn the mind or attention to; to regard, observe, or notice; with *to*; as, he *adverted to* what was said, or *to* a circumstance that occurred.

ADVERT'ED, *pp.* Attended to; regarded; with *to*.

ADVERT'ENCE, } *n.* A direction of the
ADVERT'ENCY, } mind to; attention; notice; regard; consideration; heedfulness.

ADVERT'ENT, *a.* Attentive; heedful.

ADVERT'ING, *ppr.* Attending to; regarding; observing.

ADVERTI'SE, *v. t. s* as *z*. [Fr. *avertir*; Arm. *avertisza*, to inform; from *ad* and *verto*, to turn. See *Advert*.]

1. To inform; to give notice, advice or intelligence to, whether of a past or present event, or of something future.

I will *advertise* thee what this people will do to thy people in the latter day. Num. xxiv.

I thought to *advertise* thee, saying; buy it before the inhabitants and elders of my people. Ruth iv.

In this sense, it has *of* before the subject of information; as, to *advertise* a man *of* his losses.

2. To publish a notice of; to publish a written or printed account of; as, to *advertise* goods or a farm.

ADVERTI'SED, *pp.* Informed; notified; warned; *used of persons*: published; made known; *used of things*.

ADVER'TISEMENT, *n.* Information; admonition; notice given. *More generally*, a publication intended to give notice; this may be, by a short account printed in a newspaper, or by a written account posted, or otherwise made public.

ADVERTI'SER, *n.* One who advertises. This title is often given to public prints.

ADVERTI'SING, *ppr.* Informing; giving notice; publishing notice.

2. *a.* Furnishing advertisements; as, *advertising* customers.

3. In the sense of monitory, or active in giving intelligence, as used by Shakespeare. [*Not now used.*]

ADVI'CE, *n.* [Fr. *avis*, opinion, notice; Arm. *avis*. This and the verb *aviser*, to advise, seem to be formed of *ad* and the L. *viso*, to see, to visit.]

1. Counsel; an opinion recommended, or offered, as worthy to be followed.

What *advice* give ye? 2 Ch. x.

With good *advice* make war. Prov. xx.

We may give *advice*, but we cannot give conduct. *Franklin.*

2. Prudence; deliberate consideration. *Shak.*

3. Information; notice; intelligence; as, we have late *advices* from France.

To take advice, is to consult with others.

ADVI'CE BOAT, *n.* A vessel employed to carry dispatches or information.

ADVI'SABLE, *a.* [See *Advise*.]

1. Proper to be advised; prudent; expedient; proper to be done or practiced.

It is not *advisable* to proceed, at this time, to a choice of officers.

2. Open to advice. *South.*

ADVI'SABLENESS, *n.* The quality of being advisable or expedient.

ADVI'SE, *v. t. s.* as *z*. [Fr. *aviser*; Arm. *avisa*; Sp. *avisar*; It. *avvisare*. See *Advice*.]

1. To give counsel to; to offer an opinion, as worthy or expedient to be followed; as, I *advise* you to be cautious of speculation.

2. To give information; to communicate notice; to make acquainted with; followed by *of*, before the thing communicated; as, the merchants were *advised* of the risk.

3. To deliberate, consider, or consult.

Advise thyself of what word I shall bring again to him that sent me. 1 Ch. xxi.

But in this sense, it is usually *intransitive*.

ADVI'SE, *v. i.* To deliberate, weigh well, or consider.

Advise and see what answer I shall return to him that sent me. 2 Sam. xxiv.

To advise with is to consult for the purpose of taking the opinions of others.

ADVI'SED, *pp.* Informed; counseled; also cautious; prudent; acting with deliberation.

Let him be *advised* in his answers. *Bacon.*

With the well *advised* is wisdom. Prov. xiii.

2. Done, formed, or taken with advice or deliberation; intended; as, an *advised* act or scheme.

ADVI'SEDLY, *adv.* With deliberation or advice; heedfully; purposely; by design; as, an enterprize *advisedly* undertaken.

ADVI'SEDNESS, *n.* Deliberate consideration; prudent procedure.

ADVI'SEMENT, *n.* Counsel; information; circumspection.

2. Consultation.

The action standing continued nisi for *advisement*. *Mass. Reports.*

ADVI'SER, *n.* One who gives advice or admonition; also, in a *bad sense*, one who instigates or persuades.

ADVI'SING, *ppr.* Giving counsel.

ADVI'SING, *n.* Advice; counsel. *Shak.*

ADVI'SORY, *a.* Having power to advise.

The general association has a general *advisory* superintendence over all the ministers and churches. *Trumbull's Hist. Conn.*
Madison. Ramsay, Hist. Car.

2. Containing advice; as, their opinion is merely *advisory*.

AD'VOCACY, *n.* The act of pleading for; intercession. *Brown.*

2. Judicial pleading; law-suit. *Chaucer.*

AD'VOCATE, *n.* [L. *advocatus*, from *advoco*, to call for, to plead for; of *ad* and *voco*, to call. See *Vocal*.]

1. *Advocate*, in its primary sense, signifies, one who pleads the cause of another in a court of civil law. Hence,

2. One who pleads the cause of another before any tribunal or judicial court, as a barrister in the English courts. We say, a man is a learned lawyer and an able *advocate*.

In Europe, *advocates* have different titles, according to their particular duties.

Consistorial advocates, in Rome, appear before the Consistory, in opposition to the disposal of benefices.

Elective advocates are chosen by a bishop, abbot, or chapter, with license from the prince.

Feudal advocates were of a military kind, and to attach them to the church, had grants of land, with power to lead the vassals of the church to war.

Fiscal advocates, in ancient Rome, defended causes in which the public revenue was concerned.

Juridical advocates became judges, in consequence of their attending causes in the earl's court.

Matricular advocates defended the cathedral churches.

Military advocates were employed by the church to defend it by arms, when force gave law to Europe.

Some advocates were called *nominative*, from their being nominated by the pope or king; some *regular*, from their being qualified by a proper course of study. Some were *supreme*; others, *subordinate*.

Advocate, in the German polity, is a magistrate, appointed in the emperor's name, to administer justice.

Faculty of advocates, in Scotland, is a society of eminent lawyers, who practice in the highest courts, and who are admitted members only upon the severest examination, at three different times. It consists of about two hundred members, and from this body are vacancies on the bench usually supplied.

Lord advocate, in Scotland, the principal crown lawyer, or prosecutor of crimes.

Judge advocate, in courts martial, a person who manages the prosecution.

In English and American courts, *advocates* are the same as counsel, or counselors. In England, they are of two degrees, barristers and serjeants; the former, being apprentices or learners, cannot, by ancient custom, be admitted serjeants, till of sixteen years standing. *Blackstone. Encyc.*

3. One who defends, vindicates, or espouses a cause, by argument; one who is friendly to; as, an *advocate* for peace, or for the oppressed.

In *scripture*, Christ is called an *advocate* for his people.

We have an *advocate* with the father. 1 John, ii.

AD'VOCATE, *v. t.* To plead in favor of; to defend by argument, before a tribunal; to support or vindicate.

Those who *advocate* a discrimination. *Hamilton's Report on public debt.*

The Duke of York *advocated* the amendment. *Debates on the Regency in the House of Lords*, Dec. 27, 1810.

The Earl of Buckingham *advocated* the original resolution. *Ibid.*

The idea of a legislature, consisting of a single branch, though *advocated* by some, was generally reprobated. *Ramsay, Hist. Carolina.*

How little claim persons, who *advocate* this sentiment, really possess to be considered calvinists, will appear from the following quotation. *Mackenzie's Life of Calvin.*

The most eminent orators were engaged to *advocate* his cause. *Mitford.*

A part only of the body, whose cause he *advocates*, coincide with him in judgment. *Chris. Obs.* xi. 434. *Scott.*

AD'VOCATED, *pp.* Defended by argument; vindicated.

AD'VOCATESS, *n.* A female advocate. *Taylor.*

AD'VOCATING, *ppr.* Supporting by reasons; defending; maintaining.

ADVOCA'TION, *n.* A pleading for; plea; apology.

A bill of advocation, in Scotland, is a written application to a superior court, to call an action before them from an inferior court. The order of the superior court for this purpose is called a *letter of advocation*.

ADVOU'TRESS, *n.* An adulteress. *Bacon.*

ADVOU'TRY, *n.* Adultery. [*Little used.*] *Bacon.*

ADVOWEE', *n.* He that has the right of advowson. *Cowel.*

2. The advocate of a church or religious house. *Cyc.*

ADVOW'SON, *n.* *s* as *z.* [Fr. *avouerie*, from *avouer*, to avow; Norm. *avoerie*, or *avoeson*. But the word was latinized, *advocatio*, from *advoco*, and *avow* is from *advoco.*]

In *English law*, a right of presentation to a vacant benefice; or in other words, a right of nominating a person to officiate in a vacant church. The name is derived from *advocatio*, because the right was first obtained by such as were founders, benefactors or strenuous defenders, *advocates*, of the church. Those who have this right are styled *patrons*. Advowsons are of three kinds, *presentative*, *collative*, and *donative*; *presentative*, when the patron presents his clerk to the bishop of the diocese to be instituted; *collative*, when the bishop is the patron, and institutes, or *collates* his clerk, by a single act; *donative*, when a church is founded by the king, and assigned to the patron, without being subject to the ordinary, so that the patron confers the benefice on his clerk, without presentation, institution, or induction.

Advowsons are also *appendant*, that is, annexed to a manor; or, *in gross*, that is, annexed to the person of the patron. *Blackstone.*

ADVOY'ER, or *Avoy'er*, [Old Fr. *advoes.*]

A chief magistrate of a town or canton in Switzerland.

A'DY, *n.* The *abanga*, or Thernel's restorative; a species of Palm tree, in the West Indies, tall, upright, without branches, with a thick branching head, which furnishes a juice, of which the natives make a drink by fermentation. *Encyc. Coxe.*

ADZ, *n.* [Sax. *adese*; Sp. *azuela*; formerly written in Eng. *addice.*]

An iron instrument with an arching edge, across the line of the handle, and ground from a base on its inside to the outer edge; used for chipping a horizontal surface of timber. *Encyc.*

Æ, a diphthong in the Latin language; used also by the Saxon writers. It answers to the Gr. αι. The Sax. *æ* has been changed into *e* or *ea*. In derivatives from the learned languages, it is mostly superseded by *e*, and convenience seems to require it to be wholly rejected in anglicized words. For such words as may be found with this initial combination, the reader will therefore search under the letter *E*.

ÆD, *ed*, *ead*, syllables found in names from the Saxon, signify *happy*; as, *Eadric*, happy kingdom; *Eadrig*, happy victory; *Edward*, prosperous watch; *Edgar*, successful weapon. *Gibson. Lye.*

Æ'DILE, *n.* [Lat.] In ancient Rome, an officer or magistrate, who had the care of the public buildings, [*ædes*,] streets, highways, public spectacles, &c.

Æ'GILOPS, *n.* [Gr. αιγιλωψ; αιξ, a goat, and ωψ, the eye.]

A tumor in the corner of the eye, and a plant so called. *Quincy.*

Æ'GIS, *n.* [Gr. αιγις, a goat skin, and shield; from αιξ, a goat.]

A shield, or defensive armor.

ÆL, *al*, *alh* or *eal*, in Saxon, Eng. *all*, are seen in many names; as, in *Ælfred*, Alfred, all peace; *Ælwin*, all conqueror. *Gibson.*

ÆLF, seems to be one form of *help*, but more generally written *elph* or *ulph*; as, in *Ælfwin*, victorious aid; *Æthelwulph*, illustrious help. *Gibson.*

AE'OLIST, *n.* [L. *Æolus.*]

A pretender to inspiration. *Swift.*

A'ERATE, *v. t.* [See *Air.*] To combine with carbonic acid, formerly called fixed air. [*The word has been discarded from modern chimistry.*]

A'ERATED, *pp.* Combined with carbonic acid.

A'ERATING, *ppr.* Combining with carbonic acid.

AERA'TION, *n.* The act or operation of combining with carbonic acid.

AE'RIAL, *a.* [L. *aerius.* See *Air.*]

1. Belonging to the air, or atmosphere; as, *aerial* regions.
2. Consisting of air; partaking of the nature of air; as, *aerial* particles.
3. Produced by air; as, *aerial* honey. *Pope.*
4. Inhabiting or frequenting the air; as, *aerial* songsters.
5. Placed in the air; high; lofty; elevated; as, *aerial* spires; *aerial* flight.

AE'RIANS, *n.* In *church history*, a branch of Arians, so called from Aerius, who maintained, that there is no difference between bishops and priests.

A'ERIE, *n.* [W. *eryr*, Corn. *er*, an eagle.]

The nest of a fowl, as of an eagle or hawk; a covey of birds. *Shak.*

AERIFICA'TION, *n.* The act of combining air with; the state of being filled with air. *Fourcroy.*

2. The act of becoming air or of changing into an aeriform state, as substances which are converted from a liquid or solid form into gas or an elastic vapor; the state of being aeriform. *Fourcroy.*

A'ERIFIED, *pp.* Having air infused, or combined with.

A'ERIFORM, *a.* [L. *aer*, air, and *forma*, form.]

Having the form or nature of air, or of an elastic, invisible fluid. The gases are *aeriform* fluids.

A'ERIFY, *v. t.* To infuse air into; to fill with air, or to combine air with.

AEROG'RAPHY, *n.* [Gr. αηρ, air, and γραφω, to describe.]

A description of the air or atmosphere; but *aerology* is chiefly used.

A'EROLITE, *n.* [Gr. αηρ, air, and λιθος, a stone.]

A stone falling from the air, or atmospheric regions; a meteoric stone. *Guidotte. Med. Rep.*

AEROLOG'ICAL, *a.* Pertaining to aerology.

AEROL'OGIST, *n.* One who is versed in aerology.

AEROL'OGY, *n.* [Gr. αηρ, air, and λογος, description.]

A description of the air; that branch of philosophy which treats of the air, its constituent parts, properties, and phenomena. *Encyc.*

A'EROMANCY, *n.* [Gr. αηρ, and μαντεια, divination.]

Divination by means of the air and winds. [*Little used.*]

AEROM'ETER, *n.* [Gr. αηρ, air, and μετρον, measure.]

An instrument for weighing air, or for ascertaining the mean bulk of gases. *Journ. of Science.*

AEROM'ETRY, *n.* [*as above.*] The science of measuring the air, including the doctrine of its pressure, elasticity, rarefaction, and condensation. *Encyc.*

Rather, aerometry is the art or science of ascertaining the mean bulk of the gases. *Encyc. Ure.*

A'ERONAUT, *n.* [Gr. αηρ, and ναυτης, a sailor, from ναυς, a ship.]

One who sails or floats in the air; an aerial navigator; *applied to persons who ascend in air balloons.* *Burke.*

AERONAUT'IC, *a.* Sailing or floating in the air; pertaining to aerial sailing.

AERONAUT'ICS, *n.* The doctrine, science, or art of sailing in the air, by means of a balloon.

A'ERONAUTISM, *n.* The practice of ascending and floating in the atmosphere, in balloons. *Journ. of Science.*

AEROS'COPY, *n.* [Gr. αηρ, and σκεπτομαι, to see.]

The observation of the air. [*Little used.*]

A'EROSTAT, *n.* [Gr. αηρ, and στατος, sustaining, from ιστημι, to stand.]

A machine or vessel sustaining weights in the air; a name given to air balloons. *Encyc.*

AEROSTAT'IC, *a.* Suspending in air; pertaining to the art of aerial navigation.

AEROSTA'TION, *n.* Aerial navigation; the science of raising, suspending, and guiding machines in the air, or of ascending in air balloons. *Adams.*

2. The science of weighing air.

A'ERY-LIGHT, in Milton, light as air; used for *airy light.*

AF'AR, *adv.* [*a* and *far.* See *Far.*]

1. At a distance in place; to or from a distance; used with *from* preceding, or *off* following; as, he was seen *from afar*; I saw him *afar off.*
2. In *scripture*, figuratively, estranged in affection; alienated.

My kinsmen stand *afar off.* Ps. xxxviii.

3. Absent; not assisting.

Why standest thou *afar off*, O Lord? Ps. x.

4. Not of the visible church. Eph. ii.

AFE'ARD, *a.* [Sax. *aferan*, to make afraid. *Afeard* is the participle passive. See *Fear.*]

Afraid; affected with fear or apprehension, in a more moderate degree than is expressed by *terrified*. It is followed by *of*, but no longer used in books, and even in popular use, is deemed vulgar.

AF'FA, *n.* A weight used on the Guinea coast, equal to an ounce. The half of it is called *eggeba*. *Encyc.*

AFFABIL'ITY, *n.* [See *Affable.*] The quality of being affable; readiness to converse; civility and courteousness, in receiving others, and in conversation; condescension in manners. *Affability* of countenance is that mildness of aspect, which invites to free social intercourse.

AF'FABLE, *a.* [L. *affabilis*, of *ad* and *fabulor*. See *Fable.*]

1. Easy of conversation; admitting others to free conversation without reserve; courteous; complaisant; of easy manners; condescending; usually applied to superiors; as, an *affable* prince.

2. Applied to external appearance, *affable* denotes that combination of features, which invites to conversation, and renders a person accessible, opposed to a *forbidding* aspect; mild; benign; as, an *affable* countenance.

AF'FABLENESS, *n.* Affability.

AF'FABLY, *adv.* In an affable manner; courteously; invitingly.

AFFA'IR, *n.* [Fr. *affaire*, from *faire*, to make or do; L. *facere*; Sp. *hacer;* It. *fare*. The primary sense of *facio* is to urge, drive, impel.]

1. Business of any kind; that which is done, or is to be done; *a word of very indefinite and undefinable signification.* In the plural, it denotes transactions in general; as human *affairs;* political or ecclesiastical *affairs:* also the business or concerns of an individual; as, his *affairs* are embarrassed.

2. Matters; state; condition of business or concerns.

I have sent that ye may know our *affairs.* Eph. vi.

3. In the singular, it is used for a private dispute, or duel; as, an *affair* of honor; and sometimes a partial engagement of troops.

In the phrase, *at the head of affairs*, the word means, the public concerns of executing the laws, and administering the government. *Junius.*

AFFECT' *v. t.* [L. *afficio, affectum*, of *ad* and *facio*, to make; L. *affecto*, to desire, from the same root. *Affect* is to make to, or upon, to press upon.]

1. To act upon; to produce an effect or change upon; as, cold *affects* the body; loss *affects* our interests.

2. To act upon, or move the passions; as, *affected* with grief.

3. To aim at; aspire to; desire or entertain pretension to; as, to *affect* imperial sway. [See the etymology of *Affair.*]

4. To tend to by natural affinity or disposition; as, the drops of a fluid *affect* a spherical form.

5. To love, or regard with fondness.

Think not that wars we love and strife *affect.* *Fairfax.*

[*This sense is closely allied to the third.*]

6. To make a show of; to attempt to imitate, in a manner not natural; to study the appearance of what is not natural, or real; as, to *affect* to be grave; *affected* friendship.

It seems to have been used formerly for *convict* or *attaint*, as in Ayliffe's Parergon; but this sense is not now in use.

AFFECTA'TION, *n.* [L. *affectatio.*]

1. An attempt to assume or exhibit what is not natural or real; false pretense; artificial appearance, or show; as, an *affectation* of wit, or of virtue.

2. Fondness; affection. [*Not used.*] *Hooker. Hall.*

AFFECT'ED, *pp.* Impressed; moved, or touched, either in person or in interest; having suffered some change by external force, loss, danger, and the like; as, we are more or less *affected* by the failure of the bank.

2. Touched in the feelings; having the feelings excited; as, *affected* with cold or heat.

3. Having the passions moved; as, *affected* with sorrow or joy.

4. *a.* Inclined, or disposed; followed by *to;* as, well *affected to* government.

5. *a.* Given to false show; assuming, or pretending to possess what is not natural or real; as, an *affected* lady.

6. *a.* Assumed artificially; not natural; as, *affected* airs.

AFFECT'EDLY, *adv.* In an affected manner; hypocritically; with more show than reality; formally; studiously; unnaturally; as, to walk *affectedly; affectedly* civil.

AFFECT'EDNESS, *n.* The quality of being affected; affectation.

AFFECT'ING, *ppr.* Impressing; having an effect on; touching the feelings; moving the passions; attempting a false show; greatly desiring; aspiring to possess.

2. *a.* Having power to excite, or move the passions; tending to move the affections; pathetic; as, an *affecting* address.

The most *affecting* music is generally the most simple. *Mitford.*

AFFECT'INGLY, *adv.* In an affecting manner; in a manner to excite emotions.

AFFEC'TION, *n.* The state of being affected. [*Little used.*]

2. Passion; but more generally,

3. A bent of mind towards a particular object, holding a middle place between *disposition*, which is natural, and *passion*, which is excited by the presence of its exciting object. *Affection* is a permanent bent of the mind, formed by the presence of an object, or by some act of another person, and existing without the presence of its object. *Encyc.*

4. In *a more particular sense*, a settled good will, love or zealous attachment; as, the *affection* of a parent *for* his child. It was formerly followed by *to* or *towards*, but is now more generally followed by *for.*

5. Desire; inclination; propensity, good or evil; as, virtuous or vile *affections.* Rom. i. Gal. 5.

6. In *a general sense*, an attribute, quality or property, which is inseparable from its object; as, love, fear and hope are *affections* of the mind; figure, weight, &c., are *affections* of bodies.

7. Among *physicians*, a disease, or any particular morbid state of the body; as, a gouty *affection;* hysteric *affection.*

8. In *painting*, a lively representation of passion.

Shakespeare uses the word for *affectation;* but this use is not legitimate.

AFFEC'TIONATE, *a.* [Fr. *affectionné.*]

1. Having great love, or affection; fond; as, an *affectionate* brother.

2. Warm in affection; zealous.

Man, in his love to God, and desire to please him, can never be too *affectionate.* *Sprat.*

3. Proceeding from affection; indicating love; benevolent; tender; as, the *affectionate* care of a parent; an *affectionate* countenance.

4. Inclined to; warmly attached. [*Little used.*] *Bacon.*

AFFEC'TIONATELY, *adv.* With affection; fondly; tenderly; kindly. 1. Thes. ii.

AFFEC'TIONATENESS, *n.* Fondness; goodwill; affection.

AFFEC'TIONED, *a.* Disposed; having an affection of heart.

Be ye kindly *affectioned* one to another. Rom. xii.

2. Affected; conceited. *Obs.* *Shak.*

AFFECT'IVE, *a.* That affects, or excites emotion; suited to affect. [*Little used.*]

AFFECT'IVELY, *adv.* In an affective or impressive manner.

AFFECT'OR, } *n.* One that affects; one
AFFECT'ER, } that practices affectation.

AFFECT'UOUS, *a.* Full of passion. [*Not used.*] *Leland.*

AFFEE'R, *v. t.* [Fr. *affier*, to set.]

To confirm. [*Not used.*]

AFFEE'R, *v. t.* [Fr. *afferer, affeurer*, or *afforer*, to assess or value.]

In *law*, to assess or reduce an arbitrary penalty or amercement to a precise sum; to reduce a general amercement to a sum certain, according to the circumstances of the case. *Blackstone.*

AFFEE'RED, *pp.* Moderated in sum; assessed; reduced to a certainty.

AFFEE'RMENT, *n.* The act of affeering, or assessing an amercement, according to the circumstances of the case.

AFFEE'ROR, *n.* One who affeers; a person sworn to assess a penalty, or reduce an uncertain penalty to a certainty. *Cowel.*

AFFETTUO'SO, or *con affetto*, [It., from L. *affectus.*]

In *music*, a direction to render notes soft and affecting.

AFFI'ANCE, *n.* [Norm. *affiaunce*, confidence; Fr. *fiancer*, to betroth; Sp. *fianza*, security in bail, *afianzar*, to give security or bail, from *fiar*, to trust, to bail, to confide in; Port. *id;* Fr. *fier*, to trust; It. *fidare, affidare*, to trust, *fidanza*, confidence, *fidanzare*. to betroth, from L. *fido, fides.*]

1. The marriage contract or promise; faith pledged.

2. Trust in general; confidence; reliance.

The Christian looks to God with implicit *affiance.* *Hammond.*

AFFI'ANCE, *v. t.* To betroth; to pledge one's faith or fidelity in marriage, or to promise marriage.

To me, sad maid, he was *affianced.* *Spenser.*

2. To give confidence.

Affianced in my faith. *Pope.*

AFFI'ANCED, *pp.* Pledged in marriage; betrothed; bound in faith.

AFFI'ANCER, *n.* One who makes a contract of marriage between parties.

AFFI'ANCING, *ppr.* Pledging in marriage; promising fidelity.

AFFIDA'VIT, *n.* [An old law verb in the perfect tense; *he made oath;* from *ad* and *fides*, faith.]

A declaration upon oath. In the United States, more generally, a declaration in writing, signed by the party, and sworn to, before an authorized magistrate.

AFFI'ED, *a.* or *part.* Joined by contract; affianced. [*Not used.*] *Shak.*

AFFI'LE, *v. t.* [Fr. *affiler.*]

To polish. [*Not used.*] *Chaucer.*

AFFIL'IATE, *v. t.* [Fr. *affilier*, to adopt,

to initiate into the mysteries of a religious order; L. *ad* and *filius*, a son.]

1. To adopt; to receive into a family as a son.

2. To receive into a society as a member, and initiate in its mysteries, plans, or intrigues—*a sense in which the word was much used by the Jacobins in France, during the revolution.*

AFFILIA'TION, *n.* Adoption; association in the same family or society.

AFFIN'ITY, *n.* [L. *affinitas*, from *affinis*, adjacent, related by marriage; *ad* and *finis*, end.]

1. The relation contracted by marriage, between a husband and his wife's kindred, and between a wife and her husband's kindred; in contradistinction from *consanguinity* or relation by blood.

Solomon made *affinity* with Pharaoh. 1 Kings iii.

2. Agreement; relation; conformity; resemblance; connection; as, the *affinity* of sounds, of colors, or of languages.

3. In *chimistry*, attraction; elective attraction, or that tendency which different species of matter have to unite, and combine with certain other bodies, and the power that disposes them to continue in combination. There are two kinds of affinity.

1. *Affinity of aggregation*, which is the power that causes two homogeneous bodies to tend towards each other, unite and cohere, as two drops of water, which unite in one. 2. *Affinity of composition*, which is the tendency of bodies of different kinds to unite and form new combinations of bodies with different properties. Such is the affinity which unites acids and alkalies, the results of which combination are neutral salts.

The operations of this principle are various. When heterogeneous bodies have mutually an equal attraction, it is called *compound affinity*. When one substance decomposes a combination of others, unites with one of them and precipitates the other, the power is called the *affinity of decomposition*. When bodies will not unite, but by means of a third, which enables them to combine, this is *affinity by means of a medium*.

Double affinity is when by means of four bodies, two decompositions and two new combinations are effected.

Fourcroy. Hooper.

AFFIRM, *v. t.* *afferm'.* [L. *affirmo; ad* and *firmo*, to make firm. See *Firm.*]

1. To assert positively; to tell with confidence; to aver; to declare the existence of something; to maintain as true; opposed to *deny.*

Of one Jesus whom Paul *affirmed* to be alive. Acts 25.

2. To make firm; to establish, confirm or ratify; as, the Supreme court *affirmed* the judgment.

AFFIRM' *v. i.* To declare solemnly before a court or magistrate, for confirming a fact, or to have an affirmation administered to, by way of confirmation, or as a substitute for an oath; as, the witness *affirmed* to the fact, or he was *affirmed* to the fact.

AFFIRM'ABLE, *a.* That may be asserted or declared; followed by *of;* as, an attribute *affirmable of* every just man.

AFFIRM'ANCE, *n.* Confirmation; ratification; as, the *affirmance* of a judgment; a statute in *affirmance* of common law.

2. Declaration; affirmation. [*Little used.*] *Selden. Cowper.*

AFFIRM'ANT, *n.* One who affirms.

AFFIRMA'TION, *n.* The act of affirming or asserting as true; opposed to *negation* or *denial.* *Shak.*

2. That which is asserted; position declared as true; averment. *Hammond.*

3. Confirmation; ratification; an establishing of what had been before done or decreed. *Hooker.*

4. A solemn declaration made under the penalties of perjury, by persons who conscientiously decline taking an oath; which affirmation is in law equivalent to testimony given under oath.

AFFIRM'ATIVE, *a.* That affirms, or asserts; declaratory of what exists; opposed to *negative;* as, an *affirmative* proposition.

2. Confirmative; ratifying; as, an act *affirmative* of common law.

3. In *algebra*, positive; a term applied to numbers which have the sign + *plus*, denoting addition, and opposed to *negative*, or such as have the sign — *minus*, denoting subtraction.

4. Positive; dogmatic. *Obs.* *Taylor.*

AFFIRM'ATIVE, *n.* That side of a question which affirms or maintains; opposed to *negative;* as, there were seventy votes in the *affirmative*, and thirty-five in the *negative.*

AFFIRM'ATIVELY, *adv.* In an affirmative manner; positively; on the affirmative side of a question; opposed to *negatively.*

AFFIRM'ED, *pp.* Declared; asserted; averred; confirmed; ratified.

AFFIRM'ER, *n.* One who affirms.

AFFIRM'ING, *ppr.* Asserting; declaring positively; confirming.

AFFIX', *v. t.* [L. *affigo, affixum*, of *ad* and *figo*, to fix; Gr. πηγω, πηγνυω, πηξω; Eng. *peg.* See *Fix.*]

1. To unite at the end; to subjoin, annex, or add at the close; as, to *affix* a syllable to a word; to *affix* a seal to an instrument.

2. To attach, unite, or connect with, as names *affixed* to ideas, or ideas *affixed* to things.

3. To fix or fasten in any manner. In this sense, *fix* is more generally used.

AF'FIX, *n.* A syllable or letter added to the end of a word.

AFFIX'ED, *pp.* United at the end; annexed; attached.

AFFIX'ING, *ppr.* Uniting at the end; subjoining; attaching.

AFFIX'ION, *n.* The act of uniting at the end, or state of being so united. [*Little used.*]

AFFIX'TURE, *n.* That which is affixed. *Drake.*

AFFLA'TION, *n.* [L. *afflo, afflatum*, of *ad* and *flo;* Eng. *blow.* See *Blow.*]

A blowing or breathing on.

AFFLA'TUS, *n.* [L.]

1. A breath or blast of wind.

2. Inspiration; communication of divine knowledge, or the power of prophesy. *Spence.*

AFFLICT', *v. t.* [L. *affligo, afflicto*, of *ad* and *fligo*, to strike; Eng. *flog;* Gr. Eol. φλεγω, to strike; Gr. πληγη, L. *plaga*, a stroke; Goth. *flekan*, to strike. Hence, Ger. *flegel;* D. *vlegel;* Eng. *flail, g* being suppressed; L. *flagellum.* See *Flog.*]

1. To give to the body or mind pain which is continued or of some permanence; to grieve, or distress; as, one is *afflicted* with the gout, or with melancholy, or with losses and misfortunes.

They *afflict* thy heritage, O Lord. Ps. xcv.

2. To trouble; to harass; to distress.

AFFLICT'ED, *pp.* Affected with continued or often repeated pain, either of body or mind; suffering grief or distress, of any kind; followed by *at, by* or *with;* as, afflicted *at* the loss of a child, *by* the rheumatism, or *with* losses.

AFFLICT'EDNESS, *n.* The state of being afflicted; but superseded by *affliction.*

AFFLICT'ER, *n.* One who afflicts, or causes pain of body or of mind.

AFFLICT'ING, *ppr.* Causing continued or durable pain of body or mind; grieving; distressing.

AFFLICT'ING, *a.* Grievous; distressing; as, an *afflicting* event.

AFFLIC'TION, *n.* The state of being afflicted; a state of pain, distress, or grief.

Some virtues are seen only in *affliction.*

2. The cause of continued pain of body or mind, as sickness, losses, calamity, adversity, persecution.

Many are the *afflictions* of the righteous. Ps. xxxiv.

AFFLICT'IVE, *a.* Giving pain; causing continued or repeated pain or grief; painful; distressing. *Hall.*

AFFLICT'IVELY, *adv.* In a manner to give pain or grief. *Brown.*

AF'FLUENCE, *n.* [L. *affluentia*, of *ad* and *fluo*, to *flow.* See *Flow.*]

1. *Literally*, a flowing to, or concourse. *In this sense it is rarely used.* It is sometimes written *affluency.*

2. *Figuratively*, abundance of riches; great plenty of worldly goods; wealth. *Rogers.*

AF'FLUENT, *a.* Flowing to; *more generally*, wealthy; abounding in goods or riches; abundant. *Prior.*

AF'FLUENTLY, *adv.* In abundance; abundantly.

AF'FLUX, *n.* [L. *affluxum*, from *affluo.* See *Flow.*]

The act of flowing to; a flowing to, or that which flows to; as, an *afflux* of blood to the head.

AFFLUX'ION, *n.* The act of flowing to; that which flows to. [See *Afflux.*]

AF'FORAGE, *n.* [Fr. *afforer*, to value. See *Affeer.*]

In *France*, a duty paid to the lord of a district, for permission to sell wine or other liquors, within his seignory. *Encyc.*

AFFO'RCEMENT, *n.* [*ad* and *force.*]

In *old charters*, a fortress; a fortification for defense. *Obs.* *Cyc.*

AFFO'RD, *v. t.* [*ad* and the root of *forth, further;* G. *fördern*, to further or promote; D. *voorderen;* Dan. *befordrer*, to further. The sense is to send forth. But I have not found this precise word in the exact sense of the English, in any other language.]

1. To yield or produce as fruit, profit, issues,

or result. Thus, the earth *affords* grain; a well *affords* water; trade *affords* profit; distilled liquors *afford* spirit.

2. To yield, grant or confer; as, a good life *affords* consolation in old age.

3. To be able to grant or sell with profit or without loss; as, *A* can *afford* wine at a less price than *B*.

4. To be able to expend without injury to one's estate; as, a man can *afford* a sum yearly in charity; or be able to bear expenses, or the price of the thing purchased; as, one man can *afford* to buy a farm, which another cannot.

5. To be able without loss or with profit.

The merchant can *afford* to trade for smaller profits. *Hamilton.*

AFFO'RDED, *pp.* Yielded as fruit, produce or result; sold without loss or with profit.

AFFO'RDING, *ppr.* Yielding; producing; selling without loss; bearing expenses.

AFFOR'EST, *v. t.* [*ad* and *forest.*]
To convert ground into forest, as was done by the first Norman kings in England, for the purpose of affording them the pleasures of the chase.

AFFORESTA'TION, *n.* The act of turning groud into forest or wood land. *Blackstone.*

AFFOR'ESTED, *pp.* Converted into forest.

AFFOR'ESTING, *ppr.* Converting into forest.

AFFRAN'CHISEMENT, *n.* [See *Franchise* and *Disfranchise.*]
The act of making free, or liberating from dependence or servitude. [*Little used.*]

AFFRAP', *v. t.* [Fr. *frapper*, to strike; Eng. *rap.*]
To strike. *Obs.* *Spenser.*

AFFRA'Y, AFFRA'YMENT, *n.* [Fr. *effrayer*, to frighten; *effroi*, terror; Arm. *effreyza, effrey.*]

1. In *law*, the fighting of two or more persons, in a public place, to the terror of others. A fighting in private is not, in a legal sense, an affray. *Blackstone.*

2. In *popular language*, *fray* is used to express any fighting of two or more persons; but the word is now deemed inelegant.

3. Tumult; disturbance. *Spenser.*

AFFREIGHT', *v. t.* *affra'te.* [See *Freight.*]
To hire a ship for the transportation of goods or freight. *Commerce.*

AFFREIGHT'ED, *pp.* Hired for transporting goods.

AFFREIGHT'ER, *n.* The person who hires or charters a ship or other vessel to convey goods. *Walsh, Am. Rev.*

AFFREIGHT'MENT, *n.* The act of hiring a ship for the transportation of goods. *American Review, App.*

AFFRET', *n.* [It. *affrettare*, to hasten.]
A furious onset, or attack. [*Not used.*] *Spenser.*

AFFRIC'TION, *n.* The act of rubbing. [*Not used.*] [See *Friction.*] *Boyle.*

AFFRIENDED, *a.* *affrend'ed.* Made friends; reconciled. *Obs.* *Spenser.*

AFFRI'GHT, *v. t.* *affri'te.* [Sax. *frihtan.* See *Fright.*]
To impress with sudden fear; to frighten; to terrify or alarm. It expresses a stronger impression than *fear* or *apprehend*, and perhaps less than *terror.*

AFFRI'GHT, *n.* Sudden or great fear; terror; also, the cause of terror; a frightful object.

AFFRI'GHTED, *pp.* Suddenly alarmed with fear; terrified; followed by *at* or *with*, more generally by *at*; as, *affrighted* at the cry of fire.

AFFRI'GHTER, *n.* One who frightens.

AFFRI'GHTFUL, *a.* Terrifying; terrible; that may excite great fear; dreadful.

AFFRI'GHTING, *ppr.* Impressing sudden fear; terrifying.

AFFRI'GHTMENT, *n.* Affright; terror; the state of being frightened. [*Rarely used.*]
[*In common discourse, the use of this word, in all its forms, is superseded by fright, frighted, frightful.*]

AFFRONT', *v. t.* [Fr. *affronter*, to encounter face to face, of *ad* and L. *frons*, front, face.]

1. *Literally*, to meet or encounter face to face, in a good or bad sense; as,

The seditious *affronted* the king's forces. *Hayward. Milton. Shak.*

[*The foregoing sense is obsolete.*]

2. To offer abuse to the face; to insult, dare or brave openly; to offer abuse or insult in any manner, by words or actions; as, to *affront* one by giving him the lie.

3. To abuse, or give cause of offense to, without being present with the person; to make slightly angry; *a popular use of the word.*

AFFRONT', *n.* Opposition to the face; open defiance; encounter. *Obs.*

2. Ill treatment; abuse; any thing reproachful or contemptuous, that excites or justifies resentment, as foul language, or personal abuse. It usually expresses a less degree of abuse than *insult.*

3. Shame; disgrace. [*Not usual.*] *Arbuthnot.*

4. In *popular language*, slight resentment; displeasure.

AFFRONT'ED, *pp.* Opposed face to face; dared; defied; abused.

2. In *popular language*, offended; slightly angry at ill treatment, by words or actions; displeased.

AFFRONTEE', *a.* In *heraldry*, front to front; an epithet given to animals that face each other. *Ash.*

AFFRONT'ER, *n.* One that affronts.

AFFRONT'ING, *ppr.* Opposing face to face; defying; abusing; offering abuse, or any cause of displeasure.

AFFRONT'ING, *a.* Contumelious; abusive.

AFFRONT'IVE, *a.* Giving offense; tending to offend; abusive.

AFFRONT'IVENESS, *n.* The quality that gives offense. [*Little used.*]

AFFU'SE, *v. t.* *s* as *z.* [L. *affundo, affusum, ad* and *fundo*, to pour out. See *Fuse.*]
To pour upon; to sprinkle, as with a liquid.

AFFU'SED, *pp.* Sprinkled with a liquid; sprinkled on; having a liquid poured upon.

AFFU'SING, *ppr.* Pouring upon, or sprinkling.

AFFU'SION, *n.* *affu'zhun.* The act of pouring upon, or sprinkling with a liquid substance, as water upon a diseased body, or upon a child in baptism.

AFFY', *v. t.* [Fr. *affier.*] To betroth; to bind or join. [*Not used.*]

AFFY', *v. t.* To trust or confide in. [*Not used.*]

AFIE'LD, *adv.* [*a* and *field.*]
To the field. *Milton.*

AFI'RE, *adv.* On fire. *Gower*

AFLAT', *adv.* [*a* and *flat.*] Level with the ground. *Bacon.*

AFLO'AT, *adv.* or *a.* [*a* and *float.*]

1. Borne on the water; floating; swimming; as, the ship is *afloat.*

2. *Figuratively*, moving; passing from place to place; as, a rumor is *afloat.*

3. Unfixed; moving without guide or control; as, our affairs are all *afloat.* [*As an adjective, this word always follows the noun.*]

AFOOT', *adv.* [*a* or *on* and *foot.*] On foot; borne by the feet; opposed to *riding.*

2. In action; in a state of being planned for execution; as, a design is *afoot*, or *on foot.*

AFO'RE, *adv.* or *prep.* [*a* and *fore.*] In front.

2. Between one object and another, so as to intercept a direct view or intercourse; as, to stand between a person and the light of a candle—*a popular use of the word.*

3. Prior in time; before; anterior; prior time being considered as in front of subsequent time.

The grass which withereth *afore* it groweth up. Ps. cxxix.

In all these senses it is now inelegant, and superseded by *before.*

4. In *seaman's language*, toward the head of the ship; further forward, or nearer the stem; as, *afore* the windlas. *Afore the mast*, is a phrase which is applied to a common sailor, one who does duty on the main deck, or has no office on board the ship. *Mar. Dict.*

AFO'REGOING, *a.* Going before. [See *Foregoing*, which is chiefly used.]

AFO'REHAND, *adv.* [*afore* and *hand.*]
In time previous; by previous provision; as, he is ready *aforehand.*

She is come *aforehand* to anoint my body. Mark xiv.

2. *a.* Prepared; previously provided; as, to be *aforehand* in business. Hence in *popular language*, amply provided; well supplied with the means of living; having means beyond the requirements of necessity; moderately wealthy. This word is popularly changed into *aforehanded, beforehanded*, or rather *forehanded*; as, a *forehanded* farmer.

AFO'REMENTIONED, *a.* [*afore* and *mention.*]
Mentioned before in the same writing or discourse. *Addison.*

AFO'RENAMED, *a.* [*afore* and *name.*]
Named before. *Peacham.*

AFO'RESAID, *a.* [*afore* and *say.*]
Said or recited before, or in a preceding part.

AFO'RETIME, *adv.* [*afore* and *time.*]
In time past; in a former time. *Bible.*

AFOUL', *adv.* or *a.* [*a* and *foul.*]
Not free; entangled. *Columbiad*

AFRA'ID, *a.* [The participle of *affray.*]
Impressed with fear or apprehension; fearful. This word expresses a less degree of fear than *terrified* or *frightened.* It is followed by *of* before the object of fear; as, to be *afraid of* death.

Joseph was *afraid* to sin against God.

AFRESH', *adv.* [*a* and *fresh.*]
Anew; again; recently; after intermission.

They crucify the son of God *afresh.* Heb. vi.

AF'RICA, *n.* [Qu. L. *a* neg. and *frigus*, cold.]

One of the four quarters or largest divisions of the globe; a continent separated from Europe by the Mediterranean sea.

AF'RIC, } a. Pertaining to Africa.
AF'RICAN, }

AF'RICAN, n. A native of Africa.

This name is given also to the African marygold. *Tate's Cowley.*

AFRŎNT', *adv.* In front. *Shak.*

'AFT, *a.* or *adv.* [Sax. *æft, eft,* after, behind.]

In *seaman's language,* a word used to denote the stern or what pertains to the stern of a ship; as, the *aft* part of the ship; haul *aft* the main sheet, that is, further towards the stern. *Fore and aft* is the whole length of a ship. *Right aft* is in a direct line with the stern. *Mar. Dict.*

'AFTER, *a.* [The comparative degree of *aft.* But in some Teutonic dialects it is written with *g;* D. *agter;* Dan. *agters.* The Eng. corresponds with the Sax. *æfter,* Sw. *efter,* Goth. *aftaro,* Dan. *efter.*]

1. In *marine language,* more aft, or towards the stern of the ship; as, the *after* sails; *after* hatchway.

2. In *common language,* later in time; as, an *after* period of life. *Marshall.*

In this sense, the word is often combined with the following noun; as in *afternoon.*

'AFTER, *prep.* Behind in place; as, men placed in a line one *after* another

2. Later in time; as, *after* supper. This word often precedes a sentence, as a governing preposition.

After I have arisen, I will go before you into Galilee. Math. xxvi.

3. In pursuit of, that is, moving *behind,* following; in search of.

After whom is the king of Israel come out? 1 Sam. xxiv.

Ye shall not go *after* other Gods. Deut. vi.

4. In imitation of; as, to make a thing *after* a model.

5. According to; as, consider a thing *after* its intrinsic value. *Bacon.*

6. According to the direction and influence of.

To walk *after* the flesh; to live *after* the flesh. Rom. viii.

To judge *after* the sight of the eye. Is. xi.

To inquire *after* is to seek by asking; to ask concerning.

To follow *after,* in scripture, is to pursue, or imitate; to serve, or worship.

AFTER, *adv.* Posterior; later in time; as, it was about the space of three hours *after.* In this sense, the word, however, is really a *preposition,* the object being understood; about three hours *after* the time or fact before specified.

After is prefixed to many words, forming compounds, but retaining its genuine signification. Some of the following words are of this kind, but in some of them *after* seems rather to be a separate word.

'AFTER-ACCOUNT, *n.* A subsequent reckoning. *Killingbeck.*

'AFTER-ACT, *n.* A subsequent act.

'AFTER-AGES, *n.* Later ages; succeeding times. *After-age,* in the singular, is not improper. *Addison.*

'AFTER ALL is a phrase, signifying, when all has been considered, said or done; at last; in the final result. *Pope.*

'AFTER-BAND, *n.* A future band. *Milton.*

'AFTER-BIRTH, *n.* The appendages of the fetus, called also *secundines.* *Wiseman.*

'AFTER-CLAP, *n.* An unexpected, subsequent event; something happening after an affair is supposed to be at an end. *Hubbard.*

'AFTER-CŎMER, *n.* A successor.

'AFTER-CŎMFORT, *n.* Future comfort. *Jonson.*

'AFTER-CONDUCT, *n.* Subsequent behavior. *Sherlock.*

'AFTER-CONVIC'TION, *n.* Future conviction. *South.*

'AFTER-COST, *n.* Later cost; expense after the execution of the main design. *Mortimer.*

'AFTER-COURSE, *n.* Future course. *Brown.*

'AFTER-CROP, *n.* The second crop in the same year. *Mortimer.*

'AFTER-DAYS, *n.* Future days. *Congreve.*

'AFTER-EATAGE, *n.* Part of the increase of the same year. [*Local.*] *Burn.*

'AFTER-ENDEAV'OR, *n.* An endeavor after the first or former effort. *Locke.*

'AFTER-GAME, *n.* A subsequent scheme, or expedient. *Wotton.*

'AFTER-GUARD, *n.* The seaman stationed on the poop or after part of the ship, to attend the after sails. *Mar. Dict.*

'AFTER-HOPE, *n.* Future hope. *Jonson.*

'AFTER-HOURS, *n.* Hours that follow; time following. *Shak.*

'AFTER-IGNORANCE, *n.* Subsequent ignorance. *Stafford.*

'AFTER-KING, *n.* A succeeding king. *Shuckford.*

'AFTER-LIFE, *n.* Future life or the life after this. *Dryden. Butler.*

2. A later period of life; subsequent life.

'AFTER-LIVER, *n.* One who lives in succeeding times. *Sidney.*

'AFTER-LŎVE, *n.* The second or later love. *Shak.*

'AFTER-MALICE, *n.* Succeeding malice. *Dryden.*

'AFTER-MATH, *n.* [*after* and *math.* See *Mow.*]

A second crop of grass, in the same season; rowen. *Holland.*

'AFTER-MOST, *a. Superl.* In *marine language,* nearest the stern, opposed to *foremost;* also hindmost.

'AFTER-NOON', *n.* The part of the day which follows noon, between noon and evening. *Dryden.*

'AFTER-PAINS, *n.* The pains which succeed child birth.

'AFTER-PART, *n.* The latter part. In *marine language,* the part of a ship towards the stern. *Mar. Dic.*

'AFTER-PIECE, *n.* A piece performed after a play; a farce or other entertainment. *Cumberland.*

'AFTER-PROOF, *n.* Subsequent proof or evidence; qualities known by subsequent experience. *Wotton.*

'AFTER-REPENT'ANCE, *n.* Subsequent repentance. *South.*

'AFTER-REPORT, *n.* Subsequent report, or information. *South.*

'AFTER-SAILS, *n.* The sails on the mizen-mast and stays, between the main and mizen-masts. *Mar. Dict.*

'AFTER-STATE, *n.* The future state. *Glanville.*

'AFTER-STING, *n.* Subsequent sting. *Herbert.*

'AFTER-STORM, *n.* A succeeding or future storm. *Dryden.*

'AFTER-SUPPER, *n.* The time between supper and going to bed. *Shak.*

'AFTER-SWARM, *n.* A swarm of bees which leaves the hive after the first.

'AFTER-TASTE, *n.* A taste which succeeds eating and drinking.

'AFTER-THOUGHT, *n.* [See *Thought.*] Reflections after an act; later thought, or expedient occurring too late. *Dryden.*

'AFTER-TIMES, *n.* Succeeding times. It may be used in the singular. *Dryden.*

'AFTER-TOSSING, *n.* The swell or agitation of the sea after a storm. *Addison.*

'AFTERWARD, or 'AFTERWARDS, *adv.* [See *Ward.*] In later or subsequent time. *Hooker.*

'AFTER-WISE, *a.* Wise afterwards or too late. *Addison.*

'AFTER-WIT, *n.* Subsequent wit; wisdom that comes too late. *L'Estrange.*

'AFTER-WRATH, *n.* Later wrath; anger after the provocation has ceased. *Shak.*

'AFTER-WRITER, *n.* A succeeding writer. *Shuckford.*

AGA, *n.* [Per. آق and آقا ak and aka, lord, dominus, herus; also sir, a title of respect; Tart. *aha.* Qu. the *och* in *Beloch,* and *ak* in *Balak.*]

In the Turkish dominions, a commander or chief officer. The title is given to various chief officers, whether civil or military. It is also given to great land holders, and to the eunuchs of the Sultan's seraglio. *Encyc.*

AGAIN, *adv.* agen'. [Sax. *gean, agen, agean, ongean;* D. with a different prefix, *tegen;* G. *dagegen, gegen;* Sw. *igen;* Dan. *igien;* qu. L. *con,* whence *contra;* Ir. *coinne,* opposite, a meeting. Hence Sax. *togeanes, togegnes,* against; but placed after its object; as, "hi comen heom togeanes," they come them against. D. *tegens,* against; *jegens,* towards; G. *entgegen, dagegen,* against; *begegnen,* to meet or encounter. The primary sense is to turn, or to meet in front; or the name of the face, front or forepart. So in Dan. and Sw. *mod, imod, emot,* against, is our word *meet.*]

1. A second time; once more.

I will not *again* curse the ground. Gen. viii.

2. It notes something further, or additional to one or more particulars.

For to which of the angels said he at any time, thou art my son, this day have I begotten thee? and *again,* I will be to him a father, and he shall be to me a son? and *again,* let all the angels of God worship him. Heb. i.

All the uses of this word carry in them the ideas of return or repetition; as in these phrases; give it back *again;* give him as much *again,* that is, the same quantity once more or repeated.

There is not, in the world *again,* such a commerce as in London.

Who art thou that answerest *again?*

Bring us word *again.*

Again and again, often; with frequent repetition.

AGAINST, *prep.* *agenst'.* [Sax. *togeanes.* See *Again.*]

1. In opposition; noting enmity or disapprobation.

   His hand will be *against* every man. Gen. xvi.

   I am *against* your pillows. Ez. xiii.

2. In opposition, noting contrariety, contradiction, or repugnance; as, a decree *against* law, reason or public opinion.
3. In opposition, noting competition, or different sides or parties; as, there are twenty votes in the affirmative *against* ten in the negative.
4. In an opposite direction; as, to ride *against* the wind.
5. Opposite in place; abreast; as, a ship is *against* the mouth of a river. In this sense it is often preceded by *over.*

   Aaron lighted the lamps over *against* the candlesticks. Num. viii.

6. In opposition, noting adversity, injury, or contrariety to wishes; as, this change of measures is *against* us.
7. Bearing upon; as, one leans *against* a wall.
8. In provision for; in preparation for.

   Urijah made it *against* king Ahaz came from Damascus. 2 Kings, xvi.

   In this sense *against* is a preposition, with the following part of the sentence for an object. See *After*, prep. def. 2.

In short, the sense of this word is *opposition*, variously modified according to its application to different objects.

AG'ALLOCH, AGAL'LOCHUM, *n.* [*Of oriental origin.*]

Aloes-wood, the product of a tree growing in China, and some of the Indian isles. There are three varieties, the calambac, the common lignum aloes, and the calambour. The first variety is light and porous, and so filled with a fragrant resin, that it may be molded by the fingers; the second is denser and less resinous; and the third is the aloes-wood used by cabinet makers and inlayers. *Encyc.*

AGALMAT'OLITE, *n.* [Gr. αγαλμα, image, and λιθος, stone.]

A name given by Klaproth to two varieties of the *pierre de lard*, lard stone, of China. It contains no magnesia, but otherwise has the characters of talck. It is called in German, *bildstein*, figure-stone, and by Brongniart, *steatite pagodite.* *Cyc. Ure.*

AG'APE, *adv.* or *a.* [*a* and *gape.* See *Gape.*]

Gaping, as with wonder, expectation, or eager attention; having the mouth wide open. *Milton.*

AG'APE, *n.* *ag'apy.* [Gr. αγαπη, love.]

Among the primitive christians, a love feast or feast of charity, held before or after the communion, when contributions were made for the poor. This feast was held at first without scandal, but afterwards being abused, it was condemned at the council of Carthage, A. D. 397. *Encyc.*

AG'ARIC, *n.* [Gr. αγαριχον. Qu. from Agaria, in Sarmatia. *Dioscorides.*]

In *botany*, mushroom, a genus of funguses, containing numerous species. Mushrooms grow on trees, or spring from the earth; of the latter species some are valued as articles of food; others are poisonous. The name was originally given to a fungus growing on the larch. This species is now frequent in the shops, and distinguished by the name of *female agaric.* From this fungus is extracted a turpentine, of which three fourths of its weight is a resinous substance; the rest, a slimy, mucilaginous, earthy matter, tenacious and almost insoluble in water. It is used in dyeing, but is little esteemed in medicine. *Theoph. Macquer. Quincy.*

The *Agaric* of the oak is called *touch-wood*, from its readiness to take fire. *Boletus Igniarius, Linne.*

Agaric mineral, a calcarious earth, or carbonate of lime, resembling a fungus in color and texture; found in fissures of rocks, and on the roofs of caverns. It is sometimes used as an astringent in fluxes, and a styptic in hemorrhages. It occurs in a loose semi-indurated form, white or whitish red, or yellow, light and friable. Kirwan mentions three varieties.

AG'AST or **AGH'AST**, *a.* [Qu., a contraction of *agazed*, or Goth. *agis*, Sax. *egesa*, horror. See *Aghast* and *Gaze.*]

Struck with terror, or astonishment; amazed; struck silent with horror.

   With shuddering horror pale and eyes *agast.* *Milton.*

AGA'TE, *adv.* [*a* and *gate.*]

On the way; going. *Obs.* *Gower.*

AG'ATE, *n.* [Fr. *agate*; L. *achates, gagates*; Gr. γαγατης; so called, says Pliny, 37, 10, because found near a river of that name in Sicily. So also Solinus and Isidore. But Bochart, with more probability, deduces it from the Punic and Hebrew עקר, and with a different prefix נקר, spotted. The word is used, Gen. xxx. and xxxi., to describe the speckled and spotted cattle of Laban and Jacob.]

A class of siliceous, semi-pellucid gems of many varieties, consisting of quartz-crystal, flint, horn-stone, chalcedony, amethyst, jasper, cornelian, heliotrope, and jade, in various combinations, variegated with dots, zones, filaments, ramifications, arborizations, and various figures. Agates seem to have been formed by successive layers of siliceous earth, on the sides of cavities which they now fill entirely or in part. They are esteemed the least valuable of the precious stones. Even in Pliny's time, they were in little estimation. They are found in rocks, in the form of fragments, in nodules, in small rounded lumps, rarely in stalactites. Their colors are various. They are used for rings, seals, cups, beads, boxes and handles of small utensils. *Kirwan. Encyc. Cleaveland.*

AG'ATE, *n.* An instrument used by gold-wire drawers, so called from the agate in the middle of it.

AG'ATINE, *a.* Pertaining to agate.

AG'ATINE, *n.* A genus of shells, oval or oblong.

AG'ATIZED, *a.* Having the colored lines and figures of agate. *Fourcroy.*

Agatized wood, a substance apparently produced by the petrifaction of wood; a species of hornstone. *Werner.*

AG'ATY, *a.* Of the nature of agate. *Woodward.*

AGA'VE, *n.* [Gr. αγαυος, admirable.]

1. The American aloe. The great aloe rises twenty feet, and its branches form a sort of pyramid at the top. *Encyc.*
2. A genus of univalvular shells.

AGA'ZE, *v. t.* [from *gaze.*] To strike with amazement. *Obs.* *Spenser.*

AGA'ZED, *pp.* Struck with amazement. [*Not in use.*] *Shak.*

AGE, *n.* [Fr. *age*; Arm. *oage*; deduced by Lunier from Lat. *ætas*, or *ævum.* But these are undoubtedly contracted words, Goth. *aiw*; D. *eeuw*; Gr. αιων; from the Celtic, W. *haug*, fullness, completeness, an *age*, a space of time; plu. *hogion*; the *g* being sunk in the Latin words; in the Sanscrit, *yuga.*]

1. The whole duration of a being, whether animal, vegetable, or other kind; as, the usual *age* of man is seventy years; the *age* of a horse may be twenty or thirty years; the *age* of a tree may be four hundred years.
2. That part of the duration of a being, which is between its beginning and any given time; as, what is the present *age* of a man, or of the earth?

   Jesus began to be about thirty years of *age.* Luke iii.

3. The latter part of life, or long continued duration; oldness.

   The eyes of Israel were dim for *age.* Gen. xlviii.

4. A certain period of human life, marked by a difference of state; as, life is divided into four stages or *ages*, infancy, youth, manhood, and old age; the *age* of youth; the *age* of manhood.
5. The period when a person is enabled by law to do certain acts for himself, or when he ceases to be controlled by parents or guardians; as, in our country, both males and females are of *age* at twenty-one years old.
6. Mature years; ripeness of strength or discretion.

   He is of *age*, ask him. John ix.

7. The time of life for conceiving children, or perhaps the usual time of such an event.

   Sarah was delivered of a son when she was past *age.* Heb. xi.

8. A particular period of time, as distinguished from others; as, the golden *age*, the *age* of iron, the *age* of heroes or of chivalry.
9. The people who live at a particular period; hence, a generation and a succession of generations; as, *ages* yet unborn.

   The mystery hid from *ages.* Col. i.

10. A century; the period of one hundred years.

A'GED, *a.* Old; having lived long; having lived almost the usual time allotted to that species of being; applied to animals or plants; as, an *aged* man, or an *aged* oak.

2. Having a certain age; having lived; as, a man *aged* forty years.

A'GED, *n.* Old persons.

   And the *aged* arose and stood up. Job xxix.

AGEN', for *again.* *Obs.*

A'GENCY, *n.* [L. *agens.* See *Act.*]

1. The quality of moving or of exerting power; the state of being in action; ac-

tion; operation; instrumentality; as, the *agency* of providence in the natural world.

2. The office of an agent, or factor; business of an agent entrusted with the concerns of another; as, the principal pays the charges of *agency*.

AĠEND'A, *n.* [L. things to be done.] A memorandum-book; the service or office of a church; a ritual or liturgy. *Encyc.*

A'ĠENT, *a.* Acting; opposed to *patient*, or sustaining action; as, the body *agent*. [*Little used.*] *Bacon.*

A'ĠENT, *n.* An actor; one that exerts power, or has the power to act; as, a moral *agent*.

2. An active power or cause; that which has the power to produce an effect; as, heat is a powerful *agent*.

3. A substitute, deputy, or factor; one entrusted with the business of another; an attorney; a minister.

A'ĠENTSHIP, *n.* The office of an agent. [*Not used.*] We now use *agency*.

AGĠELA'TION, *n.* [L. *gelu*.] Concretion of a fluid. [*Not used.*] *Brown.*

AGĠENERA'TION, *n.* [L. *ad* and *generatio*.] The state of growing to another. [*Not used.*] *Brown.*

AG'ĠER, *n.* [L.] A fortress, or mound. [*Not used.*] *Hearne.*

AG'ĠERATE, *v. t.* [L. *aggero*.] To heap. [*Not used.*]

AĠĠERA'TION, *n.* A heaping; accumulation; as, "*aggerations* of sand." *Ray.*

AGGLOM'ERATE, *v. t.* [L. *agglomero*, *ad* and *glomero*, to wind into a ball, from *glomus*, a ball of yarn; from the Heb. גלם, to involve; Qu. Ar. لم to go round in a circle, to be round, to collect, or condense.] To wind, or collect into a ball; to gather into a mass. *Young.*

AGGLOM'ERATE, *v. i.* To gather, grow or collect into a ball or mass. *Thomson.*

AGGLOM'ERATED, *pp.* Wound or collected into a ball.

AGGLOM'ERATING, *ppr.* Winding into a ball; gathering into a lump.

AGGLOMERA'TION, *n.* The act of winding into a ball; the state of being gathered into a ball or mass.

AGGLU'TINANT, *n.* Any viscous substance which unites other substances, by causing an adhesion; any application which tends to unite parts which have too little adhesion. *Coxe.*

AGGLU'TINANT, *a.* Uniting as glue; tending to cause adhesion.

AGGLU'TINATE, *v. t.* [Lat. *agglutino*, *ad* and *glutino*, from *gluten*; Eng. *glue*; Fr. *glu*; Arm. *glud*; W. *glyd*. See *Glue*.] To unite, or cause to adhere, as with glue or other viscous substance; to unite by causing an adhesion of substances.

AGGLU'TINATED, *pp.* Glued together; united by a viscous substance.

AGGLU'TINATING, *ppr.* Gluing together; uniting by causing adhesion.

AGGLUTINA'TION, *n.* The act of uniting by glue or other tenacious substance; the state of being thus united.

AGGLU'TINATIVE, *a.* That tends to unite, or has power to cause adhesion.

AGGRA'CE, *v. t.* To favor. [*Not used.*] *Spenser. Wiseman.*

AGGRA'CE, *n.* Kindness; favor. [*Not used.*] *Spenser.*

AGGRANDIZA'TION, *n.* The act of aggrandizing. [*Not used.*] *Waterhouse.*

AG'GRANDIZE, *v. t.* [Fr. *agrandir*, of L. *ad* and *grandis*. See *Grand*.]

1. To make great or greater in power, rank or honor; to exalt; as, to *aggrandize* a family.

2. To enlarge, applied to things; as, to *aggrandize* our conceptions. It seems to be never applied to the bulk or dimensions of material bodies.

AG'GRANDIZED, *pp.* Made great or greater; exalted; enlarged.

AGGRAND'IZEMENT, *n.* The act of aggrandizing; the state of being exalted in power, rank or honor; exaltation; enlargement.

> The Emperor seeks only the *aggrandizement* of his own family.

AG'GRANDIZER, *n.* One that aggrandizes or exalts in power, rank or honor.

AG'GRANDIZING, *ppr.* Making great; exalting; enlarging.

AGGRA'TE, *v. t.* [It.] To please. [*Not used.*] *Spenser.*

AG'GRAVATE, *v. t.* [L. *aggravo*, of *ad* and *gravis*, heavy. See *Grave*, *Gravity*.]

1. To make heavy, *but not used in this literal sense. Figuratively*, to make worse, more severe, or less tolerable; as, to *aggravate* the evils of life; to *aggravate* pain or punishment.

2. To make more enormous, or less excusable; as, to *aggravate* a crime.

3. To exaggerate.

4. To give coloring in description; to give an exaggerated representation; as, to *aggravate* a charge against an offender; to *aggravate* circumstances. *Guthrie, Quint. Paley.*

> Actions and motives maliciously *aggravated*. *Washington's Life.*

The propriety of the word in the latter passage is questionable. *Aggravate* is generally used in reference to evils, or something improper or unnatural.

AG'GRAVATED, *pp.* Increased in severity or enormity; made worse; exaggerated.

AG'GRAVATING, *ppr.* Increasing in severity, enormity, or degree, as evils, misfortunes, pain, punishment, crimes, guilt, &c.; exaggerating.

AGGRAVA'TION, *n.* The act of making worse, used of evils, natural or moral; the act of increasing severity or heinousness; addition to that which is evil or improper; as, an *aggravation* of pain or grief.

2. Exaggerated representation, or heightened description of any thing wrong, improper, or unnatural; as, an *aggravation* of features in a caricature. *Paley. Addison.*

AG'GREGATE, *v. t.* [L. *aggrego*, to collect in troops; of *ad* and *grex*, a herd or band. See *Gregarious*.] To bring together; to collect particulars into a sum, mass or body.

AG'GREGATE, *a.* Formed by a collection of particulars into a whole mass or sum; as, the *aggregate* amount of charges.

Aggregate flowers, in *botany*, are such as are composed of florets united by means of the receptacle or calyx. *Milne.*

Aggregate corporation, in *law*, is one which consists of two or more persons united, whose existence is preserved by a succession of new members. *Blackstone.*

AG'GREGATE, *n.* A sum, mass or assemblage of particulars; as, a house is an *aggregate* of stones, bricks, timber, &c. It differs from a compound in this, that the particulars of an *aggregate* are less intimately mixed than in a *compound*.

AG'GREGATED, *pp.* Collected into a sum, mass or system.

AG'GREGATELY, *adv.* Collectively; taken in a sum or mass.

AG'GREGATING, *ppr.* Collecting into a sum or mass.

AGGREGA'TION, *n.* The act of aggregating; the state of being collected into a sum or mass; a collection of particulars; an aggregate.

2. In *chimistry*, the affinity of *aggregation*, is the power which causes homogeneous bodies to tend towards each other, and to cohere, when united. The *aggregate*, in this case, differs from a *heap*, whose parts do not cohere; and from a *mixture*, which consists of parts dissimilar in their nature. The word is used of solid, fluid, or aeriform bodies.

3. The union and coherence of bodies of the same nature.

AG'GREGATIVE, *a.* Taken together; collective.

AG'GREGATOR, *n.* He that collects into a whole or mass. *Burton.*

AGGRESS', *v. i.* [L. *aggredior*, *aggressus*, of *ad* and *gradior*, to go. See *Grade*.] To make a first attack; to commit the first act of hostility or offense; to begin a quarrel or controversy; to assault first or invade. *Prior.*

AGGRESS'ING, *ppr.* Commencing hostility first; making the first attack.

AGGRESS'ION, *n.* The first attack, or act of hostility; the first act of injury, or first act leading to war or controversy. *L'Estrange.*

AGGRESS'IVE, *a.* Tending to aggress; making the first attack. *Clarkson.*

AGGRESS'OR, *n.* The person who first attacks; he who first commences hostility or a quarrel; an assaulter; an invader. *Dryden.*

> The insolence of the *aggressor* is usually proportioned to the tameness of the sufferer. *Ames.*

AGGRIE'VANCE, *n.* [See *Aggrieve*.] Oppression; hardship; injury. But *grievance* is more generally used.

AGGRIE'VE, *v. t.* [of *ad* and *grieve*, from *grief*. Perhaps the word is borrowed directly from the Sp. *agraviar*, to injure; Fr. *grever*. See *Grief* and *Grave*.] To give pain or sorrow; to afflict. *In this sense, it is nearly superseded by grieve.*

2. To bear hard upon; to oppress or injure, in one's rights; to vex or harass by civil or political injustice.

AGGRIE'VE, *v. i.* To mourn; to lament. [*Not used.* See *Grieve*.]

AGGRIE'VED, *pp.* Pained; afflicted; civilly or politically oppressed.

AGGRIE'VING, *ppr.* Afflicting; imposing hardships on; oppressing.

AGGRÖUP', AGGROOP', *v. t.* [Sp. *agrupar*; It. *aggruppare, aggroppare*, to knot or bring together. See *Group.*]

To bring together; to group; to collect many persons in a crowd, or many figures into a whole, either in statuary, painting or description. *Encyc.*

AGGRÖUP'ED, AGGROOP'ED, *pp.* Collected into a group or assemblage.

AGH'AST, or more correctly AGAST, *a* or *adv.* [Perhaps the participle of *agaze*; otherwise from the root of *ghastly* and *ghost.*]

Struck with amazement; stupified with sudden fright or horror.

AG'ILE, *a.* [Fr. *agile*; L. *agilis*, from *ago.* See *Act.*]

Nimble; having the faculty of quick motion in the limbs; apt or ready to move; brisk; active.

And bending forward, struck his *agile* heels. *Shak.*

AG'ILENESS, *n.* Nimbleness; activity; the faculty of moving the limbs quickly; agility.

AGIL'ITY, *n.* [L. *agilitas.*]

The power of moving the limbs quickly; nimbleness; briskness; activity; quickness of motion. *Watts.*

A'GIO, *n.* [Ital. *aggio*, surplus, difference.]

1. In *commerce*, the difference between bank notes and current coin. In Holland, the *agio* is three or four per cent.; in Rome, from fifteen to twenty-five per cent.; in Venice, twenty per cent.: but the agio is subject to variation. *Encyc.*

2. Premium; sum given above the nominal value. *Lunier.*

AGIST', *v. t.* [If the primary sense is to lie, or to rest, this is from Fr. *gesir*; Norm. *agiser*, to be levant and couchant, from *giser*, to lay or throw down; whence *gist*, cast; *gistance*, a casting. Class Gs. No. 18. If the primary signification is to feed, see Nos. 5, 6, 10, 12, and 56. Ch. Class Gs.]

In *law*, to take the cattle of others to graze, at a certain sum; to feed or pasture the cattle of others; used originally for the feeding of cattle in the king's forest. *Cowel. Blackstone.*

AGIST'MENT, *n.* The taking and feeding other men's cattle in the king's forest, or on one's own land; also, the price paid for such feeding. It denotes also a burden, charge or tax. [In *canon law*, a modus, or composition. *Johnson*, Qu.] *Cowel. Blackstone. Encyc.*

AGIST'OR, or AGISTA'TOR, *n.* An officer of the king's forest, who has the care of cattle agisted, and collects the money for the same; hence called *gist-taker*, which in England is corrupted into *guest-taker.* *Encyc.*

AG'ITABLE, *a.* [See *Agitate.*] That may be agitated, shaken or discussed.

AG'ITATE, *v. t.* [L. *agito*, from *ago.* See *Act.*]

1. To stir violently; to move back and forth with a quick motion; to shake or move briskly; as, to *agitate* water in a vessel.

2. To move or force into violent irregular action; as, the wind *agitates* the sea.

3. To disturb, or excite into tumult; as, to *agitate* the mind or passions.

4. To discuss; to debate; to controvert; as, to *agitate* a question.

5. To consider on all sides; to revolve in the mind, or view in all its aspects; to contrive by mental deliberation; as, politicians *agitate* desperate designs. *King Charles.*

6. To move or actuate. [*Not used.*] *Blackmore.*

AG'ITATED, *pp.* Tossed from side to side; shaken; moved violently and irregularly; disturbed; discussed; considered.

AG'ITATING, *ppr.* Shaking; moving with violence; disturbing; disputing; contriving.

AGITA'TION, *n.* The act of shaking; the state of being moved with violence, or with irregular action; commotion; as, the sea after a storm is in *agitation.* *Bacon.*

2. Disturbance of tranquility in the mind; perturbation; excitement of passion.

3. Discussion; examination of a subject in controversy. *L'Estrange.*

4. A state of being deliberated upon, with a view to contrivance, or plan to be adopted; as, a scheme is in *agitation.*

AGITA'TO, in *music*, denotes a broken style of performance, adapted to awaken surprise or perturbation. *Dict. of Music.*

AG'ITATOR, *n.* One who agitates; also, an insurgent; one who excites sedition or revolt. In *antiquity*, a chariotteer, that is, a driver. In Cromwell's time, certain officers appointed by the army to manage their concerns, were called *agitators.* *Hume.*

AG'LET, A'IGLET, *n.* [Fr. *aiguillette*, a point, from *aiguille*, a needle, from *aigu*, sharp. See *Acid.*]

1. A tag of a point curved into the representation of an animal, generally of a man; a small plate of metal.

2. In *botany*, a pendant at the ends of the chives of flowers, as in the rose and tulip.

AG'LET-BABY, *n.* A small image on the top of a lace. *Shak.*

AG'MINAL, *a.* [L. *agmen*, a troop or body of men arrayed, from *ago.*]

Pertaining to an army or troop. [*Little used.*]

AG'NAIL, *n.* [*ad* and *nail*, or Sax. *ange*, pain, and *nail.* See *Nail.*]

A disease of the nail; a whitlow; an inflammation round the nail. *Bailey.*

AG'NATE, *a.* [L. *agnatus.*] Related or akin by the father's side.

AG'NATE, *n.* [L. *agnatus, adnascor*, of *ad* and *nascor*, to be born. See *Nature.*]

Any male relation by the father's side. *Encyc.*

AGNAT'IC, *a.* Pertaining to descent by the male line of ancestors. *Blackstone.*

AGNA'TION, *n.* Relation by the father's side only, or descent in the male line, distinct from *cognation*, which includes descent in the male and female lines.

AG'NEL, *n.* [From *agnus*, a lamb, the figure struck on the coin.]

An ancient French coin, value twelve sols, six deniers. It was called also *mouton d'or* and *agnel d' or.* *Encyc.*

AGNI''TION, *n.* [L. *agnitio, agnosco.*]

Acknowledgment. [*Little used.*] *Pearson.*

AGNI'ZE, *v. t.* To acknowledge. [*Not in use.*] *Shak.*

AGNOM'INATE, *v. t.* [L. *agnomino*; *ad* and *nomino, nomen*, name.]

To name. [*Little used.*]

AGNOMINA'TION, *n.* [L. *agnomen*, a surname, of *ad* and *nomen.* See *Name.*]

1. An additional name, or title; a name added to another, as expressive of some act, achievement, &c.; a surname. *Camden. Encyc.*

2. Allusion of one word to another by sound.

AGNUS CASTUS. A species of vitex, so called from the Gr. αγνος, chaste, or from *a* negative, and γονος, seed, from its imagined virtue of preserving chastity. The Athenian ladies reposed on the leaves of this plant at the feast of Ceres. The Latin *Castus*, chaste, now added to the name, forms a duplication of the sense. *Encyc.*

AGNUS DEI. [Lamb of God.]

In the *Romish Church*, a cake of wax stamped with the figure of a lamb, supporting the banner of the cross. It is supposed to possess great virtues in preserving those who carry it, in faith and from accidents, &c. Also a part of the mass in which these words are repeated by the priest. *Encyc.*

AGNUS SCYTHICUS. [Scythian Lamb.]

A name applied to the roots of a species of fern, *Aspidium Baromez*, covered with brown wooly scales, and, in shape, resembling a lamb; found in Russia and Tartary.

AGO', *adv.* or *a.* [Sax. *agan*, or *geond*, the participle of *gan*, to go; contracted from *agone.* See *Go.*]

Past; gone; as, a year *ago.*

AGOG' *adv.* [Fr. *agogo*; *vivre à gogo*, to live in clover.]

In a state of desire; highly excited by eagerness after an object.

The gaudy gossip when she's set *agog.* *Dryden.*

AGO'ING. [The participle of *go*, with the prefix *a.*]

In motion, as to set a mill *agoing*; or about to go; ready to go; as, he is *agoing* immediately. *The latter use is vulgar.*

A'GON, *n.* [Gr.]

The contest for the prize. [*Not used.*] *Sancroft.*

AGONE, *pp. agawn'*, [See *Ago* and *Gone.*]

Ago; past; since. [*Nearly Obs.*]

AG'ONISM, *n.* [Gr. αγωνισμος.]

Contention for a prize. *Dict.*

AG'ONIST, *n.* One who contends for the prize in public games. Milton has used *Agonistes* in this sense, and so called his tragedy, from the similitude of Sampson's exertions, in slaying the Philistines, to prize fighting. In church history, the disciples of Donatus are called *agonistics.*

AGONIST'IC, AGONIST'ICAL, *a.* Pertaining to prize-fighting, contests of strength, or athletic combats. *Enfield.*

AGONIST'ICALLY, *adv.* In an agonistic manner; like prize-fighting.

AG'ONIZE, *v. t.* [Gr. αγωνιζω, to strive. See *Agony.*]

To writhe with extreme pain; to suffer violent anguish.

To smart and *agonize* at every pore. *Pope.*

AG'ONIZE, *v. t.* To distress with extreme pain; to torture. *Pope.*

AG'ONIZING, *ppr.* Suffering severe pain; writhing with torture.

AG'ONIZINGLY, *adv.* With extreme anguish.

AG'ONY, *n.* [Gr. αγων, a contest with bodily exertion; a word used to denote the athletic games, in Greece; whence αγωνια, anguish, solicitude; from αγω, L. *ago.* In Ir. *agh*, is a battle, conflict; Gr. αγωνιζω, to strive. See *Act.*]

1. In strictness, pain so extreme as to cause writhing or contortions of the body, similar to those made in the athletic contests in Greece. Hence,

2. Extreme pain of body or mind; anguish; appropriately, the pangs of death, and the sufferings of our Savior in the garden of Gethsemane. Luke xxii.

3. Violent contest or striving. *More.*

AGOOD', *adv.* In earnest. [*Not used.*] *Shak.*

AGOUTY, *n.* [Qu. Sp. *agudo*, sharp; L. *acutus.*]

A quadruped of the order *Rodentia;* arranged by naturalists in the genus *Cavia.* It is of the size of a rabbit. The upper part of the body is brownish, with a mixture of red and black; the belly yellowish. Three varieties are mentioned, all peculiar to South America and the West Indies. It burrows in the ground, or in hollow trees; lives on vegetables; is voracious like a pig, and makes a similar grunting noise. It holds its meat in its fore paws, like a squirrel. When scared or angry, its hair is erect, and it strikes the ground with its hind feet. Its flesh is white and well tasted. *Encyc.*

AGRA'RIAN, *a.* [L. *agrarius*, from *ager*, a field.]

Relating to lands. Appropriately, denoting or pertaining to an equal division of lands; as, the *agrarian* laws of Rome, which distributed the conquered and other public lands equally among all the citizens, limiting the quantity which each might enjoy. Authors sometimes use the word as a noun; an *agrarian*, for *agrarian law.* *Burke.*

An *agrarian* distribution of land or property, would make the rich, poor, but would not make the poor, rich.

AGREE', *v. i.* [Fr. *agréer*, from *gre'*, will, accord. This is contracted from Sp. *agradar*, Port. *id*, to please, to gratify, whence *agradable*, agreeable; from the root of L. *gratia*, W. *rhad*, grace, favor, that comes freely. The primary sense is advancing, from the same root as L. *gradior;* W. *rhaz*, [rhath]; Syr. ܪܕܐ radah, to go.]

1. To be of one mind; to harmonize in opinion.

In the expediency of the law, all the parties *agree.*

2. To live in concord, or without contention; as, parents and children *agree* well together.

3. To yield assent; to approve or admit; followed by *to*; *as*, to *agree to* an offer, or *to* an opinion.

4. To settle by stipulation, the minds of parties being *agreed*, as to the terms; as,

Didst thou not *agree* with me for a penny a day? Mat. xx.

To *agree* on articles of partnership.

5. To come to a compromise of differences; to be reconciled.

Agree with thy adversary quickly. Mat. v.

6. To come to one opinion or mind; to concur; as, to *agree* on a place of meeting.

This sense differs not essentially from the fourth, and it often implies a resolving to do an act. John ix.

7. To be consistent; to harmonize; not to contradict, or be repugnant.

Their witness *agreed* not together. Mark xiv.

This story *agrees* with what has been related by others.

8. To resemble; to be similar; as, the picture does not *agree* with the original.

9. To suit; to be accommodated or adapted to; as, the same food does not *agree* with every constitution.

AGREE', *v. t.* To admit, or come to one mind concerning; as, to *agree* the fact. Also, to reconcile or make friends; to put an end to variance; but these senses are unusual and hardly legitimate. Let the parties *agree* the fact, is really elliptical; let them agree *on* the fact.

AGREEABIL'ITY, *n.* Easiness of disposition. [*Not used.*] *Chaucer.*

AGREE'ABLE, *a.* Suitable; conformable; correspondent; consistent with; as, the practice of virtue is *agreeable* to the law of God and our own nature.

2. In pursuance of; in conformity with; as, *agreeable* to the order of the day, the house took up the report of the committee. It is not correctly followed by *with.* In this sense, some writers use *agreeably*, for *agreeable*, but in violation of the true principles of construction; for the word is an adjective or attribute, in agreement with the last clause of the sentence. The house took up the report of a committee, (which taking up was) *agreeable* to the order of the day. The use of *agreeably* in this sentence would pervert the sense.

3. Pleasing, either to the mind or senses; as, *agreeable* manners; fruit *agreeable* to the taste.

AGREE'ABLENESS, *n.* Suitableness; conformity; consistency; as, the *agreeableness* of virtue to the laws of God.

2. The quality of pleasing; that quality which gives satisfaction or moderate pleasure to the mind or senses; as, an *agreeableness* of manners; there is an *agreeableness* in the taste of certain fruits. This is the usual sense of the word.

3. Resemblance; likeness; with *to* or *between;* as,

The *agreeableness between* man and other parts of creation. *Obs.* *Grew.*

AGREE'ABLY, *adv.* Pleasingly; in an agreeable manner; in a manner to give pleasure; as, to be *agreeably* entertained with a discourse.

2. Suitably; consistently; conformably;

The effect of which is, that marriages grow less frequent, *agreeably* to the maxim above laid down. *Paley.*

This is a gross error, proceeding from mistake. *Agreeably* signifies, *in an agreeable manner;* but this is not the sense, nor does the word modify the verb *grow.* The sense is, marriages grow less frequent, which [fact, or whole member of the sentence, or proposition] is agreeable to the maxim above laid down. This use of *agreeably* is common, but grossly erroneous.

3. Alike; in the same manner.

Both armed *agreeably.* *Obs.* *Spenser.*

AGREE'D, *pp.* Being in concord or harmony of opinion; of one mind.

Can two walk together except they be *agreed?* Amos. iii.

2. Assented to; admitted; as, a proposition is *agreed* to.

3. Settled by consent; implying bargain or contract; as, the terms were *agreed* to, or *agreed* upon.

AGREE'ING, *ppr.* Living in concord; concurring; assenting; settling by consent.

AGREE'INGLY, *adv.* In conformity to. [*Little used.*]

AGREE'MENT, *n.* Concord; harmony; conformity.

What *agreement* hath the temple of God with idols? 2 Cor. vi.

2. Union of opinions or sentiments; as, a good *agreement* subsists among the members of the council.

3. Resemblance; conformity; similitude.

Expansion and duration have this farther *agreement.* *Locke.*

4. Union of minds in regard to a transfer of interest; bargain; compact; contract; stipulation.

Make an *agreement* with me by a present. 2 Kings xviii.

He made an *agreement* for the purchase of a house.

AGRES'TIC, **AGRES'TICAL**, } *a.* [L. *agrestis;* Fr. *agreste;* from L. *ager*, a field, or the same root.]

Rural; rustic; pertaining to fields or the country, in opposition to the city; unpolished. *Gregory.*

AG'RICULTOR, *n.* [L. *ager*, a field, and *cultor*, a cultivator.]

One whose occupation is to till the ground; a farmer; a husbandman; one skilled in husbandry.

AGRICUL'TURAL, *a.* Pertaining to husbandry, tillage, or the culture of the earth.

AG'RICULTURE, *n.* [L. *ager*, a field, and *cultura*, cultivation. See *Acre* and *Culture.*]

In *a general sense*, the cultivation of the ground, for the purpose of producing vegetables, and fruits, for the use of man and beast; or the art of preparing the soil, sowing and planting seeds, dressing the plants, and removing the crops. In this sense, the word includes gardening, or horticulture, and also the raising and feeding of cattle, or stock. But *in a more common and appropriate sense*, it is used to signify that species of cultivation which is intended to raise grain and other crops for man and beast. It is equivalent to *husbandry.*

Agriculture is the most general occupation of man.

AGRICUL'TURISM, *n.* The art or science of agriculture. [*Little used.*]

AGRICUL'TURIST, *n.* One skilled in the art of cultivating the ground; a skilful husbandman.

AG'RIMONY, *n.* [L. *argemonia*, from the Gr. Thus it is written by Pliny. But in lower Latin it is written *agrimonia.* Said to be from Gr. αργεμα, the web or pearl of the eye, from αργος, white, which this plant was supposed to cure. See Theoph. 887.]

A genus of plants, of several species. Of

these, the eupatoria or common agrimony, and the odorata or sweet scented, are the most useful. *Encyc.*

AGRIPPIN'IANS, *n.* In *Church history*, the followers of Agrippinus, bishop of Carthage, in the third century, who first taught and defended the doctrine of rebaptization. *Encyc.*

AGRÏSE, *v. i.* [Sax. *agrisan.*]
To shiver. [*Not in use.*] *Chaucer.*

AGRÏSE, *v. t.* To terrify; also, to make frightful. [*Not in use.*] *Spenser.*

A'GROM, *n.* A disease frequent in Bengal, and other parts of the E. Indies, in which the tongue chaps and cleaves, becomes rough and sometimes covered with white spots. The remedy is some chalybeate liquor, or the juice of mint. *Encyc.*

AGROSTEM'MA, *n.* A genus of plants of several species, containing the common corn cockle, wild lychnis or campion, &c.

AGROS'TIS, *n.* [Gr. αγρωςις.]
Bent grass; a genus of many species.

AGROUND', *adv.* [Of *a*, *at* or *on*, and *ground.*]
1. On the ground; a marine term, signifying that the bottom of a ship rests on the ground, for want of sufficient depth of water. When the ground is near the shore, the ship is said to be *ashore* or *stranded.*
2. *Figuratively*, stopped; impeded by insuperable obstacles.

AGUAPEÇA'ÇA, *n.* The Jacana, a Brazilian bird, about the size of a pigeon. In the extremity of each wing, it has a sharp prickle which is used for defense. *Dict. of Nat. Hist.*

A'GUE, *n.* a'gu, [Sax. *æge*, *oga*, or *hoga*, fear, horror; Arm. *hegea*, to shake; Goth. *agis*, fear, *agyan* or *ogan*, to fear; Ir. *agh*, fear, *agha* or *aghaim*, to fear. The radical idea is a shaking or shivering similar to that occasioned by terror.]
1. The cold fit which precedes a fever, or a paroxysm of fever in intermittents. It is accompanied with shivering.
2. Chilliness; a chill, or state of shaking with cold, though in health.
3. It is used for a periodical fever, an intermittent, whether quotidian, tertian, or quartan. In this case, the word, which signifies the preceding cold fit, is used for the disease.

A'GUE, *v. t.* To cause a shivering in; to strike with a cold fit. *Haywood.*

A'GUE-ÇAKE, *n.* A hard tumor on the left side of the belly, lower than the false ribs; supposed to be the effect of intermitting fevers. *Encyc.*

A'GUED, *a.* Chilly; having a fit of ague; shivering with cold or fear. *Shak.*

A'GUE-FIT, *n.* A paroxysm of cold, or shivering; chilliness.

A'GUE-PROOF, *n.* Able to resist agues; proof against agues.

AGUER'RY, *v. t.* [Fr. *aguerrir*; from *guerre*, war.]
To inure to the hardships of war; to instruct in the art of war. [*Not in use.*] *Lyttleton.*

A'GUE-SPELL, *n.* A charm or spell to cure or prevent ague. *Gay.*

A'GUE-STRUCK, *a.* Struck with ague. *Hewyt.*

A'GUE-TREE, *n.* A name sometimes applied to sassafras, on account of its febrifuge qualities. *Encyc.*

AGUI'SE, *v. t.* [See *Guise.*] To dress; to adorn. [*Not in use.*] *Spenser.*

AGUI'SE, *n.* Dress. [*Not in use.*] *More.*

A'GUISH, *a.* Chilly; somewhat cold or shivering; also, having the qualities of an ague.

Her *aguish* love now glows and burns. *Granville.*

A'GUISHNESS, *n.* Chilliness; the quality of being aguish.

AGUILLANEUF', *n.* [From *a*, to, *gui*, misleto, and *l'an neuf*, the new year.]
A form of rejoicing among the ancient Franks, on the first day of the year; derived from the druidical custom of cutting misleto, which was held sacred by the druids, and on the first day of the year, consecrating it by crying, *aguillaneuf*, the year to the misleto. This cry is said to be still observed in some parts of France; and the term came to signify also a begging of New Year's gifts. *Encyc.*

A'GUL, *n.* A species of the hedysarum.

AH, An exclamation, expressive of surprise, pity, complaint, contempt, dislike, joy, exultation, &c., according to the manner of utterance.

'AH'A. An exclamation expressing triumph, contempt, or simple surprise; but the senses are distinguished by very different modes of utterance, and different modifications of features.
2. A sunk fence, not visible, without near approach. *Mason.*

AHAN'IGER, *n.* A name of the gar-fish.

AHEAD, *adv.* *Ahed'*, [*a* and *head*, or *at head.*]
1. Further forward than another thing; in front; originally a sea term, denoting further forward than another ship, or on the point to which the stem is directed, in opposition to *astern.* *Mar. Dict.*
2. Onward; forward; towards the point before the stem or head; as, move *ahead.*
3. Headlong; without restraint; precipitantly; as, children suffered to run *ahead.* [*Not used.*] *L'Estrange.*

AHEI'GHT, *adv.* [*a* and *height.*]
Aloft; on high. [*Not used.*] *Shak.*

AHIÇCYAT'LI, *n.* A poisonous serpent of Mexico, somewhat resembling the rattlesnake, but destitute of rattles. Its poison is as fatal as that of any known species of serpent. *Encyc.*

AHI'GH, *adv.* On high. [*Not used.*]

AHO'LD, *adv.* Near the wind; as, to lay a ship *ahold.* [*Not in use.*] *Shak.*

AHOVAI, *n.* A trivial name synonymous with *Cerbera*, a very poisonous species of plum.

AHOY', *Exclam.* A sea term used in hailing.

AHRIMAN. [See *Ariman.*]

AHUIT'LA, *n.* A worm found in the lake of Mexico, four inches in length, as thick as a goose-quill; the tail, which is hard and poisonous, contains a sting. *Clavigero.*

AHUIT'ZOTE, *n.* An amphibious quadruped of the tropical climate of America, whose body is a foot long, its snout long and sharp, its skin of a mixed black and brown color. *Clavigero.*

A'IA, *n.* A Brazilian fowl of the spoon-bill kind, and resembling that bird in form and size. *Dict. of Nat. Hist.*

AIÇU'RUS, *n.* A large and beautiful species of parrot, found in Brazil; its head beautifully variegated with yellow, red and violet colors; its body green; the tips of its wings red, and its tail long and yellow. *Dict. of Nat. Hist.*

AID, *v. t.* [Fr. *aider*, to help; It. *aiutare*, which seems to be contracted from L. *adjuto.* In Ar. آاد or ايد signifies to assist or strengthen, and ادا and ادو to help. In Welsh, *ced* is a benefit, and the word was used to denote the *aids* of feudal tenants.]
To help; to assist; to support, either by furnishing strength or means to effect a purpose, or to prevent or remove evil.

AID, *n.* Help; succor; support; assistance. *Watts.*
2. The person who aids or yields support; a helper; an auxiliary; also the thing that aids or yields succor.
3. In *English law*, a subsidy or tax granted by parliament, and making a part of the king's revenue.
In *France*, *aids* are equivalent to customs, or duties on imports and exports. *Encyc.*
4. In *England*, a tax paid by a tenant to his lord; originally a mere gift, which afterwards became a right demandable by the lord. The aids of this kind were chiefly three. 1. To ransom the lord when a prisoner. 2. To make the lord's eldest son a knight. 3. To marry the lord's eldest daughter. *Blackstone.*
5. An aiddecamp, so called by abbreviation.
6. *To pray in aid*, in law, is to call in a person interested in a title, to assist in defending it. Thus a tenant for life may pray *in the aid* of him in remainder or reversion; that is, he may pray or petition that he may be joined in the suit to *aid* or help maintain the title. This act or petition is called *aid-prayer.* *Cowel. Blackstone.*
Court of aids, in France, is a court which has cognizance of causes respecting duties or customs. *Encyc.*

A'IDANCE, *n.* Aid; help; assistance. [*Little used.*] *Shak.*

A'IDANT, *a.* Helping; helpful; supplying aid. [*Not used.*]

A'IDDEÇAMP, *n.* plur. *Aiddecamps.* [Fr., but naturalized, and here anglicized.]
In *military affairs*, an officer whose duty is to receive and communicate the orders of a general officer. [The pronunciation should be English, according to the orthography, not *aid de cong.*]

A'IDED, *pp.* Assisted; supported; furnished with succor.

A'IDER, *n.* One who helps; an assistant, or auxiliary.

A'IDING, *ppr.* Helping; assisting.

A'IDLESS, *a.* Helpless; without aid; unsupported; undefended. *Shak.*

A'IGRET, AIGRETTE, *n.* In *zoology*, a name of the small white heron. *Dict. of Nat. Hist.*
2. In *botany.* [See *Egret.*]

A'IGULET, *n.* [Fr. Usually contracted into *aiglet*, which see.]
A point or tag, as at the ends of fringes.

A'IKRAW, *n.* A popular name of a species of lichen, or moss. *Fam. of Plants.*

AIL, *v. t.* [Sax. *eglian*, to be troubled, to be irksome; *egle*, trouble, grief. In the Saxon, it is impersonal.]

To trouble; to affect with uneasiness, either of body or mind; used to express some uneasiness or affection, whose cause is unknown; as, what *ails* the man? I know not what *ails* him.

What *aileth* thee, Hagar? Gen. xxi.

It is never used to express a specific disease. We never say, he *ails* a pleurisy; but it is usual to say, he *ails* something; he *ails* nothing; nothing *ails* him.

AIL, *n.* Indisposition, or morbid affection.

A'ILING, *ppr.* Diseased; indisposed; full of complaints.

A'ILMENT, *n.* Disease; indisposition; morbid affection of the body; but the word is not applied ordinarily to acute diseases.

AIM, *v. i.* [Qu. Ir. *oigham*, to eye. Skinner refers this word to the old Fr. *esmer.* If this was the orthography, I know not its affinities.]

To point at, with a missive weapon; to direct the intention or purpose; to attempt to reach, or accomplish; to tend towards; to endeavor; followed by *at* before the object; as, a man *aims at* distinction; or *aims* to be rich.

AIM, *v. t.* To direct or point as a weapon; to direct to a particular object; as, to *aim* a musket or an arrow, the fist or a blow; to *aim* a satire or a reflection at some person or vice.

AIM, *n.* The pointing or direction of a missile weapon; the direction of any thing to a particular point or object, with a view to strike or affect it; as a spear, a blow, a discourse or remark.

2. The point intended to be hit, or object intended to be affected; as, a man missed his *aim.*

3. *Figuratively*, a purpose; intention; design; scheme; as, men are often disappointed of their *aim.*

4. Conjecture; guess.

It is impossible, by *aim*, to tell it. [*Not used.*] *Spenser on Ireland.*

A'IMED, *pp.* Pointed; directed; intended to strike or affect.

A'IMER, *n.* One that aims.

A'IMING, *ppr.* Pointing a weapon at an object; directing any thing to an object; intending; purposing.

A'IMLESS, *a.* Without aim. *May.*

AIR, *n.* [Fr. *air;* L. *aer;* Gr. αηρ; It. *aria;* Sp. *ayre;* Port. *ar;* Arm. *ear, eer;* Ir. *aer;* W. *awyr;* Ch. אויר; Syr. ܐܐܪ; Eth. አየር; Ar. ايرٌ. This word, in the Shemitic languages, falls under the root אור Heb. and Ch., to shine. The radical sense is to open, expand; whence clear; or to flow, to shoot, to radiate.]

1. The fluid which we breathe. Air is inodorous, invisible, insipid, colorless, elastic, possessed of gravity, easily moved, rarefied, and condensed.

Atmospheric air is a compound fluid, consisting of oxygen gas, and nitrogen or azote; the proportion of each is stated by chimists differently; some experiments making the oxygen a twenty-eighth part of a hundred; others, not more than a twenty-third, or something less. The latter is probably the true proportion.

Oxygen gas is called vital air. The body of air surrounding the earth is called the *atmosphere.* The specific gravity of air is to that of water, nearly as 1 to 828. Air is necessary to life; being inhaled into the lungs, the oxygenous part is separated from the azotic, and it is supposed to furnish the body with heat and animation. It is the medium of sounds and necessary to combustion.

2. Air in motion; a light breeze.

Let vernal *airs* through trembling osiers play. *Pope.*

3. Vent; utterance abroad; publication; publicity; as, a story has taken *air.*

You gave it *air* before me. *Dryden.*

Wind is used in like manner.

4. A tune; a short song or piece of music adapted to words; also, the peculiar modulation of the notes, which gives music its character; as, a *soft air.* A song or piece of poetry for singing; also, the leading part of a tune, or that which is intended to exhibit the greatest variety of melody.

5. The peculiar look, appearance, manner or mien of a person; as, a heavy *air;* the *air* of youth; a graceful *air;* a lofty *air.* It is applied to manners or gestures, as well as to features.

6. *Airs*, in the plural, is used to denote an affected manner, show of pride, haughtiness; as, when it is said of a person, he puts on *airs.* The word is used also to express the artificial motions or carriage of a horse.

7. In *painting*, that which expresses the life of action; manner; gesture; attitude.

8. Any thing light or uncertain; that is light as *air.*

Who builds his hope in *air* of your fair looks. Qu. *Obs.* *Shak.*

9. Advice; intelligence; information. *Obs.* *Bacon.*

10. Different states of *air* are characterized by different epithets; as, good *air*, foul *air*, morning *air*, evening *air;* and sometimes *airs* may have been used for ill-scent or vapor, but the use is not legitimate.

To take the air, is to go abroad; to walk or ride a little distance.

To take air, is to be divulged; to be made public.

AIR, *v. t.* To expose to the air; to give access to the open air; to ventilate; as, to *air* clothes; to *air* a room.

2. To expose to heat; to warm; as, to *air* liquors.

3. To dry by a fire; to expel dampness; as, to *air* linen.

A'IRA, *n.* Hair grass, a genus of plants.

A'IR-BALLOON. [See *Balloon.*]

A'IR-BLADDER, *n.* A vesicle or cuticle filled with air; also, the bladder of a fish. *Arbuthnot.*

A'IR-BORN, *a.* Born of the air. *Congreve.*

A'IR-BRAVING, *a.* Braving the winds. *Shak.*

A'IR-BUILT, *a.* Erected in the air; having no solid foundation; chimerical; as, an *air-built* castle; *air-built* hopes.

A'IR-DRAWN, *a.* Drawn in air; imaginary. *Shak.*

A'IRED, *pp.* Exposed to air; cleansed by air; heated or dried by exposure to a fire; ventilated.

A'IRER, *n.* One who exposes to the air.

A'IR-GUN, *n.* A pneumatic engine, resembling a musket, to discharge bullets by means of the elastic force of compressed air. *Encyc.*

A'IR-HOLDER, *n.* [*Air* and *hold.*]

An instrument for holding air, for the purpose of counteracting the pressure of a decreasing column of mercury. *Clayfield. Davy.*

A'IR-HOLE, *n.* An opening to admit or discharge air.

A'IRINESS, *n.* Exposure to a free current of air; openness to the air; as, the *airiness* of a country seat.

2. Gayety; levity; as, the *airiness* of young persons.

A'IRING, *ppr.* Exposing to the air; warming; drying.

A'IRING, *n.* An exposure to the air, or to a fire, for warming or drying; also, a walk or ride in the open air; a short excursion. The exercise of horses in the open air.

A'IR-JACKET, *n.* A leather jacket, to which are fastened bags or bladders filled with air, to render persons buoyant in swimming. *Encyc.*

A'IRLESS, *a.* Not open to a free current of air; wanting fresh air, or communication with open air.

A'IRLING, *n.* A thoughtless, gay person. *Jonson.*

A'IR-PIPE, *n.* A pipe used to draw foul air from a ship's hold, by means of a communication with the furnace, and the rarefaction of the air by fire. This pipe is intended to supply the combustion with the air of the hold, by preventing the access of other air to the fire. *Encyc.*

A'IR-POISE, *n.* [*Air* and *poise.*]

An instrument to measure the weight of the air.

A'IR-PUMP, *n.* A machine for exhausting the air of a vessel. The machines for this purpose are of different constructions.

A'IR-SACS, *n.* Air bags in birds, which are certain receptacles of air, or vesicles lodged in the fleshy parts, in the hollow bones and in the abdomen, which all communicate with the lungs. These are supposed to render the body specifically lighter, and to supply the place of a muscular diaphragm. *Encyc.*

A'IR-SHAFT, *n.* A passage for air into a mine, usually opened in a perpendicular direction, and meeting the adits or horizontal passages, to cause a free circulation of fresh air through the mine. *Encyc.*

A'IR-STIRRING, *a.* Putting the air in motion. *May.*

A'IR-THREAD, *n.* A name given to the spider's webs, which are often seen floating in the air. These filaments are attached to the tops or ends of branches of shrubs or trees, and serve to support the spider when in quest of prey. *Encyc.*

A'IR-THREATENING, *a.* Threatening the air; lofty. *Todd.*

A'IR-VESSEL, *n.* A spiral duct in plants containing air, and supposed to be analogous to the lungs in animals. *Encyc.*

A'IRY, *a.* Consisting of air; as, an *airy* substance.

2. Relating or belonging to air; high in air; as, an *airy* flight; *airy* region.
3. Open to a free current of air; as, an *airy* situation.
4. Light as air; resembling air; thin; unsubstantial; without solidity; as, *airy* ghosts. An *airy* dress is one which admits air, and is cool.
5. Without reality; having no solid foundation; vain; trifling; as, an *airy* scheme; *airy* notions.
6. Gay; sprightly; full of vivacity and levity; light of heart; lively; as, an *airy* girl.

A'IRY, or *A'ery*, *n.* [See *Aery*.]
Among *sportsmen*, the nest of the hawk or eagle.

A'IRY-FLYING, *a.* Flying like air. *Thomson.*

AISLE, or AILE, *n.* Pronounced *Ile.* [Fr. *aile*, a wing; L. *ala.*]
The wing of a quire; a walk in a church.

AIZO'ON, *n.* [Sax. *aizon*, from L. *aizoon.* It seems to be composed of Gr. αει, always, Sax. *aa*, Eng. *aye*, and ζωον, living.]
A genus of plants, called by Miller *sempervive.* The name has, by some writers, been applied to the house leek and to the aloes. *Encyc.*

AJA'VA, *n.* The seed of a plant brought from Malabar, said to be an excellent carminative, and very useful in the colic. *Quincy.*

AJU'GA, *n.* Bugle, a genus of plants. *Encyc.*

AJU'RU-CATINGA, *n.* A species of American parrot, of a green color, with eyes of a fiery red, encircled with white.

AJU'RU-CURAU, *n.* An American parrot, of a lively green color, with a blue crown; the throat, and sides of the head, of a fine yellow.

AJU'RU-PARA, *n.* A small parrot of America, of a beautiful green, with the beak, legs and circlets of the eyes white. *Dict. of Nat. Hist.*

AJ'UTAGE, or AD'JUTAGE, *n.* [Fr. from *ajouter*, to join.]
A tube fitted to the mouth of a vessel, through which the water of a fountain is to be played.

AKE, *v. i.*, less properly written *ache.* [Sax. *ace*, pronounced *ake.* See *Ache.*]
1. To be in pain; usually, in pain of some continuance.
2. To feel distress of mind; to be grieved; as, the heart *akes.*

AKE, *n.* Continued pain, less severe than is expressed by pang, agony, and torment; as, the tooth-*ake*; head-*ake.* It is commonly used in composition with the name of the part affected, as *head-ake.*

A'KER, *n.* [Gr. αγρος; L. *ager*; Sax. *acer*, pronounced *aker*; Germ. *acker.* The most correct orthography is *aker.*]
Originally an open field. But in G. Britain, the quantity of land in the *aker* is fixed by statute at four thousand eight hundred and forty square yards, making one hundred and sixty square rods, perches or poles; and this is the quantity of land it contains in the United States of America. [See *Acre.*]

AKIN', *a.* [*a* or *of* and *kin.* See *Kin.*]
1. Related by blood, used of persons; as, the two families are near *akin.*
2. Allied by nature; partaking of the same properties; as, envy and jealousy are near *akin.* [*This adjective is used only after the noun.*]

A'KING, *ppr.* Having continued pain; suffering distress of mind, or grief.

A'KING, *n.* Continued pain, or distress of mind.

AL, in *Arabic*, an adjective or inseparable prefix, answering to the Italian *il*, and Sp. *el* and *la.* Its use is to render nouns definite, like the English *the*; as, *alkoran*, the koran or the book by eminence; *alcove*, *alchimy*, *alembic*, *almanac*, &c.

AL, in English, is sometimes a contraction of the Saxon *æthel*, noble or illustrious.

More generally *al*, in composition, is a contraction of *ald* or *alt*, old, and it is prefixed to many names, as *Alburg.* Sax. *eald*; Germ. *alt*, old.

Al, in the composition of Latin words, is written before *l* for *ad*, for the ease of pronunciation; as, in *allevo*, *alludo*, for *ad levo*, *ad ludo.*

AL'ABASTER, *n.* [L. from Gr. αλαβαστρον]
A sub-variety of carbonate of lime, found in large masses, formed by the deposition of calcarious particles in caverns of limestone rocks. These concretions have a foliated, fibrous or granular structure, and are of a pure white color, or more generally they present shades of yellow, red or brown, in undulating or concentric stripes, or in spots. *Cleaveland.*
Among *the ancients*, alabaster was also the name of a vessel in which odoriferous liquors were kept; so called from the stone of which it was made. Also, the name of a measure, containing ten ounces of wine or nine of oil. *Encyc. Macquer. Pliny.*

AL'ABASTER, *a.* Made of alabaster, or resembling it. *Addison.*

Alabastrum dendroide, a kind of laminated alabaster, variegated with figures of shrubs and trees, found in the province of Hohenstein. *Encyc.*

ALACK', *exclam.* [Per. هلاك halaka, perdition, destruction, and *alaksadan*, to perish.]
An exclamation expressive of sorrow.

ALACK'ADAY. An exclamation uttered to express regret or sorrow.

ALAC'RIOUSNESS, *n.* Briskness. [*Not used.*]

ALAC'RITY, *n.* [L. *alacritas*, from *alacer*, *alacris.*]
Cheerfulness; gayety; sprightliness; more usually, a cheerful readiness or promptitude to do some act; cheerful willingness; as, the soldiers advanced with *alacrity* to meet the enemy.

ALAD'INISTS. Free thinkers among the Mohammedans. *Encyc.*

AL'ALITE, *n.* A crystalized mineral; diopside; a semi-transparent pyroxene. A variety with twelve sided prisms, was found by Bonvoisin, near the village of Ala in Piedmont, and by him called Alalite. *Cleaveland.*

ALAMIRE', *n.* The lowest note but one, in Guido Aretine's scale of music. *Johnson.*

ALAMODAL'ITY, *n.* Conformity to the prevailing mode, or fashion of the times. [*Little used.*] *Encyc.*

ALAMO'DE *adv.* [Fr. *a la mode*, after the fashion.]
According to the fashion or prevailing mode. *Whitlock.*

ALAMO'DE, *n.* A thin glossy silk for hoods, scarfs, &c.

ALAND', *adv.* At or on land. *Sidney.*

AL'ARM, *n.* [Dan. *larm*, noise, bustle, *alarm*; *larmer*, to make a noise or bustle, to *alarm*; G. *lärm*, *lärmen*, id; Sw. *larm*, *larma*, id; Fr. *alarme*, *alarmer*; Sp. *alarma*, *alarmar*; It. *allarme*, *allarmare*; W. *alarm*, a great shout, compounded of *al*, very, most, and *garm*, an outcry. The Welsh gives the true origin and primary signification.]
1. Any sound, outcry or information, intended to give notice of approaching danger as, to sound an *alarm.*
2. A summon to arms. *Dryden.*
3. Sudden surprise with fear or terror; as, the fire or the enemy excited an *alarm.*
4. Terror; a sensation excited by an apprehension of danger, from whatever cause; as, we felt an *alarm* at the cry of fire.
5. In *fencing*, an appeal or challenge. *Encyc.*

AL'ARM, *v. t.* To give notice of danger; to rouse to vigilance, and exertions for safety.
2. To call to arms for defense.
3. To surprise with apprehension of danger; to disturb with terror; to fill with anxiety by the prospect of evil.

AL'ARM-BELL, *n.* A bell that gives notice of danger.

AL'ARMED, *pp.* Notified of sudden danger; surprised with fear; roused to vigilance or activity by apprehension of approaching danger; solicitous at the prospect or expectation of evil. Thus, we are *alarmed* at the approach of danger, or *alarmed* for the safety of friends at sea.

AL'ARMING, *ppr.* Giving notice of approaching danger; rousing to vigilance; exciting solicitude by a prospect of evil.

AL'ARMING, *a.* Exciting apprehension; terrifying; awakening a sense of danger; as, an *alarming message.*

AL'ARMINGLY, *adv.* With alarm; in a manner to excite apprehension.

AL'ARMIST, *n.* One that excites alarm.

AL'ARM-POST, *n.* A place to which troops are to repair in cases of an alarm.

AL'ARM-WATCH, *n.* A watch that strikes the hour by regulated movement. *Herbert.*

ALARUM, for *alarm*, is a corruption, and is not to be used.

ALAS' *ex.* [Dutch *helaas*; Fr. *helas.*]
An exclamation expressive of sorrow, grief, pity, concern, or apprehension of evil; sometimes followed by *day* or *while*; *alas the day*, like alack a day; or *alas the while*, (*Obs. Spenser.*) expressing an unhappy time.

ALA'TE, *adv.* Lately. [*Not used.*]

ALA'TED, *a.* [L. *ala*, a wing; *alatus*, winged.]
Winged; having dilatations like wings. *Botany.*

AL'ATERN, *n.* A trivial name of a species of rhamnus or buckthorn.

ALB, *n.* [L. *albus*, Gr. αλφος, white.]
A surplice or vestment of white linen, reaching to the feet, worn by the Romish clergy. Also a Turkish coin, called also an *asper*, value one hundred and twelve mills.

AL'BATROS, *n.* An aquatic fowl, belonging to the order of ansers. The bill is strait; the upper mandible crooked at the point, and the lower one truncated; the nostrils are oval, open and little prominent, and placed on the sides; the wings are pennated, and there are three webbed toes on each foot. The upper part of the body is of a spotted brown, and the belly white. It is of the size of a pelican or larger, very voracious, preying on fish and small water fowls. These fowls are seen, in great numbers, about the capes of the two continents, and on the northern shores of Asia. They are sometimes called the great gull. *Encyc.*

ALBE'IT, [This is supposed to be a compound of *all*, *be* and *it*, and is equivalent to *admit*, or *grant it all.*]
Be it so; admit all that; although; notwithstanding.

Whereas ye say, the Lord saith it, *albeit* I have not spoken. Ez. xiii.

[*This word is now antiquated.*]

AL'BELEN, *n.* A fish of the truttaceous or trout kind, found in the German lakes, weighing five or six pounds. *Dict. of Nat. Hist.*

ALBES'CENT, *a.* [L. *albesco*, to grow white.]
Becoming white, or rather, whitish; moderately white. *Encyc.*

AL'BIȻORE, *n.* [Port. *albacor; al* and *bacoro*, a little pig.]
A marine fish, like a tunny, noted for following ships.

ALBIĠEN'SES, ALBEĠEOIS, *n.* A party of Reformers, who separated from the church of Rome, in the 12th century; so called from the Albegeois, a small territory in France, where they resided. They are sometimes confounded with the *Waldenses*; but they were prior to them in time, differed from them in some of their tenets, and resided in a different part of France. The catholics made war upon them, and they gradually dwindled, till the reformation, when the remains of them fell in with the followers of Zuinglius and the Genevan Protestants. *Encyc.*

AL'BIN, *n.* [L. *albus*, white.]
A mineral, of an opake white color, consisting of aggregated crystaline lamins, found in Bohemia.
This is regarded as a variety of apophyllite. *Werner. Cleaveland.*

ALBI'NO, *n.* [L. *albus*, white.]
A white descendant of black parents, or a white person belonging to a race of blacks. A person unnaturally white.

ALBI'NOS, *n.* A name signifying white men, given by the Portuguese to the white negroes of Africa. The color of this race appears like that of persons affected with leprosy; and the negroes look upon them as monsters. *Encyc.*

AL'BION, *n.* An ancient name of England, still used in poetry. It is supposed this name was given to it on account of its white cliffs.

ALBO'RA, *n.* A sort of itch or rather leprosy, terminating without ulceration, but with fetid evacuations in the mouth and nostrils. *Quincy.*

ALBO'RO, *n.* The erythrinus, a small red fish of the Mediterranean. *Dict. of Nat. Hist.*

ALBUĠIN'EOUS, *a.* [L. *albugo*, the white spot in the eye, from *albus* white.]
Pertaining to or resembling the white of the eye, or of an egg. *Encyc.*
Albugineous humor, the aqueous humor of the eye. *Encyc. Quincy.*

ALBU'GO, *n.* The white speck in the eye, called the film, haw, dragon, pearl or cicatrice. Also a disease of the eye, occasioned by a white opake spot growing on the cornea and obstructing vision. It is called also leucoma, nebula, pannus oculi, onyx, unguis, &c. *Quincy. Encyc.*

ALBU'LA, *n.* A species of truttaceous fish, destitute of teeth. The *Albula Indica* is called by the Dutch wit-fish, and is of the size of a herring. The *Albula nobilis* is a fish caught in the lakes of Germany. *Dict. of Nat. Hist.*

AL'BUM, *n.* [L. *albus*, white.]
1. Among the Romans, a white table, board or register, on which the names of public officers and public transactions were entered. *Lat. Dict.*
2. A book, originally blank, in which foreigners or strangers insert autographs of celebrated persons, or in which friends insert pieces as memorials for each other.

ALBU'MEN, *n.* [L. from *albus*, white.]
The white of an egg. A like substance is a chief constituent in all animal solids. *Ure.*

ALBU'MINOUS, *a.* Pertaining to, or having the properties of albumen.

AL'BURN, } *n.* [L. *alburnum*, from *albus*,
ALBURN'UM, } white.]
The white and softer part of wood, between the inner bark and the wood. In America, it is popularly called the *sap*. This is annually acquiring hardness, and becoming wood. *Milne.*

AL'BURN, *n.* [L. *alburnus*, from *albus*, white.]
A fish called the *bleak*. It belongs to the order of abdominals, and the genus Cyprinus. It is five or six inches in length, and esteemed delicious food. Artificial pearls are made of its scales. *Encyc.*

AL'ȻAHEST, or AL'KA HEST, *n.* [*Arabic.*]
A pretended univer ...ssolvent, or menstruum. [See *Al hest.*]

ALȻA'IȻ, *a.* Pertaining to Alcæus, a Lyric poet of Mitylene, in Lesbos, who flourished about the forty-fourth Olympiad; or to other poets of the same name, of which three are mentioned; one an Athenian tragic poet, and another a Messenian.

ALȻA'IȻS, *n. plu.* Several kinds of verse, so called from Alcæus, their inventor. One kind consists of five feet, a spondee or iambic, an iambic, a long syllable and two dactyls. *Encyc.*

ALȻA'ID, *n.* [Sp. *alcayde;* Port. *alcaide;* Ar. قائد kaidon, with the prefix *al*, from قاد to lead, rule, govern. Hence the *Cadi* of the Turks.]
Among the Moors, Spaniards and Portuguese, a governor. In Portugal, the chief civil magistrate of a town or city; also the jurisdiction of certain judges of appeal. In Spain, the governor of a castle or fort; also a jailer. *Span. and Port. Dict.*

ALȻAN'NA, *n.* [*Arabic.*] A plant; and a powder, prepared from the leaves of the Egyptian privet, used by the Turkish females to give a golden color to the nails and hair. Infused in water, it forms a yellow color; with vinegar, it forms a red. From the berries is extracted an oil, used in medicine. In Cairo, it forms an article of commerce. *Encyc. Theophrast.*

AL'ȻATRAZ, *n.* The Spanish name of the Pelecanus Onocrotalus of Linne; a pelican; also a fish taken on the coast of India. *Span. Dict.*

ALȻAV'ALA, *n.* In Spain, a tax on every transfer of property, real or personal. *Encyc.*

ALCE'DO, *n.* [L.]
The king fisher; a genus of birds, of the order of Picæ. The species are numerous. They usually live about rivers, feeding on fish, which they take by darting into the water with surprising velocity. [See *Halcyon.*

ALȻHIM'IȻ, } *a.* Relating to alchimy,
ALȻHIM'IȻAL, } or produced by it.

ALȻHIM'IȻALLY, *adv.* In the manner of alchimy.

AL'ȻHIMIST, *n.* One who practices alchimy.

ALȻHIMIST'IȻ, } *a.* Practicing alchi-
ALȻHIMIST'IȻAL, } my, or relating to it. *Burke, Rev.*

AL'ȻHIMY, *n.* [It. *alchimia;* Ar. *al*, the, and كيميا kimia, secret, hidden, or the occult art, from كمي kamai, to hide. See *Chimistry.*]
1. The more sublime and difficult parts of chimistry, and chiefly such as relate to the transmutation of metals into gold, the finding a universal remedy for diseases, and an alkahest or universal solvent, and other things now treated as ridiculous. This pretended science was much cultivated in the sixteenth and seventeenth centuries, but is now held in contempt.
2. Formerly, a mixed metal used for utensils.

ALȻMA'NIAN, *a.* Pertaining to Alcman, a lyric poet of the twenty-seventh Olympiad, celebrated for his amorous verses. The Alcmanian *verse* consisted of two dactyls and two trochees. *Encyc.*

AL'ȻO, *n.* A quadruped of America, nearly resembling a dog, but mute and melancholy; and this circumstance seems to have given rise to the fable that dogs, transported to America, become mute. The animal was used for food by the native Americans, and the first Spanish settlers; but it is said to be now extinct. It is known also by the name of Techichi. *Clavigero.*

AL'ȻOHOL, *n.* [Ar. كحل kahala; Heb. Syr. and Eth. כחל, to paint with a preparation of powder of antimony. The oriental females still practice the painting of the eye brows with this material. The name was applied to this substance, and afterwards to other fine powders, and to highly rectified spirits.]
Pure or highly rectified spirit, obtained from fermented liquors by distillation. It con-

sists of hydrogen, carbon and oxygen. It is extremely light and inflammable, and a powerful stimulant and antiseptic. This is the usual sense of the word; but originally, in Arabic, it signified a fine impalpable powder, in which sense it is still used. *Encyc.*

ALCOHOL'IC, *a.* Pertaining to alcohol, or partaking of its qualities. *Med. Rep.*

ALCOHOLIZA'TION, *n.* The act of rectifying spirit, till it is wholly dephlegmated; or of reducing a substance to an impalpable powder.

AL'COHOLIZE, *v. t.* To convert into alcohol; to rectify spirit till it is wholly dephlegmated; also, to reduce a substance to an impalpable powder.

AL'COR, *n.* [Ar.] A small star adjoining to the large bright one in the middle of the tail of Ursa Major. *Encyc.*

ALCORAN. [See *Koran* and *Alkoran.*]

AL'COVE or ALCO'VE, *n.* [Sp. *alcoba*, composed of *al*, with the Ar. قَبَّ kabba, to arch, to construct with an arch, and its derivatives, an arch, a round house; Eng. *cubby.*]

1. A recess, or part of a room, separated by an estrade, or partition of columns, or by other corresponding ornaments; in which is placed a bed of state, and sometimes seats for company. The bed is sometimes raised two or three steps, with a rail at the foot. These are frequent in Spain. *Encyc.*

2. A recess in a library, or small lateral apartment for books.

AL'CYON, *n.* A trivial name of the kingfisher. [See *Halcyon.*]

AL'CYONITE, *n.* [*Supra.*]

A fossil zoophite, somewhat resembling a fungus. *J. of Science.*

ALCYO'NIUM, *n.* The name of a submarine plant, or bastard spunge. Also a kind of astroit or coral, a fossil found in England. *Encyc.*

AL'DER, *n.* [L. *alnus*; Fr. *aune*, *aulne*; Sax. *alr.*]

A tree, usually growing in moist land, and belonging to the genus *Alnus*. The name is applied also to some species of other genera.

ALD'ERMAN, *n. plu.* Aldermen. [Sax. *ald* or *eald*, old, comp, *alder*, older, and *man*; G. *alt*; D. *oud.*]

1. Among *our Saxon Ancestors*, a senior or superior. The title was applied to princes, dukes, earls, senators and presiding magistrates; also to archbishops and bishops, implying superior wisdom or authority. Thus, Ethelstan, duke of the East-Anglians, was called alderman of all England; and there were aldermen of cities, counties, and castles, who had jurisdiction within their respective districts.

2. In *present usage*, a magistrate or officer of a town corporate, next in rank below the mayor. The number of aldermen is different in different cities. In London the number is twenty-six, one in each ward, and the office is held for life. *Spelman. Cowel. Encyc.*

In *the United States*, the number of aldermen depends on the charters of incorporation. In general, aldermen have the powers of a justice of the peace, and, with the mayor, they constitute the court of the corporation. In most of our cities, they are annually elected by the citizens.

AL'DERMANLY, *a.* Pertaining to or like an alderman. *Swift.*

AL'DERN, *a.* Made of Alder.

ALE, *n.* [Sax. *eala*, *eale*, or *aloth*; G. *äl*; Sw. *öl*; Dan. *öl*; Ir. *ol.* Qu. Ir. *olam*, to drink.]

1. A liquor made from an infusion of malt by fermentation. It differs from beer, in having a smaller proportion of hops. It is of different sorts, chiefly *pale* and *brown*; the first made from malt slightly dried; the second, from malt more considerably dried or roasted. Ale was the common drink of the ancient inhabitants of Europe. It is usually made with barley; but sometimes with wheat, rye, millet, oats, &c. *Encyc.*

2. A merry meeting in English country places, so called from the liquor drank. *Ben Jonson.*

Medicated Ales are those which are prepared for medicinal purposes, by an infusion of herbs during fermentation. *Encyc.*

A'LE-BENCH, *n.* A bench in or before an ale house. *Homilies.*

A'LE-BERRY, *n.* A beverage, made by boiling ale with spice, sugar and sops of bread. *Johnson.*

A'LE-BREWER, *n.* One whose occupation is to brew ale.

A'LE-CONNER, *n.* [*ale* and *con*, to know or see.]

An officer in London, whose business is to inspect the measures used in public houses, to prevent frauds in selling liquors. Four of these are chosen annually by the livery men, in common hall, on midsummer's day. *Act of Parl.*

A'LE-COST, *n.* Costmary, a plant, a species of Tanacetum.

A'LE-FED, *a.* Fed with ale. *Stafford.*

A'LE-GAR, *n.* [*ale*, and Fr. *aigre*, sour.]

Sour ale; the acid of ale.

A'LE-HOOF, *n.* [D. *eiloof*, a plant used in brewing.]

Ground-ivy, the glechoma hederacea, of Linne. The leaves of this plant are used to clarify and give flavor to ale. *Lee. Encyc.*

A'LE-HOUSE, *n.* A house where ale is retailed; and hence a tipling house.

A'LE-HOUSE-KEEPER, *n.* One who keeps an ale-house.

A'LE-KNIGHT, *n.* A pot companion. *Chaucer.*

A'LE-SHOT, *n.* A reckoning to be paid for ale.

A'LE-SILVER, *n.* A duty paid to the Lord Mayor of London, by the sellers of ale within the city.

A'LE-STAKE, *n.* A stake set as a sign before an ale-house. *Chaucer.*

A'LE-TASTER, *n.* An officer appointed in every court leet, and sworn, to inspect ale, beer and bread, and examine the quality and quantity within the precincts of the lordship. *Cowel.*

A'LE-VAT, *n.* A vat in which ale is fermented.

A'LE-WASHED, *a.* Steeped or soaked in ale. *Shak.*

A'LE-WIFE, *n.* A woman who keeps an ale house.

A'LEWIFE, or A'LOOF, *n.* [This word is properly *aloof*, the Indian name of a fish. See Winthrop on the culture of maiz in America, Phil. Trans. No. 142. p. 1065, and Baddam's Memoirs, vol. 2. 131.]

An American fish, belonging to the genus Clupea, and called Clupea Serrata. It resembles the herring. The established pronunciation is alewife, *plu.* alewives.

ALECTRYOM'ANCY, *n.* [Gr. αλεκτρυων, a cock, and μαντεια, divination.]

An ancient practice of foretelling events by means of a cock. The twenty four letters were laid on the ground, and a grain of corn on each; a cock was then permitted to pick up the grains, and the letters under the grains selected, being formed into words, were supposed to foretel the event desired. *Encyc.*

ALEE', *adv.* [*a* or *at* and *lee.* See *Lee.*]

In *seaman's language*, on the side opposite to the wind, that is, opposite to the side on which it strikes. The helm of a ship is *alee*, when pressed close to the lee side.

Hard alee or *luff alee*, is an order to put the helm to the lee side.

Helm's alee, that is, *the helm is alee*, a notice given as an order to the seamen to cause the head-sails to shake in the wind, with a view to bring the ship about. *Mar. Dict.*

A'LEGER, *a.* [Fr., Sp. *alégre*; L. *alacer.*]

Gay; cheerful; sprightly. [*Not used.*] *Bacon.*

ALEGGE, *v. t.* To lighten; to lessen; to assuage. [*Not used.*]

ALEMB'DAR, *n.* In Turkey, an officer who bears the green standard of Mohammed, when the Sultan appears in public. *Encyc.*

ALEM'BIC, *n.* [Ar. *al* and اَنْبِك or اَنْبِيق a chimical vessel.]

A chimical vessel used in distillation; usually made of glass or copper. The bottom part containing the liquor to be distilled, is called the *cucurbit*; the upper part which receives and condenses the steam, is called the head, the beak of which is fitted to the neck of a receiver. The head is more properly the alembic. This vessel is not so generally used now, as the worm still and retort.

ALENGTH', *adv.* [*a* and *length.*]

At full length; along; stretched at full length. *Chaucer.*

ALEP'IDOTE, *n.* [Gr. α priv. and λεπις, a scale.]

Any fish whose skin is not covered with scales.

ALERT', *a.* [Fr. *alerte*; Sp. *alerto*, vigilant, watchful, *estar alerta*, to be on the watch.]

1. Watchful; vigilant; active in vigilance. Hence the military phrase, *upon the alert*; upon the watch, guarding against surprise or danger.

2. Brisk; nimble; moving with celerity. *Spectator.*

ALERT'NESS, *n.* Briskness; nimbleness; sprightliness; levity. *Addison.*

ALEUROM'ANCY, *n.* [Gr. αλευρον, meal, and μαντεια, divination.]
A kind of divination by meal, used by the ancients. *Encyc.*

ALEU'TIAN, or **ALEU'TIC**, *a.* Designating certain isles in the Pacific ocean, eastward of Kamtschatka, extending northeastward towards America. The word is formed from *aleut*, which, in Russian, is a bald rock. *Tooke. Pinkerton.*

ALEX'ANDERS, *n.* The name of a plant of the genus Smyrnium. *Muhlenberg.*

ALEX'ANDER'S FOOT, *n.* The name of a plant.

ALEX'ANDRIAN, *n.* Pertaining to Alexandria. There are many cities of this name, in various parts of the earth. The term is often applied as an attribute, or used as a noun, for one who professed or taught the sciences in the school of Alexandria, in Egypt; a place highly celebrated for its literature and magnificence, and whose library, it is said, consisted of 700,000 volumes. The Persians and Turks write for Alexander, *Scander*, or *Sconder;* and for Alexandria, *Scanderona;* hence Scanderoon, a sea port in Syria.

ALEX'ANDRINE, or **ALEXANDRIAN**, *n.* A kind of verse, consisting of twelve syllables, or of twelve and thirteen alternately; so called from a poem written in French on the life of Alexander. This species of verse is peculiar to modern poetry, but well adapted to epic poems. The Alexandrine in English consists of twelve syllables, and is less used than this kind of verse is among the French, whose tragedies are generally composed of Alexandrines. *Pope. Dryden.*

ALEXIPH'ARMIC, *a.* [Gr. αλεξω, to expel, and φαρμακον, poison.]
Expelling poison; antidotal; sudorific; that has the quality of expelling poison or infection by sweat.

ALEXIPH'ARMIC, *n.* A medicine that is intended to obviate the effects of poison; an antidote to poison or infection. By the Greeks, the word was used for an amulet. *Quincy. Encyc.*

ALEXITER'IC, } *a.* [Gr. αλεξω, to expel,
ALEXITE'RIAL, } and δηλητηριον, poison.]
Resisting poison; obviating the effects of venom. *Quincy. Encyc.*

ALEXITER'IC, } *n.* A medicine to re-
ALEXITER'ICAL, } sist the effects of poison, or the bite of venomous animals; nearly synonymous with *alexipharmic.* Used also by the Greeks for an amulet.

AL'GAROT, or **AL'GAROTH**, *n.* The name of an emetic powder, prepared from the regulus of antimony, dissolved in acids, and separated by repeated lotions in warm water. It is either an Arabic term, or the name of the inventor, a physician of Verona. *Quincy. Encyc.*

AL'GEBRA, *n.* [Ar. *al* and جَبْر, the reduction of parts to a whole, or fractions to whole numbers, from the verb, which signifies to consolidate; Heb. Ch. Syr. and Eth. גבר, to be strong.]
The science of quantity in general, or universal arithmetic. Algebra is a general method of computation, in which signs and symbols, which are commonly the letters of the alphabet, are made to represent numbers and quantities. It takes an unknown quantity sought, as if granted; and, by means of one or more quantities given, proceeds till the quantity supposed is discovered, by some other known quantity to which it is equal.
This science was of Oriental discovery; but whether among the Arabians or Indians, is uncertain.

ALGEBRA'IC, } *a.* Pertaining to alge-
ALGEBRA'ICAL, } bra; containing an operation of Algebra, or deduced from such operation.
Algebraic curve, a figure whose intercepted diameters bear always the same proportion to their respective ordinates. *Bailey.*

ALGEBRA'IST, *n.* One who is versed in the science of algebra.

AL'GENEB, *n.* A fixed star of the second magnitude, in the right side of Perseus; Long. 27° 46′ 12″ of Taurus; Lat. 30° 05′ 28″ North. *Encyc.*

ALGERINE', *n.* [from *Algiers.*] A native of Algiers, a city and a government on the coast of Africa.

ALGERINE', *a.* Belonging to Algiers.

AL'GID, *a.* [L. *algidus.*] Cold. [*Not used.*]

AL'GOL, *n.* A fixed star of the third magnitude, called Medusa's head, in Perseus; Long. 21° 50′ 42″ of Taurus; Lat. 23° 23′ 47″ North. *Encyc.*

AL'GOR, *n.* [Lat.] Among physicians, an unusual coldness in any part of the body.

AL'GORITHM, or **AL'GORISM**, *n.* An Arabic term, signifying numerical computation, or the six operations of arithmetic. *Johnson. Encyc.*

AL'GOUS, *a.* [L. *alga*, sea weed.]
Pertaining to sea weed; abounding with, or like sea weed.

ALHEN'NA, *n.* [See *Alkenna.*]

A'LIAS, [L.] Otherwise; as in this example, Simson *alias* Smith; a word used in judicial proceedings to connect the different names by which a person is called, who attempts to conceal his true name, and pass under a fictitious one.

A'LIAS, *n.* A second writ, or execution, issued when the first has failed to enforce the judgment.

AL'IBI, *n.* [L.] Elsewhere; in another place; a *law* term. When a person is charged with an offense, and he proves that he could not have committed it, because he was, at the time, *in another place*, he is said to prove an *alibi.* The part of a plea or allegation, which avers the party to have been in another place, is also called an *alibi.*

A'LIEN, *a.* *âlyen*, [L. *alienus*, from *alius*, another; Ir. *aile*, *eile*, *oile*, another; W. *all*, other, and *ail*, second; Arm. *eel*, *all*, *eguile;* Corn. *gele;* Gr. αλλος. Hence, L. *alieno*, to alienate; *alter*, another; whence Fr. *alterer*, to alter; L. *alterno*, to alter, to alternate, and *alterco*, *altercor*, to altercate. Eth. ከለአ kalea, to alter, to change; whence *alius*, another, the second; the first letter being lost, except in the Cornish and Armoric, as it is in *all.* See Class Gl. No. 36, and Ludolf, 387.]
1. Foreign; not belonging to the same country, land or government.
2. Belonging to one who is not a citizen.
3. Estranged; foreign; not allied; adverse to; as, principles *alien* from our religion.

A'LIEN, *n.* *âlyen.* A foreigner; one born in, or belonging to, another country; one who is not a denizen, or entitled to the privileges of a citizen.
2. In *scripture*, one who is a stranger to the church of Christ, or to the covenant of grace.

> At that time, ye were without Christ, being *aliens* from the commonwealth of Israel. Eph. ii.

In France, a child born of residents who are not citizens, is an *alien.* In Great Britain, the children of aliens born in that country, are mostly natural born subjects; and the children of British subjects, owing allegiance to the crown of England, though born in other countries, are natural subjects, and entitled to the privileges of resident citizens. *Blackstone.*
Alien-duty, a tax upon goods imported by aliens, beyond the duty on the like goods imported by citizens; a discriminating duty on the tonnage of ships belonging to aliens, or any extra duties imposed by laws or edicts on aliens.

A'LIEN, } *v. t.* [L. *alieno.*]
ALIE'NE, }
1. To transfer title or property to another; to sell.

> Nor could he *aliene* the estate, even with the consent of the Lord. *Blackstone.*

2. To estrange; to make averse or indifferent; to turn the affections from.

> The prince was *aliened* from all thoughts of the marriage. *Clarendon.*

In this sense, it is more common to use *alienate.*

ALIENABIL'ITY, *n.* The capacity of being alienated or transferred.

> The *alienability* of the domain. *Burke.*

A'LIENABLE, *a.* That may be sold, or transferred to another; as, land is *alienable* according to the laws of the State.

A'LIENAGE, *n.* The state of being an alien.

> Why restore estates, forfeitable on account of *alienage?* *Story.*

A'LIENATE, *v. t.* [L. *alieno.*]
1. To transfer title, property or right to another; as, to *alienate* lands, or sovereignty.
2. To estrange; to withdraw, as the affections; to make indifferent or averse, where love or friendship before subsisted; with *from;* as, to *alienate* the heart or affections; to *alienate* a man *from* the friends of his youth.
3. To apply to a wrong use.

> They shall not *alienate* the first fruits of the land. Ezek. xlviii.

A'LIENATE, *a.* [L. *alienatus.*]
Estranged; withdrawn from; stranger to; with *from.*

> O *alienate from* God, O spirit accurst. *Milton.*
>
> The whigs were *alienate from* truth. *Swift.*

ALIENA'TION, *n.* [L. *alienatio.*]
1. A transfer of title; or a legal conveyance of property to another.
2. The state of being alienated.
3. A withdrawing or estrangement, as of the heart or affections.
4. Delirium; derangement of mental faculties; insanity. *Hooker.*

Alienation-office, in Great-Britain, is an office to which all writs of covenant and entry, on which fines are levied and recoveries suffered, are carried, to have fines for alienation set and paid thereon. *Encyc.*

A'LIENATOR, *n.* One that alienates or transfers property. *Warton.*

ALIENEE', *n.* One to whom the title to property is transferred.

If the *alienee* enters and keeps possession. *Blackstone.*

ALI'FE, *adv.* [*a* or *on* and *life.*]
On my life. *Shak.*

ALIF'EROUS, *a.* [L. *ala*, wing, and *fero*, to bear.]
Having wings.

AL'IFORM, *a.* [L. *ala*, wing, and *forma*, shape.]
Having the shape of a wing; a term applied to a certain process and muscles of the body, as the pterygoid process, and the muscles arising from that process. *Quincy.*

ALIG'EROUS, *a.* [L. *ala* wing, and *gero*, to carry.]
Having wings.

ALI'GHT, *v. i.* [Sax. *alihtan. gelihtan, lihtan.* See *Light.*]
1. To get down or descend, as from on horseback or from a carriage.
2. To descend and settle; as, a flying bird *alights* on a tree.
3. To fall or descend and lodge; as, snow *alights* on a roof.

ALI'KE, *a.* [Sax. *gelic.* See *Like.*]
Having resemblance or similitude; similar.

The darkness and the light are both *alike* to thee. Ps. xiii.

[*This adjective never precedes the noun which it qualifies.*]

ALI'KE, *adv.* In the same manner, form or degree.

We are all *alike* concerned in religion.
He fashioneth their hearts *alike*. Ps. xxxiii.

ALI'KE-MINDED, *a.* Having the same mind; but *like-minded* is more generally used.

AL'IMENT, *n.* [L. *alimentum*, from *alo*, to feed; Ir. *alaim, ailim, olaim*, to feed or nurse.]
That which nourishes; food; nutriment; any thing which feeds or adds to a substance, animal or vegetable, in natural growth.

ALIMENT'AL, *a.* Supplying food; that has the quality of nourishing; that furnishes the materials for natural growth; as, chyle is *alimental; alimental* sap.

ALIMENT'ALLY, *adv.* So as to serve for nourishment or food.

ALIMENT'ARINESS, *n.* The quality of supplying nutriment.

ALIMENT'ARY, *a.* Pertaining to aliment or food; having the quality of nourishing; as, *alimentary* particles.
The *alimentary canal*, in animal bodies, is the great duct or intestine, by which aliments are conveyed through the body, and the useless parts evacuated.
Alimentary law, among the Romans, was a law which obliged children to support their parents. *Encyc.*
Obligation of aliment, in Scots law, is the natural obligation of parents to provide for their children. *Encyc.*

ALIMENTA'TION, *n.* The act or power of affording nutriment.
2. The state of being nourished. *Johnson. Bacon.*

ALIMO'NIOUS, *a.* [See *Alimony.*]
Nourishing; affording food. [*Little used.*]

AL'IMONY, *n.* [L. *alimonia*, of *alo*, to feed. See *Aliment.*]
An allowance made for the support of a woman, legally separated from her husband. The sum is fixed by the proper judge, and granted out of the husband's estate. *Blackstone.*

AL'IPED, *a.* [L. *ala*, wing, and *pes*, foot.]
Wing-footed; having the toes connected by a membrane, which serves as a wing.

AL'IPED, *n.* [*Supra.*]
An animal whose toes are connected by a membrane, and which thus serve for wings; a cheiropter; as, the bat. *Dumeril.*

AL'IQUANT, *a.* [L. *aliquantum*, a little.]
In *arithmetic*, an aliquant number or part is that which does not measure another number without a remainder. Thus 5 is an *aliquant* part of 16, for 3 times 5 is 15, leaving a remainder 1.

AL'IQUOT, *a.* [L.]
An aliquot part of a number or quantity is one which will measure it without a remainder. Thus 5 is the *aliquot* part of 15.

A'LISH, *a.* [From *ale.*]
Like ale; having the qualities of ale. *Mortimer.*

ALI'VE, *a.* [Sax. *gelifian*, to live, from *lifian*, to live. See *Life.*]
1. Having life, in opposition to dead; living; being in a state in which the organs perform their functions, and the fluids move, whether in animals or vegetables; as, the man or plant is *alive.*
2. In a state of action; unextinguished; undestroyed; unexpired; in force or operation; as, keep the process *alive.*
3. Cheerful; sprightly; lively; full of alacrity; as, the company were all *alive.*
4. Susceptible; easily impressed; having lively feelings, as when the mind is solicitous about some event; as, one is *alive* to whatever is interesting to a friend.
5. Exhibiting motion or moving bodies in great numbers.

The city was all *alive*, when the General entered.

6. In a *scriptural sense*, regenerated; born again.

For this my son was dead and is *alive*. Luke xv.

[*This adjective always follows the noun which it qualifies.*]

AL'KAHEST, *n.* [Arab.]
A universal dissolvent; a menstruum capable of dissolving every body, which Paracelsus and Van Helmont pretended they possessed. This pretense no longer imposes on the credulity of any man.
The word is sometimes used for fixed salts volatilized. *Encyc.*

ALKALES'CENCY, *n.* [See *Alkali.*]
A tendency to become alkaline; or a tendency to the properties of an alkali; or the state of a substance in which alkaline properties begin to be developed, or to be predominant. *Ure.*

ALKALES'CENT, *a.* Tending to the properties of an alkali; slightly alkaline.

AL'KALI, *n. plu.* Alkalies. [Ar. قلي kali, with the common prefix, the plant called glass wort, from its use in the manufacture of glass; or the ashes of the plant, which seems to be its primitive sense, for the verb signifies to fry.]
In *chimistry*, a term applied to all bodies which possess the following properties: 1. a caustic taste; 2. volatilizable by heat; 3. capability of combining with acids, and of destroying their acidity; 4. solubility in water, even when combined with carbonic acid; 5. capability of converting vegetable blues to green. *Thomson.*
The term was formerly confined to three substances: 1. potash or vegetable fixed alkali, generally obtained from the ashes of wood; 2. soda or mineral fixed alkali, which is found in the earth and procured from marine plants; and 3. ammonia or volatile alkali, an animal product.
Modern chimistry has discovered many new substances to which the term is now extended.
The alkalies were formerly considered as elementary substances; but it is now ascertained that they are all compounds.
The alkalies are used in the manufacture of glass and soap, in bleaching and in medicine.

AL'KALIFY, *v. t.* To form, or to convert into an alkali.

AL'KALIFY, *v. i.* To become an alkali.

ALKALIG'ENOUS, *a.* [*Alkali*, and γενναω, to generate.]
Producing or generating alkali.

ALKALIM'ETER, *n.* [*Alkali* and Gr. μετρον, measure.]
An instrument for ascertaining the strength of alkalies, or the quantity of alkali in potash and soda. *Ure.*

AL'KALINE, *a.* Having the properties of alkali.

ALKALIN'ITY, *n.* The quality which constitutes an alkali. *Thomson.*

AL'KALIZATE, *a.* Alkaline; impregnated with alkali. *Obs. Boyle. Newton.*

ALKALIZA'TION, *n.* The act of rendering alkaline by impregnating with an alkali.

AL'KALIZE, *v. t.* [and formerly *Alkalizate.*]
To make alkaline; to communicate the properties of an alkali to, by mixture.

AL'KANET, *n.* The plant bugloss. The root is used to impart a deep red color to oily substances, ointments, plasters, &c. *Encyc.*

ALKEKEN'GI, *n.* The winter cherry, a species of *physalis.* The plant bears a near resemblance to solanum, or nightshade. The berry is medicinal. *Chambers.*

ALKEN'NA, or ALHEN'NA, *n.* Egyptian privet, a species of Lawsonia. The pulverized leaves of this plant are much used by the eastern nations for staining their nails yellow. The powder, being wet, forms a paste, which is bound on the nails for a night, and the color thus given will last several weeks. *Encyc.*

ALKERM'ES, *n.* [Arab. See *Kermes.*]
In *pharmacy*, a compound cordial, in the form of a confection, derived from the kermes berries. Its other ingredients are said to be pippin-cider, rose water, sugar, ambergris, musk, cinnamon, aloes-wood, pearls, and leaf-gold. *Quincy. Chambers. Encyc.*

ALKER'VA, *n.* An Arabic name of the Palma Christi. *Quincy.*

AL'KORAN, *n.* [Arab. *al*, the, and *koran*, book. The book by way of eminence, as we say the *Bible.* See *Koran.* It is pronounced, I believe, by orientalists, *alkorawn.*]
The book which contains the Mohammedan doctrines of faith and practice. It was written by Mohammed, in the dialect of the Koreish, which is the purest Arabic; but the Arabian language has suffered such changes, since it was written, that the language of the Alkoran is not now intelligible to the Arabians themselves, without being learnt like other dead languages. *Niebuhr. Encyc.*

AL'KORANIST, *n.* One who adheres strictly to the letter of the Alkoran, rejecting all comments. The Persians are generally Alkoranists; the Turks, Arabs, and Tartars admit a multitude of traditions.

ALKUS'SA, *n.* A fish of the Silurus kind, with one beard only under the chin. *Dict. of Nat. Hist.*

ALL, *a. awl.* [Sax. *eal;* Dan. *al;* G. *all;* Sw. *all;* W. *oll* or *holl;* Arm. *oll;* Ir. *uile;* Gr. ολος; Shemitic כל, from כלה calah, to be ended or completed, to perfect. The Welsh retains the first radical letter. This is radically the same word as *heal;* for in Sw. *hel*, and in Dan. *hele*, signify *all*, and these words are from the root of *heal.* See *Call, Heal* and *Whole.*]

1. Every one, or the whole number of particulars.
2. The whole quantity, extent, duration, amount, quality, or degree; as, *all* the wheat; *all* the land; *all* the year; *all* the strength. This word signifies then, the whole or entire thing, or all the parts or particulars which compose it. It always *precedes* the definitive adjectives, *the, my, thy, his, our, your, their;* as, *all* the cattle; *all* my labor; *all* thy goods; *all* his wealth; *all* our families; *all* your citizens; *all* their property.

This word, not only in popular language, but in the scriptures, often signifies, indefinitely, a large portion or number, or a great part. Thus, *all* the cattle in Egypt died; *all* Judea and *all* the region round about Jordan; *all* men held John as a prophet; are not to be understood in a literal sense, but as including a large part or very great numbers.

This word is prefixed to many other words, to enlarge their signification; as *already, always, all-prevailing.*

ALL, *adv.* Wholly; completely; entirely; as *all* along; *all* bedewed; *all* over; my friend is *all* for amusement; I love my father *all.* In the ancient phrases, *all* too dear, *all* so long, this word retains its appropriate sense; as, "he thought them sixpence *all* too dear," that is, he thought them too dear by the sum of sixpence. In the sense of *although*, as "*all* were it as the rest," and in the sense of *just*, or *at the moment*, as "*all* as his straying flock he fed," it is obsolete, or restricted to poetry.

It is all one is a phrase equivalent to *the same thing in effect;* that is, it is *wholly* the same thing.

All the better is equivalent to *wholly* the better; that is, better by the whole difference.

ALL, *n.* The whole number; as, *all* have not the same disposition; that is, all men.
2. The whole; the entire thing; the aggregate amount; as, our *all* is at stake.

> And Laban said, *all* that thou seest is mine. Gen. xxxi.

This adjective is much used as a noun, and applied to persons or things.

All in all is a phrase which signifies, *all* things to a person, or every thing desired.

> Thou shalt be *all in all*, and I in thee,
> Forever. *Milton.*

When the words, *and all*, close an enumeration of particulars, the word *all* is either intensive, or is added as a general term to express what is not enumerated; as, a tree fell, nest, eagles *and all.* *L'Estrange.*

At all is a phrase much used by way of enforcement or emphasis, usually in negative or interrogative sentences. He has no ambition *at all;* that is, *not in the least degree.* Has he any property *at all?*

All and some, in Spenser, Mason interprets, *one and all.* But from Lye's Saxon Dictionary, it appears that the phrase is a corruption of the Sax. *ealle æt somne*, all together, all at once, from *somne*, together, at once. *See Lye under Somne.*

All in the wind, in seamen's language, is a phrase denoting that the sails are parallel with the course of the wind, so as to shake. *Mar. Dict.*

All is well is a watchman's phrase, expressing a state of safety.

All, in composition, enlarges the meaning, or adds force to a word; and it is generally more emphatical than *most.* In some instances, *all* is incorporated into words, as in *almighty, already, always;* but in most instances, it is an adjective prefixed to other words, but separated by a hyphen.

ALL-ABAN'DONED, *a.* Abandoned by all. *Skelton.*

ALL-ABHOR'RED, *a.* Detested by all. *Shak.*

ALL-ACCOM'PLISHED, *a.* Fully accomplished; whose education is highly finished or complete.

ALL-ADMI'RING, *a.* Wholly admiring. *Shak.*

ALL-ADVI'SED, *a.* Advised by all. *Warburton.*

ALL-APPRÖVED, *a.* Approved by all. *More.*

ALL-ATO'NING, *a.* Atoning for all; making complete atonement. *Dryden.*

ALL-BEA'RING, *a.* Producing every thing; omniparous. *Marston.*

ALL-BEAU'TEOUS, *a.* Perfectly beautiful. *Pope.*

ALL-BEHO'LDING, *a.* Beholding or seeing all things. *Drayton.*

ALL-BL'ASTING, *a.* Blasting all; defaming or destroying all. *Marston.*

ALL-BOUN'TEOUS, } *a.* Perfectly bountiful; of infinite bounty.
ALL-BOUN'TIFUL, }

ALL-CHA'NGING, *a.* Perpetually changing. *Shak.*

ALL-CHEE'RING, *a.* That cheers all; that gives gayety or cheerfulness to all. *Shak.*

ALL-COMM'ANDING, *a.* Having command or sovereignty over all. *Raleigh.*

ALL-COMPLY'ING, *a.* Complying in every respect. *More.*

ALL-COMPO'SING, *a.* That makes all tranquil or peaceful. *Crashaw.*

ALL-COMPREHEN'SIVE, *a.* Comprehending all things. *Glanville.*

ALL-CONCE'ALING, *a.* Hiding or concealing all. *Spenser.*

ALL-CON'QUERING, *a.* That subdues all. *Milton.*

ALL-CON'SCIOUS, *a.* Conscious of all; all-knowing.

ALL-CONSTRA'INING, *a.* Constraining all. *Drayton.*

ALL-CONSU'MING, *a.* That consumes or devours all. *Pope.*

ALL-DA'RING, *a.* Daring to attempt every thing. *Jonson.*

ALL-DESTROY'ING, *a.* Destroying every thing. *Fanshaw.*

ALL-DEV'ASTATING, *a.* Wasting every thing.

ALL-DEVOUR'ING, *a.* Eating or consuming all. *Pope.*

ALL-DIM'MING, *a.* Obscuring every thing. *Marston.*

ALL-DISCÖV'ERING, *a.* Discovering or disclosing every thing. *More.*

ALL-DISGRA'CED, *a.* Completely disgraced. *Shak.*

ALL-DISPENS'ING, *a.* Dispensing all things; affording dispensation or permission. *Milton. Dryden.*

ALL-DIVI'NE, *a.* Supremely excellent. *Howell.*

ALL-DIVI'NING, *a.* Foretelling all things. *Fanshaw.*

ALL-DREAD'ED, *a.* Dreaded by all. *Shak.*

ALL-EFFI''CIENT, *a.* Of perfect or unlimited efficacy or efficiency.

ALL-EL'OQUENT, *a.* Eloquent in the highest degree. *Pope.*

ALL-EMBRA'CING, *a.* Embracing all things. *Crashaw.*

ALL-END'ING, *a.* Putting an end to all things. *Shak.*

ALL-ENLI'GHTENING, *a.* Enlightening all things. *Cotton.*

ALL-ENRA'GED, *a.* Highly enraged. *Hall.*

ALL-FLA'MING, *a.* Flaming in all directions. *Beaumont.*

ALL-FOOL'S-DAY, *n.* The first of April.

ALL-FORGIV'ING, *a.* Forgiving or pardoning all. *Dryden.*

ALL-FOURS, *n.* [*all* and *four.*]
A game at cards, played by two or four persons; so called from the possession of the four honors, by one person, who is then said to have *all fours.*

To go on all fours is to move or walk on four legs, or on the two legs and two arms.

ALL-GIV'ER, *n.* The giver of all things. *Milton.*

ALL-GOOD', *a.* Completely good. *Dryden.*

ALL-GOOD', *n.* The popular name of the

plant Good-Henry, or English Mercury, *Chenopodium bonus Henricus.*

ALL-GRA'CIOUS, *a.* Perfectly gracious.

ALL-GUI'DING, *a.* Guiding or conducting all things. *Sandys.*

ALL-HA'IL, *ex.* [*all* and Sax. *hæl*, health.] All health; a phrase of salutation, expressing a wish of *all health* or safety to the person addressed.

ALL-HAL'LOW, *or* ALL-HALLOWS, *n.* All Saints day, the first of November; a feast dedicated to all the saints in general.

ALL-HALLOW-TIDE, *n.* [*tid*, in Sax., is *time.*] The time near All Saints, or November first.

ALL-HAP'PY, *a.* Completely happy.

ALL-HE'AL, *n.* The popular name of several plants.

ALL-HE'ALING, *a.* Healing all things. *Selden.*

ALL-HELP'ING, *a.* Assisting all. *Selden.*

ALL-HI'DING, *a.* Concealing all things. *Shak.*

ALL-HON'ORED, *a.* Honored by all. *Shak.*

ALL-HURT'ING, *a.* Hurting all things. *Shak.*

ALL-I'DOLIZING, *a.* Worshiping any thing. *Crashaw.*

ALL-IM'ITATING, *a.* Imitating every thing. *More.*

ALL-INFORM'ING, *a.* Actuating all by vital powers. *Sandys.*

ALL-IN'TERESTING, *a.* Interesting in the highest degree.

ALL-INTER'PRETING, *a.* Explaining all things. *Milton.*

ALL-JUDǴING, *a.* Judging all; possessing the sovereign right of judging. *Rowe.*

ALL-JUST', *a.* Perfectly just.

ALL-KI'ND, *a.* Perfectly kind or benevolent.

ALL-KNO'WING, *a.* Having all knowledge; omniscient. *Atterbury.*

ALL-LI'CENSED, *a.* Licensed to every thing. *Shak.*

ALL-LŎV'ING, *a.* Of infinite love. *More.*

ALL-MA'KING, *a.* Making or creating all; omnific. *Dryden.*

ALL-MATU'RING, *a.* Maturing all things. *Dryden.*

ALL-MER'CIFUL, *a* Of perfect mercy or compassion.

ALL-MUR'DERING, *a.* Killing or destroying every thing. *Fanshaw.*

ALL-OBE'DIENT, *a.* Entirely obedient. *Crashaw.*

ALL-OBEY'ING, *a.* [See *Obey.*] Receiving obedience from all. *Shak.*

ALL-OBLIV'IOUS, *a.* Causing total oblivion. *Shak.*

ALL-OBSCU'RING, *a.* Obscuring every thing. *King.*

ALL-PA'TIENT, *a.* Enduring every thing without murmurs. *Mitford.*

ALL-PEN'ETRATING, *a.* Penetrating every thing. *Stafford.*

ALL-PER'FECT, *a.* Completely perfect; having all perfection.

ALL-PER'FECTNESS, *n.* The perfection of the whole; entire perfection. *More.*

ALL-PIER'CING, *a.* Piercing every thing. *Marston.*

ALL-POW'ERFUL, *a.* Almighty; omnipotent. *Swift.*

ALL-PRA'ISED, *a.* Praised by all. *Shak.*

ALL-RU'LING, *a.* Governing all things. *Milton.*

ALL-SAGA'CIOUS, *a.* Having all sagacity; of perfect discernment.

ALL-SAINTS-DAY, *n.* The first day of November, called also *all hallows*; a feast in honor of all the saints.

ALL-SANC'TIFYING, *a.* Sanctifying the whole. *West.*

ALL-SA'VING, *a.* Saving all. *Selden.*

ALL-SEARCH'ING, *a.* Pervading and seaching every thing. *South.*

ALL-SEE'ING, *a.* Seeing every thing. *Dryden.*

ALL-SEE'R, *n.* One that sees every thing. *Shak.*

ALL-SHA'KING, *a.* Shaking all things. *Shak.*

ALL-SHUN'NED, *a.* Shunned by all. *Shak.*

ALL-SOULS-DAY, *n.* The second day of November; a feast or solemnity held by the church of Rome, to supplicate for the souls of the faithful deceased.

ALL'-SPICE, *n.* The berry of the pimento, a tree of the West Indies; a spice of a mildly pungent taste, and agreeably aromatic.

ALL-SUFFI''CIENCY, *n.* Complete or infinite ability. *Hall.*

ALL-SUFFI''CIENT, *a.* Sufficient to every thing; infinitely able. *Hooker.*

ALL-SUFFI''CIENT, *n.* The all-sufficient Being; God. *Whitlock.*

ALL-SURROUND'ING, *a.* Encompassing the whole.

ALL-SURVEY'ING, *n.* [See *Survey.*] Surveying every thing. *Sandys.*

ALL-SUSTA'INING, *a.* Upholding all things. *Beaumont.*

ALL-TELL'ING, *a.* Telling or divulging every thing. *Shak.*

ALL-TRI'UMPHING, *a.* Triumphant every where or over all. *Jonson.*

ALL-WATCH'ED, *a.* Watched throughout. *Shak.*

ALL-WI'SE, *a.* Possessed of infinite wisdom. *South.*

ALL-WIT'TED, *a.* Having all kinds of wit. *Jonson.*

ALL-WŎR'SHIPED, *a.* Worshiped or adored by all. *Milton.*

ALL-WŎR'THY, *a.* Of infinite worth; of the highest worth.

AL'LAGITE, *n.* A mineral, of a brown or green color, massive, with a flat conchoidal fracture, and nearly opake, found in the Hartz near Elbingerode. *Phillips.*

AL'LANITE, *n.* A mineral named from Mr. Allan, of Edinburgh, who first recognized it as a distinct species. It is massive, of a brownish black color, and conchoidal fracture. A siliceous oxyd of cerium. *Cleaveland. Jameson. Ure.*

ALLANTOIS' or ALLANTOID', *n.* [Gr. αλλας, a sausage, and ειδος, form.] A thin membrane, situated between the chorion and amnios in quadrupeds, and forming one of the membranes which invest the fetus in those animals. *Ed. Encyc.*

AL'LATRATE, *v. t.* [L. *allatro.*] To bark, as a dog. [*Not used.*] *Stubbes.*

ALLA'Y, *v. t.* [Sax. *alecgan*, *alegan*, to lay, to set, to depress, *lecgan*, to lay, to cast or strike down; G. *legen*, D. *leggen*, to lay; Gr. ληγω. The Fr. *allier*, to alloy, Sp. *ligar*, seems to be directly from the L. *ligo*, to bind; but this may be the same word differently applied, that is, to set, to fix, to make fast, to unite. *Allay* and *alloy* were formerly used indifferently; but I have recognized an entire distinction between them, applying *alloy* to metals.]

1. To make quiet; to pacify, or appease; as, to *allay* the tumult of the passions, or to *allay* civil commotions.

2. To abate, mitigate, subdue or destroy; as, to *allay* grief or pain.

Females, who soften and *allay* the bitterness of adversity. *Rawle.*

3. To obtund or repress as acrimony; as, to *allay* the acrid qualities of a substance.

4. *Formerly*, to reduce the purity of; as, to *allay* metals. But, in this sense, *alloy* is now exclusively used. [See *Alloy.*]

ALLA'Y, *n.* Formerly, a baser metal mixed with a finer; but in this sense it is now written *alloy, which see.*

2. That which allays, or abates the predominant qualities; as, the *allay* of colors. *Newton.*

Also, abatement; diminution by means of some mixture; as, joy without *allay.* But *alloy* is now more generally used.

ALLA'YED, *pp.* Layed at rest; quieted; tranquilized; abated; [reduced by mixture. *Obs.*]

ALLA'YER, *n.* He, or that, which allays.

ALLA'YING, *ppr.* Quieting; reducing to tranquillity; abating; [reducing by mixture. *Obs.*]

ALLA'YMENT, *n.* The act of quieting, or a state of tranquillity; a state of rest after disturbance; abatement; ease; as, the *allayment* of grief. *Shak.*

AL'LE, *n. ally.* The little auk, or black and white diver.

ALLEC'TIVE, *a.* Alluring. [*Not used.*] *Chaucer.*

ALLEC'TIVE, *n.* Allurement. [*Not used.*] *Eliot.*

ALLEDǴE' *v. t.* [L. *allego*, *ad* and *lego*, to send; Fr. *alleguer*; Sp. *alegar*; Port. *allegar*; It. *allegare.* This is only a modified application of the Eng. *lay*; L. *loco*, to set, or throw. See Class L g.]

1. To declare; to affirm; to assert; to pronounce with positiveness; as, to *alledge* a fact.

2. To produce as an argument, plea or excuse; to cite or quote; as, to *alledge* the authority of a judge.

ALLEDǴ'ED, *pp.* Affirmed; asserted, whether as a charge or a plea.

ALLEDǴ'ER, *n.* One who affirms or declares.

ALLEDǴ'ING, *ppr.* Asserting; averring; declaring.

ALLEGA'TION, *n.* Affirmation; positive assertion or declaration.

2. That which is affirmed or asserted; that which is offered as a plea, excuse or justification.

3. In *ecclesiastical courts*, a formal complaint, or declaration of charges.

ALLEǴE. [See *Alledge.*]

ALLEǴ'EABLE, *a.* That may be alledged. [*Not used.*] *Brown.*

ALLE'ǴEAS, or A LLE'ǴIAS, *n.* A stuff manufactured in the East Indies, of two kinds, one of cotton, the other of various plants which are spun like flax. *Encyc.*

ALLEĠ'EMENT, *n.* Allegation. [*Not in use.*]

ALLEGHA'NEAN, *a.* Pertaining to the mountains called Alleghany, or Alleghenny.

ALLEGHA'NY, *n.* The chief ridge of the great chains of mountains which run from N. East to S. West through the middle and southern states of North America; but, more appropriately, the main or unbroken ridge, which casts all the waters on one side to the east, and on the other side to the west. This ridge runs from Pennsylvania to Georgia, and chains extend through the U. States.

This name is given also to the river Ohio, above its confluence with the Monongahela; but improperly, as the Indian name of the river to its source is Ohio.

ALLE'ĠIANCE, *n.* [Old Fr. from L. *alligo*, of *ad* and *ligo*, to bind. See *Liege* and *League.*]

The tie or obligation of a subject to his Prince or government; the duty of fidelity to a king, government or state. Every native or citizen owes *allegiance* to the government under which he is born. This is called *natural* or *implied* allegiance, which arises from the connection of a person with the society in which he is born, and his duty to be a faithful subject, independent of any express promise. *Express* allegiance, is that obligation which proceeds from an express promise, or oath of fidelity.

Local or *temporary* allegiance is due from an alien to the government or state in which he resides. *Blackstone.*

ALLE'ĠIANT, *a.* Loyal. [*Not used.*] *Shak.*

ALLEGOR'IĈ, ALLEGOR'IĈAL, } *a.* In the manner of allegory; figurative; describing by resemblances.

ALLEGOR'IĈALLY, *adv.* In a figurative manner; by way of allegory.

ALLEGOR'IĈALNESS, *n.* The quality of being allegorical.

AL'LEGORIZE, *v. t.* To form an allegory; to turn into allegory; as, to *allegorize* the history of a people. *Campbell.*

2. To understand in an allegorical sense; as, when a passage in a writer may be understood literally or figuratively, he who gives it a figurative sense is said to *allegorize* it.

AL'LEGORIZE, *v. i.* To use allegory; as, a man may *allegorize*, to please his fancy.

AL'LEGORIZED, *pp.* Turned into allegory, or understood allegorically.

AL'LEGORIZING, *ppr.* Turning into allegory, or understanding in an allegorical sense.

AL'LEGORY, *n.* [Gr. αλληγορια, of αλλος, other, and αγορευω, to speak, from αγορα, a forum, an oration.]

A figurative sentence or discourse, in which the principal subject is described by another subject resembling it in its properties and circumstances. The principal subject is thus kept out of view, and we are left to collect the intentions of the writer or speaker, by the resemblance of the secondary to the primary subject. Allegory is in words what hieroglyphics are in painting. We have a fine example of an allegory in the eightieth psalm, in which God's chosen people are represented by a vineyard. The distinction in scripture between a parable and an allegory, is said to be that a parable is a *supposed* history, and an allegory, a figurative description of *real* facts. An allegory is called a continued metaphor. The following line in Virgil is an example of an allegory.

Claudite jam rivos, pueri, sat prata biberunt.

Stop the currents, young men, the meadows have drank sufficiently; that is, let your music cease, our ears have been sufficiently delighted. *Encyc.*

ALLEGRET'TO, [from *allegro*,] denotes, *in music*, a movement or time quicker than *andante*, but not so quick as *allegro*. *Rousseau. Busby.*

ALLE'GRO. [It. merry, cheerful; It. *leggiére*; Sp. *ligero*; Fr. *leger*, light, nimble. See *Light.*]

In *music*, a word denoting a brisk movement; a sprightly part or strain; the quickest except *presto*. *Piu allegro* is a still quicker movement. *Rousseau. Encyc.*

ALLELU'IAH, *n.* [Heb. הללו־יה, praise to Jah.]

Praise to Jehovah; a word used to denote pious joy and exultation, chiefly in hymns and anthems. The Greeks retained the word in their Ελελευ Ιη, praise to Io; probably a corruption of Jah. The Romans retained the latter word in their *Io triumphe.*

ALLEMAND', *n.* A slow air in common time, or grave, solemn music, with a slow movement. Also a brisk dance, or a figure in dancing. *Dict. of Music.*

ALLEMAN'NIĈ, *a.* Belonging to the *Alemanni*, ancient Germans, and to *Alemannia*, their country. The word is generally supposed to be composed of *all* and *manni*, all men. Cluver, p. 68. This is probably an error. The word is more probably composed of the Celtic *all*, other, the root of Latin *alius* and *man*, place; one of another place, a stranger. The Welsh *allman* is thus rendered, and this seems to be the original word. *Owen, Welsh Dict.*

The name, *Alemanni*, seems to have been first given to the Germans who invaded Gaul in the reign of Augustus. *Cluver, Germ. Antiq.*

ALLER'ION, *n.* In *heraldry*, an eagle without beak or feet, with expanded wings; denoting Imperialists vanquished and disarmed. *Encyc.*

ALLEVEU'R, *n.* A small Swedish coin, value about a cent. *Encyc.*

ALLE'VIATE, *v. t.* [Low L. *allevio*; *ad* and *levo*, to raise, *levis*, light; Fr. *lever*; It. *levare*, to raise; Sp. *llevar*, to carry, *levantar*, to raise, and *levante*, a rising, and the eastern coasts of the Mediterranean, the east, so called from the rising of the sun, like *oriental*, from *orior*, to rise; Sax. *hlifian*, to be eminent. See *Lift.*]

1. To make light; but always in a figurative sense, as it is not applied to material objects. To remove in part; to lessen, mitigate, or make easier to be endured; applied to evils; as, to *alleviate* sorrow, pain, care, punishment, a burden, &c.; opposed to *aggravate.*

2. To make less by representation; to lessen the magnitude or criminality; to extenuate; applied to moral conduct; as, to *alleviate* an offense. [*This sense of the word is rare.*]

ALLE'VIATED, *pp.* Made lighter; mitigated; eased; extenuated.

ALLE'VIATING, *ppr.* Making lighter, or more tolerable; extenuating.

ALLEVIA'TION, *n.* The act of lightening, allaying, or extenuating; a lessening or mitigation.

2. That which lessens, mitigates or makes more tolerable; as, the sympathy of a friend is an *alleviation* of grief.

I have not wanted such *alleviations* of life, as friendship could supply. Dr. Johnson's letter to Mr. Hector. *Boswell.*

This use of alleviation is hardly legitimate without supplying some word expressing *evil*, as *trouble*, *sorrow*, &c.

Without such *alleviations* of the cares or troubles of life.

ALLE'VIATIVE, *n.* That which mitigates. [*Not in use.*]

AL'LEY, *n.* *al'ly.* [Fr. *allée*, a passage, from *aller* to go; Ir. *alladh*. Literally, a passing or going.]

1. A walk in a garden; a narrow passage.

2. A narrow passage or way in a city, as distinct from a public street.

3. A place in London where stocks are bought and sold. *Ash.*

ALLIA'CEOUS, *a.* [L. *allium*, garlic.]

Pertaining to allium, or garlic; having the properties of garlic. *Barton.*

ALLI'ANCE, *n.* [Fr. *alliance*, from *allier*, *lier*, to tie or unite, from L. *ligo*, Gr. λυγοω; Sp. *alianza*; Port. *aliança*; It. *alleanza*; from the same root as *liege*, *league*, *allegiance*; class L. g.]

1. The relation or union between families, contracted by marriage. *Dryden.*

2. The union between nations, contracted by compact, treaty or league.

3. The treaty, league, or compact, which is the instrument of confederacy; sometimes perhaps the act of confederating.

4. Any union or connection of interests between persons, families, states or corporations; as, an *alliance* between church and state.

5. The persons or parties allied; as, men or states may secure any *alliances* in their power. *Addison.*

ALLI'ANT, *n.* An ally. [*Not used.*] *Wotton.*

ALLI''CIENCY, *n.* [Lat. *allicio*, *ad* and *lacio*; G. *locken*; D. *lokken*; Sw. *locka*; Dan. *lokker*; L. *allecto*, *elicio*. Class L g.]

The power of attracting any thing; attraction; magnetism. [*Little used.*] *Glanville.*

ALLI''CIENT, *n.* That which attracts. [*Not used.*] *Robinson.*

ALLI'ED, *pp.* Connected by marriage, treaty or similitude. [See *Ally.*]

AL'LIGATE, *v. t.* [L. *alligo*, *ad* and *ligo*, to bind. See *Allegiance*, *Liege*, *League.*]

To tie together; to unite by some tie.

ALLIGA'TION, *n.* The act of tying together; the state of being tied. [*Little used.*]

2. A rule of arithmetic, for finding the price or value of compounds consisting of ingredients of different values. Thus if a quantity of sugar, worth eight cents the pound, and another quantity worth ten cents, are mixed, the question to be solved by *alliga-*

tion is, what is the value of the mixture by the pound. Alligation is of two kinds, *medial* and *alternate*; *medial*, when the rate of a mixture is sought from the rates and quantities of the simples; *alternate*, when the quantities of the simples are sought from the rates of the simples, and the rate of the mixture.

ALLIGA'TOR, *n.* [Properly *allagarto*, from the Spanish and Portuguese *lagarto*, a lizard; L. *lacerta*. The Latin word seems to be connected with *lacertus*, the arm; and the animal may be named from the resemblance of his legs to arms.]

The American crocodile. This animal is of the lizard genus, having a long naked body, four feet, with five toes on the fore feet, and four on the hind, armed with claws, and a serrated tail. The mouth is very large, and furnished with sharp teeth; the skin is brown, tough, and, on the sides, covered with tubercles. The largest of these animals grow to the length of seventeen or eighteen feet. They live in and about the rivers in warm climates, eat fish, and sometimes catch hogs, on the shore, or dogs which are swimming. In winter, they burrow in the earth, which they enter under water and work upwards, lying torpid till spring. The female lays a great number of eggs, which are deposited in the sand, and left to be hatched by the heat of the sun. *Encyc.*

ALLIGA'TOR-PEAR, *n.* A West India fruit, resembling a pear in shape, from one to two pounds in weight, (*Laurus Persea*, Linne.) It contains within its rind a yellow butyraceous substance, which, when the fruit is perfectly ripe, constitutes an agreeable food. *Encyc.*

ALLIG'ATURE, *n.* See *Ligature*, which is the word in use.

ALLI'NEMENT, *n.* [Fr. *alignement*, a row, a squaring, from *ligne*, line; L. *linea*.]

A reducing to a line or to a square; a state of being in squares, in a line, or on a level; a line; a row. *Asiat. Res. Columbiad.*

AL'LIOTH, *n.* A star in the tail of the great bear, much used for finding the latitude at sea. *Encyc.*

ALLISION, *n.* *allizh'un.* [L. *allido*, to dash or strike against, of *ad* and *lædo*, to hurt by striking; Ir. *leas*, a sore; D. *leed*, a hurt; D. *beleedigen*; Ger. *beleidigen*, to hurt; Fr. *blesser*, to hurt. *Lædo* forms its participle *læsus*. Class. L d. L s.]

A striking against; as, the *allision* of the sea against the shore. *Woodward.*

ALLITERA'TION, *n.* [L. *ad* and *litera*, a letter.

The repetition of the same letter at the beginning of two or more words immediately succeeding each other, or at short intervals; as *f* and *g* in the following line:

Fields ever fresh, and groves forever green.

ALLIT'ERATIVE, *a.* Pertaining to, or consisting in, alliteration.

ALLOCA'TION, *n.* [L. *ad* and *locatio*, a placing, from *locus*, place. See *Local.*]

The act of putting one thing to another; hence its usual sense is the admission of an article of account, or an *allowance* made upon an account; a term used in the English Exchequer. [See *Allow.*] *Chambers. Johnson.*

AL'LOCHROITE, *n.* An amorphous, massive, opake mineral, of a grayish, yellowish or reddish color, found in Norway; considered as a variety of garnet. Its name is said to be given to it, as expressive of its changes of color before the blowpipe; Gr. αλλος, other, and χροια, color. *Cleaveland.*

ALLOCU'TION, *n.* [L. *allocutio*, of *ad* and *loquor*, to speak. See *Eloquence.*]

1. The act or manner of speaking to, or of addressing in words.

2. An address; a formal address; as, of a General to his troops; a Roman term, rarely used in English. *Addison. Encyc.*

ALLO'DIAL, *a.* Pertaining to allodium; freehold; free of rent or service; held independent of a lord paramount; opposed to *feudal*. *Blackstone.*

ALLODIAN is sometimes used, but is not well authorized. *Cowel.*

ALLO'DIUM, *n.* [Fr. *alleu*, contr. word. According to O'Brien, in his Focaloir, or Dictionary of the Irish, this word is the Celtic *allod*, ancient. According to Pontoppidan, it is composed of *all* and *odh*, all-property, or whole estate.]

Freehold estate; land which is the absolute property of the owner; real estate held in absolute independence, without being subject to any rent, service, or acknowledgment to a superior. It is thus opposed to *feud*. In England, there is no allodial land, all land being held of the king; but in the United States, most lands are allodial.

ALLONGE', *n.* *allunj'.* [Fr. *allonger*, to lengthen, to thrust, *allongé*, lengthened, of *ad* and *long*.]

1. A pass with a sword; a thrust made by stepping forward and extending the arm; a term used in fencing, often contracted into *lunge*.

2. A long rein, when a horse is trotted in the hand. *Johnson.*

ALLOO', *v. t.* or *i.* To incite dogs by a call. *Phillips.*

[See the correct word, *Halloo.*]

AL'LOPHANE, *n.* [Gr. αλλος, other, and φαινω, to appear.]

A mineral of a blue, and sometimes of a green or brown color, which occurs massive, or in imitative shapes. It gelatinizes in acids. *Ure.*

Allophane is a variety of clay, occurring in amorphous, botryoidal or reniform masses. *Cleaveland.*

ALLOT', *v. t.* [of *ad* and *lot*; Sax. *hlot.* See *Lot.*]

1. To divide or distribute by lot.

2. To distribute, or parcel out in parts or portions; or to distribute a share to each individual concerned.

3. To grant, as a portion; to give, assign or appoint in general.

Let every man be contented with that which providence *allots* to him.

ALLOT'MENT, *n.* That which is allotted; a share, part, or portion granted or distributed; that which is assigned by lot, or by the act of God.

2. A part, portion or place appropriated.

In a field, there is an *allotment* for olives. *Broome.*

ALLOT'TED, *pp.* Distributed by lot; granted; assigned.

ALLOT'TERY is used by Shakespeare for *allotment*; but is not authorized by usage.

ALLOT'TING, *ppr.* Distributing by lot; giving as portions; assigning.

ALLOW', *v. t.* [Fr. *allouer*, from *louer*; L. *loco*, to *lay*, set, place; W. *llogi*; Norm. *alluer*. See *Lay*. Class. L g.]

1. To grant, give or yield; as, to *allow* a servant his liberty; to *allow* a pension.

2. To admit; as, to *allow* the truth of a proposition; to *allow* a claim.

3. To admit; to own or acknowledge; as, to *allow* the right of the President to displace officers.

4. To approve, justify or sanction.

Ye *allow* the deeds of your fathers. Luke xi. Rom. vii.

5. To afford, or grant as a compensation; as, to *allow* a dollar a day for wages.

6. To abate or deduct; as, to *allow* a sum for tare or leakage.

7. To permit; to grant license to; as, to *allow* a son to be absent.

ALLOW'ABLE, *a.* That may be permitted as lawful, or admitted as true and proper; not forbid; not unlawful or improper; as, a certain degree of freedom is *allowable* among friends.

ALLOW'ABLENESS, *n.* The quality of being allowable; lawfulness; exemption from prohibition, or impropriety. *South.*

ALLOW'ABLY, *adv.* In an allowable manner; with propriety. *Lowth.*

ALLOW'ANCE, *n.* The act of allowing or admitting.

2. Permission; license; approbation; sanction; usually slight approbation. *Locke. Shak.*

3. Admission; assent to a fact or state of things; a granting. *Hooker.*

4. Freedom from restraint; indulgence.

5. That which is allowed; a portion appointed; a stated quantity, as of food or drink; hence, in *seamen's language*, a limited quantity of meat and drink, when provisions fall short.

6. Abatement; deduction; as, to make an *allowance* for the inexperience of youth.

7. Established character; reputation; as, a pilot of approved *allowance*. *Obs. Shak.*

ALLOW'ANCE, *v. t.* To put upon allowance; to restrain or limit to a certain quantity of provisions or drink.

Distress compelled the captain of the ship to *allowance* his crew.

ALLOW'ED, *pp.* Granted; permitted; assented to; admitted; approved; indulged; appointed; abated.

ALLOW'ING, *ppr.* Granting; permitting; admitting; approving; indulging; deducting.

ALLOY', *v. t.* [Fr. *allier*, to unite or mix; L. *alligo*, *ad* and *ligo*, to bind; Gr. λυγοω; Sp. *ligar*, to tie or bind, to *alloy* or mix base metals with gold or silver, to league or confederate; Port. *id.*; It. *legare*. We observe that *alloy* and *league*, *alliance*, *ally*, are from the same root. Class L g.]

1. To reduce the purity of a metal, by mixing with it a portion of one less valuable; as, to *alloy* gold with silver, or silver with copper.

2. To mix metals. *Lavoisier.*

3. To reduce or abate by mixture; as, to *alloy* pleasure with misfortunes.

ALLOY', *n.* A baser metal mixed with a finer.

2. The mixture of different metals; any me-

tallic compound; this is its common signification in chimistry.

3. Evil mixed with good; as, no happiness is without *alloy*.

ALLOY'AGE, *n.* [Fr. *alliage*, from *allier*.]

1. The act of alloying metals, or the mixture of a baser metal with a finer, to reduce its purity; the act of mixing metals.

2. The mixture of different metals. *Lavoisier.*

ALLOY'ED, *pp.* Mixed; reduced in purity; debased; abated by foreign mixture.

ALLOY'ING, *ppr.* Mixing a baser metal with a finer, to reduce its purity; abating by foreign mixture.

ẠLL'SPICE. [See under the compounds of *all*.]

ALLU'DE, *v. i.* [L. *alludo*, to smile upon or make sport with, of *ad* and *ludo*, to play; Sp. Port. *aludir*; It. *alludere*. Class L d.]

To refer to something not directly mentioned; to have reference; to hint at by remote suggestions; as, that story *alludes* to a recent transaction.

ALLU'DING, *ppr.* Having reference; hinting at.

ALLU'MINOR, *n.* [Fr. *allumer*, to light. See *Limner*.]

One who colors or paints upon paper or parchment, giving light and ornament to letters and figures. *Cowel. Encyc.*

This is now written *limner*.

ALLU'RE, *v. t.* [Fr. *leurrer*, to decoy, from *leurre*, a lure.]

To attempt to draw to; to tempt by the offer of some good, real or apparent; to invite by something flattering or acceptable; as, rewards *allure* men to brave danger. Sometimes used in a bad sense, to *allure* to evil; but in this sense *entice* is more common. In Hosea, ii. 14, *allure* is used in its genuine sense; in 2 Peter, ii. 18, in the sense of *entice*.

ALLU'RED, *pp.* Tempted; drawn, or invited, by something that appears desirable.

ALLU'REMENT, *n.* That which allures; any real or apparent good held forth, or operating, as a motive to action; temptation; enticement; as, the *allurements* of pleasure, or of honor.

ALLU'RER, *n.* He, or that, which allures.

ALLU'RING, *ppr.* Drawing; tempting; inviting by some real or apparent good.

2. *a.* Inviting; having the quality of attracting or tempting.

ALLU'RINGLY, *adv.* In an alluring manner; enticingly.

ALLU'RINGNESS, *n.* The quality of alluring or tempting by the prospect of some good. [*Rarely used.*]

ALLU'SION, *n.* *allúzhun.* [Fr. from *allusio*, Low L. See *Allude*.]

A reference to something not explicitly mentioned; a hint; a suggestion, by which something is applied or understood to belong to that which is not mentioned, by means of some similitude which is perceived between them. *Burnet.*

ALLU'SIVE, *a.* Having reference to something not fully expressed. *South.*

ALLU'SIVELY, *adv.* By way of allusion; by implication, remote suggestion or insinuation. *Hammond.*

ALLU'SIVENESS, *n.* The quality of being allusive. [*Rarely used.*]

ALLU'VIAL, *a.* [See *Alluvion*.]

1. Pertaining to alluvion; added to land by the wash of water.

2. Washed ashore or down a stream; formed by a current of water; as, *alluvial* ores; *alluvial* soil. *Kirwan.*

ALLU'VION, } *n.* [L. *alluvio*, of *ad* and
ALLU'VIUM, } *lavo* or *luo*, *alluo*, to wash. See *Lave*.]

1. The insensible increase of earth on a shore, or bank of a river, by the force of water, as by a current or by waves. The owner of the land thus augmented has a right to the alluvial earth.

2. A gradual washing or carrying of earth or other substances to a shore or bank; the earth thus added.

3. The mass of substances collected by means of the action of water.

In this *alluvium* was found the entire skeleton of a whale. *Buckland.*

ALLU'VIOUS, *a.* The same as *alluvial*, and less frequently used.

ALLY', *v. t.* [Fr. *allier*; reciprocal verb, *s'allier*, to match or confederate; from *ad* and *lier*, to tie or unite. L. *ligo*.]

1. To unite, or form a relation, as between families by marriage, or between princes and states by treaty, league or confederacy.

2. To form a relation by similitude, resemblance or friendship. *Note.* This word is more generally used in the passive form, as families are *allied* by blood; or reciprocally, as princes *ally themselves* to powerful states.

ALLY' *n.* A prince or state united by treaty or league; a confederate.

The *allies* of Rome were slaves. *Ames.*

2. One related by marriage or other tie; but seldom applied to individuals, except to princes in their public capacity.

ALLY'ING, *ppr.* Uniting by marriage or treaty.

AL'MACANTAR, *n.* [See *Almucantar*.]

ALMADIE, *n.* A bark canoe used by the Africans; also a long boat used at Calicut, in India, eighty feet long, and six or seven broad; called also *cathuri*. *Encyc.*

AL'MAGEST, *n.* [*al* and μεγιςη, greatest.]

A book or collection of problems in astronomy and geometry, drawn up by Ptolemy. The same title has been given to other works of the like kind. *Encyc.*

ALMA'GRA, *n.* A fine deep red ocher, with an admixture of purple, very heavy, dense but friable, with a rough dusty surface. It is the *sil atticum* of the ancients. It is austere to the taste, astringent, melting in the mouth and staining the skin. It is used as a paint and as a medicine. *Encyc.*

ẠL'MANACK, *n.* [Ar. *al* and مَنَخْ manach, manack, a calendar, or diary.]

A small book or table, containing a calendar of days, weeks and months, with the times of the rising of the sun and moon, changes of the moon, eclipses, hours of full tide, stated festivals of churches, stated terms of courts, observations on the weather, &c. for the year ensuing. This calendar is sometimes published on one side of a single sheet, and called a *sheet-almanack*. The Baltic nations formerly engraved their calendars on pieces of wood, on swords, helves of axes, and various other utensils, and especially on walking sticks. Many of these are preserved in the cabinets of the curious. They are called by different nations, *rimstocks*, *primstaries*, *runstocks*, *runstaffs*, *clogs*, &c. The characters used are generally the Runic or Gothic. *Junius. Encyc. Tooke's Russia.*

ALMANACK-MAKER, *n.* A maker of almanacks.

AL'MANDINE, *n.* [Fr. and It.] In *mineralogy*, precious garnet, a beautiful mineral of a red color, of various shades, sometimes tinged with yellow or blue. It is commonly translucent, sometimes transparent. It occurs crystalized in the rhombic dodecahedron. *Phillips.*

AL'ME, or AL'MA, *n.* Girls in Egypt, whose occupation is to amuse company with singing and dancing. *Encyc. Savary.*

ALME'NA, *n.* A weight of two pounds, used to weigh saffron in several parts of Asia. *Sp. Dict.*

ẠLMI'GHTINESS, *n.* Omnipotence; infinite or boundless power; *an attribute of God only.*

ẠLMI'GHTY, *a.* [*all* and *mighty*. See *Might*.]

Possessing all power; omnipotent; being of unlimited might; being of boundless sufficiency; *appropriately applied to the Supreme Being.*

ẠLMI'GHTY, *n.* The Omnipotent God.

AL'MOND, *n.* [Fr. *amande*; It. *mandola*; Sp. *almendra*; Germ. *mandel*.]

1. The fruit of the almond tree; an ovate, compressed nut, perforated in the pores. It is either sweet or bitter. [It is popularly pronounced *ammond*.] *Nicholson. Encyc.*

2. The tonsils, two glands near the basis of the tongue, are called almonds, from their resemblance to that nut; vulgularly, but improperly, called the *almonds of the ears*, as they belong to the throat. *Quincy. Johnson.*

3. In *Portugal*, a measure by which wine is sold, twenty-six of which make a pipe. *Encyc.*

[But in Portuguese it is written *almude*.]

4. Among *lapidaries*, almonds signify pieces of rock crystal, used in adorning branch candlesticks, so called from their resemblance to this fruit. *Encyc.*

ALMOND-FURNACE, among *refiners*, is a furnace in which the slags of litharge, left in refining silver, are reduced to lead, by the help of charcoal; that is, according to modern chimistry, in which the oxyd of lead is deoxydized, and the metal revived.

ALMOND-TREE, *n.* The tree which produces the almond. The leaves and flowers resemble those of the peach, but the fruit is longer and more compressed, the green coat is thinner and drier when ripe, and the shell is not so rugged. *Miller.*

ALMOND-WILLOW, *n.* A tree with leaves of a light green on both sides. *Mason from Shenstone.*

AL'MONER, *n.* [See *Alms*.]

An officer whose duty is to distribute charity or alms. By the ancient canons, every monastery was to dispose of a tenth of its income in alms to the poor, and all bishops were obliged to keep an almoner. This title is sometimes given to a chaplain; as, the *almoner* of a ship or regiment.

The *Lord Almoner*, or *Lord High Almoner*, in England, is an ecclesiastical officer, generally a bishop, who has the forfeiture of all deodands, and the goods of self-murderers, which he is to distribute to the poor.

The *Grand Almoner*, in France, is the first ecclesiastical dignitary, and has the superintendence of hospitals. *Encyc.*

AL'MONRY, *n.* [Corrupted into *ambry*, *aumbry*, or *aumery*.]

The place where the almoner resides, or where the alms are distributed.

ALMO'ST, *adv.* [*all* and *most*. The Saxon order of writing was thus; "*all most* who were present." Sax. Chron. p. 225. We now use a duplication, *almost all* who were present.]

Nearly; well nigh; for the greatest part.

Almost thou persuadest me to be a christian. Acts xxvi.

'ALMS, *n.* àmz. [Sax. *almes*; old Eng. *almesse*; Norm. *almoignes*; Fr. *aumônes*; D. *aalmoes*; Sw. *almosa*; Dan. *almisse*; G. *almosen*; L. *eleemosyna*; Gr. *ελεημοσυνη*. The first syllables appear to be from *ελεεω*, to pity.]

Any thing given gratuitously to relieve the poor, as money, food, or clothing, otherwise called charity.

A lame man was laid daily to ask *an alms*. Acts iii.

Cornelius gave much *alms* to the people. Acts x.

Tenure by free alms, or frank-almoign, in England, is that by which the possessor is bound to pray for the soul of the donor, whether dead or alive; a tenure by which most of the ancient monasteries and religious houses in England held their lands, as do the parochial clergy, and many ecclesiastical and eleemosynary establishments at this day. Land thus held was free from all rent or other service. *Blackstone.*

'ALMS-BASKET; 'ALMS-BOX; 'ALMS-CHEST; vessels appropriated to receive alms.

'ALMS-DEED, *n.* An act of charity; a charitable gift.

'ALMS-FOLK, *n.* Persons supporting others by alms. [*Not used.*]

'ALMS-GIVER, *n.* One who gives to the poor. *Bacon.*

'ALMS-GIVING, *n.* The bestowment of charity.

'ALMS-HOUSE, *n.* A house appropriated for the use of the poor, vho are supported by the public.

'ALMS-MEN, } *n.* Persons supported
'ALMS-PEOPLE, } by charity or by public provision.

AL'MUCANTAR, *n.* [Arabic.] A series of circles of the sphere passing through the center of the sun, or of a star, parallel to the horizon. It is synonymous with a parallel of altitude, whose common zenith is the vertical point. *Bailey. Encyc. Johnson.*

ALMUCANTAR'S STAFF. An instrument of box or pear-tree, having an arch of fifteen degrees, used to take observations of the sun, about the time of its rising or setting, to find the amplitude and the variations of the compass. *Encyc. Chambers.*

ALMU'DE, *n.* A wine measure in Portugal, of which twenty-six make a pipe. *Port. Dict.*

AL'MUG, } *n.* In *scripture*, a tree or wood
AL'GUM, } about which the learned are not agreed. The most probable conjecture is that the word denotes gummy or resinous wood in general.

The Vulgate translates it *ligna thyina*, and the Septuagint, *wrought-wood*; others, ebony, bravil or pine, and the Rabbins render it *coral*. It was used for musical instruments, stair cases, &c.

The *thyinum* is the citron tree, from Mauritania, much esteemed by the ancients for its fragrance and beauty. The *almug*, *almugim*, or *algumim*, or simply *gummim*, is most probably a gummy wood, and perhaps may be the Shittim, often mentioned in Scripture. See 1 Kings, x. 11. *Calmet. Encyc.*

AL'NAGE, *n.* [Fr. *aulnage*, now softened into *aunage*; L. *ulna*; Gr. *ωλενη*, an arm, a cubit; W. *elin*; Ir. *uelen, uile*, or *uilean*, an elbow, a nook, or corner. See *Ell.*]

A measuring by the ell.

AL'NAGER, or AL'NAGAR, *n.* A measurer by the ell; a sworn officer, whose duty was to inspect and measure woolen cloth, and fix upon it a seal. This office was abolished by Statute, 11. and 12. Will. 3. No duty or office of this kind exists in the United States.

AL'NIGHT, *n.* A cake of wax with the wick in the midst. *Bacon.*

AL'OE, *n.* *al'o*, plu. *aloes*, pronounced *aloze*, and popularly *al'oez*, in three syllables, according to the Latin. [L. *aloë*; Gr. *αλοη*; Sp. Port. It. Fr. *aloe*; Heb. plu. אהלים aloe-trees.]

In *botany*, a genus of monogynian hexanders, of many species; all natives of warm climates, and most of them, of the southern part of Africa.

Among the Mohammedans, the aloe is a symbolic plant, especially in Egypt; and every one who returns from a pilgrimage to Mecca, hangs it over his street door, as a token that he has performed the journey.

In Africa, the leaves of the Guinea aloe are made into durable ropes. Of one species are made fishing lines, bow strings, stockings and hammocs. The leaves of another species hold rain water.

ALOES, in *medicine*, is the inspissated juice of the aloe. The juice is collected from the leaves, which are cut and put in a tub, and when a large quantity is procured, it is boiled to a suitable consistence; or it is exposed to the sun, till all the fluid part is exhaled. There are several kinds sold in the shops; as the socotrine aloes from Socotora, an isle in the Indian ocean; the hepatic or common Barbadoes aloes; and the fetid or caballine aloes.

Aloes is a stimulating stomachic purgative; when taken in small doses, it is useful for people of a lax habit and sedentary life. *Encyc.*

AL'OES-WOOD, *n.* [See *Agallochum.*]

ALOET'IC, } *a.* Pertaining to aloe or
ALOET'ICAL, } aloes; partaking of the qualities of aloes.

ALOET'IC, *n.* A medicine consisting chiefly of aloes. *Quincy.*

ALOFT', *adv.* [*a* and *loft*. See *Loft* and *Luff.*]

1. On high; in the air; high above the ground; as, the eagle soars *aloft.*

2. In *seamen's language*, in the top; at the mast head; or on the higher yards or rigging. Hence on the upper part, as of a building.

ALO'GIANS, *n.* [*a* neg. and *λογος*, word.]

In *church history*, a sect of ancient heretics, who denied Jesus Christ to be the *Logos*. and consequently rejected the gospel of St. John. *Buck. Encyc.*

AL'OGOTROPHY, *n.* [Gr. *αλογος*, unreasonable, and *τροφη*, nutrition.]

A disproportionate nutrition of the parts of the body, as when one part receives more or less nourishment and growth than another. *Bailey.*

AL'OGY, *n.* [Gr. *α* and *λογος*.]

Unreasonableness; absurdity. *Obs. Brown.*

ALO'NE, *a.* [*all* and *one*; Germ. *allein*; D. *alleen*; Sw. *allena*; Dan. *allene.*]

1. Single; solitary; without the presence of another; applied to a person or thing.

It is not good that man should be *alone*. Gen. ii.

[*This adjective follows its noun.*]

2. It is applied to two or more persons or things, when separate from others, in a place or condition by themselves; without company.

And when they were *alone*, he expounded all things to his disciples. Mark, iv.

3. Only.

Thou whose name *alone* is Jehovah. Ps. lxxxiii.

This sense at first appears to be adverbial, but really is not; whose name *single*, *solitary*, *without another*, is Jehovah.

To let alone is to suffer to rest; to forbear molesting or meddling with; to suffer to remain in its present state. *Alone*, in this phrase, is an adjective, the word to which it refers being omitted; let me alone; let them alone; let it alone; that is, suffer it to be unmolested, or to remain as it is, or let it remain by itself.

ALO'NE, *adv.* Separately; by itself.

ALO'NELY, *a.* or *adv.* Only; merely; singly. [*Not used.*] *Gower.*

ALO'NENESS, *n.* That state which belongs to no other. [*Not used.*] *Montague.*

ALONG', *adv.* [Sax. *and-lang* or *ond-lang*; Fr. *au long*, *le long*. See *Long*. The Saxons always prefixed *and* or *ond*, and the sense seems to be, by the length, or opposite the length, or in the direction of the length.]

1. By the length; lengthwise; in a line with the length; as, the troops marched *along* the bank of the river, or *along* the highway. 1 Sam. vi.

2. Onward; in a line, or with a progressive motion; as, a meteor glides *along* the sky; let us walk *along*.

All along signifies the whole length; through the whole distance; in the whole way or length.

Ishmael went forth, weeping *all along* as he went. Jer. xli. 1 Sam. xxviii.

Along with signifies in company; joined with; as, Go *along with* us. Sometimes *with* is omitted;

Come then, my friend, my genius, come *along*. *Pope.*

Along side, in seamen's language, that is, by the length or in a line with the side, signifies side by side, as by another ship or by the side of a wharf.

Along shore is by the shore or coast, lengthwise, and near the shore.

Lying along is lying on the side, or pressed down by the weight of sail. *Mar. Dict.*

ALONGST′, *adv.* Along; through or by the length. *Obs.* *Knolles.*

ALOOF, *adv.* [Probably from the root of *leave*, to depart.]

1. At a distance, but within view, or at a small distance, in *a literal sense;* as, to stand *aloof.*

2. In *a figurative sense,* not concerned in a design; declining to take any share, implying circumspection; keeping at a distance from the point, or matter in debate.

AL′OPECY, *n.* [Gr. αλωπηξ, a fox, whose urine is said to occasion baldness.]

A disease, called the fox-evil or scurf, which is a falling off of the hair, from any part of the body. *Quincy. Encyc. Bailey.*

ALO′SA, *n.* A fish of passage, called the shad, or mother of herrings, a species of Clupea. It is an abdominal, and some naturalists allege it to be a different species from the shad. *Encyc. Dict. of Nat. Hist.*

ALOUD′, *adv.* [*a* and *loud;* Sax. *gehlyd,* clamor. See *Loud.*]

Loudly; with a loud voice, or great noise.

Cry *aloud*, spare not. Isa. lviii.

ALP, ALPS, *n.* [Qu. Gr. αλφος, white; L. *albus.* The Celts called all high mountains *alpes* or *olbe.* *Cluver.* Thucydides mentions a castle, in the territory of Argos, situated on a hill and called *Olpas* or *Olp.* Lib. 3. Ca. 105. Pelloutier, Hist. des Celtes, Liv. 1. 15. The derivation of the word from αλφος, white, is therefore doubtful. In Ir. or Gaelic, *ailp* is a huge mass or lump.]

A high mountain. The name, it is supposed, was originally given to mountains whose tops were covered with snow, and hence appropriately applied to the mountains of Swisserland; so that by Alps is generally understood the latter mountains. But geographers apply the name to any high mountains. *Pinkerton.*

ALPAG′NA, *n.* An animal of Peru, used as a beast of burden; the Camelus Paco of Linne, and the Pacos of Pennant. *Dict. of Nat. Hist.*

AL′PHA, *n.* [Heb. אלוף an ox, a leader.]

The first letter in the Greek alphabet, answering to A, and used to denote first or beginning.

I am *Alpha* and Omega. Rev. i.

As a numeral, it stands for one. It was formerly used also to denote *chief;* as, Plato was the Alpha of the wits.

AL′PHABET, *n.* [Gr. αλφα and Βητα, *A* and *B.*]

The letters of a language arranged in the customary order; the series of letters which form the elements of speech.

AL′PHABET, *v. t.* To arrange in the order of an alphabet; to form an alphabet in a book, or designate the leaves by the letters of the alphabet.

ALPHABETA′RIAN, *n.* A learner while in the A. B. C.

ALPHABET′IC, ALPHABET′ICAL, } *a.* In the order of an alphabet, or in the order of the letters as customarily arranged.

ALPHABET′ICALLY, *adv.* In an alphabetical manner; in the customary order of the letters.

ALPHE′NIX, *n.* [*al* and *phœnix.*]

White barley sugar, used for colds. It is common sugar boiled till it will easily crack; then poured upon an oiled marble table, and molded into various figures. *Encyc.*

AL′PHEST, *n.* A small fish, having a purple back and belly, with yellow sides, a smooth mouth, and thick fleshy lips; always caught near the shore or among rocks. *Labrus Cinædus, Linne.* *Dict. of Nat. Hist.*

ALPHON′SIN, *n.* A surgical instrument for extracting bullets from wounds, so called from its inventor, Alphonsus Ferrier of Naples. It consists of three branches, which close by a ring, and open when it is drawn back. *Encyc.*

ALPHON′SIN TABLES. Astronomical tables made by Alphonsus king of Arragon. *Bailey.*

AL′PHUS, *n.* [Gr. αλφος, white.]

That species of leprosy called vitiligo, in which the skin is rough, with white spots. *Quincy.*

AL′PINE, *a.* [L. *alpinus,* from *Alpes.*]

1. Pertaining to the Alps, or to any lofty mountain; very high; elevated.

2. Growing on high mountains; as, *alpine plants.* *Milton. Thomson.*

AL′PINE, *n.* A kind of strawberry growing on lofty hills.

AL′PIST, or AL′PIA, *n.* The seed of the fox-tail; a small seed, used for feeding birds. *Encyc.*

AL′QUIER, *n.* A measure in Portugal for dry things, as well as liquids, containing half an almude or about two gallons. It is called also *Cantar.* *Port. Dict.*

AL′QUIFOU, *n.* A sort of lead ore, which, when broke, looks like antimony. It is found in Cornwall, England; used by potters to give a green varnish to their wares, and called potters ore. A small mixture of manganese gives it a blackish hue. *Encyc.*

ALREAD′Y, *adv.* *alred′dy.* [*all* and *ready.* See *Ready.*]

Literally, a state of complete preparation; but, by an easy deflection, the sense is, at this time, or at a specified time.

Elias is come *already.* Mat. xvii.
Joseph was in Egypt *already.* Ex. i.

It has reference to past time, but may be used for a future past; as, when you shall arrive, the business will be *already* completed, or will have been completed *already.*

AL′SO, *adv.* [*all* and *so.* Sax. *eal* and *swa; eal,* all, the whole, and *swa,* so.]

Likewise; in like manner.

Where your treasure is, there will your heart be *also.* Mat. xvi.

ALT or AL′TO, *a.* [It. from L. *altus,* high; Celt, *alt, ailt,* a high place; Heb. עליח upper, על, high.]

In *music,* a term applied to high notes in the scale. In sculpture, *alto-relievo,* high relief, is when the figures project half or more, without being entirely detached from the ground. *Encyc. Cyc.*

ALTA′IC, or ALTA′IAN, *a.* [Tart. *alatau,* perhaps *al-tag,* high mountain. Tooke 1, 121.]

Pertaining to the Altai, a vast ridge of mountains extending, in an easterly direction, through a considerable part of Asia, and forming a boundary between the Russian and Chinese dominions. *Pinkerton. Encyc.*

AL′TAR, *n.* [L. *altare,* probably from the same root as *altus,* high; Celtic, *alt,* a high place.]

1. A mount; a table or elevated place, on which sacrifices were anciently offered to some deity. Altars were originally made of turf, afterwards of stone, wood or horn; some were round, others square, others triangular. They differed also in highth, but all faced the east. The principal altars of the Jews were, the altar of incense, of burnt-offerings, and of show-bread; all of shittim wood, and covered with gold or brass. *Encyc.*

2. In *modern churches,* the communion table; and, figuratively, a church; a place of worship.

3. In *scripture,* Christ is called the altar of Christians, he being the atoning sacrifice for sin.

We have an *altar,* whereof they have no right to eat, who serve tabernacles. Heb. xiii.

AL′TAR-CLOTH, *n.* A cloth to lay upon an altar in churches.

AL′TAR-PIECE, *n.* A painting placed over the altar in a church. *Warton.*

AL′TAR-WISE, *adv.* Placed in the manner of an altar. *Howell.*

AL′TARAGE, *n.* The profits arising to priests from oblations, or on account of the altar. Also, in *law,* altars erected in virtue of donations, before the reformation, within a parochial church, for the purpose of singing a mass for deceased friends. *Encyc.*

AL′TARIST, or AL′TAR-THANE, *n.* In *old laws,* an appellation given to the priest to whom the altarage belonged; also a chaplain. *Cyc.*

AL′TER, *v. t.* [Fr. *alterer;* Sp. *alterar;* It. *alterare;* from L. *alter,* another. See *Alien.* *Alter* is supposed to be a contraction of αλλοτερρος, alienus, of αλλος and ετερος.]

1. To make some change in; to make different in some particular; to vary in some degree, without an entire change.

My covenant will I not break, nor *alter* the thing that has gone out of my lips. Ps. lxxxix.

2. To change entirely or materially; as, to *alter* an opinion. In general, to *alter* is to change partially; to *change* is more generally to substitute one thing for another, or to make a material difference in a thing.

AL′TER, *v. i.* To become, in some respects, different; to vary; as, the weather *alters* almost daily.

The law which *altereth* not. Dan. vi.

AL′TERABILITY, *n.* The quality of being susceptible of alteration.

AL'TERABLE, *a.* That may become different; that may vary.

AL'TERABLENESS, *n.* The quality of admitting alteration; variableness.

AL'TERABLY, *adv.* In a manner that may be altered, or varied.

AL'TERAGE, *n.* [From *alo*, to feed.] The breeding, nourishing or fostering of a child. *Sir J. Davies.* But this is not an English word.

AL'TERANT, *a.* Altering; gradually changing.

AL'TERANT, *n.* A medicine which, without a sensible operation, gradually corrects the state of the body and changes it from a diseased to a healthy condition. An alterative. *Encyc. Quincy.*

ALTERA'TION, *n.* [L. *alteratio.*] The act of making different, or of varying in some particular; an altering or partial change; also the change made, or the loss or acquisition of qualities not essential to the form or nature of a thing. Thus a cold substance suffers an *alteration* when it becomes hot.

AL'TERATIVE, *a.* Causing alteration; having the power to alter.

AL'TERATIVE, *n.* A medicine which, without sensible operation, gradually induces a change in the habit or constitution and restores healthy functions. This word is more generally used than *alterant.*

AL'TERCATE, *v. i.* [L. *altercor, alterco,* from *alter*, another.] To contend in words; to dispute with zeal, heat or anger; to wrangle.

ALTERCA'TION, *n.* [L. *altercatio.*] Warm contention in words; dispute carried on with heat or anger; controversy; wrangle.

AL'TERN, *a.* [L. *alternus*, of *alter*, another.]
1. Acting by turns; one succeeding another; *alternate*, which is the word generally used.
2. In *chrystalography*, exhibiting, on two parts, an upper and a lower part, faces which alternate among themselves, but which, when the two parts are compared, correspond with each other. *Cleaveland.*

Altern-base, in trigonometry, is a term used in distinction from the true base. Thus in oblique triangles, the true base is the sum of the sides, and then the difference of the sides is the altern-base; or the true base is the difference of the sides, and then the sum of the sides is the altern-base. *Encyc.*

AL'TERNACY, *n.* Performance or actions by turns. [*Little used.*]

ALTERN'AL, *a.* Alternative. [*Little used.*]

ALTERN'ALLY, *adv.* By turns. [*Little used.*] *May.*

ALTERN'ATE, *a.* [L. *alternatus.*]
1. Being by turns; one following the other in succession of time or place; hence reciprocal.

And bid *alternate* passions fall and rise. *Pope.*

2. In *botany*, branches and leaves are *alternate*, when they rise higher on opposite sides alternately, come out singly, and follow in gradual order. *Encyc. Lee.*

Alternate alligation. [See *Alligation.*]

Alternate angles, in geometry, the internal angles made by a line cutting two parallels, and lying on opposite sides of the cutting line; the one below the first parallel, and the other above the second. *Johnson.*

In *heraldry*, the first and fourth quarters, and the second and third, are usually of the same nature, and are called *alternate quarters.*

ALTERN'ATE, *n.* That which happens by turns with something else; vicissitude. *Prior.*

AL'TERNATE, *v. t.* [L. *alterno.* See *Alter.* With the accent on the second syllable, the participle *alternating* can hardly be pronounced.] To perform by turns, or in succession; to cause to succeed by turns; to change one thing for another reciprocally; as, God *alternates* good and evil.

AL'TERNATE, *v. i.* To happen or to act by turns; as, the flood and ebb tides *alternate* with each other.
2. To follow reciprocally in place.

Different species *alternating* with each other. *Kirwan.*

ALTERN'ATELY, *adv.* In reciprocal succession; by turns, so that each is succeeded by that which it succeeds, as night follows day and day follows night.

ALTERN'ATENESS, *n.* The quality of being alternate, or of following in succession.

AL'TERNATING, *ppr.* Performing or following by turns.

ALTERNA'TION, *n.* The reciprocal succession of things, in time or place; the act of following and being followed in succession; as, we observe the *alternation* of day and night, cold and heat, summer and winter.
2. The different changes or alterations of orders, in numbers. Thus, if it is required to know how many changes can be rung on six bells, multiply the numbers 1, 2, 3, 4, 5, 6, continually into one another, and the last product is the number required. This is called *permutation.*
3. The answer of the congregation speaking alternately with the minister.
4. Alternate performance, in the choral sense. *Mason.*

ALTERN'ATIVE, *a.* [Fr. *alternatif.*] Offering a choice of two things.

ALTERN'ATIVE, *n.* That which may be chosen or omitted; a choice of two things, so that if one is taken, the other must be left. Thus, when *two* things offer a choice of *one* only, the two things are called *alternatives.* In strictness, then, the word can not be applied to more than *two* things, and when one thing only is offered for choice, it is said there is no *alternative.*

Between these *alternatives* there is no middle ground. *Cranch.*

ALTERN'ATIVELY, *adv.* In the manner of alternatives; in a manner that admits the choice of one out of two things.

ALTERN'ATIVENESS, *n.* The quality or state of being alternative.

ALTERN'ITY, *n.* Succession by turns; alternation.

ALTHE'A, *n.* [Gr. αλθαια, from αλθω, or αλθαινω, to heal.] In *botany*, a genus of polyandrian monadelphs, of several species; called in English *marsh-mallow.* The common species has a perennial root, and an annual stalk rising four or five feet. It abounds with mucilage, and is used as an emollient. *Encyc.*

ALTHO'UGH, *altho',* obs. verb, or used only in the Imperative. [*all* and *though;* from Sax. *thah*, or *theah;* Ir. *daighim*, to give; Ger. *doch;* D. *dog;* Sw. *doch*, and *endoch;* Dan. *dog*, though. See *Though.*] Grant all this; be it so; allow all; suppose that; admit all that; as, "*although* the fig-tree shall not blossom." Hab. iii. That is, grant, admit or suppose what follows—"the fig-tree shall not blossom." It is a transitive verb, and admits after it the definitive *that*—although *that* the fig-tree shall not blossom; but this use of the verb, has been long obsolete. The word may be defined by *notwithstanding, non obstante;* as *not opposing* may be equivalent to *admitting* or *supposing.*

ALTIL'OQUENCE, *n.* [L. *altus*, high, and *loquor, loquens*, speaking.] Lofty speech; pompous language.

ALTIM'ETER, *n.* [L. *altus*, high, and Gr. μετρον, measure. See *Measure* and *Mode.*] An instrument for taking altitudes by geometrical principles, as a geometrical quadrant.

ALTIM'ETRY, *n.* The art of ascertaining altitudes by means of a proper instrument, and by trigonometrical principles without actual mensuration.

AL'TIN, *n.* A money of account in Russia, value three kopecks, or about three cents; also a lake in Siberia, ninety miles in length. *Tooke. Encyc.*

ALTIN'CAR, *n.* A species of factitious salt or powder, used in the fusion and purification of metals, prepared in various ways. [See *Tincal.*] *Encyc.*

ALTIS'ONANT, } **ALTIS'ONOUS,** } *a.* [L. *altus*, high, and *sonans*, sounding; *sonus*, sound.] High sounding, lofty or pompous, as language. *Evelyn.*

AL'TITUDE, *n.* [L. *altitudo*, of *altus*, high, and a common termination, denoting *state*, condition or manner.]
1. Space extended upward; highth; the elevation of an object above its foundation; as, the *altitude* of a mountain, or column; or the elevation of an object or place above the surface on which we stand, or above the earth; as, the *altitude* of a cloud or a meteor; or the elevation of one object above another; as, of a bird above the top of a tree.
2. The elevation of a point, a star, or other object above the horizon. This is *true* or *apparent* altitude; *true*, when taken from the rational or real horizon; *apparent*, when taken from the sensible, or apparent horizon.
3. *Figuratively*, high degree; superior excellence; highest point of excellence.

He is proud to the *altitude* of his virtue. *Shak.*

The *altitude of the eye*, in perspective, is a right line let fall from the eye, perpendicular to the geometrical plane. *Encyc.*

Meridian altitude is an arch of the meridian between the horizon and any star or point on the meridian.

ALTIV'OLANT, *a.* [L. *altus*, high, and *volans*, flying.] Flying high.

AL'TO. [It. from L. *altus*.] High.

Alto and *Basso*, high and low, in *old law*, terms used to signify a submission of all differences of every kind to arbitration.

AL'TO-OCTA'VO. [It.]
An octave higher.

AL'TO-RELIE'VO. [It.]
High relief, in *sculpture*, is the projection of a figure half or more, without being entirely detached. *Cyc.*

AL'TO-RIPIE'NO. [It.]
The tenor of the great chorus, which sings and plays only in particular places. *Encyc.*

AL'TO-VIOLA. [It.]
A small tenor viol.

AL'TO-VIOLINO. [It.]
A small tenor violin.

ALTOGETH'ER, *adv.* [*all* and *together*. See *Together*.]
Wholly; entirely; completely; without exception.

Every man at his best estate is *altogether* vanity. Ps. xxxix.

AL'UDEL, *n.* [*a* and *lutum*, without lute. *Lunier*.]
In *chimistry*, aludels are earthern pots without bottoms, that they may be exactly fitted into each other, and used in sublimations. At the bottom of the furnace is a pot containing the matter to be sublimed, and at the top a head to receive the volatile matter. *Quincy. Encyc.*

AL'UM, *n.* [L. *alumen*.]
A triple sulphate of alumina and potassa. This substance is white, transparent and very astringent; but seldom found pure or crystalized. This salt is usually prepared by roasting and lixiviating certain clays containing pyrites, and to the lye adding a certain quantity of potassa; the salt is then obtained by crystalization. Alum is of great use in medicine and the arts. In medicine, it is used as an astringent; internally, in hemoptoe, diarrhea, and dysentery; externally, as a styptic applied to bleeding vessels, and as an escharotic. In the arts, it is used in dyeing to fix colors; in making candles, for hardening the tallow; in tanning, for restoring the cohesion of skins.
Encyc. Fourcroy. Webster's Manual.

ALUM-EARTH, *n.* A massive mineral, of a blackish brown color, a dull luster, and soft consistence. *Ure.*

AL'UMIN, } *n.* An earth, or earthy sub-
ALU'MINA, } stance, which has been considered to be elementary, and called pure clay; but recently, chemical experiments have given reason to believe it to be a metallic oxyd, to the base of which has been given the name *aluminum*. This metallic base however has not been obtained in such a state as to make its properties susceptible of examination. Alumina is destitute of taste aud smell. When moistened with water, it forms a cohesive and ductile mass, susceptible of being kneaded into regular forms.
Davy. Cyc. Webster's Manual.

ALU'MINIFORM, *a.* Having the form of alumina. *Chaptal.*

AL'UMINITE, *n.* Subsulphate of alumina; a mineral that occurs in small roundish or reniform masses. Its color is snow white or yellowish white.
Aikin. Jameson. Cleaveland.

ALU'MINOUS, *a.* Pertaining to alum or alumina, or partaking of the same properties.

ALU'MINUM, *n.* The name given to the supposed metallic base of alumina. *Davy.*

AL'UMISH, *a.* Having the nature of alum; somewhat resembling alum.

ALUM-SLATE, *n.* A mineral of two species, common and glossy.

ALUM-STONE, *n.* The siliceous subsulphate of alumina and potash. *Cleaveland.*

ALU'TA, *n.* [L.] A species of leather-stone, soft, pliable and not laminated. *Quincy.*

ALUTA'TION, *n.* [L. *aluta*, tanned leather.]
The tanning of leather.

AL'VEARY, *n.* [L. *alvearium*, *alveare*, a bee hive, from *alvus*, the belly.]
The hollow of the external ear, or bottom of the concha. *Quincy.*

AL'VEOLAR, } *a.* [L. *alveolus*, a socket,
AL'VEOLARY, } from *alveus*, a hollow vessel.]
Containing sockets, hollow cells or pits; pertaining to sockets. *Anatomy.*

AL'VEOLATE, *a.* [L. *alveolatus*, from *alveus*, a hollow vessel.]
Deeply pitted, so as to resemble a honey comb. *Martyn.*

AL'VEOLE, } *n.* [L. dim. of *alveus*.]
AL'VEOLUS, }
1. A cell in a bee hive, or in a fossil.
2. The socket in the jaw, in which a tooth is fixed.
3. A sea fossil of a conic figure, composed of a number of cells, like bee-hives, joined by a pipe of communication. *Encyc.*

AL'VEOLITE, *n.* [L. *alveolus*, and Gr. λιθος.]
In *natural history*, a kind of stony polypiers, of a globular or hemispherical shape; formed by numerous concentric beds, each composed of a union of little cells.
Dict. of Nat. Hist.

AL'VINE, *a.* [from *alvus*, the belly.]
Belonging to the belly or intestines. *Darwin.*

ALWAR'GRIM, *n.* The spotted plover, *Charadrius Apricarius*. *Pennant.*

AL'WAY or AL'WAYS, *adv.* [*all* and *way*; Sax. *eal*, and *weg*, way; properly, a going, at all goings; hence, at all times.]
1. Perpetually; throughout all time; as, God is *always* the same.
2. Continually; without variation.

I do *alway* those things which please him. John viii. Mat. xxviii.

3. Continually or constantly during a certain period, or regularly at stated intervals.

Mephibosheth shall eat bread *alway* at my table. 2 Sam. ix.

4. At all convenient times; regularly.

Cornelius prayed to God *alway*. Acts x. Luke xviii. Eph. vi.

Alway is now seldom used. The application of this compound to *time* proceeds from the primary sense of *way*, which is a going or passing; hence, continuation.

A. M. stand for *Artium Magister*, master of arts, the second degree given by universities and colleges; called in some countries, doctor of philosophy. In America, this degree is conferred without examination, on bachelors of three years standing.

A. M. stand also for *Anno Mundi*, in the year of the world.

AM, the first person of the verb *to be*, in the indicative mode, present tense. Sax. *eom*: Gr. ειμι; Goth. *im*; Pers. *am*.

I AM that I AM. Ex. iii.

A'MA, or HA'MA, *n.* [D. *aam*, a vessel.]
In *church affairs*, a vessel to contain wine for the eucharist; also, a wine measure, as a cask, a pipe, &c. *Encyc.*

AMABIL'ITY, *n.* [L. *amabilis*, from *amo*, to love.]
Loveliness; the power of pleasing, or rather the combination of agreeable qualities which win the affections. *Taylor.*

AMAD'AVAD, *n.* A small curious bird of the size of the crested wren; the upper part of the body is brown, the prime feathers of the wings black. *Dict. of Nat. Hist.*

AMADET'TO, *n.* A sort of pear, so called, it is said, from a person who cultivated it. *Skinner.*

AMAD'OGADE, *n.* A small beautiful bird in Peru; the upper part of its body and wings are of a lively green, its breast red, and its belly white. *Dict. of Nat. Hist.*

AM'ADOT, *n.* A sort of pear. *Johnson.*

AM'ADOU, *n.* A variety of the boletus igniarius, found on old ash and other trees. *Ure.*

This is written also *amadow*, and called *black match*, and *pyrotechnical spunge*, on account of its inflammability. *Cyc.*

AMA'IN, *adv.* [Sax. *a* and *mægn*, force, strength. See *May*, *Might*.]
With force, strength or violence; violently: furiously; suddenly; at once.

What, when we fled *amain*. *Milton.*

Let go amain, in seamen's language, or *strike amain*, is to let fall or lower at once. *Mar. Dict.*

AMAL'GAM, *n.* [Gr. μαλαγμα, from μαλασσω, to soften. Its usual derivation is certainly erroneous.]
1. A mixture of mercury or quicksilver with another metal; any metallic alloy, of which mercury forms an essential constituent part. *Cyc.*
2. A mixture or compound of different things. *Burke.*

AMAL'GAMATE, *v. t.* To mix quicksilver with another metal. Gregory uses *amalgamize*.
2. To mix different things, to make a compound; to unite.

AMAL'GAMATE, *v. i.* To mix or unite in an amalgam; to blend.

AMAL'GAMATED, *pp.* Mixed with quicksilver; blended.

AMAL'GAMATING, *ppr.* Mixing quicksilver with another metal; compounding.

AMALGAMA'TION, *n.* The act or operation of mixing mercury with another metal. *Encyc.*
2. The mixing or blending of different things.

AM'ALOZK, *n.* A large aquatic fowl of Mexico. *Dict. of Nat. Hist.*

AMAN'DOLA, *n.* A green marble, having the appearance of honey comb, and containing white spots; of 100 parts, 76 are mild calcarious earth, 20 shist and 2 iron. The cellular appearance proceeds from the shist. *Kirwan. Nicholson.*

AMANUEN'SIS, *n.* [L. from *manus*, hand.] A person whose employment is to write what another dictates.

AM'ARANTH, } *n.* [Gr. αμαραντος, of α
AMARANTH'US, } neg. and μαραινω, to decay; so called, it is said, because, when cropped, it does not soon wither.]

Flower-gentle; a genus of plants, of many species. Of these the tricolored has long been cultivated in gardens, on account of the beauty of its variegated leaves. *Encyc.*

AM'ARANTH, *n.* A color inclining to purple. *Cyc.*

AMARANTH'INE, *a.* Belonging to amaranth; consisting of, containing, or resembling amaranth.

AMAR'ITUDE, *n.* [L. *amaritudo*, from *amarus*, bitter; from Heb. מר bitter.] Bitterness. [*Not much used.*]

AMARYL'LIS, *n.* [The name of a country girl in Theocritus and Virgil.] In *botany*, lily-daffodil, a genus of liliaceous plants of several species, which are cultivated in gardens for the beauty of their flowers. *Encyc.*

AM'ASS, *v. t.* [Fr. *amasser*; It. *ammassare*; L. *massa*, a heap or lump; Gr. μαζα. See *Mass.*]

1. To collect into a heap; to gather a great quantity; to accumulate; as, to *amass* a treasure.

2. To collect in great numbers; to add many things together; as, to *amass* words or phrases.

AM'ASS, *n.* An assemblage, heap or accumulation. [This is superseded by *Mass.*]

AM'ASSED, *pp.* Collected in a heap, or in a great quantity or number; accumulated.

AM'ASSING, *ppr.* Collecting in a heap, or in a large quantity or number.

AM'ASSMENT, *n.* A heap collected; a large quantity or number brought together; an accumulation.

AMA'TE, *v. i.* [See *Mate.*] To accompany; also to terrify, to perplex. [*Not used.*]

AMATEU'R, *n.* [Fr., from L. *amator*, a lover, from *amo*, to love.] A person attached to a particular pursuit, study or science, as to music or painting; one who has a taste for the arts. *Burke.*

AMATO'RIAL, } *a.* [L. *amatorius*, from *amo*,
AM'ATORY, } to love.]

1. Relating to love; as, *amatorial* verses; causing love; as, *amatory* potions; produced by sexual intercourse; as, *amatorial* progeny. *Darwin.*

2. In *anatomy*, a term applied to the oblique muscles of the eye, from their use in ogling.

AMATO'RIALLY, *adv.* In an amatorial manner; by way of love. *Darwin.*

AMAURO'SIS, *n.* [Gr. αμαυρος, obscure.] A loss or decay of sight, without any visible defect in the eye, except an immovable pupil; called also *gutta serena.* Sometimes the disease is periodical, coming on suddenly, continuing for hours or days, and then disappearing. It has sometimes been cured by electricity. *Encyc. Coxe.*

AMA'ZE, *v. t.* [Qu. Ar. عمس to perplex or confuse; or from *maze.*] To confound with fear, sudden surprise, or wonder; to astonish.

They shall be afraid; they shall be *amazed* at one another. Is. xiii.

They were all *amazed* and glorified God. Mark ii. Luke v.

This word implies astonishment or perplexity, arising from something extraordinary, unexpected, unaccountable, or frightful.

AMA'ZE, *n.* Astonishment; confusion; perplexity, arising from fear, surprise or wonder. It is chiefly used in poetry, and is nearly synonymous with *amazement.*

AMA'ZED, *pp.* Astonished; confounded with fear, surprise or wonder.

AMA'ZEDLY, *adv.* With amazement; in a manner to confound. [*Little used.*]

AMA'ZEDNESS, *n.* The state of being confounded with fear, surprise or wonder; astonishment; great wonder.

AMA'ZEMENT, *n.* Astonishment; confusion or perplexity, from a sudden impression of fear, surprise or wonder. It is sometimes accompanied with fear or terror; sometimes merely extreme wonder or admiration at some great, sudden or unexpected event, at an unusual sight, or at the narration of extraordinary events.

AMA'ZING, *ppr.* Confounding with fear, surprise or wonder.

2. *a.* Very wonderful; exciting astonishment, or perplexity.

AMA'ZINGLY, *adv.* In an astonishing degree; in a manner to excite astonishment, or to perplex, confound or terrify.

AM'AZON, *n.* [This is said to be formed of α neg. and μαζος, breast. History informs us, that the Amazons cut off their right breast, that it might not incommode them in shooting and hurling the javelin. This is doubtless a fable.]

1. The Amazons are said by historians, to have been a race of female warriors, who founded an empire on the river Thermodon, in Asia Minor, on the coast of the Euxine. They are said to have excluded men from their society; and by their warlike enterprises, to have conquered and alarmed surrounding nations. Some writers treat these accounts as fables. *Herodian. Justin.*

2. By *analogy*, a warlike or masculine woman; a virago.

3. This name has been given to some American females, on the banks of the largest river in the world, who joined their husbands in attacking the Spaniards that first visited the country. This trivial occurrence gave the name Amazon to that river, whose real name is Maranon. *Garcilasso, p. 606.*

AMAZO'NIAN, *a.* Pertaining to or resembling an Amazon. *Applied to females*, bold; of masculine manners; warlike.

2. Belonging to the river Maranon in South America, or to Amazonia, the country lying on that river.

AMB, AM. About; around; used in composition. Sax. *emb*, *ymb*; W. *am*; Ir. *im*, *um*; G. *um*; D. *om*; Dan. *om*; Sw. *om*; Gr. αμφι; Lat. *am* or *amb.*

AMBA'GES, *n.* [L. *amb* and *ago*, to drive.]

1. A circumlocution; a circuit of words to express ideas which may be expressed in fewer words.

2. A winding or turning.

AMBAS'SADOR, *n.* [This is the more common orthography; but good authors write also *embassador*; and as the orthography of *embassy* is established, it would be better to write *embassador.* See *Embassador.*]

AM'BE or **AM'BI**, *n.* [Gr. αμβη, a brim; from *amb*, about.] Literally, a brim; but in *surgery*, an instrument for reducing dislocated shoulders, so called from the jutting of its extremity. Also the mango tree. *Quincy. Encyc. Coxe.*

AM'BER, *n.* [Fr. *ambre*; Sp. *ambar*; Port. *id*; It. *ambra*; an oriental word; Pers. عنبر anbar or anabar; Ar. عنبر anbaron. In 1 Kings x. 2. 10, the Arabic is rendered spices. The Arabic word is rendered by Castle, *amber*, a marine fish, a shield made of skins, crocus and fimus. In Eth. ዐንበር anbar is rendered a whale, and the word is used in Jonah, ii. 1. and Math. xii. 40. This word is placed by Castle under عنب to produce grapes, and عنب signifies grapes, Ch. and Heb. ענב. The Chaldee verb signifies to join or connect, and the sense of this word, applied to grapes, is a cluster, like *grape* in English. It signifies also in Ch. a tumor, a pustle, a mountain, the sense of which is a lump or mass collected; and this may be the sense of amber. In German, Dutch, Swedish and Danish, it has the name of *burnstone.*]

A hard semi-pellucid substance, tasteless and without smell, except when pounded or heated, when it emits a fragrant odor. It is found in alluvial soils, or on the sea shore, in many places; particularly on the shores of the Baltic, in Europe, and at Cape Sable, in Maryland, in the U. States. The ancient opinion of its vegetable origin seems now to be established, and it is believed or known to be a fossil resin. It yields by distillation an empyreumatic oil, and the succinic acid, which sublimes in small white needles. Its color usually presents some tinge of yellow. It is highly electrical, and is the basis of a varnish. *Journal of Science. Encyc. Chambers.*

AM'BER, *a.* Consisting of, or resembling amber.

AM'BER, *v. t.* To scent with amber.

AM'BER-DRINK, *n.* A drink resembling amber in color.

AM'BER-DROPPING, *a.* Dropping amber. *Milton.*

AM'BER-SEED, *n.* Musk-seed, resembling millet. It is of a bitterish taste, and brought from Egypt and the W. Indies. *Chambers.*

AM'BER-TREE, *n.* The English name of a species of *Anthospermum*, a shrub, with evergreen leaves, which, when bruised, emit a fragrant odor. *Miller.*

AM'BERGRIS, *n.* [*amber* and Fr. *gris*, gray; *gray amber.*] A solid, opake, ash-colored inflammable substance, variegated like marble, remarkably light, rugged on its surface, and when heated, it has a fragrant odor. It does not effervesce with acids; it melts easily into a kind of yellow resin, and is highly soluble in spirit of wine. Various opinions have been entertained respecting its origin; but it is well ascertained, that it is indurated fecal matter, discharged by the spermaceti whale, a species of *physeter*. It has been found in that species of whale, but usually is found floating on the surface of the ocean, in regions frequented by whales; sometimes in masses of from 60 to 225 lbs. weight. In this substance are found the beaks of the cuttle fish, on which that whale is known to feed. It is highly valued as a material in perfumery. *Encyc.*

AM'BIDEXTER, *n.* [L. *ambo*, both, and *dexter*, the right hand.]

1. A person who uses both hands with equal facility.
2. A double dealer; one equally ready to act on either side in party disputes. [*This sense is used in ludicrous language.*]
3. In *law*, a juror who takes money of both parties, for giving his verdict; an embracer. *Cowel.*

AMBIDEXTER'ITY, } AMBIDEX'TROUSNESS, } *n.* The faculty of using both hands with equal facility; double dealing; the taking of money from both parties for a verdict.

AMBIDEX'TROUS, *a.* Having the faculty of using both hands with equal ease; practicing or siding with both parties.

AM'BIENT, *a.* [L. *ambiens*, from *ambio*, to go round, from *amb*, about, and *eo*, to go.] Surrounding; encompassing on all sides; investing; applied to fluids or diffusible substances; as, the *ambient* air. *Milton.*

AMBIG'ENAL, *a.* [L. *ambo*, both, and *genu*, a knee.] An ambigenal hyperbola is one of the triple hyperbolas of the second order, having one of its infinite legs falling within an angle formed by the asymptotes, and the other without. *Encyc.*

AM'BIGU, *n.* [Fr. See *Ambiguity.*] An entertainment or feast, consisting of a medley of dishes. *King.*

AMBIGU'ITY, *n.* [L. *ambiguitas*, from *ambigo.*] Doubtfulness or uncertainty of signification, from a word's being susceptible of different meanings; double meaning.

Words should be used which admit of no *ambiguity*.

AMBIG'UOUS, *a.* [L. *ambiguus.*] Having two or more meanings; doubtful; being of uncertain signification; susceptible of different interpretations; hence, obscure. It is applied to words and expressions; not to a dubious state of mind, though it may be to a person using words of doubtful signification.

The ancient oracles were *ambiguous*, as were their answers.

AMBIG'UOUSLY, *adv.* In an ambiguous manner; with doubtful meaning.

AMBIG'UOUSNESS, *n.* The quality of being ambiguous; uncertainty of meaning; ambiguity; and hence, obscurity.

AMBIL'OGY, *n.* [*ambo*, both, and λογος, speech.] Talk or language of doubtful meaning.

AMBIL'OQUOUS, *a.* [*ambo*, both, and *loquor*, to speak.] Using ambiguous expressions.

AM'BIT, *n.* [L. *ambitus*, a circuit, from *ambio*, to go about. See *Ambient.*] The line that encompasses a thing; in *geometry*, the perimeter of a figure, or the surface of a body. The periphery or circumference of a circular body. *Johnson. Encyc.*

AMBI''TION, *n.* [L. *ambitio*, from *ambio*, to go about, or to seek by making interest, of *amb*, about, and *eo*, to go. See *Ambages.* This word had its origin in the practice of Roman candidates for office, who went about the city to solicit votes.] A desire of preferment, or of honor; a desire of excellence or superiority. It is used in a good sense; as, emulation may spring from a laudable *ambition.* It denotes also an inordinate desire of power, or eminence, often accompanied with illegal means to obtain the object. It is sometimes followed by *of*; as, a man has an *ambition of* wit. Milton has used the word in the Latin sense of *going about*, or attempting; but this sense is hardly legitimate.

AMBI''TION, *v. t.* [Fr. *ambitionner.*] Ambitiously to seek after. [*Little used.*] *King.*

AMBI''TIOUS, *a.* Desirous of power, honor, office, superiority or excellence; aspiring; eager for fame; followed by *of* before a noun; as, *ambitious of* glory.

2. Showy; adapted to command notice or praise; as, *ambitious* ornaments.
3. *Figuratively*, eager to swell or rise higher; as, the *ambitious* ocean. *Shak.*

AMBI''TIOUSLY, *adv.* In an ambitious manner; with an eager desire after preferment, or superiority.

AMBI''TIOUSNESS, *n.* The quality of being ambitious; ambition. Being nearly synonymous with *ambition*, it is not often used.

AM'BLE, *v. i.* [Fr. *ambler*, from L. *ambulo*, to walk; Qu. *amb*, about, and the root of Fr. *aller.*]

1. To move with a certain peculiar pace, as a horse, first lifting his two legs on one side, and then changing to the other. *Edin. Encyc.*
2. To move easy, without hard shocks.

Him time *ambles* withal. *Shak.*

3. In *a ludicrous sense*, to move with submission, or by direction, or to move affectedly. *Johnson.*

AM'BLE, *n.* A peculiar pace of a horse.

AM'BLER, *n.* A horse which ambles; a pacer.

AM'BLIGON, or AM'BLYGON, *n.* [Gr. αμβλυς, obtuse, and γωνια, an angle.] An obtuse angled triangle; a triangle with one angle of more than ninety degrees. *Bailey. Encyc.*

AMBLIG'ONAL, *a.* Containing an obtuse angle. *Ash.*

AM'BLIGONITE, *n.* [Gr. αμβλυγωνιος, having an obtuse angle.] A greenish colored mineral, of different pale shades, marked on the surface with reddish and yellowish brown spots. It occurs massive or crystalized in oblique four-sided prisms, in granite, with topaz and tourmalin, in Saxony. *Ure.*

AM'BLING, *ppr.* or *a.* Lifting the two legs on the same side at first going off, and then changing.

AM'BLINGLY, *adv.* With an ambling gait.

AM'BLYOPY, *n.* [Gr. αμβλυς, dull, and ωψ, eye.] Incipient amaurosis; dulness or obscurity of sight, without any apparent defect of the organs; sight so depraved that objects can be seen only in a certain light, distance, or position. *Encyc. Coxe.*

AM'BO, *n.* [Gr. αμβων, a pulpit; L. *umbo*, a boss.] A reading desk, or pulpit. *Wheler.*

AMBREA'DA, *n.* [from *amber.*] A kind of factitious amber, which the Europeans sell to the Africans. *Encyc.*

AMBRO'SIA, *n.* *ambro'zha*, [Gr. α neg. and βροτος, mortal, because it was supposed to confer immortality on them that fed on it.]

1. In *heathen antiquity*, the imaginary food of the gods. Hence,
2. Whatever is very pleasing to the taste or smell. The name has also been given to certain alexipharmic compositions.

AMBRO'SIAL, *a.* *ambro'zhal.* Partaking of the nature or qualities of ambrosia; fragrant; delighting the taste or smell; as. *ambrosial* dews. Ben Jonson uses *ambrosiac* in a like sense, and Bailey has *ambrosian*, but these seem not to be warranted by usage.

AMBRO'SIAN, *a.* Pertaining to St. Ambrose. The *Ambrosian* office, or ritual, is a formula of worship in the church of Milan, instituted by St. Ambrose, in the fourth century. *Encyc.*

AM'BROSIN, *n.* In *the middle ages*, a coin struck by the dukes of Milan, on which St. Ambrose was represented on horseback, with a whip in his right hand. *Encyc.*

AM'BRY, *n.* [contracted from Fr. *aumonerie*, almonry, from old Fr. *almoigne*, alms.]

1. An almonry; a place where alms are deposited for distribution to the poor. In ancient abbeys and priories there was an office of this name, in which the almoner lived.
2. A place in which are deposited the utensils for house keeping; also a cupboard; a place for cold victuals.

AMBS'-ACE, *n.* [L. *ambo*, both, and *ace.*] A double ace, as when two dice turn up the ace. *Johnson.*

AM'BULANT, *a.* [L. *ambulans*, from *ambulo.*] Walking; moving from place to place. *Encyc.*

Ambulant brokers, in Amsterdam, are exchange-brokers, or agents, who are not sworn, and whose testimony is not received in courts of justice. *Encyc.*

AMBULA'TION, *n.* [L. *ambulatio.*] A walking about; the act of walking.

AM'BULATOR, *n.* In *entomology*, a species of Lamia, whose thorax is armed on each side with two spines; a Cerambyx of Linne. *Cyc.*

AM'BULATORY, *a.* That has the power or faculty of walking; as, an animal is *ambulatory.*

2. Pertaining to a walk; as, an *ambulatory* view.
3. Moving from place to place; not stationary; as, an *ambulatory* court, which exercises its jurisdiction in different places. *Johnson.*

AM'BULATORY, *n.* A species of ichneumon, with a yellowish scutellum and spotted thorax. *Cyc.*

AM'BURY, or AN'BURY, *n.* [Qu. L. *umbo*, the navel; Gr. αμβων.]

Among *farriers*, a tumor, wart or swelling on a horse, full of blood and soft to the touch. *Encyc.*

AM'BUSCADE, *n.* [Fr. *embuscade;* Sp. Port. *emboscada;* It. *imboscata;* from It. *imboscare*, Sp. *emboscar*, to lie in *bushes*, or concealed; *in* and *bosco, bosque*, a wood; Eng. *bush.*]

1. *Literally*, a lying in a wood, concealed. for the purpose of attacking an enemy by surprise: hence, a lying in wait, and concealed in any situation, for a like purpose.

2. A private station in which troops lie concealed with a view to attack their enemy by surprise; ambush.

AM'BUSCADE, *v. t.* To lie in wait for, or to attack from a concealed position.

AM'BUSCADED, *pp.* Having an ambush laid against, or attacked from a private station; as, his troops were *ambuscaded.*

AM'BUSCADING, *ppr.* Lying in wait for; attacking from a secret station.

AM'BUSH, *n.* [Fr. *embûche*, of *in* and *bush;* Dan. *busk;* D. *bosch;* Germ. *busch;* Fr. *bosquet, boscage, bocage, bois.* See *Bush.*]

1. A private or concealed station, where troops lie in wait to attack their enemy by surprise.

2. The state of lying concealed, for the purpose of attacking by surprise; a lying in wait.

3. The troops posted in a concealed place for attacking by surprise.

Lay thee an *ambush* for the city. Josh. viii.

AM'BUSH, *v. t.* To lie in wait for; to surprise, by assailing unexpectedly from a concealed place.

AM'BUSH, *v. i.* To lie in wait, for the purpose of attacking by surprise.

Nor saw the snake, that *ambush'd* for his prey. *Trumbull.*

AM'BUSHED, *pp.* Lain in wait for; suddenly attacked from a concealed station.

AM'BUSHING, *ppr.* Lying in wait for; attacking from a concealed station.

AM'BUSHMENT, *n.* An ambush; *which see.*

AMBUS'TION, *n.* [L. *ambustio*, from *amburo*, to burn or scorch, of *amb*, about, and *uro*, to burn.]

Among *physicians*, a burning; a burn or scald.

AMEI'VA, *n.* A species of lizard, found in Brazil. *Dict. of Nat. Hist.*

AM'EL, *n.* [Fr. *email.*] The matter with which metallic bodies are overlaid; but its use is superseded by *enamel; which see.* *Boyle.*

AME'LIORATE, *v. t.* [Fr. *ameliorer*, from L. *melior*, better.]

To make better; to improve; to meliorate. *S. S. Smith. Christ. Obs. Buchanan.*

AME'LIORATE, *v. i.* To grow better; to meliorate.

AMELIORA'TION, *n.* A making or becoming better; improvement; melioration.

AMEN'. This word, with slight differences of orthography, is in all the dialects of the Assyrian stock. As a *verb*, it signifies to confirm, establish, verify; to trust, or give confidence; as a *noun*, truth, firmness, trust, confidence; as an *adjective*, firm, stable. In English, after the oriental manner, it is used at the beginning, but more generally at the end of declarations and prayers, in the sense of, *be it firm, be it established.*

And let all the people say *amen.* *Ps.* cvi.

The word is used also as a noun.

"All the promises of God are *amen* in Christ;" that is, firmness, stability, constancy.

AME'NABLE, *a.* [It. *menare;* Fr. *mener, amener;* Norm. *amesner*, to lead, to bring; Fr. *amener*, It. *ammainare*, in marine language, to strike sail.]

1. In *old law*, easy to be led; governable, as a woman by her husband. [*This sense is obsolete.*]

2. Liable to answer; responsible; answerable; liable to be called to account; as, every man is *amenable* to the laws.

We retain this idiom in the popular phrase, *to bring in*, to make answerable; as, a man is *brought in* to pay the debt of another.

AM'ENAGE, *v. t.* To manage. *Obs. Spenser.*

AM'ENANCE, *n.* Conduct, behavior. *Obs. Spenser.*

AMEND', *v. t.* [Fr. *amender;* L. *emendo*, of *e* neg, and *menda, mendum*, a fault; W. *mann*, a spot or blemish; Sp. Port. *emendar;* It. *ammendare.* See *Mend.*]

1. To correct; to rectify by expunging a mistake; as, to *amend* a law.

2. To reform, by quitting bad habits; to make better in a moral sense; as, to *amend* our ways or our conduct.

3. To correct; to supply a defect; to improve or make better, by some addition of what is wanted, as well as by expunging what is wrong, as to *amend* a bill before a legislature. Hence it is applied to the correction of authors, by restoring passages which had been omitted, or restoring the true reading.

AMEND', *v. i.* To grow or become better, by reformation, or rectifying something wrong in manners or morals. It differs from *improve*, in this, that to *amend* implies something previously wrong; to *improve*, does not.

AMEND', *n.* [Fr.] A pecuniary punishment, or fine. The *amende honorable*, in France, is an infamous punishment inflicted on traitors, parricides and sacrilegious persons. The offender, being led into court with a rope about his neck, begs pardon of his God, the court, &c. These words denote also a recantation in open court, or in presence of the injured person. *Encyc.*

AMEND'ABLE, *a.* That may be amended; capable of correction; as, an *amendable* writ or error.

AMEND'ATORY, *a.* That amends; supplying amendment; corrective.

AMEND'ED, *pp.* Corrected; rectified; reformed; improved, or altered for the better.

AMEND'ER, *n.* The person that amends.

AMEND'ING, *ppr.* Correcting; reforming; altering for the better.

AMEND'MENT, *n.* An alteration or change for the better; correction of a fault or faults; reformation of life, by quitting vices.

2. A word, clause or paragraph, added or proposed to be added to a bill before a legislature.

3. In *law*, the correction of an error in a writ or process.

Shakespeare uses it for the recovery of health, but this sense is unusual.

AMENDS', *n. plu.* [Fr. *amende.*]

Compensation for an injury; recompense; satisfaction; equivalent; as, the happiness of a future life will more than make *amends* for the miseries of this.

AME'NITY, *n.* [L. *amœnitas;* Fr. *aménité;* L. *amœnus;* W. *mwyn*, good, kind.]

Pleasantness; agreeableness of situation; that which delights the eye; *used of places and prospects.* *Brown.*

AM'ENT, *n.* [L. *amentum*, a thong, or strap.]

In *botany*, a species of inflorescence, from a common, chaffy receptacle; or consisting of many scales, ranged along a stalk or slender axis, which is the common receptacle; as in birch, oak, chesnut. *Martyn.*

AMENTA'CEOUS, *a.* Growing in an ament; resembling a thong; as, the chesnut has an *amentaceous* inflorescence. *Martyn.*

AMERCE, *v. t.* amers'. [A verb formed from *a* for *on* or *at*, and Fr. *merci*, mercy, or from L. *merces*, reward.]

1. To inflict a penalty *at mercy;* to punish by a pecuniary penalty, the amount of which is not fixed by law, but left to the discretion or *mercy* of the court; as, the court *amerced* the criminal in the sum of one hundred dollars.

2. To inflict a pecuniary penalty; to punish in general. Milton uses *of* after *amerce:* "Millions of spirits *amerced of* heaven;" but this use seems to be a poetic license.

AMER'CED, *pp.* Fined at the discretion of a court.

AMERCEMENT, *n.* amers'ment. A pecuniary penalty inflicted on an offender at the discretion of the court. It differs from a *fine*, in that the latter is, or was originally, a fixed and certain sum prescribed by statute for an offense; but an amercement is arbitrary. Hence the practice of *affeering.* [See *Affeer.*] But in America, the word *fine* is now used for a pecuniary penalty which is uncertain; and it is common in statutes, to enact that an offender shall be *fined*, at the discretion of the court. In England also, fines are now usually discretionary. Thus the word *fine* has, in a measure, superseded the use of *amercement.* This word, in old books, is written *amerciament.*

Amercement royal is a penalty imposed on an officer for a misdemeanor in his office.

AMER'CER, *n.* One who sets a fine at discretion, upon an offender.

AMER'ICA, *n.* [from Amerigo Vespucci, a Florentine, who pretended to have first discovered the western continent.]

One of the great continents, first discovered by Sebastian Cabot, June 11, O. S. 1498, and by Columbus, or Christoval Colon, Aug. 1, the same year. It extends from the eightieth degree of North, to the fifty-fourth degree of South Latitude; and from the thirty-fifth to the one hundred and fifty-sixth degree of Longitude West from Greenwich, being about nine thousand miles in length. Its breadth at Darien is narrowed to about forty-five miles, but at the northern extremity is nearly four thousand miles. From Darien to the *North*, the continent is called *North America*, and to the *South*, it is called *South America*.

AMER'ICAN, *a.* Pertaining to America.

AMER'ICAN, *n.* A native of America; originally applied to the aboriginals, or copper-colored races, found here by the Europeans; but now applied to the descendants of Europeans born in America.

The name *American* must always exalt the pride of patriotism. *Washington.*

AMER'ICANISM, *n.* The love which American citizens have to their own country, or the preference of its interests. *Analogically*, an American idiom.

AMER'ICANIZE, *v. t.* To render American; to naturalize in America.

AMER'ICIM, *n.* A species of lizard in South America, not more than two inches in length, and the third of an inch in diameter. Its legs are of the size of a hog's bristle. *Dict. of Nat. Hist.*

AMETH'ODIST, *n.* A quack. [*Not used.*]

AM'ETHYST, *n.* [L. *amethystus*; Gr. αμεθυσος, which the Greeks supposed to be formed from α neg. and μεθυω, to inebriate, from some supposed quality in the stone of resisting intoxication. Plin. xxxvii. 9, mentions an opinion that it takes its name from its color approaching that of wine, but not reaching it.]

A sub-species of quartz, of a violet blue color, of different degrees of intensity. It generally occurs crystalized in hexahedral prisms or pyramids; also in rolled fragments, composed of imperfect prismatic crystals. Its fracture is conchoidal or splintery. It is wrought into various articles of jewelry. *Cleaveland. Encyc.*

AM'ETHYST, in *heraldry*, signifies a purple color. It is the same, in a nobleman's escutcheon, as *purpure*, in a gentleman's, and *mercury*, in that of a prince. *Encyc.*

AMETHYST'INE, *a.* Pertaining to or resembling amethyst; anciently applied to a garment of the color of amethyst, as distinguished from the Tyrian and hyacinthine purple.

AM'IA, *n.* A genus of fish, of the abdominal order, found in the rivers of Carolina. *Pennant.*

A'MIABLE, *a.* [Fr. *amiable*; L. *amabilis*; from *amo*, to love.]

1. Lovely; worthy of love; deserving of affection; *applied usually to persons.* But in Ps. lxxxiv. 1, there is an exception, "How *amiable* are thy tabernacles, O Lord."
2. Pretending or showing love.

Lay *amiable* siege to the honesty of this Ford's wife. *Shak.*

But this use is not legitimate.

A'MIABLENESS, *n.* The quality of deserving love; loveliness.

A'MIABLY, *adv.* In an amiable manner; in a manner to excite or attract love.

AM'IANTH, AMIANTH'US, } *n.* [Gr. αμιαντος, of α neg. and μιαινω, to pollute, or vitiate; so called from its incombustibility. *Plin.* 36. 19.]

Earth-flax, or mountain flax; a mineral substance somewhat resembling flax; usually grayish, or of a greenish white; sometimes of a yellowish or silvery white, olive or mountain green, of a pale flesh red or ocher color. It is composed of delicate filaments, very flexible and somewhat elastic, often long and resembling threads of silk. It is incombustible, and has sometimes been wrought into cloth and paper. *Kirwan. Encyc. Cleaveland.*

AMIANTH'IFORM, *a.* [*Amianth* and *form.*] Having the form or likeness of amianth.

Amianthiform arseniate of copper. *Phillips.*

AMIANTH'INITE, *n.* A species of amorphous mineral, a variety of actinolite; its color ash, greenish or yellowish gray, often mixed with yellow or red; its fracture confusedly foliated and fibrous. *Kirwan.*

AMIANTH'OID, *n.* [*Amianth* and Gr. ειδος, form.]

A mineral which occurs in tufts, composed of long capillary filaments, flexible and very elastic; more flexible than the fibers of asbestus, but stiffer and more elastic than those of amianth. The color is olive green, or greenish white. *Haüy. Cleaveland.*

AMIANTH'OID, *a.* Resembling amianth in form.

AM'ICABLE, *a.* [L. *amicabilis*, from *amicus*, a friend, from *amo*, to love.]

1. Friendly; peaceable; harmonious in social or mutual transactions; usually applied to the dispositions of men who have business with each other, or to their intercourse and transactions; as, nations or men have come to an *amicable* adjustment of their differences.
2. Disposed to peace and friendship; as, an *amicable* temper. [*But rarely applied to a single person.*]

AM'ICABLENESS, *n.* The quality of being peaceable, friendly, or disposed to peace; friendliness; a disposition to preserve peace and friendship.

AM'ICABLY, *adv.* In a friendly manner; with harmony or good will; without controversy; as, the dispute was *amicably* adjusted.

AM'ICE, *n.* [L. *amictus* from *amicior*, to clothe; Fr. *amict*; Sp. *amito*; Port. *amicto.*]

A square linen cloth that a Catholic priest ties about his neck, hanging down behind under the alb, when he officiates at mass. *Sp. and Port. Dict.*

AMID', AMIDST', } *prep.* [of *a* and Sax. *midd*, the middle, L. *medius.* *Amidst* is the superlative degree *middest*, a contraction of Sax. *mid-mesta*, mid-most. See *Middle* and *Midst.*]

1. In the midst or middle.
2. Among; mingled with; as, a shepherd *amidst* his flock.
3. Surrounded, encompassed, or enveloped with; as, *amidst* the shade; *amid* the waves. *Amid* is used mostly in poetry.

AMID'-SHIPS, in *marine language*, the middle of a ship, with regard to her length and breadth.

AM'ILOT, *n.* A white fish in the Mexican lakes, more than a foot in length, and much esteemed at the table. *Clavigero.*

AMISS', *a.* [*a* and *miss.* See *Miss.*]

1. Wrong; faulty; out of order; improper; as, it may not be *amiss* to ask advice. [*This adjective always follows its noun.*]
2. *adv.* In a faulty manner; contrary to propriety, truth, law or morality.

Ye ask and receive not, because ye ask *amiss.* James, iv.

Applied to the body, it signifies indisposed; as, I am somewhat *amiss* to day.

AM'ITY, *n.* [Fr. *amitié*; It. *amistà*, *amistáde*; Sp. *amistad*, from *amistar*, to reconcile; Port. *amizade*; Norm. *amistee*, friendship, *amez*, friends, *ameis*, *ametz*, beloved. Qu. L. *amo*, *amicitia.*]

Friendship, in a general sense, between individuals, societies or nations; harmony; good understanding; as, our nation is in *amity* with all the world; a treaty of *amity* and commerce.

AM'MA, *n.* [Heb. אם mother.]

1. An abbess or spiritual mother.
2. A girdle or truss used in ruptures. [Gr. αμμα.] *Coxe.*

AM'MAN, *n.* [G. *amtmann*; D. *amptman*; Dan. *amtmand*; a compound of *ampt*, Sax. *ambaht* or *embeht*, office, duty, charge, and *man.* See *Embassador.*]

In *some European nations*, a judge who has cognizance of civil causes. In *France*, a notary or officer who draws deeds and other writings. *Encyc.*

AM'MITE or HAM'MITE, *n.* [Gr. αμμος, sand.]

A sand-stone or free-stone, of a pale brown color, very heavy, of a lax texture, composed of small round granules, cemented by an earthy sparry matter. The grit or granules are small stalagmites, composed of crusts or coats including one another. It is the roe-stone or oolite of recent authors. *Da Costa. Plin.* 37. 10.

AM'MOCETE, *n.* An obsolete name of the *ammodyte.* In *Cuvier*, the name of a genus of fish, including the lampern, *Petromyzon branchialis*, *Linne.*

AM'MOCHRYSE, *n. am'mokris*, [Gr. αμμος, sand, and χρυσος, gold.]

A yellow soft stone, found in Germany, consisting of glossy yellow particles. When rubbed or ground, it is used to strew over writing, like black sand with us. Qu. *yellow mica.* *Plin.* 37. 11. *Encyc.*

AM'MODYTE, *n.* [Gr. αμμος, sand, and δυω, to enter.]

The sand eel, a genus of fish, of the apodal order, about a foot in length, with a compressed head, a long slender body, and scales hardly perceptible. There is but one species, the *tobianus* or lance. It buries itself in the sand, and is found also in the stomach of the porpess, which indicates that the latter fish roots up the sand like a hog. *Encyc.*

This name is also given to a serpent of the size of a viper, and of a yellowish color, found in Africa; also to a large serpent of Ceylon, of a whitish ash color, and very venomous. *Dict. of Nat. Hist.*

AMMO'NIA, AM'MONY, } *n.* [The real origin of this word is not ascertained. Some authors suppose it to be from *Ammon*, a title of Jupiter, near whose temple in upper Egypt, it was generated. Others suppose it to be from *Ammonia*, a Cyrenaic territory; and others deduce it from αμμος, sand, as it was found in sandy ground. Anglicized, this forms an elegant word, *ammony.*]

Volatile alkali; a substance, which, in its purest form, exists in a state of gas. It is composed of hydrogen and nitrogen. Combined with the muriatic acid, it forms the muriate of ammonia, called also sal ammoniac and hydro-chlorate of ammonia. Native muriate of ammony is found in Egypt, where it is said to be generated in large inns and caravanseras, from the excrements of camels and other beasts. It occurs also massive and crystalized in the vicinity of volcanoes. Ammony, popularly called hartshorn, is extremely pungent and acrid, but when diluted, is an agreeable stimulant. It extinguishes flame, and is fatal to animal life. It combines with acids, and produces a class of salts, which, with few exceptions, are soluble in water. *Nicholson. Thompson. Webster's Manual.*

AMMO'NIAC, AMMONI'ACAL, } *a.* Pertaining to ammonia, or possessing its properties.

AMMO'NIAC, or AMMONIAC GUM, *n.* [See *Ammonia.*]
A gum resin, from Africa and the East, brought in large masses, composed of tears, internally white and externally yellow; supposed to be an exudation from an umbelliferous plant. It has a fetid smell, and a nauseous sweet taste, followed by a bitter one. It is inflammable, soluble in water and spirit of wine, and is used in medicine, as a deobstruent, and resolvent. *Encyc.*

AMMO'NIAN, *a.* Relating to Ammonius, surnamed Saccas, of Alexandria, who flourished at the end of the second century, and was the founder of the eclectic system of Philosophy; or rather, he completed the establishment of the sect, which originated with Potamo. *Enfield.*

AM'MONITE, *n.* [*Cornu ammonis,* from *Jupiter Ammon,* whose statues were represented with ram's horns.]
Serpent-stone, or cornu ammonis, a fossil shell, curved into a spiral, like a ram's horn; of various sizes, from the smallest grains to three feet in diameter. This fossil is found in stratums of limestone and clay, and in argillaceous iron ore. It is smooth or ridged; the ridges strait, crooked or undulated. *Cyc. Encyc. Plin.* 37. 10.

AMMO'NIUM, *n.* A name given to the supposed metallic basis of ammonia. If mercury, at the negative pole of a galvanic battery, is placed in contact with a solution of ammonia, and the circuit is completed, an amalgam is formed, which, at the temperature of 70° or 80° of Fahrenheit, is of the consistence of butter, but at the freezing point is a firm and crystalized mass. This amalgam is supposed to be formed by the metallic basis, *ammonium.* *Davy. Thomson.*

AMMONI'URET, *n.* The solution of a substance in ammonia. *Ed. Encyc.*

AMMUNI''TION, *n.* [L. *ad* and *munitio,* from *munio,* to fortify.]
Military stores, or provisions for attack or defense. In modern usage, the signification is confined to the articles which are used in the discharge of fire-arms and ordnance of all kinds; as powder, balls, bombs, various kinds of shot, &c.
Ammunition-bread, bread or other provisions to supply troops.

AM'NESTY, *n.* [Gr. αμνηστια, of α neg. and μνησις, memory, from the root of *mens,* mind. See *Mind.*]
An act of oblivion; a general pardon of the offenses of subjects against the government, or the proclamation of such pardon.

AM'NIOS or AM'NION, *n.* [Gr. αμνιον, a vessel or membrane.]
The innermost membrane surrounding the fetus in the womb. It is thin, transparent, soft and smooth on the inside, but rough on the outside. *Encyc.*

AMNIOT'IC, *a.* Obtained from the liquor of the amnios, as the *amniotic* acid. *Ure.*

AMOBE'AN, *a.* Alternately answering. *Warton.*

AMOBE'UM, *n.* [Gr. αμοιβαιος, alternate; αμοιβη, change.]
A poem in which persons are represented as speaking alternately, as the third and seventh eclogues of Virgil. *Encyc.*

AMO'MUM, *n.* [Gr. αμωμον; Ar. حماما hamauma, from حم hamma, to warm or heat; the heating plant.]
A genus of plants; all natives of warm climates, and remarkable for their pungency and aromatic properties. It includes the common ginger or *zingiber,* the zerumbet, zedoary, cardamom, and *granum paradisi* or grains of paradise. The roots of the three former, and the seeds of the two latter, are used in medicine as carminatives and stimulants, and in cookery as condiments. They are important articles of commerce. *Cyc.*
True amomum is a round fruit, from the East, of the size of a grape, containing, under a membranous cover, a number of angular seeds of a dark brown color, in three cells. Of this fruit, ten or twelve grow in a cluster, adhering, without a pedicle, to a woody stalk. It is of a pungent taste and aromatic smell, and was formerly much used in medicine, but is now a stranger to the shops. *Plin.* 12. 13. *Encyc.*

AMŎNG', AMŎNGST', } *prep.* *Amung', Amungst',* } [Sax. *onmang, ongemang,* among; *gemangan,* to mingle; D. and Ger. *mengen;* Sw. *mangia;* Dan. *mænger,* to mingle; Gr. μιγνυω. See *Mingle.*]
1. In a general or primitive sense, mixed or mingled with; as tares *among* wheat.
2. Conjoined or associated with, or making part of the number.
Blessed art thou *among* women. Luke, i.
3. Of the number; as, there is not one *among* a thousand, possessing the like qualities.

AMO'NIAN, *a.* [from *Amon* or *Hamon,* a title of Jupiter, or rather of the sun; Ar. Heb. and Ch. חם, חמה, Ham or Camah, which, as a verb, signifies to heat or warm, and as a noun, heat or the sun; and in Arabic, the supreme God.]
Pertaining to Jupiter Amon, or to his temple and worship in upper Egypt. *Bryant.*

AMORA'DO, *n.* [L. *amor,* love, *amo,* to love. But the word is ill formed.]
A lover. See *Inamorato,* which is chiefly used. *Ch. Rel. Appeal.*

AMO'RE, *n.* A name given by Marcgrave, to a tribe of fish, of three species, the pixuma, guacu, and tinga. They are found about the shores of South America, and are used for food. *Cyc. Dict. of Nat. Hist.*

AMORE'ANS, *n.* A sect of Gemaric doctors or commentators on the Jerusalem Talmud. The Amoreans were followed by the Mishnic doctors, and these by the Sebureans.

AMORET', *n.* [L. *amor,* love; Fr. *amourette.*]
A lover; an amorous woman; also a love knot or a trifling love affair.
Good's Sacred Idyls. Chaucer.

AM'ORIST, *n.* [L. *amor,* love.]
A lover; a gallant; an inamorato. *Boyle.*

AMORO'SO, *n.* [It. from *amor,* love.]
A lover; a man enamored.

AM'OROUS, *a.* [Fr. *amoreux;* It. *amoroso;* from L. *amor,* love.]
1. Inclined to love; having a propensity to love, or to sexual enjoyment; loving; fond.
2. In love; enamored. *Shak.*
3. Pertaining or relating to love; produced by love; indicating love; as, *amorous* delight; *amorous* airs. *Milton. Waller.*

AM'OROUSLY, *adv.* In an amorous manner; fondly; lovingly.

AM'OROUSNESS, *n.* The quality of being inclined to love, or to sexual pleasure; fondness; lovingness. *Sidney.*

AMORPH'A, *n.* [Gr. α neg. and μορφη, form.]
False or bastard indigo. The plant is a native of Carolina, constituting a genus. It rises, with many irregular stems, to the highth of twelve or fourteen feet; the leaves, beautifully pinnated, are of an admired green color, and its purple flowers grow in spikes of seven or eight inches long. Of this plant has been made a coarse kind of indigo. *Encyc.*

AMORPH'OUS, *a.* [Gr. α neg. and μορφη, form.]
Having no determinate form; of irregular shape; not of any regular figure. *Kirwan.*

AMORPH'Y, *n.* Irregularity of form; deviation from a determinate shape. *Swift.*

AMORT', *adv.* [L. *mors, mortuus.*]
In the state of the dead. *Shak.*

AMORTIZA'TION or AMORT'IZEMENT, *n.* The act or right of alienating lands or tenements to a corporation, which was considered formerly as transferring them to *dead hands,* as such alienations were mostly made to religious houses for superstitious uses. *Blackstone.*

AMORT'IZE, *v. t.* [Norm. *amortizer, amortir;* Sp. *amortizar,* to sell in mortmain; It. *ammortire,* to extinguish, from *morte,* L. *mors,* death. See *Mortmain.*]
In *English law,* to alienate in mortmain, that is, to sell to a corporation, sole or aggregate, ecclesiastical or temporal, and their successors. This was considered as selling to *dead hands.* This cannot be done without the king's license. [See *Mortmain.*] *Blackstone. Cowel.*

AMO'TION, *n.* [L. *amotio; amoveo.*]
Removal. *Warton.*

AMOUNT', *v. i.* [Fr. *monter,* to ascend; Norm. *amont,* upwards; Sp. Port. *montar;* It. *montare;* from L. *mons,* a mountain, or its root; W. *mynyz.*]
1. To rise or reach, by an accumulation of particulars, into an aggregate whole; to compose in the whole; as, the interest on the several sums *amounts* to fifty dollars.
2. To rise, reach, or extend to, in effect, or substance; to result in, by consequence, when all things are considered; as, the

testimony of these witnesses *amounts* to very little. *Bacon.*

AMOUNT′, *n.* The sum total of two or more particular sums or quantities; as, the amount of 7 and 9 is 16.

2. The effect, substance or result; the sum; as, the *amount* of the testimony is this.

AMOUNT′ING, *ppr.* Rising to, by accumulation or addition; coming or increasing to; resulting in effect or substance.

AMÖUR′, *n.* [Fr., from L. *amor*, love.] An unlawful connection in love; a love intrigue; an affair of gallantry. *South.*

AMÖV′AL, *n.* [L. *amoveo.*] Total removal. [*Not used.*] *Evelyn.*

AMÖVE′, *v. t.* [L. *amoveo*, *a* and *moveo*, to move.] To remove. [*Not used.*] *Hall. Spenser.*

AM′PELITE, *n.* [Gr. αμπελος, a vine. The name of an earth used to kill worms on vines. Pliny says it is like bitumen. Lib. 35, 16.] Cannel coal, or candle coal; an inflammable substance of a black color, compact texture, and resinous luster, and sufficiently hard to be cut and polished. It burns with a bright flame, of a short duration; and gives but a moderate heat. It is used like jet for making toys. It is found in France and England, where husbandmen smear vines with it to kill vermin. *Encyc. Cleaveland.*

AMPHIB′IAL, AMPHIB′IA, *n.* [Gr. αμφι, both or about, and βιος, life.] In *zoology*, amphibials are a class of animals, so formed as to live on land, and for a long time under water. Their heart has but one ventricle; their blood is red and cold; and they have such command of the lungs, as for a considerable time, to suspend respiration. This class of animals is divided into two orders, the Reptiles and the Serpents. To the first belong the testudo, or tortoise, the draco or dragon, the lacerta or lizard, and the rana or frog; to the second, the crotalus, boa, coluber, anguis, amphisbena, and cecilia. *Linne.*

The term has also been applied to such quadrupeds, as frequent the water, particularly the marine quadrupeds, such as the seal, walrus and lamantin. *Encyc.*

AMPHIB′IOLITE, *n.* [Gr. αμφιβιος, amphibious, and λιθος, stone.] A fragment of a petrified amphibious animal. *Dict. of Nat. Hist.*

AMPHIBIOLOĠ′I€AL, *a.* [*Infra.*] Pertaining to amphibiology.

AMPHIBIOL′OĠY, *n.* [Gr. αμφι, on both sides, βιος, life, and λογος, discourse.] A discourse or treatise on amphibious animals, or the history and description of such animals.

AMPHIB′IOUS, *a.* [See *Amphibial.*]

1. Having the power of living in two elements, air and water, as frogs, crocodiles, beavers, and the like.

2. Of a mixed nature; partaking of two natures; as, an *amphibious* breed.

AMPHIB′IOUSNESS, *n.* The quality of being able to live in two elements, or of partaking of two natures.

AMPHIB′IUM, *n.* That which lives in two elements, as in air and water.

AM′PHIBOLE, *n.* [Gr. αμφιβολος, equivocal; αμφι and βαλλω.] A name given by Haüy to a species of minerals, including the Tremolite, Hornblend, and Actinolite. Its primitive form is an oblique rhombic prism. *Cleaveland.*

AMPHIBOL′I€, *a.* Pertaining to amphibole; resembling amphibole, or partaking of its nature and characters. *Cooper.*

AMPHIBOLOĠ′I€AL, *a.* Doubtful; of doubtful meaning.

AMPHIBOLOĠ′I€ALLY, *adv.* With a doubtful meaning.

AMPHIBOL′OĠY, *n.* [Gr. αμφι, βαλλω and λογος, speech, αμφιβολογια.] A phrase or discourse, susceptible of two interpretations; aud hence, a phrase of uncertain meaning. Amphibology arises from the order of the phrase, rather than from the ambiguous meaning of a word, which is called equivocation. We have an example in the answer of the oracle to Pyrrhus. "Aio te Romanos vincere posse." Here *te* and *Romanos*, may either of them precede or follow *vincere posse*, and the sense may be either, *you* may conquer the *Romans*, or the *Romans* may conquer *you*. The English language seldom admits of amphibology. *Encyc. Johnson.*

AMPHIB′OLOUS, *a.* [Gr. αμφιβολος, αμφι and βαλλω, to strike.] Tossed from one to another; striking each way, with mutual blows. [*Little used.*]

AMPHIB′OLY, *n.* [Gr. αμφιβολια, αμφι, both ways, and βαλλω, to strike.] Ambiguity of meaning. [*Rarely used.*] *Spelman.*

AM′PHIBRA€H, *n.* [Gr. αμφι, and βραχυς, short.] In *poetry*, a foot of three syllables, the middle one long, the first and last short; as hăbērĕ, in Latin. In English verse, it is used as the last foot, when a syllable is added to the usual number forming a double rhyme; as,

The piece, you think, is incorrect, *why take it?* *Pope. Trumbull.*

AM′PHI€OME, *n.* [Gr. αμφι and κομη, hair.] A kind of figured stone, of a round shape, but rugged and beset with eminences; called *Erotylos*, on account of its supposed power of exciting love. Anciently, it was used in divination; but it is little known to the moderns. *Encyc.*

AMPHI€TYON′I€, *a.* Pertaining to the august council of Amphictyons.

AMPHI€′TYONS, *n.* In *Grecian history*, an assembly or council of deputies from the different states of Greece, supposed to be so called from Amphictyon, the son of Deucalion, but this opinion is probably a fable. Ten or twelve states were represented in this assembly, which sat at Thermopylæ, but ordinarily at Delphi. Each city sent two deputies, one called *Hieromnemon* and the other *Pylagoras*. The former inspected the sacrifices and ceremonies of religion; the latter, had the charge of deciding causes and differences between private persons. The former was elected by lot; the latter by a plurality of voices. They had an equal right to deliberate and vote in all matters relating to the common interests of Greece. *Paus. Plin. Strabo. Encyc.*

AM′PHIĠENE, *n.* [Gr. αμφι and γενος.] In *mineralogy*, another name of the leucite or Vesuvian.

AMPHIHEXAHE′DRAL, *a.* [Gr. αμφι, and *hexahedral.*] In *crystalography*, when the faces of the crystal, counted in two different directions, give two hexahedral outlines, or are found to be six in number. *Cleaveland.*

AMPHIM′ACER, *n.* [Gr. αμφιμακρος, long on both sides.] In *ancient poetry*, a foot of three syllables, the middle one short and the others long, as in cāstĭtās.

AMPHIS′BEN, AMPHISBE′NA, *n.* [Gr. αμφισβαινα, of αμφις and βαινω, to go; indicating that the animal moves with either end foremost.] A genus of serpents, with the head small, smooth and blunt; the nostrils small, the eyes minute and blackish, and the mouth furnished with small teeth. The body is cylindrical, destitute of scales, and divided into numerous annular segments; the tail obtuse, and scarcely to be distinguished from the head, whence the belief that it moved equally well with either end foremost. There are two species; the *fuliginosa*, black with white spots, found in Africa and America; and the *alba*, or white species, found in both the Indies, and generally in ant-hillocks. They feed on ants and earth-worms, and were formerly deemed poisonous; but this opinion is exploded. *Plin.* 8. 23. *Encyc. Cyc.*

The *aquatic amphisben*, *Gordius aquaticus*, *Linne*, is an animal resembling a horse hair, found in water, and moving with either end foremost. The vulgar opinion that this is an animated horse-hair is found to be an error. This hair worm is generated in the common black beetle, in which the parent worm lays its eggs; and is sometimes found in the earth and on the leaves of trees. *Lister, Phil. Trans. No.* 83.

AMPHIS′CII, AMPHIS′CIANS, *n.* [Gr. αμφι, on both sides, and σκια, shadow.] In *geography*, the inhabitants of the tropics, whose shadows, in one part of the year, are cast to the north, and in the other, to the south, according as the sun is in the southern or northern signs.

AM′PHITANE, *n.* A name given by ancient naturalists to a fossil, called by Dr. Hill *pyricubium.* Pliny describes it as of a square figure and a gold color. Qu. *Cubic pyrites.* *Pliny*, 37. 10. *Encyc.*

AMPHITHE′ATER, *n.* [Gr. αμφιθεατρον, of αμφι, about, and θεατρον, theater, from θεαομαι, to see or look.]

1. An edifice in an oval or circular form, having its area encompassed with rows of seats, rising higher as they recede from the area, on which people used to sit to view the combats of gladiators and of wild beasts, and other sports. The ancient theater was a semicircle, but exceeding it by a fourth part of its diameter; the amphitheater was a double theater, and its longest diameter was to its shortest as 1 1-2 to 1. It was at first of wood, but in the reign of Augustus one was erected of stone. The area or cavea being covered with sand was called *arena.* *Kennet.*

2. In *gardening*, a disposition of shrubs and trees in the form of an amphitheater, on a slope, or forming a slope, by placing the

lowest in front. An amphitheater may also be formed of turf only. *Encyc.*

AMPHITHE'ATRAL, *a.* Resembling an amphitheater. *Tooke.*

AMPHITHEAT'RICAL, *a.* Pertaining to or exhibited in an amphitheater. *Warton.*

AM'PHITRITE, *n.* [Gr. αμφιτριτη, a goddess of the sea.]

A genus of marine animals, of the Linnean order, *Mollusca.*

AM'PHOR, or **AM'PHORA**, *n.* [L. *amphora;* Gr. αμφορευς, or αμφιφορευς; αμφι and φορεω.]

Among the Greeks and Romans, a liquid measure. The amphora of the Romans contained about forty-eight sextaries, equal to seven gallons and a pint, English wine measure. The Grecian or Attic amphor contained about a third more. This was also, among the Romans, a dry measure of about three bushels. Among the Venetians, it is a liquid measure of sixteen quarts.

This name was formerly used in England; but the capacity of the Sax. *ambra* is not certainly known.

LL. Inæ. Cap. 70. Wilkins, Pref. LL. Æthelstan. Spelman. Encyc.

AM'PLE, *a.* [Fr. *ample;* L. *amplus.*]

1. Large; wide; spacious; extended; as *ample* room. This word carries with it the sense of room or space fully sufficient for the use intended.

2. Great in bulk, or size; as an *ample* tear. *Shak.*

3. Liberal; unrestrained; without parsimony; fully sufficient; as, *ample* provision for the table; *ample* justice.

4. Liberal; magnificent; as *ample* promises.

5. Diffusive; not brief or contracted; as an *ample* narrative.

AM'PLENESS, *n.* Largeness; spaciousness; sufficiency; abundance.

AMPLEX'ICAUL, *a.* [L. *amplexor*, to embrace, of *amb* about, and *plico, plexus*, to fold, and *caulis*, καυλος, a stem.]

In *botany*, surrounding or embracing the stem, as the base of a leaf.

AM'PLIATE, *v. t.* [L. *amplio.* See *Ample.*]

To enlarge; to make greater; to extend. [*Little used.*]

AMPLIA'TION, *n.* Enlargement; amplification; diffuseness. [*Little used.*]

2. In *Roman antiquity*, a deferring to pass sentence; a postponement of a decision, to obtain further evidence. *Encyc.*

AMPLIFICA'TION, *n.* [L. *amplificatio.*]

1. Enlargement; extension.

2. In *rhetoric*, diffusive description or discussion; exaggerated representation; copious argument, intended to present the subject in every view or in the strongest light; diffuse narrative, or a dilating upon all the particulars of a subject; a description given in more words than are necessary, or an illustration by various examples and proofs.

AM'PLIFIED, *pp.* Enlarged; extended; diffusively treated.

AM'PLIFIER, *n.* One who amplifies or enlarges; one who treats a subject diffusively, to exhibit it in the strongest light. *Sidney.*

AM'PLIFY, *v. t.* [Fr. *amplifier;* L. *amplifico;* of *amplus* and *facio*, to make large.]

1. To enlarge; to augment; to increase or extend, in *a general sense; applied to material or immaterial things.*

2. In *rhetoric*, to enlarge in discussion or by representation; to treat copiously, so as to present the subject in every view and in the strongest lights.

3. To enlarge by addition; to improve or extend; as, to *amplify* the sense of an author by a paraphrase.

AM'PLIFY, *v. i.* To speak largely or copiously; to be diffuse in argument or description; to dilate upon; often followed by *on;* as, to *amplify on* the several topics of discourse. *Watts.*

2. To exaggerate; to enlarge by representation or description; as,

Homer *amplifies*—not invents. *Pope.*

AM'PLIFYING, *ppr.* Enlarging; exaggerating; diffusively treating.

AM'PLITUDE, *n.* [L. *amplitudo*, from *amplus*, large.]

1. Largeness; extent, applied to bodies; as, the *amplitude* of the earth.

2. Largeness; extent of capacity or intellectual powers; as, *amplitude* of mind.

3. Extent of means or power; abundance; sufficiency. *Watts.*

Amplitude, in astronomy, is an arch of the horizon intercepted between the east and west point, and the center of the sun or star at its rising or setting. At the rising of a star, the amplitude is eastern or ortive; at the setting, it is western, occiduous, or occasive. It is also northern or southern, when north or south of the equator. *Johnson. Encyc.*

Amplitude of the range, in projectiles, is the horizontal line subtending the path of a body thrown, or the line which measures the distance it has moved. *Johnson. Chambers.*

Magnetical amplitude is the arch of the horizon between the sun or a star, at rising or setting, and the east or west point of the horizon, by the compass. The difference between this and the true amplitude is the variation of the compass. *Encyc.*

AM'PLY, *adv.* Largely; liberally; fully; sufficiently; copiously; in a diffusive manner.

AM'PUTATE, *v. t.* [L. *amputo*, of *amb*, about, and *puto*, to prune.]

1. To prune branches of trees or vines; to cut off.

2. To cut off a limb or other part of an animal body; *a term of surgery.*

AM'PUTATED, *pp.* Cut off; separated from the body.

AM'PUTATING, *ppr.* Cutting off a limb or part of the body.

AMPUTA'TION, *n.* [L. *amputatio.*]

The act or operation of cutting off a limb or some part of the body.

AM'ULET, *n.* [L. *amuletum;* Fr. *amulette;* Sp. *amuleto;* from Lat. *amolior, amolitus*, to remove.]

Something worn as a remedy or preservative against evils or mischief, such as diseases and witchcraft. Amulets, in days of ignorance, were common. They consisted of certain stones, metals or plants; sometimes of words, characters or sentences, arranged in a particular order. They were appended to the neck or body. Among some nations, they are still in use. *Encyc.*

AMU'SE, *v. t.* *s* as *z.* [Fr. *amuser*, to stop or keep at bay, to detain; from *muser*, to loiter, or trifle; It. *musare*, to gaze or stand idle; Ger. *müssig*, idle. Qu. Gr. μυζω; Lat. *musso.*]

1. To entertain the mind agreeably; to occupy or detain attention with agreeable objects, whether by singing, conversation, or a show of curiosities. Dr. Johnson remarks, that *amuse* implies something less lively than *divert*, and less important than *please.* Hence it is often said, we are *amused* with trifles.

2. To detain; to engage the attention by hope or expectation; as, to *amuse* one by flattering promises.

AMU'SED, *pp.* *s* as *z.* Agreeably entertained; having the mind engaged by something pleasing.

AMU'SEMENT, *n.* *s* as *z.* That which amuses, detains or engages the mind; entertainment of the mind; pastime; a pleasurable occupation of the senses, or that which furnishes it, as dancing, sports or music.

AMU'SER, *n.* *s* as *z.* One who amuses, or affords an agreeable entertainment to the mind.

AMU'SING, *ppr.* or *a.* *s* as *z.* Entertaining; giving moderate pleasure to the mind, so as to engage it; pleasing.

AMU'SINGLY, *adv.* *s* as *z.* In an amusing manner.

AMU'SIVE, *a.* That has the power to amuse or entertain the mind.

AMYG'DALATE, *a.* [L. *amygdalus*, an almond.] Made of almonds.

AMYG'DALATE, *n.* An emulsion made of almonds; milk of almonds. *Bailey. Coxe.*

AMYG'DALINE, *a.* Pertaining to or resembling the almond.

AMYG'DALITE, *n.* A plant; a species of spurge, with leaves resembling those of the almond. *Ash.*

AMYG'DALOID, *n.* [Gr. αμυγδαλεα, an almond, and ειδος, form; G. *mandel-stein*, almond-stone.]

Toad-stone; a compound rock, consisting of a basis of basalt, greenstone or some other variety of trap, imbedding nodules of various minerals, particularly calcarious spar, quartz, agate, zeolite, chlorite, &c. When the imbedded minerals are detached, it is porous, like lava. *Cleaveland.*

AMYG'DALOIDAL, *a.* Pertaining to amygdaloid.

AMYLA'CEOUS, *a.* [L. *amylum*, starch, of *a* priv. and μυλη, a mill, being formerly made without grinding. *Plin.* 18. vii.]

Pertaining to starch, or the farinaceous part of grain; resembling starch.

AM'YLINE, *n.* [L. *amylum;* Gr. αμυλον; αμυλος, unground, *a* and μυλη, mill.]

A farinaceous substance between gum and starch. *Webster's Manual.*

AM'YRALDISM, *n.* In *church history*, the doctrine of universal grace, as explained by Amyraldus, or Amyrault, of France, in the seventeenth century. He taught that God desires the happiness of all men, and that none are excluded by a divine decree, but that none can obtain salvation without faith in Christ; that God refuses to none the power of believing, though he does not grant to all his assistance to improve this power. *Encyc.*

AMYZ'TLI, *n.* A Mexican name of the sea-lion, an amphibious quadruped, inhabiting the shores and rivers of America, on the Pacific ocean. Its body is three feet in length, and its tail, two feet. It has a long snout, short legs and crooked nails. Its skin is valued for the length and softness of its hair. *Clavigero.*

AN, *a.* [Sax. *an, ane,* one ; D. *een ;* Ger. *ein ;* Sw. and Dan. *en ;* Fr. *on, un, une ;* Sp. *un, uno ;* It. *uno, una ;* L. *unus, una, unum ;* Gr. εν ; Ir. *ein, ean, aon ;* W. *un, yn ;* Corn. *uynyn ;* Arm. *yunan.*]

One ; noting an individual, either definitely, known, certain, specified, or understood ; or indefinitely, not certain, known, or specified. Definitely, as "Noah built *an* ark of Gopher wood." "Paul was *an* eminent apostle." Indefinitely, as "Bring me *an* orange." Before a consonant the letter *n* is dropped, as *a* man ; but our ancestors wrote *an* man, *an* king. This letter represents *an* definitely, or indefinitely. Definitely, as "I will take you to me for *a* people, and I will be to you *a* God." Ex. vi. Indefinitely, as "the province of *a* judge is to decide controversies." *An* being the same word as *one,* should not be used with it ; "such *an one*" is tautology ; the true phrase is *such one.* Although *an, a* and *one,* are the same word, and always have the same sense, yet by custom, *an* and *a* are used exclusively as a definitive adjective, and *one* is used in numbering. Where our ancestors wrote *an, twa, thry,* we now use *one, two, three.* So *an* and *a* are never used except with a noun ; but *one* like other adjectives, is sometimes used without its noun, and as a substitute for it ; "*one* is at a loss to assign a reason for such conduct."

AN, in old English authors, signifies *if ;* as, "*an* it please your honor." So in Gr. αν or εαν, Ar. ان, Sam. and L. *an,* if or whether ; Ir. *an,* Ch. אן or אין, if, whether. It is probably an imperative, like *if, gif, give.* Qu. Sax. *annan,* or *anan,* to give.

A'NA, *ăă,* or *ă.* [Gr. ανα.]

In *medical prescriptions,* it signifies an equal quantity of the several ingredients ; as, wine and honey, *ana, ăă* or *ă* ʒ ii. that is, of wine and honey each two ounces.

A'NA, as a termination, is annexed to the names of authors to denote a collection of their memorable sayings. Thus, *Scaligerana,* is a book containing the sayings of Scaliger. It was used by the Romans, as in *Collectaneus,* collected, gathered.

ANABAP'TISM, *n.* [See *Anabaptist.*]

The doctrine of the Anabaptists. *Ash.*

ANABAP'TIST, *n.* [Gr. ανα, again, and βαπτιςης, a baptist.]

One who holds the doctrine of the baptism of adults, or of the invalidity of infant baptism, and the necessity of rebaptization in an adult age. One who maintains that baptism ought always to be performed by immersion. *Encyc.*

ANABAPTIST'IC, ANABAPTIST'ICAL, } *a.* Relating to the Anabaptists, or to their doctrines. *Milton. Bull.*

ANABAP'TISTRY, *n.* The sect of Anabaptists.

ANABAPTI'ZE, *v. t.* To rebaptize. [*Not used.*] *Whitlock.*

ANACA, *n.* A species of parokeet, about the size of a lark ; the crown of the head is a dark red, the upper part of the neck, sides, back and wings are green. *Dict. of Nat. Hist.*

ANACAMP'TIC, *a.* [Gr. ανα and καμπτω, to bend.]

1. Reflecting or reflected ; a word formerly applied to that part of optics, which treats of reflection ; the same as what is now called *catoptric.* [See *Catoptrics.*]

2. *Anacamptic sounds,* among the Greeks, were sounds produced by reflection, as in echoes ; or such as proceeded downwards from acute to grave. *Rousseau. Busby.*

ANACAMP'TICS, *n.* The doctrine of reflected light. [See *Catoptrics.*]

ANACAR'DIUM, *n.* The cashew-nut, or marking nut, which produces a thickish, red, caustic, inflammable liquor, which, when used in marking, turns black, and is very durable. *Ure.*

ANACATHAR'TIC, *a.* [Gr. ανα, upward, and καθαρσις, a purging. See *Cathartic.*]

Throwing upwards ; cleansing by exciting vomiting, expectoration, &c. *Quincy.*

ANACATHAR'TIC, *n.* A medicine which excites discharges by the mouth, or nose, as expectorants, emetics, sternutatories and masticatories. *Quincy.*

ANACHORET. [See *Anchoret.*]

ANACH'RONISM, *n.* [Gr. ανα, and χρονος, time.]

An error in computing time ; any error in chronology, by which events are misplaced.

ANACHRONIS'TIC, *a.* Erroneous in date ; containing an anachronism. *Warton.*

ANACLAS'TIC, *a.* [Gr. ανα and κλασις, a breaking, from κλαω, to break.]

Refracting ; *breaking* the rectilinear course of light.

Anaclastic glasses, sonorous glasses or phials, which are flexible, and emit a vehement noise by means of the human breath ; called also *vexing* glasses, from the fright which their resilience occasions. They are low phials with flat bellies, like inverted tunnels, and with very thin convex bottoms. By drawing out a little air, the bottom springs into a concave form with a smart crack ; and by breathing or blowing into them, the bottom, with a like noise, springs into its former convex form. *Encyc.*

ANACLAS'TICS, *n.* That part of optics which treats of the refraction of light, commonly called *dioptrics,* which see. *Encyc.*

ANACOENO'SIS, *n.* [Gr. ανακοινωσις ; ανα and κοινος, common.]

A figure of rhetoric, by which a speaker applies to his opponents for their opinion on the point in debate. *Walker.*

ANACOND'A, *n.* A name given in Ceylon to a large snake, a species of Boa, which is said to devour travelers. Its flesh is excellent food. *Encyc.*

ANACREON'TIC, *a.* Pertaining to Anacreon, a Greek poet, whose odes and epigrams are celebrated for their delicate, easy and graceful air, and for their exact imitation of nature. His verse consists of three feet and a half, usually spondees and iambuses, sometimes anapests ; as in this line of Horace.

"Lydia, dic per omnes." *Encyc.*

ANACREON'TIC, *n.* A poem composed in the manner of Anacreon.

AN'ADEME, *n.* [Gr. αναδημα.] A chaplet or crown of flowers. *W. Browne.*

ANADIPLO'SIS, *n.* [Gr. ανα, again, and διπλοος, double.]

Duplication, a figure in rhetoric and poetry, consisting in the repetition of the last word or words in a line or clause of a sentence, in the beginning of the next ; as, "he retained his virtues amidst all his misfortunes, misfortunes which no prudence could foresee or prevent. *Encyc.*

ANAD'ROMOUS, *a.* [Gr. ανα, upward, and δρομος, course.]

Ascending ; a word applied to such fish as pass from the sea into fresh waters, at stated seasons. *Encyc.*

AN'AGLYPH, *n.* [Gr. ανα, and γλυφω, to engrave.]

An ornament made by sculpture.

ANAGLYP'TIC, *a.* Relating to the art of carving, engraving, enchasing or embossing plate. *Evelyn.*

AN'AGOGE, AN'AGOGY, } *n.* [Gr. αναγωγη, of ανα, upward, and αγωγη, a leading, from αγω.]

An elevation of mind to things celestial ; the spiritual meaning or application of words ; also the application of the types and allegories of the old testament to subjects of the new. *Encyc.*

ANAGOG'ICAL, *a.* Mysterious ; elevated ; spiritual ; as, the rest of the sabbath, in an *anagogical* sense, signifies the repose of the saints in heaven.

ANAGOG'ICALLY, *adv.* In a mysterious sense ; with religious elevation.

ANAGOG'ICS, *n.* Mysterious considerations. *Addison.*

AN'AGRAM, *n.* [Gr. ανα, and γραμμα, a letter.]

A transposition of the letters of a name, by which a new word is formed. Thus *Galenus* becomes *angelus ; William Noy,* (attorney general to Charles I., a laborious man,) may be turned into *I moyl in law.*

ANAGRAMMAT'IC, ANAGRAMMAT'ICAL, } *a.* Making an anagram. *Camden's Remains.*

ANAGRAMMAT'ICALLY, *adv.* In the manner of an anagram.

ANAGRAM'MATISM, *n.* The act or practice of making anagrams. *Camden.*

ANAGRAM'MATIST, *n.* A maker of anagrams.

ANAGRAM'MATIZE, *v. i.* To make anagrams. *Herbert.*

AN'AGROS, *n.* A measure of grain in Spain, containing something less than two bushels. *Encyc.*

A'NAL, *a.* [L. *anus.*] Pertaining to the anus ; as, the *anal* fin. *Encyc. Pennant.*

ANAL'CIM, ANAL'CIME, } *n.* Cubic zeolite, found in aggregated or cubic crystals. *Ure.*

This mineral is generally crystalized, but is also found amorphous, and in reniform, mammillary, laminated or radiated masses. By friction, it acquires a *weak* electricity; hence its name, Gr. αναλκις, weak. *Cleaveland.*

AN'ALECTS, *n.* [Gr. ανα and λεγω, to collect.] A collection of short essays, or remarks. *Encyc.*

AN'ALEMMA, *n.* [Gr. αναλημμα, altitude.]

1. In *geometry*, a projection of the sphere on the plane of the meridian, orthographically made by straight lines, circles and ellipses, the eye being supposed at an infinite distance, and in the east or west points of the horizon. Also,

2. An instrument of wood or brass on which this kind of projection is drawn, with a horizon and cursor fitted to it, in which the solstitial colure, and all circles parallel to it, will be concentric circles; all circles oblique to the eye will be ellipses; and all circles whose planes pass through the eye, will be right lines. *Encyc. Ash.*

ANALEP'SIS, *n.* [Gr. αναληψις, from αναλαμβανω, to receive again.] The augmentation or nutrition of an emaciated body; recovery of strength after a disease. *Quincy.*

ANALEP'TIC, *a.* Corroborating; invigorating; giving strength after disease.

ANALEP'TIC, *n.* A medicine which gives strength, and aids in restoring a body to health after sickness; a restorative.

ANAL'OGAL, *a.* Analogous. [*Not used.*] *Hale.*

ANALOG'ICAL, *a.* Having analogy; used by way of analogy; bearing some relation. Thus *analogical* reasoning is reasoning from some similitude which things known bear to things unknown. An *analogical* word is one which carries with it some relation to the original idea. Thus the word *firm* primarily denotes solidity or compactness in a material body; and by analogy, when used of the mind, it conveys the idea of qualities having a similitude to the solidity of bodies, that is, fixedness or immovability. *Watts.*

ANALOG'ICALLY, *adv.* In an analogical manner; by way of similitude, relation or agreement. Thus to reason *analogically* is to deduce inferences from some agreement or relation which things bear to each other.

ANALOG'ICALNESS, *n.* The quality of being analogical; fitness to be applied for the illustration of some analogy. *Johnson.*

ANAL'OGISM, *n.* [Gr. αναλογισμος.] An argument from the cause to the effect. *Johnson.*

Investigation of things by the analogy they bear to each other. *Crabbe.*

ANAL'OGIST, *n.* One who adheres to analogy.

ANAL'OGIZE, *v. t.* To explain by analogy; to form some resemblance between different things; to consider a thing with regard to its analogy to something else. *Cheyne.*

ANAL'OGOUS, *a.* Having analogy; bearing some resemblance or proportion; followed by *to*; as, there is something in the exercise of the mind *analogous to* that of the body.

ANAL'OGY, *n.* [Gr. αναλογια, of ανα, and λογος, ratio, proportion.]

1. An agreement or likeness between things in some circumstances or effects, when the things are otherwise entirely different. Thus a plant is said to have *life*, because its growth resembles in some degree, that of an animal. In *life* and *growth*, then, there is an *analogy* between a *plant* and an *animal*. Learning *enlightens* the mind, because it is to the mind, what *light* is to the eye, enabling it to discover things before hidden. When the things which have an analogy follow a preposition, that preposition must be *between* or *betwixt;* as there is an analogy *between* plants and animals, or *between* customs. When one of the things precedes a verb, and the other follows, the preposition used must be *to* or *with;* as, a plant has some analogy *to* or *with* an animal.

2. With *grammarians*, analogy is a conformity of words to the genius, structure or general rules of a language. Thus the general rule in English is that the plural of a noun ends in *es;* therefore all nouns which have that plural termination have an *analogy*, or are formed in *analogy* with other words of a like kind. *Johnson. Encyc.*

ANAL'YSIS, *n.* [Gr. αναλυσις, of ανα and λυσις, a loosing, or resolving, from λυω, to loosen. See *Loose.*]

1. The separation of a compound body into its constituent parts; a resolving; as, an *analysis* of water, air or oil, to discover its elements.

2. A consideration of any thing in its separate parts; an examination of the different parts of a subject, each separately; as the words which compose a sentence, the notes of a tune, or the simple propositions which enter into an argument. It is opposed to *synthesis.*

In *mathematics*, analysis is the resolving of problems by algebraic equations. The analysis of finite quantities is otherwise called algebra, or specious arithmetic. The analysis of infinites is the method of fluxions, or the differential calculus. *Encyc.*

In *logic*, analysis is the tracing of things to their source, and the resolving of knowledge into its original principles.

3. A syllabus, or table of the principal heads of a continued discourse, disposed in their natural order.

4. A brief, methodical illustration of the principles of a science. In this sense, it is nearly synonymous with *synopsis.*

AN'ALYST, *n.* One who analyzes, or is versed in analysis. *Kirwan.*

ANALYT'IC, ANALYT'ICAL, } *a.* Pertaining to analysis; that resolves into first principles; that separates into parts or original principles; that resolves a compound body or subject; as, an *analytical* experiment in chimistry, or an *analytical* investigation. It is opposed to *synthetic.*

ANALYT'ICALLY, *adv.* In the manner of analysis; by way of separating a body into its constituent parts, or a subject, into its principles.

ANALYT'ICS, *n.* The science of analysis. [See *Analysis.*]

AN'ALYZE, *v. t.* [Gr. αναλυω. See *Analysis.*] To resolve a body into its elements; to separate a compound subject into its parts or propositions, for the purpose of an examination of each separately; as, to *analyze* a fossil substance; to *analyze* an action to ascertain its morality.

AN'ALYZED, *pp.* Resolved into its constituent parts or principles, for examination.

AN'ALYZER, *n.* One who analyzes; that which analyzes or has the power to analyze.

AN'ALYZING, *ppr.* Resolving into elements, constituent parts, or first principles.

ANAMORPH'OSIS, *n.* [Gr. ανα, and μορφωσις, formation.] In *perspective drawings*, a deformed or distorted portrait or figure, which, in one point of view, is confused or unintelligible, and in another, is an exact and regular representation; or confused to the naked eye, but reflected from a plain or curved mirror, appearing regular, and in right proportion. *Johnson. Encyc.*

ANA'NAS, *n.* The name of a species of Bromelia, the pine-apple. *Encyc.*

AN'APEST, *n.* [Gr. ανα, and παιω, to strike. *Bailey.*] In *poetry*, a foot, consisting of three syllables, the two first short, the last long; the reverse of the dactyl; as,

Căn ă bŏsŏm sŏ gĕntlĕ rĕmāin
Unmoved when her Corydon sighs? *Shenstone.*

ANAPEST'IC, *n.* The anapestic measure. *Bentley.*

ANAPEST'IC, *a.* Pertaining to an anapest; consisting of anapestic feet.

ANAPH'ORA, *n.* [Gr. from αναφερω.]

1. A figure in rhetoric, when the same word or words are repeated at the beginning of two or more succeeding verses or clauses of a sentence; as, "*Where* is the wise? *Where* is the scribe? *Where* is the disputer of this world?" *Johnson.*

2. Among *physicians*, the discharge of blood or purulent matter by the mouth. *Encyc. Coxe.*

ANAPLEROT'IC, *a.* [Gr. αναπληροω, to fill.] Filling up; supplying or renovating flesh.

ANAPLEROT'IC, *n.* A medicine which renews flesh or wasted parts. *Encyc. Coxe.*

AN'ARCH, *n.* [See *Anarchy.*] The author of confusion; one who excites revolt. *Milton.*

ANARCH'IC, ANARCH'ICAL, } *a.* Without rule or government; in a state of confusion; applied to a state or society. Fielding uses *anarchial*, a word of less difficult pronunciation.

AN'ARCHIST, *n.* An anarch; one who excites revolt, or promotes disorder in a state. *Stephens.*

AN'ARCHY, *n.* [Gr. αναρχια, of α priv. and αρχη, rule.] Want of government; a state of society, when there is no law or supreme power, or when the laws are not efficient, and individuals do what they please with impunity; political confusion.

ANAR'HICHAS, *n.* The sea wolf; a genus of ravenous fish, of the order of *Apodals*, found in the northern seas.

A'NAS, *n.* [L.] A genus of water fowl of the order *Anseres;* including the swans, geese, and ducks. The species are very numerous.

ANAS'ARCA, *n.* [Gr. ανα, in or between, and σαρξ, flesh.]

A species of dropsy, from a serous humor spread between the skin and flesh; or an accumulation of lymph in the cellular membrane, occasioning a soft, pale, inelastic swelling of the skin. *Quincy. Coxe.*

ANAS'AREOUS, *a.* Belonging to anasarca, or dropsy; dropsical.

ANAS'TOMOSE, *v. i.* s as z. [Gr. ανα, and στομα, mouth.]

To inosculate; to unite the mouth of one vessel with another, as the arteries with the veins. *Darwin. Encyc.*

ANASTOM'OSY, } *n.* The inosculation of
ANASTOMO'SIS, } vessels, or the opening of one vessel into another, as an artery into a vein; a relaxation or dilatation of the mouths of vessels; also the communication of two vessels, as a vein with a vein. *Quincy. Encyc. Coxe.*

ANASTOMOT'IC, *a.* Opening the mouths of vessels, or removing obstructions.

ANASTOMOT'IC, *n.* A medicine supposed to have the power of opening the mouths of vessels, and promoting circulation, such as cathartics, deobstruents and sudorifics. *Encyc.*

ANAS'TROPHE, } *n.* [Gr. αναςροφη, a con-
ANAS'TROPHY, } version or inversion.]

In *rhetoric* and *grammar*, an inversion of the natural order of words; as *saxa per et scopulos*, for *per saxa et scopulos*. *Encyc.*

AN'ATASE, *n.* [Gr αναrασις, extension, so named from the length of its crystals.]

Octahedrite; octahedral oxyd of titanium; a mineral that shows a variety of colors by reflected light, from indigo blue to reddish brown. It is usually crystalized in acute, elongated, pyramidical octahedrons. *Ure. Cleaveland.*

ANATH'EMA, *n.* [Gr. αναθεμα, from ανατιθημι, to place behind, backward or at a distance, to separate.]

1. Excommunication with curses. Hence, a curse or denunciation by ecclesiastical authority, accompanying excommunication. This species of excommunication was practiced in the ancient churches, against notorious offenders; all churches were warned not to receive them; all magistrates and private persons were admonished not to harbor or maintain them, and priests were enjoined not to converse with them, or attend their funeral.

There are two kinds of anathemas, *judiciary* and *abjuratory*. The former is pronounced by a council, pope or bishop; the latter is the act of a convert who anathematizes the heresy which he abjures.

2. In *heathen mythology*, an offering, or present made to some deity and hung up in a temple. Whenever a person quitted his employment, he *set apart*, or dedicated his tools to his patron-deity. Persons who had escaped danger remarkably, or been otherwise very fortunate, testified their gratitude by some offering to their deity. *Encyc.*

ANATHEMAT'ICAL, *a.* Pertaining to anathema.

ANATHEMAT'ICALLY, *adv.* In the manner of anathema.

ANATHEMATIZA'TION, *n.* The act of anathematizing. *Encyc.*

ANATH'EMATIZE, *v. t.* To excommunicate with a denunciation of curses; to pronounce an anathema against. *Hammond.*

ANATH'EMATIZED, *pp.* Excommunicated with curses.

ANATH'EMATIZING, *ppr.* Pronouncing an anathema.

ANATIF'EROUS, *a.* [L. *anas*, a duck, and *fero*, to produce.] Producing ducks. *Brown.*

ANAT'OCISM, *n.* [L. *anatocismus*, from Gr. ανα, again, and τοκος, usury.]

Interest upon interest; the taking of compound interest; or the contract by which such interest is secured. [*Rarely used.*] *Johnson. Cicero.*

ANATOM'ICAL, *a.* Belonging to anatomy or dissection; produced by or according to the principles of anatomy, or natural structure of the body; relating to the parts of the body when dissected or separated.

ANATOM'ICALLY, *adv.* In an anatomical manner; by means of dissection; according to the doctrine of anatomy.

ANAT'OMIST, *n.* One who dissects bodies; more generally, one who is skilled in the art of dissection, or versed in the doctrine and principles of anatomy.

ANAT'OMIZE, *v. t.* To dissect an animal; to divide into the constituent parts, for the purpose of examining each by itself; to lay open the interior structure of the parts of a body or subject; as, to *anatomize* an animal or plant; to *anatomize* an argument.

ANAT'OMIZED, *pp.* Dissected, as an animal body.

ANAT'OMIZING, *ppr.* Dissecting.

ANAT'OMY, *n.* [Gr. ανατομη, of ανα, through, and τεμνω, to cut.]

1. The art of dissecting, or artificially separating the different parts of an animal body, to discover their situation, structure and economy.
2. The doctrine of the structure of the body, learned by dissection; as, a physician understands *anatomy.*
3. The act of dividing any thing, corporeal or intellectual, for the purpose of examining its parts; as, the *anatomy* of a plant, or of a discourse.
4. The body stripped of its integuments; a skeleton, or the corporeal frame of bones entire, without the skin, flesh and vessels; *an improper use of the word, and vulgar.*
5. *Ironically*, a meager person.

ANATREP'TIC, *a.* [Gr. ανατρεπω, to overturn.]

Overthrowing; defeating; prostrating; *a word applied to the dialogues of Plato, which represent a complete defeat in the gymnastic exercises.* *Enfield.*

AN'ATRON, *n.* [from Gr. νιτρον, niter.]

1. Soda or mineral fixed alkali.
2. Spume or glass gall, a scum which rises upon melted glass, in the furnace, and when taken off, dissolves in the air, and then coagulates into common salt.
3. The salt which collects on the walls of vaults. *Johnson. Coxe.*

AN'BURY, *n.* A disease in turneps, or an injury occasioned by a fly.

AN'CESTOR, *n.* [Fr. *ancestres, ancêtres*; L. *antecessor*, of *ante*, before, and *cedo*, to go.]

One from whom a person descends, either by the father or mother, at any distance of time, in the tenth or hundredth generation. An *ancestor* precedes in the order of nature or blood; a *predecessor*, in the order of office.

ANCES'TRAL, *a.* Relating or belonging to ancestors; claimed or descending from ancestors; as, an *ancestral* estate.

AN'CESTRY, *n.* A series of ancestors, or progenitors; lineage, or those who compose the line of natural descent. Hence, birth or honorable descent. *Addison.*

AN'CHILOPS, *n.* [Gr. αιγιλωψ, from αιξ, a goat, and ωψ, an eye. Qu.]

The goat's eye; an abscess in the inner angle of the eye; an incipient fistula lachrymalis. *Encyc. Coxe.*

AN'CHOR, *n.* [L. *anchora*; Gr. αγκυρα; It. and Port. *ancora*; Sp. *ancla*; D. G. Dan. *anker*; Sw. *anchare*; Ir. *ankaire, ancoir* or *ingir*; Corn. *ankar*; Ar. *ankar*; Pers. *anghar*; Russ. *iacor*; Fr. *ancre*; Arm. *ancor.*]

1. An iron instrument for holding a ship or other vessel at rest in water. It is a strong shank, with a ring at one end, to which a cable may be fastened; and with two arms and flukes at the other end, forming a suitable angle with the shank to enter the ground.

In seamen's language, the *anchor comes home*, when it is dislodged from its bed, so as to drag by the violence of the wind, sea or current.

Foul anchor is when the anchor hooks or is entangled with another anchor, or with a wreck or cable, or when the slack cable is entangled.

The anchor *a cock bill*, is when it is suspended perpendicularly from the cat head, ready to be let go.

The anchor *a peek*, is when it is drawn in so tight as to bring the ship directly over it.

The anchor is *a trip*, or *a weigh*, when it is just drawn out of the ground, in a perpendicular direction, either by the cable or the buoy-rope.

To back an anchor is to lay down a small anchor ahead of that by which the ship rides, with the cable fastened to the crown of the latter to prevent its coming home.

At anchor is when a ship rides by her anchor. Hence, *to lie* or *ride at anchor.*

To cast anchor, or *to anchor*, is to let go an anchor, to keep a ship at rest.

To weigh anchor is to heave or raise the anchor out of the ground.

Anchors are of different sizes. The principal, and that on which most dependence is placed, is the *sheet anchor*. Then come the *best bower*, the *small bower*, the *spare anchor*, the *stream anchor*, and the *kedge anchor*, which is the smallest. *Mar. Dict.*

2. In *a figurative sense*, that which gives stability or security; that on which we place dependence for safety.

Which hope we have as an *anchor* of the soul, both sure and stedfast. Heb. vi.

3. In *architecture*, anchors are carved work, somewhat resembling an anchor. It is commonly a part of the ornaments of the boultins of capitals in the Tuscan, Doric and Ionic orders, and on the moldings of cornices.

In *heraldry*, anchors are emblems of hope. *Encyc.*

AN'CHOR, *v. t.* To place at anchor; to moor; as to *anchor* a ship.

2. To fix or fasten on; to fix in a stable condition.

AN'CHOR, *v. i.* To cast anchor; to come to anchor; as, our ship *anchored* off the isle of Wight.

2. To stop; to fix or rest on.

AN'CHORABLE, *a.* Fit for anchorage. [*Not used.*] *Herbert.*

AN'CHORAGE, *n.* Anchor-ground; a place where a ship can anchor, where the ground is not too rocky, nor the water too deep nor too shallow.

2. The hold of a ship at anchor, or rather the anchor and all the necessary tackle for anchoring.

3. A duty imposed on ships for anchoring in a harbor.

AN'CHORED, *pp.* Lying or riding at anchor; held by an anchor; moored; fixed in safety.

AN'CHORESS, *n.* A female anchoret. *Fairfax.*

AN'CHORET, or AN'CHORITE, *n.* [Gr. αναχωρητης, from αναχωρεω, to retire, of ανα, and χωρεω, to go. Written by some authors, *anachoret.*]

A hermit; a recluse; one who retires from society into a desart or solitary place, to avoid the temptations of the world and devote himself to religious duties. Also a monk, who, with the leave of the abbot, retires to a cave or cell, with an allowance from the monastery, to live in solitude. *Encyc.*

AN'CHOR-GROUND, *n.* Ground suitable for anchoring.

AN'CHOR-HOLD, *n.* The hold or fastness of an anchor; security.

AN'CHORING, *ppr.* Mooring; coming to anchor; casting anchor.

AN'CHOR-SMITH, *n.* The maker or forger of anchors, or one whose occupation is to make anchors.

ANCHO'VY, AN'CHOVY, *n.* [Port. and Sp. *anchova*; Fr. *anchois*; It. *acciuga*; G. *anschove.*]

A small fish, about three inches in length, of the genus Clupea, found and caught, in vast numbers, in the Mediterranean, and pickled for exportation. It is used as a sauce or seasoning.

ANCHO'VY-PEAR, *n.* A fruit of Jamaica, constituting the genus Grias. It is large, contains a stone, and is esculent.

AN'CIENT, *a.* Usually pronounced most anomalously, *ancient.* The pronunciation of the first vowel ought to accord with that in *antiquity, anger, anchor,* &c. [Fr. *ancien*; It. *anziano, anzi*; from L. *ante, antiquus.*]

1. Old; that happened or existed in former times, usually at a great distance of time; as, *ancient* authors, *ancient* days. *Old*, says Johnson, relates to the duration of the thing itself, as an *old* coat; and *ancient*, to time in general, as an *ancient* dress. But this distinction is not always observed. We say, in *old* times, as well as *ancient* times; *old* customs, &c. In general, however, *ancient* is opposed to *modern*, and *old* to *new, fresh* or *recent.* When we speak of a thing that existed formerly, which has ceased to exist, we commonly use *ancient*, as *ancient* republics, *ancient* heroes, and not *old* republics, *old* heroes. But when the thing which began or existed in former times, is still in existence, we use either *ancient* or *old*; as, *ancient* statues or paintings, or *old* statues or paintings; *ancient* authors, or *old* authors, meaning books. But in these examples *ancient* seems the most correct, or best authorized. Some persons apply *ancient* to men advanced in years still living; but this use is not common in modern practice, though found in scripture.

With the *ancient* is wisdom. Job.

2. Old; that has been of long duration; as, an *ancient* forest; an *ancient* city.

3. Known from *ancient* times; as the *ancient* continent, opposed to the new continent. *Robertson.*

AN'CIENT, *n.* [*Supra.*] Generally used in the plural, *ancients.* Those who lived in former ages, opposed to *moderns.*

In *scripture*, very old men. Also, governors, rulers, political and ecclesiastical.

The Lord will enter into judgment with the *ancients* of his people. Isa. iii. Jer. xix.

God is called the *Ancient* of days from his eternal existence. Dan. vii.

Hooker uses the word for *seniors*, "They were his *ancients*," but the use is not authorized.

2. *Ancient* is also used for a flag or streamer, in a ship of war; and for an ensign or the bearer of a flag, as in Shakespeare. Cowel supposes the word, when used for a flag, to be a corruption of *end-sheet*, a flag at the stern. It is probably the Fr. *enseigne.* *Johnson. Cowel. Encyc.*

Ancient demain, in English Law, is a tenure by which all manors belonging to the crown, in the reign of William the Conqueror, were held. The numbers, names, &c. of these were all entered in a book called *Domes-day Book. Cowel. Blackstone.*

AN'CIENTLY, *adv.* In old times; in times long since past; as Rome was *anciently* more populous than at present.

AN'CIENTNESS, *n.* The state of being ancient; antiquity; existence from old times.

AN'CIENTRY, *n.* Dignity of birth; the honor of ancient lineage. *Spenser on Ireland. Shak.*

AN'CIENTY, *n.* Age; antiquity. [*Not in use.*] *Martin.*

AN'CIENTY, *n.* In some old English statutes and authors, *eldership* or seniority. 14. Hen. III.

AN'CILLARY, *a.* [L. *ancilla*, a female servant.]

Pertaining to a maid servant, or female service; subservient as a maid servant. *Blackstone.*

ANCIP'ITAL, *a.* [L. *anceps.*]

Doubtful, or double; double-faced or double-formed; applied to the stem of a plant, it signifies a two edged stem, compressed and forming two opposite angles. *Barton's Elem. of Botany. Lee.*

AN'COME, *n.* A small ulcerous swelling coming suddenly. *Boucher.*

AN'CON, *n.* [L. *ancon*; Gr. αγκων, the elbow.]

The olecranon, the upper end of the ulna, or elbow. *Coxe.*

AN'CONE, *n.* [Lat. *ancon*, Gr. αγκων.] In *architecture*, the corner of a wall, cross-beam or rafter. *Encyc.*

AN'CONY, *n.* [Probably from αγκων, the cubit, from its resemblance to the arm.]

In *iron works*, a piece of half wrought iron, in the shape of a bar in the middle, but rude and unwrought at the ends. A piece of cast iron is melted off and hammered at a forge, into a mass of two feet long and square, which is called a *bloom*; then, carried to a finery, and worked into an *ancony*; it is then sent to a chafery, where the ends are wrought into the shape of the middle, and the whole is made into a bar. *Encyc.*

AND, *conj.* [Sax. *and*; Ger. *und*; D. *ende* or *en*; and.]

And is a conjunction, connective or conjoining word. It signifies that a word or part of a sentence is to be added to what precedes. Thus, give me an apple *and* an orange; that is, give me an apple, *add* or give in addition to that, an orange. John *and* Peter *and* James rode to New-York, that is, John rode to New-York; *add* or *further*, Peter rode to New-York; *add* James rode to New-York.

AN'DALUSITE, *n.* A massive mineral, of a flesh or rose red color; sometimes found crystalized in imperfect four-sided prisms, nearly or quite rectangular. Its hardness is nearly equal to that of Corundum, and it is infusible by the blow pipe. It has its name from Andalusia, in Spain, where it was first discovered. *Werner. Brongniart.*

ANDAN'TE, [It. from *andare*, to go; Eng. to *wend*, to wander.]

In *music*, a word used to direct to a movement moderately slow, between *largo* and *allegro.* *Encyc.*

AN'DARAC, *n.* Red orpiment. *Coxe.*

AN'DEAN, *a.* Pertaining to the Andes, the great chain of mountains extending through S. America. *Columbiad*, 3, 138.

ANDI'RA, *n.* A species of bat in Brazil, nearly as large as a pigeon. *Dict. Nat. Hist.*

AND'IRON, *n.* [Teutonic, *andena*, or *andela.* In Sax. the corresponding word is *brand-isen*, brand or fire iron; D. *brandyzer.* The Fr. *landier*, Arm. *lander*, Junius thinks, is our *and-iron*, with the French *l* prefixed.]

An iron utensil used, in Great Britain, where coal is the common fuel, to support the ends of a spit; but in America, used to support the wood in fire places.

ANDORIN'HA, *n.* The Brazilian swallow. *Dict of Nat. Hist.*

ANDRANAT'OMY, *n.* [Gr. ανηρ, ανδρος, a man, and ανατομη, dissection.]

The dissection of a human body, especially of a male. *Coxe. Quincy.*

AN'DREOLITE, *n.* A mineral, the harmotome, or cross-stone. *Ure.*

ANDROG'YNAL, ANDROG'YNOUS, *a.* [Gr. ανηρ, a man, and γυνη, woman.]

Having two sexes; being male and female; hermaphroditical.

In *botany*, the word is applied to plants which bear both male and female flowers, from the same root, as birch, walnut, oak, chesnut, mulberry, &c. These plants constitute the monecian class in Linne's system, and frequently have an *amentum*, thong or catkin, for a calyx. *Milne.*

ANDROG'YNALLY, *adv.* With the parts of both sexes.

ANDROG'YNUS. *n.* A hermaphrodite. *Johnson.*

AN'DROID, *n.* [Gr. ανηρ, man, and ειδος, form.]

A machine, in the human form, which, by certain springs, performs some of the natural motions of a living man. One of these machines, invented by M. Vaucanson, appeared at Paris in 1738, representing a flute player. *Encyc.*

ANDROM'EDA, *n.* A northern constellation, behind Pegasus, Cassiopeia and Perseus, representing the figure of a woman chained. The stars in this constellation, in Ptolemy's catalogue, are 23; in Tycho's, 22; in Bayer's, 27; in Flamsted's, 84.

2. The name of a celebrated tragedy of Euripides, now lost. *Encyc.*

ANDROPH'AGI, *n.* [Gr. ανηρ, man, and φαγω, to eat.]

Man-eaters; but the word is little used, being superseded by *anthropophagi*, which see. Herodotus mentions people of this character. *Melpom*, 106.

ANE'AR, *prep.* Near. *Atterbury.*

AN'ECDOTE, *n.* [Gr. α priv. and εκδιδωμι, to publish, part. εκδοτος, given out.]

In *its original sense*, secret history, or facts not generally known. But *in more common usage*, a particular or detached incident or fact of an interesting nature; a biographical incident; a single passage of private life. Procopius gave the title of *anecdotes* to a book he published against Justinian and his wife Theodora; and similar collections of incidents in the lives of eminent men are now common. *Encyc.*

ANECDOT'ICAL, *a.* Pertaining to anecdotes. *Bolingbroke.*

ANE'LE, *v. t.* [Sax. *æll*, oil.]

To give extreme unction. [*Not used.*] *Shak.*

ANEMOG'RAPHY, *n.* [Gr. ανεμος, wind, and γραφη, description.]

A description of the winds. *Johnson.*

ANEMOL'OGY, *n.* [Gr. ανεμος, wind, and λογος, discourse.]

The doctrine of winds, or a treatise on the subject.

ANEMOM'ETER, *n.* [Gr. ανεμος, wind, and μετρεω, to measure.]

An instrument or machine for measuring the force and velocity of the wind. *Encyc.*

ANEM'ONE, } *n.* [Gr. ανεμωνη, from ανεμος,
ANEM'ONY, } wind. It was by the ancient Greeks written ανεμωλια. Theoph. Lib. 6. Ca. 7. Plin. 21, 23. Venus is said to have changed her Adonis into an *anemone*. Ovid. Metam. Lib. 10, 735.]

Wind-flower; a genus of plants of numerous species. Some of the species are cultivated in gardens, of which their double flowers are among the most elegant ornaments.

Sea Anemone. See *Animal Flower.*

ANEM'OSCOPE, *n.* [Gr. ανεμος, wind, and σκοπεω, to view.]

A machine which shows the course or velocity of the wind. *Encyc.*

ANENT', *prep.* About; concerning; over against: a Scottish word. Qu. Gr. εναντι.

AN'EURISM, *n.* [Gr. ανα, and ευρυνω, to dilate, from ευρυς, broad.]

A preternatural dilatation or rupture of the coats of an artery. This is encysted or diffused. The encysted *aneurism* is when the coats of the artery being only dilated, the blood is confined to its proper coat. Of this kind is the varicose. The diffused *aneurism* includes all those in which, from an aperture in the artery, the blood is spread about in the cellular membrane, out of its proper course. *Quincy. Coxe.*

ANEURIS'MAL, *a.* Pertaining to an aneurism.

ANEW' *adv.* [*a* and *new.*]

Over again; another time; in a new form; as, to arm *anew*; to create *anew*.

ANFRAC'TUOUS, *a.* [L. *anfractus*, of amb, about, and *fractus*, broken. See *Break.*]

Winding; full of windings and turnings; written less correctly, *anfractuose*. *Ray.*

ANFRAC'TUOUSNESS, *n.* A state of being full of windings and turnings.

ANGARIA'TION, *n.* [L. *angario*; Gr. αγγαρευω, to compel; a word of Persian origin.]

Compulsion; exertion. [*Not used.*]

ANGEIOT'OMY, *n.* See *Angiotomy.*

AN'GEL, *n.* Usually pronounced *ângel*, but most anomalously. [L. *angelus*, Gr. αγγελος, a messenger, from αγγελλω, to tell or announce; Ir. *agalla*, *agallaim*, to speak or tell; from the root of *call*, or of Ar. قال to say, to tell. Sax. *angel*; Ir. *aingeal*, or *aingiol*; D. G. Sw. Dan. *engel*; Sp. *angel*; It. *angelo*; Port. *anjo*; Fr. *ange*; Russ. *angel.*]

1. *Literally*, a messenger; one employed to communicate news or information from one person to another at a distance. But appropriately,

2. A spirit, or a spiritual intelligent being employed by God to communicate his will to man. Hence angels are ministers of God, and ministring spirits. Heb. 1.

3. In *a bad sense*, an evil spirit; as, the *angel* of the bottomless pit. Math. xxv. 1 Cor. vi. Rev. ix.

4. Christ, the mediator and head of the church. Rev. x.

5. A minister of the gospel, who is an embassador of God. Rev. ii. and iii.

6. Any being whom God employs to execute his judgments. Rev. xvi. *Cruden.*

7. In the style of love, a very beautiful person. *Shak.*

AN'GEL, *n.* A fish found on the coast of Carolina, of the thoracic order and genus Chætodon. It has a small projecting mouth; the lamens above the gills are armed with cerulean spines; the body, a foot in length, appears as if cut off, and waved, and covered with large green scales. *Pennant from Catesby.*

AN'GEL, *n.* A gold coin formerly current in England, bearing the figure of an angel. Skinner says, this device was impressed upon it in allusion to an observation of Pope Gregory the Great, who, seeing some beautiful English youths, in the market at Rome, asked who they were; being told they were *Angli*, English, he replied, they ought rather to be called *angeli*, angels. This coin had different values under different princes; but is now an imaginary sum or money of account, implying ten shillings sterling. *Encyc.*

AN'GEL, *a.* Resembling angels; angelic; as, *angel* whiteness. *Shak.*

ANGEL-AGE, *n.* The existence or state of angels. *Beaumont, &c.*

AN'GEL-FISH, *n.* A species of shark, the *squalus squatina.* It is from six to eight feet long, with a large head, teeth broad at the base, but slender and sharp above, disposed in five rows, all round the jaws. The fish takes its name from its pectoral fins, which are very large and extend horizontally, like wings when spread. This fish connects the genus of rays, with that of sharks, partaking of the characters of both; but it differs from both in this, that its mouth is placed at the extremity of the head. *Encyc.*

ANGEL'IC, } *a.* [L. *angelicus.*] Resem-
ANGEL'ICAL, } bling angels; belonging to angels, or partaking of their nature; suiting the nature and dignity of angels.

ANGEL'ICA, *n.* A genus of digynian pentanders, containing several species. The common sort is cultivated for medicinal uses. It grows naturally in northern climates, and has large umbels of a globose figure. The roots have a fragant aromatic smell, and are used in the aromatic tincture. The stalks make an agreeable sweetmeat. *Encyc.*

ANGEL'ICALLY, *adv.* Like an angel.

ANGEL'ICALNESS, *n.* The quality of being angelic; excellence more than human.

AN'GELITES, in *Church history*, so called from Angelicum in Alexandria, where they held their first meetings, a sect of heretics near the close of the 5th century, who held the persons of the trinity not to be the same, nor to exist by their own nature; but each to be a God, existing by participating of a deity common to them all. They are called also Severites, from Severus, their head; and Theodosians, from one Theodosius, whom they made their Pope. *Encyc.*

AN'GEL-LIKE, *a.* Resembling or having the manners of angels.

ANGELOL'OGY, *n.* [*Angel* and λογος.]

A discourse on angels; or the doctrine of angelic beings. *Ch. Spectator.*

AN'GELOT, *n.* [Fr. *anche*, the reed of a hautboy or other instrument of music.]

1. An instrument of music, somewhat resembling a lute. *Johnson.*

2. An ancient English coin struck at Paris while under the dominion of England; so called from the figure of an angel supporting the escutcheon of the arms of England and France. Also, a small rich sort of cheese made in Normandy. *Encyc.*

AN'GEL-SHOT, *n.* [Fr. *ange*, a chain-shot.]

Chain-shot, being two halves of a cannon ball fastened to the ends of a chain.

AN'GEL-WINGED, *a.* Winged like angels. *Thomson.*

AN'GEL-WORSHIP, *n.* The worshiping of angels. *Trapp.*

AN'GER, *n.* *ang'ger.* [L. *ango*, to choke, strangle, vex; whence *angor*, vexation, *anguish*, the quinsy, *angina*. Gr. αγχω, to strangle, to strain or draw together, to vex. The primary sense is to press, squeeze, make narrow; Gr. αγχι, near; Sax. *enge*; G. *enge*; D. Dan. *eng*, narrow, strait; W. *ing*. This word may be connected in origin with the Ar. حنق hanika, to be angry, and خنق chanaka, to strangle; Heb. Ch. Syr. Eth. חנק, to strangle. In Sax. *ange* signifies vexed; *angmod*, sad, anxious; *ang-set*, a carbuncle; *angsum*, pressed close; *anxsumian*, to vex, to make anxious; Eng. *anguish, anxious*; L. *angustus, angina*, &c. See *Anguish.*]

1. A violent passion of the mind excited by a real or supposed injury; usually accompanied with a propensity to take vengeance, or to obtain satisfaction from the offending party. This passion however varies in degrees of violence, and in ingenuous minds, may be attended only with a desire to reprove or chide the offender.

Anger is also excited by an injury offered to a relation, friend or party to which one is attached; and some degrees of it may be excited by cruelty, injustice or oppression offered to those with whom one has no immediate connection, or even to the community of which one is a member. Nor is it unusual to see something of this passion roused by gross absurdities in others, especially in controversy or discussion. Anger may be inflamed till it rises to rage and a temporary delirium.

2. Pain; smart of a sore or swelling; *the literal sense of the word*, but little used.

AN'GER, *v. t.* ang'ger. To excite anger; to provoke; to rouse resentment.

2. To make painful; to cause to smart; to inflame; as, to *anger* an ulcer. *Bacon.*

AN'GERLY, *adv.* [*anger* and *like.*]

In an angry manner; more generally written *angrily.*

ANǴI'NA, *n.* [L. from *ango*, to choke. See *Anger.*]

A quinsy; an inflammation of the throat; a tumor impeding respiration. It is a general name of the diseases called sore-throat, as quinsy, scarlet fever, croup, mumps, &c. *Coxe.*

Angina pectoris, an anomalous or spasmodic affection of the chest and organs of respiration; or a disease of the heart. *Coxe.*

ANǴIOG'RAPHY, *n.* [Gr. αγγειον, a vessel, and γραφη, description.]

A description of the vessels in the human body. *Ash.*

ANǴIOL'OǴY, *n.* [Gr. αγγειον, a vessel, and λογος, discourse.]

A treatise or discourse on the vessels of the human body, as the arteries, veins, lymphatics, &c. *Quincy.*

ANǴIOMONOSPERM'OUS, *n.* [Gr. αγγειον, a vessel, μονος, alone, and σπερμα, seed.]

Producing one seed only in a pod. *Bailey. Johnson.*

AN'ǴIOSPERM, *n.* [Gr. αγγειον, a vessel, and σπερμα, seed.]

In *botany*, a plant which has its seeds inclosed in a pericarp.

ANǴIOSPERM'OUS *a.* Having seeds inclosed in a pod or other pericarp. In Linne's system, the second order of plants in the didynamian class are called *angiospermia.* This word is opposed to *gymnospermous*, or naked-seeded.

ANǴIOT'OMY, *n.* [Gr. αγγειον, a vessel, and τεμνω, to cut.]

The opening of a vessel, whether a vein or an artery, as in bleeding. It includes both arteriotomy and phlebotomy.

AN'GLE, *n.* [Fr. *angle*; L. *angulus*, a corner; Gr. αγκυλος; W. *ongle*; G. and D. *angel*, a hook, an *angle*; Dan. *angel*, a hook, *angle*, a sting; Sax. *angel*, a hook; Sp. Port. *angulo*; It. *angolo.* The German has *angeln*, for angling with a hook; but in D. *hengel* is the rod, and *hengelen*, to *angle.* Qu. *hinge* and *hang.*]

In *popular language*, the point where two lines meet, or the meeting of two lines in a point; a corner.

In *geometry*, the space comprised between two straight lines that meet in a point, or between two straight converging lines which, if extended, would meet; or the quantity by which two straight lines, departing from a point, diverge from each other. The point of meeting is the vertex of the angle, and the lines, containing the angle, are its sides or legs.

In *optics*, the *angle of incidence* is the angle which a ray of light makes with a perpendicular to the surface, or to that point of the surface on which it falls.

The *angle of refraction* is the angle which a ray of light refracted makes with the surface of the refracting medium; or rather with a perpendicular to that point of the surface on which it falls. *Encyc.*

A *right angle*, is one formed by a right line falling on another perpendicularly, or an angle of 90 degrees, making the quarter of a circle.

An *obtuse angle* is greater than a right angle, or more than 90 degrees.

An *acute angle* is less than a right angle or less than 90 degrees.

A *rectilineal* or right-lined angle, is formed by two right lines.

A *curvilineal angle*, is formed by two curved lines.

A *mixed angle* is formed by a right line with a curved line.

Adjacent or contiguous angles are such as have one leg common to both angles, and both together are equal to two right angles.

External angles are angles of any right-lined figure without it, when the sides are produced or lengthened.

Internal angles are those which are within any right-lined figure.

Oblique angles are either acute or obtuse, in opposition to right angles.

A *solid angle* is the meeting of three or more plain angles at one point.

A *spherical angle* is one made by the meeting of two arches of great circles, which mutually cut one another on the surface of the globe or sphere. *Bailey.*

AN'GLE, *n.* A hook; an instrument to take fish, consisting of a rod, a line and a hook, or a line and hook.

AN'GLE, *v. i.* To fish with an angle, or with line and hook.

2. *v. t.* or *i.* To fish for; to try to gain by some bait or insinuation, as men angle for fish; as, to *angle* for the hearts of people, or to *angle* hearts. *Shak. Sidney.*

AN'GLED, *a.* Having angles—*used only in compounds.*

AN'GLER, *n.* One that fishes with an angle; also a fish, a species of *lophius.*

AN'GLE-ROD, *n.* The rod or pole to which a line and hook are fastened.

AN'GLIC, AN'GLICAN, *a.* [From *Angles*, Sax. *ing*, a plain or meadow, and *lic*, like, or ειxος, like, which is the root of the L. *icus*, in *publicus*, and all similar adjectives. From *ing*, was formed *Angles*, the English, to which is added this common affix, *ic.* The *Angles*, were the Ingævones, of Tacitus, *ing-woners*, dwellers on the plain or level land, near the Elbe and Weser. [See *English* and *Wont.*] *Ing* is annexed to many English names, as *Reading, Basing, Kittering*, towns situated on flat land.]

English; pertaining to England or the English nation; as the *Anglican church.* *Pinkerton.*

AN'GLICISM, *n.* An English Idiom; a form of language peculiar to the English. *Milton.*

AN'GLICIZE, *v. t.* To make English; to render conformable to the English idiom, or to English analogies.

AN'GLING, *ppr.* Fishing with an angle.

AN'GLING, *n.* A fishing with a rod and line.

ANGLO-DA'NISH, *a.* Pertaining to the English Danes, or the Danes who settled in England. *Wotton.*

ANGLO-NORM'AN, *a.* Pertaining to the English Normans. *Wotton.*

ANGLO-SAX'ON, *a.* Pertaining to the Saxons, who settled in England, or English Saxons.

ANGLO-SAX'ON, *n.* A kind of pear; also the language of the English Saxons.

ANGO'LA-PEA or PIGEON-PEA. A species of Cytisus.

AN'GOR, *n.* [L. See *Anger.*]

1. Pain; intense bodily pain.

2. The retiring of the native bodily heat to the center, occasioning head-ache, palpitation and sadness. *Encyc. Coxe.*

AN'GRED or ANG'ERED, *pp.* Made angry; provoked.

AN'GRILY, *adv.* In an angry manner; peevishly; with indications of resentment.

AN'GRY, *a.* [See *Anger.*]

1. Feeling resentment; provoked; followed generally by *with* before a person.

God is *angry with* the wicked every day. Ps. vii.

But it is usually followed by *at* before a thing.

Wherefore should God be *angry at* thy voice? Eccles. v.

2. Showing anger; wearing the marks of anger; caused by anger; as, an *angry* countenance; *angry* words.

3. Inflamed, as a sore; red; manifesting inflammation.

4. Raging; furious; tumultuous.

Or chain the *angry* vengeance of the waves. *Trumbull.*

ANGSA'NA or ANGSA'VA, *n.* A red gum of the East Indies, like that of dragon's blood. *Coxe.*

AN'GU, *n.* Bread made of the Cassada, a plant of the W. Indies.

AN'GUIFER, *n.* [L. *anguis*, a serpent, and *fero*, to bear; Sans. *agui.*]

In *astronomy*, a cluster of stars in the form of a man holding a serpent; Serpentarius, one of the twelve signs of the zodiac. *Ash.*

ANGUIL'LA, *n.* [L. an eel.]

In *zoology*, an *eel*; also the name of a Mediterranean fish used for food, called also hospetus and atherina. Qu. *Atherina Hepsetus, Linne.* *Dict. Nat. Hist.*

ANGUIL'LIFORM, *a.* [L. *anguilla*, an eel, and *forma*, shape.]

In the form of an eel, or of a serpent; resembling an eel or serpent.

AN'GUISH, *n.* [Fr. *angoisse*; It. *angoscia*; Sp. *ansia*; Port. *angustia*, showing the direct derivation of this word from L. *angustia*, narrowness, from pressure; D. and G. *angst*; Dan. *angest*. This and a numerous class of words are from the root *ang*, *eng*, denoting narrow, from pressure. See *Anger*.]

Extreme pain, either of body or mind. As bodily pain, it may differ from *agony*, which is such distress of the whole body as to cause contortion, whereas *anguish* may be a local pain as of an ulcer, or gout. But anguish and agony are nearly synonymous. As pain of the mind, it signifies any keen distress from sorrow, remorse, despair and the kindred passions.

And they hearkened not to Moses, for *anguish* of spirit, and for cruel bondage. Ex. vi.

AN'GUISH, *v. t.* To distress with extreme pain or grief. *Temple.*

AN'GUISHED, *pp.* Extremely pained; tortured; deeply distressed.

AN'GULAR, *a.* Having an angle, angles or corners; pointed; as an *angular* figure.

2. Consisting of an angle; forming an angle; as an *angular* point.

ANGULAR'ITY, *n.* The quality of having an angle or corner.

AN'GULARLY, *adv.* With angles, or corners; in the direction of the angles.

AN'GULARNESS, *n.* The quality of being angular.

AN'GULATED, *a.* Formed with angles or corners. *Woodward.*

AN'GULOUS, *a.* Angular; having corners; hooked. *Glanville.*

ANGUST', *a.* [L. *angustus.*]

Narrow; straight. [*Not used.*] *Burton.*

ANGUSTA'TION, *n.* [L. *angustus*, narrow. See *Anger*.]

The act of making narrow; a straightening, or being made narrow. *Wiseman.*

ANGUST'ICLAVE, *n.* [L. *angustus*, narrow, and *clavus*, a knob or stud.]

A robe or tunic embroidered with purple studs or knobs, or by purple stripes, worn by Roman knights. The laticlave, with broader studs, was worn by senators. *Quinctilian. Kennet.*

ANHELA'TION, *n.* [L. *anhelo*, to pant or breathe with difficulty; from *halo*, to breathe.]

Shortness of breath; a panting; difficult respiration, without fever, or with a sense of suffocation. *Encyc. Coxe.*

ANHELO'SE, *a.* Out of breath; panting; breathing with difficulty. [*Little used.*] *Dict.*

AN'HIMA, *n.* A Brazilian aquatic fowl, larger than a swan, somewhat like a crane. Its head is small, its bill black, the toes armed with long claws. But what is remarkable, is a horn growing from its forehead; and the second joint of the wing is armed with two straight triangular spurs, an inch in length. The fidelity between the male and female is so great, that when one dies, the other remains by the carcase, till it expires. *Dict. of Nat. Hist.*

AN'HYDRITE, *n.* [See *Anhydrous*.]

A species of sulphate of lime, anhydrous gypsum, of which there are several varieties; compact, granular, fibrous, radiated, sparry, siliciferous or vulpinite, and convoluted. *Jameson. Ure.*

ANHY'DROUS, *a.* [Gr. ανυδρος, dry; α priv. and υδωρ, water.]

Destitute of water. Anhydrite is so called, because it is destitute of the water of crystalization. *Cleaveland.*

ANIENT'ED, *a.* [It. *niente*, nothing; Norm. *neant*; Fr. *aneantir*, to annihilate.]

Frustrated; brought to naught. *Obs.* *Chaucer.*

ANI'GHT, *adv.* [*a* or *at*, and *night.*]

In the night time; *anights*, in the plural, is used of frequent and customary acts.

You must come in earlier *anights*. *Shak.*

AN'IL, *n.* [Sp. *añil*, indigo; Port. *anil*; D. *anyl*; Ar. نِيل nilon, slender, *nila*, blue.]

A shrub from whose leaves and stalks indigo is made; *Indigofera*, or the indigo plant. *Encyc.*

ANIL'ITY, *n.* [L. *anilis*, *anilitas*, from *anus*, an old woman; Celtic, *hen*, old.]

The state of being an old woman; the old age of a woman; dotage.

ANIMADVER'SION, *n.* [L. *animadversio.*]

Remarks by way of censure or criticism; reproof; blame. It may sometimes be used for *punishment*, or punishment may be implied in the word, but this is not common. In an ecclesiastical sense, it differs from *censure*, says Ayliffe; censure, respecting spiritual punishment, and animadversion, a temporal one. Glanville uses the word in the sense of *perception*, but this use is not authorized.

ANIMADVER'SIVE, *a.* That has the power of perceiving. *Obs.* *Glanville.*

ANIMADVERT', *v. i.* [L. *animadverto*, of *animus*, mind, and *adverto*, to turn to.]

1. To turn the mind to; to consider.

2. To consider or remark upon by way of criticism or censure. *Dryden.*

3. To inflict punishment; followed by *upon.* *Grew.*

ANIMADVERT'ER, *n.* One who animadverts or makes remarks by way of censure.

ANIMADVERT'ING, *ppr.* Considering; remarking by way of criticism or censure.

AN'IMAL, *n.* [L. *animal*, from *anima*, air, breath, soul; Gaelic *anam*, breath. The W. has *envil*, *en*, a being, soul, spirit, and *mil*, a beast; Arm. *aneval.* Qu. Dan. *aande*, Sw. *anda*, breath.]

An organized body, endowed with life and the power of voluntary motion; a living, sensitive, locomotive body; as, man is an intelligent *animal.* Animals are essentially distinguished from plants by the property of *sensation.* The contractile property of some plants, as the mimosa, has the appearance of the effect of *sensation*, but it may be merely the effect of *irritability.*

The distinction here made between animals and vegetables, may not be philosophically accurate; for we cannot perhaps ascertain the precise limit between the two kinds of beings, but this is sufficiently correct for common practical purposes.

The history of animals is called *zoology.*

By way of contempt, a dull person is called a stupid *animal.*

AN'IMAL, *a.* That belongs or relates to animals; as *animal* functions.

Animal is distinguished from *intellectual*; as *animal* appetites, the appetites of the body, as hunger and thirst.

The *animal* functions, are touch, taste, motion, &c.

Animal life is opposed to *vegetable* life.

Animal is opposed also to *spiritual* or *rational*, which respects the *soul* and *reasoning faculties*; as *animal* nature, *spiritual* nature, *rational* nature.

Animal food may signify that food which nourishes animals; but it usually denotes food consisting of animal flesh.

Animal economy is the system of laws by which the bodies of animals are governed and depending on their organic structure.

Animal spirit is a name given to the nervous fluid.

Animal spirits in the plural, life, vigor, energy.

Animal system, or *animal* kingdom denotes the whole class of beings endowed with animal life. *Encyc. Johnson.*

ANIMAL'CULE, *n.* [L. *animalculum*, *animalcula.*]

A little animal; but appropriately, an animal whose figure cannot be discerned without the aid of a magnifying glass; such as are invisible to the naked eye. *Encyc.*

AN'IMAL-FLOWER, *n.* In *zoology*, sea-anemone, sea-nettle or urtica marina, the name of several species of animals belonging to the genus actinia. They are called *sea-nettle* from their supposed property of stinging, and *sea-anemone* from the resemblance of their claws or tentacles, to the petals of some flowers. These are disposed in regular circles, and tinged with various bright colors. Some of these animals are hemispherical, others cylindrical; others are shaped like a fig. Some are stiff and gelatinous; others, fleshy and muscular; but all can alter their figure by extending their claws in search of food. These animals can move slowly, but are generally fixed by one end to rocks or stones in the sand. On the other extremity, is the mouth in the center, which is surrounded by rows of fleshy claws and capable of great dilatation. They are very voracious, and will swallow a muscle, or crab, as large as a hen's egg. *Encyc.*

The term, *Animal Flower*, is also extended to many other marine animals, from their resemblance to flowers. They belong to the *Holothurias*, which with the *Actinias*, were ranged under the *Molluscas*, by Linne; and to the *Tubularias* and *Hydras*, which were classed with the *Zoophytes*. They are all arranged under the *Zoophytes*, by Cuvier. *Cyc.*

ANIMALIZA'TION, *n.* The act of giving animal life, or endowing with the properties of an animal. *Ure. Med. Repos.*

AN'IMALIZE, *v. t.* To give animal life to; to endow with the properties of animals.

AN'IMALIZED, *pp.* Endowed with animal life.

AN'IMALIZING, *ppr.* Giving animal life to.

AN'IMATE, *v. t.* [L. *animo.* See *Animal.*]

1. To give natural life to; to quicken; to make alive; as, the soul *animates* the body.

2. To give powers to, or to heighten the

powers or effect of a thing; as, to *animate* a lyre.

3. To give spirit or vigor; to infuse courage, joy, or other enlivening passion; to stimulate or incite; as, to *animate* dispirited troops.

AN'IMATE, *a.* Alive; possessing animal life. *Milton.*

[This word is used chiefly in poetry for *animated.*]

AN'IMATED, *pp.* Being endowed with animal life, as the various classes of *animated* beings.

2. *a.* Lively; vigorous; full of spirit; indicating animation; as an *animated* discourse.

AN'IMATING, *ppr.* Giving life; infusing spirit; enlivening.

ANIMA'TION, *n.* The act of infusing life; the state of being animated.

2. The state of being lively, brisk or full of spirit and vigor; as, he recited the story with great *animation.*

AN'IMATIVE, *a.* That has the power of giving life or spirit. *Johnson.*

AN'IMATOR, *n.* One that gives life; that which infuses life or spirit.

AN'IME, *n.* [Fr.] In *heraldry*, a term denoting that the eyes of a rapacious animal are borne of a different tincture from the animal himself.

AN'IME, *n.* [Sp.] A resin exuding from the stem of a large American tree called by the natives *courbaril;* by Piso, *jetaiba.* It is of a transparent amber color, a light agreeable smell, and of little or no taste. It dissolves entirely, but not readily, in rectified spirit of wine, and is used by the Brazilians in fumigations, for pains proceeding from cold. *Encyc.*

ANIMET'TA, *n.* Among *ecclesiastical writers*, the cloth which covers the cup of the eucharist. *Encyc.*

ANIMOS'ITY, *n.* [L. *animositas;* Fr. *animosité;* from L. *animosus*, animated, courageous, enraged; from *animus*, spirit, mind, passion. So in Teutonic, *mod*, mind, signifies also pride, passion, anger. *Animus*, spirit, Gr. *ανεμος*, wind, breath, is from flowing, swelling, rushing, which gives the sense of violent action and passion. See *Animal.*]

Violent hatred accompanied with active opposition; active enmity. *Animosity* differs from *enmity* which may be secret and inactive; and it expresses a less criminal passion than *malice. Animosity* seeks to gain a cause or destroy an enemy or rival, from hatred or private interest; *malice* seeks revenge for the sake of giving pain.

ANIN'GA, *n.* A root growing in the West-Indies, like the China plant, used in refining sugar. *Encyc.*

AN'ISE, *n. an'nis.* [L. *anisum;* Gr. *ανιζον;* Ar. *ianison.* Cast. 1619.]

An annual plant, placed by Linne under the genus Pimpinella. It grows naturally in Egypt, and is cultivated in Spain and Malta, whence the seeds are imported. The stalk rises a foot and a half high, dividing into slender branches, garnished with narrow leaves, cut into three or four narrow segments. The branches terminate in large loose umbels, composed of smaller umbels or rays, on long footstalks. The flowers are small and of a yellowish white; the seeds oblong and swelling. Anise seeds have an aromatic smell, and a pleasant warm taste; they are useful in warming the stomach and expelling wind.

Encyc. Theoph. Lib. 7. 3. *Plin.* 20. 17.

AN'ISE SEED, *n.* The seed of anise.

ANK'ER, *n.* [Dutch.]

A measure of liquids used in Holland, containing about 32 gallons, English measure. *Encyc.*

Chambers says it contains two stekans; each stekan, 16 mengles; each mengle, 2 wine quarts. *Chambers. Encyc.*

ANK'LE, *n. ank'l.* [Sax. *ancleow;* D. *enkel.*]

The joint which connects the foot with the leg.

ANK'LE-BONE, *n.* The bone of the ankle.

AN'NALIST, *n.* [See *Annals.*]

A writer of annals.

AN'NALIZE, *v. t.* To record; to write annals. [*Not much used.*] *Encyc.*

AN'NALS, *n.* plu. [L. *annales, annalis*, from *annus*, a year, the root of which may be the Celtic *an, ain*, a great circle. Varro says the word *annus* signifies a great circle.]

1. A species of history digested in order of time, or a relation of events in chronological order, each event being recorded under the year in which it happened. Annals differ from history, in merely relating events, without observations on the motives, causes and consequences, which, in history, are more diffusively illustrated.

2. The books containing annals, as the *annals* of Tacitus.

AN'NATS, *n.* [L. *annus.*]

A year's income of a spiritual living; the first fruits, originally given to the Pope, upon the decease of a bishop, abbot or parish clerk, and paid by his successor. In England, they were, at the reformation, vested in the king, and in the reign of Queen Anne, restored to the church, and appropriated to the augmentation of poor livings. *Encyc.*

ANNE'AL, *v. t.* [Sax. *anælan, on-ælan*, to kindle or inflame, to heat; from *ælan*, to kindle, to heat or bake, and to anoint with oil. Sax. *æl, oil.* Hence it may be inferred that *oil* is named from inflaming or burning.]

1. To heat; to heat, as glass and iron for the purpose of rendering them less brittle, or to fix colors; vulgarly called *nealing.* This is done by heating the metal nearly to fluidity, in an oven or furnace, and suffering it to cool gradually. Metals made hard and brittle by hammering, by this process recover their malleability. The word is applied also to the baking of tiles. *Encyc. Bailey. Ash.*

2. To temper by heat; and Shenstone uses it for tempering by cold.

ANNE'ALED, *pp.* Heated; tempered; made malleable and less brittle by heat.

ANNE'ALING, *ppr.* Heating; tempering by heat.

ANNEX', *v. t.* [L. *annecto, annexum;* Fr. *annexer;* of *ad* and *necto*, to tie, or connect.]

1. To unite at the end; as to *annex* a codicil to a will. To subjoin, to affix.

2. To unite, as a smaller thing to a greater; as to *annex* a province to a kingdom.

3. To unite to something preceding, as the main object; to connect with; as to *annex* a penalty to a prohibition, or punishment to guilt.

ANNEX', *v. i.* To join; to be united. *Tooke.*

ANNEXA'TION, *n.* The act of annexing, or uniting at the end; conjunction; addition; the act of connecting; union. In *English law*, the uniting of lands or rents to the crown.

ANNEX'ED, *pp.* Joined at the end; connected with; affixed.

ANNEX'ING, *ppr.* Uniting at the end; affixing.

ANNEX'ION, *n.* The act of annexing; annexation; addition. [*Little used.*]

ANNEX'MENT, *n.* The act of annexing; the thing annexed. *Shak.*

ANNI'HILABLE, *a.* That may be annihilated.

ANNI'HILATE, *v. t.* [L. *ad* and *nihilum*, nothing, of *ne*, not, and *hilum*, a trifle.]

1. To reduce to nothing; to destroy the existence of.

No human power can *annihilate* matter.

2. To destroy the form or peculiar distinctive properties, so that the specific thing no longer exists; as, to *annihilate* a *forest* by cutting and carrying away the trees, though the timber may still exist; to *annihilate* a house by demolishing the structure.

ANNI'HILATED, *pp.* Reduced to nothing; destroyed.

ANNI'HILATING, *ppr.* Reducing to nothing; destroying the specific form of.

ANNIHILA'TION, *n.* The act of reducing to nothing or non-existence; or the act of destroying the form or combination of parts under which a thing exists, so that the name can no longer be applied to it, as the *annihilation* of a corporation.

2. The state of being reduced to nothing.

ANNIVERS'ARILY, *adv.* Annually. *Hall.*

ANNIVERS'ARY, *a.* [L. *anniversarius*, of *annus*, year, and *verto*, to turn.]

Returning with the year, at a stated time; annual; yearly; as an *anniversary* feast.

ANNIVERS'ARY, *n.* A stated day returning with the revolution of the year. The term is applied to a day on which some remarkable event is annually celebrated, or a day on which an interesting event is commemorated by solemnities of religion, or exhibitions of respect. In the Romish church, a day in which an office is yearly performed for the souls of the deceased.

2. The act of celebration; performance in honor of an event. *Dryden.*

ANNO DOMINI. [L.] In the year of our Lord, noting the time from our Savior's incarnation; as, *Anno Domini*, or *A. D.* 1800.

This was written Anno Domini, 1809, and revised A. D. 1825 and 1827. *W.*

ANNOMINA'TION, *n.* [L. *ad* and *nominatio*, from *nomino*, to name, from *nomen.*]

1. A pun; the use of words nearly alike in sound, but of different meanings; a paronomasy. *Encyc.*

2. Alliteration, or the use of two or more words successively beginning with the same letter. *Tyrwhitt.*

ANNO'NA, *n.* [L. *annona*, from *annus*, a year, and signifying a year's production or increase; hence provisions.]

The custard apple, a genus of several species, one of which, the papaw, is common in the southern and western parts of the United States. [See *Papaw.*]

AN'NOTATE, *v. i.* [L. *annoto.*]

To comment; to make remarks on a writing. *Tatler.*

ANNOTA'TION, *n.* [L. *annotatio*, of *ad* and *notatio*, a marking, from *noto*, to mark, or *nota*, a mark.]

1. A remark, note or commentary on some passage of a book, intended to illustrate its meaning; generally used in the plural, as *annotations* on the scriptures.

2. The first symptoms of a fever, or attack of a paroxysm. *Coxe.*

AN'NOTATOR, *n.* A writer of notes; a commentator; a scholiast; one who writes notes to illustrate the composition of an author.

ANNOT'TA, *n.* Orlean, or roucou; a hard, dry paste, consisting of the pellicles of the seeds of the bixa orellana, a shrub growing in S. America and the W. Indies. It is moderately hard, of a brown color on the outside, and a dull red within. It is used in dyeing to give an orange cast to a simple yellow. It is used also in coloring cheese. [See *Anotta.*] *Ure.*

ANNOUNCE, *v. t.* *announs'.* [Fr. *annoncer*; It. *annunziare*; L. *annuncio*, to deliver a message, of *ad* and *nuncio*, to tell, from *nuncius*, a messenger.]

1. To publish; to proclaim; to give notice, or first notice; as, the birth of Christ was *announced* by an angel.

2. To pronounce; to declare by judicial sentence. *Prior.*

ANNOUN'CED, *pp.* Proclaimed; first published.

ANNOUNCEMENT, *n.* *announs'ment.* The act of giving notice; proclamation; publication. *Month. Mag.*

ANNOUN'CER, *n.* One that announces, or first gives notice; a proclaimer.

ANNOUN'CING, *ppr.* Introducing notice; first publishing; proclaiming.

ANNOY', *v. t.* [Norm. *annoyer*, from *neure*, *nuire*, to hurt; Fr. *nuire*; It. *nuocere*; from L. *noceo*, to hurt, that is, to strike; Syr. ܢܟܐ, Ar. نَكَأ to strike, to hurt; Heb. and Ch. נכה to strike. Hence probably L. *neco*, to kill. See *Nuisance* and *Noxious.*]

To incommode; to injure or disturb by continued or repeated acts; to tease, vex or molest; as, to *annoy* an army by impeding their march, or by a continued cannonade.

ANNOY', *n.* Injury or molestation from continued acts or inconvenience. *Shak. Beattie.*

ANNOY'ANCE, *n.* That which annoys, or injures; the act of annoying; the state of being annoyed. It includes something more than *inconvenience.*

ANNOY'ED, *pp.* Incommoded, injured or molested by something that is continued or repeated.

ANNOY'ER, *n.* One that annoys.

ANNOY'FUL, *a.* Giving trouble; incommoding; molesting. [*Not used.*] *Chaucer.*

ANNOY'ING, *ppr.* Incommoding; hurting; molesting.

ANNOY'OUS, *a.* Troublesome. [*Not used.*] *Chaucer.*

AN'NUAL, *a.* [Fr. *annuel*; Sp. *anual*; It. *annuale*; L. *annalis*, from *annus*, a year; Gr. ενος, εννος; Sans. *anda.*]

1. Yearly; that returns every year; coming yearly; as an *annual* feast.

2. Lasting or continuing only one year or season; that requires to be renewed every year; as an *annual* plant. Leaves that grow in the spring, and perish in the autumn, are called *annual*, in opposition to *evergreens.*

3. Performed in a year; as the *annual* motion of the earth.

AN'NUAL, *n.* A plant that lives but one year, or rather but one summer. *Martyn.*

AN'NUALLY, *adv.* Yearly; returning every year; year by year.

ANNU'ITANT, *n.* [See *Annuity.*]

One who receives or is entitled to receive an annuity.

ANNU'ITY, *n.* [Fr. *annuité*, from *annus*, a year. See *Annual.*]

A sum of money, payable yearly, to continue for a given number of years, for life or for ever; an annual income, charged on the person of the grantor; or an annual allowance. Governments often borrow money upon annuities, that is, for a certain sum advanced on loan, the government contracts to pay the lender a specific sum, for life, or for a term of years. The stock created by such loans is transferable.

ANNUL', *v. t.* [Fr. *annuller*, of L. *ad nullum*, to nothing.]

1. To make void; to nullify; to abrogate; to abolish; used appropriately of laws, decrees, edicts, decisions of courts, or other established rules, permanent usages, and the like, which are made void by competent authority.

2. To reduce to nothing; to obliterate. [*Not in much use.*] *Milton.*

AN'NULAR, *a.* [L. *annulus*, a ring, from Celtic *ain*, a circle, and *ul*, young, small; *annulus*, a little circle.]

Having the form of a ring; pertaining to a ring.

Annular crystal is when a hexahedral prism has six, or an octahedral prism eight marginal faces, disposed in a ring about each base; or when these prisms are truncated on all their terminal edges. *Cleaveland.*

AN'NULARY, *a.* Having the form of a ring. *Ray.*

AN'NULATED, *a.* Furnished with rings, or circles, like rings; having belts.

AN'NULET, *n.* [L. *annulus*, a ring.]

In *architecture*, a small square member in the Doric capital, under the quarter round; also a narrow flat molding, which is common to many places, as in the bases or capitals; called also a fillet, or listil, or cincture, or a list, timea, eye brow or square rabbit. *Encyc.*

In *heraldry*, a little circle, borne as a charge in coats of arms; formerly reputed a mark of nobility and jurisdiction; it being the custom of prelates to receive their investiture per *baculum* et *annulum*, by staff and ring. It denotes also strength and eternity, by its circular form. Among the Romans, it represented liberty and distinction of rank. It denotes also difference, or mark of distinction, which the fifth brother of a family ought to bear on his coat of arms. *Encyc. Johnson.*

ANNUL'LED, *pp.* Made void; abrogated.

ANNUL'LING, *ppr.* Abrogating; abolishing.

ANNUL'MENT, *n.* The act of annulling.

ANNU'MERATE, *v. t.* [L. *annumero*, of *ad* and *numero*, to number, from *numerus*, number; W. *niver*; Ir. *nuiver* or *nuimher.* See *Number.*]

To add to a former number; to unite to something before mentioned. *Johnson.*

ANNUMERA'TION, *n.* Addition to a former number.

ANNUN'CIATE, *v. t.* [See *Announce.*]

To bring tidings; to announce. *Chaucer.*

ANNUNCIA'TION, *n.* An announcing; the tidings brought by the angel to Mary, of the incarnation of Christ. Also the day celebrated by the church, in memory of the angel's salutation of the blessed virgin, which is the 25th of March. The Jews give the title to a part of the ceremony of the passover. *Encyc.*

2. Proclamation; promulgation.

ANNUNCIA'TOR, *n.* One who announces; an officer in the church of Constantinople, whose business was to inform the people of the festivals which were to be celebrated. *Encyc.*

AN'ODYNE, *n.* [Gr. α or αν priv. and οδυνη, pain.]

Any medicine which allays pain, or causes sleep, as an opiate, paregoric, narcotic, &c. *Coxe.*

AN'ODYNE, *a.* Assuaging pain; causing sleep, or insensibility.

ANOINT', *v. t.* [Fr. *oindre*, p. *oint*; Sp. *untar*, to anoint; L. *ungo*; Sp. *ungir*; It. *ungere*, or *ugnere.*]

1. To pour oil upon; to smear or rub over with oil or unctuous substances; also to spread over, as oil. We say, the man *anoints* another, or the oil *anoints* him.

2. To consecrate by unction, or the use of oil.

> Thou shalt *anoint* the altar, and sanctify it. Ex. xxix.

3. To smear or daub.

> He *anointed* the eyes of the blind man with clay. John ix.

4. To prepare, in allusion to the consecrating use of oil.

> *Anoint* the shield. Isaiah xxi.
>
> To *anoint* the head with oil, Ps. xxiii. seems to signify to communicate the consolations of the Holy Spirit.

The use of oil in consecrations, was of high antiquity. Kings, prophets and priests were set apart or consecrated to their offices by the use of oil. Hence the peculiar application of the term *anointed* to Jesus Christ.

ANOINT'ED, *pp.* Smeared or rubbed with oil; set apart; consecrated with oil.

ANOINT'ED, *n.* The Messiah, or Son of God, consecrated to the great office of Redeemer; called the *Lord's anointed.* Cyrus is also called the *Lord's anointed.* Isaiah xlv.

ANOINT'ER, *n.* One who anoints.

ANOINT'ING, *ppr.* Smearing with oil; pouring on oil, or other oleaginous substance; consecrating.

ANOINT'ING, *n.* The act of smearing with oil; a consecrating.

ANOINT'MENT, *n.* The act of anointing, or state of being anointed.

ANO'LE, *n.* A species of lizard in the W. Indies, of a yellowish color, having several blue and green stripes running down its back. *Dict. of Nat. Hist.*

ANOM'ALIPED, *a.* [Gr. ανωμαλια, inequality, and πους, L. *pes*, foot.]

An epithet given to fowls, whose middle toe is united to the exterior by three phalanges, and to the interior by one only.

ANOM'ALIPED, *n.* An anomalous footed fowl. [See the adjective.] *Dict. Nat. Hist.*

ANOM'ALISM, *n.* An anomaly; a deviation from rule.

ANOMALIS'TIC, **ANOMALIS'TICAL**, *a.* Irregular; departing from common or established rules.

In *astronomy*, the *anomalistic year* is the time in which the earth passes through her orbit, which is longer than the tropical year, on account of the precession of the equinoxes.

ANOM'ALOUS, *a.* Irregular; deviating from a general rule, method or analogy; applied, in grammar, to words which deviate from the common rules of inflection; and in astronomy, to the seemingly irregular motions of the planets; but applied also generally to whatever is irregular; as, an *anomalous* character; *anomalous* pronunciation.

ANOM'ALOUSLY, *adv.* Irregularly; in a manner different from common rule, method or analogy.

ANOM'ALY, *n.* [Fr. *anomalie*; Sp. *anomalia*; Gr. ανωμαλια, inequality, of α priv. and ομαλος, equal, similar; Celtic, W. *hamal*, or *haval*; Ir. *amhail*, similar.]

1. Irregularity; deviation from the common rule; thus *oxen*, the plural of *ox*, is an *anomaly*, in grammar, as the regular plural would be *oxes*.
2. In *astronomy*, an irregularity in the motion of a planet, whereby it deviates from the aphelion or apogee. *Encyc.*
3. In *music*, a false scale or interval. *Busby.*

ANO'MEANS, *n.* [Gr. ανομοιος, dissimilar.] In *church history*, the pure Arians, as distinguished from the Semi-Arians. *Encyc.*

ANO'MIA, *n.* [Gr. ανομια; α priv. and νομος, rule.]

A genus of bivalve shells, so called from their unequal valves; the beaked cockle.

AN'OMITE, *n.* A fossil shell of the genus anomia. *Jameson.*

ANOMORHOM'BOID, *n.* [Gr. ανομοιος, irregular, and ρομβοειδης, of a rhomboidal figure.]

A genus of spars, pellucid, and crystaline, of no determinate form externally, but breaking into regular rhomboidal masses. The species are five, mostly of a white color. *Encyc.*

AN'OMY, *n.* [Gr. ανομια.] A violation of law. [*Rarely used.*] *Bramhall.*

ANON', *adv.* [Sax. *on an*, in one; not, as Junius supposes, in *one minute*, but in continuation, without intermission; applied originally to extension in measure, and then to time by analogy. "And sædon that hi sægon on north-east fir micel and brad with thone earthe, and weax on lengthe up *on an* to tham wolcne." Sax. Chron. A. D. 1022. And they said they saw in the north-east a great fire and broad, near the earth, and it increased in length *in continuation* to the clouds. See also An. Dom. 1127.]

1. Quickly; without intermission: soon; immediately.

   The same is he that heareth the word, and *anon* with joy receiveth it. Matt. xiii.

2. Sometimes; now and then; at other times; accompanied with *ever*, *ever* and *anon*.

ANON'YMOUS, *a.* [Fr. *anonyme*; L. *anonymus*; Gr. ανωνυμος, of α priv. and ονομα, name. See *Name*.]

Nameless; wanting a name; without the real name of the author; as, an *anonymous* pamphlet.

ANON'YMOUSLY, *adv.* Without a name.

AN'OPLOTHER, **ANOPLOTHE'RIUM**, *n.* [Gr. αν neg., οπλον, arms, and θηριον, a beast.]

This is the name which Cuvier has given to a genus of animals, whose bones are found in the gypsum quarries near Paris; a genus now extinct.

ANOP'SY, *n.* [Gr. αν neg. and ωψ, sight.] Want of sight; invision. [*Little used.*] *Brown.*

AN'OREXY, *n.* [Gr. α priv. and ορεξις, appetite.

Want of appetite, without a lothing of food. *Coxe.*

ANOTH'ER, *a.* [*an*, or *one* and *other*.]

1. Not the same; different; as, we have *one* form of government; France, *another*.
2. One more, in addition to a former number, indefinitely; as, grant one request, they will ask *another* favor, *another* and *another*.
3. Any other; any different person, indefinitely; as, "Let *another* praise thee and not thy own mouth." This word is often used without a noun, becoming a substitute for the name of the person or thing; as in the last example. It is also much used in opposition to *one*, as in the first and second passages cited. It is also frequently used with *one*, in a reciprocal sense; as, "love *one another*;" "bear *one another's* burdens;" that is, love one, or let one love another.

ANOTH'ER-GAINES, *adv.* Of another kind. *Obs.* *Sidney.*

ANOTH'ER-GATES, *adv.* Of another sort. *Obs.* *Sanderson.*

ANOTH'ER-GUISE, *a.* [*another* and *guise*, Fr. way, manner; Sax. *wise*. The Saxon manner of writing this word would be *another-wise*.]

Of a different kind; different. This is a vulgar word, and usually contracted into *other guess*.

ANOT'TA, *n.* An elegant red color, formed from the pellicles or pulp of the seeds of the bixa, a tree common in South America. This is called also Terra Orleana and Roco. The annotta is made by steeping the seeds for seven or eight days, pounding them to separate the red skins, then straining the liquor, boiling it, taking off the scum which is the coloring matter, then boiling it to a due consistence, and making it into balls. *Encyc.*

AN'SATED, *a.* [L. *ansatus*, from *ansa*, a handle.]

Having a handle or handles, or something in the form of handles. *Johnson.*

AN'SER, *n.* [L. a goose.]

1. In *zoology*, the name of the goose, whether tame or wild. The domestic goose is the gray-lag or wild goose, domesticated.
2. In *astronomy*, a small star, in the milky way, between the swan and eagle. *Encyc.*

AN'SERINE, *a.* [L. *anserinus*, from *anser*, a goose.]

1. Resembling the skin of a goose; uneven; as, an *anserine* skin. *Encyc.*
2. Pertaining to the *ansers*.

AN'SERS, *n.* In Linne's system, the third order of *aves* or fowls, whose characteristics are a smooth bill, broadest at the point, covered with a smooth skin, and furnished with teeth. The tongue is fleshy, and the toes are webbed or palmated. It includes all the web-footed water fowls, with legs and feet adapted to swimming.

AN'SLAIGHT, *n.* [See *Slay*.] An attack; an affray. [*Not in use.*]

'ANSWER, *v. t.* *ànsur.* [Sax. *andswarian*, of *anti*, against, and Sax. *swaran*, or *swerian* or *swerigan*, Goth. *swaran*, to swear. The primitive sense of *swear* was merely to speak or affirm, and hence, originally, *oath* was used after it, *to swear an oath*; which is not a pleonasm, as Lye supposes, but the primitive form of expression retained. The sense of *answer* is an opposite, a returned word or speech. Hence we observe the Saxon has *andwyrd*, *antiword*, an answer; Goth. *andawaurd*; D. *antwoord*; Ger. *antwort*.]

1. To speak in return to a call or question, or to a speech, declaration or argument of another person; as, "I have called and ye have not *answered*." "He *answered* the question or the argument." This may be in agreement and confirmation of what was said, or in opposition to it.
2. To be equivalent to; to be adequate to, or sufficient to accomplish the object. "Money *answereth* all things," noting, primarily, return.
3. To comply with, fulfill, pay or satisfy; as, he *answered* my order; to *answer* a debt.
4. To act in return, or opposition; as, the enemy *answered* our fire by a shower of grape shot.
5. To bear a due proportion to; to be equal or adequate; to suit; as, a weapon does not *answer* the size and strength of the man using it; the success does not *answer* our expectation.
6. To perform what was intended; to accomplish; as, the measure does not *answer* its end; it does not *answer* the purpose.
7. To be opposite to; to face; as, fire *answers* fire. *Shak.*
8. To write in reply; to reply to another writing, by way of explanation, refutation or justification; as, to *answer* a pamphlet.
9. To solve, as a proposition or problem in mathematics.

This word may be applied to a great variety of objects, expressing the idea of a *return*; as the notes, or sounds of birds, and other animals; an echo, &c.

'ANSWER, *v. i.* To reply; to speak by way of return; as, there is none to *answer*. 1 Kings xviii.

2. To be accountable, liable or responsible; followed by *to* before the person, and *for* before the thing for which one is liable; as, the man must *answer to* his employer *for* the money entrusted to his care; we can not *answer to* God *for* our offenses.

3. To vindicate, or give a justificatory account of; followed by *for;* as, a man cannot *answer for* his friend.
4. To correspond with; to suit with; followed by *to.*

In water face *answereth to* face, so the heart of man *to* man. Prov. 27.

5. To act reciprocally, as the strings of an instrument to the hand. *Dryden.*
6. To stand as opposite or correlative; as, allegiance in the subject *answers* to protection on the part of the prince or government.
7. To return, as sound reverberated; to echo.

The noise seems to fly away, and *answer* at a great distance. *Encyc. Art. Echo.*

8. To succeed; to effect the object intended; to have a good effect; as, gypsum *answers* as a manure on a dry soil.

ANSWER, *n.* A reply; that which is said, in return to a call, a question, an argument, or an allegation.

A soft *answer* turneth away wrath. Prov.
I called him, but he gave me no *answer.* Cant. v.

2. An account to be rendered to justice.

He will call you to so hot an *answer* for it. *Shak.*

3. In *law,* a counter-statement of facts, in a course of pleadings; a confutation of what the other party has alledged.
4. A writing, pamphlot or book, in reply to another.
5. A reverberated sound; an echo.
6. A return; that which is sent in consequence of some petition, as a blessing is sent in *answer* to prayer.
7. A solution, the result of a mathematical operation.

'ANSWERABLE, *a.* That may be answered; that to which a reply may be made, usually implying that the answer may be satisfactory; as, an *answerable* argument.
2. Obliged to give an account, or liable to be called to account; amenable; responsible; as, an agent is *answerable* to his principal.
3. Obliged or liable to pay, indemnify or make good; as, to be *answerable* for a debt or for damages.
4. Correspondent; agreeing with; in conformity with; as, the features expressed in a picture are *answerable* to the original.
5. Suitable; suited; proportionate; as, an achievement *answerable* to the preparation for it.
6. Equal; correspondent; proportionate; as, the success is *answerable* to my desires.

ANSWERABLENESS, *n.* The quality of being answerable, liable, responsible, or correspondent.

ANSWERABLY, *adv.* In due proportion, correspondence or conformity; suitably; as, continents have rivers *answerably* larger than isles.

ANSWERED, *pp.* Replied to; fulfilled; paid; complied with; accomplished; solved; confuted.

ANSWERER, *n.* One who answers; he or that which makes a return to what another has spoken; he who writes an answer.

'ANSWERING, *ppr.* Replying; corresponding to; fulfilling; solving; succeeding; reverberating; confuting.

'ANSWER-JOBBER, *n.* One who makes a business of writing answers. *Swift.*

AN'T, in old authors, is a contraction of *an it,* that is, *if it.* [See *An.*]

ĂNT, in our vulgar dialect, as in the phrases, I *ănt,* you *ănt,* he *ănt,* we *ănt,* &c., is undoubtedly a contraction of the Danish *er, ere,* the substantive verb, in the present tense of the Indicative Mode, and *not,* I *er-not,* we *ere-not,* he *er-not,* or of the Swedish *ar,* the same verb, Infinitive *vara,* to be. These phrases are doubtless legitimate remains of the Gothic dialect.

'ANT, *n.* [Sax. *æmet, emmet,* contracted into *ant;* Germ. *ameise.*]
An emmet; a pismire. Ants constitute a genus of insects of the hymenopteral order, of which the characteristics are; a small scale between the breast and belly, with a joint so deep that the animal appears as if almost cut in two. The females, and the neuter or working ants, which have no sexual characteristics, are furnished with a hidden sting; and both males and females have wings, but the neuters have none. These insects meet together in companies, and maintain a sort of republic. They raise hillocks of earth, in which they live. In these there are paths, leading to the repositories of their provisions. The large black ants, in the warm climates of America, to avoid the effects of great rains, build large nests on trees, of light earth, roundish and plastered smooth. *Encyc.*

'ANT-BEAR or 'ANT-EATER, *n.* A quadruped that feeds upon ants. This animal has no teeth, but a snout or muzzle, with a long cylindrical tongue. The body is covered with long hair. There are several species, constituting the genus, *myrmecophaga,* ant eaters. *Encyc.*

'ANT-EGGS, *n.* Little white balls found in the hillocks of ants, usually supposed to be their eggs, but found on examination to be the young brood, in their first state. They are vermicules, wrapped in a film, composed of a silky substance spun like a spider's webb. *Encyc.*

'ANT-HILL, *n.* A little tumulus or hillock, formed by ants, for their habitation.

AN'TA, *n.* In *ancient architecture,* a square column, at the corner of a building; a pilaster; written also *ante.*

ANTAC'ID, *n.* [*anti* and *acid.*]
In *pharmacy,* an alkali, or a remedy for sourness or acidity; better written *anti-acid.*

ANTAC'RID, *n.* [*anti* and *acrid.*]
That which corrects acrimony; better written *anti-acrid.*

ANTAG'ONISM, *n.* Opposition of action; counteraction of things or principles. *Good, B. of Nature.*

ANTAG'ONIST, *n.* [Gr. αντι, against, and αγωνιςης, a champion. See *Act* and *Agony.*]
1. One who contends with another in combat; used primarily in the Grecian games. An adversary.
2. An opponent in controversy. *Campbell.*
3. In *anatomy,* a muscle which acts in opposition to another; as a *flexor,* which *bends* a part, is the *antagonist* of an *extensor,* which *extends* it.

ANTAG'ONIST, *a.* Counteracting; opposing; combating; as, an *antagonist* muscle.

ANTAGONIS'TIC, *a.* Opposing in combat; contending against.

ANTAG'ONIZE, *v. i.* To contend against; to act in opposition; to oppose in argument.

ANTAG'ONY, *n.* Contest; opposition. [*Not used.*] *Milton.*

ANTAL'GIC, *a.* [Gr. αντι, against, and αλγος, pain.]
Alleviating pain; anodyne. [*Little used.*]

ANTANACLA'SIS, *n.* [Gr. ανταναχλασις, a driving back.]
1. In *rhetoric,* a figure, which consists in repeating the same word in a different sense; as, whilst we *live,* let us *live.* Learn some *craft* when young, that when old you may live without *craft.*
2. It is also a repetition of words, beginning a sentence, after a long parenthesis; as, shall that heart, (which not only feels them, but which has all motions of life placed in them,) shall that heart, &c. *Smith's Rhet.*

ANTANAGO'GE, *n.* *antanago'gy.* [Gr. αντι, against, and αναγωγη, a taking up.]
In *rhetoric,* a figure which consists in replying to an adversary, by way of recrimination; as, when the accusation of one party is unanswerable, the accused person charges him with the same or other crime. *Bailey.*

ANTAPHRODIS'IAC, *a.* [Gr. αντι, against, and αφροδισιος, venereal, from αφροδιτη, Venus.]
Antivenereal; having the quality of extinguishing or lessening venereal desire.

ANTAPHRODIS'IAC, *n.* A medicine that lessens or extinguishes the venereal appetite. *Encyc. Coxe.*

ANTAPHRODIT'IC, *a.* [Gr. See the preceding words.] Antivenereal, abating the venereal appetite, or efficacious against the venereal disease.

ANTAPHRODIT'IC, *n.* A medicine which abates the venereal appetite, or is good against the venereal disease. *Coxe. Quincy.*

ANTAPOPLEC'TIC, *a.* Good against apoplexy.

ANTARC'TIC, *a.* [Gr. αντι, against, and αρχτος, the bear, a northern constellation.]
Opposite to the northern or arctic pole; relating to the southern pole or to the region near it, and applied especially to a lesser circle, distant from the pole 23° 28′. Thus we say the *antarctic* pole, *antarctic* circle, or *antarctic* region. *Encyc.*

ANTA'RES, *n.* The name of a star of the first magnitude, called also the scorpion's heart. Its longitude is 60° 13′ 14″ of Sagittarius; and its latitude 4° 31′ 26″ South. *Encyc.*

ANTARTHRIT'IC, *a.* [Gr. αντι, against, and αρθριτις, gout.]
Counteracting the gout.

ANTARTHRIT'IC, *n.* A remedy which cures or alleviates the gout.

ANTASTHMAT'IC, *a.* [Gr. αντι, against, and ασθμα, asthma.]
Opposing the asthma.

ANTASTHMAT'IC, *n.* A remedy for the asthma.

AN'TE. A Latin preposition, the Gr. αντι, Sax. and Goth, *and;* much used in the composition of English words, especially in words from the Latin and Greek languages. It signifies *before in place,* in front; hence opposite, contrary; and figuratively, *before in time.* The Latin *ante* is generally used in the sense of *before,* and the Greek *αντι*, in that of *opposite*, or in the place of.

AN'TE or **AN'TA**, *n.* A pilaster. In *heraldry*, *ante* denotes that the pieces are let into one another, in the manner there expressed, as by dove tails, rounds, swallow tails, &c. *Encyc.*

AN'TEACT, *n.* [*ante* and *act.*] A preceding act.

ANTECEDA'NEOUS, *a.* [*Infra.*] Antecedent; preceding in time. *Owen.*

ANTECE'DE, *v. t.* [*ante* and *cedo*, to go. See *Cede.*]

To go before in time; to precede. *Hale.*

ANTECE'DENCE, *n.* The act or state of going before in time; precedence. In *astronomy*, an apparent motion of a planet towards the west, or contrary to the order of the signs. *Encyc.*

ANTECE'DENT, *a.* Going before in time; prior; anterior; preceding; as, an event *antecedent* to the deluge.

ANTECE'DENT, *n.* That which goes before in time; hence in writings, that which precedes in place. In *grammar*, the noun to which a relative or other substitute refers; as, Solomon was the *prince*, *who* built the Temple. In *logic*, the first of two propositions in an enthymeme, or argument of two propositions; as, if the sun is fixed, the earth must move. Here the first and conditional proposition is the *antecedent*; the second, the consequent. *Watts.*

In *mathematics*, the first of two terms of a ratio, or that which is compared with the other. *Encyc.*

ANTECE'DENTLY, *adv.* Previously; at a time preceding.

ANTECES'SOR, *n.* [L. whence *ancestor.* See *Antecede.*]

1. One who goes before; a leader; a principal. It was formerly a title given to those who excelled in any science; to professors of civil law; and in the Universities of France, the teachers of law take the title in their theses.

2. One that possessed land before the present possessor. *Brady.*

AN'TECHAMBER, *n.* [*Ante*, before, and *chamber.*]

A chamber or apartment before the chief apartment to which it leads, and in which persons wait for audience. *Dryden.*

ANTECHAP'EL, *n.* The part of the chapel through which is the passage to the choir or body of it. *Warton.*

ANTE'CIAN, *n.* [Gr. *αντι*, opposite, and *οικεω*, to dwell; L. *antœci.*]

In *geography*, the antecians are those inhabitants of the earth, under the same meridian, and at the same distance from the equator, but, on opposite sides, one party north, the other south. They have the same hours of day and night, but different seasons; it being winter with one, when it is summer with the other. *Encyc.*

ANTECURS'OR, *n.* [L. *ante*, before, and *cursor*, a runner, from *curro*, to run. See *Course.*]

One who runs before; a forerunner. In the Roman armies, the antecursors were a body of horse detached to obtain intelligence, get provisions, &c., for the main body. *Encyc.*

AN'TEDATE, *n.* [*Infra.*] Prior date; a date antecedent to another. *Good.*

AN'TEDATE, *v. t.* [L. *ante*, and *datum*, given. See *Date.*]

1. To date before the true time; thus, to *antedate* a deed or a bond is to express a date anterior to the true time of its execution.

2. To anticipate; to take before the true time.

And *antedate* the bliss above. *Pope.*

ANTEDILU'VIAL, } *a.* [L. *ante*, and *diluvium*, a flood. See
ANTEDILU'VIAN, } *Lave.*]

Before the flood, or deluge, in Noah's time; existing, happening, or relating to what happened before the deluge.

ANTEDILU'VIAN, *n.* One who lived before the deluge.

AN'TELOPE, *n.* [Qu. Gr. *αντι* and *ελαφος*, resembling a deer.]

In *zoology*, the gazelle; a genus of ruminant quadrupeds, intermediate between the deer and goat. Their horns are solid and permanent, straight or curved; in some species annulated; in others, surrounded by a spiral; and in others, smooth. They resemble the deer in the lightness and elegance of their forms, and in their agility. They inhabit open plains or mountains, and some species in herds of two or three thousand. Their eyes are large, black, and of exquisite beauty and vivacity; and are therefore a favorite image with the eastern poets. *Encyc. Cyc.*

ANTELU'CAN, *a.* [L. *antelucanus*, of *ante*, before, and *lux*, light.]

Being before light; a word applied to assemblies of christians, in ancient times of persecution, held before light in the morning. *Encyc.*

ANTEMERID'IAN, *a.* [*ante*, before, and *meridian.*]

Being before noon; pertaining to the forenoon.

ANTEMET'IC, *a.* [*αντι*, against, and *emetic*, from *εμεω*, to vomit.]

Restraining or allaying vomiting. *Quincy.*

ANTEMET'IC, *n.* A medicine which checks vomiting. *Quincy. Coxe.*

ANTEMUND'ANE, *a.* [*ante*, before, and *mundus*, the world.] Being before the creation of the world.

ANTENI'CENE, *a.* [*ante*, before, and *Nicene*, from *Nice.*]

Anterior to the first council of Nice; as *antenicene* faith. *Encyc.*

ANTEN'NÆ, *n. plu.* [L. *antenna*, a sail yard.]

In *zoology*, the horns or feelers of insects, projecting from the head.

ANTENUM'BER, *n.* A number that precedes another. *Bacon.*

ANTENUP'TIAL, *a.* [*ante* and *nuptial.*]

Being before marriage; as, an *antenuptial* agreement; *antenuptial* children. *Kent.*

ANTEPASCH'AL, *a.* Pertaining to the time before Easter. *Nelson.*

AN'TEPAST, *n.* [*ante*, before, and *pastum*, fed.]

A foretaste; something taken before the proper time.

ANTEPENULT', *n.* [L. *ante*, before, *pene*, almost, and *ultimus*, last.]

The last syllable of a word, except two; as *syl* in *syllable.*

ANTEPENULT'IMATE, *a.* Pertaining to the last syllable but two.

ANTEPILEP'TIC, *a.* [*αντι*, against, and *επιληπτικος*, epileptic, from *επιλαμβανω*, to seize.]

Resisting or curing epilepsy.

ANTEPILEP'TIC, *n.* A remedy for the epilepsy. *Encyc. Coxe.*

ANTEPOSI''TION, *n.* *s* as *z.* [L. *ante*, before, and *position*, from *pono*, to place.]

In *grammar*, the placing of a word before another, which, by ordinary rules, ought to follow it.

ANTEPREDIC'AMENT, *n.* [*ante* and *predicament.*]

A preliminary question in logic to illustrate the doctrine of predicaments and categories; a question which is to be first known. *Encyc.*

ANTE'RIOR, *a.* [L.] Before in time or place; prior; antecedent; preceding in time.

2. Before or in front in place.

ANTERIOR'ITY, *n.* The state of being anterior, preceding or in front; a state of being before in time, or situation.

AN'TEROOM, *n.* [*ante* and *room.*] A room before or in front of another. *Darwin.*

AN'TES, *n. plu.* [L.] Pillars of large dimensions that support the front of a building.

ANTESTAT'URE, *n.* [*ante* and *stature.*]

In *fortification*, a small retrenchment or work formed of palisades, or sacks of earth. *Encyc.*

ANTESTOM'ACH, *n.* [*ante* and *stomach.*]

A cavity which leads into the stomach, as the crop in birds. [*Not in use.*] *Ray.*

ANTEVERT', *v. t.* [L *anteverto.*] To prevent. [*Not in use.*] *Hall.*

ANTEVIRGIL'IAN, *a.* [*αντι* and *Virgil.*]

A term given to Tull's new husbandry, or method of horse hoeing. *Encyc.*

ANTHELMIN'TIC, *a.* [*αντι*, against, and *ελμινς*, a worm.] Good against worms.

ANTHELMIN'TIC, *n.* A remedy for worms in the intestines. *Encyc. Coxe.*

AN'THEM, *n.* [Gr. *αντι*, against, and *υμνος*, a hymn, from *υμνεω*, to sing. See *Hymn.*]

A hymn sung in alternate parts; but in modern usage, a sacred tune or piece of music set to words, taken from the psalms or other parts of the scriptures, first introduced into church service in Elizabeth's reign. *Encyc.*

AN'THEM-WISE, *adv.* In the manner of an anthem; alternately. *Bacon.*

AN'THEMIS, *n.* Camomile. *Tate.*

AN'THER, *n.* [L. *anthera*, a flowery plant, from the Greek *ανθηρος*, flowery, from *ανθος*, a flower.]

In *botany*, the summit or top of the stamen, connected with the flower, and elevated by means of the filament or thread, within the corol. It contains the pollen, or fertilizing dust, which, when mature, is emitted for the impregnation of the stigma. It is called by Ray, the *apex*, and by Malpighi, the *capsula staminis*. *Milne. Martyn.*

AN'THERAL, *a.* Pertaining to anthers. *Asiat. Res.* 4, 404.

ANTHERIF'EROUS, *a.* [*anther* and *fero*, to bear.] Producing anthers. *Barton*, 162.

ANTHESTE'RION, *n.* The sixth month of the Athenian year, consisting of 29 days, and answering to a part of November and a part of December. It is supposed to be so called from the Anthesteria, feasts in honor of Bacchus, celebrated in that month, and so called from ανθος, a flower; garlands of flowers being offered to Bacchus at those feasts.

ANTHOLOG'ICAL, *a.* Pertaining to anthology.

ANTHOL'OGY, *n.* [Gr. ανθος, a flower, and λογος, a discourse, or λογια, a collection.]

1. A discourse on flowers.
2. A collection of beautiful passages from authors; a collection of poems or epigrams. In *the Greek church*, a collection of devotional pieces. *Encyc.*

AN'THONY'S FIRE. A popular name of the erysipelas, supposed to have been so named from the saint in Italy, to whom those, who were affected, applied for a cure. *Encyc.*

ANTHOPH'YLLITE, *n.* [Gr. ανθος, a flower, and φυλλον, a leaf.]

A mineral in masses composed of interlaced plates, or crystalized in reed-shaped crystals, which appear to be four sided prisms longitudinally streaked. The color is between dark yellowish gray and olive brown; the luster shining and pearly. *Dict. Nat. Hist. Cleaveland.*

AN'THORISM, *n.* [Gr. αντι, opposite, and ορισμος, definition.]

In *rhetoric*, a description or definition contrary to that which is given by the adverse party. *Ash.*

AN'THRACITE, *n.* [Gr. ανθραξ, a burning coal; *infra.*]

Slaty glance-coal, or columnar glance coal; that species of coal which has a shining luster, approaching to metallic, and which burns without smoke, and with intense heat. It consists essentially of carbon.

AN'THRACOLITE. [See *Anthracite.*]

AN'THRAX, *n.* [Gr.; *supra.*]

A carbuncle; a malignant ulcer, with intense burning. The ancients gave this name to a gem, and it is sometimes used for lithanthrax or pit-coal. *Encyc.*

ANTHROP'OGLOT, *n.* [Gr. ανθρωπος, man, and γλωττα, the tongue.]

An animal which has a tongue resembling that of man, of which kind are parrots. *Encyc.*

ANTHROPOG'RAPHY, *n.* [Gr. ανθρωπος, man, and γραφη, description.]

A description of man or the human race, or of the parts of the human body. *Encyc.*

ANTHROP'OLITE, *n.* [Gr. ανθρωπος, man, and λιθος, a stone.]

A petrifaction of the human body, or skeleton. Some naturalists have asserted that skeletons of the animal frame have been found petrified in old mines; but the fact is not credited, and the existence of such petrifactions is denied. *Encyc.*

Capt. Wilford informs us, that in digging a well near the Ganga, some persons found, at the depth of 90 feet, on an old bed of that river, the bones of men and quadrupeds, supposed to be petrifactions. *Asiat. Res.* 8. 294.

The skeleton of a man has been found in a limestone rock, of recent formation, in Guadaloupe. *Ed. Encyc.*

Human bones have also been found, by Prof. Buckland, in the open cave of Paviland, Glamorganshire. He considers them postdiluvian. *Quart. Rev.* v. 29. p. 148.

ANTHROPOLOG'ICAL, *a.* Pertaining to anthropology; according to human manner of speaking. *Kirwan.*

ANTHROPOL'OGIST, *n.* One who describes, or is versed in the physical history of the human body.

ANTHROPOL'OGY, *n.* [Gr. ανθρωπος, man, and λογος, discourse.]

1. A discourse upon human nature. *Encyc.*
2. The doctrine of the structure of the human body; the natural history or physiology of the human species.
3. The word denotes that manner of expression by which the inspired writers attribute human parts and passions to God. *Encyc.*

ANTHROPOM'ANCY, *n.* [Gr. ανθρωπος, man, and μαντεια, divination.]

Divination by inspecting the entrails of a human being. *Encyc.*

ANTHROPOMORPH'ISM, *n.* The heresy of the anthropomorphites. *Encyc.*

ANTHROPOMORPH'ITE, *n.* [Gr. ανθρωπος, man, and μορφη, form.]

One who believes a human form in the Supreme Being. A sect of ancient heretics are called *anthropomorphites.* *Encyc.*

ANTHROPOMORPH'OUS, *a.* Belonging to that which has the form of man; having the figure of resemblance to a man. *Ash. Encyc.*

ANTHROPOP'ATHY, *n.* [ανθρωπος, man, and παθος, passion.]

The affections of man, or the application of human passions to the Supreme Being. *Owen. Encyc. Ash.*

ANTHROPOPH'AGI, *n. plu.* [Gr. ανθρωπος, man, and φαγω, to eat.]

Maneaters; cannibals; men that eat human flesh. *Johnson. Encyc.*

ANTHROPOPH'AGOUS, *a.* Feeding on human flesh.

ANTHROPOPH'AGY, *n.* The eating of human flesh, or the practice of eating it. *Johnson. Encyc.*

ANTHROPOS'COPY, *n.* [Gr. ανθρωπος, man, and σκοπεω, to view.]

The art of discovering or judging of a man's character, passions and inclinations from the lineaments of his body. *Encyc.*

ANTHROPOS'OPHY, *n.* [Gr. ανθρωπος, man, and σοφια, wisdom.]

Knowledge of the nature of man; acquaintance with man's structure and functions, comprehending anatomy and physiology. *Encyc.*

ANTHYPNOT'IC, *a. corrupt orthography.* [See *Antihypnotic.*]

ANTHYPOCHOND'RIAC. [See *Antihypochondriac.*]

ANTHYPOPH'ORA. [See *Antihypophora.*]

ANTHYSTER'IC. [See *Antihysteric.*]

AN'TI, [Gr. See *Ante.*] A preposition signifying *against, opposite, contrary*, or *in place of*; used in many English words.

ANTIAC'ID, *a.* Opposing or removing acidity. Often written *antacid.*

ANTIAC'ID, *n.* An alkali; a medicine proper to correct sourness, or acidity; an absorbent, as chalk, magnesia, coral, seashells, hematite, steelfilings; or an obtundent, as oil or fat; or an immutant, as lixivious salts, and soaps. *Cyc.*

ANTIAMER'ICAN, *a.* Opposed to America, or to the true interests or government of the United States; opposed to the revolution in America. *Marshall.*

ANTIARTHRIT'IC, *a.* [See *Antarthritic.*] Good against the gout.

ANTIARTHRIT'IC, *n.* A remedy for the gout.

ANTIASTHMAT'IC, *a.* [See *Antasthmatic.*] Good against asthma.

ANTIASTHMAT'IC, *n.* A remedy for the asthma.

ANTIBACCHIUS, *n.* [Gr. αντι, and βακχειος, a foot of one short and two long syllables.]

In *poetry*, a foot of three syllables, the two first long and the last short, as āmbīrĕ; opposed to the *bacchius*, in which the first syllable is short and the two last long. This foot is supposed to be so named from its use in hymns to Bacchus. *Trumbull. Encyc. Gr. Lex.*

ANTIBASIL'ICAN, *a.* s as z. [Gr. αντι, and Βασιλικη, a palace; L. *basilicus*, royal, *basilica*, a hall of justice.]

Opposed to royal state and magnificence. *Plowden, Brit. Empire.*

AN'TIC, *a.* [from Fr. *antique;* L. *antiquus;* It. *antico;* a sense derived from the grotesque figures of *antiques.*] Odd; fanciful; as, *antic* tricks.

AN'TIC, *n.* A buffoon or merry Andrew; one that practices odd gesticulations. *Shak.*

2. Odd appearance; fanciful figures. *Spenser.*
3. In *architecture, sculpture* and *painting*, such pieces as were made by the ancients; usually written *antique*, and pronounced *anteek*, but without any good reason.

AN'TIC, *v. t.* To make antic. *Shak.*

ANTICACHEC'TIC, *a.* [Gr. αντι, and καχεκτης, of an ill habit of body.]

Curing or tending to cure an ill habit of the constitution. *Johnson.*

ANTICACHEC'TIC, *n.* A medicine that tends to correct an ill habit of body. *Coxe.*

ANTICAT'ARRHAL, *a.* [αντι, against, and καταρροος, a catarrh.] Good against catarrh.

ANTICAT'ARRHAL, *n.* A remedy for catarrh. *Coxe.*

ANTICAUSOT'IC, *a.* [αντι, against, and καυσος, a burning fever.] Good against a burning fever.

ANTICAUSOT'IC, *n.* A remedy for a burning fever. *Coxe.*

AN'TI-CHAMBER, *n.* Dr. Johnson prefers *ante-chamber*, which see. But *ante* and *anti* are the same word in different dialects; and have the same radical signification. [See *Ante.*]

AN'TI-CHRIST, *n.* [Gr. αντι, against, and *Christ.*]

A great adversary of Christ; the man of sin; described 1 John, ii. 18. 2 Thess. ii. Rev. ix. Protestants generally suppose this adversary to be the Papal power; and some divines believe that, in a more general sense, the word extends to any persons who deny Christ or oppose the fundamental doctrines of christianity. *Encyc. Brown. Buck.*

ANTICHRIS'TIAN, *a.* Pertaining to antichrist; opposite to or opposing the christian religion.

ANTICHRIS'TIAN, *n.* A follower of antichrist; one opposed to the christian religion.

ANTICHRIS'TIANISM, *n.* Opposition or contrariety to the christian religion.

ANTICHRISTIAN'ITY, *n.* Opposition or contrariety to christianity.

ANTICH'RONISM, *n.* [Gr. αντι, and χρονος, time.] Deviation from the true order of time. *Selden.*

ANTIC'IPATE, *v. t.* [L. *anticipo*, of *ante*, before, and *capio*, to take.]

1. To take or act, before another, so as to prevent him; to take first possession.
2. To take before the proper time; as, the advocate has *anticipated* that part of his argument.
3. To foretaste or foresee; to have a previous view or impression of something future; as, to *anticipate* the pleasures of an entertainment; to *anticipate* the evils of life.
4. To prevent by crowding in before; to preclude. *Johnson.*

[*This sense is essentially included in the first.*]

ANTIC'IPATED, *pp.* Taken before; foretasted; foreseen; precluded; prevented.

ANTIC'IPATING, *ppr.* Taking before; foretasting; precluding; preventing.

ANTICIPA'TION, *n.* The act of taking up, placing, or considering something before the proper time, in natural order; prevention.

2. Foretaste; previous view or impression of what is to happen afterward; as, the *anticipation* of the joys of heaven.

The happy *anticipation* of a renewed existence in company with the spirits of the just. *Thodey.*

3. Previous notion; preconceived opinion, produced in the mind, before the truth is known; slight previous impression.
4. The attack of a fever before the usual time. *Coxe.*
5. In *music*, the obtrusion of a chord upon a syncopated note, to which it forms a discord. *Busby.*

ANTIC'IPATOR, *n.* One who anticipates.

ANTIC'IPATORY, *a.* Taking before the time. *More.*

ANTICLI'MAX, *n.* [Gr. αντι, opposite, and κλιμαξ, climax. See *Climate.*]

A sentence in which the ideas fall or become less important and striking at the close; opposed to *climax.* For example,

Next comes Dalhousie, the great God of war,
Lieutenant Col'nel to the Earl of Mar.

AN'TICLY, *adv.* In an antic manner; with odd postures and gesticulations; with fanciful appearance. *Shak.*

AN'TICMASK, or **AN'TIMASK**, *n.* A mask of antics. *Bacon. B. Jonson.*

ANTICONSTITU'TIONAL, *a.* Opposed to or against the constitution. *Bolingbroke.*

ANTICONSTITU'TIONALIST, *n.* One opposed to the constitution.

ANTICONTA'GIONIST, *n.* One who opposes the doctrine of contagion.

ANTICONTA'GIOUS, *a.* [αντι, and *contagious.*] Opposing or destroying contagion.

ANTICONVUL'SIVE, *a.* [αντι, and *convulsive.*] Good against convulsions. *Floyer.*

AN'TICOR, *n.* [*anti*, and Fr. *cœur*, or L. *cor*, the heart.]

Among *farriers*, an inflammation in a horse's throat, answering to the quinsy in man. *Encyc.*

ANTICOSMET'IC, *a.* [*anti* and *cosmetic.* See *Cosmetic.*] Destructive or injurious to beauty.

ANTICOSMET'IC, *n.* Any preparation which injures beauty.

AN'TICOURT, *a.* In opposition to the court. [*Not used.*] *Reresby.*

ANTICOURTIER, *n.* *anticórtyur.* [*anti* and *courtier.*]

One who opposes the court, or the measures of administration. *Ash.*

ANTICREA'TOR, *n.* One that opposes the creator.

ANTIDEMOCRAT'IC, } *a.* Opposing
ANTIDEMOCRAT'ICAL, } democracy; contrary to government by the people. *Mitford.*

AN'TIDOTAL, *a.* That has the quality of preventing the ill effects of poison, or of any thing noxious or mischievous.

AN'TIDOTE, *n.* [αντιδοτος, of αντι, against, and διδωμι, to give; W. *dodi*, to give.]

1. A medicine to counteract the effects of poison, or of any thing noxious taken into the stomach.
2. Whatever tends to prevent mischievous effects, or to counteract the evil which something else might produce.

ANTIDO'TICAL, *a.* Serving as an antidote.

ANTIDO'TICALLY, *adv.* By way of antidote. *Brown.*

ANTIDYSENTER'IC, *a.* [Gr. αντι, against, and δυσεντερικος, dysenteric.] Good against the dysentery, or bloody flux.

ANTIDYSENTER'IC, *n.* A remedy for dysentery. *Coxe.*

ANTIEMET'IC, *a.* [Gr. αντι, against, and εμετικος, emetic, from εμεω, to vomit.] Having the quality of allaying vomiting.

ANTIEMET'IC, *n.* A remedy to check or allay vomiting.

ANTIENNEAHE'DRAL, *a.* [Gr. αντι, opposite, εννεα, nine, and εδρα, side.]

In *crystalography*, having nine faces on two opposite parts of the crystal. *Cleaveland.*

ANTIENTHUSIAS'TIC, *a.* [*anti* and *enthusiastic.*] Opposing enthusiasm. *Shaftsbury.*

AN'TIENTRY, *n.* [More correctly, *ancientry.*] Cast of antiquity; that which is ancient. *Gray.*

ANTIEPISC'OPAL, *a.* Adverse to episcopacy. *K. Charles.*

ANTIEVANGEL'ICAL, *a.* Contrary to orthodoxy, or the genuine sense of the gospel. *Milner.*

AN'TIFACE, *n.* Opposite face. *Jonson.*

ANTIFANAT'IC, *n.* An opposer of fanaticism. *Milton.*

ANTIFE'BRILE, *a.* [αντι, against, and *febrile.*]

That has the quality of abating fever; opposing or tending to cure fever.

ANTIFE'BRILE, *n.* A medicine that cures, abates, or tends to allay fever.

ANTIFLAT'TERING, *a.* Opposite to flattery. *Delany.*

ANTIGUG'LER, *n.* [*anti* and *guggle.*]

A crooked tube of metal, so bent as to be introduced into the neck of a bottle, for drawing out the liquor, without disturbing the sediment. *Encyc.*

ANTIHEC'TIC, *a.* [Gr. αντι, against, and εκτικος, hectic.]

That has the quality of opposing or curing hectical disorders.

ANTIHEC'TIC, *n.* A medicine that is good in the cure of hectic disorders. *Encyc. Coxe.*

ANTIHYPNOT'IC, *a.* [Gr. αντι, and υπνος, sleep.]

Counteracting sleep; tending to prevent sleep or lethargy.

ANTIHYPNOT'IC, *n.* A medicine that prevents or tends to prevent sleep. *Coxe.*

ANTIHYPOCHOND'RIAC, *a.* [Gr. αντι, and υποχονδριακος, hypochondriac.]

That counteracts or tends to cure hypochondriac affections, and depression of spirits.

ANTIHYPOCHOND'RIAC, *n.* A remedy for hypochondriac affections and low spirits.

ANTIHYPOPH'ORA, *n.* [Gr. αντι, and υποφορα, an inference.]

In *rhetoric*, a figure which consists in refuting an objection by the opposition of a contrary sentence. *Smith. Johnson. Ash.*

ANTIHYSTER'IC, *a.* [Gr. αντι, and υςτερα, uterus.]

Counteracting hysterics.

ANTIHYSTER'IC, *n.* A medicine that cures or counteracts hysterical affections. *Coxe.*

ANTILOG'ARITHM, *n.* [*anti* and *logarithm.*]

The complement of the logarithm of any sine, tangent or secant, to 90 degrees. *Bailey.*

ANTIL'OGY, *n.* [Gr. αντι, against, and λογος, speech.]

A contradiction between any words or passages in an author.

ANTIMAGIS'TRICAL, *a.* Opposed to the office of magistrates. [*Not used.*[*South.*

ANTIMA'NIAC, } *a.* [*anti* and *maniac.*]
ANTIMANI'ACAL, }

Counteracting or curing madness or frenzy. *Beattie.*

AN'TIMASK, *n.* A lesser mask. *Bacon.*

ANTIMETAB'OLE, *n.* *antimetab'oly.* [Gr. αντι, against, and μεταβολη, mutation.]

In *rhetoric*, a setting of two things in opposition to each other; as, an honorable action may be attended with labor, but the *labor* is soon past, and the *honor* is immortal. *Encyc.*

ANTIMETATH'ESIS, *n.* [Gr. αντι, against, and μεταθεσις, a transposition.]

In *rhetoric*, an inversion of the parts or members of an antithesis; as, "Compare the arrival of this governor, with the victory of that general." "Compare this peace with that war." *Cicero in Verrem. Encyc.*

ANTIM'ETER, *n.* [Gr. αντι and μετρον, measure.]

An optical instrument for measuring angles, with greater accuracy than can be done by the usual quadrants or sextants. *Rees.*

ANTIMET'RICAL, *a.* Contrary to the rules of meter or verse. *Bailey.*

ANTIMINISTE'RIAL, *a.* [*anti* and *ministerial.*]

Opposed to the ministry, or administration of government.

ANTIMINISTE'RIALIST, *n.* One that opposes the ministry.

ANTIMONARCH'ICAL, *a.* [*anti*, against, and *monarchical.*]

Opposed to monarchy; that opposes a kingly government. *Addison.*

ANTIMONARCH′ICALNESS, *n.* The quality of being opposed to monarchy.

ANTIMO′NIAL, *a.* [from *antimony.*]
Pertaining to antimony; relating to antimony, or partaking of its qualities.

ANTIMO′NIAL, *n.* A preparation of antimony; a medicine in which antimony is a principal ingredient. *Encyc.*

ANTIMO′NIATE, *n.* A compound or salt composed of antimonic acid and a base. *Henry.*

ANTIMO′NIATED, *a.* Partaking of antimony; mixed or prepared with antimony; as *antimoniated* tartar. *Nicholson.*

ANTIMO′NIC, *a.* Pertaining to antimony; the *antimonic* acid is a peroxyd of antimony. *Henry.*

ANTIMO′NIOUS, *a.* Pertaining to antimony. The *antimonious* acid is a deutoxyd of antimony. *Henry.*

AN′TIMONITE, *n.* A compound of antimonious acid and a base. *Henry.*

AN′TIMONY, *n.* [Fr. *antimoine*; Low L. *antimonium*; It. *antimonio*; Sp. *id.* This by some writers is supposed to be composed of *anti* and Fr. *moine*, monk, from the fact that certain monks were poisoned by it. This story, reported by Furetiere, is treated by Morin, as fabulous, and by him it is said to be composed of Gr. αντι, against, and μονος, alone, and so named because it is not found alone. The real truth is not ascertained.]
Primarily, a metallic ore consisting of sulphur combined with a metal; the sulphuret of Antimony, the stibium of the Romans and the ςιμμι, of the Greeks. It is a blackish mineral, which stains the hands, hard, brittle, full of long, shining, needle-like striæ. It is found in the mines of Bohemia, and Hungary; in France and England, and in America. This word is also used for the pure metal or *regulus of antimony*, a metal of a grayish or silvery white, very brittle, and of a plated or scaly texture, and of moderate specific gravity. By exposure to air, its surface becomes tarnished, but does not rust. It is used as an ingredient in concave mirrors, giving them a finer texture. In bells, it renders the sound more clear; it renders tin more hard, white and sonorous, and gives to printing types more firmness and smoothness. It is also useful in promoting the fusion of metals, and especially in casting cannon balls. In its crude state, it is harmless to the human constitution; but many of its preparations act violently as emetics and cathartics. It has also a peculiar efficacy in promoting the secretions, particularly as a sudorific. *Chambers. Encyc. Nicholson.*

ANTIMOR′ALIST, *n.* An opposer of morality. *Warburton.*

ANTIMU′SICAL, *a.* Opposed to music; having no ear for music. *Amer. Review.*

ANTINEPHRIT′IC, *a.* [*anti*, and *nephritic*, which see.]
Counteracting diseases of the kidneys. *Coxe.*

ANTINEPHRIT′IC, *n.* A medicine that tends to remove diseases of the kidneys.

ANTINO′MIAN, *a.* [Gr. αντι, against, and νομος, law.]
Against law; pertaining to the Antinomians.

ANTINO′MIAN, *n.* One of a sect who maintain, that, under the gospel dispensation, the law is of no use or obligation; or who hold doctrines which supersede the necessity of good works and a virtuous life. This sect originated with John Agricola about the year 1538. *Encyc.*

ANTINO′MIANISM, *n.* The tenets of Antinomians. *Hall.*

AN′TINOMIST, *n.* One who pays no regard to the law, or to good works. *Sanderson.*

AN′TINOMY, *n.* A contradiction between two laws, or between two parts of the same law. *Baker.*

ANTIO′CHIAN, *a.* Pertaining to Antiochus, the founder of a sect of philosophers, cotemporary with Cicero. This sect was a branch of the academics, though Antiochus was a stoic. He attempted to reconcile the doctrines of the different schools, and was the last preceptor of the Platonic school. *Enfield. Encyc.*
The *Antiochian epoch* was a method of computing time, from the proclamation of liberty granted to the city of Antioch, about the time of the battle of Pharsalia. *Encyc.*

ANTIPA′PAL, *a.* Opposing popery.

ANTIPAPIS′TIC, } *a.* Opposed to pope-
ANTIPAPIS′TICAL, } ry or papacy. *Jortin.*

ANTIPAR′ALLEL, *a.* Running in a contrary direction. *Hammond.*

ANTIPARALYT′IC, *a.* [αντι, and *paralytic*, which see.]
Good against the palsy.

ANTIPARALYT′IC, *n.* A remedy for the palsy. *Coxe.*

ANTIPATHET′IC, } *a.* [See *Antipathy.*]
ANTIPATHET′ICAL, }
Having a natural contrariety, or constitutional aversion to a thing.

ANTIPATHET′ICALNESS, *n.* The quality or state of having an aversion or contrariety to a thing. *Johnson.*

ANTIP′ATHY, *n.* [Gr. αντι, against, and παθος, feeling.]
Natural aversion; instinctive contrariety or opposition in feeling; an aversion felt at the presence, real or ideal, of a particular object. This word literally denotes a *natural* aversion, which may be of different degrees, and in some cases may excite terror or horror at the presence of an object. Such is the aversion of animals for their natural enemies, as the *antipathy* of a mouse to a cat, or a weasel. Sometimes persons have an insuperable constitutional *antipathy* to certain kinds of food.
The word is applied also to aversion contracted by experience or habit; as when a person has suffered an injury from some food, or from an animal, which before was not an object of hatred; or when a particular kind of food or medicine is taken into a sickly stomach, and which nauseates it; the effect is *antipathy*, which is often of long continuance.
Antipathy however is often affected, as when persons pretend a great aversion to things from false delicacy.
2. In *ethics*, antipathy is hatred, aversion or repugnancy; *hatred* to persons; *aversion* to persons or things; *repugnancy* to actions. Of these *hatred* is most voluntary. *Aversion*, and *antipathy*, in its true sense, depend more on the constitution; *repugnancy* may depend on reason or education. *Encyc.*

> Inveterate *antipathies* against particular nations, and passionate attachments to others, are to be avoided. *Washington.*

3. In *physics*, a contrariety in the properties or affections of matter, as of oil and water, which will not mix.
Antipathy is regularly followed by *to*, sometimes by *against*; and is opposed to sympathy.

ANTIPATRIOT′IC, *a.* Not patriotic; opposing the interests of one's country.

> *Antipatriotic* prejudices. *Johnson.*

ANTIPEDOBAP′TIST, *n.* [Gr. αντι, against, παις, παιδος, a child, and βαπτιζω, to baptize.]
One who is opposed to the baptism of infants. *Buck.*

ANTIPERISTAL′TIC, *a.* [See *Peristaltic.*]
Opposed to peristaltic; retroverted, as in vomiting; as, the *antiperistaltic* motion of the intestines. *Cyc.*

ANTIPERIS′TASIS, *n.* [Gr. αντι, against, and περιςασις, a standing around.]
The opposition of a contrary quality, by which the quality opposed acquires strength; or the action by which a body attacked collects force by opposition; or the intension of the activity of one quality by the opposition of another. Thus quick-lime is set on fire, or sensible heat is excited in it, by mixture with water; and cold applied to the human body may increase its heat. *Johnson. Dryden. Quincy.*

ANTIPERISTAT′IC, *a.* Pertaining to antiperistasis. *Ash.*

ANTIPESTILEN′TIAL, *a.* [*anti* and *pestilential*, which see.]
Counteracting contagion or infection; having the quality of opposing or destroying pestilential diseases.

ANTIPHLOGIS′TIAN, *n.* [*anti* and *phlogiston*, which see.]
An opposer of the theory of phlogiston.

ANTIPHLOGIS′TIC, *a.* Counteracting heat or inflammation; tending to reduce arterial action; opposed to the doctrine of phlogiston. *Nicholson.*

ANTIPHLOGIS′TIC, *n.* Any medicine or diet which tends to reduce inflammation or the activity of the vital power. *Hooper. Coxe.*

AN′TIPHON, *n.* [See *Antiphony.*]
The chant or alternate singing in choirs of cathedrals.

ANTIPH′ONAL, }
ANTIPHON′IC, } *a.* [See *Antiphony.*]
ANTIPHON′ICAL, }
Pertaining to antiphony or alternate singing. *Encyc.*

ANTIPH′ONARY, *n.* [αντι, contrary, and φωνη, sound, voice.]
A service book, in the catholic church, containing all the invitatories, responsories, collects, and whatever is said or sung in the choir, except the lessons; called also a *responsary*; compiled by Gregory the Great. *Encyc.*

ANTIPH′ONER, *n.* A book of anthems or antiphons. *Chaucer.*

ANTIPH′ONY, *n.* [αντι, contrary, and φωνη, voice.]
1. The answer of one choir to another, when

an anthem or psalm is sung by two choirs; alternate singing.

2. A species of psalmody, when a congregation is divided into two parts, and each sings the verses alternately. *Encyc.*

3. The words given out at the beginning of a psalm, to which both the choirs are to accommodate their singing. *Encyc.*

4. A musical composition of several verses, extracted from different psalms. *Encyc.*

ANTIPH'RASIS, *n.* [Gr. αντι, against, and φρασις, a form of speech.]

The use of words in a sense opposite to their proper meaning; as when a court of justice is called a *court of vengeance.* *Johnson. Ash.*

ANTIPHRAS'TIC, ANTIPHRAS'TICAL, *a.* Pertaining to antiphrasis. *Ash.*

ANTIP'ODAL, *a.* Pertaining to the antipodes; having the feet directly opposite.

AN'TIPODE, *n.* [Gr. αντι, opposite, and πους, ποδος, foot.]

One who lives on the opposite side of the globe, and of course, whose feet are directly opposite.

ANTIPOI'SON, *n.* *s* as *z.* An antidote for poison. *Brown.*

AN'TIPOPE, *n.* [*anti* and *pope.*]

One who usurps the papal power, in opposition to the pope. *Addison.*

AN'TIPORT, *n.* An outward gate or door. *Smith.*

ANTIPRELAT'ICAL, *a.* Adverse to prelacy. *Morton.*

AN'TIPRIEST, *n.* An opposer or enemy of priests. *Waterland.*

ANTIPRIE'STCRAFT, *n.* Opposition to priestcraft. *Burke.*

ANTIPRIN'CIPLE, *n.* An opposite principle. *Spenser.*

ANTIPROPH'ET, *n.* An enemy or opposer of prophets. *Mede.*

ANTIP'TOSIS, *n.* [Gr. αντι and πτωσις, case.]

In *grammar,* the putting of one case for another. *Johnson.*

ANTIPU'RITAN, *n.* An opposer of puritans. *Warton.*

ANTIQUA'RIAN, *a.* Pertaining to antiquaries, or to antiquity. As a noun, this is used for antiquary.

ANTIQUA'RIANISM, *n.* Love of antiquities. *Warburton.*

AN'TIQUARY, *n.* [L. *antiquarius.*]

One who studies into the history of ancient things, as statues, coins, medals, paintings, inscriptions, books and manuscripts, or searches for them, and explains their origin and purport; one versed in antiquity.

AN'TIQUATE, *v. t.* [L. *antiquo.* See *Antiquary.*]

To make old, or obsolete; to make old in such a degree as to put out of use. Hence, when applied to laws or customs, it amounts to make void or *abrogate.*

> Christianity might reasonably introduce new laws and *antiquate* or abrogate old ones. *Hale.*

AN'TIQUATED, *pp.* Grown old; obsolete; out of use; having lost its binding force by non-observance; as an *antiquated* law.

AN'TIQUATEDNESS, *n.* The state of being old or obsolete.

ANTIQUA'TION, *n.* The state of being antiquated. *Beaumont.*

ANTÏQUE, *a.* *antee'k.* [Fr. from L. *antiquus,* probably from *ante.*]

1. Old; ancient; of genuine antiquity; in this sense it usually refers to the flourishishing ages of Greece and Rome; as an *antique* statue.

2. Old, as it respects the present age, or a modern period of time; of old fashion, as an *antique* robe.

3. Odd; wild; fanciful; more generally written *antic.*

ANTÏQUE, *n.* *antee'k.* In general, any thing very old; but in a more limited sense, the remains of ancient artists, as busts, statues, paintings and vases, the works of Grecian and Roman antiquity.

ANTÏQUENESS, *n.* *antee'kness.* The quality of being ancient; an appearance of ancient origin and workmanship. *Addison.*

ANTIQ'UITY, *n.* [L. *antiquitas.*]

1. Ancient times; former ages; times long since past; *a very indefinite term;* as, Cicero was the most eloquent orator of *antiquity.*

2. The ancients; the people of ancient times; as, the fact is admitted by all *antiquity.*

> Meaning that mankind are inclined to verify the predictions of *antiquity.* *T. Dawes.*

3. Ancientness; great age; the quality of being ancient; as, a statue of remarkable *antiquity;* a family of great *antiquity.*

4. Old age; *a ludicrous sense used by Shak.*

5. The remains of ancient times. In this sense it is usually or always plural. *Antiquities* comprehend all the remains of ancient times; all the monuments, coins, inscriptions, edifices, history and fragments of literature, offices, habiliments, weapons, manners, ceremonies; in short, whatever respects any of the ancient nations of the earth.

ANTIREVOLU'TIONARY, *a.* [See *Revolution.*]

Opposed to a revolution; opposed to an entire change in the form of government. *Burke.*

ANTIREVOLU'TIONIST, *n.* One who is opposed to a revolution in government.

ANTISABBATA'RIAN, *n.* [*anti* and *sabbath.*]

One of a sect who oppose the observance of the Christian sabbath; maintaining that the Jewish sabbath was only of ceremonial, not of moral obligation, and was consequently abolished by Christ. *Encyc.*

ANTISA'BIAN, *a.* [See *Sabian.*]

Opposed or contrary to Sabianism, or the worship of the celestial orbs. *Faber.*

ANTISACERDO'TAL, *a.* Adverse to priests. *Waterland.*

ANTIS''CIAN, ANTIS''CIANS, *n.* [L. *antiscii,* of Gr. αντι, opposite, and σκια, shadow.]

In *geography,* the inhabitants of the earth, living on different sides of the equator, whose shadows at noon are cast in contrary directions. Those who live north of the equator are *antiscians* to those on the south, and vice versa; the shadows on one side being cast towards the north; those on the other, towards the south. *Encyc.*

ANTISCORBU'TIC, *a.* [*anti* and *scorbutic,* which see.]

Counteracting the scurvy.

ANTISCORBU'TIC, *n.* A remedy for the scurvy.

ANTISCRIP'TURISM, *n.* Opposition to the Holy Scriptures. *Boyle.*

ANTISCRIP'TURIST, *n.* One that denies revelation. *Boyle.*

ANTISEP'TIC, *a.* [Gr. αντι and σηπτος, putrid, from σηπω, to putrify.]

Opposing or counteracting putrefaction. *Ash.*

ANTISEP'TIC, *n.* A medicine which resists or corrects putrefaction, as acids, stimulants, saline substances, astringents, &c. *Encyc.*

ANTISO'CIAL, *a.* [See *Social.*]

Averse to society; that tends to interrupt or destroy social intercourse. *Pascalis, Med. Rep.*

ANTIS'PASIS, *n.* [Gr. αντι, against, and σπαω, to draw.]

A revulsion of fluids, from one part of the body to another. *Quincy.*

ANTISPASMOD'IC, *a.* [Gr. αντι, against, and σπασμος, from σπαω, to draw.]

Opposing spasm; resisting convulsions; as anodynes. *Coxe.*

ANTISPASMOD'IC, *n.* A remedy for spasm or convulsions, as opium, balsam of Peru, and the essential oils of vegetables. *Coxe.*

ANTISPAS'TIC, *a.* [See *Antispasis.*]

Causing a revulsion of fluids or humors. *Johnson.*

ANTISPLENET'IC, *a.* [See *Spleen.*]

Good as a remedy in diseases of the spleen. *Johnson.*

ANTIS'TASIS, *n.* [Gr. αντι, opposite, and στασις, station.]

In *oratory,* the defense of an action from the consideration that if it had been omitted, something worse would have happened. *Encyc.*

ANTIS'TES, *n.* [L.]

The chief priest or prelate. *Milton.*

ANTIS'TROPHE, ANTIS'TROPHY, *n.* [Gr. αντι, opposite, and στροφη, a turning.]

In *grammar,* the changing of things mutually depending on each other; reciprocal conversion; as, the master of the servant, the servant of the master.

2. Among *the ancients,* that part of a song or dance, before the altar, which was performed by turning from west to east, in opposition to the *strophy.* The ancient odes consisted of stanzas called *strophies* and *antistrophies,* to which was often added the *epode.* These were sung by a choir, which turned or changed places when they repeated the different parts of the ode. The *epode* was sung, as the chorus stood still. [See *Ode.*] *West's pref. to his Pindar.*

ANTIS'TROPHON, *n.* A figure which repeats a word often. *Milton.*

ANTISTRUMAT'IC, *a.* [*anti* and *struma,* a scrophulous swelling.]

Good against scrophulous disorders. *Johnson. Wiseman.*

ANTITH'ESIS, *n.* [Gr. αντιθεσις, of αντι and θεσις, from τιθημι, to place.]

In *rhetoric,* an opposition of words or sentiments; contrast; as, "When our vices *leave us,* we flatter ourselves we *leave them.*" "The prodigal *robs his heir,* the miser *robs himself.*" "*Excess* of ceremony

shows *want* of breeding." "Liberty *with* *laws*, and government *without oppression*."
2. Opposition of opinions; controversy. *Encyc.*

ANTITHET'IC, ANTITHET'ICAL, } *a.* Pertaining to antithesis, or opposition of words and sentiments; containing or abounding with antithesis. *Enfield. Encyc.*

ANTITRINITA'RIAN, *n.* [*anti* and *trinitarian*, which see.]
One who denies the trinity or the existence of three persons in the Godhead. *Encyc.*

ANTITRINITA'RIAN, *a.* Opposing the trinity.

ANTITRINITA'RIANISM, *n.* A denial of the trinity.

AN'TITYPE, *n.* [Gr. αντιτυπον, of αντι, against, and τυπος, a type, or pattern.]
A figure corresponding to another figure; that of which the type is the pattern or representation. Thus the paschal lamb, in scripture, is the type, of which Christ is the *antitype*. An antitype then, is something which is formed according to a model or pattern, and bearing strong features of resemblance to it.
In *the Greek liturgy*, the sacramental bread and wine are called *antitypes*, that is, figures, similitudes; and the Greek fathers used the word in a like sense. *Encyc.*

ANTITYP'ICAL, *a.* Pertaining to an antitype; explaining the type. *Johnson.*

ANTIVARIO'LOUS, *a.* [*anti* and *variolous*, which see.]
Opposing the small pox. *Med. Rep.*

ANTIVENE'REAL, *a.* [*anti* and *venereal*, which see.]
Resisting venereal poison.

ANT'LER, *n.* [From the root of *ante*, before; Fr. *andouiller*. See *Ante*.]
A start or branch of a horn, especially of the horns of the cervine animals, as of the stag or moose. The branch next to the head is called the *brow-antler*, and the branch next above, the *bes-antler*. *Encyc.*

ANT'LERED, *a.* Furnished with antlers. *Encyc.*

ANTO'NIAN, *a.* Noting certain medicinal waters in Germany, at or near Tonstein. *Encyc.*

ANTONOMA'SIA, ANTONOM'ASY, } *n.* [Gr. αντι, and ονομα, name.]
The use of the name of some office, dignity, profession, science or trade, instead of the true name of the person; as when his *majesty* is used for a king, *lordship* for a nobleman. Thus instead of Aristotle, we say, the *philosopher*; a grave man is called a *Cato*; an eminent orator, a *Cicero*; a wise man, a *Solomon*. In the latter examples, a proper name is used for an appellative; the application being supported by a resemblance in character. *Encyc.*

ANTOSIAN'DRIAN, *n.* One of a sect of rigid Lutherans, so denominated from their opposing the doctrines of Osiander. This sect deny that man is made just, but is only imputatively just, that is, pronounced so. *Encyc.*

AN'VIL, *n.* [Sax. *anfilt*, *ænfilt*; D. *aanbeeld*; Old Eng. *anvelt*. The first syllable seems to be the preposition *on*, from the Belgic dialect *aan*. The last syllable is from the verb *build*; in Germ. *bilden*, to form or shape, and *bild*, an image or form, which in Dutch is *beeld*. To build is to *shape*, to *form*, and *anvil*, that is, *on build*, is that *on* which things are *shaped*. The Latin word *incus*, *incudis*, is formed by a like analogy from *in* and *cudo*, to hammer, or shape; and the same ideas are connected in the Celtic; W. *eingion*; Ir. *inneon*, anvil, and *inneonam*, to strike.]
An iron block with a smooth face, on which smiths hammer and shape their work. *Figuratively*, any thing on which blows are laid. *Shak.*
To be on the anvil, is to be in a state of discussion, formation or preparation; as when a scheme or measure is forming, but not matured. This figure bears an analogy to that of *discussion*, a shaking or beating.

ANXI'ETY, *n.* *angzi'ety.* [L. *anxietas*, from *anxius*, solicitous; L. *ango*. See *Anger*.]
1. Concern or solicitude respecting some event, future or uncertain, which disturbs the mind, and keeps it in a state of painful uneasiness. It expresses more than *uneasiness* or *disturbance*, and even more than *trouble* or *solicitude*. It usually springs from fear or serious apprehension of evil, and involves a suspense respecting an event, and often, a perplexity of mind, to know how to shape our conduct.
2. In *medical language*, uneasiness; unceasing restlessness in sickness.

ANX'IOUS, *a.* *ank'shus.* Greatly concerned or solicitous, respecting something future or unknown; being in painful suspense; *applied to persons*; as, to be *anxious* for the issue of a battle.
2. Full of solicitude; unquiet; *applied to things*; as *anxious* thoughts or labor.
3. Very careful; solicitous; as, *anxious* to please; *anxious* to commit no mistake.
It is followed by *for* or *about*, before the object.

ANX'IOUSLY, *adv.* In an anxious manner; solicitously; with painful uncertainty; carefully; unquietly.

ANX'IOUSNESS, *n.* The quality of being anxious; great solicitude. *Johnson.*

AN'Y, *a.* *en'ny.* [Sax. *anig*, *ænig*; D. *eenig*; Ger. *einig*. This word is a compound of *an*, one, and *ig*, which, in the Teutonic dialects, is the *ic* of the Latins, mus-*ic*-us. *Any* is *unic*-us, *one-like*.]
1. One indefinitely.

> Nor knoweth *any* man the Father, save the Son. Math xi.
>
> If a soul shall sin against *any* of the commandments. Lev. iv.

2. Some; an indefinite number, plurally; for though the word is formed from *one*, it often refers to *many*. Are there *any* witnesses present? The sense seems to be a small, uncertain number.
3. Some; an indefinite quantity; a small portion.

> Who will show us *any* good? Ps. iv.

4. It is often used as a substitute, the person or thing being understood.

> And when ye stand praying, forgive, if ye have aught against *any*. Mark xi.
>
> If *any* lack wisdom, let him ask it of God. James i.

It is used in opposition to *none*. Have you *any* wheat to sell? I have *none*.

ANY-WISE is sometimes used adverbially, but the two words may be separated, and used with a preposition, *in any wise*.

AO'NIAN, *a.* [From *Aonia*, a part of Bœotia, in Greece.]
Pertaining to the muses, or to Aonia, in Bœotia. The Aonian fount was *Aganippe*, at the foot of mount Helicon, not far from Thebes, and sacred to the muses. Hence the muses were called Aonides. *Dryden, Virg.* Eclogue. 10. 12. But in truth, *Aonia* itself is formed from the Celtic *aon*, a spring or fountain, [the fabled son of Neptune,] and this word gave name to *Aonia*. As the muses were fond of springs, the word was applied to the muses, and to mountains which were their favorite residence, as to Parnassus. *Milton.*

A'ORIST, *n.* [Gr. αοριςος, indefinite, of α priv. and ορος, limit.]
The name of certain tenses in the grammar of the Greek language, which express time indeterminate, that is, either past, present or future.

AORIST'IC, *a.* Indefinite; pertaining to an aorist, or indefinite tense.

AORT'A, *n.* [Gr. αορτη, the great artery; also an ark or chest.]
The great artery, or trunk of the arterial system; proceeding from the left ventricle of the heart, and giving origin to all the arteries, except the pulmonary arteries. It first rises, when it is called the ascending aorta; then makes a great curve, when it gives off branches to the head, and upper extremities; then proceeds downwards, called the descending aorta, when it gives off branches to the trunk; and finally divides into the two iliacs, which supply the pelvis and lower extremities. *Cyc. Parr.*

AORT'AL, *a.* Pertaining to the aorta, or great artery. *Darwin.*

AOU'TA, *n.* The paper-mulberry tree in Otaheite, from whose bark is manufactured a cloth worn by the inhabitants. *Encyc.*

APA'CE, *adv.* [*a* and *pace*.]
With a quick pace; quick; fast; speedily; with haste; hastily; applied to things in motion or progression; as, birds fly *apace*; weeds grow *apace*.

AP'AGOGE, AP'AGOGY, } *n.* [Gr. from απαγω, to draw aside, of απο, from, and αγω, to drive.]
1. In *logic*, abduction; a kind of argument, wherein the greater extreme is evidently contained in the medium, but the medium not so evidently in the lesser extreme, as not to require further proof. Thus, "All whom God absolves are free from sin; but God absolves all who are in Christ; therefore all who are in Christ are free from sin." The first proposition is evident; but the second may require further proof, as that God received full satisfaction for sin, by the suffering of Christ.
2. In *mathematics*, a progress or passage from one proposition to another, when the first, having been demonstrated, is employed in proving others.
3. In *the Athenian law*, the carrying a criminal, taken in the fact, to a magistrate. *Encyc.*

APAGOG'ICAL, *a.* An apagogical demonstration is an indirect way of proof, by showing the absurdity or impossibility of the contrary.

APALACH'IAN, *a.* Pertaining to the Apalaches, a tribe of Indians, in the western part of Georgia. Hence the word is applied to the mountains in or near their country, which are in fact the southern extremity of the Alleghanean ridges.

APAN'THROPY, *n.* [Gr. απο, from, and ανθρωπος, man.]

An aversion to the company of men; a love of solitude. *Encyc.*

APARITH'MESIS, *n.* [Gr.] In *rhetoric,* enumeration.

AP'ART, *adv.* [*a* and *part;* Fr. *aparté.* See *Part.*]

1. Separately; at a distance; in a state of separation, as to place.

Jesus departed thence into a desert place *apart.* Math. xiv.

2. In a state of distinction, as to purpose, use or character.

The Lord hath set *apart* him that is godly for himself. Ps. iv.

3. Distinctly; separately; as, consider the two propositions *apart.*

4. Aside; in exclusion of; as, *apart* from all regard to his morals, he is not qualified, in other respects, for the office he holds.

AP'ARTMENT, *n.* [Fr. *apartement,* or *appartement,* of *ab* or *a,* from, and *partir,* to depart. See *Part.*]

A room in a building; a division in a house, separated from others by partitions; a place separated by inclosure.

APATHET'IC, *a.* Void of feeling; free from passion; insensible. *Harris.*

AP'ATHY, *n.* [Gr. α priv. and παθος, passion.]

Want of feeling; an utter privation of passion, or insensibility to pain; *applied either to the body or the mind.* As applied to the mind, it is stoicism, a calmness of mind incapable of being ruffled by pleasure, pain or passion. In the first ages of the church, the christians adopted the term to express a contempt of earthly concerns.

Quietism is *apathy* disguised under the appearance of devotion. *Encyc.*

AP'ATITE, *n.* [from Gr. απαταω, to deceive; it having been often mistaken for other minerals.]

A variety of phosphate of lime; generally crystalized in low, flat, hexahedral prisms, sometimes even tabular. Its powder phosphoresces on burning coals.

The phosporite of Werner includes the massive and earthy varieties of the phosphate, which are distinguished from the apatite, by their containing a small portion of fluoric acid. *Cleaveland.*

APE, *n.* [D. *aap;* Dan. *abe;* Sax. Sw. and Ir. *apa;* Ice. *ape;* Germ. *affe;* W. *ab,* or *epa,* so named from the celerity of its motions.]

1. A genus of quadrupeds, found in the torrid zone of both continents, of a great variety of species. In common use, the word extends to all the tribe of monkeys and baboons; but in zoology, *ape* is limited to such of these animals as have no tails; while those with short tails are called *baboons,* and those with long ones, *monkeys.* These animals have four cutting teeth in each jaw, and two canine teeth, with obtuse grinders. The feet are formed like hands, with four fingers and a thumb, and flat nails. Apes are lively, full of frolic and chatter, generally untamable, thieving and mischievous. They inhabit the forests, and live on fruits, leaves and insects. *Encyc.*

2. One who imitates servilely, in allusion to the manners of the ape; a silly fellow.

APE, *v. t.* To imitate servilely; to mimic, as an ape imitates human actions. Weak persons are always prone to *ape* foreigners.

APE'AK, *adv.* [*a* and *peak,* a point. See *Peak.*]

1. On the point; in a posture to pierce. *Johnson.*

2. In *seamen's language,* perpendicular. The anchor is *apeak,* when the cable is drawn so as to bring the ship directly over it. *Mar. Dict.*

AP'ENNINE, *a.* [L. *apenninus; ad* and *penninus,* an epithet applied to a peak or ridge of the Alps. *Livy.* Celtic *pen* or *ben,* the peak of a mountain, or in general, a mountain.]

Pertaining to or designating a chain of mountains, which extend from the plains of Piedmont, round the gulf of Genoa, to the center of Italy, and thence south east to the extremity.

AP'ENNINE, } *n.* The mountains above
AP'ENNINES, } described.

APEP'SY, *n.* [Gr. α priv. and πεπτω, to digest.]

Defective digestion; indigestion. [*Little used.*] *Coxe. Encyc.*

A'PER, *n.* One who apes. In *zoology,* the wild boar.

APE'RIENT, *a.* [L. *aperiens, aperio;* Sp. Port. *abrir;* It. *aprire;* Fr. *ouvrir.*]

Opening; that has the quality of opening; deobstruent; laxative.

APE'RIENT, *n.* A medicine which promotes the circulation of the fluids, by removing obstructions; a laxative; a deobstruent; as, smallage, fennel, asparagus, parsley, and butcher's broom. *Encyc.*

APER'ITIVE, *a.* Opening; deobstruent; aperient. *Harvey. Fotherby.*

APERT', *a.* [L. *apertus.*] Open; evident; undisguised. [*Not used.*]

APER'TION, *n.* The act of opening; the state of being opened; an opening; a gap, aperture, or passage. [*Little used.*] *Wiseman. Wotton.*

APERT'LY, *adv.* Openly. [*Little used.*] *Bale.*

APERT'NESS, *n.* [L. *apertus.*] Openness. [*Rarely used.*] *Holder.*

APERT'OR, *n.* A muscle that raises the upper eye lid. *Quincy.*

AP'ERTURE, *n.* The act of opening; more generally, an opening; a gap, cleft or chasm; a passage perforated; a hole through any solid substance. *Holder. Newton.*

2. An opening of meaning; explanation. [*Not used.*] *Taylor.*

3. In *geometry,* the space between two right lines, forming an angle. *Encyc.*

APET'ALOUS, *a.* [Gr. α neg. and πεταλον, a flower-leaf or petal.]

In *botany,* having no petals, or flower-leaves; having no corol. *Martyn.*

APET'ALOUSNESS, *n.* A state of being without petals.

A'PEX, *n.* plu. *apexes.* [L. *apex,* plu. *apices.*]

The tip, point or summit of any thing. In *antiquity,* the cap of a flamen or priest; the crest of a helmet. In *grammar,* the mark of a long syllable. In *botany,* the anther of flowers, or tops of the stamens, like knobs. *Martyn.*

APH'ANITE, *n.* [Gr. α priv. and φαινω, to appear.]

In *mineralogy,* compact amphibole in a particular state. *Dict. of Nat. Hist.*

APHE'LION, *n.* [Gr. απο, from, and ηλιος, the sun.]

That point of a planet's orbit which is most distant from the sun; opposed to perihelion.

APHERE'SIS, *n.* [Gr. απο, from, and αιρεω, to take.]

1. The taking of a letter or syllable from the beginning of a word. Thus by an apheresis, *omittere* is written, *mittere.* *Encyc.*

2. In *the healing art,* the removal of any thing noxious. In *surgery,* amputation. *Quincy.*

APHIDIV'OROUS, *a.* [of *aphis,* the puceron or vine fretter, and *voro,* to eat.]

Eating, devouring, or subsisting on the aphis, or plant-louse. *Darwin.*

APHILAN'THROPY, *n.* [of α neg. and φιλανθρωπια, of φιλεω, to love, and ανθρωπος, man.]

Want of love to mankind. In *medicine,* the first stage of melancholy, when solitude is preferred to society. *Coxe.*

A'PHIS, *n.* In *zoology,* the puceron, vine fretter, or plant-louse; a genus of insects, belonging to the order of hemipters. The aphis is furnished with an inflected beak, and with feelers longer than the thorax. In the same species, some individuals have four erect wings, and others are entirely without wings. The feet are of the ambulatory kind, and the belly usually ends in two horns, from which is ejected the substance called honey-dew. The species are very numerous. *Encyc.*

APHLOGIS'TIC, *a.* [Gr. α priv. and φλογιςος, inflammable.]

Flameless; as an *aphlogistic* lamp, in which a coil of wire is kept in a state of continued ignition by alcohol, without flame. *Comstock.*

APH'ONY, *n.* [Gr. α priv. and φωνη, voice.]

A loss of voice; a palsy of the tongue; dumbness; catalepsy. *Johnson. Coxe.*

APH'ORISM, *n.* [Gr. αφορισμος, determination, distinction; from αφοριζω, to separate.]

A maxim; a precept, or principle expressed in few words; a detached sentence containing some important truth; as, the *aphorisms* of Hippocrates, or of the civil law. *Encyc.*

APHORISM'ER, *n.* A dealer in aphorisms. *Milton.*

APHORIS'TIC, } *a.* In the form of an
APHORIS'TICAL, } aphorism; in the form of short unconnected sentences; as an *aphoristic* style.

APHORIS'TICALLY, *adv.* In the form or manner of aphorisms.

APH'RITE, *n.* [Gr. αφρος, froth; the schaum erde, or earth scum, of Werner; the silvery chalk of Kirwan.]

A subvariety of carbonate of lime, occurring in small masses, solid or tender and friable. It is composed of lamels or scales, of a pearly luster. It is connected by insensible shades with argentine. *Jameson. Cleaveland.*

APH'RIZITE, *n.* A variety of black tourmalin. *Phillips.*

APHRODIS'IAC, } *a.* [Gr. αφροδισιος, venereal, Αφροδιτη, Venus, from αφρος, froth.]
APHRODISI'ACAL, }

Exciting venereal desire; increasing the appetite for sexual connection.

APHRODIS'IAC, *n.* A provocative to venery. *Encyc. Quincy.*

APH'RODITE, *n.* [Gr. Αφροδιτη.] A follower of Venus. *Cleaveland.*

APH'RODITE, } *n.* In *zoology*, a genus of the order of Molluscas, called also *sea-mouse*. The body is oval, with many small protuberances or tentacles on each side, which serve as feet. The mouth is cylindrical, at one end of the body, with two bristly tentacles, and capable of being retracted. *Encyc.*
APHRODI'TA, }

2. A name of Venus, so called from Gr. αφρος, froth, from which the goddess was supposed to have been produced. [See *Venus.*]

APH'THONG, *n.* [Gr. απο, without, and φθογγος, sound.]

A letter or combination of letters, which, in the customary pronunciation of a word, have no sound. *Focaloir, or Dict. of the Hiberno-Celtic Language.*

APH'THOUS, *a.* [Gr. αφθαι, ulcers in the mouth.]

Pertaining to thrush; of the nature of thrush or ulcerous affections of the mouth. *Bigelow.*

APH'YLLOUS, *a.* [Gr. α neg. and φυλλον, *folium*, a leaf.]

In *botany*, destitute of leaves, as the rush, mushrooms, garlic, some sea-weeds, &c. *Milne.*

A'PIARY, *n.* [L. *apiarium*, of *apis*, a bee.]

The place where bees are kept; a stand or shed for bees.

A'PIASTER, *n.* [From *apis*, a bee.]

The bird called a bee-eater, a species of merops. The apiaster has an iron colored back, and a belly of bluish green. *Encyc.*

A'PICES, A'PEXES. [See *Apex*, and *Anther.*]

APIE'CE, *adv.* [*a* and *piece.*]

To each; noting the share of each; as here is an orange *apiece.*

A'PIS, *n.* In *mythology*, an ox, worshiped in ancient Egypt, or a divinity or idol in the figure of an ox.

A'PIS, *n.* [L.] In *zoology*, the bee, a genus of insects, of the order of hymenopters. The mouth has two jaws, and a proboscis infolded in a double sheath; the wings are four, the two foremost covering the hinder ones when at rest. The females and working bees have a sting. *Encyc.*

A'PISH, *a.* [See *Ape.*] Having the qualities of an ape; inclined to imitate in a servile manner; hence, foolish, foppish, affected, trifling, insignificant; as, an *apish* fellow; *apish* manners.

A'PISHLY, *adv.* In an apish manner; with servile imitation; foppishly.

A'PISHNESS, *n.* The quality of being apish; mimicry; foppery.

APIT'PAT, With quick beating or palpitation; a word formed from the sound, *pit and pat*, or from *beat.*

APLANAT'IC, *a.* [Gr. α neg. and πλαναω, to wander.]

An *aplanatic* telescope is one which entirely corrects the aberration of the rays of light. It is thus distinguished from the *achromatic*, which only partially corrects the aberration. *Ed. Encyc.*

APLO'ME, *n.* [Gr. απλοος, simple.]

A mineral closely allied to garnet. It is considered by Jameson, as crystalized common garnet. It is a rare mineral, found in dodecahedrons, with rhombic faces, supposed to be derived from the cube, by one of the most *simple* laws of decrement, that of a single range of particles, parallel to all the edges of a cube. *Haüy. Cleaveland.*

APLUS'TER, } *n.* [L. from Gr. αφλαςον, the summit of the poop of a ship.]
APLUS'TRE, }

An ensign, or ornament carried by ancient ships. It was shaped like a plume of feathers, fastened on the neck of a goose or swan, and to this was attached a party-colored ribin, to indicate the course of the wind. *Addison. Encyc.*

APOC'ALYPSE, *n. apoc'alyps.* [Gr. from αποχαλυπτω, to disclose; απο and χαλυπτω, to cover.]

Revelation; discovery; disclosure. The name of a book of the New Testament, containing many discoveries or predictions respecting the future state of Christianity, written by St. John, in Patmos, near the close of the first century.

APOCALYP'TIC, } *a.* Containing or pertaining to revelation; disclosing.
APOCALYP'TICAL, }

APOCALYP'TICALLY, *adv.* By revelation; in the manner of disclosure.

APOC'OPATE, *v.t.* [See *apocope.*]

To cut off, or drop the last letter or syllable of a word.

APOC'OPATED, *pp.* Shortened by the omission of the last letter or syllable. *M. Stuart.*

APOC'OPATING, *ppr.* Cutting off, or omitting the last letter or syllable.

APOC'OPE, } *n.* [Gr. αποχοπη, abscission, of απο, and χοπτω to cut.]
APOC'OPY, }

The cutting off, or omission of the last letter or syllable of a word; as *di* for *dii.*

APOC'RISARY, *n.* [Gr. from αποχρισις, answer; αποχρινομαι, to answer.]

Anciently a resident in an imperial city, in the name of a foreign church or bishop, answering to the modern *nuncio*. He was a proctor, in the emperor's court, to negotiate, and transact business for his constituent. *Encyc. Spelman.*

APOCRUST'IC *a.* [Gr. αποχρουςιχα, from απο and χρουω, to drive from.[

Astringent; repelling.

APOCRUST'IC, *n.* A medicine which constringes, and repels the humors; a repellent. *Quincy. Coxe.*

APOC'RYPHA, *n.* [Gr. from αποχρυπτω, χρυπτω, to conceal.]

Literally such things as are not published; but in an appropriate sense, books whose authors are not known; whose authenticity, as inspired writings, is not admitted, and which are therefore not considered a part of the sacred canon of the scripture. When the Jews published their sacred books, they called them *canonical* and *divine;* such as they did not publish, were called *apocryphal.* The apocryphal books are received by the Romish Church as *canonical*, but not by Protestants. *Encyc.*

APOC'RYPHAL, *a.* Pertaining to the apocrypha; not canonical; of uncertain authority or credit; false; fictitious. *Congreve. Hooker.*

APOC'RYPHALLY, *adv.* Uncertainly; not indisputably.

APOC'RYPHALNESS, *n.* Uncertainty, as to authenticity; doubtfulness of credit, or genuineness.

AP'ODAL, *a.* [See *Apode.*]

Without feet; in *zoology*, destitute of ventral fins.

AP'ODE, *n.* [Gr. α priv. and πους, ποδος, foot.]

An animal that has no feet, applied to certain fabulous fowls, which are said to have no legs, and also to some birds that have very short legs.

In *zoology*, the apodes are an order of fishes, which have no ventral fins; the first order in Linne's system. *Encyc.*

APODIC'TIC, } *a.* [Gr. αποδειξις, evidence, of απο, and δειχνυμι, to show.]
APODIC'TICAL, }

Demonstrative; evident beyond contradiction; clearly proving. [*Little used.*] *Brown. Glanville.*

APODIC'TICALLY, *adv.* So as to be evident beyond contradiction.

APOD'OSIS, *n.* [Gr.] The application or latter part of a similitude. *Mede.*

AP'OGEE, *n.* [*apogeon, apogeum;* Gr. απο, from, and γη, the earth.]

That point in the orbit of a planet, which is at the greatest distance from the earth. The ancients regarded the earth as fixed in the center of the system, and therefore assigned to the sun, with the planets, an apogee; but the moderns, considering the sun as the center, use the terms perihelion and aphelion, to denote the least and greatest distance of the planets from that orb. The sun's apogee therefore is in strictness, the earth's aphelion. Apogee is properly applicable to the moon. *Encyc. Johnson.*

AP'OGON, *n.* A fish of the Mediterranean, the summit of whose head is elevated.

AP'OGRAPH, *n.* [Gr. απογραφον; απογραφω] An exemplar; a copy or transcript. *Ash.*

APOLLINA'RIAN, *a.* [From *Apollo.*]

The Apollinarian games, in Roman antiquity, were celebrated in honor of Apollo; instituted A. R. 542. after the battle of Cannæ. They were merely scenical, with exhibitions of music, dances and various mountebank tricks. *Encyc.*

APOLLINA'RIANS, in *Church history*, a sect, deriving their name from Apollinaris, bishop of Laodicea, in the 4th Century, who denied the proper humanity of Christ; maintaining that his body was endowed with a sensitive, and not with a rational soul; and that the divine nature supplied the place of the intellectual principle in man. *Encyc. Hooker.*

Apollo-Belvidere, an ancient statue of the first class in excellence.

APOL'LYON, *n.* [Gr. απολλυων, destroying.]

The destroyer; a name used Rev. ix. 11, for the angel of the bottomless pit, answering to the Hebrew *Abaddon.*

APOLOGET'IC, } *a.* [Gr. απολογεομαι, to speak in defense of; απο and λογος, speech.]
APOLOGET'ICAL, }

Defending by words or arguments; excusing; said or written in defense, or by way of apology; as an *apologetic* essay. *Boyle.*

APOLOGET'ICALLY, *adv.* By way of apology or excuse.

APOL'OGIST, *n.* [See *Apology.*]

One who makes an apology; one who speaks or writes in defense of another.

APOL'OGIZE, *v. i.* To make an apology; to write or speak in favor of, or to make excuse for; followed by *for;* as, my correspondent *apologized for* not answering my letter.

AP'OLOGUE, *n. ap'olog.* [Gr. απολογος, a long speech, a fable.]

A moral fable; a story or relation of fictitious events, intended to convey useful truths. An *apologue* differs from a *parable* in this; the parable is drawn from events which pass among mankind, and is therefore supported by probability; an apologue may be founded on supposed actions of brutes or inanimate things, and therefore does not require to be supported by probability. Esop's fables are good examples of *apologues.* *Encyc.*

APOL'OGY, *n.* [Gr. απολογια, of απο and λογος, discourse.]

An excuse; something said or written in defense or extenuation of what appears to others wrong, or unjustifiable; or of what may be liable to disapprobation. It may be an extenuation of what is not perfectly justifiable, or a vindication of what is or may be disapproved, but which the apologist deems to be right. A man makes an *apology* for not fulfilling an engagement, or for publishing a pamphlet. An *apology* then is a reason or reasons assigned for what *is* wrong or *may appear* to be wrong, and it may be either an extenuation or a justification of something that *is* or *may* be censured, by those who are not acquainted with the reasons.

APONEURO'SIS, } *n.* [Gr. απο, from, and APONEU'ROSY, } νευρον, a nerve; W. *nerth;* Arm. *nerz.* See *Nerve.*]

An expansion of a tendon in the manner of a membrane; the tendinous expansion or fascia of muscles; the tendon or tail of a muscle. *Encyc. Coxe.*

APOPEMP'TIC, *a.* [Gr. απο, from, and πεμπω, to send.]

Denoting a song or hymn among the ancients, sung or addressed to a stranger, on his departure from a place to his own country. It may be used as a noun for the hymn. *Encyc.*

APOPH'ASIS, *n.* [Gr. απο, from, and φασις, form of speech.]

In *rhetoric,* a waving or omission of what one, speaking ironically, would plainly insinuate; as, "I will not mention another argument, which, however, if I should, you could not refute." *Smith. Johnson.*

APOPHLEGMAT'IC *a.* [Gr. απο, from, and φλεγμα, phlegm.]

Masticatory; having the quality of exciting discharges of phlegm from the mouth or nostrils.

APOPHLEGMAT'IC, *n.* A masticatory; a medicine which excites discharges of phlegm from the mouth or nostrils. *Coxe.*

APOPHLEG'MATISM, *n.* An apophlegmatic. *Bacon.*

APOPHLEGMAT'IZANT, *n.* An apophlegmatic. *Quincy. Coxe.*

AP'OPHTHEGM, } *n.* [Gr. απο, from, and AP'OTHEM, } φθεγμα, word. It would be eligible to reduce this harsh word to *apothem.*]

A remarkable saying; a short, sententious, instructive remark, uttered on a particular occasion, or by a distinguished character; as that of Cyrus, "He is unworthy to be a magistrate, who is not better than his subjects;" or that of Cato, "Homines nihil agendo, discunt male agere;" men by doing nothing, soon learn to do mischief.

APOPH'YGE, } *n.* [Gr. απο, from, and φυγη, APOPH'YGY, } flight.]

1. In *architecture,* the part of a column, where it springs out of its base; originally a ring or ferrel to bind the extremities of columns, and keep them from splitting; afterwards imitated in stone pillars. It is sometimes called the spring of the column. *Chambers.*

2. A concave part or ring of a column, lying above or below the flat member, called by the French *le congé d'en bas,* or *d'en haut;* by the Italians, *cavo di basso,* or *di sopra;* also, *il vivo di basso.* *Encyc.*

APOPH'YLLITE, *n.* [Gr. απο, from, and φυλλον, a leaf; so called because of its tendency to exfoliate.]

A mineral occurring in laminated masses or in regular prismatic crystals, having a strong and peculiar pearly luster. Its structure is foliated, and when a fragment is forcibly rubbed against a hard body, it separates into thin lamens, like selenite. It exfoliates also before the flame of a lamp. From its peculiar luster, it is sometimes called by the harsh name, *ichthyophthalmite,* fish-eye stone. *Cleaveland.*

APOPH'YSIS, } *n.* [Gr. απο, from, and φυσις, APOPH'YSY, } growth.]

The projecting soft end or protuberance of a bone; a process of a bone. *Quincy. Encyc. Coxe.*

APOPLEC'TIC, } *a.* [See *apoplexy.*] APOPLEC'TICAL, } Pertaining to or consisting in apoplexy, as an *apoplectic* fit; or predisposed to apoplexy, as an *apoplectic* habit of body.

APOPLEC'TIC, *n.* A person affected by apoplexy. *Knatchbull.*

AP'OPLEXED, *a.* Affected with apoplexy. *Shak.*

AP'OPLEXY, *n.* [Gr. αποπληξια, of απο, from, and πλησσω, to strike.]

A sudden deprivation of all sense and voluntary motion, occasioned by repletion or whatever interrupts the action of the nerves upon the muscles. *Cullen.*

Dryden, for the sake of measure, uses *apoplex,* for *apoplexy.*

AP'ORON, } *n.* [See *Apory.*] A problem AP'ORIME, } difficult to be resolved. *Encyc.*

AP'ORY, } *n.* [Gr. απορια, from απορος, APO'RIA, } inops concilii, of α and πορος, way or passage.]

1. In *rhetoric,* a doubting or being at a loss where to begin, or what to say, on account of the variety of matter. *Smith.*

2. In *the medical art,* febrile anxiety; uneasiness; restlessness, from obstructed perspiration, or the stoppage of any natural secretion. *Coxe.*

APOSIOPE'SIS, } *n.* [Gr. αποσιωπησις, of APOSIO'PESY, } απο, and σιωπαω, to be silent.]

Reticency or suppression; as when a speaker for some cause, as fear, sorrow, or anger, suddenly breaks off his discourse, before it is ended; or speaks of a thing, when he makes a show as if he would say nothing on the subject; or aggravates what he pretends to conceal, by uttering a part and leaving the remainder to be understood. *Smith. Johnson. Encyc.*

APOS'TASY, *n.* [Gr. αποςασις, a defection, of αφιςημι, to depart, απο and ιςημι.]

1. An abandonment of what one has professed; a total desertion, or departure from one's faith or religion.

2. The desertion from a party to which one has adhered.

3. Among *physicians,* the throwing off of exfoliated or fractured bone, or the various solution of disease. *Coxe.*

4. An abscess. *Encyc.*

APOS'TATE, *n.* [Gr. αποςατης.]

One who has forsaken the church, sect or profession to which he before adhered. In its original sense, applied to one who has abandoned his religion; but correctly applied also to one who abandons a political or other party.

APOS'TATE, *a.* False; traitorous. *Spenser.*

APOSTAT'ICAL, *a.* After the manner of an apostate. *Sandys.*

APOS'TATIZE, *v. i.* To abandon one's profession or church; to forsake principles or faith which one has professed; or the party to which one has been attached. *Worthington.*

APOS'TATIZING, *ppr.* Abandoning a church, profession, sect or party.

APOS'TEMATE, *v. i.* To form into an abscess; to swell and fill with pus.

APOSTEMA'TION, *n.* The formation of an aposteme; the process of gathering into an abscess; written corruptly *imposthumation.*

APOSTEM'ATOUS, *a.* Pertaining to an abscess; partaking of the nature of an aposteme. *Journ. of Science.*

AP'OSTEME, *n.* [Gr. αποςημα, from αφιςημι, to go off, to recede; απο and ιςημι, to stand.]

An abscess; a swelling filled with purulent matter; written also corruptly *imposthume.*

A-POSTERIORI, [L. *posterior,* after.]

Arguments *a posteriori,* are drawn from effects, consequences or facts; in opposition to reasoning *a priori,* or from causes previously known.

APOS'TLE, *n. apos'l.* [L. *apostolus;* Gr. αποςολος, from αποςελλω, to send away, of απο, and ςελλω, to send; G. *stellen,* to set.]

A person deputed to execute some important business; but appropriately, a disciple of Christ commissioned to preach the gospel. Twelve persons were selected by Christ for this purpose; and Judas, one of the number, proving an apostate, his place was supplied by Matthias. Acts i.

The title of apostle is applied to Christ himself, Heb. 3. In the primitive ages of the church, other ministers were called *apostles,* Rom. xvi; as were persons sent to carry alms from one church to another,

Philip. ii. This title was also given to persons who first planted the Christian faith. Thus Dionysius of Corinth is called the *apostle* of France; and the Jesuit Missionaries are called *apostles*.

Among the Jews, the title was given to officers who were sent into distant provinces, as visitors or commissioners, to see the laws observed.

Apostle, in the Greek liturgy, is a book containing the epistles of St. Paul, printed in the order in which they are to be read in churches, through the year. *Encyc.*

APOS'TLE-SHIP, *n.* The office or dignity of an apostle.

APOS'TOLATE, *n.* A mission; the dignity or office of an apostle. Ancient writers use it for the office of a bishop; but it is now restricted to the dignity of the pope, whose see is called the *Apostolic See*. *Encyc.*

APOSTOL'IC, APOSTOL'ICAL, *a.* Pertaining or relating to the apostles, as the *apostolic* age.

2. According to the doctrines of the apostles; delivered or taught by the apostles; as *apostolic* faith or practice.

Apostolic constitutions, a collection of regulations attributed to the apostles, but generally supposed to be spurious. They appeared in the 4th century; are divided into eight books, and consist of rules and precepts relating to the duties of christians, and particularly, to the ceremonies and discipline of the church.

Apostolic Fathers, an appellation given to the christian writers of the first century.

APOSTOL'ICALLY, *adv.* In the manner of the apostles.

APOSTOL'ICALNESS, *n.* The quality of being apostolical, or according to the doctrines of the apostles.

APOSTOL'ICS, *n.* Certain sects so called from their pretending to imitate the practice of the apostles, abstaining from marriage, from wine, flesh, pecuniary reward &c., and wandering about clothed in white, with long beards, and bare heads. Sagarelli, the founder of one of these sects, was burnt at Parma in 1300. *Encyc.*

APOS'TROPHE, APOS'TROPHY, *n.* [Gr. απο, from, and ϛροφη, a turning.]

In *rhetoric*, a diversion of speech; a digressive address; a changing the course of a speech, and addressing a person who is dead or absent, as if present; or a short address introduced into a discourse, directed to some person, different from the party to which the main discourse is directed; as when an advocate, in an argument to the jury, turns and addresses a few remarks to the court. *Encyc. Smith.*

2. In *grammar*, the contraction of a word by the omission of a letter or letters, which omission is marked by a comma, as *call'd* for *called*. The comma used for this purpose may also be called an apostrophe.

APOS'TROPHIC, *a.* Pertaining to an apostrophe; noting the contraction of a word. *Murray.*

APOS'TROPHIZE, *v. i.* or *t.* To make an apostrophe, or short detached address in speaking; to address by apostrophy.

2. *v. t.* To contract a word by omitting a letter or letters.

3. To mark with a comma, indicating the omission of a letter.

APOS'TROPHIZED, *pp.* Addressed by way of digression; contracted by the omission of a letter or letters; marked by an apostrophy.

APOS'TROPHIZING, *ppr.* Addressing in a digression; contracting or marking by apostrophy.

AP'OSTUME, *n.* An aposteme, which see.

APOTAC'TITE, *n.* [Gr. αποτακτος, from αποταττω, to renounce; απο and ταττω, to ordain.]

One of a sect of ancient christians, who, in imitation of the first believers, renounced all their effects and possessions. *Encyc.*

APOTH'ECARY, *n.* [L. and Gr. *apotheca*, a repository, from αποτιθημι, to deposit or lay aside, or from θηκη, a chest.]

1. One who practices pharmacy; one who prepares drugs for medicinal uses, and keeps them for sale. In England, apothecaries are obliged to prepare medicines according to the formulas prescribed by the college of physicians, and are liable to have their shops visited by the censors of the college, who have power to destroy medicines which are not good.

2. In *the middle ages*, an apothecary was the keeper of any shop or warehouse; and an officer appointed to take charge of a magazine. *Encyc.*

AP'OTHEGM, AP'OTHEM, *n.* [See *Apophthegm*.]

A remarkable saying; a short, instructive remark.

APOTHEGMAT'IC, APOTHEGMAT'ICAL, *a.* In the manner of an apothem. *Warton.*

APOTHEG'MATIST, *n.* A collector or maker of apothems. *Pope.*

APOTHEG'MATIZE, *v. t.* To utter apothems or short instructive sentences.

AP'OTHEME, *n.* [See *Apothecary*.]

In *Russia*, an apothecary's shop, or a shop for the preparation and sale of medicines. *Tooke.*

APOTHE'OSIS, *n.* [Gr. αποθεωσις, of απο, and θεος, God.]

Deification; consecration; the act of placing a prince or other distinguished person among the heathen deities. This honor was often bestowed on illustrious men in Rome, and followed by the erection of temples, and the institution of sacrifices to the new deity. *Encyc.*

APOTH'ESIS, *n.* [Gr. απο, and τιθημι, to put back.]

1. The reduction of a dislocated bone. *Coxe.*

2. A place on the south side of the chancel in the primitive churches, furnished with shelves, for books, vestments, &c. *Wheler.*

APOT'OME, APOT'OMY, *n.* [Gr. αποτεμνω, to cut off.]

1. In *mathematics*, the difference between two incommensurable quantities. *Cyc.*

2. In *music*, that portion of a tone major which remains after deducting from it an interval, less by a comma, than a semitone major. *Busby.*

The difference between a greater and lesser semitone, expressed by the ratio 128; 125. The Greeks supposing the greater tone could not be divided into two equal parts, called the difference, or smaller part, *apotome*; the other, *limma*. *Chambers. Encyc.*

APOTREP'SIS, *n.* [Gr. απο, and τρεπω, to turn.]

The resolution of a suppurating tumor. *Coxe.*

AP'OTROPY, *n.* [Gr. απο, and τρεπω, to turn.]

In *ancient poetry*, a verse or hymn composed for averting the wrath of incensed deities. The deities invoked were called *apotropeans*. *Encyc.*

AP'OZEM, *n.* [Gr. απο, and ζεω, to boil.]

A decoction, in which the medicinal substances of plants are extracted by boiling. *Encyc. Wiseman.*

APOZEM'ICAL, *a.* Like a decoction. *Whitaker.*

APPA'IR, *v. t.* To impair. [*Not in use.*]

APPA'IR, *v. i.* To degenerate. [*Not in use.*]

APPALL', *v. t.* [Fr. *palir*; L. *palleo*, to become pale. See *Pale*.]

1. To depress or discourage with fear; to impress with fear, in such a manner that the mind shrinks, or loses its firmness; as, the sight *appalled* the stoutest heart.

2. To reduce, allay or destroy; as, to *appall* thirst. [*Unusual.*] *Thomson.*

APPALL', *v. i.* To grow faint; to be dismayed. *Lidgate.*

APPALL'ED, *pp.* Depressed or disheartened with fear; reduced.

APPALL'ING, *ppr.* Depressing with fear; reducing.

APPALL'MENT, *n.* Depression occasioned by fear; discouragement.

AP'PANAGE, *n.* [Fr. *apanage*, an estate assigned to a younger son for his maintenance; an *appendix*, dependence, appurtenance; It. *appannaggio*, an appendage. If this word is from the *panage*, *panagium* of the middle ages, it is from *panis*, food, provision; It. *panaggio*, provision. This is probably the true origin of the word.]

1. Lands appropriated by a prince to the maintenance of his younger sons, as their patrimony; but on condition of the failure of male offspring, they were to revert to the donor or his heir. From the appanage it was customary for the sons to take their surnames. *Spelman.*

2. Sustenance; means of nourishing.

Wealth—the *appanage* of wit. *Swift.*

APPARA'TUS, *n.* plu. *apparatuses*. [L. from *apparo*, to prepare, of *ad* and *paro*.]

1. Things provided as means to some end; as the tools of an artisan; the furniture of a house; instruments of war. In more technical language, a complete set of instruments or utensils, for performing any operation. *Cavallo. Encyc.*

2. In *surgery*, the operation of cutting for the stone, of three kinds, the small, the great, and the high. *Encyc. Coxe.*

Apparatus is also used as the title of several books, in the form of catalogues, bibliothecas, glossaries, dictionaries, &c. *Encyc.*

APPAR'EL, *n.* [Fr. *appareil*, from *parer*, to dress or set off; Sp. *aparejar*; L. *paro*, *apparo*, to prepare; Arm. *para*; Port. *aparelho*, Sp. *aparejo*, tackle, whence *parrel* in seamen's language; Ch. Heb. ברא, bara; Ar. برا. Class Br. No. 8. 10. 19.]

1. Clothing; vesture; garments; dress.
2. External habiliments or decorations; appearance; as, religion appears in the natural *apparel* of simplicity.
 Glorious in *apparel*. Isa. lxiii.
3. The furniture of a ship, as sails, rigging, anchors, &c.

APPAR'EL, *v. t.* To dress or clothe.
 They who are gorgeously *appareled* are in kings courts. Luke vii.
2. To adorn with dress.
 She did *apparel* her apparel. *Shak.*
3. To dress with external ornaments; to cover with something ornamental; to cover, as with garments; as, trees *appareled* with flowers; or a garden with verdure.
4. To furnish with external apparatus; as ships *appareled* for sea.

APPAR'ELED, *pp.* Dressed; clothed; covered as with dress; furnished.

APPAR'ELING, *ppr.* Dressing; clothing; covering as with dress; furnishing.

APPA'RENCE, } *n.* Appearance. [*Not in*
APPA'RENCY, } *use.*]
 Chaucer. Gower.

APPA'RENT, *a.* [See *Appear.*]
1. That may be seen, or easily seen; visible to the eye; within sight or view.
 Atterbury.
2. Obvious; plain; evident; indubitable; as, the wisdom of the creator is *apparent* in his works.
3. Visible, in opposition to *hid* or *secret*; as, a man's *apparent* conduct is good.
4. Visible; appearing to the eye; seeming, in distinction from *true* or *real*, as the *apparent* motion or diameter of the sun.
 Heirs *apparent* are those whose right to an estate is indefeasible, if they survive the ancestor; in distinction from *presumptive* heirs, who, if the ancestor should die immediately, would inherit, but whose right is liable to be defeated by the birth of other children. *Blackstone.*

APPA'RENTLY, *adv.* Openly; evidently; as, the goodness of God is *apparently* manifest in his works of providence.
2. Seemingly; in appearance; as, a man may be *apparently* friendly, yet malicious in heart.

APPARI''TION, *n.* [See *Appear.*]
1. In a general sense, an appearance; visibility. [*Little used.*] *Milton.*
2. The thing appearing; a visible object; a form. *Milton. Shak.*
3. A ghost; a specter; a visible spirit. [*This is now the usual sense of the word.*]
4. Mere appearance, opposed to reality.
 Denham.

APPAR'ITOR, *n.* [L. *apparo*, to prepare, or *appareo*, to attend.]
Among *the Romans*, any officer who attended magistrates and judges to execute their orders. In *England*, a messenger or officer who serves the process of a spiritual court, or a beadle in the university who carries the mace. *Encyc.*

APPA'Y, *v. t.* [Sp. and Port. *apagar.*]
To satisfy. *Obs.* [See *Pay.*] *Sidney.*

APPE'ACH, *v. t.* To accuse; to censure, or reproach. *Obs.* [See *Impeach.*] *Shak.*

APPE'ACHMENT, *n.* Accusation; charge exhibited. *Obs.* *Wotton.*

APPE'AL, *v. i.* [Fr. *appeler;* It. *appellare;* Sp. *apelar;* Port. *appellar;* L. *appello; ad* and *pello*, to drive or send; Gr. βαλλω. We do not see the sense of *call* in *pello*, but to drive or press out, is the radical sense of calling, naming. This word coincides in elements with L. *balo*, Eng. *bawl*, and *peal.* Class Bl.]
1. To refer to a superior judge or court, for the decision of a cause depending, or the revision of a cause decided in a lower court.
 I *appeal* to Cesar. Acts xxi.
2. To refer to another for the decision of a question controverted, or the counteraction of testimony or facts; as, I *appeal* to all mankind for the truth of what is alledged.

APPE'AL, *v. t.* To call or remove a cause from an inferior to a superior judge or court. This may be done after trial and judgment in the lower court; or by special statute or agreement, a party may appeal before trial, upon a fictitious issue and judgment. We say the cause *was appealed* before or after trial.

APPE'AL, *v. t.* In *criminal law*, to charge with a crime; to accuse; to institute a criminal prosecution, for some hainous offense; as, to *appeal* a person of felony. This process was anciently given to a private person to recover the weregild, or private pecuniary satisfaction for an injury he had received by the murder of a relation, or by some personal injury.
 Blackstone.

APPE'AL, *n.* The removal of a cause or suit from an inferior to a superior tribunal, as from a common pleas court to a superior or supreme court. Also the right of appeal.
2. An accusation; a process instituted by a private person against a man for some hainous crime by which he has been injured, as for *murder, larciny, mayhem.*
 Blackstone.
3. A summons to answer to a charge.
 Dryden.
4. A call upon a person; a reference to another for proof or decision.
 In an oath, a person makes an *appeal* to the Deity for the truth of his declaration.
5. Resort; recourse.
 Every milder method is to be tried, before a nation makes an *appeal* to arms. *Kent.*

APPE'ALABLE, *a.* That may be appealed; that may be removed to a higher tribunal for decision; as, the cause is *appealable.*
2. That may be accused or called to answer by appeal; *applied to persons;* as, a criminal is *appealable* for manslaughter.

APPE'ALANT, *n.* One who appeals. [*Not used.*] *Shak.*

APPE'ALED, *pp.* Removed to a higher court, as a cause; prosecuted for a crime by a private person, as a criminal.

APPE'ALER, *n.* One who appeals; an appellor.

APPE'ALING, *ppr.* Removing a cause to a higher tribunal; prosecuting as a private person for an offense; referring to another for a decision.

APPE'AR, *v. i.* [L. *appareo*, of *ad* and *pareo*, to appear, or be manifest; It. *apparire;* Sp. *parecer, aparecer;* Fr. *apparoir, apparoitre.* Class Br.]
1. To come or be in sight; to be in view; to be visible.
 The leprosy *appeareth* in the skin of the flesh. Lev. xiii.
 And God said, Let the dry land *appear.* Gen. i.
2. To become visible to the eye, as a spirit, or to the apprehension of the mind; *a sense frequent in scripture.*
 The Lord *appeared* to Abram, and said. Gen. xii.
 The angel of the Lord *appeared* to him in a flame of fire out of the midst of the bush. Ex. iii.
3. To stand in presence of, as parties or advocates before a court, or as persons to be tried. The defendant, being called, did not *appear.*
 We must all *appear* before the judgment seat of Christ. 2 Cor. v.
4. To be obvious; to be known, as a subject of observation or comprehension.
 Let thy work *appear* to thy servant. Ps. xc.
 It doth not yet *appear* what we shall be. 1 John iii.
5. To be clear or made clear by evidence; as, this fact *appears* by ancient records.
 But sin that it might *appear* sin. Rom. vii.
6. To seem, in opposition to reality.
 They disfigure their faces, that they may *appear* to men to fast. Mat. vi.
7. To be discovered, or laid open.
 That thy shame may *appear*. Jer. xiii.

APPE'AR, *n.* Appearance. *Obs.*

APPE'ARANCE, *n.* The act of coming into sight; the act of becoming visible to the eye; as, his sudden *appearance* surprised me.
2. The thing seen; a phenomenon; as an *appearance* in the sky.
3. Semblance; apparent likeness.
 There was upon the tabernacle as it were the *appearance* of fire. Num. ix.
4. External show; semblance assumed, in opposition to reality or substance; as, we are often deceived by *appearances;* he has the *appearance* of virtue.
 For man looketh on the outward *appearance.* 1 Sam. xvi.
5. Personal presence; exhibition of the person; as, he made his first *appearance* at court or on the stage.
6. Exhibition of the character; introduction of a person to the public in a particular character, as a person makes his *appearance* in the world, as a historian, an artist, or an orator.
7. Probability; likelihood. *Bacon.* This sense is rather an inference from the third or fourth; as *probability* is inferred from external *semblance* or *show.*
8. Presence; mien; figure; as presented by the person, dress or manners; as, the lady made a noble *appearance.*
9. A being present in court; a defendant's filing common or special bail to a process.
10. An apparition. *Addison.*

APPE'ARER, *n.* The person that appears.
 Brown.

APPE'ARING, *ppr.* Coming in sight; becoming evident; making an external show; seeming; having the semblance.

APPE'ARING, *n.* The act of becoming visible; appearance.

APPE'ASABLE, *a.* That may be appeased, quieted, calmed, or pacified.

APPE'ASABLENESS, *n.* The quality of being appeasable.

APPE'ASE, *v. t.* *s* as z. [Fr. *apaiser*, of *ad* and *paix*, peace; L. *pax*. See *Peace*.]

1. To make quiet; to calm; to reduce to a state of peace; to still; to pacify; as, to *appease* the tumult of the ocean, or of the passions; to *appease* hunger or thirst. [*This word is of a general application to every thing in a disturbed, ruffled or agitated state.*]

APPE'ASED, *pp.* Quieted; calmed; stilled; pacified.

APPE'ASEMENT, *n.* The act of appeasing; the state of being in peace.

APPE'ASER, *n.* One who appeases, or pacifies.

APPE'ASIVE, *a.* Having the power to appease; mitigating; quieting.

APPEL'LANT, *n.* [See *Appeal*.]

1. One who appeals, or removes a cause from a lower to a higher tribunal.
2. One who prosecutes another for a crime.
3. One who challenges, or summons another to single combat.
4. In *church history*, one who appeals from the Constitution Unigenitus to a general council. *Blackstone. Encyc. Milton.*

APPEL'LATE, *n.* A person appealed, or prosecuted for a crime. [*Not now used.* See *Appellee*.] *Ayliffe.*

APPEL'LATE, *a.* Pertaining to appeals; having cognizance of appeals; as "*appellate* jurisdiction." *Const. of the U. States.*

Appellate judges. *Burke, Rev. in France.*

APPELLA'TION, *n.* [L. *appellatio*. See *Appeal*.]

Name; the word by which a thing is called and known. Spenser uses it for *appeal*.

APPEL'LATIVE, *a.* Pertaining to a common name; noting the common name of a species.

APPEL'LATIVE, *n.* A *common* name in distinction from a *proper* name. A *common* name or *appellative* stands for a whole class, genus or species of beings, or for universal ideas. Thus *man* is the name of the whole human race, and *fowl* of all winged animals. *Tree* is the name of all plants of a particular class; *plant* and *vegetable* are names of things that grow out of the earth. A *proper* name, on the other hand, stands for a single thing, as, *London, Philadelphia, Washington, Boston.*

APPEL'LATIVELY, *adv.* According to the manner of nouns appellative; in a manner to express whole classes or species; as, Hercules is sometimes used *appellatively*, that is, as a common name to signify a strong man. *Johnson.*

APPEL'LATORY, *a.* Containing an appeal.

APPELLEE', *n.* The defendant in an appeal.

2. The person who is appealed, or prosecuted by a private man for a crime. *Blackstone.*

APPELLOR', *n.* The person who institutes an appeal, or prosecutes another for a crime. *Blackstone.*

This word is rarely or never used for the plaintiff in appeal from a lower court, who is called the *appellant*. *Appellee* is opposed both to *appellant* and *appellor*.

APPEND', *v. t.* [L. *appendo*, of *ad* and *pendeo*, to hang.]

1. To hang or attach to, as by a string, so that the thing is suspended; as, a seal *appended* to a record.
2. To add, as an accessory to the principal thing. *Johnson.*

APPEND'AGE, *n.* Something added to a principal or greater thing, though not necessary to it, as a portico to a house.

Modesty is the *appendage* of sobriety. *Taylor.*

APPEND'ANCE, } *n.* Something annexed.
APPEND'ENCE, } [*Not used.*] *Bp. Hall.*

APPEND'ANT, *a.* Hanging to; annexed; belonging to something; attached; as, a seal *appendant* to a paper.

2. In *law*, common *appendant*, is a right, belonging to the owners or occupiers of land, to put commonable beasts upon the lord's waste, and upon the lands of other persons within the same manor. An advowson *appendant*, is the right of patronage or presentation, annexed to the possession of a manor. So also a common of fishing may be *appendant* to a freehold. *Blackstone. Cowel.*

APPEND'ANT, *n.* That which belongs to another thing, as incidental or subordinate to it.

APPEND'ED, *pp.* Annexed; attached.

APPEND'ICATE, *v. t.* To append; to add to. *Obs.* *Hale.*

APPENDICA'TION, *n.* An appendage or adjunct. *Obs.* *Hale.*

APPEND'ICLE, *n.* A small appendage.

APPEND'ING, *n.* That which is by right annexed. *Spelman.*

APPEND'IX, *n.* plu. *appendixes*, [L. The Latin plural is *appendices*. See *Append*.]

1. Something appended or added.

Normandy became an *appendix* to England. *Hale.*

2. An adjunct, concomitant, or appendage. *Watts.*
3. More generally, a supplement or short treatise added to a book.

APPERCE'IVE, *v. t.* [Fr. *apercevoir*.] To comprehend. *Obs.* *Chaucer.*

APPERCEP'TION, *n.* [*ad* and *perception*.]

Perception that reflects upon itself; consciousness. *Leibnitz. Reid.*

APPER'IL, *n.* Peril; danger. [*Not in use.*] *Shak.*

APPERTA'IN, *v. i.* [Fr. *appartenir*; It. *appartenere*; L. *ad* and *pertineo*, to pertain, of *per* and *teneo*, to hold. *Pertineo* is *to reach to, to extend to*, hence to belong. See *Tenant*.]

To belong, whether by right, nature or appointment.

Give it to him to whom it *appertaineth*. Lev. vi.

[See *Pertain*.]

APPERTA'INING, *pp.* Belonging.

APPERTA'INMENT, *n.* That which belongs. *Shak.*

APPER'TENENCE, *n.* [See *Appurtenance*.]

APPER'TINENT, *a.* Belonging; now written *appurtenant*. *Shak.*

APPER'TINENT, *n.* That which belongs to something else. *Obs.* *Shak.*

[See *Appurtenance*.]

AP'PETENCE, } *n.* [L. *appetentia*, *appetens*,
AP'PETENCY, } from *appeto*, to desire; of *ad* and *peto*, to ask, supplicate or seek; Ch. פיט; Eth. ፈተወ to desire, to intreat; Dan. *beder*; D. *bidden*; Ger. *bitten*; Arm. *pidi*; Eng. *bid*; Sax. *bidan*; Sw. *bedja*; L. *invito*, compound. The primary sense is to strain, to urge or press, or to advance. See *Bid*. Class Bd.]

1. In *a general sense*, desire; but especially, carnal desire; sensual appetite.
2. The disposition of organized bodies to select and imbibe such portions of matter as serve to support and nourish them, or such particles as are designed, through their agency, to carry on the animal or vegetable economy.

These lacteals have mouths, and by animal selection or *appetency*, they absorb such part of the fluid as is agreeable to their palate. *Darwin.*

3. An inclination or propensity in animals to perform certain actions, as in the young to suck, in aquatic fowls to enter into water and to swim.
4. According to Darwin, animal appetency is synonymous with irritability or sensibility; as the *appetency* of the eye for light, of the paps to secrete milk, &c.
5. Attraction, or the tendency in bodies to move toward each other and unite. *Copernicus.*

AP'PETENT, *a.* Desiring; very desirous. *Buck.*

APPETIBIL'ITY, *n.* The quality of being desirable for gratification.

AP'PETIBLE, *a.* [Low L. *appetibilis*, from *appeto*.] Desirable; that may be the object of sensual desire.

AP'PETITE, *n.* [L. *appetitus*, from *appeto*. See *Appetence*.]

1. The natural desire of pleasure or good; the desire of gratification, either of the body or of the mind. *Appetites* are passions directed to general objects, as the *appetite* for fame, glory or riches; in distinction from passions directed to some particular objects, which retain their proper name, as the *passion* of love, envy or gratitude. *Passion* does not exist without an object; natural *appetites* exist first, and are then directed to objects. *Encyc.*
2. A desire of food or drink; a painful sensation occasioned by hunger or thirst.
3. Strong desire; eagerness or longing. *Clarendon.*
4. The thing desired.

Power being the natural *appetite* of princes. *Swift.*

Appetites are *natural* or *artificial*. Hunger and thirst are *natural* appetites; the appetites for olives, tobacco, snuff, &c. are *artificial*.

In old authors, appetite is followed by *to*, but regularly it should be followed by *for* before the object, as an appetite *for* pleasure.

To be given to appetite, is to be voracious or gluttonous. Prov. xxiii. 2.

APPETI''TION, *n.* [L. *appetitio*.] Desire. [*Rarely used.*]

AP'PETITIVE, *a.* That desires; that has the quality of desiring gratification; as *appetitive* power or faculty. *Hale.*

AP'PIAN, *a.* Designating something that belongs to Appius, particularly a way from Rome through Capua to Brundusium, now Brindisi, constructed by Appius Claudius, A. R. 441. It is more than 330 miles in length, formed of hard stone squared, and so wide as to admit two carriages abreast. *Livy. Lempriere.*

APPLAUD′, *v. t.* [L. *applaudo; ad* and *plaudo*, to make a noise by clapping the hands; Sp. *aplaudir;* It. *applaudire;* Fr. *applaudir.* This word is formed on the root of *laus, laudo;* Eng. *loud;* W. *clod*, praise, from *llod*, what is forcibly uttered; *llodi*, to reach out; from *llawd*, that shoots out. It coincides also with W. *bloez*, a shout, or outcry; *bloeziaw*, to shout; *blozest*, applause, acclamation. Ir. *blaodh*, a shout; *blath*, praise. These may all be of one family. Class L d. See *Loud.*]

1. To praise by clapping the hands, acclamation, or other significant sign.
2. To praise by words, actions or other means; to express approbation of; to commend; *used in a general sense.* *Pope.*

APPLAUD′ED, *pp.* Praised by acclamation, or other means; commended.

APPLAUD′ER, *n.* One who praises or commends.

APPLAUD′ING, *ppr.* Praising by acclamation; commending.

APPLAUSE′, *n.* *s* as *z.* [L. *applausus.*]

A shout of approbation; approbation and praise, expressed by clapping the hands, acclamation or huzzas; approbation expressed. In antiquity, *applause* differed from *acclamation; applause* was expressed by the hands, and *acclamation* by the voice. There were three species of applause, the *bombus*, a confused din made by the hands or mouth; the *imbrices* and *testæ*, made by beating a sort of sounding vessels in the theaters. Persons were appointed for the purpose of applauding, and masters were employed to teach the art. The applauders were divided into choruses, and placed opposite to each other, like the choristers in a cathedral. *Encyc.*

APPLAU′SIVE, *a.* Applauding; containing applause. *Jonson.*

AP′PLE, *n.* [Sax. *appl, appil;* D. *appel;* Ger. *apfel;* Dan. *æble;* Sw. *aple;* W. *aval;* Ir. *abhal* or *ubhal;* Arm. *aval;* Russ. *iabloko*, or *yabloko.* This word primarily signifies fruit in general, especially of a round form. In Pers. the same word ابهل, pronounced *ubhul*, signifies the fruit or berries of the savin or juniper. *Castle.* In Welsh, it signifies not only the *apple*, but the plum and other fruits. *Lhuyd.* *Aval melynhir*, a lemon; *aval euraid*, an orange. *Owen.*]

1. The fruit of the apple tree, [pyrus malus,] from which cider is made.
2. The *apple of the eye* is the pupil.

Apple of love, or love apple, the tomato, or lycopersicum, a species of *Solanum.* The stalk is herbaceous, with oval, pinnated leaves, and small yellow flowers. The berry is smooth, soft, of a yellow or reddish color, of the size of a plum. It is used in soups and broths. *Encyc.*

AP′PLE, *v. t.* To form like an apple. *Marshal.*

AP′PLE-GRAFT, *n.* A scion of the apple-tree engrafted.

AP′PLE-HARVEST, *n.* The gathering of apples, or the time of gathering.

AP′PLE-PIE, *n.* A pie made of apples stewed or baked, inclosed in paste, or covered with paste, as in England.

AP′PLE-SAUCE, *n.* A sauce made of stewed apples.

AP′PLE-TART, *n.* A tart made of apples baked on paste.

AP′PLE-TREE, *n.* A tree arranged by Linne under the genus *pyrus.* The fruit of this tree is indefinitely various. The crab apple is supposed to be the original kind, from which all others have sprung. New varieties are springing annually from the seeds.

AP′PLE-WOMAN, *n.* A woman who sells apples and other fruit.

AP′PLE-YARD, *n.* An orchard; an inclosure for apples.

APPLI′ABLE, *a.* [See *Apply.*] That may be applied. This word is superseded by *applicable.*

APPLI′ANCE, *n.* The act of applying, or thing applied. *Obs.* *Shak.*

APPLICABIL′ITY, *n.* [See *Apply.*] The quality of being applicable, or fit to be applied.

AP′PLICABLE, *a.* That may be applied; fit to be applied, as related to a thing; that may have relation to something else; as, this observation is *applicable* to the case under consideration.

AP′PLICABLENESS, *n.* Fitness to be applied; the quality of being applicable.

AP′PLICABLY, *adv.* In such a manner that it may be applied.

AP′PLICANT, *n.* One who applies; one who makes request; a petitioner.

The *applicant* for a cup of water declares himself to be the Messias. *Plumtree.*

The court require the *applicant* to appear in person. *Z. Swift.*

AP′PLICATE, *n.* A right line drawn across a curve, so as to be bisected by the diameter; an ordinate. *Cyc.*

AP′PLICATE-ORDINATE. A right line at right angles applied to the axis of any conic section, and bounded by the curve. *Bailey.*

APPLICA′TION, *n.* [L. *applicatio.* See *Apply.*]

1. The act of laying on; as the *application* of emollients to a diseased limb.
2. The thing applied; as, the pain was abated by the *application.*
3. The act of making request or soliciting; as, he made *application* to a court of chancery.
4. The act of applying as means; the employment of means; as, children may be governed by a suitable *application* of rewards and punishments. This is the first signification directed to moral objects.
5. The act of fixing the mind; intenseness of thought; close study; attention; as, to injure the health by *application* to study.

   Had his *application* been equal to his talents, his progress might have been greater. *J. Jay.*

6. The act of directing or referring something to a particular case, to discover or illustrate the agreement or disagreement; as, I make the remark and leave you to make the *application.*
7. In *theology*, the act by which the merits of Christ are transferred to man, for his justification.
8. In *geometry*, a division for applying one quantity to another, whose areas, but not figures, shall be the same; or the transferring a given line into a circle or other figure, so that its ends shall be in the perimeter of the figure. *Encyc.*
9. In *sermons*, that part of the discourse, in which the principles before laid down and illustrated, are applied to practical uses.

AP′PLICATIVE, *a.* That applies. *Bramhall.*

AP′PLICATORY, *a.* That includes the act of applying. *Edwards' Hist. of Redemption.*

AP′PLICATORY, *n.* That which applies. *Taylor.*

APPLI′ED, *pp.* Put on; put to: directed; employed.

APPLI′EDLY, *adv.* In a manner which may be applied. [*Not in use.*] *Montagu.*

APPLI′ER, *n.* One that applies.

APPLI′MENT, *n.* Application. [*Not in use.*] *Marston.*

APPLY′, *v. t.* [L. *applico*, of *ad* and *plico*, to fold or knit together; Fr. *appliquer;* Sp. *aplicar;* It. *applicare;* W. *plegy*, to bend or fold; Arm. *plega*, to fold or plait; *pleca*, a fold; Gr. πλεκω, to knit, or twist; Sax. *plegan, plegian, pleggan*, to *play*, to bend to or *apply*, incumbere; Dan. *fiüg*, a fold; D. *plooi*, a fold; *ploojen*, to plait; Eng. *ply, display*, and *employ.* The word *plegy, plico*, is formed from the root of *lay*, Sax. *lecgan.* The sense then is to *lay to;* and it is worthy of remark, that we use *lay to* in the precise sense of *ply* and *apply.* It is certain from the Welsh that the first consonant is a prefix.]

1. To lay on; to put one thing to another; as, to *apply* the hand to the breast; to *apply* medicaments to a diseased part of the body.
2. To use or employ for a particular purpose, or in a particular case; as, to *apply* a sum of money to the payment of a debt.
3. To put, refer or use, as suitable or relative to something; as, to *apply* the testimony to the case.
4. To fix the mind; to engage and employ with attention; as, *apply* thy heart to instruction. *Proverbs.*
5. To address or direct; as, "Sacred vows *applied* to Pluto." *Pope.*
6. To betake; to give the chief part of time and attention; as, to *apply* one's self to the study of botany. This is essentially the fourth sense.
7. To make application; to have recourse by request; as, to *apply* one's self to a counsellor for advice. This is generally used intransitively; as, to *apply* to a counsellor.
8. To busy; to keep at work; to ply. *Obs.* *Sidney. Spenser.*

[Superseded by *ply*, which see.]

APPLY′, *v. i.* To suit; to agree; to have some connection, agreement or analogy; as, this argument *applies* well to the case.

2. To make request; to solicit; to have recourse, with a view to gain something; as, to *apply* to the president for an office; I *applied* to a friend for information.

APPLY′ING, *ppr.* Laying on; making application.

APPOINT′, *v. t.* [Fr. *appointer*, to refer, to give an allowance; Sp. *apuntar*, to point or aim, to sharpen, to fasten as with points or nails; It. *appuntare*, to fix, appoint or sharpen. See *Point.*]

1. To fix; to settle; to establish; to make fast.

When he *appointed* the foundations of the earth. Prov. viii.

2. To constitute, ordain, or fix by decree, order or decision.

Let Pharaoh *appoint* officers over the land. Gen. xli.

He hath *appointed* a day in which he will judge the world. Acts xvii.

3. To allot, assign or designate.

Aaron and his sons shall *appoint* every one to his service. Num. iv.

These cities were *appointed* for all the children of Israel. Josh. xx.

4. To purpose or resolve; to fix the intention.

For so he had *appointed*. Acts xx.

5. To ordain, command or order.

Thy servants are ready to do whatever my Lord the King shall *appoint*. 2 Sam. xv.

6. To settle; to fix, name or determine by agreement; as, they *appointed* a time and place for the meeting.

APPOINT'ABLE, *a.* That may be appointed or constituted; as, officers are *appointable* by the Executive. *Federalist, Madison.*

APPOINT'ED, *pp.* Fixed; set; established; decreed; ordained; constituted; allotted.

2. Furnished; equipped with things necessary; as, a ship or an army is well *appointed.*

APPOINTEE', *n.* A person appointed. "The commission authorizes them to make appointments, and pay the *appointees.*" *Circular of Mass. Representatives*, 1768; also, *Wheaton's Reports.*

2. A foot soldier in the French army, who, for long service and bravery, receives more pay than other privates. *Encyc. Bailey.*

APPOINT'ER, *n.* Ono who appoints.

APPOINT'ING, *ppr.* Setting; fixing; ordaining; constituting; assigning.

APPOINT'MENT, *n.* The act of appointing; designation to office; as, he erred by the *appointment* of unsuitable men.

2. Stipulation; assignation; the act of fixing by mutual agreement; as, they made an *appointment* to meet at six o'clock.

3. Decree; established order or constitution; as, it is our duty to submit to the divine *appointments.*

4. Direction; order; command.

Wheat, salt, wine and oil, let it be given according to the *appointment* of the priests. Ez. vi.

5. Equipment, furniture, as for a ship, or an army; whatever is appointed for use and management.

6. An allowance to a person; a salary or pension, as to a public officer.

An *appointment* differs from wages, in being a special grant, or gratification, not fixed, whereas wages are fixed and ordinary. *Encyc.*

7. A devise or grant to a charitable use. *Blackstone.*

APPO'RTER, *n.* [Fr. *apporter*; L. *porto.*] A bringer in; one that brings into the country. [*Not in use.*] *Hale.*

APPO'RTION, *v. t.* [L. *ad* and *portio*, portion. See *Portion* and *Part.*]

To divide and assign in just proportion; to distribute among two or more, a just part or share to each; as, to *apportion* undivided rights; to *apportion* time among various employments.

APPO'RTIONED, *pp.* Divided; set out or assigned in suitable parts or shares.

APPO'RTIONER, *n.* One that apportions.

APPO'RTIONING, *ppr.* Setting out in just proportions or shares.

APPO'RTIONMENT, *n.* The act of apportioning; a dividing into just proportions or shares; a dividing and assigning to each proprietor his just portion of an undivided right or property. *Hamilton, Rep.* Feb. 13, 1793.

APPO'SE, *v. t.* *s* as *z.* [Fr. *apposer*, to set to; L. *appono.* See *Apposite.*]

1. To put questions; to examine. [See *Pose.*] *Bacon.*

2. To apply. *Harvey.*

APPO'SER, *n.* An examiner; one whose business is to put questions. In the English Court of Exchequer there is an officer called the foreign *apposer.* This is ordinarily pronounced *poser.* *Encyc.*

AP'POSITE, *a.* *s* as *z.* [L. *appositus*, set or put to, from *appono*, of *ad* and *pono*, to put or place.]

Suitable; fit; very applicable; well adapted; followed by *to*; as, this argument is very *apposite to* the case.

AP'POSITELY, *adv.* Suitably; fitly; properly. *Harvey.*

AP'POSITENESS, *n.* Fitness; propriety; suitableness. *Hale.*

APPOSI''TION, *n.* The act of adding to; addition; a setting to.

By the *apposition* of new matter. *Arbuthnot.*

2. In *Grammar*, the placing of two nouns, in the same case, without a connecting word between them; as, I admire Cicero, the orator. In this case, the second noun explains or characterizes the first.

APPRA'ISE, *v. t.* [Fr. *apprecier*; Sp. *apreciar*; It. *apprezzare*, to set a value; from L. *ad* and *pretium*, price. See *Price* and *Appreciate.*]

This word is written and often pronounced after the French and Italian manner. But generally it is pronounced more correctly *apprize*, directly from the D. *prys*; W. *pris*; Eng. *price* or *prize.* [See *Apprize.*]

To set a value; to estimate the worth, particularly by persons appointed for the purpose.

APPRA'ISEMENT, *n.* The act of setting the value; a valuation. [See *Apprizement.*]

APPRA'ISER, *n.* One who values; appropriately a person appointed and sworn to estimate and fix the value of goods and estate. [See *Apprizer.*]

APPRE'CIABLE, *a.* *appréshable.* [See *Appreciate.*]

1. That may be appreciated; valuable. *Encyc.*

2. That may be estimated; capable of being duly estimated.

APPRE'CIATE, *v. t.* *appréshate.* [Fr. *apprecier*, to set a value; L. *ad* and *pretium*, value, *price*; D. *prys*; W. *pris*; Ger. *preis.* See *Price.*]

1. To value; to set a price or value on; to estimate; as, we seldom sufficiently *appreciate* the advantages we enjoy.

2. To raise the value of.

Lest a sudden peace should *appreciate* the money. *Ramsay.*

APPRE'CIATE, *v. i.* To rise in value; to become of more value; as, the coin of the country *appreciates*; public securities *appreciated*, when the debt was funded.

APPRE'CIATED, *pp.* Valued; prized; estimated; advanced in value.

APPRE'CIATING, *ppr.* Setting a value on; estimating; rising in value.

APPRECIA'TION, *n.* A setting a value on; a just valuation or estimate of merit, weight, or any moral consideration. *Washington's Inaug. Speech*, Apr. 30, 1789.

2. A rising in value; increase of worth or value. *Marshal, L. of Washington.* *Hamilton's Report.* Feb. 13, 1793.

APPREHEND', *v. t.* [L. *apprehendo*, of *ad* and *prehendo*, to take or seize; Sax. *hendan* or *hentan.*]

1. To take or seize; to take hold of. In this literal sense, it is applied chiefly to taking or arresting persons by legal process, or with a view to trial; as to *apprehend* a thief.

2. To take with the understanding, that is, to conceive in the mind; to understand, without passing a judgment, or making an inference.

I *apprehend* not why so many and various laws are given. *Milton.*

3. To think; to believe or be of opinion, but without positive certainty; as, all this is true, but we *apprehend* it is not to the purpose.

Notwithstanding this declaration, we do not *apprehend* that we are guilty of presumption. *Encyc. Art. Metaphysics.*

4. To fear; to entertain suspicion or fear of future evil; as, we *apprehend* calamities from a feeble or wicked administration.

APPREHEND'ED, *pp.* Taken; seized; arrested; conceived; understood; feared.

APPREHEND'ER, *n.* One who takes; one who conceives in his mind; one who fears.

APPREHEND'ING, *ppr.* Seizing; taking; conceiving; understanding; fearing.

APPREHEN'SIBLE, *a.* That may be apprehended or conceived.

APPREHEN'SION, *n.* The act of taking or arresting; as, the felon, after his *apprehension*, escaped.

2. The mere contemplation of things without affirming, denying, or passing any judgment; the operation of the mind in contemplating ideas, without comparing them with others, or referring them to external objects; simple intellection. *Watts. Glanville. Encyc.*

3. An inadequate or imperfect idea, as when the word is applied to our knowledge of God. *Encyc.*

4. Opinion; conception; sentiments. In this sense, the word often denotes a belief, founded on sufficient evidence to give preponderation to the mind, but insufficient to induce certainty.

To be false, and to be thought false, is all one, in respect of men, who act not according to truth, but *apprehension.* *South.*

In our *apprehension*, the facts prove the issue.

5. The faculty by which new ideas are conceived; as, a man of dull *apprehension.*

6. Fear; suspicion; the prospect of future evil, accompanied with uneasiness of mind.

Claudius was in no small *apprehension* for his own life. *Addison*

APPREHEN'SIVE, *a.* Quick to understand; as, an *apprehensive* scholar. *Holder. South.*

2. Fearful; in expectation of evil; as, we were *apprehensive* of fatal consequences. [*This is the usual sense of the word.*]

3. Suspicious; inclined to believe; as, I am *apprehensive* he does not understand me.

4. Sensible; feeling; perceptive. [*Rarely used.*] *Milton.*

APPREHEN'SIVELY, *adv.* In an apprehensive manner.

APPREHEN'SIVENESS, *n.* The quality of being apprehensive; readiness to understand; fearfulness.

APPREN'TICE, *n.* [Fr. *apprenti*, an apprentice, from *apprendre*, to learn; L. *apprehendo.* See *Apprehend.*]

1. One who is bound by covenant to serve a mechanic, or other person, for a certain time, with a view to learn his art, mystery, or occupation, in which his master is bound to instruct him. Apprentices are regularly bound by indentures. *Blackstone.*

2. In *old law books*, a barrister; a learner of law. *Blackstone.*

APPREN'TICE, *v. t.* To bind to, or put under the care of a master, for the purpose of instruction in the knowledge of a trade or business.

APPREN'TICEHOOD, *n.* Apprenticeship. [*Not used.*] *Shak.*

APPREN'TICESHIP, *n.* The term for which an apprentice is bound to serve his master. This term in England is by statute seven years. In Paris, the term is five years; after which, the person, before he is qualified to exercise the trade as a master, must serve five years as a journeyman; during which term, he is called the *companion* of his master, and the term is called his *companionship.* *Encyc.*

2. The service, state or condition of an apprentice; a state in which a person is gaining instruction under a master.

APPREN'TISAGE, *n.* Apprenticeship. [*Not in use.*] *Bacon.*

APPREST', *a.* [*ad* and *pressed.*] In *botany*, pressed close; lying near the stem; or applying its upper surface to the stem. *Martyn. Ed. Encyc.*

APPRI'SE, *v. t.* *s* as *z.* [Fr. *appris*, participle of *apprendre*, to learn, or inform. See *Apprehend.*]

To inform; to give notice, verbal or written; followed by *of;* as, we will *apprise* the general *of* an intended attack; he *apprised* the commander *of* what he had done.

APPRI'SED, *pp.* Informed; having notice or knowledge communicated.

APPRI'SING, *ppr.* Informing; communicating notice to.

APPRI'ZE, *v. t.* [This word is usually written *appraise*, as if deduced from the Italian *apprezzare.* There is no other word, from which it can regularly be formed; the French *apprecier*, being recognized in *appreciate.* But *apprize*, the word generally used, is regularly formed, with *ad*, from *price, prize;* D. *prys;* Ger. *preis;* W. *pris;* or from the Fr. *priser*, to prize, and this is the more correct orthography.]

To value; to set a value, in pursuance of authority. It is generally used for the act of *valuing* by men appointed for the purpose, under direction of law, or by agreement of parties; as, to *apprize* the goods and estate of a deceased person. The private act of valuing is ordinarily expressed by *prize.*

APPRI'ZED, *pp.* Valued; having the worth fixed by authorized persons.

APPRI'ZEMENT, *n.* The act of setting a value under some authority or appointment; a valuation. *Statutes of Conn. Blackstone.*

2. The rate at which a thing is valued; the value fixed, or valuation; as, he purchased the article at the *apprizement.*

APPRI'ZER, *n.* A person appointed to rate, or set a value on articles. When *apprizers* act under the authority of law, they must be sworn.

APPRI'ZING, *ppr.* Rating; setting a value under authority.

APPRI'ZING, *n.* The act of valuing under authority.

APPRŌACH, *v. i.* [Fr. *approcher*, from *proche*, near. The Latin *proximus* contains the root, but the word, in the positive degree, is not found in the Latin. It is from a root in class *Brg*, signifying to drive, move, or press toward.]

1. To come or go near, in place; to draw near; to advance nearer.

> Wherefore *approached* ye so nigh the city? 2 Sam. xi.

2. To draw near in time.

> And so much the more as ye see the day *approach.* Heb. x.

3. To draw near, in a figurative sense; to advance near to a point aimed at, in science, literature, government, morals, &c.; to approximate; as, he *approaches* to the character of the ablest statesman.

4. To draw near in duty, as in prayer or worship.

> They take delight in *approaching* to God. Isaiah. li.

APPRŌACH, *v. t.* To come near to; as, Pope *approaches* Virgil in smoothness of versification. This use of the word is elliptical, *to* being omitted, so that the verb can hardly be said to be transitive. The old use of the word, as "*approach* the hand to the handle," is not legitimate.

2. To have access carnally. Lev. xviii.

3. In *gardening*, to ingraft a sprig or shoot of one tree into another, without cutting it from the parent stock. *Encyc.*

APPRŌACH, *n.* The act of drawing near; a coming or advancing near; as, he was apprised of the enemy's *approach.*

2. Access; as, the *approach* to kings. *Bacon.*

3. In *fortification*, not only the advances of an army are called *approaches*, but the works thrown up by the besiegers, to protect them in their advances towards a fortress.

APPRŌACHABLE, *a.* That may be approached; accessible.

APPRŌACHER, *n.* One who approaches or draws near.

APPRŌACHMENT, *n.* The act of coming near. [*Little used.*] *Brown.*

AP'PROBATE, *a.* [L. *approbatus.*] Approved. *Elyot.*

AP'PROBATE, *v. t.* [L. *approbo*, to approve, of *ad* and *probo*, to prove or approve. *Approbate* is a modern word, but in common use in America. It differs from *approve*, denoting not only the act of the mind, but an *expression* of the act. See *Proof, Approve* and *Prove.*]

To express approbation of; to manifest a liking, or degree of satisfaction; to express approbation officially, as of one's fitness for a public trust.

> Mr. Hutchinson *approbated* the choice. *J. Eliot.*

AP'PROBATED, *pp.* Approved; commended.

AP'PROBATING, *ppr.* Expressing approbation of.

APPROBA'TION, *n.* [L. *approbatio.* See *Proof* and *Prove.*]

1. The act of approving; a liking; that state or disposition of the mind, in which we assent to the propriety of a thing, with some degree of pleasure or satisfaction; as, the laws of God require our *approbation.*

2. Attestation; support; that is, active approbation, or action, in favor of what is approved. *Shak.*

3. The commendation of a book licensed or permitted to be published by authority, as was formerly the case in England.

AP'PROBATIVE, *a.* Approving; implying approbation. *Milner.*

AP'PROBATORY, *a.* Containing approbation; expressing approbation. *Ash. Scott.*

APPROMPT', for *Prompt.* [*Not used.*] *Bacon.*

APPROOF', *n.* Approval. [*Not used.*] *Shak.*

APPRO'PERATE, *v. t.* [L. *appropero.*] To hasten. [*Not used.*]

APPROPIN'QUATE, *v. i.* [L. *appropinquo.*] To draw near. [*Not used.*]

APPROPINQUA'TION, *n.* A drawing nigh. [*Not used.*[*Hall.*

APPROPINQUE, *v. i.* To approach. [*Not used.*] *Hudibras.*

APPRO'PRIABLE, *a.* [From *appropriate.*] That may be appropriated; that may be set apart, sequestered, or assigned exclusively to a particular use. *Brown.*

APPRO'PRIATE, *v. t.* [Fr. *approprier*, of L. *ad* and *proprius*, private, peculiar. See *Proper.*]

1. To set apart for, or assign to a particular use, in exclusion of all other uses; as, a spot of ground is *appropriated* for a garden.

2. To take to one's self in exclusion of others; to claim or use as by an exclusive right.

> Let no man *appropriate* the use of a common benefit.

3. To make peculiar; as, to *appropriate* names to ideas. *Locke.*

4. To sever an ecclesiastical benefice, and annex it to a spiritual corporation, sole or aggregate, being the patron of the living. *Blackstone.*

APPRO'PRIATE, *a.* Belonging peculiarly; peculiar; set apart for a particular use or person; as, religious worship is an *appropriate* duty to the Creator.

2. Most suitable, fit or proper; as, to use *appropriate* words in pleading.

APPRO'PRIATED, *pp.* Assigned to a particular use; claimed or used exclusively; annexed to an ecclesiastical corporation.

APPRO'PRIATENESS, *n.* Peculiar fitness; the quality of being appropriate, or peculiarly suitable. *Med. Rep.*

APPRO'PRIATING, *ppr.* Assigning to a particular person or use; claiming or using exclusively; severing to the perpetual use of an ecclesiastical corporation.

APPROPRIA'TION, *n.* The act of sequestering, or assigning to a particular use or person, in exclusion of all others; application to a special use or purpose; as, of a piece of ground for a park; of a right, to one's self; or of words, to ideas.

2. In *law*, the severing or sequestering of a benefice to the perpetual use of a spiritual corporation, sole or aggregate, being the patron of the living. For this purpose must be obtained the king's license, the consent of the bishop and of the patron. When the appropriation is thus made, the appropriator and his successors become perpetual *parsons* of the church, and must sue and be sued in that name. *Eng. Law. Blackstone.*

APPRO'PRIATOR, *n.* One who appropriates.

2. One who is possessed of an appropriated benefice. *Blackstone.*

APPRO'PRIETARY, *n.* A lay possessor of the profits of a benefice. *Spelman.*

APPRÖV'ABLE, *a.* [See *Approve.*] That may be approved; that merits approbation. *Temple.*

APPRÖV'AL, *n.* Approbation. [See *Approve.*]

APPRÖV'ANCE, *n.* Approbation. [See *Approve.*] *Thomson.*

APPRÖVE', *v. t.* [Fr. *approuver*; L. *approbo*; of *ad* and *probo*, to prove or approve. See *Approbate*, *Prove* and *Proof.*]

1. To like; to be pleased with; to admit the propriety of; as, we *approve* the measures of administration. This word may include, with the assent of the mind to the propriety, a commendation to others.

2. To prove; to show to be true; to justify.

> Would'st thou *approve* thy constancy? *Approve* first thy wisdom. *Milton.*

[*This sense, though common a century or two ago, is now rare.*]

3. To experience; to prove by trial. [*Not used.* See *Prove.*] *Shak.*

4. To make or show to be worthy of approbation; to commend.

> Jesus, a man *approved* of God. Acts ii.

This word seems to include the idea of Christ's real office, as the Messiah, and of God's love and approbation of him in that character. *Brown's Dict.*

5. To like and sustain as right; to commend.

> Yet their posterity *approve* their sayings. Ps. xlix.

This word, when it signifies *to be pleased*, is often followed by *of*, in which use, it is intransitive; as, I *approve of* the measure. But the tendency of modern usage is to omit *of*. "I approve the measure."

6. To improve. *Blackstone.*

APPRÖV'ED, *pp.* Liked; commended; shown or proved to be worthy of approbation; having the approbation and support of.

> Study to show thyself *approved* to God. 2 Tim. ii.

> Not he that commendeth himself is *approved.* 2 Cor. x.

APPRÖVE'MENT, *n.* Approbation; liking. *Hayward.*

2. In *law*, when a person indicted for felony or treason, and arraigned, confesses the fact before plea pleaded, and appeals or accuses his accomplices of the same crime, to obtain his pardon, this confession and accusation are called *approvement*, and the person an *approver*. *Blackstone.*

3. Improvement of common lands, by inclosing and converting them to the uses of husbandry. *Blackstone.*

APPRÖV'ER, *n.* One who approves. Formerly one who proves or makes trial.

2. In *law*, one who confesses a crime and accuses another. [See *Approvement.*] Also, formerly, one who had the letting of the king's demains, in small manors. In Stat. 1. Edw. 3. C. 8, sheriffs are called *approvers*. A bailiff or steward of a manor. *Encyc.*

APPRÖV'ING, *ppr.* Liking; commending; giving or expressing approbation.

APPRÖV'ING, *a.* Yielding approbation; as an *approving* conscience.

APPROX'IMANT, *a.* Approaching. [*Not used.*] *Dering.*

APPROX'IMATE, *a.* [L. *ad* and *proximus*, next. See *Approach.*] Nearest to; next; near to. [*This word is superseded by* proximate.]

APPROX'IMATE, *v. t.* To carry or advance near; to cause to approach.

> To *approximate* the inequality of riches to the level of nature. *Burke. Aikin. Shenstone.*

APPROX'IMATE, *v. i.* To come near; to approach. *Burke.*

APPROXIMA'TION, *n.* Approach; a drawing, moving or advancing near. *Hale.*

2. In *arithmetic* and *algebra*, a continual approach or coming nearer and nearer to a root or other quantity, without being able perhaps ever to arrive at it. *Encyc. Johnson.*

3. In *medicine*, communication of disease by contact. *Coxe.*

4. A mode of cure by transplanting a disease into an animal or vegetable by immediate contact. *Coxe.*

APPROX'IMATIVE, *a.* Approaching; that approaches. *Ed. Encyc.*

APPULSE, *n. appuls'.* [L. *appulsus*, of *ad* and *pello*, to drive.]

1. The act of striking against; as, in all consonants there is an *appulse* of the organs. *Holder.*

2. In *astronomy*, the approach of any planet to a conjunction with the sun, or a star.

3. Arrival; landing. *Bryant.*

APPUL'SION, *n.* The act of striking against by a moving body.

APPUL'SIVE, *a.* Striking against; driving towards; as, the *appulsive* influence of the planets. *Med. Rep.*

APPUR'TENANCE, *n.* So written for *appertenence.* [Fr. *appartenance.* See *Appertain.*] That which belongs to something else; an adjunct; an appendage. Appropriately, such buildings, rights and improvements, as belong to land, are called the *appurtenances*; as small buildings are the *appurtenances* of a mansion.

APPUR'TENANT, *a.* Belonging to; pertaining to of right.

2. In *law*, common *appurtenant* is that which is annexed to land, and can be claimed only by prescription or immemorial usage, on a legal presumption of a special grant. *Blackstone.*

A'PRICATE, *v. i.* [L. *apricor.*] To bask in the sun. [*Little used.*] *Ray.*

APRIC'ITY, *n.* Sunshine. [*Little used.*]

A'PRICOT, *n.* Old orthography, *apricock.* [W. *bricyllen*; Arm. *brigesen*; Fr. *abricot*, whence the present orthography. Junius and Skinner alledge that the Italians formerly wrote the word *bericoco, berricoccoli.* At present they write it *albicocca*, and the Spaniards *albaricoque*, which indicate the word to be formed of *albus* and *coccus*, white berry; Sp. *albar*, white. But *apricot* seems to be formed from the old orthography.] A fruit belonging to the genus *Prunus*, of the plum kind, of an oval figure, and delicious taste.

A'PRIL, *n.* [L. *aprilis*; Fr. *avril*; Sp. *abril*; Ir. *abrail*; Corn. *ebril*; W. *ebrill.*] The fourth month of the year.

A'PRON, *n.* [Ir. *aprun*; *a* or *ag*, and Celtic *bron*, the breast.]

1. A cloth or piece of leather worn on the forepart of the body, to keep the clothes clean, or defend them from injury.

2. The fat skin covering the belly of a goose. *Johnson.*

3. In *gunnery*, a flat piece of lead that covers the vent of a cannon.

4. In *ships*, a piece of curved timber, just above the foremost end of the keel. *Mar. Dict.*

5. A platform, or flooring of plank, at the entrance of a dock, on which the dock gates are shut. *Encyc.*

A'PRONED, *a.* Wearing an apron. *Pope.*

A'PRON-MAN, *n.* A man who wears an apron; a laboring man; a mechanic.

AP'ROPOS, *adv. ap'ropo.* [Fr. *a* and *propos*, purpose.]

1. Opportunely; seasonably. *Warburton.*

2. By the way; to the purpose; a word used to introduce an incidental observation, suited to the occasion, though not strictly belonging to the narration.

AP'SIS, *n.* plu. *apsides.* [Gr. αψις, connection, fron απτω, to connect.]

1. In *astronomy*, the apsides are the two points of a planet's orbit, which are at the greatest and least distance from the sun or earth; the most distant point is the aphelion, or apogee; the least distant, the perihelion or perigee. The line connecting these is called the line of the apsides. *Encyc.*

2. Apsis or absis is the arched roof of a house, room or oven; also the ring or compass of a wheel.

3. In *ecclesiastical writers*, an inner part of a church, where the altar was placed, and where the clergy sat, answering to the choir and standing opposite to the nave. Also, the bishop's seat or throne in ancient churches; called also *exedra* and *tribune.* This same name was given to a reliquary or case in which the relics of saints were kept. *Encyc.*

APT, *a.* [L. *aptus*, from *apto*, to fit; Gr. απτω, to tie; Sax. *hæp.*]

1. Fit; suitable; as, he used very *apt* metaphors.

2. Having a tendency; liable; *used of things;* as, wheat on moist land is *apt* to blast or be winter-killed.
3. Inclined; disposed customarily; *used of persons;* as, men are too *apt* to slander others.
4. Ready; quick; *used of the mental powers;* as, a pupil *apt* to learn; an *apt* wit.
5. Qualified; fit.

All the men of might, strong and *apt* for war. 2 Kings xxiv.

APT, *v. t.* To fit; to suit or adapt. *Obs.*

APT'ABLE, *a.* That may be adapted. [*Not used.*] *Sherwood.*

AP'TATE, *v. t.* To make fit. [*Not used.*] *Bailey.*

AP'TER, AP'TERA, *n.* [Gr. α priv. and πτερον, a wing.]
An insect without wings. The aptera, constituting the seventh order of insects in Linne's system, comprehend many genera. But later zoologists have made a very different distribution of these animals.

AP'TERAL, *a.* [*Supra.*] Destitute of wings.

APT'ITUDE, *n.* [of *aptus*, apt.]
1. A natural or acquired disposition for a particular purpose, or tendency to a particular action or effect; as, oil has an *aptitude* to burn; men acquire an *aptitude* to particular vices.
2. Fitness; suitableness.
3. Aptness; readiness in learning; docility.

APT'LY, *adv.* In an apt or suitable manner; with just correspondence of parts; fitly; properly; justly; pertinently.

APT'NESS, *n.* Fitness; suitableness; as, the *aptness* of things to their end.
2. Disposition of the mind; propensity; as, the *aptness* of men to follow example.
3. Quickness of apprehension; readiness in learning; docility; as, an *aptness* to learn is more observable in some children than in others.
4. Tendency, in things; as, the *aptness* of iron to rust.

AP'TOTE, *n.* [Gr. α priv. and πτωσις, case.]
In *grammar*, a noun which has no variation of termination, or distinction of cases; an indeclinable noun.

AP'YREXY, *n.* [Gr. α priv. and πυρεσσω, to be feverish, from πυρ, fire.]
The absence or intermission of fever.

AP'YROUS, *a.* [Gr. απυρος, α priv. and πυρ, fire.]
Incombustible, or that sustains a strong heat without alteration of form or properties.
Apyrous bodies differ from those simply refractory. *Refractory* bodies cannot be fused by heat, but may be altered. *Encyc.*

A'QUA, *n.* [L. *aqua;* Sp. *agua;* Port. *agoa;* It. *acqua*, water; Arm. *eagui*, to water, or steep; Goth. *ahwa*, water, which in Saxon is reduced to *ea;* G. and D. *ei*, in *eiland;* Fr. *eau;* W. *gwy* or *aw;* Ir. *oig* or *oiche;* Amh. *oge.*]
Water; a word much used in pharmacy, and the old chimistry.
Aqua fortis, in the old chimistry, is now called *nitric acid.*
Aqua marina, a name which jewelers give to the *beryl*, on account of its color.
Aqua regia, in the old chimistry, is now called *nitro-muriatic acid.*
Aqua vitæ, brandy, or spirit of wine.

AQUA'RIAN, *n.* One of a sect of christians, in the primitive church, who consecrated water in the eucharist instead of wine; either under a pretense of abstinence, or because it was unlawful to drink wine. *Encyc.*

AQUA'RIUS, *n.* [L.] The water bearer; a sign in the zodiac which the sun enters about the 21st of January; so called from the rains which prevail at that season, in Italy and the East. The stars in this constellation, according to Ptolemy, are 45; according to Tycho Brahe, 41; according to Hevelius, 47; and according to Flamstead, 108.

AQUAT'IC, *a.* [L. *aquaticus.* See *Aqua.*]
Pertaining to water; applied to animals which live in water, as fishes; or to such as frequent it, as *aquatic* fowls; applied to plants, it denotes such as grow in water. *Aquatical* is rarely used.

AQUAT'IC, *n.* A plant which grows in water, as the flag.

AQ'UATILE, *a.* That inhabits the water. [*Rarely used.*] *Brown.*

AQUATINT'A, *n.* [*aqua*, water, and It. *tinta*, dye. See *Tincture.*]
A method of etching on copper, by which a beautiful effect is produced, resembling a fine drawing in water colors or Indian ink. This is performed with a powder of asphalt and fine transparent rosin sifted on the plate, which is a little greased; the loose powder being shaken off, the plate is heated over a chafing dish; and when cool, the light places on the plate are covered with a hair pencil, dipped in turpentine varnish mixed with ivory black. A rim is then raised with bees wax, and reduced nitrous acid is poured on, and suffered to stand five minutes; then poured off, and the plate dried. This process with the pencil and the aqua fortis is to be repeated till the darkest shades are produced. *Encyc.*

AQ'UEDUCT, *n.* [L. *aqua*, water, and *ductus*, a pipe or canal, from *duco*, to lead. See *Duke.*]
A structure made for conveying water from one place to another over uneven ground; either above or under the surface. It may be either a pipe or a channel. It may be constructed above ground of stone or wood; carried through hills by piercing them, and over valleys, by a structure supported by props or arches. Some have been formed with three conduits on the same line, elevated one above another. *Encyc.*

A'QUEOUS, *a.* Watery; partaking of the nature of water, or abounding with it.

A'QUEOUSNESS, *n.* The quality of being watery; waterishness; wateriness.

AQ'UILA, *n.* [L., whence *aquilinus;* from the Oriental עקל, to be crooked. This fowl is probably named from its curving beak.]
In *ornithology*, the eagle. Also, a northern constellation containing, according to the British catalogue, 71 stars. *Encyc.*

AQ'UILINE, *a.* [L. *aquilinus.* See *Aquila.*]
1. Belonging to the eagle.
2. Curving; hooked; prominent, like the beak of an eagle.

AQ'UILON, *n.* [L. *aquilo.*]
The north wind. *Shak.*

AQUITA'NIAN, *a.* Pertaining to Aquitania, one of the great divisions of Gaul, which, according to Cesar, lay between the Garonne, the Pyrenees and the Ocean. In modern days, it has been called Gascony. The inhabitants, in Cesar's time, spoke a different dialect from that of the proper Celts, between the Garonne and Seine. This dialect bore an affinity to the *Basque*, in Biscay, to which they were contiguous; and some remains of it still exist in the Gascon. Aquitania is the *country of the Aqui;* from the name of the people, with *tan*, a Celtic word, signifying region or country. The Romans, either from their general usage, or from not understanding the Celtic *tan*, annexed another termination signifying country, *ia.* the Ir. *ai* or *aoi*, Heb. אי ai, a settlement or habitation; Gr. αια, land, country; Hindu, *eya*, the same. *Cesar, Com. Lib.* i. 1. *D'Anville.*

A. R. stand for *anno regni*, the year of the king's reign; as A. R. G. R. 20, in the 20th year of the reign of king George.

ARABESQUE, ARABESK'Y, *a.* [See *Arabian.*]
1. In the manner of the Arabians; applied to ornaments consisting of imaginary foliage, stalks, plants, &c., in which there are no figures of animals. *Encyc.*
2. The Arabic language. [*Not in use.*] *Guthrie.*

ARA'BIAN, *a.* [See the noun.] Pertaining to Arabia.

ARA'BIAN, *n.* [Arab denotes a wanderer, or a dweller in a desert.]
A native of Arabia; an Arab.

AR'ABIC, *a.* Belonging to Arabia, or the language of its inhabitants.

AR'ABIC, *n.* The language of the Arabians.

ARAB'ICALLY, *adv.* In the Arabian manner.

AR'ABISM, *n.* An Arabic idiom or peculiarity of language. *Encyc. Stuart.*

AR'ABIST, *n.* One well versed in Arabic literature. *Encyc.*

AR'ABLE, *a.* [L. *aro*, Gr. αροω, to plow; Ir. *araim.*]
Fit for plowing or tillage; hence often applied to land which has been plowed.

AR'ABY, *n.* Arabia. *Milton.*

ARACH'NOID, *a.* [Gr. αραχνη, a spider, and ειδος, form; Heb. ארג, to weave, that is, to stretch, to draw out; Eng. *reach.*]
In *anatomy*, the arachnoid tunic, or arachnoid, is a semitransparent thin membrane which is spread over the brain and piamater, and for the most part closely connected with the latter. The term has also been applied to that capsule of the crystaline lens, which is a continuation of the hyaloid membrane. *Cyc.*

ARACH'NOID, *n.* A species of madrepore found fossil. *Cyc.*

ARACHO'SIAN, *a.* Designating a chain of mountains which divide Persia from India. *As. Researches.*

ARAIGNEE' or ARRA'IGN, *n.* *arāin.* [Fr. a spider.]
In *fortification*, the branch, return or gallery of a mine. *Bailey.*

ARA'ISE, *v. t.* To raise. [*Not used.*] *Shak.*

ARAME'AN, *a.* Pertaining to Aram, a son of Shem, or to the Chaldeans.

AR'AMISM, *n.* An idiom of the Aramean or Chaldee language; a Chaldaism.

ARA'NEOUS, *a.* [L. *aranea*, a spider, or cobweb.]

Resembling a cobweb.

ARAUCA'NIAN, *a.* Pertaining to the Araucanians, a tribe of aboriginals, inhabiting Arauco, in Chili. *Molina.*

'ARBALIST, *n.* [From *arcus*, a bow, and *balista*, L., an engine to throw stones; Gr. βαλλω, to throw.]

A cross-bow. This consists of a steel bow set in a shaft of wood, furnished with a string and a trigger; and is bent with a piece of iron. It serves to throw bullets, darts, arrows, &c. *Encyc.*

'ARBALISTER, *n.* A cross-bowman. *Speed.*

'ARBITER, *n.* [L.] A person appointed, or chosen by parties in controversy, to decide their differences. This is its sense in the civil law. In modern usage, *arbitrator* is the technical word.

2. In *a general sense, now most common*, a person who has the power of judging and determining, without control; one whose power of deciding and governing is not limited.

3. One that commands the destiny, or holds the empire of a nation or state. *Mitford.*

'ARBITRABLE, *a.* Arbitrary; depending on the will. *Spelman.*

ARBIT'RAMENT, *n.* Will; determination; *Milton.*

2. The award of arbitrators. *Cowel.* In this sense *award* is more generally used.

'ARBITRARILY, *adv.* By will only; despotically; absolutely.

'ARBITRARINESS, *n.* The quality of being arbitrary; despoticalness; tyranny. *Temple.*

ARBITRA'RIOUS, *a.* Arbitrary; despotic. [*Not used.*] *Norris. More.*

ARBITRA'RIOUSLY, *adv.* Arbitrarily. [*Not used.*] *Glanville.*

'ARBITRARY, *a.* [L. *arbitrarius.*]

1. Depending on will or discretion; not governed by any fixed rules; as, an *arbitrary* decision; an *arbitrary* punishment.

Arbitrary power is most easily established on the ruins of liberty abused to licentiousness. *Washington.*

2. Despotic; absolute in power; having no external control; as, an *arbitrary* prince or government.

'ARBITRATE, *v. i.* [L. *arbitror.*]

To hear and decide, as arbitrators; as, to choose men to *arbitrate* between us.

'ARBITRATE, *v. t.* To decide; to determine; to judge of. *Milton. Shak.*

ARBITRA'TION, *n.* The hearing and determination of a cause between parties in controversy, by a person or persons chosen by the parties. This may be done by one person; but it is usual to chuse two or three; or for each party to chuse one, and these to name a third, who is called the *umpire*. Their determination is called an *award*.

2. A hearing before arbitrators, though they make no award. [*This is a common use of the word in the United States.*]

'ARBITRATOR, *n.* A person chosen by a party, or by the parties who have a controversy, to determine their differences. The act of the parties in giving power to the arbitrators is called the *submission*, and this may be *verbal* or *written*. The person chosen as umpire, by two arbitrators, when the parties do not agree, is also called an arbitrator.

2. An arbiter, governor, or president. *Milton.*

3. In *a more extensive sense*, an arbiter; one who has the power of deciding or prescribing without control. *Addison. Shak.*

'ARBITRESS, *n.* A female arbiter.

'ARBOR, *n.* [The French express the sense by *berceau*, a cradle, an *arbor*, or bower; Sp. *emparrado*, from *parra*, a vine raised on stakes, and nailed to a wall. Qu. L. *arbor*, a tree, and the primary sense.]

1. A frame of lattice work, covered with vines, branches of trees or other plants, for shade; a bower.

2. In *botany*, a tree, as distinguished from a shrub. The distinction which Linne makes, that a tree springs up with a bud on the stem, and a shrub not, is found not to hold universally; and the tree, in popular understanding, differs from the shrub only in size. *Arbor* forms the seventh family of vegetables in Linne's system. [See *Tree.*]

3. In *mechanics*, the principal part of a machine, sustaining the rest. Also the axis or spindle of a machine, as of a crane, or windmill. *Encyc.*

This in America is called the *shaft.*

'ARBORATOR, *n.* One who plants or who prunes trees. *Evelyn.*

ARBO'REOUS, *a.* [L. *arboreus*, from *arbor.*]

Belonging to a tree; resembling a tree; constituting a tree; growing on trees, as moss is *arboreous.*

ARBORES'CENCE, *n.* [L. *arboresco*, to grow to a tree.]

The figure of a tree; the resemblance of a tree in minerals, or crystalizations or groups of crystals in that form.

ARBORES'CENT, *a.* Resembling a tree; having the figure of a tree; dendritical. *Encyc.*

2. From herbaceous becoming woody. *Martyn.*

ARBORES'CENT STAR-FISH, *n.* A species of *asterias*, called also *caput Medusæ.* [See *Starfish.*]

'ARBORET, *n.* [It. *arboreto*, from *arbor*, a tree.]

A small tree or shrub; a place planted or overgrown with trees. *Milton.*

'ARBORIST, *n.* One who makes trees his study, or who is versed in the knowledge of trees. *Howell.*

ARBORIZA'TION, *n.* The appearance or figure of a tree or plant in minerals, or fossils. [See *Herborization.*]

'ARBORIZE, *v. t.* To form the appearance of a tree or plant in minerals.

'ARBUSCLE, *n.* [L. *arbusculus*, a little tree.]

A dwarf tree, in size between a shrub and a tree. *Bradley.*

ARBUS'CULAR, *a.* Resembling a shrub; having the figure of small trees. *Da Costa.*

ARBUST'IVE, *a.* [From *arbustum.*]

Containing copses of trees or shrubs; covered with shrubs. *Bartram.*

ARBUST'UM, *n.* [L. See *Arbor.*] A copse of shrubs or trees; an orchard.

'ARBUTE, *n.* [L. *arbutus.*] The strawberry tree.

ARBU'TEAN, *a.* Pertaining to the strawberry tree. *Encyc. Evelyn.*

'ARC, *n.* [L. *arcus*, a bow, vault or *arch*; *arcuo*, to bend; Gr. αρχη, beginning, origin; αρχω, to begin, to be the author or chief; Fr. *arc, arche*; Sp. *arco*, a bow and an *arch*; Port. *id*; It. *id*; Arm. *goarec.* The Greek word has a different application, but is probably from the same root as *arcus*, from the sense of springing or stretching, shooting up, rising, which gives the sense of a vault, or bow, as well as of chief or head. Heb. ארג, to weave; Syr. ܐܪܓ to desire or long for; Ar. أَرِجَ to emit odor, to diffuse fragrance; and Heb. ערג to desire, or long for, to ascend; Eth. ዐረገ to ascend, to mount; Ar. *id.* The radical sense of all these roots is, to stretch, strain, reach; Gr. ορεγω; L. *fragro*; and the sense of *arch* is from stretching upwards, ascending. From *arc* or *arch* comes the sense of bending, deviating and cunning.]

In *geometry*, any part of the circumference of a circle, or curved line, lying from one point to another; a segment, or part of a circle, not more than a semicircle. *Encyc. Johnson.*

ARCA'DE, *n.* [Fr. from *arcus*; Sp. *arcada.*]

A long or continued arch; a walk arched above. *Johnson.*

ARCA'DIAN, } *a.* Pertaining to Arcadia, a
ARCA'DIC, } mountainous district in the heart of the Peloponnesus. *Trans. of Pausanias.*

ARCA'DICS, *n.* The title of a book in Pausanias, which treats of Arcadia. *Trans. B.* 8.

ARCA'NE, *a.* [L. *arcanus.*] Hidden, secret. [*Not much used.*] *Trans. of Pausanias.*

ARCA'NUM, *n.* [L.] A secret; generally used in the plural, *arcana*, secret things, mysteries.

ARCBÖUTANT, *n.* [Fr. *arc*, and *bout.* See *About, Abutment.*] In *building*, an arched buttress. *Encyc.*

'ARCH, *n.* [See *Arc.*] A segment or part of a circle. A concave or hollow structure of stone or brick, supported by its own curve. It may be constructed of wood, and supported by the mechanism of the work. This species of structure is much used in bridges.

A vault is properly a broad arch. *Encyc.*

2. The space between two piers of a bridge, when arched; or any place covered with an arch.

3. Any curvature, in form of an arch.

4. The vault of heaven, or sky. *Shak.*

Triumphal arches are magnificent structures at the entrance of cities, erected to adorn a triumph and perpetuate the memory of the event.

'ARCH, *v. t.* To cover with an arch; to form with a curve; as to *arch* a gate.

'ARCH, *v. i.* To make an arch or arches; as, to *arch* beneath the sand. *Pope.*

'ARCH, *a.* [It. *arcare*, to bend, to arch, to cheat, or deceive, from *arco*, L. *arcus*, a bow; G. *arg*, cunning, *arch*, bad; D. *arg*, crafty, *roguish;* Sw. Dan. *arg*, id. The Teutonic *arg*, appears to be allied to *arch*, and to be the Eng. *rogue*. This circumstance, and the Arm. *goarec*, [see *arc*,] indicate that the radical letters in *arc*, *arch*, αρχη, are Rg. The radical sense of *bend* is, to strain.]

Cunning; sly; shrewd; waggish; mischievous for sport; mirthful; as we say in popular language, roguish; as an *arch* lad.

'ARCH, *a.* used also in composition. [Gr. αρχος, chief; Ir. *arg*, noble, famous.]

Chief; of the first class; principal; as, an *arch* deed. *Shak.*

Shakspeare uses this word as a noun; "My worthy *arch* and patrons;" but the use is not authorized.

'ARCHAISM, *n.* [Gr. αρχαιος, ancient, from αρχη, beginning.]

An ancient or obsolete phrase or expression. *Watts.*

ARCHAN'GEL, *n.* An angel of the highest order; an angel occupying the eighth rank in the celestial hierarchy. *Encyc.*

2. The name of several plants, as the dead-nettle, or lamium; a species of melittis; and the galeopsis or hedge-nettle.

ARCHANGEL'IC, *a.* Belonging to archangels.

ARCHAPOS'TATE, *n.* A chief apostate.

ARCHAPOS'TLE, *n.* The chief apostle. *Trapp.*

ARCH'ARCHITECT, *n.* The supreme architect. *Sylvester.*

ARCHBE'ACON, *n.* The chief beacon, place of prospect or signal.

ARCHBISH'OP, *n.* A chief bishop; a church dignitary of the first class; a metropolitan bishop, who superintends the conduct of the suffragan bishops, in his province, and also exercises episcopal authority in his own diocese. *Clarendon.*

ARCHBISH'OPRIC, *n.* [*Archbishop* and *ric*, or *rick*, territory or jurisdiction.]

The jurisdiction or place of an archbishop; the province over which an archbishop exercises authority. *Clarendon.*

ARCHBOTCH'ER, *n.* The chief botcher, or mender, ironically. *Corbet.*

ARCHBUILD'ER, } *n.* Chief builder.
ARCHBILD'ER } *Harmar.*

ARCHBUT'LER, *n.* A chief butler; an officer of the German empire, who presents the cup to the emperor, on solemn occasions. This office belongs to the king of Bohemia. *Encyc.*

ARCHCHĂMBERLAIN, *n.* A chief chamberlain; an officer of the German empire, whose office is similar to that of the great chamberlain in England. This office belongs to the elector of Brandenburg. *Encyc.*

ARCHCH'ANCELLOR, *n.* A chief chancellor; an officer in the German empire, who presides over the secretaries of the court. Under the first races of French kings, when Germany and Italy belonged to them, three archchancellors were appointed; and this institution gave rise to the three archchancellors now subsisting in Germany, who are the archbishops of Mentz, of Cologne, and of Treves. *Encyc.*

ARCHCH'ANTER, *n.* The chief chanter, or president of the chanters of a church.

ARCHCHIM'IC, *a.* Of supreme chimical powers. *Milton.*

ARCHCONSPIR'ATOR, *n.* Principal conspirator. *Maundrell.*

ARCHCOUNT', *n.* A chief count; a title formerly given to the earl of Flanders, on account of his great riches and power. *Encyc.*

ARCHCRIT'IC, *n.* A chief critic.

ARCHDAP'IFER, *n.* [*Arch*, chief, and L. *dapifer*, a food-bearer, from *daps*, meat or a feast, and *fero*, to carry.]

An officer in the German empire, whose office is, at the coronation of the emperor, to carry the first dish of meat to table on horseback. *Encyc.*

ARCHDE'ACON, *n.* [See *Deacon.*]

In *England*, an ecclesiastical dignitary, next in rank below a bishop, who has jurisdiction either over a part or over the whole diocese. He is usually appointed by the bishop, and has an authority originally derived from the bishop, but now independent of him. He has a court, the most inferior of ecclesiastical courts, for hearing ecclesiastical causes, and the punishment of offenders by spiritual censures. *Blackstone.*

ARCHDE'ACONRY, *n.* The office, jurisdiction or residence of an archdeacon. In *England*, every diocese is divided into archdeaconries, of which there are sixty, and each archdeaconry into rural deaneries, and each deanery into parishes. *Blackstone.*

ARCHDE'ACONSHIP, *n.* The office of an archdeacon.

ARCHDIVI'NE, *n.* A principal theologian.

ARCHDRU'ID, *n.* [See *Druid.*] A chief druid, or pontiff of the ancient druids. *Henry, Hist. Eng. Rowland's Mona Antiqua.*

ARCHDU'CAL, *a.* [See *Archduke.*] Pertaining to an archduke.

ARCHDUCH'ESS, *n.* [See *Duchess.*] A title given to the females of the house of Austria.

ARCHDUCH'Y, *n.* The territory of an archduke or archduchess. *Ash.*

ARCHDU'KE, [See *Duke.*] A title given to princes of the House of Austria; all the sons being archdukes, and the daughters archduchesses. *Encyc.*

ARCHDU'KEDOM, *n.* The territory or jurisdiction of an archduke or archduchess.

'ARCHED, *pp.* Made with an arch or curve; covered with an arch.

ARCHEN'EMY, *n.* A principal enemy. *Milton.*

ARCHEOLOG'ICAL, *a.* Pertaining to a treatise on antiquity, or to the knowledge of ancient things.

ARCHEOL'OGY, *n.* [Gr. αρχαιος, ancient, and λογος, discourse.]

A discourse on antiquity; learning or knowledge which respects ancient times. *Panoplist*, Dec. 1808.

'ARCHER, *n.* [Sp. *archero;* It. *arciéro;* Fr. *archer;* from *arcus*, a bow. See *Arch* and *Arc.*]

A bowman; one who uses a bow in battle; one who is skilled in the use of the bow and arrow.

'ARCHERESS, *n.* A female archer. *Markham.*

'ARCHERY, *n.* The use of the bow and arrow; the practice, art or skill of archers; the act of shooting with a bow and arrow.

'ARCHES-COURT, in England, so called from the church of St. Mary *le bow* (*de arcubus*,) whose top is raised of stone pillars built archwise, where it was anciently held, is a court of appeal, in the ecclesiastical polity, the judge of which is called the dean of the arches. This court had jurisdiction over thirteen peculiar parishes in London, belonging to the archbishop of Canterbury; but the office of *dean of the arches* being united with that of the archbishop's principal office, the dean now receives and determines appeals from the sentence of all inferior courts within the province; and from him lies an appeal to the king in chancery. This and all the principal spiritual courts are now held at Doctors' Commons. *Blackstone.*

'ARCHETYPAL, *a.* Original; constituting a model or pattern.

'ARCHETYPE, *n.* [Gr. αρχετυπον; αρχη, beginning, and τυπος, form.]

1. The original pattern or model of a work; or the model from which a thing is made; as, a tree is the *archetype* or pattern of our idea of that tree. *Watts.*

2. Among *minters*, the standard weight, by which others are adjusted.

3. Among Platonists, the *archetypal world* is the world as it existed in the idea of God, before the creation. *Encyc.*

ARCHE'US, *n.* [Gr. αρχη, beginning, or αρχος, a chief; W. *erchi.*]

A term used by the ancient chimists, to denote the internal efficient cause of all things; the anima mundi or plastic power of the old philosophers; the power that presides over the animal economy, or the vis medicatrix; the active principle of the material world. In *medicine*, good health, or ancient practice. *Johnson. Encyc. Coxe.*

ARCHFEL'ON, *n.* [See *Felon.*] A chief felon. *Milton.*

ARCHFIE'ND, *n.* [See *Fiend.*] A chief fiend or foe. *Milton.*

ARCHFLAM'EN, *n.* A chief flamen or priest *Herbert.*

ARCHFLAT'TERER, *n.* [See *Flatter.*] A chief flatterer. *Bacon.*

ARCHFO'E, *n.* [See *Foe.*] A grand or chief enemy. *Milton.*

ARCHFOUND'ER, *n.* A chief founder. *Milton.*

ARCHGŎV'ERNOR, *n.* The chief governor. *Brewer.*

ARCHHER'ESY, *n.* [See *Heresy.*] The greatest heresy. *Butler.*

ARCHHER'ETIC, *n.* A chief heretic. *Shak.*

ARCHHI'EREY, *n.* [Gr. αρχος, chief, and ιερος, priest.] A chief priest in Russia. *Tooke*, i. 530.

ARCHHYP'OCRITE, *n.* A great or chief hypocrite. *Fuller.*

ARCH'IATER, *n.* [Gr. αρχος, chief, and ιατρος, physician.] Chief physician; a word used in Russia. *Tooke*, i. 557.

ARCH'ICAL, *a.* Chief; primary. *Hallywell.*

ARCHIDIAC'ONAL, *a.* [See *Deacon.*]

Pertaining to an archdeacon; as an *archidiaconal* visitation.

ARCHIEPIS'COPAL, *a.* [See *Episcopal.*] Belonging to an archbishop; as, Canterbury is an *archiepiscopal* see. *Weever.*

'ARCHIL, *n.* A lichen, which grows on rocks, in the Canary and Cape de Verd isles, which yields a rich purple color, not durable, but very beautiful. It is bruised between stones, and moistened with strong spirit of urine mixed with quick lime. It first takes a purplish red color, and then turns to blue. In the first state it is called *archil;* and in the second, lacmas or litmase, *litmus.* *Encyc.*

ARCHILO'CHIAN, *a.* Pertaining to Archilochus, the poet, who invented a verse of seven feet, the first four dactyls or spondees, the last three, trochees.

'ARCHIMAGUS, *n.* [See *Magician.*] The high priest of the Persian Magi, or worshipers of fire. *Encyc.*

ARCHIMAND'RITE, *n.* [from *mandrite*, a Syriac word for monk.]

In *church history*, a chief of the mandrites or monks, answering to *abbot* in Europe. *Encyc. Tooke, Russ.*

'ARCHING, *ppr.* Forming an arch; covering with an arch.

'ARCHING, *a.* Curving like an arch.

ARCHIPEL'AGO, *n.* [Authors are not agreed as to the origin of this word. Some suppose it to be compounded of αρχος, chief, and πελαγος, sea; others, of Αιγαιος, and πελαγος, the Egean sea. See Gibbon, Mitford and Ed. Encyc.]

In *a general sense*, a sea interspersed with many isles; but particularly the sea which separates Europe from Asia, otherwise called the Egean Sea. It contains the Grecian isles, called Cyclades and Sporades.

'ARCHITECT, *n.* [Gr. αρχος, chief, and τεκτων, a workman. See *Technical.*]

1. A person skilled in the art of building; one who understands architecture, or makes it his occupation to form plans and designs of buildings, and superintend the artificers employed.

2. A contriver; a former or maker. *Ray.*

ARCHITECT'IVE, *a.* Used in building; proper for building. *Derham.*

ARCHITECTON'IC, *a.* That has power or skill to build. *Smellie, Ch. 13.*

ARCHITECTON'ICS, *n.* The science of architecture. *Ash.*

ARCHITECT'RESS, *n.* A female architect. *Wotton.*

ARCHITECT'URAL, *a.* Pertaining to the art of building; that is according to the rules of architecture. *Mason.*

'ARCHITECTURE, *n.* [L. *architectura.*]

1. The art of building; but in a more limited and appropriate sense, the art of constructing houses, bridges and other buildings for the purposes of civil life.

2. Frame or structure.

> The earth is a piece of divine *architecture.* *Burnet.*

Military architecture is the art of fortification.

Naval architecture is the art of building ships.

'ARCHITRAVE, *n.* [Gr. αρχος, chief, and It. *trave*, from L. *trabs*, a beam.]

In *architecture*, the lower division of an entablature, or that part which rests immediately on the column. It probably represents the beam which, in ancient buildings, extended from column to column, to support the roof.

In chimneys, the architrave is called the mantle piece; and over doors and windows, the hyperthyrion. *Johnson. Encyc. Cyc.*

'ARCHIVAL, *a.* [See *Archives.*] Pertaining to archives or records; contained in records. *Tooke.*

'ARCHIVAULT, *n.* [*arch*, chief, and *vault.*]

In *building*, the inner contour of an arch, or a band adorned with moldings, running over the faces of the arch-stones, and bearing upon the imposts. It has only a single face in the Tuscan order; two faces crowned in the Doric and Ionic, and the same moldings, as the architrave, in the Corinthian and Composite. *Encyc.*

'ARCHIVES, *n. plu.* [Gr. αρχειον; Low L. *archivum;* Fr. *archives;* It. *archivio.*]

The apartment in which records are kept; also the records and papers which are preserved, as evidences of facts.

'ARCHIVIST, *n.* [Fr. and It.] The keeper of archives or records. *Encyc.*

'ARCHLIKE, *a.* Built like an arch. *Young.*

'ARCHLUTE, } *n.* [It. *arcileuto.*]
'ARCHILUTE, }

A large lute, a theorbo, the base-strings of which are doubled with an octave, and the higher strings with a unison. *Busby.*

'ARCHLY, *adv.* Shrewdly; wittily; jestingly.

ARCHMAGI''CIAN, *n.* The chief magician. *Spenser.*

ARCHMAR'SHAL, *n.* The grand marshal of the German empire; a dignity belonging to the elector of Saxony.

'ARCHNESS, *n.* Cunning; shrewdness; waggishness.

'ARCHON, *n.* [Gr. αρχων, a prince.]

The archons in Greece were chief magistrates chosen, after the death of Codrus, from the most illustrious families, to superintend civil and religious concerns. They were nine in number; the first was properly the *archon;* the second was called *king;* the third, *polemarch*, or general of the forces. The other six were called *thesmothetæ*, or legislators. *Encyc.*

'ARCHONSHIP, *n.* The office of an archon; or the term of his office. *Mitford.*

ARCHON'TICS, *n.* In *church history*, a branch of the Valentinians, who held that the world was not created by God, but by angels, *archontes.*

ARCHP'ASTOR, *n.* Chief pastor, the shepherd and bishop of our souls. *Barrow.*

ARCHPHILOS'OPHER, *n.* A chief philosopher. *Hooker.*

ARCHPIL'LAR, *n.* The main pillar. *Harmar.*

ARCHPO'ET, *n.* The principal poet.

ARCHPOLITI''CIAN, *n.* [See *Policy.*] An eminent or distinguished politician. *Bacon.*

ARCHPON'TIFF, *n.* [See *Pontiff.*] A supreme pontiff or priest. *Burke.*

ARCHPRE'LATE, *n.* [See *Prelate.*] The chief prelate.

ARCHPRES'BYTER, *n.* [See *Presbyter.*] A chief presbyter or priest. *Encyc.*

ARCHPRES'BYTERY, *n.* The absolute dominion of presbytery, or the chief presbytery. *Milton.*

ARCHPRIE'ST, *n.* [See *Priest.*] A chief priest. *Encyc.*

ARCHPRI'MATE, *n.* The chief primate; an archbishop. *Milton.*

ARCHPROPH'ET, *n.* Chief prophet. *Warton.*

ARCHPROT'ESTANT, *n.* A principal or distinguished protestant.

ARCHPUB'LICAN, *n.* The distinguished publican. *Hall.*

ARCHREB'EL, *n.* The chief rebel. *Milton.*

ARCHTRA'ITOR, *n.* A principal traitor.

ARCHTREAS'URER, *n.* [See *Treasure.*] The great treasurer of the German empire; a dignity claimed by the elector of Hanover. *Guthrie.*

ARCHTREAS'URERSHIP, *n.* The office of archtreasurer. *Collins' Peerage.*

ARCHTY'RANT, *n.* A principal or great tyrant. *Hall.*

ARCHVIL'LAIN, *n.* [See *Villain.*] A chief or great villain. *Shak.*

ARCHVIL'LANY, *n.* Great villany.

'ARCHWISE, *adv.* [*arch* and *wise.* See *Wise.*] In the form of an arch.

ARCTA'TION, } *n.* [L. *arctus*, tight.] Preternatural straightness;
ARC'TITUDE, }

constipation from inflammation. *Coxe.*

ARC'TIC, *a.* [Gr. αρκτος, a bear, and a northern constellation so called. W. *arth;* Ir. *art*, a bear.]

Northern; pertaining to the northern constellation, called the bear; as, the *arctic* pole, circle, region or sea.

The *arctic* circle is a lesser circle parallel to the equator, 23° 28′ from the north pole. This, and the *antarctic* circle, are called the *polar circles*, and within these lie the frigid zones.

ARCTU'RUS, *n.* [Gr. αρκτος, a bear, and ουρα, tail.] A fixed star of the first magnitude, in the constellation of Bootes. *Encyc.*

'ARCUATE, *a.* [L. *arcuatus.* See *Arc.*] Bent or curved in the form of a bow. *Martyn. Bacon. Ray.*

ARCUA'TION, *n.* The act of bending; incurvation; the state of being bent; curvity; crookedness; great convexity of the thorax. *Coxe.*

2. A method of raising trees by layers; that is, by bending branches to the ground, and covering the small shoots with earth, three inches deep upon the joints; making a bason of earth to hold the water. When these have taken root, they are removed into a nursery. *Chambers. Encyc.*

'ARCUBALIST, *n.* [L. *arcus*, a bow, and *balista*, an engine for throwing stones.] A cross-bow. *Warton.*

ARCUBALIS'TER, *n.* A cross-bowman; one who used the arbalist. *Camden.*

'ARD, the termination of many English words, is the Ger. *art*, species, kind; Sw. and Dan. *art*, mode, nature, genius, form; Ger. *arten*, to take after, resemble; Sw. *arta*, to form or fashion; Ger. *artig*, of the nature of, also comely; Dan. and Sw. *artig*, beautiful; D. *aarden*, to take after, resemble; *aardig*, genteel, pretty, ingenious. We observe it in *Goddard*, a divine temper; *Giffard*, a disposition to *give*, liberality; *Bernard*, filial affection; *standard*, *drunkard*, *dotard*, &c.

'ARDENCY, *n.* [L. *ardens*, from *ardeo*, to burn.]
Warmth of passion or affection; ardor; eagerness; as, the *ardency* of love or zeal.

'ARDENT, *a.* Hot; burning; that causes a sensation of burning; as, *ardent* spirits, that is, distilled spirits; an *ardent* fever.
2. Having the appearance or quality of fire; fierce; as *ardent* eyes.
3. Warm, applied to the passions and affections; passionate; affectionate; much engaged; zealous; as, *ardent* love or vows; *ardent* zeal.

'ARDENTLY, *adv.* With warmth; affectionately; passionately.

'ARDENTNESS, *n.* Ardency.

'ARDOR, *n.* [L.] Heat, in a literal sense; as, the *ardor* of the sun's rays.
2. Warmth, or heat, applied to the passions and affections; eagerness; as, he pursues study with *ardor;* they fought with *ardor.*
Milton uses the word for person or spirit, bright and effulgent, but by an unusual license.

ARDUOUS, *a.* [L. *arduus;* Ir. *ard*, high; W. *hardh;* Ir. *airdh*, high, highth.]
1. High, lofty, in a literal sense; as, *arduous* paths. *Pope.*
2. Difficult; attended with great labor, like the ascending of acclivities; as, an *arduous* employment, task, or enterprise.

'ARDUOUSLY, *adv.* In an arduous manner; with laboriousness.

'ARDUOUSNESS, *n.* Highth; difficulty of execution.

ARE. The plural of the substantive verb; but a different word from *be*, *am* or *was.* It is from the Sw. *vara*, Dan. *værer*, to be, to exist; *v* or *w* being lost. We *are;* ye or you *are;* they *are;* past tense plural *were.* It is usually pronounced *ar.*

A-RE, ALAMIRE, } The lowest note, except one, in Guido's scale of music. *Shak.*

A'REA, *n.* [L. I suspect this to be contracted from Ch. ארעא, an area or bed; Heb. ערוגה; from a root which signifies to *reach*, stretch, lay or spread.]
1. Any plain surface, as the floor of a room, of a church or other building, or of the ground.
2. The space or site on which a building stands; or of any inclosure.
3. In *geometry*, the superficial contents of any figure; the surface included within any given lines; as the *area* of a square or a triangle.
4. Among *physicians*, baldness; an empty space; a bald space produced by alopecy; also a name of the disease. *Coxe. Parr.*
5. In *mining*, a compass of ore allotted to diggers. *Coxe.*

AREA'D, AREE'D, } *v. t.* [Sax. *aredan.*] To counsel; to advise. *Obs. Spenser.*

A'REAL, *a.* Pertaining to an area; as *areal* interstices. *Barton.*

AREE'K, *adv.* In a reeking condition. [See *Reek.*] *Swift.*

AREFAC'TION, *n.* [L. *arefacio*, to dry, from *areo.*] The act of drying; the state of growing dry. *Bacon.*

AR'EFY, *v. t.* To dry or make dry. *Bacon.*

ARE'NA, *n.* [L. sand.] An open space of ground, strewed with sand, on which the gladiators, in ancient Rome, exhibited shows of fighting for the amusement of spectators. Hence, a place for public exhibition. *Adam's Rom. Ant. Ray.*
2. Among *physicians*, sand or gravel in the kidneys.

ARENA'CEOUS, *a.* [from *arena*, sand.] Sandy; having the properties of sand. *Woodward.*
2. Brittle; as *arenaceous* limestone. *Kirwan.*

ARENA'TION, *n.* Among *physicians*, a sand bath; a sprinkling of hot sand upon a diseased person. *Coxe.*

AREN'DALITE, *n.* In *mineralogy*, another name of epidote, or pistacite; epidote being the name given to it by Haüy, and pistacite by Werner. [See *Epidote.*]

ARENDA'TOR, *n.* [Russ. *arenda*, a farm. Qu. Sp. *arrendar*, to rent.]
In Livonia and other provinces of Russia, a farmer of the farms or rents; one who contracts with the crown for the rents of the farms. He who rents an estate belonging to the crown, is called *Crown-arendator. Arende* is a term used both for the estate let to farm, and the sum for which it is rented. *Tooke's Russ.* ii. 288.

ARENILIT'IC, *a.* [*arena*, sand, and λιθος, a stone.]
Pertaining to sand stone; consisting of sandstone; as *arenilitic* mountains. *Kirwan.*

ARENO'SE, AR'ENOUS, } *a.* Sandy; full of sand. *Johnson.*

AR'EOLE, AREO'LA, } *n.* [L.] The colored circle round the nipple, or round a pustule. *Encyc. Coxe.*

AREOM'ETER, *n.* [Gr. αραιος, rare, thin, and μετρεω, to measure.]
An instrument for measuring the specific gravity of liquids. *Fourcroy.*

AREOMET'RICAL, *a.* Pertaining to an areometer.

AREOM'ETRY, *n.* The measuring or act of measuring the specific gravity of fluids.

AREOPAGIT'IC, *a.* Pertaining to the Areopagus. *Mitford.*

AREOP'AGITE, *n.* A member of the Areopagus, which see. Acts xvii. 34.

AREOP'AGUS, *n.* [Gr. Αρης, Mars, and παγος, hill.]
A sovereign tribunal at Athens, famous for the justice and impartiality of its decisions. It was originally held on a hill in the city; but afterward removed to the *Royal Portico*, an open square, where the judges sat in the open air, inclosed by a cord. Their sessions were in the night, that they might not be diverted by objects of sight, or influenced by the presence and action of the speakers. By a law of Solon, no person could be a member of this tribunal, until he had been *archon* or chief magistrate. This court took cognizance of high crimes, impiety and immorality, and watched over the laws and the public treasury. *Lempriere. Encyc. Pausanias.* Acts xvii. 19.

AREOT'IC, *a.* [Gr. αραιος, thin.] Attenuating; making thin, as in liquids; rarefying.

AREOT'IC, *n.* A medicine, which attenuates the humors, dissolves viscidity, opens the pores, and increases perspiration; an attenuant. *Quincy. Coxe.*

ARETOL'OGY, *n.* [Gr. αρετη, virtue, and λογος, discourse.]
That part of moral philosophy which treats of virtue, its nature and the means of attaining to it. [*Little used.*] *Johnson.*

'ARGAL, *n.* Unrefined or crude tartar, a substance adhering to the sides of wine casks. *Johnson. Coxe.*

ARGE'AN, *a.* Pertaining to Argo or the Ark. *Faber.*

'ARGENT, *n.* [L. *argentum;* Gr. αργυρος, silver, from αργος, white; Ir. *arg*, white; *airgiod*, silver, money; Fr. *argent*, money; Sans. *rajatam*, Qu.]
1. The white color in coats of arms, intended to represent silver, or purity, innocence, beauty, or gentleness. *Encyc.*
2. *a.* Silvery; of a pale white, like silver. *Johnson. Encyc.*
3. *a.* Bright.

Ask of yonder *argent* fields above. *Pope.*

ARGENT'AL, *a.* Pertaining to silver; consisting of silver; containing silver; combined with silver; applied to the native amalgam of silver, as *argental* mercury. *Cleaveland.*

'ARGENTATE, *n.* A combination of the argentic acid with another substance.

ARGENTA'TION, *n.* An overlaying with silver. *Johnson.*

'ARGENT-HORNED, *a.* Silver horned.

ARGENT'IC, *a.* Pertaining to silver; the *argentic* acid is a saturated combination of silver and oxygen. This is yet hypothetical. *Lavoisier.*

ARGENTIF'EROUS, *a.* [L. *argentum*, silver, and *fero*, to produce.] Producing silver; as *argentiferous* ore. *Kirwan.*

ARGENTI'NA, 'ARGENTINE, } *n.* In *ichthyology*, a genus of fishes of the order of abdominals.
Argentina is also a name of the wild tansy, silver-weed. *Encyc. Coxe.*

'ARGENTINE, *a.* Like silver; pertaining to silver, or sounding like it. *Johnson.*

'ARGENTINE, *n.* In *mineralogy*, a subspecies of carbonate of lime, nearly pure; a mineral of a lamellated or slaty structure; its lamens usually curved or undulated; its surface is shining, or of a pearly luster. It is found in primitive rocks, and frequently in metallic veins. *Cleaveland.*

'ARGIL, *n.* A species of the Ardea, or genus of cranes.

'ARGIL, *n.* [L. *argilla*, white clay, from Gr. αργος, white.]
In a general sense, clay, or potter's earth; but in a technical sense, pure clay, or *alumine.* *Fourcroy.*

ARGILLA'CEOUS, *a.* [L. *argillaceus.*] Partaking of the nature of clay; clayey; consisting of argil. *Kirwan.*

ARGILLIF'EROUS, *a.* [L. *argilla*, clay, and *fero*, to produce.] Producing clay; applied to such earths as abound with argil. *Kirwan.*

'ARGILLITE, *n.* Argillaceous shist or slate; clay-slate. Its usual color is bluish, greenish or blackish gray. *Kirwan.*

ARGILLIT'IC, *a.* Pertaining to argillite.

ARGILLOCAL'CITE, *n.* [of *argilla*, clay, and *calx*, calcarious earth.]
A species of calcarious earth, with a large proportion of clay. *Kirwan.*

ARGILLOMU'RITE, *n.* [of *argilla*, clay,

and *muria*, brine or salt water; magnesia being obtained from sea-salt.]
A species of earth consisting of magnesia, mixed with silex, alumine and lime; a variety of Magnesite. *Kirwan. Cleaveland.*

ARGIL'LOUS, *a.* Consisting of clay; clayey; partaking of clay; belonging to clay. *Brown.*

ARGIVE, *a.* Designating what belongs to Argos, the capital of Argolis in Greece, whose inhabitants were called *Argivi.* This name however is used by the poets for the Greeks in general. *Paus. Trans.*

ARGO, *n.* The name of the ship which carried Jason and his fifty-four companions to Colchis, in quest of the golden fleece.

ARGO-NAVIS, the ship Argo, is a constellation in the southern hemisphere, whose stars, in the British catalogue, are sixty-four. *Encyc.*

ARGO'AN, *a.* Pertaining to the ship Argo. *Faber.*

ARGOL'IC, *a.* Belonging to Argolis, a territory or district of Peloponnese, between Arcadia and the Egean sea; as the *Argolic* Gulf. *D'Anville.*

ARGOL'ICS, *n.* The title of a chapter in Pausanias, which treats of Argolis. *Trans. B.* ii. 15.

ARGONAUT, *n.* [of αργω, Jason's ship, and ναυτης, a sailor.]
One of the persons who sailed to Colchis with Jason, in the Argo, in quest of the golden fleece. *Cicero. Pliny. Sir W. Jones.*

ARGONAUT'A, *n.* [See *Argonaut.*]
A genus of shell-fish, of the order of vermes testacea. The shell consists of one spiral involuted valve. There are several species; one of which is the Argo, with a subdentated carina, the famous nautilus, which, when it sails, extends two of its arms, spreading a membrane, which serves for a sail, and six other arms are thrown out, for rowing or steering. *Encyc. Cuvier.*

ARGONAUT'IC, *a.* Pertaining to the Argonauts, or to their voyage to Colchis; as the *Argonautic* story. *Sir W. Jones.*

ARGONAUT'ICS, *n.* A poem on the subject of Jason's voyage, or the expedition of the Argonauts; as, the *Argonautics* of Orpheus, of V. Flaccus, and of Apollonius Rhodius. *Encyc.*

ARGOSY, *n.* [Sp. *argos*, Jason's ship.] A large merchantman; a carrac. *Shak.*

ARGUE, *v. i.* [L. *arguo*, to show, argue, accuse or convict; Fr. *arguer;* Sp. *arguir;* It. *arguire.* The radical sense of *argue* is to urge, drive, press, or struggle.]
1. To reason; to invent and offer reasons to support or overthrow a proposition, opinion or measure; as, A *argues* in favor of a measure; B *argues* against it.
2. To dispute; to reason with; followed by *with;* as, you may *argue with* your friend, a week, without convincing him.

ARGUE, *v. t.* To debate or discuss; to treat by reasoning; as, the counsel *argued* the cause before the supreme court; the cause was well *argued.*
2. To prove or evince; to manifest by inference or deduction; or to show reasons for; as, the order visible in the universe *argues* a divine cause.
3. To persuade by reasons; as, to *argue* a man into a different opinion.
4. Formerly, to accuse or charge with; a Latin sense, now obsolete; as, to *argue* one of profaneness. *Dryden.*

ARGUED, *pp.* Debated; discussed; evinced; accused.

ARGUER, *n.* One who argues; a reasoner; a disputer; a controvertist.

ARGUING, *ppr.* Inventing and offering reasons; disputing; discussing; evincing; accusing.

ARGUING, *n.* Reasoning; argumentation.
What doth your *arguing* reprove? Job. vi.

ARGUMENT, *n.* [L. *argumentum.*]
1. A reason offered for or against a proposition, opinion, or measure; a reason offered in proof, to induce belief, or convince the mind; followed by *for* or *against.*
2. In *logic*, an inference drawn from premises, which are indisputable, or at least of probable truth. *Encyc.*
3. The subject of a discourse or writing. *Milton. Shak.*
4. An abstract or summary of a book, or the heads of the subjects.
5. A debate or discussion; a series of reasoning; as, an *argument* was had before the court, in which *argument*, all the reasons were urged.
6. In *astronomy*, an arch by which we seek another unknown arch, proportional to the first. *Chambers.*

ARGUMENT'AL, *a.* Belonging to argument; consisting in argument. *Pope.*

ARGUMENTA'TION, *n.* Reasoning; the act of reasoning; the act of inventing or forming reasons, making inductions, drawing conclusions, and applying them to the case in discussion. The operation of inferring propositions, not known or admitted as true, from facts or principles known, admitted, or proved to be true. *Encyc. Watts.*

ARGUMENT'ATIVE, *a.* Consisting of argument; containing a process of reasoning; as an *argumentative* discourse.
2. Showing reasons for; as, the adaptation of things to their uses is *argumentative* of infinite wisdom in the Creator.

ARGUMENT'ATIVELY, *adv.* In an argumentative manner. *Taylor.*

ARGUS, *n.* A fabulous being of antiquity, said to have had a hundred eyes, placed by Juno to guard Io. The origin of this being may perhaps be found in the Teutonic word *arg*, crafty, cunning, of which the hundred eyes are symbolical.

ARGUS-SHELL, *n.* A species of porcelain-shell, beautifully variegated with spots, resembling, in some measure, a peacock's tail. *Encyc.*

ARGU'TE, *a.* [L. *argutus.*] Sharp; shrill; witty. [*Little used.*]

ARGU'TENESS, *n.* Acuteness; wittiness. [*Little used.*] *Dryden.*

A'RIAN, *a.* Pertaining to Arius, a presbyter of the church of Alexandria, in the fourth century; or to his doctrines.

A'RIAN, *n.* One who adheres to the doctrines of Arius, who held Christ to be a created being, inferior to God the father in nature and dignity, though the first and noblest of all created beings; and also that the Holy Spirit is not God, but created by the power of the Son. *Encyc.*

A'RIANISM, *n.* The doctrines of the Arians.

A'RIANIZE, *v. i.* To admit the tenets of the Arians. *Worthington.*

AR'ID, *a.* [L. *aridus*, dry, from *areo*, to be dry.]
Dry; exhausted of moisture; parched with heat; as an *arid* waste. *Thomson.*

AR'IDAS, *n.* A kind of taffety, from the East Indies, made of thread, from certain plants. *Encyc.*

ARID'ITY, AR'IDNESS, *n.* Dryness; a state of being without moisture. *Arbuthnot.*
2. A dry state of the body; emaciation; the withering of a limb. *Coxe.*

A'RIES, *n.* [L. from the Celtic. Ir. *reithe*, or *receith;* Corn. *urz*, a ram; W. *hwrz*, a thrust, a ram.]
The ram, a constellation of fixed stars, drawn on the globe, in the figure of a ram. It is the first of the twelve signs in the zodiac, which the sun enters about the 21st of March.

AR'IETATE, *v. i.* [L. *arieto*, from *aries.*]
To butt, as a ram. [*Not used.*] *Johnson.*

ARIETA'TION, *n.* The act of butting, as a ram. The act of battering with the aries or battering ram. *Bacon.*
2. The act of striking or conflicting. [*Rarely used.*] *Glanville.*

ARIET'TA, *n.* [It.] A short song; an air, or little air.

ARI'GHT, *adv.* [*a* and *right.* Sax. *geriht.*]
Rightly; in a right form; without mistake or crime.

AR'IL, ARIL'LUS, *n.* The exterior coat or covering of a seed, fixed to it at the base only, investing it wholly or partially, and falling off spontaneously; by some writers called, from the Greek, *Calyptra.* It is either succulent, or cartilaginous; colored, elastic, rough or knotted. *Linne. Milne. Martyn. Smith.*

AR'ILLATED, AR'ILLED, *a.* Having an exterior covering or aril, as coffee. *Encyc. Eaton.*

AR'IMAN, AR'IMA, AH'RIMAN, *n.* [Per. *ahriman.* Sans. *ari*, a foe.]
The evil genius or demon of the Persians; opposed to yezad, yezdan, ormozd, or hormizda, the good demon. The ancient magi held, that there are two deities or principles; one the author of all good, eternally absorbed in light; the other, the author of all evil, forever buried in darkness; or the one represented by light; the other by darkness. The latter answers to the *loke* of the Scandinavians, whose Celtic name, *lock*, signifies *darkness.* Originally, the Persians held these demons or principles to be equal, and from all eternity; but the moderns maintain that the evil principle is an inferior being. So the devil is called the prince of darkness. *Encyc. Gibbon. As. Researches.*

ARIOLA'TION or HARIOLA'TION, *n.* [L. *ariolus* or *hariolus*, a sooth sayer.]
A soothsaying; a foretelling. *Brown.*

ARIO'SO, *a.* [It. from *aria*, air.] Light; airy. *It. Dict.*
But according to Rousseau, applied to music, it denotes a kind of melody bordering on the majestic style of a capital air. *Cyc.*

ARI'SE, *v. i.* *s* as *z.* pret. *arose;* pp. *arisen:*

pron. *arize, aroze, arizn.* [Sax. *arisan;* D. *ryzen;* Goth. *reisan.* It may be allied to Ar. راس, to be the head or chief; Heb. Ch. Syr. Sam. Eth. ראש head, origin.]

1. To ascend, mount up or move to a higher place; as, vapors *arise* from humid places.
2. To emerge from below the horizon; as, the sun or a star *arises* or *rises.*
3. To get out of bed; to leave the place or state of rest; or to leave a sitting or lying posture.

   The king *arose* early and went to the den. Dan. vi.
4. To begin; to spring up; to originate.

   A persecution *arose* about Stephen. Acts xi.
5. To revive from death; to leave the grave.

   Many bodies of saints *arose.* Math. xxvii.

   Figuratively, to awake from a state of sin and stupidity; to repent.

   Arise from the dead, and Christ shall give thee life. Eph. v.
6. To begin to act; to exert power; to move from a state of inaction.

   Let God *arise;* let his enemies be scattered. Ps. lxviii.
7. To appear, or become known; to become visible, sensible or operative.

   To you shall the sun of righteousness *arise.* Math. iv.

   Till the day star shall *arise* in your hearts. 2 Pet. i.
8. To be put in motion; to swell or be agitated; as, the waves *arose.*
9. To be excited or provoked; as, the wrath of the king shall *arise.*
10. To emerge from poverty, depression or distress.

    By whom shall Jacob *arise?* for he is small. Amos vii.
11. To appear in a particular character; to enter upon an office.

    There *arose* a new king who knew not Joseph. Ex. i.
12. To begin sedition, insurrection, or mutiny; as, the men *arose,* or *rose* upon their officers.
13. To invade, assault or begin hostility; followed by *against.*

    When he *arose against* me, I caught him by the beard. 1 Sam. xvii.

    In this sense, the word *against* really belongs to the verb, and is necessary to give it this meaning. [See *Rise,* another form of this verb, which has the same signification, and is more generally used in popular language.]

ARI'SING, *ppr.* Ascending; moving upward; originating or proceeding; getting up; springing up; appearing.

ARIST'A, *n.* [L.] In *botany,* awn, the long pointed beard which issues from the husk, or scaly flower cup of the grasses, called the glume. *Milne.*

ARISTAR'CHY, *n.* [Gr. αριςος, best, and αρχη, rule.]

A body of good men in power, or government by excellent men. *Harington.*

ARISTOC'RACY, *n.* [Gr. αριςος, best, and κρατεω, to hold or govern.]

A form of government, in which the whole supreme power is vested in the principal persons of a state; or in a few men distinguished by their rank and opulence. When the supreme power is exercised by a small number, the government is called an *oligarchy.* The latter word however is usually applied to a corrupted form of aristocracy.

ARIST'OCRAT, *n.* One who favors an aristocracy in principle or practice; one who is a friend to an aristocratical form of government. *Burke.*

ARISTOCRAT'IC, ARISTOCRAT'ICAL, *a.* Pertaining to aristocracy; consisting in a government of nobles, or principal men; as an *aristocratic* constitution.

2. Partaking of aristocracy; as, an *aristocratic* measure; *aristocratic* pride or manners.

ARISTOCRAT'ICALLY, *adv.* In an aristocratical manner.

ARISTOCRAT'ICALNESS, *n.* The quality of being aristocratical.

ARISTOTE'LIAN, *a.* Pertaining to Aristotle, a celebrated philosopher, who was born at Stagyra, in Macedon, about 384 years before Christ. The *Aristotelian* philosophy is otherwise called *peripatetic.*

ARISTOTE'LIAN, *n.* A follower of Aristotle, who was a disciple of Plato, and founded the sect of *peripatetics.* [See *Peripatetic.*]

ARISTOTE'LIANISM, *n.* The philosophy or doctrines of Aristotle.

ARISTOTEL'IC, *a.* Pertaining to Aristotle or to his philosophy.

The pernicious effects of the *Aristotelic* system. *Schlegel, Trans.*

AR'ITHMANCY, *n.* [Gr. αριθμος, number, and μαντεια, divination.]

Divination or the foretelling of future events by the use or observation of numbers.

ARITH'METIC, *n.* [Gr. αριθμεω, to number, αριθμητικη, the art of numbering, from αριθμος, number; from ρυθμος, number, rhythm, order, agreement.]

The science of numbers, or the art of computation. The various operations of arithmetic are performed by addition, subtraction, multiplication and division.

ARITHMET'IC, ARITHMET'ICAL, *a.* Pertaining to arithmetic; according to the rules or method of arithmetic.

ARITHMET'ICALLY, *adv.* According to the rules, principles or method of arithmetic.

ARITHMETI''CIAN, *n.* One skilled in arithmetic, or versed in the science of numbers.

'ARK, *n.* [Fr. *arche;* L. *arca;* Sp. Port. It. *arca,* a chest or coffer; Ir. *airg, airk;* Sax. *erc* or *erk;* G. *arche;* D. *arke;* Ch. ארגז.]

1. A small close vessel, chest or coffer, such as that which was the repository of the tables of the covenant among the Jews. This was about three feet nine inches in length. The lid was the *propitiatory,* or mercy seat, over which were the cherubs. The vessel in which Moses was set afloat upon the Nile was an *ark* of bulrushes.
2. The large floating vessel, in which Noah and his family were preserved, during the deluge.
3. A depository.

   Arise, O Lord, into thy rest, thou and the *ark* of thy strength. Ps. cxxxii.
4. A large boat used on American rivers, to transport produce to market.

'ARKITE, *n.* A term used by Bryant to denote one of the persons who were preserved in the ark; or who, according to pagan fables, belonged to the ark.

'ARKITE, *a.* Belonging to the ark. *Bryant. Faber.*

'ARKTIZITE, 'ARCTIZITE, *n.* A mineral, now called Wernerite.

'ARM, *n.* [Sax. *arm, earm;* D. G. Sw. Dan. *arm;* L. *armus,* an *arm,* a shoulder, a wing. In Russ. a shoulder is *ramo,* which may be the same word as the L. *armus.* If so, this word belongs to the root, Rm, coinciding with L. *ramus,* a branch, that is, a shoot, like the Celtic *braich,* L. *brachium.* But if the L. *armus* is directly from the Gr. αρμος, a joint, it would seem to be formed from Gr. αρω, to fit.]

1. The limb of the human body, which extends from the shoulder to the hand.
2. The branch of a tree, or the slender part of a machine, projecting from a trunk or axis. The limbs of animals are also sometimes called arms.
3. A narrow inlet of water from the sea.
4. *Figuratively,* power, might, strength; as the secular *arm.* In this sense the word is often used in the scriptures.

   To whom is the *arm* of the Lord revealed. Isa. liii.

'ARM, *v. t.* [L. *armo;* Fr. *armer;* Sp. *armar;* It. *armare;* from L. *arma.*]

1. To furnish or equip with weapons of offense, or defense; as, to *arm* the militia.
2. To cover with a plate, or with whatever will add strength, force, or security; as, to *arm* the hilt of a sword.
3. To furnish with means of defense; to prepare for resistance; to fortify.

   Arm yourselves with the same mind. 1 Pet. iv.

'ARM, *v. i.* To provide with arms, weapons, or means of attack or resistance; to take arms; as, the nations *arm* for war.

This verb is not really intransitive in this use, but reciprocal, the pronoun being omitted. The nations *arm*—for, the nations *arm themselves.*

ARMA'DA, *n.* [Sp. from *arma.*]

A fleet of armed ships; a squadron. The term is usually applied to the Spanish fleet, called the *Invincible Armada,* consisting of 130 ships, intended to act against England in the reign of Queen Elizabeth, A. D. 1588.

ARMADIL'LO, *n.* [Sp.; so called from being *armed* with a bony shell.]

A quadruped peculiar to America, called also *tatoo,* and in zoology, the *dasypus.* This animal has neither fore-teeth, nor dog-teeth; it is covered with a hard, bony shell, divided into movable belts, except on the forehead, shoulders and haunches, where it is not movable. The belts are connected by a membrane, which enables the animal to roll itself up like a hedge hog. These animals burrow in the earth, where they lie during the day time, seldom going abroad except at night. They are of different sizes; the largest 3 feet in length, without the tail. They subsist chiefly on fruits and roots; sometimes on insects and flesh. When attacked, they roll themselves into a ball, presenting their armor on all sides to any assailant; but they are inoffensive, and their flesh is esteemed good food. *Encyc.*

ˈ**ARMAMENT**, *n.* [L. *armamenta*, utensils, tackle, from *arma.*]

A body of forces equipped for war; used of a land or naval force. It is more generally used of a naval force, including ships, men and all the necessary furniture for war.

ARMAMENT'ARY, *n.* An armory; a magazine or arsenal. [*Rarely used.*]

ˈ**ARMATURE**, *n.* [L. *armatura.*]

1. Armor; that which defends the body. It comprehends whatever is worn for *defense* of the body, and has been sometimes used for *offensive* weapons. *Armature*, like *arms* and *armor*, is used also of the furniture of animals and vegetables, evidently intended for their protection; as prickles, spines and horns.
2. In *ancient military art*, an exercise performed with missive weapons, as darts, spears and arrows. *Encyc.*

ˈ**ARMED**, *pp.* Furnished with weapons of offense or defense; furnished with the means of security; fortified, in *a moral sense.*

2. In *heraldry*, *armed* is when the beaks, talons, horns, or teeth of beasts and birds of prey are of a different color from the rest of the body. *Chambers.*
3. Capped and cased, as the load stone; that is, set in iron.

An *armed ship* is one which is taken into the service of government for a particular occasion, and armed like a ship of war.

ARME'NIA, *a.* Pertaining to Armenia, a country and formerly, a kingdom, in Asia, divided into Major and Minor. The greater Armenia is now called Turcomania.

ARME'NIAN, *n.* A native of Armenia, or the language of the country. *Sir W. Jones.*

Armenian bole is a species of clay from Armenia, and found in other countries. But the term, being of uncertain signification, is rejected in modern mineralogy. [See *Bole.*] *Cronstedt. Kirwan.*

Armenian stone, a soft blue stone, consisting of calcarious earth or gypsum, with the oxyd of copper. It is too soft to give fire with steel, loses its color when heated, and does not admit of a polish. *Nicholson.*

ARME-PUIS'SANT, *a.* [See *Puissant.*] Powerful in arms. *Weever.*

ˈ**ARMFUL**, *n.* As much as the arms can hold.

ARMGAUNT, *a.* Slender, as the arm. [*Not in use.*] *Shak.*

ˈ**ARMHOLE**, *n.* [*arm* and *hole.*] The cavity under the shoulder, or the armpit. *Bacon.*

2. A hole for the arm in a garment.

ARMIG'EROUS, *a.* [L. *armiger*; *arma* and *gero.*]

Literally, bearing arms. But in present usage, *armiger* is a title of dignity next in degree to a knight. In times of chivalry, it signified an attendant on a knight, or other person of rank, who bore his shield and rendered him other military services. So in antiquity, Abimilech, Saul, &c. had their armor bearers. Judg. ix. 1 Sam. xvi. As had Hector and Achilles. *Homer.* This title, under the French princes, in England, was exchanged, in common usage, for *esquire*, Fr. *ecuyer*, a word of similar import, from *ecu*, L. *scutum*, a shield. *Armiger* is still retained with us, as a title of respect, being the Latin word equivalent to *esquire*, which see. *Spelman.*

ˈ**ARMILLARY**, *a.* [L. *armilla*, a bracelet, from *armus*, the arm.]

Resembling a bracelet, or ring; consisting of rings or circles. It is chiefly applied to an artificial sphere, composed of a number of circles of the mundane sphere, put together in their natural order, to assist in giving a just conception of the constitution of the heavens, and the motions of the celestial bodies. This artificial sphere revolves upon its axis within a horizon, divided into degrees, and movable every way upon a brass supporter. *Encyc.*

ˈ**ARMING**, *ppr.* Equipping with arms; providing with the means of defense or attack; also, preparing for resistance in *a moral sense.*

ˈ**ARMINGS**, *n.* The same as *waist-clothes*, hung about a ship's upper works. *Chambers.*

ARMIN'IAN, *a.* Pertaining to Arminius, or designating his principles.

ARMIN'IAN, *n.* One of a sect or party of Christians, so called from Arminius, or Harmansen, of Holland, who flourished at the close of the 16th century, and beginning of the 17th. The Arminian doctrines are, 1. Conditional election and reprobation, in opposition to absolute predestination. 2. Universal redemption, or that the atonement was made by Christ for all mankind, though none but believers can be partakers of the benefit. 3. That man, in order to exercise true faith, must be regenerated and renewed by the operation of the Holy Spirit, which is the gift of God; but that this grace is not irresistible and may be lost; so that men may relapse from a state of grace and die in their sins. *Encyc.*

ARMIN'IANISM, *n.* The peculiar doctrines or tenets of the Arminians.

ARMIP'OTENCE, *n.* [*arma* and *potentia.* See *Potency.*]

Power in arms. *Johnson.*

ARMIP'OTENT, *a.* Powerful in arms; mighty in battle. *Dryden.*

ARMIS'ONOUS, *a.* [*arma* and *sonus.* See *Sound.*]

Sounding or rustling in arms. *Johnson.*

ˈ**ARMISTICE**, *n.* [L. *arma* and *sisto*, to stand still, Gr. ιςημι; Sp. *armisticio*; It. *armistizio*; Fr. *armistice.*]

A cessation of arms, for a short time, by convention; a truce; a temporary suspension of hostilities by agreement of the parties.

ˈ**ARMLESS**, *a.* Without an arm; destitute of weapons. *Beaumont.*

ˈ**ARMLET**, *n.* [dim. of *arm.*] A little arm; a piece of armor for the arm; a bracelet. *Dryden. Johnson.*

ˈ**ARMOR**, *n.* [from *arm.*]

1. Defensive arms; any habit worn to protect the body in battle; formerly called *harness.* A complete armor formerly consisted of a casque or helmet, a gorget, cuirass, gauntlets, tasses, brassets, cuishes, and covers for the legs to which the spurs were fastened. *Encyc.*

In *English statutes*, armor is used for the whole apparatus of war; including offensive as well as defensive arms. The *statutes of armor* directed what arms every man should provide, 27. Hen. II. and of Westminster. Hence *armor* includes all instruments of war.

Blackstone, B. iv. Ch. 7. B. i. Ch. 13. Hen. Hist. Brit. B. iii. Ch. 1.

2. In *a spiritual sense*, a good conscience, faith and Christian graces are called *armor.* Rom. xiii. Eph. vi. 2 Cor. vi.

Coat-armor is the escutcheon of a person or family, with its several charges and other furniture, as mantling, crest, supporters, motto, &c. *Encyc.*

ˈ**ARMOR-BEARER**, *n.* One who carries the armor of another.

ˈ**ARMORER**, *n.* A maker of armor or arms; a manufacturer of instruments of war. The armorer of a ship has the charge of the arms, to see that they are in a condition fit for service.

ARMO'RIAL, *a.* Belonging to armor, or to the arms or escutcheon of a family; as ensigns *armorial.* *Blackstone.*

ARMOR'IC, **ARMOR'ICAN**, } *a.* [Celtic *ar*, upon, and *mor*, the sea; that is, maritime.]

Designating the northwestern part of France, formerly called *Armorica*, afterward Bretagne, or Britanny. This part of France is peopled by inhabitants who speak a dialect of the Celtic. It is usually supposed their ancestors were refugees or colonists from England.

ARMOR'IC, *n.* The language of the Armoricans; one of the Celtic dialects which have remained to the present times.

ARMOR'ICAN, *n.* A native of Armorica, or Bretagne.

ˈ**ARMORIST**, *n.* One skilled in heraldry.

ˈ**ARMORY**, *n.* A place where arms, and instruments of war are deposited for safe keeping.

2. Armor; defensive arms. *Milton.*
3. Ensigns armorial. *Spenser.*
4. The knowledge of coat-armor; skill in heraldry. *Encyc.*

ˈ**ARMPIT**, *n.* [*arm* and *pit.*] The hollow place or cavity under the shoulder. *Moxon.*

ˈ**ARMS**, *n.* plu. [L. *arma*; Fr. *arme*; Sp. It. *arma.*]

1. Weapons of offense, or armor for defense and protection of the body.
2. War; hostility.

Arms and the man I sing. *Dryden.*

To be in arms, to be in a state of hostility, or in a military life.

To arms is a phrase which denotes a taking arms for war or hostility; particularly, a summoning to war.

To take arms, is to arm for attack or defense.

Bred to arms denotes that a person has been educated to the profession of a soldier.

3. The ensigns armorial of a family; consisting of figures and colors borne in shields, banners, &c., as marks of dignity and distinction, and descending from father to son.
4. In *law*, arms are any thing which a man takes in his hand in anger, to strike or assault another. *Cowel. Blackstone.*
5. In *botany*, one of the seven species of fulcra or props of plants, enumerated by Linne and others. The different species of arms or armor, are prickles, thorns, forks and stings, which seem intended to protect the plants from injury by animals. *Milne. Martyn.*

Fire arms, are such as may be charged with powder, as cannon, muskets, mortars, &c.

A *stand of arms* consists of a musket, bayonet, cartridge-box and belt, with a sword. But for common soldiers a sword is not necessary.

In *falconry*, arms are the legs of a hawk from the thigh to the foot. *Encyc.*

ARMS-END, *n.* At the end of the arms; at a good distance; *a phrase taken from boxers or wrestlers.*

ARMY, *n.* [Fr. *armée*; Ir. *arbhar*, or *armhar*; from the common root of *arm*, *armo*, *arma.*]

1. A collection or body of men armed for war, and organized in companies, battallions, regiments, brigades and divisions, under proper officers. In general, an army in modern times consists of infantry and cavalry, with artillery; although the union of all is not essential to the constitution of an army. Among savages, armies are differently formed.

2. A great number; a vast multitude; as an *army* of locusts or caterpillars. Joel ii. 25.

ARNOLDIST, *n.* A disciple of Arnold of Brescia, who in the 12th century, preached against the Romish Church, for which he was banished; but he was afterwards permitted to return. By his preaching, an insurrection was excited, for which he was condemned and executed. *Encyc.*

'ARNOT, *n.* A name of the bunium, pignut or earthnut.

ARNOT'TO, *n.* The Anotta, which see. Also a tree so called.

'ARNUTS, *n.* Tall oat grass.

ARO'MA, AR'OMA, *n.* [Gr. αρωμα.] The quality of plants which constitutes their fragrance, which is perceived by an agreeable smell, or a warm spicy taste.

AROMAT'IC, AROMAT'ICAL, *a.* Fragrant; spicy; strong-scented; odoriferous; having an agreeable odor.

AROMAT'IC, *n.* A plant which yields a spicy, fragrant smell, or a warm pungent taste; as sage, summer savory, geranium, sweet marjoram, &c. *Milne.*

AR'OMATITE, *n.* A bituminous stone, in smell and color resembling myrrh. *Coxe.*

AROMATIZA'TION, *n.* The act of impregnating or scenting with aroma, or rendering aromatic.

AR'OMATIZE, *v. t.* To impregnate with aroma; to infuse an aromatic odor; to give a spicy scent or taste; to perfume. *Bacon.*

AR'OMATIZED, *pp.* Impregnated with aroma; rendered fragrant.

AR'OMATIZER, *n.* That which communicates an aromatic quality. *Evelyn.*

AR'OMATIZING, *ppr.* Rendering spicy; impregnating with aroma.

ARO'MATOUS, *a.* Containing aroma, or the principle of fragrance.

AR'OPH, *n.* [A contraction of *aroma philosophorum.*]

1. A name by which saffron is sometimes called.

2. A chemical preparation of Paracelsus, formed by sublimation from equal quantities of hematite and sal ammoniac. The word is also used by the same writer as synonymous with *lithontriptic*, a solvent for the stone. *Encyc. Coxe.*

ARO'SE. The past or preterite tense of the verb, to *arise.*

AROUND', *prep.* [*a* and *round.* See *Round.*]

1. About; on all sides; encircling; encompassing; as, a lambent flame *around* his brows. *Dryden.*

2. In *a looser sense*, from place to place; at random.

AROUND', *adv.* In a circle; on every side.

2. In *a looser sense*, at random; without any fixed direction; as, to travel *around* from town to town. [See *Round.*]

ARÖURA, *n.* [Gr.] A Grecian measure of fifty feet. Also, a square measure of half the plethron, a measure not ascertained. The Egyptian aroura was the square of a hundred feet or a hundred cubits. *Encyc. Arbuth.*

AROUSE, *v. t.* *arouz'.* [In Heb חרץ; Ar. حرص haratza, to stir, to excite. It is often contracted into *rouse.* It may be allied to D. *raazen*; G. *brausen*, to rage, to stir, bluster; Class Rs.]

To excite into action, that which is at rest; to stir, or put in motion or exertion, that which is languid; as, to *arouse* one from sleep; to *arouse* the dormant faculties.

AROUS'ED, *pp.* Excited into action; put in motion.

AROUS'ING, *ppr.* Putting in motion; stirring; exciting into action or exertion.

ARÖW, *adv.* [*a* and *row.*] In a row; successively. *Sidney. Shak.*

AROYNT', *adv.* Be gone; away. *Obs.* *Shak.*

ARPEG'GIO, *n.* [From It. *arpa*, a harp.]

The distinct sound of the notes of an instrumental chord, accompanying the voice. *Walker.*

'ARPENT, *n.* [Fr. *arpent*; Norm. *arpen.* In Domesday, it is written *arpennus*, *arpendus*, and *arpent.* Columella mentions that the *arepennis* was equal to half the Roman *juger.* The word is supposed to be corrupted from *arvipendium*, or *aripennium*, the measuring of land with a cord. *Spelman. Lunier.*]

A portion of land in France, ordinarily containing one hundred square rods or perches, each of 18 feet. But the arpent is different in different parts of France. The arpent of Paris contains 900 square toises. It is less than the English acre, by about one seventh. *Spelman. Encyc. Cowel. Arthur Young.*

ARQUEBUSA'DE, *n.* A distilled liquor applied to a bruise. *Chesterfield.*

2. The shot of an arquebuse. *Ash.*

'ARQUEBUSE, H'ARQUEBUSE, *n.* [Fr. from *arquer*, to make crooked, and the Teutonic *bus*, a pipe, a gun; D. *bus*, a tube, pipe, gun; Sw. *bossa*, a gun or cannon. Hence the word signifies a hook gun.]

A hand gun; a species of fire arms, anciently used, which was cocked with a wheel. It carried a ball that weighed nearly two ounces. A larger kind, used in fortresses, carried a ball of three ounces and a half. *Encyc.*

ARQUEBUSIE'R, *n.* A soldier armed with an arquebuse.

AR'RACH, *n.* A plant. See *Orrach.*

ARRACK', *n.* contracted into *rack.* A spirituous liquor imported from the East Indies. The name is said to signify, in the East, any spirituous liquor; but that which usually bears this name is *toddy*, a liquor distilled from the juice of the cocoanut tree, procured by incision. Some persons alledge it to be a spirit distilled from rice or sugar, fermented with the juice of the cocoa-nut.

AR'RAGONITE, *n.* [From Molina in Arragon, Spain.]

In *mineralogy*, a species of carbonate of lime, but not pure, and said to contain 3 or 4 per cent. of carbonate of strontian. It differs from pure carbonate of lime, in hardness, specific gravity, crystaline structure, &c. It is harder than calcarious spar, and exhibits several varieties of structure and form. It is often crystalized, generally in hexahedral prisms or pyramids. The massive varieties have usually a fibrous structure, exhibiting various imitative forms, being sometimes coraloidal. *Haüy. Cleaveland. Stromeyer.*

ARRA'IGN, *v. t.* *arra'ne.* [Norm. *arraner*, *arraisoner*, and *aresner*, to put to answer, to *arraign.* The usual derivation of this word, from Sax. *wregan*, *gewregan*, to accuse, is probably incorrect. It appears to be of Norman origin, and if *s* is radical, it coincides in origin with L. *reus*, contracted from the root of *res.*]

1. To call or set a prisoner at the bar of a court, to answer to the matter charged against him in an indictment or information. When called, the indictment is read to him, and he is put to plead, guilty or not guilty, and to elect by whom he will be tried. *Blackstone.*

2. According to *Law writers*, to set in order; to fit for trial; as, to *arraign* a writ of novel disseisin. *To arraign the assize*, is to cause the tenant to be called to make the plaint, and set the cause in order, that the tenant may be brought to answer. *Cowel.*

3. To accuse; to charge with faults. *Johnson.* More correctly, to call before the bar of reason, or taste; to call in question, for faults, before any tribunal.

> They will not *arraign* you for want of knowledge. *Dryden.*

ARRA'IGN, *n.* *arra'ne.* Arraignment; as, clerk of the *arraigns.* *Blackstone.*

ARRA'IGNED, *pp.* Called before a tribunal to answer, and elect triers; accused; called in question.

ARRA'IGNING, *ppr.* Calling before a court or tribunal; accusing.

ARRA'IGNMENT, *n.* [Norm. *arresnement*, *arraynement.*]

The act of arraigning; the act of calling and setting a prisoner before a court to answer to an accusation, and to choose his triers.

2. Accusation.

3. A calling in question for faults.

ARRA'IMENT, *n.* [See *Array.*] Clothes; garments. We now use *raiment.*

ARRANGE, *v. t.* [Fr. *arranger*, of *ad* and *ranger*, to set in order; Arm. *renega*, *rang*, *rank*, a row or line. See *Rank.*]

1. To put in proper order; to dispose the parts of a whole in the manner intended, or best suited for the purpose; as troops *arranged* for battle.

2. To adjust; to settle; to put in order; to prepare; *a popular use of the word of very general application.*

ARRANĠED, *pp.* Put in order; disposed in the proper order; adjusted.

ARRANĠEMENT, *n.* The act of putting in proper order; the state of being put in order; disposition in suitable form.

2. That which is disposed in order; system of parts disposed in due order.

The interest of that portion of social *arrangement* is in the hands of all those who compose it. *Burke.*

3. Preparatory measure; previous disposition; as, we have made *arrangements* for receiving company.

4. Final settlement; adjustment by agreement; as, the parties have made an *arrangement* between themselves concerning their disputes; *a popular use of the word.*

5. Classification of facts relating to a subject, in a regular, systematic order; as the Linnean *arrangement* of plants.

ARRANĠER, *n.* One that puts in order.

ARRANĠING, *ppr.* Putting in due order or form; adjusting.

AR'RANT *a.* [I know not the origin of this word. It coincides in sense with the W. *carn*, notorious.]

Notorious, in an ill sense; infamous; mere; vile; as an *arrant* rogue or coward.

AR'RANTLY, *adv.* Notoriously, in an ill sense; infamously; impudently; shamefully.

AR'RAS, *n.* [Said to be from Arras, the capital of Artois, in the French Netherlands, where this article is manufactured.]

Tapestry; hangings wove with figures. *Shak.*

ARRA'Y, *n.* [Norm. *araie*, and *arraer*, *arair*, to *array*, settle, prepare; *ray*, a robe and the array or pannel of the Jury; Old Fr. *arroi*, a word contracted; Ir. *earradh*, a suit of armor, furniture, accouterments, wares; It. *arredo*, furniture, implements, rigging; *arredare*, to prepare or equip; Arm. *reiza*, to put in order or arrange; Sp. *arreo*, Port. *arreio*, *arreyo*, array, dress; Port. *arrear*, to dress. Class Rd., and allied to *rod*, *radius*, *ray*. The primary sense is to make straight or right. See *Dress.*]

1. Order; disposition in regular lines; as an army in battle *array*. Hence a posture of defense.

2. Dress; garments disposed in order upon the person. *Dryden.*

3. In *law*, the act of impanneling a jury; or a jury impanneled; that is, a jury set in order by the sheriff, or called man by man. *Blackstone. Cowel.*

Commission of array, in English history, was a commission given by the prince to officers in every county, to muster and *array* the inhabitants, or see them in a condition for war. *Blackstone.*

ARRA'Y, *v. t.* To place or dispose in order, as troops for battle.

2. To deck or dress; to adorn with dress; it is applied especially to dress of a splendid kind.

Array thyself with glory. Job, xl.
Pharaoh *arrayed* Joseph with fine linen. Gen. xli.

3. To set a jury in order for the trial of a cause; that is, to call them man by man. *Blackstone. Cowel.*

4. To envelop.

In gelid caves with horrid glooms *arrayed*. *Trumbull.*

ARRA'YED, *pp.* Set in order, or in lines; arranged in order for attack or defense; dressed; adorned by dress; impanneled, as a jury; enveloped.

ARRA'YER, *n.* One who arrays. In *English history*, an officer who had a commission of array, to put soldiers of a county in a condition for military service.

ARRA'YING, *ppr.* Setting in order; putting on splendid raiment; impanneling.

ARRE'AR, *adv.* [Fr. *arriere*, behind. In some of its uses it has the sense of *lower*, *inferior*. [See *Arriere-ban.*] Sp. and Port. *arriar*, to lower sail; Arm. *reor*, *revr*, or *refr*, the fundament; W. *rhevyr*, id., from *rhev*, thick. Lunier deduces *arrear* and *arriere* from L. *ad* and *retro*. But the derivation from the Celtic seems most probably correct.]

Behind; at the hinder part. *Spenser. In this sense obsolete.* But from this use, we retain the word as a noun in the phrase, *in arrear*, to signify *behind* in payment.

ARRE'AR, *n.* That which is *behind* in payment, or which remains unpaid, though due. It is generally used in the plural, as the *arrears* of rent, wages and taxes; and supposes a part of the money already paid.

ARRE'ARAĠE, *n.* [*arre r* and the common French termination *age.*]

Arrears; any sum of money remaining unpaid, after previous payment of a part. A person may be *in arrear* for the whole amount of a debt; but *arrears* and *arrearage* imply that a part has been paid.

ARREƇT', **ARREƇT'ED**, *a.* [L. *arrectus*, raised, erect, from *arrigo*. See *Reach.*]

Erect; attentive; as a person listening. *Akenside.*

ARRENTA'TION, *n.* [Sp. *arrendar*, to rent, or take by lease; of *ad* and *reddo*, to return. See *Rent.*]

In *the forest laws of England*, a licensing the owner of land in a forest, to inclose it with a small ditch and low hedge, in consideration of a yearly rent. *Cowel.*

ARREPTI''TIOUS, *a.* [L. *arreptus*, of *ad* and *rapio*, to snatch. See *Rapacious.*]

1. Snatched away.

2. [*ad* and *repo*, to creep. See *Creep.*] Crept in privily. *Johnson. Bailey.*

ARREST', *v. t.* [Fr. *arrêter*, for *arrester*; Sp. *arrestar*; It. *arrestare*; L. *resto*, to stop; W. *araws*, *arosi*, to stay, wait, dwell; Eng. to *rest*. See *Rest.*]

1. To obstruct; to stop; to check or hinder motion; as, to *arrest* the current of a river; to *arrest* the senses.

2. To take, seize or apprehend by virtue of a warrant from authority; as, to *arrest* one for debt or for a crime.

3. To seize and fix; as, to *arrest* the eyes or attention.

The appearance of such a person in the world, and at such a period, ought to *arrest* the consideration of every thinking mind. *Buckminster.*

4. To hinder, or restrain; as, to *arrest* the course of justice.

ARREST', *n.* The taking or apprehending of a person by virtue of a warrant from authority. An arrest is made by seizing or touching the body.

2. Any seizure, or taking by power, physical or moral.

3. A stop, hindrance or restraint.

4. In *law*, an *arrest* of judgment is the staying or stopping of a judgment after verdict, for causes assigned. Courts have power to arrest judgment for intrinsic causes appearing upon the face of the record; as when the declaration varies from the original writ; when the verdict differs materially from the pleadings; or when the case laid in the declaration is not sufficient in point of law, to found an action upon. The motion for this purpose is called a motion in *arrest* of judgment. *Blackstone.*

5. A mangy humor between the ham and pastern of the hind legs of a horse. *Johnson.*

ARRESTA'TION, *n.* The act of arresting; an arrest, or seizure.

ARREST'ED, *pp.* Seized; apprehended; stopped; hindered; restrained.

ARREST'ER, **ARREST'OR**, *n.* One who arrests. In *Scots law*, the person at whose suit an arrest is made.

ARREST'ING, *ppr.* Seizing; staying; hindering; restraining.

ARREST'MENT, *n.* In *Scots law*, an arrest, or detention of a criminal, till he finds caution or surety, to stand trial.

Also the order of a judge by which a debtor to the arrestor's debtor is prohibited to make payment, till the debt due to the arrestor is paid or secured.

ARRET', *n.* [Contracted from *arresté*, Fr. *arrêté*, fixed.]

The decision of a court, tribunal or council; a decree published; the edict of a sovereign prince.

ARRET', *v. t.* To assign; to allot. *Obs.* *Spenser.*

ARRI'DE, *v. t.* [L. *arrideo.*] To laugh at; to please well. [*Not in use.*] *B. Jonson.*

ARRIE'RE, *n.* The last body of an army; now called *rear*, which see.

Arriere-ban, or *ban* and *arriere ban*. This phrase is defined to be a general proclamation of the French kings, by which not only their immediate feudatories, but *their* vassals, were summoned to take the field for war. In this case, *arriere* is the French word signifying those who are last or behind, and *ban* is proclamation. [See *Ban.*]

Arriere-fee or fief. A fee or fief dependent on a superior fee, or a fee held of a feudatory.

Arriere vassal. The vassal of a vassal.

ARRI'VAL, *n.* The coming to, or reaching a place, from a distance, whether by water, as in its original sense, or by land.

2. The attainment or gaining of any object, by effort, agreement, practice or study.

ARRI'VANCE, *n.* Company coming. [*Not used.*] *Shak.*

2. Arrival; a reaching in progress. *Obs.* *Brown.*

ARRI'VE, *v. i.* [Fr. *arriver*; Arm. *arrivont*, *arrivein*; It. *arrivare*; Sp. Port. *arribar*; of *ad* and Fr. *rive*, the shore or sloping bank of a river; Sp. *ribera*; L. *ripa*; Sans. *arivi*. In Irish, *airbhe* is *ribs*. It appears that *rib*, *rive* and *ripa* are radically one word; in like manner, *costa*, a rib, and *coast* are radically the same.]

1. Literally, to come to the shore, or bank.

Hence to come to or reach in progress by water, followed by *at*. We *arrived* at Havre de Grace, July 10, 1824. N. W.

2. To come to or reach by traveling on land; as, the post *arrives* at 7 o'clock.

3. To reach a point by progressive motion; to gain or compass by effort, practice, study, enquiry, reasoning or experiment; as, to *arrive* at an unusual degree of excellence or wickedness; to *arrive* at a conclusion.

4. To happen or occur.

He to whom this glorious death *arrives*. *Waller.*

ARRI'VE, *v. t.* To reach. [*Not in use.*] *Shak.*

ARRI'VING, *ppr.* Coming to, or reaching, by water or land; gaining by research, effort or study.

ARRO'BA, *n.* [Arabic.] A weight in Portugal of thirty two pounds; in Spain, of twenty five pounds. Also a Spanish measure of thirty two Spanish pints. *Sp. Dictionary.*

AR'ROGANCE, *n.* [L. *arrogantia*, from *arrogo*, to claim; of *ad* and *rogo*, to beg, or desire; Fr. *arrogance;* Arm. *roguentez;* Sp. Port. *arrogancia;* It. *arroganza.* See *Arrogate.*]

The act or quality of taking much upon one's self; that species of pride which consists in exorbitant claims of rank, dignity, estimation or power, or which exalts the worth or importance of the person to an undue degree; proud contempt of others; conceitedness; presumption.

I will cause the *arrogance* of the proud to cease. Is. xiii. 1 Sam. ii. Prov. viii.

AR'ROGANCY, *n.* Arrogance. [*This orthography is less usual.*]

AR'ROGANT, *a.* Assuming; making or having the disposition to make exorbitant claims of rank or estimation; giving one's self an undue degree of importance; haughty; conceited; *applied to persons.*

2. Containing arrogance; marked with arrogance; proceeding from undue claims or self importance; *applied to things;* as *arrogant* pretensions or behavior.

AR'ROGANTLY, *adv.* In an arrogant manner; with undue pride or self importance.

AR'ROGANTNESS, *n.* Arrogance. [*Little used.*]

AR'ROGATE, *v. t.* [L. *arrogo*, of *ad* and *rogo;* Fr. *arroger;* Sp. Port. *arrogar*; It. *arrogare.* The primary sense of *rogo*, to ask, is to reach or stretch.]

To assume, demand or challenge more than is proper; to make undue claims, from vanity or false pretensions to right or merit; as, the Pope *arrogated* dominion over kings.

AR'ROGATED, *pp.* Claimed by undue pretensions.

AR'ROGATING, *ppr.* Challenging or claiming more power or respect than is just or reasonable.

ARROGA'TION, *n.* The act of arrogating, or making exorbitant claims; the act of taking more than one is justly entitled to.

AR'ROGATIVE, *a.* Assuming or making undue claims and pretensions. *More.*

ARROND'ISMENT, *n.* [from Fr. *arrondir*, to make round; of *ad* and *rond*, round.]

A circuit; a district; a division or portion of territory, in France, for the exercise of a particular jurisdiction.

ARRO'SION, *n.* *s* as *z.* [L. *arrodo.*] A gnawing.

AR'ROW, *n.* [Sax. *arewa.* Qu. *ray*, *radius*, a shoot.]

1. A missive weapon of offense, straight, slender, pointed and barbed, to be shot with a bow.

2. In *scripture*, the *arrows of God* are the apprehensions of his wrath, which pierce and pain the conscience. Job vi. Ps. xxxviii. In a like figurative manner, *arrows* represent the judgments of God, as thunder, lightning, tempests and famine. 2 Sam. xxii. Ez. v. Hab. iii. The word is used also for slanderous words and malicious purposes of evil men. Ps. xi. Prov. xxv. Jer. ix. Ps. lxiv. *Cruden. Brown.*

AR'ROW-GRASS, *n.* A plant or genus of plants; the Triglochin. *Muhlenberg.*

AR'ROW-HEAD, *n.* The head of an arrow.

2. Sagittaria; a genus of aquatic plants, so called from the resemblance of the leaves to the point of an arrow.

AR'ROW-ROOT, *n.* The Maranta; a genus of plants, natives of the Indies. The Indians are said to employ the roots of the *arundinacea*, in extracting the virus of poisoned arrows; whence the name. There are several species. From the root of the *arundinacea*, or starch-plant, is obtained the arrow-root of the shops. *Encyc.*

2. The starch of the maranta, or arrow-root, a nutritive medicinal food.

AR'ROWY, *a.* Consisting of arrows. *Milton.*

2. Formed like an arrow. *Cowper.*

'ARSE, *n.* *àrs.* [Sax. *earse;* D. *aars;* G. *arsch;* Persic, *arsit*, or *arst.*] The buttocks or hind part of an animal.

To hang an arse, is to lag behind; to be sluggish, or tardy.

'ARSE-SMART, *n.* The vulgar name of a species of polygonum, or knot-grass.

'ARSENAL, *n.* [Sp. Port. It. Fr. Arm. a magazine or repository of stores; in Italian and Spanish, a dock or dock-yard; probably L. *arx navalis*, a naval citadel or repository.]

A repository or magazine of arms and military stores, whether for land or naval service.

ARSE'NIAC or ARSEN'ICAL ACID. Arsenic combined with a greater proportion of oxygen, than in the arsenious acid. It is called *arsenic* acid by most authors.

ARSE'NIATE, *n.* A neutral salt, formed by arsenical acid combined with any metallic, earthy or saline base. *Lavoisier. Fourcroy.*

'ARSENIC, *n.* [Ar. زِرْنِق zirnakon; Syr. ܙܪܢܝܟܐ zarnika; Gr. αρσενικον; L. *arsenicum;* Sp. *arsenico;* Fr. *arsenic.*]

Arsenic, as it is usually seen in the shops, is not a metal, but an oxyd, from which the metal may be easily obtained by mixing it with half its weight of black flux, and introducing the mixture into a Florence flask, gradually raised to a red heat, in a sand bath. A brilliant metallic sublimate of pure arsenic collects in the upper part of the flask. Arsenic is of a steel blue color, quite brittle, and the metal with all its compounds, is a virulent poison, vulgarly called *rats-bane.* It forms alloys with most of the metals. Combined with sulphur it forms orpiment or realgar, which are the yellow and red sulphurets of arsenic. Orpiment is the true *arsenicum* of the ancients. Plin. 34, 18. Native orpiment appears in yellow, brilliant, and seemingly talcky masses of various sizes; realgar is red, of different shades, and often crystalized in needles. Arsenic is also found as a mineralizer in cobalt, antimony, copper, iron and silver ores. It is brought chiefly from the cobalt works in Saxony, where zaffer is made. *Webster's Manual. Fourcroy. Nicholson. Cyc.*

ARSEN'ICAL, *a.* Belonging to arsenic; consisting of or containing arsenic.

ARSEN'ICATE, *v. t.* To combine with arsenic.

ARSEN'ICATED, *a.* Combined with arsenic.

ARSE'NIOUS, *a.* Pertaining to, or containing arsenic. The *arsenious* acid, or white oxyd of arsenic, is a combination of arsenic with a less proportion of oxygen than in the arseniac acid.

'ARSENITE, *n.* A salt formed by the arsenious acid, with a base.

'ARSHINE, *n.* A Russian measure of two feet, four inches and 242 decimals. This seems to be the Chinese *arschin*, of which four make three yards English. *Tooke's Russia. Encyc.*

'ARSON, *n.* *àrsn.* [Norm. Fr. *arsine*, *arseun;* from L. *ardeo*, *arsum*, to burn.]

In *law*, the malicious burning of a dwelling house or outhouse of another man, which by the common law is felony. The definition of this crime is varied by statutes in different countries and states. In Connecticut, the burning not only of a dwelling house or contiguous building, but of a ship or other vessel, is declared to be arson, if human life is thereby destroyed or put to hazard.

'ART. The second person, indicative mode, present tense, of the substantive verb *am;* but from *were*, Sw. *vara*, Dan. *værer.*

'ART, *n.* [L. *ars*, *artis;* probably contracted from the root of W. *cerz*, Ir. *ceard.* The radical sense is *strength*, from *stretching*, *straining*, the primary sense of strength and power, and hence of skill. See an analogy in *can.*]

1. The disposition or modification of things by human skill, to answer the purpose intended. In this sense *art* stands opposed to *nature.* *Bacon. Encyc.*

2. A system of rules, serving to facilitate the performance of certain actions; opposed to *science*, or to speculative principles; as the *art* of building or engraving. Arts are divided into *useful* or *mechanic*, and *liberal* or *polite.* The mechanic arts are those in which the hands and body are more concerned than the mind; as in making clothes, and utensils. These arts are called *trades.* The liberal or polite arts are those in which the mind or imagination is chiefly concerned; as poetry, music and painting.

In America, literature and the elegant *arts* must grow up side by side with the coarser plants of daily necessity. *Irving.*

3. Skill, dexterity, or the power of performing certain actions, acquired by experience, study or observation; as, a man has the *art* of managing his business to advantage.

ARTEMIS'IA, *n.* Mug-wort, southern-wood, and wormwood; a genus of plants of numerous species. Of these, the absinthium or common wormwood is well known.

ARTE'RIAL, *a.* [See *Artery.*] Pertaining to an artery or the arteries; as *arterial* action.

2. Contained in an artery; as *arterial blood.*

ARTERIOT'OMY, *n.* [Gr. αρτηρια, an artery, and τομη, a cutting.]

The opening of an artery by the lancet, for the purpose of letting blood.

ARTERY, *n.* [Gr. αρτηρια, from αηρ, air, and τηρεω, to preserve or contain; so called, from the opinion of the ancients, that the arteries contained or circulated air. The term was also applied to the trachea or wind pipe, *arteria aspera.* In Ger. *luft-ader*, air-vein, is the name for artery; in Dutch, *slag-ader*, stroke-vein; in Swed. *puls-ader*, pulse-vein; Dan. *puls-aare*, pulse vein, that is, the beating vein.]

A cylindrical vessel or tube, which conveys the blood from the heart to all parts of the body. There are two principal arteries; the *aorta*, which rises from the left ventricle and ramifies through the whole body; and the *pulmonary artery*, which conveys the blood from the right ventricle to the lungs, to undergo respiration. An artery is composed of three coats; the outer consists of condensed cellular membrane, and is supplied with numerous blood vessels and nerves; the middle coat consists of circular fibers, generally supposed to be muscular; the inner coat, thin, smooth, and dense, confines the blood within its canal, and facilitates its motion. *Parr. Cyc.*

ARTFUL, *a.* [See *Art.*] Performed with art or skill. *Dryden.*

2. Artificial, as opposed to *natural.* *Johnson.*

3. Cunning; practicing art, or stratagem; crafty; as an *artful* boy. [*This is the most usual sense.*]

4. Proceeding from art or craft; as an *artful* scheme.

'ARTFULLY, *adv.* With art, or cunning; skilfully; dextrously.

'ARTFULNESS, *n.* Art; craft; cunning; address.

ARTHRIT'IC, } *a.* Pertaining to the
ARTHRIT'ICAL, } joints, or to the gout; affecting the joints.

ARTHRIT'IS, *n.* [Gr. αρθριτις, from αρθρον, a joint. It seems to be of the same family as *artus*, a limb.]

In *a general sense*, any painful disease of the joints; but more particularly, the gout, an hereditary, intermitting disease, usually affecting the small joints; sometimes the stomach. *Coxe. Quincy.*

ARTHRO'DIA, *n.* [from αρθροω, to frame or articulate.]

1. A species of articulation, in which the head of one bone is received into the shallow socket of another; as the humerus and the scapula. *Encyc.*

2. In *natural history*, a genus of imperfect crystals, found in complex masses, and forming long single pyramids, with very short and slender columns. *Encyc.*

'ARTIC. This word is by mistake used by some authors for *arctic.*

'ARTICHOKE, *n.* [Qu. the first syllable of Gr. αρτυτικα. Fr. *artichaut*; Arm. *artichauden*; Sp. *alcachofa*; Port. *alcachofra*; It. *carciofo, carciofano*, or *carciofalo.* The first syllable is probably the L. *carduus*, chard, thistle, corrupted. D. *artichok*; G. *artischoke*; Dan. *artiskok.*]

A plant somewhat resembling a thistle, with a dilated, imbricated and prickly calyx. The head is large, rough and scaly, on an upright stalk. It is composed of numerous, oval scales, inclosing the florets, sitting on a broad receptacle, which, with the fleshy base of the scales, is the eatable part of the plant. *Encyc. Miller.*

The *Jerusalem artichoke* is a species of sunflower or helianthus.

'ARTICLE, *n.* [L. *articulus*, a joint, from *artus*; Gr. αρθρον.]

1. A single clause in a contract, account, system of regulations, treaty, or other writing; a particular separate charge or item, in an account; a term, condition, or stipulation, in a contract. In short, a distinct part of a writing, instrument or discourse, consisting of two or more particulars; as, *articles* of agreement; an account consisting of many *articles.*

2. A point of faith; a doctrinal point or proposition in theology; as the thirty-nine *articles.*

3. A distinct part.

> Upon each *article* of human duty. *Paley.*

4. A particular commodity, or substance; as, an *article* of merchandize; salt is a necessary *article.* In common usage, this word is applied to almost every separate substance or material.

> The *articles* which compose the blood. *Darwin.*

5. A point of time. [*Not in use.*] *Clarendon.*

6. In *botany*, that part of a stalk or stem, which is between two joints. *Milne.*

7. In *grammar*, an adjective used before nouns, to limit or define their application; as *hic, ille, ipse*, in Latin; ο, η, το, in Greek; *the, this, that*, in English; *le, la, les*, in French; *il, la, lo*, in Italian. The primary use of these adjectives was to convert an indeterminate name into a determinate one; or to limit the application of a common name, to a specific, known, or certain individual. But *article* being an improper term to express the true signification, I make use of *definitive*, which see.

'ARTICLE, *v. t.* To draw up in distinct particulars; as, to *article* the errors or follies of a man. *Taylor.*

2. To accuse or charge by an exhibition of *articles.* "He shall be *articled* against in the High Court of admiralty." Stat. 33. George III.

3. To bind by articles of covenant or stipulation; as, to *article* an apprentice to a mechanic.

'ARTICLE, *v. i.* [*supra.*] To agree by articles; to stipulate. *Donne.*

'ARTICLED, *pp.* Drawn up in particulars; accused or bound by articles.

ARTIC'ULAR, *a.* [L. *articularis.*] Belonging to the joints; as, the gout is an *articular* disease.

ARTIC'ULATE, *a.* [L. *articulatus*, jointed, distinct.]

Formed by jointing or articulation of the organs of speech; *applied to sound.* An *articulate* sound is made by closing and opening the organs of speech. The junction or closing of the organs forms a joint or articulation, as in the syllables *ab, ad, ap*; in passing from one articulation to another, the organs are, or may be opened, and a vowel is uttered, as in *attune*; and the different articulations, with the intervening vocal sounds, form what is called *articulate sounds*; sounds distinct, separate, and modified by articulation or jointing. This articulation constitutes the prominent difference between the human voice and that of brutes. Brutes open the mouth and make vocal sounds, but have, either not at all, or very imperfectly, the power of articulation.

2. Expressed in articles, or in separate particulars. [*Not used.*] *Brown.*

3. Jointed; formed with joints. *Botany.*

ARTIC'ULATE, *v. t.* To utter articulate sounds; to utter distinct syllables or words.

2. To draw up or write in separate particulars. [*Not used.*] *Shak.*

3. To treat, stipulate or make terms. [*Not used.*] *Shak.*

4. To joint. *Smith.*

ARTIC'ULATED, *pp.* Uttered distinctly in syllables or words.

2. Jointed; having joints, as a plant.

ARTIC'ULATELY, *adv.* With distinct utterance of syllables or words.

2. Article by article; in detail. *Paley.*

ARTIC'ULATENESS, *n.* The quality of being articulate.

ARTIC'ULATING, *ppr.* Uttering in distinct syllables or words.

ARTICULA'TION, *n.* In *anatomy*, the joining or juncture of the bones. This is of three kinds: 1st, *diarthrosis*, or a movable connection, including enarthrosis, or the ball and socket joint; arthrodia, which is the same, but more superficial; ginglymus, or hinge-like joint; and trochoid, or the wheel and axle: 2d, *synarthrosis*, immovable connection, as by suture, or junction by serrated margins; harmony, or union by straight margins; and gomphosis, like a nail driven in a board, as the teeth in their sockets: 3d, *symphysis*, or union by means of another substance; as synchondrosis, union by a cartilage; syssarcosis, union by muscular fibres; synneurosis, union by a tendon; syndesmosis, union by ligaments; and synostosis, union by a bony substance. *Quincy. Coxe.*

2. In *botany*, the connection of the parts of a plant by joints; also the nodes or joints, as in cane and maize. *Encyc.*

3. The forming of words; a distinct utterance of syllables and words by the human voice, by means of closing and opening the organs.

4. A consonant; a letter noting a jointing or closing of the organs.

'ARTIFICE, *n.* [L. *artificium*, from *ars*, art, and *facio*, to make.]

Stratagem; an artful or ingenious device, in

a good or bad sense. In a bad sense, it corresponds with trick, or fraud.

2. Art; trade; skill acquired by science or practice. [*Rarely used.*]

ARTIF'ICER, *n.* [L. *artifex*, from *ars*, and *facio.*]

1. An artist; a mechanic or manufacturer; one whose occupation requires skill or knowledge of a particular kind; as a silversmith, or sadler.

2. One who makes or contrives; an inventor; as an *artificer* of fraud or lies. *Milton.*

3. A cunning, or artful fellow. [*Not used.*] *Ben Jonson.*

ARTIFI''CIAL, *a.* Made or contrived by art, or by human skill and labor, in opposition to *natural;* as *artificial* heat or light; an *artificial* magnet.

2. Feigned; fictitious; not genuine or natural; as *artificial* tears.

3. Contrived with skill or art.

4. Cultivated; not indigenous; not being of spontaneous growth; as *artificial* grasses. *Gibbon.*

Artificial arguments, in rhetoric, are arguments invented by the speaker, in distinction from laws, authorities and the like, which are called *inartificial* arguments or proofs. *Johnson.*

Artificial lines, on a sector or scale, are lines so contrived as to represent the logarithmic sines and tangents, which, by the help of the line of numbers, solve, with tolerable exactness, questions in trigonometry, navigation, &c.

Artificial numbers, the same with logarithms. *Chambers. Encyc.*

ARTIFICIAL'ITY, *n.* The quality of being artificial; appearance of art. *Shenstone.*

ARTIFI''CIALLY, *adv.* By art, or human skill and contrivance; hence, with good contrivance; with art or ingenuity.

ARTIFI''CIALNESS, *n.* The quality of being artificial.

ARTIL'LERY, *n.* This word has no plural. [Fr. *artillerie;* It. *artiglieria;* Sp. *artilleria.* In Fr. *artilleur, artillier*, is a matross; Sp. *artillar*, to mount cannon. In Armoric, *artillery* is *artilhiry*, and an artist is *artilher.* In Norm. Fr. *artillery* is written *articlarie.* The Armoric unites this word with *art, artist*, indicating that the primary sense is, instruments, things formed by *art* or rather prepared by art, preparations.]

1. In a general sense, offensive weapons of war. Hence it was formerly used for bows and arrows.

And Jonathan gave his *artillery* to his lad. 1 Sam. xx.

But in present usage, appropriately,

2. Cannon; great guns; ordnance, including guns, mortars and grenades, with their furniture of carriages, balls, bombs and shot of all kinds.

3. In a more extended sense, the word includes powder, cartridges, matches, utensils, machines of all kinds, and horses that belong to a train of artillery.

4. The men who manage cannon and mortars, including matrosses, gunners, bombardiers, cannoniers, or by whatever name they are called, with the officers, engineers and persons who supply the artillery with implements and materials. *Encyc.*

'ARTISAN, *n.* *s* as *z.* [Fr. from L. *ars.* See *Art.*]

An artist; one skilled in any art, mystery or trade; a handicrafts-man; a mechanic; a tradesman.

'ARTIST, *n.* [Fr. *artiste;* It. *artista;* from L. *ars.* See *Art.*]

1. One skilled in an art or trade; one who is master or professor of a manual art; a good workman in any trade.

2. A skilful man; not a novice.

3. In *an academical sense*, a proficient in the faculty of arts; a philosopher. *Encyc.*

4. One skilled in the fine arts; as a painter, sculptor, architect, &c.

'ARTLESS, *a.* Unskilful; wanting art, knowledge or skill. *Dryden.*

2. Free from guile, art, craft or stratagem; simple; sincere; unaffected; undesigning; as an *artless* mind.

3. Contrived without skill or art; as an *artless* tale.

'ARTLESSLY, *adv.* Without art or skill; in an artless manner.

2. Without guile; naturally; sincerely; unaffectedly. *Pope.*

'ARTLESSNESS, *n.* The quality of being void of art or guile; simplicity; sincerity; unaffectedness.

AR'TOTYRITE, *n.* [of Gr. αρτος, bread, and τυρος, cheese.]

One of a sect of heretics, in the primitive church, who celebrated the eucharist with bread and cheese, alledging that the first oblations of men were not only the fruit of the earth, but of their flocks. They admitted females to the priesthood and episcopacy. *Encyc.*

'ARTS-MAN, *n.* A learned man. *Obs.* *Shak.*

ARUNDE'LIAN, *a.* Pertaining to Arundel, as *Arundelian* marbles. The Arundelian marbles are ancient stones, containing a chronological detail of the principal events of Greece, from Cecrops, who lived about 1582 years before Christ, to the archonship of Diognetus, before Christ 264. The engraving was done in Paros, and the chronology is called the *Parian Chronicle.* These stones are called Arundelian from the Earl of Arundel, who employed William Petty to procure relics of antiquity in the East, in 1624. These, with other curiosities, were purchased, and by the Earl's grandson presented to the University of Oxford. Their antiquity and even their authenticity has been questioned. *Encyc.*

ARUNDINA'CEOUS, *a.* [L. *arundo*, a reed.]

Pertaining to a reed; resembling the reed or cane.

ARUNDIN'EOUS, *a.* Abounding with reeds.

ARU'RA, *n.* [Gr. αρουρα.] Literally, as authors suppose, a plowed field. According to Herodotus, and Suidas, the *arura* of Egypt, was a piece of ground fifty feet square. Others make it a square of 100 cubits; others of 100 feet. The Grecian aroura was a square measure of half the plethron. [See *Aroura.*] *Encyc. Herod. Euterpe.*

ARUS'PEX, *n.* [L.] A soothsayer. *Dryden.*

ARUS'PICE, *n.* written also *haruspice.* [L. *aruspex*, or *haruspex*, a soothsayer, or diviner, who attempted to foretell events by consulting the entrails of beasts slain in sacrifice. Qu. Teut. *orf, yrf;* Eth. አርዌ arwe, cattle, and L. *specio*, to view.]

A priest, in ancient Rome, whose business was to inspect the entrails of victims, killed in sacrifice, and by them to foretel future events.

ARUS'PICY, *n.* The act of prognosticating by inspection of the entrails of beasts, slain in sacrifice. *Butler.*

AS, *adv. az.* [Pers. آسا asa, like, similar, *as;* Gr. ως. Qu. Fr. *aussi.* But more probably the English word is contracted from *als*, G. and D. It corresponds in sense with the Persian.]

1. Literally, like; even; similar. "Ye shall be *as* Gods, knowing good and evil." "*As* far *as* we can see," that is, like far, equally far. Hence it may be explained by *in like manner;* as, do *as* you are commanded.

2. It was formerly used where we now use *that.* *Obs.*

The relations are so uncertain *as* they require a great deal of examination. *Bacon.*

3. It was formerly used for *as if.* *Obs.*

He lies, *as* he his bliss did know. *Waller.*

4. While; during; at the same time. "He trembled *as* he spoke." But in most of its uses, it is resolvable into *like, equal, even,* or *equally, in like manner.* In some phrases, it must be considered a nominative word, or other words must be supplied. "Appoint to office such men *as* deserve public confidence." This phrase may be elliptical for "such men *as* those who deserve public confidence."

As seems, in some cases, to imply the sense of proportion. "In general, men are more happy, *as* they are less involved in public concerns."

As, in a subsequent part of a sentence, answers to *such;* give us *such* things *as* you please; and in a preceding part of a sentence, has *so* to answer to it; *as* with the people, *so* with the priest.

AS, *n.* [L.] A Roman weight of 12 ounces, answering to the libra or pound.

2. A Roman coin, originally of a pound weight; but reduced, after the first Punic war, to two ounces; in the second Punic war, to one ounce; and by the Papirian law, to half an ounce. It was originally stamped with the figure of a sheep, sow, or ox; and afterwards with a Janus, on one side, and on the reverse, a rostrum or prow of a ship.

3. An integer; a whole or single thing. Hence the English *ace.* Hence the Romans used the word for the whole inheritance; hæres ex *asse*, an heir to the whole estate. *Encyc.*

ASA, a corruption of *lasar*, an ancient name of a gum. [See *Ooze.*]

ASA-DULCIS, the same as *benzoin.*

ASA-FET'IDA, *n.* [*Asa*, gum, and L. *fœtidus*, fetid.]

A fetid gum-resin, from the East Indies. It is the concrete juice of a large umbelliferous plant, much used in Medicine, as an antispasmodic. *Encyc.*

ASBES'TINE, *a.* [See *Asbestus.*]

Pertaining to asbestus, or partaking of its nature and qualities; incombustible.

ASBES'TINITE, *n.* [See *Asbestus.*] The actinolite or strahlstein. *Kirwan.*

Calciferous abestinite; a variety of steatite. *Kirwan.*

ASBES'TUS, ASBES'TOS, *n.* [Gr. ασβεςος, inextinguishable; of α neg. and σβεννυμι, to extinguish.]

A mineral, which has frequently the appearance of a vegetable substance. It is always fibrous, and its fibers sometimes appear to be prismatic crystals. They are sometimes delicate, flexible, and elastic; at other times, stiff and brittle. Its powder is soft to the touch; its colors are some shade of white, gray or green, passing into brown, red or black. It is incombustible, and has been wrought into a soft, flexible cloth, which was formerly used as a shroud for dead bodies. It has been also manufactured into incombustible paper, and wicks for lamps. *Kirwan. Encyc. Cleaveland.*

Ligniform asbestus is a variety of a brown color, of a splintery fracture, and if broken across, presents an irregular filamentous structure, like wood. *Kirwan.*

ASCA'RIS, *n.* plu. *ascar'ides.* [Gr.]

In *zoology*, a genus of intestinal worms. The body is cylindrical, and tapering at the ends. It includes two of the most common worms in the human intestines, the *ascarides*, and the *lumbricoides.*

ASCEND', *v. i.* [L. *ascendo*, from *scando*, to mount or climb; W. *esgyn*, to rise; *cyn*, first, chief. It has the same elements as *begin.*]

1. To move upwards; to mount; to go up; to rise, whether in air or water, or upon a material object.

2. To rise, in a figurative sense; to proceed from an inferior to a superior degree, from mean to noble objects, from particulars to generals, &c.

3. To proceed from modern to ancient times; to recur to former ages; as, our inquiries *ascend* to the remotest antiquity.

4. In a corresponding sense, to proceed in a line towards ancestors; as, to *ascend* to our first progenitors.

5. To rise as a star; to proceed or come above the horizon.

6. In *music*, to rise in vocal utterance; to pass from any note to one more acute.

ASCEND', *v. t.* To go or move upwards upon, as to *ascend* a hill or ladder; or to climb, as to *ascend* a tree.

ASCEND'ABLE, *a.* That may be ascended.

ASCEND'ANT, *n.* Superiority or commanding influence; as, one man has the *ascendant* over another.

2. An ancestor, or one who precedes in genealogy, or degrees of kindred; opposed to *descendant.*

3. Highth; elevation. [*Little used.*] *Temple.*

4. In *astrology*, that degree of the ecliptic which rises above the horizon at the time of one's birth. That part of the ecliptic at any particular time above the horizon, supposed to have influence on a person's life and fortune. *Johnson. Encyc.*

ASCEND'ANT, *a.* Superior; predominant; surpassing.

2. In *astrology*, above the horizon.

ASCEND'ED, *pp.* or *a.* Risen; mounted up; gone to heaven.

ASCEND'ENCY, *n.* Power; governing or controlling influence.

Custom has an *ascendency* over the understanding. *Watts.*

ASCEND'ING, *ppr.* Rising; moving upwards; proceeding from the less to the greater; proceeding from modern to ancient, from grave to more acute. A star is said to be *ascending*, when rising above the horizon, in any parallel of the equator.

Ascending latitude is the latitude of a planet, when moving towards the North pole.

Ascending node is that point of a planet's orbit, wherein it passes the ecliptic to proceed northward. It is also called the *northern node.*

Ascending vessels, in anatomy, are those which carry the blood upward or toward the superior parts of the body.

ASCEN'SION, *n.* [L. *ascensio.*]

1. The act of ascending; a rising. It is frequently applied to the visible elevation of our Savior to Heaven.

2. The thing rising, or ascending. [*Not authorized.*]

3. In *astronomy*, ascension is either *right* or *oblique.* *Right ascension* of the sun or of a star, is that degree of the equinoctial, counted from the beginning of Aries, which rises with the sun or star, in a right sphere. *Oblique ascension* is an arch of the equator, intercepted between the first point of Aries, and that point of the equator which rises together with a star, in an oblique sphere. *Johnson.*

ASCENSION-DAY, *n.* A festival of some christian churches, held ten days or on the Thursday but one, before Whitsuntide, which is called Holy Thursday, in commemoration of our Savior's ascension into heaven, after his resurrection.

Ascensional difference is the difference between the right and oblique ascension of the same point on the surface of the sphere. *Chambers.*

ASCEN'SIVE, *a.* Rising; tending to rise, or causing to rise. *Journ. of Science.*

ASCENT', *n.* [L. *ascensus.*]

1. The act of rising; motion upwards, whether in air, water or other fluid, or on elevated objects; rise; a mounting upwards; as the *ascent* of vapors from the earth.

2. The way by which one ascends; the means of ascending. *Bacon.*

3. An eminence, hill or high place. *Addison.*

4. The degree of elevation of an object, or the angle it makes with a horizontal line; as, a road has an *ascent* of five degrees.

5. Acclivity; the rise of a hill; as a steep *ascent.*

ASCERTA'IN, *v.t.* [from the L. *ad certum*, to a certainty.]

1. To make certain; to define or reduce to precision, by removing obscurity or ambiguity.

The divine law *ascertains* the truth. *Hooker.*

2. To make certain, by trial, examination or experiment, so as to know what was before unknown; as, to *ascertain* the weight of a commodity, or the purity of a metal.

3. To make sure by previous measures.

The ministry, in order to *ascertain* a majority in the house of lords, persuaded the queen to create twelve new peers. *Smollett.*

4. To make certain or confident, followed by a pronoun; as, to *ascertain us* of the goodness of our work. [*Unusual.*] *Dryden.*

5. To fix; to establish with certainty; to render invariable, and not subject to will.

The mildness and precision of their laws *ascertained* the rule and measure of taxation. *Gibbon.*

ASCERTA'INABLE, *a.* That may be made certain in fact, or certain to the mind; that may be certainly known or reduced to a certainty. *Kerr's Lavoisier.*

ASCERTA'INED, *pp.* Made certain; defined; established; reduced to a certainty.

ASCERTA'INER, *n.* The person who ascertains or makes certain.

ASCERTA'INING, *ppr.* Making certain; fixing; establishing; reducing to a certainty; obtaining certain knowledge.

ASCERTA'INMENT, *n.* The act of ascertaining; a reducing to certainty; certainty; fixed rule. *Swift. Burke.*

ASCESSANCY, ASCESSANT, [See *Acescency, Acescent.*]

ASCET'IC, *a.* [Gr. ασκητος, exercised, hardened; from ασκεω, to exercise.]

Retired from the world; rigid; severe; austere; employed in devotions and mortifications.

ASCET'IC, *n.* One who retires from the customary business of life, and devotes himself to the duties of piety and devotion; a hermit; a recluse.

2. The title of certain books, on devout exercises; as the *ascetics* of St. Basil.

AS'CIAN, *n.* [L. *ascii*, from Gr. α priv. and σκια, a shadow.]

A person, who, at certain times of the year, has no shadow at noon. Such are the inhabitants of the torrid zone, who have, at times, a vertical sun. *Bailey.*

AS'CITANS, *n.* [Gr. ασκος, a bag or bottle of skin.]

A sect or branch of Montanists, who appeared in the second century. They introduced into their assemblies, certain bacchanals, who danced around a bag or skin distended with air, in allusion to the bottles filled with new wine. Math ix. *Encyc.*

AS'CITES, *n.* [Gr. ασκος, a bladder.]

A dropsy or tense elastic swelling of the belly, with fluctuation, from a collection of water. *Coxe. Quincy.*

ASCIT'IC, ASCIT'ICAL, *a.* Belonging to an ascites; dropsical; hydropical.

ASCITI''TIOUS, *a.* [L. *ascitus*; Low L. *ascititius*; from *ascisco*, to take to or associate.]

Additional; added; supplemental; not inherent or original.

Homer has been reckoned an *ascititious* name. *Pope.*

ASCLE'PIAD, *n.* In *ancient poetry*, a verse of four feet, the first of which is a spondee, the second, a choriamb, and the last two, dactyls; or of four feet and a cesura, the first, a spondee, the second, a dactyl, then the cesura, followed by two dactyls; as, Mæcē | nās ătă | vis | ēditĕ | rēgibŭs. *Encyc.*

ASCRI'BABLE, *a.* [See *Ascribe.*] That may be ascribed or attributed.

ASCRI'BE, *v. t.* [L. *ascribo*, of *ad* and *scribo*, to write.]

1. To attribute, impute, or set to, as to a cause; to assign, as effect to a cause; as, losses are often to be *ascribed* to imprudence.

2. To attribute, as a quality, or an appurtenance; to consider or alledge to belong; as, to *ascribe* perfection to God, or imperfection to man. Job xxxvi. Ps. lxviii. 1 Sam. xviii.

ASCRI'BED, *pp.* Attributed or imputed; considered or alledged, as belonging.

ASCRI'BING, *ppr.* Attributing; imputing; alledging to belong.

ASCRIP'TION, *n.* The act of ascribing, imputing or affirming to belong.

ASCRIPTI''TIOUS, *a.* That is ascribed. This word is applied to villains under the feudal system, who are annexed to the freehold and transferable with it. *Spelman. Lib. Niger Scaccarii.*

ASH, *n.* [Sax. *æsc*; Dan. *ask*; Germ. *esche*; D. *essche*; Russ. *yassen.*]

1. A well known tree, of which there are many species. There is no hermaphrodite calyx, or it is quadripartite; and no corol, or it is tetrapetalous. There are two stamens; one pistil; one seed, contained in a membranous, lanceolate capsule, and the pistil of the female flower is lanceolate. The leaves are pinnate, and the capsules grow in clusters. This wood is valuable, for fuel, as well as for timber; and the tree, when it grows in an open field, often forms, with its branches, a beautiful oval figure and a thick shade. *Encyc. Linne. Miller.*

2. The wood of the ash tree.

ASH, *a.* Pertaining to or like the ash; made of ash.

ASHA'ME, *v. t.* To shame. [*Not used.*]

ASHA'MED, *a.* [from Sax. *gescamian* or *ascamian*, to be ashamed, to blush, from *scama*, shame; originally a participle. See *Shame.*]

1. Affected by shame; abashed or confused by guilt or a conviction of some criminal action or indecorous conduct, or by the exposure of some gross errors or misconduct, which the person is conscious must be wrong, and which tends to impair his honor or reputation. It is followed by *of.*

Thou shalt remember thy ways, and be *ashamed.* Ex. xvi.

Israel shall be *ashamed* of his own counsel. Hosea x.

2. Confused by a consciousness of guilt or of inferiority; by the mortification of pride; by failure or disappointment.

They shall be greatly *ashamed*, that trust in images. Isa. xlii.

[*This adjective always follows its noun.*]

ASHA'MEDLY, *adv.* Bashfully. [*Not used.*]

ASH-COLORED, *a.* Of a color between brown and gray. *Woodward.*

ASH'EN, *a.* [See *Ash.*] Pertaining to ash; made of ash.

ASH'ES, *n.* plu. without the singular number. [Sax. *asca*; Goth. *azga*; D. *asch*; G. *asche*; Sw. *aska*; Dan. *aske*; Basque, *auscua.*]

1. The earthy particles of combustible substances remaining after combustion; as of wood or coal.

2. The remains of the human body when burnt. Hence figuratively, a dead body or corpse.

3. In *scripture, ashes* is used to denote vileness, meanness, frailty, or humiliation.

I who am but dust and *ashes.* Gen. xviii.

I abhor myself and repent in dust and *ashes.* Job xlii.

ASH'-FIRE, *n.* A low fire used in chimical operations.

ASH'-HOLE, *n.* A repository for ashes; the lower part of a furnace.

ASH'LAR, *n.* Common or free stones, as they come from the quarry, of different lengths, breadths and thicknesses. *Johnson.*

ASH'LERING, *n.* Quartering for lathing to, in garrets, two or three feet high, perpendicular to the floor, and reaching to the under side of the rafters. *Encyc.*

ASHO'RE, *adv.* [*a*, *at* or *on*, and *shore.* See *Shore.*]

1. On shore; on the land adjacent to water; to the shore; as, bring the goods *ashore.*

2. On land, opposed to *aboard;* as, the captain of the ship remained *ashore.*

3. On the ground; as, the ship was driven *ashore.*

ASHWEDNESDAY, *n.* The first day of Lent; supposed to be so called from a custom in the Romish Church of sprinkling ashes, that day, on the heads of penitents, then admitted to penance.

ASH'-WEED, *n.* A plant, the small wild angelica, gout-wort, goats-foot, or herb-gerard. *Encyc.*

ASH'Y, *a.* Belonging to ashes; ash-colored; pale; inclining to a whitish gray. *Shak.*

ASHY-PALE, *a.* Pale as ashes. *Shak.*

A'SIAN, *a.* [from *Asia*, a name originally given to Asia Minor or some part of it; perhaps from the Asses, Ases or Osses, about Mount Taurus. *Mallet, North. Ant.* i. 60. *Plin.* 6. 17.]

Pertaining to Asia. *Dryden. Mitford.*

A'SIARCH, *n.* [*Asia* and αρχος, chief.]

A chief or pontiff of Asia; one who had the superintendence of the public games. Acts xix. *Milner.*

ASIAT'IC, *a.* Belonging to Asia, a quarter of the globe which extends from the strait of Constantinople and the Arabian gulf, to the Pacific ocean on the east. It is probable, the name was originally appropriated to what is now Asia Minor or rather a part of it.

ASIAT'IC, *n.* A native of Asia.

ASIAT'ICISM, *n.* Imitation of the Asiatic manner. *Warton.*

ASI'DE, *adv.* [*a* and *side.* See *Side.*]

1. On or to one side; out of a perpendicular or straight direction.

2. At a little distance from the main part or body.

Thou shalt set *aside* that which is full. 2 Kings iv.

3. From the body; as, to put or lay *aside* a garment. John xiii.

4. From the company; at a small distance or in private; as when speakers utter something by themselves, upon the stage.

5. Separate from the person, mind or attention; in a state of abandonment.

Let us lay *aside* every weight. Heb. xii.

6. Out of the line of rectitude or propriety, in a moral view.

They are all gone *aside.* Ps. xiv.

7. In a state of separation to a particular use; as, to set *aside* a thing for a future day.

To set aside, in judicial proceedings, is to defeat the effect or operation of, by a subsequent decision of a superior tribunal; as, to set *aside* a verdict or a judgment.

ASINE'GO, *n.* [Sp. *asnico*, a little ass.] A foolish fellow. *Mason.*

AS'ININE, rarely **AS'INARY**, *a.* [L. *asinus*; W. *asyn*, the ass; which see.]

Belonging to the ass; having the qualities of the ass.

'ASK, *v. t.* [Sax. *ascian*, *acsian*, or *axian*; D. *eischen*; G. *heischen*; Ir. *ascaim*; Gr. αξιοω. Qu. Eth. ለሰኰ to pray or beseech. In former times, the English word was pronounced *ax*, as in the royal style of assenting to bills in Parliament. "Be it as it is *axed.*" In Calmuc, *asoc* signifies to inquire. The sense is to urge or press.]

1. To request; to seek to obtain by words; to petition; with *of* before the person to whom the request is made.

Ask counsel *of* God. Judges xviii.

2. To require, expect or claim.

To whom men have committed much, *of* him they will *ask* the more. Luke xii.

3. To interrogate, or inquire; to put a question, with a view to an answer.

He is of age, *ask* him. John ix.

4. To require, or make claim.

Ask me never so much dowry. Gen. xxxiv. Dan. ii.

5. To claim, require or demand, as the price or value of a commodity; to set a price; as, what price do you *ask?*

6. To require, as physically necessary.

The exigence of a state *asks* a much longer time to conduct the design to maturity. *Addison.*

This sense is nearly or entirely obsolete; *ask* being superseded by *require* and *demand.*

7. To invite; as, to *ask* guests to a wedding or entertainment; *ask* my friend to step into the house.

'ASK, *v. i.* To request or petition, followed by *for;* as, *ask* for bread; or without *for.*

Ask and it shall be given you. Mat. vii.

2. To inquire, or seek by request; sometimes followed by *after.*

Wherefore dost thou *ask after* my name? Gen. xxxii.

This verb can hardly be considered as strictly intransitive, for some person or object is always understood.

Ask is not equivalent to demand, claim, and require, at least, in modern usage; much less, is it equivalent to *beg* and *beseech.* The first three words, demand, claim, require, imply a right or supposed right in the person asking, to the thing requested; and *beseech* implies more urgency, than *ask.* *Ask* and *request* imply no right, but suppose the thing desired to be a favor. The French *demander* is correctly rendered by *ask*, rather than by *demand.*

ASK'ANCE, **ASK'ANT**, *adv.* [D. *schuins*, sloping.] Sideways; obliquely; towards one corner of the eye. *Dryden.*

'ASKED, *pp.* Requested; petitioned; questioned; interrogated.

'ASKER, *n.* One who asks; a petitioner; an inquirer.

2. A water newt. *Johnson.*

ASKEW' *adv.* [G. *schief;* Dan. *skiæv;* D. *scheef*, awry, crooked, oblique.]

With a wry look; aside; askant; sometimes indicating scorn, or contempt, or envy. *Spenser.*

'ASKING, *ppr.* Requesting; petitioning; interrogating; inquiring.

2. Silently expressing request or desire.

Explain the *asking* eye. *Pope.*

ASLA′KE, *v. t.* [Sax. *aslacian.* See *Slack.*] To remit; to slacken. [*Not in use.*] *Spenser.*

ASLA′NI, *n.* A silver coin worth from 115 to 120 aspers. *Encyc.*

ASL'ANT, *a.* or *adv.* [*a* and *slant.* See *Slant.*]

On one side; obliquely; not perpendicularly or with a right angle.

The shaft drove through his neck *aslant.* *Dryden.*

ASLEE′P, *a.* or *adv.* [*a* and *sleep,* or Sax. *geslapan,* to sleep.]

1. Sleeping; in a state of sleep; at rest.

Sisera was fast *asleep.* Judges iv.

2. To a state of sleep; as to fall *asleep.*

3. Dead; in a state of death.

Concerning them who are *asleep,* sorrow not. 1 Thess. iv.

4. To death.

For since the fathers fell *asleep,* all things continue. 2 Pet. iii.

ASLO′PE, *a.* or *adv.* [*a* and *slope.* See *Slope.*]

With leaning or inclination; obliquely; with declivity or descent, as a hill; declining from an upright direction.

Set them not upright, but *aslope.* *Bacon.*

ASLUG′, *adv.* In a sluggish manner. [*Not used.*] *Fotherby.*

ASMONE′AN, *a.* Pertaining to Asmoneus, the father of Simon, and chief of the Asmoneans, a family that reigned over the Jews 126 years.

ASMONE′AN, *n.* One of the family of Asmoneus.

ASO′MATOUS, *a.* [Gr. *α* priv. and *σωμα,* body.]

Without a material body; incorporeal. [*Not used.*] *Todd.*

'ASP, ASP′IC, } *n.* [L. *aspis;* Gr. *ασπις,* a round shield and an asp; supposed to be from Heb. and Ch. אסף, to gather in, or collect; from the coil of this serpent, with his head elevated in the center, like the boss of a buckler.]

A small poisonous serpent of Egypt and Libya, whose bite occasions inevitable death, but without pain. It is said that the celebrated Cleopatra, rather than be carried a captive to Rome by Augustus, suffered death by the bite of the asp; but the fact has been questioned. Authors are not agreed, as to what species the asp of the ancients should be referred. Bruce thinks it the *coluber cerastes,* Linne.

ASPAL′ATHUS, *n.* A plant.

ASPAR′AGIN, *n.* White transparent crystals of a peculiar vegetable principle, which spontaneously form in asparagus juice evaporated to the consistence of sirup. They are in the form of rhomboidal prisms. *Ure.*

ASPAR′AGUS, *n.* [L. and Gr.; probably from *σπαρασσω,* to tear, from its lacerated appearance, or from the root of *σπειρα,* a spire, from its stem.]

Sparagus; sperage; vulgarly, sparrow-grass; a genus of plants. That which is cultivated in gardens, has an upright herbaceous stalk, bristly leaves, and equal stipulas. The roots have a bitterish mucilaginous taste; and the stalk is, in some degree, aperient and deobstruent, but not very efficacious. *Encyc.*

'ASPECT, *n.* [L. *aspectus,* from *aspicio,* to look on, of *ad* and *specio,* to see or look.]

1. Look; view; appearance to the eye or the mind; as, to present an object or a subject in its true *aspect,* or under a double *aspect.* So we say, public affairs have a favorable *aspect.*

2. Countenance; look, or particular appearance of the face; as a mild or severe *aspect.*

3. View; sight; act of seeing. [*This sense is now unusual.*]

4. Position or situation with regard to seeing, or that position which enables one to look in a particular direction; as, a house has a southern *aspect,* that is, a position which faces or looks to the south.

5. In *astronomy,* the situation of one planet with respect to another. The aspects are five; sextile, when the planets are 60° distant; quartile, or quadrate, when their distance is 90°, or the quarter of a circle; trine, when the distance is 120°; opposition, when the distance is 180°, or half a circle; and conjunction, when they are in the same degree.

ASPECT′, *v. t.* To behold. [*Not used.*] *Temple.*

ASPECT′ABLE, *a.* That may be seen. [*Not used.*] *Raleigh.*

ASPECT′ED, *a.* Having an aspect. [*Not used.*] *B. Jonson.*

ASPEC′TION, *n.* The act of viewing. [*Not used.*] *Brown.*

ASP′EN or ASP, *n.* [D. *esp;* G. *aspe, äspe;* Sax. *æspe;* Sw. *asp;* Dan. *æsp;* Qu. from the Ar. خشف gashafa, to be agitated.]

A species of the poplar, so called from the trembling of its leaves, which move with the slightest impulse of the air. Its leaves are roundish, smooth, and stand on long slender foot-stalks.

ASP′EN, *a.* Pertaining to the aspen, or resembling it; made of aspen wood.

Nor *aspen* leaves confess the gentlest breeze. *Gay.*

AS′PER, *a.* [L. See *Asperate.*] Rough; rugged. [*Little used.*] *Bacon.*

AS′PER, *n.* [L. *aspiro,* to breathe.]

In *grammar,* the Greek accent ʽ, importing that the letter over which it is placed ought to be aspirated, or pronounced as if the letter *h* preceded it. *Encyc.*

AS′PER, *n.* A Turkish coin, of which three make a medine. Its value is about a cent and 12 decimals.

AS′PERATE, *v. t.* [L. *aspero,* from *asper,* rough.]

To make rough or uneven. *Boyle.*

ASPERA′TION, *n.* A making rough.

ASPERIFO′LIATE, *a.* [L. *asper,* rough, and *folium,* a leaf.]

Having rough leaves. Plants of this kind are, by some authors, classified according to this character. They constitute the forty-first order of Linne's fragments of a natural method. In the methods of Herman, Boerhave, and Ray, this class consists of plants which have four naked seeds. Their leaves stand alternately on the stalks, and the flower is monopetalous in five divisions. *Encyc. Milne.*

ASPERIFO′LIOUS, *a.* Having leaves rough to the touch. [*See the preceding word.*]

ASPER′ITY, *n.* [L. *asperitas,* from *asper,* rough.]

1. Roughness of surface; unevenness; opposed to smoothness. *Boyle.*

2. Roughness of sound; that quality which grates the ear; harshness of pronunciation. *Warton.*

3. Roughness to the taste; sourness.

4. Roughness or ruggedness of temper; moroseness; sourness; crabbedness. *Rogers.*

5. Sharpness. *Berkeley.*

AS′PEROUS, *a.* [L. *asper,* rough.] Rough; uneven. *Boyle.*

ASPERSE, *v. t.* *aspers′.* [L. *aspergo, aspersus,* of *ad* and *spargo,* to scatter; Ar. فرج to split, divide, scatter. See Class Brg.]

1. To bespatter with foul reports or false and injurious charges; to tarnish in point of reputation, or good name; to slander or calumniate; as, to *asperse* a poet or his writings; to *asperse* a character.

2. To cast upon. *Heywood.*

ASPERS′ER, *n.* One that asperses, or vilifies another.

ASPER′SION, *n.* A sprinkling, as of water or dust, in a literal sense. *Shak.*

2. The spreading of calumnious reports or charges, which tarnish reputation, like the bespattering of a body with foul water. *Bp. Hall.*

ASPHALT′, ASPHALT′UM, } *n.* [Gr. *ασφαλτος.*] Bitumen Judaicum, Jew's pitch; a smooth, hard, brittle, black or brown substance, which breaks with a polish, melts easily when heated, and when pure, burns without leaving any ashes. It has little taste, and scarcely any smell, unless heated, when it emits a strong smell of pitch. It is found in a soft or liquid state on the surface of the Dead Sea, which, from this substance, is called *Asphaltite,* or the Asphaltic Lake. It is found also in the earth, in many parts of Asia, Europe and America. Formerly, it was used for embalming dead bodies; the solid asphalt is still employed in Arabia, Egypt, and Persia, instead of pitch for ships; and the fluid asphalt is used for varnishing, and for burning in lamps. A species found in Neufchatel is found excellent as a cement for walls and pavements; very durable in air, and not penetrable by water. A composition of asphalt, lamp black and oil is used for drawing black figures on dial-plates. *Encyc. Nicholson.*

ASPHALT′IC, *a.* Pertaining to asphalt, or containing it; bituminous. *Milton.*

ASPHALT′ITE, *a.* Pertaining to or containing asphalt. *Bryant. Wilford.*

AS′PHODEL, *n.* [L. and Gr. See Theoph. Lib. 7. Plin. Lib. 21. 17. Perhaps it is from the root of *spud;* Sw. *spyd;* Ice. *spioot,* a spear, from the shape of its leaves.]

King's-spear; a genus of liliaceous plants, cultivated for the beauty of their flowers. The ancients planted asphodels near graves, to supply the manes of the dead with nourishment. *Encyc. Johnson.*

ASPHU'RELATES, *n.* [Gr. α priv. and σφυρα, a hammer; not malleable.]
A series of semimetallic fossils, fusible by fire, and in their purest state not malleable. In their native state, they are mixed with sulphur and other adventitious matter, in the form of ore. Under this denomination are classed bismuth, antimony, cobalt, zink and quicksilver. *Coxe. Encyc.*

ASPHYX'Y, *n.* [Gr. ασφυξια, of α priv. and σφυξις, pulse.]
A temporary suspension of the motion of the heart and arteries; swooning; fainting. *Quincy. Coxe.*

ASP'IC, *n.* The asp, which see.
2. A piece of ordnance carrying a twelve pound shot.

ASP'IC, *n.* A plant growing in France, a species of lavender, which it resembles in the blue color of its flowers, and in the figure and green color of its leaves. It is called male-lavender, spica nardi, and Pseudo-nardus. The oil of this plant is used by painters, farriers and other artificers. It is very inflammable, of a white color and aromatic; and it is almost the only dissolvent of sandarac. *Nicholson. Fourcroy.*

ASPI'RANT, *n.* [See *Aspire.*] One who aspires, breathes after, or seeks with eagerness. *Faber.*

AS'PIRATE, *v. t.*]L. *aspiro*, to breathe or blow; Gr. ασπαιρω, to palpitate; from *spiro*, and σπαιρω; Ar. صفر safara, to hiss, or make a hissing by blowing on a wind instrument. See *Spire, Spirit.*]
To pronounce with a breathing or full emission of breath. We *aspirate* the words *horse* and *house*. *Dryden.*

AS'PIRATE, *v. i.* To be uttered with a strong breathing; as, the letter *h aspirates*. *Dryden.*

AS'PIRATE, *n.* A letter marked with an asper, or note of breathing; a mark of aspiration, as the Greek accent ʽ. *Bentley.*

AS'PIRATE, *a.* Pronounced with a full breath. *Holder.*

AS'PIRATED, *pp.* Uttered with a strong emission of breath.

AS'PIRATING, *ppr.* Pronouncing with a full breath.

ASPIRA'TION, *n.* The pronunciation of a letter with a full emission of breath. *Holder.*
2. A breathing after; an ardent wish or desire, chiefly of spiritual blessings. *Watts.*
3. The act of aspiring or of ardently desiring what is noble or spiritual.

ASPI'RE, *v. i.* [L. *aspiro*, to breathe. See *Aspirate.*]
1. To desire with eagerness; to pant after an object, great, noble or spiritual; followed by *to* or *after*; as to aspire *to* a crown, or *after* immortality.
2. To aim at something elevated; to rise or tower with desire.

> *Aspiring* to be Gods, if angels fell;
> *Aspiring* to be angels, men rebel. *Pope.*

ASPI'RER, *n.* One who aspires; one who aims to rise in power or consequence, or to accomplish some important object. *Milton.*

ASPI'RING *ppr.* Desiring eagerly; aiming at something noble, great, or spiritual.

ASPI'RING, *a.* Ambitious: animated with an ardent desire of power, importance, or excellencc.

ASPI'RING, *n.* Ambition; eager desire of something great. *Hammond.*
2. Points; stops. [*Not used.*] *Herbert.*

ASPORTA'TION, *n.* [L *asportatio*, of *abs* and *porto*, to carry; W. *porthi*, to carry. See *Bear.*]
A carrying away. In *law*, the felonious removal of goods from the place where they were deposited, is an asportation, and adjudged to be theft, though the goods are not carried from the house or apartment. *Blackstone.*

ASQUINT', *adv.* [D. *schuinte*, a slope; *schuins*, slopingly; Sp. *esquina*; D. *kant*, a corner. See *Askance*, and *Squint.*]
To the corner or angle of the eye; obliquely; towards one side; not in the straight line of vision; as, to look *asquint*.
2. Not with regard or due notice. *Fox.*

'ASS, *n.* [W. *asyn*; Ir. *asan*; L. *asinus*; Fr. *âne*, for *asne*; Arm. *asen*; Sp. Port. *asno*; It. *asino*. Qu. from Goth. *auso*, Gr. ους, an ear.]
1. A quadruped of the equine genus. This animal has long slouching ears, a short mane, and a tail covered with long hairs at the end. He is usually of an ash color, with a black bar across the shoulders. The tame or domestic ass is patient to stupidity, and carries a heavy burden. He is slow, but very sure footed, and for this reason very useful on rough steep hills.
2. A dull, heavy, stupid fellow; a dolt.

ASS'AI, [Ital.] A term in music; added to a word signifying slow, it denotes a little quicker; and to a word signifying quick, it denotes a little slower. *Bailey.*

ASSA'IL, *v. t.* [Fr. *assaillir*, from L. *assilio*, to leap or rush upon, of *ad* and *salio*, to leap, to rise.]
To leap or fall upon by violence; to assault; to attack suddenly, as when one person falls upon another to beat him.
2. To invade or attack, in a hostile manner, as an army, or nation. *Spenser.*
3. To attack with arguments, censure, abuse, or criticism, with a view to injure, bring into disrepute, or overthrow.
4. To attack, with a view to overcome, by motives applied to the passions.

> Nor hide the encounter of *assailing* eyes. *Shak.*

ASSA'ILABLE, *a.* That may be assailed, attacked or invaded.

ASSA'ILANT, *n.* [Fr.] One who assails, attacks or assaults.

ASSA'ILANT, *a.* Assaulting; attacking; invading with violence.

ASSA'ILED, *pp.* Assaulted; invaded; attacked with violence.

ASSA'ILER, *n.* One who assails.

ASSA'ILING, *ppr.* Assaulting; invading by force; attacking with violence.

ASSA'ILMENT, *n.* Attack. [*Little used.*] *Johnson.*

ASSAPAN'IC, *n.* The flying squirrel; an animal which flies a little distance by extending the skin between the fore and hind legs. [See *Squirrel.*] *Trevoux.*

AS'SARON, *n.* The omer or homer, a Hebrew measure of five pints. *Encyc.*

ASSART', *n.* [Old Fr. *assarter*, to grub up.]
In *ancient laws*, the offense of grubbing up trees, and thus destroying thickets or coverts of a forest. *Spelman. Cowel.*
2. A tree plucked up by the roots; also a piece of land cleared. *Ash.*

ASSART', *v. t.* To grub up trees; to commit an assart. *Ashmole.*

ASSAS'SIN, *n.* [Ar. حس hassa, to kill.]
One who kills or attempts to kill, by surprise or secret assault. The circumstance of *surprise* or *secresy* seems essential to the signification of this word; though it is sometimes used to denote one who takes any advantage, in killing or attempting to murder; as by attacking one when unarmed.

ASSAS'SINATE, *v. t.* To kill or attempt to kill, by surprise or secret assault; to murder by sudden violence. *Assassin* as a verb is not now used.
2. To way lay; to take by treachery. *Milton.*

ASSAS'SINATE, *n.* A murder or murderer. [*Not used.*] *B. Jonson.*

ASSAS'SINATED, *pp.* Murdered by surprise or secret assault.

ASSAS'SINATING, *ppr.* Murdering by surprise or secret assault.

ASSASSINA'TION, *n.* The act of killing or murdering, by surprise or secret assault; murder by violence.

ASSAS'SINATOR, *n.* An assassin, which see.

ASSAS'SINOUS, *a.* Murderous. [*Not used.*]

ASSAS'SINS, *n.* In *Syria*, a tribe or clan called Ismaelians, Batanists or Batenians. They originated in Persia about the year 1090; whence a colony migrated and settled on the mountains of Lebanon, and were remarkable for their assassinations. Their religion was a compound of magianism, judaism, and christianity. One article of their creed was, that the Holy Spirit resided in their Chief, and that his orders proceeded from God himself. He was called *Scheik*, and is better known by the denomination of *Old man of the mountain.* This barbarous chieftain and his followers spread terror among nations far and near, for almost two centuries, when the tribe was subdued by Sultan Bibaris. *Encyc.*

ASSA'TION, *n.* [Fr. from L. *assatus.*] A roasting. [*Not used.*]

ASSAULT', *n.* [Fr. *assault*, now *assaut*; It. Port. *assalto*; Sp. *asalto*; from L. *assulto*, of *ad* and *salto*, to leap, formed on *salio*, or its root. See *Assail.* We have the same root in *insult* and *result.*]
1. An attack or violent onset, whether by an individual, a company, or an army. An assault by private persons may be made with or without weapons. An assault by an army is a violent hostile attack; and when made upon a fort or fortified place is called a *storm*, as opposed to *sap* or *siege.*
2. An attack by hostile words or measures; as, an *assault* upon the prerogatives of a prince, or upon a constitution of government.
3. In *Law*, an unlawful setting upon one's person; an attempt or offer to beat another, without touching his person; as by

lifting the fist or a cane, in a threatening manner. If the blow aimed takes effect, it is a *battery*. *Blackstone*. *Finch*.

ASSAULT′, *v. t.* To attack or fall upon by violence, or with a hostile intention; as, to *assault* a man, a house or town.

2. To invade or fall on with force; as, the cry of war *assaults* our ears.

3. To attack by words, arguments or unfriendly measures, with a view to shake, impair or overthrow; as, to *assault* a character, the laws or the administration.

ASSAULT′ABLE, *a.* That may be assaulted. *Williams*.

ASSAULT′ED, *pp.* Attacked with force, arms, violence, or hostile views.

ASSAULT′ER, *n.* One who assaults, or violently attacks.

ASSAULT′ING, *ppr.* Attacking with force, or with hostile measures.

ASSA′Y, *n.* [Fr. *essai*; Sp. *ensayo*; Port. *ensaio*; It. *saggio*, an *assay*; Fr. *essayer*, to try; old Fr. *essoyer*, to endeavor. *Kelham's Norm. Dict.* It. *assaggiare*, to try; *saggiare*, to try, essay; Sp. *ensayar*, to try; Sw. *försökia*, to try; Dan. *forsöger*, to try, examine, endeavor. These words are all from the same root as *seek*, the radical sense of which is, to follow, to urge, press or strain; Sax. *secan*, to seek; L. *sequor*; *assequor*, to follow, to examine; D. *zoeken*; G. *suchen*; Dan. *söger*; Ir. *seichim*; It. *seguire*; Sp. *seguir*, to follow. *Assay* and *essay* are radically one word; but modern usage has appropriated *assay* to experiments in metallurgy, and *essay* to intellectual and bodily efforts. Class Sg. See *Essay*.]

1. The trial of the goodness, purity, weight, value, &c. of metals or metallic substances. Any operation or experiment for ascertaining the quantity of a precious metal in an ore or mineral. *Analysis* is a term of more comprehensive import, extending to an examination of the nature and quantities of all parts of the compound.

Assaying is called the *docimastic art*.

2. In *law*, an examination of weights and measures by the standard. *Cowel*.

3. Examination; trial; effort; first entrance upon any business; attempt. In these senses, which are found in old authors, now rarely used. [See *Essay*.]

4. Value; great purity. *Obs.* *Spenser*.

ASSA′Y, *v. t.* To try or prove, by examination or experiment, the quantity and purity of metallic substances.

2. To apply to the touchstone. *Milton*.

ASSA′Y, *v. i.* To attempt, try or endeavor.

He *assayed* to go. 1 Sam. xvii.

[*In this sense* essay *is now used.*]

ASSAY-BALANCE, *n.* A balance for the trial of the weight and purity of metals.

ASSA′YED, *pp.* Examined; tested; proved by experiment.

ASSA′YER, *n.* One who examines metals to find their quantity and purity. An officer of the mint, whose business is to try the weight and purity of metals.

ASSA′YING, *ppr.* Trying by some standard; examining by experiment, as metals; proving; attempting.

ASSAY-MASTER, *n.* An assayer; an officer appointed to try the weight and fineness of the precious metals.

ASSECU′RANCE, *n.* Assurance. [*Not used.*] *Sheldon*.

ASSECURA′TION, *n.* Assurance; a making secure. [*Not used.*] *Bp. Hall*.

ASSECU′RE, *v. t.* To secure. [*Not used.*] *Bullokar*.

ASSECU′TION, *n.* [L. *assequor*.] An obtaining or acquiring. *Ayliffe*.

ASSEM′BLAGE, *n.* [Fr. See *Assemble*.] A collection of individuals, or of particular things; the state of being assembled. *Locke*. *Thomson*.

2. *Rarely*, the act of assembling.

ASSEM′BLANCE, *n.* Representation; an assembling. [*Not in use.*] *Shak. Spenser*.

ASSEM′BLE, *v. t.* [Fr. *assembler*; Sw. *samla*; Dan. *samler*; D. *zamelen*; Ger. *sammeln*, to assemble. L. *simul*; Dan. *sammen*; D. *zamen*, together.]

To collect a number of individuals or particulars into one place, or body; to bring or call together; to convene; to congregate.

ASSEM′BLE, *v. i.* To meet or come together; to convene, as a number of individuals.

ASSEM′BLED, *pp.* Collected into a body; congregated.

ASSEM′BLER, *n.* One who assembles.

ASSEM′BLING, *ppr.* Coming together; collecting into one place.

ASSEM′BLING, *n.* A collection or meeting together. Heb. x.

ASSEM′BLY, *n* [Sp. *asamblea*; It. *assemblea*; Fr. *assemblée*.]

1. A company or collection of individuals, in the same place; usually for the same purpose.

2. A congregation or religious society convened.

3. In *some of the United States*, the legislature, consisting of different houses or branches, whether in session or not. In *some states*, the popular branch or House of Representatives is denominated an *assembly*. [*See the constitutions of the several states*.]

4. A collection of persons for amusement; as a dancing *assembly*.

5. A convocation, convention or council of ministers and ruling elders delegated from each presbytery; as the General *Assembly* of Scotland or of the United States. *Encyc*.

6. In *armies*, the second beating of the drum before a march, when the soldiers strike their tents. *Encyc*.

7. An assemblage. [*Not in use.*]

ASSEM′BLY-ROOM, *n.* A room in which persons assemble.

ASSENT′, *n.* [L. *assensus*, from *assentior*, to assent, of *ad* and *sentio*, to think; Eth. ሰናሰ sena or sana, concord, and its derivative, to agree, to harmonize; Sw. *sinne*, mind, sense; D. *zin*, mind; *zinnen*, to feel or mind; G. *sinn*, sense; *sinnen*, to think or consider. The Danes preserve the final consonant, *sind*, mind, sense, inclination; W. *syn*, sense; *syniaw*, to perceive.]

1. The act of the mind in admitting, or agreeing to, the truth of a proposition.

Faith is the *assent* to any proposition, on the credit of the proposer. *Locke*.

2. Consent; agreement to a proposal, respecting some right or interest; as, the bill before the house has the *assent* of a great majority of the members.

The distinction between *assent* and *consent* seems to be this: *assent* is the agreement to an abstract proposition. We *assent* to a statement, but we do not *consent* to it. *Consent* is an agreement to some proposal or measure which affects the rights or interest of the consenter. We *consent* to a proposal of marriage. This distinction however is not always observed. [See *Consent*.]

3. Accord; agreement. 2 Chron. xviii.

ASSENT′, *v. i.* To admit as true; to agree, yield or concede, or rather to express an agreement of the mind to what is alledged, or proposed.

The Jews also *assented*, saying these things are so. Acts xxiv.

It is sometimes used for *consent*, or an agreement to something affecting the rights or interest of the person assenting. But to *assent* to the marriage of a daughter is less correct than to *consent*.

ASSENTA′TION, *n.* [L. *assentatio*, from *assentor*, to comply.]

Compliance with the opinion of another, from flattery or dissimulation. *Chesterfield*.

ASSENTA′TOR, *n.* A flatterer.

ASSENTATO′RILY, *adv.* With adulation. [*Not in use.*] *Bacon*.

ASSENT′ER, *n.* One who assents, agrees to, or admits.

ASSENT′ING, *ppr.* Agreeing to, or admitting as true; yielding to.

ASSENT′INGLY, *adv.* In a manner to express assent; by agreement.

ASSENT′MENT, *a.* Assent; agreement. [*Rarely used.*] *Brown*.

ASSERT′, *v. t.* [L. *assero*, *assertum*, to claim or challenge, to maintain or assert; of *ad* and *sero*. The sense of *sero* is to sow, properly to throw or set. To *assert* is to throw or set firmly.]

1. To affirm positively; to declare with assurance; to aver. *Milton*.

2. To maintain or defend by words or measures; to vindicate a claim or title to; as, to *assert* our rights and liberties. *Dryden*.

ASSERT′ED, *pp.* Affirmed positively; maintained; vindicated.

ASSERT′ING, *ppr.* Declaring with confidence; maintaining; defending.

ASSER′TION, *n.* The act of asserting; the maintaining of a claim.

2. Positive declaration or averment; affirmation; position advanced. *Brown*.

ASSERT′IVE, *a.* Positive; affirming confidently; peremptory. *Glanville*.

ASSERT′IVELY, *adv.* Affirmatively. *Bedell*.

ASSERT′OR, *n.* One who affirms positively; one who maintains or vindicates a claim; an affirmer, supporter, or vindicator. *Dryden*.

ASSERT′ORY, *a.* Affirming; maintaining. *Bp. Hall*.

ASSESS′, *v. t.* [Fr. *asseoir*; Norm. *asser*, *asseoir*, to settle, fix, ascertain, *assess*; It. *assestare*, *assettare*; L. *assideo*, *ad* and *sedeo*; Eng. to *sit*, or *set*. See *Set* and *Sit*.]

1. To set, fix or charge a certain sum upon one, as a tax; as, to *assess* each citizen in due proportion.

2. To value; to fix the value of property, for the purpose of being taxed; as by the law of the United States. Also, to value or fix the profits of business, for the purpose of taxation.

3. To set, fix or ascertain; as, it is the province of a jury to *assess* damages.

ASSESS', *n.* Assessment. [*Not used.*]

ASSESS'ABLE, *a.* That may be assessed.

ASSESS'ED, *pp.* Charged with a certain sum; valued; set; fixed; ascertained.

ASSESS'ING, *ppr.* Charging with a sum; valuing; fixing; ascertaining.

ASSES'SION, *n.* A sitting down by a person. [*Not used.*]

ASSES'SIONARY, *a.* Pertaining to assessors. *Carew.*

ASSESS'MENT, *n.* A valuation of property or profits of business, for the purpose of taxation. An *assessment* is a valuation made by authorized persons according to their discretion, as opposed to a sum certain or determined by law. It may be a direct charge of the tax to be paid; or a valuation of the property of those who are to pay the tax, for the purpose of fixing the proportion which each man shall pay; on which valuation the law imposes a specific sum upon a given amount. *Blackstone. Laws of the U. States.*

2. A tax or specific sum charged on the person or property.

3. The act of assessing; the act of determining the amount of damages by a jury.

ASSESS'OR, *n.* One appointed to assess the person or property.

2. An inferior officer of justice, who sits to assist the judge. *Encyc.*

3. One who sits by another, as next in dignity. *Milton.*

ASSETS', *n. plu.* [Fr. *assez*, enough; It. *assai*, enough, or many; Ir. *sath*, sufficiency; *sasadh*, satisfaction; L. *sat, satis*, enough.]

Goods or estate of a deceased person, sufficient to pay the debts of the deceased. But the word *sufficient*, though expressing the original signification of *assets*, is not with us necessary to the definition. In present usage, *assets* are the money, goods or estate of a deceased person, subject by law to the payment of his debts and legacies. *Assets* are *real* or *personal*; *real assets* are lands which descend to the heir, subject to the fulfilment of the obligations of the ancestor; *personal assets* are the money or goods of the deceased, or debts due to him, which come into the hands of the executor or administrator, or which he is bound to collect and convert into money. *Blackstone.*

ASSEV'ER, } *v. t.* [L. *assevero*, from
ASSEV'ERATE, } *ad*, and the Teutonic *swear*; Sax. *swerian*; Goth. *swaran*, to swear, to affirm positively.]

To affirm or aver positively, or with solemnity. *Fotherby.*

ASSEVERA'TION, *n.* Positive affirmation or assertion; solemn declaration. This word is not, generally, if ever, used for a declaration under an official oath, but for a declaration accompanied with solemnity.

'ASS-HEAD, *n.* [*ass* and *head.*] One dull, like the ass; one slow of apprehension; a blockhead.

ASSIDE'ANS or CHASIDE'ANS. [Heb. חסד pious.]

A sect of Jews who resorted to *Mattathias* to fight for the laws of their God and the liberties of their country. They were men of great zeal, and observed the traditions of the elders. From these sprung the Pharisees and Essenes. *Encyc.*

AS'SIDENT, *a.* [L. *assideo, assidens*, of *ad* and *sedeo*, to sit.]

Assident signs, in medicine, are such as usually attend a disease, but not always; distinguished from *pathognomic* signs, which are inseparable from it. *Encyc.*

ASSID'UATE, *a.* Daily. [*Not in use.*] *K. Charles.*

ASSIDU'ITY, *n.* [L. *assiduitas*. See *Assiduous.*]

1. Constant or close application to any business or enterprise; diligence. *Addison.*

2. Attention; attentiveness to persons. *Assiduities*, in the plural, are services rendered with zeal and constancy.

ASSID'UOUS, *a.* [L. *assiduus*, from *assideo*, to sit close, *ad* and *sedeo*; Eng. to *sit*; Sax. *sittan, settan.*]

1. Constant in application; as a person *assiduous* in his occupation.

2. Attentive; careful; regular in attendance; as an *assiduous* physician or nurse.

3. Performed with constant diligence or attention; as *assiduous* labor.

ASSID'UOUSLY, *adv.* Diligently; attentively; with earnestness and care; with regular attendance.

ASSID'UOUSNESS, *n.* Constant or diligent application.

ASSIENT'O, *n.* [Sp. *asiento*, a seat, a contract or agreement; L. *assideo.*]

A contract or convention between the king of Spain and other powers, for furnishing slaves for the Spanish dominions in South America. *Treaty between G. B. and Spain, March* 26, 1713.

ASSI'GN, *v. t. assine.* [Fr. *assigner*; Sp. *asignar*; Port. *assinar*; It. *assegnare*; L. *assigno*, of *ad* and *signo*, to allot, to mark out; Ir. *sighin*; L. *signum*, a mark. The primary sense of *sign* is to send, or to set.]

1. To allot; to appoint or grant by distribution or apportionment.

The priests had a portion *assigned* them. Gen. xlvii.

2. To designate or appoint for a particular purpose.

They *assigned* Bezer, a city of refuge. Josh. xx.

3. To fix, specify or designate; as an *assigned* quantity.

4. To make or set over; to transfer, sell or convey, by writing, as by indorsing a note, or by any writing on a separate paper.

5. To alledge or show in particular; as, to *assign* a reason for one's conduct.

6. In *law*, to show or set forth with particularity; as, to *assign* error in a writ; to *assign* false judgment.

ASSI'GN, *n.* A person to whom property or an interest is or may be transferred; as, a deed to a man and his heirs and *assigns.*

ASSI'GNABLE, *a.* That may be allotted, appointed or assigned.

2. That may be transferred by writing; as an *assignable* note, or bill.

3. That may be specified, shown with precision, or designated; as an *assignable* error.

AS'SIGNAT, *n.* A public note or bill in France; paper currency. *Burke.*

ASSIGNA'TION, *n.* An appointment of time and place for meeting; used chiefly of love-meetings.

2. A making over by transfer of title. [See *Assignment.*]

3. In *Russia*, a public note or bank bill; paper currency. *Tooke.*

ASSI'GNED, *pp.* Appointed; allotted; made over; shown or designated.

ASSIGNEE', *n.* A person to whom an assignment is made; a person appointed or deputed to do some act, perform some business or enjoy some right, privilege or property; as an *assignee* of a bankrupt. An assignee may be by special appointment or deed, or be created by law; as an executor. *Cowel.*

ASSI'GNER, *n.* One who assigns, or appoints.

ASSI'GNING, *ppr.* Allotting; appointing; transferring; showing specially.

ASSI'GNMENT, *n.* An allotting, or an appointment to a particular person or use.

2. A transfer of title or interest by writing, as of a lease, bond, note, or bill of exchange.

3. The writing by which an interest is transferred.

4. The appointment or designation of causes or actions in court, for trial on particular days.

5. In *law*, the conveyance of the whole interest which a man has in an estate, usually for life or years. It differs from a *lease*, which is the conveyance of a less term than the lessor has in the estate. *Z. Swift.*

ASSIGNOR', *n.* An assigner; a person who assigns or transfers an interest; as the *assignor* of a bill of exchange.

ASSIM'ILABLE, *a.* That may be assimilated.

ASSIM'ILATE, *v. t.* [L. *assimilo*, of *ad* and *similis*, like. See *Similar.*]

1. To bring to a likeness; to cause to resemble. *Swift.*

2. To convert into a like substance; as, food is *assimilated* by conversion into animal substances, flesh, chyle, blood, &c.

ASSIM'ILATE, *v. i.* To become similar.

2. To be converted into a like substance. *Bacon.*

ASSIM'ILATED, *pp.* Brought to a likeness; changed into a like substance.

ASSIM'ILATING, *ppr.* Causing to resemble; converting into a like substance.

ASSIMILA'TION, *n.* The act of bringing to a resemblance.

2. The act or process by which bodies convert other bodies into their own nature and substance; as, flame *assimilates* oil, and the food of animals is by *assimilation* converted into the substances which compose their bodies.

Mineral assimilation is the property which substances possess, in the earth, of appropriating and assimilating to themselves other substances with which they are in contact; a property which seems to be the basis of the natural history of the earth.

ASSIM'ILATIVE, *a.* Having power of converting to a likeness, or to a like substance. *Hakewill.*

ASSIM'ULATE, *v. t.* [L. *assimulo.*] To feign. [*Not used.* See *Simulate.*]

ASSIMULA'TION, *n.* A counterfeiting. [*Not used.* See *Simulation.*]

ASSIST', *v. t.* [L. *assisto*, of *ad* and *sisto*, to stand up; Russ. *siju*, to sit, or be placed; Sp. *asistir;* It. *assistere;* Fr. *assister.* Literally, to be present, or as we still say in English, to *stand by.*]

To help; to aid; to succor; to give support to in some undertaking or effort, or in time of distress.

ASSIST', *v. i.* To lend aid.

ASSIST'ANCE, *n.* Help; aid; furtherance; succor; a contribution of support in bodily strength or other means.

ASSIST'ANT, *a.* Helping; lending aid or support; auxiliary. *Hale.*

ASSIST'ANT, *n.* One who aids, or who contributes his strength or other means to further the designs or welfare of another; an auxiliary. *Dryden.*

ASSIST'ED, *pp.* Helped; aided.

ASSIST'ER, *n.* One that lends aid.

ASSIST'ING, *ppr.* Helping; aiding; supporting with strength or means.

ASSIST'LESS, *a.* Without aid or help. *Pope.*

ASSI'ZE, ASSI'ZES, } *n.* [Fr. *assises*, and sometimes so written in English; L. *assideo*, to sit by, of *ad* and *sedeo*, to sit; Ir. *siasair*, a session. See *Assess.*]

1. Originally, an assembly of knights and other substantial men, with a bailiff or justice, in a certain place and at a certain time, for public busines. The word was sometimes applied to the general council, or *Wittenagemote*, of England. *Blackstone. Glanville.*

2. A court in *England*, held in every county by special commission to one of the judges, who is called a justice of the *assize*, and empowered to take assizes, that is, the verdict of a jury, called the assize.

3. A jury. In this sense the word was applied to the grand assize, for the trial of property, and to the petty assize, for the trial of possession. In *Scotland*, the assize consists of fifteen men, selected from a greater number.

4. A writ; as an *assize of novel disseisin*, which is given to recover the possession of lands, tenements, rents, common, &c., of which the tenant has been lately disseised; *assize of mort d' ancestor*, which lies against an abator, who enters upon land after the death of the tenant, and before the heir enters; *assize of darrein presentment*, which lies against a stranger who presents a clerk to a benefice. *Blackstone.*

5. A particular species of rents, established and not subject to be varied. *Eng. Law.*

6. The time or place of holding the court of assize.

7. In *a more general sense*, any court of justice.

8. A statute of regulation; an ordinance regulating the weight, measure and price of articles sold in market; and hence the word came to signify the weight, measure or price itself; as the *assize* of bread. *Spelman. Cowel. Encyc. Blackstone.*

This word is, in a certain sense, now corrupted into *size*, which see.

ASSI'ZE, *v. t.* To fix the weight, measure or price of commodities, by an ordinance or regulation of authority.

ASSI'ZED, *pp.* Regulated in weight, measure or price, by an assize or ordinance.

ASSI'ZER, *n.* An officer who has the care or inspection of weights and measures. *Chambers.*

ASSI'ZOR, *n.* In *Scotland*, a juror. *Bailey.*

'ASS-LIKE, *a.* Resembling an ass. *Sidney.*

ASSO'BER, *v. t.* [See *Sober.*] To keep under. [*Not used.*] *Gower.*

ASSOCIABIL'ITY, *n.* The quality of being capable of association; the quality of suffering some change by sympathy, or of being affected by the affections of another part of the body. *Darwin.*

ASSO'CIABLE, *a. assóshable.* [See *Associate.*] That may be joined to or associated.

2. In *a medical sense*, liable to be affected by sympathy, or to receive from other parts correspondent feelings and affections. "The stomach, the most *associable* of all the organs of the animal body." *Med. Rep. Darwin.*

ASSO'CIATE, *v. t. assóshate.* [Fr. *associer;* L. *associo*, of *ad* and *socio*, to join.]

1. To join in company, as a friend, companion, partner or confederate; as, to *associate* others with us in business, or in an enterprise.

It conveys the idea of intimate union.

2. To unite in the same mass; as, particles of matter *associated* with other substances.

ASSO'CIATE, *v. i.* To unite in company; to keep company, implying intimacy; as, congenial minds are disposed to *associate.*

2. To unite in action, or be affected by the action of a different part of the body. *Darwin.*

ASSO'CIATE, *a.* Joined in interest or purpose; confederate. *Milton.*

2. Joined in employment or office; as an *associate* judge.

ASSO'CIATE, *n.* A companion; one frequently in company with another, implying intimacy or equality; a mate; a fellow.

2. A partner in interest, as in business; or a confederate in a league.

3. A companion in a criminal transaction; an accomplice.

ASSO'CIATED, *pp.* United in company or in interest; joined.

ASSO'CIATESHIP, *n.* The state or office of an associate. *Encyc. art. Reynolds.*

ASSO'CIATING, *ppr.* Uniting in company or in interest; joining.

ASSOCIA'TION, *n.* The act of associating; union; connection of persons.

2. Union of persons in a company; a society formed for transacting or carrying on some business for mutual advantage; a partnership. It is often applied to a union of states or a confederacy.

3. Union of things; apposition, as of particles of matter.

4. Union or connection of ideas. An *association of ideas* is where two or more ideas constantly or naturally follow each other in the mind, so that one almost infallibly produces the other. *Encyc.*

5. An exertion or change of some extreme part of the sensory residing in the muscles or organs of sense, in consequence of some antecedent or attendant fibrous contractions. *Darwin.*

6. In *ecclesiastical affairs*, a society of the clergy, consisting of a number of pastors of neighboring churches, united for promoting the interests of religion and the harmony of the churches.

ASSOCIA'TIONAL, *a.* Pertaining to an association of clergymen.

ASSO'CIATIVE, *a.* Having the quality of associating, or of being affected by sympathy. *Darwin. Miller.*

ASSOIL', *v. t.* [Old Fr. from L. *absolvo.*] To solve; to release; to absolve. *Obs.* *Mede. Taylor.*

ASSOIL', *v. t.* [Fr. *souiller.*] To soil; to stain. *Obs.*

AS'SONANCE, *n.* [Fr. from L. *ad* and *sono*, to sound. See *Sound.*]

Resemblance of sounds. In *rhetoric* and *poetry*, a resemblance in sound or termination, without making rhyme. *Encyc.*

AS'SONANT, *a.* Having a resemblance of sounds. In Spanish poetry, *assonant* rhymes are those in which a resemblance of sounds serves instead of a natural rhyme; as, *ligera, tierra.* *Encyc.*

ASSORT', *v. t.* [Fr. *assortir;* It. *assortire;* of *ad* and *sortir, sortire*, to sally forth, and in It. to draw lots. See *Sort.*]

1. To separate and distribute into classes things of the like kind, nature or quality, or things which are suited to a like purpose. It is sometimes applied to persons as well as things.

2. To furnish with all sorts. *Burke.*

ASSORT', *v. i.* To agree; to be in accordance with; to suit. *Mitford.*

ASSORT'ED, *pp.* Distributed into sorts, kinds or classes.

2. Furnished with an assortment, or with a variety; as a well *assorted* store. *Burke.*

ASSORT'ING, *ppr.* Separating into sorts; supplying with an assortment.

ASSORT'MENT, *n.* The act of distributing into sorts, kinds or classes, or of selecting and suiting things.

2. A mass or quantity distributed into kinds or sorts; or a number of things assorted.

3. A number of things of the same kind, varied in size, color, quality, price, form, or the like, to suit the market, the wants of people, or various purposes; as an *assortment* of thread, of silks, of calicoes, &c.

An *assortment* of paintings. *W. Coxe.*

4. A variety of sorts or kinds adapted to various wants, demands or purposes; as an *assortment* of goods. *Mercantile Usage.*

ASSOT', *v. t.* [See *Sot.*] To infatuate; to besot. [*Not used.*] *Spenser.*

ASSUA'GE, *v. t.* [This word appears to be formed on the G. *schwach;* D. *zwak*, weak; or on D. *zagt*, soft, gentle, quiet, which coincides with the Sax. *swig*, silence; *swigan*, to be silent; whence *geswigean*, to be silent; D. *zwygen*, id. In Sax. also, *geswican*, is to cease, fail, rest, be quiet. But the Dutch word for *assuage* is *verzagten*, to soften.]

To soften, in *a figurative sense;* to allay, mitigate, ease or lessen, as pain or grief; to appease or pacify, as passion or tumult. In strictness, it signifies rather to *moderate*, than to quiet, tranquilize or reduce to perfect peace or ease.

ASSUA'GE, *v. i.* To abate or subside.

The waters *assuaged.* Gen. viii.

But I apprehend the sense is, the waters were checked; Heb. שך.

ASSUA'GED, *pp.* Allayed; mitigated; eased; appeased.

ASSUA'GEMENT, *n.* Mitigation; abatement.

ASSUA'GER, *n.* One who allays; that which mitigates or abates.

ASSUA'GING, *ppr.* Allaying; mitigating; appeasing; abating.

ASSUA'SIVE, *a.* [from *assuage.*] Softening; mitigating; tranquilizing. *Pope.*

ASSUEFAC'TION, *n.* [L. *assuefacio.*] The act of accustoming. [*Not used.*] *Brown.*

AS'SUETUDE, *n.* [L. *assuetudo*, from *assuetus*, p. of *assuesco*, to accustom.] Custom; habit; habitual use. *Bacon.*

ASSU'ME, *v. t.* [L. *assumo*, of *ad* and *sumo*, to take.]

1. To take or take upon one. It differs from *receive*, in not implying an offer to give.

> The God *assumed* his native form again. *Pope.*

2. To take what is not just; to take with arrogant claims; to arrogate; to seize unjustly; as, to *assume* haughty airs; to *assume* unwarrantable powers.

3. To take for granted, or without proof; to suppose as a fact; as, to *assume* a principle in reasoning.

4. To appropriate, or take to one's self; as, to *assume* the debts of another.

5. To take what is fictitious; to pretend to possess; to take in appearance; as, to *assume* the garb of humility.

ASSUME, *v. i.* To be arrogant; to claim more than is due.

2. In *law*, to take upon one's self an obligation; to undertake or promise; as, A *assumed* upon himself, and promised to pay.

ASSU'MED, *pp.* Taken; arrogated; taken without proof; pretended.

ASSU'MER, *n.* One who assumes; an arrogant person.

ASSU'MING, *ppr.* Taking; arrogating; taking for granted; pretending.

ASSU'MING, *a.* Taking or disposed to take upon one's self more than is just; haughty; arrogant.

ASSU'MING, *n.* Presumption. *Jonson.*

ASSUMP'SIT, *n.* [Pret. tense of L. *assumo.*]

1. In *law*, a promise or undertaking, founded on a consideration. This promise may be verbal or written. An assumpsit is *express* or *implied; express*, when made in words or writing; *implied*, when in consequence of some benefit or consideration accruing to one person from the acts of another, the law presumes that person has promised to make compensation. In this case, the law, upon a principle of justice, *implies* or raises a promise, on which an action may be brought to recover the compensation. Thus if A contracts with B to build a house for him, by implication and intendment of law, A *promises* to pay B for the same, without any express words to that effect.

2. An action founded on a promise. When this action is brought on a debt, it is called *indebitatus assumpsit*, which is an action on the case to recover damages for the nonpayment of a debt. *Blackstone.*

ASSUMPT', *v. t.* To take up; to raise. [*Barbarous and not used.*] *Sheldon.*

ASSUMPT', *n.* That which is assumed. [*Not used.*] *Chillingworth.*

ASSUMP'TION, *n.* [L. *assumptio.*]

1. The act of taking to one's self. *Hammond.*

2. The act of taking for granted, or supposing a thing without proof; supposition. *Norris.*

> This gives no sanction to the unwarrantable *assumption* that the soul sleeps from the period of death to the resurrection of the body. *Thodey.*

3. The thing supposed; a postulate or proposition assumed. In *logic*, the minor or second proposition in a categorical syllogism. *Encyc.*

4. A consequence drawn from the propositions of which an argument is composed. *Encyc.*

5. Undertaking; a taking upon one's self. *Kent.*

6. In *the Romish Church*, the taking up a person into heaven, as the Virgin Mary. Also a festival in honor of the miraculous ascent of Mary, celebrated by the Romish and Greek churches. *Encyc.*

7. Adoption. *Warton.*

ASSUMP'TIVE, *a.* That is or may be assumed. In heraldry, *assumptive* arms are such as a person has a right, with the approbation of his sovereign, and of the heralds, to assume, in consequence of an exploit. *Encyc.*

ASSU'RANCE, *n. ashu'rance.* [Fr. from *assurer*, of *ad* and *sûr, seur*, sure, certain. Qu. the Rab. and Talm. אשר, to make firm, confirm, verify; or is *seur* the G. *zwar*, from the root of L. *verus;* or L. *securus*, contracted.]

1. The act of assuring, or of making a declaration in terms that furnish ground of confidence; as, I trusted to his *assurances;* or the act of furnishing any ground of full confidence.

> Whereof he hath given *assurance* to all men, in that he hath raised him from the dead. Acts xvii.

2. Firm persuasion; full confidence or trust; freedom from doubt; certain expectation; the utmost certainty.

> Let us draw near with a true heart, in full *assurance* of faith. Heb. x.

3. Firmness of mind; undoubting steadiness; intrepidity.

> Brave men meet danger with *assurance.* *Knolles.*

4. Excess of boldness; impudence; as, his *assurance* is intolerable.

5. Freedom from excessive modesty, timidity or bashfulness; laudable confidence.

> Conversation with the world will give them knowledge and *assurance.* *Locke.*

6. Insurance; a contract to make good a loss. [See *Insurance.*]

7. Any writing or legal evidence of the conveyance of property. *Blackstone.*

8. Conviction. *Tillotson.*

9. In *theology*, full confidence of one's interest in Christ, and of final salvation.

ASSU'RE, *v. t. ashu're.* [Fr. *assurer.* See *Assurance.*]

1. To make certain; to give confidence by a promise, declaration, or other evidence; as, he *assured* me of his sincerity.

2. To confirm; to make certain or secure.

> And it shall be *assured* to him. Lev. xxvii.

3. To embolden; to make confident.

> And hereby we shall *assure* our hearts before him. 1 John iii.

4. To make secure, with *of* before the object secured; as, let me be *assured of* your fidelity.

5. To affiance; to betroth. *Obs.* *Shak.*

6. To insure; to covenant to indemnify for loss. [See *Insure.*]

ASSU'RED, *pp.* Made certain or confident; made secure; insured.

ASSU'RED, *a.* Certain; indubitable; not doubting; bold to excess. *Bacon. Shak.*

ASSU'REDLY, *adv.* Certainly; indubitably.

> *Assuredly* thy son Solomon shall reign. 1 Kings i.

ASSU'REDNESS, *n.* The state of being assured; certainty; full confidence. *Hakewill.*

ASSU'RER, *n.* One who assures; one who insures against loss; an insurer or underwriter.

ASSUR'GENT, *a.* [L. *assurgens, assurgo.*] Rising upwards in an arch; as an *assurgent* stem, in botany. *Eaton.*

ASSU'RING, *ppr.* Making sure or confident; giving security; confirming.

ASSWA'GE. [See *Assuage.*]

AS'TACITE, } *n.* [Gr. ασακος, a craw-
AS'TACOLITE, } fish, and λιθος, a stone.]

Petrified or fossil crawfish, and other crustaceous animals; called also *cancrites, crabites*, and *gammarolites.*

AS'TEISM, *n.* [Gr. ασειος, beautiful, polite.] In *rhetoric*, genteel irony; a polite and ingenious manner of deriding another. *Encyc.*

AS'TER, *n.* [Gr. αςηρ.] A genus of plants, with compound flowers, many of which are cultivated for their beauty, particularly the China Aster. The species are very numerous.

ASTE'RIAS, } *n.* [Gr. αςηρ, a star.] Stella
AS'TER, } marina, sea-star, or star

fish, a genus of the order of *Molluscas.* It has a depressed body with a coriaceous coat; is composed of five or more segments running out from a central part, and furnished with numerous tentacles, with a mouth below, in the center. There are many species. *Encyc.*

ASTE'RIATED, *a.* [*Supra.*] Radiated; presenting diverging rays, like a star; as *asteriated* sapphire. *Cleaveland.*

ASTE'RIATITE, *n.* Petrified asterias.

AS'TERISK, *n.* [Gr. αςερισκος, a little star, from αςηρ, a star.] The figure of a star, thus, *, used in printing and writing as a reference to a passage or note in the margin, or to fill the space when a name is omitted.

AS'TERISM, *n.* [Gr. αςερισμος, a little star, from αςηρ, a star.]

1. A constellation; a sign in the zodiac.

> The figures of the twelve *asterisms.* *As. Researches.*

2. An asterisk, or mark of reference. [*This is less proper.*]

AS'TERITE, or star stone. [See *Astrite.*]

ASTERN', *adv.* [*a* or *at*, and *stern.* See *Stern.*]

1. In or at the hinder part of a ship; or towards the hinder part, or backwards; as, to go *astern.*

2. Behind a ship, at any indefinite distance. *Mar. Dict.*

AS'TEROID, *n.* [Gr. αςηρ, a star, and ειδος, form.]

A name given by Herschel to the newly discovered planets between the orbits of Mars and Jupiter.

ASTEROID'AL, *a.* Resembling a star; or pertaining to the asteroids. *Journ. of Science.*

AS'TEROPODE, ASTEROPO'DIUM, *n.* [Gr. αςηρ, a star, and πους, ποδος, a foot.]
A kind of extraneous fossil, of the same substance with the astrite, to which it serves as the base. *Encyc.*

ASTERT', *v. t.* To startle. [*Not in use.*] *Spenser.*

ASTHEN'IC, *a.* *asten'ic.* [Gr. α priv. and σθενος, strength.]
Weak; characterized by extreme debility. *Brown.*

ASTHENOL'OGY, *n.* [Gr. α priv., σθενος, strength, and λογος, discourse.]
The doctrine of diseases arising from debility. *Coxe.*

ASTHMA, *n.* *ast'ma.* [Gr. ασθμα.]
A shortness of breath; intermitting difficulty of breathing, with cough, straitness and wheezing. *Coxe.*

ASTHMAT'IC, *a.* Pertaining to asthma; also affected by asthma; as an *asthmatic* patient.

ASTIPULATE for *Stipulate.* ASTIPULATION for *Stipulation.* [*Not in use.*]

ASTO'NE, ASTO'NY, *v. t.* [See *Astonish.*] To terrify or astonish. *Obs.* *Chaucer.*

ASTO'NED, ASTO'NIED, *pp.* Astonished. *Obs.* *Spencer.* *Milton.*

ASTON'ISH, *v. t.* [Old Fr. *estonner*, now *étonner*; L. *attono*, to astonish; *ad* and *tono*. Sax. *gestun*, noise, and *stunian*, to stun; G. *staunen*; Arm. *eston*, wonderfully. The primary sense is, to stop, to strike dumb, to fix. See *Tone* and *Stun.*]
To stun or strike dumb with sudden fear, terror, surprise or wonder; to amaze; to confound with some sudden passion.

I Daniel was *astonished* at the vision. Dan. viii.

ASTON'ISHED, *pp.* Amazed; confounded with fear, surprise, or admiration.

ASTON'ISHING, *ppr.* Amazing; confounding with wonder or fear.

ASTON'ISHING, *a.* Very wonderful; of a nature to excite great admiration, or amazement.

ASTON'ISHINGLY, *adv.* In a manner or degree to excite amazement. *Bp. Fleetwood.*

ASTON'ISHINGNESS, *n.* The quality of exciting astonishment.

ASTON'ISHMENT, *n.* Amazement; confusion of mind from fear, surprise or admiration, at an extraordinary or unexpected event.

ASTOUND', *v. t.* To astonish; to strike dumb with amazement. From Old Fr. *estonner.*

ASTRAD'DLE, *adv.* [*a* and *straddle.* See *Straddle.*]
With the legs across a thing, or on different sides; as, to sit *astraddle.*

AS'TRAGAL, *n.* [Gr. αςραγαλος, a turning joint, vertebra, spondylus.]
1. In *architecture*, a little round molding which surrounds the top or bottom of a column, in the form of a ring; representing a ring or band of iron, to prevent the splitting of the column. It is often cut into beads or berries, and is used in ornamented entablatures to separate the several faces of the architrave. *Encyc.*
2. In *gunnery*, a round molding on cannon near the mouth. *Encyc.*
3. In *anatomy*, the buckle, ankle, or sling bone; the upper bone of the foot supporting the tibia. *Coxe.*
4. In *botany*, the wood pea; the milk vetch; the liquorice vetch.

AS'TRAL, *a.* [L. *astrum*; Gr. αςηρ, a star.]
Belonging to the stars; starry. *Dryden.*

ASTRA'Y, *adv.* [*a* and *stray.* See *Stray.*]
Out of the right way or proper place, both in a literal and figurative sense. In morals and religion, it signifies wandering from the path of rectitude, from duty and happiness.

Before I was afflicted, I went *astray.* Ps. cxix.

Cattle go *astray* when they leave their proper owners or inclosures. See Deut. xxii.

ASTRE'A, *n.* [Gr. αςηρ, a star.]
The goddess of justice. A name sometimes given to the sign *virgo.* The poets feign that justice quitted heaven, in the golden age, to reside on earth; but becoming weary with the iniquities of men, she returned to heaven, and commenced a constellation of stars. *Encyc.*

ASTRICT', *v. t.* [L. *astringo, astrictus.* See *Astringe.*]
To bind fast, or compress. [*Not much used.*]

ASTRICT', *a.* Compendious; contracted. *Weever.*

ASTRICT'ED, *pp.* Bound fast; compressed with bandages.

ASTRICT'ING, *ppr.* Binding close; compressing; contracting.

ASTRIC'TION, *n.* The act of binding close, or compressing with ligatures.
2. A contraction of parts by applications; the stopping of hemorrhages. *Coxe.*

ASTRICT'IVE, *a.* Binding; compressing; styptic.

ASTRICT'ORY, *a.* Astringent; binding; apt to bind.

ASTRIF'EROUS, *a.* [L. *astrifer*; *astrum*, a star, and *fero*, to bear.]
Bearing or containing stars. [*Little used.*]

ASTRIG'EROUS, *a.* [Low L. *astriger.*]
Bearing stars. [*Not used.*]

ASTRINGE, *v. t.* *astrinj'.* [L. *astringo*, of *ad* and *stringo*, to bind fast, to *strain.* See *Strain.*]
To compress; to bind together; to contract by pressing the parts together. *Bacon.*

ASTRING'ED, *pp.* Compressed; straitened; contracted.

ASTRING'ENCY, *n.* The power of contracting the parts of the body; that quality in medicines which binds, contracts or strengthens parts which are relaxed; as the *astringency* of acids or bitters. *Bacon.*

ASTRING'ENT, *a.* Binding; contracting; strengthening; opposed to *laxative.* *Quincy.*

ASTRING'ENT, *n.* A medicine which binds or contracts the parts of the body to which it is applied, restrains profuse discharges, coagulates animal fluids, condenses and strengthens the solids. *Coxe.*
Modern practice inclines to the use of *astringent*, for internal applications, and *styptic*, for external.

ASTRING'ER, *n.* A falconer that keeps a goss hawk. *Shak.*

ASTRING'ING, *ppr.* Compressing; binding fast; contracting.

AS'TRITE, *n.* [Gr. αςηρ, a star; Fr. *astroite.*]
An extraneous fossil, called also *asteria* and *astroit.* Astrites are stones in the form of small, short, angular, or sulcated columns, about an inch and a half long, and the third of an inch in diameter, composed of several regular joints, which, when separated, resemble a radiated star. *Encyc.*
Astrites are said to be detached articulations of encrinites, a kind of marine polypier.

ASTROG'RAPHY, *n.* [Gr. αςηρ, or αςρον, a star, and γραφω, to describe.]
A description of the stars, or the science of describing them.

AS'TROIT, *n.* Star-stone. [See *Astrite.*]
2. A species of petrified madrepore often found in calcarious stones.

AS'TROLABE, *n.* [Gr. αςηρ, a star, and λαβειν, to take.]
1. An instrument formerly used for taking the altitude of the sun or stars at sea.
2. A stereographic projection of the sphere, either upon the plane of the equator, the eye being supposed to be in the pole of the world; or upon the plane of the meridian, the eye being in the point of intersection of the equinoctial and the horizon.
3. Among *the ancients*, the same as the modern armillary sphere. *Encyc.*

ASTROL'OGER, ASTROLO'GIAN, *n.* [L. *astrologus*, of αςρον, a star, and λογος, discourse.]
1. One who professes to foretell future events by the aspects and situation of the stars. *Astrologian* is little used. *Wotton.*
2. Formerly, one who understood the motions of the planets, without predicting. *Raleigh.*

ASTROLOG'IC, ASTROLOG'ICAL, *a.* Pertaining to astrology; professing or practicing astrology.

ASTROLOG'ICALLY, *adv.* In the manner of astrology.

ASTROL'OGIZE, *v. i.* To practice astrology.

ASTROL'OGY, *n.* [*Supra.*] A science which teaches to judge of the effects and influences of the stars, and to foretell future events, by their situation and different aspects. This science was formerly in great request, as men ignorantly supposed the heavenly bodies to have a ruling influence over the physical and moral world; but it is now universally exploded by true science and philosophy.

ASTRON'OMER, *n.* One who is versed in astronomy; one who has a knowledge of the laws of the heavenly orbs, or the principles by which their motions are regulated, with their various phenomena.

ASTRONOM'IC, ASTRONOM'ICAL, *a.* Pertaining to astronomy.

ASTRONOM'ICALLY, *adv.* In an astronomical manner; by the principles of astronomy.

ASTRON'OMIZE, *v. i.* To study astronomy. [*Little used.*] *Brown.*

ASTRON'OMY, *n.* [Gr. αςρον, a star, and νομος, a law or rule.]

The science which teaches the knowledge of the celestial bodies, their magnitudes, motions, distances, periods of revolution, aspects, eclipses, order, &c. This science depends on observations, made chiefly with instruments, and upon mathematical calculations.

AS'TROSCOPE, *n.* [Gr. αςρον, a star, and σκοπεω, to view.]

An astronomical instrument, composed of two cones, on whose surface the constellations, with their stars, are delineated, by means of which the stars may be easily known. *Encyc.*

AS'TROSCOPY, *n.* [See *Astroscope.*] Observation of the stars.

ASTRO-THEOL'OGY, *n.* [L. *astrum*, a star, and *theologia*, divinity.]

Theology founded on the observation of the celestial bodies. *Derham.*

ASTRUT', *adv.* [See *Strut.*] In a strutting manner.

ASTU'TE, *a.* [L. *astutus*, from *astus*, craft, subtilty; Ir. *aisde, aiste*, ingenuity.]

Shrewd; sharp; eagle-eyed; critically examining or discerning. *Sandys.*

ASUND'ER, *adv.* [Sax. *asundrian*, to divide. See *Sunder.*]

Apart; into parts; separately; in a divided state.

The Lord hath cut *asunder* the cords of the wicked. Ps. cxxix.

ASWOON', *adv.* In a swoon. *Obs.* *Gower.*

ASY'LUM, *n.* [L. from Gr. ασυλον, safe from spoil, α and συλη, spoil, συλαω, to plunder.]

1. A sanctuary, or place of refuge, where criminals and debtors shelter themselves from justice, and from which they cannot be taken without sacrilege. Temples and altars were anciently asylums; as were tombs, statues and monuments. The ancient heathens allowed asylums for the protection of the vilest criminals; and the Jews had their cities of refuge.

2. Any place of retreat and security.

ASYM'METRAL, ASYMMET'RICAL, } *a.* [See *Symmetry.*]

Not having symmetry. [*Little used.*] *More.*

ASYM'METRY, *n.* [Gr. α priv. and συμμετρια, symmetry, of συν, with, and μετρεω, to measure.]

The want of proportion between the parts of a thing. It is also used in mathematics for incommensurability, when between two quantities there is no common measure. *Johnson.*

AS'YMPTOTE, *n.* [Gr. α priv., συν, with, and πτοω, to fall; not meeting or coinciding.]

A line which approaches nearer and nearer to some curve, but though infinitely extended, would never meet it. This may be conceived as a tangent to a curve at an infinite distance. *Chambers.*

ASYMPTOT'ICAL, *a.* Belonging to an asymptote. Asymptotical lines or curves are such as continually approach, when extended, but never meet.

ASYN'DETON, *n.* [Gr. α priv. and συνδεω, to bind together.]

In *grammar*, a figure which omits the connective; as, *veni, vidi, vici.* It stands opposed to *polysyndeton*, which is a multiplication of connectives. *Campbell.*

AT, *prep.* [Sax. *æt*; Goth. *at*; L. *ad.* *At*, *ad* and *to*, if not radically the same word, often coincide in signification. In W. *at* is *to*, and in Danish it is the sign of the infinitive mode; in Amh. *od*, or *ud*, is towards. The word *at* is doubtless the oriental אתא, אתה, Ch. and Heb. to come, to approach. Hence it primarily denotes *presence, meeting, nearness, direction towards.*]

In general, *at* denotes *nearness*, or *presence*; as *at* the ninth hour, *at* the house; but it is less definite than *in* or *on*; *at* the house, may be *in* or *near* the house. It denotes also *towards, versus*; as, to aim an arrow *at* a mark.

From this original import are derived all the various uses of *at*. *At* the sight, is *with, present*, or *coming* the sight; *at* this news, *present* the news, *on* or *with* the approach or arrival of this news. *At* peace, *at* war, in a state of peace or war, peace or war existing, being present; *at* ease, *at* play, *at* a loss, &c. convey the like idea. *At* arms, furnished with arms, bearing arms, present with arms; *at* hand, within reach of the hand, and therefore *near*; *at* my cost, *with* my cost; *at* his suit, *by* or *with* his suit; *at* this declaration, he rose from his seat, that is, present, or coming this declaration; whence results the idea *in consequence of it.* *At* his command, is either *under* his command, that is, literally, coming or being come his command, in the power of, or in consequence of it. He is good *at* engraving, *at* husbandry; that is, in performing that business. He deserves well *at* our hands, that is, from us. The peculiar phrases in which this word occurs, with appropriate significations, are numerous. *At* first, *at* last, *at* least, *at* best, *at* the worst, *at* the highest or lowest, are phrases in which some noun is implied; as, at the first time or beginning; at the last time, or point of time; at the least or best degree, &c.; all denoting an extreme point or superlative degree. *At all*, is in any manner or degree.

At is sometimes used for *to*, or *towards*, noting progression or direction; as, he aims *at* perfection; he makes or runs *at* him, or points *at* him. In this phrase, he longs to be *at* him, *at* has its general sense of *approaching*, or *present*, or *with*, in contest or attack.

AT'ABAL, *n.* [Sp.] A kettle drum; a kind of tabor. *Dryden.*

ATAC'AMITE, *n.* A muriate of copper.

AT'AGAS, *n.* The red cock or moor-game. *Coxe.*

ATAMAS'CO, *n.* A species of lily of the genus *Amaryllis.*

AT'ARAXY, *n.* [Gr. αταραχος, of α priv. and ταραχη, tumult.]

Calmness of mind; a term used by the stoics and sceptics to denote a freedom from the emotions which proceed from vanity and self-conceit. *Encyc.*

ATAX'Y, *n.* [Gr. α priv. and ταξις, order.] Want of order; disturbance; irregularity in the functions of the body, or in the crises and paroxysms of disease. *Coxe. Encyc.*

ATCHE, *n.* In *Turkey*, a small silver coin, value about six or seven mills. *Encyc.*

ATE, the preterite of *eat*, which see.

A'TE, *n.* a'ty. [Gr. ατη, mischief; αταω, to hurt. *Ate* is a personification of evil, mischief or malice.]

In *pagan mythology*, the goddess of mischief, who was cast down from heaven by Jupiter. *Pope's Hom. Il.*

ATEL'LAN, *a.* Relating to the dramas at Atella in Italy. *Shaftesbury.*

ATEL'LAN, *n.* A dramatic representation, satirical or licentious. *Shaftesbury.*

A TEMP'O GIUSTO. [It.; L. *in tempore justo.*]

A direction in music, which signifies to sing or play in an equal, true or just time.

ATHANA'SIAN, *a.* Pertaining to Athanasius, bishop of Alexandria, in the fourth century. The Athanasian creed is a formulary, confession or exposition of faith, supposed formerly to have been drawn up by Athanasius, but this opinion is now rejected, and the composition is ascribed by some to Hilary, bishop of Arles. It is a summary of what was called the orthodox faith.

ATH'ANOR, *n.* [Ar. and Heb. תנור thanor, an oven or furnace.]

A digesting furnace, formerly used in chimical operations; so constructed as to maintain a uniform and durable heat. It is a furnace, with a lateral tower close on all sides, which is to be filled with fuel. As the fuel below is consumed, that in the tower falls down to supply its place. *Nicholson.*

A'THEISM, *n.* The disbelief of the existence of a God, or Supreme intelligent Being.

Atheism is a ferocious system that leaves nothing above us to excite awe, nor around us, to awaken tenderness. *Rob. Hall.*

A'THEIST, *n.* [Gr. αθεος, of α priv. and θεος, God.]

One who disbelieves the existence of a God, or Supreme intelligent Being.

A'THEIST, *a.* Atheistical; disbelieving or denying the being of a Supreme God.

ATHEIST'IC, ATHEIST'ICAL, } *a.* Pertaining to atheism.

2. Disbelieving the existence of a God; impious; *applied to persons*; as, an *atheistic* writer.

3. Implying or containing atheism; *applied to things*; as, *atheistic* doctrines or opinions.

ATHEIST'ICALLY, *adv.* In an atheistic manner; impiously.

ATHEIST'ICALNESS, *n.* The quality of being atheistical.

A'THEIZE, *v. i.* To discourse as an atheist. [*Not used.*] *Cudworth.*

ATHEL, ADEL or ÆTHEL, noble, of illustrious birth; Sax. *ædel, æthel*; G. *adel*; D. *edel*; Sw. *ædel*; Dan. *ædel*; Ar. أثل athala, to be well rooted, to be of noble origin. This word is found in many Saxon names; as in *Atheling*, a noble youth; *Ethelred*, noble counsel; *Ethelard*, noble genius; *Ethelbert*, noble bright, eminently noble; *Ethelwald*, noble government, or power; *Ethelward*, noble defender.

ATHE'NIAN, *a.* [from *Athens.*] Pertaining to Athens, the metropolis of Attica in Greece.

ATHE'NIAN, *n.* A native or inhabitant of Athens.

ATHEOLO'GIAN, *n.* One who is opposed to a theologian. *Hayward.*

ATHEOL'OGY, *n.* Atheism. [*Not in use.*] *Swift.*

A'THEOUS, *a.* Atheistic; impious. [*Not used.*] *Milton.*

ATH'ERINE, } *n.* A genus of fishes of the ATHERI'NA, } abdominal order. The characters are, the upper jaw is rather flat, the rays of the gill membrane are six, and the side belt or line shines like silver. There are four species; the best known is the *Hepsetus*, very abundant in the Mediterranean, where it is caught in large quantities. *Pennant. Ed. Encyc.*

ATHERO'MA, } *n.* [Gr. from αθηρα, pap.] ATH'EROME, }
An encysted tumor, without pain or discoloration of the skin, containing matter like pap, intermixed with hard stony particles; easily cured by incision. *Encyc. Coxe.*

ATHERO'MATOUS, *a.* Pertaining to or resembling an atherome; having the qualities of an atherome. *Wiseman.*

ATHIRST', *a. athurst'.* [*a* and *thirst.* See *Thirst.*]
1. Thirsty; wanting drink.
2. Having a keen appetite or desire.

He had a soul *athirst* for knowledge. *Ch. Observer.*

ATHLE'TE, *n.* [See *Athletic.*] A contender for victory. *A. Smith's Theory.*

ATHLET'IC, *a.* [Gr. αθλητης; L. *athleta*, a wrestler; from αεθλος, strife, contest.]
1. Belonging to wrestling, boxing, running and other exercises and sports, which were practiced by the ancients, usually called the *athletic* games. Hence,
2. Strong; lusty; robust; vigorous. An *athletic* body or constitution is one fitted for vigorous exertions.

ATHWART', *prep.* [*a* and *thwart.* See *Thwart.*]
1. Across; from side to side; transverse; as *athwart* the path.
2. In *marine language*, across the line of a ship's course; as, a fleet standing *athwart* our course.

Athwart hause, is the situation of a ship when she lies across the stem of another, whether near, or at some distance.

Athwart the fore foot, is a phrase applied to the flight of a cannon ball, across another ship's course, ahead, as a signal for her to bring to.

Athwart ships, reaching across the ship from side to side, or in that direction. *Mar. Dict.*

ATHWART', *adv.* In a manner to cross and perplex; crossly; wrong; wrongfully.

ATILT', *adv.* [*a* and *tilt.* See *Tilt.*]
1. In the manner of a tilter; in the position, or with the action of a man making a thrust; as, to stand or run *atilt.*
2. In the manner of a cask tilted, or with one end raised.

AT'IMY, *n.* [Gr. ατιμια, α and τιμη, honor.]
In *ancient Greece*, disgrace; exclusion from office or magistracy, by some disqualifying act or decree. *Mitford.*

ATLAN'TIAN, } *a.* Pertaining to the isle ATLANTE'AN, } Atlantis, which the ancients alledge was sunk and overwhelmed by the ocean. *Plato.*
2. Pertaining to Atlas; resembling Atlas.

ATLAN'TIC, *a.* [from *Atlas* or *Atlantis.*]
Pertaining to that division of the ocean, which lies between Europe and Africa on the east and America on the west.

ATLAN'TIC, *n.* The ocean, or that part of the ocean, which is between Europe and Africa on the east and America on the west.

ATLAN'TICA, } *n.* An isle mentioned by ATLAN'TIS, } the ancients, situated west of Gades, or Cadiz, on the strait of Gibraltar. The poets mention two isles and call them *Hesperides*, western isles, and *Elysian fields.* Authors are not agreed whether these isles were the Canaries, or some other isles, or the continent of America. *Homer. Horace.*

ATLAN'TIDES, *n.* A name given to the Pleiades or seven stars, which were feigned to be the daughters of Atlas, a king of Mauritania, or of his brother, Hesperus, who were translated to heaven. *Encyc.*

ATLAN'TIS, *n.* A fictitious philosophical commonwealth of Lord Bacon, or the piece describing it; composed in the manner of More's Utopia, and Campanella's *City of the Sun.* One part of the work is finished, in which the author has described a college, founded for the study of Nature, under the name of *Solomon's House.* The model of a commonwealth was never executed. *Encyc.*

AT'LAS, *n.* A collection of maps in a volume; supposed to be so called from a picture of mount Atlas, supporting the heavens, prefixed to some collection. *Johnson.*
2. A large square folio, resembling a volume of maps.
3. The supporters of a building.
4. A silk sattin, or stuff, manufactured in the east, with admirable ingenuity. Atlasses are plain, striped, or flowered; but they have not the fine gloss and luster of some French silks. *Encyc.*
5. The first verteber of the neck. *Coxe.*
6. A term applied to paper, as *atlas* fine. *Burke.*

ATMOM'ETER, *n.* [Gr. ατμος, vapor, and μετρεω, to measure.]
An instrument to measure the quantity of exhalation from a humid surface in a given time; an evaporometer. *Ure.*

AT'MOSPHERE, *n.* [Gr. ατμος, vapor, and σφαιρα, a *sphere.*]
The whole mass of fluid, consisting of air, aqueous and other vapors, surrounding the earth.

ATMOSPHER'IC } *a.* Pertaining to the ATMOSPHER'ICAL, } atmosphere; as *atmospheric* air or vapors.
2. Dependent on the atmosphere.

I am an *atmospheric* creature. *Pope.*

AT'OM, *n.* [Gr. ατομος; L. *atomus*; from α, not, and τεμνω, to cut.]
1. A particle of matter so minute as to admit of no division. Atoms are conceived to be the first principles or component parts of all bodies. *Quincy.*
2. The ultimate or smallest component part of a body. *Chimistry.*
3. Any thing extremely small. *Shak.*

ATOM'IC, } *a.* Pertaining to atoms; con- ATOM'ICAL, } sisting of atoms; extremely minute.

The *atomical* philosophy, said to be broached by Moschus, before the Trojan war, and cultivated by Epicurus, teaches that atoms are endued with gravity and motion, by which all things were formed, without the aid of a supreme intelligent Being.

The *atomic theory*, in chimistry, or the doctrine of *definite proportions*, teaches that all chimical combinations take place between the ultimate particles or *atoms* of bodies, and that these unite either atom with atom, or in proportions expressed by some simple multiple of the number of atoms. *Dalton.*

AT'OMISM, *n.* The doctrine of atoms.

AT'OMIST, *n.* One who holds to the atomical philosophy.

AT'OM-LIKE, *a.* Resembling atoms. *Browne.*

AT'OMY, *n.* A word used by Shakspeare for *atom*; also an abbreviation of *anatomy.*

ATO'NE, *adv.* [*at* and *one.*] At one; together. *Spenser.*

ATO'NE, *v. i.* [Supposed to be compounded of *at* and *one.* The Spanish has *adunar*, to unite or join, and the Ital. *adunare*, to assemble; from L. *ad* and *unus*, *unio.* In Welsh, *dyun* signifies united, accordant, agreeing; *dyunaw*, to unite or agree; from *un*, one, and *dy*, a prefix denoting iteration.]
1. To agree; to be in accordance; to accord.

He and Aufidus can no more *atone*,
Than violentest contrariety. *Shak.*

[*This sense is obsolete.*]
2. To stand as an equivalent; to make reparation, amends or satisfaction for an offense or a crime, by which reconciliation is procured between the offended and offending parties.

The murderer fell and blood *atoned* for blood. *Pope.*

By what propitiation shall I *atone* for my former gravity. *Rambler*, No. 10.

The life of a slave was deemed to be of so little value, that a very slight compensation *atoned* for taking it away. *Robertson, Charles V.*

3. *To atone for*, to make compensation or amends.

This evil was *atoned for* by the good effects of the study of the practical physics of Aristotle. *Schlegel, Trans.*

The ministry not *atoning for* their former conduct by any wise or popular measure. *Junius.*

ATO'NE, *v. t.* To expiate; to answer or make satisfaction for.

Or each *atone* his guilty love with life. *Pope.*

2. To reduce to concord; to reconcile, as parties at variance; to appease. [*Not now used.*]

ATO'NED, *pp.* Expiated; appeased; reconciled.

ATO'NEMENT, *n.* Agreement; concord; reconciliation, after enmity or controversy. Rom. v.

He seeks to make *atonement*
Between the Duke of Glo'ster and your brothers. *Shak.*

2. Expiation; satisfaction or reparation made by giving an equivalent for an injury, or by doing or suffering that which is received in satisfaction for an offense or injury; with *for.*

And Moses said to Aaron, go to the altar, and offer thy sin-offering, and thy burnt-offering, and make an *atonement* for thyself and for the people. Lev. ix.

When a man has been guilty of any vice, the best *atonement* he can make for it is, to warn others not to fall into the like. *Spect.* No. 8.

The Phocians behaved with so much gallantry, that they were thought to have made a sufficient *atonement* for their former offense. *Potter, Antiq.*

3. In *theology*, the expiation of sin made by the obedience and personal sufferings of Christ.

ATO'NER, *n.* He who makes atonement.

ATON'IC, *a.* Relaxed; debilitated.

ATO'NING, *ppr.* Reconciling. *Obs.*

2. Making amends, or satisfaction.

AT'ONY, *n.* [Gr. ατονια, defect, of α priv. and τονος, tone, from τεινω, to stretch.]

Debility; relaxation; a want of tone or tension; defect of muscular power; palsy. *Wilson. Coxe.*

ATOP' *adv.* [*a* and *top*. See *Top*.] On or at the top. *Milton.*

ATRABILA'RIAN, ATRABILA'RIOUS, } *a.* [L. *atra bilis*, black bile.]

Affected with melancholy, which the ancients attributed to the bile; replete with black bile.

ATRABILA'RIOUSNESS, *n.* The state of being melancholy, or affected with disordered bile.

ATRAMENT'AL, ATRAMENT'OUS, } *a.* [L. *atramentum*, ink, from *ater*, black.]

Inky; black like ink.

ATRAMENTA'RIOUS, *a.* Like ink; suitable for making ink. The sulphate of iron, or green copperas, is called *atramentarious*, as being the material of ink. *Fourcroy.*

ATRIP', *adv.* [*a* and *trip*. See *Trip*.]

In *nautical language*, the anchor is *atrip*, when drawn out of the ground in a perpendicular direction. The topsails are *atrip*, when they are hoisted to the top of the mast, or as high as possible. *Mar. Dict.*

ATRO'CIOUS, *a.* [L. *atrox*, *trux*, fierce, cruel.]

Extremely hainous, criminal or cruel; enormous; outrageous; as *atrocious* guilt or offense.

ATRO'CIOUSLY, *adv.* In an atrocious manner; with enormous cruelty or guilt.

ATRO'CIOUSNESS, *n.* The quality of being enormously criminal or cruel.

ATROC'ITY, *n.* Enormous wickedness; extreme hainousnes or cruelty; as the *atrocity* of murder.

AT'ROPHY, *n.* [Gr. α priv. and τρεφω, to nourish.]

A consumption or wasting of the flesh, with loss of strength, without any sensible cause or hectic fever; a wasting from defect of nourishment. *Encyc. Coxe.*

ATRO'PIA, *n.* A new vegetable alkali extracted from the *atropa belladonna*, or deadly nightshade. It is white, brilliant and crystalizes in long needles. *Ure.*

ATTACH', *v. t.* [Fr. *attacher*, to tie or fasten, to apply, to engage, to stick; Arm. *staga*; It. *attaccare*; Norm. *attacher*, to attack; *tache*, tied, fixed, tacked together; Port. Sp. *atacar*. It seems to be allied to *attack*, and the sense is to put, throw or fall on, hence to seize, and stop, coinciding with the Eng. *take*; Sw. *taga*; Dan. *tager*; Sax. *tæccan*; Gr. δεχομαι; L. *tango*, for *tago*; Eng. *tack*; &c. Class, Dg. See *Attack* and *Tack*.]

1. To take by legal authority; to arrest the person by writ, to answer for a debt; applied to a taking of the person by a *civil* process; being never used for the arrest of a criminal. It is applied also to the taking of goods and real estate by an officer, by virtue of a writ or precept, to hold the same to satisfy a judgment to be rendered in the suit.

2. To take, seize and lay hold on, by moral force, as by affection or interest; to win the heart; to fasten or bind by moral influence; as, *attached* to a friend; *attaching* others to us by wealth or flattery.

3. To make to adhere; to tie, bind or fasten; as, to *attach* substances by any glutinous matter; to *attach* one thing to another by a string.

ATTACH'ABLE, *a.* That may be legally attached; liable to be taken by writ or precept.

ATTACH'ED, *pp.* Taken by writ or precept; drawn to and fixed, or united by affection or interest.

ATTACH'ING, *ppr.* Taking or seizing by commandment or writ; drawing to, and fixing by influence; winning the affections.

ATTACH'MENT, *n.* A taking of the person, goods or estate by a writ or precept in a civil action, to secure a debt or demand.

2. A writ directing the person or estate of a person to be taken, to secure his appearance before a court. In *England*, the first notice to appear in court is by *summons*; and if the defendant disobeys this monition, a writ of attachment issues, commanding the sheriff to *attach* him, by taking gage, or security in goods, which he forfeits by non-appearance, or by making him find safe pledges or sureties for his appearance. But in trespasses, an attachment is the first process. In *this country*, *attachment* is more generally the first process, and in some states, the writ of attachment issues at first against the property or person of the defendant. In *Connecticut*, this writ issues against the person, goods or land, in the first instance, commanding to take the goods and estate of the defendant, if to be found; or otherwise, to take his body. In *England*, witnesses not appearing upon a summons, may be taken by *attachment*; a process called with us a *capias*. Attachments also issue against persons for contempt of court. The *court of attachments*, in England, is held before the verderors of the forest, to *attach* and try offenders against vert and venison.

Foreign attachment is the taking of the money or goods of a debtor in the hands of a stranger; as when the debtor is not within the jurisdiction of the court or has absconded. Any person who has goods or effects of a debtor, is considered in law as the agent, attorney, factor or trustee of the debtor; and an attachment served on such person binds the property in his hands to respond the judgment against the debtor.

3. Close adherence or affection; fidelity; regard; any passion or affection that binds a person; as, an *attachment* to a friend, or to a party.

ATTACK', *v. t.* [Fr. *attaquer*; Arm. *attacqi*; It. *attaccare*, to fasten, to engage in battle; *attacco*, a sticking; Sp. *atacar*, to assault, to fasten or make close, to cram; Port. *atacar*, to attack, to seize, to fasten; Heb. and Ch. תקע, to thrust, to drive, to strike.

It seems to be allied to *attach*; but the latter verb agrees better with the Eth. ጠወቀ to press, whence አጥወቀ to press, to make close; and the Ch. טח, to accuse, to unite. Class Dg.]

1. To assault; to fall upon with force; to assail, as with force and arms. It is the appropriate word for the commencing act of hostility between armies and navies.

2. To fall upon, with unfriendly words or writing; to begin a controversy with; to attempt to overthrow or bring into dispute, by satire, calumny or criticism; as, to *attack* a man or his opinions in a pamphlet.

ATTACK', *n.* An onset; first invasion; a falling on, with force or violence, or with calumny, satire or criticism.

ATTACK'ED, *pp.* Assaulted; invaded; fallen on by force or enmity.

ATTACK'ER, *n.* One who assaults or invades.

ATTACK'ING, *ppr.* Assaulting; invading; falling on with force, calumny or criticism.

ATTACOT'TIC, *a.* Pertaining to the Attacotti, a tribe of ancient Britons, allies of the Scots. *Pinkerton.*

AT'TAGEN, *n.* A beautiful fowl, resembling the pheasant, with a short black bill and a fine crest of yellow feathers, variegated with black and white spots, found in the mountains of Sicily. *Dict. of Nat. Hist.*

ATTA'IN, *v. i.* [Fr. and Norm. *atteindre*; L. *attingo*, to reach, come to or overtake; *ad* and *tango*, to touch, reach or strike; that is, to thrust, urge or push to. It has no connection with L. *attineo*. See Class, Dg.]

1. To reach; to come to or arrive at, by motion, bodily exertion, or efforts towards a place or object.

If by any means they might *attain* to Phenice. Acts xxvii.

2. To reach; to come to or arrive at, by an effort of mind.

Such knowledge is too wonderful for me; it is high; I cannot *attain* to it. Ps. cxxxix.

Regularly this verb should be always followed by *to*; the omission of *to*, and the use of the verb, in a transitive sense, may have originated in mistake, from the opinion that the verb is from the L. *attineo*, and equivalent to *obtain*.

ATTA'IN, *v. t.* To gain; to compass; to achieve or accomplish, that is, to reach by efforts; without *to* following.

Is he wise who hopes to *attain* the end without the means? *Tillotson.*

This use of the verb is now established; but in strictness *to* is here implied; *attain to* the end. The real sense, as in the intransitive use of the verb, is, to *reach* or *come to* the end or purpose in view. This word always implies *an effort towards* an object. Hence it is not synonymous with *obtain* and *procure*, which do not necessarily imply such effort. We *procure* or *obtain* a thing by *purchase* or *loan*, and we *obtain* by inheritance, but we do not *attain* it by such means. An inattention to this distinction has led good authors into great mistakes in the use of this word.

2. To reach or come to a place or object by progression or motion.

But ere such tidings shall his ears *attain*. *Hoole's Tasso.*

Canaan he now *attains*. *Milton.*

3. To reach in excellence or degree; to equal. *Bacon.*

ATTA'INABLE, *a.* That may be attained; that may be reached by efforts of the mind or body; that may be compassed or accomplished by efforts directed to the object; as, perfection is not *attainable* in this life. From an inattention to the true sense of this word, as explained under *attain*, authors have very improperly used this word for *obtainable, procurable;* as in the following passages. "The kind and quality of food and liquor; the species of habitation, furniture and clothing to which the common people of each country are habituated, must be *attainable* with ease and certainty." Paley, Phil. B. 6. Ch. 11. "Gen. Howe would not permit them to be purchased in Philadelphia, and they (clothes and blankets) were not *attainable* in the country." Marshall's Life of Washington, 3, 428. Each of these words should be *obtainable.*

ATTA'INABLENESS, *n.* The quality of being attainable.

ATTA'INDER, *n.* [Norm. Fr. *atteindre*, to corrupt, attaint; also conviction; L. *ad* and *tingo*, to stain; Gr. τεγγω. Class Dg. See *Tinge.*]

1. Literally a staining, corruption, or rendering impure; a corruption of blood. Hence,

2. The judgment of death, or sentence of a competent tribunal upon a person convicted of treason or felony, which judgment *attaints*, taints or corrupts his blood, so that he can no longer inherit lands. The consequences of this judgment are, forfeiture of lands, tenements and hereditaments, loss of reputation, and disqualification to be a witness in any court of law. A statute of Parliament attainting a criminal, is called an *act of attainder.*

Upon the thorough demonstration of which guilt by legal *attainder*, the feudal covenant is broken. *Blackstone.*

3. The act of attainting.

An act was made for the *attainder* of several persons. *Encyc.*

Note. By the constitution of the United States, no crime works an *attainder.*

ATTA'INMENT, *n.* The act of attaining; the act of arriving at or reaching; hence the act of obtaining by efforts; as the *attainment* of excellence.

2. That which is attained to, or obtained by exertion; acquisition; as, a man of great *attainments.*

ATTA'INT, *v. t.* [See *Attainder.*]

1. To taint or corrupt; to extinguish the pure or inheritable blood of a person found guilty of treason or felony, by confession, battle, or verdict, and consequent sentence of death, or by special act of Parliament.

No person shall be *attainted* of high treason where corruption of blood is incurred, but by the oath of two witnesses, &c. Stat. 7 and 8. W. 3.

2. To taint, as the credit of jurors, convicted of giving a false verdict. This is done by special writ of attaint. The conviction of such a crime *attaints* the reputation of jurors, and renders them infamous.

3. To disgrace; to cloud with infamy; to stain. *Spenser.*

4. To taint or corrupt. *Shak.*

ATTA'INT, *n.* A stain, spot or taint. *Shak.* [See *Taint.*]

2. Any thing injurious; that which impairs. *Obs.* *Shak.*

3. A blow or wound on the hinder feet of a horse. *Farriery.*

4. A writ which lies after judgment against a jury for giving a false verdict in any court of record.

ATTA'INTED, *pp.* Stained; corrupted; rendered infamous; rendered incapable of inheriting.

ATTA'INTING, *ppr.* Staining; corrupting; rendering infamous by judicial act; depriving of inheritable blood.

ATTA'INTMENT, *n.* The being attainted.

ATTA'INTURE, *n.* A staining or rendering infamous; reproach; imputation.

ATTASK', *v. t.* To task; to tax. [*Not used.* See *Task.*] *Shak.*

ATTA'STE, *v. t.* To taste. [*Not used.* See *Taste.*]

ATTEM'PER, *v. t.* [L. *attempero*, of *ad* and *tempero*, to temper, mix, or moderate. See *Temper.*]

1. To reduce, modify or moderate by mixture; as, to *attemper* heat by a cooling mixture, or spirit by diluting it with water.

2. To soften, mollify or moderate; as, to *attemper* rigid justice with clemency.

3. To mix in just proportion; to regulate; as, a mind well *attempered* with kindness and justice.

4. To accommodate; to fit or make suitable.

Arts *attempered* to the lyre. *Pope.*

ATTEM'PERANCE, *n.* Temperance. [*Not used.*] *Chaucer.*

ATTEM'PERATE, *a.* [L. *attemperatus.*] Tempered; proportioned; suited.

Hope must be proportioned and *attemperate* to the promise. *Hammond.*

ATTEM'PERATE, *v. t.* To attemper. [*Not in use.*] *Hammond.*

ATTEM'PERED, *pp.* Reduced in quality; moderated; softened; well mixed; suited.

ATTEM'PERING, *ppr.* Moderating in quality; softening; mixing in due proportion; making suitable.

ATTEM'PERLY, *adv.* In a temperate manner. [*Not in use.*[*Chaucer.*

ATTEMPT', *v. t.* [Fr. *attenter*, from L. *attento*, to attempt, of *ad* and *tento*, to try; Arm. *attempti.* The L. *tento* is from the same root as *tendo*, to strain; Gr. τεινω. Hence, the literal sense is to strain, urge, stretch.]

1. To make an effort to effect some object; to make trial or experiment; to try; to endeavor; to use exertion for any purpose; as, to *attempt* to sing; to *attempt* a bold flight.

2. To attack; to make an effort upon; as, to *attempt* the enemy's camp.

This verb is not always followed by an object, and appears to be intransitive; but some object is understood, or a verb in the infinitive follows in the place of an object; as, he *attempted to speak.*

ATTEMPT', *n.* An essay, trial or endeavor; an attack; or an effort to gain a point. *Bacon.*

ATTEMPT'ABLE, *a.* That may be attempted, tried or attacked; liable to an attempt, or attack. *Shak.*

ATTEMPT'ED, *pp.* Essayed; tried; attacked.

ATTEMPT'ER, *n.* One who attempts, or attacks. *Milton.*

ATTEMPT'ING, *ppr.* Trying; essaying; making an effort to gain a point; attacking.

ATTEND', *v. t.* [L. *attendo;* Fr. *attendre*, to wait, stay, hold, expect; Sp. *atender;* It. *attendere;* L. *ad* and *tendo*, to stretch, to tend. See *Tend.*]

1. To go with, or accompany, as a companion, minister or servant.

2. To be present; to accompany or be united to; as a cold *attended* with fever.

3. To be present for some duty, implying charge or oversight; to wait on; as, the physician or the nurse *attends* the sick.

4. To be present in business; to be in company from curiosity, or from some connection in affairs; as, lawyers or spectators *attend* a court.

5. To be consequent to, from connection of cause; as, a measure *attended* with ill effects.

6. To await; to remain, abide or be in store for; as, happiness or misery *attends* us after death.

7. To wait for; to lie in wait. *Shak.*

8. To wait or stay for.

Three days I promised to *attend* my doom. *Dryden.*

9. To accompany with solicitude; to regard.

Their hunger thus appeased, their care *attends*
The doubtful fortune of their absent friends. *Dryden.*

10. To regard; to fix the mind upon.

The pilot doth not *attend* the unskilful words of the passenger. *Sidney.*

This is not now a legitimate sense. To express this idea, we now use the verb intransitively, with *to, attend to.*

11. To expect. [*Not in use.*] *Raleigh.*

ATTEND' *v. i.* To listen; to regard with attention; followed by *to.*

Attend to the voice of my supplication. Ps. lxxxvi.

Hence much used in the imperative, *attend!*

2. To regard with observation, and correspondent practice.

My son, *attend to* my words.

Hence, to regard with compliance.

He hath *attended to* the voice of my prayer. Ps. lxvi.

3. To fix the attention upon, as an object of pursuit; to be busy or engaged in; as, to *attend* to the study of the scriptures.

4. To wait on; to accompany or be present, in pursuance of duty; with *on* or *upon*; as, to *attend upon* a committee; to *attend upon* business. Hence,

5. To wait on, in service or worship; to serve.

That ye may *attend upon* the Lord without distraction. 1 Cor. vii.

6. To stay; to delay. *Obs.*

For this perfection she must yet *attend*,
Till to her maker she espoused be. *Davies.*

7. To wait; to be within call. *Spenser.*

ATTEND'ANCE, *n.* [Fr.] The act of waiting on, or serving.

Of which no man gave *attendance* at the altar. Heb. vii.

2. A waiting on; a being present on business of any kind; as, the *attendance* of witnesses or persons in court; *attendance* of members of the legislature.

3. Service; ministry.

Receive *attendance*. *Shak.*

4. The persons attending; a train; a retinue. *Milton.*

5. Attention; regard; careful application of mind.

Give *attendance* to reading. 1 Tim. iv.

6. Expectation. *Obs.* *Hooker.*

ATTEND'ANT, *a.* Accompanying; being present, or in the train.

Other suns with their *attendant* moons. *Milton.*

2. Accompanying, connected with, or immediately following, as consequential; as, intemperance with all its *attendant* evils.

3. In *law*, depending on or owing service to; as, the wife *attendant* to the heir. *Cowel.*

ATTEND'ANT, *n.* One who attends or accompanies, in any character whatever, as a friend, companion, minister or servant; one who belongs to the train. *Dryden.*

2. One who is present; as an *attendant* at or upon a meeting.

3. One who owes service to or depends on another. *Cowel.*

4. That which accompanies or is consequent to.

A love of fame, the *attendant* of noble spirits. *Pope.*

Shame is the *attendant* of vice. *Anon.*

ATTEND'ED, *pp.* Accompanied; having attendants; served; waited on.

ATTEND'ER, *n.* One who attends; a companion; an associate. [*Little used.*]

ATTEND'ING, *ppr.* Going with; accompanying; waiting on; superintending or taking care of; being present; immediately consequent to; serving; listening; regarding with care.

ATTENT', *a.* Attentive. 2 Chron. vi.

ATTENT'ATES, *n.* Proceedings in a court of judicature, after an inhibition is decreed. *Ayliffe.*

ATTEN'TION, *n.* The act of attending or heeding; the due application of the ear to sounds, or of the mind to objects presented to its contemplation. [Literally, *a stretching towards.*]

They say the tongues of dying men
Enforce *attention* like deep harmony. *Shak.*

2. Act of civility, or courtesy; as *attention* to a stranger.

ATTENT'IVE, *a.* [Fr. *attentif.*]
Heedful; intent; observant; regarding with care. It is applied to the senses of hearing and seeing, as an *attentive* ear or eye; to the application of the mind, as in contemplation; or to the application of the mind, together with the senses abovementioned, as when a person is *attentive* to the words, the manner and matter of a speaker at the same time.

ATTENT'IVELY, *adv.* Heedfully; carefully; with fixed attention.

ATTENT'IVENESS, *n.* The state of being attentive; heedfulness; attention.

ATTEN'UANT, *a.* [See *Attenuate.*]
Making thin, as fluids; diluting; rendering less dense and viscid.

ATTEN'UANT, *n.* A medicine which thins the humors, subtilizes their parts, dissolves viscidity, and disposes the fluids to motion, circulation and secretion; a diluent. *Coxe.*

ATTEN'UATE, *v. t.* [L. *attenuo*, of *ad* and *tenuo*, to make thin; L. *tenuis*; W. *tenau*; Ir. *tana* or *tanaidhe*; Eng. *thin*, which see.]

1. To make thin or less consistent; to subtilize or break the humors of the body into finer parts; to render less viscid; opposed to *condense, incrassate* or *thicken.*

2. To comminute; to break or wear solid substances into finer or very minute parts.

This uninterrupted motion must *attenuate* and wear away the hardest rocks. *Trans. of Chaptal's Chimistry.*

3. To make slender; to reduce in thickness.

ATTEN'UATE, *a.* Made thin, or less viscid; made slender. *Bacon.*

ATTEN'UATED, *pp.* Made thin or less viscid; comminuted; made slender. In *botany*, growing slender towards the point.

ATTEN'UATING, *ppr.* Making thin, as fluids; making fine, as solid substances; making slender or lean.

ATTENUA'TION, *n.* The act of making thin, as fluids; as the *attenuation* of the humors.

2. The act of making fine, by comminution, or attrition.

The action of the air facilitates the *attenuation* of these rocks. *Trans. Chaptal.*

3. The act or process of making slender, thin or lean.

AT'TERATE, *v. t.* [L. *attero*, to wear.] To wear away.

2. To form or accumulate by wearing.

AT'TERATED, *pp.* Formed by wearing. *Ray.*

ATTERA'TION, *n.* The operation of forming land by the wearing of the sea, and the wearing of the earth in one place and deposition of it in another. *Ray.*

ATTEST', *v. t.* [Fr. *attester*; L. *attestor*; of *ad* and *testor*, to affirm or bear witness, from *testis*. See *Testify.*]

1. To bear witness to; to certify; to affirm to be true or genuine; to make a solemn declaration in words or writing, to support a fact; appropriately used for the affirmation of persons in their official capacity; as, to *attest* the truth of a writing; to *attest* a copy of record. Persons also *attest* writings by subscribing their names.

2. To bear witness, or support the truth of a fact, by other evidence than words; as, the ruins of Palmyra *attest* its ancient magnificence.

3. To call to witness; to invoke as conscious.

The sacred streams which heaven's imperial state
Attests in oaths, and fears to violate. *Dryden.*

ATTEST', *n.* Witness; testimony; attestation. [*Little used.*]

ATTESTA'TION, *n.* Testimony; witness; a solemn or official declaration, verbal or written, in support of a fact; evidence. The truth appears from the *attestation* of witnesses, or of the proper officer. The subscription of a name to a writing is an *attestation.*

ATTEST'ED, *pp.* Proved or supported by testimony, solemn or official; witnessed; supported by evidence.

ATTEST'ING, *ppr.* Witnessing; calling to witness; affirming in support of.

ATTEST'OR, *n.* One who attests.

AT'TIC, *a.* [L. *Atticus*; Gr. Αττικος.]
Pertaining to Attica in Greece, or to its principal city, Athens. Thus, *Attic* wit, *Attic* salt, a poignant, delicate wit, peculiar to the Athenians; *Attic* faith, inviolable faith.

Attic base, a peculiar base used by the ancient architects in the Ionic order, or column; and by Palladio and others, in the Doric. *Encyc.*

Attic order, an order of small square pillars at the uppermost extremity of a building. This had its origin in Athens, and was intended to conceal the roof. These pillars should never exceed one third of the length of the order on which they are placed, nor be less than one quarter of it. *Encyc.*

Attic story, a story in the upper part of a house, where the windows usually are square. *Encyc.*

AT'TIC, *n.* A small square pillar with its cornice on the uppermost part of a building. Attics properly form the crown of the building, or a finishing for the other orders, when they are used in the structure. *Encyc.*

2. An Athenian; an Athenian author. *Jones' Gr. Grammar.*

AT'TICISM, *n.* The peculiar style and idiom of the Greek language, used by the Athenians; refined and elegant Greek; concise and elegant expression. *Encyc. Art. Philos.*

2. A particular attachment to the Athenians. *Milford.*

AT'TICIZE, *v. t.* To conform or make conformable to the language or idiom of Attica. Adjectives in ος, when *atticized*, become ως. *Jones' Gr. Grammar.*

AT'TICIZE, *v. i.* To use atticisms, or the idiom of the Athenians.

AT'TICS, *n. plu.* The title of a book in Pausanias, which treats of Attica. *Trans. of Paus. B.* 1.

ATTI'RE, *v. t.* [Norm. *attyrer*, to provide; Fr. *atours*, dress, *attire*; *atourner*, to dress a bride, to *attire*; *atournere*sse, a *tire* woman; Arm. *atourn*, female ornaments; G. *zieren*, to adorn. We retain *tire*, the simple word, applied to the band of a wheel, and this word, in the D. *toer*, coincides with *tour*. See Class Dr.]
To dress; to array; to adorn with elegant or splendid garments.

With the linen miter shall Aaron be *attired*. Lev. xvi.

ATTI'RE, *n.* Dress; clothes; habit; but appropriately, ornamental dress.

Can a bride forget her *attire*. Jer. ii.

2. The horns of a deer.

3. In *botany*, the generative parts of plants. Florid attire, called thrums or suits, as in the flowers of marygold or tansy, consists of two or three parts, of which the outer

part is the floret. Semiform attire consists of the chives and apexes. *This language is now obsolete.*

ATTI'RED, *pp.* Dressed; decked with ornaments or attire.

ATTI'RER, *n.* One who dresses or adorns with attire.

ATTI'RING, *ppr.* Dressing; adorning with dress or attire.

ATTI'TLE, *v. t.* To entitle. [*Not in use.*] *Gower.*

AT'TITUDE, *n.* [Fr. *attitude*, posture; Sp. *actitud*, from L. *actus*, *ago*. The Italian *attitudine* is posture and fitness; *attitude* and *aptitude* being united in the same word.]

1. In *painting* and *sculpture*, the posture or action in which a figure or statue is placed; the gesture of a figure or statue; such a disposition of the parts as serves to express the action and sentiments of the person represented. *Johnson. Encyc.*

2. Posture; position of things or persons; as, in times of trouble let the prince or a nation preserve a firm *attitude.*
Washington's Farewell Address.
Hamilton. Gov. Smith. N. H.

ATTOL'LENT, *a.* [L. *attollens, attollo*, of *ad* and *tollo*, to lift.]

Lifting up; raising; as an *attollent* muscle. *Derham.*

ATTOL'LENT, *n.* A muscle which raises some part, as the ear, the tip of the nose, or the upper eye lid; otherwise called *levator* or *elevator.* *Quincy. Coxe.*

ATTŎRN', *v. i.* [L. *ad* and *torno*; Fr. *tourner*; Arm. *tuirgna, turnein*, to turn; Sp. *tornar*; Port. *id*; It. *attornare, torniare.* Hence *torniamento*, a *tournament*; Sp. *torneo.* See *Turn.*]

In *the feudal law*, to turn, or transfer homage and service from one lord to another. This is the act of feudatories, vassals or tenants, upon the alienation of the estate. *Blackstone. Encyc.*

ATTŎRN'EY, *n.* plu. *attŏrneys.* [Norm. *attournon*; *torne*, id; from *tour, tourn, turn*, change. One who takes the *turn* or place of another. See *Attorn* and *Turn.*]

One who is appointed or admitted in the place of another, to manage his matters in law. The word formerly signified any person who did business for another; but its sense is now chiefly or wholly restricted to persons who act as substitutes for the persons concerned, in prosecuting and defending actions before courts of justice, or in transacting other business in which legal rights are involved. The word answers to the *procurator*, (proctor,) of the civilians.

Attorneys are not admitted to practice in courts, until examined, approved, licensed and sworn, by direction of some court; after which they are proper officers of the court.

In G. Britain, and in some of the U. States, *attorneys* are not permitted to be advocates or counsel in the higher courts; this privilege being confined to counsellors and sergeants. In other states, there is no distinction of rank, and attorneys practice in all the courts. And in a general sense, the word *attorney* comprehends counsellors, barristers and serjeants.

In *Virginia*, the duties of *attorney*, counsellor, conveyancer and advocate, are all performed by the same individual. *Wirt.*

An attorney may have *general* powers to transact business for another; or his powers may be *special*, or limited to a particular act or acts.

Attorney General is an officer appointed to manage business for the king, the state or public; and his duty, in particular, is to prosecute persons guilty of crimes.

A letter or *warrant of attorney* is a written authority from one person empowering another to transact business for him.

ATTŎRN'EY, *v. t.* To perform by proxy; to employ as a proxy. [*Not in use.*] *Shak.*

ATTŎRN'EYSHIP, *n.* The office of an attorney; agency for another. *Shak.*

ATTŎRN'ING, *ppr.* Acknowledging a new lord, or transferring homage and fealty to the purchaser of an estate.

ATTŎRN'MENT, *n.* The act of a feudatory, vassal or tenant, by which he consents, upon the alienation of an estate, to receive a new lord or superior, and transfers to him his homage and service. *Encyc. Blackstone.*

ATTRACT', *v. t.* [L. *attraho, attractus*, of *ad* and *traho*, to draw. See *Drag* and *Draw.*]

1. To draw to; to cause to move towards, and unite with; as, electrical bodies *attract* straws, and light substances, by physical laws.

2. To draw to or incline to unite with, though some cause may prevent the union; as, the sun is supposed to *attract* the planets.

3. To draw by influence of a moral kind; to invite or allure; as, to *attract* admirers.

4. To engage; as, to *attract* attention.

ATTRACT', *n.* Attraction. [*Not in use.*] *Hudibras.*

ATTRACTABIL'ITY, *n.* The quality of being attractable, or of being subject to the law of attraction. *Asiat. Researches.*

ATTRACT'ABLE, *a.* That may be attracted; subject to attraction. *Lavoisier by Kerr.*

ATTRACT'ED, *pp.* Drawn towards; invited; allured; engaged.

ATTRACT'IC, } *a.* Having power to draw to. [*Not*
ATTRACT'ICAL, } *used.*] *Ray.*

ATTRACT'ILE, *a.* That has power to attract. *Med. Rep.*

ATTRACT'ING, *ppr.* Drawing to or towards; inviting; alluring; engaging.

ATTRACT'INGLY, *adv.* In an attracting manner.

ATTRAC'TION, *n.* The power in bodies which is supposed to draw them together; or the tendency or principle which inclines them to unite or cohere; called by Copernicus, *appetence.* *Encyc.*

This power, principle or tendency in bodies to unite, is distinguished by philosophers into *attraction of gravity* or *gravitation*, which extends to a sensible distance, such as the tendency of the planets to the sun, or of a stone, when raised in the air, to fall to the earth, and of which kind is the attraction of magnetism, and of electricity; and into *attraction of cohesion*, or that tendency which is manifested between small particles of matter, at insensible distances, or near the point of contact, to unite them in coherence.

The *attraction of gravity* is supposed to be the great principle which confines the planets in their orbits. Its power or force is *directly* as the quantity of matter in a body, and *inversely* as the square of the distances of the attracting bodies. *Newton. Encyc.*

2. The act of attracting; the effect of the principle of attraction.

Attraction may be performed by impulse or other means. *Newton's Optics.*

3. The power or act of alluring, drawing to, inviting or engaging; as the *attraction* of beauty or eloquence.

Contiguous attraction is that which is exerted between minute particles or atoms, at insensible distances. When this principle unites particles of the same kind, it is called affinity of aggregation, cohesive affinity or cohesion. When it operates on dissimilar particles, producing union, it is distinguished as heterogeneous, and called chimical attraction or affinity. *Webster's Manual.*

Elective attraction, in chimistry, is otherwise called *affinity.* It is that power in substances, which elects or selects from a mixture those elements with which they have the strongest tendency to combine.

ATTRACT'IVE, *a.* [Fr. *attractif.*]

1. Having the quality of attracting; drawing to; as the *attractive* force of bodies.

2. Drawing to by moral influence; alluring; inviting; engaging; as the *attractive* graces.

An *attractive* undertaking. *Roscoe.*

ATTRACT'IVELY, *adv.* With the power of attracting, or drawing to.

ATTRACT'IVENESS, *n.* The quality of being attractive, or engaging.

ATTRACT'OR, *n.* The person or thing that attracts.

ATTRA'HENT, *a.* [L. *attrahens.*] Drawing to; or as a noun, that which draws to. *Glanville.*

ATTRAP', *v. t.* [Qu. Fr. *drap*, cloth.] To clothe; to dress. [*Not in use.*] *Barret.*

ATTRECTA'TION, *n.* [L. *attrectatio.*] Frequent handling. *Dict.*

ATTRIB'UTABLE, *a.* [See *Attribute.*]

That may be ascribed, imputed or attributed; ascribable; imputable; as, the fault is not *attributable* to the author.

ATTRIB'UTE, *v. t.* [L. *attribuo*; *ad* and *tribuo*, to divide, to bestow, to assign; *tribus*, a *tribe*, division or ward; Fr. *attribuer*; Sp. *atribuir, tribuir*; It. *attribuire.* See *Tribe.*]

1. To allot or attach, in contemplation; to ascribe; to consider as belonging.

We *attribute* nothing to God, that contains a contradiction. *Tillotson.*

2. To give as due; to yield as an act of the mind; as, to *attribute* to God all the glory of redemption.

3. To impute, as to a cause; as, our misfortunes are generally to be *attributed* to our follies or imprudence.

AT'TRIBUTE, *n.* That which is attributed; that which is considered as belonging to, or inherent in; as, power and wisdom are *attributes* of the Supreme Being: or a quality determining something to be after

a certain manner; as, extension is an *attribute* of body. *Encyc.*
2. Quality; characteristic disposition; as bravery and generosity in men. *Bacon.*
3. A thing belonging to another; an appendant; as the arms of a warrior. In *painting* and *sculpture*, a symbol of office or character, added to the principal figure; as a club is the *attribute* of Hercules. *Encyc.*
4. Reputation; honor. *Shak.*
[*Not a proper sense of this word.*]

ATTRIB'UTED, *pp.* Ascribed; yielded as due; imputed.

ATTRIB'UTING, *ppr.* Ascribing: yielding or giving as due; imputing.

ATTRIBU'TION, *n.* The act of attributing, or the quality ascribed; commendation.

ATTRIB'UTIVE, *a.* Pertaining to or expressing an attribute. *Harris.*

ATTRIB'UTIVE, *n.* In *grammar*, a word significant of an attribute; as an adjective, verb or particle, which is the attribute of a substance. *Harris' Hermes.*

ATTRI'TE, *a.* [L. *attritus*, worn, of *ad* and *tero*, to wear; Gr. τειρω. See *Trite.*] Worn by rubbing or friction. *Milton.*
[See *Trite*, which is now generally used.]

ATTRI'TENESS, *n.* The being much worn. *Johnson.*

ATTRI''TION, *n.* Abrasion; the act of wearing by friction, or rubbing substances together.

The change of aliment is effected by the *attrition* of the stomach. *Arbuthnot.*

2. The state of being worn. *Johnson.*
3. With *divines*, grief for sin arising from fear of punishment; the lowest degree of repentance. *Wallis.*

ATTU'NE, *v. t.* [of *ad* and *tune*. See *Tone* and *Tune.*] To make musical.

Vernal airs *attune* the trembling leaves. *Milton.*

2. To tune, or put in tune; to adjust one sound to another; to make accordant; as, to *attune* the voice to a harp.

ATTU'NED, *pp.* Made musical or harmonious; accommodated in sound.

ATTU'NING, *ppr.* Putting in tune; making musical, or accordant in sound.

ATWA'IN, *adv.* In twain; asunder. *Obs.* *Shak.*

ATWEE'N, *adv.* Between. *Obs.* *Spenser.*

ATWIXT', *adv.* Betwixt. *Obs.* *Spenser.*

ATWO, *adv.* In two. *Obs.* *Chaucer.*

AUBA'INE, *n.* *aubáin.* [Fr. *aubain*, an alien.] The *droit d'aubaine*, in France, is the right of the king to the goods of an alien dying within his jurisdiction, the king standing in the place of the heirs.

AU'BURN, *a.* [This word is evidently formed from *brun*, *bruno*, Fr. and It. brown, by a transposition of the letters *r* and *n*, with a prefix, *auburn*, for *aubrun*, from *brennan*, *burn*, denoting the color made by scorching.] Brown; of a dark color.

His *auburn* locks on either shoulder flowed. *Dryden.*

AUC'TION, *n.* [L. *auctio*, a public sale; Eng. to *hawk*; G. *höken*; properly, to cry out. See *Hawk.*]
1. A public sale of property to the highest bidder, and regularly, by a person licensed and authorized for the purpose; a vendue. Contracts for services, sometimes, are sold to the lowest bidder. By the Romans, this species of sale was made by a crier, *sub hasta*, under a spear stuck in the earth.
2. The thing sold at auction. *Pope.*

AUC'TIONARY, *a.* Belonging to an auction or public sale. *Dryden.*

AUCTIONEE'R, *n.* [L. *auctionarius.*] The person who sells at auction; a person licensed by government to dispose of goods or lands by public sale to the highest bidder.

AUCTIONEE'R, *v. t.* To sell at auction. *Cowper.*

AUCUPA'TION, *n.* [L. *aucupatio*, from *aucupor*, of *avis* and *capio.*] The act or practice of taking birds; fowling; bird-catching. [*Little used.*]

AUDA'CIOUS, *a.* [L. *audax*; Fr. *audacieux*; from L. *audeo*, to dare. The sense is, advancing forward.]
1. Very bold or daring; impudent; contemning the restraints of law, religion or decorum; used for *bold in wickedness;* applied to persons; as an *audacious* wretch.
2. Committed with, or proceeding from, daring effrontery, or contempt of law; as an *audacious* crime.
3. Bold; spirited. *Jonson.*

AUDA'CIOUSLY, *adv.* In an impudent manner; with excess of boldness. *Shak.*

AUDA'CIOUSNESS, *n.* The quality of being audacious; impudence; audacity. *Sandys.*

AUDAC'ITY, *n.* Boldness, *sometimes in a good sense;* daring spirit, resolution or confidence.
2. Audaciousness; impudence; *in a bad sense;* implying a contempt of law or moral restraint.

AUD'EANISM, *n.* Anthropomorphism; or the doctrine of Audeus, who maintained that God has a human shape; from Gen. i. 26. *Encyc.*

AUD'IBLE, *a.* [L. *audibilis*, from *audio*, to hear. This word is evidently connected with the name of the ear; Gr. ουας, ουατος; Vulg. Gr. αυδια. The verb is contracted into Sp. *oir;* Port. *ouvir;* Fr. *ouïr*, to hear. Hence in law *oyer*, and from the French *oyez*, hear ye, the barbarous *O yes*, of our courts.] That may be heard; perceivable by the ear; loud enough to be heard; as an *audible* voice or whisper.

AUD'IBLENESS, *n.* The quality of being audible.

AUD'IBLY, *adv.* In an audible manner; in a manner so as to be heard.

AUD'IENCE, *n.* The act of hearing, or attending to sounds.

His bold discourse had *audience*. *Milton.*

2. Admittance to a hearing; public reception to an interview; a ceremony observed in courts, or by official characters, when embassadors or applicants to men in office are permitted to appear and state their business in person.
3. An auditory; an assembly of hearers.
4. In *the Spanish dominions*, a court; as the *audience of Seville*, which is a court of oyer and terminer; and the *audience pretorial*, in the Indies, which is a high court of judicature. The word in Spain also signifies certain law-officers, appointed to institute a judicial inquiry. *Span. Dict.*
5. In *England*, a court held by the archbishop of Canterbury, on the subject of consecrations, elections, institutions, marriages, &c. *Encyc.*

AUD'IENT, *n.* A hearer. [*Not in use.*] *Shelton.*

AUD'IT, *n.* [L. *audit*, he hears.] An examination of an account or of accounts, with a hearing of the parties concerned, by proper officers, or persons appointed for that purpose, who compare the charges with the vouchers, examine witnesses, and state the balance.
2. The result of such an examination, or account as adjusted by auditors; a final account. *Hooker.*

AUD'IT, *v. t.* To examine and adjust an account or accounts, by proper officers, or by persons legally authorized for the purpose; as, to *audit* the accounts of a treasurer, or of parties who have a suit depending in court.

AUD'IT-HOUSE, *n.* An appendage to a cathedral, in which the business belonging to it is transacted. *Wheler.*

AUD'ITIVE, *a.* Having the power of hearing. *Cotgrave.*

AUD'ITOR, [L.] A hearer; one who attends to hear a discourse.
2. A person appointed and authorized to examine an account or accounts, compare the charges with the vouchers, examine the parties and witnesses, allow or reject charges, and state the balance. It is usual with courts to refer accounts, on which an action is brought, to auditors for adjustment, and their report, if received, is the basis of the judgment.
In England, there are officers who are auditors of courts; as the auditors of the Exchequer, of the receipts, &c.

AUD'ITORSHIP, *n.* The office of auditor. *Johnson.*

AUD'ITORY, *a.* That has the power of hearing; pertaining to the sense or organs of hearing; as, the *auditory* nerve.

AUD'ITORY, *n.* [L. *auditorium.*] An audience; an assembly of hearers, as in a church or lecture room.
2. A place or apartment where discourses are delivered. In *ancient churches*, the nave, where the hearers stood to be instructed.
3. A bench on which a judge sits to hear causes. *Encyc.*

AUD'ITRESS, *n.* A female hearer. *Milton.*

AUF, *n.* A fool; a simpleton. [See *Oaf.*]

AUGE'AN, *a.* The *Augean* stable, in Grecian mythology, is represented as belonging to Augeas or Augias, one of the Argonauts, and afterwards king of Elis. This prince kept a great number of oxen, in a stable which was never cleansed, until Hercules undertook the task; a task which it seemed impracticable to execute. Hence the Augean stable came to represent what is deemed impracticable, or a place which has not, for a long time, been cleansed. *Lempriere.*

AUG'ER, *n.* [D. *avegaar.* The Saxon word is *nafe-gar* or *naue-gar*, from *nafa*, the nave of a wheel, and *gar*, a tool or a borer. It is probable that the real word is *naugar*, corrupted.] An instrument for boring large holes, chiefly used by carpenters, joiners, cabinet makers, wheelwrights and shipwrights. It consists of an iron blade, ending in a steel bit, with a handle placed at right angles with the blade. Augers, made with a straight channel or groove, in some places, are called *pod-augers*; the modern augers, with spiral channels, are called *screw-augers*.

AUG'ER-HOLE, *n.* A hole made by an auger.

AUGHT, *n. anl.* [Sax. *awiht, aht*, or *owiht, ohwit, oht*, from *wiht, wight*, a creature, animal, thing, any thing. This *wiht* seems to be our *wight* and *whit*; and I suspect the L. *qui, quæ, quod, quid, what*, to be the same word varied in orthography. This word should not be written *ought*.]

1. Any thing, indefinitely.

But go, my son, and see if *aught* be wanting. *Addison.*

2. Any part, the smallest; a jot or tittle.

There failed not *aught* of any good thing which the Lord had spoken. Josh. xxi.

AU'GITE, *n.* [Gr. αυγη, brightness. Plin. 37, 10.]

A mineral called by Haüy, pyroxene; often found in distinct crystals. Its secondary forms are all six or eight-sided prisms. Sometimes it appears in hemitrope crystals. It has a foliated structure, and is harder than hornblend. The varieties are *common augite, sahlite, fassaite*, and *coccolito*. The *omphacite* of Werner appears also to be a variety; and the common augite, found near the lake Baikal, has been called *Baikalite*. *Cleaveland.*

Werner divides augite into four sub-species; granular, foliated, conchoidal, and common; and there is a variety called slaggy augite.

AUGIT'IC, *a.* Pertaining to augite; resembling augite, or partaking of its nature and characters. *Cooper.*

AUGMENT', *v. t.* [Fr. *augmenter*; L. *augmento, augmentum*, from *augeo, auxi*, to increase; Gr. αυξω, αεξω. It seems to be the Eng. to *wax*, or to *eke*; Sax. *eacan*.]

1. To increase; to enlarge in size or extent; to swell; to make bigger; as, to *augment* an army, by reinforcement; rain *augments* a stream.

2. To increase or swell the degree, amount or magnitude; as, impatience *augments* an evil.

AUGMENT', *v. i.* To increase; to grow larger; as, a stream *augments* by rain.

AUG'MENT, *n.* Increase; enlargement by addition; state of increase.

2. In *philology*, a syllable prefixed to a word; or an increase of the quantity of the initial vowel.

AUGMENT'ABLE, *a.* That may be increased; capable of augmentation. *Walsh's Amer. Review.*

AUGMENTA'TION, *n.* The act of increasing, or making larger, by addition, expansion, or dilatation.

2. The state of being increased or enlarged.

3. The thing added by which a thing is enlarged.

4. In *music*, a doubling the value of the notes of the subject of a fugue or canon. *Busby.*

Augmentation Court, in England, a court erected by 27 Hen. VIII., to augment the revenues of the crown, by the suppression of monasteries. It was long ago dissolved. *Encyc.*

In heraldry, *augmentation* consists in additional charges to a coat-armor, often as marks of honor, borne on the escutcheon or a canton. *Encyc.*

AUGMENT'ATIVE, *a.* Having the quality or power of augmenting.

AUGMENT'ER, *n.* He that augments.

AUGMENT'ING, *ppr.* Increasing; enlarging.

AU'GUR, *n.* [L. *augur*. The first syllable is from *avis*, a fowl; but the meaning and origin of the last syllable are not obvious.]

1. Among the *Romans*, an officer whose duty was to foretell future events by the singing, chattering, flight and feeding of birds. There was a college or community of augurs, originally three in number, and afterwards nine, four patricians, and five plebeians. They bore a staff or wand, and were held in great respect. *Encyc.*

2. One who pretends to foretell future events by omens.

We all know that *augur* cannot look at *augur* without laughing. *Buckminster.*

AU'GUR, *v. i.* To guess; to conjecture by signs or omens; to prognosticate.

AU'GUR, *v. t.* To predict or foretell; as, to *augur* ill success.

AU'GURAL, *a.* [L. *auguralis*.] Pertaining to an augur, or to prediction by the appearance of birds. The Romans had their *augural* staff and *augural* books.

AU'GURATE, *v. i.* To judge by augury; to predict. [*Little used.*] *Warburton.*

AUGURA'TION, *n.* The practice of augury, or the foretelling of events by the chattering and flight of birds. It may be used for prediction by other signs and omens.

AU'GURED, *pp.* Conjectured by omens; prognosticated.

AU'GURER, *n.* An augur. [*Not legitimate.*] *Shak.*

AUGU'RIAL, *a.* Relating to augurs. *Brown.*

AU'GURIZE, *v. t.* To augur. [*Not in use.*]

AU'GUROUS, *a.* Predicting; foretelling; foreboding.

AU'GURY, *n.* [L. *augurium*.] The art or practice of foretelling events by the flight or chattering of birds.

2. An omen; prediction; prognostication. *Shak. Dryden.*

AUGUST', *a.* [L. *augustus*. The first syllable of this word is probably from the root of *augeo*, or of *awe*.]

Grand; magnificent; majestic; impressing awe; inspiring reverence.

The Trojan chief appeared, *august* in visage. *Dryden.*

It is related that this epithet was first conferred by the Roman senate upon Octavius, after confirming him in the sovereign power.

AU'GUST, *n.* The eighth month of the year, containing thirty-one days. The old Roman name was *Sextilis*, the *sixth* month from March, the month in which the primitive Romans, as well as Jews, began the year. The name was changed to *August* in honor of the Emperor Octavius Augustus, on account of his victories, and his entering on his first consulate in that month. *Gebelin.*

AUGUST'AN, *a.* Pertaining to Augustus; as the *Augustan* age.

2. The *Augustan* confession, drawn up at Augusta or Augsburg, by Luther and Melancthon, in 1530, contains the principles of the protestants, and their reasons for separating from the Romish church. *Encyc.*

AUGUSTIN'IANS, *n.* Those divines, who from St. Augustin, maintain that grace is effectual from its nature, absolutely and morally, not relatively and gradually. *Encyc.*

AUGUST'INS, } *n.* An order of monks,
AUGUSTIN'IANS, } so called from St. Augustin. They originally were hermits, and called Austin friars. They were congregated into one body by Pope Alexander IV., under Lanfranc, in 1256. They clothe in black, and make one of the four orders of mendicants. *Encyc.*

AUGUST'NESS, *n.* Dignity of mien; grandeur; magnificence.

AUK, *n.* [contracted from *Alca*.] The alca, a genus of aquatic fowls, of the order of ansers, including the northern penguin or great auk, the little auk or black and white diver, the puffin, &c.

AULA'RIAN, *n.* [L. *aula*, a hall.] At Oxford, the member of a hall, distinguished from a collegian. *Todd.*

AULET'IC, *a.* [Gr. αυλητικος, from αυλος, a pipe.]

Pertaining to pipes or to a pipe. [*Little used.*]

AU'LIC, *a.* [L. *aulicus*, from *aula*, a hall, court or palace; Gr. αυλη.]

Pertaining to a royal court. The epithet is probably confined to the German Empire, where it is used to designate certain courts or officers composing the courts. The *aulic* council is composed of a president, who is a catholic, a vice-chancellor and eighteen counsellors, nine of whom are protestants, and nine catholics. They always follow the Emperor's court, and decide without an appeal. This council ceases at the death of the Emperor.

The *Aulic*, in some European universities, is an act of a young divine, on being admitted a doctor of divinity. It begins by a harangue of the chancellor addressed to the young doctor, after which he receives the cap and presides at the *Aulic* or disputation. *Encyc.*

AUMA'IL, *v. t.* [Fr. *email*.] To figure or variegate. [*Not used.*] *Spenser.*

AUMBRY. [See *Ambry*.]

AUME, *n.* A Dutch measure for Rhenish wine, containing 40 gallons. *Encyc.*

AUNE, *n.* [A contraction of *aulne, ulna*.]

A French cloth measure, but of different lengths in different parts of the country. At Rouen, it is an Eng. ell; at Calais, 1. 52; at Lyons, 1. 061; at Paris, 0. 95. *Encyc.*

'AUNT, *n.* [L. *amita*, contracted. Qu. Fr. *tante*.]

The sister of one's father or mother, correlative to nephew or niece.

AU'RA, *n.* [L. from Heb. אור, a stream; Gr. αυρα. See *Air*.]

Literally, a breeze, or gentle current of air, but used by English writers for a stream of fine particles flowing from a body, as effluvia, aroma, or odor; an exhalation.

AU'RATE, *n.* [Supposed to be from *aurum*, gold.]
A sort of pear.
AU'RATE, *n.* [L. *aurum*, gold; Fr. *or*; from the Heb. and Ch. אור, light, fire, and to shine, from its color; Ir. *or*; W. *aur*; Corn. *our*; Basque *urrea*; Arm. *aur*, gold.]
A combination of the oxyd of gold with a base; as *aurate* of potash. *Lavoisier. Fourcroy.*
AU'RATED, *a.* Resembling gold.
AURE'LIA, *n.* [from *aurum*, or *aur*, gold, from its color. See *Chrysalis*.]
In *natural history*, the nymph or chrysalis of an insect; or the form of an animal, like a worm or maggot, covered with a hardish pellicle, and in a state of seeming insensibility. From this state, it changes to a moth, butterfly or other winged insect. *Encyc.*
AURE'LIAN, *a.* Like or pertaining to the aurelia. *Humphreys.*
AU'RIC, *a.* [from *aurum*, gold.] Pertaining to gold. The *auric* acid is a saturated combination of gold and oxygen. *Fourcroy.*
AU'RICLE, *n.* [L. *auricula*, dim. from *auris*, the ear.]
1. The external ear, or that part which is prominent from the head.
2. The auricles of the heart are two muscular bags, situated at the base, serving as diverticula for the blood, during the diastole. They resemble the auricle of the ear, and cover the ventricles of the heart, like caps. Their systole or contraction corresponds to the diastole of the heart, and *vice versa*. They receive the blood from the veins, and communicate it to the ventricles. *Encyc. Chambers.*
AURIC'ULA, *n.* That species of primrose, called, from the shape of its leaves, *bear's ear*.
AURIC'ULAR, *a.* [from L. *auricula*, the ear.]
1. Pertaining to the ear; within the sense of hearing; told in the ear; as *auricular* confession.
2. Recognized by the ear; known by the sense of hearing; as *auricular* evidence.
3. Traditional; known by report; as *auricular* traditions. *Bacon.*
AURIC'ULARLY, *adv.* In a secret manner; by way of whisper, or voice addressed to the ear.
AURIC'ULATE, *a.* Shaped like the ear. *Botany.*
AURIC'ULATED, *a.* Having large or elongated ears; as the *auriculated* vulture. *Ed. Encyc.*
AURIF'EROUS, *a.* [L. *aurifer*, from *aurum*, gold, and *fero*, to produce.]
That yields or produces gold; as *auriferous* sands or streams. *Thomson.*
AURI'GA, *n.* [L. of *aurea*, *orea*, a head-stall, a bridle, and *rego*, to govern or manage.]
Literally, the director of a car, or wagon. In *astronomy*, the wagoner, a constellation in the northern hemisphere, consisting of 23 stars, according to Tycho; 40, according to Hevelius; and 68, in the British catalogue. *Encyc.*
2. The fourth lobe of the liver; also a bandage for the sides. *Quincy.*
AURIGA'TION, *n.* [L. *auriga*.] The act or practice of driving horses harnessed to carriages.
AURIPIGMENTUM. [See *Orpiment*.]
AU'RISCALP, *n.* [L. *auris*, ear, and *scalpo*, to scrape.]
An instrument to clean the ears; used also in operations of surgery on the ear.
AU'RIST, *n.* [L. *auris*, ear.] One skilled in disorders of the ear, or who professes to cure them. *Ash.*
AU'ROCHS, *n.* [G. *urochs*, the *ure-ox*, *urus* and *ox*.]
A species of ox, whose bones are found in gravel and alluvial soil. *J. of Science.*
AURO'RA, *n.* [L. *aurora*; Sans. *arun*; Ch. and Heb. אור light, and עך to raise.]
1. The rising light of the morning; the dawn of day, or morning twilight.
2. The goddess of the morning, or twilight deified by fancy. The poets represented her as rising out of the ocean, in a chariot, with rosy fingers dropping gentle dew.
3. A species of crowfoot. *Johnson.*
Aurora Borealis, or *lumen boreale*; northern twilight. This species of light usually appears in streams, ascending towards the zenith from a dusky line a few degrees above the horizon. Sometimes it assumes a wavy appearance, as in America, in March 1782, when it overspread the whole hemisphere. Sometimes it appears in detached places; at other times, it almost covers the hemisphere. As the streams of light have a tremulous motion, they are called, in the Shetland isles, merry dancers. They assume all shapes, and a variety of colors, from a pale red or yellow to a deep red or blood color; and in the northern latitudes, serve to illuminate the earth and cheer the gloom of long winter nights. This light is sometimes near the earth. It is said to have been seen between the spectator and a distant mountain.
AURO'RAL, *a.* Belonging to the aurora, or to the northern lights; resembling the twilight. *E. Goodrich.*
AU'RUM, *n.* [L. See *Aurate*.] Gold.
Aurum fulminans, *fulminating gold*, is gold dissolved in aqua-regia or nitro-muriatic acid, and precipitated by volatile alkali. This precipitate is of a brown yellow, or orange color, and when exposed to a moderate heat, detonizes with considerable noise. It is a compound of the oxyd of gold and ammonia. *Fourcroy.*
Aurum mosaicum, or *musivum*, a sparkling gold-colored substance, from an amalgam of quick-silver and tin, mixed with sulphur and sal ammoniac, set to sublime. The mercury and part of the sulphur unite into a cinnabar, which sublimes with the sal-ammoniac, and leaves the aurum mosaicum at the bottom. It is a sulphuret of tin, and is used as a pigment. *Encyc. Nicholson.*
AUSCULTA'TION, *n.* [L. from antiq. *ause*, Gr. ους, ουας, the ear, and *cultus*, from *colo*, to use or exercise.]
1. The act of listening, or hearkening to.
2. In *medicine*, a method of distinguishing diseases, particularly in the thorax, by observing the sounds in the part, generally by means of a tube applied to the surface. *Laennec.*
AU'SPICATE, *v. t.* [L. *auspicor*.] To give a favorable turn to; a sense taken from the Roman practice of taking the *auspicium*, or inspection of birds, before they undertook any important business. *Burke's Reflections.*
2. To foreshow. *B. Jonson.*
3. To begin. *Burke.*
AU'SPICE, AU'SPICES, *n.* [L. *auspicium*, of *avis*, a bird, and *specio*, to inspect.]
1. The omens of an undertaking, drawn from birds; the same as augury, which see.
2. Protection; favor shown; patronage; influence. In this sense the word is generally plural, *auspices*.
AUSPI''CIOUS, *a.* [See *Auspice*.] Having omens of success, or favorable appearances; as an *auspicious* beginning.
2. Prosperous; fortunate; *applied to persons*; as *auspicious* chief. *Dryden.*
3. Favorable; kind; propitious; *applied to persons or things*; as an *auspicious* mistress. *Shak.*
AUSPI''CIOUSLY, *adv.* With favorable omens; happily; prosperously; favorably; propitiously.
AUSPI''CIOUSNESS, *n.* A state of fair promise; prosperity.
AUS'TER, *n.* [L.] The south wind. *Pope.*
AUSTE'RE, *a.* [L. *austerus*.] Severe; harsh; rigid; stern; *applied to persons*; as an *austere* master; an *austere* look.
2. Sour; harsh; rough to the taste; *applied to things*; as *austere* fruit, or wine.
AUSTE'RELY, *adv.* Severely; rigidly; harshly.
AUSTE'RENESS, *n.* Severity in manners; harshness; austerity.
2. Roughness in taste.
AUSTER'ITY, *n.* [L. *austeritas*.] Severity of manners or life; rigor; strictness; harsh discipline. It is particularly applied to the mortifications of a monastic life, which are called *austerities*.
AUS'TRAL, *a.* [L. *australis*, from *auster*, the south wind, or south.]
Southern; lying or being in the south; as *austral* land; *austral* signs.
AUSTRALA'SIA, *n.* [*austral* and *Asia*.] A name given to the countries situated to the south of Asia; comprehending New-Holland, New Guinea, New Zealand, &c. *Pinkerton.*
AUS'TRIAN, *a.* [from *Austria*. This word is formed with the Latin termination, *ia*, country, from *Œstreich*, the German name, which is *eastern rick*, eastern kingdom, so called in reference to the western dominions of Charlemagne.]
Pertaining to Austria, a circle or district of Germany, and an empire, lying on the Danube north of the gulf of Venice.
AUS'TRIAN, *n.* A native of Austria.
AUS'TRINE, *a.* [L. *austrinus*, from *auster*, south.]
South; southerly; southern. *Johnson.*
AUS'TROMANCY, *n.* [from *auster*, the south wind, and Gr. μαντεια, divination.]
Soothsaying, or prediction of future events, from observations of the winds. *Encyc.*
Auterfoits, a word composed of the French *autre*, another, and *foits*, *fois*, time, introduced into law language; under the Norman princes of England. It signifies, at another time, formerly; as *auterfoits*

acquit, auterfoits attaint, auterfoits convict, formerly acquitted, attainted or convicted, which being specially pleaded, is a bar to a second prosecution for the same offense. *Blackstone.*

AUTHEN'TIC, AUTHEN'TICAL, *a.* [Fr. *authentique;* It. and Sp. *autentico;* Low L. *authenticus,* from the Gr. αυθεντικος, from αυθεντης, an author or maker; one who does any thing by his own right; also one who kills himself. The first syllable is from αυτος, which is probably from the root of *author, auctor;* and the sense of self-murderer seems to indicate that the other constituent of the word is from θενω, θεινω, to kill, but the primary sense of which is, to strike, to drive or thrust with the hand, &c. In the word before us, the sense is to throw, or to set; hence *authentic* is set, fixed, made or made certain by the author, by one's own self.]

1. Having a genuine original or authority, in opposition to that which is false, fictitious, or counterfeit; being what it purports to be; genuine; true; *applied to things;* as an *authentic* paper or register.
2. Of approved authority; as an *authentic* writer.

AUTHEN'TICALLY, *adv.* In an authentic manner; with the requisite or genuine authority. *Brown.*

AUTHEN'TICALNESS, *n.* The quality of being authentic; genuineness; the quality of being of good authority; authenticity. [*The latter word is generally used.*] *Barrow.*

AUTHEN'TICATE, *v. t.* To render authentic; to give authority to, by the proof, attestation, or formalities, required by law, or sufficient to entitle to credit.

The king serves only as a notary to *authenticate* the choice of judges. *Burke.*

AUTHEN'TICATED, *pp.* Rendered authentic; having received the forms which prove genuineness.

AUTHEN'TICATING, *ppr.* Giving authority by the necessary signature, seal, attestation or other forms.

AUTHENTICA'TION, *n.* The act of authenticating; the giving of authority by the necessary formalities.

AUTHENTIC'ITY, *n.* Genuineness; the quality of being of genuine original; as the *authenticity* of the scriptures.

AUTHEN'TICNESS, *n.* Authenticity. [*Rarely used.*]

AU'THOR, *n.* [L. *auctor;* Ir. *ughdar;* W. *awdur;* Fr. *auteur;* Sp. *autor;* It. *autore.* The Latin word is from the root of *augeo,* to increase, or cause to enlarge. The primary sense is one who brings or causes to come forth.]

1. One who produces, creates, or brings into being; as, God is the *author* of the Universe.
2. The beginner, former, or first mover of any thing; hence, the efficient cause of a thing. It is appropriately applied to one who composes or writes a book, or original work, and in a more general sense, to one whose occupation is to compose and write books; opposed to compiler or translator.

AU'THOR, *v. t.* To occasion; to effect. [*Not used.*]

AU'THORESS, *n.* A female author.

AUTHOR'ITATIVE, *a.* Having due authority. *Pearson.*

2. Having an air of authority; positive; peremptory. *Wotton.*

AUTHOR'ITATIVELY, *adv.* In an authoritative manner; with a show of authority; with due authority.

AUTHOR'ITATIVENESS, *n.* The quality of being authoritative; an acting by authority; authoritative appearance.

AUTHOR'ITY, *n.* [L. *auctoritas.*]

1. Legal power, or a right to command or to act; as the *authority* of a prince over subjects, and of parents over children. Power; rule; sway.
2. The power derived from opinion, respect or esteem; influence of character or office; credit; as the *authority* of age or example, which is submitted to or respected, in some measure, as a law, or rule of action. That which is claimed in justification or support of opinions and measures.
3. Testimony; witness; or the person who testifies; as, the Gospels or the evangelists are our *authorities* for the miracles of Christ.
4. Weight of testimony; credibility; as a historian of no *authority.*
5. Weight of character; respectability; dignity; as a magistrate of great *authority* in the city.
6. Warrant; order; permission.

By what *authority* dost thou these things. Mat. xxi. Acts ix.

7. Precedents, decisions of a court, official declarations, respectable opinions and sayings, also the books that contain them, are called *authorities,* as they influence the opinions of others; and in *law,* the decisions of supreme courts have a binding force upon inferior courts, and are called *authorities.*
8. Government; the persons or the body exercising power or command; as the local *authorities* of the states. *Marshall.* 1 Pet. iii.

In *Connecticut,* the justices of the peace are denominated the *civil authority.*

AUTHORIZA'TION, *n.* The act of giving authority, or legal power; establishment by authority.

AU'THORIZE, *v. t.* [Fr. *autoriser;* Sp. *autorizar.*]

1. To give authority, warrant or legal power to; to give a right to act; to empower; as, to *authorize* commissioners to settle the boundary of the state.
2. To make legal; as, to *authorize* a marriage.
3. To establish by authority, as by usage, or public opinion; as an *authorized* idiom of language.
4. To give authority, credit or reputation to; as to *authorize* a report, or opinion.
5. To justify; to support as right. Suppress desires which reason does not *authorize.*

AU'THORIZED, *pp.* Warranted by right; supported by authority; derived from legal or proper authority; having power or authority.

AU'THORIZING, *ppr.* Giving authority to, or legal power, credit, or permission.

AU'THORSHIP, *n.* [*author* and *ship.*] The quality or state of being an author. *Shaftesbury.*

AUTOBIOG'RAPHY, *n.* [Gr. αυτος, and *biography.*]

Biography or memoirs of one's life written by himself. *Walsh.*

AUTOC'RASY, *n.* [Gr. αυτος, self, and κρατος, power, or κρατεω, to govern, to take or hold.]

Independent power; supreme, uncontrolled, unlimited authority or right of governing, in a single person.

AU'TOCRAT, AU'TOCRATER, AU'TOCRATOR, *n.* An absolute prince or sovereign; a ruler or monarch who holds and exercises the powers of government by inherent right, not subject to restriction; a title assumed by the Emperors of Russia. *Tooke.*

2. This title was sometimes conferred by the Athenians on their embassadors and generals, when invested with unlimited powers. *Encyc.*

AUTOCRAT'IC, AUTOCRAT'ICAL, *a.* Pertaining to autocracy; absolute; holding independent and unlimited powers of government. *Eton.*

AU'TOCRATRIX, *n.* A female sovereign, who is independent and absolute; a title given to the Empresses of Russia. *Tooke.*

Auto da fe. [Port. *act of faith.*]

1. In *the Romish church,* a solemn day held by the Inquisition, for the punishment of heretics, and the absolution of the innocent accused. Span. *Auto de fe.* *Encyc.*
2. A sentence given by the Inquisition, and read to a criminal, or heretic, on the scaffold, just before he is executed. *Sp. Dict.*
3. The session of the court of inquisition.

AU'TOGRAPH, AUTOG'RAPHY, *n.* [Gr. αυτος, self, and γραφη, writing.]

A person's own hand writing; an original manuscript.

AUTOGRAPH'IC, AUTOGRAPH'ICAL, *a.* Pertaining to an autograph, or one's own hand writing.

AUTOM'ALITE, *n.* A mineral called by Haüy, spinelle zincifère. It is classed with the spinel ruby. It occurs imbedded in talcky slate; the color, a dark green. It is crystalized in regular octahedrons, or in tetrahedrons with truncated angles. It is harder than quartz, but not so hard as spinel. It is sometimes called gahnite, from Gahn, its discoverer. *Cyc. Thomson. Cleaveland.*

AU'TOMATH, *n.* [Gr. αυτος, and μανθανω, to learn.] One who is self taught. *Young.*

AUTOMAT'IC, AUTOMAT'ICAL, *a.* Belonging to an automaton; having the power of moving itself; mechanical. *Johnson. Stewart.*

2. Not voluntary; not depending on the will. Dr. Hartley has demonstrated that all our motions are originally *automatic,* and generally produced by the action of tangible things on the muscular fiber.

AUTOM'ATON, *n.* [Gr. αυτοματος; αυτος, self, and μαω, *moveo, motus.* The Greek plural, *automata,* is sometimes used; but the regular English plural, *automatons,* is preferable.]

A self-moving machine, or one which moves by invisible springs.

AUTOM'ATOUS, *a.* Having in itself the power of motion. *Brown.*

AUTON'OMOUS, *a.* [*Infra.*] Independent

in government; having the right of self government. *Mitford.*

AUTON'OMY, *n.* [Gr. αυτος, self, and νομος, law, rule.]

This word is rarely used. It signifies the power or right of self government, whether in a city which elects its own magistrates and makes its own laws, or in an individual who lives according to his own will. *Johnson. Encyc.*

AU'TOPSY, *n.* [Gr. αυτοψια, αυτος, self, and οψις, sight.] Personal observation; ocular view. *Ray.*

AUTOP'TICAL, *a.* Seen with one's own eyes. *Johnson.*

AUTOP'TICALLY, *adv.* By means of ocular view, or one's own observation. *Brown.*

[*Autopsy* and its derivatives are rarely used.]

AU'TUMN, *n.* *áutum.* [L. *autumnus*, "Etymon multum torquetur." *Ainsworth.*]

The third season of the year, or the season between summer and winter. Astronomically, it begins at the equinox, when the sun enters libra, and ends at the winter solstice; but in popular language, autumn comprises September, October and November.

The golden pomp of *autumn*. *Irving.*

AUTUM'NAL, *a.* Belonging to autumn; produced or gathered in autumn; as *autumnal* fruits.

AUTUM'NAL, *n.* A plant that flowers in Autumn. The autumnals form the third division of plants in Du Pas' arrangement. *Milne.*

AUXE'SIS, *n.* [Gr. αυξησις, increase.]

In *rhetoric*, a figure by which any thing is magnified too much; an increasing, or exornation, when, for amplification, a more grave and magnificent word is put for the proper word. *Smith. Encyc.*

AUXIL'IAR, } *a.* [L. *auxiliaris*, from *auxilium*, aid, *auxilior*, to
AUXIL'IARY, } aid.]

Helping; aiding; assisting; subsidiary; conferring aid or support by joint exertion, influence or use; as *auxiliary* troops.

AUXIL'IARIES, *n. plu.* Foreign troops in the service of nations at war.

AUXIL'IARY, *n.* A helper; an assistant; a confederate in some action, enterprise or undertaking.

2. In *grammar*, a verb which helps to form the modes and tenses of other verbs; as, *have, be, may, can, do, must, shall* and *will*, in English; *être* and *avoir*, in French; *avére* and *essere*, in Italian; *estar* and *haber*, in Spanish.

AVA'IL, *v. t.* [Fr. *valoir*, to be worth; L. *valeo*, to be strong or able, to profit, to be of force or authority; Sp. *valer*, to be valuable, to avail or prevail, to be binding, to be worth; It. *valere*, to be worth, to be useful; Eng. *well*; Ar. بلا balla. The primary sense is, to stretch or extend, whence strength, value.]

1. To profit one's self; to turn to advantage; followed by the pronouns, *myself, thyself, himself, herself, ourselves, yourselves, themselves*, with *of* before the thing used; as, let him *avail himself of* his license.

2. To assist or profit; to effect the object, or bring to a succesful issue; as, what will skill *avail* us against numbers. Artifices will not *avail* the sinner in the day of judgment.

AVA'IL, *v. i.* To be of use, or advantage; to answer the purpose; as, strength without judgment will rarely *avail.* Generally, it signifies to have strength, force or efficacy sufficient to accomplish the object; as, the plea in bar must *avail*, that is, be sufficient to defeat the suit; this scheme will not *avail*; medicines will not *avail* to check the disease; suppositions, without proof, will not *avail.*

AVA'IL, *n.* Profit; advantage towards success; benefit; as, labor without economy is of little *avail*. It seems usually to convey the idea of efficacious aid or strength.

AVA'ILABLE, *a.* Profitable; advantageous; having efficacy; as, a measure is more or less *available.* *Atterbury.*

2. Having sufficient power, force, or efficacy, for the object; valid; as an *available* plea.

Laws are *available* by consent. *Hooker.*

AVA'ILABLENESS, *n.* Power or efficacy, in promoting an end in view.

2. Competent power; legal force; validity; as the *availableness* of a title.

AVA'ILABLY, *adv.* Powerfully; profitably; advantageously; validly; efficaciously.

AVA'ILING, *pp.* Turning to profit: using to advantage or effect.

AVA'ILMENT, *n.* Profit; efficacy; successful issue. [*Little used.*]

AVA'ILS, *n. plu.* Profits or proceeds. It is used in New-England, for the proceeds of goods sold, or for rents, issues or profits.

AVALANCHE, } *n.* [Fr. from *avaler*, to
AVALANGE, } fall.]

A snow-slip; a vast body of snow sliding down a mountain.

AVANT', *n.* The front of an army. [*Not used.*] [See *Van.*]

AVANT'GUARD, *n.* The van or advanced body of an army. [See *Vanguard.*]

AVANT'URINE, *n.* A variety of quartz rock containing spangles. *Ure.*

AV'ARICE, *n.* [L. *avaritia*, from *avarus*, from *aveo*, to covet.]

An inordinate desire of gaining and possessing wealth; covetousness; greediness or insatiable desire of gain. *Shak.*

Avarice sheds a blasting influence over the finest affections and sweetest comforts of mankind. *Buckminster.*

AVARI''CIOUS, *a.* Covetous; greedy of gain; immoderately desirous of accumulating property.

AVARI''CIOUSLY, *adv.* Covetously; with inordinate desire of gaining wealth. *Goldsmith.*

AVARI''CIOUSNESS, *n.* The quality of being avaricious; insatiable or inordinate passion for property.

AV'AROUS, *a.* Covetous. [*Not used.*] *Gower.*

AV'AST, *exclam.* [Ger. *basta*, stop; *bastant*, sufficient; from It. *basta*, enough; Per. *bas*, enough.]

In *seamen's language*, cease; stop; stay.

AVAUNT', *excl.* [W. *ibant*, begone.]

Begone; depart; a word of contempt or abhorrence, equivalent to the phrase, "Get thee behind me."

A'VE MARY, *n.* [from the first words of Gabriel's salutation to the Virgin Mary; L. *ave*, hail.]

A form of devotion in the Romish Church. Their chaplets and rosaries are divided into a certain number of ave-marys and paternosters.

AVENA'CEOUS, *a.* [L. *avenaceus*, from *avena*, oats; Fr. *avoine.*]

Belonging to, or partaking of the nature of oats.

AV'ENAGE, *n.* [Fr.] A certain quantity of oats paid by a tenant to a landlord in lieu of rent or other duty. *Spelman.*

AV'ENER, } *n.* [Norm. French.]
AV'ENOR, }

In *English feudal law*, an officer of the king's stable whose duty was to provide oats.

AVENGE, *v. t.* *avenj'.* [Fr. *venger*; Sp. *vengar*; Port. *vingar*; L. *vindex.* In Sax. *winnan*, to contend, to gain, to *win.*]

1. To take satisfaction for an injury by punishing the injuring party; to vindicate by inflicting pain or evil on the wrong doer.

Shall not God *avenge* his own elect. Luke xviii.

Avenge me of my adversary. Id. v. 3.

In these examples, *avenge* implies that the evil inflicted on the injuring party is a satisfaction or justice done to the injured, and the party vindicated is the object of the verb.

2. To take satisfaction for, by pain or punishment inflicted on the injuring party.

He will *avenge* the blood of his servants. Deut. xxxii.

Here the thing for which satisfaction is taken is the object of the verb.

3. To revenge. To *avenge* and *revenge*, radically, are synonymous. But modern usage inclines to make a valuable distinction in the use of these words, restricting *avenge* to the taking of just punishment, and *revenge* to the infliction of pain or evil, maliciously, in an illegal manner.

4. In the *passive form*, this verb signifies to have or receive just satisfaction, by the punishment of the offender.

Shall not my soul be *avenged* on such a nation as this? Jer. 5.

AVENG'EANCE, *n.* Punishment. [*Not used.*] [See *Vengeance.*]

AVENG'ED, *pp.* Satisfied by the punishment of the offender; vindicated; punished.

AVENG'EMENT, *n.* Vengeance; punishment; the act of taking satisfaction for an injury by inflicting pain or evil on the offender; satisfaction taken; revenge.

AVENG'ER, *n.* One who avenges or vindicates; a vindicator; a revenger.

AVENG'ERESS, *n.* A female avenger. *Spenser.*

AVENG'ING, *ppr.* Executing vengeance; taking satisfaction for an injury by the punishment of the offender; vindicating.

AV'ENS, *n.* The herb bennet. *Miller.*

AV'ENTINE, *a.* Pertaining to *Mons Aventinus*, one of the seven hills on which Rome stood. *Bryant.*

AVEN'TURE, *n.* [Fr. *aventure*, from L. *venio*, to come.]

A mischance causing a person's death without felony; as by drowning, or falling from a house. [See *Adventure.*] *Cowel.*

AV'ENUE, *n.* [Fr. from *venir*, to come or go; L. *venio.*]

1. A passage; a way or opening for entrance into a place; any opening or passage by which a thing is or may be introduced.
2. An alley, or walk in a garden, planted with trees, and leading to a house, gate, wood, &c., and generally terminated by some distant object. The trees may be in rows on the sides, or, according to the more modern practice, in clumps at some distance from each other. *Encyc.*
3. A wide street, as in Washington, Columbia.

AVER' *v. t.* [Fr. *averer*; It. *avverare*, to aver or verify; Arm. *quirya*, from the root of *verus*, true; Ir. *feor*, or *fir*; W. *gwir*; Corn. *uir*; Ger. *wahr*; D. *waar*. See *Verify*.]
To affirm with confidence; to declare in a positive or peremptory manner, as in confidence of asserting the truth. *Prior.*

AV'ERAGE, *n.* [Norm. *aver*, *avers*, cattle, money, goods, Sp. *averio*, from *aver* or *haber*, Fr. *avoir*, to *have* or possess. In *ancient law*, a duty or service which a tenant was bound to render to his lord, by his beasts and carriages or instruments of husbandry. *Spelman.* But *averagium* signifies also the loss of goods in transportation; Sp. *averia*, damage sustained by goods or ships; Port. *avaria*, an allowance out of freight to the master of a ship, for damage sustained; contribution by insurers, to make good a loss; It. *avaria*; Dan. *haverie*, damage of a ship or waste of goods, extraordinary charges during a voyage. If *avaria* signifies damage, and is from *aver* or *haber*, Spanish, to have, the sense of the word is probably that which happens or falls, a misfortune, for the verb *have* and *happen* are radically the same word; Spanish, *haber*, to have, and to happen or befall; also fortune, property. This would give the sense of damage, or of proportion, lot, share, that which falls to each of a number. But the primary sense is not very obvious.]
1. In *commerce*, a contribution to a general loss. When for the safety of a ship in distress, any destruction of property is incurred, either by cutting away the masts, throwing goods overboard, or other means, all persons who have goods on board, or property in the ship, contribute to the loss according to their average, that is, the goods of each on board. This principle, introduced into the commerce of Europe, from the Rhodian laws, and recognized by the regulations of Wisby, is now an established rule in the maritime laws of Europe; for it is most reasonable, that when one man's property is sacrificed to save a ship, all persons whose property is saved, or in like hazard, should bear their proportion of the loss. *Spelman. Park. Beawes.*
2. From the practice of contributing to bear losses, in proportion to each man's property, this word has obtained the present popular sense, which is, that of a mean proportion, medial sum or quantity, made out of unequal sums or quantities. Thus, if A loses 5 dollars, B 9 and C 16, the sum is 30, and the average, 10.
3. A small duty payable by the shippers of goods, to the master of the ship, over and above the freight, for his care of the goods. Hence the expression in bills of lading, "paying so much freight, with primage and *average* accustomed." *Cowel. Encyc.*
4. In *England*, the breaking up of cornfields, eddish or roughings. *Ash. Spelman.*
Upon, or *on an average*, is taking the mean of unequal numbers or quantities.

AV'ERAGE, *a.* Medial; containing a mean proportion. *Price. Beddoes. Kirwan. Edwards' W. Indies.*

AV'ERAGE, *v. t.* To find the mean of unequal sums or quantities; to reduce to a medium; to divide among a number, according to a given proportion; as, to *average* a loss.

AV'ERAGE, *v. i.* To form a mean or medial sum or quantity; as, the losses of the owners will *average* 25 dollars each.

These spars *average* 10 feet in length. *Belknap. Ch. Obs.* x. 522. xi. 302.

AV'ERAGED, *pp.* Reduced or formed into a mean proportion, or into shares proportioned to each man's property. *Jefferson.*

AV'ERAGING, *ppr.* Forming a mean proportion out of unequal sums or quantities, or reducing to just shares according to each man's property.

AVER'MENT, *n.* [See *Aver*.] Affirmation; positive assertion; the act of averring.
2. Verification; establishment by evidence. *Bacon.*
3. In *pleading*, an offer of either party to justify or prove what he alledges. In any stage of pleadings, when either party advances new matter, he *avers* it to be true, and concludes with these words, "and this he is ready to verify." This is called an *averment*. *Blackstone.*

AVER'NAT, *n.* A sort of grape. *Ash. Johnson.*

AVER'NIAN, *a.* Pertaining to Avernus, a lake of Campania in Italy, famous for its poisonous qualities, which the poets represent as so malignant, as to kill fowls flying over. Hence, as authors tell us, its name, αορνος, without birds. *Virgil. Mela. Strabo.*

AV'ERPENNY, *n.* Money paid towards the king's carriages by land, instead of service by the beasts in kind. *Burn.*

AVER'RED, *pp.* Affirmed; laid with an averment.

AVER'RING, *ppr.* Affirming; declaring positively; offering to justify or verify.

AVERROIST, *n.* One of a sect of peripatetic philosophers, who were so denominated from Averroes, a celebrated Arabian author. They held the soul to be mortal, though they pretended to submit to the christian theology. *Encyc.*

AVERRUNC'ATE, *v. t.* [L. *averrunco*, of *ab* and *erunco*, from *runco*, to weed, or rake away.]
To root up; to scrape or tear away by the roots. *Hudibras.*

AVERRUNCA'TION, *n.* The act of tearing up or raking away by the roots.

AVERSA'TION, *n.* [L. *aversor*. See *Avert*.]
A turning from with disgust or dislike; aversion; hatred; disinclination. *South.*
It is nearly superseded by *aversion*.

AVERSE, *a.* *avers'* [See *Avert*.] The literal sense of this word is, *turned from*, in manifestation of dislike. Hence the real sense is,
1. Disliking; unwilling; having a repugnance of mind.

Averse alike to flatter or offend. *Pope*

2. Unfavorable; indisposed; malign.

And Pallas now *averse* refused her aid. *Dryden.*

This word and its derivatives ought to be followed by *to*, and never by *from*. This word includes the idea of *from*; but the literal meaning being lost, the affection of the mind signified by the word, is exerted *towards* the object of dislike, and like its kindred terms, *hatred*, *dislike*, *contrary*, *repugnant*, &c., should be followed by *to*. Indeed it is absurd to speak of an affection of the mind exerted *from* an object. *Averse* expresses a less degree of opposition in the mind, than *detesting* and *abhorring*.
Milton once uses *averse* in its literal sense, with *from*, but it is not according to the English idiom.

AVERSELY, *adv.* *avers'ly.* With repugnance; unwillingly. *Brown.*

AVERSENESS, *n.* *avers'ness.* Opposition of mind; dislike; unwillingness; backwardness. *Herbert.*

AVER'SION, *n.* [Fr. *aversion*, from L. *averto*.]
1. Opposition or repugnance of mind; dislike; disinclination; reluctance; hatred. Usually this word expresses moderate hatred, or opposition of mind, not amounting to *abhorrence* or *detestation*. It ought generally to be followed by *to* before the object. [See *Averse*.] Sometimes it admits of *for*.

A freeholder is bred with an *aversion to* subjection. *Addison.*

2. Opposition or contrariety of nature; *applied to inanimate substances.*

Magnesia, notwithstanding this *aversion* to solution, forms a kind of paste with water. *Fourcroy, Trans.*

3. The cause of dislike.

Pain their *aversion*, pleasure their desire. *Pope.*

AVERT', *v. t.* [L. *averto*, *a*, from, and *verto*, to turn, anciently, *vorto*; hence *vertex*, *vortex*, *averto*; probably allied to L. *vario*; Eng. *veer*; Sp. *birar*; Eth. በረ bari. Class Br.]
1. To turn from; to turn off or away; as, to *avert* the eyes from an object. *Shak.*
2. To keep off, divert or prevent; as, to *avert* an approaching calamity. *Hooker.*
3. To cause to dislike. *Hooker.* But this sense seems to be improper, except when *heart* or some equivalent word is used; as, to *avert* the heart or affections, which may signify to alienate the affections. *Thomson.*

AVERT', *v. i.* To turn away. *Thomson.*

AVERT'ER, *n.* One that turns away; that which turns away.

AVERT'ING, *ppr.* Turning from; turning away.

A'VIARY, *n.* [L. *aviarium*, from *avis*, a fowl.]
A bird cage; an inclosure for keeping birds confined. *Wotton.*

AVID'IOUSLY, *adv.* [See *Avidity*.] Eagerly; with greediness. *Bale.*

AVID'ITY, *n.* [L. *aviditas*, from *avidus*, and this from *aveo*, to desire, to have appetite; Heb. and Ch. אוה, to desire, or covet.]
1. Greediness; strong appetite; *applied to the senses.*

2. Eagerness; intenseness of desire; *applied to the mind.*

AVIGA'TO, } *n.* The Persea, or alligator-
AVOCA'DO, } pear, a species ranked under the genus *Laurus*, a native of the W. Indies. The tree has a straight trunk, long oval pointed leaves, and flowers of six petals disposed like a star, produced in clusters, on the extremities of the branches. The fruit is insipid. *Encyc. Miller.*

Avignon-berry, the fruit of a species of lycium, so called from the city, Avignon, in France. The berry is less than a pea, of a yellowish green color, and bitter astringent taste; used by dyers and painters for staining yellow. *Encyc.*

AVI'LE, *v. t.* [Fr. *avilir.* See *Vile.*] To depreciate. [*Not in use.*] *B. Jonson.*

AVI'SE, } *n.* [Fr. *avis.*] Advice; intelligence.
AVI'SO, } [*Not in use.*]

AVI'SE, *v. i.* *s* as *z.* To consider. [*Not in use.*] *Spenser.*

AVI'SEMENT, *n.* Advisement. [See *Advice* and *Advise.*]

AV'OCATE, *v. t.* [L. *avoco*, from *a* and *voco*, to call. See *Voice* and *Vocal.*]

To call off, or away. [*Not used.*] *Boyle.*

AVOCA'TION, *n.* [See *Vocation, Voice, Vocal.*]

1. The act of calling aside, or diverting from some employment; as an *avocation* from sin or from business.

2. The business which calls aside. The word is generally used for the smaller affairs of life, or occasional calls which summon a person to leave his ordinary or principal business. The use of this word for *vocation* is very improper.

AVO'CATIVE, *a.* Calling off. [*Not used.*]

AVOID', *v. t.* [Fr. *vuider*, or *vider; vuide*, void, empty; Eng. *wide, void, widow;* L. *vidua.* See *Void.* It coincides also with L. *vito, evito;* Fr. *eviter.* See Class Bd.]

1. To shun; to keep at a distance from; that is, literally, to go or be *wide* from; as, to *avoid* the company of gamesters.

2. To shift off, or clear off; as, to *avoid* expense.

3. To quit; to evacuate; to shun by leaving; as, to *avoid* the house.

4. To escape; as, to *avoid* danger. *Shak.*

5. To emit or throw out; as, to *avoid* excretions. For this, *void* is now generally used.

6. To make void; to annul or vacate.

The grant cannot be *avoided* without injustice to the grantee. *Anon.*

7. In *pleading*, to set up some new matter or distinction, which shall *avoid*, that is, defeat or evade the allegation of the other party. Thus, in a replication, the plaintiff may deny the defendant's plea, or confess it, and *avoid* it by stating new matter. *Blackstone.*

AVOID', *v. i.* To retire; to withdraw.

David *avoided* out of his presence. 1 Sam. xviii. [*Improper.*]

2. To become void, vacant or empty.

A benefice *avoids* by common law. *Ayliffe.*

AVOID'ABLE, *a.* That may be avoided, left at a distance, shunned or escaped.

2. That may be vacated; liable to be annulled.

AVOID'ANCE, *n.* The act of avoiding, or shunning.

2. The act of vacating, or the state of being vacant. It is appropriately used for the state of a benefice becoming void, by the death, deprivation, or resignation of the incumbent. *Cowel. Encyc.*

3. The act of annulling.

4. The course by which any thing is carried off. *Bacon.*

AVOID'ED, *pp.* Shunned; evaded; made void; ejected.

AVOID'ER, *n.* One who avoids, shuns or escapes.

2. The person who carries any thing away; the vessel in which things are carried away. *Johnson.*

AVOID'ING, *ppr.* Shunning; escaping; keeping at a distance; ejecting; evacuating; making void, or vacant.

AVOID'LESS, *a.* That cannot be avoided; inevitable. *Dryden.*

AVOIRDUPOIS', *n.* *s* as *z.* [Fr. *avoir du poids*, to have weight. See *Poise.*]

A weight, of which a pound contains 16 ounces. Its proportion to a pound Troy is as 17 to 14. This is the weight for the larger and coarser commodities, as hay, iron, cheese, groceries, &c. *Chambers.*

AVOLA'TION, *n.* [L. *avolo*, to fly away, of *a* and *volo.* See *Volatile.*]

The act of flying away; flight; escape. [*Little used.*]

AV'OSET, } *n.* In *ornithology*, a species
AVOSET'TA, } of fowls, arranged under the genus, *recurvirostra*, and placed by Linne in the grallic order, but by Pennant and Latham, among the palmipeds. The bill is long, slender, flexible and bent upward towards the tip. This bird is of the size of a lapwing, with very long legs, and the feathers variegated with black and white. It is found both in Europe and America. *Encyc.*

AVOUCH', *v. t.* [Norm. *voucher*, to call, to *vouch;* L. *voco, advoco.* See *Voice.*]

1. To affirm; to declare or assert with positiveness. *Hooker.*

2. To produce or call in; to affirm in favor of, maintain or support.

Such antiquities could be *avouched* for the Irish. *Spenser.*

3. To maintain, vindicate or justify. *Skak.*

AVOUCH', *n.* Evidence; testimony; declaration. [*Little used.*] *Shak.*

AVOUCH'ABLE, *a.* That may be avouched. [*Little used.*]

AVOUCH'ED, *pp.* Affirmed; maintained; called in to support.

AVOUCH'ER, *n.* One who avouches.

AVOUCH'ING, *ppr.* Affirming; calling in to maintain; vindicating.

AVOUCH'MENT, *n.* Declaration; the act of avouching. *Shak.*

AVOW', *v. t.* [Fr. *avouer;* Arm. *avoei;* Norm. *avower;* L. *voveo.*]

1. To declare openly, with a view to justify, maintain or defend; or simply to own, acknowledge or confess frankly; as, a man *avows* his principles or his crimes.

2. In *law*, to acknowledge and justify; as when the distrainer of goods defends in an action of replevin, and *avows* the taking, but insists that such taking was legal. *Blackstone.*

AVOW', *n.* A vow or determination. [*Not used.*] *Gower.*

AVOW'ABLE, *a.* That may be avowed, or openly acknowledged with confidence. *Donne.*

AVOW'AL, *n.* An open declaration; frank acknowledgment. *Hume.*

AVOW'ANT, *n.* The defendant in replevin, who *avows* the distress of the goods, and justifies the taking. *Cowel.*

AVOW'ED, *pp.* Openly declared; owned; frankly acknowledged.

AVOW'EDLY, *adv.* In an open manner; with frank acknowledgment.

AVOW'EE, *n.* Sometimes used for *advowee*, the person who has a right to present to a benefice, the patron. [See *Advowson.*] *Cowel.*

AVOW'ER, *n.* One who avows, owns, or asserts.

AVOW'ING, *ppr.* Openly declaring; frankly acknowledging; justifying.

AVOW'RY, *n.* In *law*, the act of the distrainer of goods, who, in an action of replevin, *avows* and justifies the taking; the act of maintaining the right to distrain, by the distrainer, or defendant in replevin. *Blackstone.*

AVOW'TRY, [See *Advowtry.*]

AVULS'ED, *a.* [See *Avulsion.*] Plucked or pulled off. *Shenstone.*

AVUL'SION, *n.* [L. *avulsio*, from *avello*, *a* and *vello*, to pull, coinciding with Heb. and Ar. פלה, to separate; Eng. *pull.*]

A pulling or tearing asunder; a rending or violent separation.

AWA'IT, *v. t.* [*a* and *wait.* See *Wait.* Fr. *guetter*, to watch; *guet*, a watch; It. *guatare*, to look or watch.]

Literally, to remain, hold or stay.

1. To wait for; to look for, or expect.

Betwixt the rocky pillars, Gabriel sat,
Chief of the Angelic guards, *awaiting* night. *Milton.*

2. To be in store for; to attend; to be ready for; as, a glorious reward *awaits* the good.

AWA'IT, *n.* Ambush; in a state of waiting for. *Spenser.*

AWA'ITING, *ppr.* Waiting for; looking for; expecting; being ready or in store for.

AWA'KE, *v. t.* pret. *awoke, awaked;* pp. *awaked.* [Sax. *gewæcan, wacian*, or *weccan;* D. *wekken;* Ger. *wecken;* Sw. *upväcka;* Dan. *vækker.* The L. *vigilo* seems to be formed on this root. See *Wake.*]

1. To rouse from sleep.

I go that I may *awake* him out of sleep. John xi.

2. To excite from a state resembling sleep, as from death, stupidity or inaction; to put into action, or new life; as, to *awake* the dead; to *awake* the dormant faculties.

AWA'KE, *v. i.* To cease to sleep; to come from a state of natural sleep.

Jacob *awaked* out of sleep. Gen. xxviii.

2. To bestir, revive or rouse from a state of inaction; to be invigorated with new life; as, the mind *awakes* from its stupidity.

Awake, O sword, against my shepherd. Zech. xiii.

3. To rouse from spiritual sleep.

Awake thou that sleepest, and arise from the dead, and Christ shall give thee light. Eph. v.

Awake to righteousness. 1 Cor. xv.

4. To rise from the dead. Job xiv.

AWA'KE, *a.* Not sleeping; in a state of vigilance or action.

AWA'KEN, *v. t.* *awákn.* This is the word *awake*, with its Saxon infinitive. It is transitive or intransitive; but more frequently transitive, as *awake* is more frequently intransitive. Its significations are the same as those of *awake.*

AWA'KENED, *pp.* Roused from sleep, in a natural or moral sense.

AWA'KENER, *n.* He or that which awakens.

AWA'KENING, *n.* A revival of religion, or more general attention to religion, than usual.

AWARD', *v. t.* [Scot. *warde*, determination; Norm. *garda*, award, judgment; *agardetz*, awarded. See *Guard* and *Regard.*]

To adjudge; to give by sentence or judicial determination; to assign by sentence. This word is appropriately used to express the act of arbitrators in pronouncing upon the rights of parties; as, the arbitrators *awarded* damages to A. B.

AWARD', *v. i.* To judge; to determine; to make an *award.*

AWARD', *n.* The judgment, or determination of arbitrators, or the paper containing it.

2. Judgment; sentence; determination of points submitted to arbitrators.

AWARD'ED, *pp.* Adjudged, or given by judicial sentence, or by the decision of arbitrators.

AWARD'ER, *n.* One that awards, or assigns by sentence or judicial determination; a judge. *Thomson.*

AWARD'ING, *ppr.* Adjudging; assigning by judicial sentence; determining.

AWA'RE, *a.* [Sax. *gewarian*, to take care, provide, avoid; to preserve or defend; also covered, protected; *warian*, to beware; *war*, aware. See *Ware* and *Wary.*]

Watchful; vigilant; guarded; but more strictly in modern usage, apprised; expecting an event from information, or probability; as, the general was *aware* of the enemy's designs.

AWA'RE, *v. i.* To beware; to be cautious. [*Not legitimate.*] *Milton.*

AWARN', *v. t.* To warn, which see. *Spenser.*

AWAT'CHA, *n.* A bird of Kamtchatka, enumerated by Pennant, among the warblers. The upper parts of the body are of a deep brown color; the throat and breast white, with black spots.

AWA'Y, *adv.* [Sax. *aweg*, absent, *a* and *weg*, way; also *onweg*, away, and *awegan*, to avert. See *Way.*]

1. Absent; at a distance; as, the master is *away* from home.

> Have me *away*, for I am wounded. 2 Chron. xxxv.

2. It is much used with words signifying moving or going from; as, go *away*, send *away*, run *away*, &c.; all signifying departure, or separation to a distance. Sometimes without the verb; as, whither *away* so fast. *Shak.*

> Love hath wings and will *away*. *Waller.*

3. As an exclamation, it is a command or invitation to depart; *away*, that is, be gone, or let us go. "*Away* with him." Take him *away.*

4. With verbs, it serves to modify their sense and form peculiar phrases; as,

To throw away, to cast from, to give up, dissipate or foolishly destroy.

To trifle away, to lose or expend in trifles, or in idleness.

To drink away, *to squander away*, &c., to dissipate in drinking or extravagance.

To make away, is to kill or destroy.

5. *Away with* has a peculiar signification in the phrase, "I cannot *away* with it." Isa. i. The sense is, "I cannot bear or endure it."

AWE, *n.* *aw.* [Dan. *ave*, fear, awe, chastisement, discipline; *aver*, to chastise or correct; Gr. αγαω, to be astonished. Qu. Ir. *agh*; Sax. *ege*, or *oga*, fear; Goth. *agjan*, or *ogan*, to dread. It would appear that the primary sense of the Dan. is to strike, or check.]

1. Fear mingled with admiration or reverence; reverential fear.

> Stand in *awe* and sin not. Ps. iv.

2. Fear; dread inspired by something great, or terrific.

AWE, *v. t.* To strike with fear and reverence; to influence by fear, terror or respect; as, his majesty *awed* them into silence.

AWE'ARY, *a.* Weary, which see. *Shak.*

AWEATH'ER, *adv.* *aweth'er.* [*a* and *weather.*]

On the weather-side, or towards the wind; as, the helm is *aweather*; opposed to *alee.* *Mar. Dict.*

AWE-COMMAND'ING, *a.* Striking or influencing by awe. *Gray.*

AW'ED, *pp.* Struck with fear; influenced by fear or reverence.

AWEIGH', *adv.* [*a* and *weigh.*] Atrip. The anchor is *aweigh*, when it is just drawn out of the ground, and hangs perpendicular. [See *Atrip.*]

AWE-INSPI'RING, *a.* Impressing with awe. *Bp. Hobart.*

AWE'-STRUCK, *a.* Impressed or struck with awe. *Milton.*

AW'FUL, *a.* [*awe* and *full.*]

1. That strikes with awe; that fills with profound reverence; as the *awful* majesty of Jehovah.

2. That fills with terror and dread; as the *awful* approach of death.

3. Struck with awe; scrupulous.

> A weak and *awful* reverence for antiquity. *Watts.*

Shakspeare uses it for worshipful, inspiring respect by authority or dignity.

Our common people use this word in the sense of frightful, ugly, detestable.

AW'FULLY, *adv.* In a manner to fill with awe; in a reverential manner.

AW'FULNESS, *n.* The quality of striking with awe, or with reverence; solemnity; as, "the *awfulness* of this sacred place."

2. The state of being struck with awe.

> A help to prayer, producing in us reverence and *awfulness.* *Taylor.*

[*Not legitimate.*]

AWHAPE, *v. t.* *awhap'.* [W. *cwapiaw*, to strike smartly.] To strike; to confound. *Obs.* *Spenser.*

[This is our vulgar *whop.*]

AWH'ILE, *adv.* [*a* and *while*, time, or interval.]

A space of time; for some time; for a short time.

AWK, *a.* Odd; out of order. *L'Estrange.*

2. Clumsy in performance, or manners; unhandy; not dextrous. [*Vulgar.*]

AWK'WARD, *a.* [*awk* and *ward.*] Wanting dexterity in the use of the hands or of instruments; unready; not dextrous; bungling; untoward. *Dryden.*

2. Inelegant; unpolite; ungraceful in manners; clumsy; unnatural; bad. *Shak.*

AWK'WARDLY, *adv.* Clumsily; in a rude or bungling manner; inelegantly; badly.

AWK'WARDNESS, *n.* Clumsiness; ungracefulness in manners; want of dexterity in the use of the hands or instruments; unsuitableness. *Addison.*

AWL, *n.* [Sax. *æl*, an *awl*, and an eel; Ger. *ahl*, an awl, and *aal*, an eel; D. *els*, an awl; *aal*, an eel; Dan. *aal*, an eel; Ir. *ail*, a sting or prickle.]

An iron instrument for piercing small holes in leather, for sewing and stitching; used by shoemakers, sadlers, &c. The blade is either straight, or a little bent and flattened.

AW'LESS, *a.* [*awe* and *less.*] Wanting reverence; void of respectful fear; as *awless* insolence. *Dryden.*

2. Wanting the power of causing reverence; not exciting awe; as an *awless* throne. *Shak.*

AWL'WORT, *n.* [*awl* and *wort.* See *Wort.*]

The popular name of the *Subularia aquatica*, or rough leaved alyssum; so called from its awl-shaped leaves, which grow in clusters round the root. It is a native of Britain and Ireland. *Encyc.*

AWM, AUM, } *n.* [D. *aam*; G. *ahm.*]

A Dutch liquid measure, containing eight steckans or twenty verges or verteels, equal to the English tierce, the sixth of a French tun, and the seventh of an English tun, or thirty-six gallons. *Encyc.* *Arbuthnot.*

AWN, *n.* [Sw. *agne*; Gr. αχνα, αχνη.]

The beard of corn or grass, as it is usually understood. But technically, a slender sharp process issuing from the chaff or glume in corn and grasses. *Martyn.*

AWN'ING, *n.* [Goth. *hulyan*, to cover.]

1. A cover of canvas, usually a sail or tarpauling, spread over a boat or ship's deck, to shelter from the sun's rays, the officers and crew, and preserve the decks.

2. That part of the poop deck which is continued forward beyond the bulk head of the cabin. *Mar. Dict.*

AWN'LESS, *a.* Without awn or beard.

AWN'Y, *a.* Having awns; full of beard.

AWO'KE. The preterit of *awake.*

AWŎRK', *adv.* [Sax. *geweorcan*, to work.]

At work; in a state of labor or action. [*Not used.*] *Shak.*

AWŎRK'ING, *adv.* At work; into a state of working or action. *Hubbard's Tale.*

AWRY', *a.* or *adv.* [Dan. *vrider*, to twist; *vrien*, twisted; Sw. *vrida*; Sax. *writhan*, to *writhe.*]

1. Turned or twisted towards one side; not in a straight or true direction, or position; asquint; with oblique vision; as, "to glance a look *awry*;" the lady's cap is *awry.*

2. In *a figurative sense*, turned aside from the line of truth, or right reason; perverse or perversely. *Sidney.* *Milton.*

AX, *n.* improperly written *axe.* [Sax. *æx, eax, æse*; Sw. *yxe*; L. *ascia*; Gr. *αξινη*; It. *azza*; Eth. ሐጸይ hatzi, an ax; or Ar. حز hazza, to cut; Ch. and Syr. חצינא an ax.]

An instrument usually of iron, for hewing timber and chopping wood. It consists of a head with an arching edge, and a helve or handle. The ax is of two kinds, the broad ax for hewing, and the narrow ax for rough-hewing and cutting. The hatchet is a small ax to be used with one hand.

AXAYA'CAT, *n.* A fly in Mexico, whose eggs, deposited on rushes and flags, in large quantities, are sold and used as a sort of caviare, called ahuauhtli. This was a dish among the Mexicans, as it now is among the Spaniards. *Clavigero.*

AXESTONE, } *n.* A mineral, a subspecies
AXSTONE, } of jade; less hard than nephrite; of a leek or grass green, olive green or greenish gray color. It occurs amorphous, or in rolled fragments. It is found chiefly in New-Zealand and the S. Sea isles, where it is used by the rude natives for axes and other instruments. *Ure. Cleaveland.*

AX'IFORM, *a.* [L. *axis*, and *forma.*] In the form of an axis. *Encyc.*

AX'IL, *n.* [L. *axilla*; Ir. *asgal*; Fr. *aisselle*; D. *oxel*, the armpit; Ch. and Heb. אצל, to separate or set apart; whence אצילי, armpits.]

1. The armpit; a cavity under the upper part of the arm or shoulder.

2. In *botany*, the space or angle formed by a branch with the stem, or by a leaf with the stem or branch. *Milne. Darwin.*

AX'ILLAR, } *a.* Pertaining to the arm-
AX'ILLARY, } pit, or to the axil of plants. *Axillary* leaves are those which proceed from the angle formed by the stem and branch. *Martyn. Milne.*

AX'INITE, *n.* A mineral which sometimes occurs in lamellar masses, but commonly in crystals, whose general form is that of a very oblique rhomb, or rather, four-sided prism, so flattened that some of its edges become thin and sharp, like that of an ax; whence its name, Gr. *αξινη*. This is the thumerstone of Kirwan. It has been sometimes called yanolite and violet shorl. *Haüy. Brongniart. Cleaveland.*

AXINOM'ANCY, *n.* [Gr. *αξινη*, an ax, and *μαντεια*, divination.]

Among *the ancients*, a species of divination, by means of an ax or hatchet, performed by laying an agate-stone on a red hot hatchet, or by fixing a hatchet on a round stake, so as to be poised; then the names of those suspected were repeated, and he at whose name the hatchet moved, was pronounced guilty. *Encyc.*

AX'IOM, *n.* [Gr. *αξιωμα*, authority, an authoritative sentence, or that which is assumed, from *αξιος*, worthy, *αξιοω*, to think worthy, to esteem; Eng. to *ask*, [to *ax*;] that which is asked, sought or esteemed.]

1. A self evident truth, or a proposition whose truth is so evident at first sight, that no process of reasoning or demonstration can make it plainer; as, "the whole is greater than a part." *Johnson. Encyc.*

2. An established principle in some art or science; a principle received without new proof; as, "things which are equal to the same thing, are equal to one another." *Encyc.*

AXIOMAT'IC, } *a.* Pertaining to an ax-
AXIOMAT'ICAL, } iom; having the nature of self evident truths or received principles. *Pref. to Bacon's Aphorisms.*

AX'IS, *n.* plu. *axes.* [L.; Gr. *αξων*; Russ. *os*, or *osi*; Sax. *æx*; Fr. *axe*, or *aissieu*; G. *achse*; D. *as*; It. *asse*; Sp. *exe*; Port. *exo*, *eixo.*]

1. The straight line, real or imaginary, passing through a body, on which it revolves, or may revolve; as the *axis* of the earth.

2. In *geometry*, a straight line in a plain figure, about which it revolves to produce a solid.

3. In *conic sections*, a right line dividing the section into two equal parts, and cutting all its ordinates at right angles.

4. In *mechanics*, the axis of a balance is that line about which it moves, or rather turns.

The *axis of oscillation* is a right line parallel to the horizon passing through the center, about which a pendulum vibrates.

The *axis in peritrochio* is a wheel concentric with the base of a cylinder, and movable with it about its axis.

5. In *optics*, a particular ray of light from any object which falls perpendicularly on the eye.

6. In *architecture*, spiral axis is the axis of a twisted column spirally drawn in order to trace the circumvolutions without.

Axis of the Ionic capital is a line passing perpendicularly through the middle of the eye of the volute.

The axis of a vessel is an imaginary line passing through the middle of it, perpendicular to its base, and equally distant from its sides.

In *botany*, axis is a taper column in the center of some flowers or catkins, about which the other parts are disposed.

In *anatomy*, axis is the name of the second verteber of the neck; it has a tooth which enters into the first verteber, and this tooth is by some called the axis. *Encyc.*

AX'LE, } *n.* [Sax. *æx* and *tree.* See
AX'LE-TREE, } *Axis.*]

A piece of timber or bar of iron, fitted for insertion in the hobs or naves of wheels, on which the wheels turn.

AX'OLOTE, *n.* A water lizard found in the Mexican lake, about eight inches in length, sometimes much larger. The skin is black and soft. It swims with its feet, which resemble those of a frog. It has a periodical evacuation of blood, like the human female. *Clavigero.*

AY, } *adv.* [G. D. Dan. Sw. *ja*, pron. *ya*;
AYE, } Dan. *eja*; Corn. *ia*; Ar. *ya*; Fr. *oui.* It may be a contracted word.]

Yes, yea, a word expressing assent, or an affirmative answer to a question. It is used also to enforce the sense of what is asserted, equivalent to *even so, truly, certainly.*

AYE, *adv.* [Sax. *aa, a*, or *awa*; Gr. *αει*; Amh. *ai*, continually; D. *eeuw*, an age; Goth. *aiw*, an age, eternity; L. *ævum*, which, without its termination, is *æv, æw*; probably a contracted word, W. *haug.*]

Always; forever; continually; for an indefinite time; used in poetry.

AYLE, *n.* In *law*, a grandfather. [See *Besayle.*]

A'YRY. [See *Aerie.*]

AZ'AROLE, *n.* [Fr.] A species of thorn; the three grained medlar, a species of cratægus.

AZ'ERIT, }
AZERI'TA, } *n.* A species of plum or pru-
AZERI'RA, } nus. *Fam. of Plants.*

AZ'IMUTH, *n.* [Ar. سمت samatha, to move or go towards; سَمْت, (L. *semita*,) a way or path; with a prefix.]

1. In *astronomy*, an arch of the horizon intercepted between the meridian of the place, and the azimuth or vertical circle, passing through the center of the object.

2. *Magnetical azimuth*, an arch of the horizon, intercepted between the azimuth or vertical circle, passing through the center of any heavenly body, and the magnetic meridian. This is found by observing the object with an azimuth compass.

3. *Azimuth compass*, an instrument for finding either the magnetic azimuth or amplitude of an heavenly object.

4. *Azimuth dial*, a dial whose stile or gnomon is at right angles to the plane of the horizon.

5. *Azimuths* or vertical circles, are great circles intersecting each other in the zenith and nadir, and cutting the horizon at right angles. *Encyc. Chambers. Bailey. Johnson.*

On charts, these azimuths are represented by rhumbs, and on the globe, by the quadrant of altitude, when screwed in the zenith.

AZ'OTE, *n.* [Gr. *α* priv. and *ζωη*, life, or *ζωτικος*, vital.]

A species of gas, called also mephitic air, and atmospheric mephitis, on account of its fatal effects upon animal life. It is tasteless, and inodorous: it exists in common air, mixed with oxygen, and constitutes about seventy-nine hundredth parts of atmospheric air. It may be obtained, in large quantities, from the muscular fibers of animals. Combined with hydrogen, it forms volatile alkali; and it enters into the composition of most animal substances. It is the radical of nitric acid, and is now called nitrogen gas, or nitrogen.

AZ'OTH, *n.* Among alchimists, the first principle of metals; the mercury of metals; a universal medicine. *Obs.* *Ash.*

2. The liquor of sublimated quicksilver; brass. *Coxe.*

AZOT'IC, *a.* Pertaining to azote; fatal to animal life.

AZ'OTITE, *n.* A salt formed by a combination of the protoxyd of azote, or nitrous oxyd, with an alkali. *Thomson.*

AZ'URE, *a. azh'ur.* [Persic, *lazurd*, blue; Fr. *azur*; Sp. *azul*, or *azur*; It. *azzurro*; W. *asur*, blue. Hence *lazuli*, in Lapis Lazuli.]

Of a sky-blue; resembling the clear blue color of the sky.

AZ'URE, *n. azh'ur.* The fine blue color of

the sky. This word was formerly applied to the *lapis lazuli*, and the color prepared from it. But it is now applied to the blue extracted from cobalt, though somewhat a different color; the blue of the lapis is called ultramarine. Azure is applied also to the blue glass made of the oxyd of cobalt and vitrifiable substances, reduced to fine powder. In large masses it is called *smalt*. *Encyc.*

2. The sky, or azure vault of heaven.

3. In *heraldry*, a blue color in coats of all persons under the degree of baron. *Jones.*

AZ'URE, *v. t.* To color blue.

AZ'URED, *a. azh'ured.* Colored azure; being of an azure color. *Sidney.*

AZ'URE-STONE, } *n.* Another name of the
AZ'URITE, } lazulite.

AZ'URN, *a.* Of a blue color. [*Little used.*] *Milton.*

AZ'YME, *n.* [See *Azymous.*] Unleavened bread. [*Not in use.*]

AZ'YMITE, *n.* [See *Azymous.*] In *church history*, azymites are christians who administer the eucharist with unleavened bread. *Encyc.*

AZ'YMOUS, *a.* [Gr. α priv. and ζυμη, leaven.]

Unleavened; unfermented; as sea-biscuit. *Encyc. Ash.*

B.

B is the second letter, and the first articulation, or consonant, in the English, as in the Hebrew, Greek, Latin, and most other alphabets. In the Ethiopic, it is the ninth letter, and its shape is that of a hut. Perhaps from this or other like figure, it received its Hebrew name, *beth*, a house. It is a *mute* and a *labial*, being formed by pressing the whole length of the lips together, as in pronouncing *eb*. It is less perfectly mute than *p*, as may be perceived by pronouncing the syllables *ab* and *ap*. It is convertible, 1st, with *p*, as in the Celtic, *ben* or *pen*, a mountain; in the English, *beak* and *peak*, *beck* and *peck*; 2d, with *v*, as in the German, *silber* for *silver*; and in Spanish, *b* and *v* are used indifferently; 3d, with *f*, as in *bore* and *perforo*; Eng. *bear*, L. *fero*; in the Celtic *bun*, *bunadh*, *bunait*, stock, origin, foundation; English, *found*; L. *fundamentum*; with the Gr. φ, as *Bilip*, for φιλιππος; 4th, with *v* and *w*; as, Ir. *fior*, L. *verus*; *fear*, *vir*; Ir. *buaic*, the *wick* of a candle.

The Greek B is always pronounced like the English V, and the Russian B corresponds with the Greek.

In composition, the letter B is changed into *p* before the letter *p*; as in *opprimo*, from *ob* and *premo*; *oppono*, from *ob* and *pono*; into *f*, before *f*, as in *offero*, from *ob* and *fero*; into *c* before *c*, as in *occido*, from *ob* and *cado*, and *cædo*.

As a numeral, B was used by the Hebrews and Greeks, as now by the Arabians, for 2; by the Romans for 300, and with a dash over it thus B̄, for 3000. B is used also as an abbreviation; thus B. A. stand for bachelor of arts; B. L. for bachelor of laws; B. D. for bachelor of divinity; B. F. before the decrees of the old Romans, for *bonum factum*. In music, B stands for the tone above A; B♭, for B flat, or the semitone major above A. B also stands for base, and B. C. for *basso continuo*, or thorough base.

B'AA, *n.* The cry or appropriate bleating of sheep.

B'AA, *v. i.* To cry or bleat as sheep.

BA'AL, *n.* [Oriental, בעל, lord.]

An idol among the ancient Chaldeans and Syrians, representing the sun. The word signifies also lord, or commander; and the character of the idol was varied by different nations, at different times. Thus Baal Berith is supposed to signify the Lord of the Covenant; Baal Peor, or rather Baal Phegor, the Lord of the dead. Ps. cvi. Baal Zebub, the god of flies, &c.

BAB'BLE, *v. i.* [D. *babbelen*; Fr. *babiller*; properly to throw out.]

1. To utter words imperfectly or indistinctly, as children. *Prior.*

2. To talk idly or irrationally; to talk thoughtlessly. *Arbuthnot.*

3. To talk much; to prate; hence to tell secrets. *Shak.*

4. To utter sounds frequently, incessantly, or indistinctly; as, a *babbling* echo; a *babbling* stream.

BAB'BLE, *v. t.* To prate; to utter.

BAB'BLE, *n.* Idle talk; senseless prattle. *Shak.*

BAB'BLEMENT, *n.* Idle talk; senseless prate; unmeaning words. *Milton.*

BAB'BLER, *n.* An idle talker; an irrational prattler; a teller of secrets.

BAB'BLING, *ppr.* Talking idly; telling secrets.

2. Uttering a succession of murmuring sounds; as a *babbling* stream.

3. In hunting, *babbling* is when the hounds are too busy after they have found a good scent.

BAB'BLING, *n.* Foolish talk. 1 Tim. vi.

BABE, *n.* [Ger. *bube*, a boy; Ir. *baban*; D. *babyn*; Syr. *babia*; Phenician, *babion*; Ar. *babah*, a babe, an infant. Ar. بابوس babos or baboson, the young of man or beast; Syr. *babosa*, a little child. It is remarkable that this Syriac and Arabic word for an infant, is retained by the natives of America, who call an infant *pappoos*. L. *pupus*, a word of endearment; *pupa*, little girl; whence *pupillus*, *pupilla*, *pupil*. Ar. *bobohon*, the beginning of youth; Gr. βαβαι, and παπαι; Ar. بابا, baba, to say *baba*, that is, father; *papa*, a word taken from the first attempts of children to pronounce the name of a parent.]

An infant; a young child of either sex.

BA'BEL, *n.* [Heb.] Confusion; disorder. *Beaumont.*

BA'BERY, *n.* Finery to please a child; any trifling toy for children. *Sidney.*

BA'BISH, *a.* Like a babe; childish. *Ascham.*

BA'BISHLY, *adv.* Childishly.

BABOON', *n.* [Fr. *babouin*, so called from its resemblance to a babe. This name seems to have originated in the oriental *babion*, *papio*. See *Babe.*]

A monkey of the largest species; a quadruped belonging to the genus *Simia*, in the class *Mammalia*, and order *Primates*, according to the system of Linne; but by Pennant arranged under the digitated quadrupeds. Baboons have short tails; a long face; a broad high muzzle; dog-like tusks, or canine teeth; and naked callosities on the buttocks. They are found only on the eastern continent. *Encyc.*

BA'BY, *a.* Like a young child; pertaining to an infant.

BA'BY, *n.* [See *Babe.*] An infant or young child of either sex; a babe; [*used in familiar language.*]

2. A small image in form of an infant, for girls to play with; a doll.

BA'BY, *v. t.* To treat like a young child. *Young.*

BA'BYHOOD, *n.* The state of being a baby. *Ash.*

BA'BY-HOUSE, *n.* A place for children's dolls and babies. *Swift.*

BABYLO'NIAN, } *a.* Pertaining to Baby-
BABYLO'NISH, } lon, the capital of the ancient kingdom of *Babylonia*, or to the kingdom. The city stood on the river *Frat*, or Euphrates, and it is supposed, on the spot where the tower of Babel was founded.

2. Like the language of Babel; mixed; confused.

BABYLO'NIAN, *n.* An inhabitant of Babylonia. In ancient writers, an astrologer, as the Chaldeans were remarkable for the study of astrology.

BABYLON'IC, } *a.* Pertaining to Baby-
BABYLON'ICAL, } lon, or made there; as *Babylonic* garments, carpets or hangings. *Encyc.*

2. Tumultuous; disorderly. *Harrington.*

BABYLON'ICS, *n. plu.* The title of a fragment of the history of the world, ending 267 years before Christ, composed by Berosus, a priest of Babylon. *Encyc.*

BABYROÜS'SA, *n.* In *zoology*, the Indian hog, a native of Celebes, and of Buero, but not found on the continent of Asia or of Africa. This quadruped belongs to the genus *Sus*, in the class *Mammalia*, and order *Bellua*. From the outside of the upper jaw, spring two teeth twelve inches long, bending like horns, and almost touching the forehead. Along the back are some weak bristles, and on the rest of the body only a sort of wool. These animals live in herds, feed on herbage, are sometimes tamed, and their flesh is well tasted. When pursued hard, they rush into the sea, swim or dive and pass from isle to isle. In the forest, they rest their heads by hooking their upper tusks on a bough. *Encyc.*

BAC or **BACK**, *n.* [D. *bak*, a bowl or cistern.]

1. In *navigation*, a ferry-boat or praam.
2. In *brewing*, a large flat tub, or vessel, in which wort is cooled before boiling; hence called a *cooler*.
3. In *distilleries*, a vessel into which the liquor to be fermented is pumped, from the cooler, in order to be worked with the yeast.

BAC'CA, *n.* [L.] In *botany*, a berry; a fruit which consists of a pulpy pericarp, without valves, inclosing several naked seeds. *Milne.*

BACCALAU'REATE, *n.* [The first part of this word is from the same root as bachelor; or as Bailey supposes, from *bacca*, berry; and the latter part, from *laurea*, a laurel, from the practice of wearing a garland of bay berries.]

The degree of bachelor of arts.

BAC'CATED, *a.* [L. *baccatus*, garnished with pearls, from *bacca*, a berry.]

Set or adorned with pearls; having many berries. [*Little used.*]

BAC'CHANAL, **BACCHANA'LIAN**, *n.* [from *Bacchus*, Gr. βακχος, the deity of wine and revelling. Qu. Ir. *back*, drunk; or D. *bak*, bowl, L. *poculum*; Gyp. *bechari*, a cup; or from raging, revelling.]

One who indulges in drunken revels; a drunkard; one who is noisy and riotous, when intoxicated.

BAC'CHANAL, **BACCHANA'LIAN**, *a.* Revelling in intemperate drinking; riotous; noisy.

BACCHANA'LIAN, *a.* Pertaining to revelling and drunkenness.

Even *bacchanalian* madness has its charms. *Cowper.*

BAC'CHANALS, *n. plu.* Drunken feasts; the revels of bacchanalians. In *antiquity*, feasts in honor of Bacchus, the god of wine. These were celebrated in spring and autumn, with games and shows. *Encyc.*

BAC'CHIC, *a.* Jovial; drunken; mad with intoxication.

2. Relating to Bacchus, the god of wine; as, a *bacchic* feast or song; *bacchic* mysteries. *Faber. Encyc.*

BAC'CHIUS, *n.* In *ancient poetry*, a foot composed of a short syllable and two long ones; as in ăvārī. *Encyc.*

BACCIF'EROUS, *a.* [L. *baccifer*, of *bacca*, a berry, and *fero*, to bear.]

That produces berries. [See *Bacca*.] Bacciferous plants formerly included all such plants as have a pulpy fruit, whether of the apple, berry or cherry kind; but the modern systems of botany comprehend under this description such plants only as bear the pulpy pericarp, called *bacca*, or berry. *Milne.*

BACCIV'OROUS, *a.* [L. *bacca*, berry, and *voro*, to eat.]

Eating or subsisting on berries; as *baccivorous* birds.

BACH'ELOR, *n.* [Fr. *bachelier*; Sp. *bachiller*, a bachelor of arts and a babbler; Port. *bacharel*, id. and *bacello*, a shoot or twig of the vine; It. *baccelliere*, a bachelor of arts; *bacchio*, a staff; *bacchetta*, a rod; L. *baculus*, a stick, that is, a shoot; Fr. *bachelette*, a damsel or young woman; Scot. *baich*, a child; W. *bacgen*, a boy, a child; *bacgenes*, a young girl; from *bac*, small. This word has its origin in the name of a child or young person of either sex, whence the sense of *babbling* in the Spanish. Or both senses are rather from shooting, protruding.]

1. A young man who has not been married.
2. A man of any age, who has not been married; often with the word *old*.
3. A person who has taken the first degree in the liberal arts and sciences, at a college or university. This degree or honor is called the *baccalaureate*. This title is given also to such as take the first degree in divinity, law or physic, in certain European universities.
4. A knight of the lowest order, or more correctly, a young knight, styled, a *knight bachelor*. The Germans anciently constituted their young men knights or soldiers, by presenting to them a shield and a lance, in a great council. This ceremony answered to that of the *toga virilis* of the Romans. In the livery companies of London, those persons not yet admitted to the livery are called *bachelors*.

BACH'ELORSHIP, *n.* The state of being a bachelor.

2. The state of one who has taken his first degree in a college or university.

BACK, *n.* [Sax. *bac*, *bæc*; Dan. *bag*; Sw. *bak*; and Sw. *backe*, *bakke*, a hill, a clod or lump. The sense probably is a *ridge*, like the Ger. *rücken*, D. *rug*, applied to the shoulders or to the back of a beast.]

1. The upper part of an animal, particularly of a quadruped, whose back is a ridge. In human beings, the hinder part of the body.
2. The outward or convex part of the hand, opposed to the inner, concave part, or palm.
3. As the back of man is the part on the side opposite to the face; hence the part opposed to the front; as the *back* of a book and of a chimney, or the *back* of a house.
4. The part opposite to or most remote from that which fronts the speaker or actor, or the part out of sight; as the *back* of an isle, of a wood, of a village.
5. As the back is the strongest part of an animal, and as the back is behind in motion; hence the thick and strong part of a cutting tool; as the *back* of a knife, or of a saw.
6. The place behind or nearest the back; as, on the *back* of a hill or of a village.
7. The outer part of the body, or the whole body; a part for the whole; as, he has not clothes to his *back*.
8. *To turn the back on one*, is to forsake, or neglect him. *South.*
9. *To turn the back to one*, to acknowledge to be superior.
10. *To turn the back*, is to depart, or to leave the care or cognizance of; to remove or be absent. *Davies.*
11. *Behind the back*, is in secret, or when one is absent.
12. *To cast behind the back*, in scripture, is to forget and forgive, Is. xxxviii. 17; or to treat with contempt. Ez. xxiii. 35. Neh. ix. 26.
13. *To plow the back*, is to oppress and persecute. Ps. cxxix.
14. *To bow the back*, is to submit to oppression. Rom. xi. 10.

BACK, *adv.* To the place from which one came; as, to go *back* is to return.

2. In *a figurative sense*, to a former state, condition or station; as, he cannot go *back* from his engagements.
3. Behind; not advancing; not coming or bringing forward; as, to keep *back* a part; to keep one's self *back*.
4. Towards times or things past; as, to look *back* on former ages.
5. Again; in return; as, give *back* the money.
6. *To go* or *come back*, is to return, either to a former place, or state.
7. *To go* or *give back*, is to retreat, to recede.

BACK, *v. t.* To mount; to get upon the back; sometimes perhaps to place upon the back; as, to *back* a horse. *Shak.*

2. To support; to maintain; to second or strengthen by aid; as, the Court was *backed* by the House of Commons. *Dryden.*
3. To put backward; to cause to retreat or recede; as, to *back* oxen.
4. *To back a warrant*, is for a justice of the peace in the county where the warrant is to be executed, to sign or indorse a warrant, issued in another county, to apprehend an offender. *Blackstone.*
5. In seamanship, *to back an anchor* is to lay down a small anchor ahead of a large one, the cable of the small one being fastened to the crown of the large one, to prevent its coming home.
6. *To back astern*, in rowing, is to manage the oars in a direction contrary to the usual method, to move a boat stern foremost.
7. *To back the sails*, is to arrange them so as to cause the ship to move astern. *Mar. Dict.*

BACK, *v. i.* To move or go back; as, the horse refuses to *back*. *Encyc.*

BACK'BITE, *v. t.* [*back* and *bite.*] To censure, slander, reproach, or speak evil of the absent. Prov. xxv.

BACK'BITER, *n.* One who slanders, calumniates or speaks ill of the absent.

BACK'BITING, *n.* The act of slandering the absent; secret calumny. 2 Cor. xii.

BACKBI'TINGLY, *adv.* With secret slander. *Barret.*

BACK'BOARD, *n.* [*back* and *board.*] A board placed across the after part of a boat.

BACKBO'NE, *n.* [*back* and *bone.*] The bone of the back; or the spine.

BACK'CARRY, *n.* A having on the back; *a term of law.*

BACKDOOR, *n.* [*back* and *door.*] A door on the back part of a building; a private passage; an indirect way.

BACK'ED, *pp.* Mounted; having on the back; supported by aid; seconded; moved backward.

BACK'ED, *a.* Having a back; a word used in composition; as *broad-backed*, *hump-backed.*

BACK'FRIEND, *n.* [*back* and *friend.* A secret enemy. *South.*

BACKGAM'MON, *n.* [W. *bac*, small, and *cammaun*, conflict, battle; *camp*, a game.]
A game played by two persons, upon a table, with box and dice. The table is in two parts, on which are 24 black and white spaces, called points. Each player has 15 men of different colors for the purpose of distinction. *Encyc.*

BACK'GROUND, *n.* [*back* and *ground.*] Ground in the rear or behind, as opposed to the front.
2. A place of obscurity, or shade; a situation little seen, or noticed.

BACK'HANDED, *a.* [*back* and *hand.*] With the hand turned backward; as a *backhanded* blow.

BACK'HANDED, *adv.* With the hand directed backward; as, to strike *backhanded.*

BACK'HOUSE, *n.* [*back* and *house.*] A building behind the main or front building.

BACK'ING, *ppr.* Mounting; moving back, as a horse; seconding.

BACK'PAINTING, *n.* [*back* and *paint.*] The method of painting mezzotinto prints, pasted on glass of a size to fit the print. *Encyc.*

BACK'PIECE, *n.* [*back* and *piece.*] The piece of armor which covers the back.

BACK'RETURN, *n.* Repeated return. *Shak.*

BACK'ROOM, *n.* [*back* and *room.*] A room behind the front room, or in the back part of the house.

BACKS, *n.* Among dealers in leather, the thickest and best tanned hides. *Encyc.*

BACK'SET, *a.* [*back* and *set.*] Set upon in the rear. *Anderson.*

BACK'SIDE, *n.* [*back* and *side.*] The back part of any thing; the part behind that which is presented to the face of a spectator. Ex. iii.
2. The hind part of an animal.
3. The yard, ground or place behind a house.

BACKSLI'DE, *v. i.* [*back* and *slide.*] To fall off; to apostatize; to turn gradually from the faith and practice of christianity. Jer. iii. Hos. iv.

BACKSLI'DER, *n.* An apostate; one who falls from the faith and practice of religion. Prov. xiv.
2. One who neglects his vows of obedience and falls into sin.

BACKSLI'DING, *n.* The act of apostatizing from faith or practice; a falling insensibly from religion into sin or idolatry. Jer. v. 6.

BACK'STAFF, *n.* [*back* and *staff*, so called from its being used with the observer's back toward the sun.]
A quadrant; an instrument for taking the sun's altitude at sea; called also, from its inventor, Davis's quadrant. *Encyc.*

BACK'STAIRS, *n.* [*back* and *stairs.*]
Stairs in the back part of a house; private stairs; and *figuratively*, a private or indirect way.

BACK'STAYS, *n.* [*back* and *stay.*]
Long ropes or stays extending from the topmast heads to both sides of a ship, to assist the shrouds in supporting the mast, when strained by a weight of sail, and prevent it from giving way and falling overboard. *Mar. Dict.*

BACK'SWORD, *n.* [*back* and *sword.*]
A sword with one sharp edge. In Engtand, a stick wth a basket handle used in rustic amusements. *Arbuthnot.*

BACK'WARD, } *adv.* [*back* and *ward.* See
BACK'WARDS, } *Ward.*] With the back in advance; as, to move *backward.*
2. Toward the back; as, to throw the arms *backward;* to move *backwards* and forwards.
3. On the back, or with the back downwards; as, to fall *backward.*
4. Toward past times or events; as to look *backward* on the history of man.
5. By way of reflection; reflexively. *Davies.*
6. From a better to a worse state; as, public affairs go *backward.*
7. In time past; as, let us look some ages *backward.*
8. Perversely; from a wrong end.

> I never yet saw man but she would spell him *backward.* *Shak.*

9. Towards the beginning; in an order contrary to the natural order; as, to read *backward.*
10. In a scriptural sense, *to go or turn backward*, is to rebel, apostatize, or relapse into sin, or idolatry. Is. i.
11. Contrarily; in a contrary manner. *Swift.*

To be driven or *turned backward*, is to be defeated, or disappointed. Ps. xl.

To turn judgment backward, is to pervert justice and laws. Is. lix.

BACK'WARD, *a.* Unwilling; averse; reluctant; hesitating.

> For wiser brutes are *backward* to be slaves. *Pope.*

2. Slow; sluggish; dilatory.

> The mind is *backward* to undergo the fatigue of weighing every argument. *Watts.*

3. Dull; not quick of apprehension; behind in progress; as a *backward* learner.
4. Late; behind in time; coming after something else, or after the usual time; as *backward* fruits; the season is *backward.*

BACK'WARD *n.* The things or state behind or past.

> In the dark *backward* or abysm of time. *Shak.*

[*Not proper, nor in use.*]

BACK'WARDLY, *adv.* Unwillingly; reluctantly; aversely; perversely.

BACK'WARDNESS, *n.* Unwillingness; reluctance; dilatoriness, or dullness in action.
2. A state of being behind in progress; slowness; tardiness; as the *backwardness* of the spring.

BACK'WŎRM, *n.* [*back* and *worm.*] A small worm, in a thin skin, in the reins of a hawk. [See *Filanders.*] *Encyc.*

BA'€ON, *n.* *ba'kn.* [W. *baccun;* Ir. *bogun.* In old charters, *boca. Cowel.* In Ger. *bache*, is a wild sow.]
Hog's flesh, salted or pickled and dried, usually in smoke.

To save one's bacon, is to preserve one's self from harm.

BA€'ULE, *n.* [Fr. *bascule.*]
In *fortification*, a kind of portcullis or gate, made like a pit-fall, with a counterpoise, and supported by two great stakes. *Encyc.*

BA€'ULITE, *n.* [L. *baculus.*]
A genus of fossil shells, of a straight form, in their cellular structure resembling the ammonites. *Edin. Encyc.*

BA€ULOM'ETRY, *n.* [L. *baculus*, a staff, and Gr. *μετρον*, measure.]
The act of measuring distance or altitude by a staff or staves. *Bailey. Johnson.*

BAD, *a.* [Pers. بَدْ bad, evil, depraved; allied perhaps to Ar. بَادَ; Heb. Ch. Syr. Sam. אבד to perish or destroy.]
1. Ill; evil; opposed to good; a word of general use, denoting physical defects and moral faults, in men and things; as a *bad* man, a *bad* heart, a *bad* design, *bad* air, *bad* water, *bad* books.
2. Vicious; corrupt; depraved, in a moral sense; as a *bad* life; a *bad* action.
3. Unwholesome; as *bad* provisions.
4. Unfortunate; unprosperous; as a *bad* state of affairs.
5. Unskilful; as a *bad* player.
6. Small; poor; as a *bad* crop.
7. Infirm; as a *bad* state of health.
8. Feeble, corrupt, or oppressive; as a *bad* government.
9. Hurtful; pernicious; as, fine print is *bad* for the eyes.
10. Unfavorable; as a *bad* season.
11. Poor; steril; as a *bad* soil.
12. Rough or muddy; as a *bad* road.

In short, *bad* expresses whatever is injurious, hurtful, inconvenient, unlawful or immoral; whatever is offensive, painful or unfavorable; or what is defective.

BAD, BADE, the past tense of *bid.* [See *Bid.*]

BADĠE, *n.* [I know not the affinities of this word, not having found it in any other language. Probably it belongs to class Bg.]
1. A mark, sign, token or thing, by which a person is distinguished, in a particular place or employment, and designating his relation to a person or to a particular occupation; as the *badge* of authority.
2. The mark or token of any thing; as the *badge* of bitterness. *Shak.*
3. An ornament on ships, near the stern, decorated with figures.

BADĠE, *v. t.* To mark, or distinguish with a badge. *Shak.*

BADĠ'ER, *n.* [Qu. *badge*, supra; or Sax. *bygan, bycgan*, to buy; Norm. *bugge.*]
In *law*, a person who is licensed to buy corn in one place and sell it in another, without incurring the penalties of engrossing. *Cowel.*

BADĠ'ER, *n.* A quadruped of the genus *Ursus*, of a clumsy make, with short, thick legs, and long claws on the fore feet. It inhabits the north of Europe and Asia, burrows, is indolent and sleepy, feeds by night on vegetables, and is very fat. Its skin is used for pistol furniture; its flesh makes good bacon, and its hair is used for brushes to soften the shades in painting. *Encyc.*

The American badger is called the ground hog, and is sometimes white. *Pennant.*

BADG'ER-LEGGED, *a.* Having legs like a badger. Johnson says having legs of unequal length; but, qu. short thick legs. *Shak.*

BADIA'GA, *n.* A small spunge, common in the North of Europe, the powder of which is used to take away the livid marks of bruises. *Encyc.*

BAD'IANE, } *n.* The seed of a tree in China, which smells like anise seeds; used by the Chinese and Dutch to give their tea an aromatic taste. *Encyc.*
BAN'DIAN, }

BADIGE'ON, *n.* A mixture of plaster and free stone, ground together and sifted, used by statuaries to fill the small holes and repair the defects of the stones, of which they make their statues. *Encyc.*

BAD'INAGE, *n.* [Fr.] Light or playful discourse. *Chesterfield.*

BAD'LY, *adv.* [from *bad.*]
In a bad manner; not well; unskilfully; grievously; unfortunately; imperfectly.

BAD'NESS, *n.* The state of being bad, evil, vicious or depraved; want of good qualities, natural or moral; as the *badness* of the heart, of the season, of the roads, &c.

BAF'FETAS, }
BAF'TAS, } *n.* An India cloth or plain muslin. That of Surat is said to be the best. *Encyc.*
BAS'TAS, }

BAF'FLE, *v. t.* [Fr. *befler*, to make, or play the fool with; Sp. *befar*; It. *beffare*, id. It coincides in origin with *buffoon*. In Scottish, *beff*, *baff*, signifies to *strike*.]
To mock or elude by artifice; to elude by shifts and turns; hence to defeat, or confound; as, to *baffle* the designs of an enemy.

Fashionable follies *baffle* argument. *Anon.*

BAF'FLE, *v. i.* To practice deceit. *Barrow.*

BAF'FLE, *n.* A defeat by artifice, shifts and turns. *South.*

BAF'FLED, *pp.* Eluded; defeated; confounded.

BAF'FLER, *n.* One that baffles.

BAF'FLING, *ppr.* Eluding by shifts and turns, or by stratagem; defeating; confounding. A *baffling* wind, among seamen, is one that frequently shifts, from one point to another.

BAG, *n.* [Norm. *bage*, a bag, a coffer; *bagnes*, baggage. This word seems to be from the root of *pack*, *pouch*, Fr. *poche*, or of the same family; or it is from the sense of tying, binding; Sp. *baga*, a rope or cord for fastening loads on beasts of burden. Hence *baggage*; It. *bagaglia*; Sp. *bagage*; Port. *bagagem*; Fr. *bagage*; Arm. *pacq*, a *pack*, and *bagaich.*]
1. A sack; a pouch, usually of cloth or leather, used to hold, preserve or convey corn, and other commodities.
2. A sack in animal bodies containing some fluid or other substance.
3. Formerly, a sort of silken purse tied to the hair.
4. In *commerce*, a certain quantity of a commodity, such as it is customary to carry to market in a sack; as a *bag* of pepper or hops; a *bag* of corn.
5. Among *farriers*, a bag of asafœtida and savin is tied to the bits of horses to restore their appetites. *Encyc.*

BAG, *v. t.* To put into a bag.
2. To load with bags.

BAG, *v. i.* To swell like a full bag, as sails when filled with wind.

BAGATELLE, *n. bagatel'.* [Fr.; Sp. *bagatela*; It. *bagatella*; Arm. *bagauh.*]
A trifle; a thing of no importance.

BAG'GAGE, *n.* [Fr. *bagage.* Qu. Eng. *package*; D. *pakkaadje*, baggage, that which is *packed.* See *Bag.*]
1. The tents, clothing, utensils, and other necessaries of an army.
2. The clothing and other conveniencies which a traveller carries with him, on a journey.

Having dispatched my *baggage* by water to Altdorf. *Coxe, Switz.*

[The English now call this *luggage.*]

BAG'GAGE, *n.* [Fr. *bagasse*; It. *bagascia*; Sp. *bagazo*, a catamite; Pers. *baga*, a strumpet.]
A low worthless woman; a strumpet.

BAG'GING, *ppr.* Swelling; becoming protuberant.

BAG'GING, *n.* The cloth or materials for bags. *U. States. Edwards' W. Indies.*

BAGNIO, *n. ban'yo.* [It. *bagno*; Sp. *baño*; Port. *banho*; Fr. *bain*; L. *balneum.*]
1. A bath; a house for bathing, cupping, sweating and otherwise cleansing the body. In Turkey, it is the name of prisons where slaves are kept; so called from the baths which they contain. *Encyc.*
2. A brothel.

BAG'PIPE, *n.* [*bag* and *pipe.*]
A musical wind instrument, used chiefly in Scotland and Ireland. It consists of a leathern bag, which receives the air by a tube, which is stopped by a valve; and pipes, into which the air is pressed by the performer. The base-pipe is called the *drone*, and the tenor or treble is called the *chanter.* The pipes have eight holes like those of a flute, which the performer stops and opens at pleasure. There are several species of bag-pipes, as the soft and melodious Irish bag-pipe, with two short drones and a long one; the Highland bag-pipe, with two short drones, the music of which is very loud; the Scot's Lowland bag-pipe, which is played with a bellows and is also a loud instrument. There is also a small pipe, with a chanter about eight inches in length. *Encyc.*
In seamanship, *to bag-pipe the mizen*, is to lay it aback by bringing the sheet to the mizen shrouds. *Mar. Dict.*

BAG'PIPER, *n.* One who plays on a bag-pipe.

BAG'RE, *n.* A small bearded fish, a species of Silurus, anguilliform, of a silvery hue, without scales, and delicious food. *Dict. of Nat. Hist.*

BAG'REEF, *n.* [*bag* and *reef.*]
A fourth and lower reef used in the British navy. *Mar. Dict.*

BAGUET', *n.* [Fr. *baguette*, from *bague*, a ring; Ir. *beacht*; Sax. *beag.*]
In *architecture*, a little round molding, less than an astragal, sometimes carved and enriched. *Encyc.*

BAHAR', } *n.* Weights used in the E. Indies. The great bahar, for weighing pepper, cloves, nutmegs, &c., is 524lb. 9oz. avoirdupoise. The little bahar, for weighing quicksilver, vermilion, ivory, silk, &c., is 437 lbs. 9oz. *Encyc.*
BAR'RE, }

BAIGNE, *v. t.* [Fr. *baigner.*]
To soak or drench. [*Not used.*] *Carew.*

BA'IKALITE, *n.* [From Baikal, a lake in Northern Asia.]
A mineral occurring in acicular prisms, sometimes long, and either confusedly grouped or radiating from a center. Its color is greenish, or yellowish white. It is regarded as a variety of Tremolite. This name is given also to an olive-green variety of augite and also of epidote. *Cleaveland*

BAIL, *v. t.* [Fr. and Norm. *bailler*, to deliver, to lease; Arm. *bahailhat*; Ar. بَهَلَ bahala; Eth. በለሐ baleah, to deliver, free, liberate, permit to go.]
1. To set free, deliver, or liberate from arrest and imprisonment, upon security given that the person bailed shall appear and answer in court. The word is applied to the magistrate, or the surety. The magistrate *bails* a man, when he liberates him from arrest or imprisonment, upon bond given with sureties. The surety *bails* a person, when he procures his release from arrest, by giving bond for his appearance. *Blackstone.*
2. To deliver goods in trust, upon a contract, expressed or implied, that the trust shall be faithfully executed on the part of the bailee or person entrusted; as, to *bail* cloth to a tailor to be made into a garment, or to *bail* goods to a carrier. *Blackstone.*
3. To free from water, as to *bail* a boat. This word is improperly written *bale.* The word is probably the same as *bail* in law, to *free*, or *liberate*, and signifies to throw out water, as with a bucket or shovel.

BAIL, *n.* The person or persons who procure the release of a prisoner from custody, by becoming surety for his appearance in court.

The *bail* must be real substantial bondsmen. *Blackstone.*

B and B were *bail* to the arrest in a suit at law. *Kent.*

Bail is not used with a plural termination.
2. The security given for the release of a prisoner from custody; as, the man is out upon *bail.*

Excessive *bail* ought not to be required. *Blackstone.*

Bail is *common* or *special.* *Common* bail are imaginary persons, who are pledges for the plaintiff's prosecution; as John Doe and Richard Roe.
Special bail must be men of real substance, sufficient to pay their bond or recognizance. To *perfect* or *justify* bail is to prove by the oath of the person that he is worth the sum for which he is surety beyond his debts. To *admit* to bail, is to release upon security given by bondsmen.
3. The handle of a kettle or other vessel.
4. In *England*, a certain limit within a forest.

BA'ILABLE, *a.* That may be set free upon bond with sureties; that may be admitted to bail; *used of persons.*
2. That admits of bail; as a *bailable* offense. *Blackstone.*

BA'ILBOND, *n.* A bond or obligation given

by a prisoner and his surety, to insure the prisoner's appearance in court, at the return of the writ.

BA'ILED, *pp.* Released from custody on bonds for appearance in court.

2. Delivered in trust, to be carried and deposited, redelivered, or otherwise accounted for.

3. Freed from water, as a boat.

BAILEE', *n.* The person to whom goods are committed in trust, and who has a temporary possession and a qualified property in them, for the purposes of the trust. *Blackstone.*

BA'ILER, } *n.* One who delivers goods to
BA'ILOR, } another in trust, for some particular purpose.

BA'ILIFF, *n.* [Fr. *baillif*; Arm. *belly*; Scot. *bailli*; It. *bailo*, a magistrate; *balia*, power, authority. Ch. Ar. Heb. Syr. בעל, lord, chief. Class, Bl.]

In *England*, an officer appointed by the sheriff. Bailiffs are either special, and appointed, for their adroitness, to arrest persons; or bailiffs of hundreds, who collect fines, summon juries, attend the assizes, and execute writs and process. The sheriff in England is the king's bailiff.

There are also *bailiffs* of liberties, appointed by the lords in their respective jurisdictions, to execute process, and perform other duties; *bailiffs* of forests and of manors, who direct the husbandry, collect rents, &c.; and *water bailiffs* in each port, to search vessels, gather toll for anchorage, arrest persons for debt on the water, &c. *Blackstone. Encyc.*

The office of bailiff formerly was high and honorable in England, and officers under that title on the continent are still invested with important functions.

BA'ILIWICK, *n.* [*bailli*, an officer, see *bailiff*, and Sax. *wic.*]

The precincts in which a bailiff has jurisdiction; the limits of a bailiff's authority; as a hundred, a liberty, a forest, over which a bailiff is appointed. In the liberties and franchises of lords, the bailiff has exclusive jurisdiction. *Encyc.*

BA'ILMENT, *n.* [from *bail.*]

A delivery of goods, in trust, upon a contract, expressed or implied, that the trust shall be faithfully executed. *Blackstone.*

BA'ILPIECE, *n.* A slip of parchment or paper containing a recognizance of bail *above* or bail to *the action. Blackstone.*

BAIRN, } *n.* [Sax. *bearn*; Scot. *bairn*; prob-
BARN, } ably, Eng. *born.*] A child. [*Little used in English.*]

BAIT, *n.* [W. *abwyd*, *bwyd*; Arm. *boet*; Ir. *abadh*; Sw. *bete*, food; *beta*, to feed; Sax. *batan*, to bait; Russ. *pitayu*; Dan. *beder*, to rest for refreshment.]

1. Any substance for food, proper to be used or actually used, to catch fish, or other animals, by alluring them to swallow a hook, or to be caught in snares, or in an inclosure or net.

2. A portion of food and drink, or a refreshment taken on a journey.

3. An allurement; enticement; temptation.

BAIT, *v. t.* To put meat on a hook or line, or in an inclosure, or among snares, to allure fish, fowls and other animals into human power.

2. To give a portion of food and drink to man or beast upon the road; as, to *bait* horses.

BAIT, *v. i.* To take a portion of food and drink for refreshment on a journey; as, we stopped to *bait*.

BAIT, *v. t.* [Goth. *beitan*. In Sax. *bate* is contention. See *Make-bate.*]

1. To provoke and harass by dogs; to harass by the help of others; as, to *bait* a bull or a boar.

2. To attack with violence; to harass in the manner of small animals. *Shak.*

BAIT, *v. i.* To clap the wings; to flutter as if to fly; or to hover as a hawk, when she stoops to her prey. *Bailey. Shak.*

BAIT, *n.* White Bait, a small fish of the Thames.

BA'ITED, *pp.* Furnished with bait; allured; tempted.

2. Fed, or refreshed, on the road.

3. Harassed by dogs or other small animals; attacked.

BA'ITING, *ppr.* Furnishing with bait; tempting; alluring.

2. Feeding; refreshing at an inn.

3. Harassing, with dogs; attacking.

BAIZE, *n.* [Per. *pozah*, the nap or down of cloth; Sp. *bausan*, the same.]

A coarse woolen stuff, with a long nap, sometimes frized on one side, without wale, being wove with two treadles like flannel. *Chambers.*

BAKE, *v. t.* [Sax. *bacan*; Sw. *baka*; Dan. *bager*; D. *bakken*; Ger. *backen*; Gypsey, *pekgum*; Russ. *peku*, to bake; *pekar*, a baker; Per. *pochtan*, to bake or cook.]

1. To heat, dry and harden, as in an oven or furnace, or under coals of fire; to dress and prepare for food, in a close place heated; as, to *bake* bread.

2. To dry and harden by heat, either in an oven, kiln or furnace, or by the solar rays; as, to *bake* bricks; to *bake* the ground.

BAKE, *v. i.* To do the work of baking; as, she brews, washes and *bakes*.

2. To be baked; to dry and harden in heat; as, the bread *bakes*; the ground *bakes* in a hot sun.

BA'KED, *pp.* Dried and hardened by heat; dressed in heat; as *baked* meat.

BA'KEHOUSE, *n.* [*bake* and *house.*] A house or building for baking.

BA'KEMEATS, *n.* Meats prepared for food in an oven. Gen. xl.

BA'KEN, *pp.* The same as *baked*, and nearly obsolete.

BA'KER, *n.* One whose occupation is to bake bread, biscuit, &c.

BA'KER-FOOT, *n.* An ill-shaped or distorted foot. *Taylor.*

BA'KER-LEGGED, *a.* One who has crooked legs, or legs that bend inward at the knees.

BA'KERY, *n.* The trade of a baker.

2. A place occupied with the business of baking bread, &c. *Smollett.*

BA'KING, *ppr.* Drying and hardening in heat; dressing or cooking in a close place, or in heat.

BA'KING, *n.* The quantity baked at once; as a *baking* of bread.

BAL'AN, *n.* A fish of a beautiful yellow, variegated with orange, a species of wrasse, caught on the shores of England. *Dict. of Nat. Hist.*

BAL'ANCE, *n.* [Fr. *balance*; Sp. *balanza*; It. *bilancia*; L. *bilanx*, *bis*, twice, and *lanx*, a dish, the double dish.]

1. A pair of scales, for weighing commodities. It consists of a beam or lever suspended exactly in the middle, with a scale or basin hung to each extremity, of precisely equal weight. The Roman balance, our steel-yard, consists of a lever or beam, movable on a center, and suspended near one of its extremities. Hence,

2. One of the simple powers in mechanics, used for determining the equality or difference of weight in heavy bodies, and consequently their masses or quantity of matter. *Encyc.*

3. *Figuratively*, an impartial state of the mind, in deliberating; or a just estimate of the reasons and arguments on both sides of a question, which gives to each its due *weight*, or force and importance.

4. As *balance* signifies equal weight, or equality, it is by custom used for the *weight* or *sum necessary to make two unequal weights or sums equal*; that which is necessary to bring them to a balance or equipoise. Hence, in accounts, *balance* is the *difference of two sums*; as upon an adjustment of accounts, a *balance* was found against A, in favor of B. Hence, to *pay a balance*, is to *pay the difference* and make the two accounts *equal*.

5. *Balance of trade* is an equal exportation of domestic productions, and importation of foreign. But, usually, the term is applied to the *difference* between the amount or value of the commodities exported and imported. Hence the common expression, the *balance* of trade is against or in favor of a country.

6. Equipoise, or an equal state of power between nations; as the "*balance* of power."

7. Equipoise, or an equal state of the passions.

> The *balance* of the mind. *Pope.*

8. That which renders weight or authority equal.

> The only *balance* attempted against the ancient kings, was a body of nobles. *J. Adams.*

9. The part of a clock or watch which regulates the beats.

10. In *astronomy*, a sign in the zodiac, called in Latin Libra, which the sun enters at the equinox in September.

The *hydrostatic balance* is an instrument to determine the specific gravity of fluid and solid bodies.

The *assay balance* is one which is used in docimastic operations, to determine the weight of minute bodies.

BAL'ANCE, *v. t.* To adjust the weights in the scales of a balance so as to bring them to an equipoise. Hence,

2. To weigh reasons; to compare, by estimating the relative force, importance, or value of different things; as, to *balance* good and evil.

3. To regulate different powers, so as to keep them in a state of just proportion; as, to *balance* Europe, or the powers of Europe.

4. To counterpoise; to make of equal weight or force; to make equipollent; as, one species of attraction *balances* another.

> One expression in the letter must check and *balance* another. *Kent.*

5. To settle and adjust, as an account; to find the difference of two accounts, and to pay the balance, or difference, and make them equal.

6. In *seamanship*, to contract a sail, by rolling up a small part of it at one corner. *Mar. Dict.*

BAL'ANCE, *v. i.* To have on each side equal weight; to be on a poise.

2. To hesitate; to fluctuate between motives which appear of equal force, as a balance plays when poised by equal weights.

> Between right and wrong, never *balance* a moment. *Anon.*

BAL'ANCED, *pp.* Charged with equal weights; standing on an equipoise; regulated so as to be equal; settled; adjusted; made equal in weight or amount.

BAL'ANCE FISH, *n.* The zygæna, or marteau; a fish of the genus squalus, or shark kind. It is 6 feet long, and weighs 500 lbs. It has three or four rows of broad pointed and serrated teeth; has a horrible aspect, and is very voracious. *Encyc.*

BAL'ANCER, *n.* The person who weighs, or who uses a balance.

2. A member of an insect useful in balancing the body.

3. One skilled in balancing.

BAL'ANCE-REEF, *n.* A reef band that crosses a sail diagonally, used to contract it in a storm. *Mar. Dict.*

BAL'ANCING, *ppr.* Charging with equal weights; being in a state of equipoise; bringing to a state of equality; regulating respective forces or sums to make them equal; settling; adjusting; paying a difference of accounts; hesitating; contracting a sail by rolling up one corner of it.

BAL'ANCING, *n.* Equilibrium; poise. *Spenser.*

BAL'ANITE, *n.* A fossil shell of the genus Balanus. *Jameson.*

BAL'ASS, BAL'AS, *n.* [Sp. *balax*; Fr. *balais.*]
A variety of spinel ruby, of a pale rose red, or inclining to orange. Its crystals are usually octahedrons, composed of two four-sided pyramids, applied base to base. [See *Spinel.*] *Cleaveland. Kirwan.*

BALAUS'TINE, *n.* The wild pomegranate tree. *Coxe.*

BAL'ƐONY, *n.* [Fr. *balcon*; It. *balcone*; Sp. *balcon*; Port. *balcam*; probably a jutting, as in *bulk*, *belly*, W. *balc.* In Pers. بالكانه balkanah, is a cancellated window.]
In *architecture*, a frame of wood, iron or stone, in front of a house or other building, supported by columns, pillars or consoles, and encompassed with a balustrade. Balconies are common before windows. *Encyc.*

BALD, *a. bauld.* [Sp. *baldio*, untilled, vacant, unfurnished; Port. *baldio*, open, common; *baldar*, to frustrate.]

1. Destitute of hair, especially on the top and back of the head.

2. Destitute of the natural covering; as a *bald* oak.

3. Without feathers on the head; as a *bald* vulture.

4. Destitute of trees on the top; as a *bald* mountain.

5. Unadorned; inelegant; as a *bald* translation. *Dryden.*

6. Mean; naked; base; without dignity or value. *Shak.*

7. In *popular language*, open, bold, audacious.

8. Without beard or awn; as *bald* wheat.

BALD'AƐHIN, BALD'AQUIN, *n.* [It. *baldacchino*; Sp. *baldaquino*, a rich silk or canopy, carried over the host. *Du Cange.* Lunier deduces it from the name of a city in Babylonia.]
In *architecture*, a building in form of a canopy, supported by columns, and often used as a covering to insulated altars; sometimes used for a shell over a door. *Encyc. Johnson.*

BALD'ERDASH, *n.* [Qu. Sp. *balda*, a trifle, or *baldonar*, to insult with abusive language; W. *baldorz*, to prattle; D. *bulderen.*]
Mean, senseless prate; a jargon of words; ribaldry; any thing jumbled together without judgment.

BALD'ERDASH, *v. t.* To mix or adulterate liquors. *Johnson.*

BALD'LY, *adv.* Nakedly; meanly; inelegantly; openly.

BALD'NESS, *n.* Want of hair on the top and back of the head; loss of hair; meanness or inelegance of writing; want of ornament.

BALD'PATE, *n.* A pate without hair. *Shak.*

BALD'PATED, *a.* Destitute of hair; shorn of hair. *Shak.*

BALD'RICK, *n.* [from Sw. *balt*, Ir. *balta*, L. *balteus*, a belt, and *rick*, rich. See these words.]

1. A girdle, or richly ornamented belt; a war girdle.

> A radiant *baldrick* o'er his shoulders tied. *Pope.*

2. The zodiac. *Spenser.*

BALE, *n.* [Fr. *balle*; Ger. *ballen*; D. *baal*; It. *balla*, a bale; Ch. Ar. Heb. חבל, to bind, to pledge, and its derivative, in Ar. and Eth., a rope.]

1. A bundle or package of goods in a cloth cover, and corded for carriage or transportation.

2. Formerly, a pair of dice.

BALE, *v. t.* To make up in a bale.

BALE, *n.* [Sax. *beal*, *bealo.* Qu. Heb. Ch. Syr. and Ar. אבל, to grieve or mourn, to be desolate, or חבל, to destroy. In Ir. *beala* is to die, and *abail*, death.] Misery; calamity. *Obs.*

BALEAR'IƐ, *a.* [from *Balearis*, the denomination given to Majorca and Minorca. Qu. from Gr. βαλλω, to throw, because the inhabitants were good slingers.]
Pertaining to the isles of Majorca and Minorca, in the Mediterranean sea.

BA'LEFUL, *a.* [See *Bale.*] Woeful; sad; sorrowful; full of grief; producing misery; as, a *baleful* smart; *baleful* eyes. *Spenser. Milton.*

2. Mischievous; destructive; pernicious; calamitous; deadly; as, *baleful* enemies; *baleful* war.

BA'LEFULLY, *adv.* Sorrowfully; perniciously; in a calamitous manner.

BALIS'TER, *n.* [L. *balista*, from Gr. βαλλω, to throw.] A cross bow. *Blount.*

BALÏZE', *n.* [Fr. *balise*; Sp. *valiza*, a beacon.] A sea-mark; a pole raised on a bank.

BALK, *n. bauk.* [Sax. *balc*; W. *balc*, a ridge between furrows; *balc*, prominent, swelling, proud; said to be from *bal*, a prominence; *bala*, eruption; *balau*, to shoot, spring or drive out.]

1. A ridge of land, left unplowed, between furrows, or at the end of a field.

2. A great beam, or rafter. [G. *balken*; D. *balk.*]

3. Any thing left untouched, like a ridge in plowing. *Spenser.*

4. A frustration; disappointment. *South.*

BALK, *v. t. bauk.* To disappoint; to frustrate. *Locke.*

2. To leave untouched; to miss or omit. *Drayton.*

3. To pile, as in a heap or ridge. *Shak.*

4. To turn aside; to talk beside one's meaning. *Obs.* *Spenser.*

5. To plow, leaving balks.

BALK'ED, *pp.* Plowed in ridges between furrows, as in American husbandry.

2. Frustrated; disappointed.

BALK'ER, *n.* One who balks. In *fishery*, balkers are persons who stand on rocks and eminences to espy the sholes of herring, and to give notice to the men in boats, which way they pass. *Encyc. Cowel.*

BALK'ING, *ppr.* Plowing in ridges; frustrating.

BALL, *n.* [G. *ball*; D. *bal*; Sw. *ball*; Dan. *ballon*; Russ. *bal*; Sp. *bala*, *bola*; It. *palla*; L. *pila*; W. *pêl*, *pellen*; Arm. *bolat*; Fr. *balle*, *boule.* A *ball* may signify a mass from collecting, or it may be that which is driven, from the root of L. *pello*; probably the former.]

1. A round body; a spherical substance, whether natural or artificial; or a body nearly round; as, a *ball* for play; a *ball* of thread; a *ball* of snow.

2. A bullet; a *ball* of iron or lead for cannon, muskets, &c.

3. A printer's ball, consisting of hair or wool, covered with leather or skin, and fastened to a stock, called a ball-stock, and used to put ink on the types in the forms.

4. The globe or earth, from its figure.

5. A globe borne as an ensign of authority; as, to hold the *ball* of a kingdom. *Bacon.*

6. Any part of the body that is round or protuberant; as, the eye *ball*; the *ball* of the thumb or foot.

7. The weight at the bottom of a pendulum.

8. Among *the Cornish miners in England*, a tin mine.

9. In *pyrotechnics*, a composition of combustible ingredients, which serve to burn, smoke or give light.

Ball-stock, among printers, a stock somewhat hollow at one end, to which balls of skin, stuffed with wool, are fastened, and which serves as a handle.

Ball-vein, among miners, a sort of iron ore, found in loose masses, of a circular form, containing sparkling particles. *Encyc.*

Ball and socket, an instrument used in surveying and astronomy, made of brass, with a perpetual screw, to move horizontally, obliquely, or vertically.

Puff-ball, in botany, the Lycoperdon, a genus of funguses.

Fire-ball, a meteor; a luminous globe darting through the atmosphere; also, a bag of canvas filled with gunpowder, sulphur, pitch, saltpeter, &c., to be thrown by the hand, or from mortars, to set fire to houses.

BALL, *n.* [Fr. *bal*; It. *ballo*; Sp. *bayle*, a dance; It. *ballare*, to dance, to shake; Gr. βαλλω, to toss or throw; or παλλω, to leap.]

An entertainment of dancing; originally and peculiarly, at the invitation and expense of an individual; but the word is used in America, for a dance at the expense of the attendants.

BALL, *v. i.* To form into a ball, as snow on horses' hoofs, or on the feet. We say the horse *balls*, or the snow *balls*.

BAL'LAD, *n.* [It. *ballata*, a ball, a dance, a ballad; Fr. *ballade*, a song, and *baladin*, a dancer. See *Ball*.]

A song; originally, a solemn song of praise; but now a meaner kind of popular song. *Watts.*

BAL'LAD, *v. i.* To make or sing ballads. *Shak.*

BAL'LADER, *n.* A writer of ballads. *Overbury.*

BAL'LAD-MAKER, *n.* A maker or composer of ballads. *Shak.*

BAL'LAD-MONGER, *n.* [See *Monger*.] A dealer in writing ballads. *Shak.*

BAL'LADRY, *n.* The subject or style of ballads. *B. Jonson.*

BAL'LAD-SINGER, *n.* One whose employment is to sing ballads.

BAL'LAD-STYLE, *n.* The air or manner of a ballad.

BAL'LAD-TUNE, *n.* The tune of a ballad. *Warton.*

BAL'LAD-WRITER, *n.* A composer of ballads. *Warton.*

BAL'LARAG, *v. t.* To bully; to threaten. [*Not in use.*] *Warton.*

BAL'LAST, *n.* [Sax. *bat*, a boat, with *last*, a load; D. Ger. and Dan. *last*; W. *llwyth*; Arm. *lastr*, a load; *bat-last*, boat-load, corrupted into *ballast*; Russ. *ballast*; Fr. *lest*; Sp. *lastre*.]

1. Heavy matter, as stone, sand or iron, laid on the bottom of a ship or other vessel, to sink it in the water, to such a depth, as to enable it to carry sufficient sail, without oversetting.

Shingle ballast is ballast of coarse gravel. *Mar. Dict.*

2. *Figuratively*, that which is used to make a thing steady. *Swift.*

BAL'LAST, *v. t.* To place heavy substances on the bottom of a ship or vessel, to keep it from oversetting.

2. To keep any thing steady, by counterbalancing its force. *Dryden.*

BAL'LASTED, *pp.* Furnished with ballast; kept steady by a counterpoising force.

BAL'LASTING, *ppr.* Furnishing with ballast; keeping steady.

BAL'LASTING, *n.* Ballast; that which is used for ballast. *Shak.*

BAL'LATED, *a.* Sung in a ballad. [*Little used.*]

BALLATOON', *n.* A heavy luggage boat employed on the rivers about the Caspian Lake. *Encyc.*

BAL'LATRY, *n.* A song; a jig. *Milton.*

BAL'LET, *n.* [Fr. *ballet*; It. *balletto*. See *Ball*, a dance.]

1. A kind of dance; an interlude; a comic dance, consisting of a series of several airs, with different movements, representing some subject or action.

2. A kind of dramatic poem, representing some fabulous action or subject, in which several persons appear and recite things, under the name of some deity or personage. *Encyc.*

In *heraldry*, ballets or balls, a bearing in coats of arms, denominated according to their color, bezants, plates, hurts, &c. *Encyc.*

BAL'LIAGE, or more correctly *bàilage*, *n.* [Ir. *baile*, a town.]

A small duty paid to the city of London by aliens, and even by denizens, for certain commodities exported by them. *Encyc.*

BALLIARDS. [See *Billiards*.]

BALLISTER. [See *Baluster*.]

BALLIS'TIC, *a.* [L. *balista*, an engine to throw stones, or shoot darts, from Gr. βαλλω, to throw or shoot.]

Pertaining to the *balista*, or to the art of shooting darts, and other missive weapons, by means of an engine.

BALLIS'TICS, *n.* The science or art of throwing missive weapons, by the use of an engine. The balista was a machine resembling a cross-bow. *Encyc. Math. Dict. Ash.*

BALLOON', *n.* [Fr. *ballon*, a foot-ball; Sp. *balon*; It. *pallone*; W. *pelhen*, from *pêl*, a ball. See *Ball*.]

1. In *general*, any spherical hollow body. *Encyc.*

2. In *chimistry*, a round vessel with a short neck, to receive whatever is distilled; a glass receiver of a spherical form.

3. In *architecture*, a ball or globe, on the top of a pillar.

4. In *fireworks*, a ball of pasteboard, or kind of bomb, stuffed with combustibles, to be played off, when fired, either in the air, or in water, which, bursting like a bomb, exhibits sparks of fire like stars. *Johnson. Encyc.*

5. A game, somewhat resembling tennis, played in an open field, with a large ball of leather, inflated with wind. *Encyc.*

6. A bag or hollow vessel, made of silk or other light material, and filled with hydrogen gas or heated air, so as to rise and float in the atmosphere; called for distinction, an air-balloon.

7. In *France*, a quantity of paper, containing 24 reams. [See *Bale*.]

8. In *France*, balloon, ballon or ballot, a quantity of glass plates; of white glass, 25 bundles of six plates each; of colored glass, 12 1-2 bundles of three plates each. *Encyc.*

BALLOON', } *n.* A state barge of Siam,
BAL'LOEN, } made of a single piece of timber, very long, and managed with oars. *Encyc.*

BAL'LOT, *n.* [Fr. *ballotte*; Sp. *balota*, a little ball. See *Ball*.]

1. A ball used in voting. Ballots are of different colors; those of one color give an affirmative; those of another, a negative. They are privately put into a box or urn.

2. A ticket or written vote, being given in lieu of a ballot, is now called by the same name.

3. The act of voting by balls or tickets.

BAL'LOT, *v. i.* To vote by ballot, that is, by putting little balls of different colors into a box, the greater number of one color or the other determining the result.

2. To vote by written papers or tickets.

BAL'LOTADE, } *n.* In *the menage*, a leap of
BAL'OTADE, } a horse between two pillars, or upon a strait line, so that when his fore feet are in the air, he shews nothing but the shoes of his hind feet, without jerking out. In a capriole, the horse yerks out his hind legs. *Farrier's Dict. Encyc.*

BALLOTA'TION, *n.* A voting by ballot. [*Little used.*] *Wotton.*

BAL'LOT-BOX, *n.* A box for receiving ballots.

B'ALM, *n.* *bàm.* [Fr. *baume*, a contraction of *balsam*, which see.]

1. The sap or juice of trees or shrubs remarkably odoriferous or aromatic. *Dryden.*

2. Any fragrant or valuable ointment. *Shak.*

3. Any thing which heals, or which soothes or mitigates pain. *Shak. Young.*

4. In *botany*, the name of several plants, particularly of the genus Melissa. They are aromatic and used as corroborants.

Balm of Gilead. A plant of the genus Amyris. Its leaves yield, when bruised, a strong aromatic scent; and from this plant is obtained the *balm of Gilead* of the shops, or balsam of Mecca or of Syria. It has a yellowish or greenish color, a warm bitterish aromatic taste, and an acidulous fragrant smell. It is valued as an odoriferous unguent, and cosmetic, by the Turks, who possess the country of its growth, and hence it is adulterated for market. *Encyc.*

B'ALM, *v. t.* To anoint with balm, or with any thing medicinal.

2. To soothe; to mitigate; to assuage. *Shak.*

B'ALMY, *a.* Having the qualities of balm; aromatic. *Milton.*

2. Producing balm; as the *balmy* tree. *Pope.*

3. Soothing; soft; mild; as *balmy* slumbers. *Dryden.*

4. Fragrant; odoriferous; as *balmy* wings. *Dryden.*

5. Mitigating; easing; assuaging; as *balmy* breath. *Shak.*

BAL'NEAL, *a.* [L. *balneum*.] Pertaining to a bath. *Howell.*

BAL'NEARY, *n.* [L. *balnearium*, from *balneum*. Syr. *balna*, bath.]

A bathing room. *Brown.*

BALNEA'TION, *n.* The act of bathing. *Brown.*

BAL'NEATORY, *a.* Belonging to a bath or stove. *Johnson.*

BAL'SAM, *n.* [Gr. βαλσαμον; L. *balsamum*.]

An oily, aromatic, resinous substance, flowing spontaneously or by incision, from certain plants. A great variety of substances pass under this denomination. But in modern chimistry, the term is confined to such vegetable juices, as are liquid or spontaneously become concrete, and consist of a resinous substance, combined with benzoic acid, or capable of affording it by decoction or sublimation. The balsams are either liquid or solid; of the former, are the balm of Gilead and the balsams of copaiba,

Peru and tolu; of the latter, benzoin, dragon's blood, and storax. *Encyc. Nicholson. Ure.*

Balsam apple, an annual Indian plant, included under the genus *Momordica*. A water and a subtil oil are obtained from it, which are commended as deobstruents.

Balsam tree. This name is given to a genus of plants called *Clusia;* to another, called *Copaifera*, which produces the balsam of *Copaiba;* and to a third, called *Pistacia*, turpentine tree or mastich tree.

Balsam of Sulphur is a solution of sulphur in oil.

Balsam of Tolu is the produce of the *Toluifera*, or *Tolu tree*, of South America. It is of a reddish yellow color, transparent, thick and tenacious, but growing hard and brittle by age. It is very fragrant, and like the Balsam of Peru, is a stimulant, and used as a pectoral. *Encyc. Linne.*

Balsam of Peru, the produce of a tree in Peru, possessing strong stimulant qualities.

BALSAMA'TION, *n.* The act of rendering balsamic.

BALSAM'IC, BALSAM'ICAL, } *a.* Having the qualities of balsam; stimulating; unctuous; soft; mitigating; mild. *Arbuthnot.*

BALSAM'IC, *n.* A warm, stimulating, demulcent medicine, of a smooth and oily consistence. *Coxe.*

BAL'SAMINE, *n.* Touch-me-not, or Impatiens, a genus of plants. *Encyc.*

BAL'SAM-SWEATING, *a.* Yielding balsam. *Crashaw.*

BALT'IC, *n.* [From *balte*, belt, from certain straits or channels, surrounding its isles, called *belts*. See *Belt.*]

The sea which separates Norway and Sweden from Jutland, Holstein and Germany.

BALT'IC, *a.* Pertaining to the sea of that name; situated on the Baltic sea.

> Each *Baltic* state to join the righteous cause. *Barlow.*

BAL'USTER, *n.* [It. *balaustro;* Sp. *balaustre;* Fr. *balustre;* from L. *palus;* Eng. *pole, pale.* This is corrupted into *bannister*, which I have rejected.]

A small column or pilaster, of various forms and dimensions, often adorned with moldings, used for balustrades.

BAL'USTERED, *a.* Having balusters. *Soames.*

BAL'USTRADE, *n.* [Sp. *balaustrado;* It. *balaustrata;* Fr. *balustrade;* from *baluster.*]

A row of balusters, joined by a rail, serving as a fence or inclosure, for altars, balconies, stair-cases, terraces, tops of buildings, &c. *Encyc. Johnson.*

BAM or BEAM, as an initial syllable in names of places, signifies *wood;* implying that the place took its name from a grove, or forest. Ger. *baum*, a tree.

BAM'BOO, *n.* A plant of the reed kind, or genus *Arundo*, growing in the East Indies, and in some other warm climates, and sometimes attaining to the height of 60 feet. From the main root, which is long, thick and jointed, spring several round, jointed stalks, which at 10 or 12 feet from the ground, send out from their joints several stalks which are united at their base. These are armed, at their joints, with one or two sharp rigid spines, and furnished with oblong, oval leaves, eight or nine inches long, on short footstalks. The flowers grow in large panicles, from the joints of the stalk, placed three in a parcel, close to their receptacles. Old stalks grow to five or six inches in diameter, and are so hard and durable, as to be used for building and for all sorts of furniture, for water-pipes, and for poles to support palanquins. The smaller stalks are used for walking sticks, flutes, &c. *Encyc.*

BAMBOO'ZLE, *v. t.* To confound; to deceive; to play low tricks. [*A low word.*] *Arbuthnot.*

BAMBOO'ZLER, *n.* A cheat; one who plays low tricks. *Arbuthnot.*

BAN, *n.* [Sax. *bannan, abannan*, to proclaim; It. *bando*, a proclamation; Sp. and Port. *bando;* Fr. *ban;* Arm. *ban;* D. *ban, bannen;* Ger. *id;* Sw. *banna*, to revile; Dan. *band*, ban, outlawry; *forbander*, to curse. Hence *banish*. The radical sense is to send, thrust or drive. Class Bn. No. 3.]

1. A public proclamation or edict; a public order or notice, mandatory or prohibitory.
   In a more particular sense,
2. Notice of a marriage proposed, or of a matrimonial contract, proclaimed in a church, that any person may object, if he knows of any kindred between the parties, of any precontract or other just cause, why the marriage should not take place.
3. An edict of interdiction or proscription. Hence to put a prince under the *ban* of the empire, is to divest him of his dignities, and to interdict all intercourse and all offices of humanity with the offender. Sometimes whole cities have been put under the *ban*, that is, deprived of their rights and privileges. *Encyc.*
4. Interdiction; prohibition. *Milton.*
5. Curse; excommunication; anathema. *Raleigh.*
6. A pecuniary mulct or penalty laid upon a delinquent for offending against a ban.
7. A mulct paid to the bishop by one guilty of sacrilege and other crimes.
8. In *military affairs*, a proclamation by beat of drum, requiring a strict observance of discipline, either for declaring a new officer, or for punishing an offender.
9. In *commerce*, a smooth fine muslin, imported from the E. Indies. *Encyc.*

BAN, *v. t.* To curse; to execrate. *Shak. Knolles.*

BAN, *v. i.* To curse. *Spenser.*

BAN'ANA, *n.* A species of the genus *Musa*, or plantain tree, and its fruit. It rises 15 or 20 feet high, with a soft stalk, marked with dark purple stripes and spots, with leaves six feet long, and a foot broad. The flowers grow in bunches, covered with a sheath of a fine purple color. The fruit is four or five inches long, and an inch or more in diameter; the pulp soft and of a luscious taste. When ripe, it is eaten raw, or fried in slices. Bananas grow in large bunches weighing a dozen pounds or more. This tree is the native of tropical countries, and on many isles, constitutes an important article of food. *Encyc.*

BAND, *n.* [Sax. *banda;* Sw. *band;* Dan. *baand;* D. *band;* G. *band, binde;* Sp. *banda, venda;* Port. It. *banda;* Ir. *banna;* Pers. بَنْد band; Sans. *bande, bunda;* Fr. *bande.* See *Bind* and *Bend.*]

1. A fillet; a cord; a tie; a chain; any narrow ligament with which a thing is bound, tied or fastened, or by which a number of things are confined together.
2. In *architecture*, any flat low member or molding, broad but not deep, called also *fascia*, face or plinth. *Johnson. Encyc.*
3. *Figuratively*, any chain; any means of restraint; that which draws or confines. *Dryden.*
4. Means of union or connection between persons; as, *Hymen's bands.* *Shak.*
5. Any thing bound round or encircling another. *Bacon.*
6. Something worn about the neck; as the *bands* of clergymen. *Addison.*
7. A company of soldiers; the body of men united under one flag or ensign. Also, indefinitely, a troop, a body of armed men. 2 Kings vi.
8. A company of persons united in any common design; as a *band* of brothers.
9. A slip of canvas, sewed across a sail to strengthen it. *Mar. Dict.*

The *band* of pensioners in England, is a company of 120 gentlemen, who receive a yearly allowance of £100 st., for attending the king on solemn occasions. *Encyc.*

The *bands* of a saddle are two pieces of iron nailed upon the bows, to hold them in their proper situation. *Johnson.*

BAND, *v. t.* To bind together; to bind over with a band. *Dryden.*

2. To unite in a troop, company or confederacy. *Milton.*

BAND, *v. i.* To unite; to associate; to confederate for some common purpose. Acts xxiii.

BAND'AGE, *n.* [Fr.] A fillet, roller, or swath, used in dressing and binding up wounds, restraining hemorrhages, and joining fractured and dislocated bones. Sometimes, the act or practice of applying bandages.

2. Something resembling a bandage; that which is bound over another. *Addison.*

BANDAN'A, *n.* A species of silk handkerchief.

BAND'BOX, *n.* A slight paper box for bands, caps, bonnets, muffs, or other light articles. *Addison.*

BAND'ED, *pp.* Bound with a band; united in a band.

BAND'ER, *n.* One that bands or associates with others.

BAND'ERET, *n.* [from *band.*] In *Swisserland*, a general in chief of military forces.

BAND'IED, *pp.* Beat or tossed to and fro; agitated; controverted without ceremony.

BAND'ING, *ppr.* Binding with a band; uniting in a band or company.

BAN'DIT, *n.* plu. BAN'DITS or BANDIT'TI, [It. *bandito*, from *bandire*, to proclaim, to banish or proscribe by proclamation. *Bandito*, is the participle. Sp. *bandido.* See *Ban.*]

An outlaw; also in *a general sense*, a robber; a highwayman; a lawless or desperate fellow.

BAN'DLE, *n.* An Irish measure of two feet in length. *Bailey.*

BAND'LET, } n. [Fr. *bandelette.*]
BAND'ELET, }
Any little band or flat molding, as that which crowns the Doric architrave. *Encyc.*

BAN'DOG, n. A large species of dog. *Shak. Spenser.*

BANDOLEE'RS, n. [Sp. *bandolera*; It. *bandoliera*; Fr. *bandouliere*; *band* and D. *leer*, leather.]
A large leathern belt, thrown over the right shoulder, and hanging under the left arm; worn by ancient musketeers for sustaining their fire arms, and their musket charges, which being put into little wooden cases, and coated with leather, were hung, to the number of twelve, to each bandoleer. *Encyc.*

BAN'DON, n. Disposal; license. [*Not in use.*] *Chaucer.*

BAN'DORE, n. [Sp. *bandurria*; Gr. πανδυρα.]
A musical stringed instrument, like a lute. *Encyc.*

BAND'ROL, n. [Fr. *banderole*; It. *banderuola*; Sp. *banderolas*; literally, a little *banner.* See *Banner.*]
1. A little flag or streamer, in form of a guidon, used to be hung on the masts of vessels. *Encyc.*
2. The little fringed silk flag that hangs on a trumpet. *Johnson.*

BAND' STRING, n. A string appendant to a band. *Taylor.*

BAND'Y, n. [Fr. *bander*, to tie, *bind, bend, bandy*; L. *pando.*]
A club for striking a ball at play. *Johnson.*

BAND'Y, v. t. To beat to and fro, as a ball in play.
2. To exchange; to give and receive reciprocally; as, to *bandy* looks. *Shak.*
3. To agitate; to toss about, as from man to man.

> Let not known truth be *bandied* in disputation. *Watts.*

BAND'Y, v. i. To contend, as at some game, in which each strives to drive the ball his own way. *Shak.*

BAND'YING, *ppr.* Beating, impelling or tossing from one to another; agitating in controversy without ceremony.

BAND'Y-LEG, n. [*bandy* and *leg.* See *Bend.*]
A crooked leg; a leg bending inward or outward. *Encyc.*

BAND'Y-LEGGED, a. Having crooked legs.

BANE, n. [Qu. the affinities. In Sax. *bana*, is a murderer; in Gr. φενω, is to kill; in L. *venenum* is poison; Fr. *venin*; Arm. *benym* or *vinym.*]
Poison of a deadly quality; hence, any fatal cause of mischief, injury or destruction; as, vice is the *bane* of society.

BANE, v. t. To poison. *Shak.*

BA'NE BERRY, n. A name of the herb christopher, actæa, or aconitum racemosum.

BA'NEFUL, a. Poisonous; pernicious; destructive.

BA'NEFULLY, *adv.* Perniciously; destructively.

BA'NEFULNESS, n. Poisonousness; destructiveness.

BA'NE WORT, n. [See *Wort.*] A plant, called also deadly nightshade. *Johnson.*

BANG, v. t. [Dan. *banker*, to beat; G. *bängel*, a club, and the clapper of a bell; D. *bengel*, a bell; Ir. *beanaim*, to beat.]
1. To beat, as with a club or cudgel; to thump; to cudgel. [*A low word.*]
2. To beat or handle roughly; to treat with violence. *Shak.*

BANG, n. A blow with a club; a heavy blow. *Shak.*

BAN'GLE, v. t. To waste by little and little; to squander carelessly. *Johnson.*

BAN'IAN, n. A man's undress or morning gown, as worn by the Banians in the E. Indies. *Johnson.*
2. A Gentoo servant, employed as an agent in commerce. *Herbert.*
3. A tree in India. *Milton.*

Banian days, in seamen's language, are three days in a week, in which the sailors have no flesh meat served out to them. This use of the term seems to be borrowed from the Banians in Asia, who, believing in a metempsychosis, will eat no flesh, nor even kill noxious animals.

BAN'ISH, v. t. [Fr. *bannir, bannissant*; whence *bannissement, banishment*; Arm. *embanna*, to publish; *forbana* and *forbaniza*, to banish; It. *bandire*; D. *bannen*; G. *verbannen, ausbannen.* See *Ban.*]
1. To condemn to exile, or compel to leave one's country, by authority of the prince or government, either for life or for a limited time. It is common for Russians to be *banished* to Siberia.
2. To drive away; to compel to depart; as, to *banish* sorrow.
3. To quit one's country voluntarily, and with a view to reside abroad; as, he *banished* himself.

BAN'ISHED, *pp.* Compelled to leave one's country; driven away.

BAN'ISHER, n. One who compels another to quit his country.

BAN'ISHING, *ppr.* Compelling to quit one's country; driving away.

BAN'ISHMENT, n. The act of a prince or government, compelling a citizen to leave his country, either for a limited time or forever, as for some crime.
2. A voluntary forsaking of one's country upon oath, called *abjuration.* [*This practice has now ceased in G. Britain.*]
3. The state of being banished; exile.
4. The act of driving away or dispelling; as the *banishment* of care from the mind.

BANK, n. [Sax. *banc*; D. and G. *bank*; Sw. *banck*; Dan. *banke*; It. *banco*; Sp. Port. *banca, banco*; Fr. *banc, banque*; W. *banc*; Arm. *bancq*; Ar. بنق bank, a *bench.* *Bank* and *bench* are radically the same word. The sense is, that which is set, laid or extended. Applied to a mass of earth, it is a collection, that which is thrown or laid together.]
1. A mound, pile or ridge of earth, raised above the surrounding plain, either as a defense or for other purposes. 2 Sam. xx. 15.
2. Any steep acclivity, whether rising from a river, a lake, or the sea, or forming the side of a ravine, or the steep side of a hillock on a plain. When we speak of the earth in general adjoining a lake or the sea, we use the word shore; but a particular steep acclivity on the side of a lake, river or the sea, is called a *bank.*
3. A bench, or a bench of rowers, in a galley; so called from their seat.

> Placed on their *banks*, the lusty Trojans sweep. *Waller.*

4. By *analogy*, a collection or stock of money, deposited, by a number of persons, for a particular use; that is, an aggregate of particulars, or a fund; as, to establish a *bank*, that is a joint fund.
5. The place where a collection of money is deposited; a common repository of the money of individuals or of companies; also a house used for a bank.
6. A company of persons concerned in a bank, whether a private association, or an incorporated company; the stockholders of a bank, or their representatives, the directors, acting in their corporate capacity.
7. An elevation, or rising ground, in the sea; called also flats, shoals, shelves or shallows. These may rise to the surface of the water or near to it; but the word *bank* signifies also elevated ground at the bottom of the sea, when many fathoms below the surface, as the *banks* of Newfoundland.

BANK, v. t. To raise a mound or dyke; to inclose, defend or fortify with a bank; as, to *bank* a house.
2. To pass by the banks of.

> As I have *bank'd* their towns. *Shak.*

[*Not in use.*]
3. To lay up or deposit money in a bank. [*Little used.*] *Johnson.*

BANK'ABLE, a. Receivable at a bank, as bills; or discountable, as notes. [*Of recent origin.*]

BANK-BILL, } n. A promissory note, is-
BANK-NOTE, } sued by a banking company, signed by their President and countersigned by the Cashier, payable to the *bearer* in gold or silver at the bank, on demand. If payable to *order*, the note is called a *post-note.*

BANK'ED, *pp.* Raised in a ridge or mound of earth; inclosed, or fortified with a bank.

BANK'ER, n. One who keeps a bank; one who trafficks in money, receives and remits money, negotiates bills of exchange, &c.
2. A vessel employed in the codfishery on the banks of Newfoundland. *Mar. Dict.*

BANK'ING, *ppr.* Raising a mound or bank; inclosing with a bank. When we speak of restraining water, we usually call it *banking*; when we speak of defending the land, we call it *imbanking.* *Encyc.*

BANK'ING, n. The business or employment of a banker; the business of establishing a common fund for lending money, discounting notes, issuing bills, receiving deposits, collecting the money on notes deposited, negotiating bills of exchange, &c.

BANK'RUPT, n. [Fr. *banqueroute*; Sp. *bancarrota*, bankruptcy, *bank* and Sp. *roto*, Port. *roto*, It. *rotto*, broken; Eng. *rout*, defeat. This may signify *bench*-broken, or *bank*-broken; most probably the latter, referring to the fund or stock. The last syllable is the Latin *ruptus* contracted; Norm. *roupt, rous*, broken.]
1. A trader who secretes himself, or does certain other acts tending to defraud his creditors. *Blackstone.*
2. In *a less technical sense*, a trader who fails or becomes unable to pay his just debts; an insolvent trader. In strictness, no per-

son but a trader can be a bankrupt. *Bankruptcy* is applied to merchants and traders; *insolvency*, to other persons.

BANK'RUPT, *a.* Having committed acts of bankruptcy; unable to pay just debts; insolvent.

BANK'RUPT, *v. t.* To break one in trade; to make insolvent.

BANK'RUPTCY, *n.* The state of being a bankrupt, or insolvent; inability to pay all debts.

2. The act of becoming a bankrupt; the act of rendering one's self a bankrupt, as by absconding, or otherwise; failure in trade.

BANK'RUPTED, *pp.* Rendered insolvent.

BANK'RUPTING, *ppr.* Breaking in trade; rendering insolvent.

BANK'RUPT-LAW, *n.* A law, which, upon a bankrupt's surrendering all his property to commissioners for the benefit of his creditors, discharges him from the payment of his debts, and all liability to arrest or suit for the same, and secures his future acquired property from a liability to the payment of his past debts.

BANKRUPT-SYSTEM, *n.* A system of laws and legal proceedings in regard to bankrupts and their property.

BANK-STOCK, *n.* A share or shares in the capital stock of a bank.

BAN'NER, *n.* [Fr. *banniere*; W. *baner*; It. *bandiera*; Sp. *bandera*; G. *fahne* and *panier*; D. *vaan* and *vaandel*; from Goth. *fana*, cloth; Sax. *fana*; L. *pannus*; Ir. *fuan*, cloth.]

1. A square flag; a military ensign; the principal standard of a prince or state. *Encyc.*

2. A streamer borne at the end of a lance or elsewhere. *Johnson.*

3. In *botany*, the upper petal of a papilionaceous corol. *Martyn.*

BAN'NERED, *a.* Furnished with or bearing banners. *Milton.*

> Shield the strong foes, and rake the *bannered* shore. *Barlow.*

BAN'NERET, *n.* [Fr. from *banner.*] A knight made in the field. Bannerets formerly constituted an order of knights or feudal lords, who led their vassals to battle under their own flags. On the day of battle, the candidates presented their flags to the king or general, who cut off the train or skirt, and made it square. They were then called *knights of the square flag*. They were a middle order between barons and simple knights. *Spelman. Encyc.*

BAN'NEROL. [See *Bandrol.*]

BAN'NOCK, *n.* [Ir. *boinneog.*] A cake made of oatmeal or peas-meal, baked on an iron plate over the fire; used in Scotland, and the northern counties of England. *Johnson.*

BAN'OY, *n.* A species of hawk, somewhat larger than the English sparrow hawk; the back and wings yellow, and the belly white; a native of the Philippine isles. *Dict. of Nat. Hist.*

BAN'QUET, *n.* [Fr. *banquet*; Arm. *bancqed*, or *banvez*; It. *banchetto*, a little seat, a feast; Sp. *banqueta*, a stool with three legs; *banquete*, a banquet. From these words, it would appear that *banquet* is a sitting and hence a feast, and not, as supposed, from the oriental פנק, فنق to feed or bring up delicately.]

A feast; a rich entertainment of meat and drink. Esther v. Job xli. Amos vi.

BAN'QUET, *v. t.* To treat with a feast, or rich entertainment. *Shak.*

BAN'QUET, *v. i.* To feast; to regale one's self with good eating and drinking. *Shak.*

BAN'QUETED, *pp.* Feasted; richly entertained at the table.

BAN'QUETER, *n.* A feaster; one who lives deliciously.

2. One who makes feasts, or rich entertainments.

BAN'QUETING, *ppr.* Feasting; entertaining with rich fare.

2. Partaking of rich fare.

BAN'QUETING, *n.* A feast; luxurious living; rich entertainment. 1 Pet. iv.

BAN'QUETING-HOUSE, } *n.* A house where entertainments are made. Cant. xxiv. Dan. v.
BAN'QUET-HOUSE, }

BAN'QUETING-ROOM, *n.* A saloon, or spacious hall for public entertainments. *Encyc.*

BANQUETTE or BANQUET, *n.* *banket'.* [Fr.] In *fortification*, a little raised way or foot bank, running along the inside of a parapet, on which musketeers stand to fire upon the enemy in the moat or covered way. *Encyc.*

BAN'SHEE or BEN'SHI, *n.* An Irish fairy. *Todd.*

BAN'STICKLE, *n.* A small fish, called also stickle-back. This fish falls under the genus *Gasterosteus.*

BAN'TER, *v. t.* [Gr. φεναξ, whence φεναχιζω, to mock, or deride.]

To play upon in words and in good humor; to rally; to joke, or jest with. *Banter* hardly amounts to ridicule, much less to derision. It consists in being pleasant and witty with the actions of another, and raising a humorous laugh at his expense, often attended with some degree of sarcasm.

BAN'TER, *n.* A joking or jesting; raillery; wit or humor; pleasantry.

BAN'TERED, *pp.* Rallied; laughed at in good humor.

BAN'TERER, *n.* One who banters, or laughs at with pleasantry.

BAN'TERING, *ppr.* Joking; laughing at with good humor.

BANT'LING, *n.* [G. *bankart.* Qu.] A young child; an infant.

BAP'TISM, *n.* [Gr. βαπτισμα, from βαπτιζω, from βαπτω, to baptize; Sp. *bautizar*; It. *battezzare*; Port. *bautizar*, or *baptizar*. These seem to be from the Greek, by contraction. But the Arm. *badeza*, *badein*, may be from *bath*, *bad*, water.]

1. The application of water to a person, as a sacrament or religious ceremony, by which he is initiated into the visible church of Christ. This is usually performed by sprinkling or immersion.

2. The sufferings of Christ. Matt. xx. 22. 23.

3. So much of the gospel as was preached by John, the Baptist. Acts xviii. *Cruden.*

BAPTIS'MAL, *a.* Pertaining to baptism; as a *baptismal* vow.

BAP'TIST, *n.* One who administers baptism. This appellation is appropriately given to John, the forerunner of Christ.

2. As a contraction of *Anabaptist*, one who denies the doctrine of infant baptism, and maintains that baptism ought to be administered only to adults by immersing the body in water.

BAP'TISTERY, *n.* [L. *baptisterium.*] A place where the sacrament of baptism is administered. Primitively, baptisteries were in buildings separate from the church; but in the sixth century, they were taken into the church-porch, and afterwards into the church itself. *Encyc.*

BAPTIS'TIC, } *a.* Pertaining to baptism. *Bramhall.*
BAPTIS'TICAL, }

BAPTI'ZE, *v. t.* [See *Baptism.*] To administer the sacrament of baptism to; to christen. By some denominations of christians, baptism is performed by plunging, or immersing the whole body in water, and this is done to none but adults. More generally the ceremony is performed by sprinkling water on the face of a person, whether an infant or an adult, and in the case of an infant, by giving him a name, in the name of the Father, Son and Holy Spirit, which is called *Christening.*

BAPTI'ZED, *pp.* Having received baptism; christened.

BAPTI'ZER, *n.* One who christens, or administers baptism.

BAPTI'ZING, *ppr.* Administering baptism to; christening.

B'AR, *n.* [W. *bar*; Ir. *barra*; Fr. *barre*; Sp. *barra*; Port. *id*; It. *barra*, *sbarra*; Arm. *barren*, *sparl*; Heb. בריח; Ch. עברא. If these words are the Eng. *bar*, the sense is a shoot, that which shoots, passes or is driven.]

1. A piece of wood, iron or other solid matter, long in proportion to its diameter, used for various purposes, but especially for a hindrance or obstruction; as the *bars* of a fence or gate; the *bar* of a door or hatchway. Numb. iii. 36. Ex. xxvi. 26.

2. Any obstacle which obstructs, hinders or defends; an obstruction; a fortification. Amos i.

> Must I new *bars* to my own joy create. *Dryden.*

3. The shore of the sea, which restrains its waters. Job xxxviii.

4. The railing that incloses the place which counsel occupy in courts of justice. Hence the phrase, *at the bar of the court*, signifies in open court. Hence also licensed lawyers are called *barristers*; and hence the whole body of lawyers licensed in a court, are customarily called the *bar*. *A trial at bar*, in England, is a trial in the courts of Westminster, opposed to a trial at Nisi Prius, in the circuits.

5. *Figuratively*, any tribunal; as the *bar* of public opinion. Thus the final trial of men is called the *bar* of God.

6. The inclosed place of a tavern, inn or coffee house, where the landlord or his servant delivers out liquors, and waits upon customers. *Addison.*

7. A bank of sand, gravel or earth, forming a shoal at the mouth of a river or harbor, obstructing entrance, or rendering it difficult.

8. A rock in the sea, according to Brown; or any thing by which structure is held to-

gether, according to Johnson; used in Jonah ii.

9. Any thing laid across another, as *bars* in heraldry, stripes in color, and the like.

10. In *the menage*, the highest part of the place in a horse's mouth between the grinders and tusks, so that the part of the mouth which lies under and at the side of the bars, retains the name of the gum. *Encyc.* The upper part of the gums, which bears no teeth, and to which the bit is applied. *Johnson.*

11. In *music*, *bars* are lines drawn perpendicularly across the lines of the staff, including between each two, a certain quantity of time, or number of beats.

12. In *law*, a peremptory exception sufficient to destroy the plaintiff's action. It is divided into a bar to common intendment, and bar special; bar temporary and bar perpetual. Bar to common intendment is an ordinary or general bar, which disables the declaration of the plaintiff. A *special* bar is more than ordinary, as a fine, release, or justification. A *temporary* bar is that which is good for a time, but may afterwards cease. A *perpetual* bar overthrows the action of the plaintiff forever. *Blackstone. Cowel.*

13. A bar of gold or silver, is an ingot, lump or wedge, from the mines, run in a mold, and unwrought. A bar of iron is a long piece, wrought in the forge and hammered from a pig.

14. Among *printers*, the iron with a wooden handle, by which the screw of the press is turned.

15. In *the African trade*, a denomination of price; payment formerly being made to the Africans in iron bars. *Johnson.*

B'AR, *v. t.* To fasten with a bar; as, to *bar* a door, or gate.

2. To hinder; to obstruct, or prevent; as, to *bar* the entrance of evil.

3. To prevent; to exclude; to hinder; to make impracticable; as, the distance between us *bars* our intercourse. In this sense, the phrase is often varied, thus: the distance *bars me from his* aid, or *bars him from my* aid.

4. To prohibit; to restrain or exclude by express or implied prohibition; as, the statute *bars* my right; the law *bars* the use of poisoned weapons.

5. To obstruct, prevent or hinder by any moral obstacle; as, the right is *barred* by time, or by statute; a release *bars* the plaintiff's recovery.

6. To except; to exclude by exception; as, I *bar* to night. *Shak.*

7. To cross with stripes of a different color.

8. *To bar a vein*, in farriery, is an operation upon the legs of a horse, or other parts, to stop malignant humors. This is done by opening the skin above a vein, disengaging it and tying it both above and below, and striking between the two ligatures. *Johnson.*

9. To adorn with trappings; a contraction of *barb*. [See *Barb.*] *Drayton. Haywood.*

B'ARB, *n.* [L. *barba*; W. *barv*; Corn. *bar*; Arm. *baro.* This is *beard*, with a different ending. The sense may be, that which shoots out.]

1. Beard, or that which resembles it, or grows in the place of it; as the *barb* of a fish, the smaller claws of the polypus, &c. *Johnson. Coxe.*

2. The down, or pubes, covering the surface of some plants; or rather, a tuft or bunch of strong hairs terminating leaves. *Linne. Milne.*

3. Anciently, armor for horses; formerly, *barbe* or *barde.* *Hayward.*

4. A common name of the barbary pigeon, a bird of a black or dun color. *Dict. of Nat. Hist.*

5. A horse from *Barbary*, of which it seems to be a contraction.

6. The points that stand backward in an arrow, fish-hook or other instrument for piercing, intended to prevent its being extracted.

7. In *botany*, a straight process armed with teeth pointing backward like the sting of a bee. This is one sort of pubescence. *Martyn.*

B'ARB, *v. t.* To shave; to dress the beard. *Obs.* *Shak.*

2. To furnish with *barbs*, as an arrow, fish hook, spear, or other instrument.

3. To put armor on a horse. *Milton.*

B'ARBACAN, *n.* [Fr. *barbacane*; Sp. *barbacana*; It. *barbacane.* Qu. a projecting work.]

1. A fortification or outer defense to a city or castle, consisting of an elevation of earth about three feet high, along the foot of the rampart. *Encyc. Johnson. Sp. Dict.*

2. A fortress at the end of a bridge, or at the outlet of a city, having a double wall with towers. *Encyc.*

3. An opening in the wall of a fortress through which guns are leveled and fired upon an enemy. *Johnson. Encyc.*

The French use the word also for an aperture in a wall to let in or drain off water; and the Spaniards, for a low wall round a church yard. *Fr. and Sp. Dict.*

BARBA'DOES-CHERRY, *n.* The Malpighia, a tree growing in the W. Indies, fifteen feet high and producing a pleasant tart fruit. *Johnson.*

BARBA'DOES TAR, *n.* A mineral fluid, of the nature of the thicker fluid bitumens, of a nauseous bitterish taste, a very strong disagreeable smell, viscid, of a brown, black or reddish color; it easily melts, and burns with much smoke, but is not soluble in ardent spirits. It contains a portion of acid of amber. It trickles down the sides of mountains in some parts of America, and sometimes is found on the surface of the waters. It is recommended in coughs and disorders of the breast and lungs. *Encyc. Nicholson.*

BARBA'RIAN, *n.* [L. *barbarus*; Gr. βαρϐαρος; Ir. *barba*, or *beorb*; Russ. *varvar*; Ch. ברבר. See Class Br. No. 3 and 7. The sense is, foreign, wild, fierce.]

1. A man in his rude, savage state; an uncivilized person. *Denham.*

2. A cruel, savage, brutal man; one destitute of pity or humanity. *Philips.*

3. A foreigner. The Greeks and Romans denominated most foreign nations *barbarians*; and many of these were less civilized than themselves, or unacquainted with their language, laws and manners. But with them the word was less reproachful than with us.

BARBA'RIAN, *a.* Belonging to savages; rude; uncivilized. *Pope.*

2. Cruel; inhuman.

BARBAR'IC, *a.* [L. *barbaricus.* See *Barbarian.* The Romans applied this word to designate things foreign; *Barbaricum aurum*, gold from Asia, Virg. Æn. 2. 504; *Barbaricæ vestes*, embroidered garments from foreign nations. English writers use the word in a like sense.]

Foreign; imported from foreign nations. *Milton. Pope.*

B'ARBARISM, *n.* [L. *barbarismus.* See *Barbarian.*]

1. An offense against purity of style or language; any form of speech contrary to the pure idioms of a particular language. *Dryden.*

2. Ignorance of arts; want of learning. *Shak. Dryden.*

3. Rudeness of manners; savagism; incivility; ferociousness; a savage state of society. *Spenser. Davies.*

4. Brutality; cruelty; barbarity. [*In this sense little used, being superseded by* barbarity.]

BARBAR'ITY, *n.* [See *Barbarian.*]

The manners of a barbarian; savageness; cruelty; ferociousness; inhumanity. *Clarendon.*

2. Barbarism; impurity of speech. *Dryden. Swift.*

[*The use of the word in this sense, is now superseded by* barbarism.]

B'ARBARIZE, *v. t.* To make barbarous.

Hideous changes have *barbarized* France. *Burke.*

B'ARBAROUS, *a.* Uncivilized; savage; unlettered; untutored; ignorant; unacquainted with arts; stranger to civility of manners.

Thou art a Roman; be not *barbarous.* *Shak.*

2. Cruel; ferocious; inhuman; as *barbarous* usage. *Clarendon.*

B'ARBAROUSLY, *adv.* In the manner of a barbarian; ignorantly; without knowledge or arts; contrary to the rules of speech. *Dryden.*

2. In a savage, cruel, ferocious or inhuman manner.

B'ARBAROUSNESS, *n.* Rudeness or incivility of manners. *Temple.*

2. Impurity of language. *Brerewood.*

3. Cruelty; inhumanity; barbarity. *Hall.*

B'ARBARY, *n.* A barbary horse; a barb. *Beaum.*

B'ARBASTEL, *n.* A bat with hairy lips.

B'ARBATE, } *a.* [L. *barbatus*, from *barba.*
B'ARBATED, } See *Barb.*]

In *botany*, bearded; also gaping or ringent. *Barbatus flos*, a gaping or ringent flower; synonymous with the *ringent* flower of Linne, and the *labiate* of Tournefort. *Milne. Lee.*

B'ARBE. In *the military art*, to fire *in barbe*, is to fire the cannon over the parapet, instead of firing through the embrasures. *Encyc.*

B'ARBECUE, *n.* In *the West Indies*, a hog roasted whole. It is, with us, used for an ox or perhaps any other animal dressed in like manner.

B'ARBECUE, *v. t.* To dress and roast a

hog whole, which is done by splitting the hog to the back bone, and roasting it on a gridiron; to roast any animal whole.

B'ARBED, *pp.* [See *Barb.*]

1. Furnished with armor; as *barbed* steeds. *Shak.*

2. Bearded; jagged with hooks or points; as *barbed* arrows.

3. Shaved or trimmed; having the beard dressed. *Encyc.*

B'ARBEL, *n.* [L. *barba*; Fr. *barbeau*; D. *barbeel.*]

1. A fish of the genus Cyprinus, of the order of abdominals. The mouth is toothless; the gill has three rays; the body is smooth and white. This fish is about three feet long, and weighs 18 pounds. It is a very coarse fish, living in deep still rivers and rooting like swine in the soft banks. Its dorsal fin is armed with a strong spine, sharply serrated, from which circumstance it probably received its name. *Encyc.*

2. A knot of superfluous flesh, growing in the channels of a horse's mouth; written also *barble*, or *barb. Encyc. Farrier's Dict.*

B'ARBER, *n.* [Persian, *barbr.* See *Barb.*] One whose occupation is to shave men, or to shave and dress hair. *Shak.*

B'ARBER, *v. t.* To shave and dress hair. *Shak.*

B'ARBER-CHIRURGEON, *n.* One who joins the practice of surgery with that of a barber; a practice now unusual. A low practitioner of surgery. *Wiseman.*

B'ARBERESS, *n.* A female barber. [*Not used.*]

B'ARBER-MONGER, *n.* A man who frequents the barber's shop, or prides himself in being dressed by a barber; a fop. *Shak.*

B'ARBERRY, *n.* [L. *berberis*; Ir. *barbrog*; D. *berberis*; Sp. *berbero.* In Eth. *abarbar*, is the nettle, urtica major; in Amh., a species of thistle. Lud. Eth. 233; Amh. 39. It is probable therefore that this plant is so named from its spines or *barbs.* Its other name, *oxyacanthus*, indicates a like origin.]

1. A plant of the genus *berberis*, common in hedges; called in England, pipperidge-bush. The berries are used in housewifery, and are deemed efficacious in fluxes and fevers. The bark dyes a fine yellow, especially the bark of the root. This plant is pernicious to wheat, the ears of which will not fill, if within the effluvia of the plant; and the influence of this has been known to extend three or four hundred yards. *Miller. Encyc.*

B'ARBET, *n.* A name given by some French writers to a peculiar species of those worms which feed on the puceron or aphis. [See *Aphis.*] *Encyc.*

2. The Bucco, a genus of birds found in the warm climates of both continents.

3. A dog, so called from his long hair.

B'ARD, *n.* [W. *bardh*, or *barz*; Ir. *bard*; Fr. *barde*; a poet; Ir. *bardas*, a satire or lampoon; W. *bardhas*, philosophy; *bardgan*, a song.]

1. A poet and a singer among the ancient Celts; one whose occupation was to compose and sing verses, in honor of the heroic achievements of princes and brave men. The bards used an instrument of music like a lyre or guitar, and not only praised the brave, but reproached the cowardly. *Diod. Sic. Am. Marcel. Lucan. Festus.*

2. In modern usage, a poet. *Pope. Dryden.*

B'ARD, *n.* The trappings of a horse.

B'ARDED, *a.* In *heraldry*, caparisoned. *Encyc.*

BARDES'ANISTS, *n.* A sect of heretics, who sprung from Bardesanes, of Edessa, in Mesopotamia, in the 2d century, who taught that the actions of men depend on fate, to which God himself is subject. His followers went farther, and denied the incarnation of Christ and the resurrection. *Encyc.*

B'ARDIC, *a.* Pertaining to bards, or to their poetry. *Owen.*

B'ARDISH, *a.* Pertaining to bards; written by a bard.

B'ARDISM, *n.* The science of bards; the learning and maxims of bards. *Owen.*

BARE, *a.* [Sax. *bar*, or *bær*; Sw. and Dan. *bar*; G. *bar.* This word is from opening, separating, stripping. In Ch. Syr. Sam. באר signifies to open, or explain; Ar. to dig; also ברר is to separate, to purify. Ch. Syr. בור to lay waste; Ar. *id.*]

1. Naked; without covering; as, the arm is *bare*; the trees are *bare.*

2. With the head uncovered, from respect. *Clarendon.*

3. Plain; simple; unadorned; without the polish of refined manners. *Spenser.*

4. Laid open to view; detected; no longer concealed. *Milton.*

5. Poor; destitute; indigent; empty; unfurnished. *Hooker. Dryden.*

> I have made Esau bare. Jer. xlix.

6. Alone; unaccompanied. *Shak. South.*

7. Thread-bare; much worn. *Shak.*

8. Wanting clothes; or ill supplied with garments. *Johnson.*

Under bare poles, at sea, signifies having no sail set. *Mar. Dict.*

It is often followed by of; as, the country is *bare of* money. *Locke.*

BARE, *v. t.* [Sax. *abarian.* See *Bare*, adj.] To strip off the covering; to make naked; as, to *bare* the breast. *Bacon. Pope.*

BARE, the old preterit of *bear*, now *bore.*

BA'REBONE, *n.* [See *Bone.*] A very lean person.

BA'REBONED, *a.* Lean, so that the bones appear, or rather, so that the bones show their forms. *Shak.*

BA'RED, *pp.* Made bare; made naked.

BA'REFACED, *a.* [See *Face.*]

1. With the face uncovered; not masked. *Shak.*

2. Undisguised; unreserved; without concealment; hence shameless; impudent; audacious; as a *barefaced* falsehood.

BA'REFACEDLY, *adv.* Without disguise or reserve; openly; impudently.

BA'REFACEDNESS, *n.* Effrontery; assurance; audaciousness.

BA'REFOOT, *a.* [See *Foot.*] With the feet bare; without shoes and stockings. 2 Sam. xv. Isaiah xx.

BA'REFOOT, *a.* or *adv.* With the feet bare; as, to dance *barefoot.* *Shak.*

BA'REFOOTED, *a.* Having the feet bare.

BA'REGNAWN, *a.* [See *Gnaw.*] Eaten bare. *Shak.*

BA'REHEADED, *a.* [See *Head.*] Having the head uncovered, either from respect or other cause. *Bacon. Dryden.*

BA'RELEGGED, *a.* Having the legs bare. *Burton.*

BA'RELY, *adv.* Nakedly; poorly; indigently; without decoration; merely; only; without any thing more; as a prince *barely* in title. *Barret. Hooker.*

BA'RENECKED, *a.* Having the neck uncovered; exposed. *Shak.*

BA'RENESS, *n.* Nakedness; leanness; poverty; indigence; defect of clothes, or the usual covering. *Shak. South.*

BA'REPICKED, *a.* Picked to the bone. *Shak.*

BA'RERIBBED, *a.* Lean. *Shak.*

B'ARGAIN, *n.* [Fr. *barguigner*, to haggle, to hum and haw; Arm. *barguignour*, a haggler; It. *bargagnare*, to cavil, contend, *bargain*; Ir. *braighean*, debate. It seems to accord with It. *briga*, Sp. *brega*, Fr. *brigue.*]

An agreement between parties concerning the sale of property; or a contract by which one party binds himself to transfer the right to some property, for a consideration, and the other party binds himself to receive the property and pay the consideration.

2. Stipulation: interested dealing.

3. Purchase or the thing purchased. *Locke.*

4. In *popular language*, final event; upshot.

> We must make the best of a bad *bargain.*

To sell bargains, is a vulgar phrase.

To strike a bargain, is to ratify an agreement, originally by *striking*, or shaking hands. The Latin *ferire fœdus*, may represent a like ceremony, unless it refers to the practice of killing a victim, at the solemn ratification of oaths.

Bargain and sale, in law, a species of conveyance, by which the bargainer contracts to convey the lands to the bargainee, and becomes by such contract a trustee for and seised to the use of the bargainee. The statute then completes the purchase; that is, the bargain vests the use, and the statute vests the possession. *Blackstone.*

B'ARGAIN, *v. i.* To make a contract or conclusive agreement, for the transfer of property; often with *for* before the thing purchased; as, to *bargain for* a house. A *bargained* with B *for* his farm.

B'ARGAIN, *v. t.* To sell; to transfer for a consideration; as, A *bargained* away his farm; *a popular use of the word.*

BARGAINEE', *n.* The party in a contract who receives or agrees to receive the property sold. *Blackstone.*

B'ARGAINER, *n.* The party in a contract who stipulates to sell and convey property to another. *Blackstone.*

B'ARGE, *n.* *bàrj.* [D. *bargie*; It. and Sp. *barca*; Ir. *barc. Barge*, and *bark* or *barque*, a ship, are radically one word.]

1. A pleasure boat; a vessel or boat of state, furnished with elegant apartments, canopies and cushions, equipped with a band of rowers, and decorated with flags and streamers; used by officers and magistrates. *Encyc.*

2. A flat-bottomed vessel of burthen, for loading and unloading ships. *Mar. Dict.*

B'ARGE-COUPLES, *n.* In *architecture*, a beam mortised into another, to strengthen the building. *Encyc.*

B'ARGE-COURSE, *n.* In *bricklaying*, a

part of the tiling which projects beyond the principal rafters, in buildings where there is a gable, or kirkinhead. *Encyc.*

B'ARGEMAN, *n.* The man who manages a barge.

B'ARGEMASTER, *n.* The proprietor of a barge, conveying goods for hire. *Blackstone.*

B'ARGER, *n.* The manager of a barge.

BARIL'LA, *n.* [Sp.] A plant cultivated in Spain for its ashes, from which the purest kind of mineral alkali is obtained; used in making glass and soap, and in bleaching linen. The plant is cut and laid in heaps, and burnt, the salts running into a hole in the ground where they form a vitrified lump. *Encyc.*

2. The alkali procured from this plant.

BAR'ITONE, [See *Barytone.*]

BAR'IUM, *n.* The metallic basis of baryte or baryta, which is an oxyd of *barium.* *Davy.*

B'ARK, *n.* [Dan. *bark*; Sw. *barck*; G. *borke*; probably from stripping, separating.]

1. The rind or exterior covering of a tree, corresponding to the skin of an animal. This is composed of the cuticle or epidermis, the outer bark or cortex, and the inner bark or liber. The rough broken matter on bark is, by the common people of New-England, called *ross.*

2. By way of distinction, Peruvian Bark.

B'ARK, *v. t.* To peel; to strip off bark. Also to cover or inclose with bark.

B'ARK, } *n.* [Ir. *barc*; Fr. *barque*; Russ.
BARQUE, } *barka*; It. and Sp. *barca.*]

A small ship; but appropriately, a ship which carries three masts without a mizen top sail. The English mariners, in the coal trade, apply this name to a broad-sterned ship without a figure-head. *Encyc. Mar. Dict.*

Water-barks, in Holland, are small vessels, for conveying fresh water from place to place, the hold of which is filled with water. *Encyc.*

B'ARK, *v. i.* [Sax. *beorcan*, *byrcan*, to bark.]

1. To make the noise of dogs, when they threaten or pursue.

2. To clamor at; to pursue with unreasonable clamor or reproach. It is followed by *at.*

To *bark at* sleeping fame. *Spenser.*

B'ARK-BARED, *a.* Stripped of the bark. *Mortimer.*

B'ARK-BOUND, *a.* Having the bark too firm or close, as with trees. This disease is cured by slitting the bark. *Encyc.*

B'ARKED, *pp.* Stripped of the bark; peeled; also covered with bark.

B'ARKER, *n.* One who barks, or clamors unreasonably; one who strips trees of their bark.

B'ARK-GALLED, *a.* Having the bark galled, as with thorns. This defect is cured by binding on clay. *Encyc.*

B'ARKING, *ppr.* Stripping off bark; making the noise of dogs; clamoring; covering with bark.

B'ARKY, *a.* Consisting of bark; containing bark. *Shak.*

B'ARLEY, *n.* [W. *barlys*; Sax. *bere.* Qu. L. *far*, Gr. πυρος, Heb. בר bar, corn. In the Saxon chronicle, An. 1124, it is written *bærlie.* Owen renders it bread-corn, from *bara*, bread.]

A species of valuable grain, used especially for making malt, from which are distilled liquors of extensive use, as *beer*, *ale* and *porter.* It is of the genus *hordeum*, consisting of several species. Those principally cultivated in England, are the common spring barley, the long eared barley, the winter or square barley, by some called *big*, and the sprat or battledore barley. This grain is used in medicine, as possessing emollient, diluent, and expectorant qualities. *Encyc. Miller. Arbuthnot.*

B'ARLEY-BRAKE, *n.* A rural play; a trial of swiftness. *Sidney.*

B'ARLEY-BROTH, *n.* A low word for strong beer. *Shak.*

B'ARLEY-CORN, *n.* [See *Corn.*] A grain of barley; the third part of an inch in length; hence originated our measures of length. *Johnson.*

B'ARLEY-MOW, *n.* A mow of barley, or the place where barley is deposited. *Gay.*

B'ARLEY-SUGAR, *n.* Sugar boiled till it is brittle, formerly with a decoction of barley.

B'ARLEY-WATER, *n.* A decoction of barley, which is reputed soft and lubricating, and much used in medicine.

French barley and *pearl barley* are used for making decoctions. These are made by separating the grain from its coat. The pearl barley is reduced to the size of a small shot.

B'ARM, *n.* [Sax. *beorm.* Qu. L. *fermentum*, from *ferveo*; or *beer-rahm*, beer cream; or W. *berwi*, to boil.]

Yeast; the scum rising upon beer, or other malt liquors, when fermenting, and used as leaven in bread to make it swell, causing it to be softer, lighter, and more delicate. It may be used in liquors to make them ferment or work. *Johnson. Encyc.*

B'ARMY, *a.* Containing barm, or yeast. *Bacon. Shak.*

B'ARN, *n.* [Sax. *berern*, from *bere*, barley, and *ærn*, or *ern*, a close place or repository.]

A covered building for securing grain, hay, flax, and other productions of the earth. In *the northern states of America*, the farmers generally use barns for stabling their horses and cattle; so that among them, a barn is both a cornhouse or grange, and a stable.

B'ARNACLE, *n.* [Port. *bernaca*, the Solan goose; Fr. *barnacle* or *barnaque*; L. *perna*, a shell-fish.]

1. A shell which is often found on the bottoms of ships, rocks and timber, below the surface of the sea.

2. A species of goose, found in the northern seas, but visiting more southern climates in winter. The forehead and cheeks are white, but the upper part of the body and neck is black. Formerly, a strange notion prevailed, that these birds grew out of wood, or rather out of the barnacles attached to wood in the sea. Hence the name. It is written also *Bernacle.* *Pennant.*

3. In the plural, an instrument consisting of two branches joined at one end with a hinge, to put upon a horse's nose, to confine him, for shoeing, bleeding, or dressing. *Encyc.*

BAR'OLITE, *n.* [Gr. βαρος, weight, and λιθος, a stone.]

Carbonate of baryte. Its color is usually a light yellowish gray; sometimes whitish, or with a tinge of green. It is strongly translucent. It usually occurs in small masses, which have a fibrous structure; sometimes in distinct crystals.

This mineral is called also Witherite, from Dr. Withering, the discoverer. *Cleaveland. Kirwan. Ure.*

BAROM'ETER, *n.* [Gr. βαρος, weight, and μετρον, measure.]

An instrument for measuring the weight or pressure of the atmosphere, consisting of a glass tube, hermetically sealed at one end, filled with quicksilver, well defecated and purged of air, and inverted in a basin of quicksilver. A column of quicksilver is then supported in the tube, of equal weight with the incumbent atmosphere. This instrument was invented by Torricelli, of Florence, in 1643. Its uses are to indicate changes of weather, and to determine the altitude of mountains, by the falling and rising of the mercury. For this purpose, the tube is fixed to a graduated scale, so that the smallest variation in the column is visible. *Encyc. Johnson.*

BAROMET'RICAL, *a.* Pertaining or relating to the barometer; made by a barometer; as *barometrical* experiments.

BAROMET'RICALLY, *adv.* By means of a barometer. *Pinkerton.*

BAR'ON, *n.* [Fr. *baron*; Sp. *baron* or *varon*; It. *barone*; Sans. *bareru*, *bharta*, a husband. This word, in the middle ages, was written *bar*, *ber*, *var*, *baro*, *paro*, *viro*, *virro*, *viron.* It is the *vir* of the Latins; Sax. *wer*; Ir. *fir*, *fear*; W. *gwr*, for *guir*, *gevir.* See *Spelman's Glossary*, and *Hirt. Pansa. De Bell. Alex.* 42: *Hicks' Sax. Grammar*, 113, 146. The Sax. *wer*, L. *vir*, is doubtless the Shemitic גבר, a man, so named from strength.]

1. In *Great Britain*, a title or degree of nobility; a lord; a peer; one who holds the rank of nobility next below that of a viscount, and above that of a knight or baronet. Originally, the barons, being the feudatories of princes, were the proprietors of land held by honorable service. Hence, in ancient records, the word *barons* comprehends all the nobility. All such in England had, in early times, a right to sit in parliament. As a *baron* was the proprietor of a manor, and each manor had its *court-baron*; hence the *barons* claimed, and to this day enjoy, the right of judging in the last resort; a right pertaining to the house of lords, or peers, as the representatives of the ancient *barons*, *land-holders*, *manor-holders.*

Anciently, *barons* were greater, or such as held their lands of the king *in capite*; or lesser, such as held their lands of the greater barons by military service *in capite.*

The title of *baron* is no longer attached to the possession of a manor, but given by the king's letters patent, or writ of summons to parliament; that is, the dignity is personal, and not territorial.

The radical word, *vir, fir*, a man, is Celtic, as well as Teutonic; but the word *baron* was not known in the British isles, till introduced from the continent under the Norman princes. *Spelman. Blackstone. Encyc. Cowel.*

2. Baron is a title of certain officers, as *barons of the exchequer*, who are the four judges who try cases between the king and his subjects, relating to the revenue. *Barons of the Cinque Ports* are members of the House of Commons, elected by the seven Cinque Ports, two for each port. These ports are Dover, Sandwich, Romney, Hastings, Hythe, Winchelsea, and Rye. *Blackstone.*

3. In *law*, a husband; as *baron* and *feme*, husband and wife.

BAR'ONAGE, *n.* The whole body of barons or peers.

2. The dignity of a baron.

3. The land which gives title to a baron. *Johnson.*

BAR'ONESS, *n.* A baron's wife or lady.

BAR'ONET, *n.* [Fr. dimin of *baron.*]

A dignity or degree of honor, next below a baron, and above a knight; having precedency of all knights except those of the garter, and being the only knighthood that is hereditary. The order was founded by James I. in 1611, and is given by patent. *Johnson. Blackstone.*

BARO'NIAL, *a.* Pertaining to a baron. *Encyc.*

BAR'ONY, *n.* The lordship, honor, or fee of a baron, whether spiritual or temporal. This lordship is held in chief of the king, and gives title to the possessor, or baron. *Johnson. Encyc.*

BAR'OSCOPE, *n.* [Gr. βαρος, weight, and σκοπεω, to view.]

An instrument to show the weight of the atmosphere; superseded by the *Barometer.*

BAROSCOP'IC, *a.* Pertaining to or determined by the baroscope.

BAROSEL'ENITE, *n.* [Gr. βαρος, weight, or βαρυς, heavy, and *selenite.*]

A mineral; sulphate of baryte; heavy spar. *Kirwan. Cleaveland.*

BAR'RA, *n.* In *Portugal* and *Spain*, a long measure for cloths. In Valencia, 13 barras make $12\frac{4}{7}$ yards English; in Castile, 7 are equal to $6\frac{4}{7}$ yards; in Arragon, 3 make $2\frac{4}{7}$ yards. *Encyc.*

BARRACA'DA, *n.* A fish, about fifteen inches in length, of a dusky color on the back, and a white belly, with small black spots. *Dict. of Nat. Hist.*

BAR'RACAN, *n.* [It. *baracane;* Sp. *barragan;* Fr. *bouracan.*]

A thick, strong stuff, something like camelot; used for clokes, surtouts, and other outer garments.

BAR'RACK, *n.* [Sp. *barraca;* Fr. *baraque.* It seems to be formed like Sax. *parruc*, a park, an inclosure.]

A hut or house for soldiers, especially in garrison. In *Spain*, a hut or cabin for fishermen.

BAR'RACK-MASTER, *n.* The officer who superintends the barracks of soldiers. *Swift.*

BARRACU'DA, *n.* A species of fish of the pike kind, found in the seas about the Bahamas and W. Indies, of ten feet in length. The color is deep brown, and the fish is very voracious. The flesh is disagreeable and sometimes poisonous. *Catesby. Pennant.*

BAR'RATOR, *n.* [Old Fr. *barat*, strife, deceit; Cimbric, *baratton;* Ice. and Scandinavian, *baratta*, contest; It. *baratta*, strife, quarrel; *barattare*, to barter, to cheat; Sp. *barato*, fraud, deceit; *baratar*, to barter, to deceive. The radical sense is to *turn, wind* and *twist*, whence to strive; L. *verto;* Eng. *barter.* See *Barter.*]

1. One who frequently excites suits at law; a common mover and maintainer of suits and controversies; an encourager of litigation. *Coke. Blackstone.*

2. The master of a ship, who commits any fraud, in the management of the ship, or in relation to his duties as master, by which the owner or insurers are injured.

BAR'RATRY, *n.* The practice of exciting and encouraging lawsuits and quarrels. *Coke. Blackstone.*

2. In *commerce*, any species of cheating or fraud, in a shipmaster, by which the owners or insurers are injured; as by running away with the ship, sinking or deserting her, by wilful deviation, or by embezzling the cargo. *Park.*

B'ARRED, *pp.* Fastened with a bar; hindered; restrained; excluded; forbid; striped; checkered.

BAR'REL, *n.* [W. Fr. *baril;* Sp. *barril;* It. *barile;* Arm. *baraz.*]

1. A vessel or cask, of more length than breadth, round and bulging in the middle, made of staves and heading, and bound with hoops.

2. The quantity which a barrel contains. Of wine measure, the English barrel contains $31\frac{1}{2}$ gallons; of beer measure, 36 gallons; of ale, 32 gallons; and of beer-vinegar, 34 gallons.

Of weight, a barrel of Essex butter is 106 pounds; of Suffolk butter, 256; a barrel of herring should contain 32 gallons wine measure, and hold 1000 herrings; a barrel of salmon should contain 42 gallons; a barrel of soap should weigh 256 lbs. *Johnson. Encyc.*

In *America*, the contents of a barrel are regulated by statutes.

In Connecticut, the barrel for liquors must contain $31\frac{1}{2}$ gallons, each gallon to contain 231 cubic inches. In New-York, a barrel of flour by statute must contain either 196 lb. or 228 lb. nett weight. The barrel of beef and pork in New-York and Connecticut, is 200 lbs. In general, the contents of barrels, as defined by statute, in this country, must be from 28 to $31\frac{1}{2}$ gallons.

3. Any thing hollow and long, as the *barrel* of a gun; a tube.

4. A cylinder; as the *barrel* of a watch, within which the spring is coiled, and round which is wound the chain.

5. A cavity behind the tympanum of the ear is called *the barrel of the ear.* It is four or five lines deep, and five or six wide, and covered with a fine membrane. It is more usually called *the cavity of the tympanum.* *Encyc. Johnson.*

BAR'REL, *v. t.* To put in a barrel; to pack in a barrel with salt for preservation, as to *barrel* beef, pork or fish.

BAR'REL-BELLIED, *a.* [See *Belly.*] Having a large belly. *Dryden.*

BAR'RELED, *pp.* Put or packed in a barrel.

BAR'RELING, *ppr.* Putting or packing in a barrel.

BAR'REN, *a.* [from the same root as *bare.*]

1. Not producing young, or offspring; *applied to animals.*

2. Not producing plants; unfruitful; steril; not fertile; or producing little; unproductive; *applied to the earth.*

3. Not producing the usual fruit; *applied to trees*, &c.

4. Not copious; scanty; as a scheme *barren* of hints. *Swift.*

5. Not containing useful or entertaining ideas; as a *barren* treatise.

6. Unmeaning; uninventive; dull; as *barren* spectators. *Shak. Johnson. Qu.*

7. Unproductive; not inventive; as a *barren* mind.

BAR'REN, *n.* In *the States west of the Alleghany*, a word used to denote a tract of land, rising a few feet above the level of a plain, and producing trees and grass. The soil of these *barrens* is not *barren*, as the name imports, but often very fertile. It is usually alluvial, to a depth sometimes of several feet. *Atwater, Journ. of Science.*

2. Any unproductive tract of land; as the pine *barrens* of South Carolina. *Drayton.*

BAR'RENLY, *adv.* Unfruitfully.

BAR'RENNESS, *adv.* The quality of not producing its kind; want of the power of conception; *applied to animals.*

2. Unfruitfulness; sterility; infertility. The quality of not producing at all, or in small quantities; as the *barrenness* of soil.

3. Want of invention; want of the power of producing any thing new; *applied to the mind.*

4. Want of matter; scantiness; as the *barrenness* of a cause. *Hooker.*

5. Defect of emotion, sensibility or fervency; as the *barrenness* of devotion. *Taylor.*

BAR'RENWORT, *n.* [See *Wort.*] A plant, constituting the genus Epimedium, of which the alpinum is the only species; a low herbaceous plant, with a creeping root, having many stalks, each of which has three flowers. *Encyc.*

B'ARRFUL, *a.* Full of obstructions. *Shak.*

BARRICA'DE, *n.* [Fr. *barricade;* It. *barricata;* from It. *barrare*, Sp. *barrear*, to bar.]

1. A fortification made in haste, of trees, earth, palisades, wagons, or any thing that will obstruct the progress of an enemy, or serve for defense or security, against his shot.

2. Any bar or obstruction; that which defends.

3. In *naval architecture*, a strong wooden rail, supported by stanchions, extending across the foremost part of the quarter deck, in ships of war, and filled with rope, mats, pieces of old cable, and full hammocks, to prevent the effect of small shot in time of action. *Encyc.*

BARRICA'DE, *v. t.* To stop up a passage; to obstruct.

2. To fortify with any slight work that prevents the approach of an enemy.

BARRICA'DO. The same as *barricade.*

BAR'RIER, [Fr. *barriere;* It. *barriera;* Sp. *barrera*, a barrier; Sp. *barrear*, to bar or barricade. See *Bar.*]

1. In *fortification*, a kind of fence made in a passage or retrenchment, composed of great stakes, with transums or overthwart rafters, to stop an enemy. *Encyc.*
2. A wall for defense.
3. A fortress or fortified town on the frontier of a country. *Swift.*
4. Any obstruction; any thing which confines, or which hinders approach, or attack; as constitutional *barriers.* *Hopkinson.*
5. A bar to mark the limits of a place; any limit, or boundary; a line of separation. *Pope.*

B'ARRING, *ppr.* Making fast with a bar; obstructing; excluding; preventing; prohibiting; crossing with stripes.

BAR'RISTER, *n.* [from *bar.*] A counselor, learned in the laws, qualified and admitted to plead at the bar, and to take upon him the defense of clients; answering to the advocate or licentiate of other countries. Anciently, barristers were called, in England, apprentices of the law. Outer barristers are pleaders without the bar, to distinguish them from inner barristers, benchers or readers, who have been sometime admitted to plead within the bar, as the king's counsel are. *Johnson. Encyc.*

BAR'ROW, *n.* [Sax. *berewe;* W. *berva;* Ger. *bahre;* D. *berri;* from the root of *bear*, to carry. See *Bear.*]

1. A light small carriage. A *hand-barrow* is a frame covered in the middle with boards, and borne by and between two men.
   A *wheel-barrow*, is a frame with a box, supported by one wheel, and rolled by a single man.
2. A wicker case, in salt works, where the salt is put to drain. *Encyc.*

BAR'ROW, *n.* [Sax. *berga, or beorgh*, a hog; D. *barg*, a *barrow* hog.]

1. In *England*, a hog; and according to Ash, *obsolete. Barrow-grease* is hog's lard.
2. In *America*, a male hog castrated; *a word in common use.*

BAR'ROW, *n.* [Sax. *beara*, or *bearewe*, a grove.]
In the names of places, *barrow* is used to signify a wood or grove.

BAR'ROW, *n.* [Sax. *beorg*, a hill or hillock; *byrgen*, a tomb; G. and D. *bergen*, to conceal, to save.]
A hillock or mound of earth, intended as a repository of the dead. Such barrows are found in England, in the North of the European continent, and in America. They sometimes were formed of stones, and in England called *cairns.* The barrow answers to the *tumulus* of the Latins. [See *Tomb.*]

B'ARSE, *n.* An English name for the common perch. *Dict. of Nat. Hist.*

B'ARSHOT, *n.* [See *Bar* and *Shoot.*]
Double headed shot, consisting of a bar, with a half ball or round head at each end; used for destroying the masts and rigging in naval combat. *Mar. Dict.*

B'ARTER, *v. i.* [Sp. *baratar;* It. *barattare*, to exchange. The primary sense is probably to turn or change, and this gives the sense of deceiving, barratry, as well as of bartering. L. *vario, verto.* Class Br.]
To traffick or trade, by exchanging one commodity for another, in distinction from a sale and purchase, in which money is paid for the commodities transferred.

B'ARTER, *v. t.* To give one thing for another in commerce. It is sometimes followed by *away;* as, to *barter away* goods or honor.

B'ARTER, *n.* The act or practice of trafficking by exchange of commodities; sometimes, perhaps, the thing given in exchange.

B'ARTERED, *pp.* Given in exchange.

B'ARTERER, *n.* One who trafficks by exchange of commodities.

B'ARTERING, *ppr.* Trafficking or trading by an exchange of commodities.

B'ARTERY, *n.* Exchange of commodities in trade. [*Not used.*] *Camden.*

B'ARTON, *n.* [Sax. *bere-ton*, barley-town.]
The demain lands of a manor; the manor itself; and sometimes the out-houses. *Johnson. Blount.*

B'ARTRAM, *n.* [L. *pyrethrum;* Gr. πυρ, fire.]
A plant; pellitory. *Bailey. Johnson.*

BARYSTRON'TIANITE, *n.* [Gr. βαρυς, heavy, and *strontian.*]
A mineral, called also stromnite, from Stromness, in Orkney. It has been found in masses of a grayish white color internally, but externally of a yellowish white. *Traill. Cleaveland. Phillips.*

BARY'TA, BAR'YTE, *n.* [Gr. βαρυς, heavy; βαρυτης, weight.]
Ponderous earth; so called from its great weight, it being the heaviest of the earths. Spec. grav. about 4. Recent discoveries have shown that *baryte* is an oxyd, the basis of which is a metallic substance called *barium.* It is generally found in combination with the sulphuric and carbonic acids, forming the sulphate and carbonate of baryte, the former of which is called *heavy spar.* *Cleaveland. Thomson.*

BARYT'IC, *a.* Pertaining to baryte; formed of baryte, or containing it. *Kirwan.*

BARYTO-CAL'CITE, *n.* [*baryte* and *calx.* See *Calx.*]
A mixture of carbonate of lime with sulphate of baryte, of a dark or light gray color, of various forms. *Kirwan.*

BAR'YTONE, *a.* [Gr. βαρυς, heavy, and τονος, tone.]
Pertaining to or noting a grave deep sound, or male voice. *Walker. Arbuthnot.*

BAR'YTONE, *n.* In *music*, a male voice, the compass of which partakes of the common base and the tenor, but which does not descend so low as the one, nor rise as high as the other.
2. In *Greek Grammar*, a verb which has no accent marked on the last syllable, the grave accent being understood.

BA'SAL, *a.* Pertaining to the base; constituting the base. *Say.*

BASALT', *n. bazalt'.* [Pliny informs us that the Egyptians found in Ethiopia, a species of marble, called *basaltes*, of an iron color and hardness, whence it received its name. Nat. Hist. Lib. 36. Ca. 7. But according to Da Costa, that stone was not the same which now bears the name of *basalt.* Hist. of Fossils. p. 263. If named from its color, it may be allied to the Fr. *basané*, tawny. Lunier refers it to the Ethiopic *basal*, iron, a word I cannot find.]
A dark, grayish black mineral or stone, sometimes bluish or brownish black, and when withered, the surface is grayish or reddish brown. It is amorphous, columnar, tabular or globular. The columnar form is straight or curved, perpendicular or inclined, sometimes nearly horizontal; the diameter of the columns from three inches to three feet, sometimes with transverse semi-spherical joints, in which the convex part of one is inserted in the concavity of another. The forms of the columns generally are pentagonal, hexagonal, or octagonal. It is sometimes found also in rounded masses, either spherical, or compressed and lenticular. These rounded masses are sometimes composed of concentric layers, with a nucleus, and sometimes of prisms radiating from a center. It is heavy and hard. The pillars of the Giant's causey in Ireland, composed of this stone and exposed to the roughest sea for ages, have their angles as perfect as those at a distance from the waves. The English miners call it *cockle;* the German, *shorl*, or *shœrl.* It is called by Kirwan, *Figurate Trap*, from its prismatic forms. *Kirwan. Jameson. Cleaveland.*

BASALT'IC, *a.* Pertaining to basalt; formed of or containing basalt.

BASALT'IFORM, *a.* In the form of basalt; columnar.

BASALT'INE, *n.* Basaltic Hornblend; a variety of common hornblend, so called from its being often found in Basalt. It is also found in lavas and volcanic scoriæ. It is generally in distinct crystals, and its color is a pure black, or slightly tinged with green. It is more foliated than the other varieties, and has been mistaken for mica. *Kirwan. Cleaveland.*
2. A column of basalt. *Kirwan.*

BAS'ANITE, *n. s* as *z.* [Gr. βασανος, the trier. Plin. Lib. 36. Ca. 22. See *Basalt.*]
Lydian stone, or black jasper; a variety of siliceous or flinty slate. Its color is a grayish or bluish black, interspersed with veins of quartz. It is employed to test the purity of gold. *Kirwan. Ure. Cleaveland.*

BASE, *a.* [Fr. *bas*, low; W. *bas;* It. *basso;* Sp. *baxo*, low; W. *basu*, to fall, or lower. See *Abase.*]

1. Low in place. *Obs.* *Spenser.*
2. Mean; vile; worthless; that is, *low* in value or estimation; *used of things.*
3. Of low station; of mean account; without rank, dignity or estimation among men; *used of persons.*
   The *base* shall behave proudly against the honorable. Is. iii.
4. Of mean spirit; disingenuous; illiberal; low; without dignity of sentiment; as a *base* and abject multitude.
5. Of little comparative value; *applied to metals, and perhaps to all metals, except gold and silver.*
6. Deep; grave; *applied to sounds;* as the *base* sounds of a viol. *Bacon.*
7. Of illegitimate birth; born out of wedlock. *Shak.*
8. Not held by honorable tenure. A *base* estate is an estate held by services not honorable, not *in capite*, or by villenage.

Such a tenure is called *base*, or low, and the tenant, a *base* tenant. So writers on the laws of England use the terms, a *base* fee, a *base* court. *Encyc.*

BASE, *n.* [Gr. βασις; L. *basis*; It. *basa*, *base*; Sp. *basa*; Fr. *base*; that which is set, the foundation or bottom.]

1. The bottom of any thing, considered as its support or the part of a thing on which it stands or rests; as the *base* of a column, the pedestal of a statue, the foundation of a house, &c.

In *architecture*, the base of a pillar properly is that part which is between the top of a pedestal and the bottom of the shaft; but when there is no pedestal, it is the part between the bottom of the column and the plinth. Usually it consists of certain spires or circles. The pedestal also has its base. *Encyc.*

2. In *fortification*, the exterior side of the polygon; or that imaginary line which is drawn from the flanked angle of a bastion to the angle opposite to it.

3. In *gunnery*, the least sort of ordnance, the diameter of whose bore is 1 1-4 inch. *Encyc.*

4. The part of any ornament which hangs down, as housings. *Sidney.*

5. The broad part of any thing, as the bottom of a cone.

6. In *old authors*, stockings; armor for the legs. *Hudibras.*

7. The place from which racers or tilters start; the bottom of the field; the carcer or starting post. *Dryden.*

9. The lowest or gravest part in music; improperly written *bass*.

10. A rustic play, called also *bays*, or *prison bars*. *Shak.*

11. In *geometry*, the lowest side of the perimeter of a figure. Any side of a triangle may be called its base, but this term most properly belongs to the side which is parallel to the horizon. In rectangled triangles, the base, properly, is the side opposite to the right angle. The *base* of a solid figure is that on which it stands. The *base* of a conic section is a right line in the hyperbola and parabola, arising from the common intersection of the secant plane and the base of the cone. *Encyc.*

12. In *chimistry*, any body which is dissolved by another body, which it receives and fixes. Thus any alkaline, earthy or metallic substance, combining with an acid, forms a compound or neutral salt, of which it is the *base*. Such salts are called salts with alkaline, earthy or metallic *bases*. *Encyc.*

13. *Thorough base*, in music, is the part performed with base viols or theorbos, while the voices sing and other instruments perform their parts, or during the intervals when the other parts stop. It is distinguished by figures over the notes.

Counter base is a second or double base, when there are several in the same concert. *Encyc.*

BASE, *v. t.* To embase; to reduce the value by the admixture of meaner metals. [*Little used.*] *Bacon.*

2. To found; to lay the base or foundation.

> To *base* and build the commonwealth of man. *Columbiad.*

BA'SE-BORN, *a.* [*base* and *born.*] Born out of wedlock. *Gay.*

2. Born of low parentage.

3. Vile; mean. *Milton.*

BA'SE-COURT, *n.* [Fr. *basse-cour.* See *Court.*]

The back yard, opposed to the chief court in front of a house; the farm yard. *Shak.*

BA'SED, *pp.* Reduced in value; founded.

BA'SELESS, *a.* Without a base; having no foundation, or support.

> The *baseless* fabric of a vision. *Shak.*
>
> The fame how poor that swells our *baseless* pride. *Trumbull.*

BA'SELY, *adv.* In a base manner; meanly; dishonorably. *Dryden.*

2. Illegitimately; in bastardy. *Knolles.*

BA'SEMENT, *n.* In *architecture*, the ground floor, on which the order or columns which decorate the principal story, are placed. *Encyc.*

BA'SE-MINDED, *a.* Of a low spirit or mind; mean. *Camden.*

BA'SE-MINDEDNESS, *n.* Meanness of spirit. *Sandys.*

BA'SENESS, *n.* Meanness; vileness; worthlessness. *Dryden.*

2. Vileness of metal; the quality of being of little comparative value. *Swift.*

3. Bastardy; illegitimacy of birth. *Shak.*

4. Deepness of sound. *Bacon.*

BA'SENET, *n.* A helmet. *Spenser.*

BA'SE-STRING, *n.* The lowest note. *Shak.*

BA'SE-VIOL, *n.* [See *Viol.*] A musical instrument, used for playing the base or gravest part.

BASH, *v. i.* [Heb. בוש, bosh, to be cast down, or confounded. Qu. D. *verbaazen*, to confound. See *Abash.*]

To be ashamed; to be confounded with shame. *Spenser.*

BASHAW', *n.* [Ar. باشا basha; Pers. *pasha*; Sp. *baxa*; It. *bascia*; Turk. *basch*, the head. Qu. D. *baas*, master, and the *bassus* of the *Alemanni* and *Longobards*, in the middle ages. This word is often written most absurdly *pasha*, both by the English and Americans. It should be written and pronounced *pashaw.*]

1. A title of honor in the Turkish dominions; appropriately, the title of the prime vizer, but given to viceroys or governors of provinces, and to generals and other men of distinction. The Turkish bashaws exercise an oppressive authority in their provinces. Hence,

2. A proud, tyrannical, overbearing man.

BASH'FUL, *a.* [See *Bash* and *Abash.*]

1. Properly, having a downcast look; hence very modest.

2. Modest to excess; sheepish. *Shak.*

3. Exciting shame.

BASH'FULLY, *adv.* Very modestly; in a timorous manner.

BASH'FULNESS, *n.* Excessive or extreme modesty; a quality of mind often visible in external appearance, as in blushing, a downcast look, confusion, &c.

2. Vicious or rustic shame. *Sidney.*

BASH'LESS, *a.* Shameless; unblushing. *Spenser.*

BAS'IL, *n.* *s* as *z.* The slope or angle of a tool or instrument, as of a chisel or plane; usually of 12 degrees, but for hard wood, 18 degrees. *Encyc.*

BAS'IL, *v. t.* To grind or form the edge of a tool to an angle. *Moxon.*

BAS'IL, *n.* *s* as *z.* [Fr. *basilic*; It. *basilico.*]

1. A plant of the genus *Ocymum*, of which there are many species, all natives of warm climates. They are fragrant aromatic plants, and one species, the sweet basil, is much used in cookery, especially in France.

BAS'IL, *n.* [Orient. בזן to strip.]

The skin of a sheep tanned; written also *basan*.

BAS'IL-WEED, *n.* Wild basil, a plant of the genus Clinopodium. *Muhlenburg.*

BAS'ILAR, } *a.* *s* as *z.* [See *Basilic.*]
BAS'ILARY,

Chief; an anatomical term applied to several bones, and to an artery of the brain. *Coxe.*

Basilian monks, monks of the order of St. Basil, who founded the order in Pontus. The order still exists, but has less power and celebrity than formerly. *Encyc.*

BAS'ILIC, *n.* *s* as *z.* [Gr. βασιλικη; L. *basilica*; Gr. βασιλευς, a king.]

Anciently, a public hall or court of judicature, where princes and magistrates sat to administer justice. It was a large hall, with aisles, porticoes, tribunes, and tribunals. The bankers also had a part allotted for their residence. These edifices, at first, were the palaces of princes, afterwards courts of justice, and finally converted into churches. Hence *basilic* now signifies a church, chapel, cathedral or royal palace. *Encyc. Sp. and It. Dict.*

BAS'ILIC, *n.* [See *Basil.*] The middle vein of the arm, or the interior branch of the axillary vein, so called by way of eminence. *Encyc. Quincy.*

BAS'ILIC, } *a.* Belonging to the middle vein of the arm.
BASIL'ICAL,

2. Noting a particular nut, the walnut, *basilica nux*.

BASIL'ICON, *n.* *s* as *z.* [Gr. βασιλικος, royal.]

An ointment. This name is given to several compositions in ancient medical writers. At present it is confined to three officinal ointments, distinguished into black, yellow and green basilicon. *Encyc.*

BAS'ILISK, *n.* *s* as *z.* [Gr. βασιλισκος; L. *basiliscus.*]

1. A fabulous serpent, called a cockatrice, and said to be produced from a cock's egg brooded by a serpent. The ancients alledged that its hissing would drive away all other serpents, and that its breath and even its look was fatal. Some writers suppose that a real serpent exists under this name.

2. In *military affairs*, a large piece of ordnance, so called from its supposed resemblance to the serpent of that name, or from its size. This cannon carried a ball of 200 pounds weight, but is not now used. Modern writers give this name to cannon of a smaller size, which the Dutch make 15 feet long, and the French 10, carrying a 48 pound ball. *Encyc.*

BA'SIN, *n.* *básn.* [Fr. *bassin*; Ir. *baisin*; Arm. *baçzin*; It. *bacino*, or *bacile*; Port.

bacia. If the last radical is primarily a palatal letter, this is the German *becken*; D. *bekken.*]

1. A hollow vessel or dish, to hold water for washing, and for various other uses.
2. In *hydraulics*, any reservoir of water.
3. That which resembles a basin in containing water, as a pond, a dock for ships, a hollow place for liquids, or an inclosed part of water, forming a broad space within a strait or narrow entrance; a little bay.
4. Among *glass grinders*, a concave piece of metal by which convex glasses are formed.
5. Among *hatters*, a large shell or case, usually of iron, placed over a furnace, in which the hat is molded into due shape.
6. In *anatomy*, a round cavity between the anterior ventricles of the brain.
7. The scale of a balance, when hollow and round.
8. In *Jewish antiquities*, the laver of the tabernacle.

BA'SIS, *n.* plu. *bases.* [L. and Gr.; the same as *base*, which see.]

1. The foundation of any thing; that on which a thing stands or lies; the bottom or foot of the thing itself, or that on which it rests. *See a full explanation under base.*
2. The ground work or first principle; that which supports.
3. Foundation; support.

The *basis* of public credit is good faith. *Hamilton.*

The *basis* of all excellence is truth. *Johnson.*

4. Basis, in chemistry. See *Base.* No. 12.

B'ASK, *v. i.* [The origin of this word is not obvious. Qu. Ir. *basgaim*, to rest or repose.]

To lie in warmth; to be exposed to genial heat; to be at ease and thriving under benign influences; as, to *bask* in the blaze of day; to *bask* in the sunshine of royal favor. The word includes the idea of some continuance of exposure.

B'ASK, *v. t.* To warm by continued exposure to heat; to warm with genial heat. *Dryden.*

B'ASKED, *pp.* Exposed to warmth, or genial heat.

B'ASKET, *n.* [W. *basged*, or *basgawd*; Ir. *bascaid*; probably from weaving or texture; W. *basg*, a netting or plaiting of splinters.]

1. A domestic vessel made of twigs, rushes, splinters or other flexible things interwoven. The forms and sizes of baskets are very various, as well as the uses to which they are applied; as corn-baskets, clothes-baskets, fruit-baskets, and work-baskets.
2. The contents of a basket; as much as a basket will contain; as, a *basket* of medlars is two bushels. But in general, this quantity is indefinite.

In *military affairs*, baskets of earth sometimes are used on the parapet of a trench, between which the soldiers fire. They serve for defense against small shot. *Encyc.*

B'ASKET, *v. t.* To put in a basket. *Cowper.*

B'ASKET-FISH, *n.* A species of sea-star, or star-fish, of the genus Asterias, and otherwise called the Magellanic star-fish. It has five rays issuing from an angular body, and dividing into innumerable branches. These when extended form a circle of three feet diameter. [See *Asterias.*] *Encyc.*

B'ASKET-HILT, *n.* [See *Hilt.*] A hilt which covers the hand, and defends it from injury, as of a sword. *Hudibras.*

B'ASKET-HILTED, *a.* Having a hilt of basket-work. *Warton.*

B'ASKET-SALT, *n.* Salt made from salt-springs, which is purer, whiter and finer, than common brine salt. *Encyc.*

B'ASKET-WOMAN, *n.* A woman who carries a basket, to and from market.

B'ASKING, *ppr.* Exposing or lying exposed to the continued action of heat or genial warmth.

B'ASKING-SHARK, *n.* The sun-fish of the Irish; a species of *squalus* or shark. This fish is from three to twelve yards in length, or even longer. The upper jaw is much longer than the lower one; the tail is large and the upper part much longer than the lower; the skin is rough, of a deep leaden color on the back, and white on the belly. The fish weighs more than a thousand pounds, and affords a great quantity of oil, which is used for lamps, and to cure bruises, burns, and rheumatic complaints. It is viviparous, and frequents the northern seas. [See *Squalus.*] *Pennant. Encyc.*

B'ASQUISH, *a.* *bàskish.* Pertaining to the people or language of Biscay. *Brown.*

B'ASS, *n.* [It has no plural.] The name of several species of fish. In *England*, this name is given to a species of perch, called by some the sea-wolf, from its voracity, and resembling, in a degree, the trout in shape, but having a larger head. It weighs about fifteen pounds. In *the northern states of America*, this name is given to a striped fish which grows to the weight of 25 or 30 pounds, and which enters the rivers; the *perca ocellata.*

A species of striped fish, of a darker color, with a large head, is called sea-bass, as it is never found in fresh water. This fish grows to two or three pounds weight. Both species are well tasted, but the proper bass is a very white and delicious food. *Prince. Belknap.*

B'ASS, *n.* The linden, lime or tiel tree; called also *bass-wood.* [See *Bast.*]

2. [pron. *bas.*] A mat to kneel on in churches.

BASS, *n.* In *music*, the *base*; the deepest or gravest part of a tune. This word is thus written in imitation of the Italian *basso*, which is the Eng. *base*, low; yet with the pronunciation of *base* and plural *bases*, a gross error that ought to be corrected; as the word used in pronunciation is the English word *base.*

BASS, *v. t.* To sound in a deep tone. *Shak.*

BASS-RELIE'F, *n.* In English, *base-relief.* [From It. *basso*, low, and *rilevare*, to raise; whence *rilievo*, raised work. See *Lift* and *Relief.*]

Sculpture, whose figures do not stand out far from the ground or plane on which they are formed. When figures do not protuberate so as to exhibit the entire body, they are said to be done *in relief*; and when they are low, flat or little raised from the plane, the work is said to be in *low relief.* When the figures are so raised as to be well distinguished, they are said to be *bold, strong*, or *high, alto relievo.* [See *Relief.*] *Encyc.*

BASS-VIOL, *n.* [See *Base-viol.*]

BAS'SA. [See *Bashaw.*]

BAS'SET, *n.* [Fr. *bassette.*] A game at cards, said to have been invented at Venice, by a nobleman, who was banished for the invention. The game being introduced into France by the Venetian embassador, Justiniani, in 1674, it was prohibited by severe edicts. *Encyc.*

BAS'SET, *v. i.* [See *Basil.*] Among coal diggers, to incline upwards. Thus a vein of coal *bassets*, when it takes a direction towards the surface of the earth. This is called *cropping*, and is opposed to *dipping.* *Encyc.*

BAS'SETING, *ppr.* Having a direction upwards.

BAS'SETING, *n.* The upward direction of a vein in a coal mine.

BASSO-CONCERTANTE, in *music*, is the base of the little chorus, or that which plays throughout the whole piece. *Bailey.*

BASSO-CONTINUO, thorough base, which see under *base.* *Bailey.*

BASSO-REPIENO, is the base of the grand chorus, which plays only occasionally, or in particular parts. *Bailey.*

BASSO-RELIEVO. [See *Base relief.*]

BASSO-VIOLINO, is the base of the base-viol. *Bailey.*

BAS'SOCK, *n.* The same as *bass*, a mat.

BASSOON', *n.* [Fr. *basson*; It. *bassone*, from *basso*, low.]

A musical wind instrument, blown with a reed, and furnished with eleven holes, which are stopped, as in other large flutes. Its compass comprehends three octaves. Its diameter at bottom is nine inches, and for convenience of carriage it is divided into two parts; whence it is called also a *fagot.* It serves for the base in a concert of hautboys, flutes, &c. *Johnson. Encyc. Busby.*

BASSOON'IST, *n.* A performer on the bassoon. *Busby.*

B'AST, *n.* [Qu. D. and Dan. *bast*, bark, or from twisting.]

A rope or cord, made of the bark of the lime tree, bass-wood or linden; or the bark made into ropes and mats. *Ash. Bailey.*

B'ASTARD, *n.* [Arm. *bastard*; Ir. *basdard*; Fr. *bâtard*; D. *bastaard*; G. *bastart*; It. and Sp. *bastardo*; W. *bastarz*; *basu*, to fall, whence *base*, and *tarz*, growth, issue, a sprout.]

A natural child; a child begotten and born out of wedlock; an illegitimate or spurious child. By the civil and canon laws, a bastard becomes a legitimate child, by the intermarriage of the parents, at any future time. But by the laws of this country, as by those of England, a child, to be legitimate, must at least be *born* after the lawful marriage. *Blackstone.*

Bastard eigne', or bastard elder, in law, is when a man has a bastard son, and afterward marries the mother, and has a legitimate son, called *mulier puisne*, or younger. *Blackstone.*

B'ASTARD, *n.* A kind of sweet wine. [*Not in use.*] *Shak.*

B'ASTARD, *a.* Begotten and born out of lawful matrimony; illegitimate.

2. Spurious; not genuine; false; supposititious; adulterate. In this sense, it is applied to things which resemble those which are genuine, but are really not genuine; as a *bastard* hope, *bastard* honors. *Shak. Temple.*

In military affairs, *bastard* is applied to pieces of artillery which are of an unusual make or proportion, whether longer or shorter, as the double culverin extraordinary, half or quarter culverin extraordinary. *Encyc.*

Bastard-Flower-fence, a plant, a species of *Adenanthera.*

Bastard-hemp, a plant, a species of *Datisca*, false hemp.

Bastard-Rocket, dyers-weed, or wild woad, a species of *Reseda.*

Bastard-Star of Bethlehem, a plant, a species of *Albuca.*

Bastard-Scarlet, a red color dyed with bale-madder.

B'ASTARD, *v. t.* To make or determine to be a bastard. *Bacon.*

B'ASTARDISM, *n.* The state of a bastard.

B'ASTARDIZE, *v. t.* To make or prove to be a bastard; to convict of being a bastard; to declare legally, or decide a person to be illegitimate.

> The law is so indulgent as not to *bastardize* the child, if born, though not begotten, in lawful wedlock. *Blackstone.*

2. To beget a bastard. *Shak.*

B'ASTARDLY, *adv.* In the manner of a bastard; spuriously. *Donne.*

B'ASTARDS, an appellation given to a faction or troop of bandits, who ravaged Guienne in France in the 14th century; supposed to have been headed by the illegitimate sons of noblemen, who were excluded from the rights of inheritance. *Mezeray.*

B'ASTARDY, *n.* A state of being a bastard, or begotten and born out of lawful wedlock, which condition disables the person from inheriting an estate. *Blackstone.*

BASTARN'IC, *a.* Pertaining to the Basternæ, ancient inhabitants of the Carpathian mountains. *D'Anville.*

Bastarnic Alps, the Carpathian mountains, between Poland, Hungary and Transylvania; so called from the ancient inhabitants, the *Bastarnæ.* *D'Anville.*

BÂSTE, *v. t.* [Arm. *baz;* Fr. *bâton*, for *baston;* Sp. *baston;* It. *bastone*, a stick or club.]

1. To beat with a stick.

2. To drip butter or fat upon meat, as it turns upon the spit, in roasting; to moisten with fat or other liquid. *Swift.*

BÂSTE, *v. t.* [Sp. *bastear;* It. *imbastire*, to baste; It. *basta*, a long stitch.]

To sew with long stitches; to sew slightly.

BÂSTED, *pp.* Beat with a stick; moistened with fat or other matter in roasting; sewed together with long stitches, or slightly.

BAS'TILE, *n.* [Fr., from *bâtir, bastir*, to build.]

An old castle in Paris, built between 1369 and 1383, used as a state prison, and converted to the purpose of confining men for life, who happened to incur the resentment or jealousy of the French monarchs. It was demolished by the enraged populace in 1789.

BASTINA'DE, BASTINA'DO, *n.* [Fr. *bastonnade;* Sp. *bastonada;* It. *bastonata*, from *bastone*, a stick or staff. See *Baste.*]

A sound beating with a stick or cudgel; the blows given with a stick or staff. This name is given to a punishment in use among the Turks, of beating an offender on the soles of his feet.

BASTINA'DE, BASTINA'DO, *v. t.* To beat with a stick or cudgel.

BÂSTING, *ppr.* Beating with a stick; moistening with dripping; sewing together with long stitches.

BÂSTING, *n.* A beating with a stick; a moistening with dripping; a sewing together slightly with long stitches.

BAS'TION, *n. bas'chun.* [Fr. and Sp. *bastion;* It. *bastione;* probably from *bastir, bâtir*, to build, to set or found.]

A huge mass of earth, usually faced with sods, sometimes with brick, or stones, standing out from a rampart, of which it is a principal part; formerly called a *bulwark.* Bastions are solid or hollow. A *flat* bastion is made in the middle of the curtain, when it is too long to be defended by the bastions in its extremes. A *cut* bastion has its point cut off and instead of it a re-entering angle, or an angle inwards, with two points outward. A *composed* bastion has two sides of the interior polygon unequal, which makes the gorges unequal. A *demibastion* is composed of one face only, with one flank and a demigorge. A *double* bastion is one raised on the plane of another. *Encyc.*

BAS'TO, *n.* The ace of clubs at quadrille.

BAS'TON, or **BATOON'**, *n.* [Sp. See *Baste.*]

In *architecture*, a round molding in the base of a column; called also a *tore*, [torus.] *Encyc.*

BAT, *n.* [Sax. *bat;* Ir. *bat, bata;* Russ. *bot;* allied to *beat.*]

1. A heavy stick or club; a piece of wood with one end thicker or broader than the other.

2. Bat or bate, a small copper coin of Germany, with a small mixture of silver, worth four crutzers. Also a coin of Switzerland, worth five livres. *Encyc.*

3. A term given by miners to shale or bituminous shale. *Kirwan.*

BAT, *v. i.* To manage a bat, or play with one. *Mason.*

BAT, *n.* [Rab. and Tal. באות, בותא, or בואת *Buxtorf.* I have not found this word in any European language, except in English.]

A race of quadrupeds, technically called *Vespertilio*, of the order *primates*, in Linne's system. The fore feet have the toes connected by a membrane, expanded into a kind of wings, by means of which the animals fly. The species are numerous. Of these, the vampire or Ternate bat inhabits Africa and the Oriental Isles. These animals fly in flocks from isle to isle, obscuring the sun by their numbers. Their wings when extended measure five or six feet. They live on fruits; but are said sometimes to draw blood from persons when asleep. The bats of the northern latitudes are small; they are viviparous and suckle their young. Their skin resembles that of a mouse. They enter houses in pleasant summer evenings, feed upon moths, flies, flesh, and oily substances, and are torpid during the winter. *Encyc.*

BAT'-FOWLER, *n.* One who practices, or is pleased with bat-fowling. *Barrington.*

BAT'-FOWLING, *n.* A mode of catching birds at night, by holding a torch or other light, and beating the bush or perch where they roost. The birds flying to the light are caught with nets or otherwise. *Cowel. Encyc.*

BA'TABLE, *a.* [See *Bate* and *Debate.*] Disputable. The land between England and Scotland, which, when the kingdoms were distinct, was a subject of contention, was called *batable* ground. *Cowel. Encyc.*

BATA'TAS, *n.* A species of tick or mite, found on the potatoes of Surinam. Also the Peruvian name of the *sweet potatoe.* *Encyc.*

BATA'VIAN, *a.* [from *Batavi*, the people who inhabited the isle.]

Pertaining to the isle of Betaw in Holland, between the Rhine and the Waal. But more generally, the word denotes what appertains to Holland in general.

BATA'VIAN, *n.* A native of Betaw, or of the Low Countries.

BATCH, *n.* [D. *bakzel;* G. *gebäck;* from *bake.*]

1. The quantity of bread baked at one time; a baking of bread.

2. Any quantity of a thing made at once, or so united as to have like qualities. *B. Jonson.*

BATE, *n.* [Sax. *bate*, contention. It is probably from the root of *beat.* See *Debate.*]

Strife; contention; retained in *make-bate.*

BATE, *v. t.* [Fr. *battre*, to *beat*, to *batter;* but perhaps from *abattre*, to *beat* down. The literal sense is, to beat, strike, thrust; to force down. See *Beat.*]

To lessen by retrenching, deducting or reducing; as, to *bate* the wages of the laborer; to *bate* good cheer. *Locke. Dryden.*

[We now use *abate.*]

BATE, *v. i.* To grow or become less; to remit or retrench a part; with *of.*

> Abate thy speed and I will *bate of* mine. *Dryden.*

Spenser uses *bate* in the sense of sinking, driving in, penetrating; a sense regularly deducible from that of *beat*, to thrust.

> Yet there the steel staid not, but inly *bate*
> Deep in the flesh, and open'd wide a red flood gate.

BATE-BREEDING, *a.* Breeding strife. [*Not used.*] *Shak.*

BA'TEFUL, *a.* Contentious; given to strife; exciting contention. *Sidney.*

BA'TELESS, *a.* Not to be abated. *Shak.*

BA'TEMENT, *n.* Abatement; deduction; diminution.

[*Bate*, with its derivatives, is, I believe, little used, or wholly obsolete in the U. States.]

BATEAU, *n. batto'.* [Fr. from L. *batillum.*] A light boat, long in proportion to its breadth, and wider in the middle than at the ends.

BAT'ENITES, BAT'ENISTS, or **BATE'-NIANS,** *n.* A sect of apostates from Mohammedism, who professed the abominable practices of the Ismaelians and Kirmatians. The word signifies *esoteric,* or persons of inward light. [See *Assassins.*]

BAT'FUL, *a.* [See *Batten.*] Rich, fertile, as land. [*Not in use.*] *Mason.*

B'ATH, *n.* [Sax. *bæth, batho,* a bath; *bathian,* to bathe; W. *badh,* or *baz;* D. G. Sw. Dan. *bad,* a *bath;* Ir. *bath,* the sea; Old Phrygian *bedu,* water. Qu. W. *bozi,* to immerse.]

1. A place for bathing; a convenient vat or receptacle of water for persons to plunge or wash their bodies in. Baths are warm or tepid, hot or cold, more generally called *warm* and *cold.* They are also *natural* or *artificial. Natural* baths are those which consist of spring water, either hot or cold, which is often impregnated with iron, and called chalybeate, or with sulphur, carbonic acid, and other mineral qualities. These waters are often very efficacious in scorbutic, bilious, dyspeptic and other complaints.

2. A place in which heat is applied to a body immersed in some substance. Thus,

A *dry* bath is made of hot sand, ashes, salt, or other matter, for the purpose of applying heat to a body immersed in them.

A *vapor* bath is formed by filling an apartment with hot steam or vapor, in which the body sweats copiously, as in Russia; or the term is used for the application of hot steam to a diseased part of the body. *Encyc. Tooke.*

A *metalline* bath is water impregnated with iron or other metallic substance, and applied to a diseased part. *Encyc.*

In *chimistry,* a wet bath is formed by hot water in which is placed a vessel containing the matter which requires a softer heat than the naked fire.

In *medicine,* the *animal* bath is made by wrapping the part affected in a warm skin just taken from an animal. *Coxe.*

3. A house for bathing. In some eastern countries, baths are very magnificent edifices.

4. A Hebrew measure containing the tenth of a homer, or seven gallons and four pints, as a measure for liquids; and three pecks and three pints, as a dry measure. *Calmet.*

B'ATH-ROOM, *n.* An apartment for bathing. *Tooke.*

BATHE, *v. t.* [Sax. *bathian,* to wash. See *Bath.* Qu. W. *bozi,* to immerse.]

1. To wash the body, or some part of it, by immersion, as in a bath; it often differs from ordinary washing in a longer application of water, to the body or to a particular part, as for the purpose of cleansing or stimulating the skin.

2. To wash or moisten, for the purpose of making soft and supple, or for cleansing, as a wound.

3. To moisten or suffuse with a liquid; as, to *bathe* in tears or blood.

BATHE, *v. i.* To be or lie in a bath; to be in water, or in other liquid, or to be immersed in a fluid, as in a bath; as, to *bathe* in fiery floods. *Shak.*

BA'THED, *pp.* Washed as in a bath; moistened with a liquid; bedewed.

BA'THER, *n.* One who bathes; one who immerses himself in water, or who applies a liquid to himself or to another. *Tooke.*

BA'THING, *ppr.* Washing by immersion, or by applying a liquid; moistening; fomenting.

BA'THING, *n.* The act of bathing, or washing the body in water. *Mason.*

BA'THING-TUB, *n.* A vessel for bathing, usually made either of wood or tin. In the Royal Library at Paris, I saw a bathing-tub of porphyry, of beautiful form and exquisite workmanship.

BA'THOS, *n.* [Gr. βαθος; allied to Eng. *bottom,* and perhaps to W. *bozi,* to immerse.]

The art of sinking in poetry. *Arbuthnot.*

BA'TING, *ppr.* [from *bate.*] Abating; taking away; deducting; excepting.

Children have few ideas, *bating* some faint ideas of hunger and thirst. *Locke.*

BAT'INIST. [See *Batenites.*]

BAT'IST, *n.* A fine linen cloth made in Flanders and Picardy, of three different kinds or thicknesses. *Encyc*

BAT'LET, *n.* [from *bat.*] A small bat, or square piece of wood with a handle, for beating linen when taken out of the buck. *Johnson.*

BAT'MAN, *n.* A weight used in Smyrna, of six okes, each of 400 drams; equal to 16 lbs. 6 oz. 15 dr. English.

BATOON' or **BAT'ON,** *n.* [Fr. *bâton* from *baston.* See *Baste.*]

A staff or club; a marshal's staff; a truncheon; a badge of military honors. *Johnson.*

BAT'RACHITE, *n.* [Gr. βατραχος, a frog.] A fossil or stone in color resembling a frog. *Ash.*

BAT'RACHOMYOM'ACHY, *n.* [Gr. βατραχος, a frog, μυς, a mouse, and μαχη, a battle.]

The battle between the frogs and mice; a burlesque poem ascribed to Homer.

BATRA'CIAN, *a.* [Gr. βατραχος, a frog.] Pertaining to frogs; an epithet designating an order of animals, including frogs, toads and similar animals. *Barnes.*

BATRA'CIAN, *n.* An animal of the order above mentioned.

BAT'TABLE, *a.* Capable of cultivation. [*Not in use.*] *Burton.*

BAT'TAILANT, *n.* [See *Battle.*] A combatant. [*Not used.*] *Shelton.*

BAT'TAILOUS, *a.* [See *Battle.*] Warlike; having the form or appearance of an army arrayed for battle; marshaled, as for an attack. *Milton. Fairfax.*

BATTAL'IA, *n.* [Sp. *batalla;* It. *battaglia,* battle. See *Battle.*]

1. The order of battle; troops arrayed in their proper brigades, regiments, battalions, &c., as for action.

2. The main body of an army in array, distinguished from the wings. *Johnson.*

BATTAL'ION, *n.* [Fr. *bataillon.* See *Battle.*]

A body of infantry, consisting of from 500 to 800 men; so called from being originally a body of men arrayed for battle. A battalion is generally a body of troops next below a regiment. Sometimes a battalion composes a regiment; more generally a regiment consists of two or more battalions. *Johnson. Encyc.*

Shakspeare uses the word for an army.

BATTAL'IONED, *a.* Formed into battalions. *Barlow.*

BAT'TEL, *n.* [See *Battle.*]

In *law,* wager of battel, a species of trial for the decision of causes between parties. This species of trial is of high antiquity, among the rude military people of Europe. It was introduced into England, by William, the Norman Conqueror, and used in three cases only; in the court martial, or court of chivalry or honor; in appeals of felony; and in issues joined upon a writ of right. The contest was had before the judges, on a piece of ground inclosed, and the combatants were bound to fight till the stars appeared, unless the death of one party or victory sooner decided the contest. It is no longer in use. *Blackstone.*

BATTEL, *v. i.* To grow fat. [*Not in use.*] [See *batten.*]

2. To stand indebted in the college books at Oxford, for provisions and drink, from the buttery. Hence a *batteler* answers to a *sizer* at Cambridge.

BAT'TEL, *n.* An account of the expenses of a student at Oxford.

BAT'TEL, *a.* [See *Batten.*] Fertile; fruitful. [*Not used.*] *Hooker.*

BAT'TELER, } *n.* A student at Oxford.
BAT'TLER, }

BAT'TEMENT, *n.* [Fr.] A beating; striking; impulse. [*Not in use.*] *Darwin, Zoon.*

BAT'TEN, *v. t.* *bat'n.* [Russ. *botiayu.* Qu. Ar. بَدَنَ badana, to be fat; or فَدَّنَ faddana, to fatten. See *Fat.*]

1. To fatten; to make fat; to make plump by plenteous feeding. *Milton.*

2. To fertilize or enrich land. *Philips.*

BAT'TEN, *v. i.* To grow or become fat; to live in luxury, or to grow fat in ease and luxury. *Dryden.*

The pampered monarch *battening* in ease. *Garth.*

BAT'TEN, *n.* A piece of board or scantling, of a few inches in breadth, used in making doors and windows. It is not as broad as a pannel. *Encyc.*

BAT'TEN, *v. t.* To form with battens.

BAT'TER, *v. t.* [Fr. *battre;* Sp. *batir;* It. *battere;* L. *batuo,* to beat. See *Beat.*]

1. To beat with successive blows; to beat with violence, so as to bruise, shake, or demolish; as, to *batter* a wall.

2. To wear or impair with beating; as a *battered* pavement; a *battered* jade. *Dryden. Pope.*

3. To attack with a battering ram.

4. To attack with heavy artillery, for the purpose of making a breach in a wall or rampart.

BAT'TER, *v. i.* To swell, bulge or stand out, as a timber or side of a wall from its foundation. *Moxon.*

BAT'TER, *n.* [from *beat* or *batter.*]

A mixture of several ingredients, as flour, eggs, salt, &c., beaten together with some liquor, used in cookery. *King.*

BAT'TERED, *pp.* Beaten; bruised, broken, impaired by beating or wearing.

BAT'TERER, *n.* One who batters or beats.

BAT'TERING, *ppr.* Beating; dashing against; bruising or demolishing by beating.

BAT'TERING-RAM, *n.* In *antiquity*, a military engine used to beat down the walls of besieged places. It was a large beam, with a head of iron somewhat resembling the head of a ram, whence its name. It was suspended by ropes in the middle to a beam which was supported by posts, and balanced so as to swing backwards and forwards, and was impelled by men against the wall. It was sometimes mounted on wheels.

BAT'TERY, *n.* [Fr. *batterie*; Sp. *bateria*; It. *batteria.* See *Beat.*]

1. The act of battering, or beating.
2. The instrument of battering.
3. In the *military art*, a parapet thrown up to cover the gunners and others employed about them, from the enemy's shot, with the guns employed. Thus, *to erect a battery*, is to form the parapet and mount the guns. The term is applied also to a number of guns ranged in order for battering, and to mortars used for a like purpose.

Cross batteries are two batteries which play athwart each other, forming an angle upon the object battered.

Battery d'enfilade, is one which scours or sweeps the whole line or length.

Battery en echarpe, is that which plays obliquely.

Battery de revers, is that which plays upon the enemy's back.

Camerade battery, is when several guns play at the same time upon one place. *Encyc.*

4. In *law*, the unlawful beating of another. The least violence or the touching of another in anger is a battery. *Blackstone.*
5. In *electrical apparatus and experiments*, a number of coated jars placed in such a manner, that they may be charged at the same time, and discharged in the same manner. This is called *an electrical battery.*
6. *Galvanic battery*, a pile or series of plates of copper and zink, or of any substances susceptible of galvanic action.

BAT'TING, *n.* The management of a bat play. *Mason.*

BAT'TISH, *a.* [from *bat*, an animal.] Resembling a *bat*; as a *battish* humor. *Vernon.*

BAT'TLE, *n.* [Fr. *bataille*; W. *batel*, a drawing of the bow, a battle; Sp. *batalla*; It. *battaglia*, from *beating.* See *Beat.* Owen supposes the Welsh *batel*, to be from *tel*, tight, stretched, compact, and the word primarily to have expressed the drawing of the bow. This is probably an error. The first battles of men were with clubs, or some weapons used in *beating*, striking. Hence the club of Hercules. And although the moderns use different weapons, still a battle is some mode of beating or striking.]

1. A fight, or encounter between enemies, or opposing armies; an engagement. It is usually applied to armies or large bodies of men; but in popular language, the word is applied to an encounter between small bodies, between individuals, or inferior animals. It is also more generally applied to the encounters of land forces than of ships; the encounters of the latter being called *engagements.* But *battle* is applicable to any combat of enemies.
2. A body of forces, or division of an army. *Bacon.*

The main body, as distinct from the van and rear. *Obs.* *Hayward.*

To give battle, is to attack an enemy; *to join battle*, is properly to meet the attack; but perhaps this distinction is not always observed.

A pitched battle is one in which the armies are previously drawn up in form, with a regular disposition of the forces.

To turn the battle to the gate, is to fight valiantly, and drive the enemy, who hath entered the city, back to the gate. Is. xxviii.

BAT'TLE, *v. i.* [Fr. *batailler*; Sp. *batallar.*] To join in battle; to contend in fight; sometimes with *it*; as, to *battle it.* *Addison.*

BAT'TLE, *v. t.* To cover with armed force. *Fairfax.*

BATTLE-ARRA'Y, *n.* [*battle* and *array.*] Array or order of battle; the disposition of forces preparatory to a battle.

BAT'TLE-AX, **BAT'TLE-AXE**, } *n.* An ax anciently used as a weapon of war. It has been used till of late years by the highlanders in Scotland; and is still used by the city guards in Edinburg, in quelling mobs, &c. *Encyc.*

BAT'TLE-DOOR, *n. bat'tl-dore.* An instrument of play, with a handle and a flat board or palm, used to strike a ball or shuttle-cock; a racket. *Locke.*

2. A child's horn book. [*Not in use in U. S.*]

BAT'TLEMENT, *n.* [This is said to have been *bastillement*, from *bastille*, a fortification, from Fr. *bâtir*, *bastir*, to build. Qu.] A wall raised on a building with openings or embrasures, or the embrasure itself. *Encyc. Johnson.*

BAT'TLEMENTED, *a.* Secured by battlements. *Herbert.*

BAT'TLING, *n.* Conflict. *Thomson.*

BATTOL'OGIST, *n.* [See *Battology.*] One that repeats the same thing in speaking or writing. [*Little used.*] *Whitlock.*

BATTOL'OGIZE, *v. t.* To repeat needlessly the same thing. [*Little used.*] *Herbert.*

BATTOL'OGY, *n.* [Gr. βαττολογια, from βαττος, a garrulous person, and λογος, discourse.] A needless repetition of words in speaking. *Ash. Encyc.*

BAT'TON, *n.* [from *bat.*] In *commerce*, pieces of wood or deal for flooring, or other purposes. *Encyc.*

BAT'TORY, *n.* Among *the Hans-Towns*, a factory or magazine which the merchants have in foreign countries. *Encyc.*

BAT'TULATE, *v. t.* To interdict commerce. [*A word used by the Levant company.*] *Eton.*

BATTULA'TION, *n.* A prohibition of commerce. *Eton.*

BAT'TY, *a.* [from *bat*, an animal.] Belonging to a bat. *Shak.*

BATZ, *n.* A small copper coin with a mixture of silver, current in some parts of Germany and Switzerland. *Encyc.*

BAUBEE', *n.* [Qu. Fr. *bas-billon.*] In Scotland and the North of England, a half penny. *Johnson.*

BAUGE, *n.* A drugget manufactured in Burgundy, with thread spun thick, and of coarse wool. *Encyc.*

BAULK. [See *Balk.*]

BAV'AROY, *n.* A kind of cloke or surtout. *Johnson.*

BAV'IN, *n.* A stick like those bound up in faggots; a piece of waste wood. In *war*, brush, faggots. *Johnson. Encyc.*

BAW'BLE, *n.* [Fr. *babiole*, a toy, or *baby-thing*; according to Spelman, *baubella* are gems or jewels.] A trifling piece of finery; a gew-gaw; that which is gay or showy without real value. *Dryden.*

BAWB'LING, *a.* Trifling; contemptible. *Obs.* *Shak.*

BAW'-COCK, *n.* A fine fellow. [Qu. *beaucock.*] *Shak.*

BAWD, *n.* [I know not the origin of this word; but in French, *baudir* is a term in hunting, signifying to excite or encourage dogs to the chase; formed, according to Lunier, from the Low Latin, *baldire*, or *exbaldire*, to enliven, to quicken; which, from the Italian, *baldo*, *baldanza*, appears to be from the root of Eng. *bold*, the primary sense of which is, to project, to push or rush forward. In W. *pud* is what tends to allure. But one author quotes Hesychius, as giving Gr. βαδας, a procurer or procuress.] A procurer or procuress. A person who keeps a house of prostitution, and conducts criminal intrigues. [*Usually applied to females.*]

BAWD, *v. i.* To procure; to provide women for lewd purposes.

2. To foul or dirty. [*Not in use.*] *Skelton.*

BAWD'-BORN, *a.* Descended from a bawd. *Shak.*

BAWD'ILY, *adv.* Obscenely; lewdly.

BAWD'INESS, *n.* Obscenity; lewdness.

BAWD'RICK, *n.* [See *Baldrick.*] A belt. *Chapman.*

BAWD'RY, *n.* [See *Bawd.*] The abominable practice of procuring women for the gratification of lust.

2. Obscenity; filthy, unchaste language.

BAWD'Y, *a.* Obscene; filthy; unchaste; *applied to language.*

BAWD'Y-HOUSE, *a.* A house of lewdness and prostitution.

BAWL, *v. i.* [Sax. *bellan*; Sw. *bola*, to low or *bellow*; W. *ballaw*; G. *bellen*, to bark; D. *balderen*, to roar; L. *balo*, to bleat; Fr. *piailler*, to bawl, to *pule*; Heb. יבל the blast of a trumpet; Per. *bala*, a cry or clamor; and Ar. and Heb. אבל, to weep, to wail. These all coincide in elements with L. *pello*, *appello*, Eng. *peal*, and the primary sense is the same.]

1. To cry out with a loud full sound; to hoot; to cry with vehemence, as in calling, or in pain or exultation.
2. To cry loud, as a child from pain or vexation.

BAWL, *v. t.* To proclaim by outcry, as a common crier. *Swift.*

BAWL'ED, *pp.* Proclaimed by outcry.

BAWL'ING, *ppr.* Crying aloud.

BAWL'ING, *n.* The act of crying with a loud sound.

BAWN, *n.* An inclosure with mud or stone walls for keeping cattle; a fortification. [*Not used.*] *Spenser.*

BAW'REL, *n.* A kind of hawk. *Todd.*

BAW'SIN, *n.* A badger. *B. Jonson.*

BAXTE'RIAN, *a.* Pertaining to Baxter, a celebrated English divine; as the *Baxterian* scheme. *Encyc.*

BAY, *a.* [Fr. *bai* or *baie*; It. *baio*; Sp. *bayo*; L. *badius*. Class Bd.]

Red, or reddish, inclining to a chesnut color; applied to the color of horses. The shades of this color are called *light bay, dark bay, dappled bay, gilded bay, chesnut bay.* In popular language, in England, all bay horses are called *brown.* *Johnson. Encyc.*

BAY, *n.* [Fr. *baie*; Sp. Port. *bahia*; It. *baia*; D. *baai*; contracted from the root of Sax. *byge*, an angle, *bygan*, D. *boogen*, to bend, whence *bow.*]

1. An arm of the sea, extending into the land, not of any definite form, but smaller than a gulf, and larger than a creek. The name however is not used with much precision, and is often applied to large tracts of water, around which the land forms a curve, as Hudson's *Bay.* Nor is the name restricted to tracts of water with a narrow entrance, but used for any recess or inlet between capes or head lands, as the *bay* of Biscay.
2. A pond-head, or a pond formed by a dam, for the purpose of driving mill-wheels. [*I believe not used in U. S.*]
3. In *a barn*, a place between the floor and the end of the building, or a low inclosed place, for depositing hay.

In *England*, says Johnson, if a barn consists of a floor and two heads, where they lay corn, they call it a barn of *two bays.* These bays are from 14 to 20 feet long, and floors from 10 to 12 feet broad, and usually 20 feet long, which is the breadth of the barn. *Builder's Dict.*

4. In *ships of war*, that part on each side between decks which lies between the bitts. *Mar. Dict.*
5. Any kind of opening in walls. *Chambers.*

BAY, *n.* [Qu. Gr. βαιον, a branch of the palm tree. In Sp. *baya* is a berry, the fruit of the laurel.]

1. The laurel tree. Hence,
2. Bays, in the plural, an honorary garland or crown, bestowed as a prize for victory or excellence, anciently made or consisting of branches of the laurel.

The patriot's honors, and the poet's *bays.* *Trumbull.*

3. In *some parts of the U. States*, a tract of land covered with bay trees. *Drayton, S. Carolina.*

BAY, *n.* [Goth. *beidan*, to expect; It. *bada*; "*tenere a bada*," to keep at bay; "*star a bada*," to stand trifling; *badare*, to stand trifling, to amuse one's self, to take care, to watch, to covet; *abbadare*, to mind; Fr. *bayer*, to gape or stand gaping. Qu. *aboyer.*]

A state of expectation, watching or looking for; as, to keep a man *at bay.* So a stag *at bay* is when he turns his head against the dogs. Whence *abeyance*, in law, or a state of expectancy.

BAY, *v. i.* [Fr. *aboyer*; It. *baiare*, to bark.]

1. To bark, as a dog at his game. *Spenser.*
2. To encompass, or inclose, from *bay.* We now use *embay.* *Shak.*

BAY, *v. t.* To bark at; to follow with barking. *Shak.*

BAY-SALT, is salt which crystalizes or receives its consistence from the heat of the sun or action of the air. It forms in pits or basins, and from this circumstance receives its denomination. It appears first in a slight incrustation upon the surface of the water, which may be sea water, or any other water in which salt is dissolved. This crust thickens and hardens, till the crystalization is perfected, which takes place, in eight, ten or fifteen days. *Encyc. Chambers.*

BAY-WINDOW, *n.* A window jutting out from the wall, as in shops.

BAY-YARN, *n.* A denomination sometimes used promiscuously with woolen yarn. *Chambers.*

BA'YARD, *n.* [*bay* and *ard*, kind.]

1. A bay horse. *Philips.*
2. An unmannerly beholder. *B. Jonson.*

BA'YARDLY, *a.* Blind; stupid. *Taylor.*

BA'YED, *a.* Having bays, as a building.

BA'YONET, *n.* [Fr. *baïonette*; Sp. *bayoneta*; It. *baionetta*; so called, it is said, because the first bayonets were made at Bayonne. *Vieyra's Portuguese Dict.*]

A short pointed instrument of iron or broad dagger, formerly with a handle fitted to the bore of a gun, where it was inserted for use, after the soldier had fired; but now made with an iron handle and ring which go over the muzzle of the piece, so that the soldier fires with his bayonet fixed. *Encyc.*

BA'YONET, *v. t.* To stab with a bayonet.

2. To compel or drive by the bayonet. *Burke.*

BAYS, or **BAYZE**. [See *Baize.*]

BAZ'AR, *n.* [Pers. بَازَار bazar; Russ. *bazari*, a market.]

Among the Turks and Persians, an exchange, market-place, or place where goods are exposed to sale. Some bazars are open, others are covered with lofty ceilings or domes, pierced to give light. The bazar at Tauris will contain 30,000 men. *Encyc.*

BAZ'AT, } *n.* A long, fine spun cotton from **BAZ'A**, } Jerusalem, whence it is called *Jerusalem cotton.* *Encyc.*

BDEL'LIUM, *n. dell'yum.* [L.; Gr. βδελλιον; Syr. Ch. Heb. ברלח. Bochart and Parkhurst translate it, pearl. Gen. ii. But it is doubtful whether the bdellium of the scriptures is that now used.]

A gummy resinous juice, produced by a tree in the East Indies, of which we have no satisfactory account. It is brought from the E. Indies and from Arabia, in pieces of different sizes and figures, externally of a dark reddish brown, internally, clear and not unlike to glue. To the taste, it is slightly bitterish and pungent; its odor is agreeable. In the mouth, it becomes soft and sticks to the teeth; on a red hot iron, it readily catches flame and burns with a crackling noise. It is used as a perfume and a medicine, being a weak deobstruent. *Encyc.*

BE, *v. i. substantive; ppr. being; pp. been.* [Sax. *beon*, to be. G. *bin, bist*; D. *ben*; Indic. pres. tense. Qu. Pers. بُودَن bodan, to be, and W. *bôd, byzu, bydiaw.* The sense is to stand, remain or be fixed; hence to continue. This verb is defective, and its defects are supplied by verbs from other roots, *am, is, was, were,* which have no radical connection with *be.* The case is the same with the substantive verb in most languages.]

1. To be fixed; to exist; to have a real state or existence, for a longer or shorter time.

Let this mind *be* in you, which was in Christ Jesus. Phil. ii.

To *be*, contents his natural desire. *Pope.*

2. To be made to be; to become.

And they twain shall *be* one flesh. Math. xix. Jer. xxxii.

3. To remain. Let the garment *be* as it was made.
4. To be present in a place. Where *was* I at the time? When will you *be* at my house?
5. To have a particular manner of being or happening; as, how *is* this affair? how *was* it? what *were* the circumstances?

This verb is used as an auxiliary in forming the tenses of other verbs, and particularly in giving to them the passive form; as, he has *been* disturbed. It forms, with the infinitive, a particular future tense, which often expresses duty, necessity or purpose; as, government *is to be* supported; we *are to pay* our just debts.

Let be is to omit, or leave untouched; to let alone.

Let be, said he, my prey. *Dryden.*

BE, a prefix, as in *because, before, beset, bedeck,* is the same word as *by*; Sax. *be, big*; Goth. *bi.* It is common to the English, Saxon, Gothic, German, Dutch, Danish and Swedish languages. It occurs probably in the Russian, but is written *po*, as it is in *possideo* and a few other words in the Latin. It denotes nearness, closeness, about, on, at, from some root signifying to pass or to press. [See *By.*]

That this word is the Shemitic ב, used as a prefix, is certain, not only from its general applications, which may be seen by comparing the uses of the word, in the Heb. for instance, with those in the Saxon; but from its use in particular phrases, particularly in its use before the name of the Supreme being in swearing. Hence we find that ב is not from בה nor from בית, as Parkhurst supposes, but is a contraction of *big*, which is used in the Saxon, *bigspell*, a proverb, a *by*-word; *bigstandan*, to stand *by.*

BEACH, *n.* [Qu. Russ. *bok*, coast.]

The shore of the sea, or of a lake, which is washed by the tide and waves; the strand. It may be sometimes used for the shore of large rivers.

BE'ACHED, *a.* Exposed to the waves; washed by the tide and waves. *Shak.*

BE'ACHY, *a.* Having a beach or beaches. *Shak.*

BE'ACON, *n. beékn.* [W. *pigwn*, a beacon, cone, or turret, from *pig*, a point. See *Pike.* Sax. *beacen, becen*, a signal; D. *baak, baaken*; Ger. *bake.*]

1. A signal erected on a long pole, upon an eminence, consisting of a pitch barrel, or some combustible matter, to be fired at night, or to cause a smoke by day, to notify the approach of an enemy.
2. A light-house; a house erected on a point

of land, or other place on the sea-coast, with lamps which burn at night, to direct navigators, and preserve vessels from running upon rocks, sand banks, or the shore. In general, a *beacon* may be any light or mark intended for direction and security against danger.

3. *Figuratively*, that which gives notice of danger.

BE'ACONAGE, *n.* Money paid for the maintenance of a beacon. *Encyc. Ash.*

BEAD, *n.* [Ger. *bethe*, a bead; supposed from *beten*, *biddan*, to pray, from the use of beads in Catholic countries; Sax. *bead*, a praying. In Spanish and Portuguese, the word answering to *count* is used for a bead.]

1. A little perforated ball, to be strung on a thread, and worn about the neck, for ornament. A string of beads is called a necklace. Beads are made of gold, pearl, amber, steel, garnet, coral, diamond, crystal, pastes, glasses, &c. The Romanists use strings of beads in rehearsing their prayers. Hence the phrase, *to tell beads*, and *to be at one's beads*, is to be at prayer. *Encyc. Johnson.*

2. Any small globular body; hence the glass globules, used in traffick with savages, and sold in strings, are called beads; also a bubble on spirit.

3. In *architecture*, a round molding, commonly made upon the edge of a piece of stuff, in the Corinthian and Roman orders, cut or carved in short embossments, like beads in necklaces. *Encyc.*

Bidding of beads, is a charge given by a priest to his parishioners, to repeat certain pater-nosters upon their beads for a departed soul. *Bailey.*

BE'AD-MAKER, *n.* One who makes beads. In French, *paternostrier* is one who makes, strings, and sells beads. In Paris are three companies of paternostriers; one that works in glass or crystal; one, in wood and horn; a third, in amber, coral, &c. *Encyc.*

BE'AD-PROOF, *a.* Spirit is *bead-proof*, when, after being shaken, a crown of bubbles will stand, for some time after, on the surface, manifesting a certain standard of strength. *Encyc.*

BE'AD-ROLL, *n.* Among *Catholics*, a list or catalogue of persons, for the rest of whose souls, they are to repeat a certain number of prayers, which they count by their beads. *Encyc.*

BE'AD-TREE, *n.* The azedarach, a species of Melia, a native of the Indies, growing about 20 feet high, adorned with large pinnated or winged leaves, and clusters of pentapetalous flowers. *Encyc.*

BE'ADS-MAN, *n.* A man employed in praying, generally in praying for another. *Johnson.*

BE'ADS-WOMAN, *n.* A praying woman; a woman who resides in an alms-house. *Ash.*

BE'ADLE, *n.* [Sax. *bydel*, or *bœdel*; Fr. *bedeau*; Sp. *bedel*; It. *bidello*; Ger. *büttel*, *pedell*; Sw. *bodel*, a beadle, or lictor; from the root of *bid*, Sax. *beodan*, to order or command. See *Bid*.]

1. A messenger or crier of a court; a servitor; one who cites persons to appear and answer; called also an apparitor or summoner. *Encyc.*

2. An officer in a university, whose chief business is to walk with a mace, before the masters, in a public procession; or as in America, before the president, trustees, faculty and students of a college, in a procession, at public commencements. *Encyc.*

3. A parish officer, whose business is to punish petty offenders. *Johnson.*

BE'ADLESHIP, *n.* The office of a beadle. *Wood.*

BE'AGLE, *n.* [Fr. *bigle*, so named from littleness; W. *bac*, little; Ir. *pig*; It. *piccolo*. We have from the same root *boy*, and the Danes *pige*, a little girl, and probably *pug* is the same word. Qu. Gr. πυγμαιος, a pygmy.]

A small hound, or hunting dog. Beagles are of different sorts; as the *southern beagle*, shorter and less, but thicker, than the deep-mouthed hound; the *fleet northern*, or *cat beagle*, smaller, and of a finer shape than the southern. From these species united, is bred a third, still preferable; and a smaller sort is little larger than the lap-dog. *Encyc.*

BEAK, *n.* [D. *bek*; W. *pig*; Ir. *peac*; Arm. *bek*; Fr. *bec*; Sp. *pico*; It. *becco*; Dan. *pig*, *pik*; Sw. *pigg*, *pik*; Sax. *piic*; Fr. *pique*; Eng. *peak*, *pike*, &c. The sense is, a shoot, or a point, from thrusting; and this word is connected with a numerous family. See Class Bg.]

1. The bill, or nib of a bird, consisting of a horny substance, either straight or curving, and ending in a point.

2. A pointed piece of wood, fortified with brass, resembling a beak, fastened to the end of ancient gallies; intended to pierce the vessels of an enemy. In modern ships, the *beak-head* is a name given to the forepart of a ship, whose forecastle is square, or oblong; a circumstance common to all ships of war, which have two or more tiers of guns. *Mar. Dict.*

Beak or *beak-head*, that part of a ship, before the forecastle, which is fastened to the stem, and supported by the main knee. *Encyc.*

3. In *farriery*, a little shoe, at the toe, about an inch long, turned up and fastened in upon the fore part of the hoof. *Farrier's Dict.*

4. Any thing ending in a point, like a beak. This in America is more generally pronounced *peak*.

BEAK, *v. t.* Among cock fighters, to take hold with the beak. *Ash.*

BE'AKED, *a.* Having a beak; ending in a point, like a beak.

BE'AKER, *n.* [Ger. *becher*.] A cup or glass. *Johnson.*

BE'AKIRON, *n.* A bickern; an iron tool, ending in a point, used by blacksmiths. *Ash.*

BEAL, *n.* [See *Boil*. W. *bal*, a prominence.] A pimple; a whelk; a small inflammatory tumor; a pustule. *Johnson. Ash.*

BEAL, *v. i.* To gather matter; to swell and come to a head, as a pimple. *Johnson. Ash.*

BEAM, *n.* [Goth. *bagms*, a tree; Sax. *beam*; G. *baum*; D. *boom*, a tree; Dan. *bom*, a bar or rail; Ir. *beim*, a beam. We see by the Gothic, that the word belongs to Class Bg. It properly signifies the stock or stem of a tree; that is, the fixed, firm part.]

1. The largest, or a principal piece in a building, that lies across the walls, and serves to support the principal rafters. *Encyc.*

2. Any large piece of timber, long in proportion to its thickness, and squared, or hewed for use.

3. The part of a balance, from the ends of which the scales are suspended; sometimes used for the whole apparatus for weighing. *Encyc.*

4. The part on the head of a stag, which bears the antlers, royals and tops.

5. The pole of a carriage, which runs between the horses. *Dryden.*

6. A cylinder of wood, making part of a loom, on which weavers wind the warp before weaving; and this name is given also to the cylinder on which the cloth is rolled, as it is wove.

7. The straight part or shank of an anchor.

8. In *ships*, a great main cross timber, which holds the sides of a ship from falling together. The beams support the decks and orlops. The main beam is next the mainmast. *Mar. Dict.*

9. The main piece of a plow, in which the plow-tails are fixed, and by which it is drawn.

10. *Beam compass*, an instrument consisting of a square wooden or brass beam, having sliding sockets, that carry steel or pencil points; used for describing large circles, and in large projections for drawing the furniture on wall-dials. *Encyc. Johnson.*

On the beam, in navigation, signifies any distance from the ship, on a line with the beams, or at right angles with the keel. *Mar. Dict.*

Before the beam, is an arch of the horizon between a line that crosses the ship at right angles, or the line of the beam, and that point of the compass which she steers. *Mar. Dict.*

Beam ends. A vessel is said to be on her beam ends, when she inclines so much on one side that her beams approach a vertical position. *Mar. Dict.*

Beam-feathers, in falconry, the long feathers of a hawk's wing. *Bailey.*

BE'AM-BIRD, *n.* In *Yorkshire*, *England*, the petty chaps, a species of Motacilla, called in Dorsetshire, the *hay-bird*. *Encyc.*

The spotted fly-catcher, a species of Muscicapa. *Ed. Encyc.*

BE'AM-TREE, *n.* A species of wild service. *Johnson.*

The Cratægus Aria. *Cyc.*

BEAM, *n.* [Sax. *beam*, a ray of the sun; *beamian*, to shine or send forth beams; Sam. *bahmah*, splendor; Ir. *beim*, a stroke, and *solbheim*, a thunderbolt.]

A ray of light, emitted from the sun, or other luminous body.

BEAM, *v. t.* To send forth; to emit.

BEAM, *v. i.* To emit rays of light, or beams; to shine.

> He beam'd, the day star of the rising age. *Trumbull.*

BE'AMING, *ppr.* Emitting rays of light or beams.

BE'AMING, *n.* Radiation; the emission or darting of light in rays.

2\. The issuing of intellectual light; dawn; prophetic intimation; first indication.

Such were the *beamings* of an original and gifted mind. *T. Dawes.*

BE'AMLESS, *a.* Emitting no rays of light.

BE'AMY, *a.* Emitting rays of light; radiant; shining.

2\. Resembling a beam in size and weight; massy. *Dryden.*

3\. Having horns, or antlers. *Dryden.*

BEAN, *n.* [Sax. *bean;* Dan. *bönne;* Sw. *bőna;* Gr. πυανον; D. *boon;* Ger. *bohne;* Ch. אפון, apun, a vetch. Qu. Arm. *favon;* Corn. *id.;* W. *faen.*]

A name given to several kinds of pulse, or leguminous seeds, and the plants producing them. They belong to several genera, particularly Vicia, Phaseolus and Dolichos. The varieties most usually cultivated are, the horse bean, the mazagan, the kidney bean, the cranberry bean, the lima bean, the frost bean, &c. The stalk is erect or climbing, and the fruit generally roundish, oval or flat, and of various colors.

Malacca-beans. Anacardia, the fruit of a tree growing in Malabar, and other parts of the Indies. This fruit is of a shining black color, of the shape of a heart flattened, about an inch long, terminating at one end in an obtuse point, and at the other, adhering to a wrinkled stalk. It contains, within two shells, a kernel of a sweetish taste; and betwixt the shells is lodged a thick acrid juice. *Encyc.*

BE'AN-CAPER, *n.* A plant, a species of zygophyllum, a native of warm climates. *Encyc.*

BE'AN-COD, *n.* A small fishing vessel or pilot boat, used in the rivers of Portugal. It is sharp forward, having its stem bent above into a great curve, and plated with iron. *Encyc.*

BE'AN-FED, *a.* Fed with beans. *Shak.*

BE'AN-FLY, *n.* A beautiful fly, of a pale purple color, found on bean flowers, produced from a maggot called *mida.* *Encyc.*

BE'AN-GOOSE, *n.* A species of Anas; a migratory bird, which arrives in England in autumn, and retires to the north in summer. It is so named, from the likeness of the nail of the bill to a horse-bean. *Encyc.*

Bean-tree of America, a name given to the Erythrina.

Kidney-Bean-tree, a name given to the Glycine.

Binding-bean-tree, a name given to the Mimosa.

Bean-trefoil, the Cytisus. *Fam. of Plants.*

BEAR, *v. t.* pret. *bore;* pp. *born, borne.* [Sax. *bæran, beran, beoran, byran, gebæran, geberan, gebyran, abæran, aberan,* to bear, carry, bring, sustain, produce, bring forth; *gebyrian, gebyrigan,* to pertain to, to belong to, to happen, to become, or be suitable; answering to the Latin *fero, porto, pario* and *oporteo.* Hence, probably, Sax. *barn, bearn,* a son, coinciding with *born.* Goth. *bairan,* to bear, or carry; *gabairan,* to bear; G. *führen,* to carry, and *gebären,* to bring forth; D. *beuren,* to lift; *voeren,* to carry or *bear; baaren,* to bring forth; Sw. *bära,* to carry; *bära fram,* to bring forth; *barn,* a son; Dan. *bærer,* to carry, bear, produce; L. *fero, pario, porto;* Gr. φερω, φορεω; Sp. Port. *parir,* to bring forth; *portar,* to carry; It. *portare,* to carry; Ir. *bearadh, beirim,* to bear or bring forth, to tell or relate, whence Fr. *parler;* Russ. *beru,* to take, to carry; Sans. *bharadi,* to bear. This verb I suppose to be radically the same as the Shemitic ברא to produce; L. *pario.* The primary sense is to throw out, to bring forth, or in general, to thrust or drive along. It includes the proper significations, both of L. *fero* and *pario;* Shemitic פרה and ፈረየ. Hence, probably, Gr. βαρος, βαρυς, and a great family of words. See Class Br. No. 15, 22, 33, 35.]

1\. To support; to sustain; as, to *bear* a weight or burden.

2\. To carry; to convey; to support and remove from place to place; as, "they *bear* him upon the shoulder;" "the eagle *beareth* them on her wings." *Isaiah. Deuteronomy.*

3\. To wear; to bear as a mark of authority or distinction; as, to *bear* a sword, a badge, a name; to *bear* arms in a coat.

4\. To keep afloat; as, the water *bears* a ship.

5\. To support or sustain without sinking or yielding; to endure; as, a man can *bear* severe pain or calamity; or to sustain with proportionate strength, and without injury; as, a man may *bear* stronger food or drink.

6\. To entertain; to carry in the mind; as, to *bear* a great love for a friend; to *bear* inveterate hatred to gaming.

7\. To suffer; to undergo; as, to *bear* punishment.

8\. To suffer without resentment, or interference to prevent; to have patience; as, to *bear* neglect or indignities.

9\. To admit or be capable of; that is, to suffer or sustain without violence, injury, or change; as, to give words the most favorable interpretation they will *bear.*

10\. To bring forth or produce, as the fruit of plants, or the young of animals; as, to *bear* apples; to *bear* children.

11\. To give birth to, or be the native place of.

Here dwelt the man divine whom Samos *bore.* *Dryden.*

12\. To possess and use as power; to exercise; as, to *bear* sway.

13\. To gain or win.

Some think to *bear* it by speaking a great word. *Bacon.*

[Not now used. The phrase now used is, *to bear away.*]

14\. To carry on, or maintain; to have; as, to *bear* a part in conversation.

15\. To show or exhibit; to relate; as, to *bear* testimony or witness. This seems to imply *utterance,* like the Latin *fero,* to relate or utter.

16\. To sustain the effect, or be answerable for; as, to *bear* the blame.

17\. To sustain, as expense; to supply the means of paying; as, to *bear* the charges, that is, to pay the expenses.

18\. To be the object of.

Let me but *bear* your love, and I'll *bear* your cares. [*Unusual.*] *Shak.*

19\. To behave; to act in any character; as, "hath he *borne* himself penitent?" [*Not usual.*] *Shak.*

20\. To remove, or to endure the effects of; and hence to give satisfaction for.

He shall *bear* their iniquities. Is. liii. Heb. ix.

To bear the infirmities of the weak, to bear one another's burdens, is to be charitable towards their faults, to sympathize with them, and to aid them in distress. *Brown.*

To bear off, is to restrain; to keep from approach; and in seamanship, to remove to a distance; to keep clear from rubbing against any thing; as, to *bear off* a blow; to *bear off* a boat; also, to *carry away;* as, to *bear off* stolen goods.

To bear down, is to impel or urge; to overthrow or crush by force; as, to *bear down* an enemy.

To bear down upon, to press to overtake; to make all sail to come up with.

To bear hard, is to press or urge.

Cesar doth *bear* me *hard.* *Shak.*

To bear on, is to press against; also to carry forward, to press, incite or animate.

Confidence hath *borne* thee *on.* *Milton.*

To bear through, is to conduct or manage; as, "to *bear through* the consulship." *B. Jonson.* Also, to maintain or support to the end; as, religion will *bear* us *through* the evils of life.

To bear out, is to maintain and support to the end; to defend to the last.

Company only can *bear* a man *out* in an ill thing. *South.*

To bear up, to support; to keep from falling.

Religious hope *bears up* the mind under sufferings. *Addison.*

To bear up, to keep afloat.

To bear a body. A color is said to *bear a body* in painting, when it is capable of being ground so fine, and mixed so entirely with the oil, as to seem only a very thick oil of the same color. *Johnson.*

To bear date, is to have the mark of time when written or executed; as, a letter or bond *bears date,* Jan. 6, 1811.

To bear a price, is to have a certain price. In common mercantile language, it often signifies or implies, to bear a good or high price.

To bear in hand, to amuse with false pretenses; to deceive. *Bacon. South. Shak.*

I believe this phrase is obsolete, or never used in America.

To bear a hand, in seamanship, is to make haste, be quick.

BEAR, *v. i.* To suffer, as with pain.

But man is born to *bear.* *Pope.*

This is unusual in prose; and though admissible, is rendered intransitive, merely by the omission of pain, or other word expressive of evil.

2\. To be patient; to endure.

I cannot, cannot *bear.* *Dryden.*

This also seems to be elliptical.

3\. To produce, as fruit; to be fruitful, in opposition to barrenness.

This age to blossom, and the next to *bear.* *Dryden.*

Here *fruit* must be understood.

4\. To take effect; to succeed; as, to bring matters to *bear.* *Guardian.*

5\. To act in any character.

Instruct me how I may *bear* like a true friar [*Unusual.*] *Shak.*

6\. To be situated as to the point of compass,

with respect to something else; as, the land *bore* E. N. E. from the ship.

7. *To bear away*, in navigation, is to change the course of a ship, when close hauled, or sailing with a side wind, and make her run before the wind. *To bear up*, is used in a like sense, from the act of *bearing up* the helm to the windward. *Mar. Dict.*

Hence, perhaps, in other cases, the expression may be used to denote *tending* or *moving* from.

8. *To bear down*, is to drive or tend to; to approach with a fair wind; as, the fleet *bore down* upon the enemy.

9. *To bear in*, is to run or tend towards; as, a ship *bears in* with the land; opposed to *bear off*, or keeping at a greater distance.

10. *To bear up*, is to tend or move towards; as, to *bear up* to one another: also, to be supported; to have fortitude; to be firm; not to sink; as, to *bear up* under afflictions.

11. *To bear upon*, or *against*, is to lean upon or against; to act on as weight or force, in any direction, as a column upon its base, or the sides of two inclining objects against each other.

12. *To bear against*, to approach for attack or seizure; as, "a lion *bears against* his prey." *Dryden.*

13. *To bear upon*, to act upon; as, the artillery *bore* upon the *center*: or to be pointed or situated so as to affect; as, to bring or plant guns so as to *bear upon* a fort, or a ship.

14. *To bear with*, to endure what is unpleasing; to be indulgent; to forbear to resent, oppose, or punish.

Reason would I should *bear with* you. Acts xviii.

Shall not God avenge his elect, though he *bear* long *with* them? Luke xviii.

BEAR CLOTH, BEARING-CLOTH, *n.* A cloth in which a new born child is covered when carried to church to be baptized. *Shak.*

BEAR, *n.* [Sax. *bera*; Ger. *bär*; D. *beer*; Sw. Dan. and Ice. *biörn*; Ir. *bear*; allied perhaps to *fierce*, L. *ferus*, *fera*, or to *barbarus*.]

1. A wild quadruped, of the genus Ursus. The marks of the genus are, six fore teeth in the upper jaw, alternately hollow on the inside; and six in the under jaw, the two lateral ones lobated; the dog teeth are solitary and conical; the eyes have a nictitating membrane, and the nose is prominent.

The *arctos*, or black bear, has his body covered with long shaggy hair. Some are found in Tartary, of a pure white color. The polar, or white bear, has a long head and neck; short, round ears; the hair long, soft, and white, tinged in some parts with yellow. He grows to a great size, the skins of some being 13 feet long. This bear lives in cold climates only, and frequently swims from one isle of ice to another. *Encyc.*

2. The name of two constellations in the northern hemisphere, called the greater and lesser bear. In the tail of the lesser bear is the pole star.

BEAR-BAITING, *n.* The sport of baiting bears with dogs. *Shak.*

BEAR-BERRY, *n.* A plant, a species of Arbutus.

BEAR-BIND, *n.* A species of bind weed, or Convolvulus.

BEAR'S-BREECH, *n.* Brank-ursine or Acanthus, a genus of plants.

BEAR'S-EAR, *n.* The trivial name of *primula auricula.*

BEAR'S EAR SANICLE, *n.* A species of Cortusa.

BEAR-FLY, *n.* An insect. *Bacon.*

BEAR'S-FOOT, *n.* A plant, a species of hellebore.

BEAR-GARDEN, *n.* A place where bears are kept for diversion. *Ash.*

BEAR-GARDEN, *a.* Rude; turbulent; as *bear-garden* sport. *Todd.*

BEAR-WHELP, *n.* The whelp of a bear. *Shak.*

BEAR'S WÖRT, *n.* A plant. *Shak.*

BEARD, *n. berd.* [Sax. *beard*; D. *baard*; Ger. *bart*; Dan. *bart*; L. *barba*; Russ. *boroda*, the beard and the chin; probably from *bear.*]

1. The hair that grows on the chin, lips and adjacent parts of the face, chiefly of male adults; hence a mark of virility. A *gray beard*, *long beard* and *reverend beard*, are terms for old age.

2. Beard is sometimes used for the face, and to do a thing to a man's beard, is to do it in defiance, or to his face. *Johnson.*

3. The awn or sharp prickles on the ears of corn. But more technically, parallel hairs or a tuft of stiff hairs terminating the leaves of plants, a species of pubescence. By some authors the name is given to the lower lip of a ringent corol. *Martyn.*

4. A barb or sharp point of an arrow, or other instrument, bent backward from the end to prevent its being easily drawn out.

5. The *beard* or chuck of a horse, is that part which bears the curb of a bridle, underneath the lower mandible and above the chin. *Farrier's Dict. Encyc.*

6. The rays of a comet, emitted towards that part of the heaven to which its proper motion seems to direct it. *Encyc.*

7. The threads or hairs of an oyster, muscle or similar shell-fish, by which they fasten themselves to stones. *Encyc.*

8. In *insects*, two small, oblong, fleshy bodies, placed just above the trunk, as in gnats, moths and butterflies. *Encyc.*

BEARD, *v. t. berd.* To take by the beard; to sieze, pluck or pull the beard, in contempt or anger.

2. To oppose to the face; to set at defiance.

I have been *bearded* by boys. *More.*

BEARD'ED, *a. berd'ed.* Having a beard, as a man. Having parallel hairs or tufts of hair, as the leaves of plants. *Martyn.*

2. Barbed or jagged, as an arrow. *Dryden.*

BEARD'ED, *pp. berd'ed.* Taken by the beard; opposed to the face.

BEARD'-GRASS, *n.* A plant, the Andropogon.

BEARD'ING, *ppr. berd'ing.* Taking by the beard; opposing to the face.

BEARD'LESS, *a. berd'less.* Without a beard; young; not having arrived to manhood. In *botany*, not having a tuft of hairs.

BEARD'LESSNESS, *n.* The state or quality of being destitute of beard. *Lawrence, Lect.*

BEARER, *n.* [See *Bear.*] One who bears, sustains, or carries; a carrier, especially of a corpse to the grave.

2. One who wears any thing, as a badge or sword.

3. A tree or plant that yields its fruit; as a good *bearer.*

4. In *architecture*, a post or brick wall between the ends of a piece of timber, to support it. In *general*, any thing that supports another thing.

5. In *heraldry*, a figure in an achievement, placed by the side of a shield, and seeming to support it; generally the figure of a beast. The figure of a human creature for a like purpose is called a *tenant.* *Encyc.*

BEARHERD, *n.* [*bear* and *herd.*] A man that tends bears. *Shak.*

BEARING, *ppr.* Supporting; carrying; producing.

BEARING, *n.* Gesture; mien; behavior.

I know him by his *bearing.* [*Unusual.*] *Shak.*

2. The situation of an object, with respect to another object, by which it is supposed to have a connection with it or influence upon it, or to be influenced by it.

But of this frame, the *bearings* and the ties. *Pope.*

3. In *architecture*, the space between the two fixed extremes of a piece of timber, or between one extreme and a supporter. *Builder's Dict.*

4. In *navigation*, the situation of a distant object, with regard to a ship's position, as on the bow, on the lee quarter, &c. Also, an arch of the horizon intercepted between the nearest meridian and any distant object, either discovered by the eye and referred to a point on the compass, or resulting from sinical proportion. *Mar. Dict.*

5. In *heraldry*, bearings are the coats of arms or figures of armories, by which the nobility and gentry are distinguished from common persons. *Encyc.*

BEARISH, *a.* Partaking of the qualities of a bear. *Harris.*

BEARLIKE, *a.* Resembling a bear. *Shak.*

BEARN, *n.* [Sax. *bearn*; Goth. *barn*; from *bear*; Goth. *gabaurans*, born.]

A child. In Scotland, *bairn.* *Shak.*

BEARWARD, *n.* A keeper of bears. *Shak.*

BEAST, *n.* [Ir. *biast*, *piasd*; Corn. *bêst*; D. *beest*; L. *bestia*; Fr. *bête*, from *beste*; Dan. *bæst*, *beest*; W. *bwyst*, wild, savage, ferocious. See *Boisterous.*]

1. Any four footed animal, which may be used for labor, food or sport; distinguished from fowls, insects, fishes and man; as *beasts* of burden, *beasts* of the chase, *beasts* of the forest. It is usually applied to large animals.

2. Opposed to man, it signifies any irrational animal, as in the phrase "*man* and *beast.*" So wild *beast.*

3. *Figuratively*, a brutal man; a person rude, coarse, filthy, or acting in a manner unworthy of a rational creature. *Johnson.*

4. A game at cards. Hence *to beast.* *Encyc.*

BE'ASTLIKE, *a.* Like a beast; brutal. *Titus Andronicus.*

BE'ASTLINESS, *n.* [from *beastly.*] Brutality; coarseness; vulgarity; filthiness; a practice contrary to the rules of humanity.

BE'ASTLY, *a.* Like a beast; brutal; coarse; filthy; contrary to the nature and dignity of man.

2. Having the form or nature of a beast. *Prior.*

BEAT, *v. t.* pret. *beat*; pp. *beat*, *beaten*. [Sax. *beatan*, *gebeotan*, to beat; *gebeaten*, beaten; W. *bæzu*; Fr. *battre*, or *batre*; Sp. *batir*; Port. *bater*; It. *battere*; L. *batuo*; Russ. *botayu*; Ar. خَبَطَ gabata, and كَبَتَ kabata; Heb. Ch. Syr. חבט. Perhaps, Hindoo, *pata*, to kill; Burman, *potai*, id; as we say, to smite and to slay. Hence, the *oir-pata*, man killers, in Herodotus. Class Bd. No. 20. 23. 33. See *Abate.*]

1. To strike repeatedly; to lay on repeated blows, with a stick, with the hand or fist, or with any instrument, and for any cause, just or unjust, or for punishment. Luke xii. Deut. xxv.

2. To strike an instrument of music; to play on, as a drum. *Shak.*

3. To break, bruise, comminute, or pulverize by beating or pounding, as pepper or spices. Ex. xxx.

4. To extend by beating, as gold or other malleable substance; or to hammer into any form; to forge. Ex. xxxix.

5. To strike bushes; to shake by beating, or to make a noise to rouse game. *Prior.*

6. To thresh; to force out corn from the husk by blows. *Ruth.*

7. To break, mix or agitate by beating; as, to *beat* an egg with any other thing. *Boyle.*

8. To dash or strike, as water; to strike or brush, as wind. *Milton.*

9. To tread, as a path. *Blackmore.*

10. To overcome in a battle, contest or strife; to vanquish or conquer; as, one *beats* another at play.

Pyrrhus *beat* the Carthaginians at sea. *Arbuthnot.*

11. To harass; to exercise severely; to overlabor; as, to *beat* the brains about logic. *Hakewill.*

To beat down, to break, destroy, throw down, by beating or battering, as a wall.

Also, to press down or lay flat, as by treading, by a current of water, by violent wind, &c. *Shak.*

Also, to lower the price by importunity or argument.

Also, to depress or crush; as, to *beat down* opposition.

Also, to sink or lessen the price or value.

Usury *beats down* the price of land. *Bacon.*

To beat back, to compel to retire or return.

To beat into, to teach or instill, by repetition of instruction.

To beat up, to attack suddenly; to alarm or disturb; as, to *beat up* an enemy's quarters.

To beat the wing, to flutter; to move with fluttering agitation.

To beat off, to repel or drive back.

To beat the hoof, to walk; to go on foot.

To beat time, to measure or regulate time in music by the motion of the hand or foot.

In *the manege*, a horse *beats the dust*, when at each motion he does not take in ground enough with his fore legs; and at curvets, when he does them too precipitately, or too low. He *beats upon a walk*, when he walks too short. *Encyc.*

To beat out, to extend by hammering. In *popular use*, *to be beat out*, is to be extremely fatigued; to have the strength exhausted by labor or exertion.

BEAT, *v. i.* To move with pulsation, as the pulse *beats*; or to throb, as the heart *beats*.

2. To dash with force, as a storm, flood, passion, &c.; as, the tempest *beats* against the house.

3. To knock at a door. Judges xix.

4. To fluctuate; to be in agitation. *Shak.*

To beat about, to try to find; to search by various means or ways. *Addison.*

To beat upon, to act upon with violence. *Jonah.*

Also, to speak frequently; to enforce by repetition. *Hooker.*

To beat up for soldiers, is to go about to enlist men into the army.

In seamanship, *to beat*, is to make progress against the direction of the wind, by sailing in a zigzag line or traverse. *Mar. Dict.*

With hunters, a stag *beats up and down*, when he runs first one way and then another. *Encyc.*

BEAT, *n.* A stroke; a striking; a blow, whether with the hand, or with a weapon.

2. A pulsation; as the *beat* of the pulse.

3. The rise or fall of the hand or foot, in regulating the divisions of time in music.

4. A transient grace-note in music, struck immediately before the note it is intended to ornament. *Busby.*

In the military art, the *beat of drum*, is a succession of strokes varied, in different ways, for particular purposes; as to regulate a march, to call soldiers to their arms or quarters, to direct an attack or retreat, &c.

The *beat* of a watch or clock, is the stroke made by the fangs or pallets of the spindle of the balance, or of the pads in a royal pendulum. *Encyc.*

BEAT, BE'ATEN, } *pp.* Struck; dashed against; pressed or laid down; hammered; pounded; vanquished; made smooth by treading; worn by use; tracked.

BE'ATER, *n.* One who beats, or strikes; one whose occupation is to hammer metals.

2. An instrument for pounding, or comminuting substances.

BE'ATER-UP, *n.* One who beats for game; *a sportsman's term.* *Butler.*

BEATH, *v. t.* To bathe. [*Not in use.*] *Spenser.*

BEATIF'IC, BEATIF'ICAL, } *a.* [L. *beatus*, blessed, from *beo*, to bless, and *facio*, to make. See *Beatify.*]

That has the power to bless or make happy, or the power to complete blissful enjoyment; used only of heavenly fruition after death; as *beatific vision.* *Milton.*

BEATIF'ICALLY, *adv.* In such a manner as to complete happiness.

BEATIFICA'TION, *n.* In *the Romish church*, an act of the Pope by which he declares a person beatified or blessed after death. This is the first step towards canonization, or the raising of one to the dignity of a saint. No person can be beatified till 50 years after his death. All certificates or attestations of his virtues and miracles are examined by the congregation of rites, and this examination continues often for years; after which his Holiness decrees the beatification, and the corpse and relics of the intended saint are exposed to the veneration of all good christians. *Encyc.*

BEAT'IFY, *v. t.* [L. *beatus*, happy, from *beo*, to bless, and *facio*, to make.]

1. To make happy; to bless with the completion of celestial enjoyment.

2. In *the Romish church*, to declare, by a decree or public act, that a person is received into heaven, and is to be reverenced as blessed, though not canonized.

BE'ATING, *ppr.* Laying on blows; striking; dashing against; conquering; pounding; sailing against the direction of the wind; &c.

BE'ATING, *n.* The act of striking or giving blows; punishment or chastisement by blows.

The *beating* of flax and hemp is an operation which renders them more soft and pliable. For this purpose, they are made into rolls and laid in a trough, where they are beat, till no roughness or hardness can be felt. *Encyc.*

In *book binding*, *beating* is performed by laying the book in quires or sheets folded, on a block, and beating it with a heavy broad-faced hammer. On this operation the elegance of the binding and the easy opening of the book chiefly depend. *Encyc.*

Beating the wind, was a practice in the ancient trial by combat. If one of the combatants did not appear on the field, the other was to *beat the wind*, by making flourishes with his weapons; by which he was entitled to the advantages of a conqueror.

Beatings, in music, the regular pulsative swellings of sound, produced in an organ by pipes of the same key, when not in unison, and their vibrations not simultaneous or coincident. *Busby.*

BEAT'ITUDE, *n.* [L. *beatitudo*, from *beatus*, *beo*. See *Beatify.*]

1. Blessedness; felicity of the highest kind; consummate bliss; *used of the joys of heaven.*

2. The declaration of blessedness made by our Savior to particular virtues.

BEAU, *n. bo.* plu. *beaux*, boze. [Fr. *beau*, contracted from *bel*, L. *bellus*, Sp. It. *bello*, fine, gay, handsome.]

A man of dress; a fine, gay man; one whose great care is to deck his person. In *familiar language*, a man who attends a lady.

BEAUISH, *a. bo'ish.* Like a beau; foppish; fine.

BEAU-MONDE, *n. bomond'.* [Fr. *beau*, fine, and *monde*, world.]

The fashionable world; people of fashion and gaiety. *Prior.*

BEAU'TEOUS, *a. bu'teous.* [See *Beauty.*] Very fair; elegant in form; pleasing to the sight; beautiful; very handsome. It expresses a greater degree of beauty than handsome, and is chiefly used in poetry.

BEAU'TEOUSLY, *adv. bu'teously.* In a

beauteous manner; in a manner pleasing to the sight; beautifully.

BEAU'TEOUSNESS, *n. bu'teousness.* The state or quality of being beauteous; beauty.

BEAU'TIFIER, *n. bu'tifier.* He or that which makes beautiful.

BEAU'TIFUL, *a. bu'tiful.* [*beauty* and *full.*]

1. Elegant in form; fair; having the form that pleases the eye. It expresses more than *handsome.*

A *beautiful* woman is one of the most attractive objects in all nature's works. *Anon.*

A circle is more *beautiful* than a square; a square is more *beautiful* than a parrallelogram. *Lord Kames.*

2. Having the qualities which constitute beauty, or that which pleases the senses other than the sight; as a *beautiful* sound. *Encyc.*

BEAU'TIFULLY, *adv. bu'tifully.* In a beautiful manner.

BEAU'TIFULNESS, *n. bu'tifulness.* Elegance of form; beauty; the quality of being beautiful.

BEAU'TIFȲ, *v. t. bu'tify.* [*beauty* and L. *facio.*]

To make or render beautiful; to adorn; to deck; to grace; to add beauty to; to embellish. *Hayward.*

BEAU'TIFȲ, *v. i. bu'tify.* To become beautiful; to advance in beauty. *Addison.*

BEAU'TY, *n. bu'ty.* [Fr. *beauté*, from *beau.* See *Beau.*]

1. An assemblage of graces, or an assemblage of properties in the form of the person or any other object, which pleases the eye. In *the person,* due proportion or symmetry of parts constitutes the most essential property to which we annex the term *beauty.* In *the face,* the regularity and symmetry of the features, the color of the skin, the expression of the eye, are among the principal properties which constitute *beauty.* But as it is hardly possible to define all the properties which constitute beauty, we may observe in general, that beauty consists in whatever pleases the eye of the beholder, whether in the human body, in a tree, in a landscape, or in any other object.

Beauty is *intrinsic,* and perceived by the eye at first view, or *relative,* to perceive which the aid of the understanding and reflection is requisite. Thus, the beauty of a machine is not perceived, till we understand its uses, and adaptation to its purpose. This is called the beauty of utility. By an easy transition, the word beauty is used to express what is pleasing to the other senses, or to the understanding. Thus we say, the *beauty* of a thought, of a remark, of sound, &c.

So *beauty,* armed with virtue, bows the soul
With a commanding, but a sweet control.
Percival.

2. A particular grace, feature or ornament; any particular thing which is beautiful and pleasing; as the *beauties* of nature.

3. A particular excellence, or a part which surpasses in excellence that with which it is united; as the *beauties* of an author.

4. A beautiful person. In *scripture,* the chief dignity or ornament. 2 Sam. i.

5. In the *arts,* symmetry of parts; harmony; justness of composition. *Encyc.*

6. Joy and gladness. Is. lxi. Order, prosperity, peace, holiness. Ezek. xvi.

BEAU'TY, *v. t. bu'ty.* To adorn; to beautify or embellish. *Obs. Shak.*

BEAU'TY-SPOT, *n. bu'ty-spot.* A patch; a foil; a spot placed on the face to heighten beauty.

BEAU'TY-WANING, *a.* Declining in beauty. *Shak.*

BE'AVER, *n.*]Sax. *befor, biofor;* Fr. *bièvre;* L. *fiber;* Ir. *beabhar;* Sw. *bafwer;* Dan. *bæver;* Ger. *biber;* D. *bever;* Russ. *bobr;* Pers. بَبر babir.]

1. An amphibious quadruped, of the genus Castor. It has short ears, a blunt nose, small fore feet, large hind feet, with a flat ovate tail. It is remarkable for its ingenuity in constructing its lodges or habitations, and from this animal is obtained the castor of the shops, which is taken from cods or bags in the groin. Its fur, which is mostly of a chesnut brown, is the material of the best hats.

2. The fur of the beaver, and a hat made of the fur; also, a part of a helmet that covers the face.

BE'AVERED, *a.* Covered with or wearing a beaver. *Pope.*

BEBLEE'D, *v. t.* [*be* and *bleed.*] To make bloody. *Obs. Chaucer.*

BEBLŎOD', BEBLŎOD'Y, } *v. t.* [*be* and *blood.*] To make bloody. *Obs. Sheldon.*

BEBLOT', *v. t.* [*be* and *blot.*] To blot; to stain. *Obs. Chaucer.*

BEBLUB'BERED, *a.* [*be* and *blubber.*] Foul or swelled with weeping. *Shelton.*

BEƐABUN'GA, *n.* [Sax. *becc;* G. *bach,* a brook.]

Brooklime speedwell; veronica becabunga; a plant common in ditches and shallow streams. *Hooper.*

BEƐAFI'ƐO, *n.* [It. from the root of *pica, peck, beck,* and *fico,* a fig. See *Beak.*]

A fig-pecker; a bird like a nightingale which feeds on figs and grapes. *Johnson. Prior. Bailey.*

BEƐALM, *v. t. becàm.* [*be* and *calm.* See *Calm.*]

1. To still; to make quiet; to appease; to stop, or repress motion in a body; used of the elements and of the passions; as, to *becalm* the ocean, or the mind. But *calm* is generally used.

2. To intercept the current of wind, so as to prevent motion; to keep from motion for want of wind; as, high lands *becalm* a ship.

BEƐALMED, *pp. becàmed.* Quieted; appeased.

2. *a.* Hindered from motion or progress by a calm; as a ship *becalmed.*

BEƐALMING, *ppr. becàming.* Appeasing; keeping from motion or progress.

BEƐALMING, *n. becàming.* A calm at sea. *Herbert.*

BEƐA'ME, *pret.* of *become.* [See *Become.*]

BEƐAUSE, *becauz',* a compound word. [Sax. *be* for *by* and *cause.* See *By* and *Cause.*]

By cause, or by the cause; on this account; for the cause which is explained in the next proposition; for the reason next explained. Thus, I fled, *because* I was afraid, is to be thus resolved; I fled, *by the cause, for the cause,* which is mentioned in the next affirmation, viz. I was afraid. Hence, cause being a noun, *because* may be regularly followed by *of.*

The spirit is life, *because of* righteousness.

Because of these cometh the wrath of God upon the children of disobedience.

BECH'ARM, *v. t.* [*be* and *charm.*] To charm; to captivate. *Beaum.*

BECH'ANCE, *v. i.* [*be, by,* and *chance.*] To befall; to happen to. *Shak.*

BE'ƐHIƐ, *n.* [Gr. βηχικα, from βηξ, a cough.]

A medicine for relieving coughs, synonymous with *pectoral,* which is now the term mostly used. *Quincy.*

BECK, *n.* A small brook. *Gray.* This word, Sax. *becc,* Ger. *bach,* D. *beek,* Dan. *bæk,* Sw. *back,* Pers. بَج bak, a brook or rivulet, is found in the Ir. Ar. Ch. Syr. Sam. Heb. and Eth., in the sense of *flowing,* as tears, weeping. Gen. xxxii. 22. It is obsolete in English, but is found in the names of towns situated near streams, as in *Walbeck;* but is more frequent in names on the continent, as in *Griesbach,* &c.

BECK, *n.* [Sax. *beacn,* a sign; *beacnian, bycnian,* to beckon. The Sw. *peka,* Dan. *peger,* signifies to point with the finger.]

A nod of the head; a significant nod, intended to be understood by some person, especially as a sign of command.

BECK, *v. i.* To nod or make a sign with the head.

BECK, *v. t.* To call by a nod; to intimate a command to; to notify by a motion of the head. *Shak.*

BECK'ED, *pp.* Called or notified by a nod.

BECK'ET, *n.* A thing used in ships to confine loose ropes, tackles or spars; as a large hook, a rope, with an eye at one end, or a wooden bracket. *Mar. Dict.*

BECK'ING, *ppr.* Nodding significantly; directing by a nod.

BECK'ON, *v. i. bek'n.* [See *Beck.*]

To make a sign to another, by nodding, winking, or a motion of the hand or finger, &c., intended as a hint or intimation. Acts xix.

BECK'ON, *v. t. bek'n.* To make a significant sign to. *Dryden.*

BECK'ONED, *pp.* Having a sign made to.

BECK'ONING, *ppr.* Making a significant sign, as a hint.

BEƐLIP', *v. t.* [Sax. *beclyppan.*] To embrace. [*Not in use.*] *Wickliffe.*

BEƐLOUD', *v. t.* [See *Cloud.*] To cloud; to obscure; to dim. *Sidney.*

BEƐŎME, *v. i. becum'.* pret. *became,* pp. *become.* [Sax. *becuman,* to fall out or happen; D. *bekoomen;* G. *bekommen,* to get or obtain; Sw. *bekomma;* Dan. *bekommer,* to obtain; *be* and *come.* These significations differ from the sense in English. But the sense is, to *come to,* to arrive, to reach, to fall or pass to. [See *Come.*] Hence the sense of suiting, agreeing with. In Sax. *cuman,* Goth. *kwiman,* is to come, and Sax. *cweman,* is to please, that is, to suit or be agreeable.]

1. To pass from one state to another; to enter into some state or condition, by a change from another state or condition, or by assuming or receiving new properties or qualities, additional matter, or a new character; as, a cion *becomes* a tree.

The Lord God breathed into his nostrils the breath of life and man *became* a living soul.

To the Jew, I *became* a Jew.

2. *To become of*, usually with *what* preceding; to be the fate of; to be the end of; to be the final or subsequent condition; as, *what* will *become of* our commerce? *what* will *become of* us?

In the present tense, it applies to *place* as well as *condition*. What has *become of* my friend? that is, where is he? as well as, what is his condition? *Where is he become?* used by Shakspeare and Spenser, is obsolete; but this is the sense in Saxon, where has he fallen?

BECOME, *v. t.* In general, to suit or be suitable; to be congruous; to befit; to accord with, in character or circumstances; to be worthy of, decent or proper. It is used in the same sense applied to persons or things.

If I *become* not a cart as well as another man. *Shak.*

This use of the word however is less frequent, the verb usually expressing the suitableness of *things*, to persons or to other things; as, a robe *becomes* a prince.

It *becomes* me so to speak of an excellent poet. *Dryden.*

BECOM'ING, *ppr.*, but used rarely or never except as an adjective. Fit; suitable; congruous; proper; graceful; belonging to the character, or adapted to circumstances; as, he speaks with *becoming* boldness; a dress is very *becoming*.

Some writers formerly used *of*, after this word.

Such discourses as are *becoming of* them. *Dryden.*

But this use is inelegant or improper.

BECOM'ING, *a.* Ornament. *Obs.* *Shak.*

BECOM'INGLY, *adv.* After a becoming or proper manner.

BECOM'INGNESS, *n.* Fitness; congruity; propriety; decency; gracefulness arising from fitness. *Grew.*

BECRIP'PLE, *v. t.* [See *Cripple.*] To make lame; to cripple. [*Little used.*]

BECURL', *v. t.* To curl. [*Not used.*]

BED, *n.* [Sax. *bed*; D. *bed*; G. *bett* or *beet*; Goth. *badi*. The sense is a lay or spread, from laying or setting.]

1. A place or an article of furniture to sleep and take rest on; in modern times, and among civilized men, a sack or tick filled with feathers or wool; but a bed may be made of straw or any other materials. The word *bed* includes often the bedstead.
2. Lodging; a convenient place for sleep.
3. Marriage; matrimonial connection.

George, the eldest son of his second *bed*. *Clarendon.*

4. A plat or level piece of ground in a garden, usually a little raised above the adjoining ground. *Bacon.*
5. The channel of a river, or that part in which the water usually flows. *Milton.*
6. Any hollow place, especially in the arts; a hollow place, in which any thing rests; as the *bed* of a mortar.
7. A layer; a stratum; an extended mass of any thing, whether upon the earth or within it; as a *bed* of sulphur; a *bed* of sand or clay.
8. Pain, torment. Rev. ii. The grave. Is. lvii. The lawful use of wedlock. Heb. xiii.

The *bed* of the carriage of a gun is a thick plank which lies under the piece, being, as it were, the body of the carriage.

The *bed* of a mortar is a solid piece of oak, hollow in the middle, to receive the britch and half the trunnions.

In *masonry*, *bed* is a range of stones, and the joint of the bed is the mortar between two stones placed over each other. *Encyc.*

Bed of justice, in France, was a throne on which the king was seated when he went to parliament. Hence the phrase, *to hold a bed of justice*.

To make a bed, is to put it in order after it has been used.

To bring to bed, to deliver of a child, is rarely used. But in the passive form, *to be brought to bed*, that is, *to be delivered of a child*, is common. It is often followed by *of*; as, to be brought to bed *of* a son.

To put to bed, in midwifery, is to deliver of a child.

Dining bed, or discubitory bed, among the ancients, a bed on which persons lay at meals. It was four or five feet high, and would hold three or four persons. Three of these beds were ranged by a square table, one side of the table being left open, and accessible to the waiters. Hence the Latin name for the table and the room, *triclinium*, or three beds. *Encyc.*

From bed and board. In law, a separation of man and wife, without dissolving the bands of matrimony, is called a separation from *bed* and *board*, *a mensa et thoro*. In this case the wife has a suitable maintenance allotted to her out of the husband's estate, called alimony. *Blackstone.*

BED, *v. t.* To place in a bed. *Bacon.*

2. To go to bed with. [*Unusual.*] *Shak.*
3. To make partaker of the bed. *Bacon.*
4. To plant and inclose or cover; to set or lay and inclose; as, to *bed* the roots of a plant in soft mold.
5. To lay in any hollow place, surrounded or inclosed; as, to *bed* a stone.
6. To lay in a place of rest or security, covered, surrounded or inclosed; as a fish *bedded* in sand, or under a bank.
7. To lay in a stratum; to stratify; to lay in order, or flat; as *bedded* clay, *bedded* hairs. *Shak.*

BED, *v. i.* To cohabit; to use the same bed.

If he be married and *bed* with his wife. *Wiseman.*

BEDAB'BLE, *v. t.* [*be* and *dabble.*] To wet; to sprinkle.

Bedabbled with the dew. *Shak.*

BEDAB'BLED, *pp.* Wet; sprinkled.

BEDAB'BLING, *ppr.* Wetting; sprinkling.

BEDAFF', *v. t.* To make a fool of. [*Not in use.*] *Chaucer.*

BEDAG'GLE, *v. t.* [*be* and *daggle.*] To soil, as clothes, by drawing the ends in the mud, or spattering them with dirty water.

BEDAG'GLED, *pp.* Soiled by reaching the mud in walking; bespattering.

BEDA'RE, *v. t.* [*be* and *dare.*] To dare; to defy. [*Not used.*] *Peele.*

BEDARK', *v. t.* [*be* and *dark.*] To darken. [*Not used.*] *Gower.*

BEDASH', *v. t.* [*be* and *dash.*] To wet, by throwing water, or other liquor upon; to bespatter, with water or mud.

BEDASH'ED, *pp.* Bespattered with water or other liquid.

BEDASH'ING, *ppr.* Bespattering; dashing water upon, or other liquid.

BEDAUB', *v. t.* [*be* and *daub.*] To daub over; to besmear with viscous, slimy matter; to soil with any thing thick and dirty. *Shak.*

BEDAUB'ED, *pp.* Daubed over; besmeared.

BEDAUB'ING, *ppr.* Daubing over; besmearing.

BEDAZ'ZLE, *v. t.* [*be* and *dazzle.*] To confound the sight by too strong a light; to make dim by luster. *Shak*

BEDAZ'ZLED, *pp.* Having the sight confounded by too strong a light.

BEDAZ'ZLING, *ppr.* Confounding or making dim by a too brilliant luster.

BED'CHAMBER, *n.* [*bed* and *chamber.*] An apartment or chamber intended or appropriated for a bed, or for sleep and repose.

BED'-CLOTHES, *n. plu.* [*bed* and *clothes.*] Blankets, or coverlets, &c., for beds. *Shak.*

BED'DED, *pp.* Laid in a bed; inclosed as in a bed.

BED'DER, } *n.* [from *bed.*] The nether stone of an oil mill.
BEDET'TER, } *Todd.*

BED'DING, *ppr.* Laying in a bed; inclosing as in a bed.

BED'DING, *n.* A bed and its furniture; a bed; the materials of a bed, whether for man or beast. *Spenser.*

BEDECK', *v. t.* [*be* and *deck.*] To deck; to adorn; to grace. *Shak.*

BEDECK'ED, *pp.* Adorned; ornamented.

BEDECK'ING, *ppr.* Adorning; decking.

BE'DEHOUSE, *n.* [Sax. *bead*, a prayer, and *house.*]

Formerly, a hospital or alms house, where the poor prayed for their founders and benefactors.

BE'DEL, *n.* An officer in the universities of England. [A peculiar orthography of *beadle.*]

BE'DELRY, *n.* The extent of a bedel's office. *Blount.*

BEDEW', *v. t.* [*be* and *dew.*] To moisten, as with dew; to moisten in a gentle manner with any liquid; as, tears *bedew* her face. *Shak.*

BEDEW'ED, *pp.* Moistened, as if with dew; gently moistened.

BEDEW'ER, *n.* That which bedews. *Sherwood.*

BEDEW'ING, *ppr.* Moistening gently, as with dew; wetting.

BEDEW'Y, *a.* Moist with dew. [*Little used.*]

BED'FELLOW, *n.* [*bed* and *fellow.*] One who lies in the same bed. *Shak.*

BED-HANGINGS, *n.* Curtains. *Shak.*

BEDI'GHT, *v. t. bedi'te.* [*be* and *dight.*]

To adorn; to dress; to set off with ornaments. [*Little used.*] *More.*

BEDI'GHTED, *pp.* Adorned; set off with ornaments.

BEDI'GHTING, *ppr.* Adorning.

BEDIM', *v. t.* [*be* and *dim.*] To make dim; to obscure or darken. *Sidney.*

BEDIM'MED, *pp.* Made dim; obscured.

BEDIM'MING, *ppr.* Making dim; obscuring; darkening.

BEDIZ'EN, *v. t. bediz'n.* [*be* and *dizen.*] To adorn; to deck; *a low word.*

BEDIZ'ENED, *pp.* Bedecked; adorned.

BEDIZ′ENING, *ppr.* Adorning.

BED′LAM, *n.* [Corrupted from *Bethlehem*, the name of a religious house in London, afterward converted into a hospital for lunatics.]
1. A mad house; a place appropriated for lunatics. *Spelman.*
2. A madman; a lunatic; one who lives in *Bedlam.* *Shak.*
3. A place of uproar.

BED′LAM, *a.* Belonging to a mad house; fit for a mad house. *Shak.*

BED′LAMITE, *n.* An inhabitant of a mad-house; a madman. *B. Jonson.*

BED′MAKER, *n.* [*bed* and *maker.*] One whose occupation is to make beds, as in a college or university. *Spectator.*

BED′MATE, *n.* [*bed* and *mate.*] A bed-fellow. *Shak.*

BED′-MOLDING, *n.* [*bed* and *molding.*] In *architecture*, the members of a cornice, which are placed below the coronet, consisting of an ogee, a list, a large boultine, and another list under the coronet. *Encyc.*

BEDO′TE, *v. t.* [*be* and *dote.*] To make to dote. [*Not in use.*] *Chaucer.*

BED′POST, *n.* [*bed* and *post.*] The post of a bedstead.

BED′PRESSER, *n.* [*bed* and *press.*] A lazy fellow; one who loves his bed. *Shak.*

BEDRAG′GLE, *v. t.* [*be* and *draggle.*] To soil, as garments which are suffered, in walking, to reach the dirt; to soil by drawing along on mud. *Swift.*

BEDRAG′GLED, *pp.* Soiled by reaching the dirt, in walking.

BEDRAG′GLING, *ppr.* Soiling by drawing along in dirt or mud.

BEDRENCH′, *v. t.* [*be* and *drench.*] To drench; to soak; to saturate with moisture: *applied to things which imbibe moisture.* *Shak.*

BEDRENCH′ED, *pp.* Drenched; soaked.

BEDRENCH′ING, *ppr.* Soaking; drenching.

BED′RID, } *a.* [*bed* and *ride*; Sax. *bed-*
BED′RIDDEN, } *rida.*]
Confined to the bed, by age or infirmity. *Shak.*

BED′RITE, *n.* [*bed* and *rite.*] The privilege of the marriage bed.

BED′ROOM, *n.* [*bed* and *room.*] A room or apartment intended or used for a bed; a lodging room.
2. Room in a bed. [*Not in use.*] *Shak.*

BEDROP′, *v. t.* [*be* and *drop.*] To sprinkle, as with drops. *Chaucer.*

BEDROP′PED, *pp.* Sprinkled as with drops; speckled; variegated with spots.

BED′SIDE. *n.* The side of the bed. *Middleton.*

BED′STAFF, *n.* [*bed* and *staff.*] A wooden pin anciently inserted on the sides of bedsteads, to keep the clothes from slipping on either side. *Johnson.*

BED′STEAD, *n.* *bed′sted.* [*bed* and *stead.*] A frame for supporting a bed.

BED′STRAW, *n.* [*bed* and *straw.*] Straw laid under a bed to make it soft; also the name of a plant, a species of *galium.*

BED′SWERVER, *n.* [*bed* and *swerve.*] One that swerves from his bed; that is, one who is false and unfaithful to the marriage vow. *Shak.*

BED′TIME, *n.* [*bed* and *time.*] The time to go to rest; the usual hour of going to bed. *Shak.*

BEDUCK′, *v. t.* [*be* and *duck.*] To duck; to put the head under water; to immerse. *Spenser.*

BEDUST′, *v. t.* [*be* and *dust.*] To sprinkle, soil or cover with dust. *Sherwood.*

BED′WARD, *adv.* [*bed* and *ward.*] Toward bed. *Shak.*

BEDWARF′, *v. t.* [*be* and *dwarf.*] To make little; to stunt or hinder growth. *Donne.*

BED′WORK, *n.* [*bed* and *work.*] Work done in bed, without toil of the hands or with ease. *Shak.*

BEDY′E, *v. t.* [*be* and *dye.*] To dye; to stain. *Spenser.*

BEDY′ED, *pp.* Dyed; stained.

BEE, *n.* [Sax. *beo*; D. *bye*; Ger. *biene*; Sw. *bij*; Dan. *bie*; Ir. *beach*; It. *pecchia*; Sp. *abeja.* Class Bg.]
An insect of the genus Apis. [See *Apis.*] The species are numerous, of which the honey-bee is the most interesting to man. It has been cultivated from the earliest periods, for its wax and honey. It lives in swarms or societies, of from 10,000 to 50,000 individuals. These swarms contain three classes of bees, the females or queen bees, the males or drones, and the neuters or working bees. Of the former, there is only one in each hive or swarm, whose sole office is to propagate the species. It is much larger than the other bees. The drones serve merely for impregnating the queen, after which they are destroyed by the neuters. These last are the laborers of the hive. They collect the honey, form the cells, and feed the other bees and the young. They are furnished with a proboscis by which they suck the honey from flowers, and a mouth by which they swallow it, and then convey it to the hive in their stomachs, where they disgorge it into the cells. The pollen of flowers settles on the hairs with which their body is covered, whence it is collected into pellets, by a brush on their second pair of legs, and deposited in a hollow in the third pair. It is called *bee bread*, and is the food of the *larvæ* or young. The adult bees feed on honey. The wax was supposed to be formed from pollen by a digestive process, but it is now ascertained that it is formed from the honey by a similar process. The females and neuters have a barbed sting, attached to a bag of poison, which flows into the wound inflicted by the sting. When a hive is overstocked, a new colony is sent out under the direction of a queen bee. This is called *swarming.* *Cyc. Ed. Encyc.*

BEE′-BREAD, *n.* [*bee* and *bread.*] The pollen of flowers collected by bees, as food for their young. [See *Bee.*]

BEE′-EATER, *n.* [*bee* and *eat.*] A bird that feeds on bees. There are several species included in the genus *merops*, of which the *apiaster* of Europe is remarkable for the brilliancy of its plumage. *Encyc.*

BEE′-FLOWER, *n.* [*bee* and *flower.*] A plant; a species of *Ophrys* or *twyblade*, whose flowers represent singular figures of bees, flies and other insects. *Encyc.*

BEE′-GARDEN, *n.* [*bee* and *garden.*] A garden, or inclosure to set bee-hives in. *Johnson.*

BEE′-GLUE, *n.* [*bee* and *glue.*] A soft, unctuous matter with which bees cement the combs to the hives, and close up the cells; called also *propolis.* *Encyc.*

BEE′-HIVE, *n.* [*bee* and *hive.*] A case, box, or other hollow vessel, which serves as a habitation for bees. Hives are made of various materials, as of boards, the hollow trunk of a tree, and withes of straw, or of glass.

BEE′-MASTER, *n.* [*bee* and *master.*] One who keeps bees. *Mortimer.*

BEECH, *n.* [Sax. *bece*, *boc*; D. *beuke*, or *beukenboom*; Ger. *buche*, or *buchbaum*; Slav. *boku*; Russ. *buk*; Gr. *φαγος*; L. *fagus*; It. *faggio*; Sp. *haya*; Port. *faia.* In Saxon *bec* and *boc* is a book. It is probable that *beech* is properly the name of bark, and this being used, by our rude ancestors, as the material for writing, the word came to signify a book.]
A tree arranged by Linne under the genus *fagus*, with the chesnut. The beech grows to a large size, with branches forming a beautiful head, with thick foliage. The bark is smooth and of a silvery cast. The mast or nuts are the food of swine, and of certain wild animals, and yield a good oil for lamps. When eaten by man, they are said to occasion giddiness and headach. *Encyc.*

BEE′CH-COAL, *n.* [*beech* and *coal.*] Charcoal from beech wood.

BEE′CHEN, *a.* *bee′chn.* Consisting of the wood or bark of the beech; belonging to the beech; as a *beechen* vessel. *Dryden.*

BEE′CHMAST, *n.* The fruit or nuts of the beech.

BEE′CH-OIL, *n.* [*beech* and *oil.*] Oil expressed from the mast or nuts of the beech-tree. It is used in Picardy, and in other parts of France, instead of butter; but is said to occasion heaviness and pains in the stomach. *Encyc.*

BEE′CH-TREE, *n.* [*beech* and *tree.*] The beech.

BEEF, *n.* [Fr. *bœuf*, *beuf*, an ox; Arm. *bevin*; It. *bue*; Sp. *buey*; Port. *boy*; W. *buw*; Corn. *byuh*, an ox; Ir. *bo*, a cow, plu. *buaibh*; L. *bos*, *bovis*; Gr. *βους.*]
1. An animal of the bovine genus, whether ox, bull or cow; but used of those which are full grown or nearly so. In this, which is the original sense, the word has a plural, *beeves.*
2. The flesh of an ox, bull, or cow, when killed. In *popular language*, the word is often applied to the live animal; as, an ox is good *beef*; that is, is well fattened. In this sense, the word has no plural.

BEEF, *a.* Consisting of the flesh of the ox, or bovine kind; as a *beef*-steak. *Swift.*

BEE′F-EATER, *n.* [*beef* and *eat.*] One that eats beef.
2. A yeoman of the guards, in England.
3. The Buphaga, an African bird that feeds on the larvas which nestle under the hides of oxen.
4. In *popular use*, a stout fleshy man.

BEE′F-STEAK, *n.* [*beef* and *steak.*] A steak or slice of beef for broiling.

BEE′F-WITTED, *a.* [*beef* and *wit.*] Dull in intellects; stupid; heavy-headed. *Shak.*

BEELD, *n.* [Sax. *behlydan*, to cover.] Protection; refuge. [*Not in use.*] *Fairfax.*

BEEN, [Sax. *beon.*] Part. perf. of *be;* pronounced *bin.* In old authors, it is also the present tense plural of *be.*

BEEN, *n.* A fretted stringed instrument of music of the guitar kind, having nineteen frets; used in India. *As. Researches.*

BEER, *n.* [W. *bir;* Fr. *biere;* Arm. *byer, bir, ber;* D. and Ger. *bier;* It. *birra.*]

1. A spirituous liquor made from any farinaceous grain; but generally from barley, which is first malted and ground, and its fermentable substance extracted by hot water. This extract or infusion is evaporated by boiling in caldrons, and hops or some other plant of an agreeable bitterness added. The liquor is then suffered to ferment in vats. *Beer* is of different degrees of strength, and is denominated *small beer, ale, porter, brown stout,* &c., according to its strength, or other peculiar qualities. *Encyc.*

2. Beer is a name given in America to fermenting liquors made of various other materials; and when a decoction of the roots of plants forms a part of the composition, it is called *spring-beer,* from the season in which it is made.

BEE'R-BARREL, *n.* A barrel for holding beer.

BEE'R-HOUSE, *n.* A house where malt liquors are sold; an ale house.

BEESTINGS, [See *Biestings.*]

BEET, *n.* [D. *biet;* Ger. *beete;* It. *bietola;* W. *betysen;* L. *beta;* Fr. *bette.*]

A plant of the genus *Beta.* The species cultivated in gardens are the *cicla* and *vulgaris,* or white and red beet. There are many varieties; some with long taper roots, and others with flat roots, like turneps. The root furnishes a large portion of sugar, which has been recently manufactured in France on a great scale. *Cyc.*

BEE'TLE, *n.* [Sax. *bitl,* or *bytl,* a mallet; *betel,* the insect, *beetle.*]

1. A heavy mallet or wooden hammer, used to drive wedges, beat pavements, &c.; called also a stamper, or rammer.

2. In *zoology,* a genus of insects, the scarabæus, of many species. The generic characters are, clavated antennæ, fissile longitudinally, legs frequently dentated, and wings which have hard cases, or sheaths. The bones of these insects are placed externally, and their muscles within. They are of different sizes, from that of a pin's head, to that of a man's fist. Some are produced in a month, and go through their existence in a year; in others, four years are required to produce them, and they live as winged insects a year more. They have various names, as the may-bug, the dorr-beetle, the cock-chaffer, the tumble-dung, the elephant-beetle, &c. The latter, found in South America, is the largest species, being four inches long. *Encyc.*

BEE'TLE, *v. i. bee'tl.* To jut; to be prominent; to hang or extend out; as, a cliff that *beetles* over its base. *Shak.*

BEE'TLE-BROW, *n.* [*beetle* and *brow.*] A prominent brow. *Shak.*

BEE'TLE-BROWED, *a.* Having prominent brows. *Swift.*

BEE'TLE-HEAD, *n.* [*beetle* and *head.*] A stupid fellow. *Scot.*

BEE'TLE-HEADED, *a.* Having a head like a beetle; dull; stupid. *Shak.*

BEE'TLE-STOCK, *n.* [*beetle* and *stock.*] The handle of a beetle. *Spenser.*

BEE'TLING, *ppr.* Jutting; being prominent; standing out from the main body. *Thomson.*

BEET-RAVE, } *n.* A kind of beet, used
BEE'T-RADISH, } for sallad. *Ash.*

BEEVES, *n.* plu. of *beef.* Cattle; quadrupeds of the bovine genus, called in England, *black* cattle.

BEFALL', *v. t.* pret. *befell;* part. *befallen.* [Sax. *befællan,* of *be* and *fall.*]

To happen to; to occur to; as, let me know the worst that can *befall* me. It usually denotes ill. It is generally transitive in form, but there seems to be an ellipsis of *to,* and *to* sometimes follows it.

BEFALL', *v. i.* To happen; to come to pass.

> I have reveal'd this discord which *befell.* *Milton.*

To *befall of* is not legitimate.

BEFALL'ING, *ppr.* Happening to; occurring to; coming to pass.

BEFELL', *pret.* of *befall.*

BEFIT', *v. t.* [*be* and *fit.*] To suit; to be suitable to; to become.

> That name best *befits* thee. *Milton.*

BEFIT'TING, *ppr.* or *a.* Suiting; becoming.

BEFOAM, *v. t.* [*be* and *foam.*] To cover with foam. [*Little used.*]

BEFOOL', *v. t.* [*be* and *fool.*] To fool; to infatuate; to delude or lead into error.

> Men *befool* themselves. *South.*

BEFOOL'ED, *pp.* Fooled; deceived; led into error.

BEFOOL'ING, *ppr.* Fooling; making a fool of; deceiving; infatuating.

BEFO'RE, *prep.* [*be* and *fore,* that is *by fore, near* the fore part. Sax. *before,* or *beforan,* retained by Chaucer in *beforn.*]

1. In front; on the side with the face, at any distance; used of persons. *Milton.*

2. In presence of, with the idea of power, authority, respect.

> Abraham bowed *before* the people of the land. Gen. xxiii.
>
> Wherewithal shall I come *before* the Lord. Micah vi.

3. In sight of; as *before* the face.

4. In the presence of, noting cognizance or jurisdiction.

> Both parties shall come *before* the judge. Ex. xxii.

5. In the power of, noting the right or ability to choose or possess; free to the choice.

> The world was all *before* them. *Milton.*
>
> My land is *before* thee. Gen. xx.

6. In front of any object; as *before* the house; *before* the fire.

7. Preceding in time.

> *Before* I was afflicted, I went astray. Ps. cxix.
>
> *Before* Abraham was, I am. John viii.

Here the preposition has a sentence following for an object.

8. In preference to.

> And he set Ephraim *before* Manasseh. Gen. xlviii.
>
> Poverty is desirable *before* torments. *Taylor.*

9. Superior; preceding in dignity.

> He that cometh after me is preferred *before* me, for he was before me. John i.

10. Prior to; having prior right; preceding in order; as, the eldest son is *before* the younger in succession.

11. Previous to; in previous order; in order to.

> *Before* this treatise can become of use, two points are necessary. *Swift.* [See No. 7.]

12. *Before the wind,* is to move in the direction of the wind by its impulse.

BEFO'RE, *adv.* In time preceding.

> You tell me what I knew *before.* *Dryden.*

2. In time preceding, to the present, or to this time; hitherto; as, tumults then arose which *before* were unknown.

3. Further onward in place, in progress, or in front.

> Reaching forth to those things which are *before.* Phil. iii.

4. In front; on the fore part.

> The battle was *before* and behind. 2 Chron. xiii.

In some of the examples of the use of *before,* which Johnson places under the adverb, the word is a preposition governing a sentence; as, "*Before* the hills appeared." This is the real construction, however overlooked or misunderstood.

BEFO'REHAND, *adv.* [*before* and *hand.*] In a state of anticipation or preoccupation; often followed by *with;* as, you are *before hand with* me.

2. Antecedently; by way of preparation or preliminary; aforetime. Math. xiii. 1 Tim. v.

3. In a state of accumulation, so as that more has been received than expended. A man is *beforehand. In this use it is more properly an adjective.*

4. At first; before any thing is done. *L'Estrange.*

BEFO'RE-TIME, *adv.* [*before* and *time.*] Formerly; of old time. 1 Sam. 9. Josh. xx. *Obs.*

BEFOR'TUNE, *v. t.* [*be* and *fortune.*] To happen to; to betide. *Shak.*

BEFOUL', *v. t.* [Sax. *befylan, be* and *foul.*] To make foul; to soil.

BEFRIEND, *v. t. befrend'.* [*be* and *friend.*] To favor; to act as a friend to; to countenance, aid or benefit. *Shak.*

BEFRIEND'ED, *pp.* Favored; countenanced.

BEFRIEND'ING, *ppr.* Favoring; assisting as a friend; showing kindness to.

BEFRINGE, *v. t. befrinj'.* [*be* and *fringe.*] To furnish with a fringe; to adorn as with fringe. *Fuller.*

BEFRING'ED, *pp.* Adorned as with a fringe.

BEG, } *n.* [The Turks write this word *begh*
BEY, } or *bek,* but pronounce it *bey.*]

In the *Turkish dominions,* a governor of a town or country; more particularly, the lord of a sangiac or banner. Every province is divided into seven sangiacs or banners, each of which qualifies a bey; and these are commanded by the governor of the province, called *begler-beg* or lord of all the beys. Each beg has the command of a certain number of spahis, or horse, denominated timariots.

In *Tunis,* the *beg* or bey is the prince or king, answering to the *dey* of Algiers.

In *Egypt,* the *begs* are twelve generals

who command the militia, or standing forces of the kingdom. *Encyc.*

BEG, *v. t.* [In Italian, *piccaro* is a beggar. This word is from some root in Class Bg, which signifies to make towards or to press, to urge, or to cry out. The Ger. *begehren*, to which Skinner refers this word, is a compound of *be* and *gieren* to desire, D. *begeeren*, Sax. *giernan*, whence *yearn*. With this, *beg* has no connection.]

1. To ask earnestly; to beseech; to entreat or supplicate with humility. It implies more urgency than *ask* or *petition*.

Joseph *begged* the body of Jesus. Math. xxvii.

2. To ask or supplicate in charity; as, we may yet be reduced to *beg* our bread.

3. To take for granted; to assume without proof; as, to *beg* the question in debate.

BEG, *v. i.* To ask alms or charity; to practice begging; to live by asking alms.

I cannot dig; I am ashamed to *beg*. Luke xvi.

BEGET′, *v. t.* pret. *begot*, *begat*; pp. *begot*, *begotten*. [Sax. *begetan*, of *be* and *getan*, to get. See *Get*.]

1. To procreate, as a father or sire; to generate; as, to *beget* a son.

2. To produce, as an effect; to cause to exist; to generate; as, luxury *begets* vice.

BEGET′TER, *n.* One who begets or procreates; a father.

BEG′GABLE, *a.* That may be begged. *Butler.*

BEG′GAR, *n.* [See *Beg*.] One that lives by asking alms, or makes it his business to beg for charity.

2. One who supplicates with humility; a petitioner; but in this sense rarely used, as the word has become a term of contempt. *Johnson.*

3. One who assumes in argument what he does not prove. *Tillotson.*

BEG′GAR, *v. t.* To reduce to beggary; to impoverish. *Shak.*

2. To deprive or make destitute; to exhaust; as, to *beggar* description.

BEG′GARED, *pp.* Reduced to extreme poverty.

BEG′GARING, *ppr.* Reducing to indigence or a state of beggary.

BEG′GARLINESS, *n.* The state of being beggarly; meanness; extreme poverty. *Barret.*

BEG′GARLY, *a.* Mean; poor; in the condition of a beggar; extremely indigent. *Shak.*

BEG′GARLY, *adv.* Meanly; indigently; despicably. *Hooker.*

BEG′GAR-MAID, *n.* A maid that is a beggar. *Shak.*

BEG′GAR-MAN, *n.* A man that is a beggar. *Shak.*

BEG′GAR-WÖMAN, *n.* A female beggar. *Shak.*

BEG′GARY, *n.* A state of extreme indigence. *Sidney.*

BEG′GED, *pp.* Entreated; supplicated; asked in charity.

BEG′GING, *ppr.* Asking alms; supplicating: assuming without proof.

BEG′GING, *n.* The act of soliciting alms; the practice of asking alms; as, he lives by *begging*.

BEGHARDS′, } *n.* A religious order of St.
BEGUARDS′, } Francis in Flanders, established at Antwerp in 1228, and so named from *St. Begghe*, their patroness. They at first employed themselves in making linen cloth, united in bonds of charity, without any rule; but in 1290, they embraced that of the third order of St. Francis. The name has been transferred to all the other religious of the convent of Antwerp. *Encyc.*

BEGILT′, *a.* Gilded. *B. Jonson.*

BEGIN′, *v. i.* pret. *began*; pp. *begun*. [Sax. *gynnan*, *aginnan*, *beginnan*, and *onginnan*, to begin, *ongin*, a beginning; Goth. *duginnan*; Sw. *begynna*; Dan. *begynder*; D. and Ger. *beginnen*, to begin; D. and Ger. *beginn*, a beginning, origin; W. *cycwnu*, to begin, *cy*, a prefix, and *cwn*, a head. The radical word is *gin* or *gyn*, to which are prefixed *be*, *on*, and *du* which is *to*. This appears to be the root of the Gr. *γινομαι*, *γενναω*, L. *genero*, *gigno*, coinciding with Syr. ܟܢ Kōn, to begin to be; in Aph. to plant, to confirm, to create; Eth. ከወነ Kōn, to be, to become or be made; Ar. كَانَ to be or become, to make, to create, to generate; Heb. Ch. Sam. כון, to make ready, to adapt, prepare, establish; Sam. to create. The primary sense is, to throw, thrust, stretch forward, hence to set, or to produce, according to its connection or application.]

1. To have an original or first existence; to take rise; to commence.

As he spake by the mouth of his holy prophets, who have been since the world *began*. Luke 1.

Judgment must *begin* at the house of God. 1 Pet. 4.

From Nimrod first the savage race *began*. *Pope.*

And tears *began* to flow. *Dryden.*

2. To do the first act; to enter upon something new; to take the first step; as, *begin*, my muse.

Begin every day to repent. *Taylor.*

When I *begin*, I will also make an end. 1 Sam. iii.

BEGIN′, *v. t.* To do the first act of any thing; to enter on; to commence.

Ye nymphs of Solyma, *begin* the song. *Pope.*

And this they *begin* to do. Gen. xi.

2. To trace from any thing, as the first ground; to lay the foundation.

The apostle *begins* our knowledge in the creatures, which leads us to the knowledge of God. *Locke.*

To begin with, to enter upon first; to use or employ first; as, to *begin with* the Latin Grammar; to *begin business with* a small capital.

BEGIN′NER, *n.* The person who begins; he that gives an original; the agent who is the cause; an author.

2. One who first enters upon any art, science or business; one who is in his rudiments; a young practitioner; often implying want of experience.

BEGIN′NING, *ppr.* First entering upon; commencing; giving rise or original; taking rise or origin.

BEGIN′NING, *n.* The first cause; origin.

I am the *beginning* and the ending. Rev. i.

2. That which is first; the first state; commencement; entrance into being.

In the *beginning*, God created the heaven and the earth. Gen. 1.

3. The rudiments, first ground or materials.

Mighty things from small *beginnings* grow. *Dryden.*

BEGIN′NINGLESS, *a.* That hath no beginning. [*A bad word and not used.*] *Barrow.*

BEGIRD, *v. t. begurd′.* pret. *begirt*, *begirded*; pp. *begirt*. [*be* and *gird*; Sax. *begyrdan*.]

1. To bind with a band or girdle.

2. To surround; to inclose; to encompass.

Begird the Almighty throne. *Milton.*

3. To besiege. *Clarendon.*

To begirt, used by B. Jonson, is a corrupt orthography.

BEGIRD′ED, } *pp.* Bound with a girdle;
BEGIRT, } surrounded; inclosed; besieged.

BEGIRD′ING, *ppr.* Binding with a girdle; surrounding; besieging.

BEG′LERBEG, *n.* [See *Beg*.] The governor of a province in the Turkish empire, next in dignity to the grand vizier. Each has three ensigns or staves, trimmed with a horse tail, to distinguish him from a bashaw, who has two, and a beg, who has one. His province is called *beglerbeglik*. *Encyc.*

BEGNAW′, *v. t. benaw′.* [Sax. *begnagan*; *be* and *gnaw*.]

To bite or gnaw; to eat away; to corrode; to nibble. *Shak.*

BEGONE. Go away; depart. These two words have been improperly united. *Be* retains the sense of a verb, and *gone*, that of a participle.

BEGO′RED, *a.* [*be* and *gore*.] Besmeared with gore. *Spenser.*

BEGOT′, **BEGOT′TEN**, *pp.* of *get*. Procreated; generated.

BEGRA′VE, *v. t.* To deposit in the grave; to bury. [*Not used.*]

2. To engrave. [*Not used.*] *Gower.*

BEGRE′ASE, *v. t.* *s* as *z*. [*be* and *grease*.] To soil or daub with grease, or other oily matter.

BEGRI′ME, *v. t.* [*be* and *grime*.] To soil with dirt deep-impressed, so that the natural hue cannot easily be recovered. *Shak.*

BEGRI′MED, *pp.* Deeply soiled.

BEGRUDGE, *v. t. begrudj′.* [See *Grudge*.] To grudge; to envy the possession of.

BEGUI′LE, *v. t. begi′le.* [*be* and *guile*.] To delude; to deceive; to impose on by artifice or craft.

The serpent *beguiled* me and I did eat. Gen. iii.

2. To elude by craft.

When misery could *beguile* the tyrant's rage. *Shak.*

3. To elude any thing disagreeable by amusement, or other means; to pass pleasingly; to amuse; as, to *beguile* the tedious day with sleep. *Shak.*

BEGUI′LED, *pp.* Deluded; imposed on; misled by craft; eluded by stratagem; passed pleasingly.

BEGUI′LER, *n.* He or that which beguiles or deceives.

BEGUI′LING, *ppr.* Deluding; deceiving by craft; eluding by artifice; amusing.

BEGUIL′TY, *v. t.* To render guilty. [*A barbarous word.*] *Sanderson.*

BE′GUIN, *n.* The Beguins are a congregation of nuns in Flanders, so called from their founder, or from their head dress. *Beguin*, in French, is a linen cap. From this order sprung the Beguinages in Flanders. *Encyc. Mason.*

BEGUN′, *pp.* of *begin*. Commenced; originated.

BEHALF, *n.* behȧf. [This word is probably a corruption. If composed of *be* and *half*, it is a word of modern origin: but I take it to be the Sax. *behefe*, profit, need, or convenience; G. *behuf*; D. *behoef*, necessaries, business; *behoeve*, behalf; Sw. *behof*; Dan. *behov*, need, necessity, sufficiency, or what is required, sustenance or support; from the verb *behoove*, *behofwa*, *behöver*, to need. The spelling is therefore corrupt: it should be *behof* or *behoof*. See *Behoof*.]

1. Favor; advantage; convenience; profit; support; defense; vindication. The advocate pleads in *behalf* of the prisoner. The patriot suffers in *behalf* of his country.
2. Part; side; noting substitution, or the act of taking the part of another; as, the agent appeared in *behalf* of his constituents, and entered a claim.

BEHAP′PEN, *v.i.* [*be* and *happen*.] To happen to. *Spenser.*

BEHA′VE, *v.t.* [G. *gehaben*; Sax. *gehabban*, and *behabban*; *be* and *have*.]

1. To restrain; to govern; to subdue. [The Saxon sense of the word.]

> He did *behave* his anger e'er 'twas spent. *Shak.*

This sense is obsolete. Yet it often seems to be implied; for to *behave one's self*, is really, to *govern* one's self; to have in command.

2. To carry; to conduct; used with the reciprocal pronoun; as, he *behaves himself* manfully. But the tendency of modern usage is to omit the pronoun; as, he *behaves* well.

BEHA′VE, *v. i.* To act; to conduct; generally applied to manners, or to conduct in any particular business; and in a good or bad sense. He *behaves* well or ill.

BEHA′VED, *pp.* Conducted.

BEHA′VING, *ppr.* Carrying; conducting.

BEHA′VIOR, *n.* behávyur. [See *Behave*.] Manner of behaving, whether good or bad; conduct; manners; carriage of one's self, with respect to propriety, or morals; deportment. It expresses external appearance or action; sometimes in a particular character; more generally in the common duties of life; as, our future destiny depends on our *behavior* in this life. It may express correct or good manners, but I doubt whether it ever expresses the idea of *elegance of manners*, without another word to qualify it.

To be upon one's behavior, is to be in a state of trial, in which something important depends on propriety of conduct. The modern phrase is, *to be* or *to be put, upon one's good behavior*.

BEHEAD′, *v. t.* behed′. [*be* and *head*.] To cut off the head; to sever the head from the body, with a cutting instrument; appropriately used of the execution of men for crimes.

BEHEAD′ED, *pp.* behed′ed. Having the head cut off.

BEHEAD′ING, *ppr.* behed′ing. Severing the head from the body.

BEHEAD′ING, *n.* behed′ing. The act of separating the head from the body by a cutting instrument: decollation.

BEHELD′, *pret.* and *pp.* of *behold*, which see.

BE′HEMOTH, *n.* [Heb. בהמות, from בהמה, a beast or brute; from an Arabic verb, which signifies, to shut, to lie hid, to be dumb. In Eth. dumb.]

Authors are divided in opinion as to the animal intended in scripture by this name; some supposing it to be an ox, others, an elephant; and Bochart labors to prove it the hippopotamus, or river horse. The latter opinion is most probable. [See *Hippopotamus*.] The original word in Arabic signifies a brute or beast in general, especially a quadruped.

BE′HEN, BEN, or BEK′EN, *n.* A plant. The white behen is a species of Cucubalus, called Swedish Lychnis, or gum sepungar. The empalement of its flower resembles net-work, and its leaves have somewhat of the flavor of pease. *Family of Plants. Encyc.*

The *behen* of the shops, or white behen, is spatling poppy. *Red behen* is sea lavender. *Lee. Bailey. Coxe.*

BEHEST′, *n.* [*be* and Sax. *hæse*, a command; Ger. *geheiss*, command, from *heissen*, to call, tell, or command. See *Heat*.] Command; precept; mandate. [*Antiquated, except in poetry*.]

BEHI′GHT, *v. t.* behite; pret. *behot*. [Sax. *behetan*, to promise.] To promise; to entrust; to call, or name; to command; to adjudge; to address; to inform; to mean; to reckon. The orthography is corrupt; it should be *behite*. *Obs.* *Spenser. Chaucer.*

BEHIND, *prep.* [Sax. *behindan*, of *be* and *hindan*, behind; Goth. *hindar*, beyond, behind; *hindar-leithan*, to pass, præterire; Ger. *hinter*.]

1. At the back of another; as, to ride *behind* a horseman.
2. On the back part, at any distance; in the rear; as, to walk *behind* another.
3. Remaining; left after the departure of another, whether by removing to a distance, or by death; as, a man leaves his servant *behind* him, or his estate at his decease.
4. Left at a distance, in progress or improvement; as, one student is *behind* another in mathematics.
5. Inferior to another in dignity and excellence.

> For I suppose I was not a whit *behind* the very chiefest apostles. 2 Cor. xi.

6. On the side opposite the front or nearest part, or opposite to that which fronts a person; on the other side; as *behind* a bed; *behind* a hill; *behind* a house, tree, or rock.

Behind the back, in scripture, signifies, out of notice, or regard; overlooked; disregarded.

> They cast thy laws *behind their backs*. Neh. xix. Is. xxxviii.

BEHIND, *adv.* [*be* and *hind*.] Out of sight; not produced, or exhibited to view; remaining; as, we know no what evidence is *behind*.

2. Backwards; on the back-part; as, to look *behind*.
3. Past in the progress of time.

> Forgetting those things which are *behind*. Phil. iii.

4. Future, or remaining to be endured.

> And fill up that which is *behind* of the afflictions of Christ in my flesh. Col. i.

5. Remaining after a payment; unpaid; as, there is a large sum *behind*.
6. Remaining after the departure of; as, he departed and left us *behind*.

BEHINDHAND, *a.* [*behind* and *hand*.] In arrear; in an exhausted state; in a state in which rent or profit has been anticipated, and expenditures precede the receipt of funds to supply them. In *popular use*, a state of poverty, in which the means of living are not adequate to the end. Also, in a state of backwardness, in which a particular business has been delayed beyond the proper season for performing it; as, he is *behindhand* in his business.

Behindhand with, is *behind* in progress; not upon equal terms in forwardness; as, to be *behindhand with* the fashionable world.

This word is really an adjective, as it is applied to the *person* rather than to the *verb*; but like *adrift*, *aloft*, *ashamed*, and several other words, never precedes the noun. Shakspeare's "behindhand slackness," therefore, according to present usage, is not a legitimate phrase.

BEHO′LD, *v.t.* pret. and pp. *beheld′*. [Sax. *behealdan*, *beheoldan*, *gehealdan*, *gehaldan*, from *healdan*, to hold. The sense is, to hold, or rather to reach with the eye, to have in sight, from straining, or extending. In Saxon, the verb signifies not only to look or see, but to guard; so in Latin, *observo*, from *servo*, to keep. This explication leads us to an understanding of the participle *beholden*, which retains the primitive sense of the verb, *bound*, *obliged*. The Germans retain the original sense in *behalten*, to hold or keep; as the Dutch do in *gehouden*, held, bound; and the Danes in *beholder*, to keep, retain; *behold*, a retreat, refuge, reservation. See *Observe* and *Regard*.]

1. To fix the eyes upon; to see with attention; to observe with care.

> *Behold* the lamb of God which taketh away the sin of the world. John i.

2. In *a less intensive sense*, to look upon; to see.

> When he *beheld* the serpent of brass, he lived. Num. xxi.

BEHO′LD, *v. i.* To look; to direct the eyes to an object.

> And I *beheld*, and lo, in the midst of the throne, a lamb, as it had been slain. Rev. 5.

2. To fix the attention upon an object; to attend; to direct or fix the mind.

> *Behold*, I stand at the door and knock. Rev. iii.

This word is much used in this manner for exciting attention, or admiration. It is in the imperative mode, expressing command, or exhortation; and by no means a mere exclamation.

BEHO′LDEN, *pp.* or *a.* *beholdn*. [The participle of *behold*, to keep, guard, or bind. See *Behold*.] Obliged; bound in gratitude; indebted.

> Little are we *beholden* to your love. *Shak.*

BEHO′LDER, *n.* One who beholds; a spectator; one who looks upon, or sees.

BEHO′LDING, *ppr.* Fixing the eyes upon; looking on; seeing.

2. Fixing the attention; regarding with attention.

3. Obligation. [*Not used.*] *Carew.*

4. Obliged. *Bacon on Love.* A mistaken use of the word for *beholden.*

BEHO′LDINGNESS, *n.* The state of being obliged. *Donne. Sidney.* [*An error, and not in use.*]

BEHON′EY, *v. t.* To sweeten with honey. *Sherwood.*

BEHOOF′, *n.* [Sax. *behofian*, to want, to be necessary, to be expedient; hence, to be a duty; D. *behoeven*, to need; Ger. *behuf*, behoof; Dan. *behöver*, to need, to lack; *behov*, need, necessity, sufficiency, maintenance, that is, things needed; Sw. *behof*, need; *behofwa*, to need.]

1. *Radically,* need, necessity; whence, by an easy analogy, the word came to signify that which supplies want. Hence, in present usage,

2. That which is advantageous; advantage; profit; benefit.

> No mean recompense it brings to your *behoof.* *Milton.*

BEHOOV′ABLE, *a.* Needful; profitable.

BEHOOVE, *v. t.* *behoov′.* [Sax. *behofian*, to want, to be necessary, or expedient. *Supra.*]

To be necessary for; to be fit for; to be meet for, with respect to necessity, duty, or convenience.

> And thus it *behooved* Christ to suffer. Luke xxiv.

It may perhaps be used intransitively; as, let him behave as it *behooveth;* but I believe such use is rare.

BEHOOVEFUL, *a.* *behoov′ful.* Needful; useful; profitable; advantageous.

BEHOOVEFULLY, *adv.* *behoov′fully.* Usefully; profitably. [*Obs.* or *nearly so.*]

BEHOT′, *pret.* of *behight. Obs.*

BEHOVE, and its derivatives. [See *Behoove.*]

BEHOWL′, *v. i.* [*be* and *howl.*] To howl at. [*Not used.*] *Shak.*

BE′ING, *ppr.* [See *Be.*] Existing in a certain state.

> Man, *being* in honor, abideth not. Ps. xlix.

BE′ING, *n.* Existence; as, God is the author of our *being.*

> In God we live, and move, and have our *being.* Acts xvii.

2. A particular state or condition. [*This is hardly a different sense.*]

3. A person existing; *applied to the human race.*

4. An immaterial, intelligent existence, or spirit.

> Superior *beings,* when of late they saw
> A mortal man unfold all nature's law— *Pope.*

5. An animal; any living creature.

> Animals are such *beings,* as are endowed with sensation and spontaneous motion.

BEJA′DE, *v. t.* [*be* and *jade.*] To tire. [*Not used.*] *Milton.*

BEJA′PE, *v. t.* To laugh at; to deceive. [*Not used.*] *Chaucer.*

BEKISS′, *v. t.* [*be* and *kiss.*] To kiss or salute. [*Not in use.*] *Jonson.*

BEKNA′VE, *v. t.* [*be* and *knave.*] To call knave. [*Not used.*] *Pope.*

BEKNOW′, *v. t.* [*be* and *know.*] To acknowledge. [*Not used.*] *Chaucer.*

BELA′BOR, *v. t.* [perhaps from *be* and *labor;* but in Russ. *bulava* is a club.] To beat soundly; to thump.

> Ajax *belabors* there a harmless ox. *Dryden.*

BELA′CE, *v. t.* [*be* and *lace.*] To fasten, as with a lace or cord.

2. To beat; to whip.

BELA′CED, *a.* Adorned with lace. *Beaumont.*

BEL′AMÖUR, *n.* [Fr. *bel-amour.*] A gallant; a consort. [*Not used.*] *Spenser.*

BEL′AMY, *n.* [Fr. *bel-ami.*] A good friend; an intimate. [*Not used.*] *Spenser.*

BELA′TE, *v. t.* [*be* and *late.*] To retard or make too late. [*Not used.*]

BELA′TED, *a.* [*be* and *lated.*] Benighted; abroad late at night.

2. Too late for the hour appointed or intended; later than the proper time.

BELA′TEDNESS, *n.* A being too late. *Milton.*

BELA′VE, *v. t.* [*be* and *lave.*] To wash. [*Not used.*]

BELAW′GIVE, *v. t.* To give a law to. [*Barbarous and not used.*] *Milton.*

BELA′Y, *v. t.* [This word is composed of *be* and *lay,* to lay to, lay by, or close. See *Beleaguer.*]

1. To block up, or obstruct. *Dryden. Gower.*

2. To place in ambush. *Spenser.*

3. To adorn, surround, or cover. *Spenser.*

4. In *seamanship,* to fasten, or make fast, by winding a rope round a cleat, kevil, or belaying-pin. It is chiefly applied to the running rigging. *Mar. Dict.*

BELA′YED, *pp.* Obstructed; ambushed; made fast.

BELA′YING, *ppr.* Blocking up; laying an ambush; making fast.

BELCH, *v. t.* [Sax. *bealcan,* to belch, that is, to push out, to swell or heave; *belgan,* to be angry, that is, to swell with passion; Eng. *bulge, bilge, bulk;* allied to W. *balc,* prominent.]

1. To throw or eject wind from the stomach with violence.

2. To eject violently from a deep hollow place; as, a volcano *belches* flames and lava.

BELCH, *n.* The act of throwing out from the stomach, or from a hollow place; eructation.

2. A cant name for malt liquor. *Dennis.*

BELCH′ED, *pp.* Ejected from the stomach, or from a hollow place.

BELCH′ING, *ppr.* Ejecting from the stomach or any deep hollow place.

BELCH′ING, *n.* Eructation. *Barret.*

BEL′DAM, *n.* [Fr. *belle,* fine, handsome, and *dame,* lady. It seems to be used in contempt, or as a cant term.]

1. An old woman. *Shak.*

Spenser seems to have used the word in its true sense for *good dame.*

2. A hag. *Dryden. Shak.*

BELE′AGUER, *v. t.* *belee′ger.* [Ger. *belagern,* from *be,* by, near, and *lagern,* to lay; D. *belegeren,* to besiege, to convene, to belay; Sw. *belægra,* to besiege; Dan. *beligger;* Russ. *oblegayu.*]

To besiege; to block up; to surround with an army, so as to preclude escape. *Dryden.*

BELE′AGUERED, *pp.* Besieged.

BELE′AGUERER, *n.* One who besieges. *Sherwood.*

BELE′AGURING, *ppr.* Besieging; blocking up.

BELE′AVE, *v. t.* [*be* and *leave.*] To leave. [*Not used.*] *May*

BELEE′, *v. t.* [*be* and *lee.*] To place on the lee, or in a position unfavorable to the wind. [*Not used.*] *Shak.*

BELEM′NITE, *n.* [Gr. βελεμνον, a dart, or arrow, from βελος, from the root of βαλλω, *pello,* to throw.]

Arrow-head, or finger stone; vulgarly called thunder-bolt, or thunder stone. A genus of fossil shells, common in chalk and limestone. These shells consist of an interior cone, divided into partitions connected by a syphon, as in the nautilus, and surrounded by a number of concentric layers, made up of fibers radiating from the axis. These layers are somewhat transparent, and when burnt, rubbed or scraped, give the odor of rasped horn. The species are now extinct. *Encyc. Ed. Encyc.*

BELEP′ER, *v. t.* To infect with leprosy. [*Not used.*] *Beaumont.*

BEL′FRY, *n.* [Fr. *befroy;* barb. L. *belfredus.*]

1. Among military writers of the middle age, a tower erected by besiegers to overlook the place besieged, in which sentinels were placed to watch the avenues, and to prevent surprise from parties of the enemy, or to give notice of fires, by ringing a bell. *Encyc.*

2. That part of a steeple, or other building, in which a bell is hung, and more particularly, the timber work which sustains it. *Encyc.*

BELGARD′, *n.* [Fr. *bel* and *egard.*] A soft look or glance. [*Not used.*] *Spenser.*

BEL′ĠIAN, *a.* [See *Belgic.*] Belonging to Belgica, or the Netherlands.

BEL′ĠIAN, *n.* A native of Belgica, or the Low Countries.

BEL′ĠIC, *a.* [L. *belgicus,* from *Belgae,* the inhabitants of the Netherlands and the country bordering on the Rhine, from that river to the Seine and the ocean. The name may have been given to them from their *bulk* or large stature; W. *balc,* prominent, proud, from *bal,* a shooting out; Eng. *bulge;* Russ. *velikai,* great. See Pomp. Mela. Lib. 3. 3, and 3. 5: Tac. Agric: Joseph. De Bell. Jud. 2. 16: Herod. L. 6: Strabo. L. 4. Owen supposes the Welch name, *Belgiad,* to have been given them, from their bursting forth and ravaging Britain and Ireland. But they had the name on the continent, before their irruption into Britain.]

Pertaining to the *Belgae,* who, in Cesar's time, possessed the country between the Rhine, the Seine and the ocean. They were of Teutonic origin, and anterior to Cesar's invasion of Gaul and Britain, colonies of them had established themselves in the southern part of Britain. The country was called from its inhabitants *Belgica,* not *Belgium,* which was the town of *Beauvais.* See Cluv. Germ. Ant. 2. 2.

Belgic is now applied to the Netherlands, called also Flanders, or that part of the Low Countries which formerly belonged to the house of Austria.

BE'LIAL, *n.* [Heb. בליעל.] As a noun, unprofitableness; wickedness. As an adjective, worthless; wicked. In a collective sense, wicked men. *Parkhurst.*

BELI'BEL, *v. t.* [*be* and *libel.*] To libel or traduce. [*Not used.*] *Fuller.*

BELI'E, *v. t.* [*be* and *lie.* Sax. *belecgan*, of *be* and *leogan*, to lie, *lig*, or *lyg*, a lie; D. *beliegen*; Ger. *belügen*, to belie. See *Lie.*]

1. To give the lie to; to show to be false; to charge with falsehood; as, the heart *belies* the tongue. It is rarely used of declarations; but of appearances and facts which show that declarations, or certain appearances and pretences are false and hypocritical. Hence,

2. To counterfeit; to mimic; to feign resemblance.

With dust, with horse's hoofs, that beat the ground,
And martial brass, *belie* the thunder's sound. *Dryden.*

3. To give a false representation.

Should I do so, I should *belie* my thoughts. *Shak.*

4. To tell lies concerning; to calumniate by false reports.

Thou dost *belie* him, Percy. *Shak.*

5. To fill with lies.

Slander doth *belie* all corners of the world.
[*Not legitimate.*] *Shak.*

BELI'ED, *pp.* Falsely represented either by word or obvious evidence and indication; counterfeited; mimicked.

BELIE'F, *n.* [Sax. *geleaf*, leave, license, permission, consent, assent, belief, faith or trust; *geleafan, gelefan, geliefan, gelyfan*, to believe; *leofan*, to leave and to live. From these words, it appears that *belief* is from the root of *leave*, permission, assent; Sax. *leaf*, leave and *belief*, fides; *leofa*, permission, license; written also *lif* and *lufa*; *lyfan*, to permit; D. *geloof*, G. *glaube*, belief, credit, faith; *gelooven, glauben*, to believe; Dan. *belover*, to promise; D. *oorlof, verlof*, leave, permission; G. *urlaub*, leave, *furlow.* The primary sense of *believe* is to throw or put to, or to assent to; to leave with or to rest on; to rely. See *Leave* and *Live.*]

1. A persuasion of the truth, or an assent of mind to the truth of a declaration, proposition or alledged fact, on the ground of evidence, distinct from personal knowledge; as the *belief* of the gospel; *belief* of a witness. *Belief* may also be founded on internal impressions, or arguments and reasons furnished by our own minds; as the *belief* of our senses; a train of reasoning may result in *belief. Belief* is opposed to *knowledge* and *science.*

2. In *theology*, faith, or a firm persuasion of the truths of religion.

No man can attain [to] *belief* by the bare contemplation of heaven and earth. *Hooker.*

3. Religion; the body of tenets held by the professors of faith.

In the heat of persecution, to which christian *belief* was subject, upon its first promulgation. *Hooker.*

4. In some cases, the word is used for persuasion or opinion, when the evidence is not so clear as to leave no doubt; but the shades of strength in opinion can hardly be defined, or exemplified. Hence the use of qualifying words; as a *firm, full* or *strong belief.*

5. The thing believed; the object of belief.

Superstitious prophecies are the *belief* of fools. *Bacon.*

6. A creed; a form or summary of articles of faith. In this sense, we generally use *Creed.*

BELIE'VABLE, *a.* That may be believed; credible. *Sherwood.*

BELIE'VE, *v. t.* To credit upon the authority or testimony of another; to be persuaded of the truth of something upon the declaration of another, or upon evidence furnished by reasons, arguments, and deductions of the mind, or by other circumstances, than personal knowledge. When we *believe* upon the authority of another, we always put confidence in his veracity. When we *believe* upon the authority of reasoning, arguments, or a concurrence of facts and circumstances, we rest our conclusions upon their strength or probability, their agreement with our own experience, &c.

2. To expect or hope with confidence; to trust.

I had fainted, unless I had *believed* to see the goodness of the Lord in the land of the living. Ps. xxvii.

BELIE'VE, *v. i.* To have a firm persuasion of any thing. In some cases, to have full persuasion, approaching to certainty; in others, more doubt is implied. It is often followed by *in* or *on*, especially in the scriptures. *To believe in*, is to hold as the object of faith. "Ye *believe in* God, *believe* also *in* me." John xiv. *To believe on*, is to trust, to place full confidence in, to rest upon with faith. "To them gave he power to become the sons of God, even to them that *believe on* his name." John i. *Johnson.* But there is no ground for much distinction.

In *theology*, to *believe* sometimes expresses a mere assent of the understanding to the truths of the gospel; as in the case of Simon. Acts viii. In others, the word implies, with this assent of the mind, a yielding of the will and affections, accompanied with a humble reliance on Christ for salvation. John i. 12. iii. 15.

In *popular use*, and *familiar discourse*, to *believe* often expresses an opinion in a vague manner, without a very exact estimate of evidence, noting a mere preponderance of opinion, and is nearly equivalent to *think* or *suppose.*

BELIE'VED, *pp.* Credited; assented to, as true.

BELIE'VER, *n.* One who believes; one who gives credit to other evidence than that of personal knowledge.

2. In *theology*, one who gives credit to the truth of the scriptures, as a revelation from God. In a more restricted sense, a professor of christianity; one who receives the gospel, as unfolding the true way of salvation, and Christ, as his Savior.

In *the primitive church*, those who had been instructed in the truths of the gospel and baptized, were called *believers*; in distinction from the *catechumens*, who were under instruction, as preparatory to baptism and admission to church privileges. *Encyc.*

BELIE'VING, *ppr.* Giving credit to testimony or to other evidence than personal knowledge.

BELIE'VINGLY, *adv.* In a believing manner.

BELI'KE, *adv.* [*be* and *like.*] Probably; likely; perhaps. [*Nearly antiquated.*]

BELI'KELY, *adv.* Probably. [*Not used.*] *Hall.*

BELI'VE, *adv.* [See *Live.*] Speedily; quickly. *Obs.* *Spenser.*

BELL, *n.* [Sax. *bell, bella, belle*, so named from its sound; Sax. *bellan*, to *bawl*, or *bellow*; W. *ballaw*; G. *bellen*; D. *id.*; coinciding with βαλλω and *pello.* See *Peal.*]

1. A vessel or hollow body, used for making sounds. Its constituent parts are a barrel or hollow body, enlarged or expanded at one end, an ear or cannon by which it is hung to a beam, and a clapper on the inside. It is formed of a composition of metals. Bells are of high antiquity. The blue tunic of the Jewish High Priest was adorned with golden bells; and the kings of Persia are said to have the hem of their robe adorned with them in like manner. Among the Greeks, those who went the nightly rounds in camps or garrisons, used to ring a bell, at each sentinel-box, to see that the soldier on duty was awake. Bells were also put on the necks of criminals, to warn persons to move out of the way of so ill an omen, as the sight of a criminal or his executioner; also on the necks of beasts and birds, and in houses. In churches and other public buildings, bells are now used to notify the time of meeting of any congregation or other assembly. *Encyc.*

In private houses, bells are used to call servants, either hung and moved by a wire, or as hand-bells. Small bells are also used in electrical experiments.

2. A hollow body of metal, perforated, and containing a solid ball, to give sounds when shaken; used on animals, as on horses or hawks.

3. Any thing in form of a bell, as the cup or calix of a flower.

To bear the bell, is to be the first or leader, in allusion to the bell-wether of a flock, or the leading horse of a team or drove, that wears bells on his collar.

To shake the bells, a phrase of Shakspeare, signifies to move, give notice or alarm.

BELL, *v. i.* To grow in the form of bells, as buds or flowers.

BELL'-FASHIONED, *a.* Having the form of a bell. *Mortimer.*

BELL'-FLOWER, *n.* [*bell* and *flower.*] A genus of plants, so named from the shape of the corol or flower which resembles a bell, L. *Campanula*, a genus of monogynian pentanders, comprehending many species.

BELL'-FOUNDER, *n.* [*bell* and *founder.*] A man whose occupation is to found or cast bells.

BELL'-MAN, *n.* [*bell* and *man.*] A man who rings a bell, especially to give notice of any thing in the streets.

BELL'-METAL, *n.* [*bell* and *metal.*] A mixture of copper and tin, in the proportion of about ten parts of copper to one of tin, or according to Thomson, three parts to one, and usually a small portion of brass or zink; used for making bells. *Encyc.*

BELL'-PEPPER, *n.* [*bell* and *pepper.*] A name of the Guinea pepper, a species of Capsicum. This is the red pepper of the gardens, and most proper for pickling. *Encyc.*

BELL'-RINGER, *n.* One whose business is to ring a church or other bell.

BELL'-SHAPED, *a.* [*bell* and *shape.*] Hàving the form of a bell. *Botany.*

BELL'-WETHER, *n.* [*bell* and *wether.*] A wether or sheep which leads the flock, with a bell on his neck.

BELL'-WÖRT, *n.* A plant, the Uvularia. *Muhlenberg.*

BEL'LADONNA, *n.* A plant, a species of Atropa, or deadly nightshade. *Lee.*

BEL'LATRIX, *n.* [L.] A ruddy, glittering star of the second magnitude, in the left shoulder of Orion; so named from its imagined influence in exciting war. *Encyc.*

BELLE, *n. bel.* [Fr., from L. *bellus*, It. *bello*, Sp. *bello*, handsome, fine, whence to *embellish;* allied perhaps to Russ. *bielo*, white.]

A young lady. In *popular use*, a lady of superior beauty and much admired.

BELL'ED, *a.* Hung with bells.

BELLES-LETTRES, *n. plu. bel' letter*, or anglicised, *bell-letters.* [Fr. See *Belle* and *Letter.*]

Polite literature; a word of very vague signification. It includes poetry and oratory; but authors are not agreed to what particular branches of learning the term should be restricted. *Encyc.*

BELL'IBONE, *n.* [Fr.*belle* and *bonne.*] A woman excelling both in beauty and goodness. [*Not in use.*] *Spenser.*

BELLIG'ERENT, *a.* [L. *belliger*, warlike; *belligero*, to wage war; from *bellum*, war, and *gero*, to wage; part. *gerens, gerentis*, waging. Gr. πολεμος, war; W. *bel*, war, tumult; *bela*, to war, to wrangle.]

Waging war; carrying on war; as a *belligerent* nation.

BELLIG'ERENT, *n.* A nation, power or state carrying on war.

BELLIG'EROUS, *a.* The same as *belligerent.* [*Not used.*]

BELL'ING, *n.* [Sax. *bellan*, to bellow.] The noise of a roe in rutting time; *a huntsman's term.* *Dict.*

2. *a.* Growing or forming like a bell; growing full and ripe; used of hops; from *bell.* *Ash.*

BELLIP'OTENT, *a.* [L. *bellum*, war, and *potens*, powerful, *bellipotens.*]

Powerful or mighty in war. [*Little used.*] *Dict.*

BELLIQUE, *a. bellee'k.* [Old Fr.] Warlike. [*Not used.*] *Feltham.*

BEL'LON, *n.* A disease, attended with languor and intolerable griping of the bowels, common in places where lead ore is smelted. *Encyc.*

BELLO'NA, *n.* [from L. *bellum*, war.] The goddess of war. *Ant. Mythol.*

BEL'LŌW, *v. i.* [Sax. *bulgian, bylgean;* W. *ballaw;* L. *balo;* D. *bulken;* Sw. *bȯla;* Sax. *bellan*, to bawl. See *Bawl.*]

1. To make a hollow, loud noise, as a bull; to make a loud outcry; to roar. In *contempt*, to vociferate or clamor.

2. To roar, as the sea in a tempest, or as the wind when violent; to make a loud, hollow, continued sound. *Dryden.*

BEL'LŌW, *n.* A loud outcry; roar.

BEL'LŌWING, *ppr.* Making a loud hollow sound, as a bull, or as the roaring of billows.

BEL'LŌWING, *n.* A loud hollow sound or roar. *Herbert.*

BEL'LŌWS, *n. sing.* and *plu.* [Sax. *bilig* or *bylig*, bellows; and *bilig, bylg*, a blown bladder, a bottle; Goth. *balgs, bylg, bylga*, a mail or budget; L. *bulga;* Ir. *builg, bolg*, a bellows; Ger. *balg*, a skin; *blasebalg*, a bellows, that is, a blow-skin; D. *blaasbalg;* Sw. *blåsbalg;* Dan. *blæsebelg.* See *Blaze.* The word is properly in the singular number, Goth *balgs*, but is used also in the plural. It seems to be the same word as the L. *follis*, and probably from shooting out, swelling or driving, W. *bal.*]

An instrument, utensil or machine for blowing fire, either in private dwellings or in forges, furnaces and shops. It is so formed as by being dilated and contracted, to inhale air by a lateral orifice which is opened and closed with a valve, and to propel it through a tube upon the fire.

BEL'LŌWS-FISH, *n.* The trumpet-fish, about four inches long, with a long snout; whence its name. *Dict. of Nat. Hist.*

BEL'LUINE, *a.* [L. *belluinus*, from *bellua*, a beast.]

Beastly; pertaining to or like a beast; brutal. [*Little used.*] *Atterbury.*

BEL'LY, *n.* [Ir. *bolg*, the *belly*, a bag, pouch, budget, blister, bellows; W. *boly*, the belly, whence *boliaw*, to belly, to gorge; Arm. *boelcu*, bowels. The primary sense is swelled, or a swell.]

1. That part of the human body which extends from the breast to the thighs, containing the bowels. It is called also the abdomen or lower belly, to distinguish it from the head and breast, which are sometimes called *bellies*, from their cavity. *Quincy.*

2. The part of a beast, corresponding to the human belly.

3. The womb. Jer. i. 5.

4. The receptacle of food; that which requires food, in opposition to the back.

> Whose god is their *belly.* Phil. iii.

5. The part of any thing which resembles the human belly in protuberance or cavity, as of a harp or a bottle.

6. Any hollow inclosed place; as the *belly* of hell, in *Jonah.*

7. In *scripture*, *belly* is used for the heart. Prov. xviii. 8. xx. 30. John vii. 38. Carnal lusts, sensual pleasures. Rom. xvi. 18. Phil. iii. 19. The whole man. Tit. i. 12. *Brown. Cruden.*

BEL'LY, *v. t.* To fill; to swell out. *Shak.*

BEL'LY, *v. i.* To swell and become protuberant, like the belly; as, *bellying* goblets; *bellying* canvas. *Dryden. Phillips.*

2. To strut. *Bailey.*

BEL'LY-ACHE, *n.* [*belly* and *ache.*] Pain in the bowels; the colic. [*Vulgar.*]

BEL'LY-ACHE BUSH or **WEED**, *n.* A species of Jatropha.

BEL'LY-BAND, *n.* A band that encompasses the belly of a horse, and fastens the saddle; a girth. *Sherwood.*

BEL'LY-BOUND, *a.* Diseased in the belly, so as to be costive, and shrunk in the belly. *Johnson.*

BEL'LY-CHEER, *n.* Good cheer. [*Not used.*] *Chaucer.*

BEL'LY-FRETTING, *n.* The chafing of a horse's belly, with a fore girt.

2. A violent pain in a horse's belly, caused by worms. *Dict.*

BEL'LYFUL, *n.* [*belly* and *full.*] As mnch as fills the belly, or satisfies the appetite. In *familiar* and *ludicrous language*, a great abundance; more than enough. [*Vulgar.*] *Johnson.*

BEL'LY-GOD, *n.* [*belly* and *god.*] A glutton; one who makes a god of his belly; that is, whose great business or pleasure is to gratify his appetite.

BEL'LYING, *ppr.* Enlarging capacity; swelling out, like the belly.

BEL'LY-PINCHED, *a.* [See *Pinch.*] Starved; pinched with hunger. *Shak.*

BEL'LY-ROLL, *n.* [See *Roll.*] A roller protuberant in the middle, to roll land between ridges, or in hollows. *Mortimer.*

BEL'LY-SLAVE, *n.* A slave to the appetite. *Homily.*

BEL'LY-TIMBER, *n.* [See *Timber.*] Food; that which supports the belly. [*Vulgar.*] *Prior. Hudibras.*

BEL'LY-WÖRM, *n.* [See *Worm.*] A worm that breeds in the belly or stomach. *Johnson.*

BELOCK', *v. t.* [Sax. *belucan*, from *loc*, a lock, with *be.*]

To lock or fasten as with a lock. *Shak.*

BEL'OMANCY, *n.* [Gr. βελος, an arrow, and μαντεια, divination.]

A kind of divination, practiced by the ancient Scythians, Babylonians and other nations, and by the Arabians. A number of arrows, being marked, were put into a bag or quiver, and drawn out at random; and the marks or words on the arrow drawn determined what was to happen. See Ezek. xxi. 21. *Encyc.*

BELO'NE, *n.* [Gr. βελονη, a needle.] The gar, garfish, or sea-needle, a species of Esox. It grows to the length of two or three feet, with long pointed jaws, the edges of which are armed with small teeth. *Encyc.*

BELONG', *v. i.* [D. *belangen*, to concern, *belang*, concern, interest, importance, of *be* and *lang;* Ger. *belangen*, to attain to, or come to; *anlangen*, to arrive, to come to, to concern, touch or belong; Dan. *anlanger*, to arrive at, to belong. In Sax. *gelangian* is to call or bring. The radical sense of *long* is to extend or draw out, and with *be* or *an*, it signifies to *extend to*, to reach.]

1. To be the property of; as, a field *belongs* to Richard Roe; Jamaica *belongs* to G. Britain.

2. To be the concern or proper business of; to appertain; as, it *belongs* to John Doe to prove his title.

3. To be appendant to.

> He went into a desert place *belonging* to Bethsaida. Luke ix.

4. To be a part of, or connected with, though detached in place; as, a beam or rafter

belongs to such a frame, or to such a place in the building.

5. To have relation to.

And David said, to whom *belongest* thou? 1 Sam. xxx.

6. To be the quality or attribute of.

To the Lord our God *belong* mercies and forgiveness. Dan. ix.

7. To be suitable for.

Strong meat *belongeth* to them of full age. Heb. v.

8. To relate to, or be referred to.

He careth for things that *belong* to the Lord. 1 Cor. vii.

9. To have a legal residence, settlement, or inhabitancy, whether by birth or operation of law, so as to be entitled to maintenance by the parish or town.

Bastards also are settled in the parishes to which the mothers *belong*. *Blackstone.*

Hence,

10 To be the native of; to have original residence.

There is no other country in the world to which the Gipeys could *belong*. *Grellman.* Pref. 12.

11. In *common language*, to have a settled residence; to be domiciliated.

BELONG'ING, *ppr.* Pertaining; appertaining; being the property of; being a quality of; being the concern of; being appendant to; being a native of, or having a legal or permanent settlement in.

BELONG'ING, *n.* A quality. [*Not in use.*] *Shak.*

BELŎV'ED, *ppr.* [*be* and *loved*, from *love*. *Belove*, as a verb, is not used.]

Loved; greatly loved; dear to the heart. *Paul.*

BELŌW, *prep.* [*be* and *low.*] Under in place; beneath; not so high; as, *below* the moon; *below* the knee.

2. Inferior in rank, excellence or dignity. *Felton.*

3. Unworthy of; unbefitting. *Dryden.*

BELŌW, *adv.* In a lower place, with respect to any object; as, the heavens above and the earth *below*.

2. On the earth, as opposed to the heavens.

The fairest child of Jove *below*. *Prior.*

3. In hell, or the region of the dead; as the realms *below*. *Dryden.*

4. In a court of inferior jurisdiction; as, at the trial *below*. *Wheaton.*

BELOWT', *v. t.* [See *Lowt.*] To treat with contemptuous language. [*Not in use.*] *Camden.*

BEL'SWAGGER, *n.* A lewd man. *Dryden.*

BELT, *n.* [Sax. *belt*; Sw. *bålt*; Dan. *bælte*; L. *balteus*. Qu. Ir. *balt*, a *welt*. Class Bl.]

1. A girdle; a band, usually of leather, in which a sword or other weapon is hung.

2. A narrow passage, or strait between the isle of Zealand and that of Funen at the entrance of the Baltic, usually called the *Great Belt*. The *Lesser Belt* is the passage between the isle of Funen, and the coast of Jutland.

3. A bandage or band used by surgeons for various purposes.

4. In *astronomy*, certain girdles or rings, which surround the planet Jupiter, are called *belts*.

5. A disease among sheep, cured by cutting off the tail, laying the sore bare, then casting mold on it, and applying tar and goose-grease. *Encyc.*

BELT, *v. t.* To encircle. *Warton.*

BELU'GA, *n.* [Russ. signifying white fish.] A fish of the cetaceous order, and genus *Delphinus*, from 12 to 18 feet in length. The tail is divided into two lobes, lying horizontally, and there is no dorsal fin. In swimming, this fish bends its tail under its body like a lobster, and thrusts itself along with the rapidity of an arrow. This fish is found in the arctic seas and rivers, and is caught for its oil and its skin. *Pennant.*

BEL'VIDERE, *n.* [L. *bellus*, fine, and *video*, to see.]

1. A plant, a species of chenopodium, goose-foot or wild orach, called scoparia or annual mock cypress. It is of a beautiful pyramidical form, and much esteemed in China, as a salad, and for other uses. *Encyc.*

2. In *Italian architecture*, a pavilion on the top of an edifice; an artificial eminence in a garden. *Encyc.*

BELYE. [See *Belie.*]

BE'MA, *n.* [Gr. βημα.] A chancel. [*Not in use.*] *Beaumont.*

2. In *ancient Greece*, a stage or kind of pulpit, on which speakers stood when addressing an assembly. *Mitford.*

BEMAD', *v. t.* [*be* and *mad.*] To make mad. [*Not in use.*] *Shak.*

BEMAN'GLE, *v. t.* [*be* and *mangle.*] To mangle; to tear asunder. [*Little used.*] *Beaumont.*

BEM'ASK, *v. t.* [*be* and *mask.*] To mask; to conceal. *Shelton.*

BEMA'ZE, *v. t.* To bewilder. [See *Maze.*] [*Little used.*] *Cowper.*

BEME'TE, *v. t.* [*be* and *mete.*] To measure. [*Not in use.*] *Shak.*

BEMIN'GLE, *v. t.* [*be* and *mingle.*] To mingle; to mix. [*Little used.*]

BEMI'RE, *v. t.* [*be* and *mire.*] To drag or incumber in the mire; to soil by passing through mud or dirty places. *Swift.*

BEMIST', *v. t.* [*be* and *mist.*] To cover or involve in mist. [*Not used.*] *Felton.*

BEMŌAN, *v. t.* [*be* and *moan.*] To lament; to bewail; to express sorrow for; as, to *bemoan* the loss of a son. *Jeremiah.*

BEMŌANABLE, *a.* That may be lamented. [*Not used.*] *Sherwood.*

BEMŌANED, *pp.* Lamented; bewailed.

BEMŌANER, *n.* One who laments.

BEMŌANING, *ppr.* Lamenting; bewailing.

BEMOCK', *v. t.* [*be* and *mock.*] To treat with mockery. [*Little used.*] *Shak.*

BEMOCK', *v. i.* To laugh at.

BEMOIL', *v. t.* [*be* and *moil.* Fr. *mouiller*, to wet.]

To bedraggle; to bemire; to soil or incumber with mire and dirt. [*Not in use.*] *Shak.*

BEMŌL, *n.* In *music*, a half note. *Bacon.*

BEMON'STER, *v. t.* [*be* and *monster.*] To make monstrous. [*Not in use.*] *Shak.*

BEMŌURN, *v. t.* To weep or mourn over. [*Little used.*]

BEMU'SED, *a.* [*be* and *muse.*] Overcome with musing; dreaming; *a word of contempt.* *Johnson. Pope.*

BEN or BEN'-NUT, *n.* A purgative fruit or nut, the largest of which resembles a filbert, yielding an oil used in pharmacy. *Encyc.*

BENCH, *n.* [Ir. *binse*; Corn. *benk*; Sax. *benc*; Fr. *banc*. See *Bank.*]

1. A long seat, usually of board or plank, differing from a stool in its greater length.

2. The seat where judges sit in court; the seat of justice. Hence,

3. The persons who sit as judges; the court. *Shak. Dryden.*

Free bench, in England, the estate in copyhold lands, which the wife, being espoused a virgin, has for her dower, after the decease of her husband. This is various in different manors, according to their respective customs.

King's Bench, in England, a court in which the king formerly sat in person, and which accompanied his household. The court consists of the Lord Chief Justice, and three other justices, who have jurisdiction over all matters of a criminal or public nature. It has a crown side and a plea side; the former determining criminal, the latter, civil causes. *Blackstone.*

BENCH, *v. t.* To furnish with benches. *Dryden.*

2. To seat on a bench. *Shak.*

3. *v. i.* To sit on a seat of justice. *Shak.*

BENCH'ER, *n.* In *England*, the benchers in the inns of court, are the senior members of the society who have the government of it. They have been readers, and being admitted to plead within the bar, are called inner barristers. They annually elect a treasurer. *Encyc. Johnson.*

2. The alderman of a corporation. *Ashmole.*

3. A judge. *Shak.*

BEND, *v. t.* pret. *bended* or *bent*: pp. *bended* or *bent*. [Sax. *bendan*, to bend; Fr. *bander*, to bend, bind or tie; Ger. *binden*, to wind, bind or tie; D. *binden*, the same; Sw. *banda*, to bind; Dan. *binder*, to bind; L. *pando*, *pandare*, to bend in; *pando*, *pandere*, to open; *pandus*, bent, crooked; It. *banda*, sidewise; *benda*, a fillet or band; *bendare*, to crown; Sp. *pandear*, to bend or be inclined, to bulge out, to belly; *pandeo*, a bulge or protuberance; *pando*, jutting out. The primary sense is, to stretch or strain. *Bend* and *bind* are radically the same word.]

1. To strain, or to crook by straining; as, to *bend* a bow.

2. To crook; to make crooked; to curve; to inflect; as, to *bend* the arm.

3. To direct to a certain point; as, to *bend* our steps or course to a particular place.

4. To exert; to apply closely; to exercise laboriously; to intend or stretch; as, to *bend* the mind to study.

5. To prepare or put in order for use; to stretch or strain.

He hath *bent* his bow and made it ready. Ps. vii.

6. To incline; to be determined; that is, to stretch towards, or cause to tend; as, to be *bent* on mischief.

It expresses disposition or purpose.

7. To subdue; to cause to yield; to make submissive; as, to *bend* a man to our will.

8. In *seamanship*, to fasten, as one rope to another or to an anchor; to fasten, as a sail to its yard or stay; to fasten, as a cable to the ring of an anchor. *Mar. Dict.*

9. *To bend the brow*, is to knit the brow; to scowl; to frown. *Camden.*

BEND, *v. i.* To be crooked; to crook, or be curving. *Sandys.*
2. To incline; to lean or turn; as, a road *bends* to the west.
3. To jut over; as a *bending* cliff.
4. To resolve, or determine. [See *Bent on.*] *Dryden.*
5. To bow or be submissive. Is. lx.

BEND, *n.* A curve; a crook; a turn in a road or river; flexure; incurvation.
2. In *marine language*, that part of a rope which is fastened to another or to an anchor. [See *To bend.* No. 8.]
3. *Bends* of a ship, are the thickest and strongest planks in her sides, more generally called *wales.* They are reckoned from the water, *first, second* or *third bend.* They have the beams, knees, and foot hooks bolted to them, and are the chief strength of the ship's sides. *Encyc. Mar. Dict.*
4. In *heraldry*, one of the nine honorable ordinaries, containing a third part of the field, when charged, and a fifth, when plain. It is made by two lines drawn across from the dexter chief, to the sinister base point. It sometimes is indented, ingrailed, &c. *Johnson. Encyc.*

BEND, *n.* A band. [*Not in use.*] *Spenser.*

BEND'ABLE, *a.* That may be bent or incurvated. *Sherwood.*

BEND'ED, BENT, } *pp.* Strained; incurvated: made crooked; inclined; subdued.

BEND'ER, *n.* The person who bends, or makes crooked; also, an instrument for bending other things.

BEND'ING, *ppr.* Incurvating; forming into a curve; stooping; subduing; turning as a road or river; inclining; leaning; applying closely, as the mind; fastening.

BEND'LET, *n.* In *heraldry*, a little bend, which occupies a sixth part of a shield. *Bailey.*

BEND'-WITH, *n.* A plant. *Dict.*

BEND'Y, *n.* In *heraldry*, the field divided into four, six or more parts, diagonally, and varying in metal and color. *Encyc. Ash.*

BENE, *n. ben'y.* The popular name of the sesamum orientale, called in the West Indies vangloe, an African plant. *Mease.*

BENE'APED, *a.* [*be* and *neap.*] Among *seamen*, a ship is *beneaped*, when the water does not flow high enough to float her from a dock or over a bar. *Encyc.*

BENE'ATH, *prep.* [Sax. *beneath, beneothan, benythan*; of *be* and *neothan*, below, under. See *Nether.*]
1. Under; lower in place, with something directly over or on, as to place a cushion *beneath* one; often with the sense of *pressure* or *oppression*, as to sink *beneath* a burden, in *a literal sense.*
2. Under, in *a figurative sense;* bearing heavy impositions, as taxes, or oppressive government.

Our country sinks *beneath* the yoke. *Shak.*

3. Lower in rank, dignity or excellence; as, brutes are *beneath* man; man is *beneath* angels, in the scale of beings.
4. Unworthy of; unbecoming; not equal to; as, he will do nothing *beneath* his station or character.

BENE'ATH, *adv.* In a lower place; as, the earth from *beneath* will be barren. *Mortimer.*
2. Below, as opposed to heaven, or to any superior region; as, in heaven above, or in earth *beneath.*

BEN'EDICT, *a.* [L. *benedictus.*] Having mild and salubrious qualities. [*Not in use.*] *Bacon.*

BENEDIC'TINE, *a.* Pertaining to the order or monks of St. Benedict, or St. Benet.

BENEDIC'TINES, *n.* An order of monks, who profess to follow the rules of St. Benedict; an order of great celebrity. They wear a loose black gown, with large wide sleeves, and a cowl on the head, ending in a point. In the canon law, they are called *black friars.*

BENEDIC'TION, *n.* [L. *benedictio*, from *bene*, well, and *dictio*, speaking. See *Boon* and *Diction.*]
1. The act of blessing; a giving praise to God or rendering thanks for his favors; a blessing pronounced; hence grace before and after meals.
2. Blessing, prayer, or kind wishes, uttered in favor of any person or thing; a solemn or affectionate invocation of happiness; thanks; expression of gratitude.
3. The advantage conferred by blessing. *Bacon.*
4. The form of instituting an abbot, answering to the consecration of a bishop. *Ayliffe.*
5. The external ceremony performed by a priest in the office of matrimony is called the *nuptial benediction.* *Encyc.*
6. In *the Romish Church*, an ecclesiastical ceremony by which a thing is rendered sacred or venerable. *Encyc.*

BENEFAC'TION, *n.* [L. *benefacio*, of *bene*, well, and *facio*, to make or do.]
1. The act of conferring a benefit.

More generally,

2. A benefit conferred, especially a charitable donation. *Atterbury.*

BENEFAC'TOR, *n.* He who confers a benefit, especially one who makes charitable contributions either for public institutions or for private use.

BENEFAC'TRESS, *n.* A female who confers a benefit. *Delany.*

BEN'EFICE, *n.* [L. *beneficium*; Fr. *benefice.* See *Benefaction.*]
1. *Literally*, a benefit, advantage or kindness. But in *present usage*, an ecclesiastical living; a church endowed with a revenue, for the maintenance of divine service, or the revenue itself. All church preferments are called benefices, except bishoprics, which are called *dignities.* But ordinarily, the term *dignity* is applied to bishoprics, deaneries, arch-deaconries, and prebendaries; and *benefice*, to parsonages, vicarages, and donatives. *Encyc.*
2. In the middle ages, *benefice* was used for a fee, or an estate in lands, granted at first for life only, and held *ex mero beneficio* of the donor. The estate afterwards becoming hereditary, took the appellation of *feud*, and *benefice* became appropriated to church livings. *Encyc.*

BEN'EFICED, *a.* Possessed of a benefice or church preferment. *Ayliffe.*

BEN'EFICELESS, *a.* Having no benefice. [*Not used.*] *Sheldon.*

BENEF'ICENCE, *n.* [L. *beneficentia*, from the participle of *benefacio.*]
The practice of doing good; active goodness, kindness, or charity.

BENEF'ICENT, *a.* Doing good; performing acts of kindness and charity. It differs from *benign*, as the *act* from the *disposition; beneficence* being *benignity* or kindness exerted in action. *Johnson.*

BENEF'ICENTLY, *adv.* In a beneficent manner.

BENEFI''CIAL, *a.* Advantageous; conferring benefits; useful; profitable; helpful; contributing to a valuable end; followed by *to;* as, industry is *beneficial to* the body, as well as *to* the property.
2. Receiving or entitled to have or receive advantage, use or benefit; as the *beneficial* owner of an estate. *Kent.*

BENEFI''CIALLY, *adv.* Advantageously; profitably; helpfully.

BENEFI''CIALNESS, *n.* Usefulness; profitableness. *Hale.*

BENEFI''CIARY, *a.* [L. *beneficiarius.* See *Benefaction.*]
Holding some office or valuable possession, in subordination to another; having a dependent and secondary possession. *Bacon.*

BENEFI''CIARY, *n.* One who holds a benefice. A beneficiary is not the proprietor of the revenues of his church; but he has the administration of them, without being accountable to any person. The word was used, in the middle ages, for a feudatory, or vassal. *Encyc.*
2. One who receives any thing as a gift, or is maintained by charity. *Blackstone.*

BENEFI''CIENCY, *n.* Kindness or favor bestowed. *Brown.*

BENEFI''CIENT, *a.* Doing good. *Adam Smith.*

BEN'EFIT, *n.* [Primarily from L. *beneficium*, or *benefactum;* but perhaps directly from the Fr. *bienfait*, by corruption.]
1. An act of kindness; a favor conferred.

Bless the Lord, O my soul, and forget not all his *benefits.* Ps. ciii.

2. Advantage; profit; a word of extensive use, and expressing whatever contributes to promote prosperity and personal happiness, or add value to property.

Men have no right to what is not for their *benefit.* *Burke.*

3. In law, *benefit of clergy.* [See *Clergy.*]

BEN'EFIT, *v. t.* To do good to; to advantage; to advance in health, or prosperity; *applied either to persons or things;* as, exercise *benefits* health; trade *benefits* a nation.

BEN'EFIT, *v. i.* To gain advantage; to make improvement; as, he has *benefited* by good advice; that is, he has been benefited.

BEN'EFITED, *pp.* Profited; having received benefit.

BEN'EFITING, *ppr.* Doing good to; profiting; gaining advantage.

BENE'ME, *v. t.* [Sax. *be* and *naman.*] To name. [*Not in use.*] *Spenser.*
2. To promise; to give. [*Not in use.*] *Spenser.*

BENEMP'NE, *v. t.* To name. [*Not in use.*] *Spenser.*

BENEPLAC'ITURE, *n.* [L. *beneplacitum*, *bene*, well, and *placitum*, from *placeo*, to please.]
Will; choice. [*Not in use.*] *Glanville.*

BENET', *v. t.* [*be* and *net.*] To catch in a net; to ensnare. [*Not used.*] *Shak.*

BENEV'OLENCE, *n.* [L. *benevolentia*, of *bene*, well, and *volo*, to will or wish. See *Will.*]

1. The disposition to do good; good will; kindness; charitableness; the love of mankind, accompanied with a desire to promote their happiness.

The *benevolence* of God is one of his moral attributes; that attribute which delights in the happiness of intelligent beings. "God is love." 1 John iv.

2. An act of kindness; good done; charity given.

3. A species of contribution or tax illegally exacted by arbitrary kings of England. *Blackstone.*

BENEV'OLENT, *a.* [L. *benevolens*, of *bene* and *volo.*]

Having a disposition to do good; possessing love to mankind, and a desire to promote their prosperity and happiness; kind.

BENEV'OLENTLY, *adv.* In a kind manner; with good will.

BENGAL', *n.* A thin stuff made of silk and hair, for women's apparel, so called from Bengal in the E. Indies. *Bailey. Johnson.*

BENGALEE', *n.* The language or dialect spoken in Bengal.

BENGALE'SE, *n. sing.* and *plu.* A native or the natives of Bengal. *As. Res.* vii. 171.

BENI'GHT, *v. t.* [*be* and *night.*] To involve in darkness; to shroud with the shades of night.

The clouds *benight* the sky. *Garth.*

2. To overtake with night; as a *benighted* traveler.

3. To involve in moral darkness, or ignorance; to debar from intellectual light; as *benighted* nations, or heathen.

BENI'GHTED, *pp.* Involved in darkness, physical or moral; overtaken by the night.

BENI'GN, *a. beni'ne.* [L. *benignus*, from the same root, as *bonus*, *bene*, ancient L. *benus*, Eng. *boon.*]

1. Kind; of a kind disposition; gracious; favorable.

Our Creator, bounteous and *benign*. *Milton.*

2. Generous; liberal; as a *benign* benefactor.

3. Favorable; having a salutary influence; as the *benign* aspect of the seasons.

The *benign* light of revelation. *Washington.*

4. Wholesome; not pernicious; as a *benign* medicine. *Arbuthnot.*

5. Favorable; not malignant; as a *benign* disease.

BENIG'NANT, *a.* Kind; gracious; favorable.

BENIG'NITY, *n.* Goodness of disposition or heart; kindness of nature; graciousness.

2. Actual goodness; beneficence.

3. Salubrity; wholesome quality; or that which tends to promote health. *Wiseman.*

BENI'GNLY, *adv. beni'nely.* Favorably; kindly; graciously.

BEN'ISON, *n.* *s* as *z.* [Fr. *benir*, to bless; *benissant*, blessing; from the root of *bene*, *bonus*, *boon.* See *Boon.*]

Blessing; benediction. [Nearly antiquated.] *Johnson.*

BEN'JAMIN, *n.* A tree, the *Laurus Benzoin*, a native of America, called also *spice-bush.* It grows to the height of 15 or 20 feet, with a very branchy head.

2. A gum or resin, or rather a balsam. [See *Benzoin.*] *Encyc.*

BEN'NET, *n.* The herb bennet, or avens, known in botany by the generic term *Geum.* *Fam. of Plants.*

BEN'NET FISH, *n.* A fish of two feet in length, caught in the African seas, having scales of a deep purple, streaked with gold. *Dict. of Nat. Hist.*

BENT, *pp.* of *bend.* Incurvated; inflected; inclined; prone to or having a fixed propensity; determined.

Bent on, having a fixed inclination; resolved or determined on.

BENT, *n.* The state of being curving, crooked, or inclined from a straight line; flexure; curvity.

2. Declivity; as the *bent* of a hill. [*Unusual.*] *Dryden.*

2. Inclination; disposition; a leaning or bias of mind; propensity; as the *bent* of the mind or will; the *bent* of a people towards an object. This may be natural or artificial, occasional or habitual, with indefinite degrees of strength.

4. Flexion; tendency; particular direction; as the *bents* and turns of a subject. *Locke.*

5. Application of the mind; a *bending* of the mind in study or investigation. *Locke.*

BENT, } *n.* A kind of grass, called
BENT'-GRASS, } in botany, *Agrostis*, of several species. *Encyc.*

BENT'ING-TIME, *n.* The time when pigeons feed on bents, before peas are ripe. *Johnson. Dryden.*

BENUM', corruptly **BENUMB'**, *v. t.* [Sax. *beniman*, *benyman*, pp. *benumen*, to seize, of *be* and *niman*, Sax. and Goth., to take or seize. This root is retained in *withernam.* It is to be observed, that *b* after *m*, in *numb*, *thumb*, *dumb*, &c., is an arbitrary addition of modern writers.]

1. To make torpid; to deprive of sensation; as, a hand or foot *benummed* by cold.

2. To stupify; to render inactive; as, to *benum* the senses. *Dryden.*

BENUM'MED, *pp.* Rendered torpid; deprived of sensation; stupified.

BENUM'MING, *ppr.* Depriving of sensation; stupifying.

BEN'ZOATE, *n.* [See *Benzoin.*] A salt formed by the union of the benzoic acid with any salifiable base.

BENZO'IC, *a.* Pertaining to benzoin.

Benzoic acid, or flowers of Benzoin, is a peculiar vegetable acid, obtained from Benzoin and other balsams, by sublimation or decoction. It is a fine light white matter in small needles; its taste pungent and bitterish, and its odor slightly aromatic. *Thomson.*

BENZOIN', } *n.* Gum benjamin; a con-
BEN'JAMIN, } crete resinous juice flowing from the *Styrax Benzoin*, a tree of Sumatra, &c. It is properly a balsam, as it yields benzoic acid. It flows from incisions made in the stem or branches. It is solid and brittle, sometimes in yellowish white tears joined together by a brown substance, and sometimes of a uniform brown substance like resin. It has little taste, but its smell, especially when rubbed or heated, is extremely fragrant and agreeable. It is chiefly used in cosmetics and perfumes. *Encyc. Thomson.*

BEPA'INT, *v. t.* [*be* and *paint.*] To paint; to cover with paint. [*Little used.*] *Shak.*

BEPA'LE, *v. t.* [*be* and *pale.*] To make pale. [*Not in use.*] *Carew.*

BEPINCH', *v. t.* [*be* and *pinch.*] To mark with pinches.

BEPINCH'ED, } *pp.* Marked with pinches.
BEPINCHT', } *Chapman.*

BEPOW'DER, *v. t.* [*be* and *powder.*] To powder; to sprinkle or cover with powder.

BEPRA'ISE, *v. t.* [*be* and *praise.*] To praise greatly or extravagantly. *Goldsmith.*

BEPUR'PLE, *v. t.* [*be* and *purple.*] To tinge or dye with a purple color.

BEQUE'ATH, *v. t.* [Sax. *becwœthan*; *be* and *cwethan*, to say; *cwid*, a saying, opinion, will, testament; *cythan*, to testify; Eng. *quoth.*]

To give or leave by will; to devise some species of property by testament; as, to *bequeath* an estate or a legacy.

BEQUE'ATHED, *pp.* Given or left by will.

BEQUE'ATHING, *ppr.* Giving or devising by testament.

BEQUE'ATHMENT, *n.* The act of bequeathing; a bequest.

BEQUEST', *n.* Something left by will; a legacy.

BERA'IN, *v. t.* To rain upon. [*Not in use.*] *Chaucer.*

BERA'TE, *v. t.* [*be* and *rate.*] To chide vehemently; to scold.

BERAT'TLE, *v. t.* [*be* and *rattle.*] To fill with rattling sounds or noise. *Shak.*

BERA'Y, *v. t.* To make foul; to soil. [*Not in use.*] *Milton.*

BER'BERRY, *n.* [L. *berberis.*] [See *Barberry.*]

BERE, *n.* [Sax. *ber*, barley.] The name of a species of barley in Scotland. *Gray.*

BERE'AVE, *v. t.* pret. *bereaved*, *bereft*: pp. *bereaved*, *bereft.* [Sax. *bereafian*, of *be* and *reafian*, to deprive. See *Rob* and *Reap.*]

1. To deprive; to strip; to make destitute; with *of* before the thing taken away.

Me have ye *bereaved of* my children. Gen. xlii.

It is sometimes used without *of*, and is particularly applied to express the loss of friends by death.

2. To take away from. *Shak.*

BERE'AVED, *pp.* Deprived; stripped and left destitute.

BERE'AVEMENT, *n.* Deprivation, particularly by the loss of a friend by death.

BERE'AVING, *ppr.* Stripping bare; depriving.

BEREFT', *pp.* of *bereave.* Deprived; made destitute.

BERENGA'RIANISM, *n.* The opinions or doctrines of Berengarius, archdeacon of St. Mary at Anjou, and of his followers, who deny the reality of the body and blood of Christ in the Eucharist. *Encyc.*

BERG, *n.* [Sax. *beorg*, *beorh*, a hill, a castle.]

A borough; a town that sends burgesses to Parliament; a castle. [See *Burg.*] *Obs.* *Ash.*

BERG'AMOT, *n.* [Fr. *bergamote*; Sp. *bergamota.*]

1. A species of pear.

2. A species of citron, at first casually produced by an Italian, who grafted a citron on the stock of a bergamot pear tree. The fruit has a fine taste and smell, and its essential oil is in high esteem as a perume. This oil is extracted from the yellow rind of the fruit. Hence,

3. An essence or perfume from the citron thus produced.

4. A species of snuff perfumed with bergamot.

5. A coarse tapestry, manufactured with flocks of wool, silk, cotton, hemp and ox or goat's hair, said to have been invented at Bergamo in Italy. *Encyc.*

BERG'ANDER, *n.* [*berg*, a cliff, and Dan. *and*, G. *ente*, Sax. *ened*, a duck.]

A burrow duck; a duck that breeds in holes under cliffs. *Thomson.*

BER'GERET, *n.* [Fr. *berger*, a shepherd.] A song. [*Not used.*] *Chaucer.*

BERG'MANITE, *n.* [from *Bergman*, the mineralogist.]

A mineral classed with scapolite, in the family of felspath. It occurs massive, with gray and red quartz in Norway. Its colors are greenish and grayish white. *Cyc.*

BERG'MASTER, *n.* [Sax. *beorg*, a hill or castle, and *master.*]

The bailiff or chief officer among the Derbyshire miners. *Johnson.*

BERG'MOTE, *n.* [Sax. *beorg*, a hill, and *mote*, a meeting.]

A court held on a hill in Derbyshire, in England, for deciding controversies between the miners. *Blount. Johnson.*

BERHY'ME, *v. t.* [*be* and *rhyme.*] To mention in rhyme or verse; *used in contempt.* *Shak.*

BER'LIN, *n.* A vehicle of the chariot kind, supposed to have this name from Berlin, the chief city of Prussia, where it was first made, or from the Italian *berlina*, a sort of stage or pillory, and a coach. *Encyc.*

BERLUC'CIO, *n.* A small bird, somewhat like the yellow hammer, but less and more slender. *Dict. of Nat. Hist.*

BERME, *n.* In *fortification*, a space of ground of three, four or five feet in width, left between the rampart and the moat or foss, designed to receive the ruins of the rampart, and prevent the earth from filling the foss. Sometimes, it is palisaded, and in Holland, it is generally planted with quick-set hedge. *Encyc.*

BER'NACLE, [See *Barnacle.*]

BER'NARDINE, *a.* Pertaining to St. Bernard, and the monks of the order.

BER'NARDINS, *n.* An order of monks, founded by Robert, abbot of Moleme, and reformed by St. Bernard. The order originated about the beginning of the 12th century. They wear a white robe, with a black scapulary; and when they officiate, they are clothed with a large white gown, with great sleeves, and a hood of the same color. *Encyc.*

BEROB', *v. t.* [*be* and *rob.*] To rob. [*Not in use.*] *Spenser.*

BER'OE, *n.* A marine animal of an oval or spherical form, nearly an inch in diameter, and divided into longitudinal ribs, like a melon. *Dict. of Nat. Hist.*

BER'RIED, *a.* Furnished with berries.

BER'RY, *n.* [Sax. *beria*, a grape or cluster of grapes; *berga*, a grape stone, a berry.]

1. A succulent or pulpy fruit, containing naked seeds. Or in more technical language, a succulent pulpy pericarp, or seed vessel, without valves, containing several seeds, which are naked, that is, which have no covering but the pulp and rind. It is commonly round or oval. This botanical definition includes the orange and other like fruits. But in popular language, *berry* extends only to the smaller fruits, as strawberry, gooseberry, &c., containing seeds or granules.

2. A mound. [for *barrow.*] *W. Browne.*

BER'RY, *v. i.* To bear or produce berries.

BER'RY-BEARING, *a.* Producing berries.

BERT. Sax. *beorht*, *berht*; Eng. *bright.* This word enters into the name of many Saxon princes and noblemen; as Egbert, Sigbert. The *Bertha* of the northern nations was by the Greeks called *Eudoxia*, an equivalent word. Of the same sort were *Phædrus*, *Epiphanius*, *Photius*, *Lampridius*, *Fulgentius*, *Illustris.* *Camden.* [See *Bright.*]

BERTH, *n.* [from the root of *bear.*]

1. A station in which a ship rides at anchor, comprehending the space in which she ranges. In more familiar usage, the word signifies any situation or place, where a vessel lies or can lie, whether at anchor or at a wharf.

2. A room or apartment in a ship, where a number of officers or men mess and reside.

3. The box or place for sleeping at the sides of a cabin; the place for a hammoc, or a repository for chests, &c.

To berth, in seamen's language, is to allot to each man a place for his hammoc.

BER'TRAM, *n.* [L. *pyrethrum*, said to be from πυρ, fire, from its acrid quality.]

Bastard pellitory, a plant.

BER'YL, *n.* [L. *beryllus*; Gr. βηρυλλος; Ch. Syr. Eth. a gem, beryl, and in Syr. crystal, and a *pearl*; the latter word being a different orthography of *beryl*; probably from the root of the Fr. *briller*, to shine, Eng. *brilliant*, Eth. በረሀ bareah, to shine.]

A mineral, considered by Cleaveland as a subspecies of Emerald. Its prevailing color is green of various shades, but always pale. Its crystals are usually longer and larger than those of the precious emerald, and its structure more distinctly foliated. It is harder than the apatite, with which it has been confounded; harder and less heavy than the pycnite. The best beryls are found in Brazil, in Siberia and Ceylon, and in Dauria, on the frontiers of China. They are found in many parts of the United States. *Silliman. Cleaveland.*

BER'YL-CRYSTAL, *n.* A species of imperfect crystal, of a very pure, clear, and equal texture. It is always of the figure of a long and slender column, irregularly hexangular, and tapering at the top. Its color is a pale brown, of a fine transparency. *Encyc.*

BER'YLLINE, *a.* Like a beryl; of a light or bluish green.

BESA'INT, *v. t.* [*be* and *saint.*] To make a saint. [*Not in use.*]

BESA'YLE, *n.* [Norm. *ayle*; Fr. *aïeul*, a grandfather.] A great grandfather.

If the abatement happened on the death of one's grandfather or grandmother, a writ of *ayle* lieth; if on the death of the great grandfather, then a writ of *besayle*; but if it mounts *one* degree higher, to the *tresayle*, or grandfather's grandfather, &c., the writ is called a writ of *cosinage*, or *de consanguineo.* *Blackstone.*

BESCAT'TER, *v. t.* [*be* and *scatter.*] To scatter over. [*Not used.*] *Spenser.*

BESCORN', *v. t.* [*be* and *scorn.*] To treat with scorn; to mock at. [*Not used.*] *Chaucer.*

BESCRATCH', *v. t.* [*be* and *scratch.*] To scratch; to tear with the nails. [*Not in use.*] *Chaucer.*

BESCRAWL', *v. t.* [*be* and *scrawl.*] To scrawl; to scribble over. *Milton.*

BESCREE'N, *v. t.* [*be* and *screen.*] To cover with a screen; to shelter; to conceal. *Shak.*

BESCREE'NED, *pp.* Covered; sheltered; concealed.

BESCRIB'BLE, *v. t.* To scribble over. *Milton.*

BESCUM'BER, *v. t.* [from *cumber.*] To encumber. [*Not legitimate nor used.*] *B. Jonson.*

BESEE', *v. i.* [*be* and *see.*] To look; to mind. [*Not in use.*] *Wickliffe.*

BESEE'CH, *v. t.* pret. and pp. *besought.* [Sax. *be* and *secan*, to seek, enquire, follow; D. *verzoeken*; Ger *ersuchen*; from *seek*, *sequor*, to follow, with *be*, by, near, about; that is, to follow close, to press. See *Seek* and *Essay.* The Saxon has *gesecan.*]

To entreat; to supplicate; to implore; to ask or pray with urgency; followed by *a person*; as, "I Paul *beseech you* by the meekness of Christ," 2 Cor. x.; or by a *thing*; as, I *beseech* your patience.

BESEE'CHER, *n.* One who beseeches.

BESEE'CHING, *ppr.* Entreating.

BESEE'K, *v. t.* To beseech. [*Not used.*] *Chaucer.*

BESEE'M, *v. t.* [*be* and *seem.*] To become; to be fit for, or worthy of; to be decent for.

What form of speech or behavior *beseemeth* us, in our prayers to God? *Hooker.*

BESEE'MING, *ppr.* or *a.* Becoming; fit; worthy of.

BESEE'MING, *n.* Comeliness. *Barret.*

BESEE'MLY, *a.* Becoming; fit; suitable.

BESEE'N, *a.* Adapted; adjusted. [*Not used.*] *Spenser.*

BESET', *v. t.* pret. and pp. *beset.* [Sax. *besettan*, to place, of *be* and *settan*, to set; D. *bezetten*; Ger. *besetzen.* See *Set.*]

1. To surround; to inclose; to hem in; to besiege; as, we are *beset* with enemies; a city is *beset* with troops. Hence,

2. To press on all sides, so as to perplex; to entangle, so as to render escape difficult or impossible.

Adam sore *beset* replied. *Milton.*

3. To waylay. *Shak.*

4. To fall upon. *Spenser.*

BESET'TING, *ppr.* Surrounding; besieging; waylaying.

BESET'TING, *a.* Habitually attending, or pressing; as a *besetting* sin.

BESHI'NE, *v. t.* To shine upon. [*Not used.*]

BESHREW', *v. t.* [*be* and *shrew.*] To wish a curse to; to execrate. *Dryden.*

2. To happen ill to. [*Not in use.*] *Shak.*

BESHUT′, *v. t.* To shut up. [*Not used.*] *Chaucer.*

BESI′DE, *prep.* [*be* and *side*, by the side.]

1. At the side of a person or thing; near; as, sit down *beside* me, or *beside* the stream.
2. Over and above; distinct from.

Beside all this, between us and you, there is a great gulf fixed. Luke xvi.

3. On one side; out of the regular course or order; not according to, but not contrary.

It is *beside* my present business to enlarge upon this speculation. *Locke.*

4. Out of; in a state deviating from; as, to put one *beside* his patience. Hence,
5. With the reciprocal pronoun, *beside one's self* is out of the wits or senses; out of the order of reason, or of rational beings.

Paul, thou art *beside* thyself. Acts xxvi.

BESI′DES, *prep.* Over and above; separate or distinct from.

And there was a famine in the land, *besides* the first famine. Gen. xxvi.

Note. This word, though radically the same as *beside*, and a corruption of it, ought not to be confounded with it, for it is never used in the senses explained under *beside*, except in the second.

BESI′DE, BESI′DES, } *adv.* Moreover; more than that; over and above; distinct from; not included in the number, or in what has been mentioned.

Besides, you know not what is the fate of your friend.

The men said to Lot, hast thou here any *besides?* Gen. xix.

To all *beside*, as much an empty shade,
An Eugene living, as a Cesar dead. *Pope.*

These sentences may be considered as elliptical.

BESID′ERY, *n.* A species of pear. *Johnson.*

BESIE′GE, *v. t.* [*be* and *siege;* Fr. *siege*, and *assieger*, to *besiege.* See *Siege.*]

1. To lay siege to; to beleaguer; to beset, or surround with armed forces, for the purpose of compelling to surrender, either by famine or by violent attacks; as, to *besiege* a castle or city.
2. To beset; to throng round.

BESIE′GED, *pp.* Surrounded or beset with hostile troops.

BESIE′GER, *n.* One who lays siege, or is employed in a siege.

BESIE′GING, *ppr.* Laying siege; surrounding with armed forces.

BESIE′GING, *a.* Surrounding in a hostile manner; employed in a siege; as a *besieging* army.

BESIT′, *v. t.* [*be* and *sit.*] To suit; to become. [*Not used.*] *Spenser.*

BESLA′VE, *v. t.* To subjugate; to enslave. [*Not used.*] *Bp. Hall.*

BESLI′ME, *v. t.* To daub with slime; to soil. [*Not used.*] *B. Jonson.*

BESLUB′BER, *v. t.* [*be* and *slubber, slabber.*] To soil or smear with spittle, or any thing running from the mouth or nose. [*Vulgar.*]

BESME′AR, *v. t.* [*be* and *smear.*] To bedaub; to overspread with any viscous, glutinous matter, or with any soft substance that adheres. Hence, to foul; to soil.

BESME′ARED, *pp.* Bedaubed; overspread with any thing soft, viscous, or adhesive; soiled.

BESME′ARER, *n.* One that besmears.

BESME′ARING, *ppr.* Bedaubing; soiling.

BESMIRCH′ *v. t.* [*be* and *smirch.*] To soil; to foul; to discolor. [*Little used.*] *Shak.*

BESMO′KE, *v. t.* [*be* and *smoke.*] To foul with smoke; to harden or dry in smoke. [*Little used.*]

BESMO′KED, *pp.* Fouled or soiled with smoke; dried in smoke.

BESMUT′, *v. t.* [*be* and *smut.*] To blacken with smut; to foul with soot.

BESMUT′TED, *pp.* Blackened with smut or soot.

BESNOW, *v. t.* [*be* and *snow.* Sax. *besniwed*, participle.] To scatter like snow. [*Little used.*] *Gower.*

BESNÔWED, *a.* or *pp.* [*be* and *snow.*] Covered or sprinkled with snow, or with white blossoms. *Hanbury.*

BESNUFF′, *v. t.* To befoul with snuff.

BESNUFF′ED, *pp.* Foul with snuff. *Young.*

BE′SOM, *n.* *s* as z. [Sax. *besm*, a brush or broom; *besman*, twigs. Orosius, 2. 3. Ger. *besen;* D. *bezem;* Arm. *bezo*, birch. The *besom* was a little bundle of twigs used for sweeping.]

A broom; a brush of twigs for sweeping.

I will sweep it with the *besom* of destruction, saith the Lord of Hosts. Is. xiv.

BE′SOM, *v. t.* To sweep, as with a besom.

Rolls back all Greece, and *besoms* wide the plain. *Barlow.*

BESORT′, *v. t.* [*be* and *sort.*] To suit; to fit; to become. *Shak.*

BESORT′, *n.* Company; attendance; train. *Obs.* *Shak.*

BESOT′, *v. t.* [*be* and *sot.*] To make sottish; to infatuate; to stupify; to make dull or senseless. *Milton.*

2. To make to dote. *Shak.*

BESOT′TED, *pp.* Made sottish or stupid.

Besotted on, infatuated with foolish affection. *Dryden.*

BESOT′TEDLY, *adv.* In a foolish manner. *Milton.*

BESOT′TEDNESS, *n.* Stupidity; arrant folly; infatuation. *Milton.*

BESOT′TING, *ppr.* Infatuating; making sottish or foolish.

BESOUGHT′, *besaut′. pp.* of *beseech.* Entreated; implored; sought by entreaty.

BESPAN′GLE, *v. t.* [*be* and *spangle.*] To adorn with spangles; to dot or sprinkle with something brilliant; as, the heavens *bespangled* with stars.

BESPAN′GLED, *pp.* Adorned with spangles or something shining.

BESPAN′GLING, *ppr.* Adorning with spangles or glittering objects.

BESPAT′TER, *v. t.* [*be* and *spatter.*] To soil by spattering; to sprinkle with water, or with dirt and water.

2. To asperse with calumny or reproach. *Swift.*

BESPAT′TERED, *pp.* Spattered over; soiled with dirt and water; aspersed; calumniated.

BESPAT′TERING, *ppr.* Spattering with water; soiling with dirt and water; aspersing.

BESPAWL′, *v. t.* [*be* and *spawl.*] To soil or make foul with spittle. *Milton.*

BESPE′AK, *v. t.* pret. *bespoke;* pp. *bespoke, bespoken.* [*be* and *speak.*]

1. To speak for beforehand; to order or engage against a future time; as, to *bespeak* a seat in a public coach.

My lady is *bespoke.* *Shak.*

2. To forebode; to foretell.

They started fears, and *bespoke* dangers, to scare the allies. *Swift.*

3. To speak to; to address. This sense is mostly poetical.

He thus the queen *bespoke.* *Dryden.*

4. To betoken; to show; to indicate by external marks or appearances; as, his manners *bespeak* him a gentleman.

BESPE′AKER, *n.* One who bespeaks.

BESPE′AKING, *ppr.* Speaking for or ordering beforehand; foreboding; addressing; showing; indicating.

BESPE′AKING, *n.* A previous speaking or discourse, by way of apology, or to engage favor. *Dryden.*

BESPECK′LE, *v. t.* [*be* and *speckle.*] To mark with speckles or spots. *Milton.*

BESPI′CE, *v. t.* [*be* and *spice.*] To season with spices. *Shak.*

BESPIRT′, BESPURT′, } *v. t.* To spurt out, or over; to throw out in a stream or streams. [*Not used.*] *Milton.*

BESPIT′, *v. t.* pret. *bespit;* pp. *bespit, bespitten.* [*be* and *spit.*] To daub or soil with spittle. *Johnson.*

BESPO′KE, *pret.* and *pp.* of bespeak.

BESPOT′, *v. t.* [*be* and *spot.*] To mark with spots. *Mortimer.*

BESPOT′TED, *pp.* Marked with spots.

BESPOT′TING, *ppr.* Marking with spots.

BESPREAD′, *v. t.* *bespred′.* pret. and pp. *bespread.* [*be* and *spread.*] To spread over; to cover over; as, to *bespread* with flowers.

BESPRINK′LE, *v. t.* [*be* and *sprinkle.*] To sprinkle over; to scatter over; as, to *besprinkle* with dust.

BESPRINK′LED, *pp.* Sprinkled over.

BESPRINK′LER, *n.* One that sprinkles over.

BESPRINK′LING, *ppr.* Sprinkling over.

BEST, *a. superlative.* [Sax. *best*, contracted from *betest*, from *bet*, more, or better; *betre* is also used; *betan*, to amend, or restore, correct, heal; *bote*, reparation, compensation; Eng. *boot*, to *boot;* Goth. *botyan*, to profit, aid, assist; Eng. *but;* G. *bass*, good, *besser*, better, *beste*, best; D. *beter, best;* Dan. *beste;* Sw. *båst.* This word has no connection in origin with *good.* See *Better.*]

Literally, most advanced. Hence,

1. Most good; having good qualities in the highest degree; applied indifferently to physical or moral subjects; as, the *best* man; the *best* road; the *best* cloth; the *best* abilities. This, like *most*, and other attributes, is often used without its noun, when the noun is obvious; as, men are all sinners; the *best* of them fail in the performance of duty.
2. Most advanced; most accurate; as the *best* scholar.
3. Most correct or complete; as the *best* view of a landscape, or of a subject.
4. *The best.* This phrase is elliptical, and may be variously interpreted; as, the utmost power; the strongest endeavor; the most, the highest perfection; as, let a man do his *best;* let him do a thing to *the best* of his power.
5. *At best*, in the best manner; in the utmost

degree or extent, applicable to the case; as, life is *at best* very short.

To make the best of, to carry to its greatest perfection; to improve to the utmost; as, *to make the best of* a sum of money, or a piece of land. Also, to permit the least possible inconvenience; as, *to make the best of* ill fortune or a bad bargain.

The best of the way. We had made *the best of our way* to the city; that is, the most, the greatest part of the distance. [*This is the primary sense of the word.*]

BEST, *adv.* In the highest degree; beyond all other; as, to love one *best*; to like this *best*; to please *best.*

2. To the most advantage; with the most ease; as, "which instrument can you *best* use?"

3. With most profit or success; as, money is *best* employed in manufactures; this medicine will answer *best* in the present case.

4. Most intimately or particularly; most correctly; as, what is expedient is *best* known to himself.

BEST-TEM′PERED, *a.* Having the most kind or mild temper.

BESTA′IN, *v. t.* [*be* and *stain.*] To mark with stains; to discolor, either the whole surface of a thing, or in spots. *Shak.*

BESTEAD′, *v. t. bested′.* pret. and pp. *bested.* [*be* and *stead.*] To profit.

How little you *bestead.* *Milton.*

2. To accommodate.

They shall pass through it, *hardly bestead.* Is. 8.

That is, distressed; perplexed.

3. To dispose. *Spenser.*

BES′TIAL, *a.* [from *beast.*]

1. Belonging to a beast, or to the class of beasts.

2. Having the qualities of a beast; brutal; below the dignity of reason or humanity; carnal; as a *bestial* appetite. *Shak.*

BESTIAL′ITY, *n.* The quality of beasts; the state or manners of man which resemble those of brutes.

2. Unnatural connection with a beast.

BES′TIALIZE, *v. t.* To make like a beast.

BES′TIALLY, *adv.* Brutally; in a manner below humanity.

BESTICK′, *v. t.* pret. and pp. *bestuck.* [*be* and *stick.*]

To stick over, as with sharp points; to mark, by infixing points or spots here and there.

Truth shall retire, *bestuck* with slanderous darts. *Milton.*

BESTIR′, *v. t. bestur′.* [*be* and *stir.*] To put into brisk or vigorous action; to move with life and vigor; usually with the reciprocal pronoun; as, rise and *bestir yourselves.*

BESTIR′RED, *pp.* Roused into vigorous action; quickened in action.

BESTIR′RING, *ppr.* Moving briskly; putting into vigorous action.

BEST′NESS, *n.* The state of being best. [*Not used.*] *Morton.*

BESTORM′, *v. i.* [*be* and *storm.*] To storm; to rage. [*Not used.*] *Young.*

BESTOW, *v. t.* [*be* and *stow,* a place. See *Stow.* Literally, to set or place.]

1. To give; to confer; to impart; with the sense of gratuity, and followed by *on* or *upon.*

Consecrate yourselves to the Lord, that he may *bestow* on you a blessing. Ex. xxxii.

Though I *bestow* all my goods to feed the poor. 1 Cor. xiii. 3.

This word should never be followed by *to.*

2. To give in marriage; to dispose of.

I could have *bestowed* her upon a fine gentleman. *Tatler.*

3. To apply; to place for the purpose of exertion, or use; as, to *bestow* our whole force upon an object.

4. To lay out, or dispose of; to give in payment for; as, to *bestow* money for what we desire. Deut. xiv. 26.

5. To lay up in store; to deposit for safe keeping; to stow; to place.

I have no room where to *bestow* my fruits. Luke xii.

BESTOWAL, *n.* A conferring; disposal. [*Little used.*]

BESTOWED, *pp.* Given gratuitously; conferred; laid out; applied; deposited for safe-keeping.

BESTOWER, *n.* One who bestows; a giver; a disposer.

BESTOWING, *ppr.* Conferring gratuitously; laying out; applying; depositing in store.

BESTOWMENT, *n.* The act of giving gratuitously; a conferring.

God the father had committed the *bestowment* of the blessings purchased, to his son. *Edwards on Redemp.* 372.

If we consider this *bestowment* of gifts in this view. *Chauncey, U. Sal.* 155.

Whatever may be the secret counsel of his will respecting his own *bestowment* of saving grace. *Smalley, Serm.* p. 37.

2. That which is conferred, or given; donation.

They strengthened his hands by their liberal *bestowments* on him and his family. *Christ. Mag.* iii. 665.

The free and munificent *bestowment* of the Sovereign Judge. *Thodey.*

BESTRAD′DLE, *v. t.* To bestride. [See *Straddle.*]

BESTRAUGHT′, *a.* Distracted; mad. [*Not used.*] *Shak.*

BESTREW′, *v. t.* pret. *bestrewed*; pp. *bestrewed, bestrown.* [*be* and *strew.*] To scatter over; to besprinkle; to strow. *Milton.*

BESTREW′ED, *pp.* of *bestrew.*

BESTRI′DE, *v. t.* pret. *bestrid*; pp. *bestrid, bestridden.* [*be* and *stride.*]

1. To stride over; to stand or sit with any thing between the legs, or with the legs extended across; as, to *bestride* the world, like a colossus; to *bestride* a horse. *Shak.*

2. To step over; as, to *bestride* a threshold. *Shak.*

Bestriding sometimes includes *riding,* or *defending,* as Johnson remarks; but the particular purposes of the act, which depend on the circumstances of the case, can hardly be reduced to definition.

BESTRI′DING, *ppr.* Extending the legs over any thing, so as to include it between them.

BESTROWN, *pp.* of *bestrew.* Sprinkled over.

BESTUCK′, *pp.* of *bestick.* Pierced in various places with sharp points.

BESTUD′, *v. t.* [*be* and *stud.*] To set with studs; to adorn with bosses; as, to *bestud* with stars. *Milton.*

BESTUD′DED, *pp.* Adorned with studs.

BESTUD′DING, *ppr.* Setting with studs; adorning as with bosses.

BESWIKE, *v. t. beswik′.* [Sax. *beswican.*] To allure. [*Not used.*] *Gower.*

BET, *n.* [Sax. *bad,* a pledge; *badian,* to give or take a pledge.]

A wager; that which is laid, staked or pledged in a contest, to be won, either by the victorious party himself, or by another person, in consequence of his victory. At a race, a man lays a *bet* on his own horse, or on the horse of another man.

BET, *v. t.* To lay a bet; to lay a wager; to stake or pledge something upon the event of a contest.

BET, the old participle of *beat,* is obsolete or vulgar.

BETA′KE, *v. t.* pret. *betook*; pp. *betaken.* [*be* and *take.* Sax. *betæcan.*]

1. To take to; to have recourse to; to apply; to resort; with the reciprocal pronoun; as, to *betake ourselves* to arms, or to action. It generally implies a motion towards an object, as to *betake ourselves* to a shady grove; or an application of the mind or faculties, corresponding with such motion, as to *betake ourselves* to study or to vice.

2. *Formerly,* to take or seize. *Obs.* *Spenser.*

BETA′KEN, *part.* of *betake.*

BETA′KING, *ppr.* Having recourse to; applying; resorting.

BETAUGHT′, *pret.* of *betake.* [*Not used.*] *Chaucer.*

BETEE′M, *v. t.* [*be* and *teem.*] To bring forth; to produce; to shed; to bestow. [*Not used.*] *Spenser. Shak.*

BE′TEL, BE′TLE, *n.* A species of pepper, the leaves of which are chewed by the inhabitants of the East Indies. It is a creeping or climbing plant like the ivy, the leaves somewhat resembling those of the citron. It is planted by a tree, or supported by props. In India, betel is taken after meals; during a visit, it is offered to friends when they meet, and when they separate; in short, nothing is to be done without betel. To correct the bitterness of the leaves, a little *areca* is wrapped in them with the *chinam,* a kind of burnt lime made of shells. *Encyc.*

BETHINK′, *v. t.* pret. and pp. *bethought.* [*be* and *think.*]

To call to mind; to recall or bring to recollection, reflection, or consideration; generally followed by a reciprocal pronoun, with *of* before the subject of thought.

I have *bethought* myself *of* another fault. *Shak.*

BETHINK′, *v. i.* To have in recollection; to consider. *Spenser.*

BETH′LEHEM, *n.* [Heb. *the house of food or bread.*]

1. A town or village in Judea, about six miles south-east of Jerusalem; famous for its being the place of Christ's nativity.

2. A hospital for lunatics; corrupted into *bedlam.*

BETH′LEMITE, *n.* An inhabitant of Bethlehem; a lunatic.

2. In *church history,* the Bethlemites were a sort of Monks, introduced into England in the year 1257, who were habited like the Dominicans, except that they wore a star with five rays, in memory of the comet or

star which appeared over Bethlehem at the nativity of our Savior. There is an order of Bethlemites also in Peru. *Encyc.*

BETHOUGHT', *bethaut'*, *pret.* and *pp.* of *bethink.*

BETHRALL', *v. t.* [*be* and *thrall.*] To enslave; to reduce to bondage; to bring into subjection. [*Little used.*] *Shak.*

BETHUMP', *v. t.* [*be* and *thump.*] To beat soundly. [*Little used.*] *Shak.*

BETI'DE, *v. t.* pret. *betid*, or *betided*; pp. *betid.* [*be* and *tide.* Sax. *tidan*, to happen. See *Tide.*]

To happen; to befall; to come to; *used of good* or *evil.*

What will *betide* the few? *Milton.*

BETI'DE, *v. i.* To come to pass; to happen.

What news else *betideth* here? *Shak.*

Shakspeare has used it with *of.* What would *betide of* thee? but this is unusual or improper.

BETI'ME, } *adv.* [*be* and *time*, that is, by
BETI'MES, } the time.]

1. Seasonably; in good season or time; before it is late.

To measure life learn thou *betimes.* *Milton.*

2. Soon; in a short time.

He tires *betimes*, that spurs too fast *betimes.* *Shak.*

BETO'KEN, *v. t.* *beto'kn.* [*be* and *token.* Sax. *betæcan.*]

1. To signify by some visible object; to show by signs.

A dewy cloud, and in the cloud a bow
Betokening peace from God. *Milton.*

2. To foreshow by present signs; to indicate something future by that which is seen or known; as, a dark cloud often *betokens* a storm. *Thomson.*

BETO'KENED, *pp.* Foreshown; previously indicated.

BETO'KENING, *ppr.* Indicating by previous signs.

BET'ONY, *n.* [L. *betonica.*] A genus of plants, of several species. The purple or wood betony grows in woods and shady places, and is deemed useful as a mild corroborant. *Encyc.*

BETOOK', *pret.* of *betake.*

BETO'RN, *a.* Torn in pieces.

BETOSS', *v. t.* [*be* and *toss.*] To toss; to agitate; to disturb; to put in violent motion. *Shak. Shelton.*

BETRAP', *v. t.* [from *trap.*] To entrap; to ensnare. [*Not used.*] *Occleve.*

BETRA'Y, *v. t.* [Chaucer wrote *betrass*, *betraiss*, and the Fr. *traître* is a contraction of *traistre*; Arm. *trayçza*, to betray; Norm. *trahir*, to draw in, to betray; *treitre*, a traitor; Fr. *trahir*, which seems to be the L. *traho.* From *trahir*, is formed *trahissant*, and *trahison*, treason. If *traho* is the root, the sense is, to draw aside, to withdraw, or lead away; which would agree with the D. *bedriegen*, G. *betriegen*, Sw. *bedraga*, Dan. *bedrager*, to deceive; and *treachery*, Fr. *tricherie*, is from the root of *trick.* I do not find *betrogan* in the Saxon, but *bedrog* is rendered *fefellit*, and this is from *dragan*, to draw. *Betray* then seems to be a compound of *be* and *dragan*, to draw; and *betrass*, supra, may be from a different root. In strictness, to fail in duty; to be guilty of breach of trust; to violate the confidence reposed. The word does not in itself import to *deliver up*; but by usage, either with or without the word *enemies*, it signifies to deliver up, in breach of trust.]

1. To deliver into the hands of an enemy by treachery or fraud, in violation of trust; as, an officer *betrayed* the city.

The son of man shall be *betrayed* into the hands of men. Matt. xvii.

2. To violate by fraud, or unfaithfulness; as, to *betray* a trust.

If the people of America ever *betray* their trust, their guilt will merit even greater punishment than other nations have suffered, and the indignation of heaven. *J. Adams.*

3. To violate confidence by disclosing a secret, or that which was intrusted; to expose; followed by the person, or the thing; as, my friend *betrayed me*, or *betrayed the secret.*

4. To disclose, or permit to appear, what is intended to be kept secret, or what prudence would conceal.

Be swift to hear, but cautious of your tongue, lest you *betray* your ignorance. *Watts.*

Hence,

5. To mislead or expose to inconvenience not foreseen; as, great confidence *betrays* a man into errors.

6. To show; to discover; to indicate what is not obvious at first view, or would otherwise be concealed.

Nor, after length of years, a stone *betray*
The place where once the very ruins lay. *Addison.*

This river *betrays* its original in its name. *Holwell.*

All the names in the country *betray* great antiquity. *Bryant.*

7. To fail, or deceive.

But when I rise, I shall find my legs *betraying* me. *Johnson, Boswell.*

BETRA'YED, *pp.* Delivered up in breach of trust; violated by unfaithfulness; exposed by breach of confidence; disclosed contrary to expectation or intention; made known; discovered.

BETRA'YER, *n.* One who betrays; a traitor.

BETRA'YING, *ppr.* Delivering up treacherously; violating confidence; disclosing contrary to intention; exposing; discovering.

BETRIM', *v. t.* [*be* and *trim.*] To deck; to dress; to adorn; to grace; to embellish; to beautify; to decorate. *Shak.*

BETRIM'MED, *pp.* Adorned; decorated.

BETRIM'MING, *ppr.* Decking; adorning; embellishing.

BETROTH', *v. t.* [*be* and *troth*, truth, faith. See *Truth*, and *Troth.*]

1. To contract to any one, in order to a future marriage; to promise or pledge one to be the future spouse of another; to affiance; used of either sex. "The father *betroths* his daughter."

2. To contract with one for a future spouse; to espouse; as, a man *betroths* a lady.

3. To nominate to a bishopric, in order to consecration. *Ayliffe.*

BETROTH'ED, *pp.* Contracted for future marriage.

BETROTH'ING, *ppr.* Contracting to any one, in order to a future marriage, as the father or guardian; contracting with one for a future wife, as the intended husband; espousing.

BETROTH'MENT, *n.* A mutual promise or contract between two parties, for a future marriage between the persons betrothed; espousals. *Encyc.*

BETRUST', *v. t.* [*be* and *trust.*] To entrust; to commit to another in confidence of fidelity; to confide. This is less used than *entrust.* *Hall.*

BETRUST'ED, *pp.* Entrusted; confided; committed in trust.

BETRUST'ING, *ppr.* Entrusting; committing in trust.

BETRUST'MENT, *n.* The act of entrusting; the thing entrusted. *Chipman.*

BET'SO, *n.* The smallest Venetian coin. *Mason.*

BET'TER, *a. comp.* of *bet.* See *Best.* [Sax. *bet*, more, better; *betere*, *betera*, better; Sw. *bätter*; D. *beter*; G. *besser*; D. *baat*, profit; *baaten*, to *boot*, to avail; Sans. *bhadra*, good. The primary sense is, more, or advanced further; and in America, this is a common popular signification. This vessel contains *better* than half, that is, more than half; he walked *better* than a mile, that is, more than a mile.]

1. Having good qualities in a greater degree than another; applied to physical, acquired or moral qualities; as a *better* soil, a *better* man, a *better* physician, a *better* house, a *better* air, a *better* harvest.

2. More advantageous.

Were it not *better* for us to return to Egypt? Ex. xiv.

3. More acceptable.

To obey is *better* than sacrifice. 1 Sam. xv.

4. More safe.

It is *better* to trust in the Lord, than to put confidence in man. Ps. cxviii.

5. Improved in health; less affected with disease; as, the patient is *better.*

6. *To be better off*, to be in a better condition. *Beddoes, Hygeia.* This is a very common phrase; but ought not *off*, to be *of*? It is not elegant.

7. *To have the better*, is to have the advantage or superiority, followed by *of* before him or that over which the advantage is enjoyed; as, the English *had the better of* the Spaniards.

8. *To get or gain the better*, is to obtain the advantage, superiority or victory; as, to *get the better of* an enemy.

9. *For the better*, is for the advantage or improvement.

BET'TER, *adv.* In a more excellent manner; with more skill and wisdom, virtue, advantage or success; as, to perform work *better*; to plan a scheme *better*; land *better* cultivated; laws *better* executed; government *better* administered.

2. More correctly, or fully; as, to understand a subject *better* than another.

3. With superior excellence; as, to write or speak *better* than another.

4. With more affection; in a higher degree; as, to love one *better* than another.

It is not easy to specify and exemplify the various applications of *better.* In general, it implies what is more excellent, advantageous, useful, or virtuous, than something else.

BET'TER, *v. t.* [Sax. *beterian*, *betrian.* See *Better.*]

1. To improve; to meliorate; to increase the good qualities of; as, manure *betters* land; discipline may *better* the morals.
2. To surpass; to exceed.

The works of nature do always aim at that which cannot be *bettered*. *Hooker.*

Qu. is not the sense, *made better?*

3. To advance; to support; to give advantage to; as, to *better* a party; to *better* a cause.

BET'TER, *n.* A superior; one who has a claim to precedence on account of his rank, age, or office; as, give place to your *betters*. It is generally or always used in the plural.

BET'TERED, *pp.* Improved; meliorated; made better.

BET'TERING, *ppr.* Making better; improving.

BET'TOR, *n.* [from *bet.*] One who bets or lays a wager. *Addison.*

BET'TY, *n.* [Supposed to be a cant word from the name of a maid; but qu. is it not from the root of *beat* or L. *peto?*]
An instrument to break open doors. *Arbuthnot.*

BETUM'BLED, *a.* [*be* and *tumble.*] Rolled about; tumbled; disordered. *Shak.*

BETWEE'N, *prep.* [Sax. *betweonan, betwynan*; of *be* and *twain*, two, Sax. *tweg, twegen*. The Saxons used, in the same sense, *betuh* and *betweoh*, betwo. *See Twain, Twin.*]

1. In the intermediate space, without regard to distance; as, New-York is *between* Boston and Philadelphia; the Delaware river runs *between* Pennsylvania and New-Jersey.
2. From one to another; passing from one to another, noting exchange of actions or intercourse; as, things go well *between* the parties.
3. Belonging to two or more, in common or partnership; as, two friends have but one soul *between* them; twenty proprietors own a tract of land *between* them. We observe that *between* is not restricted to *two.*
4. Having mutual relation to two or more; as, discords exist *between* the families.
5. Noting difference, or discrimination of one from another; as, to distinguish *between* right and wrong.

BETWIXT', *prep.* [Sax. *betwyx, betwyxt, betweox, betweoh*; *be* and *tweg*, two.]

1. Between; in the space that separates two persons or things; as, *betwixt* two oaks.
2. Passing between; from one to another, noting intercourse. [See *Between.*]

BEV'EL, *n.* [Fr. *buveau.* Qu. It. *bieca livella*, oblique level.]
Among masons, carpenters, joiners, &c., an instrument, or kind of square, one leg of which is frequently crooked, according to the sweep of an arch or vault. It is movable on a point or center, and so may be set to any angle. An angle that is not square is called a *bevel angle*, whether obtuse or acute. *Bailey. Johnson. Encyc.*

2. A curve or inclination of a surface from a right line; as, the proper *bevel* of a piece of timber. *Encyc.*

BEV'EL, *a.* Crooked; awry; oblique. *Bailey.*

BEV'EL, *v. t.* To cut to a bevel angle. *Moxon.*

BEV'EL, *v. i.* To curve; to incline towards a point, or from a direct line.

BEV'ELED, *pp.* Formed to a bevel angle. *Kirwan.*

BEV'ELING, *ppr.* Forming to a bevel angle.

BEV'ELING, *a.* Curving; bending from a right line.

BEV'ELING, *n.* A hewing of timber with a proper and regular curve, according to a mold laid on one side of its surface.

2. The curve or bevel of timber. *Encyc.*

BEV'ELMENT, *n.* In *mineralogy*, bevelment supposes the removal of two contiguous segments from the edges, angles or terminal faces of the predominant form, thereby producing two new faces, inclined to each other at a certain angle and forming an edge. *Cleaveland.*

BEV'ER, *n.* [It. *bevere*, to drink.] A collation or small repast between meals. [*Not used.*] *Morison.*

BEV'ER, *v. i.* To take a small repast between meals. *Wallis.*

BEV'ERAĠE, *n.* [It. *bevere*, or *bere*, to drink; *beveraggio*, drink; Sp. *beber*, from L. *bibo*; Fr. *buveur*, a tipler; *buvette*, a tavern; *buvotter*, to sip, to tipple; Arm. *beuvrauh*, beverage.]
Drink; liquor for drinking. It is generally used of a mixed liquor. Nectar is called the *beverage* of the gods.

In the middle ages, *beverage, beveragium*, or *biberagium* was money for drink given to an artificer or other person over and above his hire or wages. The practice has existed, to a certain extent, in America, within my memory, and I know not but it still exists in some parts of this country. A person who had a new garment, was called on to *pay beverage*, that is, to treat with liquor. Hence,

2. A treat on wearing a new suit of clothes, or on receiving a suit from the tailor; also a treat on first coming into prison; a garnish.
3. In *England*, water-cider, a mixture of cider and water, made by putting water into pumice before it is pressed. *Mortimer. Johnson.*

BEV'ILE, *n.* [See *Bevel.*] In *heraldry*, a thing broken or opening, like a carpenter's bevel. *Encyc.*

BEV'Y, *n.* [I know not the origin or affinities of this word. The etymologies I have seen are not worth notice.]
A flock of birds; hence, a company; an assembly or collection of persons; *usually applied to females.*

BEWA'IL, *v. t.* [*be* and *wail.*] To bemoan; to lament; to express sorrow for. It expresses deep sorrow; as, to *bewail* the loss of a child.

The true penitent *bewails* his ingratitude to God. *Anon.*

BEWA'IL, *v. i.* To express grief. *Shak.*

BEWA'ILABLE, *a.* That may be lamented. *Sherwood.*

BEWA'ILED, *pp.* Lamented; bemoaned.

BEWA'ILING, *ppr.* Lamenting; bemoaning; expressing grief for.

BEWA'ILING, *n.* Lamentation. *Raleigh.*

BEWA'KE, *v. t.* [*be* and *wake.*] To keep awake. [*Not used.*] *Gower.*

BEWA'RE, *v. i.* [Sax. *bewerian, bewarian, gewarian*, to guard, defend, restrain, prohibit, fortify, be cautious; Sw. *bevara*; D. *bewaaren*; Ger. *bewahren*; Dan. *bevarer*, to keep, guard, preserve. See *Ware, Wary.*]

1. Literally, to restrain or guard one's self from. Hence, to regard with caution; to restrain one's self from any thing that may be dangerous, injurious or improper; to avoid; to take care; followed by *of* before the thing that is to be avoided.

Beware of all, but most *beware* of man. *Pope.*

Beware of false prophets; *beware* of the leaven of the Pharisees; *beware* of the concision. *Scripture.*

2. To have a special regard to.

Behold, I send an angel before thee—*beware* of him, and obey his voice. Ex. xxiii.

[*This is unusual and hardly legitimate.*]

This word though here admitted as a verb, from the Saxon, is rarely used as a verb in fact; or if a verb, is now never used except in the imperative mode. It is a compound of *be* and the Old Eng. *ware*, now *wary*. *Be wary* of danger. Hence it cannot be used with *did*, like a regular verb, nor with *be*, in any of its inflections, he is *beware*; for this would be to use the substantive verb twice before *ware* and *wary*, *is* and *be*. Ben Jonson however has used the word in the third person. He *bewares* to act. But it has no past tense or participle, and therefore, if admitted as a verb, it is defective, and used only in the imperative mode, or after an auxiliary.

We must *beware* of excess.

BEWEE'P, *v. t.* [*be* and *weep.*] To weep over; to bedew with tears. [*Little used.*] *Shak.*

BEWEE'P, *v. i.* To make lamentation. [*Little used.*] *Shak.*

BEWEPT', *pp.* Wept over; bedewed with tears. [*Little used.*]

BEWET', *v. t.* [*be* and *wet.*] To wet; to moisten. [*Not used.*]

BEWIL'DER, *v. t.* [Dan. *forvilder, vilder*; D. *verwilderen*; G. *verwildern*; from *wild.*]
To lead into perplexity or confusion; to lose in pathless places; to confound for want of a plain road; to perplex with mazes; or in general, to perplex.

Lost and *bewildered* in the fruitless search. *Addison.*

BEWIL'DERED, *pp.* Lost in mazes; perplexed with disorder, confusion, or intricacy.

BEWIL'DERING, *ppr.* Losing in a pathless place; perplexing with confusion or intricacy.

BEWIN'TER, *v. t.* To make like winter. [*Not used.*] *Cowley.*

BEWITCH', *v. t.* [*be* and *witch.*] To fascinate; to gain an ascendancy over by charms or incantation; an operation which was formerly supposed to injure the person bewitched, so that he lost his flesh, or behaved in a strange unaccountable manner; ignorant people being inclined to ascribe to evil spirits what they could not account for.

Look, how I am *bewitched*; behold, mine arm
Is like a blasted sapling withered up. *Shak.*

2. To charm; to fascinate; to please to such a degree as to take away the power of resistance.

The charms of poetry our souls *bewitch*. *Dryden.*

3. To deceive and mislead by juggling tricks or imposture. Acts viii. 9.

BEWITCH'ED, *pp.* Fascinated; charmed.

BEWITCH'ER, *n.* One that bewitches or fascinates. *Stafford.*

BEWITCH'ERY, *n.* Fascination; charm; resistless power of any thing that pleases. *South.*

BEWITCH'FUL, *a.* Alluring; fascinating. *Milton.*

BEWITCH'ING, *ppr.* Fascinating; charming.

BEWITCH'ING, *a.* That has power to bewitch or fascinate; that has power to control by the arts of pleasing.

BEWITCH'INGLY, *adv.* In a fascinating manner. *Hallywell.*

BEWITCH'MENT, *n.* Fascination; power of charming. *Shak.*

BEWŎN'DERED, *a.* [*be* and *wonder.*] Amazed. [*Not used.*] *Fairfax.*

BEWRAP', *v. t. berap'.* [*be* and *wrap.*] To wrap up.

BEWRA'Y, *v. t. beráy.* [Chaucer has *wraie*, *wreye*, *wray*, and in the infinitive, *bewrien*, to discover, as if from Sax. *wrecan*, to tell. In Sax. *awreon*, *onwreon*, signify to reveal, as if the negative of *wrigan*, to cover.]

To disclose perfidiously; to betray; to show or make visible.

Thy speech *bewrayeth* thee. Matt. xxiii.

[*This word is nearly antiquated.*]

BEWRA'YED, *pp.* Disclosed; indicated; betrayed; exposed to view.

BEWRA'YER, *n.* A divulger of secrets; a discoverer.

BEWRA'YING, *ppr.* Disclosing; making known or visible.

BEWRECK', *v. t. bereck'.* [*be* and *wreck.*] To ruin; to destroy. [*Not used.*]

BEWROUGHT', *a. beraut'.* [*be* and *work.*] Worked. [*Not used.*] *B. Jonson.*

BEY, *n.* In *the Turkish dominions*, a governor of a town or particular district of country; also, in some places, a prince; the same as the Arabic *Beg.* [See *Beg.*] *Eton. Encyc.*

BEYOND', *prep.* [Sax. *begeond*, *begeondan*, of *be* and *geond*, yond, yonder. This is the participle of the verb *gan*, to go, to pass. It coincides with the D. *gaande*, the participle of the present tense of the same verb *gaan*, to go; Dan. *gaaende.* Literally, then, it signifies *by-passing*, or *bypast*; or as we now say, *past by*, *gone by.*]

1. On the further side of; on the side most distant, at any indefinite distance from that side; as *beyond* a river, or the sea, either a mile *beyond*, or a hundred miles *beyond* the river.

2. Before; at a place not yet reached.

A thing *beyond* us, even before our death. *Pope.*

3. Past; out of reach of; further than any given limit; further than the extent of any thing else; as, *beyond* our power; *beyond* comprehension; *beyond* dispute; *beyond* our care.

4. Above; in a degree exceeding or surpassing; proceeding to a greater degree, as in dignity, excellence, or quality of any kind; as, one man is great or good *beyond* another.

To go beyond is a phrase which expresses an excess in some action or scheme; to exceed in ingenuity, in research, or in any thing else; hence, in a bad sense, to deceive or circumvent.

Let no man *go beyond* and defraud his brother in any matter. *St. Paul.*

BEYOND', *adv.* At a distance; yonder. *Spenser.*

BEZ'AN, *n.* A cotton cloth from Bengal, white or striped. *Encyc.*

BEZ'ANT, *n.* A gold coin of Byzantium. [See *Byzant.*]

BEZANT'LER, *n.* [from *antler.*] The branch of a deer's horn, next above the brow antler. *Encyc.*

BEZ'EL, *n.* [Qu. Ch. בזל, limits, confines; Sw. *betzel*, a rein; *betzla*, to curb.]

The upper part of the collet of a ring, which encompasses and fastens the stone. *Bailey.*

BE'ZŌAR, *n.* [Pers. بادزهر badzhar, which Castle interprets "ventus, i. e. dissipator veneni, alexipharmicum omne, quod venenum pellit, et spirituum facultates retinet," from باد wind, breath, spirit, and زهر poison. Others make it *pazahar*, against poison, an antidote for poison.]

1. An antidote; a general name for certain animal substances supposed to be efficacious in preventing the fatal effects of poison. Bezoar is a calcarious concretion found in the stomach of certan ruminant animals, composed of concentric coats surrounding each other, with a little cavity in the middle, containing a bit of wood, straw, hair, or the like substance. There are two sorts; the *oriental*, from Persia and the East Indies, of a shining dark green or olive color, with a smooth surface; and the *occidental*, from the Spanish West Indies, which has a rough surface, is less green, much heavier, more brittle, and of a looser texture. The oriental is generally less than a walnut; the occidental is larger, and sometimes as large as a goose egg. *Encyc.*

The oriental bezoars are generally of a resinous composition and combustible. *Thomson.*

2. In *a more general sense*, any substance formed, stratum upon stratum, in the stomach or intestines of animals. *Encyc.*

This name is also given to the *biliary calculi* of certain animals. *Cyc.*

Fossil-bezoar is a figured stone, formed, like the animal bezoar, with several coats round some extraneous body, which serves as a nucleus; found chiefly in Sicily, in sand and clay pits. It is of a purple color, and of the size of a walnut. It seems to be of the nature of bole armenian, and is called Sicilian earth. *Encyc.*

Bezoar-mineral. This preparation is an oxyd of antimony, produced by distilling the nitrous acid several times to dryness from the sublimated muriate of antimony. *Nicholson.*

BEZOAR'DIC, *a.* Pertaining to or compounded of bezoar.

BEZOAR'DIC, *n.* A medicine compounded with bezoar. *Johnson.*

BEZ'OLA, *n.* A fish of the truttaceous kind, of a dusky blue color, nearly of the size of a herring. *Dict. of Nat. Hist.*

BEZ'ZLE, *v. t.* To waste in riot. [*Not used.*] [See *Embezzle.*] *Milton.*

BHUCHAMP'AC, *n.* [Hindu, *bhu*, ground, and *champac*, a plant.]

A beautiful plant of India, known in Linne's system, under the name of *Kæmpferia rotunda.* The blossoms rise from the ground with a short scape, and scarce live a whole day. *As. Res.* iii. 254.

BI'A, *n.* In *commerce*, a small shell called a *cowry*, much valued in the East Indies. *Encyc.*

BIAN'GULATE, **BIAN'GULATED**, **BIAN'GULOUS**, *a.* [L. *bis*, twice, and *angulus*, an angle.]

Having two angles or corners. [*Little used.*]

BIARM'IAN, *a.* Noting a race of Finns in Perme, in the north of Europe, on the Dvina, and about the White Sea; written also *Permian.* The Biarmians or Permians are said to be the most wealthy and powerful of the Finnish tribes. *Tooke.*

BI'AS, *n.* [Arm. *bihays* or *vies*; Fr. *biais*, a slope; *biaiser*, to use shifts, evasions or tricks.]

1. A weight on the side of a bowl which turns it from a straight line.

2. A leaning of the mind; inclination; prepossession; propensity towards an object, not leaving the mind indifferent; as, education gives a *bias* to the mind.

3. That which causes the mind to lean or incline from a state of indifference, to a particular object or course.

BI'AS, *v. t.* To incline to one side; to warp; to give a particular direction to the mind; to prejudice; to prepossess. The judgment is often *biassed* by interest.

This word is used by Shakspeare as an adverb, *bias* and thwart, i. e. *aslope*; and as an adjective.

Blow till thy *bias* cheek
Outswell the cholic of puft Aquilon.

BI'AS-DRAWING, *n.* Partiality. [*Not used.*] *Shak.*

BI'ASED, *pp.* Inclined from a right line; warped; prejudiced.

BI'ASING, *ppr.* Giving a bias, particular direction or propensity; warping; prejudicing.

BIB, *n.* A small piece of linen or other cloth worn by children over the breast.

2. A fish about a foot in length, the back of a light olive, the sides yellow, and the belly white. *Dict. of Nat. Hist.*

BIB, *v. t.* [L. *bibo*; Sp. *beber*; It. *bevere*; Gypsey, *piava*, to drink; Slav. *pibo*, *piba*, drink.]

To sip; to tipple; to drink frequently. [*Little used.*] *Locke.*

BIBA'CIOUS, *a.* [L. *bibax.* See *Bib.*] Addicted to drinking; disposed to imbibe.

BIBAC'ITY, *n.* The quality of drinking much. [*Not used.*]

BIB'BER, *n.* A tippler; a man given to drinking; chiefly used in composition, as *winebibber.*

BIB'BLE-BABBLE, *n.* Idle talk; prating to no purpose. [*A low word, and not used.*] *Shak.*

BIB'IO, *n.* A name of the wine fly, a small insect found in empty wine casks. *Dict. of Nat. Hist.*

BI'BLE, *n.* [Gr. βιβλιον, βιβλος, a book.]

THE BOOK, by way of eminence; the sacred volume, in which are contained the revelations of God, the principles of Christian faith, and the rules of practice. It consists of two parts, called the Old and New Testaments.

The *Bible* should be the standard of language as well as of faith. *Anon.*

BIB'LER, *n.* [See *Bib.*] A tipler; a great drinker.

BIB'LICAL, *a.* Pertaining to the Bible, or to the sacred writings; as *biblical* criticism.

BIBLIOG'RAPHER, *n.* [Gr. βιβλος, a book, and γραφω, to write.]
One who composes or compiles the history of books; one skilled in literary history; a transcriber. *Bailey. Johnson. Ash.*

BIBLIOGRAPH'IC, } *a.* Pertaining to
BIBLIOGRAPH'ICAL, } the history of books. *Kett.*

BIBLIOG'RAPHY, *n.* A history or description of books; the perusal of books, and manuscripts, with notices of the different editions, the times when they were printed, and other information tending to illustrate the history of literature. *Encyc. Pinkerton.*

BIB'LIOLITE, *n.* [Gr. βιβλιον, a book, and λιθος, a stone; called also *phytobiblia* and *lithobiblia.*]
Bookstone; a species of shistous stones, mostly calcarious, which present, between their lamens, the figures of leaves, or sometimes simple dendrites.

BIBLIOM'ANCY, *n.* [Gr. βιβλος, a book, and μαντεια, divination.]
A kind of divination, performed by means of the bible; consisting in selecting passages of scripture at hazard, and drawing from them indications concerning things future. *Encyc. Southey.*

BIBLIOMA'NIA, *n.* [Gr. βιβλιον, book, and μανια, madness.]
Book-madness; a rage for possessing rare and curious books.

BIBLIOMA'NIAC, *n.* One who has a rage for books.

BIBLIOP'OLIST, *n.* [Gr. βιβλιον, book, and πωλεω, to sell.] A bookseller.

BIBLIOTH'ECAL, *a.* [L. *bibliotheca*, a library; βιβλος, and *theca*, θηκη, a repository.]
Belonging to a library.

BIBLIOTH'ECARY, *n.* A librarian. *Hall.*

BIBLIOTHE'KE, *n.* A library. *Bale.*

BIB'LIST, *n.* [from *bible.*] With the Romanists, one who makes the scriptures the sole rule of faith. *Encyc.*
2. One who is conversant with the bible. *Ash.*

BIBRAC'TEATE, *a.* Doubly bracteate. *Eaton.*

BIB'ULOUS, *a.* [L. *bibulus*, from *bibo*, to drink.]
Spungy; that has the quality of imbibing fluids or moisture. *Thomson.*

BICAP'SULAR, *a.* [L. *bis*, double, and *capsula*, a little chest, from *capsa*, a chest. See *Capsular.*]
In *botany*, having two capsules containing seeds, to each flower; as a *bicapsular* pericarp. *Martyn.*

BIC'ARBONATE, *n.* Supercarbonate; a carbonate containing two primes of carbonic acid. *Ure.*

BICAU'DA, *n.* A fish of the sword-fish kind, about five feet in length; its back and sides of a brown color, and its belly white. *Dict. of Nat. Hist.*

BICE or **BISE**, *n.* Among painters, a blue color prepared from the *lapis armenus*, Armenian stone. *Encyc.*

Bice is smalt reduced to a fine powder by levigation. *Cyc.*

BICIP'ITAL, } *a.* [L. *biceps*, of *bis*, twice,
BICIP'ITOUS, } and *caput*, head.]
Having two heads. Applied to the muscles, it signifies having two heads or origins; and any such muscle is denominated *biceps.*

BICK'ER, *v. i.* [W. *bicra*, to fight, to bicker; Scot. *bicker*, to fight by throwing stones, to move quickly, to skirmish; allied perhaps to It. *picchiare*, to beat; *picchiarsi*, to fight; *picchiere*, a soldier armed with a *pike; picchio*, a blow or stroke, a woodpecker; *beccare*, to peck. This verb is from the root of *beak*, *peck*, *pike*, and primarily signifies to beat, to strike, to thrust at, or to make at by repeated thrusts or blows.]
1. To skirmish; to fight off and on; that is, to make repeated attacks. [*But in this sense I believe rarely used.*]
2. To quarrel; to contend in words; to scold; to contend in petulant altercation. [*This is the usual signification.*]
3. To move quickly; to quiver; to be tremulous, like flame or water; as the *bickering* flame; the *bickering* stream. *Milton. Thomson.*

BICK'ERER, *n.* One who bickers, or engages in a petty quarrel.

BICK'ERING, *ppr.* Quarreling; contending; quivering.

BICK'ERMENT, *n.* Contention. [*Not used.*] *Spenser.*

BICK'ERN, *n.* [of W. *pig*, a beak, or *beak* and *iron.*]
An iron ending in a beak or point.

BI'CORN, *n.* [L. *bis*, twice, and *cornu*, a horn, *bicornis.*]
A plant whose anthers have the appearance of two horns. *Milne.*

BI'CORN, } *a.* Having two horns.
BICORN'OUS, } *Browne.*

BID, *v. t.* pret. *bid*, or *bade*; pp. *bid*, *bidden.* [Sax. *biddan*; Goth. *bidyan*, to ask, request or pray; Sax. *beodan*, to command; *bead*, one who persuades or exhorts; Sw. *bidia*, to ask or entreat; D. *bieden*, to offer, or bid; *gebieden*, to command; G. *bieten*, to offer; *gebieten*, *entbieten*, to command; Dan. *beder*, to pray, or desire; *byder*, to command, to bid, to offer, to invite; L. *peto*, to drive at, to attack, to ask, to desire, to beseech, anciently *beto*; Ir. *impidhim*, to beseech; Sp. Port. *pedir*, to ask or beg; Sans. *badi*, *padi*, *petir*, *botti*, a commander; Ch. פיט, to pray or beseech; Eth. ፈተወ fato, or fatho, to desire. The primary sense is, to press forward, to drive, to urge; hence, L. *impetus.* Applied to the voice, it denotes utterance, a driving of sounds, which is applied to asking, prayer, and command. Class Bd.]
1. To ask; to request; to invite.

Go ye into the highways, and as many as ye shall find, *bid* to the marriage. Math. xxii.

This sense is antiquated, but we have the same word from the Latin, in *invite*, [*in* and *bid.*]
2. To command; to order or direct.

And Peter answered him and said, Lord, if it be thou, *bid* me come to thee on the water. Mat. xiv.

3. To offer; to propose; as, to *bid* a price at an auction.
4. To proclaim; to make known by a public voice. *Obs.*

Our bans thrice *bid.* *Shak.*

5. To pronounce or declare; as, to *bid* a welcome.
6. To denounce, or threaten; as, to *bid* defiance.
7. To wish or pray.

Neither *bid* him good speed. 2 John 10.

To bid beads, is to pray with beads, as the Catholics; to distinguish each bead by a prayer. *Johnson.*

Also, to charge parishioners to say a number of paternosters. *Encyc.*

To bid fair, is to open or offer a good prospect; to appear fair.

BID or **BID'DEN**, *pp.* of *bid.* Invited; offered; commanded.

BID, *n.* An offer of a price; *a word much used at auctions.*

BID'ALE, *n.* [*bid* and *ale.*] In England, an invitation of friends to drink ale at some poor man's house, and there to contribute in charity; an ancient and still a local custom. *Encyc.*

BID'DER, *n.* One who offers a price.

Bidders at the auction of popularity. *Burke.*

BID'DING, *ppr.* Inviting; offering; commanding.

BID'DING, *n.* Invitation; command; order; a proclamation or notifying. *Shak.*

BIDE, *v. i.* [Sax. *bidan.* See *Abide.*] To dwell; to inhabit. *Milton.*
2. To remain; to continue or be permanent, in a place or state. [*Nearly antiquated.*] *Shak.*

BIDE, *v. t.* To endure; to suffer. [See *Abide.*] *Shak.*

BI'DENS, *n.* A plant, bur marigold. *Muhlenberg.*

BIDENT'AL, *a.* [L. *bidens*, of *bis*, twice, and *dens*, a tooth.] Having two teeth. *Swift.*

BIDET', *n.* [Fr.] A small horse, formerly allowed to each trooper or dragoon for carrying his baggage. *B. Jonson. Encyc.*

BI'DING, *ppr.* Dwelling; continuing; remaining. [See *Abiding.*]

BI'DING, *n.* Residence; habitation. *Rowe.*

BID'ON, *n.* A measure of liquids, of about five quarts, wine measure, used by seamen. *Encyc.*

BIEN'NIAL, *a.* [L. *biennis*, of *bis*, twice, and *annus*, a year.]
1. Continuing for two years; or happening, or taking place once in two years; as a *biennial* election.
2. In *botany*, continuing for two years and then perishing; as plants, whose root and leaves are formed the first year, and which produce fruit the second. *Martyn.*

BIEN'NIALLY, *adv.* Once in two years; at the return of two years.

BIER, *n.* [Sax. *bær*; D. *baar*; Ger. *bahre*; Dan. *baare*; Ir. *fier*; from the same root as *bear*; L. *feretrum*, from *fero.* See *Bear.*]
A carriage or frame of wood for conveying dead human bodies to the grave.

BIE'R-BALK, *n.* The church road for burials. [*Not used in America.*] *Homilies.*

BIE'STINGS, *n. plu.* [Sax. *byst*, or *bysting*; D. *biest*; Ger. *biestmilch.*]
The first milk given by a cow after calving. *B. Jonson.*

BIFA'RIOUS, *a.* [L. *bifarius*; *bis* and *fero*, or Teutonic, *faran*, to go.]
Two-fold. In *botany*, pointing two ways, as leaves that grow only on opposite sides of a branch. *Martyn.*

BIFA'RIOUSLY, *adv.* In a bifarious manner. A stem or branch is bifariously hairy, when the hairs between any two joints come out on the front and back, and in the two adjoining internodes, on the right and left side. *Martyn.*

BIF'EROUS, *a.* [L. *bifer*, *biferus*; of *bis*, twice, and *fero*, to bear.
Bearing fruit twice a year, as plants do in warm climates. *Martyn.*

BIF'ID, } *a.* [L. *bifidus*, *bifidatus*, of *bis*,
BIF'IDATE, } twice, and *findo*, *fidi*, to split or cleave. See *Divide* and *Wide.*]
In *botany*, two-cleft; divided; opening with a cleft; divided by a linear sinus, with straight margins. *Martyn.*

BIF'LOROUS, *a.* [L. *bis*, twice, and *floreo.*]
Bearing two flowers. *Martyn.*

BI'FOLD, *a.* [L. *bis*, twice, and *fold.*] Two-fold; double; of two kinds, degrees, &c.

BI'FORM, *a.* [L. *biformis*, of *bis*, twice, and *forma*, form.]
Having two forms, bodies or shapes. *Croxall.*

BI'FORMED, *a.* Compounded of two forms. *Johnson.*

BIFORM'ITY, *n.* A double form. *More.*

BI'FURCATE, } *a.* [L. *bifurcus*, of *bis*,
BI'FURCATED, } twice, and *furca*, a fork.]
Forked; divided into two branches. *Johnson.*

BIFURCA'TION, *n.* A forking, or division into two branches. *Brown.*

BIG, *a.* [In W. *baic* is a load; *beiciaw*, to load, or lay on; *beiciawg*, pregnant; and *bog* is a swelling; *buciaw*, to bellow; Dan. *bug*, the belly. These words seem to be allied to *big*, but I have not found this word in any other language.]

1. Bulky; protuberant; pregnant, *applied to females*. *Big*, in the sense of pregnant, is followed by *with*; as, big *with* child. The use of *of*, big *of* child, is not good English.
2. Great; large; in a more general sense; *applied to any body or object.*
3. Full; fraught, and about to have vent, or be brought forth.
   The important day, *big* with the fate of Rome. *Addison.*
4. Distended; full, as with grief or passion.
   Thy heart is *big*, get thee apart and weep. *Shak.*
5. Swelled; tumid; inflated, as with pride; hence, haughty in air or mien, or indicating haughtiness; proud; as *big* looks; *big* words; to look *big*.
6. Great in spirit; lofty; brave.
   Have not I a heart as *big* as thine? *Shak.*

BIG, *n.* A kind of barley.

BIG'AM, *n.* A bigamist. [*Not used.*] *Bp. Peacock.*

BIG'AMIST, *n.* [See *Bigamy.*] One who has committed bigamy, or had two wives at once.

BIG'AMY, *n.* [L. *bis*, twice, and Gr. γαμεω, to marry, γαμος, marriage. In Ar. جمع is to collect; to come together; to agree, or be in accord; to sleep together; to bind.]
The crime of having two wives at once. But the term is ordinarily used as synonymous with Polygamy, and may be more justly defined, the crime of having a plurality of wives. *Blackstone.*
In *the canon law*, bigamy was the marrying a second wife after the death of the first, or once marrying a widow. This disqualified a man for orders, and holding ecclesiastical offices. *Blackstone.*

BIG'BELLIED, *a.* Having a great belly; advanced in pregnancy.

BIGBO'NED, *a.* Having large bones. *Herbert.*

BIG'CORNED, *a.* Having large grains. *Dryden.*

BIGEM'INATE, *a.* [L. *bis*, twice, and *geminus*, double.]
Twin-forked; used of a decompound leaf having a forked petiole, with several leaflets, at the end of each division. *Martyn.*

BIG'GEL, *n.* A quadruped of the East Indies, somewhat like a rane or rein-deer, but its head resembles that of a horse. It has two horns, cloven feet and a mane like an ass. *Dict. of Nat. Hist.*

BIG'GIN, *n.* [Fr. *beguin*; Sp. *beca*, a tippet, or cap.]
1. A child's cap, or something worn about the head.
2. A building. *Obs.* [Sax. *byggan*, to build.] *Shak.*

BIGHT, *n.* [D. *bogt*, a bend, a turning, a coil, a bay; Dan. *bugt*, a bend, a bow, a bay. It is the participle of *boogen*, *buigen*, *bugan*, to bend; W. *bac*, *bacu*. See *Bow.*]
1. A bend, or small bay between two points of land.
2. The double part of a rope when folded, in distinction from the end; that is, a round, bend or coil any where except at the ends. *Mar. Dict.*
3. The inward bent of a horse's chambrel, and the bent of the fore knees. *Bailey.*

BIG'LY, *adv.* [from *big.*] In a tumid, swelling, blustering manner; haughtily.

BIG'NAMED, *a.* Having a great or famous name. *Crashaw.*

BIG'NESS, *n.* Bulk; size; largeness; dimensions. It is used of any object, animate or inanimate, and with or without comparison. Thus we speak of the *bigness* of a tree, of a rock, of a house, without instituting a comparison with other objects of the kind. Yet in this case there is always some reference in the mind to known measure. We also say, one thing is as *big* as another; in which case we give the idea of unknown size, by a known object. *Big* and *bigness* always imply expansion, more or less, in breadth, and are thus distinguished from *tall* and *tallness.*

BIG'OT, *n.* [Fr. *bigot*, and *cagot*, a bigot or hypocrite; Arm. *bigod*. In Italian, *bacchettone* is a hypocrite. In Spanish, *bigote* is a whisker; *hombre de bigote*, a man of spirit; *tener bigotes*, to be firm or undaunted. If the French *cagot* is connected with *bigot*, the first syllable in both is a prefix. But I am not able to ascertain the real origin and primary sense of the word. The etymologies I have seen are not satisfactory.]
1. A person who is obstinately and unreasonably wedded to a particular religious creed, opinion, practice or ritual. The word is sometimes used in an enlarged sense, for a person who is illiberally attached to any opinion, or system of belief; as a *bigot* to the Mohammedan religion; a *bigot* to a form of government.
2. A Venetian liquid measure containing the fourth part of the amphor, or half the boot. *Encyc.*

BIG'OT, } *a.* Obstinately and blindly
BIG'OTED, } attached to some creed, opinion, practice or ritual; unreasonably devoted to a system or party, and illiberal towards the opinions of others.

BIG'OTEDLY, *adv.* In the manner of a bigot; pertinaciously.

BIG'OTRY, *n.* Obstinate or blind attachment to a particular creed, or to certain tenets; unreasonable zeal or warmth in favor of a party, sect or opinion; excessive prejudice.
2. The practice or tenet of a bigot. *Pope.*

BIG'SOUNDING, *a.* Having a pompous sound. *Hall.*

BIG'SWOLN, *a.* [*big* and *swoln*. See *Swell.*]
Swelled to a large size; turgid; greatly swelled; ready to burst. *Addison.*

BIG-UDDERED, *a.* [*big* and *udder.*]
Having large udders, or udders swelled with milk. *Pope.*

BIHYDROG'URET, *n.* A double hydroguret, or with two atoms of hydrogen. *Thomson.*

BIJU'GOUS, *a.* [L. *bis*, twice, and *jugum*, a yoke, a pair.]
Having two pairs of leaflets; used of pinnated leaves. *Martyn.*

BILA'BIATE, *a.* [L. *bis*, twice, and *labium*, a lip.]
Having two lips, as the corols of flowers. *Martyn.*

BILAM'ELLATE, *a.* [L. *bis*, twice, and *lamella*, a plate.]
Having the form of a flatted sphere, longitudinally bifid; used of the stigma of plants. *Martyn.*

BI'LANDER, *n.* [D. *bylander*; Fr. *belande*, *belandre*; Sp. *bilandra*; from *be*, by, and *land*; Ger. *binnenlander.*]
A small merchant vessel with two masts, distinguished from other vessels of two masts, by the form of the main-sail, which is bent to the whole length of a yard, hanging fore and aft, and inclined to the horizon in an angle of about 45 degrees; the foremost lower corner, called the tack, being secured to a ring-bolt in the deck, and the aftermost or sheet, to the tafferel. Few vessels are now rigged in this manner. *Encyc. Mar. Dict.*
The bilander is a kind of hoy, manageable by four or five men and used chiefly in the canals of the Low Countries. *Johnson.*

BILAT'ERAL, *a.* [L. *bis* and *latus*, side.]
Having two sides. *Dict.*

BIL'BERRY, *n.* [I know not the meaning of *bil* in this word. The Dutch word is *blaauwbes*, blue-berry; the Ger. *heidelbeere*, heath-berry.]

The name of a shrub and its fruit; a species of Vaccinium or whortle-berry. The name with us is given to the taller shrub and its fruit which is of a bluish color.

BIL'BO, *n.* [from *Bilboa*, in Spain.]

A rapier; a sword; so named, it is said, from Bilboa in Spain, where the best are made. *Ash. Johnson.*

BIL'BOES, *n. plu.* On board of ships, long bars or bolts of iron with shackles sliding on them, and a lock at the end, used to confine the feet of prisoners or offenders. Hence the punishment of offenders in this manner is called by the same name. *Mar. Dict. Encyc.*

BILD, *v. t.* pret. *bilded*, *bilt*; pp. *id.* [G. *bilden*; Dan. *bilder*; Sw. *bilda*.]

To construct; to erect; to set up and finish; as, to *bild* a house or ship; to *bild* a wall. [This is the true orthography; the common spelling is incorrect. See *Build*.]

BILD'STEIN, *n.* [G. *bild*, shape, and *stein*, stone.]

Agalmatolite, or figure-stone. A massive mineral, with sometimes a slaty structure; of a color gray, brown, flesh red, sometimes spotted, or with blue veins. It fuses into a transparent glass. Brongniart calls it steatite pagodite, from its coming from China in grotesque figures. *Ure.*

This mineral resembles steatite in its physical characters, but differs from it essentially in its composition. It is soft, easily cut with a knife, and reducible to a fine unctuous powder. *Cleaveland.*

BILE, *n.* [L. *bilis*; Fr. *bile*.] A yellow bitter liquor, separated from the blood in the liver, collected in the *pori biliarii* and gall bladder, and thence discharged by the common duct into the duodenum. *Encyc.*

BILE, *n.* An inflamed tumor. [See *Boil*, the correct orthography.]

BI'LEDUCT, *n.* [*bile* and L. *ductus*, a conduit.] A vessel or canal to convey bile. *Darwin.*

BI'LESTONE, *n.* [*bile* and *stone*.] A concretion of viscid bile. *Darwin.*

BILGE, *n.* [A different orthography of *bulge*, and *belly*, a protuberance.]

1. The protuberant part of a cask, which is usually in the middle.

2. The breadth of a ship's bottom, or that part of her floor which approaches to a horizontal direction, on which she would rest, if aground. Hence, when this part of a ship is fractured, she is said to be *bilged*. *Encyc. Mar. Dict.*

BILGE, *v. i.* To suffer a fracture in the bilge; to spring a leak by a fracture in the bilge. The term is used also when a ship has some of her timbers struck off by a rock or an anchor, and springs a leak. *Encyc. Mar. Dict.*

BILG'ED, *pp.* or *a.* Having a fracture in the bilge. This participle is often used, as if the verb were transitive; and perhaps it is sometimes so used.

BILGE-PUMP, *n.* A burr-pump; a pump to draw the bilge-water from a ship.

BILGE-WATER, *n.* Water which enters a ship, and lies upon her bilge or bottom.

BIL'IARY, *a.* [from L. *bilis*.] Belonging to the bile; conveying the bile; as a *biliary* duct.

BIL'INGSGATE, *n.* [from a place of this name in London frequented by low people who use foul language.]

Foul language; ribaldry. *Pope.*

BILIN'GUOUS, *a.* [L. *bis*, and *lingua*, tongue.]

Having two tongues, or speaking two languages.

BIL'IOUS, *a.* [L. *biliosus*, from *bilis*, the bile.]

Pertaining to bile; consisting or partaking of bile; caused by a redundancy, or bad state of the bile; as a *bilious* fever.

BILIT'ERAL, *a.* [L. *bis*, twice, and *litera*, letter.]

Consisting of two letters; as a *biliteral* root in language. *Sir W. Jones.*

BILK, *v. t.* [Goth. *bilaikan*, to mock or deride. This Gothic word appears to be compound, *bi* and *laikan*, to leap or exult.]

To frustrate or disappoint; to deceive or defraud, by non-fulfilment of engagement; as, to *bilk* a creditor. *Dryden.*

BILK'ED, *pp.* Disappointed; deceived; defrauded.

BILK'ING, *ppr.* Frustrating; defrauding.

BILL, *n.* [Sax. *bile*, a beak, that is, a shoot.]

1. The beak of a fowl.

2. An instrument used by plumbers, basket-makers and gardeners, made in the form of a crescent, and fitted with a handle. When short, it is called a *hand-bill*; when long, a *hedge-bill*. It is used for pruning trees, &c.

BILL, *n.* [Sax. *bil*; G. *beil*, an ax or hatchet; D. *byl*; Dan. *bile*; W. *bwyell*; Pers. بیل bil, a mattock, or pick-ax, and a shovel.]

A pick-ax, or mattock; a battle-ax; an ax or hatchet with a crooked point.

BILL, *n.* [Norm. *bille*, a label or note; Fr. *billet*, *bil*; Arm. *bilked*; Sp. *billete*; It. *biglietto*, *bulletta*, *bollettino*. The primary sense probably is a roll or folded paper, Sp. *boleta*, a *billet*, a ticket, and a paper of tobacco, coinciding with *bola*, a ball; or it is from cutting off, and signifies a piece.]

1. In *law*, a declaration in writing, expressing some wrong the complainant has suffered from the defendant, or a fault committed by some person against a law. It contains the fact complained of, the damage sustained, and a petition or process against the defendant for redress. It is used both in civil and criminal cases.

In *Scots law*, every summary application in writing, by way of petition to the court of session, is called a *bill*. *Encyc.*

2. In *law* and in *commerce*, in England, an obligation or security given for money under the hand, and sometimes the seal of the debtor, without a condition or forfeiture for non-payment. In the latter circumstance, it differs from a bond. In the United States, this species of security is usually called a note, a note of hand, or a promissory note.

3. A form or draft of a law, presented to a legislature, but not enacted. In some cases, *statutes* are called *bills*; but usually they are qualified by some description, as a *bill of attainder*.

4. A paper written or printed, and posted in some public place, advertising the proposed sale of goods, or particular things; an advertisement posted.

5. An account of goods sold or delivered, services rendered or work done, with the price or value annexed to each article.

6. Any written paper, containing a statement of particulars; as a *bill* of charges or expenditures; a physician's *bill* of prescriptions; a *bill* of fare or provisions, &c.

7. A *bill of exchange* is an order drawn on a person, in a distant place, requesting or directing him to pay money to some person assigned by the drawer, or to his order, in consideration of the same sum received by the drawer. Bills of exchange are either *foreign* or *inland*; *foreign*, when drawn by a person in one country upon one residing in another; *inland*, when both the drawer and drawee reside in the same country. The person who draws the bill is called the *drawer*; the person on whom the request or demand is made, is called the *drawee*; and the person to whom the money is directed to be paid, is called the *payee*.

8. A *bill of entry* is a written account of goods entered at the custom house, whether imported or intended for exportation.

9. A *bill of lading* is a written account of goods shipped by any person, on board of a vessel, signed by the master of the vessel, who acknowledges the receipt of the goods, and promises to deliver them safe at the place directed, dangers of the sea excepted. It is usual for the master to sign two, three or four copies of the bill; one of which he keeps in possession, one is kept by the shipper, and one is sent to the consignee of the goods.

10. A *bill of parcels* is an account given by the seller to the buyer, of the several articles purchased, with the price of each.

11. A *bill of sale* is when a person borrows money and delivers goods to the lender as security, and at the same time, gives him a bill, empowering him to sell the goods, if the money is not repaid at the appointed time with interest. *Encyc.*

In the United States, a *bill of sale* is a writing given by the seller of personal property, to the purchaser, answering to a deed of real estate, but without seal.

12. A *bill of mortality* is an account of the number of deaths in a place, in a given time. In these bills it is not unusual to insert registers of births and christenings, as in London.

13. *Bank-bill.* [See *Bank*.]

14. A *bill of rights* is a summary of rights and privileges, claimed by a people. Such was the declaration presented by the lords and commons of England to the prince and princess of Orange in 1688. In America, a *bill* or declaration of rights is prefixed to most of the constitutions of the several states.

15. A *bill of divorce*, in the Jewish law, was a writing given by the husband to the wife,

by which the marriage relation was dissolved.

16. [See *Indictment.*]

BILL, *v. i.* [from *bill*, a beak.] To join bills, as doves; to caress in fondness. *Dryden.*

BILL, *v. t.* [from *bill*, a writing.] To advertise by a bill or public notice; *a cant word.* *L'Estrange.*

BILL'ARD, *n.* A bastard or imperfect capon; also a fish of the cod kind. *Ash.*

BILL'ET, *n.* [dim. of *bill*; Fr. *billet*; It. *bulletta.*]

A small paper or note in writing, used for various purposes; sometimes it is a short letter, addressed to some person; sometimes a ticket directing soldiers at what house to lodge.

In heraldry, *billet* is a bearing in the form of a long square. *Encyc.*

Billet-doux, *bil'le-doo.* [Fr.] A love billet.

BILL'ET, *n.* [Fr. *billot.*] A small stick of wood.

BILL'ET, *v. t.* [from *billet*, a ticket.] To direct a soldier by a ticket or note where to lodge; hence, to quarter, or place in lodgings, as soldiers in private houses.

BILL'ETING, *ppr.* Quartering, as soldiers in private houses.

BILL'IARD, *a. bil'yard.* Pertaining to the game of billiards.

BILL'IARDS, *n. plu. bil'yards.* [Fr. *billard*, a mace or billiard-table; It. *bigliardo*; Sp. *villar.* According to the ancient orthography, *balyard*, this word is composed of *ball* and *yard*, a ball-stick.]

A game played on a rectangular table, covered with a green cloth, with small ivory balls, which the players aim to drive into hazard-nets or pockets at the sides and corners of the tables, by impelling one ball against another, with maces, or cues, according to certain rules of the game.

BILL'ION, *n. bil'yun.* [*bis* and *million.*]

A million of millions; as many millions as there are units in a million.

BIL'LOW, *n.* [Dan. *bölge*, Sw. *bölja*, a swell, or rolling swell, allied to *bilge*, *bulge.*]

A great wave or surge of the sea, occasioned usually by violent wind. It can hardly be applied to the waves of a river, unless in poetry, or when the river is very large.

BIL'LOW, *v. i.* To swell; to rise and roll in large waves, or surges. *Prior.*

BIL'LOW-BEATEN, *a.* Tossed by billows.

BIL'LOWING, *ppr.* Swelled into large waves or surges.

BIL'LOWY, *a.* Swelling, or swelled into large waves; wavy; full of billows, or surges.

BILO'BED, } *a.* [L. *bis*, twice, and Gr. λοβος. See *Lobe.*] Divided into two lobes; as a *bilobate* leaf.
BILO'BATE, } *Martyn.*

BILOC'ULAR, *a.* [L. *bis*, twice, and *loculus*, from *locus*, a place.]

Divided into two cells, or containing two cells internally; as a *bilocular* pericarp. *Martyn.*

BIL'VA, *n.* The Hindu name of a plant, the Cratæva Marmelos of Linne. *As. Res.* iii. 256.

BIMA'NOUS, *a.* [*bis* and *manus.*] Having two hands. Man is *bimanous.* *Lawrence.*

BIME'DIAL, *a.* [L. *bis*, twice, and *medial.*] In *mathematics*, if two medial lines, A B and B C, commensurable only in power, and containing a rational rectangle, are compounded, the whole line A C will be irrational, and is called a first *bimedial* line. *Encyc.*

2. Belonging to a quantity arising from a particular combination of two other quantities. *Ash.*

BIN, *n.* [Sax. *binn*, or *binne.*] A wooden box or chest used as a repository of corn or other commodities.

BIN'ACLE, *n.* [Formerly *bittacle*, supposed to be a corruption of Fr. *habitacle*; but more probably, *boite d'aiguille*, needle box.]

A wooden case or box in which the compass and lights are kept on board a ship. It is sometimes divided into three apartments, with sliding shutters; the two sides contain each a compass, and the middle division, a lamp or candle.

BI'NARY, *a.* [L. *binus*, two and two.]

Binary arithmetic, the invention of Leibnitz, is that in which two figures only, 0 and 1, are used, in lieu of ten; the cypher multiplying every thing by two, as in common arithmetic by 10. Thus, 1 is one; 10 is two; 11 is three; 100 is four; 101 is five; 110 is six; 111, is seven; 1000 is eight; 1001 is nine; 1010 is ten. It is said this species of arithmetic has been used by the Chinese for 4000 years, being left in enigma by Fohi. *Encyc.*

Binary measure, in music, is that used in common time, in which the time of rising in beating, is equal to the time of falling. *Encyc.*

Binary number is that which is composed of two units. *Encyc.*

BI'NARY, *n.* The constitution of two. *Fotherby.*

BI'NATE, *a.* [L. *binus.* See *Binary.*] Being double or in couples; growing in pairs. A *binate* leaf has a simple petiole, connecting two leaflets on the top; a species of digitate leaf. *Martyn.*

BIND, *v. t.* pret. *bound*; pp. *bound*, and obs. *bounden.* [Sax. *bindan*, *gebindan*, pret. *band*, *bund*, or *bunden*; Goth. *bindan*, *gabindan*; D. *binden*, *verbinden*; Ger. the same; Sw. *binda*, *förbinda*; Dan. *binder*, to bind, and *bind*, a band; also *baand*, a band; Hindu, *bandna*; Gypsey, *bandopen*; Pers. بَنْدَن bandan, and بَنْدِيدَن bandidan, to bind; the former signifies also, to apply, to *bend* the mind; and the latter, to shut, close, make fast. The sense is, to strain.]

1. To tie together, or confine with a cord, or any thing that is flexible; to fasten as with a band, fillet or ligature.

2. To gird, inwrap or involve; to confine by a wrapper, cover or bandage; sometimes with *up*; as, to *bind up* a wound.

3. To confine or restrain, as with a chain, fetters or cord; as, *bind* him hand and foot.

4. To restrain in any manner.

> He *bindeth* the floods from overflowing. Job xxviii.

5. To oblige by a promise, vow, stipulation, covenant, law, duty or any other moral tie; to engage.

> If a man shall swear an oath to *bind* his soul with a bond. Numbers xxx.

> We are *bound* by the laws of kindness, of nature, of a state, &c.

6. To confirm or ratify.

> Whatsoever thou shalt *bind* on earth, shall be *bound* in heaven. Matth. xvi.

7. To distress, trouble, or confine by infirmity.

> Whom Satan hath *bound* these eighteen years. Luke xiii.

8. To constrain by a powerful influence or persuasion.

> I go *bound* in the spirit to Jerusalem. Acts xx.

9. To restrain the natural discharges of the bowels; to make costive; as, certain kinds of food *bind* the body or bowels.

10. To form a border; to fasten with a band, ribin, or any thing that strengthens the edges; as, to *bind* a garment or carpet.

11. To cover with leather or any thing firm; to sew together and cover; as, to *bind* a book.

12. To cover or secure by a band; as, to *bind* a wheel with tire.

13. To oblige to serve, by contract; as, to *bind* an apprentice; often with *out*; as, to *bind out* a servant.

14. To make hard or firm; as, certain substances *bind* the earth.

The uses of this word are too various and numerous to be reduced to exact definitions.

To bind to is to contract; as, to *bind* one's self *to* a wife.

To bind over is to oblige by bond to appear at a court.

BIND, *v. i.* To contract; to grow hard or stiff; as, clay *binds* by heat. *Mortimer.*

2. To grow or become costive.

3. To be obligatory.

BIND, *n.* A stalk of hops, so called from its winding round a pole or tree, or being bound to it.

2. A *bind of eels*, is a quantity consisting of 10 strikes, each containing 25 eels, or 250 in the whole. *Encyc.*

3. Among *miners*, indurated clay, when much mixed with the oxyd of iron. *Kirwan.*

BI'NDER, *n.* A person who binds; one whose occupation is to bind books; also, one who binds sheaves.

2. Any thing that binds, as a fillet, cord, rope, or band.

BI'NDERY, *n.* A place where books are bound.

BI'NDING, *ppr.* Fastening with a band; confining; restraining; covering or wrapping; obliging by a promise or other moral tie; making costive; contracting; making hard or stiff.

BI'NDING, *a.* That obliges; obligatory; as the *binding* force of a moral duty or of a command.

BI'NDING, *n.* The act of fastening with a band or obliging; a bandage; the cover of a book, with the sewing and accompanying work; any thing that binds; something that secures the edge of cloth.

2. In *the art of defense*, a method of securing or crossing the adversary's sword with a pressure, accompanied with a spring of the wrist. *Encyc.*

Binding-joists, in *architecture*, are the joists of a floor into which the trimmers of staircases, or well holes of the stairs and chimney ways, are framed. *Encyc.*

BI'ND-WEED, *n.* A genus of plants, called *Convolvulus*, comprehending many species, as the white, the blue, the Syrian bind-weed, &c. The *black briony* or *Tamus* is called *black bind-weed*; and the *Smilax* is called *rough bind-weed*. *Encyc. Fam. of Plants.*

BING, *n.* In *alum works*, a heap of alum thrown together in order to drain. *Encyc.*

BIN'OCLE, *n.* [*binus*, double, and *oculus*, an eye.]
A dioptric telescope, fitted with two tubes joining, so as to enable a person to view an object with both eyes at once. *Harris.*

BINOC'ULAR, *a.* [See *Binocle.*] Having two eyes; also, having two apertures or tubes, so joined that one may use both eyes at once in viewing a distant object; as a *binocular* telescope. *Encyc.*

BINO'MIAL, *a.* [L. *bis*, twice, and *nomen*, name.]
In *algebra*, a root consisting of two members connected by the sign plus or minus; as $a+b$, or $7-3$. *Encyc.*

BINOM'INOUS, *a.* [L. *bis*, twice, and *nomen*, name.]
Having two names. *Johnson.*

BINOT'ONOUS, *a.* [*bis* and *note.*] Consisting of two notes; as a *binotonous* cry. *Montague.*

BIOG'RAPHER, *n.* [See *Biography.*] One who writes an account or history of the life and actions of a particular person; a writer of lives, as Plutarch.

BIOGRAPH'IC, BIOGRAPH'ICAL, *a.* Pertaining to biography, or the history of the life of a person; containing biography.

BIOG'RAPHY, *n.* [Gr. βιος, life, and γραφω, to write.]
The history of the life and character of a particular person.

BIOTINA, *n.* [from *Biot*, a French naturalist.]
A newly discovered Vesuvian mineral, whose primitive form is that of an obtuse rhomboid. *Journ. of Science.*

BIP'AROUS, *a.* [L. *bis*, twice, and *pario*, to bear.]
Bringing forth two at a birth.

BIPART'IBLE, BIP'ARTILE, *a.* [L. *bis*, twice, and *partio*, to divide.] That may be divided into two parts. *Martyn.*

BIPAR'TIENT, *a.* [L. *bis*, twice, and *partio, partiens*, to divide.] Dividing into two parts. *Ash.*

BIP'ARTITE, *a.* [L. *bis*, twice, and *partitus*, divided.]
1. Having two correspondent parts, as a legal contract or writing, one for each party.
2. In *botany*, divided into two parts to the base, as a leaf. *Martyn.*

BIPARTI''TION, *n.* The act of dividing into two parts, or of making two correspondent parts. *Johnson.*

BI'PED, *n.* [L. *bipes*, of *bis*, twice, and *pes, pedis*, a foot.]
An animal having two feet, as man.

BIP'EDAL, *a.* Having two feet, or the length of two feet.

BIPEN'NATE, *a.* [L. *bis*, and *penna*, a wing or feather.] Having two wings.
2. In *botany*, having pinnate leaves on each side of the petiole, as a leaf or frond. *Martyn.*

BIPET'ALOUS, *a.* [L. *bis*, twice, and Gr. πεταλον, a leaf.]
Consisting of two flower leaves; having two petals.

BIPIN'NATIFID, BIPEN'NATIFID, *a.* [L. *bis*, twice, *pinna*, a wing or feather, and *findo*, to divide.]
Doubly-pinnatifid; having pinnatifid leaves on each side of the petiole. *Martyn.*

BIQUAD'RATE, *n.* [L. *bis*, twice, and *quadratus*, squared.]
In *mathematics*, the fourth power, arising from the multiplication of a square number or quantity by itself. Thus $4\times4=16$, which is the square of 4, and $16\times16=256$, the biquadrate of that number.

BIQUADRAT'IC, *n.* The same as *biquadrate*. *Encyc.*

BIQUADRAT'IC, *a.* Pertaining to the biquadratic or fourth power.
Biquadratic equation, in algebra, is an equation raised to the fourth power, or where the unknown quantity of one of the terms has four dimensions.
Biquadratic parabola, in geometry, is a curve line of the third order, having two infinite legs tending the same way.
Biquadratic root of a number, is the square root of the square root of that number. Thus the square root of 81 is 9, and the square root of 9 is 3, which is the *biquadratic* root of 81. *Encyc.*

BIQUIN'TILE, *n.* [L. *bis*, twice, and *quintus*, fifth.]
An aspect of the planets, when they are distant from each other, by *twice the fifth* part of a great circle, that is 144 degrees or twice 72 degrees.

BIRA'DIATE, BIRA'DIATED, *a.* [L. *bis*, twice, and *radiatus*, set with rays.] Having two rays; as a *biradiate* fin. *Encyc.*

BIRCH, *n. burch.* [Sax. *birce*; D. *berken*, or *berkeboom*; Ger. *birke*; Dan. *birk.*]
A genus of trees, the *Betula*, of which there are several species; as the white or common birch, the dwarf birch, the Canada birch, of which there are several varieties, and the common black birch.
Birch of Jamaica, a species of the Pistacia or turpentine tree. *Fam. of Plants.*

BIRCH, BIRCH'EN, *a.* Made of birch; consisting of birch.

BIRD, *n. burd.* [Sax. *bird*, or *bridd*, a chicken; from the root of *bear*, or W. *bridaw*, to break forth.]
1. Properly, a chicken, the young of fowls, and hence a small fowl.
2. In *modern use*, any fowl or flying animal. It is remarkable that a nation should lay aside the use of the proper generic name of flying animals, *fowl*, Sax. *fugel*, D. *vogel*, the flyer, and substitute the name of the young of those animals, as the generic term. The fact is precisely what it would be to make *lamb*, the generic name of sheep, or *colt*, that of the equine genus.

BIRD, *v. t.* To catch birds. *Shak.*
Bird of paradise, a genus of birds, found in the Oriental isles, and in New Guinea; some of them remarkably beautiful. The beak is covered with a belt or collar of downy feathers at the base, and the feathers on the sides are very long. The largest species is two feet four inches in length. The head and back part of the neck are lemon-colored; the neck of the brightest emerald green, soft like velvet; the breast is black; the wings of a chesnut color. The back part of the body is covered with long straight narrow feathers, of a pale brown color, similar to the plumes of the ostrich. These are spread when the bird flies, for which reason he cannot keep long on the wing. From the rump proceed two long stiff shafts, feathered at the extremities. *Encyc.*

BIRD'BOLT, *n.* [*bird* and *bolt.*] An arrow, broad at the end, for shooting birds. *Shak.*

BIRD'-CAGE, *n.* [*bird* and *cage.*] A box or case with wires, small sticks, or wicker, forming open work, for keeping birds.

BIRD'CALL, *n.* [*bird* and *call.*] A little stick, cleft at one end, in which is put a leaf of some plant for imitating the cry of birds. A laurel leaf counterfeits the voice of lapwings; a leek, that of nightingales; &c. *Encyc.*

BIRD'-CATCHER, *n.* [*bird* and *catch.*] One whose employment is to catch birds; a fowler.

BIRD'-CATCHING, *n.* [*bird* and *catch.*]
The art of taking birds or wild fowls, either for food, for pleasure, or for their destruction, when pernicious to the husbandman.

BIRD'-CHERRY, *n.* [*bird* and *cherry.*] A tree, a species of Prunus, called *padus*; there are other species called by the same name. *Encyc. Fam. of Plants.*

BIRD'ER, *n.* A bird-catcher.

BIRD'-EYE, BIRD'S-EYE, *a.* [*bird* and *eye.*] Seen from above, as if by a flying bird; as a *bird-eye* landscape. *Burke.*

BIRD'EYED, *a.* Of quick sight.

BIRD'ING-PIECE, *n.* [*bird* and *piece.*] A fowling-piece. *Shak.*

BIRD'-LIKE, *a.* Resembling a bird.

BIRD'-LIME, *n.* [*bird* and *lime.*] A viscous substance, usually made of the juice of holly-bark, extracted by boiling, mixed with a third-part of nut oil or thin grease, used to catch birds. For this purpose, the twigs of a bush are smeared over with this viscid substance. *Encyc.*

BIRD'-LIMED, *a.* Smeared with bird-lime; spread to ensnare. *Howell.*

BIRD'-MAN, *n.* [*bird* and *man.*] A fowler or bird-catcher.

BIRD'-PEPPER, *n.* [*bird* and *pepper.*] A species of Capsicum or Guinea-pepper; a shrubby plant, bearing a small oval fruit, more biting than the other sorts. *Encyc.*

BIRDS'EYE, *n.* [*bird* and *eye.*] A genus of plants, called also *pheasant's eye*, known in botany by the generic term *Adonis*. There are several species, some of which produce beautiful flowers. *Encyc.*

BIRDS'FOOT, *n.* [*bird* and *foot.*] A plant, the Ornithopus, whose legumen is articulated, cylindrical, and bent in the form of a bow. *Encyc.*

BIRDSFOOT-TREFOIL, *n.* A genus of plants, the Lotus, of several species. *Encyc.*

BIRDS'NEST, *n.* [*bird* and *nest.*] The nest in which a bird lays eggs and hatches her young.

2. A plant, a species of Ophrys or twyblade; also a species of Orchis. *Encyc.*

3. In *cookery*, the nest of a small swallow, of China, and the neighboring countries, delicately tasted, and mixed with soups. This nest is found in the rocks; it is of a hemispherical figure, of the size of a goose egg, and in substance resembles isinglass. In the East, these nests are esteemed a great luxury, and sell at a very high price. *Encyc.*

BIRDSTARES and **BIRDSTŎNGUE**; names of plants.

BIRD′-WITTED, *a.* Not having the faculty of attention. *Bacon.*

BI′REME, *n.* [L. *biremis, bis* and *remus*, an oar.]
A vessel with two banks or tiers of oars. *Mitford.*

BIRG′ANDER, *n.* The name of a wild goose. Qu. *Bergander.*

BIRHOMBOID′AL, *a.* [*bis* and *rhomboid.*]
Having a surface composed of twelve rhombic faces, which, being taken six and six, and prolonged in idea, till they intercept each other, would form two different rhombs. *Cleaveland.*

BIRK′EN, *v. t.* [from *birch*, Sax. *birce, byrc.*]
To beat with a birch or rod. *Obs.* *Ch. Relig. Appeal.*

BIROS′TRATE, } *a.* [L. *bis*, twice, and
BIROS′TRATED, } *rostrum*, a beak.]
Having a double beak, or process resembling a beak.

The capsule is bilocular and *birostrated.* *Encyc.*

BIRT, *n. burt.* A fish, called also turbot.

BIRTH, *n. berth.* [Sax. *byrd, beorth*; D. *geboorte*; Ger. *geburt*; Ir. *beirthe*; L. *partus*, the participle of *pario*, to *bear.*]

1. The act of coming into life, or of being born. Except in poetry, it is generally applied to human beings; as the *birth* of a son.

2. Lineage; extraction; descent; as, Grecian *birth.* *Denham.*
It is used of high or low extraction; but is often used by way of distinction for a descent from noble or honorable parents and ancestors; as a man of *birth.*

3. The condition in which a person is born.
A foe by *birth* to Troy. *Dryden.*

4. That which is born; that which is produced, whether animal or vegetable. *Milton. Addison.*

5. The act of bringing forth; as, she had two children at a *birth.*

6. In *a theological sense*, regeneration is called the *new birth.*

7. Origin; beginning; as the *birth* of an empire.

BIRTH, BERTH, *n.* A station in which a ship rides. [See *Berth.*]

BIRTH′DAY, *n.* [*birth* and *day.*] The day in which any person is born.

2. The same day of the month, in which a person was born, in every succeeding year; often celebrated as a joyful anniversary. It sometimes has the form of an attribute; as a *birth-day* ode.

BIRTH′DOM, *n.* [*birth* and *dom.* See *Dom* and *Doom.*] Privilege of birth. [*Not used.*] *Shak.*

BIRTH′ING, *n.* Any thing added to raise the sides of a ship. *Ash. Bailey.*

BIRTH′NIGHT, *n.* [*birth* and *night.*] The night in which a person is born; and the anniversary of that night in succeeding years.

BIRTH′PLACE, *n.* [*birth* and *place.*] The town, city or country, where a person is born; more generally, the particular town, city, or other local district.

BIRTH′RIGHT, *n.* [*birth* and *right.*] Any right or privilege, to which a person is entitled by birth, such as an estate descendible by law to an heir, or civil liberty under a free constitution.

Esau, for a morsel, sold his *birthright.* Heb. xii.

It may be used in the sense of primogeniture, or the privilege of the first born, but is applicable to any right which results from descent.

BIRTH′-SONG, *n.* A song sung at the birth of a person.

BIRTH′-STRANGLED, *a.* [*birth* and *strangle.*] Strangled or suffocated in being born. *Shak.*

BIRTH′WŎRT, *n.* [*birth* and *wort.*] A genus of plants, Aristolochia, of many species. Of these are the snake root of America, and the contrayerva of Jamaica. *Encyc.*

BISA, } *n.* A coin of Pegu, of the value of half
BIZA, } a ducat; also, a weight. *Encyc.*

BIS′€OTIN, *n.* [Fr.] A confection, made of flour, sugar, marmelade and eggs.

BIS′€UIT, *n. bis′kit.* [Fr. compounded of L. *bis*, twice, and *cuit*, baked; It. *biscotto*; Sp. *bizcocho.*]

1. A kind of bread, formed into cakes, and baked hard for seamen.

2. A cake, variously made, for the use of private families. The name, in England, is given to a composition of flour, eggs, and sugar. With us the name is given to a composition of flour and butter, made and baked in private families. But the compositions under this denomination are very various.

3. The body of an earthern vessel, in distinction from the glazing. *Thomson.*

BISE€T′, *v. t.* [L. *bis*, twice, and *seco, sectum*, to cut. See *Section.*]
To cut or divide into two parts. In *geometry*, one line *bisects* another when it crosses it, leaving an equal part of the line on each side of the point where it is crossed.

BISE€T′ED, *pp.* Divided into two equal parts.

BISE€T′ING, *ppr.* Dividing into two equal parts.

BISE€′TION, *n.* The act of cutting into two equal parts; the division of any line or quantity into two equal parts.

BISEG′MENT, *n.* [*bis* and *segment.*] One of the parts of a line, divided into two equal parts.

BISEX′OUS, *a.* Consisting of both sexes. *Brown.*

BISH′OP, *n.* [L. *episcopus*; Gr. ἐπισκοπος, of ἐπι, over, and σκοπος, inspector, or visitor; σκοπεω, to view, or inspect; whence ἐπισκεπτομαι, to visit or inspect; also ἐπισκοπεω, to view. This Greek and Latin word accompanied the introduction of christianity into the west and north of Europe, and has been corrupted into Saxon *biscop, bisceop*, Sw. and Dan. *biskop*, D. *bisschop*, Ger. *bischof*, It. *vescovo*, Fr. *evêque*, Sp. *obispo*, Port. *bispo*, W. *esgob*, and Ir. *easgob.* In Ar. and Pers. أُسْقُف oskof. This title the Athenians gave to those whom they sent into the provinces subject to them, to *inspect* the state of affairs; and the Romans gave the title to those who were *inspectors* of provisions.]

1. An overseer; a spiritual superintendent, ruler or director; *applied to Christ.*

Ye were as sheep going astray, but are now returned to the shepherd and *bishop* of your souls. 1 Pet. ii.

2. In *the primitive church*, a spiritual overseer; an elder or presbyter; one who had the pastoral care of a church.

The same persons are in this chapter called elders or presbyters, and overseers or *bishops.* *Scott, Comm.* Acts xx.

Till the churches were multiplied, the *bishops* and presbyters were the same. *Ib.* Phil. i. 1. 1 Tim. iii. 1. Tit. i. 7.

Both the Greek and Latin fathers do, with one consent, declare, that *bishops* were called presbyters, and presbyters *bishops*, in apostolic times, the name being then common. *Whitby.*

3. In the Greek, Latin, and some Protestant churches, a prelate, or person consecrated for the spiritual government and direction of a diocese. In *Great Britain*, bishops are nominated by the king, who, upon request of the dean and chapter, for leave to elect a bishop, sends a *conge d'elire*, or license to elect, with a letter missive, nominating the person whom he would have chosen. The election, by the chapter, must be made within twelve days, or the king has a right to appoint whom he pleases. Bishops are consecrated by an archbishop, with two assistant bishops. A bishop must be thirty years of age; and all bishops, except the bishop of Man, are peers of the realm. *Blackstone.*

By the canons of the Protestant Episcopal church in the United States, no diocese or state shall proceed to the election of a bishop, unless there are at least six officiating presbyters residing therein, who shall be qualified, according to the canons, to vote for a bishop; a majority of whom at least must concur in the election. But the conventions of two or more dioceses, or states, having together nine or more such presbyters, may join in the election of a bishop. A convention is composed of the clergy, and a lay delegation, consisting of one or more members from each parish. In every state, the bishop is to be chosen according to such rules as the convention of that state shall ordain. The mode of election, in most or all of the states, is by a concurrent vote of the clergy and laity, in convention, each body voting separately. Before a bishop can be consecrated, he must receive a testimonial of approbation from the General Convention of the church; or if that is not in session, from a majority of the standing committee in the several dioceses. The mode of consecrating bishops and ordaining priests and deacons differs not essentially from the practice in England. *Bishop Brownell.*

BISH′OP, *n.* A cant word for a mixture of wine, oranges, and sugar. *Swift.*

BISH'OP, *v. t.* To confirm; to admit solemnly into the church. *Johnson.*
2. Among *horse-dealers*, to use arts to make an old horse look like a young one, or to give a good appearance to a bad horse. *Ash. Encyc.*
BISH'OPLIKE, *a.* Resembling a bishop; belonging to a bishop. *Fulke.*
BISH'OPRIC, *n.* [*bishop* and *ric*, jurisdiction.]
1. A diocese; the district over which the jurisdiction of a bishop extends. In *England*, are twenty-four bishoprics, besides that of Sodor and Man; in *Ireland*, eighteen.
2. The charge of instructing and governing in spiritual concerns; office. Acts i. 20.
BISH'OPSWEED, *n.* [*bishop* and *weed.*] A genus of plants, with the generic name *Ammi.*
BISH'OPSWŎRT, *n.* A plant.
BISK, *n.* [Fr. *bisque.*] Soup or broth, made by boiling several sorts of flesh together. *King.*
BISK'ET, *n.* A biscuit. This orthography is adopted by many respectable writers.
BIS'MUTH, *n. s* as *z.* [G. *wissmuth.*] A metal of a yellowish or reddish white color, and a lamellar texture. It is somewhat harder than lead, and scarcely, if at all, malleable, being so brittle as to break easily under the hammer, and it is reducible to powder. Its internal face or fracture exhibits large shining plates, variously disposed. It melts at 476° Fahr. and may be fused in the flame of a candle. It is often found in a native state, crystalized in rhombs or octahedrons, or in the form of dendrites, or thin lamens investing the ores of other metals, particularly cobalt. *Nicholson. Encyc.*
BIS'MUTHAL, *a.* Consisting of bismuth, or containing it. *Cleaveland.*
BIS'MUTHIC, *a.* Pertaining to bismuth; as *bismuthic* acid. *Lavoisier.*
BIS'ON, *n.* [L.] A quadruped of the bovine genus, usually but improperly called the buffalo. The proper buffalo is a distinct species, peculiar to the warmer climates of the Eastern Continent. The bison is a wild animal, with short, black, rounded horns, with a great interval between their bases. On the shoulders is a large hunch, consisting of a fleshy substance. The head and hunch are covered with a long undulated fleece, of a rust-color, divided into locks. In winter, the whole body is covered in this manner; but in summer, the hind part of the body is naked, and wrinkled. The tail is about a foot long, naked, except a tuft of hairs at the end. The fore parts of the body are very thick and strong; the hind parts are slender and weak. These animals inhabit the interior parts of North America, and some of the mountainous parts of Europe and Asia. *Pennant.*
Pennant alledges that the bison of America is the same species of animal as the bison and aurochs of Europe, the *bonasus* of Aristotle, the *urus* of Cesar, the *bos ferus* or wild ox of Strabo, the *bison* of Pliny, and the *biston* of Oppian.
Cuvier has not separated the bison of America from that of Europe. He considers their identity as doubtful. The former has the legs and tail shorter, and the hairs of its head and neck longer than in the latter. *Regne Anim.*
BISSEX'TILE, *n.* [L. *bissextilis*, leap year, from *bissextus*, [*bis* and *sextus*] the *sixth* of the calends of March, or twenty-fourth day of February, which was reckoned *twice* every fourth year, by the intercalation of a day. *Ainsworth.*]
Leap year; every fourth year, in which a day is added to the month of February, on account of the excess of 6 hours, which the civil year contains, above 365 days. This excess is 11 minutes 3 seconds too much; that is, it exceeds the real year, or annual revolution of the earth. Hence at the end of every century, divisible by 4, it is necessary to retain the bissextile day, and to suppress it at the end of those centuries which are not divisible by 4. *Encyc.*
BISSEX'TILE, *a.* Pertaining to the leap year.
BIS'SON, *a.* [Sax. *bisen.*] Blind. [*Not used.*] *Shak.*
BIS'TER, *n.* [Fr. *bistre*, from *bis*, brown.] Among painters, the burnt oil extracted from the soot of wood; a brown pigment. To prepare it, soot [that of beach is the best] is put into water, in the proportion of two pounds to a gallon, and boiled half an hour; after standing to settle, and while hot, the clearer part of the fluid must be poured off from the sediment, and evaporated to dryness; the remainder is bister. *Encyc.*
BIS'TORT, *n.* [L. *bistorta*, *bis* and *tortus*, twisted.]
A plant, a species of *polygonum*, or many-knotted or angled. In popular language, it is called *snake-weed.*
BIS'TOURY, *n. bis'tury.* [Fr. *bistouri*, from *Pistoia*, a city.]
A surgical instrument for making incisions. It is either straight and fixed in a handle like a knife, or its blade turns like a lancet, or it is crooked, with the sharp edge on the inside. *Encyc.*
BISULC'OUS, *a.* [L. *bisulcus*, of *bis* and *sulcus*, a furrow.] Cloven footed, as swine or oxen. *Brown.*
BISUL'PHURET, *n.* [*bis* and *sulphuret.*] In *chimistry*, a sulphuret, with a double proportion of sulphur. *Silliman.*
BIT, *n.* [Sax. *bitol*, *gebæte*, *gebætel*, a bit; *bætan*, to bit or curb.]
The iron part of a bridle which is inserted in the mouth of a horse, and its appendages, to which the reins are fastened. It includes the bit mouth, the branches, the curb, the sevel holes, the tranchefil and cross chains. Bits are of various kinds, as the musrol, snaffle, or watering bit; the canon mouth, jointed in the middle; the canon or fast mouth, all of a piece, kneed in the middle; the scatch-mouth; the masticador, or slavering bit; &c. *Johnson. Encyc.*
BIT, *v. t.* To put a bridle upon a horse; to put the bit in the mouth.
BIT, *pret.* and *pp.* of *bite.* Seized or wounded by the teeth.
BIT, *n.* [Sax. *bita*, a bite or mouthful; *bitan*, to bite; D. *bit*; G. *biss.*] A small piece; a mouthful, or morsel; a *bite.*
2. A small piece of any substance.
3. A small coin of the West Indies, a half pistareen, about ten cents, or five pence sterling.
4. The point of an auger, or other borer; the *bite.*
This word is used, like *jot* and *whit*, to express the smallest degree; as, he is not a *bit* wiser or better.
BITCH, *n.* [Sax. *bicca*, *bicce*, *bice*; Dan. *bikke.* Qu. Ger. *betze*; Basque, *potzoa.* This word probably signifies a female, for the French *biche* is a *hind.*]
1. The female of the canine kind, as of the dog, wolf, and fox.
2. A name of reproach for a woman. *Pope. Arbuthnot.*
BITE, *v. t.* pret. *bit*; pp. *bit*, *bitten.* [Sax. *bitan*; Sw. *bita*; Dan. *bider*; Ger. *beissen*, to bite.]
1. To break or crush with the teeth, as in eating; to pierce with the teeth, as a serpent; to seize with the teeth, as a dog.
2. To pinch or pain, as with cold; as a *biting* north wind; the frost *bites.*
3. To reproach with sarcasm; to treat with severity by words or writing; as, one poet praises, another *bites.*
4. To pierce, cut, or wound; as a *biting* faulchion. *Shak.*
5. To make to smart; as, acids *bite* the mouth.
6. To cheat; to trick.

> The rogue was *bit.* *Pope.*

[*Not elegant, but common.*]
7. To enter the ground and hold fast, as the bill and palm of an anchor. *Mar. Dict.*
8. To injure by angry contention.

> If ye *bite* and devour one another. Gal. 5.

BITE, *n.* The seizure of any thing by the teeth of an animal, as the *bite* of a dog; or with the mouth, as of a fish.
2. The wound made by the teeth.
3. A morsel; as much as is taken at once by *biting*; a mouthful.
4. A cheat; a trick; a fraud. [*A low word.*]
5. A sharper; one who cheats.
BI'TER, *n.* One who bites; that which bites; a fish apt to take bait.
2. One who cheats or defrauds.
BITERN'ATE, *a.* [L. *bis* and *ternus*, three.] In *botany*, doubly ternate, as when a petiole has three ternate leaflets. *Martyn.*
BI'TING, *ppr.* Seizing, wounding, or crushing with the teeth; pinching, paining, causing to smart with cold; reproaching with severity, or treating sarcastically; cheating.
BI'TING, *a.* Sharp; severe; sarcastic.
BI'TINGLY, *adv.* In a sarcastic or jeering manner.
BIT'LESS, *a.* Not having a bit or bridle. *Fanshaw.*
BIT'MOUTH, *n.* [*bit* and *mouth.*] The bit, or that part of a bridle which is put in a horse's mouth. *Bailey. Ash. Encyc.*
BIT'TACLE, *n.* [Qu. Fr. *boite d'aiguille*, needle box.]
The box for the compasses and lights on board a ship. [See *Binnacle.*]
BIT'TEN, *pp.* of *bite.* *bit'tn.* Seized or wounded by the teeth; cheated.
BIT'TER, *a.* [Sax. *biter*; Sw. D. Ger. and Dan. *bitter*; from *bite.*]
1. Sharp, or biting to the taste; acrid; like wormwood.
2. Sharp; cruel; severe; as *bitter* enmity. Heb. i.

3. Sharp, as words; reproachful; sarcastic.
4. Sharp to the feeling; piercing; painful; that makes to smart; as a *bitter* cold day, or a *bitter* blast.
5. Painful to the mind; calamitous; poignant; as a *bitter* fate.
6. Afflicted; distressed.

The Egyptians made their lives *bitter*. Ex. i.

7. Hurtful; very sinful.

It is an evil and *bitter* thing. Jer. ii.

8. Mournful; distressing; expressive of misery; as a *bitter* complaint or lamentation. Job xxiii. Jer. vi. xxxi.

BIT'TER, *n.* A substance that is bitter. [See *Bitters*.]

BIT'TER, *n.* [See *Bitts*.] In *marine language*, a turn of the cable which is round the bitts.

Bitter-end, that part of a cable which is abaft the bitts, and therefore within board, when the ship rides at anchor. *Mar. Dict.*

BIT'TER-GŌURD, *n.* [*bitter* and *gourd*.] A plant, a species of Cucumis, called Colocynthis, Colocynth, Coloquintada. The fruit is of the gourd kind, having a shell inclosing a bitter pulp, which is a very drastic purgative. It is brought from the Levant, and is the bitter apple of the shops. *Encyc.*

BIT'TERISH, *a.* Somewhat bitter; bitter in a moderate degree. *Goldsmith.*

BIT'TERISHNESS, *n.* The quality of being moderately bitter. *Encyc.*

BIT'TERLY, *adv.* With a bitter taste.

2. In a severe manner; in a manner expressing poignant grief; as, to weep *bitterly*.
3. In a manner severely reproachful; sharply; severely; angrily; as, to censure *bitterly*.

BIT'TERN, *n.* [D. *butoor;* Fr. *butor;* Corn. *klabitter*.]

A fowl of the grallic order, the *Ardea stellaris*, a native of Europe. This fowl has long legs and neck, and stalks among reeds and sedge, feeding upon fish. It makes a singular noise, called by Dryden *bumping*, and by Goldsmith *booming*. *Encyc.*

BIT'TERN, *n.* [from *bitter*.] In *salt works*, the brine remaining after the salt is concreted. This being laded off, and the salt taken out of the pan, is returned, and being again boiled, yields more salt. It is used in the preparation of Epsom salt, the sulphate of magnesia, and of Glauber's salt, the sulphate of soda. *Johnson. Encyc.*

BIT'TERNESS, *n.* [from *bitter*.] A bitter taste; or rather a quality in things which excites a *biting* disagreeable sensation in the tongue.

2. In *a figurative sense*, extreme enmity, grudge, hatred; or rather an excessive degree or implacableness of passions and emotions; as the *bitterness* of anger. Eph. iv.
3. Sharpness; severity of temper.
4. Keenness of reproach; piquancy; biting sarcasm.
5. Keen sorrow; painful affliction; vexation; deep distress of mind.

Hannah was in *bitterness* of soul. 1 Sam. i. Job vii.

In *the gall of bitterness*, in a state of extreme impiety or enmity to God. Acts viii.

Root of bitterness, a dangerous error, or schism, tending to draw persons to apostasy. Heb. xii.

BIT'TERS, *n.* A liquor in which bitter herbs or roots are steeped; generally a spirituous liquor, *the bitter cause of intemperance, of disease, and of premature death!*

BIT'TER-SALT, *n.* Epsom salt.

BIT'TER-SPAR, *n.* Rhombspar, a mineral that crystalizes in rhomboids. It is the crystalized variety of magnesian limestone. *Ure.*

BIT'TER-SWEET, *n.* [*bitter* and *sweet*.] A species of *Solanum*, a slender climbing plant, whose root, when chewed, produces first a bitter, then a sweet taste. *Encyc.*

BIT'TERVETCH, *n.* [*bitter* and *vetch*.] A species of Ervum, or lentil, cultivated for fodder. *Encyc.*

2. A genus of plants, known by the generic name *Orobus*, remarkable for their beautiful papilionaceous flowers. The tubercles of one species are in great esteem among the Highlanders of Scotland, who chew them, when dry, to give a better relish to their liquors.

BIT'TER-WŎRT, *n.* [*bitter* and *wort*.] The plant called gentian, *Gentiana*, which has a remarkably bitter taste.

BIT'TOUR or **BIT'TOR**, *n.* The *bittern*. *Dryden.*

BITTS, *n. plu.* [from the same root as *bite*.] A frame of two strong pieces of timber fixed perpendicularly in the fore part of a ship, on which to fasten the cables, when she rides at anchor. There are also *topsail sheet bitts, paul-bitts, carrick-bitts*, &c. *Mar. Dict.*

BITT, *v. t.* To put round the bitts; as, to *bitt the cable*, in order to fasten it or to slacken it out gradually, which is called *veering away*. *Mar. Dict.*

BITU'ME, *n.* Bitumen, so written for the sake of the rhyme. *May.*

BIT'UMEN, } *n.* [L.; Fr. *bitume;* Sp. *betun;*
BITU'MEN, } It. *bitume*.]

This name is used to denote various inflammable substances, of a strong smell, and of different consistencies, which are found in the earth. There are several varieties, most of which evidently pass into each other, proceeding from Naphtha, the most fluid, to Petroleum, a viscid fluid, Maltha, more or less cohesive, elastic bitumen or mineral caoutchouc, and Asphalt, which is sometimes too hard to be scratched by the nail. *Nicholson. Cleaveland.*

BITU'MINATE, *v. t.* To impregnate with bitumen.

BITU'MINATED, *a.* Impregnated with bitumen.

BITUMINIF'EROUS, *a.* [*bitumen* and *fero*, to produce.]

Producing bitumen. *Kirwan.*

BITU'MINIZE, *v. t.* To form into, or impregnate with bitumen. *Lit. Mag.*

BITU'MINOUS, *a.* Having the qualities of bitumen; compounded with bitumen; containing bitumen. *Milton.*

Bituminous Limestone is of a lamellar structure, susceptible of polish, of a brown or black color, and when rubbed emitting an unpleasant smell. That of Dalmatia is so charged with bitumen, that it may be cut like soap. *Ure.*

BI'VALVE, *n.* [L. *bis*, twice, and *valve*, L. *valva*.]

An animal having two valves, or a shell consisting of two parts which open and shut. Also a pericarp in which the seed-case opens or splits into two parts. *Encyc.*

BI'VALVE, } Having two shells or
BIVALV'ULAR, } *a.* valves which open and
BIVALV'OUS, } shut, as the oyster and the seed cases of certain plants. *Martyn. Coxe.*

BIVAULT'ED, *a.* [L. *bis*, twice, and *vault*.] Having two vaults or arches. *Barlow.*

BIVENT'RAL, *a.* [L. *bis* and *venter*, belly.] Having two bellies; as a *biventral* muscle. *Bailey.*

BIV'IOUS, *a.* [L. *bivius;* *bis* and *via*, way.] Having two ways, or leading two ways. *Brown.*

BIVOUAC, *n.* [Fr. This word is probably composed of *be* and the Teutonic root of *wake, watch;* Sax. *wacian*, to wake, to watch; L. *vigilo;* G. *wache*, a guard; *wachen*, to watch.]

The guard or watch of a whole army, as in cases of great danger of surprise or attack.

BIVOUAC, *v. t.* To watch or be on guard, as a whole army.

[This word anglicised would be *bewatch*.]

BIX'WŎRT, *n.* A plant.

BIZANTINE. [See *Byzantine*.]

BLAB, *v. t.* [W. *llavaru*, to speak; D. *labbery*, prattle; Ir. *clabaire*, a babbler; *labhraim*, to speak; Chaucer, *labbe*, a blabber.]

1. To utter or tell in a thoughtless manner; to publish secrets or trifles without discretion. It implies, says Johnson, rather thoughtlessness than treachery, but may be used in either sense. *Dryden.*
2. To tell, or utter; *in a good sense*. *Shak.*

BLAB, *v. i.* To tattle; to tell tales. *Shak.*

BLAB, *n.* A babbler; a telltale; one who betrays secrets, or tell things which ought to be kept secret.

BLAB'BER, *n.* A tattler; a tell-tale.

BLAB'BING, *ppr.* Telling indiscreetly what ought to be concealed; tattling.

BLACK, *a.* [Sax. *blac*, and *blæc*, black, pale, wan, livid; *blacian, blæcan*, to become pale, to turn white, to become black, to blacken; *blæc*, ink; Sw. *blek*, pale, wan, livid; *bleck*, ink; *bleka*, to insolate, to expose to the sun, or to bleach; also to lighten, to flash; D. *bleek*, pale; *bleeken*, to bleach; G. *bleich*, pale, wan, bleak; *bleichen*, to bleach; Dan. *blæk*, ink; *bleeg*, pale, wan, bleak, sallow; *bleeger*, to bleach. It is remarkable that *black, bleak* and *bleach* are all radically one word. The primary sense seems to be, pale, wan or sallow, from which has proceeded the present variety of significations.]

1. Of the color of night; destitute of light; dark.
2. Darkened by clouds; as the heavens *black* with clouds.
3. Sullen; having a cloudy look or countenance. *Shak.*
4. Atrociously wicked; horrible; as a *black* deed or crime. *Dryden.*
5. Dismal; mournful; calamitous. *Shak.*

Black and blue, the dark color of a bruise in the flesh, which is accompanied with a mixture of blue.

BLACK, *n.* That which is destitute of light

or whiteness; the darkest color, or rather a destitution of all color; as, a cloth has a good *black*.
2. A negro; a person whose skin is *black*.
3. A black dress, or mourning; as, to be clothed in *black*.

BLACK, *v. t.* To make black; to blacken; to soil. *Boyle.*

BLACK'-ACT, *n.* [*black* and *act.*] The English statute 9. Geo. I. which makes it felony to appear armed in any park or warren, &c., or to hunt or steal deer, &c., with the face *blacked* or disguised. *Blackstone.*

BLACK'-BALL, *n.* [*black* and *ball.*] A composition for blacking shoes.

BLACK'-BALL, *v. t.* To reject or negative in choosing, by putting black balls into a ballot-box.

BLACK'-BAR, *n.* [*black* and *bar.*] A plea obliging the plaintiff to assign the place of trespass. *Ash.*

BLACK'-BERRY, *n.* [Sax. *blacberian*, *black* and *berry.*]
The berry of the bramble or *rubus*; a popular name applied, in different places, to different species, or varieties of this fruit.

BLACK'-BIRD, *n.* [*black* and *bird.*] In *England*, the *merula*, a species of *turdus*, a singing bird with a fine note, but very loud. In *America*, this name is given to different birds, as to the gracula quiscula, or crow black-bird, and to the oriolus phæniceus, or red winged black-bird, [*Sturnus predatorius*, Wilson.]

BLACK'-BOOK, *n.* [*black* and *book.*] The Black Book of the Exchequer in England, is a book said to have been composed in 1175, by Gervais of Tilbury. It contains a description of the Court of Exchequer, its officers, their ranks and privileges, wages, perquisites and jurisdiction, with the revenues of the crown, in money, grain and cattle. *Encyc.*
2. Any book which treats of necromancy. *Encyc.*
3. A book compiled by order of the visitors of monasteries, under Henry VIII., containing a detailed account of the enormities practised in religious houses, to blacken them and to hasten their dissolution. *Encyc.*

BLACK'-BROWED, *a.* [*black* and *brow.*] Having black eye-brows; gloomy; dismal; threatening; as a *black-browed* gust. *Dryden.*

BLACK-BRY'ONY, *n.* [*black* and *bryony.*] A plant, the Tamus. *Encyc.*

BLACK-CAP, *n.* [*black* and *cap.*] A bird, the *Motacilla atricapilla*, or mock-nightingale; so called from its black crown. It is common in Europe. *Encyc. Pennant.*
2. In *cookery*, an apple roasted till black, to be served up in a dish of boiled custard. *Mason.*

BLACK'-CATTLE, *n.* [*black* and *cattle.*] Cattle of the bovine genus, as bulls, oxen and cows. [English.] *Johnson.*

BLACK-CHALK, *n.* A mineral of a bluish black color, of a slaty texture, and soiling the fingers when handled; a variety of argillaceous slate. *Ure.*

BLACK'-COCK, *n.* [*black* and *cock.*] A fowl, called also *black-grous* and *black-game*, the *Tetrao tetrix* of Linne.

BLACK'-EAGLE, *n.* [*black* and *eagle.*] In *Scotland*, a name given to the *Falco fulvus*, the white tailed eagle of Edwards.

BLACK'-EARTH, *n.* Mold; earth of a dark color. *Woodward.*

BLACK'ED, *pp.* Made black; soiled.

BLACK'EN, *v. t.* [Sax. *blæcan.* See *Black.*]
1. To make black.
The importation of slaves that has *blackened* half America. *Franklin.*
2. To make dark; to darken; to cloud.
3. To soil.
4. To sully reputation; to make infamous; as, vice *blackens* the character.

BLACK'EN, *v. i.* To grow black, or dark.

BLACK'ENER, *n.* He that blackens.

BLACK'-EYED, *a.* Having black eyes. *Dryden.*

BLACK'-FACED, *a.* Having a black face. *Shak.*

BLACK'-FISH, *n.* [*black* and *fish.*] A fish in the Orontes, about twenty inches long, in shape resembling the sheat-fish. Its eyes are placed near the corners of its mouth on the edge of the lower jaw. *Dict. of Nat. Hist.*
2. In the U. States, a fish caught on the rocky shores of New-England.

BLACK-FOREST, *n.* [*black* and *forest.*] A forest in Germany, in Swabia; a part of the ancient Hercynian forest.

BLACK-FRIAR, *n.* Black-friars is a name given to the Dominican Order, called also Predicants and preaching friars; in France, Jacobins. *Encyc.*

BLACK'-GUARD, *n.* [said to be of *black* and *guard*; but is it not a corruption of *black-ard*, black-kind?]
A vulgar term applied to a mean fellow, who uses abusive, scurrilous language, or treats others with foul abuse.

BLACK'ING, *ppr.* Making black.

BLACK'ING, *n.* A substance used for blacking shoes, variously made; any factitious matter for making things black. *Encyc. Ash.*

BLACK'ISH, *a.* Somewhat black; moderately black or dark.

BLACK'-JACK, *n.* A name given by miners to blend, a mineral called also *false galena*, and *blend.* It is an ore of zink, in combination with iron and sulphur, sulphuret of zink. *Nicholson.*
2. A leathern cup of old times.

BLACK'-LEAD, *n.* A mineral of a dark steel-gray color, and of a scaly texture, composed of carbon, with a small portion of iron. This name, *black-lead*, is improper, as it contains no lead. It is called plumbago, and technically graphite, as it is used for pencils. *Cleaveland.*

BLACK'-LEGS, *n.* In some parts of England, a disease among calves and sheep. It is a sort of jelly which settles in the legs and sometimes in the neck. *Encyc.*

BLACK'LY, *adv.* Darkly; atrociously.

BLACK'-MAIL, *n.* A certain rate of money, corn, cattle or other thing, anciently paid, in the north of England, to certain men, who were allied to robbers, to be by them protected from pillage. *Cowel. Encyc.*
2. Black rent, or rents paid in corn or flesh. *Bailey. Encyc.*

BLACK'-MONDAY, *n.* Easter Monday, in 34. Ed. III., which was misty, obscure, and so cold that men died on horseback. *Stowe.*

BLACK'-MONKS, a denomination given to the Benedictines. *Encyc.*

BLACK'-MOOR, *n.* [*black* and *moor.*] A negro; a black man.

BLACK'-MOUTHED, *a.* Using foul or scurrilous language. *Killingbeck.*

BLACK'NESS, *n.* The quality of being black; black color; darkness; atrociousness or enormity in wickedness.

BLACK'-PUDDING, *n.* A kind of food made of blood and grain. *Johnson.*

BLACK'-ROD, *n.* [*black* and *rod.*] In *England*, the usher belonging to the order of the garter; so called from the black rod which he carries. He is of the king's chamber and usher of Parliament. *Cowel.*

Black row grains, a species of iron stone or ore, found in the mines about Dudley in Staffordshire, England. *Encyc.*

BLACK' SEA, *n.* [*black* and *sea.*] The Euxine Sea, on the eastern border of Europe.

BLACK'-SHEEP, *n.* [*black* and *sheep.*] In *oriental history*, the ensign or standard of a race of Turkmans in Armenia and Mesopotamia. *Encyc.*

BLACK'SMITH, *n.* [*black* and *smith.*] A smith who works in iron, and makes iron utensils; more properly, an iron-smith.

Black'-strakes, in a ship, are a range of planks immediately above the wales in a ship's side, covered with tar and lamp-black. *Encyc.*

BLACK'-TAIL, *n.* [*black* and *tail.*] A fish, a kind of perch, called also a *ruff* or *pope.* *Johnson.*

BLACK'-THORN, *n.* [*black* and *thorn.*] A species of prunus, called also *sloe.* It grows ten or twelve feet high, very branchy, and armed with sharp, strong spines, and bearing small, round, black cherries. It is much cultivated for hedges. *Encyc.*

BLACK'-TIN, *n.* [*black* and *tin.*] Tin ore, when dressed, stamped and washed ready for melting. It is the ore comminuted by beating into a black powder, like fine sand. *Encyc.*

BLACK'-VISAGED, *a.* Having a dark visage or appearance. *Marston.*

BLACK'-WADD, *n.* [*black* and *wadd.*] An ore of manganese, found in Derbyshire, England, and used as a drying ingredient in paints. It is remarkable for taking fire, when mixed with linseed oil in a certain proportion. *Encyc.*

BLACK'-WORK, *n.* [*black* and *work.*] Iron wrought by black-smiths; so called in distinction from that wrought by white-smiths. *Encyc.*

BLAD'-APPLE, *n.* In *botany*, the cactus or a species of it. *Fam. of Plants.*

BLAD'DER, *n.* [Sax. *blædr*, *blædra*, *bleddra*, a bladder, and *blæd*, a puff of wind, also a goblet, fruit, the branch of a tree; W. *pledren*, a bladder; Sw. and Dan. *blad*, a page, a leaf, Eng. a *blade*; D. *blad*, a leaf, page, sheet, a board, a *blade*, a *plate*; G. *blatt*, a leaf; *blatter*, a blister, which is our *bladder*. The Germans express *bladder* by *blase*, D. *blaas*, which is our *blaze.* Hence we observe that the sense is taken from swelling, extending, dilating, blowing; Sax. *blawan*, to blow; W. *blot* or *bloth*, a puff or blast; W. *pled*, extension, from *lled*, breadth; L. *latus.*]

1. A thin membranous bag in animals, which serves as the receptacle of some secreted fluid, as the *urinary bladder*, the *gall bladder*, &c. By way of eminence, the word, in common language, denotes the urinary bladder, either within the animal, or when taken out and inflated with air. *Encyc. Johnson.*

2. Any vesicle, blister or pustule, especially if filled with air, or a thin, watery liquor.

3. In *botany*, a distended membranaceous pericarp. *Martyn.*

BLAD'DERED, *a.* Swelled like a bladder. *Dryden.*

BLAD'DER-NUT, *n.* [*bladder* and *nut.*] A genus of plants, with the generic name of *Staphylœa.* They have three capsules, inflated and joined by a longitudinal suture. *Encyc.*

2. The *African bladder nut* is the *Royena.*

3. The *laurel-leaved bladder-nut* is a species of *Ilex*, holm or holly. *Fam. of Plants.*

BLAD'DER-SENNA, or *bastard-senna*, a genus of plants, called in botany *Colutea.* *Fam. of Plants.*

The *jointed-podded bladder-senna* is the *Coronilla.* *Fam. of Plants.*

BLAD'DERY, *a.* Resembling a bladder; containing bladders.

BLADE, *n.* [Sax. *blæd*, *bled*, a branch, fruit, herbs, goblet, a phial, the broad part or blade of an oar; Gr. πλατυς, broad. The radical sense is to shoot, extend, dilate. See *Bladder.*]

1. The stalk or spire of a plant, particularly of grass and corn; but applicable to the stalk of any herbaceous plant, whether green or dry.

2. A leaf. *In this sense much used in the Southern States of N. America, for the leaves of maize, which are used as fodder.*

3. The cutting part of an instrument, as the *blade* of a knife, or sword, so named from its length or breadth. Usually, it is made of iron or steel, but may be of any other metal, cast or wrought to an edge or point. Also, the broad part of an oar.

4. The *blade of the shoulder*, *shoulder-blade*, or *blade-bone*, is the scapula, or scapular bone. It is the broad upper bone of the shoulder, so called from its resemblance to a blade or leaf.

5. A brisk man; a bold, forward man; a rake.

BLADE, *v. t.* To furnish with a blade.

BLA'DE-BONE, *n.* The scapula, or upper bone in the shoulder.

BLA'DED, *pp.* Having a blade or blades. It may be used of blade in the sense of a leaf, a spire, or the cutting part of an instrument.

2. In *mineralogy*, composed of long and narrow plates, like the blade of a knife. *Cleaveland.*

BLA'DE-SMITH, *n.* A sword cutler.

BLAIN, *n.* [Sax. *blegene*; D. *blein.*]

A pustule; a botch; a blister. In *farriery*, a bladder growing on the root of the tongue, against the wind pipe, which swells so as to stop the breath. *Encyc.*

BLA'MABLE, *a.* [See *Blame.*] Faulty; culpable; reprehensible; deserving of censure. *Dryden.*

BLA'MABLENESS, *n.* Culpableness; fault; the state of being worthy of censure. *Whitlock.*

BLA'MABLY, *adv.* Culpably; in a manner deserving of censure.

BLAME, *v. t.* [Fr. *blâmer*, for *blasmer*; It. *biasmare*, to blame; *biasmo*, for *blasmo*, blame. The Greeks have the root of this word in βλασφημεω, to *blaspheme*, and it seems to be of the same family as Fr. *blesser*, to injure, that is, to strike. See *Blemish.* But it is not clear that the noun ought not to be arranged before the verb.]

1. To censure; to express disapprobation of; to find fault with; opposed to *praise* or *commend*, and *applicable* most *properly* to *persons*, but *applied* also to *things.*

> I withstood him, because he was to be *blamed.* Gal. ii.

I must *blame* your conduct; or I must *blame* you *for* neglecting business. Legitimately, it cannot be followed by *of.*

2. To bring reproach upon; to blemish; to injure. [See *Blemish.*]

> She had *blamed* her noble blood. [*Obs.*] *Spenser.*

BLAME, *n.* Censure; reprehension; imputation of a fault; disapprobation; an expression of disapprobation for something deemed to be wrong.

> Let me bear the *blame* forever. Gen. xliii.

2. Fault; crime; sin; that which is deserving of censure or disapprobation.

> That we should be holy and without *blame* before him in love. Eph. i.

3. Hurt; injury.

> And glancing down his shield, from *blame* him fairly blest. *Spenser.*

The sense of this word, as used by Spenser, proves that it is a derivative from the root of *blemish.*

To blame, in the phrase, he is *to blame*, signifies *blamable*, to be blamed.

Blame is not strictly a *charge* or *accusation* of a fault; but it implies an opinion in the censuring party, that the person censured is faulty. *Blame* is the act or expression of disapprobation for what is supposed to be wrong.

BLA'MED, *pp.* Censured; disapproved.

BLA'MEFUL, *a.* Faulty; meriting blame; reprehensible.

BLA'MELESS, *a.* Without fault; innocent; guiltless; not meriting censure.

> A bishop then must be *blameless.* 1 Tim. iii.

Sometimes followed by *of.*

> We will be *blameless of* this thine oath. Josh. ii.

BLA'MELESSLY, *adv.* Innocently; without fault or crime. *Hammond.*

BLA'MELESSNESS, *n.* Innocence; a state of being not worthy of censure. *Hammond.*

BLA'MER, *n.* One who blames, finds fault or censures.

BLA'MEWÖRTHINESS, *n.* The quality of deserving censure.

BLA'MEWÖRTHY, *a.* [*blame* and *worthy.*] Deserving blame; censurable; culpable; reprehensible. *Martin.*

BLA'MING, *ppr.* Censuring; finding fault.

BLANC'ARD, *n.* [Fr. *blanc*, white, and *ard*, kind.]

A kind of linen cloth, manufactured in Normandy, so called because the thread is half blanched before it is wove. *Encyc.*

BL'ANCH, *v. t.* [Fr. *blanchir*; It. *bianchire*, the *l* suppressed as in *blame*; Sp. *blanquear*; Port. *branquear*, *l* changed into *r*; Eng. *blank.* See *Bleach.*]

1. To whiten; to take out the color, and make white; to obliterate. *Dryden.*

2. To slur; to balk; to pass over; that is, to avoid; to make empty. *Obs.* *Bacon.*

3. To strip or peel; as, to *blanch* almonds. *Wiseman.*

BL'ANCH, *v. i.* To evade; to shift; to speak softly. *Johnson.*

Rather, to fail or withhold; to be reserved; to remain *blank*, or empty.

> Books will speak plain, when counselors *blanch.* *Bacon.*

BL'ANCHED, *pp.* Whitened.

BL'ANCHER, *n.* One who whitens; also, one who anneals, and cleanses money.

BLANCHIM'ETER, *n.* [*blanch*, and Gr. μετρον, measure.]

An instrument for measuring the bleaching power of oxymuriate [chloride] of lime, and potash. *Ure.*

BL'ANCHING, *ppr.* Whitening. In *coinage*, the operation of giving brightness to pieces of silver, by heating them on a peel, and afterwards boiling them successively in two pans of copper, with aqua fortis, common salt, and tartar of Montpelier; then draining off the water in a sieve: sand and fresh water are then thrown over them, and when dry, they are rubbed with a towel. *Encyc.*

The covering of iron plates with a thin coat of tin is also called *blanching.* *Encyc.*

Blanch-ferm, or blank farm, in ancient law, a white farm, was one, where the rent was paid in silver, not in cattle. *Encyc.*

Blanch-holding, in law, a tenure by which the tenant is bound to pay only an elusory yearly duty to his superior, as an acknowledgment to his right. *Encyc.*

BLANC-MANGER, pron. *blomonge.* [Fr. white food.] In *cookery*, a preparation of dissolved isinglass, milk, sugar, cinnamon, &c., boiled into a thick consistence, and garnished for the table with *blanched* almonds. *Encyc.*

BLAND, *a.* [L. *blandus*; Fr. *blond*; G. *linde*, *gelinde*, mild, soft; Sw. *lindra*; G. *lindern*; D. *linderen*; Dan. *lindrer*; to soften or mitigate; Dan. *lind*, soft, mild, gentle; L. *lenis*, *lentus*; Ar. لَانَ lana, to be mild, soft, gentle, placid, smooth, *lenient.* See *Relent.*]

Mild; soft; gentle; as *bland* words; *bland* zephyrs. *Milton. Thomson.*

BLANDIL'OQUENCE, *n.* [L. *blandus*, mild, and *loquor*, to speak.] Fair, mild, flattering speech.

BLAND'ISH, *v. t.* [L. *blandior*; It. *blandire*; Sp. *blandiar*, *blandir*; Old Eng. *blandise.* *Chaucer.*]

To soften; to caress; to flatter by kind words or affectionate actions. *Milton.*

BLAND'ISHER, *n.* One that flatters with soft words.

BLAND'ISHING, *ppr.* Soothing or flattering with fair words.

BLAND'ISHING, *n.* Blandishment.

BLAND'ISHMENT, *n.* Soft words; kind speeches; caresses; expression of kindness; words or actions expressive of affection or kindness, and tending to win the heart. *Milton. Dryden.*

BLANK, *a.* [Fr. *blanc*; It. *bianco*; Sp. *blanco*; D. and Ger. *blank*; Dan. *blank*;

shining; Sw. *blanck*, white, shining; *blankia*, to shine. See *Bleach*.]
1. Void; empty; consequently white; as a *blank* paper.
2. White or pale; as the *blank* moon. *Milton.*
3. Pale from fear or terror; hence confused; confounded; dispirited; dejected.
Adam—astonished stood, and *blank*. *Milton.*
4. Without rhyme; as *blank* verse, verse in which rhyme is *wanting*.
5. Pure; entire; complete. *Beddoes.*
6. Not containing balls or bullets; as *blank* cartridges.
This word is applied to various other objects, usually in the sense of destitution, emptiness; as a *blank* line; a *blank* space, in a book, &c.
BLANK, *n.* Any void space; a void space on paper, or in any written instrument.
2. A lot by which nothing is gained; a ticket in a lottery which draws no prize.
3. A paper unwritten; a paper without marks or characters.
4. A paper containing the substance of a legal instrument, as a deed, release, writ or execution, with vacant spaces left to be filled with names, date, descriptions, &c.
5. The point to which an arrow is directed, marked with white paper. [*Little used.*] *Shak.*
6. Aim; shot. *Obs.* *Shak.*
7. Object to which any thing is directed. *Shak.*
8. A small copper coin formerly current in France, at the rate of 5 deniers Tournois. There were also pieces of three blanks, and of six; but they are now become moneys of account. *Encyc.*
9. In *coinage*, a plate or piece of gold or silver, cut and shaped, but not stamped. *Encyc.*
Blank-bar, in law, a common bar, or a plea in bar, which, in an action of trespass, is put in to oblige the plaintiff to assign the place where the trespass was committed. *Encyc.*
Point-blank, in gunnery, the shot of a gun leveled horizontally. The distance between the piece, and the point where the shot first touches the ground, is called the *point-blank range*; the shot proceeding on a straight line, without curving. *Encyc.*
BLANK, *v. t.* To make void; to annul. *Spenser.*
2. To deprive of color, the index of health and spirits; to damp the spirits; to dispirit or confuse; as, to *blank* the face of joy. *Shak.* *Tillotson.*
BLANK'ED, *pp.* Confused; dispirited.
BLANK'ET, *n.* [Fr. *blanchet*, the blanket of a printing press.]
1. A cover for a bed, made of coarse wool loosely woven, and used for securing against cold. Blankets are used also by soldiers, and seamen, for covering.
2. A kind of pear, sometimes written after the French, *blanquet*.
3. Among *printers*, woolen cloth or white baize, to lay between the tympans. *Print. Guide.*
BLANK'ET, *v. t.* To toss in a blanket by way of punishment; *an ancient custom.* The Emperor Otho used to sally forth in dark nights, and if he found a drunken man, he administered the discipline of the blanket. *Encyc.*
2. To cover with a blanket.
BLANK'ETING, *ppr.* Tossing in a blanket.
BLANK'ETING, *n.* The punishment of tossing in a blanket.
2. Cloth for blankets.
BLANK'LY, *adv.* In a blank manner; with paleness or confusion.
BLARE, *v. i.* [Old Belgic *blaren*; Teut. *blarren*; L. *ploro*, to cry out, to bawl, to weep; Ir. *blor*, or *glor*, a noise, or voice. The radical sense is to shoot or drive forth, or to spread.]
1. To roar; to bellow. [*Little used.*] *Johnson.*
2. To sweal or melt away, as a candle. *Bailey.*
This is, I believe, usually called *flare*.
BLARE, *n.* Roar; noise. [*Little used.*]
And sigh for battle's *blare*. *Barlow.*
2. A small copper coin of Bern, nearly of the same value as the ratz. *Encyc.*
BLASPHE'ME, *v. t.* [Gr. βλασφημεω. The first syllable is the same as in *blame*, *blasme*, denoting injury; probably, Fr. *blesser*, to hurt, that is, to strike; L. *lædo*, *læsus*. Hence in Sp. *blasfemable* is *blamable*. The last syllable is the Gr. φημι, to speak.]
1. To speak of the Supreme Being in terms of impious irreverence; to revile or speak reproachfully of God, or the Holy Spirit. 1 Kings xxi. Mark iii.
2. To speak evil of; to utter abuse or calumny against; to speak reproachfully of. *Pope.*
BLASPHE'ME, *v. i.* To utter blasphemy.
He that shall *blaspheme* against the Holy Spirit shall not be forgiven. Mark iii.
2. To arrogate the prerogatives of God.
This man *blasphemeth*. Who can forgive sins but God? Math. ix. Mark ii.
BLASPHE'MER, *n.* One who blasphemes; one who speaks of God in impious and irreverent terms. 1 Tim. i.
BLASPHE'MING, *ppr.* Uttering impious or reproachful words concerning God.
BLAS'PHEMOUS, *a.* Containing blasphemy; calumnious; impiously irreverent or reproachful towards God. *Sidney.*
BLAS'PHEMOUSLY, *adv.* Impiously; with impious irreverence to God.
BLAS'PHEMY, *n.* An indignity offered to God by words or writing; reproachful, contemptuous or irreverent words uttered impiously against Jehovah.
Blasphemy is an injury offered to God, by denying that which is due and belonging to him, or attributing to him that which is not agreeable to his nature. *Linwood.*
In the middle ages, blasphemy was used to denote simply the blaming or condemning of a person or thing. Among the Greeks, to *blaspheme* was to use words of ill omen, which they were careful to avoid. *Encyc.*
2. That which derogates from the prerogatives of God. Mark ii.
BL'AST, *n.* [Sax. *blæst*, a puff of wind, a blowing; Sw. *blåst*; Dan. *blæst*; Ger. *blasen*; D. *blaazen*; Dan. *blæser*; Sw. *blåsa*, to blow; whence Ger. *blase*, D. *blaas*, Sw. *blåsa*, a bladder. Hence Eng. *blaze*, which is primarily a *blowing* or *swelling*. Ice. *bloes*, to blow. Qu. Fr. *blaser*, to burn up, to consume. The primary sense is to rush or drive; hence to strike.]
1. A gust or puff of wind; or a sudden gust of wind.
2. The sound made by blowing a wind instrument. *Shak.*
3. Any pernicious or destructive influence upon animals or plants.
4. The infection of any thing pestilential; a blight on plants.
5. A sudden compression of air, attended with a shock, caused by the discharge of cannon.
6. A forcible stream of air from the mouth, from a bellows or the like.
7. A violent explosion of gunpowder, in splitting rocks, and the explosion of inflammable air in a mine.
8. The whole blowing of a forge necessary to melt one supply of ore; a common use of the word among workmen in forges in America.
BL'AST, *v. t.* [Literally, to strike.] To make to wither by some pernicious influence, as too much heat or moisture, or other destructive cause; or to check growth and prevent from coming to maturity and producing fruit; to blight, as trees or plants.
2. To affect with some sudden violence, plague, calamity, or destructive influence, which destroys or causes to fail; as, to *blast* pride or hopes. The figurative senses of this verb are taken from the *blasting* of plants, and all express the idea of checking growth, preventing maturity, impairing, injuring, destroying, or disappointing of the intended effect; as, to *blast* credit, or reputation; to *blast* designs.
3. To confound, or strike with force, by a loud blast or din. *Shak.*
4. To split rocks by an explosion of gunpowder.
They did not stop to *blast* this ore. *Forster's Kalm's Travels.*
BL'ASTED, *pp.* Affected by some cause that checks growth, injures, impairs, destroys, or renders abortive; split by an explosion of gunpowder.
BL'ASTER, *n.* He or that which blasts or destroys.
BL'ASTING, *ppr.* Affecting by a blast; preventing from coming to maturity; frustrating; splitting by an explosion of gunpowder.
BL'ASTING, *n.* A blast; destruction by a pernicious cause; explosion.
BL'ASTMENT, *n.* Blast; sudden stroke of some destructive cause. [Superseded by *blast* and *blasting*.] *Shak.*
BLA'TANT, *a.* [See *Bleat*.] Bellowing as a calf. [*Not used.*] *Dryden.*
BLAT'TER, *v. i.* [from the root of *bleat*.] To make a senseless noise.
BLAT'TERER, *n.* A noisy blustering boaster. [*Not used.*] *Spenser.*
BLAY, *n.* [See *Bleak*.] A small river fish, the bleak. *Ainsworth.* *Johnson.*
BLAZE, *n.* [Sw. *blåsa*; G. *blasen*; D. *blaazen*; Dan. *blæser*, to blow, and Dan. *blusser*, to burn, *blaze*, glisten; Eng. to *blush*; Sax. *blaze*, a lamp or torch; Dan. *blus*; Fr. *blaser*. The word seems primarily to express rushing or flowing, or violent agitation, and expansion.]
1. Flame; the stream of light and heat from any body when burning, proceeding from the combustion of inflammable gas.
2. Publication; wide diffusion of report. In

this sense, we observe the radical sense of *dilatation*, as well as that of *light*.

3. A white spot on the forehead or face of a horse, descending nearly to the nose.
4. Light; expanded light; as the *blaze* of day.
5. Noise; agitation; tumult.

BLAZE, *v. i.* To flame; as, the fire *blazes*.

2. To send forth or show a bright and expanded light.

The third fair morn now *blazed* upon the main. *Pope.*

3. To be conspicuous.

BLAZE, *v. t.* To make public far and wide.

To *blaze* those virtues which the good would hide. *Pope.*

2. To blazon. [*Not used.* See *Blazon.*] *Peacham.*
3. To set a white mark on a tree, by paring off a part of the bark. *Todd.*

BLA'ZED, *pp.* Published far and wide.

BLA'ZER, *n.* One who publishes and spreads reports.

BLA'ZING, *ppr.* Flaming; publishing far and wide.

BLA'ZING, *a.* Emitting flame, or light; as a *blazing* star.

BLA'ZING-STAR, *n.* A comet; a star that is accompanied with a coma or train of light.

BLA'ZON, *v. t.* bla'zn. [Fr. *blasonner*; It. *blasonare*; Sp. *blasonar*, to blazon; *blason*, heraldry. It is a derivative of *blaze*.]

1. To explain, in proper terms, the figures on ensigns armorial. *Addison.*
2. To deck; to embellish; to adorn.

She *blazons* in dread smiles her hideous form. *Garth.*

3. To display; to set to show; to celebrate by words or writing. *Shak.*
4. To blaze about; to make public far and wide.
5. To display; to exhibit conspicuously.

There pride sits *blazon'd* on th' unmeaning brow. *Trumbull.*

BLA'ZON, *n.* The art of drawing, describing or explaining coats of arms; perhaps a coat of arms, as used by the French. *Peacham.*

2. Publication; show; celebration; pompous display, either by words or by other means.

BLA'ZONED, *pp.* Explained, decyphered in the manner of heralds; published abroad; displayed pompously.

BLA'ZONER, *n.* One that blazons; a herald; an evil speaker, or propagator of scandal.

BLA'ZONING, *ppr.* Explaining, describing as heralds; showing; publishing; blazing abroad; displaying.

BLA'ZONRY, *n.* The art of describing coats of arms, in proper terms.

BLEA, *n.* The part of a tree, which lies immediately under the bark. [*I believe not used.*] *Chambers.*

BLEACH, *v. t.* [Sax. *blæcan*; D. *bleeken*; G. *bleichen*; Sw. *bleka*; Dan. *bleeger*; to whiten or *bleach*; D. *blyken*, to appear, to show; Dan. *blik*, a white plate of iron, or tin plate; *bleeg*, pale, wan, Eng. *bleak*; Sw. *blek*, id.; *bleka*, to shine. Ar. بلق balaka, to open or be opened, to shine; بلج balaja, id. It is not improbable that *blank* and *blanch* are this same word, with a nasal sound casually uttered and afterwards written before the final consonant.]

To whiten; to make white or whiter; to take out color; *applied to many things*, but *particularly* to *cloth and thread.* Bleaching is variously performed, but in general by steeping the cloth in lye, or a solution of pot or pearl ashes, and then exposing it to the solar rays.

Bleaching is now generally performed, on the large scale, by means of chlorine or the oxymuriatic acid, which has the property of whitening vegetable substances. *Cyc.*

BLEACH, *v. i.* To grow white in any manner. *Shak.*

BLE'ACHED, *pp.* Whitened; made white.

BLE'ACHER, *n.* One who whitens, or whose occupation is to whiten cloth.

BLE'ACHERY, *n.* A place for bleaching; as a wax *bleachery*. *Tooke.*

BLE'ACHING, *ppr.* Whitening; making white; becoming white.

BLE'ACHING, *n.* The act or art of whitening, especially cloth.

BLEAK, *a.* [Sax. *blac*, *blæc*, black, and pale, or wan; niger, pallidus, fuscus, pullus. It appears that originally this word did not denote perfect whiteness, but a wan or brown color. This is from the same root as *black* and *bleach*. See *Bleach.*]

1. Pale. [*But not often used in this sense, in America, as far as my observations extend.*] *Gower.*
2. Open; vacant; exposed to a free current of air; as a *bleak* hill or shore. This is the true sense of the word; hence cold and cheerless. A *bleak* wind is not so named merely from its coldness, but from its blowing without interruption, on a wide waste; at least this is the sense in America. So in Addison. "Her desolation presents us with nothing but *bleak* and barren prospects."

BLEAK, *n.* A small river fish, five or six inches long, so named from its whiteness. It belongs to the genus Cyprinus, and is known to the Londoners by the name of *white bait.* It is called also by contraction *blay.* *Encyc.*

BLE'AKNESS, *n.* Openness of situation; exposure to the wind; hence coldness. *Addison.*

BLE'AKY, *a.* Bleak; open; unsheltered; cold; chill. *Dryden.*

BLEAR, *a.* [D. *blaar*; Dan. *blære*, a blister, a bladder or bubble.]

Sore, with a watery rheum; applied only to the eyes; as the *blear*-eyed owl. *L'Estrange.*

BLEAR, *v. t.* To make sore; to affect with soreness of eyes, or a watery humor; to make dim or partially obscure the sight. *Raleigh. Dryden.*

BLE'AREDNESS, *n.* The state of being bleared, or dimmed with rheum. *Wiseman.*

BLE'AR-EYED, *a.* Having sore eyes; having the eyes dim with rheum; dim-sighted. *Butler.*

BLEAT, *v. i.* [Sax. *blætan*; L. *blatero*; D. *blaeten*; Sw. *bladra, pladdra*; Dan. *pludrer*. It coincides in elements with L. *plaudo.*]

To make the noise of a sheep; to cry as a sheep.

BLEAT, *n.* The cry of a sheep.

BLE'ATING, *ppr.* or *a.* Crying as a sheep.

BLE'ATING, *n.* The cry of a sheep.

BLEB, *n.* [This word belongs to the root of *blab*, *blubber.*]

A little tumor, vesicle or blister.

Arsenic abounds with air *blebs*. *Kirwan.*

BLED, *pret.* and *pp.* of *bleed.*

BLEED, *v. i.* pret. and pp. *bled.* [Sax. *bledan*; D. *bloeden*; G. *bluten*; to bleed: allied perhaps to Gr. βλυζω.]

1. To lose blood; to run with blood, by whatever means; as, the arm *bleeds*.
2. To die a violent death, or by slaughter.

The lamb thy riot dooms to *bleed* to day. *Pope.*

3. To issue forth, or drop as blood, from an incision; to lose sap, gum or juice; as, a tree or a vine *bleeds*.

For me the balm shall *bleed*. *Pope.*

The heart bleeds, is a phrase used to denote extreme pain from sympathy or pity.

BLEED, *v. t.* To let blood; to take blood from, by opening a vein.

BLEE'DING, *ppr.* Losing blood; letting blood; losing sap or juice.

BLEE'DING, *n.* A running or issuing of blood, as from the nose; a hemorrhage; the operation of letting blood, as in surgery; the drawing of sap from a tree or plant.

BLEIT, } *a.* [Ger. *blöde*; D. *bloode.*] Bashful; used in Scotland and the
BLATE, } northern counties of England. *Johnson.*

BLEM'ISH, *v. t.* [In Fr. *blemir*, is to grow pale, and *blême*, from the ancient *blesme*, is pale, wan; Arm. *blem*; Norman, *blasme*, blamed; *blemish*, and *blesmys*, broken; *blemishment*, *blemissment*, infringement, prejudice; *blesme*, pale, wan; from *blesser*, to injure, or its root, from which was formed the noun *blesme*, pale, wan, or *black* and *blue*, as we should now say; and the *s* being dropped, *blamer* and *blemir*, were formed. See *Blame.*]

1. To mark with any deformity; to injure or impair any thing which is well formed, or excellent; to mar, or make defective, either the body or mind. *Sidney.*
2. To tarnish, as reputation or character; to defame. *Dryden.*

BLEM'ISH, *n.* Any mark of deformity; any scar or defect that diminishes beauty, or renders imperfect that which is well formed.

2. Reproach; disgrace; that which impairs reputation; taint; turpitude; deformity. *Hooker.*

BLEM'ISHED, *pp.* Injured or marred by any mark of deformity; tarnished; soiled.

BLEM'ISHING, *ppr.* Marking with deformity; tarnishing.

BLEM'ISHLESS, *a.* Without blemish; spotless.

BLEM'ISHMENT, *n.* Disgrace. [*Little used.*] *Morton.*

BLENCH, *v. i.* [This evidently is the *blanch* of Bacon [see *Blanch*,] and perhaps the modern *flinch.*]

To shrink; to start back; to give way. *Shak.*

BLENCH, *v. t.* To hinder or obstruct, says Johnson. But the etymology explains the passage he cites in a different manner. "The rebels carried great trusses of hay before them, to *blench* the defendants' fight." *Carew.* That is, to render the combat *blank*; to render it ineffectual; to break the force of the attack; to deaden the shot. *Obs.*

BLENCH, *n.* A start. *Shak.*

BLENCH'ER, *n.* That which frustrates.

BLENCH'-HOLDING, *n.* A tenure of lands upon the payment of a small sum in silver, *blanch*, that is, white money. *Blackstone.*

BLEND, *n.* [Ger. *blenden*, to blind; *blende*, a blind or skreen.]

An ore of zink, called also mock-lead, false galena and black jack. Its color is mostly yellow, brown and black. There are several varieties, but in general, this ore contains more than half its weight of zink, about one fourth sulphur, and usually a small portion of iron. In chemical language, it is a sulphuret of zink. *Fourcroy. Cleaveland. Thomson.*

BLEND, *v. t.* [Sax. *blendian*, to blend and to blind; *geblendan*, to mix, to stain or dye; *blindan*, to blind; D. *blinden*; Ger. *blenden*, to blind; Dan. *blander*, to blend or mix; *blinder*, to blind.]

1. To mix or mingle together; hence to confound, so that the separate things mixed cannot be distinguished.

2. To pollute by mixture; to spoil or corrupt. *Obs.* *Spenser.*

3. To blind. *Obs.*

BLEND, *v. i.* To be mixed; to be united.

There is a tone of solemn and sacred feeling that *blends* with our conviviality. *Irving.*

BLEND'ED, *pp.* Mixed; confounded by mixture.

BLEND'ER, *n.* One that mingles or confounds.

BLEND'ING, *ppr.* Mingling together; confounding by mixture.

BLEND'OUS, *a.* Pertaining to blend.

BLEND'-WATER, *n.* A distemper incident to cattle, called also more-hough. *Encyc.*

BLEN'NY, *n.* [Sax. *blinnan*, to cease.] A genus of fishes, of the order of *Jugulars*, in Ichthyology called *Blennius*. There are several species; the size from five inches to a foot in length. *Encyc. Dict. of Nat. Hist.*

BLENT, the obsolete participle of *blend*. *Spenser.*

BLESS, *v. t.* pret. and pp. *blessed* or *blest*. [Sax, *bledsian*, *bletsian*, *bletsigan* and *blessian*; whence, *bletsung*, *bledsung*, a blessing or benediction. W. *llâd*, a gift, a favor, a blessing.]

1. To pronounce a wish of happiness to one; to express a wish or desire of happiness.

And Isaac called Jacob and *blessed* him. Gen. xxviii.

2. To make happy; to make successful; to prosper in temporal concerns; as, we are *blest* with peace and plenty.

The Lord thy God shall *bless* thee in all thou doest. Deut. xv.

3. To make happy in a future life.

Blessed are the dead who die in the Lord. Rev. xiv.

4. To set apart or consecrate to holy purposes; to make and pronounce holy.

And God *blessed* the seventh day and sanctified it. Gen. 2.

5. To consecrate by prayer; to invoke a blessing upon.

And Jesus took the five loaves and the two fishes, and looking up to heaven he *blessed* them. Luke ix.

6. To praise; to glorify, for benefits received.

Bless the Lord, O my soul, and all that is within me. Ps. ciii.

7. To praise; to magnify; to extol, for excellencies. Ps. civ.

8. To esteem or account happy; with the reciprocal pronoun.

The nations shall *bless themselves* in him. Jer. iv.

9. To pronounce a solemn prophetical benediction upon. Gen. xxvii. Deut. xxxiii.

10. In this line of Spenser, it may signify to *throw*, for this is nearly the primary sense.

His sparkling blade about his head he *blest*.

Johnson supposes the word to signify to *wave* or *brandish*, and to have received this sense from the old rite of blessing a field, by directing the hands to all parts of it.

Bless in Spenser for *bliss*, may be so written, not for rhyme merely, but because *bless* and *bliss* are from the same root.

BLESS'ED, *pp.* Made happy or prosperous; extolled; pronounced happy.

BLESS'ED, *a.* Happy; prosperous in worldly affairs; enjoying spiritual happiness and the favor of God; enjoying heavenly felicity.

BLESSED-THISTLE. A plant of the genus *Cnicus*, sometimes used in decoctions, for a bitter.

BLESS'EDLY, *adv.* Happily; in a fortunate manner.

BLESS'EDNESS, *n.* Happiness; felicity; heavenly joys; the favor of God.

2. Sanctity. *Shak.*

BLESS'ER, *n.* One that blesses or prospers; one who bestows a blessing.

BLESS'ING, *ppr.* Making happy; wishing happiness to; praising or extolling; consecrating by prayer.

BLESS'ING, *n.* Benediction; a wish of happiness pronounced; a prayer imploring happiness upon another.

2. A solemn prophetic benediction, in which happiness is desired, invoked or foretold.

This is the *blessing* wherewith Moses—*blessed* the children of Israel. Deut. xxxiii.

3. Any means of happiness; a gift, benefit or advantage; that which promotes temporal prosperity and welfare, or secures immortal felicity. A just and pious magistrate is a public *blessing*. The divine favor is the greatest *blessing*.

4. Among *the Jews*, a present; a gift; either because it was attended with kind wishes for the welfare of the giver, or because it was the means of increasing happiness.

Take, I pray thee, my *blessing* that is brought to thee. Gen. xxxiii.

BLEST, *pp.* of *bless*.

BLEST, *a.* Made happy.

2. Making happy; cheering.

While these *blest* sounds my ravish'd ear assail. *Trumbull.*

BLE'TONISM, *n.* The faculty of perceiving and indicating subterraneous springs and currents by sensation; so called from one Bleton of France who possessed this faculty. *Encyc.*

BLE'TONIST, *n.* One who possesses the faculty of perceiving subterraneous springs by sensation. *Encyc.*

BLEW, *pret.* of *blow*.

BLEYME, *n.* An inflammation in the foot of a horse, between the sole and the bone. *Farrier's Dict.*

BLICE'A, *n.* A small fish caught in the German seas, somewhat resembling the English sprat. *Dict. of Nat. Hist.*

BLIGHT, *n.* [Qu. Sax. *blæctha*, scurf, leprosy.]

1. A disease incident to plants, affecting them variously. Sometimes the whole plant perishes; sometimes only the leaves and blossoms, which will shrivel, as if scorched.

2. Any thing nipping or blasting.

In *America*, I have often heard a cutaneous eruption on the human skin called by the name of *blights*.

BLIGHT, *v. t.* To affect with blight; to blast; to prevent growth, and fertility; to frustrate.

BLIN, *v. t.* [Sax. *blinnan*.] To stop or cease. *Obs.* *Spenser.*

BLIND, *a.* [Sax. *blind*; Ger. D. Sw. and Dan. *blind*; Sax. *blendan*, to blend and to blind. This is the same word as *blend*, and was so written by Spenser. See *Blend*. Obscurity is from mixture.]

1. Destitute of the sense of seeing, either by natural defect, or by deprivation; not having sight.

2. Not having the faculty of discernment; destitute of intellectual light; unable to understand or judge; ignorant; as, authors are *blind* to their own defects. *Blind* should be followed by *to*; but it is followed by *of*, in the phrase, *blind of an eye*.

3. Unseen; out of public view; private; dark; sometimes implying contempt or censure; as a *blind* corner. *Hooker.*

4. Dark; obscure; not easy to be found; not easily discernible; as a *blind* path.

5. Heedless; inconsiderate; undeliberating.

This plan is recommended neither to *blind* approbation nor *blind* reprobation. *Federalist, Jay.*

6. In *scripture*, *blind* implies not only want of descernment, but moral depravity.

BLIND, *v. t.* To make blind; to deprive of sight.

2. To darken; to obscure to the eye.

Such darkness *blinds* the sky. *Dryden.*

3. To darken the understanding; as, to *blind* the mind.

4. To darken or obscure to the understanding.

He endeavored to *blind* and confound the controversy. *Stillingfleet.*

5. To eclipse. *Fletcher.*

BLIND, or BLINDE, See *Blend*, an ore.

BLIND, *n.* Something to hinder the sight.

Civility casts a *blind* over the duty. *L'Estrange.*

2. Something to mislead the eye or the understanding; as, one thing serves as a *blind* for another.

3. A skreen; a cover; as a *blind* for a window, or for a horse.

BLINDED, *pp.* Deprived of sight; deprived of intellectual discernment; made dark or obscure.

BLINDFŌLD, *a.* [*blind* and *fold*.] Having the eyes covered; having the mental eye darkened.

BLINDFŌLD, *v. t.* To cover the eyes; to hinder from seeing.

BLINDFŌLDED, *pp.* Having the eyes covered; hindered from seeing.

BLINDFŌLDING, *ppr.* Covering the eyes; hindering from seeing.

BLINDING. *ppr.* Depriving of sight, or of understanding; obscuring.

BLINDLY, *adv.* Without sight, or understanding.

2. Without discerning the reason; implicitly; without examination; as, to be *blindly* led by another. *Dryden.*

3. Without judgment or direction. *Dryden.*

BLINDMAN'S BALL, *n.* A species of fungus, Lycoperdon, or puff-ball. *Fam. of Plants.*

BLINDMAN'S BUFF, *n.* A play in which one person is blindfolded, and hunts out the rest of the company. *Johnson.*

BLINDNESS, *n.* Want of bodily sight; want of intellectual discernment; ignorance. *Locke.*

BLINDNETTLE, *n.* A plant.

BLINDS, *n.* In *the military art*, a defense made of osiers or branches interwoven, and laid across two rows of stakes, four or five feet asunder, of the highth of a man, to shelter the workmen, and prevent their being overlooked by the enemy. *Encyc.*

BLIND SERPENT, *n.* A reptile of the Cape of Good Hope, covered with black scales, but spotted with red, white and brown. *Dict. of Nat. Hist.*

BLINDSIDE, *n.* [*blind* and *side.*] The side which is most easily assailed; or the side on which the party is least able or disposed to see danger; weakness; foible; weak part. *Swift.*

BLIND VESSEL, with chimists, a vessel with an opening on one side only. *Johnson.*

BLINDWŎRM, *n.* [*blind* and *worm.*] A small reptile, called also slow worm, a species of *Anguis*, about eleven inches long, covered with scales, with a forked tongue, but harmless. *Dict. of Nat. Hist.*

BLINK, *v. i.* [Sax. *blican*, to shine, to twinkle; *bliciend*, clothed in white; *ablican*, to appear, to whiten; D. *blikken*, to glance, to twinkle, and *blinken*, to shine, to glitter; *blyken*, to appear or show; Sw. *blincha*, to wink, to connive; *bleka*, to shine, to twinkle; Ger. *blicken*, to look, to glance; *blinken*, to glance, to shine, to twinkle, to wink; Dan. *blinker*, to blink, to glance, to wink, to shine, to glitter. This contains the same radical letters as *light.*]

1. To wink; to twinkle with the eye.

2. To see obscurely. *Johnson.* Is it not to see with the eyes half shut, or with frequent winking, as a person with weak eyes?

> One eye was *blinking* and one leg was lame. *Pope.*

BLINK, *n.* A glimpse or glance. *Hall.*

BLINK, *n.* *Blink of ice*, is the dazzling whiteness about the horizon, occasioned by the reflection of light from fields of ice at sea. *Mar. Dict.*

BLINK'ARD, *n.* [*blink* and *ard*, kind.] A person who blinks or has bad eyes; that which twinkles, or glances, as a dim star, which appears and disappears. *Hakewill.*

BLINK'ING, *ppr.* Winking; twinkling.

BLISS, *n.* [Sax. *bliss*, joy, alacrity, exultation; *blissian*, to rejoice, to exult, to congratulate, to applaud; also *blithsian*, to rejoice. See *Bless* and *Blithe.*]

The highest degree of happiness; blessedness; felicity; used of felicity in general, when of an exalted kind, but appropriately, of heavenly joys. *Hooker. Pope.*

BLISS'FUL, *a.* Full of joy and felicity; happy in the highest degree. *Spenser.*

BLISS'FULLY, *adv.* In a blissful manner. *Sherwood.*

BLISS'FULNESS, *n.* Exalted happiness; felicity; fulness of joy. *Barrow.*

BLISS'LESS, *a.* Destitute of bliss. *Hawkins.*

BLIS'SOM, *v. i.* [W. *blys*, *blysiaw*, to crave, that is, to reach forward.]

To be lustful; to caterwaul. [*Little used.*]

BLIS'TER, *n.* [Ger *blase*, and *blatter.* It is radically the same word as *bladder*, in a different dialect. See *Bladder*, *Blast*, and *Blaze.*]

1. A pustule; a thin bladder on the skin, containing watery matter or serum, whether occasioned by a burn, or other injury, or by a vesicatory. It is formed by raising the cuticle.

2. Any tumor made by the separation of the film or skin, as on plants; or by the swelling of the substance at the surface, as on steel.

3. A vesicatory; a plaster of flies, or other matter, applied to raise a vesicle.

BLIS'TER, *v. i.* To rise in blisters. *Dryden.*

BLIS'TER, *v. t.* To raise a blister, by any hurt, burn or violent action upon the skin; to raise a blister by a medical application, or vesicatory.

2. To raise tumors on iron bars in a furnace, in the process of converting iron into steel.

BLIS'TERED, *pp.* Having blisters or tumors.

BLIS'TERING, *ppr.* Raising a blister; applying a blistering plaster, or vesicatory.

BLITE, *n.* [L. *blitum*; Gr. βλιτον.] A genus of plants, called strawberry spinach. *Encyc.*

2. A species of amaranth, or flower gentle. *Fam. of Plants.*

BLITHE, *a.* [Sax. *blithe* and *bleatha*, *bleathe*, gay, joyful. This is probably the same word as *bliss*; L. *lætus*; Eng. *glad.* See *Bliss* and *Glad.* The Ir. *lith*, happiness, seems to be the original word without the prefix.]

Gay; merry; joyous; sprightly; mirthful.

> For that fair female troop thou sawest, that seemed
> Of goddesses, so *blithe*, so smooth, so gay. *Milton.*

BLI'THEFUL, *a.* Gay; full of gayety.

BLI'THELY, *adv.* In a gay, joyful manner.

BLI'THENESS, *n.* Gayety; sprightliness; the quality of being blithe.

BLI'THESŎME, *a.* Gay; merry; cheerful. *Philips.*

BLI'THESŎMENESS, *n.* The quality of being blithesome; gayety.

BLŌAT, *v. t.* [This word may be allied to *bladder*, from the sense of inflating, swelling; W. *blwth*, a puff, a blast; *blythaç*, a fat paunch, a bloated person.]

1. To swell or make turgid, as with air; to inflate; to puff up; hence, to make vain; followed by *up*, but without necessity. To *bloat up* with praise is less elegant than to *bloat* with praise. *Dryden.*

2. To swell or make turgid with water, or other means; as a *bloated* limb. It is used to denote a morbid enlargement, often accompanied with softness.

BLŌAT, *v. i.* To grow turgid; to dilate. *Arbuthnot.*

BLŌAT, *a.* Swelled; turgid. [*Not used.*]

BLŌATED, *pp.* Swelled; grown turgid; inflated.

BLŌATEDNESS, *n.* A turgid state; turgidness; dilatation from inflation, debility, or any morbid cause. *Arbuthnot.*

BLŌATING, *ppr.* Swelling; inflating.

BLOB'BER, *n.* [Ir. *plub*, or *pluibin*, from swelling, pushing out, as in *bleb*, *blubber*; W. *llwb*, a bulging out. Qu. *bulb*, by transposition. See *Blubber.*]

A bubble: pronounced by the common people in America, *blubber.* It is a legitimate word, but not elegant. *Carew.*

BLOB'BERLIP, *n.* [*blobber* and *lip.*] A thick lip. *Dryden.*

BLOB'BERLIPPED, *a.* Having thick lips. *L'Estrange.*

BLOCK, *n.* [D. *blok*; Ger. *block*; Fr. *bloc*; W. *ploc*, from *lloc*, a mound; *plociaw*, to block, to *plug*; Russ. *placha*, a block. The primary sense is, set, fixed, or a mass.]

1. A heavy piece of timber or wood, usually with one plain surface; or it is rectangular, and rather thick than long.

2. Any mass of matter with an extended surface; as a *block* of marble, a piece rough from the quarry.

3. A massy body, solid and heavy; a mass of wood, iron, or other metal, with at least one plain surface, such as artificers use.

4. The wood on which criminals are beheaded.

5. Any obstruction, or cause of obstruction; a stop; hindrance; obstacle.

6. A piece of wood in which a pulley runs; used also for the pulley, or the block itself and the sheaves, or wheels.

7. A blockhead; a stupid fellow.

8. Among *cutters in wood*, a form made of hard wood, on which they cut figures in relief with knives, chisels, &c. *Encyc.*

9. In *falconry*, the perch whereon a bird of prey is kept. *Encyc.*

BLOCK, *v. t.* [Fr. *bloquer*; Port. and Sp. *bloquear*; It. *bloccare.*]

To inclose or shut up, so as to hinder egress or passage; to stop up; to obstruct, by placing obstacles in the way: often followed by up; as, to *block* up a town, or a road.

BLOCKA'DE, *n.* [It. *bloccato*; Port. *bloqueado*, blocked up; Sp. *bloqueo*; Fr. *blocus.*]

The siege of a place, formed by surrounding it with hostile troops or ships, or by posting them at all the avenues, to prevent escape, and hinder supplies of provisions and ammunition from entering, with a view to compel a surrender, by hunger and want, without regular attacks.

To constitute a *blockade*, the investing power must be able to apply its force to every point of practicable access, so as to render it dangerous to attempt to enter; and there is no *blockade* of that port, where its force cannot be brought to bear. *Kent's Commentaries.*

BLOCKA'DE, *v. t.* To shut up a town or fortress, by posting troops at all the avenues, to compel the garrison or inhabitants to surrender by means of hunger and want, without regular attacks; also, to station ships of war to obstruct all intercourse with a town or nation.

BLOCKA'DED, *pp.* Shut up or inclosed by an enemy.

BLOCKA'DING, *ppr.* Besieging by a blockade.

BLOCK'HEAD, *n.* [*block* and *head.*] A stupid fellow; a dolt; a person deficient in understanding.

BLOCK'HEADED, *a.* Stupid; dull. *Shak.*

BLOCK'HEADLY, *a.* Like a blockhead.

BLOCK'HOUSE, *n.* [*block* and *house.*] A house or fortress, erected to block up a pass, and defend against the entrance of an enemy.

BLOCK'ISH, *a.* Stupid; dull; deficient in understanding. *Shak.*

BLOCK'ISHLY, *adv.* In a stupid manner. *Harmar.*

BLOCK'ISHNESS, *n.* Stupidity; dullness.

BLOCK'LIKE, *a.* Like a block; stupid. *Hakewill.*

BLOCK'-TIN, *n.* [*block* and *tin.*] Tin which is pure, unmixed, and unwrought. *Johnson. Ash.*

BLŌ'MARY, *n.* [See *Bloom*, a mass of iron.] The first forge through which iron passes, after it is melted from the ore.

BLONK'ET, *a.* Gray. [*Not used.*] *Spenser.*

BLŎOD, *n.* [Sax. Sw. and Dan. *blod;* Ger. *blut*, blood; *bluten*, to bleed; D. *bloed*, blood; *bloeden*, to bleed; allied perhaps to Gr. βλυζω.]

1. The fluid which circulates through the arteries and veins of the human body, and of other animals, which is essential to the preservation of life. This fluid is generally red. If the blood of an animal is not red, such animal is called *exsanguious*, or white-blooded; the blood being white, or white tinged with blue.

2. Kindred; relation by natural descent from a common ancestor; consanguinity.

God hath made of one *blood*, all nations of the earth. Acts xvii.

Hence the word is used for a child; a family; a kindred; descent; lineage; progeny; descendants; &c.

3. Royal lineage; blood royal; as a prince of the *blood*.

4. Honorable birth; high extraction; as a gentleman of *blood*. *Shak.*

5. Life.

Shall I not require his *blood* at your hands? 2 Sam. iv.

6. Slaughter; murder, or bloodshedding.

I will avenge the *blood* of Jezreel upon the house of Jehu. Hosea i.

The voice of thy brother's *blood* crieth to me from the ground. Gen. iv.

7. Guilt, and punishment.

Your *blood* be upon your own heads. Acts xviii.

8. Fleshly nature; the carnal part of man; as opposed to spiritual nature, or divine life.

Who were born, not of flesh and *blood*, nor of the will of the flesh, nor of the will of man, but of God. John i.

9. Man, or human wisdom, or reason.

Flesh and *blood* hath not revealed it to thee, but my Father who is in heaven. Matt. xvi.

10. A sacramental symbol of the *blood* of Christ.

This is my *blood* of the New Testament, which is shed for the remission of sins. Matt. xxvi.

11. The death and sufferings of Christ.

Being now justified by his *blood*, we shall be saved from wrath through him. Rom. v. iii. Eph. i.

12. The price of blood; that which is obtained by shedding blood, and seizing goods.

Wo to him that buildeth a town with *blood*. Hab. ii. Acts i.

13. Temper of mind; state of the passions; but in this sense, accompanied with *cold* or *warm*, or other qualifying word. Thus to commit an act in *cold* blood, is to do it deliberately, and without sudden passion. *Warm blood* denotes a temper inflamed or irritated; to *warm* or *heat the blood*, is to excite the passions.

14. A hot spark; a man of fire or spirit; a rake.

15. The juice of any thing, especially if red; as, "the *blood* of grapes." Gen. xlix.

Whole blood. In *law*, a kinsman of the *whole blood* is one who descends from the same couple of ancestors; of the *half blood*, one who descends from either of them singly, by a second marriage. *Encyc.*

BLŎOD, *v. t.* To let blood; to bleed by opening a vein.

2. To stain with blood. *Addison. Dryden.*

3. To enter; to inure to blood; as a hound. *Spenser.*

4. To heat the blood; to exasperate. [*Unusual.*] *Bacon.*

BLŎOD-BESPOT'TED, *a.* Spotted with blood. *Shak.*

BLŎOD-BŌLTERED, *a.* [*blood* and *bolter.*] Sprinkled with blood. [*Not used.*] *Macbeth.*

BLŎOD-CONSU'MING, *a.* Wasting the blood. *Shak.*

BLŎOD'ED, *pp.* Bled; stained with blood; inured to blood.

BLŎOD'-FLOWER, *n.* [*blood* and *flower.*] Hæmanthus, a genus of plants, natives of the Cape of Good Hope. *Encyc.*

BLŎOD-FRŌZEN, *a.* Having the blood chilled. *Spenser.*

BLŎOD-GUILTINESS, *n.* [*blood* and *guilt.*] The guilt or crime of shedding blood. Ps. li.

BLŎOD-HOT, *a.* [*blood* and *hot.*] As warm as blood in its natural temperature.

BLŎOD'-HOUND, *n.* [*blood* and *hound.*] A species of canis or dog, with long, smooth and pendulous ears, remarkable for the acuteness of its smell, and employed to recover game which had escaped wounded from the hunter, by tracing the lost animal by the blood it had spilt; whence the name of the dog. *Encyc.*

BLŎOD'ILY, *adv.* In a bloody manner; cruelly; with a disposition to shed blood. *Shak.*

BLŎOD'INESS, *n.* The state of being bloody; disposition to shed blood.

BLŎOD'ING, *ppr.* Letting blood; staining with blood; inuring to blood, as a hound.

BLŎOD'LESS, *a.* Without blood; dead.

2. Without shedding of blood or slaughter; as a *bloodless* victory. *Shak. Waller.*

3. Without spirit or activity. *Shak.*

BLŎOD-LET, *v. t.* To bleed; to let blood. *Arbuthnot.*

BLŎOD'-LETTER, *n.* One who lets blood, as in diseases; a phlebotomist. *Wiseman.*

BLŎOD'LETTING, *n.* [*blood* and *let.*] The act of letting blood, or bleeding by opening a vein.

BLŎOD'PU̇DDING, *n.* [*blood* and *pudding.*] A pudding made with blood and other materials.

BLŎOD'-RED, *n.* Red as blood.

BLŎOD'-ROOT, *n.* A plant so named from its color; a species of sanguinaria, called also puccoon, turmeric and red root. *Bigelow.*

BLŎOD'SHED, *n.* [*blood* and *shed.*] The shedding or spilling of blood; slaughter; waste of life; the crime of shedding blood. *Spenser.*

BLŎOD'SHEDDER, *n.* One who sheds blood; a murderer.

BLŎOD'SHEDDING, *n.* The shedding of blood; the crime of shedding blood. *Homilies.*

BLŎOD'SHOT, *a.* [*blood* and *shoot.*] Red and inflamed by a turgid state of the blood vessels, as in diseases of the eye. *Garth.*

BLŎOD'SNAKE, *n.* A species of snake, the hæmorrhus. *Ash.*

BLŎOD'-SPAVIN, *n.* [*blood* and *spavin.*] A dilatation of the vein that runs along the inside of the hock of a horse, forming a soft swelling. *Encyc.*

BLŎOD'-STAINED, *a.* Stained with blood; also, guilty of murder.

BLŎOD'STONE, *n.* [*blood* and *stone.*] A stone, imagined, if worn as an amulet, to be a good preventive of bleeding at the nose. [See *Hematite.*]

BLŎOD'-SUCKER, *n.* [*blood* and *suck.*] Any animal that sucks blood, as a leech, a fly, &c. A cruel man; a murderer.

BLŎOD'-SUCKING, *a.* That sucks or draws blood. *Shak.*

BLŎOD'-THIRSTY, *a.* [*blood* and *thirst.*] Desirous to shed blood; murderous.

BLŎOD'-VESSEL, *n.* [*blood* and *vessel.*] Any vessel in which blood circulates in an animal body; an artery or a vein.

BLŎOD'-WARM, *a.* Warm as blood; luke warm. *Addison.*

BLŎOD'-WITE, *n.* [*blood* and *wite*, a fine or penalty.]

In *ancient law*, a fine or amercement, paid as a compositon for the shedding of blood.

BLŎOD'-WO̤OD, *n.* [*blood* and *wood.*] A name given to log-wood, from its color.

BLŎOD'-WŎRT, *n.* [*blood* and *wort.*] A plant, a species of Rumex.

BLŎOD'Y, *a.* Stained with blood.

2. Cruel; murderous; given to the shedding of blood; or having a cruel, savage disposition; *applied to animals.*

3. Attended with bloodshed; marked by cruelty; *applied to things;* as a *bloody* battle.

BLŎOD'Y, *v. t.* To stain with blood. *Overbury.*

BLŎODY', *adv.* Very; as *bloody* sick, *bloody* drunk. [*This is very vulgar.*]

BLŎOD'Y-EYED, *a.* Having bloody or cruel eyes.

BLŎOD'Y-FACED, *a.* Having a bloody face or appearance. *Shak.*

BLŎOD'Y-FLUX, *n.* [*blood* and *flux.*] The dysentery, a disease in which the discharges from the bowels have a mixture of blood. *Arbuthnot.*

BLŎOD'Y-HAND, *n.* [*blood* and *hand.*] A hand stained with the blood of a deer, which, in the old forest laws of England, was sufficient evidence of a man's trespass in the forest against venison. *Ash.*

BLŎOD'Y-HUNTING, *a.* Hunting for blood. *Shak.*

BLŎOD'Y-MINDED, *a.* [*blood* and *mind.*] Having a cruel, ferocious disposition; barbarous; inclined to shed blood. *Dryden.*

BLŎOD'Y-RED, *a.* Having the color of blood.

BLŎODY-SCEP'TERED, *a.* Having a scepter obtained by blood or slaughter. *Shak.*

BLŎOD'Y-SWEAT, *n.* [*blood* and *sweat.*] A sweat, accompanied by a discharge of blood; also a disease, called sweating sickness, which formerly prevailed in England and other countries.

BLOOM, *n.* [Goth. *bloma;* D. *bloem;* G. *blume;* Sw. *blomme;* Dan. *blomster;* W. *bloden, blawd,* from the root of *blow;* Sax. *blowan,* contracted from *blodan,* or *blothan. Blossom* is a dialectical form of the word, from the same root. See *Blossom.*]

1. Blossom; the flower of a plant; an expanded bud.

While opening *blooms* diffuse their sweets around. *Pope.*

2. The opening of flowers in general; flowers open, or in a state of blossoming; as, the trees are clothed with *bloom.*

3. The state of youth, resembling that of blossoms; a state of opening manhood, life, beauty, and vigor; a state of health and growth, promising higher perfection; as the *bloom* of youth.

4. The blue color upon plums and grapes newly gathered. *Johnson.*

BLOOM, *v. i.* To produce or yield blossoms; to flower.

2. To be in a state of healthful, growing youth and vigor; to show the beauty of youth; as *blooming* graces.

BLOOM, *v. t.* To put forth as blossoms.

Charitable affection *bloomed* them.
[*Not in use.*] *Hooker.*

BLOOM, *n.* [Sax. *bloma,* a mass or lump; W. *plwm;* Arm. *plom, plowm,* or *bloum;* Fr. *plomb;* Sp. *plomo;* It. *piombo;* L. *plumbum,* lead, properly a *lump.*]

A mass of iron that has passed the blomary, or undergone the first hammering.

BLOOM'ING, *ppr.* Opening in blossoms; flowering; thriving in the health, beauty, and vigor of youth; showing the beauties of youth.

His *blooming* laurels graced the muse's seat. *Trumbull.*

BLOOM'INGLY, *adv.* In a blooming manner.

BLOOM'Y, *a.* Full of bloom; flowery; flourishing with the vigor of youth; as a *bloomy* spray; *bloomy* beauties.

BLORE, *n.* [This is a different orthography of *blare,* which see.]

The act of blowing; a blast. [*Not used.*] *Chapman.*

BLOS'SOM, *n.* [Sax. *blosm, blosma, blostm, blostma,* and *blosan,* a blossom; *blosmian, blostmian,* to blossom; D. *bloessem,* a blossom; G. *blüthe,* a blossom; allied perhaps to G. *bloss,* Dan. *blot,* naked; G. *blössen,* Dan. *blotter,* to uncover; W. *bloden,* a flower, *blodeuaw,* to blossom, from *blawd,* meal, bloom; Gr. βλαςημα, a bud, probably from the same root; Syr. ܒܠܨ to germinate, to flourish, to put forth leaves.]

1. The flower or corol of a plant; a general term, applicable to every species of tree or plant, but more generally used than flower or bloom, when we have reference to the fruit which is to succeed. Thus we use *flowers,* when we speak of shrubs cultivated for ornament; and *bloom,* in a more general sense, as flowers in general, or in reference to the beauty of flowers.

2. This word is used to denote the color of a horse, that has his hair white, but intermixed with sorrel and bay hairs; otherwise, *peach-colored.* *Encyc.*

BLOS'SOM, *v. i.* To put forth blossoms or flowers; to bloom; to blow; to flower.

2. To flourish and prosper.

The desert shall *blossom* as the rose. Is. xxxv.

BLOS'SOMING, *ppr.* Putting forth flowers; blowing.

BLOS'SOMING, *n.* The blowing or flowering of plants.

BLOT, *v. t.* [Goth. *blauthjan;* Sw. *plottra;* Dan. *plet,* a spot, stain, *blot;* *pletter,* to blot or stain; L. *litura,* [whence *lituro, oblitero,*] without the prefix; and D. *kladden,* with a different one.]

1. To spot with ink; to stain or bespatter with ink; as, to *blot* a paper.

2. To obliterate writing or letters with ink, so as to render the characters invisible, or not distinguishable; generally with *out;* as, to *blot out* a word or a sentence.

3. To efface; to erase; to cause to be unseen, or forgotten; to destroy; as, to *blot out* a crime, or the remembrance of any thing.

4. To stain with infamy; to tarnish; to disgrace; to disfigure.

Blot not thy innocence with guiltless blood. *Rowe.*

5. To darken.

He sung how earth *blots* the moon's gilded wane. *Cowley.*

6. In *scripture,* to *blot one out of the book of life,* is to reject him from the number of those who are to be saved. To *blot out a name,* a person or a nation, is to destroy the person or nation; to exterminate or consume. To *blot out sins,* is to forgive them. *Sins* are compared to debts, which are recorded in God's book of remembrance, and when paid, are crossed or cancelled.

BLOT, *n.* A spot or stain on paper, usually applied to ink.

2. An obliteration of something written or printed. *Dryden.*

3. A spot in reputation; a stain; a disgrace; a reproach; a blemish. *Shak.*

4. Censure; scorn; reproach.

He that rebuketh the wicked getteth a *blot.* Prov. ix.

5. In *backgammon,* when a single man lies open to be taken up. *Johnson.*

BLOTCH, *n.* [Sax. *blæctha,* a scab or leprous affection.]

A pustule upon the skin; an eruption, usually of a large kind.

BLOTCH, *v. t.* To blacken. *Harmar.*

BLOTE, *v. t.* [The affinities of this word are not clearly ascertained. In Sax. *blotan* is to sacrifice; in Goth. to serve or worship; in Arm. *bloda* is to soften; W. *plyz,* soft; *plyzaw,* to soften; Dan *blöder,* Sw. *blöta,* to soften.]

To dry and smoke; as, to *blote* herrings.

BLO'TED, *pp.* Smoked and dried.

BLOT'TED, *pp.* Stained; spotted; erased.

BLOT'TER, *n.* In *counting houses,* a waste book.

BLOT'TING, *ppr.* Spotting with ink; obliterating; staining.

BLOW, *n.* [This probably is a contracted word, and the primary sense must be, to strike, thrust, push, or throw, that is, to drive. I have not found it in the cognate dialects. If *g* or other palatal letter is lost, it corresponds in elements with the L. *plaga,* Gr. πληγη, L. *fligo,* Eng. *flog.* But *blow,* a stroke, is written like the verb to *blow,* the Latin *flo,* and *blow,* to blossom. The letter lost is probably a dental, and the original was *blod* or *bloth,* in which case, the word has the elements of *loud, laudo, claudo, lad,* &c.]

1. The act of striking; more generally the stroke; a violent application of the hand, fist, or an instrument to an object.

2. The fatal stroke; a stroke that kills; hence, death.

3. An act of hostility; as, the nation which strikes the first *blow.* Hence, to come to *blows,* is to engage in combat, whether by individuals, armies, fleets or nations; and when by nations, it is war.

4. A sudden calamity; a sudden or severe evil. In like manner, *plaga* in Latin gives rise to the Eng. *plague.*

5. A single act; a sudden event; as, to gain or lose a province at a *blow,* or by one *blow.* At a *stroke* is used in like manner.

6. An ovum or egg deposited by a fly, on flesh or other substance, called a *fly-blow.*

BLŌW, *v. i.* pret. *blew;* pp. *blown.* [Sax. *blawen, blowan,* to blow as wind; *blowan,* to blossom or blow, as a flower; D. *bloeyen,* to blossom; G. *blähen,* to swell or inflate; L. *flo,* to blow. This word probably is from the same root as *bloom, blossom, blow,* a flower; W. *bloden.* See *Blossom.*]

1. To make a current of air; to move as air; as, the wind *blows.* Often used with *it;* as, *it blows* a gale.

2. To pant; to puff; to breathe hard or quick.

Here is Mrs. Page at the door, sweating and *blowing.* *Shak.*

3. To breathe; as, to *blow* hot and cold. *L'Estrange.*

4. To sound with being blown, as a horn or trumpet. *Milton.*

5. To flower; to blossom; to bloom; as plants.

How *blows* the citron grove. *Milton.*

To blow over, to pass away without effect; to cease or be dissipated; as, the storm or the clouds are *blown over.*

To blow up, to rise in the air; also, to be broken and scattered by the explosion of gunpowder.

BLŌW, *v. t.* To throw or drive a current of air upon; as, to *blow* the fire; also, to fan.

2. To drive by a current of air; to impel; as, the tempest *blew* the ship ashore.
3. To breathe upon, for the purpose of warming; as, to *blow* the fingers in a cold day. *Shak.*
4. To sound a wind instrument; as, *blow* the trumpet.
5. To spread by report.

And through the court his courtesy was *blown*. *Dryden.*

6. To deposit eggs, as flies.
7. To form bubbles by blowing.
8. To swell and inflate, as veal; *a practice of butchers.*
9. To form glass into a particular shape by the breath, as in glass manufactories.
10. To melt tin, after being first burnt to destroy the mundic. *Encyc.*

To blow away, to dissipate; to scatter with wind.

To blow down, to prostrate by wind.

To blow off, to shake down by wind, as to *blow off* fruit from trees; to drive from land, as to *blow off* a ship.

To blow out, to extinguish by a current of air, as a candle.

To blow up, to fill with air; to swell; as, to *blow up* a bladder or a bubble.
2. To inflate; to puff up; as, to *blow up* one with flattery.
3. To kindle; as, to *blow up* a contention.
4. To burst, to raise into the air, or to scatter, by the explosion of gunpowder. Figuratively, to scatter or bring to naught suddenly; as, to *blow up* a scheme.

To blow upon, to make stale; as, to *blow upon* an author's works. *Addison.*

BLŌW, *n.* A flower; a blossom. This word is in general use in the U. States, and legitimate. In the Tatler, it is used for blossoms in general, as we use *blowth.*
2. Among seamen, a gale of wind. This also is a legitimate word, in general use in the U. States.

BLŌW-BALL, *n.* [*blow* and *ball.*] The flower of the dandelion. *B. Jonson.*

BLŌWER, *n.* One who blows; one who is employed in melting tin.
2. A plate of iron for drawing up a fire in a stove chimney. *Mason.*

BLŌWING, *ppr.* Making a current of air; breathing quick; sounding a wind instrument; inflating; impelling by wind; melting tin.

BLŌWING, *n.* The motion of wind or act of blowing.

BLŌWN, *pp.* Driven by wind; fanned; sounded by blowing; spread by report; swelled; inflated; expanded as a blossom.

BLŌW-PIPE, *n.* [*blow* and *pipe.*] An instrument by which a blast or current of air is driven through the flame of a lamp or candle, and that flame directed upon a mineral substance, to fuse or vitrify it.

Blow-pipe of the artist, a conical tube of brass, glass or other substance, usually a quarter of an inch in diameter at one end, and capillary or nearly so at the other, where it is bent nearly to a right angle. This is used to propel a jet of air from the lungs, through the flame of a lamp or candle, upon the substance to be fused.

Blow-pipe of the mineralogist, the same instrument substantially as the foregoing, but usually fitted with an ivory or silver mouth-piece, and with several movable jets to produce flames of different sizes. Its office is to produce instantly a furnace heat, on minute fragments of mineral substances, supported on charcoal, by platina forceps, &c.

Compound Blow-pipe of Dr. Hare, invented in 1821, an instrument in which oxygen and hydrogen, propelled by hydrostatic or other pressure, coming from separate reservoirs, in the proportions requisite to form water, are made to unite in a capillary orifice, at the moment when they are kindled. The heat produced, when the focus is formed on charcoal or any non-conducting substance, is such as to melt every thing but the diamond, to burn the metals, and to dissipate in vapor, or in gaseous forms, most known substances.

The blow-pipe of Newman, Clarke, &c., is the compound blow-pipe of Dr. Hare, with some unimportant modifications. *Silliman.*

BLŌW-POINT, *n.* [*blow* and *point.*] A kind of play among children. *Johnson.*

BLŌWTH, *n.* [Ir. *blath, blaith*, a flower or blossom; D. *bloeizel;* Ger. *blüthe.*]

Bloom, or blossom, or that which is expanded. It signifies bloom or blossoms in general, or the state of blossoming. Thus we say, trees are now in their *blowth*, or they have a full *blowth.*

BLOWZE, *n. blowz.* [From the same root as *blush*, which see.]

A ruddy fat-faced woman. *Hall.*

BLOWZ'Y, *a.* Ruddy-faced; fat and ruddy; high colored.

BLUB, *v. t.* To swell. [*Not in use.* See *Bleb.*]

BLUB'BER, *n.* [See *Blobber, Blob* and *Bleb.*]
1. A blobber, or bubble; *a common vulgar word, but legitimate.*
2. The fat of whales and other large sea animals, of which is made train-oil. It lies immediately under the skin and over the muscular flesh.
3. Sea nettle, or sea blubber, the medusa. *Encyc.*

BLUB'BER, *v. i.* To weep in such a manner as to swell the cheeks. *Johnson.*

If I mistake not, this word carries with it the idea of weeping, so as to slaver.

BLUB'BER, *v. t.* To swell the cheeks or disfigure the face with weeping.

BLUB'BERED, *pp.* Swelled; big; turgid; as a *blubbered* lip.

BLUB'BERING, *ppr.* Weeping so as to swell the cheeks.

BLUD'GEON, *n.* [Goth. *blyggwan*, to strike.]

A short stick, with one end loaded or thicker and heavier than the other, and used as an offensive weapon by low persons.

BLUE, *a. blu.* [Sax. *bleo, bleoh, bleow*, color; D. *blaauw;* Ger. *blau;* Dan. *blaae;* Sw. *blå*, blue; Sw. *bly*, Dan. *blye*, Ger. *blei*, lead, so named from its color; Slav. *plavu;* Fr. *bleu;* Corn. *blou.*]

One of the seven colors, into which the rays of light divide themselves, when refracted through a glass prism. There are various shades of blue, as *sky-blue*, or *azure, Prussian blue, indigo blue, smalt blue*, &c. *Kirwan. Encyc.*

Prussian blue, a combination of the oxyd of iron with an acid called *ferro-prussic.* *Ure.*

BLU'E, *v. t.* To make blue; to dye of a blue color; to make blue by heating, as metals, &c.

BLU'E-BIRD, *n.* [*blue* and *bird.*] A small bird, a species of Motacilla, very common in the U. States. The upper part of the body is blue, and the throat and breast, of a dirty red. It makes its nest in the hole of a tree.

BLU'E-BONNET, *n.* [*blue* and *bonnet.*] A plant, a species of Centaurea. *Fam. of Plants.*

BLU'E-BOTTLE, *n.* [*blue* and *bottle.*] A plant, a species of Centaurea, called Cyanus, which grows among corn. This and the former plant receive their names from their blue funnel-shaped flowers.
2. A fly with a large blue belly. *Johnson.*

BLU'E-CAP, *n.* [*blue* and *cap.*] A fish of the salmon kind, with blue spots on its head. *Dict. of Nat. Hist.*

BLU'E-EYED, *a.* Having blue eyes. *Dryden.*

BLU'E-FISH, *n.* [*blue* and *fish.*] A fish, a species of Coryphæna, of the order of *thoracics*, found about the Bahamas, and on the coast of Cuba. *Encyc.*

BLU'E-HAIRED, *a.* Having hair of a blue color. *Milton.*

BLU'E-JOHN, *n.* Among *miners*, fluor spar, a mineral, found in the mines of Derbyshire, and fabricated into vases and other ornamental figures. *Encyc.*

BLU'ELY, *adv.* With a blue color. *Swift.*

BLU'ENESS, *n.* The quality of being blue; a blue color. *Boyle.*

BLU'E-THROAT, *n.* [*blue* and *throat.*] A bird with a tawny breast, marked with a sky-blue crescent, inhabiting the northern parts of Europe and Asia.

BLU'E-VEINED, *a.* Having blue veins or streaks. *Shak.*

BLUFF, *a.* [Perhaps allied to W. *llwf*, Eng. *leap*, from shooting forward.] Big; surly; blustering. *Dryden.*

BLUFF, *n.* A high bank, almost perpendicular, projecting into the sea; a high bank presenting a steep front. *Belknap. Mar. Dict.*

BLUFF'-BOWED, *a.* [*bluff* and *bow.*] Having broad and flat bows. *Mar. Dict.*

BLUFF'-HEADED, *a.* [*bluff* and *head.*] Having an upright stem. *Mar. Dict.*

BLUFF'NESS, *n.* A swelling or bloatedness; surliness. *World.*

BLU'ISH, *a.* Blue in a small degree. *Pope.*

BLU'ISHNESS, *n.* A small degree of blue color. *Boyle.*

BLUN'DER, *v. i.* [This word seems to be allied to the Gr. πλαναω, to err, and to *flounder.* The sense of the latter is to move with sudden jerks, and irregular motions. In Dan. *blunder* is to wink, twinkle or dissemble; allied to Fr. *loin.*]
1. To mistake grossly; to err widely or stupidly. *Johnson.*
2. To move without direction, or steady guidance; to plunge at an object; to move, speak or write with sudden and blind precipitance; as, to *blunder* upon a reason; to *blunder* round a meaning. *Pope.*
3. To stumble, as a horse; *a common use of the word.*

BLUN'DER, *n.* A mistake through precipitance, or without due exercise of judgment; a gross mistake.

BLUN'DERBUSS, *n.* [*blunder*, and D. *bus*, a tube; Dan. *bösse;* Sw. *bössa*, a gun.]

A short gun or fire-arm, with a large bore, capable of holding a number of balls, and intended to do execution without exact aim.

BLUN'DERER, *n.* One who is apt to blunder, or to make gross mistakes; a careless person.

BLUN'DERHEAD, *n.* [*blunder* and *head.*] A stupid fellow; one who blunders. *L'Estrange.*

BLUN'DERING, *ppr.* Moving or acting with blind precipitance; mistaking grossly; stumbling.

BLUN'DERINGLY, *adv.* In a blundering manner. *Lewis.*

BLUNT, *a.* [from the root of Gr. ἀμβλυνω, to dull.]

1. Having a thick edge or point, as an instrument; dull; not sharp.
2. Dull in understanding; slow of discernment. *Shak.*
3. Abrupt in address; plain; unceremonious; wanting the forms of civility; rough in manners or speech. *Bacon.*
4. Hard to penetrate. [*Unusual.*] *Pope.*

BLUNT, *v. t.* To dull the edge or point, by making it thicker.

2. To repress or weaken any appetite, desire or power of the mind; to impair the force of any passion which affects the mind, or of any evil or good which affects the body; as, to *blunt* the edge of love, of pain, or of suffering.

Your ceaseless endeavors will be exerted to *blunt* the stings of pain. *Dwight.*

BLUNT'ED, *pp.* Made dull; weakened; impaired; repressed.

BLUNT'ING, *ppr.* Making dull; repressing; impairing.

BLUNT'ING, *n.* Restraint. *Taylor.*

BLUNT'LY, *adv.* In a blunt manner; coarsely; plainly; abruptly; without delicacy, or the usual forms of civility.

BLUNT'NESS, *n.* Want of edge or point; dullness; obtuseness; want of sharpness.

2. Coarseness of address; roughness of manners; rude sincerity or plainness.

BLUNT'WITTED, *a.* [*blunt* and *wit.*] Dull; stupid. *Shak.*

BLUR, *n.* [I have not found this word in any other language, but probably it is allied to the W. *llur*, black and blue, livid, L. *luridus.*]

A dark spot; a stain; a blot, whether upon paper or other substance, or upon reputation. *South.*

BLUR, *v. t.* To obscure by a dark spot, or by any foul matter, without quite effacing.

2. To sully; to stain; to blemish; as, to *blur* reputation. *Butler.*

BLUR'RED, *pp.* Darkened or stained; obscured.

BLUR'RING, *ppr.* Darkening or staining; spotting.

BLURT, *v. t.* [Allied probably to *flirt*, to throw.]

To throw out, or throw at random, hastily, or unadvisedly; to utter suddenly or inadvertently; commonly with *out*, and applied to words. *Young.*

BLUSH, *v. i.* [D. *bloozen;* Sw. *blyas*, to blush; Dan. *blusser*, to blaze or glisten; *blussel*, blushing; D. *blos*, a blush; Sw. *bloss;* Dan. *blus*, a torch; Dan. *blues ved*, to blush or be ashamed; Ir. *loise*, *loisi*, flame. It implies a throwing out, or spreading. *Flash* may be from the same root. See *Blaze.*]

1. To redden in the cheeks or face; to be suddenly suffused with a red color in the cheeks or face, from a sense of guilt, shame, confusion, modesty, diffidence or surprise; followed by *at* or *for*, before the cause of blushing; as, *blush at* your vices; *blush for* your degraded country.

In the presence of the shameless and unblushing, the young offender is ashamed to *blush.* *Buckminster.*

2. To bear a blooming red color, or any soft bright color; as the *blushing* rose.

He bears his *blushing* honors thick upon him. *Shak.*

Shakspeare has used this word in a transitive sense, *to make red*, and it may be allowable in poetry.

BLUSH, *n.* A red color suffusing the cheeks only, or the face generally, and excited by confusion, which may spring from shame, guilt, modesty, diffidence or surprise.

The rosy *blush* of love. *Trumbull.*

2. A red or reddish color.
3. Sudden appearance; a glance; a sense taken from the sudden suffusion of the face in blushing; as, a proposition appears absurd at first *blush.* *Locke.*

BLUSH'ET, *n.* A young modest girl. [*Not used.*]

BLUSH'ING, *ppr.* Reddening in the cheeks or face; bearing a bright color.

BLUSH'LESS, *a.* Unblushing; past blushing; impudent. *Marston.*

BLUSH'Y, *a.* Like a blush; having the color of a blush. *Harvey.*

BLUS'TER, *v. i.* [Probably allied to *blaze*, *blast;* Dan. *blusser*, to blaze, to rage.]

1. To be loud, noisy or swaggering; to bully; to puff; to swagger; as a turbulent or boasting person.
2. To roar, and be tumultuous, as wind; to be boisterous; to be windy; to hurry.

BLUS'TER, *n.* Noise; tumult; boasting; boisterousness; turbulence; roar of a tempest; violent wind; hurry; any irregular noise and tumult from wind, or from vanity.

BLUS'TERER, *n.* A swaggerer; a bully; a noisy, tumultuous fellow, who makes great pretensions from vanity.

BLUS'TERING, *ppr.* Making a noise; puffing; boasting.

BLUS'TERING, *a.* Noisy; tumultuous; windy.

BLUS'TROUS, *a.* Noisy; tumultuous; boastful. *Hudibras.*

BO, *exclam.* [W. *bw.*] A word of terror; a customary sound uttered by children to frighten their fellows.

BO'A, *n.* A genus of serpents, of the class Amphibia, the characters of which are, the belly and tail are furnished with scuta. It includes the largest species of serpent, the *constrictor*, sometimes 30 or 40 feet long. *Cyc.*

BOAR, *n.* [Sax. *bar;* Corn. *bora*, a boar; D. *beer*, a bear or *boar;* Ger. *eber*, a boar, and a gimlet or auger; also, *eberschwein*, boar-swine. Qu. L. *aper*, and *verres;* Sans. *varaha.*]

The male of swine not castrated.

BOAR-SPEAR, *n.* A spear used in hunting boars. *Spenser.*

BOAR, *v. i.* In *the manege*, a horse is said *to boar*, when he shoots out his nose, raising it as high as his ears, and tosses his nose in the wind. *Encyc.*

BOARD, *n.* [Sax. *bord* and *bred*, a *board*, or table; Goth. *baurd;* Sw. *bord*, and *bräde;* D. *boord*, a *board*, a hem, *border*, margin; Ger. *bord*, a *board*, a brim, bank, border; and *bret*, a *board*, or plank; Dan. *bord*, a *board*, a table; *bræde*, a *board*, or plank; and *bred*, a *border;* W. *bwrz*, a board or table; Ir. *bord*, a table, a *border.* This word and *broad* seem to be allied in origin, and the primary sense is to open or spread, whence broad, dilated.]

1. A piece of timber sawed thin and of considerable length and breadth, compared with the thickness, used for building and other purposes.
2. A table. The table of our rude ancestors was a piece of board, perhaps originally laid upon the knees. "Lauti cibum capiunt; separata singulis sedes, et sua cuique mensa." The Germans wash before they eat, and each has a separate seat, and his own table. *Tacitus. De Mor. Germ.* 22.
3. Entertainment; food; diet; as, the price of *board* is two, five, or seven dollars a week.
4. A table at which a council or court is held; hence a council, convened for business, or any authorized assembly or meeting; as a *board* of directors.
5. The deck of a ship; the interior part of a ship or boat; used in the phrase, *on board*, *aboard.* In this phrase however the sense is primarily the side of the ship. *To go aboard* is to go over the side.
6. The side of a ship. [Fr. *bord;* Sp. *borda.*]

Now *board* to *board*, the rival vessels row. *Dryden.*

To fall *over board*, that is, over the side; the mast went by the *board.*

Board and board, side by side.

7. The line over which a ship runs between tack and tack. *To make a good board*, is to sail in a straight line, when close hauled. *To make short boards*, is to tack frequently. *Mar. Dict.*
8. A table for artificers to sit or work on.
9. A table or frame for a game; as a *chess board*, &c.
10. A body of men constituting a quorum in session; a court, or council; as a *board* of trustees; a *board* of officers.

BOARD, *v. t.* To lay or spread with boards; to cover with boards.

2. To enter a ship by force in combat, which answers to storming a city or fort on land.
3. To attack; to make the first attempt upon a man. In Spenser, to accost. [Fr. *aborder.*] *Obs.* *Bacon. Shak.*
4. To place at board, for a compensation, as a lodger.
5. To furnish with food, or food and lodging, for a compensation; as, a man *boards* ten students.

BOARD, *v. i.* To receive food or diet as a lodger or without lodgings, for a compensation; as, he *boards* at the moderate price of two dollars a week.

BOARDABLE, *a.* That may be boarded, as a ship.

BŌARDED, *pp.* Covered with boards; entered by armed men, as a ship; furnished with food for a compensation.

BŌARDER, *n.* One who has food or diet and lodging in another's family for a reward.

2. One who boards a ship in action; one who is selected to board ships. *Mar. Dict.*

BŌARDING, *ppr.* Covering with boards; entering a ship by force; furnishing or receiving board, as a lodger, for a reward.

BŌARDING-SCHOOL, *n.* A school, the scholars of which *board* with the teacher.

BŌARD-WAGES, *n.* Wages allowed to servants to keep themselves in victuals. *Dryden.*

BŌARISH, *a.* [from *boar.*] Swinish; brutal; cruel. *Shak.*

BŌAST, *v. i.* [W. *bostiaw*, to boast, to toss or throw; G. *pausten*, to blow, swell, bounce; Sw. *pŏsa*, Dan. *puster*, id. Qu. Gr. φυσαω, to inflate; Russ. *chvastayu*, to boast; L. *fastus.*]

1. To brag, or vaunt one's self; to make an ostentatious display, in speech, of one's own worth, property, or actions.

Not of works, lest any man should *boast*. Eph. ii. 9.

2. To glory; to speak with laudable pride and ostentation of meritorious persons or things.

I *boast* of you to them of Macedonia. *St. Paul.* 2 Cor. ix.

Usually, it is followed by *of*; sometimes by *in*.

3. To exalt one's self.

With your mouth you have *boasted* against me. Ezek.

BŌAST, *v. t.* To display in ostentatious language; to speak of with pride, vanity or exultation, with a view to self-commendation.

Lest men should *boast* their specious deeds. *Milton.*

2. To magnify or exalt.

They *boast* themselves in the multitude of their riches. Ps. xlix.

3. To exult in confident expectation.

Boast not thyself of to-morrow. Prov. xxvii.

BŌAST, *n* Expression of ostentation, pride or vanity; a vaunting.

Thou makest thy *boast* of the law. Rom. ii.

2. The cause of boasting; occasion of pride, vanity, or laudable exultation.

Trial by peers is the *boast* of the British nation.

BŌASTER, *n.* One who boasts, glories or vaunts ostentatiously. *Boyle.*

BŌASTFUL, *a.* Given to boasting; ostentatious of personal worth or actions. *Shak.*

BŌASTING, *ppr.* Talking ostentatiously; glorying; vaunting.

BŌASTING, *n.* Ostentatious display of personal worth, or actions; a glorying or vaunting.

Where is *boasting* then? Rom. iii.

BŌASTINGLY, *adv.* In an ostentatious manner; with boasting.

BŌASTIVE, *a.* Presumptuous. [*Unusual.*] *Shenstone.*

BŌASTLESS, *a.* Without ostentation. *Thomson.*

BŌAT, *n.* [Sax. and Sw. *bat*; Dan. *baad*; W. *bâd*; Ir. *bad*; D. *boot*; G. *bot*, a boat; It. dim. *battello*, a little boat, whence Fr. *bateau*; Sp. *bote*, a boat.]

1. A small open vessel, or water craft, usually moved by oars, or rowing. The forms, dimensions and uses of boats are very various, and some of them carry a light sail. The different kinds of boats have different names; as, *long-boat, lanch, barge, pinnace, jolly-boat, cutter, yawl, ferry-boat, wherry, Moses-boat, punt, felucca, fishing-boat, perogue,* &c.

2. A small vessel carrying a mast and sails; but usually described by another word, as a *packet-boat, passage-boat, advice-boat,* &c. *Johnson.*

BŌAT, *v. t.* To transport in a boat; as, to *boat* goods across a lake. *Report on Canals. Ash.*

BŌATABLE, *a.* Navigable for boats, or small river craft. *Ramsay.*

BŌAT-BILL, *n.* [*boat* and *bill.*] A genus of birds, the Cancroma, of two species, the crested and the brown; but by some ornithologists, they are considered as varieties of the same species. They are of the grallic order, with a bill four inches long, not unlike a boat with the keel uppermost, or like the bowls of two spoons, with the hollow parts placed together. *Encyc.*

BŌAT-FLY or BŌAT-INSECT, *n.* A genus of insects, hemipters, known in zoology by the generic term Notonecta. *Encyc.*

BŌAT-HOOK, *n.* [*boat* and *hook.*] An iron hook with a point on the back, fixed to a long pole, to pull or push a boat. *Mar. Dict.*

BŌATING, *ppr.* Transporting in boats.

BŌATING, *n.* The act or practice of transporting in boats.

2. In *Persia*, a punishment of capital offenders by laying them on the back in a boat which is covered, where they perish. *Encyc.*

BOA'TION, *n.* [L. *boo.*] A crying out; a roar. [*Not used.*] *Derham.*

BŌATMAN, } *n.* [*boat* and *man.*] A man who manages a boat; a rower of a boat.
BŌATSMAN, } *Dryden. Prior.*

BŌAT-ROPE, *n.* [*boat* and *rope.*] A rope to fasten a boat, usually called a painter.

BŌAT-SHAPED, *a.* Having the shape of a boat; navicular; cymbiform; hollow like a boat; as the valve of some pericarps. *Martyn.*

BŌATSWAIN, *n.* In *seamen's language*, bŏsn. [Sax. *batswein*, from *bat*, boat, and *swein*, swain, a boy or servant.]

An officer on board of ships, who has charge of the boats, sails, rigging, colors, anchors, cables and cordage. His office is also, to summon the crew to their duty, to relieve the watch, assist in the necessary business of the ship, seize and punish offenders, &c. He has a mate who has charge of the long-boat, for setting forth and weighing anchors, warping, towing and mooring. *Mar. Dict. Encyc. Johnson.*

BOB, *n.* Any little round thing, that plays loosely at the end of a string, cord, or movable machine; a little ornament or pendant that hangs so as to play loosely. *Dryden.*

Our common people apply the word to a knot of worms, on a string, used in fishing for eels.

2. The words repeated at the end of a stanza. *L'Estrange.*

3. A blow; a shake or jog; a jeer or flout. *Ainsworth. Ascham.*

4. The ball of a short pendulum. *Encyc.*

5. A mode of ringing. *Johnson.*

6. A bob-wig. *Shenstone.*

BOB, *v. t.* To beat; to shake or jog. *Shak.*

2. To cheat; to gain by fraud. *Shak.*

3. To mock or delude. *Ainsworth.*

4. To cut short.

BOB, *v. i.* To play backward and forward; to play loosely against any thing. *Dryden.*

2. To angle, or fish for eels, or to catch eels with a bob. *Encyc.*

BOBANCE, *n. bobans'.* A boasting. [*Not in use.*] *Chaucer.*

BOB'BED, *pp.* Beat or shaken; cheated; gained by fraud; deluded.

BOB'BIN, *n.* [Fr. *bobine*; D. *babyn.*] A small pin or cylindrical piece of wood, with a head, on which thread is wound for making lace. A similar instrument, bored through to receive an iron pivot, and with a border at each end, is used in spinning, to wind thread or silk on; a spool.

BOB'BING, *ppr.* Playing back and forth; striking; cheating; angling for eels.

BOB'BINWŌRK, *n.* [*bobbin* and *work.*] Work woven with bobbins. *Grew.*

BOB'-CHERRY, *n.* [*bob* and *cherry.*] Among *children*, a play in which a cherry is hung so as to bob against the mouth. *Johnson.*

BO'BO, *n.* A Mexican fish, two feet long, in high esteem for food. *Clavigero.*

BOB'STAYS, *n.* [*bob* and *stay.*] Ropes to confine the bowsprit of a ship downward to the stem. *Mar. Dict.*

BOB'TAIL, *n.* [*bob* and *tail.*] A short tail, or a tail cut short. *Shak.*

2. The rabble; used in contempt. *Bramston.*

BOB'-TAILED, *a.* Having the hair cut short. *L'Estrange.*

BOB-WIG, *n.* [*bob* and *wig.*] A short wig. *Spectator.*

BOCAQUE or BOCAKE, *n.* An animal found on the banks of the Nieper, resembling a rabbit, except that its ears are shorter, and it has no tail. *Dict. of Nat. Hist.*

BOC'ASÏNE, *n.* [Fr.] A sort of fine linen or buckram. *Johnson.*

BOCE, *n.* The sparus, a beautiful fish. *Ash.*

BOCK'ELET, } *n.* A kind of long-winged hawk. *Johnson.*
BOCK'ERET, }

BOCKLAND. [See *Bookland.*] *Encyc.*

BODE, *v. t.* [Sax. *bodian, bodigan*, to foretell, to utter or announce; *bod*, an order, mandate or edict; *boda*, a messenger, or preacher; Sw. *bod*, a message, an embassy; *beboda*, to tell or relate; Sax. *gebodian*, to offer or *bid*, to relate, tell or announce, to command, to show, to promise. Radically, this is the same word as *bid*, which see. The radical sense is, to utter, to drive out the voice.]

To portend; to foreshow; to presage; to indicate something future by signs; to be the omen of; *most generally applied to things*; as, our vices *bode* evil to the country.

BODE, *v. i.* To foreshow; to presage.

This *bodes* well to you. *Dryden.*

BODE, *n.* An omen. *Chaucer.*

2. A stop. [See *Abide.*]

BO'DEMENT, *n.* An omen; portent; prognostic; a fore-showing. *Obs.* *Shak.*

BODǴE, *v. i.* [See *Boggle.*] To boggle; to stop. [*Not used.*] *Shak.*

BODǴE, *n.* A botch. [*Not used.*] *Whitlock.*

BOD'ICE, *n.* Stays; a waistcoat, quilted with whalebone; worn by women. *Johnson.*

BOD'IED, *a.* [from *body.*] Having a body. *Shak.*

BOD'ILESS, *a.* [See *Body.*] Having no body or material form; incorporeal. *Davies.*

BOD'ILY, *a.* Having or containing a body or material form; corporeal; as *bodily* dimensions. *South.*

2. Relating or pertaining to the body, in distinction from the mind; as *bodily* defects; *bodily* pain. *Locke.*

3. Real; actual; as *bodily* act. *Shak.*

BOD'ILY, *adv.* Corporeally; united with a body or matter.

It is his human nature, in which the Godhead dwells *bodily.* *Watts.*

BO'DING, *ppr.* [from *bode.*] Foreshowing; presaging.

BO'DING, *n.* An omen. *Bp. Ward.*

BOD'KIN, *n.* [Ir. *bod*, a limb, that is, a point, a shoot, with the termination *kin*, used as a diminutive; Gr. βατος, a thorn.]

1. An instrument of steel, bone, ivory or the like, with a small blade, and a sharp point, for making holes by piercing. A like instrument with an eye, for drawing thread, tape, or ribin through a loop, &c. An instrument to dress the hair. *Johnson.*

2. A dagger. [*Not in use.*] *Chaucer.*

BODLE'IAN, *a.* Pertaining to Sir Thomas Bodley, who founded a celebrated library in the 16th century.

BOD'Y, *n.* [Sax. *bodig*, stature, trunk, spine, *body;* that which is set or fixed.]

1. The frame of an animal; the material substance of an animal, in distinction from the living principle of beasts, and the soul of man.

Be not anxious for your *body.* *Matthew. Luke.*

2. Matter, as opposed to spirit. *Hooker.*

3. A person; a human being; sometimes alone; more generally, with *some* or *no;* as, *somebody; nobody.*

4. Reality, as opposed to representation.

A shadow of things to come, but the *body* is of Christ. Col. ii.

5. A collective mass; a number of individuals or particulars united; as the *body* of mankind. Christians united or the Church is called the *body,* of which each Christian is a member, and Christ the head. 1 Cor. xii. 12. 27.

6. The main army, in distinction from the wings, van or rear. Also, any number of forces under one commander. *Clarendon.*

7. A corporation; a number of men, united by a common tie, by one form of government, or by occupation; as the legislative *body;* the *body* of the clergy; *body* corporate; *body* politic.

8. The main part; the bulk; as the *body* of a tree; the *body* of a coach, of a ship, &c.

9. Any extended solid substance; matter; any substance or mass distinct from others; as a metaline *body;* a floating *body;* a moving *body;* a light *body;* a heavy *body.*

10. A pandect; a general collection; a code; a system; as a *body* of laws; a *body* of divinity.

11. Strength; as wine of a good *body.*

12. Among painters, colors *bear a body,* when they are capable of being ground so fine, and of being mixed so entirely with oil, as to seem only a very thick oil of the same color. *Encyc.*

13. The unrenewed part of man, or sensual affections.

But I keep under my *body.* 1 Cor. ix.

14. The extent; the limits.

Cause to come here on such a day, twelve free and lawful men—from the *body* of your county. *Form of a venire facias.*

BOD'Y, *v. t.* To produce in some form.

Imagination *bodies* forth the forms of things. *Shak.*

BOD'Y-ȻLOTHES, *n. plu.* [*body* and *cloth.*] Clothing or covering for the body, as for a horse. *Addison.*

BOD'Y-GUARD, *n.* The guard that protects or defends the person; the life guard. Hence, security. *Porteus.*

BOG, *n.* [Ir. *bog*, soft; *bogach*, a marsh; *bogha*, a bow; *boghaim*, to bend; Sax. *bugan;* D. *boogen*, to bend. *Soft* is flexible, yielding to pressure, bending. See *Bow.*]

1. A quagmire covered with grass or other plants. It is defined by *marsh*, and *morass*, but differs from a marsh, as a part from the whole. Wet grounds are *bogs*, which are the softest and too soft to bear a man; *marshes* or fens, which are less soft, but very wet; and *swamps*, which are soft spongy land, upon the surface, but sustain man and beast, and are often mowed.

2. A little elevated spot or clump of earth, in marshes and swamps, filled with roots and grass. [*This is a common use of the word in New-England.*]

BOG, *v. t.* To whelm or plunge, as in mud and mire. *Jonson.*

BOG'-BEAN, *n.* [*bog* and *bean;* called *buckbean.*]

Menyanthes, a plant, the marsh-trefoil, which grows in moist and marshy places. *Fam. of Plants.*

BOG'-BERRY, *n.* [*bog* and *berry.*] Vaccinium, a name of the cranberry growing in low lands and marshy places. *Fam. of Plants.*

BOG'GLE, *v. i.* [Qu. W. *bwgwl*, a terrifying.]

1. To doubt; to hesitate; to stop, as if afraid to proceed, or as if impeded by unforeseen difficulties; to play fast and loose.

We *boggle* at every unusual appearance. *Granville.*

2. To dissemble. *Howell.*

BOG'GLE, *v. t.* To embarrass with difficulties; *a popular or vulgar use of the word in the United States.*

BOG'GLED, *pp.* Perplexed and impeded by sudden difficulties; embarrassed.

BOG'GLER, *n.* A doubter; a timorous man. *Shak.*

BOG'GLING, *ppr.* Starting or stopping at difficulties; hesitating.

BOG'GLISH, *a.* Doubtful. [*Not used.*] *Taylor.*

BOG'GY, *a.* [from *bog.*] Containing bogs; full of bogs.

BOG'HOUSE, *n.* [*bog* and *house.*] A house of office.

BOG'-LAND, *a.* [*bog* and *land.*] Living in or pertaining to a marshy country. *Dryden.*

BO'GLE or **BOG'GLE**, *n.* [W. *bwg*, a bugbear or goblin.] A bugbear.

BOG'-ORE, *n.* An ore of iron found in boggy or swampy land.

BOG'-RUSH, *n.* [*bog* and *rush.*] A rush that grows in bogs, the Schœnus. *Pennant.*

2. A bird, a species of warbler, of the size of a wren, of a testaceous brown color, seen among the bog-rushes of Schonen in Sweden. *Pennant.*

BOG'-SPAVIN, *n.* [*bog* and *spavin.*] In *horses*, an encysted tumor on the inside of the hough, containing a gelatinous matter. *Encyc.*

BOG'-TROTTER, *n.* [*bog* and *trot.*] One who lives in a boggy country. *Johnson.*

BOG'-WHŎRT, *n.* [*bog* and *whort.*] The bilberry or whortleberry growing in low lands. *Fam. of Plants.*

BOHE'A, *n.* [Grosier informs us that this is named from a mountain in China, called *Vou-y* or *Voo-y.* Vol. i. 467.]

A species of coarse or low priced tea from China; a species of black tea.

BOI'AR or **BOY'AR**, *n.* In the *Russian Empire*, a nobleman; a lord; a person of quality; a soldier. This word answers nearly to Baron in Great Britain, and other countries in the west of Europe. *Tooke. Eton.*

BOI'ARIN, *n.* In *Russia*, a gentleman; a person of distinction; the master of a family. *Tooke. Russ. Dict.*

BOIGU'AȻU, *n.* The largest of the serpent kind, and said to be forty feet long. *Bailey.*

BOIL, *v. i.* [Fr. *bouillir;* L. *bullio;* It. *bollire;* Sp. *bullir*, to boil; L. *bulla*, a bubble; Russ. *bul*, the noise of boiling water; It. *bolla*, a bubble or blister; Eth. ፈለሐ Amh. ፈለ to boil; W. *balau*, to spring. Qu. Sax. *weallan*, to well, to boil.]

1. To swell, heave, or be agitated by the action of heat; to bubble; to rise in bubbles; as, the water *boils.* In a chimical sense, to pass from a liquid to an aeriform state or vapor, with a bubbling motion.

2. To be agitated by any other cause than heat; as, the *boiling* waves which roll and foam.

3. To be hot or fervid; to swell by native heat, vigor or irritation; as the *boiling* blood of youth; his blood *boils* with anger.

4. To be in boiling water; to suffer boiling heat in water or other liquid, for cookery or other purpose.

5. To bubble; to effervesce; as a mixture of acid and alkali.

To boil away, to evaporate by boiling.

To boil over, is to run over the top of a vessel, as liquor when thrown into violent agitation by heat or other cause of effervescence.

BOIL, *v. t.* To dress or cook in boiling water; to seethe; to extract the juice or quality of any thing by boiling.

2. To prepare for some use in boiling liquor; as, to *boil* silk, thread or cloth. To form by boiling and evaporation. This word is applied to a variety of processes for different purposes; as, to *boil* salt, or su-

gar, &c. In general, *boiling* is a violent agitation, occasioned by heat; to *boil* a liquor is to subject it to heat till it bubbles, and to *boil* any solid substance is to subject it to heat in a boiling liquid.

BOIL, *n.* [D. *buil;* Ger. *beule;* Dan. *bylde;* Sax. *bile;* Arm. *buil,* a blister; Sw. *bula,* a protuberance; D. *bol,* plump; Ger. *bolle,* a bud, a gem; Ir. *buile,* rage, madness; Pers. *pallo,* a wart, an ulcer, a boil; W. *bal,* a prominence.]
A tumor upon the flesh, accompanied with soreness and inflammation; a sore angry swelling.

BOIL'ED, *pp.* Dressed or cooked by boiling; subjected to the action of boiling liquor.

BOIL'ER, *n.* A person who boils.
2. A vessel in which any thing is boiled. A large pan, or vessel of iron, copper or brass, used in distilleries, pot-ash works and the like, for boiling large quantities of liquor at once.

BOIL'ERY, *n.* A place for boiling and the apparatus.

BOIL'ING, *ppr.* Bubbling; heaving in bubbles; being agitated as boiling liquor; swelling with heat, ardor or passion; dressing or preparing for some purpose by hot water.

BOIL'ING, *n.* The act or state of bubbling; agitation by heat; ebullition; the act of dressing by hot water; the act of preparing by hot water, or of evaporating by heat.

BOIO'BI, *n.* A green snake, found in America, an ell in length, called by the Portuguese, *cobra de verb.* It is harmless, unless provoked; but its bite is noxious. *Encyc.*

BOIS'TEROUS, *a.* [Dan. *pust,* a puff, a blast; *puster,* and Sw. *pusta,* to blow; D. *byster;* Dan. *bister,* furious, raging; W. *bwyst,* wild, savage, whence, *beast.*]
1. Loud; roaring; violent; stormy; as a *boisterous* wind.
2. Turbulent; furious; tumultuous; noisy; as a *boisterous* man.
3. Large; unwieldy; huge; clumsily violent; as a *boisterous* club. *Obs. Spenser.*
4. Violent; as a *boisterous* heat. *Woodward.*

BOIS'TEROUSLY, *adv.* Violently; furiously; with loud noise; tumultuously.

BOIS'TEROUSNESS, *n.* The state or quality of being boisterous; turbulence; disorder; tumultuousness.

BOITI'APO, *n.* A Brazilian serpent, about eight feet long, covered with triangular scales, of an olive or yellowish color, whose bite is mortal. *Dict. of Nat. Hist.*

BO'LARY, *a.* [See *Bole.*] Pertaining to bole or clay, or partaking of its nature and qualities. *Brown.*

BOL'BITINE, *a.* An epithet given to one of the channels of the Nile, by which its waters are discharged into the Mediterranean. It is the second from West to East, but nearly filled with sand. *D'Anville. Encyc.*

BŌLD, *a.* [Sax. *bald, beald;* D. *bout,* contracted; It. *baldo,* bold; *baldanza,* presumption; *imbaldanzire,* to embolden. The sense is, open, forward, rushing forward.]
1. Daring; courageous; brave; intrepid; fearless; *applied to men or other animals;* as, *bold* as a lion.
2. Requiring courage in the execution; executed with spirit or boldness; planned with courage and spirit; as a *bold* enterprise.
3. Confident; not timorous.

We were *bold* in our God to speak to you. 1 Thess. ii.

4. In *an ill sense,* rude, forward, impudent.
5. Licentious; showing great liberty of fiction or expression; as, the figures of an author are *bold.*
6. Standing out to view; striking to the eye; as *bold* figures in painting, sculpture and architecture.
7. Steep; abrupt; prominent; as a *bold* shore, which enters the water almost perpendicularly, so that ships can approach near to land without danger.

Where the *bold* cape its warning forehead rears. *Trumbull.*

To make bold, to take freedoms; a common, but not a correct phrase. *To be bold* is better.

BŌLD, *v. t.* To make daring. [*Not used.*] *Hall.*

BŌLDEN, *v. t.* To make bold; to give confidence. This is nearly disused; being superseded by *embolden.* *Ascham.*

BŌLD-FACE, *n.* [*bold* and *face.*] Impudence; sauciness; a term of reprehension, and reproach. *L'Estrange.*

BŌLD-FACED, *a.* Impudent. *Bramhall.*

BŌLDLY, *adv.* In a bold manner; courageously; intrepidly; without timidity or fear; with confidence. Sometimes, perhaps, in a bad sense, for impudently.

BŌLDNESS, *n.* Courage; bravery; intrepidity; spirit; fearlessness. I cannot, with Johnson, interpret this word by *fortitude* or *magnanimity.* Boldness does not, I think, imply the *firmness* of mind, which constitutes fortitude, nor the *elevation* and *generosity* of magnanimity.
2. Prominence; the quality of exceeding the ordinary rules of scrupulous nicety and caution; *applied to style, expression, and metaphors in language; and to figures in painting, sculpture and architecture.*
3. Freedom from timidity; liberty.

Great is my *boldness* of speech towards you. 2 Cor. vii.

4. Confidence; confident trust.

We have *boldness* and access with confidence. Eph. iii.

5. Freedom from bashfulness; assurance; confident mien. *Bacon.*
6. Prominence; steepness; as the *boldness* of the shore.
7. Excess of freedom, bordering on impudence. *Hooker.*

BOLE, *n.* [Sw. *bol;* Dan. *bul.*]
1. The body, or stem of a tree. [*Not in use.*] *Dryden.*
2. A measure of corn, containing six bushels. *Mortimer.*

BOLE, *n.* A kind of fine clay, often highly colored by iron. Its color is reddish yellow of various shades, often with a tinge of brown, sometimes passing to reddish, yellowish, or blackish brown, flesh red, or yellowish white. It is opake or a little translucid, especially at the edges, in the red and yellow varieties. It is compact and its fracture conchoidal. It is brittle, smooth, a little unctuous, and receives a polish from the finger nail. It adheres to the tongue, melts by degrees in the mouth, and impresses a slight sense of astringency. *Cleaveland.*
Armenian bole is of a bright red color, with a tinge of yellow, harder than the other kinds, and of a rough dusty surface.
Bole of Blois is yellow, lighter than the other kinds, and it effervesces with acids.
Bohemian bole is of a yellow color, with a cast of red, and of a flaky texture.
French bole is of a pale red color, variegated with specks of white and yellow.
Lemnian bole is of a pale red color.
Silesian bole is of a pale yellow color. *Encyc.*

BOLET'IC, *a.* *Boletic acid* is the acid of Boletus, a genus of mushrooms.

BOLE'TUS, *n.* [L.] A genus of mushrooms, containing many species.

BO'LIS, *n.* [L. from Gr. βολις, a dart; βαλλω, to throw.]
A fire-ball darting through the air, followed by a train of light or sparks.

BŌLL, *n.* [W. *bul,* a seed vessel; Sax. *bolla,* a bowl.]
The pod or capsule of a plant, as of flax; a pericarp. *Bole,* a measure of six bushels, is sometimes written in this manner.

BŌLL, *v. i.* To form into a pericarp or seed-vessel.

The barley was in the ear and the flax was *bolled.* Exodus ix.

Heb. נבעל, Gr. σπερματιζον, as translated by the seventy.

Bollard timbers, in a ship, or knight-heads, are two timbers, rising just within the stem, one on each side of the bowsprit, to secure its end. *Mar. Dict.*

In *docks,* bollards are large posts set in the ground on each side, to which are lashed large blocks, through which are reeved the transporting hawsers for docking and undocking ships. *Encyc.*

BOLO'GNIAN STONE. *bolo'nian stone.* Radiated sulphate of barytes; found in roundish masses, composed of radiating fibers; first discovered near Bologna. It is phosphorescent, when calcined.

BŌLSTER, *n.* [Sax. and Sw. *bolster;* Ger. *polster;* Dan. *bolster-dyne,* a feather bed; Pers. بالشت balisht. In Dutch, *bolster* is a husk, cod or shell.]
1. A long pillow or cushion, used to support the head of persons lying on a bed; generally laid under the pillows.
2. A pad, or quilt, used to hinder pressure, support any part of the body, or make a bandage sit easy upon a wounded part a compress.
3. In *sadlery,* a part of a saddle raised upon the bows or hinder part, to hold the rider's thigh. *Farrier's Dict.*
4. In *ships,* a cushion or bag, filled with tarred canvas, used to preserve the stays from being worn or chafed by the masts. *Mar. Dict.*

BŌLSTER, *v. t.* To support with a bolster, pillow or any soft pad or quilt.
2. To support; to hold up; to maintain. *Hooker. South.*
3. To afford a bed to. [*Unusual.*] *Shak.*

BŌLSTERED, *a.* Swelled out.

BŌLSTERER, *n.* A supporter.

BOLSTERING, *n.* A prop or support. *Taylor.*

BŎLT, *n.* [Dan. *bolt*; Russ. *bolt*; D. *bout*; G. *bolzen*; Sax. *bolta*, catapulta, that which is driven, from the root of Gr. βαλλω, L. *pello.*]

1. An arrow; a dart; a pointed shaft. *Dryden.*

2. A strong cylindrical pin, of iron or other metal, used to fasten a door, a plank, a chain, &c. In *ships*, bolts are used in the sides and decks, and have different names, as rag-bolts, eye-bolts, ring-bolts, chain-bolts, &c. In *gunnery*, there are prise-bolts, transom-bolts, traverse-bolts, and bracket-bolts.

3. A thunder-bolt; a stream of lightning, so named from its darting like a bolt.

4. The quantity of twenty-eight ells of canvas. *Encyc.*

BŎLT, *v. t.* To fasten or secure with a bolt, or iron pin, whether a door, a plank, fetters or any thing else.

2. To fasten; to shackle; to restrain. *Shak.*

3. To blurt out; to utter or throw out precipitately.

I hate when vice can *bolt* her arguments. *Milton.*

In this sense it is often followed by *out.*

4. [Norm. *bulter*, a bolting sieve. Qu. Fr. *bluter.*] To sift or separate bran from flour. *In America this term is applied only to the operation performed in mills.*

5. Among sportsmen, to start or dislodge, used of coneys.

6. To examine by sifting; to open or separate the parts of a subject, to find the truth; generally followed by *out.* "Time and nature will *bolt out* thetruth of things." [*Inelegant.*] *L'Estrange.*

7. To purify; to purge. [*Unusual.*] *Shak.*

8. To discuss or argue; as at Gray's inn, where cases are privately discussed by students and barristers. *Encyc.*

BŎLT, *v. i.* To shoot forth suddenly; to spring out with speed and suddenness; to start forth like a bolt; commonly followed by *out;* as, to *bolt out* of the house, or *out* of a den. *Dryden.*

BŎLT-AUGER, *n.* [*bolt* and *auger.*] A large borer, used in ship-building. *Ash.*

BŎLT-BOAT, *n.* [*bolt* and *boat.*] A strong boat that will endure a rough sea. *Ash.*

BŎLTED, *pp.* Made fast with a bolt; shot forth; sifted; examined.

BŎLTER, *n.* An instrument or machine for separating bran from flour or the coarser part of meal from the finer.

2. A kind of net. *Johnson.*

BŎLT-HEAD, *n.* [*bolt* and *head.*] A long straight-necked glass vessel for chimical distillations, called also a matrass or receiver. *Johnson.*

BŎLTING, *ppr.* Fastening with a bolt, or bolts; blurting out; shooting forth suddenly; separating bran from flour; sifting; examining; discussing; dislodging.

BŎLTING, *n.* The act of fastening with a bolt or bolts; a sifting; discussion.

BŎLTING-CLOTH, *n.* [*bolt* and *cloth.*] A linen or hair cloth of which bolters are made for sifting meal. *Encyc.*

BŎLTING-HOUSE, *n.* [*bolt* and *house.*] The house or place where meal is bolted. *Johnson.*

BŎLTING-HUTCH, *n.* A tub for bolted flour.

BŎLTING-MILL, *n.* [*bolt* and *mill.*] A machine or engine for sifting meal. *Encyc.*

BŎLTING-TUB, *n.* A tub to sift meal in.

BŎLT-ROPE, *n.* [*bolt* and *rope.*] A rope to which the edges of sails are sewed to strengthen them. That part of it on the perpendicular side is called the *leech-rope*; that at the bottom, the *foot-rope*; that at the top, the *head-rope.* *Mar. Dict.*

BŎLT-SPRIT, *n.* [From the universal popular pronunciation of this word, this may have been the original word; but I doubt it. See *Bowsprit.*]

BO'LUS, *n.* [L. *bolus*; Gr. βωλος, a mass.] A soft mass of any thing medicinal to be swallowed at once, like a pill. It may be of any ingredients, made a little thicker than honey. *Encyc.*

BOM, *n.* A large serpent found in America, of a harmless nature, and remarkable for uttering a sound like *bom.* *Dict. of Nat. Hist.*

BŎMB, *n.* [L. *bombus*; Gr. βομβος.] A great noise. *Bacon.*

2. A large shell of cast iron, round and hollow, with a vent to receive a fusee, which is made of wood. This being filled with gunpowder and the fusee driven into the vent, the fusee is set on fire and the bomb is thrown from a mortar, in such a direction as to fall into a fort, city or enemy's camp, when it bursts with great violence and often with terrible effect. The inventor of bombs is not known; they came into common use about the year 1634. *Encyc.*

3. The stroke upon a bell.

BŎMB, *v. t.* To attack with bombs; to bombard. [*Not used.*] *Prior.*

BŎMB, *v. i.* To sound. *B. Jonson.*

BŎM'BARD, *n.* [*bomb* and *ard*, kind. Fr. *bombarde*; Sp. It. *bombarda.*]

1. A piece of short thick ordnance with a large mouth, formerly used; some of them carrying a ball of three hundred pounds weight. It is called also *basilisk*, and by the Dutch, *donderbuss*, thunder-gun. But the thing and the name are no longer in use. *Encyc.*

2. An attack with bombs; bombardment. *Barlow.*

3. A barrel; a drinking vessel. *Obs.* *Johnson. Ash.*

BŎMB'ARD, *v. t.* To attack with bombs thrown from mortars.

BŎMB'ARDED, *pp.* Attacked with bombs.

BŎMBARDIE'R, *n.* One whose business is to attend the loading and firing of mortars.

2. Carabus, a genus of insects of the beetle kind. *Encyc.*

BŎMB'ARDING, *ppr.* Attacking with shells or bombs.

BŎMB'ARDMENT, *n.* An attack with bombs; the act of throwing bombs into a town, fort or ship. *Addison.*

BŎMB'ARDO, *n.* A musical instrument of the wind kind, much like the bassoon, and used as a base to the hautboy. *Encyc.*

BŎMBASI'N, *n.* *s* as *z.* A name given to two sorts of stuffs, one of silk, the other crossed of cotton. *Encyc.*

BŎM'BAST, *n.* Originally a stuff of soft loose texture, used to swell garments. Hence, high sounding words; an inflated style; fustian; a serious attempt, by strained description, to raise a low or familiar subject beyond its rank, which, instead of being sublime, never fails to be ridiculous. *Encyc.*

BŎM'BAST, *a.* High-sounding; inflated; big without meaning. *Swift.*

BŎMBAS'TIC, *a.* Swelled; high sounding; bombast. *Shaftesbury.*

BŎM'BASTRY, *n.* Swelling words without much meaning; fustian. *Swift.*

BŎMB'-CHEST, *n.* [*bomb* and *chest.*] A chest filled with bombs or only with gun powder, placed under ground, to make destruction by its displosion.

BOM'BIAT, *n.* A salt formed by the bombic acid and any base saturated. *Lavoisier.*

BOM'BIC, *a.* [L. *bombyx*, a silk worm.] Pertaining to the silk worm; as *bombic* acid.

BOMBILA'TION, *n.* [L. *bombilo.*] Sound; report; noise. [*Little used.*] *Brown.*

BŎMB'-KETCH, / **BŎMB'-VESSEL**, } *n.* A small ship or vessel, constructed for throwing bombs into a fortress from the sea, and built remarkably strong, in order to sustain the shocks produced by the discharge of the mortars. They generally are rigged as ketches. *Mar. Dict.*

BOMBYC'INOUS, *a.* [L. *bombycinus*, from *bombyx*, a silk worm.]

1. Silken; made of silk.

2. Being of the color of the silk worm; transparent, with a yellow tint. *Darwin.*

BO'NA-FIDE, [L.] With good faith; without fraud or deception.

BONA-ROBA, *n.* [It. a fine gown.] A showy wanton. *Shak.*

BONA'IR, *a.* [It. *bonario*, from L. *bonus.*] Complaisant; yielding. [*Not used.*]

BONA'SUS, *n.* [L.] A species of Bos, or wild ox, with a long mane; a native of Asia and Africa. It is of the size of a bull. *Encyc.*

BON CHRETIEN, *n.* [Fr. good christian.] A species of pear.

BOND, *n.* [Sax. *bond.* See *Band* and *Bind.*]

1. Any thing that binds, as a cord, a chain, a rope; a band.

2. Ligament; that which holds things together.

3. Union; connection; a binding.

Let walls be so constructed as to make a good *bond.* *Mortimer.*

4. In *the plural*, chains; imprisonment; captivity.

He hath done nothing worthy of death or of *bonds.* Acts.

5. Cause of union; cement which unites; link of connection; as the *bonds* of affection.

Charity is the *bond* of perfectness. Col. 3.

6. An obligation imposing a moral duty, as by a vow, or promise, by law or other means.

7. In *law*, an obligation or deed by which a person binds himself, his heirs, executors, and administrators, to pay a certain sum, on or before a future day appointed. This is a single bond. But usually a condition is added, that if the obligor shall do a certain act, or pay a certain sum of money, on or before a time specified, the obligation shall be void; otherwise it shall

remain in full force. If the condition is not performed, the bond becomes forfeited, and the obligor and his heirs are liable to the payment of the whole sum. *Blackstone.*

BOND, *a.* [for *bound.*] In a state of servitude, or slavery; captive.

Whether we be Jews or Gentiles; whether we be *bond* or free. 1 Cor. xii.

BOND, *v. t.* To give bond for, as for duties or customs at a custom house; to secure payment of, by giving a bond.

On their reshipment and exportation, official clearances were given, in which no mention was made that the cargo consisted of *bonded* or debentured goods. *War in disguise.*

In the U. States, it is applied to the goods on which the customs arise, and to the duties secured by bond.

BOND'AĠE, *n.* Slavery or involuntary servitude; captivity; imprisonment; restraint of a person's liberty by compulsion. In *ancient English law*, villenage.

2. Obligation; tie of duty.

He must resolve not to be brought under the *bondage* of observing oaths. *South.*

3. In *scripture*, spiritual subjection to sin and corrupt passions, or to the yoke of the ceremonial law; servile fear. Heb. ii. Gal. ii. Rom. viii.

BOND'ED, *pp.* Secured by bond, as duties. *Bonded* goods are those for the duties on which bonds are given at the custom house.

BOND'MAID, *n.* [*bond* and *maid.*] A female slave, or one bound to service without wages, in opposition to a hired servant.

BOND'MAN, *n.* [*bond* and *man.*] A man slave, or one bound to service without wages. In *old English law*, a villain, or tenant in villenage.

BOND'SERVANT, *n.* [*bond* and *servant.*] A slave; one who is subjected to the authority of another, or whose person and liberty are restrained.

BOND'SERVICE, *n.* [*bond* and *service.*] The condition of a bond-servant; slavery.

BOND'SLAVE, *n.* [*bond* and *slave.*] A person in a state of slavery; one whose person and liberty are subjected to the authority of a master.

BONDS'MAN, *n.* [*bond* and *man.*] A slave. *Obs.* *Derham.*

2. A surety; one who is bound, or who gives security, for another.

BONDS'WŎMAN, } *n.* [*bond* and *woman.*]
BOND'-WŎMAN, } A woman slave. *B. Jonson.*

BON'DU€, *n.* A species of Guilandina, or *nickar tree*, the yellow nickar, a climbing plant, a native of the West Indies, bearing a pod containing two hard seeds of the size of a child's marble. *Encyc.*

BONE, *n.* [Sax. *ban*; Sw. *ben*; D. *been*, bone or leg; Ger. *bein*, a leg; Dan. *been*, leg or bone. The sense probably is, that which is set or fixed.]

1. A firm hard substance, of a dull white color, composing some part of the frame of an animal body. The bones of an animal support all the softer parts, as the flesh and vessels. They vary in texture in different bones, and in different parts of the same bone. The long bones are compact in their middle portion, with a central cavity occupied by a network of plates and fibers, and cellular or spongy at the extremities. The flat bones are compact externally, and cellular internally. The bones in a fetus are soft and cartilaginous, but they gradually harden with age. The ends of the long bones are larger than the middle, which renders the articulations more firm, and in the fetus are distinct portions, called epiphyses. Bones are supplied with blood vessels, and in the fetus, or in a diseased state, are very vascular. They are probably also furnished with nerves and absorbents, though less easily detected in a sound state. They are covered with a thin, strong membrane, called the periosteum, which, together with the bones, has very little sensibility in a sound state, but when inflamed, is extremely sensible. Their cells and cavities are occupied by a fatty substance, called the medulla or marrow. They consist of earthy matter, rather more than half, gelatin, one sixteenth, and cartilage, about one third of the whole. The earthy matter gives them their solidity, and consists of phosphate of lime, with a small portion of carbonate of lime and phosphate of magnesia. *Cyc. Wistar. Thomson.*

2. A piece of bone, with fragments of meat adhering to it.

To be upon the bones, is to attack. [*Little used, and vulgar.*]

To make no bones, is to make no scruple; a metaphor taken from a dog who greedily swallows meat that has no bones. *Johnson.*

Bones, a sort of bobbins, made of trotter bones, for weaving lace; also dice. *Johnson.*

BONE, *v. t.* To take out bones from the flesh, as in cookery. *Johnson.*

2. To put whale bone into stays. *Ash.*

BO'NE-ACE, *n.* [*bone* and *ace.*] A game at cards, in which he who has the highest card turned up to him, wins the *bone*, that is, one half the stake. *Encyc.*

BO'NE-A€HE, *n.* Pain in the bones. *Shak.*

BO'NED, *pp.* Deprived of bones, as in cookery.

BO'NED, *a.* Having bones; used in composition; as *high-boned; strong-boned.*

BO'NELACE, *n.* [*bone* and *lace.*] A lace made of linen thread, so called because made with bobbins of bone, or for its stiffness. *Obs.*

BO'NELESS, *a.* Without bones; wanting bones; as *boneless* gums. *Shak.*

BO'NE-SET, *v. t.* [*bone* and *set.*] To set a dislocated bone; to unite broken bones. *Wiseman.*

BO'NE-SET, *n.* A plant, the thoroughwort, a species of *Eupatorium.*

BO'NE-SETTER, *n.* [*bone* and *set.*] One whose occupation is to set, and restore broken and dislocated bones.

BO'NE-SETTING, *n.* That branch of surgery which consists in replacing broken and luxated bones; the practice of setting bones.

BO'NE-SPAVIN, *n.* [*bone* and *spavin.*] A bony excrescence, or hard swelling, on the inside of the hock of a horse's leg; usually cured by blistering and firing, or caustic blisters. *Encyc.*

BONET'TA, *n.* A sea fish. Qu. *bonito.* *Herbert.*

BON'FIRE, *n.* [Fr. *bon*, good, and *fire.*] A fire made as an expression of public joy and exultation.

BON'GRACE, *n.* [Fr. *bonne*, and *grace.*] A covering for the forehead. [*Not used.*] *Beaum.*

BO'NIFŶ, *v. t.* To convert into good. [*Not used.*] *Cudworth.*

BONĪTO, *n.* [Sp.] A fish of the tunny kind, growing to the length of three feet, and found on the American coast, and in the tropical climates. It has a greenish back, and a white silvery belly. *Hawksworth. Pennant. Dict. Nat. Hist.*

BON'MOT, *n.* [Fr. *bon*, good, and *mot*, a word.]

A jest; a witty repartee. This word is not anglicized, and may be pronounced *bomo.*

BON'NET, *n.* [Fr. *bonnet*; Sp. *bonete*; Ir. *boinead*; Arm. *boned.*]

1. A covering for the head, in common use before the introduction of hats. The word, as now used, signifies a cover for the head, worn by females, close at the sides, and projecting over the forehead.

2. In *fortification*, a small work with two faces, having only a parapet, with two rows of palisades about 10 or 12 feet distant. Generally it is raised above the salient angle of the counterscarp, and communicates with the covered way. *Encyc.*

Bonnet à prêtre, or priest's bonnet, is an outwork, having at the head three salient angles and two inwards. *Johnson.*

3. In *sea language*, an addition to a sail, or an additional part laced to the foot of a sail, in small vessels, and in moderate winds. *Mar. Dict.*

BON'NET-PEPPER, *n.* A species of Capsicum, or guinea pepper. *Fam. of Plants.*

BON'NIBEL, *n.* [Fr. *bonne*, and *belle.*] A handsome girl. *Spenser.*

BON'NILASS, *n.* [*bonny* and *lass.*] A beautiful girl. *Spenser.*

BON'NILY, *adv.* [See *Bonny.*] Gayly; handsomely; plumply.

BON'NINESS, *n.* Gayety; handsomeness; plumpness. [*Little used.*]

BON'NY, *a.* [Fr. *bon, bonne*, good; L. *bonus.* See *Boon.*]

1. Handsome; beautiful.

Till *bonny* Susan sped across the plain. *Gay.*

2. Gay; merry; frolicksome; cheerful; blithe.

Blithe and *bonny.* *Shak.*

3. In *familiar language*, plump, as plump and healthful persons are most inclined to mirth.

[*This word is much used in Scotland.*]

BON'NY, *n.* Among *miners*, a bed of ore, differing from a squat in being round, whereas a squat is flat; or a distinct bed of ore, that communicates with no vein. *Bailey. Encyc.*

BON'NY-€LABBER, *n.* [Qu. *bonny*, or Ir. *baine*, milk, and *clabber*; Ar. لبا biestings; G. *lab*, D. *leb*, rennet.]

A word used in Ireland for sour buttermilk. *Johnson.*

It is used, in America, for any milk that is *turned* or become thick in the process of souring, and applied only to that part which is thick.

BON'TEN, *n.* A narrow woolen stuff.

BONUM MAGNUM, [L.] A species of plum. *Johnson.*

BO'NY, *a.* [from *bone.*] Consisting of bones; full of bones; pertaining to bones.

2. Having large or prominent bones; stout; strong.

BON'ZE, *n.* *bon'zy.* An Indian priest; a name used in China, Tunkin and the neighboring countries. In China, the Bonzes are the priests of the Fohists, or sect of Fohi. They are distinguished from the laity by their dress. In Japan, they are gentlemen of family. In Tunkin, every pagoda has at least two bonzes belonging to it, and some have thirty or forty. In China, the number of bonzes is estimated at fifty thousand, and they are represented as idle dissolute men. *Encyc.*

BOO'BY, *n.* [Sp. *bobo*, a dunce or ideot, a ruff for the neck, a buffoon, the bird *bobo.*]

1. A dunce; a stupid fellow; a lubber; one void of wisdom, or intellect. *Prior.*

2. A fowl of the pelican genus, of a brown and white color, much varied in different individuals. This fowl is found among the Bahama isles, feeds upon fish and lays its eggs on the bare rocks. It has a joint in the upper mandible, by which it can raise it without opening the mouth. *Encyc.*

BOOK, *n.* [Sax. *boc*, a book and the beech-tree; Goth. *boka*; Icelandic *book*; D. *boek*, a book, and the mast of beech; *beuke*, a beech tree; G. *buch*, a book, and *buche*, a beech; Dan. *bog*; Sw. *bok*; Russ. *buk*; Gypsey, *buchos*. Like the Latin liber, *book* signifies primarily bark and *beech*, the tree being probably named from its bark.]

A general name of every literary composition which is printed; but appropriately, a printed composition bound; a volume. The name is given also to any number of written sheets when bound or sewed together, and to a volume of blank paper, intended for any species of writing, as for memorandums, for accounts, or receipts.

2. A particular part of a literary composition; a division of a subject in the same volume.

3. A volume or collection of sheets in which accounts are kept; a register of debts and credits, receipts and expenditures, &c.

In books, in kind remembrance; in favor.

I was so much *in his books*, that at his decease he left me his lamp. *Addison.*

Without book, by memory; without reading; without notes; as, a sermon was delivered *without book.* This phrase is used also in the sense of *without authority*; as, a man asserts *without book.*

BOOK, *v. t.* To enter, write or register in a book.

BOOK-ACCOUNT', *n.* [*book* and *account.*] An account or register of debt or credit in a book.

BOOK'BINDER, *n.* [*book* and *bind.*] One whose occupation is to bind books.

BOOK'BINDING, *n.* The art or practice of binding books; or of sewing the sheets, and covering them with leather or other material.

BOOK'ED, *pp.* Written in a book; registered.

BOOK'FUL, *a.* [*book* and *full.*] Full of notions gleaned from books; crowded with undigested learning. *Pope.*

BOOK'ING, *ppr.* Registering in a book.

BOOK'ISH, *a.* Given to reading; fond of study; more acquainted with books than with men. *Shak.*

BOOK'ISHLY, *adv.* In the way of being addicted to books or much reading. *Thurlow.*

BOOK'ISHNESS, *n.* Addictedness to books; fondness for study. *Whitlock.*

BOOK'-KEEPER, *n.* [*book* and *keep.*] One who keeps accounts, or the accounts of another; the officer who has the charge of keeping the books and accounts in a public office.

BOOK'-KEEPING, *n.* [*book* and *keep.*] The art of recording mercantile transactions in a regular and systematic manner; the art of keeping accounts in such a manner, that a man may know the true state of his business and property, or of his debts and credits, by an inspection of his books. The books for this purpose are, 1. a *Waste Book*, or *blotter*, in which are registered all accounts or transactions in the order in which they take place; 2. the *Journal*, which contains the accounts transferred from the waste book, in the same order, but expressed in a technical style; 3. the *Leger*, in which articles of the same kind are collected together, from the journal, and arranged under proper titles.

In addition to these, several others are used; as *cash-book*; *book of charges of merchandize*; *book of house-expenses*; *invoice-book*; *sales-book*; *bill-book*; *receipt-book*; *letter-book*; *pocket-book*; the use of which may be understood from the names. *Encyc.*

BOOK'LAND, } *n.* [*book* and *land.*] In *old*
BOCK'LAND, } *English laws*, charter land, held by deed under certain rents and free-services, which differed nothing from free socage lands. This species of tenure has given rise to the modern freeholds. *Blackstone.*

BOOK'LEARNED, *a.* [*book* and *learn.*] Versed in books; acquainted with books and literature; a term sometimes implying *an ignorance of men*, or of the common concerns of life. *Dryden.*

BOOK'LEARNING, *n.* Learning acquired by reading; acquaintance with books and literature; sometimes implying want of practical knowledge. *Sidney.*

BOOK'LESS, *a.* [*book* and *less.*] Without books; unlearned. *Shenstone.*

BOOK'MAKING, *n.* The practice of writing and publishing books.

BOOK'MAN, *n.* [*book* and *man.*] A man whose profession is the study of books. *Shak.*

BOOK'MATE, *n.* [*book* and *mate.*] A school-fellow. *Shak.*

BOOK'OATH, *n.* The oath made on the book, or Bible. *Shak.*

BOOK'SELLER, *n.* [*book* and *sell.*] One whose occupation is to sell books.

BOOK'WORM, *n.* [*book* and *worm.*] A worm or mite that eats holes in books.

2. A student closely attached to books, or addicted to study; also, a reader without judgment. *Pope.*

BOO'LEY, *n.* In *Ireland*, one who has no settled habitation, but wanders from place to place, with his flocks and herds, living on their milk, like the Tartars. *Spenser.*

BOOM, *n.* [D. *boom*, a tree, a pole, a *beam*, a bar, a rafter; Goth. *bagms*; Ger. *baum*; Eng. *beam*; D. *boomen*, to push forward with a pole; Dan. *bom*, a rail or bar.]

A long pole or spar, run out from various parts of a ship, or other vessel, for the purpose of extending the bottom of particular sails; as the *jib-boom*, *studding-sail boom*, *main-boom*, *square-sail boom*, &c. *Mar. Dict.*

2. A strong iron chain, fastened to spars, and extended across a river, or the mouth of a harbor, to prevent an enemy's ships from passing.

3. A pole set up as a mark to direct seamen how to keep the channel, in shallow water.

BOOM, *v. i.* [Sax. *byma*, *byme*, a trumpet; *bymian*, to blow or sound a trumpet; D. *bomme*, a drum; *bommen*, to drum; W. *bwmp*, a hollow sound. We see the senses of *sounding*, *uttering the voice*, *swelling* and *rushing forward*, are connected.]

1. In *marine language*, to rush with violence, as a ship under a press of sail.

2. To swell; to roll and roar, as waves.

The hoarse waves *booming* to the ocean shore. *Hillhouse.*

3. To cry as the bittern. *Goldsmith.*

Tho Dutch use *bom* for the sound of an empty barrel, and *bommen* is to drum.

BOON, *n.* [L. *bonus*; Fr. *bon*; Norm. *boon*; It. *buono*; Sp. *bueno*; Port. *bom*, good.]

1. A gift; a grant; a benefaction; a present; a favor granted. *Addison.*

2. [Dan. *bön*, Sw. *bon*, a petition.] A prayer, or petition. *Ash.*

BOON, *a.* [Fr. *bon*; L. *bonus.*] Gay; merry; kind; bountiful; as a *boon* companion. *Milton.*

BO'OPS, *n.* The pike-headed whale, with a double pipe in its snout, and a hard horny ridge on its back; so named from its sharp pointed nose. *Encyc.*

BOOR, *n.* [Sax. *gebur*, a countryman or farmer; D. *boer*, a rustic, or farmer; G. *bauer*, a countryman and a builder, from *bauen*, to build, to cultivate; Sax. *byan*, or *bugian*, and *gebugian*; D. *bouwen*; Dan. *bygger*; Sw. *byggia*, to build. Boor is a contracted word.]

A countryman; a peasant; a rustic; a plowman; a clown; hence, one who is rude in manners, and illiterate. *Dryden.*

BOOR'ISH, *a.* Clownish; rustic; awkward in manners; illiterate. *Shak.*

BOOR'ISHLY, *adv.* In a clownish manner.

BOOR'ISHNESS, *n.* Clownishness; rusticity, coarseness of manners.

BOOSE, *n.* [Sax. *bosig*, *bosg*; Heb. Ch. אבוס, a stall or crib; Ar. أبس abasa, to shut up or imprison.]

A stall or inclosure for an ox, cow or other cattle. [*Not used* or *local.*]

BOOSE, } *v. i.* *booz.* [W. *bozi*, to immerse.]
BOUSE, }

To drink hard; to guzzle. [*Vulgar.*]

BOO'SY, *a.* *boo'zy.* A little intoxicated; merry with liquor. [*Vulgar.*]

BOOST, *v. t.* To lift or raise by pushing; to push up. [*A common vulgar word in N. England.*]

BOOT, *v. t.* [Sax. *bot*, *bote*, reparation, satisfaction, a making good, amends; Goth. *botyan*, to profit or help; Sw. *bōt*, a fine; D. *boete*, fine, penalty, repentance; *boeten*, to amend, or repair; G. *busse*, boot, fine, penance; *büssen*, to amend; Dan. *bödder*, to repair, or requite; *böder*, to expiate, or make atonement; W. *buz*, profit; *buziaw*, to profit. We observe this word is from the root of *better*, denoting more, or advance; Eng. *but*. The primary sense of the root is to advance, or carry forward.]

1. To profit; to advantage.

It shall not *boot* them. *Hooker.*

But more generally followed by *it*, what *boots it?* Indeed it is seldom used, except in the latter phrase.

2. To enrich; to benefit.

I will *boot* thee. *Obs.* *Shak.*

BOOT, *n.* Profit; gain; advantage; that which is given to make the exchange equal, or to supply the deficiency of value in one of the things exchanged. *Shak.*

2. *To boot*, in addition to; over and above; besides; a compensation for the difference of value between things bartered; as, I will give my house for yours, with one hundred dollars *to boot*. [Sax. *to bote*. The phrase is pure Saxon.]

3. Spoil; plunder. [See *Booty.*] *Shak.*

BOOT, *n.* [Fr. *botte*, a boot, a bunch; Ir. *butais*; W. *botasen*, *botas*; Sp. *bota*, a boot, a *butt*, or cask, a leather bag to carry liquors; Port. *bota*; It. *botte*, boots, a cask.]

1. A covering for the leg, made of leather, and united with a shoe. This garment was originally intended for horsemen, but is now generally worn by gentlemen on foot. The different sorts are *fishing-boots*, worn in water; *hunting-boots*, a thinner kind for sportsmen; *jack-boots*, a strong kind for horsemen; and *half-boots.*

2. A kind of rack for the leg, formerly used to torture criminals. This was made of boards bound fast to the legs by cords; or a boot or buskin, made wet and drawn upon the legs and then dried by the fire, so as to contract and squeeze the legs. *Encyc.*

3. A box covered with leather in the fore part of a coach. Also, an apron or leathern cover for a gig or chair, to defend persons from rain and mud. *This latter application is local and improper.*

BOOT, *v. t.* To put on boots.

BOOT'CATCHER, *n.* [*boot* and *catch.*] The person at an inn whose business is to pull off boots. *Obs.* *Swift.*

BOOT'ED, *pp.* Having boots on. *Dryden.*

BOOTEE', *n.* A word sometimes used for a half or short boot.

BOO'TES, *n.* A northern constellation, consisting, according to Flamstead's catalogue, of fifty-four stars.

BOOTH, *n.* [W. *bwth*; Ir. *boith* or *both*; G. *bude*; Russ. *budka*; Ch. בית, bith, a house, and to lodge for a night; also in the Ar. Sam. Syr. Eth. and Heb. beth, a house or booth, a nest for birds. Probably the sense is, a dwelling, from lodging, abiding.]

A house or shed built of boards, boughs of trees, or other slight materials, for a temporary residence. *Bible.* *Camden.*

BOOT'-HOSE, *n.* [*boot* and *hose.*] Stocking-hose or spatterdashes, in lieu of boots. *Shak.*

BOOT'LEG, *n.* [*boot* and *leg.*] Leather cut out for the leg of a boot. *Ash.*

BOOT'LESS, *a.* [from *boot.*] Unavailing; unprofitable; useless; without advantage or success. *Shak.*

BOOT'LESSLY, *adv.* Without use or profit.

BOOT'-TOPPING, *n.* [*boot* and *top.*] The operation of cleansing a ship's bottom, near the surface of the water, by scraping off the grass, slime, shells, &c., and daubing it with a mixture of tallow, sulphur and rosin. *Mar. Dict.*

BOOT'-TREE, or **BOOT'-LAST**, *n.* An instrument to stretch and widen the leg of a boot, consisting of two pieces, shaped like a leg, between which, when put into the boot, a wedge is driven. *Encyc.*

BOOT'Y, *n.* [Sw. *byte*; Dan. *bytte*; D. *buit*; G. *beute*; It. *bottino*; Sp. *botin*; Fr. *butin*; D. *buiten*, to rove. See *But.*]

1. Spoil taken from an enemy in war; plunder; pillage. *Milton.*

2. That which is seized by violence and robbery. *Shak.*

To play booty is to play dishonestly with an intent to lose. *Johnson.*

BOPEE'P, *n.* [*bo*, an exclamation, and *peep.*] The act of looking out or from behind something and drawing back, as children in play, for the purpose of frightening each other. *Shak.* *Dryden.*

BO'RABLE, *a.* [See *Bore.*] That may be bored. [*Little used.*]

BORACH'IO, *n.* [Sp. *borracho*, drunk.] A drunkard. *Congreve.*

2. A bottle or cask. [*Not used.*] *Dryden.*

BORAC'IC, *a.* [See *Borax.*] Pertaining to or produced from borax.

Boracic acid, a compound of a peculiar base, *boron*, with oxygen. It is generally obtained from borax, by adding sulphuric acid. It it also found native, in certain mineral springs in Italy. *Webster.*

BO'RACITE, *n.* Borate of magnesia; magnesian earth combined with boracic acid. It is generally of a cubic form, and remarkable for its electrical properties when heated. *Cleaveland.*

BO'RACITED, *a.* Combined with boracic acid.

BO'RACOUS ACID, the base of boracic acid, partially saturated with oxygen. *Lavoisier.*

BORAGE, *n. bur'rage.* A plant of the genus *Borago.*

BO'RATE, *n.* A salt formed by a combination of boracic acid with any base saturated. *Fourcroy.*

BO'RAX, *n.* [Pers. بوره; Ar. بورق borakon, from برق baraka, to shine; Russ. *bura.*]

Sub-borate of soda; a salt formed by the combination of boracic acid with the marine alkali or soda. It is brought from the East Indies, where it is said to be found at the bottom or on the margin of certain lakes, particularly in Thibet. It is said to be artificially prepared in Persia, like niter. It comes in three states. 1. Crude borax, tinkal, or chrysocolla, from Persia, in greenish masses of a greasy feel, or in opake crystals. 2. Borax of China, somewhat purer, in small plates or masses, irregularly crystalized, and of a dirty white. 3. Dutch or purified borax, in portions of transparent crystals, which is the kind generally used. It is an excellent flux in docimastic operations, a styptic in medicine, and useful in sodering metals. *Encyc.* *Cleaveland.* *Hooper.*

BŌRDAGE, *n.* [See *Bordlands.*]

BORD'EL, / **BORDEL'LO**, *n.* [Fr. *bordel*, a brothel; D. *bordeel*; Ger. *bordell*; It. *bordello*; Sp. *burdel*; Arm. *bordell*; from *bord*, a house. This is the Eng. *brothel.*]

A brothel; a bawdy-house; a house devoted to prostitution. *B. Jonson.*

BORD'ELLER, *n.* The keeper of a brothel. *Gower.*

BORD'ER, *n.* [Fr. *bord*; Arm. *id*; Sp. *bordo*; Port. *borda*; It. *bordo*. See *Board.*]

The outer edge of any thing; the extreme part or surrounding line; the confine or exterior limit of a country, or of any region or tract of land; the exterior part or edge of a garment, or of the corol of plants; the rim or brim of a vessel, but not often applied to vessels; the exterior part of a garden, and hence a bank raised at the side of a garden, for the cultivation of flowers, and a row of plants; in short, the outer part or edge of things too numerous to be specified.

BORD'ER, *v. i.* To confine; to touch at the edge, side or end; to be contiguous or adjacent; with *on* or *upon*; as, Connecticut on the north *borders on* or *upon* Massachusetts.

2. To approach near to.

Wit, which *borders upon* profaneness, deserves to be branded as folly. *Tillotson.*

BORD'ER, *v. t.* To make a border; to adorn with a border of ornaments; as, to *border* a garment or a garden.

2. To reach to; to touch at the edge or end; to confine upon; to be contiguous to.

Sheba and Raamah *border* the Persian gulf. *Raleigh.*

3. To confine within bounds; to limit. [*Not used.*] *Shak.*

BORD'ERED, *pp.* Adorned or furnished with a border.

BORD'ERER, *n.* One who dwells on a border, or at the extreme part or confines of a country, region or tract of land; one who dwells near to a place. *Bacon.*

BORD'ERING, *ppr.* Lying adjacent to; forming a border.

BŌRD-HALFPENNY, *n.* Money paid for setting up boards or a stall in market. *Burn.*

BŌRD-LAND, *n.* [*bord* and *land.* See *Board.*]

In *old law*, the demain land which a lord kept in his hands for the maintenance of his *bord*, board, or table. *Spelman.*

BŌRD-LODE, / **BOARD-LŌAD**, *n.* [*bord* and *load.*] The service required of a tenant to carry timber from the woods to the lord's house; also, the quantity of provision paid by a bord-man for bord-land. *Bailey.*

BŌRD-MAN, *n.* [*bord* and *man.*] A tenant of bord-land, who supplied his lord with provisions. *Encyc.*

BORD'-RAGING, *n.* An incursion upon the borders of a country. *Obs.* *Spenser.*

BŌRD'-SERVICE, *n.* [*board* and *service.*] The tenure by which bord-land was held, which was the payment of a certain quantity of provisions to the lord. In lieu of this, the tenant now pays six pence an acre. *Encyc.*

BORD'URE, *n.* In *heraldry*, a tract or compass of metal, color or fur, within the escutcheon, and around it. *Bailey.*

BORE, *v. t.* [Sax. *borian*; Sw. *bora*; D. *booren*; Ger. *bohren*; Dan. *borer*, to bore; D. *boor*; Ger. *bohrer*; Dan. *borre*, a borer; L. *foro* and *perforo*, to bore, to *perforate*; Russ. *burav*, a borer; Gr. *πειρω*, to pierce or transfix; also, to pass over, in which sense it coincides with *ferry*. The Celtic *ber*, *bear*, a spit, L. *veru*, from thrusting or piercing, coincide in elements with this root. Pers. بيره a borer.]

1. To perforate or penetrate a solid body and make a round hole by turning an auger, gimlet, or other instrument. Hence, to make hollow; to form a round hole; as, to *bore* a cannon.
2. To eat out or make a hollow by gnawing or corroding, as a worm.
3. To penetrate or break through by turning or labor; as, to *bore* through a crowd. *Gay.*

BORE, *v. i.* To be pierced or penetrated by an instrument that turns; as, this timber does not *bore* well or is hard to *bore*.

2. To pierce or enter by boring; as, an auger *bores* well.
3. To push forward toward a certain point.

Boring to the west. *Dryden.*

4. With *horsemen*, a horse *bores*, when he carries his nose to the ground. *Dict.*
5. In *a transitive* or *intransitive sense*, to pierce the earth with scooping irons, which, when drawn out, bring with them samples of the different stratums, through which they pass. This is a method of discovering veins of ore and coal without opening a mine. *Encyc.*

BORE, *n.* The hole made by boring. Hence, the cavity or hollow of a gun, cannon, pistol or other fire-arm; the caliber; whether formed by boring or not.

2. Any instrument for making holes by boring or turning, as an auger, gimlet or wimble.

BORE, *n.* A tide, swelling above another tide. *Burke.*

A sudden influx of the tide into a river or narrow strait. *Cyc.*

BORE, *pret.* of *bear*. [See *Bear*.]

BO'RE-COLE, *n.* A species of Brassica or cabbage. *Fam. of Plants.*

BO'REAL, *a.* [L. *borealis*. See *Boreas*.] Northern; pertaining to the north or the north wind. *Pope.*

BO'REAS, *n.* [L. *boreas*; Gr. *βορεας*, the north wind; Russ. *boria*, boreas, and *buria*, a storm or tempest; *buran*, a tempest with snow. The Russ. gives the radical sense.]

The northern wind; a cold northerly wind. *Milton.*

BO'RED, *pp.* Perforated by an auger or other turning instrument; made hollow.

BOREE', *n.* [Fr.] A certain dance, or movement in common time, of four crotchets in a bar; always beginning in the last quaver or last crotchet of the measure. *Busby.*

BO'RER, *n.* One who bores; also an instrument to make holes with by turning.

2. Terebella, the piercer, a genus of sea worms, that pierce wood.

BORN, *pp.* of *bear*. *baurn.* Brought forth, as an animal. A very useful distinction is observed by good authors, who, in the sense of *produced* or brought forth, write this word *born*; but in the sense of *carried*, write it *bōrne*. This difference of orthography renders obvious the difference of pronunciation.

1. *To be born*, is to be produced or brought into life. "Man is *born* to trouble." A man *born* a prince or a beggar. It is followed by *of*, before the mother or ancestors.

Man that is *born of woman* is of few days and full of trouble. Job xiv.

2. *To be born*, or *born again*, is to be regenerated and renewed; to receive spiritual life. John iii.

BŌRNE, *pp.* of *bear*. Carried; conveyed; supported; defrayed.

BŌRNE, *n.* The more correct orthography of *bourn*, a limit or boundary. [See *Bourn*.]

BO'RON, *n.* The combustible base of boracic acid. *Ure.*

BOROUGH, *n.* *bur'ro.* [Goth. *bairgs*; Sax. *burg*, *burh*, *beorh*, *beorg*, *byrig*; Ir. *brog*; Fr. *bourg*; It. *borgo*; Sp. *burgo*; D. *burg* and *borg*; Dan. *borg*; Arm. *bourg*; G. *burg* and *berg*; Gr. *πυργος*; Ar. برج Sans. *bura*. This word, in Saxon, is interpreted a hill, heap, mountain, fortification, castle, tower, city, house and tomb. Hence *Perga*, in Pamphylia, *Bergen*, in Norway, *Burgos*, in Spain, and probably *Prague*, in Bohemia. In W. *bwr*, *bwrc*, signifies a wall, rampart, or work for defense, and *bwrdais* is a burgess. But the original sense probably is found in the verb, Sax. *beorgan*, D. and G. *bergen*, Russ. *beregu*, to keep, or save, that is, to make close or secure. Hence it coincides with *park*, and L. *parcus*, saving. See the next word. If the noun is the primary word, denoting hill, this is from throwing together, collecting; a sense allied to that of making fast or close.]

Originally, a fortified city or town; hence a hill, for hills were selected for places of defense. But in later times, the term *city* was substituted to denote an episcopal town, in which was the see of a bishop, and that of *borough* was retained for the rest. At present, the name is given appropriately to such towns and villages as send representatives or burgesses to Parliament. Some boroughs are incorporated, others are not. *Blackstone. Encyc.*

BOROUGH, *n.* *bur'ro.* [Sax. *borhoe*, a surety; *borgian*, to borrow; *borg*, interest; *borga*, a debtor, a surety; *borgwed*, a promise or bond for appearance, a pledge; *borg-bryce*, burg-break, violation of pledge; *borghand*, *borhhand*, a surety or bail; *beorgan*, to keep, guard or preserve; G. *borgen*, D. *id.*, to borrow. See the preceding word.]

In *Saxon times*, a main pledge, or association of men, who were sureties or free pledges to the king for the good behavior of each other, and if any offense was committed in their district, they were bound to have the offender forthcoming. The association of ten men was called a *tithing*, or *decenary*; the presiding man was called the *tithing man*, or *head-borough*; or in some places, *borsholder*, *borough's elder*. This society was called also *friburg*, free burg, frank pledge. Ten tithings formed a *hundred*, consisting of that number of sureties, and this denomination is still given to the districts, comprehended in the association. The term seems to have been used both for the society and for each surety. The word *main*, hand, which is attached to this society, or their mutual assurance, indicates that the agreement was ratified by shaking hands. *Spelman. Blackstone. Cowel.*

Some writers have suggested that the application of this word to towns sprung from these associations, and of course was posterior to them in time. See *Encyc.* Art. *Borough.* But the word was used for a town or castle in other nations, and in Asia, doubtless long before the origin of the *frank pledge*.

In Connecticut, this word, *borough*, is used for a town or a part of a town, or a village, incorporated with certain privileges, distinct from those of other towns and of cities; as the *Borough* of Bridgeport.

In Scotland, a borough is a body corporate, consisting of the inhabitants of a certain district, erected by the Sovereign, with a certain jurisdiction.

Boroughs are erected to be held of the sovereign, as is generally the case of royal boroughs; or of the superior of the lands included, as in the case of boroughs of regality and barony. Royal boroughs are generally erected for the advantage of trade. *Encyc.*

Borough English, is a customary descent of lands and tenements to the youngest son, instead of the eldest; or if the owner leaves no son, to the youngest brother. *Blackstone. Cowel.*

Borough-head, the same as *head-borough*, the chief of a borough. *Ash.*

BOROUGH-HŌLDER, *n.* A head-borough; a borsholder. *Ash.*

BOROUGH-MASTER, *n.* The mayor, governor or baliff of a borough. *Ash.*

BORRACH'IO, *n.* The caoutchouc, India rubber, or elastic gum. [See *Caoutchouc*.]

BOR'RELISTS, *n.* In *church history*, a sect of Christians in Holland, so called from Borrel, their founder, who reject the use of the sacraments, public prayer and all external worship. They lead a very austere life. *Encyc.*

BOR'RŌW, *v. t.* [Sax. *borgian*, to borrow; D. *borgen*, to borrow, lend or trust; Ger. *borgen*, the same; Dan. *borger*, to borrow; *borgen*, bail, surety, pledge, warranter, main-pernor; *borg*, trust, credit; Sw. *borgan*, a giving bail; *borg*, a fortress. The primary sense is, to make fast or secure.]

1. To take from another by request and consent, with a view to use the thing taken for a time, and return it, or if the thing taken is to be consumed or transferred in the use, then to return an equivalent in kind; as, to *borrow* a book, a sum of money, or a loaf of bread. It is opposed to *lend*.

2. To take from another, for one's own use; to copy or select from the writings of another author; as, to *borrow* a passage from a printed book; to *borrow* a title.

3. To take or adopt for one's own use, sentiments, principles, doctrines and the like; as, to *borrow* instruction.

4. To take for use something that belongs to another; to assume, copy or imitate; as, to *borrow* a shape; to *borrow* the manners of another, or his style of writing.

BOR'RŌW, *n.* A borrowing; the act of borrowing. [*Not used.*]

> But of your royal presence I'll adventure
> The *borrow* of a week. *Shak.*

BOR'ROWED, *pp.* Taken by consent of another, to be returned or its equivalent in kind; copied; assumed.

BOR'RŌWER, *n.* One who borrows; opposed to *lender*. [See the verb.]

2. One who takes what belongs to another to use as one's own.

BOR'RŌWING, *ppr.* Taking by consent to use and return, or to return its equivalent; taking what belongs to another to use as one's own; copying; assuming; imitating.

BOR'RŌWING, *n.* The act of borrowing. [*See the verb.*]

BORS'HŌLDER, *n.* [A contraction of *burh's ealdor*, borough's elder, the elder or chief of a borough.]

The head or chief of a tithing or *burg* of ten men; the head-borough. *Lambert. Spelman.*

BOS, *n.* [L.] In *zoology*, the technical name of a genus of quadrupeds. The characters are, the horns are hollow within and turned outward in the form of crescents; there are eight fore teeth in the under jaw, but none in the upper; there are no dog teeth. The species are, the *Taurus* or common ox, the *Urus*, aurochs or bison of Europe, the *Bison* or buffalo of North America, the *Bubalus* or proper buffalo of the Eastern continent, the *Caffer* or Cape buffalo, the *Grunniens* or yak of Thibet, and the *Moschatus* or musk ox of Arctic America. *Encyc. Cuvier.*

BOSC'AĠE, *n.* [Fr. *boscage*, now *bocage*, a grove; It. *bosco*; Dan. *busk*; Ger. *busch*, a wood, or properly a thicket or underwood; Eng. *bush*.]

1. Wood; under-wood; perhaps, sometimes, lands covered with underwood; also, a thicket.

2. In *old laws*, food or sustenance for cattle, which is yielded by bushes and trees. *Cowel.*

3. With *painters*, a landscape, representing thickets of wood. *Encyc.*

BOS'CHAS, *n.* The common wild duck, or mallard, belonging to the genus Anas. *Encyc.*

BOSH, *n.* Outline; figure. *Todd.*

BOSK'ET, **BOS'QUET**, **BUSK'ET**, *n.* [It. *boschetto*, a little wood, from *bosco*. See *Boscage*.]

In *gardening*, a grove; a compartment formed by branches of trees, regularly or irregularly disposed, according to fancy. *Encyc.*

BOSK'Y, *a.* [See *Boscage*.] Woody; covered with thickets. *Milton.*

BŌ'SOM, *n.* *s* as *z*. [Sax. *bosm*, *bosum*; D. *boezem*; G. *busen*. Qu. Ch. ביזה or בוזא, the breast, uber, mamma.]

1. The breast of a human being and the parts adjacent.

2. The folds or covering of clothes about the breast.

> Put thy hand in thy *bosom*. Ex. iv.

3. Embrace, as with the arms; inclosure; compass; often implying friendship or affection; as, to live in the *bosom* of a church.

4. The breast, as inclosing the heart; or the interior of the breast, considered as the seat of the passions.

> Anger resteth in the *bosom* of fools. Eccles. vii.

> Their soul was poured into their mother's *bosom*. Lam. ii.

5. The breast, or its interior, considered as a close place, the receptacle of secrets.

> If I covered my transgressions as Adam, by hiding my iniquity in my *bosom*. Job xxxi.

6. Any inclosed place; the interior; as the *bosom* of the earth or of the deep.

7. The tender affections; kindness; favor; as the son of his *bosom*; the wife of thy *bosom*.

> He shall carry the lambs in his *bosom*. Is. xl.

8. The arms, or embrace of the arms. Ps. cxxix.

9. Inclination; desire. [*Not used.*] *Shak.*

Bosom, in composition, implies intimacy, affection and confidence; as a *bosom-friend*, an intimate or confidential friend; *bosom-lover*, *bosom-interest*, *bosom-secret*, &c. In such phrases, *bosom* may be considered as an attribute equivalent to intimate, confidential, dear.

BŌ'SOM, *v. t.* To inclose in the bosom; to keep with care.

> *Bosom* up my counsel. *Shak.*

2. To conceal; to hide from view.

> To happy convents *bosom'd* deep in vines. *Pope.*

BŌ'SOMED, *pp.* Inclosed in the breast; concealed.

BO'SON, *n.* A boatswain; a popular, but corrupt pronunciation.

> The merry *boson*. *Dryden.*

BOSPO'RIAN, *a.* [from *Bosporus*.] Pertaining to a bosporus, a strait or narrow sea between two seas, or a sea and a lake.

> The Alans forced the *Bosporian* kings to pay them tribute, and exterminated the Taurians. *Tooke.*

BOS'PORUS, *n.* [Gr. βους, an ox, and πορος, a passage.]

A narrow sea or a strait, between two seas or between a sea and a lake, so called, it is supposed, as being an ox-passage, a strait over which an ox may swim. So our northern ancestors called a strait, a *sound*, that is, a *swim*. The term Bosporus has been particularly applied to the strait between the Propontis and the Euxine, called the *Thracian Bosporus*; and to the strait of Caffa, called the *Cimmerian Bosporus*, which connects the Palus Mæotis or sea of Azof, with the Euxine. *D'Anville.*

BOSS, *n.* [Fr. *bosse*; Arm. *boçz*. In D. *bos* is a bunch, a bundle, a truss, a tuft, a bush, a sheaf, whence *bosch*, G. *busch*, a bush, or thicket. In W. *bôth* is the boss of a buckler, the nave of a wheel, and a *bottle*, and hence W. *bothel*, a rotundity, a bottle or any round vessel, a wheal or blister. A *boss* is a protuberance, either from shooting, projecting, or from collecting and forming a mass.]

1. A stud or knob; a protuberant ornament, of silver, ivory, or other material, used on bridles, harness, &c.

2. A protuberant part; a prominence; as the *boss* of a buckler.

3. A round or swelling body of any kind; as a *boss* of wood. *Moxon.*

4. A water-conduit, in form of a *tun-bellied* figure. *Ash. Bailey.*

BOSS'AĠE, *n.* [from *boss*; Fr. *bossage*.]

1. A stone in a building which has a projecture, and is laid rough, to be afterwards carved into moldings, capitals, coats of arms, &c. *Encyc.*

2. Rustic work, consisting of stones which advance beyond the naked or level of the building, by reason of indentures or channels left in the joinings; chiefly in the corners of edifices, and called *rustic quoins*. The cavities are sometimes round, sometimes beveled or in a diamond form, sometimes inclosed with a cavetto, and sometimes with a listel. *Encyc.*

BOSS'ED, *pp.* Studded; ornamented with bosses. *Shak.*

BOSS'IVE, *a.* Crooked; deformed. *Osborne.*

BOSS'Y, *a.* Containing a boss; ornamented with bosses.

> His head reclining on his *bossy* shield. *Pope.*

BOS'TRYCHITE, *n.* [Gr. βοςρυχος.] A gem in the form of a lock of hair. *Ash.*

BOS'VEL, *n.* A plant, a species of crow-foot. *Johnson.*

BOT. [See *Bots*.]

BOTAN'IC, **BOTAN'ICAL**, *a.* [See *Botany*.] Pertaining to botany; relating to plants in general; also, containing plants, as a *botanic* garden.

BOTAN'ICALLY, *adv.* According to the system of botany.

BOT'ANIST, *n.* One skilled in botany; one versed in the knowledge of plants or vegetables, their structure, and generic and specific differences.

> The *botanist* is he who can affix similar names to similar vegetables, and different names to different ones, so as to be intelligible to every one. *Linne.*

BOT'ANIZE, *v. i.* To seek for plants; to investigate the vegetable kingdom; to study plants.

> He could not obtain permission to *botanize* upon mount Sabber. *Niebuhr, Trans.*

BOTANOL'OGY, *n.* [Gr. βοτανη, a plant, and λογος, discourse.] A discourse upon plants. *Dict.*

BOTANOM'ANCY, *n.* [βοτανη, a plant, and μαντεια, divination.]

An ancient species of divination by means of plants, especially sage and fig leaves. Persons wrote their names and questions on leaves, which they exposed to the wind, and as many of the letters as remained in their places were taken up, and being joined together, contained an answer to the question. *Encyc.*

BOT'ANY, *n.* [Gr. βοτανη, a plant; Pers. بوته a shrub; probably allied to *bud*, to shoot.]

That branch of natural history which treats of vegetables; a science which treats of the different plants, and of the distinguishing marks by which each individual species may be known from every other. *Martyn. Encyc.*

Or, botany is the science of the structure, functions, properties, habits and arrangement of plants, and of the technical characters by which they are distinguished. *Cyc.*

BOTAR'GO, *n.* [Sp.] A relishing sort of food, made of the roes of the mullet, much used on the coast of the Mediterranean, as an incentive to drink. *Johnson. Chambers.*

BOTCH, *n.* [It. *bozza*, [*botza*,] a swelling, or rather *pezzo*, a piece; the latter is the Eng. *patch*.]

1. A swelling on the skin; a large ulcerous affection.

   Botches and blains must all his flesh imboss. *Milton.*

2. A patch, or the part of a garment patched or mended in a clumsy manner; ill-finished work in mending.

3. That which resembles a botch; a part added clumsily; adventitious or ill-applied words.

   If those words are not notorious *botches*, I am deceived. *Dryden.*

BOTCH, *v. t.* To mend or patch with a needle or awl, in a clumsy manner, as a garment; to mend or repair awkwardly, as a system of government. *Hudibras.*

2. To put together unsuitably, or unskilfully; to make use of unsuitable pieces.

   For treason *botched* in rhyme will be thy bane. *Dryden.*

3. To mark with botches.

   Young Hylas *botched* with stains. *Garth.*

BOTCH'ED, *pp.* Patched clumsily; mended unskilfully; marked with botches.

BOTCH'ER, *n.* A clumsy workman at mending; a mender of old clothes, whether a tailor or cobler. *Elyot.*

BOTCH'Y, *a.* Marked with botches; full of botches.

BOTE, *n.* [The old orthography of *boot*, but retained in law, in composition. See *Boot.*]

1. In *law*, compensation; amends; satisfaction; as *manbote*, a compensation for a man slain. Also, payment of any kind.

2. A privilege or allowance of necessaries, used in composition as equivalent to the French estovers, supplies, necessaries; as *house-bote*, a sufficiency of wood to repair a house or for fuel, sometimes called *fire-bote*; so *plow-bote*, *cart-bote*, wood for making or repairing instruments of husbandry; *hay-bote* or *hedge-bote*, wood for hedges or fences, &c. These were privileges enjoyed by tenants under the feudal system. *Blackstone.*

BO'TELESS, *a.* In vain. [See *Bootless.*]

BOTET'TO, *n.* A small thick fish of Mexico, about eight inches long, with a flat belly, and convex back. When taken out of the water it swells, and if kicked, will burst. Its liver is deadly poison. *Clavigero.*

BŌTH, *a.* [Sax. *butu*, *butwu*, or *batwa*, (qu. Goth. *bayoths*;) Ir. *beit*; Sw. *båda*; Dan. *baade*; D. and Ger. *beide*; in Ancient African, בת bet, beth, two. *Buxt.* 1866.]

Two, considered as distinct from others or by themselves; the one and the other; Fr. *tous les deux*; *l' un et l' autre*; as, here are two books, take them *both.*

This word is often placed before the nouns with which it is connected.

He understands how to manage *both* public and private concerns. *Guth. Quintilian*, p. 4.

It is often used as a substitute for nouns.

And Abraham took sheep and oxen, and gave them to Abimelech: and *both* of them made a covenant. Gen. xxi.

Both often represents two members of a sentence.

He will not bear *the loss of his rank*, because he can bear *the loss of his estate*; but he will bear *both*, because he is prepared for *both*. *Bolingbroke on Exile.*

Both often pertains to adjectives or attributes, and in this case generally precedes them in construction; as, he endeavored to render commerce *both* disadvantageous and infamous. *Mickle's Lusiad.*

BOTH'ER, the vulgar pronunciation of *pother*. [See *Pother.*]

BOTH'NIC, **BOTH'NIAN**, *a.* Pertaining to Bothnia, a province of Sweden, and to a gulf of the Baltic sea, which is so called from the province, which it penetrates. Pinkerton uses *Bothnic*, as a noun for the gulf, and Barlow uses *Bothnian*, in the same manner.

Pink. Art. *Sweden. Columb.* 9. 564.

BOTO'TOE, *n.* A bird of the parrot kind, of a fine blue color, found in the Philippine isles. *Dict. of Nat. Hist.*

BO'TRYOID, **BOTRYOI'DAL**, *a.* [Gr. βοτρυς, a bunch of grapes, and ειδος, form; Fr. *botte*, a bunch or bundle; Arm. *bod*, *bot*, a grape.]

Having the form of a bunch of grapes; like grapes; as a mineral presenting an aggregation of small globes. *Kirwan. Phillips.*

BO'TRYOLITE, *n.* [Gr. βοτρυς, supra, and λιθος, stone.]

Literally, grape-stone. This mineral occurs in mammillary or botryoidal concretions, in a bed of magnetic iron in gneiss, near Arendal in Norway. Its colors are pearl-gray, grayish or reddish white, and pale rose-red, and form concentric stripes. *Cyc.*

Botryolite is a variety of siliceous borate of lime. It is found near the Passaic falls in New-Jersey. *Cleaveland.*

BOTS, *n.* generally used in the plural. [Qu. Pers. *pot*, teredo, a worm that eats wood.]

A species of small worms found in the intestines of horses. They are the *larvas* of a species of *Œstrus* or gad-fly, which deposits its eggs on the tips of the hairs, generally of the fore-legs and mane, whence they are taken into the mouth and swallowed. This word is also applied to the *larvas* of other species of Œstrus, found under the hides of oxen, in the nostrils of sheep, &c. *Cyc.*

BOT'TLE, *n.* [Fr. *bouteille*; Arm. *boutailh*; Ir. *boid*, *buideal*; W. *bôth*, a boss, a bottle, the nave of a wheel; *bot*, a round body; *botas*, from *bot*, a boot, a buskin; *botwm*, a button; and from *bôth*, the W. has also *bothell*, a bottle, a round vessel, a wheal or blister; Sp. *botella*, a bottle, and *botilla*, a small wine bag, from *bota*, a leather bag for wine, a *butt* or cask, a *boot*; It. *bottiglia*, a bottle; *botte*, a butt, a cask, and boots; Russ. *butilka*, a bottle. In G. *beutel*, a bag, a purse, seems to be the Sp. *botilla*. In Fr. *botte* is a boot, a bunch or bundle, *botte de foin*, a bottle of hay. It would seem that *bottle* is primarily a bag, and from the sense of swelling, bulging, or collecting into a bunch; if so, the word was originally applied to the bags of skins used as bottles in Asia. Yet the primary sense is not easily ascertained. The Arabic has بطّ a duck, Sp. *pato*, and urceus coriaceus in quo liquidiora circumferunt viatores. *Cast.*]

1. A hollow vessel of glass, wood, leather or other material, with a narrow mouth, for holding and carrying liquors. The oriental nations use skins or leather for the conveyance of liquors; and of this kind are the bottles mentioned in scripture. "Put new wine into new *bottles*." In Europe and America, glass is used for liquors of all kinds; and farmers use small cags or hollow vessels of wood. The small kinds of glass bottles are called vials or phials.

2. The contents of a bottle; as much as a bottle contains; but from the size of bottles used for wine, porter and cyder, a bottle is nearly a quart; as a *bottle* of wine or of porter.

3. A quantity of hay in a bundle; a bundle of hay.

BOT'TLE, *v. t.* To put into bottles; as, to *bottle* wine or porter. This includes the stopping of the bottles with corks.

BOT'TLE-ALE, *n.* Bottled ale. *Shak.*

BOT'TLE-COMPANION, **BOT'TLE-FRIEND**, *n.* A friend or companion in drinking.

BOT'TLED, *pp.* Put into bottles; inclosed in bottles.

2. Having a protuberant belly. *Shak.*

BOT'TLE-FLOWER, *n.* A plant, the cyanus, or blue bottle, a species of *Centaurea*. *Fam. of Plants.*

BOT'TLE-SCREW, *n.* A screw to draw corks out of bottles.

BOT'TLING, *ppr.* Putting into bottles.

BOT'TLING, *n.* The act of putting into bottles and corking.

BOT'TOM, *n.* [Sax. *botm*; Sw. *botn*; D. *bodem*; G. *boden*. It seems to be allied to Gr. βαθος, and to the Russ. *pad*, a valley, *padayu*, to fall. The sense is from throwing down, setting, laying or beating down; a dialect perhaps of basis. Class Bd.]

1. The lowest part of any thing; as the *bottom* of a well, vat or ship; the *bottom* of a hill.

2. The ground under any body of water; as the *bottom* of the sea, of a river or lake.

3. The foundation or ground work of any thing, as of an edifice, or of any system or moral subject; the base, or that which supports any superstructure.

4. A low ground; a dale; a valley; *applied in the U. States to the flat lands adjoining rivers, &c. It is so used in some parts of England.* *Mitford.*

5. The deepest part; that which is most remote from the view; as, let us examine this subject to the *bottom.*

6. Bound; limit.

   There is no *bottom* in my voluptuousness. *Shak.*

7. The utmost extent or depth of cavity, or of intellect, whether deep or shallow.

   I do see the *bottom* of justice Shallow. *Shak.*

8. The foundation, considered as the cause,

spring or origin; the first moving cause; as, a foreign prince is at the *bottom* of the confederacy.

9. A ship or vessel. Goods imported in foreign *bottoms* pay a higher duty, than those imported in our own. Hence, a state of hazard, chance or risk; but in this sense it is used chiefly or solely in the singular. We say, venture not too much in *one bottom*; that is, do not hazard too much at a single risk.

10. A ball of thread. [W. *botwm*, a button; Corn. *id.* See *Bottle.*]

11. The *bottom of a lane or alley*, is the lowest end. This phrase supposes a declivity; but it is often used for the most remote part, when there is very little declivity.

12. The *bottom of beer*, or other liquor, is the grounds or dregs.

13. In *the language of jockeys*, stamina, native strength; as a horse of good *bottom*.

BOT'TOM, *v. t.* To found or build upon; to fix upon as a support; followed by *on*; as, sound reasoning is *bottomed on* just premises.

2. To furnish with a seat or bottom; as, to *bottom* a chair.

3. To wind round something, as in making a ball of thread. *Shak.*

BOT'TOM, *v. i.* To rest upon, as its ultimate support.

Find on what foundation a proposition *bottoms.* *Locke.*

BOT'TOMED, *pp.* Furnished with a bottom; having a bottom.

This word is often used in composition, as a *flat-bottomed boat*, in which case the compound becomes an adjective.

BOT'TOMING, *ppr.* Founding; building upon; furnishing with a bottom.

BOT'TOMLESS, *a.* Without a bottom; applied to water, caverns &c., it signifies fathomless, whose bottom cannot be found by sounding; as a *bottomless* abyss or ocean.

BOT'TOMRY, *n.* [from *bottom.*] The act of borrowing money, and pledging the keel or *bottom* of the ship, that is, the ship itself, as security for the repayment of the money. The contract of bottomry is in the nature of a mortgage; the owner of a ship borrowing money to enable him to carry on a voyage, and pledging the ship as security for the money. If the ship is lost, the lender loses the money; but if the ship arrives safe, he is to receive the money lent, with the interest or premium stipulated, although it may exceed the legal rate of interest. The tackle of the ship also is answerable for the debt, as well as the person of the borrower. When a loan is made upon the goods shipped, the borrower is said to take up money at *respondentia*, as he is bound personally to answer the contract. *Blackstone. Park.*

BOT'TONY, *n.* [from the same root as *bud, button.*]

In *heraldry*, a cross bottony terminates at each end in three buds, knots or buttons, resembling in some measure the three-leaved grass. *Encyc.*

BOUCHET', *n.* [Fr.] A sort of pear.

BOUD, *n.* An insect that breeds in malt or other grain; called also a weevil. *Dict.*

BÖUGE, *v. i. booj.* [Fr. *bouge*, a lodge, the bilge of a cask; from the root of *bow*, which see.] To swell out. [*Little used.*]

BOUGE, *n.* Provisions. [*Not in use.*] *Jonson.*

BOUGH, *n. bou.* [Sax. *bog, boh* or *bogh*, the shoulder, a branch, an arm, the body of a tree, a stake, a tail, an arch, or bow; Sw. *bog*; Dan. *bov*; from the same root as *bow*, to bend, to throw; Sax. *bugan.*]

The branch of a tree; *applied to a branch of size*, not to a small shoot.

BOUGHT, *bawt, pret.* and *pp.* of *buy*. [See *Buy.*]

BOUGHT, *n. bawt.* [D. *bogt*, a bend, a coil; from *boogen* to bend. See *Bight.*]

1. A twist; a link; a knot; a flexure, or bend. *Milton. Brown.*

2. The part of a sling that contains the stone.

BOUGHT'Y, *a. baw'ty.* Bending. *Sherwood.*

BÖUGIE, *n. boogee'.* [Fr. a wax-candle; Sp. *bugia.*]

In *Surgery*, a long slender instrument, that is introduced through the urethra into the bladder, to remove obstructions. It is usually made of slips of waxed linen, coiled into a slightly conical form by rolling them on any hard smooth surface. It is also made of catgut, elastic gum and metal; but those of waxed linen are generally preferred. *Hooper. Dorsey.*

BÖUILLON, *n.* [Fr. from *bouillir*, to boil. See *Boil.*] Broth; soup.

BÖULDER-WALL, *n.* [rather *bowlder-wall.* See *Bowlder.*]

A wall built of round flints or pebbles laid in a strong mortar, used where the sea has a beach cast up, or where there is a plenty of flints. *Builder's Dict.*

BÖULET', *n.* [from the root of *ball*, or *bowl*; Fr. *boule.*]

In *the manege*, a horse is so called, when the fetlock or pastern joint bends forward, and out of its natural position. *Encyc.*

BOULT, *an incorrect orthography.* [See *Bolt.*]

BÖULTIN, *n.* [from the root of *bolt*; Sp. *bulto*, a protuberance.]

In *architecture*, a molding, the convexity of which is just one fourth of a circle, being a member just below the plinth in the Tuscan and Doric capital. *Encyc.*

BOUNCE, *v. i.* [D. *bonzen*, to bounce; *bons*, a bounce; allied probably to *bound*; Arm. *boundiçza*; Fr. *bondir.*]

1. To leap or spring; to fly or rush out suddenly.

Out *bounced* the mastiff. *Swift.*

2. To spring or leap against any thing, so as to rebound; to beat or thump by a spring.

Against his bosom *bounced* his heaving heart. *Dryden.*

3. To beat hard, or thump, so as to make a sudden noise.

Another *bounced* as hard as he could knock. *Swift.*

4. To boast or bully; *used in familiar speech.* *Johnson.*

5. To be bold or strong. *Shak.*

BOUNCE, *n.* A heavy blow, thrust or thump with a large solid body.

The *bounce* burst open the door. *Dryden.*

2. A loud heavy sound, as by an explosion. *Shak. Gay.*

3. A boast; a threat; *in low language.* *Johnson.*

4. A fish; a species of squalus or shark. *Encyc.*

BOUN'CER, *n.* A boaster; a bully; *in familiar language.* *Johnson.*

BOUN'CING, *ppr.* Leaping; bounding with violence, as a heavy body; springing out; thumping with a loud noise; boasting; moving with force, as a heavy bounding body.

BOUN'CING, *a.* Stout; strong; large and heavy; *a customary sense in the U States*; as a *bouncing* lass.

BOUN'CINGLY, *adv.* Boastingly.

BOUND, *n.* [Norm. *bonne, boune*, a bound; *bond*, limited; *bundes*, limits; from *bind*, *bond*, that which binds; or from French *bondir*, to spring, and denoting the utmost extent.]

1. A limit; the line which comprehends the whole of any given object or space. It differs from *boundary.* See the latter. *Bound* is applied to kingdoms, states, cities, towns, tracts of land, and to territorial jurisdiction.

2. A limit by which any excursion is restrained; the limit of indulgence or desire; as, the love of money knows no *bounds.*

3. A leap; a spring; a jump; a rebound: [Fr. *bondir*, to spring.]

4. In *dancing*, a spring from one foot to the other.

BOUND, *v. t.* To limit; to terminate; to fix the furthest point of extension, whether of natural or moral objects, as of land, or empire, or of passion, desire, indulgence. Hence, to restrain or confine; as, to *bound* our wishes. *To bound in* is hardly legitimate.

2. To make to bound. *Shaks.*

BOUND, *v. i.* [Fr. *bondir*; Arm. *boundiçza.*] To leap; to jump; to spring; to move forward by leaps.

Before his lord the ready spaniel *bounds.* *Pope.*

2. To rebound—*but the sense is the same.*

BOUND, *pret.* and *pp.* of *bind.* As *a participle*, made fast by a band, or by chains or fetters; obliged by moral ties; confined; restrained.

2. As *a participle* or perhaps more properly *an adj.*, destined; tending; going, or intending to go; with *to* or *for*; as, a ship is *bound to* Cadiz, or *for* Cadiz.

The application of this word, in this use, is taken from the orders given for the government of the voyage, implying obligation, or from tending, stretching. So *destined* implies *being bound.*

Bound is used in composition, as in *ice-bound, wind-bound*, when a ship is confined or prevented from sailing by ice or by contrary winds.

BOUND'ARY, *n.* A limit; a bound. *Johnson.* This word is thus used as synonymous with *bound.* But the real sense is, a visible mark designating a limit. *Bound* is the limit itself or furthest point of extension, and may be an imaginary line; but *boundary* is the thing which ascertains the limit; *terminus*, not *finis.* Thus by a statute of Connecticut, it is enacted that the inhabitants of every town shall procure its *bounds* to be set out by such marks and *boundaries* as may be a plain direction for the future; which marks and *boundaries* shall be a great heap of stones or a ditch of six feet long, &c. This distinction is observed also in the statute of Massachusetts. But the two words are, in ordinary use, confounded.

Bound-bailiff, *n.* An officer appointed by a sheriff to execute process; so denominated from the *bond* given for the faithful discharge of his trust. *Blackstone.*

BOUND'ED, *pp.* Limited; confined; restrained.

BOUND'EN, *pp.* of *bind.* [See *Bind*, and *pp. Bound.*]

BOUND'ER, *n.* One that limits; a boundary. *Herbert.*

BOUND'ING, *ppr.* Limiting; confining; restraining; leaping; springing; rebounding; advancing with leaps.

BOUND'ING-STONE, BOUND'-STONE, } *n.* A stone to play with. *Dryden.*

BOUND'LESS, *a.* Unlimited; unconfined; immeasurable; illimitable; as *boundless* space; *boundless* power.

BOUND'LESSNESS, *n.* The quality of being without limits. *South.*

BOUN'TEOUS, *a.* [See *Bounty.*] Liberal in charity; disposed to give freely; generous; munificent; beneficent; free in bestowing gifts; as *bounteous* nature. It is used chiefly in poetry for *bountiful.* *Johnson.*

BOUN'TEOUSLY, *adv.* Liberally; generously; largely; freely.

BOUN'TEOUSNESS, *n.* Liberality in bestowing gifts or favors; munificence; kindness.

BOUN'TIFUL, *a.* [*bounty* and *full.*] Free to give; liberal in bestowing gifts and favors; munificent; generous.

God, the *bountiful* author of our being. *Locke.*

It is followed by *of* before the thing given, and *to* before the person receiving.

BOUN'TIFULLY, *adv.* Liberally; largely; in a bountiful manner.

BOUN'TIFULNESS, *n.* The quality of being bountiful; liberality in the bestowment of gifts and favors.

BOUN'TIHEDE, BOUN'TIHEAD, } *n.* Goodness. *Obs.*

BOUN'TY, *n.* [Fr. *bonté*, goodness, excellence, favor; It. *bontà*; L. *bonitas*, from *bonus*, good.]

1. Liberality in bestowing gifts and favors; generosity; munificence. The word includes the gift or favor and the kindness of disposition with which it is bestowed; or a favor bestowed with a benevolent disposition. This distinguishes it from a mere gift. It is also observed by Johnson, that it differs from *charity*, as a *present* from an *alms*, in not being bestowed upon persons absolutely necessitous. This is often the case; but *bounty* includes *charity*, as the genus comprehends the species; *charity* however does not necessarily include *bounty*, for *charity* or an *alms* may be given with reluctance.

The word may be used also for a free gift, 2 Cor. ix. 5; or a disposition to give, without the gift; goodness in general. *Spenser.*

2. A premium offered or given, to induce men to enlist into the public service; or to encourage any branch of industry, as husbandry, manufactures or commerce.

BÖUQUET, *n.* *booka'y.* [Fr. a plume, a nosegay; Arm. *boged*; It. *boschetto.* See *Bush.*]

A nosegay; a bunch of flowers.

BÖURD, *n.* A jest. *Obs.* *Spenser.*

BÖURD'ER, *n.* A jester. *Obs.*

BOURĠEOIS', *n.* *burjois'.* [It appears to be a French word, but I know not the reason of its application to types.]

A small kind of printing types, in size between long primer and brevier. The type on which the main body of this work is printed.

BOUR'ĠEON, *v. i.* *bur'jun.* [Fr. *bourgeon*, a bud; Arm. *bourgeon*, a button, or a bud.]

To sprout; to put forth buds; to shoot forth as a branch. *Goldsmith.*

BÖURN, rather **BÕRNE**, *n.* [Fr. *borne*, a limit; *borner*, to bound. In the sense of a stream, Sax. *burn*; Sw. *brunn*; D. *bron*; G. *brunnen*; Dan. *brönd.*]

1. A bound; a limit.

That undiscovered country, from whose *bourn*
No traveller returns.——— *Shak.*

2. A brook; a torrent; a rivulet. [*In this sense obsolete; but retained in many names of towns, seated on the banks of streams. In Scotland, it is still used in the sense of a brook, but they write it* burn.]

BÖURNONITE, *n.* Antimonial sulphuret of lead. *Ure.*

BÖUSE, BOOZE, } *v. i.* *booz.* [Arm. *beuzi*, to overflow, to drown; W. *bozi*; Old D. *buysen.* In Russ. *busa* is a drink brewed from millet. *Tooke.*]

To drink freely; to tope; to guzzle. [*A vulgar word.*] *Spenser.*

BÖUS'Y, *a.* *booz'y.* Drunken; intoxicated. [*Vulgar.*] *Dryden.*

BOUT, *n.* [Fr. *bout*, end, or It. *botta*, a stroke.]

A turn; as much of an action as is performed at one time; a single part of an action carried on at successive intervals; essay; attempt. *Sidney. Dryden.*

BOUT, *n.* [It. *beuita*, or *bevuta*, a drinking, from *bere*, or *bevere*, to drink; L. *bibo*; Fr. *boire*; Sp. *beber.*]

We use this word tautologically in the phrase, a drinking-*bout*; or the word is the same as the preceding.

BÖUTA'DE, *n.* [Fr. from *bouter*, Sp. *botar*, It. *buttare*, to thrust; Eng. *put*; allied to *bud.*]

Properly, a start; hence, a whim. [*Not English.*] *Swift.*

BÖUTEFEU, *n.* [Fr. from *bouter*, to throw, and *feu*, fire; or according to Thomson, from *boute*, a match. Qu. from the root of Eng. *bate* or *better.*]

An incendiary; a make-bate. [*Not English.*] *Bacon.*

BÖUTISALE, *n.* [Qu. *sale of booty*, or from *boute*, a match. *Thomson.*]

A cheap sale; or according to others, a sale by a lighted match, during the burning of which a man may bid. [*Not used.*] *Hayward.*

BO'VATE, *n.* [In Law L. *bovata*, from *bos*, *bovis*, an ox.]

An ox-gate, or as much land as an ox can plow in a year; Cowell says 28 acres.

BO'VEY-COAL, *n.* Brown lignite, an inflammable fossil, resembling, in many of its properties, bituminous wood. Its structure is a little slaty; its cross fracture, even or conchoidal, with a resinous luster, somewhat shining. It is brittle, burns with a weak flame, and exhales an odor, which is generally disagreeable. *Cleaveland.*

BO'VINE, *a.* [Low L. *bovinus*, from *bos*, *bovis*, an ox; W. *bu*, *buw*, *buç*, *buwç*, and the verb, *buçiaw*, to bellow.]

Pertaining to oxen and cows, or the quadrupeds of the genus Bos.

This animal is the strongest and fiercest of the *bovine* genus. *Barrow's Trav.*

The ox-born souls mean nothing more than the eight living souls, who issued from their allegorical mother, the *bovine* ark. *Faber.*

BOW, *v. t.* [Sax. *bugan*, *bygan*; W. *bwan*, and *bacu*, to bend, to grapple; G. *biegen*, *beugen*; D. *boogen*, *buigen*; Sw. *böya*; Dan. *böyer*, to bend.]

1. To bend; to inflect; as, to *bow* vines.
2. To bend the body in token of respect or civility; as, to *bow* the head.
3. To bend or incline towards, in condescension.

Bow down thine ear to the poor. Eccles.

4. To depress; to crush; to subdue.

His heavy hand hath *bowed* you to the grave.

He *bows* the nations to his will.

BOW, *v. i.* To bend; to curve; to be inflected; to bend, in token of reverence, respect or civility; often with *down.*

This is the idol to which the world *bows.*

2. To stoop; to fall upon the knees.

The people *bowed* upon their knees. Judges.

3. To sink under pressure.

They stoop: they *bow down* together. Isaiah.

BOW, *n.* An inclination of the head, or a bending of the body, in token of reverence, respect, civility, or submission.

BŌW, *n.* [See *bow*, to bend.] An instrument of war, and hunting, made of wood, or other elastic matter, with a string fastened to each end. The bow being bent by drawing the string, and suddenly returning to its natural state by its elastic force, throws an arrow to a great distance, and with force sufficient to kill an animal. It is of two kinds, the *long-bow*, and the *cross-bow*, arbalet or arbalest. The use of the bow is called *archery.*

2. Any thing bent, or in form of a curve; the rainbow; the doubling of a string in a knot; the part of a yoke which embraces the neck; &c.
3. A small machine, formed with a stick and hairs, which being drawn over the strings of an instrument of music, causes it to sound.
4. A beam of wood or brass, with three long screws that direct a lathe of wood or steel to any arch; used in forming drafts of ships, and projections of the sphere, or wherever it is necessary to draw large arches. *Harris.*
5. An instrument for taking the sun's altitude at sea, consisting of a large arch of ninety degrees graduated, a shank or staff, a side-vane, a sight-vane, and a horizon-vane; *now disused.* *Encyc.*
6. An instrument in use among smiths for turning a drill; with turners, for turning wood; with hatters, for breaking fur and wool.
7. *Bōws* of a saddle, are the two pieces of wood laid archwise to receive the upper

part of a horse's back, to give the saddle its due form, and to keep it tight. *Farrier's Dict.*

8. *Bow* of a ship, is the rounding part of her side forward, beginning where the planks arch inwards, and terminating where they close, at the stem or prow. A narrow bow is called a *lean* bow; a broad one, a *bold* or *bluff* bow.

On the bow, in navigation, is an arch of the horizon, not exceeding 45 degrees, comprehended between some distant object, and that point of the compass which is right ahead. *Mar. Dict.*

BŌW-BEARER, *n.* [*bow* and *bear.*] An under officer of the forest, whose duty is to inform of trespasses. *Cowel.*

BŌW-BENT, *a.* [*bow* and *bend.*] Crooked. *Milton.*

BŌW-DYE, *n.* A kind of scarlet color, superior to madder, but inferior to the true scarlet grain for fixedness, and duration; first used at Bow, near London. *Encyc.*

BOW'-GRACE, *n.* In *sea language*, a frame or composition of junk, laid out at the sides, stem, or bows of ships to secure them from injury by ice. *Encyc.*

BŌW-HAND, *n.* [*bow* and *hand.*] The hand that draws a bow. *Spenser.*

BŌW-LEGGED, *a.* [*bow* and *leg.*] Having crooked legs. *Johnson.*

BŌWMAN, *n.* [*bow* and *man.*] A man who uses a bow; an archer. Jerem. iv. 29.

BOW'MAN, *n.* The man who rows the foremost oar in a boat. *Mar. Dict.*

BŌWNET, *n.* [*bow* and *net.*] An engine for catching lobsters and crawfish, called also *bow-wheel.* It is made of two round wicker baskets, pointed at the end, one of which is thrust into the other, and at the mouth is a little rim bent inwards. *Encyc.*

BOW'-PIECE *n.* [*bow* and *piece.*] A piece of ordnance carried at the bow of a ship. *Encyc.*

BŌW-SHOT, *n.* [*bow* and *shot.*] The space which an arrow may pass when shot from a bow. Gen. xxi, 16. *Boyle.*

BŌWSPRIT, *n.* [*bow* and *sprit*; D. *boegspriet*; Dan. *boug-sprid*; G. *bugspriet.* See *Sprit.*]

A large boom or spar, which projects over the stem of a ship or other vessel, to carry sail forward. [*This is probably the true orthography.*] *Mar. Dict.*

BŌW-STRING, *n.* [*bow* and *string.*] The string of a bow.

BŌW-WINDOW. [See *Bay-window.*]

BOW'ABLE, *a.* Of a flexible disposition. [*Not in use.*]

BOW'ED, *pp.* Bent; crushed; subdued.

BŌWED, *pp.* Bent; like a bow.

BOW'ELS, *n. plu.* [G. *bauch*; D. *buik*; Sw. *buk*; Dan. *bug*; Fr. *boyau*; W. *bog*, a swelling; *bogel*, the navel. The sense is protuberance.]

1. The intestines of an animal; the entrails, especially of man. The heart. 2. Cor. vi. 12.

2. The interior part of any thing; as the *bowels* of the earth.

3. The seat of pity or kindness; hence, tenderness, compassion, *a scriptural sense.*

Bowel, in the singular, is sometimes used for *gut.*

BOW'EL, *v. t.* To take out the bowels; to eviscerate; to penetrate the bowels. *Ainsworth. Ash.*

BOW'ELLESS, *a.* Without tenderness or pity.

BOW'ER, *n.* [from *bow.*] An anchor carried at the bow of a ship. There are generally two bowers, called *first* and *second*, *great* and *little*, or *best* and *small.* *Encyc.*

BOW'ER, *n.* [Sax. *bur*, a chamber or private apartment, a hut, a cottage; W. *bwr*, an inclosure.]

1. A shelter or covered place in a garden, made with boughs of trees bent and twined together. It differs from *arbor* in that it may be round or square, whereas an arbor is long and arched. *Milton. Encyc.*

2. A bed-chamber; any room in a house except the hall. *Spenser. Mason.*

3. A country seat; a cottage. *Shenstone. B. Jonson.*

4. A shady recess; a plantation for shade. *W. Brown.*

BOW'ER, *v. t.* To embower to inclose. *Shaks.*

BOW'ER, *v. i.* To lodge. *Spenser.*

BOW'ERS, } *n.* [from *bow.*] Muscles that
BOW'RS, } bend the joints. *Spenser. Mason.*

BOW'ERY, *a.* Covering; shading as a bower; also, containing bowers. *Thomson.*

A *bowery* maze that shades the purple streams. *Trumbull.*

BOW'ESS, BOW'ET, *n.* A young hawk, when it begins to get out of the nest; a term in falconry. *Encyc. Ash.*

BOWĠE, *v. i.* To swell out. [See *Bouge.*]

BOWĠE, *v. t.* To perforate; as, to *bowge* a ship. *Ainsworth.*

[*I do not find this word in any other author.*]

BOW'ING, *ppr.* Bending; stooping; making a bow.

BOW'INGLY, *adv.* In a bending manner.

BŌWL, *n.* [Sax. *bolla.* In Latin, *vola* is the hollow of the hand.]

1. A concave vessel to hold liquors, rather wide than deep, and thus distinguished from a cup, which is rather deep than wide.

2. The hollow part of any thing; as the *bowl* of a spoon.

3. A basin; a fountain. *Bacon.*

BŌWL, *n.* [D. *bol*; Fr. *boule*; Sp. *bola*; Arm. *boul*, a ball; W. *pel.*]

A ball of wood used for play on a level plat of ground.

BŌWL, *v. i.* To play with bowls, or at bowling.

BŌWL, *v. t.* To roll as a bowl; also, to pelt with any thing rolled. *Shak.*

BŌWLDER, *n.* [from *bowl.*] A small stone of a roundish form, and of no determinate size, found on the sea shore and on the banks or in the channels of rivers, &c., worn smooth or rounded by the action of water; a pebble. *Johnson. Encyc.*

The term *bowlder* is now used in Geology for rounded masses of any rock, found out of place, and apparently transported from their original bed by water. Bowlders of Granite, often of great size, are very common on the surface of the most recent formations.

BŌWLDER-STONE. [See *Bowlder.*]

BŌWLDER-WALL, *n.* A wall constructed of pebbles or bowlders of flint or other siliceous stones, which have been rounded by the action of water. *Builder's Dict.*

BŌWLER, *n.* One who plays at bowls.

BŌWLINE, *n.* [Sp. and Port. *bolina*; Arm. *bouline*, "voile de biais pour recevoir le vent de côté," a slanting sail to receive a side wind, *Gregoire*; Fr. *bouline*, a tack; *bouliner*, to tack, to turn one way and the other, to dodge or shift. But in Danish it is *bougline*, the line of the bow or bend.]

A rope fastened near the middle of the leech or perpendicular edge of the square sails, by subordinate parts, called *bridles*, and used to keep the weather edge of the sail tight forward, when the ship is close hauled. *Mar. Dict.*

Bōwline-bridles, are the ropes by which the bowline is fastened to the leech of the sail. *Encyc.*

BŌWLING, *ppr.* Playing at bowls.

BŌWLING-GREEN, *n.* [*bowl* and *green.*] A level piece of ground kept smooth for bowling.

2. In *gardening*, a parterre in a grove, laid with fine turf, with compartments of divers figures, with dwarf trees and other decorations. It may be used for bowling; but the French and Italians have such greens for ornament. *Encyc.*

BOWSE, *v. i.* In *seaman's language*, to pull or haul; as, to *bowse upon a tack*; to *bowse away*, to pull all together. *Encyc.*

BOWSS'EN, *v. t.* To drink; to drench. [*Not used.*] Qu. *bouse.*

BŌWYER, *n.* [from *bow*, a corruption of *bower*, like sawyer.]

An archer; one who uses a bow; one who makes bows. [*Little used.*] *Johnson.*

BOX, *n.* [Sax. *box*, a coffer and the box-tree; Lat. *buxus*, the tree, and *pyxis*, a box; Gr. *πυξις*, a box, and *πυξος*, the tree; *πυξ*, the fist; Ir. *bugsa*, *buksa*; Sw. *buxbom*; Ger. *buchsbaum*; Dan. *buxbom*, the box tree; Ger. *büchse*, a box; It. *bosso*, the box tree; *bossolo*, a box; Sp. *box*, the tree; Port. *buxo*, the tree; *buxa*, a stopple; Pers. بقش buxus, box tree; Ar. the same. Box may be from closeness, applied to the shrub, the fist and the case.]

A coffer or chest, either of wood or metal. In general, the word *box* is used for a case of rough boards, or more slightly made than a chest, and used for the conveyance of goods. But the name is applied to cases of any size and of any materials; as a wooden *box*, a tin *box*, an iron *box*, a strong *box*.

2. The quantity that a box contains; as a *box* of quicksilver; a *box* of rings. In some cases, the quantity called a *box* is fixed by custom; in others, it is uncertain, as a *box* of tea or sugar.

3. A certain seat in a play-house, or in any public room.

4. The case which contains the mariner's compass.

5. A money chest.

6. A tree or shrub, constituting the genus *buxus*, used for bordering flower-beds. The *African box* is the *myrsine.*

7. A blow on the head with the hand, or on the ear with the open hand.

8. A cylindrical hollow iron used in wheels, in which the axle-tree runs. Also, a hollow tube in a pump, closed with a valve.

BOX, *v. i.* To fight with the fist; to combat with the hand or fist.

BOX, *v. t.* To inclose in a box; also, to furnish with boxes, as a wheel or block.

2. To strike with the hand or fist, especially the ear or side of the head.

3. To rehearse the several points of the compass in their proper order. *Encyc.*

4. To make a hole or cut in a tree, to procure the sap; as, to *box* a maple.

5. To sail round. [Sp. *boxar.*]

BOX'ED, *pp.* Inclosed in a box; struck on the head with the fist or hand; furnished with a box or hollow iron, as a wheel.

BOX'EN, *a.* Made of box-wood; resembling box. *Dryden. Gay.*

BOX'ER, *n.* One who fights with his fist.

BOX'-HAUL, *v. t.* To veer a ship in a particular manner, when it is impracticable to tack. *Chambers.*

BOX'ING, *ppr.* Inclosing in a box; striking with the fist; furnishing with a box.

BOX'ING, *n.* The act of fighting with the fist; a combat with the fist.

BOX'-THORN, *n.* [*box* and *thorn.*] A plant, the Lycium, or a species of it. *Fam. of Plants.*

BOY, *n.* [Pers. *bach*, a boy; W. *bacgen*, from *bac*, little; Arm. *buguel*, a child, *bugale*, boyish; Sw. *poike*, a young boy; Dan. *pog*; Fr. *page*. See *Beagle* and *Pug*. *Boy* is a contracted word, and probably the L. *puer* for *puger*, for we see by *puella*, that *r* is not radical. So the Gr. παις probably is contracted, for the derivative verb, παιζω, forms παιξω, παιχθεις. The radical letters probably are Bg or Pg.]

A male child, from birth to the age of puberty; but in general, applied to males under ten or twelve years of age; a lad. Sometimes it is used in contempt for a young man, indicating immaturity, want of vigor or judgment.

BOY, *v. t.* To treat as a boy. *Johnson.*

Rather, to act as a boy; to imitate a boy in action. The passage in Shakspeare, in which this word is found, is supposed to allude to the practice of boys acting women's parts, on the stage.

I shall see some squeaking Cleopatra *boy* my greatness. *See Mason's Sup. to Johnson.*

BOY'AR, *n.* A Russian nobleman. [See *Boiar.*]

BOY'AU, *n. boy'o.* [Fr. *boyau*, a gut, and a branch of a tree.]

In *fortification*, a ditch covered with a parapet, serving as a communication between two trenches. *Encyc.*

BOY'-BLIND, *a.* Blind as a boy; undiscerning. *Obs.* *Beaum.*

BOY'ER, *n.* A Flemish sloop, with a castle at each end. *Encyc.*

BOY'HOOD, *n.* [*boy* and *hood.*] The state of a boy, or of immature age. *Swift.*

BOY'ISH, *a.* Belonging to a boy; childish; trifling; resembling a boy in manners or opinions; puerile. *Shak.*

BOY'ISHLY, *adv.* Childishly; in a trifling manner. *Sherwood.*

BOY'ISHNESS, *n.* Childishness; the manners or behavior of a boy.

BOY'ISM, *n.* Childishness; puerility. *Dryden.*

2. The state of a boy. *Warton.*

BOYS-PLAY, *n.* Childish amusement; any thing trifling.

BOYU'NA, *n.* A large serpent of America, black and slender, having an intolerable smell. Also, a harmless reptile. *Dict. of Nat. Hist.*

BP. An abbreviation of Bishop.

BRABANT'INE, *a.* Pertaining to Brabant, a province of the Netherlands, of which Brussels is the capital. *State Papers*, V. ii.

BRAB'BLE, *n.* [D. *brabbelen*, to stammer.] A broil; a clamorous contest; a wrangle. *Obs.* *Shak.*

BRAB'BLE, *v. i.* To clamor; to contest noisily. *Obs.* *Beaum.* and *Fletcher.*

BRAB'BLER, *n.* A clamorous, quarrelsome, noisy fellow; a wrangler. *Obs.* *Shak.*

BRAB'BLING, *ppr.* Clamoring; wrangling. *Obs.*

BRACE, *n.* [Fr. *bras*; Sp. *brazo*; Port. *braço*; Arm *breach*, or *breh*; Ir. *brac* and *raigh*; W. *braic*; Corn. *breck*, or *breh*; L. *brachium*; Gr. βραχιων, the arm. This word furnishes clear and decisive evidence of the change of a palatal letter into a sibilant. The change comes through the Spanish or other Celtic dialect, *brach*, *brazo*, the Sp. *z* being originally a palatal or guttural; thence to the Fr. *bras*, and Eng. *brace*. In like manner, *Durazzo* is formed from *Dyrrachium*. The Greek verbs furnish a multitude of similar changes. This word furnishes also a proof that *b* is a prefix, for in Irish *brac* is written also *raigh*. The sense of arm is, that which breaks forth, a shoot. From *bras*, the French have *embrasser*, to *embrace*, and in Sp. *brazas* is braces, and *bracear* is to *brace*, and to swing the arms. Brace, in naval affairs, is in D. *bras*; Dan. *bras*, and *braser*, to brace. Qu. is this the same word as the Fr. *bras*, an arm.]

1. In *architecture*, a piece of timber framed in with bevel joints, to keep the building from swerving either way. It extends like an arm from the post or main timber.

2. That which holds any thing tight; a cincture or bandage. The *braces* of a drum are not *bands*.

3. A pair; a couple; as a *brace* of ducks. It is used of persons only in contempt, or in the style of drollery.

4. In *music*, a double curve at the beginning of stave.

5. A thick strap, which supports a carriage on wheels.

6. A crooked line in printing, connecting two or more words or lines; thus, boll. } bowl. }

It is used to connect triplets in poetry.

7. In *marine language*, a rope reeved through a block at the end of a yard, to square or traverse the yard. The name is given also to pieces of iron which are used as supports; such as of the poop lanterns, &c. *Mar. Dict.*

8. Brace, or brasse, is a foreign measure answering to our fathom.

9. Harness; warlike preparation; as we say, *girded* for battle. *Shak.*

10. Tension; tightness. *Holder.*

11. Braces, *plu.*, suspenders, the straps that sustain pantaloons, &c.

12. The *braces* of a drum, are the cords on the sides of it, for tightening the heads and snares.

BRACE, *v. t.* To draw tight; to tighten; to bind or tie close; to make tight and firm.

2. To make tense; to strain up; as, to *brace* a drum.

3. To furnish with braces; as, to *brace* a building.

4. To strengthen; to increase tension; as, to *brace* the nerves.

5. In *marine language*, to bring the yards to either side.

To brace about is to turn the yards round for the contrary tack.

To brace sharp is to cause the yards to have the smallest possible angle with the keel.

To brace to is to check or ease off the lee braces, and round-in the weather ones, to assist in tacking. *Mar. Dict.*

BRA'CED, *pp.* Furnished with braces; drawn close and tight; made tense.

BRA'CELET, *n.* [Fr. *brasselet*, and *bracelet*; It. *bracciale*, *braccialetto*; Sp. *brazalete*. See *Brace.*]

1. An ornament for the wrist, worn by ladies. This ornament seems anciently to have been worn by men as well as women.

2. A piece of defensive armor for the arm. *Johnson.*

BRA'CER, *n.* That which braces, binds or makes firm; a band or bandage; also, armor for the arm. *Chaucer.*

2. An astringent medicine, which gives tension or tone to any part of the body.

BRAȻH, *n.* [Fr. *braque*; D. *brak*; It. *bracco*, a setting dog; Sp. *braco*, pointing or setting as a pointer.] A bitch of the hound kind. *Shak.*

BRAȻH'IAL, *a.* [L. *brachium*, from the Celtic *braic*, *brac*, the arm.] Belonging to the arm; as the *brachial* artery. *Hooper.*

BRAȻH'IATE, *a.* [See *Brachial.*] In *botany*, having branches in pairs, decussated, all nearly horizontal, and each pair at right angles with the next. *Martyn.*

BRAȻH'MAN, } *n.* An ancient philosopher
BRAM'IN, } of India. The brachmans are a branch of the ancient gymnosophists, and remarkable for the severity of their lives and manners. *Encyc.*

BRAȻHYG'RAPHER, *n.* [See *the next word.*] A writer in short hand. *Gayton.*

BRAȻHYG'RAPHY, *n.* [Gr. βραχυς, short, and γραφη, a writing.]

The art or practice of writing in short hand; stenography. *B. Jonson.*

BRAȻHYL'OĠY, *n.* [Gr. βραχυς, short, and λογος, expression.]

In *rhetoric*, the expressing of any thing in the most concise manner. *Encyc.*

BRACK, *n.* [G. *bruch*; Dan. *bræk*; Norm. *brek*; from *break*, which see.]

An opening caused by the parting of any solid body; a breach; a broken part.

BRACK'EN, *n.* Fern. [See *Brake.*]

BRACK'ET, *n.* [Fr. *braquer*, to bend. Qu. Oriental ברך, Ar. Ch. Heb. Syr. Sam. and Eth., to bend the knee; hence it signifies the knee.]

1. Among *workers in timber*, an angular wooden stay, in form of the knee bent, to support shelves, scaffolds and the like.

2. The cheek of a mortar carriage, made of strong plank. *Encyc.*

3. In *printing*, hooks; thus, [ ].

BRACK'ISH, *a.* [D. *brak*, overflowed; qu. from *break* or Gr. βρεχω, to water. Perhaps applied to land on which salt water has flowed.]
Salt, or salt in a moderate degree; it is applied to any water partially saturated with salt. *Bacon.*

BRACK'ISHNESS, *n.* The quality of being brackish; saltness in a small degree. *Cheyne.*

BRACK'Y, *a.* Brackish. [*Not used.*]

BRAC'TEA, **BRACTE**, *n.* [L. Ainsworth writes, *bractea*, or *brattea.*]
In *botany*, a floral leaf, one of the seven fulcrums or props of plants. It differs from other leaves in shape and color, and is generally situated on the peduncle, so near the corol, as easily to be mistaken for the calyx. *Martyn.*
In the Asiatic Researches, iv. 354, this word is anglicized, and written *bract.*

BRAC'TEATE, *a.* [from *bractea.*] Furnished with bractes. *Barton.*

BRAC'TED, *a.* Furnished with bractes. *Martyn.*

BRAC'TEOLE, *n.* A little bract. *De Candolle.*

BRAC'TEOLATE, *a.* Furnished with bracteoles.

BRAD, in Sax., is *broad*, and occurs in names; as in *Bradford*, *broadford.*

BRAD, *n.* [Arm. *broud*, a point; Ir. *brod*, or *braid;* Dan. *braad*, a goad or sting; Ch. ברט a dart, a borer.]
A particular kind of nail, used in floors and other work, where it is deemed proper to drive nails entirely into the wood. For this purpose, it is made without a broad head or shoulder over the shank. *Moxon.*

BRAD'YPUS, *n.* The sloth, which see.

BRAG, *v. i.* [W. *bragiaw*, to swell, to shoot up, to brag; *brag*, a sprouting, malt; *bragu*, to malt. It coincides with Dan. *brager*, to crackle, Gr. βραχω, Eng. to *brag*, and many other words signifying to *break* or shoot forth. See *Brave.*]
To boast; to display one's actions, merits or advantages ostentatiously; to tell boastful stories; followed by *of;* as, to *brag of* a good horse, or *of* a feat. *Sidney. Shak.*
To brag on is vulgar; indeed the word itself is become low, and is not to be used in elegant composition.

BRAG, *n.* A boast, or boasting; ostentatious verbal display of one's deeds, or advantages; the thing boasted. *Milton. Bacon.*
Spenser has used this word as an adverb for *proudly.*

BRAG, *n.* A game at cards. *Chesterfield.*

BRAGGADO'CIO, *n.* A puffing, boasting fellow. *Dryden.*

BRAG'GARDISM, *n.* Boastfulness; vain ostentation.

BRAG'GART, *n.* [*brag* and *art*, *ard*, kind.] A boaster; a vain fellow. *Shak.*

BRAG'GART, *a.* Boastful; vainly ostentatious. *Donne.*

BRAG'GER, *n.* One who brags; a boaster.

BRAG'GET, *n.* [W. *bragawd.* See *Brag.*] A liquor made by fermenting the wort of ale and mead. *Owen.*

BRAG'GING, *ppr.* Boasting.

BRAG'GINGLY, *adv.* Boastingly.

BRAG'LESS, *a.* Without bragging, or ostentation. [*Unusual.*] *Shak.*

BRAG'LY, *adv.* Finely; so as it may be bragged of. [*Not used.*] *Spenser.*

BRAHMAN'IC, *a.* Pertaining to the Brachmans or Bramins of India. *Vallancey.*

BRAID, *v. t.* [Sax. *bredan*, to braid; Old Eng. *brede;* Dan. *breider*, to upbraid.]
1. To weave or infold three or more strands to form one.
2. To reproach. *Obs.* [See *Upbraid.*]

BRAID, *n.* A string, cord or other texture, formed by weaving together different strands.
2. A start. *Sackville.*

BRAID, *a.* Deceitful. *Shak.*
Chaucer used the Saxon word *brede*, to deceive. This is the figurative sense of *braid. Obs.*

BRAIL, *n.* [Fr. *brayer*, a *brail*, or truss, a contracted word.]
1. A piece of leather to bind up a hawk's wing. *Bailey.*
2. In *navigation*, brails are ropes passing through pulleys, on the mizen mast and yard, and fastened to the aftmost leech of the sail in different places, to truss it up close. Also, all ropes employed to haul up the bottoms, lower corners and skirts of the other great sails, for the more ready furling of them. *Mar. Dict.*

BRAIL, *v. t. To brail up*, is to haul up into the brails, or to truss up with the brails. *Mar. Dict.*

BRAIN, *n.* [Sax. *brægan*, *bregen*, *bragen;* D. *brein;* Gr. βρεγμα, properly the fore part of the head or sinciput, also the brain.]
1. That soft whitish mass, or viscus, inclosed in the cranium or skull, in which the nerves and spinal marrow terminate, and which is supposed to be the seat of the soul or intelligent principle in man. It is divided above into a right and left hemisphere, and below into six lobes. It is composed of a *cortical* substance, which is external, and a *medullary*, which is internal. From the brain proceed nine pair of nerves, which are distributed principally to the head and neck. *Hooper. Encyc.*
2. The understanding. *Hale.*
3. The affections; fancy; imagination. [*Unusual.*] *Shak. Sandys.*

BRAIN, *v. t.* To dash out the brains; to kill by beating out the brains. *Pope. Dryden.*
2. To conceive; to understand. [*Not used.*] *Shak.*

BRA'INISH, *a.* Hot-headed; furious; as L. *cerebrosus.* *Shak.*

BRA'INLESS, *a.* Without understanding; silly; thoughtless; witless. *Tickel. Shak.*

BRA'INPAN, *n.* [*brain* and *pan.*] The skull which incloses the brain. *Dryden.*

BRA'INSICK, *a.* [*brain* and *sick.*] Disordered in the understanding; giddy; thoughtless. *Shak. Knolles.*

BRA'INSICKLY, *adv.* Weakly; with a disordered understanding. *Shak.*

BRA'INSICKNESS, *n.* Disorder of the understanding; giddiness; indiscretion.

BRAIT, *n.* Among *jewelers*, a rough diamond.

BRAKE, *pp.* of *break. Obs.* [See *Break.*]

BRAKE, *n.* [W. *brwg;* Ir. *fraoch;* Port. *brejo;* Sp. *brezo;* Dan. *bregne;* G. *breche;* L. *erica;* Gr. ερικω, ερεικω, to break. So named probably from its roughness or broken appearance.]
1. Brake is a name given to fern, or rather to the female fern, a species of cryptogamian plants, of the genus Pteris, whose fructification is in lines under the margin of the leaf or frond. *Fam. of Plants. Encyc.*
2. A place overgrown with brake. *Encyc.*
3. A thicket; a place overgrown with shrubs and brambles. *Johnson.*
4. In *the U. States*, a thicket of canes, as a *cane-brake;* but I believe used only in composition. *Ellicott.*

BRAKE, *n.* [See *Break.*] An instrument to break flax or hemp.
2. The handle or lever by which a pump is worked; that is, *brac*, *brachium*, an arm.
3. A baker's kneading trough.
4. A sharp bit, or snaffle.
5. A machine for confining refractory horses, while the smith is shoeing them. *Johnson.*
6. That part of the carriage of a movable battery or engine which enables it to turn. *Fairfax.*
7. A large heavy harrow for breaking clods after plowing; called also a drag.

BRA'KY, *a.* Full of brakes; abounding with brambles or shrubs; rough; thorny. *B. Jonson.*

BRAM'A, *n.* The bream, a fish. [See *Bream.*]

BRAM'A, **BRUM'A**, **BRAH'MA**, *n.* [*Broum*, Piromis. Herodotus. Qu. L. *primus*, Ir. *priomh*, first, chief, Goth. *frum*, origin, beginning.]
The chief deity of the Indian nations, considered as the creator of all things. *As. Researches.*

BRAM'BLE, *n.* [Sax. *brembel*, *brembr*, *bremel*, a bramble, rubus, vepres; D. *braam*, *braambosch*, *braamstruik*, bramble; Ger. *brombeer*, blackberry; *brombeerstaude*, bramble. This plant probably is named from its berry or its prickles. See *Broom.*]
The raspberry bush or blackberry bush; a general name of the genus *rubus*, of which there are several species. They are armed with prickles; hence in common language, any rough, prickly shrub.

BRAM'BLEBUSH, *n.* [*bramble* and *bush.*] The bramble, or a collection of brambles growing together. *Ash.*

BRAM'BLED, *a.* Overgrown with brambles.

BRAM'BLE-NET, *n.* [*bramble* and *net.*] A hallier, or a net to catch birds. *Encyc. Ash.*

BRAM'BLING, **BRAM'BLE**, *n.* A bird, a species of fringilla, the mountain finch. *Encyc.*

BRAM'IN, **BRAH'MIN**, *n.* [See *Brachman.*]
A priest among the Hindoos and other nations of India. There are several orders of Bramins, many of whom are very corrupt in their morals; others live sequestered from the world devoted to superstition and indolence. They are the only persons who understand the Sanscrit, or ancient language of the country, in which

their sacred books are written; and to them are European nations indebted for their knowledge of the language. They worship Brama, the supposed creator of the world, but have many subordinate deities.

BRAM'INESS, BRAMINEE', } *n.* The wife of a Bramin.

BRAMIN'ICAL, *a.* Pertaining to the Bramins, or their doctrines and worship; as the *Braminical* system. *Asiat. Researches.*

BRAM'INISM, *n.* The religion, or system of doctrines of the Bramins.

BRAN, *n.* [W. *bran*, composed of *b* and *rhan*, a piece, from *rhanu*, to rend or tear; Arm. *brenn;* Ir. and Fr. *bran.* In Italian, *brano*, is a piece or bit. Arm. *ranna;* Ir. *rannam*, to tear.]

The outer coat of wheat, rye or other farinaceous grain, separated from the flour by grinding.

BRAN-NEW, properly *brand-new, a.* [G. *brennen*, to burn; *brand*, burning.] Quite new, [fire new]; bright or shining.

BRANC'ARD, *n.* [Fr.] A horse litter. [*Not in use.*]

BR'ANCH, *n.* [Fr. *branche;* Arm. *brancq.* If *n* is not radical, this word coincides with W. *braic*, the arm, a shoot. This is probably the fact.]

1. The shoot of a tree or other plant; a limb; a bough shooting from the stem, or from another branch or bough. Johnson restricts the word to a *shoot from a main bough;* but the definition is warranted neither by etymology nor usage.

A division of a main stem, supporting the leaves and fructification. *Martyn.*

An arm of a tree sprouting from the stem. *Encyc.*

2. Any arm or extended part shooting or extended from the main body of a thing; as the *branch* of a candlestick or of an artery. Hence, from similitude, a smaller stream running into a larger one, or proceeding from it. Also, the shoot of a stag's horn; an antler.
3. Any member or part of a body, or system; a distinct article; a section or subdivision; as, charity is a *branch* of christian duty.
4. Any individual of a family descending in a collateral line; any descendant from a common parent or stock.
5. *Branches of a bridle*, two pieces of bent iron which bear the bit, the cross chains and the curb. *Encyc.*
6. In *architecture, branches of ogives* are the arches of Gothic vaults, traversing from one angle to another diagonally, and forming a cross between the other arches, which make the sides of the square, of which these arches are diagonals. *Harris.*
7. A warrant or commission given to a pilot. *Laws of Massachusetts.*
8. A chandelier. *Ash.*

BR'ANCH, *v. i.* To shoot or spread in branches; to ramify, as a plant, or as horns.

2. To divide into separate parts, or subdivisions, as a mountain, a stream, or a moral subject; to ramify.
3. To speak diffusively; to make many distinctions or divisions in a discourse.
4. To have horns shooting out. *Milton.*

BR'ANCH, *v. t.* To divide as into branches; to make subordinate divisions. *Bacon.*

2. To adorn with needle work, representing branches, flowers, or twigs. *Spenser.*

BR'ANCHED, *pp.* Divided or spread into branches; separated into subordinate parts; adorned with branches; furnished with branches.

BR'ANCHER, *n.* One that shoots forth branches.

2. A young hawk when it begins to leave the nest and take to the branches.

BR'ANCHERY, *n.* The ramifications or ramified vessels dispersed through the pulpy part of fruit. *Encyc. Ash.*

BR'ANCHINESS, *n.* Fulness of branches. *Johnson.*

BR'ANCHING, *ppr.* Shooting in branches; dividing into several subordinate parts.

BR'ANCHING, *a.* Furnished with branches; shooting out branches.

BRANCHIOS'TEGOUS, *a.* [Gr βραγχια, gills, and ςεγος, a covering.] Having gill-covers, or covered gills, as a *branchiostegous* fish; covering the gills, as the *branchiostegous* membrane. The *branchiostegi* are an order of fish in the Linnean system, the rays of whose fins are bony, but whose gill-covers are destitute of bony rays.

BR'ANCH-LEAF, *n.* A leaf growing on a branch. *Martyn.*

BR'ANCHLESS, *a.* Destitute of branches, or shoots; without any valuable product; barren; naked. *Shak.*

BR'ANCHLET, *n.* A little branch; a twig; the subdivision of a branch. *Martyn. Asiat. Researches.*

BR'ANCH-PEDUNCLE, *n.* A peduncle springing from a branch. *Martyn.*

BR'ANCH-PILOT, *n.* A pilot who has a branch or public commission. *Laws of Massachusetts and N. York.*

BR'ANCHY, *a.* Full of branches; having wide spreading branches. *Pope.*

BRAND, *n.* [Sax. *brand;* D. *brand;* G. *brand;* Dan. *brænde;* Sw. *brand;* from *brånna, brennen*, to burn. See *Burn.*]

1. A burning piece of wood; or a stick or piece of wood partly burnt, whether burning or after the fire is extinct.
2. A sword, either from brandishing, Fr. *brandir*, or from its glittering brightness; *now obsolete, unless in poetry.* *Milton.*
3. A thunder-bolt. *Granville.*
4. A mark made by burning with a hot iron, as upon a criminal, or upon a cask; a stigma; any note of infamy. *Bacon. Dryden.*

BRAND, *v. t.* To burn or impress a mark with a hot iron; as, to *brand* a criminal, by way of punishment; or to *brand* a cask or any thing else, for the purpose of fixing a mark upon it.

2. To fix a mark or character of infamy, in allusion to the branding of criminals; to stigmatize as infamous; as, to *brand* a vice with infamy. *Rowe. Addison.*

BRAND'ED, *pp.* Marked with a hot iron; stigmatized.

BRAND'-GOOSE, *n.* A species of Anas, or the goose kind; usually called in America *brant* or *brent.*

BRAND'ING, *ppr.* Impressing a mark with a hot iron; fixing a stigma or mark of reproach.

BRAND'-IRON, BRAND'ING-IRON, } *n.* An iron to brand with.

BRAND'ISH, *v. t.* [Fr. *brandir;* Port. *brandir;* Sp. *blandir, r* changed into *l;* It. *brandire;* probably allied to Fr. *branler*, to shake.]

1. To move or wave, as a weapon; to raise, and move in various directions; to shake or flourish; as, to *brandish* a sword or a cane. It often indicates *threatening.*
2. To play with; to flourish; as, to *brandish* syllogisms. *Locke.*

BRAND'ISHED, *pp.* Raised and waved in the air with a flourish.

BRAND'ISHER, *n.* One who brandishes.

BRAND'ISHING, *ppr.* Raising and waving in the air; flourishing.

BRAND'LING, *n.* A kind of worm. *Walton.*

BRAND'-NEW, *a.* Quite new; bright as a brand of fire. *Tatler.*

BRAN'DY, *n.* [D. *branden;* Ger. *brennen*, to distil; *branden*, to boil; *brenner*, a distiller; G. *branntwein;* Fr. *brandevin*, brandy. See *Burn.*]

An ardent spirit distilled from wine. The same name is now given to spirit distilled from other liquors, and in the U. States particularly to that which is distilled from cyder and peaches.

BRAN'DY-WINE, *n.* Brandy. *Wiseman.*

BRAN'GLE, *n.* [Russ. *bran*, war, strife, noise, broil; *branyu*, to hinder, to scold; L. *frendeo.* Qu. *wrangle.* Brangle, in Scottish, signifies to shake, or to threaten; Fr. *branler.*]

A wrangle; a squabble; a noisy contest or dispute. *Swift.*

BRAN'GLE, *v. i.* To wrangle; to dispute contentiously; to squabble. *Swift.*

BRAN'GLEMENT, *n.* Wrangle; brangle.

BRAN'GLING, *n.* A quarrel. *Whitlock.*

BRANK, *n.* [So named probably from its joints, *breaks.* "Galliæ quoque suum genus farris dedere; quod illic *brance* vocant, apud nos sandalum, nitidissimi grani." Plin. 18. 7.]

1. Buckwheat, a species of polygonum; a grain cultivated mostly for beasts and poultry; but in the U. States, the flour is much used for making breakfast cakes.
2. In some parts of England and Scotland, a *scolding-bridle*, an instrument for correcting scolding women. It consists of a headpiece, which incloses the head of the offender, and of a sharp iron which enters the mouth and restrains the tongue. *Plott. Encyc.*

BRANK'URSINE, *n.* [*brank* and *ursus*, a bear.]

Bear's-breech, or acanthus, a genus of plants, of several species. The leaves of the common sort are said to have furnished the model of the Corinthian capitals.

BRAN'LIN, *n.* A species of fish of the salmon kind, in some places called the *fingry*, from five or six black lines or marks on each side resembling fingers. It is found in rapid streams. *Dict. of Nat. Hist.*

BRAN'NY, *a.* [from *bran.*] Having the appearance of bran; consisting of bran. *Wiseman.*

BRAN'SLE, *n.* A brawl, or dance. [*Not used.*] *Spenser.*

BRANT, *n.* [Qu. *brand*, burnt or brown.] A species of anas or the goose kind; called also *brent* and *brand-goose*, which see.

BRANT, *a.* Steep. *Todd.*

BRA'SEN, *a. brázn.* Made of brass. [See *Brass* and *Brazen.*]

BRA'SIER, *n. brázhur.* An artificer who works in brass. *Franklin.*

2. A pan for holding coals. [See *Brass.*]

BRASIL. [See *Brazil.*]

BR'ASS, *n.* [Sax. *bræs*; W. *prês*; Corn. *brest*; Ir. *pras.* In Welsh, *prês* signifies *brass* and what is quick, ready, sharp, smart, also haste, fuel, and *presu*, to render imminent, to hasten, to render *present.* The latter sense indicates that it is from the Latin. But I see no connection between these senses and *brass.* This word may be named from its bright color, and be allied to Port. *braza*, Sp. *brasas*, live coals, *abrazar*, *abrasar*, to burn or inflame; but the real origin and primary sense are not evident.]

1. An alloy of copper and zink, of a yellow color; usually containing about one third of its weight of zink, but the proportions are variable. The best brass is made by cementation of calamine or the oxyd of zink with granulated copper. *Thomson. Encyc.*

2. Impudence; a brazen face.

BR'ASSE, *n.* The pale spotted perch, with two long teeth on each side; the *lucioperca.* *Ash.*

BRAS'SICA, *n.* [L.] Cabbage. *Pope.*

BR'ASSINESS, *n.* A quality of brass; the appearance of brass.

BR'ASS-PAVED, *a.* Hard as brass. *Spenser.*

BR'ASS-VISAGED, *a.* Impudent. *Todd.*

BR'ASSY, *a.* Pertaining to brass; partaking of brass; hard as brass; having the color of brass.

2. Impudent; impudently bold.

BRAST, *a.* Burst. [*Not in use.*] *Spenser.*

BRAT, *n.* A child, so called in contempt.

2. Offspring: progeny.

BRAUL, *n.* Indian cloth with blue and white stripes, called *turbants.* *Encyc.*

BRAVA'DO, *n.* [Sp. *bravata*; Fr. *bravade.* See *Brave.*]

A boast or brag; an arrogant menace, intended to intimidate.

BRAVE, *a.* [Fr. *brave*; Arm. *brao*; Sp. Port. It. *bravo*; D. *braaf*; Sw. *braf*; Dan. *brav*; Ger. *brav*, whence *braviren*, to look big, to bully or hector. In Sp. and Port. *bravo* signifies *brave*, valiant, strenuous, bullying, fierce, wild, savage, rude, unpolished, excellent, fine; *bravear*, to bully, to menace in an arrogant manner; *brava* is a swell of the sea; *braveza*, valor, and fury of the elements. The word *brave* expresses also a showy dress; Arm. *bragal*, to be well dressed, fine, spruce, of which *brao* seems to be a contraction. The word bears the sense of open, bold, expanding, and rushing, vaunting. It is doubtless contracted, and probably from the root of *brag.*]

1. Courageous; bold; daring; intrepid; fearless of danger; as a *brave* warrior. It usually unites the sense of *courage* with *generosity* and *dignity* of mind; qualities often united. *Bacon.*

The *brave* man will not deliberately do an injury to his fellow man. *Anon.*

2. Gallant; lofty; graceful; having a noble mien. *Shak.*

3. Magnificent; grand; as a *brave* place. *Denham.*

4. Excellent; noble; dignified. *But in modern usage, it has nearly lost its application to things.*

5. Gaudy; showy in dress. [Ar. برق to adorn.] *Obs.* *Spenser.*

BRAVE, *n.* A hector; a man daring beyond discretion or decency.

Hot *braves* like these may fight. *Dryden.*

2. A boast; a challenge; a defiance. *Shak.*

BRAVE, *v. t.* To defy; to challenge; to encounter with courage and fortitude, or without being moved; to set at defiance.

The ills of love I can *brave.*

The rock that *braves* the tempest. *Dryden.*

2. To carry a boasting appearance of; as, to *brave* that which they believe not. *Bacon.*

BRA'VED, *pp.* Defied; set at defiance; met without dismay, or being moved.

BRA'VELY, *adv.* Courageously; gallantly; splendidly; in a brave manner; heroically. In Spenser, finely; gaudily.

BRA'VERY, *n.* Courage; heroism; undaunted spirit; intrepidity; gallantry; fearlessness of danger; often united with generosity or dignity of mind which despises meanness and cruelty, and disdains to take advantage of a vanquished enemy.

The duellist, in proving his *bravery*, shows that he thinks it suspected. *Anon.*

2. Splendor; magnificence; showy appearance.

The *bravery* of their tinkling ornaments. Is. iii. *Spenser.*

3. Show; ostentation; fine dress. *Bacon.*

4. Bravado; boast. *Bacon. Sidney.*

5. A showy person. *Spenser.*

[*In the last four senses, this word is nearly antiquated.*]

BRA'VING, *ppr.* Setting at defiance; challenging.

BRA'VO, *n.* [It. and Sp.] A daring villain; a bandit; one who sets law at defiance; an assassin or murderer. *Gov't of the Tongue.*

BRAWL, *v. i.* [G. *brüllen*; D. *brullen*; Dan. *vraaler* and *bröler*; Sw. *vråla*, to roar or bellow; Fr. *brailler*; Arm. *brailhat*, to brawl or be noisy; L. *prælior*; W. *broliaw*, to boast, to brag; *brawl*, a shooting out, a boast.]

1. To quarrel noisily and indecently. *Watts.*

2. To speak loud and indecently. *Shak.*

3. To roar as water; to make a noise. *Shak.*

BRAWL, *v. t.* To drive or beat away. *Shak.*

BRAWL, *n.* [Norm. *braul.*] Noise; quarrel; scurrility; uproar. *Hooker.*

2. Formerly, a kind of dance. *Shak. B. Jonson. Gray.*

BRAWL'ER, *n.* A noisy fellow; a wrangler. *Ayliffe.*

BRAWL'ING, *n.* The act of quarreling.

BRAWL'INGLY, *adv.* In a quarrelsome manner. *Huloet.*

BRAWN, *n.* [L. *aprugnus*, caro *aprugna.*]

1. The flesh of a boar, or the animal.

2 The fleshy, protuberant, muscular part of the body. *Peacham.*

3. Bulk; muscular strength. *Dryden.*

4. The arm, from its muscles or strength. *Shak.*

BRAWN'ED, *a.* Brawny; strong. *Spenser.*

BRAWN'ER, *n.* A boar killed for the table. *Johnson. King.*

BRAWN'INESS, *n.* The quality of being brawny; strength; hardiness. *Locke.*

BRAWN'Y, *a.* Musculous; fleshy; bulky; having large, strong muscles; strong. *Dryden.*

BRAY, *v. t.* [Sax. *bracan*; Fr. *broyer*, to pound, or bruise; *braire*, to roar, or bray as an ass; Arm. *bregui*, to roar; Norm. *brair*, to cry, to *brag*; Gr. βραχω; W. *briwaw*, to break in pieces, to rub, or grind; *breyan*, a quern; Ir. *bra*, a handmill. See *Brag* and *Break.*]

1. To pound, beat or grind small; as, to *bray* a fool in a mortar. Prov. xxvii.

2. To make a harsh sound, as of an ass. *Dryden.*

3. To make a harsh, disagreeable grating sound. *Milton.*

BRAY, *n.* The harsh sound or roar of an ass; a harsh grating sound.

2. Shelving ground. *Fairfax.*

BRAY, *n.* [W. *bre*, a mount or peak.] A bank or mound of earth. *Obs.* *Herbert.*

BRA'YER, *n.* One that brays like an ass. *Pope.*

2. A instrument to temper ink in printing offices. *Bailey. Johnson.*

BRA'YING, *ppr.* Pounding or grinding small; roaring.

BRA'YING, *n.* Roar; noise; clamor. *Smith.*

BRAZE, *v. t.* [Fr. *braser.*] To soder with brass. *Moxon.*

2. To harden to impudence; to harden as with brass. *Shak.*

BRA'ZEN, *a. brázn.* Made of brass; as a *brazen* helmet. *Dryden.*

2. Pertaining to brass; proceeding from brass; as a *brazen* din. *Shak.*

3. Impudent; having a front like brass.

Brazen age, or age of brass, in mythology, the age which succeeded the *silver age*, when men had degenerated from primitive purity.

Brazen dish, among miners, is the standard by which other dishes are guaged, and is kept in the king's hall. *England.*

Brazen sea, in Jewish antiquity, a huge vessel of brass, cast on the plain of Jordan, and placed in Solomon's temple. It was ten cubits from brim to brim, five in height, thirty in circumference, and contained 3000 baths. It was designed for the priests to wash themselves in, before they performed the service of the temple. *Encyc.*

BRA'ZEN, *v. i. brázn.* To be impudent; to bully. *Arbuthnot.*

BRA'ZEN-FACE, *n.* [*brazen* and *face.*] An impudent person; one remarkable for effrontery. *Shak.*

BRA'ZEN-FACED, *a.* Impudent; bold to excess; shameless. *Dryden.*

BRA'ZENLY, *adv.* In a bold impudent manner.

BRA'ZENNESS, *n.* Appearance like brass. In this sense, *brassiness* is the more correct word.

2. Impudence; excess of assurance.

BRAZIER. [See *Brasier.*]

BRAZIL', **BRAZIL'-WOOD**, *n.* [Port. *braza*, a live coal, or glowing fire. This name was given to the wood for its color, and it is said that King Emanuel of Portugal gave this name to the country in America on account of its producing this wood. It was first named Santa Cruz, by its discoverer, Pedro Alvares Cabral. *Lindley's Narrative of a voyage to Brazil. Med. Rep.* Hex. 2. vol. 3. 200.]

Brazil, or brazil-wood, or braziletto, is a very heavy wood of a red color, growing in Brazil, and other tropical countries. It is used in manufactures for dyeing red. It is a species of Cæsalpina.

BRAZILET'TO, *n.* The same as Brazil-wood.

BRAZIL'IAN, *a.* Pertaining to Brazil; as, *Brazilian* strand. *Barlow.*

BREACH, *n.* [Fr. *breche;* D. *breuk;* Ger. *bruch;* Sw. *bråck;* Dan. *brœk;* Sp. and Port. *brecha.* See *Break.*]

1. The act of breaking; or state of being broken; a rupture; a break; a gap; the space between the severed parts of a solid body parted by violence; as a *breach* in a garment, or in a wall.

2. The violation of a law; the violation or non-fulfilment of a contract; the non-performance of a moral duty; non-performance of duty being a *breach* of obligation, as well as a positive transgression or violation.

> Every *breach* of the public engagements is hurtful to public credit. *Hamilton.*

3. An opening in a coast. [*Not usual.*] *Spenser.*

4. Separation between friends by means of enmity; difference; quarrel. *Clarendon.*

5. Infraction; injury; invasion; as a *breach* upon kingly power. *Clarendon.*

6. Bereavement; loss of a friend and its consequent affliction.

7. A violation of the public peace, as by a riot, affray, or any tumult which is contrary to law, and destructive to the public tranquillity, is called a *breach of the peace.*

BREACH, *v. t.* To make a breach, or opening. *Life of Wellington.*

BREAD, *n. bred.* [Sax. *breod;* G. *brot;* D. *brood;* Sw. *brod;* Dan. *bröd.* Qu. Gr. βρωτος, any thing esculent. If the word signifies food in general, or that which is eaten, probably it is the Heb. and Ch. ברות, from ברה barah, to eat or feed. But in German, it signifies loaf as well as bread. "Zehen brot," ten loaves. It may therefore signify primarily a lump or portion.]

1. A mass of dough, made by moistening and kneading the flour or meal of some species of grain, and baked in an oven, or pan.

2. Food in general.

> In the sweat of thy face shalt thou eat *bread.* Gen. iii.

> Give us this day our daily *bread.* *Lord's Prayer.*

3. Support of life in general; maintenance.

> Is the reward of virtue, *bread?* *Pope.*

Bee-bread. [See *Bee.*]

Ship-bread, bread for ships; hard biscuits.

Cassada-bread. [See *Cassada.*]

BREAD, *v. t.* [Sax. *brœdan.* See *Broad.*] To spread. [*Not used.*] *Ray.*

BREAD'-CHIPPER, *n.* [*bread* and *chip.*] One who chips bread; a baker's servant; an under butler. *Shak.*

BREAD'-CORN, *n.* [*bread* and *corn.*] Corn of which bread is made. This in most countries is wheat and rye; but in some countries bread is made of other grain, as of maize in some parts of America.

BREAD'EN, *a.* Made of bread. [*Little used.*] *Rogers.*

BREAD'LESS, *a.* Without bread; destitute of food.

BREAD'-ROOM, *n.* An apartment in a ship's hold, where the bread is kept.

BREAD'-TREE, *n.* [*bread* and *tree.*] The *bread-fruit tree*, or Artocarpus, a tree which grows in the isles of the Pacific ocean, of the size of an apple-tree, producing a fruit shaped like a heart, and as large as a small loaf of bread, which is eaten as food. *Encyc.*

BREADTH, *n. bredth.* [Sax. *brœd* and *bred.* See *Board* and *Broad.*]

The measure or extent of any plain surface from side to side; a geometrical dimension, which, multiplied into the length, constitutes a surface; as, the length of a table is five feet, and the *breadth*, three; 5 × 3 = 15 foot, the whole surface.

BREADTH'LESS, *a.* Having no breadth. *More.*

BREAK, *v. t.* pret. *broke*, [*brake. Obs.*]; pp. *broke* or *broken.* [Sax. *brœcan*, *brecan*, to break, and *bracan*, to bray, as in a mortar; Sw. *bråka;* Dan. *brœkker;* D. *braaken*, *breeken;* G. *brechen;* W. *bregu*, to break; *breg*, a rent or rupture; *breç*, a breaking out, a *freckle;* Goth. *brikan;* Ir. *bracaim*, to break, to harrow; Sp. and Port. *brecha*, a breach; L. *frango*, *fregi*, *n* casual; Arm. *fricga;* Fr. *fracas;* Heb. Ch. Syr. Sam. Ar. פרק to break, to free or deliver, to separate; Gr. φρασσω, φραγμα. These words seem also to be allied to ברך and פרך. If the first consonant is a prefix, which is probable, then connected with these words are the Gr. ρηγνυω, and ερειχω, W. *rhwygaw*, Arm. *roga*, *rega*, to rend. *Wreck* is probably of the same family. The primary sense is to strain, stretch, *rack*, drive; hence, to strain and burst or break. It should be noted that the Greek ρηγη, in the Æolic dialect, is βρηγη.]

1. To part or divide by force and violence, as a solid substance; to rend apart; as, to *break* a band; to *break* a thread or a cable.

2. To burst or open by force.

> The fountains of the earth were *broke* open. *Burnet.*

3. To divide by piercing or penetrating; to burst forth; as, the light *breaks* through the clouds. *Dryden.*

4. To make breaches or gaps by battering, as in a wall. *Shak.*

5. To destroy, crush, weaken, or impair, as the human body or constitution. *Milton.*

6. To sink; to appall or subdue; as, to *break* the spirits, or the passions. *Philips.*

7. To crush; to shatter; to dissipate the strength of, as of an army. *Dryden.*

8. To weaken, or impair, as the faculties. *Shak.*

9. To tame; to train to obedience; to make tractable; as, to *break* a horse. *Addison.*

10. To make bankrupt. *South.*

11. To discard, dismiss or cashier; as, to *break* an officer. *Swift.*

12. To crack, to part or divide, as the skin; to open, as an aposteme.

13. To violate, as a contract or promise, either by a positive act contrary to the promise, or by neglect or non-fulfilment.

14. To infringe or violate, as a law, or any moral obligation, either by a positive act or by an omission of what is required. *Dryden.*

15. To stop; to interrupt; to cause to cease; as, to *break* conversation; to *break* sleep. *Shak.*

16. To intercept; to check; to lessen the force of; as, to *break* a fall, or a blow. *Bacon.*

17. To separate; to part; as, to *break* company or friendship. *Atterbury.*

18. To dissolve any union; sometimes with *off;* as, to *break off* a connection.

19. To cause to abandon; to reform or cause to reform; as, to *break* one of ill habits or practices. *Grew.*

20. To open as a purpose; to propound something new; to make a first disclosure of opinions; as, to *break* one's mind. *Bacon.*

21. To frustrate; to prevent.

> If plagues or earthquakes *break* not heaven's design. *Pope.*

22. To take away; as, to *break* the whole staff of bread. Ps. cv.

23. To stretch; to strain; to rack; as, to *break* one on the wheel.

To break the back, to strain or dislocate the vertebers with too heavy a burden; also, to disable one's fortune. *Shak.*

To break bulk, to begin to unload. *Mar. Dict.*

To break a deer, to cut it up at table. *Johnson.*

To break fast, to eat the first meal in the day, but used as a compound word.

To break ground, to plow. *Carew.*

To break ground, to dig; to open trenches. *Encyc.*

To break the heart, to afflict grievously; to cause great sorrow or grief; to depress with sorrow or despair. *Dryden.*

To break a jest, to utter a jest unexpected. *Johnson.*

To break the neck, to dislocate the joints of the neck. *Shak.*

To break off, to put a sudden stop to; to interrupt; to discontinue.

> *Break off* thy sins by righteousness. Dan. iv.

2. To sever; to divide; as, to *break off* a twig.

To break sheer, in marine language. When a ship at anchor is in a position to keep clear of the anchor, but is forced by wind or current out of that position, she *breaks her sheer.* *Mar. Dict.*

To break up, to dissolve or put an end to; as, to *break up* house-keeping.

2. To open or lay open; as, to *break up* a bed of earth.

3. To plow ground the first time, or after lying long unplowed; *a common use in the U. States.*

4. To separate; as, to *break up* a company.

5. To disband; as, to *break up* an army.

To break upon the wheel, to stretch and break the bones by torture upon the wheel.

To break wind, to give vent to wind from the body backward.

BREAK, *v. i.* To part; to separate; to divide in two; as, the ice *breaks*; a band *breaks*.

2. To burst; as, a storm or deluge *breaks*. *Dryden.*

3. To burst, by dashing against something; as, a wave *breaks* upon a rock. *Pope.*

4. To open, as a tumor or aposteme. *Harvey.*

5. To open, as the morning; to show the first light; to dawn. *Addison.*

6. To burst forth; to utter or exclaim. *Shak.*

7. To fail in trade or other occupation; to become bankrupt. *Pope.*

8. To decline in health and strength; to begin to lose the natural vigor. *Swift.*

9. To issue out with vehemence. *Pope.*

10. To make way with violence or suddenness; to rush; often with a particle; as, to *break in*; to *break in upon*, as calamities; to *break over*, as a flood; to *break out*, as a fire; to *break forth*, as light or a sound.

11. To come to an explanation.

> I am to *break* with thee upon some affairs. [*I believe, antiquated.*] *Shak.*

12. To suffer an interruption of friendship; to fall out.

> Be not afraid to *break* with traitors. *B. Jonson.*

13. To faint, flag or pant.

> My soul *breaketh* for longing to thy judgments. Ps. cxix.

To break away, to disengage itself from; to rush from; also, to dissolve itself or dissipate, as fog or clouds.

To break forth, to issue out.

To break from, to disengage from; to depart abruptly, or with vehemence. *Roscommon.*

To break in, to enter by force; to enter unexpectedly; to intrude. *Addison.*

To break loose, to get free by force; to escape from confinement by violence; to shake off restraint. *Milton. Tillotson.*

To break off, to part; to divide; also, to desist suddenly. *Bacon.*

To break off from, to part from with violence. *Shak.*

To break out, to issue forth; to discover itself by its effects, to arise or spring up; as, a fire *breaks out*; a sedition *breaks out*; a fever *breaks out*. *Dryden. Milton.*

2. To appear in eruptions, as pustules; to have pustules, or an efflorescence on the skin, as a child *breaks out*. Hence we have *freckle* from the root of *break*; Welsh *breç*.

3. To throw off restraint, and become dissolute. *Dryden.*

To break up, to dissolve itself and separate; as a company *breaks up*; a meeting *breaks up*; a fog *breaks up*; but more generally we say, fog, mist or clouds *break away*.

To break with, to part in enmity; to cease to be friends; as, to *break with* a friend or companion. *Pope.*

This verb carries with it its primitive sense of *straining*, *parting*, *severing*, *bursting*, often with violence, with the consequential senses of *injury*, *defect*, and *infirmity*.

BREAK, *n.* A state of being open, or the act of separating; an opening made by force; an open place. It is the same word as *brack*, differently written and pronounced.

2. A pause; an interruption.

3. A line in writing or printing, noting a suspension of the sense, or a stop in the sentence.

4. In a ship, the *break of the deck* is the part where it terminates, and the descent on to the next deck below commences.

5. The first appearance of light in the morning; the dawn; as the *break* of day. Ar. فَرَقٌ farakon, id.

6. In *architecture*, a recess.

BREĀKAĠE, *n.* A breaking; also, an allowance for things broken, in transportation.

BREĀKER, *n.* The person who breaks any thing; a violator or transgressor; as a *breaker* of the law. *South.*

2. A rock which breaks the waves; or the wave itself which breaks against a rock, a sand bank, or the shore, exhibiting a white foam. *Mar. Dict. Johnson.*

3. A pier, mound or other solid matter, placed in a river, to break the floating ice, and prevent it from injuring a bridge below; called also *ice-breaker*.

4. One that breaks up ground.

5. A destroyer. Micah ii.

BREAK′FAST, *n.* brek′fast. [*break* and *fast.*]

1. The first meal in the day; or the thing eaten at the first meal.

2. A meal, or food in general. *Dryden.*

BREAK′FAST, *v. i.* brek′fast. To eat the first meal in the day.

BREAK′FASTING, *ppr.* Eating or taking the first meal in the day.

BREAK′FASTING, *n.* A party at breakfast. *Chesterfield.*

BREĀKING, *ppr.* Parting by violence; rending asunder; becoming bankrupt.

BREĀKNECK, *n.* [*break* and *neck.*] A fall that breaks the neck; a steep place endangering the neck. *Shak.*

BREĀKPROMISE, *n.* [*break* and *promise.*] One who makes a practice of breaking his promise. [*Not used.*] *Shak.*

BREĀKVOW, *n.* [*break* and *vow.*] One who habitually breaks his vows. [*Not used.*] *Shak.*

BREĀKWATER, *n.* [*break* and *water.*] The hull of an old vessel sunk at the entrance of a harbor, to break or diminish the force of the waves, to secure the vessels in harbor. *Mar. Dict.*

2. A small buoy fastened to a large one, when the rope of the latter is not long enough to reach the surface of the water. *Mar. Dict.*

3. A mole, at the mouth of a harbor, intended to break the force of the waves.

BREAM, *n.* [Fr. *breme*; Ch. אברומה, abrumah; Sp. *brema.*]

A fish, the *Cyprinus brama*, an inhabitant of lakes and deep water, extremely insipid and little valued. *Encyc. Walton.*

BREAM, *v. t.* In *sea language*, to burn off the filth, such as grass, sea weed, ooze, &c., from a ship's bottom. *Mar. Dict.*

BREAST, *n.* brest. [Sax. *breast*; Sw. *brôst*; D. *borst*, the breast, a lad, a notch; G. *brust*, breast, and *brüsten*, to hold up the head, to look big; Dan. *bröst*, breast; also default, defect, blemish; also, *bryst*, breast, pap; *bryster sig*, to strut; *brister*, to burst. The sense seems to be, a protuberance.]

1. The soft, protuberant body, adhering to the thorax, which, in females, furnishes milk for infants.

> His *breasts* are full of milk. Job xxi. 24.

2. The fore part of the thorax, or the fore part of the human body between the neck and the belly.

3. The part of a beast which answers to the breast in man. This, in quadrupeds, is between the fore legs, below the neck.

4. *Figuratively*, the heart; the conscience; the disposition of the mind; the affections; the seat of the affections and passions. *Cowley. Dryden.*

5. Formerly, the power of singing. *Tusser.*

BREAST, *v. t.* brest. To meet in front; to oppose breast to breast. *Goldsmith. Dwight.*

> The court *breasted* the popular current by sustaining the demurrer. *Wirt.*

BREAST′BONE, *n.* [*breast* and *bone.*] The bone of the breast; the sternum. *Peacham.*

BREAST′-C̀ASKET, *n.* [*breast* and *casket.*]

One of the largest and longest of the caskets or strings on the middle of the yard of a ship. *Johnson.* [*I do not find this word in the Mariner's Dictionary.*]

BREAST′DEEP, *a.* Breast high; as high as the breast.

BREAST′ED, *a.* Having a broad breast; having a fine voice. *Fiddes.*

BREAST′F̀AST, *n.* [*breast* and *fast.*] A large rope to confine a ship sidewise to a wharf or key. *Mar. Dict.*

BREAST′HIGH, *a.* [*breast* and *high.*] High as the breast. *Sidney.*

BREAST′HO̱OK, *n.* [*breast* and *hook.*] A thick piece of timber placed directly across the stem of a ship to strengthen the fore part and unite the bows on each side. *Mar. Dict.*

BREAST′ING, *ppr.* Meeting with the breast; opposing in front.

BREAST′KNOT, *n.* [*breast* and *knot.*] A knot of ribins worn on the breast. *Addison.*

BREAST′PLATE, *n.* [*breast* and *plate.*]

1. Armor for the breast. *Cowley.*

2. A strap that runs across a horse's breast. *Ash.*

3. In *Jewish antiquity*, a part of the vestment of the high priest, consisting of a folded piece of the rich embroidered stuff of which the ephod was made. It was set with twelve precious stones, on which were engraved the names of the twelve tribes. *Encyc.*

BREAST′PLOW, *n.* [*breast* and *plow.*] A plow, driven by the breast, used to cut or pare turf. *Johnson.*

BREAST′ROPE, *n.* [*breast* and *rope.*] In a ship, *breast ropes* are used to fasten the yards to the parrels, and with the parrels, to hold the yards fast to the mast; now called *parrel ropes*.

BREAST'-WŎRK, *n.* [*breast* and *work.*] In *fortification*, a work thrown up for defense; a parapet, which see.

BREATH, *n. breth.* [Sax. *bræth*, odor, scent, breath; G. *brodem*, steam, vapor, breath.]

1. The air inhaled and expelled in the respiration of animals.

2. Life.

No man has more contempt than I of *breath.* *Dryden.*

3. The state or power of breathing freely; opposed to a state of exhaustion from violent action; as, I am out of *breath;* I am scarce in *breath.* *Shak.*

4. Respite; pause; time to breathe; as, let me take *breath*; give me some *breath.* *Shak.*

5. Breeze; air in gentle motion.

Calm and unruffled as a summer's sea,
When not a *breath* of wind flies o'er its surface. *Addison.*

6. A single respiration; as, he swears at every *breath.*

7. An instant; the time of a single respiration; a single act.

He smiles and he frowns in a *breath.* *Dryden.*

8. A word.

A *breath* can make them, as a *breath* has made. *Goldsmith.*

BRE'ATHABLE, *a.* That may be breathed.

BREATHE, *v. i.* To respire; to inspire and expire air. Hence, to live. *Pope. Shak.*

2. To take breath; to rest from action; as, let them have time to *breathe.*

3. To pass as air.

To whose foul mouth no wholesome air *breathes* in. *Shak.*

BREATHE, *v. t.* To inhale as air into the lungs and expel it; as, to *breathe* vital air. *Dryden.*

2. To inject by breathing; to infuse; followed by *into.*

And the Lord God *breathed into* his nostrils the breath of life. Gen. ii.

3. To expire; to eject by breathing; followed by *out;* as, to *breathe out* threatenings and slaughter. *Acts.*

4. To exercise; to keep in breath.

The greyhounds are as swift as *breathed* stags. *Shak.*

5. To inspire or blow into; to cause to sound by breathing; as, to *breathe* the flute. *Prior.*

6. To exhale; to emit as breath; as, the flowers *breathe* odors or perfume.

7. To utter softly or in private; as, to *breathe* a vow. *Shak.*

8. To give air or vent to; to open; as, to *breathe* a vein. [W. *brathu*, to pierce.] *Johnson. Dryden.*

9. To express; to manifest.

Other articles *breathe* the same severe spirit. *Milner.*

BRE'ATHED, *pp.* Inhaled and exhaled; respired; uttered.

BRE'ATHER, *n.* One that breathes or lives; one that utters; an inspirer, one who animates or infuses by inspiration.

BREATH'FUL, *a. breth'ful.* Full of breath; full of odor. *Spenser.*

BRE'ATHING, *ppr.* Respiring; living; uttering.

2. *a.* Exhibiting to the life; as *breathing* paint. *Pope.*

BRE'ATHING, *n.* Respiration; the act of inhaling and exhaling air.

2. Aspiration; secret prayer. *Prior.*

3. Breathing-place; vent. *Dryden.*

4. Accent; aspiration.

BRE'ATHING-PLACE, *n.* A pause.

2. A vent.

BRE'ATHING-TIME, *n.* Pause; relaxation. *Hall.*

BREATH'LESS, *a. breth'less.* Being out of breath; spent with labor or violent action.

2. Dead; as a *breathless* body. *Shak.*

BREATH'LESSNESS, *n.* The state of being exhausted of breath. *Hall.*

BREC'CIA, *n.* [It. a *breach.*] In *mineralogy*, an aggregate composed of angular fragments of the same mineral, or of different minerals, united by a cement, and presenting a variety of colors. Sometimes a few of the fragments are a little rounded. The varieties are the siliceous, calcarious and trap breccias. *Cleaveland.*

When rounded stones and angular fragments are united by a cement, the aggregate is usually called coarse conglomerate.

BREC'CIATED, *a.* Consisting of angular fragments, cemented together.

BRECH'ITE, *n.* A fossil allied to the Alcyons. It is cylindrical, striated, and its thick end conical, pierced with holes, and crested. *Fr. Dict. Nat. Hist.*

BRED, *pp.* of *breed.* Generated; produced; contrived; educated.

BREDE, *n.* A braid. [*Not used.*] *Addison.*

BREECH, *n. brich.* [See *Breach* and *Break.*] The lower part of the body behind.

2. Breeches; *but rarely used in the singular.* *Shak.*

3. The hinder part of any thing. *Johnson.*

BREECH, *v. t.* To put into breeches. *Johnson.*

2. To whip on the breech. *Massinger.*

3. See *Britch.*

BREECHES, *n. plu. brich'es.* [Sax *bræc*, *bræccæ;* D. *broek;* Arm. *braga*, *brages*; It. *brace*, *brachesse* or *braghesse;* Port. Sp. *bragas;* Fr. *braies*; Ir. *brog;* Low L. *braccæ;* Dan. *brog*, breeches, and *broged*, of various colors, mixed, variegated; W. *bryçan*, a spotted covering, scotch plaid; *bryc*, variegated with colors. "Sarmatæ totum *braccati* corpus." Mela, 2. 1. See Plin. 3. 4. Herod. Lib. 7. Strabo, Lib. 15. Ovid. Trist. 5. 7. Cluv. Germ. Ant. 1. 16. Pelloutier, Hist. Celt. 1. 30. The word seems to be from the root of *break*, and to denote, diverse in color, variegated, like *freckled.* See *Freckle.*]

A garment worn by men, covering the hips and thighs. It is now a close garment; but the word formerly was used for a loose garment, now called trowsers, *laxæ braccæ.* *Ovid.*

To wear the breeches is, in the wife, to usurp the authority of the husband. *Johnson.*

BREECHING, *ppr. brich'ing.* Furnishing with breeches, or with a breech. [See *Britch.*]

2. Whipping the breech; and as a noun, a whipping. *Marlow.*

BREECHING, in gunnery on board of ships. [See *Britching.*]

BREED, *v. t.* pret. and pp. *bred.* [Sax. *bredan*, *brædan*, to warm, to dilate, to open, to spread; D. *broeden*, to brood; Ger. *brüten*, to brood; Dan. *breder*, to spread, dilate, unfold; W. *brwd*, warm; *brydiaw*, to warm, to heat. Class Rd. See *Broad.*]

1. To generate; to engender; to hatch; to produce the young of any species of animals. I think it is never used of plants, and in animals is always applied to the mother or dam.

2. To produce within or upon the body; as, to *breed* teeth; to *breed* worms.

3. To cause; to occasion; to produce; to originate.

Intemperance and lust *breed* infirmities. *Tillotson.*

Ambition *breeds* factions. *Anon.*

4. To contrive; to hatch; to produce by plotting.

Had he a heart and a brain to *breed* it in? *Shak.*

5. To give birth to; to be the native place of; as, a pond *breeds* fish; a northern country *breeds* a race of stout men.

6. To educate; to instruct; to form by education; often, but unnecessarily, followed by *up;* as, to *breed* a son to an occupation; a man *bred* at a university. *To breed up* is vulgar.

7. To bring up; to nurse and foster; to take care of in infancy, and through the age of youth; to provide for, train and conduct; to instruct the mind and form the manners in youth.

To bring thee forth with pain, with care to *breed.* *Dryden.*

BREED, *v. i.* To produce, as a fetus; to bear and nourish, as in pregnancy; as, a female *breeds* with pain.

2. To be formed in the parent or dam; to be generated, or to grow, as young before birth; as, children or young *breed* in the matrix.

3. To have birth; to be produced; as, fish *breed* in rivers.

4. To be increased by a new production.

But could youth last and love still *breed.* *Raleigh.*

5. To raise a breed; as, to choose the best species of swine to *breed* from.

BREED, *n.* A race or progeny from the same parents or stock.

2. A cast; a kind; a race of men or other animals, which have an alliance by nativity, or some distinctive qualities in common; as a *breed* of men in a particular country; a *breed* of horses or sheep. *Applied to men, it is not elegant.* We use *race.*

3. Progeny; offspring; applied to other things than animals. *Shak.*

4. A number produced at once; a hatch; a brood; but for this, *brood* is generally used. *Grew.*

BREE'D-BATE, *n.* One that breeds or originates quarrels. [*Not in use.*] *Shak.*

BREE'DER, *n.* The female that breeds or produces, whether human or other animal.

2. The person who educates or brings up; that which brings up.

Italy and Rome have been the best *breeders* of worthy men. *Ascham.*

3. That which produces.

Time is the nurse and *breeder* of all good. *Shak.*

4. One who raises a breed; one who takes care to raise a particular breed, or breeds, as of horses or cattle. *Temple.*

BREE'DING, *ppr.* Bearing and nourishing,

as a fetus; engendering; producing; educating.

BREE'DING, *n.* The act of generating or of producing.

2. The raising of a breed or breeds; as, the farmer attends to the *breeding* of sheep.

3. Nurture; education; instruction; formation of manners.

She had her *breeding* at my father's charge. *Shak.*

4. *By way of eminence*, manners; knowledge of ceremony; deportment or behavior in the external offices and decorums of social life. Hence *good breeding* is politeness, or the qualifications which constitute genteel deportment. *Encyc.*

BREEZE, *n.* [Sax. *briosa*, from its sound, resembling a breeze.]

A genus of flies or insects, technically called *Tabanus*. There are many species, but the most noted is the *bovinus*, great horse-fly, whose mouth is armed with two hooks which penetrate the skin of an animal, while with a proboscis, like a sting, it sucks the blood.

BREEZE, *n.* [It. *brezza*, a cold, windy mist; Sp. *brisa*, a breeze; Sw. *brusa*, to be fervid, to boil, to murmur; Dan. *bruser*, to rush, roar or foam, to rise in waves; *bruusen*, the rustling of the wind, a humming or buzzing, fermentation. In French sea language, *brise*, a breeze; Gr. βραζω, and βρασσω, to boil; Fr. *brasser*, to brew; W. *brys* hasty, from *rhys*, a rushing. These words seem all to have a common root. See *Rush.*]

1. A light wind; a gentle gale.

From land a gentle *breeze* arose at night. *Dryden.*

2. A shifting wind, that blows from the sea or from the land, for a certain time, by night or by day. Such breezes are common in the tropical regions, and in a good degree regular. The wind from the sea is called a *sea breeze*, and that from the land, a *land breeze*. In general, the sea breeze blows in the day time, and the land breeze at night. The like breezes are common, in the summer months, in the temperate latitudes.

BREEZE, *v. i.* To blow gently; *a word common among seamen.*

For now the breathing airs, from ocean born,
Breeze up the bay, and lead the lively morn. *Barlow.*

BREE'ZELESS, *a.* Motionless; destitute of breezes. *Shenstone.*

BREE'ZY, *a.* Fanned with gentle winds or breezes; as the *breezy* shore. *Pope.*

2. Subject to frequent breezes. *Gray.*

BRE'HON, *n.* In *Irish*, a judge. In ancient times, the general laws of Ireland were called Brehon laws, unwritten like the common law of England. These laws were abolished by statute of Edward III. *Encyc. Blackstone.*

BRE'ISLAKITE, *n.* A newly discovered Vesuvian mineral, resembling a brownish or reddish brown down, which lines the small bubbles found in the lava of Scalla, and is found in cavities of the lava of Olebano; named from Breislak, a celebrated Italian naturalist. *Journal of Science.*

BREME, *a.* [Sax. *bremman*, to murmur, to fret; L. *fremo.*] Cruel; sharp. [*Not used.*] *Chaucer.*

BREN, *v. t.* [Sax. *brennan*, to burn.] To burn. *Obs.* *Spenser.*

BREN'NAGE, *n.* [from *bran.*] In the *middle ages*, a tribute or composition which tenants paid to their lord, in lieu of bran which they were obliged to furnish for his hounds. *Encyc.*

BRENT or BRANT, *a.* [W. *bryn*, a hill.] Steep; high. *Obs.* *Ascham.*

BRENT, *n.* A brant, or brand-goose, a fowl with a black neck and a white collar or line round it. [See *Brant.*]

2. Burnt. [See *Bren. Obs.*] *Spenser.*

BREST or BREAST, *n.* In *architecture*, the member of a column, more usually called *torus* or *tore.* [See *Torus.*] *Encyc.*

BREST'-SUMMER, *n.* In *architecture*, a piece in the outward part of a wooden building, into which the girders are framed. This, in the ground floor, is called a *sill*, and in the garret floor, a *beam.* *Encyc.*

BRET, *n.* A local name of the turbot, called also *burt* or *brut.*

BRET'FUL, *a.* Brimful. *Obs.* *Chaucer.*

BRETH'REN, *n. plu.* of *brother.* It is used almost exclusively in solemn and scriptural language, in the place of *brothers.* [See *Brother.*]

BREVE, *n.* [It. *breve*; L. *brevis*; Sp. *breve*; Fr. *bref*, short. See *Brief.*]

1. In *music*, a note or character of time, equivalent to two semibreves or four minims. When dotted, it is equal to three semibreves.

2. In *law*, a writ directed to the chancellor, judges, sheriffs or other officers, whereby a person is summoned, or attached, to answer in the king's court. *Encyc.*

This word, in the latter sense, is more generally written *brief.*

BREVET', *n.* [from *breve.*] In *the French customs*, the grant of a favor or donation from the king, or the warrant evidencing the grant; a warrant; a brief, or commission. More particularly, a commission given to a subaltern officer, written on parchment, without seal. *Encyc.*

2. A commission to an officer which entitles him to a rank in the army above his pay. Thus a brevet major serves as a captain and receives pay as such. Such commissions were given to the officers of the American Army at the close of the war, giving them a grade of rank above that which they had held during service. *Encyc. Marshall's Life of Wash.*

BRE'VIARY, *n.* [Fr. *breviaire*; L. *breviarium*, from *brevis*, short. See *Brief.*]

1. An abridgment; a compend; an epitome. *Ayliffe.*

2. A book containing the daily service of the Romish church. It is composed of matins, lauds, first, third, sixth and ninth vespers, and the compline or post communio. The Greeks also have a breviary. *Encyc.*

BRE'VIAT, *n.* [See *Breve* and *Brief.*] A short compend; a summary. *Decay of Piety.*

BRE'VIATE, *v. t.* To abridge. [*Not used.*] [See *Abbreviate.*]

BRE'VIATURE, *n.* An abbreviation. [See *Brief.*] *Johnson.*

BREVIE'R, *n.* [Fr. *breviaire*; so called, says Johnson, from being originally used in printing a breviary.]

A small kind of printing types, in size between bourgeois and minion. It is much used in printing marginal notes.

BREV'IPED, *a.* [L. *brevis*, short, and *pes*, foot.] Having short legs, as a fowl.

BREV'IPED, *n.* A fowl having short legs.

BREV'ITY, *n.* [L. *brevitas*, from *brevis*, short. See *Brief.*]

1. Shortness; *applied to time*; as the *brevity* of human life.

2. Shortness; conciseness; contraction into few words; *applied to discourses or writings.* *Dryden.*

BREW, *v. t.* [Sax. *briwan*, to brew; *briw*, broth; D. *brouwen*, to brew, to contrive, to mix; G. *brauen.* These seem to be contractions of the Gothic; Sw. *briggia*; Dan. *brygger*, to brew. The Russ. has *burchu.* The Welch has *brwc*, a boiling, stir, tumult, from *rhwc*, something *rough*; and it has also *berwi*, to boil, or bubble, whence *berwezu*, to brew, from *bar*, fury, impulse. Our word *brew* seems to be directly from the Saxon. The sense is, to stir, boil, or agitate with violence.]

1. In *a general sense*, to boil, and mix; hence in Saxon, it signifies broth or pottage; Old Eng. *brewis.*

2. In *a more restricted sense*, to make beer, ale or other similar liquor from malt; or to prepare a liquor from malt and hops, and in private families, from other materials, by steeping, boiling and fermentation.

3. To mingle.

Brew me a pottle of sack. *Shak.*

4. To contrive; to plot; as, to *brew* mischief.

5. To put in a state of preparation. Qu.

BREW, *v. i.* To be in a state of preparation; to be mixing, forming or collecting; as, a storm *brews* in the west. In this sense I do not recollect the use of the verb, in a transitive sense, and generally the participle only is used; as, a storm is *brewing.*

2. To perform the business of brewing or making beer; as, she can *brew*, wash and bake.

BREW, *n.* The mixture formed by brewing; that which is brewed. *Bacon.*

BREW'AGE, *n.* Malt liquor; drink brewed. *Shak.*

BREW'ED, *pp.* Mixed, steeped and fermented; made by brewing.

BREW'ER, *n.* One whose occupation is to prepare malt liquors; one who brews.

BREW'ERY, *n.* A brew-house; the house and apparatus where brewing is carried on.

BREW'-HOUSE, *n.* [*brew* and *house.*] A brewery; a house appropriated to brewing.

BREW'ING, *ppr.* Preparing malt liquor.

2. In a state of mixing, forming or preparing; as, a storm is *brewing.* *Pope.*

3. Contriving; preparing; as, a scheme is *brewing.* *Wotton.*

BREW'ING, *n.* The act or process of preparing liquors from malt and hops.

2. The quantity brewed at once. *Bacon.*

3. Among *seamen*, a collection of black clouds portending a storm. *Mar. Dict.*

BREW'IS, *n.* Broth; pottage. *Obs.*

2. A piece of bread soaked in boiling fat pottage, made of salted meat. *Bailey. Johnson.*

BRIAR, [See *Brier*.]

BRIBE, *n*. [Ir. *breab*. In Pers. پاره parah, is a bribe, a half, piece, bit, segment, a morsel. Fr. *bribe*, a piece of bread.]
1. A price, reward, gift or favor bestowed or promised with a view to pervert the judgment, or corrupt the conduct of a judge, witness or other person. A bribe is a consideration given or promised to a person, to induce him to decide a cause, give testimony, or perform some act contrary to what he knows to be truth, justice or rectitude. It is not used in a good sense, unless in familiar language.
2. That which seduces.

Not the *bribes* of sordid wealth can seduce to leave these ever blooming sweets. *Akenside.*

BRIBE, *v. t.* To give or promise a reward or consideration, with a view to pervert the judgment, or corrupt the conduct. To hire for bad purposes; to purchase the decision of a judge, the testimony of a witness, or the performance of some act contrary to known truth, justice or rectitude.
2. To gain by a bribe.

In *familiar language*, it is sometimes used in a good sense; as, to *bribe* a child to take a medicine. Dryden has used the word in a good sense, in solemn language; but such use is rare, and hardly legitimate.

BRIBE-DEVOUR'ING, *a*. Greedy of bribes or presents; as *bribe-devouring* kings. *Mitford.*

BRI'BER, *n*. One who bribes, or pays for corrupt practices. *South.*

BRI'BERY, *n*. The act or practice of giving or taking rewards for corrupt practices; the act of paying or receiving a reward for a false judgment, or testimony, or for the performance of that which is known to be illegal, or unjust. It is applied both to him who gives, and to him who receives the compensation, but appropriately to the giver.

BRIBE-WȮRTHY, *a*. [*bribe* and *worthy*.] Worth bribing to obtain. *Mason.*

BRICK, *n*. [Fr. *brique*, a brick, and a little loaf; Ir. *brice*, or *brike*; Arm. *brigen*; supposed to be a contraction of L. *imbrex*, a gutter-tile, from *imber*, a shower, which is probably a compound, of which the last syllable is from βρεχω, whence It. *imbriacarsi*, to get drunk. See *Ebriety*.]

A mass of earth, chiefly clay, first moistened and made fine by grinding or treading, then formed into a long square in a mold, dried and baked or burnt in a kiln; used in buildings and walls.
2. A loaf shaped like a brick.

BRICK, *v. t.* To lay or pave with bricks. *Swift.*
2. To imitate or counterfeit a brick wall on plaster, by smearing it with red ocher and making the joints with an edge-tool, filling them with fine plaster. *Encyc.*

BRICK'BAT, *n*. [*brick* and *bat*.] A piece or fragment of a brick. *Bacon.*

BRICK'-BUILT, *a*. Built with bricks. *Dryden.*

BRICK'ȻLAY, *n*. [*brick* and *clay*.] Clay used or suitable for making bricks. *Woodward.*

BRICK'DUST, *n*. [*brick* and *dust*.] Dust of pounded bricks. *Spectator.*

BRICK'EARTH, *n*. [*brick* and *earth*.] Clay or earth used, or suitable for bricks.

BRICK'KILN, *n*. [*brick* and *kiln*.] A kiln, or furnace, in which bricks are baked or burnt, or a pile of bricks, laid loose, with arches underneath to receive the wood or fuel.

BRICK'LAYER, *n*. [*brick* and *lay*.] One whose occupation is to build with bricks; a mason.

BRICKLE, *a*. [from *break*.] Brittle; easily broken. [*Not used*.] *Spenser.*

BRICK'MAKER, *n*. [*brick* and *make*.] One who makes bricks, or whose occupation is to make bricks.

BRICK'WȮRK, *n*. The laying of bricks, or a wall of bricks.

BRICK'Y, *a*. Full of bricks, or formed of bricks. *Spenser.*

BRI'DAL, *a*. [See *Bride*.] Belonging to a bride, or to a wedding; nuptial; connubial; as *bridal* ornaments. *Milton. Pope.*

BRI'DAL, *n*. The nuptial festival. *Dryden.*

BRIDAL'ITY, *n*. Celebration of the nuptial feast. [*Not used*.] *Jonson.*

BRIDE, *n*. [Sax. *bryd*; Sw. *brud*; D. *bruid*; Ger. *braut*; Dan. *brud*; Arm. *pryed, pried*; W. *priod*-verch, *priodas*-verch, a bride; Ir. *brideog*; W. *priodi* o verch, to be married; Ar. *prietaat*, to marry; Corn. *benen-priot*, a bride; W. *priod-vab*, a bride-mab, bridegoom; Arm. *pridolidh*, wedlock. It seems, by the Celtic dialects, that *bride* is primarily an adjective used with the name of maid or woman, as *bridegoom* is the same word with the name of a man. In W. *priawd*, the root of *priodas*, signifies appropriate, proper, fit; *priodi*, to render appropriate, to espouse, to marry.]
1. A woman new married. *Johnson.*

But the name is applied to a woman at the marriage festival, before she is married, as well as after the ceremony.
2. A woman espoused, or contracted to be married. The case of Lewellyn, prince of Wales. *Henry's Hist. of Britain*, B. iv. ch. i. sect. 2. [*This is the true original sense of the word*.]

BRI'DEBED, *n*. [*bride* and *bed*.] The marriage bed. *Prior.*

BRI'DEȻAKE, *n*. [*bride* and *cake*.] The cake which is made for the guests at a wedding; called, in the U. States, *wedding cake*.

BRI'DECHAMBER, *n*. The nuptial apartment. Matt. ix.

BRI'DEGOOM, *n*. [Sax. *brydguma*; Sw. *brudgumme*; D. *bruidegom*; Ger. *bräutigam*; Dan. *brudgom*; a compound of *bride*, and *gum, guma*, a man, which, by our ancestors, was pronounced *goom*. This word, by a mispronouncing of the last syllable, has been corrupted into *bridegroom*, which signifies a *bride's hostler*; groom being a Persian word, signifying a man who has the care of horses. Such a gross corruption or blunder ought not to remain a reproach to philology.]

A man newly married; or a man about to be married. The passage of Shakspeare cited by Johnson proves that the last definition is just.

As are those dulcet sounds in break of day,
That creep into the dreaming *bridegroom's* ear,
And summon him to marriage.

BRI'DEGROOM, *n*. [See *Bridegoom*.]

BRI'DEMAID, *n*. [*bride* and *maid*.] A woman who attends on a bride at her wedding.

BRI'DEMAN, *n*. [*bride* and *man*.] A man who attends upon a bridegoom and bride at their marriage. I have generally heard these words pronounced *bride's man* and *bride's maid*.

BRI'DESTAKE, *n*. A stake or post set in the ground to dance round. *B. Jonson.*

BRI'DEWELL, *n*. A house of correction, for the confinement of disorderly persons; so called from the palace built near *St. Bride's* or *Bridget's well*, in London, which was turned into a workhouse. *Johnson.*

BRIDĠE, *n*. [Sax. *bric, bricg, brigg*, or *bryc, brycg*; Dan. *broe*; Sw. *bryggia, bro*; D. *brug*; Ger. *brücke*; Prus. *brigge*.]
1. Any structure of wood, stone, brick, or iron, raised over a river, pond, or lake, for the passage of men and other animals. Among rude nations, bridges are sometimes formed of other materials; and sometimes they are formed of boats, or logs of wood lying on the water, fastened together, covered with planks, and called floating bridges. A bridge over a marsh is made of logs or other materials laid upon the surface of the earth.

Pendent or *hanging bridges* are not supported by posts, but by the peculiar structure of the frame, resting only on the abutments.

A *draw bridge* is one which is made with hinges, and may be raised or opened. Such bridges are constructed in fortifications, to hinder the passage of a ditch or moat; and over rivers, that the passage of vessels need not be interrupted.

A *flying bridge* is made of pontoons, light boats, hollow beams, empty casks or the like. They are made, as occasion requires, for the passage of armies.

A *flying bridge* is also constructed in such a manner as to move from one side of a river to the other, being made fast in the middle of the river by a cable and an anchor. *Encyc.*
2. The upper part of the nose. *Johnson.*
3. The part of a stringed instrument of music, over which the strings are stretched, and by which they are raised.
4. In *gunnery*, the two pieces of timber which go between the two transums of a gun-carriage. *Encyc.*

BRIDĠE, *v. t.* To build a bridge or bridges over; as, to *bridge* a river.
2. To erect bridges on; to make a passage by a bridge or bridges. *Milton.*

BRIDĠ'ED, *pp*. Covered or furnished with a bridge.

BRIDĠ'ING, *ppr*. Erecting a bridge; building a bridge over.

BRIDĠ'Y, *a*. Full of bridges. [*Not used*.] *Sherwood.*

BRI'DLE, *n*. [Sax. *bridl*, or *bridel*; Fr. *bride*; Arm. *brid*; D. *breidel*, a bridle; Sp. *brida*, the reins of a bridle; Port. *brida*.]
1. The instrument with which a horse is governed and restrained by a rider; consisting of a head-stall, a bit, and reins, with other appendages, according to its particular form and uses.
2. A restraint; a curb; a check. *Watts.*
3. A short piece of cable well served, attached to a swivel on a chain, laid in a

harbor, and the upper end drawn into a ship and secured to the bitts. The use is to enable a ship, when moored, to veer with the wind and tide. *Mar. Dict.*

Bowline bridles are short legs or pieces of rope, running through iron thimbles, by which the bowline attaches to different places on the leech or edge of a large sail. *Mar. Dict.*

BRI′DLE, *v. t.* To put on a bridle; as, to *bridle* a horse.

2. To restrain, guide or govern; to check, curb or control; as, to *bridle* the passions; "to *bridle* a muse." *Pope.*

Bridle the excursions of youth. *Dwight.*

BRI′DLE, *v. i.* To hold up the head, and draw in the chin.

BRI′DLED, *pp.* Having a bridle on; restrained.

BRI′DLE-HAND, *n.* [*bridle* and *hand.*] The hand which holds the bridle in riding. *Sidney.*

BRI′DLER, *n.* One that bridles; one that restrains and governs. *Milton.*

BRI′DLING, *ppr.* Putting on a bridle; restraining; curbing.

2. Holding up the head, and drawing in the chin.

The *bridling* frown of wrinkled brows. *Trumbull.*

BRIEF, *a.* [Fr. *bref;* It. Sp. Port. *breve;* L. *brevis*, whence *brevio*, to shorten, *abbreviate*. *Brevis*, in Latin, is doubtless contracted from the Gr. βραχυς, whence to *abridge*. The Greek word coincides in elements with *break.*]

Short; concise; it is used chiefly of language, discourses, writings and time; as a *brief* space, a *brief* review of a book. Shakspeare applies it to *wars*, to *nature*, &c. A little *brief* authority, is authority very limited.

BRIEF, *n.* [In this sense the word has been received into most of the languages of Europe.]

1. An epitome; a short or concise writing. This is the general sense of the word, as explained by Zonaras on the council of Carthage. It was thus used as early as the third century after Christ. *Spelman.*

In modern times, an *apostolical brief* is a letter which the pope dispatches to a prince or other magistrate, relating to public affairs. A *brief* is distinguished from a *bull*, in being more concise, written on paper, sealed with red wax, and impressed with the seal of the fisherman or Peter in a boat. A *bull* is more ample, written on parchment, and sealed with lead or green wax. *Encyc.*

2. In *law*, an abridgment of a client's case, made out for the instruction of council on a trial at law. *Encyc. Johnson.*

Also, a writ summoning a man to answer to any action; or any precept of the king in writing, issuing from any court, whereby he commands a thing to be done. *Cowel.*

In *Scots law*, a writ issuing from the chancery, directed to any judge ordinary, commanding and authorizing that judge to call a jury to inquire into the case, and upon their verdict to pronounce sentence. *Encyc.*

3. A letter patent, from proper authority, authorizing a public collection or charitable contribution of money for any public or private purpose. *New-England.*

4. A writing in general. *Shak.*

In *music*, the word, if I mistake not, is now written *breve.*

BRIE′FLY, *adv.* Concisely; in few words. *Bacon.*

BRIE′FNESS, *n.* Shortness; conciseness in discourse or writing. *Camden.*

BRI′ER, *n.* [Sax. *brær;* Ir. *briar*, a prickle; Fr. *bruyere*, heath; Arm. *brug.* The latter shows this word to be from the root of *rough.*]

1. In *a general sense*, a prickly plant or shrub. Is. v. 6. Judges viii. 7.

2. In *a limited sense*, the sweet-brier and the wild-brier, species of the rose.

BRI′ERY, *a.* Full of briers; rough; thorny. *Johnson.*

BRIG, the termination of names, signifies a *bridge*, or perhaps, in some cases, a town, or *burg.*

BRIG, *n.* [from *brigantine.*] A vessel with two masts, square rigged, or rigged nearly like a ship's mainmast and foremast. The term however is variously applied by the mariners of different nations. *Mar. Dict.*

BRIGA′DE, *n.* [Fr. *brigade;* It. *brigata;* Sp. and Port. *brigada*; perhaps from Ar. فَرِيقٌ farikon, agmen, turba hominum major, that is, a division, from فَرَقَ faraka, to *break.* This word comes to us from the south of Europe, and may have been introduced into Spain by the Moors. If this conjecture is not well founded, I know not the origin of the word. See *Cast. Hept. Col.* 3084.]

A party or division of troops, or soldiers, whether cavalry or infantry, regular or militia, commanded by a brigadier. It consists of an indeterminate number of regiments, squadrons, or battalions. A brigade of horse is a body of eight or ten squadrons; of infantry, four, five, or six battalions, or regiments.

BRIGA′DE, *v. t.* To form into a brigade, or into brigades.

BRIGA′DE-MAJOR, *n.* [See *Major.*] An officer appointed by the brigadier, to assist him in the management and ordering of his brigade.

BRIGADIE′R, *n.* [Fr. from *brigade.*] The general officer who commands a brigade, whether of horse or foot, and in rank next below a major-general.

BRIG′AND, *n.* [Fr. *brigand;* W. *brigant*, a mountaineer, a plunderer, from W. *brig*, a top or summit.]

A robber; a free booter; a lawless fellow who lives by plunder, or who belongs to a band of robbers. *Warburton.*

BRIG′ANDAGE, *n.* Theft; robbery; plunder. *Warburton.*

BRIG′ANDINE, *n.* [Qu. the origin of this word. In Pers. *praghe* is a helmet.]

Anciently, a coat of mail. The name has ceased to be used, with the disuse of the thing. It consisted of thin jointed scales of plate, pliant and easy to the body. *Encyc.*

BRIG′ANTINE, *n.* [Fr. *brigantin;* Arm. *bringantine;* It. *brigantino;* Sp. *bergantin;* Port. *bargantim;* D. *berkantyn.* Qu. from L. *aphractum*, Gr. αφρακτος, a vessel without a deck, uncovered. It is usually derived from *brigand.*] [See *Brig.*]

BRIGHT, *a. brite.* [Sax. *beorht, briht, byrht*, or *bryht*, clear, shining, whence *beorhtnes*, brightness, *beorhtian*, Goth. *bairtiyan*, to shine or be clear, or to manifest; Ar. Ch. Heb. Syr. Eth. ברק to shine, or more probably, Eth. በረሀ bareah, to shine, as the Eth. participle ብረህተ berht or bereht, corresponds exactly with the Saxon. I have not found this word in any other Teutonic or Gothic language, and the original verb is lost in the Saxon. In Saxon, *beorhthwile*, or *brihthwile*, signifies a moment, the twinkling of an eye. This directs us to the primary sense of the verb to shine, which is, to shoot, to dart, to glance. That this is the primary sense, we have evidence from the Sax. *bryhtm*, which is a derivative from *bryht*, and which signifies a *moment*, that is, the time of a shoot, or darting, like *glance.*]

1. Shining; lucid; luminous; splendid; as a *bright* sun or star; a *bright* metal.

2. Clear; transparent; as liquors. *Thomson.*

3. Evident; clear; manifest to the mind, as light is to the eyes.

The evidence of this truth is *bright.* *Watts.*

4. Resplendent with charms; as a *bright* beauty; the *brightest* fair. *Pope.*

5. Illuminated with science; sparkling with wit; as the *brightest* of men. *Pope.*

6. Illustrious; glorious; as the *brightest* period of a kingdom. *Cotton.*

7. In *popular language*, ingenious; possessing an active mind.

8. Promising good or success; as *bright* prospects.

9. Sparkling; animated; as *bright* eyes.

BRIGHT-BURNING, *a.* Burning with a bright flame.

BRIGHTEN, *v. t. britn.* To make bright or brighter; to make to shine; to increase luster.

2. To make luminous by light from without, or by dispelling gloom; as, to *brighten* sorrow or prospects. *Philips.*

3. To cheer; to make gay or cheerful.

Joy *brightens* his crest. *Milton.*

4. To make illustrious, or more distinguished; as, to *brighten* a character. *Swift.*

5. To make acute or witty. *Johnson.*

BRIGHTEN, *v. i. britn.* To grow bright, or more bright; to clear up; as, the sky *brightens.*

2. To become less dark or gloomy; as, our prospects *brighten.*

BRIGHT-EYED, *a.* Having bright eyes. *Gray.*

BRIGHT-HAIRED, *a.* Having bright hair. *Milton.*

BRIGHT-HARNESSED, *a.* Having glittering armor. *Milton.*

BRIGHTLY, *adv. britely.* Splendidly; with luster.

BRIGHTNESS, *n. briteness.* Splendor; luster; glitter. *South.*

2. Acuteness, applied to the faculties; sharpness of wit; as the *brightness* of a man's parts. *Prior.*

BRIGHT-SHINING, *a.* Shining with splendor. *Spenser.*

BRIGO'SE, *a.* [from *brigue.*] Contentious. [*Not used.*] *Fuller.*

BRĬGUE, *n. breeg.* [Fr. *brigue;* Sp. *brega;* It. *briga,* strife, disquiet; Ir. *breaghean,* to debate, to quarrel.]
A cabal; intrigue; faction; contention. [*Little used.*] *Chaucer. Chesterfield.*

BRĬGUE, *v. i. breeg.* To canvass; to solicit. [*Little used.*] *Hurd.*

BRILL'IANCY, *n.* [See *Brilliant.*] Splendor; glitter; great brightness.

BRILL'IANT, *a.* [Fr. *brillant,* sparkling, from *briller,* to shine or sparkle; It. *brillante,* sparkling; *brillo,* joy, gladness, also tipsey; Sp. *brillar,* to glitter; *brillador,* brilliant; *brillo,* splendor; Ger. and Dan. *brille,* a pair of spectacles; hence Eng. *beryl* and *pearl.*]
1. Sparkling with luster; glittering; as a *brilliant* gem; a *brilliant* dress.
2. Splendid; shining; as a *brilliant* achievement.

Washington was more solicitous to avoid fatal mistakes, than to perform *brilliant* exploits. *Ames.*

BRILL'IANT, *n.* A diamond of the finest cut, formed into angles, so as to refract the light, by which it is rendered more glittering. *Dryden. Encyc.*
2. In *the manege,* a brisk, high-spirited horse, with a stately carriage. *Encyc.*

BRILL'IANTLY, *adv.* Splendidly. *Warton.*

BRILL'IANTNESS, *n.* Brilliancy; splendor; glitter. *Johnson.*

BRILLS, *n.* The hair on the eyelids of a horse.

BRIM, *n.* [Sax. *brymm;* Sw. *bråm;* Dan. *bræmme;* probably the extent or extreme.]
1. The rim, lip or broad border of any vessel or other thing; as the *brim* of a hat, or of a vessel.
2. The upper edge of a vessel, whether broad or not; as the *brim* of a cup or glass.
3. The top of any liquor; the edge or that next the border at the top.

The feet of the priests were dipped in the *brim* of the water. Josh. iii.

4. The edge or brink of a fountain; the verge. *Drayton.*

BRIM, *a.* [Sax. *bryme.*] Public; well known; celebrated. [*Not in use.*] *Warner.*

BRIM, *v. t.* To fill to the brim, upper edge, or top. *Milton.*

BRIM, *v. i.* To be full to the brim. *Philips.*

BRIM'FUL, *a.* [*brim* and *full.*] Full to the top; completely full; as a glass *brimful;* a heart *brimful* of tears.

BRIM'FULNESS, *n.* Fulness to the top. [*Not used.*] *Shak.*

BRIM'LESS, *a.* Having no brim. *Addison.*

BRIM'MER, *n.* A bowl full to the top. *Dryden.*

BRIM'MING, *a.* Full to the top or brim; as a *brimming* pail. *Dryden.*

BRIM'STONE, *n.* [Sax. *bryne,* combustion, and *stone, burn-stone,* or *burning* stone. See *Brand* and *Burn.*]
Sulphur; a hard, brittle, inflammable substance, of a lemon yellow color, which has no smell, unless heated, and which becomes negatively electric by heat and friction. It is found, in great quantities, and sometimes pure, in the neighborhood of volcanoes. It is an ingredient in a variety of minerals and ores. The sulphur of commerce is procured from its natural beds, or artificially extracted from pyrites. *Hooper. Nicholson.*

BRIM'STONY, *a.* Full of brimstone, or containing it; resembling brimstone; sulphurous.

BRIND'ED, *a.* [It. *brinato,* spotted.] Marked with spots; tabby; having different colors. *Milton.*

BRIN'DLE, *n.* [from *brind,* the root of *brinded.*]
The state of being brinded; spottedness. *Richardson.*

BRIN'DLED, *a.* Spotted; variegated with spots of different colors. *Addison.*

BRINE, *n.* [Sax. *bryne,* brine, and a burning, from *brennan,* to burn.]
1. Water saturated or strongly impregnated with salt, like the water of the ocean. Artificial brine is used for the preservation of the flesh of animals, fish, vegetables, &c.
2. The ocean or sea. *Milton.*
3. Tears, so called from their saltness. *Shak.*

Leach brine is brine which drops from corned salt in drying, which is preserved to be boiled again. *Encyc.*

BRINE, *v. t.* To steep in brine, as corn to prevent smut; also, to mix salt with, as to *brine* hay. *Encyc.*

BRI'NE-PAN, *n.* [*brine* and *pan.*] A pit of salt water, where, by the action of the sun, salt is formed by crystalization.

BRI'NE-PIT, *n.* [*brine* and *pit.*] A brine-pan, or a salt spring from which water is taken to be boiled or evaporated for making salt. *Encyc.*

BRI'NE-SPRING, *n.* [*brine* and *spring.*] A spring of salt water. *Encyc.*

BRING, *v. t.* pret. and pp. *brought.* [Sax. *bringan;* Sw. *bringa;* Dan. *bringer;* D. *brengen;* G. *bringen;* Goth. *briggan.* We see by *brought,* D. *bragt,* and the Gothic *briggan,* that *n* is not radical.]
1. To fetch; to bear, convey or lead from a distant to a nearer place, or to a person; as, *bring* me a book from the shelf; *bring* me a morsel of bread. In this sense, it is opposed to *carry,* and it is applied to the *person bearing* or *leading,* in opposition to *sending* or *transmitting* by another.
2. To produce; to procure as a cause; to draw to.

Nothing *brings* a man more honor than to be invariably just.

3. To attract or draw along.

In distillation the water *brings* over with it another substance.

4. To cause to come; to cause to proceed from a distant place, in company, or at the same time; as, to *bring* a boat over a river; to *bring* a horse or carriage; to *bring* a cargo of dry goods.
5. To cause to come to a point, by moral influence; used of the mind, and implying previous remoteness, aversion, alienation, or disagreement; as, to *bring* the mind to assent to a proposition; or to *bring* a man to terms, by persuasion or argument. In this sense, it is nearly equivalent to *persuade, prevail upon,* or *induce.* The same process is effected by custom, and other causes. Habit *brings* us to relish things at first disagreeable; reflection *brings* a man to his senses, and whether the process is slow or rapid, the sense of the verb is the same. To *bring* to the mind any thing before and forgotten, is to *recall;* but the sense of *bring* is the same.

The primary sense is to *lead, draw* or *cause to come;* the sense of *conveying* or *bearing* is secondary.

The use of this verb is so extensive, and incorporated into so many peculiar phrases, that it is not easy to reduce its significations within any precise limits. In general, the verb *bring* implies motion from a place remote, either in a literal or figurative sense. It is used with various modifying words.

To bring back is to recall, implying previous departure, either in a literal or figurative sense.

To bring about, to bring to pass; to effect; to accomplish; to bring to the desired issue.

To bring forth is to produce, as young or fruit; also, to bring to light; that is, to make manifest; to disclose.

To bring forward, to cause to advance; to produce to view.

To bring in, to import; to introduce; to bear from a remote place within a certain precinct; to place in a particular condition; to collect things dispersed; to reduce within the limits of law and government; to produce, as income, rent or revenue; to induce to join; &c.

To bring off, to bear or convey from a distant place, as to *bring off* men from an isle; also, to procure to be acquitted; to clear from condemnation; to cause to escape.

To bring on, to cause to begin, as to *bring on* an action; also, to originate or cause to exist, as to *bring on* a disease; also, to bear or convey from a distance, as to *bring on* a quantity of goods; also, to attend, or to aid in advancing, as to *bring* one *on* his way.

To bring over, to bear across, as to *bring over* dispatches, to *bring over* passengers in a boat; also, to convert by persuasion or other means; to draw to a new party; to cause to change sides, or an opinion.

To bring out, to expose; to detect; to bring to light from concealment; as, to *bring out* an accomplice or his crimes.

To bring under, to subdue; to repress; to restrain; to reduce to obedience: also, to bring beneath any thing.

To bring up, to nurse; to educate; to instruct; to feed and clothe; to form the manners, and furnish the mind with knowledge. The phrase may comprehend all these particulars. Also, to introduce to practice, as to *bring up* a fashion or ceremony; also, to cause to advance near, as to *bring up* forces, or the body of reserve: also, to bear or convey upwards. In navigation, to cast anchor.

To bring down, to cause to come down; also, to humble or abase, as to *bring down* high looks.

To bring to, in navigation, to check the course of a ship, by arranging the sails in such a manner, that they shall counteract each other, and keep her nearly stationary. She is then said to *lie to.* The phrase is used also in applying a rope to the capstan.

To bring by the lee, to incline so rapidly to leeward of the course, when a ship sails large, as to bring the lee side suddenly to the windward, and by laying the sails aback, expose her to the danger of oversetting. *Mar. Dict.*

BRING'ER, *n.* One who brings, or conveys to.

Bringer in, the person who introduces.

Bringer up, an instructor; one who feeds, clothes, and educates; also, one who is in the rear of an army. *Ascham.*

BRING'ING, *ppr.* Bearing to; conveying; persuading; causing to come.

BRING'ING FORTH, *n.* Production. *Shak.*

BRI'NISH, *a.* [from *brine.*] Like brine; salt; somewhat salt; saltish.

BRI'NISHNESS, *n.* Saltness; the quality of being saltish.

BRINK, *n.* [Dan. Sw. *brink*; W. *bryncyn*; Ir. *breoch*, *bruach*; from *break.*]
The edge, margin or border of a steep place, as of a precipice, or the bank of a river.

BRI'NY, *a.* [from *brine.*] Pertaining to brine, or to the sea; partaking of the nature of brine; salt; as a *briny* taste; the *briny* flood. *Dryden. Addison.*

BRISK, *a.* [This word may be of the same family with *frisk*, and *fresh*, which see. W. *brysg*, from *brys*, quick; *brysiaw*, to hasten, coinciding with *press*; from W. *rhys*, a *rushing*. See *Rush.*]
1. Lively; active; nimble; gay; sprightly; vivacious; *applied to animals*; as a *brisk* young man; a *brisk* horse.
2. Full of spirit or life; effervescing, as liquors; as *brisk* cyder.
3. Lively; burning freely; as a *brisk* fire.
4. Vivid; bright; as, a glass makes an object appear *brisk.* [*Not used.*] *Newton.*

BRISK UP, *v. t.* To make lively; to enliven; to animate.

BRISK UP, *v. i.* To come up with life and speed; to take an erect, or bold attitude.

BRISK'ET, *n.* [Qu. Fr. *brechet.*] The breast of an animal; or that part of the breast that lies next to the ribs. The fore part of the neck of a horse, at the shoulder down to the fore legs. *Bailey.*

BRISK'LY, *adv.* Actively; vigorously; with life and spirit. *Boyle. Ray.*

BRISK'NESS, *n.* Liveliness; vigor in action; quickness; gayety; vivacity; effervescence of liquors. *South. Dryden.*

BRIS'TLE, *n.* *bris'l.* [Sax. *bristl*, and *byrst*; Sw. *borst*; D. *borstel*, a bristle, a brush; G. *borste*, bristle; *borsten*, to bristle up; Dan. *bryster*, to strut. The sense is, a shoot.]
1. The stiff glossy hair of swine, especially that growing on the back, used for making brushes; similar hair on other animals.
2. A species of pubescence on plants, in form of stiff roundish hair. *Martyn.*

BRIS'TLE, *v. t.* To erect in bristles; to erect in defiance or anger, like a swine; as, to *bristle* the crest. *Shak.*
2. To fix a bristle; as, to *bristle* a thread. *Johnson.*

BRIS'TLE, *v. i.* To rise or stand erect: as, the hair *bristles.* *Dryden.*
2. To raise the head and strut, as in anger or defiance; as, a man *bristles* up to another. In this sense the word is common in the U. States, but generally pronounced *brustle.*

BRIS'TLE-SHAPED, *a.* [*bristle* and *shape.*] Of the thickness and length of a bristle, as a leaf. *Martyn.*

BRIS'TLY, *a.* *bris'ly.* Thick set with bristles, or with hairs like bristles; rough. *Bacon.*

BRIS'TOL-FLOWER, *n.* A species of Lychnis, bachelor's button or catch fly. *Fam. of Plants.*

BRIS'TOL-STONE, *n.* Rock crystal or crystals of quartz, found in a rock near the city of Bristol in England.

BRIS'TOL-WATER, *n.* The water of a warm spring near the city of Bristol in England. *Ash. Encyc.*

BRIT, *n.* A fish; probably a different orthography of *bret*, or *burt.* *Carew.*

BRITAN'NIC, *a.* Pertaining to Britain; or in its present use, to Great Britain. It is applied almost exclusively to the title of the king; as his *Britannic* Majesty. In the Encyclopedia, article *Argo Navis*, it is applied to *catalogue*, the *Britannic* catalogue.

BRITCH, *n.* [G. *britsche*, a club or mace.]
The large end of a cannon or of a musket; the club or thick part of the stock of a musket or other fire arm.

BRITCH', *v. t.* To fasten with britching.

BRITCH'ING, *n.* A strong rope, fastened to the cascabel or pummelion of a cannon, by a thimble, and clinched to ring bolts in the ship's side, to prevent it from recoiling too much in battle. *Mar. Dict.*

BRITE, or BRIGHT, *v. i.* To be or become over ripe, as wheat, barley or hops. *Johnson.*

[*I know not that this word is used in the U. States.*]

BRIT'ISH, *a.* Pertaining to Great Britain or its inhabitants. It is sometimes applied to the language of the Welsh.

BRIT'ON, *n.* A native of Britain.

BRIT'ON, *a.* British. *Spenser.*

BRIT'TLE, *a.* [Sax. *brittan*, *brytan*, to break; Sw. *bryta*; Dan. *bryder*, id.; W. *brad*, a breaking; Sam. ࠐࠓࠕ; Ch. פרת; Ar. فَرَثَ; Syr. ܦܪܬ; Heb. פרד, to *part*, to break. See *Part.*]
Easily broken, or easily breaking short, without splinters or loose parts rent from the substance; fragile; not tough or tenacious; as *brittle* stone or glass. *Arbuthnot.*

BRIT'TLELY, *adv.* In a brittle manner. *Sherwood.*

BRIT'TLENESS, *n.* Aptness to break; fragility; opposed to toughness and tenacity. *Boyle.*

BRIZE, *n.* The gad fly. [See *Breeze.*]

BRŌACH, *n.* [Fr. *broche*, a spit, faucet or quill; W. *proc*, a thrust, a stab; It. *brocco*, a peg; *brocciare*, to prick; Sp. *broca*, a drill, a tack. It denotes a shoot, a sharp pointed thing.]
1. A spit, and in some parts of the English dominions, an awl, and a bodkin. *Encyc.*
2. A musical instrument played by turning a handle. *Johnson.*
3. A clasp or small utensil to fasten a vest. [See *Brooch.*]
4. A start of the head of a young stag. *Johnson.*

BRŌACH, *v. t.* [W. *prociaw*, to thrust or stab.]
1. To spit; to pierce as with a spit. *Shak. Hakewill.*
2. To tap; to pierce, as a cask, in order to draw the liquor; hence, to let out. *Hudibras.*
3. To open, as a store. [*Unusual.*] *Knolles.*
4. To utter; to give out; to publish first; to make public what was before unknown; as, to *broach* an opinion. *Swift.*
To broach to, in navigation, to incline suddenly to windward, so as to lay the sails aback and expose the vessel to the danger of oversetting. *Mar. Dict.*

BRŌACHED, *pp.* Spitted; tapped; opened; uttered; first published.

BRŌACHER, *n.* A spit; one who broaches, opens or utters; a first publisher. *Dryden. L'Estrange.*

BROAD, *a.* *brawd.* [Sax. *brad*; Sw. *bred*; D. *breed*; Ger. *breit*; Dan. *breed*, broad; Arm. *brudi*, *brudein*, to publish. This word and *spread* seem to be formed on the root רדד or רדה to open, expand, spread; in Syr. to go, L. *gradior*; a root of extensive use.]
1. Wide; extended in breadth, or from side to side, as distinguished from *long*, or extended from end to end. It is opposed to *narrow*; as a *broad* street; a *broad* table. *Dryden. Temple.*
2. Wide; extensive; vast; as the *broad* expanse of ocean.
3. Large; as a *broad* mixture of falsehood. *Locke.*
4. Open; clear; not covered, confined or concealed; as in *broad* sunshine.
5. Gross; coarse; as *broad* mirth; *broad* nonsense. *Pope. Dryden.*
6. Plain; tending to obscenity; as a *broad* comment. *Dryden.*
7. Bold; not delicate; not reserved; as *broad* words. *Shak.*
8. Comprehensive.

It may be urged that the *words* in the constitution are *broad* enough to include the case. *D. Daggett, Wheaton's Rep.*

Broad as long, equal upon the whole. *L'Estrange.*

BROAD-AX, *n.* [*broad* and *ax.*] Formerly, a military weapon. In *modern usage*, an ax for hewing timber.

BROAD-BACKED, *a.* [*broad* and *back.*] Having a broad back. *Barlow.*

BROAD-BLŌWN, *a.* [*broad* and *blow.*] Full blown. *Shak.*

BROAD-BREASTED, *a.* Having a broad breast.

BROAD-BRIMMED, *a.* [*broad* and *brim.*] Having a broad brim. *Bramston.*

BROAD-CAST, *n.* [*broad* and *cast.*] Among *farmers*, a casting or throwing seed from the hand for dispersion in sowing.

BROAD-CAST, *adv.* By scattering or throwing at large from the hand; as, to sow *broad-cast.*

BROAD-CAST, *a.* Cast or dispersed upon

the ground with the hand, as seed in sowing; opposed to planting in hills or rows.

BROAD-CLOTH, *n.* A species of woolen cloth, so called from its breadth.

BROADEN, *v. i.* *brawd'n.* To grow broad. [*Unusual.*] *Thomson.*

BROAD-EYED, *a.* [*broad* and *eye.*] Having a wide view or survey; as *broad-eyed* day. *Shak.*

BROAD-FRONTED, *a.* Having a broad front; *applied to cattle.* *Chapman.*

BROAD-HORNED, *a.* Having large horns. *Huloet.*

BROAD'ISH, *a.* Rather broad. *Russel.*

BROAD-LEAVED, BROAD-LEAFED, } *a.* [*broad* and *leaf.*] Having broad leaves. *Woodward.*

BROADLY, *adv.* In a broad manner.

BROADNESS, *n.* Breadth; extent from side to side; coarseness; grossness; fulsomeness. *Dryden.*

BROAD-PIECE, *n.* [*broad* and *piece.*] A piece of gold coin broader than a guinea. *Encyc.*

BROAD-SEAL, *n.* The great seal of England; as a verb, not used.

BROAD-SHOULDERED, *a.* [*broad* and *shoulder.*] Broad across the shoulders. *Spectator.*

BROAD-SIDE, *n.* [*broad* and *side.*] A discharge of all the guns on one side of a ship, above and below, at the same time. *Mar. Dict.*

2. The side of a ship, above the water, from the bow to the quarter. *Mar. Dict.*

3. In *printing*, a sheet of paper containing one large page, or printed on one side only. *Ash. Johnson.*

BROAD-SPREADING, *a.* Spreading widely. *Shak.*

BROAD-SWORD, *n.* [*broad* and *sword.*] A sword with a broad blade, and a cutting edge. *Ash. Wiseman.*

BROAD-TAILED, *a.* Having a broad tail. *Sandys.*

BROAD-WISE, *adv.* [*broad* and *wise.*] In the direction of the breadth. *Boyle.*

BROCA'DE, *n.* [Sp. *brocado*; probably from *broche*, the instrument used in embroidery; so Fr. *brochure*, a pamphlet or stitched book.]

Silk stuff, variegated with gold and silver, or raised and enriched with flowers, foliage and other ornaments. *Encyc. Span. Dict.*

BROCA'DED, *a.* Woven or worked, as brocade, with gold and silver.

2. Drest in brocade. *Johnson.*

BROCADE-SHELL, *n.* The trivial name of the *Conus geographicus.* *Cyc.*

BRO'CAGE, *n.* [See *Broke, Broker.*]

1. The premium or commission of a broker; the gain or profit derived from transacting business for other men, as brokers, either in a good or bad sense. *Spenser.*

2. The hire given for any unlawful office. *Bacon.*

3. The trade of a broker; a dealing in old things.

4. The business of a broker; the transactions of commercial business, as buying and selling, for other men. [See *Broke, Broker.*]

5. The act of pimping. *Ash.*

BRO'CATEL, BROCATEL'LO, } *n.* [Sp. *brocatel.*] A calcarious stone or species of marble, composed of fragments of four colors, white, gray, yellow and red. *Fourcroy. Nicholson. Sp. Dict.*

2. A kind of coarse brocade, used chiefly for tapestry. Newman says it is made of hemp and silk. *Encyc. Newman's Sp. Dict.*

BROC'COLI, *n.* [It. *broccolo*, sprouts; Fr. *brocoli.*]

A variety of cabbage or Brassica.

BROCHE, the true, but not the common orthography of *broach.*

BROCK, *n.* [Sax. *broc*; Ir. *broc*; Corn. *id*; W. *broc*, a badger, and noise, din, tumult, foam, anger; *broçi*, to chafe, fume, wax fierce, from *rhoc*, a rough sound; *rhoçain*, to grunt. *Owen.*]

A badger; an animal of the genus Ursus, found in the northern parts of Europe and Asia. The Russians call it *barsuk.* In Ir. *brech* is a wolf, a wild savage and a badger.

BROCK'ET, *n.* [See *Brock.*] A red deer two years old. Bailey writes this *brock* or *brocket.* The French write it *brocard.*

BRO'DEKIN, *n.* [Fr. *brodequin.*] A buskin or half boot. *Echard.*

BROG'GLE, *v. i.* To fish for eels. [*Not used.*]

BROGUE, *n.* *brōg.* [Ir. *brog*, a shoe, a house.]

1. A shoe. "Clouted *brogues*," in Shakspeare, signify shoes whose soles are studded with nails, or clouts.

2. A cant word for a corrupt dialect or manner of pronunciation. *Farquhar.*

3. Brogues is used by Shenstone for *breeches*, from the Irish *brog.*

BROGUE-MAKER, *n.* A maker of brogues. *Johnson.*

BROID, *v. t.* To braid. *Obs.* [See *Braid.*]

BROID'ER, *v. t.* [Fr. *broder*; Sp. and Port. *bordar*, *to embroider*; Arm. *brouda*, to prick; D. *borduuren*, to embroider; W. *brodiaw*, to make compact, to darn, to embroider; *brwyd*, a broach, an embroidering frame.]

To adorn with figures of needle work.

A robe, a *broidered* coat, and a girdle. Exod.

BROID'ERER, *n.* One that embroiders.

BROID'ERY, *n.* Embroidery; ornamental needle work wrought upon cloth. [See *Embroider.*] *Tickel.*

BROIL, *n.* [Fr. *brouillerie*, from *brouiller*, to mix, confound, embroil; It. *broglia*, tumult; *brogliare*, to embroil. From this verb, we have *roil*, to disturb, as lees. See *Roil.* The primary sense is, to stir, to agitate. It may be allied to *brawl* and the French *bruler.*]

A tumult; a noisy quarrel; contention; discord, either between individuals or in the state. *Shak. Granville.*

BROIL, *v. t.* [Qu. Fr. *bruler.* I believe this is from *brouiller.*]

To agitate with heat; to dress or cook over coals, before the fire; but more generally upon a gridiron over coals. *Dryden.*

BROIL, *v. i.* To be subjected to the action of heat, like meat over the fire; to be greatly heated or to sweat with heat.

Where have you been *broiling?* *Shak.*

BROIL'ED, *pp.* Agitated or dressed by heat.

BROIL'ER, *n.* One that excites broils; that which dresses by broiling.

BROIL'ING, *ppr.* Agitating by heat; sweating.

BROKE, *v. i.* [Sax. *brucan*, to use, employ, enjoy; to eat or chew; to *brook*; to profit; *broce*, use; *brec*, use, gain; *bryce*, gain, profit, fruit, *fructus*; a violation, or breaking; Sw. *bruka*; G. *brauchen*; Dan. *bruger*; D. *gebruiken*, to use or employ; L. *fruor*, for *frucor*, whence *fructus*, *fruit*; Gr. *πρασσω, πραξω, πραγμα.* See *Practice.*]

To transact business for another in trade; to act as agent in buying and selling, and other commercial business; to transact business by an agent. *Bacon. Shak.*

[*This word is little used, at least in America; and English writers seem to have used it in a low sense.*]

BROKE, *pret.* and *pp.* of *break.*

BRO'KEN, *pp.* of *break.* *bro'kn.* Parted by violence; rent asunder; infirm; made bankrupt.

BRO'KEN-BACKED, *a.* A *broken-backed ship* is one which is so weakened in her frame as to droop at each end. *Mar. Dict.*

BRO'KEN-BELLIED, *a.* Having a ruptured belly. *Sandys.*

BRO'KEN-HEARTED, *a.* [*break* and *heart.*] Having the spirits depressed or crushed by grief or despair.

BRO'KENLY, *adv.* In a broken interrupted manner; without a regular series. *Hakewill.*

BRO'KENNESS, *n.* A state of being broken; unevenness.

2. Contrition; as *brokenness* of heart.

BRO'KENWIND, *n.* [*break* and *wind.*] A disease in horses, often accompanied with a preternatural enlargement of the lungs and heart, which disables them from bearing fatigue. *Encyc.*

BRO'KENWINDED, *a.* Having short breath, as a horse.

BRO'KER, *n.* [from *broke.*]

1. An agent or negotiator, who is employed by merchants to make and conclude bargains for them, for a fee or rate per cent., or who transacts other business for his employers.

Brokers are of several kinds.

1. *Exchange-brokers*, who make and conclude bargains for others in matters of money or merchandize, learn the rate of exchange and notify their employers.

2. *Stock-brokers*, who are employed to buy and sell shares in the stocks, whether of the public funds, of banks or of other corporations.

3. *Pawn-brokers*, who make it their business to lend money upon *pawns*, that is, property deposited in pledge.

4. *Insurance-brokers*, whose business is to procure the insurance of vessels at sea or bound on a voyage.

In *the U. States*, the business of a stock-broker and an insurance-broker is often or generally carried on by the same person.

2. One who deals in old household goods. *Johnson.*

3. A pimp or procurer. *Shak. Johnson.*

[*In the two latter senses, the word, I believe, is never used in America, unless in cant language.*]

BRO'KERAGE, *n.* The fee, reward or commission given or charged for transacting business as a broker. *Anderson's Comm.*

BRO'KERLY, *a.* Mean; servile. *Jonson.*

BRO'KERY, *n.* The business of a broker. [*Not used.*] *Hall.*

BRO'KING, *ppr.* Transacting business as a broker; practiced by brokers. *Shak.*

BROME, *n.* [Gr. βρωμος, fœtor.] A liquid of a deep red-brown color, very volatile, and having an ill smell, obtained from the mother-water of salt-works, and from the lixivia of the ashes of sea plants, by treating these solutions with chlorine. It has three times the density of water. *Journ. of Science.*

BROME-GRASS, *n.* A plant, the Bromus. *Muhlenberg.*

BRONCH'IAL, *a.* [Gr. βρογχος, the wind-pipe.] Belonging to the bronchia, or ramifications of the wind-pipe in the lungs.

The *bronchial arteries* are branches of the superior descending aorta accompanying the bronchia, or branches of the trachea.

Bronchial glands, glands at the division of the bronchia. *Quincy. Coxe.*

BRONCH'IC, *a.* The same as bronchial.

BRONCH'OCELE, *n.* [Gr. βρογχος, the wind-pipe, and κηλη, a tumor.]

An enlarged thyroid gland; a tumor on the fore part of the neck, called *goiter;* the Derbysbire neck. *Quincy. Coxe.*

BRONCHOT'OMY, *n.* [Gr. βρογχος, the wind-pipe, and τομη, a cutting.]

An incision into the wind pipe or larynx, between the rings; called also *tracheotomy.* *Quincy. Coxe.*

BROND, *n.* A sword. [See *Brand.*]

BRONTOL'OGY, *n.* [Gr. βροντη, thunder, and λογος, discourse.]

A discourse or dissertation upon thunder, containing an explanation of its causes and phenomena. *Encyc.*

BRONZ, } *n.* [Fr. *bronze;* Arm. *bronçz;*
BRONZE, } It. *bronzo;* Sp. *bronce.* In Ital. *bronzino* is sun burnt. It may take its name from its color, from *burn, brown.*]

1. A compound of copper and tin, to which other metallic substances are sometimes added, especially zink. It is brittle, hard, and sonorous, and used for statues, bells and cannon, the proportions of the respective ingredients being varied to suit the particular purposes. *Nicholson. Encyc.*

2. A color prepared for the purpose of imitating bronze, of two kinds, the yellow and the red. The yellow is made of fine copper-dust; the red, of copper-dust with a little pulverized red ocher. *Encyc.*

3. Among *antiquaries*, any figure of men, beasts, urns, or other piece of sculpture, which the ancients made of bronze. *Encyc.*

4. Any statue or bust cast of bronze, whether original or a copy of an antique. *Encyc.*

5. Among *medalists*, any copper medal. *Encyc.*

BRONZE, *v. t.* To imitate bronze, by means of copper-dust or leaf fastened on the outside, as gold-leaf is in gilding. *Encyc.*

2. To harden, or make like brass. *Young.*

BRONZ'ING, *ppr.* Imitating bronze.

BRONZ'ING, *n.* The act or art of imitating bronze, by means of copper-dust or leaf. *Encyc.*

BRONZ'ITE, *n.* [from *bronze.*] A mineral, called by Haüy *diallage metalloïde*, nearly allied to Labrador hornblend, or hyperstene. It has a yellowish brown color and semi-metallic luster, approaching to that of bronze. *Dict.*

Bronzite is regarded by Cleaveland as a subspecies of diallage.

BROOCH, *n. broche.* [Slav. *obrutsh*, or *obruch*, a ring, a circle, a bracelet.]

1. An ornamental utensil for fastening the vest, or the bosom of a shirt, as formerly used in America. It is usually made of silver, often round, with a tongue crossing its diameter, sometimes with two tongues. It formerly was used in England, as it was in America, and is still in the highlands of Scotland. *Encyc.*

2. A jewel.

3. With *painters*, a painting all of one color. *Dict.*

BROOCH, *v. t.* To adorn or furnish with brooches or jewels. *Shak.*

BROOD, *v. i.* [Sax. *brod*, a brood; and *brædan, bredan*, to dilate or extend, to warm, to divulge, to spread; D. *broeden*, to brood; Ger. *brüten*, to brood; *brut*, brood; W. *brwd*, warm; *brydiaw*, to warm. The sense is, to *warm*, or to *cover*, to *spread over.*]

1. To sit on and cover, as a fowl on her eggs for the purpose of warming them and hatching chickens, or as a hen over her chickens, to warm and protect them.

2. To sit on; to spread over, as with wings; as, to sit *brooding* over the vast abyss. *Milton.*

3. To remain a long time in anxiety or solicitous thought; to have the mind uninterruptedly dwell a long time on a subject; as, the miser *broods* over his gold. *Dryden.*

4. To mature any thing with care. *Bacon.*

BROOD, *v. t.* To sit over, cover and cherish; as, a hen *broods* her chickens.

2. To cherish.

> You'll *brood* your sorrows on a throne. *Dryden.*

BROOD, *n.* [Sax. *brod.*] Offspring; progeny; formerly used of human beings in elegant works, and we have *brother*, from this word; but it is now more generally used in contempt.

2. A hatch; the young birds hatched at once; as a *brood* of chickens or of ducks.

3. That which is bred; species generated; that which is produced.

> Lybia's *broods* of poison. *Addison.*

4. The act of covering the eggs, or of brooding. [*Unusual.*] *Shak.*

BROOD'ED, *pp.* Covered with the wings; cherished.

BROOD'ING, *ppr.* Sitting on; covering and warming; dwelling on with anxiety.

BROOD'Y, *a.* In a state of sitting on eggs for hatching; inclined to sit. [*Unusual.*] *Ray.*

BROOK, *n.* [Sax. *broc*, or *brooc.* As the sense is a stream or flowing, it may be the D. *broek*, G. *bruch*, a marsh, and allied to Gr. βρεχω, or βρυω, to rain, to pour, to flow, Eolic βρυαξ, a brook. Near the site of ancient Troy is a stream called *Thymbrec, Thymbrius.*]

A small natural stream of water, or a current flowing from a spring or fountain less than a river. In some parts of America, *run* is used in a like sense; but *run* is also applied to larger streams than *brook.*

BROOK, *v. t.* [Sax. *brucan*, to use, employ or perform, to eat or chew; *bræcan, brecan*, to break; Gr. βρυχω, to eat, to grind the teeth.]

Literally, to chew or digest, as the Fr. *digerir.* Hence,

To bear; to endure; to support; as, young men cannot *brook* restraint. *Hooker. Dryden.*

BROOK'-LIME, *n.* [*brook* and *lime.*] A plant, a species of Veronica, called becabunga, with blue flowers in loose lateral spikes. *Encyc.*

BROOK'-MINT. *n.* The water mint.

BROOK'-WEED, *n.* A plant, water pimpernel, the Samolus. *Muhlenberg.*

BROOK'Y, *a.* Abounding with brooks. *Dyer.*

BROOM, *n.* [Sax. *brum;* D. *brem, braam;* Ir. *brum.* This is the simple root of bramble.]

1. A plant of several species, called *dyer's weed*, being used by dyers to give a yellow color, *dyer's broom, green wood*, or *wood waxen, dwarf broom*, all belonging to the genus *Genista. Broom rape* is *Orobanche*, and with large purple flowers, *Lathræa.* *Fam. of Plants.*

Spanish Broom is a species of Spartium, and *Butcher's broom* is the Ruscus.

2. A besom, or brush with a long handle for sweeping floors; so called from being originally made of the broom-plant. In *America*, brooms are made of the tops of broom-corn, or of some species of wood splintered, chiefly ash. The latter species of broom is furnished by the natives of the country. The original broom, made of shrubs or twigs, is still used in stables.

BROOM. [See *Bream.*]

BROOM'CORN, *n.* [*broom* and *corn.*] A species of Holcus or Guinea-corn, with a jointed stem, like a reed, or the stem of maize, rising to the highth of eight or ten feet, bearing a head of which brooms are made.

BROOMING a ship. [See *Bream.*]

BROOM'LAND, *n.* [*broom* and *land.*] Land producing broom. *Mortimer.*

BROOM'RAPE, *n.* [See *Broom.*]

BROOM'STAFF, } *n.* [See *Staff* and *Stick.*]
BROOM'STICK, } The staff or handle of a broom. *Shak. Swift.*

BROOM'Y, *a.* Full of broom; containing broom. *Mortimer. Swift.*

BROTH, *n. brauth.* [Sax. *broth;* It. *brodo;* Ir. *broth;* Sp. *brodio;* Ir. *bruithim*, to boil. Qu. D. *braaden*, to roast; W. *broth*, a stirring or tumult.]

1. Liquor in which flesh is boiled and macerated, usually with rice and herbs, or some ingredient to give it a better relish.

2. In *America*, the word is often applied to foaming water, and especially to a mixture of snow and water in the highways which is called *snow-broth.*

BROTH'EL, *n.* [A dialectical orthography of *bordel*, which see.]

A house of lewdness; a house appropriated to the purposes of prostitution; a bawdy house; a stew.

BROTH'ELER, *n.* One that frequents brothels.

BROTH'EL-HOUSE, *n.* A brothel.

BROTH'ELRY, *n.* Lewdness; obscenity. *Hall. Jonson.*

BRŎTHER, *n.* plu. *brŏthers* or *brethren.* [Goth. *brothar*; Sax. *brother.* or *brether*; Sw. and Dan. *broder*; D. *broeder*, from *broeden*, to *brood*, to *breed*; G. *bruder*; Sans. *brader*; Russ. *brat*; Dalmatian *brath*; L. *frater*; Gr. φρατηρ, φρατωρ; Pers. برادر boradar; Corn. *bredar*; Ir. *brathair*; W. *brawd*; Sam. *abrat*; Fr. *frère*, from L. *frater*; Sp. *frayle*, a friar; It. *fratello*, brother, and *frate*, friar; Arm. *breuzr*. By the Dutch, it appears that this word signifies one of the brood or breed. The common plural is *brothers*; in the solemn style *brethren* is used.]

1. A human male born of the same father and mother. A male by one of the parents only is called a half-brother, or brother of the half blood. *Blackstone.*
2. Any one closely united; an associate; as a band of *brothers*.
3. One that resembles another in manners.

He that is slothful in his work is *brother* to him that is a great waster. *Proverbs* xviii.

In *scripture*, the term *brother* is applied to a kinsman by blood more remote than a son of the same parents; as in the case of Abraham and Lot, Jacob and Laban. Persons of the same profession call each other brother, as judges, clergymen, professors of religion, members of societies united in a common cause, monks and the like.

Kings give to each other the title of *brother*.

Clergymen address their congregations by the title of *brethren*. In a more general sense, *brother* or *brethren* is used for man in general; all men being children of the same primitive ancestors, and forming one race of beings.

Brother-german is a brother by the father's and mother's side, in contradistinction to a uterine brother, or by the mother only. *Encyc.*

BRŎTH'ERHOOD, *n.* [*brother* and *hood.*] The state or quality of being a brother. *Locke.*

2. An association of men for any purpose, as a society of monks; a fraternity. *Davies.*
3. A class of men of the same kind, profession, or occupation. *Addison.*

BRŎTH'ERLESS, *a.* Without a brother. *Shak.*

BRŎTH'ERLIKE, *a.* Becoming a brother. *Shak.*

BRŎTH'ERLŎVE, *n.* Brotherly affection. *Shak.*

BRŎTH'ERLY, *a.* Pertaining to brothers; such as is natural for brothers; becoming brothers; kind; affectionate; as *brotherly* love. *Bacon.*

Shakspeare uses this word as an adverb. "I speak but *brotherly*." But the use is not authorized.

BROUGHT, *pret.* and *pp.* of *bring*; pronounced *braut.* [See *Bring.*]

BROW, *n.* [Sax. *brœw*, *bruwa*; D. *braauw*; G. *braue*; Russ. *brov*; Ir. *bra*, *brai*, eyebrow, and *abhra*, the eyelid; Sans. *bruwan*, *bru*; Gr. οφρυη, οφρυς; Pers. برو or ابرو; and the last syllable of L. *palpebra*. It is probably contracted from *brg*, and signifies an edge, border or projection.]

1. The prominent ridge over the eye, forming an arch above the orbit. The skin of this arch or ridge is moved by muscles, which contract it in a frown and elevate it in joy or surprize. Hence, to *knit the brows*, is to frown. *Encyc.*
2. The hair that covers the brow forming an arch, called the *eye brow*.
3. The forehead. Hence, the general air of the countenance. *Shak. Waller.*
4. The edge of a steep place, as the brink of a river or precipice; as the *brow* of a hill. *Bacon.*
5. A fringe of coppice, adjoining to the hedge of a field. *Mason.*

BROW, *v t.* To bound; to limit; to form the edge or border of. *Milton.*

BROW'-ANTLER, *n.* [*brow* and *antler.*] The first start that grows on a deer's head. *Bailey.*

2. The branch of a deer's horn next the tail. *Encyc.*

BROW'-BEAT, *v. t.* [*brow* and *beat.*] To depress or bear down with haughty, stern looks, or with arrogant speech and dogmatic assertions; or in general to bear down by impudence.

BROW'BEATEN, *pp.* Overborne by impudence.

BROW'BEATING, *ppr.* Overbearing with severe brows, stern looks, or positive assertions.

BROW'BEATING, *n.* A bearing down with stern looks, supercilious manners, or confident assertions.

BROW'BOUND, *a.* [*brow* and *bound.*] Crowned; having the head encircled as with a diadem. *Shak.*

BROW'LESS, *a.* Without shame. *Addison.*

BROW'-PŎST, *n.* [*brow* and *post.*] Among *builders*, a beam that goes across a building. *Encyc.*

BROW'-SICK, *a.* [*brow* and *sick.*] Dejected; hanging the head. [*Not used.*] *Suckling.*

BROWN, *a.* [Sax. *brun*; D. *bruin*; Ger. *braun*; Dan. *bruun*; Fr. *brun*; Sp. and It. *bruno*; from the verb, to *burn.*]

Dusky; of a dark or dusky color, inclining to redness; but the shades are various, as Spanish *brown*, London *brown*, clove *brown*, tawny *brown*. *Brown* results from a mixture of red, black and yellow. *Kirwan.*

BROWN, *v. t.* To make brown or dusky.

A trembling twilight o'er the welkin moves,
Browns the dim void, and darkens deep the groves. *Barlow.*

BROWN'-BILL, *n.* [*brown* and *bill.*] A weapon formerly used by the English foot soldiers. The origin of the name is not stated; but from it *brown musket* is said to have derived its appellation. *Johnson.*

BROWN'ISH, *a.* Somewhat brown; inclined to brown. *Kirwan.*

BROWN'ISM, *n.* The doctrines or religious creed of the Brownists, who maintained that any body of professing Christians united under one pastor, or communing together, constitute a church independent of any other. *Encyc.*

BROWN'IST, *n.* A follower of Robert Brown, a puritan, or dissenter from the Church of England, who left England with his congregation and settled at Middleburgh in Zealand. He was the head of a party of Independents in Church government. *Encyc.*

BROWN'NESS, *n.* A brown color. *Sidney.*

BROWN-SPAR, *n.* Pearl spar, or siderocalcite. *Ure.*

BROWN'-STUDY, *n.* [*brown* and *study.*] Gloomy study; dull thoughtfulness; meditation directed to no certain object. *Norris.*

BROWN'-WŎRT, *n.* [*brown* and *wort.*] A plant, prunella.

2. A species of Scrophularia, the vernalis, or yellow figwort, with brown stalks. *Encyc. Fam. of Plants.*

BROWN'Y, *a.* Brown. [*Not used.*] *Shak.*

BROWSE, *v. t.* *s* as *z*. [Gr. βροσκω, to eat or browse, βρωσις, food, but probably these words may be from *sprouts*; Arm. *brouz*, *brouez*, or *broust*, sprouts, buds; Fr. *brout*, *brouter*; Arm. *brousta*, or *brouza*, to browze. It is allied to *brush*; W. *brwys*, luxuriant growth; *rhwys*, vigor, luxuriance, wantonness.]

To eat the ends of branches of trees and shrubs or the young shoots, as cattle, or deer. *Spenser. Shak.*

BROWSE, *v. i.* *s* as *z*. To feed on the tender branches or shoots of shrubs and trees, as cattle, sheep and goats. *Arbuthnot. Shak.*

BROWSE, *n.* *brows.* The tender branches or twigs of trees and shrubs, fit for the food of cattle and other animals.

BROWS'ING, *ppr.* *s* as *z*. Feeding on branches, shrubs, or shoots of trees.

BRU'CIA, } *n.* A new vegetable alkali, extracted from the bark of the false angustura. *Ure.*
BRU'CINE, }

BRU'CITE, *n.* A mineral, the chondrodite of Berzelius, which sometimes occurs in grains or imperfect crystals, sometimes in four-sided prisms with rhombic bases. It is so named from the late Dr. Bruce, a distinguished mineralogist of New York. *Cleaveland.*

BRŪISE, *v. t.* *s* as *z*. [Sax. *brysan*, to bruise; Fr. *briser*, to break or bruise; *froisser*, to *bruise*; Arm. *brousta.*]

To crush by beating or pounding with an instrument not edged or pointed. When applied to animal flesh or to vegetables, a bruise is a contusion that impairs the natural solidity and texture of the part, but often without breaking the skin. When applied to minerals and similar substances, it signifies to break them, and often to reduce them to a coarse powder.

BRŪISE. *n.* A contusion; a hurt upon the flesh of animals, upon plants or other bodies, with a blunt or heavy instrument.

BRŪISED, *pp.* Crushed; hurt or broken by a blunt or heavy instrument.

BRŪISER, *n.* A concave tool for grinding the specula of telescopes. *Chambers.*

2. In *vulgar language*, a boxer.

BRŪISEWŎRT, *n.* [*bruise* and *wort.*] A plant; comfrey. *Johnson.*

BRŪISING, *ppr.* Crushing; breaking or wounding by a blunt or heavy instrument.

BRŪISING, *n.* In *popular language*, a beating or boxing.

BRŪIT, *n.* [Fr.] Report; rumor; fame. *Obs.* *Shak.*

BRUIT, *v. t.* To report; to noise abroad. *Obs.* *Raleigh.*

BRU'MAL, *n.* [L. *bruma*, winter, *brumalis*; Span. *bruma*, winter, fog or mist.]
Belonging to the winter. *Brown.*

BRUME, *n.* [Fr. *brume*; Sp. *bruma*. See *Brumal.*]
Mist; fog; vapors. [*Little used.*] *Barlow.*

BRUN, BURN. A river or stream. *Obs.*

BRUNET', **BRUNETTE**, *n.* [Fr. from *brun*, brown. See *Brown.*] A woman with a brown or dark complexion.

BRUN'ION, *n.* [Fr. *brugnon.*] A sort of fruit between a plum and a peach. *Trevoux.*

Brunswick green. An ammoniaco-muriate of copper, used for paper hangings and in oil painting. *Ure.*

BRUNT, *n.* [Dan. *brynde*, and *brunst*, ardor, ardency, burning heat. It is the Dutch *brand*, fire, flame, ardor, from the common root of *burn*, *brennan*, *brand*. This shows the radical sense of *burn*. See *Burn.*]
1. The heat, or utmost violence of an onset; the strength or violence of any contention; as the *brunt* of a battle.
2. The force of a blow; violence; shock of any kind. *Hudibras.*
3. A sudden effort. *Bp. Hall.*

BRUSH, *n.* [Fr. *brosse*; It. *brusca*; Sp. *brusca*, *bruza*; probably allied to *browze*, W. *brwys*, thick, branching, from *rhwys*, vigor, luxuriance, or *prys*, brushwood. A *brush* is primarily sprouts, shoots.]
1. An instrument for cleaning any thing of dust and dirt by light rubbing, as floors, furniture, boots, &c. Brushes originally were made of shrubs or small branches of trees tied together, and such are yet used for coarse purposes. But the materials most used are bristles set in wood. Painters use a small brush to lay colors on their large pieces. Silver smiths use a wire-brush for scrubbing silver, copper or brass, in order to gilding; and there is a method of staining leather by rubbing the color on the skin with a brush. *Encyc.*
2. Branches of trees lopped off; brushwood; *a sense common in the U. States.*
3. The small trees and shrubs of a wood; or a thicket of small trees. *Encyc.*
4. A skirmish; a slight encounter; also, an assault; a shock, or rude treatment, from collision; as we say a *scouring*, a *rub*.
5. In *electricity*, the luminous appearance of electric matter issuing in diverging rays from a point. *Encyc.*
6. A tail; as the *brush* of a fox.

BRUSH, *v. t.* To sweep or rub with a brush; as, to *brush* a hat.
2. To strike as with a brush; to strike lightly, by passing over the surface, without injury, or impression; as, to *brush* the arm in passing; to *brush* the briny flood. *Dryden.*
3. To paint with a brush; hence, to *brush up* is often used for cleansing in general. *Pope.*
4. With *off*, to remove by brushing, as to *brush off* dust; also, to carry away by an act like that of brushing, or by passing over lightly, as by wind. *Bentley.*
5. To move as a brush; to pass over with a light contact. *Dryden.*

BRUSH, *v. i.* To move nimbly in haste; to move so lightly as scarcely to be perceived; as, to *brush* by. *Prior.*
2. To move or skim over, with a slight contact, or without much impression. *Dryden.*

BRUSH'ED, *pp.* Rubbed with a brush; struck lightly.

BRUSH'ER, *n.* One who brushes.

BRUSH'ING, *ppr.* Sweeping or rubbing with a brush; striking gently; moving nimbly in haste; skimming over lightly.

BRUSH'ING, *a.* Brisk; light; as a *brushing* gallop. *Encyc.*

BRUSH'LIKE, *a.* [*brush* and *like.*] Resembling a brush *Asiat. Res.*

BRUSH'WOOD, *n.* [*brush* and *wood.*]
Brush; a thicket or coppice of small trees and shrubs; also, branches of trees cut off. *Dryden.*

BRUSH'Y, *a.* Resembling a brush; rough; shaggy; having long hair. *Boyle.*

BRUSK, *a.* [Fr. *brusque.*] Rude; rough. *Wotton.*

BRUS'TLE, *v. i.* *brus'l.* [Sax. *brastlian*, to crackle; G. *brausen*; Dan. *bruser*; Sw. *brusa*; from the root of *rustle.*]
To crackle; to make a small crackling noise; to *rustle*, as a silk garment; to vapor, as a bully.

BRUS'TLING, *ppr.* Crackling; rustling; vaporing.

BRUT, *v. i.* [Fr. *brouter.*] To browse. [*Not in use.*] *Evelyn.*

BRU'TAL, *a.* [See *Brute.*] Pertaining to a brute; as *brutal* nature.
2. Savage; cruel; inhuman; brutish; unfeeling like a brute; merciless; as *brutal* courage; *brutal* manners.

BRUTAL'ITY, *n.* Inhumanity; savageness; churlishness; insensibility to pity or shame. *Locke.*

BRU'TALIZE, *v. t.* To make brutal, churlish or inhuman.

All cruel punishments *brutalize* the heart. *Z. Swift.*

BRU'TALIZE, *v. i.* To become brutal, inhuman, or coarse and beastly. *Addison.*

BRU'TALLY, *adv.* Cruelly; inhumanly; in a coarse, churlish, or brutal manner. *Arbuthnot.*

BRUTE, *a.* [Fr. *brut*, from L. *brutus*, senseless, irrational; It. and Sp. *bruto*. This word may be the Ch. ברותא foreign, strange, as the ancients expressed wildness and savageness by verbs which signify to depart or be distant.]
1. Senseless; unconscious; as the *brute* earth. *Bentley.*
2. Irrational; ferine; as a *brute* beast. *South.*
3. Bestial; in common with beasts; as *brute* violence. *Milton.*
4. Rough; uncivilized; insensible; as a *brute* philosopher. *Pope.*

BRUTE, *n.* A beast; any animal destitute of reason, and of course the word comprehends all animals except *man*, but is applied mostly to the larger beasts.
2. A brutal person; a savage in heart or manners; a low bred, unfeeling man.

BRUTE, *v. t.* for *bruit*, to report. [*Not used.*]

BRU'TELY, *adv.* In a rude manner. *Milton.*

BRU'TENESS, *n.* Brutality. *Obs.* *Spenser.*

BRU'TIFY, *v. t.* To make a person a brute; to make senseless, stupid or unfeeling. *Congreve.*

BRU'TISH, *a.* Like a brute or beast; as a *brutish* form. *Milton.*
2. Insensible; stupid; as *brutish* men. *Grew.*
3. Unfeeling; savage; ferocious; brutal.
4. Gross; carnal; bestial. *Shak.* *South.*
5. Ignorant; uncivilized; untaught. *Hooker.*

BRU'TISHLY, *adv.* In the manner of a brute; grossly; irrationally; stupidly; savagely. *South.*

BRU'TISHNESS, *n.* Stupidity; insensibility; brutality; savageness; the qualities of a brute. *Spratt.*

BRY'ONY, *n.* [L. *bryonia*; Gr. βρυωνια.]
White jalap; a genus of plants of several species. The root of the rough or white bryony is a strong irritating cathartic. *Encyc.* *Coxe.*

Black-bryony is a genus of plants, called Tamus. *Encyc.*

BUB, *n.* A cant word for strong malt liquor. *Prior.*

BUB, *v. t.* To throw out in bubbles. [*Not used.*] *Sackville.*

BUB'BLE, *n.* [D. *bobbel*; Sw. *bubla*; from swelling, inflation.]
1. A small bladder or vesicle of water or other fluid inflated with air. *Newton.*
2. Any thing that wants firmness or solidity; a vain project; that which is more specious than real. Hence, a false show; a cheat or fraud. *Bacon.* *Dryden.*
3. A delusive scheme of speculation; an empty project to raise money on imaginary grounds; as the South Sea *bubble*. *Swift.*
4. A person deceived by an empty project. *Prior.*

BUB'BLE, *v. i.* To rise in bubbles, as liquors when boiling or agitated. *Shak.* *Dryden.*
2. To run with a gurgling noise; as a *bubbling* stream. *Pope.*

BUB'BLE, *v. t.* To cheat; to deceive or impose on. *Addison.*

BUB'BLER, *n.* One who cheats. *Digby.*

BUB'BY, *n.* [from the same root as *bubble* and *bubo.*] A woman's breast. *Arbuthnot.*

BU'BO, *n.* [Gr. βουβων, L. *bubo*, a swelling.]
A tumor or abscess with inflammation, which rises in certain glandular parts of the body, as in the groin, or armpit. *Encyc.* *Coxe.*

BU'BONOCELE, *n.* [Gr. βουβων, the groin, and κηλη, a tumor.]
Hernia inguinalis, or inguinal rupture; a tumor in the groin, formed by a prolapsus of the intestines or omentum or both, through the processes of the peritoneum and rings of the abdominal muscles. *Encyc.*

BU'BUKLE, *n.* A red pimple. [*Not used.*] *Shak.*

BUBUL'CA, *n.* A flat fresh-water fish, of a circular form and a silvery color. *Dict. of Nat. Hist.*

BUCANEE'R, **BUCANIE'R**, *n.* [Fr. *boucaner*, to broil fish or flesh, to hunt oxen for their skins.]
Primarily, a bucaneer is said to be one who dries and smokes flesh or fish after the manner of the Indians. The name was first given to the French settlers in Haiti or Hispaniola, whose business was to hunt wild cattle and swine. It was afterwards

applied to the piratical adventurers, English and French, who combined to make depredations on the Spaniards in America. *Encyc.*

BUCA'O, *n.* A species of owl, in the Philippine isles, of a beautiful plumage, and size of a peacock, but remarkable for a hideous nocturnal scream. *Dict. of Nat. Hist.*

BUC'CAL, *a.* [L. *bucca*, the cheek; W. *boc.*]
Pertaining to the cheek. The *buccal* glands are the small glands of the mouth, under the cheek, which secrete saliva. *Hooper.*

BUCCELLA'TION, *n.* [L. *buccella*, *buccea*, a mouthful.]
The act of breaking into large pieces.

BUC'CINITE, *n.* Fossil remains or petrifactions of the shells called buccinum. *Jameson.*

BUCENT'AUR, *n.* The state barge of Venice.

BUCEPH'ALUS, *n.* An animal of the gazelle tribe, of the size of a hind.

BU'CEROS, *n.* The hornbill or Indian raven; a genus of birds, common in the East Indies.

BUCH'OLZITE, *n.* A newly discovered mineral, whose colors are white and black, appearing in spots. *Cleaveland.*

BUCK, *n.* [G. *bauche*, *beuche*; Sp. *bugada.*]
Lye in which clothes are soaked in the operation of bleaching; the liquor in which clothes are washed. *Encyc. Johnson.*
2. The cloth or clothes soaked or washed in lye. *Shak.*

BUCK, *v. t.* [G. *beuchen*; Dan. *böger*; Sw. *byka*; Arm. *bugad*; Norm. *buer.* This verb is retained in the L. *imbuo*, for *imbuco* or *imbugo*, to steep, tinge, imbue.]
To soak or steep in lye, a process in bleaching; to wash or steep in lye or suds. *Encyc. Shak.*

BUCK, *n.* [Sax. *buc*, *bucca*; D. *bok*; Ger. Sw. *bock*; Sp. *boque*; W. *bwç*; It. *becco.* This Italian word signifies a bill or *beak*, the mouth, the helm of a ship, the pipe of a still and a *buck.* We see it is the same word as *beak*, from thrusting; Dan. *buk*, whence *bukker*, to ram or thrust piles. Ir. *boc* or *poc*; Corn. *byk*; Fr. *bouc*; Arm. *bouch*; Kalmuc, *bugn*, a stag. Qu. Eth. በሐከ bahak, the male of sheep or goats.]
The male of the fallow deer, of the goat, the sheep, the rabbit and hare. It is applied only to the smaller quadrupeds.

BUCK, *v. i.* To copulate as bucks and does. *Mortimer.*

BUCK'-BASKET, *n.* [*buck* and *basket.*] A basket in which clothes are carried to the wash. *Shak.*

BUCK'BEAN, *n.* This is properly *bogbean*, which see.

BUCK'ED, *pp.* Soaked in lye. *Ash.*

BUCK'ET, *n.* [Sax. *buc*; Fr. *baquet*; Ir. *buicead*; Sw. *buc*; Dan. *bak.*]
1. The vessel in which water is drawn out of a well; it is nearly in the form of a pail.
2. A vessel or pail used at sea to draw water up at the side of a ship, for washing the decks, &c. *Mar. Dict.*
3. A vessel made of leather, nearly in the form of a pail, but narrower and deeper, used to convey water by hand for extinguishing fires.

BUCK'ING, *ppr.* Soaking in lye, in the process of bleaching; washing.

BUCK'ING, *n.* The act or process of soaking cloth in lye for bleaching; also, the lye or liquor; a washing. *Encyc. Ash.*

BUCK'ING-STOOL, *n.* A washing block.

BUCK'LE, *n.* [Fr. *boucle*, a buckle, a ring, a knocker; *boucler*, to curl, to ring, to buckle; Ir. *bucla*; Arm. *boucl.* In Sp. *bucle* is hair curled. In W. *baçu*, *baçellu*, and *baglu* signify, to bend, hook or grapple. Sax. *bugan*, to bow.]
1. An instrument made of some kind of metal, for fastening together certain parts of dress, as the straps of shoes, kneebands &c., or other straps and bands, as in a harness. The forms are various, but it consists of a ring or rim with a chape and tongue.
2. A curl, or a state of being curled or crisped, as hair. *Spectator.*
3. In *coats of arms*, a token of the surety, faith and service of the bearer. *Encyc.*

BUCK'LE, *v. t.* To fasten with a buckle, or buckles.
2. To prepare for action; a metaphor, taken from buckling on armor. *Spenser.*
3. To join in battle. *Hayward.*
4. To confine or limit.

A span *buckles* in his sum of age. *Shak.*

BUCKLE, *v. i.* To bend; to bow; as, to *buckle* under life. *Skak.*
To buckle to, to bend to; to apply with vigor; to engage with zeal. *Locke.*
To buckle in, to close in; to embrace or seize the body, as in a scuffle; *a popular use in America.*
To buckle with, to encounter with embrace; to join in close combat. *Dryden.*

BUCK'LER, *n.* [W. *bwccled*; Fr. *bouclier*; Ir. *buicleir.*]
A kind of shield, or piece of defensive armor, anciently used in war. It was composed of wood, or wickers woven together, covered with skin or leather, fortified with plates of brass or other metal, and worn on the left arm. On the middle was an umbo, boss or prominence, very useful in causing stones and darts to glance off. The buckler often was four feet long, and covered the whole body. *Encyc.*

BUCK'LER, *v. t.* To support; to defend. [*Not used.*] *Shak.*

BUCK'LER-THORN, *n.* Christ's thorn. *Johnson.*

BUCK'MAST, *n.* [*buck*, that is, *beach*, and *mast.*]
The mast or fruit of the beach tree. *Johnson.*

BUCK'RAM, *n.* [Fr. *bougran*; It. *bucherame*; qu. from It. *bucare*, to make holes.]
A coarse linen cloth, stiffened with glue, used in garments to keep them in the form intended, and for wrappers to cover cloths, and other merchandize. *Encyc.*

BUCK'RAM, *a.* Stiff; precise. *Fulke.*

BUCK'RAMS, *n.* The same as wild garlic. *Johnson.*

BUCKS'HORN, *n.* [*buck* and *horn.*] A plant, a species of *Plantago*, or plantain, called *coronopus.*
The *warted buckshorn* is a species of Cochlearia, or scurvy grass. *Fam. of Plants.*

BUCK'SKIN, *n.* The skin of a buck. As an adjective, made of leather prepared from the skin of a buck. *Ash.*

BUCK'STALL, *n.* [*buck* and *stall.*] A toil or net to take deer. *Encyc.*

BUCK'THORN, *n.* [*buck* and *thorn.*] A genus of plants, called *Rhamnus*, of many species. The common purging buck-thorn grows to the height of 12 or 14 feet, and bears a black berry, which, when green, is used to dye yellow, and when ripe, green. The bark also dyes yellow. The *sea buck-thorn* is a genus of plants, called *Hippophae.* *Encyc. Fam. of Plants.*

BUCK'WHEAT, *n.* [D. *boek-weit*; Ger. *buchweitzen.*]
A plant and a species of grain; called also brank. It belongs to the genus *polygonum*, or knot-grass. It is cultivated as food for beasts, and the flour is much used in America for breakfast cakes.

BUCOL'IC, *a.* [Gr. βουκολος, a herdsman; βουκολικος, pastoral; L. *buculus*, an ox; *bucolicus*, pertaining to cattle, pastoral; W. and Corn. *bugail* or *bygel*; Ir. *buachail*, a shepherd. See *Bovine.*]
Pastoral; relating to country affairs and to a shepherd's life and occupation. *Johnson.*

BUCOL'IC, *n.* A pastoral poem, representing rural affairs, and the life, manners and occupation of shepherds; as the *bucolics* of Theocritus and Virgil. *Dryden. Encyc.*
2. A writer of pastorals. *Warton.*

BUD, *n.* [D. *bot*; Fr. *bouton*; It. *bottone*, a *bud* or *button*; Ir. *abaidh*, a bud; Sp. *boton*; Arm. *bouton*, literally a push; Sp. *botar*, to push or thrust, to vow; Gr. φυτον; φυω, to plant or beget, contracted from φυτω; Ch. נבט; Ar. نَبَتَ nabata; allied to pout, Fr. *bouder.* See class Bd, No. 34.]
A gem; the shoot of a plant; a small protuberance on the stem or branches of a plant, containing the rudiments of future leaves or a flower. It is called by botanists the *hybernacle*, the winter lodge or receptacle of the leaves or flowers of plants, and is an epitome of a flower, or of a shoot, which is to be unfolded the succeeding summer. It is covered with scales, which are intended to defend the inclosed rudiments from cold and other external injuries.
Buds are of three kinds; that containing the flower; that containing the leaves; and that containing both flower and leaves. *Milne. Martyn.*

BUD, *v. i.* To put forth or produce buds or gems. Job xiv. 9.
2. To put forth shoots; to grow as a bud into a flower or shoot. *Dryden.*
3. To begin to grow, or to issue from a stock in the manner of a bud, as a horn. *Dryden.*
4. To be in bloom, or growing like a young plant. *Shak.*

BUD, *v. t.* To inoculate a plant; to insert the bud of a plant under the bark of another tree, for the purpose of raising, upon any stock, a species of fruit different from that of the stock.

BUD'DED, *pp.* Put forth in buds; inoculated.

BUD'DHISM, *n.* The doctrines of the Buddhists in Asia.

BUD'DING, *ppr.* Putting forth buds; inoculating.

BUD'DLE, *n.* In *mining*, a large square frame of boards, used in washing tin ore. *Ash. Encyc.*

BUD'DLE, *v. i.* Among *miners*, to wash ore. *Bailey. Ash.*

BUDĠE, *v. t.* [Fr. and Norm. *bouger*, to stir or wag.]

To move off; to stir; to wag. In America, *wag* is much used as equivalent to *budge*; but the use of both words is vulgar. *Shak.*

BUDĠE, *n.* The dressed skin or fur of lambs. *Bailey.*

BUDĠE, *a.* Brisk; jocund. *Bailey.*

2. Surly; stiff; formal. *Obs. Johnson.*

BUDĠE-BACHELORS, a company of men clothed in long gowns lined with lamb's fur, who accompany the Lord Mayor of London at his inauguration. *Bailey. Ash.*

BUDĠE-BARREL, *n.* A small barrel with only one head; on the other end, a piece of leather is nailed, which is drawn together upon strings like a purse. It is used for carrying powder, with a gun or mortar. *Encyc.*

BUDĠENESS, *n.* Sternness; severity. [*Not used.*]

BUDĠ'ER, *n.* One who moves or stirs from his place. *Shak.*

BUDĠ'ET, *n.* [Fr. *bougette*; Arm. *bougeden*; Norm. *bouge*; perhaps from the root of *bag*.]

1. A bag; a little sack, with its contents. Hence, a stock or store; as a *budget* of inventions. *L'Estrange.*

2. The papers respecting the finances of the British nation.

To open the budget, to lay before a legislative body the papers of the Executive Government. *Price.*

BUDĠ'Y, *a.* Consisting of fur. [*Not used.*]

BUD'LET, *n.* [from *bud*.] A little bud springing from a parent bud.

We have a criterion to distinguish one bud from another, or the parent bud from the numerous *budlets* which are its offspring. *Darwin.*

BUFF, *n.* [contracted from *buffalo*, or *buffskin*.]

1. Buffskin; a sort of leather, prepared from the skin of the buffalo, dressed with oil, like shammy. It is used for making bandoliers, belts, pouches, gloves and other articles. The skins of oxen, elks and other animals, dressed in like manner, are also called *buffs*. *Encyc.*

2. A military coat made of buff-skin or similar leather. *Shak.*

3. The color of buff; a light yellow.

4. A yellow viscid substance formed on the surface of blood drawn in inflammatory diseases. *Parr.*

BUFF, *v. t.* To strike. [See *Buffet*.]

BUFF'ALO, *n.* [It. and Sp. *bufalo*; Fr. *buffle*; L. *bubalus*.]

The Bubalus, a species of the bovine genus, originally from India, but now found in most of the warmer countries of the Eastern Continent. It is larger and less docile than the common ox, and is fond of marshy places and rivers. The name is also applied to wild oxen in general, and particularly to the Bison of North America. [See *Bison*.] *Cyc. Cuvier.*

BUFF'EL, *n.* Buffel's head duck, anas bucephala, a bird with a short blue bill, and a head whose apparent size is greatly increased by the fulness of its feathers, found in winter in the rivers of Carolina. *Catesby. Pennant.*

BUFF'ET, *n.* [Fr. *buffet*; It. *buffetto*; Sp. *bufete*.]

A cupboard, or set of shelves, for plates, glass, china and other like furniture. It was formerly and is still in some parts of the country, an apartment erected on one side of a room; but in more fashionable houses, it has been laid aside, and a side board substituted, which is now considered as the buffet. But as far as my knowledge extends, the name has become, in a great measure, obsolete, except among the common people, by whom it is pronounced *bofat*.

BUFF'ET, *n.* [It. *buffetto*; Sp. Port. *bufar*, to blow, to *puff*; Norm. *buffe*, a blow; W. *pafiaw*, to thump. See *Buffoon* and *Puff*.]

A blow with the fist; a box on the ear or face; a slap. *Milton.*

BUFF'ET, *v. t.* To strike with the hand or fist; to box; to beat.

They spit in his face and *buffetted* him. Math. xxvi.

2. To beat in contention; to contend against; as, to *buffet* the billows. *Otway.*

BUFF'ET, *v. i.* To exercise or play at boxing. *Shak.*

BUFF'ETED, *pp.* Struck; beaten. 1 Cor. iv. 11. 1 Pet. ii. 20.

BUFF'ETER, *n.* One who buffets; a boxer. *Johnson.*

BUFF'ETING, *ppr.* Striking with the hand; boxing; contending against.

BUFF'ETING, *n.* A striking with the hand.

2. Contention; attack; opposition.

He seems to have been a plant of slow growth, but formed for duration, and fitted to endure the *buffetings* of the rudest storm. *Wirt.*

BUFF'IN, *n.* A sort of coarse stuff; as, *buffin* gowns. *Massinger.*

BUFF'LE, *n.* [Fr.] The buffalo.

BUFF'LE, *v. i.* To puzzle; to be at a loss. *Swift.*

This is probably the same word as baffle

BUFF'LE-HEAD, *n.* [*buffle* and *head*.] One who has a large head.

BUFF'LE-HEADED, *a.* Having a large head, like a buffalo; dull; stupid; foolish.

BUFF'ON, *n.* The Numidian crane, an African fowl. *Dict. of Nat. Hist.*

BUFFOON', *n.* [Fr. *bouffon*; It. *buffo*; Sp. *bufon*, a buffoon, comical; It. *beffare* and *buffare*, to trifle, joke, play the fool; Sp. *befar*, to mock or ridicule; *bufar*, to blow, or *puff* with anger, to snort; Port. *id.* These verbs indicate the origin of buffoonery. The root of *buffet*, *puff*, signifies to drive, to push, to strike. See *Puff*.]

1. A man who makes a practice of amusing others by low tricks, antic gestures and postures, jokes and other vulgar pleasantries. A droll; a mimic. *Johnson. Encyc.*

2. He that uses indecent raillery. *Garth.*

BUFFOON', *v. t.* To make ridiculous. *Glanville.*

BUFFOON'ERY, *n.* The arts and practices of a buffoon; low jests; ridiculous pranks; vulgar tricks and postures. *Johnson.*

Dryden has placed the accent improperly on the first syllable.

BUFFOON'ING, *n.* Buffoonery. *Dryden. Guthrie's Quint.*

BUFFOON'ISH, *a.* Like a buffoon; consisting in low jests or gestures.

BUFFOON'ISM, *n.* The practices of a buffoon.

BUFFOON'-LIKE, *a.* Resembling a buffoon. *Sherwood.*

BUFFOON'LY, *a.* Consisting of low vulgar tricks. [*Little used.*]

BU'FONITE, *n.* [L. *bufo*, a toad.] Toadstone, or fossil-teeth of the anarrhicas or sea-wolf, formerly much esteemed for its imaginary virtues and worn in rings. It was named from an opinion that it was found in the head of a toad. *Encyc.*

BUG, *n.* [Qu. W. *bac*, *byçan*, small.] In *common language*, the name of a vast multitude of insects, which infest houses and plants. In *zoology*, this word is applied to the insects arranged under the genus *Cimex*, of which several hundred species are described. Bugs belong to the order of hemipters. They are furnished with a rostrum or beak, with antennæ longer than the thorax, and the wings are folded together crosswise. The back is flat, the throat margined, and the feet are formed for running. Some species have no wings. The house-bug, or bed-bug, is a troublesome and disgusting insect. *Encyc.*

BUG, or **BUG'BEAR**, *n.* [W. *bwg*, a hobgoblin or scarecrow; *bugadu*, to terrify; Russ. *buka*, a sprite or goblin. In Pers. بُاكَ is fear.]

A frightful object; a walking specter; any thing imaginary that is considered as frightful. *Locke. Pope.*

BUG'BEAR, *v. t.* To alarm or frighten with idle phantoms. *Archb'p. King.*

BUGEE', *n.* A species of monkey found in India, of a beaver color. *Dict. of Nat. Hist.*

BU'GELUGEY, *n.* A large species of lizard, four feet long. *Dict. of Nat. Hist.*

BUG'GER, *n.* [Fr. *bougre*; Sp. *bujarron*; D. *boggeren*, verb.]

One guilty of the crime against nature. A vile wretch; *a term of reproach.*

BUG'GERY, *n.* The unnatural and detestable crime of carnal intercourse of man or woman with a beast; or of human beings unnaturally with each other. Sodomy. *Encyc.*

BUG'GINESS, *n.* [from *buggy*.] The state of being infected with bugs.

BUG'GY, *a.* [from *bug*.] Abounding with bugs. *Johnson.*

BU'GLE, } *n.* [W. *bugail*, a shepherd. See *Bucolic*.
BU'GLE-HORN, }

The shepherd's horn, or from the same root as the Fr. *beugler*, to bellow, from its sound.] A hunting horn. *Spenser. Shak.*

2. A military instrument of music.

BU'GLE, *n.* A shining bead of black glass. *Shak.*

BU'GLE, *n.* [L. *bugula*, or *bugillo.*] A genus of plants, Ajuga, of several species. *Encyc.*

BU'GLE, *n.* [L. *buculus*, an ox.] A sort of wild ox. *Philips.*

BU'GLE-WEED, *n.* A plant, the lycopus virginicus, valued as a remedy for hæmoptysis, or spitting of blood.

BU'GLOSS, *n.* [L. *buglossus* ; Gr. βȣγλωσσος, of βους, an ox, and γλωσσα, tongue.]

A genus of plants, called alkanet ; in botany, *anchusa.*

The *small wild bugloss*, is the *Asperugo.*

The *viper's bugloss*, is the *Echium.*

BUG'WORT, *n.* A plant, the Cimicifuga. *Muhlenberg.*

BUHR'STONE, *n.* A subspecies of silex or quartz, occurring in amorphous masses, partly compact, but containing many irregular cavities. It is used for mill-stones. *Cleaveland.*

This word is often written *burr-stone.*

BUILD, } *v. t. bild* ; pret. *built* ; pp. *built*,
BILD, } pronounced *bilt.* The regular pret. and pp. *builded*, is sometimes used. [Sax. *byldan*, to confirm ; *byld, bylde, byldo*, constancy, firmness ; *bilith*, a model, an image ; Sw. *bilda* ; D. *afbeelden, verbeelden* ; Ger. *bilden, abbilden* ; Dan. *bilder, afbilder*, to shape, form, design, delineate, represent, counterfeit ; Sw. and Ger. *bild* ; D. *beeld*, image, statue, figure, representation. The primary sense is to set, fix or make, and the true orthography is *bild.*]

1. To frame, construct, and raise, as an edifice or fabric of almost any kind, as a house, barn, shop, ship or vessel, a wall, or other structure of art ; to unite materials into a regulär structure for use or convenience.
2. To raise by art ; to frame or shape into a particular form ; as, to *build up* a head dress in a cone. *Spectator.*
3. To raise any thing on a support or foundation ; as, to *build* our hopes on air.
4. In *scripture*, to increase and strengthen ; to cement and knit together ; to settle or establish and preserve. Acts xx. 32. Eph. ii. 22. 1 Sam. ii. 35.

BUILD, *v. i. bild.* To exercise the art, or practice the business of building.

To *build*, to plant, whatever you intend. *Pope.*

2. To construct, rest or depend on as a foundation ; as, to *build* on the opinions of others. *Addison.*

BUILD'ER, *n. bild'er.* One who builds ; one whose occupation is to build ; an architect, a ship-wright, a mason, &c.

2. A creator.

Whose *builder* and maker is God. Heb. xi.

BUILD'ING, *ppr. bild'ing.* Framing and erecting ; resting on.

BUILD'ING, *n. bild'ing.* A fabric or edifice constructed for use or convenience, as a house, a church, a shop, &c.

BUILT, *pp. bilt.* Framed and raised ; constructed.

BUILT, *n. bilt.* Form ; shape ; general figure of a structure ; as the *built* of a ship. *Dryden. Mar. Dict.*

2. Species of building. *Temple.*

BUL, *n.* The common flounder. *Chambers.*

BULB, *n.* [Gr. βολβος ; L. *bulbus*, a bulb or round root ; Fr. *bulbe* ; It. *bulbo* ; Sp. *bulbo*, an onion, or bulbous root ; W. *bal, bol*, protuberance.]

A round body, applied to many objects. But in *botany*, it is appropriately a bud formed under ground, upon or near the roots of certain herbaceous plants, which are hence called *bulbous* plants, as the *tulip, onion* and *lily.* The bulb under ground is what the bud is upon the stem or branches, a hybernacle or winter receptacle of a future plant, containing the plant in embryo, covered with a bark or rind, generally consisting of scales placed over each other, to defend the tender rudiments of the plant from cold and other external injuries. A bulb is scaly in the lily, solid in the tulip, coated in the onion, and jointed in the tuberous moschatel. *Milne. Martyn.*

BULB, *v. i. To bulb out* is to project or be protuberant. [*Little used.*] *Evelyn.*

BULBA'CEOUS, *a.* Bulbous. [*I believe, not used.*] *Johnson.*

BULB'ED, *a.* Round headed.

BULBIF'EROUS, *a.* Producing bulbs ; as *bulbiferous* stems. *Eaton.*

BULB'OUS, *a.* Containing bulbs or a bulb ; growing from bulbs ; round or roundish. *Martyn. Milne.*

2. Containing a knob, or protuberant part ; swelling out ; presenting rounded elevations. *Kirwan.*

BULCHIN, *n.* A young male calf. *Dekker. Marston.*

BULGE, *n.* A different orthography of *bilge.* [W. *bwlg*, bulk ; *balc*, prominent ; Sax. *bulgian*, to bellow, from *swelling out.*]

The bilge or protuberant part of a cask ; protuberance.

BULGE, *v. i.* To swell out ; to be protuberant. *Moxon.*

2. To bilge as a ship. [See *Bilge.*] *Dryden.*

BULG'ING, *ppr.* or *a.* Swelling out ; bilging.

As an adjective, protuberant.

BU'LIMY, *n.* [Gr. βȣλιμια, βȣ, great, and λιμος, hunger.]

A voracious appetite ; a disease in which the patient has a perpetual and insatiable appetite for food, and often faints, if not indulged. It is attended with various symptoms ; sometimes with heart burn ; sometimes with vomiting or convulsions. *Encyc. Coxe.*

BULK, *n.* [W. *bwlg*, bulk ; *balciaw*, to swell, to be proud ; Ir. *balc*, great, strong ; Russ. *bulikayu*, to boil, to bubble ; D. *bulken*, to low or bellow ; Dan. *bulk*, a bunch on the back ; Sax. *bulgian*, to low.]

1. Magnitude of material substance ; whole dimensions ; size of a thing ; as an ox or a ship of great *bulk.*
2. The gross ; the majority ; the main mass or body ; as the *bulk* of a debt ; the *bulk* of a nation. *Swift. Addison.*
3. Main fabric. *Shak.*
4. The whole content of a ship's hold for the stowage of goods. *Encyc.*
5. A part of a building jutting out. *Shak.*

To break bulk, in seamen's language, is to begin to unload. *Mar. Dict.*

Laden in bulk, having the cargo loose in the hold, or not inclosed in boxes, bales or casks.

BULK'-HEAD, *n.* [*bulk* and *head.*] A partition in a ship made with boards, to form separate apartments. *Encyc. Mar. Dict.*

BULK'INESS, *n.* Greatness in bulk, size or stature. *Locke.*

BULK'Y, *a.* Large ; of great dimensions ; of great size. *Dryden.*

BULL, *n.* [G. *bull* ; W. *bwla* ; Russ. *vol.* Qu. from his sex, or from bellowing ; Sw. *bola*, or *bóla* ; Dan. *boler.*]

1. The male of the Bos, or bovine genus of quadrupeds, of which *cow* is the female.
2. In *a scriptural sense*, an enemy, powerful, fierce and violent.

Many *bulls* have compassed me. Psalms.

3. Taurus, one of the twelve signs of the zodiac.

BULL, *n.* [It. *bolla*, a bubble, a blister, a seal or stamp, the Pope's bull ; Fr. *bulle* ; L. *bulla*, a boss, and an ornament worn on a child's neck. This name was given to the seal which was appended to the edicts and briefs of the Pope, and in process of time, applied to the edict itself. *Spelman.*]

1. A letter, edict or rescript of the Pope, published or transmitted to the churches over which he is head, containing some decree, order or decision. It is used chiefly in matters of justice or of grace. If the former, the lead or seal is hung by a hempen cord ; if the latter, by a silken thread. The lead or bull is impressed on one side with the heads of St. Peter and St. Paul ; on the other with the name of the Pope and the year of his pontificate. The writing is in the old, round Gothic letter ; and the instrument has about it a cross with some text of scripture, or religious motto. *Lunier. Encyc.*

The Golden Bull, so called from its golden seal, is an edict or imperial constitution, made by the Emperor Charles V., containing the fundamental law of the German Empire.

Leaden Bulls were sent by the Emperors of Constantinople to patriarchs and princes ; and by the grandees of the Empire, of France, Sicily, &c., and by patriarchs and bishops.

Waxen bulls were in frequent use with the Greek Emperors, who thus sealed letters to their relations. *Encyc.*

2. A blunder or contradiction. *Pope.*

BULL, a prefix, signifies a *bull*, or large, or having a large head.

BULL'-BAITING, *n.* [*bull* and *bait.*] The practice of baiting or exciting bulls with dogs. *Addison.*

BULL'-BEEF, *n.* [*bull* and *beef.*] The flesh of a bull ; coarse beef. *Shak.*

BULL'-BEGGAR, *n.* [*bull* and *beggar.*] Something terrible, or frightful. *Ayliffe.*

BULL'-CALF, *n.* [*bull* and *calf.*] A male-calf ; a stupid fellow. *Shak.*

BULL'-DOG, *n.* [*bull* and *dog.*] A species of dog of a particular form and of remarkable courage ; so named probably from being employed in baiting bulls, or from the size of the head.

BULL'S-EYE, *n.* [*bull* and *eye.*] Among *seamen*, a piece of wood in the form of a ring, answering the purpose of a thimble. *Mar. Dict.*

2. Aldebaran, a star of the first magnitude in the constellation Taurus. *Ash.*
3. A small obscure cloud, ruddy in the middle, portending a great storm. *Encyc.*

BULL'-FACED, *a.* Having a large face. *Dryden.*

BULL'-FEAST, *n.* [See *Bull-fight.*]

BULL'-FIGHT, *n.* [*bull* and *fight.*] A combat with a bull; an amusement among the Spaniards and Portuguese. A horseman, called a *toreador* or *picador* attacks a bull in a circus or inclosed arena, in presence of multitudes of spectators, irritating him with a spear, till the bull rushes upon the horseman, and perhaps dismounts the rider. After the bull has been tormented a long time, the horseman leaves him, and some persons on foot attack him and plunge darts into his neck; and at a signal given by the president, the barbarous sport is ended by the dagger of a *matador.* *Encyc.*

BULL'-FINCH, *n.* [*bull* and *finch.*] A bird of the Sparrow kind, whose breast, cheeks and throat are of a crimson color; the *rubicilla.* *Dict. of Nat. Hist.*

BULL'-FLY, or BULL'-BEE, *n.* An insect. *Philips.*

BULL'-FROG, *n.* [*bull* and *frog.*] The rana ocellata, a large species of frog, found in North America, of a dusky brown color, mixed with a yellowish green, and spotted with black. These frogs live in stagnant water, and utter a loud croaking sound, from which they probably received their name.

BULL'-HEAD, *n.* [*bull* and *head.*] A genus of fishes, the Cottus, with a head broader than the body, whence the name. This fish is called by some the *Miller's thumb.* *Encyc.*

2. A stupid fellow; a lubber. *Johnson.*

3. A small black water vermin. *Philips.*

BULL'-TROUT, *n.* [*bull* and *trout.*] A large species of trout, called also *sea-trout*, thicker than the common sort, and weighing about three pounds. Its back has a bluish green gloss, and there are several black spots on the sides. *Dict. of Nat. Hist.*

BULL'-WEED, *n.* Knap weed. *Johnson.*

BULL'-WORT, *n.* Bishopsweed. *Johnson.*

BULL'ACE, *n.* The *bully*-tree, or Chrysophyllum, a plant of two species, natives of the West Indies. *Fam. of Plants. Encyc.*

2. The wild plum, a species of Prunus. *Fam. of Plants. Encyc.*

BULLAN'TIC, *a.* [from *bull.*] Designating certain ornamental capital letters, used in Apostolic bulls. It is used also as a noun. *Fry.*

BULL'ARY, *n.* A collection of Papistical bulls. *South.*

BUL'LATE, *a.* [L. *bullatus.*] Having elevations, like blisters; as a *bullate* leaf. *Martyn.*

BULL'ET, *n.* [Fr. *boulet*, dim. of *boule*, a ball. See *Ball.*]

A ball of iron or lead, called also *shot*, used to load guns for killing man or beast. Balls for cannon are made of iron; musket-balls are made of lead.

BULL'ETIN, *n.* [Fr. *bulletin*, a ballot, a packet, a certificate; Sp. *boletin*, a ticket or warrant; *boleta*, a ticket, a *billet*; Port. *boleta*; It. *bulletta, bullettino*; properly, a roll.]

A French word denoting

1. An official report from an officer to his commander or superior.

2. An official report of a physician respecting the king's health.

3. A little note given by a banking company.

4. It is sometimes used for a notice, or public announcement; as a *bibliographical bulletin.*

BULL'ION, *n.* [Fr. *billon*, base coin.] Uncoined gold or silver in the mass. The precious metals are called bullion, when smelted and not perfectly refined, or when refined, but in bars, ingots, or in any form uncoined, as in plate. *Encyc.*

BULL'ISH, *a.* Partaking of the nature of a bull or blunder. *Milton.*

BULL'IST, *n.* A writer of papal bulls. *Harmar.*

BUL'LITE, *n.* A petrified shell, or the fossil remains of shells, of the genus Bulla. *Jameson.*

BULLI"TION, *n.* [L. *bullio*, to boil. See *Boil.*]

The act or state of boiling. *Superseded by ebullition.* *Bacon.*

BULL'OCK, *n.* [Sax. *bulluca*; G. *bullochs.*] An ox, or castrated bull. In America, it is applied to a full grown ox.

BULL'Y, *n.* [Sw. *bola*, to bellow; *buller*, a tumult; Dan. *bullen*, swelled, puffed up; or more directly from Sax. *bulgian*, to *bellow.*]

A noisy, blustering, overbearing fellow, more distinguished for insolence and empty menaces, than for courage, and disposed to provoke quarrels. *Addison.*

BULL'Y, *v. t.* To insult and overbear with noise and blustering menaces. *King.*

BULL'Y, *v. i.* To be noisy and quarrelsome. *Johnson.*

BUL'RUSH, *n.* [*bole*, or *boll*, and *rush.*] A large kind of rush, growing in wet land or water, and without knots, says Johnson, but Dryden calls it, the knotty *bulrush.* It is not a technical word.

BUL'TEL, *n.* [See *Bolt.*] A *bolter* or bolting cloth; also, bran. [*Not used.*]

BUL'WARK, *n.* [Sw. *bolvärck*; D. *bolwerk*; Ger. *bollwerk*; Dan. *bolværk*; from D. *bol*, plump and a ball, Sw. *bula*, W. *bal*, a protuberance, and *work*; a projecting or outwork. Fr. *boulevard*; Sp. and Port. *baluarte*; It. *baluardo.*]

1. In *fortification*, a bastion, or a rampart; a mound of earth round a place, capable of resisting cannon shot, and formed with bastions, curtains, &c. *Encyc.*

2. A fortification; also, any means of defense; as, a navy is the *bulwark* of a nation.

3. That which secures against an enemy or external annoyance; a screen or shelter; means of protection and safety.

> Salvation will God appoint for walls and *bulwarks.* Is. xxvi.

BUL'WARK, *v. t.* To fortify with a rampart; to secure by a fortification; to protect. *Addison. Barlow.*

BUM, *n.* The buttocks; the part on which we sit. *Johnson.*

BUM, *v. i.* To make a noise. *Marston.*

BUMBA'ILIFF, *n.* [A corruption of *bound bailiff.*]

In England, an under-bailiff; a subordinate civil officer, appointed to serve writs, and to make arrests and executions, and bound with sureties for a faithful discharge of his trust. [*A vulgar word.*] *Blackstone.*

BUM'BARD, *n.* [See *Bombard.*]

BUM'BAST, *n.* [A different orthography of *bombast*, which see.]

1. A cloth made by sewing one stuff upon another; patchwork. *Grew.*

2. Linen stuffed with cotton; stuffing; wadding. *Shak.*

BUM'BLE BEE, *n.* [L. *bombus*, a buzzing.] A large bee, sometimes called humble bee; so named from its sound.

BUM'BOAT, *n.* A small boat, for carrying provisions to a ship at a distance from shore. *Mar. Dict.*

BUM'KIN, *n.* [See *Bumpkin.*] A short boom projecting from each bow of a ship, to extend the clue of the foresail to windward.

2. A small out-rigger over the stern of a boat, to extend the mizen. *Mar. Dict.*

BUMP, *n.* [W. *pwmp*, a round mass; *pwmpiaw*, to thump; allied to L. *bombus*, and Eng. *pomp*, from swelling, thrusting out.]

1. A swelling or protuberance. *Dryden.*

2. A thump; a heavy blow.

BUMP, *v. i.* To make a loud, heavy or hollow noise, as the bittern. It is also written *boom.* [W. *bwmp.*] *Dryden.*

BUMP, *v. t.* To strike as with or against any thing large or solid, as to *bump* the head against a wall; to thump.

BUMP'ER, *n.* A cup or glass filled to the brim, or till the liquor runs over. *Dryden.*

BUMP'KIN, *n.* [*bump*, large, swelling, and *kin*, Sax. *cyn*, kind, genus.]

An awkward heavy rustic; a clown, or country lout. *Locke.*

BUMP'KINLY, *a.* Clownish. [*Not used.*] *Richardson.*

BUNCH, *n.* [W. *pwng*; Dan. *bunke, bynke*, a heap or heaped measure.]

1. A protuberance; a hunch; a knob or lump; as the *bunch* on a camel's back. *Isaiah.*

2. A cluster; a number of the same kind growing together; as a *bunch* of grapes. *Dryden.*

3. A number of things tied together; as a *bunch* of keys; a *bunch* of rods. *Locke.*

4. A collection of things; a knot; as a *bunch* of hair; a *bunch* of trees. *Spenser.*

BUNCH, *v. i.* To swell out in a protuberance; to be protuberant or round. *Woodward.*

BUNCH, *v. t.* To form or tie in a bunch or bunches.

BUNCH'-BACKED, *a.* [*bunch* and *back.*] Having a bunch on the back; crooked. *Shak.*

BUNCH'INESS, *n.* The quality of being bunchy, or growing in bunches. *Johnson.*

BUNCH'Y, *a.* Growing in bunches; like a bunch; having tufts. *Grew.*

BUN'DLE, *n.* [Sax. *byndel*; D. *bondel*; G. *bund, bundel*; Sw. *bindel* and *bunt.* This word is formed from the root of *bind, band, bond.*]

1. A number of things put together.

2. A roll; any thing bound or rolled into a convenient form for conveyance; as a *bundle* of lace; a *bundle* of hay. *Spectator.*

BUN'DLE, *v. t.* To tie or bind in a bundle or roll; often followed by *up*; as, to *bundle up* clothes. *Locke. Swift.*

BUNG, *n.* [Fr. *bondon*; G. *spund*; D. *sponds*; W. *bwng*, a bung hole.]

1. The stopple of the orifice in the bilge of a cask. *Mortimer.*
2. The hole or orifice in the bilge of a cask.

BUNG, *v. t.* To stop the orifice in the bilge of a cask with a bung; to close up.

BUNG'-HOLE, *n.* [*bung* and *hole*.] The The hole or orifice in the bilge of a cask.

BUNG'LE, *v. i. bung'gl.* To perform in a clumsy, awkward manner; as, to *bungle* in making shoes. *Dryden.*

BUNG'LE, *v. t.* To make or mend clumsily; to botch; to manage awkwardly; with *up*. *Dryden.*

BUNG'LE, *n.* A botch; inaccuracy; gross blunder; clumsy performance. *Ray.*

BUNG'LER, *n.* A clumsy awkward workman; one who performs without skill. *Peacham.*

BUNG'LING, *ppr.* Performing awkwardly.

BUNG'LING, *a.* Clumsy; awkwardly done. *Dryden.*

BUNG'LINGLY, *adv.* Clumsily; awkwardly. *Bentley.*

BUNK, *n.* [Dan. *bynke*, a meal tub; Sw. *miolk-bunck*, a milk pan.]

A case or cabin of boards for a bed; *a word used in some parts of America.*

BUNN or **BUN**, *n.* [Scot. *bun*, *bunn*; Ir. *bunna*; Gr. βουνος, a hill, and a cake offered to deities. It signifies a mass or collection.]

A small cake, or a kind of sweet bread. *Gay.*

BUN'SING, *n.* An animal found at the Cape of Good Hope, resembling the ferret, but twice as large. When pursued, it emits an intolerable stench. *Dict. of Nat. Hist.*

BUNT, *n.* The middle part, cavity, or belly of a sail. *Mar. Dict.*

BUNT, *v. i.* To swell out; as, the sail *bunts*.

2. In *popular language*, to push with the horns; to butt. [See *Point*.]

BUNT'ER, *n.* A cant word for a woman who picks up rags in the streets; hence, a low vulgar woman. *Johnson.*

BUNT'ING, *n.* A bird of the genus Emberiza. The name is applied to different species, as the English bunting and the rice bunting.

BUNT'ING or **BUN'TINE**, *n.* [Ger. *bunt*, D. *bont*, streaked, or of different colors.]

A thin woolen stuff, of which the colors or flags and signals of ships are made. *Mar. Dict.*

BUNT'LINES, *n.* Ropes fastened to cringles on the bottoms of square sails, to draw them up to their yards. *Mar. Dict.*

BUOY, *n.* [Fr. *bouée*, a buoy; D. *boei*, a buoy, a lodge or hut, a fetter, or shackle, a handcuff; *boeijen*, to fetter, to *buoy*; Ger. *boy*; Dan. *boy*; Russ. *bui*; Sp. *boya*, a buoy; probably from the root of Sax. *byan*, to dwell, that is, to set, be fixed, or stationary; Dan. *boe*, *boende*.]

A close empty cask, or a block of wood or cork, fastened by a rope to an anchor, and floating on the water, to show where the anchor is situated. Buoys are of various kinds, as *can-buoys*, in the form of a cone; *nun-buoys*, which are large in the middle, and tapering nearly to a point at each end; *cable-buoys*, empty casks, employed to buoy up the cable, in rocky anchorage. Buoys are used also as marks, to point out the situation of rocks, shoals, or a channel.

To stream the buoy, is to let it fall by the ship's side into the water, before letting go the anchor. *Mar. Dict.*

BUOY'ROPE, *n.* [*buoy* and *rope*.] The rope which fastens a buoy to an anchor.

BUOY, *v. t.* To keep afloat in a fluid; to bear up, or keep from sinking in a fluid, as in water or air; with *up*. *Woodward.*

2. To support, or sustain; to keep from sinking into ruin or despondency. *King Charles.*
3. To fix buoys, as a direction to mariners.

BUOY, *v. i.* To float; to rise by specific lightness. *Pope.*

BUOY'ANCY, *n.* The quality of floating on the surface of water, or in the atmosphere; specific lightness.

BUOY'ANT, *a.* Floating; light; that will not sink; having the quality of rising or floating in a fluid. *Thomson.*

2. Bearing up, as a fluid; sustaining another body. [*Unusual.*] *Dryden.*

BUPRES'TES, *n.* A species of cantharides, of a nauseous scent, and biting severely. *Dict. of Nat. Hist.*

BUR, **BOUR**, **BOR**, } Sax. *bur*, signifies a chamber or a cottage.

BUR, *n.* [Sax. *burre*, burdock; W. *bar*, a bushy head or bunch; Ir. *borr*, a bunch or knob; Fr. *bourrée*, bush.]

1. A rough prickly covering of the seeds of certain plants, as of the chesnut, and burdock.
2. A broad ring of iron behind the place for the hand on a spear, used in tilting. *Encyc.*

BUR'BOT, *n.* [from L. *barbatus*, so named from its beard.]

A fish of the genus Gadus, shaped like an eel, but shorter, with a flat head, and on the nose it has two small beards, and another on the chin. It is disgusting in appearance, but delicate food. It is called also *eel-pout*. *Encyc.*

BURD'ELAIS, *n.* A sort of grape. *Johnson.*

BURD'EN, *n. burd'n*; written also *burthen*. [Sax. *byrden*, *byrthen*; Sw. *börda*; Dan. *byrde*; G. *bürde*; Ir. *beart* or *beirt*; Gr. φορτος; Fr. *fardeau*; Arm. *fard*; from *bear*; L. *fero*, or *porto*; Pers. بردن burdan, to carry. See *Bear*.]

1. That which is borne or carried; a load. Hence,
2. That which is borne with labor or difficulty; that which is grievous, wearisome or oppressive. *Milton.*
3. A birth. *Shak.*
4. [Fr. *bourdon*, a drone.] The verse repeated in a song, or the return of the theme at the end of each verse; the chorus; so called from the application of this word to the drone or base, and the pipe or string which plays it, in an instrument. A chord which is to be divided, to perform the intervals of music, when open and undivided, is also called the *burden*. *Encyc.*
5. In *common language*, that which is often repeated; a subject on which one dwells.
6. A fixed quantity of certain commodities; as a *burden* of gad steel, 120 pounds.
7. The contents of a ship; the quantity or number of tuns, a vessel will carry; as a ship of a hundred tuns *burden*.
8. A club. [*Not in use.*] *Spenser.*

BURD'EN, *v. t. burd'n.* To load; to lay on a heavy load; to incumber with weight. Hence,

2. To oppress with any thing grievous; as, to *burden* a nation with taxes.
3. To surcharge; as, to *burden* the memory.

BURD'ENED, *pp.* Loaded with weight; incumbered; oppressed.

BURD'ENER, *n.* One who loads; an oppressor.

BURD'ENOUS, *a.* Grievous; heavy to be borne; oppressive. *Sidney.*

2. Cumbersome; useless. *Milton.*

BURD'ENSOME, *a.* Heavy; grievous to be borne; causing uneasiness or fatigue; oppressive. *Dryden.*

BURD'ENSOMENESS, *n.* The quality of being burdensome; heaviness; oppressiveness.

BUR'DOCK, *n.* [*bur* and *dock*.] A genus of plants, called *Arctium*. They are troublesome weeds.

The lesser burdock is a species of *xanthium*.

BU'REAU, *n. búro.* [Fr. *bureau*, an office, a table, a court, a chest of drawers; Sp. *bureo*, a court of justice; Arm. *burell*; Fr. *bure*, a cloth. The primary sense is a cloth covering a table, like *exchequer*. *Lunier.*]

1. A chest of drawers, for keeping papers or clothes.
2. An embassador's or secretary's office.

In Spanish, this word *bureo* is a court of justice for the trial of persons belonging to the king's household.

BURG, *n.* [This is the same word as *borough*, the only difference being in the pronunciation of the final letter.]

A borough; originally a fortified town, but now a city or town, which sends members to parliament, whether incorporated or not. [See *Borough*.]

BURG'AGE, *n.* [from *burg*.] In *English law*, tenure in burgage, or burgage tenure, is tenure in socage, applied to cities or towns, or where houses, or lands which were formerly the site of houses, in an ancient borough, are held of some lord in common socage by a certain established rent; a remnant of Saxon liberty. *Blackstone.*

BURG'AMOT, *n.* A species of pear. [See *Bergamot*.]

2. A kind of perfume. [See *Bergamot*.]

BURG'ANET, **BURG'ONET**, } *n.* [Fr. *bourguignote*, from *burg*, in the sense of *covering* or *guarding*.]

A kind of helmet, the Spanish murrion. *Spenser. Shak.*

BURĠEOIS', *n.* [Fr. *bourgeois*, pronounced *boorzhwá*, from *bourg*, *burg*.] A burgess.

BURĠEOIS', **BOURĠEOIS'**, } *n. burjois'.* A species of type, or printing letter, smaller than long primer, and larger than brevier.

BURĠEON. [See *Bourgeon*.]

BURG'ER-MASTER, *n.* An aquatic fowl which builds its nest on cliffs near the water. *Dict. of Nat. Hist.*

BURG'ESS, *n.* [Fr. *bourgeois*, from *bourg*, *burg*.]
1. An inhabitant of a borough, or walled town; or one who possesses a tenement therein; a citizen or freeman of a borough. *Blackstone.*
2. A representative of a borough in parliament. *Ib.*
3. A magistrate of certain towns. *Encyc.*
4. Before the revolution, the representatives in the popular branch of the legislature of Virginia, were called *burgesses*, as the *House of Burgesses*. It is now called the *House of Delegates*.

BURG'ESS-SHIP, *n.* The state or quality of a burgess. *South.*

BURGH, *n. burg.* A different orthography of *burg*, *borough*, which see.

BURGH'-BOTE, *n.* [*burgh* and *bote.*] In *old laws*, a contribution towards the building or repairing of castles, or walls, for the defense of a city or town. *Encyc.*

BURGH'-BRECH, *n.* [*burgh* and *break.*] A fine imposed on a burgh, for a breach of the peace. *English.*

BURGH'ER, *n.* [from *burg.*] An inhabitant of a burgh or borough, who enjoys the privileges of the borough of which he is a freeman. In *America*, it is applied to any native citizen, especially in the state of New-York.

BURGH'ER-SHIP, *n.* The state or privilege of a burgher.

BURGH'-M'ASTER, *n.* [*burgh* and *master.*] A burgomaster; also, an officer in the tin-mines, who directs and lays out the meers for the workmen, called also bailiff and bar-master. *Encyc.*

BURGH'MOTE, *n.* [*burgh* and *mote*, meeting.] The court of a *burgh* or borough. *Encyc.*

BURG'LAR, *n.* [*burgh* or *burg*, a house, and Arm. *laer*, a thief; whence Fr. *larron.*]
One guilty of nocturnal house breaking; one who breaks and enters a mansion house, with intent to commit a felony. *Coke.*

BURGLA'RIOUS, *a.* Pertaining to burglary; constituting the crime of burglary.

To come down a chimney is held a *burglarious* entry. *Blackstone.*

BURGLA'RIOUSLY, *adv.* With an intent to commit burglary; in the manner of a burglar. *Blackstone.*

BURG'LARY, *n.* The act or crime of nocturnal house breaking, with an intent to commit a felony. To constitute this crime, the act must be committed in the night, or when there is not day-light enough to discern a man's face. It must be in a mansion house, or in an adjoining building which is a part or parcel of the mansion. There must be an actual breaking and an entry; but an opening made by the offender, as by taking out a pane of glass, or lifting a window, raising a latch, picking a lock, or removing any fastening, amounts to a breaking; and a putting in of the hand, after such breaking, is an entry. The act must also be done with an intent to commit felony. *Blackstone.*

BURG'OMASTER, *n.* [*burg* and *master.*] A burgh-master; a magistrate or one employed in the government of a city. The *burgomasters* are the chief magistrates of the great towns, in Holland, Flanders and Germany.

BUR'GRAVE, *n.* [*burg* and G. *graf*, D. *graaf*, an earl.]
In some European countries, an hereditary governor of a town or castle.

BUR'GUNDY, *n.* A kind of wine, so called from Burgundy in France. *Shenstone.*
Burgundy pitch is turpentine boiled down to a firmer consistence.

BURH, is the same as *burg*, *burgh*, with the aspirate. It is Saxon, and signifies a city, a castle, a house, or tower. Hence in composition it signifies defense, protection; as *cwenburh, (queen-burh)* a woman ready to assist; *Cuthburh*, eminent for assistances. *Gibson's Camden.*

BURIAL, *n. ber'rial.* [See *Bury.*] The act of burying a deceased person; sepulture; interment; the act of depositing a dead body in the earth, in a tomb or vault, or in the water.
2. The act of placing any thing under earth or water; as, to *bury* seed in the earth.
3. The church service for funerals. *Johnson.*

BURIAL-PLACE, *n.* A place appropriated to the burial of the dead; a grave-yard.

BURIER, *n. ber'rier.* One who buries a deceased person. *Shak.*

BU'RIN, *n.* [Fr. *burin*; Port. *boril*; It. *bulino.*]
A graver; an instrument for engraving. *Johnson.*

BURL, *v. t.* [See *Burly.*] To dress cloth as fullers do. *Johnson.*
2. To pick knots and loose threads off from cloth. *Ash.*

BUR'LACE, *n.* [A contraction of *burdelais.*] A sort of grape. *Johnson.*

BURL'ER, *n.* A dresser of cloth.

BURLESQUE, BURLESK', *a.* [Fr.; It. *burlesco*, from *burlare*, to ridicule; *burla*, mockery, raillery; Port. and Sp. *burlar*, to jest or scoff; *burlesco*, a wag, a jester. The termination *esque* answers to Eng. *ish.*]
Jocular; tending to excite laughter by ludicrous images, or by a contrast between the subject and the manner of treating it, as when a trifling subject is treated with gravity.

BURLESQUE, BURLESK', *n.* Ludicrous representation; a contrast between the subject and the manner of treating it, which tends to excite laughter or ridicule.
2. A composition in which a trifling subject or low incident is treated with great gravity, as a subject of great dignity or importance; or a composition in which the contrast between the subject and the manner of considering it renders it ludicrous or ridiculous; as in Virgil Travestie, the Lutrin of Boileau, Butler's Hudibras and Trumbull's McFingal.

BURLESQUE, BURLESK', *v. t.* To turn into ridicule; or to make ludicrous by representation; as by treating a low or trifling subject with great gravity.

BURLESQ'UER, BURLESK'ER, *n.* One who burlesques, or turns to ridicule.

BURLET'TA, *n.* [Italian. See *Burlesque*, *Burly.*]
A comic opera; a musical entertainment.

BUR'LINESS, *n.* [See *Burly.*] Bulk; bluster. *Johnson.*

BURL'Y, *a.* [The sense probably is *swelled.* Hence it accords with Russ. *burlyu*, to be noisy, to swell as sound. Qu. W. *broliaw.* See *Burlesque.*]
Great in size; bulky; tumid; falsely great; boisterous. *Dryden. Cowley.*

This word is obsolete or nearly so in America; but *hurly-burly* is common in vulgar use, for noise, confusion, uproar.

BURN, *v. t.* pret. and pp. *burned* or *burnt.* [Sax. *bernan*, *bœrnan* or *byrnan*, to burn; *bryne*, a burning, fire, ardor; Sw. *brinna*, *bränna*; G. *brennen*; D. *branden*; Dan. *brœnder*, from *brand*; L. *pruna*, and perhaps, *furnus*, *fornax*, a *furnace.* The primary sense is, to rage, to act with violent excitement.]
1. To consume with fire; to reduce to ashes by the action of heat or fire; frequently with *up*; as, to *burn up* wood.
2. To expel the volatile parts and reduce to charcoal by fire; as, to *burn* wood into coal. Hence, in popular language, to *burn a kiln* of wood, is to char the wood.
3. To cleanse of soot by burning; to inflame; as, to *burn* a chimney; *an extensive use of the word.*
4. To harden in the fire; to bake or harden by heat; as, to *burn* bricks or a brickkiln.
5. To scorch; to affect by heat; as, to *burn* the clothes or the legs by the fire; to *burn* meat or bread in cookery.
6. To injure by fire; to affect the flesh by heat.
7. To dry up or dissipate; with *up*; as, to *burn up* tears. *Dryden.*
8. To dry excessively; to cause to wither by heat; as, the sun *burns* the grass or plants.
9. To heat or inflame; to affect with excessive stimulus; as, ardent spirits *burn* the stomach.
10. To affect with heat in cookery, so as to give the food a disagreeable taste. Hence the phrase *burnt to.*
11. To calcine with heat or fire; to expel the volatile matter from substances, so that they are easily pulverized; as, to *burn* oyster shells, or lime-stone.
12. To affect with excess of heat; as, the fever *burns* a patient.
13. To subject to the action of fire; to heat or dry; as, to *burn* colors. *Encyc.*

To burn up, to consume entirely by fire.
To burn out, to burn till the fuel is all consumed.

BURN, *v. i.* To be on fire; to flame; as, the mount *burned* with fire. *Exodus.*
2. To shine; to sparkle.

O prince! O wherefore *burn* your eyes? *Rowe.*

3. To be inflamed with passion or desire; as, to *burn* with anger or love. *Thomson.*
4. To act with destructive violence, as fire.

Shall thy wrath *burn* like fire? *Psalm* lxxxix.

5. To be in commotion; to rage with destructive violence.

The groan still deepens and the combat *burns.* *Pope.*

6. To be heated; to be in a glow; as, the face *burns.*
7. To be affected with a sensation of heat, pain or acidity; as, the heart *burns.*
8. To feel excess of heat; as, the flesh *burns* by a fire; a patient *burns* with a fever.

To burn out, to burn till the fuel is exhausted and the fire ceases.

BURN, *n.* A hurt or injury of the flesh caused by the action of fire.

2. The operation of burning or baking, as in brickmaking; as, they have a good *burn.*

BURN'ABLE, *a.* That may be burnt. [*Little used.*]

BURN'-COW or **BURST'-COW**, *n.* A genus of insects, with filiform feelers, of several species; very obnoxious to cattle. *Dict. of Nat. Hist.*

BURN'ED, BURNT, *pp.* Consumed with fire; scorched or dried with fire or heat; baked or hardened in the fire.

BURN'ER, *n.* A person who burns or sets fire to any thing.

BURN'ET, *n.* A plant, Poterium or garden burnet.

BURNET-SAXIFRAGE, *n.* A plant, Pimpinella.

BURN'ING, *ppr.* Consuming with fire; flaming; scorching; hardening by fire; calcining; charring; raging as fire; glowing.

BURN'ING, *n.* Combustion; the act of expelling volatile matter and reducing to ashes, or to a calx; a fire; inflammation; the heat or raging of passion. In *surgery,* actual cautery; cauterization.

BURN'ING, *a.* Powerful; vehement; as a *burning* shame; a *burning* scent. *Shak.*

2. Much heated; very hot; scorching.

The *burning* plains of India. *S. S. Smith.*

BURN'ING-GLASS, *n.* [*burn* and *glass.*] A convex glass which, when exposed to the direct rays of the sun, collects them into a small space, called a *focus,* producing an intense heat. The name is given also to a concave mirror which condenses the sun's rays. *Encyc.*

BURNING-THORNY-PLANT. A species of Euphorbia or spurge. *Fam. of Plants.*

BURN'ISH, *v. t.* [Fr. *brunir*; D. *bruineeren*; It. *brunire*; Sp. *brunir.* This word undoubtedly is of secondary formation, from the color of flame. See *Burn.*]

To polish by friction; to make smooth, bright and glossy; as, to *burnish* steel. *Dryden.*

BURN'ISH, *v. i.* To grow bright or glossy. *Swift.*

BURN'ISH, *n.* Gloss; brightness; luster. *Christ. Observ.*

BURN'ISHED, *pp.* Polished; made glossy.

BURN'ISHER, *n.* The person who polishes, or makes glossy.

2. An instrument used in polishing, of different kinds. It may be a piece of round polished steel, a dog's or wolf's tooth, a piece of copper, agate or pebble, &c. It is used for giving a gloss or smoothness to metals, to the edges of books, &c.

BURN'ISHING, *ppr.* Polishing; making smooth and glossy.

BURN'OOSE, BURN'OS, } *n.* [Sp. *albornoz*; Port. *albernoz*; Pers. بروان; Syr. ܒܝܪܘܢܐ biruna.]

An upper cloke or garment. *Parkhurst.*

BURNT, *pp.* of *burn.* Consumed; scorched; heated; subjected to the action of fire.

BURNT-OFFERING, *n.* [*burnt* and *offer.*] Something offered and burnt on an altar, as an atonement for sin; a sacrifice; called also *burnt-sacrifice.* The offerings of the Jews were a clean animal, as an ox, a calf, a goat, or sheep; or some species of vegetable substance, as bread and ears of wheat or barley. *Brown.*

BURR, *n.* The lobe or lap of the ear. *Dict.*

2. The round knob of a horn next a deer's head. *Encyc.*

3. The sweetbread.

Burr-pump, or *bilge-pump.* A pump, having a staff of 6, 7 or 8 feet long with a bar of wood to which the leather is nailed, which serves instead of a box. This staff is worked by men who pull it up and down, with a rope fastened to the middle of it. *Encyc.*

BUR'RAS-PIPE, *n.* An instrument or vessel used to keep corroding powders in. *Johnson.*

BUR'-REED, *n.* A plant, the Sparganium. *Muhlenberg.*

BUR'REL, *n.* A sort of pear, called also the red butter pear, from its smooth, delicious, soft pulp. *Philips.*

BURREL-FLY, *n.* The ox-fly, gad-bee, or breeze. *Johnson.*

BURREL-SHOT, *n.* [Fr. *bourreler,* to torment, and *shot.*]

Small shot, nails, stones, pieces of old iron, &c., put into cases, to be discharged among enemies.

BUR'ROCK, *n.* A small wier or dam where wheels are laid in a river, for catching fish. *Philips.*

BUR'ROW, *n.* A different orthography of *burgh, borough,* which see.

BUR'ROW, *n.* [Sax. *byrgen,* a sepulcher, *byrian,* to *bury,* or *beorgan,* to keep.]

A hollow place in the earth or in a warren, where small animals lodge, and sometimes deposit their provisions. Some animals excavate the earth, by scratching, and form these lodges.

BUR'ROW, *v. i.* To lodge in a hole excavated in the earth, as coneys or rabbits. In *a more general sense,* to lodge in any deep or concealed place. The word seems to include the idea of excavating a hole for a lodge, as well as lodging in it; but the verb is not often used transitively, as to *burrow* the earth.

BUR'ROWING, *ppr.* Lodging in a burrow.

BURS'AR, *n.* [See *Burse.*] A treasurer, or cash-keeper, as the *bursar* of a college, or of a monastery; a purser.

2. A student to whom a stipend is paid out of a burse or fund appropriated for that purpose, as the exhibitioners sent to the universities in Scotland by each presbytery. *Encyc. Johnson.*

BURS'AR-SHIP, *n.* The office of a bursar. *Hales.*

BURS'ARY, *n.* The treasury of a college, or monastery.

2. In Scotland, an exhibition. *Encyc.*

BURSE, *n. burs.* [Fr. *bourse,* a purse, the vesicle of the gall, the hull or skin of seeds, an exchange; D. *beurs,* a purse, an exchange, scrotum; Ger. *börse,* a purse, an exchange; D. *börs,* the same; It. *borsa*; Sp. and Port. *bolsa,* a purse or bag, *r* being changed into *l.*]

1. A public edifice in certain cities, for the meeting of merchants to consult on matters of trade and money, and to negotiate bills of exchange. This is the name used in many cities in Europe, but in England and America, such building is called an exchange. The new *Burse* in Paris is one of the most elegant buildings in the city.

2. In *France,* a fund or foundation for the maintenance of poor scholars in their studies. In the middle ages, it signified a little college, or a hall in a university. *Encyc.*

BURST, *v. i.* pret. and pp. *burst.* The old participle *bursten* is nearly obsolete. [Sax. *byrstan, burstan*; D. *barsten*; G. *bersten*; Dan. *brister*; Sw. *brista,* to burst. The word *bristle* seems to belong to *burst,* denoting a *shoot.*]

1. To fly or break open with force, or with sudden violence; to suffer a violent disruption. The peculiar force of this word is, in expressing a sudden rupture, with *violence,* or *expansion,* or both. Hence it is generally used to signify the sudden rupture of a thing by internal force, and a liberation from confinement; as, to *burst* from a prison; the heart *bursts* with grief. *Milton.*

2. To break away; to spring from; as, to *burst* from the arms. *Pope.*

3. To come or fall upon suddenly or with violence; to rush upon unexpectedly; as, a sound *bursts* upon our ears.

4. To issue suddenly, or to come from a hidden or retired place into more open view; as, a river *bursts* from a valley; a spring *bursts* from the earth.

5. To break forth into action suddenly; as, to *burst* into tears.

6. To break or rush in with violence; as, to *burst* into a house or a room.

It is often followed by an intensive particle; as, *out, forth, away, from,* or *asunder.*

BURST, *v. t.* To break or rend by force or violence; to open suddenly; as, to *burst* a chain or a door; to *burst* a cannon.

BURST, *n.* A sudden disruption; a violent rending; *more appropriately,* a sudden explosion or shooting forth; as a *burst* of thunder; a *burst* of applause; a *burst* of passion.

2. A rupture, a hernia, or the unnatural protrusion of the contents of the abdomen.

BURST, or BURST'EN, *pp.* or *a.* Affected with a rupture or hernia.

BURST, *pp.* Opened or rent asunder by violence.

BURST'ENNESS, *n.* The state of having a rupture; the hernia.

BURST'ER, *n.* One that bursts.

BURST'ING, *ppr.* Rending or parting by violence; exploding.

BURST'-WORT, *n.* The Herniaria, a plant said to be good against hernia or ruptures.

BURT, *n.* A flat fish of the turbot kind. *Johnson.*

BURTHEN. [See *Burden.*]

BUR'TON, *n.* A small tackle formed by two blocks or pulleys, used to set up or tighten the topmost shrouds, and for various other purposes; called also *top-burton-tackle.* *Mar. Dict.*

BURY, *n. ber'ry.* This word is a different orthography of *burg, burh, borough.* It signifies a house, habitation or castle, and is retained in many names of places, as in

Shrewsbury, Danbury, Aldermanbury. The word is used by Grew, for *burrow.*

BURY, *v. t.* ber'ry. [Sax. *byrian, burgan,* to bury; *byrgen,* a tomb or sepulcher; allied to *beorgan,* to save.]

1. To deposit a deceased person in the grave; to inter a corpse; to entomb.
2. To cover with earth, as seed sown.
3. To hide; to conceal; to overwhelm; to cover with any thing; as, to *bury* any one in the ruins of a city.
4. To withdraw or conceal in retirement; as, to *bury* one's self in a monastery or in solitude.
5. To commit to the water; to deposit in the ocean; as dead bodies *buried* in the deep.
6. To place one thing within another.

   Thy name so *buried* in her. *Shak.*

7. To forget and forgive; to hide in oblivion; as, to *bury* an injury.

To bury the hatchet, in the striking metaphorical language of American Indians, is to lay aside the instruments of war, forget injuries, and make peace.

BURYING, *ppr.* Interring; hiding; covering with earth; overwhelming.

BURYING, *n.* The act of interring the dead; sepulture. John xii. 7.

BURYING-PLACE, *n.* A grave-yard; a place appropriated to the sepulture of the dead; a church-yard.

BUSH, *n.* [D. *bosch;* G. *busch;* Dan. *busk;* Sw. *buska;* It. *bosco;* Sp. *bosque;* Port. *bosque;* whence Sp. *boscage,* Fr. *bocage,* It. *boscata,* a grove or cluster of trees. Qu. Gr. βοσκω, L. *pasco,* originally, to feed on sprouts.]

1. A shrub with branches; a thick shrub; also, a cluster of shrubs. With hunters, a fox tail. *Spenser. Waller. Encyc. Ash.*
2. An assemblage of branches interwoven. *Encyc.*
3. A branch of a tree fixed or hung out as a tavern sign. Hence, since the branch has been discontinued, a coronated frame of wood hung out as a tavern sign, is so called. Hence the English proverb, "Good wine needs no bush." *Encyc.*

   [*I know not that this word is thus used in the U. States.*]

4. A circle of metal let into the sheaves of such blocks as have iron pins, to prevent their wearing. *Mar. Dict.*

   This word when applied to sheaves is called *bush,* but when applied to the circular iron of a cart wheel is, in America, called a *box.* Qu. It. *bosso,* the box-tree; *bossolo,* a little box. Johnson writes it *bushel.*

BUSH, *v. i.* To grow thick or bushy. *Milton.*

BUSH, *v. t.* To furnish a block with a bush.

BUSH'EL, *n.* [Fr. *boisseau;* Arm. *boesel;* Norm. *bussel;* probably from *boiste, boîte,* a box; It. *bossolo,* that is, a little box.]

A dry measure, containing eight gallons, or four pecks. The standard English bushel, by Stat. 12. Henry VII., contains eight gallons of wheat, each gallon eight pounds of wheat, troy weight, the pound, twelve ounces troy, the ounce, twenty sterlings, and the sterling, thirty two grains of wheat growing in the middle of the ear. The contents are 2145. 6 solid inches, equivalent to 1131 ounces and 14 pennyweights troy. *Encyc.*

The English bushel is used also in the U. States.

Bushel signifies both the quantity or capacity, and the vessel which will contain the quantity.

2. In *popular language,* a large quantity indefinitely. *Johnson.*
3. The circle of iron in the nave of a wheel; in America, called a box. [See *Bush.*]

BUSH'ELAGE, *n.* A duty payable on commodities by the bushel. [*Not used in the U. States.*]

BUSH'INESS, *n.* [from *bush, bushy.*] The quality of being bushy, thick or intermixed, like the branches of a bush.

BUSH'-MAN, *n.* [D. *bosch-man.*] A woodsman; a name which the Dutch give to the wild and ferocious inhabitants of Africa, near the Cape of Good Hope.

BUSH'MENT, *n.* [from *bush.*] A thicket; a cluster of bushes. [*Not used.*] *Raleigh.*

BUSH'Y, *a.* [from *bush.*] Full of branches; thick and spreading, like a bush; as a *bushy* beard or brier. *Bacon.*

2. Full of bushes; overgrown with shrubs. *Dryden.*

BUSIED, *pp.* of *busy;* pron. *biz'zied.*

BUSILESS, *a. biz'ziless.* [See *Busy.*] Without business; at leisure; unemployed. *Shak.*

BUSILY, *adv. biz'zily.* With constant occupation; actively; earnestly; as, to be *busily* employed.

2. With an air of hurry or importance; with too much curiosity; importunately; officiously. *Dryden.*

BUSINESS, *n. biz'ness.* [See *Busy.*] Employment; that which occupies the time, attention and labor of men, for the purpose of profit or improvement—*a word of extensive use and indefinite signification.* *Business* is a particular occupation, as agriculture, trade, mechanic art, or profession, and when used of a particular employment, the word admits of the plural number, *businesses. Business* is also any temporary employment.

2. Affairs; concerns; as, a man leaves his *business* in an unsettled state.
3. The subject of employment; that which engages the care and attention.

   You are so much the *business* of our souls. *Dryden.*

4. Serious engagement; important occupation, in distinction from trivial affairs.

   It should be the main *business* of life to serve God, and obey his commands.

5. Concern; right of action or interposing. "What *business* has a man with the disputes of others?"
6. A point; a matter of question; something to be examined or considered.

   Fitness to govern is a perplexed *business.* *Bacon.*

7. Something to be done; employment of importance to one's interest, opposed to amusement; as, we have no *business* in town.

   They were far from the Zidonians and had no *business* with any one. *Judges.*

8. Duty, or employment that duty enjoins. A lawyer's *business* is to do justice to his clients.

To do the business for a man, is to kill, destroy or ruin him.

BUSK, *n.* [Fr. *busque.*] A piece of steel or whale bone, worn by women to strengthen their stays; *a word dependent on fashion.* *Donne.*

BUSK, *n.* A bush. [*Not used.*]

BUSK, *v. i.* To be active or busy. This is probably the Saxon word *bysgian,* to busy, or the Sp. *buscar,* to search. *Busk* is still used in America. [See *Busy.*] Fairfax uses it in the sense of *prepare,* transitively, "to *busk* them for the battle."

BUSK'ET, *n.* A small bush, or a compartment of shrubs in a garden. *Spenser.*

BUSK'IN, *n.* A kind of half boot, or high shoe, covering the foot and leg to the middle and tied underneath the knee, worn by actors in tragedy on the stage. The buskins of the ancients had very thick soles, to raise the actors and actresses to the stature of the persons they represented. *Encyc.*

2. In classic authors, the word is used for tragedy.

BUSK'INED, *a.* Dressed in buskins. *Milton. Pope.*

BUSK'Y, *a.* Bushy; wooded; shaded or overgrown with trees or shrubs; generally written *bosky.* [See *Bush.*] *Shak.*

BUSS, *n.* [Per. بوسيدن bosidan; Ar. باس bausa, to kiss; L. *basio;* Fr. *baiser;* Norm. *beser;* Sp. *besar;* Port. *beijar;* It. *baciare;* D. *poezen;* to kiss. The verb may be from the noun, and perhaps from the name of the lip; at any rate, from the same radical sense, to push; Per. *puz,* the lip; W. and Ir. *bus,* the lip; D. *poes,* a kiss, a puss, a fur-tippet, a girl; Sp. *beso,* a kiss; Port. *beiço,* the lip; *beijo,* a kiss; It. *bacio.* This word, so venerable for its antiquity and general use, has fallen into disrepute.]

A kiss; a salute with the lips.

2. [D. *buis;* G. *büse;* Russ. *busa.*] A small vessel, from 50 to 70 tons burthen, carrying two masts, and two sheds or cabins, one at each end; used in the herring fishery. *Encyc. Mar. Dict.*

BUSS, *v. t.* To kiss; to salute with the lips. *Shak.*

BUST, *n.* [It. and Sp. *busto;* Fr. *buste;* L. *bustum.*]

In *sculpture,* the figure of a person in relief, showing only the head, shoulders and stomach; ordinarily placed on a pedestal or console. In speaking of an antique, we say the head is marble and the *bust* porphyry or bronze; that is, the shoulders and stomach. The Italians use the word for the trunk of the body from the neck to the hips. *Encyc.*

BUST'ARD, *n.* [*bus* and *tarda;* It. *otarda;* Fr. *outarde.* Ancient Celtic, *tarda.* Plin. 10. 22.]

The *tarda,* a species of fowl of the grallic order, and genus *Otis.* This fowl grows to the weight of 25 or 27 pounds, with a breadth of wing of six or seven feet. It inhabits England, feeding on green corn and other vegetables, and on earth-worms. It runs fast and takes flight with difficulty. *Encyc.*

BUS'TLE, *v. i. bus'l.* [This word may be allied to *busy,* or to L. *festino.*]

To stir quick; to be very active; to be

very quick in motion, often or usually with the sense of noise or agitation.

And leave the world for me to *bustle* in. *Shak.*

BUS'TLE, *n. bus'l.* Hurry; great stir; rapid motion with noise and agitation; tumult from stirring or agitation; combustion.

All would have been well without this *bustle.* *Spectator.*

BUS'TLER, *n. bus'ler.* An active stirring person.

BUS'TLING, *ppr. bus'ling.* Stirring; moving actively with noise or agitation.

BUST'O, *n.* A bust; sometimes perhaps used for a statue. *Ashmole.*

BUSY, *a. biz'zy.* [Sax. *bysi, bysig;* whence, *byseg*, business, *bysgian*, to busy; D. *bezig*, busy; *bezigen*, to busy, to use. This word appears, from the Dutch, to be composed of *be*, the prefix, and *zig*, the root of *see*, contracted in Inf. to *zien*, but retained in the pret. *zag*, and in the derivatives, *zigt*, sight, *zigtbaar*, visible. We find *bezigtigen* signifies to view. If this opinion is correct, the primary sense is seeing, or closely inspecting.]

1. Employed with constant attention; engaged about something that renders interruption inconvenient; as, a man is *busy* in posting his books.

My mistress is *busy* and cannot come. *Shak.*

2. Actively employed; occupied without cessation; constantly in motion; as a *busy* bee. *Shak.*

3. Active in that which does not concern the person; meddling with or prying into the affairs of others; officious; importunate; hence, troublesome; vexatious. *Waller.*

4. Much occupied with employment; as a *busy* day.

BUSY, *v. t. biz'zy.* To employ with constant attention; to keep engaged; to make or keep busy; as, to *busy* one's self with books.

To be *busied* with genus and species. *Locke.*

BUSY-BODY, *n. biz'zy-body.* [*busy* and *body.*]

A meddling person; one who officiously concerns himself with the affairs of others. *Taylor.*

BUT, *part.* for *butan.* [Sax. *butan, buton, buta, bute*, without, on the outside, abroad; hence, except or excepting, besides; that is, separated, not included. The verb is not in the Saxon; but in Dutch we have the verb in its primary sense, *buiten*, to rove, or wander, to go freebooting; *buit*, booty; *buiten*, out, without, abroad, besides, except; *buiten boord*, over board; *buiten deur*, out of doors; *buiten huis*, an out-house; *buiten man*, an out-man, a stranger; G. *beute*, booty; Sw. *byte*, booty; *byta*, to exchange; Dan. *bytte*, booty, a parting, division, distribution; *bytter*, to part, divide, exchange, barter; Sp. *botin*; It. *bottino*; Fr. *butin*, booty. The primary sense of *booty* is to rove or wander, to part or separate from; applied to persons, it is to wander; applied to things, it may include stripping. *But* then is a contraction of *butan*, and primarily a participle.]

1. Except; besides; unless.

Who can it be, *but* perjured Lycon? *Smith.*

That is, removed, separated, excepted. Lycon being separated, or excepted, who can it be?

And *but* infirmity,
Which waits upon worn times, hath something seized
His wish'd ability, he had himself
The lands and waters measured. *Shak.*

That is, except, unless, separate this fact, that infirmity had seized his ability, he had measured the lands and waters.

In this use *but, butan*, is a participle equivalent to *excepting*, and may be referred to the person speaking, or more naturally, it is equivalent to excepted, and with the following words, or clause, forming the case absolute.

Who can it be, Lycon being excepted?

And *but* my noble Moor is true of mind, it were enough to put him to ill thinking. *Shak.*

It cannot be *but* nature hath some director, of infinite power, to guide her in all her ways. *Hooker.*

There is no question *but* the King of Spain will reform most of the abuses. *Addison.*

It is not impossible *but* I may alter the complexion of my play. *Dryden.*

In the last three examples, *that* is omitted after *but.*

It is not impossible *but that* I may alter the complexion of my play.

In these and all similar phrases, *but* denotes separation, exception.

2. Only.

A formidable man, *but* to his friends. *Dryden.*

There is *but* one man present.

This use of *but* is a modern innovation; but perhaps too firmly established to be corrected. In all such phrases, a negative, *not, nothing*, or other word, is omitted. He is *not* a formidable man, *but* to his enemies, that is, except. There is *not but* one one man present, that is, there is *not except* or *besides* one present. So also, "Our light affliction is *but* for a moment." 2 Cor. iv. Our affliction is *not, except* for a moment.

If they kill us, we shall *but* die. 2 Kings vii.

The common people in America retain the original and correct phrase; usually employing a negative. They do not say, I have *but* one. On the other hand, they say, I have *not but* one, that is, I have not except one; except one, and I have none. This word *but* for *butan* is not a conjunction, nor has it the least affinity to that part of speech.

BUT, *conj.* [Sax. *bote*, reparation, satisfaction, compensation, and adverbially, moreover, further, that is, something added to make good, to supply what is wanted, from *betan*, to make *better*, or more, to amend, that is, to advance; D. *boete*; Sw. *böte*; Dan. *baade*; W. *buz*, advantage. So in Ger. *aber*, but, is the Eng. *over.* In some of these languages it denotes a fine or penance, that which makes satisfaction. In Danish, profit; *baader*, to gain or profit; W. *buziaw*; Goth. *botyan*, id; G. *busse, büssen.* We use this word as a noun, in the phrase, he gives a guinea to *boot*, that is, to make good, to satisfy, or by way of addition; and as a verb, in the phrase, what *boots* it, what gain or profit is it. It is radically the same word as *bet* in *better*; and the radical sense is to advance.]

More; further; noting an addition to supply what is wanting to elucidate, or modify the sense of the preceding part of a sentence, or of a discourse, or to continue the discourse, or to exhibit a contrast.

Now abide faith, hope, charity, these three; *but*, the greatest of these is charity. 1 Cor. xiii.

When pride cometh, then cometh shame; *but* with the lowly is wisdom. Prov. xi.

Our wants are many and grievous; *but* quite of another kind.

The house of representatives were well agreed in passing the bill; *but* the senate dissented.

This word is in fact a noun equivalent to addition or supply; but in grammatical construction, no inconvenience results from considering it to be a connective.

BUT, *n.* [Fr. *bout*, end, extremity, and *but*, end, aim, design; Arm. *but* or *baut.* It is sometimes written *butt*, especially when applied to the end of a plank. It coincides, in sense and elements, with L. *peto*, Sp. *bote*, a thrust, *botar*, to cast, It. *botta, botto, botare*, Fr. *botte, bouder*, Eng. *pout*, and many other words. See *Butt.*]

1. An end; a limit; a bound. It is used particularly for the larger end of a thing, as of a piece of timber, or of a fallen tree; that which grows nearest the earth. It is not often applied to the *bound* or limit of land; yet *butted*, for bounded, is often used.

2. The end of a plank in a ship's side or bottom, which unites with another; generally written *butt.*

BUT, *v. i.* To be bounded by; to lie contiguous to; *a word used in America.* [See *Abut.*]

BUT-END, *n.* [*but* and *end.*] The largest or blunt end of a thing; as the *but-end* of a musket or of a piece of timber. This word is tautological, *but* and *end* signifying the same thing; unless *but* is considered as equivalent to *swelling, protuberant.*

BUTCH'ER, *n.* [Fr. *boucher;* Arm. *boçzer*, a butcher; Fr. *boucherie;* It. *beccheria*, butchery, shambles. The primary sense probably is to stick or stab, as the Fr. *boucher* signifies to stop, that is, to set, to thrust.]

1. One who slaughters animals for market; or one whose occupation is to kill animals for the table. The word may and often does include the person who cuts up and sells meat.

2. One who kills men, or commands troops to kill them; one who sheds, or causes to be shed human blood in abundance; *applied to princes and conquerors who delight in war, or are remarkable for destroying human life.* *Locke.*

BUTCH'ER, *v. t.* To kill or slaughter animals for food, or for market.

2. To murder; but emphatically applied to murder committed with unusual cruelty, or circumstances of uncommon barbarity.

BUTCH'ER-BIRD, *n.* The shrike; a genus of birds, called *Lanius.* One species of this genus is called *king-bird*, from its courage in attacking hawks and crows. *Encyc.*

The *king-bird* is now arranged under the genus *Muscicapa.* *Ed. Encyc.*

BUTCH'ERLINESS, *n.* A cruel, savage, butcherly manner. *Johnson.*

BUTCH'ERLY, *a.* [from *butcher.*] Cruel; savage; murderous; grossly and clumsily barbarous. *Ascham. Shak.*

BUTCH'ER'S-BROOM, *n.* Ruscus; a genus of plants, called also knee-holly. It is used by butchers for brooms to sweep their blocks. *Encyc.*

BUTCH'ERY, *n.* The business of slaughtering cattle for the table or for market. *Pope.*

2. Murder, especially murder committed with unusual barbarity; great slaughter. *Shak. Dryden.*

3. The place where animals are killed for market; a shambles, or slaughter-house; also, a place where blood is shed. *Shak.*

BUT'LER, *n.* [Fr. *bouteillier*, from *bouteille*, a bottle, that is, the *bottler*; Ir. *buitleir*, a butler, from *buidel*, *boide*, a bottle.]

A servant or officer in the houses of princes and great men, whose principal business is to take charge of the liquors, plate, &c. Formerly, an officer in the court of France, being the same as the grand echanson or great cup-bearer of the present times. *Encyc.*

BUT'LERAGE, *n.* A duty of two shillings on every tun of wine imported into England by foreigners or merchant strangers. It was a composition for the privileges granted to them by king John and Edward I., and originally received by the crown; but it has been granted to certain noblemen. It was called *butlerage*, because originally paid to the king's butler for the king. *Blackstone. Encyc.*

BUT'LERSHIP, *n.* The office of a butler. Gen. xl. 21.

BUT'MENT, *n.* [Old Fr. *aboutement*, from *bout*, *but*, end.]

1. A buttress of an arch; the supporter, or that part which joins it to the upright pier. *Johnson. Encyc.*

2. The mass of stone or solid work at the end of a bridge, by which the extreme arches are sustained. The mass of stone at the end of a timber bridge, without arches, is called by the same name. It is written also *abutment.*

BUT'SHAFT, *n.* [*but* and *shaft.*] An arrow to shoot at butts with. *B. Jonson.*

BUTT, *n.* [See *But.*] Literally, end, furthest point. Hence, a mark to be shot at; the point where a mark is set or fixed to be shot at. *Dryden.*

2. The point to which a purpose or effort is directed. *Shak.*

3. The object of aim; the thing against which an attack is directed. *Clarendon.* Hence,

4. The person at whom ridicule, jests or contempt are directed; as the *butt* of ridicule. *Spectator.*

5. A push or thrust given by the head of an animal, as the *butt* of a ram; also, a thrust in fencing.

6. A cask whose contents are 126 gallons of wine, or two hogsheads; called also a pipe. A butt of beer is 108 gallons, and from 1500 to 2200 weight of currants is a *butt.* [Sax. *butte* or *bytt*; Sp. *bota.*] *Johnson.*

7. The end of a plank in a ship's side or bottom. *Mar. Dict.*

8. A particular kind of hinge for doors, &c.

BUTT, *v. i.* [W. *pwtiaw*, to butt, to thrust; It. *buttare*; Sp. *botar*; Port. *botar*, to thrust, or throw; Fr. *botte*, a thrust; from the same root probably as *but*, *bout*, L. *peto.*]

To thrust the head forward; to strike by thrusting the head against, as an ox or a ram. *Wotton. Dryden.*

BUT'TER, *n.* [Sax. *buter*, *butera*; D. *boter*; Ger. *butter*; L. *butyrum*; Gr. *βουτυρον.*]

An oily substance obtained from cream or milk by churning. Agitation separates the fat or oily part of milk from the thin or serous part, called *butter-milk.*

Butter, in the old chimistry, was applied to various preparations; as,

Butter of antimony, now called the sublimated muriate of antimony, and made by distilling a mixture of corrosive sublimate and the regulus.

Butter of arsenic, sublimated muriate of arsenic, made by a like process.

Butter of bismuth, sublimated muriate of bismuth.

Butter of tin, sublimated muriate of tin.

Butter of zink, sublimated muriate of zink. *Fourcroy.*

Butter of cacao, is an oily concrete white matter obtained from the cacao nut, made by bruising the nut and boiling it in water. *Nicholson.*

Butter of wax, the oleaginous part of wax, obtained by distillation, and of a butyraceous consistence. *Nicholson.*

BUT'TER, *v. t.* To smear with butter.

2. To increase the stakes at every throw or every game; *a cant term among gamesters.* *Johnson.*

BUT'TER-BUMP, *n.* The bittern. *Johnson.*

BUT'TER-BURR, *n.* A plant, a species of Tussilago, or Colt's-foot, called *petasites*, growing in wet land, with large leaves. *Fam. of Plants. Encyc.*

BUT'TER-CUPS, *n.* A name given to a species of Ranunculus or crow-foot, with bright yellow flowers; called also golden-cup. *Fam. of Plants. Lee.*

BUT'TER-FLOWER, *n.* A yellow flower. *Gay.*

BUT'TERFLY, *n.* [from the color of a yellow species.]

Papilio, a genus of insects, of the order of lepidopters. They have four wings imbricated with a kind of downy scales; the tongue is convoluted in a spiral form; and the body is hairy. The species are numerous. Butter-flies proceed from the crysalids of caterpillars; caterpillars proceed from eggs deposited by butterflies; they then change into crysalids, which produce butterflies, which again deposit their eggs.

BUTTERFLY-SHELL, *n.* A genus of testaceous molluscas, with a spiral unilocular shell; called *voluta.* *Encyc.*

BUT'TERIS, *n.* An instrument of steel set in wood, for paring the hoof of a horse. *Farrier's Dict.*

BUT'TER-MILK, *n.* The milk that remains after the butter is separated from it. Johnson calls this *whey*; but whey is the thin part of the milk after the curd or cheese is separated. Butter-milk in America is not called *whey.*

BUT'TERNUT, *n.* [*butter* and *nut.*]

The fruit of an American tree, the Juglans cinerea; so called from the oil it contains. The tree bears a resemblance, in its general appearance, to the walnut, or black walnut, so called. It is sometimes called oilnut and white walmut. The tree is called also butternut or butternut-tree. Dr. M. Cutler calls it Juglans Cathartica. *Belknap.*

BUT'TER-PRINT, } *n.* A piece of carved wood, used to mark cakes of butter.
BUT'TER-STAMP, }

BUT'TER-TOOTH, *n.* A broad fore tooth. *Johnson.*

BUT'TER-WIFE, } *n.* A woman who sells butter. *Johnson.*
BUT'TER-WÖMAN, }

BUT'TERWÖRT, *n.* A species of Pinguicula, a plant growing on bogs or soft grounds. The leaves are covered with soft pellucid prickles, which secrete a glutinous liquor; and milk, in which these are steeped, or washed, acquires, in a day or two, consistency, and is an agreeable food, used in the north of Sweden. *Encyc.*

BUT'TERY, *a.* [from *butter.*] Having the qualities or appearance of butter. *Harvey.*

BUT'TERY, *n.* An apartment in a house, where butter, milk, provisions and utensils are kept. In some colleges, a room where liquors, fruit and refreshments are kept for sale to the students.

BUT'TOCK, *n.* The rump, or the protuberant part behind.

2. The convexity of a ship behind, under the stern. *Mar. Dict.*

BUT'TON, *n.* *but'n.* [Fr. *bouton*, a button, a bud; W. *buttun*, or *botwm*; Corn. *bottum*; It. *bottone*; Sp. *boton*, a button or bud; from the root of *bud*, that is, a push or protuberance. See *Butt.*]

1. A knob; a small ball; a catch, used to fasten together the different parts of dress, made of metal, silk, mohair, wood, &c.

2. Any knob or ball fastened to another body; a small protuberant body. *Boyle. Pope.*

3. A bud; a gem of a plant. *Shak.*

4. The button of the reins of a bridle, is a ring of leather, with the reins passed through, which runs along the length of the reins. *Encyc.*

5. A flat piece of wood, turning on a nail or screw, to fasten doors.

6. A small round mass of metal, found at the bottom of a crucible, in chimical experiments. *Nicholson.*

7. The sea-urchin, an animal which has prickles instead of feet. *Ainsworth.*

BUT'TON, *v. t.* *but'n.* To fasten with a button, or buttons; to inclose, or make secure with buttons; often followed with *up*, as to *button up* a waistcoat.

2. To dress or clothe. [*Not used.*]

BUT'TON-HOLE, *n.* The hole or loop in which a button is caught.

BUT'TON-MAKER, *n.* One whose occupation is to make buttons.

BUT'TON-STONE, *n.* A species of figured stone, or hard flint, resembling a button, consisting of two bodies which appear to be the filling up of holes in a shell. A species has been found finely striated, like a mohair button. This name is given also to a species of slate found in the marquisate of Bareith. *Encyc.*

BUT'TON-TREE, *n.* The Conocarpus, called also button-wood, a genus of plants, natives of the West-Indies. *Fam. of Plants. Encyc.*

BUT'TON-WEED, *n.* A genus of plants, the Spermacoce. *Fam. of Plants.*

BUT'TON-WOOD, *n.* The Cephalanthus, a shrub of N. America, growing five or six feet high. *Encyc.*

2. The Platanus Occidentalis, Western plane-tree, a large tree growing in N. America, producing rough balls, from which it is named. The wood is hard, and used for windlasses, wheels and blocks. *Belknap. Mease.*

BUT'TRESS, *n.* [This word appears to be composed of *but*, end, and *truss*, or some word of that family.]

1. A prop; a wall or abutment built archwise, serving to support another wall on the outside, when very high or loaded with a heavy superstructure. *Encyc.*

2. Any prop or support. *South.*

BUT'TRESS, *v. t.* To support by a buttress; to prop.

BUT'TRESSED, *a.* Supported with a buttress. *Ward.*

BUTTS, *n. plu.* [from *butt.*] A place where archers meet to shoot at mark. Also, short pieces of land in arable ridges and furrows. *Encyc.*

BUT'-WINK, *n.* A bird. *Johnson.*

BUTYRA'CEOUS, **BUT'YROUS**, *a.* [from *butyrum*, butter.] Having the qualities of butter; resembling butter. *Encyc. Nicholson. Floyer.*

BUX'OM, *a.* [Sax. *bocsum*, from *bog*, a bow, *bugan*, to bend, and *sum*, some.]

1. Obedient; obsequious; ready to obey. *Obs.* *Milton.*

2. Gay; lively; brisk. *Milton.*

3. Wanton; jolly. *Dryden.*

BUX'OMLY, *adv.* Obediently. *Obs.*

2. Wantonly; amorously. *Johnson.*

BUX'OMNESS, *n.* Meekness; obedience. *Obs.* *Chaucer.*

2. Briskness; amorousness.

BUY̆, *v. t.* pret. and pp. *bought*, pron. *bawt.* [Sax. *bigan*, or *bycgan*, *bygan*; Goth. *bugyan*, to buy.]

1. To acquire the property, right or title to any thing, by paying a consideration or an equivalent in money. It differs from *barter* only in this, that in *barter* the consideration or equivalent is some species of commodity; in *purchase*, the consideration is money paid or promised. To purchase; to acquire by paying a price to the satisfaction of the seller; opposed to *sell.*

2. To procure by a consideration given, or by something that is deemed worth the thing bought; to procure at a price; as, to *buy* pleasure with praise; to *buy* favor with flattery. *Denham.*

3. To bribe; to corrupt or pervert the judgment, by paying a consideration.

To buy off, to influence to compliance; to cause to bend or yield by some consideration, as to *buy off* conscience; to detach by a consideration given, as to *buy off* one from a party.

To buy out, to buy off, or detach from. *Shak.*

2. To purchase the share or shares of a person in a stock, fund, or partnership, by which the seller is separated from the company, and the purchaser takes his place; as, A *buys out* B. To purchase stock in any fund or partnership, is to *buy in.*

To buy on credit, is to purchase a thing, on a promise in fact or in law, to make payment at a future day.

To buy the refusal, is to give money for the right of purchasing at a fixed price at a future time.

To buy the small pox, in South Wales, is to receive it by inoculation. *Encyc.*

In popular language, *to buy* is to pay dear for, as in Chaucer.

BUY̆, *v. i.* To negotiate, or treat about a purchase.

I will *buy* with you and sell with you. *Shak.*

BUY̆ER, *n.* One who buys; a purchaser. *Wotton.*

BUY̆ING, *ppr.* Purchasing.

BUZZ, *v. i.* [It. *buzzicare*, to whisper; Pers. بزيدن bazidan, to blow as wind.]

1. To make a low hissing sound, as bees; to make the sound of *z*, with an expiration of breath between the tongue and the roof of the mouth or upper teeth.

2. To whisper; to speak with a low hissing voice; to make a low hissing sound. *Shak. Hayward.*

BUZZ, *v. t.* To whisper; to spread, as report, by whispers, or to spread secretly. *Bentley.*

BUZZ, *n.* The noise of bees; also, a whisper. *South. Bacon.*

BUZZ'ARD, *n.* [D. *buzaard*; G. *bussaar*, *busshard*; It. *bozzago*; Fr. *buze*, *buse* or *busard*; Pers. باز a hawk.]

1. A species of falco, or hawk, the *buteo*; a rapacious, but sluggish bird; the breast usually of a yellowish white; the upper parts of a deep brown. In some parts of America, it is called the great *Hen-hawk*, from its feeding on poultry. *Pennant. Encyc.*

2. A block-head; a dunce. *Johnson.*

BUZZ'ARD, *a.* Senseless; stupid. *Milton.*

BUZZARDET', *n.* A species of Falco or hawk, resembling the buzzard in most respects; but its legs are in proportion rather longer. *Pennant.*

BUZZ'ER, *n.* A whisperer; one who is busy in telling tales secretly. *Shak.*

BUZZ'ING, *ppr.* Making a low hissing sound; whispering; tattling in secret.

BY̆, *prep.* [Sax. *be* or *big*; Goth. *bi*; Sw. and Dan. *be*; D. *by*; G. *bei*; all contracted from *big*. This word in composition is often written *be*, as in *because*, *besiege*. In Sw. and Dan. it is used only in composition. The Sw. and Dan. *paa*, and Russ. *po*, may be from a different root, although they are nearly allied in signification, and may be the same word differently written. This preposition occurs as a prefix in all the Shemitic languages, contracted indeed into ב. See the Introduction. The primary sense is, *pressing*, *close*, *near*, *at*; but in Goth. and Sax. it signifies also, *about*, *according to*, *on*, *with*, *against*, *after*, &c. In some of these senses, it coincides with the Russ. *po*. The original verb to which this word belongs, most probably signifies to pass, to go, or come, to drive, to press.]

1. Near; close; as, sit *by* me; that house stands *by* a river. So in It. *presso*, from L. *pressus*; Fr. *près*, *auprès*.

2. Near, in motion; as, to move, go or pass *by* a church. But it seems, in other phrases, or with a verb in the past time, to signify *past*, gone beyond. "The procession is gone *by*;" "the hour is gone *by*;" "John went *by*." We now use *past* as an equivalent word. The procession is gone *past*. *Gone by* is in strictness tautology, as now used; but I apprehend *by* signifies primarily *near*.

3. Through, or with, denoting the agent, means, instrument or cause; as, "a city is destroyed *by* fire;" "profit is made *by* commerce;" "to take *by* force." This use answers to that of the Latin *per*, through, denoting a passing, acting, agency, or instrumentality.

4. "Day *by* day;" "year *by* year" "article *by* article." In these phrases, *by* denotes passing from one to another, or each particular separately taken.

5. "*By* the space of seven years." In this phrase, *by* denotes through, passing or continuing, during.

6. "*By* this time, the sun had risen." The word here seems to denote, *at*, *present* or *come to*.

7. According to; as, "this appears *by* his own account;" "these are good rules to live *by*."

8. On; as, "to pass *by* land or water;" "great battles *by* sea and land." In the latter phrase, *at* or *on* might be substituted for *by*.

9. It is placed before words denoting quantity, measure or proportion; as, to sell *by* the pound; to work *by* the rod or perch; this line is longer *by* a tenth.

10. It is used to represent the means or instrument of swearing, or affirming; as, to swear *by* heaven, or *by* earth; to affirm *by* all that is sacred.

11. In the phrase, "he has a cask of wine *by* him," *by* denotes nearness or presence.

12. "To sit *by* one's self," is to sit alone, or without company.

13. "To be present *by* attorney." In this phrase, *by* denotes means or instrument; through or in the presence of a substitute.

14. In the phrase, "North *by* West," the sense seems to be north *passing* to the west, inclining or going westward, or near west.

As an adverb, *by* denotes also nearness, or presence; as, there was no person *by*, at the time. But some noun is understood. So in the phrase, "to pass or go *by*," there is a noun understood.

By and *by* is a phrase denoting nearness in time; in a short time after; presently; soon.

When persecution ariseth, because of the word, *by and by*, he is offended. Math. xiii.

By the *by* signifies, as we proceed or pass, [Fr. *en passant*,] noting something interposed in the progress of a discourse, which is distinct from the main subject. The old phrase, "on the *by*," on the passage, is now obsolete.

To stand by, is to stand near, or to support.

By, in *lullaby*, and in the nursery, a word used in lulling infants to sleep, is evidently allied to words found in many languages, signifying to rest, or be quiet, or to appease; that is, to press, to stop, as the Gr. παυω, L. *paco*. It is used in Russia, as with us, *bayu*, *bai*. This probably is the same word as the foregoing.

By or *bye*, in *by-law*, Sax. *bilage*, is probably the Sw. *by*, Dan. *bye*, a village, town, borough or city, from Sw. *byggia*, Dan. *bygger*, G. *bauen*, D. *bouwen*, to build, Sax. *byan*, to inhabit; that is, a town-law, a municipal law.

In the common phrase, *good-bye*, *bye* signifies *passing*, *going*. The phrase signifies, a good going, a prosperous passage, and it is precisely equivalent to *farewell*, Sax. *faran*, to go, *go well*, may you have a good going, equivalent to *good speed*, in the phrase, "to bid one good speed." [Not *God speed*, as is generally read and understood.]

By is used in many compound words, in most of which we observe the sense of nearness, closeness, or a withdrawing or seclusion.

BȲ-COFFEE-HOUSE, *n.* A coffee house in an obscure place. *Addison.*

BȲ-CONCERN'MENT, *n.* An affair distinct from the main business. *Dryden.*

BY'-CORNER, *n.* A private corner.

BȲ-DEPEND'ENCE, *n.* An appendage; that which depends on something else, or is distinct from the main dependence. *Shak.*

BȲ-DESI'GN, *n.* An incidental design, or purpose. *Hudibras.*

BY'-DRINKING, *n.* A private drinking.

BY'-END, *n.* Private end; secret purpose or advantage. *L'Estrange.*

BY'-GONE, *a.* Past; gone by. (*Scots dialect.*) *Grew.*

BY'-INTEREST, *n.* Self interest: private advantage. *Atterbury.*

BY'-LANE, *n.* A private lane, or one out of the usual road.

BY'-LAW, *n.* A town law; the law of a city, town or private corporation. *Bacon.*

BY'-MATTER, *n.* Something incidental. *Bacon.*

BY'-NAME, *n.* Nickname; an incidental appellation. *Camden.*

BY'-PAST, *a.* Past; gone by. (*Scots dialect.*) *Cheyne.*

BY'-PATH, *n.* A private path; an obscure way. *Shak.*

BȲ-RESPECT', *n.* Private end, or view. *Bacon. Dryden.*

BY'-RŌAD, *n.* A private or obscure road. *Swift.*

BY'-ROOM, *n.* A private room or apartment. *Shak.*

BY'-SPEECH, *n.* An incidental or casual speech, not directly relating to the point. *Hooker.*

BY'-SPELL, *n.* [Sax. *bigspell.*] A proverb. [*Not used.*] *Coles.*

BY'-STANDER, *n.* [Sax. *bigstandan*, to stand by.] One who stands near; a spectator; one who has no concern with the business transacting. *Locke.*

BY'-STREET, *n.* A separate, private or obscure street. *Gay.*

BY'-TURNING, *n.* An obscure road. *Sidney.*

BY'-VIEW, *n.* Private view; self interested purpose. *Atterbury.*

BY'-WALK, *n.* A secluded or private walk. *Dryden.*

BY'-WAY, *n.* A secluded, private or obscure way. *Addison.*

BȲ-WEST', *adv.* Westward; to the west of. *Davies.*

BY'-WIPE, *n.* A secret stroke or sarcasm. *Milton.*

BY'-WŎRD, *n.* [Sax. *bi*, or *big*, and *word*, as in *bigcwid*, and *bigspell*. Either a passing word, or a town-saying.]

A common saying; a proverb; a saying that has a general currency. *Bacon.*

BYE, *n.* [Sax.] A dwelling. *Gibson.*

BYS'SIN, BYS'SUS, *n.* [Gr. βυσσος, infra.] A silk or linen hood. [*Not in use.*] *Gower.*

BYS'SINE, *a.* Made of silk. *Coles.*

BYS'SOLITE, *n.* [Gr. βυσσος, fine flax, and λιθος, stone; so called from its resemblance to moss.]

A rare mineral, occurring in very delicate filaments, short, flexible and elastic. Their color is olive green, or brownish yellow, and their luster a little silky. Jameson places byssolite under actinolite; Haüy arranges it under amianthoid. *Hausman. Saussure. Cleaveland.*

BYS'SUS, *n.* [L. *byssus*; Gr. βυσσος, fine linen, or cotton.]

The asbestus, composed of parallel fibers, is by some called by this name. *Nicholson.*

BYZ'ANT, BYZ'ANTINE, *n.* [from *Byzantium.*] A gold coin of the value of fifteen pounds sterling, so called from being coined at Byzantium. Also, a piece of gold offered by the king on certain festivals. *Johnson. Camden. Ash.*

BYZAN'TINE, BYZAN'TIAN, *a.* Pertaining to Byzantium, an ancient city of Thrace situated on the Bosporus. In the year 330, Constantine the Great took possession of Byzantium, enlarged and embellished it, and changed its name to Constantinople. *D'Anville. Encyc.*

C.

C, the third letter in the English alphabet, and the second articulation or consonant, is a palatal, nearly corresponding in sound with the Greek κ, kappa, and with the Hebrew כ, caph. It bears a middle place in pronunciation, between the aspirate ה, and the palatal ג. It is a Roman character, borrowed from the Gr. κ, or from the oriental כ, which was used in languages written from right to left, and when inverted and the corners rounded, becomes C. In the old Etruscan, it was written Ɔ, with the corners rounded, but not inverted; in Arcadian, C, as now written. That its sound in Latin was the same, or nearly the same, as that of kappa, may be known from the fact, that the Greeks, while the Latin was a living language, wrote kappa for the Roman C. Perhaps the same character may be the basis of the Arabic ج.

As an abbreviature, C stands for Caius, Carolus, Cæsar, *condemno*, &c., and CC for *consulibus*. As a numeral C stands for 100; CC for 200; &c. In *music*, C after the cliff, is the mark of common time. *Encyc.*

In English, C has two sounds, or rather it represents two very different articulations of the organs; one close, like K, which occurs before *a*, *o* and *u*; the other, a sibilant, precisely like *s*, which occurs before *e*, *i* and *y*. The former is distinguished in this vocabulary by Ꞓ, which may be called *ke*. In Russ. C is precisely the English *s*, as it was in the old Greek alphabet.

ꞒAB, *n.* [Heb. Ch. קב kab.] An oriental dry measure, being the sixth part of a seah or satum, and the eighteenth of an ephah; containing two pints and five sixths English and American corn measure.

ꞒABAL', *n.* [Fr. *cabale*, a club, society or combination; It. *cabala*, knowledge of secret things; Sp. *cabala*, secret science; *cabal*, perfect, just, exact; Heb. קבל to take, receive, accept; Ch. to cry out, to *bawl*; also to take or receive; also to be dark, to obscure; Syr. to accuse, oppose, or censure, to *cavil*; Eth. to accept, to pour out; Sam. to accept, and to darken; Ar. to admit or accept, as agreeable; to come to be surety; to give *bail*. See Class Bl. This word seems to include the significations of several biliteral roots. Qu. W. *cafael*, to get or obtain; or *gavaelu*, to hold. The primary sense of the root seems to be to catch or seize by rushing on, or in general, to press, to drive; hence the sense of collection, combination and accusation.]

1. A number of persons united in some close design; usually to promote their private views in church or state by intrigue. A junto. It is sometimes synonymous with *faction*, but a *cabal* usually consists of fewer men than a party, and the word generally implies close union and secret intrigues. This name was given to the ministry of Charles II., Clifford, Ashley, Buckingham, Arlington, and Lauderdale, the initials of whose names compose the word.

2. Intrigue; secret artifices of a few men united in a close design. *Dryden.*

ꞒABAL', ꞒAB'ALA, *n.* [See the preceding word. It is from the sense of reception.]

Tradition, or a mysterious kind of science among Jewish Rabbins, pretended to have been delivered to the ancient Jews by revelation, and transmitted by oral tradition; serving for the interpretation of difficult passages of scripture. This science consists chiefly in understanding the combination of certain letters, words and numbers, which are alledged to be significant. Every letter, word, number and accent of the law is supposed to contain a mystery, and the cabalists pretend even to foretell future events by the study of this science. *Encyc. Buck.*

CABAL′, *v. i.* To unite in a small party to promote private views by intrigue; to intrigue; to unite in secret artifices to effect some design. *Dryden.*

CAB′ALISM, *n.* The secret science of the cabalists.

CAB′ALIST, *n.* A Jewish doctor who professes the study of the cabala, or the mysteries of Jewish traditions.

2. In *French commerce*, a factor or agent. *Encyc.*

CABALIST′IC, CABALIST′ICAL, } *a.* Pertaining to the cabala, or mysterious science of Jewish traditions; containing an occult meaning.

CABALIST′ICALLY, *adv.* In the manner of the cabalists. *Herbert.*

CAB′ALIZE, *v. i.* To use the manner or language of the cabalists. [*Not much used.*]

CABAL′LER, *n.* One who unites with others in close designs to effect an object by intrigue; one who cabals.

CAB′ALLINE, *a.* [L. *caballinus*, from *caballus*, a horse; Russ. *kobila, kobiela*, a mare; Ir. *capall;* Fr. *cheval*, a horse; *cavale*, a mare; It. *cavallo;* Sp. *caballo.*]
Pertaining to a horse; as *caballine* aloes, so called from its being given to horses as a purge. *Encyc.*

CABAL′LING, *ppr.* Uniting in a cabal; intriguing in a small party.

CAB′ARET, *n.* [Fr. allied probably to *cabin.*]
A tavern; a house where liquors are retailed. *Bramhall.*

CAB′BAGE, *n.* [It. *cappuccio;* Corn. *kavatsh;* Ir. *gabaisde, gabaiste.* This word is probably from the root of *caput*, a head; It. *capuccio*, a head; Sp. *cabeza;* Fr. *caboche*, a head. Hence D. *kabuis-kool, head-cole*, or *headed-cole.* In Fr. *choux-cabus*, is *cabbage-headed*, or *cabbage-head.* See *Cap, Cope.*]
A genus of plants, called in botany Brassica, of several species; some of which are cultivated for food. The leaves are large and fleshy, the pods long and slender, and the seeds globular. The kinds most cultivated are the common cabbage, called with us the *drum-head*, the *Savoy*, the *broccoli*, the *cauliflower*, the *sugar-loaf*, and the *cole-wort.*
Dog's cabbage, a name given to the *Thelygonum cynocrambe.* *Fam. of Plants.*
Sea-cabbage, n. The sea-beach kale, or sea-colewort, a genus of plants, called *crambe.* They are herbaceous esculents, with perennial roots, producing large leaves like those of cabbage, spreading on the ground. *Encyc.*

CAB′BAGE, *v. i.* To form a head in growing; as, a plant *cabbages.* *Johnson.*

CAB′BAGE, *v. t.* [D. *kabassen*, to steal; *kabas*, a hand basket; Old Fr. *cabasser.*]
To purloin or embezzle, as pieces of cloth, after cutting out a garment. *Arbuthnot.*

CAB′BAGE-NET, *n.* A small net to boil cabbage in. *Shenstone.*

CAB′BAGE-TREE, *n.* The cabbage-palm, a species of Areca, the oleracea, a native of warm climates. This tree grows with a straight stem to the highth of 170 or 200 feet. Its branches grow in a circular manner, and the lowermost ones spread horizontally with great regularity. The fibers of the leaves are used for making cordage and nets. On the top grows a substance called *cabbage*, lying in thin, snow-white, brittle flakes, in taste resembling an almond, but sweeter. This is boiled and eaten with flesh, like other vegetables. When this is cut out, the tree is destroyed. *Encyc.*

CAB′BAGE-WORM, *n.* An insect. *Johnson.*

CAB′IAI, *n.* An animal of South America resembling a hog, living on the margins of lakes and rivers, and feeding on fish. It is a species of Cavy, called also thick-nosed tapir. *Dict. of Nat. Hist. Encyc.*

CAB′IN, *n.* [Fr. *cabane*, a cabin, a cottage; *caban*, a cloke; It. *capanna*, a cottage; Sp. and Port. *cabana*, a hut or cottage; Ir. *caban;* W. *caban*, from *cab*, a hut, cot, or booth made in the form of a cone, with rods set in the ground, and tied at the top; Gr. καπανη, from καπη, a stable or inclosed place.]
1. A small room; an inclosed place. *Spenser.*
2. A cottage; a hut, or small house. *Swift.*
3. A tent; a shed; any covered place for a temporary residence. *Fairfax.*
4. An apartment in a ship for officers and passengers. In large ships there are several cabins, the principal of which is occupied by the commander. In small vessels, there is one cabin in the stern for the accommodation of the officers and passengers. The bed-places in ships are also called cabins. *Encyc. Mar. Dict.*

CAB′IN, *v. i.* To live in a cabin; to lodge. *Shak.*

CAB′IN, *v. t.* To confine in a cabin. *Shak.*

CAB′IN-BOY, *n.* A boy whose duty is to wait on the officers and passengers on board of a ship.

CAB′INED, *pp.* Inclosed; covered. *Milton.*

CAB′INET, *n.* [Fr. *cabinet;* It. *gabinetto;* Sp. *gabinete.* See *Cabin.*]
1. A closet; a small room, or retired apartment. *Bacon.*
2. A private room, in which consultations are held. *Dryden.*
3. The select or secret council of a prince or executive government; so called from the apartment in which it was originally held. *Encyc.*
4. A piece of furniture, consisting of a chest or box, with drawers and doors. A private box. *Swift.*
5. Any close place where things of value are reposited for safe keeping. *Taylor.*
6. A hut; a cottage; a small house. *Obs.* *Spenser.*

CAB′INET, *v. t.* To inclose. [*Little used.*] *Howel.*

CAB′INET-COUNCIL, *n.* A council held with privacy; the confidential council of a prince or executive magistrate. *Bacon.*
2. The members of a privy council; a select number of confidential counselors. *Gay.*

CAB′INETED, *pp.* Inclosed in a private apartment, or in a cabinet.

CAB′INET-MAKER, *n.* A man whose occupation is to make cabinets, tables, bureaus, bed-steads, and other similar furniture.

CAB′IN-MATE, *n.* One who occupies the same cabin with another. *Beaum.*

CABIRE′AN, *n.* [See the words below.] One of the Cabiri. *Faber.*

CABIR′IAN, CABIR′IC, CABIRIT′IC, } *a.* [Oriental גבר to be strong or powerful, to be great; whence it signifies man, a lord, and in some languages, a giant. It is common to all the Shemitic dialects. Perhaps L. *vir*, with a prefix.]
Pertaining to the Cabiri, certain deities greatly venerated by the ancient Pagans, in Greece and Phenicia. The accounts of these deities are confused and contradictory. Some authors limit their number to four; some to three; others to two; while Sanchoniathon makes them to be eight. They were worshiped with particular honors in the isle of Samothrace; and their worship and mysteries are said to have been introduced into Greece by the Pelasgians. They were supposed to have a particular influence over the sea and maritime affairs.

In truth, the name which signifies *great*, or the *mighty ones*, seems to have been applied to the supposed beings that presided over the more striking operations of nature. Herod. ii. 51. Paus. ix. 25.
Bryant. Faber. Asiat. Researches.

CA′BLE, *n. cábl.* [Sp. Fr. *cable;* D. Dan. G. *kabel;* Arm. *chabl;* Ir. *cabla* or *gabla;* Russ. *kabala*, a bond; Heb. Ch. Syr. Ar. כבל a chain; as a verb, to tie or bind; or חבל to tie or make fast, and a rope. If the first letter of the oriental word is a prefix, this coincides with *bale*, a package, that is, a tie.]
A large strong rope or chain, used to retain a vessel at anchor. It is made usually of hemp or iron, but may be made of other materials. Cables are of different sizes, according to the bulk of the vessel for which they are intended, from three to twenty inches in circumference. A cable is composed of three strands; each strand of three ropes; and each rope of three twists. A ship's cable is usually 120 fathom, or 720 feet, in length. Hence the expression, *a cable's length.*
Stream cable is a hawser or rope, smaller than the bower cables, to moor a ship in a place sheltered from wind and heavy seas.
To pay out, or *to veer out the cable*, is to slacken it that it may run out of the ship.
To serve the cable, is to bind it round with ropes, canvas, &c., to prevent its being worn or galled in the hawse.
To slip the cable, is to let it run out end for end. *Mar. Dict.*

CA′BLED, *a.* Fastened with a cable. *Dyer.*

CAB'LET, *n.* A little cable. *Mar. Dict.*

CA'BLE-TIER, *n.* The place where the cables are coiled away. *Mar. Dict.*

CABO'CHED, } *a.* In *heraldry*, having the
CABO'SHED, } head cut close, so as to have no neck left. *Dict.*

CABOOSE', *n.* [G. *kabuse*, a little room or hut; Dan. *kabyse*, a cook's room in a ship. Qu. Ch. כבש to hide or cover, or Heb. Ch. כבשן a kiln or furnace. In Dutch, *kombuis* is an oven, furnace or cook's room.]

1. The cook-room or kitchen of a ship. In smaller vessels, it is an inclosed fire-place, hearth or stove for cooking, on the main deck. In a ship of war, the cook room is called a galley. *Mar. Dict.*

2. A box that covers the chimney in a ship. *Encyc.*

CAB'OS, *n.* A species of eel-pout, about two feet long, whose flesh is well tasted. *Dict. of Nat. Hist.*

CAB'RIOLE, } *n.* [Fr. *cabriolet*, from *ca-*
CAB'RIOLET, } *briole*, a goat-leap; L. *capra*.]

A gig; a one horse chair, a light carriage.

CAB'URE, *n.* A Brazilian bird of the owl kind, of the size of a thrush, of a beautiful umber color, spotted with white. *Dict. of Nat. Hist.*

CAB'URNS, *n.* Small lines made of spun yarn, to bind cables, seize tackles, and the like. *Encyc.*

CAC'AO or **CO'COA**, *n.* The chocolate-tree, a species of the Theobroma, a native of the West Indies. This tree grows about twenty feet high, bearing pods which are oval and pointed. The nuts or seeds are numerous, and lodged in a white pithy substance. *Encyc.*

CACCOONS', *n.* A plant called in botany *Flevillea*. *Encyc.*

CACH'ALOT, *n.* A cetaceous fish, the physeter or spermaceti whale. The principal species are, the black headed with a dorsal fin, and the round-headed, without a fin on the back, and with a fistula in the snout. From this whale is obtained the spermaceti. *Encyc.*

CACHEC'TIC, } *a.* [See *Cachexy*.] Hav-
CACHEC'TICAL, } ing an ill habit of body; of a deranged or vitiated state of the body without fever. *Coxe.*

CACHEX'Y, *n.* [Gr. καχεξια, from κακος, ill, and εξις, habit, from εχω, to have.]

A vicious state of the powers of the body; a deranged state of the constitution, without fever or nervous disease. *Encyc. Coxe.*

CACHINNA'TION, *n.* [L. *cachinnatio*.] Loud laughter. [*Little used.*]

CACH'OLONG, *n.* [said to be from *Cach*, the name of a river in Bucharia, and *cholon*, a Calmuc word for stone.]

A variety of chalcedony, which is a subspecies of quartz, usually milk white, sometimes grayish or yellowish white; opake or slightly translucent at the edges. Its fracture is even, or conchoidal with large cavities, sometimes dull, sometimes pearly or glossy. It often envelops common chalcedony; the two minerals being united by insensible shades. It also associates with flint and semi-opal. *Cleaveland.*

CACK, *v. i.* [L. *caco.*] To ease the body by stool. *Pope.*

CACK'EREL, *n.* [said to be from L. *caco.*] A fish which is said to void excrements when pursued. Others say, a fish which eaten produces lax bowels. *Skinner. Johnson.*

CACK'LE, *v. i.* [D. *kaakelen*, to chatter; Ger. *gackern*, to cackle, to gaggle; D. *gaggelen*, to chatter; Eng. *gaggle* and *giggle*; Dan. *kagler*, to cluck, as a hen; Sp. *cacarear*, to cackle or crow.]

1. To make a particular noise, as a goose or a hen. *Dryden. Shak.*

2. To laugh with a broken noise, like the cackling of a goose; to *giggle*, which is a word from the same root. *Arbuthnot.*

3. To prate; to prattle; to tattle; to talk in a silly manner. *Johnson.*

CACK'LE, *n.* The broken noise of a goose or hen. *Dryden.*

2. Idle talk; silly prattle. *Johnson.*

CACK'LER, *n.* A fowl that cackles.

2. A tell-tale; a tattler. *Johnson.*

CACK'LING, *ppr.* Making the noise of a goose or hen. *Johnson.*

CACK'LING, *n.* The broken noise of a goose or hen. Rome was saved by the *cackling* of a goose.

CACOCHYM'IC, } *a.* [See *Cacochymy*.]
CACOCHYM'ICAL, } Having the fluids of the body vitiated, especially the blood. *Encyc.*

CAC'OCHYMY, *n.* [Gr. κακοχυμια, of κακος, ill, and χυμος, juice.]

A vicious state of the vital humors, especially of the blood, arising from a disorder of the secretions or excretions, or from contagion. *Encyc.*

CACODE'MON, *n.* [Gr. κακος, evil, and δαιμων, a demon.] An evil spirit. *Shak.*

CACOE'THES, *n.* [Gr. κακοηθεια; κακος, vicious, and ηθος, manners.]

1. A bad custom or habit; a bad disposition.

2. In *medicine*, an incurable ulcer. *Coxe.*

CACOPH'ONY, *n.* [Gr. κακος, ill, and φωνη, voice.]

1. In *rhetoric*, an uncouth or disagreeable sound of words, proceeding from the meeting of harsh letters or syllables. *Encyc.*

2. In *medicine*, a depraved voice; an altered state of the voice. *Coxe. Encyc.*

3. In *music*, a combination of discordant sounds.

CAD'AVER, *n.* [L.] A corpse.

CADAV'EROUS, *a.* [L. *cadaver*, a dead carcase.]

1. Having the appearance or color of a dead human body; pale; wan; ghastly; as a *cadaverous* look.

2. Having the qualities of a dead body. *Arbuthnot.*

CAD'DIS, *n.* [Qu. L. *cadus*, a cask.] A kind of tape or ribin. *Shak.*

2. A kind of worm or grub found in a case of straw. *Johnson.*

CAD'DOW, *n.* A chough; a jack daw. *Ray.*

CAD'DY, *n.* A small box for keeping tea.

CADE, *a.* [Qu. W. *cadw*, to keep or guard; or Ar. قاد to lead or govern, to be led, to be submissive.]

Tame; bred by hand; domesticated; as a *cade* lamb.

CADE, *v. t.* To bring up or nourish by hand, or with tenderness; to tame.

CADE, *n.* [L. *cadus*; Gr. καδος, a cask; καδιον, a purse or little cask; allied perhaps to W. *cadw*, to hold, to keep.]

A barrel or cask. A *cade* of herrings is the quantity of five hundred; of sprats, a thousand. *Encyc.*

CA'DE-OIL, *n.* In *the materia medica*, an oil used in Germany and France, made of the fruit of the oxycedrus, called in those countries, *cada*. *Encyc.*

CADE-WORM, *n.* The same as *caddis*.

CA'DENCE, } *n.* [Fr. *cadence*; Sp. Port.
CA'DENCY, } *cadencia*; L. *cadens*, from *cado*, to fall; W. *cwyzaw*; Corn. *kodha*; Arm. *kuedha*, or *kueza*; Ir. *cadam*, *cudaim*; It. *cadere*; Sp. *caer*; Port. *cahir*; Fr. *cheoir*.]

1. A fall; a decline; a state of sinking. *Milton.*

2. A fall of the voice in reading or speaking, as at the end of a sentence; also, the falling of the voice in the general modulation of tones in reciting. In reading or speaking, a certain tone is taken, which is called the key, or key-note, on which most of the words are pronounced, and the fall of the voice below this tone is called *cadence*. *Encyc.*

The ordinary cadence is a fall of the last syllable of a sentence only.

3. The general tone of reading verse. The *cadence* of one line must be a rule to that of the next; as the sound of the former must slide gently into that which follows. *Dryden.*

4. Tone; sound; as, hoarse *cadence*. *Milton.*

5. In *music*, repose; the termination of a harmonical phrase on a repose or on a perfect chord. *Encyc.*

Also, the manner of closing a song; embellishment at the close. *Busby.*

6. In *horsemanship*, an equal measure or proportion observed by a horse in all his motions. *Encyc.*

7. In *heraldry*, the distinction of families. *Todd.*

CA'DENCE, *v. t.* To regulate by musical measure. *Smith.*

CA'DENCED, *pp.* or *a.* Having a particular cadence; as well *cadenced* music. *Rousseau.*

CADE'NE, *n.* A species of inferior carpet imported from the Levant. *Encyc.*

CA'DENT, *a.* [L. *cadens*.] Falling down; sinking. *Johnson.*

CADEN'ZA, *n.* [It. See *Cadence*.] The fall or modulation of the voice in singing.

CADET', *n.* [Fr. *cadet*; It. *cadetto*; Sp. *cadete*. In French properly the second son. *Gebelin.* But in general, the younger son or brother, or the youngest.]

1. The younger or youngest son. *Brown.*

2. A gentleman who carries arms in a regiment, as a private man, with a view to acquire military skill, and obtain a commission. His service is voluntary, but he receives pay, and thus is distinguished from a volunteer. *Encyc.*

3. A young man, in a military school.

CADEW', *n.* A straw worm. [See *Caddis*.]

CADGE, *v. t.* To carry a burden. [*Not in use.*] *Ray.*

CADG'ER, *n.* One who brings butter, eggs

and poultry to the market, from the country; a huckster. *Johnson.*

[*I believe not used in the U. States.*]

CA'DI, *n.* [Ar. قاضى a governor, from قضى to lead, rule or govern; Eng. *guide.* Hence *Alcaide.*]

In *the Turkish dominions,* a judge in civil affairs; usually the judge of a town or village, for the judge of a city or province is called Moula. *Encyc.*

CADIL'LAC, *n.* A sort of pear. *Johnson.*

CADME'AN, CAD'MIAN, *a.* Relating to Cadmus, a reputed prince of Thebes, who introduced into Greece, the sixteen simple letters of the alphabet—α, β, γ, δ, ε, ι, κ, λ, μ, ν, ο, π, ρ, σ, τ, υ. These are called Cadmean letters. *Bryant.*

This personage may be a fabulous being, or if such a person ever existed, he may have been named from his knowledge of letters, for in the ancient Persian, *kadeem* signified language; Ir. *cuadham,* to tell or relate; *ceadach,* talkative; *ceadal,* a story. Or he may have been named from his eminence or antiquity, קדם kadam, to precede; Arabic, to excel; whence the sense of priority and antiquity; or his name may denote a man from the East.

CAD'MIA, *n.* An oxyd of zink which collects on the sides of furnaces where zink is sublimed, as in brass founderies. This substance is readily volatilized on charcoal, by the oxy-hydrogen blowpipe, and it burns with the usual beautiful combustion of zink. Pulverized, mixed with charcoal powder, wrapped in sheet copper, and heated with the compound blowpipe, it readily forms brass. *Silliman.*

CAD'MIUM, *n.* A metal discovered by M. Stromeyer, in 1817, in carbonate of zink, at Hanover. Its color is a fine white, with a shade of bluish gray, resembling that of tin. Its texture is compact, its fracture hackly, and it is susceptible of polish. It is ductile and malleable, and when fused, crystalizes in octahedrons. It melts below a red heat, and suffers no change in air. *Ure. Cleaveland.*

CADU'CEUS, *n.* [L.] In *antiquity,* Mercury's rod; a wand entwisted by two serpents, borne by Mercury as an ensign of quality and office. On medals, the Caduceus is a symbol of good conduct, peace and prosperity. The rod represents power; the serpents, wisdom; and the two wings, diligence and activity. *Encyc.*

CADU'CITY, *n.* [L. *caducus,* from *cado,* to fall.] Tendency to fall. [*Little used.*] *Chesterfield.*

CADU'COUS, *a.* [L. supra.] In *botany,* falling early; as *caducous* leaves, which fall before the end of summer, A *caducous* calyx falls before the corol is well unfolded. *Martyn.*

CÆ'CIAS, *n.* [L.] A wind from the northeast, [and in Latin, according to Ainsworth, from the north-west.] *Milton.*

CÆSARIAN. [See *Cesarian.*]

CÆSURA. [See *Cesura.*]

CAF'FEIN, *n.* A substance obtained from an infusion of unroasted coffee, by treating it with the muriate of tin. *Ure.*

CAF'TAN, *n.* [Persic.] A Persian or Turkish vest or garment. *Johnson.*

CAG, *n.* [Fr. *caque;* Dan. *kag;* allied probably to *cage,* that which holds.]

A small cask, or barrel, differing from the barrel only in size, and containing a few gallons, but not of any definite capacity. It is generally written *Keg.*

CAGE, *n.* [Fr. *cage;* D. *kouw* and *kooi.* See *Cag.*]

1. A box or inclosure, made of boards, or with lattice work of wood, wicker or wire, for confining birds or beasts. For the confinement of the more strong and ferocious beasts, a cage is sometimes made of iron. *Encyc.*

2. An inclosure made with pallisades for confining wild beasts. *Johnson.*

3. A prison for petty criminals. *Johnson.*

4. In *carpentry,* an outer work of timber, inclosing another within it; as the *cage* of a wind mill or of a stair case. *Encyc.*

CAGE, *v. t.* To confine in a cage; to shut up, or confine. *Donne.*

CA'GIT, *n.* A beautiful green parrot of the Philippine isles. *Dict. of Nat. Hist.*

CAG'UI, *n.* A monkey of Brazil, of two species, one of them called the pongi, the other not more than six inches long. They are called also jacchus and œdipus. *Encyc. Dict. of Nat. Hist.*

CAIC or CAIQUE, *n.* [Fr.] A skiff belonging to a galley.

CAIMAN. [See *Cayman.*]

CAIRN, *n.* [Welsh, *carn.*] A heap of stones.

CA'ISSON, or CAISSOON', *n.* [Fr. from *caisse,* a chest. See *Case.*]

1. A wooden chest into which several bombs are put, and sometimes gunpowder, to be laid in the way of an enemy, or under some work of which the enemy intend to possess themselves, and to be fired when they get possession. *Encyc.*

2. A wooden frame or chest used in laying the foundation of the pier of a bridge. *Encyc.*

3. An ammunition chest, or waggon.

CA'ITIFF, *n.* [It. *cattivo,* a captive, a slave, a rascal; *cattivare,* to master, to enslave. This word is from the L. *captivus,* a captive, from *capio* or *capto,* to take. The sense of *knavery* is from the natural connection between the degradation of a slave and vice.]

A mean villain; a despicable knave: it implies a mixture of wickedness and misery. *Johnson.*

CAJ'EPUT, *n.* An oil from the East Indies, resembling that of cardamoms, obtained from the *Melaleuca leucodendron.* *Encyc.*

CAJO'LE, *v. t.* [Fr. *cajoler, enjoler;* Arm. *cangeoli.* See *Gull.*]

To flatter; to soothe; to coax; to deceive or delude by flattery. *Hudibras.*

CAJO'LER, *n.* A flatterer; a wheedler.

CAJO'LERY, *n.* Flattery; a wheedling to delude. *Burke.*

CAJO'LING, *ppr.* Flattering; wheedling; deceiving.

CAJO'TA, *n.* A Mexican animal resembling a wolf and a dog. *Clavigero.*

CAKE, *n.* [D. *koek;* G. *kuchen;* Dan. *kage;* Sw. *kaka;* Ch. כעך; Pers. كاك; Syr. ܟܥܟܐ. The sense seems to be, a mass or lump.]

1. A small mass of dough baked; or a composition of flour, butter, sugar, or other ingredients, baked in a small mass. The name is applied to various compositions, baked or cooked in different shapes.

2. Something in the form of a cake, rather flat than high, but roundish; as a *cake* on a tree. *Bacon.*

3. A mass of matter concreted; as a *cake* of ice. *Dryden.*

In *New England,* a piece of floating ice in a river or lake.

4. A hard swelling on the flesh; or rather a concretion without such swelling.

CAKE, *v. t.* To form into a cake or mass.

CAKE, *v. i.* To concrete, or form into a hard mass, as dough in an oven, or as flesh or any other substance. *Addison.*

CAKE, *v. i.* To cackle. [*Not used.*] *Ray.*

CAL'ABASH, *n.* [Sp. *calabaza,* a pumpkin, a gourd, a calabash; Port. *calabaça.* Qu. Gr. χαλπη, a water-pot or pitcher.]

1. A vessel made of a dried gourd-shell or of the shell of a calabash tree, used for containing liquors, or goods, as pitch, rosin and the like. *Encyc.*

2. A popular name of the gourd-plant, or Cucurbita. *Fam. of Plants.*

CAL'ABASH-TREE, *n.* A tree of two species, known in botany by the generic name *Crescentia.* The cujete has narrow leaves, but a large round or oval fruit. The latifolia has broad leaves. The shell of the fruit is used for cups, bowls, dishes and other utensils. *Encyc.*

CALA'DE, *n.* The slope or declivity of a rising manege-ground. *Encyc.*

CÁLA'ITE, *n.* A name given to the turquois; which see.

CALAMANC'O, *n.* [Fr. *callimanque, calmande;* D. *kalmink;* G. *kalmank;* Sp. *calamaco.* Qu. Sp. *maca,* a spot.]

A woolen stuff, of a fine gloss, and checkered in the warp. *Encyc.*

CAL'AMAR, *n.* [Sp. *id.;* It. *calamaia,* an ink-horn, and this animal.]

An animal, having an oblong body and ten legs. On the belly are two bladders containing a black fluid, which the animal emits when pursued. It is called also sea-sleeve and cuttle-fish. *Sp. Dict. Dict. of Nat. Hist.*

CAL'AMBAC, *n.* [Sp. *calambuco.*] Aloes-wood, xyloe-aloes, a drug, which is the product of a tree growing in China and some of the Indian isles. It is of a light spungy texture, very porous, and the pores so filled with a soft fragrant resin, that it may be indented by the fingers and chewed like mastich. It is also called tambac. The two coarser kinds are called lignum aloes, and calambour. *Encyc.*

CAL'AMBOUR, *n.* A species of the aloes-wood, of a dusky or mottled color, of a light, friable texture, and less fragrant than calambac. This wood is used by cabinet-makers and inlayers. *Encyc.*

CALAMIF'EROUS, *a.* [*calamus* and *fero.*] Producing plants having a long, hollow, knotted stem. *Chambers.*

CAL'AMINE, or CAL'AMIN, *n.* Lapis calaminaris, or cadmia fossilis; an ore of zink, much used in the composition of brass. This term is applied both to the siliceous oxyd and the native carbonate of zink. They can scarcely be distinguished by their external characters. They are generally compact, often stalactitic, and sometimes crystalized. Most of the calamines of England and Scotland are said to be carbonates. *Encyc. Cleaveland.*

ȻAL'AMINT, *n.* [L. *calamintha;* Gr. καλαμινθη; μινθα, mentha, menta, *mint.*]

A plant, a species of Melissa, or baum, an aromatic plant, and a weak corroborant. *Encyc.*

Water-calamint is a species of Mentha, or mint.

ȻAL'AMISTRATE, *v. t.* To curl or frizzle the hair. [*Not used.*] *Cotgrave.*

ȻALAMISTRA'TION, *n.* The act of curling the hair. [*Not used.*]

ȻAL'AMIT, *n.* [L. *calamus,* a reed.] A mineral, probably a variety of Tremolite. It occurs in imperfect or rounded prismatic crystals, longitudinally striated, and sometimes resembling a reed. Its structure is foliated; its luster vitreous, and more or less shining. *Cleaveland. Werner.*

ȻALAM'ITOUS, *a.* [Fr. *calamiteux.* See *Calamity.*]

1. Very miserable; involved in deep distress; oppressed with infelicity; wretched from misfortune; *applied to men.* *Johnson. Calamy.*

2. Producing distress and misery; making wretched; *applied to external circumstances;* as a *calamitous* event. *Milton.*

3. Full of misery; distressful; wretched; *applied to state or condition.* *South.*

ȻALAM'ITOUSLY, *adv.* In a manner to bring great distress.

ȻALAM'ITOUSNESS, *n.* Deep distress; wretchedness; misery; the quality of producing misery.

ȻALAM'ITY, *n.* [L. *calamitas.* Qu. Ar. كَلَمَ kalama, to wound; Heb. Ch. כלם to make ashamed. Under this root, the Syriac has *calamity.* The sense of the verb is, to strike, to beat down. But the origin of the word is uncertain.]

Any great misfortune, or cause of misery; generally applied to events or disasters which produce extensive evils, as loss of crops, earthquakes, conflagrations, defeat of armies, and the like. But it is applied also to the misfortunes which bring great distress upon individuals. *Milton. Prior.*

The deliberations of *calamity* are rarely wise. *Burke.*

ȻAL'AMUS, *n.* [L. from Gr. καλαμος, a stalk or stem, a reed, stubble; Eth. and Ar. قَلَمٌ calamus scriptorius, a writing reed or pen. The verb in Arabic signifies to cut or pare. But qu., for it would seem to be allied to *culmus.*]

1. The generic name of the Indian cane, called also *rotang.* It is without branches, has a crown at the top, and is beset with spines. *Encyc.*

2. In *antiquity,* a pipe or fistula, a wind instrument, made of a reed or oaten stalk. *Encyc.*

3. A rush or reed used anciently as a pen to write on parchment or papyrus. *Encyc.*

4. A sort of reed, or sweet-scented cane, used by the Jews as a perfume. It is a knotty root, reddish without and white within, and filled with a spungy substance. It has an aromatic smell. *Brown. Calmet.*

5. The sweet flag, called by Linne *Acorus.* *Encyc.*

ȻALAN'DRA, *n.* A species of lark, with a thick bill, the upper part of the body of a reddish brown, spotted with black, with a body thicker than the sky-lark. *Pennant.*

ȻALAN'DRE or **ȻAL'ANDER,** *n.* The French name of a species of insect of the beetle kind, very destructive in granaries. *Encyc.*

ȻALAN'GAY, *n.* A species of white parrot. *Ash.*

ȻALASH', *n.* [Fr. *caleche;* D. *kales;* Sp. *calesa;* Russ. *koliaska.*]

1. A light chariot or carriage with very low wheels, used for taking the air in parks and gardens. It is open, or covered with mantlets of cloth, that are let down at pleasure. *Encyc.*

2. A cover for the head sometimes used by ladies.

ȻALȻ'AR, *n.* In glass works, a kind of oven, or reverberating furnace, used for the calcination of sand and salt of potash, and converting them into frit. *Encyc.*

ȻALȻ'ARATE, *a.* [L. *calcar,* a spur; *calx,* the heel; Ir. *calg,* a sting or goad.]

Furnished with a spur; as a *calcarate* corol, in larkspur; a *calcarate* nectary, a nectary resembling a cock's spur. *Martyn.*

ȻALȻA'RIO-SUL'PHUROUS, *a.* [See *Calx* and *Sulphur.*]

Having lime and sulphur in combination, or partaking of both. *Kirwan.*

ȻALȻA'RIOUS, *a.* [L. *calcarius.* See *Calx.*] Partaking of the nature of lime; having the qualities of lime; as *calcarious* earth or stone. *Encyc. Kirwan.*

ȻALȻAVAL'LA, *n.* A kind of sweet wine from Portugal. *Mason.*

ȻAL'CEATED, *a.* [L. *calceatus,* from *calceus,* a shoe.]

Shod; fitted with or wearing shoes. *Johnson.*

ȻAL'CEDON, *n.* [See *Chalcedony.*] With jewelers, a foul vein, like chalcedony, in some precious stones. *Ash.*

ȻALCEDON'IȻ, }
ȻALCEDO'NIAN, } *a.* [See *Chalcedony.*]

Pertaining to or resembling chalcedony. *Encyc. Kirwan.*

ȻALCEDONY. See *Chalcedony,* the more correct orthography.

ȻALCIF'EROUS, *a.* [of *calx,* lime, and *fero,* to produce.] Producing calx or lime.

ȻAL'CIFORM, *a.* [of *calx,* lime, and *forma,* form.] In the form of calx.

ȻALCIMU'RITE, *n.* [of *calx,* lime, and *muria,* salt water.]

A species of earth, of the muriatic genus, of a blue or olive green color, of the consistence of clay. It consists of calcarious earth and magnesia tinged with iron. *Kirwan.*

ȻALCI'NABLE, *a.* [See *Calcine.*] That may be calcined; capable of being reduced to a friable state by the action of fire. *Encyc.*

ȻAL'CINATE, *v. t.* To calcine. [See *Calcine.*] *Bacon.*

ȻALCINA'TION, *n.* [from *calcine.*] The operation of expelling from a substance by heat, some volatile matter with which it is combined, or which is the cementing principle, and thus reducing it to a friable state. Thus chalk and carbonate of lime are reduced to lime by *calcination,* or the expulsion of carbonic acid.

2. The operation of reducing a metal to an oxyd, or metallic calx. This in modern chimistry is called oxydation.

ȻAL'CINATORY, *n.* A vessel used in calcination.

ȻAL'CINE, *v. t.* [Fr. *calciner;* It. *calcinare;* Sp. *calcinar;* from *calx.* See *Calx.*]

1. To reduce a substance to a powder or to a friable state, by the action of heat; or to expel from a substance some volatile matter, combined with it, or forming its cementing principle, as the carbonic acid from limestone, or the water of crystalization from salts.

2. To oxydize, as a metal; to reduce to a metallic calx.

3. To dissolve; to destroy the principles which unite. *Denham.*

ȻAL'CINE, *v. i.* To be converted into a powder or friable substance, or into a calx, by the action of heat. *Newton.*

ȻAL'CIUM, *n.* [from L. *calx.*] The metallic basis of lime. *Davy.*

ȻALȻOGRAPH'IȻAL, *a.* [See *Calcography.*] Pertaining to calcography.

ȻALȻOG'RAPHY, *n.* [L. *calx,* chalk, and Gr. γραφω, to engrave.] An engraving in the likeness of chalk.

ȻALȻ-SINTER, *n.* Stalactitic carbonate of lime. *Ure.*

ȻALȻ-TUFF, *n.* An alluvial formation of carbonate of lime. *Ure.*

ȻALȻ'ULABLE, *a.* [See *Calculate.*] That may be calculated, or ascertained by calculation.

ȻALȻ'ULARY, *n.* [L. *calculus,* a pebble.] A congeries of little stony knots dispersed through the parenchyma of the pear and other fruits, formed by concretions of the sap. *Encyc.*

ȻALȻ'ULATE, *v. t.* [Fr. *calculer;* It. *calculare;* Sp. *calcular;* Lat. *calculo;* from *calculus,* a pebble. Ar. Syr. قلقي gravel.]

To compute; to reckon; to add, subtract, multiply or divide any sums, for the purpose of finding the amount, difference, or other result. Thus, to *calculate* the expenses of erecting a house, is to estimate and add together the several sums which each part of the materials and the work will cost.

2. To ascertain by the use of tables or numbers; as, to *calculate* an eclipse.

3. To form tables upon mathematical principles, as logarithms, ephemerides, &c.

4. To compute the situation of the planets at a certain time, for astrological purposes; as, to *calculate* the *birth* of a person. *Shak.*

5. To adjust by computation; to fit or prepare by the adaptation of the means to the end; as, to *calculate* a system of laws for a free people.

Religion is *calculated* for our benefit. *Tillotson.*

CAL'CULATE, *v. i.* To make a computation; as, we *calculate* better for ourselves than for others.

In *popular use*, this word is often equivalent to *intend* or *purpose*, that is, to make arrangements, and form a plan; as, a man *calculates* to go a journey. This use of the word springs from the practice of *computing* or *estimating* the various circumstances which concur to influence the mind in forming its determinations.

CAL'CULATED, *pp.* Computed; reckoned; suited; adapted by design.

CAL'CULATING, *ppr.* Computing; reckoning; adapting by design; adjusting.

CALCULA'TION, *n.* The art, practice or manner of computing by numbers. The use of numbers, by addition, subtraction, multiplication, or division, for the purpose of arriving at a certain result. Thus computations in astronomy and geometry for making tables of numbers are called *calculations*. *Encyc.*

2. The result of an arithmetical operation; computation; reckoning. *Hooker.*

3. Estimate formed in the mind by comparing the various circumstances and facts which influence its determination.

CAL'CULATIVE, *a.* Pertaining to calculation; tending to calculate. *Burke.*

CAL'CULATOR, *n.* One who computes or reckons; one who estimates or considers the force and effect of causes, with a view to form a correct estimate of the effects.

CAL'CULATORY, *a.* Belonging to calculation. *Johnson.*

CAL'CULE, *n.* Reckoning; computation. *Obs.* *Howel.*

CAL'CULOUS, *a.* [Supra.] Stony; gritty; hard like stone; as a *calculous* concretion *Brown.*

2. Affected with the gravel or stone; as a *calculous* person. *Sharp.*

CAL'CULUS, *n.* [L. See *Calculate.*] The stone in the bladder or kidneys. The calculus in the bladder is called *lithiasis*; in the kidneys, *nephritis*. *Encyc.*

2. In mathematics; *Differential calculus*, is the arithmetic of the infinitely small differences of variable quantities; the method of differencing quantities, or of finding an infinitely small quantity, which, being taken infinite times, shall be equal to a given quantity. This coincides with the doctrine of fluxions. *Encyc.*

3. *Exponential calculus*, is a method of differencing exponential quantities; or of finding and summing up the differentials or moments of exponential quantities; or at least of bringing them to geometrical constructions. *Encyc.*

4. *Integral calculus*, is a method of integrating or summing up moments or differential quantities; the inverse of the differential calculus. *Encyc.*

5. *Literal calculus*, is specious arithmetic or algebra. *Encyc.*

CALDRON, *n. cawl'dron.* [Old Fr. *chauldron*, now *chaudron*; Basque, *galda*, to heat; *galdarea*, a great kettle; It. *caldaia*, or *caldaro*, a caldron; *caldo*, heat and hot; Sp. *calda*, heat; *caldear*, to heat, to weld iron; *caldera*, a caldron; Port. *caldeira*, a caldron; L. *caldarium*, id; *calda*, hot water; *calidus*, hot; from *caleo*, to be hot. This is from the root of Eng. *scald.*]

A large kettle or boiler, of copper, or other metal, furnished with a movable handle or bail, with which to hang it on a chimney hook. *Addison.*

CALECHE, [See *Calash.*]

CALEDO'NIAN, *a.* Pertaining to Caledonia, an ancient name of Scotland. The termination *ia*, signifies a country, and was added by the Romans. *Caledon* signifies probably, the hill or town of the *Gaels*, or *Caels*, the primitive inhabitants.]

CALEDO'NIAN, *n.* A native of Caledonia, now Scotland.

CALEFA'CIENT, *a.* [See *Calefaction*, *Calefy.*] Warming; heating.

CALEFA'CIENT, *n.* That which warms or heats.

CALEFAC'TION, *n.* [L. *calefactio*, from *calefacio*, to make warm. See *Calefy.*]

The act or operation of warming or heating; the production of heat in a body by the action of fire, or by the communication of heat from other bodies. *Encyc.*

2. The state of being heated. *Johnson.*

CALEFAC'TIVE, } *a.* [See *Calefaction.*]
CALEFAC'TORY, } That makes warm or hot; that communicates heat.

CAL'EFȲ, *v. i.* [L. *calefio*, to become warm, or hot; from *caleo* and *fio* or *facio.*]

To grow hot or warm; to be heated. *Brown.*

CAL'EFȲ, *v. t.* To make warm or hot. *Johnson.*

CAL'ENDAR, *n.* [L. *calendarium*, an account book. See *Calends.*]

1. A register of the year, in which the months, weeks, and days are set down in order, with the feasts observed by the church, &c.; an almanack. It was so named from the Roman *Calendæ*, the name given to the first day of the month, and written, in large letters, at the head of each month. [See *Calends.*] *Encyc.*

2. A list of prisoners in the custody of the sheriff. *Eng.*

3. An orderly table or enumeration of persons or things. *Encyc.*

Calendar-month, a solar month as it stands in Almanacks.

CAL'ENDAR, *v. t.* To enter or write in a calendar.

CAL'ENDER, *v. t.* [Fr. *calendrer*; Sp. *calentar*, to heat, to urge or press forward; from *caleo*, to be hot.]

To press between rollers, for the purpose of making smooth, glossy and wavy; as woolen and silk stuffs and linens.

CAL'ENDER, *n.* A machine or hot press, used in manufactories to press cloths, for the purpose of making them smooth, even and glossy, laying the nap, watering them and giving them a wavy appearance. It consists of two thick rollers or cylinders, placed between boards or planks, the lower one being fixed, the upper one movable, and loaded with a great weight. *Encyc.*

CAL'ENDRER, *n.* The person who calenders cloth.

CAL'ENDS, *n. plu.* [L. *calendæ*, from *calo*, Gr. καλεω, Eng. to *call*. See *Call.*]

Among the Romans, the first day of each month. The origin of this name is differently related. Varro supposes it to have originated in the practice of notifying the time of the new moon, by a priest who *called* out or proclaimed the fact, to the people, and the number of the calends, or the day of the nones. Others alledge that the people being convened, the pontifex proclaimed the several feasts or holidays in the month; a custom which was discontinued in the year of Rome 450, when the fasti or calendar was set up in public places, to give notice of the festivals. *Encyc.* *Adam's Rom. Ant.*

CAL'ENTURE, *n.* [Sp. *calentura*, heat, a fever with irregular pulse; *calentur*, to heat; from L. *caleo*, to be hot. Russ. *kalyu*, to heat, to make red or red hot.]

A violent ardent fever, incident to persons in hot climates, especially natives of cooler climates. It is attended with delirium, and one of the symptoms is, that the person affected imagines the sea to be a green field, and sometimes attempting to walk in it, is lost. *Encyc.* *Coxe.*

C'ALF, *n. c'aff*, plu. *calves*, pron. *c'avz.* [Sax. *cealf*; Sw. *kalf*; Dan. *kalv*; D. *kalf*; and the verb *kalven*, to calve, to vomit; G. *kalb*; *kalben*. The primary sense is issue, from throwing out. Hence the word is applied to the protuberant part of the leg, a push, a swell.]

1. The young of the cow, or of the bovine genus of quadrupeds.

2. In *contempt*, a dolt; an ignorant, stupid person; a weak or cowardly man. *Drayton.*

3. The thick fleshy part of the leg behind; so called from its protuberance. *Wiseman.*

4. *The calves of the lips*, in Hosea, signify the pure offerings of prayer, praise and thanksgiving. *Brown.*

C'ALF-LIKE, *a.* Resembling a calf. *Shak.*

C'ALF-SKIN, *n.* The hide or skin of a calf; or leather made of the skin.

CAL'IBER, *n.* [Fr. and Sp. *calibre.*]

1. The diameter of a body; as the *caliber* of a column, or of a bullet. *Encyc.*

2. The bore of a gun, or the extent of its bore.

Caliber-compasses, *calibers*, or *callipers*, a sort of compasses made with arched legs, to take the diameter of round bodies, as masts, shot, &c. The legs move on an arch of brass, on which are marked the inches and half inches, to show how far the points of the compasses are opened asunder. *Encyc.*

Caliber-rule, Gunner's Callipers, an instrument in which a right line is so divided as that the first part being equal to the diameter of an iron or leaden ball of one pound weight, the other parts are to the first as the diameters of balls of two, three, four, &c. pounds, are to the diameter of a ball of one pound. It is used by engineers, to determine, from a ball's weight, its diameter or caliber and *vice versa*. *Encyc.*

CAL'ICE, *n.* [L. *calix*; Fr. *calice*; Sax. *calic*, a cup; Gr. κυλιξ. It is usually written *chalice*; but incorrectly.]

A cup; appropriately, a communion cup, or vessel used to administer the wine in the sacrament of the Lord's supper. It is used by the Roman Catholics in the mass.

CAL'ICO, *n.* [said to be from *Calicut*, in India.] Cotton cloth. In England, white or unprinted cotton cloth is called calico.

In the United States, calico is printed cotton cloth, having not more than two colors. I have never heard this name given to the unprinted cloth. Calico was originally imported from India, but is now manufactured in Europe and the United States.

CAL'ICO-PRINTER, *n.* One whose occupation is to print calicoes.

CAL'ID, *a.* [L. *calidus*, from *caleo*, to be hot.] Hot; burning; ardent. *Johnson.*

CALID'ITY, *n.* Heat. *Brown.*

CAL'IDUCT, *n.* [L. *caleo*, to be hot, *calor*, heat, and *duco*, to lead.]

Among *the Ancients*, a pipe or canal used to convey heat from a furnace to the apartments of a house.

CA'LIF, *n.* written also *caliph* and *kalif.* [from Ar. خَلَفَ calafa, to succeed. Hence a *calif* is a successor, a title given to the successors of Mohammed.]

A successor or vicar; a representative of Mohammed, bearing the same relation to him as the Pope pretends to bear to St. Peter. Among the Saracens, or Mohammedans, a calif is one who is vested with supreme dignity and power in all matters relating to religion and civil policy. This title is borne by the Grand Signior in Turkey, and by the Sophi of Persia. *Encyc.*

CA'LIFATE, } The office or dignity of
CA'LIPHATE, } *n.* a calif; or the govern-
KA'LIFATE, } ment of a calif. *Harris.*

CALIGA'TION, *n.* [L. *caligatio*, dimness, from *caligo*, to be dark.] Darkness; dimness; cloudiness.

In *medical authors*, caligation or caligo, is an opakeness or cloudiness of the anterior surface of the crystaline lens, causing dimness of sight; impaired sight from obstruction to the passage of light, or cataract. *Coxe. Encyc.*

CALIG'INOUS, *a.* Dim; obscure; dark.

CALIG'INOUSNESS, *n.* Dimness; obscurity.

CALIGRAPH'IC, *a.* [Infra.] Pertaining to elegant penmanship. *Warton.*

CALIG'RAPHY, } *n.* [Gr. καλος, fair, and
CALLIG'RAPHY, } γραφω, to write; καλλιγραφια.]

Fair or elegant writing, or penmanship. *Prideaux.*

CA'LIN, *n.* A compound metal, of which the Chinese make tea canisters and the like. The ingredients seem to be lead and tin. *Encyc.*

CAL'IVER, *n.* [from *caliber.*] A kind of handgun, musket or arquebuse. *Shak.*

CA'LIX, *n.* [L. *calix*; Gr. κυλιξ.]

1. A cup.
2. The membrane which covers the papillæ in the pelvis of the human kidney. *Coxe.*

But it seems to be erroneously used for *calyx*, which see.

CALK, *v. t. cauk.* [Qu. the connection of this word with the Sp. *calafetear*; It. *calafatare*; Port. *calafetar*; Arm. *calefeti*; Fr. *calfater*, to smear with cement or mortar; Ar. قَلَفَ kalafa, to stop the seams of ships with fine moss, &c., and pay them over with pitch; Sam. *id.* It may be corrupted from this word; if not, it may be from the Dan. *kalk*, calx, lime or mortar; but this seems not probable. The Germans and Danes have borrowed the Spanish and French word to express the idea. Skinner deduces the word from Fr. *calage*, tow.]

1. To drive oakum or old ropes untwisted, into the seams of a ship or other vessel, to prevent their leaking, or admitting water. After the seams are filled, they are covered with hot melted pitch or rosin, to keep the oakum from rotting.
2. In *some parts of America*, to set upon a horse or ox shoes armed with sharp points of iron, to prevent their slipping on ice; that is, to *stop* from slipping.

CALK, *n. cauk.* In *New-England*, a sharp pointed piece of iron on a shoe for a horse or an ox, called in Great Britain *calkin*; used to prevent the animal from slipping.

CALK'ER, *n. cauk'er.* A man who calks; sometimes perhaps a *calk* or pointed iron on a horse-shoe.

CALK'ED, *pp. cauk'ed.* Having the seams stopped; furnished with shoes with iron points.

CALK'IN, *n.* A calk.

CALK'ING, *ppr. cauk'ing.* Stopping the seams of a ship; putting on shoes with iron points.

CALK'ING, *n. cauk'ing.* In *painting*, the covering of the back side of a design with black lead, or red chalk, and tracing lines through on a waxed plate or wall or other matter, by passing lightly over each stroke of the design with a point, which leaves an impression of the color on the plate or wall. *Chambers.*

CALK'ING-IRON, *n. cauk'ing-iron.* An instrument like a chisel, used in calking ships.

CALL, *v. t.* [L. *calo*; Gr. χαλεω; Sw. *kalla*; Dan. *kalder*; W. *galw*, to call; D. *kallen*, to talk; Ch. כלא in Aph. to *call*, to thunder; Heb. to *hold* or restrain, which is the Gr. χωλυω, L. *caula*; Syr. Sam. Eth. to *hold*, or restrain; Ar. to keep; L. *celo*. The primary sense is to press, drive or strain. We find the like elements and signification in Sax. *giellan*, or *gyllan*, to yell; Dan. *galer*, to crow. Class Gl. The W. *galw* is connected in origin with *gallu*, to be able, to have power, may, can, Eng. *could*, the root of *gallant*, L. *gallus*, &c.]

In *a general sense*, to drive; to strain or force out sound. Hence,

1. To name; to denominate or give a name.

   And God *called* the light day, and the darkness he *called* night. Gen. i.

2. To convoke; to summon; to direct or order to meet; to assemble by order or public notice; often with *together*; as, the king *called* his council *together*; the president *called together* the congress.
3. To request to meet or come.

   He sent his servants to *call* them that were bidden. Math. xxii.

4. To invite.

   Because I have *called* and ye refused. Prov. i.

5. To invite or summon to come or be present; to invite, or collect.

   Call all your senses to you.

6. To give notice to come by authority; to command to come; as, *call* a servant.
7. To proclaim; to name, or publish the name.

   Nor parish clerk, who *calls* the psalm so clear. *Gay.*

8. To appoint or designate, as for an office, duty or employment.

   See, I have *called* by name Bezaleel. Ex. xxxi.

   Paul *called* to be an apostle. Rom. i.

9. To invite; to warn; to exhort. Is. xxii. 12. *Cruden.*
10. To invite or draw into union with Christ; to bring to know, believe and obey the gospel. Rom. viii. 28.
11. To own and acknowledge. Heb. ii. xi.
12. To invoke or appeal to.

    I *call* God for a record. 2 Cor. i.

13. To esteem or account. Is. lviii. 5. Mat. iii. 15.

To call down, to invite, or to bring down.

To call back, to revoke, or retract; to recall; to summon or bring back.

To call for, to demand, require or claim, as a crime *calls for* punishment; or to cause to grow. Ezek. xxxvi. Also, to speak for; to ask; to request; as, to *call for* a dinner.

To call in, to collect, as to *call in* debts or money; or to draw from circulation, as to *call in* clipped coin; or to summon together; to invite to come together; as, to *call in* neighbors or friends.

To call forth, to bring or summon to action; as, to *call forth* all the faculties of the mind.

To call off, to summon away; to divert; as, to *call off* the attention; to *call off* workmen from their employment.

To call up, to bring into view or recollection; as, to *call up* the image of a deceased friend; also, to bring into action, or discussion; as, to *call up* a bill before a legislative body.

To call over, to read a list, name by name; to recite separate particulars in order, as a roll of names.

To call out, to summon to fight; to challenge; also, to summon into service; as, to *call out* the militia.

To call to mind, to recollect; to revive in memory.

CALL, *v. i.* To utter a loud sound, or to address by name; to utter the name; sometimes with *to*.

The angel of God *called to* Hagar. Gen. xxi.

2. To stop, without intention of staying; to make a short stop; as, to *call* at the inn. This use Johnson supposes to have originated in the custom of denoting one's presence at the door by a *call*. It is common, in this phrase, to use *at*, as to *call at* the inn; or *on*, as to *call on* a friend. This application seems to be equivalent to *speak*, D. *kallen*. Let us *speak* at this place.

To call on, to make a short visit to; also, to solicit payment, or make a demand of a debt. In a *theological sense*, to pray to or worship; as, to *call on* the name of the Lord. Gen. iv. To repeat solemnly. *Dryden.*

To call out, to utter a loud voice; to bawl; *a popular use of the phrase.*

CALL, *n.* A vocal address, of summons or invitation; as, he will not come at a *call.*

2. Demand; requisition; public claim; as, listen to the *calls* of justice or humanity.
3. Divine vocation, or summons; as the *call* of Abraham.
4. Invitation; request of a public body or society; as, a clergyman has a *call* to settle in the ministry.
5. A summons from heaven; impulse.

St. Paul believed he had a *call*, when he persecuted the christians. *Locke.*

6. Authority; command. *Denham.*

7. A short visit; as, to make a *call*; to give one a *call;* that is, a speaking to; D. *kallen.* To give one a call, is to stop a moment and speak or say a word; or to have a short conversation with.

8. Vocation; employment. In this sense *calling* is generally used.

9. A naming; a nomination. *Bacon.*

10. Among *hunters*, a lesson blown on the horn, to comfort the hounds. *Encyc.*

11. Among *seamen*, a whistle or pipe, used by the boatswain and his mate, to summon the sailors to their duty. *Encyc.*

12. The English name of the mineral called by the Germans tungsten or wolfram. *Encyc.*

13. Among *fowlers*, the noise or cry of a fowl, or a pipe to call birds by imitating their voice. *Encyc. Bailey.*

14. In *legislative bodies*, the *call of the house*, is a calling over the names of the members, to discover who is absent or for other purpose; a calling of names with a view to obtain answers from the persons named.

CALL'ED, *pp.* Invited; summoned; addressed; named; appointed; invoked; assembled by order; recited.

CALL'ER, *n.* One who calls.

CAL'LET, CAL'LAT, *n.* A trull, or a scold. [*Not used.*] *Shak.*

CAL'LET, *v. i.* To rail; to scold. [*Not in use.*]

CALL'ING, *ppr.* Inviting; summoning; naming; addressing; invoking.

CALL'ING, *n.* A naming, or inviting; a reading over or reciting in order, or a call of names with a view to obtain an answer, as in legislative bodies.

2. Vocation; profession; trade; usual occupation, or employment. *Pope. Swift.* 1 Cor. vii. 20.

3. Class of persons engaged in any profession or employment. *Hammond.*

4. Divine summons, vocation, or invitation.

Give all diligence to make your *calling* and election sure. 2 Pet. i.

CAL'LIOPE, *n.* *cal'liopy.* In Pagan mythology, the muse that presides over eloquence and heroic poetry.

CAL'LIPERS. [See *Caliber.*]

CALLOS'ITY, *n.* [Fr. *callosité;* L. *callositas.* See *Callous.*]

Hardness, or bony hardness; the hardness of the cicatrix of ulcers. *Coxe.*

CAL'LOUS, *a.* [L. *callus*, hardness; *calleo*, to be hard, to know or be skilled; Eng. *could*, which see.]

1. Hard; hardened; indurated; as an ulcer or some part of the body. *Wiseman.*

2. Hardened in mind; insensible; unfeeling. *Dryden.*

CAL'LOUSLY, *adv.* In a hardened or unfeeling manner.

CAL'LOUSNESS, *n.* Hardness, induration, applied to the body; insensibility, applied to the mind or heart. *Cheyne. Bentley.*

CAL'LOW, *a.* [Ir. *calbh;* L. *calvus*, bald; G. *kahl;* D. *kaal;* Fr. *chauve;* Pers. كَلْ kal; Russ. *golei*, bald, naked; *goleyu*, to be stripped.]

Destitute of feathers; naked; unfledged; as a young bird. *Milton.*

CAL'LUS, *n.* [L. *callus*, from *calleo*, to be hard; Sans. *kalla*, stone.]

Any cutaneous, corneous, or bony hardness, but generally the new growth of osseous matter between the extremities of fractured bones, serving to unite them; also, a hardness in the skin; a hard, dense, insensible knob on the hands, feet, &c. *Encyc. Coxe.*

C'ALM, *a.* *càm.* [Fr. *calme;* Sp. *calma;* It. *calma;* D. *kalm.* Qu. Gr. χαλαω; It. *calare*, to decrease or abate; Sp. *calar*, to sink.]

1. Still; quiet; being at rest; as the air. Hence not stormy or tempestuous; as a *calm* day.

2. Undisturbed; not agitated; as a *calm* sea.

3. Undisturbed by passion; not agitated or excited; quiet; tranquil; as the mind, temper, or attention.

C'ALM, *n.* Stillness; tranquillity; quiet; freedom from motion, agitation, or disturbance; *applied to the elements, or to the mind and passions.* *South.*

C'ALM, *v. t.* To still; to quiet; as the wind, or elements; to still, appease, allay or pacify, as the mind, or passions. *Dryden. Atterbury.*

C'ALMER, *n.* The person or thing that calms, or has the power to still, and make quiet; that which allays or pacifies.

C'ALMING, *ppr.* Stilling; appeasing.

C'ALMLY, *adv.* In a quiet manner; without disturbance, agitation, tumult, or violence; without passion; quietly.

C'ALMNESS, *n.* Quietness; stillness; tranquillity; *applied to the elements.*

2. Quietness; mildness; unruffled state; *applied to the mind, passions or temper.*

C'ALMY, *a.* Calm; quiet; peaceable. *Spenser. Cowley.*

CAL'OMEL, *n.* [Qu. Gr. χαλος, fair, and μελας, black, or Æthiops mineral.]

A preparation of mercury, much used in medicine. It is called the submuriate or protochloride of mercury, and is prepared in various ways, by sublimation or precipitation, and also in the dry way. The following are the directions given in the last *London Pharmacopœia.* Take of muriated quicksilver one pound, and of purified quicksilver, nine ounces; rub them together till the globules disappear; then sublime, and repeat the sublimation twice more successively. *Webster.*

CALOR'IC, *n.* [L. *calor*, heat.] The principle or matter of heat, or the simple element of heat. *Lavoisier.*

Caloric may be defined, the agent to which the phenomena of heat and combustion are ascribed. *Ure.*

Caloric expands all bodies. *Henry.*

CALOR'IC, *a.* Pertaining to the matter of heat.

CALORIF'IC, *a.* That has the quality of producing heat; causing heat; heating.

CALORIM'ETER, *n.* [L. *calor*, heat, and Gr. μετρον, measure.]

An apparatus for measuring relative quantities of heat, or the specific caloric of bodies; or an instrument for measuring the heat given out by a body in cooling, from the quantity of ice it melts, invented by *Lavoisier* and *Laplace.*

CAL'ORIMOTOR, *n.* [*caloric* and L. *motor*, mover.]

A galvanic instrument, in which the calorific influence or effects are attended by scarcely any electrical power. *Hare.*

CALO'TTE, CALO'TE, *n.* [Fr. *calotte.*] A cap or coif, of hair, satin or other stuff, worn in popish countries, as an ecclesiastical ornament.

2. In *architecture*, a round cavity or depression, in form of a cup or cap, lathed and plastered, used to diminish the elevation of a chapel, cabinet, alcove, &c., which would otherwise be too high for other pieces of the apartment. *Harris. Encyc.*

CALOY'ERS, or CALOGERI, *n.* Monks of the Greek church, of three orders; *archari*, or novices; ordinary professed, or *microchemi;* and the more perfect, called *megalochemi.* They are also divided into *cenobites*, who are employed in reciting their offices, from midnight to sunrise; *anchorets*, who retire and live in hermitages; and *recluses*, who shut themselves up in grottos and caverns, on the mountains, and live on alms furnished to them by the monasteries. *Encyc.*

CALP, *n.* A subspecies of carbonate of lime, of a bluish black, gray or grayish blue, but its streak is white, called also argillo-ferruginous limestone. It is intermediate between compact limestone and marl. *Kirwan. Cleaveland. Phillips.*

CAL'TROP, *n.* [Sax. *coltrœppe*, a species of thistle, rendered by Lye, *rhamnus*, and *carduus stellatus.* The French has *chaussetrape.* The Italian *calcatreppolo* is from *calcare*, to tread, and *tribolo*, a thistle; L. *tribulus.*]

1. A kind of thistle, the Latin *tribulus*, with a roundish prickly pericarp; on one side, gibbous, often armed with three or four daggers; on the other side, angular, converging with transverse cells. It grows in France, Italy and Spain, among corn, and is very troublesome, as the prickles run into the feet of cattle. *Fam. of Plants. Miller.*

2. In *military affairs*, an instrument with four iron points, disposed in a triangular form, so that three of them being on the ground, the other points upward. These are scattered on the ground where an enemy's cavalry are to pass, to impede their progress by endangering the horses' feet. *Encyc. Dr. Addison.*

CAL'UMET, *n.* Among the *aboriginals of America*, a pipe, used for smoking tobacco, whose bowl is usually of soft red marble, and the tube a long reed, ornamented with feathers. The calumet is used as a symbol or instrument of peace and war. To accept the calumet, is to agree to the terms of peace, and to refuse it, is to reject them. The calumet of peace is used to seal or ratify contracts and alliances, to receive strangers kindly, and to travel with safety. The calumet of war, differently made, is used to proclaim war.

CALUM'NIATE, *v. t.* [See *Calumny.*] To accuse or charge one falsely, and knowingly, with some crime, offense, or something disreputable; to slander.

CALUM'NIATE, *v. i.* To charge falsely and knowingly with a crime or offense; to propagate evil reports with a design to injure the reputation of another.

CALUM'NIATED, *pp.* Slandered; falsely and maliciously accused of what is criminal, immoral, or disgraceful.

CALUM'NIATING, *ppr.* Slandering.

CALUMNIA'TION, *n.* False accusation of a crime or offense, or a malicious and false representation of the words or actions of another, with a view to injure his good name.

CALUM'NIATOR, *n.* One who slanders; one who falsely and knowingly accuses another of a crime or offense, or maliciously propagates false accusations or reports.

CALUM'NIATORY, *a.* Slanderous. *Montagu.*

CALUM'NIOUS, *a.* Slanderous; bearing or implying calumny; injurious to reputation.

CALUM'NIOUSLY, *adv.* Slanderously.

CALUM'NIOUSNESS, *n.* Slanderousness. *Bp. Morton.*

CAL'UMNY, *n.* [L. *calumnia*; Fr. *calomnie*; It. *calunnia*. If *m* is radical, this word may be allied to *calamity*, both from the sense of falling upon, rushing, or throwing on. If *m* is not radical, this word may be the Gothic *holon*, to calumniate, Saxon *holan*, to rush upon. The word is found in Ir. *guilimne*, calumny, *guilimnighim*, to calumniate or reproach].

Slander; false accusation of a crime or offense, knowingly or maliciously made or reported, to the injury of another; false representation of facts reproachful to another, made by design, and with knowledge of its falsehood; sometimes followed by *on*.

Neglected *calumny* soon expires. *Murphy's Tacitus.*

CAL'VARY, *n.* [L. *calvaria*, from *calva*, a skull or scalp; Ir. *calb*, the head; Sp. *calvario*, *calva*; It. *calvo*.]

1. A place of skulls; particularly, the place where Christ was crucified, on a small hill west of Jerusalem. In *catholic countries*, a kind of chapel raised on a hillock near a city, as a place of devotion, in memory of the place where our Savior suffered.

2. In *heraldry*, a cross so called, set upon steps, resembling the cross on which our Saviour was crucified.

C'ALVE, *v. i.* *càv.* [from *calf*; Sax. *calfian*.] To bring forth young, as a cow.

2. In *a metaphorical sense, and sometimes by way of reproach, as when applied to the human race*, to bring forth; to produce.

C'ALVES-SNOUT, *n.* A plant, snap-dragon, antirrhinum.

CAL'VER, *v. t.* To cut in slices. [*Not in use.*] *B. Jonson.*

CAL'VER, *v. i.* To shrink by cutting, and not fall to pieces. [*Not in use.*] *Cotton.*

CAL'VILLE, *n.* [Fr.] A sort of apple.

CAL'VINISM, *n.* The theological tenets or doctrines of Calvin, who was born in Picardy in France, and in 1536, chosen professor of divinity, and minister of a church in Geneva. The distinguishing doctrines of this system are, original sin, particular election and reprobation, particular redemption, effectual grace in regeneration, or a change of heart by the spirit of God, justification by free grace, perseverance of the saints, and the trinity.

CAL'VINIST, *n.* A follower of Calvin; one who embraces the theological doctrines of Calvin.

CALVINIST'IC, **CALVINIST'ICAL**, *a.* Pertaining to Calvin, or to his opinions in theology.

C'ALVISH, *a.* [from *calf*.] Like a calf. [More properly, *calfish*.] *Sheldon.*

CALX, *n.* plu. *calxes* or *calces*. [L. *calx*; Sax. *cealc*, a stone, *calculus*, and *chalk*; D. *kalk*; G. *kalk*; Sw. *kalck*; Dan. *kalk*; Fr. *chaux*. The same word signifies *chalk*, lime, mortar, and the heel, and from that is formed *calculus*, a little stone. The word then signifies primarily, a lump, or clod, or hard mass, and is allied to *callus*. If *calx* is from χαλιξ, the usual orthography was not observed by the Latins. See *Calculate*.]

Properly lime or chalk; but more appropriately, the substance of a metal or mineral which remains after being subjected to violent heat, burning, or calcination, solution by acids, or detonation by niter, and which is or may be reduced to a fine powder. Metallic calxes are now called oxyds. They are heavier than the metal from which they are produced, being combined with oxygen. *Coxe. Encyc.*

Calx nativa, native calx, a kind of marly earth, of a dead whitish color, which, in water, bubbles or hisses, and without burning, will make a cement, like lime or *gypsum*.

Calx viva, quick-lime, is lime not slaked.

CALYC'INAL, **CAL'YCINE**, *a.* Pertaining to a calyx; situated on a calyx. *Martyn.*

CAL'YCLE, *n.* [L. *calyculus*. See *Calyx*.]

In *botany*, a row of small leaflets, at the base of the calyx, on the outside. The *calycle* of the seed is the outer proper covering or crown of the seed, adhering to it, to facilitate its dispersion. *Martyn.*

CALYC'ULATE or **CAL'YCLED**, *a.* Having a calycle at the base on the outside; used of the *calyx*.

CALYP'TER, *n.* [Gr. καλυπτηρ, a cover.]

The calyx of mosses, according to Linne; but not properly a calyx. It is a kind of vail, or cowl, which covers or is suspended over the tops of the stamens, like an extinguisher. *Milne.*

The *calyptra* of mosses is an appendage of the capsule or female flower. It at first closely invests the capsule, and its summit is the stigma. As the capsule approaches maturity, the *calyptra* is detached below, and appended to the stigma like a hood. *Cyc. Smith.*

CA'LYX, *n.* plu. *calyxes*. [L. *calyx*; Gr. καλυξ, a flower not opened, a husk or shell. It has been confounded with κυλιξ, calix, a cup.]

The outer covering of a flower, being the termination of the cortical epidermis or outer bark of the plant, which, in most plants, incloses and supports the bottom of the corol. In Linne's system, it comprehends the perianth, the involucrum, the ament, the spath, the glume, the calyptra, and the volva. But in general it signifies the perianth, and the leaves are generally green *Milne. Martyn. Encyc*

The opinion of Linne that the calyx is the continuation of the epidermis is now considered erroneous. *Ed. Encyc. Smith.*

CALZOONS', *n.* [Sp. *calzones*.] Drawers. [*Not English.*] *Herbert.*

CAM'BER, *n.* [Fr. *cambrer*, to arch, to vault, to bend, from L. *camera*, a vault, a chamber.]

Among *builders*, camber or camber-beam is a piece of timber cut archwise, or with an obtuse angle in the middle, used in platforms, where long and strong beams are required. As a verb, this word signifies to bend, but I know not that it is used.

A *cambered-deck*, is one which is higher in the middle, or arched, but drooping or declining towards the stem and stern; also, when it is irregular.

CAM'BERING, *ppr.* or *a.* Bending; arched; as, a deck lies *cambering*.

CAM'BIST, *n.* [It. *cambista*, from *cambio*, exchange; Sp. *id.*]

A banker; one who deals in notes, and bills of exchange. *Christ. Obs.*

CAMBRIC, *n.* A species of fine white linen, made of flax, said to be named from Cambray in Flanders, where it was first manufactured.

CAME, *pret.* of *come*, which see.

CAME, *n.* A slender rod of cast lead, of which glaziers make their turned lead. *Encyc.*

CAM'EL, *n.* [L. *camelus*; Gr. καμηλος; D. Dan. *kameel*; G. *kamel*; Heb. Syr. Eth. גמל; Ch. גמלא; Ar. جَمَلَ The Arabic verb, to which this word belongs, signifies to be beautiful or elegant, to please or to behave with kindness and humanity. In Sax. *gamele*, or *gamol*, is a camel, and an old man; *gamol-feax*, one that has long hair; *gamol-ferhth*, a man of a great mind. In W. the word is *cammarc*, a crooked horse.]

1. A large quadruped used in Asia and Africa for carrying burdens, and for riders. As a genus, the camel belongs to the order of Pecora. The characteristics are; it has no horns; it has six fore teeth in the under jaw; the canine teeth are wide set, three in the upper and two in the lower jaw; and there is a fissure in the upper lip. The dromedary or Arabian camel has one bunch on the back, four callous protuberances on the fore legs and two on the hind legs. The Bactrian camel has two bunches on the back. The Llama of South America is a smaller animal, with a smooth back, small head, fine black eyes, and very long neck. The Pacos or sheep of Chili has no bunch. Camels constitute the riches of an Arabian, without which he could neither subsist, carry on trade nor travel over sandy desarts. Their milk is his common food. By the camel's power of sustaining abstinence from drink, for many days, and of subsisting on a few coarse shrubs, he is peculiarly fitted for the parched and barren lands of Asia and Africa.

2. In Holland, Camel, [or Kameel, as Coxe writes it,] is a machine for lifting ships, and bearing them over the Pampus, at the mouth of the river Y, or over other bars. It is also used in other places, and particularly at the dock in Petersburg, to bear vessels over a bar to Cronstadt. *Coxe. Encyc.*

CAM'EL-BACKED, *a.* Having a back like a camel. *Fuller.*

Came'leon mineral. [See *Chameleon.*] A compound of pure potash and black oxyd of manganese, fused together, whose solution in water, at first green, passes spontaneously through the whole series of colored rays to the red; and by the addition of potash, it returns to its original green. *Ure.*

ЄAM'ELOPARD, *n.* [*camelus* and *pardalis.*] The giraff, a species constituting the genus *Camelopardalis.* This animal has two straight horns, without branches, six inches long, covered with hair, truncated at the end and tufted. On the forehead, is a tubercle, two inches high, resembling another horn. The fore legs are not much longer than the hind ones, but the shoulders are of such a vast length, as to render the fore part of the animal much higher than the hind part. The head is like that of a stag; the neck is slender and elegant, furnished with a short mane. The color of the whole animal is a dirty white marked with large broad rusty spots. This animal is found in the central and eastern parts of Africa. It is timid and not fleet. *Encyc.*

ЄAM'EO, ЄAMA'IEU, or **ЄAMAY'EU**, *n.* [It. *cammeo;* Fr. *camayeu;* Sp. and Port. *camafeo.*]

A peculiar sort of onyx; also, a stone on which are found various figures and representations of landscapes, a kind of lusus naturæ, exhibiting pictures without painting. The word is said to be the oriental *camehuia*, a name given to the onyx, when they find, in preparing it, another color; as who should say, another color.

The word is applied by others to those precious stones, onyxes, carnelians and agates, on which lapidaries employ their art, to aid nature and perfect the figures.

The word is also applied to any gem on which figures may be engraved.

The word signifies also a painting in which there is only one color, and where the lights and shadows are of gold, wrought on a golden or azure ground. When the ground is yellow, the French call it *cirage;* when gray, *grisaille.* This work is chiefly used to represent basso-relievos. These pieces answer to the *μονοχρωματα* of the Greeks. *Encyc. Chambers. Lunier.*

Camera obscura, or dark chamber, in optics, an apparatus representing an artificial eye, in which the images of external objects, received through a double convex glass, are exhibited distinctly, and in their native colors, on a white matter, placed within the machine, in the focus of the glass.

ЄAM'ERADE, *n.* [L. *camera*, a chamber.] One who lodges or resides in the same apartment; now *comrade*, which see.

ЄAMERALIS'TIЄ, *a.* [Infra.] Pertaining to finance and public revenue.

ЄAMERALIS'TIЄS, *n.* [G. *cameralist*, a financier. In Sp. *camarista*, is a minister of state; *camarilla*, a small room. The word seems to be from L. *camera*, a chamber.]

The science of finance or public revenue, comprehending the means of raising and disposing of it. *Grimke.*

ЄAM'ERATE, *v. t.* [L. *camero*, from *camera*, a chamber, properly an arched roof.] To vault; to ceil. [*Little used.*]

ЄAM'ERATED, *a.* [L. *cameratus*, from *camera.*] Arched; vaulted.

ЄAMERA'TION, *n.* An arching or vaulting.

ЄAM'IS, *n.* [It. *camice.*] A thin dress. [*Not English.*]

ЄAMISA'DE, *n.* [Fr. from *chemise*, a shirt; It. *camicia;* Sp. *camisa.*]

An attack by surprise, at night, or at break of day, when the enemy is supposed to be in bed. This word is said to have taken its rise from an attack of this kind, in which the soldiers, as a badge to distinguish each other by, bore a shirt over their arms. *Encyc.*

ЄAM'ISATED, *a.* Dressed with a shirt outwards. *Johnson.*

ЄAM'LET, *n.* [from *camel*, sometimes written *camelot.*]

A stuff originally made of camel's hair. It is now made, sometimes of wool, sometimes of silk, sometimes of hair, especially that of goats, with wool or silk. In some, the warp is silk and wool twisted together, and the woof is hair. The pure oriental camlet is made solely from the hair of a sort of goat, about Angora. Camlets are now made in Europe. *Encyc.*

ЄAM'LETED, *a.* Colored or veined. *Herbert.*

ЄAM'MOЄ, *n.* [Sax. *cammoc*, or *cammec.*] A plant, petty whin or rest-harrow, Ononis.

ЄAM'OMILE, *n.* [Fr. *camomille;* Arm. *cramamailh;* D. *kamille;* G. *id.;* Dan. *kameel-blomster;* L. *chamæmelon*, which seems to be the Gr. *χαμαι*, earth, and *μηλον*, an apple.]

A genus of plants, Anthemis, of many species. It has a chaffy receptacle; the calyx is hemispheric and subequal, and the florets of the ray are more than five. The common sort is a trailing perennial plant, has a strong aromatic smell, and a bitter nauseous taste. It is accounted carminative, aperient, and emollient.

ЄAM'OUS, ЄAMOYS', *a.* [Fr. *camus;* W. *cam*, crooked.]

Flat; depressed; *applied only to the nose*, and *little used.*]

ЄAM'OUSED, *a.* Depressed; crooked. *B. Jonson.*

ЄAM'OUSLY, *adv.* Awry. *Skelton.*

ЄAMP', *n.* [L. *campus;* Fr. *camp* and *champ;* Arm. *camp;* It. Sp. Port. *campo;* Sax. *camp.* The sense is, an open level field or plain. See *Champion* and *Game.*]

1. The ground on which an army pitch their tents, whether for a night or a longer time.

2. The order or arrangement of tents, or disposition of an army, for rest; as, to pitch a *camp.* Also, the troops encamped on the same field.

3. An army. *Hume.*

ЄAMP, *v. t.* or *i.* To rest or lodge, as an army, usually in tents; to pitch a camp; to fix tents; but seldom used. [See *Encamp.*]

ЄAMP'-FIGHT, *n.* In *law writers*, a trial by duel, or the legal combat of two champions, for the decision of a controversy. [*Camp* in W. is a game, and *campiaw* is to contend.]

ЄAMPA'IGN, ЄAMPA'IN, *n. campáne.* [Fr. *campagne;* It. *campagna;* Sp. *compaña;* Port. *campanha;* from *camp.* This should be written *campain*, as Mitford writes it.]

1. An open field; a large open plain; an extensive tract of ground without considerable hills. [See *Champaign.*]

2. The time that an army keeps the field, either in action, marches, or in camp, without entering into winter quarters. A campaign is usually from spring to autumn or winter; but in some instances, armies make a winter campaign.

ЄAMPA'IGN, *v. i.* To serve in a campaign. *Musgrave.*

ЄAMPA'IGNER, *n.* One who has served in an army several campaigns; an old soldier; a veteran.

ЄAMPA'NA, *n.* [L.] The pasque-flower.

ЄAMPAN'IFORM, *a.* [L. *campana*, a bell, and *forma*, form.]

In the shape of a bell; *applied to flowers.* *Botany.*

ЄAMPAN'ULA, *n.* [L.] The bell-flower.

ЄAMPAN'ULATE, *a.* [L. *campanula*, a little bell.] In the form of a bell. *Botany.*

ЄAMPE'ACHY-WOOD, from Campeachy in Mexico. [See *Logwood.*]

ЄAMPES'TRAL, ЄAMPES'TRIAN, *a.* [L. *campestris*, from *campus*, a field.]

Pertaining to an open field; growing in a field or open ground. *Mortimer.*

ЄAM'PHOR, *n.* properly *cafor.* [Low L. *camphora;* Fr. *camphre;* It. *canfora;* Sp. *alcanfor;* Port. *canfora;* D. and G. *kamfer;* Ar. كافور kafor, kaforon, from كفر kafara, Heb. Ch. Syr. כפר kafar, to drive off, remove, separate, wipe away; hence, to cleanse, to make atonement. It seems to be named from its purifying effects, or from exudation. It will be seen that the letter *m* in this word is casual.]

A solid concrete juice or exudation, from the laurus camphora, or Indian laurel-tree, a large tree growing wild in Borneo, Sumatra, &c. It is a whitish translucent substance, of a granular or foliated fracture, and somewhat unctuous to the feel. It has a bitterish aromatic taste, and a very fragrant smell, and is a powerful diaphoretic. *Encyc. Lunier. Aikin.*

ЄAM'PHOR, *v. t.* To impregnate or wash with camphor. [*Little used.*]

ЄAM'PHORATE, *n.* In *chimistry*, a compound of the acid of camphor, with different bases.

ЄAM'PHORATE, *a.* Pertaining to camphor, or impregnated with it.

ЄAM'PHORATED, *a.* Impregnated with camphor.

ЄAMPHOR'IЄ, *a.* Pertaining to camphor, or partaking of its qualities.

ЄAMPHOR-OIL. [See *Camphor-tree.*]

ЄAM'PHOR-TREE, *n.* The tree from which camphor is obtained. According to Miller, there are two sorts of trees that produce camphor; one, a native of Borneo, which produces the best species; the other, a native of Japan, which resembles the bay-tree, bearing black or purple berries. But the tree grows also in Sumatra. The stem is thick, the bark of a brownish color, and the ramification strong, close and extended. The wood is soft, easily worked, and useful for domestic purposes. To obtain camphor, the tree is cut down, and divided into pieces, and the camphor taken out; it being found in small whitish flakes, situated perpendicularly, in irregular veins, in and near the center of the tree. It is then repeatedly soaked and washed in soapy water, to separate from it all extraneous matter. It is then passed through three sieves of different texture, to divide it into three sorts, head, belly and foot camphor. Camphor oil is camphor, before the operations of nature have reduced it to a concrete form; and concrete camphor may be reduced to oil, by the nitric acid. *Asiat. Res.* iv. 1.

ȻAMPIL'LA, *n.* A plant of a new genus, used by dyers. *Asiat. Res.*

ȻAMP'ING, *ppr.* Encamping.

ȻAMP'ING, *n.* A playing at football. *Bryant.*

ȻAMP'ION, *n.* A plant, the popular name of the lychnis.

ȻAM'US, ȻAM'IS, } *n.* [L. *camisa.*] A thin dress. [*Not Eng.*] *Spenser.*

ȻAN, *n.* [D. *kan*; Sax. *canna*; G. *kanne*; Dan. *kande*; Sw. *kanna*; Corn. *hannath*; Sans. *kundha*; probably from holding, containing, W. *cannu* or *ganu*, to contain, *gan*, capacity, a mortise, Eng. *gain*, in carpentry. Hence W. *cant*, a circle, a hoop, a fence round a yard, a hundred, L. *centum*, Teut. *hund*, in hundred. See *Cent* and *Hundred*, and *Can*, infra.]

A cup or vessel for liquors, in modern times made of metal; as a *can* of ale.

ȻAN, *v. i.* pret. *could*, which is from another root. [See *Could.*] [*Can* is from the Sax. *cennan*, to know, to bear or produce; Goth. *kunnan*, Sax. *cunnan*, to know, to be able; *cunnian*, to try, to attempt, to prove; *cind*, *cyn*, *gecynd*, kind; L. *genus*; D. *kunnen*, to know, to understand, to hold, to contain, to be able, like the Fr. *savoir*; Dan. *kan*, to be able; *kiender*, to know; Sw. *känna*, to know; *kunna*, to be able; G. *kennen*, to know; *können*, to be able. Hence *cunning*, that is, knowing, skilful, experienced; G. *können*, a being able, ability, knowledge; *kund*, public; *kunde*, knowledge, *acquaintance*. The Teutonic and Gothic words unite with the Greek γενναω, to beget, as a male, and to bear, as a female, which is connected with γινομαι, to be born or produced. *Can*, *cennan*, and γενναω, are probably the same word; and the Sax. *ginnan*, in the compounds, *aginnan*, *beginnan*, *onginnan*, to *begin*, is from the same root. The primary sense is, to strain, to stretch, to urge or thrust with force, which gives the sense of producing, and of holding, containing, which is the primary sense of *knowing*, comprehending; and straining gives the sense of power. The Sax. *cunnian*, to try, is to *strain*. See *Ken*. Ar. كَانَ to be, the substantive verb; also, to become, to be made, to endure; also, to create, to generate, to form; يَقِنَ to know; Heb. and Ch. כון, to fit or prepare, to form or fashion; whence right, fit; as we have *right*, Sax. *reht*, L. *rectus*, from *rego*, to rule, that is, to strain, stretch, make straight; Syr. ܟܢ to *begin* to be, and its derivatives, to plant or establish, to create, to be prepared; Eth. ከወነ kun, to be, to become, to be made; Ch. Sam. as the Hebrew. See Class Gn. No. 29. 38. and 58. 42. 45. &c. *Can* in English is treated as an auxiliary verb, the sign of the infinitive being omitted, as in the phrases, *I can go*, instead of, *I can to go*; thou *canst* go; he *can* go.]

1. To be able; to have sufficient strength or physical power. One man *can* lift a weight which another *can* not. A horse *can* run a certain distance in a given time.

2. To have means, or instruments, which supply power or ability. A man *can* build a house, or fit out a ship, if he has the requisite property. A nation *cannot* prosecute a war, without money or credit. I will lend you a thousand dollars, if I *can*.

3. To be possible.

> Nicodemus said, How *can* these things be? John iii.

4. To have adequate moral power. A man *can* indulge in pleasure, or he *can* refrain. He *can* restrain his appetites, if he will.

5. To have just or legal competent power, that is, right; to be free from any restraint of moral, civil or political obligation, or from any positive prohibition. We *can* use a highway for travel, for this is permitted by law. A man *can* or *cannot* hold an office. The Jews *could* not eat certain kinds of animals which were declared to be unclean. The House of Commons in England *can* impeach, but the House of Lords only *can* try impeachments. In general, we *can* do whatever neither the laws of God nor of man forbid.

> How *can* I do this great wickedness and sin against God. Gen. xxxix.
>
> I *cannot* go beyond the word of the Lord, my God, to do less or more. Numb. xxii.

6. To have natural strength, or capacity; to be susceptible of; to be able or free to undergo any change, or produce any effect, by the laws and constitution of nature, or by divine appointment. Silver *can* be melted, but *cannot* be changed into gold.

> *Can* the rush grow without mire? Job viii.
> *Can* the fig tree bear olive berries? James iii.
> *Can* faith save him? James ii.

7. To have competent strength, ability, fortitude, patience, &c., in a passive sense. He *cannot* bear reproof. I *cannot* endure this impertinence.

> This is a hard saying; who *can* hear it? John vi.

8. To have the requisite knowledge, experience or skill. Young men are not admitted members of college, till they *can* translate Latin and Greek. An astronomer *can* calculate an eclipse, though he *can* not make a coat.

9. To have strength of inclination or motives sufficient to overcome obstacles, impediments, inconvenience or other objection.

> I have married a wife, and therefore I *cannot* come. Luke xiv.
>
> I *cannot* rise and give thee—yet because of his importunity, he will rise and give him. Luke xi.

10. To have sufficient capacity; as, a vessel *can* not hold or contain the whole quantity.

ȻAN, *v. t.* To know. [*Not in use.*] *Spenser.*

ȻAN'-BUOY, *n.* In *seamanship*, a buoy in form of a cone, made large, and sometimes painted, as a mark to designate shoals, &c. *Mar. Dict.*

ȻAN'-HOOK, *n.* An instrument to sling a cask by the ends of its staves, formed by reeving a piece of rope through two flat hooks, and splicing its ends together. *Mar. Dict.*

ȻANA'DIAN, *a.* Pertaining to Canada, an extensive country on the north of the United States.

ȻANA'DIAN, *n.* An inhabitant or native of Canada.

ȻANA'IL, *n.* [Fr. *canaille*; Sp. *canalla*; Port. *canalha*; It. *canaglia.*]

The coarser part of meal; hence, the lowest people; lees; dregs; offscouring.

ȻAN'AKIN, *n.* A little can or cup. *Shak.*

ȻANAL', *n.* [L. *canalis*, a *channel* or *kennel*; these being the same word differently written; Fr. *canal*; Arm. *can*, or *canol*; Sp. Port. *canal*; It. *canale*. See *Cane*. It denotes a passage, from shooting, or passing.]

1. A passage for water; a water course; properly, a long trench or excavation in the earth for conducting water, and confining it to narrow limits; but the term may be applied to other water courses. It is chiefly applied to artificial cuts or passages for water, used for transportation; whereas *channel* is applicable to a natural water course.

> The *canal* from the Hudson to Lake Erie is one of the noblest works of art.

2. In *anatomy*, a duct or passage in the body of an animal, through which any of the juices flow, or other substances pass; as the neck of the bladder, and the alimentary *canal*.

3. A surgical instrument; a splint. *Coxe.*

ȻANAL-COAL. [See *Cannel-coal.*]

ȻANALIȻ'ULATE, ȻANALIȻ'ULATED, } *a.* [L. *canaliculatus*, from *canaliculus*, a little pipe, from *canalis*, *canna*, a pipe.]

Channelled; furrowed. In *botany*, having a deep longitudinal groove above, and convex underneath; *applied to the stem, leaf, or petiole of plants.* *Martyn.*

ȻANA'RY, *n.* Wine made in the Canary isles.

2. An old dance. Shakspeare has used the word as a verb in a kind of cant phrase.

ȻANA'RY-BIRD, *n.* A singing bird from the Canary isles, a species of Fringilla. The bill is conical and straight; the body is yellowish white; the prime feathers of the wings and tail are greenish. These birds are now bred in other countries.

ȻANA'RY-GRASS, *n.* A plant, the Phalaris, whose seeds are collected for canary-birds.

ȻAN'CEL, *v. t.* [Fr. *canceller*; Port. *cancellar*; L. *cancello*, to deface, properly to make cross bars or lattice-work, hence to make cross lines on writing, from *cancelli*, cross bars or lattice-work; Gr. κιγκλις; Syr. Ch. קנקל kankel, id.]

1. To cross the lines of a writing, and deface them; to blot out or obliterate.

2. To annul, or destroy; as, to *cancel* an obligation or a debt.

ÇAN'CELATED, *a.* [L. *cancellatus*, *cancello.*] Cross-barred; marked with cross lines. *Grew. Martyn.*

ÇANCELA'TION, *n.* The act of defacing by cross lines; a canceling.

ÇAN'CELED, *pp.* Crossed; obliterated; annulled.

ÇAN'CELING, *ppr.* Crossing; obliterating; annulling.

ÇAN'CER, *n.* [L. *cancer;* Sax. *cancre;* Fr. *cancre;* D. *kanker;* Sp. *cangrejo, cancro;* It. *cancro, canchero;* Gr. *κογχη*. This seems to be the same word, though applied to the shell; *καρκινος*, a cancer, is a different word. From the Greek, the Latins have *concha*, Eng. *conch.* But *n* is not radical; for this is undoubtedly the W. *cocos*, Eng. *cockle*, Fr. *coquille, coque*, It. *coccia.* These words are probably from the same root as Sp. *cocar*, to wrinkle, twist, or make wry faces; Ir. *cuachaim*, to fold; Eng. *cockle*, to shrink or pucker; verbs which give the primary sense. It is to be noted that *cancer* and *canker* are the same word; *canker* being the original pronunciation.]

1. The crab or crab-fish. This genus of animals have generally eight legs, and two claws which serve as hands; two distant eyes, supported by a kind of peduncles, and they are elongated and movable. They have also two clawed palpi, and the tail is jointed. To this genus belong the lobster, shrimp, cray-fish, &c.

2. In *astronomy*, one of the twelve signs of the zodiac, represented by the form of a crab, and limiting the sun's course northward in summer; hence, the sign of the summer solstice.

3. In *medicine*, a roundish, hard, unequal, scirrous tumor of the glands, which usually ulcerates, is very painful, and generally fatal.

ÇAN'CERATE, *v. i.* To grow into a cancer; to become cancerous. *L'Estrange.*

ÇANCERA'TION, *n.* A growing cancerous, or into a cancer.

ÇAN'CEROUS, *a.* Like a cancer; having the qualities of a cancer. *Wiseman.*

ÇAN'CEROUSNESS, *n.* The state of being cancerous.

ÇAN'ÇRIFORM, *a.* Cancerous.

2. Having the form of a cancer or crab.

ÇAN'ÇRINE, *a.* Having the qualities of a crab.

ÇAN'ÇRITE, *n.* [from *cancer.*] A fossil or petrified crab. *Fourcroy.*

ÇAN'DENT, *a.* [L. *candens*, from *candeo*, to be white or hot. See the verb, to *cant.*]

Very hot; heated to whiteness; glowing with heat.

ÇAN'DIÇANT. *a.* Growing white. *Dict.*

ÇAN'DID, *a.* [L. *candidus*, white, from *candeo*, to be white; W. *canu*, to bleach. See *Cant.*] White. *Dryden.*

[*But in this sense rarely used.*]

2. Fair; open; frank; ingenuous; free from undue bias; disposed to think and judge according to truth and justice, or without partiality or prejudice; *applied to persons.*

3. Fair; just; impartial; *applied to things*; as a *candid* view, or construction.

ÇAN'DIDATE, *n.* [L. *candidatus*, from *candidus*, white; those who sought offices in Rome being obliged to wear a white gown.]

1. A man who seeks or aspires to an office; one who offers himself, or is proposed for preferment, by election or appointment; usually followed by *for;* as a *candidate for* the office of sheriff.

2. One who is in contemplation for an office, or for preferment, by those who have power to elect or appoint, though he does not offer himself.

3. One who, by his services or actions, will or may justly obtain preferment or reward, or whose conduct tends to secure it; as a *candidate* for praise.

4. A man who is qualified, according to the rules of the church, to preach the gospel, and take the charge of a parish or religious society, and proposes to settle in the ministry. *U. States.*

5. One who is in a state of trial or probation for a reward, in another life; as a *candidate* for heaven or for eternity.

ÇAN'DIDLY, *adv.* Openly; frankly; without trick or disguise; ingenuously.

ÇAN'DIDNESS, *n.* Openness of mind; frankness; fairness; ingenuousness.

ÇAN'DIED, *pp.* or *a.* [from *candy.*] Preserved with sugar, or incrusted with it; covered with crystals of sugar or ice, or with matter resembling them; as *candied* raisins.

ÇAN'DLE, *n.* [L. Sp. It. *candela;* Fr. *chandelle;* Sax. *candel;* Pers. *kandil;* Arm. *cantol;* W. *canwyll;* Ir. *cainneal*; from L. *candeo*, to shine, to be white, or its root. The primary sense of the root is, to shoot, to throw, to radiate. See *Cant* and *Chant.*]

1. A long, but small cylindrical body of tallow, wax or spermaceti, formed on a wick composed of linen or cotton threads, twisted loosely; used for a portable light of domestic use.

2. A light.

3. A light; a luminary. In scripture, the *candle of the Lord* is the divine favor and blessing, Job xxix. 3.; or the conscience or understanding. Prov. xx. 27.

Excommunication by inch of candle, is when the offender is allowed time to repent, while a candle burns, and is then excommunicated.

Sale by inch of candle, is an auction in which persons are allowed to bid, only till a small piece of candle burns out.

Medicated candle, in medicine, a bougie.

Rush-candles are used in some countries; they are made of the pith of certain *rushes*, peeled except on one side, and dipped in grease. *Encyc.*

ÇAN'DLE-BERRY TREE, *n.* The *Myrica cerifera*, or wax-bearing myrtle; a shrub common in North America, from the berries of which a kind of wax or oil is procured, of which candles are made. The oil is obtained by boiling the berries in water; the oil rising to the surface is skimmed off, and when cool, is of the consistence of wax, and of a dull green color. In popular language, this is called *bayberry tallow.*

ÇAN'DLE-BŎMB, *n.* A small glass bubble, filled with water, placed in the wick of a candle, where it bursts with a report.

ÇAN'DLE-HŌLDER, *n.* [*candle* and *hold.*] A person that holds a candle. Hence, one that remotely assists another, but is otherwise not of importance. *Shak.*

ÇAN'DLE-LIGHT, *n.* [*candle* and *light.*] The light of a candle; the necessary candles for use. *Molineux.*

ÇAN'DLEMAS, *n.* [*candle* and *mass*, Sax. *mæssa; candle-feast.*]

The feast of the church celebrated on the second day of February, in honor of the purification of the Virgin Mary; so called from the great number of lights used on that occasion. This feast is supposed to have originated in the declaration of Simeon, that our Savior was "to be a light to lighten the Gentiles." On this day, the Catholics consecrate all the candles and tapers which are to be used in their churches during the whole year. In Rome, the pope performs the ceremony himself, and distributes wax candles to the cardinals and others, who carry them in procession through the great hall of the pope's palace. The ceremony was prohibited in England by an order of council in 1548. But candlemas is one of the four terms for paying and receiving rents and interest; and it gives name to a law term, beginning Jan. 15, and ending Feb. 3. *Encyc.*

ÇAN'DLE-STICK, *n.* [*candle* and *stick;* Sax. *candel-sticca.*] An instrument or utensil to hold a candle, made in different forms and of different materials; originally a stick or piece of wood.

ÇAN'DLE-STUFF, *n.* [*candle* and *stuff.*] A material of which candles are made, as tallow, wax, &c. *Bacon.*

ÇAN'DLE-WASTER, *n.* [*candle* and *waste.*] One who wastes or consumes candles; a hard student, or one who studies by candle-light; a spendthrift. *B. Jonson. Shak.*

ÇAN'DLES-ENDS, *n.* Scraps; fragments. *Beaum.*

ÇAN'DOÇ, *n.* A plant or weed that grows in rivers. *Walton.*

ÇAN'DOR, *n.* [L. *candor*, from *candeo*, to be white.]

Openness of heart; frankness; ingenuousness of mind; a disposition to treat subjects with fairness; freedom from tricks or disguise; sincerity. *Watts.*

ÇAN'DY, *v. t.* [It. *candire*, to candy, to preserve; *candito*, candied; Fr. *candir.* This seems not to be the Latin *condio*, for the Italian has also *condire.* Possibly it may be from L. *candeo*, to be white. But in Ar. قَنْدٌ *kand, kandon*, is the saccharine matter of the sugar cane, or concrete sugar, and it is the same in Persian; Sans. *khand.*]

1. To conserve or dress with sugar; to boil in sugar.

2. To form into congelations or crystals. *Shak.*

3. To cover or incrust with congelations, or crystals of ice. *Dryden.*

ÇAN'DY, *v. i.* To form into crystals, or become congealed; to take on the form of candied sugar.

ÇAN'DYING, *ppr.* Conserving with sugar.

ÇAN'DYING, *n.* The act of preserving

simples in substance, by boiling then in sugar. *Encyc.*

CAN'DY-TUFTS, *n.* A plant, the Iberis. *Fam. of Plants.*

2. A Cretan flower. *Tate.*

CANE, *n.* [L. *canna*; Gr. κάννα; Fr. *canne*; W. *cawn*; Sp. *caña*; Port. *cana* or *canna*; It. *canna*; Arm. *canen*; Heb. Ch. Syr. Ar. קנה. In the Arabic, a word of this family signifies a subterraneous passage for water, or canal. It probably signifies a shoot.]

1. In *botany*, this term is applied to several species of plants belonging to different genera, such as Arundo, Calamus, Saccharum, &c. Among these is the *bamboo* of the East Indies, with a strong stem, which serves for pipes, poles, and walking sticks. The sugar cane, a native of Asia, Africa and America, furnishes the juice from which are made, sugar, melasses and spirit. [See *Sugar Cane.*]

2. A walking stick.

3. A lance, or dart made of cane. *Dryden.*

4. A long measure, in several countries of Europe; at Naples, the length is 7 feet 3¼ inches; in Thoulouse in France, 5 feet 8½ inches; in Provence, &c., 6 feet 5¼ inches.

CANE, *v. t.* To beat with a cane or walking stick.

CA'NE-BRAKE, *n.* [*cane* and *brake.*] A thicket of canes. *Ellicott.*

CA'NE-HOLE, *n.* [*cane* and *hole.*] A hole or trench for planting the cuttings of cane, on sugar plantations. *Edwards' W. Indies.*

CA'NE-TRASH, *n.* [*cane* and *trash.*] Refuse of canes, or macerated rinds of cane, reserved for fuel to boil the cane-juice. *Edwards' W. Indies*

CANES'CENT, *a.* [L. *canescens.*] Growing white or hoary.

CANIC'ULA, } *n.*
CA'NICULE, } [L. *canicula*, a little dog, from *canis*, a dog.]

A star in the constellation of Canis Major, called also the dog-star, or Sirius; a star of the first magnitude, and the largest and brightest of all the fixed stars. From the rising of this heliacally, or at its emersion from the sun's rays, the ancients reckoned their *dog-days.*

CANIC'ULAR, *a.* [L. *canicularis.*] Pertaining to the dog-star.

CANINE, *a.* [L. *caninus*, from *canis*, a dog.] Pertaining to dogs; having the properties or qualities of a dog; as a *canine* appetite, insatiable hunger; *canine* madness, or hydrophobia.

Canine teeth are two sharp pointed teeth in each jaw of an animal, one on each side, between the incisors and grinders; so named from their resemblance to a dog's teeth.

CA'NING, *n.* A beating with a stick or cane.

CAN'ISTER, *n.* [L. *canistrum*; Gr. κανασρον, κανης or κανεον; Fr. *canastre*; Port. *canastra*; Sp. *canasta.*]

Properly, a small basket, as in Dryden; but more generally, a small box or case, for tea, coffee, &c.

CANK'ER, *n.* [L. *cancer*; Sax. *cancere* or *cancre*; D. *kanker*; Fr. *chancre*; It. *canchero.* This is the Latin *cancer*, with the Roman pronunciation. See *Cancer.*]

1. A disease incident to trees, which causes the bark to rot and fall.

2. A popular name of certain small eroding ulcers in the mouth, particularly of children. They are generally covered with a whitish slough. *Cyc.*

3. A virulent, corroding ulcer; or any thing that corrodes, corrupts or destroys.

> Sacrilege may prove an eating *canker.* *Atterbury.*
>
> And their word will eat as doth a *canker.* 2 Tim. ii.

4. An eating, corroding, virulent humor; corrosion. *Shak.*

5. A kind of rose, the dog rose. *Peacham. Shak.*

6. In *farriery*, a running thrush of the worst kind; a disease in horses' feet, discharging a fetid matter from the cleft in the middle of the frog. *Encyc.*

CANK'ER, *v. t.* To eat, corrode, corrupt, consume, in the manner that a cancer affects the body. *Herbert.*

2. To infect or pollute. *Addison.*

CANK'ER, *v. i.* To grow corrupt; to decay, or waste away by means of any noxious cause; to grow rusty, or to be oxydized, as a metal. *Bacon.*

CANK'ERBIT, *a.* Bitten with a cankered or envenomed tooth. *Shak.*

CANK'ERED, *pp.* Corrupted.

2. *a.* Crabbed; uncivil. *Spenser.*

CANK'EREDLY, *adv.* Crossly; adversely.

CANK'ER-FLY, *n.* A fly that preys on fruit. *Walton.*

CANK'ER-LIKE, *a.* Eating or corrupting like a canker.

CANK'EROUS, *a.* Corroding like a canker. *Thomson.*

CANK'ER-WŎRM, *n.* A worm, destructive to trees or plants. In *America*, this name is given to a worm that, in some years, destroys the leaves and fruit of apple trees. This animal springs from an egg deposited by a miller, that issues from the ground.

CANK'ERY, *a.* Rusty.

CAN'NABINE, *a.* [L. *cannabinus*, from *cannabis*, hemp.] Pertaining to hemp; hempen.

CAN'NEL-CŌAL, **CAN'DLE-CŌAL**, *n.* A hard, opake, inflammable fossil coal of a black color, sufficiently solid to be cut and polished. On fire it decrepitates and breaks into angular fragments. It is sometimes used for inkholders and toys. *Cleaveland.*

CAN'NEQUIN, *n.* White cotton cloth from the East Indies, suitable for the Guinea trade. *Encyc.*

CAN'NIBAL, *n.* A human being that eats human flesh; a man-eater, or anthropophagite. *Bacon. Bentley.*

CAN'NIBALISM, *n.* The act or practice of eating human flesh, by mankind.

2. Murderous cruelty; barbarity. *Burke.*

CAN'NIBALLY, *adv.* In the manner of a cannibal. *Shak.*

CAN'NON, *n.* [Fr. *canon*; Arm. *canon* or *canol*; D. *kanon*; G. *kanone*; Sp. *cañon*; Port. *canham*; It. *cannone.* Probably from L. *canna*, a tube. See *Cane.*]

A large military engine for throwing balls, and other instruments of death, by the force of gunpowder. Guns of this kind are made of iron or brass and of different sizes, carrying balls from three or four pounds, to forty eight pounds weight. In some countries, they have been made of much larger size. The smaller guns of this kind are called field pieces.

CANNONA'DE, *n.* The act of discharging cannon and throwing balls, for the purpose of destroying an army, or battering a town, ship or fort. The term usually implies an attack of some continuance.

CANNONA'DE, *v. t.* To attack with heavy artillery; to throw balls, or other deadly weapons, as chain-shot or langrage, against an enemy's army, town, fortress or ship; to batter with cannon shot.

CANNONA'DE, *v. i.* To discharge cannon; to play with large guns.

CAN'NON-BALL, *n.* A ball, usually made of cast iron, to be thrown from cannon. *Cannon bullet*, of the like signification, is not now used. Cannon balls were originally of stone.

CANNONEE'R, } *n.*
CANNONIE'R, } A man who manages cannon; an engineer.

CAN'NON-PROOF, *a.* Proof against cannon shot.

CAN'NON-SHOT, *n.* A ball for cannon; also, the range or distance a cannon will throw a ball.

CANNOT, [*can* and *not.*] These words are usually united, but perhaps without good reason; *canst* and *not* are never united.

CAN'NULAR, *a.* [L. *canna*, a tube.] Tubular; having the form of a tube. *Encyc.*

CANŎE, *n.* *canoo'.* [Fr. *canot*; Sp. *canoa*; It. *canoe* or *canon*; from L. *canna*, a tube or cane, or the same root.]

1. A boat used by rude nations, formed of the body or trunk of a tree, excavated, by cutting or burning, into a suitable shape. Similar boats are now used by civilized men, for fishing and other purposes. It is impelled by a paddle, instead of an oar.

2. A boat made of bark or skins, used by savages.

CAN'ON, *n.* [Sax. Fr. Sp. Port. *canon*; It. *canone*; L. *canon*; Gr. κανων. Dr. Owen deduces the word from the Heb. קנה a cane, reed or measuring rod. In Eth. ቀነነ kanan, signifies to set, to establish, to form a rule, whence canon, a rule. But this verb is probably from the noun. The word is from one of the roots in Class Gn, which signifies to set, or to strain. The Welsh unites it with the root of *can*, L. *cano*, to sing, W. *canon*, a song, a rule, a canon, from *canu* to sing, L. *cano.* The sense of *canon* is that which is set or established.]

1. In *ecclesiastical affairs*, a law, or rule of doctrine or discipline, enacted by a council and confirmed by the sovereign; a decision of matters in religion, or a regulation of policy or discipline, by a general or provincial council.

2. A law or rule in general.

3. The genuine books of the Holy Scriptures, called the sacred *canon*, or general rule of moral and religious duty, given by inspiration.

4. A dignitary of the church; a person who possesses a prebend or revenue allotted for the performance of divine service in a cathedral or collegiate church.

A *cardinal canon* is one attached to a church, *incardinatus*, as a priest to a parish.

Domicellary canons, are young canons,

not in orders, having no right in any particular chapters.

Expectative canons, having no revenue or prebend, but having the title and dignities of canons, a voice in the chapter and a place in the choir, till a prebend should fall.

Foreign canons, such as did not officiate in their canonries; opposed to mansionary or residentiary canons.

Lay, secular or *honorary canons*, laymen admitted out of honor or respect, into some chapter of canons.

Regular canons, who live in monasteries or in community, and who, to the practice of their rules, have added the profession of vows.

Tertiary canons, who have only the third part of the revenue of the canonicate. *Encyc.*

5. In *monasteries*, a book containing the rules of the order.
6. A catalogue of saints acknowledged and canonized in the Romish Church.
7. The secret words of the mass from the preface to the Pater, in the middle of which the priest consecrates the host. The people are to rehearse this part of the service, on their knees, and in a voice lower than can be heard. *Romish Church.*
8. In *ancient music*, a rule or method for determining the intervals of notes, invented by Ptolemy. *Encyc.*
9. In *modern music*, a kind of perpetual fugue, in which the different parts, beginning one after another, repeat incessantly the same air. *Busby.*
10. In *geometry* and *algebra*, a general rule for the solution of cases of a like nature with the present inquiry. Every last step of an equation is a canon.
11. In *pharmacy*, a rule for compounding medicines.
12. In *surgery*, an instrument used in sewing up wounds.

Canon-law, is a collection of ecclesiastical laws, serving as the rule of church government.

ЄAN'ON-BIT, *n.* That part of a bit let into a horse's mouth.

ЄAN'ONESS, *n.* A woman who enjoys a prebend, affixed, by the foundation, to maids, without obliging them to make any vows or renounce the world. *Encyc.*

ЄANON'IЄAL, *a.* [L. *canonicus.*] Pertaining to a canon; according to the canon or rule.

Canonical books or *canonical scriptures*, are those books of the scriptures which are admitted by the canons of the church, to be of divine origin. The Roman catholic church admits the Apocryphal books to be canonical; the Protestants reject them.

Canonical hours, are certain stated times of the day, fixed by the ecclesiastical laws, or appropriated to the offices of prayer and devotion. In Great Britain, these hours are from eight o'clock to twelve in the forenoon, before and after which marriage cannot be legally performed in the church. *Encyc.*

Canonical obedience, is submission to the canons of a church, especially the submission of the inferior clergy to their bishops. and other religious orders to their superiors.

Canonical punishments, are such as the church may inflict, as excommunication, degradation, penance, &c.

Canonical life, is the method or rule of living prescribed by the ancient clergy who lived in community, a course of living prescribed for clerks, less rigid than the monastic and more restrained than the secular.

Canonical sins, in the ancient church, were those for which capital punishment was inflicted; as idolatry, murder, adultery, heresy, &c.

Canonical letters, anciently, were letters which passed between the orthodox clergy, as testimonials of their faith, to keep up the catholic communion, and to distinguish them from heretics.

Canonical epistles, is an appellation given to those epistles of the New Testament which are called general or catholic. *Encyc.*

ЄANON'IЄALLY, *adv.* In a manner agreeable to the canon.

ЄANON'IЄALNESS, *n.* The quality of being canonical.

ЄANON'IЄALS, *n. plu.* The full dress of the clergy, worn when they officiate.

ЄANON'IЄATE, *n.* The office of a canon. *Encyc.*

ЄAN'ONIST, *n.* A professor of canon law; one skilled in the study and practice of ecclesiastical law.

ЄANONIS'TIЄ, *a.* Having the knowledge of a canonist.

ЄANONIZA'TION, *n.* [See *Canonize.*] The act of declaring a man a saint, or rather the act of ranking a deceased person in the catalogue of saints, called a canon. This act is preceded by beatification, and by an examination into the life and miracles of the person; after which the Pope decrees the canonization. *Addison. Encyc.*

2. The state of being sainted.

ЄAN'ONIZE, *v. t.* [from *canon.*] To declare a man a saint and rank him in the catalogue, called a canon.

ЄAN'ONRY, ЄAN'ONSHIP, } *n.* An ecclesiastical benefice, in a cathedral or collegiate church, which has a prebend or stated allowance out of the revenues of the church commonly annexed to it. The benifice filled by a canon. A prebend may subsist without a canonry; but a canonicate is inseparable from a prebend. *Ayliffe. Encyc.*

ЄAN'OPIED, *a.* [See *Canopy.*] Covered with a canopy. *Milton.*

ЄAN'OPY, *n.* [Gr. κωνωπειον, a pavilion or net spread over a bed to keep off gnats, from κωνωψ, a gnat.]

1. A covering over a throne, or over a bed; more generally, a covering over the head. So the sky is called a *canopy*, and a canopy is borne over the head in processions.
2. In *architecture* and *sculpture*, a magnificent decoration serving to cover and crown an altar, throne, tribunal, pulpit, chair or the like. *Encyc.*

ЄAN'OPY, *v. t.* To cover with a canopy. *Dryden.*

ЄANO'ROUS, *a.* [L. *canorus*, from *cano*, to sing.] Musical; tuneful. *Brown.*

ЄANO'ROUSNESS, *n.* Musicalness.

ЄANT, *v. t.* [L. *canto*, to sing; Sp. *cantar*, Port. *id.*, to sing, to chant, to recite, to creak, to chirp, to whistle; It. *cantare*, to sing, to praise, to crow; Fr. *chanter*; Arm. *cana*; from L. *cano*, to sing. The primary sense is to throw, thrust or drive, as in *can*; a sense retained in the phrase, to *cant* over any thing. In singing, it implies a modulation or inflexion of voice. In Welsh, *can*, with a different sound of the vowel, signifies a song and white, L. *cano*, *canus*, and *caneo*. These are from the same root and have the same radical sense, to throw or shoot as rays of light, to shine, probably applied to the sun's morning rays. W. *canu*, to sing; Sanscrit, *gana*; Persic, *kandam.*]

1. In *popular usage*, to turn about, or to turn over, by a sudden push or thrust; as, to *cant* over a pail or a cask. *Mar. Dict.*
2. To toss; as, to *cant* a ball.
3. To speak with a whining voice, or an affected singing tone.

[*In this sense, it is usually intransitive.*]

4. To sell by auction, or to bid a price at auction. *Swift.*

ЄANT, *n.* A toss; a throw, thrust or push with a sudden jerk; as, to give a ball a *cant.* [*This is the literal sense.*]

2. A whining, singing manner of speech; a quaint, affected mode of uttering words either in conversation or preaching.
3. The whining speech of beggars, as in asking alms and making complaints of their distresses.
4. The peculiar words and phrases of professional men; phrases often repeated, or not well authorized.
5. Any barbarous jargon in speech.
6. Whining pretension to goodness. *Johnson.*
7. Outcry, at a public sale of goods; a call for bidders at an auction. *Swift.*

This use of the word is precisely equivalent to *auction*, auctio, a *hawking*, a crying out, or in the vulgar dialect, a singing out, but I believe not in use in the U. States.

ЄANT, *n.* [D. *kant*, a corner.] A nich; a corner or retired place. *B. Jonson.*

Cant-timbers, in a ship, are those which are situated at the two ends. *Mar. Dict.*

ЄANTA'BRIAN, *a.* Pertaining to Cantabria, on the Bay of Biscay, in Spain.

ЄAN'TALIVER, *n.* [*cantle* and *eaves.*] In *architecture*, a piece of wood, framed into the front or side of a house, to suspend the moldings and eaves over it. *Encyc.*

ЄAN'TAR, ЄAN'TARO, } *n.* An eastern weight; at Acra in Turkey, 603 pounds; at Tunis and Tripoli, 114 pounds. In Egypt, it consists of 100 or 150 rotolos; at Naples, it is 25 pounds; at Genoa, 150; at Leghorn, 150, 151, or 160. *Encyc.*

At Alicant in Spain, the cantaro is a liquid measure of 3 gallons. In Cochin, a measure of capacity, of 4 rubies; the rubi, 32 rotolos.

ЄANTA'TA, *n.* [Italian, from *cantare*, to sing; L. *canto.*]

A poem set to music; a composition or song, intermixed with recitatives and airs, chiefly intended for a single voice.

CANTA'TION, *a.* A singing. [*Not used.*]

ЄANTEE'N, *n.* [It. *cantina.*] A tin vessel used by soldiers for carrying liquor for drink. *Chambers.*

CAN'TELEUP, *n.* A variety of muskmelon.

CANT'ER, *v. i.* [Arm. *cantreal* or *cantren*, to run, to rove or ramble, from tossing or leaping, *canting*. See *Cant.*]
To move as a horse in a moderate gallop, raising the two fore feet nearly at the same time, with a leap or spring.

CANT'ER, *v. t.* To ride upon a canter.

CANT'ER, *n.* A moderate gallop.
2. One who cants or whines.

CANTERBURY BELL, *n.* A species of Campanula. [See *Bell-Flower.*]

CANTERBURY TALE, *n.* A fabulous story; so called from the tales of Chaucer.

CANT'ERING, *ppr.* Moving or riding with a slow gallop.

CANTHAR'IDIN, *n.* [Infra.] That peculiar substance existing in the Meloe vesicatorius, or cantharides, which causes vesication. *Thomson.*

CANTHA'RIS or *plu.* **CANTHAR'IDES**, *n.* [Gr. κανθαρις.] Spanish flies; a species of Meloe. This fly is nine or ten lines in length, of a shining green color, mixed with azure, and has a nauseous smell. It feeds upon the leaves of trees and shrubs, preferring the ash. These flies, when bruised, are universally used as a vesicatory, or blistering plaster. The largest come from Italy, but the best from Spain.

CANTH'US, *n.* [Gr. κανθος; D. *kant*, a corner.]
An angle of the eye; a cavity at the extremities of the eyelids; the greater is next to the nose; the lesser, near the temple. *Encyc.*

CAN'TICLE, *n.* [Sp. and It. *cantico*; L. *canticum*, from *canto*. See *Cant.*]
1. A song. In the plural, *canticles*, the Song of Songs or Song of Solomon, one of the books of the Old Testament.
2. A canto; a division of a song. *Obs.* *Spenser.*

CAN'TILLATE, *v. t.* [L. *cantillo*. See *Cant.*] To chant; to recite with musical tones. *M. Stuart.*

CANTILLA'TION, *n.* A chanting; recitation with musical modulations.

CANT'ING, *ppr.* Throwing with a sudden jerk; tossing.
2. Speaking with a whine or song-like tone.

CANT'INGLY, *adv.* With a cant.

CAN'TION, *n.* A song or verses. [*Not used.*] *Spenser.*

CAN'TLE, *n.* [Arm. *chantell*; Fr. *chanteau*, whence *echantillon*; Eng. *scantling*.]
A fragment; a piece; a portion. *Obs.* *Shak.*

CAN'TLE, *v. t.* To cut into pieces; to cut out a piece. *Obs.* *Dryden.*

CANT'LET, *n.* A piece; a little corner; a fragment. *Dryden.*

CAN'TO, *n.* [It. *canto*, a song; L. *cantus*. See *Cant.*]
A part or division of a poem, answering to what in prose is called a book. In Italian, canto is a song, and it signifies also the treble part, first treble, or highest vocal part.

CAN'TON, *n.* [It. *cantone*, a corner-stone, and a canton; Sp. *canton*; Port. *canto*, a corner; Fr. *canton*, a corner, a part of a country, a district; Arm. *canton*; D. *kant*; G. *kante*; Dan. *kandt*, a corner, point, edge, border. The Welsh unites *canton* with *cant*, a hundred, L. *centum*, Sax. *hund*, for *cantrev* is a circuit or division of a country, from *cant*, a hundred.]
1. A small portion of land, or division of territory; originally, a portion of territory on a border; also, the inhabitants of a canton.
2. A small portion or district of territory, constituting a distinct state or government; as in Switzerland.
3. In *heraldry*, a corner of the shield.
4. A distinct part, or division; as the *cantons* of a painting or other representation. *Burnet.*

CAN'TON, *v. t.* [Sp. *acantonar.*] To divide into small parts or districts, as territory; to divide into distinct portions. *Locke. Addison.*
2. To allot separate quarters to each regiment of an army or body of troops. *Marshall. Encyc.*

CAN'TONAL, *a.* Pertaining to a canton; divided into cantons.

CAN'TONED, *pp.* Divided into distinct parts, or quarters; lodged in distinct quarters, as troops.

CAN'TONING, *ppr.* Dividing into distinct districts; allotting separate quarters to each regiment.

CAN'TONIZE, *v. t.* To canton, or divide into small districts. *Davies.*

CAN'TONMENT, *n.* A part or division of a town or village, assigned to a particular regiment of troops; separate quarters. *Marshall.*

CAN'TRED, } *n.* [L. *centum.*] A hundred
CAN'TREF, } villages, as in Wales. *Encyc.*

CAN'VAS, *n.* [Fr. *canevas*, canvas, and *chanvre*, hemp; Arm. *canavas*; Sp. *cañamazo*; Port. *canamo*; It. *canavaccio*, canvas, and *canapa*, hemp; D. *kanefas*, canvas, and *hennep*, hemp; G. *kanefass*, canvas, and *hanf*, hemp; Dan. *canefas*; L. *cannabis*, hemp; Gr. κανναβις; Ir. *canbhas*, canvas, and *canaib*, hemp; Russ. *kanephas*. It is from the root of *canna*, *cane*; perhaps a diminutive.]
1. A coarse cloth made of hemp, or flax, used for tents, sails of ships, painting and other purposes.
2. A clear unbleached cloth, wove regularly in little squares, used for working tapestry with the needle.
3. Among *the French*, the rough draught or model on which an air or piece of music is composed, and given to a poet to finish. The canvas of a song contains certain notes of the composer, to show the poet the measure of the verses he is to make.
4. Among *seamen*, cloth in sails, or sails in general; as, to spread as much *canvas* as the ship will bear.

CANVAS-CLIMBER, *n.* A sailor that goes aloft to handle sails. *Shak.*

CAN'VASS, *v. t.* [Old Fr. *cannabasser*, to beat about or shake, to examine. *Junius. Skinner.*]
1. To discuss; literally, to beat or shake out, to open by beating or shaking, like the L. *discutio*. This is the common use of the word, as to *canvass* a subject, or the policy of a measure.
2. To examine returns of votes; to search or scrutinize; as, to *canvass* the votes for senators.

CAN'VASS, *v. i.* To seek or go about to solicit votes or interest; to use efforts to obtain; to make interest in favor of; followed by *for*; as, to *canvass for* an office, or preferment; to *canvass for* a friend.

CAN'VASS, *n.* Examination; close inspection to know the state of; as a *canvass* of votes.
2. Discussion; debate.
3. A seeking, solicitation, or efforts to obtain.

CAN'VASSED, *pp.* Discussed; examined.

CAN'VASSER, *n.* One who solicits votes, or goes about to make interest. *Burke.*
2. One who examines the returns of votes for a public officer.

CAN'VASSING, *ppr.* Discussing; examining; sifting; seeking.

CAN'VASSING, *n.* The act of discussing, examining, or making interest.

CA'NY, *a.* [from *cane.*] Consisting of cane, or abounding with canes. *Milton.*

CAN'ZONE, *n.* [It. a song. See *Cant.*] A song or air in two or three parts, with passages of fugue and imitation; or a poem to which music may be composed in the style of a cantata. When set to a piece of instrumental music, it signifies much the same as cantata; and when set to a sonata, it signifies allegro, or a brisk movement. *Bailey. Busby.*

CAN'ZONET, *n.* [It. *canzonetta.*] A little or short song, in one, two or three parts. It sometimes consists of two strains, each of which is sung twice. Sometimes it is a species of jig. *Encyc. Busby.*

CAP, *n.* [Sax. *cæppe*, a cap, and a cape, a cloke; D. *kap*; G. *kappe* and *haube*; Dan. *kappe*, a robe or coat; Sw. *kappa*, id; It. *cappa*, a cap, a cloke; W. *cap*; Fr. *chape*, *chapeau*; Arm. *chap* or *cap*. The sense is probably that which is put on. Class Gb. No. 70. also 31. 36.]
1. A part of dress made to cover the head.
2. The ensign of a cardinalate. *Shak.*
3. The top, or the uppermost; the highest.
Thou art the *cap* of fools. *Shak.*
4. A vessel in form of a cap. *Wilkins.*
5. An act of respect, made by uncovering the head. *L'Estrange.*

Cap of cannon, a piece of lead laid over the vent to keep the priming dry; now called an apron.

Cap of maintenance, an ornament of state, carried before the Kings of England at the coronation. It is also carried before the mayors of some cities.

In *ship-building*, a cap is a thick strong block of wood, used to confine two masts together, when one is erected at the head of another.

CAP, *v. t.* To cover the top, or end; to spread over; as, a bone is *capped* at the joint with a cartilaginous substance.
The *cloud-capped* towers. *Shak.*
2. To deprive of the cap, or take off a cap.

To cap verses, is to name alternately verses beginning with a particular letter; to name in opposition or emulation; to name alternately in contest. *Johnson.*

CAP, *v. i.* To uncover the head in reverence or civility. [*Not used.*] *Shak.*

Cap-a-pie, [Fr.] From head to foot; all over; as, armed *cap-a-pie*.

Cap-paper, *n.* A coarse paper, so called from

being used to make caps to hold commodities. *Boyle.*

Cap-sheaf, n. The top sheaf of a stack of grain; the crowner.

CAPABIL'ITY, *n.* [See *Capable.*] The quality of being capable; capacity; capableness. *Shak. Lavoisier, Trans.*

CA'PABLE, *a.* [Fr. *capable*, from L. *capio*, to take. See Class Gb. No. 68. 69. 75. 83.]

1. Able to hold or contain; able to receive; sufficiently capacious; often followed by *of*; as, the room is not *capable of* receiving, or *capable of* holding the company.
2. Endued with power competent to the object; as, a man is *capable* of judging, or he is not *capable.*
3. Possessing mental powers; intelligent; able to understand, or receive into the mind; having a capacious mind; as a *capable* judge; a *capable* instructor.
4. Susceptible; as, *capable* of pain or grief. *Prior.*
5. Qualified for; susceptible of; as, a thing is *capable* of long duration; or it is *capable* of being colored or altered.
6. Qualified for, in a moral sense; having legal power or capacity; as, a bastard is not *capable* of inheriting an estate.
7. Hollow. [*Not now used.*] *Shak.*

CA'PABLENESS, *n.* The state or quality of being capable; capacity; power of understanding; knowledge. *Killingbeck.*

CAPAC'IFY, *v. t.* To qualify. [*Unusual.*] *Barrow. Good.*

CAPA'CIOUS, *a.* [L. *capax*, from *capio*, to take or hold.]

1. Wide; large; that will hold much; as a *capacious* vessel.
2. Broad; extensive; as a *capacious* bay or harbor.
3. Extensive; comprehensive; able to take a wide view; as a *capacious* mind.

CAPA'CIOUSNESS, *n.* Wideness; largeness; as of a vessel.

2. Extensiveness; largeness; as of a bay.
3. Comprehensiveness; power of taking a wide survey; *applied to the mind.*

CAPAC'ITATE, *v. t.* [See *Capacity.*] To make capable; to enable; to furnish with natural power; as, to *capacitate* one for understanding a theorem.

2. To endue with moral qualifications; to qualify; to furnish with legal powers; as, to *capacitate* one for an office.

CAPAC'ITATED, *pp.* Made capable; qualified.

CAPACITA'TION, *n.* The act of making capable.

CAPAC'ITY, *n.* [L. *capacitas*, from *capax*, *capio*; Fr. *capacité.*]

1. Passive power; the power of containing, or holding; extent of room or space; as the *capacity* of a vessel, or a cask.
2. The extent or comprehensiveness of the mind; the power of receiving ideas or knowledge.

   Let instruction be adapted to the *capacities* of youth.

3. Active power; ability; *applied to men or things; but less common, and correct.*

   The world does not include a cause endued with such *capacities.* *Blackmore.*

4. State; condition; character; profession; occupation. A man may act in the *capacity* of a mechanic, of a friend, of an attorney, or of a statesman. He may have a natural or a political *capacity.*
5. Ability, in a moral or legal sense; qualification; legal power or right; as, a man or a corporation may have a *capacity* to give or receive and hold estate.
6. In *geometry*, the solid contents of a body.
7. In *chimistry*, that state, quality or constitution of bodies, by which they absorb and contain, or render latent, any fluid; as the *capacity* of water for caloric.

CAPAR'ISON, *n.* [Sp. *caparazon*; Port. *caparazam*, a cover put over the saddle of a horse, a cover for a coach; Fr. *caparaçon.*]

A cloth or covering laid over the saddle or furniture of a horse, especially a sumpter horse or horse of state. *Milton.*

CAPAR'ISON, *v. t.* To cover with a cloth, as a horse. *Dryden.*

2. To dress pompously; to adorn with rich dress. *Shak.*

CAP'CASE, *n.* A covered case. [*Little used.*] *Burton.*

CAPE, *n.* [Sp. Port. *cabo*; It. *capo*; Fr. *cap*; D. *kaap*; Dan. *kap*; L. *caput*; Gr. κεφαλη; Sans. *cabala*, head. It signifies end, furthest point, from extending, shooting.]

1. A head land; properly the head, point or termination of a neck of land, extending some distance into the sea, beyond the common shore, and hence the name is applied to the neck of land itself, indefinitely, as in *Cape-Cod, Cape-Horn, Cape of Good Hope.* It differs from a promontory in this, that it may be high or low land; but a promontory is a high bold termination of a neck of land.
2. The neck-piece of a cloke or coat.

CAP'ELAN, *n.* A small fish, about six inches in length, sholes of which appear off the coasts of Greenland, Iceland and Newfoundland. They constitute a large part of the food of the Greenlanders. *Pennant.*

CAPEL'LA, *n.* A bright fixed star in the left shoulder of the constellation Auriga. *Encyc.*

CAP'ELLET, *n.* A kind of swelling, like a wen, growing on the heel of the hock on a horse, and on the point of the elbow. *Encyc.*

CA'PER, *v. i.* [Fr. *cabrer*, to prance; *cabriole*, a goat-leap, a caper; It. *capriola*, a wild goat, a caper in dancing; Sp. *cabriola*; L. *caper*, a goat. But probably *caper* is from the root of *capio*, which signifies not merely to seize, but to shoot or reach forward, or to leap and seize. Hence it is probable that this word coincides in origin with Dan. *kipper*, to leap, whence Eng. to *skip.*]

To leap; to skip or jump; to prance; to spring. *Shak.*

CA'PER, *n.* A leap; a skip; a spring; as in dancing or mirth, or in the frolick of a goat or lamb.

CA'PER, *n.* [Fr. *capre*; Arm. *capresen*; Sp. Port. *alcaparra*; It. *cappero*; L. *capparis*; D. *kapper*; G. *kaper*; Syr. *kapar*; Ar. كبر kabaron. The Ar. verb signifies to increase.]

The bud of the caper-bush, which is much used for pickling. The buds are collected before the flowers expand, and preserved in vinegar. The bush is a low shrub, generally growing from the joints of old walls, from fissures in rocks and amongst rubbish, in the southern parts of Europe. *Encyc.*

CA'PER-BUSH. [See *Caper.*]

CA'PER-CUTTING, *n.* A leaping or dancing in a frolicksome manner. *Beaum.*

CA'PERER, *n.* One who capers, leaps and skips about, or dances.

CA'PERING, *ppr.* Leaping; skipping.

CA'PIAS, *n.* [L. *capio*, to take.] In *law*, a writ of two sorts; one before judgment, called a *capias ad respondendum*, where an original is issued, to take the defendant, and make him answer to the plaintiff; the other, which issues after judgment, is of divers kinds; as a *capias ad satisfaciendum*, or writ of execution; a *capias pro fine*; a *capias utlagatum*; a *capias in withernam.* *Blackstone.*

CAP'IBAR, *n.* An animal partaking of the form of a hog and of a rabbit, the cabiai.

CAPILLA'CEOUS, *a.* [L. *capillaceus*, hairy.] Hairy; resembling a hair. [See *Capillary.*]

CAPILLA'IRE, *n.* [Fr.] A kind of sirrup, extracted from maiden-hair. *Mason.*

CAPIL'LAMENT, *n.* [L. *capillamentum*, from *capillus*, hair, probably a little shoot.]

1. The filament, a small fine thread, like a hair, that grows in the middle of a flower, with a little knob at the top; a chive.
2. A fine fiber, or filament, of which the nerves are composed.

CAP'ILLARY, *a.* [L. *capillaris*, from *capillus*, hair.]

1. Resembling a hair, fine, minute, small in diameter, though long; as a *capillary* tube or pipe; a *capillary* vessel in animal bodies, such as the ramifications of the blood vessels. *Arbuthnot.*
2. In botany, *capillary* plants are hair-shaped, as the ferns; a term used by Ray, Boerhaave and Morison. This class of plants corresponds to the order of Filices, in the Sexual method, which bear their flower and fruit on the back of the leaf or stalk. *Milne.*

This term is applied also to leaves which are longer than the setaceous or bristle-shaped leaf, to glands resembling hairs, to the filaments, to the style, and to the pappus or down affixed to some seeds. *Martyn.*

CAP'ILLARY, *n.* A fine vessel or canal. *Darwin.*

CAPILLA'TION, *n.* A blood vessel like a hair. [*Not in use.*] *Brown.*

CAPIL'LIFORM, *a.* [L. *capillus*, a hair, and *forma*, form.]

In the shape or form of a hair, or of hairs. *Kirwan.*

CAP'ITAL, *a.* [L. *capitalis*, from *caput*, the head. See *Cape.*]

1. Literally, pertaining to the head; as a *capital* bruise, in Milton, a bruise on the head. [*This use is not common.*]
2. *Figuratively, as the head is the highest part of a man*, chief; principal; first in importance; as a *capital* city or town; the *capital* articles of religion.
3. Punishable by loss of the head or of life; incurring the forfeiture of life; punishable with death; as, treason and murder are *capital* offenses or crimes.

4. Taking away life, as a *capital* punishment; or affecting life, as a *capital* trial.
5. Great, important, though perhaps not chief; as, a town possesses *capital* advantages for trade.
6. Large; of great size; as *capital* letters, which are of different form, and larger than common letters.

Capital stock, is the sum of money or stock which a merchant, banker or manufacturer employs in his business; either the original stock, or that stock augmented. Also, the sum of money or stock which each partner contributes to the joint fund or stock of the partnership; also, the common fund or stock of the company, whether incorporated or not.

A *capital* city or town is the metropolis or chief city of an empire, kingdom, state or province. The application of the epithet indicates the city to be the largest, or to be the seat of government, or both. In many instances, the capital, that is, the largest city, is not the seat of government.

ꞒAP'ITAL, *n.* [L. *capitellum.*] The uppermost part of a column, pillar or pilaster, serving as the head or crowning, and placed immediately over the shaft, and under the entablature. *Encyc.*

By the customary omission of the noun, to which the adjective, *capital*, refers, it stands for,
1. The chief city or town in a kingdom or state; a metropolis.
2. A large letter or type, in printing.
3. A stock in trade, in manufactures, or in any business requiring the expenditure of money with a view to profit.

ꞒAP'ITALIST, *n.* A man who has a capital or stock in trade, usually denoting a man of large property, which is or may be employed in business. *Burke. Stephens.*

ꞒAP'ITALLY, *adv.* In a capital manner; nobly; finely.
2. With loss of life; as, to punish *capitally*.

ꞒAP'ITALNESS, *n.* A capital offense. [*Little used.*] *Sherwood.*

ꞒAP'ITATE, *a.* [L. *capitatus*, from *caput*, a head.]
In *botany*, growing in a head, applied to a flower, or stigma. *Martyn. Lee.*

ꞒAPITA'TION, *n.* [L. *capitatio*, from *caput*, the head.]
1. Numeration by the head; a numbering of persons. *Brown.*
2. A tax, or imposition upon each head or person; a poll-tax. Sometimes written *Capitation-tax*. *Encyc.*

ꞒAP'ITE. [L. *caput*, the head, abl.] In *English law*, a tenant *in capite*, or in *chief*, is one who holds lands immediately of the king, *caput*, the head or Lord Paramount of all lands in the kingdom, by knight's service or by soccage. This tenure is called tenure *in capite*; but it was abolished in England, by 12 Charles II. 24. *Blackstone.*

ꞒAP'ITOL, *n.* [L. *capitolium*, from *caput*, the head.]
1. The temple of Jupiter in Rome, and a fort or castle, on the Mons Capitolinus. In this, the Senate of Rome anciently assembled; and on the same place, is still the city hall or town-house, where the conservators of the Romans hold their meetings. The same name was given to the principal temples of the Romans in their colonies. *Encyc.*
2. The edifice occupied by the Congress of the United States in their deliberations. In some states, the State-house, or house in which the legislature holds its sessions; a government house.

ꞒAPITO'LIAN, *a.* Pertaining to the capitol in Rome. *D'Anville.*

ꞒAP'ITOLINE, *a.* Pertaining to the capitol in Rome. The *Capitoline Games* were annual games instituted by Camillus in honor of Jupiter Capitolinus, and in commemoration of the preservation of the capitol from the Gauls, and other games instituted by Domitian and celebrated every five years. *Encyc.*

ꞒAPIT'ULAR, } *n.* [L. *capitulum*, a head or chapter.]
ꞒAPIT'ULARY, }
1. An act passed in a chapter, either of knights, canons or religious.
2. The body of laws or statutes of a chapter, or of an ecclesiastical council. This name is also given to the laws, civil and ecclesiastical, made by Charlemagne, and other princes, in general councils and assemblies of the people. Some indeed have alledged that these are supplements to laws. They are so called, because they are divided into chapters or sections. *Encyc.*
3. The member of a chapter.

ꞒAPIT'ULARLY, *adv.* In the form of an ecclesiastical chapter. *Swift.*

ꞒAPIT'ULARY, *a.* Relating to the chapter of a cathedral. *Warton.*

ꞒAPIT'ULATE, *v.i.* [from *capitulum*, supra.]
1. To draw up a writing in chapters, heads or articles. *Shak.*
[*But this sense is not usual.*]
2. To surrender, as an army or garrison, to an enemy, by treaty, in which the terms of surrender are specified and agreed to by the parties. The term is applicable to a garrison or to the inhabitants of a besieged place, or to an army or troops in any situation in which they are subdued or compelled to submit to a victorious enemy.

ꞒAPITULA'TION, *n.* The act of capitulating, or surrendering to an enemy upon stipulated terms or conditions.
2. The treaty or instrument containing the conditions of surrender.
3. A reducing to heads. [*Not much used.*]
4. In *German polity*, a contract which the Emperor makes with the electors, in the names of the princes and states of the empire, before he is raised to the imperial dignity.

ꞒAPIT'ULATOR, *n.* One who capitulates. *Sherwood.*

ꞒAP'ITULE, *n.* A summary. [*Not in use.*] *Wickliffe.*

ꞒAPĪVI, *n.* A balsam of the Spanish West-Indies. [See *Copaiba.*]

ꞒAP'NOMANCY, *n.* [Gr. καπνος, smoke, and μαντεια, divination.] Divination by the ascent or motion of smoke. *Spenser.*

ꞒAPO'CH, *n.* [Sp. *capucho*, a hood; Fr. *capuce.*] A monk's hood.

ꞒA'PON, *n.* [Sp. *capon*; Port. *capam*; It. *cappone*; Fr. *chapon*; L. *capo*; Ir. *cabun*; D. *kapoen*; G. *kapaun*; Arm. *cabon*; Sw. Dan. *kapun*; Gr. καπων. Qu. the root of Fr. *couper.*] A castrated cock; a cock-chicken gelded as soon as he quits his dam, or as soon as he begins to crow.

ꞒA'PON, *v. t.* To castrate, as a cock. *Birch.*

ꞒAPONNIE'RE, *n.* [Fr., Sp. *caponera*, It. *capponiera*, a little cut or trench, and it seems to be allied to *capon*, Sp. *caponar*, to cut or curtail.]
In *fortification*, a covered lodgment, sunk four or five feet into the ground, encompassed with a parapet, about two feet high, serving to support several planks, laden with earth. It is large enough to contain 15 or 20 soldiers, and is placed in the glacis, at the extremity of the counterscarp, and in dry moats, with embrasures or loop holes, through which the soldiers may fire. *Harris. Encyc.*

ꞒAPO'T, *n.* [Fr., probably from L. *capio*, to seize.]
A winning of all the tricks of cards at the game of piquet. *Johnson.*

ꞒAPO'T, *v. t.* To win all the tricks of cards at picquet.

ꞒAP'PER, *n.* [from *cap.*] One whose business is to make or sell caps.

ꞒAP'REOLATE, *a.* [L. *capreolus*, a tendril, properly a shoot, from the root of *capra*, a goat.]
In *botany*, having tendrils, or filiform spiral claspers, by which plants fasten themselves to other bodies, as in vines, peas, &c. *Harris. Martyn.*

ꞒAPRĪCE, *n.* [Fr. *caprice*; Sp. Port. *capricho*; It. *capriccio*, a shaking in fever, rigors; also, whim, freak, fancy. I suspect this word to be formed, with a prefix *ca*, on the root of *freak*, *break*; denoting primarily a sudden bursting, breaking, or starting. So we see in Italian, *maglio*, and *camaglio*, a *mail*. In early English writers, it is written, according to the Spanish, *capricho*. If formed from the root of *capio*, *caper*, the primary sense is the same.]
A sudden start of the mind; a sudden change of opinion, or humor; a whim, freak, or particular fancy.

ꞒAPRI''CIOUS, *a.* Freakish; whimsical; apt to change opinions suddenly, or to start from one's purpose; unsteady; changeable; fickle; fanciful; subject to change or irregularity; as a man of a *capricious* temper.

ꞒAPRI''CIOUSLY, *adv.* In a capricious manner; whimsically.

ꞒAPRI''CIOUSNESS, *n.* The quality of being led by caprice; whimsicalness; unsteadiness of purpose or opinion.
2. Unsteadiness; liableness to sudden changes; as the *capriciousness* of fortune.

ꞒAP'RIꞒORN, *n.* [L. *capricornus*, *caper*, a goat, and *cornu*, a horn.]
One of the twelve signs of the zodiac, the winter solstice; represented on ancient monuments, by the figure of a goat, or a a figure having the fore part like a goat and the hind part like a fish. *Encyc.*

ꞒAPRIFIꞒA'TION, *n.* [L. *caprificatio.*] A method of ripening figs by means of a gnat or insect that pricks the bud. *Encyc.*

ꞒAP'RIFOLE, *n.* [L. *caprifolium.*] Honeysuckle; woodbine. *Spenser.*

ꞒAP'RIFORM, *a.* [L. *caper*, a goat, and *forma*, form.] Having the form of a goat. *Eclectic Review.*

ꞒAP'RIOLE, *n.* [Fr., now *cabriole*; Sp. Port. *cabriola*; It. *capriola*, a *caper.*]
In *the manege*, caprioles are leaps that a

horse makes in the same place without advancing, in such a manner that when he is at the highth of the leap, he jerks out with his hind legs, even and near. It differs from the croupade in this, that, in a croupade, a horse does not show his shoes, and from a balotade, in which he does not jerk out. *Farrier's Dict.*

ĈAP'RIPED, *a.* [L. *caper*, a goat, and *pes*, foot.]

Having feet like those of a goat.

ĈAP'SIĈUM, *n.* Guinea pepper. *Chambers.*

ĈAPSI'ZE, *v. t.* To upset or overturn; *a seaman's phrase.* *Mar. Dict.*

ĈAP'STAN, *n.* sometimes written *capstern.* [Fr. *cabestan*; Sp. *cabestrante*; Port. *cabrestante*, from *cabresto*, Sp. *cabestro*, a halter; L. *capistrum*; Sax. *cæpster*, or *cæbestr*, a halter. The Spanish has also *cabria*, an axle-tree, and *cabrio*, a rafter. *Capstan* is probably from L. *capio*, to hold, with some other word.]

A strong massy column of timber, formed like a truncated cone, and having its upper extremity pierced to receive bars or levers, for winding a rope round it, to raise great weights, or perform other extraordinary work, that requires a great power. It may be let down through the decks of a ship, and so fixed that the work is performed by a horizontal motion. *Mar. Dict.*

CAP'SULAR, } *a.* Hollow like a chest.
ĈAP'SULARY, }

2. *Capsular ligament*, is that which surrounds every movable articulation, and contains the synovia like a bag. *Hooper.*

ĈAP'SULATE, } *a.* Inclosed in a capsule, or as in a chest or box. *Botany.*
ĈAP'SULATED, }

ĈAP'SULE, *n.* [L. *capsula*, a little chest, perhaps from *capio*, to take.]

The seed vessel of a plant; a dry membranaceous hollow pericarp, opening differently in different plants. It is composed of valves or outer covering, partitions, the columella or central pillar, and cells. *Martyn. Milne.*

ĈAP'TAIN, *n.* [Fr. *capitaine*; Sp. *capitan*; Port. *capitam*; It. *capitano*; from L. *caput*, the head. In the feudal laws of Europe, the term was applied to tenants *in capite*, who were bound to attend their prince in his wars, at the head of soldiers, and from this practice the name had its origin, or from their command.]

1. Literally, a head or chief officer; appropriately, the military officer who commands a company, whether of infantry, cavalry, artillery or matrosses.
2. The commander of a ship of war, or of a merchantman. But the latter is often called a master.
3. The commander of a military band, a sense that occurs in the scriptures; as a *captain* of fifty.
4. A man skilled in war or military affairs; as, Lord Wellington is a great *captain.*
5. A chief commander. *Shak.* But in this sense rarely used, but in composition.

Captain-general, is the commander in chief of an army, or of the militia. The governor of a state is *Captain-General* of the militia. *U. States.*

Captain-Lieutenant, is an officer, who with the rank of captain and pay of lieutenant, commands a company or troop. Thus the colonel of a regiment being the captain of the first company, that company is commanded by a Captain-Lieutenant.

Captain-Bashaw, or *Capudan Bashaw*, in Turkey, is the High Admiral.

ĈAP'TAIN, *a.* Chief; valiant. *Shak.*

ĈAP'TAINCY, *n.* The rank, post or commission of a captain. *Washington.*

2. The jurisdiction of a captain, or commander, as in South America.

ĈAP'TAINRY, *n.* The power or command over a certain district; chieftainship. *Spenser. Johnson.*

ĈAP'TAINSHIP, *n.* The condition or post of a captain or chief commander. *Shak.*

2. The rank, quality or post of a captain. In lieu of this *captaincy* is now used.
3. The command of a clan, or government of a certain district. *Davies.*
4. Skill in military affairs.

ĈAPTA'TION, *n.* [L. *captatio*, from *capto*, to catch.]

The act or practice of catching favor or applause, by flattery or address. *King Charles.*

ĈAP'TION, *n.* [L. *captio*, from *capio*, to seize.]

1. The act of taking, or apprehending by a judicial process. [*Little used.*]
2. A certificate signed by commissioners in Chancery, declaring when and where the commission was executed. *Ash.*
3. A preamble.
4. In *Scots law*, a writ issued at the instance of a creditor, commanding an officer to take and imprison the debtor, till he pays the debt.

ĈAP'TIOUS, *a.* [L. *captiosus*, from *capto*, to catch.]

1. Disposed to find fault, or raise objections; apt to cavil, as in popular language, it is said, *apt to catch at*; as a *captious* man.
2. Fitted to catch or ensnare; insidious; as a *captious* question. *Locke.*
3. Proceeding from a caviling disposition; as a *captious* objection or criticism.

ĈAP'TIOUSLY, *adv.* In a captious manner; with an inclination or intention to object, or censure. *Locke.*

ĈAP'TIOUSNESS, *n.* Disposition to find fault; inclination to object; peevishness. *Locke.*

ĈAP'TIVATE, *v. t.* [L. *captivo*, from *captivus*, a prisoner, from *capto*, to take; Fr. *captiver*; Sp. *cautivar*; Port. *cativar*; It. *cattivare.*]

1. To take prisoner; to seize by force; as an enemy in war. *Shak. Locke. B. Trumbull.*
2. To subdue; to bring into bondage. *King Charles.*
3. To overpower and gain with excellence or beauty; to charm; to engage the affections; to bind in love. *Addison.*
4. To enslave; with *to*; as, *captivated to* error. *Locke.*

ĈAP'TIVATE, *a.* Taken prisoner. *Shak.*

ĈAP'TIVATED, *pp.* Made prisoner; charmed.

ĈAP'TIVATING, *ppr.* Taking prisoner; engaging the affections.

2. *a.* Having power to engage the affections.

ĈAPTIVA'TION, *n.* The act of taking a prisoner; a taking one captive.

ĈAP'TIVE, *n.* [Fr. *captif*; Sp. *cautivo*; It. *cattivo*, whence Eng. *caitiff*; L. *captivus*, from *capto*, to seize.]

1. A prisoner taken by force or stratagem in war, by an enemy; followed by *to*; as a *captive to* the victor.
2. One who is charmed or subdued by beauty or excellence; one whose affections are seized, or who is held by strong ties of love.
3. One who is ensnared by love or flattery, or by wiles. 2 Tim. ii, 26.
4. A slave. Anciently captives were enslaved by their conquerors. But in modern times, they are not made slaves in christian countries; and the word *captive*, in a literal sense, rarely signifies a slave.

ĈAP'TIVE, *a.* Made prisoner in war; kept in bondage, or confinement; as *captive* souls. *Dryden.*

2. Holding in confinement; as *captive* chains.

ĈAP'TIVE, *v. t.* To take prisoner; to bring into subjection. *Obs.* *Dryden. Prior.*

ĈAPTIV'ITY, *n.* [Fr. *captivité*; L. *captivitas*, from *capto* to seize.]

1. The state of being a prisoner, or of being in the power of an enemy by force or the fate of war. *Dryden.*
2. Subjection to love. *Addison.*
3. Subjection; a state of being under control.

   Bringing into *captivity* every thought to the obedience of Christ. 2 Cor. x.

4. Subjection; servitude; slavery.

   But I see another law in my members—bringing me into *captivity* to the law of sin. Rom. vii.

To lead captivity captive, in scripture, is to subdue those who have held others in slavery, or captivity. Ps. lxviii.

ĈAP'TOR, *n.* [L. *capio*, to take.] One who takes, as a prisoner or a prize. It is appropriately one who takes a prize at sea.

ĈAP'TURE, *n.* [L. *captura*; Fr. *capture*; from L. *capio*, to take.]

1. In a general sense, the act of taking or seizing; as the *capture* of an enemy, of a ship, or of booty, by force, surprise or stratagem.
2. The thing taken; a prize; prey taken by force, surprise or stratagem.
3. Seizure; arrest; as the *capture* of a criminal or debtor.

ĈAP'TURE, *v. t.* To take or seize by force, surprise or stratagem, as an enemy or his property; to take by force under the authority of a commission; as to *capture* a ship.

ĈAP'TURED, *pp.* Taken as a prize.

ĈAP'TURING, *ppr.* Seizing as a prize.

ĈAPU'CCIO, *n.* [It.] A capuchin or hood.

ĈAPU'CHED, *a.* Covered with a hood. [*Little used.*] *Brown.*

ĈAPUČHI'N, *n.* [Fr. *capucine*, from *capuce*, a hood or cowl.]

1. A garment for females, consisting of a cloke and hood, made in imitation of the dress of capuchin monks. *Johnson.*
2. A pigeon whose head is covered with feathers.

ĈAPUČHI'NS, *n.* Monks of the order of St. Francis, who cover their heads with a *capuce*, *capuchon*, a stuff-cap or cowl. They are clothed in brown or gray, go bare-footed, and never shave their faces. *Encyc.*

CAP'UCINE, *n.* A species of monkey, the *sagoo* or *saï*.

CAP'ULIN, *n.* The Mexican cherry.

CAR, CAER, CHAR, in names of places, is sometimes the Celtic *Caer*, a town or city, as in *Caermarthen*.

C'AR, *n.* [W. *car*; Ir. *carr, carra*, or *cairt*; Arm. *qarr*; D. and G. *karre*; Sw. *kärra*; Dan. *karre*; Sp. It. Port. *carro*; L. *carrus*, or *currus*; Fr. *char*, whence *chariot*; Sax. *cræt*, a cart. The sense is probably taken from running on wheels. See *Current*.]

1. A small vehicle moved on wheels, usually drawn by one horse. *Johnson.*
2. In *poetical language*, any vehicle of dignity or splendor; a chariot of war, or of triumph. *Milton. Prior.*
3. The constellation called Charles's wain or the bear. *Dryden.*

CAR'ABINE, CARBINE, *n.* [Fr. *carabine*; Sp. *carabina*; It. *id.*]
A short gun or fire arm, carrying a ball of 24 to the pound, borne by light horsemen, and hanging by a belt over the left shoulder. The barrel is two feet and a half long, and sometimes furrowed.

CARABINEE'R, *n.* A man who carries a carabine; one who carries a longer carabine than others, which is sometimes used on foot. *Encyc.*

CAR'AC, CAR'ACK, *n.* [Port. *carraca*; Fr. *caraque*; Sp. *carraca*; allied to It. *carico*, a burden, cargo.]
A large ship of burden; a Portuguese Indiaman.

CAR'ACOL, *n.* [Fr. *caracole*, a wheeling about; Sp. *caracol*, a small cone, a winding staircase, a snail; It. *caracollo*, a wheeling.]

1. In *the manege*, a semi-round, or half turn which a horseman makes, either to the right or left. In the army, the cavalry make a caracol after each discharge, in order to pass to the rear of the squadron. *Encyc.*
2. In *architecture*, a staircase in a helix or spiral form. *Encyc.*

CAR'ACOL, *v. i.* To move in a caracol; to wheel.

CAR'ACOLY, *n.* A mixture of gold, silver and copper, of which are made rings, pendants and other toys for the savages.

CAR'AT, *n.* [It. *carato*; Fr. *carat*; D. *karaat*; G. *karat*; Gr. κερατιον, a little horn, a pod, and the berry of a pod, used for a weight of four grains. From the Greeks, it is said, the Arabians borrowed their قيراط karat, a weight used in Mecca, equal to the twenty-fourth of a denarius, or denier. See *Castell*, Col. 3448, and *Ludolf*, 199.]

1. The weight of four grains, used by goldsmiths and jewelers in weighing precious stones and pearls. *Encyc.*
2. The weight that expresses the fineness of gold. The whole mass of gold is divided into 24 equal parts, and as many 24th parts as it contains of pure gold, it is called gold of so many carats. Thus gold of twenty-two parts of pure metal, is gold of twenty-two *carats*. The *carat* in Great Britain is divided into four grains; among the Germans into twelve parts; and among the French into thirty-two. *Encyc.*
3. The value of any thing. *Obs. B. Jonson.*

CAR'AVAN, *n.* [Ar. قيروان from قرا karau, to stretch along, to follow, to proceed from place to place. Sp. *caravana*; Fr. *caravane*. Pers. as Ar.]
A company of travellers, pilgrims or merchants, marching or proceeding in a body over the deserts of Arabia, or other region infested with robbers.

CARAVAN'SARY, *n.* A place appointed for receiving and loading caravans; a kind of inn, where the caravans rest at night, being a large square building, with a spacious court in the middle. *Encyc.*

CAR'AVEL, C'ARVEL, *n.* [Sp. *caravela*; It. *caravello*; Fr. *caravelle*.]

1. A small vessel on the coast of France, used in the herring fishery. These vessels are usually from 25 to 30 tons burden.
2. A light, round, old-fashioned ship. *Johnson.*

CAR'AWAY, *n.* [Gr. καρος, καρον; L. *caros*, *careum*; Fr. *carvi*; Sp. *alcaravea* or *alcarahueya*; D. *kerwe*; Ar. كرويا karawia.]
A plant of the genus Carum, a biennial plant, with a taper root like a parsnip, which, when young, is good eating. The seeds have an aromatic smell and a warm pungent taste. They are used in cakes, incrusted with sugar, and distilled with spirituous liquors. *Encyc.*

C'ARBON, *n.* [L. *carbo*, a coal; Sp. *carbon*; It. *carbone*; Fr. *charbon*. Qu. Gr. καρφω, to dry, or the root of *char*, Russ. *charyu*, to burn.]
Pure charcoal; a simple body, black, brittle, light and inodorous. It is usually the remains of some vegetable body, from which all its volatile matter has been expelled by heat. When crystalized, it forms the diamond; and by means of a galvanic apparatus, it is found to be capable of fusion.

CARBONA'CEOUS, *a.* Pertaining to charcoal. [See *Carbonic*.]

C'ARBONADE, CARBONA'DO, *n.* [from *carbo*, supra.] In *cookery*, flesh, fowl or the like, cut across, seasoned and broiled on coals. *Obs. Shak.*

C'ARBONADE, CARBONA'DO, *v. t.* To cut or hack. *Obs. Shak.*

C'ARBONATE, *n.* In *chimistry*, a compound formed by the union of carbonic acid with a base; as the *carbonate* of lime; a *carbonate* of copper.

C'ARBONATED, *a.* Combined with carbon. *Lavoisier.*

CARBON'IC, *a.* Pertaining to carbon, or obtained from it. The *carbonic acid* is a saturated combination of carbon and oxygen. It has been called *fixed air, aerial acid, mephitic gas*, and *cretaceous acid*, or acid of chalk. It is found, in some places, in a state of gas; it exists in the atmosphere, and is disengaged from fermenting liquors, and from decomposing vegetable and animal substances. It is heavier than common air, and subsides into low places, vaults and wells. *Hooper.*

CARBONIF'EROUS, *a.* [*carbo* and *fero*, to bear.] Producing carbon, or coal. *Kirwan, Geol.*

CARBONIZA'TION, *n.* The act or process of carbonizing.

C'ARBONIZE, *v. t.* To convert into carbon by combustion or the action of fire; to expel from wood or other substance all volatile matter.

C'ARBONIZED, *pp.* Converted into carbon or charcoal.

CARBONOHY'DROUS, *a.* [*carbon* and Gr. υδωρ, water.] Composed of carbon and hydrogen.

C'ARBONOUS, *a.* *Carbonous acid* is carbon not fully saturated with oxygen. *Lavoisier.*

C'ARBUNCLE, *n.* [L. *carbunculus*, a little coal, from *carbo*.]

1. An *anthrax*; an inflammatory tumor, or painful gangrenous boil or ulcer. *Coxe. Hooper.*
2. A beautiful gem, of a deep red color, with a mixture of scarlet, called by the Greeks *anthrax*, found in the East Indies. It is found pure, and adhering to a heavy ferruginous stone, of the emery kind. It is usually a quarter of an inch in length, and two-thirds of that in diameter, of an angular figure. When held up to the sun, it loses its deep tinge, and becomes exactly of the color of a burning coal. *Encyc.*
The carbuncle of the ancients is supposed to have been a garnet. *Cleaveland.*
3. In *heraldry*, a charge or bearing consisting of eight radii, four of which make a common cross, and the other four, a saltier. *Encyc.*

C'ARBUNCLED, *a.* Set with carbuncles; spotted.

CARBUNC'ULAR, *a.* Belonging to a carbuncle; resembling a carbuncle; red; inflamed.

CARBUNCULA'TION, *n.* [L. *carbunculatio*, from *carbunculo*, to burn to a coal, to blast. See *Carbon*.]
The blasting of the young buds of trees or plants, by excessive heat or cold. *Harris.*

C'ARBURET, *n.* A combination of carbon with a metal, earth or alkali. *Lavoisier.*
A combination of carbon with a simple inflammable or a metal. *Webster.*

C'ARBURETED, *a.* Combined with carbon, or holding carbon in solution; as *carbureted* hydrogen gas.
Carbureted hydrogen consists of one prime equivalent of each. *Ure.*
Carbureted hydrogen gas is called hydro-carbonate, being resolvable into carbonic acid and water, by combustion with oxygen. *Aiken.*
Carbureted is applied to gaseous compounds. Thus we say *carbureted* hydrogen, instead of *carburet of hydrogen*. *Silliman.*

C'ARCAJO, *n.* The glutton, a voracious carnivorous animal.

C'ARCANET, *n.* [Fr. *carcan*, a chain; It. *carcame*.] A chain or collar of jewels. *Shak. Hakewell.*

C'ARCASS, *n.* [Fr. *carcasse*; It. *carcame*; Norm. *carkoys*, a mast, and a carcass. Qu. Gr. καρχησιον.]

1. The body of an animal; usually the body when dead. It is not applied to the living body of the human species, except in low or ludicrous language.
2. The decaying remains of a bulky thing, as of a boat or ship.
3. The frame or main parts of a thing, unfin-

ished or without ornament. This seems to be the primary sense of the word. [See the next word.] *Hale.*

C'ARCASS, *n.* [It. *carcassa*; Sp. *carcax*; Fr. *carcasse*; D. *karkas.*]

An iron case or hollow vessel, about the size of a bomb, of an oval figure, filled with combustible and other substances, as meal-powder, salt-peter, sulphur, broken glass, turpentine, &c., to be thrown from a mortar into a town, to set fire to buildings. It has two or three apertures, from which the fire blazes, and the light sometimes serves as a direction in throwing shells. It is equipped with pistol-barrels, loaded with powder to the muzzle, which explode as the composition burns down to them. This instrument is probably named from the ribs of iron that form it, which resemble the ribs of a human carcass. *Encyc. Mar. Dict.*

C'ARCELAGE, *n.* [L. *carcer.*] Prison fees. [*Not in use.*]

C'ARCERAL, *a.* Belonging to a prison.

CARCINO'MA, *n.* [Gr. καρκινωμα, from καρκινοω, καρκινος, a cancer.]

A cancer; also, a turgesence of the veins of the eye. *Coxe.*

CARCINO'MATOUS, *a.* Cancerous; like a cancer, or tending to it.

C'ARD *n.* [Fr. *carte*; Sp. Port. It. *carta*; L. *charta*, Gr. χαρτης; D. *kaart*; G. *karte*; Dan. *kort*; Ir. *cairt*; perhaps from bark, L. *cortex*, Ir. *coirt* or *cairt*, or the same root.]

1. A paper or pasteboard of an oblong figure, on which are painted figures or points; *used in games.*

2. A blank piece of paper, or the like paper with some writing upon it, used in messages of civility, or business.

3. The paper on which the points of the compass are marked.

> Reason the *card*, but passion is the gale. *Pope.*

C'ARD, *v. i.* To play much at cards; to gain. *Johnson.*

C'ARD, *n.* [D. *kaard*; G. *kardetsche*; Dan. *karde*; Sw. *karda*; Fr. *carde*; Arm. *encardoner*; Sp. *carda*, teasel, and a card; Port. *carda*, a card, and *cardo*, a thistle; L. *carduus*; It. *cardo*, a thistle and a card; L. *caro*, to card; Ir. *cir*, a comb. It seems that *card*, and L. *carduus*, are the same word, and probably the plant, *teasel*, is the original word, or both are from a common root. The French *carde* is a *card*, and the stalks of the artichoke. *Artichoke* is so written for *cardichoke.*]

An instrument for combing, opening and breaking wool or flax, freeing it from the coarser parts, and from extraneous matter. It is made by inserting bent teeth of wire in a thick piece of leather, and nailing this to a piece of oblong board, to which a handle is attached.

C'ARD, *v. t.* To comb, or open wool, flax, hemp, &c., with a card, for the purpose of cleansing it of extraneous matter, separating the coarser parts, and making it fine and soft for spinning.

C'ARDAMINE, *n.* [Gr.] The plant, meadow cresses, or cuckow flower.

C'ARDAMOM, *n.* [Gr. καρδαμωμον.] A plant of the genus *Amomum*, and its seeds, a native of India. The seeds of this plant, which grow in a pod, have a warm aromatic flavor, and are used in medicine. *Encyc.*

C'ARDED, *pp.* Combed; opened; cleansed with cards.

C'ARDER, *n.* One who cards wool; also, one who plays much at cards. *Wotton.*

C'ARDIAC, C'ARDIACAL, *a.* [L. *cardiacus*; Gr. καρδιακος, from καρδια, the heart.]

1. Pertaining to the heart.

2. Exciting action in the heart, through the medium of the stomach; having the quality of stimulating action in the system, invigorating the spirits, and giving strength and cheerfulness. *Med. Dict.*

C'ARDIAC, *n.* A medicine which excites action in the stomach, and animates the spirits.

C'ARDIALGY, *n.* [Gr. καρδια, the heart, and αλγος, pain.]

The heart-burn, a violent sensation of heat and acrimony in the upper or left orifice of the stomach, seemingly at the heart, but rising into the œsophagus. It is called also the *cardiac passion.*

C'ARDINAL, *a.* [L. *cardinalis*, said to be from *cardo*, a hinge.]

Chief, principal, preeminent, or fundamental; as the *cardinal* virtues, which Pagans supposed to be justice, prudence, temperance and fortitude.

C'ARDINAL, *n.* An ecclesiastical prince in the Romish church, who has a voice in the conclave at the election of a Pope, who is taken from their number. The cardinals are divided into three classes or orders, containing six bishops, fifty priests, and fourteen deacons, making seventy. These constitute the sacred college, and compose the Pope's council. Originally they were subordinate in rank to bishops; but they have now the precedence. The dress of a cardinal is a red soutaine or cassock, a rocket, a short purple mantle and a red hat. *Encyc. Spelman.*

2. A woman's cloke.

Cardinal-flower, a plant of the genus *Lobelia*, of many species. They are fibrous-rooted perennials, rising from two to five or six feet high, with erect stalks, ornamented with oblong, oval, spear-shaped simple leaves, and spikes of beautiful monopetalous flowers of scarlet, blue and violet colors. The natives of this country use a decoction of one species, the siphilitica, as a remedy in the venereal disease. *Encyc.*

Cardinal numbers, are the numbers, *one*, *two*, *three*, &c., in distinction from *first*, *second*, *third*, &c., which are called ordinal numbers.

Cardinal points, in cosmography, are the four intersections of the horizon with the meridian, and the prime vertical circle, or North and South, East and West. In *astrology*, the cardinal points are the rising and setting of the sun, the zenith and nadir.

Cardinal signs, in astronomy, are Aries, Libra, Cancer and Capricorn.

Cardinal winds, are those which blow from the cardinal points.

C'ARDINALATE, C'ARDINALSHIP, *n.* The office, rank or dignity of a cardinal.

C'ARDINALIZE, *v. t.* To make a cardinal. [*Little used.*] *Sheldon.*

C'ARDING, *ppr.* Combing, as flax, wool, &c.

2. The act of playing at cards. [*Little used.*]

C'ARDING-MACHINE, *n.* A machine lately invented, for combing, breaking and cleansing wool and cotton. It consists of cylinders, thick set with teeth, and moved by the force of water, steam, &c.

C'ARDIOID, *n.* [Gr. καρδια, heart, and ειδος, form.]

An algebraic curve, so called from its resemblance to a heart. *Chambers.*

C'ARDITE, *n.* Fossil or petrified shells of the genus Cardium. *Jameson.*

C'ARD-MAKER, *n.* [*card* and *maker.*] A maker of cards.

C'ARD-MATCH, *n.* [*card* and *match.*] A match made by dipping pieces of card in melted sulphur. *Addison.*

CARDOON', *n.* [Sp. *cardon*; L. *carduus.*] A species of Cynara, resembling the artichoke, but larger. *Chambers.*

C'ARD-TABLE, *n.* The table appropriated to the use of gamesters, or used for playing cards on.

CARE, *n.* [Sax. *car*, *cara*; Goth. *kar*, *kara*; Ir. *car*; L. *cura.* In Welch, *cur* is care, anxiety; also, a blow or beating, a throb; *curaw*, to beat, strike or throb, to fight; *curiaw*, to trouble, vex, pine, or waste away. In L. *curo* signifies to care, and to cure. In Sp. *curar* is to prescribe medicine; to salt or cure, as flesh; to season, as timber; to bleach, as cloth; intransitively, to recover from sickness; and reciprocally, to take care of one's self. In Italian, *curare* is to *cure*, attend, protect, defend, and to value or esteem. In French, *curer* is to cleanse; "curer les dens," to pick the teeth; *cure* is a benefice. The primary sense is, to strain, or stretch, as in care, attention, and *curious* is stretching forward; but the sense of separating, or driving off, is comprehended, which gives the French sense, and the sense of *prying into* is included in *curious.* The sense of healing is from that of care, or making sound and strong. The Welch sense of beating is from driving, thrusting, coinciding with straining. See *Cark* and *Cure.*]

1. Concern; anxiety; solicitude; noting some degree of pain in the mind, from apprehension of evil.

> They shall eat bread by weight and with *care.* Ezek. iv.

2. Caution; a looking to; regard; attention, or heed, with a view to safety or protection, as in the phrase, "take care of yourself."

> A want of *care* does more damage than a want of knowledge. *Franklin.*

3. Charge or oversight, implying concern for safety and prosperity; as, he was under the *care* of a physician.

> That which cometh upon me daily, the *care* of all the churches. 2 Cor. xi.

4. The object of care, or watchful regard and attention; as, "Is she thy care?" *Dryden.*

CARE, *v. i.* To be anxious or solicitous; to be concerned about.

> Master, *carest* thou not that we perish? Mark iv.

2. To be inclined or disposed; to have regard

to; with *for* before a noun, and *to* before a verb. "Not *caring to* observe the wind." "Great masters in painting never *care for* drawing people in the fashion." In this sense the word implies a less degree of concern. The different degrees of anxiety expressed by this word constitute the chief differences in its signification or applications.

CA'RE-CRAZED, *a.* [*care* and *craze.*] Broken or disordered by care, or solicitude; as a *care-crazed* mother. *Shak.*

CARE-DEFY'ING, *a.* Bidding defiance to care. *Shenstone.*

CA'RE-TUNED, *a.* Tuned by care; mournful. *Shak.*

CA'RE-WOUNDED, *a.* Wounded with care. *May.*

CAREE'N, *v. t.* [Fr. *carener*, from *carene*, the side and keel of a ship, L. *carina*; Sp. *carenar*; Port. *querenar*; It. *carenare.*]

1. In *sea language*, to heave or bring a ship to lie on one side, for the purpose of calking, repairing, cleansing, or paying over with pitch, the other side. *Mar. Dict.*

CAREE'N, *v. i.* To incline to one side, as a ship under a press of sail. *Mar. Dict.*

CAREE'NED, *pp.* Laid on one side; inclined.

CAREE'NING, *ppr.* Heaving down on one side; inclining.

CAREE'NING, *n.* The act of heaving down on one side, as a ship.

CAREE'R, *n.* [Fr. *carriere*; Sp. *carrera*; Port. *carreira*; It. *carriera*. It is from the root of *car*, and L. *curro*, from the sense of running.]

1. A course; a race, or running; a rapid running; speed in motion. *Wilkins. Prior.*
2. General course of action or movement; procedure; course of proceeding.

 Continue and proceed in honor's fair *career*. *Dryden.*

3. The ground on which a race is run. *Johnson.*
4. In *the manege*, a place inclosed with a barrier, in which they run the ring. *Encyc.*
5. In *falconry*, a flight or tour of the hawk, about 120 yards. *Encyc.*

CAREE'R, *v. i.* To move or run rapidly.

 When a ship is decked out in all her canvas, every sail swelled, and *careering* gayly over the curling waves, how lofty, how gallant she appears! *Irving.*

CAREE'RING, *pp.* Running or moving with speed.

CA'REFUL, *a.* [See *Care.*] Full of care; anxious; solicitous.

 Martha, thou art *careful* and troubled about many things. Luke x.

2. Provident; attentive to support and protect; with *of* or *for*.

 Thou hast been *careful for* us with all care. 2 Kings iv.

 What could a *careful* father more have done. *Dryden.*

 In present usage *careful* is generally followed by *of*; as, *careful of* health.

3. Watchful; cautious; giving good heed; as, be *careful* to maintain good works; be *careful* of your conversation.
4. Filling with care or solicitude; exposing to concern, anxiety or trouble; full of cares.

 Raised to a *careful* height. *Shak.*

CA'REFULLY, *adv.* With care, anxiety, or solicitude.

 Though he sought it *carefully* with tears. Heb. xii.

2. Heedfully; watchfully; attentively; as, consider these precepts *carefully*.

 If thou *carefully* hearken to the Lord. Deut. xv.

3. In a manner that shows care.

 Envy, how *carefully* does it look. *Collier.*

4. Providently; cautiously. *Johnson.*

CA'REFULNESS, *n.* Anxiety; solicitude.

 Drink thy water with trembling and with *carefulness*. Ezek. xii.

2. Heedfulness; caution; vigilance, in guarding against evil, and providing for safety.

CA'RELESS, *a.* [*care* and *less*, Sax. *leas*, Goth. *laus*. See *Loose.*]

1. Having no care; heedless; negligent; unthinking; inattentive; regardless; unmindful; followed by *of* or *about*; as a *careless* mother; a mother *careless of* or *about* her children, is an unnatural parent.
2. Free from care or anxiety; whence, undisturbed; cheerful.

 Thus wisely *careless*, innocently gay. *Pope.*

3. Done or said without care; unconsidered; as a *careless* throw; a *careless* expression.
4. Not regarding with care; unmoved by; unconcerned for; as, *careless of* money; *careless of* consequences.
5. Contrived without art. *Bp. Taylor.*

CA'RELESSLY, *adv.* In a careless manner or way; negligently; heedlessly; inattentively; without care or concern.

CA'RELESSNESS, *n.* Heedlessness; inattention; negligence; manner without care.

CAR'ENTANE, *n.* [Fr. *quarantaine*, forty.] A papal indulgence, multiplying the remission of penance by forties. *Taylor.*

CARESS', *v. t.* [Fr. *caresser*; Arm. *cherisza*, to *caress*, and to *cherish*; W. *caredigaw*; It. *carezza*, flattery, a *caressing*; *careggiare*, to coax, flatter, esteem; Sp. *caricia*, a caress; *acariciar*, to *caress*, *cherish*, fondle; Port. *id.* It may be from the common root of L. *carus*, Fr. *cher*, *cherir*, W. *car*. But some difficulties attend this hypothesis.]

To treat with fondness, affection, or kindness; to fondle; to embrace with tender affection; as a parent a child. *South.*

CARESS', *n.* An act of endearment; any act or expression of affection; an embracing with tenderness; as conjugal *caresses*. *Milton.*

CARESS'ED, *pp.* Treated or embraced with affection.

CARESS'ING, *ppr.* Treating with endearment, or affection.

CA'RET, *n.* [L. *caret*, there is wanting, from *careo*, to want.]

In writing, this mark ʌ, which shows that something, omitted in the line, is interlined above, or inserted in the margin, and should be read in that place.

C'ARGASON, *n.* A cargo; which see. *Howell.*

C'ARGO, *n.* [W. *carg*, a load, *cargu*, to load, from *car*, a vehicle; Port. *carga*, Sp. *carga*, a load, burden, *charge*; Sp. *cargo*, a load; *cargazon*, id.; *cargar*, to load, to *charge*; It. *carico*, a load or *charge*; *caricare*, to load, to *charge*; Fr. *cargaison*, a *cargo*; *charge*, a charge or load; *charger*, to load, burden, *charge*; Arm. *carg*. See *Charge.*]

The lading or freight of a ship; the goods, merchandize, or whatever is conveyed in a ship or other merchant vessel. The lading within the hold is called the *inboard cargo*, in distinction from horses, cattle and other things carried on deck. The person employed by a merchant to proceed with, oversee and dispose of the lading, is called a *supercargo*.

C'ARGOOSE, *n.* A fowl belonging to the genus *Colymbus*, called the crested diver. The cheeks and throat are surrounded with a long pendant ruff, of a bright tawny color, edged with black. The breast and belly are of a silvery white. It weighs two pounds and a half.

CA'RIATED, *a.* Carious. [*Not used.* See *Carious.*]

CAR'IBOO, *n.* A quadruped of the stag kind.

CAR'ICA, *n.* The papaw, a tree bearing a fleshy fruit of the size of a small melon.

CAR'ICATURE, *n.* [It. *caricatura*, formed from *carica*, a load, *caricare*, to load. See *Cargo.*]

A figure or description in which beauties are concealed and blemishes exaggerated, but still bearing a resemblance to the object. *Encyc.*

CAR'ICATURE, *v. t.* To make or draw a caricature; to represent as more ugly than the life. *Lyttelton.*

CAR'ICATURIST, *n.* One who caricatures others.

CARICOG'RAPHY, *n.* [*carex*, sedge, and γραφω, to describe.]

A description of the plants of the genus Carex or sedge. *Dewey, Journ. of Science.*

CAR'ICOUS, *a.* [L. *carica*, a fig.] Resembling a fig; an epithet given to tumors that resemble a fig, such as occur often in the piles. *Encyc.*

CA'RIES, *n.* [L.] The corruption or mortification of a bone; an ulcerated bone. *Coxe.*

CAR'ILLON, *n.* [Fr.] A little bell. Also, a simple air in music, adapted to the performance of small bells or clocks. [See *Carol.*] *Busby.*

CAR'INATE, **CAR'INATED**, *a.* [L. *carinatus*, from *carina*, a keel.]

In *botany*, shaped like the keel of a ship; having a longitudinal prominency on the back like a keel; applied to a calyx, leaf or nectary. *Martyn.*

CARIN'THIN, *n.* A mineral from Carinthia, regarded as a variety of hornblend. *Cleaveland.*

CARIOS'ITY, *n.* [See *Caries.*] Mortification, or ulceration of a bone. *Wiseman.*

CA'RIOUS, *a.* Mortified; corrupted; ulcerated; as a bone. *Wiseman.*

C'ARK, *n.* [W. *carc*, care, restraint; *carcar*, a prison, L. *carcer*; Sax. *cearc*, care; *cearcian*, to cark, to creak, to grumble. The primary sense is, to *strain.*]

Care; anxiety; concern; solicitude; distress. *Obs.* *Sidney.*

C'ARK, *v. i.* To be careful, anxious, solicitous, concerned. *Obs.* *Sidney.*

C'ARKING, *pp.* Distressing; perplexing; giving anxiety. *Obs.*

C'ARLE, *n.* *carl.* [Sax. *carl*, a male, whence *Carolus*, *Charles*. The word signifies primarily, strong, robust. Whence the English, *carl-cat*, and *carl-hemp*; *house-carl*, a domestic servant; Ger. *kerl*, a fellow; *kerlhaft*, masculine, stout. See *Churl*.]

1. A rude, rustic, rough, brutal man. *Obs.* [See *Churl*.]
2. A kind of hemp. *Tusser.*

C'ARLE, *v. i.* To act like a churl. [*Not in use.*] *Burton.*

C'ARLINE, or CAR'OLINE, *n.* A silver coin in Naples.

C'ARLINE, } *n.* [Fr. *carlingue*, or *escar-*
C'ARLING, } *lingue.*]
A piece of timber in a ship, ranging fore and aft, from one deck beam to another, directly over the keel, serving as a foundation for the body of the ship. On these rest the ledges, on which the planks of the deck are made fast. *Encyc. Mar. Dict.*

Carline-knees are timbers in a ship, lying across from the sides to the hatchway, and serving to sustain the deck. *Encyc.*

C'ARLINE-THISTLE, *n.* A genus of plants growing in the south of France, and one a native of Great Britain.

CARLISH, CARLISHNESS. [See *Churlish.*]

C'ARLOCK, *n.* A sort of isinglass from Russia, made of the sturgeon's bladder, and used in clarifying wine. *Encyc.*

C'ARLOT, *n.* A countryman. [See *Carle. Not used.*] *Shak.*

CARLOVIN'GIAN, *a.* Pertaining to Charlemagne; as the *Carlovingian* race of kings.

C'ARMAN, *n.* [*car* and *man.*] A man whose employment is to drive a cart, or to convey goods and other things in a cart.

C'ARMELIN, } *a.* Belonging to the order
C'ARMELITE, } of Carmelites. *Weever.*

C'ARMELITE, *n.* [from Mount *Carmel.*] A mendicant friar. The Carmelites have four tribes, and they have now thirty-eight provinces, besides the congregation in Mantua, in which are fifty-four monasteries, under a vicar general, and the congregations of barefooted Carmelites in Italy and Spain. They wear a scapulary, or small woolen habit, of a brown color, thrown over the shoulders. *Encyc.*

2. A sort of pear.

CARMIN'ATIVE, *a.* [Fr. *carminatif*; Sp. *carminativo*, from *carminar*, to expel wind backward, from L. *carmino*, to card or tease.]
Expelling wind from the body; warming; antispasmodic.

CARMIN'ATIVE, *n.* A medicine, which tends to expel wind, or to remedy colic and flatulencies.

C'ARMINE, *n.* [Fr. *carmin*; Sp. *carmin*; Port. *carmim*; It. *carminio*; from the same root as *crimson*; Port. *carmesim*, crimson; Sp. *carmesi*, crimson and cochineal powder; It. *chermisi*, crimson, and *chermes*, cochineal, *kermes*; Ar. قِرْمِزٌ kirmiz, kirmizon, a berry, and an insect, used in dyeing.]
A powder or pigment, of a beautiful red or crimson color, bordering on purple, and used by painters in miniature, though rarely, on account of its great price. It is prepared by dissolving cochineal in an alkaline lye, and precipitating it by alum. *Encyc. Nicholson.*

C'ARNAGE, *n.* [Fr. *carnage*; Sp. *carniceria*, carnage, and shambles; It. *carnaggio*, flesh-meat, and *carnaccia*, carrion; Port. *carnagem*; from L. *caro*, flesh.]

1. Literally, flesh, or heaps of flesh, as in shambles.
2. Slaughter; great destruction of men; havock; massacre. *Hayward.*

C'ARNAL, *a.* [Fr. *charnel*; L. *carnalis*, from *caro*, flesh.]

1. Pertaining to flesh; fleshly; sensual; *opposed to spiritual*; as *carnal* pleasure.
2. Being in the natural state; unregenerate.

> The *carnal* mind is enmity against God. Rom. viii.

3. Pertaining to the ceremonial law; as *carnal* ordinances. Heb. ix. 10.
4. Lecherous; lustful; libidinous; given to sensual indulgence. *Shak.*

Carnal-knowledge, sexual intercourse.

C'ARNALIST, *n.* One given to the indulgence of sensual appetites. *Burton.*

C'ARNALITE, *n.* A worldly-minded man. *Anderson.*

CARNAL'ITY, *n.* Fleshly lust, or desires, or the indulgence of those lusts; sensuality. *South.*

2. Grossness of mind or desire; love of sensual pleasures. *Tillotson.*

C'ARNALIZE, *v. t.* To make carnal; to debase to carnality. *Scott.*

C'ARNALLY, *adv.* In a carnal manner; according to the flesh; in a manner to gratify the flesh or sensual desire. Lev. xviii. 20. Rom. viii. 6.

CARNAL-MINDED, *a.* Worldly-minded. *More.*

CARNAL-MINDEDNESS, *n.* Grossness of mind. *Ellis.*

CARNA'TION, *n.* [Fr. *carnation*, the naked part of a picture, flesh color; It. *incarnatino*; *carnagione*, complexion; Sp. *carnaza*; Port. *carnaz*; from L. *caro*, flesh.]

1. Flesh color; the parts of a picture which are naked, or without drapery, exhibiting the natural color of the flesh. *Encyc.*
2. A genus of plants, Dianthus, so named from the color of the flower. Among these are the clove-gilliflower, sweet-william, Indian pink, &c.

CARNA'TIONED, *a.* Made like carnation color.

CARNE'LIAN, *n.* [Fr. *cornaline*; Sp. *cornerina.*]
A siliceous stone, a variety of chalcedony, of a deep red, flesh-red, or reddish white color. It is tolerably hard, capable of a good polish, and used for seals. *Encyc. Cleaveland.*

Carnel-work, in ship-building, is the putting together the timbers, beams and planks, as distinguished from clinch-work. *Encyc.*

C'ARNEOUS, *a.* [L. *carneus*, from *caro*, flesh.]
Fleshy; having the qualities of flesh. *Ray.*

C'ARNEY, *n.* A disease of horses, in which the mouth is so furred that they cannot eat. *Chambers.*

CARNIFICA'TION, *n.* [Infra.] A turning to flesh. *Chambers.*

C'ARNIFY, *v. i.* [from L. *caro*, *carnis*, flesh.]
To form flesh; to receive flesh in growth. *Hale.*

C'ARNIVAL, } *n.* [Sp. Port. *carnaval*; Fr.
C'ARNAVAL, } *carnaval*; It. *carnovale*; from L. *caro*, flesh.]
The feast or season of rejoicing, before Lent, observed, in Catholic countries, with great solemnity, by feasts, balls, operas, concerts, &c. *Encyc.*

CARNIVORAC'ITY, *n.* [Infra.] Greediness of appetite for flesh. *Pope.*

CARNIV'OROUS, *a.* [L. *caro*, flesh, and *voro*, to eat.]
Eating or feeding on flesh; an epithet applied to animals which naturally seek flesh for food, as the lion, tiger, dog, wolf, &c.

CARNOS'ITY, *n.* [Fr. *carnosité*, from L. *caro*, flesh.]
A little fleshy excrescence in the urethra, the neck of the bladder, &c.

C'ARNOUS, *a.* Fleshy. [See *Carneous.*]

CAR'OB, *n.* [Sp. *algarroba*; It. *carruba.*]
The carob-tree, *Ceratonia siliqua*, a native of Spain, Italy, and the Levant. It is an evergreen, growing in hedges, and producing long, flat, brown-colored pods, filled with a mealy, succulent pulp, of a sweetish taste. In times of scarcity, these pods are eaten by poor people, but they are apt to cause griping and lax bowels. *Miller. Encyc.*

CARO'CHE, *n.* [It. *carrozza.* See *Car.*] A carriage of pleasure. *Burton.*

CARO'CHED, *a.* Placed in a caroche. *Beaum.*

CAR'OL, *n.* [It. *carola*; W. *carawl*; Arm. *coroll*, a dance; W. *cor*, Corn. *karol*, a choir.]
A song of joy and exultation; a song of devotion; or a song in general. *Dryden. Spenser. Bacon. Milton.*

CAR'OL, *v. i.* [It. *carolare*; W. *caroli*; Arm. *carolli*, to dance, to sing love songs.]
To sing; to warble; to sing in joy or festivity. *Prior. Shak.*

CAR'OL, *v. t.* To praise or celebrate in song. *Milton.*

CAROLI'NA, *n.* [from *Carolus*, Charles II.]
The name of two of the Atlantic States in North America, called North Carolina and South Carolina.

CAR'OLING, *n.* A song of praise or devotion. *Spenser.*

CAROLIN'IAN, *a.* Pertaining to Carolina.

CAROLIN'IAN, *n.* A native or inhabitant of Carolina.

CAR'OMEL, *n.* The smell exhaled by sugar, at a calcining heat. *Ure.*

CAROT'ID, *a.* [Gr. χαρωτιδες.] The carotid arteries, in the body, are two arteries, the right and left, which convey the blood from the aorta to the head and brain. The ancients supposed drowsiness to be seated in these arteries. Gr. χαρος.

CAROUS'AL, *n.* *s* as *z.* [See *Carouse.*] A feast or festival. *Johnson.*

But in America it signifies a noisy drinking bout, or reveling.

CAROUSE, *v. i.* *carouz'.* [Fr. *carrouse*, hard drinking. I know not the real original of this word. In Per. كروز karoz signifies hiliarity, singing, dancing. In Germ. *rauschen* signifies to rush, to fuddle. In Ir. *craosal* is drunkenness, from *craos*, excess, revelling.]
To drink hard; to guzzle. In the U. States,

it signifies also to be noisy, as bacchanalians.

ȻAROUSE, *n.* *carouz'.* A drinking match; a hearty drink or full draught of liquor; a noisy drinking match.

ȻAROUS'ER, *n.* A drinker; a toper; a noisy reveler, or bacchanalian.

ȻAROUS'ING, *ppr.* Drinking hard; reveling.

Ȼ'ARP, *v. i.* [L. *carpo*, to seize, catch, pick; It. *carpire;* Sp. Port. *carpir*, to tear or scratch. See *Carve.*]

Literally, to snap or catch at, or to pick. Hence, to censure, cavil, or find fault, particularly without reason, or petulantly; followed by *at.*

No, not a tooth or nail to scratch
And *at* my actions *carp* and catch. *Herbert.*

Ȼ'ARP, *n.* [Fr. Port. *carpe;* Sp. *carpa;* It. *carpione;* Arm. *carpen;* Russ. *karp;* D. *karper;* G. *karpfen;* Dan. *karpe;* Sw. *karp;* Low L. *carpio*, from *carpo*, to sieze.]

A fish, a species of *cyprinus*, an excellent fish for ponds. These fishes breed rapidly, grow to a large size, and live to a great age. *Encyc.*

Ȼ'ARPAL, *a.* [L. *carpus*, the wrist.] Pertaining to the wrist. *Encyc.*

ȻARPA'THIAN, *a.* Pertaining to the *Carpates*, a range of mountains between Poland, Hungary and Transylvania.

Ȼ'ARPENTER, *n.* [Fr. *charpentier;* Sp. *carpintero;* Port. *carpenteiro;* It. *carpentiere*, a cart-wright, or coach-maker; L. *carpentarius*, from *carpentum*, a chariot.]

An artificer who works in timber; a framer and builder of houses, and of ships. Those who build houses are called *house-carpenters*, and those who build ships are called *ship-carpenters.*

In New England, a distinction is often made between the man who frames, and the man who executes the interior wood-work of a house. The framer is the *carpenter*, and the finisher is called a *joiner.* This distinction is noticed by Johnson, and seems to be a genuine English distinction. But in some other parts of America, as in New-York, the term *carpenter* includes both the framer and the joiner; and in truth both branches of business are often performed by the same person. The word is never applied, as in Italy and Spain, to a coach-maker.

Ȼ'ARPENTRY, *n.* The art of cutting, framing, and joining timber, in the construction of buildings; divided into *house-carpentry* and *ship-carpentry.*

Ȼ'ARPER, *n.* One who carps; a caviler.

Ȼ'ARPET, *n.* [I know not the origin of this word.]

1. A covering for floors, tables, stairs, &c. This covering is usually made of wool, wrought with a needle, or more generally in a loom, but is sometimes made of other materials. The manufacture is of Asiatic origin, but has been introduced into many parts of Europe, and into the U. States.

2. Level ground covered, as with grass; as a grassy *carpet;* a *carpet* of green grass. *Shak. Ray.*

To be on the carpet, is to be under consideration; to be the subject of deliberation. The French phrase, *to be on the tapis*, is used in the like sense.

Carpet-knight, in Shakspeare, is a knight who enjoys ease and security, or luxury, and has not known the hardships of the field.

Carpet-monger is used in a like sense.

Ȼ'ARPET, *v. t.* To cover with a carpet; to spread with carpets. *Bacon. Derham.*

Ȼ'ARPETED, *pp.* Covered with a carpet.

Ȼ'ARPETING, *n.* Cloth for carpets; carpets in general.

Ȼ'ARPET-WALK, *n.* A walk on smooth turf. *Evelyn.*

Ȼ'ARPING, *ppr.* Caviling; captious; censorious. *Watts.*

Ȼ'ARPING, *n.* The act of caviling; a cavil; unreasonable censure.

Ȼ'ARPINGLY, *adv.* Captiously; in a carping manner. *Camden.*

Ȼ'ARPMEALS, *n.* A kind of coarse cloth made in the North of England. *Phillips.*

Ȼ'ARPOLITE, *n.* [Gr. χαρπος, fruit, and λιθος, stone.]

Petrified fruits, of which the most remarkable are nuts converted into silex.

ȻARPOL'OĠIST, *n.* [Gr. χαρπος, fruit, and λεγω, to speak.] One who describes fruits.

ȻARPOL'OĠY, *n.* [Supra.] A description of fruits. *Cyc.*

Ȼ'ARPUS, *n.* [L.] The wrist, but not an English word.

ȻAR'RAWAY, *n.* A kind of apple. *Mason.*

ȻAR'RIABLE, *a.* That may be carried. [*Not in use.*] *Sherwood.*

ȻAR'RIAĠE, *n.* [Fr. *charriage*, from *charrier*, to *carry;* It. *carreggio*, or *carriaggio.* See *Carry.*]

1. The act of carrying, bearing, transporting, or conveying; as the *carriage* of sounds. *Bacon.*

2. The act of taking by an enemy; conquest; acquisition. *Obs.* *Knolles.*

3. That which carries, especially on wheels; a vehicle. This is a general term for a coach, chariot, chaise, gig, sulkey, or other vehicle on wheels, as a *cannon-carriage* on trucks, a *block-carriage* for mortars, and a *truck-carriage.* Appropriately the word is applied to a coach; and carts and wagons are rarely or never called *carriages.*

4. The price or expense of carrying.

5. That which is carried; burden; as baggage, vessels, furniture, &c.

And David left his *carriage* in the hands of the keeper of the *carriage.* 1 Sam. xvii.

[*Little used.*] *Spenser.*

6. In *a moral sense*, the manner of carrying one's self; behavior; conduct; deportment; personal manners. *Bacon. Dryden.*

7. Measures; practices; management. *Shak.*

ȻAR'RIBOO. [See *Cariboo.*]

ȻAR'RICK-BEND, *n.* A particular kind of knot.

ȻAR'RICK-BITTS, *n.* In a ship, the bitts which support the windlass. *Mar. Dict.*

ȻAR'RIER, *n.* [See *Carry.*] One who carries; that which carries or conveys; also, a messenger.

2. One who is employed to carry goods for others for a reward; also, one whose occupation is to carry goods for others, called a *common carrier;* a porter.

3. A pigeon that conveys letters from place to place, the letters being tied to the neck.

ȻAR'RION, *n.* [It. *carogna;* Sp. *carroña;* Fr. *charogne;* Arm. *caroan;* D. *karonje.*]

The dead and putrefying body or flesh of animals; flesh so corrupted as to be unfit for food. *Dryden. Pope.*

2. A worthless woman; *a term of reproach.* *Shak.*

ȻAR'RION, *a.* Relating to dead and putrefying carcasses; feeding on carrion, as a *carrion-crow.* *Shak.*

ȻARRONA'DE, *n.* [It is said to be from *Carron*, in Scotland, where it was first made.]

A short piece of ordnance, having a large caliber, and a chamber for the powder, like a mortar. This species of cannon is carried on the upper works of ships, as the poop and forecastle, and is very useful in close engagements. *Mar. Dict. Encyc.*

ȻARROON', *n.* In *London*, a rent received for the privilege of driving a cart. *Ash.*

2. A species of cherry. *Tooke, Russ.*

ȻAR'ROT, *n.* [It. *carota;* Fr. *carotte;* Low L. *carota.*]

An esculent root, of the genus *Daucus*, cultivated for the table and for cattle.

ȻAR'ROTY, *a.* Like a carrot in color; an epithet given to red hair.

ȻAR'RÖWS, *n.* In *Ireland*, people who wander about and get their living by cards and dice; strolling gamesters. *Spenser.*

ȻAR'RY, *v. t.* [W. *cariaw*, from *car*, a dray, drag, or wagon; Fr. *charrier;* Arm. *charreat* or *charreein;* Sp. *acarrear;* Dan. *kiörer;* Sw. *kiöra;* G. *karren.* These verbs signify primarily to carry on a *cart* or *car*, and are evidently from the noun. But the English *carry* coincides also with the Latin *gero*, our vulgar *kerry;* for the sense of *behavior* can hardly proceed from the moving of a wheel-carriage, nor indeed can some other senses of this word. But the primary sense, in both cases, is to move.]

1. To bear, convey, or transport, by sustaining and moving the thing carried, either by bodily strength, upon a beast, in a vehicle, or in any kind of water-craft. In general, it implies a moving *from* the speaker or the place present or near, to a place more distant, and so is opposed to *bring* and *fetch*, and it is often followed by *from, away, off, out.*

He shall *carry* the lambs in his bosom. Is. xl.

When he dieth, he shall *carry* nothing away. Ps. xlix.

2. To convey; as, sound is *carried* in the air.

3. To effect; to accomplish; to prevail; to gain the object; as, to *carry* a point, measure, or resolution; to *carry* a prize; to *carry* a fortified town by force of arms; sometimes followed by *it.*

Whose wills will *carry it* over the rest. *Locke. Burke.*

4. To bear out; to face through.

If a man *carries it* off, there is so much money saved. *L'Estrange.*

5. To urge, impel, lead or draw, noting moral impulse.

Pride or passion will *carry* a man to great lengths.

Men are *carried* away with imaginary prospects. See Eph. iv. 14. Heb. xiii. 9.

6. To bear; to have.

In some vegetables, we see something that *carries* a kind of analogy to sense. *Hale.*

7. To bear; to show, display or exhibit to view.

The aspect of every one in the family *carries* satisfaction. *Addison.*

8. To imply or import.

To quit former tenets *carries* an imputation of ignorance. *Locke.*

9. To contain or comprise.

He thought it *carried* something of argument in it, to prove that doctrine. *Watts.*

10. To extend or continue in time, as to *carry* a historical account to the first ages of the world; but usually with a particle, as to *carry up* or *carry back*, to *carry forward.*

11. To extend in space, as to *carry* a line or a boundary; or in a moral sense, as to *carry* ideas very far.

12. To support or sustain.

Carry camomile on sticks. *Bacon.*

13. To bear or produce, as trees.

Set them a reasonable depth, and they will *carry* more shoots upon the stem. *Bacon.*

14. To manage or transact, usually with *on*; as, to *carry on* business.

15. *To carry one's self*, to behave, conduct or demean.

He *carried himself* insolently. *Clarendon.*

Sometimes with *it*; as, he *carried it* high.

16. To remove, lead or drive.

And he *carried* away all his cattle. Gen. xxxi.

17. To remove; to cause to go.

And the king of Assyria did *carry* away Israel to Assyria. 2 Kings xviii.

18. To transport; to affect with extraordinary impressions on the mind. Rev. xvii.

19. To fetch and bring.

Young whelps learn easily to *carry.* *Ascham.*

20. To transfer; as, to *carry* an account to the ledger.

War was to be diverted from Greece by being *carried* into Asia. *Mitford.*

To carry coals, to bear injuries. *Mason.*

To carry off, to remove to a distance; also, to kill, as to be *carried off* by sickness.

To carry on, to promote, advance, or help forward; to continue; as, to *carry on* a design; to *carry on* the administration of grace.

2. To manage or prosecute; as, to *carry on* husbandry.

3. To prosecute, continue or pursue; as, to *carry on* trade or war.

To carry through, to support to the end; to sustain or keep from failing, or being subdued.

Grace will *carry* a man *through* all difficulties. *Hammond.*

To carry out, to bear from within; also, to sustain to the end; to continue to the end.

To carry away, in seamanship, is to break; to carry sail till a spar breaks; as, to *carry away* a fore-topmast.

CAR'RY, *v. i.* To run on rotten ground, or on frost, which sticks to the feet, as a hare. *Johnson.*

2. To bear the head in a particular manner, as a horse. When a horse holds his head high, with an arching neck, he is said to *carry well.* When he lowers his head too much, he is said to *carry low.*

3. To convey; to propel; as, a gun or mortar *carries* well; *but this is elliptical.*

CAR'RYING, *ppr.* Bearing, conveying, removing, &c.

CAR'RYING, *n.* A bearing, conveying, removing, transporting.

Carrying trade, the trade which consists in the transportation of goods by water from country to country, or place to place.

We are rivals with them in navigation and the *carrying trade.* *Federalist, Jay.*

Carrying wind, among horsemen, is a tossing of the nose, as high as the horse's ears. *Encyc.*

CAR'RY-TALE, *n.* A tale-bearer. [*Not used.*] *Shak.*

C'ART, *n.* [W. *cart*; Sax. *cræt*, *crat*; Ir. *cairt*; Russ. *karet.* See *Car.*]

1. A carriage with two wheels, fitted to be drawn by one horse, or by a yoke of oxen, and used in husbandry or commercial cities for carrying heavy commodities. In Great Britain, *carts* are usually drawn by horses. In America, horse-carts are used mostly in cities, and ox-carts in the country.

2. A carriage in general. *Temple. Dryden.*

C'ART, *v. t.* To carry or convey on a cart; as, to *cart* hay.

2. To expose in a cart, by way of punishment.

C'ARTAGE, *n.* The act of carrying in a cart, or the price paid for carting.

C'ART-BOTE, *n.* In *English law*, wood to which a tenant is entitled for making and repairing carts and other instruments of husbandry.

C'ARTED, *pp.* Borne or exposed in a cart.

C'ART-HORSE, *n.* A horse that draws a cart.

C'ARTING, *ppr.* Conveying or exposing in a cart.

C'ARTING, *n.* The act of carrying in a cart.

C'ART-JADE, *n.* A sorry horse; a horse used in drawing, or fit only for the cart. *Sidney.*

C'ART-LOAD, *n.* A load borne on a cart; as much as is usually carried at once on a cart, or as is sufficient to load it.

C'ART-ROPE, *n.* A rope for binding hay, or other articles on a cart.

C'ART-RUT, *n.* The cut or track of a cart-wheel. [See *Route.*]

C'ART-TIRE, *n.* The tire, or iron bands, used to bind the wheels of a cart.

C'ART-WAY, *n.* A way that is or may be passed with carts, or other wheel carriages.

C'ART-WHEEL, *n.* The wheel of a cart.

C'ART-WRIGHT, *n.* An artificer who makes carts.

Carte-blanche. [Fr. white paper.] A blank paper, signed at the bottom with a person's name, and sometimes sealed with his seal, given to another person with permission to superscribe what conditions he pleases. *Encyc.*

C'ARTEL, *n.* [It. *cartello*; Fr. Sp. Port. *cartel*; from L. *chartula.*]

1. A writing or agreement between states at war, for the exchange of prisoners, or for some mutual advantage; also, a vessel employed to convey the messenger on this occasion.

2. A letter of defiance or challenge; a challenge to single combat. This sense the word has still in France and Italy; but with us it is obsolete.

Cartel-ship, is a ship employed in the exchange of prisoners, or in carrying propositions to an enemy.

C'ARTEL, *v. i.* To defy. *Obs.* *B. Jonson.*

C'ARTER, *n.* The man who drives a cart, or whose occupation is to drive a cart.

CARTE'SIAN, *a.* *cartézhun.* Pertaining to the philosopher Des Cartes, or to his philosophy, which taught the doctrine of vortexes round the sun and planets.

CARTE'SIAN, *n.* One who adopts the philosophy of Des Cartes.

CARTHAGIN'IAN, *a.* Pertaining to ancient Carthage, a celebrated city on the Northern Coast of Africa, about twelve miles from the modern Tunis. It was founded by the Phenicians, and destroyed by the Romans.

CARTHAGIN'IAN, *n.* An inhabitant or native of Carthage.

C'ARTHAMUS, *n.* The generic name of Bastard Saffron. [See *Safflower.*]

CARTHU'SIAN, *n.* *carthúzhun.* One of an order of monks, so called from Chartreuse, the place of their institution. They are remarkable for their austerity. They cannot go out of their cells, except to church, nor speak to any person without leave. *Encyc.*

C'ARTILAGE, *n.* [L. *cartilago*; Fr. *cartilage.* I suspect this and the English *gristle* to be the same word; the *r* being transposed, *cartil* for *cratil.*]

Gristle; a smooth, solid, elastic substance, softer than bone, of a pearly color and homogeneous texture, without cells or cavities. It is invested with a particular membrane called *perichondrium*, which in the articular cartilages, is a reflexion of the synovial membrane. *Cyc. Wistar.*

CARTILAG'INOUS, *a.* Pertaining to or resembling a cartilage; gristly; consisting of cartilage. *Ray.*

2. In *ichthyology*, cartilaginous fishes are those whose muscles are supported by cartilages instead of bones, or whose skeleton is cartilaginous. Many of these are viviparous, as the ray and shark, whose young are excluded from an egg hatched within them. Others are oviparous, as the sturgeon. Some of them have no gill-covers, but breathe through apertures, on the sides of the neck or top of the head; others have gill-covers, but destitute of bony rays. *Encyc. Ed. Encyc.*

CARTOON', *n.* [It. *cartone*, paste-board; Sp. Fr. *carton*; from L. *charta*, paper.]

In *painting*, a design drawn on strong paper, to be afterward calked through and transferred on the fresh plaster of a wall, to be painted in fresco. Also, a design colored for working in Mosaic, tapestry &c. *Encyc.*

CARTOUCH', *n.* [Fr. *cartouche*; Sp. *cartucho*; Port. *cartuxo*; It. *cartuccia*, a cartridge, a bit of paper, from *carta*, paper.]

1. A case of wood, about three inches thick at the bottom, girt with marlin, holding about four hundred musket balls, and six or eight iron balls of a pound weight, to be fired out of a howitz, for defending a pass. A cartouch is sometimes made of a globular form, and filled with a ball of a pound weight; and sometimes for guns, being of a ball of a half or quarter of a pound weight, tied in the form of a bunch of grapes, on a tompion of wood and coated over. *Encyc.*

2. A portable box for charges. [See *Cartridge-box.*]
3. A roll or scroll on the cornice of a column. *Coles.*

CARTRIDGE, *n.* [a corruption of *cartouch.*] A case of pasteboard or parchment, holding the charge of powder or powder and ball, for a cannon, mortar, musket or pistol. The cartridges for small arms, prepared for battle, contain the powder and ball; those for cannon and mortars are made of paste-board, or tin. Cartridges, without balls, are called blank cartridges.

CARTRIDGE-BOX, *n.* A case, usually of wood, covered with leather, with cells for cartridges. It is worn upon a belt thrown over the left shoulder, and hangs a little below the pocket-hole on the right side.

CARTULARY, *n.* [Fr. *cartulaire;* Sp. *cartulario;* from *carta,* paper.]
A register-book, or record, as of a monastery. Blackstone writes it *chartulary;* and primarily it signifies the officer who has the care of charters and other public papers. *Cyc.*

CAR'UCATE, *n.* [L. *caruca.*] As much land as one team can plow in the year. *Eng. Law. Kelham.*

CAR'UNCLE, *n.* [L. *caruncula,* from *caro,* flesh.]
1. A small fleshy excrescence, either natural or morbid. *Coxe.*
2. The fleshy comb on the head of a fowl.

CARUNC'ULAR, *a.* In the form of a caruncle.

CARUNC'ULATED, *a.* Having a fleshy excrescence, or soft fleshy protuberance. *Encyc.*

C'ARVE, *v. t.* c'*arv.* [Sax. *ceorfan, cearfan;* D. *kerven;* G. *kerben;* Dan. *karver;* L. *carpo.* See Ar. حرب and خرف, Heb. חרף and Ch. כרב. Class Rb. No. 26. 27. 30.]
1. To cut into small pieces or slices, as meat at table.
2. To cut wood, stone or other material into some particular form, with an instrument, usually a chisel; to engrave; to cut figures or devices on hard materials.
3. To make or shape by cutting; as, to *carve* an image.
4. To apportion; to distribute; to provide at pleasure; to select and take, as to one's self, or to select and give to another. *South.*
5. To cut; to hew. *Shak.*
To carve out, is to cut out, or to lay out, by design; to plan.

C'ARVE, *v. i.* c'*arv.* To cut up meat; followed sometimes by *for;* as, to *carve for* all the guests.
2. To exercise the trade of a sculptor.
3. To engrave or cut figures.

C'ARVE, *n.* A carucate. [*Not in use.*]

C'ARVED, *pp.* Cut or divided; engraved; formed by carving.

C'ARVEL, *n.* [See *Caravel.*]
2. The urtica marina, or sea blubber.

C'ARVER, *n.* One who cuts meat at table; a sculptor; one who apportions or distributes at will, or one who takes or gives at pleasure. *Dryden. Shak.*
2. A large table knife for carving.

C'ARVING, *ppr.* Cutting, dividing, as meat; cutting in stone, wood or metal; apportioning; distributing.

C'ARVING, *n.* The act of cutting, as meat; the act or art of cutting figures in wood or stone; sculpture; figures carved.

CARYA'TES, } *n.* In *architecture,* figures of women dressed in long robes, after the Asiatic manner, serving to support entablatures. The Athenians had been long at war with the Caryans; the latter being at length vanquished and their wives led captive, the Greeks, to perpetuate this event, erected trophies, in which figures of women, dressed in the Caryatic manner, were used to support entablatures. Other female figures were afterwards used in the same manner, but they were called by the same name. *Encyc.*
CARYAT'IDES, }

They were called *Caryatides,* from Carya, a city in the Peloponnesus, which sided with the Persians, and on that account was sacked by the other Greeks, its males butchered, and its females reduced to slavery. *Cyc.*

CARYAT'IC, *a.* Pertaining to the Caryans or Caryatides.

CARYOPHYL'LEOUS, *a.* [Gr. χαρυον, a nut, and φυλλον, a leaf.] Having five petals with long claws, in a tubular calyx; applied to flowers. *Eaton.*

CARYOPH'YLLOID, *n.* [Gr. χαρυοφυλλον, clove-gilliflower. Infra.]
A species of mica, the scales of which are concentric and perpendicular. *Obs.* *Cronstedt. Nicholson.*

CASARC'A, *n.* A fowl of the genus *Anas,* called also ruddy-goose, larger than a mallard, found in Russia and Siberia. *Encyc.*

CASC'ABEL, *n.* [Port. *cascavel;* Sp. *cascabel,* a little bell, a button or knob at the end of a cannon.] The knob or pummelion of a cannon. *Mar. Dict.*

CASCA'DE, *n.* [Fr. *cascade;* Sp. *cascada;* It. *cascata,* from *cascare,* to fall.]
A waterfall; a steep fall or flowing of water over a precipice, in a river or natural stream; or an artificial fall in a garden. The word is applied to falls that are less than a cataract.

CASCAL'HO, *n.* [Port.] In *Brazil,* a deposit of pebbles, gravel and sand in which the diamond is usually found. *Port. Dict. Cleaveland.*

CASE, *n.* [Fr. *caisse;* Sp. Port. *caxa,* a box or chest; It. *cassa;* D. *kas;* Dan. *kasse.* The French *caisse* is the Sp. *caxa.* The Spanish *caxeta,* a gasket, seems to be a derivative of *caxa,* and if so, the fact indicates that *caxa* is from an oriental root, signifying to tie or bind, and that the word originally denoted a bag made of skin, like a bottle, or a basket made of osiers interwoven, like *fisc, fiscus.* Qu. Syr. ܟܫܐ casha, to bind or tie.]
1. A covering, box or sheath; that which incloses or contains; as a *case* for knives; a *case* for books; a watch *case;* a printer's *case;* a pillow *case.*
2. The outer part of a building. *Addison.*
3. A certain quantity; as a *case* of crown glass.
4. A building unfurnished. [*Not used.*]

CASE, *v. t.* To cover with a case; to surround with any material that shall inclose or defend.
2. To put in a case or box.
3. To strip off a case, covering, or the skin. [*Unusual.*] *Shak.*

CASE, *n.* [Fr. *cas;* It. *caso;* Sp. Port. *caso;* Ir. *cas;* L. *casus,* from *cado,* to fall.]
1. Literally, that which falls, comes, or happens; an event. Hence, the particular state, condition, or circumstances that befall a person, or in which he is placed; as, make the *case* your own; this is the *case* with my friend; this is his present *case.*
2. The state of the body, with respect to health or disease; as a *case* of fever; he is in a consumptive *case;* his *case* is desperate.
To be in good case, is to be fat, and this phrase is customarily abridged, *to be in case;* applied to beasts, but not to men, except in a sense rather ludicrous.
3. A question; a state of facts involving a question for discussion or decision; as, the lawyer stated the *case.*
4. A cause or suit in court; as, the *case* was tried at the last term. In this sense, *case* is nearly synonymous with *cause,* whose primary sense is nearly the same.
5. In *grammar,* the inflection of nouns, or a change of termination, to express a difference of relation in that word to others, or to the thing represented. The variation of nouns and adjectives is called declension; both *case* and *declension* signifying *falling* or *leaning* from the first state of the word. Thus, *liber* is a book; *libri,* of a book; *libro,* to a book. In other words, *case* denotes a variation in the termination of a noun, to show how the noun acts upon the verb with which it is connected, or is acted upon by it, or by an agent. The cases, except the nominative, are called oblique cases.
In case, is a phrase denoting condition or supposition; literally, in the event or contingency; if it should so fall out or happen.
Put the case, suppose the event, or a certain state of things.
Action on the case, in law, is an action in which the whole cause of complaint is set out in the writ. *Blackstone.*

CASE, *v. i.* To put cases. [*Not in use.*] *L'Estrange.*

CA'SED, *pp.* Covered with a case.

CASE-HARDEN, *v. t.* To harden the outer part or superficies, as of iron, by converting it into steel. This may be done by putting the iron into an iron box, with a cement, and exposing it, for some hours, to a red heat. *Encyc.*

CA'SEIC, *a.* [L. *caseus,* cheese.] The *caseic acid* is the acid of cheese, or a substance so called, extracted from cheese. *Proust.*

CASE-KNIFE, *n.* A large table knife, often kept in a case.

CA'SEMATE, *n.* [Fr. *casemate;* It. *casamatta;* Sp. Port. *casamata;* from *casa,* a house.]
1. In *fortification,* a vault of mason's work in the flank of a bastion, next to the curtain, somewhat inclined toward the capital of the bastion, serving as a battery to defend the face of the opposite bastion, and the moat or ditch. *Chambers.*

2. A well, with its subterraneous branches, dug in the passage of the bastion, till the miner is heard at work, and air given to the mine. *Harris.*

CA'SEMENT, *n.* [It. *casamento*, a large house.]

1. A hollow molding, usually one sixth or one fourth of a circle. *Encyc.*

2. A little movable window, usually within a larger, made to turn and open on hinges. *Encyc.*

CA'SEOUS, *a.* [L. *caseus*, cheese.] Like cheese; having the qualities of cheese.

CAS'ERN, *n.* [Fr. *caserne*; Sp. *caserna*, from *casa*, a shed or house.]

A lodging for soldiers in garrison towns, usually near the rampart, containing each two beds. *Encyc.*

CASE-SHOT, *n.* Musket balls, stones, old iron, &c., put in cases, to be discharged from cannon.

CA'SE-WORM, *n.* A worm that makes itself a case. *Johnson.*

CASH, *n.* [Fr. *caisse*; Sp. Port. *caxa*, a chest, box, coffer. See *Case.*]

Money; primarily, ready money, money in chest or on hand, in bank or at command. It is properly silver and gold; but since the institution of banks, it denotes also bank notes equivalent to money. *To pay in cash* is opposed to payment in goods, commodities, or labor, as in barter.

CASH, *v. t.* To turn into money, or to exchange for money; as, to *cash* a note or an order.

2. To pay money for; as, the clerks of a bank *cash* notes when presented. *Mercantile usage.*

CASH, *v. t.* To discard. [for *cashier. Not used.*]

CASH-ACCOUNT', *n.* An account of money received, paid, or on hand.

CASH'-BOOK, *n.* A book in which is kept a register or account of money.

CASH'-KEEPER, *n.* One entrusted with the keeping of money.

CASH'EW-NUT, *n.* A tree of the West-Indies, *Anacardium*, bearing a kidney-shaped nut. The fruit is as large as an orange, and full of an acid juice, which is often used to make punch. To the apex of this fruit grows a nut, of the size of a hare's kidney, the shell of which is hard, and the kernel, which is sweet, is covered with a thin film. *Encyc.*

CASHIE'R, *n.* [Fr. *caissier*; It. *cassiere*; Sp. *caxero*; Port. *caxeiro*; from *caxa*, a box, whence *cash.*]

One who has charge of money; a cash-keeper. In a banking institution, the cashier is the officer who superintends the books, payments and receipts of the bank. He also signs or countersigns the notes, and superintends all the transactions, under the order of the directors.

CASHIE'R, *v. t.* [Fr. *casser*, to break; It. *cassare*, to annul, blot out, erase.]

1. To dismiss from an office or place of trust, by annulling the commission; to break, as for mal-conduct, and therefore with reproach; as, to *cashier* an officer of the army.

2. To dismiss or discard from service or from society. *Addison. Dryden. Swift.*

3. To reject; to annul or vacate. *Locke. South.*

CASHIE'RED, *pp.* Dismissed; discarded; annulled.

CASHIE'RER, *n.* One who rejects, discards or breaks; as a *cashierer* of monarchs. *Burke.*

CASHIE'RING, *ppr.* Discarding; dismissing from service.

CASH'OO, *n.* The juice or gum of a tree in the East Indies.

CA'SING, *ppr.* Covering with a case.

CA'SING, *n.* The act or operation of plastering a house with mortar on the outside, and striking it while wet, by a ruler, with the corner of a trowel, to make it resemble the joints of free-stone. *Encyc.*

2. A covering; a case.

C'ASK, *n.* [Sp. Port. *casco*; Fr. *casque*; Arm. *casquen*, *casqed*; L. *cassis*. See *Case.*]

A head-piece; a helmet; a piece of defensive armor, to cover and protect the head and neck, in battle.

C'ASK, *n.* [Sp. Port. *casco.*] A close vessel for containing liquors, formed by staves, heading and hoops. This is a general term comprehending the pipe, hogshead, butt, barrel, &c.

C'ASKET, *n.* [dim. of *cask*. See *Case.*] A small chest or box, for jewels or other small articles. *Shak.*

2. In *seamen's language*, a small rope, fastened to gromets or little rings upon the yards, used to fasten the sail to the yard in furling. *Encyc.*

This is usually written *gasket.*

C'ASKET, *v. t.* To put in a little chest. *Shak.*

CAS'PIAN, *a.* [*Caspiæ*, a word applied to a pass in the range of Mount Taurus. Plin. 5. 27. *D'Anville.*]

An epithet given to a large lake between Persia and Astracan, called the Caspian Sea.

CASS, *v. t.* [Fr. *casser*, L. *quasso.*] To quash; to defeat; to annul. [*Not now used.*] *Raleigh.*

CASS'ADA, } *n.* A plant, of the genus *Jatropha*, of different species.
CASS'AVI, }

The roots of the manihot or bitter cassada, and of the janipha, are made into a kind of bread which serves for food to the natives of Africa and the West Indies, and they are also roasted and eaten like potatoes. They yield also a great quantity of starch, which the Brasilians export in small lumps under the name of *tapioca.*

CASSAMUNA'IR, *n.* An aromatic vegetable brought from the East. *Todd.*

CAS'SATE, *v. t.* [Fr. *casser*. See *Cashier.*] To vacate, annul, or make void. *Obs. Ray.*

CASSA'TION, *n.* The act of annulling. In France there is a court of *Cassation.*

CASSIA, *n. cash'ia.* [Fr. *casse*; It. *cassia*; Gr. and L. *id.* Qu. Heb. קדה.]

A genus of plants of many species, among which are the fistula, or purging cassia, and the senna. The former is a native of Egypt and both Indies; the latter is a native of Persia, Syria and Arabia. The latter is a shrubby plant, the leaves of which are much used in medicine. The purging cassia is the pulp of the pods, and is a gentle laxative.

Cassia is also the name of a species of Laurus, the bark of which usually passes under the name of cinnamon, differing from real cinnamon chiefly in the strength of its qualities. From a plant of this kind was extracted an aromatic oil, used as a perfume by the Jews. Ex. xxx. Ps. xlv, 8. *Encyc.*

CAS'SIDONY, *n.* [Fr. *cassidoine.*] A species of plant, Gnaphalium, cotton-weed, cudweed or goldylocks; also, *Lavandula stœchas* or French lavender. *Encyc. Fam. of Plants.*

CAS'SIMER, *n.* [Sp. *casimira.*] A thin twilled woolen cloth. *Encyc.*

CASSI'NO, *n.* A game at cards. *Todd.*

CAS'SIOBURY, *n.* A species of plant, of the genus *Cassine*, of which the most remarkable species is the Yapon of the Southern States of America. The berries are of a beautiful red color. *Fam. of Plants. Encyc.*

The Yapon is now arranged in the genus *Ilex.* *Cyc.*

CASSIOPE'IA, *n.* A constellation in the Northern Hemisphere, situated near to Cepheus, as the fabulous Cassiopeia was wife to Cepheus, king of Ethiopia. It contains fifty five stars. *Encyc.*

CASSITE'RIA, *n.* [L. *cassiteron*, tin.] A kind of crystals which appear to have an admixture of tin. The color is brown or whitish. *Encyc.*

CAS'SOCK, *n.* [Sp. *casaca*; It. *casacca*; Fr. *casaque.*]

A robe or gown worn over the other garments, particularly by the clergy. *Encyc.*

A close garment, now generally that which clergymen wear under their gowns. *Johnson.*

CAS'SOCKED, *a.* Clothed with a cassock.

The *cassock'd* huntsman. *Cowper.*

CASSONA'DE, *n.* [Fr.] Cask-sugar; sugar not refined. *Encyc.*

CAS'SOWARY, *n.* [Sp. *casuel.*] A large fowl of the genus *Struthio*, nearly as large as the ostrich, but its legs are thicker and stronger in proportion. The wings are so small as not to appear, being hid under the feathers. The head is armed with a helmet of horny substance, consisting of plates one over another. It runs with great rapidity, outstripping the swiftest racer. *Encyc.*

It is now arranged in a separate genus, *Casuarius.* *Cuvier.*

C'AST, *v. t.* pret. and pp. *cast.* [Dan. *kaster*; Sw. *kasta.* Qu. Arm. *caçz*, pp. *caçzet*, to send, to throw. See Class Gs. No. 1. 56. In Dan. *et blind kast*, is a *guess*, and to cast is the radical sense of *guess.* In Norman, *gistes* signifies *cast up*, and this seems to be the participle of *gesir*, to lie down; to lie down may be to throw one's self down. This verb coincides in sense with the W. *cothi*, to throw off.]

1. To throw, fling or send; that is, to drive from, by force, as from the hand, or from an engine.

Hagar *cast* the child under a shrub. Gen. xxi.
Uzziah prepared slings to *cast* stones. 2 Ch. xxvi.

2. To sow; to scatter seed.

If a man should *cast* seed into the ground. Mark iv.

3. To drive or impel by violence.

A mighty west wind *cast* the locusts into the sea. Ex. x.

4. To shed or throw off; as, trees *cast* their fruit; a serpent *casts* his skin.
5. To throw or let fall; as, to *cast* anchor. Hence, *to cast anchor* is to moor, as a ship, the effect of casting the anchor.
6. To throw, as dice or lots; as, to *cast* lots.
7. To throw on the ground, as in wrestling. *Shak.*
8. To throw away, as worthless.
His carcase was *cast* in the way. I Kings xiii.
9. To emit or throw out.
This *casts* a sulphurous smell. *Woodward.*
10. To throw, to extend, as a trench or rampart, including the sense of digging, raising, or forming.
Thy enemies shall *cast* a trench about thee. Luke xix.
11. To thrust; as, to *cast* into prison.
12. To put, or set, in a particular state.
Both chariot and horse were *cast* into a dead sleep. Ps. lxxvi.
13. To condemn; to convict; as a criminal.
Both tried and both were *cast*. *Dryden.*
14. To overcome in a civil suit, or in any contest of strength or skill; as, to *cast* the defendant or an antagonist.
15. To cashier or discard. *Shak.*
16. To lay aside, as unfit for use; to reject; as a garment. *Addison.*
17. To make to preponderate; to throw into one scale, for the purpose of giving it superior weight; to decide by a vote that gives a superiority in numbers; as, to *cast* the balance in one's favor; a *casting* vote or voice.
18. To throw together several particulars, to find the sum; as, to *cast* accounts. Hence, to throw together circumstances and facts, to find the result; to compute; to reckon; to calculate; as, to *cast* the event of war.
To *cast* and see how many things there are which a man cannot do himself. *Bacon.*
19. To contrive; to plan. *Temple.*
20. To judge, or to consider, in order to judge. *Milton.*
21. To fix, or distribute the parts of a play among the actors. *Addison.*
22. To throw, as the sight; to direct, or turn, as the eye; to glance; as, to *cast* a look, or glance, or the eye.
23. To found; to form into a particular shape, by pouring liquid metal into a mold; to run; as, to *cast* cannon.
Thou shalt *cast* four rings of gold for it. Ex. xxv.
24. *Figuratively*, to shape; to form by a model. *Watts.*
25. To communicate; to spread over; as, to *cast* a luster upon posterity; to *cast* splendor upon actions, or light upon a subject.
To cast aside, to dismiss or reject as useless or inconvenient.
To cast away, to reject. Lev. xxvi. Is. v. Rom. xi. Also, to throw away; to lavish or waste by profusion; to turn to no use; as, to *cast away* life. *Addison.*
Also, to wreck, as a ship.
To cast by, to reject; to dismiss or discard with neglect or hate, or as useless. *Shak. Locke.*
To cast down, to throw down; to deject or depress the mind.
Why art thou *cast down*, O my soul. Ps. xlii.
To cast forth, to throw out, or eject, as from an inclosed place; to emit, or send abroad; to exhale.
To cast off, to discard or reject; to drive away; to put off; to put away; to disburden. Among *huntsmen*, to leave behind, as dogs; to set loose, or free. Among *seamen*, to loose, or untie.
To cast out, to send forth; to reject or turn out; to throw out, as words; to speak or give vent to.
To cast up, to compute; to reckon; to calculate; as, to *cast up* accounts, or the cost. Also, to eject; to vomit.
To cast on, to refer or resign to. *South.*
To cast one's self on, to resign or yield one's self to the disposal of, without reserve.
To cast young, to miscarry; to suffer abortion. Gen. xxxi.
To cast in the teeth, to upbraid; to charge; to twit. So in Danish, "*kaster en i næsen*," to cast in the nose.

€'AST, *v. i.* To throw forward, as the thoughts, with a view to some determination; or to turn or revolve in the mind; to contrive; sometimes followed by *about*.
I *cast* in careful mind to seek her out. *Spenser.*
To *cast about* how to perform or obtain. *Bacon. Bentley.*
2. To receive form or shape.
Metal will *cast* and mold. *Woodward.*
3. To warp; to twist from regular shape.
Stuff is said to *cast* or warp, when it alters its flatness or straightness. *Moxon.*
Note. *Cast*, like *throw* and *warp*, implies a winding motion.
4. In *seamen's language*, to fall off, or incline, so as to bring the side of a ship to the wind; applied particularly to a ship riding with her head to the wind, when her anchor is first loosened.

€'AST, *n.* The act of casting; a throw; the thing thrown; the form or state of throwing; kind or manner of throwing.
2. The distance passed by a thing thrown; or the space through which a thing thrown may ordinarily pass; as, about a stone's *cast*. Luke xxii.
3. A stroke; a touch.
This was a *cast* of Wood's politics. *Swift.*
4. Motion or turn of the eye; direction, look or glance; a squinting.
They let you see by one *cast* of the eye. *Addison.*
5. A throw of dice; hence, a state of chance or hazard.
It is an even *cast*, whether the army should march this way or that way. *South.*
Hence the phrase, *the last cast*, is used to denote that all is ventured on one throw, or one effort.
6. Form; shape.
A heroic poem in another *cast*. *Prior.*
7. A tinge; a slight coloring, or slight degree of a color; as a *cast* of green. Hence, a slight alteration in external appearance, or deviation from natural appearance.
The native hue of resolution
Is sicklied o'er with the pale *cast* of thought. *Shak.*
8. Manner; air; mien; as, a peculiar *cast* of countenance. This sense implies, the turn or manner of throwing; as, the neat *cast* of verse. *Pope.*
9. A flight; a number of hawks let go at once. *Sidney.*
10. A small statue of bronze. *Encyc.*
11. Among *founders*, a tube of wax, fitted into a mold, to give shape to metal.
12. A cylindrical piece of brass or copper, slit in two lengthwise, to form a canal or conduit, in a mold, for conveying metal.
13. Among *plumbers*, a little brazen funnel, at one end of a mold, for casting pipes without sodering, by means of which the melted metal is poured into the mold. *Encyc.*
14. [Sp. Port. *casta.*] A breed, race, lineage, kind, sort.
15. In *Hindoostan*, a tribe or class of the same rank or profession; as the *cast* of *Bramins*, or priests; of *rajahs*, or princes; of *choutres*, or artificers; and of *parias*, or poor people. Or according to some writers, of *Bramins;* of *cuttery*, or soldiers; of *shuddery*, or merchants; and of *wyse*, or mechanics. *Encyc.*
The four casts of the Hindoos are the *Brahmins* or sacred order; the *Chehteres* or soldiers and rulers; the *Bice*, *Vaissya*, or husbandmen and merchants; and the *Sooders*, *Sudras*, or laborers and mechanics. *Cyc. Ed. Encyc.*
16. A trick. *Martin.*

CASTA'LIAN, *a.* Pertaining to Castalia, a cool spring on Parnassus, sacred to the muses; as *Castalian* fount. *Poetry.*

€AST'ANET, *n.* [Sp. *castañeta*, *castañuela;* Port. *castanheta;* Fr. *castagnette;* It. *castagnetta.* This word seems to be from *castaña*, a chestnut, so named from the resemblance to two chestnuts.]
An instrument of music formed of small concave shells of ivory or hard wood, shaped like spoons, placed together, fastened to the thumb and beat with the middle finger. This instrument is used by the Spaniards, Moors and Bohemians, as an accompaniment to their dances, sarabands and guitars. *Span. Dict. Encyc.*

€'ASTAWAY, *n.* [*cast* and *away.*] That which is thrown away. A person abandoned by God, as unworthy of his favor; a reprobate. 1 Cor. ix. 27.

€'ASTAWAY, *a.* Rejected; useless; of no value. *Raleigh.*

€'ASTED, *pp.* for *cast*, is not in use.

€AS'TELLAN, *n.* [Sp. *castellan;* Fr. *chatelain.* See *Castle.*]
A governor or constable of a castle. In Poland, the name of a dignity or charge; a kind of lieutenant of a province, commanding part of a palatinate under a palatine. The castellans are senators, of the lower class, sitting, in the diets, on low seats behind the palatines. *Encyc.*

€AS'TELLANY, *n.* [See *Castle.*] The lordship belonging to a castle; or the extent of its land and jurisdiction. *Phillips.*

€AS'TELLATED, *a.* Inclosed in a building, as a fountain or cistern. *Johnson.*
2. Adorned with turrets, and battlements, like a castle.

€ASTELLA'TION, *n.* The act of fortifying a house and rendering it a castle.

€'ASTER, *n.* [from *cast.*] One who throws or casts; one who computes; a calculator; one who calculates fortunes. *Addison.*
2. A small phial or vessel for the table; as a set of *casters*.
3. A small wheel on a swivel, on which furniture is *cast*, or rolled, on the floor.

CAS'TIGATE, *v. t.* [L. *castigo*, from *castus*, chaste. Qu. Eth. ገሠጸ gasts, to chasten, correct, chide. The French use *châtier*, from *castus*, chaste; Arm. *castiza*; Sp. Port. *castigar*; It. *castigare*.]
To chastise; to punish by stripes; to correct; to chasten; to check. *Shak.*

CAS'TIGATED, *pp.* Punished; corrected.

CAS'TIGATING, *ppr.* Punishing; correcting; chastising.

CASTIGA'TION, *n.* Punishment; correction; penance; discipline; emendation; restraint. *Boyle. Hale.*

2. Among *the Romans*, a military punishment inflicted on offenders, by beating with a wand or switch. *Encyc.*

CAS'TIGATOR, *n.* One who corrects.

CAS'TIGATORY, *a.* Tending to correction; corrective; punitive. *Bramhall.*

CAS'TIGATORY, *n.* An engine formerly used to punish and correct arrant scolds, called also a ducking stool, or trebucket. *Blackstone.*

CAS'TĪLE-SOAP, *n.* A kind of pure, refined soap.

CASTIL'IAN, *a.* Pertaining to Castile in Spain.

CASTIL'IAN, *n.* An inhabitant or native of Castile in Spain.

C'ASTING, *ppr.* Throwing; sending; computing; calculating, turning; giving a preponderancy; deciding; running, or throwing into a mold to give shape. [See *Cast.*]

C'ASTING, *n.* The act of casting or founding.

2. That which is cast in a mold; any vessel formed by casting melted metal into a mold, or in sand.

3. The taking of casts and impressions of figures, busts, medals, &c.

C'ASTING-NET, *n.* A net which is cast and drawn, in distinction from a net that is set and left. *May.*

C'ASTING-VOTE, } *n.* The vote of a pre-
C'ASTING-VOICE, } siding officer, in an assembly or council, which decides a question, when the votes of the assembly or house are equally divided between the affirmative and negative. *U. States. Coxe.*

When there was an equal vote, the Governor had the *casting voice*. *B. Trumbull.*

CAS'TLE, *n.* *kas'l.* [Sax. *castel*; L. *castellum*; D. *kasteel*; Arm. *gastell*; Norm. *chaxtel*; Fr. *château*; Port. *castello*; It. *id*; W. *cast*, envelopment, from *cás*, a being separated or insulated, hatred, envy, a castle; *castell*, a castle, whence *castellu*, to surround; *casul*, a cloke, a chasuble. The Welch *cás* gives the primary sense, which is to separate, to drive off; hence, to defend. It is probably from this root the Latins had *casa*. We observe in the Welch, *cás* signifies, separated, a castle, and hatred, envy; also, hateful, odious; and *casnawr*, a hater, a persecutor; *casnori*, to persecute, to chase. Hence we see the radical sense of hatred is a *driving off*.]

1. A house fortified for defense against an enemy; a fortress. The term seems to include the house and the walls or other works around it. In old writers, the word is used for a town or village fortified.

2. The house or mansion of a nobleman or prince.

3. In a *ship*, there are two parts called by this name; the *forecastle*, a short deck in the fore part of the ship, above the upper deck; and the *hindcastle*, at the stern.

Castle in the air, a visionary project; a scheme that has no solid foundation.

CAS'TLE, *v. t.* In the game of chess, to cover the king with a castle, by a certain move. *Encyc.*

CAS'TLE-BUILDER, *n.* One who forms visionary schemes.

CAS'TLE-BUILDING, *n.* The act of building castles in the air.

CAS'TLE-CROWNED, *a.* Crowned with a castle.

CAS'TLED, *a.* Furnished with castles; as a *castled* elephant. *Dryden.*

CAS'TLE-GUARD, *n.* A feudal tenure, or knight service, which obliged the tenant to perform service within the realm, without limitation of time. *Lyttelton.*

CAS'TLERY, *n.* The government of a castle. *Blount.*

CAS'TLET, *n.* A small castle. *Leland.*

CAS'TLE-WARD, *n.* An imposition laid upon subjects dwelling within a certain distance of a castle, for the purpose of maintaining watch and ward in the castle. *Encyc.*

C'ASTLING, *n.* An abortion or abortive. *Brown.*

C'ASTOR, *n.* [L. *castor*; Fr. Sp. Port. *id.*; Gr. *καςωρ*. See Ar. Class Gs. No. 42.]

1. A beaver, an amphibious quadruped, with a flat ovate tail, short ears, a blunt nose, small fore feet, and large hind feet.

2. A reddish brown substance, of a strong penetrating smell, taken from bags or cods in the groin of the beaver; a powerful antispasmodic. *Nicholson.*

3. In *astronomy*, a moiety of the constellation *Gemini*, called also Apollo.

Castor and Pollux, in *meteorology*, a fiery meteor, which, at sea, appears sometimes adhering to a part of a ship, in the form of one, two and even three or four balls. When one is seen alone, it is called *Helena*, which portends that the severest part of the storm is yet to come. Two appearing at once are denominated *Castor and Pollux*, or *Tyndaridæ*, and portend a cessation of the storm. *Chambers.*

C'ASTORIN, } *n.* An animal principle dis-
C'ASTORINE, } covered in castor, and prepared by boiling castor in six times its weight of alcohol, and filtering the liquor. From this is deposited the Castorin. *Webster's Manual.*

CASTOR-OIL, *n.* The oil of the Ricinus, or Palma Christi, a plant of the West Indies, which grows to the highth of twenty feet, in one season. The oil is obtained from the nuts or seeds by expression or decoction. That obtained by decoction is preferred, as less liable to become rancid, being free from the mucilage and acrid matter, which is mixed with the oil when expressed. It is a mild cathartic. *Encyc.*

CASTRAMETA'TION, *n.* [L. *castrametor*, to encamp, *castra*, camp, and *metior*, to measure or survey.]
The art or act of encamping; the marking or laying out of a camp. *Murphy's Tacitus.*

CAS'TRATE, *v. t.* [L. *castro*; Fr. *châtrer*, for *chastrer*; Sp. Port. *castrar*; It. *castrare*; Ar. خَصَى, Eth. ኀጸወ to castrate; Ch. חצא to cut out or off. Class Gs. No. 41. 42.]

1. To geld; to deprive of the testicles; to emasculate.

2. To take away or retrench, as the obscene parts of a writing.

3. To take out a leaf or sheet from a book, and render it imperfect.

CAS'TRATED, *pp.* Gelded; emasculated; purified from obscene expressions.

CAS'TRATING, *ppr.* Gelding; taking away the obscene parts of a writing.

CASTRA'TION, *n.* The act of gelding; the act or practice of making eunuchs; the act of taking away the obscene parts of a writing; the act of taking out a leaf or sheet of a book. In *botany*, the cutting off of the anthers, or tops of the stamens of flowers, before the ripening of the pollen.

CASTRA'TO, *n.* [It. See *Castrate.*] A male person emasculated for the purpose of improving his voice for a singer. *Swift.*

CAS'TREL or **KES'TREL,** *n.* A kind of hawk, resembling the lanner in shape and the hobby in size.

CASTREN'SIAN, *a.* [L. *castrensis*, from *castra*, a camp.] Belonging to a camp.

CAS'UAL, *a.* *cazh'ual.* [Fr. *casuel*; Sp. Port. *casual*; It. *casuale*; from L. *casus*, a fall. See *Case* and *Accident*.]

1. Falling; happening or coming to pass, without design in the person or persons affected, and without being foreseen, or expected; accidental; fortuitous; coming by chance; as, the parties had a *casual* rencounter.

2. Occasional; coming at certain times, without regularity, in distinction from stated, or regular; as *casual* expenses.

3. Taking place, or beginning to exist without an efficient intelligent cause, and without design.

Atheists assert that the existence of things is *casual*. *Dwight.*

CAS'UALLY, *adv.* Accidentally; fortuitously; without design; by chance.

CAS'UALNESS, *n.* Accidentalness; the quality of being casual.

CAS'UALTY, *n.* Accident; that which comes by chance or without design, or without being foreseen; contingency.

2. An accident that produces unnatural death; and by a metonymy, death, or other misfortune, occasioned by an accident.

3. In *Scots law*, an emolument due from a vassal to his superior, beyond the stated yearly duties, upon certain casual events. *Encyc.*

CAS'UIST, *n.* [It. Sp. Port. *casuista*; Fr. *casuiste*; from L. *casus*, a *case*.]
One who studies and resolves cases of conscience.

The judgment of any *casuist* or learned divine is not sufficient to give him confidence. *South.*

CAS'UIST, *v. i.* To play the part of a casuist. *Milton.*

CASUIS'TIC, } *a.* Relating to cases of
CASUIS'TICAL, } conscience, or to cases of doubtful propriety. *South.*

CAS'UISTRY, *n.* The science or doctrine of cases of conscience; the science of resolving cases of doubtful propriety, or of determining the lawfulness or unlawfulness of what a man may do, by rules and principles drawn from the scriptures, from the laws of society, or from equity and natural reason. *Pope.*

Casus fœderis. [L.] The case stipulated by treaty; that which comes within the terms of compact. *Law of Nations.*

CAT, *n.* [Ir. *cat;* Fr. *chat;* D. *kat;* Dan. *kat;* Sw. *katt;* G. *kater,* or *katze;* L. *catus;* Vulgar Greek, *κατις,* or *γατος;* It. *gatto;* Port. and Sp. *gato;* Lap. *id.;* Pol. *kot;* Russ. *kots;* Turkish *keti;* W. *cath;* Corn. *kath;* Arm. *gaz* or *kaz;* Basque *catua.* In Ar. قطّ kitta, is a male cat. Class Gd. No. 56.]

1. A name applied to certain species of carnivorous quadrupeds, of the genus *Felis.* The domestic cat needs no description. It is a deceitful animal, and when enraged, extremely spiteful. It is kept in houses, chiefly for the purpose of catching rats and mice. The wild cat is much larger than the domestic cat. It is a strong, ferocious animal, living in the forest, and very destructive to poultry and lambs.

The wild cat of Europe is of the same species with the domestic cat; the catamount, of N. America, is much larger and a distinct species. *Ed. Encyc.*

2. A ship formed on the Norwegian model, having a narrow stern, projecting quarters, and a deep waist. It is strong built, from four to six hundred tons burthen, and employed in the coal trade.

3. A strong tackle or combination of pulleys, to hook and draw an anchor perpendicularly up to the cat-head of a ship.

4. A double tripod having six feet.

Cat of nine tails, an instrument of punishment, consisting of nine pieces of line or cord fastened to a piece of thick rope, and having three knots at intervals, used to flog offenders on board of ships.

CAT'AMOUNT, *n.* Cat of the mountain, the wild cat.

CAT'-BLOCK, *n.* A two or three fold block with an iron strop and large hook, used to draw up an anchor to the cat-head. *Mar. Dict.*

CAT'S'-EYE, *n.* Sun-stone, a subspecies of quartz, called in Latin *oculus cati* or *onycopalus,* from its white zones or rings like onyx, and its variable colors like opal. It is very hard and semitransparent, and from certain points exhibits a yellowish radiation, or chatoyant appearance, somewhat resembling a cat's eye. *Encyc. Cleaveland.*

CAT'-EYED, *a.* Having eyes like a cat. *Dryden.*

CAT'-FISH, *n.* A species of the Squalus, or shark. The cat-fish of the N. American rivers is a species of *Cottus,* or bull-head.

CAT'S'-FOOT, *n.* A plant of the genus Glechoma, ground ivy, or gill.

CAT'-GUT, *n.* The intestines of sheep or lambs, dried and twisted together, used as strings for violins and other instruments, and for other purposes. Great quantities are imported from Lyons and Italy.

CAT'-HARPINGS, *n.* Ropes serving to brace in the shrouds of the lower masts behind their respective yards, to tighten the shrouds and give more room to draw in the yards, when the ship is close hauled. *Mar. Dict.*

CAT'-HEAD, *n.* A strong beam projecting horizontally over a ship's bows, carrying two or three sheaves, about which a rope called the *cat-fall* passes, and communicates with the cat-block. *Mar. Dict.*

CAT'S'-HEAD, *n.* A kind of apple.

CAT'-HOOK, *n.* A strong hook fitted to the *cat-block.* *Mar. Dict.*

CAT'-MINT, *n.* A plant of the genus Nepeta, so called because cats eat it.

CAT'S'-PAW, *n.* Among *seamen,* a light air perceived, in a calm, by a rippling of the surface of the water; also, a particular turn in the bight of a rope, made to hook a tackle on. *Mar. Dict.*

2. A dupe; the instrument which another uses.

CAT'-SALT, *n.* A sort of salt beautifully granulated, formed out of the bittern or leach-brine, used for making hard soap.

CAT'SILVER, *n.* A fossil, a species of mica.

CAT'-TAIL, *n.* [*cat* and *tail.*] A species of reed, of the genus *Typha,* the downy substance of which is used for stuffing mattresses, &c. *Bailey.*

2. A substance growing on nut-trees, pines, &c. *Bailey.*

CATABAP'TIST, *n.* [Gr. *κατα* and *βαπτιςης.*] One who opposes baptism. *Featley.*

CATACAUS'TIC, *a.* [Gr. *κατακαυσις,* a burning.] Catacaustic curves, in *geometry,* are that species of caustic curves, which are formed by reflection. *Bailey. Encyc.*

CATACHRE'SIS, *n.* [Gr. *καταχρησις,* abuse, from *κατα,* against, and *χραομαι,* to use.]

An abuse of a trope or of words; a figure in rhetoric, when one word is abusively put for another, or when a word is too far wrested from its true signification; as, a voice *beautiful* to the *ear.* *Smith. Bailey. Johnson.*

A catachresis is a trope which borrows the name of one thing to express another, or a harsh trope; as when Milton, speaking of Raphael's descent from heaven, says, he "sails between worlds and worlds." Here the novelty of the word *sails* enlivens the image. So in scripture we read of the "*blood* of the grape." Deut. xxxii.

CATACHRES'TIC, **CATACHRES'TICAL**, } *a.* Belonging to a catachresis; forced; far-fetched; wrested from its natural sense. *Johnson. Brown.*

CATACHRES'TICALLY, *adv.* In a forced manner. *Evelyn.*

CAT'ACLYSM, *n.* [Gr. *κατακλυσμος,* a deluge, from *κατακλυζω,* to inundate.]

A deluge, or overflowing of water; particularly, the flood in Noah's days. [*Little used.*] *Hall.*

CAT'ACOMB, *n.* [probably from Gr. *κατα,* and *κυμβος,* a hollow or recess.]

A cave, grotto or subterraneous place for the burial of the dead. It is said to have been originally applied to the chapel of St. Sebastian in Rome, where the ancient Roman Calendars say, the body of St. Peter was deposited. It is now applied to a vast number of subterraneous sepulchers, about three miles from Rome, in the Appian way; supposed to be the cells and caves in which the primitive christians concealed themselves, and in which were deposited the bodies of the primitive martyrs. These are visited by devout people, and relics are taken from them, baptized by the Pope and dispersed through Catholic countries. Each catacomb is three feet broad and eight or ten high; along the side walls are sepulchral niches, closed with thick tiles or pieces of marble. Catacombs are found also at Naples and in other places. *Encyc.*

CATACOUS'TICS, *n.* [Gr. *κατακουω,* to hear.]

That part of acoustics or the doctrine of sounds, which treats of reflected sounds. But the distinction is deemed of little use. *Encyc.*

CATADIOP'TRIC, **CATADIOP'TRICAL**, } *a.* [Gr. *κατα,* and *διοπτομαι,* to see through.] Reflecting light.

CAT'ADUPE, *n.* [Gr. *κατα,* and *δουπεω,* to sound.]

A cataract or waterfall. [*Not in use.*] *Brewer.*

CATAGMAT'IC, *a.* [Gr. *καταγμα,* a fragment.]

That has the quality of consolidating broken parts; promoting the union of fractured bones. *Wiseman. Coxe.*

CAT'AGRAPH, *n.* [Gr. *κατα,* and *γραφω,* to describe.]

The first draught of a picture; also, a profile. *Chambers.*

CATALEC'TIC, *a.* [Gr. *κατα,* and *λεγω.*] Pertaining to metrical composition, or to measure. *Tyrwhitt.*

Catalectic verses, are such as want either feet or syllables. *Cyc.*

CATALEP'SIS, **CAT'ALEPSY**, } *n.* [Gr. *καταληψις,* a seizing, from *καταλαμβανω,* to take, seize, or invade.]

A sudden suppression of motion and sensation, a kind of apoplexy, in which the patient is speechless, senseless, and fixed in one posture, with his eyes open, without seeing or understanding. The word is applied also to a retention of the breath or of the humors, and to the interception of the blood by bandages. *Encyc. Coxe.*

CATALEP'TIC, *a.* Pertaining to catalepsy.

CAT'ALOGIZE, *v. t.* To insert in a catalogue. [*Not used.*] *Coles.*

CAT'ALOGUE, *n.* *kat'alog.* [Gr. *καταλογος;* *κατα* and *λογος,* according to words.]

A list or enumeration of the names of men or things disposed in a certain order, often in alphabetical order; as a *catalogue* of the students of a college, or of books, or of the stars.

CAT'ALOGUE, *v. t.* [*as above.*] To make a list of. *Herbert.*

CATAL'PA, *n.* A large tree of Carolina and the South, which in blossom has a beautiful appearance. It belongs to the genus *Bignonia,* or trumpet flower. *Drayton. Encyc.*

CATAL'YSIS, *n.* [Gr. *καταλυσις.*] Dissolution. [*Little used.*] *Taylor.*

CATAME'NIAL, *a.* [Gr. *καταμηνιος;* *κατα* and *μην,* a month.]

Pertaining to the catamenia, or menstrual discharges.

ƇAT'AMITE, *n.* [L. *catamitus.*] A boy kept for unnatural purposes.

ƇAT'APASM, *n.* [Gr. καταπασμα.] A dry powder for sprinkling the body. *Coxe.*

ƇAT'APELT, or ƇAT'APULT, *n.* [Gr. καταπελτης; L. *catapulta*; κατα and πελτη, a target, or more probably from παλλω or βαλλω, to throw or drive, L. *pello.*]
A military engine used by the ancient Greeks and Romans for throwing stones, darts and arrows upon an enemy. Some of these would throw a stone of a hundred pounds weight. *Mitford.*

ƇATAPEL'TIƇ, *a.* Pertaining to the catapelt. As a noun, the catapelt.

ƇATAPHON'IƇS, *n.* [Gr. κατα, and φωνη, sound.]
The doctrine of reflected sounds, a branch of acoustics. *Encyc.*

ƇAT'APHRAƇT, *n.* [L. *cataphracta*; Gr. καταφρακτος, from καταφρασσω, to arm or fortify.]
1. In *the ancient military art*, a piece of heavy defensive armor, formed of cloth or leather, strengthened with scales or links, used to defend the breast, or whole body, or even the horse as well as the rider. *Encyc.*
2. A horseman in complete armor. *Milton.*

ƇAT'APLASM, *n.* [Gr. καταπλασμα, from καταπλασσω, to anoint, or to spread as a plaster.]
A poultice; a soft and moist substance to be applied to some part of the body, to excite or repel heat, or to relax the skin, &c. When mustard is an ingredient, it is called a *sinapism.* *Encyc.*

ƇAT'APUCE, *n.* The herb spurge. *Obs.* *Chaucer.*

ƇAT'ARAƇT, *n.* [L. *cataracta*; Gr. καταρακτης, from καταρασσω, to break or fall with violence, from ρασσω, ραξω, to strike or dash.]
1. A great fall of water over a precipice; as that of Niagara, of the Rhine, Danube and Nile. It is a cascade upon a great scale.
The tremendous *cataracts* of America thundering in their solitudes. *Irving.*
2. In *medicine* and *surgery*, an opacity of the crystaline lens, or its capsule; a disorder in the eye, by which the pupil, which is usually black and transparent, becomes opake, blue, gray, brown, &c., by which vision is impaired or destroyed. *Encyc.*

ƇAT'ARRH, *n.* catàr. [L. *catarrhus*; Gr. καταρροος, from καταρρεω, to flow down.]
A defluxion, or increased secretion of mucus from the membranes of the nose, fauces and bronchiæ, with fever, sneezing, cough, thirst, lassitude and loss of appetite, and sometimes an entire loss of taste; called also a cold, *coryza.* An epidemic catarrh is called *Influenza.* *Hooper. Coxe. Encyc.*

ƇAT'ARRHAL, } *a.* Pertaining to catarrh,
ƇAT'ARRHOUS, } produced by it or attending it; as a *catarrhal* fever.

ƇATAS'TERISM, *n.* [Gr. καταςερισμος, from καταςεριζω, to distinguish with stars, or to place among the stars; κατα and αςηρ, a star.]
A constellation, or a placing among the stars.

ƇATAS'TROPHE, } *n.* [Gr. καταςροφη, an
ƇATAS'TROPHY, } end or overthrowing, from καταςρεφω, to subvert; κατα and ςρεφω.]
1. The change or revolution which produces the final event of a dramatic piece; or the unfolding and winding up of the plot, clearing up difficulties, and closing the play. The ancients divided a play into the protasis, epitasis, catastasis, and catastrophe; the introduction, continuance, heightening, and development or conclusion. *Johnson. Encyc.*
2. A final event; conclusion; generally, an unfortunate conclusion, calamity, or disaster.

ƇAT'ƇALL, *n.* [*cat* and *call.*] A squeaking instrument, used in play-houses to condemn plays. *Johnson. Pope.*

ƇATCH, *v. t.* pret. and pp. *catched* or *caught.* [Sp. *coger*, to catch, coinciding in elements with Gr. κιχεω. The orthography of *caught* determines the radical letters to be Cg. The popular or common pronunciation is *ketch.*]
1. To seize or lay hold on with the hand; carrying the sense of pursuit, thrusting forward the hand, or rushing on.
And they came upon him and *caught* him. Acts vi.
2. To seize, in a general sense; as, to *catch* a ball; to *catch* hold of a bough.
3. To seize, as in a snare or trap; to ensnare; to entangle.
They sent certain of the Pharisees and of the Herodians, to *catch* him in his words. Mark xii.
4. To seize in pursuit; hence simply to overtake, *a popular use of the word.*
He ran, but could not *catch* his companion.
5. To take hold; to communicate to.
The fire *caught* the adjoining building.
6. To seize the affections; to engage and attach to; as, to *catch* the fair. *Dryden.*
7. To take or receive by contagion or infection; as, to *catch* the measles or small pox.
8. To snatch; to take suddenly; as, to *catch* a book out of the hand.
9. To receive something passing.
The swelling sails no more
Catch the soft airs and wanton in the sky. *Trumbull.*
To catch at, to endeavor to seize suddenly.
To *catch at* all opportunities of subverting the state. *Addison.*
To catch up, to snatch; to take up suddenly.

ƇATCH, *v. i.* To communicate; to spread by infecting; as, a disease will *catch* from man to man.
2. To seize and hold; as, a hook *catches.*

CATCH, *n.* Seizure; the act of seizing.
2. Any thing that seizes or takes hold, as a hook.
3. The posture of seizing; a state of preparation to catch, or of watching an opportunity to seize; as, to lie upon the *catch.* *Addison.*
4. A sudden advantage taken. *Dryden.*
5. The thing caught, considered as an object of desire; profit; advantage.
Hector shall have a great *catch.* *Shak.*
6. A snatch; a short interval of action.
It has been writ by *catches.* *Locke.*
7. A little portion.
We retain a *catch* of a pretty story. *Glanville.*
8. In *music*, a fugue in the unison, wherein to humor some conceit in the words, the melody is broken, and the sense is interrupted in one part, and *caught* and supported by another, or a different sense is given to the words; or a piece for three or more voices, one of which leads and the others follow in the same notes. *Encyc. Busby.*

ƇATCH'ABLE, *a.* That may be caught. [*Not well authorized.*]

ƇATCH'ER, *n.* One who catches; that which catches, or in which any thing is caught.

ƇATCH'-FLY̆, *n.* A plant of the genus Lychnis; campion.

ƇATCH'ING, *ppr.* Seizing; taking hold; ensnaring; entangling.

ƇATCH'ING, *a.* Communicating, or that may be communicated, by contagion; infectious; as, a disease is *catching.*

ƇATCH'PENNY, *n.* [*catch* and *penny.*] Something worthless, particularly a book or pamphlet, adapted to the popular taste, and intended to gain money in market.

ƇATCH'-PŌLL, *n.* [*catch* and *poll*, the head.] A bailiff's assistant, so called by way of reproach.

ƇATCH'UP, } *n.* A liquor extracted from
ƇAT'SUP, } mushrooms, used as a sauce.

ƇATCH'-WŎRD, *n.* Among *printers*, the word placed at the bottom of each page, under the last line, which is to be inserted as the first word on the following page.

ƇATE, *n.* [See *Cates.*]

ƇATEƇHET'IƇAL, *a.* [See *Catechise.*] Relating to oral instruction, and particularly in the first principles of the christian religion.
2. Relating to or consisting in asking questions and receiving answers, according to the ancient manner of teaching pupils.
Socrates introduced a *catechetical* method of arguing. *Addison.*

ƇATEƇHET'IƇALLY, *adv.* By question and answer; in the way of oral instruction.

ƇAT'EƇHISE, *v. t.* *s* as *z.* [Gr. κατηχιζω, and κατηχεω, to sound, to utter sound, to teach by the voice; from κατα, and ηχεω, to sound, whence *echo.* Hence κατηχησις, κατηχισμος, *catechise, catechism*, instruction.]
1. To instruct by asking questions, receiving answers, and offering explanations and corrections.
2. To question; to interrogate; to examine or try by questions, and sometimes with a view to reproof, by eliciting answers from a person, which condemn his own conduct.
3. *Appropriately*, to ask questions concerning the doctrines of the christian religion; to interrogate pupils and give instruction in the principles of religion.

ƇAT'EƇHISED, *pp.* Instructed.

ƇAT'EƇHISER, *n.* One who catechises; one who instructs by question and answer, and particularly in the rudiments of the christian religion.

ƇAT'EƇHISING, *ppr.* Instructing in rudiments or principles.

ƇAT'EƇHISM, *n.* [Gr. κατηχισμος.] A form of instruction by means of questions and answers, particularly in the principles of religion.
2. An elementary book containing a summary of principles in any science or art, but appropriately in religion, reduced to the form of questions and answers, and sometimes with notes, explanations, and references to authorities.

CAT'ECHIST, *n.* [Gr. κατηχιςης.] One who instructs viva voce, or by question and answer; a catechiser; one appointed by the church to instruct in the principles of religion.

CATECHIS'TIC, CATECHIS'TICAL, *a.* Pertaining to a catechist, or catechism.

CAT'ECHU, *n.* Terra Japonica, a dry extract, or brown astringent substance, obtained by decoction and evaporation from a species of Mimosa in India. It consists chiefly of tannin. *Thomson. Ure.*

CATECHU'MEN, *n.* [Gr. κατηχουμενα, places where hearers stood to be instructed, or buildings adjoining a church where the catechist taught the doctrines of religion.]
One who is in the first rudiments of christianity; one who is receiving instruction and preparing himself for baptism. These were anciently the children of believing parents, or pagans not fully initiated in the principles of the christian religion. They were admitted to this state by the imposition of hands, and the sign of the cross. *Encyc.*

CATECHUMEN'ICAL, *a.* Belonging to catechumens.

CATECHU'MENIST, *n.* A catechumen. *Bp. Morton.*

CATEGOR'ICAL, *a.* [See *Category.*] Pertaining to a category.
2. Absolute; positive; express; not relative or hypothetical; as a *categorical* proposition, syllogism or answer.

CATEGOR'ICALLY, *adv.* Absolutely; directly; expressly; positively; as, to affirm *categorically.*

CAT'EGORY, *n.* [Gr. κατηγορια, from κατηγορεω, to accuse, show, demonstrate; κατα and αγορεω, to speak in an assembly, to harangue or denounce, from αγορα, a forum, judicial tribunal or market.]
In *logic*, a series or order of all the predicates or attributes contained under a genus. The school philosophers distributed all the objects of our thoughts and ideas into genera or classes. Aristotle made ten categories, viz. substance, quantity, quality, relation, action, passion, time, place, situation and habit. *Encyc.*

CATENA'RIAN, CAT'ENARY, *a.* [L. *catenarius*, from *catena*, a chain.]
Relating to a chain; like a chain. The *catenarian curve*, in geometry, is formed by a rope or chain hanging freely between two points of suspension, whether the points are horizontal or not. *Harris. Encyc.*

CAT'ENATE, *v. t.* [L. *catena*, a chain; G. *kette*; Sans. *ketta*, whence *kettenu*, to bind.]
To chain, or rather to connect in a series of links or ties. *Darwin.*

CATENA'TION, *n.* Connection of links, union of parts, as in a chain; regular connection. [See *Concatenation.*]

CAT'ENULATE, *a.* Consisting of little links or chains.

CA'TER, *v. i.* [In It. *cattare* is to get; *accattare*, to beg or borrow. In Fr. *acheter* is to buy; Norm. *acat*, a buying. The Fr. *quêter*, for *quester*, to beg, seems to be a different word. See *Caterer.*]
To provide food; to buy or procure provisions; followed by *for*; as, to *cater for* the the sparrow. *Shak.*

CA'TER, *n.* A provider. [See *Caterer.*] Old Eng. *achator.* *Chaucer.*

CA'TER, *n.* The four of cards or dice; so written for Fr. *quatre.*

CA'TER-COUSIN, *n.* A quatre-cousin, a remote relation. *Shak.*

CA'TERER, *n.* [from *cater.* In Chaucer, *achator*, a purchaser or caterer, is evidently from *acheter*, to buy.]
A provider, buyer or purveyor of provisions. *Chaucer*, Cant. Tales. 570. *South.*

CA'TERESS, *n.* A woman who caters; a female provider of food.

CAT'ERPILLAR, *n.* [The etymology of this word is uncertain. Perhaps it may be from Fr. *chatte pelue*, hairy cat.]
The colored and often hairy larva of the *lepidopterous* insects. This term is also applied to the larvas of other insects, such as the *Tenthredo*, or saw-fly; but is more generally confined to the *lepidopters.* Caterpillars are produced immediately from the egg; they are furnished with several pairs of feet, and have the shape and appearance of a worm. They contain the embryo of the perfect insect, inclosed within a muscular envelop, which is thrown off, when the insect enters the nymph or chrysalis state, in which it remains for sometime as if inanimate. It then throws off its last envelop, and emerges a perfect insect. Caterpillars generally feed on leaves or succulent vegetables, and are sometimes very destructive. *Ed. Encyc. Kirby.*

CAT'ERPILLAR-EATER, *n.* A worm bred in the body of a caterpillar, which eats it. *Encyc.*

CAT'ERWAUL, *v. i.* [probably from *cat* and *wawl*, It. *guaiolare*, Eng. *wail.*]
To cry or wawl, as cats in rutting time; to make a harsh offensive noise.

CAT'ERWAULING, *n.* The cry of cats; a harsh disagreeable noise or cry.

CA'TERY, *n.* The place where provisions are deposited.

CATES, *n.* Delicious food or viands; dainties.

CATH'ARIST, *n.* [Gr. χαραθος, pure.] One who pretends to more purity than others possess.

CATH'ARTIC, CATH'ARTICAL, *a.* [Gr. χαθαρτιχος, from χαθαρενω, χαθαιρω, to purge, χαθαρος, clean, χατα and αιρω, to remove.]
Purging; cleansing the bowels; promoting evacuations by stool; purgative.

CATH'ARTIC, *n.* A medicine that promotes alvine discharges, and thus cleanses the stomach and bowels; a purge; a purgative.

CATH'ARTICALNESS, *n.* The quality of promoting discharges from the bowels.

CATHE'DRAL, *n.* [L. *cathedra*; Gr. χαθεδρα, a chair or seat, from χατα and εδρα, a seat.]
The see or seat of a bishop; the principal church in a diocese.

CATHE'DRAL, *a.* Pertaining to the church which is the bishop's seat, or head church of a diocese; containing the see of a bishop; as a *cathedral* church; *cathedral* service.
2. Resembling the aisles of a cathedral; as, *cathedral* walks. *Pope.*

CATH'EDRATED, *a.* Relating to the authority of the chair or office of a teacher. *Whitlock.*

CATH'ETER, *n.* [Gr. χαθετηρ, from χαθιημι, to thrust in; χατα and ιημι, to send.]
In *surgery*, a tubular instrument, usually made of silver, to be introduced into the bladder, to draw off the urine when the natural discharge is suppressed; also, a sound to search for the stone, or a bougie made of silver or elastic gum. *Encyc. Coxe.*

CATH'ETUS, *n.* [Gr. χαθετος. See *Catheter.*]
In *geometry*, a line or radius, falling perpendicularly on another line or surface; as the two sides of a right-angled triangle. *Encyc.*
Cathetus of incidence, in catoptrics, is a right line drawn from a point of the object, perpendicular to the reflecting line.
Cathetus of reflection, or *of the eye*, a right line drawn from the eye, perpendicular to the reflecting plane.
Cathetus of obliquation, a right line drawn perpendicular to the speculum, in the point of incidence or reflection.
In *architecture*, a cathetus is a perpendicular line, supposed to pass through the middle of a cylindrical body. *Encyc.*

CATH'OLIC, *a.* [Gr. χαθολιχος, χατα and ολιχος, from ολος, the whole; L. *catholicus*; Fr. *catholique*; Sp. *catolico*; It. *cattolico.*]
Universal or general; as the *Catholic* church. Originally this epithet was given to the Christian church in general, but is now appropriated to the Romish church, and in strictness there is no Catholic church, or universal Christian communion. The epithet is sometimes set in opposition to heretic, sectary or schismatic.
2. Liberal; not narrow minded, partial or bigoted; as a *catholic* man.
3. Liberal; as *catholic* principles.
Catholic epistles, the epistles of the apostles which are addressed to all the faithful, and not to a particular church.

CATH'OLIC, *n.* A papist.

CATH'OLICISM, *n.* Adherence to the Catholic church.
2. Universality, or the orthodox faith of the whole church. *Pearson.*
3. More generally, liberality of sentiments.
This is the renowned seat of *Catholicism.* *E. D. Griffin.*

CATH'OLICIZE, *v. i.* To become a catholic. [*Little used.*]

CATH'OLICLY, *adv.* Generally; in a catholic manner. *Sir L. Cary.*

CATH'OLICNESS, *n.* Universality. *Brevint.*

CATHOL'ICON, *n.* [Gr. χοθολιχον ιαμα, universal remedy.]
A remedy for all diseases; a universal remedy; a remedy supposed to be efficacious in purging away all humors; a panacea; a kind of soft purgative electuary so called.

CAT'ILINISM, *n.* The practices of Catiline, the Roman conspirator; conspiracy.

CAT'KIN, *n.* [from *cat* and *kin.*] In *botany*, a species of calyx or rather of inflorescence, from a common chaffy gemmaceous receptacle, or consisting of many chaffy scales ranged along a stalk, slender as a thread, which is the common receptacle, as in hazle, birch, oak, willow, poplar, &c.; so called from its resemblance to a cat's tail. *Martyn.*

ȻAT'-LIKE. *a.* Resembling a cat. *Shak.*

ȻAT'LING, *n.* A dismembering knife, used by surgeons. *Harris.*

2. The down or moss growing about walnut trees, resembling the hair of a cat. *Harris.*

3. Catgut. Qu. *Shak.*

ȻATO'NIAN, *a.* Pertaining to or resembling Cato, the Roman, who was remarkable for his severity of manners; grave; severe; inflexible.

ȻATOP'TER, } *n.* [Gr. κατοπτρον. See
ȻATOP'TRON, } *Catoptrics.*] An optical glass or instrument. *Dict.*

ȻATOP'TRIȻ, } *a.* [See *Catoptrics.*]
ȻATOP'TRIȻAL, }
Relating to catoptrics, or vision by reflection.

ȻATOP'TRIȻS, *n.* [Gr. κατοπτρικος, from κατοπτρον, a mirror, from κατα, against, and οπτομαι, to see.]

That part of optics which explains the properties of reflected light, and particularly that which is reflected from mirrors or polished bodies. *Encyc.*

ȻATOP'TROMANCY, *n.* [Gr. κατοπτρομαντεια; κατοπτρον, a mirror, and μαντεια, divination.]

A species of divination among the ancients, which was performed by letting down a mirror into water, for a sick person to look at his face in it. If his countenance appeared distorted and ghastly, it was an ill omen; if fresh and healthy, it was favorable. *Encyc.*

ȻAT'-PIPE, *n.* [See *Catcall.*]

ȻAT'SUP, *n.* [See *Catchup, Ketchup.*]

ȻAT'TLE, *n. sing.* or *plu.* [Norm. *catal, chastel,* and *chatters,* goods, commodities, movables; Arm. *chetal,* beasts; Port. *gado,* cattle. In Syr. and Ch. נת and גית signify a flock, herd, possession, goods. But Spelman alledges that the word *chattel* is contracted from *capitalia, captal,* from *caput,* a word used in the middle ages for all goods, movable and immovable, answering nearly to the use of Gr. κεφαλαιον, Acts xxii. 28. πολλου κεφαλαιου, "with a great price or sum I obtained this freedom." Qu. Sp. *caudal,* wealth, property, capital sum.]

Beasts or quadrupeds in general, serving for tillage, or other labor, and for food to man. In its primary sense, the word includes camels, horses, asses, all the varieties of domesticated horned beasts or the bovine genus, sheep of all kinds and goats, and perhaps swine. In this general sense, it is constantly used in the scriptures. See Job i. 3. Hence it would appear that the word properly signifies possessions, goods. But whether from a word originally signifying a beast, for in early ages beasts constituted the chief part of a man's property, or from a root signifying to *get* or possess, Gr. κτaομαι, It. *cattare,* or from *capitalia,* it is not easy to determine. This word is restricted to domestic beasts; but in England it includes horses, which it ordinarily does not, in the United States, at least not in New-England.

2. In the United States, cattle, in common usage, signifies only beasts of the bovine genus, oxen, bulls, cows and their young. In the laws respecting domestic beasts, horses, sheep, asses, mules and swine are distinguished from *cattle,* or neat cattle. Thus the law in Connecticut, requiring "that all the owners of any cattle, sheep or swine, shall ear-mark or brand *all their cattle,* sheep and swine," does not extend to horses. Yet it is probable that a law, giving damages for a trespass committed by *cattle* breaking into an inclosure, would be adjudged to include horses.

In Great Britain, beasts are distinguished into *black cattle,* including bulls, oxen, cows and their young; and *small cattle,* including sheep of all kinds and goats.

3. In reproach, human beings are called cattle. *Shak.*

ȻAUȻA'SIAN, } *a.* Pertaining to Mount
ȻAUȻASE'AN, } Caucasus in Asia. *As. Researches. Pinkerton.*

ȻAUȻ'US, *n.* A word used in America to denote a meeting of citizens to agree upon candidates to be proposed for election to offices, or to concert measures for supporting a party. The origin of the word is not ascertained.

ȻAUD'AL, *a.* [L. *cauda,* a tail.] Pertaining to a tail; or to the thread which terminates the seed of a plant. *Botany.*

ȻAUD'ATE, } *a.* [L. *cauda,* a tail.] Ha-
ȻAUD'ATED, } ving a tail. *Fairfax.*

ȻAUD'EX, *n.* plu. *caudexes.* [L.] In *botany,* the stem of a tree. Linne uses the word for the stock which proceeds from a seed, one part ascending and forming the body above ground, the other descending and putting forth roots. *Martyn. Darwin.*

ȻAU'DLE, *n.* [Fr. *chaudeau,* from *chaud,* warm or hot, by contraction from L. *calidus* or its root; It. *caldo.*]

A kind of warm broth, a mixture of wine and other ingredients prepared for the sick. *Wiseman.*

ȻAU'DLE, *v. t.* To make or prepare caudle, or to dress with caudle. *Shak.*

ȻAUF, *n.* [probably from the root of *coffer.*]

A chest with holes for keeping fish alive in water. *Ash.*

ȻAUGHT, *pret.* and *pp.* of *catch,* pronounced *caut.*

ȻAUK, } *n.* A name given by miners to
ȻAWK, } certain specimens of the compact sulphate of baryte. These are of a white, gray or fawn color, often irregular in figure, but sometimes resembling a number of small convex lenses set in a ground. *Nicholson. Ure.*

This name is sometimes given to masses composed of concentric lamellar concretions. *Cleaveland.*

ȻAUK'Y, *a.* Pertaining to cauk; like cauk. *Woodward.*

ȻAUL, *n.* [L. *caula,* a fold, from the root of *hold.* See *Hold.*]

1. In *anatomy,* a membrane in the abdomen, covering the greatest part of the lower intestines, called from its structure, reticulum, a net, but more generally, the omentum; also, a little membrane sometimes encompassing the head of a child when born. *Encyc.*

2. A kind of net in which females inclose their hair; the hinder part of a cap. *Dryden.*

3. Any kind of net. *Grew.*

ȻAULES'CENT, *a.* [L. *caulis,* a stalk; Gr. καυλος. See *Cole.*]

In *botany,* having a stem different from that which produces the flower; as a *caulescent* plant. Linne applies this term to the root also, as in cabbage and turnep. *Martyn. Lee.*

ȻAULIF'EROUS, *a.* [L. *caulis,* a stem, and *fero,* to bear.]

In *botany,* having a stem or stalk.

ȻAUL'IFLOWER, *n.* [It. *cavolfiore;* L. *caulis,* W. *cawl,* D. *kool,* and *flower.*]

A variety of Brassica or cabbage, well known and much esteemed.

ȻAUL'IFORM, *a.* [L. *caulis,* a stem, and *forma,* form.]

Having the form of a stalk or of stems. *Kirwan.*

ȻAUL'INE, *a.* [L. *caulis,* a stalk.] In *botany,* growing immediately on the stem, without the intervention of branches; as a *cauline* leaf, bulb, peduncle or scape. *Martyn.*

ȻAULK, [See *Calk.*]

ȻAUP'ONATE, *v. i.* [L. *cauponor.*] To keep a victualling house. [*Not in use.*]

ȻAUP'ONISE, *v. t.* To sell wine or victuals. [*Not in use.*] *Warburton.*

CAUS'ABLE, *a.* [See *Cause.*] That may be caused, produced or effected. *Ash.*

ȻAUS'AL, *a.* [See *Cause.*] Relating to cause or causes; implying or containing a cause or causes; expressing a cause.

Causal propositions are where two propositions are joined by *causal* words, as *that* or *because.* *Watts.*

ȻAUS'AL, *n.* In *grammar,* a word that expresses a cause, or introduces the reason. *Harris.*

ȻAUSAL'ITY, *n.* The agency of a cause; the action or power of a cause, in producing its effect. *Encyc. Glanville.*

ȻAUS'ALLY, *adv.* According to the order or series of causes. *Johnson. Brown.*

ȻAUS'ALTY, *n.* Among *miners,* the lighter, earthy parts of ore, carried off by washing. *Encyc.*

ȻAUSA'TION, *n.* The act of causing or producing; the act or agency by which an effect is produced. *Brown.*

ȻAUS'ATIVE, *a.* That expresses a cause or reason; also, that effects as a cause. *Johnson.*

ȻAUS'ATIVELY, *adv.* In a causative manner.

ȻAUSA'TOR, *n.* One who causes or produces an effect. *Brown.*

ȻAUSE, *n. s* as *z.* [Fr. *cause;* Sp. Port. It. *causa;* L. *causa,* from the Celtic; Welsh *acaws,* effecting power, allied to *cais,* effort, *ceisiaw,* to seek or go after, to attempt; Arm. *caus* or *cos.* The primary sense is to urge, press, impel, like *sequor,* whence *suit;* hence, to *accuse,* to attack or follow with a charge. The root of this word coincides with that of *castle, cast,* &c., which express a driving. A *cause* is that which moves, excites or impels to action or effect; in law, a pressing for a claim. See *Question. Cause, sake* and *thing* have the like radical sense.]

1. A suit or action in court; any legal pro-

cess which a party institutes to obtain his demand, or by which he seeks his right or his supposed right. This is a legal, scriptural and popular use of the word, coinciding nearly with *case* from *cado*, and *action* from *ago*, to urge or drive.

The *cause* of both parties shall come before the judges. Ex. xxii.

2. That which produces an effect; that which impels into existence, or by its agency or operation produces what did not before exist; that by virtue of which any thing is done; that from which any thing proceeds, and without which it would not exist.

Cause is a substance exerting its power into act, to make a thing begin to be. *Locke.*

3. The reason or motive that urges, moves, or impels the mind to act or decide.

For this *cause* have I raised up Pharaoh. Ex. ix.

And David said, is there not a *cause?* 1 Sam. xvii.

4. Sake; account.

I did it not for his *cause* that had done the wrong. 2. Cor. vii. [See *Sake*.]

5. That which a party or nation pursues; or rather pursuit, prosecution of an object. We say, Bible Societies are engaged in a noble *cause*. [See the first definition.] Hence the word *cause* is used to denote that which a person or thing favors; that to which the efforts of an intelligent being are directed; as, to promote religion is to advance the *cause* of God. So we say, the *cause* of truth or of justice. In all its applications, *cause* retains something of its original meaning, struggle, impelling force, contest, effort to obtain or to effect something.

6. *Without cause*, without good reason; without a reason or motive to justify the act.

They hate me *without cause*. Ps. xxxv. lxix.

CAUSE, *v. t.* To produce; to bring into existence.

They *caused* great joy to all the brethren. Acts xv.

2. To effect by agency, power or influence.

I will *cause* it to rain on the earth forty days. Gen. vii.

I will *cause* him to fall by the sword. 2 Kings xix.

CAUSE, *v. i.* To assign insufficient cause. *Obs.* *Spenser.*

CAUS'ED, *pp.* Produced; effected; brought about.

CAUSELESS, *a.* *cauz'less.* Having no cause, or producing agent. *Blackmore.*

2. Without just ground, reason or motive; as *causeless* hatred; *causeless* fear. *Fairfax. Waller.* Prov. xxvi.

CAUSELESSLY, *adv. cauz'lessly.* Without cause or reason. *Taylor.*

CAUSELESSNESS, *n. cauz'lessness.* The state of being causeless. *Hammond.*

CAUS'ER, *n.* He that causes; the agent by which an effect is produced. *Johnson. Sidney.*

CAUS'EY, *n. cauz'y.* [Norm. *calsay*; Fr. *chaussée* for *chaulsée*, a bank, or raised way; Arm. *chauçzer*, the bank or mole of a pond. The Spanish has *calzada*, a causey, or way paved and raised; Port. *calçada*, a pavement, and stones used in paving. Both these words are evidently from the same root as Sp. *calzas*, Port. *calçado*, Sp. *calzado*, hose, loose breeches, trowsers, shoes, Fr. *chausse*, and the French word is evidently the same with the loss of *l*. The sense is probably taken from putting on, covering, Port. *calçar*, to put on shoes, or stockings, to pave, Sp. *calzar*, id, L. *calceo*, *calceus*.]

A way raised above the natural level of the ground, by stones, earth, timber, fascines, &c., serving as a dry passage over wet or marshy ground, or as a mole to confine water to a pond or restrain it from overflowing lower ground. Most generally it is a way raised in a common road.

CAUSID'ICAL, *a.* [L. *causidicus*, *causa* and *dico*.]

Pertaining to an advocate, or to the maintenance and defense of suits.

CAUS'ING, *ppr.* Producing; effecting; bringing into being.

CAUS'TIC, **CAUS'TICAL**, *a.* [Gr. καυςικος, from καιω, καυσω, to burn.]

Burning; corroding; destroying the texture of animal flesh.

CAUS'TIC, *n.* In *medicine*, any substance which applied to living animals, acts like fire, in corroding the part and dissolving its texture; an escharotic. [See *Causticity*.] *Coxe. Encyc.*

Lunar caustic, a preparation of crystals of silver, obtained by solution in nitric acid, and afterwards fused in a crucible. It is a nitrate of silver. *Nicholson.*

Caustic curve, in geometry, a curve formed by a coincidence of rays of light reflected from another curve. *Encyc.*

CAUSTIC'ITY, *n.* The quality of acting like fire on animal matter, or the quality of combining with the principles of organized substances, and destroying their texture. This quality belongs to concentrated acids, pure alkalis, and some metallic salts. *Nicholson.*

CAU'TEL, *n.* [L. *cautela*, from *caveo*, to take care.] Caution. [*Not used.*] *Shak.*

CAU'TELOUS, *a.* [Fr. *cauteleux*, from L. *cautela*.] Cautious; wary; provident. *Wotton.*

2. Cunning; treacherous; wily. *Spenser.*

CAU'TELOUSLY, *adv.* Cunningly; slily; treacherously. *Bacon.*

2. Cautiously; warily. *Brown.*

CAU'TELOUSNESS, *n.* Cautiousness.

CAU'TERISM, *n.* The application of cautery. *Ferrand.*

CAUTERIZA'TION, *n.* [See *Cauterize*.]

In *surgery*, the act of burning or searing some morbid part, by the application of fire. This is done by burning tow, cotton, moxa, Spanish wax, pyramidical pieces of linen, &c., or more generally by a hot iron. *Encyc.*

CAU'TERIZE, *v. t.* [Fr. *cauteriser*; Sp. Port. *cauterizar*; It. *cauterizzare*; Gr. καυτηριαζω, from καυτηρ, a burning or branding iron, from καιω, to burn.]

To burn or sear with fire or a hot iron, as morbid flesh.

CAU'TERIZED, *pp.* Burnt or seared with a hot iron.

CAU'TERIZING, *ppr.* Burning, as with a hot iron.

CAU'TERIZING, *n.* The act of burning, as with a hot iron.

CAU'TERY, *n.* [Gr. καυτηριον; L. *cauterium*. See *Cauterize*.]

A burning or searing, as of morbid flesh, by a hot iron or by caustic medicines that burn, corrode or destroy any solid part of an animal body. The burning by a hot iron is called *actual* cautery; that by caustic medicines, *potential* cautery.

CAU'TION, *n.* [L. *cautio*; Fr. *caution*; Sp. *caucion*; from L. *caveo*, to take care. See Class Gb. No. 3. 52. 53. 83. The sense of *caveo* is probably to retire, or to stop, check or hold.]

1. Provident care; prudence in regard to danger; wariness, consisting in a careful attention to the probable effects of a measure, and a judicious course of conduct to avoid evils and the arts of designing men.

Caution is the armor to defend us against imposition and the attacks of evil.

2. Security for, nearly the sense of the French *caution*, bail.

The parliament would give his majesty sufficient *caution* that the war should be prosecuted. *Clarendon.*

3. Provision or security against; measures taken for security; as the rules and *cautions* of government.

4. Precept; advice; injunction; warning; exhortation, intended as security or guard against evil.

CAU'TION, *v. t.* To give notice of danger; to warn; to exhort to take heed.

You *cautioned* me against their charms. *Swift.*

CAU'TIONARY, *a.* Containing caution, or warning to avoid danger; as *cautionary* advice.

2. Given as a pledge or in security; as a *cautionary* town.

CAU'TIONED, *pp.* Warned; previously admonished.

CAU'TIONER, *n.* In *Scots law*, the person who is bound for another, to the performance of an obligation.

CAU'TIONING, *ppr.* Warning; giving previous notice of danger.

CAU'TIONRY, *n.* In *Scots law*, the act of giving security for another, or the obligation by which one person becomes engaged as security for another, that he shall pay a sum of money or perform a deed. *Encyc.*

CAU'TIOUS, *a.* Wary; watchful; careful to avoid evils; attentive to examine probable effects and consequences of measures, with a view to avoid danger or misfortune; prudent; circumspect.

CAU'TIOUSLY, *adv.* With caution; in a wary, scrupulous manner.

CAU'TIOUSNESS, *n.* The quality of being cautious; watchfulness; provident care; circumspection; prudence with regard to danger. *Addison.*

CAV'ALCADE, *n.* [Fr. *cavalcade*; Sp. *cabalgada*; It. *cavalcata*. See *Cavalry*.]

A procession of persons on horseback; a formal, pompous march of horsemen and equipage, by way of parade, or to grace a triumph, the public entry of a person of distinction, &c.

CAVALIE'R, *n.* [Fr. See *Cavalry*.] A horseman, especially an armed horseman; a knight.

2. A gay, sprightly, military man.

3. The appellation of the party of king Charles I. *Swift.*

4. In *fortification*, an elevation of earth, situ-

ated ordinarily in the gorge of a bastion, bordered with a parapet, with embrasures. *Encyc.*

4. In *the manege*, one who understands horsemanship; one skilled in the art of riding.

CAVALIE'R, *a.* Gay; sprightly; warlike; brave; generous.

2. Haughty; disdainful.

CAVALIE'RLY, *adv.* Haughtily; arrogantly; disdainfully. *Warburton.*

CAVALIE'RNESS, *n.* Haughtiness; a disdainful manner.

CAV'ALRY, *n.* [Fr. *cavalerie*, from *cavalier*, a horseman, and this from *cheval*, a horse, whence *cavalcade*; It. *cavallo*, a horse, *cavaliere*, *cavalcata*; Sp. *caballo*, *caballero*, *cabalgada*; from L. *caballus*, a horse; Ir. *capall* and *peall*; Russ. *kobila*, a mare; Gr. *χαβαλλης*, a pack-horse.]

A body of military troops on horses; a general term, including light-horse, dragoons, and other bodies of men, serving on horseback. *Encyc.*

CA'VATE, *v. t.* [L. *cavo*, to make hollow.] To dig out and make hollow; but superseded by *excavate*.

CAVATI'NA, *n.* [It.] In *music*, a short air, without a return or second part, which is sometimes relieved by recitative. *Busby.*

CAVA'ZION, *n.* [L. *cavo*, to hollow.] In *architecture*, the underdigging or hollowing of the earth for the foundation of a building, or for cellarage; allowed to be the sixth part of the highth of the building. *Johnson. Bailey.*

CAVE, *n.* [Fr. *cave*; L. *cavea*; Sp. *cueva*; It. *cava*; Arm. *caff*, or *cau*; W. *ogov*; Hindoo, *gopa*; Ar. قَاَب to dig out or excavate, or جَاَف to be hollow. Class Gb. No. 8. 71.]

A hollow place in the earth; a subterraneous cavern; a den. This may be natural or artificial. The primitive inhabitants of the earth, in many countries, lived in caves; and the present inhabitants of some parts of the earth, especially in the high northern latitudes, occupy caves, particularly in winter.

> Lot dwelt in a *cave*, he and his daughters. Gen. xix.

Caves were also used for the burial of the dead.

> Abraham buried Sarah in the *cave* of the field of Machpelah. Gen. xxiii.

Bacon applies the word to the ear, "the cave of the ear;" but this application is unusual.

CAVE, *v. t.* To make hollow. *Spenser.*

CAVE, *v. i.* To dwell in a cave. *Shak.*

To cave in, to fall in and leave a hollow, as earth on the side of a well or pit. When in digging into the earth, the side is excavated by a falling of a quantity of earth, it is said *to cave in*.

CA'VEAT, *n.* [L. *caveat*, let him beware, from *caveo*.]

In *law*, a process in a court, especially in a spiritual court, to stop proceedings, as to stop the proving of a will; also to prevent the institution of a clerk to a benefice. *Blackstone.*

In America, it is used in courts of common law. *Cranch's Reports.*

2. Intimation of caution; hint; warning; admonition.

CA'VEAT, *v. t.* To enter a caveat. *Judge Innes, Cranch's Rep.*

CA'VEATING, *n.* In *fencing*, is the shifting the sword from one side of that of your adversary to the other. *Encyc.*

CA'VEATOR, *n.* One who enters a caveat. *Judge Innes, Cranch's Rep.*

CAV'ERN, *n.* [L. *caverna*; Sp. Port. It. *id.* This word seems to be composed of *cavus*, and the Sax. *ærn*, a secret place.]

A deep hollow place in the earth. In general, it differs from *cave* in greater depth, and in being applied most usually to natural hollows, or chasms.

> Earth with its *caverns* dark and deep. *Watts.*

CAV'ERNED, *a.* Full of caverns, or deep chasms; having caverns.

2. Inhabiting a cavern. *Pope.*

CAV'ERNOUS, *a.* [L. *cavernosus*.] Hollow; full of caverns. *Woodward.*

[Faber uses *cavernal*, which is less regularly formed.]

CAVERN'ULOUS, *a.* [L. *cavernula*.] Full of little cavities; as *cavernulous* metal. *Black.*

CAVET'TO, *n.* [from It. *cavo*.] In *architecture*, a hollow member, or round concave molding, containing the quadrant of a circle; used as an ornament in cornices. *Encyc.*

CAV'EZON, } *n.* [Fr. *caveçon*, or *cavesson*;
CAV'ESSON, } It. *cavezzone*, a muzzle for a horse, from *cavare*, to draw.]

A sort of nose-band, of iron, leather or wood, sometimes flat, and sometimes hollow or twisted, which is put on the nose of a horse to wring it, and thus to forward the suppling and breaking of him. *Farrier's Dict.*

CAVIAR, *n.* *cavee'r* [Sp. *cabial*; It. *caviale*; Ar. خبيار gabiar. The Arabic verb خبر gabara, from which this word is formed, signifies to try, to strain or press, and to season with fat. It may coincide with the Gr. *πειραω*, L. *experior*.]

The roes of certain large fish, prepared and salted. The best is made from the roes of the sterlet, sturgeon, sevruga, and beluga, caught in the lakes or rivers of Russia. The roes are put into a bag with a strong brine, and pressed by wringing, and then dried and put in casks, or into cisterns, perforated at bottom, where they are pressed by heavy weights. The poorest sort is trodden with the feet. *Tooke.*

CAV'IL, *v. i.* [Sp. *cavilar*; Port. *cavillar*; It. *cavillare*; L. *cavillor*; D. *kibbelen*; Oriental קבל; Ch. to cry out or complain; Syr. to accuse, oppose, censure.]

1. To raise captious and frivolous objections; to find fault without good reason; followed by *at*.

> It is better to reason than to *cavil*. *Anon.*

2. To advance futile objections, or to frame sophisms, for the sake of victory in an argument.

CAV'IL, *v. t.* To receive or treat with objections.

> ——Wilt thou enjoy the good,
> Then *cavil* the conditions. *Milton.*

[*Not usual.*]

CAV'IL, *n.* False or frivolous objections; also, a fallacious kind of reason, bearing some resemblance to truth, advanced for the sake of victory. *Johnson. Encyc.*

CAV'ILER, *n.* One who cavils; one who is apt to raise captious objections; a captious disputant. *Addison.*

CAV'ILING, *ppr.* Raising frivolous objections.

CAV'ILINGLY, *adv.* In a caviling manner. *Sherwood.*

CAVILLA'TION, *n.* [L. *cavillatio*.] The act or practice of *caviling*, or raising frivolous objections. *Hooker.*

CAV'ILOUS, *a.* Captious; unfair in argument; apt to object without good reason. *Ayliffe.*

CAV'ILOUSLY, *adv.* In a cavilous manner; captiously. *Milton.*

CAV'ILOUSNESS, *n.* Captiousness; disposition or aptitude to raise frivolous objections.

CAV'IN, *n.* [Fr. from L. *cavus*, hollow.]

In *the military art*, a hollow way or natural hollow, adapted to cover troops and facilitate their approach to a place. *Johnson. Bailey.*

CAV'ITY, *n.* [L. *cavitas*; Fr. *cavité*; from L. *cavus*, hollow.]

A hollow place; hollowness; an opening; as the *cavity* of the mouth or throat. *This is a word of very general signification.*

CAV'OLINITE, *n.* [from *Cavolini*, a Neapolitan naturalist.]

A newly discovered Vesuvian mineral, of a hexahedral form, occurring in the interior of calcarious balls, accompanied with garnets, idocrase, mica, and granular pyroxene, lining the cavity of the geode, &c. *Journ. of Science.*

CA'VY, *n.* A genus of quadrupeds, holding a middle place between the murine and leporine tribes. *Encyc.*

CAW, *v. i.* [probably from the sound; Sax. *ceo*, a crow or a jay.]

To cry like a crow, rook or raven.

CAX'OU, *n.* [Sp. *caxa*, *caxon*.] A chest of ores of any metal that has been burnt, ground and washed, and is ready to be refined. [*Local.*] *Todd.*

CA'YMAN, *n.* An animal of the genus Lacerta, found in the West Indies, the alligator.

CAZI'C, or **CAZI'QUE**, *n.* *cazeék.* The title of a king or chief among several tribes of Indians in America.

CEASE, *v. i.* [Fr. *cesser*; Sp. *cesar*; Port. *cessar*; It. *cessare*; L. *cesso*.]

1. To stop moving, acting or speaking; to leave off; to give over; followed by *from* before a noun.

> It is an honor for a man to *cease* from strife. Prov. xx.

2. To fail; to be wanting.

> The poor shall never *cease* out of the land. Deut. xv.

3. To stop; to be at an end; as, the wonder *ceases*; the storm has *ceased*.

4. To be forgotten.

> I would make the remembrance of them to *cease*. Deut. xxxii.

5. To abstain; as, *cease* from anger. Ps. xxxvii.

To cease from labor, is to rest; *to cease from strife*, is to be quiet; but in such phrases, the sense of *cease* is not varied.

CEASE, *v. t.* To put a stop to; to put an end to.

Cease this impious rage. *Milton.*

[*But in this use the phrase is generally elliptical.*]

CEASE, *n.* Extinction. [*Not in use.*] *Shak.*

CE′ASELESS, *a.* Without a stop or pause; incessant; continual; without intermission.

All these with *ceaseless* praise his works behold. *Milton.*

2. Endless; enduring for ever; as the *ceaseless* joys of heaven.

CE′ASELESSLY, *adv.* Incessantly; perpetually. *Donne.*

CE′ASING, *ppr.* Stopping; ending; desisting; failing.

CECCH N, *n.* A coin of Italy and Barbary. [See *Zechin.*]

CE′CITY, *n.* [L. *cæcitas*, from *cæcus*, blind.] Blindness. *Brown.*

CE′DAR, *n.* [L. *cedrus*; Fr. *cedre*; Sp. It. *cedro*; from Gr. κεδρος; Syr. ܩܕܪ; Heb. קדר kadar, to be dark.]

A tree. This name is given to different species of the juniper, and to a species of Pinus. The latter is that which is mentioned in scripture. It is an evergreen, grows to a great size, and is remarkable for its durability.

CE′DAR-LIKE, *a.* Resembling a cedar. *B. Jonson.*

CE′DARN, *a.* Pertaining to the cedar. *Milton.*

CEDE, *v. t.* [Fr. *ceder*; Sp. Port. *ceder*; It. *cedere*; L. *cedo*; W. *gadu, gadaw*; Eng. to *quit*. See *Quit* and *Conge*. This coincides also with the Gr. χαζω, εχαδον.]

1. To yield; to surrender; to give up; to resign; as, to *cede* a fortress, a province or country, by treaty. This word is appropriately used to denote the relinquishment of a conquered city, fortress, or territory, to the former sovereign or proprietor.

2. To relinquish and grant; as, to *cede* all claims to a disputed right or territory.

The people must *cede* to the government some of their natural rights. *Jay.*

CE′DED, *pp.* Yielded; surrendered; given up.

CE′DING, *ppr.* Yielding; giving up.

CE′DRAT, *n.* A species of citron-tree. *Pallas. Tooke.*

CE′DRINE, *a.* Belonging to cedar.

CE′DRY, *a.* Having the color or properties of cedar. *Evelyn.*

CED′UOUS, *a.* Fit to be felled. *Evelyn.*

CEIL, *v. t.* [Sp. *cielo*, heaven, a roof or ceiling; It. *cielo*; Fr. *ciel*, heaven, a canopy, a tester; L. *cælum*. Qu. Gr. κοιλος. This word indicates its original application to vaulted buildings, without divisions into stories; such as many of the public edifices in Europe, but which are rarely seen in America.]

To overlay or cover the inner roof of a building; or to cover the top or roof of a room.

And the greater house he *ceiled* with fir-tree. 2 Chron. iii.

CE′ILED, *pp.* Overlaid with timber, or with plastering.

CE′ILING, *ppr.* Covering the top of a room or building.

CE′ILING, *n.* The covering which overlays the inner roof of a building, or the timbers which form the top of a room. This covering may be of boards, or of lath and plastering. Hence ceiling is used for the upper part of a room.

2. In *ship building*, the inside planks of a ship.

CEL′ANDINE, *n.* [D. *celedonie*; It. *celidonia*; L. *chelidonia*; Gr. χελιδονιον, from χελιδων, a swallow.]

A plant, swallow-wort, horned or prickly poppy, growing on old walls, among rubbish, and in waste places. The lesser celandine is called pile-wort, a species of Ranunculus. The name is also given to the Bocconia, a plant of the West Indies, called the greater tree-celandine. The true orthography would be *Chelidine*. *Coxe. Fam. of Plants.*

CE′LATURE, *n.* [L. *cælatura*, from *cælo*, to engrave or emboss.]

1. The act or art of engraving or embossing.

2. That which is engraved. *Hakewill.*

CEL′EBRATE, *v. t.* [Ir. *ceileabradh*; Fr. *celebrer*; Sp. Port. *celebrar*; It. *celebrare*; L. *celebro*, from *celeber*, famous. The Russ. has *slavlyu*. Qu. the root of *call.*]

1. To praise; to extol; to commend; to give praise to; to make famous; as, to *celebrate* the name of the Most High.

The grave cannot *celebrate* thee. Is. xxxviii.

2. To distinguish by solemn rites; to keep holy.

From even to even shall ye *celebrate* your sabbath. Lev. xxiii.

3. To honor or distinguish by ceremonies and marks of joy and respect; as, to *celebrate* the birth day of Washington; to *celebrate* a marriage.

4. To mention in a solemn manner, whether of joy or sorrow. *Johnson.*

CEL′EBRATED, *pp.* Praised; extolled; honored.

CEL′EBRATING, *ppr.* Praising; honoring.

CELEBRA′TION, *n.* Solemn performance; a distinguishing by solemn rites; as the *celebration* of a marriage, or of a religious festival.

2. A distinguishing by ceremonies, or by marks of joy or respect; as the *celebration* of a birth day, or other anniversary.

3. Praise; renown; honor or distinction bestowed, whether by songs, eulogies, or rites and ceremonies. *Clarendon.*

CEL′EBRATOR, *n.* One who celebrates. *Boyle.*

CELE′BRIOUS, *a.* Famous; renowned. [*Little used.*] *Grew.*

CELE′BRIOUSLY, *adv.* With praise or renown. [*Little used.*]

CELE′BRIOUSNESS, *n.* Fame; renown. [*Little used.*]

CELEB′RITY, *n.* [L. *celebritas.*] Fame; renown; the distinction or honor publicly bestowed on a nation or person, on character or exploits; the distinction bestowed on whatever is great or remarkable, and manifested by praises or eulogies; as the *celebrity* of the duke of Wellington; the *celebrity* of Homer, or of the Iliad.

England acquired *celebrity* from the triumphs of Marlborough. *T. Dawes.*

2. Public and splendid transaction; as the *celebrity* of a marriage. In this sense, as used by Bacon, we now use *celebration*.

CEL′ERI. [See *Celery.*]

CELE′RIAC, *n.* A variety of celery, called also the *turnep-rooted celery*. [See *Celery.*]

CELER′ITY, *n.* [L. *celeritas*; Fr. *celerité*; Sp. *celeridad*; It. *celerità*; from L. *celer*, swift; Oriental קל swift, light; Gr. κελλω.]

1. Rapidity in motion; swiftness; speed; applied most generally to bodies moving on or near the earth; as the *celerity* of a horse or of a fowl. We speak of the *velocity* of sound or of light, or of a planet in its orbit. This distinction however is not general, nor can the different uses of the two words be precisely defined. We apply *celerity* rather than *velocity* to *thought*; but there seems to be no reason, except usage, why the two words should not be synonymous.

2. An affection of motion by which a movable body runs through a given space in a given time. *Encyc.*

CEL′ERY, *n.* [Fr. *celeri*; D. *seldery*; G. *selleri*; Gr. σελινον.]

A plant, a species of Apium, cultivated for the table.

CELES′TIAL, *a.* [L. *cælestis*, from *cælum*, heaven.]

1. Heavenly; belonging or relating to heaven; dwelling in heaven; as *celestial* spirits; *celestial* joys. Hence the word conveys the idea of superior excellence, delight, purity, &c. *Dryden.*

2. Belonging to the upper regions, or visible heaven; as *celestial* signs; the *celestial* globe.

3. Descending from heaven; as a suit of *celestial* armor. *Pope.*

CELES′TIAL, *n.* An inhabitant of heaven. *Pope.*

CELES′TIALLY, *adv.* In a heavenly or transporting manner.

CELES′TIFY, *v. t.* To communicate something of a heavenly nature to any thing. [*Not used.*] *Brown.*

CEL′ESTIN, } *n.* In *mineralogy*, native
CEL′ESTINE, } sulphate of strontian, a mineral so named from its occasional delicate blue color. *Ure.*

CEL′ESTINS, *n.* A religious order, so named from Pope Celestin. They have ninety-six convents in Italy, and twenty-one in France. They rise two hours after midnight to say matins. They eat no flesh, except when sick, and fast often. Their habit is a white gown, a capuche and a black scapulary. *Encyc.*

CE′LIAC, *a.* [L. *cæliacus*; Gr. κοιλιακος, from κοιλια, the belly.]

Pertaining to the lower belly, or intestines. *Arbuthnot.*

CELIB′ACY, *n.* [L. *cælebs*, an unmarried person; *cælibatus*, a single life.]

An unmarried state; a single life. It is most frequently if not always applied to males, or to a voluntary single life.

They look on *celibacy* as an accursed state. *Spectator.*

CEL′IBATE, *n.* A single life; celibacy; chiefly used when speaking of the single life of the Popish clergy. *Encyc.*

CELL, *n.* [L. *cella*; Ir. *ceall*; Sp. *celda*; Port. It. *cella*; D. *kelder*, a *cellar*; G. *keller*; Sw. *kellare*; Dan. *kelder*; W. *cell*. It has the elements of the Latin *celo*, to conceal, and of the English *hold.*]

1. A small or close apartment, as in a prison, or a bath.
2. A cottage; a cave; a small or mean place of residence. *Prior.*
3. A small cavity or hollow place, variously applied; as the *cells* of the brain; the *cells* of a honey comb, &c.
4. In *botany*, a hollow place in a pericarp, particularly in a capsule, in which seeds are lodged. According to the number of these cells, pericarps are called unilocular, bilocular, trilocular, &c. *Martyn.*
5. In *anatomy*, a little bag, or bladder, containing fluid or other matter; as the *adipose cells*, containing fat. *Encyc.*
6. A religious house. *Chaucer.*

CEL'LAR, *n.* [L. *cellarium.* See *Cell.*]
A room under a house or other building, used as a repository of liquors, provisions, and other stores for a family.

CEL'LARAGE, *n.* The room for a cellar; a cellar, or cellars.

CEL'LARET, *n.* A case of cabinet work, for holding bottles of liquors. [*Local.*]

CEL'LARIST, CEL'LARER, *n.* An officer in a monastery who has the care of the cellar, or the charge of procuring and keeping the provisions; also, an officer in chapters, who has the care of the temporals, and particularly of distributing bread, wine, and money to canons, an account of their attendance in the choir. *Encyc.*

CELLIF'EROUS, *a.* [L. *cella*, and *fero*, to bear.] Bearing or producing cells. *Encyc.*

CEL'LULAR, *a.* [L. *cellula*, a little *cell.*] Consisting of cells, or containing cells. *Kirwan.*
The *cellular membrane*, in animal bodies, is composed of an infinite number of minute cells, communicating with each other. It invests every fiber, and seems to be the medium of connection between all parts of the body. The cells serve as reservoirs for fat. *Encyc.*

CELLULIF'EROUS, *a.* [L. *cellula*, a little cell, and *fero*, to bear.] Bearing or producing little cells. *Dict. Nat. Hist.*

CELS'ITUDE, *n.* [L. *celsitudo.*] Highth; elevation. *Chaucer.*

CELT, *n.* One of the primitive inhabitants of the South of Europe. [See *Celtic.*]

CELTIBE'RIAN, *a.* Pertaining to Celtiberia, and its inhabitants, the Celtiberi, or Celts of the Iberus, a river in Spain.

CELTIBE'RIAN, *n.* An inhabitant of Celtiberia.

CELT'IC, *a.* [W. *celt*, a covert or shelter; *celtiad*, one that dwells in a covert, an inhabitant of the forest, a Celt; *celu*, to conceal, L. *celo*; Gr. Κελτοι, Celts.]
Pertaining to the primitive inhabitants of the South and West of Europe, or to the early inhabitants of Italy, Gaul, Spain and Britain. We say, *Celtic* nations; *Celtic* customs; *Celtic* origin.

CELT'IC, *n.* The language of the Celts.

CELT'ICISM, *n.* The manners and customs of the Celts. *Warton.*

CELT'IS, *n.* The nettle-tree, of several species; among which are the australis or southern, a native of Africa and the South of Europe; the oriental, growing in Armenia and Taurica; and the western, growing in Virginia. *Encyc. Tooke.*

CEM'ENT, *n.* [L. *cæmentum*; Fr. *ciment*; Arm. *cimant*; Sp. *cimiento*, the ground work of a building; It. *cimento*, an essay or experiment.]
1. Any glutinous or other substance capable of uniting bodies in close cohesion, as mortar, glue, soder, &c. In *building*, cement denotes a stronger kind of mortar than that which is ordinarily used. *Encyc.*
2. Bond of union; that which unites firmly, as persons in friendship, or men in society.
3. Powders or pastes, surrounding bodies in pots and crucibles, for chimical purposes.

CEMENT', *v. t.* To unite by the application of glutinous substances, by mortar which hardens, or other matter that produces cohesion of bodies.
2. To unite firmly or closely; as, to *cement* all parts of the community; to *cement* friendship.

CEMENT', *v. i.* To unite or become solid; to unite and cohere. *Sharp.*

CEMENTA'TION, *n.* The act of cementing; the act of uniting by a suitable substance.
2. In *chimistry*, the act of applying cements to substances, or the corroding and changing of them by cement. This is done by surrounding them with the powder of another body, and exposing them, in a close vessel, to a heat not sufficient to fuse them. *Encyc. Ure.*

CEMENT'ATORY, *a.* Cementing; having the quality of uniting firmly. *Encyc.*

CEMENT'ED, *pp.* United by cement; changed by cement; firmly united; consolidated

CEMENT'ER, *n.* The person or thing that cements.

CEMENT'ING, *ppr.* Uniting by cement; changing by means of a cement; uniting closely; consolidating.

CEMENTI''TIOUS, *a.* Uniting as cement; conglutinating; tending to unite or consolidate.

CEM'ETERY, *n.* [L. *cæmeterium*; Gr. κοιμητηριον, from κοιμαω, to sleep.]
A place where the dead bodies of human beings are buried. *Addison.*

CEN'ATORY, *a.* [L. *cænatorius*, from *cœna*, supper, *cœno*, to sup.]
Pertaining or relating to supper. *Brown.*

CE'NOBITE, *n.* [Gr. κοινοβιοτης, a community, from κοινος, common, and βιος, life, βιοω, to live.]
One of a religious order, who live in a convent, or in community; in opposition to an anchoret, or hermit, who lives in solitude. *Encyc.*

CENOBIT'IC, } *a.* Living in communi-
CENOBIT'ICAL, } ty, as men belonging to a convent. *Stillingfleet.*

CE'NOBY, *n.* A place where persons live in community. *Buck.*

CEN'OTAPH, *n.* [Gr. κενοταφιον, from κενος, empty, and ταφος, a tomb.]
An empty tomb erected in honor of some deceased person; a monument erected to one who is buried elsewhere. *Johnson. Encyc.*

CENSE, *n. cens.* [L. *census*, a valuation, a registering, a tax; *censeo*, to enroll, to tax. Qu. Ch. קנס to impose a fine.]
1. A public rate or tax. *Bacon.*
2. Condition; rank. *Obs.* *B. Jonson.*

CENSE, *v. t.* [Fr. *encenser.* See *Incense.*]
To perfume with odors from burning substances. *Dryden.*

CENS'ER, *n.* [Fr. *encensoir*; Sp. *incensario*; It. *incensiere.* See *Incense.*]
A vase or pan in which incense is burned. Among the Jews, a kind of chafing-dish, covered by a dome, and suspended by a chain, used to offer perfumes in sacrifices. *Encyc.*

CENS'ING, *ppr.* Perfuming with odors.

CEN'SION, *n.* [L. *censio.* See *Cense.*] A rate, tax, or assessment. [*Not used.*] *J. Hall.*

CENS'OR, *n.* [L. *censor.* See *Cense.*]
An officer, in ancient Rome, whose business was to register the effects of the citizens, to impose taxes according to the property which each man possessed, and to inspect the manners of the citizens, with power to censure vice and immorality, by inflicting a public mark of ignominy on the offender.
2. One who is empowered to examine all manuscripts and books, before they are committed to the press, and to see that they contain nothing heretical or immoral. *Encyc.*
3. One who is given to censure. *Roscommon. Dryden.*

CENSO'RIAL, } *a.* Belonging to a censor,
CENSO'RIAN, } or to the correction of public morals; as, *censorial* power.
2. Full of censure. See *Censorious*, the proper word.

CENSO'RIOUS, *a.* Addicted to censure; apt to blame or condemn; severe in making remarks on others, or on their writings or manners; often implying ill-nature, illiberality, or uncharitableness; as a *censorious* critic.
2. Implying or expressing censure; as, *censorious* remarks.

CENSO'RIOUSLY, *adv.* In a censorious manner.

CENSO'RIOUSNESS, *n.* Disposition to blame and condemn; the habit of censuring or reproaching. *Taylor.*
2. The quality of being censorious.

CENS'ORSHIP, *n.* The office or dignity of a censor; the time during which a censor holds his office.

CENS'UAL, *a.* [L. *censualis.*] Relatingt o, or containing a census; liable to be rated. *Whitaker. Encyc.*

CENS'URABLE, *a.* [See *Censure.*] Worthy of censure; blamable; culpable; reprehensible; faulty; as a *censurable* person, or *censurable* conduct or writings. *Locke.*

CENS'URABLENESS, *n.* Blamableness; fitness to be censured. *Whitlock.*

CENS'URABLY, *adv.* In a manner worthy of blame.

CENS'URE, *n. cen'shur.* [L. *censura*; Fr. *censure*; Sp. Port. It. *censura*; from L. *censeo, censor.*]
1. The act of blaming or finding fault and condemning as wrong; applicable to the moral conduct, or to the works of men. When applied to persons, it is nearly equivalent to blame, reproof, reprehension, reprimand. It is an expression of disapprobation, which often implies reproof.
2. Judicial sentence; judgment that condemns. An ecclesiastical *censure* is a sentence of condemnation, or penalty inflicted on a member of a church for mal-conduct, by which he is deprived of the com-

munion of the church, or prohibited from executing the sacerdotal office. *Encyc.*

CENS'URE, *v. t.* *cen'shur.* [Fr. *censurer;* Sp. *censurar.*] To find fault with and condemn as wrong; to blame; to express disapprobation of; as, to *censure* a man, or his manners, or his writings.

> We laugh at vanity, oftener than we *censure* pride. *Buckminster.*

2. To condemn by a judicial sentence, as in ecclesiastical affairs.
3. To estimate. [*Not in use.*] *Shak.*

CENS'URE, *v. i.* To judge. [*Not in use.*]

CENS'URED, *pp.* Blamed; reproved; condemned.

CENS'URING, *ppr.* Blaming; finding fault with; condemning.

CENS'US, *n.* [L. from *censeo.* See *Cense.*]

In *ancient Rome*, an authentic declaration made before the censors, by the citizens, of their names and places of abode. This declaration was registered, and contained an enumeration of all their lands and estates, their quantity and quality, with the wives, children, domestics, tenants, and slaves of each citizen. Hence the word signifies this enumeration or register, a man's whole substance, and the tax imposed according to each man's property.

2. In *the United States of America*, an enumeration of the inhabitants of all the States, taken by order of the Congress, to furnish the rule of apportioning the representation among the States, and the number of represensatives to which each State is entitled in the Congress; also, an enumeration of the inhabitants of a State, taken by order of its legislature.

CENT, *n.* [Fr. *cent;* Sp. *ciento;* Port. *cento;* It. *cento;* from L. *centum*, formed on the Celtic, W. *cant*, Arm. *cant*, Corn. *kanz.* The Welch *cant* signifies a circle, hoop, wheel, or rim, a wattled fence round a yard or corn floor; hence, a complete circle, a hundred. It is probable that the Teutonic and Gothic *hund*, in hundred, is the same word. Ar. هند handon, a hundred, and the same root gives *India, Hindu.* See *Hundred.*]

1. A hundred. In commerce, *per cent.* denotes a certain rate by the hundred; as, *ten per cent.* is *ten in the hundred*, whether profit or loss. This rate is called *percentage.*
2. In *the United States of America*, a copper coin whose value is the hundredth part of a dollar.

CENT'AGE, *n.* Rate by the cent or hundred.

CEN'TAUR, *n.* [L. *centaurus;* Gr. κενταυρος. Qu. κεντεω, to spur, and ταυρος, a bull.]

In *mythology*, a fabulous being, supposed to be half man and half horse. It has been supposed that this fancied monster originated among the Lapithæ, a tribe in Thessaly, who first invented the art of breaking horses. But the origin of the fable and of the name is doubtful.

2. Part of a southern constellation, in form of a centaur, usually joined with the wolf, containing thirty-five stars; the archer. *Encyc.*

CEN'TAURLIKE, *a.* Having the appearance of a centaur. *Sidney.*

CEN'TAURY, *n.* [L. *centaurea;* Gr. κενταυρεον.]

The name of a plant, and a genus of plants, of numerous species. The *lesser centaury* is a species of *Gentiana.* Centaury bears the popular names of knapweed, bluebottle, sultan, and star-thistle. *Encyc.*

CENT'ENARY, *n.* [L. *centenarius*, from *centum*, a hundred.]

The number of a hundred; as a *centenary* of years.

CENT'ENARY, *a.* Relating to a hundred; consisting of a hundred.

CENTEN'NIAL, *a.* [L. *centum*, a hundred, and *annus*, a year.]

1. Consisting of a hundred years, or completing that term. *Mason.*
2. Pertaining to a hundred years.
3. Happening every hundred years.

CEN'TER, *n.* [Gr. κεντρον, a point, goad or spur, from κεντεω, to prick; L. *centrum;* Fr. *centre;* Sp. *centro;* Port. It. *id.*]

1. A point equally distant from the extremities of a line, figure or body; the middle point or place.
2. The middle or central object. In an *army*, the body of troops occupying the place in the line between the wings. In a *fleet*, the division between the van and rear of the line of battle, and between the weather division and lee, in the order of sailing. *Mar. Dict.*
3. A single body or house.

> These institutions collected all authority into one *center*, kings, nobles and people. *J. Adams.*

Center of gravity, in mechanics, the point about which all the parts of a body exactly balance each other.

Center of motion, the point which remains at rest, while all the other parts of a body move round it. *Encyc.*

CEN'TER, *v. t.* To place on a center; to fix on a central point. *Milton.*

2. To collect to a point.

> Thy joys are *centered* all in me alone. *Prior.*

CEN'TER, *v. i.* To be collected to a point.

> Our hopes must *center* on ourselves alone. *Dryden.*

2. To be collected to a point; to rest on.
3. To be placed in the middle. *Milton.*

CEN'TERED, *pp.* Collected to a point or center; fixed on a central point.

CEN'TERING, *ppr.* Placing on the center; collecting to a point.

CENTES'IMAL, *a.* [L. *centesimus*, from *centum*, a hundred.]

The hundredth. As a noun, the next step of progression after decimal in the arithmetic of fractions. *Johnson.*

CENTESIMA'TION, *n.* [L. *centesimus*, *supra.*]

A military punishment, for desertion, mutiny or the like, where one person in a hundred is selected for execution. *Encyc.*

CEN'TESM, *n.* [L. *centesimus.*] The hundredth part of an integer or thing. [*Not used.*] *Bailey.*

CENTIFO'LIOUS, *a.* [L. *centum*, a hundred, and *folium*, a leaf.] Having a hundred leaves. *Bailey. Johnson.*

CEN'TIGRADE, *a.* [L. *centum*, a hundred, and *gradus*, a degree.]

Consisting of a hundred degrees; graduated into a hundred divisions or equal parts; as a *centigrade* thermometer. *Medical Repository.*

CEN'TIGRAM, *n.* [L. *centum* and *gram.*] In *French Measure*, the hundredth part of a gram. [See *Gram.*]

CEN'TILITER, *n.* [L. *centum*, and Fr. *litre* or *litron.*] The hundredth part of a *liter*, a little more than 6-10 of a cubic inch.

CENTIM'ETER, *n.* [L. *centum*, a hundred, and Gr. μετρον, measure.]

In *French measure*, the hundreth part of a meter, rather more than 39-100 of an inch, English measure. *Christ. Obs.* x. 192.

CEN'TINODY, *n.* Knotgrass. [*Not used.*]

CEN'TIPED, *n.* [L. *centipeda;* *centum*, a hundred, and *pes*, a foot.]

An insect having a hundred feet, but the term is applied to insects that have many feet, though not a hundred. Insects of this kind are called generically *Scolopendra.* In warm climates, some of them grow to the length of six inches or more, and their bite is poisonous. *Encyc.*

CENTIPEE, for *centiped*, is not used.

CENT'NER, *n.* [L. *centum, centenarius.*]

In *metallurgy* and *assaying*, a docimastic hundred; a weight divisible first into a hundred parts, and then into smaller parts. The metallurgists use a weight divided into a hundred equal parts, each one pound; the whole they call a *centner:* the pound is divided into thirty-two parts or half ounces; the half ounce into two quarters, and each of these into two drams. But the assayers use different weights. With them a *centner* is one dram, to which the other parts are proportioned. *Encyc.*

CEN'TO, *n.* [L. *cento*, patched cloth, a rhapsody.]

A composition formed by verses or passages from other authors, disposed in a new order. *Johnson. Encyc.*

CEN'TRAL, *a.* [L. *centralis.*] Relating to the center; placed in the center or middle; containing the center, or pertaining to the parts near the center.

Central forces, in mechanics, the powers which cause a moving body to tend towards or recede from the center of motion.

CENTRAL'ITY, *n.* The state of being central.

CEN'TRALLY, *adv.* With regard to the center; in a central manner.

CEN'TRIC, *a.* Placed in the center or middle.

CEN'TRICALLY, *adv.* In a central position.

CEN'TRICALNESS, *n.* Situation in the center.

CENTRIF'UGAL, *a.* [L. *centrum*, and *fugio*, to flee.]

Tending to recede from the center. The *centrifugal force* of a body, is that force by which all bodies moving round another body in a curve, tend to fly off from the axis of their motion, in a tangent to the periphery of the curve. *Encyc.*

CENTRIP'ETAL, *a.* [L. *centrum*, and *peto*, to move towards.]

Tending towards the center. *Centripetal force* is that force which draws or impels a body towards some point as a center; as in case of a planet revolving round the sun, the center of the system.

[Note. The common accentuation of *cen-*

trifugal and *centripetal* is artificial and harsh. The accent on the first and third syllables, as in *circumpolar*, would be natural and easy.]

CEN'TUMVIR, *n.* [L. *centum*, a hundred, and *vir*, a man.]
One of a hundred and five judges, in ancient Rome, appointed to decide common causes among the people.

CENTUM'VIRAL, *a.* Pertaining to the centumvirs.

CEN'TUPLE, *a.* [Fr. from L. *centuplex*, *centum*, and *plico*, to fold.]
A hundred fold.

CEN'TUPLE, *v. t.* To multiply a hundred fold. *Beaum.*

CENTU'PLICATE, *v. t.* [L. *centum*, and *plicatus*, folded; Sp. *centuplicar*, to make a hundred fold.]
To make a hundred fold.

CENTU'RIAL, *a.* [from *century.*] Relating to a century, or a hundred years; as a *centurial* sermon.

When the third *centurial* jubilee of New-England shall come, who of us will then be living to participate the general joy? *J. Woodbridge.*

CENTU'RIATE, *v. t.* [L. *centurio*, to divide into hundreds or companies.]
To divide into hundreds. *Johnson. Bailey.*

CENTURIA'TORS, } *n.* [Fr. *centuriateur*,
CEN'TURIST, } from L. *centuria*, a *century*, or from *centurio*, to divide into hundreds.]
A historian who distinguishes time into centuries; as in the Universal Church History of Magdeburg. *Ayliffe.*

CENTU'RION, *n.* [L. *centurio*, from *centum*, a hundred.]
Among *the Romans*, a military officer who commanded a hundred men, a century or company of infantry, answering to the captain in modern armies.

CEN'TURY, *n.* [L. *centuria*, from *centum*, a hundred.]
1. In *a general sense*, a hundred; any thing consisting of a hundred parts.
2. A division of the Roman people for the purpose of electing magistrates and enacting laws, the people voting by centuries; also, a company consisting of a hundred men.
3. A period of a hundred years. This is the most common signification of the word; and as we begin our modern computation of time from the incarnation of Christ, the word is generally applied to some term of a hundred years subsequent to that event; as the *first* or *second century*, or the *tenth century*. If we intend to apply the word to a different era, we use an explanatory adjunct; as the third *century* before the Christian era, or after the reign of Cyrus.
4. The *Centuries of Magdeburg*, a title given to an ecclesiastical history, arranged in 13 centuries, compiled by a great number of Protestants at Magdeburg.

CENTZONT'LI, *n.* The Mexican name of the Turdus Polyglottus, or mocking thrush. *Clavigero.*

CEOL, Sax. a ship, L. *celox*, or Eng. *keel.* This word is sometimes found prefixed to names.

CEPHALAL'GIC, *n.* [Infra.] A medicine good for the headache. *Swift.*

CEPH'ALALGY, *n.* [Gr. κεφαλαλγια, κεφαλη, the head, and αλγος, pain.] The headache.

CEPHAL'IC, *a.* [Gr. κεφαλικος, from κεφαλη, the head.]
Pertaining to the head; as *cephalic* medicines, remedies for disorders in the head. The *cephalic* vein, which runs along the arm, was so named because the ancients used to open it for disorders of the head. *Encyc.*

CEPHAL'IC, *n.* A medicine for headache or other disorder in the head.

CEPH'EUS, *n.* A constellation in the Northern hemisphere.

CE'PHUS, *n.* A fowl of the duck kind; also, a species of monkey, the mona. *Dict. Nat. Hist.*

CERASEE', *n.* The male balsam apple.

CER'ASIN, *n.* [L. *cerasus.*]
Any gummy substance which swells in cold water, but does not readily dissolve in it. *Ure. Dr. John.*

CER'ASITE, *n.* [L. *cerasum*, cherry.] A petrifaction resembling a cherry. *Cyc.*

CERAS'TES, *n.* [Gr. κεραςης, from κερας, a horn.]
In *zoology*, the name of a serpent, of the genus Coluber, which the ancients supposed to have horns.

CE'RATE, *n.* [L. *ceratum*, from *cera*, wax.]
A thick kind of ointment, composed of wax and oil, with other ingredients; applied externally in various diseases. *Cyc.*

CE'RATED, *a.* [L. *ceratus.*] Covered with wax.

CERE, *n.* The naked skin that covers the base of a hawk's bill. *Encyc.*

CERE, *v. t.* [L. *cera*, wax.] To wax or cover with wax. *Wiseman.*

CER'EBEL, } *n.* [L. *cerebellum.*] The
CEREBEL'LUM, } hinder part of the head, or the little brain. *Coxe.*

CER'EBRAL, } *a.* [from L. *cerebrum*, the
CER'EBRINE, } brain.]
Pertaining to the cerebrum or brain.

CE'RECLOTH, *n.* [L. *cera*, wax, and *cloth.*]
A cloth smeared with melted wax, or with some gummy or glutinous matter. *Bacon.*
[But the English word for a cloth used to cover wounds is *sear-cloth*, Sax. *sar-cloth*, a sore-cloth.]

CE'REMENT, *n.* [L. *cera*, wax.] Cloths dipped in melted wax, with which dead bodies were infolded, when embalmed. *Johnson.*

CEREMO'NIAL, *a.* [See *Ceremony.*]
1. Relating to ceremony, or external rite; ritual; according to the forms of established rites; as *ceremonial* exactness. It is particularly applied to the forms and rites of the Jewish religion; as the *ceremonial* law or worship, as distinguished from the *moral* and *judicial* law.
2. Formal; observant of old forms; exact; precise in manners. *Dryden.*
[In this sense, *ceremonious* is now used.]

CEREMO'NIAL, *n.* Outward form; external rite, or established forms or rites, including all the forms prescribed; a system of rules and ceremonies, enjoined by law or established by custom, whether in religious worship, in social intercourse, or in the courts of princes.
2. The order for rites and forms in the Romish church, or the book containing the rules prescribed to be observed on solemn occasions.

CEREMO'NIOUS, *a.* Consisting of outward forms and rites; as the *ceremonious* part of worship. [In this sense, *ceremonial* is now used.]
2. Full of ceremony or solemn forms. *Shak.*
3. According to the rules and forms prescribed or customary; civil; formally respectful. "*Ceremonious* phrases." *Addison.*
4. Formal; according to the rules of civility; as, to take a *ceremonious* leave.
5. Formal; exact; precise; too observant of forms.

CEREMO'NIOUSLY, *adv.* In a ceremonious manner; formally; with due forms.

CEREMO'NIOUSNESS, *n.* The use of customary forms; the practice of too much ceremony; great formality in manners.

CER'EMONY, *n.* [L. Sp. It. Port. *ceremonia*; Fr. *ceremonie.*]
1. Outward rite; external form in religion.
2. Forms of civility; rules established by custom for regulating social intercourse.
3. Outward forms of state; the forms prescribed or established by order or custom, serving for the purpose of civility or magnificence, as in levees of princes, the reception of embassadors, &c.
Master of ceremonies, an officer who superintends the reception of embassadors. A person who regulates the forms to be observed by the company or attendants on a public occasion.

CER'EOLITE, *n.* [L. *cera*, wax, and Gr. λιθος, a stone.]
A substance which in appearance and softness resembles wax; sometimes confounded with steatite. *Cyc. Cleaveland.*

CE'REOUS, *a.* [L. *cereus*, from *cera*, wax.]
Waxen; like wax. *Gayton.*

CE'RES, *n.* In *mythology*, the inventor or goddess of corn, or rather the name of corn deified.
2. The name of a planet discovered by M. Piozzi, at Palermo in Sicily, in 1801.

CE'RIN, *n.* [L. *cera*, wax.] A peculiar substance which precipitates on evaporation, from alcohol, which has been digested on grated cork. *Ure.*
2. The part of common wax which dissolves in alcohol. *Dr. John.*
3. A variety of the mineral allanite.

CERINTH'IANS, *n.* A set of heretics, so called from Cerinthus, one of the first heresiarchs in the church. They denied the divinity of Christ, but they held that, in his baptism, a celestial virtue descended on him in the form of a dove, by means of which he was consecrated by the Holy Spirit and made Christ. *Encyc.*

CE'RITE, *n.* [See *Cerium.*] The siliceous oxyd of Cerium, a rare mineral of a pale rose red color, with a tinge of yellow. *Haüy. Jameson. Cleaveland.*
2. A fossil shell.

CE'RIUM, *n.* A metal recently discovered in Sweden, in the mineral cerite, and so called from the planet Ceres. It is of great specific gravity. Its color a grayish white and its texture lamellar. *Dict. Nat. Hist.*

CEROON', *n.* [from the Spanish.] A bale or package made of skins.

CER'RIAL, *a.* Pertaining to the Cerrus, or bitter oak. *Chaucer.*

CER'RUS, *n.* [L.] The bitter oak.

CER'TAIN, *a.* *cer'tin.* [Fr. *certain*; Sp. *cierto*; It. Port. *certo*; from L. *certus.*]

1. Sure; true; undoubted; unquestionable; that cannot be denied; existing in fact and truth.

The dream is *certain* and the interpretation sure. Dan. ii.

2. Assured in mind; having no doubts; followed by *of*, before a noun.

However I with thee have fixed my lot,
Certain to undergo like doom of death,
Consort with thee. *Milton.*

To make her *certain of* the sad event. *Dryden.*

3. Unfailing; always producing the intended effect; as, we may have a *certain* remedy for a disease.

4. Not doubtful or casual; really existing.

Virtue that directs our ways
Through *certain* dangers to uncertain praise. *Dryden.*

5. Stated; fixed; determinate; regular.

Ye shall gather a *certain* rate every day. Ex. xvi.

6. Particular.

There came a *certain* poor widow. Mark xii.

In the plural number, a particular part or number; some; an indefinite part, number, or quantity. "Hanani came, he and *certain* men of Judah." "I mourned *certain* days." Neh. i. 2. 6.

In the latter sense, it is used as a noun; as, "*certain* also of your own poets have said." Acts xvii.

CER'TAINLY, *adv.* Without doubt or question; in truth and fact.

Certainly this was a righteous man. Luke xxiii.

2. Without failure.

He said, I will *certainly* return to thee. Gen. xviii.

CER'TAINNESS, *n.* Certainty, which see.

CER'TAINTY, *n.* A fixed or real state; truth; fact.

Know for a *certainty*, that the Lord your God will no more drive out these nations. Josh. xxiii. Luke i.

2. Full assurance of mind; exemption from doubt.

Certainty is the perception of the agreement or disagreement of our ideas. *Locke.*

3. Exemption from failure; as the *certainty* of an event, or of the success of a medicine.

The *certainty* of punishment is the truest security against crimes. *Ames.*

4. Regularity; settled state.

CER'TES, *adv.* Certainly; in truth; verily. *Obs.* *Chaucer.*

CERTIF'ICATE, *n.* [Fr. *certificat*; It. *certificato.* See *Certify.*]

1. In *a general sense*, a written testimony not sworn to; a declaration in writing, signed by the party, and intended to verify a fact.

2. In *a more particular sense*, the written declaration, under the hand or seal or both, of some public officer, to be used as evidence in a court, or to substantiate a fact. A certificate of this kind may be considered as given under the oath of office.

3. *Trial by certificate*, is where the evidence of the person certifying is the only proper criterion of the point in dispute; as when the issue is whether a person was absent in the army, this is tried by the certificate of the Mareschall of the army, in writing under his seal. *Blackstone.*

CERTIF'ICATE, *v. t.* or *i.* To give a certificate; to lodge a certificate with the proper officer, for the purpose of being exempted from the payment of taxes to support the ministry, in a parish or ecclesiastical society. *New England.*

2. To give a certificate to, acknowledging one to be a parishioner.

But such *certificated* person can gain no settlement. *Blackstone.* B. 1. Ch. 9.

CERTIFICA'TION, *n.* The act of certifying.

CER'TIFIED, *pp.* [See *Certify.*] Assured; made certain; informed.

CER'TIFIER, *n.* One who certifies, or assures.

CER'TIFY, *v. t.* [Fr. *certifier*; Sp. *certificar*; It. *certificare*; Low L. *certifico*; from *certus*, certain, and *facio*, to make.]

1. To testify to in writing; to make a declaration in writing, under hand, or hand and seal, to make known or establish a fact.

The judges shall *certify* their opinion to the chancellor, and upon such certificate, the decree is usually founded.

The judge shall *certify* under his hand, that the freehold came chiefly in question. *Blackstone.*

2. To give certain information *to*; *applied to persons.*

We have sent and *certified* the king. Ezra iv.

3. To give certain information *of*; *applied to things.*

This is designed to *certify* those things that are confirmed of God's favor. *Hammond.*

It is followed by *of*, after the person, and before the thing told; as, I *certified* you *of* the fact.

CER'TIFYING, *ppr.* Giving a written testimony, or certificate; giving certain notice; making certainly known.

CERTIORA'RI, *n.* [Low L. *certioror*, from *certus, certior.*]

A writ issuing out of Chancery, King's Bench or other superior court, to call up the records of an inferior court, or remove a cause there depending, that it may be tried in the superior court. This writ is obtained upon complaint of a party, that he has not received justice, or that he cannot have an impartial trial, in the inferior court. *Encyc.*

CER'TITUDE, *n.* [Low L. *certitudo*, from *certus*, certain.] Certainty; assurance; freedom from doubt. *Dryden.*

CERU'LEAN, } *a.* [L. *cæruleus*; It. Sp.
CERU'LEOUS, } *ceruleo.*] Sky-colored; blue. *Thomson.*

CERULIF'IC, *a.* Producing a blue or sky-color.

CERU'MEN, *n.* [L. *cera*, wax.] The wax or yellow matter secreted by the ear.

CER'USE, *n.* [Fr. *ceruse*; L. It. *cerussa*; Sp. *cerusa.*]

White-lead; a carbonate of lead, produced by exposing the metal in thin plates to the vapor of vinegar. Lead is sometimes found native in the form of ceruse.

Ceruse of antimony is a white oxyd of antimony, which separates from the water in which diaphoretic antimony has been washed. *Nicholson.*

CER'USED, *a.* Washed with a preparation of white lead. *Beaum.*

CER'VICAL, *a.* [L. *cervix*, the neck, whence *cervicalis.*]

Belonging to the neck; as the *cervical* nerves; *cervical* vessels. *Encyc.*

CERV'IN, } *a.* [L. *cervinus*; Sp. *cervino*;
CERV'INE, } from L. *cervus*, a deer; W. *carw*; Corn. and Arm. *karu*; Kamtchatka, *karo.*]

Pertaining to the deer, or to animals of the genus Cervus.

CESA'REAN, *a.* The *Cesarean* operation is the taking of a child from the womb by cutting; an operation, which, it is said, gave name to Cæsar, the Roman emperor.

CESPITI''TIOUS, *a.* [L. *cespes*, turf.] Pertaining to turf; made of turf. *Gough.*

CES'PITOUS, *a.* Pertaining to turf; turfy.

A *cespitous* or turfy plant, has many stems from the same root, usually forming a close thick carpet or matting. *Martyn.*

CESS, as a noun, a rate or tax, and as a verb, to rate or lay a tax, is probably a corruption of *assess*, or from the same root. It is not used. *Spenser.*

CESS, *v. i.* [L. *cesso*, to cease.] To neglect a legal duty. *Obs.* *Cowel.*

CESSA'TION, *n.* [L. *cessatio*, from *cesso*, to cease.]

1. A ceasing; a stop; a rest; the act of discontinuing motion or action of any kind, whether temporary or final.

2. A ceasing or suspension of operation, force or effect; as a *cessation* of the laws of nature.

A *cessation of arms*, an armistice or truce, agreed to by the commanders of armies, to give time for a capitulation, or for other purposes.

CESSA'VIT, *n.* [L. *cesso*, to cease, *cessavit*, he hath ceased.]

In *law*, a writ given by statute, to recover lands, when the tenant or occupier has *ceased* for two years to perform the service, which constitutes the condition of his tenure, and has not sufficient goods or chattels to be distrained, or the tenant has so inclosed the land that the lord cannot come upon it to distrain. *Blackstone.*

CES'SER, *n.* [See *Cess.*] A ceasing; a neglect to perform services or payment for two years. [See *Cessavit.*] *Blackstone.*

CESSIBIL'ITY, *n.* [See *Cede* and *Cession.*] The act of giving way or receding. [*Little used.*] *Digby.*

CES'SIBLE, *a.* [See *Cede.*] Giving way; yielding; easy to give way. *Digby.*

CES'SION, *n.* [L. *cessio*; Fr. *cession*; from L. *cedo, cessum.* See *Cede.*]

1. The act of giving way; a yielding to force or impulse. *Bacon.*

2. A yielding, or surrender, as of property or rights, to another person; particularly, a surrender of conquered territory to its former proprietor or sovereign, by treaty.

3. In *the civil law*, a voluntary surrender of a person's effects to his creditors, to avoid imprisonment. *Encyc.*

4. In *ecclesiastical law*, the leaving of a benefice without dispensation or being otherwise qualified. When an ecclesiastical person is created a bishop, or when the parson of a parish takes another benefice, without dispensation, the benefices are void by *cession*, without resignation. *Encyc.*

CES′SIONARY, *a.* Having surrendered effects; as a *cessionary* bankrupt. *Martin.*

CESS′MENT, *n.* An assessment or tax. [*Not used.*]

CES′SOR, *n.* [L. *cesso*, to *cease.*] In *law*, he that neglects, for two years, to perform the service by which he holds lands, so that he incurs the danger of the writ of cessavit. [See *Cessavit.*] *Cowel.*

2. An assessor, or taxer.

CEST, *n.* [Infra.] A lady's girdle. *Collins.*

CEST′US, *n.* [L. from Gr. κεϛος.] The girdle of Venus, or marriage-girdle, among the Greeks and Romans.

CESU′RA, } *n.* [Fr. *cesure*; It. *cesura*; L.
CE′SURE, } *cæsura*, from *cædo*, *cæsum*, to cut off.]

A pause in verse, so introduced as to aid the recital, and render the versification more melodious. It divides a verse or line into equal or unequal parts. Its most pleasing effect is produced, when it is placed at the end of the second foot, or in the middle, or at the end of the third foot. *Sheridan.*

CE′SURAL, *a.* Pertaining to the cesure.

CETA′CEOUS, *a.* [L. *cete*; Gr. κητος, a whale.]

Pertaining to the whale; belonging to the whale kind. The *cetaceous* fishes include the genera *monodon*, *balæna*, *physeter* and *delphinus*. They have no gills, but an aperture on the top of the head, and a flat or horizontal tail. *Encyc.*

CE′TATE, *n.* A compound of cetic acid, with a base. *Chevreul.*

CET′ERACH, *n.* A trivial name of a species of Asplenium, or spleen-wort.

CE′TIC, *a.* [L. *cetus*, a whale.] Pertaining to the whale. The *cetic acid* is a peculiar substance obtained from the spermaceti. *Ure.*

CE′TIN, *n.* [L. *cetus*, a whale.] A name given to spermaceti by Chevreul.

CETOLOG′ICAL, *a.* [from *cetology.*] Pertaining to cetology.

CETOL′OGIST, *n.* One who is versed in the natural history of the whale and its kindred animals.

CETOL′OGY, *n.* [Gr. κητος, a whale, and λογος, discourse.]

The doctrine or natural history of cetaceous animals. *Ed. Encyc.*

CE′TUS, *n.* [Supra.] In *astronomy*, the whale, a large constellation of the southern hemisphere, containing ninety-seven stars. *Encyc.*

CE′YLANITE, *n.* [from *Ceylon.*] A mineral, classed with the ruby family; called also *pleonaste*. Its color is a muddy, dark blue, and grayish black, approaching to iron black. It occurs in grains, or small crystals, either perfect octahedrons, or truncated on the edges, or with the angles acuminated by four planes. It occurs also in rhomboidal dodecahedrons. *Cyc. Ure.*

CHAB′ASIE, } *n.* [*Schabasit.* Werner.] A
CHAB′ASITE, } mineral which has been regarded as a variety of zeolite. It is divisible into very obtuse rhomboids. *Dict. Nat. Hist.*

This mineral occurs in crystals, whose primitive form is nearly a cube. *Ure.*

Chabasie has a foliated structure; its fracture is somewhat conchoidal or uneven, with a glistening vitreous luster. It is translucent, sometimes transparent. Its color is white or grayish white, sometimes with a rosy tinge. Before the blowpipe, it intumesces a little, and easily melts into a white spongy mass. *Cleaveland.*

CHAD, *n.* A kind of fish; pronounced *shad.* *Carew.*

CHAFE, *v. t.* [Fr. *echauffer*; Sp. *escalfar*, to warm; Port. *escalfar*, to poach or boil slightly; from the root of L. *caleo*, whence *calefio*, *calfacio.*]

1. To excite heat or inflammation by friction, as to *chafe* the skin; also, to fret and wear by rubbing, as to *chafe* a cable.

2. To excite heat in the mind; to excite passion; to inflame; to make angry; to cause to fret; to provoke or incense. 2 Sam. xvii. 8.

3. To excite violent action; to cause to rage; as, the wind *chafes* the ocean.

4. To perfume; rather, to stimulate, or agitate; to excite by pungent odors.

> Lilies, whose scent *chafed* the air. *Suckling.*

CHAFE, *v. i.* To be excited or heated; to rage; to fret; to be in violent action. *Pope.*

2. To act violently upon, by rubbing; to fret against, as waves against a shore.

> The troubled Tyber *chafing* with his shores. *Shak.*

3. To be fretted and worn by rubbing; as, a cable *chafes.*

CHAFE, *n.* Heat, excited by friction.

2. Violent agitation of the mind or passions; heat; fret; passion. *Camden.*

CHA′FED, *pp.* Heated or fretted by rubbing; worn by friction.

CHA′FER, *n.* One who chafes.

CHA′FER, *n.* [Sax. *ceafor*; D. *kever*; G. *käfer.*] An insect, a species of Scarabæus, or beetle.

CHA′FERY, *n.* [from *chafe.*] In *Iron works*, a forge in which an ancony or square mass of iron, hammered into a bar in the middle, with its ends rough, is reduced to a complete bar, by hammering down the ends to the shape of the middle. *Encyc.*

CHA′FE-WAX, *n.* In *England*, an officer belonging to the Lord Chancellor, who fits the wax for the sealing of writs. *Harris.*

CH′AFF, *n.* [Sax. *ceaf*; D. *kaf*; G. *kaff.*]

1. The husk, or dry calyx of corn, and grasses. In common language, the word is applied to the husks when separated from the corn by thrashing, riddling or winnowing. The word is sometimes used rather improperly to denote straw cut small for the food of cattle. *Martyn. Encyc.*

2. Refuse; worthless matter; especially that which is light, and apt to be driven by the wind. In *scripture*, false doctrines, fruitless designs, hypocrites and ungodly men are compared to chaff. Ps. i. 4. Jer. xxiii. 28. Is. xxxiii. 11. Math. iii. 12.

CHAF′FER, *v. i.* [Sax. *ceapian*; D. *koopen*; G. *kaufen*; Sw. *köpa*; Dan. *kiöber*, to bargain or buy. It seems to be radically the same word as *cheap*, *cheapen*, and *chap* in *chapman*. See *Cheap.*]

To treat about a purchase; to bargain; to haggle; to negotiate; to chop and change; as, to *chaffer* for preferments. *Dryden.*

CHAF′FER, *v. t.* To buy; to exchange. *Spenser.*

[*In this sense it is obsolete.*]

CHAF′FER, *n.* Merchandize. [*Not in use.*] *Skelton.*

CHAF′FERER, *n.* One who chaffers; a bargainer; a buyer.

CHAF′FERN, *n.* A vessel for heating water. [*Local.*]

CHAF′FERY, *n.* Trafick; buying and selling. *Obs.* *Spenser.*

CHAF′FINCH, *n.* [*chaff* and *finch.*] A species of birds of the genus *Fringilla*, which are said to delight in chaff, and are admired for their song.

CH′AFFLESS, *n.* Without chaff. *Shak.*

CH′AFFWEED, *n.* A plant, cud-weed, a species of Gnaphalium; but this name is given also to the Centunculus. *Muhlenberg.*

CH′AFFY, *a.* Like chaff; full of chaff; light; as, *chaffy* straws; *chaffy* opinions. *Brown. Glanville.*

CHA′FING, *ppr.* Heating or fretting by friction.

CHA′FING-DISH, *n.* [*chafe* and *dish.*] A dish or vessel to hold coals for heating any thing set on it; a portable grate for coals.

CHAGRIN′, *n.* [Fr. This word, applied to a particular kind of skin, or leather, is said to be derived from a Turkish word, *sagri*, Fr. *croupe*. The skin is dressed so as to present on its surface little eminences. See *Shagreen.*]

Ill-humor; vexation; peevishness; fretfulness. *Pope.*

CHAGRIN′, *v. t.* [Fr. *chagriner.*] To excite ill-humor in; to vex; to mortify.

CHAGRIN′ED, *pp.* Vexed; fretted; displeased.

CHAIN, *n.* [Fr. *chaîne*, for *chaisne*; Norm. *cadene*, and *cheyne*; Arm. *chaden*, *cadenn*, or *jadenn*; Sp. *cadena*; Port. *cadea*; It. *catena*; L. *catena*; D. *keten*; G. *kette*; Sw. *kädia*; Dan. *kede*; W. *cadwen*. Qu. Ar. أكاد from أكد akada, to bind or make fast.]

1. A series of links or rings connected, or fitted into one another, usually made of some kind of metal, as a *chain* of gold, or of iron; but the word is not restricted to any particular kind of material. It is used often for an ornament about the person.

2. That which binds; a real chain; that which restrains, confines, or fetters; a bond.

> If God spared not the angels that sinned, but delivered them into *chains* of darkness. 2 Peter ii.

3. Bondage; affliction.

> He hath made my *chain* heavy. Lam. iii.

4. Bondage; slavery.

> In despotism the people sleep soundly in their *chains.* *Ames.*

5. Ornament. Prov. i. 9.

6. A series of things linked together; a series of things connected or following in succession; as a *chain* of causes, of ideas, or events; a *chain* of being.

7. A range, or line of things connected; as a *chain* of mountains.

8. A series of links, forming an instrument to measure land.

9. A string of twisted wire, or something similar, to hang a watch on, and for other purposes.
10. In *France*, a measure of wood for fuel, and various commodities, of various length.
11. In *ship-building*, chains are strong links or plates of iron, bolted at the lower end to the ship's side, used to contain the blocks called dead eyes, by which the shrouds of the mast are extended.
12. The warp in weaving, as in French.

Chain-pump. This consists of a long chain, equipped with a sufficient number of valves, moving on two wheels, one above, the other below, passing downward through a wooden tube and returning through another. It is managed by a long winch, on which several men may be employed at once. *Encyc.*

Chain-shot, two balls connected by a chain, and used to cut down masts, or cut away shrouds and rigging.

Chain-wales of a ship, broad and thick planks projecting from a ship's side, abreast of and behind the masts, for the purpose of extending the shrouds, for better supporting the masts, and preventing the shrouds from damaging the gunwale. *Encyc.*

Chain-work, work consisting of threads, cords and the like, linked together in the form of a chain; as lineal chaining or tambour work, reticulation or net work, &c. *Ed. Encyc.*

Top-chain, on board a ship, a chain to sling the sail-yards in time of battle, to prevent their falling, when the ropes that support them are shot away. *Encyc.*

CHAIN, *v. t.* To fasten, bind or connect with a chain; to fasten or bind with any thing in the manner of a chain.
2. To enslave; to keep in slavery.

> And which more blest? Who *chain'd* his country, say,
> Or he whose virtue sighed to lose a day? *Pope.*

3. To guard with a chain, as a harbor or passage.
4. To unite; to form chain-work.

CHA'INED, *pp.* Made fast, or bound by a chain; connected by a chain; bound; enslaved.

CHA'INING, *ppr.* Binding, fastening or connecting with a chain; binding, or attaching to; enslaving.

CHAIR, *n.* [Fr. *chaire*, a pulpit, contracted from Norm. *cadiere*, as *chain* from *catena*; Arm. *cadarn*, or *cador*; Ir. *cathaoir*; L. *cathedra*; Gr. χαθεδρα, connected with χαθεζομαι, to sit, χατα and εζομαι; W. *cadair*, a seat or stool.]

1. A movable seat; a frame with a bottom made of different materials, used for persons to sit in; originally a stool, and anciently a kind of pulpit in churches.
2. A seat of justice or of authority; as a *chair* of state.
3. A seat for a professor, or his office; as the professor's *chair*.
4. The seat for a speaker or presiding officer of a public council or assembly, as the speaker's *chair*; and by a metonymy, the speaker himself; as, to address the *chair*.
5. A sedan; a vehicle on poles borne by men.
6. A pulpit. *Burnet.*
7. A two-wheeled carriage, drawn by one horse; a gig.
8. Supreme office or magistracy.

> When Governor Shute came to the *chair*, several of the old councilors were laid aside. *Belknap.*

Curule chair, an ivory seat placed on a car, used by the prime magistates of Rome.

CHA'IR-MAN, *n.* The presiding officer or speaker of an assembly, association or company, particularly of a legislative house; also, the president or senior member of a committee.
2. One whose business is to carry a chair. *Dryden.*

CHAISE, *n. s* as *z.* [Fr. *chaise*, a seat or chair. Qu. It. *seggia.*]
A two-wheeled carriage drawn by one horse; a gig. It is open or covered.

CHALCEDON'IC, *a.* Pertaining to chalcedony.

CHAL'CEDONY, *n.* [from *Chalcedon*, a town in Asia Minor, opposite to Byzantium, now Constantinople. Pliny informs us that Chalcedon signifies the *town* of blind men. The last syllable then is the Celtic *dun*, English *town*, a fact that the historian should not overlook. Plin. Lib. 5. 32.]
A subspecies of quartz, a mineral called also white agate, resembling milk diluted with water, and more or less clouded or opake, with veins, circles and spots. It is used in jewelry. *Cleaveland. Nicholson. Encyc.*
The varieties of chalcedony are common chalcedony, heliotrope, chrysoprase, plasma, onyx, sard and sardonyx. *Ure.*

CHAL'CEDONYX, *n.* A variety of agate, in which white and gray layers alternate. *Cleaveland.*

CHAL'CITE, *n.* [Gr. χαλκος, brass.] Sulphate of iron of a red color, so far calcined as to have lost a considerable part of its acid. *Fourcroy.*

CHALCOG'RAPHER, *n.* [Infra.] An engraver in brass.

CHALCOG'RAPHY, *n.* [Gr. χαλκος, brass, and γραφω, to write.] The act or art of engraving in brass.

CHALDA'IC, *a.* Pertaining to Chaldea, anciently a country on the Frat or Euphrates, in Asia, called in scripture Shinar. Of this Babylon was the principal city.

CHALDA'IC, *n.* The language or dialect of the Chaldeans.

CHAL'DAISM, *n.* An idiom or peculiarity in the Chaldee dialect. *Parkhurst.*

CHALDE'AN, *n.* An inhabitant of Chaldea.

CHAL'DEE, *a.* Pertaining to Chaldea.

CHAL'DEE, *n.* The language or dialect of the Chaldeans.

CHAL'DRON, } *n.* [Fr. *chaudron*; Sp. *calderon*; It. *calderone*, a
CHAL'DER, } kettle. The same word as *caldron*. *Chalder* is not in use in the United States.]
A measure of coals consisting of thirty six bushels. *Chambers.*

CHAL'ICE, *n.* [Fr. *calice*; Sp. *caliz*; It. *calice*; D. *kelk*; G. *kelch*; L. *calix*; Gr. χυλιξ. It should have been written *calice.*]
A cup, or bowl; usually, a communion cup.

CHAL'ICED, *a.* Having a cell or cup; applied by Shakspeare to a flower; *but I believe little used.*

CHALK, *n. chauk.* [Sax. *cealc*; D. Dan. G. *kalk*; Sw. *kalck*; W. *calc*; Corn. *kalch*; Ir. *cailk*; L. *calx*; Fr. *chaux*. The Latin *calx* is lime-stone, chalk-stone, and the heel, and *calco* is to kick and to tread. In Italian *calca* is a crowd. The sense then is a mass made compact, a clod or lump. If the Gr. χαλιξ, flint, gravel, is the same word, the Latins deviated from their usual practice in writing *calx*, for *chalx*. These words are probably connected in origin with *callus.*]
A well known calcarious earth, of an opake white color, soft and admitting no polish. It contains a large portion of carbonic acid, and is a subspecies of carbonate of lime. It is used as an absorbent and anti-acid. *Cleaveland. Nicholson. Kirwan. Aikin.*

Black-chalk is a species of earth used by painters for drawing on blue paper.

Red-chalk is an indurated clayey ocher used by painters and artificers.

CHALK, *v. t.* To rub with chalk; to mark with chalk.
2. To manure with chalk, as land.
3. From the use of chalk in marking lines, the phrase *to chalk out* is used to signify, to lay out, draw out or describe; as, to *chalk out* a plan of proceeding.

CHALK-CUTTER, *n.* A man that digs chalk. *Woodward.*

CHALKINESS, *n. chauk'iness.* The state of being chalky.

CHALK-PIT, *n.* A pit in which chalk is dug. *Johnson.*

CHALK-STONE, *n.* In *medicine*, a calcarious concretion in the hands and feet of men violently affected by the gout. *Encyc.*
2. A small lump of chalk. *Isaiah.*

CHALKY, *a. chauk'y.* Resembling chalk; as a *chalky* taste.
2. White with chalk; consisting of chalk; as, *chalky* cliffs. *Rowe.*
3. Impregnated with chalk; as, *chalky* water.

CHAL'LENGE, *n.* [Norm. *calenge*, an accusation; *chalunge*, a claim; *challenger*, to claim; from the root of *call*, Gr. χαλεω, χελλω, L. *calo*. See *Call.*]
Literally, a calling, or crying out, the primary sense of many words expressing a demand, as *claim*, L. *clamo*. Hence appropriately,
1. A calling upon one to fight in single combat; an invitation or summons, verbal or written, to decide a controversy by a duel. Hence the letter containing the summons is also called a challenge.
2. A claim or demand made of a right or supposed right.

> There must be no *challenge* of superiority. *Collier.*

3. Among *hunters*, the opening and crying of hounds at first finding the scent of their game. *Encyc.*
4. In *law*, an exception to jurors; the claim of a party that certain jurors shall not sit in trial upon him or his cause; that is, a calling them off. The right of challenge is given both in civil and criminal trials, for certain causes which are supposed to disqualify a juror to be an impartial judge. The right of challenge extends either to the whole panel or array, or only to par-

ticular jurors, called a challenge to the polls. A principal challenge is that which the law allows without cause assigned. A challenge to the favor, is when the party alledges a special cause. In criminal cases, a prisoner may challenge twenty jurors, without assigning a cause. This is called a peremptory challenge. *Blackstone.*

CHAL'LENGE, *v. t.* To call, invite or summon to answer for an offense by single combat, or duel.

2. To call to a contest; to invite to a trial; as, I *challenge* a man to prove what he asserts, implying defiance.

3. To accuse; to call to answer. *Spenser. Shak.*

4. To claim as due; to demand as a right; as, the Supreme Being *challenges* our reverence and homage.

5. In *law*, to call off a juror, or jurors; or to demand that jurors shall not sit in trial upon a cause. [See the noun.]

6. To call to the performance of conditions.

CHAL'LENGEABLE, *a.* That may be challenged; that may be called to account. *Sadler.*

CHAL'LENGED. *pp.* Called to combat or to contest; claimed; demanded, as due; called from a jury.

CHAL'LENGER, *n.* One who challenges; one who invites to a single combat; one who calls on another by way of defiance. *Shak.*

2. One who claims superiority; one who claims any thing as his right, or makes pretensions to it. *Hooker.*

3. One who calls a juror, or a jury, from the trial of his cause.

CHAL'LENGING, *ppr.* Summoning to a duel, or to contest; claiming as a right; defying; calling off from a jury.

CHALYB'EAN, *a.* [Infra.] Pertaining to steel well tempered. *Milton.*

CHALYB'EATE, *a.* [L. *chalybs*; Gr. χαλυψ, steel. Qu. from *Chalybs*, a town near the Euxine.]

Impregnated with particles of iron; as *chalybeate* waters.

CHALYB'EATE, *n.* Any water or other liquor into which iron enters.

CHAM, *n. kam.* The sovereign prince of Tartary. Usually written *Khan.*

CHAMA'DE, *n.* [Fr. from It. *chiamata*, a calling; *chiamare*, to call; L. *clamo*; Sp. *llamada*; Port. *chamada*, from *chamar*, to call. See *Claim.*]

In *war*, the beat of a drum or sound of a trumpet, inviting an enemy to a parley; as for making a proposition for a truce, or for a capitulation. *Encyc.*

CHĀMBER, } *n.* The first pronunciation is
CH'AMBER, } most common; the last, most analagous and correct. [Fr. *chambre*; Arm. *campr*, *cambr*; It. *camera*; Port. Sp. *camara*; L. *camera*; Gr. καμαρα, an arched roof, vault or upper gallery, a chamber; D. *kamer*; G. *kammer*; Sw. *kammare*; Dan. *kammer*; Ch. קמר to arch; Eth. ቀመረ kamare, an arch or vault.]

1. An apartment in an upper story, or in a story above the lower floor of a dwelling house; often used as a lodging room.

2. Any retired room; any private apartment which a person occupies; as, he called on the judge at his *chamber.*

Joseph entered into his *chamber* and wept. Gen. xliii.

3. Any retired place.

Her house is the way to hell, going down to the *chambers* of death. Prov. vii.

4. A hollow or cavity; as the *chamber* of the eye. *Sharp.*

5. A place where an assembly meets, and the assembly itself; as *star-chamber*; imperial *chamber*; *chamber* of accounts; ecclesiastical *chamber*; privy *chamber*; *chamber* of commerce, &c.

6. In *military affairs*, the *chamber* of a mortar is that part of the chase, where the powder lies.

7. A *powder-chamber*, or *bomb-chamber*, a place under ground for holding powder and bombs, where they may be safe and secured from rains.

8. The *chamber of a mine*, a place, generally of a cubical form, where the powder is confined.

9. A species of ordnance. Qu. *Camden.*

10. The clouds. Ps. civ.

11. Certain southern constellations which are hid from us.

The *chambers* of the south. Job ix.

Chamber-council, a private or secret council. *Shak.*

Chamber-counsel, a counselor, who gives his opinion in a private apartment, but does not advocate causes in court.

CHĀMBER, } *v. i.* To reside in or occupy
CH'AMBER, } as a chamber.

2. To be wanton; to indulge in lewd or immodest behavior. Rom. xiii.

CHĀMBER, } *v. t.* To shut up as in a
CH'AMBER, } chamber. *Shak.*

CHĀMBERER, } *n.* One who intrigues, or
CH'AMBERER, } indulges in wantonness. *Shak.*

CHĀMBER-FELLOW, } *n.* One who
CH'AMBER-FELLOW, } sleeps in the same apartment. *Spectator.*

CHAMBER-HANGING, *n.* Tapestry or hangings for a chamber.

CHĀMBERING, } *n.* Wanton, lewd, im-
CH'AMBERING, } modest behavior. Rom. xiii.

CHĀMBERLAIN, } *n.* [Fr. *chambellan*;
CH'AMBERLAIN, } Arm. *cambrelan*; Sp. *camarero*; Port. *camareiro*; It. *camerlingo*; D. *kamerling*; Dan. *kammer-herre*; L. *camerarius.*]

1. An officer charged with the direction and management of a chamber, or of chambers. The Lord Chamberlain of Great Britain is the sixth officer of the crown. To him belong livery and lodging in the king's court; on coronation day he brings to the king his apparel, his sword, scabbard, &c. He dresses and undresses the king on that day, and waits on him before and after dinner. To him also belongs the care of providing all things in the house of lords, in time of parliament. Under him are the gentleman usher of the black rod, and other officers. The Lord Chamberlain of the household has the oversight of all officers belonging to the king's chambers, except the precinct of the bed-chamber, of the wardrobe, physicians, chaplains, barbers, &c., and administers the oath to all officers above stairs.

The chamberlains of the exchequer, of London, of Chester, of North Wales, &c., are receivers of rents and revenues. *Encyc. Johnson.*

2. A servant who has the care of the chambers in an inn or hotel.

CHĀMBERLAINSHIP, } *n.* The office of
CH'AMBERLAINSHIP, } a chamberlain.

CHAMBER-LYE, *n.* Urine.

CHĀMBER-MAID, } *n.* A woman who
CH'AMBER-MAID, } has the care of chambers, making the beds, and cleaning the rooms, or who dresses a lady and waits upon her in her apartment.

CHAMBER-POT, *n.* A vessel used in bedrooms.

CHĀMBER-PRACTICE, } *n.* The prac-
CH'AMBER-PRACTICE, } tice of counselors at law, who give their opinions in private, but do not appear in court.

CHAM'BREL, *n.* The joint or bending of the upper part of a horse's hind leg. In New England pronounced *gambrel*, which see.

CHAME'LEON, *n.* [L. *chamæleon*; Gr. χαμαιλεων.]

An animal of the genus Lacerta, or lizard, with a naked body, a tail and four feet. The body is six or seven inches long, and the tail five inches; with this it clings to the branches of trees. The skin is cold to the touch, and contains small grains or eminences, of a bluish gray color, in the shade, but in the light of the sun, all parts of the body become of a grayish brown, or tawny color. It is a native of Africa and Asia. *Encyc.*

CHAME'LEONIZE, *v. t.* To change into various colors. *Dict.*

CHAM'FER, *v. t.* [corrupted from Fr. *echancrer*, to hollow, to cut sloping; Arm. *chancra*; said to be from *cancer.*]

1. To channel; to cut a furrow, as in a column, or to cut into a sloping form. *Johnson. Bailey. Encyc.*

2. To wrinkle. *Shak.*

CHAM'FER, } *n.* A small gutter or furrow
CHAM'FRET, } cut in wood or other hard material; a slope.

CHAM'FERED, *pp.* Cut into furrows, or cut sloping.

CHAM'FERING, *ppr.* Cutting a gutter in; cutting in a slope.

CHAM'ITE, *n.* Fossil remains of the Chama, a shell.

CHAMLET, [See *Camlet.*]

CHAMOIS, *n.* [Fr. from It. *camozza*; Sp. *gamuza*, from *gamo*, a buck.]

An animal of the goat kind, whose skin is made into soft leather, called *shammy.* *Johnson.*

It is now arranged with the Antelopes. *Cuvier.*

CHAM'OMILE, [See *Camomile.*]

CHAMP, *v. t.* [Fr. *champayer*, I have not found. Qu. Gr. καπτω, for *m* is often casual before a labial, and in Gr. γαμφαι is the jaws.]

1. To bite with repeated action of the teeth; as, a horse *champs* the bit.

2. To bite into small pieces; to chew; to masticate; to devour. *Dryden.*

CHAMP, *v. i.* To chew; to perform the action of biting by repeated motion of the teeth; as, to *champ* upon the bit. *Hooker.*

ČHAMPA'GNE, } n. A kind of brisk, sparkling wine, from Champagne in France.
ČHAMPA'NE, }

ČHAMPA'IGN, } n. [from *camp* or the same root.] A flat open country. *Bacon. Milton.*
ČHAMPA'IN, }

ČHAMPA'IN, *n.* In *heraldry*, champain or point champain, is a mark of dishonor in the coat of arms of him who has killed a prisoner of war after he has asked for quarter. *Encyc.*

CHAMP'ED, *pp.* Bitten; chewed.

CHAMP'ER, *n.* One that champs or bites.

CHAM'PERTOR, *n.* [See *Champerty.*] In *law*, one who is guilty of *champerty*, which see.

CHAM'PERTY, *n.* [Fr. *champart*, field-rent; *champ*, L. *campus*, a field, and *part*, a share, or *partir*, to divide, *campum partire.*]

A species of maintenance, being a bargain with a plaintiff or defendant, to divide the land or other matter in suit, between them, if they prevail; whereupon the champertor is to carry on the party's suit at his own expense. The purchase of a suit, or of the right of suing. *Blackstone.*

ČHAMPIGN'ON, *n. shampin'yon.* [Fr.] A kind of mushroom.

CHAMP'ING, *pp.* Biting with repeated action.

CHAM'PION, *n.* [Fr. *champion*; Arm. *campyon*; Sp. *campeon*; Port. *campeam*, or *campiam*; It. *campione*; D. *kamper*, or *kampvegter*; G. *kampfer*. In all the Teutonic dialects, *camp* or *kamp* signifies a combat, and in some of them, a *camp*; Sax. *campa*, a camp and a combat; *cempa*, a soldier, warrior or gladiator; W. *camp*, a game, a feat; *campiaw*, to contend in a game. Here we have the origin of the Latin *campus*. It was originally the plain or open place appropriated to games, sports and athletic exercises.]

1. A man who undertakes a combat in the place or cause of another. *Bacon.*
2. A man who fights in his own cause n a duel.
3. A hero; a brave warrior. Hence, one who is bold in contest; as a *champion* for the truth.

CHAM'PION, *v. t.* To challenge to a combat. *Shak.*

CHAM'PIONESS, *n.* A female champion. *Fairfax.*

CH'ANCE, *n.* [Fr. *chance*; Norm. *cheaunce*; Arm. *chancz*; D. *kans*; G. *schanze*. This seems to be from the participle of the French verb *cheoir*, to fall, Sp. *caer*, from the L. *cado*, or directly from the Latin *cadens*, *cadentia.*]

1. An event that happens, falls out or takes place, without being contrived, intended, expected or foreseen; the effect of an unknown cause, or the unusual or unexpected effect of a known cause; accident; casualty; fortuitous event; as, time and *chance* happen to all.

> By *chance* a priest came down that way. Luke x.

2. Fortune; what fortune may bring; as, they must take their *chance*.
3. An event, good or evil; success or misfortune; luck. *Shak.*
4. Possibility of an occurrence; opportunity.

> Your ladyship may have a *chance* to escape this address. *Swift.*

CH'ANCE, *v. i.* To happen; to fall out; to come or arrive without design, or expectation.

> If a bird's nest *chance* to be before thee. Deut. xxii.
>
> Ah Casca, tell us what hath *chanced* to day. *Shak.*

CH'ANCE, *a.* Happening by chance; casual; as a *chance* comer.

CH'ANCEABLE, *a.* Accidental; casual; fortuitous. *Sidney.*

CH'ANCE-ČOMER, *n.* One who comes unexpectedly. *Addison.*

CH'ANCEFUL, *a.* Hazardous. *Spenser.*

CH'ANCE-MEDLEY, *n.* [*chance* and *medley*, a mixture.]

In *law*, the killing of a person by chance, when the killer is doing a lawful act; for if he is doing an unlawful act, it is felony. As if a man, when throwing bricks from a house into a street where people are continually passing, after giving warning to passengers to take care, should kill a person, this is chance-medley. But if he gives no warning, and kills a man, it is manslaughter.

CH'ANCEL, *n.* [Fr. *chancel* or *chanceau*; L. *cancelli*, lattices or cross bars, inclosing the place; Sp. *cancel*, *cancilla*, a wooden screen, a wicker gate; It. *cancello*, balustrades; Gr. κιγκλις; Ch. קנקל kankel or kankail, net work; Syr. *id.* See *Cancel.*]

That part of the choir of a church, between the altar or communion table and the balustrade or railing that incloses it, or that part where the altar is placed; formerly inclosed with lattices or cross bars, as now with rails. *Encyc. Johnson.*

CH'ANCELLOR, *n.* [Fr. *chancelier*; Arm. *chanceilher*, or *canceller*; Sp. *canciller*; Port. *chanceller*; It. *cancelliere*; D. *kanselier*; G. *kanzler*; Sw. *cantsler*; Dan. *kantsler* or *cantsler*; L. *cancellarius*, a scribe, secretary, notary, or chancellor; from *cancello*, to make lattice work, to *cancel*, or blot out by crossing the lines; or from *cancelli*, lattices, because the secretary sat behind lattices.]

Originally, a chief notary or scribe, under the Roman Emperors; but in England, in later times, an officer invested with judicial powers, and particularly with the superintendance of all charters, letters and other official writings of the crown, that required to be solemnly authenticated. Hence this officer became the keeper of the great seal. From the Roman Empire, this office passed to the church, and hence every bishop has his chancellor.

The Lord High Chancellor of Great Britain, or *Keeper of the Great Seal*, is the highest officer of the crown. He is a privy counselor by his office, and prolocutor of the house of lords by prescription. To him belongs the appointment of all justices of the peace; he is keeper of the king's conscience, visitor of all hospitals and colleges founded by the king, guardian of all charitable uses, and judge of the high court of chancery

Chancellor of an Ecclesiastical Court, is the bishop's lawyer, versed in the civil and canon law, to direct the bishop in causes of the church, civil and criminal.

Chancellor of a Cathedral, is an officer who hears lessons and lectures in the church, by himself or his vicar, inspects schools, hears causes, applies the seal, writes and dispatches letters of the chapter, keeps the books, &c.

Chancellor of the Exchequer, is an officer who presides in that court, and takes care of the interest of the crown. He has power, with the lord treasurer, to lease the crown lands, and with others, to compound for forfeitures on penal statutes. He has a great authority in managing the royal revenues, and in matters relating to the first fruits.

Chancellor of a University, is an officer who seals the diplomas, or letters of degree, &c. The chancellor of Oxford is usually one of the prime nobility, elected by the students in convocation, and he holds the office for life. He is the chief magistrate in the government of the university. The chancellor of Cambridge is also elected from among the prime nobility; he does not hold his office for life, but may be elected every three years.

Chancellor of the Order of the Garter, and other military orders, is an officer who seals the commissions and mandates of the chapter and assembly of the knights, keeps the register of their proceedings, and delivers their acts under the seal of their order. *Johnson. Encyc.*

In *France*, a secretary is, in some cases, called a chancellor.

In *the United States*, a chancellor is the judge of a court of chancery or equity, established by statute.

In *scripture*, a master of the decrees, or president of the council. Ezra iv.

CH'ANCELLORSHIP, *n.* The office of a chancellor; the time during which one is chancellor.

CH'ANCERY, *n.* [Fr. *chancellerie*; Arm. *cancellery*; Sp. *chancilleria*; It. *cancelleria*; L. *cancellaria*, from *cancelli*, lattices, or from the judge, who presided in the court.]

1. In *Great Britain*, the highest court of justice, next to the parliament, consisting of two distinct tribunals; one *ordinary*, being a court of common law; the other *extraordinary*, or a court of equity. The ordinary legal court holds pleas of recognizances acknowledged in the chancery, writs of scire facias, for repeal of letters patent, writs of partition, and all personal actions by or against any officer of the court. But if the parties come to issue, in fact, this court cannot try it by a jury; but the record must be delivered to the king's bench. From this court issue all original writs that pass under the great seal, commissions of charitable uses, bankruptcy, idiocy, lunacy, &c.

The extraordinary court, or court of equity, proceeds upon rules of equity and conscience, moderates the rigor of the common law, and gives relief in cases where there is no remedy in the common law courts.

2. In *the United States*, a court of equity.

ČHAN'ČRE, *n.* [Fr. *chancre*; Arm. *chancr.* The same as *cancer*, *canker.*] A venereal ulcer.

ČHAN'ČROUS, *a.* Ulcerous; having the qualities of a chancre.

CHANDELIE'R, *n.* [Fr. *id.; Sp. candelero;* It. *candeliere;* Arm. *cantolozr*, or *cantuler;* from L. *candela*, a *candle*, from *caneo*, to shine.]
1. A frame with branches to hold a number of candles, to illuminate a public or large room.
2. In *fortification*, a movable parapet, serving to support fascines to cover pioneers.

CH'ANDLER, *n.* [Qr. Fr. *chandelier*, or rather Teutonic *handler*. See *Corn-chandler.*]
An artisan whose trade is to make candles, or one who sells candles. *Johnson.*
In America, I believe the word never signifies a seller of candles, unless he is the maker. A corn-chandler is a seller of corn, but I believe not used in the U. States.

CH'ANDLERLY, *a.* Like a chandler. *Milton.*

CH'ANDLERY, *n.* The commodities sold by a chandler.

CH'ANDRY, *n.* The place where candles are kept. *B. Jonson.*

CHANGE, *v. t.* [Fr. *changer;* It. *cangiare;* Arm. *eceinch;* Norm. *chainant*, exchanging. Qu. Is this radically the same word as It. *cambio, cambiare*, Sp. *id.*?]
1. To cause to turn or pass from one state to another; to alter, or make different; to vary in external form, or in essence; as, to *change* the color or shape of a thing; to *change* the countenance; to *change* the heart or life.
2. To put one thing in the place of another; to shift; as, to *change* the clothes.

> Be clean and *change* your garments. Gen. xxxv.

3. To quit one thing or state for another; followed by *for;* as, persons educated in a particular religion do not readily *change* it *for* another.
4. To give and take reciprocally; as, will you *change* conditions *with* me?
5. To barter; to exchange goods; as, to *change* a coach for a chariot.
6. To quit, as one place for another; as, to *change* lodgings.
7. To give one kind of money for another; to alter the form or kind of money, by receiving the value in a different kind, as to *change* bank notes *for* silver; or to give pieces of a larger denomination for an equivalent in pieces of smaller denomination, as to *change* an eagle *for* dollars, or a sovereign *for* sixpences, or to *change* a dollar *into* cents; or on the other hand, to *change* dollars *for* or *into* eagles, giving money of smaller denomination for larger.
8. To become acid or tainted; to turn from a natural state of sweetness and purity; as, the wine is *changed;* thunder and lightning are said to *change* milk.
To change a horse, or *to change hand*, is to turn or bear the horse's head from one hand to the other, from the left to the right, or from the right to the left. *Farrier's Dict.*

CHANGE, *v. i.* To be altered; to undergo variation; as, men sometimes *change* for the better, often for the worse.

> I am Jehovah; I *change* not. Mal. iii.

2. To pass the sun, as the moon in its orbit; as, the moon will *change* the 14th of this month.

CHANGE, *n.* Any variation or alteration in form, state, quality, or essence; or a passing from one state or form to another; as a *change* of countenance; a *change* of habits or principles.
2. A succession of one thing in the place of another; vicissitude; as a *change* of seasons; a *change* of objects on a journey; a *change* of scenes.
3. A revolution; as a *change* of government.
4. A passing by the sun, and the beginning of a new monthly revolution; as a *change* of the moon.
5. A different state by removal; novelty; variety.

> Our fathers did, for *change*, to France repair. *Dryden.*

6. Alteration in the order of ringing bells; variety of sounds.

> Four bells admit twenty-four *changes* in ringing. *Holder.*

7. That which makes a variety, or may be substituted for another.

> Thirty *changes* of raiment. Judges xiv.

8. Small coins of money, which may be given for larger pieces.
9. The balance of money paid beyond the price of goods purchased.

> I gave the clerk a bank note for his cloth, and he gave me the *change*.

10. The dissolution of the body; death.

> All the days of my appointed time will I wait, till my *change* come. Job xiv.

11. *Change* for *exchange*, a place where merchants and others meet to transact business; a building appropriated for mercantile transactions.
12. In *arithmetic*, permutation; variation of numbers. Thirteen numbers admit of 6,227,020,800 changes, or different positions.

CHANGEABIL'ITY, *n.* Changeableness, *which is generally used.* *Fleming.*

CHANGEABLE, *a.* That may change; subject to alteration; fickle; inconstant; mutable; variable; as a person of a *changeable* mind.
2. Having the quality of suffering alteration of external appearance; as *changeable* silk.

CHANGEABLENESS, *n.* The quality of being changeable; fickleness; inconstancy; instability; mutability.
2. Susceptibility of change, or alteration. *Hooker.*

CHANGEABLY, *adv.* Inconstantly.

CHANGED, *pp.* Altered; varied; turned; converted; shifted.

CHANGEFUL, *a.* Full of change; inconstant; mutable; fickle; uncertain; subject to alteration. *Pope.*

CHANGELESS, *a.* Constant; not admitting alteration.

CHANGELING, *n.* [*change* and *ling*. It is said this word originated in a superstitious opinion that fairies steal children and put others that are ugly and stupid in their places. *Johnson.*]
1. A child left or taken in the place of another. *Spenser.*
2. An idiot; a fool. *Dryden. Locke.*
3. One apt to change; a waverer. *Shak.*
4. Any thing changed and put in the place of another. *Shak.*

CHANGER, *n.* One who alters the form of any thing.
2. One that is employed in changing and discounting money; a money-changer.
3. One given to change.

CHANGING, *ppr.* Altering; turning; putting one thing for another; shifting.

CHAN'NA, *n.* A fish taken in the Mediterranean, resembling the sea-perch. *Dict. of Nat. Hist.*

CHAN'NEL, *n.* [Ir. *cainneal;* Fr. *canal;* L. *canalis;* Arm. *can*, or *canol*. It is a different spelling of *canal.*]
1. In *a general sense*, a passage; a place of passing or flowing; particularly, a water-course.
2. The place where a river flows, including the whole breadth of the river. But more appropriately, the deeper part or hollow in which the principal current flows.
3. The deeper part of a strait, bay, or harbor, where the principal current flows, either of tide or fresh water, or which is the most convenient for the track of a ship.
4. That through which any thing passes; means of passing, conveying, or transmitting; as, the news was conveyed to us by different *channels*.
5. A gutter or furrow in a column.
6. An arm of the sea; a straight or narrow sea, between two continents, or between a continent and an isle; as the British or Irish *channel*.
7. Channels of a ship. [See *Chain-wales.*]

CHAN'NEL, *v. t.* To form a channel; to cut channels in; to groove; as, to *channel* a field or a column. *Wotton.*

CHAN'NELED, *pp.* Having channels; grooved longitudinally.

CHAN'NELING, *ppr.* Cutting channels; grooving longitudinally.

CHAN'SON, *n.* [Fr.] A song. *Shak.*

CH'ANT, *v. t.* [Fr. *chanter;* L. *canto, cantus;* W. *açanu;* Arm. *cana, cannein;* It. *cantare;* Sp. Port. *cantar;* L. *cano*. See *Cant.*]
1. To sing; to utter a melodious voice; that is, to *cant* or throw the voice in modulations.

> The cheerful birds do *chant* sweet music. *Spenser.*

2. To celebrate in song; as, to *chant* the praises of Jehovah.
3. To sing, as in church-service; to repeat words in a kind of canting voice, with modulations.

CH'ANT, *v. i.* To sing; to make melody with the voice.

> They *chant* to the sound of the viol. Amos vi.

2. To repeat words in the church-service with a kind of singing.

CH'ANT, *n.* Song; melody; church-service.

CH'ANTED, *pp.* Sung; uttered with modulations of voice.

CH'ANTER, *n.* One who chants; a singer or songster. *Pope.*
2. The chief singer, or priest of the chantry. *Gregory.*
3. The pipe which sounds the tenor or treble in a bagpipe.

CH'ANTICLEER, *n.* [*chant* and *clear*, Fr. *clair.*]
A cock, so called from the clearness or loudness of his voice in crowing. *Dryden.*

CH'ANTING, *ppr.* Singing; uttering a melodious voice; repeating words with a singing voice.

CH'ANTING, *n.* The act of singing, or uttering with a song.

CH'ANTRESS, *n.* A female singer. *Milton.*

CH'ANTRY, *n.* [Fr. *chantrerie*, from *chant.*] A church or chapel endowed with lands, or other revenue, for the maintenance of one or more priests daily to sing or say mass for the souls of the donors, or such as they appoint. *Cowell.*

€HA'OS, *n.* [L. *chaos;* Gr. *χαος.*] That confusion, or confused mass, in which matter is supposed to have existed, before it was separated into its different kinds and reduced to order, by the creating power of God. "Rudis, indigestaque moles." *Ovid.*

2. Any mixed mass, without due form or order; as a *chaos* of materials.

3. Confusion; disorder; a state in which the parts are undistinguished. *Donne.*

€HAOT'I€, *a.* Resembling chaos; confused; as, the earth was originally in a *chaotic* state.

CHAP, *v. t.* [Ar. جَبَّ jabba, to cut off or out, to castrate; جَابَ to split, rend, tear, or cleave, to cut. It seems to be allied to the G. and D. *kappen*, Dan. *kapper*, Fr. *couper;* but these agree better with Ar. كبج or كيف to cut. See *Chop* and *Gape*. *Chap* is sometimes pronounced *chop.*]

To cleave, split, crack, or open longitudinally, as the surface of the earth, or the skin and flesh of the hand. Dry weather *chaps* the earth; cold dry winds *chap* the hands.

CHAP, *v. i.* To crack; to open in long slits; as, the earth *chaps;* the hands *chap.*

CHAP, *n.* A longitudinal cleft, gap or chink, as in the surface of the earth, or in the hands or feet.

CHAP, *n.* [Sax. *ceafl*, a beak, or chap; plu. *ceaflas*, the chaps.]

The upper and lower part of the mouth; the jaw. It is applied to beasts, and vulgarly to men; generally in the plural, the *chaps* or mouth.

CHAP, *n.* A man or a boy; a youth. It is used also in the sense of a buyer. "If you want to sell, here is your *chap.*" In this sense it coincides with *chapman.* [See *Cheap.*] *Steele.*

CHAP, *v. i.* [Sax. *ceapian.*] To cheapen. [*Not used.*]

CHAP'BOOK, *n.* [See *Chapman* and *Cheap.*] A small book or pamphlet, carried about for sale by hawkers.

CHAPE, *n.* [Fr. *chape*, the tongue of a buckle, a cover, a churchman's cope, the head of an alembic; Arm. *chap;* Sp. *chapa*, a thin plate of metal covering some kind of work. Qu. *cap.*]

1. The catch of any thing, as the hook of a scabbard, or the catch of a buckle, by which it is held to the back strap.

2. A brass or silver tip or case, that strengthens the end of a scabbard. *Johnson. Phillips.*

ČHAPEAU, *n. shappo.* [Fr.] A hat; in *heraldry*, a cap or bonnet.

CHAP'EL, *n.* [Fr. *chapelle;* L. *capella;* Arm. *chapel;* Sp. *capilla*, a chapel, a hood or cowl, a chapter of collegians, a proof-sheet; Port. *capella;* It. *cappella;* D. *kapel;* from the same root as *cap.* It is said that the kings of France, in war, carried St. Martin's hat into the field, which was kept in a tent as a precious relic, whence the place took the name *capella*, a little hat, and the priest who had the custody of the tent was called *capellanus*, now *chaplain.* Hence the word *chapel* came to signify a private oratory. *Encyc. Lunier.*]

1. A house for public worship; primarily, a private oratory, or house of worship belonging to a private person. In Great Britain there are several sorts of chapels; as *parochial chapels*, distinct from the mother church; *chapels* which adjoin to and are a part of the church; such were formerly built by honorable persons for burying places; *chapels of ease*, built in large parishes for the accommodation of the inhabitants; *free chapels*, which were founded by the kings of England; *chapels in the universities*, belonging to particular colleges; *domestic chapels*, built by noblemen or gentlemen for the use of their families. *Encyc.*

2. A printer's workhouse; said to be so called because printing was first carried on in a chapel. *Bailey. Encyc.*

CHAP'EL, *v. t.* To deposit in a chapel. *Beaum.*

CHA'PELESS, *a.* Without a chape.

CHAP'ELET, CHAP'LET, *n.* [Fr. *chapelet.*] A pair of stirrup leathers, with stirrups, joined at the top in a sort of leather buckle, by which they are made fast to the pommel of the saddle, after they have been adjusted to the length and bearing of the rider. *Farrier's Dict.*

CHAP'ELLANY, *n.* A place founded within some church and dependent thereon. *Ayliffe.*

CHAP'ELLING, *n.* The act of turning a ship round in a light breeze of wind, when close hauled, so that she will lie the same way as before. *Mar. Dict.*

CHAP'ELRY, *n.* The bounds or jurisdiction of a chapel.

ČHAP'ERON, *n.* [Fr.] A hood or cap worn by the knights of the garter in their habits. It was anciently worn by men, women, nobles and populace; afterwards appropriated to doctors and licentiates in colleges. The name then passed to certain devices placed on the foreheads of horses which drew the herse in pompous funerals. *Johnson. Encyc*

ČHAP'ERON, *v. t.* To attend on a lady in a public assembly. *Todd.*

CHAP'-FALLEN, *a.* [*chap* and *fall.*] Having the lower chap depressed; hence, dejected; dispirited; silenced. *B. Jonson.*

CHAP'ITER, *n.* [Fr. *chapiteau;* It. *capitello;* L. *capitellum*, from *caput*, a head. This is a different word for *capital.*]

1. The upper part or capital of a column or pillar; a word used in the scriptures. [See *Capital.*]

2. That which is delivered by the mouth of the justice in his charge to the inquest. *Encyc.*

CHAP'LAIN, *n.* [Fr. *chapelain;* Sp. *capellan;* It. *cappellano;* L. *capellanus;* from *chapel.*]

1. An ecclesiastic who has a chapel, or who performs service in a chapel. The king of Great Britain has forty-eight chaplains, who attend, four each month, to perform divine service for the royal family. Princes also, and persons of quality have chaplains, who officiate in their chapels.

2. A clergyman who belongs to a ship of war, or to a regiment of land forces, for performing divine service.

3. A clergyman who is retained to perform divine service in a family.

Chaplains of the Pope, are auditors or judges of causes in the sacred palace. *Encyc.*

CHAP'LAINCY, *n.* The office or station of a chaplain.

CHAP'LAINSHIP, *n.* The office or business of a chaplain.

2. The possession, or revenue of a chapel. *Johnson.*

CHAP'LESS, *a.* Without any flesh about the mouth. *Bailey. Shak.*

CHAP'LET, *n.* [Fr. *chapelet.*] A garland or wreath to be worn on the head; the circle of a crown.

2. A string of beads used by the Roman Catholics, by which they count the number of their prayers. They are made sometimes of coral, of wood, of diamonds, &c., and are called *paternosters.* The invention is ascribed to Peter the hermit, who probably learnt it in the East, as the Orientals use a kind of chaplet, called a chain, rehearsing one of the perfections of God on each link, or head. The Great Mogul is said to have eighteen of these chains, all precious stones. The Turks also use a kind of chaplet in reciting their prayers. *Encyc.*

3. In *architecture*, a little molding, carved into round beads, pearls, olives or the like.

4. In *horsemanship*, a chapelet, which see.

5. A tuft of feathers on a peacock's head. *Johnson.*

6. A small chapel or shrine. *Hammond.*

CHAP'MAN, *n.* plu. *chapmen.* [Sax. *ceapman;* D. *koopman;* G. *kaufmann;* Dan. *kiöbmand.* See *Cheap.*]

1. A cheapener; one that offers as a purchaser.

> Their *chapmen* they betray. *Dryden.*

2. A seller; a market-man. *Shak.*

CHAP'PED, *pp.* Cleft; opened, as the surface or skin.

CHAP'PING, *ppr.* Cleaving, as the surface or skin.

CHAP'PY, *a.* Full of chaps; cleft.

CHAPS, the mouth or jaws. [See *Chap.*]

CHAPT. [See *Chapped.*]

CHAP'TER, *n.* [Fr. *chapitre;* L. *capitulum*, a head; It. *capitolo;* Sp. *capitulo;* from L. *caput*, the head.]

1. A division of a book or treatise; as, Genesis contains fifty *chapters.* Hence the phrase, *to the end of the chapter*, that is, throughout; to the end. *Johnson.*

2. In *ecclesiastical polity*, a society or community of clergymen, belonging to a cathedral or collegiate church. *Encyc.*

3. A place where delinquents receive discipline and correction. *Ayliffe.*

4. A decretal epistle. *Ayliffe.*

CHAP'TER, *v. t.* To tax; to correct. *Dryden*

CHAP'TER-HOUSE, *n.* A house where a chapter meets. *Bailey.*

CHAP′TREL, *n.* [from *chapiter.*] The capitals of pillars and pilasters, which support arches, commonly called imposts. *Moxon.*

CH`AR, *n.* A fish.

CHĀR, *n.* In *England*, work done by the day; a single job, or task. In *New England*, it is pronounced *chore*, which see. I know not the origin of the word. In Sax. *cerre*, *cyrr*, signifies a time, a turn, occasion, from *cerran*, *cyrran*, to turn, or return.

CHĀR, *v. t.* To perform a business. *May.*

CHĀR, *v. i.* To work at others houses by the day, without being a hired servant; to do small jobs. *Bailey. Johnson.*

CHĀR-WÖMAN, *n.* A woman hired for odd work, or for single days. *Johnson.*

[*Char-man and Char-woman are, I believe, not used in America.*]

CH`AR, *v. t.* [Russ. *jaryu* or *charyu*, to roast, or burn; or *goryu* to burn, or be burnt; and with a prefix, *sgarayu* or *sgorayu*, to burn; Fr. *charrée*, ashes. Qu. Heb. Ch. Eth. חרר. Class Gr. No. 22. 23. This seems to be the root of L. *carbo.* See *Chark.*]

1. To burn or reduce to coal or carbon; to reduce to charcoal, by expelling all volatile matter from wood. This is done by burning wood slowly under a covering of turf and earth.

2. To expel all volatile matter from stone or earth, by heat.

The stone or earth *charred* from all foreign visible ingredients. *Kirwan.*

CHAR′ACT, CHAR′ECT, } *n.* [See *Character.*] An inscription. [*Not in use.*] *Skelton.*

CHAR′ACTER, *n.* [L. *character*; Fr. *caractere*; Sp. *caracter*; It. *carattere*; Gr. χαρακτηρ, from the verb χαρασσω, χαραττω, χαραξω, to scrape, cut, engrave.]

1. A mark made by cutting or engraving, as on stone, metal or other hard material; hence, a mark or figure made with a pen or style, on paper, or other material used to contain writing; a letter, or figure used to form words, and communicate ideas. Characters are *literal*, as the letters of an alphabet; *numeral*, as the arithmetical figures; *emblematical* or *symbolical*, which express things or ideas; and *abbreviations*, as C. for *centum*, a hundred; *lb.* for *libra*, a pound; A. D. Anno Domini; &c.

2. A mark or figure made by stamping or impression, as on coins.

3. The manner of writing; the peculiar form of letters used by a particular person.

You know the *character* to be your brother's. *Shak.*

4. The peculiar qualities, impressed by nature or habit on a person, which distinguish him from others; these constitute *real character*, and the qualities which he is supposed to possess, constitute his *estimated character*, or reputation. Hence we say, a *character* is not formed, when the person has not acquired stable and distinctive qualities.

5. An account, description or representation of any thing, exhibiting its qualities and the circumstances attending it; as, to give a bad *character* to a town, or to a road.

6. A person; as, the assembly consisted of various *characters*, eminent *characters*, and low *characters.*

All the *characters* in the play appeared to advantage.

The friendship of distinguished *characters.* *Roscoe.*

7. By way of eminence, distinguished or good qualities; those which are esteemed and respected; and those which are ascribed to a person in common estimation. We enquire whether a stranger is a man of *character.*

8. Adventitious qualities impressed by office, or station; the qualities that, in public estimation, belong to a person in a particular station; as when we ask how a magistrate, or commander supports his *character.*

9. In *natural history*, the peculiar discriminating qualities or properties of animals, plants and minerals.

These properties, when employed for the purpose of discriminating minerals, are called *characters.* *Cleaveland.*

CHAR′ACTER, *v. t.* To engrave; to inscribe. *Milton. Shak.*

2. To describe; to distinguish by particular marks or traits. *Mitford.*

CHAR′ACTERED, *pp.* Engraved; inscribed; distinguished by a particular character. *Mitford.*

CHAR′ACTERISM, *n.* The distinction of character. *Bp. Hall.*

2. A particular aspect or configuration of the heavens. *Encyc.*

CHARACTERIS′TIC, CHARACTERIS′TICAL, } *a.* [Gr. χαρακτηριςικος, from χαρακτηρ.]

That constitutes the character; that marks the peculiar, distinctive qualities of a person or thing.

Generosity is often a *characteristic* virtue of a brave man.

It is followed by *of.*

Generosity is *characteristic of* true bravery.

CHARACTERIS′TIC, *n.* That which constitutes a character; that which characterizes; that which distinguishes a person or thing from another.

Invention is the *characteristic* of Homer. *Pope.*

2. In *grammar*, the principal letter of a word, which is preserved in most of its tenses, in its derivatives and compounds.

The *characteristic of a logarithm*, is its index or exponent.

The *characteristic triangle of a curve*, in geometry, is a rectilinear right-angled triangle, whose hypotenuse makes a part of the curve, not sensibly different from a right line. *Encyc.*

CHARACTERIS′TICALLY, *adv.* In a manner that distinguishes character.

CHARACTERIS′TICALNESS, *n.* The state or qualities of being characteristic.

CHAR′ACTERIZE, *v. t.* [Gr. χαρακτηριζω.] To give a character, or an account of the personal qualities of a man; to describe by peculiar qualities.

2. To distinguish; to mark, or express the character; to exhibit the peculiar qualities of a person or thing; as, humility *characterizes* the true christian; the hero is *characterized* by bravery and magnanimity.

The system of mediation has *characterized* the entire scheme of divine dispensation. *Thodey.*

3. To engrave or imprint. [*Little used.*] *Hale.*

4. To mark with a peculiar stamp, or figure.

European, Asiatic, and African faces are all *characterized.* *Arbuthnot.*

CHAR′ACTERIZED, *pp.* Described or distinguished by pecular qualities.

CHAR′ACTERIZING, *ppr.* Describing or distinguishing by peculiar qualities.

CHAR′ACTERLESS, *a.* Destitute of any peculiar character. *Shak.*

CHAR′ACTERY, *n.* Impression; mark; distinction. [*Not used.*] *Shak.*

CHARA′DE, *n.* [Said to be from the name of the inventor.]

A composition, in which the subject must be a word of two syllables, each forming a distinct word; and these syllables are to be concealed in an enigmatical description, first separately and then together. Example.

My *first*, when a Frenchman in learning English, serves him to swear by. My *second* is either hay or corn. My *whole* is the delight of the age. *Gar-rick.* *Encyc.*

CH`ARCOAL, *n.* [*char* and *coal.* See *Char.*]

Coal made by charring wood; the remains of wood burnt under turf, and from which all watery and other volatile matter has been expelled by heat. It makes a strong heat, and is used in furnaces, forges, private families, &c. It is black, brittle, light and inodorous, and not being decomposable by water or air, will endure for ages without alteration.

CH`ARD, *n.* [Fr. *charde*; L. *carduus.*]

The leaves of artichokes tied and wrapped all over, except the top, in straw, during autumn and winter. This makes them grow white and lose some of their bitterness. *Chambers.*

Chards of beet are plants of white beet transplanted, producing great tops, which, in the midst, have a large, white, thick, downy, cotton-like main shoot, which is the true chard. *Mortimer.*

CH`ARGE, *v. t.* charj. [Fr. *charger*; Arm. *carga*; Sp. *cargar*; It. *caricare*, or *carcare*; Port. *carregar.* It would seem from the Welsh that this word is from *car*, a cart or other vehicle, and that the noun *charge* or *cargo* was first formed, and therefore ought in arrangement to precede the verb. If the verb was first formed, the primary sense would be to load, to throw or put on or in. I think the fact to be otherwise. See *Cargo.*]

1. To rush on; to fall on; to attack, especially with fixed bayonets; as, an army *charges* the enemy.

2. To load, as a musket or cannon; to thrust in powder, or powder and ball or shot.

3. To load or burden; to throw on or impose that which oppresses; as, to *charge* the stomach with indigestible food; or to lay on, or to fill, without oppressing; as, to *charge* the memory with rules and precepts; to *charge* the mind with facts.

4. To set or lay on; to impose, as a tax; as, the land is *charged with* a quit rent; a rent is *charged on* the land.

5. To lay on or impose, as a task.

The gospel *chargeth* us *with* piety towards God. *Tillotson.*

6. To put or lay on; as, to *charge* a building with ornaments, often implying superfluity.

7. To lay on, as a duty; followed by *with.*

The commander *charged* the officer *with* the execution of the project. See Gen. xl. 4.

8. To entrust to; as, an officer is *charged with* dispatches.
9. To set to, as a debt; to place on the debit side of an account; as, to *charge* a man with the price of goods sold to him.
10. To load or lay on in words, something wrong, reproachful or criminal; to impute to; as, to *charge* a man *with* theft.
11. To lay on in words; to impute to; followed by *on* before the person; as, to *charge* a crime *on* the offender; to *charge* evil consequences *on* the doctrines of the stoics.
12. To censure; to accuse.

In all this, Job sinned not, nor *charged* God foolishly. Job i.

13. To lay on, give or communicate, as an order, command or earnest request; to enjoin; to exhort.

Charge them that are rich in this world, that they be not high-minded. 1 Tim. vi.

In this sense, when the command is given in the name of God, or with an oath, the phrase amounts to an adjuration.

To adjure; to bind by an oath. 1 Sam. xiv. 28.

14. To give directions to; to instruct authoritatively; as, the judge *charged* the grand jury to inquire respecting breaches of the peace.
15. To communicate electrical matter to, as to a coated vial, or an electrical battery.

CH'ARGE, *v. i.* To make an onset. Thus Glanville says, "like your heroes of antiquity, he *charges* in iron;" and we say, to *charge* with fixed bayonets. But in this application, the object is understood; to *charge* the enemy.

CH'ARGE, *n.* [Fr. *charge*; Arm. and W. *carg*; Sp. *carga*, *cargo*; Port. *carga*, *carrega*; It. *carica*, *carco*; Eng. *cargo*.]

1. That which is laid on or in; in *a general sense*, any load or burden. It is the same word radically as *cargo*.
2. The quantity of powder, or of powder and ball or shot, used to load a musket, cannon or other like instrument.
3. An onset; a rushing on an enemy; attack; especially by moving troops with fixed bayonets. But it is used for an onset of cavalry as well as of infantry.
4. An order, injunction, mandate, command.

Moses gave Joshua a *charge*. Numbers xxvii.

The king gave *charge* concerning Absalom. 2 Sam. xviii.

Hence,

5. That which is enjoined, committed, entrusted or delivered to another, implying care, custody, oversight, or duty to be performed by the person entrusted.

I gave Hanani *charge* over Jerusalem. Neh. vii.

Hence the word includes any trust or commission; an office, duty, employment. It is followed by *of* or *over*; more generally by *of*. Hence,

6. The person or thing committed to another's custody, care or management; a trust. Thus the people of a parish are called the minister's *charge*.

The starry guardian drove his *charge* away
To some fresh pasture. *Dryden.*

7. Instructions given by a judge to a jury, or by a bishop to his clergy. The word may be used as synonymous with command, direction, exhortation or injunction, but always implies solemnity.
8. Imputation in a bad sense; accusation.

Lay not this sin to their *charge*. Acts vii.

9. That which constitutes debt, in commercial transactions; an entry of money or the price of goods, on the debit side of an account.
10. Cost; expense; as, the *charges* of the war are to be borne by the nation.
11. Imposition on land or estate; rent, tax, or whatever constitutes a burden or duty.
12. In *military affairs*, a signal to attack; as, to sound the *charge*.
13. The posture of a weapon fitted for an attack or combat.

Their armed slaves in *charge*. *Shak.*

14. Among *farriers*, a preparation of the consistence of a thick decoction, or between an ointment and a plaster, used as a remedy for sprains and inflammations.
15. In *heraldry*, that which is borne upon the color; or the figures represented on the escutcheon, by which the bearers are distinguished from one another.
16. In *electrical experiments*, a quantity of electrical fluid, communicated to a coated jar, vial or pane of glass.

A *charge of lead*, is thirty-six pigs, each containing six stone, wanting two pounds.

CH'ARGEABLE, *a.* That may be charged; that may be set, laid, imposed; as, a duty of forty per cent. is *chargeable on* wine.

2. Subject to be charged; as, wine is *chargeable with* a duty of forty per cent.
3. Expensive; costly; as a *chargeable* family.
4. Laying or bringing expense.

Because we would not be *chargeable* to any of you. 1 Thess. ii.

5. Imputable; that may be laid or attributed as a crime, fault or debt; as a fault *chargeable on* a man.
6. Subject to be charged or accused; as a man *chargeable with* a fault, or neglect.

CH'ARGEABLENESS, *n.* Expensiveness; cost; costliness. *Boyle.*

CH'ARGEABLY, *adv.* Expensively; at great cost. *Ascham.*

CH'ARGED, *pp.* Loaded; burdened; attacked; laid on; instructed; imputed; accused; placed to the debt; ordered; commanded.

CH'ARGEFUL, *a.* Expensive; costly. [*Not used.*] *Shak.*

CH'ARGELESS, *a.* Not expensive; free from expense.

CH'ARGER, *n.* In *Scots law*, one who charges another in a suit.

2. A large dish. Num. vii.
3. A horse used for attack.

CH'ARGING, *ppr.* Loading; attacking; laying on; instructing; commanding; accusing; imputing.

CHA'RILY, *adv.* [See *Chary.*] Carefully; warily; frugally. [*Little used.*] *Shak.*

CHA'RINESS, *n.* Caution; care; nicety; scrupulousness. [*Little used.*] *Shak.*

CHAR'IOT, *n.* [Fr. *chariot*, from *char*, a car, which see; Sp. It. *carro*; It. *carretta*.]

1. A half coach; a carriage with four wheels and one seat behind, used for convenience and pleasure.
2. A car or vehicle used formerly in war, drawn by two or more horses, and conveying two men each. These vehicles were sometimes armed with hooks or sythes.

CHAR'IOT, *v. t.* To convey in a chariot. *Milton.*

CHAR'IOTED, *pp.* Borne in a chariot. *Cowper.*

CHARIOTEE'R, *n.* The person who drives or conducts a chariot. It is used in speaking of military chariots and those in the ancient games, but not of modern drivers. *Johnson. Addison.*

CHAR'IOT-MAN, *n.* The driver of a chariot. 2 Chron. xviii.

CHAR'IOT-RACE, *n.* A race with chariots; a sport in which chariots were driven in contest for a prize. *Addison.*

CHAR'ITABLE, *a.* [Fr. See *Charity.*] Benevolent and kind; as a *charitable* disposition.

2. Liberal in benefactions to the poor, and in relieving them in distress; as a *charitable* man.
3. Pertaining to charity; springing from charity, or intended for charity; benevolent; as a *charitable* institution, or society; a *charitable* purpose.
4. Formed on charitable principles; favorable; dictated by kindness; as a *charitable* construction of words or actions.

CHAR'ITABLENESS, *n.* The disposition to be charitable; or the exercise of charity.

2. Liberality to the poor.

CHAR'ITABLY, *adv.* Kindly; liberally; benevolently; with a disposition to help the poor; favorably.

CHAR'ITY, *n.* [Fr. *charité*; L. *charitas*, or *caritas*; W. *cariad*; Sp. *caridad*; Port. *caridade*; It. *carità*, *caritade*. Qu. Gr. χαρις. The Latin *caritas* is from *carus*, dear, costly, whence beloved, and the word was sometimes written *charitas*, as if from the Gr. χαρις. The Lat. *carus* would seem to be from the verb *careo*, to want, as dearness arises from scarcity. Of this we have an example in the English *dear*, whence *dearth*, which shows the primary sense of *dear* to be *scarce*. But qu. the Oriental יקר. Class Gr. No. 56.]

1. In *a general sense*, love, benevolence, good will; that disposition of heart which inclines men to think favorably of their fellow men, and to do them good. In *a theological sense*, it includes supreme love to God, and universal good will to men. 1 Cor. xiii. Col. iii. 1 Tim. i.
2. In *a more particular sense*, love, kindness, affection, tenderness, springing from natural relations; as the *charities* of father, son and brother. *Milton.*
3. Liberality to the poor, consisting in almsgiving or benefactions, or in gratuitous services to relieve them in distress.
4. Alms; whatever is bestowed gratuitously on the poor for their relief.
5. Liberality in gifts and services to promote public objects of utility, as to found and support bible societies, missionary societies, and others.
6. Candor; liberality in judging of men and their actions; a disposition which inclines men to think and judge favorably, and to put the best construction on words and actions which the case will admit.

The highest exercise of *charity*, is charity towards the uncharitable. *Buckminster.*

7. Any act of kindness, or benevolence; as the *charities* of life.

8. A charitable institution. *D. Webster.*

Charity-school, is a school maintained by voluntary contributions for educating poor children.

CH'ARK, *v. t.* [Qu. *char*, or Ch. חרך, Ar. حرق haraka, to burn.]

To burn to a coal; to char. [*Not used.* See *Char.*] *Grew.*

ČH'ARLATAN, *n.* [Fr. from It. *ciarlatano*, a quack, from *ciarlare*, to prate; Sp. *charlatan*, from *charlar*, to prate; Port. *charlar*, id.; L. *garrulo, garrio*; Gr. γηρυω.]

One who prates much in his own favor, and makes unwarrantable pretensions to skill; a quack; an empiric; a mountebank. *Brown. Butler.*

ČHARLATAN'ICAL, *a.* Quackish; making undue pretensions to skill; ignorant. *Cowley.*

ČH'ARLATANRY, *n.* Undue pretensions to skill; quackery; wheedling; deception by fair words. *Johnson.*

CH'ARLES'S-WAIN, *n.* [*Charles*, Celtic *karl*, a man, or brave man. See *Wain.*]

In *astronomy*, seven stars in the constellation called Ursa Major, or the Great Bear. *Encyc.*

CH'ARLOCK, *n.* [Sax. *cerlice. Leac*, in Saxon, is a *leek*, but the same word occurs in *hemlock*, and it probably signifies, a plant or root.]

The English name of the Raphanus raphanistrum and Sinapis arvensis, very pernicious weeds among grain. One kind has yellow flowers; another, white, with jointed pods. *Lee. Encyc.*

CH'ARM, *n.* [Fr. *charme*; Norm. *carme* or *garme*; Arm. *chalm*; L. *carmen*, a song, a verse, an outcry, a charm. It coincides with the W. *garm*, an outcry, *garmiaw*, to shout, Sax. *cirm*, or *cyrm*, outcry, noise. See *Alarm.*]

1. Words, characters or other things imagined to possess some occult or unintelligible power; hence, a magic power or spell, by which with the supposed assistance of the devil, witches and sorcerers have been supposed to do wonderful things. Spell; enchantment. Hence,

2. That which has power to subdue opposition, and gain the affections; that which can please irresistibly; that which delights and attracts the heart; generally in the plural.

The smiles of nature and the *charms* of art. *Addison.*

Good humor only teaches *charms* to last. *Pope.*

CH'ARM, *v. t.* To subdue or control by incantation or secret influence.

I will send serpents among you—which will not be *charmed.* Jer. viii.

2. To subdue by secret power, especially by that which pleases and delights the mind; to allay, or appease.

Music the fiercest grief can *charm.* *Pope.*

3. To give exquisite pleasure to the mind or senses; to delight.

We were *charmed* with the conversation.

The aerial songster *charms* us with her melodious notes. *Anon.*

4. To fortify with charms against evil.

I have a *charmed* life, which must not yield. [*Not in use.*] *Shak.*

5. To make powerful by charms. *Johnson.*

6. To summon by incantation. *Shak. Johnson.*

7. To temper agreeably. *Spenser.*

CH'ARM, *v. i.* To sound harmonically. *Milton.*

CH'ARMA, *n.* A fish resembling the sea-wolf.

CH'ARMED, *pp.* Subdued by charms; delighted; enchanted.

CH'ARMER, *n.* One that charms, or has power to charm; one that uses or has the power of enchantment. Deut. xviii. 11.

2. One who delights and attracts the affections.

CH'ARMERESS, *n.* An enchantress. *Chaucer.*

CH'ARMFUL, *a.* Abounding with charms. *Cowley.*

CH'ARMING, *ppr.* Using charms; enchanting.

2. *a.* Pleasing in the highest degree; delighting.

Music is but an elegant and *charming* species of elocution. *E. Porter.*

CH'ARMINGLY, *adv.* Delightfully; in a manner to charm, or to give delight.

She smiled very *charmingly.* *Addison.*

CH'ARMINGNESS, *n.* The power to please. *Johnson.*

CH'ARMLESS, *a.* Destitute of charms. *Swift.*

CH'ARNEL, *a.* [Fr. *charnel*, carnal, fleshly; *charnier*, a charnel-house, a larder; Arm. *carnell*; Sp. *carnero*; It. *carnaio*; L. *carnalis*, carnal, from *caro*, flesh.]

Containing flesh or carcasses. *Milton.*

CH'ARNEL-HOUSE, *n.* A place under or near churches, where the bones of the dead are reposited. Anciently, a kind of portico or gallery, in or near a church-yard, over which the bones of the dead were laid, after the flesh was consumed. *Encyc.*

ČHA'RON, *n.* In *fabulous history*, the son of Erebus and Nox, whose office was to ferry the souls of the deceased over the waters of Acheron and Styx, for a piece of money.

CH'ARR, *n.* A fish, a species of Salmo.

CH'ARRED, *pp.* [from *char.*] Reduced to a coal.

CH'ARRING, *ppr.* Reducing to coal; depriving of volatile matter.

CH'ARRY, *a.* [See *Char.*] Pertaining to charcoal; like charcoal, or partaking of its qualities. *Lavoisier.*

CH'ART, *n.* [L. *charta*, the same as *card*, which see.]

A hydrographical or marine map; a draught or projection of some part of the earth's superficies on paper, with the coasts, isles, rocks, banks, channels or entrances into harbors, rivers, and bays, the points of compass, soundings or depth of water, &c., to regulate the courses of ships in their voyages. The term *chart* is applied to a marine map; *map* is applied to a draught of some portion of land.

A *plane chart* is a representation of some part of the superficies of the globe, in which the meridians are supposed parallel to each other, the parallels of latitude at equal distances, and of course the degrees of latitude and longitude are every where equal to each other.

Mercator's chart, is one on which the meridians are straight lines, parallel and equidistant; the parallels are straight lines and parallel to each other, but the distance between them increases from the equinoctial towards either pole, in the ratio of the secant of the latitude to the radius.

Globular chart, is a meridional projection in which the distance of the eye from the plane of the meridian, on which the projection is made, is supposed to be equal to the sine of the angle of forty-five degrees.

Selenographic charts, represent the spots and appearances of the moon.

Topographic charts, are draughts of particular places, or small parts of the earth. *Encyc.*

CH'ARTER, *n.* [Fr. *chartre*, from L. *charta.* See *Card.*]

A written instrument, executed with usual forms, given as evidence of a grant, contract, or whatever is done between man and man. In its more usual sense, it is the instrument of a grant conferring powers, rights and privileges, either from a king or other sovereign power, or from a private person, as a *charter of exemption*, that no person shall be empannelled on a jury, a *charter of pardon*, &c. The charters under which most of the colonies in America were settled, were given by the king of England, and incorporated certain persons, with powers to hold the lands granted, to establish a government, and make laws for their own regulation. These were called *charter-governments.*

2. Any instrument, executed with form and solemnity, bestowing rights or privileges. *Dryden. South.*

3. Privilege; immunity; exemption.

My mother,
Who has a *charter* to extol her blood,
When she does praise me, grieves me. *Shak.*

CH'ARTER, *v. t.* To hire, or to let a ship by charter. [See *Charter-party.*]

2. To establish by charter. *Buchanan.*

CH'ARTER-LAND, *n.* Land held by charter, or in soccage. *Coke.*

CH'ARTER-PARTY, *n.* [Fr. *charte-partie*, a divided charter; from the practice of cutting the instrument in two, and giving one part to each of the contractors.]

In *commerce*, an agreement respecting the hire of a vessel and the freight. This is to be signed by the proprietor or master of the ship and by the merchant who hires or freights it. It must contain the name and burden of the vessel, the names of the master and freighter, the price or rate of the freight, the time of loading and unloading, and other stipulated conditions. *Encyc.*

CH'ARTERED, *pp.* Hired or let, as a ship.

2. Invested with privileges by charter; privileged. *Shak.*

3. Granted by charter; as *chartered* rights; *chartered* power. *D. Ramsay.*

CH'ARTERING, *ppr.* Giving a charter; establishing by charter.

2. Hiring or letting by charter.

CH'ARTLESS, *a.* Without a chart; of which no chart has been made; not delineated on paper; as the *chartless* main. *Barlow.*

CH'ARTULARY, *n.* [Fr. *chartulaire.* See *Cartulary.*]
An officer in the ancient Latin church, who had the care of charters and other papers of a public nature. Blackstone uses this word for a record or register, as of a monastery.

CHA'RY, *a.* [Sax. *cearig.* See *Care.*] Careful; wary; frugal. *Shak.*

CHA'SABLE, *a.* That may be chased; fit for the chase. *Gower.*

CHASE, *v. t.* [Fr. *chasser;* Arm. *chaçzeal;* Sp. *cazar;* Port. *caçar;* It. *cacciare.* The elements are Cg or Ck; and the change of a palatal to a sibilant resembles that in *brace.*]
1. Literally to drive, urge, press forward with vehemence; hence, to pursue for the purpose of taking, as game; to hunt.
2. To pursue, or drive, as a defeated or flying enemy. Lev. xxvi. 7. Deut. xxxii. 30.
3. To follow or pursue, as an object of desire; to pursue for the purpose of taking; as, to *chase* a ship.
4. To drive; to pursue.

Chased by their brother's endless malice. *Knolles.*

To chase away, is to compel to depart; to disperse.
To chase metals. [See *Enchase.*]

CHASE, *n.* Vehement pursuit; a running or driving after; as game, in hunting; a flying enemy, in war; a ship at sea, &c.
2. Pursuit with an ardent desire to obtain, as pleasure, profit, fame, &c.; earnest seeking.
3. That which may be chased; that which is usually taken by chase; as beasts of *chase.*
4. That which is pursued or hunted; as, seek some other *chase.* So at sea, a ship chased is called the *chase.*
5. In *law,* a driving of cattle to or from a place.
6. An open ground, or place of retreat for deer and other wild beasts; differing from a forest, which is not private property and is invested with privileges, and from a park which is inclosed. A chase is private property, and well stored with wild beasts or game.
7. [Fr. *chasse;* Sp. *caxa;* It. *cassa.* See *Case* and *Cash.*] An iron frame used by printers to confine types, when set in columns.
8. *Chase of a gun,* is the whole length of the bore.
9. A term in the game of tennis.
Chase guns, in a ship of war, guns used in chasing an enemy or in defending a ship when chased. These have their ports at the head or stern. A gun at the head is called a *bow-chase;* at the stern, a *stern-chase.*

CHA'SED, *pp.* Pursued; sought ardently; driven.

CHA'SER, *n.* One who chases; a pursuer; a driver; a hunter.
2. An enchaser. [See *Enchase.*]

CHA'SING, *ppr.* Pursuing; driving; hunting.

CHASM, *n.* [Gr. χασμα, L. *chasma,* from Gr. χαω, χασκω, χαινω, to open.]
1. A cleft; a fissure; a gap; properly, an opening made by disrupture, as a breach in the earth or a rock.
2. A void space; a vacuity.

Between the two propositions, that the gospel is true and that it is false, what a fearful *chasm!* The unsettled reason hovers over it in dismay. *Buckminster.*

CHAS'MED, *a.* Having gaps or a chasm.

CHAS'SELAS, *n.* A sort of grape.

CHASTE, *a.* [Fr. *chaste;* Arm. *chast;* It. Sp. Port. *casto;* from L. *castus.* Sax. *cusc,* D. *kuisch,* G. *keusch,* Sw. *kysk,* Russ. *chistei,* are probably from the same root. Qu. Ir. *caidh.* I suppose the primary sense to be, separate, from the oriental practice of sequestering females. If so, *castus* accords with the root of *castle,* W. *cás;* and at any rate, the word denotes purity, a sense taken from separation.]
1. Pure from all unlawful commerce of sexes. *Applied to persons before marriage,* it signifies pure from all sexual commerce, undefiled; *applied to married persons,* true to the marriage bed.
2. Free from obscenity.

While they behold your *chaste* conversation. 1 Peter iii.

3. In *language,* pure; genuine; uncorrupt; free from barbarous words and phrases, and from quaint, affected, extravagant expressions.

CHA'STE-EYED, *a.* Having modest eyes. *Collins.*

CHA'STE-TREE, *n.* The agnus castus, or vitex; a tree that grows to the highth of eight or ten feet, producing spikes of flowers at the end of every strong shoot in autumn. *Miller.*

CHA'STELY, *adv.* In a chaste manner; without unlawful commerce of sexes; without obscenity; purely; without barbarisms or unnatural phrases.

CHA'STEN, *v. t. cha'sn.* [Fr. *châtier,* for *chastier;* Arm. *castien;* Russ. *chischu.*]
1. To correct by punishment; to punish; to inflict pain for the purpose of reclaiming an offender; as, to *chasten* a son with a rod.

I will *chasten* him with the rod of men. 2 Sam. vii.

2. To afflict by other means.

As many as I love I rebuke and *chasten.* Rev. iii.

I *chastened* my soul with fasting. Ps. lxix.

3. To purify from errors or faults.

CHA'STENED, *pp.* Corrected; punished; afflicted for correction.

CHA'STENER, *n.* One who punishes, for the purpose of correction.

CHA'STENESS, *n.* Chastity; purity.

CHA'STENING, *ppr.* Correcting; afflicting for correction.

CHA'STENING, *n.* Correction; punishment for the purpose of reclaiming.

No *chastening* for the present seemeth to be joyous but grievous. Heb. xii.

CHASTI'SABLE, *a.* Deserving of chastisement. *Sherwood.*

CHASTI'SE, *v. t. s* as *z.* [Fr. *châtier;* Arm. *castiza;* from *chaste, castus.* The Latin *castigo,* Sp. Port. *castigar,* It. *gastigare,* are formed with a different termination. We have *chastise* from the Armoric dialect.]
1. To correct by punishing; to punish; to inflict pain by stripes, or in other manner, for the purpose of punishing an offender and recalling him to his duty.

I will *chastise* you seven times for your sins. Lev. xxvi.

2. To reduce to order or obedience; to restrain; to awe; to repress.

The gay social sense,
By decency *chastis'd.* *Thomson.*

3. To correct; to purify by expunging faults; as, to *chastise* a poem.

CHASTI'SED, *pp.* Punished; corrected.

CHAS'TISEMENT, *n.* [Fr. *châtiment;* Arm. *castiz;* from *chaste.*]
Correction; punishment; pain inflicted for punishment and correction, either by stripes or otherwise.

Shall I so much dishonour my fair stars,
On equal terms to give him *chastisement.* *Shak.*

I have borne *chastisement,* I will not offend any more. Job xxxiv.

The chastisement of our peace, in Scripture, was the pain which Christ suffered to purchase our peace and reconciliation to God. Is. liii.

CHASTI'SER, *n.* One who chastises; a punisher; a corrector.

CHASTI'SING, *ppr.* Punishing for correction; correcting.

CHAS'TITY, *n.* [L. *castitas;* Fr. *chasteté;* Sp. *castidad;* It. *castità;* from L. *castus,* chaste.]
1. Purity of the body; freedom from all unlawful commerce of sexes. *Before marriage,* purity from all commerce of sexes; *after marriage,* fidelity to the marriage bed.
2. Freedom from obscenity, as in language or conversation.
3. Freedom from bad mixture; purity in words and phrases.
4. Purity; unadulterated state; as the *chastity* of the gospel. *Gibbon.*

CHAT, *v. i.* [G. *kosen,* to talk or prattle; Ir. *ceadach,* talkative; *ceadac,* a story or narrative; Sp. *cotorra,* a magpie; *cotorrera,* a hen-parrot, a talkative woman; Gr. κωτιλλω, to prate; D. *koeteren,* to jabber, and *kwetteren,* to *chatter; kouden,* id.]
1. To talk in a familiar manner; to talk without form or ceremony. *Milton. Dryden.*
2. To talk idly; to prate. *Johnson.*

CHAT, *v. t.* To talk of. [*Not in use.*] *Shak.*

CHAT, *n.* Free, familiar talk; idle talk; prate.

CHAT, *n.* A twig, or little stick. [See *Chit.*]

CHAT'EAU, *n. shat'o.* [Fr. a *castle.* See *Castle.*] A castle; a seat in the country.

CHAT'ELET, *n.* A little castle. *Chambers.*

CHAT'ELLANY, *n.* [Fr. *chatellenie.*] The lordship or jurisdiction of a castellan, or governor of a castle. [See *Castellany.*]

CHATOY'ANT, *a.* [Fr. *chat,* cat, and *œil,* eye.]
Having a changeable, undulating luster, or color, like that of a cat's eye in the dark.

CHATOY'ANT, *n.* A hard stone, a little transparent, which being cut smooth presents on its surface and in the interior, an undulating or wavy light. It is of a yellowish gray color or verging to an olive green. It rarely exceeds the size of a filbert. *Dict. of Nat. Hist.*

CHATOY'MENT, *n.* Changeable colors, or changeableness of color, in a mineral; play of colors. *Cleaveland.*

CHAT'TEL, *n. chat'l.* [See *Cattle.*] Prima

rily, any article of movable goods. In modern usage, the word *chattels* comprehends all goods, movable or immovable, except such as have the nature of freehold. "Chattels are real or personal. *Chattels real*, are such as concern or savor of the realty, as a term for years of land, wardships in chivalry, the next presentation to a church, estates by statute merchant, elegit and the like. *Chattels personal*, are things movable, as animals, furniture of a house, jewels, corn, &c." *Blackstone.*

CHAT'TER, *v. i.* [See *Chat.*]
1. To utter sounds rapidly and indistinctly, as a magpie, or a monkey.
2. To make a noise by collision of the teeth. We say, the teeth *chatter*, when one is chilly and shivering.
3. To talk idly, carelessly or rapidly; to jabber.

CHAT'TER, *n.* Sounds like those of a pie or monkey; idle talk.

CHAT'TER-BOX, *n.* One that talks incessantly.

CHAT'TERER, *n.* A prater; an idle talker.

CHAT'TERING, *ppr.* Uttering rapid, indistinct sounds, as birds; talking idly; moving rapidly and clashing, as the teeth.

CHAT'TERING, *n.* Rapid, inarticulate sounds, as of birds; idle talk; rapid striking of the teeth, as in chilliness.

CHAT'TING, *ppr.* Talking familiarly.

CHAT'TY, *a.* Given to free conversation; talkative.

CHAT'WOOD, *n.* Little sticks; fuel. *Bailey. Johnson.*

CHAUMONTELLE, *n.* [Fr.] A sort of pear.

CHAUN, *n.* A gap. [*Not in use.* See *Yawn.*]

CHAUN, *v. i.* To open; to yawn. [*Not in use.*]

CHAV'ENDER, } *n.* [Fr. *chevesne.*] The
CHEV'EN, } chub, a fish.

CHAW, *v. t.* [Sax. *ceowan;* D. *kaauwen;* G. *kauen;* Ir. *cagnaim*, or *cognaim;* Arm. *jaoga*, or *chaguein;* coinciding with *jaw*, which in Arm. is *javed*, *gaved* or *chagell*, and as *cheek* and *jaw* are often united, this word coincides with Sax. *ceac*, *ceoca.* It is most correctly written and pronounced *chaw;* but *chew* is deemed most elegant.]
1. To grind with the teeth; to masticate, as food in eating; to ruminate, or to chew as the cud.
2. To ruminate in thought; to revolve and consider. *Obs.*

CHAW, *n.* [a different spelling of *jaw.* See *Chaw*, supra.]
1. The jaw. Ezek. xxix. 4. But in modern editions of the Bible it is printed *jaw.*
2. In *vulgar language*, a cud; as much as is put in the mouth at once.

CHAW'DRON, *n.* Entrails. *Shak.*

CHAY, *n.* Chaya-root; the root of the Oldenlandia umbellata, used in dyeing red.

CHEAP, *a.* [Sax. *ceap*, cattle, business, or trade, a price, a pledge or pawn, a selling any thing that may be bought or sold; *ceapian*, *cypan*, to buy, to sell, to negotiate, to gain; D. *koop*, a bargain or purchase; "te koop zetten," to set to sale; "goed koop," *cheap*, good purchase; *koopen*, to buy; G. *kaufen;* Dan. *kiöber;* Sw. *kåpa;* Russ. *kupayu;* L. *caupo;* Eng. to *cheapen*, to *chaffer*, *chap-man*, *chap-book*, to *chop* and *change.* The sense is a purchase, and *good cheap* is a good purchase or bargain. Hence probably, omitting *good*, we have *cheap.*]
1. Bearing a low price, in market; that may be purchased at a low price; that is, at a price as low or lower than the usual price of the article or commodity, or at a price less than the real value. The sense is always comparative; for a price deemed *cheap* at one time is considered *dear* at another.

> It is a principle which the progress of political science has clearly established; a principle that illustrates at once the wisdom of the creator and the blindness of human cupidity, that it is *cheaper* to hire the labor of freemen than to compel the labor of slaves. *L. Bacon.*

2. Being of small value; common; not respected; as *cheap* beauty.

> Make not yourself *cheap* in the eyes of the world. *Anon.*

CHEAP, *n.* Bargain; purchase; as in the phrases, good *cheap*, better *cheap;* the original phrases from which we have *cheap.*

CHE'APEN, *v. t. che'apn.* [Sax. *ceapian.* See *Cheap*, supra.]
1. To attempt to buy; to ask the price of a commodity; to chaffer.

> To shops in crowds the daggled females fly,
> Pretend to *cheapen* goods, but nothing buy. *Swift.*

2. To lessen value. *Dryden.*

CHE'APENER, *n.* One who cheapens or bargains.

CHE'APLY, *adv.* At a small price; at a low rate.

CHE'APNESS, *n.* Lowness in price, considering the usual price, or real value.

CHEAR, [See *Cheer.*]

CHEAT, *v. t.* [Sax. *ceatt.* In Ar. خدع gadaa, signifies to deceive, circumvent, seduce; to fail, to hide, to disguise, to defraud; كاد kaida, signifies to deceive, to lay snares; Eth. ኀየጠ chiet or hiet, signifies to cheat, to deceive, to defraud.]
1. To deceive and defraud in a bargain; to deceive for the purpose of gain in selling. Its proper application is to commerce, in which a person uses some arts, or misrepresentations, or withholds some facts, by which he deceives the purchaser.
2. To deceive by any artifice, trick or device, with a view to gain an advantage contrary to common honesty; as, to *cheat* a person at cards.
3. To impose on; to trick. It is followed by *of* or *out of*, and colloquially by *into*, as to *cheat* a child *into* a belief that a medicine is palatable.

CHEAT, *n.* A fraud committed by deception; a trick; imposition; imposture.
2. A person who cheats; one guilty of fraud by deceitful practices.

CHE'ATABLENESS, *n.* Liability to be cheated. *Hammond.*

CHE'AT-BREAD, *n.* Fine bread purchased, or not made in the family. [*Little used.*]

CHE'ATED, *pp.* Defrauded by deception.

CHE'ATER, *n.* One who practices a fraud in commerce.

CHE'ATING, *ppr.* Defrauding by deception; imposing on.

CHE'ATING, *n.* The act of defrauding by deceitful arts.

CHECK, *v. t.* [Fr. *echec*, plu. *echecs*, which we have changed into *chess;* Sp. *xaque*, a move at chess; *xaque de mate*, check-mate; Port. *xaque*, a check; *xagoate*, a rebuke. Sp. and Port. *xaquima*, a halter; It. *scacco* the squares of a chess-board; *scacchi*, chess-men; *scacco-matto*, check-mate; *scaccato*, checkered; Low L. *scaccarium*, an exchequer, Fr. *echiquier;* G. *schach*, chess; *schachmatt*, check-mate; D. *schaak*, chess; *schaak-mat*, check-mate; Dan. *skak*, chess, crooked, curving; *skak-mat*, check-mate; *skakrer*, to barter, chaffer, chop and change; Sw. *schach*, chess; *schach-matt*, check-mate; Russ. *schach*, check, chess; *schach-mat*, check-mate. In Spanish *xaque*, *xeque*, is an old man, a *shaik*, and *xaco*, a *jacket.* These latter words seem to be the Ar. شاح or شاخ; the latter is rendered to grow old, to be old, to blame or rebuke, under which we find *shaik;* the former signifies to use diligence, quasi, to bend to or apply; also, to abstain or turn aside. In Arabic we find also شكّ to doubt, hesitate, halt, and in Heb. the same word שכן signifies to still, allay, sink, stop or check, to obstruct or hedge; שך a hedge. We have, in these words, clear evidence of the manner, in which several modern nations express the Shemitic ש, or ش.]
1. To stop; to restrain; to hinder; to curb. It signifies to put an entire stop to motion, or to restrain its violence, and cause an abatement; to moderate.
2. To rebuke; to chide or reprove. *Shak.*
3. To compare any paper with its counterpart or with a cipher, with a view to ascertain its authenticity; to compare corresponding papers; to control by a counter-register.
4. In *seamenship*, to ease off a little of a rope, which is too stiffly extended; also, to stopper the cable. *Mar. Dict.*

CHECK, *v. i.* To stop; to make a stop; with *at.*

> The mind *checks at* any vigorous undertaking. *Locke.*

2. To clash or interfere.

> I love to *check* with business. *Bacon.*

3. To strike with repression. *Dryden.*
[*These applications are not frequent.*]

CHECK, *n.* A stop; hindrance; rebuff; sudden restraint, or continued restraint; curb; control; government.
2. That which stops or restrains, as reproof, reprimand, rebuke, slight or disgust, fear, apprehension, a person; any stop or obstruction. *Shak. Dryden. Clarendon.*
3. In *falconry*, when a hawk forsakes her proper game, to follow rooks, pies, or other fowls, that cross her in her flight. *Bailey. Encyc.*
4. The correspondent cipher of a bank note; a corresponding indenture; any counter-register. *Johnson.*
5. A term in chess, when one party obliges

the other either to move or guard his king.

6. An order for money, drawn on a banker or on the cashier of a bank, payable to the bearer.

This is a sense derived from that in definition 4.

7. In popular use, *checkered* cloth; *check*, for *checkered*.

Check or *check-roll*, a roll or book containing the names of persons who are attendants and in the pay of a king or great personage, as domestic servants. *Bailey. Encyc.*

Clerk of the check, in the British King's household, has the check and control of the yeomen of the guard, and all the ushers belonging to the royal family, the care of the watch, &c. *Bailey. Encyc.*

Clerk of the check, in the British Royal Dock-Yards, is an officer who keeps a register of all the men employed on board his majesty's ships and vessels, and of all the artificers in the service of the navy, at the port where he is settled.

CHECK'ED, CHECKT, *pp.* Stopped; restrained; repressed; curbed; moderated; controlled; reprimanded.

CHECK'ER, *v. t.* [from *check*, or perhaps directly from the Fr. *echiquier*, a chess board. Norm. *eschegir*, or *chekere*, exchequer.]

1. To variegate with cross lines; to form into little squares, like a chess board, by lines or stripes of different colors. Hence,

2. To diversify; to variegate with different qualities, scenes, or events.

Our minds are, as it were, *checkered* with truth and falsehood. *Addison.*

CHECK'ER, *n.* One who checks or restrains; a rebuker.

2. A chess-board.

CHECK'ER, CHECK'ER-WÖRK, *n.* Work varied alternately as to its colors or materials; work consisting of cross lines.

CHECK'ERS, *n. plu.* A common game on a checkered board.

CHECK'ING, *ppr.* Stopping; curbing; restraining; moderating; controlling; rebuking.

CHECK'LESS, *a.* That cannot be checked, or restrained.

CHECK'-MATE, *n.* [See *Check*. *Mate* is from the root of the Sp. and Port. *matar*, to kill. Ar. Ch. Syr. Heb. Eth. Sam. מות moth, to die, to kill.]

1. The movement on a chess board or in the game of chess that kills the opposite men, or hinders them from moving, so that the game is finished.

2. Defeat; overthrow. *Spenser.*

CHECK'-MATE, *v. t.* To finish. *Skelton.*

CHECK'Y, *n.* In *heraldry*, a border that has more than two rows of checkers, or when the bordure or shield is checkered, like a chess-board. *Bailey. Encyc.*

CHEEK, *n.* [Sax. *ceac*, *ceoca*; D. *kaak*; this is probably the same word as *jaw*, Fr. *joue*, Arm. *gaved*, *javed*, connected with *jaoga*, *chaguein*, to chaw, or chew, for the words *chin*, *cheek* and *jaw*, are confounded, the same word which, in one dialect, signifies the cheek, in another, signifies the jaw. *Gena* in Latin is the English *chin.*]

1. The side of the face below the eyes on each side.

2. Among mechanics, *cheeks* are those pieces of a machine which form corresponding sides, or which are double and alike; as the *cheeks* of a printing press, which stand perpendicular and support the three sommers, the head, shelves and winter; the *cheeks* of a turner's lathe; the *cheeks* of a glazier's vise; the *cheeks* of a mortar, and of a gun-carriage; the *cheeks* of a mast, which serve to sustain the trestle trees, &c.

Cheek by jowl, closeness, proximity. *Beaum.*

CHEE'K-BONE, *n.* The bone of the cheek.

CHEE'KED, *a.* Brought near the cheek. *Cotton.*

CHEE'K-TOOTH, *n.* The hinder tooth or tusk. Joel i. 6.

CHEEP, *v. i.* To chirp, as a small bird.

CHEER, *v. t.* [Fr. *chère*; Arm. *cher*, cheer, entertainment; Ir. *gairim*, to call, shout, extol, rejoice; Gr. χαιρω, to rejoice, to hail or salute. The primary sense is to call out or shout, as in joy; a sense retained in jovial companies, to *give cheers*, and among seamen, to salute a ship by *cheers*. Orient. קרא kara.]

1. To salute with shouts of joy, or cheers. *Mar. Dict.*

2. To dispel gloom, sorrow, silence or apathy; to cause to rejoice; to gladden; to make cheerful; as, to *cheer* a lonely desert; the *cheering* rays of the sun; good news *cheers* the heart.

3. To infuse life, spirit, animation; to incite; to encourage; as, to *cheer* the hounds.

CHEER, *v. i.* To grow cheerful; to become gladsome, or joyous.

At sight of thee my gloomy soul *cheers* up. *Phillips.*

Cheer up, my lads.

CHEER, *n.* A shout of joy; as, they gave three *cheers*.

2. A state of gladness or joy; a state of animation, above gloom and depression of spirits, but below mirth, gayety and jollity.

Son, be of good *cheer*, thy sins are forgiven thee. Mat. ix.

Then were they all of good *cheer*, and they also took some meat. Acts xxvii.

3. Mirth; gayety; jollity; as at a feast.

4. Invitation to gayety. *Shak.*

5. Entertainment; that which makes cheerful; provisions for a feast. *Shak.*

The table was loaded with good *cheer*. *Irving.*

6. Air of countenance, noting a greater or less degree of cheerfulness.

His words their drooping *cheer*
Enlightened. *Milton.*

CHEE'RED, *pp.* Enlivened; animated; made glad.

CHEE'RER, *n.* One who cheers; he or that which gladdens.

Thou *cheerer* of our days. *Wotton.*
Prime *cheerer*, light. *Thomson.*

CHEE'RFUL, *a.* Lively; animated; having good spirits; moderately joyful. This is the most usual signification of the word, expressing a degree of animation less than mirth and jollity.

2. Full of life; gay; animated; mirthful; musical; as the *cheerful* birds.

3. Expressive of good spirits or joy; lively; animated.

A merry heart maketh a *cheerful* countenance. Prov. xv.

CHEE'RFULLY, *adv.* In a cheerful manner; with alacrity or willingness; readily; with life, animation or good spirits.

CHEE'RFULNESS, *n.* Life; animation; good spirits; a state of moderate joy or gayety; alacrity.

He that showeth mercy, with *cheerfulness*. Rom. xii.

CHEE'RILY, *adv.* With cheerfulness; with spirit.

CHEE'RING, *ppr.* Giving joy or gladness; enlivening; encouraging; animating.

CHEE'RISHNESS, *n.* State of cheerfulness. [*Not in use.*] *Milton.*

CHEE'RLESS, *a.* Without joy, gladness, or comfort; gloomy; destitute of any thing to enliven or animate the spirits. *Spenser.*

CHEE'RLY, *a.* Gay; cheerful; not gloomy.

CHEE'RLY, *adv.* Cheerfully; heartily; briskly.

CHEE'RY, *a.* Gay; sprightly; having power to make gay.

Come, let us hie, and quaff a *cheery* bowl. *Gay.*

CHEESE, *n.* *s* as *z*. [Sax. *cese*, or *cyse*; Ir. *cais*; W. *caws*; Corn. *kes*; Arm. *caus*; L. *caseus*; Sp. *queso*; Port. *queijo*; D. *kaas*; G. *käse*; Basque, *gasna* or *gazta*. The primary sense is to curdle, to congeal, from collecting, drawing or driving, W. *casiaw*, to curdle. Perhaps it is allied to *squeeze.*]

1. The curd of milk, coagulated by rennet, separated from the serum or whey, and pressed in a vat, hoop or mold.

2. A mass of pumice or ground apples placed on a press. *New England.*

CHEE'SE-CAKE, *n.* A cake made of soft curds, sugar and butter. *Prior.*

CHEE'SE-MÖNGER, *n.* One who deals in or sells cheese. *B. Jonson.*

CHEE'SE-PARING, *n.* The rind or paring of cheese. *Beaum.*

CHEE'SE-PRESS, *n.* A press, or engine for pressing curd in the making of cheese. *Gay.*

CHEE'SE-RENNET, *n.* A plant, ladies bed-straw, Galium verum.

CHEE'SE-VAT, *n.* The vat or case in which curds are confined for pressing. *Glanville.*

CHEE'SY, *a.* Having the nature, qualities, taste or form of cheese.

CHEG'OE, *n.* A tropical insect that enters the skin of the feet and multiplies incredibly, causing an itching. *Encyc.*

CHEI'ROPTER, *n.* [Gr. χειρ, the hand, and πτερον, wing.]

An animal whose anterior toes are connected by a membrane, and whose feet thus serve for wings, as the bat. *Lunier.*

CHEL'IDON, *n.* [Gr.] A brown fly with silvery wings.

CHELIF'EROUS, *a.* [Gr. χηλη, a claw, and L. *fero*, to bear.] Furnished with claws, as an animal.

CHEL'IFORM, *a.* [L. *chela*, a claw, and *form.*] Having the form of a claw.

CHELMS'FORDITE, *n.* A mineral arranged as a subspecies of schaalstein; found in Chelmsford, Massachusetts. *Cleaveland.*

CHELO'NIAN, *a.* [Gr. χελυς, χελωνη, a tortoise.] Pertaining to or designating animals of the tortoise kind.

ȻHEL'Y, *n.* [L. *chela*, Gr. χηλη, a claw.] The claw of a shell-fish. *Brown.*

ȻHEMIȻAL. [See *Chimical.*]

ȻHEMIȻALLY. [See *Chimically.*]

ȻHEMISE, *n.* [Fr. *chemise*; Ir. *caimse*, *caimis*; Sp. *camisa*; It. *camicia*; Ar. قميص kamitzon; Amh. *id.*]

1. A shift, or under garment worn by females.
2. A wall that lines the face of any work of earth. *Bailey.*

ȻHEMIST. [See *Chimist.*]

ȻHEMISTRY. [See *Chimistry.*]

CHEQUER. [See *Checker.*]

CHER'IFF, *n.* written also *Sheriff.* The prince of Mecca; a high priest among the Mohammedans.

CHER'ISH, *v. t.* [Fr. *cherir*; Arm. *cheriçza*; from Fr. *cher*, dear; W. *cir*, bounty; *ciriaw*, to pity, to cherish. See *Caress.*]

1. To treat with tenderness and affection; to give warmth, ease or comfort to.

   We were gentle among you, even as a nurse *cherisheth* her children. 1 Thess. ii.

   The damsel was fair and *cherished* the king. 1 Kings i.
2. To hold as dear; to embrace with affection; to foster, and encourage; as, to *cherish* the principles of virtue; to *cherish* religion in the heart.
3. To treat in a manner to encourage growth, by protection, aid, attendance, or supplying nourishment; as, to *cherish* tender plants.
4. To harbor; to indulge and encourage in the mind; as, to *cherish* ill will, or any evil passion.

CHER'ISHED, *pp.* Treated with tenderness; warmed; comforted; fostered.

CHER'ISHER, *n.* One who cherishes; an encourager; a supporter.

CHER'ISHING, *ppr.* Warming; comforting; encouraging; fostering; treating with affection.

CHER'ISHING, *n.* Support; encouragement.

CHER'ISHMENT, *n.* Encouragement; comfort. [*Not used.*] *Spenser.*

ȻHERMES. [See *Kermes.*]

CHER'RY, *n.* [Fr. *cerise*; L. *cerasus*; It. *ciriegia*; Port. *cereja*; Sp. *cereza*; Arm. *geresen*; D. *kars*, or *kriek*; G. *kirsche*; Sw. *kirsbar*; Dan. *kirsebær*; so named, it is said, from *Cerasus*, a city in Pontus, near the Euxine, whence the tree was imported into Italy.]

The fruit of a tree, a species of Prunus, of which there are many varieties, as the red or garden cherry, the red heart, the white heart, the black cherry, the black heart, and several others. The fruit is a pulp inclosing a kernel. It is related that this fruit was brought from Cerasus in Pontus to Italy, after the defeat of Mithridates by Lucullus, A R. 680., and introduced into England by the Romans, about 120 years afterwards, A. D. 55.

Barbadoes cherry, is the genus Malpighia, of several species. The berries are red, cherry-shaped, acid and eatable.

Bird cherry, is a species of Prunus, the common laurel or *lauro-cerasus*. *Lee.*

Also, the *Prunus padus*. *Encyc.*

Cornelian cherry, is the fruit of the Cornus, cornel-tree or dogwood. It is a small, acid, cherry-like, eatable berry.

Dwarf cherry, is the fruit of a species of Lonicera, or honey-suckle.

Hottentot-cherry, is the fruit of a species of Cassine. The fruit is a trispermous berry of a dark purple color.

Winter-cherry, is a name of the fruit of the Physalis, a genus of many species. It is a berry of the size of a small cherry, inclosed in an inflated, bladder-like calyx. This name is also given to a species of Solanum. *Fam. of Plants.*

CHER'RY, *a.* Like a red cherry in color; red, ruddy, blooming; as a *cherry* lip; *cherry* cheeks.

CHER'RY, *n.* A cordial composed of cherry juice and spirit, sweetened, and diluted. The wild cherry is most generally used for this purpose, being steeped for some days in spirit, which extracts the juice of the fruit; the tincture is then sweetened and diluted to the taste. This cordial is moderately bitter and astringent. It is sometimes made of the mazzard.

CHER'RY-CHEEKED, *a.* Having ruddy cheeks. *Congreve.*

CHER'RY-PIT, *n.* A child's play, in which cherry stones are thrown into a hole. *Shak.*

CHER'RY-TREE, *n.* A tree whose fruit is cherries, in the more appropriate sense of the word. The name is mostly given to the common cultivated trees, and to that which produces the black wild cherry. The wood of the latter is valued for cabinet work.

ȻHER'SONESE, *n.* [Gr. χερσονησος; χερσος, land or uncultivated land, and νησος, an isle.]

A peninsula; a tract of land of any indefinite extent, which is nearly surrounded by water, but united to a larger tract by a neck of land or isthmus; as the *Cimbric Chersonese* or Jutland; the *Tauric Chersonese*, or Crimea.

CHERT, *n.* In *mineralogy*, a subspecies of rhomboidal quartz; called also hornstone, petrosilex or rock flint. It is less hard than common quartz; its fracture usually dull and splintery, sometimes more or less conchoidal. It is more or less translucent, sometimes at the edges, and sometimes the whole mass, if thin, has the strong translucency of certain horns. Its colors are numerous and usually dull. It is usually amorphous, sometimes globular, or in nodules. It occurs often in veins, especially metallic, in primitive mountains. *Jameson. Cleaveland.*

Chert is also applied to other minerals besides hornstone. Aikin calls a variety of flint, *flinty chert*, and the Derbyshire miners apply the term, *black chert*, to a fusible mineral, whereas the hornstone above described is infusible.

CHERT'Y, *a.* Like chert; flinty. *Pennant.*

CHER'UB, *n.* plu. *cherubs*, but the Hebrew plural *cherubim* is also used. [Heb. כרוב kerub. In Ch. and Syr. the corresponding verb signifies to plow; and the word is said to signify properly any image or figure; if so, it may have been named from engraving. But this is uncertain, and the learned are not agreed on the signification.]

A figure composed of various creatures, as a man, an ox, an eagle or a lion. The first mention of cherubs is in Gen. iii. 24, where the figure is not described, but their office was, with a flaming sword, to keep or guard the way of the tree of life. The two cherubs which Moses was commanded to make at the ends of the Mercy seat, were to be of beaten work of gold; and their wings were to extend over the Mercy seat, their faces towards each other, and between them was the residence of the Deity. Ex. xxv. The cherubs, in Ezekiel's vision, had each four heads or faces, the hands of a man and wings. The four faces were, the face of a bull, that of a man, that of a lion, and that of an eagle. They had the likeness of a man. Ezek. iv. and x. In 2 Sam. xxii. 11. and Psalm xviii., Jehovah is represented as riding on a cherub, and flying on the wings of the wind. In the celestial hierarchy, cherubs are represented as spirits next in order to seraphs. The hieroglyphical and emblematical figures embroidered on the vails of the tabernacle are called cherubs of curious or skilful work. Ex. xxvi.

CHER'UBIȻ, CHERU'BIȻ, *a.* [The accent is usually laid on the second syllable, but improperly.]

Pertaining to cherubs; angelic. *Sheldon.*

CHER'UBIM, *n.* The Hebrew plural of *cherub.*

CHER'UBIN, *a.* Cherubic; angelic. *Shak.*

CHER'UBIN, *n.* A cherub. *Dryden.*

CHER'UP, a corruption of *chirp*, which see.

CHER'VIL, *n.* [Sax. *cerfille*, a contraction of L. *chærophyllum*; Gr. χαιρεφυλλον, χαιρω to rejoice, and φυλλον, leaf.]

A genus of plants, two species of which are called cow-weed.

CHES'APEAK, *n.* A bay of the U. States, whose entrance is between Cape Charles and Cape Henry, in Virginia, and which extends northerly into Maryland 270 miles. It receives the waters of the Susquehannah, Potomack, Rappahannock, York, and James Rivers.

CHES'IBLE, *n.* [Old Fr. *casuble.*] A short vestment without sleeves, worn by a popish priest at mass. *Bale.*

CHES'LIP, *n.* A small vermin that lies under stones and tiles. *Skinner.*

CHESS, *n.* [Fr. *echecs.* See *Check.*] An ingenious game performed by two parties with different pieces, on a *checkered* board, that is, a board divided into sixty four squares or houses. The success of the game depends almost entirely on skill. Each gamester has eight dignified pieces, called a king, a queen, two bishops, two knights, and two rooks or castles; also eight pawns. The pieces of the parties are of different colors. *Encyc.*

CHESS, *n.* [I do not find this word in any English Dictionary; nor do I know its origin or affinities. In Persian, خس chas or gas, signifies evil, depraved, and a useless weed.]

In New England, that weed which grows among wheat, and is supposed to be wheat degenerated or changed, as it abounds most in fields where the wheat is winter-killed. It bears some resemblance to oats. This fact is mentioned by Pliny, Nat. Hist. Lib. 18. Ca. 17. Primum omnium frumenti vitium avena est: et hordeum in eam degenerat. This change of wheat and barley into oats, he ascribes to a moist soil, wet weather, bad seed, &c. This opinion coincides with observations in America, as wheat is most liable to perish in moist land, and often in such places, almost all the wheat is killed, and instead of it chess often appears.

CHESS′-APPLE, *n.* A species of wild service.

CHESS′-BOARD, *n.* The board used in the game of chess, and from the squares of which *chess* has its name.

CHESS′-MAN, *n.* A piece or puppet, for the game of chess.

CHESS′-PLAYER, *n.* One who plays chess; one skilled in the game of chess.

CHESS′-TREE, *n.* In *ships*, a piece of wood bolted perpendicularly on the side to confine the clews of the main sail.

CHESS′OM, *n.* Mellow earth. *Bacon.*

CHEST, *n.* [Sax. *cest* or *cyst*; L. *cista*; W. *cist*; Ir. *cisde*; Gr. κιϛη; G. *kiste*; D. *kist*; Sw. *kista*; Dan. *kiste*. See *Chestnut.*]

1. A box of wood or other material, in which goods are kept or transported. It differs from a trunk in not being covered with skin or leather.
2. The trunk of the body from the neck to the belly; the thorax. Hence, *broad-chested*, *narrow-chested*, having a broad or narrow chest.
3. In *commerce*, a certain quantity; as a *chest* of sugar; a *chest* of indigo; &c.

Chest of drawers is a case of movable boxes called drawers.

CHEST, *v. t.* To reposit in a chest; to hoard. *Johnson.*

CHEST′-FOUNDERING, *n.* A disease in horses, like the pleurisy or peripneumony in the human body. *Farrier's Dict.*

CHEST′NUT, *n.* [Sax. *cystel*, and the tree in Sax. is *cystbeam* or *cystenbeam*; L. *castanea*, the tree and the nut; Fr. *chataigne*; Arm. *gistenen*, or *gestenen*; W. *castan*; Sp. *castaña*; Port. *castanha*; It. *castagna*; G. *kastanie*; Sw. Dan. *kastanie*; from Welsh *cast*, envelopment, the root of *castle*, from separating, defending; so named from its shell or cover.]

The fruit, seed or nut of a tree belonging to the genus Fagus. It is inclosed in a prickly pericarp, which contains two or more seeds.

CHEST′NUT, *a.* Being of the color of a chestnut; of a brown color. It is perhaps rarely used as a noun.

CHEST′NUT-TREE, *n.* The tree which produces the chestnut. This tree grows to a great size, with spreading branches. It is one of the most valuable timber trees, as the wood is very durable, and forms in America the principal timber for fencing. The timber is also used in building, and for vessels of various kinds.

Dwarf-chestnut, or chinkapin, is another species of Fagus.

Horse-chestnut, is a tree of the genus Æsculus. The common tree of this sort is a native of the North of Asia, and admired for the beauty of its flowers. It is used for shade and ornament, and its nuts are esteemed good food for horses. The scarlet-flowering horse-chestnut is a native of Carolina, Brazil and the East, and is admired for its beauty.

The *Indian Rose-chestnut*, of the genus Mesua, bears a nut, roundish, pointed and marked with four elevated longitudinal sutures. *Encyc. Fam. of Plants.*

CHES′TON, *n.* A species of plum. *Johnson.*

ČHEV′AČHIE, *n.* An expedition with cavalry. [*Not used.*] *Chaucer.*

ČHEVAL DE FRISE, generally used in the plural, *chevaux de frise*, pronounced *shevo de freez.* [Fr. *cheval*, a horse, and *frise*, any thing curled, rough, entangled; the horse of frise, or frizzled horse. Hence called also *turnpike, tourniquet.*]

1. A piece of timber traversed with wooden spikes, pointed with iron, five or six feet long; used to defend a passage, stop a breach, or make a retrenchment to stop cavalry.
2. A kind of trimming.

ČHEVALIE′R, *n.* [Fr. from *cheval*, a horse; Sp. *caballero*. See *Cavalry.*]

1. A knight; a gallant young man. *Shak.*
2. In *heraldry*, a horseman armed at all points. *Encyc.*

CHEV′EN, *n.* [Fr. *chevesne.*] A river fish, the chub.

CHEV′ERIL, *n.* [Fr. *chevreau*, a kid, from *chevre*, a goat, L. *caper*, W. *gavar*, Arm. *gavricq, gavr.*]

A kid, or rather leather made of kid-skin; used as a noun or adjective. *Shak.*

CHEV′ERILIZE, *v. t.* To make as pliable as kid-leather. *Montagu.*

ČHEV′ISANCE, *n.* *s* as *z.* [Fr. *chevir*, to come to the end, to perform, to prevail, from *chef*, the head, literally the end. See *Chief* and *Achieve.*]

1. Achievement; deed; performance; enterprize accomplished. *Obs.* *Spenser.*
2. In *law*, a making of contracts; a bargain. Stat. 13 Eliz. 7.
3. An unlawful agreement or contract. 21 James. 17.
4. An agreement or composition, as an end or order set down between a creditor and his debtor. *Encyc.*

ČHEV′RON, *n.* [Fr. a rafter; W. *ceber*; Arm. *gebr.*]

In *heraldry*, an honorable ordinary, representing two rafters of a house meeting at the top. *Bailey.*

ČHEV′RONED, *a.* Having a chevron, or the form of it. *B. Jonson.*

ČHEVROTA′IN, *n.* [from Fr. *chevre*, a goat.] The smallest of the antelope kind.

CHEW, *v. t.* [Sax. *ceowan*; D. *kaauwen*; G. *kauen*. See *Chaw.*]

1. To bite and grind with the teeth; to masticate, as food, to prepare it for deglutition and digestion.
2. To ruminate in the thoughts; to meditate; as, to *chew* revenge. *Shak.*
3. To champ; to bite, hold or roll about in the mouth; as, to *chew* tobacco.
4. To taste, without swallowing. *Shak.*

CHEW, *v. i.* To champ upon; to ruminate.

Old politicians *chew* on wisdom past. *Pope.*

CHEW, *n.* That which is chewed; that which is held in the mouth at once; a cud. [*Vulgar.*]

CHEW′ED, *pp.* Ground by the teeth; masticated.

CHEW′ET, *n.* A kind of pie, made with chopped substances.

CHEW′ING, *ppr.* Grinding with the teeth; masticating; ruminating; meditating; champing.

CHI′A, *n.* A beautiful Mexican plant.

ČHI′AN, *a.* Pertaining to *Chios*, an isle in the Levant.

Chian earth, a medicinal, dense, compact kind of earth, from Chios, used anciently as an astringent, and a cosmetic. *Encyc.*

Chian turpentine, or Cyprus turpentine, is procured from the Pistacia Terebinthus. It is of the consistence of honey, clear and of a yellowish white.

ČHIAS′TOLITE, *n.* [Gr. χιαςος, decussated.]

A mineral, called also *macle*, whose crystals are arranged in a peculiar manner. The form of the crystals is a four-sided prism, whose bases are rhombs, differing little from squares. But each crystal, when viewed at its extremities, or on a transverse section, is obviously composed of two very different substances; and its general aspect is that of a black prism, passing longitudinally through the axis of another prism which is whitish. The term *macle*, as the name of a distinct species, applies to the whitish prisms only. *Cleaveland.*

CHIB′BAL, *n.* [Fr. *ciboule.*] A small sort of onion. *Beaum.*

ČHIČA′NE, *n.* [Fr. *chicane*; Arm. *cican* or *cicanerez*. Qu. Gr. Σικανος, a Sicilian, a cheat. *Lunier.*]

1. In *law*, shift; turn; trick; cavil; an abuse of judiciary proceedings, by artifices, unfair practices, or idle objections, which tend to perplex a cause, puzzle the judge, or impose on a party, and thus to delay or pervert justice.
2. In *disputes*, sophistry; distinctions and subtleties, that tend to perplex the question and obscure the truth. *Locke.*
3. Any artifice or stratagem. *Prior.*

ČHIČA′NE, *v. i.* [Fr. *chicaner.*] To use shifts, cavils or artifices.

ČHIČA′NER, *n.* [Fr. *chicaneur.*] One who uses shifts, turns, evasions or undue artifices, in litigation or disputes; a caviller; a sophister; an unfair disputant. *Locke.*

ČHIČA′NERY, *n.* [Fr. *chicanerie.*] Sophistry; mean or unfair artifices to perplex a cause and obscure the truth.

CHICH′ES, *n. plu.* Dwarf peas.

CHICH′LING, } *n.* A vetch or pea,
CHICKLING-VETCH, } of the genus Lathyrus, used in Germany for food, but inferior to other kinds. *Miller.*

CHICK, *v. i.* To sprout, as seed in the ground; to vegetate. *Todd.*

CHICK, } *n.* [Sax. *cicen*; D. *kuiken*;
CHICK′EN, } G. *küchlein*. Qu. Russ. *chikayu*, to peep.]

1. The young of fowls, particularly of the domestic hen, or gallinaceous fowls.
2. A person of tender years.
3. A word of tenderness.

CHICK′EN-HEARTED, *a.* Timid; fearful; cowardly.

CHICK′EN-POX, *n.* A mild contagious

eruptive disease, generally appearing in children.

CHICK'LING, *n.* A small chick or chicken.

CHICK'-PEA, *n.* [L. *cicer;* G. *kicher;* Sp. *chicharo.*]

A plant or pea, constituting the genus Cicer; a native of Spain, where it is used in olios. It is smaller than the common pea.

CHICK'-WEED, *n.* A plant of the genus *Alsine*, which includes many species. The common chick-weed, with white blossoms, affords a remarkable instance of the sleep of plants; for, at night, the leaves approach in pairs, and inclose the tender rudiments of the young shoots. The leaves are cooling and nutritive, and are deemed excellent food for persons of a consumptive habit. They are deemed useful also for swelled breasts. *Encyc. Wiseman.*

CHIDE, *v. t.* pret. *chid,* [*chode* is obs.]; part. *chid, chidden.* [Sax. *cidan, chidan,* to chide, to scold; W. *cozi,* to chide, to press, to straiten; Ch. קטט, to scold, to brawl, to fight. Qu. W. *cad,* a battle.] Literally, to scold; to clamor; to utter noisy words; that is, to drive. Hence,

1. To scold at; to reprove; to utter words in anger, or by way of disapprobation; to rebuke; as, to *chide* one for his faults.

2. To blame; to reproach; as, to *chide* folly or negligence.

To chide from or *chide away,* is to drive away by scolding or reproof.

CHIDE, *v. i.* To scold; to clamor; to find fault; to contend in words of anger; sometimes followed by *with.*

The people did *chide with* Moses. Ex. xvii.

2. To quarrel. *Shak.*

3. To make a rough, clamorous, roaring noise; as the *chiding* flood. *Shak.*

CHIDE, *n.* Murmur; gentle noise. *Thomson.*

CHI'DER, *n.* One who chides, clamors, reproves or rebukes.

CHI'DERESS, *n.* A female who chides. [*Not used.*] *Chaucer.*

CHI'DING, *ppr.* Scolding; clamoring; rebuking; making a harsh or continued noise.

CHI'DING, *n.* A scolding or clamoring; rebuke; reproof.

CHI'DINGLY, *adv.* In a scolding or reproving manner.

CHIEF, *a.* [Fr. *chef,* the head, that is, the top or highest point; Norm. *chief;* Sp. *xefe;* Ir. *ceap;* It. *capo.* It is evidently from the same root as the L. *caput,* Gr. κεφαλη, and Eng. *cape,* but through the Celtic, probably from shooting, extending.]

1. Highest in office or rank; principal; as a *chief* priest; the *chief* butler. Gen. xl. 9.

Among the *chief* rulers, many believed on him. John xii.

2. Principal or most eminent, in any quality or action; most distinguished; having most influence; commanding most respect; taking the lead; most valuable; most important; a word of extensive use; as a country *chief* in arms.

The hand of the princes and rulers hath been *chief* in this trespass. Ezra ix.

Agriculture is the *chief* employment of men.

3. First in affection; most dear and familiar.

A whisperer separateth *chief* friends. Prov. xvi.

CHIEF, *n.* A commander; particularly a military commander; the person who heads an army; equivalent to the modern terms, commander or general in chief, captain general, or generalissimo. 1 Ch. xi.

2. The principal person of a tribe, family, or congregation, &c. Num. iii. Job xxix. Math. xx.

3. *In chief,* in English law, *in capite.* To hold land *in chief* is to hold it directly from the king by honorable personal services. *Blackstone.*

4. In *heraldry,* chief signifies the head or upper part of the escutcheon, from side to side, representing a man's head. *In chief,* imports something borne in this part. *Encyc.*

5. In Spenser, it seems to signify something like achievement, a mark of distinction; as, chaplets wrought with a *chief.* *Johnson.*

6. This word is often used, in the singular number, to express a plurality.

I took the *chief* of your tribes, wise men and known, and made them heads over you. Deut. i. 15.

These were the *chief* of the officers, that were over Solomon's work. 1 Kings 9.

In these phrases, *chief* may have been primarily an adjective, that is, *chief men, chief persons.*

7. The principal part; the most or largest part, of one thing or of many.

The people took of the spoil, sheep and oxen, the *chief* of the things which should have been utterly destroyed. 1 Sam. xv.

He smote the *chief* of their strength. Ps. lxviii.

The *chief* of the debt remains unpaid.

CHIEF, *adv.* Chiefly.

CHIE'FAGE, CHE'VAGE, *n.* A tribute by the head. *Obs.* *Chambers.*

CHIE'FDOM, *n.* Sovereignty. *Spenser.*

CHIE'FLESS, *a.* Without a chief or leader. *Pope.*

CHIE'FLY, *adv.* Principally; eminently; in the first place.

It *chiefly* concerns us to obey the divine precepts.

2. For the most part.

In the parts of the kingdom where the estates of the dissenters *chiefly* lay. *Swift.*

CHIE'FRIE, *n.* A small rent paid to the lord paramount. *Spenser's Ireland.*

CHIE'FTAIN, *n.* [from *chief,* Norm. *cheventeins,* formed like *captain, capitaine.*]

A captain, leader or commander; a chief; the head of a troop, army or clan. It is most commonly used in the latter sense. The chieftains of the Highland clans in Scotland, were the principal noblemen and gentlemen. *Encyc.*

CHIE'FTAINRY, CHIE'FTAINSHIP, *n.* Headship; captaincy; the government over a clan. *Johnson. Smollett.*

CHIE'VANCE, *n.* [Norm. *chivisance.* See *Chevisance.*]

An unlawful bargain; traffick in which money is extorted. *Obs.* *Bacon.*

CHIEVE or CHIVE, *v. i.* [Fr. *chevir.* See *Achieve.*] To come to an end; to issue; to succeed. *Obs.* *Chaucer.*

CHIL'BLAIN, *n.* [*chill,* Sax. *cele,* cold, and *blain.*]

A blain or sore produced by cold; a tumor affecting the hands and feet, accompanied with inflammation, pain, and sometimes ulceration. *Encyc.*

CHILD, *n.* plu. *chil'dren.* [Sax. *cild;* in Dan. *kuld* is progeny, *kulde* is coldness, and *kuler* is to blow strong. *Child* is undoubtedly issue, that which is produced.]

1. A son or a daughter; a male or female descendant, in the first degree; the immediate progeny of parents; applied to the human race, and chiefly to a person when young. The term is applied to infants from their birth; but the time when they cease ordinarily to be so called, is not defined by custom. In strictness, a child is the shoot, issue or produce of the parents, and a person of any age, in respect to the parents, is a child.

An infant.

Hagar cast the *child* under one of the shrubs. Gen. xxi.

It signifies also a person of more advanced years.

Jephtha's daughter was his only *child.* Judges xi.

The *child* shall behave himself proudly. Is. iii.

A curse will be on those who corrupt the morals of their *children.* *J. Clarke.*

The application of *child* to a female in opposition to a male, as in *Shakspeare,* is not legitimate.

2. One weak in knowledge, experience, judgment or attainments; as, he is a mere *child.*

Behold, I cannot speak, for I am a *child.* Jer. i.

3. One young in grace. 1 John ii.

One who is humble and docile. Math. xviii.

One who is unfixed in principles. Eph. iv.

4. One who is born again, spiritually renewed and adopted; as a *child* of God.

5. One who is the product of another; or whose principles and morals are the product of another.

Thou *child* of the devil. Acts xiii.

That which is the product or effect of something else.

This noble passion, *child* of integrity. *Shak.*

6. In *the plural,* the descendants of a man however remote; as the *children* of Israel; the *children* of Edom.

7. The inhabitants of a country; as the *children* of Seir. 2 Chron. xxv.

To be with child, to be pregnant. Gen. xvi. 11. xix. 36.

CHILD, *v. i.* To bring children. [*Not used.*] *Shak.*

CHILD-BEARING, *a.* or *ppr.* [See *Bear.*] Bearing or producing children.

CHILD-BEARING, *n.* The act of producing or bringing forth children; parturition. *Milton. Addison.*

CHILDBED, *n.* [*child* and *bed.*] The state of a woman bringing forth a child or being in labor; parturition.

CHILDBIRTH, *n.* [*child* and *birth.*] The act of bringing forth a child; travail; labor; as the pains of *childbirth.* *Taylor.*

CHILDED, *a.* Furnished with a child. [*Not used.*] *Shak.*

CHILD'ERMAS DAY, *n.* [*child, mass* and *day.*]
An anniversary of the church of England, held on the 28th of December, in commemoration of the children of Bethlehem slain by Herod; called also *Innocents' Day.* *Bailey. Encyc.*

CHILD'HOOD, *n.* [Sax. *cildhad.* See *Hood.*]
1. The state of a child, or the time in which persons are children, including the time from birth to puberty. But in a more restricted sense, the state or time from infancy to puberty. Thus we say, *infancy, childhood, youth* and *manhood.*
Childhood and youth are vanity. Eccl. xi.
2. The properties of a child. *Dryden.*

CHILDING, *ppr.* [The verb *to child* is not now used.] Bearing children; producing; as *childing* women. *Arbuthnot.*

CHILDISH, *a.* Belonging to a child; trifling; puerile.
When I became a man, I put away *childish* things. 1 Cor. xiii.
2. Pertaining to a child; as *childish* years or age; *childish* sports.
3. Pertaining to children; ignorant; silly; weak; as *childish* fear.

CHILDISHLY, *adv.* In the manner of a child; in a trifling way; in a weak or foolish manner.

CHILDISHNESS, *n.* Triflingness, puerility, the state or qualities of a child, in reference to manners. But in reference to the mind, simplicity, harmlessness, weakness of intellect.

CHILDLESS, *a.* Destitute of children or offspring. 1 Sam. xv. 33.

CHILDLIKE, *a.* Resembling a child or that which belongs to children; becoming a child; meek; submissive; dutiful; as *childlike* obedience.

CHILDLY, *a.* Like a child.

CHIL'DREN, *n.* plu. of *child.*

CHIL'IAD, *n.* [Gr. χιλιας, from χιλια, a thousand.]
1. A thousand; a collection or sum, containing a thousand individuals or particulars. *Holder.*
2. The period of a thousand years. *Encyc.*

CHIL'IAGON, *n.* [Gr. χιλια, a thousand, and γωνια, a corner.]
A plain figure of a thousand angles and sides. *Math. Dict.*

CHILIAHE'DRON, *n.* [Gr. χιλια, a thousand, and ἑδρα, a base.]
A figure of a thousand equal sides.

CHIL'IARCH, *n.* [Gr. χιλια, a thousand, and αρχος, a chief.]
The military commander or chief of a thousand men.

CHIL'IARCHY, *n.* A body consisting of a thousand men. *Mitford.*

CHIL'IAST, *n.* [Supra.] One of the sect of Millenarians.

CHILIFAC'TIVE. [See *Chylifactive.*]

CHILIOL'ITER. [See *Kiloliter.*]

CHILIOM'ETER. [See *Kilometer.*]

CHILL, *n.* [Sax. *cele, cyle, cyl,* cold; *celan,* to be cold; D. *kil;* allied to Fr. *geler,* L. *gelo, gelidus.* See *Cold,* which appears to be radically the same word. The word *cele* in Saxon is a noun.]
1. A shivering with cold; rigors, as in an ague; the cold fit that precedes a fever; sensation of cold in an animal body; chilliness. [See *Cold* and *Heat.*]
2. A moderate degree of cold; chilliness in any body; that which gives the sensation of cold.

CHILL, *a.* Cool; moderately cold; tending to cause shivering; as the *chill* vapors of night.
2. Shivering with cold.
My *chill* veins freeze with despair. *Rowe.*
3. Cool; distant; formal; dull; not warm, animated or affectionate; as a *chill* reception.
4. Depressed; dispirited; dejected; discouraged.

CHILL, *v. t.* To cause a shivering, or shrinking of the skin; to check circulation or motion; as, to *chill* the blood, or the veins. The force of this word lies in expressing the shivering and shrinking caused by cold.
2. To make cold, or cool; as, the evening air *chills* the earth.
3. To blast with cold; to check the circulation in plants, and stop their growth. *Blackmore.*
4. To check motion, life or action; to depress; to deject; to discourage; as, to *chill* the gayety of the spirits. *Rogers.*

CHILL'ED, *pp.* Made cool; made to shiver; dejected.

CHIL'LI, *n.* A Mexican plant, Guinea pepper.

CHILL'INESS, *n.* A sensation of shivering; rigors.
2. A moderate degree of coldness; as the *chilliness* of the air, which tends to cause a shivering.

CHILL'ING, *ppr.* Cooling; causing to shiver.

CHILL'NESS, *n.* Coolness; coldness; a shivering.

CHILL'Y, *a.* Cool; moderately cold, such as to cause shivering; as a *chilly* day, night, or air.

CHIL'OGRAM. [See *Kilogram.*]

CHIMB, *n.* [See *Chime.*]

CHIME, *n.* [Chaucer, *chimbe;* Dan. *kimer,* to tinkle, to tingle, to toll a bell; L. *campana,* a bell, from its sound, whence It. *scampanare,* to chime.]
1. The consonant or harmonic sounds of several correspondent instruments.
Instruments that made melodious *chime.* *Milton.*
2. Correspondence of sound.
Love—harmonized the *chime.* *Dryden.*
3. The musical sounds of bells, struck with hammers. *Shak.*
4. Correspondence of proportion or relation. *Grew.*
5. A kind of periodical music, or tune of a clock, produced by an apparatus annexed to it.
6. A set of bells which chime, or ring in harmony.

CHIME, *v. i.* To sound in consonance or harmony; to accord.
To make the rough recital aptly *chime.* *Prior.*
2. To correspond in relation or proportion.
Father and son, husband and wife, correlative terms, do readily *chime.* *Locke.*
3. To agree; to fall in with.
He often *chimed* in with the discourse. *Arbuthnot.*
4. To agree; to suit with. *Locke.*
5. To jingle; to clatter. *Smith.*
The sely tonge may wel ringe and *chimbe.* *Chaucer.*

CHIME, *v. t.* To move, strike, or cause to sound in harmony. *Dryden.*
2. To strike or cause to sound, as a set of bells.

CHIME, *n.* [D. *kim;* G. *kimme,* edge, brim.]
The edge or brim of a cask or tub, formed by the ends of the staves.

CHI'MER, *n.* One who chimes.

CHIME'RA, *n.* [L. *chimæra;* Gr. χιμαιρα, a goat, a monstrous beast.]
1. In *fabulous history,* a monster with three heads, that of a lion, of a goat, and of a dragon, vomiting flames. The foreparts of the body were those of a lion, the middle was that of a goat, and the hinder parts were those of a dragon; supposed to represent a volcanic mountain in Lycia, whose top was the resort of lions, the middle, that of goats, and the foot, that of serpents. Hence,
2. In *modern usage,* a vain or idle fancy; a creature of the imagination, composed of contradictions or absurdities, that can have no existence except in thought. *Encyc.*

CHIMER'ICAL, *a.* Merely imaginary; fanciful; fantastic; wildly or vainly conceived; that has, or can have no existence except in thought.

CHIMER'ICALLY, *adv.* Wildly; vainly; fancifully; fantastically.

CHIM'ICAL, *a.* [See *Chimistry.*] Pertaining to chimistry; as a *chimical* operation.
2. Resulting from the operation of the principles of bodies by decomposition, combination, &c.; as *chimical* changes.
3. According to the principles of chimistry; as a *chimical* combination.

CHIM'ICALLY, *adv.* According to chimical principles; by chimical process or operation.

CHIM'INAGE, *n.* [Fr. *chemin;* Sp. *camino,* a way.]
In *law,* a toll for passage through a forest. *Cowel. Bailey.*

CHI'MING, *ppr.* [from *chime.*] Causing to chime; sounding in accordance.

CHIM'IST, *n.* A person versed in chimistry; a professor of chimistry.

CHIM'ISTRY, *n.* [Fr. *chimie;* Sp. *chimia;* It. and Port. *chimica.* The orthography of this word has undergone changes through a mere ignorance of its origin, than which nothing can be more obvious. It is the Arabic كيميا kimia, the occult art or science, from كَمَى kamai, to conceal. This was originally the art or science now called alchimy; the art of converting baser metals into gold. The order of Diocletian, directing search to be made for books treating of the wonderful art of making gold and silver, and all that should be found to be committed to the flames, proves the origin of this art to be as remote as the close of the third century, and it was probably somewhat earlier. *Gibbon,* Ch. 13. It is not improbable that this art was used in counterfeiting coins. The common orthography is from χεω, to melt or fuse; the old orthography was from χνω, the same word, differently written; both having no foundation, but a random guess. If lexicographers and writers had been contented to take the orthography of the nations in the south of Europe, where the origin of the word was doubtless understood, and through whom the word was introduced into England, the orthography would have been settled, uniform, and corresponding exactly with the pronunciation.]

Chimistry is a science, the object of which is to discover the nature and properties of all bodies by analysis and synthesis. *Macquer.*

Chimistry is that science which explains the intimate mutual action of all natural bodies. *Fourcroy.*

Analysis or decomposition, and synthesis or combination, are the two methods which chimistry uses to accomplish its purposes. *Fourcroy. Hooper.*

Chimistry may be defined, the science which investigates the composition of material substances, and the permanent changes of constitution which their mutual actions produce. *Ure.*

Chimistry may be defined, that science, the object of which is to discover and explain the changes of composition that occur among the integrant and constituent parts of different bodies. *Henry.*

Chimistry is the science which treats of those events and changes in natural bodies, which are not accompanied by sensible motions. *Thomson.*

Chimistry is justly considered as a science, but the practical operations may be denominated an art.

CHIM'NEY, *n.* plu. *chimneys.* [Fr. *cheminée*; Arm. *ciminal*, or *cheminal*; G. *kamin*; Corn. *chimbla*; Ir. *simileur*; Sp. *chimenea*; It. *cammino*; L. *caminus*; Ch. קמין; Ar. قمين; Gr. χαμινος; Russ. *kamin.* It seems originally to have been a furnace, a stove, or a hearth.]

1. In *architecture*, a body of brick or stone, erected in a building, containing a funnel or funnels, to convey smoke, and other volatile matter through the roof, from the hearth or fire-place, where fuel is burnt. This body of materials is sometimes called *a stack of chimneys*, especially when it contains two or more funnels, or passages.

2. A fireplace; the lower part of the body of brick or stone which confines and conveys smoke.

CHIM'NEY-CORNER, *n.* The corner of a fire-place, or the space between the fire and the sides of the fire-place. In the Northern States of America, fire-places were formerly made six or eight feet wide, or even more, and a stool was placed by the side of the fire, as a seat for children, and this often furnished a comfortable situation for idlers. As fuel has become scarce, our fire-places are contracted, till, in many or most of our dwellings, we have no chimney-corners.

2. In *a more enlarged sense*, the fire-side, or a place near the fire.

CHIM'NEY-HOOK, *n.* A hook for holding pots and kettles over a fire.

CHIM'NEY-MONEY, *n.* Hearth-money, a duty paid for each chimney in a house. *Eng.*

CHIM'NEY-PIECE, *n.* An ornamental piece of wood or stone set round a fire-place.

CHIM'NEY-SWEEPER, *n.* One whose occupation is to sweep and scrape chimneys, to clean them of the soot that adheres to their sides.

CHIMPAN'ZEE, *n.* An animal of the ape kind, a variety of the ourang-outang. *Dict. Nat. Hist.*

It is now considered a distinct species. *Cuvier.*

CHIN, *n.* [Sax. *cinne*; Pers. چان; D. *kin*; G. *kinn*; Dan. *kind*, the cheek; Sw. *kind*; L. *gena*; Gr. γενυς. The sense is probably an edge or side, and allied to *chine.*]

The lower extremity of the face below the mouth; the point of the under jaw.

CHI'NA, *n.* A species of earthern ware made in China, and so called from the country; called also *china ware* and *porcelain.* [See *Porcelain.*]

CHI'NA-ORANGE, *n.* The sweet orange, said to have been originally brought from China.

CHI'NA-ROOT, *n.* The root of a species Smilax, brought from the East Indies, of a pale reddish color, with no smell, and very little taste.

CHINCH, *n.* [Qu. It. *cimice*, L. *cimex*, corrupted.]

A genus of insects, resembling the featherwing moths. These insects live in the flowers of plants, and wander from flower to flower, but prefer those which are sweetest. *Dict. Nat. Hist.*

CHIN'-COUGH, *n.* [D. *kink-hoest*, from *kink*, a twist or bend, and *hoest*, a cough; G. *keichhusten*, from *keichen*, to pant. Qu. for in Pers. خنه chonah is a cough.]

A contagious disease, often epidemic among children. It increases for some weeks, is attended with a difficulty of breathing, and in its worst stage, with a degree of convulsion. From a particular noise made in coughing, it is also called hooping cough.

CHINE, *n.* [Fr. *echine*; It. *schiena*; Arm. *chein.* It may be allied to *chin.* In German, *schiene* is the *shin*, also a clout, a splint; and *rad-schiene* is the band of a wheel; Russ. *schina.*]

1. The back-bone, or spine of an animal.

2. A piece of the back-bone of an animal, with the adjoining parts, cut for cooking.

3. The chime of a cask, or the ridge formed by the ends of the staves. *Stat. of Pennsylvania.*

CHINE, *v. t.* To cut through the back-bone, or into chine-pieces.

CHI'NED, *a.* Pertaining to the back. *Beaum.*

CHINE'SE, *a.* Pertaining to China.

CHINE'SE, *n. sing.* and *plu.* A native of China; also, the language of China.

CHIN'GLE, *n.* Gravel free from dirt. [See *Shingle.*] *Donne.*

CHINK, *n.* [This word may be a derivative from the Saxon *cinan*, or *ginian*, *geonan*, to gape, to *yawn*, Gr. χαινω; or from the common root of these words. Sax. *cina*, or *cinu*, a fissure.]

A small aperture lengthwise; a cleft, rent, or fissure, of greater length than breadth; a gap or crack; as the *chinks* of a wall.

CHINK, *v. i.* To crack; to open. *Barret.*

CHINK, *v. t.* To open or part and form a fissure.

CHINK, *v. t.* [See *Jingle.*] To cause to sound by shaking coins or small pieces of metal, or by bringing small sonorous bodies in collision; as, to *chink* a purse of money. *Pope.*

CHINK, *v. i.* To make a small sharp sound, as by the collision of little pieces of money, or other sonorous bodies. *Arbuthnot.*

CHINK'APIN, *n.* The dwarf chestnut, Fagus pumila, a tree that rises eight or ten feet, with a branching shrubby stem, producing a nut.

CHINK'Y, *a.* Full of chinks, or fissures; gaping; opening in narrow clefts. *Dryden.*

CHIN'NED, *a.* Having a long chin. *Kersey.*

CHINSE, *v. t.* In *naval affairs*, to thrust oakum into the seams or chinks of a ship with a chisel or point of a knife, as a temporary expedient for calking. *Mar. Dict.*

CHINTS, *n.* [D. *chits*; G. *zitz*; Sans. *cheet*; Hindoo, *cheent*; Per. *chinz*, spotted, stained.]

Cotton cloth, printed with more than two colors.

CHIOPPI'NE, *n.* [Sp. *chapin*; Port. *chapim.* It is said to be of Arabian origin. It cannot be the L. *crepis*, Gr. χρηπις, unless a letter has been lost.]

A high shoe, formerly worn by ladies. *Shak.*

CHIP, CHEAP, CHIPPING, in the names of places, imply a market; from Sax. *ceapan*, *cypan*, to buy or sell. [See *Cheap.*]

CHIP, *n.* [from the root of *chop.* Fr. *coupeau.*]

1. A piece of wood or other substance, separated from a body by a cutting instrument, particularly by an ax. It is used also for a piece of stone separated by a chisel or other instrument, in hewing.

2. A fragment or piece broken off; a small piece.

CHIP, *v. t.* To cut into small pieces, or chips; to diminish by cutting away a little at a time, or in small pieces; to hew. *Shak.*

CHIP, *v. i.* To break or fly off in small pieces, as in potter's ware.

CHIP-AX, *n.* An ax for chipping.

CHIP'PED, *pp.* Cut in chips, or small pieces; hewed.

CHIP'PING, *ppr.* Cutting off in small pieces.

CHIP'PING, *n.* A chip; a piece cut off or separated by a cutting or engraving instrument; a fragment.

2. The flying or breaking off in small pieces, of the edges of potter's ware, and porcelain. *Encyc.*

CHIRAG'RICAL, *a.* [from *chiragra*, hand-gout, Gr. χειρ, the hand, and αγρα, seizure.]

Having the gout in the hand, or subject to that disease. *Brown.*

CHIRK, *a. churk.* [Probably allied to *chirp*; D. *circken*, obs. Chaucer uses the verb, to *chirk*, in the sense of *chirp* or chatter. The word is found in the Russ. *chirkayu*, to chirp. It is in popular use in New-England.]

Lively; cheerful; in good spirits; in a comfortable state.

CHIRK, *v. i.* To chirp. *Obs.* *Chaucer.*

CHIRM, *v. i.* [Sax. *cyrman.*] To sing as a bird. [*Not in use.*]

CHI'ROGRAPH, *n.* [Gr. χειρ, the hand, and γραφω, to write.]

1. Anciently a deed, which, requiring a counterpart, was engrossed twice on the same piece of parchment, with a space between, in which was written *chirograph*, through which the parchment was cut, and one part given to each party. It answered to what is now called a *charter-party*. *Encyc.*

2. A fine, so called from the manner of engrossing, which is still retained in the chirographer's office in England. *Ibm.*

CHIROG'RAPHER, *n.* [See *Chirograph.*] He that exercises or professes the art or business of writing. In England, the chirographer of fines is an officer in the common pleas, who engrosses fines acknowledged in that court, and delivers the indentures to the parties. *Encyc.*

CHIROGRAPH'IC, CHIROGRAPH'ICAL, } *a.* Pertaining to chirography.

CHIROG'RAPHIST, *n.* One who tells fortunes by examining the hand. [*Not a legitimate word.*] *Arbuthnot.*

CHIROG'RAPHY, *n.* [See *Chirograph.*] The art of writing, or a writing with one's own hand.

CHIROLOĠ'ICAL, *a.* Pertaining to chirology.

CHIROL'OĠIST, *n.* [Gr. χειρ, the hand, and λογος, discourse.]

One who communicates thoughts by signs made with the hands and fingers.

CHIROL'OĠY, *n.* [See *Chirologist.*] The art or practice of communicating thoughts by signs made by the hands and fingers; a substitute for language or discourse, much used by the deaf and dumb, and by others who communicate with them. *Bailey.*

CHIR'OMANCER, *n.* [See *Chiromancy.*] One who attempts to foretell future events, or to tell the fortunes and dispositions of persons, by inspecting the hands. *Dryden.*

CHIR'OMANCY, *n.* [Gr. χειρ, the hand, and μαντεια, divination.]

Divination by the hand; the art or practice of attempting to foretell events, or to discover the dispositions of a person, by inspecting the lines and lineaments of his hand. *Brown.*

CHIROMAN'TIC, *a.* Pertaining to chiromancy, or divination by the hand.

Chiromantic deception. *Grellman.*

CHIRP, *v. i. cherp.* [Ger. *zirpen.*] To make the noise of certain small birds, or of certain insects; as a *chirping* lark, or cricket. *Thomson.*

CHIRP, *v. t.* To make cheerful. *Pope.*

CHIRP, *n.* A particular voice of certain birds or insects. *Spectator.*

CHIRP'ER, *n.* One that chirps, or is cheerful.

CHIRP'ING, *ppr.* Making the noise of certain small birds.

CHIRP'ING, *n.* The noise of certain small birds and insects.

CHIRUR'ĠEON, *n.* [Gr. χειρουργος, one who operates with the hand, χειρ, the hand, and εργον, work; L. *chirurgus;* Fr. *chirurgien;* Sp. *cirujano;* Port. *surgiam*, or *cirurgiam;* It. *chirurgo;* Arm. *surgyan.*]

A surgeon; one whose profession is to heal diseases by manual operations, instruments or external applications. [This ill-sounding word is obsolete, and it now appears in the form of *surgeon*, which see.]

CHIRUR'ĠERY, *n.* [Gr. χειρουργια. See *Chirurgeon.*]

That part of the medical art which consists in healing diseases and wounds by instruments and external applications; now written *surgery.*

CHIRUR'ĠIC, CHIRUR'ĠICAL, } *a.* Pertaining to surgery, or to the art of healing diseases and wounds by manual operations, instruments or external applications.

2. Having qualities useful in external applications, for healing diseases or injuries.

It is now written *surgical.*

CHIS'EL, *n. s* as *z.* [Fr. *ciseau*, a chisel; *ciseler*, to engrave; Arm. *gisell;* Sp. *cincel;* Heb. גזז, Ch. גזם, or גזא, or Ar. جَزَّ chazza, to cut, hew, carve. See Class Gs.]

An instrument of iron or steel, used in carpentry, joinery, cabinet work, masonry, sculpture, &c., either for paring, hewing or gouging. Chisels are of different sizes and shapes, fitted for particular uses.

CHIS'EL, *v. t.* To cut, pare, gouge, or engrave with a chisel.

CHIS'ELED, *pp.* Cut or engraved with a chisel.

CHIS'ELING, *ppr.* Cutting with a chisel.

CHIS'LEU, *n.* [Heb. כסלו, from the Ar. كَسَلَ kasila, to be torpid or cold.]

The ninth month of the Jewish year, answering to a part of November and a part of December, in the modern division of the year.

CHIT, *n.* [Sax. *cith*, a shoot or twig, from thrusting out.]

1. A shoot or sprout; the first shooting or germination of a seed or plant. Hence,

2. A child or babe, in *familiar language.*

3. A freckle, that is, a push.

CHIT, *v. i.* To sprout; to shoot, as a seed or plant.

CHIT'-CHAT, *n.* [See *Chat, Chatter.*]

Prattle; familiar or trifling talk.

CHIT'TERLING, *n.* The frill to the breast of a shirt. *Gascoigne.*

CHIT'TERLINGS, *n. plu.* [G. *kuttel*, probably from the root of *gut.*]

The guts or bowels; sausages.

Johnson. Bailey.

CHIT'TY, *a.* Childish; like a babe. *Johnson.*

2. Full of chits or warts.

CHIV'ALROUS, *a.* [See *Chivalry.*] Pertaining to chivalry, or knight errantry; warlike; bold; gallant. *Spenser.*

CHIV'ALRY, *n.* [Fr. *chevalerie*, from *chevalier*, a knight or horseman, from *cheval*, a horse; Sp. *caballeria;* It. *cavalleria.* See *Cavalry.*]

1. Knighthood; a military dignity, founded on the service of soldiers on horseback, called knights; a service formerly deemed more honorable than service in infantry. *Bacon.*

2. The qualifications of a knight, as valor and dexterity in arms. *Shak.*

3. The system of knighthood; the privileges, characteristics or manners of knights; the practice of knight-errantry, or the heroic defense of life and honor. *Dryden.*

4. An adventure or exploit, as of a knight. *Sidney.*

5. The body or order of knights. *Shak.*

6. In *English law*, a tenure of lands by knight's service; that is, by the condition of performing service on horseback, or of performing some noble or military service to his lord. This was general or special; *general*, when the tenant held *per servitium militare*, without specification of the particular service; *special*, when the particular service was designated. When the tenant held only of the king, the tenure was *regal;* when he held of a common person, it was called *common.* This service was also *grand sergeantry*, as when the tenant was bound to perform service to the king in his own person; and *petit sergeantry*, when he was bound to yield to the king annually some small thing, as a sword or dagger. Chivalry that might be held of a common person, was called *escuage, scutagium*, or shield service. *Blackstone.*

Court of chivalry, a court formerly held before the Lord High Constable and Earl Marshal of England, having cognizance of contracts and other matters relating to deeds of arms and war. It had jurisdiction both of civil and criminal causes, but no power to enforce its decisions by fine or imprisonment, not being a court of record. It is now nearly extinct. *Blackstone.*

CHIVE, *n.* [Fr. *cive;* L. *cepa.*] A species of small onion.

CHIVES, *n. plu.* In *botany*, slender threads or filaments in the blossoms of plants. [See *Stamen.*]

CHLO'RATE, *n.* [See *Chlorine.*] A compound of chloric acid with a salifiable base. *Ure.*

CHLO'RIC, *a.* Pertaining to chlorine, or obtained from it; as *chloric* acid. *Ure.*

CHLO'RIDE, CHLO'RID, } *n.* [See *Chlorine.*] A compound of chlorine with a combustible body. *Ure.*

CHLORID'IC, *a.* Pertaining to a chloride. *Ure.*

CHLO'RINE, CHLO'RIN, } *n.* [Gr. χλωρος, green; so named from its color.]

Chloric gas; a new name given to what has been called oxymuriatic gas. This substance has hitherto resisted all efforts to decompose it, and as it is not known to contain oxygen, and is apparently a simple substance, it has been denominated from its color, *chlorine*, or chloric gas. *Davy.*

CHLORIOD'IC, *a.* Consisting of chlorine and iodine, or obtained from them. *Davy.*

CHLO'RIS, *n.* [Gr. χλωρος, green.] The green finch, a small bird.

CHLO'RITE, *n.* [Gr. χλωρος, green.]

A mineral of a grass green color, opake, usually friable or easily pulverized, composed of little spangles, scales, prisms or shining small grains. It is classed by Kirwan with the muriatic genus. There are four subspecies, chlorite earth, common chlorite, chlorite slate, and foliated chlorite. *Ure. Kirwan.*

ЄHLORO-ЄARBON'IЄ, } *a.* The terms, ЄHLORO-Є'ARBONOUS, } *chloro-carbonic acid* and *chloro-carbonous acid*, are applied, the former by Thomson, and the latter by Ure, to a compound of chlorine and carbonic oxyd, formed by exposing a mixture of the two gases to the direct solar rays. It was discovered by Dr. J. Davy, and called by him *phosgene gas.*

ЄHLORO'PAL, *n.* [green opal.] A newly observed mineral, of two varieties, the conchoidal and the earthy; the conchoidal is of a pistachio green color; the other has an earthy fracture, and both varieties are possessed of magnetic properties. *Phillips.*

ЄHLO'ROPHANE, *n.* [Gr. χλωρος, green, and φαινω, to show.]
A variety of fluor spar, from Siberia. When placed on a heated iron, it gives a beautiful emerald green light. *Cleaveland. Cyc.*

ЄHLO'ROPHEITE, *n.* [Gr. χλωρος, green, and φαιος, blackish.]
A rare mineral found in small nodules. *Cleaveland.*

ЄHLO'ROPHYL, *n.* [Gr. χλωρος, green, and φυλλον, leaf.]
The green matter of the leaves of vegetables. *Pelletier.*

ЄHLORO'SIS, *n.* [Gr. χλωρος, green.] The green sickness; a disease of females, characterized by a pale or greenish hue of the skin, weakness, palpitation, dyspepsy, &c. *Coxe.*

ЄHLOROT'IЄ, *a.* Pertaining to chlorosis; as, *chlorotic* affections. *Medical Repository.*
2. Affected by chlorosis; as, *chlorotic* nuns. *Battie.*

ЄHLO'ROUS, *a.* Pertaining to chlorine; as *chlorous* oxyd.

CHOAK, [See *Choke.*]

CHOCK, *n.* [from *choke.*] In *marine language*, a kind of wedge for confining a cask or other body, to prevent it from moving.
Chocks of the rudder, are pieces of timber kept in readiness to stop the motion of the rudder, in case of an accident, &c. *Mar. Dict.*

CHOCK, an encounter. [See *Shock.*]

CHOЄ'OLATE, *n.* [Fr. *chocolat;* Sp. Port. *chocolate;* It. *cioccolata;* from *cacao.*]
1. A paste or cake composed of the kernel of cacao, with other ingredients, usually a little sugar, cinnamon or vanilla. The nut is first ground fine, mixed with the ingredients, and put in a mold.
2. The liquor made by dissolving chocolate in boiling water.

CHOЄ'OLATE-HOUSE, *n.* A house where company may be served with chocolate.

CHOЄ'OLATE-NUT. [See *Cacao.*]

CHODE, the old preterit of *chide*, which see.

CHOICE, *n.* [Fr. *choix;* Arm. *choas;* Sax. *cyse;* D. *keus.* See *Choose.*]
1. The act of choosing; the voluntary act of selecting or separating from two or more things that which is preferred; or the determination of the mind in preferring one thing to another; election.

Ye know how that a good while ago God made *choice* among us, that the Gentiles by my mouth should hear the word of the gospel, and believe. Acts xv.

2. The power of choosing; option.

Where there is force, there can be no *choice.*
Of these alternatives we have our own *choice.* *Anon.*

3. Care in selecting; judgment or skill in distinguishing what is to be preferred, and in giving a preference.

I imagine Cesar's apothems were collected with judgment and *choice.* *Bacon.*

4. The thing chosen; that which is approved and selected in preference to others; selection.

Nor let thy conquests only be her *choice.* *Prior.*

5. The best part of any thing; that which is preferable, and properly the object of choice.

In the *choice* of our sepulchers bury thy dead. Gen. xxiii.

6. The act of electing to office by vote; election.
To make choice of, to choose; to select; to separate and take in preference.

CHOICE, *a.* Worthy of being preferred; select; precious; very valuable.

My *choicest* hours of life are lost. *Swift.*
My revenue is better than *choice* silver. Prov. viii.

2. Holding dear; preserving or using with care, as valuable; frugal; as, to be *choice* of time or of advantages.
3. Selecting with care, and due attention to preference; as, to be *choice* of one's company.

CHOICE-DRAWN, *a.* Selected with particular care. *Shak.*

CHOICE'LESS, *a. chois'less.* Not having the power of choosing; not free. *Hammond.*

CHOICE'LY, *adv. chois'ly.* With care in choosing; with nice regard to preference; with exact choice; as a band of men *choicely* collected.
2. Valuably; excellently; preferably; curiously.
3. With great care; carefully; as a thing *choicely* preserved.

CHOICE'NESS, *n. chois'ness.* Valuableness; particular value or worth; as the *choiceness* of a plant or of wine.

ЄHOIR, *n. quire.* [L. *chorus;* Gr. χορος; Fr. *chœur;* Sp. Port. It. *coro;* Sax. *chor;* D. *choor;* G. *chor;* Ar. كَرَ to go round, to collect or bind. See *Chorus.*]
1. A collection of singers, especially in divine service, in a church.
2. Any collection of singers.
3. That part of a church appropriated for the singers, separated from the chancel and the nave. In congregational and some other churches, the singers are placed in certain seats in the galleries.
4. In *nunneries*, a large hall adjoining to the body of the church, separated by a grate, where the nuns sing the office.

ЄHOIR-SERVICE, *n.* The service of singing performed by a choir. *Warton.*

CHOKE, *v. t.* [Sax. *aceocan.* In Arm. *coucq* or *goucq* is the neck, with which *choke* may be connected, in the sense of narrowness or compression. The sense of *choke* is to stuff, thrust down or stop; or to compress, or bind tight. [The Sp. *ahogar* is the Port. *afogar*, L. *suffoco.*] It is probably allied to the Sp. *cegar*, to shut, L. *cæcus*, Eng. *key*, Sax. *cæg.*]
1. To stop the passage of the breath, by filling the windpipe or compressing the neck. The word is used to express a temporary or partial stoppage, as to *choke* with dirt or smoke; or an entire stoppage that causes death; to suffocate; to strangle. Mark v.
2. To stop by filling; to obstruct; to block up; as, to *choke* the entrance of a harbor, or any passage.
3. To hinder by obstruction or impediments; to hinder or check growth, expansion, or progress; as, to *choke* plants; to *choke* the spreading of the fruit. *Bacon.*

Thorns *choke* them. Matt. xiii. Luke viii.

4. To smother or suffocate, as fire. *Dryden.*
5. To suppress or stifle; as, to *choke* the strong conception. *Shak.*
6. To offend; to cause to take an exception; as, I was *choked* at this word. *Swift.*
We observe that this word generally implies crowding, stuffing or covering. A channel is *choked* by stones and sand, but not by a boom.

CHOKE, *v. i.* To have the wind-pipe stopped; as, cattle are apt to *choke* when eating potatoes.
2. To be offended; to take exceptions.

CHOKE, *n.* The filamentous or capillary part of the artichoke. *Johnson.*

CHO'KE-CHERRY, *n.* The popular name of a species of wild cherry, remarkable for its astringent qualities.

CHO'KED, *pp.* Suffocated; strangled; obstructed by filling; stifled; suppressed; smothered.

CHO'KE-FULL, *a.* [*choke* and *full.*] Full as possible; quite full.

CHO'KE-PEAR, *n.* A kind of pear that has a rough astringent taste, and is swallowed with difficulty, or which contracts the parts of the mouth.
2. An aspersion or sarcasm by which a person is put to silence. [*A low term.*] *Clarissa.*

CHO'KER, *n.* One that chokes another; one that puts another to silence; that which cannot be answered. *Johnson.*

CHO'KE-WEED, *n.* A plant so called.

CHO'KY, *a.* That tends to suffocate, or has power to suffocate.

ЄHOL'AGOGUE, *n. col'agog.* [Gr. χοληγαγος, from χολη, bile.]
A medicine that has the specific quality of evacuating the bile.

ЄHOL'ER, *n.* [L. *cholera;* Gr. χολερα, from χολη, bile.]
1. The bile. By the superabundance of this fluid, anger was formerly supposed to be produced; or perhaps the opinion was that the bile caused the inflamed appearance of the face in anger. Hence,
2. Anger; wrath; irritation of the passions.
Cholera Morbus, a sudden evacuation of bile, both upwards and downwards.

ЄHOL'ERIЄ, *a.* Abounding with choler. *Dryden.*
2. Easily irritated; irascible; inclined to anger; as a *choleric* man.

3. Angry; indicating anger; excited by anger; as a *choleric* speech. *Raleigh*

ȻHOL'ERIȻNESS, *n.* Irascibility; anger; peevishness.

ȻHOLES'TERIȻ, *a.* Pertaining to cholesterin, or obtained from it; as *cholesteric* acid. *Ure.*

ȻHOLES'TERINE, } *n.* [Gr. χολη, bile, and
ȻHOLES'TERIN, } γερεος, solid.]
A name given by M. Chevreul, to the pearly or crystaline substance of human biliary calculi.

ȻHOLIAM'BIȻ, *n.* [L. *choliambi.*] A verse in poetry having an iambic foot in the fifth place, and a spondee in the sixth or last. *Bentley.*

ȻHON'DRODITE, *n.* A mineral, called also Brucite. It occurs in grains or imperfect crystals, or in four-sided prisms with rhombic bases, truncated on the two acute lateral edges. It is translucent; and its color varies from reddish or amber yellow to grayish brown. *Cleaveland.*

CHOOSE, *v. t. s* as *z.* pret. *chose*; pp. *chosen, chose.* [Sax. *ceosan*; D. *kiezen*; G. *kiesen*; Sw. *kesa*; Ice. *kioosa*; Fr. *choisir*; Arm. *choasa*; Pers. *ghozidan.* The Hebrew has קשש to collect. See Class Gs. No. 40. 70. 71.]

1. To pick out; to select; to take by way of preference from two or more things offered; to make choice of.

The man the Lord doth *choose* shall be holy. Num. xvi.

Refuse the evil and *choose* the good.

2. To take in preference.

Let us *choose* to us judgment. Job xxxiv.

3. To prefer; to choose for imitation; to follow.

Envy not the oppressor, and *choose* none of his ways. Prov. iii.

4. To elect for eternal happiness; to predestinate to life.

Many are called but few *chosen.* Matt. xx.

For his elect's sake, whom he hath *chosen.* Mark xiii.

5. To elect or designate to office or employment by votes or suffrages. In *the United States*, the people *choose* representatives by votes, usually by ballot.

CHOOSE, *v. i.* To prefer; as, I *choose* to go.

2. To have the power of choice. The phrase, he cannot *choose* but stay, denotes that he has not the power of choice, whether to stay or not.

The verb, in these phrases, is really transitive; the following verb standing as the object, instead of a noun.

CHOOS'ER, *n.* He that chooses; he that has the power or right of choosing; an elector.

CHOOS'ING, *ppr.* Selecting; taking in preference; electing.

CHOOS'ING, *n.* Choice; election.

CHOP, *v. t.* [G. and D. *kappen*; Dan. *kapper*; Gr. κοπτω; Fr. *couper*; Norm. *copper*, or *couper*; Ar. كبح or كيف to cut. Class Gb. No. 47. 51.]

1. To cut off or separate, by striking with a sharp instrument, either by a single blow or by repeated blows; as, to *chop* off a head; to *chop* wood.

2. To cut into small pieces; to mince; as, to *chop* meat; to *chop* straw.

3. To grind and mince with the teeth; to devour eagerly; with *up*; as, to *chop up* an entertainment. *Dryden.*

4. To break or open into chinks or fissures; to crack; to *chap.* [See *Chap.*]

CHOP, *v. i.* To catch or attempt to seize with the mouth. [*Not used.*]

To *chop* at the shadow and lose the substance. *L'Estrange.*

2. To light or fall on suddenly. *Johnson.*

[If this is a legitimate sense, it indicates that the primary sense is, to throw, thrust, or strike. It is not in common use.]

To chop in, to become modish. [*Not used.*] *Wilson.*

To chop out, to give vent to. [*Not used.*] *Beaum.*

CHOP, *v. t.* [Sax. *ceapian*, *cypan*, to buy or sell. See *Cheap.*]

1. To buy, or rather to barter, truck, exchange.

2. To exchange; to put one thing in the place of another; as, to *chop* and change our friends. *L'Estrange.*

3. To bandy; to altercate; to return one word or thing for another.

Let not the council *chop* with the judge. *Bacon.*

CHOP, *v. i.* To turn, vary, change or shift suddenly; as in the seaman's phrase, the wind *chops*, or *chops about.*

[The various senses of this verb seem to center in that of thrusting, driving, or a sudden motion or exertion of force.]

CHOP, *n.* A piece chopped off; a small piece of meat; as a mutton *chop.*

2. A crack or cleft. See *Chap*, which, with the broad sound of *a*, is often pronounced *chop.*

3. The chap; the jaw: plu. the jaws; the mouth; the sides of a river's mouth or channel. [See *Chap.*]

CHOP'-CHURCH, *n.* An exchange or an exchanger of benefices.

CHOP'-FALLEN, *a.* Dejected; dispirited.

CHOP'-HOUSE, *n.* A house where provision ready dressed is sold.

CHO'PIN, *n.* [Fr. *chopine.*] A liquid measure in France, containing nearly a pint Winchester measure. In Scotland, a quart of wine measure.

CHOP'PED, *pp.* Cut; minced.

CHOP'PING, *ppr.* Cutting; mincing; buying; bartering.

CHOP'PING, *a.* Stout; lusty; plump.

CHOP'PING, *n.* [Sp. *chapin.*] A high-heeled shoe, worn by ladies in Italy. [See *Chioppine.*]

2. A cutting; a mincing; from *chop.*

CHOP'PING-BLOCK, *n.* A block on which any thing is laid to be chopped.

CHOP'PING-KNIFE, *n.* A knife for mincing meat.

CHOP'PY, *a.* Full of clefts or cracks.

CHOPS, [See *Chop.*]

ȻHO'RAL, *a.* [from *chorus.*] Belonging to or composing a choir or concert; as, *choral* symphonies. *Milton.*

2. Singing in a choir; as, *choral* seraphs. *Amhurst.*

ȻHO'RALLY, *adv.* In the manner of a chorus. *Mason.*

ȻHORD, *n.* [L. *chorda*; Gr. χορδη, an intestine, of which strings were made. When it signifies a string or small rope, in general, it is written *cord.* See *Cord.*]

1. The string of a musical instrument. *Milton.*

2. In *music*, the union of two or more sounds uttered at the same time, forming an entire harmony; as a third, fifth and eighth, which are *perfect* chords, or consonancies. The fourth and sixth are *imperfect* chords.

3. In *geometry*, a right line drawn or supposed to extend from one end of an arch of a circle to the other. Hence the chord of an arch is a right line joining the extremities of that arch. *Encyc.*

ȻHORD, *v. t.* To string. *Dryden.*

ȻHORDEE', *n.* [See *Chord.*] In *medicine* and *surgery*, an inflammatory or spasmodic contraction of the frænum, attending gonorrhea and accompanied with pain. *Coxe. Encyc.*

CHORE, *n.* [Eng. *char.*] In America, this word denotes small work of a domestic kind, as distinguished from the principal work of the day. It is generally used in the plural, *chores*, which includes the daily or occasional business of feeding cattle and other animals, preparing fuel, sweeping the house, cleaning furniture, &c. [See *Char.*]

ȻHOREPIS'ȻOPAL, *a.* [Gr. χωρος, place, and επισκοπος, bishop.]
Pertaining to the power of a suffragan or local bishop. *Fell.*

ȻHORE'US, *n.* [Gr. χορειος.] In *ancient poetry*, a foot of two syllables, the first long and the second short; the trochee.

ȻHOR'IAMB, } *n.* [Gr. χορειος, a trochee,
ȻHORIAM'BUS, } and ιαμβος, iambus.]
In *ancient poetry*, a foot consisting of four syllables, of which the first and last are long, and the others short; that is, a choreus or trochee and an iambus united; as, *nobilitas, anxietas.* *Encyc.*

ȻHORIAM'BIȻ, *n.* A choriamb.

ȻHORIAM'BIȻ, *a.* Pertaining to a choriamb. *Mason.*

ȻHO'RION, *n.* [Gr. χοριον, or χωριον; the latter seems to be allied to χωρεω, to hold, or contain.]
In *anatomy*, the exterior membrane which invests the fetus in utero.

ȻHO'RIST, *n.* [Fr. *choriste.*] A singing man in a choir.

ȻHOR'ISTER, *n.* [from *chorus, choir.*]
Literally, a singer; one of a choir; a singer in a concert. *Dryden.*

2. One who leads a choir in church music. This is the sense in the United States.

ȻHOROG'RAPHER, *n.* [See *Chorography.*] A person who describes a particular region or country; or one who forms a map or maps of particular regions or countries. *Encyc.*

ȻHOROGRAPH'IȻAL, *a.* Pertaining to chorography; descriptive of particular regions or countries; laying down or marking the bounds of particular countries. *Encyc.*

ȻHOROGRAPH'IȻALLY, *adv.* In a chorographical manner; in a manner descriptive of particular regions.

ȻHOROG'RAPHY, *n.* [Gr. χωρος, a place or region, and γραφω, to describe.]
The art or practice of making a map of a particular region, country, or province; or of marking its limits, bounds or position. *Chorography* differs from *geography*, as the description of a particular country differs

from that of the whole earth; and from *topography*, as the description of a country differs from that of a town, city or district. *Encyc.*

ϾHO'ROID, *n.* [Gr. χοριον, a particular membrane, and ειδος, likeness.]

In *anatomy*, a term applied to several parts of the body that resemble the chorion; as the inner membrane investing the brain, or the pia mater; the second coat of the eye; the fold of the carotid artery in the brain, in which is the pineal gland. *Coxe. Encyc.*

ϾHO'RUS, *n.* [L. *chorus;* Gr. χορος; Sax. *chor;* Fr. *chœur;* D. *choor* or *koor;* Sp. It. *coro;* Ir. *cora;* W. *côr.* In Welsh, the word signifies a round or circle, a choir. If the primary sense is a circle, or a company, the word may be referred to the Ar. كار kaura, to go round, to collect, to bind, or to كر karra, to return, to repeat. Class Gr. No. 32. 34. If the radical sense is to sing or shout, it may be allied to Gr. χαιρω. The former is most probable.]

1. A number of singers; a company of persons singing in concert. *Dryden. Pope. Addison.*
2. The persons who are supposed to behold what passes in the acts of a tragedy, and sing their sentiments between the acts. *Shak. Johnson.*
3. The song between the acts of a tragedy. *Johnson.*
4. Verses of a song in which the company join the singer; or the union of a company with a singer, in repeating certain couplets or verses, at certain periods in a song. *Johnson. Encyc.*
5. A musical composition of two or more parts.
6. Among the Greeks, a chorus consisted of a number of singers and dancers.

ČHOSE, *n.* [Fr. *chose;* Sp. *cosa,* suit, cause, thing; It. *cosa;* Port. *cousa;* L. *causa.* See *Cause.* The primary sense is, action, urging, prosecution. See *Thing* and *Cause.*]

In *law*, property in action; a right to possession; or that which may be demanded and recovered by suit or action at law. Thus, money due on a bond or note is a *chose in action;* a recompense for damage done is a *chose in action;* the former proceeding from an *express,* the latter from an *implied* contract. A contract executed is a *chose in possession;* a contract executory conveys only a *chose in action.* A *chose local* is annexed to a place, as a mill or the like; a *chose transitory* is a thing which is movable. *Blackstone. Encyc.*

CHOSE, *s* as *z*, *pret.* and *pp.* of *choose.*

CHO'SEN, *pp. cho'zn.* Selected from a number; picked out; taken in preference; elected; predestinated; designated to office.

2. *a.* Select; distinguished by preference; eminent.

> His *chosen* captains are drowned in the sea. Ex. xv.
>
> Ye are a *chosen* generation, a royal priesthood. 1 Pet. ii.

CHOUGH, *n. chuff.* [Fr. *choucas;* Ir. *cag;* Sax. *ceo* or *ceogh.* This word may be the same as *jack*, in jackdaw. It appears to be a Cornish word.]

The *Cornish chough* is a fowl of the genus *Corvus*, nearly of the size of the crow, and mischievous, like the magpie. It is black, except the bill, legs and feet, which are red. It is a native of the west of England. *Dict. of Nat. Hist.*

Chough is also applied to the jackdaw. *Cyc.*

CHOULE. [See *Jowl.*]

CHOUSE, *v. t.* [This word may be from the root of *cozen*, Arm. *couçzein*, or *conche-za.* Ar. خاس gausa, to deceive or defraud; Eth. ሐሰወ chaso, to lie, deceive or cheat.]

To cheat, trick, defraud; followed by *of*, in Hudibras; but in America, by *out of;* as, to *chouse* one *out of* his money. [*It is now vulgar.*] *Dryden. Swift.*

CHOUSE, *n.* One who is easily cheated; a tool; a simpleton.

A trick; sham; imposition. *Johnson.*

CHOUS'ED, *pp.* Cheated; defrauded; imposed on.

CHOUS'ING, *ppr.* Cheating; imposing on.

CHOW'DER, *n.* In *New England*, a dish of fish boiled with biscuit, &c. In Spanish, *chode* is a paste made of milk, eggs, sugar and flour. In the west of England, *chowder-beer* is a liquor made by boiling black spruce in water and mixing with it melasses.

CHOW'DER, *v. t.* To make a chowder.

CHOW'TER, *v. t.* To grumble like a frog or a froward child. *Phillips.*

ϾHRISM, *n.* [Gr. χρισμα, from χριω, to anoint.]

Unguent; unction. In the Romish and Greek churches, oil consecrated by the bishop, and used in the administration of baptism, confirmation, ordination, and extreme unction. It is prepared on holy Thursday with much ceremony, and in some cases, mixed with balsam. *Encyc.*

ϾHRIS'MAL, *a.* Pertaining to chrism. *Brevint.*

ϾHRISMA'TION, *n.* The act of applying the chrism, or consecrated oil; in baptism, by the priest; in confirmation, by the bishop. In ordination, it is usually styled *unction.* *Encyc.*

ϾHRIS'MATORY, *n.* A vessel to hold the oil for chrism.

ϾHRIS'OM, *n.* [See *Chrism.*] A child that dies within a month after its birth; so called from the chrisom-cloth, a linen cloth anointed with holy oil, which was formerly laid over a child's face when it was baptized. Also, the cloth itself. *Encyc.*

ϾHRIST, *n.* [Gr. χριςος, anointed, from χριω, to anoint.]

The anointed; an appellation given to the Savior of the world, and synonymous with the Hebrew Messiah. It was a custom of antiquity to consecrate persons to the sacerdotal and regal offices by anointing them with oil.

ϾHRIS'TEN, *v. t. kris'n.* [Sax. *cristnian;* D. *kerstenen.* See *Christ.*]

1. To baptize, or rather to baptize and name; to initiate into the visible church of Christ by the application of water; *applied to persons.* And as a name is given to the person in the ceremony, hence,
2. To name; to denominate; *applied to things.* *Burnet.*

ϾHRIS'TENDOM, *n. kris'ndom.* [Sax. *cristendom, cristen,* christian, and *dom,* power, judgment, rule, jurisdiction. See *Christ.*]

1. The territories, countries or regions inhabited by christians, or those who profess to believe in the christian religion.
2. The whole body of christians. *Hooker.*
3. Christianity; the christian religion; as, while *christendom* prevailed. [*Unusual.*] *Milner.*

ϾHRIS'TENED, *pp. kris'nd.* Baptized and named; initiated into christianity.

ϾHRIS'TENING, *ppr. kris'ening.* Baptizing and naming.

ϾHRIS'TENING, *n.* The act or ceremony of baptizing and naming; initiation into the christian religion.

ϾHRIS'TIAN, *n. kryst'yan.* [Gr. χριςιανος; L. *christianus;* Sax. *cristen;* D. *kristen;* Fr. *chrétien;* Sp. *christiano;* Arm. *cristen;* W. *cristian.* See *Christ.*]

1. A believer in the religion of Christ.
2. A professor of his belief in the religion of Christ.
3. A real disciple of Christ; one who believes in the truth of the christian religion, and studies to follow the example, and obey the precepts, of Christ; a believer in Christ who is characterized by real piety.
4. In *a general sense,* the word *christians* includes all who are born in a christian country or of christian parents.

ϾHRIS'TIAN, *a.* [See the Noun.] Pertaining to Christ, taught by him, or received from him; as the *christian* religion; *christian* doctrines.

2. Professing the religion of Christ; as a *christian* friend.
3. Belonging to the religion of Christ; relating to Christ, or to his doctrines, precepts and example; as *christian* profession and practice.
4. Pertaining to the church; ecclesiastical; as courts *christian.* *Blackstone.*

ϾHRIS'TIAN, *v. t.* To baptize. [*Not used.*] *Fulke.*

ϾHRIS'TIANISM, *n.* [Gr. χριςιανισμος. See *Christ.*]

1. The christian religion.
2. The nations professing christianity. *Johnson.*

ϾHRIS'TIANITE, *n.* A newly discovered Vesuvian mineral; its primitive form is that of an oblique rectangular prism; its colors brown, yellow or reddish. *Journ. of Science.*

ϾHRISTIAN'ITY, *n.* [See *Christian*, from *Christ.*]

The religion of christians; or the system of doctrines and precepts taught by Christ, and recorded by the evangelists and apostles.

> Whilst politicians are disputing about monarchies, aristocracies, and republics, *christianity* is alike applicable, useful and friendly to them all. *Paley.*

ϾHRIS'TIANIZE, *v. t.* To make christian; to convert to christianity; as, to *christianize* pagans.

ϾHRIS'TIANLIKE, *a.* Becoming a christian. *Shak.*

ϾHRIS'TIANLY, *adv.* In a christian manner; in a manner becoming the principles of the christian religion, or the profession of that religion.

ЄHRIS'TIAN-NAME, *n.* The name given in baptism, as distinct from the gentilitious or surname.

ЄHRISTIANOG'RAPHY, *n.* A description of christian nations. [*Not used.*] *Pagitt.*

ЄHRIST'MAS, *n.* [*Christ* and *mass*, Sax. *mæssa*, a holy day or feast; D. *kersmis.*]

1. The festival of the christian church observed annually on the 25th day of December, in memory of the birth of Christ, and celebrated by a particular church service. The festival includes twelve days.

2. Christmas-day.

ЄHRIST'MAS-BOX, *n.* A box in which little presents are deposited at christmas.

ЄHRIST'MAS-DAY, *n.* The twenty fifth day of December, when christmas is celebrated.

ЄHRISTMAS-FLOWER, *n.* Hellebore.

ЄHRIST'MAS-ROSE, *n.* A plant of the genus Helleborus, producing beautiful white flowers about Christmas.

ЄHRIST'S-THORN, *n.* The *Rhamnus paliurus*, a deciduous shrub, a native of Palestine and the South of Europe. It has two thorns at each joint, and is supposed to have been the sort of which the crown of thorns for our Savior was made. *Encyc. Hanbury.*

ЄHROAS'TACES, *n.* [Gr. χροα, color.] In *natural history*, a genus of pellucid gems, comprehending all those of variable colors, as viewed in different lights. [*Not technical.*] *Encyc.*

ЄHRO'MATE, *n.* [See *Chrome.*] A salt or compound formed by the chromic acid with a base.

ЄHROMAT'IЄ *a.* [Gr. χρωματικος, from χρωμα, color, from χρωζω, to color. Χροα, χροιζω, seem to be a dialectical orthography of the same word.]

1. Relating to color. *Dryden.*

2. Noting a particular species of music, which proceeds by several semitones in succession. *Encyc. Busby.*

ЄHROMAT'IЄ, *n.* [Supra.] A kind of music that proceeds by several consecutive semitones, or semitonic intervals. *Rousseau.*

ЄHROMAT'IЄALLY, *adv.* In the chromatic manner.

ЄHROMAT'IЄS, *n.* The science of colors; that part of optics which treats of the properties of the colors of light and of natural bodies. *Encyc.*

ЄHROME, *n.* [Gr. χρωμα, color.] A metal consisting of a porous mass of agglutinated grains, very hard, brittle, and of a grayish white color. Its texture is radiated. In its highest degree of oxydation, it passes into the state of an acid, of a ruby red color. It takes its name from the various and beautiful colors which its oxyd and acid communicate to minerals into whose composition they enter. Chrome is employed to give a fine deep green to the enamel of porcelain, to glass, &c.

The oxyd of Chrome is of a bright grass green or pale yellow color. *Cleaveland.*

ЄHRO'MIЄ, *a.* Pertaining to chrome, or obtained from it; as *chromic* acid.

Chromic yellow, the artificial chromate of lead, a beautiful pigment.

ЄHRON'IЄ, ЄHRON'IЄAL, } *a.* [Fr. *chronique*; It. Sp. *cronico*; Gr. χρονικος, from χρονος, time, duration. See Ar. قرن. Class Rn. No. 15.]

Continuing a long time, as a disease. A *chronic* disease is one which is inveterate or of long continuance, in distinction from an *acute* disease, which speedily terminates.

ЄHRON'IЄLE, *n.* [See *Chronic.*] A historical account of facts or events disposed in the order of time. It is nearly synonymous with annals. In general, this species of writing is more strictly confined to chronological order, and is less diffuse than the form of writing called *history*.

2. In a more general sense, a history. *Dryden.*

3. That which contains history.

> Europe—her very ruins tell the history of times gone by, and every moldering stone is a *chronicle.* *Irving.*

4. Chronicles, *plu.* Two books of the Old Testament.

ЄHRON'IЄLE, *v.t.* To record in history, or chronicle; to record; to register. *Spenser. Shak.*

ЄHRON'IЄLER, *n.* A writer of a chronicle; a recorder of events in the order of time; a historian.

ЄHRONIQUE, *n.* *chron'ik.* A chronicle. *Addison.*

ЄHRON'OGRAM, *n.* [Gr. χρονος, time, and γραμμα, a letter or writing, from γραφω, to write.]

An inscription in which a certain date or epoch is expressed by numeral letters; as in the motto of a medal struck by Gustavus Adolphus in 1632.

ChrIstVs DVX; ergo trIVMphVs.

ЄHRONOGRAMMAT'IЄ, ЄHRONOGRAMMAT'IЄAL, } *a.* Belonging to a chronogram, or containing one.

ЄHRONOGRAM'MATIST, *n.* A writer of chronograms.

ЄHRONOG'RAPHER, *n.* [Gr. χρονος, time, and γραφω, to describe.]

One who writes concerning time or the events of time; a chronologer. *Tooke.*

ЄHRONOG'RAPHY, *n.* The description of time past. [*Little used.*]

ЄHRONOL'OĠER, ЄHRONOL'OĠIST, } *n.* [See *Chronology.*] A person who attempts to discover the true dates of past events and transactions, and to arrange them under their proper years, or divisions of time, in the order in which they happened.

2. One who studies chronology, or is versed in the science.

ЄHRONOLOĠ'IЄ, ЄHRONOLOĠ'IЄAL, } *a.* Relating to chronology; containing an account of events in the order of time; according to the order of time.

ЄHRONOLOĠ'IЄALLY, *adv.* In a chronological manner; in a manner according with the order of time, the series of events, or rules of chronology.

ЄHRONOL'OĠY, *n.* [Gr. χρονολογια; χρονος, time, and λογος, discourse or doctrine.]

The science of time; the method of measuring, or computing time by regular divisions or periods, according to the revolutions of the sun, or moon; of ascertaining the true periods or years when past events or transactions took place; and arranging them in their proper order according to their dates.

> If history without *chronology* is dark and confused; *chronology* without history is dry and insipid. *A. Holmes.*

ЄHRONOM'ETER, *n.* [Gr. χρονος, time, and μετρον, measure.]

Any instrument that measures time or that divides time into equal portions, or that is used for that purpose, as a clock, watch or dial; particularly an instrument that measures time with great exactness. *Chronoscope* is now rarely used.

ЄHRYS'ALID, *n.* [See *Chrysalis.*]

ЄHRYS'ALIS, *n.* [L. *chrysalis*, Gr. χρυσαλλις, a grub, from its golden color, χρυσος, gold.]

The particular form which butterflies, moths, and some other insects assume, before they arrive at their winged or perfect state. It is called also *aurelia*, from *aurum*, gold. In this form, the animal is in a state of rest or insensibility; having no organs for taking nourishment, nor wings, nor legs. The external covering is cartilaginous, and usually smooth and glossy; sometimes hairy. The name is taken from the yellow color of certain species: but they are of different colors, as green, black, &c.

ЄHRYS'OBERYL, *n.* [Gr. χρυσος, gold, and βηρυλλιον, beryl.]

A siliceous gem, of a dilute yellowish green color. *Kirwan.*

Chrysoberyl, the cymophane of Haüy, is a mineral usually found in round pieces, about the size of a pea; but it is also found crystalized in eight-sided prisms. It is next to the sapphire in hardness, and employed in jewelry. *Ure. Cleaveland.*

ЄHRYS'OЄOLLA, *n.* [Gr. χρυσοκολλα, glue of gold, χρυσος and κολλα; a name given by the Greeks to borax and to mountain green.]

Carbonate of copper, of two subspecies, the blue and the green; formerly called blue and green chrysocolla, also mountain blue and mountain green. It occurs in crystals, stalactites and other forms. *Fourcroy. Cleaveland.*

ЄRYS'OLITE, *n.* [Gr. χρυσος, gold, and λιθος, stone.]

A mineral, called by Haüy and Brongniart, peridote, and by Jameson, prismatic chrysolite. Its prevailing color is some shade of green. It is harder than glass, but less hard than quartz; often transparent, sometimes only translucent. It occurs sometimes in crystals, sometimes in small amorphous masses or grains, and sometimes in rolled pieces. *Cleaveland.*

ЄHRYS'OPRASE, *n.* [Gr. χρυσοπρασος; χρυσος, gold, and πρασον, a leek.]

A mineral, a subspecies of quartz. Its color is commonly apple green, and often extremely beautiful. It is translucent, or sometimes semi-transparent; its fracture even and dull, sometimes a little splintery, sometimes smooth and slightly conchoidal; its hardness little inferior to that of flint. *Cleaveland.*

CHUB, *n.* [This word seems to signify thick head, or a mass or lump. In Pers. *chub* or *chob* is a club. See Class Gb. No. 1 and 2.]

A river fish, called also *cheven*, of the genus Cyprinus. The body is oblong, nearly round; the head and back, green; the sides silvery, and the belly white. It frequents deep holes in rivers shaded by trees; but in warm weather floats near the surface, and furnishes sport for anglers. It is indifferent food. *Dict. Nat. Hist. Encyc.*

CHUB'BED, } *a.* Like a chub; short and
CHUB'BY, } thick.

CHUB'-FACED, *a.* Having a plump round face. *Addison.*

CHUCK, *v. i.* To make the noise of a hen or partridge, when she calls her chickens.

CHUCK, *v. t.* To call, as a hen her chickens.

CHUCK, *v. i.* To jeer; to laugh. [See *Chuckle.*]

CHUCK, *v. t.* [Fr. *choquer;* Russ. *chokayu*, to strike gently; Port. Sp. *chocar.*]

1. To strike, or give a gentle blow; as, to *chuck* one under the chin.

2. To throw, with quick motion, a short distance; to pitch. [*Vulgar.*]

CHUCK, *n.* The voice or call of a hen.

2. A sudden small noise.

3. A word of endearment, corrupted from *chick, chicken.*

CHUCK-FARTHING, *n.* A play in which a farthing is pitched into a hole.

CHUCK'LE, *v. t.* [from *chuck.*] To call, as a hen her chickens.

2. To fondle; to cocker. [Qu. W. *cocru.* See *Cocker.*]

CHUCK'LE, *v. i.* [Ch. חוך chuk or huk, to laugh. See Class Gk. No. 18. and *Giggle.*]

To laugh heartily, or convulsively; to shake with laughter, or to burst into fits of laughter.

CHUCK'LE-HEAD, *n.* A vulgar word in America, denoting a person with a large head, a dunce. Bailey says, a rattling, noisy, empty fellow.

CHUD, *v. t.* To champ; to bite. [*Not in use.*] *Stafford.*

CHU'ET, *n.* Forced meat. *Bacon.*

CHUFF, *n.* [Perhaps W. *cyf*, a stock or stem; *cyfiaw*, to become torpid.]

A clown; a coarse, heavy, dull or surly fellow.

CHUFF'ILY, *adv.* In a rough, surly manner; clownishly.

CHUFF'INESS, *n.* Surliness.

CHUFF'Y, *a.* Blunt; clownish; surly; angry; stomachful. In N. England, this word expresses that displeasure which causes a swelling or surly look and grumbling, rather than heat and violent expressions of anger.

CHUK, *n.* A word used in calling swine. It is the original name of that animal, which our ancestors brought with them from Persia, where it is still in use, Pers. *chuk*, Zend, *chuk*, a hog; Sans. *sugara.* Our ancestors, while in England, adopted the Welsh *hwc*, hog, but *chuck* is retained in our popular name of *woodchuck*, that is, wood hog. This is a remarkable proof of the original seat of the Teutonic nations. I have taken *chuk* from Adelung. The French *cochon* may be the same word.

CHUM, *n.* [Arm. *chomm*, or *chommein*, or *ham*, to dwell, stay, or lodge; Fr. *chômer*, to rest. Qu. Sax. *ham*, home.]

A chamber-fellow; one who lodges or resides in the same room; *a word used in colleges.*

CHUMP, *n.* A short, thick, heavy piece of wood, less than a block. *Johnson.*

CHURCH, *n.* [Sax. *circe, circ* or *cyric;* Scots, *kirk*, which retains the Saxon pronunciation; D. *kerk;* G. *kirche;* Sw. *kyrckia;* Dan. *kirke;* Gr. κυριακον, a temple of God, from κυριακος, pertaining to a Lord, or to our Lord Jesus Christ, from κυριος, a Lord; Russ. *tzerkov.*]

1. A house consecrated to the worship of God, among christians; the Lord's house. This seems to be the original meaning of the word. The Greek εκκλησια, from εκκαλεω, to call out or call together, denotes an assembly or collection. But κυριακος, κυριακον, are from κυριος, Lord, a term applied by the early christians to Jesus Christ; and the house in which they worshipped was named from that title. So κυριακα signifies church goods, bona ecclesiastica; κυριακη, sc. ημερα, the Lord's day, dies dominica.

2. The collective body of christians, or of those who profess to believe in Christ, and acknowledge him to be the Savior of mankind. In this sense, the church is sometimes called the *Catholic* or *Universal Church.* *Johnson. Encyc.*

3. A particular number of christians, united under one form of ecclesiastical government, in one creed, and using the same ritual and ceremonies; as the English *church;* the Gallican *church;* the Presbyterian *church;* the Romish *church;* the Greek *church.*

4. The followers of Christ in a particular city or province; as the *church* of Ephesus, or of Antioch.

5. The disciples of Christ assembled for worship in a particular place, as in a private house. Col. iv. [See No. 9.]

6. The worshipers of Jehovah or the true God, before the advent of Christ; as the Jewish *church.*

7. The body of clergy, or ecclesiastics, in distinction from the laity. Hence, ecclesiastical authority. *Encyc.*

8. An assembly of sacred rulers convened in Christ's name to execute his laws. *Cruden. Brown.*

9. The collective body of christians, who have made a public profession of the christian religion, and who are united under the same pastor; in distinction from those who belong to the same parish, or ecclesiastical society, but have made no profession of their faith.

CHURCH, *v. t.* To perform with any one the office of returning thanks in the church, after any signal deliverance, as from the dangers of childbirth. *Johnson.*

CHURCH-ALE, *n.* A wake or feast commemoratory of the dedication of the church. *Johnson.*

CHURCH-ATTIRE, *n.* The habit in which men officiate in divine service. *Hooker.*

CHURCH-AUTHORITY, *n.* Ecclesiastical power; spiritual jurisdiction. *Atterbury.*

CHURCH-BENCH, *n.* The seat in the porch of a church.

CHURCH-BURIAL, *n.* Burial according to the rites of the church. *Ayliffe.*

CHURCH-DISCIPLINE, *n.* Discipline of the church, intended to correct the offenses of its members.

CHURCH'DOM, *n.* The government or authority of the church.

CHURCH-FOUNDER, *n.* He that builds or endows a church. *Hooker.*

CHURCH-HISTORY, *n.* History of the christian church; ecclesiastical history.

CHURCH'ING, *n.* The act of offering thanks in church after childbirth.

CHURCH-LAND, *n.* Land belonging to a church. *Yelverton.*

CHURCH'LIKE, *a.* Becoming the church.

CHURCH'MAN, *n.* An ecclesiastic or clergyman; one who ministers in sacred things.

2. An episcopalian, as distinguished from a presbyterian or congregationalist, &c.

CHURCH-MEM'BER, *n.* A member in communion with a church; a professor of religion.

CHURCH-MU'SIC, *n.* The service of singing or chanting in a church.

2. Music suited to church service.

CHURCH'SHIP, *n.* Institution of the church. *South.*

CHURCH-WARDEN, *n.* A keeper or guardian of the church, and a representative of the parish. Church-wardens are appointed by the minister, or elected by the parishioners, to superintend the church, its property and concerns, and the behavior of the parishioners. For these and many other purposes, they possess corporate powers. *Johnson. Encyc.*

CHURCH'-WAY, *n.* The way, street or road that leads to the church.

CHURCH'-WORK, *n.* Work carried on slowly. *Todd.*

CHURCH-YARD, *n.* The ground adjoining to a church in which the dead are buried; a cemetery. *ohnson.*

CHURL, *n.* [Sax. *ceorl;* D. *kaerel;* G. *kerl;* Dan. *karl.* It signifies primarily, a man, or rather a male, for it was applied to other animals, as a *carl-cat*, a male-cat; and males are named from their strength, or the sex implies it; hence, *carl-hemp* denoted strong hemp. *Huscarla*, a *house-carl*, or servant; *buscarla*, a *ship's-carl.* See *Spelman.* Hence the name, *Charles, Carolus.*]

1. A rude, surly, ill-bred man. *Sidney.*

2. A rustic; a countryman, or laborer. *Dryden.*

3. A miser; a niggard. Is. xxxii.

CHURL'ISH, *a.* Rude; surly; austere; sullen; rough in temper; unfeeling; uncivil.

2. Selfish; narrow-minded; avaricious. *King.*

3. [Of things.] Unpliant; unyielding; cross-grained; harsh; unmanageable; as *churlish* metal. *Bacon.*

4. Hard; firm; as a *churlish* knot. *Shak.*

5. Obstinate; as a *churlish* war. *Bacon.*

CHURL'ISHLY, *adv.* Rudely; roughly; in a churlish manner.

CHURL'ISHNESS, *n.* Rudeness of manners or temper, but generally the word refers to the temper or disposition of mind; sullenness; austerity; indisposition to kindness or courtesy.

CHURL'Y, *a.* Rude; boisterous.

CHURME, or CHIRM, *n.* [Sax. *cyrm*, clamor; *cyrman*, to cry out; W. *garm.*] Noise; clamor, or confused noise. *Obs.* *Bacon.*

CHURN, *n.* [Sax. *ciern*, *cyrin*, or *cerene*, a churn; *cernan*, to churn; D. *karn*, *karnen*; Dan. *kierne*, *kierner.*]
A vessel in which cream or milk is agitated for separating the oily part from the caseous and serous parts, to make butter.

CHURN, *v. t.* To stir or agitate cream for making butter.
2. To shake or agitate with violence or continued motion, as in the operation of making butter.

CHURN'ED, *pp.* Agitated; made into butter.

CHURN'ING, *ppr.* Agitating to make butter; shaking; stirring.

CHURN'ING, *n.* The operation of making butter from cream by agitation; a shaking or stirring.
2. As much butter as is made at one operation.

CHURN'-STAFF, *n.* The staff or instrument used in churning.

CHURR'WORM, *n.* [Sax. *cyrran*, to turn, and *worm.*]
An insect that turns about nimbly, called also a fancricket. *Johnson. Bailey.*

CHUSE, [See *Choose.*]

CHU'SITE, *n.* A yellowish mineral found by Saussure in the cavities of porphyries in the environs of Limbourg. *Ure.*

CHYLA'CEOUS, *a.* [See *Chyle.*] Belonging to chyle; consisting of chyle.

CHYLE, *n.* [Gr. χυλος, juice, humor.] In *animal bodies*, a white or milky fluid separated from aliments by means of digestion. It is absorbed by the lacteal vessels, by which it is conveyed into the circulation, assimilated into blood, and converted into nutriment. *Encyc. Quincy. Coxe.*

CHYLIFAC'TION, *n.* [*chyle* and L. *facio.*] The act or process by which chyle is formed from food in animal bodies. *Arbuthnot.*

CHYLIFAC'TIVE, *a.* Forming or changing into chyle; having the power to make chyle.

CHYLOPOET'IC, *adv.* [Gr. χυλος, chyle, and ποιεω, to make.]
Chylifactive; having the power to change into chyle; making chyle. *Arbuthnot.*

CHY'LOUS, *a.* [from *chyle.*] Consisting of chyle, or partaking of it. *Arbuthnot.*

CHYME, *n.* [Gr. χυμος, juice.] That particular modification which food assumes after it has undergone the action of the stomach. *Cyc.*
Among the older authors, juice; chyle, or the finest part of the chyle contained in the lacteals and thoracic duct; any humor incrassated by concoction, whether fit or unfit for preserving and nourishing the body. *Encyc. Coxe. Bailey.*

CHYMIC, CHYMIST, CHYMISTRY. [See *Chimical, Chimist, Chimistry.*]

CIBA'RIOUS, *a.* [L. *cibarius*, from *cibus*, food.]
Pertaining to food; useful for food; edible. *Johnson.*

CIB'OL, *n.* [Fr. *ciboule*; L. *cepula.*] A sort of small onion.

CICA'DA, *n.* [L. See *Cigar.*] The frog-hopper, or flea locust; a genus of insects of many species.

CIC'ATRICLE, *n.* [L. *cicatricula*, from *cicatrix.*]
The germinating or fetal point in the embryo of a seed or the yelk of an egg; as, "germinating *cicatricle.*" *Barton.*

CIC'ATRISIVE, *a.* Tending to promote the formation of a cicatrix.

CIC'ATRIX, } *n.* [L. *cicatrix*; Fr. *cicatrice.*] A scar; a little seam or elevation of flesh remaining after a wound or ulcer is healed. *Encyc.*
CIC'ATRICE, }

CIC'ATRIZANT, *n.* [from *cicatrize.*] A medicine or application that promotes the formation of a cicatrix, such as Armenian bole, powder of tutty, &c. It is called also an escharotic, epulotic, incarnative, agglutinant, &c. *Encyc.*

CICATRIZA'TION, *n.* The process of healing or forming a cicatrix; or the state of being healed, cicatrized or skinned over.

CIC'ATRIZE, *v. t.* To heal, or induce the formation of a cicatrix, in wounded or ulcerated flesh; or to apply medicines for that purpose.

CIC'ATRIZE, *v. i.* To heal or be healed; to skin over; as wounded flesh *cicatrizes.*

CIC'ATRIZED, *pp.* Healed, as wounded flesh; having a cicatrix formed.

CIC'ATRIZING, *ppr.* Healing; skinning over; forming a cicatrix.

CIC'ELY, *n.* A plant, a species of Chærophyllum. The sweet cicely is a species of Scandix.

CICERO'NE, *n.* [from *Cicero.*] A guide; one who explains curiosities. *Addison.*

CICERO'NIAN, *a.* [from *Cicero*, the Roman orator.]
Resembling Cicero, either in style or action; in style, diffuse and flowing; in manner, vehement.

CICERO'NIANISM, *n.* Imitation or resemblance of the style or action of Cicero.

CICHORA'CEOUS, *a.* [from L. *cichorium*, succory or wild endive.] Having the qualities of succory. *Floyer.*

CICISBE'ISM, *n.* The practice of dangling about females.

CICISBE'O, *n.* [It.] A dangler about females. *Smollett.*

CIC'URATE, *v. t.* [L. *cicur*, tame; *cicuro*, to tame.]
To tame; to reclaim from wildness. [*Little used.*]

CICURA'TION, *n.* The act of taming wild animals. [*Little used.*]

CICU'TA, *n.* [L. *cicuta*; W. *cegid*; Fr. *cigue*; Arm. *chagud*. The Welsh is from *ceg*, a choking.]
Water-hemlock, a plant whose root is poisonous. This term was used by the ancients and by medical writers for the Conium maculatum, or common hemlock, the expressed juice of which was used as a common poison. Socrates and Phocion perished by it. It is now used medicinally in moderate doses, with good effect.

CI'DER, *n.* [Fr. *cidre* or *sidre*; It. *sidro*; Sp. *sidra*; Arm. *cistr*; Port. *cidra*, a citron and cider. This cannot be the Gr. σικερα, unless the radical letter has been changed.]
The juice of apples expressed, a liquor used for drink. The word was formerly used to signify the juice of other fruits, and other kinds of strong liquor; but it is now appropriated to the juice of apples, before and after fermentation.

CI'DERIST, *n.* A maker of cider. *Mortimer.*

CI'DERKIN, *n.* The liquor made of the gross matter of apples, after the cider is pressed out, and a quantity of boiled water is added; the whole steeping forty eight hours. *Phillips.*
[*The two last words, I believe, are little used in America.*]

CIERGE, *n.* [Fr. Qu. L. *cera.*] A candle carried in processions.

CIGAR', *n.* [Sp. *cigarro*, a small roll of tobacco for smoking. In Sp. *cigarra* is the L. *cicada*, the balm-cricket or locust, Port. *cigarra*; and in Sp. *cigarron* is a large species of that animal, and a large roll of tobacco.]
A small roll of tobacco, so formed as to be tubular, used for smoking. *Cigars* are of Spanish origin.

CIL'IARY, *a.* [L. *cilium*, the eye-lashes, or edge of the eyelid.] Belonging to the eyelids. *Ray.*

CIL'IATED, *a.* [from L. *cilium*, as above.] In *botany*, furnished or surrounded with parallel filaments, or bristles, resembling the hairs of the eye-lids, as a *ciliated* leaf, &c. *Encyc. Martyn.*

CILI''CIOUS, *a.* [from L. *cilium*, whence *cilicium*, hair cloth.] Made or consisting of hair. *Brown.*

CIMA, [See *Cyma.*]

CIM'BAL, *n.* [It. *ciambella.*] A kind of cake.

CIM'BRIC, *a.* Pertaining to the Cimbri, the inhabitants of the modern Jutland, in Denmark, which was anciently called the Cimbric Chersonese. Hence the modern names, *Cymru*, Wales, Cambria; *Cymro*, a Welshman; *Cymreig*, Welsh, or the Welsh language; names indicating the Welsh to be a colony of the Cimbri or from the same stock.

CIM'BRIC, *n.* The language of the Cimbri.

CIM'ITER, *n.* [Fr. *cimiterre*; Sp. and Port. *cimitarra*; It. *scimitarra.*]
A short sword with a convex edge or recurvated point, used by the Persians and Turks. [This word is variously written; but it is a word of foreign origin, and it is not material which orthography is used, provided it is uniform. I have adopted that which is most simple.]

CIMME'RIAN, *a.* Pertaining to *Cimmerium*, a town at the mouth of the Palus Mæotis. The ancients pretended that this country was involved in darkness; whence the phrase *Cimmerian* darkness, to denote a deep or continual obscurity. The country is now called Crimea, or Krim-Tartary.

CIM'OLITE, *n.* [Gr. κιμωλια; L. *cimolia*, so called by Pliny; said to be from *Cimolus*, an isle in the Cretan Sea, now Argentiera.]
A species of clay, used by the ancients, as a remedy for erysipelas and other inflammations. It is white, of a loose, soft texture, molders into a fine powder, and effervesces with acids. It is useful in taking spots from cloth. Another species, of a purple color, is the steatite or soap-rock. From another species, found in the isle of Wight, tobacco pipes are made.
Pliny. Lib. 35. 17. *Encyc.*

CINCHO'NA, *n.* The Peruvian bark, quinquina, of which there are three varieties, the red, yellow and pale.

CINC'TURE, *n.* [L. *cinctura*, from *cingo*, to surround, to gird; It. *cintura*; Fr. *ceinture*.]

1. A belt, a girdle, or something worn round the body. *Pope.*
2. That which encompasses, or incloses. *Bacon.*
3. In *architecture*, a ring or list at the top and bottom of a column, separating the shaft at one end from the base; at the other, from the capital. It is supposed to be in imitation of the girths or ferrils anciently used to strengthen columns. *Chambers.*

CIN'DER, *n.* chiefly used in the plu. *cinders.* [Fr. *cendre*; It. *cenere*; Sp. *ceniza*; L. *cinis*, ashes. In W. *sindw*, is the cinders or scoria of a forge; Sax. *sinder*, the scoria of metals; D. *zindel*; Sw. *sinder.* Qu. Gr. χονις, χονιὰ, dust, ashes.]

1. Small coals or particles of fire mixed with ashes; embers. [*This is the usual sense of the word in America.*]
2. Small particles of matter, remaining after combustion, in which fire is extinct; as the *cinders* of a forge.

[*I believe this word is never used as synonymous with ashes.*]

CINDER-WENCH, } *n.* A woman whose
CINDER-WOMAN, } business is to rake into heaps of ashes for cinders.
[*Not known in America.*] *Johnson.*

CINERA'TION, *n.* [from L. *cinis*, ashes.] The reducing of any thing to ashes by combustion.

CINE'REOUS, *a.* [L. *cinereus*, from *cinis*, ashes.] Like ashes; having the color of the ashes of wood. *Martyn.*

CINERI''TIOUS, *a.* [L. *cinericius*, from *cinis*, ashes.] Having the color or consistence of ashes. *Cheyne.*

CIN'GLE, *n.* [Ir. *ceangal*; L. *cingulum*, from *cingo*, to gird.] A girth; but the word is little used. [See *Surcingle.*]

CIN'NABAR, *n.* [Gr. κινναβαρι; L. *cinnabaris*; Pers. كنبار kanbar.]

Red sulphuret of mercury. *Native* cinnabar is an ore of quicksilver, moderately compact, very heavy, and of an elegant striated red color. It is called native vermilion, and its chief use is in painting. The intensity of its color is reduced by bruising and dividing it into small parts. It is found amorphous, or under some imitative form, or crystalized. *Factitious* cinnabar is a mixture of mercury and sulphur sublimed, and thus reduced into a fine red glebe. *Encyc. Cleaveland. Hooper.*

CIN'NABARINE, *a.* Pertaining to cinnabar; consisting of cinnabar, or containing it; as, *cinnabarine* sand. *Journ. of Science.*

CIN'NAMON, *n.* [Gr. κινναμον, or κινναμωμον; L. *cinnamomum.* Qu. It. *cannella*; Sp. *canela*; D. *kaneel*; Fr. *cannelle.* It is in the Heb. קנמון.]

The bark of two species of Laurus. The true cinnamon is the inner bark of the Laurus Cinnamomum, a native of Ceylon. The base cinnamon is from the Laurus Cassia. The true cinnamon is a most grateful aromatic, of a fragrant smell, moderately pungent taste, accompanied with some degree of sweetness and astringency. It is one of the best cordial, carminative and restorative spices. The essential oil is of great price. *Encyc. Hooper.*

Cinnamon stone, called by Haüy, *Essonite*, is a rare mineral from Ceylon, of a hyacinth red color, yellowish brown or honey yellow; sometimes used in jewelry. *Cleaveland.*

Cinnamon-water, is made by distilling the bark, first infused in barley water, in spirit of wine, brandy or white wine.

Clove-cinnamon, is the bark of a tree growing in Brazil, which is often substituted for real cloves.

White-cinnamon, or Winter's bark, is the bark of a tree, growing in the West Indies, of a sharp biting taste, like pepper.

CINQUE, *n.* *cink.* [Fr. five.] A five; a word used in games.

CINQUE-FOIL, *n.* [Fr. *cinque*, five, and *feuille*, a leaf, L. *folium.*] Five-leaved clover, a species of Potentilla.

CINQUE-PACE, *n.* [Fr. *cinque*, five, and *pas*, pace.] A kind of grave dance. *Shak.*

CINQUE-PORTS, *n.* [Fr. *cinque*, five, and *ports.*]

Five havens on the eastern shore of England, towards France, viz. Hastings, Romney, Hythe, Dover and Sandwich. To these ports, Winchelsea and Rye have been added. These were anciently deemed of so much importance, in the defense of the kingdom against an invasion from France, that they received royal grants of particular privileges, on condition of providing a certain number of ships in war at their own expense. Over these is appointed a warden, and each has a right to send two barons to Parliament. *Cowel. Blackstone. Encyc.*

CINQUE-SPOTTED, *a.* Having five spots. *Shak.*

CI'ON, *n.* [Fr. *cion* or *scion.* Different modes of spelling the same word are very inconvenient; and whatever may have been the original orthography of this word, *cion*, the most simple, is well established, and is here adopted.]

1. A young shoot, twig or sprout of a tree, or plant, or rather the cutting of a twig, intended for ingrafting on another stock; also, the shoot or slip inserted in a stock for propagation.

CI'PHER, *n.* [Fr. *chiffre*; Arm. *chyfr* or *cyfr*; It. *cifera* or *cifra*; Sp. and Port. *cifra*; D. *cyffer*; G. *ziffer*; Dan. *ciffer*; Sw. *ziffra*; Russ. *tsiphir*; Ar. صفر empty, and a cipher.]

1. In *arithmetic*, an Arabian or Oriental character, of this form 0, which, standing by itself, expresses nothing, but increases or diminishes the value of other figures, according to its position. In whole numbers, when placed at the right hand of a figure, it increases its value ten fold; but in decimal fractions, placed at the left hand of a figure, it diminishes the value of that figure ten fold.
2. A character in general. *Raleigh.*
3. An intertexture of letters, as the initials of a name, engraved on a seal, box, plate, coach or tomb; a device; an enigmatical character. Anciently, merchants and tradesmen, not being permitted to bear family arms, bore, in lieu of them, their cyphers, or initials of their names, artfully interwoven about a cross. *Encyc.*
4. A secret or disguised manner of writing; certain characters arbitrarily invented and agreed on by two or more persons, to stand for letters or words, and understood only by the persons who invent, or agree to use them. This is a mode of communicating information by letters, in time of war, with a view to conceal facts from an enemy, in case the letters should be intercepted. This art has given rise to another art, that of *decyphering*; and hence *cipher* is used for a key to unravel the characters. To *have*, or to *learn a cipher*, is to be able to interpret it.

CI'PHER, *v. i.* In *popular language*, to use figures, or to practice arithmetic.

CI'PHER, *v. t.* To write in occult characters. *Hayward.*

2. To designate; to characterize. *Shak.*

CI'PHERING, *ppr.* Using figures, or practicing arithmetic.

2. Writing in occult characters.

CIP'OLIN, *n.* [Qu. It. *cipolla*, an onion, *cipollina*, a shalot.]

A green marble from Rome, containing white zones. It consists chiefly of carbonate of lime, with quartz, shistus, and a small portion of iron. *Nicholson.*

CIRC, [See *Circus.*]

CIRCE'AN, *a.* Pertaining to Circe, the fabled daughter of Sol and Perseis, who was supposed to possess great knowledge of magic and venomous herbs, by which she was able to charm and fascinate. *Bryant.*

CIRCEN'SIAN, *a.* [L. *circenses*, games of the *circus.*]

Pertaining to the Circus, in Rome, where were practiced games of various kinds, as running, wrestling, combats, &c. The Circensian games accompanied most of the feasts of the Romans; but the grand games were held five days, commencing on the 15th of September. *Lempriere. Encyc.*

CIR'CINAL, *a.* [L. *circinus*, a compass; *circino*, to go round. See *Circle.*]

Rolled in spirally downwards, the tip occupying the center; a term in foliation or leafing, as in ferns. *Martyn.*

CIR'CINATE, *v. t.* [L. *circino*, to go round.] To make a circle; to compass.

CIRCINA'TION, *n.* An orbicular motion. [*Not used.*] *Bailey.*

CIR'CLE, *n.* *sur'kl.* [Fr. *cercle*; It. *circolo*; L. *circulus*, from *circus*; Gr. κιρκος; Sp. *cerco*; It. *cerchio*; from the Celtic, W. *cyrc*, from *cwr*, a circle, a limit; Ar. كار to go round. Class Gr. No. 32. 34.]

1. In *geometry*, a plane figure comprehended by a single curve line, called its circumference, every part of which is equally distant from a point called the center. Of course all lines drawn from the center to the circumference or periphery, are equal to each other.
2. In *popular use*, the line that comprehends the figure, the plane or surface compre-

hended, and the whole body or solid matter of a round substance, are denominated a *circle*; a ring; an orb; the earth.

He that sitteth on the *circle* of the earth. Is. xl.

3. Compass; circuit; as the *circle* of the forest. *Shak.*
4. An assembly surrounding the principal person. Hence, any company, or assembly; as a *circle* of friends, or of beauties. Hence the word came to signify indefinitely a number of persons of a particular character, whether associated or not; as a political *circle;* the *circle* of one's acquaintance; having however reference to a primary association.
5. A series ending where it begins, and perpetually repeated; a going round.

Thus in a *circle* runs the peasant's pain. *Dryden.*

6. Circumlocution; indirect form of words. *Fletcher.*
7. In *logic*, an inconclusive form of argument, when the same terms are proved *in orbem* by the same terms, and the parts of the syllogism alternately by each other, directly and indirectly; or when the foregoing proposition is proved by the following, and the following is inferred from the foregoing; as, "that heavy bodies descend by gravity, and that gravity is a quality by which a heavy body descends." *Encyc. Glanville. Watts.*
8. *Circles of the sphere*, are such as cut the mundane sphere, and have their periphery either on its movable surface, as the meridians; or in another immovable, conterminous and equidistant surface, as the ecliptic, equator, and its parallels.
9. *Circles of altitude* or *almucantars*, are circles parallel to the horizon, having their common pole in the zenith, and diminishing as they approach the zenith.
10. *Circles of latitude*, are great circles perpendicular to the plane of the ecliptic, passing through its poles and through every star and planet.
11. *Circles of longitude*, are lesser circles parallel to the ecliptic, diminishing as they recede from it.
12. *Circle of perpetual apparition*, one of the lesser circles, parallel to the equator, described by any point of the sphere touching the northern point of the horizon, and carried about with the diurnal motion. The stars within this circle never set.
13. *Circle of perpetual occultation*, another lesser circle at a like distance from the equator, which includes all the stars which never appear in our hemisphere.
14. *Diurnal circles*, are immovable circles supposed to be described by the several stars and other points in the heavens, in their diurnal rotation round the earth, or rather in the rotation of the earth round its axis.
15. *Horary circles*, in dialing, are the lines which show the hours on dials.
16. *Circles of the empire*, the provinces or principalities of the German empire, which have a right to be present at the diets. Maximilian I. divided the empire into six circles at first, and afterwards into ten; Austria, Burgundy, Lower Rhine, Bavaria, Upper Saxony, Franconia, Swabia, Upper Rhine, Westphalia, and Lower Saxony.
17. *Druidical circles*, in British Topography, are certain ancient inclosures formed by rude stones circularly arranged; as Stonehenge near Salisbury. *Encyc.*

CIR'CLE, *v. t.* To move round; to revolve round.

And other planets *circle* other suns. *Pope.*

2. To encircle; to encompass; to surround; to inclose. *Prior. Pope.*
3. *To circle in*, to confine; to keep together. *Digby.*

CIR'CLE, *v. i.* To move circularly; as, the bowl *circles;* the *circling* years.

CIR'CLED, *pp.* Surrounded; encompassed; inclosed.

CIR'CLED, *a.* Having the form of a circle; round; as the moon's *circled* orb. *Shak.*

CIR'CLER, *n.* A mean poet, or circular poet. *B. Jonson.*

CIR'CLET, *n.* A little circle; a circle; an orb. *Pope.*

CIR'CLING, *ppr.* Surrounding; going round; inclosing.

CIR'CLING, *a.* Circular; round. *Milton.*

CIR'COCELE, *n.* [Gr. κρισσος or κρισος, a dilated vein, and κηλη, a tumor. But the same Greek word seems to be written κιρσος, which would give the orthography, *cirsocele.*]

A varix, or dilatation of the spermatic vein; a varicocele; hernia varicosa. *Quincy. Coxe.*

CIR'CUIT, *n. sur'kit.* [Fr. *circuit;* L. *circuitus;* of *circa, circum*, and *eo*, to go.]

1. The act of moving or passing round; as the periodical *circuit* of the earth round the sun, or of the moon round the earth. *Watts.*
2. The space inclosed in a circle, or within certain limits. *Milton.*
3. Any space or extent measured by traveling round. *Addison.*
4. That which encircles; a ring; a diadem. *Shak.*
5. In *England*, the journey of judges through several counties or boroughs, for the purpose of holding courts. In *the United States*, the journey of judges through certain states or counties for the same purpose.
6. The counties or states in which the same judge or judges hold courts and administer justice. It is common to designate a certain number of counties to form a circuit, and to assign one or more judges to each circuit. The courts in the circuits are called *circuit courts.* In the government of the United States, a certain number of states form a circuit.
7. A long deduction of reason. *Donne.*
8. In *law*, a longer course of proceedings than is necessary to recover the thing sued for. *Cowel. Encyc. Johnson.*

Bailey gives this as the definition of *circuity.*

CIR'CUIT, *v. i.* To move in a circle; to go round. *Philips.*

CIR'CUIT, *v. t.* To move or go round. *Warton.*

CIRCUITEE'R *n.* One that travels a circuit. *Pope.*

CIRCUI"TION, *n.* [L. *circuitio.*] The act of going round; compass; circumlocution. [*Little used.*] *Hooker.*

CIR'CUITOUS, *a. sur'kitous.* Going round in a circuit; not direct; as a *circuitous* road or course.

CIR'CUITOUSLY, *adv.* In a circuit.

CIRCU'ITY, *n.* A going round; a course not direct. *Ash.*

CIR'CULAR, *a.* [L. *circularis.* See *Circle.*]

1. In the form of a circle; round; circumscribed by a circle; spherical; as, the sun appears to be *circular.*
2. Successive in order; always returning. *Roscommon.*
3. Vulgar; mean; circumforaneous; as a *circular* poet. *Dennis.*
4. Ending in itself; used of a paralogism, where the second proposition at once proves the first, and is proved by it. *Johnson. Baker.*
5. Addressed to a circle, or to a number of persons having a common interest; as a *circular* letter.
6. *Circular lines*, such straight lines as are divided from the divisions made in the arch of a circle; as the lines of sines, tangents and secants, on the plain scale and sector. *Johnson.*
7. *Circular numbers*, are those whose powers terminate in the roots themselves; as 5 and 6, whose squares are 25 and 36. *Bailey.*
8. *Circular sailing*, is the method of sailing by the arch of a great circle. *Encyc.*

CIR'CULAR, *n.* A circular letter, or paper.

CIRCULAR'ITY, *n.* A circular form.

CIR'CULARLY, *adv.* In a circular manner; in the form of a circle; in the form of going and returning.

CIR'CULATE, *v. i. sur'culate.* [Fr. *circuler;* L. *circulo.*]

1. To move in a circle; to move or pass round; to move round and return to the same point; as, the blood *circulates* in the body.
2. To pass from place to place, from person to person, or from hand to hand; to be diffused; as, money *circulates* in the country; a story *circulates* in town.
3. To move round; to run; to flow in veins or channels, or in an inclosed place; as, the sap of plants *circulates;* water *circulates* in the earth, or air in a city or house.

CIR'CULATE, *v. t.* To cause to pass from place to place, or from person to person; to put about; to spread; as, to *circulate* a report; to *circulate* bills of credit.

CIRCULA'TION, *n.* The act of moving round, or in a circle, or in a course which brings or tends to bring the moving body to the point where its motion began; as the *circulation* of the blood in the body.

2. A series in which the same order is preserved and things return to the same state.
3. The act of going and returning; or of passing from place to place, or from person to person; as the *circulation* of money.
4. Currency; circulating coin, or notes or bills current for coin.
5. In *chimistry*, circulation is an operation by which the same vapor, raised by fire, falls back to be returned and distilled several times.

CIRCULATO'RIOUS, *a.* Travelling in a circuit, or from house to house. [*Little used.*] *Barrow.*

CIR'CULATORY, *a.* Circular; as a *circulatory* letter.

2. Circulating.

CIR'CULATORY, *n.* A chemical vessel, in which that which rises from the vessel on the fire is collected and cooled in another fixed upon it, and falls down again. *Johnson.*

CIRCUMAM'BIENCY, *n.* [L. *circum*, around, and *ambio*, to go about. See *Ambient.*]
The act of surrounding, or encompassing. *Brown.*

CIRCUMAM'BIENT, *a.* Surrounding; encompassing; inclosing or being on all sides; used particularly of the air about the earth.

CIRCUMAM'BULATE, *v. i.* [L. *circumambulo*, to walk round; *circum* and *ambulo.*]
To walk round about. [*Little used.*]

CIRCUMAMBULA'TION, *n.* The act of walking round. [*Little used.*]

CIRCUMCEL'LION, *n.* [L. *circum*, about, and *cella*, a cell, or cellar. Hence, a vagrant.]
In *church history*, a set of illiterate peasants that adhered to the Donatists in the fourth century. *Milner.*

CIR'CUMCISE, *v. t.* *sur'cumcize.* [L. *circumcido, circum*, around, and *cido*, to cut; Fr. *circoncire*; Sp. *circuncidar*; It. *circoncidere.*]
To cut off the prepuce or foreskin of males; a ceremony or rite in the Jewish and Mohammodan religions. The word is applied also to a practice among some nations of performing a like operation upon females.

CIR'CUMCISER, *n.* One who performs circumcision. *Milton.*

CIRCUMCIS'ION, *n.* The act of cutting off the prepuce or foreskin,

CIRCUMCURSA'TION, *n.* [L. *circum*, about, and *curso*, to run.]
The act of running about. [*Not used.*] *Barrow.*

CIRCUMDUCT', *v. t.* [L. *circumduco*; *circum*, round, and *duco*, to lead.]
To contravene; to nullify; *a term of civil law.* [*Little used.*] *Ayliffe.*

CIRCUMDUC'TION, *n.* A leading about. [*Little used.*] *Hooker.*
2. An annulling; cancellation. [*Little used.*] *Ayliffe.*

CIR'CUMFER, *v. t.* [L. *circumfero.*] To bear or carry round. [*Not in use.*] *Bacon.*

CIRCUM'FERENCE, *n.* [L. *circumferentia*, from *circum*, round, and *fero*, to carry.]
1. The line that bounds a circle; the exterior line of a circular body; the whole exterior surface of a round body; a periphery. *Newton. Milton.*
2. The space included in a circle. *Milton. Dryden.*
3. An orb; a circle; any thing circular or orbicular; as in Milton, speaking of a shield,

The broad *circumference*
Hung on his shoulders like the moon.

CIRCUM'FERENCE, *v. t.* To include in a circular space. [*Not used.*] *Brown.*

CIRCUMFEREN'TIAL, *a.* Pertaining to the circumference. *Parkhurst.*

CIRCUMFEREN'TOR, *n.* An instrument used by surveyors for taking angles. It consists of a brass index, and circle, all of a piece; on the circle is a chart, divided into 360 degrees. There are also two sights to screw on and slide up and down the index; also a spangle and socket screwed on the back side of the circle to put the head of the staff in. *Encyc.*

CIR'CUMFLEX, *n.* [L. *circumflexus*; *circum*, round, and *flecto*, to bend.]
In *grammar*, an accent serving to note or distinguish a syllable of an intermediate sound between acute and grave; marked in Greek thus ~. It is a kind of undulation in the voice, but not used in English.

CIR'CUMFLEX, *v. t.* To mark or pronounce with the accent called a circumflex. *Walker.*

CIRCUM'FLUENCE, *n.* [L. *circumfluens*; *circum*, round, and *fluo*, to flow.]
A flowing round on all sides; an inclosure of waters.

CIRCUM'FLUENT, *a.* Flowing round; surrounding as a fluid; as, *circumfluent* waves. *Pope.*

CIRCUM'FLUOUS, *a.* [L. *circumfluus.* See *Circumfluence.*] Flowing round; encompassing as a fluid; circumfluent. *Milton. Pope.*

CIRCUMFORA'NEAN, CIRCUMFORA'NEOUS, } *a.* [L. *circumforaneus*; *circum*, around, and *foris*, a door, or abroad.]
Going about; walking or wandering from house to house; as a *circumforaneous* fidler or piper; *circumforaneous* wits. *Addison, Spect.* 47.
Circumforaneous musicians, male and female, are daily seen at the doors of hotels, in France; and sometimes they enter the room, where a company is dining, and entertain them with music; expecting a franc or a few sous as a reward. W.

CIRCUMFU'SE, *v. t.* *s* as *z.* [L. *circumfusus*; *circum* and *fundo, fusus*, to pour.]
1. To pour round; to spread round, as a fluid. *Bacon.*
2. To spread round; to surround. *Milton.*

CIRCUMFU'SILE, *a.* [L. *circum*, and *fusilis*, that may be melted.]
That may be poured or spread round; as, *circumfusile* gold. *Pope.*

CIRCUMFU'SION, *n.* [See *Circumfuse.*]
The act of pouring or spreading round; the state of being poured round. *Johnson.*

CIRCUMGESTA'TION, *n.* [L. *circum* and *gestatio.*] A carrying about. *Taylor.*

CIRCUM'GYRATE, CIRCUMGY'RE, } *v. t.* [L. *circum*, and *gyrus*, a turning round.]
To roll or turn round. [*Little used.*] *Ray.*

CIRCUMGYRA'TION, *n.* The act of turning, rolling or whirling round; the turning of a limb in its socket. *Quincy. Cheyne.*

CIRCUMJA'CENT, *a.* [L. *circumjacens*; *circum* and *jaceo*, to lie.]
Lying round; bordering on every side. *Johnson.*

CIRCUMLIGA'TION, *n.* [L. *circumligo*, to bind round; *circum* and *ligo*, to bind.]
The act of binding round; the bond with which any thing is encompassed. *Johnson.*

CIRCUMLOCU'TION, *n.* [L. *circumlocutio*; *circum* and *locutio*, a speaking, *loquor*, to speak.]
A circuit or compass of words; a periphrase; the use of a number of words to express an idea, when a suitable term is not at hand, or when a speaker chooses to avoid the use of a single term, either from delicacy or respect, or with a view to soften the force of a direct expression, or for other reason.

CIRCUMLOC'UTORY, *a.* Pertaining to circumlocution; consisting or contained in a compass of words; periphrastic. *Shenstone.*

CIRCUMMU'RED, *a.* [L. *circum* and *murus*, a wall.]
Walled round; encompassed with a wall. *Shak.*

CIRCUMNAV'IGABLE, *a.* [See *Circumnavigate.*] That may be sailed round. *Ray.*

CIRCUMNAV'IGATE, *v. t.* [L. *circumnavigo*; *circum* and *navigo*, to sail, from *navis*, a ship.]
To sail round; to pass round by water; as, to *circumnavigate* the globe.

CIRCUMNAVIGA'TION, *n.* The act of sailing round. *Arbuthnot.*

CIRCUMNAV'IGATOR, *n.* One who sails round.

CIRCUMPLICA'TION, *n.* [L. *circumplico*; *circum* and *plico*, to fold.]
A folding, winding or wrapping round; or a state of being enwrapped. [*Little used.*] *Bailey.*

CIRCUMPO'LAR, *a.* [L. *circum*, and Eng. *polar.*]
About the pole; an appellation given to stars, which are so near the north pole, as to revolve round it without setting. The number of these depends on the latitude of the spectator. We apply it to the north polar region and stars, but the word is applicable to either pole.

CIRCUMPOSI''TION, *n.* *s* as *z.* [L. *circum*, and *positio.*]
The act of placing in a circle; or the state of being so placed. *Evelyn.*

CIRCUMRA'SION, *n.* *s* as *z.* [L. *circumrasio*; *circum* and *rado*, to shave.]
The act of shaving or paring round. [*Little used.*]

CIRCUMRO'TARY, *a.* Turning, rolling or whirling round. *Shenstone.*

CIRCUMROTA'TION, *n.* [L. *circum* and *rotatio*, rotation, from *roto*, to turn round.]
The act of rolling or revolving round, as a wheel; circumvolution; the state of being whirled round. *Gregory.*

CIRCUMSCRI'BE, *v. t.* [L. *circumscribo*; *circum* and *scribo*, to draw.] Literally, to draw a line round. Hence,
1. To inclose within a certain limit; to limit, bound, confine.

You are above
The little forms which *circumscribe* your sex. *Southern.*

2. To write round. [*Little used.*]

CIRCUMSCRI'BED, *pp.* Drawn round as a line; limited; confined.
In *geometry*, this word is applied to a figure which is drawn round another figure, so that all its sides or planes touch the inscribed figure. *Encyc.*

CIRCUMSCRI'BING, *ppr.* Drawing a line round; inclosing; limiting; confining.

CIRCUMSCRIP'TIBLE, *a.* That may be circumscribed or limited by bounds.

CIRCUMSCRIP'TION, *n.* The line that limits; limitation; bound; confinement. *Shak.*
2. In *natural philosophy*, the termination or

limits of a body; the exterior line which determines the form or magnitude of a body. *Ray.*

3. A circular inscription. *Ashmole.*

CIRCUMSCRIP'TIVE, *a.* Defining the external form; marking or inclosing the limits or superficies of a body. *Grew.*

CIRCUMSCRIP'TIVELY, *adv.* In a limited manner. *Montagu.*

CIR'CUMSPECT, *a.* [L. *circumspectus; circum* and *specio*, to look.]

Literally, looking on all sides; looking round. Hence,

Cautious; prudent; watchful on all sides; examining carefully all the circumstances that may affect a determination, or a measure to be adopted. *Boyle. Haywood.*

CIRCUMSPEC'TION, *n.* [L. *circumspectio.*] Caution; attention to all the facts and circumstances of a case, and to the natural or probable consequences of a measure, with a view to a correct course of conduct, or to avoid danger. *Clarendon. Milton.*

CIRCUMSPEC'TIVE, *a.* Looking round every way; cautious; careful of consequences; watchful of danger. *Pope.*

CIRCUMSPEC'TIVELY, *adv.* Cautiously; vigilantly; heedfully; with watchfulness to guard against danger.

CIR'CUMSPECTLY, *adv.* Cautiously; with watchfulness every way; with attention to guard against surprise or danger. *Ray.*

CIR'CUMSPECTNESS, *n.* Caution; circumspection; vigilance in guarding against evil from every quarter. *Wotton.*

CIR'CUMSTANCE, *n.* [L. *circumstantia*, from *circumstans*, standing about; *circum* and *sto*, to stand.]

Literally, that which stands around or near. Hence,

1. Something attending, appendant, or relative to a fact, or case; a particular thing, which, though not essential to an action, in some way affects it; the same to a moral action, as accident to a natural substance; as, the *circumstances* of time, place and persons, are to be considered.
2. The adjuncts of a fact, which make it more or less criminal, or make an accusation more or less probable; accident; something adventitious; incident; event. *Johnson.*
3. Circumstances, *in the plural*, condition, in regard to worldly estate; state of property; as a man in low *circumstances*, or in easy *circumstances.*

CIR'CUMSTANCED, *pp.* or *a.* Placed in a particular manner, with regard to attending facts or incidents; as, *circumstanced* as we were, we could not escape.

CIR'CUMSTANT, *a.* Surrounding. [*Little used or not at all.*]

CIRCUMSTAN'TIAL, *a.* Attending; relating to; but not essential.

2. Consisting in or pertaining to circumstances, or to particular incidents.

> The usual character of human testimony is substantial truth under *circumstantial* variety. *Paley.*

3. Incidental; casual. *Donne.*
4. Abounding with circumstances, or exhibiting all the circumstances; minute; particular; as a *circumstantial* account or recital.
5. In *law, circumstantial* evidence is that which is obtained from circumstances, which necessarily or usually attend facts of a particular nature, from which arises presumption. *Blackstone.*

CIRCUMSTANTIAL'ITY, *n.* The appendage of circumstances; the state of any thing as modified by circumstances. *Johnson.*

2. Particularity in exhibiting circumstances; minuteness; as the *circumstantiality* of a story or description.

CIRCUMSTAN'TIALLY, *adv.* According to circumstances; not essentially; accidentally. *Glanville.*

2. Minutely; exactly; in every circumstance or particular. *Broome.*

CIRCUMSTAN'TIATE, *v. t.* To place in particular circumstances; to invest with particular accidents or adjuncts. *Bramhall.*

2. To place in a particular condition with regard to power or wealth. *Swift.*

[*This word is little used.*]

CIRCUMTERRA'NEOUS, *a.* [*circum*, about, and *terra*, earth.] Around the earth. *Halywell.*

CIRCUMVAL'LATE, *v. t.* To surround with a rampart. [*Little used.*]

CIRCUMVALLA'TION, *n.* [L. *circumvallo*, to wall round; *circum*, and *vallo*, to fortify with a rampart.]

1. In *the art of war*, a surrounding with a wall or rampart; also, a wall, rampart, or parapet with a trench, surrounding the camp of a besieging army, to prevent desertion, and guard the army against any attempt of an enemy to relieve the place besieged. *Encyc.*
2. The rampart, or fortification surrounding a besieged place.

> [Note. This word, from the Latin, *vallo*, or *vallum, vallus*, denotes properly the *wall* or rampart thrown up; but as the rampart is formed by entrenching, and the trench makes a part of the fortification, the word is applied to both. See Eng. *Wall.*]

CIRCUMVEC'TION, *n.* [L. *circum*, and *veho*, to carry.] A carrying about. [*Not used.*]

CIRCUMVENT', *v. t.* [L. *circumvenio; circum*, and *venio*, to come.] Literally, to come round; hence,

To gain advantage over another, or to accomplish a purpose, by arts, stratagem, or deception; to deceive; to prevail over another by wiles or fraud; to delude; to impose on. *Milton. Dryden.*

CIRCUMVENT'ED, *pp.* Deceived by craft or stratagem; deluded.

CIRCUMVENT'ING, *ppr.* Deceiving; imposing on.

CIRCUMVEN'TION, *n.* The act of prevailing over another by arts, address, or fraud; deception; fraud; imposture; delusion. *South.*

2. Prevention; preoccupation *Obs. Shak.*

CIRCUMVENT'IVE, *a.* Deceiving by artifices; deluding.

CIRCUMVEST', *v. t.* [L. *circumvestio; circum*, and *vestio*, to clothe.]

To cover round, as with a garment. *Wotton.*

CIRCUMVOLA'TION, *n.* [L. *circumvolo; circum*, and *volo*, to fly.]

The act of flying round. [*Little used.*]

CIRCUMVOLU'TION, *n.* The act of rolling round; the state of being rolled; also, the thing rolled round another. *Arbuthnot. Wilkins.*

2. In *architecture*, the torus of the spiral line of the Ionic order. *Encyc.*

CIRCUMVOLVE, *v. t. circumvolv'.* [L. *circumvolvo; circum*, and *volvo*, to roll.]

To roll round; to cause to revolve; to put into a circular motion. *Glanville.*

CIRCUMVOLVE, *v. i.* To roll round; to revolve.

CIRCUMVOLV'ED, *pp.* Rolled round; moved in a circular manner.

CIRCUMVOLV'ING, *ppr.* Rolling round; revolving.

CIRC'US, *n.* plu. *circuses.* [L. *circus;* Fr. *cirque;* It. *circo;* Sp. *circo;* Gr. κιρκος; whence *circle*, which see.]

1. In *antiquity*, a round or oval edifice, used for the exhibition of games and shows to the people. The Roman circus was encompassed with porticos, and furnished with rows of seats, rising one above another for the accommodation of spectators. The Circus Maximus was nearly a mile in circumference. *Adam. Encyc.*
2. The open area, or space inclosed, in which were exhibited games and shows; as wrestling, fighting with swords, staves or pikes, running or racing, dancing, quoits, &c.
3. In *modern times*, a circular inclosure for the exhibition of feats of horsemanship.

CIRL, *n.* An Italian bird about the size of a sparrow. *Dict. Nat. Hist.*

CIRRIF'EROUS, *a.* [L. *cirrus*, a tendril, and *fero*, to bear.]

Producing tendrils or claspers, as a plant.

CIR'ROUS, *a.* [L. *cirrus*, a curl.] Terminating in a cirrus, curl or tendril; as a *cirrous* leaf. *Martyn.*

CISALP'INE, *a.* [L. *cis*, on this side, and *Alpes*, Alps, whence *alpinus, alpine.*]

On this side of the Alps, with regard to Rome; that is, on the south of the Alps; opposed to *transalpine.*

CIS'PADANE, *a.* [L. *cis*, on this side, and *Padus*, the river Po, whence *padanus.*]

On this side of the Po, with regard to Rome; that is, on the south side. *Stephens.*

CISSOID', *n.* [Gr. κισσος, ivy, and ειδος, form.] A curve of the second order, invented by Diocles. *Bailey. Encyc.*

CIST, *n.* A case. [See *Cyst*, the proper orthography.]

CIST'ED, *a.* Inclosed in a cyst. [See *Cysted.*]

CISTER'CIAN, *n.* [*Cisteaux*, in France.] A monk, a reformed Benedictine.

CIS'TERN, *n.* [L. *cisterna; cista*, and Sax. *ærn*, place, repository.]

1. An artificial reservoir or receptacle for holding water, beer or other liquor, as in domestic uses, distilleries, and breweries.
2. A natural reservoir; a hollow place containing water; as a fountain or lake.

CIST'IC, *a.* [See *Cystic.*]

CIST'US, *n.* [Gr. κιςος.] The rock-rose, a genus of plants of many species, most of them natives of the southern parts of Europe. Some of them are beautiful evergreen flowering shrubs, and ornamental in gardens. *Encyc.*

CIT, *n.* [contracted from *citizen.*] A citizen, *in a low sense;* an inhabitant of a city; a pert townsman; a pragmatical trader. *Pope.*

CIT'ADEL, *n.* [Fr. *citadelle*; It. *cittadella*; Sp. *ciudadela*; from the It. *citta*, city.]
A fortress or castle, in or near a city, intended for its defense; a place of arms. *Johnson. Encyc.*

CI'TAL, *n.* [from *cite*.] Reproof; impeachment. [*Little used.*] *Shak.*
2. Summons; citation; quotation. [*Little used.*] *Johnson.*

CITA'TION, *n.* [L. *citatio*, from *cito*, to *cite*, which see.]
1. A summons; an official call or notice, given to a person, to appear in a court, and answer to a demand; a call or notice to appear, in various other cases, and the paper containing such notice or call.
2. Quotation; the act of citing a passage from a book; or from another person, in his own words; also, the passage or words quoted. *Watts. Atterbury.*
3. Enumeration; mention. *Harvey.*

CI'TATORY, *a.* Citing; calling; having the power or form of citation; as, letters *citatory*. *Ayliffe.*

CITE, *v. t.* [L. *cito*, to call; Fr. *citer*; It. *citare*; Sp. Port. *citar*; Goth. *haitan*; Sax. *hætan*, or *hatan*, to call, order, command; G. *heissen*, whence Eng. *behest*; D. *heeten*; Sw. *heta*; Dan. *heder*. The same word in Dutch and Danish signifies to *heat*. The sense then is to rouse, push, drive, stimulate. See *Excite, Incite*.]
1. To call upon officially, or authoritatively; to summon; to give legal or official notice, as to a defendant to appear in court, to answer or defend. *Milton.*
2. To enjoin; to direct; to summon; to order or urge. *Prior.*
3. To quote; to name or repeat, as a passage or the words of another, either from a book or from verbal communication; as, to *cite* a passage from scripture, or to *cite* the very words a man utters. *Bacon. Dryden.*
4. To call or name, in support, proof or confirmation; as, to *cite* an authority to prove a point in law.

CI'TER, *n.* One who cites or summons into court.
2. One who quotes a passage or the words of another.

CIT'ESS, *n.* [See *Cit*.] A city woman. [*Little used.*]

CITHARIS'TIC, *a.* [L. *cithara*, a harp or lyre.]
Pertaining to or adapted to the harp; or appropriated to the accompaniment of the harp. *Mus. Dict.*

CITH'ERN, *n.* [L. *cithara*; It. *citara*; Sp. *citara*; D. *cyter*; Gr. κιθαρα.]
A stringed musical instrument, among the ancients, the precise form of which is not known, but it bore some resemblance to the modern *guitar*, the name of which is evidently from this ancient word.

CIT'ICISM, *n.* [from *cit*.] The manners of a cit or citizen. *B. Johnson.*

CIT'IED, *a.* Belonging to a city. *Drayton.*

CIT'ISIN, *n.* A substance of a yellow color, obtained from the seeds of the *Cytisus Laburnum*. *Webster's Manual.*

CIT'IZEN, *n.* cit'izn. [Fr. *citoyen*; It. *cittadino*; Sp. *ciudadano*; Port. *cidadam*; from It. *citta*, Sp. *ciudad*, a city. See *City*.]
1. The native of a city, or an inhabitant who enjoys the freedom and privileges of the city in which he resides; the freeman of a city, as distinguished from a foreigner, or one not entitled to its franchises.
2. A townsman; a man of trade; not a gentleman. *Shak.*
3. An inhabitant; a dweller in any city, town or place. *Dryden.*
4. In *a general sense*, a native or permanent resident in a city or country; as the *citizens* of London or Philadelphia; the *citizens* of the United States.
5. In *the U. States*, a person, native or naturalized, who has the privilege of exercising the elective franchise, or the qualifications which enable him to vote for rulers, and to purchase and hold real estate.

If the *citizens* of the U. States should not be free and happy, the fault will be entirely their own. *Washington.*

CIT'IZEN, *a.* Having the qualities of a citizen.

CIT'IZENIZE, *v. t.* To make a citizen; to admit to the rights and privileges of a citizen.

Talleyrand was *citizenized* in Pennsylvania, when there in the form of an emigrant. *Pickering.*

CIT'IZENSHIP, *n.* The state of being vested with the rights and privileges of a citizen. *Bp. Horne.*

CIT'RATE, *n.* [L. *citrus*, a *citron* or lemon.] In *chimistry*, a neutral salt, formed by a union of the citric acid, or acid of lemons, with a base.

The onion yields *citrate* of lime. *Ure.*

CIT'RIC, *a.* Belonging to lemons or limes; as *citric* acid.

CIT'RIL, *n.* A beautiful song bird of Italy. *Dict. Nat. Hist.*

CITRINA'TION, *n.* [See *Citrine*.] The turning to a yellow green color.

CIT'RINE, *a.* [L. *citrinus*.] Like a citron or lemon; of a lemon color; yellow, or greenish yellow.

CIT'RINE, *n.* [L. *citrinus*.] A species of very fine sprig crystal, of a beautiful yellow color, found in columns, and terminating in a hexangular pyramid. *Hill. Encyc.*

CIT'RON, *n.* [Fr. *citron*; L. *citreum*, or *citrum*.]
The fruit of the citron tree, a large species of lemon.

CIT'RON-TREE, *n.* The tree which produces the citron, of the genus Citrus. It has an upright smooth stem, with a branchy head, rising from five to fifteen feet, adorned with large, oval, spear-shaped leaves. To the same genus belong the lemon-tree, orange-tree, &c. *Encyc.*

CIT'RON-WATER, *n.* A liquor distilled with the rind of citrons. *Pope.*

CIT'RUL, *n.* The pompion or pumpkin, so named from its yellow color. [*I believe not used.*]

CIT'Y, *n.* [Fr. *cité*; It. *citta*, *cittade* or *cittate*; Sp. *ciudad*; Port. *cidade*; from the Latin *civitas*.]
1. In *a general sense*, a large town; a large number of houses and inhabitants, established in one place.
2. In *a more appropriate sense*, a corporate town; a town or collective body of inhabitants, incorporated and governed by particular officers, as a mayor and aldermen. This is the sense of the word in the United States. In Great Britain, a city is said to be a town corporate that has a bishop and a cathedral church; but this is not always the fact.
3. The collective body of citizens, or the inhabitants of a city; as when we say, the *city* voted to establish a market, and the *city* repealed the vote.

CIT'Y, *a.* Pertaining to a city; as *city* wives; a *city* feast; *city* manners. *Shak.*

CITY-COURT, *n.* The municipal court of a city, consisting of the mayor or recorder and aldermen. *U. States.*

CIVES, *n.* [Fr. *cive*; L. *cepa*.] A species of leek, of the genus Allium.

CIV'ET, *n.* [Fr. *civette*; It. *zibetto*; Pers. زباد zabad, the sweet scent of any beast; Ar. زباد cream, and civet; زبادة a civet-cat. The Arabic verb signifies to make butter, and this substance may be named from its resemblance to it.]
A substance, of the consistence of butter or honey, taken from a bag under the tail of the civet-cat. It is of a clear, yellowish, or brownish color; of a strong smell, and offensive when undiluted, but agreeable when a small portion is mixed with another substance. It is used as a perfume. *Encyc.*

CIV'ET-CAT, *n.* The animal that produces civet, a species of Viverra. This animal bears a resemblance to a cat or to a fox; it is of a cinereous color, tinged with yellow, marked with dusky spots disposed in rows. It inhabits India, Guinea, Ethiopia, and Madagascar. *Encyc.*

CIV'IC, *a.* [L. *civicus*, from *civis*, a citizen.] Literally, pertaining to a city or citizen; relating to civil affairs or honors. *Pope.*
The *civic* crown, in Roman affairs, was a crown or garland of oak boughs, bestowed on a soldier who had saved the life of a citizen in battle.

CIV'IL, *a.* [L. *civilis*, from *civis*, a citizen; Fr. *civil*; It. *civile*; Sp. *civil*. Qu. the Welsh *cau*, to shut, inclose, fence, hedge; for the rude inhabitants of antiquity fortified their towns with hedges, stakes or palisades.]
1. Relating to the community, or to the policy and government of the citizens and subjects of a state; as in the phrases, *civil* rights, *civil* government, *civil* privileges, *civil* war, *civil* justice. It is opposed to *criminal*; as a *civil* suit, a suit between citizens alone; whereas a *criminal* process is between the state and a citizen. It is distinguished from *ecclesiastical*, which respects the church; and from *military*, which respects the army and navy.
2. Relating to any man as a member of a community; as *civil* power, *civil* rights, the power or rights which a man enjoys as a citizen.
3. Reduced to order, rule and government; under a regular administration; implying some refinement of manners; not savage or wild; as *civil* life; *civil* society.
4. Civilized; courteous; complaisant; gentle and obliging; well-bred; affable; kind; having the manners of a city, as opposed

to the rough, rude, coarse manners of a savage or clown.

Where *civil* speech and soft persuasion hung. *Prior.*

5. Grave; sober; not gay or showy.

Till *civil* suited morn appear. *Milton.*

6. Complaisant; polite; *a popular colloquial use of the word.*

7. *Civil death*, in law, is that which cuts off a man from *civil* society, or its rights and benefits, as banishment, outlawry, excommunication, entering into a monastery, &c., as distinguished from *natural* death.

8. *Civil law*, in a general sense, the law of a state, city or country; but in an appropriate sense, the Roman law; the municipal law of the Roman empire, comprised in the Institutes, Code and Digest of Justinian and the Novel Constitutions. *Blackstone.*

9. *Civil list*, the officers of civil government, who are paid from the public treasury; also, the revenue appropriated to support the civil government. *Blackstone.*

The army of James II. was paid out of his *civil list*. *Hamilton.*

10. *Civil state*, the whole body of the laity or citizens, not included under the military, maritime, and ecclesiastical states.

11. *Civil war*, a war between people of the same state or city; opposed to *foreign* war.

12. *Civil year*, the legal year, or annual account of time which a government appoints to be used in its own dominions, as distinguished from the natural year, which is measured by the revolution of the heavenly bodies. *Bailey. Encyc.*

13. *Civil architecture*, the architecture which is employed in constructing buildings for the purposes of civil life, in distinction from military and naval architecture; as private houses, palaces, churches, &c.

CIVIL'IAN, *n.* [from *civil.*] One who is skilled in the Roman law; a professor or doctor of civil law. *Encyc.*

2. In *a more extended sense*, one who is versed in law and government.

3. A student of the civil law at the university. *Graves.*

CIV'ILIST, *n.* A civilian. [*Not in use.*]

CIVIL'ITY, *n.* [L. *civilitas*, from *civilis*, civil; It. *civilita*; Sp. *civilidad.*]

1. The state of being civilized; refinement of manners; *applied to nations;* as distinguished from the rudeness of barbarous nations. [*This sense is obsolescent or obsolete.*] *Spenser. Davies. Denham.*

2. Good breeding; politeness; complaisance; courtesy; decorum of behavior in the treatment of others, accompanied with kind offices, and attention to their wants and desires. Civility respects manners or external deportment, and in the plural, *civilities* denote acts of politeness. *Clarendon. South. Dryden.*

CIVILIZA'TION, *n.* [See *Civilize.*] The act of civilizing, or the state of being civilized; the state of being refined in manners, from the grossness of savage life, and improved in arts and learning.

2. The act of rendering a criminal process civil. [*Not used.*]

CIV'ILIZE, *v. t.* [It. *civilizzare;* Fr. *civiliser;* Sp. Port. *civilizar;* from *civil.*] To reclaim from a savage state; to introduce civility of manners among a people, and instruct them in the arts of regular life. *Locke. Waller. Denham.*

CIV'ILIZED, *pp.* Reclaimed from savage life and manners; instructed in arts, learning and civil manners.

Such sale of conscience and duty in open market is not reconcilable with the present state of *civilized* society. *J. Quincy.*

CIV'ILIZER, *n.* One who civilizes; he that reclaims others from a wild and savage life, and teaches them the rules and customs of civility.

2. That which reclaims from savageness.

CIV'ILIZING, *ppr.* Reclaiming from savage life; instructing in arts and civility of manners.

CIV'ILLY, *adv.* In a manner relating to government, or to the rights or character of a member of the community. *Hooker.*

2. In a manner relating to private rights; opposed to *criminally;* as a process *civilly* commenced for the private satisfaction of a party injured. *Ayliffe.*

3. Not naturally, but in law; as a man *civilly* dead.

4. Politely; complaisantly; gently; with due decorum; courteously; as, we were *civilly* treated. *Dryden. Prior.*

5. Without gaudy colors, or finery; as chambers furnished *civilly*. *Obs.* *Bacon.*

CIV'ISM, *n.* [L. *civis*, a citizen.] Love of country; patriotism.

CIZ'AR, *v. t.* To clip with scissors. [*Not in use nor correct.*] *Beaum.*

CIZE, for *size*, is not in use.

ClAB'BER or BONNY-ClABBER, *n.* Milk turned, become thick or inspissated. [G. *lab*, D. *leb*. rennet.]

ClACK, *v. i.* [Fr. *claquer*, to flap or snap; *cliquet*, a mill-clapper; *cliqueter*, to *clack;* W. *cleca*, *clegyr;* Ir. *clagaim;* D. *klakken;* Sax. *cloccan*, to *cluck*, L. *glocio.* Probably from the root of the Lat. *loquor*, Gr. λακω, ληκεω. See *Cluck*, and Class Lg. No 27.]

1. To make a sudden sharp noise, as by striking or cracking; to clink; to click.

2. To utter words rapidly and continually, or with sharp, abrupt sounds; to let the tongue run.

ClACK, *n.* [W. *clec*, a sharp noise, a crack, tale-bearing; *cleca*, *clecian*, *clegyr*, to clack, to crack, to tattle. See the Verb.]

1. A sharp, abrupt sound continually repeated, such as is made by striking an object, or by bursting or cracking; continual talk; as, we do not wish to hear his *clack;* a common expression. Hence the word is used for the tongue, the instrument of clacking. *Butler. Prior.*

2. The instrument that strikes the hopper of a grist-mill, to move or shake it, for discharging the corn. And according to Johnson, a bell that rings when more corn is required to be put in.

To clack wool, is to cut off the sheep's mark, which makes it weigh less, and yield less duty. [*Not used, I believe, in America.*]

ClACK'ER, *n.* One that clacks; that which clacks.

ClACK'ING, *ppr.* Making a sharp, abrupt sound, continually repeated; talking continually; tattling; rattling with the tongue.

ClACK'ING, *n.* A prating.

ClAD, *pp.* [See *Clothe.*] Clothed; invested; covered as with a garment.

Jeroboam had *clad* himself with a new garment. 1 Kings xi.

The fields are *clad* in cheerful green.

ClAIM, *v. t.* [L. *clamo*, to cry out, to call upon; It. *clamare*, or *chiamare;* Port. *clamar;* Sp. *llamar;* Sax. *hlemman;* Sw. *glamma;* Ir. *glamaim.*]

1. To call for; to ask or seek to obtain, by virtue of authority, right or supposed right; to challenge as a right; to demand as due; as, to *claim* a debt; to *claim* obedience, or respect.

2. To assert, or maintain as a right; as, he *claims* to be the best poet of the age.

3. To have a right or title to; as, the heir *claims* the estate by descent; he *claims* a promise.

4. To proclaim. *Obs.* *Spenser.*

5. To call or name. *Obs.*

ClAIM, *n.* A demand of a right or supposed right; a calling on another for something due, or supposed to be due; as a *claim* of wages for services. A claim implies a right or supposed right in the claimant to something which is in another's possession or power. A claim may be made in words, by suit, and by other means. The word is usually preceded by *make* or *lay;* to *make claim;* to *lay claim.*

2. A right to claim or demand; a title to any debt, privilege or other thing in possession of another; as, a prince has a *claim* to the throne.

Homer's *claims* to the first rank among Epic poets have rarely been disputed. *Anon.*

3. The thing claimed, or demanded.

4. A loud call. *Spenser*

[*This original sense of the word is now obsolete.*]

ClA'IMABLE, *a.* That may be demanded as due.

ClA'IMANT, *n.* A person who claims; one who demands any thing as his right.

2. A person who has a right to claim, or demand.

ClA'IMED, *pp.* Demanded as due; challenged as a right; asserted; maintained.

ClA'IMER, *n.* A claimant; one who demands as due.

ClA'IMING, *ppr.* Demanding as due; challenging as a right; asserting; maintaining; having a right to demand.

ClAIR-OBSCURE. [See *Clare-obscure.*]

ClAM, *n.* [See the Verb.] The popular name of certain bivalvular shell-fish, of many species.

ClAM'-SHELL, *n.* The shell of a clam.

ClAM, *v. t.* [Sax. *clæmian*, to glue; D. *klam*, clammy; *lym*, glue; G. *klamm*, close, clammy; *klemmen*, to pinch; Dan. *klammer*, to cling; *klemmer*, to squeeze, or pinch; *lim*, glue; *limer*, to glue; *limagtig*, clammy. Qu. W. *clymu*, to bind or tie a knot. See *Lime* and Class Lm. No. 1. 5. 9. 13.]

To clog with glutinous or viscous matter. *L'Estrange.*

ClAM, *v. i.* To be moist. [*Little used.*] *Dryden.*

ClA'MANT, *a.* [See *Claim.*] Crying, beseeching. *Thomson.*

ClAM'BER, *v. i.* [from *climb*, or D. *klampen*, to grapple.]

To climb with difficulty, or with hands and feet. *Addison.*

ȻLAM'BERING, *ppr.* Climbing with effort and labor.

ȻLAM'MINESS, *n.* [See *Clammy.*] The state of being viscous; viscosity; stickiness; tenacity of a soft substance. *Moxon.*

ȻLAM'MY, *a.* [See *Clam.*] Thick, viscous, adhesive; soft and sticky; glutinous; tenacious; as, bodies *clammy* and cleaving. *Bacon.*

Cold sweat, in *clammy* drops, his limbs o'erspread. *Dryden.*

ȻLAM'OR, *n.* [L. *clamor;* Fr. *clameur;* Ir. *glam;* Sax. *hlem.* See *Claim.*]

1. A great outcry; noise; exclamation; vociferation, made by a loud human voice continued or repeated, or by a multitude of voices. It often expresses complaint and urgent demand. *Shak. Prior.*

2. *Figuratively,* loud and continued noise, as of a river or other inanimate things. *Addison.*

ȻLAM'OR, *v. t.* To stun with noise. *Bacon.*

To clamor bells, is to multiply the strokes. *Warburton.*

ȻLAM'OR, *v. i.* To utter loud sounds, or outcries; to talk loud; to utter loud voices repeatedly; to vociferate, as an individual; to utter loud voices, as a multitude; to complain; to make importunate demands. *Shak. Bacon.*

Those who most loudly *clamor* for liberty do not most liberally grant it. *Anon.*

"*Clamor* your tongues" in Shakspeare, if intended to mean, "stop from noise," is not English. Perhaps the word was *clam,* or intended for a derivative.

ȻLAM'ORER, *n.* One who clamors. *Chesterfield.*

ȻLAM'ORING, *ppr.* Uttering and repeating loud words; making a great and continued noise; particularly in complaint or importunate demands.

ȻLAM'OROUS, *a.* Speaking and repeating loud words; noisy; vociferous; loud; turbulent. *Hooker. Pope. Swift.*

ȻLAM'OROUSLY, *adv.* With loud noise, or words.

ȻLAM'OROUSNESS, *n.* The state or quality of being loud or noisy.

ȻLAMP, *n.* [D. *klamp;* G. *klammer, klemmen;* Dan. *klamp;* W. *clymu,* to tie.]

1. In *general,* something that fastens or binds; a piece of timber or of iron, used to fasten work together; or a particular manner of uniting work by letting boards into each other.

2. In *ship-building,* a thick plank on the inner part of a ship's side, used to sustain the ends of the beams.

3. A smooth crooked plate of iron forelocked on the trunnions of a cannon to keep it fast to the carriage. Clamps are also used to strengthen masts, and to fasten the masts and bowsprits of small vessels and of boats. *Mar. Dict.*

4. A pile of bricks laid up for burning, in which the end of one brick is laid over another, and a space is left between the bricks for the fire to ascend. *Encyc.*

Clamp-irons, irons used at the ends of fires to keep the fuel from falling. *Bailey.*

Clamp-nails, nails used to fasten on clamps in ships.

ȻLAMP, *v. t.* To fasten with clamps.

2. In *joinery,* to fit a piece of board with the grain, to the end of another piece of board across the grain; as, to *clamp* a table to prevent its warping. *Moxon.*

ȻLAMP'ED, *pp.* United or strengthened with a clamp.

ȻLAMP'ING, *ppr.* Fastening or strengthening with a clamp.

ȻLAN, *n.* [Ir. *clann,* or *cland,* children, posterity; a tribe, breed, generation, family. Erse. *clan* or *klaan.*]

1. A race; a family; a tribe. Hence, an association of persons under a chieftain. *Milton. Dryden.*

2. In *contempt,* a sect, society, or body of persons closely united by some common interest or pursuit. *Swift.*

NOTE. In Russ. *kolieno* signifies a knee, and a family, race or tribe. Irish *glun,* the knee, and a generation.

ȻLAN'ȻULAR, *a.* [L. *clancularius.*] Clandestine; secret; private; concealed. [*Little used.*]

ȻLAN'ȻULARLY, *adv.* Privately; secretly. [*Little used.*]

ȻLANDES'TINE, *a.* [L. *clandestinus.*] Secret; private; hidden; withdrawn from public view. It often bears an ill sense, as implying craft or deception, or evil design.

ȻLANDES'TINELY, *adv.* Secretly; privately; in secret.

ȻLANDES'TINENESS, *n.* Secrecy; a state of concealment.

ȻLANG, *v. t.* [L. *clango,* to sound; G. *klang;* D. *klank;* Sw. *klang;* Dan. *klang;* Gr. κλαγγω, κλαζω, κλαγξω, εκλαγον. It appears from the Greek, that *n* is not radical, and that this word belongs to Class Lg, coinciding with *clink, clank,* and probably with *clack.*]

To make a sharp, shrill sound, as by striking metallic substances; or to strike with a sharp sound.

They *clanged* their sounding arms. *Prior.*

ȻLANG, *n.* [L. *clangor;* G. *klang;* D. *klank.* See the Verb.]

A sharp, shrill sound, made by striking together metallic substances, or sonorous bodies, as the *clang* of arms; or any like sound, as the *clang* of trumpets. This word implies a degree of harshness in the sound, or more harshness than *clink.* *Milton.*

ȻLAN'GOR, *n.* [L.] A sharp, shrill, harsh sound. [See *Clang.*] *Dryden.*

ȻLAN'GOROUS, *a.* Sharp, or harsh in sound. *Spectator.*

ȻLAN'GOUS, *a.* Making a clang, or a shrill, or harsh sound. *Brown.*

ȻLAN'ISH, *a.* Closely united, like a clan; disposed to adhere closely, as the members of a clan.

ȻLAN'ISHNESS, *n.* Close adherence or disposition to unite, as a clan.

ȻLANK, *n.* [See *Clang.*] The loud, shrill, sharp sound, made by a collision of metallic or other sonorous bodies. *Spectator.*

ȻLANK, *v. t.* To make a sharp, shrill sound; to strike with a sharp sound; as, the prisoners *clank* their chains.

ȻLAN'SHIP, *n.* A state of union, as in a family, or clan; an association under a chieftain. *Robertson. Encyc.*

ȻLAP, *v. t.* pret. and pp. *clapped* or *clapt.* [D. *klappen, kloppen;* Dan. *klapper;* Sw. *klappa;* G. *klappen* or *klaffen;* Russ. *kleplyu.* The Dutch and German words signify to *clap* or strike, and to talk, clatter, prate. Sax. *cleopian* or *clypian,* to call, to speak, whence *ycleped,* obs. W. *clepian,* to clack, to babble, from *llep,* a lapping, *llepiaw,* to *lap,* to lick. The sense is to send, drive or strike, L. *alapa,* a *slap.*]

1. To strike with a quick motion, so as to make a noise by the collision; to strike with something broad, or having a flat surface; as, to *clap* the hands; to *clap* the wings. *Locke. Dryden.*

2. To thrust; to drive together; to shut hastily; followed by *to;* as, to *clap to* the door or gate. *Locke. Shak.*

3. To thrust or drive together; to put one thing to another by a hasty or sudden motion; followed by *to, on* or *in;* as, to *clap* the hand *to* the mouth; to *clap* spurs *to* a horse; to *clap on* a saddle. *Watts. Addison. Dryden.*

4. To thrust; to put, place or send; followed by *in, into, under, over,* &c.; as, to *clap* one *under* the hatches; to *clap* one *into* Bedlam; to *clap* a board *over* a pit. *Shak. Spectator.*

5. To applaud; to manifest approbation or praise by striking the hands together; as, to *clap* a performance on the stage.

6. To infect with venereal poison. *Wiseman.*

To clap up, to make or complete hastily; as, to *clap up* a peace. *Shak. Howel.*

2. To imprison hastily, or with little delay. *Sandys.*

ȻLAP, *v. i.* To move or drive together suddenly with noise.

The doors around me *clapt.* *Dryden.*

2. To enter on with alacrity and briskness; to drive or thrust on; as we say to reapers or mowers, *clap in,* or *clap to,* that is, enter on the work, begin without delay, begin briskly.

3. To strike the hands together in applause.

Bid them *clap.* *Shak.*

ȻLAP, *n.* A driving together; a thrust and collision of bodies with noise, usually bodies with broad surfaces.

Give the door a *clap.* *Swift.*

2. A sudden act or motion; a thrust.

Pay all debts at one *clap.* *Swift.*

3. A burst of sound; a sudden explosion; as a *clap* of thunder.

4. An act of applause; a striking of hands to express approbation. *Addison.*

5. A venereal infection. [Fr. *clapoir;* D. *klapoor.*] *Pope.*

6. With falconers, the nether part of the beak of a hawk. *Bailey.*

ȻLAP'-BOARD, *n.* A thin narrow board for covering houses. In England, according to Bailey, a clapboard is also what in America is called a stave for casks.

ȻLAP'-DISH, *n.* A wooden bowl or dish.

ȻLAP'-DOȻTOR, *n.* One who is skilled in healing the clap. *Tatler.*

ȻLAP'-NET, *n.* A net for taking larks, united with a looking glass. *Bailey. Encyc.*

ȻLAP'PED, *pp.* Thrust or put on or together; applauded by striking the hands together; infected with the venereal disease.

ƇLAP'PER, *n.* A person who claps, or applauds by clapping.

2. That which strikes, as the tongue of a bell, or the piece of wood that strikes a mill-hopper.

ƇLAP'PER-ƇLAW, *v. t.* [*clap* and *claw.*] To scold; to abuse with the tongue; to revile. *Shak. Hudibras.*

ƇLAP'PING, *ppr.* Driving or putting on, in, over, or under, by a sudden motion; striking the hands together.

ƇLARE, *n.* A nun of the order of St. Clare. *Todd.*

ƇLAR'ENCEUX, ƇLAR'ENCIEUX, } *n.* In Great Britain, the second king at arms, so called from the duke of Clarence, and appointed by Edward IV. His office is to marshal and dispose the funerals of all baronets, knights and esquires, on the south of the river Trent. *Bailey. Encyc.*

ƇLARE-OBSƇU'RE, *n.* [L. *clarus,* clear, and *obscurus,* obscure.]

Light and shade in painting; or the particular distribution of the lights and shades of a piece, with respect to the ease of the eye and the effect of the whole piece; also, a design of two colors. *Encyc.*

ƇLAR'ET, *n.* [Fr. *clairet,* from *clair,* clear; It. *claretto.*]

A species of French wine, of a clear pale red color. *Thomson.*

ƇLAR'IƇHORD, *n.* [L. *clarus,* clear, and *chorda,* a string. See *Chord.*]

A musical instrument in form of a spinet, called also *manichord.* It has forty nine or fifty stops or keys, and seventy strings; some of the latter being in unison. There are several little mortises for passing the jacks, armed with brass hooks, which stop and raise the chords, instead of the feather used in virginals and spinets. The chords are covered with pieces of cloth, which deaden the sound and render it sweeter. Hence it is particularly used by nuns. *Encyc.*

ƇLARIFIƇA'TION, *n.* [See *Clarify.*] The act of clearing; particularly the clearing or fining of liquid substances from all feculent matter. *Bacon.*

ƇLAR'IFIED, *pp.* Purified; made clear or fine; defecated.

ƇLAR'IFIER, *n.* That which clarifies or purifies; as, whites of eggs, blood and isinglass are *clarifiers* of liquors. *Edwards.*

2. A vessel in which liquor is clarified. *Higgins, Med. Repos.*

ƇLAR'IFȲ, *v. t.* [Fr. *clarifier;* It. *chiarificare;* from L. *clarus,* clear, and *facio,* to make.[

To make clear; to purify from feculent matter; to defecate; to fine; *applied particularly to liquors;* as, to *clarify* wine, or syrup.

2. To make clear; to brighten or illuminate; *applied to the mind or reason.* [*Rarely used.*] *South.*

ƇLAR'IFȲ, *v. i.* To clear up; to grow clear or bright.

His understanding *clarifies,* in discoursing with another. *Bacon.*

2. To grow or become clear or fine; to become pure, as liquors. Cider *clarifies* by fermentation.

ƇLAR'IFȲING, *ppr.* Making clear, pure or bright; defecating; growing clear.

ƇLAR'INET, *n.* [Fr. *clarinette.*] A wind instrument of music.

ƇLAR'ION, *n.* [Fr. *clairon;* Sp. *clarin;* It. *chiarina;* Port. *clarim;* from L. *clarus,* clear, from its shrill sound.]

A kind of trumpet, whose tube is narrower and its tone more acute and shrill than that of the common trumpet. *Encyc.*

ƇLAR'ITUDE, *n.* Clearness; splendor. [*Little used.*] *Beaum.*

ƇLAR'ITY, *n.* [Fr. *clarté;* L. *claritas,* from *clarus,* clear.]

Clearness, brightness; splendor. [*Little used.*] *Bacon. Brown.*

ƇLAR'Y, *v. i.* To make a loud or shrill noise. [*Not used.*] *Golding.*

ƇLA'RY, *n.* A plant of the genus Salvia, or sage.

ƇLA'RY-WATER, *n.* A composition of brandy, sugar, clary-flowers, and cinnamon, with a little ambergris dissolved in it. It is a cardiac and helps digestion. *Encyc.*

ƇLASH, *v. i.* [D. *kletsen;* G. *klatschen, klitschen;* Dan. *klatsker.*]

To strike against; to drive against with force.

Note. The sense of this word is simply to strike against or meet with force; but when two sounding bodies strike together, the effect is a sound. Hence the word often implies, to strike with a noise, as *clashing* arms. *Denham.*

2. To meet in opposition; to be contrary; to act in a contrary direction; to interfere, as opposing persons, minds, views, interests, &c.; as, the opinions of men *clash; clashing* interests. *South. Bacon.*

Independent jurisdictions—could not fail to *clash.* *Dwight's Theol.*

ƇLASH, *v. t.* To strike one thing against another, with sound. *Dryden.*

ƇLASH, *n.* A meeting of bodies with violence; a striking together with noise; collision, or noisy collision of bodies; as the *clash* of arms. *Pope. Denham.*

2. Opposition; contradiction; as between differing or contending interests, views, purposes, &c. *Atterbury. Denham.*

ƇLASH'ING, *ppr.* Striking against with noise; meeting in opposition; opposing; interfering.

ƇLASH'ING, *n.* A striking against; collision of bodies; opposition. *Howel.*

ƇL'ASP, *n.* [Ir. *clasba.*]

1. A hook for fastening; a catch; a small hook to hold together the covers of a book, or the different parts of a garment, of a belt, &c. *Addison.*

2. A close embrace; a throwing of the arms round. *Shak.*

ƇL'ASP, *v. t.* To shut or fasten together with a clasp. *Pope.*

2. To catch and hold by twining; to surround and cling to; as the *clasping* ivy. *Milton.*

3. To inclose and hold in the hand; or simply to inclose or encompass with the fingers. *Bacon.*

4. To embrace closely; to throw the arms round; to catch with the arms. *Milton. Dryden.*

5. To inclose, and press.

ƇL'ASPED, *pp.* Fastened with a clasp; shut; embraced; inclosed; encompassed; caught.

ƇL'ASPER, *n.* He or that which clasps; usually the tendril of a vine or other plant, which twines round something for support.

ƇL'ASPERED, *a.* Furnished with tendrils.

ƇL'ASPING, *ppr.* Twining round; catching and holding; embracing; inclosing; shutting or fastening with a clasp.

2. In *botany,* surrounding the stem at the base, as a leaf. *Martyn.*

ƇL'ASP-KNIFE, *n.* A knife which folds into the handle. *Johnson.*

ƇL'ASS, *n.* [L. *classis,* a class, a fleet, a troop, that is, a collection; It. *classe;* Fr. *classe;* Sp. *clase;* Arm. *claçz,* and *sclaçz;* Dan. *klasse,* a class, and *klase,* a cluster, a bunch. This seems to be a branch of the root of L. *claudo, clausus.*]

1. An order or rank of persons; a number of persons in society, supposed to have some resemblance or equality, in rank, education, property, talents, and the like; as in the phrase, all *classes* of men in society.

The readers of poetry may be distinguished into three *classes,* according to their capacity of judging. *Dryden.*

2. A number of students in a college or school, of the same standing, or pursuing the same studies. In colleges, the students entering or becoming members the same year, and pursuing the same studies. In academies and schools, the pupils who learn the same lesson, and recite together. In some cases, students of different standings, pursuing the same studies and reciting together, or attending the same professor, or the same course of lectures.

3. Scientific division or arrangement; a set of beings or things, having something in common, or ranged under a common denomination. Hence in zoology, animals are divided into classes; as quadrupeds, fowls, fishes, &c. So in botany, plants are arranged in classes. Classes are natural or artificial; natural, when founded on natural relations, or resemblances; artificial, when formed arbitrarily, for want of a complete knowledge of natural relations. *Martyn.*

ƇL'ASS, *v. t.* To arrange in a class or classes; to arrange in sets, or ranks, according to some method founded on natural distinctions; to place together, or in one division, men or things which have or are supposed to have something in common.

2. To place in ranks or divisions students that are pursuing the same studies; to form into a class or classes.

ƇLAS'SIƇ, ƇLAS'SIƇAL, } *a.* [L. *classicus;* Fr. *classique;* It. *classico;* Sp. *clasico;* from L. *classis,* the first order of Roman citizens.]

1. Relating to ancient Greek and Roman authors of the first rank or estimation, which, in modern times, have been and still are studied as the best models of fine writing. Thus, Aristotle, Plato, Demosthenes, Thucydides, &c., among the Greeks, and Cicero, Virgil, Livy, Sallust, Cesar, and Tacitus, among the Latins, are *classical* authors. Hence,

2. Pertaining to writers of the first rank among the moderns; being of the first order; constituting the best model or au-

thority as an author; as, Addison and Johnson are English *classical* writers. Hence *classical* denotes pure, chaste, correct, refined; as a *classical* taste; a *classical* style.

At Liverpool, Roscoe is like Pompey's column at Alexandria, towering alone in *classic* dignity. *Irving.*

3. Denoting an order of presbyterian assemblies. *Milton. Mason.*

ЄLAS'SIЄ, *n.* An author of the first rank; a writer whose style is pure, correct, and refined; primarily, a Greek or Roman author of this character; but the word is applied to writers of a like character in any nation. *Pope.*

2. A book written by an author of the first class.

ЄLAS'SIЄALLY, *adv.* In the manner of classes; according to a regular order of classes, or sets.

It would be impossible to bear all its specific details in the memory, if they were not *classically* arranged. *Kerr's Lavoisier.*

2. In a classical manner; according to the manner of classical authors.

ЄLASSIF'IЄ, *a.* Constituting a class or classes; noting classification, or the order of distribution into sets. *Med. Repos. Hex.* 2.

ЄLASSIFIЄA'TION, *n.* [See *Classify.*] The act of forming into a class or classes; distribution into sets, sorts or ranks. *Enfield's Phil. Encyc.*

ЄLAS'SIFIED, *pp.* Arranged in classes; formed into a class or classes.

ЄLAS'SIFY, *v. t.* [L. *classis*, a class, and *facio*, to make; a word of modern coinage.] To make a class or classes; to distribute into classes; to arrange in sets according to some common properties or characters.

The diseases and casualties are not scientifically *classified*. *Tooke, Russ. Emp.* i. 531.

See also, *Aikin's Letters.* 106. *Black's Chimistry.* i. 345. *Walsh.* iii. 44. *Stewart, El. Phil.* i.187.

ЄLAS'SIFYING, *ppr.* Forming a class or classes; arranging in sorts or ranks.

ЄLAS'SIS, *n.* Class; order; sort. *Clarendon.*

2. A convention or assembly. *Milton.*

ЄLAT'TER, *v. i.* [D. *klateren, kletteren*; W. *clewtiaw*; Sax. *clatninge*, a clattering. Qu. Fr. *eclater*; L. *latro*; Sax. *hlyd*, loud. It seems to be a diminutive.]

1. To make rattling sounds; to make repeated sharp sounds, as by striking sonorous bodies; as, to *clatter* on a shield. *Dryden.*

2. To utter continual or repeated sharp sounds, or rattling sounds, by being struck together; as *clattering* arms.

3. To talk fast and idly; to run on; to rattle with the tongue. *Spenser.*

ЄLAT'TER, *v. t.* To strike and make a rattling noise.

You *clatter* still your brazen kettle. *Swift.*

2. To dispute, jar or clamor. [*A low word.*] *Martin.*

ЄLAT'TER, *n.* A rapid succession of abrupt, sharp sounds, made by the collision of metallic or other sonorous bodies; rattling sounds. *Swift.*

2. Tumultuous and confused noise; a repetition of abrupt, sharp sounds. *Swift. Shak.*

ЄLAT'TERER, *n.* One who clatters; a babbler.

ЄLAT'TERING, *ppr.* Making or uttering sharp, abrupt sounds, as by a collision of sonorous bodies; talking fast with noise; rattling.

ЄLAT'TERING, *n.* A rattling noise.

ЄLAUD'ENT, *a.* [L. *claudens*; *claudo*, to shut.] Shutting; confining; drawing together; as a *claudent* muscle. [*Little used.*]

ЄLAUD'IЄANT, *a.* Halting; limping. [*Little used.*]

ЄLAUD'IЄATE, *v. i.* [L. *claudico*, to limp, from *claudus*, lame.] To halt or limp. [*Little used, or not at all.*]

ЄLAUDIЄA'TION, *n.* A halting or limping. [*Little used.*]

ЄLAUSE, *n. s* as *z.* [Fr. *clause*; L. *clausura*, from *claudo*, to shut; Gr. κλειω, κλειςος; W. *claws*; Eng. *close*; Sax. *hlidan*, to cover; *hlid*, a cover, a *lid*, which see. Class Ld. No. 1. 8. 9.]

Literally, a close, or inclosure. Hence, that which is included, or contained, within certain limits.

1. In *language* or *grammar*, a member of a period or sentence; a subdivision of a sentence, in which the words are inseparably connected with each other in sense, and cannot, with propriety, be separated by a point; as, "there is reason to think that he afterwards rose to favor, and obtained several honors civil and military." In this sentence are two clauses.

2. An article in a contract or other writing; a distinct part of a contract, will, agreement, charter, commission, or other writing; a distinct stipulation, condition, proviso, grant, covenant, &c. *South.*

ЄLAUS'TRAL, *a.* [L. *claustrum*, an inclosure, from *claudo*. See *Clause.*] Relating to a cloister, or religious house; as a *claustral* prior. *Ayliffe.*

ЄLAUS'URE, *n. s* as *z.* [See *Clause.*] The act of shutting up or confining; confinement. [*Little used.*] *Geddes.*

2. In *anatomy*, an imperforated canal. *Coxe. Quincy.*

ЄLAV'ATED, *a.* [L. *clava*; Eng. a *club*; W. *clwpa.*]

1. Club-shaped; having the form of a club; growing gradually thicker towards the top, as certain parts of a plant. *Martyn.*

2. Set with knobs. *Woodward.*

ЄLAVE, *pret.* of *cleave.*

ЄLAV'ELLATED, *a.* *Clavellated* ashes, potash and pearlash. *Coxe.*

ЄLAV'IARY, *n.* [L. *clavis*, a key; Gr. κλεις, contracted from κλειδοω; L. *claudo.*] A scale of lines and spaces in music. *Encyc.* art. *Clef.*

ЄLAV'IЄHORD, *n.* [L. *clavis*, a key, and *chorda*, a string.] A musical instrument of an oblong figure, of the nature of a spinet. The strings are muffled with small bits of fine woolen cloth, to soften the sounds; *used in nunneries.* [See *Clarichord.*] *Encyc.*

ЄLAV'IЄLE, *n.* [L. *clavicula*, a tendril, that is a little key or fastener, from *clavis*, a key or lock.] The collar bone. There are two *clavicles*, or channel bones, joined at one end to the scapula or shoulder bone, and at the other, to the sternum or breast bone. *Quincy.*

ЄLAV'IGER, *n.* [L. *clavis*, a key, and *gero*, to carry.] One who keeps the keys of any place. *Ch. Relig. Appeal.*

ЄLAW, *n.* [Sax. *claw*; G. *klaue*; D. *klaauw*; Dan. *klov*; Sw. *klof*, or *klo.*]

1. The sharp hooked nail of a beast, bird or other animal.

Every beast that parteth the hoof, and cleaveth the cleft into two *claws*, and cheweth the cud—ye shall eat. Deut. xiv.

His nails were grown like birds *claws*. Dan. iv.

2. The whole foot of an animal armed with hooked nails.

3. The hand, in contempt.

ЄLAW, *v. t.* [Sax. *clawen.*] To pull, tear or scratch with the nails. *Shak. South.*

2. To scratch or tear in general; to tickle. *Shak. Hudibras.*

3. To flatter. *Obs.* *Shak.*

To claw off or *away*, to scold or rail at. *L'Estrange.*

2. In *seamanship*, to turn to windward and beat, to prevent falling on a lee shore.

3. In *vulgar language*, to scratch away; to get off or escape.

ЄLAW'BACK, *n.* [*claw* and *back.*] One who flatters; a sycophant; a wheedler. *Jewel.*

ЄLAW'ED, *pp.* Scratched, pulled or torn with claws.

2. *a.* Furnished with claws. *Grew.*

ЄLAW'ING, *ppr.* Pulling, tearing or scratching with claws or nails.

ЄLAW'LESS, *a.* Destitute of claws. *Journ. of Science.*

ЄLAY, *n.* [Sax. *clæg*; G. *klei*; D. *klei*; W. *clai*; Dan. *klæg*, viscous, sticky.]

1. The name of certain substances which are mixtures of silex and alumin, sometimes with lime, magnesia, alkali and metallic oxyds. A species of earths which are firmly coherent, weighty, compact, and hard when dry, but stiff, viscid and ductile when moist, and smooth to the touch; not readily diffusible in water, and when mixed, not readily subsiding in it. They contract by heat. Clays absorb water greedily, and become soft, but are so tenacious as to be molded into any shape, and hence they are the materials of bricks and various vessels, domestic and chimical. *Encyc. Cleaveland*

2. In *poetry* and in *scripture*, earth in general. *Donne.*

I also am formed out of the *clay*. Job xxxiii.

3. In scripture, *clay* is used to express frailty, liableness to decay and destruction.

They that dwell in houses of *clay*. Job iv.

ЄLAY, *v. t.* To cover or manure with clay. *Mortimer.*

2. To purify and whiten with clay, as sugar. *Edwards, W. Ind.*

ЄLAY-ЄOLD, *a.* Cold as clay or earth; lifeless. *Rowe.*

ЄLA'YED, *pp.* Covered or manured with clay.

2. Purified and whitened with clay; as *clayed* sugar. *Edwards.*

ЄLAYES, *n. plu.* [Fr. *claie*, a hurdle; W. *clwyd.*] In *fortification*, wattles or hurdles made with stakes interwoven with osiers, to cover lodgments. *Chambers.*

ЄLA'YEY, *a.* Consisting of clay; abounding with clay; partaking of clay; like clay.

CLAY-GROUND, *n.* Ground consisting of clay, or abounding with it.

CLA'YISH, *a.* Partaking of the nature of clay, or containing particles of it.

CLAY-LAND, } *n.* Land consisting of clay,
CLAY-SOIL, } or abounding with it.

CLAY-MARL, *n.* A whitish, smooth, chalky clay. *Mortimer.*

CLAY-PIT, *n.* A pit where clay is dug. *Woodward.*

CLAY-SLATE, *n.* In *mineralogy,* argillaceous shist; argillite.

CLAY-STONE, *n.* A mineral, the *thonstein* of Werner, and *indurated clay* of Kirwan. It resembles compact limestone or calcarious marl. Its texture is porous, compact or slaty. Its color is gray, often tinged with yellow or blue; also rose or pale red, or brownish red, and sometimes greenish. *Cleaveland.*

CLEAN, *a.* [Sax. *clæne;* W. *glan,* or *glain;* Ir. *glan;* Arm. *glan.* The primary sense seems to be, to open or to remove, to separate.]

In *a general sense,* free from extraneous matter, or whatever is injurious or offensive; hence its signification depends on the nature and qualities of the substances to which it is applied.

1. Free from dirt, or other foul matter; as *clean* water; a *clean* cup; a *clean* floor.
2. Free from weeds or stones; as *clean* land; a *clean* garden or field.
3. Free from knots or branches; as *clean* timber. In America, *clear* is generally used.
4. Free from moral impurity; innocent.

> Who can bring a *clean* thing out of an unclean? Job xiv. Acts xviii.

5. Free from ceremonial defilement. Lev. x. Numb. xix.
6. Free from guilt; sanctified; holy. John xiii. Ps. li.
7. That might be eaten by the Hebrews. Gen. vii. viii.
8. That might be used. Luke xi.
9. Free from a foul disease; cured of leprosy. 2 Kings v. Math. viii.
10. Dextrous; adroit; not bungling; free from awkwardness; as a *clean* feat; a *clean* boxer.
11. Free from infection; as a *clean* ship. A *clean* bill of health is a certificate that a ship is *clean,* or free from infection.

CLEAN, *adv.* Quite; perfectly; wholly; entirely; fully; indicating separation or complete removal of every part. "The people passed *clean* over Jordan." Josh. iii. "Is his mercy *clean* gone forever?" Ps. lxxvii. This use of *clean* is not now elegant, and not used except in vulgar language.

2. Without miscarriage; dextrously.

> Pope came off *clean* with Homer. *Henley.*

CLEAN, *v. t.* [Sax. *clænan;* W. *glanau.* See the Adjective.]

To remove all foreign matter from; to separate from any thing whatever is extraneous to it, or whatever is foul, noxious, or offensive, as dirt or filth from the hands, body or clothes, foul matter from a vessel, weeds, shrubs and stones from a meadow; to purify. Thus, a house is *cleaned* by sweeping and washing; a field is *cleaned* by plowing and hoeing.

CLEAN'LINESS, *n.* *clen'liness.* [from *cleanly.*] Freedom from dirt, filth, or any foul, extraneous matter. *Addison.*

2. Neatness of person or dress; purity. *Swift.*

CLEAN'LY, *a.* *clen'ly.* [from *clean.*] Free from dirt, filth, or any foul matter; neat; carefully avoiding filth. *Dryden. Addison.*

2. Pure; free from mixture; innocent; as *cleanly* joys. *Glanville.*
3. Cleansing; making clean; as *cleanly* powder. *Prior.*
4. Nice; artful; dextrous; adroit; as a *cleanly* play; a *cleanly* evasion. *Obs.* *Spenser. L'Estrange.*

CLEAN'LY, *adv.* *clen'ly.* In a clean manner; neatly; without filth. *Shak.*

CLE'ANNESS, *n.* Freedom from dirt, filth, and foreign matter; neatness.

2. Freedom from infection or a foul disease.
3. Exactness; purity; justness; correctness; *used of language or style;* as, *cleanness* of expression. *Dryden.*
4. Purity; innocence.

In scripture, *cleanness* of hands denotes innocence. *Cleanness* of teeth denotes want of provisions. Amos iv. 6.

CLEANS'ABLE, *a.* *clenz'able.* That may be cleansed. *Sherwood.*

CLEANSE, *v. t.* *clenz.* [Sax. *clænsian,* from *clæne,* clean.]

1. To purify; to make clean; to remove filth, or foul matter of any kind, or by any process whatever, as by washing, rubbing, scouring, scraping, purging, ventilation, &c.; as, to *cleanse* the hands or face; to *cleanse* a garment; to *cleanse* the bowels; to *cleanse* a ship; to *cleanse* an infected house.
2. To free from a foul or infectious disease; to heal. Lev. xiv. 4. 8. Mark i. 42.
3. To free from ceremonial pollution, and consecrate to a holy use. Numb. viii. 15. Ezek. xliii. 20.
4. To purify from guilt. 1 John i. 7.
5. To remove; as, to *cleanse* a crime. *Dryden.*

CLEANS'ED, *pp.* *clenz'ed.* Purified; made clean; purged; healed.

CLEANS'ER, *n.* *clenz'er.* He or that which cleanses; in medicine, a detergent. *Arbuthnot.*

CLEANS'ING, *pp.* *clenz'ing.* Purifying; making clean; purging; removing foul or noxious matter from; freeing from guilt.

CLEANS'ING, *n.* *clenz'ing.* The act of purifying, or purging. Mark i. 44. Luke v. 14.

CLE'AN-TIMBERED, *a.* Well-proportioned. [*Not in use.*] *Shak.*

CLEAR, *a.* [W. *claer,* clear, bright, from *llaer,* a reflux, *llaeru,* to ebb, to clear, or W. *eglur,* clear, from *llur,* extended, [like floor;] Ir. *gleair, lear, leir* and *glor;* Arm. *sclear;* L. *clarus;* Fr. *clair;* Sp. Port. *claro;* It. *chiaro;* D. *klaar;* G. *klar;* Sw. and Dan. *klar.* See *Glare* and *Glory.*]

1. Open; free from obstruction; as a *clear* plat of ground; the way is *clear.*
2. Free from clouds, or fog; serene; as a *clear* day.
3. Free from foreign matter; unmixed; pure; as *clear* water; *clear* sand; *clear* air; *clear* glass.
4. Free from any thing that creates doubt or uncertainty; apparent; evident; manifest; not obscure; conspicuous; that is, open to the mind; as, the reason is *clear.*
5. Unclouded; luminous; not obscured; as a *clear* sun; a *clear* shining after a rain. 2 Sam. xxiii.
6. Unobstructed; unobscured; as a *clear* view.
7. Perspicacious; sharp; as a *clear* sight.
8. Not clouded with care, or ruffled by passion; cheerful; serene; as a *clear* aspect. *Milton.*
9. Evident; undeniable; indisputable; as the victory was *clear.* *Milton.*
10. Quick to understand; prompt; acute.

> Mother of science, now I feel thy power
> Within me *clear.* *Milton.*

11. Free from guilt or blame; innocent; unspotted; irreproachable. 2 Cor. vii.

> In action faithful, and in honor *clear.* *Pope.*

12. Free from bias; unprepossessed; not preoccupied; impartial; as a *clear* judgment. *Sidney.*
13. Free from debt, or obligation; not liable to prosecution; as, to be *clear* of debt or responsibility. *Gay.*
14. Free from deductions, or charges; as, *clear* gain or profit. *Locke.*
15. Not entangled; unembarrassed; free; as, the cable is *clear.* A ship is *clear,* when she is so remote from shore or other object, as to be out of danger of striking, or to have sea room sufficient.
16. Open; distinct; not jarring, or harsh; as a *clear* sound; a *clear* voice.
17. Liberated; freed; acquitted of charges; as, a man has been tried and got *clear.*
18. Free from spots or any thing that disfigures; as a *clear* skin.

Clear is followed by *from* or by *of.*

> Thou shalt be *clear from* this my oath. Gen. xxiv.
>
> The air is *clear of* damp exhalations. *Temple.*

CLEAR, *adv.* Plainly; not obscurely; manifestly.

2. Clean; quite; entirely; wholly; indicating entire separation; as, to cut a piece *clear* off; to go *clear* away; but in this sense its use is not elegant.

Clear or *in the clear,* among joiners and carpenters, denotes the space within walls, or length and breadth *clear* or exclusive of the thickness of the wall.

CLEAR, *v. t.* To make clear; to fine; to remove any thing foreign; to separate from any foul matter; to purify; to clarify; as, to *clear* liquors.

2. To free from obstructions; as, to *clear* the road.
3. To free from any thing noxious or injurious; as, to *clear* the ocean of pirates; to *clear* the land of enemies.
4. To remove any incumbrance, or embarrassment; often followed by *off* or *away;* as, to *clear off* debts; to *clear away* rubbish.
5. To free; to liberate, or disengage; to exonerate; as, to *clear* a man from debt, obligation, or duty.
6. To cleanse; as, to *clear* the hands from filth; to *clear* the bowels.
7. To remove any thing that obscures, as

clouds or fog; to make bright; as, to *clear* the sky; sometimes followed by *up*. *Dryden. Milton.*

8. To free from obscurity, perplexity or ambiguity; as, to *clear* a question or theory; to *clear up* a case or point. *Prior.*

9. To purge from the imputation of guilt; to justify or vindicate.

How shall we *clear* ourselves? Gen. xliv.
That will by no means *clear* the guilty. Ex. xxxiv.

10. In *a legal sense*, to acquit on trial, by verdict; as, the prisoner has been tried and *cleared.*

11. To make gain or profit, beyond all expenses and charges; as, to *clear* ten per cent. by a sale of goods, or by a voyage.

12. To remove wood from land; to cut down trees, remove or burn them, and prepare land for tillage or pasture; as, to *clear* land for wheat.

To clear a ship at the custom house, is to exhibit the documents required by law, give bonds or perform other acts requisite, and procure a permission to sail, and such papers as the law requires.

To clear the land, in seamen's language, is to gain such a distance from shore, as to have open sea room, and be out of danger from the land.

To clear the hold, is to empty or unload a ship.

To clear a ship for action, or *to clear for action*, is to remove all incumbrances from the decks, and prepare for an engagement.

ЄLEAR, *v. i.* To become free from clouds or fog; to become fair; often followed by *up*, *off*, or *away*; as, the sky *clears*; the weather *clears up*; it *clears away*; it *clears off*.

2. To be disengaged from incumbrances, distress or entanglements; to become free or disengaged.

He that *clears* at once will relapse. *Bacon.*

ЄLE'ARAĠE, *n.* The removing of any thing. [*Little used.*]

ЄLE'ARANCE, *n.* A certificate that a ship or vessel has been *cleared* at the custom house; permission to sail.

ЄLE'ARED, *pp.* Purified; freed from foreign matter, or from incumbrance; made manifest; made luminous; cleansed; liberated; acquitted.

ЄLE'ARER, *n.* That which clears, purifies, or enlightens; that which brightens. *Addison.*

ЄLE'ARING, *ppr.* Purifying; removing foul matter, incumbrances, or obstructions; making evident, or luminous; cleansing; liberating; disengaging; acquitting; making gain beyond all costs and charges.

ЄLE'ARING, *n.* A defense; justification; vindication. 2 Cor. vii.

2. A place or tract of land cleared of wood for cultivation; *a common use of the word in America.*

3. The act of making clear.

ЄLE'ARLY, *adv.* Plainly; evidently; fully; as, the fact is *clearly* proved.

2. Without obstruction; luminously; as, to shine *clearly.*

3. With clear discernment; as, to understand *clearly.*

4. Without entanglement, or confusion. *Bacon.*

5. Plainly; honestly; candidly.

Deal *clearly* and impartially with yourselves. *Tillotson.*

6. Without reserve, evasion or subterfuge. *Davies.*

ЄLE'ARNESS, *n.* Freedom from foul or extraneous matter; purity; as the *clearness* of water, or other liquor.

2. Freedom from obstruction or incumbrance; as the *clearness* of the ground.

3. Freedom from fogs or clouds; openness; as the *clearness* of the sky. It generally expresses less than brightness or splendor. Ex. xxiv.

4. Distinctness; perspicuity; luminousness; as the *clearness* of reason, of views, of arguments, of explanations.

5. Plainness, or plain dealing; sincerity; honesty; fairness; candor. *Bacon.*

6. Freedom from imputation of ill. *Shak.*

7. Freedom from spots, or any thing that disfigures; as the *clearness* of the skin.

ЄLE'AR-SHINING, *a.* [*clear* and *shine.*] Shining with brightness, or unobstructed splendor. *Shak.*

ЄLE'AR-SIGHTED, *a.* [*clear* and *sight.*] Seeing with clearness; having acuteness of sight; discerning; perspicacious; as *clear-sighted* reason; a *clear-sighted* judge.

ЄLEAR-SIGHTEDNESS, *n.* Acute discernment. *Bp. Barlow.*

ЄLE'AR-STARCH, *v. t.* [*clear* and *starch.*] To stiffen and clear with starch, and by clapping with the hands; as, to *clear-starch* muslin.

ЄLE'AR-STARCHER, *n.* One who clear-starches.

ЄLE'AR-STARCHING, *ppr.* Stiffening and clearing with starch.

2. *n.* The act of stiffening and clearing with starch.

ЄLEAT, *n.* [Qu. the root of L. *claudo*, Gr. *κλειθρον*, the fastener.]

A piece of wood used in a ship to fasten ropes upon. It is formed with one arm or two, or with a hollow to receive a rope, and is made fast to some part of a vessel. Cleats are belaying-cleats, deck-cleats or thumb-cleats. *Mar. Dict.*

ЄLE'AVAĠE, *n.* The act of cleaving or splitting.

2. In *mineralogy*, the manner of cleaving, or of mechanical division. It is used in relation to the fracture of minerals which have natural joints and possess a regular structure. *Phillips.*

ЄLEAVE, *v. i.* pret. *clave* or *cleaved.* [Sax. *cleofian*, *cliofian*, to split and to adhere; *clyfian*, to adhere; D. *kleeven*; G. *kleben* or *kleiben*; Dan. *klæber*, *kleber*; Sw. *klibba*; Russ. *lipnu.* The old preterit *clave* is obsolescent.]

1. To stick; to adhere; to hold to.

My bones *cleave* to my skin. Ps. cii.
Let my tongue *cleave* to the roof of my mouth. Ps. cxxxvii.
Cleave to that which is good. Rom. xii.

2. To unite aptly; to fit; to sit well on. *Shak.*

3. To unite or be united closely in interest or affection; to adhere with strong attachment.

A man shall leave father and mother, and *cleave* to his wife. Gen. ii. Math. xix.
Cleave to Jehovah your God. Josh. xxiii.

ЄLEAVE, *v. t.* pret. *cleft*; pp. *cleft* or *cleaved.* The old pret. *clove* is obsolete; *clave* is obsolescent. The old participle, *cloven*, is obsolescent, or rather used as an adjective. [Sax. *cleofian*, or *clifian*; D. *klooven*; G. *klieben*; Sw. *klyfwa*; Dan. *klöver*; Russ. *lopayu*; Gr. λεπω. This word seems to be connected with the L. *liber*, free, and bark, book, *libero*, to free, Fr. *livrer*, whence *deliver.*]

1. To part or divide by force; to split or rive; to open or sever the cohering parts of a body, by cutting or by the application of force; as, to *cleave* wood; to *cleave* a rock; to *cleave* the flood. Ps. lxxiv. *Milton. Dryden.*

2. To part or open naturally.

Every beast that *cleaveth* the cleft into two claws. Deut. xiv.

ЄLEAVE, *v. i.* To part; to open; to crack; to separate, as parts of cohering bodies; as, the ground *cleaves* by frost.

The mount of Olives shall *cleave* in the midst thereof. Zech. xiv.

ЄLE'AVED, *pp.* Split; rived; divided.

ЄLE'AVELANDITE, *n.* [from *Professor Cleaveland.*] A mineral, generally of a white or grayish white color, sometimes blue or bluish or reddish; called also siliceous felspar, or albite. *Phillips.*

ЄLE'AVER, *n.* One who cleaves; that which cleaves; a butcher's instrument for cutting animal bodies into joints or pieces. *Arbuthnot.*

ЄLE'AVING, *ppr.* Sticking; adhering; uniting to. Also, splitting; dividing; riving.

ЄLECHE, *n.* In *heraldry*, a kind of cross, charged with another cross of the same figure, but of the color of the field. *Encyc.*

ЄLEDĠE, *n.* Among *miners*, the upper stratum of fuller's earth.

ЄLEF, *n.* [Fr. *clef*; L. *clavis*, a key, the fastener.]

A character in music placed at the beginning of a stave, to determine the degree of elevation occupied by that stave in the general claviary or system, and to point out the names of all the notes which it contains in the line of that clef. *Rousseau.*

ЄLEFT, *pp.* of *cleave.* Divided; split; parted asunder. *Milton.*

ЄLEFT, *n.* A space or opening made by splitting; a crack; a crevice; as the *cleft* of a rock. Is. ii. 21. *Addison.*

2. A disease in horses; a crack on the bought of the pastern. *Farrier's Dict.*

3. A piece made by splitting; as a *cleft* of wood.

[This word is sometimes written *clift.*]

ЄLEFT-GRAFT, *v. t.* [*cleft* and *graft.*]

To engraft by cleaving the stock and inserting a cion. *Mortimer.*

ЄLEG, *n.* The horse fly; Dan. *klæg.*

ЄLEM, *v. t.* [G. *klemmen.*] To starve. [*Not in use.*] *Jonson.*

ЄLEM'ENCY, *n.* [L. *clementia*, from *clemens*, mild, smooth; whence Fr. *clemence*, It. *clemenza*, Sp. *clemencia*; W. *llim*, smooth; Heb. לחם to be soft, mild, gentle.]

1. Mildness; softness; as the *clemency* of the air. *Dryden.*

2. Mildness of temper; gentleness or lenity of disposition; disposition to treat with favor and kindness.

I pray thee that thou wouldest hear us of thy *clemency* a few words. Acts xxiv.

3. Mercy; disposition to treat with lenity, to forgive or to spare, as offenders; tenderness in punishing; opposed to severity, harshness, or rigor. *Addison.*

ƇLEM'ENT, *a.* Mild in temper and disposition; gentle; lenient; merciful; kind; tender; compassionate.

ƇLEM'ENTINE, *a.* Pertaining to St. Clement, or to his compilations; or to the constitutions of Clement the fifth.

ƇLEM'ENTLY, *adv.* With mildness of temper; mercifully. *Taylor.*

ƇLENCH. [See *Clinch.*]

ƇLEPE, *v. t.* or *i.* [Sax. *clepan, cleopan, clypan*, to cry out; W. *clepiaw*, to clack.] To call, or name. *Obs.* *Shak.*

ƇLEPSAM'MIA, *n.* [Gr. κλεπτω, to hide, to steal, and αμμος, sand.]

An instrument for measuring time by sand, like an hour glass. *Brown.*

ƇLEP'SYDRA, *n.* [L. from Gr. κλεψυδρα; κλεπτω, to steal, to hide, and υδωρ, water.]

1. A time piece used by the Greeks and Romans, which measured time by the discharge of a certain quantity of water. Also, a fountain in Greece.

2. A chimical vessel.

ƇLER'ĠIƇAL, *a.* Pertaining to the clergy. [*Not used.*] [See *Clerical.*] *Milton.*

ƇLER'ĠY, *n.* [Fr. *clergé*; Norm. *clerkus, clerex*, clergy, or clerks, and *clergie*, literature; Arm. *cloer*, the plural of *cloarecq*, a clerk; Corn. *cloireg*; Ir. *cleir*, clergy, and *cleirioch*, a clerk or clergyman; L. *clerus, clericus*, which would seem to be from the Gr. κληρος, lot or portion, inheritance, estate, and the body of those who perform sacred duties; whence κληροω, to choose by lot, to make a clerk, clericum facere. In 1 Peter v. 3. the word in the plural seems to signify the church or body of believers; it is rendered God's heritage. In W. *cler* signifies teachers or learned men of the druidical order; *clerig*, belonging to the *cler*, clerical. It. Sp. *clero*, from the Latin. The application of this word to ministers or ecclesiastical teachers seems to have originated in their possessions, or separate allotments of land; or from the Old Testament denomination of the priests, for the tribe of Levi is there called the lot, heritage, or inheritance of the Lord.]

The body of men set apart, and consecrated, by due ordination, to the service of God, in the christian church; the body of ecclesiastics, in distinction from the laity. *Hooker. Encyc.*

2. The privilege or benefit of clergy.

If convicted of a clergyable felony, he is entitled equally to his *clergy* after as before conviction. *Blackstone.*

Benefit of clergy, in English law, originally the exemption of the persons of clergymen from criminal process before a secular judge; or a privilege by which a clerk or person in orders claimed to be delivered to his ordinary to purge himself of felony. But this privilege has been abridged and modified by various statutes. See Blackstone, B. 4. Ch. 28. In the United States, no benefit of clergy exists.

ƇLER'ĠYABLE, *a.* Entitled to or admitting the benefit of clergy; as a *clergyable* felony. *Blackstone.*

ƇLER'ĠYMAN, *n.* A man in holy orders; a man licensed to preach the gospel, according to the forms and rules of any particular denomination of christians.

ƇLER'IƇ, *n.* A clerk or clergyman. *Horsley.*

ƇLER'IƇAL, *a.* [L. *clericus*; Gr. κληρικος. See *Clergy* and *Clerk.*]

Relating or pertaining to the clergy as *clerical* tonsure; *clerical* robes; *clerical* duties. *Blackstone.*

ƇLERK, *n.* [Sax. *cleric, clerc, clerc*; L. *clericus*; Gr. κληρικος. See *Clergy.*]

1. A clergyman, or ecclesiastic; a man in holy orders. *Ayliffe.*

2. A man that can read.

Every one that could read—being accounted a *clerk.* *Blackstone.*

3. A man of letters; a scholar. *Sidney. South.*

The foregoing significations are found in the English laws, and histories of the church; as in the rude ages of the church, learning was chiefly confined to the clergy. In modern usage,

4. A writer; one who is employed in the use of the pen, in an office public or private, for keeping records, and accounts; as the *clerk* of a court. In some cases *clerk* is synonymous with secretary; but not always. A clerk is always an officer subordinate to a higher officer, board, corporation or person; whereas, a secretary may be either a subordinate officer, or the head of an office or department.

5. A layman who is the reader of responses in church service. *Johnson.*

ƇLERK'-ALE, *n.* [*clerk* and *ale.*] In *England*, the feast of the parish clerk. *Warton.*

ƇLERK'LIKE, *a.* Like a clerk; learned. *Shak.*

ƇLERK'LY, *a.* Scholarlike. *Cranmer.*

ƇLERK'LY, *adv.* In a learned manner. *Gascoigne.*

ƇLERK'SHIP, *n.* A state of being in holy orders. *Blackstone.*

2. Scholarship. *Johnson.*

3. The office or business of a clerk or writer. *Swift.*

ƇLER'OMANCY, *n.* [Gr. κληρος, lot, and μαντεια, divination.]

A divination by throwing dice or little bones, and observing the points or marks turned up. *Bailey.*

ƇLEVE, ƇLIF, ƇLIVE, } in the composition of names, denote a place situated on or near a cliff, on the side of a hill, rock or precipice; as *Cleveland, Clifton.*

ƇLEV'ER, *a.* [I know not the radical letters of this word. If the elements are *clb*, or *lb*, the affinities may be Russ. *lovkie*, convenient, dextrous, *ulovka*, dexterity, craft, *lovlyu*, to take or seize, as if allied to Gothic *lofa*, Ir. *lamh*, W. *llaw*, the hand. In Ir. *lub* is a thong or *loop*, a plait or fold, and craft, cunning; *lubach*, sly, crafty; *lubam* to bend. In Eth. ለበዎ labawi, signifies ingenious, ready, skilful, and the verb, to understand, or be skilful. If *v* in *clever* is from *g*, as in many other words, the affinities may be Sax. *gleaw*, knowing, skilful, industrious, wise, which is the G. *klug*, D. *kloek*, Dan. *klog*, Sw. *klok.* Let the reader judge.]

1. Fit; suitable; convenient; proper; commodious. *Pope.*

2. Dextrous; adroit; ready; that performs with skill or address. *Addison.*

3. In *New England*, good-natured, possessing an agreeable mind or disposition. In *Great Britain*, this word is applied to the body or its movements, in its literal sense; in *America*, it is applied chiefly to the mind, temper, disposition. In Great Britain, a *clever man* is a dextrous man, one who performs an act with skill or address. In *New-England*, a *clever man* is a man of a pleasing obliging disposition, and amiable manners, but often implying a moderate share of talents. Fitness, suitableness, gives both senses analogically; the former applied to the body; the latter, to the mind, or its qualities. It is a colloquial word, but sometimes found in respectable writings.

In some of the United States, it is said this word is applied to the intellect, denoting ingenious, knowing, discerning.

ƇLEV'ERLY, *adv.* Fitly; dextrously; handsomely. *Butler.*

ƇLEV'ERNESS, *n.* Dexterity; adroitness; skill. *Johnson.*

2. Mildness or agreeableness of disposition; obligingness; good nature. *New England.*

ƇLEV'Y, ƇLEV'IS, } *n.* [Qu. L. *clavis.*] An iron bent to the form of an ox bow, with the two ends perforated to receive a pin, used on the end of a cart-neap to hold the chain of the forward horse or oxen; or a draft iron on a plow. *New England.*

ƇLEW, *n.* [Sax. *cleow, cliwe*; D. *kluwen*; G. *kloben*; L. *globus.* The word signifies a ball or a lump. In Welsh, *clob* is a knob or boss; *clwpa* is a club or knob; *clap* is a lump; all from roots in *lb*; *llob*, a lump, a lubber.]

1. A ball of thread. *Spenser.*

2. The thread that forms a ball; the thread that is used to guide a person in a labyrinth. Hence, any thing that guides or directs one in an intricate case. *Watts.*

3. The lower corner of a square sail, and the aftmost corner of a stay sail. *Mar. Dict.*

ƇLEW, *v. t.* In *seamanship*, to truss up to the yard, by means of clew-garnets or clew-lines, in order to furling.

2. To direct.

ƇLEW-GARNETS, *n.* In *marine language*, a sort of tackle, or rope and pulley, fastened to the clews of the main and foresails to truss them up to the yard.

ƇLEW'-LINES, *n.* These are the same tackle, and used for the like purpose as clew-garnets, but are applied to the smaller square sails, as the top-sail, top-gallant and sprit-sails. *Mar. Dict.*

ƇLICK, *v. i.* [D. *klikken*; Fr. *cliqueter*, to *crack*; *cliquet*, a mill-clapper. See *Clack*, to the root of which this word belongs.]

Literally, to strike; hence,

To make a small sharp noise, or rather a succession of small sharp sounds, as by a gentle striking.

The solemn death-watch *clicked.* *Gay.*

ƇLICK, *n.* In *seamen's language*, a small piece of iron falling into a notched wheel attached to the winches in cutters, &c. *Mar. Dict.*

ƇLICK, *n.* The latch of a door. [*Local.*]

ƇLICK'ER, *n.* The servant of a salesman, who stands at the door to invite customers; *a low word and not used in the United States.*

ƇLICK'ET, *n.* The knocker of a door. [*Not used in the United States.*]

ƇLICK'ING, *ppr.* Making small sharp noises.

ƇLI'ENT, *n.* [Fr. *client;* It. *cliente;* Sp. *id.*; L. *cliens.*]

1. Among the Romans, a citizen who put himself under the protection of a man of distinction and influence, who, in respect to that relation, was called his *patron.* Hence in modern usage,

2. One who applies to a lawyer or counselor for advice and direction in a question of law, or commits his cause to his management in prosecuting a claim, or defending against a suit, in a court of justice. *Bacon. Taylor.*

3. A dependent. *B. Jonson.*

ƇLI'ENTAL, *a.* Dependent. [*Unusual.*] *Burke.*

ƇLI'ENTED, *a.* Supplied with clients. *Carew.*

ƇLI'ENTSHIP, *n.* The condition of a client; a state of being under the protection of a patron. [*Clientele* is not used.] *Dryden.*

ƇLIFF, *n.* [Sax. *clif, clyf,* or *cleof;* D. *klif,* or *klip;* G. and Dan. *klippe;* Sw. *klippa;* W. *clip;* L. *clivus;* probably from *cleaving,* Sax. *clifian, cleofian.*]

1. A steep bank; as the *cliffs* of Dover. So in Saxon, the *cliffs* of the Red Sea. *Orosius,* supposed by Alfred.

2. A high and steep rock; any precipice. *Bacon. Dryden.*

This word has been sometimes written *clift,* and if from *cleaving,* rending, coincides with *cleft* in origin.

ƇLIFF, in music. [See *Clef.*]

ƇLIFF'Y, *a.* Having cliffs; broken; craggy. *Harmar.*

ƇLIFT'ED, *a.* Broken. *Congreve.*

ƇLIMAƇ'TER, *n.* [Gr. κλιμακτηρ, the step of a ladder, from κλιμαξ, a ladder or scale; L. *climacter.*]

1. A critical year in human life; but *climacteric* is more generally used.

2. A certain space of time. [*Not used.*] *Brown.*

ƇLIMAƇ'TERIƇ, *a.* [Gr. κλιμακτηρικος; L. *climactericus,* from *climax,* a ladder. See *Climax.*]

Literally, noting a scale, progression, or gradation; appropriately, denoting a critical period of human life, or a certain number of years, at the end of which a great change is supposed to take place in the human constitution. [See the Noun.]

ƇLIMAƇ'TERIƇ, *n.* A critical period in human life, or a period in which some great change is supposed to take place in the human constitution. The critical periods are supposed by some persons to be the years produced by multiplying 7 into the odd numbers 3, 5, 7, and 9; to which others add the 81st year. The 63d year is called the grand climacteric. It has been supposed that these periods are attended with some remarkable change in respect to health, life or fortune. *Brown. Dryden. Pope.*

ƇLIMATARƇH'IƇ, *a.* [Gr. κλιμα, climate, and αρχη, dominion.] Presiding over climates. *Paus. Trans. Note.*

ƇLI'MATE, *n.* [Gr. κλιμα; whence L. *clima;* It. Sp. *clima;* Fr. *climat.* Qu. from Gr. κλινω, to lean or incline, or the root of *climax.*]

1. In *geography,* a part of the surface of the earth, bounded by two circles parallel to the equator, and of such a breadth that the longest day in the parallel nearest the pole is half an hour longer than that nearest to the equator. The beginning of a climate is a parallel circle in which the longest day is half an hour shorter than that at the end. The climates begin at the equator, where the day is 12 hours long; and at the end of the first climate the longest day is 12½ hours long, and this increase of half an hour constitutes a climate, to the polar circles; from which climates are measured by the increase of a month. *Johnson. Encyc.*

2. In *a popular sense,* a tract of land, region or country, differing from another in the temperature of the air; or any region or country with respect to the temperature of the air, the seasons, and their peculiar qualities, without any regard to the length of the days, or to geographical position. Thus we say, a warm or cold *climate;* a moist or dry *climate;* a happy *climate;* a genial *climate;* a mountainous *climate.*

ƇLI'MATE, *v. i.* To dwell; to reside in a particular region. *Shak. Hist. of St. Domingo.* [*Little used, and hardly legitimate.*]

ƇLIMAT'IƇ, ƇLIMAT'IƇAL, *a.* Pertaining to a climate or climates; limited by a climate. *S. S. Smith.*

ƇLI'MATURE, *n.* A climate. [*Little used.*] *Shak.*

ƇLI'MAX, *n.* [Gr. κλιμαξ, a scale or ladder; L. *climax;* perhaps from the root of the W. *llamu,* to step, stride, leap, *llam,* a step, stride, leap, Ir. *leimim, leim,* or from the root of *climb.*]

1. Gradation; ascent; a figure of rhetoric, in which a sentence rises as it were, step by step; or in which the expression which ends one member of the period, begins the second, and so on, till the period is finished; as in the following: "When we have practiced good actions a while, they become easy; and when they are easy, we begin to take pleasure in them; and when they please us, we do them frequently; and by frequency of acts, they grow into a habit." *Tillotson.*

2. A sentence, or series of sentences, in which the successive members or sentences rise in force, importance or dignity, to the close of the sentence or series. *Dryden.*

ƇLIMB, *v. i. clime.* pret. and pp. *climbed,* or *clomb,* but the latter is not elegant. [Sax. *climan,* or *climban;* D. *klimmen;* G. *id.* The corresponding word in Dan. is *klyver;* Sw. *klifwa.*]

1. To creep up by little and little, or step by step; to mount or ascend, by means of the hands and feet; to rise on any fixed object, by seizing it with the hands and lifting the body, and by thrusting with the feet; as, to *climb* a tree or a precipice.

> And he ran before and *climbed* up into a sycamore tree. Luke xix.

2. To mount or ascend with labor and difficulty. *Shak.*

3. To rise or ascend with a slow motion.

> Black vapors *climb* aloft. *Dryden.*

ƇLIMB, *v. t.* To ascend by means of the hands and feet, implying labor, difficulty and slow progress; as, to *climb* a wall, or a steep mountain. *Prior.*

2. To mount or ascend, with labor or a slow motion; as, to *climb* the ascents of fame. *Prior.*

ƇLIMBABLE, *a.* That may be climbed. *Sherwood.*

ƇLIMBED, *pp.* Ascended by the use of the hands and feet; ascended with labor.

ƇLIMBER, *n.* One who climbs, mounts or rises, by the hands and feet; one who rises by labor or effort.

2. A plant that creeps and rises on some support. *Mortimer.*

ƇLIM'BER, *v. i.* [from *climb,* or a different orthography of *clamber.*]

To climb; to mount with effort. [*Not used.*] *Tusser.*

ƇLIMBING, *ppr.* Ascending by the use of the hands and feet; ascending with difficulty.

ƇLIMBING, *n.* The act of ascending.

ƇLIME, *n.* [from *climate,* or directly from Gr. and L. *clima.*]

A climate; a tract or region of the earth; *a poetical word,* but sometimes used in prose. [See *Climate.*]

> Whatever *clime* the sun's bright circle warms. *Milton.*

ƇLINCH, *v. t.* [D. *klinken,* to clink or rivet; *klink,* a latch, a rivet; Dan. *klinke,* a latch; Sw. *klinka;* Fr. *clenche;* allied to *cling, link,* W. *clicied,* a latch.]

1. To gripe with the hand; to make fast by bending over, folding, or embracing closely. Thus, to *clinch* a nail, is to bend the point and drive it closely. To *clinch* the hand or fist, is to contract the fingers closely into the palm of the hand. To *clinch* an instrument, is to close the fingers and thumb round it, and hold it fast.

2. To fix or fasten; to make firm; as, to *clinch* an argument.

ƇLINCH, *n.* A word used in a double meaning; a pun; an ambiguity; a duplicity of meaning, with identity of expression. *Johnson.*

> Here one poor word a hundred *clinches* makes. *Pope.*

2. A witty, ingenious reply. *Bailey.*

3. In *seamen's language,* the part of a cable which is fastened to the ring of an anchor; a kind of knot and seizings, used to fasten a cable to the ring of an anchor, and the britching of a gun to the ring bolts in a ship's side. *Mar. Dict.*

ƇLINCH'ED, *pp.* Made fast by doubling or embracing closely.

ƇLINCH'ER, *n.* That which clinches; a cramp or piece of iron bent down to fasten any thing. *Pope.*

2. One who makes a smart reply. *Bailey.*

3. That which makes fast.

ƇLINCH'ER-BUILT, ƇLINK'ER-BUILT, *a.* Made of clincher work.

ƇLINCH'ER-WŎRK, *n.* In *ship building,* the disposition of the planks in the side of a boat or vessel, when the lower edge of every plank overlays the next below it, like slates on the roof a house. *Mar. Dict.*

CLINCH'ING, *ppr.* Making fast by doubling over or embracing closely; griping with the fist.

CLING, *v. i.* pret. and pp. *clung.* [Sax. *clingan*, to adhere and to wither; Dan. *klynger*, to grow in clusters; *klynge*, a heap or cluster. See the transitive verb below.]

1. To adhere closely; to stick to; to hold fast upon, especially by winding round or embracing; as, the tendril of a vine *clings* to its support.

> Two babes of love close *clinging* to her waist. *Pope.*

2. To adhere closely; to stick to; as a viscous substance. *Wiseman.*

3. To adhere closely and firmly, in interest or affection; as, men of a party *cling* to their leader.

CLING, *v. t.* To dry up, or wither.

> Till famine *cling* thee. *Shak.*

In Saxon, *clingan* is rendered to fade or wither, *marcesco*, as well as to *cling.* In this sense is used *forclingan*, pp. *forclungen.* The radical sense then appears to be, to contract or draw together; and drying, withering, is expressed by shrinking. [*The latter use of the word is obsolete.*]

CLING'ING, *ppr.* Adhering closely; sticking to; winding round and holding to.

CLING'Y, *a.* Apt to cling; adhesive.

CLIN'IC, **CLIN'ICAL**, *a.* [Gr. χλινιχος, from χλινη, a bed, from χλινω, to recline. See *Lean.*]

In a general sense, pertaining to a bed. A *clinical* lecture is a discourse delivered at the bed-side of the sick, or from notes taken at the bed-side, by a physician, with a view to practical instruction in the healing art. *Clinical* medicine is the practice of medicine on patients in bed, or in hospitals. A *clinical* convert is a convert on his death-bed. Anciently persons receiving baptism on their death-beds were called *clinics.* *Coxe. Encyc. Taylor.*

CLIN'IC, *n.* One confined to the bed by sickness.

CLIN'ICALLY, *adv.* In a clinical manner; by the bed-side.

CLINK, *v. t.* [Sw. *klinga*; Dan. *klinger*, *klinker*; D. *klinken*; G. *klingen.* This seems to be a dialectical orthography of *clang*, *clank*, L. *clango*, and if *n* is not radical, they coincide with *clack*, *click*, with the radical sense, to strike.]

To ring or jingle; to utter or make a small sharp sound, or a succession of such sounds, as by striking small metallic or other sonorous bodies together. *Prior. Gay.*

CLINK, *n.* A sharp sound, made by the collision of small sonorous bodies. Spenser, according to Johnson, uses the word for a knocker.

CLINK'ING, *ppr.* Making a small sharp sound, or succession of sounds.

CLINK'STONE, *n.* [*clink* and *stone*, from its sonorousness. See *Phonolite.*]

A mineral which has a slaty structure, and is generally divisible into tabular masses, usually thick, sometimes thin like those of argillite. The cross fracture is commonly splintery. Its colors are dark greenish gray, yellowish, bluish, or ash gray; and it is usually translucent at the edges, sometimes opake. It occurs in extensive masses, often composed of columnar or tabular distinct concretions, more or less regular. It is usually found among secondary rocks; sometimes resting on basalt, and covered by greenstone. *Cleaveland.*

CLINOM'ETER, *n.* [Gr. χλινω, to lean, and μετρον, measure.]

An instrument for measuring the dip of mineral strata. *Ure.*

CLINQ'UANT, *a.* [Fr.] Dressed in tinsel finery. [*Not English.*] *Shak.*

CLIP, *v. t.* [Sax. *clypan*; Dan. *klipper*; Sw. *klippa.* The sense seems to be, to strike, to cut off by a sudden stroke. The Danish word signifies not only to cut off with scissors, but to wink or twinkle with the eyes. In our popular dialect, a *clip* is a blow or stroke; as, to hit one a *clip.* *Cut* is used in a like sense. The radical sense then is, to strike or drive with a sudden effort, thrust or spring.]

1. To cut off with shears or scissors; to separate by a sudden stroke; especially to cut off the ends or sides of a thing, to make it shorter or narrower, in distinction from shaving and paring, which are performed by rubbing the instrument close to the thing shaved; as, to *clip* the hair; to *clip* wings.

> But love had *clipped* his wings and cut him short. *Dryden.*

2. To diminish coin by paring the edge. *Locke.*

3. To curtail; to cut short. *Addison.*

4. To confine, limit, restrain, or hold; to hug. [*Little used.*] *Shak.*

To clip it, is a vulgar phrase in New England for to run with speed. So *cut* is used; *cut on*, run fast. This seems to be the meaning in Dryden.

> Some falcon stoops at what her eye designed,
> And with her eagerness the quarry missed,
> Straight flies at check, and *clips it* down the wind.

This sense would seem to be allied to that of *leap.*

CLIP, *n.* A blow or stroke with the hand; as, he hit him a *clip.* *New-England.*

2. An embrace; that is, a throwing the arms round. *Sidney.*

CLIP'PED, **CLIPT**, *pp.* Cut off; cut short; curtailed; diminished by paring.

CLIP'PER, *n.* One who clips; especially one who cuts off the edges of coin. *Addison.*

CLIP'PING, *ppr.* Cutting off or shortening with shears or scissors; diminishing coin by paring off the edges; curtailing.

CLIP'PING, *n.* The act of cutting off, curtailing or diminishing.

2. That which is clipped off; a piece separated by clipping. *Locke.*

CLIV'ERS, *n.* A plant, the *Galium aparine*; called also goose-grass, or hairiff. It has a square, rough, jointed stem; the joints hairy at the base; with eight or ten narrow leaves at each joint. *Encyc. Fam. of Plants.*

CLOAK. [See *Cloke.*]

CLO'CHARD, *n.* [from *clock*, Fr. *cloche.*] A belfry. [*Not used.*] *Weever.*

CLOCK, *n.* [Sax. *clugga*, *clucga*; D. *klok*; G. *klocke*; Dan. *klokke*; Sw. *klocka*; Fr. *cloche*; Arm. *cloch*, or *clech*; Ir. *clog*; W. *clôc*; properly a bell, and named from its sound, from striking. It coincides in origin with *clack* and *cluck*, L. *glocio*, Ch. גלג. Class Lg. No. 27. See *Cluck.*]

1. A machine, consisting of wheels moved by weights, so constructed that by a uniform vibration of a pendulum, it measures time, and its divisions, hours, minutes and seconds, with great exactness. It indicates the hour by the stroke of a small hammer on a bell.

The phrases, what o'clock is it? it is nine o'clock, seem to be contracted from *what of the clock? it is nine of the clock.*

2. A figure or figured work in the ankle of a stocking. *Swift.*

CLOCK, *v. t.* To call. [See *Cluck.*]

CLOCK'-MAKER, *n.* An artificer whose occupation is to make clocks.

CLOCK'-SETTER, *n.* One who regulates the clock. [*Not used.*] *Shak.*

CLOCK'-WORK, *n.* The machinery and movements of a clock; or that part of the movement which strikes the hours on a bell, in distinction from that part which measures and exhibits the time on the face or dial plate, which is called watch-work. *Encyc.*

2. Well adjusted work, with regular movement. *Prior.*

CLOD, *n.* [D. *kluit*, a clod; G. *klots*; Dan. *klods*; Sw. *klot*, a log, stock, or stump; Dan. *klode*, D. *kloot*, a ball; G. *loth*, a ball; D. *lood*, lead, a ball; Sw. and Dan. *lod*, id.; W. *cluder*, a heap. *Clod* and *clot* seem to be radically one word, signifying a mass or lump, from collecting or bringing together, or from condensing, setting, fixing. In Sax. *clud*, a rock or hill, may be from the same root. See Class Ld. No. 8. 9. 10. 16. 26. 35. 36. 40. Qu. Gr. χλωθω, to form a ball.]

1. A hard lump of earth, of any kind; a mass of earth cohering. *Bacon. Dryden.*

2. A lump or mass of metal. [*Little used.*] *Milton.*

3. Turf; the ground. *Swift.*

4. That which is earthy, base and vile, as the body of man compared to his soul. *Milton. Glanville. Burnet.*

5. A dull, gross, stupid fellow; a dolt. *Dryden.*

6. Any thing concreted. *Carew.*

CLOD, *v. i.* To collect into concretions, or a thick mass; to coagulate; as *clodded* gore. *Milton.*

[See *Clot*, which is more generally used.]

CLOD, *v. t.* To pelt with clods.

CLOD'DY, *a.* Consisting of clods; abounding with clods.

2. Earthy; mean; gross. *Shak.*

CLOD'HOPPER, *n.* A clown; a dolt.

CLOD'PATE, *n.* A stupid fellow; a dolt; a thickskull.

CLOD'PATED, *a.* Stupid; dull; doltish. *Arbuthnot.*

CLOD'POLL, *n.* A stupid fellow; a dolt; a blockhead. *Shak.*

CLOG, *v. t.* [W. *cleg*, a lump; *clug*, a swelling, roundness; *clog*, a large stone; *lloc*, a mound, a dam; *llog*, an augment; *llogi*, to make compact, to hire, L. *loco*; Ir. *loc*, a stop; *locaim*, to hinder. These coincide with Eng. *lock*, in primary sense, or may be from the same root. But *clog*, though of the same family, seems not to be directly derived from either of these words.]

1. To load or fill with something that retards or hinders motion; as, to *clog* the channel of a river; to *clog* a passage.
2. To put on any thing that encumbers, with a view to hinder or restrain leaping; to shackle; as, to *clog* a beast.
3. To load with any thing that encumbers; to burden; to embarrass; as, to *clog* commerce with impositions or restrictions. *Addison.*
4. To obstruct natural motion, or render it difficult; to hinder; to impede.

ƇLOG, *v. i.* To coalesce; to unite and adhere in a cluster or mass.

Move it sometimes with a broom, that the seeds *clog* not together. *Evelyn.*

2. To form an accretion; to be loaded or encumbered with extraneous matter.

The teeth of the saw will begin to *clog*. *Sharp.*

ƇLOG, *n.* Any thing put upon an animal to hinder motion, or leaping, as a piece of wood fastened to his leg.
2. An encumbrance; that which hinders motion, or renders it difficult; hindrance; impediment.

Slavery is the greatest *clog* to speculation. *Swift.*

3. [Qu. Fr. *claque;* Sp. Port. *galocha;* Arm. *galoig.*] A wooden shoe; also, a sort of patten worn by ladies to keep their feet dry in wet weather.

ƇLOG'GED, *pp.* Wearing a clog; shackled; obstructed; loaded with incumbrance.

ƇLOG'GINESS, *n.* The state of being clogged.

ƇLOG'GING, *ppr.* Putting on a clog; loading with incumbrance; obstructing; impeding.

ƇLOG'GY, *a.* That clogs, or has power to clog; thick; gross.

ƇLOIS'TER, *n.* [Fr. *cloître;* Sax. *claustr,* or *cluster;* Arm. *claustr,* or *cloestr;* Sp. *claustro;* It. *claustro,* or *chiostro;* D. *klooster;* G. *kloster;* Dan. and Sw. *kloster;* W. *claws, clwys;* Ir. *clabhstur;* L. *claustrum,* from *clausus,* pp. of *claudo.* See Eng. *Close.*]
1. Literally, a close; a close, or inclosed place. A monastery or nunnery; a house inhabited by monks or nuns. In a more limited sense, the principal part of a regular monastery, consisting of a square, erected between the church, the chapter-house and the refectory, and over which is the dormitory. The proper use of the cloister is for the monks to meet in for conversation. The cloister is square, and has its name from being inclosed on its four sides with buildings. Hence in *architecture,* a building is said to be in the form of a cloister, when there are buildings on each of the four sides of the court. *Encyc.*
2. A peristyle; a piazza. *Johnson.*

ƇLOIS'TER, *v. t.* To confine in a cloister or monastery.
7. To shut up; to confine closely within walls; to immure; to shut up in retirement from the world. *Bacon.*

ƇLOIS'TERAL, *a.* Confined to a cloister; retired from the world; recluse. *Walton.*

ƇLOIS'TERED, *pp.* Shut up in a cloister; inhabiting a monastery.
2. *a.* Solitary; retired from the world. *Shak.*
3. Built with peristyles or piazzas; inclosed. *Wotton.*

ƇLOIS'TERING, *ppr.* Shutting up in a monastery; confining; secluding from the world.

ƇLOIS'TRESS, *n.* A nun; a woman who has vowed religious retirement. [*Little used.*] *Shak.*

ƇLOKE, *n.* [Sax. *lach.* In D. *laken,* Chaucer, *lake* is cloth.]
1. A loose outer garment worn over other clothes both by men and women.

He was clad with zeal as a *cloke.* Is. lix.

2. A cover; that which conceals; a disguise or pretext; an excuse; a fair pretense.

Not using your liberty for a *cloke* of maliciousness. 1 Peter ii.

They have no *cloke* for their sin. John xv.

ƇLOKE, *v. t.* To cover with a cloke.
2. To hide; to conceal; to use a false covering. *Spenser.*

ƇLO'KE-BAG, *n.* A bag in which a cloke or other clothes are carried; a portmanteau. *Shak.*

ƇLO'KED, *pp.* Covered with a cloke; concealed under a cover.

ƇLO'KING, *ppr.* Covering with a cloke; hiding under an external covering.

ƇLOMB, *pret.* of *climb.*

ƇLONG, old part. of *cling.*

ƇLON'IƇ, *a.* [Gr. κλονος, a shaking or irregular motion.] Shaking; convulsive; irregular; as *clonic* spasm. *Coxe.*

ƇLOOM, *v. t.* [Sax. *clæman.*] To close with glutinous matter. [*Local.*] *Mortimer.*

ƇLOSE, *v. t. s* as *z.* [Fr. *clos;* Arm. verb *closa,* or *closein;* part. *closet;* from the L. participle *clausus,* of *claudo,* to shut; Fr. *clorre;* It. *chiudere, chiuso;* D. *kluis,* an inclosure. The D. *sluiten,* G. *schliessen, schloss,* Dan. *slutter,* Sw. *sluta,* are from the same root, with a prefix. Gr. κλειω, for κλειδοω, whence κλεις, a key, *clavis,* that which shuts or fastens; W. *claws, clwys,* a close, a cloister; Sax. *hlid,* a lid, the shutter; *hlidan,* to cover; Ir. *cleithim, cludaim.* See Class Ld. No. 1. 8. 9. 10.]
1. To shut; to make fast, by pressing together, or by stopping an open place, so as to intercept a passage, in almost any manner; as, to *close* the eyes; to *close* a gate, door or window. In these and other cases, *closing* is performed by bringing an object before the opening. To *close* a book, is to bring the parts together.

The Lord hath *closed* your eyes. Is. xxix.

He *closed* the book. Luke iv.

2. To end; to finish; to conclude; to complete; to bring to a period; as, to *close* a bargain, or contract.

One frugal supper did our studies *close.* *Dryden.*

3. To unite, as the parts of a breach or fracture; to make whole; to consolidate; often followed by *up.*

The Lord *closed up* the flesh instead thereof. Gen. ii.

4. To cover; to inclose; to encompass; to overwhelm.

The depths *closed* me round about. Jonah ii.

5. To inclose; to confine. [See *Inclose.*]
6. To move or bring together; to unite separate bodies or parts; as, to *close* the ranks of an army.

ƇLOSE, *v. i. s* as *z.* To unite; to coalesce; to come together; as the parts of a wound or fracture, or parts separated; often followed by *on* or *upon.*

The fat *closed upon* the blade. Judges iii.

The earth *closed upon* them. Num. xvi.

2. To end; to terminate, or come to a period; as, the debate *closed* at six o'clock.

To close on or *upon,* to come to a mutual agreement; to agree on or join in.

France and Holland might *close upon* some measures to our disadvantage. *Temple.*

To close with, to accede to; to consent or agree to; as, to *close with* the terms proposed. When followed by the person with whom an agreement is made, to make an agreement with; to unite with; as, to *close with* an enemy.

He took the time when Richard was deposed,
And high and low *with* happy Harry *closed.* *Dryden.*

In this sense, to *close in with* is less elegant.

To close with, } to unite; to join closely;
To close in with, } to grapple, as persons in a contest; applied to wrestlers, when they come to close embrace for scuffling.

ƇLOSE, *n. s* as *z.* An inclosed place; any place surrounded by a fence or other body which defends or confines it, particularly a field, or portion of land.
2. Conclusion; termination; final end; as the *close* of life; the *close* of day or night.
3. A temporary finishing; a pause; rest; cessation; intermission.

At every *close* she made, th' attending throng
Replied, and bore the burden of the song. *Dryden.*

4. The manner of shutting.

The doors of plank were; their *close* exquisite. *Chapman.*

5. A grapple in wrestling. *Bacon.*

ƇLOSE, *a.* Shut fast; tight; made fast, so as to have no opening; as a *close* box; a *close* vizard.
2. Having parts firmly united; compact; dense; applied to solid substances of any kind; as the *close* texture of wood or metal.
3. Having parts firmly adhering; viscous; tenacious; as oil, or glue. *Wilkins.*
4. Confined; stagnant; without ventilation or motion; as *close* air.
5. Confined; retired.

While David kept himself *close.* 1 Chron. xii.

6. Hid; private; secret; as, to keep a purpose *close.* Numb. v. Luke ix.
7. Confined within narrow limits; narrow; as a *close* alley.
8. Near; within a small distance; as a *close* fight or action.
9. Joined; in contact or nearly so; crowded; as, to sit *close.*
10. Compressed, as thoughts or words; hence, brief; concise; opposed to loose or diffuse.

Where the original is *close,* no version can reach it in the same compass. *Dryden.*

11. Very near, in place or time; adjoining, or nearly so.

I saw him come *close* to the ram. Dan. viii.

They sailed *close* by Crete. Acts xxvii.

Some dire misfortune follows *close* behind. *Pope.*

12. Having the quality of keeping secrets, thoughts or designs; cautious; as a *close*

minister. Hence in friendship, trusty; confidential. *Shak.*

13. Having an appearance of concealment; implying art, craft or wariness; as a *close* aspect. *Shak.*

14. Intent; fixed; attentive; pressing upon the object; as, to give *close* attention.

Keep your mind or thoughts *close* to the business or subject. *Locke.*

15. Full to the point; home; pressing; as a *close* argument; bring the argument *close* to the question. *Dryden.*

16. Pressing; earnest; warm; as a *close* debate.

17. Confined; secluded from communication; as a *close* prisoner.

18. Covetous; penurious; not liberal; as a *close* man.

19. Applied to the weather or air, *close*, in popular language, denotes warm and damp, cloudy or foggy, or warm and relaxing, occasioning a sense of lassitude and depression. Perhaps originally, confined air.

20. Strictly adhering to the original; as a *close* translation.

21. In *heraldry*, drawn in a coat of arms with the wings close, and in a standing posture. *Bailey.*

ЄLOSE, *adv.* Closely; nearly; densely; secretly; pressingly.

Behind her death
Close followed, pace for pace. *Milton.*

ЄLOSE-BANDED, *a.* Being in close order; closely united. *Milton.*

ЄLOSE-BODIED, *a.* Fitting the body exactly; setting close; as a garment. *Ayliffe.*

ЄLOSE-ЄOMPAЄT'ED, *a.* Being in compact order; compact. *Addison.*

ЄLOSE-ЄOUCHED, *a.* Quite concealed. *Milton.*

ЄLOSE-ЄURTAINED, *a.* Inclosed or surrounded with curtains. *Milton.*

ЄLOSE-FISTED, *a.* Covetous; niggardly. *Berkeley.*

ЄLOSE-HANDED, *a.* Covetous; penurious. *Hale.*

ЄLOSE-HANDEDNESS, *n.* Covetousness. *Holyday.*

ЄLOSE-HAULED, *a.* In *seamanship*, having the tacks or lower corners of the sails drawn close to the side to windward, and the sheets hauled close aft, in sailing near the wind. *Encyc.*

ЄLOSE-PENT, *a.* Shut close. *Dryden.*

ЄLOSE-QUARTERS, *n.* Strong barriers of wood used in a ship for defense when the ship is boarded. *Mar. Dict.*

ЄLOSE-STOOL, *n.* A chamber utensil for the convenience of the sick and infirm.

ЄLOSE-TONGUED, *a.* Keeping silence; cautious in speaking. *Shak.*

ЄLO'SED, *pp.* *s* as *z.* Shut; made fast; ended; concluded.

ЄLO'SELY, *adv.* In a close, compact manner; with the parts united, or pressed together, so as to leave no vent; as a crucible *closely* luted.

2. Nearly; with little space intervening; *applied to space or time;* as, to follow *closely* at one's heels; one event follows *closely* upon another.

3. Intently; attentively; with the mind or thoughts fixed; with near inspection; as, to look or attend *closely.*

4. Secretly; slyly. [*Not much used.*] *Carew.*

5. With near affection, attachment or interest; intimately; as, men *closely* connected in friendship; nations *closely* allied by treaty.

6. Strictly; within close limits; without communication abroad; as a prisoner *closely* confined.

7. With strict adherence to the original; as, to translate *closely.*

ЄLO'SENESS, *n.* The state of being shut, pressed together, or united. Hence according to the nature of the thing to which the word is applied,

2. Compactness; solidity; as the *closeness* of texture in wood or fossils. *Bacon.*

3. Narrowness; straitness; as of a place.

4. Tightness in building, or in apartments; firmness of texture in cloth, &c.

5. Want of ventilation; applied to a close room, or to the air confined in it. *Swift.*

6. Confinement or retirement of a person; recluseness; solitude. *Shak.*

7. Reserve in intercourse; secrecy; privacy; caution. *Bacon.*

8. Covetousness; penuriousness. *Addison.*

9. Connection; near union; intimacy, whether of friendship, or of interest; as the *closeness* of friendship, or of alliance.

10. Pressure; urgency; variously applied; as the *closeness* of an agreement, or of debate; the *closeness* of a question or inquiry.

11. Adherence to an original; as the *closeness* of a version.

ЄLO'SER, *n.* *s* as *z.* A finisher; one who concludes.

ЄLO'SER, *a.* comp. of *close.* More close.

ЄLO'SEST, *a.* superl. of *close.* Most close. In these words, *s* has its proper sound.

ЄLOS'ET, *n.* *s* as *z.* A small room or apartment for retirement; any room for privacy.

When thou prayest, enter into thy *closet.* Mat. vi.

2. An apartment for curiosities or valuable things. *Dryden.*

3. A small close apartment or recess in the side of a room for repositing utensils and furniture.

ЄLOS'ET, *v. t.* *s* as *z.* To shut up in a closet; to conceal; to take into a private apartment for consultation. *Herbert. Swift.*

ЄLOS'ETED, *pp.* *s* as *z.* Shut up in a closet; concealed.

ЄLOS'ETING, *ppr.* *s* as *z.* Shutting up in a private room; concealing.

ЄLOS'ET-SIN, *n.* *cloz'et-sin.* Sin committed in privacy. *Bp. Hall.*

ЄLOSH, *n.* A disease in the feet of cattle, called also the *founder.* *Bailey.*

ЄLO'SING, *ppr.* *s* as *z.* Shutting; coalescing; agreeing; ending.

ЄLO'SING, *a.* *s* as *z.* That ends or concludes; as a *closing* word or letter.

ЄLO'SING, *n.* *s* as *z.* End; period; conclusion.

ЄLO'SURE, *n.* *clo'zhur.* The act of shutting; a closing. *Boyle.*

2. That which closes, or shuts; that by which separate parts are fastened or made to adhere. *Pope.*

3. Inclosure; that which confines. *Shak.*

4. Conclusion. *Shak.*

ЄLOT, *n.* [See *Clod.*] A concretion, particularly of soft or fluid matter, which concretes into a mass or lump; as a *clot* of blood. *Clod* and *clot* appear to be radically the same word; but we usually apply *clod* to a hard mass of earth, and *clot* to a mass of softer substances, or fluids concreted.

ЄLOT, *v. i.* To concrete; to coagulate, as soft or fluid matter into a thick, inspissated mass; as, milk or blood *clots.*

2. To form into clots or clods; to adhere; as, *clotted* glebe. *Philips.*

ЄLOT'-BIRD, *n.* The common œnanthe or English ortolan.

ЄLOT'-BUR, *n.* [G. *klette.*] Burdock.

ЄLOTH, *n.* *clawth.* [Sax. *clath;* D. *kleed,* cloth, and *kleeden,* to clothe; G. *kleid, kleiden;* Sw. *klåde, klåda;* Dan. *klæde, klæder.* The plural is regular, *cloths;* but when it signifies garments, it is written *clothes.*]

1. A manufacture or stuff of wool or hair, or of cotton, flax, hemp or other vegetable filaments, formed by weaving or intertexture of threads, and used for garments or other covering and for various other purposes; as *woolen cloth, linen cloth, cotton cloth, hair cloth.*

2. The covering of a table; usually called a *tablecloth.* *Pope.*

3. The canvas on which pictures are drawn. *Dryden.*

4. A texture or covering put to a particular use; as a *cloth* of state. *Hayward.*

5. Dress; raiment. [See *Clothes.*]

I'll ne'er distrust my God for *cloth* and bread. *Quarles.*

6. The covering of a bed. [*Not used.*] *Prior.*

ЄLOTHE, *v. t.* pret. and pp. *clothed,* or *clad.* [See *Cloth.*]

1. To put on garments; to invest the body with raiment; to cover with dress, for concealing nakedness and defending the body from cold or injuries.

The Lord God made coats of skin and *clothed* them. Gen. iii.

2. To cover with something ornamental.

Embroidered purple *clothes* the golden beds. *Pope.*

But *clothe,* without the aid of other words, seldom signifies to adorn. In this example from Pope, it signifies merely to cover.

3. To furnish with raiment; to provide with clothes; as, a master is to feed and *clothe* his apprentice.

4. To put on; to invest; to cover, as with a garment; as, to *clothe* thoughts with words.

I will *clothe* her priests with salvation. Ps. cxxxii.

Drowsiness shall *clothe* a man with rags. Prov. xxiii.

Let them be *clothed* with shame. Ps. xxxv.

5. To invest; to surround; to encompass.

The Lord is *clothed* with majesty. Ps. xciii.

Thou art *clothed* with honor and majesty. Ps. civ.

6. To invest; to give to by commission; as, to *clothe* with power or authority.

7. To cover or spread over; as, the earth is *clothed* with verdure.

ЄLOTHE, *v. i.* To wear clothes.

Care no more to *clothe* and eat *Shak.*

ЄLOTHED, *pp.* Covered with garments; dressed; invested; furnished with clothing.

ЄLOTHES, *n.* plu. of *cloth;* pronounced *cloze.* Garments for the human body;

dress; vestments; vesture; a general term for whatever covering is worn, or made to be worn, for decency or comfort.

If I may touch but his *clothes*, I shall be whole. Mark v.

2. The covering of a bed; bed-clothes. *Prior.*

CLŌTHIER, *n.* *clōthyer.* In English authors, a man who makes cloths; a maker of cloth. *Johnson. In this sense, I believe it is not used in the U. States; certainly not in New England.*

2. In *America*, a man whose occupation is to full and dress cloth.

CLŌTHING, *ppr.* Covering with or putting on vestments of any kind; providing with garments; investing; covering.

CLŌTHING, *n.* Garments in general; clothes; dress; raiment; covering.

As for me—my *clothing* was sackcloth. Ps. xxxv.

2. The art or practice of making cloth. [*Unusual.*]

The king took measures to instruct the refugees from Flanders in the art of *clothing*. *Ray.*

CLOTH-SHEARER, *n.* One who shears cloth, and frees it from superfluous nap.

CLOTH-WŎRKER, *n.* A maker of cloth. *Scott.*

CLOT′PŎLL, *n.* A thickskull; a blockhead. [See *Clod-poll.*]

CLOT′TED, *pp.* Concreted into a mass; inspissated; adhering in a lump.

CLOT′TER, *v. i.* [from *clot.*] To concrete or gather into lumps. *Dryden.*

CLOT′TING, *ppr.* Concreting; inspissating; forming into clots.

CLOT′TY, *a.* [from *clot.*] Full of clots, or small hard masses; full of concretions, or clods.

CLOUD, *n.* [I have not found this word in any other language. The sense is obvious—a collection.]

1. A collection of visible vapor, or watery particles, suspended in the atmosphere, at some altitude. A like collection of vapors near the earth is usually called *fog*. *Locke.*

I do set my bow in the *cloud*. Gen. ix.
Behold, a white *cloud*. Rev. xiv.

2. A state of obscurity or darkness. *Waller. Addison.*

3. A collection of smoke, or a dense collection of dust, rising or floating in the air; as a *cloud* of dust.

A *cloud* of incense. Ezek. viii.

4. The dark or varied colors, in veins or spots, on stones or other bodies, are called *clouds*.

5. A great multitude; a vast collection.

Seeing we are encompassed with so great a *cloud* of witnesses. Heb. xii.

CLOUD, *v. t.* To overspread with a cloud or clouds; as, the sky is *clouded; clouds* intercept the rays of the sun. Hence,

2. To obscure; to darken; as, to *cloud* the day, or truth, or reason.

3. To darken in veins or spots; to variegate with colors; as *clouded* marble.

4. To make of a gloomy aspect; to give the appearance of sullenness.

What sullen fury *clouds* his scornful brow. *Pope.*

5. To sully; to tarnish. *Shak.*

CLOUD, *v. i.* To grow cloudy; to become obscure with clouds; sometimes followed by *over;* as, the sky *clouds over.*

CLOUD-ASCEND′ING, *a.* Ascending to the clouds. *Sandys.*

CLOUD′-BERRY, *n.* A plant, called also knot-berry; Rubus chamæmorus.

CLOUD′-BORN, *a.* Born of a cloud. *Dryden.*

CLOUD′-CAPT, *a.* [*cloud* and *cap.*] Capped with clouds; touching the clouds; lofty.

The *cloud-capt* towers. *Shak.*

CLOUD-COMPEL′LER, *n.* He that collects clouds; Jove.

CLOUD-COMPEL′LING, *a.* Collecting clouds; or driving clouds; as *cloud-compelling* Jove. *Waller. Dryden.*

CLOUD′-COVERED, *a.* Enveloped with clouds. *Young.*

CLOUD-DISPEL′LING, *a.* Having power to disperse clouds. *Dryden.*

CLOUD-ECLIP′SED, *a.* Eclipsed by a cloud. *Shak.*

CLOUD′ED, *pp.* Overcast; overspread with clouds; obscured; darkened; rendered gloomy or sullen; variegated with colored spots or veins.

CLOUD′ILY, *adv.* [from *cloudy.*] With clouds; darkly; obscurely. *Dryden.*

CLOUD′INESS, *n.* The state of being overcast with clouds; as the *cloudiness* of the atmosphere. *Harvey.*

2. Obscurity; gloom; want of brightness.

3. Darkness of appearance; variegation of colors in a fossil or other body.

4. Appearance of gloom or sullenness; as *cloudiness* of aspect.

CLOUD′ING, *ppr.* Overspreading with clouds; obscuring; giving an appearance of gloom or sullenness.

CLOUD′-KISSING, *a.* Touching the clouds. *Shak.*

CLOUD′LESS, *a.* Being without a cloud; unclouded; clear; bright; luminous; as *cloudless* skies. *Pope.*

CLOUD′-PIERCING, *a.* Penetrating or rising above the clouds. *Philips.*

CLOUD′-TOPT, *a.* Having the top covered with a cloud. *Gray.*

CLOUD′-TOUCHING, *a.* Touching the clouds. *Sandys.*

CLOUD′Y, *a.* Overcast with clouds; obscured with clouds; as a *cloudy* day; a *cloudy* sky; a *cloudy* night.

2. Consisting of a cloud or clouds; as a *cloudy* pillar. Ex. xxxiii. 9.

3. Obscure; dark; not easily understood; as *cloudy* and confused notions. *Watts.*

4. Having the appearance of gloom; indicating gloom, anxiety, sullenness, or ill-nature; not open or cheerful; as *cloudy* looks. *Spenser. Shak.*

5. Indicating gloom or sullenness; as *cloudy* wrath.

6. Marked with veins or spots of dark or various hues, as marble.

7. Not bright; as a *cloudy* diamond. *Boyle.*

CLOUGH, *n.* *cluf.* [Sax. *clough*, a cleft.] A cleft in a hill. In commerce, an allowance of two pounds in every hundred weight, for the turn of the scale, that the commodity may hold out in retailing. [*Not used in America.*]

CLOUT, *n.* [Sax. *clut*, a patch, a plaster, a plate, a seam or joint; Sw. *klut;* W. *clwt*, a patch, a clout; *clwtiaw*, to patch; Sax. *gecluted*, sewed together, clouted, patched; *gesceod mid gecludedum scon*, shod with clouted shoes. This undoubtedly signifies patched shoes, for *clut* in Saxon does not signify a nail. The word *clout*, a nail, may be from the French, *clou, clouter*, from L. *clavus*, from the root of L. *claudo, cludo.* Whether *clouted brogues* in Shakspeare signify patched shoes or shoes studded with nails, let the critic determine. Such shoes are common in England, and were formerly worn in America. The primary sense is, to thrust or put on; hence the sense of *blow.*]

1. A patch; a piece of cloth or leather, &c., to close a breach.

2. A piece of cloth for mean purposes. *Spenser.*

3. A piece of white cloth, for archers to shoot at. [*Not now used.*] *Shak.*

4. An iron plate on an axle tree, to keep it from wearing.

5. [Fr. *clou, clouter.*] A small nail.

6. In *vulgar language*, a blow with the hand. *New-England. Todd.*

CLOUT, *v. t.* To patch; to mend by sewing on a piece or patch; as *clouted shoon*, in Milton. This is the sense as understood by Johnson. Mason understands the word *clouted* to signify *nailed*, studded with small nails, from the French *clouter*, and the following words in Shakspeare, "whose rudeness answered my steps too loud," give some countenance to Mason's interpretation. In this case, the verb *clout* must signify, to nail, or fasten with nails; to stud.

2. To cover with a piece of cloth. *Spenser.*

2. To join clumsily; as *clouted* sentences. *Ascham.*

4. To cover or arm with an iron plate.

5. To strike; to give a blow. *Beaum.*

Clouted cream, in Gay, is evidently a mistake for *clotted* cream.

CLOUT′ED, *pp.* Patched; mended clumsily; covered with a clout.

CLOUT′ERLY, *a.* Clumsy; awkward. *Mortimer.*

CLOUT′ING, *ppr.* Patching; covering with a clout.

CLOVE, *pret.* of *cleave. Obs.* *Spenser.*

CLOVE, *n.* [D. *kloof.* See *Cleave.*] A cleft; a fissure; a gap; a ravine. This word, though properly an appellative, is not often used as such in English; but it is appropriated to particular places, that are real clefts, or which appear as such; as the *Clove* of Kaaterskill, in the state of New-York, and the Stony *Clove.* It is properly a Dutch word. *Journ. of Science.*

CLOVE, *n.* [Sax. *clufe;* Fr. *clou;* Sp. *clavo;* Port. *cravo;* from L. *clavus*, a nail; so called from its resemblance to a nail. So in D. *kruidnagel*, herb-nail, or spice-nail.]

1. A very pungent aromatic spice, the flower of the clove-tree, Caryophyllus, a native of the Molucca isles. The tree grows to the size of the laurel, and its bark resembles that of the olive. No verdure is seen under it. At the extremities of its branches are produced vast numbers of flowers, which are at first white, then green, and at last red and hard. These are called *cloves*. *Encyc.*

2. [from *cleave.*] The parts into which garlic separates, when the outer skin is removed. *Tate.*

3. A certain weight; seven pounds of wool; eight pounds of cheese or butter. [*Not used in America.*]

ȻLOVE-ĠILLY-FLOWER, *n.* A species of Dianthus, bearing a beautiful flower, cultivated in gardens; called also Carnation pink.

Note. Some writers suppose that *gilly-flower* should be written *July-flower*. But qu. is it not a corruption of the French *girofle, clou de girofle*, cloves; *giroflée*, a gilliflower; *giroflier*, a stock gilliflower; L. *caryophyllus*. Chaucer wrote *cloue gilofre*. Cant.Tales. 13692. The Italians write *garofano*, probably for *garofalo*; Arm. *genofles, genoflen*. Johnson supposes the plant so called from the smell of the flower, resembling that of cloves; but it is probably from its shape, the nail-flower, as in Dutch. [See *Clove*.]

ȻLO'VEN, *pp.* of *cleave*. Divided; parted; pronounced *clovn*.

ȻLO'VEN-FOOTED, ȻLO'VEN-HOOFED, } *a.* Having the foot or hoof divided into two parts, as the ox; bisulcous.

ȻLO'VER, ȻLO'VER-GRASS, } *n.* [Sax. *clæfer-wyrt*, clover-wort; G. *klee*; D. *klaver*; Dan. *klever* or *klee*. The Saxon word is rendered also marigold and violet. The Dutch word signifies a *club*. The name then signifies *club-grass, club-wort*, L. *clava*, from its flower.]

A genus of plants, called *Trifolium*, trefoil, or three-leafed, Fr. *trefle*. The species are numerous. The red clover is generally cultivated for fodder and for enriching land. The white clover is also excellent food for cattle, either green or dry, and from its flowers the bee collects no small portion of its stores of honey.

To live in clover, is to live luxuriously, or in abundance; a phrase borrowed from the luxuriant growth of clover, and the feeding of cattle in clover.

ȻLO'VERED, *a.* Covered with clover. *Thomson.*

ȻLOWN, *n.* [L. *colonus*, a husbandman.] A countryman; a rustic; hence, one who has the manners of a rustic; a churl; a man of coarse manners; an ill-bred man. *Sidney. Dryden. Swift.*

ȻLOWN'AGE, *n.* The manners of a clown. [*Not in use.*] *B. Jonson.*

ȻLOWN'ERY, *n.* Ill-breeding; rustic behaior; rudeness of manners. [*Little used.*] *L'Estrange.*

ȻLOWN'ISH, *a.* Containing clowns; consisting of rustics; as a *clownish* neighborhood. *Dryden.*

2. Coarse; hard; rugged; rough; as *clownish* hands. *Spenser.*

3. Of rough manners; ill-bred; as a *clownish* fellow.

4. Clumsy; awkward; as a *clownish* gait. *Prior.*

ȻLOWN'ISHLY, *adv.* In the manner of clowns; coarsely; rudely.

ȻLOWN'ISHNESS, *n.* The manners of a clown; rusticity; coarseness or rudeness of behavior; incivility; awkwardness. *Dryden. Locke.*

ȻLOY, *v. t.* [from Fr. *clouer*, or the root of the word, the L. *cludo, claudo*; coinciding in elements with *glut*.]

Strictly, to fill; to glut. Hence, to satisfy, as the appetite; to satiate. And as the appetite when satisfied rejects additional food, hence, to fill to lothing; to surfeit.

Who can *cloy* the hungry edge of appetite
By bare imagination of a feast? *Shak.*

2. To spike up a gun; to drive a spike into the vent. *Bailey. Johnson.*

3. In *farriery*, to prick a horse in shoeing. *Ash.*

[*In the two latter senses, I believe the word is little used, and not at all in America.*]

ȻLOY'ED, *pp.* Filled; glutted; filled to satiety and lothing; spiked; pricked in shoeing.

ȻLOY'ING, *ppr.* Filling; filling to satiety, or disgust.

ȻLOY'LESS, *a.* That cannot cloy, or fill to satiety.

ȻLOY'MENT, *n.* Surfeit; repletion beyond the demands of appetite. [*Little used.*] *Shak.*

ȻLUB, *n.* [W. *clopa, clwpa*, coinciding with *clap*, a lump, and *clob, clobyn*; G. *klöpfel*; D. *klaver*; Sw. *klubba*; Dan. *klubbe*; L. *clava*. The sense is probably a knob or lump, W. *llwb, llob*, whence *lubber*.]

1. Properly, a stick or piece or wood with one end thicker and heavier than the other, and no larger than can be wielded with the hand.

2. A thick heavy stick, that may be managed with the hand, and used for beating, or defense. In early ages, a club was a principal instrument of war and death; a fact remarkably perpetuated in the accounts which history relates of the achievements of Hercules with his club. Plin. Lib. 7. Ca. 56. This use of the club was the origin of the *scepter*, as a badge of royalty.

3. The name of one of the suits of cards; so named from its figure.

4. A collection or assembly of men; usually a select number of friends met for social or literary purposes. Any small private meeting of persons. *Dryden.*

5. A collection of expenses; the expenses of a company, or unequal expenses of individuals, united for the purpose of finding the average or proportion of each individual. Hence the share of each individual in joint expenditure is called his *club*, that is, his proportion of a club, or joint charge.

6. Contribution; joint charge. *Hudibras.*

ȻLUB, *v. i.* [W. *clapiaw*, to form into a lump.]

1. To join, as a number of individuals, to the same end; to contribute separate powers to one end, purpose or effect.

Till grosser atoms, tumbling in the stream
Of fancy, madly met, and *clubbed* into a dream. *Dryden.*

2. To pay an equal proportion of a common reckoning or charge.

ȻLUB, *v. t.* To unite different sums of expense, in a common sum or collection, to find the average, that each contributor may pay an equal share. *Pope.*

2. In *common parlance*, to raise or turn uppermost the britch or club of a musket; as, the soldiers *clubbed* their muskets.

ȻLUB'BED, *pp.* Collected into a sum and averaged, as different expenses.

2. United to one end or effect.

3. Shaped like a club. *Asiat. Researches.* v. 213.

4. Having the britch turned upwards, as a musket.

5. Heavy like a club. *Chaucer.*

ȻLUB'BER, ȻLUB'BIST, } *n.* One who belongs to a party, club or association. *Burke.*

ȻLUB'BING, *ppr.* Joining in a club; uniting to a common end.

ȻLUB'-FIST, *n.* A large heavy fist.

ȻLUB'-FISTED, *a.* Having a large fist. *Howell.*

ȻLUB'-FOOTED, *a.* Having short or crooked feet.

ȻLUB'-HEADED, *a.* Having a thick head. *Derham.*

ȻLUB'-LAW, *n.* Government by clubs, or violence; the use of arms, or force, in place of law; anarchy. *Addison.*

ȻLUB'-ROOM, *n.* The apartment in which a club meets. *Addison.*

ȻLUB'-RUSH, *n.* A genus of plants, the Scirpus. *Muhlenberg.*

ȻLUB'-SHAPED, *a.* Shaped like a club; growing thicker towards the top; clavated. *Martyn.*

ȻLUCK, *v. i.* [Sax. *cloccan*; Dan. *klukker*; Sw. *klycka*; G. *glucken*; D. *klokken*; W. *clwcian, clocian*; Arm. *clochat*; L. *glocio*; It. *chiocciare*; Sp. *clocar, cloquear*; Ch. גלג. Class Lg. No. 27. See *Clack* and *Clock*. The Gr. κλωζω seems to be the same word, as it gives κλωγμος; the guttural passing into ζ, as in many Greek verbs; and hence Fr. *glousser*. See *Brace*.]

To make the noise, or utter the voice of the domestic hen, when sitting on eggs for hatching, and when conducting her chickens. This voice, with the change of the vowel, is precisely our word *clack* and *clock*, and is probably an onomatopy. [See *Clack* and *Clock*.]

ȻLUCK, *v. t.* To call chickens by a particular sound. *Shak.*

ȻLUCK'ING, *ppr.* Uttering the voice of a sitting hen; calling chickens.

ȻLUE. [See *Clew*.]

ȻLUMP, *n.* [G. *klump*; D. *klomp*; Sw. *klimp*; Dan. *klump*, a *lump*; W. *clamp*. It is *lump* with a prefix. It coincides with *plump*, and L. *plumbum*, lead; as the D. *lood*, G. *loth*, Dan. *lod*, Eng. *lead*, coincide with *clod*. It signifies a mass or collection. If *m* is the final radical, see Class Lm. No. 1. 4. 5. 9. L. *glomus*.]

1. A thick, short piece of wood, or other solid substance; a shapeless mass. Hence *clumper*, a clot or clod.

2. A cluster of trees or shrubs; formerly written *plump*. In some parts of England, it is an adjective signifying lazy, unhandy. *Bailey.*

ȻLUMPS, *n.* [from *clump*.] A stupid fellow; a numskull. *Bailey.*

ȻLUM'SILY, *adv.* [from *clumsy*.] In a clumsy manner; awkwardly; in an unhandy manner; without readiness, dexterity or grace.

ȻLUM'SINESS, *n.* The quality of being short and thick, and moving heavily; awkwardness; unhandiness; ungainliness; want of readiness, nimbleness or dexterity. *Collier.*

ȻLUM'SY, *a.* *s* as *z*. [from *clump, lump*.]

1. Properly, short and thick, like a *clump* or *lump*. Hence,

2. Moving heavily, slowly or awkwardly; as *clumsy* fingers.

3. Awkward; ungainly; unhandy; artless; without readiness, dexterity or grace; as a *clumsy* man; a *clumsy* fellow.

4. Ill-made; badly constructed; as a *clumsy* garment; *clumsy* verse,

CLUNCH, *n.* Among *miners*, indurated clay, found in coal pits next to the coal. *Kirwan. Bailey.*

CLUNG, *pret.* and *pp.* of *cling*, which see.

CLUNG, *v. i.* To shrink. [*Not used.*] See *Cling.*

CLU'NIAC, *n.* One of a reformed order of Benedictine monks, so called from Cluni in Burgundy.

CLUS'TER, *n.* [Sax. *cluster.* It seems to be from the root of *close*, L. *clausus, claustrum, claudo*, a collecting or crowding together; Sw. *klasa*, a cluster of grapes; Dan. *klase.* The latter in orthography coincide nearly with *class.* In Welsh, *clws* is compact, neat; *clysa*, to make compact; *clwys* is a close.]

1. A bunch; a number of things of the same kind growing or joined together; a knot; as a *cluster* of raisins.

2. A number of individuals or things collected or gathered into a close body; as a *cluster* of bees; a *cluster* of people. *Milton. Dryden.*

3 A number of things situated near each other; as a *cluster* of governments in Italy. *J. Adams.*

CLUS'TER, *v. i.* To grow in clusters; to gather or unite in a bunch, or bunches; as, *clustering* grapes. *Milton.*

2. To form into flakes; as, *clustering* snow. *Thomson.*

3. To collect into flocks or crowds.

CLUS'TER, *v. t.* To collect into a bunch or close body.

CLUS'TERED, *pp.* Collected into a cluster, or crowd; crowded.

CLUS'TER-GRAPE, *n.* A small black grape. *Mortimer.*

CLUS'TERING, *ppr.* Growing in a cluster or in bunches; uniting in a bunch, or in a flock, crowd, or close body.

CLUS'TERY, *a.* Growing in clusters. *Johnson.*
Full of clusters. *Bailey.*

CLUTCH, *v.t.* [This seems to be from the root of Sax. *laeccan*, to seize, whence *gelaeccan*, id. If not, I know not its origin. It may be allied to *lock* and *latch.*]

1. To double in the fingers and pinch or compress them together; to clinch. [If *n* is not radical in *clinch*, this may be from the same root.]

2. To seize, clasp or gripe with the hand; as, to *clutch* a dagger; to *clutch* prey. *Shak. Herbert.*

3. To seize, or grasp; as, to *clutch* the globe at a grasp. *Collier.*

CLUTCH, *n.* A griping or pinching with the fingers; seizure; grasp.

CLUTCH'ES, *plu.* The paws or talons of a rapacious animal, as of a cat or dog.

2. The hands, in the sense of rapacity or cruelty, or of power. *Hudibras. Stillingfleet.*

CLUT'TER, *n.* [W. *cluder*, a heap or pile, from *cludaw*, to bear, to bring together, to heap. It has the elements of L. *claudo.*]

1. A heap or assemblage of things lying in confusion; *a word of domestic application.*
He saw what a *clutter* there was with huge pots, pans and spits. *L'Estrange.*

2. Noise; bustle. [This sense seems allied to *clatter*, but it is not the sense of the word in N. England.]

CLUT'TER, *v. t.* To crowd together in disorder; to fill with things in confusion; as, to *clutter* a room; to *clutter* the house.

CLUT'TER, *v. i.* To make a bustle, or fill with confusion.
[The English lexicographers explain this word by *noise* and *bustle*; but probably by mistake.]

CLUT'TERED, *pp.* Encumbered with things in disorder.

CLUT'TERING, *ppr.* Encumbering with things in confusion.

CLYS'TER, *n.* [Gr. κλυςηρ, from κλυζω, to wash or cleanse; L. *clyster*; D. *klisteer*; G. *klystier*; Fr. *clistere*; Dan. *klisteer.*]
An injection; a liquid substance injected into the lower intestines, for the purpose of promoting alvine discharges, relieving from costiveness, and cleansing the bowels. Sometimes it is administered to nourish and support patients who cannot swallow aliment.

CLYS'TER-PIPE, *n.* A tube, or pipe used for injections.

CLYS'TERWISE, *adv.* In the manner of a clyster.

CO, a prefix, signifying *with*, in conjunction. [See *Con.*]

COACERV'ATE, *v. t.* [L. *coacervo*; *con* and *acervo*, to heap up; *acervus*, a heap.] To heap up; to pile. [*Little used.*]

COACERV'ATE, *a.* [L. *coacervatus.*] Heaped; raised into a pile; collected into a crowd. [*Little used.*] *Bacon.*

COACERVA'TION, *n.* The act of heaping, or state of being heaped together. [*Little used.*] *Bacon.*

CÔACH, *n.* [Fr. *coche*; Arm. *coich*; It. *cocchio*, a coach or coach-box; Sp. *coche*, a coach and a coasting barge; Port. *coche*; D. *koets*, a *coach* and a *couch*; G. *kutsche.* This word seems to be radically a *couch* or bed, [Fr. *couche, coucher*,] a covered bed on wheels, for conveying the infirm.]
A close vehicle for commodious traveling, borne on four wheels, and drawn by horses or other animals. It differs from a chariot in having seats in front, as well as behind. It is a carriage of state, or for pleasure, or for travelling.
Hackney-coach, a coach kept for hire. In some cities, they are licensed by authority, and numbered, and the rates of fare fixed by law.
Mail-coach, a coach that carries the public mails.
Stage-coach, a coach that regularly conveys passengers from town to town. [See *Stage.*]

CÔACH or COUCH, *n.* An apartment in a large ship of war near the stern, the roof of which is formed by the poop. *Mar. Dict.*

CÔACH, *v. t.* To carry in a coach. *Pope.*

CÔACH-BOX, *n.* The seat on which the driver of a coach sits. *Arbuthnot.*

CÔACH-HIRE, *n.* Money paid for the use of a hired coach. *Dryden.*

CÔACH-HORSE, *n.* A horse used in drawing coaches.

CÔACH-HOUSE, *n.* A house to shelter a coach from the weather. *Swift.*

CÔACH-MAKER, *n.* A man whose occupation is to make coaches. *Swift.*

CÔACHMAN, *n.* The person who drives a coach. *Prior.*

CÔACHMANSHIP, *n.* Skill in driving coaches. *Jenyns.*

COACT', *v. i.* To act together. [*Not used.*] *Shak.*

COACT'ED, *pp.* or *a.* Forced; compelled. [*Not used.*] *B. Jonson.*

COAC'TION, *n.* [L. *coactio, coactus, cogo*; *con* and *ago*, to drive.]
Force; compulsion, either in restraining or impelling. *South.*

COACT'IVE, *a.* Forcing; compulsory; having the power to impel or restrain. *Raleigh.*

2. Acting in concurrence. *Shak.*

COACT'IVELY, *adv.* In a compulsory manner. *Bramhall.*

COADJU'TANT, *a.* [L. *con* and *adjutans*, helping.]
Helping; mutually assisting or operating. *Philips.*

COADJU'TOR, *n.* [L. *con* and *adjutor*, a helper; *adjuto*, to help.]

1. One who aids another; an assistant; a fellow-helper; an associate in operation.

2. In *the canon law*, one who is empowered or appointed to perform the duties of another. *Johnson.*

COADJU'TRIX, *n.* A female assistant. *Smollet.*

COADJU'VANCY, *n.* [L. *con* and *adjuvans*; *adjuvo*, to assist.]
Joint help; assistance; concurrent aid; cooperation. [*Little used.*] *Brown.*

COAD'UNATE, *a.* [L. *coadunatus*; *con, ad* and *unus.*]
In *botany*, *coadunate* leaves are several united at the base. The word is used also to denote one of the natural orders of plants in Linne's system. *Martyn.*

COADUNI''TION, *n.* [L. *con, ad* and *unitio*, from *unus*, one.]
The union of different substances in one mass. [*Little used.*] *Hale.*

COADVENT'URER, *n.* A fellow adventurer. *Howell.*

COAFFOR'EST, *v. t.* To convert ground into a forest. *Howell.*

COA'GENT, *n.* An assistant or associate in an act. *Beaum.*

COAGMENT', *v. t.* [L. *coagmento*, to join or cement; *con* and *agmen*, a compact body, from *ago*, to drive.]
To congregate or heap together. [*Not used.*] *Glanville.*

COAGMENTA'TION, *n.* Collection into a mass or united body; union; conjunction. [*Little used.*] *B. Jonson.*

COAGMENT'ED, *a.* Congregated; heaped together; united in one mass. [*Little used.*] *Glanville.*

COAGULABIL'ITY, *n.* The capacity of being coagulated. *Ure.*

COAG'ULABLE, *a.* [See *Coagulate.*] That may be concreted; capable of congealing or changing from a liquid to an inspissated state; as *coagulable* lymph. *Boyle.*

COAG'ULATE, *v. t.* [L. *coagulo*; Fr. *coaguler*; It. *coagulare*; Sp. *coagular.* Usually considered as from *cogo, con* and *ago.* But probably the last component part of the word is the W. *ceulaw*, to curdle, the root of *gelid* and *congeal.*]
To concrete; to curdle; to congeal; to change from a fluid into a fixed substance, or solid mass; as, to *coagulate* blood; rennet *coagulates* milk. This word is generally applied to the change of fluids into

substances like curd or butter, of a moderate consistence, but not hard or impenetrable. *Bacon. Arbuthnot.*

COAG'ULATE, *v. i.* To curdle or congeal; to turn from a fluid into a consistent state, or fixed substance; to thicken. *Bacon. Boyle.*

COAG'ULATED, *pp.* Concreted; curdled.

COAG'ULATING, *ppr.* Curdling; congealing.

COAGULA'TION, *n.* The act of changing from a fluid to a fixed state; concretion; the state of being coagulated; the body formed by coagulating. *Arbuthnot.*

COAG'ULATIVE, *a.* That has the power to cause concretion. *Boyle.*

COAG'ULATOR, *n.* That which causes coagulation. *Arbuthnot.*

COAG'ULUM, *n.* Rennet; curd; the clot of blood, separated by cold, acid, &c. *Encyc. Coxe.*

COA'ITI, *n.* A species of monkey in South America.

COAK. [See *Coke.*]

COAL, *n.* [Sax. *col* or *coll;* G. *kohle;* D. *kool;* Dan. *kul;* Sw. *kol;* Ir. *gual;* Corn. *kolan;* Russ. *ugol.* Qu. Heb. גחל. It is from the sense of glowing, raging, for in Dan. *kuler* signifies to blow strong.]

1. A piece of wood, or other combustible substance, ignited, burning, or charred. When burning or ignited, it is called a live coal, or burning coal, or coal of fire. When the fire is extinct, it is called charcoal.
2. In the language of chimists, any substance containing oil, which has been exposed to a fire in a close vessel, so that its volatile matter is expelled, and it can sustain a red heat without further decomposition. *Encyc.*
3. In *mineralogy*, a solid, opake, inflammable substance, found in the earth, and by way of distinction called *fossil* coal. It is divided by recent mineralogists into three species, anthracite or glance coal, black or bituminous coal, and brown coal or lignite; under which are included many varieties, such as cannel coal, bovey coal, jet, &c.

COAL, *v. t.* To burn to coal, or charcoal; to char. *Carew. Bacon.*

2. To mark or delineate with charcoal. *Camden.*

[*As a verb, this word is little used.*]

COAL-BLACK, *a.* Black as a coal; very black. *Dryden.*

COAL-BOX, *n.* A box to carry coal to the fire. *Swift.*

COAL-FISH, *n.* A species of Gadus or cod, named from the color of its back. It grows to the length of two feet, or two and a half, and weighs about thirty pounds. This fish is found in great numbers about the Orkneys, and the northern parts of Britain. *Dict. Nat. Hist.*

COAL-HOUSE, *n.* A house or shed for keeping coal.

COAL-MINE, *n.* A mine or pit in which coal is dug.

COAL-MINER, *n.* One who works in a coal-mine.

COAL-MOUSE, *n.* A small species of titmouse, with a black head.

COAL-PIT, *n.* A pit where coal is dug. In America, a place where charcoal is made.

COAL-SHIP, *n.* A ship employed in transporting coal.

COAL-STONE, *n.* A kind of cannel-coal.

COAL-WORK, *n.* A coalery; a place where coal is dug, including the machinery for raising the coal.

COALERY, *n.* A coal-mine, coal-pit, or place where coals are dug, with the engines and machinery used in discharging the water and raising the coal. *Encyc.*

COALESCE, *v. i. coaless'.* [L. *coalesco*, from *coaleo; con* and *alesco*, from *aleo* or *oleo*, to grow.]

1. To grow together; to unite, as separate bodies, or separate parts, into one body, as separate bones in an infant, or the fingers or toes. *Encyc.*
2. To unite and adhere in one body or mass, by spontaneous approximation or attraction; as, vapors *coalesce.* *Newton.*
3. To unite in society, in a more general sense.

The Jews were incapable of *coalescing* with other nations. *Campbell, Prelim. Dissert.*

COALES'CENCE, *n.* The act of growing together; the act of uniting by natural affinity or attraction; the state of being united; union; concretion.

COALES'CING, *ppr.* Growing or coming together; uniting in a body or mass; uniting and adhering together.

COALIER. } [See *Collier.*]
COALLIER. }

CO'ALITE, *v. t.* To unite or coalesce. [*Not in use.*] *Bolingbroke.*

COALI''TION, *n.* Union in a body or mass; a coming together, as of separate bodies or parts, and their union in one body or mass; as, a *coalition* of atoms or particles. *Bentley.*

2. Union of individual persons, parties or states.

CO-ALLY', *n.* A joint ally; as the subject of a *co-ally.* *Kent.*

COALY, *a.* Like coal; containing coal. *Milton.*

COAMINGS, *n.* In *ships*, the raised borders or edges of the hatches, made to prevent water from running into the lower apartments from the deck. *Mar. Dict.*

COAPPREHEND', *v. t.* To apprehend with another. [*Little used.*] *Brown.*

COAPTA'TION, *n.* [L. *con* and *apto*, to fit.] The adaptation or adjustment of parts to each other. *Boyle.*

CO'ARCT, } *v. t.* [L. *coarcto; con* and *arcto.*]
CO'ARCTATE, }

1. To press together; to crowd; to straiten; to confine closely. *Bacon.*
2. To restrain; to confine. *Ayliffe.*

COARCTA'TION, *n.* Confinement; restraint to a narrow space. *Bacon.*

2. Pressure; contraction. *Ray.*
3. Restraint of liberty. *Bramhall.*

COARSE, *a.* [This word may be allied to *gross*, and the Latin *crassus*, for similar transpositions of letters are not uncommon.]

1. Thick; large or gross in bulk; comparatively of large diameter; as *coarse* thread or yarn; *coarse* hair; *coarse* sand. This seems to be the primary sense of the word; opposed to fine or slender. Hence,
2. Thick; rough; or made of coarse thread or yarn; as *coarse* cloth.
3. Not refined; not separated from grosser particles, or impurities; as *coarse* metal; *coarse* glass. *Shak.*
4. Rude; rough; unrefined; uncivil; as *coarse* manners.
5. Gross; not delicate.

The *coarser* tie of human law. *Thomson.*

6. Rude; rough; unpolished; inelegant; *applied to language.* *Dryden.*
7. Not nicely expert; not accomplished by art or education; as a *coarse* practitioner. *Arbuthnot.*
8. Mean; not nice; not refined or elegant; as a *coarse* perfume; a *coarse* diet.

COARSELY, *adv.* Roughly; without fineness or refinement; rudely; inelegantly; uncivilly; meanly; without art or polish. *Brown. Dryden.*

COARSENESS, *n.* Largeness of size; thickness; as the *coarseness* of thread.

2. The quality of being made of coarse thread or yarn; whence thickness and roughness; as the *coarseness* of cloth.
3. Unrefined state; the state of being mixed with gross particles or impurities; as the *coarseness* of glass. *Bacon.*
4. Roughness; grossness; rudeness; *applied to manners;* as the *coarseness* of a clown. *Garth.*
5. Grossness; want of refinement or delicacy; want of polish; as the *coarseness* of expression or of language. *L'Estrange.*
6. Meanness; want of art in preparation; want of nicety; as the *coarseness* of food or of raiment.

COASSES'SOR, *n.* [See *Assess.*] A joint assessor.

COASSU'ME, *v. t.* [*con* and *assume.*] To assume something with another. *Walsall.*

COAST, *n.* [L. *costa*, a rib, side or coast; W. *côst;* Fr. *côte* for *coste;* It. *costa;* Sp. *costa;* Port. *id.;* D. *kust;* G. *küste.* Hence to *accost.* See Class Gs. No. 18. 25. 67. The word properly signifies a side, limit, border, the exterior part, from extension.]

1. The exterior line, limit or border of a country, as in Scripture. "From the river to the uttermost sea shall your *coast* be." Deut. xi. "And ships shall come from the *coast* of Chittim." Numb. xxiv. Hence the word may signify the whole country within certain limits. Ex. x. 4.
2. The edge or margin of the land next to the sea; the sea-shore. This is the more common application of the word; and it seems to be used for sea-coast, the border of the sea. Hence it is never used for the bank of a river.
3. A side; *applied to objects indefinitely, by Bacon and Newton. This is a correct use of the word, but now obsolete.*
4. The country near the sea-shore; as, populous towns along the *coast.*

The coast is clear, is a proverbial phrase signifying, the danger is over; the enemies have marched off, or left the coast. *Dryden.*

COAST, *v. i.* To sail near a coast; to sail by or near the shore, or in sight of land.

The ancients *coasted* only in their navigation. *Arbuthnot.*

2. To sail from port to port in the same country.

COAST, *v. t.* To sail by or near to; as, to *coast* the American shore.

2. To draw near; to approach; to follow. *Obs.* *Spenser.*

ЄŌASTED, *pp.* Sailed by.

ЄŌASTER, *n.* One who sails near the shore. *Dryden.*

2. A vessel that is employed in sailing along a coast, or is licensed to navigate or trade from port to port in the same country. In the United States, coasting vessels of twenty tuns burthen and upwards must be enrolled at the custom house.

ЄŌASTING, *ppr.* Sailing along or near a coast.

ЄŌASTING-PILOT, *n.* A pilot who conducts vessels along a coast.

ЄŌASTING-TRADE, *n.* The trade which is carried on between the different ports of the same country, or under the same jurisdiction, as distinguished from foreign trade.

ЄŌASTING-VESSEL, *n.* A vessel employed in coasting; a coaster.

ЄŌAT, *n.* [Fr. *cotte*; It. *cotta*; Ir. *cota*; Corn. *kota*; Pol. *kotz.* It may be from the root of the Russ. *kutayu*, to cover, and be allied to *hut.* The primary sense may be, that which is spread over or put on. But such words are sometimes from verbs which signify to strip, or to repel. The Gr. κευθω has the like elements, but the sense seems to be, to withdraw. I question whether *coat* has any connection with the Shemitic כתן, Gr. χιτων, a tunic. This word in Ch. Syr. and Ar. signifies flax.]

1. An upper garment, of whatever material it may be made. The word is, in modern times, generally applied to the garment worn by men next over the vest.

God made *coats* of skin and clothed them. Gen. iii.

Jacob made Joseph a *coat* of many colors. Gen. xxxvii.

He shall put on the holy linen *coat*. Levit. xvi.

Goliath was armed with a *coat* of mail. 1 Sam. xvii.

2. A petticoat; a garment worn by infants or young children. *Locke.*

3. The habit or vesture of an order of men, indicating the order or office.

Men of his *coat* should be minding their prayers. *Swift.*

So we say, "men of his *cloth.*"

4. External covering, as the fur or hair of a beast, the skin of serpents, the wool of sheep, &c. *Milton.*

5. A tunic of the eye; a membrane that serves as a cover; a tegument. *Derham.*

6. The division or layer of a bulbous root; as the *coats* of an onion.

7. A cover; a layer of any substance covering another; as a *coat* of tar, pitch or varnish; a *coat* of canvas round a mast; a *coat* of tin-foil.

8. That on which ensigns armorial are portrayed; usually called a *coat of arms.* Anciently knights wore a habit over their arms, reaching as low as the navel, open at the sides, with short sleeves, on which were the armories of the knights, embroidered in gold and silver, and enameled with beaten tin of various colors. This habit was diversified with bands and fillets of several colors, placed alternately, and called devises, as being divided and composed of several pieces sewed together. The representation of these is still called a coat of arms.

9. A *coat of mail* is a piece of armor, in form of a shirt, consisting of a net-work of iron rings.

10. A card; a *coat-card* is one on which a king, queen or knave is painted.

ЄŌAT, *v. t.* To cover or spread over with a layer of any substance; as, to *coat* a retort; to *coat* a ceiling; to *coat* a vial.

2. To cover with cloth or canvas; as, to *coat* a mast or a pump.

ЄŌAT-ARMOR, *n.* A coat of arms; armorial ensigns. *Blackstone. Shenstone.*

ЄŌATED, *pp.* Covered with a coat; loricated; covered or overspread with any thing that defends; clothed with a membrane.

2. Having concentric coats or layers, as a bulbous root. *Martyn.*

ЄOATI, *n.* An animal of South America, resembling the raccoon, but with a longer body and neck, shorter fur and smaller eyes; the *Viverra nasua* of Linne.

ЄŌATING, *ppr.* Covering with a coat; overspreading.

ЄŌATING, *n.* A covering, or the act of covering; lorication; any substance spread over for cover or defense; as the *coating* of a retort or of a vial.

2. Cloth for coats; as, merchants advertise an assortment of *coatings.*

ЄŌAX, *v. t.* [W. *cocru*, to fondle, to cocker; *cocyr*, a coaxing, indulgence; Sp. *cocar*, to make wry faces, to coax.]

To wheedle; to flatter; to soothe, appease or persuade by flattery and fondling. [*A low word.*] *L'Estrange.*

ЄŌAXED, *pp.* Soothed or persuaded by flattery.

ЄŌAXER, *n.* A wheedler; a flatterer.

ЄŌAXING, *ppr.* Wheedling; flattering.

ЄOB, *n.* [W. *cob* or *cop*, a top or tuft, a thump; Gr. κυβη; G. *kopf*, the head; D. *kop*; Sax. *cop.*]

1. The top or head; a covetous wretch; a foreign coin. *Bailey.*

[*In these senses not used in America.*]

2. In *America*, the receptacle of the maiz, or American corn; a shoot in form of a pin or spike, on which grows the corn in rows. This receptacle, with the corn, is called the ear.

3. A sea-fowl, the sea-cob. [It. *gabbiano*, a cob, sea-mew or gull.]

4. A ball or pellet for feeding fowls. *Bailey.*

5. In some parts of England, a spider. Old Dutch, *kop* or *koppe*, a spider, retained in *koppespin*, *spinnekop*, a spider.

6. A horse not castrated; a strong poney.

ЄOB, *v. t.* In *seamen's language*, to punish by striking the breech with a flat piece of wood, or with a board. *Mar. Dict.*

ЄO'BALT, *n.* [D. *cobalt.* This is said to be the G. *kobold*, a goblin, the demon of the mines; so called by miners, because cobalt was troublesome to miners, and at first its value was not known.]

A mineral of a reddish gray or grayish white color, very brittle, of a fine close grain, compact, but easily reducible to powder. It crystalizes in bundles of needles, arranged one over another. It is never found in a pure state; but usually as an oxyd, or combined with arsenic or its acid, with sulphur, iron, &c. Its ores are arranged under the following species, viz. arsenical cobalt, of a white color, passing to steel gray; its texture is granular, and when heated it exhales the odor of garlic: gray cobalt, a compound of cobalt, arsenic, iron, and sulphur, of a white color, with a tinge of red; its structure is foliated, and its crystals have a cube for their primitive form: sulphuret of cobalt, compact and massive in its structure: oxyd of cobalt, brown or brownish black, generally friable and earthy: sulphate and arseniate of cobalt, both of a red color, the former soluble in water. The impure oxyd of cobalt is called *zaffer*; but when fused with three parts of siliceous sand and an alkaline flux, it is converted into a blue glass, called *smalt.* The great use of cobalt is to give a permanent blue color to glass and enamels upon metals, porcelain and earthern wares. *Fourcroy. Encyc. Cleaveland.*

Cŏbalt-bloom, acicular arseniate of cobalt.

Cŏbalt-crust, earthy arseniate of cobalt.

ЄOBALT'IЄ, *a.* Pertaining to cobalt, or consisting of it; resembling cobalt, or containing it.

ЄOB'BLE, } *n.* [Eng. *copple.* This
ЄOB'BLE-STONE, } seems to be of Welsh origin, W. *cub*, a mass, a cube, or *cob*, *cop*, head, top.]

A roundish stone; a pebble; supposed to be a fragment, rounded by the attrition of water. We give this name to stones of various sizes, from that of a hen's egg or smaller, to that of large paving stones. These stones are called by the English *copple-stones* and *bowlder-stones* or *bowlders.* The latter name is among us known only in books.

ЄOB'BLE, *v. t.* [In Persic, كوبال kobal, is a shoemaker.]

1. To make or mend coarsely, as shoes; to botch. *Shak.*

2. To make or do clumsily or unhandily; as, to *cobble* rhymes. *Dryden.*

ЄOB'BLER, *n.* A mender of shoes. *Addison.*

2. A clumsy workman. *Shak.*

3. A mean person. *Dryden.*

ЄOB'BLING, *ppr.* Mending coarsely.

ЄOB'BY, *a.* Stout; brisk. [*Not in use.*] *Chaucer.*

ЄOB'ЄAL, *n.* A sandal worn by ladies in the east.

ЄOB'ЄOALS, *n.* Large round coals.

ЄOBELLIĠ'ERENT, *a.* [See *Belligerent.*] Carrying on war in conjunction with another power.

ЄOBELLIĠ'ERENT, *n.* A nation or state that carries on war in connection with another.

ЄOB'IRON, *n.* [See *Cob.*] An andiron with a knob at the top. *Bacon.*

ЄOBISH'OP, *n.* A joint or coadjutant bishop. *Ayliffe.*

ЄO'BLE, *n.* [Sax. *cuople.*] A boat used in the herring fishery.

ЄOB'LOAF, *n.* A loaf that is irregular, uneven or crusty. Qu. Is it not a round loaf?

ЄOB'NUT, *n.* A boy's play, or a hazle-nut

so called, used in play; the conquering nut. *Ash. Barret.*

COBOOSE, *n.* [See *Caboose.*]

COB′STONE, *n.* [See *Cobble.*]

COB′SWAN, *n.* [*cob*, head, and *swan.*] The head or leading swan. *B. Jonson.*

COB′WEB, *n.* [*cob* or *koppe*, a spider; D. *spinnekop*; Sax. *atter-coppa*, poison spider. In Ch. כובי is a spider's web.]

1. The line, thread or filament which a spider spins from its abdomen; the net-work spread by a spider to catch its prey. Hence,
2. Any snare, implying insidiousness and weakness. *Johnson.*

In this sense it is used adjectively or in composition, for thin, flimsy; as a *cobweb* law. *Dryden. Swift.*

Or slender, feeble; as the *cobweb* thread of life. *Buckminster.*

COB′WEBBED, *a.* In *botany*, covered with a thick interwoven pubescence. *Martyn.*

2. Covered with cobwebs.

CO′CALON, *n.* A large cocoon, of a weak texture. *Encyc.*

COCCIF′EROUS, *a.* [L. *coccus*, and *fero*, to bear; Gr. κοκκος, a berry, grain or seed, or a red berry used in dyeing; W. *côc*, red.]

Bearing or producing berries; as *cocciferous* trees or plants. *Quincy.*

COC′COLITE, *n.* [Gr. κοκκος, a berry, and λιθος, a stone.]

A variety of augite or pyroxene; called by Haüy, granuliform pyroxene. Its color is usually some shade of green. It is composed of granular distinct concretions, easily separable, some of which present the appearance of crystals whose angles and edges have been obliterated. *Cleaveland. Dict. Nat. Hist.*

Cocculus Indicus, the fruit of the Menispermum cocculus, a poisonous berry, often used in adulterating malt liquors. *Encyc.*

COCH′INEAL, *n.* [Sp. *cochinilla*, a woodlouse, and an insect used in dyeing; It. *coccíniglia*; Fr. *cochenille*; from the Gr. κοκκος, as the cochineal was formerly supposed to be the grain or seed of a plant, and this word was formerly defined to be the grain of the *ilex glandifera*. See *Gregoire's Armoric Dictionary.*]

An insect, the *Coccus cacti*, of the genus *Coccus*, a native of the warmer climates of America, particularly of Oaxaca, in Mexico. It is found on a plant called nopal or Indian fig-tree. The female, which alone is valued for its color, is ill-shaped, tardy and stupid; the male is small, slender and active. It is of the size of a tick. At a suitable time, these insects are gathered and put in a pot, where they are confined for some time, and then killed by the application of heat. These insects thus killed form a mass or drug, which is the proper *cochineal* of the shops. It is used in giving red colors, especially crimson and scarlet, and for making carmine. It has been used in medicine, as a cardiac, sudorific, alexipharmic and febrifuge; but is now used only to give a color to tinctures, &c. *Encyc.*

COCH′LEARY, COCH′LEATE, COCH′LEATED, *a.* [L. *cochlea*, a screw, the shell of a snail; Gr. κοχλος, from κοχλω, to turn or twist.] Having the form of a screw; spiral; turbinated; as a *cochleate* pod. *Martyn.*

COCH′LITE, *n.* [Gr. κοχλιας, a snail.] A fossil shell having a mouth like that of a snail. *Morin.*

COCK, *n.* [Sax. *coc*; Fr. *coq*; Arm. *gocq*; Sans. *kuka*; Slav. *kokosch.* The sense is, that which shoots out or up; It. *cocca*, the tip of a spindle, the top or crown; L. *cacumen.*]

1. The male of birds, particularly of gallinaceous or domestic fowls, which having no appropriate or distinctive name, are called dunghill fowls or barn-door fowls.
2. A weather-cock; a vane in shape of a cock. *Shak.*

   [It is usually called a *weather-cock.*]
3. A spout; an instrument to draw out or discharge liquor from a cask, vat or pipe; so named from its projection.
4. The projecting corner of a hat. *Addison.*
5. A small conical pile of hay, so shaped for shedding rain; called in England a *cop.* When hay is dry and rolled together for carting, the heaps are not generally called *cocks*, at least not in New England. A large conical pile is called a stack.
6. The style or gnomon of a dial. *Chambers.*
7. The needle of a balance. *Bailey. Johnson.*
8. The piece which covers the balance in a clock or watch. *Bailey.*
9. The notch of an arrow. [It. *cocca.*] *Johnson.*
10. The part of a musket or other fire arm, to which a flint is attached, and which, being impelled by a spring, strikes fire, and opens the pan at the same time.
11. A small boat. [W. *cwc*, Ir. *coca*, D. and Dan. *kaag*, It. *cocca.*] It is now called a *cock-boat*, which is tautology, as *cock* itself is a boat.
12. A leader; a chief man.

    Sir Andrew is the *cock* of the club. *Addison.*
13. Cock-crowing; the time when cocks crow in the morning. *Shak.*

Cock a hoop, or *cock on the hoop*, a phrase denoting triumph; triumphant; exulting. [Qu. Fr. *coq à huppe. Bailey.*] *Camden. Shak. Hudibras.*

Cock and a bull, a phrase denoting tedious trifling stories.

COCK, *v. t.* To set erect; to turn up; as, to *cock* the nose or ears. *Addison.*

2. To set the brim of a hat so as to make sharp corners or points; or to set up with an air of pertness. *Prior.*
3. To make up hay in small conical piles.
4. To set or draw back the cock of a gun, in order to fire. *Dryden.*

COCK, *v. i.* To hold up the head; to strut; to look big, pert, or menacing. *Dryden. Addison.*

2. To train or use fighting cocks. [*Little used.*] *B. Jonson.*
3. To cocker. [*Not in use.*]

COCKA′DE, *n.* [Fr. *cocarde*; Sp. *cocarda*; Port. *cocar*, or *cocarda.*]

A ribin or knot of ribin, or something similar, worn on the hat, usually by officers of the army or navy, sometimes by others. It most usually designates the military character; sometimes political parties.

COCKA′DED, *a.* Wearing a cockade. *Young.*

COCK′AL, *n.* A game called huckle bone. *Kinder.*

COCKATOO′, *n.* A bird of the parrot kind. *Herbert.*

COCK′ATRICE, *n.* [Fr. *cocatrix*, from *coc.* Junius mentions the word as in D. *kocketras.* The Irish call it *riogh-nathair*, the king-serpent, answering to *basilisk.*]

A serpent imagined to proceed from a cock's egg. *Bacon. Taylor.* Is. xi. 8. lix. 5.

COCK-BILL. In *seamen's language*, the anchor is *a cock-bill*, when it is suspended perpendicularly from the cat-head, ready to be let go in a moment. *Mar. Dict.*

COCK′-BOAT, *n.* A small boat. [See *Cock*, No. 11.]

COCK′-BRAINED, *a.* Giddy; rash. *Milton.*

COCK′-BROTH, *n.* Broth made by boiling a cock. *Harvey.*

COCK′-CHAFFER, *n.* The May-bug or dorr-beetle, a species of Scarabæus.

COCK′-CROWING, *n.* The time at which cocks crow; early morning. Mark xiii.

COCK′ER, *v. t.* [W. *cocru.* See *Coax.*]

To fondle; to indulge; to treat with tenderness; to pamper. *Locke. Swift.*

COCK′ER, *n.* One who follows cock-fighting. *Johnson.*

2. A sort of spatter-dash. *Bp. Hall.*

COCK′EREL, *n.* A young cock. *Dryden.*

COCK′ERING, *n.* Indulgence. *Milton.*

COCK′ET, *a.* Brisk; pert. *Sherwood.*

COCK′ET, *n.* [Qu. Fr. *cachet*, Arm. *cacheot*, a seal.]

A seal of the custom-house; a royal seal; rather a scroll of parchment, sealed and delivered by the officers of the custom-house, to merchants, as a warrant that their merchandize is entered. The office of entry. *Spelman. Cowel. Encyc.*

COCK′ET-BREAD, *n.* The finest sort of wheat bread. Qu. *stamped-bread.*

COCK′-FIGHT, COCK′-FIGHTING, *n.* A match or contest of cocks; a barbarous sport of the ancients, and moderns, in which cocks are set to fight with each other, till one or the other is conquered. *Bacon. Addison.*

COCK′-HORSE, *a.* On horse back; triumphant; exulting. *Prior.*

COCK′ING, *n.* Cock-fighting. *Beaum.*

COCK′LE, *n.* [Sax. *coccel*, *cocel*, or *cocle*; Ir. *cagal*; Sp. and Port. *joyo*; Fr. *coquelicot.*]

A plant or weed that grows among corn, the cornrose, a species of Agrostemma. It is also applied to the Lolium or darnel.

COCK′LE, *n.* [Fr. *coque*, *coquille*; L. *cochlea*; W. *cocos*, plu.; Gr. κοχλος, κοχλιας, from κοχλω, to turn or roll. Probably by giving the χ a nasal sound, Gr. κογχη, L. *concha*, are from the same root, whence κογχυλιον, L. *conchylium*, It. *conchiglia.* See *Conch.*]

1. A small testaceous shell; or rather a genus of shells, the Cardium. The general characteristics are; shells nearly equilateral and equivalvular; hinge with two small teeth, one on each side near the beak, and two larger remote lateral teeth, one on each side; prominent ribs running from the hinge to the edge of the valve. *Cuvier. Linne.*
2. A mineral; a name given by the Cornish miners to *shirl* or *shorl.* *Nicholson.*
3. A young cock. *Obs.* [See *Cockerel.*] *Spenser.*

ȻOCK'LE, *v. i.* or *t.* To contract into wrinkles; to shrink, pucker, or wrinkle, as cloth. *Bailey.*

ȻOCK'LED, *pp.* Contracted into folds or wrinkles; winding.

2. Having shells.

ȻOCK'LER, *n.* One that takes and sells cockles. *Gray.*

ȻOCK'LE-STAIRS, *n.* Winding or spiral stairs. *Chambers.*

ȻOCK'-LOFT, *n.* [See *Cock.*] The top-loft; the upper room in a house or other building; a lumber room. *Dryden. Swift.*

ȻOCK'-MASTER, *n.* One who breeds game cocks. *L'Estrange.*

ȻOCK'-MATCH, *n.* A match of cocks; a cock-fight. *Addison.*

ȻOCK'NEY, *n.* [Most probably from L. *coquina*, a kitchen, or *coquino*, to cook; Fr. *coquin*, idle; Fr. *cocagne*, It. *cuccagna*, an imaginary country of idleness and luxury. In some ancient poetry, the word seems to signify a cook.

"And yet I say by my soul I have no salt bacon,
Ne no *cokeney* by Christe coloppes to make."
"At that feast were they served in rich array;
Every five and five had a *cokeney*."

See note on Chaucer, Canterbury Tales, Line, 4206. Edinburgh, 1782. Hence, a citizen who leads an idle life or never leaves the city.]

1. A nativo of London, by way of contempt. *Watts. Shak.*

2. An effeminate, ignorant, despicable citizen. *Shak.*

ȻOCK'NEYLIKE, *a.* Resembling the manners of a cockney. *Burton.*

ȻOCK'-PADDLE, *n.* The lump fish or sea-owl. *Encyc.*

ȻOCK'PIT, *n.* A pit or area, where game cocks fight. *Shak.*

2. In *ships of war*, a room or apartment, in which the wounded men are dressed; situated near the after-hatchway, under the lower gun-deck. The fore-cockpit is a place leading to the magazine passage and the store room of the boatswain, gunner and carpenter. *Mar. Dict.*

ȻOCK'ROACH, *n.* A genus of insects, the Blatta, of several species. They have four semicrustaceous wings, and resemble the beetle; the head is inflected towards the breast; the feelers are hard like bristles; the elytra and wings are plain and resemble parchment. These animals are very troublesome, as they enter chests of clothes, meal-tubs, pantries, and infest beds. They avoid the light, and have a very unsavory smell. *Encyc.*

ȻOCKS'ȻOMB, *n.* The caruncle or comb of a cock.

2. A plant. This name is given to the *Celosia cristata*, the *Pedicularis* or *louse-wort*, and the *Rhinanthus*, or *yellow rattle*. *Fam. of Plants. Lee.*

3. A fop, or vain silly fellow. [See *Coxcomb.*]

ȻOCKS'HEAD, *n.* A plant, the Hedysarum or sainfoin. *Fam. of Plants.*

ȻOCK'SHUT, *n.* The close of the day, when fowls go to roost. *Shak.*

COCK'SPUR, *n.* Virginia hawthorn, a species of medlar. *Miller.*

ȻOCK'SURE, *a.* Confidently certain. [*A low word.*] *Pope.*

COCK'SWAIN, *n.* contracted into *coxen.* [See *Swain.*] An officer on board of a ship who has the care of the boat and the boat's crew. *Mar. Dict.*

ȻOCK'-WEED, *n.* A plant called also dittander and pepperwort. *Johnson.*

ȻOȻOA, *n. co'co.* [Sp. *coco;* Port. *coco*, the nut, and *coqueiro*, the tree; It. *cocco;* Fr. *coco.*]

A tree belonging to the genus *Cocos*, of the order of Palmæ; and the fruit or nut of the tree. This tree grows in the warm climates of both the Indies. It rises to the highth of 60 feet, and the stem is like an apothecary's pestle, of equal thickness at the ends, but somewhat smaller in the middle. The bark is smooth, of a pale brown color, and the tree often leans to one side. The leaves or branches are 14 or 15 feet long, about 28 in number, winged, of a yellow color, straight and tapering. The nuts hang in clusters of a dozen each, on the top of the tree. The husk of this nut consists of strong, tough, stringy filaments, resembling coarse oakum. This covers a hard shell, which contains a white kernel that is wholesome food, and a liquor which is a cooling beverage. *Encyc.*

ȻO'ȻOA-NUT, *n.* The nut or fruit of the cocoa-tree.

ȻOȻOON', *n.* [Fr. *cocon.*] An oblong ball or case in which the silk-worm involves itself, formed by threads which compose silk.

ȻOȻ'TILE, *a.* [L. *coctilis*, from *coquo*, to cook.]

Made by baking, or exposing to heat, as a brick.

ȻOȻ'TION, *n.* [L. *coctio*, from *coquo*, to cook.]

The act of boiling or exposing to heat in liquor. In *medicine*, that alteration in the crude matter of a disease, which fits it for a discharge; digestion. *Coxe. Encyc.*

ȻOD, ⎫
ȻOD'FISH, ⎭ *n.* A species of fish, of the genus *Gadus*, inhabiting northern seas, but particularly the banks of Newfoundland, and the shores of New England. [See *Haddock.*]

ȻOD, *n.* [Sax. *codd;* W. *cod*, *cwd;* G. *hode.* Probably in a different dialect, Fr. *cosse*, or *ecosse.*]

1. Any husk, envelop or case, containing the seeds of a plant; a pod. *Mortimer.*

2. A bag; the scrotum.

3. A pillow. [*Not in use.*]

ȻOD'DED, *a.* Inclosed in a cod. *Mortimer.*

ȻOD'DER, *n.* A gatherer of cods or peas. *Johnson.*

ȻOD'DY, *a.* Husky. *Sherwood.*

ȻODE, *n.* [L. *codex*, or *caudex;* Fr. *code;* It. *codice;* Sp. *codigo.* The Latin word signifies the stem of a tree, and a board or number of boards united, on which accounts were kept. So the Greeks used σχεδη, a board, for a like purpose, from σχιζω, to cut or split; whence L. *scheda*, a sheet.]

1. A collection of the laws and constitutions of the Roman emperors, made by order of Justinian, containing twelve books. The name is also given to other collections of Roman laws; as the Theodosian *code.* Hence in general,

2. Any collection or digest of laws. *Pope. Blackstone.*

ȻOD'ǴER, *n.* [Sp. *coger*, to catch, says Todd. Hence he defines the word by *miser.* But the primary sense is by no means obvious. I take it to be a corruption of *cottager*, Norm. *cotier.*]

A rustic; a clown; a miserly man.

ȻOD'ICIL, *n.* [L. *codicillus*, dim. of *codex.*]

A writing by way of supplement to a will. *Prior.*

ȻODILLE, *n. codill'.* [Fr. *codille;* Sp. *codillo*, the knee, a joint; *codo*, the elbow, that is, a turn or a fastening.]

A term at ombre, when the game is won. *Pope.*

ȻOD'LE, ⎫
ȻOD'DLE, ⎭ *v. t.* To parboil, or soften by the heat of water.

ȻOD'LE, *v. t.* To make much of. [*Not in use.*]

ȻOD'LING, ⎫
ȻOD'LIN, ⎭ *n.* An apple codled; or one suitable for codling, or used for that purpose. *Bacon. Mortimer.*

ȻOD'LING, *n.* A young cod.

ȻOEF'FIȻACY, *n.* [*con* and *efficacy*, L. *efficio.*]

Joint efficacy; the power of two or more things acting together to produce an effect. *Brown.*

ȻOEFFI''CIENCY, *n.* [*con* and *efficiency*, L. *efficio.*]

Cooperation; joint power of two or more things or causes, acting to the same end. *Glanville.*

ȻOEFFI''CIENT, *a.* [*con* and L. *efficiens.*] Cooperating; acting in union to the same end.

ȻOEFFI''CIENT, *n.* That which unites in action with something else to produce the same effect.

2. In *algebra*, a number or known quantity put before letters, or quantities, known or unknown, and into which it is supposed to be multiplied; as in $3x$ and ax, 3 and a are the coefficients of x.

3. In *fluxions*, the *coefficient* of any generating term is the quantity which arises from the division of that term by the generated quantity. *Chambers. Bailey.*

ȻOEFFI''CIENTLY, *adv.* By cooperation.

ȻO-ELD'ER, *n.* An elder of the same rank. *Trapp.*

ȻŒ'LIAȻ, ⎫
CE'LIAȻ, ⎭ *a.* [Gr. κοιλιακος, from κοιλια, the belly; allied perhaps to κοιλος, hollow.]

Pertaining to the belly, or to the intestinal canal.

Cœliac artery is the artery which issues from the aorta just below the diaphragm. *Encyc.*

Cœliac passion, the lientery, a flux or diarrhœa of undigested food. *Coxe.*

Cœliac vein, a vein of the intestinum rectum. *Coxe.*

ȻOEMP'TION, *n.* [L. *coemptio;* *con* and *emo*, to buy.]

The act of purchasing the whole quantity of any commodity. *Bacon.*

ȻOENJOY', *v. t.* To enjoy together. *Howell.*

ȻOE'QUAL, *a.* [L. *con* and *equalis*, equal.] Equal with another person or thing; of the same rank, dignity or power. *Shak.*

ȻOE'QUAL, *n.* One who is equal to another.

ȻOEQUAL'ITY, *n.* The state of being equal with another; equality in rank, dignity or power.

ȻOE'QUALLY, *adv.* With joint equality.

COERCE′, *v. t.* coers′. [L. *coerceo*; *con* and *arceo*, to drive, or press.]

1. To restrain by force; to keep from acting, or transgressing, particularly by moral force, as by law or authority; to repress. *Ayliffe.*

2. To compel; to constrain.

These causes—*coerced* by those which preceded and *coercing* those which followed. *Dwight, Theol.*

COER′CED, *pp.* Restrained by force; compelled.

COER′CIBLE, *a.* That may or ought to be restrained or compelled.

COER′CING, *ppr.* Restraining by force; constraining.

COER′CION, *n.* Restraint, check, particularly by law or authority; compulsion; force. *South.*

COER′CIVE, *a.* That has power to restrain, particularly by moral force, as of law or authority. *Hooker. Dryden.*

2. Compulsory; constraining; forcing.

COER′CIVELY, *adv.* By constraint.

COESSEN′TIAL, *a.* [*con* and *essential*, from L. *essentialis.* See *Essence.*]

Partaking of the same essence.

We bless and magnify that *coessential* spirit, eternally proceeding from the father and son. *Hooker.*

COESSENTIAL′ITY, *n.* Participation of the same essence. *Johnson.*

COESSEN′TIALLY, *adv.* In a coessential manner.

COESTAB′LISHMENT, *n.* Joint establishment. *Bp. of Landaff.*

COETA′NEOUS, *a.* [L. *coætaneus*; *con* and *ætas*, age. *Coetanean* is rarely used.]

Of the same age with another; beginning to exist at the same time; with *to.* "Every fault has penal effects, *coetaneous to* the act." But *with* may be preferable to *to.* This word is sometimes used as synonymous with *cotemporary*; but *coetaneous* seems properly to denote cotemporary in origin, rather than cotemporary in existence at any other period. It may however be used in both senses.

COETERN′AL, *a.* [L. *con* and *æternus.*] Equally eternal with another. *Milton.*

COETERN′ALLY, *adv.* With equal eternity. *Hooker.*

COETERN′ITY, *n.* Existence from eternity equal with another eternal being; equal eternity. *Hammond.*

COE′VAL, *a.* [L. *coævus*; *con* and *ævum*, age.]

Of the same age; beginning to exist at the same time; of equal age; usually and properly followed by *with.* *Hale. Pope. Bentley.*

COE′VAL, *n.* One of the same age; one who begins to exist at the same time. It is not properly used as synonymous with *cotemporary.*

COE′VOUS, *a.* The same as *coeval*, but not used. *South.*

CO-EXEC′UTOR, *n.* A joint executor.

COEXIST′, *v. i.* [L. *con* and *existo.* See *Exist.*]

To exist at the same time with another; followed by *with.* *Hale. Locke.*

COEXIST′ENCE, *n.* Existence at the same time with another; followed regularly by *with.* *Locke. Grew.*

COEXIST′ENT, *a.* Existing at the same time with another; regularly followed by *with.* *Locke. Bentley.*

COEXTEND′, *v. i.* [L. *con* and *extendo.* See *Extend.*]

To extend through the same space or duration with another; to extend equally; as, one line *coextends* with another; or perhaps in a transitive sense, to *coextend* a line with another.

COEXTEND′ED, *pp.* Being equally extended. *Grew.*

COEXTEND′ING, *ppr.* Extending through the same space or duration with another.

COEXTEN′SION, *n.* The act of extending equally, or the state of being equally extended. *Hale.*

COEXTEN′SIVE, *a.* Equally extensive; having equal extent.

COEXTEN′SIVENESS, *n.* Equal extension or extent.

COF′FEE, *n.* [Fr. *caffé*; It. *caffe*; Sp. *café*; Port. *id.*; G. *kaffee*; D. *koffy*; Ar. *cahuah.*]

The berry of a tree belonging to the genus Coffea, growing in Arabia, Persia, and in other warm climates of Asia and America. It will grow to the highth of 16 or 18 feet, but its growth is generally stinted to five feet, for the convenience of gathering the fruit. The stem is upright, and covered with a light brown bark; the branches are horizontal and opposite, crossing each other at every joint, and forming a sort of pyramid. The flowers grow in clusters at the root of the leaves, and close to the branches; they are of a pure white and of an agreeable odor. The fruit which is a berry, grows in clusters, along the branches, under the axils of the leaves. *Encyc.*

2. A drink made from the berry of the coffee-tree, by decoction. The berry is first roasted, and then ground in a mill, and boiled. The use of it is said to have been introduced into France by Thevenot, the traveler, and into England, in 1652, by a Greek servant, called Pasqua. The best coffee is said to be the Mocha coffee from Arabia Felix. The coffee of Java, Bourbon and the West Indies constitutes an important article of commerce.

COF′FEE-CUP, *n.* A cup from which coffee is drank.

COF′FEE-HOUSE, *n.* A house of entertainment, where guests are supplied with coffee and other refreshments, and where men meet for conversation. *Prior. Swift.*

2. A house of entertainment; an inn; which in some cities is also an exchange where merchants meet to transact business.

COF′FEE-MAN, *n.* One who keeps a coffee-house. *Addison.*

COF′FEE-POT, *n.* A covered pot in which coffee is boiled, or in which it is brought upon the table for drinking.

COF′FER, *n.* [Fr. *coffre*; Arm. *couffr*, *coffr*; Ir. *cofra*; Sp. *cofre*; Port. *id.*; D. and G. *koffer*; Dan. *koffert*; Sw. *id*; W. *cofawr*, from *cof*, a hollow trunk. The same French word *coffre* signifies a *coffer*, and the trunk of the body, and a *coffin.* In Ar. قفير is a chest or basket. The primary sense is probably a holder, or a hollow place.]

1. A chest or trunk; and as a chest is customarily used for keeping money, hence

2. A chest of money; a treasure. *Bacon.*

3. In *architecture*, a square depression or sinking in each interval between the modillions of the Corinthian cornice, ordinarily filled with a rose, a pomegranate or other enrichment. *Chambers. Encyc.*

4. In *fortification*, a hollow lodgment across a dry moat, from 6 to 7 feet deep and from 16 to 18 broad; the upper part made of pieces of timber, raised two feet above the level of the moat; which little elevation has hurdles laden with earth for its covering, and serves as a parapet with embrasures. It is raised by the besieged to repulse besiegers when they endeavor to pass the ditch. *Chambers. Encyc.*

COF′FER, *v. t.* To reposit or lay up in a coffer. *Bacon.*

COF′FERED, *pp.* Laid up in a coffer.

COF′FERER, *n.* The Cofferer of the king's household in Great Britain, a principal officer of the court, next under the Controller. He was also a white-staff officer, and a member of the privy council. He had the special charge and oversight of the other officers of the household. This office is now suppressed, and the business is transacted by the lord steward and paymaster of the household. *Cowel. Encyc.*

COF′FIN, *n.* [Fr. *coffre.* See *Coffer.* In French, *coffin* is a candle-basket; Gr. κοφινος; Norm. French, *cofin*, a basket; Sp. *cofin*; radically the same word as *coffer.*]

1. The chest or box in which a dead human body is buried, or deposited in a vault.

2. A mold of paste for a pie. *Johnson.*

3. A paper case, in the form of a cone, used by grocers. *Johnson.*

4. In *farriery*, the hollow part of a horse's hoof; or the whole hoof above the coronet, including the coffin-bone, which is a small spungy bone in the midst of the hoof, and possessing the whole form of the hoof. *Bailey. Farrier's Dict.*

COF′FIN, *v. t.* To put in or inclose in a coffin. *Shak. Donne.*

COF′FINED, *pp.* Inclosed in a coffin.

COF′FIN-MAKER, *n.* One who makes, or whose occupation is to make coffins. *Tatler.*

COFOUND′ER, *n.* A joint founder. *Weever.*

COG, *v. t.* [W. *coegiaw*, to make void, to deceive, from *coeg*, empty, vain.]

1. To flatter; to wheedle; to seduce or draw from, by adulation or artifice.

I'll *cog* their hearts from them. *Shak.*

2. To obtrude or thrust in, by falsehood or deception; as, to *cog* in a word to serve a purpose. *Stillingfleet. Tillotson. Dennis.*

To cog a die, to secure it so as to direct its fall; to falsify; to cheat in playing dice. *Dryden. Swift.*

COG, *v. i.* To deceive; to cheat; to lie. *Tusser. Shak.*

2. To wheedle.

COG, *n.* [W. *cocos*, cogs of a wheel. Qu. Sp. *coger*, to catch, or Welsh *cocw*, a mass or lump, *cog*, a mass, a short piece of wood.]

The tooth of a wheel, by which it drives another wheel or body.

COG, *v. t.* To fix a cog; to furnish with cogs.

ĈOG, } n. A boat; a fishing boat. It is
ĈOG'GLE, } probably the W. *cwc*, Ir. *coca*. [See *Cock*.]

ĈO'ĠENCY, n. [L. *cogens*, from *cogo*; *con* and *ago*, to drive.]
Force; strength; power of compelling; literally, urgency, or driving. It is used chiefly of moral subjects, and in relation to force or pressure on the mind; as the *cogency* of motives or arguments. *Locke.*

ĈOGE'NIAL, for *congenial*. [*Not used*.] *Warton.*

ĈO'ĠENT, a. [See *Cogency*.]
1. Forcible, in *a physical sense*; as the *cogent* force of nature. *Prior.*
2. Urgent; pressing on the mind; forcible; powerful; not easily resisted; as a *cogent* reason, or argument.

The harmony of the universe furnishes *cogent* proofs of a deity. *Anon.*

ĈO'ĠENTLY, *adv.* With urgent force; with powerful impulse; forcibly. *Locke.*

ĈOG'GED, *pp.* Flattered; deceived; cheated; thrust in deceitfully; falsified; furnished with cogs.

ĈOG'GER, n. A flatterer, or deceiver.

ĈOG'GERY, n. Trick; falsehood. *Watson.*

ĈOG'GING, *ppr.* Wheedling; deceiving; cheating; inserting deceitfully; fixing cogs.

ĈOG'GING, n. Cheat; deception; fallacy; *Beaum.*

ĈOĠ'ITABLE, a. [See *Cogitate*.] That may be thought on; that may be meditated on. *Johnson.*

ĈOĠ'ITATE, v. i. [L. *cogito*. Varro says from *cogo*, quasi *coagito*, to agitate in the mind. But the Gothic *hugyan*, and Sax. *hogian*, signify to think.]
To think; to meditate. [*Little used*.]

ĈOĠITA'TION, n. The act of thinking; thought; meditation; contemplation. *Hooker. Bentley. Milton.*
2. Thought directed to an object; purpose. *Bacon.*

ĈOĠ'ITATIVE, a. Thinking; having the power of thinking, or meditating; as a *cogitative* substance. *Bentley.*
2. Given to thought, or contemplation. *Wotton.*

ĈOG'NATE, a. [L. *cognatus*; *con* and *nascor*, to be born.]
1. Allied by blood; kindred by birth.
2. Related in origin; proceeding from the same stock; of the same family; as a *cognate* dialect.
3. Allied in the manner of formation or utterance; uttered by the same organs; as a *cognate* letter or sound.

ĈOG'NATE, n. In *Scots law*, any male relation through the mother. *Encyc.*

ĈOGNA'TION. n. [L. *cognatio*. See *Cognate*.]
1. In *the civil law*, kindred or natural relation between males and females, both descended from the same father; as *agnation* is the relation between males only descended from the same stock. *Encyc.*
2. Kindred; relation by descent from the same original.

Pride and hardheartedness are of near *cognation* to ingratitude. *Wotton.*

3. Relation; participation of the same nature. *Brown.*

ĈOGNI''TION, n. [L. *cognitio*; *cognosco*, *cognitus*; *con* and *nosco*, to know.]
Knowledge or certain knowledge, as from personal view or experience. *Shak. Brown.*

ĈOG'NITIVE, a. Knowing, or apprehending by the understanding; as *cognitive* power. [*Little used*.] *South.*

ĈOGN'IZABLE, a. *con'izable*. [Fr. *connoissable*, from *connoître*, to know; It. *cognoscere*; Sp. *conocer*, *conocible*; Port. *conhecer*; from L. *cognosco*, *con* and *nosco*, to know personally; Gr. γινωσκω, id.]
1. That falls or may fall under judicial notice; that may be heard, tried, and determined; as, a cause or action is *cognizable* before the circuit court.

These wrongs are *cognizable* by the ecclesiastical courts. *Blackstone.*

2. That falls or may fall under notice or observation; that may be known, perceived or apprehended.

The cause of many phenomena is not *cognizable* by the senses. *Anon.*

ĈOGN'IZANCE, n. *con'izance*. [Fr. *connoissance*; It. *cognoscenza*; Sp. *conocencia*; Port. *conhecença*.]
1. Judicial notice or knowledge; the hearing, trying and determining of a cause or action in court.

The court of king's bench takes *cognizance* of civil and criminal causes. *Blackstone.*

In the United States, the district courts have *cognizance* of maritime causes.
2. Jurisdiction, or right to try and determine causes.

The court of king's bench has original jurisdiction and *cognizance* of all actions of trespass vi et armis. *Blackstone.*

3. In *law*, an acknowledgment or confession; as in fines, the acknowledgment of the cognizor or deforciant, that the right to the land in question is in the plaintiff or cognizee, by gift or otherwise; in replevin, the acknowledgment of the defendant, that he took the goods, but alledging that he did it legally as the bailiff of another person who had a right to distrain. *Blackstone.*
4. A badge on the sleeve of a waterman or servant, by which he is known to belong to this or that nobleman or gentleman. *Encyc.*
5. Knowledge or notice; perception; observation; as the *cognizance* of the senses.
6. Knowledge by recollection. *Spenser.*

ĈOGNIZEE', n. *conizee'*. In *law*, one to whom a fine is acknowledged, or the plaintiff in an action for the assurance of land by fine. *Blackstone.*

ĈOGNIZOR', n. *conizor'*. One who acknowledges the right of the plaintiff or cognizee, in a fine; otherwise called the defendant or deforciant. *Blackstone.*

ĈOGNOM'INAL, a. [L. *cognomen*, a surname; *con* and *nomen*, name.]
1. Pertaining to a surname.
2. Having the same name. [*Little used*.] *Brown.*

ĈOGNOMINA'TION, n. [L. *cognomen*.] A surname; the name of a family; a name given from any accident or quality; as Alexander the *Great*. *Brown.*

ĈOGNOS'CENCE, n. [See *Cognition*.]
Knowledge; the act or state of knowing. [*Little used*.]

ĈOGNOS'CIBLE, a. That may be known. [*Little used*.] *Hale.*

ĈOGNOS'CITIVE, a. Having the power of knowing. *Cudworth.*

ĈOGUAR, n. A carnivorous quadruped of America.

ĈO-GUARD'IAN, n. A joint guardian. *Kent.*

ĈOHAB'IT, v. i. [L. *con* and *habito*, to dwell.]
1. To dwell with; to inhabit or reside in company, or in the same place, or country. *Stiles. South.*
2. To dwell or live together as husband and wife; usually or often applied to persons not legally married.

ĈOHAB'ITANT, n. One who dwells with another or in the same place. *Decay of piety.*

ĈOHABITA'TION, n. The act or state of dwelling together or in the same place with another. *Stiles, Elect. Serm.*
2. The state of living together as man and wife, without being legally married. *Bacon.*

ĈOHEIR, n. *coa'ir*. [L. *cohæres*; *con* and *hæres*, an *heir*. See *Heir*.]
A joint heir; one who succeeds to a share of an inheritance, which is to be divided among two or more.

ĈOHEIRESS, n. *coa'iress*. A female who inherits a share of an estate, which is to be divided among two or more heirs or heiresses; a joint heiress.

ĈOHE'RE, v. i. [L. *cohæreo*; *con* and *hæreo*, to stick or cleave together.]
1. To stick together; to cleave; to be united; to hold fast, as parts of the same mass, or as two substances that attract each other. Thus, particles of clay *cohere*; polished surfaces of bodies *cohere*.
2. To be well connected; to follow regularly in the natural order; to be suited in connection; as the parts of a discourse, or as arguments in a train of reasoning.
3. To suit; to be fitted; to agree. *Shak.*

ĈOHE'RENCE, } n. A sticking, cleaving or
ĈOHE'RENCY, } hanging together; union of parts of the same body, or a cleaving together of two bodies, by means of attraction; *applied to all substances, solid or fluid*. *Locke. Bentley.*
2. Connection; suitable connection or dependence, proceeding from the natural relation of parts or things to each other, as in the parts of a discourse, or of any system; consistency. *Hooker. Locke.*

ĈOHE'RENT, a. Sticking together; cleaving; as the parts of bodies, solid or fluid. *Arbuthnot.*
2. Connected; united, by some relation in form or order; followed by *to*, but rather by *with*. *Locke.*
3. Suitable or suited; regularly adapted. *Shak.*
4. Consistent; having a due agreement of parts; as a *coherent* discourse. Or observing due agreement; as a *coherent* thinker or reasoner.

ĈOHE'RENTLY, *adv.* In a coherent manner; with due connection or agreement of parts.

ĈOHE'SION, n. *s* as *z*. [It. *coesione*; from L. *cohæsi*, pret. of *cohæreo*.]
1. The act of sticking together; the state of being united by natural attraction, as the constituent particles of bodies which unite

in a mass, by a natural tendency; one of the different species of attraction. *Newton. Arbuthnot.*

2. Connection; dependence; as the *cohesion* of ideas. But in this sense, see *Coherence.* *Locke.*

COHE'SIVE, *a.* That has the power of sticking or cohering; tending to unite in a mass, and to resist separation. *Nicholson.*

COHE'SIVELY, *adv.* With cohesion.

COHE'SIVENESS, *n.* The quality of being cohesive; the quality of adhering together, as particles of matter.

CO'HOBATE, *v. t.* [Port. *cohorar.*] Among *chimists*, to repeat the distillation of the same liquor or that from the same body, pouring the liquor back upon the matter remaining in the vessel. *Bailey. Encyc.*

CO'HOBATED, *pp.* Repeatedly distilled.

CO'HOBATING, *ppr*, Distilling repeatedly.

COHOBA'TION, *n.* [Sp. *cohobacion.*] The operation of repeatedly distilling the same liquor, or that from the same substance. *Encyc.*

COHÖES, or **COHO'ZE**, *n.* A fall of water, or falls; a word of Indian origin in America.

CO'HORT, *n.* [L. *cohors;* Fr. *cohorte;* It. *coorte;* Sp. *cohorte;* Port. *id.*]

1. Among *the Romans*, a body of about five or six hundred men; each cohort consisted of three maniples, and each maniple, of two centuries; and ten cohorts constituted a legion. *Adam, Rom. Ant.*

2. In *poetry*, a band or body of warriors. *Milton.*

COHORTA TION, *n.* Exhortation; encouragement. [*Not used.*] *Dict.*

COIF, *n.* [Fr. *coiffe;* Arm. *coeff;* It. *cuffia*, a cap; Sp. *cofia*, a net of silk or thread worn on the head; Port. *coifa*, a caul.] A kind of caul, or cap, worn on the head, by sergeants at law, and others. Its chief use was to cover the clerical tonsure. *Encyc.*

COIF, *v. t.* To cover or dress with a coif.

COIF'ED, *a.* Wearing a coif.

COIF'FURE, *n.* [Fr.] A head-dress. *Addison.*

COIGNE, for *coin.* [See *Coin*, a corner.] *Shak.*

COIGNE or **COIN'Y**, *v. i.* To live by extortion. [*An Irish word.*] *Bryskett.*

COIL, *v. t.* [Fr. *cueillir;* perhaps Gr. ειλεω, or κυλιω. See the roots, גלל and קהל, Class Gl. No. 5. 48.] To gather, as a line or cord into a circular form; to wind into a ring, as a serpent, or a rope.

COIL, *n.* A rope gathered into a ring; on shipboard, a single turn or winding is called a *fake*, and a range of fakes is called a *tier.*

2. A noise, tumult, bustle. [*Not used.*] *Bailey. Johnson.*

COIL'ED, *pp.* Gathered into a circular form, as a rope or a serpent.

COIL'ING, *ppr.* Gathering or winding into a ring or circle.

COIN, *n.* [Fr. *coin*, a corner, a wedge; Arm. *coign;* Sp. *esquina*, a corner, and *cuña*, a wedge; Port. *quina;* L. *cuneus;* Gr. γωνια; Ir. *cuinne;* W. *gaing*, or *cyn*, a wedge. The pronunciation of this word, by our common people, is *quine*, or *quoin*, when applied to a wedging stone, in masonry. See the next word.]

1. A corner; a jutting point, as of a wall. *Shak.*

Rustic coins, stones jutting from a wall for new buildings to be joined to. *Bailey.*

2. A wedge for raising or lowering a piece of ordnance. *Bailey.*

3. A wedge or piece of wood to lay between casks on shipboard. *Bailey.*

COIN, *n.* [Sp. *cuña;* Port. *cunho*, a die to stamp money; Sp. *acuñar*, to coin or impress money, to wedge; Port. *cunhar;* It. *conio*, a die; *coniare*, to coin; Fr. *coin;* Ar. قَانَ to hammer, forge or stamp. The sense is, to strike, beat, or drive, coinciding with the French *coigner*, or *cogner.* Hence we see that *coin*, whether it signifies a corner, a wedge or a die, is from the same root, from thrusting, driving.] Primarily, the die employed for stamping money. Hence,

1. Money stamped; a piece of metal, as gold, silver, copper, or other metal, converted into money, by impressing on it marks, figures or characters. To make good money, these impressions must be made under the authority of government. That which is stamped without authority is called false or counterfeit coin. Formerly, all coin was made by hammering; but it is now impressed by a machine or mill.

Current coin is coin legally stamped and circulating in trade.

Ancient coins are chiefly those of the Jews, Greeks and Romans, which are kept in cabinets as curiosities.

2. In *architecture*, a kind of die cut diagonally, after the manner of a flight of a stair case, serving at bottom to support columns in a level, and at top to correct the inclination of an entablature supporting a vault. *Encyc.*

3. That which serves for payment.

The loss of present advantage to flesh and blood is repaid in a nobler *coin.* *Hammond.*

COIN, *v. t.* To stamp a metal, and convert it into money; to mint.

2. To make; as, to *coin* words. *Shak.*

3. To make; to forge; to fabricate; in *an ill sense;* as, to *coin* a lie; to *coin* a fable. *Hudibras. Dryden.*

COIN'AGE, **COIN'ING**, *n.* The act, art or practice of stamping money. *Arbuthnot.*

2. Coin; money coined: stamped and legitimated metal for a circulating medium.

3. Coins of a particular stamp; as the *coinage* of George III.

4. The charges or expense of coining money.

5. A making; new production; formation; as the *coinage* of words.

6. Invention; forgery; fabrication.

This is the very *coinage* of your brain. *Shak.*

COINCI'DE, *v. i.* [L. *con* and *incido*, to fall on; *in* and *cado*, to fall. See *Cadence, Case.* Low L. *coincido;* Sp. *coincidir;* Fr. *coincider.*]

1. To fall or to meet in the same point, as two lines, or bodies; followed by with.

If the equator and the ecliptic had *coincided*, it would have rendered the annual revolution of the earth useless. *Cheyne.*

2. To concur; to be consistent with; to agree.

The rules of right judgment and of good ratiocination often *coincide* with each other. *Watts.*

The judges did not *coincide* in opinion.

COIN'CIDENCE, *n.* The falling or meeting of two or more lines, surfaces, or bodies in the same point. *Bentley.*

2. Concurrence; consistency; agreement; as the *coincidence* of two or more opinions; *coincidence* of evidences. *Hale.*

3. A meeting of events in time; concurrence; a happening at the same time; as *coincidence* of events.

COIN'CIDENT, *a.* Falling on the same point; meeting as lines, surfaces or bodies; followed by *with.* *Newton.*

2. Concurrent; consistent; agreeable to; followed by *with.*

Christianity teaches nothing but what is perfectly *coincident* with the ruling principles of a virtuous man. *South.*

COINCI'DER, *n.* He or that which coincides or concurs.

COINCI'DING, *ppr.* Meeting in the same point; agreeing; concurring.

COINDICA'TION, *n.* [L. *con* and *indicatio*, from *indico*, to show.] In *medicine*, a sign or symptom, which, with other signs, assists to show the nature of the disease, and the proper remedy; a concurrent sign or symptom.

COIN'ED, *pp.* Struck or stamped, as money; made; invented; forged.

COIN'ER, *n.* One who stamps coin; a minter; a maker of money. *Addison.*

2. A counterfeiter of the legal coin; a maker of base money.

3. An inventor or maker, as of words. *Camden.*

COIN'ING, *ppr.* Stamping money; making; inventing; forging; fabricating.

COIN'QUINATE, *v. t.* [L. *coinquino.*] To pollute. [*Not used.*]

COINQUINA'TION, *n.* Defilement. [*Not used.*]

COIS'TRIL, *n.* [Said to be from *kestrel*, a degenerate hawk.] A coward; a runaway. *Shak. Johnson.*

2. A young lad. *Bailey.*

COIT, *n.* A quoit, which see.

COIT'ING. [See *Quoit.*]

COI''TION, *n.* [L. *coitio*, from *coeo*, to come together; *con* and *eo*, to go.] A coming together; chiefly the venereal intercourse of the sexes; copulation. *Grew.*

COJOIN', *v. t.* [L. *conjungo.* See *Conjoin.*] To join with another in the same office. [*Little used.*] *Shak.*

COJU'ROR, *n.* One who swears to another's credibility. *Wotton.*

COKE, *n.* Fossil coal charred, or deprived of its bitumen, sulphur or other extraneous or volatile matter by fire, and thus prepared for exciting intense heat. *Encyc. Cleaveland.*

CŎL'ANDER, *n.* [L. *colo*, to strain; Fr. *couler*, to flow, to trickle down; *coulant*, flowing; *couloir*, a colander.] A vessel with a bottom perforated with little holes for straining liquors. In America, this name is given, I believe, exclusively to a vessel of tin, or other metal. In Great Britain, the name is given to vessels, like sieves, made with hair, osiers or twigs. *May. Ray. Dryden.*

COLA'TION, *n.* The act of straining, or purifying liquor, by passing it through a perforated vessel. [*Little used.*]

COL'ATURE, *n.* The act of straining; the matter strained. [*Little used.*]

COL'BERTINE, *n.* A kind of lace worn by women. *Johnson.*

COL'COTHAR, *n.* The brown red oxyd of iron which remains after the distillation of the acid from sulphate of iron; used for polishing glass and other substances. It is called by artists crocus, or crocus martis. *Encyc. Ure.*

The sulphate of iron is called *colcothar* or *chalcite*, when the calcination has been carried so far as to drive off a considerable part of the acid. *Fourcroy.*

[See *Chalcite.*]

COLD, *a.* [Sax. *cald*; G. *kalt*; D. *koud*, contracted; Goth. *calds*; Basque, *galda*; Sw. *kall*; Dan. *kold*, and the noun, *kulde*. The latter seems to be connected with *kul*, a coal, and *kuler*, to blow strong. But the connection may be casual. In Swedish, *kyla* signifies to cool, and to burn; thus connecting *cool, cold*, with the L. *caleo*, to be hot. Both cold and heat may be from rushing, raging, and this word may be from the same root as *gale*. If not, *cool* would seem to be allied to L. *gelo.*]

1. Not warm or hot; gelid; frigid; a relative term. A substance is *cold* to the touch, when it is less warm than the body, and when in contact, the heat of the body passes from the body to the substance; as *cold* air; a *cold* stone; *cold* water. It denotes a greater degree of the quality than *cool.* [See the Noun.]
2. Having the sensation of cold; chill; shivering, or inclined to shiver; as, I am *cold.*
3. Having cold qualities; as a *cold* plant. *Bacon.*
4. Frigid; wanting passion, zeal or ardor; indifferent; unconcerned; not animated, or easily excited into action; as a *cold* spectator; a *cold* christian; a *cold* lover, or friend; a *cold* temper. *Hooker. Addison.*

Thou art neither *cold* nor hot. Rev. iii.

5. Not moving; unaffecting; not animated; not able to excite feeling; spiritless; as a *cold* discourse; a *cold* jest. *Addison.*
6. Reserved; coy; not affectionate, cordial or friendly; indicating indifference; as a *cold* look; a *cold* return of civilities; a *cold* reception. *Clarendon.*
7. Not heated by sensual desire. *Shak.*
8. Not hasty; not violent. *Johnson.*
9. Not affecting the scent strongly. *Shak.*
10. Not having the scent strongly affected. *Shak.*

COLD, *n.* [Sax. *cele, cyl, cyle*; D. *koelte, koude*; G. *kälte.* See *Cool.*]

1. The sensation produced in animal bodies by the escape of heat, and the consequent contraction of the fine vessels. Also, the cause of that sensation. Heat expands the vessels, and cold contracts them; and the transition from an expanded to a contracted state is accompanied with a sensation to which, as well as to the cause of it, we give the denomination of *cold.* Hence *cold* is a privation of heat, or the cause of it. *Encyc. Bacon.*
2. A shivering; the effect of the contraction of the fine vessels of the body; chilliness, or chillness. *Dryden.*
3. A disease; indisposition occasioned by cold; catarrh.

COLD-BLOODED, *a.* Having cold blood.

2. Without sensibility, or feeling.

COLD-FINCH, *n.* A species of Motacilla, a bird frequenting the west of England, with the head and back of a brownish gray, the belly white, and the quill feathers and tail black. *Dict. Nat. Hist.*

COLD-HEARTED, *a.* Wanting passion or feeling; indifferent.

COLD-HEARTEDNESS, *n.* Want of feeling or sensibility.

COLDLY, *adv.* In a cold manner; without warmth; without concern; without ardor or animation; without apparent passion, emotion or feeling; with indifference or negligence; as, to answer one *coldly*; a proposition is *coldly* received.

COLDNESS, *n.* Want of heat; as the *coldness* of water or air. When the heat or temperature of any substance is less than that of the animal body exposed to it, that state or temperature is called *coldness.*

2. Unconcern; indifference; a frigid state of temper; want of ardor, zeal, emotion, animation, or spirit; negligence; as, to receive an answer with *coldness*; to listen with *coldness.*
3. Want of apparent affection, or kindness; as, to receive a friend with *coldness.*
4. Coyness; reserve; indifference; as, to receive addresses with *coldness.*
5. Want of sensual desire; frigidity; chastity. *Pope.*

COLD-SHORT, *a.* Brittle when cold, as a metal.

COLE, *n.* [Sax. *caul, cawl* or *cawel*; L. *caulis*; Gr. *χαυλος*; D. *kool*; G. *kohl*; Sw. *kål*; Dan. *kaal*; W. *cawl*; Ir. *colis, coilis*; It. *cavolo*; Sp. *col*; Port. *couve*; Arm. *caulin, colen*; Fr. *chou.*]

The general name of all sorts of cabbage or brassica; but we generally use it in its compounds, *cole-wort, cauliflower*, &c.

CO'LE-MOUSE, *n.* [See *Coal-mouse.*]

COL'EOPTER, } *n.* [Gr. *χολεος*, a sheath,
COLEOP'TERA, } and *πτερον*, a wing.]

The coleopters, in Linne's system of entomology, are an order of insects, having crustaceous elytra or shells, which shut and form a longitudinal suture along the back, as the beetle.

COLEOP'TERAL, *a.* Having wings covered with a case or sheath, which shuts as above.

CO'LE-PERCH, *n.* A small fish, less than the common perch. *Dict. Nat. Hist.*

CO'LE-SEED, *n.* The seed of the navew, napus sativa, or long-rooted, narrow-leafed rapa; reckoned a species of brassica or cabbage. *Encyc.*

2. Cabbage seed. *Mortimer.*

CO'LE-WORT, *n.* [*cole* and *wort*, Sax. *wyrt*, an herb.] A particular species of cole, brassica, or cabbage.

COL'IC, *n.* [L. *colicus*; Gr. *χωλικος*, from *χωλον*, the colon.]

In *general*, a severe pain in the bowels, of which there are several varieties; as bilious colic, hysteric colic, nervous colic and many others. *Coxe. Quincy.*

COL'IC, } *a.* Affecting the bowels.
COL'ICAL, } *Milton.*

COL'IN, *n.* A bird of the partridge kind, found in America and the West Indies, called also a quail.

COLL, *v. t.* To embrace. [*Not in use.* See *Collar.*] *Spenser.*

COLLAPSE, *v. i.* *collaps'.* [L. *collabor, collapsus*; *con* and *labor*, to slide or fall.]

To fall together, as the two sides of a vessel; to close by falling together; as, the fine canals or vessels of the body *collapse* in old age. *Arbuthnot.*

COLLAPS'ED, *pp.* Fallen together; closed.

COLLAP'SION, *n.* A state of falling together; a state of vessels closed.

COL'LAR, *n.* [L. *collare*; Fr. *collier, collet*; Arm. *colyer*; It. *collare*; Sp. *collar*; from L. *collum*, the neck.]

1. Something worn round the neck, as a ring of metal, or a chain. The knights of several orders wear a chain of gold, enameled, and sometimes set with ciphers or other devices, to which the badge of the order is appended. *Encyc.*
2. The part of a garment which surrounds the neck. Job xxx. 18.
3. A part of a harness for the neck of a horse or other beast, used in draught.
4. Among *seamen*, the upper part of a stay; also, a rope in form of a wreath to which a stay is confined. *Mar. Dict.*

To slip the collar, is to escape or get free; to disentangle one's self from difficulty, labor, or engagement. *Johnson.*

A *collar of brawn*, is the quantity bound up in one parcel. [*Not used in America.*] *Johnson.*

COL'LAR, *v. t.* To seize by the collar.

2. To put a collar on.

To collar beef or other meat, is to roll it up and bind it close with a string. [*English.*]

COL'LARAGE, *n.* A tax or fine laid for the collars of wine-drawing horses. [*Eng.*] *Bailey. Encyc.*

COLLAR-BONE, *n.* The clavicle.

COL'LARED, *pp.* Seized by the collar.

2. Having a collar on the neck.

COLLA'TE, *v. t.* [L. *collatum, collatus*; *con* and *latum, latus*; considered to be the supine and participle of *fero, confero*, but a word of distinct origin.]

Literally, to bring or lay together. Hence,

1. To lay together and compare, by examining the points in which two or more things of a similar kind agree or disagree; *applied particularly to manuscripts and books*; as, to *collate* copies of the Hebrew Scriptures.
2. To confer or bestow a benefice on a clergyman, by a bishop who has it in his own gift or patronage; or more strictly, to present and institute a clergyman in a benefice, when the same person is both the ordinary and the patron; followed by *to.*

If the patron neglects to present, the bishop may *collate* his clerk *to* the church. *Blackstone.*

3. To bestow or confer; *but now seldom used, except as in the second definition.* *Taylor.*

COLLA'TE, *v. i.* To place in a benefice, as by a bishop.

If the bishop neglects to *collate* within six

months, the right to do it devolves on the arch-bishop. *Encyc.*

COLLA'TED, *pp.* Laid together and compared; examined by comparing; presented and instituted, as a clergyman, to a benefice.

COLLAT'ERAL, *a.* [L. *collateralis*; *con* and *lateralis*, from *latus*, a side.]

1. Being by the side, side by side, on the side, or side to side.

> In his bright radiance and *collateral* light
> Must I be comforted, not in his sphere. *Shak.*

Collateral pressure is pressure on the side. So we say, *collateral* circumstances, circumstances which accompany a principal event.

2. In *genealogy*, descending from the same stock or ancestor, but not one from the other; as distinguished from *lineal*. *Lineal* descendants proceed one from another in a direct line; *collateral* relations spring from a common ancestor, but from different branches of that common stirps or stock. Thus the children of brothers are *collateral* relations, having different fathers, but a common grandfather. *Blackstone.*

3. *Collateral security*, is security for the performance of covenants or the payment of money, besides the principal security.

4. Running parallel. *Johnson.*

5. Diffused on either side; springing from relations; as, *collateral* love. *Milton.*

6. Not direct, or immediate.

> If by direct or *collateral* hand. *Shak.*

7. Concurrent; as, *collateral* strength. *Atterbury.*

COLLAT'ERAL, *n.* A collateral relation or kinsman.

COLLAT'ERALLY, *adv.* Side by side; or by the side.

2. Indirectly. *Dryden.*

3. In collateral relation; not in a direct line; not lineally.

COLLAT'ERALNESS, *n.* The state of being collateral.

COLLA'TING, *ppr.* Comparing; presenting and instituting.

COLLA'TION, *n.* The act of bringing or laying together, and comparing; a comparison of one copy or thing of a like kind with another. *Pope.*

2. The act of conferring or bestowing; a gift. *Ray.*

3. In *the canon law*, the presentation of a clergyman to a benefice by a bishop, who has it in his own gift or patronage. Collation includes both presentation and institution. When the patron of a church is not a bishop, he presents his clerk for admission, and the bishop institutes him; but if a bishop is the patron, his presentation and institution are one act and are called *collation*. *Blackstone.*

4. In *common law*, the presentation of a copy to its original, and a comparison made by examination, to ascertain its conformity; also, the report of the act made by the proper officers. *Encyc.*

5. In *Scots law*, the right which an heir has of throwing the whole heritable and movable estates of the deceased into one mass, and sharing it equally with others who are of the same degree of kindred.

6. A repast between full meals; as a cold *collation*.

Collation of seals, denotes one seal set on the same label, on the reverse of another. *Encyc.*

COLLA'TIVE, *a.* Advowsons are presentative, *collative* or donative. An advowson *collative* is where the bishop and patron are one and the same person; in which case the bishop cannot present to himself, but he does, by one act of collation or conferring the benefice, the whole that is done, in common cases, by both presentation and institution. *Blackstone.*

COLLA'TOR, *n.* One who collates or compares manuscripts or copies of books. *Addison.*

2. One who collates to a benefice, as when the ordinary and patron are the same person. *Ayliffe.*

COLLAUD', *v. t.* [L. *collaudo.*] To unite in praising. [*Little used.*] *Howell.*

COL'LEAGUE, *n.* col'leeg. [L. *collega*; Fr. *collegue*; It. *collega*; Sp. *colega*; L. *con* and *lego*, to choose, or *lego* to send, or *ligo* to bind. This word is differently accented by different speakers and lexicographers. I have followed the latest authorities.]

A partner or associate in the same office, employment or commission, civil or ecclesiastical. *Milton. Swift.*

It is never used of partners in trade or manufactures.

COLLE'AGUE, *v. t.* or *i.* collee'g. To unite with in the same office.

COLLE'AGUED, *pp.* United as an associate in the same office.

COL'LEAGUESHIP, *n.* Partnership in office. *Milton.*

COLLECT', *v. t.* [L. *colligo*, *collectum*; *con* and *lego*, to gather; Gr. λεγω.]

1. To gather, as separate persons or things, into one body or place; to assemble or bring together; as, to *collect* men into an army; to *collect* ideas; to *collect* particulars into one sum.

2. To gain by observation or information.

> From all that can be *collected*, the public peace will not soon be interrupted.

3. To gather from premises; to infer as a consequence.

> Which consequence, I conceive, is very ill *collected*. *Locke.*

4. To gather money or revenue from debtors; to demand and receive; as, to *collect* taxes; to *collect* the customs; to *collect* accounts, or debts.

5. To gather, as crops; to reap, mow or pick, and secure in proper repositories; as, to *collect* hay, corn or fruits.

6. To draw together; to bring into united action; as, to *collect* all the strength, or all the powers of the mind.

7. To obtain from contribution.

To collect one's self, is to recover from surprise, or a disconcerted state; to gain command over the thoughts, when dispersed; over the passions, when tumultuous; or the mind, when dismayed. *Shak. Milton.*

COLLECT', *v. i.* To run together; to accumulate; as, pus *collects* in an abscess; sand or snow *collects* in banks.

COL'LECT, *n.* A short comprehensive prayer; a prayer adapted to a particular day or occasion. *Taylor.*

2. A collection or gathering of money. [*Little used.*] *Encyc.*

COLLECTA'NEOUS, *a.* [L. *collectaneus.*] Gathered; collected.

COLLECT'ED, *pp.* Gathered; assembled; congregated; drawn together.

2. *a.* Recovered from surprise or dismay; not disconcerted; cool; firm; prepared.

COLLECT'EDLY, *adv.* In one view; together; in one body.

COLLECT'EDNESS, *n.* A collected state of the mind; recovery from surprise.

COLLECT'IBLE, *a.* That may be collected or gathered; that may be inferred.

2. That may be gathered or recovered; as, the debts or taxes are or are not *collectible*.

COLLECT'ING, *ppr.* Gathering; drawing together; assembling.

COLLEC'TION, *n.* The act of gathering, or assembling.

2. The body formed by gathering; an assemblage, or assembly; a crowd; as a *collection* of men.

3. A contribution; a sum collected for a charitable purpose.

> Now concerning the *collection* for the saints. 1 Cor. xvi.

4. A gathering, as of matter in an abscess.

5. The act of deducing consequences; reasoning; inference. [*Little used.*] *Johnson. Hooker.*

6. A corollary; a consectary; a deduction from premises; consequence. *Johnson. Hooker.*

7. A book compiled from other books, by the putting together of parts; a compilation; as a *collection* of essays or sermons.

COLLECT'IVE, *a.* [L. *collectivus*; Fr. *collectif*; It. *collettivo.*]

1. Formed by gathering; gathered into a mass, sum, or body; congregated, or aggregated. *Watts. Swift.*

2. Deducing consequences; reasoning; inferring. *Brown.*

3. In *grammar*, expressing a number or multitude united; as a *collective* noun or name, which, though in the singular number itself, denotes more than one; as, *company*, *army*, *troop*, *assembly*.

COLLECT'IVELY, *adv.* In a mass, or body; in a collected state; in the aggregate; unitedly; in a state of combination; as the citizens of a state *collectively* considered.

COLLECT'IVENESS, *n.* A state of union; mass.

COLLECT'OR, *n.* One who colleets or gathers things which are scattered or separate.

2. A compiler; one who gathers and puts together parts of books, or scattered pieces, in one book. *Addison.*

3. In *botany*, one who gathers plants, without studying botany as a science. *Encyc.*

4. An officer appointed and commissioned to collect and receive customs, duties, taxes or toll. *Temple.*

5. A bachelor of arts in Oxford, who is appointed to superintend some scholastic proceedings in Lent. *Todd.*

COLLECT'ORSHIP, *n.* The office of a collector of customs or taxes.

2. The jurisdiction of a collector. *Asiat. Researches.*

COLLEG'ATARY, *n.* [L. *con* and *lego*, to send.]

In *the civil law*, a person who has a legacy

left to him in common with one or more other persons. *Chambers. Johnson.*

COL'LEGE, *n.* [L. *collegium; con* and *lego*, to gather.]

In its primary sense, a collection, or assembly. Hence,

1. In *a general sense*, a collection, assemblage or society of men, invested with certain powers and rights, performing certain duties, or engaged in some common employment, or pursuit.

2. In *a particular sense*, an assembly for a political or ecclesiastical purpose; as the *college* of Electors or their deputies at the diet in Ratisbon. So also, the *college* of princes, or their deputies; the *college* of cities, or deputies of the Imperial cities; the *college* of Cardinals, or sacred college. In Russia, the denomination, *college*, is given to councils of state, courts or assemblies of men intrusted with the administration of the government, and called *Imperial colleges*. Of these some are supreme and others subordinate; as the Supreme Imperial *College*; the *college* of foreign affairs; the *college* of war; the admiralty *college*; the *college* of justice; the *college* of commerce; the medical *college*. *Tooke* ii. 335. 356.

In *Great Britain* and *the United States of America*, a society of physicians is called a *college*. So also there are *colleges* of surgeons; and in Britain, a *college* of philosophy, a *college* of heralds, a *college* of justice, &c. Colleges of these kinds are usually incorporated or established by the supreme power of the state.

3. An edifice appropriated to the use of students, who are acquiring the languages and sciences.

4. The society of persons engaged in the pursuits of literature, including the officers and students. Societies of this kind are incorporated and endowed with revenues.

5. In foreign universities, a public lecture.

COL'LEGE-LIKE, *n.* Regulated after the manner of a college.

COLLE'GIAL, *a.* Relating to a college; belonging to a college; having the properties of a college.

COLLE'GIAN, *n.* A member of a college, particularly of a literary institution so called; an inhabitant of a college. *Johnson.*

COLLE'GIATE, *a.* Pertaining to a college; as *collegiate* studies.

2. Containing a college; instituted after the manner of a college; as a *collegiate* society. *Johnson.*

3. A *collegiate* church is one that has no bishop's see; but has the ancient retinue of a bishop, canons and prebends. Of these some are of royal, others of ecclesiastical foundation; and each is regulated, in matters of divine service, as a cathedral. Some of these were anciently abbeys which have been secularized. *Encyc.*

COLLE'GIATE, *n.* The member of a college. *Burton.*

COL'LET, *n.* [Fr. *collet*, a collar, or neck, from L. *collum.*]

1. Among *jewelers*, the horizontal face or plane at the bottom of brilliants; or the part of a ring in which the stone is set. *Encyc. Johnson.*

2. In *glass-making*, that part of glass vessels which sticks to the iron instrument used in taking the substance from the melting-pot. *Encyc.*

3. Anciently, a band or collar.

4. A term used by turners. *Johnson.*

COLLET'IC, *a.* Having the property of gluing; agglutinant. *Encyc.*

COLLET'IC, *n.* [Gr. κολλητικος.] An agglutinant. *Encyc.*

COLLI'DE, *v. i.* [L. *collido; con* and *lædo*, to strike.]

To strike or dash against each other. *Brown.*

COL'LIER, *n. col'yer.* [from *coal.*] A digger of coal; one who works in a coal-mine. *Johnson.*

2. A coal-merchant or dealer in coal. *Bacon.*

3. A coasting vessel employed in the coal trade, or in transporting coal from the ports where it is received from the mines, to the ports where it is purchased for consumption.

COL'LIERY, *n. col'yery.* The place where coal is dug. [See *Coalery.*]

2. The coal trade. Qu.

COLLIFLOWER. [See *Cauliflower.*]

COL'LIGATE, *v. t.* [L. *colligo; con* and *ligo*, to bind.] To tie or bind together.

The pieces of isinglass are *colligated* in rows. *Nich. Dict.*

COL'LIGATED, *pp.* Tied or bound together.

COL'LIGATING, *ppr.* Binding together.

COLLIGA'TION, *n.* A binding together. *Brown.*

COLLIMA'TION, *n.* [L. *collimo; con* and *limes*, a limit. Ainsworth suggests that it may be an error, and that *collineo, con* and *linea*, is the real reading; but *collimo* is in perfect analogy with other words of like signification. To *aim* is to direct to the limit or end.]

The act of aiming at a mark; aim; the act of leveling, or of directing the sight to a fixed object. *Asiat. Research.*

COLLINEA'TION, *n.* [L. *collineo; con* and *linea*, a line.]

The act of aiming, or directing in a line to a fixed object. *Johnson.*

COL'LING, *n.* [L. *collum*, the neck.] An embrace; dalliance. [*Not used.*] *Chaucer.*

COLLIQ'UABLE, *a.* [See *Colliquate.*] That may be liquefied, or melted; liable to melt, grow soft, or become fluid.

COLLIQ'UAMENT, *n.* The substance formed by melting; that which is melted. *Bailey. Johnson.*

2. Technically, the fetal part of an egg; the transparent fluid in an egg, containing the first rudiments of the chick. *Coxe. Encyc.*

3. The first rudiments of an embryo in generation. *Coxe.*

COL'LIQUANT, *a.* That has the power of dissolving or melting.

COL'LIQUATE, *v. i.* [L. *colliqueo; con* and *liqueo*, to melt. See *Liquid.*]

To melt; to dissolve; to change from solid to fluid; to become liquid. *Brown.*

COL'LIQUATE, *v. t.* To melt or dissolve.

COL'LIQUATED, *pp.* Melted; dissolved; turned from a solid to a fluid substance. *Boyle. Harvey.*

COL'LIQUATING, *ppr.* Melting; dissolving.

COLLIQUA'TION, *n.* The act of melting. *Boyle.*

2. A dissolving, flowing or wasting; applied to the blood, when it does not readily coagulate, and to the solid parts, when they waste away by excessive secretion, occasioning fluxes and profuse, clammy sweats. *Coxe. Encyc. Quincy.*

COLLIQ'UATIVE, *a.* Melting; dissolving; appropriately indicating a morbid discharge of the animal fluids; as a *colliquative* fever, which is accompanied with diarrhœa, or profuse sweats; a *colliquative* sweat is a profuse clammy sweat.

COLLIQUEFAC'TION, *n.* [L. *colliquefacio.*] A melting together; the reduction of different bodies into one mass by fusion. *Bacon.*

COLLI''SION, *n. s* as *z.* [L. *collisio*, from *collido, collisi; con* and *lædo*, to strike or hurt.]

1. The act of striking together; a striking together of two hard bodies. *Milton.*

2. The state of being struck together; a clashing. Hence,

3. Opposition; interference; as a *collision* of interests or of parties.

4. A running against each other, as ships at sea. *Marshal on Insurance. Walsh.*

COL'LOCATE, *v. t.* [L. *colloco; con* and *loco*, to set or place.] To set or place; to set; to station.

COL'LOCATE, *a.* Set; placed. *Bacon.*

COL'LOCATED, *pp.* Placed.

COL'LOCATING, *ppr.* Setting; placing.

COLLOCA'TION, *n.* [L. *collocatio.*] A setting; the act of placing; disposition in place.

2. The state of being placed, or placed with something else. *Bacon.*

COLLOCU'TION, *n.* [L. *collocutio; con* and *locutio*, from *loquor*, to speak.]

A speaking or conversing together; conference; mutual discourse. *Bailey. Johnson.*

COLLOCU'TOR, *n.* One of the speakers in a dialogue.

COLLO'GUE, *v. t.* To wheedle. [*Not in use.*]

COL'LOP, *n.* A small slice of meat; a piece of flesh. *Dryden.*

2. In burlesque, a child. *Shak.*

In Job xv. 27. it seems to have the sense of a thick piece or fleshy lump. "He maketh *collops* of fat on his flanks." This is the sense of the word in N. England.

COLLO'QUIAL, *a.* [See *Colloquy.*] Pertaining to common conversation, or to mutual discourse; as *colloquial* language; a *colloquial* phrase.

COL'LOQUIST, *n.* A speaker in a dialogue. *Malone.*

COL'LOQUY, *n.* [L. *colloquium; con* and *loquor*, to speak.]

Conversation; mutual discourse of two or more; conference; dialogue. *Milton. Taylor.*

COLLOW. [See *Colly.*]

COLLUC'TANCY, *n.* [L. *colluctor; con* and *luctor*, to struggle.]

A struggling to resist; a striving against; resistance; opposition of nature.

COLLUCTA'TION, *n.* A struggling to resist; contest; resistance; opposition; contrariety. *Woodward.*

COLLU'DE, *v. i.* [L. *colludo ; con* and *ludo*, to play, to banter, to mock.]

To play into the hand of each other; to conspire in a fraud; to act in concert. *Johnson.*

COLLU'DER, *n.* One who conspires in a fraud.

COLLU'DING, *ppr.* Conspiring with another in a fraud.

COLLU'DING, *n.* A trick; collusion.

COLLU'SION, *n. s* as *z.* [L. *collusio.* See *Collude.*]

1. In *law*, a deceitful agreement or compact between two or more persons, for the one party to bring an action against the other, for some evil purpose, as to defraud a third person of his right. *Cowel.*

A secret understanding between two parties, who plead or proceed fraudulently against each other, to the prejudice of a third person. *Encyc.*

2. In general, a secret agreement for a fraudulent purpose.

COLLU'SIVE, *a.* Fraudulently concerted between two or more; as a *collusive* agreement.

COLLU'SIVELY, *adv.* By collusion; by secret agreement to defraud.

COLLU'SIVENESS, *n.* The quality of being collusive.

COLLU'SORY, *a.* Carrying on a fraud by a secret concert; containing collusion.

COL'LY, COL'LOW, *n.* [Supposed to be from *coal.*] The black grime or soot of coal or burnt wood. *Woodward. Burton.*

COL'LY, *v. t.* To make foul; to grime with the smut of coal. *Shak.*

COL'LYRITE, *n.* [Gr. κολλυριον, infra.] A variety of clay, of a white color, with shades of gray, red, or yellow. *Cleaveland.*

COLLYR'IUM, *n.* [L.; Gr. κολλυριον. Qu. from κωλυω, to check, and ρεος, defluxion.]

Eye-salve; eye-wash; a topical remedy for disorders of the eyes. *Coxe. Encyc.*

COL'MAR, *n.* [Fr.] A sort of pear.

COL'OCYNTH, *n.* [Gr. κολοκυνθις.] The coloquintida, or bitter apple of the shops, a kind of gourd, from Aleppo and from Crete. It contains a bitter pulp, which is a drastic purge. *Encyc.*

COLOGNE-EARTH, *n.* A kind of light bastard ocher, of a deep brown color, not a pure native fossil, but containing more vegetable than mineral matter; supposed to be the remains of wood long buried in the earth. *Hill.*

It is an earthy variety of lignite or brown coal. *Cleaveland.*

COLOM'BO, *n.* A root from Colombo in Ceylon. Its smell is aromatic, and its taste pungent and bitter. It is much esteemed as a tonic in dyspeptic and bilious diseases. *Hooper.*

CO'LON, *n.* [Gr. κωλον, the colon, a member or limb.]

1. In *anatomy*, the largest of the intestines, or rather the largest division of the intestinal canal; beginning at the cœcum, and ascending by the right kidney, it passes under the hollow part of the liver, and the bottom of the stomach, to the spleen; thence descending by the left kidney, it passes, in the form of an S, to the upper part of the os sacrum, where, from its straight course, the canal takes the name of rectum. *Encyc. Quincy.*

2. In *grammar*, a point or character formed thus [:], used to mark a pause, greater than that of a semicolon, but less than that of a period; or rather it is used when the sense of the division of a period is complete, so as to admit a full point; but something is added by way of illustration, or the description is continued by an additional remark, without a necessary dependence on the foregoing members of the sentence. Thus,

> A brute arrives at a point of perfection he can never pass: in a few years he has all the endowments he is capable of. Spect. No. iii.

The colon is often used before an address, quotation or example. "Mr. Gray was followed by Mr. Erskine, who spoke thus: 'I rise to second the motion of my honorable friend.'" But the propriety of this depends on the pause, and this depends on the form of introducing the quotation; for after *say, said*, or a like word, the colon is not used, and seems to be improper. Thus in our version of the scriptures, such members are almost invariably followed by a comma. "But Jesus said to them, 'Ye know not what ye ask.'"

The use of the colon is not uniform; nor is it easily defined and reduced to rules. Indeed the use of it might be dispensed with without much inconvenience.

COL'ONEL, *n. cur'nel.* [Fr. *colonel;* It. *colonnello ;* Arm. *coronal ;* Sp. *coronel;* Port. *coronel ;* from It. *colonna*, Fr. *colonne*, a column, It. *colonnello*, the column of a book.]

The chief commander of a regiment of troops, whether infantry or cavalry. He ranks next below a brigadier-general. In England, *colonel-lieutenant* is the commander of a regiment of guards, of which the king, prince or other person of eminence is colonel. *Lieutenant-colonel* is the second officer in a regiment, and commands it in the absence of the colonel.

COLONELCY, *n. cur'nelcy.* **COLONELSHIP,** *n. cur'nelship.* The office, rank or commission of a colonel. *Swift. Washington.*

COLO'NIAL, *a.* [See *Colony.*] Pertaining to a colony; as *colonial* government; *colonial* rights. [*Colonical* is not in use.]

COL'ONIST, *n.* [See *Colony.*] An inhabitant of a colony. *Blackstone. Marshall, Life of Washington.*

COLONIZA'TION, *n.* The act of colonizing, or state of being colonized.

COL'ONIZE, *v. t.* [See *Colony.*] To plant or establish a colony in; to plant or settle a number of the subjects of a kingdom or state in a remote country, for the purpose of cultivation, commerce or defense, and for permanent residence. *Bacon.*

> The Greeks *colonized* the South of Italy and of France.

2. To migrate and settle in, as inhabitants.

> English Puritans *colonized* New England.

COL'ONIZED, *pp.* Settled or planted with a colony.

COL'ONIZING, *ppr.* Planting with a colony.

COL'ONIZING, *n.* The act of establishing a colony.

> This state paper has been adopted as the basis of all her later *colonizings.* *Tooke*, i. 622.

COLONNA'DE, *n.* [It. *colonnata*, from *colonna*, a column; Sp. *colunata ;* Fr. *colonnade.* See *Column.*]

1. In *architecture*, a peristyle of a circular figure, or a series of columns, disposed in a circle, and insulated within side. *Builder's Dict. Addison.*

2. Any series or range of columns. *Pope.*

A *polystyle colonnade* is a range of columns too great to be taken in by the eye at a single view; as that of the palace of St. Peter at Rome, consisting of 284 columns of the Doric order. *Encyc.*

COL'ONY, *n.* [L. *colonia*, from *colo*, to cultivate.]

1. A company or body of people transplanted from their mother country to a remote province or country to cultivate and inhabit it, and remaining subject to the jurisdiction of the parent state; as the British *colonies* in America or the Indies; the Spanish *colonies* in South America. When such settlements cease to be subject to the parent state, they are no longer denominated *colonies.*

> The first settlers of New England were the best of Englishmen, well educated, devout christians, and zealous lovers of liberty. There was never a *colony* formed of better materials. *Ames.*

2. The country planted or colonized; a plantation; also, the body of inhabitants in a territory colonized, including the descendants of the first planters. The people, though born in the territory, retain the name of *colonists*, till they cease to be subjects of the parent state.

3. A collection of animals; as *colonies* of shell-fish. *Encyc.*

COL'OPHON, *n.* [from a city of Ionia.] The conclusion of a book, formerly containing the place or year, or both, of its publication. *Warton.*

COL'OPHONITE, *n.* [Supra, from the city or its resin color.]

A variety of garnet, of a reddish yellow or brown color, occurring in small amorphous granular masses. *Dict. Nat. Hist.*

COL'OPHONY, *n.* In *pharmacy*, black resin or turpentine boiled in water and dried; or the residuum, after distillation of the etherial oil of turpentine, being further urged by a more intense and long continued fire. It is so named from Colophon in Ionia, whence the best was formerly brought. *Nicholson. Encyc.*

COLOQUINT'IDA, *n.* [Gr. κολοκυνθις; L. *colocynthis.*]

The colocynth or bitter apple, the fruit of a plant of the genus Cucumis, a native of Syria and of Crete. It is of the size of a large orange, containing a pulp which is violently purgative, but sometimes useful as a medicine. *Chambers.*

CŎL'OR, *n.* [L. *color;* It. *colore ;* Sp. Port. *color ;* Fr. *couleur.*]

1. In *physics*, a property inherent in light, which, by a difference in the rays and the laws of refraction, or some other cause, gives to bodies particular appearances to the eye. The principal colors are red, orange, yellow, green, blue, indigo and violet. *White* is not properly a color; as a white body reflects the rays of light without separating them. *Black* bodies, on the contrary, absorb all the rays, or nearly

all, and therefore *black* is no distinct color. But in common discourse, *white* and *black* are denominated *colors;* and all the colors admit of many shades of difference.

2. Appearance of a body to the eye, or a quality of sensation, caused by the rays of light; hue; dye; as the *color* of gold, or of indigo.

3. A red color; the freshness or appearance of blood in the face.

> My cheeks no longer did their *color* boast. *Dryden.*

4. Appearance to the mind; as, prejudice puts a false *color* upon objects.

5. Superficial cover; palliation; that which serves to give an appearance of right; as, their sin admitted no *color* or excuse. *King Charles.*

6. External appearance; false show; pretense; guise.

> Under the *color* of commending him,
> I have access my own love to prefer. *Shak.*
> [See Acts xxvii. 30.]

7. Kind; species; character; complexion.

> Boys and women are, for the most part, cattle of this *color.* *Shak.*

8. That which is used for coloring; paint; as red lead, ocher, orpiment, cinnabar, or vermilion, &c.

9. *Colors,* with a plural termination, in the military art, a flag, ensign or standard, borne in an army or fleet. [See *Flag.*]

10. In *law, color* in pleading is when the defendant in assize or trespass, gives to the plaintiff a *color* or appearance of title, by stating his title specially; thus removing the cause from the jury to the court. *Blackstone.*

Water-colors are such as are used in painting with gum-water or size, without being mixed with oil. *Encyc.*

COL'OR, *v. t.* To change or alter the external appearance of a body or substance; to dye; to tinge; to paint; to stain; as, to *color* cloth. Generally, to *color* is to change from white to some other color.

2. To give a specious appearance; to set in a fair light; to palliate; to excuse.

> He *colors* the falsehood of Æneas by an express command of Jupiter to forsake the queen. *Dryden.*

3. To make plausible; to exaggerate in representation. *Addison.*

To color a stranger's goods, is when a freeman allows a foreigner to enter goods at the custom house in his name, to avoid the alien's duty.

COL'OR, *v. i.* To blush.

COL'ORABLE, *a.* Specious; plausible; giving an appearance of right or justice; as a *colorable* pretense; a *colorable* excuse. *Spenser. Hooker.*

COL'ORABLY, *adv.* Speciously; plausibly; with a fair external appearance. *Bacon.*

COL'ORATE, *a.* [L. *coloratus,* from *coloro,* to color.]

Colored; dyed; or tinged with some color. [*Little used.*] *Ray.*

COLORA'TION, *n.* [L. *coloro.*] The art or practice of coloring, or the state of being colored. *Bacon.*

COL'ORATURE, *n.* In *music,* all manner of variations, trills, &c., intended to make a song agreeable. *Encyc.*

COL'ORED, *pp.* Having the external appearance changed; dyed; tinged; painted or stained.

2. Streaked; striped; having a diversity of hues. *Bacon.*

3. Having a specious appearance.

Colored people, black people, Africans or their descendants, mixed or unmixed.

COLORIF'IC, *a.* [*color,* and L. *facio.*] That has the quality of tinging; able to give color, or tint to other bodies. *Kirwan.*

COLOR'ING, *ppr.* Dying; staining; tinging.

2. Giving a fair external appearance; palliating; excusing.

COL'ORING, *n.* The act or art of dyeing; the state of being colored; color.

2. A specious appearance; fair artificial representation; as, the story has a *coloring* of truth.

3. Among *painters,* the manner of applying colors; or the mixture of light and shade, formed by the various colors employed.

COL'ORIST, *n.* [Supra.] One who colors; a painter who excels in giving the proper colors to his designs. *Dryden.*

COL'ORLESS, *a.* [Supra.] Destitute of color; not distinguished by any hue; transparent; as *colorless* water, glass or gas. *Newton.*

COLOS'SAL, COLOSSE'AN, *a.* [See *Colossus.*] Like a colossus; very large; huge; gigantic.

COLOS'SUS, *n.* [L. and Gr.] A statue of a gigantic size. The most remarkable colossus of antiquity was one at Rhodes, a statue of Apollo, so high that it is said ships might sail between its legs.

COLOS'SUS-WISE, *adv.* In the manner of a colossus. *Shak.*

COL'STAFF, *n.* A staff for carrying burdens by two on their shoulders. [*Local.*]

COLT, *n.* [Sax. *colt.*] The young of the equine genus of animals or horse kind. In America, *colt* is equally applied to the male or female, and this is unquestionably correct. The male is called a *horse-colt,* and the female is called a *filly.*

2. A young foolish fellow; a person without experience or stability. *Shak.*

COLT, *v. i.* To frisk, riot or frolick, like a colt; to be licentious. [*Not used.*] *Spenser.*

COLT, *v. t.* To befool. [*Not used.*] *Shak.*

COLT'S-FOOT, *n.* A genus of plants, the Tussilago. The name is also given to a species of Cacalia. *Fam. of Plants.*

COLT'S-TOOTH, *n.* An imperfect or superfluous tooth in young horses. *Johnson.*

2. A love of youthful pleasure.

> Well said, Lord Sands;
> Your *colt's-tooth* is not yet cast? *Shak.*

[*Little used.*]

COLTER, *n.* [L. *culter,* a colter or knife, that is, the *cutter;* Fr. *coutre;* It. *coltro;* W. *cylltawr;* D. *kouter;* G. *kolter.*]

The fore iron of a plow, with a sharp edge, that cuts the earth or sod.

COLTISH, *a.* Like a colt; wanton; frisky; gay. *Chaucer.*

COL'UBER, *n.* [L. a serpent or adder.] In *zoology,* a genus of serpents, distinguished by scuta or hard crusts on the belly, and scales on the tail. Under this genus are ranked many species, as the viper, black snake, &c.

COL'UBRINE, *a.* [L. *colubrinus.*] Relating to the coluber, or to serpents; cunning; crafty. [*Little used.*] *Johnson.*

COL'UMBARY, *n.* [L. *columbarium,* from *columba,* a pigeon; W. *colomen;* Ir. *colm* or *colum;* Arm. *coulm;* Russ. *golub,* a pigeon or dove. In Russ. *golubei* signifies, of a sky-blue, azure.]

A dove-cot; a pigeon-house.

COLUM'BATE, *n.* A salt or compound of columbic acid, with a base.

COLUM'BIAN, *a.* Pertaining to the United States, or to America, discovered by Columbus.

COLUM'BIC, *a.* Pertaining to columbium; as *columbic* acid.

COLUMBIF'EROUS, *a.* Producing or containing columbium. *Phillips.*

COL'UMBINE, *a.* Like or pertaining to a pigeon or dove; of a dove-color, or like the neck of a dove.

COL'UMBINE, *n.* [L. *columbina.*] Aquilegia, a genus of plants of several species. The Thalictrum or meadow-rue is also called feathered columbine. *Fam. of Plants.*

COLUM'BITE, *n.* [See *Columbium.*] The ore of columbium.

COLUM'BIUM, *n.* [from *Columbia,* America.]

A metal first discovered in an ore or oxyd, found in Connecticut, at New-London, near the house of Gov. Winthrop, and by him transmitted to Sir Hans Sloane, by whom it was deposited in the British museum. The same metal was afterwards discovered in Sweden, and called *tantalum,* and its ore *tantalite.* *Cleaveland.*

COLUMBO. [See *Colombo.*]

COL'UMEL, *n.* In *botany,* the central column in a capsule, taking its rise from the receptacle, and having the seeds fixed to it all round. *Martyn.*

COL'UMN, *n. col'um.* [L. *columna, columen;* W. *colov,* a stalk or stem, a prop; *colovyn,* a column; Ir. *colbh,* a stalk, a column; Arm. *coulouenn;* Fr. *colonne;* It. *colonna;* Sp. *columna;* Port. *columna* or *coluna.* This word is from the Celtic, signifying the stem of a tree, such stems being the first columns used. The primary sense is a shoot, or that which is set.]

1. In *architecture,* a long round body of wood or stone, used to support or adorn a building, composed of a base, a shaft and a capital. The shaft tapers from the base, in imitation of the stem of a tree. There are five kinds or orders of columns. 1. The Tuscan, rude, simple and massy; the highth of which is fourteen semidiameters or modules, and the diminution at the top from one sixth to one eighth of the inferior diameter. 2. The Doric, which is next in strength to the Tuscan, has a robust, masculine aspect; its highth is sixteen modules. 3. The Ionic is more slender than the Tuscan and Doric; its highth is eighteen modules. 4. The Corinthian is more delicate in its form and proportions, and enriched with ornaments; its highth should be twenty modules. 5. The Composite is a species of the Corinthian, and of the same highth. *Encyc.*

In strictness, the shaft of a column consists of one entire piece; but it is often composed of different pieces, so united, as to have the appearance of one entire piece. It differs in this respect from a *pillar,* which primarily signifies a *pile,* composed of small pieces. But the two things are unfortunately confounded; and a column consisting of a single piece of timber is absurdly called a *pillar* or pile.

2. An erect or elevated structure resembling a column in architecture; as the *astronomical column* at Paris, a kind of hollow tower with a spiral ascent to the top; *gnomonic column*, a cylinder on which the hour of the day is indicated by the shadow of a style; *military column*, among the Romans; *triumphal column*; &c.

3. Any body pressing perpendicularly on its base, and of the same diameter as its base; as a *column* of water, air or mercury.

4. In *the military art*, a large body of troops drawn up in order; as a solid *column*.

5. Among *printers*, a division of a page; a perpendicular set of lines separated from another set by a line or blank space. In manuscript books and papers, any separate perpendicular line or row of words or figures. A page may contain two or more *columns;* and in arithmetic, many *columns* of figures may be added.

COLUM'NAR, *a.* Formed in columns; having the form of columns; like the shaft of a column; as *columnar* spar.

COLUM'NARISH, *a.* Somewhat resembling a column. [*A bad word.*] *Fam. of Plants.* Vol. ii. 454.

COLU'RE, *n.* [Gr. κολουρος; κολος, mutilated, and ουρα, a tail; so named because a part is always beneath the horizon.]

In *astronomy* and *geography*, the colures are two great circles supposed to intersect each other at right angles, in the poles of the world, one of them passing through the solstitial and the other through the equinoctial points of the ecliptic, viz. Cancer and Capricorn, Aries and Libra, dividing the ecliptic into four equal parts. The points where these lines intersect the ecliptic are called cardinal points. *Encyc. Harris.*

COM, in composition as a prefix, Ir. *comh*, or *coimh*, W. *cym* or *cyv*, L. *com* or *cum*, denotes *with*, *to* or *against*.

CO'MA, *n.* [Gr. κωμα, lethargy.] Lethargy; dozing; a preternatural propensity to sleep; a kind of stupor of diseased persons. *Coxe.*

CO'MA, *n.* [L. from Gr. κομη, a head of hair.] In *botany*, a species of bracte, terminating the stem of a plant, in a tuft or bush; as in crown-imperial. *Martyn.*

2. In *astronomy*, hairiness; the hairy appearance that surrounds a comet, when the earth or the spectator is between the comet and the sun.

CO'MART, *n.* [*con* and *mart.*] A treaty; article; agreement. *Obs.* *Shak.*

CO'MATE, *a.* [L. *comatus*, from *coma;* Ir. *ciamh*, *ciabh.*] Hairy; encompassed with a coma, or bushy appearance, like hair. *Shak.*

CO-MA'TE, *n.* [*co* and *mate.*] A fellow mate, or companion. *Shak.*

CO'MATOSE, CO'MATOUS, *a.* [See *Coma.*] Preternaturally disposed to sleep; drowsy; dozing, without natural sleep; lethargic. *Coxe. Grew.*

COMB, *n.* [Sax.] A valley between hills or mountains. [*Not in use.*] *Brown.*

COMB, *n. b* silent. [Sax. *camb*, a comb; *cemban*, to comb; G. *kamm;* D. *kam;* Sw. *kamm;* Dan. *kam*, a comb: Ir. *ciomaim*, to comb or card. Qu. L. *como*, to dress, trim or comb, which seems to be allied to the Gr. κομψος. But the noun may be the radical word in our language, and from scratching, scraping; Eth. ገመዐ gamea, to shave or scrape.]

1. An instrument, with teeth, for separating, cleansing and adjusting hair, wool, or flax. Also, an instrument of horn or shell, for keeping the hair in its place when dressed.

2. The crest, caruncle or red fleshy tuft, growing on a cock's head; so called from its indentures which resemble the teeth of a comb.

3. The substance in which bees lodge their honey, in small hexagonal cells.

4. A dry measure of four bushels. [*Not used in U. States.*]

COMB, *v. t.* To separate, disentangle, cleanse, and adjust with a comb, as to *comb* hair; or to separate, cleanse and lay smooth and straight, as to *comb* wool.

COMB, *v. i.* In *the language of seamen*, to roll over, as the top of a wave; or to break with a white foam. [Qu. Sp. *combar*, to bend, or from the English *comb.*]

COMB-BIRD, *n.* A gallinaceous fowl of Africa, of the size of a turkey-cock.

COMB-BRUSH, *n.* A brush to clean combs.

COMB-MAKER, *n.* One whose occupation is to make combs.

COM'BAT, *v. i.* [Fr. *combattre*, *com* and *battre*, to beat with or against; It. *combattere;* Sp. *combatir;* Port. *combater;* Arm. *combadti* or *combatein.* See *Beat.*]

1. To fight; to struggle or contend with an opposing force.

> Pardon me; I will not *combat* in my shirt. *Shak.*

This word is particularly used to denote private contest, or the fighting of two persons in a duel; but it is used in a general sense for the contention of bodies of men, nations, armies, or any species of animals.

> After the fall of the republic, the Romans *combated* only for the choice of masters. *Gibbon.*

2. To act in opposition. *Milton.*

It is followed by *with* before the person, and *for* before the thing sought.

> A *combats with* B *for* his right

COM'BAT, *v. t.* To fight with; to oppose by force; as, to *combat* an antagonist.

2. To contend against; to oppose; to resist; as, to *combat* arguments or opinions.

COM'BAT, *n.* A fighting; a struggling to resist, overthrow or conquer; contest by force; engagement; battle; as the *combat* of armies.

2. A duel; a fighting between two men; formerly, a formal trial of a doubtful cause, or decision of a controversy between two persons, by swords or bastons.

COM'BATANT, *a.* Contending; disposed to contend. *B. Jonson.*

COM'BATANT, *n.* A person who combats; any person who fights with another, or in an army, or fleet.

2. A duellist; one who fights or contends in battle, for the decision of a private quarrel or difference; a champion.

3. A person who contends with another in argument, or controversy.

COM'BATED, *pp.* Opposed; resisted. *Locke.*

COM'BATER, *n.* One who fights or contends. *Sherwood.*

COM'BATING, *ppr.* Striving to resist; fighting; opposing by force or by argument.

COMBED, *pp.* Separated, cleaned, or dressed with a comb.

COMBER, *n.* One who combs; one whose occupation is to comb wool, &c.

COM'BER, *n.* Incumbrance. [*Not used.*]

COM'BER, *n.* A long slender fish with a red back, found in Cornwall, England.

COMBI'NABLE, *a.* Capable of combining. *Chesterfield.*

COM'BINATE, *a.* [See *Combine.*] Espoused; betrothed. [*Not used.*] *Shak.*

COMBINA'TION, *n.* [Fr. *combinaison.* See *Combine.*] In *general*, close union or connection. Hence,

1. Intimate union, or association of two or more persons or things, by set purpose or agreement, for effecting some object, by joint operation; in a *good sense*, when the object is laudable; in an *ill sense*, when it is illegal or iniquitous. It is sometimes equivalent to league, or to conspiracy. We say, a *combination* of men to overthrow government, or a *combination* to resist oppression.

2. An assemblage; union of particulars; as a *combination* of circumstances.

3. Commixture; union of bodies or qualities in a mass or compound; as, to make new compounds by new *combinations*. *Boyle.*

4. Chemical union; union by affinity.

> Mix dry acid of tartar with dry carbonate of potash; no *combination* will ensue, till water is added. *Henry.*

5. In *mathematics*, the union of numbers or quantities in every possible manner; or the variation or alteration of any number of quantities, letters, sounds, or the like, in all the different manners possible. The number of possible changes or *combinations* is found by multiplying the terms 1. 2. 3. 4. 5 continually into each other. Thus $1\times2=2$: $2\times3=6$: $6\times4=24$: $24\times5=120$. &c. So the permutations of five quantities amount to 120. The changes that may be rung on twelve bells amount to 479,001,600. And the twenty four letters of the alphabet admit of 62,044,840,173,323,943,936,000 changes or combinations. *Encyc.*

COMBI'NE, *v. t.* [Fr. *combiner;* It. *combinare;* Sp. *combinar;* from the Low Latin *combino*, of *com* and *binus*, two and two, or double.]

1. To unite or join two or more things; to link closely together.

> Friendship *combines* the hearts of men. *Anon.*

2. To agree; to accord; to settle by compact. [*Not usual.*] *Shak.*

3. To join words or ideas together; opposed to *analyze*. *Johnson.*

4. To cause to unite; to bring into union or confederacy.

> The violences of revolutionary France *combined* the powers of Europe in opposition.

COMBI'NE, *v. i.* To unite, agree or coalesce.

> Honor and policy *combine* to justify the measure.

2. To unite in friendship or design; to league together.

> You with your foes *combine.* *Dryden.*

3. To unite by affinity, or natural attraction.

Two substances which will not *combine* of themselves, may be made to *combine*, by the intervention of a third.

4. To confederate; to unite as nations.

The powers of Europe *combined* against France.

COMBI'NED, *pp.* United closely; associated; leagued; confederated; chimically united.

COMBING, *ppr.* Separating and adjusting hair, wool, &c.

COMBING, *n.* Borrowed hair combed over a bald part of the head. [*Local.*] *Bp. Taylor.*

COMBI'NING, *ppr.* Uniting closely; joining in purpose; confederating; uniting by chimical affinity.

COMBLESS, *a.* Without a comb or crest; as a *combless* cock. *Shak.*

COMBUST', *a.* [L. *combustus, comburo.*] When a planet is in conjunction with the sun or apparently very near it, it is said to be *combust* or in combustion. The distance within which this epithet is applicable to a planet, is said by some writers to be 8½ degrees; others say, within the distance of half the sun's disk.

COMBUST'IBLE, *a.* [Fr. *combustible;* Sp. *id.*; from L. *comburo, combustum.*] That will take fire and burn; capable of catching fire; thus, wood and coal are *combustible* bodies.

COMBUST'IBLE, *n.* A substance that will take fire and burn; a body which, in its rapid union with others, disengages heat and light. *Ure.*

COMBUST'IBLENESS, } *n.* The quality
COMBUSTIBIL'ITY, } of taking fire and burning; the quality of a substance which admits the action of fire upon it; capacity of being burnt, or combined with oxygen. *Lavoisier.*

The quality of throwing out heat and light, in the rapid combination of its substance with another body. *Ure.*

COMBUS'TION, *n. combus'chun.* [Low L. *combustio.* See *Combust.*]

1. The operation of fire on inflammable substances; or according to modern chimistry, the union of an inflammable substance with oxygen, attended with light, and in most instances, with heat. In the combustion of a substance, heat or caloric is disengaged, and oxygen is absorbed. *Lavoisier.*

This theory of Lavoisier being found somewhat defective, the following definition is given. Combustion is the disengagement of heat and light which accompanies chimical combination. *Ure.*

Combustion cannot be regarded as dependent on any peculiar principle or form of matter, but must be considered as a general result of intense chimical action. *Webster's Man. of Chim.*

2. In *popular language*, a burning; the process or action of fire in consuming a body, attended with heat, or heat and flame; as the *combustion* of wood or coal.

3. Conflagration; a great fire. Hence, from the violent agitation of fire or flame,

4. Tumult; violent agitation with hurry and noise; confusion; uproar. *Hooker. Milton. Dryden.*

COME, *v. i.* pret. *came*, part. *come.* [Sax. *cuman*, or *cwiman;* Goth. *cwiman*, pret. *cwom;* D. *koomen*, pret. *kwam;* G. *kommen;* Sw. *komma;* Dan. *kommer*, to come. Qu. W. *cam*, Ir. *ceim*, a step. And qu. the Ar. قوم Heb. Ch. קום to rise, or stand erect; to set or establish; to subsist, consist, remain; to rectify, or set in order; and in Arabic, to be thick, stiff or congealed. The senses of the words appear to be very different; but we use *come* in the sense of rising or springing, applied to corn; the corn *comes* or *comes up*, G. *keimen.* So the butter *comes*, when it separates from the whey and becomes thick or stiff. And is not our common use of *come*, when we invite another to begin some act, or to move, equivalent to *rise*, being originally directed to persons sitting or reclining, in the oriental manner? *Coming* implies moving, driving, shooting along, and so we use *set:* we say, to *set forward;* the tide *sets* northerly.]

1. To move towards; to advance nearer, in any manner, and from any distance. We say, the men *come* this way, whether riding or on foot; the wind *comes* from the west; the ship *comes* with a fine breeze; light *comes* from the sun. It is applicable perhaps to every thing susceptible of motion, and is opposed to *go.*

2. To draw nigh; to approach; to arrive; to be present.

Come thou and all thy house into the ark. Gen. vii.

All my time will I wait, till my change *come.* Job xiv.

When shall I *come* and appear before God? Ps. xlii.

Then shall the end *come.* Math. xxiv.

Thy kingdom *come;* thy will be done. Math. vi.

The time has *come.*

3. To advance and arrive at some state or condition; as, the ships *came* to action; the players *came* to blows; is it *come* to this?

His sons *come* to honor and he knoweth it not. Job xiv.

I wonder how he *came* to know what had been done; how did he *come* by his knowledge? the heir *comes* into possession of his estate; the man will *come* in time to abhor the vices of his youth, or he will *come* to be poor and despicable, or to poverty.

In these and similar phrases, we observe the process or advance is applied to the body or to the mind, indifferently; and to persons or events.

4. To happen or fall out; as, how *comes* that? let *come* what will. Hence when followed by an object or person, with *to* or *on*, to befall; to light on.

After all that has *come* on us for our evil deeds. Ezra ix.

All things *come* alike to all. Eccles. ix.

5. To advance or move into view; to appear; as, blood or color *comes* and goes in the face. *Spenser. Shak.*

6. To sprout, as plants; to spring. The corn *comes* or *comes up.* "In the *coming* or sprouting of malt, as it must not *come* too little, so it must not *come* too much." *Mortimer.* So Bacon uses the word; and this use of it coincides nearly with the sense of קום, quom, 2 Kings xix. 26. and in the same chapter inserted in Isaiah xxxvii. 27. It is the G. *keimen*, Icelandic *keima*, to bud, or germinate.

7. To become.

So *came* I a widow. *Shak.*

8. To appear or be formed, as butter; to advance or change from cream to butter; a common use of the word; as, the butter *comes.* *Hudibras.*

9. *Come*, in the imperative, is used to excite attention, or to invite to motion or joint action; *come*, let us go.

This is the heir; *come*, let us kill him.

When repeated, it sometimes expresses haste; *come, come.* Sometimes it expresses or introduces rebuke.

As the sense of *come* is to move, in almost any manner, in its various applications, that sense is modified indefinitely by other words used in connection with it. Thus with words expressing *approach*, it denotes *advancing nearer;* with words expressing departure, as *from, of, out of*, &c., it denotes *motion from*, &c.

To come about, to happen; to fall out; to come to pass; to arrive. How did these things *come about?* So the French *venir à bout*, to come to the end, that is, to arrive.

To come about, to turn; to change; to come round. The wind will *come about* from west to east. The ship *comes about.* It is applied to a change of sentiments.

On better thoughts, and my urged reasons,
They are *come about*, and won to the true side. *B. Jonson.*

To come again, to return. Gen. xxviii. Lev. xiv.

To come after, to follow. Math. xvi. Also, to come to obtain; as, to *come after* a book.

To come at, to reach; to arrive within reach of; to gain; to come so near as to be able to take or possess. We prize those most who are hardest to *come at.* To *come at* a true knowledge of ourselves. *Addison.*

Also, to come towards, as in attacking.

To come away, to depart from; to leave; to issue from.

To come back, to return.

To come by, to pass near; a popular phrase. Also, to obtain, gain, acquire; that is, to *come near, at* or *close.*

Examine how you *came by* all your state. *Dryden.*

This is not an irregular or improper use of this word. It is precisely equivalent to *possess*, to *sit by.* [See *Possess.*] So in Ger. *bekommen*, D. *bekoomen*, to get or obtain; the *by* or *be* prefixed.

To come down, to descend.

The Lord will *come down* on mount Sinai. Ex. xix.

Also, to be humbled or abased.

Your principalities shall *come down.* Jer. xiii.
Come down from thy glory. Jer. xlviii.

To come for, to come to get or obtain; to come after.

To come forth, to issue or proceed from. Gen. xv. Is. xi. Micah v.

Also, to depart from; to leave. Mark ix.
Also, to come abroad. Jer. iv.

To come from, to depart from; to leave. In popular language, this phrase is equivalent to, where is his native place or former place of residence; where did this man, this animal or this plant originate.

To come home, that is, *to come to home*, or

the house; to arrive at the dwelling. Hence, to come close; to press closely; to touch the feelings, interest, or reason. [See *Home.*]

To come in, to enter, as into an inclosure.

Also, to comply; to yield; as, *come in* and submit.

Also, to arrive at a port, or place of rendezvous; as, the fleet has *come in.*

Also, to become fashionable; to be brought into use.

Silken garments did not *come in* till late. *Arbuthnot.*

Also, to enter as an ingredient or part of a composition.

A nice sense of propriety *comes in* to heighten the character.

Also, to grow and produce; to come to maturity and yield. If the corn *comes in* well, we shall have a supply, without importation. Crops *come in* light.

Also, to lie carnally with. Gen. xxxviii.

To come in for, to arrive in time to take a share. Johnson says this phrase is taken from hunting, where the slow dogs take nothing. Qu. But the sense in which we now use the phrase has no reference to time or slow movement. It is, to unite with others in taking a part.

The rest *came in for* subsidies. *Swift.*

To come into, to join with; to bring help.

Also, and more generally, to agree to; to comply with; to unite with others in adopting; as, to *come into* a measure or scheme.

To come near, to approach in place. Hence metaphorically, to approach in quality; to arrive at nearly the same degree in a quality, or accomplishment; to resemble. *Temple.*

To come nigh, is popularly used in like senses.

To come no near, in seamanship, is an order to the helmsman not to steer so close to the wind.

To come of, to issue from; to proceed from, as a descendant.

Of Priam's royal race my mother *came.* *Dryden.*

Also, to proceed from, as an effect from a cause.

This *comes of* judging by the eye. *L'Estrange.*

Whence come wars—*come* they not *of* your lusts? James iv.

To come off, to depart from; to remove from on.

Also, to depart or deviate from a line or point; to become wider; to dilate. *Bacon.*

Also, to escape; to get free.

If they *come off* safe, call their deliverance a miracle. *Addison.*

Hence, to end; to arrive at the final issue; as, to *come off* with honor or disgrace.

To come off from, to leave; to quit. *Felton.*

To come on, to advance; to proceed; as, *come on*, brave boys; night is *coming on.* So we say, the young man *comes on* well in his studies, and the phrase often denotes a prosperous advance, successful improvement. So we say of plants, they *come on* well, they grow or thrive—that is, they proceed.

Also, to fall on; to happen to.

Lest that *come on* you, which is spoken of in the prophets. Acts xiii.

Also, to invade; to rush on.

To come over, to pass above or across, or from one side to another. In distillation, to rise and pass over, as vapor.

Also, to pass from one party, side or army to another; to change sides.

To come out, to depart or proceed from.

They shall *come out* with great substance. Gen. xv.

Also, to become public; to escape from concealment or privacy; to be discovered; as, the truth is *come out* at last.

Also, to be published, as a book. The work *comes out* in quarto.

Also, to end or come to an issue; as, how will this affair *come out;* he has *come out* well at last.

To come out of, to issue forth, as from confinement, or a close place; to proceed or depart from.

Also, to issue from, as descendants.

Kings shall *come out of* thee. Gen. xvii.

To come out with, to give publicity to; to disclose. *Boyle.*

To come short, to fail; not to accomplish.

All have sinned and *come short* of the glory of God. Rom. iii.

To come to, to consent or yield. *Swift.*

Also, to amount to; as, the taxes *come to* a large sum.

Also, to recover, as from a swoon.

To come together, to meet or assemble.

To come to pass, to be; to happen; to fall out; to be effected. The phrase is much used in the common version of the scriptures, but is seldom found in modern English writings.

To come up, to ascend; to rise.

Also, to spring; to shoot or rise above the earth, as a plant. *Bacon.*

Also, to come into use, as a fashion.

To come up the capstern, in seamanship, is to turn it the contrary way, so as to slacken the rope about it.

To come up the tackle fall, is to slacken it gently.

To come up to, to approach near.

Also, to amount to.

Also, to advance to; to rise to.

To come up with, to overtake, in following or pursuit.

To come upon, to fall on; to attack or invade.

To come, in futurity; to happen hereafter. In times *to come.* Success is yet *to come.*

Take a lease for years *to come.* *Locke.*

Come is an intransitive verb, but the participle *come* is much used with the substantive verb, in the passive form. "The end of all flesh *is* come." I *am* come, thou *art* come, he *is* come, we *are* come, &c. This use of the substantive verb, for *have*, is perhaps too well established to be rejected; but *have* or *has* should be used in such phrases. In the phrase, "*come* Friday, *come* Candlemas," there is an ellipsis of certain words, as *when Friday shall come.*

Come, come, the repetition of *come*, expresses haste, or exhortation to hasten. Sometimes it introduces a threat.

ĈŎME, *n.* A sprout. [*Not used.*] *Mortimer.*

ĈŎME-OFF, *n.* Means of escape; evasion; excuse.

We do not want this *come-off.* *Grellman*, 172.

ĈOME'DIAN, *n.* [See *Comedy.*] An actor or player in comedy; or a player in general, male or female. *Camden.*

2. A writer of comedy. *Peacham.*

ĈOM'EDY, *n.* [L. *comœdia;* Gr. κωμωδια. Qu. from κωμη, a village, and ωδη, or rather αειδω, to sing, and denoting that the comedian was a strolling singer; or whether the first syllable is from κωμος, a merry feast, whence *comic, comical*, the latter indicating that the comedian was characterized by buffoonery. The latter coincides in elements with the English *game.*]

A dramatic composition intended to represent human characters, which are to be imitated in language, dress and manner, by actors on a stage, for the amusement of spectators. The object of comedy is said to be to recommend virtue and make vice ridiculous; but the real effect is amusement.

ĈŎMELILY, *adv. cum'lily.* In a suitable or decent manner. [*Little used.*] *Sherwood.*

ĈŎMELINESS, *n. cum'liness.* [See *Comely.*] That which is becoming, fit or suitable, in form or manner. *Comeliness* of person implies symmetry or due proportion of parts; *comeliness* of manner implies decorum and propriety. "It signifies something less forcible than *beauty*, less elegant than *grace*, and less light than *prettiness.*" *Johnson.*

A careless *comeliness* with comely care. *Sidney.*

He hath no form nor *comeliness.* Is. liii. 2.

ĈŎMELY, *a. cum'ly.* [from *come.* The sense of suitableness is often from meeting, coming together, whence adjusting, putting in order. So in Latin, *conveniens*, from *convenio.*]

Properly, becoming; suitable: whence, handsome; graceful. *Applied to person or form*, it denotes symmetry or due proportion, but it expresses less than *beautiful* or *elegant.*

I have seen a son of Jesse—a *comely* person. 1 Sam. xvi.

I will not conceal his *comely* proportion. Job xli.

2. Decent; suitable; proper; becoming; suited to time, place, circumstances or persons.

Praise is *comely* for the upright. Ps. xxxiii.

Is it *comely* that a woman pray to God uncovered? 1 Cor. xi.

O what a world is this, when what is *comely*
Envenoms him that bears it. *Shak.*

ĈŎMELY, *adv. cum'ly.* Handsomely; gracefully. *Ascham.*

ĈŎMER, *n.* One that comes; one who approaches; one who has arrived and is present.

ĈOMESSA'TION, *n.* [L. *comessatio.*] Feasting or reveling. *Hall.*

ĈOMES'TIBLE, *a.* [Fr.] Eatable. [*Not used.*] *Wotton.*

ĈOM'ET, *n.* [L. *cometa;* Gr. κομητης; from κομη, *coma*, hair; a hairy star.]

An opake, spherical, solid body, like a planet, but accompanied with a train of light, performing revolutions about the sun, in an elliptical orbit, having the sun in one of its foci. In its approach to its perihelion, it becomes visible, and after passing its perihelion, it departs into remote regions and disappears. In popular language, comets are *tailed, bearded* or *hairy*, but these terms are taken from the appearance of the light which attends them, which, in different positions with respect to the sun, exhibits the form of a tail or train, a beard, or a border of hair. When the comet is westward of the sun and rises or sets before it, the light appears in the morning like a train beginning at the body of the comet and extending westward and diverging in proportion to its extent. Thus the comet of 1769, [which I saw,] when it rose in the morning, presented a luminous train that extended nearly from the horizon to the meridian. When the comet and the sun are opposite, the earth being between them, the comet is, to the view, immersed in its train and the light appears around its body like a fringe or border of hair. From the train of a comet, this body has obtained the popular name of a *blazing star*.

Herschel observed several comets, which appeared to have no nucleus, but to be merely collections of vapor condensed about a center. *Cyc.*

COM'ET, *n.* A game at cards. *Southerne.*

COMETA'RIUM, COM'ETARY, *n.* A machine exhibiting an idea of the revolution of a comet round the sun. *Encyc.*

COM'ETARY, *a.* Pertaining to a comet. *Cheyne.*

COMET'IC, *a.* Relating to a comet.

COM'ET-LIKE, *a.* Resembling a comet. *Shak.*

COMETOG'RAPHY, *n.* [*comet* and Gr. γραφω, to describe.] A description or treatise of comets.

COM'FIT, COM'FITURE, *n.* [D. *konfyt*; G. *confect*; Dan. *confect*; Fr. *confit, confiture*; It. *confetto, confettura*, or *confezione*; Sp. *confite*; Port. *confeito*; from the L. *confectura, confectus, conficio, con* and *facio*, to make.]
A dry sweet-meat; any kind of fruit or root preserved with sugar and dried. *Johnson.*

COM'FIT, *v. t.* To preserve dry with sugar. *Cowley.*

COM'FIT-MAKER, *n.* One who makes or prepares comfits.

COM'FORT, *v. t.* [Low L. *conforto*; Fr. *conforter*; Arm. *conforti*, or *conforta*; It. *confortare*; Sp. and Port. *confortar*; Ir. *comh-fhurtach*, comfort, and *furtachd*, id.; *furtaighim*, to relieve or help; from the L. *con* and *fortis*, strong.]

1. To strengthen; to invigorate; to cheer or enliven.

   Light excelleth in *comforting* the spirits of men. *Bacon.*

   Comfort ye your hearts. Gen. xviii.

2. To strengthen the mind when depressed or enfeebled; to console; to give new vigor to the spirits; to cheer, or relieve from depression, or trouble.

   His friends came to mourn with him and to *comfort* him. Job ii.

3. In *law*, to relieve, assist or encourage, as the accessory to a crime after the fact. *Blackstone.*

COM'FORT, *n.* Relief from pain; ease; rest or moderate pleasure after pain, cold or distress or uneasiness of body. The word signifies properly new strength, or animation; and relief from pain is often the effect of strength. In a popular sense, the word signifies rather negatively the absence of pain and the consequent quiet, than positive animation.

2. Relief from distress of mind; the ease and quiet which is experienced when pain, trouble, agitation or affliction ceases. It implies also some degree of positive animation of the spirits; or some pleasureable sensations derived from hope, and agreeable prospects; consolation.

   Let me alone, that I may take *comfort* a little. Job x.

   Daughter, be of good *comfort;* thy faith hath made thee whole. Mat. ix.

3. Support; consolation under calamity, distress or danger.

   Let thy merciful kindness be for my *comfort.* Ps. cxix.

4. That which gives strength or support in distress, difficulty, danger, or infirmity.

   Pious children are the *comfort* of their aged parents.

5. In *law*, support; assistance; countenance; encouragement; as, an accessory affords aid or *comfort* to a felon.

6. That which gives security from want and furnishes moderate enjoyment; as the *comforts* of life.

COM'FORTABLE, *a.* Being in a state of ease, or moderate enjoyment; as a person after sickness or pain. *This is the most common use of the word in the U. States.*

2. Admitting comfort; that may afford comfort.

   Who can promise him a *comfortable* appearance before his dreadful judge? *South.*

3. Giving comfort; affording consolation.

   The word of my lord the king shall now be *comfortable.* 2 Sam. xiv.

4. Placing above want and affording moderate enjoyment; as a *comfortable* provision for old age.

COM'FORTABLENESS, *n.* The state of enjoying comfort.

COM'FORTABLY, *adv.* In a manner to give comfort or consolation.

   Speak ye *comfortably* to Jerusalem. Is. xl.

2. With comfort, or cheerfulness; without despair.

   Hope *comfortably* and cheerfully for God's performance. *Hammond.*

COM'FORTED, *pp.* Strengthened; consoled; encouraged.

COM'FORTER, *n.* One who administers comfort or consolation; one who strengthens and supports the mind in distress or danger.

   I looked for *comforters*, but found none. Ps. lxix.

   Miserable *comforters* are ye all. Job xvi.

2. The title of the Holy Spirit, whose office it is to comfort, and support the christian.

   But the *Comforter*, the Holy Spirit, whom the Father will send in my name—he shall teach you all things. John xiv.

COM'FORTING, *ppr.* Giving strength or spirits; giving ease; cheering; encouraging; consoling.

COM'FORTLESS, *a.* Without comfort; without any thing to alleviate misfortune, or distress.

   I will not leave you *comfortless.* John xiv.

COM'FORTRESS, *n.* A female that affords comfort.

COM'FREY, COM'FRY, *n.* [Qu. L. *confirmo*, equivalent to *consolida.*] A genus of plants, the Symphytum.

COM'IC, *a.* [L. *comicus*; Gr. κωμικος. See *Comedy.*]

1. Relating to comedy, as distinct from tragedy. *Waller.*

2. Raising mirth; fitted to excite merriment. *Shak.*

COM'ICAL, *a.* Relating to comedy; comic. *Gay.*

2. Exciting mirth; diverting; sportive; droll. *Addison.*

   We say, a buffoon is a *comical* fellow, or his story or his manners are *com ica.*

COM'ICALLY, *adv.* In a manner befitting comedy.

2. In a comical manner; in a manner to raise mirth.

COM'ICALNESS, *n.* The quality of being comical; the power or quality of raising mirth. *Johnson.*

COM'ING, *ppr.* [See *Come.*] Drawing nearer or nigh; approaching; moving towards; advancing.

2. *a.* Future; yet to come; as, in *coming* ages.

3. Forward; ready to come.

   How *coming* to the poet every muse. *Pope.*

   [*The latter sense is now unusual.*]

COM'ING, *n.* The act of coming; approach.

2. The state of being come; arrival.

   The Lord hath blessed thee since my *coming.* Gen. xxx.

COM'ING-IN, *n.* Entrance.

   I know thy going-out and thy *coming-in.* 2 Kings xix.

2. Beginning; commencement; as the *coming-in* of the year. 2 Kings xiii.

3. Income; revenue. [*Not now used.*] *Shak.*

4. Compliance; submission. [*Not in use,*] *Massinger.*

COMI''TIAL, *a.* [L. *comitia*, an assembly of the Romans; probably formed from *cum* and *eo*, Ir. *coimh*, W. *cym* or *cyv.*]

1. Relating to the comitia or popular assemblies of the Romans, for electing officers and passing laws. *Middleton.*

2. Relating to an order of presbyterian assemblies. *Bp. Bancroft.*

COM'ITY, *n.* [L. *comitas*, from *comes*, mild, affable; Ir. *caomh.*]
Mildness and suavity of manners; courtesy; civility; good breeding. Wellbred people are characterized by *comity* of manners.

COM'MA. *n.* [Gr. κομμα, a segment, from κοπτω, to cut off.]

1. In *writing* and *printing*, this point [,] denoting the shortest pause in reading, and separating a sentence into divisions or members, according to the construction. Thus, "There is not a just man upon earth, that doeth good, and sinneth not." "Virtue, wit, knowledge, are excellent accomplishments." "Live soberly, righteously, and piously, in the present world."

2. In *music*, an enharmonic interval, being the eighth part of a tone, or the difference between a major and a minor semitone; a term used in theoretic music to show the exact proportions between concords. *Encyc. Harris.*

3. Distinction. *L. Addison.*

COMM'AND, *v. t.* [It. *comandare; Sp. comandar, mandar;* Arm. *coumandi;* Fr. *commander; con,* or *com,* and L. *mando,* to command, to commit to, Basque *manatu;* literally, to send to, to send forth, from the same root as *commend, demand,* and L. *moneo.* See Class Mn.]

1. To bid; to order; to direct; to charge; implying authority, and power to control, and to require obedience.

We will sacrifice to the Lord our God, as he shall *command* us. Ex. viii.

I know that he [Abraham] will *command* his children and his household after him, and they shall keep the way of the Lord. Gen. xviii.

2. To govern, lead or direct; to have or to exercise supreme authority over.

Lord Wellington *commanded* an army in Spain; he *commanded* the army at the battle of Waterloo.

3. To have in power; to be able to exercise power or authority over; as, a military post *commands* the surrounding country; a fort *commands* the harbor.

5. To overlook, or have in the power of the eye, without obstruction.

One side *commands* a view of the finest garden in the world. *Addison.*

5. To direct; to send.

The Lord shall *command* the blessing on thee. Deut. xxviii.

The Lord will *command* his loving kindness. Ps. xlii.

6. To have or to exercise a controlling influence over.

A good magistrate *commands* the respect and affections of the people.

COMM'AND, *v. i.* To have or to exercise supreme authority; to possess the chief power; to govern; as, the general *commands* with dignity and humanity. What general *commands* in Canada?

COMM'AND, *n.* The right or power of governing with chief or exclusive authority; supreme power; control; as, an officer has a brigade under his *command;* he takes *command* of the army in France; *an appropriate military term.*

2. The power of controlling; governing influence; sway.

He assumed an absolute *command* over his readers. *Dryden.*

3. Cogent or absolute authority.

Command and force may often create, but can never cure, an aversion. *Locke.*

4. The act of commanding; the mandate uttered; order given.

The captain gives *command.* *Dryden.*

5. The power of overlooking, or surveying, without obstruction.

The steepy strand,
Which overlooks the vale with wide *command.* *Dryden.*

6. The power of governing or controlling by force, or of defending and protecting.

The fortress has complete *command* of the port.

7. That which is commanded; control; as a body of troops under *command.* *Marshall.*

COMM'ANDABLE, *a.* That may be commanded.

COMMANDANT', *n.* [Fr.] A commander; a commanding officer of a place or of a body of forces. *Smollett.*

COMM'ANDATORY, *a.* Having the force of a command.

COMM'ANDED, *pp.* Ordered; directed; governed; controlled.

COMM'ANDER, *n.* A chief; one who has supreme authority; a leader; the chief officer of an army, or of any division of it. The term may also be applied to the admiral of a fleet, or of a squadron, or to any supreme officer; as the *commander* of the land or of the naval force; the *commander* of a ship.

2. One on whom is bestowed a benefice or commandry.

3. A heavy beetle or wooden mallet, used in paving, &c. [This gives us the primary sense of L. *mando,* to send, to drive.]

4. An instrument of surgery. *Wiseman.*

COMM'ANDERY, } *n.* [Fr. *commanderie.*]
COMM'ANDRY, } A kind of benefice or fixed revenue, belonging to a military order, conferred on knights of merit. There are strict and regular commandries, obtained by merit, or in order; and others are of grace and favor, bestowed by the Grand Master. There are also commandries for the religious, in the orders of St. Bernard and St. Anthony. *Encyc.*

COMM'ANDING, *ppr.* Bidding; ordering; directing with authority; governing; bearing rule; exercising supreme authority; having in power; overlooking without obstruction.

2. *a.* Controlling by influence, authority, or dignity; as a man of *commanding* manners; a *commanding* eloquence.

COMM'ANDINGLY, *adv.* In a commanding manner.

COMM'ANDMENT, *n.* A command; a mandate; an order or injunction given by authority; charge; precept.

Why do ye transgress the *commandment* of God. Math. xv.

This is the first and great *commandment.* Math. xxii.

A new *commandment* I give to you, that ye love one another. John xiii.

2. By way of eminence, a precept of the decalogue, or moral law, written on tables of stone, at Mount Sinai; one of the *ten commandments.* Ex. xxxiv.

3. Authority; coercive power. *Shak.*

COMM'ANDRESS, *n.* A woman invested with supreme authority. *Hooker.*

COM'MARK, *n.* [Fr. *comarque;* Sp. *comarca.*] The frontier of a country. *Shelton.*

COMMATE'RIAL, *a.* [*con* and *material.*] Consisting of the same matter with another thing. *Bacon.*

COMMATERIAL'ITY, *n.* Participation of the same matter. *Johnson.*

COM'MATISM, *n.* [from *comma.*] Briefness; conciseness in writing. *Bp. Horsley.*

COMMEAS'URABLE, *a.* [See *Measure.*] Reducible to the same measure. But *commensurable* is generally used.

COM'MELINE, *n.* A genus of herbaceous plants, Commelina, natives of warm climates. This name was given to this genus by Linne, in honor of the Commelins, distinguished botanists of Holland. These plants have flowers with three petals, two large and one small; the large petals representing John and Gaspard Commelin, who published catalogues of plants; the smaller petal representing another of the name who published nothing. *Gloss. de Botanique, De Theis.*

COMMEM'ORABLE, *a.* Memorable; worthy to be remembered, or noticed with honor. [See *Memorable.*]

COMMEM'ORATE, *v. t.* [L. *commemoro; con* and *memoro,* to mention. See *Memory.*]

To call to remembrance by a solemn act; to celebrate with honor and solemnity; to honor, as a person or event, by some act of respect or affection, intended to preserve the remembrance of that person or event.

The Lord's supper is designed to *commemorate* the sufferings and dying love of our Savior.

COMMEM'ORATED, *pp.* Called to remembrance by some act of solemnity.

COMMEM'ORATING, *ppr.* Celebrating with honor by some solemn act.

COMMEMORA'TION, *n.* The act of calling to remembrance, by some solemnity; the act of honoring the memory of some person or event, by solemn celebration. The feast of shells at Plymouth in Massachusetts is an annual *commemoration* of the first landing of our ancestors in 1620.

COMMEM'ORATIVE, *a.* Tending to preserve the remembrance of something. *Atterbury.*

COMMEM'ORATORY, *a.* Serving to preserve the memory of.

COMMENCE, *v. i.* *commens'.* [Fr. *commencer;* Port. *começar;* Sp. *comenzar;* It. *cominciare;* Arm. *coumançz.* Perhaps *com* and *initio.*]

1. To begin; to take rise or origin; to have first existence; as, a state of glory to *commence* after this life; this empire *commenced* at a late period.

2. To begin to be, as in a change of character.

Let not learning too *commence* its foe. *Pope.*

3. To take a degree or the first degree in a university or college. *Bailey.*

COMMENCE, *v. t.* To begin; to enter upon; to perform the first act; as, to *commence* operations.

2. To begin; to originate; to bring; as, to *commence* a suit, action or process in law.

COMMEN'CED, *pp.* Begun; originated.

COMMENCEMENT, *n.* *commens'ment.* Beginning; rise; origin; first existence; as the *commencement* of New Style in 1752; the *commencement* of hostilities in 1775.

2. The time when students in colleges *commence* bachelors; a day in which degrees are publicly conferred on students who have finished a collegiate education. In Cambridge, Eng., the day when masters of arts and doctors complete their degrees. *Worthington.*

COMMEN'CING, *ppr.* Beginning; entering on; originating.

COMMEND', *v. t.* [L. *commendo; con* and *mando;* It. *commendare;* Port. *encommendar;* Fr. *recommander;* Sp. *comandar,* to *command,* and formerly to *commend.* This is the same word as *command,* differently applied. The primary sense is, to send to or throw; hence, to charge, bid, desire or intreat.]

1. To represent as worthy of notice, regard, or kindness; to speak in favor of; to recommend.

I *commend* to you Phebe our sister. Rom. xvi.

2. To commit; to entrust or give in charge.

Father, into thy hands I *commend* my spirit. Luke xxiii.

3. To praise; to mention with approbation.

The princes *commended* Sarai before Pharaoh. The Lord *commended* the unjust steward. *Bible.*

4. To make acceptable or more acceptable.

But meat *commendeth* us not to God. 1 Cor. viii.

5. To produce or present to favorable notice.

The chorus had an occasion of *commending* their voices to the king. *Dryden.*

6. To send or bear to.

These draw the chariot which Latinus sends,
And the rich present to the prince *commends.* *Dryden.*

COMMEND, *n.* Commendation. [*Not used.*] *Shak.*

COMMEND'ABLE, *a.* [Fr. *recommandable*; It. *commendabile.* Formerly accented improperly on the first syllable.]
That may be commended or praised; worthy of approbation or praise; laudable.

Order and decent ceremonies in the church are *commendable.* *Bacon.*

COMMEND'ABLENESS, *n.* State of being commendable.

COMMEND'ABLY, *adv.* Laudably; in a praise-worthy manner.

COMMEND'AM, *n.* In *ecclesiastical law*, in England, a benefice or living *commended*, by the king or head of the church, to the care of a clerk, to hold till a proper pastor is provided. This may be temporary or perpetual. *Blackstone.*
The trust or administration of the revenues of a benefice given to a layman, to hold as a deposit for six months in order to repairs, &c., or to an ecclesiastic, to perform the pastoral duties, till the benefice is provided with a regular incumbent. *Encyc.*

COMMEND'ATARY, *n.* [Fr. *commendataire*; It. *commendatario, commendatore.*]
One who holds a living in commendam.

COMMENDA'TION, *n.* [L. *commendatio.*] The act of commending; praise; favorable representation in words; declaration of esteem.

Need we, as some others, letters of *commendation.* 2 Cor. xxxi.

2. Ground of esteem, approbation or praise; that which presents a person or thing to another in a favorable light, and renders worthy of regard, or acceptance.

Good-nature is the most godlike *commendation* of a man. *Dryden.*

3. Service; respects; message of love. *Shak.*

COMMEND'ATORY, *a.* Which serves to commend; presenting to favorable notice or reception; containing praise; as a *commendatory* letter. *Bacon. Pope.*

2. Holding a benefice in commendam; as a *commendatory* bishop.

COMMEND'ATORY, *n.* A commendation; eulogy. *South.*

COMMEND'ED, *pp.* Praised; represented favorably; committed in charge.

COMMEND'ER, *n.* One who commends or praises.

COMMEND'ING, *ppr.* Praising; representing favorably; committing, or delivering in charge.

Note. In imitation of the French, we are accustomed to use *recommendation*, &c., for *commendation.* But in most instances, it is better to use the word without the prefix *re.* A letter of commendation, is the preferable phrase.

COMMENS'AL, *n.* [L. *con* and *mensa*, table.] One that eats at the same table. *Obs.* *Chaucer.*

COMMENSAL'ITY, *n.* [Sp. *comensalia*; L. *commensalis*; *con* and *mensa*, a table.]
Fellowship at table; the act or practice of eating at the same table. [*Little used.*] *Brown. Gillies.*

COMMENSURABIL'ITY, **COMMEN'SURABLENESS**, *n.* [Fr. *commensurabilité.*] The capacity of being compared with another in measure, or of being measured by another, or of having a common measure. *Brown. Hale.*

COMMEN'SURABLE, *a.* [Fr. from *con* and L. *mensura*, measure. See *Measure.*]
That have a common measure; reducible to a common measure. Thus a yard and a foot are *commensurable*, as both may be measured by inches. Commensurable numbers are those which may be measured or divided by another number without a remainder; as 12 and 18 which may be measured by 6 and 3.
Commensurable surds are those which, being reduced to their least terms, become true figurative quantities of their kind; and are therefore as a rational quantity to a rational one. *Encyc.*

COMMEN'SURATE, *a.* [It. *commensurare*; Sp. *conmensurar*, whence *conmensurativo*; *con* and L. *mensura*, measure.]

1. Reducible to one and the same common measure.

2. Equal; proportional; having equal measure or extent.

We find nothing in this life *commensurate* to our desires.

COMMEN'SURATE, *v. t.* To reduce to a common measure.

COMMEN'SURATELY, *adv.* With the capacity of measuring or being measured by some other thing. *Holder.*

2. With equal measure or extent.

COMMENSURA'TION, *n.* Proportion, or proportion in measure; a state of having a common measure.

All fitness lies in a particular *commensuration*, or proportion, of one thing to another. *South.*

COM'MENT, *v. i.* [L. *commentor*, to cast in the mind, to think, to devise, to compose; from *con* and *mens*, mind, or the same root. It. *comentare*; Fr. *commenter*; Sp. *comentar*; Port. *commentar.* See *Mind.*]

1. To write notes on the works of an author, with a view to illustrate his meaning, or to explain particular passages; to explain; to expound; to annotate; followed by *on.* We say, to *comment on* an author or *on* his writings. *Dryden. Pope.*

2. To make verbal remarks, or observations, either on a book, or writing, or on actions, events, or opinions. *Shak.*

COM'MENT, *v. t.* To explain. *Fuller.*

2. To feign; to devise. *Obs.* *Spenser.*

COM'MENT, *n.* A note, intended to illustrate a writing, or a difficult passage in an author; annotation; explanation; exposition; as the *comments* of Scott on the Scriptures.

2. That which explains or illustrates; as, a man's conduct is the best *comment* on his declarations. Poverty and disgrace are very significant *comments* on lewdness, gambling and dissipation.

3. Remark; observation.

In such a time as this, it is not meet
That every nice offense should bear its *comment.* *Shak.*

COM'MENTARY, *n.* A comment; exposition; explanation; illustration of difficult and obscure passages in an author.

2. A book of comments or annotations.

3. A historical narrative; a memoir of particular transactions; as the *commentaries* of Cesar.

COM'MENTARY, *v. t.* To write notes upon. [*Little used.*]

COM'MENTATOR, *n.* One who comments; one who writes annotations; an expositor; an annotator. [The accent on the first syllable and that on the third are nearly equal.]

COM'MENTER, *n.* One that writes comments; an annotator.

2. One who makes remarks.

COM'MENTING, *ppr.* Making notes or comments on something said or written.

COMMENTI''TIOUS, *a.* [L. *commentitius.*] Invented; feigned; imaginary. *Glanville.*

COM'MERCE, *n.* [Fr. *commerce*; L. *commercium*; *con* and *mercor*, to buy; *merx, mereo.* See Class Mr. No. 3. It. *commercio*; Sp. *comercio*; Port. *commercio.* Formerly accented on the second syllable.]

1. In *a general sense*, an interchange or mutual change of goods, wares, productions, or property of any kind, between nations or individuals, either by barter, or by purchase and sale; trade; traffick. Commerce is *foreign* or *inland.* *Foreign commerce* is the trade which one nation carries on with another; *inland commerce*, or inland trade, is the trade in the exchange of commodities between citizens of the same nation or state. *Active* commerce. [See *Active.*]

2. Intercourse between individuals; interchange of work, business, civilities or amusements; mutual dealings in common life.

3. Familiar intercourse between the sexes.

4. Interchange; reciprocal communications; as, there is a vast *commerce* of ideas. *D. Webster.*

COM'MERCE, *v. i.* To traffick; to carry on trade. *Raleigh.*

2. To hold intercourse with.

And looks *commercing* with the skies. *Milton.*

COMMER'CIAL, *a.* Pertaining to commerce or trade; as *commercial* concerns; *commercial* relations.

2. Carrying on commerce; as a *commercial* nation.

3. Proceeding from trade; as *commercial* benefits or profits.

COMMER'CIALLY, *adv.* In a commercial view. *Burke.*

COM'MIGRATE, *v. i.* [L. *commigro*; *con* and *migro*, to migrate.]
To migrate together; to move in a body from one country or place to another for permanent residence. [*Little used.*]

COMMIGRA'TION, *n.* The moving of a body of people from one country or place to another with a view to permanent residence. *Woodward.*

COMMINA'TION, *n.* [L. *comminatio*; *con* and *minatio*, a threatening, from *minor*, to threaten. See *Menace.*]

1. A threat or threatening; a denunciation of punishment or vengeance.
2. The recital of God's threatenings on stated days; an office in the Liturgy of the Church of England, appointed to be read on Ash Wednesday or on the first day of Lent. *Encyc.*

COMMIN'ATORY, *a.* Threatening; denouncing punishment. *B. Jonson.*

COMMIN'GLE, *v. t.* [*con* and *mingle.*] To mix together; to mingle in one mass, or intimately; to blend. [See *Mingle.*] *Shak.*

COMMIN'GLE, *v. i.* To mix or unite together, as different substances. *Bacon.*

COMMIN'UATE, *v. t.* To grind. [*Not used.*] [See *Comminute.*]

COMMIN'UIBLE, *a.* Reducible to' powder. *Brown.*

COM'MINUTE, *v. t.* [L. *comminuo*; *con* and *minuo*, to lessen, from the root of *minor*; Ir. *mion*, *min*, fine, small, tender; W. *main*, *man*; Ar. مَنَّ manna, to diminish. Class Mn. No. 5.]

To make small or fine; to reduce to minute particles, or to a fine powder, by breaking, pounding, rasping, or grinding; to pulverize; to triturate; to levigate. It is chiefly or wholly applied to substances, not liquid. *Bacon.*

COM'MINUTED, *pp.* Reduced to fine particles; pulverized; triturated.

COM'MINUTING, *ppr.* Reducing to fine particles; pulverizing; levigating.

COMMINU'TION, *n.* The act of reducing to a fine powder or to small particles; pulverization. *Ray. Bentley.*

2. Attenuation; as *comminution* of spirits. *Bacon.*

COMMIS'ERABLE, *a.* [See *Commiserate.*] Deserving of commiseration or pity; pitiable; that may excite sympathy or sorrow.

This *commiserable* person, Edward.

[*Little used.*] *Bacon.*

COMMIS'ERATE, *v. t.* [L. *commiseror*; *con* and *misereor*, to pity. See *Miserable.*]

1. To pity; to compassionate; to feel sorrow, pain or regret for another in distress; *applied to persons.*

We should *commiserate* those who groan beneath the weight of age, disease or want. *Denham.*

2. To regret; to pity; to be sorry for; as, to *commiserate* our mutual ignorance. *Locke.*

COMMIS'ERATED, *pp.* Pitied.

COMMIS'ERATING, *ppr.* Pitying; compassionating; feeling sorrow for.

COMMISERA'TION, *n.* Pity; compassion; a sympathetic suffering of pain or sorrow for the wants, afflictions or distresses of another.

I cannot think of these poor deluded creatures, but with *commiseration.*

COMMIS'ERATIVELY, *adv.* From compassion. *Overbury.*

COMMIS'ERATOR, *n.* One who pities. *Brown.*

COMMISSA'RIAL, *a.* [See *Commissary.*] Pertaining to a commissary.

Smollett uses *commissorial*; but this is not regular nor authorized.

COMMISSA'RIATE, *n.* [Sp. *comisariato.* See *Commissary.*]

The office or employment of a commissary; or the whole body of officers in the commissary's department. *Tooke, Russ.* i. 575.

COM'MISSARY, *n.* [Fr. *commissaire*; It. and Port. *commissario*; Sp. *comisario*; Low L. *commissarius*; from *commissus*, *committo*; *con* and *mitto*, to send.]

1. In *a general sense*, a commissioner; one to whom is *committed* some charge, duty or office, by a superior power; one who is sent or delegated to execute some office or duty, in the place, or as the representative, of his superior.
2. In *ecclesiastical law*, an officer of the bishop, who exercises spiritual jurisdiction in places of the diocese, so far distant from the episcopal see, that the chancellor cannot call the people to the bishop's principal consistory court, without putting them to inconvenience. *Ayliffe. Encyc.*
3. In *a military sense*, an officer who has the charge of furnishing provisions, clothing, &c., for an army. Commissaries are distinguished by different names, according to their duties; as *commissary-general*, who is at the head of the department of supplies, and has under him *deputy commissaries*, and *issuing commissaries*; the latter to issue or distribute the supplies.
4. An officer who musters the army, receives and inspects the muster-rolls, and keeps an account of the strength of the army. He is called, the *commissary-general of musters.* The *commissary of horses* has the inspection of the artillery horses; and the *commissary of stores* has charge of all the stores of the artillery. *Encyc.*

COM'MISSARYSHIP, *n.* The office of a commissary. *Ayliffe.*

COMMIS'SION, *n.* [Fr. *commission*; It. *commisione*; Sp. *comision*; L. *commissio*, with a different application, from *committo*; *con* and *mitto*, to send.]

1. The act of committing, doing, performing, or perpetrating; as the *commission* of a crime.
2. The act of committing or sending to; the act of entrusting, as a charge or duty. Hence,
3. The thing committed, entrusted or delivered; letters patent, or any writing from proper authority, given to a person as his warrant for exercising certain powers, or the performance of any duty, whether civil, ecclesiastical, or military. Hence,
4. Charge; order; mandate; authority given.

He bore his great *commission* in his look. *Dryden.*

5. By *a metonymy*, a number of persons joined in an office or trust.
6. The state of that which is entrusted, as the great seal was put *into commission*; or the state of being authorized to act or perform service, as a ship is put *into commission.*
7. In *commerce*, the state of acting under authority in the purchase and sale of goods for another. To trade or do business *on commission*, is to buy or sell for another by his authority. Hence,
8. The allowance made to a factor or commission-merchant for transacting business, which is a certain rate per cent. of the value of the goods bought or sold.

Commission of bankruptcy, is a commission issuing from the Chancellor in Great Britain, and in other countries, from some proper authority, appointing and empowering certain persons to examine into the facts relative to an alledged bankruptcy, and to secure the bankrupt's lands and effects for the creditors.

Commission of lunacy, is a commission issuing from the court of chancery, to authorize an inquiry whether a person is a lunatic or not.

Commission-officer, in the army or navy, is an officer who has a commission, in distinction from subaltern officers.

COMMIS'SION-MERCHANT, *n.* A merchant who transacts business as the agent of other men, in buying and selling, and receives a rate per cent. as his commission or reward.

COMMIS'SION, *v. t.* To give a commission to; to empower or authorize by commission. The president and senate appoint, but the president *commissions.* *United States.*

2. To send with a mandate or authority.

———A chosen band
He first *commissions* to the Latian land. *Dryden.*

3. To authorize or empower.

Note. *Commissionate*, in a like sense, has been used, but rarely.

COMMIS'SIONAL, **COMMIS'SIONARY**, } *a.* Appointed by warrant. [*Little used.*]

COMMIS'SIONED, *pp.* Furnished with a commission; empowered; authorized.

COMMIS'SIONER, *n.* A person who has a commission or warrant from proper authority, to perform some office, or execute some business, for the person or government which employs him, and gives him authority; as *commissioners* for settling the bounds of a state, or for adjusting claims.

COMMIS'SIONING, *ppr.* Giving a commission to; furnishing with a warrant; empowering by letters patent or other writing; authorizing.

COM'MISSURE, *n.* [L. *commissura*, from *committo*, *commissus*; literally, a sending or thrusting together.]

1. A joint, seam or closure; the place where two bodies or parts of a body meet and unite; an interstice or cleft between particles or parts, as between plates or lamellæ.
2. In *architecture*, the joint of two stones, or application of the surface of one to that of another. *Encyc.*
3. In *anatomy*, a suture of the cranium or skull; articulation; the corners of the lips. Also, certain parts in the ventricles of the brain, uniting the two hemispheres. *Coxe.*

COMMIT', *v. t.* [L. *committo*, to send to, or thrust together; *con* and *mitto*, to send; Fr. *mettre*, to put, set or lay; *commettre*, to commit; It. *mettere*, *commettere*; Sp. *meter*, *cometer*; Port. *meter*, *cometer.*]

Literally, to send to or upon; to throw, put or lay upon. Hence,

1. To give in trust; to put into the hands or power of another; to entrust; with *to*.

Commit thy way *to* the Lord. Ps. xxxvii.

The things thou hast heard of me, *commit to* faithful men. 2 Tim. ii.

2. To put into any place for preservation; to deposit; as, to *commit* a passage in a book to memory; to *commit* the body to the grave.

3. To put or send to, for confinement; as, to *commit* an offender to prison. Hence for the sake of brevity, *commit* is used for *imprison*. The sheriff has *committed* the offender.

These two were *committed*, at least restrained of their liberty. *Clarendon.*

4. To do; to effect or perpetrate; as, to *commit* murder, treason, felony, or trespass.

Thou shalt not *commit* adultery. Ex. xx.

5. To join or put together, for a contest; to match; followed by *with*; a latinism.

How does Philopolis *commit* the opponent *with* the respondent. [*Little used.*] *More.*

6. To place in a state of hostility or incongruity. "*Committing* short and long words." But this seems to be the same signification as the foregoing.

7. To expose or endanger by a preliminary step or decision which cannot be recalled; as, to *commit* the peace of a country by espousing the cause of a belligerent.

You might have satisfied every duty of political friendship without *committing* the honor of your sovereign. *Junius.*

8. To engage; to pledge; or to pledge by implication.

The general—addressed letters to Gen. Gates and to Gen. Heath, cautioning them against any sudden assent to the proposal, which might possibly be considered as *committing* the faith of the United States. *Marshall.*

And with the reciprocal pronoun, to *commit one's self*, is to do some act, or make some declaration, which may bind the person in honor, good faith, or consistency, to pursue a certain course of conduct, or to adhere to the tenor of that declaration.

9. To refer or entrust to a committee, or select number of persons, for their consideration and report; *a term of legislation*; as, the petition or the bill is *committed*. Is it the pleasure of the house to *commit* the bill?

COMMIT'MENT, *n.* The act of committing; a sending to prison; a putting into prison; imprisonment. It is equivalent to *sending* or *putting in* simply; as a *commitment* to the tower, or to Newgate; or for the sake of brevity, omitting the name of the place, it is equivalent to *putting into prison*; as, the offender is secured by *commitment*.

2. An order for confining in prison. But more generally we use *mittimus*.

3. The act of referring or entrusting to a committee for consideration; *a term in legislation*; as the *commitment* of a petition or a bill to a select number of persons for consideration and report.

4. The act of delivering in charge or entrusting.

5. A doing, or perpetration, as of sin or a crime; commission. *Clarendon.*

6 The act of pledging or engaging; or the act of exposing or endangering. [See the Verb, No. 7 and 8.] *Hamilton.*

COMMIT'TED, *pp.* Delivered in trust; given in charge; deposited; imprisoned; done; perpetrated; engaged; exposed; referred to a committee.

COMMIT'TEE, *n.* One or more persons, elected or appointed, to whom any matter or business is referred, either by a legislative body or either branch of it, or by a court, or by any corporation, or by any society, or collective body of men acting together. In legislative bodies, a house or branch of that body may resolve or form itself into a committee, called a *committee of the whole house*, when the speaker leaves the chair, and one of the members acts as chairman. *Standing committees* are such as continue during the existence of the legislature, and to these are committed all matters that fall within the purposes of their appointment; as the *committee of elections*, or *of privileges*, &c. *Special committees* are appointed to consider and report on particular subjects.

COMMIT'TEESHIP, *n.* The office and profit of committees. *Milton.*

COMMIT'TER, *n.* One who commits; one who does or perpetrates. *South.*

COMMIT'TIBLE, *a.* That may be committed. [*Little used.*] *Brown.*

COMMIT'TING, *ppr.* Giving in trust; depositing; imprisoning; perpetrating; engaging; referring to a committee; exposing.

COMMIX', *v. t.* [L. *commisceo*, *commixtus*; *con* and *misceo*, to mix. See *Mix*.]

To mix or mingle; to blend; to mix, as different substances. *Bacon. Newton.*

COMMIX', *v. i.* To mix; to mingle. *Shak.*

COMMIX'ED, *pp.* Mixed; blended.

COMMIX'ING, *ppr.* Mixing; blending.

COMMIX'TION, *n.* Mixture; a blending of different ingredients in one mass or compound. *Brown.*

Mixion is used by Shakspeare, but is hardly legitimate.

COMMIX'TURE, *n.* The act of mixing; the state of being mingled; the blending of ingredients in one mass or compound. *Bacon.*

2. The mass formed by mingling different things; composition; compound. *Bacon. Shak. Wotton.*

3. In *Scots law*, a method of acquiring property, by blending different substances belonging to different proprietors. *Encyc.*

COMMO'DE, *n.* [Fr. from L. *commodus*, convenient; *con* or *com* and *modus*, manner. See *Mode*.]

A kind of head dress formerly worn by ladies. *Addison.*

COMMO'DIOUS, *a.* [Fr. *commode*; It. *comodo*; Sp. *id.*; L. *commodus*. See *Mode*.]

Convenient; suitable; fit; proper; adapted to its use or purpose, or to wants and necessities; as a *commodious* house or room.

The haven was not *commodious* to winter in. Acts xxvii. 12.

It is followed by *for* before a noun; as a place *commodious for* a camp.

COMMO'DIOUSLY, *adv.* Conveniently; in a commodious manner; suitably; in a manner to afford ease, or to prevent uneasiness; as a house *commodiously* situated; we may pass life *commodiously* without the restraints of ceremony.

COMMO'DIOUSNESS, *n.* Convenience fitness; suitableness for its purpose; as the *commodiousness* of a house or an apartment; the *commodiousness* of a situation for trade.

COMMOD'ITY, *n.* [L. *commoditas*; It. *comodità*; Fr. *commodité*; Sp. *comodidad*; Port. *commodidade*. See *Commode*.]

1. Primarily, convenience; profit; advantage; interest. "Men seek their own *commodity*." In this sense it was used by *Hooker*, *Sidney*, &c; but this is nearly or wholly obsolete.

2. That which affords ease, convenience or advantage; any thing that is useful, but particularly in commerce, including every thing movable that is bought and sold, goods, wares, merchandize, produce of land and manufactures. Unless perhaps animals may be excepted, the word includes all the movables which are objects of commerce.

Commodities are movables, valuable by money, the common measure. *Locke.*

The principal use of money is to save the commutation of more bulky *commodities*. *Arbuthnot.*

Staple commodities are those which are the produce or manufacture of a country, and constitute the principal articles of exportation. Thus flour is the staple commodity of New-York and Pennsylvania; flour and tobacco, of Maryland and Virginia; cotton and rice, of S. Carolina and Georgia; cotton and sugar, of Louisiana.

COM'MODORE, *n.* [This word is probably a corruption of the Italian *comandatore*, a commander; or the Spanish *comendador*, a superior of a monastery, or a knight who holds a commandry.]

1. The officer who commands a squadron or detachment of ships, destined on a particular enterprise. In the British marine, he bears the rank of a brigadier-general in the army, and his ship is distinguished by a broad red pendant, tapering to the outer end, and sometimes forked. *Encyc.*

2. A title given by courtesy to the senior captain, when three or more ships of war are cruising in company. *Mar. Dict.*

3. The convoy or leading ship in a fleet of merchantmen, which carries a light in her top to conduct the other ships.

COMMODULA'TION, *n.* [L. *con* and *modulatio*.] Measure; agreement. [*Little used.*] *Hakewill.*

COMMOIGNE, *n.* [Fr.] A monk of the same convent. [*Not in use.*] *Selden.*

COM'MON, *a.* [L. *communis*; Fr. *commun*; Arm. *coumun*; It. *comune*; Sp. *comun*; Port. *commum*; Goth. *gamains*; Sax. *gemæn*; G. *gemein*; D. *gemeen*; Sw. *gemen*; Dan. *gemeen*; Ir. *cumann*; Goth. *gamana*, a fellow, fellowship. This word may be composed of *cum* and *man*, *men*, the plural *men* being equivalent to *people* and *vulgus*. The last syllable is clearly from the root of *many*, which seems to belong to the root of *man*, and *mean* is of the same family. Hence we see the connection between *common* and *mean*, as *vulgar*, from *vulgus*, Eng. *folks*.]

1. Belonging equally to more than one, or to many indefinitely; as, life and sense are

common to man and beast; the *common* privileges of citizens; the *common* wants of men.

2. Belonging to the public; having no separate owner. The right to a highway is *common.*

3. General; serving for the use of all; as the *common* prayer.

4. Universal; belonging to all; as, the earth is said to be the *common* mother of mankind.

5. Public; general; frequent; as *common* report.

6. Usual; ordinary; as the *common* operations of nature; the *common* forms of conveyance; the *common* rules of civility.

7. Of no rank or superior excellence; ordinary. *Applied to men,* it signifies, not noble, not distinguished by noble descent, or not distinguished by office, character or talents; as a *common* man; a *common* soldier. *Applied to things,* it signifies, not distinguished by excellence or superiority; as a *common* essay; a *common* exertion. It however is not generally equivalent to *mean,* which expresses something lower in rank or estimation.

8. Prostitute; lewd; as a *common* woman.

9. In *grammar,* such verbs as signify both action and passion, are called *common;* as *aspernor,* I despise or am despised; also, such nouns as are both masculine and feminine, as *parens.*

10. A *common bud,* in botany, is one that contains both leaves and flowers; a *common peduncle,* one that bears several flowers; a *common perianth,* one that incloses several distinct fructifications; a *common receptacle,* one that connects several distinct fructifications. *Martyn.*

Common divisor, in mathematics, is a number or quantity that divides two or more numbers or quantities without a remainder.

Common Law, in Great Britain and the United States, the *unwritten* law, the law that receives its binding force from immemorial usage and universal reception, in distinction from the *written* or statute law. That body of rules, principles and customs which have been received from our ancestors, and by which courts have been governed in their judicial decisions. The evidence of this law is to be found in the reports of those decisions, and the records of the courts. Some of these rules may have originated in edicts or statutes which are now lost, or in the terms and conditions of particular grants or charters; but it is most probable that many of them originated in judicial decisions founded on natural justice and equity, or on local customs.

Common pleas, in Great Britain, one of the king's courts, now held in Westminster-Hall. It consists of a chief justice and three other justices, and has cognizance of all civil causes, real, personal or mixed, as well by original writ, as by removal from the inferior courts. A writ of error, in the nature of an appeal, lies from this court to the court of king's bench. *Blackstone.*

In some of the American states, a *court of common pleas* is an inferior court, whose jurisdiction is limited to a county, and it is sometimes called a county court. This court is variously constituted in different states, and its powers are defined by statutes. It has jurisdiction of civil causes, and of minor offenses; but its final jurisdiction is very limited; all causes of magnitude being removable to a higher Court by appeal or by writ of error.

Common prayer, the liturgy of the Church of England, which all the clergy of the Church are enjoined to use, under a penalty. *Encyc.*

Common recovery, a legal process for recovering an estate or barring entails.

Common time, in music, duple or double time, when the semibreve is equal to two minims.

In common, equally with another, or with others; to be equally used or participated by two or more; as tenants *in common;* to provide for children *in common;* to assign lands to two persons *in common,* or to twenty *in common;* we enjoy the bounties of providence *in common.*

ƇOM'MON, *n.* A tract of ground, the use of which is not appropriated to an individual, but belongs to the public or to a number. Thus we apply the word to an open ground or space in a highway, reserved for public use.

2. In *law,* an open ground, or that soil the use of which belongs equally to the inhabitants of a town or of a lordship, or to a certain number of proprietors; or the profit which a man has in the land of another; or a right which a person has to pasture his cattle on land of another, or to dig turf, or catch fish, or cut wood, or the like; called *common* of pasture, of turbary, of piscary, and of estovers.

Common, or right of common, is *appendant, appurtenant, because of vicinage,* or *in gross.*

Common appendant is a right belonging to the owners or occupiers of arable land to put commonable beasts upon the lord's waste, and upon the lands of other persons within the same manor. This is a matter of most universal right.

Common appurtenant may be annexed to lands in other lordships, or extend to other beasts, besides those which are generally commonable; this is not of common right, but can be claimed only by immemorial usage and prescription.

Common because of vicinage or neighborhood, is where the inhabitants of two townships, lying contiguous to each other, have usually intercommoned with one another, the beasts of the one straying into the other's fields; this is a permissive right.

Common in gross or at large, is annexed to a man's person, being granted to him and his heirs by deed; or it may be claimed by prescriptive right, as by a parson of a church or other corporation sole. *Blackstone.*

ƇOM'MON, *v. i.* To have a joint right with others in common ground. *Johnson.*

2. To board together; to eat at a table in common. *Encyc.*

ƇOM'MON, *adv.* Commonly. *Shak.*

ƇOMMON-ƇOUNCIL, *n.* The council of a city or corporate town, empowered to make by-laws for the government of the citizens. The common council of London consists of two houses; the upper house, composed of the Lord Mayor and Aldermen; and the lower house, of the common-council-men, elected by the several wards. In most of the American cities, the Mayor, Aldermen and common-council-men constitute one body, called a *Court of Common-Council.*

ƇOMMON-ƇRIER, *n.* A crier whose occupation is to give notice of lost things.

ƇOMMON-HALL, *n.* A hall or house in which citizens meet for business.

ƇOMMON-LAWYER, *n.* One versed in Common Law. *Spelman.*

ƇOM'MONPLACE, *n.* A memorandum; a common topic.

ƇOM'MONPLACE, *v. t.* To enter in a commonplace-book, or to reduce to general heads. *Felton.*

Commonplace-book, a book in which are registered such facts, opinions or observations as are deemed worthy of notice or remembrance, so disposed that any one may be easily found. Hence *commonplace* is used as an epithet to denote what is common or often repeated, or trite; as a *commonplace* observation.

ƇOM'MONABLE, *a.* Held in common. *Bacon.*

2. That may be pastured on common land.

Commonable beasts are either beasts of the plow, or such as manure the ground. *Blackstone.*

ƇOM'MONAGE, *n.* The right of pasturing on a common; the joint right of using any thing in common with others. *Johnson.*

ƇOM'MONALTY, *n.* The common people. In Great Britain, all classes and conditions of people, who are below the rank of nobility.

The *commonalty,* like the nobility, are divided into several degrees. *Blackstone.*

In the United States, *commonalty* has no very definite signification. It is however used to denote that part of the people who live by labor, and are not liberally educated, nor elevated by office or professional pursuits.

2. The bulk of mankind. *Hooker.*

ƇOM'MONER, *n.* One of the lower rank, or common people; one under the degree of nobility. *Addison.*

2. A member of the house of commons. *Swift.*

3. One who has a joint right in common ground. *Bacon.*

4. A student of the second rank in the universities in England; one who eats at a common table. *Johnson.*

5. A prostitute. *Shak.*

6. A partaker. *Fuller.*

ƇOMMONI''TION, *n.* [L. *commonitio.* See *Monition.*] Advice; warning; instruction. [*Little used.*]

ƇOMMON'ITIVE, *a.* Warning; monitory. [*Little used.*]

ƇOM'MONLY, *adv.* Usually; generally; ordinarily; frequently; for the most part; as, confirmed habits *commonly* continue through life.

ƇOM'MONNESS, *n.* Frequent occurrence; a state of being common or usual.

2. Equal participation by two or more. [*Little used.*]

ƇOM'MONS, *n. plu.* The common people, who inherit or possess no honors or titles; the vulgar. *Chaucer. Shak. Dryden.*

2. In *England,* the lower house of Parliament, consisting of the representatives of

cities, boroughs and counties, chosen by men possessed of the property or qualifications required by law. This body is called the *House of Commons.* The House of Representatives in North Carolina bears the same name.

3. Common grounds; land possessed or used by two or more persons in common. [See *Common.*]
4. Food provided at a common table, as in colleges, where many persons eat at the same table or in the same hall.

Their *commons*, though but coarse, were nothing scant. *Dryden.*

Doctors Commons, in London, a college founded by Dr. Harvey, for the professors of the civil law, where the civilians *common* together. The house was consumed in the great fire in 1666, but rebuilt in 1672. To this college belong thirty four proctors. *Encyc.*

COM'MONTY, *n.* In *Scots law*, land belonging to two or more common proprietors; or a heath or muir, of which there has been a promiscuous possession by pasturage. *Encyc.*

COMMONWE'AL, **COMMONWEALTH'**, *n.* [See *Weal* and *Wealth.*]

1. An established form of government, or civil polity; or more generally, a state; a body politic, consisting of a certain portion of men united by compact or tacit agreement, under one form of government and system of laws. This term is applied to the government of Great Britain, which is of a mixed character, and to other governments which are considered as free or popular, but rarely or improperly, to an absolute government. A commonwealth is properly a free state; a popular or representative government; a republic; as the *commonwealth* of Massachusetts. The word signifies strictly, the *common good* or *happiness;* and hence, the form of government supposed best to secure the public good.
2. The whole body of people in a state; the public. *Shak.*
3. The territory of a state; as, all the land within the limits of the *commonwealth.* *Massachusetts.*

COMMONWEALTH'S'MAN, *n.* One who favors the commonwealth, or a republican government.

COM'MORANCE, **COM'MORANCY**, *n.* [L. *commorans, commoror; con* and *moror*, to stay or delay.]

A dwelling or ordinary residence in a place; abode; habitation.

Commorancy consists in usually lying there. *Blackstone.*

COM'MORANT, *a.* Dwelling; ordinarily residing; inhabiting.

All freeholders within the precinct—and all persons *commorant* therein—are obliged to attend the court-leet. *Blackstone.*

COMMO'RIENT, *a.* [L. *commoriens.*] Dying at the same time.

COM'MOTHER, *n.* A godmother. [*Little used.*]

COMMO'TION, *n.* [L. *commotio, commoveo; con* and *moveo.* See *Move.*]

1. Agitation; as the *commotion* of the sea.
2. Tumult of people; disturbance; disorder, which may amount at times to sedition or insurrection; as the *commotions* of a state.

When ye hear of wars and *commotions*, be not terrified. Luke xxi.

3. Agitation; perturbation; disorder of mind; heat; excitement.

He could not debate without *commotion.* *Clarendon.*

COMMO'TIONER, *n.* One who excites commotion. [*Little used.*] *Bacon.*

COMMÖVE, *v. t.* [L. *commoveo.* See *Move.*] To put in motion; to disturb; to agitate; to unsettle; *a poetic word.* *Thomson.*

COMMU'NE, *v. i.* [Fr. *communier;* W. *cymunaw;* Arm. *communya.* The Welsh word is by Owen considered as a compound of *cy*, a prefix equivalent to *co* and *con* in Latin, and *ymun; ym*, noting identity, and *unaw*, to unite. If the word is formed from *cy* or *cum* and *unus*, it is radically different from *common.* But the Latin *communico* accords with this word, and with *common.*]

1. To converse; to talk together familiarly; to impart sentiments mutually, in private or familiar discourse; followed by *with* before the person.

And there will I meet and *commune with* thee. Ex. xxv.

2. To have intercourse in contemplation or meditation.

Commune with your own heart on your bed. Ps. iv.

3. To partake of the sacrament or Lord's supper; to receive the communion; *a common use of the word in America, as it is in the Welsh.*

COMMU'NE, *n.* A small territorial district in France—one of the subordinate divisions of the country introduced in the late revolution.

Communibus annis, one year with another; on an average.

Communibus locis, one place with another; on a medium.

COMMUNICABIL'ITY, *n.* [See *Communicate.*] The quality of being communicable; capability of being imparted from one to another. *Johnson.*

COMMU'NICABLE, *a.* [Fr.] That may be communicated; capable of being imparted from one to another; as, knowledge is *communicable* by words.

Lost bliss, to thee no more *communicable.* *Milton.*

Eternal life is *communicable* to all. *Hooker.*

2. That may be recounted. *Milton.*
3. Communicative; ready to impart. [*Not used.*] *B. Jonson.*

COMMU'NICANT, *n.* One who communes at the Lord's table; one who is entitled to partake of the sacrament, at the celebration of the Lord's supper. *Hooker. Atterbury.*

COMMU'NICATE, *v. t.* [L. *communico*, from *communis, common;* It. *comunicare;* Sp. *comunicar;* Fr. *communiquer.*]

1. To impart; to give to another, as a partaker; to confer for joint possession; to bestow, as that which the receiver is to hold, retain, use or enjoy; with *to.*

Where God is worshiped, there he *communicates* his blessings and holy influences. *Taylor.*

Let him that is taught in the word *communicate to* him that teacheth in all good things. Gal. vi.

2. To impart reciprocally, or mutually; to have or enjoy a share of; followed by *with.*

Common benefits are to be *communicated with* all, but peculiar benefits *with* choice. *Bacon.*

But Diomede desires my company,
And still *communicates* his praise *with* me. *Dryden.*

3. To impart, as knowledge; to reveal; to give, as information, either by words, signs or signals; as, to *communicate* intelligence, news, opinions, or facts.

Formerly this verb had *with* before the person receiving; as, "he *communicated* those thoughts only *with* the Lord Digby." *Clarendon.* But now it has *to* only.

4. To deliver, as to *communicate* a message; to give, as to *communicate* motion.

COMMU'NICATE, *v. i.* To partake of the Lord's supper. *Taylor.*

Instead of this, in America, at least in New England, *commune* is generally or always used.

2. To have a communication or passage from one to another; to have the means of passing from one to another; as, two houses *communicate* with each other; a fortress *communicates* with the country; the canals of the body *communicate* with each other. *Arbuthnot.*
3. To have intercourse; *applied to persons.*
4. To have, enjoy or suffer reciprocally; to have a share with another.

Ye have done well that ye did *communicate* with my affliction. Phil. iv.

COMMU'NICATED, *pp.* Imparted from one to another; bestowed; delivered.

COMMU'NICATING, *ppr.* Imparting; giving or bestowing; delivering.

2. Partaking of the sacrament of the Lord's supper.
3. Leading or conducting from place to place, as a passage; connected by a passage or channel, as two lakes *communicating* with each other.
4. Having intercourse by words, letters or messages; corresponding.

COMMUNICA'TION, *n.* The act of imparting, conferring, or delivering, from one to another; as the *communication* of knowledge, opinions or facts.

2. Intercourse by words, letters or messages; interchange of thoughts or opinions, by conference or other means.

Abner had *communication* with the elders of Israel, saying, Ye sought for David in times past to be king over you. 2 Sam. iii.

Let your *communication* be, yea, yea; nay, nay. Mat. v.

In 1 Cor. xv. 33, "Evil *communications* corrupt good manners," the word may signify conversation, colloquial discourses, or customary association and familiarity.

3. Intercourse; interchange of knowledge; correspondence; good understanding between men.

Secrets may be carried so far as to stop the *communication* necessary among all who have the management of affairs. *Swift.*

4. Connecting passage; means of passing from place to place; as a strait or channel between seas or lakes, a road between cities or countries, a gallery between apartments in a house, an avenue between streets, &c.

Keep open a *communication* with the besieged place.

5. That which is communicated or imparted.

The house received a *communication* from the Governor, respecting the hospital.

6. In *rhetoric*, a trope by which a speaker or writer takes his hearer or speaker as a partner in his sentiments, and says *we*, instead of *I* or *you*. *Beattie.*

COMMU'NICATIVE, *a.* Inclined to communicate; ready to impart to others. In the sense of *liberal of benefits*, though legitimate, it is little used.

2. Disposed to impart or disclose, as knowledge, opinions, or facts; free to communicate; not reserved.

We have paid for our want of prudence, and determine for the future to be less *communicative*. *Swift.*

COMMU'NICATIVENESS, *n.* The quality of being communicative; readiness to impart to others; freedom from reserve. *Norris.*

COMMU'NICATORY, *a.* Imparting knowledge. *Barrow.*

COMMU'NING, *ppr.* Conversing familiarly; having familiar intercourse.

COM'MUNING, *n.* Familiar converse; private intercourse. *E. T. Fitch.*

COMMU'NION, *n.* *commu'nyon.* [L. *communio;* Fr. *communion;* It. *comunione;* Sp. *comunion;* Port. *communham.* See *Common.*]

Fellowship; intercourse between two persons or more; interchange of transactions, or offices; a state of giving and receiving; agreement; concord.

We are naturally led to seek *communion* and fellowship with others. *Hooker.*

What *communion* hath light with darkness? 2 Cor. vi.

The *communion* of the Holy Spirit be with you all. 2 Cor. xiii.

2. Mutual intercourse or union in religious worship, or in doctrine and discipline.

The Protestant churches have no *communion* with the Romish church.

3. The body of christians who have one common faith and discipline. The three grand *communions* into which the christian church is divided, are those of the Greek, the Romish and the Protestant churches.

4. The act of communicating the sacrament of the eucharist; the celebration of the Lord's supper; the participation of the blessed sacrament. The fourth council of Lateran decrees that every believer shall receive the *communion* at least at Easter. *Encyc.*

5. Union of professing christians in a particular church; as, members in full *communion.*

Communion-service, in the liturgy of the Episcopal church, is the office for the administration of the holy sacrament.

COMMU'NITY, *n.* [L. *communitas;* It. *comunità;* Sp. *comunidad;* Fr. *communauté.* See *Common.*]

1. Properly, common possession or enjoyment; as a *community* of goods.

It is a confirmation of the original *community* of all things. *Locke.*

2. A society of people, having common rights and privileges, or common interests, civil, political or ecclesiastical; or living under the same laws and regulations. This word may signify a commonwealth or state, a body politic, or a particular society or order of men within a state, as a *community* of monks; and it is often used for the public or people in general, without very definite limits.

3. Commonness; frequency. *Obs.* *Shak.*

COMMUTABIL'ITY, *n.* [See *Commute.*] The quality of being capable of being exchanged, or put, one in the place of the other.

COMMU'TABLE, *a.* [L. *commutabilis.* See *Commute.*]

That may be exchanged, or mutually changed; that may be given for another. In *philology*, that may pass from one into another; as, the letter *b* is *commutable* with *v;* or in Celtic, *b* and *mh* are *commutable.*

COMMUTA'TION, *n.* [L. *commutatio.* See *Commute.*]

1. Change; alteration; a passing from one state to another. *South.*

2. Exchange; the act of giving one thing for another; barter.

The use of money is to save the *commutation* of more bulky commodities. *Arbuthnot.*

3. In *law*, the change of a penalty or punishment from a greater to a less; as banishment instead of death.

Suits are allowable in the spiritual courts for money agreed to be given as a *commutation* for penance. *Blackstone.*

COMMU'TATIVE, *a.* [Fr. *commutatif;* It. *commutativo.* See *Commute.*]

Relative to exchange; interchangeable; mutually passing from one to another; as *commutative* justice, justice which is mutually done and received, between men in society.

To cultivate an habitual regard to *commutative* justice. *Burke.*

COMMU'TATIVELY, *adv.* By way of reciprocal exchange. *Brown.*

COMMU'TE, *v. t.* [L. *commuto;* *con* and *muto*, to change. See *Mutable* and *Mutation.*]

1. To exchange; to put one thing in the place of another; to give or receive one thing for another; as, to *commute* our labors; to *commute* pain for pleasure.

2. In *law*, to exchange one penalty or punishment for another of less severity; as, to *commute* death for transportation.

COMMU'TE, *v. i.* To atone; to compensate; to stand in the place of; as, one penalty *commutes* for another.

COMMU'TUAL, *a.* [*con* and *mutual.*] Mutual; reciprocal; *used in poetry.*

There, with *commutual* zeal, we both had strove
In acts of dear benevolence and love. *Pope.*

COMPACT', *a.* [L. *compactus, compingo;* *con* and *pango, pactus*, to thrust, drive, fix, make fast or close; antiq. *pago, paco;* Gr. *πηγνυω.* See *Pack.*] Literally, driven, thrust or pressed together. Hence,

1. Closely and firmly united, as the particles of solid bodies; firm; close; solid; dense. Stone, iron and wood are *compact* bodies. A *compact* leaf, in botany, is one having the pulp of a close firm texture.

2. Composed; consisting.

A wandering fire,
Compact of unctuous vapor. *Milton. Shak.*

This sense is not common. [See the Verb.] *Compact* seems to be used for *compacted.* So in the following example.

3. Joined; held together. [*Little used.*]

A pipe of seven reeds, *compact* with wax together. *Peacham.*

4. Brief; close; pithy; not diffuse; not verbose; as a *compact* discourse.

COM'PACT, *n.* [L. *compactum.*] An agreement; a contract between parties; a word that may be applied, in a general sense, to any covenant or contract between individuals; but it is more generally applied to agreements between nations and states, as treaties and confederacies. So the constitution of the United States is a political contract between the States; a national *compact.* Or the word is applied to the agreement of the individuals of a community.

The law of nations depends on mutual *compacts*, treaties, leagues, &c. *Blackstone*

In the beginnings of speech there was an implicit *compact*, founded on common consent. *South.*

COMPACT', *v. t.* To thrust, drive or press closely together; to join firmly; to consolidate; to make close; as the parts which compose a body.

Now the bright sun *compacts* the precious stone. *Blackmore.*

This verb is not much used. The participle is more frequent; as, the earth's *compacted* sphere. *Roscommon.*

The solids are more strict and *compacted.* *Arbuthnot.*

2. To unite or connect firmly, as in a system.

The whole body fitly joined together and *compacted.* Eph. 4.

3. To league with.

Thou pernicious woman,
Compact with her that's gone. *Shak.*

4. To compose or make out of.

If he, *compact* of jars, grow musical. *Shak.*

In the two last examples, *compact* is used for *compacted.*

COMPACT'ED, *pp.* Pressed close; firmly united, or connected.

COMPACT'EDNESS, *n.* A state of being compact; firmness; closeness of parts; density, whence results hardness. *Digby.*

COMPACT'ING, *ppr.* Uniting closely; consolidating.

COMPAC'TION, *n.* The act of making compact; or the state of being compact. *Bacon.*

COMPACT'LY, *adv.* Closely; densely; with close union of parts.

COMPACT'NESS, *n.* Firmness; close union of parts; density. *Boyle.*

COMPACT'URE, *n.* Close union or connection of parts; structure well connected; manner of joining. *Spenser.*

COMPA'GES, COM'PAGES, *n.* [L.] A system or structure of many parts united. *Ray.*

COMPAGINA'TION, *n.* [L. *compago.* See *Compact.*]

Union of parts; structure; connection; contexture. [*Little used.*] *Brown.*

COM'PANABLE, *a.* Companionable. *Obs.* *Chaucer.*

COM'PANABLENESS, *n.* Sociableness. *Obs.* *Sidney.*

COMPAN'IABLE, *a.* Social. *Obs.* *Bacon.*

COMPAN'IABLENESS, *n.* Sociableness. *Obs.* *Bp. Hall.*

COMPAN'ION, *n.* *compan'yun.* [Fr. *com-*

pagnon; Arm. *compaignun*; It. *compagno*; Sp. *compañero*; Port. *companheiro*; Ir. *companach*. See *Company*.]

1. One who keeps company with another; one with whom a person frequently associates, and converses. "It differs from *friend*, says Johnson, as *acquaintance* from *confidence*." The word does not necessarily imply friendship; but a *companion* is often or generally a *friend*.

A *companion* of fools shall be destroyed. Prov. xiii.

2. One who accompanies another; as two persons meeting casually and traveling together are called *companions*. So soldiers are called *companions* in arms.

3. A partner; an associate.

Epaphroditus, my brother, and *companion* in labor, and fellow soldier. Phil. ii.

4. A fellow; a mate. *Shak.*

5. A sort of wooden porch placed over the entrance or stair case of the cabin in merchant ships. Hence the ladder by which officers ascend to and descend from the quarter deck is called the *companion ladder*. *Mar. Dict.*

COMPAN'IONABLE, *a.* Fit for good fellowship; qualified to be agreeable in company; sociable; agreeable as a companion. *Clarendon.*

COMPAN'IONABLY, *adv.* In a companionable manner.

COMPAN'IONSHIP, *n.* Fellowship; association. *Shak.*

2. Company; train. *Shak.*

COM'PANY, *n.* [It. *compagnia*; Sp. *compañia*; Port. *companhia*; Fr. *compagnie*; not from *cum* and *panis*, bread, a mess or number of men eating together, as is commonly supposed; but from *cum* and *pannus*, cloth, Teutonic *fahne* or *vaan*, a flag. The word denotes a band or number of men under one flag or standard. What decides this question is, the Spanish mode of writing the word with *n* tilde, titled *n*, *compañia*, for this is the manner of writing *paño*, cloth; whereas *panis*, bread, is written *pan*. The orthography of the word in the other languages is confirmatory of this opinion.]

1. In *military affairs*, the soldiers united under the command of a captain; a subdivision of a regiment, consisting usually of a number from 60 to 100 men. But the number is indefinite.

2. Any assemblage of persons; a collection of men, or other animals, in a very indefinite sense. It may be applied to a small number, or any multitude whatever; as in scripture we read of a *company* of priests, a *company* of prophets, and an innumerable *company* of angels; also, a *company* of horses.

3. An assemblage of persons for entertainment or festivity; a party collected by invitation or otherwise.

4. Persons that associate with others for conversation or pleasure; society; as, let your children keep good *company*.

5. The state of being a companion; the act of accompanying; fellowship; society.

I will keep thee *company*. *Dryden.*
We cannot enjoy the *company* of licentious men.

6. A number of persons united for the same purpose, or in a joint concern; as a *company* of merchants or mechanics; a *company* of players. The word is applicable to private partnerships or to incorporated bodies of men. Hence it may signify a firm, house or partnership; or a corporation, as the East India *Company*, a banking or insurance *company*.

7. The crew of a ship, including the officers; also, a fleet.

To bear company, to accompany; to attend; to go with; denoting a temporary association.

His faithful dog shall *bear him company*. *Pope.*

To keep company, to accompany; to attend; also, to associate with frequently or habitually; hence, to frequent public houses. Prov. xxix.

COM'PANY, *v. t.* To accompany; to attend; to go with; to be companion to. [But *accompany* is generally used.]

COM'PANY, *v. i.* To associate with; to frequent the company of.

I wrote you not to *company* with fornicators. 1 Cor. v.

2. To be a gay companion. *Obs.* *Spenser.*

3. To have commerce with the other sex. *Bp. Hall.*

COM'PARABLE, *a.* [L. *comparabilis*. See *Compare*.]

That may be compared; worthy of comparison; being of equal regard; that may be estimated as equal.

There is no blessing of life *comparable* to the enjoyment of a discreet and virtuous friend. *Addison.*

The precious sons of Zion, *comparable* to fine gold. Lam. iv.

COM'PARABLY, *adv.* In a manner or degree worthy to be compared, or of equal regard. *Wotton.*

COM'PARATES, *n.* In *logic*, the two things compared to one another.

COMPAR'ATIVE, *a.* [L. *comparativus*; It. *comparativo*; Fr. *comparatif*. See *Compare*.]

1. Estimated by comparison; not positive or absolute. The *comparative* weight of a body, is that which is estimated by comparing it with the weight of another body. A body may be called heavy, when compared with a feather, which would be called light, when compared with iron. So of *comparative* good, or evil.

2. Having the power of comparing different things; as a *comparative* faculty. Qu. *Glanville.*

3. In *grammar*, expressing more or less. The *comparative* degree of an adjective expresses a greater or less degree of a quantity, or quality, than the positive; as *brighter*, or *more bright*; *smaller*; *finer*; *stronger*; *weaker*.

Comparative anatomy, that branch of anatomy which treats of the anatomy of other animals than man, with a view to *compare* their structure with that of human beings, and thus to illustrate the animal functions, and particularly with reference to a more perfect knowledge of the functions of several parts of the human body. *Encyc.*

COMPAR'ATIVE, *n.* One who is equal or pretends to be an equal. [*Not now used.*] *Shak.*

COMPAR'ATIVELY, *adv.* In a state of comparison; by comparison; according to estimate made by comparison; not positively, absolutely or in itself. A thing is *comparatively* heavy, when it is compared with something less heavy. Paper is *comparatively* light or heavy; *light*, when compared with *lead*; and *heavy*, when compared with *air*.

How few, *comparatively*, are the instances of a wise application of time and talents! *Anon.*

COMPA'RE, *v. t.* [L. *comparo*, to prepare, to provide or procure, to make equal, to compare; *con* and *paro*, to prepare; It. *parare*, to dress, trim, adorn; also, to *parry*; Sp. *parar*, to prepare, to halt, to stop, to prevent, to detain, to stake at cards; Port. *parar*, to stop or cease to go forward; to meet or confine upon; to touch or be bounded; to tend; to drive at some end; to aim at; to come to; to hinder; to *parry*, or ward off; to turn or change in inclination or morals; to lay or stake as a wager; Sp. *parada*, a halt, stop, pause; a fold for cattle; a relay of horses or mules; a dam or bank; a bet, stake or wager; a *parade*, or place of exercise for troops; Port. *id.* Arm. *para*; W. *parodi*, to prepare. This seems to be the ברא bara, of the Shemitic languages. The primary sense is, to throw, drive, or strike; hence, to drive or force off, to separate, to *pare*; hence, to trim, or dress, which may be from separating, as in the French *parer des cuirs*, to dress or curry leather; or from *setting off*, as we express the idea, that is, by enlargement, or display; or from setting in order, as we say, to fix. The sense of *compare* is allied to the Portuguese application of the word, to come to, to meet; and the L. *par*, equal, belongs to the same root, and seems to be included in *comparo*. One of the principal significations is, to stop; that is, to set; to fix. In fencing, it is to intercept by thrusting the weapon aside. In gaming, it is to lay or throw down. All the senses unite in that of extending, thrusting, or driving. W. *par*, that is contiguous, *preparedness*, a *pair*, a fellow, Eng. *peer*, L. *par*. The latter word seems to signify, extended, or reaching to, and to be closely allied to the Portuguese sense of contiguity.]

1. To set or bring things together in fact or in contemplation, and to examine the relations they bear to each other, with a view to ascertain their agreement or disagreement; as, to *compare* two pieces of cloth, two tables, or coins; to *compare* reasons and arguments; to *compare* pleasure *with* pain.

In comparing movable things, it is customary to bring them together, for examination. In comparing things immovable or remote, and abstract ideas, we bring them together in the mind, as far as we are able, and consider them in connection. Comparison therefore is really collation, or it includes it.

2. To liken; to represent as similar, for the purpose of illustration.

Solon *compared* the people *to* the sea, and orators and counselors *to* the winds; for that the sea would be calm and quiet, if the winds did not trouble it. *Bacon.*

In this sense *compare* is followed by *to*.

3. To examine the relations of things to each other, with a view to discover their relative proportions, quantities or qualities; as, to *compare* two kingdoms, or two mountains *with* each other; to *compare* the number ten *with* fifteen; to *compare* ice *with* crystal; to *compare* a clown *with* a dancing master or a dandy.

In this sense *compare* is followed by *with*.

4. In *grammar*, to form an adjective in the degrees of comparison; as *blackish, black, blacker, blackest*.

4. To get; to procure; to obtain; as in Latin. *Obs.* *Spenser.*

COMPA'RE, *v. i.* To hold comparison; to be like or equal.

2. To vie. *Obs.* *Spenser.*

COMPA'RE, *n.* The state of being compared; comparative estimate; comparison; possibility of entering into comparison, or being considered as equal.

> Their small gallies may not hold *compare*
> With our tall ships. *Waller.*

2. Simile; similitude; illustration by comparison. *Johnson.*

[*This noun is in use, but cannot be considered as elegant.*]

COMPA'RED, *pp.* Set together and examined with respect to likeness or unlikeness, agreement or disagreement; likened; represented as similar.

COMPA'RER, *n.* One who compares or makes a comparison.

COMPA'RING, *ppr.* Examining the relations of things to each other; likening.

COMPAR'ISON, *n.* [It. *comparazione*; Sp. *comparacion*; Fr. *comparaison*; Port. *comparaçam*; L. *comparatio*. See *Compare*.]

1. The act of comparing; the act of considering the relation between persons or things, with a view to discover their agreement or resemblance, or their disagreement or difference.

> We learn to form a correct estimate of men and their actions by *comparison*. *Anon.*

2. The state of being compared.

> If we rightly estimate what we call good and evil, we shall find it lies much in *comparison*. *Locke.*

3. Comparative estimate; proportion.

> Who is left among you that saw this house in its first glory? And how do you see it now? Is it not in your eyes in *comparison* of it as nothing? Hag. ii.

4. In *grammar*, the formation of an adjective in its several degrees of signification; as *strong, stronger, strongest; greenish, green, greener, greenest; glorious, more glorious, most glorious*. In English, there are strictly four degrees of *comparison*.

5. A simile, similitude, or illustration by similitude.

> Whereto shall we liken the kingdom of God? Or with what *comparison* shall we compare it? Mark iv.

6. In *rhetoric*, a figure by which two things are considered with regard to a third, which is common to them both; as, "a hero is like a lion in courage." Here courage is common to hero and lion, and constitutes the point of resemblance. *Encyc.*

> The distinction between *similitude* and *comparison* is, that the *former* has reference to the *quality*; the *latter*, to the *quantity*. *Comparison* is between *more* and *less*; *similitude* is between *good* and *bad*. Hannibal—hung like a tempest on the declivities of the Alps—is a likeness by *similitude*. The sublimity of the scriptural prophets exceeds that of Homer, as much as thunder is louder than a whisper—is a likeness by *comparison*. *J. Q. Adams. Lecture* ix.

But comparison has reference to quality as well as quantity.

COMP'ART, *v. t.* [Fr. *compartir*; It. *compartire*; Sp. *compartir*, *con* or *com* and *partir*, L. *partio*, to divide. See *Part*.]

To divide; to mark out a plan or design into its several parts, or subdivisions. *Wotton.*

COMP'ARTED, *pp.* Divided into parts or apartments.

COMP'ARTING, *ppr.* Dividing or disposing into parts.

COMPARTI''TION, *n.* The act of dividing into parts. In *architecture*, the division or disposition of the whole ground-plot of an edifice, into its various apartments. *Encyc.*

2. Division; part divided; a separate part; as, amphitheaters needed no *compartitions*. *Wotton.*

COMP'ARTMENT, *n.* [Fr. *compartiment*; It. *compartimento*.]

1. A division or separate part of a general design, as of a picture, or of a ground-plot. *Pope. Peacham.*

2. A design composed of several different figures, disposed with symmetry, for ornament; as a *compartment* of tiles or bricks, duly arranged, of various colors and varnished, to decorate a building. In gardening, *compartments* are assemblages of beds, plots, borders, walks, &c. In heraldry, a *compartment* is called also a partition. *Encyc.*

COMP'ARTNER, *n.* A sharer. *Pearson.*

CÔM'PASS, *n.* [Fr. *compas*; Sp. *compas*; It. *compasso*; Port. *compasso*; *con* or *com* and Fr. *pas*, Sp. *paso*, It. *passo*, a *pace* or step, L. *passus*, which coincides with the participle of *pando*, to open or stretch. See *Pace* and *Pass*. A *compass* is a *stepping* together. So in Spanish and Portuguese, it signifies a beating of time in music.]

1. Stretch; reach; extent; the limit or boundary of a space, and the space included; *applied to time, space, sound*, &c. Our knowledge lies within a very narrow *compass*. The universe extends beyond the *compass* of our thoughts. So we say, the *compass* of a year, the *compass* of an empire, the *compass* of reason, the *compass* of the voice.

> And in that *compass* all the world contains. *Dryden.*

2. A passing round; a circular course; a circuit.

> Time is come round;
> And where I did begin, there shall I end:
> My life has run its *compass*. *Shak.*
>
> They fetched a *compass* of seven days journey. 2 Kings iii. 2 Sam. v. Acts xxviii.

3. Moderate bounds; limits of truth; moderation; due limits.

> In two hundred years, (I speak within *compass*,) no such commission had been executed. *Davies.*

This sense is the same as the first, and the peculiar force of the phrase lies in the word *within*.

4. The extent or limit of the voice or of sound. [See No. 1.]

5. An instrument for directing or ascertaining the course of ships at sea, consisting of a circular box, containing a paper card marked with the thirty two points of direction, fixed on a magnetic needle, that always points to the north, the variation excepted. The needle with the card turns on a pin in the center of the box. In the center of the needle is fixed a brass conical socket or cap, by which the card hanging on the pin turns freely round the center. The box is covered with glass, to prevent the motion of the card from being disturbed by the wind. *Encyc.*

6. *Compass* or *compasses*, [or a pair of compasses, so named from its legs, but *pair* is superfluous or improper, and the singular number *compass* is the preferable name,] an instrument for describing circles, measuring figures, &c., consisting of two pointed legs or branches, made of iron, steel or brass, joined at the top by a rivet, on which they move. There are also compasses of three legs or triangular compasses, cylindrical and spherical compasses with four branches, and various other kinds. *Encyc.*

7. An instrument used in surveying land, constructed in the main like the mariner's compass; but with this difference, that the needle is not fitted into the card, moving with it, but plays alone; the card being drawn on the bottom of the box, and a circle divided into 360 degrees on the limb. This instrument is used in surveying land, and in directing travelers in a desert or forest, miners, &c. *Encyc.*

Compass-saw, a saw with a broad edge and thin back, to cut in a circular form. *Moxon.*

CÔM'PASS, *v. t.* Literally, to measure with a compass. Hence,

1. To stretch round; to extend so as to embrace the whole; hence, to inclose, encircle, grasp or seize; as, to *compass* with the arms.

2. To surround; to environ; to inclose on all sides; sometimes followed by *around*, *round* or *about*.

> Now all the blessings
> Of a glad father *compass* thee *about*. *Shak.*
>
> With favor wilt thou *compass* him as with a shield. Ps. v.
>
> The willows of the brook *compass* him *about*. Job 40.

3. To go or walk round.

> Ye shall *compass* the city—and the seventh day ye shall *compass* the city seven times. Josh. vi.
>
> For ye *compass* sea and land. Math. xxiii.

4. To besiege; to beleaguer; to block up. This is not a different sense, but a particular application.

> Thine enemies shall cast a trench about thee, and *compass* thee round, and keep thee in on every side. Luke xix.

5. To obtain; to attain to; to procure; to bring within one's power; to accomplish.

> If I can check my erring love, I will;
> If not, to *compass* her I'll use my skill. *Shak.*
>
> How can you hope to *compass* your designs? *Denham.*

6. To purpose; to intend; to imagine; to plot; to contrive; as we say, to go about to perform, but in mind only; as, to *compass* the death of the king.

Compassing and *imagining* the death of the king are synonymous terms; *compass* signifying the purpose or design of the mind or will, and not, as in common speech, the carrying such design to effect. *Blackstone.*

ÇOM'PASSED, *pp.* Embraced; surrounded; inclosed; obtained; imagined.

ÇOM'PASSING, *ppr.* Embracing; going round; inclosing; obtaining; accomplishing; imagining; intending.

2. In *ship-building*, incurvated; arched. *Mar. Dict.*

ÇOMPAS'SION, *n.* [It. *compassione*; Sp. *compasion*; Fr. *compassion*; Low L. *compassio, compatior*; *con* and *patior, passus*, to suffer. See *Patience.*]

1. A suffering with another; painful sympathy; a sensation of sorrow excited by the distress or misfortunes of another; pity; commiseration. Compassion is a mixed passion, compounded of love and sorrow; at least some portion of love generally attends the pain or regret, or is excited by it. Extreme distress of an enemy even changes enmity into at least temporary affection.

He, being full of *compassion*, forgave their iniquity. Ps. lxxviii.

His father had *compassion*, and ran, and fell on his neck, and kissed him. Luke xv.

ÇOMPAS'SION, *v. t.* To pity. [*Not used.*] *Shak.*

ÇOMPAS'SIONABLE, *a.* Deserving of pity. [*Little used.*] *Barrow.*

ÇOMPAS'SIONATE, *a.* Having a temper or disposition to pity; inclined to show mercy; merciful; having a heart that is tender, and easily moved by the distresses, sufferings, wants and infirmities of others.

There never was a heart truly great and generous, that was not also tender and *compassionate.* *South.*

ÇOMPAS'SIONATE, *v. t.* To pity; to commiserate; to have compassion for.

Compassionates my pains and pities me. *Addison.*

ÇOMPAS'SIONATELY, *adv.* With compassion; mercifully. *Clarendon.*

ÇOMPAS'SIONATENESS, *n.* The quality of being compassionate.

ÇOMPATERN'ITY, *n.* [*con* and *paternity.*] The relation of a godfather to the person for whom he answers. *Davies.*

ÇOMPATIBIL'ITY, *n.* [See *Compatible.*] Consistency; the quality or power of coexisting with something else; suitableness; as a *compatibility* of tempers.

ÇOMPAT'IBLE, *a.* [Fr. *compatible*; Sp. *id.*; Port. *compativel*; from the L. *competo*, to sue or seek for the same thing, to agree; *con* and *peto*, to seek.]

1. Consistent; that may exist with; suitable; not incongruous; agreeable; followed by *with*; sometimes by *to*, but less properly.

The poets have joined qualities which by nature are the most *compatible.* *Broome.*

The office of a legislator and of a judge are deemed not *compatible.*

To pardon offenders is not always *compatible with* public safety.

ÇOMPAT'IBLENESS, *n.* Consistency; fitness; agreement; the same as *compatibility*, which is generally used.

ÇOMPAT'IBLY, *adv.* Fitly; suitably; consistently.

ÇOMPA'TIENT, *a.* [L. *con* and *patior.*] Suffering together. [*Little used.*] *Buck.*

ÇOMPAT'RIOT, *n.* [It. *compatriotta*; Sp. *compatriota*; *con* or *com* and *patriot.*] A fellow patriot; one of the same country.

ÇOMPAT'RIOT, *a.* Of the same country. *Akenside.*

ÇOMPEE'R, *n.* [L. *compar*; *con* and *par*, equal. See *Peer.*] An equal; a companion; an associate; a mate. *Philips.*

ÇOMPEE'R, *v. t.* To equal; to match; to be equal with. *Shak.*

ÇOMPEL', *v. t.* [L *compello, compellere*; *con* and *pello*, to drive; Sp. *compeler*; Port. *compellir.* See *Peal* and *Appeal.*]

1. To drive or urge with force, or irresistibly; to constrain; to oblige; to necessitate, either by physical or moral force.

Thou shalt not *compel* him to serve as a bond servant. Levit. 25.

And they *compel* one Simon—to bear his cross. Mark xv.

Go out into the highways and hedges, and *compel* them to come in, that my house may be filled. Luke xiv.

Circumstances *compel* us to practice economy.

2. To force; to take by force, or violence; to seize.

The subjects' grief
Comes through commissions, which *compel* from each
A sixth part of his substance. *Shak.*

[*This sense is harsh, and not very common.*] *Johnson.*

3. To drive together; to gather; to unite in a crowd or company. A Latinism, compellere gregem.

In one troop *compelled.* *Dryden.*

4. To seize; to overpower; to hold.

And easy sleep their weary limbs *compelled.* [*Unusual.*] *Dryden.*

5. To call forth, L. *compellare.* *Obs.* *Spenser.*

ÇOMPEL'LABLE, *a.* That may be driven, forced or constrained.

ÇOMPEL'LABLY, *adv.* By compulsion.

ÇOMPELLA'TION, *n.* [L. *compellatio*; *compello, compellare*, the same word as the preceding, applied to the voice; to send or drive out the voice.] Style or manner of address; the word of salutation.

The *compellation* of the Kings of France is by *sire.* *Temple.*

ÇOMPEL'LED, *pp.* Forced; constrained; obliged.

ÇOMPEL'LER, *n.* One who compels or constrains.

ÇOMPEL'LING, *ppr.* Driving by force; constraining; obliging.

ÇOM'PEND, } *n.* [L. *compendium.*] In
ÇOMPEND'IUM, } *literature*, an abridgment; a summary; an epitome; a brief compilation or composition, containing the principal heads, or general principles, of a larger work or system.

ÇOMPENDIA'RIOUS, *a.* Short; contracted. [*Little used.*]

ÇOMPEND'IATE, *v. t.* To sum or collect together. [*Not used.*]

ÇOMPEND'IOUS, *a.* Short; summary; abridged; comprehensive; containing the substance or general principles of a subject or work in a narrow compass; as a *compendious* system of chimistry; a *compendious* grammar.

2. Short; direct; near; not circuitous; as a *compendious* way to acquire science.

ÇOMPEND'IOUSLY, *adv.* In a short or brief manner; summarily; in brief; in epitome.

The substance of christian belief is *compendiously* expressed in a few articles. *Anon.*

ÇOMPEND'IOUSNESS, *n.* Shortness; brevity; comprehension in a narrow compass. *Bentley.*

ÇOMPENS'ABLE, *a.* [See *Compensate.*] That may be compensated. [*Little used.*]

ÇOM'PENSATE, *v. t.* [L. *compenso*; *con* and *penso*, to prize or value, from *pendo*, to weigh, to value. See *Pendent.*]

1. To give equal value to; to recompense; to give an equivalent for services, or an amount lost or bestowed; to return or bestow that which makes good a loss, or is estimated a sufficient remuneration; as, to *compensate* a laborer for his work, or a merchant for his losses.

2. To be equivalent in value or effect to; to counterbalance; to make amends for.

The length of the night and the dews do *compensate* the heat of the day. *Bacon.*

The pleasures of sin never *compensate* the sinner for the miseries he suffers, even in this life. *Anon.*

ÇOM'PENSATE, *v. i.* To make amends; to supply an equivalent; followed by *for.*

Nothing can *compensate for* the loss of reputation.

This word is generally accented on the second syllable, most unfortunately, as any ear will determine by the feebleness of the last syllables in the participles, *compens'ated, compens'ating.*

Each seeming want *compensated* of course. *Pope.*

With the primary accent on the first syllable and the secondary accent on the third, this defect and the difficulty of uttering distinctly the last syllables are remedied.

ÇOM'PENSATED, *pp.* Recompensed; supplied with an equivalent in amount or effect; rewarded.

ÇOM'PENSATING, *ppr.* Giving an equivalent; recompensing; remunerating.

ÇOMPENSA'TION, *n.* That which is given or received as an equivalent for services, debt, want, loss, or suffering; amends; remuneration; recompense.

All other debts may *compensation* find. *Dryden.*

The pleasures of life are no *compensation* for the loss of divine favor and protection.

2. In *law*, a set-off; the payment of a debt by a credit of equal amount.

ÇOMPENS'ATIVE, *a.* Making amends or compensation.

ÇOMPENS'ATORY, *a.* Serving for compensation; making amends.

ÇOMPENSE, *v. t.* to recompense, is found in Bacon; but is not now in use.

ÇOMPE'TE, *v. i.* [L. *competo*; *con* and *peto.*]

1. To seek, or strive for the same thing as another; to carry on competition or rivalry.

Our manufacturers *compete* with the English in making cotton cloths.

2. To strive or claim to be equal.

The sages of antiquity will not dare to *compete* with the inspired authors. *Milner.*

ÇOM'PETENCE, } *n.* [L. *competens, compe-*
ÇOM'PETENCY, } *to*, to be meet or fit; *con* and *peto*, to seek; properly, to press,

urge or come to.] Primarily, fitness; suitableness; convenience. Hence,

1. Sufficiency; such a quantity as is sufficient; property or means of subsistence sufficient to furnish the necessaries and conveniencies of life, without superfluity.

Reason's whole pleasure, all the joys of sense,
Lie in three words, health, peace, and *competence*. *Pope.*

2. Sufficiency, applied to other things than property; *but this application is less common.*

3. Legal capacity or qualifications; fitness; as the *competence* of a witness, which consists in his having the qualifications required by law, as age, soundness of mind, impartiality, &c.

4. Right or authority; legal power or capacity to take cognizance of a cause; as the *competence* of a judge or court to examine and decide. *Kent.*

5. Fitness; adequacy; suitableness; legal sufficiency; as the *competency* of evidence. *Sewall.*

COM'PETENT, *a.* Suitable; fit; convenient; hence, sufficient, that is, fit for the purpose; adequate; followed by *to*; as, *competent* supplies of food and clothing; a *competent* force; an army *competent to* the preservation of the kingdom or state; a *competent* knowledge of the world. This word usually implies a moderate supply, a sufficiency without superfluity.

2. Qualified; fit; having legal capacity or power; as a *competent* judge or court; a *competent* witness. In a judge or court, it implies right or authority to hear and determine; in a witness, it implies a legal right or capacity to testify.

3. Incident; belonging; having adequate power or right.

That is the privilege of the infinite author of things, who never slumbers nor sleeps, but is not *competent* to any finite being. *Locke.*

It is not *competent* to the defendant to allege fraud in the plaintiff.

COM'PETENTLY, *adv.* Sufficiently; adequately; suitably; reasonably; as, the fact has been *competently* proved; a church is *competently* endowed.

COMPET'IBLE, *a.* [Not now used. See *Compatible.*]

COMPE'TING, *ppr.* Striving in rivalry.

COMPETI''TION, *n.* [Low L. *competitio.* See *Compete* and *Competence.*]

1. The act of seeking, or endeavoring to gain, what another is endeavoring to gain, at the same time; rivalry; mutual strife for the same object; also, strife for superiority; as the *competition* of two candidates for an office, or of two poets for superior reputation.

2. A state of rivalship; a state of having equal claims.

A portrait, with which one of Titian's could not come in *competition.* *Dryden.*

3. Double claim; claim of more than one to the same thing; formerly with *to*, now with *for*.

Competition to the crown there is none nor can be. *Bacon.*

There is no *competition* but *for* the second place. *Dryden.*

COMPET'ITOR, *n.* One who seeks and endeavors to obtain what another seeks; or one who claims what another claims; a rival.

They cannot brook *competitors* in love. *Shak.*

2. An opponent. *Shak.*

COMPET'ITORY, *a.* Rivaling; acting in competition. *Dangers of the country.*

COMPET'ITRESS, COMPET'ITRIX, *n.* A female competitor.

COMPILA'TION, *n.* [See *Compile.*]

1. A collection of certain parts of a book or books, into a separate book or pamphlet.

2. A collection or assemblage of other substances; or the act of collecting and forming an aggregate. *Woodward.*

COMPILA'TOR, *n.* A collector. [*Not used.*] *Chaucer.*

COMPI'LE, *v. t.* [L. *compilo*, to pilfer or plunder; *con* and *pilo*, to pillage, to *peel*, and to drive close; *compilatio*, a pillaging; It. *compilare*; Fr. *compiler*; Sp. Port. *compilar.* The L. *pilo* is the English, to *peel*, to strip; but *pilo*, to make thick, or drive together, is the Gr. πιλοω, lanas cogo, coarcto, constipo. *Compile* is probably from *peeling*, picking out, selecting and putting together.]

1. To collect parts or passages of books or writings into a book or pamphlet; to select and put together parts of an author, or to collect parts of different authors; or to collect and arrange separate papers, laws, or customs, in a book, code or system.

2. To write; to compose.

In poetry, they *compile* the praises of virtuous men and actions. *Temple.*

3. To contain; to comprise. [*Not used.*] *Spenser.*

4. To make up; to compose. [*Not used.*] *Shak.*

5. To put together; to build. [*Not used.*] *Spenser.*

COMPI'LED, *pp.* Collected from authors; selected and put together.

COMPI'LEMENT, *n.* The act of piling together or heaping; coacervation. [*Little used.*] *Woodward.*

COMPI'LER, *n.* A collector of parts of authors, or of separate papers or accounts; one who forms a book or composition from various authors or separate papers. *Bacon. Swift.*

COMPI'LING, *ppr.* Collecting and arranging parts of books, or separate papers, in a body or composition.

COMPLA'CENCE, COMPLA'CENCY, *n.* [L. *complacens*, *complaceo*; *con* and *placeo*, to please; Fr. *complaire*, *complaisant*; It. *compiacere*, *compiacente*; Sp. *complacer.*]

1. Pleasure; satisfaction; gratification. It is more than *approbation*, and less than *delight* or *joy*.

Others proclaim the infirmities of a great man with satisfaction and *complacency*, if they discover none of the like in themselves. *Addison.*

2. The cause of pleasure or joy. *Milton.*

3. Complaisance; civility; softness of manners; deportment and address that afford pleasure.

Complacency, and truth, and manly sweetness,
Dwell ever on his tongue, and smooth his thoughts. *Addison.*

In the latter sense, *complaisance*, from the French, is now used. [See *Complaisance.*]

COMPLA'CENT, *a.* Civil; complaisant.

They look up with a sort of *complacent* awe to kings. *Burke.*

COMPLACEN'TIAL, *a.* Marked by complacence; accommodating. *Ch. Relig. Appeal.*

COMPLA'CENTLY, *adv.* Softly; in a complacent manner.

COMPLA'IN, *v. i.* [Fr. *complaindre*; *con* or *com* and *plaindre*, *plaint*, to lament, to bewail; Sp. *plañir*; It. *compiagnere*, or *compiangere*; from the L. *plango*, to strike, to lament. If *n* is not radical, the original word was *plago*, coinciding with *plaga*, Gr. πληγη. But this is doubtful. The primary sense is to drive, whence to strike and to lament, that is, to strike the hands or breasts, as in extreme grief, or to drive forth the voice, as in *appello.*]

1. To utter expressions of grief; to lament.

I will *complain* in the bitterness of my spirit. Job vii.

I *complained* and my spirit was overwhelmed. Ps. lxxvii.

2. To utter expressions of censure or resentment; to murmur; to find fault.

And when the people *complained*, it displeased the Lord. Num. xi.

3. To utter expressions of uneasiness, or pain. He *complains* of thirst. He *complains* of a head-ache.

4. To charge; to accuse of an offense; to present an accusation against a person to a proper officer.

To A B, one of the justices of the peace for the county of S, *complains* C D.

This verb is regularly followed by *of*, before the cause of grief or censure; as, to *complain of* thirst, *of* ignorance, *of* vice, *of* an offender.

5. To represent injuries, particularly in a writ of Audita Querela.

COMPLA'IN, *v. t.* To lament; to bewail.

They might the grievance inwardly *complain.*

This use of *complain* is uncommon, and hardly legitimate. The phrase is properly elliptical.

COMPLA'INABLE, *a.* That may be complained of. [*Not in use.*] *Feltham.*

COMPLA'INANT, *n.* [Fr. *complaignant.*] A prosecutor; one who prosecutes by complaint, or commences a legal process against an offender for the recovery of a right or penalty.

He shall forfeit one moiety to the use of the town; and the other moiety to the use of the *complainant.* *Stat. of Massachusetts.*

2. The plaintiff in a writ of Audita Querela. *Ibm.*

COMPLA'INER, *n.* One who complains, or expresses grief; one who laments; one who finds fault; a murmurer.

These are murmurers, *complainers*, walking after their own lusts. Jude 16.

COMPLA'INFUL, *a.* Full of complaint. [*Not used.*]

COMPLA'INING, *ppr.* Expressing grief, sorrow, or censure; finding fault; murmuring; lamenting; accusing of an offense.

COMPLA'INING, *n.* The expression of regret, sorrow, or injury.

COMPLA'INT, *n.* [Fr. *complainte*; It. *compianto.*] Expression of grief, regret, pain, censure, or resentment; lamentation; murmuring; a finding fault.

Even to day is my *complaint* bitter. Job xxiii.

I mourn in my *complaint* and make a noise. Ps. lv.

The Jews laid many and grievous *complaints* against Paul. Acts xxv.

I find no cause of *complaint*. *Hooker.*

2. The cause or subject of complaint, or murmuring.

The poverty of the clergy hath been the *complaint* of all who wish well to the church. *Swift.*

3. The cause of complaint, or of pain and uneasiness in the body; a malady; a disease; usually applied to disorders not violent; as a *complaint* in the bowels or breast.

4. Accusation; a charge against an offender, made by a private person or informer to a justice of the peace or other proper officer, alledging that the offender has violated the law, and claiming the penalty due to the prosecutor. It differs from an *information*, which is the prosecution of an offender by the Attorney or Solicitor General; and from a *presentment* and *indictment*, which are the accusation of a Grand Jury.

5. Representation of injuries, in a general sense; and appropriately, in a writ of Audita Querela.

COM'PLAISANCE, *n.* *com'plazance.* [Fr. *complaisance*, from *complaisant*, the participle of *complaire; con* or *com* and *plaire*, to please, whence *plaisant*, pleasing, *plaisir*, pleasure, L. *placeo, placere*, the infinitive changed into *plaire*; It. *compiacenza*, from *compiacere, piacere*; Sp. *complacencia, complacer.* This is the same word as *complacence;* the latter we have from the Latin orthography. This word affords an example of a change of a palatal letter in the Latin into a sibilant in French, c into *s*.]

1. A pleasing deportment; courtesy; that manner of address and behaviour in social intercourse which gives pleasure; civility; obliging condescension; kind and affable reception and treatment of guests; exterior acts of civility; as, the gentleman received us with *complaisance*.

2. Condescension; obliging compliance with the wishes or humors of others.

In *complaisance* poor Cupid mourned. *Prior.*

3. Desire of pleasing; disposition to oblige; the *principle* for the *act*.

Your *complaisance* will not permit your guests to be incommoded. *Anon.*

COM'PLAISANT, *a.* *com'plazant.* Pleasing in manners; courteous; obliging; desirous to please; as a *complaisant* gentleman.

2. Civil; courteous; polite; as *complaisant* deportment or treatment.

COM'PLAISANTLY, *adv.* *com'plazantly.* In a pleasing manner; with civility; with an obliging, affable address or deportment. *Pope.*

COM'PLAISANTNESS, *n.* Civility; complaisance. [*Little used.*]

COM'PLANATE, } *v. t.* [L. *complano; con*
COMPLA'NE, } and *planus*, plain. See *Plane* and *Plain*.]

To make level; to reduce to an even surface. *Derham.*

COM'PLEMENT, *n.* [L. *complementum*, from *compleo*, to fill; *con* and *pleo*, to fill. Literally, a filling.]

1. Fulness; completion; whence, perfection.

They as they feasted had their fill,
For a full *complement* of all their ill.
Hub. Tales.

2. Full quantity or number; the quantity or number limited; as, a company has its *complement* of men; a ship has its *complement* of stores.

3. That which is added, not as necessary, but as ornamental; something adventitious to the main thing; ceremony. [See *Compliment.*]

Garnished and decked in modest *complement*. *Shak.*

4. In *geometry*, what remains of the quadrant of a circle, or of ninety degrees, after any arch has been taken from it. Thus if the arch taken is thirty degrees, its complement is sixty. *Bailey. Johnson.*

5. In *astronomy*, the distance of a star from the zenith. *Johnson.*

6. *Arithmetical complement* of a logarithm, is what the logarithm wants of 10,000,000. *Chambers.*

7. In *fortification*, the *complement of the curtain* is that part in the interior side which makes the demigorge.

COMPLEMENT'AL, *a.* Filling; supplying a deficiency; completing.

COMPLEMENT'ARY, *n.* One skilled in compliments. [*Not in use.*] *B. Jonson.*

COMPLE'TE, *a.* [L. *completus*, from *compleo; con* and *pleo*, inusit., to fill; It. *compiere.* The Greek has πλαω, to approach, to fill, contracted from πελαω, the primary sense of which is, to thrust or drive; and if the Latin *pleo* is from the Greek, which is probable, then the original orthography was *peleo, compeleo;* in which case, πλαω, πελαω, *pleo*, is the same word as the English *fill*. The Greek πληθω is said to be a derivative. Literally, filled; full.]

1. Having no deficiency; perfect.

And ye are *complete* in him who is the head of all principality and power. Col. ii.

2. Finished; ended; concluded; as, the edifice is *complete*.

This course of vanity almost *complete*. *Prior.*

In strict propriety, this word admits of no comparison; for that which is *complete*, cannot be more or less so. But as the word, like many others, is used with some indefiniteness of signification, it is customary to qualify it with *more, most, less* and *least*. *More complete, most complete, less complete*, are common expressions.

3. In *botany*, a *complete* flower is one furnished with a calyx and corolla. *Vaillant.* Or having all the parts of a flower. *Martyn.*

COMPLE'TE, *v. t.* To finish; to end; to perfect; as, to *complete* a bridge, or an edifice; to *complete* an education.

2. To fill; to accomplish; as, to *complete* hopes or desires.

3. To fulfil; to accomplish; to perform; as, the prophecy of Daniel is *completed*.

COMPLE'TED, *pp.* Finished; ended; perfected; fulfilled; accomplished.

COMPLE'TELY, *adv.* Fully; perfectly; entirely. *Swift.*

COMPLE'TEMENT, *n.* The act of completing; a finishing. *Dryden.*

COMPLE'TENESS, *n.* The state of being complete; perfection. *Watts.*

COMPLE'TING, *ppr.* Finishing; perfecting; accomplishing.

COMPLE'TION, *n.* Fulfilment; accomplishment.

There was a full entire harmony and consent in the divine predictions, receiving their *completion* in Christ. *South.*

2. Act of completing; state of being complete; utmost extent; perfect state; as, the gentleman went to the university for the *completion* of his education or studies.

The *completion* of a bad character is to hate a good man. *Anon.*

COMPLE'TIVE, *a.* Filling; making complete. *Harris.*

COM'PLETORY, *a.* Fulfilling; accomplishing. *Barrow.*

COM'PLETORY, *n.* The evening service; the complin of the Romish church. *Hooper.*

COM'PLEX, } *a.* [L. *complexus*, complex,
COMPLEX'ED, } embracing, from *complector*, to embrace; *con* and *plecto*, to weave, or twist; Gr. πλεκω; L. *plico;* W. *plygu;* Arm. *plega*; Fr. *plier;* It. *piegare;* Sp. *plegar;* D. *plooijen*, to fold, bend, or double.]

1. Composed of two or more parts or things; composite; not simple; including two or more particulars connected; as a *complex* being; a *complex* idea; a *complex* term.

Ideas made up of several simple ones, I call *complex*, such as beauty, gratitude, a man, the universe. *Locke.*

2. Involved; difficult; as a *complex* subject.

COM'PLEX, *n.* Assemblage; collection; complication. [*Little used.*]

This parable of the wedding supper comprehends in it the whole *complex* of all the blessings and privileges of the gospel. *South.*

COMPLEX'EDNESS, *n.* Complication; involution of parts in one integral; compound state; as the *complexedness* of moral ideas. *Locke.*

COMPLEX'ION, *n.* *complex'yon.* Involution; a complex state. [*Little used.*] *Watts.*

2. The color of the skin, particularly of the face; the color of the external parts of a body or thing; as a fair *complexion;* a dark *complexion;* the *complexion* of the sky.

3. The temperament, habitude, or natural disposition of the body; the peculiar cast of the constitution, which gives it a particular physical character; *a medical term, but used to denote character, or description;* as, men of this or that *complexion*.

'Tis ill, though different your *complexions* are,
The family of heaven for men should war.
Dryden.

COMPLEX'IONAL, *a.* Depending on or pertaining to complexion; as *complexional* efflorescencies; *complexional* prejudices. *Brown. Fiddes.*

COMPLEX'IONALLY, *adv.* By complexion. *Brown.*

COMPLEX'IONARY, *a.* Pertaining to the complexion, or to the care of it. *Taylor.*

COMPLEX'IONED, *a.* Having a certain temperament or state. *Addison.*

COMPLEX'ITY, *n.* The state of being complex; complexness. *Burke.*

COM'PLEXLY, *adv.* In a complex manner; not simply.

COM'PLEXNESS, *n.* The state of being complex or involved. *Smith.*

COMPLEX'URE, *n.* The involution or complication of one thing with others.

COMPLI'ABLE, *a.* [See *Comply.*] That can bend or yield. *Milton.*

COMPLI'ANCE, *n.* [See *Comply.*] The act of complying; a yielding, as to a request, wish, desire, demand or proposal; concession; submission.

Let the king meet *compliance* in your looks,
A free and ready yielding to his wishes. *Rowe.*

2. A disposition to yield to others.

He was a man of few words and great *compliance.* *Clarendon.*

3. Obedience; followed by *with;* as *compliance with* a command, or precept.

4. Performance; execution; as a *compliance with* the conditions of a contract.

COMPLI'ANT, *a.* Yielding, bending; as the *compliant* boughs. [See *Pliant,* which is generally used.] *Milton.*

2. Yielding to request or desire; civil; obliging.

COMPLI'ANTLY, *adv.* In a yielding manner.

COM'PLICACY, *n.* A state of being complex or intricate. *Mitford.*

COM'PLICATE, *v. t.* [L. *complico; con* and *plico,* to fold, weave or knit. See *Complex.*]

1. Literally, to interweave; to fold and twist together. Hence, to make complex; to involve; to entangle; to unite or connect mutually or intimately, as different things or parts; followed by *with.*

Our offense against God hath been *complicated with* injury to men. *Tillotson.*

So we say, a *complicated* disease; a *complicated* affair.

Commotion in the parts may *complicate* and dispose them after the manner requisite to make them stick. *Boyle.*

2. To make intricate.

COM'PLICATE, *a.* Complex; composed of two or more parts united.

Though the particular actions of war are *complicate* in fact, yet they are separate and distinct in right. *Bacon.*

2. In *botany,* folded together, as the valves of the glume or chaff in some grasses. *Martyn.*

COM'PLICATED, *pp.* Interwoven; entangled; involved; intricate; composed of two or more things or parts united.

COM'PLICATELY, *adv.* In a complex manner.

COM'PLICATENESS, *n.* The state of being complicated; involution; intricacy; perplexity. *Hale.*

COM'PLICATING, *ppr.* Interweaving; infolding; uniting.

COMPLICA'TION, *n.* The act of interweaving, or involving two or more things or parts; the state of being interwoven, involved or intimately blended.

The notions of a confused knowledge are always full of perplexity and *complications.* *Wilkins.*

2. The integral consisting of many things involved or interwoven, or mutually united.

By admitting a *complication* of ideas—the mind is bewildered. *Watts.*

COM'PLICE, *n.* [It. *complice;* Fr. Port. Sp. *id.;* L. *complico, complicitum, complices.* See *Complicate* and *Complex.*]

One who is united with another in the commission of a crime, or in an ill design; an associate or confederate in some unlawful act or design; an *accomplice.* The latter is now used. [See *Accomplice.*] *Shak. Clarendon.*

COMPLI'ED, *pret.* of *comply.*

COMPLI'ER, *n.* One who complies, yields or obeys; a person of ready compliance; a man of an easy, yielding temper. *Swift.*

COM'PLIMENT, *n.* [Fr. *id.;* It. *complimento;* Sp. *cumplimiento,* completion, perfection, compliment; Port. *comprimento,* length, fulfilment, compliment, obliging words, from the verb *comprir,* to fulfil, to perform; Sp. *cumplir;* It. *compiere;* L. *compleo.* See *Complete.*]

1. An expression of civility, respect or regard; as, to send, or make one's *compliments* to an absent friend. In this application, the plural is always used.

He observed few *compliments* in matter of arms. *Sidney.*

2. A present or favor bestowed. My friend made me a *compliment* of Homer's Iliad.

COM'PLIMENT, *v. t.* To praise; to flatter by expressions of approbation, esteem or respect.

Monarchs——
Should *compliment* their foes, and shun their friends. *Prior.*

She *compliments* Menelaus very handsomely. *Pope.*

2. To congratulate; as, to *compliment* a prince on the birth of a son.

3. To bestow a present; to manifest kindness or regard for, by a present or other favor.

He *complimented* us with tickets for the exhibition.

COM'PLIMENT, *v. i.* To pass compliments; to use ceremony, or ceremonious language.

I make the interlocutors upon occasion *compliment* with each other. *Boyle.*

COMPLIMENT'AL, *a.* Expressive of civility or respect; implying compliments.

Languages—grow rich and abundant in *complimental* phrases, and such froth. *Wotton.*

COMPLIMENT'ALLY, *adv.* In the nature of a compliment; by way of civility, or ceremony. *Broome.*

COM'PLIMENTER, *n.* One who compliments; one given to compliments; a flatterer. *Johnson.*

COM'PLINE, COM'PLIN, *n.* [Fr. *complie;* It. *compieta;* from L. *compleo, complendo, completus.*]

The last division of the Romish breviary; the last prayer at night, to be recited after sun-set; so called because it closes the service of the day.

Johnson. Encyc. Taylor.

COMPLISH, for *accomplish,* is not now used. *Spenser.*

COM'PLOT, *n.* [*con* or *com* and *plot.*] A plotting together; a joint plot; a plot; a confederacy in some evil design; a conspiracy.

I know their *complot* is to have my life. *Shak.*

COMPLOT', *v. t.* To plot together; to conspire; to form a plot; to join in a secret design, generally criminal.

We find them *complotting* together, and contriving a new scene of miseries to the Trojans. *Pope.*

COMPLOT'MENT, *n.* A plotting together; conspiracy. *King.*

COMPLOT'TED, *pp.* Plotted together; contrived.

COMPLOT'TER, *n.* One joined in a plot; a conspirator. *Dryden.*

COMPLOT'TING, *ppr.* Plotting together; conspiring; contriving an evil design or crime.

COMPLY', *v. i.* pret. *complied.* [The Italian *compiacere,* to humor, to comply, is the Latin *complaceo,* Fr. *complaire.* The Sp. *cumplir* is from *compleo,* for it is rendered, to discharge one's duty, to provide or supply, to reach one's birth day, to fulfil one's promise, to be fit or convenient, to suffice. The Portuguese changes *l* into *r; comprir,* to fulfil, to perform; hence, *comprimento,* a *complement,* and a *compliment.* *Comply* seems to be from the Spanish *cumplir,* or L. *compleo;* formed like *supply,* from *suppleo.* It is followed by *with.*]

1. *To comply with,* to fulfil; to perfect or carry into effct; to complete; to perform or execute; as, to *comply with* a promise, with an award, with a command, with an order. So to *comply with* one's expectations or wishes, is to fulfil them, or complete them.

2. To yield to; to be obsequious; to accord; to suit; followed by *with;* as, to *comply with* a man's humor.

The truth of things will not *comply with* our conceits. *Tillotson.*

COMPLY'ING *with, ppr.* Fulfilling; performing; yielding to.

COMPO'NE. COMPO'NED. In *heraldry,* a bordure compone is that formed or composed of a row of angular parts or checkers of two colors.

COMPO'NENT, *a.* [L. *componens, compono; con* and *pono,* to place.]

Literally, setting or placing together; hence, composing; constituting; forming a compound; as the *component* parts of a plant or fossil substance; the *component* parts of a society.

COMPO'RT, *v. i.* [It. *comportare:* Fr. *comporter;* Sp. Port. *comportar; con* and L. *porto,* to bear. See *Bear.* It is followed by *with.*]

To comport with, literally, to bear to or with; to carry together. Hence, to agree with; to suit; to accord; as, to consider how far our charity may *comport with* our prudence. His behavior does not *comport with* his station.

COMPO'RT, *v. t.* With the reciprocal pronoun, to behave; to conduct.

It is curious to observe how lord Somers—*comported himself* on that occasion. *Burke.*

[*Little used.*]

2. To bear; to endure; as in French, Spanish and Italian. [*Not used.*] *Daniel.*

COM'PORT, *n.* Behavior; conduct; manner of acting.

I knew them well, and marked their rude *comport.* *Dryden.*

This word is rarely or never used, but may he admissible in poetry. We now use *deportment.* The accent, since Shakspeare's time, has been transferred to the first syllable.

COMPO'RTABLE, *a.* Suitable; consistent.

We cast the rules of this art into some *comportable* method. *Wotton.*

COMPO'RTANCE, *n.* Behavior; deportment. *Obs.* *Spenser.*

COMPORTA'TION, *n.* An assemblage. [*Not used.*] *Bp. Richardson.*

COMPO'RTMENT, *n.* Behavior; demeanor; manner of acting. [*Not now used.*] *Hale. Addison.*

Compos mentis. [L. *con* and *pos*, from the root of *possum, potis.*] Possessed of mind; in a sound state of mind.

COMPO'SE, *v. t.* *s* as *z.* [Fr. *composer*; Arm. *composi*; from the participle of the L. *compono, compositus; con* and *pono, positus*, to set, put or lay, Fr. *poser*, and in a different dialect, Eng. to *put*; Sp. *componer*; It. *comporre.*] Literally, to place or set together. Hence,

1. To form a compound, or one entire body or thing, by uniting two or more things, parts, or individuals; as, to *compose* an army of raw soldiers; the parliament of G. Britain is *composed* of two houses, lords and commons; the senate of the U. States is *composed* of two senators from each state.

Zeal ought to be *composed* of the highest degrees of all pious affections. *Spratt.*

2. To invent and put together words and sentences; to make, as a discourse or writing; to write, as an author; as, to *compose* a sermon, or a book.

3. To constitute, or form, as parts of a whole; as, letters *compose* syllables, syllables *compose* words, words *compose* sentences.

A few useful things, confounded with many trifles, fill their memories, and *compose* their intellectual possessions. *Watts.*

4. To calm; to quiet; to appease; to tranquilize; that is, to set or lay; as, to *compose* passions, fears, disorders, or whatever is agitated or excited.

5. To settle; to adjust; as, to *compose* differences.

6. To place in proper form, or in a quiet state.

In a peaceful grave my corpse *compose.* *Dryden.*

7. To settle into a quiet state.

The sea *composes* itself to a level surface. It requires about two days to *compose* it after a gale.

8. To dispose; to put in a proper state for any purpose.

The army seemed well *composed* to obtain that by their swords which they could not by their pen. *Clarendon.*

9. In *printing*, to set types or characters in a composing stick, from a copy, arranging the letters in the proper order.

10. In *music*, to form a tune or piece of music with notes, arranging them on the stave in such a manner as when sung to produce harmony.

COMPO'SED, *pp.* Set together, or in due order; formed; constituted; calmed; quieted; settled; adjusted.

2. *a.* Calm; sedate; quiet; tranquil; free from agitation.

The Mantuan there in sober triumph sat,
Composed his posture, and his look sedate. *Pope.*

COMPO'SEDLY, *adv.* Calmly; seriously; sedately.

The man very *composedly* answered, I am he. *Clarendon.*

COMPO'SEDNESS, *n.* A state of being composed; calmness; sedateness; tranquility. *Wilkins.*

COMPO'SER, *n.* One who composes; one who writes an original work, as distinguished from a compiler; an author; also, one who forms tunes, whether he adapts them to particular words or not.

2. One who quiets or calms; one who adjusts a difference.

COMPO'SING, *ppr.* Placing together; forming; constituting; writing an original work; quieting; settling; adjusting; setting types.

COMPO'SING-STICK, *n.* Among *printers*, an instrument on which types are set from the cases, adjusted to the length of the lines.

COMPOS'ITE, *a.* In *architecture*, the Composite order is the last of the five orders of columns; so called because its capital is *composed* out of those of the other orders or columns, borrowing a quarter-round from the Tuscan and Doric, a row of leaves from the Corinthian, and volutes from the Ionic. Its cornice has simple modillions or dentils. It is called also the *Roman* or the *Italic* order. *Encyc.*

Composite numbers are such as can be measured exactly by a number exceeding unity, as 6 by 2 or 3; so that 4 is the lowest composite number. Composite numbers between themselves, are those which have a common measure besides unity; as 12 and 15, both which are measured by 3. *Encyc.*

COMPOSI''TION, *n.* *s* as *z.* In *a general sense*, the act of composing, or that which is composed; the act of forming a whole or integral, by placing together and uniting different things, parts or ingredients; or the whole body, mass or compound, thus formed. Thus we speak of the *composition* of medicines, by mixing divers ingredients, and call the whole mixture a *composition.* A *composition* of sand and clay is used for luting chimical vessels.

Vast pillars of stone, cased over with a *composition* that looks like marble. *Addison.*

Heat and vivacity, in age, is an excellent *composition* for business. *Bacon.*

2. In *literature*, the act of inventing or combining ideas, clothing them with words, arranging them in order, and in general, committing them to paper, or otherwise writing them. Hence,

3. A written or printed work; a writing, pamphlet or book. *Addison.*

4. In *music*, the act or art of forming tunes; or a tune, song, anthem, air, or other musical piece.

5. The state of being placed together; union; conjunction; combination.

Contemplate things first in their simple natures, and then view them in *composition.* *Watts.*

6. The disposition or arrangement of figures connected in a picture.

By *composition* is meant the distribution and orderly placing of things, both in general and particular. *Dryden.*

7. Adjustment; orderly disposition. Ben Jonson speaks of the *composition* of gesture, look, pronunciation and motion, in a preacher.

8. Mutual agreement to terms or conditions for the settlement of a difference or controversy.

Thus we are agreed;
I crave our *composition* may be written. *Shak.*

9. Mutual agreement for the discharge of a debt, on terms or by means different from those required by the original contract, or by law, as by the payment of a different sum, or by making other compensation. Hence, the sum so paid, or compensation given, in lieu of that stipulated or required.

A real *composition* is when an agreement is made between the owner of lands and the parson or vicar, with the consent of the ordinary and the patron, that such lands shall for the future be discharged from the payment of tithes, by reason of some land or other real recompense given to the parson, in lieu and satisfaction thereof. *Blackstone.*

A bankrupt is cleared by a commission of bankruptcy, or by *composition* with his creditors.

10. Consistency; congruity. [*Little used.*] *Shak.*

11. The act of uniting simple ideas in a complex idea or conception; *opposed to analysis.* *Newton.*

12. The joining of two words in a compound, as in *book-case;* or the act of forming a word with a prefix or affix, which varies its signification; as *return*, from *turn; preconcert*, from *concert; endless* from *end.*

13. The synthetical method of reasoning; synthesis; a method of reasoning from known or admitted truths or principles, as from axioms, postulates or propositions previously demonstrated, and from these deducing a clear knowledge of the thing to be proved; or the act of collecting scattered parts of knowledge, and combining them into a system, so that the understanding is enabled distinctly to follow truth through its different stages of gradation. This method of reasoning is opposed to *analysis* or *resolution.* It begins with first principles, and by a train of reasoning from them, deduces the propositions or truths sought. *Composition* or *synthesis* proceeds by collecting or combining; *analysis* or *resolution*, by separating or unfolding. *Harris. Encyc.*

14. In *printing*, the act of setting types or characters in the composing-stick, to form lines, and of arranging the lines in a galley, to make a column or page, and from this to make a form.

15. In *chimistry*, the combination of different substances, or substances of different natures, by affinity; from which results a compound substance, differing in properties from either of the component parts. Thus *water* is a *composition* of hydrogen and oxygen, which are invisible gases.

COMPOS'ITOR, *n.* *s* as *z.* In *printing*, one who sets types, and makes up the pages and forms.

2. One who sets in order.

COMPOS'SIBLE, *a.* [*con* and *possible.*] Consistent. [*Not used.*] *Chillingworth.*

COM'POST, *n.* [It. *composta;* L. *compositum*, from *compono.* See *Compose.*] In *agriculture*, a mixture or composition of various manuring substances for fertilizing land. Compost may be made by almost every animal and vegetable substance in nature, with lime or other earthy matter.

COM'POST, *v. t.* To manure with compost. *Bacon.*

COMPOS'TURE, *n.* Soil; manure. [*Not used.*] *Shak.*

COMPO'SURE, *n.* *compózhur.* [See *Compose.*]

1. The act of composing, or that which is composed; a composition; as a form of prayer of public *composure;* a hasty *composure.*

In the *composures* of men, remember you are a man. *Watts.*

In this use, this word has given way to *composition.*

2. Composition; combination; arrangement; order. [*Little used.*]

When such a *composure* of letters, such a word, is intended to signify a certain thing. *Holder.*

3. The form, adjustment, or disposition of the various parts.

In *composure* of his face,
Lived a fair but manly grace. *Crashaw.*

The outward form and *composure* of the body. *Duppa.*

4. Frame; make; temperament.

His *composure* must be rare indeed,
Whom these things cannot blemish. *Shak.*

5. A settled state of the mind; sedateness; calmness; tranquility.

When the passions are silent, the mind enjoys its most perfect *composure.* *Watts.*

[*This is the most common use of this word.*]

6. Agreement; settlement of differences; composition. [*Little used.*]

The treaty at Uxbridge gave the fairest hopes of a happy *composure.* *King Charles.*

COMPOTA'TION, *n.* [L. *compotatio; con* and *potatio,* from *poto,* to drink.]

The act of drinking or tippling together. *Brown. Philips.*

COM'POTATOR, *n.* One who drinks with another. *Pope.*

COMPOUND', *v. t.* [L. *compono; con* and *pono,* to set or put; Sp. *componer;* It. *comporre,* for *componere;* Port. *compor.*]

1. To mix or unite two or more ingredients in one mass or body; as, to *compound* drugs.

Whoever *compoundeth* any like it—shall be cut off from his people. Ex. xxx.

2. To unite or combine.

We have the power of altering and *compounding* images into all the varieties of picture. *Addison.*

3. To compose; to constitute. [*Not used.*] *Shak.*

4. In *grammar,* to unite two or more words; to form one word of two or more.

5. To settle amicably; to adjust by agreement; as a difference or controversy. *Bacon. Shak.*

[*In this sense we now use* compose.]

6. To pay by agreement; to discharge, as a debt, by paying a part, or giving an equivalent different from that stipulated or required; as, to *compound* debts. *Gay.*

But we now use, more generally, to *compound with.* [See the Verb Intransitive.]

To compound felony, is for a person robbed to take the goods again, or other compensation, upon an agreement not to prosecute the thief or robber. This offense is, by the laws of England, punishable by fine and imprisonment. *Blackstone.*

COMPOUND', *v. i.* To agree upon concession; to come to terms of agreement, by abating something of the first demand; followed by *for* before the thing accepted or remitted.

They were glad to *compound for* his bare commitment to the tower. *Clarendon.*

2. To bargain in the lump; to agree; followed by *with.*

Compound with this fellow by the year. *Shak.*

3. To come to terms, by granting something on each side; to agree.

Cornwall *compounded* to furnish ten oxen for thirty pounds. *Carew.*

Paracelsus and his admirers have *compounded* with the Galenists, and brought into practice a mixed use of chimical medicines. *Temple.*

4. To settle with a creditor by agreement, and discharge a debt by paying a part of its amount; or to make an agreement to pay a debt by means or in a manner different from that stipulated or required by law. A bankrupt may *compound with* his creditors for ten shillings on the pound, or fifty cents on the dollar. A man may *compound with* a parson to pay a sum of money in lieu of tithes. [See *Composition,* No. 9.]

To compound with a felon, is to take the goods stolen, or other amends, upon an agreement not to prosecute him. *Blackstone.*

COM'POUND, *a.* Composed of two or more ingredients.

Compound substances are made up of two or more simple substances. *Watts.*

2. In *grammar,* composed of two or more words. *Ink-stand, writing-desk, carelessness,* are *compound* words.

3. In *botany,* a *compound flower* is a species of aggregate flower, containing several florets, inclosed in a common perianth, on a common receptacle, with the anthers connected in a cylinder, as in the sunflower and dandelion. *Martyn. Harris.*

A *compound stem* is one that divides into branches.

A *compound leaf* connects several leaflets in one petiole, called a common petiole.

A *compound raceme* is composed of several racemules or small racemes.

A *compound spike* is composed of several spicules or spikelets.

A *compound corymb* is formed of several small corymbs.

A *compound umbel* is one which has all its rays or peduncles bearing umbellules or small umbels at the top.

A *compound fructification* consists of several confluent florets; opposed to *simple.*

4. *Compound interest,* is interest upon interest; when the interest of a sum is added to the principal, and then bears interest; or when the interest of a sum is put upon interest.

5. *Compound motion,* is that which is effected by two or more conspiring powers, acting in different but not in opposite directions.

6. *Compound number,* is that which may be divided by some other number besides unity, without a remainder; as 18, which may be divided by 2, 6 and 9.

7. *Compound ratio,* is that which the product of the antecedents of two or more ratios has to the product of their consequents. Thus 6 to 72 is in a ratio *compounded* of 2 to 6, and of 3 to 12.

8. *Compound quantities,* in algebra, are such as are joined by the signs + and — plus and minus, and expressed by more letters than one, or by the same letters unequally repeated. Thus $a+b-c$, and $bb-b$, are compound quantities. *Bailey.*

9. *Compound larceny,* is that which is accompanied with the aggravation of taking goods from one's house or person. *Blackstone.*

COM'POUND, *n.* A mass or body formed by the union or mixture of two or more ingredients or different substances; the result of composition.

Man is a *compound* of flesh and spirit. *South.*

Mortar is a *compound* of lime, sand and water.

COMPOUND'ABLE, *a.* Capable of being compounded. *Sherwood.*

COMPOUND'ED, *pp.* Made up of different materials; mixed; formed by union of two or more substances.

COMPOUND'ER, *n.* One who compounds or mixes different things.

2. One who attempts to bring parties to terms of agreement. [*Little used.*] *Swift.*

COMPOUND'ING, *ppr.* Uniting different substances in one body or mass; forming a mixed body; agreeing by concession, or abatement of demands; discharging a debt by agreement to pay less than the original sum, or in a different manner.

COMPREHEND', *v. t.* [L. *comprehendo; con* and *prehendo,* to seize or grasp; It. *comprendere, prendere;* Sp. Port. *comprehender, prender;* Fr. *comprendre, prendre.* This word is a compound of the Latin *con* and *præ,* and the Saxon *hendan* or *hentan,* to take or seize; *ge-hentan,* id. Hence *forehend,* in Spenser.]

Literally, to take in; to take with, or together.

1. To contain; to include; to comprise.

The empire of Great Britain *comprehends* England, Scotland and Ireland, with their dependencies.

2. To imply; to contain or include by implication or construction.

If there be any other commandment, it is briefly *comprehended* in this saying, thou shalt love thy neighbor as thyself. Rom. xiii.

3. To understand; to conceive; that is, to take, hold or contain in the mind; to possess or to have in idea; according to the popular phrase, "I *take* your meaning."

God doeth great things, which we cannot *comprehend.* Job xxxvii.

It is not always safe to disbelieve a proposition or statement, because we do not *comprehend* it.

COMPREHEND'ED, *pp.* Contained; included; implied; understood.

COMPREHEND'ING, *ppr.* Including; comprising; understanding; implying.

COMPREHEN'SIBLE, *a.* [L. *comprehensibilis.*]

1. That may be comprehended, or included; possible to be comprised.

2. Capable of being understood; intelligible; conceivable by the mind.

COMPREHEN'SIBLENESS, *n.* Capability of being understood. *More.*

COMPREHEN'SIBLY, *adv.* With great extent of embrace, or comprehension; with large extent of signification; in a manner to comprehend a large circuit.

The words wisdom and righteousness are commonly used very *comprehensibly*, so as to signify all religion and virtue. *Tillotson.*

This word is rarely used. [See *Comprehensively.*]

COMPREHEN'SION, *n.* [L. *comprehensio.*] The act or quality of comprehending, or containing; a comprising.

In the *Old* Testament there is a close *comprehension* of the *New*; in the *New*, an open discovery of the *Old*. *Hooker.*

2. An including or containing within a narrow compass; a summary; an epitome or compend.

This wise and religious aphorism in the text, is the sum and *comprehension* of all the ingredients of human happiness. *Rogers.*

3. Capacity of the mind to understand; power of the understanding to receive and contain ideas; capacity of knowing.

The nature of spirit is not within our *comprehension.*

4. In *rhetoric*, a trope or figure, by which the name of a whole is put for a part, or that of a part for a whole, or a definite number for an indefinite. *Harris.*

COMPREHEN'SIVE, *a.* Having the quality of comprising much, or including a great extent; extensive; as a *comprehensive* charity; a *comprehensive* view. It seems sometimes to convey the sense of comprehending much in a small compass.

2. Having the power to comprehend or understand many things at once; as a *comprehensive* head. *Pope.*

COMPREHEN'SIVELY, *adv.* In a comprehensive manner; with great extent of embrace.

COMPREHEN'SIVENESS, *n.* The quality of being comprehensive, or of including much extent; as the *comprehensiveness* of a view.

2. The quality of including much in a few words or narrow compass.

Compare the beauty and *comprehensiveness* of legends on ancient coins. *Addison.*

COMPREHEN'SOR, *n.* One who has obtained knowledge. [*Not in use.*] *Hall.*

COMPRESBYTE'RIAL, *a.* Pertaining to the presbyterian form of ecclesiastical ministration. *Milton.*

COMPRESS', *v. t.* [L. *compressus, comprimo; con* and *premo, pressus*, to press. But the verb *premo* and participle *pressus* may be from different roots. Fr. *presser;* D. *pressen;* Sp. *apretar*, and *prensar*. See *Press.*]

1. To press together by external force; to force, urge or drive into a narrower compass; to crowd; as, to *compress* air.

The weight of a thousand atmospheres will *compress* water twelve and a half per cent. *Perkins.*

2. To embrace carnally. *Pope.*

3. To crowd; to bring within narrow limits or space.

Events of centuries—*compressed* within the compass of a single life. *D. Webster.*

COM'PRESS, *n.* In *surgery*, a bolster of soft linen cloth, with several folds, used by surgeons to cover a plaster or dressing, to keep it in its place and defend the part from the external air. *Encyc.*

COMPRESS'ED, *pp.* Pressed or squeezed together; forced into a narrow or narrower compass; embraced carnally.

2. In *botany*, flatted; having the two opposite sides plane or flat; as a *compressed* stem. *Martyn.*

COMPRESSIBIL'ITY, *n.* The quality of being compressible, or yielding to pressure; the quality of being capable of compression into a smaller space or compass; as the *compressibility* of elastic fluids, or of any soft substance.

COMPRESS'IBLE, *a.* Capable of being forced or driven into a narrower compass; yielding to pressure; giving way to a force applied.

Elastic fluids are *compressible*. Water is *compressible* in a small degree.

COMPRESS'IBLENESS, *n.* Compressibility; the quality of being compressible.

COMPRES'SION, *n.* The act of compressing, or of pressing into a narrower compass; the act of forcing the parts of a body into closer union, or density, by the application of force.

2. The state of being compressed.

COMPRES'SIVE, *a.* Having power to compress. *Smith.*

COMPRES'SURE, *n.* The act or force of one body pressing against another; pressure. *Boyle.*

COM'PRIEST, *n.* A fellow priest. [*Not in use.*] *Milton.*

COMPRINT', *v. i.* [See *Print.*] To print together. It is taken, in law, for the deceitful printing of another's copy, or book, to the prejudice of the proprietor. [*Little used.*] *Philips.*

COMPRI'SAL, *n.* The act of comprising or comprehending. *Barrow.*

COMPRI'SE, *v. t.* *s* as *z*. [Fr. *compris*, participle of *comprendre*, L. *comprehendo*. See *Comprehend.*]

To comprehend; to contain; to include; as, the substance of a discourse may be *comprised* in a few words.

COMPRI'SED, *pp.* Comprehended; contained.

COMPRI'SING, *ppr.* Containing; including; comprehending.

COM'PROBATE, *v. i.* To agree in approving; to concur in testimony. *Elyot.*

COMPROBA'TION, *n.* [L. *comprobatio, comprobo; con* and *probo*, to prove.]

Proof; joint attestation. [*Little used.*] *Brown.*

COM'PROMISE, *n.* *s* as *z*. [L. *compromissum*, from *compromitto*, to give bond to stand to an award; *con* and *promitto*, to promise; It. *compromesso;* Fr. *compromis;* Sp. *compromiso*. See *Promise.*]

1. A mutual promise or contract of two parties in controversy, to refer their differences to the decision of arbitrators.

2. An amicable agreement between parties in controversy, to settle their differences by mutual concessions.

3. Mutual agreement; adjustment. *Chipman.*

[*This is its usual signification.*]

COM'PROMISE, *v. t.* To adjust and settle a difference by mutual agreement, with concessions of claims by the parties; to compound.

2. To agree; to accord. *Shak.*

3. To commit; to put to hazard; to pledge by some act or declaration.

[*In this sense, see* Compromit, *which is generally used.*]

COM'PROMISED, *pp.* Settled by agreement with mutual concessions.

COM'PROMISER, *n.* One who compromises.

COM'PROMISING, *ppr.* Adjusting by agreement.

COMPROMISSO'RIAL, *a.* Relating to a compromise. *Todd.*

COM'PROMIT, *v. t.* [Fr. *compromettre;* It. *compromettere;* Sp. *comprometer;* L. *compromitto, com* and *promitto*, to promise.]

To pledge or engage, by some act or declaration, which may not be a direct promise, but which renders necessary some future act. Hence, to put to hazard, by some previous act or measure, which cannot be recalled; as, to *compromit* the honor or the safety of a nation.

COM'PROMITED, *pp.* Pledged by some previous act or declaration.

COM'PROMITING, *ppr.* Pledging; exposing to hazard.

COMPROVIN'CIAL, *n.* [*con* and *provincial.*]

One belonging to the same province or archiepiscopal jurisdiction. *Aylitfe.*

COMPT, *n.* [Fr. *compte*, from *computo.*] Account; computation. *Obs.* *Shak.*

COMPT, *v. t.* To compute. *Obs.* [See *Count.*]

COMPT, *a.* [L. *comptus.*] Neat; spruce. [*Not used.*]

COMPT'IBLE, *a.* Accountable; subject; submissive. *Obs.* *Shak.*

COMPT'LY, *adv.* Neatly. [*Not in use.*] *Sherwood.*

COMPT'NESS, *n.* Neatness. [*Not in use.*] *Sherwood.*

COMP'TONITE, *n.* A newly discovered mineral, found in drusy cavities of masses ejected from Mount Vesuvius; so called from Lord Compton, who brought it to England in 1818. *Ure.*

COMPTROLL, from Fr. *compter*, L. *computo*, to count or compute, and *rolle*, a register. If this word were of genuine origin, both the verb and its derivative, *comptroller*, as applied to a public officer, would not be sense. But there is no such legitimate word in English, nor in any other known language. [See *Control.*]

COMPULS'ATIVE, **COMPULS'ATORY**, } *a.* [L. *compulsus*, from *compello;* Low L. *compulso*. See *Compel.*]

Compelling; forcing; constraining; operating by force. *Shak.*

COMPULS'ATIVELY, *adv.* By constraint or compulsion.

COMPUL'SION, *n.* [Low L. *compulsio*. See *Compel.*]

1. The act of driving or urging by force, physical or moral; force applied; constraint of the will; the application of a force that is irresistible.

If reasons were as plenty as blackberries, I would give no man a reason on *compulsion*. *Shak.*

A man is excused for acts done through unavoidable force and *compulsion*. *Blackstone.*

2. The state of being compelled or urged by violence.

ꞒOMPUL'SIVE, *a.* Having power to compel; driving; forcing; constraining; applying force.

Uniformity of opinions cannot be effected by *compulsive* measures.

ꞒOMPUL'SIVELY, *adv.* By compulsion; by force.

ꞒOMPUL'SIVENESS, *n.* Force; compulsion.

ꞒOMPULS'ORILY, *adv.* In a compulsory manner; by force or constraint.

ꞒOMPULS'ORY, *a.* Having the power or quality of compelling; applying force; driving by violence; constraining.

In the correction of vicious propensities, it may be necessary to resort to *compulsory* measures.

ꞒOMPUNꞒ'TION, *n.* [L. *compunctio, compungo; con* and *pungo*, to prick or sting; It. *compunzione, compugnere*, or *compungere;* Sp. *compuncion;* Fr. *componction.* See *Pungency.*]

1. A pricking; stimulation; irritation; *seldom used in a literal sense.* *Brown.*

2. A pricking of heart; poignant grief or remorse proceeding from a consciousness of guilt; the pain of sorrow or regret for having offended God, and incurred his wrath; the sting of conscience proceeding from a conviction of having violated a moral duty.

He acknowledged his disloyalty to the king, with expressions of great *compunction.* *Clarendon.*

ꞒOMPUNꞒ'TIOUS, *a.* Pricking the conscience; giving pain for offenses committed.

Let no *compunctious* visitings of nature
Shake my fell purpose. *Shak.*

ꞒOMPUNꞒ'TIVE, *a.* Causing remorse. *Johnson.*

ꞒOMPU'PIL, *n.* A fellow-pupil. [*Little used.*] *Walton.*

ꞒOMPURGA'TION, *n.* [L. *compurgo; con* and *purgo*, to purify.]

In *law*, the act or practice of justifying a man by the oath of others who swear to their belief of his veracity; wager of law, in which a man who has given security to make his law, brings into court eleven of his neighbors, and having made oath himself that he does not owe the plaintiff, the eleven neighbors, called compurgators, avow on their oaths that they believe in their consciences he has affirmed the truth. *Blackstone.*

ꞒOMPURGA'TOR, *n.* One who bears testimony or swears to the veracity or innocence of another. [See *Compurgation.*]

ꞒOMPU'TABLE, *a.* [See *Compute.*] Capable of being computed, numbered or reckoned. *Hale.*

ꞒOMPUTA'TION, *n.* [L. *computatio*, from *computo.* See *Compute.*]

1. The act of computing, numbering, reckoning or estimating; the process by which different sums or particulars are numbered, estimated, or compared, with a view to ascertain the amount, aggregate, or other result depending on such sums or particulars. We find by *computation* the quantity of provisions necessary to support an army for a year, and the amount of money to pay them; making the ration and pay of each man the basis of the *computation.* By *computations* of time or years, we ascertain the dates of events.

2. The sum, quantity or amount ascertained by computing, or reckoning.

We pass for women of fifty: many additional years are thrown into female *computations* of this nature. *Addison.*

3. Calculation.

ꞒOMPU'TE, *v.t.* [L. *computo; con* and *puto*, to lop or prune; to think, count, reckon; to cast up. The sense is probably to cast or throw together.]

1. To number; to count; to reckon; to cast together several sums or particulars, to ascertain the amount or aggregate. *Compute* the quantity of water that will fill a vessel of certain dimensions, or that will cover the surface of the earth. *Compute* the expenses of a campaign. *Compute* time by weeks or days.

2. To cast or estimate in the mind; to estimate the amount by known or supposed data.

3. To calculate.

ꞒOMPU'TE, *n.* Computation. [*Not used.*] *Brown.*

ꞒOMPU'TED, *pp.* Counted; numbered; reckoned; estimated.

ꞒOMPU'TER, *n.* One who computes; a reckoner; a calculator. *Swift.*

ꞒOMPU'TING, *ppr.* Counting; numbering; reckoning; estimating.

ꞒOM'PUTIST, *n.* A computer. [*Not used.*] *Wotton.*

ꞒOM'RADE, *n.* [Fr. *camarade;* It. *camerata;* Sp. *camarada;* Port. *camarada;* from *camara, camera*, a *chamber.*]

Literally, one who lodges in the same room. Hence in a more general sense, a fellow, a mate or companion; an associate in occupation.

ꞒOM'ROGUE, *n.* A fellow rogue. [*Not in use.*] *B. Jonson.*

ꞒON. A Latin inseparable preposition or prefix to other words. Ainsworth remarks that *con* and *cum* have the same signification, but that *cum* is used separately, and *con* in composition. *Con* and *cum* may be radically distinct words. The Irish *comh*, or *coimh*, is equivalent to the Latin *con;* and the Welsh *cym*, convertible into *cyv*, appears to be the same word, denoting, says Owen, a mutual act, quality or effect. It is precisely equivalent to the Latin *com*, in *comparo, compono*, and the Latin *com*, in composition, may be the Celtic *comh* or *cym.* But generally it seems to be *con*, changed into *com.* Ainsworth deduces *cum* from the Greek *συν;* for originally it was written *cyn.* But this is probably a mistake.

Con coincides in radical letters and in signification with the Teutonic *gain, gen, gean, igen, igien*, in the English *again, against;* Sax. *gean, ongean;* Sw. *igen;* Dan. *igien.* Whatever may be its origin or affinities, the primary sense of the word is probably from some root that signifies to *meet* or *oppose*, or turn and meet; to approach to, or to be with. This is the radical sense of most prepositions of the like import. See the English *with, again.* So in Irish, *coinne*, a meeting; *os coinne*, opposite.

Con, in compounds, is changed into *l* before *l*, as in *colligo*, to *collect*, and into *m* before a labial, as in *comparo*, to compare. Before a vowel or *h*, the *n* is dropped; as in *coalesco*, to *coalesce*, to *cooperate; cohibeo*, to restrain. It denotes union, as in *conjoin;* or opposition, as in *conflict, contend.* Qu. W. *gan*, with.

ꞒON, [abbreviated from Latin *contra*, against.] In the phrase, *pro* and *con*, for and against, *con* denotes the negative side of a question. As a noun, a person who is in the negative; as the *pros* and *cons.*

ꞒON, *v. t.* [Sax. *cennan, connan, cunnan*, to know, to be able, to be skilful or wise; and *cennan*, to bear or bring forth, Gr. *γενναω;* and *cunnian*, to try, to attempt, to prove, L. *conor;* whence *cunning*, skilful, experienced, or skill, experience; the latter word, *cunnian*, coincides in sense with Sax. *anginnan, onginnan*, to begin, to try, to attempt, L. *conor.* D. *kennen*, to know, understand or be acquainted; *kunnen*, to be able, *can*, to know or understand, to hold or contain; the last signification coinciding with the W. *ganu*, to contain. G. *kennen*, to know; and *können*, to be able. Dan. *kan*, to be able, pret. *kunde*, whence *kundskab*, knowledge, skill, experience. Sw. *kånna*, to know; *kuna*, to be able, to be skilled, to know. The primary sense is, to strain or stretch, which gives the sense of strength, power, as in *can*, and of holding, containing, comprehending, as *contain*, from *contineo, teneo*, Gr. *τεινω*, L. *tendo.* And this signification connects these words with *gin*, in its compounds, *begin*, Sax. *beginnan, anginnan*, &c., to strain, to try, to stretch forward and make an effort; also with the Greek *γενναω*, L. *gignor*, to beget or to bring forth. See Class Gn. No. 29. 36. 40. 42. 45. 58. In the sense of know, *con* signifies to hold or to reach.]

1. To know. *Obs.*

"I *conne* no skill." *Spenser.*

"I shall not *conne* answer." I shall not know or be able to answer. *Chaucer.*

2. To make one's self master of; to fix in the mind or commit to memory; as, to *con* a lesson. *Milton. Holder.*

To con thanks, to be pleased or obliged, or to thank. *Obs.* *Chaucer. Shak.*

ꞒONA'TUS, *n.* [L.] Effort; attempt. *Paley.*

2. The tendency of a body towards any point, or to pursue its course in the same line of direction. *Paley.*

ꞒONꞒAM'ERATE, *v. t.* [L. *concamero*, to arch; *con* and *camera*, an arch, arched roof, or *chamber.*]

To arch over; to vault; to lay a concave over; as a *concamerated* bone. *Grew.*

ꞒONꞒAM'ERATED, *pp.* Arched over.

ꞒONꞒAMERA'TION, *n.* An arching; an arch or vault. *Glanville.*

ꞒONꞒAT'ENATE, *v. t.* [It. *concatenare*, to link together; *concatenato;* Low Lat. *concatenatus; con* and *catena*, a chain; Sp. *concadenar*, and *encadenar*, from *cadena*, Fr. *cadene*, a chain.]

To link together; to unite in a successive series or chain, as things depending on each other. *Harris.*

ꞒONꞒAT'ENATED, *pp.* Linked together; united in a series.

ꞒONꞒATENA'TION, *n.* A series of links

united; a successive series or order of things connected or depending on each other; as a *concatenation* of causes.

CONCAUSE, *n.* Joint cause. [*Not used.*] *Fotherby.*

CONCAVA'TION, *n.* [See *Concave.*] The act of making concave.

CON'CAVE, *a.* [L. *concavus; con* and *cavus*, hollow. See *Cave.*]

1. Hollow, and arched or rounded, as the inner surface of a spherical body: opposed to *convex;* as a *concave* glass.
2. Hollow, in *a general sense;* as the *concave* shores of the Tiber. *Shak.*
3. In *botany*, a *concave* leaf is one whose edge stands above the disk. *Martyn.*

CON'CAVE, *n.* A hollow; an arch, or vault; as the ethereal *concave.*

CON'CAVE, *v. t.* To make hollow. *Seward.*

CON'CAVENESS, *n.* Hollowness.

CONCAV'ITY, *n.* [It. *concavità;* Fr. *concavité;* Sp. *concavidad.*]

Hollowness; the internal surface of a hollow spherical body, or a body of other figure; or the space within such body. *Wotton.*

CONCA'VO-CON'CAVE, *a.* Concave or hollow on both surfaces.

CONCA'VO-CON'VEX, *a.* Concave on one side, and convex on the other. [See *Convex.*]

CONCA'VOUS, *a.* [L. *concavus.*] Concave, *which see.*

CONCA'VOUSLY, *adv.* With hollowness; in a manner to discover the internal surface of a hollow sphere.

CONCE'AL, *v. t.* [Low L. *concelo; con* and *celo*, to withhold from sight; Sax. *helan, hælan, gehælan, gehelan*, to heal and to conceal; G. *hehlen*, to conceal, and *heilen*, to heal; D. *heelen*, to heal and to conceal; Dan. *hæler*, to conceal; W. *celu*, to hide; Fr. *celer;* It. *celare;* Sp. *callar*, to keep silence, to dissemble, to abate, to grow calm; Port. *calar*, to conceal or keep close, to pull or let down, "cala a boca," hold your peace; also intransitive, to be still or quiet, to keep silence; coinciding in origin with *whole, all, holy, hold*, &c. The primary sense is to strain, hold, stop, restrain, make fast or strong, all from the same root as the Shemitic כול, כלא, كَلَّ, ከለለ, Gr. κωλυω. Class Gl. No. 32. 36.]

1. To keep close or secret; to forbear to disclose; to withhold from utterance or declaration; as, to *conceal* one's thoughts or opinions.

   I have not *concealed* the words of the Holy One. Job vi.

2. To hide; to withdraw from observation; to cover or keep from sight.

   What profit is it if we slay our brother and *conceal* his blood? Gen. xxxvii.

   A party of men *concealed* themselves behind a wall. A mask *conceals* the face.

CONCE'ALABLE, *a.* That may be concealed, hid or kept close. *Brown.*

CONCE'ALED, *pp.* Kept close or secret; hid; withdrawn from sight; covered.

CONCE'ALER, *n.* One who conceals; as the *concealer* of a crime. *Clarendon.*

CONCE'ALING, *ppr.* Keeping close or secret; forbearing to disclose; hiding; covering.

CONCE'ALING, *n.* A hiding; a withholding from disclosure.

CONCE'ALMENT, *n.* Forbearance of disclosure; a keeping close or secret; as the *concealment* of opinions or passions.

2. The act of hiding, covering, or withdrawing from sight; as the *concealment* of the face by a mask, or of the person by any cover or shelter.
3. The state of being hid or concealed; privacy; as a project formed in *concealment.*
4. The place of hiding; a secret place; retreat from observation; cover from sight.

   The cleft tree
   Offers its kind *concealment* to a few,
   Their food its insects, and its moss their nests. *Thomson.*

CONCE'DE, *v. t.* [L. *concedo; con* and *cedo*, to yield, give way, depart, desist; It. *concedere, cedere;* Sp. *conceder, ceder;* Fr. *conceder, ceder;* Ir. *ceadaighim;* W. *gadael*, and *gadaw*, to quit or leave, to permit. The preterite *cessi* indicates that this word may be from a root in Class Gs. See that Class No 67. Samaritan. See also Class Gd., and *Cede*, and *Conge.*]

1. To yield; to admit as true, just or proper; to grant; to let pass undisputed; as, this must not be *conceded* without limitation. *Boyle.*

   The advocate *concedes* the point in question.

2. To allow; to admit to be true.

   We *concede* that their citizens were those who lived under different forms. *Burke.*

CONCE'DED, *pp.* Yielded; admitted; granted; as, a question, proposition, fact or statement is *conceded.*

CONCE'DING, *ppr.* Yielding; admitting; granting.

CONCE'IT, *n.* [It. *concetto;* Sp. *concepto;* Port. *conceito;* L. *conceptus*, from *concipio*, to *conceive; con* and *capio*, to take or seize.]

1. Conception; that which is conceived, imagined, or formed in the mind; idea; thought; image.

   In laughing there ever precedeth a *conceit* of somewhat ridiculous, and therefore it is proper to man. *Bacon.*

2. Understanding; power or faculty of conceiving; apprehension; as a man of quick *conceit.* [*Nearly antiquated.*]

   How often did her eyes say to me, that they loved! yet I, not looking for such a matter, had not my *conceit* open to understand them. *Sidney.*

3. Opinion; notion; fancy; imagination; fantastic notion; as a strange or odd *conceit.*

   Seest thou a man wise in his own *conceit?* there is more hope of a fool than of him. Prov. xxvi.

4. Pleasant fancy; gayety of imagination.

   On the way to the gibbet, a freak took him in the head to go off with a *conceit. L'Estrange.*

5. A striking thought; affected or unnatural conception.

   Some to *conceit* alone their works confine. *Pope.*

6. Favorable or self-flattering opinion; a lofty or vain conception of one's own person or accomplishments.

   By a little study and a great *conceit* of himself, he has lost his religion. *Bentley.*

Out of conceit with, not having a favorable opinion of; no longer pleased with; as, a man is *out of conceit with* his dress. Hence to *put one out of conceit with*, is to make him indifferent to a thing, or in a degree displeased with it. *Tillotson. Swift.*

CONCE'IT, *v. t.* To conceive; to imagine; to think; to fancy

   The strong, by *conceiting* themselves weak, are thereby rendered inactive. *South.*

CONCE'ITED, *pp.* Conceived; imagined: fancied.

2. *part. a.* Endowed with fancy, or imagination. *Obs. Knolles.*
3. *a.* Entertaining a flattering opinion of one's self; having a vain or too high conception of one's own person or accomplishments; vain.

   If you think me too *conceited*,
   Or to passion quickly heated. *Swift.*

   Followed by *of* before the object of conceit.

   The Athenians were *conceited of* their own wit, science and politeness. *Bentley.*

CONCE'ITEDLY, *adv.* In a conceited manner; fancifully; whimsically.

   Conceitedly dress her. *Donne.*

CONCE'ITEDNESS, *n.* The state of being conceited; conceit; vanity; an overweening fondness of one's own person or endowments. *Collier.*

CONCE'ITLESS, *a.* Of dull conception; stupid; dull of apprehension. [*Not in use.*] *Shak.*

CONCE'IVABLE, *a.* [Fr. *concevable;* It. *concepibile;* Sp. *conceptible.* See *Conceive.*]

1. That may be imagined, or thought; capable of being framed in the mind by the fancy or imagination.

   If it were possible to contrive an invention, whereby any *conceivable* weight may be moved by any *conceivable* power. *Wilkins.*

2. That may be understood or believed.

   It is not *conceivable*, that it should be the very person, whose shape and voice it assumed. *Atterbury.*

CONCE'IVABLENESS, *n.* The quality of being conceivable.

CONCE'IVABLY, *adv.* In a conceivable or intelligible manner.

CONCE'IVE, *v. t.* [Fr. *concevoir;* It. *concepire;* Sp. *concebir;* Port. *conceber;* L. *concipio; con* and *capio*, to take.]

1. To receive into the womb, and breed; to begin the formation of the embryo or fetus of an animal.

   Then shall she be free and *conceive* seed. Num. v. Heb. xi.

   Elisabeth hath *conceived* a son in her old age. Luke i.

   In sin did my mother *conceive* me. Ps. li.

2. To form in the mind; to imagine; to devise.

   They *conceive* mischief and bring forth vanity. Job xv.

   Nebuchadnezzar hath *conceived* a purpose against you. Jer. xlix.

3. To form an idea in the mind; to understand; to comprehend.

   We cannot *conceive* the manner in which spirit operates upon matter.

4. To think; to be of opinion; to have an idea; to imagine.

   You can hardly *conceive* this man to have been bred in the same climate. *Swift.*

CONCE'IVE, *v. i.* To have a fetus formed in the womb; to breed; to become pregnant.

   Thou shalt *conceive* and bear a son. Judges xiii.

2. To think; to have a conception or idea.

Conceive of things clearly and distinctly in their own natures. *Watts.*

The grieved commons
Hardly *conceive* of me. *Shak.*

3. To understand; to comprehend; to have a complete idea of; as, I cannot *conceive* by what means this event has been produced.

CONCE'IVED, *pp.* Formed in the womb; framed in the mind; devised; imagined; understood.

CONCE'IVER, *n.* One that conceives; one that comprehends.

CONCE'IVING, *ppr.* Forming a fetus in the womb; framing in the mind; imagining; devising; thinking; comprehending.

CONCE'IVING, *n.* Apprehension; conception. *Shak.*

CONCEL'EBRATE, *v. t.* To celebrate together. [*Not used.*] *Sherwood.*

CONCENT', *n.* [L. *concentus*, from *concino*, to sing in accordance; *con* and *cano*, to sing.]

1. Concert of voices; concord of sounds; harmony; as a *concent* of notes. *Bacon.*

2. Consistency; accordance; as, in *concent* to a man's own principles. *Atterbury.*

CONCENT'ED, *part. a.* Made to accord. *Spenser.*

CONCEN'TER, *v. i.* [Fr. *concentrer*; It. *concentrare*; Sp. and Port. *concentrar*; *con* and L. *centrum*, a *center*; Gr. κεντρον, a goad, a sharp point, a *center*; κεντεω, to prick or goad. The primary sense is a point.]

To come to a point, or to meet in a common center; used of converging lines, or other things that meet in a point.

All these are like so many lines drawn from several objects, that in some way relate to him, and *concenter* in him. *Hale.*

CONCEN'TER, *v. t.* To draw, or direct to a common center; to bring to a point; as two or more lines or other things.

The having a part less to animate, will serve to *concenter* the spirits, and make them more active in the rest. *Decay of Piety.*

CONCEN'TERED, *pp.* Brought to a common center; united in a point.

CONCEN'TERING, *ppr.* Tending to a common center; bringing to a center.

CONCENT'FUL, *a.* Harmonious. *Fotherby.*

CONCEN'TRATE, *v. t.* [See *Concenter.*]

To bring to a common center, or to a closer union; to cause to approach nearer to a point, or center; to bring nearer to each other; as, to *concentrate* particles of salt by evaporating the water that holds them in solution; to *concentrate* the troops in an army; to *concentrate* rays of light into a focus.

CONCEN'TRATED, *pp.* Brought to a point or center; brought to a closer union; reduced to a narrow compass; collected into a closer body.

CONCEN'TRATING, *ppr.* Bringing to a point or to closer union; collecting into a closer body, or narrow compass.

CONCENTRA'TION, *n.* The act of concentrating; the act of bringing nearer together; collection into a central point; compression into a narrow space; the state of being brought to a point.

Note. The verb *concentrate* is sometimes accented on the first syllable. The reason is, with the primary accent on the first syllable, and a secondary accent on the third, the pronunciation of the participles, *concentrating*, *concentrated*, is much facilitated.

CONCEN'TRIC, *a.* [It. *concentrico*; Fr. *concentrique*; L. *concentricus*; *con* and *centrum*, center.]

Having a common center; as the *concentric* coats of an onion; the *concentric* orbits of the planets.

CONCENT'UAL, *a.* [from *concent.*] Harmonious; accordant. *Warton.*

CONCEP'TACLE, *n.* [L. *conceptaculum*, from *concipio*. See *Conceive.*]

1. That in which any thing is contained; a vessel; a receiver, or receptacle. *Woodward.*

2. In *botany*, a follicle; a pericarp of one valve, opening longitudinally on one side and having the seeds loose in it. *Martyn.*

CONCEP'TIBLE, *a.* [See *Conceivable.*]

That may be conceived; conceivable; intelligible. [*Not used.*] *Hale.*

CONCEP'TION, *n.* [L. *conceptio*, from *concipio*. See *Conceive*. It. *concezione*; Sp. *concepcion*; Fr. *conception.*]

1. The act of conceiving; the first formation of the embryo or fetus of an animal.

I will greatly multiply thy sorrow and thy *conception*. Gen. iii.

2. The state of being conceived.

Joy had the like *conception* in our eyes. *Shak.*

3. In *pneumatology*, apprehension of any thing by the mind; the act of conceiving in the mind; that mental act or combination of acts by which an idea or notion is formed of an absent object of perception, or of a sensation formerly felt. When we see an object with our eyes open, we have a *perception* of it; when the same object is presented to the mind with the eyes shut, in idea only or in memory, we have a *conception* of it. *Kaims. Stewart. Encyc.*

4. Conception may be sometimes used for the power of conceiving ideas, as when we say, a thing is not within our *conception*. Some writers have defined conception as a distinct faculty of the mind; but it is considered by others as memory, and perhaps with propriety.

5. Purpose conceived; conception with reference to the performance of an act. *Shak.*

6. Apprehension; knowledge.

And as if beasts conceived what reason were,
And that *conception* should distinctly show. *Davies.*

7. Conceit; affected sentiment, or thought.

He is too full of *conceptions*, points of epigram, and witticisms. *Dryden.*

CONCEP'TIOUS, *a.* Apt to conceive; fruitful; pregnant. [*Not now used.*] *Shak.*

CONCEP'TIVE, *a.* Capable of conceiving. [*Little used.*] *Brown.*

CONCERN', *v. t.* [Fr. *concerner*; It. *concernere*; Sp. *concernir*; to concern, to regard, to belong to; L. Latin, *concerno*; *con* and *cerno*, to separate, sift, divide; to see. If this is the true origin, as I suppose, the primary sense is, to reach or extend to, or to look to, as we use *regard.*]

1. To relate or belong to.

Preaching the kingdom of God and teaching those things which *concern* the Lord Jesus Christ. Acts xxviii.

2. To relate or belong to, in an emphatical manner; to affect the interest of; to be of importance to.

Our wars with France have affected us in our most tender interests, and *concerned* us more than those with any other nation. *Addison.*

It much *concerns* us to secure the favor and protection of God. *Anon.*

3. To interest or affect the passions; to take an interest in; to engage by feeling or sentiment.

A good prince *concerns* himself in the happiness of his subjects.

A kind parent *concerns* himself in the virtuous education of his children.

They think themselves out of the reach of Providence, and no longer *concerned* to solicit his favor. *Rogers.*

4. To disturb; to make uneasy. [*Little used.*] *Derham.*

5. To intermeddle.

We need not *concern* ourselves with the affairs of our neighbors.

CONCERN', *n.* That which relates or belongs to one; business; affair; a very general term, expressing whatever occupies the time and attention, or affects the interests of a person.

Intermeddle not in the private *concerns* of a family. Religion is the main *concern* of a rational being. We have no *concern* in the private quarrels of our neighbors. The industrious and prudent occupy their time with their own *concerns.*

2. Interest; importance; moment; that which affects the welfare or happiness.

To live in peace, is a matter of no small *concern* to a nation.

Mysterious secrets of a high *concern*,
And weighty truths, solid convincing sense,
Explained by unaffected eloquence. *Roscommon.*

3. Affection; regard; careful regard; solicitude; anxiety.

Why all this *concern* for the poor things of this life?

O Marcia, let me hope thy kind *concerns*,
And gentle wishes, follow me to battle. *Addison.*

An impenitent man feels no *concern* for his soul. *Anon.*

4. Persons connected in business; or their affairs in general; as a debt due to the whole *concern*; a loss affecting the whole *concern*. *Mercantile Usage.*

CONCERN'ED, *pp.* or *a.* Interested; engaged; having a connection with that which may affect the interest, welfare or happiness.

All men are *concerned* in the propagation of truth.

We are *concerned* in the virtuous education of our children.

2. Interested in business; having connection in business; as, A is *concerned* with B in the East India trade. Of an advocate or counselor we say, he is *concerned* in the cause of A against B.

3. Regarding with care; solicitous; anxious; as, we are *concerned* for the fate of our fleet.

CONCERN'EDLY, *adv.* With affection or interest. *Clarendon.*

CONCERN'ING, *ppr.* Pertaining to; regarding; having relation to.

The Lord hath spoken good *concerning* Israel. Num. x.

I have accepted thee *concerning* this thing. Gen. xix.

This word has been considered as a preposition, but most improperly: *concerning*, when so called, refers to a verb, sentence or proposition; as in the first example, the word applies to the preceding affirmation. The Lord hath spoken good, which speaking good is *concerning* Israel. *Concerning*, in this case, refers to the first clause of the sentence.

CONCERN'MENT, *n.* The thing in which one is concerned or interested; concern; affair; business; interest.

To mix with thy *concernments* I desist. *Milton.*

Propositions which extend only to the present life, are small, compared with those that have influence upon our everlasting *concernments*. *Watts.*

The great *concernment* of men is with men. *Locke.*

2. A particular bearing upon the interest or happiness of one; importance; moment.

Experimental truths are matters of great *concernment* to mankind. *Boyle.*

3. Concern; interposition; meddling; as, the father had no *concernment* in the marriage of his daughter. In this sense, we generally use *concern*.

4. Emotion of mind; solicitude; as, their ambition is manifest in their *concernment*. In this sense, *concern* is generally used.

CONCERT', *v. t.* [It. *concertare*, to contrive; Sp. *concertar*, to agree, to adjust, to covenant; Port. *id.*; Fr. *concerter*; from L. *concerto*, to strive together; *con* and *certo*, to strive. The primary sense is to set or act together.]

To contrive and settle by mutual communication of opinions or propositions; to settle or adjust, as a plan or system to be pursued, by conference or agreement of two or more parties; as, to *concert* measures; to *concert* a plan of operations.

CON'CERT, *n.* Agreement of two or more in a design or plan; union formed by mutual communication of opinions and views; accordance in a scheme; harmony.

The allies were frustrated for want of *concert* in their operations.

The Emperor and the Pope acted in *concert*.

2. A number or company of musicians, playing or singing the same piece of music at the same time; or the music of a company of players or singers, or of both united.

3. A singing in company.

4. Accordance; harmony.

CONCERTA'TION, *n.* Strife; contention. [*Little used.*]

CONCERT'O, *n.* [It.] A piece of music for a concert. *Mason.*

CONCES'SION, *n.* [L. *concessio*, from *concedo*. See *Concede*.]

1. The act of granting or yielding; usually implying a demand, claim, or request from the party to whom it is made, and thus distinguished from *giving*, which is voluntary or spontaneous.

The *concession* of these charters was in a parliamentary way. *Hale.*

2. The thing yielded; as, in the treaty of peace, each power made large *concessions*.

3. In *rhetoric* or *debate*, the yielding, granting, or allowing to the opposite party some point or fact that may bear dispute, with a view to obtain something which cannot be denied, or to show that even admitting the point conceded, the cause is not with the adverse party, but can be maintained by the advocate on other grounds.

4. Acknowledgment by way of apology; confession of a fault.

CONCES'SIONARY, *a.* Yielding by indulgence or allowance.

CONCES'SIVE, *a.* Implying concession; as a *concessive* conjunction. *Lowth.*

CONCES'SIVELY, *adv.* By way of concession or yielding; by way of admitting what may be disputable. *Brown.*

CONCET'TO, *n.* [It. See *Conceit.*] Affected wit; conceit. [*Not English, nor in use.*] *Shenstone.*

CONCH, *n.* [L. *concha*; Gr. κογχη; It. *conca*; Sp. *concha*; Fr. *conque*; probably W. *cocos*, cockles, and perhaps allied to *cociaw*, to frown, to knit the brows, that is, to wrinkle. See *Cancer.*]

A marine shell.

Adds orient pearls, which from the *conchs* he drew. *Dryden.*

CONCHIF'EROUS, *a.* [L. *concha*, shell, and *fero*, to bear.] Producing or having shells.

CONCH'ITE, *n.* A fossil or petrified conch or shell. *Nat. Hist.*

CONCH'OID, *n.* [*conch*, supra, and Gr. ειδος, form.]

The name of a curve, given to it by its inventor Nicomedes.

CONCHOID'AL, *a.* In *mineralogy*, resembling a conch or marine shell; having convex elevations and concave depressions, like shells; as a *conchoidal* fracture. *Kirwan.*

CONCHOLOG'ICAL, *a.* [See *Conchology.*] Pertaining to conchology.

CONCHOL'OGIST, *n.* One versed in the natural history of shells and shell-fish; one who studies the nature, properties and habits of shells and their included animals.

CONCHOL'OGY, *n.* [Gr. κογχη, a shell, and λογος, discourse.]

The doctrine or science of shells and shell-fish.

CONCHOM'ETER, *n.* [Gr. κογχη, a shell, and μετρεω, to measure.]

An instrument for measuring shells. *Barnes.*

CONCHYLA'CEOUS, *a.* [from *conch.*] Pertaining to shells; resembling a shell; as *conchylaceous* impressions. *Kirwan.*

CONCHYLIOL'OGIST, } from L. *conchylium*, a shell-fish,
CONCHYLIOL'OGY, } are sometimes used as synonyms of the preceding words; but they are words of inconvenient length, and useless.

CON'CIATOR, *n.* In *glass-works*, the person who weighs and proportions the salt on ashes and sand, and who works and tempers them. *Encyc.*

CONCIL'IABLE, *n.* [L. *conciliabulum.*] A small assembly. [*Not in use.*] *Bacon.*

CONCIL'IAR, *a.* [from L. *concilium*, a council.] Pertaining or relating to a council. [*Little used.*] *Baker.*

CONCIL'IATE, *v. t.* [L. *concilio*, to draw or bring together, to unite; a compound of *con* and *calo*, Gr. καλεω, to call; Ch. אכלי in Aph., from כלי, כלא or כלה, to hold or keep, to trust, to finish, to *call*, to thunder; W. *galw*. The primary sense of the root is to strain, stretch, drive or draw. *Calling* is a straining or driving of voice. See Class Gl. No. 32. 36. 48. 49. and see *Council.*]

1. To lead or draw to, by moral influence or power; to win, gain or engage, as the affections, favor or good will; as, politeness and hospitality *conciliate* affection.

2. To reconcile, or bring to a state of friendship, as persons at variance. We say, an attempt has been made to *conciliate* the contending parties.

CONCIL'IATED, *pp.* Won; gained; engaged by moral influence, as by favor or affection; reconciled.

CONCIL'IATING, *ppr.* Winning; engaging; reconciling.

2. *a.* Winning; having the quality of gaining favor; as a *conciliating* address.

CONCILIA'TION, *n.* The act of winning or gaining, as esteem, favor or affection; reconciliation.

CONCILIA'TOR, *n.* One who conciliates or reconciles.

CONCIL'IATORY, *a.* Tending to conciliate, or reconcile; tending to make peace between persons at variance; pacific.

The General made *conciliatory* propositions to the insurgents.

The Legislature adopted *conciliatory* measures.

CONCIN'NITY, *n.* [L. *concinnitas*, from *concinnus*, fit, *concinno*, to fit or prepare; either from *con* and *cano*, to sound in accord; or the last constituent of the word may be the Heb. and Ch. כון to fit or adapt.]

1. Fitness; suitableness; neatness. [*Little used.*]

2. A jingling of words. *Tyrwhitt.*

CONCIN'NOUS, *a.* [L. *concinnus*. See *Concinnity.*]

Fit; suitable; agreeable; becoming; pleasant; as a *concinnous* interval in music; a *concinnous* system. *Encyc.*

CONCIONA'TOR, *n.* [Infra.] A preacher. [*Not in use.*]

CON'CIONATORY, *a.* [L. *concionatorius*, from *concio*, an assembly.]

Used in preaching or discourses to public assemblies. *Howel.*

CONCI'SE, *a.* [L. *concisus*, cut off, brief, from *concido*; *con* and *cædo*, to cut. See Class Gd. No. 2. 4. 8. 49. 59.]

Brief; short, applied to language or stile; containing few words; comprehensive; comprehending much in few words, or the principal matters only.

The *concise* stile, which expresseth not enough, but leaves somewhat to be understood. *B. Jonson.*

Where the author is too brief and *concise*, amplify a little. *Watts.*

In Genesis, we have a *concise* account of the creation.

CONCI'SELY, *adv.* Briefly; in few words; comprehensively.

CONCI'SENESS, *n.* Brevity in speaking or writing.

Conciseness should not be studied at the expense of perspicuity.

CONCIS'ION, *n.* *s* as *z*. [Low L. *concisio*, from *concisum*, *concido*, to cut off; It. *concisione.*] Literally, a cutting off. Hence, In *scripture*, the Jews or those who adhered to circumcision, which, after our Savior's death, was no longer a seal of the covenant, but a mere cutting of the flesh.

Beware of dogs; beware of the *concision*. Phil. iii.

CONCITA'TION, *n.* [L. *concitatio*, from *concito*, to stir or disturb; *con* and *cito*, to stir.]

The act of stirring up, exciting or putting in motion. *Brown.*

CONCI'TE, *v. t.* [L. *concito.*] To excite. [*Not in use.*]

CONCLAMA'TION, *n.* [L. *conclamatio*, from *conclamo*; *con* and *clamo*, to cry out. See *Claim.*]

An outcry or shout of many together. *Dict.*

CON'CLAVE, *n.* [L. *conclave*, an inner room; *con* and *clavis*, a key, or from the same root, to make fast.]

1. A private apartment, particularly the room in which the Cardinals of the Romish church meet in privacy, for the election of a Pope. It consists of a range of small cells or apartments, standing in a line along the galleries and hall of the Vatican. *Encyc.*

2. The assembly or meeting of the Cardinals, shut up for the election of a Pope. *Encyc.*

3. A private meeting; a close assembly. *Garth.*

CONCLU'DE, *v. t.* [L. *concludo*; *con* and *claudo* or *cludo*, to shut; Gr. κλειδοω, or κλειω, contracted; It. *conchiudere*; Sp. *concluir*; Port. *id.*; Fr. *conclure*. The sense is to stop, make fast, shut, or rather to thrust together. Hence in Latin, *claudo* signifies to halt, or limp, that is, to stop, as well as to shut. See *Lid.*]

1. To shut.

The very person of Christ—was only, touching bodily substance, *concluded* in the grave. *Hooker.*

[*This use of the word is uncommon.*]

2. To include; to comprehend.

For God hath *concluded* them all in unbelief. Rom. xi.

The scripture hath *concluded* all under sin. Gal. iii.

The meaning of the word in the latter passage may be to declare irrevocably or to doom.

3. To collect by reasoning; to infer, as from premises; to close an argument by inferring.

Therefore we *conclude*, that a man is justified by faith without the deeds of the law. Rom. iii.

4. To decide; to determine; to make a final judgment or determination.

As touching the Gentiles who believe, we have written and *concluded* that they observe no such thing. Rom. xi.

5. To end; to finish.

I will *conclude* this part with the speech of a counselor of state. *Bacon.*

6. To stop or restrain, or as in law, to estop from further argument or proceedings; to oblige or bind, as by authority or by one's own argument or concession; generally in the passive.

If they will appeal to revelation for their creation, they must be *concluded* by it. *Hale.*

The defendant is *concluded* by his own plea.

I do not consider the decision of that motion, upon affidavits, to amount to a *res judicata*, which ought to *conclude* the present inquiry. *Kent.*

CONCLU'DE, *v. i.* To infer, as a consequence; to determine.

The world will *conclude* I had a guilty conscience. *Arbuthnot.*

But this verb is really transitive. The world will *conclude that I had a guilty conscience—that* is here the object, referring to the subsequent clause of the sentence. [See Verb Transitive, No. 3.]

2. To settle opinion; to form a final judgment.

Can we *conclude* upon Luther's instability, as our author has done. *Atterbury.*

3. To end.

A train of lies,
That, made in lust, *conclude* in perjuries. *Dryden.*

The old form of expression, to *conclude of*, is no longer in use.

CONCLU'DED, *pp.* Shut; ended; finished; determined; inferred; comprehended; stopped, or bound.

CONCLU'DENCY, *n.* Inference; logical deduction from premises. *Hale.*

CONCLU'DENT, *a.* Bringing to a close; decisive. *Bacon.*

CONCLU'DER, *n.* One who concludes. *Mountagu.*

CONCLU'DING, *ppr.* Shutting; ending; determining; inferring; comprehending.

2. *a.* Final; ending; closing; as the *concluding* sentence of an essay.

CONCLU'DINGLY, *adv.* Conclusively; with incontrovertible evidence. [*Little used.*] *Digby.*

CONCLU'SIBLE, *a.* That may be concluded or inferred; determinable. [*Little used.*] *Hammond.*

CONCLU'SION, *n. s* as *z.* [L. *conclusio.*] End; close; the last part; as the *conclusion* of an address.

2. The close of an argument, debate or reasoning; inference that ends the discussion; final result.

Let us hear the *conclusion* of the whole matter; fear God, and keep his commandments; for this is the whole of man. Eccles. xii.

3. Determination; final decision.

After long debate, the house of commons came to this *conclusion*.

4. Consequence; inference; that which is collected or drawn from premises; particular deduction from propositions, facts, experience, or reasoning.

5. The event of experiments; experiment.

We practice all *conclusions* of grafting and inoculating. [*Little used.*] *Bacon.*

6. Confinement of the thoughts; silence. [*Not used.*] *Shak.*

CONCLU'SIONAL, *a.* Concluding. [*Not used.*] *Hooper.*

CONCLU'SIVE, *a.* [It. *conclusivo.*] Final; decisive; as a *conclusive* answer to a proposition.

2. Decisive; giving a final determination; precluding a further act.

The agreeing votes of both houses were not, by any law or reason, *conclusive* to my judgment. *King Charles.*

3. Decisive; concluding the question; putting an end to debate; as a *conclusive* argument.

4. Regularly consequential.

Men, not knowing the true forms of syllogisms, cannot know whether they are made in right and *conclusive* modes and figures. *Locke.*

CONCLU'SIVELY, *adv.* Decisively; with final determination; as, the point of law is *conclusively* settled.

CONCLU'SIVENESS, *n.* The quality of being conclusive, or decisive; the power of determining the opinion, or of settling a question; as the *conclusiveness* of evidence or of an argument. *Hale.*

CONCOAG'ULATE, *v. t.* [*con* and *coagulate.*] To curdle or congeal one thing with another. *Boyle.*

CONCOAG'ULATED, *pp.* Curdled; concreted.

CONCOAG'ULATING, *ppr.* Concreting; curdling.

CONCOAGULA'TION, *n.* A coagulating together, as different substances, or bodies, in one mass. Crystalization of different salts in the same menstruum. *Coxe.*

[*This word is little used.*]

CONCOCT', *v. t.* [L. *concoquo*, *concoctum*; *con* and *coquo*, to *cook*. See *Cook.*]

1. To digest by the stomach, so as to turn food to chyle or nutriment.

The vital functions are performed by general and constant laws; the food is *concocted*. *Cheyne.*

2. To purify or sublime; to refine by separating the gross or extraneous matter; as, *concocted* venom. *Thomson.*

3. To ripen.

Fruits and grains are half a year in *concocting*. *Bacon.*

CONCOCT'ED, *pp.* Digested; purified; ripened.

CONCOCT'ING, *ppr.* Digesting; purifying; ripening.

CONCOC'TION, [L. *concoctio.*] Digestion or solution in the stomach; the process by which food is turned into chyle, or otherwise prepared to nourish the body; the change which food undergoes in the stomach. *Coxe. Encyc.*

2. Maturation; the process by which morbid matter is separated from the blood or humors, or otherwise changed and prepared to be thrown off. *Coxe.*

3. A ripening; the acceleration of any thing towards perfection. *Johnson.*

CONCOC'TIVE, *a.* Digesting; having the power of digesting or ripening. *Milton.*

CONCŎL'OR, *a.* Of one color. [*Not in use.*] *Brown.*

CONCOM'ITANCE, } *n.* [L. *con* and *comitor*, to accompany,
CONCOM'ITANCY, } from *comes*, a companion. See *Count.*]

A being together, or in connection with another thing.

The secondary action subsisteth not alone, but in *concomitancy* with the other. *Brown.*

CONCOM'ITANT, *a.* Accompanying; conjoined with; concurrent; attending.

It has pleased our wise creator to annex to several objects—a *concomitant* pleasure. *Locke.*

CONCOM'ITANT, *n.* A companion; a person or thing that accompanies another, or is collaterally connected. *It is seldom applied to persons.*

The other *concomitant* of ingratitude is hardheartedness. *South.*

Reproach is a *concomitant* to greatness. *Addison.*

CONCOM'ITANTLY, *adv.* In company with others. *Pearson.*

CONCOM'ITATE, *v. t.* To accompany or attend; to be collaterally connected. [*Not used.*] *Harvey.*

CON'CORD, *n.* [Fr. *concorde*; L. *concordia*, from *concors*, of *con* and *cor*, *cordis*, the heart. See *Accord.*]

1. Agreement between persons; union in opinions, sentiments, views or interests; peace; harmony.

What *concord* hath Christ with Belial? 2 Cor. vi.

2. Agreement between things; suitableness; harmony.

If, nature's *concord* broke,
Among the constellations war were sprung. *Milton.*

3. In *music*, consent of sounds; harmony; the relation between two or more sounds which are agreeable to the ear. [See *Chord.*]

The man who hath not music in himself,
Nor is not moved with *concord* of sweet sounds,
Is fit for treasons. *Shak.*

4. A compact; an agreement by stipulation; treaty. *Davies.*

5. In *law*, an agreement between the parties in a fine, made by leave of the court. This is an acknowledgment from the deforciants that the land in question is the right of the complainant. *Blackstone.*

6. In *grammar*, agreement of words in construction; as adjectives with nouns in gender, number and case; or verbs with nouns or pronouns in number and person. Or *concord* may signify the system of rules for construction called *syntax.*

Form of concord, in ecclesiastical history, is a book among the Lutherans containing a system of doctrines to be subscribed as a condition of communion, composed at Torgaw in 1576. *Encyc.*

CONCORD'ANCE, *n.* [Fr. *concordance*; It. *concordanza*; L. *concordans*, from *concordo*, to agree. See *Concord.*]

1. Agreement. In this sense, *accordance* is generally used.
2. In *grammar*, concord. [*Not used.*]
3. A dictionary in which the principal words used in the scriptures are arranged alphabetically, and the book, chapter and verse in which each word occurs are noted; designed to assist an inquirer in finding any passage of scripture, by means of any leading word in a verse which he can recollect.

CONCORD'ANCY, *n.* Agreement. *Mountagu.*

CONCORD'ANT, *a.* Agreeing; agreeable; correspondent; harmonious. *Brown.*

CONCORD'ANT, *n.* That which is accordant. *Mountagu.*

CONCORD'ANTLY, *adv.* In conjunction.

CONCORD'AT, *n.* In *the canon law*, a compact, covenant, or agreement concerning some beneficiary matter, as a resignation, permutation, promotion and the like. In particular, an agreement made by a prince with the Pope relative to the collation of benefices; such as that between the Emperor Frederic III., the German princes, and the Pope's legate, A. D. 1448. *Encyc. Span. Dict. Lunier.*

CONCORD'IST, *n.* The compiler of a concordance. *Ch. Observer, March,* 1811.

CONCOR'PORATE, *v. t.* [L. *concorporo*, of *con* and *corpus*, a body.]

To unite different things in one mass or body; to incorporate. [*Little used.*] *Taylor.*

CONCOR'PORATE, *v. i.* To unite in one mass or body. *Cleaveland.*

CONCORPORA'TION, *n.* Union of things in one mass or body.

CON'COURSE, *n.* [Fr. *concours*; Sp. *concurso*; It. *concorso*; L. *concursus*, from *concurro*, to run together; *con* and *curro*, to run.]

1. A moving, flowing or running together; confluence; as a fortuitous *concourse* of atoms; a *concourse* of men.
2. A meeting; an assembly of men; an assemblage of things; a collection formed by a voluntary or spontaneous moving and meeting in one place. Acts xix.
3. The place or point of meeting, or a meeting; the point of junction of two bodies.

The drop will begin to move towards the *concourse* of the glasses. *Newton.*

[*This application is unusual.*]

CONCREA'TE, *v. t.* [*con* and *create*; It. *concreare.*]

To create with, or at the same time.

Dr. Taylor—insists that it is inconsistent with the nature of virtue, that it should be *concreated* with any person. *Edwards, Orig. Sin.*

CONCREA'TED, *pp.* Created at the same time, or in union with.

CONCRED'IT, *v. t.* To entrust. [*Not used.*] *Barrow.*

CONCREMA'TION, *n.* [L. *concremo*, to burn together; *con* and *cremo*, to burn.]

The act of burning different things together. [*Little used.*]

CON'CREMENT, *n.* [Low L. *concrementum*, from *concresco*, to grow together. See *Concrete.*]

A growing together; the collection or mass formed by concretion, or natural union. *Hale.*

CONCRES'CENCE, *n.* [L. *concrescentia*, *concresco*. See *Concrete.*]

Growth or increase; the act of growing or increasing by spontaneous union, or the coalescence of separate particles. *Raleigh.*

CONCRES'CIBLE, *a.* Capable of concreting; that may congeal or be changed from a liquid to a solid state.

They formed a genuine, fixed, *concrescible* oil. *Fourcroy.*

CON'CRETE, *a.* [L. *concretus*, from *concresco*, to grow together; *con* and *cresco*, to grow. See *Grow.*]

1. Literally, united in growth. Hence, formed by coalition of separate particles in one body; consistent in a mass; united in a solid form.

The first *concrete* state or consistent surface of the chaos. *Burnet.*

2. In *logic*, applied to a subject; not abstract; as the *whiteness* of *snow*. Here whiteness is used as a concrete term, as it expresses the quality of snow.

Concrete terms, while they express the quality, do also express, or imply, or refer to a subject to which they belong. *Watts.*

A *concrete* number expresses or denotes a particular subject, as *three* men; but when we use a number without reference to a subject, as *three*, or *five*, we use the term in the abstract. *Bailey.*

CON'CRETE, *n.* A compound; a mass formed by concretion, spontaneous union or coalescence of separate particles of matter in one body.

Gold is a porous *concrete.* *Bentley.*

2. In *philosophy*, a mass or compound body, made up of different ingredients; a mixed body or mass.

Soap is a factitious *concrete.* *Encyc.*

3. In *logic*, a concrete term; a term that includes both the quality and the subject in which it exists; as *nigrum*, a black thing. *Ainsworth.*

CONCRE'TE, *v. i.* To unite or coalesce, as separate particles, into a mass or solid body, chiefly by spontaneous cohesion, or other natural process; as, saline particles *concrete* into crystals; blood *concretes* in a bowl. Applied to some substances, it is equivalent to *indurate*; as, metallic matter *concretes* into a hard body. Applied to other substances, it is equivalent to *congeal*, *thicken*, *inspissate*, *coagulate*; as in the concretion of blood. *Arbuthnot. Woodward. Newton.*

CONCRE'TE, *v. t.* To form a mass by the cohesion or coalescence of separate particles. *Hale.*

CONCRE'TED, *pp.* United into a solid mass; congealed; inspissated; clotted.

CONCRE'TELY, *adv.* In a concrete manner; in a manner to include the subject with the predicate; not abstractly. *Norris.*

CONCRE'TENESS, *n.* A state of being concrete; coagulation.

CONCRE'TING, *ppr.* Coalescing or congealing in a mass; becoming thick; making solid.

CONCRE'TION, *n.* The act of concreting; the process by which soft or fluid bodies become thick, consistent, solid or hard; the act of growing together, or of uniting, by other natural process, the small particles of matter into a mass.

2. The mass or solid matter formed by growing together, by congelation, condensation, coagulation or induration; a clot; a lump; a solid substance formed in the soft parts or in the cavities of animal bodies.

CONCRE'TIVE, *a.* Causing to concrete; having power to produce concretion; tending to form a solid mass from separate particles; as, *concretive* juices. *Brown.*

CONCRE'TURE, *n.* A mass formed by concretion. [*Not used.*]

CONCREW', *v. i.* To grow together. [*Not used.*] *Spenser.*

CONCU'BINAGE, *n.* [Fr. See *Concubine.*] The act or practice of cohabiting, as man and woman, in sexual commerce, without the authority of law, or a legal marriage. In a more general sense, this word is used to express any criminal or prohibited sexual commerce, including adultery, incest, and fornication.

In some countries, concubinage is a marriage of an inferior kind, or performed with less solemnity than a true or formal marriage; or marriage with a woman of inferior condition, to whom the husband does not convey his rank or quality. This is said to be still in use in Germany. *Encyc.*

In *law*, concubinage is used as an exception against her that sueth for dower; in which it is alledged that she was not lawfully married to the man in whose lands she seeks to be endowed, but that she was his concubine. *Cowel.*

CONCU'BINATE, *n.* Whoredom; lewdness. [*Not in use.*] *Taylor.*

CON'CUBINE, *n.* [Fr. from L. *concubina*, from *concumbo*, to lie together; *con* and *cumbo*, or *cubo*, to lie down.]

1. A woman who cohabits with a man, without the authority of a legal marriage; a woman kept for lewd purposes; a kept mistress. *Bacon. Shak. Dryden.*

2. A wife of inferior condition; a lawful wife, but not united to the man by the usual ceremonies, and of inferior condition. Such were Hagar and Keturah, the concubines of Abraham; and such concubines were allowed by the Roman laws. *Encyc. Cruden.*

CONCUL'CATE, *v. t.* [L. *conculco.*] To tread on; to trample under foot. *Mountagu.*

CONCULCA'TION, *n.* A trampling under foot. [*Not much used.*]

CONCU'PISCENCE, *n.* [L. *concupiscentia*, from *concupisco*, to covet or lust after; *con* and *cupio*, to desire or covet.]

Lust; unlawful or irregular desire of sexual pleasure. In a more general sense, the coveting of carnal things, or an irregular appetite for worldly good; inclination for unlawful enjoyments.

We know even secret *concupiscence* to be sin. *Hooker.*

Sin, taking occasion by the commandment, wrought in me all manner of *concupiscence.* Rom. vii.

CONCU'PISCENT, *a.* Desirous of unlawful pleasure; libidinous. *Shak.*

CONCU'PISCIBLE, *a.* Exciting or impelling to the enjoyment of carnal pleasure; inclining to the attainment of pleasure or good; as *concupiscible* appetite. *South.*

CONCUR', *v. i.* [L. *concurro*, to run together; *con* and *curro*, to run; It. *concorrere;* Sp. *concurrir;* Port. *concorrer;* Fr. *concourir.*]

1. To meet in the same point; to agree.

Reason and sense *concur.* *Temple.*

2. To agree; to join or unite, as in one action or opinion; to meet, mind with mind; as, the two houses of parliament *concur in* the measure.

It has *with* before the person with whom one agrees.

Mr. Burke *concurred with* Lord Chatham in opinion.

It has *to* before the effect.

Extremes in man *concur to* general use. *Pope.*

3. To unite or be conjoined, with the consequential sense of aiding, or contributing power or influence to a common object.

Various causes may *concur* in the changes of temperature.

CONCUR'RENCE, *n.* A meeting or coming together; union; conjunction.

We have no other measure but of our own ideas, with the *concurrence* of other probable reasons, to persuade us. *Locke.*

2. A meeting of minds; agreement in opinion; union in design; implying joint approbation.

Tarquin the proud was expelled by the universal *concurrence* of nobles and people. *Swift.*

3. A meeting or conjunction, whether casual or intended; combination of agents, circumstances or events.

Struck with these great *concurrences* of things. *Crashaw.*

4. Agreement; consent; approbation. See No. 2.

5. Agreement or consent, implying joint aid or contribution of power or influence.

From these sublime images we collect the greatness of the work, and the necessity of the divine *concurrence* to it. *Rogers.*

6. A meeting, as of claims, or power; joint rights; implying equality in different persons or bodies; as a *concurrence* of jurisdiction in two different courts.

CONCUR'RENCY, *n.* The same as *concurrence; but little used.*

CONCUR'RENT, *a.* Meeting; uniting; accompanying; acting in conjuction; agreeing in the same act; contributing to the same event or effect; operating with.

I join with these laws the personal presence of the King's son, as a *concurrent* cause of this reformation. *Davies.*

All combined,
Your beauty, and my impotence of mind,
And his *concurrent* flame, that blew my fire. *Dryden.*

2. Conjoined; associate; concomitant.

There is no difference between the *concurrent* echo and the iterant, but the quickness or slowness of the return. *Bacon.*

3. Joint and equal; existing together and operating on the same objects. The courts of the United States, and those of the States have, in some cases, *concurrent* jurisdiction.

CONCUR'RENT, *n.* That which concurs; joint or contributory cause.

To all affairs of importance there are three necessary *concurrents*—time, industry and faculties. *Decay of Piety.*

CONCUR'RENTLY, *adv.* With concurrence; unitedly.

CONCUR'RING, *ppr.* Meeting in the same point; agreeing; running or acting together; uniting in action; contributing to the same event or effect; consenting.

A *concurring* figure, in geometry, is one which, being laid on another, exactly meets every part of it, or one which corresponds with it in all its parts.

CONCUSSA'TION, *n.* [See *Concussion.*] A violent shock or agitation.

CONCUS'SION, *n.* [L. *concussio*, from *concutio*, to shake, from *con* and *quatio*, *quasso*, to shake or shatter. From the sense of *discutio*, and *percutio*, we may infer that the primary sense is to beat, to strike, or to beat in pieces, to bruise, to beat down, Fr. *casser*, Eng. to *quash*, L. *cædo*, *cudo.* See Class Gd. No. 38. 40. 76. and Class Gs. No. 17.]

1. The act of shaking, particularly and properly, by the stroke or impulse of another body.

It is believed that great ringing of bells, in populous cities, hath dissipated pestilent air, which may be from the *concussion* of the air. *Bacon.*

2. The state of being shaken; a shock; as the *concussion* of the brain by a stroke. It is used also for shaking or agitation in general; as the *concussion* of the earth. *Woodward.*

CONCUS'SIVE, *a.* Having the power or quality of shaking. *Johnson.*

COND, *v. t.* [Fr. *conduire.*] In *seamen's language*, to conduct a ship; to direct the man at helm how to steer. *Bailey. Encyc.*

CONDEMN, *v. t. condem'.* [L. *condemno; con* and *damno*, to condemn, to disapprove, to doom, to devote; It. *condannare*, *dannare;* Port. *condenar;* Sp. *id.;* Fr. *condamner;* Arm. *condauni;* D. *doemen*, *verdoemen;* G. *verdammen;* Sw. *dôma*, *fördôma;* Dan. *dömmer*, *fordömmer;* Sax. *deman*, *fordeman*, to *deem*, to *doom*, to judge, to condemn. See *Damn*, *Deem*, *Doom.*]

1. To pronounce to be utterly wrong; to utter a sentence of disapprobation against; to censure; to blame. But the word often expresses more than *censure* or *blame*, and seems to include the idea of utter rejection; as, to *condemn* heretical opinions; to *condemn* one's conduct.

We *condemn* mistakes with asperity, where we pass over sins with gentleness. *Buckminster.*

2. To determine or judge to be wrong, or guilty; to disallow; to disapprove.

Beloved, if our heart *condemn* us not, we have confidence towards God. 1 John iii.

3. To witness against; to show or prove to be wrong, or guilty, by a contrary practice.

The men of Nineveh shall rise in judgment with this generation, and shall *condemn* it. Matth. xii.

4. To pronounce to be guilty; to sentence to punishment; to utter sentence against judicially; to doom; opposed to *acquit* or *absolve;* with *to* before the penalty.

The son of man shall be betrayed to the chief priests, and to the scribes, and they shall *condemn* him *to* death. Matth. xx.

He that believeth on him is not *condemned.* John iii.

5. To doom or sentence to pay a fine; to fine.

And the king of Egypt—*condemned* the land in a hundred talents of silver. 2 Chron. xxxvi.

6. To judge or pronounce to be unfit for use or service; as, the ship was *condemned* as not sea-worthy.

To judge or pronounce to be forfeited; as, the ship and her cargo were *condemned.*

CONDEM'NABLE, *a.* That may be condemned; blamable; culpable. *Brown.*

CONDEMNA'TION, *n.* [L. *condemnatio.*] The act of condemning; the judicial act of declaring one guilty, and dooming him to punishment.

For the judgment was by one to *condemnation.* Rom. v.

2. The state of being condemned.

Dost thou not fear God, seeing thou art in the same *condemnation.* Luke xxiii.

3. The cause or reason of a sentence of condemnation. John iii.

CONDEM'NATORY, *a.* Condemning; bearing condemnationn or censure; as a *condemnatory* sentence or decree.

CONDEM'NED, *pp.* Censured; pronounced to be wrong, guilty, worthless or forfeited; adjudged or sentenced to punishment.

CONDEM'NER, *n.* One who condemns or censures. *Taylor.*

CONDEM'NING, *ppr.* Censuring; disallowing; pronouncing to be wrong, guilty, worthless or forfeited; sentencing to punishment.

CONDENS'ABLE, *a.* [See *Condense.*] Capable of being condensed; that may be compressed into a smaller compass, and into a more close, compact state; as, vapor is *condensable.*

CONDENS'ATE, *v. t.* [See *Condense.*] To condense; to compress into a closer form to cause to take a more compact state; to make more dense.

CONDENS'ATE, *v. i.* To become more dense, close or hard.

CONDENS'ATE, *a.* Made dense; condensed; made more close or compact. *Peacham.*

CONDENSA'TION, *a.* [L. *condensatio.* See *Condense.*]
The act of making more dense or compact; or the act of causing the parts that compose a body to approach or unite more closely, either by mechanical pressure, or by a natural process; the state of being condensed. Dew and clouds are supposed to be formed by the *condensation* of vapor. It is opposed to *rarefaction* and *expansion.* Condensation is applicable to any compressible matter; and from condensation proceeds increased hardness, solidity, and weight.

CONDENS'ATIVE, *a.* Having a power or tendency to condense.

CONDENSE, *v. t. condens'.* [L. *condenso; con* and *denso*, to make thick or close; It. *condensare;* Sp. Port. *condensar;* Fr. *condenser.* See *Dense.*]
1. To make more close, thick or compact; to cause the particles of a body to approach, or to unite more closely, either by their own attraction or affinity, or by mechanical force. Thus, vapor is said to be *condensed* into water by the application of cold; and air is *condensed* in a tube by pressure. Hence the word is sometimes equivalent to *compress.*
2. To make thick; to inspissate; *applied to soft compressible substances.*
3. To compress into a smaller compass, or into a close body; to crowd; *applied to separate individuals.* Thus we say, *to condense* ideas into a smaller compass. *Dryden.*

CONDENSE, *v. i. condens'.* To become close or more compact, as the particles of a body; to approach or unite more closely; to grow thick.

Vapors *condense* and coalesce into small parcels. *Newton.*

CONDENSE, *a. condens'.* Close in texture or composition; compact; firm; dense; condensated. [See *Dense*, which is generally used.] *Milton.*

CONDENS'ED, *pp.* Made dense, or more close in parts; made or become compact; compressed into a narrower compass.

CONDENS'ER, *n.* He or that which condenses; particularly a pneumatic engine or syringe in which air may be compressed. It consists of a cylinder, in which is a movable piston to force the air into a receiver, and a valve to prevent the air from escaping. *Encyc.*

CONDENS'ITY, *n.* The state of being condensed; denseness; density. [*The latter are generally used.*]

COND'ER, *n.* [Fr. *conduire;* L. *conduco.* See *Cond.*]
1. A person who stands upon a cliff, or elevated part of the sea-coast, in the time of the herring fishery, to point out to the fishermen by signs, the course of the shoals of fish. *Cowel.*
2. One who gives directions to a helmsman how to steer the ship. *Encyc.*

CONDESCEND', *v. i.* [It. *condescendere;* Sp. *condescender;* Fr. *condescendre; con* and L. *descendo.* See *Descend.*]
1. To descend from the privileges of superior rank or dignity, to do some act to an inferior, which strict justice or the ordinary rules of civility do not require. Hence, to submit or yield, as to an inferior, implying an occasional relinquishment of distinction.

Mind not high things, but *condescend* to men of low estate. Rom. xii.

2. To recede from one's rights in negotiation, or common intercourse, to do some act, which strict justice does not require.

Spain's mighty monarch,
In gracious clemency does *condescend*,
On these conditions, to become your friend. *Dryden.*

3. To stoop or descend; to yield; to submit; implying a relinquishment of rank, or dignity of character, and sometimes a sinking into debasement.

Can they think me so broken, so debased,
With corporal servitude, that my mind ever
Will *condescend* to such absurd commands? *Milton.*

CONDESCEND'ENCE, *n.* A voluntary yielding or submission to an inferior.

You will observe [in the Turks] an insulting *condescendence* which bespeaks their contempt of you. *Eton.*

CONDESCEND'ING, *ppr.* Descending from rank or distinction in the intercourse of life; receding from rights or claims; yielding.
2. *a.* Yielding to inferiors; courteous; obliging.

CONDESCEND'INGLY, *adv.* By way of yielding to inferiors; with voluntary submission; by way of kind concession; courteously. *Atterbury.*

CONDESCEN'SION, *n.* Voluntary descent from rank, dignity or just claims; relinquishment of strict right; submission to inferiors in granting requests or performing acts which strict justice does not require. Hence, courtesy.

It forbids pride and commands humility, modesty and *condescension* to others. *Tillotson.*

Raphael, amidst his tenderness, shows such a dignity and *condescension* in all his behavior, as are suitable to a superior nature. *Addison.*

CONDESCEN'SIVE, *a.* Condescending; courteous. *Barrow.*

CONDESCENT', *n.* Condescension. [*Not used.*] *Bp. Hall.*

CONDI'GN, *a. condi'ne.* [L. *condignus; con* and *dignus*, worthy. See *Dignity.*]
1. Deserved; merited; suitable; *applied usually to punishment;* as, the malefactor has suffered *condign* punishment.
2. Worthy; merited; as *condign* praise. *Spenser. Shak.*

[*In the latter sense, seldom used.*]

CONDIG'NITY, *n.* Merit; desert. In *school divinity*, the merit of human actions which claims reward, on the score of justice. *Milner.*

CONDI'GNLY, *adv. condi'nely.* According to merit.

CONDI'GNNESS, *n. condi'neness.* Agreeableness to deserts; suitableness.

CON'DIMENT, *n.* [L. *condimentum*, from *condio*, to season, pickle or preserve.]
Seasoning; sauce; that which is used to give relish to meat or other food, and to gratify the taste.

As for radish and the like, they are for *condiments*, and not for nourishment. *Bacon.*

CONDISCI'PLE, *n.* [L. *condiscipulus; con* and *discipulus.* See *Disciple.*]
A school fellow; a learner in the same school, or under the same instructor.

CONDI'TE, *v. t.* [L. *condio, conditum.*] To prepare and preserve with sugar, salt, spices, or the like; to pickle; as, to *condite* pears, plums, quinces, mushrooms, &c. [*Little used.*] *Grew. Taylor.*

CONDI'TEMENT, *n.* A composition of conserves, powders, and spices, in the form of an electuary. [*Little used.*] *Bailey.*

CONDI'TING, *ppr.* Preserving. [*Little used.*] *Grew.*

CONDI''TION, *n.* [L. *conditio*, from *condo*, to build or make, to ordain; properly, to set or fix, or to set together or in order; *con* and *do*, to give; properly, to send.]
1. State; a particular mode of being; *applied to external circumstances, to the body, to the mind, and to things.* We speak of a good *condition* or a bad *condition*, in reference to wealth and poverty; in reference to health and sickness; in reference to a cheerful or depressed disposition of mind; and with reference to a sound or broken, perishing state of things. The word signifies a setting or fixing, and has a very general and indefinite application, coinciding nearly with *state*, from *sto*, to stand, and denotes that particular frame, form, mode or disposition, in which a thing exists, at any given time. A man is in a good *condition*, when he is thriving. A nation, with an exhausted treasury and burthened with taxes, is not in a *condition* to make war. A poor man is in a humble *condition.* Religion affords consolation to man in every *condition* of life. Exhortations should be adapted to the *condition* of the mind.

Condition, circumstance, is not the thing;
Bliss is the same in subject or in king. *Pope.*

2. Quality; property; attribute.

It seemed to us a *condition* and property of divine powers and beings to be hidden and unseen to others. *Bacon.*

3. State of the mind; temper; temperament; complexion. [See No. 1.] *Shak.*
4. Moral quality; virtue or vice. *Raleigh. South.*

[*These senses however fall within the first definition.*]

5. Rank, that is, state with respect to the orders or grades of society, or to property; as, persons of the best *condition.* *Clarendon.*
6. Terms of a contract or covenant; stipulation; that is, that which is set, fixed, established or proposed. What are the *conditions* of the treaty?

Make our *conditions* with yon captive king. *Dryden.*

He sendeth and desireth *conditions* of peace. Luke xiv.

7. A clause in a bond, or other contract containing terms or a stipulation that it is to be performed, and in case of failure, the penalty of the bond is to be incurred.
8. Terms given, or provided, as the ground of something else; that which is established, or to be done, or to happen, as requisite to another act; as, I will pay a sum of money, on *condition* you will engage to refund it.

A *condition* is a clause of contingency, on the happening of which the estate granted may be defeated. *Blackstone.*

CONDI''TION, *v. i.* To make terms; to stipulate.

It is one thing to *condition* for a good office, and another to execute it.

CONDI''TION, *v. t.* To contract; to stipulate.

It was *conditioned* between Saturn and Titan, that Saturn should put to death all his male children. *Raleigh.*

CONDI''TIONAL, *a.* Containing or depending on a condition or conditions; made with limitations; not absolute; made or granted on certain terms. A *conditional* promise is one which is to be performed, when something else stipulated is done or has taken place. A *conditional* fee, in law, is one which is granted upon *condition*, that if the donee shall die without such particular heirs as are specified, the estate shall revert to the donor. Hence it is a fee restrained to particular heirs, to the exclusion of others.

2. In *grammar* and *logic*, expressing a condition or supposition; as a *conditional* word, mode, or tense; a *conditional* syllogism.

CONDI''TIONAL, *n.* A limitation. *Bacon.*

CONDITIONAL'ITY, *n.* The quality of being conditional, or limited; limitation by certain terms.

CONDI''TIONALLY, *adv.* With certain limitations; on particular terms or stipulations; not absolutely or positively.

We see large preferments tendered to him, but *conditionally*, upon his doing wicked offices. *South.*

CONDI''TIONARY, *a.* Conditional; stipulated. [*Not used.*] *Norris.*

CONDI''TIONATE, *a.* Conditional; established on certain terms. [*Not used.*] *Hammond.*

CONDI''TIONATE, *v. t.* To qualify; to regulate. [*Not in use.*] *Brown.*

CONDI''TIONED, *pp.* Stipulated; containing terms to be performed.

2. *a.* Having a certain state or qualities. This word is usually preceded by some qualifying term; as *good-conditioned; ill-conditioned; best-conditioned.*

CONDI''TIONLY, *adv.* On certain terms. [*Not used.*] *Sidney.*

CONDO'LE, *v. i.* [L. *condoleo; con*, with, and *doleo*, to ache, or to grieve.]

To feel pain, or to grieve, at the distress or misfortunes of another.

Your friends would have cause to rejoice, rather than *condole with* you.

It is followed by *with* before the person for whom we feel grief.

CONDO'LE, *v. t.* To lament or bewail with another, or on account of another's misfortune. [*Unusual.*]

Why should our poet petition Isis for her safe delivery, and afterwards *condole* her miscarriage? *Dryden. Milton.*

CONDO'LEMENT, *n.* Grief; pain of mind, at another's loss or misfortune; sorrow; mourning. *Shak.*

CONDO'LENCE, *n.* Pain of mind, or grief excited by the distress, or misfortune of another. *Arbuthnot.*

CONDO'LER, *n.* One who condoles.

CONDO'LING, *ppr.* Grieving at another's distress.

CONDO'LING, *n.* Expression of grief for another's loss.

CON'DOMA, *n.* An animal of the goat kind, as large as a stag, and of a gray color. *Dict. Nat. Hist.*

It is a species of Antelope, the *A. strepsiceros.*

CONDONA'TION, *n.* [L. *condono.*] The act of pardoning. [*Little used.*]

CON'DOR, *n.* The largest species of fowl hitherto discovered; a native of South America. Some naturalists class it with the vulture; others, with the eagle. The wings of the largest, when expanded, are said to extend 15 or 18 feet; and the fowl has strength to bear off a calf or a deer. *Dict. Nat. Hist.*

The size of the Condor has been greatly exaggerated. It is about the size of the *Lämmer-geyer* or vulture of the Alps, which it resembles in its habits. It is properly a vulture. *Humboldt. Cuvier.*

CONDU'CE, *v. i.* [L. *conduco; con* and *duco*, to lead; Sp. *conducir;* It. *condurre.*]

To lead or tend; to contribute; followed by *to.*

They may *conduce to* farther discoveries for completing the theory of light. *Newton.*

To conduce to includes the sense of aiding, tending to produce, or furnishing the means; hence it is sometimes equivalent to *promote*, advance, or further. Virtue *conduces to* the welfare of society. Religion *conduces to* temporal happiness. Temperance *conduces to* health and long life.

In the transitive sense, to *conduct*, it is not authorized.

CONDU'CEMENT, *n.* A leading or tending to; tendency. *Gregory.*

CONDU'CENT, *a.* Tending or contributing to. *Laud.*

CONDU'CIBLE, *a.* [L. *conducibilis.*] Leading or tending to; having the power of conducing; having a tendency to promote or forward.

Our Savior hath enjoined us a reasonable service; all his laws are in themselves *conducible* to the temporal interest of them that observe them. *Bentley.*

[*This word is less used than* conducive.]

CONDU'CIBLENESS, *n.* The quality of leading or contributing to any end. *More.*

CONDU'CIVE, *a.* That may conduce or contribute; having a tendency to promote.

An action, however *conducive* to the good of our country, will be represented as prejudicial to it. *Addison.*

CONDU'CIVENESS, *n.* The quality of conducing or tending to promote. *Boyle.*

CON'DUCT, *n.* [Sp. *conducta;* It. *condotta;* Fr. *conduite;* from the L. *conductus*, but with a different sense, from *conduco*, to lead; *con* and *duco.* See *Duke.*]

1. Literally, the act of leading; guidance; command. So Waller has used it.

Conduct of armies is a prince's art.

2. The act of convoying, or guarding; guidance or bringing along under protection. *Shak.*

3. Guard on the way; convoy; escort. *Shak.*

[*These senses are now unusual, though not improper.*]

4. In *a general sense*, personal behavior; course of actions; deportment; *applicable equally to a good or bad course of actions;* as laudable *conduct;* detestable *conduct.* The word seems originally to have been followed with *life, actions, affairs*, or other term; as the *conduct of life;* the *conduct of actions;* that is, the leading along of life or actions.

Young men in the *conduct* and *manage of actions* embrace more than they can hold. *Bacon.*

What in the *conduct of our life* appears. *Dryden.*

But by custom, *conduct* alone is now used to express the idea of behavior or course of life and manners.

5. Exact behavior; regular life. [*Unusual.*] *Swift.*

6. Management; mode of carrying on.

Christianity has humanized the *conduct* of war. *Paley.*

7. The title of two clergymen appointed to read prayers at Eton College in England. *Mason.*

CONDUCT', *v. t.* [Sp. *conducir;* Port. *conduzir*, to conduct, and to conduce; Fr. *conduire;* It. *condurre;* L. *conduco.* But the English verb is from the noun *conduct*, or the Lat. participle.]

1. To lead; to bring along; to guide; to accompany and show the way.

And Judah came to Gilgal—to *conduct* the king over Jordan. 2 Sam. xix.

2. To lead; to direct or point out the way.

The precepts of Christ will *conduct* us to happiness.

3. To lead; to usher in; to introduce; to attend in civility.

Pray receive them nobly, and *conduct* them Into our presence. *Shak.*

4. To give a direction to; to manage; *applied to things;* as, the farmer *conducts* his affairs with prudence.

5. To lead, as a commander; to direct; to govern; to command; as, to *conduct* an army or a division of troops.

6. With the reciprocal pronoun, to *conduct one's self*, is to behave. Hence, by a customary omission of the pronoun, to *conduct*, in an intransitive sense, is to behave; to direct personal actions. [See the Noun.]

7. To escort; to accompany and protect on the way.

CONDUCT'ED, *pp.* Led; guided; directed; introduced; commanded; managed.

CONDUCT'ING, *ppr.* Leading; escorting; introducing; commanding; behaving; managing.

CONDUC'TION, *n.* The act of training up. [*Not in use.*] *B. Jonson.*

CONDUCTI''TIOUS, *a.* [L. *conductitius*, from *conduco*, to hire.]

Hired; employed for wages. *Ayliffe.*

CONDUCT'OR, *n.* A leader; a guide; one who goes before or accompanies, and shows the way.

2. A chief; a commander; one who leads an army or a people.

3. A director; a manager. *Addison.*

4. In *surgery*, an instrument which serves to direct the knife in cutting for the stone, and in laying up sinuses and fistulas; also, a machine to secure a fractured limb. *Coxe. Encyc.*

5. In *electrical experiments*, any body that receives and communicates electricity; such

as metals and moist substances. Bodies which repel it, or into which it will not pass, are called *non-conductors*. Hence,

6. A metallic rod erected by buildings or in ships, to conduct lightning to the earth or water, and protect the building from its effects.

CONDUCT'RESS, *n.* A female who leads or directs; a directress.

CON'DUIT, *n.* [Fr. *conduit*, the participle of *conduire*, L. *conducere*, to conduct; Sp. *conducto*; It. *condotto*; Port. *conducta*.]

1. A canal or pipe for the conveyance of water; an aqueduct. Conduits are made of lead, stone, cast iron, wood, &c., above or below the surface of the earth.

2. A vessel that conveys the blood or other fluid.

> The *conduits* of my blood. *Shak.*

3. A conductor.

> These organs are the nerves which are the *conduits* to convey them from without to their audience in the brain. *Locke.*

4. A pipe or cock for drawing off liquor. *Shak.*

5. Any channel that conveys water or fluids; a sink, sewer or drain.

CONDU'PLICATE, *a.* [L. *conduplicatus*, from *conduplico*, to double or fold; *con* and *duplico*. See *Double*.]

Doubled or folded over or together; as the leaves of a bud. *Martyn.*

CONDU'PLICATE, *v.t.* To double; to fold together.

CONDU'PLICATED, *a.* Doubled; folded together.

CONDUPLICA'TION, *n.* [L. *conduplicatio*.] A doubling; a duplicate. *Johnson.*

CON'DYL, *n.* [L. *condylus*; Gr. κονδυλος.] A protuberance on the end of a bone; a knot, or joint; a knuckle. *Coxe.*

CON'DYLOID, *a.* [Gr. κονδυλος, and ειδος, form.]

The condyloid process is the posterior protuberance at the extremities of the under jaw; an oblong rounded head, which is received into the fossa of the temporal bone, forming a movable articulation. The anterior is called the coronoid process. *Encyc.*

CON'DYLOID, *n.* The apophysis of a bone; the projecting soft end, or process of a bone. *Coxe.*

CONE, *n.* [Fr. *cone*; It. and Sp. *cono*; from L. *conus*; Gr. κωνος; W. *con*, that which shoots to a point, from extending; W. *connyn*, a tail; *conyn*, a stalk; *cono*, a spruce fellow. It coincides in radical sense with the root of *can* and *begin*.]

1. A solid body or figure having a circle for its base, and its top terminated in a point or vertex, like a sugar loaf.

2. In *botany*, the conical fruit of several evergreen trees, as of the pine, fir, cedar and cypress. It is composed of woody scales, usually opening, and has a seed at the base of each scale. *Martyn.*

A *cone of rays*, in optics, includes all the rays of light which proceed from a radiant point and fall upon the surface of a glass. *Encyc.*

A *right cone*, is when its axis is perpendicular to its base, and its sides equal. It is formed by the revolution of a right-angled plane triangle about one of its sides.

A *scalene cone*, is when its axis is inclined to its base and its sides unequal. *Bailey.*

CO'NEPATE or **CO'NEPATL**, *n.* An animal of the weasel kind in America, resembling the pole-cat in form and size, and in its fetid stench. *Dict. Nat. Hist.*

CONEY. [See *Cony*.]

CONFAB'ULATE, *v. i.* [L. *confabulor*; *con* and *fabulor*, to tell. See *Fable*.]

To talk familiarly together; to chat; to prattle.

> If birds *confabulate* or no. [*Little used.*] *Cowper.*

CONFABULA'TION, *n.* [L. *confabulatio*.] Familiar talk; easy, unrestrained, unceremonious conversation. [*Not an elegant word, and little used.*]

CONFAB'ULATORY, *a.* Belonging to familiar talk. [*Little used.*]

CONFAMIL'IAR, *a.* Very familiar. [*Not in use.*]

CONFARREA'TION, *n.* [L. *confarreatio*; *con* and *farreo*, to join in marriage with a cake, from *far*, corn or meal.]

The solemnization of marriage among the Romans, by a ceremony in which the bridegoom and bride tasted a cake made of flour with salt and water, called *far* or *panis farreus*, in presence of the high priest and at least ten witnesses. *Ayliffe. Adam.*

CONFA'TED, *a.* Fated together. [*Not in use.*]

CONFECT', *v. t.* To make sweetmeats. [*Not used.* See *Comfit*.]

CON'FECT, *n.* [L. *confectus*, *conficio*. See *Comfit*.]

Something prepared with sugar or honey, as fruit, herbs, roots and the like; a sweetmeat. *Harvey.*

CONFEC'TION, *n.* [L. *confectio*, from *conficio*; *con* and *facio*, to make.]

1. Any thing prepared with sugar, as fruit; a sweetmeat; something preserved. *Bacon. Encyc.*

2. A composition or mixture. *Bacon.*

3. A soft electuary. *Encyc.*

CONFEC'TIONARY, } *n.* One whose occupation is to make, or to sell sweetmeats, &c.
CONFEC'TIONER, } *Boyle. Shak.*

[*The latter word is most generally used.*]

CONFEC'TIONARY, *n.* A place for sweetmeats; a place where sweetmeats and similar things are made or sold.

2. Sweetmeats in general; things prepared or sold by a confectioner.

CONFEC'TOR, *n.* [L.] An officer in the Roman games, whose business was to kill any beast that was dangerous. *Milner.*

CONFEC'TORY, *a.* Pertaining to the art of making sweetmeats. *Beaum.*

CONFED'ERACY, *n.* [Low L. *confœderatio*; *con* and *fœderatio*, from *fœdus*, a league. See *Federal* and *Wed*.]

1. A league, or covenant; a contract between two or more persons, bodies of men or states, combined in support of each other, in some act or enterprise; mutual engagement; federal compact.

> The friendships of the world are oft
> *Confederacies* in vice. *Addison.*

> A *confederacy* of princes to check innovation. *Anon.*

2. The persons, states or nations united by a league.

> Virgil has a whole *confederacy* against him *Dryden.*

3. In *law*, a combination of two or more persons to commit an unlawful act. *Encyc.*

CONFED'ERATE, *a.* [Low L. *confœderatus*.]

United in a league; allied by treaty; engaged in a confederacy.

> These were *confederate* with Abram. Gen. xiv.

> Syria is *confederate* with Ephraim. Is. vii.

CONFED'ERATE, *n.* One who is united with others in a league; a person or nation engaged in a confederacy; an ally. *Shak. Dryden.*

CONFED'ERATE, *v. i.* [Fr. *confederer*; Low L. *confœdero*. But the English verb seems to be directly from the adjective, supra.]

To unite in a league; to join in a mutual contract or covenant.

> By words men come to know one another's minds; by these they covenant and *confederate* *South.*

> The colonies of America *confederated* in 1775.

> Several States of Europe have sometimes *confederated* for mutual safety.

CONFED'ERATE, *v. t.* To unite in a league; to ally.

> With these the Piercies them *confederate.* *Daniel.*

CONFED'ERATED, *pp.* United in a league.

CONFED'ERATING, *ppr.* Uniting in a league.

CONFEDERA'TION, *n.* [Fr. *confederation*; It. *confederazione*; Low L. *confœderatio*; *con* and *fœderatio*.]

1. The act of confederating; a league; a compact for mutual support; alliance; particularly of princes, nations or states.

> The three princes enter into a strict league and *confederation.* *Bacon.*

2. The United States of America are sometimes called the *confederation.*

CONFER', *v. i.* [Fr. *conferer*; It. *conferire*; Sp. *conferir*; L. *confero*; *con* and *fero*, to bear, to bring forth, to show, to declare. See *Bear*.]

To discourse; to converse; to consult together; implying conversation on some serious or important subject, in distinction from mere talk or light familiar conversation; followed by *with*.

> Adonijah *conferred with* Joab and Abiathar. 1 Kings i.

> Festus *conferred with* the council. Acts xxv.

CONFER', *v. t.* To give, or bestow; followed by *on*.

> Coronation *confers on* the king no royal authority. *South.*

This word is particularly used to express the grant of favors, benefits and privileges to be enjoyed, or rights which are to be permanent; as, to *confer* on one the privileges of a citizen; to *confer* a title or an honor.

2. To compare; to examine by comparison; literally, to bring together. [See *Compare*.]

> If we *confer* these observations with others of the like nature. *Boyle.*

[*This sense, though genuine, is now obsolete.*]

3. To contribute; to conduce to; that is, to bring to. The closeness of parts *confers* much to the strength of the union, or in-

transitively, *confers to* the strength of the union. *Obs.* *Glanville.*

CON'FERENCE, *n.* [Fr. *conference*; Sp. *conferencia*; It. *conferenza.* See *Confer.*]

1. The act of conversing on a serious subject; a discoursing between two or more, for the purpose of instruction, consultation, or deliberation; formal discourse; oral discussion.

For they who seemed to be somewhat, in *conference* added nothing to me. Gal. ii.

The ministers had a *conference* at Ratisbon.

2. A meeting for consultation, discussion or instruction.

3. Comparison; examination of things by comparison.

The mutual *conference* of observations. The *conference* of different passages of scripture. *Hooker.*

[*This sense is, I believe, now obsolete.*]

CONFER'RED, *pp.* Given; imparted; bestowed.

CONFER'RER, *n.* One who confers; one who converses; one who bestows.

CONFER'RING, *ppr.* Conversing together; bestowing.

CONFER'RING, *n.* The act of bestowing.

2. Comparison; examination.

CONFESS', *v. t.* [Fr. *confesser*; It. *confessare*; Sp. *confesar*; Port. *confessar*; from L. *confiteor*, *confessum*; *con* and *fateor*, to own or acknowledge; Ir. *faoisdin.*]

1. To own, acknowledge or avow, as a crime, a fault, a charge, a debt, or something that is against one's interest, or reputation.

Human faults with human grief *confess.* *Prior.*

I *confess* the argument against me is good and not easily refuted.

Let us frankly *confess* our sins.

"*Confess thee* freely of thy sins," used by Shakspeare, is not legitimate, unless in the sense of Catholics.

2. In *the Catholic Church*, to acknowledge sins and faults to a priest; to disclose the state of the conscience to a priest, in private, with a view to absolution; sometimes with the reciprocal pronoun.

The beautiful votary *confessed herself* to this celebrated father. *Addison.*

3. To own, avow or acknowledge; publicly to declare a belief in and adherence to.

Whoever shall *confess* me before men. Math. x.

4. To own and acknowledge, as true disciples, friends or children.

Him will I *confess* before my father who is in heaven. *Ibm.*

5. To own; to acknowledge; to declare to be true, or to admit or assent to in words; opposed to deny.

Then will I *confess* to thee, that thine own right hand can save thee. Job xl.

These—*confessed* that they were strangers and pilgrims on earth. Heb. xi.

6. To show by the effect; to prove; to attest.

Tall thriving trees *confessed* the fruitful mold. *Pope.*

7. To hear or receive the confession of another; as, the priest *confessed* the nuns.

CONFESS', *v. i.* To make confession; to disclose faults, or the state of the conscience; as, this man went to the priest to *confess.*

CONFESS'ANT, *n.* One who confesses to a priest. *Bacon.*

CONFESS'ARY, *n.* One who makes a confession. [*Not used.*] *Hall.*

CONFESS'ED, *pp.* Owned; acknowledged; declared to be true; admitted in words; avowed; admitted to disclose to a priest.

CONFESS'EDLY, *adv.* By confession, or acknowledgment; avowedly; undeniably. Demosthenes was *confessedly* the greatest orator in Greece.

2. With avowed purpose; as, his object was *confessedly* to secure to himself a benefice.

CONFESS'ING, *ppr.* Owning; avowing; declaring to be true or real; granting or admitting by assent; receiving disclosure of sins, or the state of the conscience of another.

CONFES'SION, *n.* The acknowledgment of a crime, fault or something to one's disadvantage; open declaration of guilt, failure, debt, accusation, &c.

With the mouth *confession* is made to salvation. Rom. x.

2. Avowal; the act of acknowledging; profession.

Who before Pontius Pilate witnessed a good *confession.* 1 Tim. vi.

3. The act of disclosing sins or faults to a priest; the disburdening of the conscience privately to a confessor; sometimes called *auricular confession.*

4. A formulary in which the articles of faith are comprised; a creed to be assented to or signed, as a preliminary to admission into a church.

5. The acknowledgment of a debt by a debtor before a justice of the peace, &c., on which judgment is entered and execution issued.

CONFES'SIONAL, *n.* The seat where a priest or confessor sits to hear confessions; a confession-chair.

CONFES'SIONARY, *n.* [Sp. *confesionario.*] A confession-chair, as above.

CONFES'SIONARY, *a.* Pertaining to auricular confession.

CONFES'SIONIST, *n.* One who makes a profession of faith. *Mountagu.*

CONFESS'OR, *n.* [Fr. *confesseur*; Sp. *confesor.*]

1. One who confesses; one who acknowledges his sins.

2. One who makes a profession of his faith in the christian religion. The word is appropriately used to denote one who avows his religion in the face of danger, and adheres to it, in defiance of persecution and torture. It was formerly used as synonymous with *martyr*; afterwards it was applied to those who, having been persecuted and tormented, were permitted to die in peace. It was used also for such christians as lived a good life, and died with the reputation of sanctity. *Encyc.*

3. A priest; one who hears the confessions of others, and has power to grant them absolution. *Romish Church.*

CONFEST', *pp.* [for *confessed.*] Owned; open; acknowledged; apparent; not disputed.

CONFEST'LY, *adv.* [for *confessedly.*] Avowedly; indisputably. [*Little used.*]

CON'FIDANT, *n.* [See *Confident.*]

CONFI'DE, *v. t.* [L. *confido*; *con* and *fido*, to trust; It. *confidare*; Sp. Port. *confiar*; Fr. *confier*; Arm. *fizyout.* See *Faith.*] To trust; to rely on, with a persuasion of faithfulness or veracity in the person trusted or of the reality of a fact; to give credit to; to believe in, with assurance; followed by *in.* The prince *confides in* his ministers. The minister *confides in* the strength and resources of the nation. We *confide in* the veracity of the sacred historians. We *confide in* the truth of a report.

CONFI'DE, *v. t.* To entrust; to commit to the charge of, with a belief in the fidelity of the person entrusted; to deliver into possession of another, with assurance of safe keeping, or good management; followed by *to.* We *confide* a secret *to* a friend. The prince *confides* a negotiation *to* his envoy. The common interests of the United States are *confided to* the Congress.

They would take the property out of the hands of those to whom it was *confided* by the charter. *Hopkinson.*

Congress may, under the constitution, *confide* to the circuit court, jurisdiction of all offenses against the U. States. *Story.*

CONFI'DED, *pp.* Entrusted; committed to the care of, for preservation, or for performance or exercise.

CON'FIDENCE, *n.* [L. *confidentia*; It. *confidenza*; Sp. *confianza*; Fr. *confiance*, *confidence.* See *Confide.*]

1. A trusting, or reliance; an assurance of mind or firm belief in the integrity, stability or veracity of another, or in the truth and reality of a fact.

It is better to trust in the Lord, than to put *confidence* in man. Ps. cxviii.

I rejoice that I have *confidence* in you in all things. 2 Cor. vii.

Mutual *confidence* is the basis of social happiness.

I place *confidence* in a statement, or in an official report.

2. Trust; reliance; *applied to one's own abilities, or fortune*; belief in one's own competency.

His times being rather prosperous than calm, had raised his *confidence* by success. *Bacon.*

3. That in which trust is placed; ground of trust; he or that which supports.

Israel was ashamed of Beth-el their *confidence.* Jer. xlviii.

Jehovah shall be thy *confidence.* Prov. iii.

4. Safety, or assurance of safety; security.

They shall build houses and plant vineyards; yea, they shall dwell with *confidence.* Ezek. xxviii.

5. Boldness; courage.

Preaching the kingdom of God with all *confidence.* Acts xxviii.

6. Excessive boldness; assurance, proceeding from vanity or a false opinion of one's own abilities, or excellencies.

Their *confidence* ariseth from too much credit given to their own wits. *Hooker.*

CON'FIDENT, *a.* Having full belief; trusting; relying; fully assured.

I am *confident* that much may be done towards the improvement of philosophy. *Boyle.*

The troops rush on, *confident* of success.

2. Positive; dogmatical; as a *confident* talker.

3. Trusting; without suspicion.

Rome, be as just and gracious unto me,
As I am *confident* and kind to thee. *Shak.*

4. Bold to a vice; having an excess of assurance.

The fool rageth and is *confident.* Prov. xiv.

CON'FIDENT, *n.* One entrusted with secrets; a confidential or bosom friend. *Dryden. Coxe. Mitford.*

[*This word has been usually, but improperly, written* confidant. *I have followed the regular English orthography, as Coxe and Mitford have done.*]

CONFIDEN'TIAL, *a.* Enjoying the confidence of another; trusty; that may be safely trusted; as a *confidential* friend.

2. That is to be treated or kept in confidence; private: as a *confidential* matter.

3. Admitted to special confidence.

CONFIDEN'TIALLY, *adv.* In confidence; in reliance or secrecy.

CON'FIDENTLY, *adv.* With firm trust; with strong assurance; without doubt or wavering of opinion; positively; as, to believe *confidently;* to assert *confidently.*

CON'FIDENTNESS, *n.* Confidence; the quality or state of having full reliance.

CONFI'DER, *n.* One who confides; one who entrusts to another.

CONFIG'URATE, *v. i.* [L. *configuro.* See *Configure.*]

To show like the aspects of the planets towards each other. *Jordan.*

CONFIGURA'TION, *n.* [Fr. from L. *configuro.*]

1. External form, figure, shape; the figure which bounds a body, and gives it its external appearance, constituting one of the principal differences between bodies. *Encyc.*

2. Aspects of the planets; or the face of the horoscope, according to the aspects of the planets toward each other at any time. *Bailey. Johnson.*

3. Resemblance of one figure to another. *Bailey. Jones.*

CONFIG'URE, *v. t.* [L. *configuro; con* and *figuro,* to form; *figura,* figure.]

To form; to dispose in a certain form, figure or shape. *Bentley.*

CONFI'NABLE, *a.* That may be confined or limited. *Bp. Hall.*

CON'FINE, *n.* [L. *confinis,* at the end or border, adjoining; *confinium,* a limit; *con* and *finis,* end, border, limit; It. *confine, confino;* Sp. *confin;* Fr. Port. *confins.* See *Fine.*]

Border; edge; exterior part; the part of any territory which is at or near the end or extremity. It is used generally in the plural, and applied chiefly to countries, territory, cities, rivers, &c. We say, the *confines* of France, or of Scotland, and figuratively, the *confines* of light, of death, or the grave; but never, the *confines* of a book, table or small piece of land.

CON'FINE, *a.* Bordering on; lying on the border; adjacent; having a common boundary. *Johnson.*

CON'FINE, *v. i.* [Fr. *confiner;* Sp. *confinar;* It. *confinare.*]

To border on; to touch the limit; to be adjacent or contiguous, as one territory, kingdom or state to another; usually followed by *on;* sometimes by *with.* England *confines on* Scotland. Connecticut *confines on* Massachusetts, New-York, Rhode Island and the sound.

CONFI'NE, *v. t.* [Sp. *confinar;* Fr. *confiner.* See Supra.]

1. To bound or limit; to restrain within limits; hence, to imprison; to shut up; to restrain from escape by force or insurmountable obstacles, in *a general sense;* as, to *confine* horses or cattle to an inclosure; to *confine* water in a pond, to dam; to *confine* a garrison in a town; to *confine* a criminal in prison.

2. To immure; to keep close, by a voluntary act; to be much at home or in retirement; as, a man *confines* himself to his studies, or to his house.

3. To limit or restrain voluntarily, in some act or practice; as, a man may *confine* himself to the use of animal food.

4. To tie or bind; to make fast or close; as, to *confine* air in a bladder, or corn in a bag or sack.

5. To restrain by a moral force; as, to *confine* men by laws. The constitution of the United States *confines* the states to the exercise of powers of a local nature.

CONFI'NED, *pp.* Restrained within limits; imprisoned; limited; secluded; close.

CON'FINELESS, *a.* Boundless; unlimited; without end. *Shak.*

CONFI'NEMENT, *n.* Restraint within limits; imprisonment; any restraint of liberty by force or other obstacle or necessity; as the *confinement* of a debtor or criminal to a prison, or of troops to a besieged town.

2. Voluntary restraint; seclusion; as the *confinement* of a man to his house, or to his studies.

3. Voluntary restraint in action or practice; as *confinement* to a particular diet.

4. Restraint from going abroad by sickness, particularly by child-birth.

CONFI'NER, *n.* He or that which limits or restrains.

CON'FINER, *n.* A borderer; one who lives on confines, or near the border of a country. *Shak.*

2. He or that which is near the limit; a near neighbor; he or that which is adjacent or contiguous; as *confiners* in art; *confiners* between plants and animals, as oysters. *Wotton. Bacon.*

CONFI'NING, *ppr.* Restraining; limiting; imprisoning.

CONFIN'ITY, *n.* [L. *confinitas.*] Contiguity; nearness; neighborhood. *Dict.*

CONFIRM', *v. t. conferm'.* [L. *confirmo; con* and *firmo,* to make firm. See *Firm.*]

1. To make firm, or more firm; to add strength to; to strengthen; as, health is *confirmed* by exercise.

2. To fix more firmly; to settle or establish.

Confirming the souls of the disciples. Acts xiv.

I *confirm* thee in the priesthood. *Maccabees.*

Confirm the crown to me and to mine heirs. *Shak.*

3. To make firm or certain; to give new assurance of truth or certainty; to put past doubt.

The testimony of Christ was *confirmed* in you. 1 Cor. 1.

4. To fix; to radicate; as, the patient has a *confirmed* dropsy.

5. To strengthen; to ratify; as, to *confirm* an agreement, promise, covenant or title.

6. To make more firm; to strengthen; as, to *confirm* an opinion, a purpose or resolution.

7. To admit to the full privileges of a christian, by the imposition of hands. *Johnson.*

CONFIRM'ABLE, *a. conferm'able.* That may be confirmed, established or ratified; capable of being made more certain. *Brown.*

CONFIRMA'TION, *n.* The act of confirming or establishing; a fixing, settling, establishing or making more certain or firm; establishment.

In the defense and *confirmation* of the gospel, ye are all partakers of my grace. Phil. i.

2. The act of ratifying; as the *confirmation* of a promise, covenant, or stipulation.

3. The act of giving new strength; as the *confirmation* of health.

4. The act of giving new evidence; as the *confirmation* of opinion or report.

5. That which confirms; that which gives new strength or assurance; additional evidence; proof; convincing testimony; as, this fact or this argument is a *confirmation* of what was before alledged.

6. In *law,* an assurance of title, by the conveyance of an estate or right *in esse,* from one man to another, by which a voidable estate is made sure or unavoidable, or a particular estate is increased, or a possession made perfect. *Blackstone.*

7. In *church affairs,* the act of ratifying the election of an archbishop or bishop, by the king, or by persons of his appointment. *Blackstone.*

8. The act or ceremony of laying on of hands, in the admission of baptized persons to the enjoyment of christian privileges. The person to be confirmed brings his godfather and godmother, and takes upon himself the baptismal vows. This is practiced in the Greek, Roman and Episcopal churches. *Hammond. Encyc.*

CONFIRM'ATIVE, *a. conferm'ative.* Having the power of confirming; tending to establish.

CONFIRMA'TOR, *n.* He or that which confirms. *Brown.*

CONFIRM'ATORY, *a. conferm'atory.* That serves to confirm; giving additional strength, force or stability, or additional assurance or evidence.

2. Pertaining to the rite of confirmation. *Bp. Compton.*

CONFIRM'ED, *pp. conferm'ed.* Made more firm; strengthened; established.

2. Admitted to the full privileges of the church.

CONFIRM'EDNESS, *n. conferm'edness.* A fixed state.

CONFIRM'ER, *n. conferm'er.* He or that which confirms, establishes or ratifies; one that produces new evidence; an attester. *Shak.*

CONFIRM'ING, *ppr. conferm'ing.* Making firm or more firm; strengthening; ratifying; giving additional evidence or proof; establishing.

CONFIRM'INGLY, *adv. conferm'ingly.* In a manner to strengthen or make firm. *B. Jonson.*

CONFIS'CABLE, *a.* [See *Confiscate.*] That may be confiscated; liable to forfeiture. *Browne.*

CON'FISCATE, *v. t.* [L. *confisco; con* and *fiscus,* a basket, hamper or bag; hence, revenue or the Emperor's treasure; It. *confiscare;* Fr. *confisquer;* Sp. *confiscar.*]

To adjudge to be forfeited to the public treasury, as the goods or estate of a traitor or other criminal, by way of penalty; or to condemn private forfeited property to public use.

The estate of the rebels was seized and *confiscated*. *Anon.*

CON'FISCATE, *a.* Forfeited and adjudged to the public treasury, as the goods of a criminal.

CON'FISCATED, *pp.* Adjudged to the public treasury, as forfeited goods or estate.

CON'FISCATING, *ppr.* Adjudging to the public use.

CONFISCA'TION, *n.* The act of condemning as forfeited, and adjudging to the public treasury; as the goods of a criminal who has committed a public offense. Ezra vii. 26.

CON'FISCATOR, *n.* One who confiscates. *Burke.*

CONFIS'CATORY, *a.* Consigning to forfeiture. *Burke.*

CON'FIT, *n.* A sweetmeat. [See *Confect.*]

CON'FITENT, *n.* [L. *confitens.* See *Confess.*] One who confesses his sins and faults. [*Not much used.*]

CON'FITURE, *n.* [Fr. from *confire, confit*; L. *confectura, conficio; con* and *facio.* This word is corrupted into *comfit*, which is now used.]
A sweetmeat; confection; comfit. *Bacon.*

CONFIX', *v. t.* [L. *configo, confixum; con* and *figo*, to fix, to thrust to or on. See *Fix.*]
To fix down; to fasten. *Shak.*

CONFIX'ED, *pp.* Fixed down or to; fastened.

CONFIX'ING, *ppr.* Fixing to or on; fastening.

CONFIX'URE, *n.* The act of fastening. *Mountagu.*

CONFLA'GRANT, *a.* [L. *conflagrans, conflagro; con* and *flagro*, to burn. See *Flagrant.*]
Burning together; involved in a common flame. *Milton.*

CONFLAGRA'TION, *n.* [L. *conflagratio.* See *Flagrant.*]
1. A great fire or the burning of any great mass of combustibles, as a house, but more especially a city or a forest. *Bentley.*
2. The burning of the world at the consummation of things, when "the elements shall melt with fervent heat."

CONFLA'TION, *n.* [L. *conflatio*, from *conflo; con* and *flo*, to blow. See *Blow.*]
1. The act of blowing two or more instruments together. *Bacon.*
2. A melting or casting of metal. [*Little used.*]

CONFLEX'URE *n.* A bending. [*Not used.*]

CON'FLICT, *n.* [L. *conflictus*, from *confligo; con* and *fligo*, to strike, Eng. to *flog*, to *lick*; Sp. *conflicto*; It. *conflitto*; Fr. *conflit.*]
1. A striking or dashing against each other, as of two moving bodies in opposition; violent collision of substances; as a *conflict* of elements, or waves; a *conflict* of particles in ebullition.
2. A fighting; combat, as between men, and applicable to individuals or to armies; as, the *conflict* was long and desperate.
3. Contention; strife; contest.

In our last *conflict*, four of his five wits went halting off. *Shak.*

4. A struggling with difficulties; a striving to oppose, or overcome.

The good man has a perpetual *conflict* with his evil propensities.

5. A struggling of the mind; distress; anxiety. Col. ii.
6. The last struggle of life; agony; as the *conflict* with death. *Thomson.*
7. Opposing operations; countervailing action; collision; opposition.

In exercising the right of freemen, the man of religion experiences no *conflict* between his duty and his inclination. *J. Appleton.*

CONFLICT', *v. i.* To strike or dash against; to meet and oppose, as bodies driven by violence; as *conflicting* waves or elements.
2. To drive or strike against, as contending men, or armies; to fight; to contend with violence; as *conflicting* armies.
3. To strive or struggle to resist and overcome; as men *conflicting* with difficulties.
4. To be in opposition or contradictory.

The laws of the United States and of the individual States, may, in some cases, *conflict* with each other. *Ogden, Wheaton's Rep.*

CONFLICT'ING, *ppr.* Striking, or dashing together; fighting; contending; struggling to resist and overcome.
2. *a.* Being in opposition; contrary; contradictory.

In the absence of all *conflicting* evidence. *Story.*

CON'FLUENCE, *n.* [L. *confluentia*, from *confluo; con* and *fluo*, to flow. See *Flow.*]
1. A flowing together; the meeting or junction of two or more streams of water, or other fluid; also, the place of meeting; as the *confluence* of the Tigris and the Frat, or of the Ohio and Mississippi.
2. The running together of people; the act of meeting and crowding in a place; a crowd; a concourse; *the latter word is more generally used.* *Temple. Shak.*
3. A collection; meeting; assemblage. *Boyle.*

CON'FLUENT, *a.* [L. *confluens.*] Flowing together; meeting in their course, as two streams; as *confluent* streams. *Blackmore.*
2. In *medical science*, running together, and spreading over a large surface of the body; as the *confluent* small-pox. *Encyc.*
3. In *botany*, united at the base; growing in tufts, as *confluent* leaves; running into each other, as *confluent* lobes. *Martyn.*

CON'FLUX, *n.* [Low L. *confluxio*, from *confluo.* See *Confluence.*]
1. A flowing together; a meeting of two or more currents of a fluid. *Shak.*
2. A collection; a crowd; a multitude collected; as a general *conflux* of people. *Clarendon.*

CONFLUXIBIL'ITY, *n.* The tendency of fluids to run together. [*Little used.*] *Boyle.*

CONFORM', *a.* [L. *conformis; con* and *forma*, form.]
Made to resemble; assuming the same form; like; resembling. [*Little used.*] *Bacon.*

CONFORM', *v. t.* [L. *conformo; con* and *formo*, to form, or shape, from *forma*, form.]
1. To make like, in external appearance; to reduce to a like shape, or form, with something else; with *to*; as, to *conform* any thing *to* a model.
2. *More generally*, to reduce to a likeness or correspondence in manners, opinions or moral qualities.

For whom he did foreknow, he also did predestinate to be *conformed* to the image of his son. Rom. viii.

Be not *conformed* to this world. Rom. xii.

3. To make agreeable to; to square with a rule or directory.

Demand of them why they *conform* not themselves to the order of the church? *Hooker.*

CONFORM', *v. i.* To comply with or yield to; to live or act according to; as, to *conform* to the fashion or to custom.
2. To comply with; to obey; as, to *conform* to the laws of the state.

CONFORM'ABLE, *a.* Correspondent; having the same or similar external form, or shape; like; resembling; as an edifice *conformable* to a model or draft.
2. Having the same or similar manners, opinions or moral qualities.

The Gentiles were not made *conformable* to the Jews, in that which was to cease at the coming of Christ. *Hooker.*

3. Agreeable; suitable; consistent; as, nature is *conformable* to herself. *Newton.*
4. Compliant; ready to follow directions; submissive; obsequious; peaceable; disposed to obey.

I have been to you a true and humble wife,
At all time to your will *conformable*. *Shak.*

It is generally followed by *to*, but good writers have used *with.* In its etymological sense, *that may be conformed, capable of being conformed*, it seems not to be used.

CONFORM'ABLY, *adv.* With or in conformity; suitably; agreeably.

Let us settle, in our own minds, what rules to pursue and act *conformably.*

CONFORMA'TION, *n.* The manner in which a body is formed; the particular texture or structure of a body, or disposition of the parts which compose it; form; structure; often with relation to some other body, and with adaptation to some purpose or effect.

Light of different colors is reflected from bodies, according to their different *conformation.* Varieties of sound depend on the *conformation* of the organs.

2. The act of conforming; the act of producing suitableness, or conformity; with *to*; as the *conformation* of our hearts and lives *to* the duties of true religion. *Watts.*
3. In *medical science*, the particular make or construction of the body peculiar to an individual; as a good or bad *conformation.* *Encyc.*

CONFORM'ED, *pp.* Made to resemble; reduced to a likeness of; made agreeable to; suited.

CONFORM'ER, *n.* One who conforms; one who complies with established forms or doctrines.

CONFORM'ING, *ppr.* Reducing to a likeness; adapting; complying with.

CONFORM'IST, *n.* One who conforms or complies; appropriately, one who complies with the worship of the church of England or of the established church, as distinguished from a dissenter, or nonconformist.

CONFORM'ITY, *n.* Likeness; correspondence with a model in form or manner;

resemblance; agreement; congruity with something else; followed by *to* or *with*.

A ship is constructed in *conformity to* a model, or in *conformity with* a model.

True happiness consists in *conformity* of life *to* the divine law.

2. Consistency; agreement.

Many instances prove the *conformity* of the essay *with* the notions of Hippocrates. *Arbuthnot.*

3. In *theology*, correspondence in manners and principles; compliance with customs.

Live not in *conformity with* the world. *Anon.*

CONFORTA'TION, *n.* [See *Comfort.*] The act of comforting or giving strength. [*Not used.*] *Bacon.*

CONFOUND', *v. t.* [Fr. *confondre*; L. *confundo*; *con* and *fundo*, to pour out; It. *confondere*; Sp. Port. *confundir.* Literally, to pour or throw together.]

1. To mingle and blend different things, so that their forms or natures cannot be distinguished; to mix in a mass or crowd, so that individuals cannot be distinguished.

2. To throw into disorder.

Let us go down, and there *confound* their language. Gen. xi.

3. To mix or blend, so as to occasion a mistake of one thing for another.

A fluid body and a wetting liquor, because they agree in many things, are wont to be *confounded.* *Boyle.*

Men may *confound* ideas with words.

4. To perplex; to disturb the apprehension by indistinctnes of ideas or words.

Men may *confound* each other by unintelligible terms or wrong application of words.

5. To abash; to throw the mind into disorder; to cast down; to make ashamed.

Be thou *confounded* and bear thy shame. Ezek. xvi.

Saul *confounded* the Jews at Damascus. Acts ix.

6. To perplex with terror; to terrify; to dismay; to astonish; to throw into consternation; to stupify with amazement.

So spake the Son of God; and Satan stood
A while as mute, *confounded* what to say. *Milton.*

The multitude came together and were *confounded.* Acts ii.

7. To destroy; to overthrow.

So deep a malice to *confound* the race
Of mankind in one root. *Milton.*

CONFOUND'ED, *pp.* Mixed or blended in disorder; perplexed; abashed; dismayed; put to shame and silence; astonished.

2. *a.* Enormous; as a *confounded* tory. [*Vulgar.*]

CONFOUND'EDLY, *adv.* Enormously; greatly; shamefully; as, he was *confoundedly* avaricious. [*A low word.*]

CONFOUND'EDNESS, *n.* The state of being confounded. *Milton.*

CONFOUND'ER, *n.* One who confounds; one who disturbs the mind, perplexes, refutes, frustrates and puts to shame or silence; one who terrifies.

CONFOUND'ING, *ppr.* Mixing and blending; putting into disorder; perplexing; disturbing the mind; abashing, and putting to shame and silencc; astonishing.

CONFRATER'NITY, *n.* [It. *confraternità*; Fr. *confraternité*; *con* and L. *fraternitas*, fraternity, from *frater*, brother.]

A brotherhood; a society or body of men, united for some purpose or in some profession; as the *confraternity* of Jesuits.

CONFRICA'TION, *n.* [It. *confricazione*, friction; L. *confrico*; *con* and *frico*, to rub. See *Friction.*]

A rubbing against; friction. *Bacon.*

CONFRI'ER, *n.* [Fr. *confrere.*] One of the same religious order. *Weever.*

CONFRONT', *v. t.* [It. *confrontare*; Sp. Port. *confrontar*; Fr. *confronter*; *con* and *front*, the forehead, or *front*, L. *frons.*]

To stand face to face in full view; to face; to stand in front.

He spoke and then *confronts* the bull. *Dryden.*

2. To stand in direct opposition; to oppose.

The East and West churches did both *confront* the Jews, and concur with them. *Hooker.*

3. To set face to face; to bring into the presence of; as an accused person and a witness, in court, for examination and discovery of the truth; followed by *with.*

The witnesses are *confronted with* the accused, the accused *with* one another, or the witnesses *with* one another. *Encyc.*

4. To set together for comparison; to compare one thing with another.

When I *confront* a medal with a verse, I only show you the same design executed by different hands. *Addison.*

CONFRONTA'TION, *n.* The act of bringing two persons into the presence of each other for examination and discovery of truth.

CONFRONT'ED, *pp.* Set face to face, or in opposition; brought into the presence of.

CONFRONT'ING, *ppr.* Setting or standing face to face, or in opposition, or in presence of.

CONFU'SE, *v. t.* *s* as *z.* [L. *confusus*; Fr. *confus*; from L. *confundo.* See *Confound.*]

1. To mix or blend things, so that they cannot be distinguished.

Stunning sounds and voices all *confused.* *Milton.*

Every battle of the warrior is with *confused* noise. Is. ix.

2. To disorder; as, a sudden alarm *confused* the troops; a careless bookkeeper has *confused* the accounts.

3. To perplex; to render indistinct; as, the clamor *confused* his ideas.

4. To throw the mind into disorder; to cast down or abash; to cause to blush; to agitate by surprise, or shame; to disconcert.

A sarcastic remark *confused* the gentleman and he could not proceed in his argument.

Confused and sadly she at length replied. *Pope.*

CONFU'SED, *pp.* Mixed; blended, so that the things or persons mixed cannot be distinguished.

Some cried one thing, and some another: for the assembly was *confused.* Acts xix.

2. Perplexed by disorder, or want of system; as a *confused* account.

3. Abashed; put to the blush or to shame; agitated; disconcerted.

CONFU'SEDLY, *adv.* In a mixed mass; without order or separation; indistinctly; not clearly; tumultuously; with agitation of mind; without regularity or system.

CONFU'SEDNESS, *n.* A state of being confused; want of order, distinction or clearness.

The cause of the *confusedness* of our notions is want of attention. *Norris.*

CONFU'SION, *n.* In a general sense, a mixture of several things promiscuously; hence, disorder; irregularity; as the *confusion* of tongues at Babel.

2. Tumult; want of order in society.

The whole city was filled with *confusion.* Acts xix.

God is not the author of *confusion.* 1 Cor. xiv.

3. A blending or confounding; indistinct combination; opposed to distinctness or perspicuity; as a *confusion* of ideas.

4. Abashment; shame.

O Lord, let me never be put to *confusion.* Ps. lxxi.

We lie in shame and our *confusion* covereth us. Jer. iii.

5. Astonishment; agitation; pertubation; distraction of mind.

Confusion dwelt in every face. *Spectator.*

6. Overthrow; defeat; ruin.

The makers of idols shall go to *confusion* together. Is. xlv.

7. A shameful blending oi natures, a snocking crime. Levit. xviii. 23. xx. 12.

CONFU'TABLE, *a.* [See *Confute.*] That may be confuted, disproved or overthrown; that may be shown to be false, defective or invalid; as, an argument or a course of reasoning is *confutable.*

CONFU'TANT, *n.* One who confutes or undertakes to confute. *Milton.*

CONFUTA'TION, *n.* The act of confuting, disproving, or proving to be false, or invalid; refutation; overthrow; as of arguments, opinions, reasoning, theory, or error.

CONFU'TE, *v. t.* [L. *confuto*; *con* and ant. *futo*; Sp. *confutar*; It. *confutare.* Class Bd.]

1. To disprove; to prove to be false, defective or invalid; to overthrow; as, to *confute* arguments, reasoning, theory, error.

2. To prove to be wrong; to convict of error, by argument or proof; as, to *confute* an advocate at the bar; to *confute* a writer.

CONFU'TED, *pp.* Disproved; proved to be false, defective or unsound; overthrown by argument, fact or proof.

CONFU'TER, *n.* One who disproves, or confutes. *Morton.*

CONFU'TING, *ppr.* Disproving; proving to be false, defective or invalid; overthrowing by argument or proof.

CON'GE, *n.* *con'jee.* [Fr. *congé*, leave, permission, discharge, contracted from *conged*; verb, *congedier*, to dismiss; It. *congedo*, leave, permission; *congedare*, to give leave; Arm. *congea.* The verb is a compound of *con* and *ged*; W. *gadaw*, to *quit*, to leave, to permit; *gad*, leave. *Gadaw* is the Celtic form of the L. *cedo.* *Conged* is therefore *concedo.*]

1. Leave; farewell; parting ceremony. *Spenser.*

2. The act of respect performed at the parting of friends. Hence, the customary act of civility, on other occasions; a bow or a courtesy.

The captain salutes you with *conge* profound. *Swift.*

CONGE', *v. i.* To take leave with the customary civilities; to bow or courtesy.

The preterite *congeed* is tolerable in English; but *congeing* will not be admitted, and *congeeing* is an anomaly.

Conge d' elire, in ecclesiastical affairs, the king's license or permission to a dean and chapter, to choose a bishop; or to an abbey or priory of his own foundation, to choose their abbot or prior. The king of Great Britain, as sovereign patron, had formerly the appointment of all ecclesiastical dignities; investing by crosier and ring, and afterwards by letters patent. But now the king, on demand, sends his *conge d' elire* to the dean and chapter, with a letter missive, containing the name of the person he would have them elect, and if they delay the election twelve days, the nomination devolves on the king, who may appoint by letters patent. *Encyc. Cowel. Blackstone.*

CON'ĠE, *n.* In *architecture*, a mold in form of a quarter round, or a cavetto, which serves to separate two members from one another; such as that which joins the shaft of the column to the cincture, called also *apophyge*. Also, a ring or ferrule, formerly used on the extremities of columns to keep them from splitting; afterwards imitated in stone-work. *Encyc.*

CONĠE'AL, *v. t.* [L. *congelo; con* and *gelo*, to freeze; Fr. *congeler;* It. *congelare;* Sp. *congelar;* Arm. *caledi.* This may be connected with the W. *ceulaw*, to curdle or coagulate, from *caul*, a calf's maw; also, rennet, curd and *chyle.* The L. *gelo* has the elements of *cool*, but it may be a different word.]

1. To change from a fluid to a solid state, as by cold, or a loss of heat, as water in freezing, liquid metal or wax in cooling, blood in stagnating or cooling, &c.; to harden into ice, or into a substance of less solidity. Cold *congeals* water into ice, or vapor into hoar frost or snow, and blood into a less solid mass, or clot.

2. To bind or fix with cold. Applied to the circulating blood, it does not signify absolutely to *harden*, but to cause a sensation of cold, a shivering, or a receding of the blood from the extremities; as, the frightful scene *congealed* his blood.

CONĠE'AL, *v. i.* To grow hard, stiff or thick; to pass from a fluid to a solid state; to concrete into a solid mass. Melted lead *congeals;* water *congeals;* blood *congeals.*

CONĠE'ALABLE, *a.* That may be congealed; capable of being converted from a fluid to a solid state. *Bacon.*

CONĠE'ALED, *pp.* Converted into ice, or a solid mass, by the loss of heat or other process; concreted.

CONĠE'ALING, *ppr.* Changing from a liquid to a solid state; concreting.

CONĠE'ALMENT, *n.* A clot or concretion; that which is formed by congelation. Also, congelation.

CONĠELA'TION, *n.* [L. *congelatio.*] The process of passing, or the act of converting, from a fluid to a solid state; or the state of being congealed; concretion. It differs from crystalization in this: in congelation the whole substance of a fluid may become solid; in crystalization, when a salt is formed, a portion of liquid is left. But the congelation of water is a real crystalization. *Encyc.*

CONĠE'NER, *n.* [L. *congener; con* and *gener*, kind, race.]

A thing of the same kind or nature.

> The cherry tree has been often grafted on the laurel, to which it is a *congener.* *Miller.*

CONĠE'NER, CONĠEN'EROUS, *a.* Of the same kind or nature; allied in origin or cause; as *congenerous* bodies; *congenerous* diseases. *Brown. Arbuthnot.*

CONĠEN'ERACY, *n.* Similarity of origin.

CONĠENER'IC, *a.* Being of the same kind or nature.

CONĠEN'EROUSNESS, *n.* The quality of being from the same original, or of belonging to the same class. *Dict.*

CONĠE'NIAL, *a.* [L. *con* and *genus*, whence *genialis, genial.* See *Generate.*]

1. Partaking of the same genus, kind or nature; kindred; cognate; as *congenial* souls.

2. Belonging to the nature; natural; agreeable to the nature; usually followed by *to;* as, this severity is not *congenial to* him.

3. Natural; agreeable to the nature; adapted; as a soil *congenial* to a plant.

CONĠENIAL'ITY, CONĠE'NIALNESS, *n.* Participation of the same genus, nature or original; cognation; natural affinity; suitableness. *Wotton.*

CONĠEN'ITE, CONĠEN'ITAL, *a.* [L. *congenitus; con* and *genitus*, born, from *gigno*, to beget, *gignor*, to be born.]

Of the same birth; born with another; connate; begotten together.

> Many conclusions of moral and intellectual truths seem to be *congenite* with us. *Hale.*

> Native or *congenital* varieties of animals. *Lawrence.*

CON'GER, *n.* cong'gur. [L. *conger* or *congrus;* Gr. κογγρος, or γογγρος; It. *gongro;* Fr. *congre.*]

The sea-eel; a large species of eel, sometimes growing to the length of ten feet, and weighing a hundred pounds. In Cornwall, England, it is an article of commerce, being shipped to Spain and Portugal. *Encyc.*

CONĠE'RIES, *n.* [L. from *congero*, to bring together, to amass; *con* and *gero*, to bear.]

A collection of several particles or bodies in one mass or aggregate. *Boyle.*

CONĠEST', *v. t.* [L. *congero, congestum; con* and *gero*, to bear.]

To collect or gather into a mass or aggregate. *Raleigh.*

CONĠEST'IBLE, *a.* That may be collected into a mass.

CONĠES'TION, *n.* [L. *congestio.*] A collection of humors in an animal body, hardened into a tumor. An accumulation of blood in a part. *Encyc. Coxe.*

CON'ĠIARY, *n.* [L. *congiarium*, from *congius*, a measure; Fr. *congiaire.*]

Properly, a present made by the Roman emperors to the people; originally in corn or wine measured out to them in a congius, a vessel holding a gallon or rather more. In present usage, a gift or a donative represented on a medal. *Encyc. Addison.*

CONGLA'CIATE, *v. i.* [L. *conglacio; con* and *glacio*, to freeze; *glacies*, ice.]

To turn to ice; to freeze. *Brown.*

CONGLACIA'TION, *n.* The act of changing into ice, or the state of being converted to ice; a freezing; congelation. *Brown.*

CONGLO'BATE, *a.* [L. *conglobatus*, from *conglobo; con* and *globo*, to collect or to make round; *globus*, a ball. See *Globe.*]

Formed or gathered into a ball. A *conglobate* gland is a single or lymphatic gland, a small smooth body, covered in a fine skin, admitting only an artery and a lymphatic vessel to pass in, and a vein and a lymphatic vessel to pass out. *Parr. Coxe.*

CONGLO'BATE, *v. t.* To collect or form into a ball or hard, round substance. *Grew.*

CONGLO'BATED, *pp.* Collected or formed into a ball.

CONGLO'BATELY, *adv.* In a round or roundish form.

CONGLOBA'TION, *n.* The act of forming into a ball; a round body.

CONGLO'BE, *v. t.* [L. *conglobo; con* and *globo*, from *globus*, a round body.]

To gather into a ball; to collect into a round mass. *Milton.*

CONGLO'BE, *v. i.* To collect, unite or coalesce in a round mass. *Milton.*

CONGLO'BED, *pp.* Collected into a ball.

CONGLO'BING, *ppr.* Gathering into a round mass or ball.

CONGLOB'ULATE, *v. i.* To gather into a little round mass, or globule. *Johnson.*

CONGLOM'ERATE, *a.* [L. *conglomero; con* and *glomero*, to wind into a ball, from *glomus*, a ball, a clew. See *Glomerate.*]

1. Gathered into a ball or round body. A *conglomerate* gland is composed of many smaller glands, whose excretory ducts unite in a common one, as the liver, kidneys, pancreas, parotids, &c. Each little granulated portion furnishes a small tube, which unites with other similar ducts, to form the common excretory duct of the gland. *Coxe. Encyc.*

2. In botany, *conglomerate* flowers grow on a branching peduncle or foot stalk, on short pedicles, closely compacted together without order; opposed to *diffused.* *Martyn.*

3. Conglomerate rocks. [See *Pudding-stone.*]

CONGLOM'ERATE, *v. t.* To gather into a ball or round body; to collect into a round mass. *Grew.*

CONGLOM'ERATE, *n.* In *mineralogy*, a sort of pudding-stone, or coarse sandstone, composed of pebbles of quartz, flint, siliceous slate, &c. *Cleaveland.*

CONGLOM'ERATED, *pp.* Gathered into a ball or round mass.

CONGLOM'ERATING, *ppr.* Collecting into a ball.

CONGLOMERA'TION, *n.* The act of gathering into a ball; the state of being thus collected; collection; accumulation.

CONGLU'TINANT, *a.* [See *Conglutinate.*] Gluing; uniting; healing. *Bacon.*

CONGLU'TINANT, *n.* A medicine that heals wounds.

CONGLU'TINATE, *v. t.* [L. *conglutino; con* and *glutino*, from *gluten*, glue. See *Glue.*]

1. To glue together; to unite by some glutinous or tenacious substance.

2. To heal; to unite the separated parts of a wound by a tenacious substance.

CONGLU'TINATE, *v. i.* To coalesce; to unite by the intervention of a callus. *Johnson.*

CONGLU'TINATED, *pp.* Glued together; united by a tenacious substance.

CONGLU'TINATING, *ppr.* Gluing together; uniting or closing by a tenacious substance.

CONGLUTINA'TION, *n.* The act of gluing together; a joining by means of some tenacious substance; a healing by uniting the parts of a wound; union. *Arbuthnot.*

CONGLU'TINATIVE, *a.* Having the power of uniting by glue or other substance of like nature.

CONGLU'TINATOR, *n.* That which has the power of uniting wounds. *Woodward.*

CON'GO, *n. cong'go.* A species of tea from China.

CONGRAT'ULANT, *a.* Rejoicing in participation. *Milton.*

CONGRAT'ULATE, *v. t.* [L. *congratulor*; *con* and *gratulor*, from *gratus*, grateful, pleasing. See *Grace.*]

To profess one's pleasure or joy to another on account of an event deemed happy or fortunate, as on the birth of a child, success in an enterprise, victory, escape from danger, &c.; to wish joy to another. We *congratulate* the nation on the restoration of peace.

Formerly this verb was followed by *to.* "The subjects of England may congratulate *to* themselves." *Dryden.* But this use of *to* is entirely obsolete. The use of *with* after this verb, "I congratulate *with* my country," is perhaps less objectionable, but is rarely used. The intransitive sense of the verb may therefore be considered as antiquated, and no longer legitimate.

CONGRAT'ULATED, *pp.* Complimented with expressions of joy at a happy event.

CONGRAT'ULATING, *ppr.* Professing one's joy or satisfaction on account of some happy event, prosperity or success.

CONGRATULA'TION, *n.* The act of professing one's joy or good wishes at the success or happiness of another, or on account of an event deemed fortunate to both parties or to the community.

CONGRAT'ULATOR, *n.* One who offers congratulation. *Milton.*

CONGRAT'ULATORY, *a.* Expressing joy for the good fortune of another, or for an event fortunate for both parties or for the community.

CONGREE', *v. i.* To agree. [*Not in use.*] *Shak.*

CONGREE'T, *v. t.* To salute mutually. [*Not in use.*] *Shak.*

CON'GREGATE, *v. t.* [L. *congrego*; *con* and *grex*, a herd, W. *gre.* See *Gregarious.*]

To collect separate persons or things into an assemblage; to assemble; to bring into one place, or into a crowd or united body; as, to *congregate* men or animals; to *congregate* waters or sands. *Hooker. Milton. Shak.*

CON'GREGATE, *v. i.* To come together; to assemble; to meet.

Equals with equals often *congregate.* *Denham.*

CON'GREGATE, *a.* Collected; compact; close. [*Little used.*] *Bacon.*

CON'GREGATED, *pp.* Collected; assembled in one place.

CON'GREGATING, *ppr.* Collecting; assembling; coming together.

CONGREGA'TION, *n.* The act of bringing together, or assembling.

2. A collection or assemblage of separate things; as a *congregation* of vapors. *Shak.*

3. *More generally,* an assembly of persons; and appropriately, an assembly of persons met for the worship of God, and for religious instruction. *Hooker.*

4. An assembly of rulers. Numb. xxxv.

5. An assembly of ecclesiastics or cardinals appointed by the pope; as the *congregation* of the holy office, &c. Also, a company or society of religious cantoned out of an order. *Encyc.*

6. An academical assembly for transacting business of the university. *England.*

CONGREGA'TIONAL, *a.* Pertaining to a congregation; appropriately used of such christians as hold to church government by consent and election, maintaining that each congregation is independent of others, and has the right to choose its own pastor and govern itself; as a *congregational* church, or mode of worship.

CONGREGA'TIONALISM, *n.* Ecclesiastical government in the hands of each church, as an independent body.

CONGREGA'TIONALIST, *n.* One who belongs to a congregational church or society; one who holds to the independence of each congregation or church of christians, in the right of electing a pastor, and in governing the church.

CON'GRESS, *n.* [L. *congressus*, from *congredior*, to come together; *con* and *gradior*, to go or step; *gradus*, a step. See *Grade* and *Degree.*]

1. A meeting of individuals; an assembly of envoys, commissioners, deputies, &c., particularly a meeting of the representatives of several courts, to concert measures for their common good, or to adjust their mutual concerns. *Europe.*

2. The assembly of delegates of the several British Colonies in America, which united to resist the claims of Great Britain in 1774, and which declared the colonies independent.

3. The assembly of the delegates of the several United States, after the declaration of Independence, and until the adoption of the present constitution, and the organization of the government in 1789. During these periods, the congress consisted of one house only.

4. The assembly of senators and representatives of the several states of North America, according to the present constitution, or political compact, by which they are united in a federal republic; the legislature of the United States, consisting of two houses, a senate and a house of representatives. Members of the senate are elected for six years, but the members of the house of representatives are chosen for two years only. Hence the united body of senators and representatives for the two years, during which the representatives hold their seats, is called *one congress.* Thus we say the first or second session of the *sixteenth* congress.

5. A meeting of two or more persons in a contest; an encounter; a conflict. *Dryden.*

6. The meeting of the sexes in sexual commerce.

CONGRES'SION, *n.* A company. [*Not in use.*]

CONGRES'SIONAL, *a.* Pertaining to a congress, or to the congress of the United States; as *congressional* debates.

The *congressional* institution of Amphictyons in Greece. *Barlow.*

CONGRES'SIVE, *a.* Meeting, as the sexes. *Brown.*

2. Encountering.

CONGRU'E, *v. i.* To agree. [*Not used.*] *Shak.*

CON'GRUENCE, } *n.* [L. *congruentia*, from
CONGRU'ENCY, } *congruo*, to agree, or suit.]

Suitableness of one thing to another; agreement; consistency. *More.*

CON'GRUENT, *a.* Suitable; agreeing; correspondent. *Davies.*

CONGRU'ITY, *n.* Suitableness; the relation of agreement between things.

There is no *congruity* between a mean subject and a lofty style; but an obvious *congruity* between an elevated station and dignified deportment.

2. Fitness; pertinence.

A whole sentence may fail of its *congruity* by wanting a particle. *Sidney.*

3. Reason; consistency; propriety. *Hooker.*

4. In *school divinity*, the good actions which are supposed to render it meet and equitable that God should confer grace on those who perform them. The merit of congruity is a sort of imperfect qualification for the gift and reception of God's grace. *Milner.*

5. In *geometry*, figures or lines, which when laid over one another, exactly correspond, are in *congruity.* *Johnson.*

CON'GRUOUS, *a.* [L. *congruus.*] Suitable; consistent; agreeable to. Light airy music and a solemn or mournful occasion are not *congruous.* Obedience to God is *congruous* to the light of reason. *Locke.*

2. Rational; fit.

It is not *congruous* that God should be always frightening men into an acknowledgment of the truth. *Atterbury.*

CON'GRUOUSLY, *adv.* Suitably; pertinently; agreeably; consistently. *Boyle.*

CON'IC, } *a.* [L. *conicus*; Gr. κωνικος.
CON'ICAL, } See *Cone.*]

1. Having the form of a cone; round and decreasing to a point; as a *conic* figure; a *conical* vessel.

2. Pertaining to a cone; as *conic* sections.

Conic Section, a curve line formed by the intersection of a cone and plane. The conic sections are the parabola, hyperbola, and ellipsis. *Bailey.*

CON'ICALLY, *adv.* In the form of a cone. *Boyle.*

CON'ICALNESS, *n.* The state or quality of being conical.

CON'ICS, *n.* That part of geometry which treats of the cone and the curves which arise from its sections. *Johnson.*

CONIF'EROUS, *a.* [L. *conifer*, *coniferus*; from *conus* and *fero*, to bear.]

Bearing cones; producing hard, dry, scaly seed-vessels of a conical figure, as the pine, fir, cypress and beech. *Martyn. Encyc.*

ƆO'NIFORM, *a.* [*cone* and *form.*] In form of a cone; conical; as a *coniform* mountain of Potosi. *Kirwan.*

ƆO'NITE, *n.* [Gr. κονις, dust.] A mineral of an ash or greenish gray color, which becomes brown by exposure to the air, occurring massive or stalactitic; found in Saxony and in Iceland. *Ure.*

ƆONJEƆT', *v. t.* To throw together, or to throw. [*Not used.*] *Mountagu.*

ƆONJEƆT', *v. i.* To guess. [*Not used.*] *Shak.*

ƆONJEƆ'TOR, *n.* [L. from *conjicio*, to cast together; *con* and *jacio*, to throw.] One who guesses or conjectures. [See *Conjecture.*] *Swift.*

ƆONJEƆ'TURABLE, *a.* That may be guessed or conjectured.

ƆONJEƆ'TURAL, *a.* Depending on conjecture; done or said by guess; as a *conjectural* opinion.

ƆONJEƆ'TURALLY, *adv.* Without proof, or evidence; by conjecture; by guess; as, this opinion was given *conjecturally.*

ƆONJEƆ'TURE, *n.* [L. *conjectura;* Fr. *conjecture;* It. *congettura*, or *conghiettura;* Sp. *conjetura;* Port. *conjectura* or *conjeitura.* See *Conjector.*]

1. Literally, a casting or throwing together of possible or probable events; or a casting of the mind to something future, or something past but unknown; a guess, formed on a supposed possibility or probability of a fact, or on slight evidence; preponderance of opinion without proof; surmise. We speak of future or unknown things by *conjecture*, and of probable or unfounded *conjectures.*

2. Idea; notion. *Shak.*

ƆONJEƆ'TURE, *v. t.* To guess; to judge by guess, or by the probability or the possibility of a fact, or by very slight evidence; to form an opinion at random. What will be the issue of a war, we may *conjecture*, but cannot know. He *conjectured* that some misfortune had happened.

ƆONJEƆ'TURED, *pp.* Guessed; surmised.

ƆONJEƆ'TURER, *n.* One who guesses; a guesser; one who forms or utters an opinion without proof. *Addison.*

ƆONJEƆ'TURING, *ppr.* Guessing; surmising.

ƆONJOIN', *v. t.* [Fr. *conjoindre;* It. *congiugnere*, or *congiungere;* L. *conjungo;* *con* and *jungo*, to *join.* See *Join.*]

1. To join together, without any thing intermediate; to unite two or more persons or things in close connection; as, to *conjoin* friends; to *conjoin* man and woman in marriage. *Dryden. Shak.*

2. To associate, or connect.

> Let that which he learns next be nearly *conjoined* with what he knows already. *Locke.*

ƆONJOIN', *v. i.* To unite; to join; to league. *Shak.*

ƆONJOIN'ED, *pp.* Joined to or with; united; associated.

ƆONJOIN'ING, *ppr.* Joining together; uniting; connecting.

ƆONJOINT', *a.* United; connected; associate.

Conjoint degrees, in music, two notes which follow each other immediately in the order of the scale; as *ut* and *re.* *Johnson.*

Conjoint tetrachords, two tetrachords or fourths, where the same chord is the highest of one and the lowest of the other. *Encyc.*

ƆONJOINT'LY, *adv.* Jointly; unitedly; in union; together. *Dryden.*

ƆON'JUGAL, *a.* [L. *conjugalis*, from *conjugium*, marriage; *conjugo*, to yoke or couple; *con* and *jugo*, id. See *Join* and *Yoke.*]

1. Belonging to marriage; matrimonial; connubial; as *conjugal* relation; *conjugal* ties.

2. Suitable to the married state; becoming a husband in relation to his consort, or a consort in relation to her husband; as *conjugal* affection.

ƆON'JUGALLY, *adv.* Matrimonially; connubially.

ƆON'JUGATE, *v. t.* [L. *conjugo, conjugatus*, to couple; *con* and *jugo*, to yoke, to marry. See *Join* and *Yoke.*]

1. To join; to unite in marriage. [*Not now used.*] *Wotton.*

2. In *grammar*, to distribute the parts or inflections of a verb, into the several voices, modes, tenses, numbers and persons, so as to show their connections, distinctions, and modes of formation. Literally, to connect all the inflections of a verb, according to their derivation, or all the variations of one verb. In *English*, as the verb undergoes few variations, conjugation consists chiefly in combining the words which unitedly form the several tenses in the several persons.

ƆON'JUGATE, *n.* A word agreeing in derivation with another word, and therefore generally resembling it in signification.

> We have learned in logic, that *conjugates* are sometimes in name only, and not in deed. *Bramhall.*

ƆON'JUGATE, *a.* In *botany*, a *conjugate* leaf is a pinnate leaf which has only one pair of leaflets; a *conjugate* raceme has two racemes only, united by a common peduncle. *Martyn.*

Conjugate diameter or *axis*, in geometry, a right line bisecting the transverse diameter; the shortest of the two diameters of an ellipsis. *Chambers. Encyc.*

ƆONJUGA'TION, *n.* [L. *conjugatio.*] A couple or pair; as a *conjugation* of nerves. [*Little used.*] *Brown.*

2. The act of uniting or compiling; union; assemblage. *Bentley. Taylor.*

3. In *grammar*, the distribution of the several inflections or variations of a verb, in their different voices, modes, tenses, numbers and persons; a connected scheme of all the derivative forms of a verb.

ƆONJUNƆT', *a.* [L *conjunctus*, from *conjungo.* See *Conjoin.*] Conjoined; united; concurrent. *Shak.*

ƆONJUNƆ'TION, *n.* [L. *conjunctio.* See *Conjoin.*]

1. Union; connection; association by treaty or otherwise. *Bacon. South.*

2. In *astronomy*, the meeting of two or more stars or planets in the same degree of the zodiac; as the *conjunction* of the moon with the sun, or of Jupiter and Saturn.

3. In *grammar*, a connective or connecting word; an indeclinable word which serves to unite sentences or the clauses of a sentence and words, joining two or more simple sentences into one compound one, and continuing it at the pleasure of the writer or speaker.

> This book cost one dollar *and* ten cents.
> God called the light day *and* the darkness he called night.
> Virtue *and* vice are not compatible.
> The hope of the righteous shall be gladness, *but* the expectation of the wicked shall perish. Prov. x.

4. The copulation of the sexes. *Smith's Tour.*

ƆONJUNƆ'TIVE, *a.* Closely united. *Shak.*

2. Uniting; serving to unite.

3. In *grammar*, the *conjunctive* mode is that which follows a conjunction, or expresses some condition, or contingency. It is more generally called *subjunctive.*

ƆONJUNƆ'TIVELY, *adv.* In conjunction, or union; together. *Brown.*

ƆONJUNƆ'TIVENESS, *n.* The quality of conjoining or uniting.

ƆONJUNƆT'LY, *adv.* In union; jointly; together.

ƆONJUNƆ'TURE, *n.* [Fr. *conjoncture.* See *Conjoin.*]

1. A joining; a combination or union, as of causes, events or circumstances; as an unhappy *conjuncture* of affairs.

2. An occasion; a critical time, proceeding from a union of circumstances. *Juncture* is used in a like sense.

> At that *conjuncture*, peace was very desirable.

3. Union; connection; mode of union; as the *conjunctures* of letters in words. *Holder.*

4. Connection; union; consistency.

> I was willing to grant to presbytery what with reason it can pretend to in a *conjuncture* with episcopacy. *King Charles.*

ƆŎNJURA'TION, *n.* [See *Cŏnjure.*] The act of using certain words or ceremonies to obtain the aid of a superior being; the act of summoning in a sacred name; the practice of arts to expel evil spirits, allay storms, or perform supernatural or extraordinary acts.

ƆONJU'RE, *v. t.* [L. *conjuro*, to swear together, to conspire; *con* and *juro*, to swear; It. *congiurare;* Sp. *conjurar;* Fr. *conjurer.*]

1. To call on or summon by a sacred name, or in a solemn manner; to implore with solemnity. It seems originally to have signified, to bind by an oath.

> I *conjure* you! let him know,
> Whate'er was done against him, Cato did it. *Addison.*

2. To bind two or more by an oath; to unite in a common design. Hence intransitively, to conspire. [*Not usual.*] *Milton.*

ƆŎN'JURE, *v. t.* To expel, to drive or to affect, in some manner, by magic arts, as by invoking the Supreme Being, or by the use of certain words, characters or ceremonies to engage supernatural influence; as, to *conjure up* evil spirits, or to *conjure down* a tempest; to *conjure* the stars.

> Note. It is not easy to define this word, nor any word of like import; as the practices of conjurors are little known, or various and indefinite. The use of this word indicates that an oath or solemn invocation originally formed a part of the ceremonies.

ƆŎN'JURE, *v. i.* To practice the arts of a conjurer; to use arts to engage the aid of spirits in performing some extraordinary act. *Shak.*

2. In *a vulgar sense*, to behave very strangely; to act like a witch; to play tricks.

CONJU′RED, *pp.* Bound by an oath.

CONJU′REMENT, *n.* Serious injunction; solemn demand. *Milton.*

CON′JURER, *n.* One who practices conjuration; one who pretends to the secret art of performing things supernatural or extraordinary, by the aid of superior powers; an impostor who pretends, by unknown means, to discover stolen goods, &c. Hence ironically, a man of shrewd conjecture; a man of sagacity. *Addison. Prior.*

CONJU′RING, *ppr.* Enjoining or imploring solemnly.

CONNAS′CENCE, *n.* [L. *con* and *nascor*, to be born.]

1. The common birth of two or more at the same time; production of two or more together.
2. A being born or produced with another. *Brown.*
3. The act of growing together, or at the same time. *Wiseman.*

CON′NATE, *a.* [L. *con* and *natus*, born, from *nascor*.]

1. Born with another; being of the same birth; as *connate* notions. *South.*
2. In *botany*, united in origin; growing from one base, or united at their bases; united into one body; as *connate* leaves or anthers. *Martyn.*

CONNAT′URAL, *a.* [*con* and *natural*.]

1. Connected by nature; united in nature; born with another.

> These affections are *connatural* to us, and as we grow up, so do they. *L'Estrange.*

2. Participating of the same nature.

> And mix with our *connatural* dust. *Milton.*

CONNATURAL′ITY, *n.* Participation of the same nature; natural union. *Johnson. Hale.*

CONNAT′URALLY, *adv.* By the act of nature; originally. *Hale.*

CONNAT′URALNESS, *n.* Participation of the same nature; natural union. *Johnson. Pearson.*

CONNECT′, *v. t.* [L. *connecto; con* and *necto;* It. *connettere.* See Class Ng. No. 32. 38. 40. 41.]

1. To knit or link together; to tie or fasten together, as by something intervening, or by weaving, winding or twining. Hence,
2. To join or unite; to conjoin, in almost any manner, either by junction, by any intervening means, or by order and relation. We *connect* letters and words in a sentence; we *connect* ideas in the mind; we *connect* arguments in a discourse. The strait of Gibraltar *connects* the Mediterranean with the Atlantic. A treaty *connects* two nations. The interests of agriculture are *connected* with those of commerce. Families are *connected* by marriage or by friendship.

CONNECT′, *v. i.* To join, unite or cohere; to have a close relation. This argument *connects* with another. [*This use is rare and not well authorized.*]

CONNEC′TION, *n.* [L. *connexio;* It. *connessione.* See *Connect.*]

The act of joining or state of being joined; a state of being knit or fastened together; union by junction, by an intervening substance or medium, by dependence or relation, or by order in a series; *a word of very general import.* There is a *connection* of links in a chain; a *connection* between all parts of the human body; a *connection* between virtue and happiness, and between this life and the future; a *connection* between parent and child, master and servant, husband and wife; between motives and actions, and between actions and their consequences. In short, the word is applicable to almost every thing that has a dependence on or relation to another thing.

CONNEC′TIVE, *a.* Having the power of connecting.

CONNEC′TIVE, *n.* In *grammar*, a word that connects other words and sentences; a conjunction. Harris uses the word for conjunctions and prepositions. *Hermes.*

CONNEC′TIVELY, *adv.* In union or conjunction; jointly. *Swift.*

CONNEX′, *v. t.* [L. *connexum.*] To link together; to join. [*Not in use.*] *Hall.*

CONNEX′ION, *n.* Connection. But for the sake of regular analogy, I have inserted *connection*, as the derivative of the English *connect*, and would discard *connexion.*

CONNEX′IVE, *a.* Connective; having the power to connect; uniting; conjunctive; as *connexive* particles. [*Little used.*] *Watts.*

CONNI′VANCE, *n.* [See *Connive.*] Properly, the act of winking. Hence *figuratively*, voluntary blindness to an act; intentional forbearance to see a fault or other act, generally implying consent to it.

> Every vice interprets a *connivance* to be approbation. *South.*

CONNI′VE, *v. i.* [L. *conniveo, connivi* or *connixi; con* and the root of *nicto*, to wink. Class Ng.]

1. To wink; to close and open the eyelids rapidly. *Spectator.*
2. In *a figurative sense*, to close the eyes upon a fault or other act; to pretend ignorance or blindness; to forbear to see; to overlook a fault or other act, and suffer it to pass unnoticed, uncensured or unpunished; as, the father *connives* at the vices of his son.

CONNI′VENCY, *n.* Connivance, which see. *Bacon.*

CONNI′VENT, *a.* Shutting the eyes; forbearing to see. *Milton.*

2. In *anatomy*, the *connivent* valves are those wrinkles, cellules and vascules, which are found on the inside of the two intestines, ilium and jejunum. *Encyc.*
3. In *botany*, closely united; converging together. *Eaton.*

CONNI′VER, *n.* One who connives.

CONNI′VING, *ppr.* Closing the eyes against faults; permitting faults to pass uncensured.

CONNOISSEU′R, *n. connissu're.* [Fr. from the verb *connoitre*, from L. *cognosco*, to know.]

A person well versed in any subject; a skilful or knowing person; a critical judge or master of any art, particularly of painting and sculpture.

CONNOISSEU′RSHIP, *n.* The skill of a connoisseur.

CON′NOTATE, *v. t.* [*con* and *note*, L. *noto, nota us.*]

To designate with something else; to imply. [*Little used.*] *Hammond.*

CONNOTA′TION, *n.* The act of making known or designating with something; implication of something beside itself; inference. [*Little used.*] *Hale.*

CONNO′TE, *v. t.* [L. *con* and *nota*; *noto*, to mark. See *Note.*]

To make known together; to imply; to denote or designate; to include. [*Little used.*] *South.*

CONNU′BIAL, *a.* [L. *connubialis*, from *connubium; con* and *nubo*, to marry.]

Pertaining to marriage; nuptial; belonging to the state of husband and wife; as, *connubial* rites; *connubial* love.

CONNUMERA′TION, *n.* A reckoning together. *Porson.*

CON′NUSANCE, *n.* [Fr. *connoissance*, from *connoitre*, to know, L. *cognosco.*] Knowledge. [See *Cognizance.*]

CON′NUSANT, *a.* Knowing; informed; apprised.

> A neutral vessel, breaking a blockade, is liable to confiscation, if *connusant* of the blockade. *Browne.*

CON′NY, *a.* [W. *cono.*] Brave; fine. [*Local.*] *Grose.*

CO′NOID, *n.* [Gr. κωνοειδης; κωνος, a cone, and ειδος, form.]

In *geometry*, a solid formed by the revolution of a conic section about its axis. If the conic section is a parabola, the resulting solid is a parabolic conoid, or paraboloid; if a hyperbola, the solid is a hyperbolic conoid, or hyperboloid; if an ellipse, an elliptic conoid, a spheroid, or an ellipsoid. *Edin. Encyc.*

2. In *anatomy*, a gland in the third ventricle of the brain, resembling a cone or pine-apple, and called the pineal gland. *Encyc.*

CONOID′IC, } *a.* Pertaining to a conoid;
CONOID′ICAL, } having the form of a conoid.

CONQUAS′SATE, *v. t.* [L. *conquasso.*] To shake. [*Little used.*] *Harvey.*

CON′QUER, *v. t. con'ker.* [Fr. *conquerir*, from the L. *conquiro; con* and *quæro*, to seek, to obtain, to conquer; Arm. *conqeuri.* As *quæro* is written, it belongs to Class Gr. and its preterit to Class Gs. See Ar. قَرَا Karau or quarau, and Heb. Ch. חקר to seek. Class Gr. No. 51. 55.]

1. To subdue; to reduce, by physical force, till resistance is no longer made; to overcome; to vanquish. Alexander *conquered* Asia. The Romans *conquered* Carthage.
2. To gain by force; to win; to take possession by violent means; to gain dominion or sovereignty over, as the subduing of the power of an enemy generally implies possession of the person or thing subdued by the conqueror. Thus, a king or an army *conquers* a country, or a city, which is afterward restored.
3. To subdue opposition or resistance of the will by moral force; to overcome by argument, persuasion or other influence.

> Anna *conquers* but to save,
> And governs but to bless. *Smith.*
> He went forth *conquering*, and to *conquer.* Rev. vi.

4. To overcome, as difficulties; to surmount, as obstacles; to subdue whatever oppo-

ses; as, to *conquer* the passions; to *conquer* reluctance.

5. To gain or obtain by effort; as, to *conquer* freedom; to *conquer* peace; *a French application of the word.*

ȻON'QUER, *v. i.* To overcome; to gain the victory.

The champions resolved to *conquer* or to die. *Waller.*

ȻON'QUERABLE, *a.* That may be conquered, overcome or subdued. *South.*

ȻON'QUERED, *pp.* Overcome; subdued; vanquished; gained; won.

ȻON'QUERESS, *n.* A female who conquers; a victorious female. *Fairfax.*

ȻON'QUERING, *ppr.* Overcoming; subduing; vanquishing; obtaining.

ȻON'QUEROR, *n.* One who conquers; one who gains a victory; one who subdues and brings into subjection or possession, by force or by influence. The man who defeats his antagonist in combat is a *conqueror*, as is the general or admiral who defeats his enemy.

ȻON'QUEST, *n.* [Fr. *conquête*; It. *conquista*; Sp. *id.*; L. *conquisitus*, *quæsitus*, *quæstus*, from *quæro*, to seek. The L. *quæsivi*, *quæsitus*, coincides in elements with the W. *ceisiaw*, Eth. [Ethiopic]. Class Gs. No. 35. The primary sense is to seek, to press or drive towards.]

1. The act of conquering; the act of overcoming or vanquishing opposition by force, physical or moral. *Applied to persons, territory and the like,* it usually implies or includes a taking possession of; as the *conquest* of Canada by the British troops. So we speak of the *conquest* of the heart, the passions, or the will.

2. Victory; success in arms; the overcoming of opposition.

In joys of *conquest* he resigns his breath. *Addison.*

3. That which is conquered; possession gained by force, physical or moral; as, Jamaica was a valuable *conquest* for England.

4. In *a feudal sense,* acquest; acquisition; the acquiring of property by other means than by inheritance, or the acquisition of property by a number in community or by one for all the others. *Blackstone. Encyc.*

5. In *the law of nations,* the acquisition of sovereignty by force of arms.

The right of *conquest* is derived from the laws of war. *Encyc.*

6. The act of gaining or regaining by effort; as the *conquest* of liberty or peace; *a French phrase.*

ȻONSANGUIN'EOUS, *a.* [L. *consanguineus*, infra.] Of the same blood; related by birth; descended from the same parent or ancestor. *Shak.*

ȻONSANGUIN'ITY, *n.* [L. *consanguinitas*; *con* and *sanguis*, blood.]

The relation of persons by blood; the relation or connection of persons descended from the same stock or common ancestor, in distinction from affinity or relation by marriage. It is lineal or collateral. *Blackstone.*

ȻON'SCIENCE, *n. con'shens.* [Fr. from L. *conscientia*, from *conscio*, to know, to be privy to; *con* and *scio*, to know; It. *coscienza*, or *coscienza*; Sp. *conciencia.*]

1. Internal or self-knowledge, or judgment of right and wrong; or the faculty, power or principle within us, which decides on the lawfulness or unlawfulness of our own actions and affections, and instantly approves or condemns them.

Conscience is called by some writers the *moral sense*, and considered as an original faculty of our nature. Others question the propriety of considering conscience as a distinct faculty or principle. They consider it rather as the general principle of moral approbation or disapprobation, applied to one's own conduct and affections; alledging that our notions of right and wrong are not to be deduced from a single principle or faculty, but from various powers of the understanding and will. *Encyc. Hucheson. Reid. Edin. Encyc.*

Being convicted by their own *conscience*, they went out one by one. John viii.

The *conscience* manifests itself in the feeling of obligation we experience, which precedes, attends and follows our actions. *E. T. Fitch.*

Conscience is first occupied in ascertaining our duty, before we proceed to action; then in judging of our actions when performed. *J. M. Mason.*

2. The estimate or determination of conscience; justice; honesty.

What you require cannot, in *conscience*, be deferred. *Milton.*

3. Real sentiment; private thoughts; truth; as, do you in *conscience* believe the story?

4. Consciousness; knowledge of our own actions or thoughts.

The sweetest cordial we receive at last,
Is *conscience* of our virtuous actions past. *Denham.*

[*This primary sense of the word is nearly, perhaps wholly obsolete.*]

5. Knowledge of the actions of others. *B. Jonson.*

6. In *ludicrous language,* reason or reasonableness.

Half a dozen fools are, in all *conscience*, as many as you should require. *Swift.*

To make conscience or *a matter of conscience*, is to act according to the dictates of conscience, or to scruple to act contrary to its dictates. *Locke.*

Court of conscience, a court established for the recovery of small debts in London and other trading cities and districts. *Blackstone.*

ȻON'SCIENCED, *a.* Having conscience. *South.*

ȻON'SCIENT, Conscious. [*Not used.*] *Bacon.*

ȻONSCIEN'TIOUS, *a.* Influenced by conscience; governed by a strict regard to the dictates of conscience, or by the known or supposed rules of right and wrong; as a *conscientious* judge.

2. Regulated by conscience; according to the dictates of conscience; as a *conscientious* probity. *L'Estrange.*

ȻONSCIEN'TIOUSLY, *adv.* According to the direction of conscience; with a strict regard to right and wrong. A man may err *conscientiously.*

ȻONSCIEN'TIOUSNESS, *n.* A scrupulous regard to the decisions of consoience; a sense of justice, and strict conformity to its dictates. *Locke.*

All his conduct seemed marked with an exact and unvarying *conscientiousness.* *J. L. Kingsley, Eulogy on Prof. Fisher.*

ȻON'SCIONABLE, *a.* According to conscience; reasonable; just.

Let my debtors have *conscionable* satisfaction. *Wotton.*

ȻON'SCIONABLENESS, *n.* Reasonableness; equity. *Dict.*

ȻON'SCIONABLY, *adv.* In a manner agreeable to conscience; reasonably; justly. *Taylor.*

ȻON'SCIOUS, *a.* [L. *conscius.*] Possessing the faculty or power of knowing one's own thoughts, or mental operations. Thus, man is a *conscious* being.

2. Knowing from memory, or without extraneous information; as, I am not *conscious* of the fact.

The damsel then to Tancred sent,
Who, *conscious* of the occasion, feared the event. *Dryden.*

3. Knowing by conscience, or internal perception or persuasion; as, I am not *conscious* of having given any offense. Sometimes followed by *to*; as, I am not *conscious to* myself.

Æneas only, *conscious to* the sign,
Presaged the event. *Dryden.*

So we say, *conscious* of innocence, or of ignorance, or of a crime.

ȻON'SCIOUSLY, *adv.* With knowledge of one's own mental operations or actions.

If these perceptions, with their consciousness, always remained in the mind, the same thinking thing would be always *consciously* present. *Locke.*

ȻON'SCIOUSNESS, *n.* The knowledge of sensations and mental operations, or of what passes in one's own mind; the act of the mind which makes known an internal object. *Locke. Reid. Encyc.*

Consciousness of our sensations, and *consciousness* of our existence, seem to be simultaneous. *Edin. Encyc.*

Consciousness must be an essential attribute of spirit. *Watts.*

2. Internal sense or knowledge of guilt or innocence.

A man may betray his *consciousness* of guilt by his countenance.

3. Certain knowledge from observation or experience. *Gibbon.*

ȻON'SȻRIPT, *a.* [L. *conscriptus*, from *conscribo*, to enroll; *con* and *scribo*, to write.]

Written; enrolled; as *conscript* fathers, the senators of Rome, so called because their names were written in the register of the senate.

ȻON'SȻRIPT, *n.* An enrolled soldier; *a word used in France.*

ȻONSȻRIP'TION, *n.* [L. *conscriptio.*] An enrolling or registering.

2. Soldiers or forces levied by enrolling.

ȻON'SEȻRATE, *v. t.* [L. *consecro*; *con* and *sacro*, to consecrate, from *sacer*, sacred. See *Sacred.*]

1. To make or declare to be sacred, by certain ceremonies or rites; to appropriate to sacred uses; to set apart, dedicate, or devote, to the service and worship of God; as, to *consecrate* a church.

Thou shalt *consecrate* Aaron and his sons. Ex. xxix.

All the silver, and gold, and vessels of brass and iron, are *consecrated* to the Lord. Josh. vi.

2. To canonize; to exalt to the rank of a saint; to enroll among the gods, as a Roman emperor.

3. To set apart and bless the elements in the eucharist.

4. To render venerable; to make respected; as, rules or principles *consecrated* by time.

CON'SE€RATE, *a.* Sacred; consecrated; devoted; dedicated.

They were assembled in that *consecrate* place. *Bacon.*

[*This word is now seldom used, unless in poetry.*]

€ON'SE€RATED, *pp.* Made sacred by ceremonies or solemn rites; separated from a common to a sacred use; devoted or dedicated to the service and worship of God; made venerable.

€ON'SE€RATING, *ppr.* Making sacred; appropriating to a sacred use; dedicating to the service of God; devoting; rendering venerable.

€ONSE€RA'TION, *n.* The act or ceremony of separating from a common to a sacred use, or of devoting and dedicating a person or thing to the service and worship of God, by certain rites or solemnities. Consecration does not make a person or thing really *holy*, but declares it to be *sacred*, that is, devoted to God or to divine service; as the *consecration* of the priests among the Israelites; the *consecration* of the vessels used in the temple; the *consecration* of a bishop.

2. Canonization; the act of translating into heaven, and enrolling or numbering among the saints or gods; the ceremony of the apotheosis of an emperor. *Hale.*

3. The benediction of the elements in the eucharist; the act of setting apart and blessing the elements in the communion. *Encyc.*

€ON'SE€RATOR, *n.* One who consecrates; one who performs the rites by which a person or thing is devoted or dedicated to sacred purposes. *Atterbury.*

€ON'SE€RATORY, *a.* Making sacred. *Bp. Morton.*

€ON'SE€TARY, *a.* [L. *consectarius*, from *consector*, to follow; *con* and *sector*, *sequor*. See *Seek.*]

Following; consequent; consequential; deducible. *Brown.*

€ON'SE€TARY, *n.* That which follows; consequence; deduction from premises; corollary. *Woodward.*

€ONSE€U'TION, *n.* [L. *consecutio*, from *consequor*, to follow; *con* and *sequor*, to follow. See *Seek.*]

1. A following or sequel; train of consequences from premises; series of deductions. *Hale.*

2. Succession; series of things that follow each other; as a *consecution* of colors. *Newton.*

3. In astronomy, *consecution month* is the space between one conjunction of the moon with the sun and another. *Bailey.*

€ONSE€'UTIVE, *a.* [It. *consecutivo*; Fr. *consecutif.* See *Consecution.*]

1. Following in a train; succeeding one another in a regular order; successive; uninterrupted in course or succession; as, fifty *consecutive* years. *Arbuthnot.*

2. Following; consequential; succeeding; as, the actions of men *consecutive* to volition. *Locke.*

3. *Consecutive chords*, in music, imply a succession or repetition of the same consonance in similar motion. *Encyc.*

€ONSE€'UTIVELY, *adv.* By way of consequence or succession, in opposition to *antecedently* or *casually.* *Dict.*

€ONSENES'CENCE, } *n.* [L. *consenesco*,
€ONSENES'CENCY, } to grow old.]

A growing old; decay from age; as the *consenescence* of the world. *Ray.*

€ONSEN'SION, *n.* [L. *consensio.* See *Consent.*]

Agreement; accord. [*Little used.*] *Bentley.*

€ONSENT', *n.* [L. *consensus*; It. *consenso*; Fr. *consentement*; Sp. *consentimiento*; from L. *consentio*, to be of one mind, to agree; *con* and *sentio*, to think, feel or perceive; Sp. *consentir*; Port. Fr. *id.*; It. *consentire.* See *Sense* and *Assent.*]

1. Agreement of the mind to what is proposed or stated by another; accord; hence, a yielding of the mind or will to that which is proposed; as, a parent gives his *consent* to the marriage of his daughter.

We generally use this word in cases where power, rights and claims are concerned. We give *consent*, when we yield that which we have a right to withhold; but we do not give *consent* to a mere opinion, or abstract proposition. In this case, we give our *assent.* But *assent* is also used in conceding what we may withhold. We give our *assent* to the marriage of a daughter. Consequently, *assent* has a more extensive application than *consent.* But the distinction is not always observed. *Consent* often amounts to *permission.*

Defraud ye not one another, except with *consent* for a time. 1 Cor. vii.

2. Accord of minds; agreement; unity of opinion.

All with one *consent* began to make excuse. Luke xiv.

The company of priests murder by *consent.* Hos. vi.

3. Agreement; coherence; correspondence in parts, qualities, or operation.

Such is the world's great harmony that springs
From union, order, full *consent* of things. *Pope.*

4. In *the animal economy*, an agreement, or sympathy, by which one affected part of the system affects some distant part. This *consent* is supposed to exist in, or be produced by the nerves; and the affections to be communicated from one part to another by means of their ramifications and distribution through the body. Thus, the stone in the bladder, by vellicating the fibers, will produce spasms and colic in the bowels; a shameful thing seen or heard will produce blushing in the cheeks. *Quincy. Encyc.*

But many facts indicate that other causes than nervous communication produce sympathy.

€ONSENT', *v. i.* [L. *consentio.* See the Noun.]

Literally, to think with another. Hence, to agree or accord. More generally, to agree in mind and will; to yield to what one has the power, the right, or the disposition to withhold, or refuse to grant.

If sinners entice thee, *consent* thou not. Prov. i.

And Saul was *consenting* to Stephen's death. Acts viii.

Only let us *consent* to them, and they will dwell with us. Gen. xxxiv.

2. To agree.

When thou sawest a thief, thou *consentedst* with him. Ps. l.

3. To assent.

I *consent* to the law that it is good. Rom. vii. 1 Tim. vi.

€ONSENTA'NEOUS, *a.* [L. *consentaneus.* See *Consent.*]

Agreeable; accordant; consistent with; suitable.

The practice of virtue is not *consentaneous* to the unrenewed heart. *Anon.*

€ONSENTA'NEOUSLY, *adv.* Agreeably; consistently; suitably.

€ONSENTA'NEOUSNESS, *n.* Agreement; accordance; consistency. *Dict.*

€ONSENT'ER, *n.* One who consents.

€ONSEN'TIENT, *a.* [L. *consentiens*, *consentio.*]

Agreeing in mind; accordant in opinion.

The authority due to the *consentient* judgment of the church. *Pearson.*

€ON'SEQUENCE, *n.* [L. *consequentia*, from *consequor*; *con* and *sequor*, to follow. See *Seek.*]

1. That which follows from any act, cause, principle, or series of actions. Hence, an event or effect produced by some preceding act or cause.

Shun the bitter *consequence*; for know,
The day thou eatest thereof, thou shalt die. *Milton.*

The *consequences* of intemperance are disgrace, poverty, disease and premature death.

2. In *logic*, a proposition collected from the agreement of other previous propositions; the conclusion which results from reason or argument; inference; deduction.

Every rational being is accountable to his maker; man is a rational being; the *consequence* then must be, that man is accountable to his maker.

From this train of argument, the *consequence* is obvious.

3. Connection of cause and effect; consecution.

I felt
That I must after thee, with this my son;
Such fatal *consequence* unites us three. *Milton.*

4. Influence; tendency, as to effects. The sense of *consequence*, in this use, is modified by the words connected with it; as, "it is of *little consequence*," that is, of little importance, small effects will follow; "it is of *no consequence*," of no moment, no effect of importance will follow; "it is of *great consequence*," of great importance, great effects will follow.

5. Importance; extensive influence; distinction; as a man of great *consequence* in society.

In consequence, by means of; as the effect of.

€ON'SEQUENT, *a.* [L. *consequens.*] Following, as the natural effect; with *to* or *on.*

The right was *consequent to*, and built on, an act perfectly personal. *Locke.*

His poverty was *consequent on* his vices.

2. Following by necessary inference or rational deduction; as a proposition *consequent to* other propositions.

€ON'SEQUENT, *n.* Effect; that which follows a cause.

They were ill governed, which is always a *consequent* of ill payment. *Davies.*

2. That which follows from propositions by rational deduction; that which is deduced from reasoning or argumentation; a conclusion or inference.

CONSEQUEN'TIAL, *a.* Following as the effect; produced by the connection of effects with causes; as a *consequential* evil.

2. Having the consequence justly connected with the premises; conclusive.

These arguments are highly *consequential* and concludent to my purpose. *Hale.*

3. Important.

4. Conceited; pompous; *applied to persons.*

CONSEQUEN'TIALLY, *adv.* With just deduction of consequences; with right connection of ideas. *Addison.*

2. By consequence; not immediately; eventually. *South.*

3. In a regular series; in the order of cause and effect. *Addison.*

4. With assumed importance; with conceit. *Campbell.*

CONSEQUEN'TIALNESS, *n.* Regular consecution in discourse. *Dict.*

CON'SEQUENTLY, *adv.* By consequence; by necessary connection of effects with their causes; in consequence of something.

CON'SEQUENTNESS, *n.* Regular connection of propositions, following each other; consecution of discourse. [*Little used.*] *Digby.*

CONSER'TION, *n.* [L. *consero, consertum.*] Junction; adaptation. *Young.*

CONSERV'ABLE, *a.* [See *Conserve.*] That may be kept or preserved from decay or injury.

CONSERV'ANCY, *n.* [L. *conservans.* See *Conserve.*]

A *court of conservancy* is held by the Lord Mayor of London, for the preservation of the fishery on the Thames. *Johnson.*

CONSERV'ANT. *a.* Preserving; having the power or quality of preserving from decay or destruction.

CONSERVA'TION, *n.* [L. *conservatio.* See *Conserve.*]

The act of preserving, guarding or protecting; preservation from loss, decay, injury, or violation; the keeping of a thing in a safe or entire state; as the *conservation* of bodies from perishing; the *conservation* of the peace of society; the *conservation* of privileges.

CONSERV'ATIVE, *a.* Preservative; having power to preserve in a safe or entire state, or from loss, waste or injury. *Peacham.*

CONSERVA'TOR, *n.* A preserver; one who preserves from injury or violation. *Appropriately*, an officer who has the charge of preserving the public peace, as judges and sheriffs; also, an officer who has the charge of preserving the rights and privileges of a city, corporation or community, as in catholic universities. It is a word of extensive application.

2. In *Connecticut*, a person appointed to superintend idiots, lunatics, &c., manage their property, and preserve it from waste.

CONSERV'ATORY, *a.* Having the quality of preserving from loss, decay or injury.

CONSERV'ATORY, *n.* A place for preserving any thing in a state desired, as from loss, decay, waste or injury. Thus a fish-pond for keeping fish, a granary for corn, an ice-house for ice and other things, a receptacle for water, &c., are called *conservatories.*

2. A large green-house for exotics, in which the plants are planted in beds and borders, and not in tubs or pots, as in the common green-house.

CONSERVE, *v. t.* *conserv'.* [L. *conservo; con* and *servo*, to hold, keep or guard; Fr. *conserver;* It. *conservare;* Sp. *conservar.* See Class Sr. No. 34. 38. 39. 40. 45. and Class Dr. No. 32.]

To keep in a safe or sound state; to save; to preserve from loss, decay, waste, or injury; to defend from violation; as, to *conserve* bodies from perishing; to *conserve* the peace of society; to *conserve* fruits, roots and herbs, with sugar, &c.

CON'SERVE, *n.* A sweetmeat made of the inspissated juice of fruit, boiled with sugar. *Johnson.*

2. In *pharmacy*, a form of medicine contrived to preserve the flowers, herbs, roots or fruits of simples, as nearly as possible, in their natural fresh state. Fresh vegetables and sugar of the consistence of honey. *Encyc. Coxe.*

3. A conservatory. [*Not usual.*] *Evelyn.*

CONSERV'ED, *pp.* Preserved in a safe and sound state; guarded; kept; maintained; protected; prepared with sugar.

CONSERV'ER, *n.* One who conserves; one who keeps from loss or injury; one who lays up for preservation; a preparer of conserves. *Hayward. Temple.*

CONSERV'ING, *ppr.* Keeping in safety; defending; maintaining; preparing with sugar.

CONSES'SION, *n.* [L. *consessio.* See *Session.*]

A sitting together. [*Little used.*]

CONSES'SOR, *n.* One that sits with others. [*Little used.*]

CONSID'ER, *v. t.* [L. *considero*, to consider, to view attentively, from *consido* or *considео*, to sit by; *con* and *sedeo*, to sit. See *Sit.* The literal sense is, to *sit by or close*, or to *set the mind* or *the eye to;* hence, to view or examine with attention.]

1. To fix the mind on, with a view to a careful examination; to think on with care; to ponder; to study; to meditate on.

Know, therefore, this day, and *consider* it in thy heart. Deut. iv.

Hast thou *considered* my servant Job? Job i.

Consider the lilies of the field how they grow. Matth. vi.

2. To view attentively; to observe and examine.

The priest shall *consider* the leprosy. Lev. xiii.

3. To attend to; to relieve.

Blessed is he that *considereth* the poor. Ps. xli.

4. To have regard to; to respect.

Let us *consider* one another, to provoke to love, and to good works. Heb. x.

5. To take into view in examination, or into account in estimates.

In adjusting accounts, services, time, and expense ought to be *considered.*

6. In the imperative, *consider* is equivalent to, think with care, attend, examine the subject with a view to truth or the consequences of a measure. So we use *see, observe, think, attend.*

7. To requite; to reward; particularly for gratuitous services.

CONSID'ER, *v. i.* To think seriously, maturely or carefully; to reflect.

None *considereth* in his heart, neither is there knowledge or understanding. Is. xliv.

In the day of adversity *consider.* Eccles. vii.

2. To deliberate; to turn in the mind; as in the case of a single person; to deliberate or consult, as numbers; sometimes followed by *of;* as, I will *consider* your case, or *of* your case.

The apostles and elders come together to *consider of* this matter. Acts xv.

3. To doubt; to hesitate. *Dryden.*

CONSID'ERABLE, *a.* [Fr. Sp. See *Consider.*] That may be considered; that is to be observed, remarked or attended to.

It is *considerable*, that some urns have had inscriptions on them, expressing that the lamps were burning. *Wilkins.*

[*This primary use of the word is obsolescent or very rarely used.*]

2. Worthy of consideration; worthy of regard or attention.

Eternity is infinitely the most *considerable* duration. *Tillotson.*

As that which is worthy of regard is in some measure important, hence

3. Respectable; deserving of notice; of some distinction; *applied to persons.*

Men *considerable* in all worthy professions, eminent in many ways of life. *Spratt.*

4. Important; valuable; or moderately large, according to the subject. *Considerable* aid was expected from the allies. A man has a *considerable* estate in Norfolk. A *considerable* sum of money was collected. Sometimes followed by *to.* He thought his aid *considerable to* him.

CONSID'ERABLENESS, *n.* Some degree of importance, moment or dignity; a degree of value or importance that deserves notice.

The *considerableness* of things is to be estimated by their usefulness, or by their effects on society.

CONSID'ERABLY, *adv.* In a degree deserving notice; in a degree not trifling, or unimportant.

And Europe still *considerably* gains
Both by their good examples and their pains. *Roscommon.*

CONSID'ERANCE, *n.* Consideration; reflection; sober thought. [*Not used.* See *Consideration.*] *Shak.*

CONSID'ERATE, *a.* [L. *consideratus.* See *Consider.*]

1. Given to consideration, or to sober reflection; thoughtful; hence, serious; circumspect; careful; discreet; prudent; not hasty or rash; not negligent.

Æneas is patient, *considerate*, and careful of his people. *Dryden.*

2. Having respect to; regardful; as, *considerate* of praise. [*Little used.*]

3. Moderate; not rigorous. *Johnson.*

CONSID'ERATELY, *adv.* With deliberation; with due consideration; calmly; prudently. *Bacon.*

CONSID'ERATENESS, *n.* Prudence; calm deliberation.

CONSIDERA'TION, *n.* [L. *consideratio.* See *Consider.*]

1. The act of considering; mental view; regard; notice.

Let us take into *consideration* the consequences of a hasty decision.

2. Mature thought; serious deliberation.

Let us think with *consideration*. *Sidney.*

3. Contemplation; meditation.

The love you bear to Mopsa hath brought you to the *consideration* of her virtues. *Sidney.*

4. Some degree of importance; claim to notice, or regard; a moderate degree of respectability.

Lucan is an author of *consideration* among the Latin poets. *Addison.*

5. That which is considered; motive of action; influence; ground of conduct.

He was obliged, antecedent to all other *considerations*, to search an asylum. *Dryden.*

6. Reason; that which induces to a determination.

He was moved by the *considerations* set before him.

7. In *law*, the reason which moves a contracting party to enter into an agreement; the material cause of a contract; the price or motive of a stipulation. In all contracts, each party gives something in exchange for what he receives.

A contract is an agreement, upon sufficient *consideration*. This consideration is *express* or *implied; express*, when the thing to be given or done is specified; *implied*, when no specific consideration is agreed upon, but justice requires it and the law implies it; as when a man labors for another, without stipulating for wages, the law infers that he shall receive a reasonable *consideration*. A good *consideration* is that of blood, or natural love; a valuable *consideration* is such as money, marriage, &c. Hence a *consideration* is an equivalent or recompense; that which is *given* as of equal estimated value with that which is *received*.

CONSID'ERATIVE, *a.* Taking into consideration. [*Little used.*]

CONSID'ERED, *pp.* Thought of with care; pondered; viewed attentively; deliberated on; examined.

CONSID'ERER, *n.* A thinker; one who considers; a man of reflection. [*Considerator* is not in use.]

CONSID'ERING, *ppr.* Fixing the mind on; meditating on; pondering; viewing with care and attention; deliberating on.

Note. We have a peculiar use of this word, which may be a corruption for *considered*, or which may be a deviation from analogy by an insensible change in the structure of the phrase. "It is not possible for us to act otherwise, *considering* the weakness of our nature." As a participle, this word must here refer to *us*, or the sentence cannot be resolved by any rule of English syntax. It would be correct to say, "It is not possible for us to act otherwise, the weakness of our nature being *considered*;" or "We, considering the weakness of our nature, cannot act otherwise." But the latter phrase is better grammar, than it is sense. We use other participles in like manner; as, "*Allowing* for tare, the weight could not be more than a hundred pounds." These and similar phrases are anomalous. But *considering* is no more a *kind of conjunction*, in such phrases, than it is a *noun.*

CONSID'ERING, *n.* The act of deliberating, or carefully attending to; hesitation; as, many mazed *considerings*. *Shak.*

CONSID'ERINGLY, *adv.* With consideration or deliberation. *Whole Duty of Man.*

CONSI'GN, *v. t.* *consi'ne.* [L. *consigno*, to seal or sign; *con* and *signo*, to seal or stamp; *signum*, a sign, seal or mark; It. *consegnare*, to deposit, deliver, consign; Sp. *consignar;* Fr. *consigner*. See *Sign.* The sense is to *set to*, to *thrust* or *send.*]

1. To give, send or set over; to transfer or deliver into the possession of another, or into a different state, with the sense of fixedness in that state, or permanence of possession.

At the day of general account, good men are to be *consigned over to* another state. *Atterbury.*

At death the body is *consigned to* the grave.

2. To deliver or transfer, as a charge or trust; to commit; as, to *consign* a youth to the care of a preceptor; to *consign* goods to a factor.

3. To set over or commit, for permanent preservation; as, to *consign* a history to writing. *Addison.*

4. To appropriate. *Dryden.*

CONSI'GN, *v. i.* *consi'ne.* To submit to the same terms with another; also, to sign; to agree or consent. *Obs.* *Shak.*

CONSIGNA'TION, *n.* The act of consigning; the act of delivering or committing to another person, place or state.

Despair is a certain *consignation* to eternal ruin. *Taylor. Park.*

[*Little used.* See *Consignment.*]

CONSIG'NATURE, *n.* Full signature; joint signing or stamping.

CONSI'GNED, *pp.* Delivered; committed for keeping, or management; deposited in trust.

CONSIGNEE', *n.* The person to whom goods or other things are delivered in trust, for sale or superintendance; a factor.

CONSI'GNER, } *n.* The person who con-
CONSI'GNOR, } signs; one who sends, delivers, or commits goods to another for sale, or a ship for superintendence, bills of lading, papers, &c.

CONSIGNIFICA'TION, *n.* [See *Signify.*] Joint signification. *Harris.*

CONSIGNIF'ICATIVE, *a.* [See *Signify.*] Having a like signification, or jointly significative. *Vallancey, Gram.* 57.

CONSI'GNING, *ppr.* Delivering to another in trust; sending or committing, as a possession or charge.

CONSI'GNMENT, *n.* The act of consigning; consignation; the act of sending or committing, as a charge for safe-keeping or management; the act of depositing with, as goods for sale.

2. The thing consigned; the goods sent or delivered to a factor for sale; as, A received a large *consignment* of goods from B.

3. The writing by which any thing is consigned.

CONSIM'ILAR, *a.* Having common resemblance. [*Little used.*]

CONSIMIL'ITUDE, *n.* Resemblance. [*Little used.*]

CONSIST', *v. i.* [L. *consisto; con* and *sisto*, to stand; Sp. *consistir;* It. *consistere;* Fr. *consister.*]

1. To stand together; to be in a fixed or permanent state, as a body composed of parts in union or connection. Hence, to be; to exist; to subsist; to be supported and maintained.

He was before all things, and by him all things *consist.* Col. i.

2. To stand or be; to lie; to be contained; followed by *in*.

The beauty of epistolary writing *consists in* ease and freedom.

3. To be composed; followed by *of*.

A landscape should *consist of* a variety of scenery.

To consist together, to coexist; to have being concurrently.

Necessity and election cannot *consist together* in the same act. *Bramhall.*

To consist with, to agree; to be in accordance with; to be compatible.

Health *consists with* temperance alone. *Pope.*

CONSIST'ENCE, } *n.* A standing togeth-
CONSIST'ENCY, } er; a being fixed in union, as the parts of a body; that state of a body, in which its component parts remain fixed.

The *consistency* of bodies is divers; dense, rare, tangible, pneumatical, volatile, &c. *Bacon.*

2. A degree of density or spissitude, but indefinite.

Let the juices or liquor be boiled into the *consistency* of syrup. *Arbuthnot.*

3. Substance; make; firmness of constitution; as, friendship of a lasting *consistency;* resolutions of durable *consistence.* *South. Hammond.*

4. A standing together, as the parts of a system, or of conduct, &c.; agreement or harmony of all parts of a complex thing among themselves, or of the same thing with itself at different times; congruity; uniformity; as the *consistency* of laws, regulations or judicial decisions; *consistency* of opinions; *consistency* of behavior or of character.

There is harmony and *consistency* in all God's works. *J. Lathrop.*

5. A standing; a state of rest, in which things capable of growth or decrease, remain for a time at a stand. *Chambers.*

CONSIST'ENT, *a.* [L. *consistens.* See *Consist.*] Fixed; firm; not fluid; as the *consistent* parts of a body, distinguished from the *fluid.* *Harvey.*

2. Standing together or in agreement; compatible; congruous; uniform; not contradictory or opposed; as, two opinions or schemes are *consistent;* let a man be *consistent with* himself; the law is *consistent with* justice and policy.

So two *consistent* motions act the soul. *Pope.*

CONSIST'ENTLY, *adv.* In a consistent manner; in agreement; agreeably; as, to command confidence, a man must act *consistently.*

CONSISTO'RIAL, } *a.* [See *Consistory.*]
CONSIST'ORY, } Pertaining or relating to a *consistory*, or ecclesiastical court of an archbishop or bishop. *Ayliffe.*

Every archbishop and bishop of a diocese hath a *consistory* court. *Encyc.*

CONSISTO'RIAN, *a.* Relating to an order of presbyterian assemblies. *Bp. Bancroft.*

CONSIST'ORY, *n.* [L. *consistorium*, from *consisto.* See *Consist.*] Primarily, a place of meeting; a council-house, or place of justice. Hence,

1. A place of justice in the spiritual court, or the court itself; the court of every diocesan bishop, held in their cathedral churches, for the trial of ecclesiastical

causes, arising within the diocese. The bishop's chancellor or his commissary is the judge. *Blackstone.*

2. An assembly of prelates; the college of cardinals at Rome.

Pius was then hearing causes in *consistory*. *Bacon.*

3. A solemn assembly or council. *Milton. Pope.*

4. A place of residence. [*Not used.*] *Shak.*

5. In the Reformed churches, an assembly or council of ministers and elders.

CONSO'CIATE, *n.* [L. *consociatus.* See the next word.]

An associate; a partner or confederate; an accomplice. *Hayward.*

CONSO'CIATE, *v. t.* [L. *consociatus*, from *consocio; con* and *socio*, to unite; *socius*, a companion. See *Social.*]

1. To unite; to join; to associate. *Wotton.*

2. To cement, or hold in close union. *Burnet.*

3. To unite in an assembly or convention, as pastors and messengers or delegates of churches. *Saybrook Platform.*

CONSO'CIATE, *v. i.* To unite; to coalesce. *Bentley.*

2. To unite, or meet in a body; to form a consociation of pastors and messengers. *Saybrook Platform.*

CONSOCIA'TION, *n.* Intimate union of persons; fellowship; alliance; companionship; union of things. [*This word is less used than* association.] *Wotton.*

2. Fellowship or union of churches by their pastors and delegates; a meeting of the pastors and delegates of a number of congregational churches, for aiding and supporting each other, and forming an advisory council in ecclesiastical affairs. *Trumbull, Hist. of Connecticut.*

CONSOCIA'TIONAL, *a.* Pertaining to a consociation. *Trumbull.*

CON'SOL, *n.* [from *consolidate.*] Consols, in England, are the funds or stocks formed by the consolidation of different annuities. *Crabbe.*

CONSO'LABLE, *a.* [See *Console.*] That admits comfort; capable of receiving consolation.

CON'SOLATE, *v. t.* To comfort. *Obs.* [See *Console.*]

CONSOLA'TION, *n.* [L. *consolatio.* See *Console.*]

1. Comfort; alleviation of misery, or distress of mind; refreshment of mind or spirits; a comparative degree of happiness in distress or misfortune, springing from any circumstance that abates the evil, or supports and strengthens the mind, as hope, joy, courage and the like.

Against such cruelties,
With inward *consolations* recompens'd. *Milton.*

We have great joy and *consolation* in thy love. Philem. 7.

2. That which comforts, or refreshes the spirits; the cause of comfort; as the *consolation* of Israel. Luke ii.

CON'SOLATOR, *n.* One who comforts.

CONSOL'ATORY, *a.* [L. *consolatorius.*] Tending to give comfort; refreshing to the mind; assuaging grief. *Howell.*

CONSOL'ATORY, *n.* A speech or writing containing topics of comfort. *Milton.*

CONSO'LE, *v. t.* [L. *consolor;* It. *consolare;* Sp. *consolar;* Fr. *consoler.* The primary sense is either to set or allay, to give rest or quiet, Ar. سلا, Heb. שלה; or the sense is to strengthen, in which case it coincides with the root of *solid.* The latter is most probable.]

To comfort; to cheer the mind in distress or depression; to alleviate grief, and give refreshment to the mind or spirits; to give contentment or moderate happiness by relieving from distress.

The promises of the gospel may well *console* the christian in all the afflictions of life.

It is a *consoling* reflection that the evils of life are temporary.

I am much *consoled* by the reflection that the religion of Christ has been attacked in vain by all the wits and philosophers, and its triumph has been complete. *P. Henry.*

CON'SOLE, *n.* [Fr.] In *architecture*, a bracket or shoulder-piece; or an ornament cut upon the key of an arch, which has a projecture, and on occasion serves to support little cornices, figures, busts and vases. *Encyc.*

CONSO'LED, *pp.* Comforted; cheered.

CONSO'LER, *n.* One that gives comfort.

CONSOL'IDANT, *a.* [See *Consolidate.*] Having the quality of uniting wounds or forming new flesh.

CONSOL'IDANT, *n.* A medicine that heals or unites the parts of wounded flesh. *Coxe.*

CONSOL'IDATE, *v. t.* [It. *consolidare;* Fr. *consolider;* Sp. *consolidar; con* and L. *solidus*, solid. See *Solid.*]

1. To make solid; to unite or press together loose or separate parts, and form a compact mass; to harden or make dense and firm.

He fixed and *consolidated* the earth above the waters. *Burnet.*

2. To unite the parts of a broken bone or the lips of a wound, by means of applications. *Encyc.*

3. To unite two parliamentary bills in one. *Johnson.*

4. In *law*, to combine two benefices in one. *Encyc.*

CONSOL'IDATE, *v. i.* To grow firm and hard; to unite and become solid.

In hurts and ulcers of the head, dryness maketh them more apt to *consolidate*. *Bacon.*

Moist clay *consolidates* by drying.

CONSOL'IDATE, *a.* Formed into a solid mass. *Elyot.*

CONSOL'IDATED, *pp.* Made solid, hard, or compact; united.

CONSOL'IDATING, *ppr.* Making solid; uniting.

CONSOLIDA'TION, *n.* The act of making or process of becoming solid; the act of forming into a firm compact mass, body or system.

2. The annexing of one bill to another in parliament or legislation.

3. The combining of two benefices in one. *Cowel.*

4. The uniting of broken bones or wounded flesh.

CON'SONANCE, *n.* [Fr. from L. *consonantia, consonans*, from *consono*, to sound together; *con* and *sono*, to sound. See *Sound* and *Tone.*]

1. Accord or agreement of sounds. In *music*, consonance is an accord of sounds which produces an agreeable sensation in the ear, as the third, fifth and eighth. It denotes also the according intervals. When the interval of a consonance is invariable, it is called perfect; but when it may be either major or minor, it is termed imperfect. *Busby.*

2. Agreement; accord; congruity; consistency; agreeableness; suitableness; as the *consonance* of opinions among judges; the *consonance* of a ritual to the scriptures.

CON'SONANT, *a.* Agreeing; according; congruous; consistent; followed generally by *to;* sometimes by *with;* as, this rule is *consonant to* scripture and reason.

2. In *music*, composed of consonances; as *consonant* intervals.

CON'SONANT, *n.* A letter, so named because it is considered as being sounded only in connection with a vowel. But some consonants have no sound, even when united with a vowel, and others have a very imperfect sound. The consonants are better called *articulations*, as they are the names given to the several closings or junctions of the organs of speech, which precede and follow the openings of the organs, with which the vowels are uttered. These closings are perfect, and wholly intercept the voice, as in the syllables *ek, ep, et;* or imperfect, and admitting some slight sound, as in *em, en.* Hence some articulations are called *mutes*, and others, *semivowels.* The consonants begin or end syllables, and their use is to determine the manner of beginning or ending the vocal sounds. These closings or configurations of the organs being various, serve to diversify the syllables, as in uttering *ba, da, pa*, or *ab, ad, ap;* and although *b* and *p* may be considered as representing no sounds at all, yet they so modify the utterance of *ab, ap*, or *ba, pa*, that the slight difference between these articulations may be perceived as far as the human voice can be distinctly heard.

CON'SONANTLY, *adv.* Consistently; in agreement.

CON'SONANTNESS, *n.* Agreeableness; consistency.

CON'SONOUS, *a.* [L. *consonus.*] Agreeing in sound; symphonious.

CONSO'PIATE, *v. t.* To lull asleep. [*Not used.*]

CONSOPIA'TION, *n.* A lulling asleep. [*Not used.*]

CON'SOPITE, *v. t.* [L. *consopio.*] To compose; to lull to sleep. [*Not used.*]

CON'SOPITE, *a.* Calm; composed. [*Not used.*] *More.*

CON'SORT, *n.* [L. *consors; con* and *sors*, sort, state, kind.]

1. A companion; a partner; an intimate associate; particularly, a partner of the bed; a wife or husband.

He single chose to live, and shunn'd to wed,
Well pleased to want a *consort* of his bed. *Dryden.*

2. An assembly or association of persons, convened for consultation. *Spenser.*

3. Union; conjunction; concurrence. *Atterbury.*

4. A number of instruments played together; a symphony; a concert. In this sense, *concert* is now used.

5. In *navigation*, any vessel keeping company with another.

Queen consort, the wife of a king, as distinguished from a *queen regent*, who rules alone, and a *queen dowager*, the widow of a king.

ƇONSORT′, *v. i.* To associate; to unite in company; to keep company; followed by *with.*

Which of the Grecian chiefs *consorts with* thee. *Dryden.*

ƇONSORT′, *v. t.* To join; to marry.

With his *consorted* Eve. *Milton.*

2. To unite in company.

He begins to *consort* himself with men. *Locke.*

3. To accompany. [*Not used.*] *Shak.*

ƇONSORT′ABLE, *a.* Suitable. *Wotton.*

ƇONSORT′ED, *pp.* United in marriage. *Milton.*

ƇONSORT′ING, *ppr.* Uniting in company with; associating.

ƇONSOR′TION, *n.* Fellowship. [*Not used.*] *Brown.*

ƇON′SORTSHIP, *n.* Fellowship; partnership. *Bp. Hall.*

ƇON′SOUND, *n.* The name of several species of plants.

ƇONSPIƇU′ITY, *n.* Conspicuousness; brightness. [*Little used.*] *Shak.*

ƇONSPIƇ′UOUS, *a.* [L. *conspicuus*, from *conspicio*, to look or see; *con* and *specio*, to see. See *Species.*]

1. Open to the view; obvious to the eye; easy to be seen; manifest; as, to stand in a *conspicuous* place.

Or come I less *conspicuous.* *Milton.*

2. Obvious to the mental eye; clearly or extensively known, perceived or understood. Hence, eminent; famous; distinguished; as a man of *conspicuous* talents; a lady of *conspicuous* virtues.

ƇONSPIƇ′UOUSLY, *adv.* In a conspicuous manner; obviously; in a manner to be clearly seen; eminently; remarkably.

ƇONSPIƇ′UOUSNESS, *n.* Openness or exposure to the view; a state of being visible at a distance; as the *conspicuousness* of a tower.

2. Eminence; fame; celebrity; renown; a state of being extensively known and distinguished; as the *conspicuousness* of an author.

ƇONSPIR′ACY, *n.* [L. *conspiratio*, from *conspiro.* See *Conspire.*]

1. A combination of men for an evil purpose; an agreement between two or more persons, to commit some crime in concert; particularly, a combination to commit treason, or excite sedition or insurrection against the government of a state; a plot; as a *conspiracy* against the life of a king; a *conspiracy* against the government.

More than forty had made this *conspiracy.* Acts xxiii.

2. In *law*, an agreement between two or more persons, falsely and maliciously to indict, or procure to be indicted, an innocent person of felony. *Blackstone.*

3. A concurrence; a general tendency of two or more causes to one event. *Sidney.*

ƇONSPI′RANT, *a.* [L. *conspirans.*] Conspiring; plotting; engaging in a plot to commit a crime. *Shak.*

ƇONSPIRA′TION, *n.* Conspiracy; agreement or concurrence of things to one end.

ƇONSPIR′ATOR, *n.* One who conspires; one who engages in a plot to commit a crime, particularly treason.

2. In *law*, one who agrees with another falsely and maliciously to indict an innocent person of felony. By the British statute, a conspirator is defined to be one who binds himself by oath, covenant, or other alliance, to assist another falsely and maliciously to indict a person, or falsely to maintain pleas. *Encyc.*

ƇONSPI′RE, *v. i.* [L. *conspiro*, to plot; *con* and *spiro*, to breathe. But the primary sense is to throw, to wind; hence *spira*, a fold, circle, wreath or band; and the sense of the verb is, to breathe together, or more probably, to wind or band together.]

1. To agree, by oath, covenant or otherwise, to commit a crime; to plot; to hatch treason.

The servants of Ammon *conspired* against him, and slew the king in his own house. 2 Kings xxi.

They *conspired* against Joseph to slay him. Gen. xxxvii.

2. In *law*, to agree falsely and maliciously to indict an innocent person of felony.

3. To agree; to concur to one end.

The press, the pulpit, and the stage,
Conspire to censure and expose our age. *Roscommon.*

All things *conspire* to make us prosperous.

ƇONSPI′RER, *n.* One who conspires or plots; a conspirator. *Shak.*

ƇONSPI′RING, *ppr.* Agreeing to commit a crime; plotting; uniting or concurring to one end.

2. In mechanics, *conspiring powers* are such as act in a direction not opposite to one another; cooperating powers. *Harris.*

ƇONSPI′RINGLY, *adv.* In the manner of a conspiracy; by conspiracy. *Milton.*

ƇONSPISSA′TION, *n.* [L. *conspissatus.*] The act of making thick or viscous; thickness. *More.*

ƇONSPURƇA′TION, *n.* [L. *conspurco; con* and *spurco*, to defile.]

The act of defiling; defilement; pollution. [*Not in use.*] *Bp. Hall.*

ƇON′STABLE, *n.* [Sp. *condestable;* Port. *id.;* It. *conestabile;* Fr. *connetable;* Sp. *conde*, It. *conte*, a count, and L. *stabulum*, a stable; L. *comes stabuli*, count of the stable.]

1. The Lord High Constable of England, the seventh officer of the crown. He had the care of the common peace, in deeds of arms, and matters of war; being a judge of the court of chivalry, now called the court of honor. To this officer and to the Earl Marshal belonged the cognizance of contracts, deeds of arms, without the realm, and combats and blazonry within the realm. The power of this officer was so great and so improperly used, that it was abridged by the 13th Richard II., and was afterwards forfeited in the person of Edward Stafford, duke of Buckingham, in 1521. It has never been granted to any person, since that time, except *pro hac vice*, or on a particular occasion. *Encyc.*

2. An officer of the peace. In *England*, there are high constables, petty constables, and constables of London. The high constables are chosen at the court leets of the franchise or hundred over which they preside, or in default of that, by the justices of the quarter sessions, and are removable by the same authority that appoints them. The petty constables are chosen by the jury of the court leet, or if no court is held, they are appointed by two justices of the peace. In London, a constable is nominated in each precinct by the inhabitants, and confirmed at the court of wardmote. The duty of constables is to keep the peace, and for this purpose they are invested with the power of arresting and imprisoning, and of breaking open houses.

In *the United States*, constables are town or city officers of the peace, with powers similar to those possessed by the constables in Great Britain. They are invested also with powers to execute civil as well as criminal process, and to levy executions. In *New England*, they are elected by the inhabitants of towns in legal meeting.

To overrun the constable, to spend more than a man is worth or can pay; *a vulgar phrase.*

ƇON′STABLESHIP, *n.* The office of a constable.

ƇON′STABLEWICK, *n.* The district to which a constable's power is limited. *Hale.*

ƇON′STANCY, *n.* [L. *constantia*, from *consto; con* and *sto*, to stand.]

1. Fixedness; a standing firm; hence, applied to God or his works, immutability; unalterable continuance; a permanent state. *Hooker.*

2. Fixedness or firmness of mind; persevering resolution; steady, unshaken determination; particularly applicable to firmness of mind under sufferings, to steadiness in attachments, and to perseverence in enterprise. Lasting affection; stability in love or friendship.

3. Certainty; veracity; reality. *Shak. Johnson.*

ƇON′STANT, *a.* [L. *constans.*] Fixed; firm; opposed to *fluid.*

To turn two fluid liquors into a *constant* body. *Boyle.*

[*In this sense, not used.*]

2. Fixed; not varied; unchanged; permanent; immutable.

The world's a scene of changes, and to be
Constant, in nature were inconstancy. *Cowley.*

3. Fixed or firm in mind, purpose, affection or principle; unshaken; unmoved; as a *constant* friend or lover.

4. Certain; steady; firmly adherent; with *to;* as a man *constant to* his purpose, or *to* his duties.

ƇONSTANTINOPOL′ITAN, *a.* Relating to Constantinople, the metropolis of Turkey in Europe.

ƇON′STANTLY, *adv.* Firmly; steadily; invariably; continually; perseveringly.

Rhoda *constantly* affirmed that it was even so. Acts xii.

These things I will that thou affirm *constantly.* Tit. iii.

ƇON′STAT, *n.* [L. it appears.] In *England*, a certificate given by the clerk of the pipe and auditors of the exchequer, to a person who intends to plead or move for a discharge of any thing in that court. The effect of it is to show what appears upon the record, respecting the matter in question.

2. An exemplification under the great seal of the enrollment of any letters patent. *Encyc.*

CON'STELLATE, *v. i.* [Low L. *constellatus; con* and *stello*, to shine, *stella*, a star.] To join luster; to shine with united radiance or one general light. [*Little used.*]

The several things which engage our affections shine forth and *constellate* in God. *Boyle.*

CON'STELLATE, *v. t.* To unite several shining bodies in one splendor. [*Little used.* *Brown.*

CON'STELLATED, *pp.* United in one splendor. *Brown.*

2. Starry; set or adorned with stars or constellations. *J. Barlow.*

CONSTELLA'TION, *n.* A cluster of fixed stars; an asterism; a number of stars which appear as if situated near each other in the heavens, and are considered as forming a particular division. The constellations are reduced mostly to the figures of certain animals or other known things, as the bear, the bull, the ram, the balance, &c.

For the stars of heaven, and the *constellations* thereof, shall not give their light. Is. xiii.

2. An assemblage of splendors or excellencies. *Hammond.*

CONSTERNA'TION, *n.* [L. *consternatio*, from *consterno; con* and *sterno*, to throw or strike down.]

Astonishment; amazement or horror that confounds the faculties, and incapacitates a person for consultation and execution; excessive terror, wonder or surprise. *South.*

CON'STIPATE, *v. t*, [L. *constipo; con* and *stipo*, to crowd, or cram, Eng. to *stuff*, to *stop*. See *Stuff* and *Stop*.]

1. To crowd or cram into a narrow compass; to thicken or condense. *Bacon.*

2. To stop, by filling a passage, and preventing motion; as, to *constipate* capillary vessels. *Arbuthnot.*

3. To fill or crowd the intestinal canal, and make costive. *Brown.*

CONSTIPA'TION, *n.* The act of crowding any thing into a less compass; a pressing together; condensation; as a close *constipation* of particles. *Bentley.*

2. More generally, a crowding or filling to hardness the intestinal canal, from defective excretion; costiveness; obstipation. *Encyc. Coxe.*

CONSTIT'UENT, *a.* [L. *constituens, constituo; con* and *statuo*, to set. See *Statue, Statute.*]

Setting; constituting; *applied to parts of a thing that are essential to it.* Hence, necessary or essential; elemental; forming, composing or making as an essential part.

Body, soul, and reason, are the three *constituent* parts of a man. *Dryden.*

Oxygen and hydrogen are the *constituent* parts of water.

CONSTIT'UENT, *n.* He or that which sets, fixes or forms; he or that which constitutes or composes.

Their first composure and origination requires a higher and nobler *constituent* than chance. *Hale.*

2. That which constitutes or composes, as a part, or an essential part.

The lymph in those glands is a necessary *constituent* of the aliment. *Arbuthnot.*

3. One who appoints or elects another to an office or employment. *Burke.*

CON'STITUTE, *v. t.* [L. *constituo; con* and *statuo*, to set. See *Statue, Statute.* It. *constituire;* Sp. *constituir;* Fr. *constituer.*]

1. To set; to fix; to enact; to establish.

We must obey laws appointed and *constituted* by lawful authority, not against the law of God. *Taylor.*

2. To form or compose; to give formal existence to; to make a thing what it is.

Perspicuity *constitutes* the prime excellence of style.

Truth and reason *constitute* that intellectual gold that defies destruction. *Johnson.*

3. To appoint, depute or elect to an office or employment; to make and empower.

A sheriff is *constituted* a conservator of the peace.

A has *constituted* B his attorney or agent.

CON'STITUTED, *pp.* Set; fixed; established; made; elected; appointed.

CON'STITUTER, *n.* One who constitutes or appoints.

CON'STITUTING, *ppr.* Setting; establishing; composing; electing; appointing.

CONSTITU'TION, *n.* The act of constituting, enacting, establishing, or appointing.

2. The state of being; that form of being or peculiar structure and connection of parts which makes or characterizes a system or body. Hence the particular frame or temperament of the human body is called its *constitution.* We speak of a robust or feeble *constitution;* a cold, phlegmatic, sanguine or irritable *constitution.* We speak of the *constitution* of the air, or other substance; the *constitution* of the solar system; the *constitution* of things.

3. The frame or temper of mind, affections or passions.

4. The established form of government in a state, kingdom or country; a system of fundamental rules, principles and ordinances for the government of a state or nation. In free states, the constitution is paramount to the statutes or laws enacted by the legislature, limiting and controlling its power; and in the United States, the legislature is created, and its powers designated, by the constitution.

5. A particular law, ordinance, or regulation, made by the authority of any superior, civil or ecclesiastical; as the *constitutions* of the churches; the novel *constitutions* of Justinian and his successors.

6. A system of fundamental principles for the government of rational and social beings.

The New Testament is the moral *constitution* of modern society. *Grimke.*

CONSTITU'TIONAL, *a.* Bred or inherent in the constitution, or in the natural frame of body or mind; as a *constitutional* infirmity; *constitutional* ardor or dulness.

2. Consistent with the constitution; authorized by the constitution or fundamental rules of a government; legal.

An act of congress prohibiting the importation of slaves into the United States is *constitutional.*

3. Relating to the constitution; as a *constitutional* doubt. *Paley.*

CONSTITU'TIONALIST, *n.* An adherent to the constitution of government.

2. An innovator of the old constitution, or a framer or friend of the new constitution in France. *Burke.*

CONSTITUTIONAL'ITY, *n.* The state of being constitutional; the state of being inherent in the natural frame; as the *constitutionality* of disease. *Coxe. Med. Repository.*

2. The state of being consistent with the constitution or frame of government, or of being authorized by its provisions.

The judges of the supreme court of the United States have the power of determining the *constitutionality* of laws.

CONSTITU'TIONALLY, *adv.* In consistency with the constitution or frame of government.

CONSTITU'TIONIST, *n.* One who adheres to the constitution of the country. *Bolingbroke.*

CON'STITUTIVE, *a.* That constitutes, forms or composes; elemental; essential.

The *constitutive* parts of a schismatic, being the esteem of himself and contempt of others. *Decay of Piety.*

2. Having power to enact or establish; instituting.

CONSTRA'IN, *v. t.* [Fr. *contraindre;* It. *constrignere*, or *costringere;* Sp. *constreñir;* Port. *constringir;* from L. *constringo; con* and *stringo*, to strain, to bind. See *Strain.*]

In *a general sense*, to strain; to press; to urge; to drive; to exert force, physical or moral, either in urging to action or in restraining it. Hence,

1. To compel or force; to urge with irresistible power, or with a power sufficient to produce the effect.

The spirit within me *constraineth* me. Job xxxii.

I was *constrained* to appeal to Cesar. Acts xxviii.

For the love of Christ *constraineth* us. 2 Cor. v.

2. To confine by force; to restrain from escape or action; to repress.

My sire in caves *constrains* the winds. *Dryden.*

3. To hold by force; to press; to confine.

How the strait stays the slender waist *constrain.* *Gay.*

4. To constringe; to bind.

When winter frosts *constrain* the field with cold. *Dryden.*

5. To tie fast; to bind; to chain; to confine.

He binds in chains
The drowsy prophet, and his limbs *constrains.* *Dryden.*

6. To necessitate.

Did fate or we the adulterous act *constrain?* *Pope.*

7. To force; to ravish. [*Not used.*] *Shak.*

8. To produce in opposition to nature; as a *constrained* voice; *constrained* notes. *Waller.*

CONSTRA'INABLE, *a.* That may be constrained, forced, or repressed; liable to constraint, or to restraint. *Hooker.*

CONSTRA'INED, *pp.* Urged irresistibly or powerfully; compelled; forced; restrained; confined; bound; imprisoned; necessitated.

CONSTRA'INEDLY, *adv.* By constraint; by compulsion. *Hooker.*

CONSTRA'INER, *n.* One who constrains.

CONSTRA'INING, *ppr.* Urging with irresistible or powerful force; compelling; forcing; repressing; confining; holding by force; pressing; binding.

CONSTRA'INT, *n.* [Fr. *contrainte.*] Irresistible force, or its effect; any force, or power, physical or moral, which compels to act or to forbear action, or which urges so strongly as to produce its effect upon the body or mind; compulsion; restraint; confinement.

Not by *constraint*, but by my choice, I came. *Dryden.*

Feed the flock of God, taking the oversight thereof, not by *constraint*, but willingly. 1 Pet. v.

CONSTRA'INTIVE, *a.* Having power to compel. [*Ill.*] *Carew.*

CONSTRICT', *v. t.* [L. *constringo, constrictum.* See *Constrain.*]

To draw together; to bind; to cramp; to draw into a narrow compass; hence, to contract or cause to shrink. *Arbuthnot.*

CONSTRICT'ED, *pp.* Drawn together; bound; contracted.

CONSTRICT'ING, *ppr.* Drawing together; binding; contracting.

CONSTRIC'TION, *n.* A drawing together or contraction by means of some inherent power, or by spasm, as distinguished from compression, or the pressure of extraneous bodies; as the *constriction* of a muscle or fiber. It may perhaps be sometimes used as synonymous with *compression.*

CONSTRICT'OR, *n.* That which draws together or contracts. In *anatomy*, a muscle which draws together or closes an orifice of the body; as the *constrictor labiorum*, a muscle of the lips. *Encyc.*

2. A species of serpents, the black snake of the United States. *Encyc.*

Also, the *Boa constrictor*, the largest of known serpents.

CONSTRINGE, *v. t.* constrinj'. [L. *constringo.* See *Constrain.*]

To draw together; to strain into a narrow compass; to contract; to force to contract itself.

Strong liquors *constringe*, harden the fibers, and coagulate the fluids. *Arbuthnot.*

CONSTRIN'GED, *pp.* Contracted; drawn together.

CONSTRIN'GENT, *a.* Having the quality of contracting, binding or compressing. *Bacon. Thomson.*

CONSTRIN'GING, *ppr.* Drawing or compressing into a smaller compass; contracting; binding.

CONSTRUCT', *v. t.* [L. *construo, constructum; con* and *struo*, to lay, dispose or set in order; Sp. *construir;* Fr. *construire;* It. *id.* See *Structure.*]

1. To put together the parts of a thing in their proper place and order; to build; to form; as, to *construct* an edifice.

2. To devise and compose, as to *construct* a new system; or simply to frame or form, as to *construct* a telescope. The word may include the invention, with the formation, or not, at the pleasure of the writer. A man *constructs* a ship according to a model; or a grammar by a new arrangement of principles; or a planetarium of a new form.

3. To interpret or understand. [See *Construe.*]

CONSTRUCT'ED, *pp.* Built; formed; composed; compiled.

CONSTRUCT'ER, *n.* One who constructs or frames.

CONSTRUCT'ING, *ppr.* Building; framing; composing.

CONSTRUC'TION, *n.* [L. *constructio.*]

1. The act of building, or of devising and forming; fabrication.

2. The form of building; the manner of putting together the parts of a building, a machine, or a system; structure; conformation.

The sailing of a ship and its capacity depend chiefly on its *construction.*

3. In *grammar*, syntax, or the arrangement and connection of words in a sentence, according to established usages, or the practice of good writers and speakers.

4. Sense; meaning; interpretation; explanation; or the manner of understanding the arrangement of words, or of understanding facts. Let us find the true *construction;* or let us give the author's words a sound, rational, consistent *construction.* What *construction* can be put upon this affair, or upon the conduct of a man?

5. The manner of describing a figure or problem in geometry. *Johnson.*

The drawing of such lines, such figure, &c., as are previously necessary for making any demonstration appear more plain and undeniable. *Encyc.*

6. In *algebra*, the construction of equations is the method of reducing a known equation into lines and figures, in order to a geometrical demonstration. *Johnson.*

CONSTRUC'TIONAL, *a.* Pertaining to construction; deduced from construction or interpretation. [*Unusual.*] *Waterland.*

CONSTRUC'TIVE, *a.* By construction; created or deduced by construction, or mode of interpretation; not directly expressed, but inferred; as *constructive* treason. *Blackstone.*

Stipulations, expressed or implied, formal or *contructive.* *Paley.*

CONSTRUC'TIVELY, *adv.* In a constructive manner; by way of construction or interpretation; by fair inference. *Chauncey. U. States.*

A neutral must have notice of a blockade, either actually by a formal information, or *constructively* by notice to his government. *Kent.*

CONSTRUC'TURE, *n.* An edifice; pile; fabric. [For this, *structure* is more generally used.] *Blackmore.*

CON'STRUE, *v. t.* [L. *construo.* See *Construct.*]

1. To arrange words in their natural order; to reduce from a transposed to a natural order, so as to discover the sense of a sentence; hence, to interpret; and when applied to a foreign language, to translate; to render into English; as, to *construe* Greek, Latin or French.

2. To interpret; to explain; to show or to understand the meaning.

I pray that I may not be so understood or *construed.* *Hooker.*

Thus we are put to *construe* and paraphrase our own words. *Stillingfleet.*

CON'STRUED, *pp.* Arranged in natural order; interpreted; understood; translated.

CON'STRUING, *ppr.* Arranging in natural order; expounding; interpreting; translating.

CON'STUPRATE, *v. t.* [L. *constupro; con* and *stupro*, to ravish.] To violate; to debauch; to defile.

CONSTUPRA'TION, *n.* The act of ravishing; violation; defilement. *Bp. Hall.*

CONSUBSIST', *v. i.* To subsist together. [See *Subsist.*]

CONSUBSTAN'TIAL, *a.* [L. *consubstantialis; con* and *substantia.* See *Substance.*]

1. Having the same substance or essence; co-essential.

The orthodox believe the Son to be *consubstantial* with the Father. *Encyc.*

2. Of the same kind or nature.

It continueth a body *consubstantial* with ours. *Hooker.*

CONSUBSTAN'TIALIST, *n.* One who believes in consubstantiation. *Barrow.*

CONSUBSTANTIAL'ITY, *n.* The existence of more than one in the same substance; as, the co-eternity and *consubstantiality* of the Son with the Father. *Hammond.*

2. Participation of the same nature. *Johnson.*

CONSUBSTAN'TIATE, *v. t.* [L. *con* and *substantia*, substance.]

To unite in one common substance or nature. *Johnson.*

CONSUBSTAN'TIATE, *v. i.* To profess consubstantiation. *Dryden.*

CONSUBSTANTIA'TION, *n.* The union of the body of our blessed Savior with the sacramental elements. The Lutherans maintain that after consecration of the elements, the body and blood of Christ are substantially present with the substance of the bread and wine, which is called *consubstantiation* or impanation. *Encyc.*

CON'SUL, *n.* [L. *consul*, from *consulo*, to *consult.*]

1. The chief magistrate of the Ancient Roman Republic, invested with regal authority for one year. There were two consuls, annually chosen in the Campus Martius. In the first ages of Rome, they were elected from Patrician families or noblemen; but in the year of Rome 388, the people obtained the privilege of electing one of the consuls from their own body, and sometimes both were plebeians. *Encyc.*

2. In *modern usage*, the name *consul* is given to a person commissioned by a king or state to reside in a foreign country as an agent or representative, to protect the rights, commerce, merchants and seamen of the state, and to aid the government in any commercial transactions with such foreign country.

3. An adviser. [*Not well authorized.*] *Bacon.*

CON'SULAGE, *n.* A duty laid by the British Levant Company on imports and exports for the support of the company's affairs. *Eton.*

CON'SULAR, *a.* Pertaining to a consul; as *consular* power; *consular* dignity, or privileges.

CON'SULATE, *n.* [L. *consulatus.*] The office of a consul. *Addison.*

[*This is applicable to modern consuls, as well as to the Roman.*]

2. The jurisdiction or extent of a consul's authority. *Kent.*

CON'SULSHIP, *n.* The office of a consul; or the term of his office; *applicable only to Roman consuls.*

CONSULT', *v. i.* [L. *consulto*, from *consulo*, to consult, to ask counsel. The last syllable may be from the Ar. سال, Heb. Ch. Sam. Eth. שאל to ask.]

1. To seek the opinion or advice of another, by a statement of facts, and suitable inquiries, for the purpose of directing one's own judgment; followed by *with*.

Rehoboam *consulted with* the old men. 1 Kings xii.

David *consulted with* the captains of thousands. 1 Chron. xiii.

2. To take counsel together; to seek opinions and advice by mutual statements, enquiries and reasonings; to deliberate in common.

The chief priests *consulted* that they might put Lazarus to death. John xii.

3. To consider with deliberation. Luke xiv.

CONSULT′, *v. t.* To ask advice of; to seek the opinion of another, as a guide to one's own judgment; as, to *consult* a friend or parent.

2. To seek for information, or facts, in something; as by examining books or papers. Thus, I *consulted* several authors on the subject; I *consulted* the official documents.

3. To regard; to have reference or respect to, in judging or acting; to decide or to act in favor of. We are to *consult* the necessities, rather than the pleasures of life. We are to *consult* public as well as private interest. He *consulted* his own safety in flight.

Ere fancy you *consult, consult* your purse. *Franklin.*

4. To plan, devise or contrive.

Thou hast *consulted* shame to thy house, by cutting off many people. Hab. ii.

[*This sense is unusual and not to be countenanced.*]

CONSULT′, *n.* The act of consulting; the effect of consultation; determination; a council, or deliberating assembly. *Dryden. Bacon.*

This word is, I believe, entirely obsolete, except in poetry. It would be naturally accented on the first syllable, but the poets accent the last.

CONSULTA′TION, *n.* The act of consulting; deliberation of two or more persons, with a view to some decision.

The chief priests held a *consultation* with the elders and scribes. Mark xv.

2. The persons who consult together; a number of persons seeking mutually each others opinions and advice; a council for deliberation; as, a *consultation* of physicians was called. *Wiseman.*

Writ of consultation, in law, a writ awarded by a superior court, to return a cause, which had been removed by prohibition from the court christian, to its original jurisdiction; so called because the judges on *consultation* find the prohibition ill founded. *Blackstone.*

CONSULT′ATIVE, *a.* Having the privilege of consulting. *Bramhall.*

CONSULT′ED, *pp.* Asked; enquired of, for opinion or advice; regarded.

CONSULT′ER, *n.* One who consults, or asks counsel or information; as a *consulter* with familiar spirits. Deut. xviii.

CONSULT′ING, *ppr.* Asking advice; seeking information; deliberating and enquiring mutually; regarding.

CONSU′MABLE, *a.* [See *Consume.*] That may be consumed; possible to be destroyed, dissipated, wasted or spent; as, asbestos is not *consumable* by fire. *Wilkins.*

The importation and exportation of *consumable* commodities. *Locke.*

CONSU′ME, *v. t.* [L. *consumo; con* and *sumo*, to take. So in English we say, it *takes up* time, that is, it *consumes* time. Sp. *consumir;* It. *consumare;* Fr. *consumer.* Class Sm.]

1. To destroy, by separating the parts of a thing, by decomposition, as by fire, or by eating, devouring, and annihilating the form of a substance. Fire *consumes* wood, coal, stubble; animals *consume* flesh and vegetables.

2. To destroy by dissipating or by use; to expend; to waste; to squander; as, to *consume* an estate.

Ye ask, and receive not, because ye ask amiss, that ye may *consume* it upon your lusts. James iv.

3. To spend; to cause to pass away, as time; as, to *consume* the day in idleness.

Their days did he *consume* in vanity. Ps. lxxviii.

4. To cause to disappear; to waste slowly.

My flesh is *consumed* away. Job xxxviii.

5. To destroy; to bring to utter ruin; to exterminate.

Let me alone—that I may *consume* them. Ex. xxxii.

CONSU′ME, *v. i.* To waste away slowly; to be exhausted.

Their flesh—their eyes—their tongue shall *consume* away. Zech. xiv.

The wicked shall perish—they shall *consume.* Ps. xxxvii.

CONSU′MED, *pp.* Wasted; burnt up; destroyed; dissipated; squandered; expended.

CONSU′MER, *n.* One who consumes, spends, wastes or destroys; that which consumes.

CONSU′MING, *ppr.* Burning; wasting; destroying; expending; eating; devouring.

2. *a.* That destroys.

The Lord thy God is a *consuming* fire. Deut. iv.

CON′SUMMATE, *v. t.* [L. *consummo, consummatus; con* and *summo*, from *summa*, sum; Fr. *consommer;* Sp. *consumar.* See *Sum.*]

To end; to finish by completing what was intended; to perfect; to bring or carry to the utmost point or degree.

He had a mind to *consummate* the happiness of the day. *Tatler.*

CONSUM′MATE, *a.* Complete; perfect; carried to the utmost extent or degree; as *consummate* greatness or felicity.

CON′SUMMATED, *pp.* Completed; perfected; ended.

CONSUM′MATELY, *adv.* Completely; perfectly. *Warton.*

CON′SUMMATING, *ppr.* Completing; accomplishing; perfecting.

CONSUMMA′TION, *n.* [L. *consummatio.*] Completion; end; perfection of a work, process or scheme. *Addison.*

2. The end or completion of the present system of things; the end of the world. *Hooker.*

3. Death; the end of life. *Shak.*

Consummation of marriage, the most intimate union of the sexes, which completes the connubial relation.

CONSUMP′TION, *n.* [L. *consumptio.* See *Consume.*]

1. The act of consuming; waste; destruction by burning, eating, devouring, scattering, dissipation, slow decay, or by passing away, as time; as the *consumption* of fuel, of food, of commodities or estate, of time, &c.

2. The state of being wasted, or diminished.

Etna and Vesuvius have not suffered any considerable diminution or *consumption.* *Woodward.*

3. In *medicine*, a wasting of flesh; a gradual decay or diminution of the body; *a word of extensive signification.* But particularly, the disease called *phthisis pulmonalis*, pulmonic consumption, a disease seated in the lungs, attended with hectic fever, cough, &c.

CONSUMP′TIVE, *a.* Destructive; wasting; exhausting; having the quality of consuming, or dissipating; as a long *consumptive* war. *Addison.*

2. Affected with a consumption or pulmonic disease, as *consumptive* lungs; or inclined to a consumption; tending to the phthisis pulmonalis; *applied to the incipient state of the disease, or to a constitution predisposed to it.*

CONSUMP′TIVELY, *adv.* In a way tending to consumption. *Beddoes.*

CONSUMP′TIVENESS, *n.* A state of being consumptive, or a tendency to a consumption.

CONTAB′ULATE, *v. t.* [L. *contabulo; con* and *tabula.*] To floor with boards. *Gayton.*

CONTABULA′TION, *n.* The act of laying with boards, or of flooring.

CON′TACT, *n.* [L. *contactus*, from *contingo*, to touch; *con* and *tango*, to touch, originally *tago.* See *Touch.*]

A touching; touch; close union or juncture of bodies. Two bodies come in *contact*, when they meet without any sensible intervening space; the parts that touch are called the points of *contact.*

CONTAC′TION, *n.* The act of touching. *Brown.*

CONTA′GION, *n.* [L. *contagio*, from the root of *contingo, tango*, primarily *tago*, to touch.]

1. *Literally*, a touch or touching. Hence, the communication of a disease by contact, or the matter communicated. *More generally*, that subtil matter which proceeds from a diseased person or body, and communicates the disease to another person; as in cases of small pox, measles, anginas, and malignant fevers; diseases which are communicated without contact. This contagion proceeds from the breath of the diseased, from the perspiration or other excretions.

2. That which communicates evil from one to another; infection; that which propagates mischief; as the *contagion* of vice or of evil examples. *Milton.*

3. Pestilence; a pestilential disease; venomous exhalations. *Shak.*

CONTA′GIOUS, *a.* Containing or generating contagion; catching; that may be communicated by contact, or by a subtil excreted matter; as a *contagious* disease.

2. Poisonous; pestilential; containing con-

tagion; as *contagious* air; *contagious* clothing.

3. Containing mischief that may be propagated; as *contagious* example.

4. That may be communicated from one to another, or may excite like affections in others.

His genius rendered his courage more *contagious*. *Wirt.*

CONTA'GIOUSNESS, *n.* The quality of being contagious.

CONTA'IN, *v. t.* [L. *contineo; con* and *teneo*, to hold; It. *contenere;* Fr. *contenir;* Sp. *contener.* See *Tenet, Tenure.*]

1. To hold, as a vessel; as, the vessel *contains* a gallon. Hence, to have capacity; to be able to hold; *applied to an empty vessel.*

2. To comprehend; to hold within specified limits.

Behold, the heaven and the heaven of heavens cannot *contain* thee. 1 Kings viii.

3. To comprehend; to comprise. The history of Livy *contains* a hundred and forty books.

4. To hold within limits prescribed; to restrain; to withhold from trespass or disorder.

The King's person *contains* the unruly people from evil occasions. *Obs.* *Spenser.*

Fear not, my Lord, we can *contain* ourselves. *Shak.*

5. To include. This article is not *contained* in the account. This number does not *contain* the article specified.

6. To inclose; as, this cover or envelop *contains* a letter.

CONTA'IN, *v. i.* To live in continence or chastity. *Arbuthnot and Pope.* 1 Cor. vii.

CONTA'INABLE, *a.* That may be contained, or comprised. *Boyle.*

CONTA'INED, *pp.* Held; comprehended; comprised; included; inclosed.

CONTA'INING, *ppr.* Holding; having capacity to hold; comprehending; comprising; including; inclosing.

CONTAM'INATE, *v. t.* [L. *contamino; con* and ant. *tamino.* Qu. Heb. Ch. Syr. טמא to defile. Class Dm. No. 19.]

To defile; to pollute; usually in a figurative sense; to sully; to tarnish; to taint. Lewdness *contaminates* character; cowardice *contaminates* honor.

Shall we now
Contaminate our fingers with base bribes? *Shak.*

CONTAM'INATE, *a.* Polluted; defiled; corrupt. *Shak.*

CONTAM'INATED, *pp.* Polluted; defiled; tarnished.

CONTAM'INATING, *ppr.* Polluting; defiling; tarnishing.

CONTAMINA'TION, *n.* The act of polluting; pollution; defilement; taint.

CON'TECK, *n.* Quarrel; contention. [*Not English.*]

CONTEC'TION, *n.* [L. *contego.*] A covering. [*Not used.*] *Sir T. Browne.*

CONTEMN', *v. t. contem'.* [L. *contemno; con* and *temno*, to despise; It. *contennere;* Ar. ذَأَمَ to drive away, to despise. Class Dm. No. 1. 4.]

1. To despise; to consider and treat as mean and despicable; to scorn.

In whose eyes a vile person is *contemned.* Ps. xv.

2. To slight; to neglect as unworthy of regard; to reject with disdain.

Wherefore do the wicked *contemn* God. Ps. x.

They *contemn* the counsel of the Most High. Ps. cvii.

CONTEM'NED, *pp.* Despised; scorned; slighted; neglected, or rejected with disdain.

CONTEM'NER, *n.* One who contemns; a despiser; a scorner.

CONTEM'NING, *ppr.* Despising; slighting as vile or despicable; neglecting or rejecting, as unworthy of regard.

CONTEM'PER, *v. t.* [Low L. *contempero; con* and *tempero*, to mix or temper. See *Temper.*]

To moderate; to reduce to a lower degree by mixture with opposite or different qualities; to temper.

The leaves qualify and *contemper* the heat. *Ray.*

CONTEM'PERAMENT, *n.* Moderated or qualified degree; a degree of any quality reduced to that of another; temperament. *Derham.*

CONTEM'PERATE, *v. t.* [See *Contemper.*] To temper; to reduce the quality of, by mixing something opposite or different; to moderate. *Brown. Wiseman.*

CONTEMPERA'TION, *n.* The act of reducing a quality by admixture of the contrary; the act of moderating or tempering. *Brown.*

2. Temperament; proportionate mixture; as the *contemperament* of humors in different bodies. *Hale.*

[Instead of these words, *temper* and *temperament* are now generally used.]

CON'TEMPLATE, *v. t.* [L. *contemplor.* If *m* is radical, see Class Dm. No. 3. 4. 35.]

1. To view or consider with continued attention; to study; to meditate on. This word expresses the attention of the mind, but sometimes in connection with that of the eyes; as, to *contemplate* the heavens. More generally, the act of the mind only is intended; as, to *contemplate* the wonders of redemption; to *contemplate* the state of the nation and its future prospects.

2. To consider or have in view, in reference to a future act or event; to intend.

A decree of the National Assembly of France, June 26, 1792, *contemplates* a supply from the United States of four millions of livres.

There remain some particulars to complete the information *contemplated* by those resolutions. *Hamilton's Report.*

If a treaty contains any stipulations which *contemplate* a state of future war. *Kent's Commentaries.*

CON'TEMPLATE, *v. i.* To think studiously; to study; to muse; to meditate.

He delights to *contemplate* on the works of creation.

CON'TEMPLATED, *pp.* Considered with attention; meditated on; intended.

CON'TEMPLATING, *ppr.* Considering with continued attention; meditating on; musing.

CONTEMPLA'TION, *n.* [L. *contemplatio.*] The act of the mind in considering with attention; meditation; study; continued attention of the mind to a particular subject.

Contemplation is keeping the idea, brought into the mind, some time actually in view. *Locke.*

2. Holy meditation; attention to sacred things; *a particular application of the foregoing definition.*

To have in contemplation, to intend or purpose, or to have under consideration.

CONTEM'PLATIVE, *a.* Given to contemplation, or continued application of the mind to a subject; studious; thoughtful; as a *contemplative* philosopher, or mind.

2. Employed in study; as a *contemplative* life. *Bacon.*

3. Having the appearance of study, or a studious habit; as a *contemplative* look. *Denham.*

4. Having the power of thought or meditation; as the *contemplative* faculty of man. *Ray.*

CONTEM'PLATIVELY, *adv.* With contemplation; attentively; thoughtfully; with deep attention.

CON'TEMPLATOR, *n.* One who contemplates; one employed in study or meditation; an inquirer after knowledge. *Raleigh. Brown.*

CONTEMPORA'NEOUS, *a.* [See *Cotemporary.*] Living or being at the same time.

CONTEM'PORARY, *a.* [It. Sp. *contemporaneo;* Fr. *contemporain;* L. *contemporalis; con* and *temporalis, temporarius*, from *tempus*, time. For the sake of easier pronunciation and a more agreeable sound, this word is often changed to *cotemporary.*]

Coetaneous; living at the same time, *applied to persons;* being or existing at the same time, *applied to things;* as *contemporary* kings; *contemporary* events. [See *Cotemporary*, the preferable word.]

CONTEM'PORARY, *n.* One who lives at the same time with another.

Socrates and Plato were *contemporaries.*

CONTEM'PORISE, *v. t.* To make contemporary; to place in the same age or time. [*Not used.*] *Brown.*

CONTEMPT', *n.* [L. *contemptus.* See *Contemn.*]

1. The act of despising; the act of viewing or considering and treating as mean, vile and worthless; disdain; hatred of what is mean or deemed vile. This word is one of the strongest expressions of a mean opinion which the language affords.

Nothing, says Longinus, can be great, the *contempt* of which is great. *Addison.*

2. The state of being despised; whence in a scriptural sense, shame, disgrace.

Some shall awake to everlasting *contempt.* Dan. xii.

3. In *law*, disobedience of the rules and orders of a court, which is a punishable offense.

CONTEMPT'IBLE, *a.* [L. *contemptibilis.*]

1. Worthy of contempt; that deserves scorn, or disdain; despicable; mean; vile. Intemperance is a *contemptible* vice. No plant or animal is so *contemptible* as not to exhibit evidence of the wonderful power and wisdom of the Creator.

The pride that leads to duelling is a *contemptible* passion.

2. Apt to despise; contemptuous. [*Not legitimate.*] *Shak.*

CONTEMPT'IBLENESS, *n.* The state of

being contemptible, or of being despised; despicableness; meanness; vileness.

CONTEMPT'IBLY, *adv.* In a contemptible manner; meanly; in a manner deserving of contempt.

CONTEMPT'UOUS, *a.* Manifesting or expressing contempt or disdain; scornful; as *contemptuous* language or manner; a *contemptuous* opinion. *Applied to men*, apt to despise; haughty; insolent; as a nation, proud, severe, *contemptuous.* *Milton.*

CONTEMPT'UOUSLY, *adv.* In a contemptuous manner; with scorn or disdain; despitefully.

The apostles and most eminent christians were poor, and treated *contemptuously.* *Taylor.*

CONTEMPT'UOUSNESS, *n.* Disposition to contempt; act of contempt; insolence; scornfulness; haughtiness.

CONTEND', *v. i.* [L. *contendo*; *con* and *tendo*, to stretch, from *teneo*, Gr. τεινω. See *Tend, Tenet.*]

1. To strive, or to strive against; to struggle in opposition.

Distress not the Moabites, nor *contend with* them in battle. Deut. ii.

2. To strive; to use earnest efforts to obtain, or to defend and preserve.

You sit above, and see vain men below
Contend for what you only can bestow. *Dryden.*

Ye should earnestly *contend for* the faith once delivered to the saints. Jude 3.

3. To dispute earnestly; to strive in debate.

They that were of the circumcision *contended with* him. Acts xi. Job ix.

4. To reprove sharply; to chide; to strive to convince and reclaim.

Then *contended* I with the rulers. Neh. xiii.

5. To strive in opposition; to punish.

The Lord God called to *contend* by fire. Amos vii.

6. To quarrel; to dispute fiercely; to wrangle. The parties *contend about* trifles.

To contend for, to strive to obtain; as, two competitors *contend for* the prize.

CONTEND', *v. t.* To dispute; to contest.

When Carthage shall *contend* the world with Rome. *Dryden.*

This transitive use of *contend* is not strictly legitimate. The phrase is elliptical, *for* being understood after *contend*; but it is admissible in poetry.

CONTEND'ED, *pp.* Urged in argument or debate; disputed; contested.

CONTEND'ENT, *n.* An antagonist or opposer. *L'Estrange.*

CONTEND'ER, *n.* One who contends; a combatant; a champion. *Locke. Watts.*

CONTEND'ING, *ppr.* Striving; struggling to oppose; debating; urging in argument; quarreling.

2. *a.* Clashing; opposing; rival; as *contending* claims or interests.

CONTEN'EMENT, *n.* [*con* and *tenement.*] Land, or freehold contiguous to a tenement. *Blackstone. Norm. Dict.*

CONTENT', *a.* [L. *contentus*, from *contineor*, to be held; *con* and *teneo*, to hold.]

Literally, held, contained within limits; hence, quiet; not disturbed; having a mind at peace; easy; satisfied, so as not to repine, object, or oppose.

Content with science in the vale of peace. *Pope.*

Having food and raiment, let us be therewith *content.* 1 Tim. vi.

CONTENT', *v. t.* To satisfy the mind; to make quiet, so as to stop complaint or opposition; to appease; to make easy in any situation; *used chiefly with the reciprocal pronoun.*

Do not *content* yourselves with obscure and confused ideas, where clearer are to be obtained. *Watts.*

Pilate, willing to *content* the people, released Barabbas. Mark xv.

2. To please or gratify.

It doth much *content* me,
To hear him so inclined. *Shak.*

CONTENT', *n.* Rest or quietness of the mind in the present condition; satisfaction which holds the mind in peace, restraining complaint, opposition, or further desire, and often implying a moderate degree of happiness.

A wise *content* his even soul secur'd;
By want not shaken, nor by wealth allur'd. *Smith.*

2. Acquiescence; satisfaction without examination.

The style is excellent;
The sense they humbly take upon *content.* *Pope.*

3. The term used in the House of Lords in England, to express an assent to a bill or motion.

CON'TENT, *n.* often in the plural, *contents.* That which is contained; the thing or things held, included or comprehended within a limit or line; as the *contents* of a cask or bale; of a room or a ship; the *contents* of a book or writing.

2. In *geometry*, the area or quantity of matter or space included in certain lines.

3. The power of containing; capacity; extent within limits; as a ship of great *content.* *Bacon.*

[*But in this sense the plural is generally used.*]

CONTENTA'TION, *n.* Content; satisfaction. *Obs.* *Arbuthnot.*

CONTENT'ED, *pp.* or *a.* Satisfied; quiet; easy in mind; not complaining, opposing or demanding more. The good man is *contented* with his lot. It is our duty to be *contented* with the dispensations of providence.

CONTENT'EDLY, *adv.* In a contented manner; quietly; without concern.

CONTENT'EDNESS, *n.* State of resting in mind; quiet; satisfaction of mind with any condition or event. *Walton.*

CONTENT'FUL, *a.* Full of contentment. [*Not used.*] *Barrow.*

CONTEN'TION, *n.* [L. *contentio.* See *Contend.*]

1. Strife; struggle; a violent effort to obtain something, or to resist a person, claim or injury; contest; quarrel.

Multitudes lost their lives iu a tumult raised by *contention* among the partizans of the several colors. *Adam.*

2. Strife in words or debate; quarrel; angry contest; controversy.

Avoid foolish questions, and genealogies, and *contentions*, and strivings about the law. Tit. iii.

A fool's lips enter into *contention.* Prov. xviii.

3. Strife or endeavor to excel; emulation. *Shak.*

4. Eagerness; zeal; ardor; vehemence of endeavor. *Obs.*

This is an end worthy of our utmost *contention* to obtain. *Rogers.*

CONTEN'TIOUS, *a.* [Fr. *contentieux*; It. *contenzioso.*]

1. Apt to contend; given to angry debate; quarrelsome; perverse.

A continual dropping in a rainy day, and a *contentious* woman are alike. Prov. xxvii.

2. Relating to contention in law; relating to litigation; having power to decide causes between contending parties; as a court of *contentious* jurisdiction. *Blackstone.*

3. Exciting or adapted to provoke contention or disputes; as a *contentious* subject. *Milner.*

CONTEN'TIOUSLY, *adv.* In a contentious manner; quarrelsomely; perversely. *Brown.*

CONTEN'TIOUSNESS, *n.* A disposition to contend; proneness to contest; perverseness; quarrelsomeness. *Bentley.*

CONTENT'LESS, *a.* Discontented; dissatisfied; uneasy. *Shak.*

CONTENT'LY, *adv.* In a contented way. *Obs.*

CONTENT'MENT, *n.* [Fr. *contentement.*]

1. Content; a resting or satisfaction of mind without disquiet; acquiescence.

Contentment, without external honor, is humility. *Grew.*

Godliness with *contentment* is great gain. 1 Tim. vi.

2. Gratification.

At Paris the prince spent a day, to give his mind some *contentment.* *Wotton.*

CONTERM'INABLE, *a.* [L. *con* and *terminus.*] Capable of the same bounds. *Wotton.*

CONTERM'INATE, *a.* Having the same bounds. *B. Jonson.*

CONTERM'INOUS, *a.* [L. *conterminus*; *con* and *terminus*, a border.]

Bordering upon; touching at the boundary; contiguous; as a people *conterminous* to the Roman territory.

CONTERRA'NEAN, CONTERRA'NEOUS, } *a.* [L. *conterraneus*; *con* and *terra*, country.]

Being of the same country. [*Not used.*] *Dict.*

CONTEST', *v. t.* [Fr. *contester*, to dispute. The Sp. and Port. *contestar*, and L. *contestor*, have a different sense, being equivalent to the Eng. *attest.* See *Test.*]

1. To dispute; to strive earnestly to hold or maintain; to struggle to defend. The troops *contested* every inch of ground.

2. To dispute; to argue in opposition to; to controvert; to litigate; to oppose; to call in question; as, the advocate *contested* every point.

None have *contested* the proportion of these ancient pieces. *Dryden.*

CONTEST', *v. i.* To strive; to contend; followed by *with.*

The difficulty of an argument adds to the pleasure of *contesting with* it, when there are hopes of victory. *Burnet.*

2. To vie; to emulate.

Of man who dares in pomp *with* Jove *contest.* *Pope.*

CON'TEST, *n.* Strife; struggle for victory, superiority, or in defense; struggle in arms. All Europe engaged in the *contest* against France. The *contest* was furious.

2. Dispute; debate; violent controversy; strife in argument.

Leave all noisy *contests*, all immodest clamors, and brawling language. *Watts.*

ɆONTEST′ABLE, *a.* That may be disputed or debated; disputable; controvertible.

ɆONTEST′ABLENESS, *n.* Possibility of being contested.

ɆONTESTA′TION, *n.* The act of contesting; strife; dispute.

After years spent in domestic *contestations*, she found means to withdraw. *Clarendon.*

2. Testimony; proof by witnesses. *Barrow.*

ɆONTEST′INGLY, *adv.* In a contending manner. *Mountagu.*

ɆON′TESTLESS, *a.* Not to be disputed. *Hill.*

ɆONTEX′, *v. t.* To weave together. [*Not used.*] *Boyle.*

ɆON′TEXT, *n.* [L. *contextus*, from *contexo*; *con* and *texo*, to weave.]

The general series or composition of a discourse; more particularly, the parts of a discourse which precede or follow the sentence quoted; the passages of scripture which are near the text, either before it or after it. The sense of a passage of scripture is often illustrated by the *context*.

ɆONTEXT′, *a.* Knit or woven together; close; firm. *Derham.*

ɆONTEXT′, *v. t.* To knit together. [*Not used.*]

ɆONTEX′TURE, *n.* The manner of interweaving several parts into one body; the disposition and union of the constituent parts of a thing, with respect to each other; composition of parts; constitution; as a silk of admirable *contexture*.

He was not of any delicate *contexture*; his limbs rather sturdy than dainty. *Wotton.*

ɆONTEX′TURAL, *a.* Pertaining to contexture, or to the human frame. *Smith.*

ɆONTIGNA′TION, *n.* [L. *contignatio*; *con* and *tignum*, a beam.] A frame of beams; a story. *Wotton.*

2. The act of framing together, or uniting beams in a fabric. *Burke.*

ɆONTIGU′ITY, *n.* [See *Contiguous.*] Actual contact of bodies; a touching. *Hale.*

ɆONTIG′UOUS, *a.* [L. *contiguus*; *con* and *tango*, *tago*, to touch.]

Touching; meeting or joining at the surface or border; as two *contiguous* bodies or countries.

The houses in ancient Rome were not *contiguous*. *Encyc.*

Usually followed by *to*. Bacon uses *with*, but he has not been followed.

ɆONTIG′UOUSLY, *adv.* In a manner to touch; without intervening space. *Dryden.*

ɆONTIG′UOUSNESS, *n.* A state of contact; close union of surfaces or borders.

ɆON′TINENCE, ɆON′TINENCY, *n.* [L. *continentia*, from *contineo*, to hold, or withhold; *con* and *teneo*, to hold. See *Tenet.*]

1. In *a general sense*, the restraint which a person imposes upon his desires and passions; self-command.

2. *Appropriately*, the restraint of the passion for sexual enjoyment; resistance of concupiscence; forbearance of lewd pleasures; hence, chastity. But the term is usually applied to males, as *chastity* is to females. Scipio the younger exhibited the noblest example of *continence* recorded in Pagan history; an example surpassed only by that of Joseph in sacred history.

3. Forbearance of lawful pleasure.

Content without lawful venery, is *continence*; without unlawful, is chastity. *Grew.*

4. Moderation in the indulgence of sexual enjoyment.

Chastity is either abstinence or *continence*: abstinence is that of virgins or widows; *continence*, that of married persons. *Taylor.*

5. Continuity; uninterrupted course. [*Not now used.*] *Ayliffe.*

ɆON′TINENT, *a.* [L. *continens.*] Refraining from unlawful sexual commerce, or moderate in the indulgence of lawful pleasure; chaste.

2. Restrained; moderate; temperate.

Have a *continent* forbearance. *Shak.*

3. Opposing; restraining. *Shak.*

4. Continuous; connected; not interrupted.

The North East part of Asia, if not *continent* with America— *Brerewood.*

A *continent* fever. More generally we now say a *continued* fever.

ɆON′TINENT, *n.* In *geography*, a great extent of land, not disjoined or interrupted by a sea; a connected tract of land of great extent; as the Eastern and Western *continent*. It differs from an isle only in extent. New Holland may be denominated a *continent*. Britain is called a *continent*, as opposed to the isle of Anglesey. *Henry, Hist. Brit.* i. 34.

In Spenser, *continent* is used for ground in general.

2. That which contains any thing. [*Not used.*] *Shak.*

ɆONTINENT′AL, *a.* Pertaining or relating to a continent; as the *continental* powers of Europe. In America, pertaining to the United States, as *continental* money, in distinction from what pertains to the separate states; *a word much used during the revolution.*

ɆON′TINENTLY, *adv.* In a continent manner; chastely; moderately; temperately.

ɆONTIN′ǴENCE, ɆONTIN′ǴENCY, *n.* [L. *contingens*; *contingo*, to fall or happen to; *con* and *tango*, to touch. See *Touch.*]

1. The quality of being contingent or casual; a happening; or the possibility of coming to pass.

We are not to build certain rules on the *contingency* of human actions. *South.*

2. Casualty; accident; fortuitous event. The success of the attempt will depend on *contingencies*. [See *Accident* and *Casualty.*]

ɆONTIN′ǴENT, *a.* Falling or coming by chance, that is, without design or expectation on our part; accidental; casual. On our part, we speak of chance or *contingencies*; but with an infinite being, nothing can be *contingent*.

2. In *law*, depending on an uncertainty; as a *contingent* remainder. *Blackstone.*

ɆONTIN′ǴENT, *n.* A fortuitous event; that which comes without our design, foresight or expectation.

2. That which falls to one in a division or apportionment among a number; a quota; an equal or suitable share; proportion. Each prince furnishes his *contingent* of men, money and munitions.

ɆONTIN′ǴENTLY, *adv.* Accidentally; without design or foresight.

ɆONTIN′ǴENTNESS, *n.* The state of being contingent; fortuitousness.

ɆONTIN′UAL, *a.* [Fr. *continuel*; L. *continuus*. See *Continue.*]

1. Proceeding without interruption or cessation; unceasing; not intermitting; used in reference to time.

He that hath a merry heart hath a *continual* feast. Prov. xv.

I have great heaviness and *continual* sorrow of heart. Rom. ix.

2. Very frequent; often repeated; as, the charitable man has *continual* applications for alms.

3. *Continual* fever, or continued fever, a fever that abates, but never entirely intermits, till it comes to a crisis; thus distinguished from remitting and intermitting fever.

4. *Continual* claim, in law, a claim that is made from time to time within every year or day, to land or other estate, the possession of which cannot be obtained without hazard. *Cowel.*

5. Perpetual.

ɆONTIN′UALLY, *adv.* Without pause or cessation; unceasingly; as, the ocean is *continually* rolling its waves on the shore.

2. Very often; in repeated succession; from time to time.

Thou shalt eat bread at my table *continually*. 2 Sam. ix.

ɆONTIN′UALNESS, *n.* Permanence. *Hales.*

ɆONTIN′UANCE, *n.* [See *Continue.*] A holding on or remaining in a particular state, or in a course or series. Applied to time, duration; a state of lasting; as the *continuance* of rain or fair weather for a day or a week. Sensual pleasure is of short *continuance*.

2. Perseverance; as, no excuse will justify a *continuance* in sin.

By patient *continuance* in well doing. Rom. ii.

3. Abode; residence; as, during our *continuance* in Paris.

4. Succession uninterrupted; continuation; a prolonging of existence; as, the brute regards the *continuance* of his species. *Addison.*

5. Progression of time.

In thy book all my members were written, which in *continuance* were fashioned. Ps. cxxxix.

6. In *law*, the deferring of a suit, or the giving of a day for the parties to a suit to appear. After issue or demurrer joined, as well as in some of the previous stages of proceeding, a day is *continually* given, and entered upon record, for the parties to appear on from time to time. The giving of this day is called a *continuance*. *Blackstone.*

7. In *the United States*, the deferring of a trial or suit from one stated term of the court to another.

8. Continuity; resistance to a separation of parts; a holding together. [*Not used.*] *Bacon.*

ɆONTIN′UATE, *v. t.* To join closely together. *Potter*

CONTIN'UATE, *a.* [L. *continuatus.*] Immediately united; holding together. [*Little used.*] *Hooker.*

2. Uninterrupted; unbroken. [*Little used.*] *Peacham.*

CONTIN'UATELY, *adv.* With continuity; without interruption. [*Little used.*] *Wilkins.*

CONTINUA'TION, *n.* [L. *continuatio.*] Extension of existence in a series or line; succession uninterrupted.

These things must be the works of providence, for the *continuation* of the species. *Ray.*

2. Extension or carrying on to a further point; as the *continuation* of a story.

3. Extension in space; production; a carrying on in length; as the *continuation* of a line in surveying.

CONTIN'UATIVE, *n.* An expression noting permanence or duration.

To these may be added *continuatives:* as, Rome remains to this day; which includes at least two propositions, viz. Rome was, and Rome is. *Watts.*

2. In *grammar*, a word that continues. *Harris.*

CONTINUA'TOR, *n.* One who continues or keeps up a series or succession.

CONTIN'UE, *v. i.* [Fr. *continuer;* L. *continuo; con* and *teneo*, to hold; It. *continuare;* Sp. *continuar.* See *Tenet.*]

1. To remain in a state, or place; to abide for any time indefinitely.

The multitude *continue* with me now three days, and have nothing to eat. Matt. xv.

2. To last; to be durable; to endure; to be permanent.

Thy kingdom shall not *continue.* 1 Sam. xiii.

3. To persevere; to be steadfast or constant in any course.

If ye *continue* in my word, then are ye my disciples indeed. John viii.

CONTIN'UE, *v. t.* To protract; not to cease from or to terminate.

O *continue* thy loving kindness to them that know thee. Ps. xxxvi.

2. To extend from one thing to another; to produce or draw out in length. *Continue* the line from A to B. Let the line be *continued* to the boundary.

3. To persevere in; not to cease to do or use; as, to *continue* the same diet.

4. To hold to or unite. [*Not used.*]

The navel *continues* the infant to its mother. *Brown.*

CONTIN'UED, *pp.* Drawn out; protracted; produced; extended in length; extended without interruption.

2. *a.* Extended in time without intermission; proceeding without cessation; unceasing; as a *continued* fever, which abates but never entirely intermits. A *continued* base is performed through the whole piece.

Continued proportion, in arithmetic, is where the consequent of the first ratio is the same with the antecedent of the second, as 4 : 8 : : 8 : 16, in contradistinction from discrete proportion. *Encyc.*

CONTIN'UEDLY, *adv.* Without interruption; without ceasing. *Norris.*

CONTIN'UER, *n.* One who continues; one that has the power of perseverance. *Shak.*

CONTIN'UING, *ppr.* Remaining fixed or permanent; abiding; lasting; enduring; persevering; protracting; producing in length.

2. *a.* Permanent.

Here we have no *continuing* city. Heb. xiii.

CONTINU'ITY, *n.* [L. *continuitas.*] Connection uninterrupted; cohesion; close union of parts; unbroken texture.

Philosophers talk of the solution of *continuity.*

CONTIN'UOUS, *a.* [L. *continuus.*] Joined without intervening space; as *continuous* depth. *Thomson.*

CONTORT', *v. t.* [L. *contorqueo, contortus; con* and *torqueo, tortus.*] To twist together; to writhe.

CONTORT'ED, *pp.* Twisted together. A *contorted* corol, in botany, has the edge of one petal lying over the next, in an oblique direction. *Martyn.*

CONTOR'TION, CONTOR'SION, *n.* [Fr. *contorsion;* L. *contortio.*]

1. A twisting; a writhing; a wresting; a twist; wry motion; as the *contorsion* of the muscles of the face. *Swift.*

2. In *medicine*, a twisting or wresting of a limb or member of the body out of its natural situation; the iliac passion; partial dislocation; distorted spine; contracted neck. *Encyc. Coxe.*

CONTÖUR', *n.* [Fr. *contour;* It. *contorno;* Sp. *id.; con* and *tour, torno*, a turn.]

The outline; the line that defines or terminates a figure. *Encyc. Johnson.*

CONTÖUR'NIATED, *a.* Having edges appearing as if turned in a lathe. *Encyc.*

CON'TRA. A Latin preposition signifying *against, in opposition*, entering into the composition of some English words. It appears to be a compound of *con* and *tra*, like *intra; tra* for W. *tras.* Fr. *contre.*

CON'TRABAND, *a.* [It. *contrabbando*, contrary to proclamation, prohibited; Sp. *contrabando;* Fr. *contrebande.* See *Ban.*]

Prohibited. Contraband goods are such as are prohibited to be imported or exported, either by the laws of a particular kingdom or state, or by the law of nations, or by special treaties. In time of war, arms and munitions of war are not permitted by one belligerent, to be transported to the other, but are held to be *contraband* and liable to capture and condemnation.

CON'TRABAND, *n.* Prohibition of trading in goods, contrary to the laws of a state or of nations.

2. Illegal traffick.

CON'TRABANDIST, *n.* One who trafficks illegally.

CONTRACT', *v. t.* [L. *contraho, contractum; con* and *traho*, to draw; It. *contrarre;* Sp. *contraer;* Port. *contrahir;* Fr. *contracter.* See *Draw.*]

1. To draw together or nearer; to draw into a less compass, either in length or breadth; to shorten; to abridge; to narrow; to lessen; as, to *contract* an inclosure; to *contract* the faculties; to *contract* the period of life; to *contract* the sphere of action.

2. To draw the parts together; to wrinkle; as, to *contract* the brow.

3. To betroth; to affiance. A *contracted* his daughter to B. The lady was *contracted* to a man of merit.

4. To draw to; to bring on; to incur; to gain. We *contract* vicious habits by indulgence. We *contract* debt by extravagance.

5. To shorten by omission of a letter or syllable; as, to *contract* a word.

6. To epitomize; to abridge; as, to *contract* an essay.

CONTRACT', *v. i.* To shrink; to become shorter or narrower.

Many bodies *contract* by the application of cold.

A hempen cord *contracts* by moisture.

2. To bargain; to make a mutual agreement, as between two or more persons. We have *contracted for* a load of flour; or we have *contracted with* a farmer *for* a quantity of provisions.

CONTRACT', for *contracted, pp.* Affianced; betrothed. *Shak.*

CON'TRACT, *n.* An agreement or covenant between two or more persons, in which each party binds himself to do or forbear some act, and each acquires a right to what the other promises; a mutual promise upon lawful consideration or cause, which binds the parties to a performance; a bargain; a compact. *Contracts* are executory or executed. *Sup. Court, Cranch's Rep.*

2. The act by which a man and woman are betrothed, each to the other. *Shak.*

3. The writing which contains the agreement of parties with the terms and conditions, and which serves as a proof of the obligation.

CONTRACT'ED, *pp.* Drawn together, or into a shorter or narrower compass; shrunk; betrothed; incurred; bargained.

2. *a.* Narrow; mean; selfish; as a man of a *contracted* soul or mind.

CONTRACT'EDLY, *adv.* In a contracted manner. *Bp. Newton.*

CONTRACT'EDNESS, *n.* The state of being contracted.

2. Narrowness; meanness; excessive selfishness.

CONTRACTIBIL'ITY, *n.* Possibility of being contracted; quality of suffering contraction; as the *contractibility* and dilatibility of air. *Arbuthnot.*

CONTRACT'IBLE, *a.* Capable of contraction.

Small air bladders, dilatable and *contractible.* *Arbuthnot.*

CONTRACT'IBLENESS, *n.* The quality of suffering contraction; contractibility. *Dict.*

CONTRACT'ILE, *a.* Tending to contract; having the power of shortening or of drawing into smaller dimensions; as the *contractile* force of certain elastic bodies. *Darwin.*

CONTRACTIL'ITY, *n.* The inherent quality or force by which bodies shrink or contract. *Beddoes.*

CONTRACT'ING, *ppr.* Shortening or narrowing; drawing together; lessening dimensions; shrinking; making a bargain; betrothing.

2. *a.* Making or having made a contract or treaty; stipulating; as the *contracting parties* to a league.

CONTRAC'TION, *n.* [L. *contractio.*] The act of drawing together, or shrinking; the act of shortening, narrowing or lessening extent or dimensions, by causing the parts of a body to approach nearer to each other; the state of being contracted.

Oil of vitriol will throw the stomach into involuntary *contractions*. *Arbuthnot.*

The *contraction* of the heart is called systole.

Some things induce a *contraction* of the nerves. *Bacon.*

2. The act of shortening, abridging, or reducing within a narrower compass by any means. A poem may be improved by omissions or *contractions*.

3. In *grammar*, the shortening of a word, by the omission of a letter or syllable; as, *can't* for *cannot*; *burst* for *bursted* or *bursten*; Swedish and Danish *ord*, a word.

4. A contract; marriage contract. [*Not used.*] *Shak.*

5. Abbreviation.

CONTRACT'OR, *n.* One who contracts; one of the parties to a bargain; one who covenants to do any thing for another. *Taylor.*

2. One who contracts or covenants with a government to furnish provisions or other supplies or to perform any work or service for the public, at a certain price or rate.

CON'TRA-DANCE, COUN'TER-DANCE, *n.* [Fr. *contre-danse*; It. *contraddanza*; Sp. *contradanza.*]

A dance in which the partners are arranged in opposition, or in opposite lines.

CONTRADICT', *v. t.* [L. *contradico*; *contra* and *dico*, to speak.]

1. To oppose by words; to assert the contrary to what has been asserted, or to deny what has been affirmed.

It is not lawful to *contradict* a point of history known to all the world. *Dryden.*

The Jews—spoke against those things which were spoken by Paul, *contradicting* and blaspheming. Acts xiii.

2. To oppose; to be directly contrary to.

No truth can *contradict* another truth. *Hooker.*

CONTRADICT'ED, *pp.* Opposed in words; opposed; denied.

CONTRADICT'ER, *n.* One who contradicts or denies; an opposer. *Swift.*

CONTRADICT'ING, *ppr.* Affirming the contrary to what has been asserted; denying; opposing.

CONTRADIC'TION, *n.* [L. *contradictio.*] An assertion of the contrary to what has been said or affirmed; denial; contrary declaration.

2. Opposition, whether by words, reproaches or attempts to defeat.

Consider him that endured such *contradiction* of sinners against himself. Heb. xii.

3. Direct opposition or repugnancy; inconsistency with itself; incongruity or contrariety of things, words, thoughts or propositions. These theorems involve a *contradiction.*

If we perceive truth, we thereby perceive whatever is false in *contradiction* to it. *Grew.*

CONTRADIC'TIONAL, *a.* Inconsistent. [*Not in use.*] *Milton.*

CONTRADIC'TIOUS, *a.* Filled with contradictions; inconsistent. *Collier.*

2. Inclined to contradict; disposed to deny or cavil.

3. Opposite; inconsistent.

CONTRADIC'TIOUSNESS, *n.* Inconsistency; contrariety to itself. *Norris.*

2. Disposition to contradict or cavil.

CONTRADICT'ORILY, *adv.* In a contradictory manner; in a manner inconsistent with itself, or opposite to others. *Brown.*

CONTRADICT'ORINESS, *n.* Direct opposition; contrariety in assertion or effect. *Baxter.*

CONTRADICT'ORY, *a.* Affirming the contrary; implying a denial of what has been asserted; as *contradictory* assertions.

2. Inconsistent; opposite; contrary; as *contradictory* schemes.

CONTRADICT'ORY, *n.* A proposition which denies or opposes another in all its terms; contrariety; inconsistency.

It is common with princes to will *contradictories.* *Bacon.*

CONTRADISTINCT', *a.* Distinguished by opposite qualities. *Smith.*

CONTRADISTINC'TION, *n.* [*contra* and *distinction.*] Distinction by opposite qualities.

We speak of sins of infirmity, in *contradistinction* to those of presumption. *South.*

CONTRADISTINC'TIVE, *a.* Distinguishing by opposites. *Harris.*

CONTRADISTIN'GUISH, *v. t.* [*contra* and *distinguish.*]

To distinguish not merely by differential, but by opposite qualities.

These are our complex ideas of soul and body, as *contradistinguished.* *Locke.*

CONTRADISTIN'GUISHED, *pp.* Distinguished by opposites.

CONTRADISTIN'GUISHING, *ppr.* Distinguishing by opposites.

CONTRAFIS'SURE, *n.* [*contra* and *fissure.*] In *surgery*, a fissure or fracture in the cranium, on the side opposite to that which received the blow, or at some distance from it. *Coxe. Encyc.*

CONTRAIN'DICANT, *n.* A symptom that forbids to treat a disorder in the usual way. *Burke.*

CONTRAIN'DICATE, *v. t.* [*contra* and *indicate.*] In *medicine*, to indicate some method of cure, contrary to that which the general tenor of the disease requires; or to forbid that to be done which the main scope of the malady points out. *Harvey. Encyc.*

CONTRAINDICA'TION, *n.* An indication, from some peculiar symptom or fact, that forbids the method of cure which the main symptoms or nature of the disease requires. *Arbuthnot.*

CON'TRAMURE, *n.* An out wall. [See *Countermure.*]

CONTRANAT'URAL, *a.* Opposite to nature. [*Little used.*] *Bp. Rust.*

CONTRANI'TENCY, *n.* [L. *contra* and *nitor*, to strive.] Reaction; resistance to force.

CONTRAPOSI''TION, *n.* [*contra* and *position.*] A placing over against; opposite position.

CONTRAPUNT'IST, *n.* One skilled in counterpoint. *Mason.*

CONTRAREGULAR'ITY, *n.* [*contra* and *regularity.*] Contrariety to rule, or to regularity. *Norris.*

CONTRA'RIANT, *a.* [Fr. from *contrarier*, to contradict, or run counter.]

Contradictory; opposite; inconsistent. [*Little used.*] *Ayliffe.*

CON'TRARIES, *n. plu.* [See *Contrary.*] In *logic*, propositions which destroy each other, but of which the falsehood of one does not establish the truth of the other.

If two universals differ in quality, they are *contraries*; as, *every vine is a tree*; *no vine is a tree.* These can never be both true together; but they may be both false. *Watts.*

CONTRARI'ETY, *n.* [L. *contrarietas.* See *Contrary.*]

1. Opposition in fact, essence, quality or principle; repugnance. The expedition failed by means of a *contrariety* of winds. There is a *contrariety* in the nature of virtue and vice; of love and hatred; of truth and falsehood. Among men of the same profession, we find a *contrariety* of opinions.

2. Inconsistency; quality or position destructive of its opposite.

How can these *contrarieties* agree. *Shak.*

CON'TRARILY, *adv.* In an opposite manner; in opposition; on the other side; in opposite ways.

CON'TRARINESS, *n.* Contrariety; opposition. *Dict.*

CONTRA'RIOUS, *a.* Contrary; opposite; repugnant. *Milton.*

CONTRA'RIOUSLY, *adv.* Contrarily; opposite[l]y. *Shak.*

CON'TRARIWISE, *adv.* [*contrary* and *wise*, manner.]

On the contrary; oppositely; on the other hand.

Not rendering evil for evil, nor railing for railing, but *contrariwise*, blessing. 1 Pet iii

CON'TRARY, *a.* [L. *contrarius*, from *contra*, against; Fr. *contraire*; Sp. It. *contrario.*]

1. Opposite; adverse; moving against or in an opposite direction; as *contrary* winds.

2. Opposite; contradictory; not merely different, but inconsistent or repugnant.

The flesh lusteth against the spirit, and the spirit against the flesh; and these are *contrary*, the one to the other. Gal. v.

This adjective, in many phrases, is to be treated grammatically as an adverb, or as an adjective referring to a sentence or affirmation; as, this happened *contrary* to my expectations. The word here really belongs to the affirmation or fact declared, *this happened*; for *contrary* does not, like an adverb, express the *manner* of happening, but that the fact itself was contrary to my expectation. *According*, *agreeable*, *pursuant*, *antecedent*, *prior*, *anterior*, *&c.*, are often used in the like manner.

CON'TRARY, *n.* A thing that is contrary or of opposite qualities.

No *contraries* hold more antipathy,
Than I and such a knave. *Shak.*

2. A proposition contrary to another, or a fact contrary to what is alledged; as, this is stated to be a fact, but I will endeavor to show the *contrary.*

On the contrary, in opposition; on the other side. *Swift.*

To the contrary, to an opposite purpose, or fact.

They did it, not for want of instruction *to the contrary.* *Stillingfleet.*

He said it was just, but I told him *to the contrary.*

CON'TRARY, *v. t.* [Fr. *contrarier.*] To contradict or oppose. *Obs.*

CONTRARY-MINDED, *a.* Of a different mind or opinion. *Hall.*

CONTRAST', *v. t.* [Fr. *contraster*, Norm. *id.*, to *contrast*; It. *contrastare*, Sp. Port.

contrastar, to resist, withstand, strive, debate, quarrel. The primary sense is to set against, or to strain, to strive.]

1. To set in opposition two or more figures of a like kind, with a view to show the difference or dissimilitude, and to manifest the superior excellence of the one by the inferiority of the other, or to exhibit the excellence of the one and the defects of the other in a more striking view; as, to *contrast* two pictures or statues.
2. To exhibit differences or dissimilitude in painting and sculpture, by position or attitude, either of the whole figure or of its members; or to show to advantage by opposition or difference of position.
3. To set in opposition different things or qualities, to show the superior excellence of one to advantage.

To *contrast* the *goodness of God* with *our rebellion*, will tend to make us humble and thankful. *Clark, Serm.* July 4, 1814.

CON'TRAST, *n.* Opposition or dissimilitude of figures, by which one contributes to the visibility or effect of the other. *Johnson.*

Contrast, in this sense, is applicable to things of a similar kind. We never speak of a *contrast* between a man and a mountain, or between a dog and a tree; but we observe the *contrast* between an oak and a shrub, and between a palace and a cottage.

2. Opposition, or difference of position, attitude, &c., of figures, or of their several members; as in painting and sculpture.
3. Opposition of things or qualities; or the placing of opposite things in view, to exhibit the superior excellence of one to more advantage. What a *contrast* between modesty and impudence, or between a wellbred man and a clown!

CONTRAST'ED, *pp.* Set in opposition; examined in opposition.

CONTRAST'ING, *ppr.* Placing in opposition, with a view to discover the difference of figures or other things, and exhibit the advantage or excellence of one beyond that of the other.

CON'TRA-TENOR, *n.* In *music*, a middle part between the tenor and treble; counter.

CON'TRATE-WHEEL, *n.* In *watch-work*, the wheel next to the crown, the teeth and hoop of which lie *contrary* to those of the other wheels, whence its name.

CONTRAVALLA'TION, *n.* [L. *contra* and *vallo*, to fortify; Fr. *contrevallation.*]
In *fortification*, a trench guarded with a parapet, thrown round a place by the besiegers, to secure themselves, and check the sallies of the garrison.

CONTRAVE'NE, *v.t.* [L. *contravenio; contra* and *venio*, to come.]
Literally, to come against; to meet. Hence, to oppose, but used in a figurative or moral sense; to oppose in principle or effect; to contradict; to obstruct in operation; to defeat; as, a law may *contravene* the provisions of the constitution.

CONTRAVE'NED, *pp.* Opposed; obstructed.

CONTRAVE'NER, *n.* One who opposes.

CONTRAVE'NING, *ppr.* Opposing in principle or effect.

CONTRAVEN'TION, *n.* Opposition; obstruction; a defeating of the operation or effect.

The proceedings of the allies were in direct *contravention* of the treaty.

CONTRAVER'SION, *n.* [L. *contra* and *versio*, a turning.]
A turning to the opposite side; antistrophe. *Congreve.*

CONTRAYER'VA, *n.* [Sp. *contrayerba;* Port. *contraherva; contra* and *yerba, herva*, an *herb*, L. *herba;* a *counter herb*, an antidote for poison, or in general, an antidote.]
The genus of plants, Dorstenia; all low herbaceous plants, natives of the warm climates of America, and useful as diaphoretics. *Encyc.*

CONTRECTA'TION, *n.* [L. *contrectatio, tracto.*] A touching or handling. *Ferrand.*

CONTRIB'UTARY, *a.* [See *Contribute.*] Paying tribute to the same sovereign; contributing aid to the same chief or principal.

It was situated on the Ganges, at the place where this river received a *contributary* stream. *D'Anville, An. Geog.*

CONTRIB'UTE, *v. t.* [L. *contribuo; con* and *tribuo*, to grant, assign, or impart; It. *contribuire;* Sp. *contribuir;* Fr. *contribuer.* See *Tribe, Tribute.*]

1. To give or grant in common with others; to give to a common stock or for a common purpose; to pay a share.

England *contributes* much more than any other of the allies. *Addison.*

It is the duty of christians to *contribute* a portion of their substance for the propagation of the gospel.

2. To impart a portion or share to a common purpose.

Let each man *contribute* his influence to correct public morals.

CONTRIB'UTE, *v. i.* To give a part; to lend a portion of power, aid or influence; to have a share in any act or effect.

There is not a single beauty in the piece, to which the invention must not *contribute*. *Pope.*

CONTRIB'UTED, *pp.* Given or advanced to a common fund, stock or purpose; paid as a share.

CONTRIB'UTING, *ppr.* Giving in common with others to some stock or purpose; imparting a share.

CONTRIBU'TION, *n.* The act of giving to a common stock, or in common with others; the act of lending a portion of power or influence to a common purpose; the payment of each man's share of some common expense.

2. That which is given to a common stock or purpose, either by an individual or by many. We speak of the *contribution* of one person, or the *contribution* of a society. *Contributions* are *involuntary*, as taxes and imposts; or *voluntary*, as for some undertaking.
3. In *a military sense*, impositions paid by a frontier country, to secure themselves from being plundered by the enemy's army; or impositions upon a country in the power of an enemy, which are levied under various pretenses, and for various purposes, usually for the support of the army.

CONTRIB'UTIVE, *a.* Tending to contribute; contributing; having the power or quality of giving a portion of aid or influence; lending aid to promote, in concurrence with others.

This measure is *contributive* to the same end. *Taylor.*

CONTRIB'UTOR, *n.* One who contributes; one who gives or pays money to a common stock or fund; one who gives aid to a common purpose in conjunction with others.

CONTRIB'UTORY, *a.* Contributing to the same stock or purpose; promoting the same end; bringing assistance to some joint design, or increase to some common stock.

CONTRIS'TATE, *v. t.* [L. *contristo.*] To make sorrowful. [*Not used.*] *Bacon.*

CONTRISTA'TION, *n.* The act of making sad. [*Not used.*] *Bacon.*

CON'TRITE, *a.* [L. *contritus*, from *contero*, to break or bruise; *con* and *tero*, to bruise, rub or wear. See *Trite.*]
Literally, worn or bruised. Hence, brokenhearted for sin; deeply affected with grief and sorrow for having offended God; humble; penitent; as a *contrite* sinner.

A broken and a *contrite* heart, O God, thou wilt not despise. Ps. li.

CON'TRITELY, *adv.* In a contrite manner; with penitence.

CON'TRITENESS, *n.* Deep sorrow and penitence for sin.

CONTRI''TION, *n.* [L. *contritio.*] The act of grinding or rubbing to powder. *Newton.*

2. Penitence; deep sorrow for sin; grief of heart for having offended an infinitely holy and benevolent God. The word is usually understood to mean genuine penitence, accompanied with a deep sense of ingratitude in the sinner, and sincere resolution to live in obedience to the divine law.

Fruits of more pleasing savor, from thy seed
Sown with *contrition* in his heart. *Milton.*

Imperfect repentance is by some divines called *attrition*.

CONTRI'VABLE, *a.* [See *Contrive.*] That may be contrived; capable of being planned, invented, or devised.

Perpetual motion may seem easily *contrivable*. *Wilkins.*

CONTRI'VANCE, *n.* [See *Contrive.*] The act of inventing, devising or planning.

There is no work impossible to these *contrivances*. *Wilkins.*

2. The thing invented or planned; a scheme; plan; disposition of parts or causes by design.

Our bodies are made according to the most orderly *contrivance*. *Glanville.*

3. Artifice; plot; scheme.

He has managed his *contrivance* well.

CONTRI'VE, *v. t.* [Fr. *controuver; con* and *trouver*, to find; It. *controvare.*]

1. To invent; to devise; to plan.

Our poet has always some beautiful design, which he first establishes, and then *contrives* the means which will naturally conduct him to his end. *Dryden.*

2. To wear out. *Obs.* *Spenser.*

[This must be from the L. *contero, contrivi*, and if the French *controuver*, and Italian *controvare*, are the same word differently applied, the primary sense is, to invent by rubbing, that is, by ruminating; or to strike out, as in *forge*. But the word is probably from *trouver*, to find.]

CONTRI'VE, *v. i.* To form or design; to plan; to scheme.

How shall we *contrive* to hide our shame?

This verb is really transitive, but followed by a verb, in the place of an object or name.

CONTRI'VED, *pp.* Invented; planned; devised.

CONTRI'VEMENT, *n.* Contrivance; invention.

CONTRI'VER, *n.* An inventor; one who plans or devises; a schemer. *Swift. Shak.*

CONTRI'VING, *ppr.* Planning; forming in design.

CONTRŌL, **CONTRŌLL**, *n.* [Fr. *controlle*, a counter-register; *contre* and *rolle*, a roll, list or catalogue; Arm. *counter roll.*]

1. Primarily, a book, register or account, kept to correct or check another account or register; a counter-register. Hence, check; restraint; as, to speak, or to act without *control*. The wind raged without *control*. Our passions should be under the *control* of reason.

2. Power; authority; government; command. Children should be under the *control* of their parents. The events of life are not always under our *control*.

3. He or that which restrains. *Burke.*

CONTRŌL, **CONTRŌLL**, *v. t.* To keep under check by a counter-register or double account. The proper officer *controls* the accounts of the treasury.

2. To check; to restrain; to govern.

I feel my virtue struggling in my soul:
But stronger passion does its power *control*. *Dryden.*

3. To overpower; to subject to authority; to counteract; to have under command. The course of events cannot be *controlled* by human wisdom or power.

4. To direct or govern in opposition; to have superior force, or authority over.

A recital cannot *control* the plain words in the granting part of a deed. *Johnson's Reports.*

CONTRŌLLABLE, *a.* That may be controlled, checked or restrained; subject to command.

Passion is the drunkenness of the mind, and not always *controllable* by reason. *South.*

CONTRŌLLED, *pp.* Checked; restrained; governed.

CONTRŌLLER, *n.* [Norm. *countre-rouler.*] One who controls, or restrains; one that has the power or authority to govern or control.

The great *controller* of our fate
Deign'd to be man, and lived in low estate. *Dryden.*

2. An officer appointed to keep a counter-register of accounts, or to oversee, control or verify the accounts of other officers; as in Great Britain, the *controller* of the hanaper, of the household, of the pipe, and of the pells. In the United States, the duty of the *controller* of the treasury is to superintend the adjustment and preservation of the public accounts; to examine all accounts settled by the auditor, and certify to the register the balances due thereon; to countersign all warrants drawn by the secretary of the treasury which shall be warranted by law; to report to the secretary the official forms of all papers to be issued in the different offices for collecting the public revenue, and the manner and form of keeping and stating the accounts of the persons employed in them, &c. *Stat. of United States.*

CONTRŌLLERSHIP, *n.* The office of a controller.

CONTRŌLMENT, **CONTRŌLLMENT**, *n.* The power or act of controlling; the state of being restrained; control; restraint.

2. Opposition; resistance; counteraction; refutation.

For this word, *control* is now generally used.

CON'TROVERSE, *n.* and *v.* Controversy, and to dispute. *Obs.*

CON'TROVERSER, **CON'TROVERSOR**, *n.* A disputant. *Obs. Mountagu.*

CONTROVER'SIAL, *a.* [See *Controvert*, *Controversy.*]

Relating to disputes; as a *controversial* discourse.

CONTROVER'SIALIST, *n.* One who carries on a controversy; a disputant.

CON'TROVERSY, *n.* [L. *controversia.* See *Controvert.*]

1. Dispute; debate; agitation of contrary opinions. A *dispute* is commonly oral, and a *controversy* in writing. *Johnson.* Dispute is often or generally a debate of short duration, a temporary debate; a *controversy* is often oral and sometimes continued in books or in law for months or years.

This left no room for *controversy*, about the title. *Locke.*

Without *controversy*, great is the mystery of godliness. 1 Tim. iii.

2. A suit in law; a case in which opposing parties contend for their respective claims before a tribunal.

And by their word shall every *controversy* and every stroke be tried. Deut. xxi.

3. Dispute; opposition carried on.

The Lord hath a *controversy* with the nations. Jer. xxv.

4. Opposition; resistance.

And stemming [the torrent] with hearts of *controversy*. *Shak.*

CON'TROVERT, *v. t.* [L. *controverto*, *controversor; contra* and *verto*, *verso*, to turn. Literally, to turn against.]

To dispute; to oppose by reasoning; to contend against in words or writings; to deny and attempt to disprove or confute; to agitate contrary opinions; as, to *controvert* opinions, or principles; to *controvert* the justness of a conclusion.

CON'TROVERTED, *pp.* Disputed; opposed in debate.

CON'TROVERTER, *n.* One who controverts; a controversial writer. *B. Jonson.*

CONTROVERT'IBLE, *a.* That may be disputed; disputable; not too evident to exclude difference of opinion; as, this is a *controvertible* point of law.

CON'TROVERTING, *pp.* Disputing; denying and attempting to refute.

CON'TROVERTIST, *n.* One who controverts; a disputant; a man versed or engaged in controversy, or disputation.

How unfriendly is the spirit of the *controvertist* to the discernment of the critic. *Campbell.*

CONTUMA'CIOUS, *a.* [L. *contumax*, from *con* and *tumeo*, to swell.]

1. Literally, swelling against; haughty. Hence, obstinate; perverse; stubborn; inflexible; unyielding; disobedient; as a *contumacious* child.

2. In *law*, wilfully disobedient to the orders of a court. *Blackstone.*

CONTUMA'CIOUSLY, *adv.* Obstinately; stubbornly; perversely; in disobedience of orders.

CONTUMA'CIOUSNESS, *n.* Obstinacy; perverseness; stubbornness; contumacy.

CON'TUMACY, *n.* [L. *contumacia.*] Stubbornness; unyielding obstinacy; inflexibility. *Milton.*

2. In *law*, a wilful contempt and disobedience to any lawful summons or order of court; a refusal to appear in court when legally summoned, or disobedience to its rules and orders. *Ayliffe.*

CONTUME'LIOUS, *a.* [L. *contumeliosus.* See *Contumely.*]

1. Haughtily reproachful; contemptuous; insolent; rude and sarcastic; as *contumelious* language. *Swift.*

2. Haughty and contemptuous; disposed to utter reproach, or to insult; insolent; proudly rude; as a *contumelious* person. *Shak.*

3. Reproachful; shameful; ignominious. *Decay of Piety.*

CONTUME'LIOUSLY, *adv.* In a contumelious manner; with pride and contempt; reproachfully; rudely; insolently.

CONTUME'LIOUSNESS, *n.* Reproach; rudeness; contempt.

CON'TUMELY, *n.* [L. *contumelia*, from *contumeo; con* and *tumeo*, to swell.]

Rudeness or reproach compounded of haughtiness and contempt; contemptuousness; insolence; contemptuous language.

The oppressor's wrong; the proud man's *contumely.* *Shak.*

CONTUND', *v. t.* [L. *contundo.*] To beat; to bruise by beating. [*Little used.*] *Gayton.*

CONTU'SE, *v. t.* *s* as *z.* [L. *contusus*, *contundo.*]

To beat; to bruise; to injure the flesh or substance of a living being or other thing without breaking the skin or substance, sometimes with a breach of the skin or substance. *Bacon.*

CONTU'SION, *n.* *s* as *z.* [L. *contusio*, from *contundo; con* and *tundo*, to beat.]

1. The act of beating and bruising, or the state of being bruised.

2. The act of reducing to powder or fine particles by beating. *Bacon.*

3. In *surgery*, a bruise; a hurt or injury to the flesh or some part of the body by a blunt instrument, or by a fall.

CONUN'DRUM, *n.* A low jest; a mean conceit.

CON'USANCE, *n.* [Fr. *connoissance.*] Cognizance; knowledge; notice. [See *Connusance.*]

CON'USANT, *a.* Knowing; having notice of.

CONVALES'CENCE, **CONVALES'CENCY**, *n.* [L. *convalesco*, to grow stronger; *con* and *valesco*, to get strength, *valeo*, to be strong, Eng. *well.* See *Well* and *Avail.*]

Renewal of health; the insensible recovery of health and strength after disease; the state of a body renewing its vigor after sickness or weakness.

CONVALES'CENT, *a.* Recovering health and strength after sickness or debility.

CON'VALLARY, *n.* A genus of plants, Convallaria. *Muhlenberg.*

CONVE'NABLE, *a.* [See *Convene.*] That may be convened, or assembled. *Panoplist, May* 1809.

2. Consistent. *Obs.* *Spenser.*

CONVE'NE, *v. i.* [L. *convenio ; con* and *venio*, to come.]

1. To come together; to meet; to unite; as things. [*Unusual.*]

The rays of light converge and *convene* in the eyes. *Newton.*

2. To come together; to meet in the same place; to assemble; as persons. Parliament will *convene* in November. The two houses of the legislature *convened* at twelve o'clock. The citizens *convened* in the state-house.

CONVE'NE, *v. t.* To cause to assemble; to call together; to convoke. The President has power to *convene* the Congress, on special occasions.

2. To summon judicially to meet or appear.

By the papal canon law, clerks can be *convened* only before an ecclesiastical judge. *Ayliffe.*

CONVE'NED, *pp.* Assembled; convoked.

CONVE'NER, *n.* One who convenes or meets with others; one who calls together.

CONVE'NIENCE, CONVE'NIENCY, *n.* [L. *convenientia*, from *convenio.*] Literally, a coming together; a meeting. Hence,

1. Fitness; suitableness; propriety; adaptation of one thing to another, or to circumstances. *Hooker.*

2. Commodiousness; ease; freedom from difficulty.

Every man must want something for the *convenience* of his life. *Calamy.*

There is another *convenience* in this method. *Swift.*

3. That which gives ease; accommodation; that which is suited to wants or necessity. A pair of spectacles is a great *convenience* in old age.

4. Fitness of time or place. *Shak.*

CONVE'NIENT, *a.* Fit; suitable; proper; adapted to use or to wants; commodious; followed by *to* or *for ;* usually by *for.*

Some arts are peculiarly *convenient to* particular nations. *Tillotson.*

Feed me with food *convenient for* me. Prov. xxx.

CONVE'NIENTLY, *adv.* Fitly; suitably; with adaptation to the end or effect. That house is not *conveniently* situated for a tradesman.

2. Commodiously; with ease; without trouble or difficulty. He cannot *conveniently* accept the invitation.

CONVE'NING, *ppr.* Coming together; calling together.

CONVE'NING, *n.* The act of coming together; convention.

CON'VENT, *n.* [L. *conventus*, from *convenio*, to assemble ; Fr. *couvent.*]

1. An assembly of persons devoted to religion; a body of monks or nuns.

2. A house for persons devoted to religion; an abbey; a monastery; a nunnery.

CONVENT', *v. t.* [L. *conventus, convenio.*] To call before a judge or judicature. *Shak. Bacon.*

CONVENT', *v. i.* To meet; to concur. [*Not used.*] *Beaum.*

CONVENT'ICLE, *n.* [L. *conventiculum*, dim. of *conventus.*]

1. An assembly or meeting; usually applied to a meeting of dissenters from the established church, for religious worship. In this sense it is used by English writers and in English statutes. Hence, an assembly, in contempt. *Atterbury.*

In the United States, this word has no appropriate application, and is little used, or not at all.

2. A secret assembly or cabal; a meeting for plots. *Shak.*

CONVENT'ICLE, *v. i.* To belong to a conventicle. *South.*

CONVENT'ICLER, *n.* One who supports or frequents conventicles. *Dryden.*

CONVEN'TION, *n.* [L. *conventio.* See *Convene.*]

1. The act of coming together; a meeting of several persons or individuals. *Boyle.*

2. Union; coalition.

3. An assembly. In this sense, the word includes any formal meeting or collection of men for civil or ecclesiastical purposes; particularly an assembly of delegates or representatives for consultation on important concerns, civil, political or ecclesiastical.

In *Great Britain*, convention is the name given to an extraordinary assembly of the estates of the realm, held without the king's writ; as the assembly which restored Charles II. to the throne, and that which declared the throne to be abdicated by James II.

In *the United States*, this name is given to the assembly of representatives which forms a constitution of government, or political association; as the *convention* which formed the constitution of the United States in 1787.

4. An agreement or contract between two parties, as between the commanders of two armies; an agreement previous to a definitive treaty.

CONVEN'TIONAL, *a.* [Fr. *conventionnel.*] Stipulated; formed by agreement.

Conventional services reserved by tenures on grants, made out of the crown or knights service. *Hale.*

CONVEN'TIONARY, *a.* Acting under contract; settled by stipulation; conventional; as *conventionary* tenants. *Carew.*

CONVEN'TIONER, *n.* One who belongs to a convention.

CONVEN'TIONIST, *n.* One who makes a contract. *Sterne.*

CONVEN'TUAL, *a.* [Fr. *conventuel.*] Belonging to a convent; monastic; as *conventual* priors.

CONVEN'TUAL, *n.* One that lives in a convent; a monk or nun. *Addison.*

CONVERGE, *v. i. converj'.* [Low L. *convergo ; con* and *vergo*, to incline. See *Verge.*] To tend to one point; to incline and approach nearer together, as two lines which continually approach each other; opposed to *diverge.* Lines which *converge* in one direction, *diverge* in the other.

The mountains *converge* into a single ridge. *Jefferson.*

CONVERG'ENCE, CONVERG'ENCY, *n.* The quality of converging; tendency to one point. *Gregory.*

CONVERG'ENT, *a.* Tending to one point; approaching each other, as they proceed or are extending.

CONVERG'ING, *ppr.* Tending to one point; approaching each other, as lines extended.

Converging rays, in optics, those rays of light, which proceeding from different points of an object, approach, meet and cross, and become diverging rays. *Encyc.*

Converging series, in mathematics, is that in which the magnitude of the several terms gradually diminishes. *Encyc.*

CONVERS'ABLE, *a.* [It. *conversabile ;* Fr. *conversable.* See *Converse.*] Qualified for conversation, or rather disposed to converse; ready or inclined to mutual communication of thoughts; sociable; free in discourse. *Addison.*

CONVERS'ABLENESS, *n.* The quality of being free in conversation; disposition or readiness to converse; sociability.

CONVERS'ABLY, *adv.* In a conversable manner.

CON'VERSANT, *a.* [It. *conversante.* See *Converse.*]

1. Keeping company; having frequent or customary intercourse; intimately associating; familiar by fellowship or cohabitation; acquainted.

But the men were very good to us—as long as we were *conversant with* them. 1 Sam. xxv.

Never to be infected with delight,
Nor *conversant with* ease and idleness. *Shak.*

2. Acquainted by familiar use or study. We correct our style, and improve our taste, by being *conversant with* the best classical writers.

In the foregoing applications, this word is most generally followed by *with*, according to present usage. *In* was formerly used; and both *in* and *among* may be used.

3. Concerning; having concern, or relation to; having for its object; followed by *about.*

Education is *conversant about* children. *Wotton.*

CONVERSA'TION, *n.* General course of manners; behavior; deportment; especially as it respects morals.

Let your *conversation* be as becometh the gospel. Phil. i.

Be ye holy in all manner of *conversation.* 1 Pet. i.

2. A keeping company; familiar intercourse; intimate fellowship or association; commerce in social life. Knowledge of men and manners is best acquired by *conversation* with the best company.

3. Intimate and familiar acquaintance; as a *conversation* with books, or other object.

4. Familiar discourse; general intercourse of sentiments; chat; unrestrained talk; opposed to a formal conference.

What I mentioned in *conversation* was not a new thought. *Swift.*

[*This is now the most general use of the word.*]

CONVERSA'TIONED, *a.* Acquainted with the manner of acting in life. [*Not used.*] *Beaum.*

ȻONVERS'ATIVE, *a.* Relating to an intercourse with men; opposed to *contemplative.*

She chose to endue him with *conversative* qualities of youth. *Wotton.*

ȻONVERSAZIO'NE, *n.* [It.] A meeting of company. *Gray.*

ȻONVERSE, *v. i. convers'.* [L. *conversor; con* and *versor*, to be turned; Fr. *converser;* It. *conversare;* Sp. *conversar.* Literally, to be turned to or with; to be turned about.]

1. To keep company; to associate; to cohabit; to hold intercourse and be intimately acquainted; followed by *with.*

For him who lonely loves
To seek the distant hills, and there *converse*
With nature. *Thomson.*

2. To have sexual commerce. *Guardian.*

3. To talk familiarly; to have free intercourse in mutual communication of thoughts and opinions; to convey thoughts reciprocally; followed by *with* before the person addressed, and *on* before the subject. *Converse* as friend *with* friend. We have often *conversed with* each other *on* the merit of Milton's poetry.

[*This is now the most general use of the word.*]

ȻON'VERSE, *n.* Conversation: familiar discourse or talk; free interchange of thoughts or opinions.

Formed by thy *converse* happily to steer
From grave to gay, from lively to severe. *Pope.*

2. Acquaintance by frequent or customary intercourse; cohabitation; familiarity. In this sense, the word may include discourse, or not; as, to hold *converse* with persons of different sects; or to hold *converse* with terrestrial things.

3. In *mathematics*, an opposite proposition; thus, after drawing a *conclusion* from something *supposed*, we invert the order, making the conclusion the supposition or premises, and draw from it what was first supposed. Thus, if two sides of a triangle are equal, the angles opposite the sides are equal: and the *converse* is true; if these angles are equal, the two sides are equal. *Chambers. Bailey.*

ȻON'VERSELY, *adv.* With change of order; in a contrary order; reciprocally. *Johnson.*

ȻONVER'SION, *n.* [L. *conversio.* See *Convert.*]

1. In *a general sense*, a turning or change from one state to another; with regard to substances, transmutation; as a *conversion* of water into ice, or of food into chyle or blood.

2. In *military affairs*, a change of front, as when a body of troops is attacked in the flank, and they change their position to face the enemy.

3. In a *theological* or *moral sense*, a change of heart, or dispositions, in which the enmity of the heart to God and his law and the obstinacy of the will are subdued, and are succeeded by supreme love to God and his moral government, and a reformation of life.

4. Change from one side or party to another.

That *conversion* will be suspected that apparently concurs with interest. *Johnson.*

5. A change from one religion to another; as the *conversion* of the Gentiles. Acts xv.

6. The act of appropriating to private use; as in trover and *conversion.*

Conversion of equations, in algebra, the reduction of equations by multiplication, or the manner of altering an equation, when the quantity sought or any member of it is a fraction; the reducing of a fractional equation into an integral one. *Encyc. Bailey. Johnson.*

Conversion of propositions, in logic, is a changing of the subject into the place of the predicate, and still retaining the quality of the proposition. *Bailey.*

Conversion of the ratios, in arithmetic, is the comparing of the antecedent with the difference of the antecedent and consequent, in two equal ratios or proportions. *Bailey.*

ȻONVERT', *v. t.* [L. *converto; con* and *verto*, to turn; coinciding in elements and signification with *barter*, and probably from the root of *vary, vario, veer*, Sp. *birar*, Port. *virar*, to turn. Class Br.]

1. To change or turn into another substance or form; as, to *convert* gases into water, or water into ice.

2. To change from one state to another; as, to *convert* a barren waste into a fruitful field; to *convert* a wilderness into a garden; to *convert* rude savages into civilized men.

3. To change or turn from one religion to another, or from one party or sect to another; as, to *convert* pagans to christianity; to *convert* royalists into republicans.

4. To turn from a bad life to a good one; to change the heart and moral character, from enmity to God and from vicious habits, to love of God and to a holy life.

Repent ye therefore, and be *converted*, that your sins may be blotted out. Acts iii.

He that *converteth* a sinner from the error of his way, shall save a soul from death. James v.

5. To turn toward a point.

Crystal will callify into electricity, and *convert* the needle freely placed. [*Unusual.*] *Brown.*

6. To turn from one use or destination to another; as, to *convert* liberty into an engine of oppression.

7. To appropriate or apply to one's own use, or to personal benefit; as, to *convert* public property to our own use.

8. To change one proposition into another, so that what was the subject of the first becomes the predicate of the second; as, all sin is a transgression of the law; but every transgression of the law is sin. *Hale.*

9. To turn into another language. *B. Jonson.*

ȻONVERT', *v. i.* To turn or be changed; to undergo a change.

The love of wicked friends *converts* to fear:
That fear, to hate. *Shak.*

ȻON'VERT, *n.* A person who is converted from one opinion or practice to another; a person who renounces one creed, religious system or party, and embraces another; applied particularly to those who change their religious opinions, but applicable to political or philosophical sects.

2. In a more strict sense, one who is turned from sin to holiness.

Zion shall be redeemed with judgment, and her *converts* with righteousness. Is. i.

3. In *monasteries*, a lay-friar or brother, admitted to the service of the house, without orders, and not allowed to sing in the choir. *Encyc.*

ȻONVERT'ED, *pp.* Turned or changed from one substance or state to another; turned from one religion or sect to another; changed from a state of sin to a state of holiness; applied to a particular use; appropriated.

ȻONVERT'ER, *n.* One who converts; one who makes converts.

ȻONVERTIBIL'ITY, *n.* [from *convertible.*]

1. The quality of being possible to be converted or changed from one substance, form or state to another; as the *convertibility* of land into money. *Burke.*

2. The quality of being changeable from one letter to another; as the *convertibility* of *m* with *b*, or of *d* into *t*. *As. Researches.*

ȻONVERT'IBLE, *a.* [Fr. from *convertir.*]

1. That may be changed; susceptible of change; transmutable; transformable.

Minerals are not *convertible* into another species, though of the same genus. *Harvey.*

2. So much alike that one may be used for another. Usury and interest are not now *convertible* terms, though formerly they were.

3. That may be changed, as one letter for another; as *b, p* and *f* are *convertible* letters.

ȻONVERT'IBLY, *adv.* Reciprocally; with interchange of terms. *South.*

ȻON'VERTITE, *n.* A convert. [*Not in use.*]

ȻON'VEX, *a.* [L. *convexus;* It. *convesso.*] Rising or swelling on the exterior surface into a spherical or round form; gibbous; opposed to concave, which expresses a round form of the interior surface; as a *convex* mirror or lens.

ȻON'VEX, *n.* A convex body; as heaven's *convex.* *Tickel.*

ȻON'VEXED, *a.* Made convex; protuberant in a spherical form. *Brown.*

ȻONVEX'EDLY, *adv.* In a convex form. *Brown.*

ȻONVEX'ITY, *n.* [L. *convexitas.*] The exterior surface of a convex body; a gibbous or globular form; roundness. *Newton. Bentley.*

ȻON'VEXLY, *adv.* In a convex form; as a body *convexly* conical.

ȻON'VEXNESS, *n.* Convexity, which see.

ȻONVEX'O-ȻON'ȻAVE, *a.* Convex on one side and concave on the other; having the hollow on the inside corresponding to the convex surface.

ȻONVEX'O-ȻON'VEX, *a.* Convex on both sides.

ȻONVEY', *v. t.* [L. *conveho; con* and *veho*, to carry, Sax. *wægan, wegan*, Eng. to *weigh.* See *Weigh* and *Way.*]

1. To carry, bear or transport, either by land or water, or in air; as, to *convey* a letter or a package; to *convey* goods from England to France.

2. To pass or cause to pass; to transmit; as, to *convey* a right or an estate from father to son.

3. To transfer; to pass a title to any thing from one person to another, as by deed,

assignment or otherwise; as, to *convey* lands by bargain and sale.
4. To cause to pass; to transmit; to carry, by any medium; as, air *conveys* sound; words *convey* ideas.
5. To manage; to carry on. [*Not used.*]

I will *convey* the business as I shall find means. *Shak.*

6. To impart; to communicate.

CONVEY'ABLE, *a.* That may be conveyed or transferred. *Burke on the Sublime.*

CONVEY'ANCE, *n.* The act of conveying; the act of bearing, carrying, or transporting, by land or water, or through any medium.
2. The act of transmitting, or transferring, as titles, estates or claims from one person to another; transmission; transferrence; assignment.
3. The instrument or means of passing a thing from place to place, or person to person; as, a vehicle is a *conveyance* for persons or goods; a canal or aqueduct is a *conveyance* for water; a deed is a *conveyance* of land.
4. Removal; the act of removing or carrying. *Shak.*
5. Management; artifice; secret practices. [*In this sense, obsolete.*] *Spenser.*

CONVEY'ANCER, *n.* One whose occupation is to draw conveyances of property, deeds, &c.

CONVEY'ANCING, *n.* The act or practice of drawing deeds, leases or other writings for transferring the title to property from one person to another.

CONVEY'ER, *n.* One who conveys; he or that which conveys, carries, transports, transmits or transfers from one person or place to another.
2. A juggler. *Shak.*

CONVEY'ING, *ppr.* Carrying; transporting; transferring.

CONVICIN'ITY, *n.* Neighborhood; vicinity. *Warton.*

CONVICT', *v. t.* [L. *convinco, convictum; con* and *vinco*, to vanquish or subdue; Sp. *convencer*; It. *convincere*; Fr. *convaincre*. See *Convince*. The verb *vinco* is allied to *vincio*, to bind, the primary sense of which is to strain, force, make fast, hence to subdue; and as *n* appears to be casual, the root is *Vg* or *Vc*.]
1. To determine the truth of a charge against one; to prove or find guilty of a crime charged; to determine or decide to be guilty, as by the verdict of a jury, by confession, or other legal decision. The jury *convicted* the prisoner of felony.
2. To convince of sin; to prove or determine to be guilty, as by the conscience.

They who heard it, being *convicted* by their own conscience, went out one by one. John viii.

3. To confute; to prove or show to be false. *Obs.* *Brown.*
4. To show by proof or evidence. *Obs.* *Hooker.*

CONVICT', *pp.* for *convicted*. Proved or found guilty. *Shak.*

CON'VICT, *n.* A person proved or found guilty of a crime alledged against him, either by the verdict of a jury or other legal decision.

CONVICT'ED, *pp.* Proved or determined to be guilty, either by verdict of a jury or by the decision of conscience.

CONVICT'ING, *ppr.* Proving or finding guilty.

CONVIC'TION, *n.* The act of proving, finding or determining to be guilty of an offense charged against a person before a legal tribunal; as by confession, by the verdict of a jury, or by the sentence of other tribunal, as in the summary *convictions* before commissioners of the revenue.
2. The act of convincing, or compelling one to admit the truth of a charge; the act of convincing of sin or sinfulness; the state of being convinced or convicted by conscience; the state of being sensible of guilt; as, the *convictions* of a sinner may be temporary, or lasting and efficacious. By *conviction*, a sinner is brought to repentance. Men often sin against the *conviction* of their own consciences.
3. The act of convincing of error; confutation; the act of compelling one to acknowledge his error, or the truth of what is alledged; as, the *conviction* of a heretic may induce him to abandon his errors.

CONVIC'TIVE, *a.* Having the power to convince or convict.

CONVIC'TIVELY, *adv.* In a convincing manner. *More.*

CONVINCE, *v. t. convins'*. [L. *convinco; con* and *vinco*, to vanquish; Sp. *convencer*; It. *convincere*; Fr. *convaincre*.]
1. To persuade or satisfy the mind by evidence; to subdue the opposition of the mind to truth, or to what is alledged, and compel it to yield its assent; as, to *convince* a man of his errors; or to *convince* him of the truth.

For he mightily *convinced* the Jews—showing by the scriptures that Jesus was the Christ. Acts xviii.

2. To convict; to prove guilty; to constrain one to admit or acknowledge himself to be guilty.

If ye have respect to persons, ye commit sin, and are *convinced* of [by] the law as transgressors. James ii.

To *convince* all that are ungodly among them of all their ungodly deeds. Jude 15.

3. To envince; to prove. *Obs.* *Shak.*
4. To overpower; to surmount; to vanquish. *Obs.* *Shak.*

CONVIN'CED, *pp.* Persuaded in mind; satisfied with evidence; convicted.

CONVINCEMENT, *n. convins'ment.* Conviction. [*Little used.*]

CONVIN'CER, *n.* He or that which convinces; that which makes manifest. *More.*

CONVIN'CIBLE, *a.* Capable of conviction.
2. Capable of being disproved or refuted. [*Little used.*] *Brown.*

CONVIN'CING, *ppr.* Persuading the mind by evidence; convicting.
2. *a.* Persuading the mind by evidence; capable of subduing the opposition of the mind and compelling its assent. We have *convincing* proof of the truth of the scriptures, and of God's moral government of the world.

CONVIN'CINGLY, *adv.* In a convincing manner; in a manner to leave no room to doubt, or to compel assent. *Clarendon.*

CONVIN'CINGNESS, *n.* The power of convincing.

CONVI''TIOUS, *a.* [L. *convitior.*] Reproachful. *Obs.*

CONVI'VE, *v. t.* To entertain; to feast. [*Not in use.*] *Shak.*

CONVIV'IAL, *a.* [L. *convivalis*, from *conviva*, a guest, or *convivo*, to live or eat and drink together; *con* and *vivo*, to live. See *Victuals.*]
Relating to a feast or entertainment; festal; social; jovial; as a *convivial* meeting. *Denham.*

CONVIVIAL'ITY, *n.* The good humor or mirth indulged at an entertainment.
2. A convivial spirit or disposition.

CON'VOCATE, *v. t.* [L. *convoco*, to convoke; *con* and *voco*, to call. See *Voice.*]
To convoke; to call or summon to meet; to assemble by summons. [See *Convoke.*]

CONVOCA'TION, *n.* [L. *convocatio.*] The act of calling or assembling by summons.
2. An assembly.

In the first day there shall be a holy *convocation*. Ex. xii.

3. In *England*, an assembly of the clergy, by their representatives, to consult on ecclesiastical affairs. It is held during the session of parliament, and consists of an upper and lower house. In the upper house sit the archbishops and bishops; in the lower house sit the inferior clergy, represented by their proctors, consisting of all the deans and arch-deacons, of one proctor for every chapter, and two for the clergy of every diocese, in all one hundred and forty-three divines, viz. twenty-two deans, fifty-three arch-deacons, twenty-four prebendaries, and forty-four proctors of the diocesan clergy. *Encyc.*
4. An academical assembly, in which the business of the university is transacted. *Laud.*

CONVO'KE, *v. t.* [L. *convoco*; Fr. *convoquer*. See *Voice.*]
To call together; to summon to meet; to assemble by summons.

It is the prerogative of the President of the U. States to *convoke* the senate.

CONVO'KED, *pp.* Summoned or assembled by order.

CONVO'KING, *ppr.* Summoning to convene; assembling.

CON'VOLUTE, **CON'VOLUTED**, } *a.* Rolled together, or one part on another; as the sides or margins of nascent leaves in plants, or as the petals and stigmas in Crocus. *Martyn.* *Lee.*

CONVOLU'TION, *n.* [L. *convolutio.*] The act of rolling or winding together, or one thing on another; the state of being rolled together.
2. A winding or twisting; a winding motion; as the *convolution* of certain vines; the *convolution* of an eddy. *Thomson.*

CONVOLVE, *v. t. convolv'.* [L. *convolvo; con* and *volvo*, to roll. See *Wallow.*]
To roll or wind together; to roll one part on another.

CONVOLV'ULUS, *n.* [L. from *convolvo.*] Bindweed, a genus of plants of many species.

CONVOY', *v. t.* [Fr. *convoyer*; It. *conviare*; Sp. *convoyar*; Port. *comboyar*; *con* and *voie, via*, way, or the same root; or more directly from the root of L. *veho*, to carry, Sax. *wægan, wegan*, to bear or carry, to bring along.]
To accompany on the way for protection, either by sea or land; as, ships of war *con*

voyed the Jamaica fleet; the troops *convoyed* the baggage wagons.

When *persons* are to be protected, the word *escort* is used.

CON'VOY, *n.* A protecting force accompanying ships or property on their way from place to place, either by sea or land. By sea, a ship or ships of war which accompany merchantmen for protection from an enemy. By land, any body of troops which accompany provisions, ammunition or other property for protection.

2. The ship or fleet conducted and protected; that which is conducted by a protecting force; that which is convoyed. The word sometimes includes both the protecting and protected fleets. *Admiralty Reports. Anderson. Burchett. Encyc. State Papers.*

3. The act of attending for defense. *Shak. Milton.*

4. Conveyance. *Obs.* *Shak.*

CONVOY'ED, *pp.* Attended on a passage by a protecting force.

CONVOY'ING, *ppr.* Attending on a voyage or passage for defense from enemies; attending and guarding.

CONVULSE, *v. t.* *convuls'.* [L. *convello, convulsum, convulsus; con* and *vello*, to pull or pluck.]

1. To draw or contract, as the muscular parts of an animal body; to affect by irregular spasms; as, the whole frame may be *convulsed* by agony.

2. To shake; to affect by violent irregular action.

Convulsing heaven and earth. *Thomson.*

CONVULS'ED, *pp.* Contracted by spasms; shaken violently.

CONVULS'ING, *ppr.* Affecting by spasmodic contractions; shaking with violence.

CONVUL'SION, *n.* [L. *convulsio.*] A preternatural, violent and involuntary contraction of the muscular parts of an animal body. *Encyc.*

2. Any violent and irregular motion; tumult; commotion; as political *convulsions.*

CONVUL'SIVE, *a.* That produces convulsion; as *convulsive* rage; *convulsive* sorrow. *Dryden. Prior.*

2. Attended with convulsion or spasms; as *convulsive* motions; *convulsive* strife. *Dryden. Hale.*

CONVUL'SIVELY, *adv.* With violent shaking or agitation.

CO'NY, CO'NEY, *n.* [D. *konyn*; G. *kanin*; Sw. *kanin*; Dan. *kanine*; Fr. *conin* or *conil*; L. *cuniculus*; It. *coniglio*; Sp. *conejo*; Ir. *cuinin*; W. *cwning.* The primary sense is a shoot, or a shooting along.]

A rabbit; a quadruped of the genus Lepus, which has a short tail and naked ears. In a wild state the fur is brown, but the color of the domestic rabbit is various.

CO'NY-BURROW, *n.* A place where rabbits burrow in the earth.

CO'NY-CATCH, *v. i.* [*cony* and *catch.*] In *the cant of thieves*, to cheat; to bite; to trick. *Shak.*

CO'NY-CATCHER, *n.* A thief; a cheat; a sharper. *Obs.*

CO'NY-CATCHING, *n.* Banter. *Obs.* *Shak.*

COO, *v. i.* [probably from the sound.]

To cry, or make a low sound, as pigeons or doves. *Thomson.*

COO'ING, *ppr.* Uttering a low sound, as a dove.

COO'ING, *n.* Invitation, as the note of the dove. *Young.*

COOK, *v. t.* [Sax. *gecocnian*; Sw. *koka*; Dan. *koger*; D. *kooken*; G. *kochen*; It. *cuocere*; Sp. *cocer*, and *cocinar*; Port. *cozinhar*; L. *coquo.*]

1. To prepare, as victuals for the table, by boiling, roasting, baking, broiling, &c. To dress, as meat or vegetables, for eating.

2. To prepare for any purpose. *Shak.*

3. To throw. [*Obs. or local.*] *Grose.*

COOK, *v. i.* To make the noise of the cuckoo.

COOK, *n.* [Sax. *coc*; D. *kok*; G. *koch*; Sw. *kock*; Dan. *kok*; It. *cuoco*; Ir. *coca*; L. *coquus.*]

One whose occupation is to prepare victuals for the table; a man or woman who dresses meat or vegetables for eating.

COOK'ED, *pp.* Prepared for the table.

COOK'ERY, *n.* The art or the practice of dressing and preparing victuals for the table.

COOK'ING, *ppr.* Preparing victuals for the table.

COOK'MAID, *n.* [*cook* and *maid.*] A female servant or maid who dresses provisions.

COOK'ROOM, *n.* [*cook* and *room.*] A room for cookery; a kitchen. On board of ships, a galley or caboose.

COOL, *a.* [Sax. *col*; D. *koel*; G. *kühl*; Sw. *kall*; Dan. *kold*, cold; *kiöler*, to cool; *kulde*, chilliness; *kuler*, to blow strong.]

1. Moderately cold; being of a temperature between hot and cold; as *cool* air; *cool* water.

2. Not ardent or zealous; not angry; not fond; not excited by passion of any kind; indifferent; as a *cool* friend; a *cool* temper; a *cool* lover.

3. Not hasty; deliberate; calm; as a *cool* purpose.

4. Not retaining heat; light; as a *cool* dress.

COOL, *n.* A moderate state of cold; moderate temperature of the air between hot and cold; as the *cool* of the day; the *cool* of the morning or evening.

COOL, *v. t.* [Sax. *colian, acolian*; D. *koelen*; G. *kühlen*; Dan. *kiöler.*]

1. To allay heat; to make cool or cold; to reduce the temperature of a substance; as, ice *cools* water.

Send Lazarus, that he may dip the tip of his finger in water, and *cool* my tongue. Luke xvi.

2. To moderate excitement of temper; to allay, as passion of any kind; to calm, as anger; to abate, as love; to moderate, as desire, zeal or ardor; to render indifferent.

COOL, *v. i.* To become less hot; to lose heat. Let tea or coffee *cool* to the temperature of the blood, before it is drank.

2. To lose the heat of excitement or passion; to become less ardent, angry, zealous, or affectionate; to become more moderate. Speak not in a passion; first let your temper *cool.*

COOL-CUP, *n.* A beverage that is cooling.

COOL'ED, *pp.* Made less hot, or less ardent.

COOL'ER, *n.* That which cools; any substance which abates heat or excitement; as, acids are *coolers* to the body.

2. A vessel in which liquors or other things are cooled.

COOL-HEADED, *a.* Having a temper not easily excited; free from passion. *Burke.*

COOL'ING, *ppr.* Abating heat or excitement; making or becoming cool.

COOL'ISH, *a.* Somewhat cool. *Goldsmith.*

COOL'LY, *adv.* Without heat or sharp cold.

2. In a cool or indifferent manner; not cordially; without passion or ardor. He was *coolly* received at court.

3. Without haste; calmly; deliberately. The design was formed *coolly*, and executed with firmness.

COOL'NESS, *n.* A moderate degree of cold; a temperature between cold and heat; as the *coolness* of the summer's evening.

2. A moderate degree, or a want of passion; want of ardor, or zeal; indifference; want of affection; as, they parted with *coolness.*

COOM, *n.* [Fr. *cambouis*; Sw. *kim*, soot.] Soot that gathers over an oven's mouth; also, the matter that works out of the naves or boxes of carriage wheels. In Scotland, the useless dust which falls from coals.

COOMB or **COMB**, *n.* [Qu. L. *cumulus*, or Gr. κυμβος.]

A dry measure of four bushels, or half a quarter.

COOP, *n.* [D. *kuip*, a tub; *kuiper*, a cooper; G. *kufe*; Fr. *cuve*; L. *cupa*, from bending, hollowness, or containing, holding. Qu. Gr. κυφος. The Latin *cupa* seems to be both *coop* and *cup.* See *Cup.*]

1. A box of boards, grated or barred on one side, for keeping fowls in confinement. It is usually applied to long boxes for keeping poultry for fattening or conveyance on board of ships, as *cage* is used for a small box to keep singing birds in houses. I do not know that it is ever used in America for a *pen* to confine other animals.

2. A pen; an inclosed place for small animals. *Johnson.*

3. A barrel or cask for the preservation of liquors. *Johnson.*

4. A tumbrel or close cart. *Encyc. Jamieson's Dict.*

[*The three last senses, not American.*]

COOP, *v. t.* To put in a coop; to confine in a coop. Hence, to shut up or confine in a narrow compass; usually followed by *up*, to *coop up*; sometimes by *in.*

The Trojans *cooped within* their walls. *Dryden.*

They are *cooped in* close by the laws of the country. *Locke.*

COOP'ED, *pp.* Shut up in a coop; confined to narrow limits.

COOP'ER, *n.* [from *coop*; D. *kuiper*; G. *küfer.*]

One whose occupation is to make barrels, hogsheads, butts, tubs and casks of various kinds.

COOP'ERAGE, *n.* The price paid for cooper's work; also, a place where cooper's work is done.

CO-OP'ERATE, *v. i.* [L. *con* and *opero*, to work; Fr. *cooperer*; It. *cooperare*; Sp. *cooperar.*]

1. To act or operate jointly with another or others, to the same end; to work or labor with mutual efforts to promote the same object. It has *with* before the agent, and *to* before the end. Russia *cooperated with* Great Britain, Austria and Prussia, to reduce the power of Buonaparte.

2. To act together; to concur in producing the same effect. Natural and moral events *cooperate* in illustrating the wisdom of the Creator.

CO-OP'ERATING, *ppr.* Acting or operating together.

CO-OPERA'TION, *n.* The act of working, or operating together, to one end; joint operation; concurrent effort or labor; as the *cooperation* of the combined powers; the *cooperation* of the understanding and the will.

CO-OP'ERATIVE, *a.* Operating jointly to the same end.

CO-OP'ERATOR, *n.* One who endeavors jointly with others to promote the same end.

CO-OP'TATE, *v. t.* [L. *coopto.*] To choose, or choose with another. [*Not used.*]

CO-OPTA'TION, *n.* Adoption; assumption. *Howell.*

CO-OR'DINATE, *a.* [L. *con* and *ordinatus*, from *ordino*, to regulate. See *Order.*]
Being of equal order, or of the same rank or degree; not subordinate; as, two courts of *co-ordinate* jurisdiction.

CO-OR'DINATELY, *adv.* In the same order or rank; in equal degree; without subordination.

CO-OR'DINATENESS, *n.* The state of being coordinate; equality of rank and authority.

CO-ORDINA'TION, *n.* The state of holding equal rank, or of standing in the same relation to something higher.

In the high court of Parliament there is a rare *coordination* of power. *Howell.*

COOT, *n.* [D. *koet*; W. *cwtiar*, from *cwta*, short, bob-tailed.]
A fowl of the genus *Fulica*, frequenting lakes and other still waters. The common coot has a bald forehead, a black body, and lobated toes, and is about fifteen inches in length. It makes its nest among rushes, with grass and reeds, floating on the water.

COP, *n.* [Sax. *cop*, or *copp*; W. *cop*, *cob*; D. *kop*; G. *kopf*; Fr. *coupeau*; Gr. *κυϐη*.]
The head or top of a thing, as in *cob-castle* for *cop-castle*, a castle on a hill; a tuft on the head of birds. This word is little used in America, unless *cob*, the spike of maize, may be the same word. *Chaucer.*

COP'AIBA, *n.* [Sp. Port.] Balsam of copaiba or capivi, is a liquid resinous juice, flowing from incisions made in the stem of a tree called *Copaifera officinalis*, growing in Spanish America, in the province of Antiochia. This juice is clear, transparent, of a whitish or pale yellowish color, an agreeable smell, and a bitterish pungent taste. It is of the consistence of oil, or a little thicker. As a medicine, it is corroborating and detergent. *Encyc.*

CO'PAL, *n.* [Mexican *copalli*, a generic name of resins. *Clavigero.*]
The concrete juice of a tree growing in Mexico or New Spain, hard, shining, transparent, citron-colored, and odoriferous. It is not strictly a gum nor a resin, as it has not the solubility in water common to gums, nor that in spirit of wine common to resins. In these respects it rather resembles amber. It may be dissolved by digestion in lintseed oil, with a heat little less than sufficient to boil or decompose the oil. This solution, diluted with spirit of turpentine, forms a beautiful transparent varnish. *Encyc. Nicholson.*

COP'ARCENARY, *n.* [*co* or *con* and Norm. *parcenier*, parcenary. See *Coparcener.*]
Partnership in inheritance; joint heirship; joint right of succession or joint succession to an estate of inheritance.

COP'ARCENER, *n.* [*con* and *parcener*, from *part*, Fr. *parti*, L. *pars*, or the verb *partir*, to divide.]
A coheir; one who has an equal portion of the inheritance of his or her ancestor with others.

All the *coparceners* together make but one heir, and have but one estate among them. *Blackstone.*

Coparceners take by descent; *joint-tenants*, by purchase. *Id.*

COP'ARCENY, *n.* An equal share of an inheritance.

COP'ARTMENT, *n.* The same as *compartment.* [*Not in use.*] *Warton.*

COP'ARTNER, *n.* [*con* and *partner.* See *Coparcener.*]
1. One who has a share in a common stock for transacting business, or who is jointly concerned with one or more persons, in carrying on trade or other business; a partner; an associate, particularly in trade or manufactures.
2. A sharer; a partaker; as, *copartners* of our loss. *Milton.*

COP'ARTNERSHIP, *n.* Joint concern in business; a state of having a joint share in a common stock, or a joint interest and concern in business, particularly in trade and manufactures.
2. The persons who have a joint concern.

CO'PATAN, *n.* [See *Cop.*] High raised; pointed. [*Not in use.*] *Shak.*

COPE, *n.* [W. *côb*; Sax. *cæppe*; D. *kap*; Dan. *kappe*, *kaabe*; Sw. *kappa* or *kåpa*; Fr. *chape*, whence *chapeau*, a hat; Sp. *capa*; It. *cappa*; Port. *capa.*]
1. A cover for the head.
2. A sacerdotal ornament or vestment worn in sacred ministrations. An ornament worn by chanters and subchanters, when they officiate in solemnity. It reaches from the shoulders to the feet.
3. Any thing spread or extended over the head; the arch or concave of the sky; the roof or covering of a house; the arch over a door, &c.
4. An ancient tribute due to the king or lord of the soil, out of the lead mines in some part of Derbyshire. *Encyc.*

COPE, *v. t.* To cover as with a cope. *Addison.*
2. To pare the beak or talons of a hawk. *Bailey.*
4. To embrace. *Obs.* *Shak.*

COPE, *v. i.* [Dan. *kiv*, contention; *kives*, to strive; *kappes*, to strive, to equal, to envy; Sw. *kif*, strife; *kifwa*, to contend or quarrel; *kåppas*, to strive, to emulate; Ar. كفا kafaa, to turn back, to drive away, to thrust, to oppose, to equal; كفى kafai, to be sufficient, to be equal, to be like, to be a substitute. Class Gb. No. 53. 55.]
1. To strive or contend on equal terms, or with equal strength; to equal in combat; to match; to oppose with success.

Their Generals have not been able to *cope with* the troops of Athens. *Addison.*

Till Luther rose, no power could *cope* with the pope. *D. A. Clark.*

He was too open and direct in his conduct, and possessed too little management—to *cope* with so cool and skilful an adversary. *Wirt.*

2. To contend; to strive or struggle; to combat.

Host *cop'd* with host, dire was the din of war. *Philips.*

3. To encounter; to interchange kindness or sentiments. *Shak.*
4. To make return; to reward. *Obs.* *Shak.*
5. To exchange, or barter. [*Not in use.*] *Bailey.*

CO'PEMAN, *n.* A chapman. [*Not used.*] *Shak.*

COPER'NICAN, *a.* Pertaining to Copernicus, a Prussian by birth, who taught the world the solar system now received, called the *Copernican* system.

CO'PESMATE, *n.* [*cope* and *mate.*] A companion or friend. *Obs.* *Hubberd.*

COP'IED, *pp.* [See *Copy.*] Taken off; written or transcribed from an original or form; imitated.

COP'IER, } *n.* One who copies; one who
COP'YIST, } writes or transcribes from an original or form; a transcriber; an imitator; also, a plagiary. *Addison. Dryden.*

CO'PING, *n.* [See *Cope*, *n.*] The top or cover of a wall, made sloping to carry off the water. 1 Kings vii. 9. A *coping over*, is a projecting work beveling on its under side.

CO'PIOUS, *a.* [Fr. *copieux*; It. *copioso*; Sp. *id.*; L. *copiosus*, from *copia*, abundance, Ir. *coib.* Qu. Ch. גבב to collect, gather, accumulate; Ar. جبا jabau, id. Class Gb. No 2. 5. 55.]
1. Abundant; plentiful; in great quantities; full; ample; furnishing full supplies.

The tender heart is peace,
And kindly pours its *copious* treasures forth
In various converse. *Thomson.*

2. Furnishing abundant matter; not barren; rich in supplies.

The redemption of man is a *copious* subject of contemplation.

Hail, Son of God, Savior of men! thy name
Shall be the *copious* matter of my song. *Milton.*

CO'PIOUSLY, *adv.* Abundantly; plentifully; in large quantities.
2. Largely; fully; amply; diffusely.

The remains of antiquity have been *copiously* described by travelers. *Addison.*

CO'PIOUSNESS, *n.* Abundance; plenty; great quantity; full supply.
2. Diffusiveness of style or manner of treating a subject; as the *copiousness* of Homer. *Dryden.*

CO'PIST, *n.* A copier; *an ill formed word.*

COP'LAND, *n.* A piece of ground terminating in a *cop* or acute angle. [*Not used in America.*] *Dict.*

CO-PLANT', *v. t.* To plant together. [*Not in use.*] *Howel.*

CO-PORTION, *n.* Equal share. [*Not used.*] *Spenser.*

COP'PED, COP'PLED, *a.* [See *Cop.*] Rising to a point, or head.

Copped like a sugar loaf. *Wiseman.*

COP'PEL. [See *Cupel.*]

COP'PER, *n.* [D. *koper*; G. *kupfer*; Sw. *koppar*; Ir. *copar*; Corn. *cober*; L. *cuprum*; Fr. *cuivre*; Sp. *cobre*; Port. *id.*; Arm. *cuevr*, *coevr*; supposed to be so called from *Cyprus*, an isle in the Mediterranean. This opinion is probable, as the Greeks called it χαλκος κυπριος, *Cyprian* brass, brass of Cyprus. In this case, *copper* was originally an adjective.]

A metal, of a pale red color, tinged with yellow. Next to gold, silver and platina, it is the most ductile and malleable of the metals, and it is more elastic than any metal, except steel, and the most sonorous of all the metals. It is found native in lamins or fibers, in a gangue almost always quartzous; it is also found crystalized, and in grains or superficial lamins on stones or iron. It is not altered by water, but is tarnished by exposure to the air, and is at last covered with a green carbonated oxyd. Copper in sheets is much used for covering the bottoms of ships, for boilers and other utensils: mixed with tin and zink, it is used in enamel-painting, dyeing, &c.: mixed with tin, it forms bell-metal; with a smaller proportion, bronze; and with zink, it forms brass, pinchbeck, &c. When taken into the body it operates as a violent emetic, and all its preparations are violent poisons. *Fourcroy. Encyc. Hooper.*

COP'PER, *a.* Consisting of copper. *Cleaveland.*

COP'PER, *n.* A vessel made of copper, particularly a large boiler.

2. Formerly, a small copper coin.

My friends filled my pocket with *coppers.* *Franklin.*

COP'PER, *v. t.* To cover or sheathe with sheets of copper; as, to *copper* a ship.

COP'PERAS, *n.* [Fr. *couperose*; D. *koperrood*, that is, red copper, and *koperroest* is copper rust, verdigris; Arm. *couperosa*, or *couperos.*]

Sulphate of iron, or green vitriol; a salt of a peculiar astringent taste, and of various colors, green, gray, yellowish, or whitish, but more usually green. It is much used in dyeing black and in making ink, and in medicine, as a tonic. The copperas of commerce is usually made by the decomposition of iron pyrites. The term *copperas* was formerly synonymous with *vitriol*, and included the green, blue and white vitriols, or the sulphates of iron, copper and zink. *Cleaveland. Fourcroy.*

COP'PER-BOTTOMED, *a.* Having a bottom sheathed with copper.

COP'PERED, *pp.* Covered with sheets of copper; sheathed.

COP'PER-FASTENED, *a.* Fastened with copper bolts.

COP'PERISH, *a.* Containing copper; like copper or partaking of it.

COP'PER-NOSE, *n.* A red nose. *Shak.*

COP'PER-PLATE, *n.* A plate of copper on which concave lines are engraved or corroded, according to some delineated figure or design. This plate, when charged with any colored fluid, imparts an impression of the figure or design to paper or parchment. *Encyc.*

COP'PER-SMITH, *n.* One whose occupation is to manufacture copper utensils.

COP'PER-WORK, *n.* A place where copper is wrought or manufactured. *Woodward.*

COP'PER-WORM, *n.* A little worm in ships; a worm that frets garments; a worm that breeds in one's hand. *Ainsworth.*

COP'PERY, *a.* Mixed with copper; containing copper, or made of copper; like copper in taste or smell. *Woodward.*

COP'PICE, COPSE, *n.* [Norm. *coupiz*, from *couper*, to cut, Gr. κοπτω.]

A wood of small growth, or consisting of underwood or brushwood; a wood cut at certain times for fuel.

The rate of *coppice* lands will fall on the discovery of coal-mines. *Locke.*

COP'PLED, *a.* [from *cop.*] Rising to a point; conical. *Woodward.*

COP'PLE-DUST, *n.* Powder used in purifying metals.

COP'PLE-STONES, *n.* Lumps and fragments of stone broke from the adjacent cliffs, rounded by being bowled and tumbled to and again by the action of water. *Johnson. Woodward.*

In New England, we pronounce this word *cobble*, *cobble-stones*, and if the word is a diminutive of *cob*, *cop*, a head, or *cub*, a heap, we follow the Welsh *cob*, as the English do the same word, *cop*, in the Saxon dialect. We apply the word to small round stones, from the size of an inch or two, to five or six inches or more, in diameter, wherever they may be found.

COPSE, *n.* [See *Coppice.*]

COPSE, *v. t.* To preserve underwoods. *Swift.*

COP'SY, *a.* Having copses. *Dyer.*

COP'TIC, *a.* Pertaining to the descendants of the ancient Egyptians, called Copts, or Cophti, as distinct from the Arabians and other inhabitants of modern Egypt. The name is supposed to be taken from *Coptos*, the metropolis of the Thebaid; as *Egypt*, Αιγυπτος, is probably from that name; Sanscrit, *agupta*, inclosed, fortified. So *Misraim* and *Mazor* are from צרר to inclose, to bind, to fortify. Whatever may be the origin of *Copt*, the adjective *Coptic* now refers to the people called *Copts*, who are christians, and to their language. Hence,

COP'TIC, *n.* The language of the *Copts.* [See Class Gb. No. 8. 14.]

COP'ULA, *n.* [L. See *Copulation* and *Couple.*] In *logic*, the word which unites the subject and predicate of a proposition. Religion *is* indispensable to happiness. Here *is* is the copula joining *religion*, the subject, with *indispensable to happiness*, the predicate.

COP'ULATE, *a.* Joined. [*Little used.*]

COP'ULATE, *v. t.* [L. *copulo*, to *couple*; Sp. *copular*; It. *copulare*; Fr. *coupler.* See *Couple.*]

To unite; to join in pairs. [*Little used.*]

COP'ULATE, *v. i.* To unite in sexual embrace; *applied to animals in general.*

COPULA'TION, *n.* [L. *copulatio.*] The act of coupling; the embrace of the sexes in the act of generation; coition.

COP'ULATIVE, *a.* That unites or couples. In *grammar*, the *copulative* conjunction connects two or more subjects or predicates, in an affirmative or negative proposition; as, riches *and* honors are temptations to pride; the Romans conquered Spain *and* Gaul *and* Britain; neither wealth *nor* honors will purchase immortal happiness.

COP'ULATIVE, *n.* A copulative conjunction.

2. Connection. [*Not in use.*]

COP'Y, *n.* [Fr. *copie*; Arm. *copy*; It. *copia*; Sp. and Port. *copia*; Ir. *coib*, *coibeadh.* This word is from the root of *cope*, in the sense of likeness, resemblance, Ar. كَفَي to be like; or it is from doubling, and the root of *cuff*, Ar. كَافَ. Class Gb. No. 50. See *Cope* and *Cuff.*]

Literally, a likeness, or resemblance of any kind. Hence,

1. A writing like another writing; a transcript from an original; or a book printed according to the original; hence, any single book, or set of books, containing a composition resembling the original work; as the *copy* of a deed, or of a bond; a *copy* of Addison's works; a *copy* of the laws; a *copy* of the scriptures.

2. The form of a picture or statue according to the original; the imitation or likeness of any figure, draught, or almost any object.

3. An original work; the autograph; the archetype. Hence, that which is to be imitated in writing or printing. Let the child write according to the *copy.* The *copy* is in the hands of the printer. Hence, a pattern or example for imitation. His virtues are an excellent *copy* for imitation.

4. Abundance. [L. *copia.*] *Obs.*

COP'Y, *v. t.* To write, print or engrave, according to an original; to form a like work or composition by writing, printing or engraving; to transcribe; often followed by *out*, but the use is not elegant.

The men of Hezekiah *copied* certain proverbs of Solomon.

2. To paint or draw according to an original.

3. To form according to a model, as in architecture.

4. To imitate or attempt to resemble; to follow an original or pattern, in manners or course of life. *Copy* the Savior in his humility and obedience.

COP'Y, *v. i.* To imitate or endeavor to be like; to do any thing in imitation of something else. A painter *copies from* the life. An obedient child *copies after* his parent.

They never fail, when they *copy*, to follow the bad as well as the good. *Dryden.*

COP'YBOOK, *n.* A book in which copies are written or printed for learners to imitate.

COP'YED, *pp.* Transcribed; imitated; usually written *copied.*

COP'YER, *n.* One who copies or transcribes; usually written *copier.*

COP'YHOLD, *n.* In England, a tenure of estate by copy of court roll; or a tenure for which the tenant hath nothing to show, except the rolls made by the steward of the lord's court. *Blackstone.*

COP'YHOLDER, *n.* One who is possessed of land in copyhold.

COP'YIST, *n.* A copier; a transcriber.

COP'YRIGHT, *n.* The sole right which an author has in his own original literary compositions; the exclusive right of an author to print, publish and vend his own literary works, for his own benefit; the like right in the hands of an assignee.

COQUAL'LIN, *n.* A small quadruped of the squirrel kind, but incapable of climbing trees. *Dict. of Nat. Hist.*

CO'QUELICOT, } *n.* [Fr.] Wild poppy;
CO'QUELICO, } corn rose; hence, the color of wild poppy.

COQUET', } *n.* [Fr. *coquet*, a beau, a gen-
COQUETTE, } eral lover, a cock-boat; *coquette*, a jilt; from the Welsh or Celtic *coegen*, a vain saucy wench, a coquet, from *coeg*, vain; Sp. *coqueta;* It. *civetta*, an owl; *civettare*, to play the wag, to trifle, to coquet; *civetteria*, coquetry; *civettino*, a vain young fellow.]

A vain, airy, trifling girl, who endeavors to attract admiration and advances in love, from a desire to gratify vanity, and then rejects her lover; a jilt.

> The light *coquettes* in sylphs aloft repair,
> And sport and flutter in the fields of air. *Pope.*

NOTE. In French, *coquet* is masculine and *coquette* feminine: but as our language has no such termination for gender, it may be better to write *coquet* for both sexes, and for distinction prefix *male* to the word when applied to a man.

COQUET', *v. t.* To attempt to attract notice, admiration or love, from vanity; to entertain with compliments and amorous tattle; to treat with an appearance of amorous tenderness.

> You are *coquetting* a maid of honor. *Swift.*

COQUET', *v. i.* To trifle in love; to act the lover from vanity; to endeavor to gain admirers.

COQUET'ISH, *a.* Practicing coquetry.

CO'QUETRY, *n.* [Fr. *coquetterie.*] Attempts to attract admiration, notice or love, from vanity; affectation of amorous advances; trifling in love. *Addison.*

COR'ACLE, *n.* [W. *cwrwgle.*] A boat used in Wales by fishermen, made by covering a wicker frame with leather or oil-cloth. *Johnson.*

COR'ACOID, *n.* [Gr. κοραξ, a crow, and ειδος, form.]

A small sharp process of the scapula, shaped like a crow's beak. *Hooper.*

COR'ACOID, *a.* Shaped like a beak. *Buckland.*

COR'AL, *n.* [L. *corallium;* Gr. κοραλλιον; Fr. *corail*, or *coral;* It. *corallo;* Sp. *coral;* D. *koraal;* G. *koralle;* Dan. *koral.*]

1. In *zoology*, a genus belonging to the order of vermes zoophyta. The trunk is radicated, jointed and calcarious. The species are distinguished by the form of their branches, and are found in the ocean adhering to stones, bones, shells, &c. Coral was formerly supposed to be a vegetable substance, but is now known to be composed of a congeries of animals. Coral is red, white and black. It is properly the shells of marine animals of the polype kind, consisting of calcarious earth combined with gelatine and other animal matter. In the South Sea, the isles are mostly coral rocks covered with earth. *Encyc. Nicholson.*

> Corals seem to consist of carbonate of lime and animal matter, in equal proportions. *Ure.*

2. A piece of coral worn by children about their necks.

COR'AL, *a.* Made of coral; resembling coral.

COR'AL-TREE, *n.* A genus of plants, Erythrina, of several species, natives of Africa and America. They are all shrubby flowering plants, adorned chiefly with trifoliate or three-lobed leaves, and scarlet spikes of papilionaceous flowers.

COR'AL-WORT, *n.* A genus of plants, Dentaria, called also *tooth-wort* or tooth-violet. *Fam. of Plants.*

CORALLA'CEOUS, *a.* Like coral, or partaking of its qualities.

COR'ALLIFORM, *a.* [*coral* and *form.*] Resembling coral; forked and crooked. *Kirwan.*

COR'ALLINE, *a.* Consisting of coral; like coral; containing coral.

COR'ALLINE, *n.* A submarine plant-like body, consisting of many slender, jointed branches, resembling some species of moss; or animals growing in the form of plants, having their stems fixed to other bodies. These stems are composed of capillary tubes, which pass through a calcarious crust and open on the surface. In the Linnean system, corallines are classed with the zoophytes. They have been distributed by Ellis into *vesiculated*, furnished with small bodies like bladders; *tubular*, composed of simple tubes; *celliferous*, which, when magnified, appear to be fine thin cells, the habitations of small animals; and *articulated*, consisting of short pieces of stony or cretaceous brittle matter, covered with pores or cells, joined by a tough, membranous, flexible substance, composed of many small tubes. But in this arrangement of Ellis, the term *coralline* is synonymous with the more ancient term *lithophyta*, including all the polype-bearing animals, and nearly coinciding with the *zoophyta* of Linne, and the *polypiers* of the French naturalists. *Encyc. Cyc.*

COR'ALLINITE, *n.* A fossil polypier or coralline. *Dict. Nat. Hist.*

COR'ALLITE, *n.* A mineral substance or petrifaction, in the form of coral; or a fossil polypier, larger than a corallinite. *Kirwan. Dict. Nat. Hist.*

COR'ALLOID, } *a.* [*coral*, and ειδος,
CORALLOID'AL, } form.]

Having the form of coral; branching like coral. *Dict. Nat. Hist.*

COR'ALLOID, *n.* Eschara or hornwrack, a species of coralline, resembling woven cloth in texture, consisting of arrangements of very small cells. One species is called narrow-leaved hornwrack; another, the broad-leaved hornwrack. This name is given also to the keratophyta, horn-plant, or sea-shrub, a species of *Gorgonia.* *Encyc.*

CORANT', *n.* [Fr. *courant*, running; *courir*, to run, L. *curro.*]

A lofty sprightly dance. *Johnson. Temple.*

CORB, *n.* [L. *corbis.* See the next word.]

1. A basket used in coaleries.

2. An ornament in a building. *Spenser.*

CORB'AN, *n.* [L. *corbis;* D. *korf;* G. *korb;* Sw. *korg;* Dan. *kurv;* Fr. *corbeille;* Eth. ከረበ karbo, a wicker basket; Russ. *korban*, a chuch box or chest, a treasury. But in Ethiopic, korban is an oblation, that which is offered to God, a gift, a sacrifice, coinciding with the Heb. קרבן, from קרב to approach, to cause to approach, to bring or offer.]

1. In *Jewish antiquity*, an offering which had life; an animal offered to God; in opposition to the *mincha*, which was an offering without life.

> It is a gift, *corban*, by whatsoever thou mightest be profited by me; that is, I have devoted that to God which you ask of me, and it is no longer mine to give. *Encyc.*

2. An alms-basket; a vessel to receive gifts of charity; a gift; an alms; a treasury of the church, where offerings are deposited. *Calmet.*

3. Among Mohammedans, a ceremony performed at the foot of mount Arrarat in Arabia, near Mecca. It consists in killing a number of sheep, and distributing them among the poor. *Encyc.*

CORBE, *a.* [Fr. *courbe.*] Crooked. [*Not in use.*] *Spenser.*

CORB'EIL, *n.* [Fr. *corbeille;* It. *corbello.* See *Corban.*]

In *fortification*, a little *basket*, to be filled with earth, and set upon a parapet, to shelter men from the fire of besiegers. *Johnson.*

CORB'EL, *n.* [See the preceding words.]

1. In *architecture*, the representation of a basket, sometimes set on the heads of caryatides.

2. The vase or tambour of the Corinthian column; so called from its resemblance to a basket. *Encyc.*

CORB'EL, *n.* A short piece of timber in a wall, jutting six or eight inches, as occasion requires, in the manner of a shoulder-piece; sometimes placed for strength under the semigirder of a platform. The under part is sometimes cut into the form of a boultin; sometimes of an ogee, or of a face, &c. *Encyc. Johnson.*

2. A niche or hollow left in walls for images, figures or statues. *Chambers.*

COR'BY, *n.* A raven. [*Not in use.*]

CORCELET, } *n. cors'let.* [Fr. *corselet*, from
CORSELET, } *corps*, L. *corpus*, body.]

In *natural history*, that part of winged insects, which answers to the breast of other animals. *Encyc.*

CORC'ULE, } *n.* [L. *corculum*, but in a dif-
CORC'LE. } ferent sense. It is a diminutive from *cor*, the heart.]

In *botany*, the heart of the seed, or rudiment of a future plant, attached to and involved in the cotyledons. It consists of the plume or ascending part, and the rostel, or radicle, the simple descending part. *Martyn.*

ꞒORD, *n.* [W. *cord;* Fr. *corde;* It. *corda;* Sp. *cuerda;* D. *koord;* L. *chorda;* Gr. χορδη. According to the Welsh, this word signifies a twist, from *côr*, the root of *chorus.*]

1. A string, or small rope, composed of several strands twisted together. Rahab let down the spies by a *cord* through the window. Josh. ii.
2. A quantity of wood, or other material, originally measured with a cord or line. The cord is a pile containing 128 cubic feet; or a pile eight feet long, four feet high, and four feet broad.
3. In *scripture*, the *cords of the wicked* are the snares with which they catch the unwary. Ps. cxxix.

The *cords of sin* are bad habits, or the consequences of sin. Prov. v.

The *cords of a man* are the fair, gentle or natural means of alluring men to obedience. Hos. xi.

The *cords of vanity* are worldly vanities and pleasures, profit or preferment; or vain and deceitful arguments and pretenses, which draw men to sin. Is. v.

To stretch a line or *cord about a city*, is to level it, or utterly to destroy it. Lam. ii.

The *cords of a tent* denote stability. To *loosen or break the cords*, is to weaken or destroy; to *lengthen the cords*, is to enlarge. Job xxx. Is. liv. Jer. x.

ꞒORD, *v. t.* To bind with a cord or rope; to fasten with cords.

2. To pile wood or other material for measurement and sale by the cord.

ꞒORD'MAKER, *n.* One whose occupation is to make ropes; but in America, called *rope-maker.*

ꞒORD'WOOD, *n.* Wood cut and piled for sale by the cord, in distinction from long wood; properly, wood cut to the length of four feet; but in this respect, the practice is not uniform. In Scotland, *cord-wood* is wood conveyed to market on board of vessels, in opposition to that which is floated. *Encyc.*

ꞒORD'AGE, *n.* [Sp. *cordage;* Fr. *id.;* from *cord.*]

All sorts of cords or ropes, used in the running rigging of a ship, or kept in reserve to supply the place of that which may be rendered unserviceable. In a more general sense, the word includes all ropes and lines used on board of ships.

ꞒORD'ATE, ꞒORD'ATED, *a.* [L. *cordatus*, with a different signification, from *cor*, the heart.]

Having the form of a heart; heart-shaped; a term used by naturalists; as a *cordate* leaf in botany, resembling the longitudinal section of the heart. Hence, *cordate-oblong*, heart-shaped lengthened; *cordate-lanceolate*, heart-shaped, gradually tapering towards each extremity, like the head of a lance; *cordate-sagittate*, heart-shaped, but resembling the head of an arrow. *Martyn.*

ꞒORD'ATELY, *adv.* In a cordate form.

ꞒORD'ED, *pp.* Bound or fastened with cords.

2. Piled in a form for measurement by the cord.
3. Made of cords; furnished with cords. *Shak.*
4. In heraldry, a *cross corded* is one wound with cords, or made of two pieces of wood. *Encyc.*

ꞒORDELIE'R, *n.* [Fr. from *corde*, a girdle or cord worn by the order.]

A Franciscan friar; one of the order of religious founded by St. Francis; a gray friar. The cordeliers wear a thick gray cloth, a little cowl, a chaperon, and a cloke, with a girdle of rope or cord, tied with three knots. *Encyc.*

ꞒORD'IAL, *a.* [Fr. and Sp. *cordial;* It. *cordiale;* from L. *cor*, the heart.]

1. Proceeding from the heart; hearty; sincere; not hypocritical; warm; affectionate.

With looks of *cordial* love. *Milton.*

We give our friends a *cordial* reception.

2. Reviving the spirits; cheering; invigorating; giving strength or spirits; as *cordial* waters. *Wiseman.*

ꞒORD'IAL, *n.* In *medicine*, that which suddenly excites the system, and increases the action of the heart or circulation when languid; any medicine which increases strength, raises the spirits, and gives life and cheerfulness to a person when weak and depressed.

2. Any thing that comforts, gladdens and exhilarates; as, good news is a *cordial* to the mind.

ꞒORDIAL'ITY, *n.* Relation to the heart. [*Not used.*] *Brown.*

2. Sincerity; freedom from hypocrisy; sincere affection and kindness.

Our friends were received with *cordiality.*

ꞒORD'IALLY, *adv.* Heartily; sincerely; without hypocrisy; with real affection.

The christian *cordially* receives the doctrines of grace.

ꞒORD'IERITE, *n.* The mineral called otherwise iolite and dichroite.

ꞒORD'IFORM, *a.* [L. *cor*, the heart, and *forma*, form.]

Heart-shaped; having the form of the human heart.

ꞒORD'INER, *n.* [*Not used.* See *Cordwainer.*]

ꞒORD'ON, *n.* [Fr. Sp. *cordon;* It. *cordone;* Port. *cordam.* See *Cord.*]

1. In *fortification*, a row of stones jutting before the rampart, and the basis of the parapet; or a row of stones between the wall of a fortress which lies aslope, and the parapet which is perpendicular; serving as an ornament, and used only in fortifications of stone-work. *Johnson. Encyc.*
2. In *military language*, a line or series of military posts; as a *cordon* of troops.

ꞒORD'OVAN, *n.* Spanish leather.

ꞒORDUROY', *n.* A thick cotton stuff ribbed.

ꞒORD'WAIN, *n.* [Sp. *cordoban;* Port. *cordovam;* Fr. *cordouan;* from *Cordova*, or *Cordoba*, in Spain.]

Spanish leather; goat-skin tanned and dressed. *Spenser. Sp. Dict.*

ꞒORD'WAINER, *n.* [from *cordwain.*] A shoemaker. This word was formerly written *cordiners.* It is evidently from the French *cordouan, cordouannier;* properly, a worker in cordwain, or cordovan leather.

ꞒORE, *n.* [Fr. *cœur;* Norm. *core;* Sp. *corazon;* Port. *coraçam;* It. *cuore;* from L. *cor*, the heart, Gr. κεαρ. See Class Gr.]

1. The heart or inner part of a thing; particularly, the central part of fruit, containing the kernels or seeds; as the *core* of an apple or quince. It was formerly applied to place; as, in the *core* of a square. *Raleigh.*
2. The inner part of an ulcer or boil. *Dryden.*
3. A body. Fr. *corps.* [*Not used.*] *Bacon.*
4. A disorder of sheep, occasioned by worms in the liver. *Chambers.*

ꞒO'RED, *a.* In the herring fishery, rolled in salt and prepared for drying. *Ash.*

ꞒO-RE'GENT, *n.* A joint regent or ruler. *Wraxall.*

ꞒORIA'CEOUS, *a.* [L. *coriaceus*, from *corium*, leather.]

1. Consisting of leather, or resembling leather; tough; as *coriaceous* concretions. *Arbuthnot.*
2. In *botany*, stiff, like leather or parchment; *applied to a leaf, a calyx or capsule.* *Martyn.*

ꞒORIAN'DER, *n.* [L. *coriandrum;* Gr. κοριον, κοριαννον.]

A genus of plants of two species. The seeds of one species, the *sativum*, have a strong smell, and in medicine are considered as stomachic and carminative.

ꞒORIN'DON, *n.* [See *Corundum.*]

ꞒOR'INTH, *n.* A city of Greece. Hence,

2. A small fruit, now called *currant*, which see. *Philips. Broome.*

ꞒORINTH'IAꞒ, *a.* Pertaining to Corinth. *D'Anville.*

ꞒORINTH'IAN, *a.* Pertaining to Corinth, a celebrated city of Greece; as *Corinthian* column; *Corinthian* order; *Corinthian* brass. The *Corinthian* order, in architecture, is the most delicate of all the orders, and enriched with a profusion of ornaments. The capital is usually adorned with olive leaves or acanthus. *Encyc.*

ꞒO-RI'VAL, *n.* [*con* and *rival;* written improperly *corrival.*]

A rival, or fellow rival; a competitor. *Shak.*

ꞒORI'VAL, *v. t.* To rival; to pretend to equal. *Shak.*

ꞒORK, *n.* [D. *kurk;* G. *kork;* Sw. *korck;* Dan. *kork;* Sp. *corcho;* Russ. *korka;* Fr. *ecorce;* L. *cortex*, bark, rind, shell, crust.]

1. A glandiferous tree, a species of Quercus, growing in Spain and Portugal, having a thick, rough, fungous, cleft bark.
2. The outer bark of the tree, or epidermis, of which stopples for bottles and casks are made. This outer bark is taken off, and a new epidermis is formed, which, in six or seven years, becomes fit for use. This bark is also burnt to make a kind of light black, called *Spanish black.*
3. A stopple for a bottle or cask, cut out of cork.

ꞒORK, *v. t.* To stop bottles or casks with corks; to confine or make fast with a cork.

ꞒORK'ING-PIN, *n.* A pin of a large size. *Swift.*

ꞒORK'-SꞒREW, *n.* A screw to draw corks from bottles.

ꞒORK'Y, *a.* Consisting of cork; resembling cork; made of cork; tough.

ꞒOR'MORANT, *n.* [Fr. *cormoran;* Sp. *corvejon.* *Cormorant* is supposed to be corrupted from *corvus marinus*, sea raven. The Welsh also call the fowl *morvran*, sea crow.]

1. The water raven, a large fowl of the pelican kind: the head and neck are black; the coverts of the wings, the scapulars and the back are of a deep green, edged with black and glossed with blue. The base of the lower mandible is covered with a naked yellow skin, which extends under the chin and forms a sort of pouch. This fowl occupies the cliffs by the sea, feeds on fish, and is extremely voracious. *Encyc.*

2. A glutton.

CORN, *n.* [Sax. *corn;* D. *koorn;* G. *korn;* Dan. Sw. *korn.* Not improbably this word is the L. *granum.* Such transpositions are not uncommon. The word signifies not only the hard seeds of certain plants, but hail and shot, L. *grando,* Ir. *gran,* grain, hail, shot. Johnson quotes an old Runic rhyme.

Hagul er kaldastur *korna.*
Hail is the coldest *corn.* See *Grain.*]

1. A single seed of certain plants, as wheat, rye, barley and maiz; a grain. In this sense, it has a plural; as, three barley *corns* make an inch. It is generally applied to edible seeds, which, when ripe, are hard.
2. The seeds of certain plants in general, in bulk or quantity; as, *corn* is dear or scarce. In this sense, the word comprehends all the kinds of grain which constitute the food of men and horses. In *Great Britain*, *corn* is generally applied to wheat, rye, oats and barley. In *the United States,* it has the same general sense, but by custom, it is appropriated to maiz. We are accustomed to say, the crop of wheat is good, but the *corn* is bad; it is a good year for wheat and rye, but bad for *corn.* In this sense, *corn* has no plural.
3. The plants which produce corn, when growing in the field; the stalks and ears, or the stalks, ears and seeds, after reaping and before thrashing. We say, a field of *corn,* a sheaf or a shock of *corn,* a load of *corn.* The plants or stalks are included in the term corn, until the seed is separated from the ears.
4. In *surgery,* a hard excrescence, or induration of the skin, on the toes or some part of the feet, occasioned by the pressure of the shoes; so called from its hardness and resemblance to a corn.
5. A small hard particle. [See *Grain.*]

CORN, *v. t.* To preserve and season with salt in grains; to sprinkle with salt; as, to *corn* beef.

2. To granulate; to form into small grains.

CORN'BIND, *n.* Climbing buck-wheat. [*Local.*] *Grose.*

CORN'BLADE, *n.* The leaf of the maiz. Cornblades are collected and preserved as fodder, in some of the southern states of America.

CORN'-CHANDLER, *n.* [*Chandler,* a dealer in candles, is supposed to be from the French *chandelier;* but what has this word to do with *corn* and *ship,* in *corn-chandler* and *ship-chandler?* In these words, *chandler* seems to be a corruption of the Teutonic *handler,* a trader; Sw. *kornhandlare,* a corn-dealer; Dan. *handler;* G. *id.;* D. *handelaar.*] A dealer in corn.

CORN'CLAD, *a.* Covered with growing corn. *Barlow.*

CORN'CRAKE, *n.* The crake or land rail; the corn-crow, for *kråka,* in Sw., and *krage,* in Dan., is our word *crow,* and the name is probably taken from its cry. The Dutch *kraai,* a crow, is contracted from *kraag,* and *kraaijen* is to crow, to vaunt, to tell tales; G. *krähe, krähen.*

CORN'-CUTTER, *n.* [*corn* and *cut.*] One who cuts corns, or indurations of the skin.

CORN'FIELD, *n.* A field where corn is growing.

CORN'FLAG, *n.* A genus of plants, the Gladiolus, of several species, bearing red or white flowers.

CORN'FLOOR, *n.* A floor for corn, or for thrashing corn. Is. xxi. Hos. ix.

CORN'FLOWER, *n.* A flower or plant growing among corn; as the blue-bottle, wild poppy, &c. *Bacon.*

CORN'HEAP, *n.* A heap of corn. *Hall.*

CORN'LAND, *n.* Land appropriated or suitable to the production of corn, or grain.

CORN'LOFT, *n.* An apartment for corn; a granary. *Sherwood.*

CORN-MARYGOLD, *n.* A genus of plants, the Chrysanthemum.

CORN'MASTER, *n.* One who cultivates corn for sale. [*Not used.*] *Bacon.*

CORN'METER, *n.* One who measures corn.

CORN'MILL, *n.* A mill for grinding corn, more generally called a *grist-mill.*

CORN'-PARSLEY, *n.* A genus of plants, the Sison.

CORN'PIPE, *n.* A pipe made by slitting the joint of a green stalk of corn. *Johnson.*

CORN'-ROCKET, *n.* A genus of plants, the Bunias.

CORN'ROSE, *n.* A species of poppy, or Papaver.

CORN'-SALLAD, *n.* A plant, a species of Valeriana, whose top leaves are said to be a good sallad.

CORN'STALK, *n.* A stalk of corn, particularly a stalk of the maiz. *America.*

CORN'-VIOLET, *n.* A species of Campanula. *Tate.*

CORN'AGE, *n.* [from Fr. *corne,* L. *cornu,* a horn.]

An ancient tenure of lands, which obliged the tenant to give notice of an invasion by blowing a horn. *Blackstone.*

CORN'EA, *n.* [from L. *cornu,* a horn.] The transparent membrane in the fore-part of the eye, through which the rays of light pass; situated in the *sclerotica,* and considered by some as a portion of it.

CORN'EL, **CORN'EL-TREE**, **CORNE'LIAN-TREE**, *n.* [L. *cornus,* from *cornu,* a horn, or its root, from the hardness of the wood; Sp. *corno;* It. *corniolo;* Fr. *cornouiller.*]

The cornelian cherry or dog-wood, a genus of plants of several species. The *mascula,* or cornelian cherry tree, has a stem of twenty feet high, branching and forming a large head, garnished with oblong leaves and small umbels of yellowish-green flowers, succeeded by small, red, acid, eatable, cherry-like fruit. *Encyc.*

CORNE'LIAN. [See *Carnelian.*]

CORN'EMUSE, **CORN'AMUTE**, *n.* [Fr. *cornemuse; corne,* a horn, and *muse;* It. *cornamusa.*]

A kind of rustic flute. *Drayton.*

CORN'EOUS, *a.* [L. *corneus,* from *cornu,* a horn. See *Horn.*]

Horny; like horn; consisting of a horny substance, or substance resembling horn; hard. *Brown.*

CORN'ER, *n.* [W. *cornel,* from *corn,* a point or projection, a horn; Corn. *kornal;* Arm. *corn;* Ir. *cearna;* Sw. *hörn.* See *Horn* and *Grain.* Qu. Heb. Ch. Syr. Ar. קרן karan, to shoot.

1. The point where two converging lines meet; properly, the external point; an angle; as, we meet at the *corner* of the state-house, or at the *corner* of two streets.
2. The interior point where two lines meet; an angle.
3. The space between two converging lines or walls which meet in a point. Hence,
4. An inclosed place; a secret or retired place.

   This thing was not done in a *corner.* Acts xxvi.

5. Indefinitely any part; a part. They searched every *corner* of the forest. They explored all *corners* of the country.
6. The end, extremity or limit; as the *corners* of the head or beard. Lev. xxi. xix.

Corner-teeth of a horse, the foreteeth between the middling teeth and the tushes, two above and two below, on each side of the jaw, which shoot when the horse is four years and a half old. *Farrier's Dict.*

CORN'ERED, *a.* Having corners; having three or more angles.

CORN'ER-STONE, *n.* The stone which lies at the corner of two walls, and unites them; the principal stone, and especially the stone which forms the corner of the foundation of an edifice.

Who laid the *corner-stone* thereof? Job xxxviii.

Christ himself being the chief *corner-stone.* Eph. ii.

CORN'ER-WISE, *adv.* Diagonally; with the corner in front; not parallel.

CORN'ET, *n.* [Fr. *cornet, cornette;* It. *cornetta, cornetto;* Sp. *corneta;* from L. *cornu,* a horn. See *Horn.*]

1. An instrument of music, in the nature of a trumpet, sounded by blowing with the mouth. It was of a winding shape like a horn; used in armies and on occasions of joy.

   David played before the Lord on *cornets.* 2 Sam. vi.

2. In *modern usage,* an officer of cavalry, who bears the ensign or colors of a troop. He is the third officer in the company. *Encyc.*
3. A company of cavalry; a troop of horse. [*Not used.*] *Clarendon. Bacon.*
4. *The cornet of a horse* [coronet] is the lowest part of his pastern, that runs round the coffin and is distinguished by the hair that joins and covers the upper part of the hoof. *Farrier's Dict.*
5. A little cap of paper in which retailers inclose small wares.
6. A scarf anciently worn by doctors. *Dict.*
7. A head dress. *Dict.*

CORN'ETCY, *n.* The commission or rank of a cornet. *Chesterfield. Stephens.*

CORN'ETTER, **CORN'ETER**, *n.* One who blows a cornet. *Hakewill.*

COR'NICE, *n.* [It. *cornice;* Fr. *corniche;* Sp. *cornisa;* from L. *coronis,* Gr. *χορωνις, χορωνη,* a summit, a *crown.*]

1. In *architecture*, the uppermost member of the entablature of a column, or the highest projecture; that which crowns an order. *Johnson. Encyc.*

2. A little projecture in joinery or masonry; as the *cornice* of a chimney. *Encyc.*

Cornice-ring of a cannon, is the ring next from the muzzle-ring backward. *Encyc.*

CORN'ICLE, *n.* [L. *corniculum*, from *cornu*, a horn.] A little horn. *Brown.*

CORNIC'ULATE, *a.* [from L. *cornu*, a horn.]

1. Horned; having horns. *More.*

2. In *botany*, producing horned pods; bearing a little spur or horn. *Chambers.*

CORNIG'EROUS, *a.* [L. *corniger*; *cornu*, a horn, and *gero*, to bear.]

Horned; having horns; as *cornigerous* animals. *Brown.*

CORN'ING-HOUSE, *n.* A house or place where powder is granulated.

CORN'ISH, *a.* Pertaining to Cornwall, in England; and as a noun, the language of Cornwall.

CORN'IST, *n.* A performer on the cornet or horn.

CORN'LESS, *a.* Destitute of corn; as *cornless* dwelling places. *Tooke's Russia.*

CORNUCO'PIA, *n.* [L. *cornu*, a horn, and *copia*, plenty.]

1. The horn of plenty, an emblem of abundance of fruits.

2. In *architecture* and *sculpture*, the figure of a horn, from which fruits and flowers are represented as proceeding.

CORNU'TE, *v. t.* [L. *cornutus*, from *cornu*, a horn.] To bestow horns; to cuckold. *Burton.*

CORNU'TED, *pp.* or *a.* Grafted with horns; horned; cuckolded.

2. In *botany*, horn-shaped.

CORNU'TO, *n.* [It.] A man that wears the horns; a cuckold.

CORNU'TOR, *n.* A cuckold-maker. *Jordan.*

CORN'Y, *a.* [L. *cornu*, a horn.] Horny; strong, stiff or hard like horn; resembling horn. *Milton.*

CORN'Y, *a.* [from *corn.*] Producing corn; containing corn. *Prior. Dryden.*

COR'ODY, COR'RODY, *n.* [It. *corredo*, provision; *corredare*, to furnish.] An allowance of meat, drink or clothing, due to the king from an abbey or other religious house, for the sustenance of such one of his servants, as he thinks good to bestow on it. An allowance for the maintenance of any of the king's servants living in an abbey. *Cowel.*

Corodies are a right of sustenance, or to receive certain allotments of victuals and provision for one's maintenance. In lieu of which, a pension or sum of money is sometimes substituted. *Blackstone.*

The king is entitled to a *corody* out of every bishopric, that is, to send one of his chaplains to be maintained by the bishop, or to have a pension allowed, till the bishop promotes him to a benefice. [*This has fallen into disuse.*] *Blackstone.*

According to the Italian, the latter word is the correct orthography.

COR'OL, COROL'LA, *n.* [L. *corolla*, a little crown.] In *botany*, the inner covering of a flower. The corol surrounds the parts of fructification, and is composed of one or more flower leaves, called petals. It is distinguished from the perianth, by the fineness of its texture and the gayness of its colors; but there are many exceptions. It is sometimes inaccurately called *blossom* and *flower*. *Martyn. Encyc. Darwin.*

COROLLA'CEOUS, *a.* Pertaining to a corol; inclosing and protecting like a wreath.

A *corrollaceous* covering. *Lee.*

COR'OLLARY, *n.* [L. *corollarium*, a coronet, from *corolla*, a crown. *Finis coronat opus. Johnson.* Fr. *corollaire.*]

1. A conclusion or consequence drawn from premises, or from what is advanced or demonstrated. If it is demonstrated that a triangle which has equal sides, has also equal angles, it follows as a *corollary* that a triangle which has three equal sides, has its three angles equal. *Encyc.*

A *corollary* is an inference from a preceding proposition. *J. Day.*

2. A surplus. *Shak.*

COR'OLLET, COR'OLLULE, *n.* One of the partial flowers which make a compound one; the floret in an aggregate flower. *Martyn. Encyc.*

CORO'NA, *n.* [L. a crown.] In *architecture*, a large flat member of a cornice, crowning the entablature, and the whole order; called by workmen the *drip*. *Chambers.*

2. In *anatomy*, the upper surface of the molar teeth or grinders.

3. In *botany*, the circumference or margin of a radiated compound flower. *Encyc.*

Also, the appendage to the top of seeds, which enables them to disperse. *Martyn.*

4. In *optics*, a halo or luminous circle around the sun, moon or stars. *Encyc.*

COR'ONAL, *a.* Belonging to the crown or top of the head; as the *coronal* suture.

COR'ONAL, *n.* A crown; wreath; garland. *Spenser.*

2. The first suture of the skull. *Encyc.*

COR'ONARY, *a.* Relating to a crown; seated on the top of the head; or placed as a crown. *Brown.*

Coronary vessels, in anatomy, certain vessels which furnish the substance of the heart with blood. *Encyc.*

Coronary arteries, two arteries which spring from the aorta, before it leaves the pericardium, and supply the substance of the heart with blood. *Coxe. Encyc.*

Coronary vein, a vein diffused over the exterior surface of the heart, receiving the blood from the heart. *Coxe. Encyc.*

Stomachic coronary, a vein inserted into the trunk of the splenic vein, which, by uniting with the mesenteric, forms the vena porta. *Encyc.*

CORONA'TION, *n.* [from *corona*, a crown.] The act or solemnity of crowning a king or emperor; the act of investing a prince with the insignia of royalty, on his succeeding to the sovereignty.

2. The pomp or assembly attending a coronation. *Pope.*

Coronation-oath, the oath taken by a king at his coronation.

COR'ONEL, *n. kur'nel.* [Sp. *coronel*; Port. *id.*; Fr. *colonel*; It. *colonnello.* We follow the Sp. and Port. orthography in our pronunciation.]

The officer who commands a regiment. *Obs.* *Spenser.*

COR'ONER, *n.* [Law Lat. *coronator*, from *corona*, a crown.]

An officer whose office is concerned principally with pleas of the crown. One chief part of his duty is, when a person is slain or dies suddenly or in prison, to inquire into the manner of his death. This must be done by a jury, on sight of the body, and at the place where the death happened. In *England*, the coroner is to inquire also concerning shipwrecks, and certify whether wrecks or not, and who is in possession of the goods; also concerning treasure-trove. As a ministerial officer, the coroner is the sheriff's substitute; and when an exception can be taken to the sheriff, for suspicion of partiality, process is awarded to the coroner. *Blackstone.*

In some of the States, in America, there is a coroner, but his principal or only duty is to inquire into the causes of untimely death. In Connecticut there is no such officer, the duty being performed by a constable or justice of the peace.

COR'ONET, *n.* [from *corona*, a crown.] An inferior crown worn by noblemen. The coronet of a duke is adorned with strawberry leaves; that of a marquis has leaves with pearls interposed; that of an earl raises the pearls above the leaves; that of a viscount is surrounded with pearls only; that of a baron has only four pearls. *Johnson.*

2. In *poetical language*, an ornamental head dress.

Coronet of a horse. [See *Cornet.*]

COR'ONIFORM, *a.* [L. *corona*, a crown, and *forma*, form.] Having the form of a crown.

COR'ONOID, *a.* [Gr. κορωνη, a crow, and ειδος, form.]

Noting the upper and anterior process of the end of the lower jaw, called the *coronoid* process. *Coxe.*

COR'ONULE, *n.* [from *corona*, a crown.] A coronet or little crown of a seed; the downy tuft on seeds. *Martyn.*

COR'PORAL, *n.* [It. *caporale*; Fr. *caporal*; Sp. *caporal*; from L. *caput*, head, or more directly from the Celtic root of *caput*, Sp. *cabo*, It. *capo*, Eng. *cape*. Our orthography is a corruption.]

1. The lowest officer of a company of infantry, next below a sergeant. He has charge over one of the divisions, places and relieves sentinels, &c.

2. The *corporal of a ship of war*, is an officer under the master at arms, employed to teach the sailors the use of small arms; to attend at the gangways or entering ports, and see that no spirituous liquors are brought, except by permission; to extinguish fire and candles, &c.

COR'PORAL, *a.* [L. *corporalis*, from *corpus*, body.]

1. Belonging or relating to the body; as *corporal* pain, opposed to *mental*.

2. Material; not spiritual. [See *Corporeal.*] *Shak.*

COR'PORAL, COR'PORALE, *n.* A fine linen cloth, used to cover the sacred elements in the eucharist or in which the sacrament is put. *Paley. Todd.*

Corporal oath, a solemn oath, so called from

the ancient usage of touching the *corporale*, or cloth that covered the consecrated elements. *Paley.*

CORPORAL'ITY, *n.* The state of being a body or embodied; opposed to spirituality.

If this light hath any *corporality*, it is most subtile and pure. *Raleigh.*

COR'PORALLY, *adv.* Bodily; in or with the body; as, to be *corporally* present.

COR'PORALSHIP, *n.* [from *corporal.*] A corporal's command in a Russian company, or a division of twenty-three men.

Each squadron consists of two companies, and each of these, of three *corporalships* or sixty nine men who come in the front. *Tooke.*

COR'PORAS, *n.* The old name of the corporal or communion cloth.

COR'PORATE, *a.* [L. *corporatus*, from *corporor*, to be shaped into a body, from *corpus*, body.]

1. United in a body, or community, as a number of individuals, who are empowered to transact business as an individual; formed into a body; as a *corporate* assembly, or society; a *corporate* town. *Swift.*

2. United; general; collectively one.

They answer in a *corporate* voice. *Shak.*

COR'PORATENESS, *n.* The state of a corporate body. *Dict.*

CORPORA'TION, *n.* A body politic or corporate, formed and authorized by law to act as a single person; a society having the capacity of transacting business as an individual. Corporations are *aggregate* or *sole*. *Corporations aggregate* consist of two or more persons united in a society, which is preserved by a succession of members, either forever, or till the corporation is dissolved by the power that formed it, by the death of all its members, by surrender of its charter or franchises, or by forfeiture. Such corporations are the mayor and aldermen of cities, the head and fellows of a college, the dean and chapter of a cathedral church, the stockholders of a bank or insurance company, &c. A *corporation sole* consists of one person only and his successors, as a king or a bishop. *Blackstone.*

CORPORA'TOR, *n.* The member of a corporation. *Sergeant.*

COR'PORATURE, *n.* The state of being embodied. [*Not in use.*] *More.*

CORPO'REAL, } *a.* Having a body; consisting of a material
CORPO'REOUS, } body; material; opposed to *spiritual* or *immaterial;* as our *corporeal* frame; *corporeal* substance

CORPO'REALIST, *n.* One who denies the existence of spiritual substances.

CORPO'REALLY, *adv.* In body; in a bodily form or manner. *Richardson.*

CORPORE'ITY, *n.* The state of having a body, or of being embodied; materiality.

The one attributed *corporeity* to God. *Stillingfleet.*

CORPO'RIFY, *v. t.* To embody; to form into a body. [*Not used.*] *Boyle.*

COR'POSANT, *n.* [Sp. *cuerpo santo*, holy body.]

A name given by seamen to a luminous appearance often beheld, in dark tempestuous nights, about the decks and rigging of a ship, but particularly at the mastheads and yard-arms, supposed to be electrical. *Mar. Dict.*

CORPS, *n.* [Fr. from L. *corpus*, body. It is pronounced *kore*, and is an ill word in English.]

1. In *military language*, a body of troops; any division of an army; as a *corps de reserve*.

2. A body, in contempt, as used by Milton and Dryden, but probably pronounced in the English manner, as *corpse*.

3. A carcase; a dead body. [See *Corpse.*] *Shak.*

4. In *architecture*, any part that projects beyond a wall, serving as the ground of some decoration. *Encyc.*

CORPSE, *n. corps.* [L. *corpus*, a body; Ir. *corp;* W. *corv;* Arm. *corf;* It. *corpo;* Sp. *cuerpo.*] The dead body of a human being. *Addison.*

COR'PULENCE, } *n.* [L. *corpulentia*, from
COR'PULENCY, } *corpus*, body.]

1. Fleshiness; excessive fatness; a state of being loaded with flesh; as the body of a human being. *Arbuthnot.*

2. Spissitude; grossness of matter; as *corpulence* of water. [*Little used.*] *Ray.*

COR'PULENT, *a.* Fleshy; having a great or excessive quantity of fat or flesh, in proportion to the frame of the body; as a *corpulent* child.

Corpus Christi. [Body of Christ.] A festival of the church of England, kept on the next Thursday after Trinity-Sunday, in honor of the Eucharist. *Encyc.*

COR'PUSCLE, *n.* [L. *corpusculum*, dim. of *corpus*, body.]

A minute particle, or physical atom; corpuscles are the very small bodies which compose large bodies, not the elementary principles of matter, but such small particles simple or compound, as are not dissolved or dissipated by ordinary heat.

It will add much to our satisfaction, if those *corpuscles* can be discovered by microscopes. *Newton.*

CORPUS'CULAR, *a.* Relating to corpuscles, or small particles, supposed to be the constituent materials of all large bodies. The *corpuscular* philosophy attempts to account for the phenomena of nature, by the motion, figure, rest, position, &c., of the minute particles of matter. *Encyc.*

CORPUSCULA'RIAN, *a.* Corpuscular, as above.

CORPUSCULA'RIAN, *n.* An advocate for the *corpuscular* philosophy.

CORRADIA'TION, *n.* [L. *con* and *radiatio*. See *Ray.*] A conjunction of rays in one point. *Bacon.*

CORRECT', *a.* [L. *correctus*, from *corrigo;* *con* and *rego*, to set right; *rectus*, right, straight. See *Right.*]

Literally, set right, or made straight. Hence, right; conformable to truth, rectitude or propriety, or conformable to a just standard; not faulty; free from error. A *correct* edition of a book is exactly according to the original copy. *Correct* manners correspond with the rules of morality and received notions of decorum. *Correct* principles coincide with the truth. *Correct* language is agreeable to established usage.

CORRECT', *v. t.* [L. *correctus, corrigo;* *con* and *rego*. See *Right.*]

1. To make right; to rectify; to bring to the standard of truth, justice, or propriety; as, to *correct* manners or principles. Hence,

2. To amend; to remove or retrench faults or errors; to set right; as, to *correct* a book; to *correct* a copy for the press; or in printing, to *correct* the press, or errors of the press.

3. To bring back or attempt to bring back to propriety in morals; to punish for faults or deviations from moral rectitude; to chastise; to discipline; as, a child should be *corrected* for lying.

Correct thy son, and he shall give thee rest. Prov. xxix.

4. To obviate or remove whatever is wrong or inconvenient; to reduce or change the qualities of any thing by mixture, or other application; to counteract whatever is injurious; as, to *correct* the acidity of the stomach by alkaline preparations; to *correct* the relaxing quality of water by boiling it with animal substances. *Arbuthnot.*

CORRECT'ED, *pp.* Set right; freed from errors; amended; punished.

CORRECT'ING, *ppr.* Bringing to the standard of truth, justice or propriety; amending; chastising.

CORREC'TION, *n.* [L. *correctio.*] The act of correcting; the act of bringing back, from error or deviation, to a just standard, as to truth, rectitude, justice or propriety; as the *correction* of opinions or manners.

All scripture is profitable for *correction.* 2 Tim. iii.

2. Retrenchment of faults or errors; amendment; as the *correction* of a book, or of the press.

3. That which is substituted in the place of what is wrong; as the *corrections* of a copy are numerous; set the *corrections* in the margin of a proof-sheet.

4. That which is intended to rectify, or to cure faults; punishment; discipline; chastisement; that which corrects.

Withhold not *correction* from the child. Prov. xxiii.

5. In *scriptural language*, whatever tends to correct the moral conduct, and bring back from error or sin, as afflictions.

They have refused to receive *correction*. Jer. v.

My son, despise not the chastening of the Lord, nor be weary of his *correction*. Prov. iii.

6. Critical notice; animadversion. *Brown.*

7. Abatement of noxious qualities; the counteraction of what is inconvenient or hurtful in its effects; as the *correction* of acidity in the stomach.

House of correction, a house where disorderly persons are confined; a bridewell.

CORREC'TIONAL, *a.* Tending to or intended for correction. *Walsh.*

CORREC'TIONER, *n.* One that has been in the house of correction. [*Not used.*] *Shak.*

CORRECT'IVE, *a.* Having the power to correct; having the quality of removing or obviating what is wrong, or injurious; tending to rectify; as *corrective* penalties.

Mulberries are pectoral, *corrective* of bilious alkali. *Arbuthnot.*

CORRECT'IVE, *n.* That which has the power of correcting; that which has the quality of altering or obviating what is wrong, or injurious; as, alkalies are *correctives* of acids; penalties are *correctives* of immoral conduct.

2. Limitation; restriction. [*Little used.*] *Hale.*

CORRECT'LY, *adv.* In a correct manner; in conformity with truth, justice, rectitude, or propriety; according to a standard; agreeable to a copy or original; exactly; accurately; without fault, or error; as, to behave *correctly;* to write, speak or think *correctly;* to judge *correctly.*

CORRECT'NESS, *n.* Conformity to truth, justice, or propriety; as the *correctness* of opinions, of judgment, or of manners.
2. Conformity to settled usages or rules; as *correctness* in writing or speaking.
3. Conformity to a copy or original; as the *correctness* of a book.
4. Conformity to established rules of taste or proportion; as the *correctness* of design in painting, sculpture or architecture.

CORRECT'OR, *n.* One who corrects; one who amends faults, retrenches error, and renders conformable to truth or propriety, or to any standard; as a *corrector* of the press; a *corrector* of abuses.
2. One who punishes for correction; one who amends or reforms by chastisement, reproof or instruction.
3. That which corrects; that which abates or removes what is noxious or inconvenient; an ingredient in a composition which abates or counteracts the force of another; as, an alkali is a *corrector* of acids.

Turpentine is a *corrector* of quicksilver. *Quincy.*

CORREG'IDOR, *n.* [Sp.] A Spanish magistrate. *Smollett.*

COR'RELATE, *n.* [L. *con* and *relatus.* See *Relate.*]
One who stands in an opposite relation, as father and son. *South.*

CORRELA'TION, *n.* Reciprocal relation. *Paley.*

CORREL'ATIVE, *a.* [L. *con* and *relativus.* See *Relate* and *Relative.*]
Having a reciprocal relation, so that the existence of one in a certain state depends on the existence of another; as father and son, husband and wife, are *correlative* terms. The term *son* is *correlative* to that of *father.*

CORREL'ATIVE, *n.* That which is opposed to something else in a certain relation. The son is the *correlative* of his father. Darkness and light are *correlatives.* Rest is the *correlative* of motion.

CORREL'ATIVELY, *adv.* In a correlative relation.

CORREL'ATIVENESS, *n.* The state of being correlative.

CORREP'TION, *n.* [L. *corripio.*] Chiding; reproof; reprimand. *Hammond.*

CORRESPOND', *v. i.* [It. *corrispondere;* Fr. *correspondre;* Sp. *corresponder;* from L. *con* and *respondeo,* to answer; *re* and *spondeo,* to promise. See *Sponsor.*]
1. To suit; to answer; to agree; to fit; to be congruous; to be adapted to. Levity of manners does not *correspond with* the dignity of the clerical character. The length of a room should *correspond with* the breadth. Actions should *correspond with* words.
2. To be equal; to be adequate or proportioned. Let the means of prosecuting a war *correspond with* the magnitude of the contest.
3. To communicate by letters sent and received; to hold intercourse with a person at a distance by sending and receiving letters. We delight to *correspond with* those we love and respect.

CORRESPOND'ENCE, CORRESPOND'ENCY, } *n.* Relation; fitness; congruity; mutual adaptation of one thing to another. There is no *correspondence* between a polite education and clownish manners.
2. Intercourse between persons at a distance, by means of letters sent and answers received. The ministers of the two courts have had a *correspondence* on the subject of commerce. Hence,
3. The letters which pass between correspondents. The *correspondence* of the ministers is published.
4. Friendly intercourse; reciprocal exchange of offices or civilities; connection.

Let military persons hold good *correspondence* with the other great men in the state. *Bacon.*

CORRESPOND'ENT, *a.* Suitable; fit; congruous; agreeable; answerable; adapted. Let behavior be *correspondent* to profession, and both be *correspondent* to good morals.

CORRESPOND'ENT, *n.* One who corresponds; one with whom an intercourse is carried on by letters or messages. When A is the *correspondent* of B, B is the *correspondent* of A.

CORRESPOND'ENTLY, *adv.* In a corresponding manner.

CORRESPOND'ING, *ppr.* Carrying on intercourse by letters.
2. *a.* Answering; agreeing; suiting.

CORRESPON'SIVE, *a.* Answerable; adapted. *Shak.*

COR'RIDOR, *n.* [Fr.; Sp. *corredor,* from *correr,* It. *correre,* L. *curro,* to run, to flow. The termination *dor* may perhaps be the L. *tor,* as in *curator, cursitor. Corridor* signifies a runner; hence, a running, flowing, or long line.]
1. In *architecture,* a gallery or long aisle round a building, leading to several chambers at a distance from each other. *Harris.*
2. In *fortification,* the covered way lying round the whole compass of the fortifications of a place. *Harris.*

COR'RIGIBLE, *a.* [Fr. from L. *corrigo,* to correct.]
1. That may be set right, or amended; as a *corrigible* defect.
2. That may be reformed; as, the young man may be *corrigible.*
3. Punishable; that may be chastised for correction. He was adjudged *corrigible* for abusive words.

CORRI'VAL, *n.* A fellow rival; a competitor. More correctly *co-rival,* which see.

COR'RIVATE, *v. t.* [L. *con* and *rivus.*] To draw water out of several streams into one. [*Little used.*] *Burton.*

CORRIVA'TION, *n.* The running of different streams into one. [*Not much used.*] *Burton.*

CORROB'ORANT, *a.* [See *Corroborate.*] Strengthening; having the power or quality of giving strength; as a *corroborant* medicine.

CORROB'ORANT, *n.* A medicine that strengthens the human body when weak.

CORROB'ORATE, *v. t.* [L. *corroboro; con* and *roboro,* to strengthen, from *robur,* strength. Class Rb.]
1. To strengthen; to make strong, or to give additional strength to; as, to *corroborate* the nerves; to *corroborate* the judgment, authority or habits. *Watts. Wotton.*
2. To confirm; to make more certain. The news was doubtful, but is *corroborated* by recent advices.

CORROB'ORATED, *pp.* Strengthened; confirmed; rendered more certain.

CORROB'ORATING, *ppr.* Strengthening; giving firmness or additional assurance.

CORROBORA'TION, *n.* The act of strengthening, or confirming; addition of strength, assurance, or security; confirmation; as the *corroboration* of an argument, or of intelligence.

CORROB'ORATIVE, *a.* Having the power of giving strength, or additional strength; tending to confirm.

CORROB'ORATIVE, *n.* A medicine that strengthens; a corroborant.

CORRO'DE, *v. t.* [L. *corrodo; con* and *rodo,* to gnaw, Ar. أرض aradha, to eat or gnaw, [qu. *raw* and *crude;*] It. *corrodere, rodere;* Fr. *corroder;* Sp. *corroer;* W. *rhwtiaw,* to corrode, to rub or fret.]
1. To eat away by degrees; to wear away, or diminish, by gradually separating small particles from a body, in the manner an animal gnaws a substance. Thus, nitric acid *corrodes* copper.
2. To wear away by degrees; to prey upon; to impair; to consume, or diminish by slow degrees. Jealousy and envy *corrode* the constitution. Substances are *corroded* by time. The anxious man is a victim to *corroding* care.

CORRO'DED, *pp.* Eaten away gradually; worn, diminished, impaired, by slow degrees.

CORRO'DENT, *a.* Having the power of corroding, or wasting by degrees.

CORRO'DENT, *n.* Any substance or medicine that corrodes. *Coxe.*

CORRODIBIL'ITY, *n.* The quality of being corrodible.

CORRO'DIBLE, *a.* That may be corroded. *Brown.*

CORRO'DING, *ppr.* Eating away gradually; impairing; wasting.

COR'RODY. [See *Corody.*] But *corrody* is the most correct orthography.

CORRO'SIBLE, *a.* [See *Corrodible.*]

CORROSIBIL'ITY, *n.* [See *Corrodibility.*]

CORRO'SION, *n.* *s* as *z.* [from *corrode.*] The action of eating or wearing away by slow degrees, as by the action of acids on metals, by which the substance is gradually changed. This is effected by the affinity of the menstruum with the component parts of the substance, in consequence of which the two substances unite and form new combinations.

CORRO'SIVE, *a.* Eating; wearing away; having the power of gradually wearing, consuming or impairing; as *corrosive* sublimate; *corrosive* care; a *corrosive* ulcer.
2. Having the quality of fretting or vexing.
Corrosive sublimate, the corrosive muriate or perchloride of mercury.

CORRO'SIVE, *n.* That which has the quality of eating or wearing gradually.

2. That which has the power of fretting. *Hooker.*

CORRO'SIVELY, *adv.* Like a corrosive; with the power of corrosion; in a corrosive manner.

CORRO'SIVENESS, *n.* The quality of corroding, eating away or wearing; acrimony. *Boyle.*

COR'RUGANT, *a.* [See *Corrugate.*] Having the power of contracting into wrinkles.

COR'RUGATE, *v. t.* [L. *corrugo; con* and *rugo*, to wrinkle, in our vulgar language, to *ruck*, W. *rhyçu*, to furrow.]
To wrinkle; to draw or contract into folds; as, to *corrugate* the skin. *Bacon.*

COR'RUGATE, *a.* Wrinkled. *Young.*

COR'RUGATED, *pp.* Wrinkled.

COR'RUGATING, *ppr.* Contracting into wrinkles.

CORRUGA'TION, *n.* A wrinkling; contraction into wrinkles.

COR'RUGATOR, *n.* A muscle which contracts the skin of the forehead into wrinkles. *Coxe.*

CORRUPT', *v. t.* [L. *corruptus*, from *corrumpo; con* and *rumpo*, for *rupo*, to break; Fr. *corrompre;* It. *corrompere;* Sp. *corromper.* Class Rb.]
Literally, to break, separate or dissolve. Hence,
1. To change from a sound to a putrid or putrescent state; to separate the component parts of a body, as by a natural process, which is accompanied by a fetid smell.
2. To vitiate or deprave; to change from good to bad.
Evil communications *corrupt* good manners. 1 Cor. xv.
3. To waste, spoil or consume.
Lay not up for yourselves treasures on earth, where moth and rust doth *corrupt.* Math. vi.
4. To defile or pollute. Ex. xxxii.
5. To entice from good and allure to evil. 2 Cor. xi.
6. To pervert; to break, disobey or make void. Mal. ii.
7. To pervert or vitiate integrity; to bribe; as, to *corrupt* a judge.
8. To debase or render impure, by alterations or innovations; as, to *corrupt* language.
9. To pervert; to falsify; to infect with errors; as, to *corrupt* the sacred text.

CORRUPT', *v. i.* To become putrid; to putrefy; to rot. Animal and vegetable substances speedily *corrupt* in a warm and moist air.
2. To become vitiated; to lose purity.

CORRUPT', *a.* [L. *corruptus;* It. *corrotto.*]
1. Changed from a sound to a putrid state, as by natural decomposition.
2. Spoiled; tainted; vitiated; unsound; as *corrupt* air, or bread. *Knolles.*
3. Depraved; vitiated; tainted with wickedness.
They are *corrupt;* they have done abominable works. Ps. xiv.
The earth was *corrupt* before God. Gen. vi.
4. Debased; rendered impure; changed to a worse state; as *corrupt* language.
5. Not genuine; infected with errors or mistakes. The text is *corrupt.*

CORRUPT'ED, *pp.* Putrefied; vitiated; depraved; spoiled; marred; bribed; infected with errors.

CORRUPT'ER, *n.* One who corrupts; one who vitiates, or taints; as a *corrupter* of morals, or of christianity.
2. One who bribes; that which depraves or destroys integrity.
3. One who introduces errors.

CORRUPTIBIL'ITY, *n.* The possibility of being corrupted.

CORRUPT'IBLE, *a.* [Fr. *corruptible;* It. *corruttibile.*]
1. That may be corrupted; that may become putrid; subject to decay and destruction. Our bodies are *corruptible.*
2. That may be vitiated in qualities or principles; susceptible of depravation. Manners are *corruptible* by evil example.

CORRUPT'IBLE, *n.* That which may decay and perish; the human body.
This *corruptible* must put on incorruption. 1 Cor. xv.

CORRUPT'IBLENESS, *n.* Susceptibility of corruption; corruptibility.

CORRUPT'IBLY, *adv.* In such a manner as to be corrupted or vitiated.

CORRUPT'ING, *ppr.* Putrefying; depraving; vitiating.

CORRUP'TION, *n.* [L. *corruptio.*] The act of corrupting, or state of being corrupt or putrid; the destruction of the natural form of bodies, by the separation of the component parts, or by disorganization, in the process of putrefaction.
Thou wilt not suffer thy holy One to see *corruption.* Ps xvi.
2. Putrid matter; pus.
3. Putrescence; a foul state occasioned by putrefaction.
4. Depravity; wickedness; perversion or deterioration of moral principles; loss of purity or integrity.
Having escaped the *corruption* that is in the world through lust. 2 Pet. i.
Corruption in elections is the great enemy of freedom. *J. Adams.*
5. Debasement; taint; or tendency to a worse state.
Keep my honor from *corruption.* *Shak.*
6. Impurity; depravation; debasement; as a *corruption* of language.
7. Bribery. He obtained his suit by *corruption.*
8. In *law*, taint; impurity of blood, in consequence of an act of attainder of treason or felony, by which a person is disabled to inherit lands from an ancestor, nor can retain those in his possession, nor transmit them by descent to his heirs.
Corruption of blood can be removed only by act of parliament. *Blackstone.*

CORRUPT'IVE, *a.* Having the quality of corrupting, tainting or vitiating.
It should be endued with some *corruptive* quality. *Ray.*

CORRUPT'LESS, *a.* Not susceptible of corruption, or decay. *Dryden.*

CORRUPT'LY, *adv.* In a corrupt manner; with corruption; viciously; wickedly; without integrity.
We have dealt very *corruptly* against thee. Neh. i.
2. By bribery. A judgment was obtained *corruptly.*

CORRUPT'NESS, *n.* The state of being corrupt; putrid state or putrescence.
2. A state of moral impurity; as the *corruptness* of a judge.
3. A vicious state; debasement; impurity; as the *corruptness* of language.

CORRUPT'RESS, *n.* A female that corrupts others. *Beaum.*

COR'SAIR, *n.* [Fr. *corsaire;* Sp. *corsario*, a cruising by a privateer; *corsear*, to cruise; It. *corsare*, a pirate, from *corso*, a course or career, L. *cursus*, from *curro*, to run.]
A pirate; one who cruises or scours the ocean, with an armed vessel, without a commission from any prince or state, to seize and plunder merchantmen.

COR'SAK, *n.* A species of fox. *Pennant.*

CORSE, *n.* [Fr. *corps;* L. *corpus.*] A corpse; the dead body of a human being: *a poetical word.* *Addison.*

CORSE-ENCUM'BERED, *a.* Loaded with dead bodies; as the *corse-encumbered* plains. *Barlow.*

CORSE-PRESENT, *n.* A mortuary or present paid at the interment of a dead body. *Blackstone.*

CORSELET, *n.* *cors'let.* [Fr. *corselet;* It. *corsaletto;* from *corse.*]
1. A little cuirass, or an armor to cover the body for protection, worn formerly by pike-men. *Encyc.*
2. [See *Corcelet.*]

CORSELET, *v. t.* *cors'let.* To encircle with a corselet. *Beaum.*

CORS'ET, *n.* [Fr. from *corse.*] A boddice; jumps; something worn to give shape to the body; used by ladies and dandies.

CORS'NED, *n.* [Sax. *corsnæde*, comp. of *corse*, curse, and *snæd*, a mouthful, piece or bit. It is called also *ned-bread*, need-bread, bread of necessity.]
The morsel of execration, or curse; a piece of bread consecrated by exorcism, and to be swallowed by a suspected person, as a trial of his innocence. If guilty, it was supposed the bread would produce convulsions and paleness, and find no passage. If innocent, it was believed it would turn to nourishment. *Blackstone.*

CORTE'GE, *n.* [Fr. from the It. *corteggio*, from *corte*, court.] A train of attendants.

CORT'ES, *n. plu.* [from *corte*, court.] The Spanish name of the States of the kingdom, composed of nobility, clergy and representatives of cities; the assembly of the States, answering, in some measure, to the parliament of Great Britain.

COR'TICAL, *a.* [from L. *cortex*, bark. See *Chart.*] Belonging to bark; consisting of bark or rind; resembling bark or rind; external; belonging to the external covering; as the *cortical* part of the brain. *Cheyne.*
A *cortical* bud in plants proceeds from the scales of the bark. *Martyn.*

COR'TICATE, COR'TICATED, *a.* [L. *corticatus*, from *cortex*, bark.] Resembling the bark or rind of a tree. *Brown.*

CORTICIF'EROUS, *a.* [*cortex* and *fero*, to produce.]
Producing bark, or that which resembles it. *Dict.*

CORTIC'IFORM, *a.* [*cortex* and *form.*] Resembling bark.

CORT'ICOSE, CORT'ICOUS, *a.* Barky; full of bark. *Dict.*

CORUND'UM, *n.* The corindon-harmophane of Haüy, corindon adamantin of Brongniart, the korund of Werner, and the adamantine spar of Kirwan. It is octahedral, rhomboidal or prismatic. *Cleaveland. Ure.*

CORUS'CANT, *a.* [See *Coruscate.*] Flashing; glittering by flashes.

COR'USCATE, *v. i.* [L. *corusco*, to flash.] To flash; to lighten; to glitter. *Barlow.*

CORUSCA'TION, *n.* [L. *coruscatio.*] A flash; a sudden burst of light in the clouds or atmosphere. *Bacon.*

2. The light produced by the combustion of imflammable gas in the earth. *Newton.*

Artificial coruscations are produced by phosporus and sulphuric acid, or by sulphuric acid and iron filings. *Encyc.*

COR'VET, *n.* [Fr. *corvette*; Sp. *corveta*, a leap, a curvet, a boat.] A sloop of war; an advice boat.

CORV'US, *n.* [L. *corvus*, a raven.] In *astronomy*, a constellation of the southern hemisphere, containing nine stars.

2. A military engine or gallery used by the Romans for boarding ships in war. It was a strong platform of boards at the prow, movable as on a spindle, and thrown over the side of the enemy's vessel, when grappled. *Encyc.*

CORYBAN'TIC, *a.* Madly agitated; inflamed like the Corybantes, the frantic priests of Cybele. *Cudworth.*

COR'YMB, *n.* [L. *corymbus*; Gr. κυρυμβος.] Primarily, a top, head or cluster. In *modern botany*, a species of inflorescence, in which the lesser or partial flower-stalks are produced along the common stalk on both sides, and though of unequal length, rise to the same highth, so as to form an even surface; as in spiræa opulifolia, scurvy-grass, &c. *Milne. Martyn.*

CORYM'BIATED, *a.* Garnished with corymbs.

CORYMBIF'EROUS, *a.* [L. *corymbifer*; *corymbus* and *fero*, to bear.]
Producing corymbs; bearing fruit or berries in clusters, or producing flowers in clusters. *Milne.*

CORYM'BOUS, *a.* Consisting of corymbs; in clusters. *Barton. Lee.*

CORYM'BULOUS, *a.* Having or consisting of little corymbs. *Barton.*

COR'YPHENE, *n.* A fish with a sloping truncated head, and the dorsal fin extending the whole length of the back. *Pennant.*

CORYPHE'US, *n.* [Gr.] The chief of a chorus; the chief of a company. *South.*

COSCINOM'ANCY, *n.* [Gr. κοσκινον, a sieve, and μαντεια, divination.]
The art or practice of divination, by suspending a sieve and taking it between two fingers, or by fixing it to the point of a pair of shears, then repeating a formula of words, and the names of persons suspected. If the sieve trembles, shakes or turns, when any name is repeated, the person is deemed guilty. This divination is mentioned by Theocritus, and is said to be still practiced in some parts of England. The practice and the name are strangers in America.

CO-SE'CANT, *n.* [See *Secant.*] In *geometry*, the secant of an arc which is the complement of another to ninety degrees. *Encyc.*

CO'SIER, *n.* [Fr. *cousu*, *coudre.*] A botcher. [*Not used.*] *Shak.*

COS'INAGE, *n. s* as z. [Fr. *cousinage*, kindred. See *Cousin.*]
In *law*, a writ to recover possession of an estate in lands, when a stranger has entered and abated, after the death of the tresail, or the grandfather's grandfather, or other collateral relation. *Blackstone.*

CO'-SINE, *n.* [See *Sine.*] In *geometry*, the sine of an arc which is the complement of another to ninety degrees. *Encyc.*

COSMET'IC, *a. s* as z. [Gr. κοσμητικος, from κοσμος, order, beauty.]
Beautifying; improving beauty, particularly the beauty of the skin.

COSMET'IC, *n.* Any preparation that renders the skin soft, pure and white, and helps to beautify and improve the complexion. *Encyc.*

COS'MICAL, *a. s* as z. [Gr. κοσμικος, from κοσμος, order, the world.]

1. Relating to the world, or to the whole system of visible bodies, including the earth and stars.

2. In *astronomy*, rising or setting with the sun; not acronical. *Encyc.*

COS'MICALLY, *adv.* With the sun at rising or setting; a star is said to rise or set *cosmically*, when it rises or sets with the sun.

COSMOG'ONIST, *n.* [See *Cosmogony.*] One who treats of the origin or formation of the universe. *Enfield.*

COSMOG'ONY, *n. s* as z. [Gr. κοσμογονια; κοσμος, world, and γονη, generation.]
The generation, origin or creation of the world or universe. In *physics*, the science of the origin or formation of the universe. *Enfield. Encyc.*

COSMOG'RAPHER, *n.* [See *Cosmography.*] One who describes the world or universe, including the heavens and the earth.

COSMOGRAPH'IC, **COSMOGRAPH'ICAL**, } *a.* Relating to the general description of the universe.

COSMOGRAPH'ICALLY, *adv.* In a manner relating to the science of describing the universe, or corresponding to cosmography.

COSMOG'RAPHY, *n. s* as z. [Gr. κοσμογραφια; κοσμος, the world, and γραφω, to describe.]
A description of the world or universe; or the art which teaches the construction of the whole system of worlds, or the figure, disposition and relation of all its parts, and the manner of representing them on a plane. *Encyc.*

COS'MOLABE, *n. s* as z. [Gr. κοσμος, world, and λαμβανω, to take.]
An ancient instrument for measuring distances in the heavens or on earth, much the same as the astrolabe, and called also *pantacosm.* *Encyc.*

COSMOL'ATORY, *n. s* as z. [Gr. κοσμος, world, and λατρευω, to worship.]
The worship paid to the world or its parts by heathens. *Cudworth.*

COSMOLOG'ICAL, *a.* [See *Cosmology.*] Relating to a discourse or treatise of the world, or to the science of the universe.

COSMOL'OGIST, *n.* One who describes the universe.

COSMOL'OGY, *n. s* as z. [Gr. κοσμολογια; κοσμος, the universe, and λογος, discourse.]
The science of the world or universe; or a treatise relating to the structure and parts of the system of creation, the elements of bodies, the modifications of material things, the laws of motion, and the order and course of nature. *Encyc. Enfield.*

COSMOPLAS'TIC, *a.* [Gr. κοσμος, world, and πλασσω, to form.]
World-forming; pertaining to the formation of the world. *Hallywell.*

COSMOPOL'ITAN, **COSMOP'OLITE**, } *n. s* as z. [Gr. κοσμος, world, and πολιτης, a citizen.]
A person who has no fixed residence; one who is no where a stranger, or who is at home in every place; a citizen of the world. *Howell.*

COSS, *n.* A Hindoo measure of one English mile and a quarter nearly. *Asiat. Res.*

COS'SACK, *n.* The Cossacks inhabit the Ukraine, in the Russian empire.

COS'SAS, *n.* Plain India muslins, of various qualities and breadths.

COS'SET, *n.* [Qu. G. *kossat*, like D. *huislam*, and from the root of *cot*, or *house*; It. *casiccio*, from *casa*, a house.]
A lamb brought up by hand, or without the aid of the dam.

COS'SIC, *a.* Relating to algebra. *Bp. Hall.*

COST, *n.* *caust.* [G. D. Sw. Dan. *kost*; Ir. *cosdas*; W. *cost*, coast and cost; Fr. *coût*; Arm. *coust*. See the Verb.]

1. The price, value or equivalent of a thing purchased; the amount in value paid, charged or engaged to be paid for any thing bought or taken in barter. The word is equally applicable to the price in money or commodities; as the *cost* of a suit of clothes; the *cost* of a house or farm.

2. Expense; amount in value expended or to be expended; charge; that which is given or to be given for another thing.

> I will not offer burnt offerings without *cost.* 1 Chron. xxi.
>
> Have we eaten at all at the king's *cost?* 2 Sam. xix.
>
> The *cost* of maintaining armies is immense and often ruinous. *Anon.*

3. In *law*, the sum fixed by law or allowed by the court for charges of a suit awarded against the party losing, in favor of the party prevailing, &c. The jury find that the plaintiff recover of the defendant ten dollars with *costs* of suit or with his *cost.*

4. Loss or expense of any kind; detriment; pain; suffering. The vicious man indulges his propensities at a great *cost.*

5. Sumptuousness; great expense. *Shak.*

COST, *v. t.* pret. and pp. *cost.* [G. and D. *kosten*; Dan. *koster*; Sw. *kosta*; Fr. *coûter*, for *couster*; Arm. *cousta*, *coustein*; W. *costiaw*; It. *costare*; Sp. *costar*; Port. *custar*; Ir. *cosnam.* The noun *cost* coincides in most of these languages with *coast* and L. *costa*, a rib, the exterior part. The primary sense of the verb is, to throw or send out, to *cast*, as we say, to *lay out.* Qu. the Ar. and Pers. قسطاس a balance, or pair of scales, from قسط to distribute. I call this a transitive verb. In the phrase, a hat *costs* six dollars, the sense is, it expends, lays out, or causes to be laid out six dollars.]

1. To require to be given or expended in barter or purchase; to be bought for; as, this book *cost* a dollar; the army and navy *cost* four millions a year.

2. To require to be laid out, given, bestowed or employed; as, Johnson's Dictionary *cost* him seven years labor.

3. To require to be borne or suffered. Our sins *cost* us many pains. A sense of ingratitude to his maker *costs* the penitent sinner many pangs and sorrows.

ЄOST'AL, *a.* [Fr. *costal*, from L. *costa*, a *coast*, side or rib; Sp. *costa*, cost, and a coast; *costear*, to pay *costs*, to *coast* along. A coast or side is the extreme part, a limit, from extending, throwing or shooting out, Eng. to *cast*.]

Pertaining to the side of the body or the ribs; as *costal* nerves.

ЄOST'ARD, *n.* A head. [*Not used.*] *Shak.*

2. An apple, round and bulky, like the head. *Johnson.*

ЄOST'ARD-MŎNGER, *n.* An apple-seller. *Burton.*

ЄOST'ER-MŎNGER, *n.* An apple-seller.

ЄOS'TIVE, *a.* [contracted from It. *costipato*, *costipare*, from the L. *constipo*, to cram, to *stuff; con* and *stipo*, to cram.]

1. Literally, crowded, stuffed, as the intestines; hence, bound in body; retaining fecal matter in the bowels, in a hard and dry state; having the excrements obstructed, or the motion of the bowels too slow.

2. Dry and hard; as *costive* clay. [*Not used.*] *Mortimer.*

ЄOS'TIVENESS, *n.* A preternatural detention of the fecal matter of the bowels, with hardness and dryness; an obstruction or preternatural slowness of evacuations from the bowels. *Medicine.*

ЄOST'LINESS, *n.* [See *Costly.*] Expensiveness; great cost, or expense; sumptuousness. Rev. xviii. 19. *Sidney.*

ЄOST'LESS, *a.* Costing nothing. *Barrow.*

ЄOST'LY, *a.* [from *cost.*] Of a high price; sumptuous; expensive; purchased at a great expense; as a *costly* habit; *costly* furniture.

> Mary took a pound of spikenard, very *costly*. John xii.

ЄOST'MARY, *n.* [Gr. κοςος, L. *costus*, an aromatic plant, and *Maria*. Ar. and Pers. قسط kost.]

A species of tansy, or Tanacetum; alecost.

ЄOS'TREL, *n.* A bottle. [*Not in use.*]

ЄOS'TUME, *n.* [Fr. *costume*, custom.] In *painting*, a rule or precept by which an artist is enjoined to make every person and thing sustain its proper character, observing the scene of action, the country or place, and making the habits, arms, manners, and proportions correspond. Hence, the observance of this rule in execution. *Encyc.*

2. An established mode of dress.

ЄO-SUF'FERER, *n.* One who suffers with another.

ЄO-SUPRE'ME, *n.* A partaker of supremacy. *Shak.*

ЄO-SU'RETY, *n.* One who is surety with another. *Mass. Rep.*

ЄOT, } *n.* [Sax. *cot*, *cote*, *cyte*; G. *koth*; D. *kot*; W. *cwt*. In Welsh, the
ЄOTE, }

word signifies a *cot*, a hovel or stye, an abrupt termination, a rump, a tail, a skirt. *Cwta*, short, abrupt, bob-tailed; *cwtau*, to shorten. This indicates that *cot* is from cutting off, and hence defending.]

1. A small house; a hut; a mean habitation; also, a shed or inclosure for beasts. 2 Chron. xxxii.

2. A leathern cover for a sore finger.

3. An abridgement of *cotquean*.

4. A cade lamb. [*Local.*] *Grose.*

5. A little boat.

ЄO-TAN'ĠENT, *n.* The tangent of an arc which is the complement of another to ninety degrees. *Harris.*

ЄOTE, *n.* A sheepfold. [See *Cot.*]

ЄOTE, *v. t.* To pass by and turn before; to gain ground in coursing and give a competitor the turn. [*Little used.*] *Shak. Chapman.*

ЄOTEMPORA'NEOUS, *a.* [infra.] Living or being at the same time.

ЄOTEM'PORARY, *a.* [L. *con*, *co*, and *tempus*, time.]

Living or being at the same time; as *cotemporary* authors. Josephus was *cotemporary* with Vespasian. *Locke. Blackstone.*

ЄOTEM'PORARY, *n.* One who lives at the same time with another.

[I consider this word as preferable to *contemporary*, as being more easily pronounced.]

ЄO-TEN'ANT, *n.* A tenant in common. *Kent.*

ЄOTERIE', *n.* [Fr.] A friendly party, or fashionable association.

ЄOTIЄ'ULAR, *a.* [L. *coticula*, from *cos*, a whetstone.]

Pertaining to whetstones; like or suitable for whetstones. *Kirwan.*

ЄOTIL'LON, *n.* *cotil'yun.* [Fr. a petticoat.] A brisk dance, performed by eight persons together; also, a tune which regulates the dance.

ЄOT'LAND, *n.* Land appendant to a cottage. *Johnson.*

ЄOT'QUEAN, *n.* A man who busies himself with the affairs which properly belong to women.

ЄO-TRUSTEE', *n.* A joint trustee. *Kent.*

ЄOTS'WŎLD, *n.* [Sax. *cote* and *wold.*] Sheepcotes in an open country.

ЄOTT, *n.* [Sax. *cot*, *cote*, a bed. Qu. Gr. κοιτη.] A small bed; on board of ships, a bed frame suspended from the beams, for the officers to sleep in, between the decks; a piece of canvas, extended by a frame. *Mar. Dict.*

ЄOT'TAĠE, *n.* [from *cot.*] A cot; a hut; a small mean habitation.

> The sea coast shall be dwellings and *cottages* for shepherds. Zeph. ii.

ЄOT'TAĠED, *a.* Set or covered with cottages. *Collins.*

ЄOT'TAĠER, *n.* One who lives in a hut or cottage.

2. In *law*, one who lives on the common, without paying any rent, or having land of his own. *Johnson.*

ЄOT'TER, ЄOT'TAR or ЄOT'TIER, *n.* A cottager.

ЄOT'TON, *n.* *cot'n.* [Fr. *coton*; It. *cotone*; Ir. *cadas*; Sp. *algodon*, the cotton-plant or the wool; *coton*, printed cotton; Port. *algodam*; D. *katoen*; W. *cotwm*, cotton, dag-wool, as if from *cot*, a short tail. But it seems to be an Arabic word, قُطْن, corresponding with a word in Ethiopic and Syriac, which signifies to be thin or fine. And with a common dialectical variation, it may coincide with the first syllable of *gossypium* and *gossamer.*]

1. A soft downy substance, resembling fine wool, growing in the capsules or pods of a shrub, called the cotton-plant. It is the material of a large proportion of cloth for apparel and furniture.

2. Cloth made of cotton.

Lavender-cotton, a genus of plants, Santolina, of several species; shrubs cultivated in gardens. One species, the *chamæcyparyssus* or abrotanum fœmina, female southernwood, is vulgarly called *brotany*. *Encyc.*

Philosophic cotton, flowers of zink, which resemble cotton.

Silk-cotton tree, a genus of plants, the Bombax, growing to a great size in the Indies, and producing a kind of cotton in capsules. *Encyc.*

ЄOT'TON, *a.* Pertaining to cotton; made of cotton; consisting of cotton; as *cotton* cloth; *cotton* stockings.

ЄOT'TON, *v. i.* To rise with a nap. *Johnson.*

2. To cement; to unite with; *a cant word.* *Swift.*

ЄOT'TON-ĠIN, *n.* A machine to separate the seeds from cotton, invented by that celebrated mechanician, E. Whitney.

ЄOT'TON-GRASS, *n.* A genus of plants, the Eriophorum. *Muhlenberg.*

ЄOTTON-MAЄHĪNE, *n.* A machine for carding or spinning cotton.

ЄOT'TON-MILL, *n.* A mill or building, with machinery for carding, roving and spinning cotton, by the force of water or steam.

ЄOT'TON-PLANT, } *n.* A plant or shrub of the genus Gossypium, of several species, all growing in warm climates. The principal species are, 1. the herbaceous cotton, with smooth leaves and yellow flowers, succeeded by roundish capsules, full of seeds and cotton; 2. the hairy American cotton, with hairy stalks and leaves, and yellow flowers succeeded by oval pods; 3. the Barbadoes shrub-by cotton, has a shrubby stalk, yellow flowers and oval pods; 4. the arboreum or tree cotton, with a woody perennial stalk, bears yellow flowers and large pods. The first three species are annual plants; the last is perennial. *Encyc.*
ЄOT'TON-SHRUB, }

In the southern states of America, the cotton cultivated is distinguished into three kinds; the *nankeen cotton*, so called from its color; the *green seed cotton*, producing white cotton with green seeds. These grow in the middle and upper country, and are called short staple cotton. The *black seed cotton*, cultivated in the lower country near the sea, and on the isles near the shore, produces cotton of a fine, white, silky appearance, very strong and of a long staple. The seeds of the long staple cotton are separated by roller-gins. The seeds of the short staple cotton are separated with more difficulty, by a saw-gin invented by E. Whitney. *Ramsay. Drayton.*

COT'TON-THISTLE, *n.* A plant, the Onopordum. *Muhlenberg.*

COT'TON-WEED, *n.* A plant, the Filago. The name is given also to the Gnaphalium, cud-weed, or goldy-locks.

COT'TONY, *a.* Downy; nappy; covered with hairs or pubescence like cotton. *Martyn.*

2. Soft like cotton.

CO'TYLE, *n.* [Gr. κοτυλη.] The cavity of a bone which receives the end of another in articulation.

COTYL'EDON, *n.* [Gr. κοτυληδων, from κοτυλη, a hollow or cavity.]

1. In *botany*, the perishable lobe or placenta of the seeds of plants. It involves and nourishes the embryo plant, and then perishes. Some seeds have two lobes; others one only, and others none. *Milne. Martyn. Encyc.*

2. In *anatomy*, a little glandular body adhering to the chorion of some animals. *Coxe. Encyc.*

3. A genus of plants, navel-wort, or kidney-wort, of several species. *Encyc.*

COTYLED'ONOUS, *a.* Pertaining to cotyledons; having a seed-lobe.

COUCH, *v. i.* [Fr. *couche*, a bed; *coucher*, to lay down; Norm. *couche*, a couch, and laid double; Sp. *gacho*, bent down, slouching; *agacharse*, to stoop, to crouch; Port. *agacharse*, *acaçaparse*, to stoop, crouch, or squat; Arm. *coacha* and *scoacha*, our vulgar *scooch*; D. *hukken*; G. *hocken*; Dan. *huger*. The primary sense is to lay or throw down. See Class Cg. Gk. No. 7. 8. 9.]

1. To lie down, as on a bed or place of repose.

2. To lie down on the knees; to stoop and recline on the knees, as a beast.

Fierce tigers *couched* around. *Dryden.*

3. To lie down in secret or in ambush; to lie close and concealed.

The earl of Angus *couched* in a furrow. *Hayward.*

Judah *couched* as a lion. Gen. xlix.

4. To lie; to lie in a bed or stratum.

Blessed of the Lord be his land—for the dew, and for the deep that *coucheth* beneath. Deut. xxxiii.

5. To stoop; to bend the body or back; to lower in reverence, or to bend under labor, pain, or a burden.

Issachar is a strong ass, *couching* down between two burdens. Gen. xlix.

These *couchings*, and these lowly courtesies. *Shak.*

COUCH, *v. t.* To lay down; to repose on a bed or place of rest.

Where unbruised youth, with unstuffed brain, Doth *couch* his limbs. *Shak.*

3. To lay down; to spread on a bed or floor; as, to *couch* malt. *Mortimer.*

3. To lay close, or in a stratum.

The waters *couch* themselves, as close as may be, to the center of the globe. *Burnet.*

4. To hide; to lay close, or in another body.

It is in use at this day, to *couch* vessels in walls, to gather the wind from the top, and pass it down in spouts into rooms. *Bacon.*

5. To include secretely; to hide; or to express in obscure terms, that imply what is to be understood; with *under*.

All this, and more, lies *couched under* this allegory. *L'Estrange.*

Hence,

6. To involve; to include; to comprise; to comprehend or express.

This great argument for a future state, which St. Paul hath *couched* in the words read. *Atterbury.*

7. To lie close. *Spenser.*

8. To fix a spear in the rest, in the posture of attack.

They *couched* their spears. *Milton. Dryden.*

9. To depress the condensed crystaline humor or film that overspreads the pupil of the eye. *Johnson.*

To remove a cataract, by entering a needle through the coats of the eye, and pushing the lens to the bottom of the vitreous humor, and then downwards and outwards, so as to leave it in the under and outside of the eye. *Encyc.*

The true phrase is, to *couch* a cataract; but we say, to *couch* the eye, or the patient.

COUCH, *n.* A bed; a place for rest or sleep. *Milton. Dryden.*

2. A seat of repose; a place for rest and ease, on which it is common to lie down undressed. *Milton. Dryden.*

3. A layer or stratum; as a *couch* of malt. *Mortimer.*

4. In *painting*, a lay or impression of color, in oil or water, covering the canvas, wall, or other matter to be painted. *Encyc.*

5. Any lay, or impression, used to make a thing firm or consistent, or to screen it from the weather. *Encyc.*

6. A covering of gold or silver leaf, laid on any substance to be gilded or silvered. *Encyc.*

COUCH'ANT, *a.* [Fr. See *Couch.*] Lying down; squatting. In *heraldry*, lying down with the head raised, which distinguishes the posture of *couchant* from that of *dormant*, or sleeping; applied to a lion or other beast. *Encyc.*

Levant and *couchant*, in law, rising up and lying down; applied to beasts, and indicating that they have been long enough on land to lie down and rise up to feed, or one night at least. *Blackstone.*

COUCH'ED, *pp.* Laid down; laid on; hid; included or involved; laid close; fixed in the rest, as a spear; depressed or removed, as a cataract.

COUCH'EE, *n.* [Fr.] Bedtime; late visiting at night. *Dryden.*

COUCH'ER, *n.* One who couches cataracts.

2. In *old English statutes*, a factor; a resident in a country for traffick. *Encyc.*

3. A book in which a religious house register their acts. *Encyc.*

COUCH'-FELLOW, *n.* A bed fellow; a companion in lodging.

COUCH'-GRASS, *n.* A species of grass, very injurious to other plants.

COUCH'ING, *ppr.* Lying down; laying down; lying close; involving; including; expressing; depressing a cataract.

COUCH'ING, *n.* The act of stooping or bowing. *Shak.*

COUGH, *n.* *kauf.* [Qu. D. *kuch.* The elements are not both of the same organ; but *gh* and *f* are sometimes interchanged, as in *rough*, *ruff.* See Class Cg. No. 29. 36. In Pers. خفته chaftah, and خفه chafa, is a cough.]

A violent effort of the lungs to throw off offending matter; a violent, sometimes involuntary, and sonorous expiration, suddenly expelling the air through the glottis. The convulsion of the muscles serving for expiration gives great force to the air, while the contraction of the glottis produces the sound. The air forced violently carries along with it the phlegm or irritating matter which causes the convulsion or effort of the muscles. *Encyc.*

COUGH, *v. i.* To have the lungs convulsed; to make a violent effort with noise to expel the air from the lungs, and evacuate any offending matter that irritates the parts or renders respiration difficult.

COUGH, *v. t.* To expel from the lungs by a convulsive effort with noise; to expectorate; followed by *up*; as, to *cough up* phlegm.

COUGH'ER, *n.* One that coughs.

COUGH'ING, *ppr.* Expelling from the lungs by a violent effort with noise; expectorating.

COULD, pron. COOD. [The past tense of *can*, according to our customary arrangement in grammar; but in reality a distinct word, *can* having no past tense. *Could*, we receive through the Celtic dialects, W. *gallu*, Corn. *gally*, Arm. *gallout*, to be able; Heb. יכל, Ch. כהל, Eth. ከሀለ to be able, to prevail; L. *calleo*. Either of the Oriental verbs may be the root, and all may be of one family. In the past tense, *could* signifies, was able, had power.]

1. Had sufficient strength or physical power. A sick man *could* not lift his hand. Isaac was old and *could* not see. Alexander *could* easily conquer the effeminate Asiatics.

2. Had adequate means or instruments. The men *could* defray their own expenses. The country was exhausted and *could* not support the war.

3. Had adequate moral power. We heard the story, but *could* not believe it. The intemperate man *could* have restrained his appetite for strong drink. He *could* have refrained, if he would.

My mind *could* not be towards this people. Jer. xv.

4. Had power or capacity by the laws of its nature. The tree *could* not grow for want of water.

5. Had competent legal power; had right, or had the requisite qualifications. Formerly, a citizen *could* not vote for officers of government without the possession of some property. AB *could* not be elected to the office of senator, for want of estate. BC, not being of the blood of the ancestor, *could* not inherit his estate.

6. Had sufficient capacity. The world *could* not contain the books. John xxi.

7. Was capable or susceptible, by its nature or constitution, as of some change. He found a substance that *could* not be fused.

8. Had adequate strength or fortitude; as, he *could* not endure the pain or the reproach.

9. Had motives sufficient to overcome ob-

jections. He thought at first he *could* not comply with the request; but after consideration he determined to comply.

10. Had competent knowledge or skill. He *could* solve the most difficult problems.

COUL'TER. [See *Colter.*]

COUN'CIL, *n.* [Fr. *concile;* Sp. *concilio;* It. *conciglio, concilio;* from L. *concilium; con* and *calo,* to call, Gr. *καλεω,* W. *galw,* Ch. כלא in Aph., to call. See *Hold.* Class Gl. This word is often confounded with *counsel,* with which it has no connection. *Council* is a collection or assembly.]

1. An assembly of men summoned or convened for consultation, deliberation and advice.

> The chief priests and all the *council* sought false witness. Matth. xx.

> The kings of England were formerly assisted by a grand *council* of peers.

The word is applicable to any body of men, appointed or convened for consultation and advice, in important affairs; as, a *council* of divines or clergymen, with their lay delegates; a *council* of war, consisting of the principal officers, to advise the commander in chief or admiral; a *council* of physicians, to consult and advise in difficult cases of disease.

2. A body of men specially designated to advise a chief magistrate in the administration of the government, as in Great Britain.

3. In some of the American states, a branch of the legislature, corresponding with the senate in other states, and called legislative *council.* *New Jersey.*

4. An assembly of prelates and doctors, convened for regulating matters of doctrine and discipline in the church.

5. Act of deliberation; consultation of a council. *Milton.*

Common-Council of a city. In London, a court consisting of the lord mayor and aldermen in one house, and of representatives of the several wards, called *common-council-men,* in the other. But more generally the common-council is considered as the body of representatives of the citizens, as distinct from the mayor and aldermen. Thus in Connecticut, the cities are incorporated by the name of "The Mayor, Aldermen, *Common-Council* and Freemen, of the city of Hartford, New-Haven, &c."

Ecumenical Council, in church history, a general council or assembly of prelates and doctors, representing the whole church; as the *council* of Nice, of Ephesus, and of Chalcedon. *Encyc.*

Privy Council, a select council for advising a king in the administration of the government.

AULIC COUNCIL. [See *Aulic.*]

COUN'CIL-BOARD, *n.* Council-table; the table round which a council holds consultation. Hence, the council itself in deliberation or session.

COUN'CILOR, *n.* The member of a council. [See *Counselor.*]

COUN'CIL-TABLE, *n.* Council-board.

CO-UNI'TE, *v. t.* To unite. [*Not used.*] *More.*

COUN'SEL, *n.* [Fr. *conseil;* Arm. *consailh;* It. *consiglio;* Sp. *consejo;* Port. *conselho;* from L. *consilium,* from the root of *consulo,* to *consult,* which is probably the Heb. Ch. Syr. Sam. Eth. שאל, Ar. سال to ask. Class Sl. No. 16. 42. The radical sense of the verb, to ask, is to set upon, urge, or press. Hence the Oriental verb is probably the root of the L. *salio, assilio,* or from the same root. See the like analogies in L. *peto,* to ask, to assail.]

1. Advice; opinion, or instruction, given upon request or otherwise, for directing the judgment or conduct of another; opinion given upon deliberation or consultation.

> Every purpose is established by *counsel.* Prov. xx.

> Thou hast not hearkened to my *counsel.* 2 Chron. xxv.

2. Consultation; interchange of opinions.

> We took sweet *counsel* together. Ps. lv.

3. Deliberation; examination of consequences.

> They all confess that, in the working of that first cause, *counsel* is used, reason followed, and a way observed. *Hooker.*

4. Prudence; deliberate opinion or judgment, or the faculty or habit of judging with caution.

> O how comely is the wisdom of old men, and understanding and *counsel* to men of honor. Ecclus. xxv.

> The law shall perish from the priest, and *counsel* from the ancients. Ezek. vii.

5. In *a bad sense,* evil advice or designs; art; machination.

> The *counsel* of the froward is carried headlong. Job v.

6. Secresy; the secrets entrusted in consultation; secret opinions or purposes. Let a man keep his own *counsel.*

7. In *a scriptural sense,* purpose; design; will; decree.

> What thy *counsel* determined before to be done. Acts iv.

> To show the immutability of his *counsel.* Heb. vi.

8. Directions of God's word.

> Thou shalt guide me by thy *counsel.* Ps. lxxiii.

9. The will of God or his truth and doctrines concerning the way of salvation.

> I have not shunned to declare to you all the *counsel* of God. Acts xx.

10. Those who give counsel in law; any counselor or advocate, or any number of counselors, barristers or serjeants; as the plaintiff's *counsel,* or the defendant's *counsel.* The attorney-general and solicitor-general are the king's *counsel.* In this sense, the word has no plural; but in the singular number, is applicable to one or more persons.

COUN'SEL, *v. t.* [L. *consilior.*] To give advice or deliberate opinion to another for the government of his conduct; to advise.

> I *counsel* thee to buy of me gold tried in the fire. Rev. iii.

2. To exhort, warn, admonish, or instruct. We ought frequently to *counsel* our children against the vices of the age.

> They that will not be *counseled,* cannot be helped. *Franklin.*

3. To advise or recommend; as, to *counsel* a crime. [*Not much used.*] *Dryden.*

COUN'SEL-KEEPER, *n.* One who can keep a secret. *Shak.*

COUN'SEL-KEEPING, *a.* Keeping secrets. *Shak.*

COUN'SELABLE, *a.* Willing to receive counsel; disposed to follow the advice or opinions of others. *Clarendon.*

COUN'SELED, *pp.* Advised; instructed; admonished.

COUN'SELING, *ppr.* Advising; instructing; admonishing.

COUN'SELOR, *n.* Any person who gives advice; but properly one who is authorized by natural relationship, or by birth, office or profession, to advise another in regard to his future conduct and measures. Ahithophel was David's *counselor.* His mother was his *counselor* to do wickedly. 2 Chron. xxii. In Great Britain, the peers of the realm are hereditary *counselors* of the crown.

2. The members of a counsel; one appointed to advise a king or chief magistrate, in regard to the administration of the government.

3. One who is consulted by a client in a law-case; one who gives advice in relation to a question of law; one whose profession is to give advice in law, and manage causes for clients.

Privy Counselor, a member of a privy counsel.

COUN'SELORSHIP, *n.* The office of a counselor, or privy counselor.

COUNT, *v. t.* [Fr. *conter;* It. *contare;* Sp. Port. *contar;* Arm. *counta* or *contein.* Qu. the root. The Fr. has *compter,* also, from the L. *computo;* the Sp. and Port. *computar,* and the It. *computare.* The Eng. *count* is directly from *conter;* and it may be a question whether *conter* and *contar* are from the L. *computo.*]

1. To number; to tell or name one by one, or by small numbers, for ascertaining the whole number of units in a collection; as, to *count* the years, days and hours of a man's life; to *count* the stars.

> Who can *count* the dust of Jacob? Numb. xxiii.

2. To reckon; to preserve a reckoning; to compute.

> Some tribes of rude nations *count* their years by the coming of certain birds among them at certain seasons, and leaving them at others. *Locke.*

3. To reckon; to place to an account; to ascribe or impute; to consider or esteem as belonging.

> Abraham believed in God, and he *counted* it to him for righteousness. Gen. xv.

4. To esteem; to account; to reckon; to think, judge or consider.

> I *count* them my enemies. Ps. cxxxix.

> Neither *count* I my life dear to myself. Acts xx.

> I *count* all things loss. Phil. iii.

5. To impute; to charge. *Rowe.*

COUNT, *v. i.* To *count on* or *upon,* to reckon upon; to found an account or scheme on; to rely on. We cannot *count on* the friendship of nations. *Count* not *on* the sincerity of sycophants.

COUNT. *n.* [Fr. *conte* and *compte;* Sp. *cuenta* and *cuento;* It. *conto.* The Spanish has also *computo,* and the It. *id.*]

1. Reckoning; the act of numbering; as, this is the number according to my *count.*

2. Number. *Spenser.*

3. In *law,* a particular charge in an indictment, or narration in pleading, setting forth the cause of complaint. There may

be different *counts* in the same declaration.

ȻOUNT, *n.* [Fr. *comte;* It. *conte;* Sp. *conde;* Port. *id.;* Arm. *condt;* from L. *comes, comitis,* a companion or associate, a fellow traveler. Qu. *con* and *eo.*]

A title of foreign nobility, equivalent to the English earl, and whose domain is a *county.* An earl; the alderman of a shire, as the Saxons called him. The titles of English nobility, according to their rank, are Duke, Marquis, *Earl,* Viscount, and Baron. *Blackstone. Encyc.*

ȻOUNT-WHEEL, *n.* The wheel in a clock which moves round and causes it to strike.

ȻOUNT'ABLE, *a.* That may be numbered. *Spenser.*

ȻOUNT'ED, *pp.* Numbered; told; esteemed; reckoned; imputed.

ȻOUN'TENANCE, *n.* [Fr. *contenance,* from *contenant,* containing, from *contenir,* to contain, L. *contineo; con* and *teneo,* to hold.]

1. Literally, the contents of a body; the outline and extent which constitutes the whole figure or external appearance. Appropriately, the human face; the whole form of the face, or system of features; visage.

A merry heart maketh a cheerful *countenance.* Prov. xv.

Be not, as the hypocrites, of a sad *countenance.* Matt. vi.

2. Air; look; aspect; appearance of the face; as in the phrase, to change or alter the *countenance.*

3. The face or look of a beast; as a horse of a good *countenance.*

4. Favor; good will; kindness.

Thou hast made him glad with thy *countenance.* Ps. xxi.

Hence in scriptural language, the *light of God's countenance* is his smiles or favorable regards, his favor and grace; and *to hide his face* or *countenance* is to manifest his displeasure, and withdraw his gracious aids. So the *rebuke of his countenance* indicates his anger and frowns. Ps. lxxx.

This application of face or *countenance,* which seems to be of high antiquity, proceeded probably from the practice of turning away the face to express anger, displeasure and refusal; a practice still common, but probably universal among rude nations. The opposite conduct would of course express favor. The grant of a petition is accompanied with a look directed to the petitioner; the refusal or denial, with an averted face. Hence,

5. Support; aid; patronage; encouragement; favor in promoting and maintaining a person or cause.

It is the province of the magistrate, to give *countenance* to piety and virtue. *Atterbury.*

Let religion enjoy the *countenance* of the laws.

Give no *countenance* to violations of moral duty.

5. Show; resemblance; superficial appearance.

The election being done, he made *countenance* of great discontent thereat. *Ascham.*

7. In *law,* credit or estimation. *Cowel.*

To keep the countenance, is to preserve a calm, composed or natural look, unruffled by passion; to refrain from expressing laughter, joy, anger or other passion, by an unchanged countenance.

In countenance, in favor; in estimation.

If the profession of religion were *in countenance* among men of distinction, it would have a happy effect on society.

To keep in countenance, to give assurance or courage to; to support; to aid by favor; to prevent from shame or dismay.

To put in countenance, to give assurance; to encourage; or to bring into favor; to support.

Out of countenance, confounded; abashed; with the countenance cast down; not bold or assured.

To put out of countenance, to cause the countenance to fall; to abash; to intimidate; to disconcert.

ȻOUN'TENANCE, *v. t.* To favor; to encourage by opinion or words.

The design was made known to the minister, but he said nothing to *countenance* it. *Anon.*

2. To aid; to support; to encourage; to abet; to vindicate; by any means.

Neither shalt thou *countenance* a poor man in his cause. Ex. xxiii.

3. To encourage; to appear in defense.

He *countenanced* the landing in his long boat. *Wotton.*

4. To make a show of.

Each to these ladies love did *countenance.* *Spenser.*

5. To keep an appearance. *Shak.*

ȻOUN'TENANCED, *pp.* Favored; encouraged; supported.

ȻOUN'TENANCER, *n.* One who countenances, favors or supports.

ȻOUN'TENANCING, *ppr.* Favoring; encouraging; supporting.

ȻOUNT'ER, *n.* [from *count.*] A false piece of money or stamped metal, used as means of reckoning; any thing used to keep an account or reckoning, as in games.

2. Money, in contempt. *Shak.*

3. A table or board on which money is counted; a table on which goods in a shop are laid for examination by purchasers.

In lieu of this, we sometimes see written the French *comptoir,* from *compter, computo;* but *counter* is the genuine orthography.

4. The name of certain prisons in London.

5. One that counts or reckons; also, an auditor.

6. Encounter. [*Not used.*]

7. In *ships,* an arch or vault, whose upper part is terminated by the bottom of the stern. The upper or second counter is above the former, but not vaulted.

Counter of a horse, that part of a horse's forehand which lies between the shoulder and under the neck. *Farrier's Dict.*

ȻOUN'TER, *adv.* [Fr. *contre;* L. *contra;* Sp. It. *contra;* probably a compound of *con* and *tra,* as in *extra, ultra.*]

1. Contrary; in opposition; in an opposite direction; used chiefly with *run* or *go;* as, to *run counter* to the rules of virtue; he *went counter* to his own interest.

2. The wrong way; contrary to the right course. *Shak.*

3. Contrariwise; in a contrary manner. *Locke.*

4. The face, or at the face. [*Not used.*] *Sandys.*

This word is prefixed to many others, chiefly verbs and nouns, expressing *opposition.*

ȻOUNTERAȻT', *v. t.* [*counter* and *act.*] To act in opposition to; to hinder, defeat or frustrate by contrary agency. Good precepts will sometimes *counteract* the effects of evil example; but more generally good precepts are *counteracted* by bad examples.

ȻOUNTERAȻT'ED, *pp.* Hindered; frustrated; defeated by contrary agency.

ȻOUNTERAȻT'ING, *ppr.* Hindering; frustrating.

ȻOUNTERAȻ'TION, *n.* Action in opposition; hindrance.

ȻOUNTER-ATTRAȻ'TION, *n.* [*counter* and *attraction.*] Opposite attraction. *Shenstone.*

ȻOUNTERBAL'ANCE, *v. t.* [*counter* and *balance.*]

To weigh against; to weigh against with an equal weight; to act against with equal power or effect; to countervail. A column of thirty inches of quicksilver, and a column of thirty-two feet of water, *counterbalance* the weight of a like column of the whole atmosphere. The pleasures of sin never *counterbalance* the pain, misery and shame which follow the commission of it.

ȻOUNTERBAL'ANCE, *n.* Equal weight, power or agency acting in opposition to any thing.

Money is the *counterbalance* of all things purchasable. *Locke.*

ȻOUNTERBAL'ANCED, *pp.* Opposed by equal weight, power or effect.

ȻOUNTERBAL'ANCING, *ppr.* Opposing by equal weight, power or operation.

ȻOUN'TERBOND, *n.* [*counter* and *bond.*] A bond to save harmless one who has given bond for another.

ȻOUNTERBUFF', *v. t.* [*counter* and *buff.*] To strike back or in an opposite direction; to drive back; to stop by a blow or impulse in front. *Dryden.*

ȻOUN'TERBUFF, *n.* A blow in an opposite direction; a stroke that stops motion or causes a recoil. *Sidney.*

ȻOUNTERBUFF'ED, *pp.* Struck with a blow in opposition.

ȻOUN'TERȻAST, *n.* Delusive contrivance; contrary cast. *Spenser.*

ȻOUN'TERȻASTER, *n.* [*counter* and *caster.*] A caster of accounts; a reckoner; a bookkeeper, in contempt. *Shak.*

ȻOUN'TERCHANĠE, *n.* [*counter* and *change.*] Exchange; reciprocation.

ȻOUNTERCHA'NĠE, *v. t.* To give and receive; or to cause to change places.

ȻOUNTERCHA'NĠED, *pp.* Exchanged. In *heraldry,* intermixed, as the colors of the field and charge.

ȻOUN'TERCHARM, *n.* [*counter* and *charm.*] That which has the power of dissolving or opposing the effect of a charm. *Pope.*

ȻOUNTERCH'ARM, *v. t.* To destroy the effect of enchantment.

ȻOUNTERCHECK', *v. t.* [*counter* and *check.*] To oppose or stop by some obstacle; to check.

ȻOUN'TERCHECK, *n.* Check; stop; rebuke; or a censure to check a reprover. *Bailey.*

COUNTERCUR'RENT, *a.* [*counter* and *current.*] Running in an opposite direction. *Kirwan.*

COUN'TERCURRENT, *n.* A current in an opposite direction.

COUNTERDISTINC'TION, *n.* Contradistinction. *More.*

COUNTERDRAW', *v. t.* [*counter* and *draw.*] In *painting*, to copy a design or painting, by means of a fine linen cloth, an oiled paper, or other transparent matter, whereon the strokes appearing through, they are traced with a pencil. The same is done on glass, and with frames or nets divided into squares with silk or thread, or by means of instruments, as the parallelogram. *Encyc.*

COUNTERDRAW'ING, *ppr.* Copying by means of lines drawn on some transparent matter.

COUNTERDRAW'N, *pp.* Copied from lines drawn on something else.

COUNTER-EV'IDENCE, *n.* [*counter* and *evidence.*] Opposite evidence; evidence or testimony which opposes other evidence. *Burnet.*

COUN'TERFEIT, *v. t.* coun'terfit. [Fr. *contrefaire*, *contrefait*; *contre* and *faire*, to make; L. *contra* and *facio*; It. *contraffare*, *contraffatto*; Sp. *contrahacer*, *contrahecho.*]

1. To forge; to copy or imitate, without authority or right, and with a view to deceive or defraud, by passing the copy or thing forged, for that which is original or genuine; as, to *counterfeit* coin, bank notes, a seal, a bond, a deed or other instrument in writing, the hand writing or signature of another, &c. To make a likeness or resemblance of any thing with a view to defraud.

2. To imitate; to copy; to make or put on a resemblance; as, to *counterfeit* the voice of another person; to *counterfeit* piety.

COUN'TERFEIT, *v. i.* To feign; to dissemble; to carry on a fiction or deception. *Shak.*

COUN'TERFEIT, *a.* Forged; fictitious; false; fabricated without right; made in imitation of something else, with a view to defraud, by passing the false copy for genuine or original; as *counterfeit* coin; a *counterfeit* bond or deed; a *counterfeit* bill of exchange.

2. Assuming the appearance of something; false; hypocritical; as a *counterfeit* friend.

3. Having the resemblance of; false; not genuine; as *counterfeit* modesty.

COUN'TERFEIT, *n.* A cheat; a deceitful person; one who pretends to be what he is not; one who personates another; an impostor.

2. In *law*, one who obtains money or goods by counterfeit letters or false tokens. *Encyc.*

3. That which is made in imitation of something, but without lawful authority, and with a view to defraud, by passing the false for the true. We say, the note is a *counterfeit.*

COUN'TERFEITED, *pp.* Forged; made in imitation of something, with a view to defraud; copied; imitated; feigned.

COUN'TERFEITER, *n.* One who counterfeits; a forger.

2. One who copies or imitates; one who assumes a false appearance.

3. One who endeavors to set off a thing in false colors.

COUN'TERFEITLY, *adv.* By forgery; falsely; fictitiously.

COUNTERFER'MENT, *n.* [*counter* and *ferment.*] Ferment opposed to ferment. *Addison.*

COUNTERFE'SANCE, *n.* [Fr. *contrefaisance.*] The act of forging; forgery. *Obs.*

COUN'TERFOIL, } *n.* That part of a tal-
COUN'TERSTOCK, } ly struck in the Exchequer, which is kept by an officer in that court, the other being delivered to the person who has lent the king money on the account, and is called the *stock.* *Bailey.*

COUN'TERFORT, *n.* [*counter* and *fort.*] A buttress, spur or pillar serving to support a wall or terrace subject to bulge. *Chambers.*

COUN'TERGAGE, *n.* [*counter* and *gage.*] In *carpentry*, a method used to measure the joints, by transferring the breadth of a mortise to the place where the tenon is to be, in order to make them fit each other. *Chambers.*

COUN'TERGUARD, *n.* [*counter* and *guard.*] In *fortification*, a small rampart or work raised before the point of a bastion, consisting of two long faces parallel to the faces of the bastion, making a salient angle, to preserve the bastion. It is sometimes of a different shape, or differently situated. *Encyc.*

COUNTER-IN'FLUENCE, *v. t.* To hinder by opposing influence. [*Little used.*] *Scott.*

COUN'TERLIGHT, *n.* [*counter* and *light.*] A light opposite to any thing, which makes it appear to disadvantage. *Chambers.*

COUNTERM'AND, *v. t.* [Fr. *contremander*; *contre* and *mander*, L. *mando*, to command.]

1. To revoke a former command; or to give an order contrary to one before given, which annuls a former command and forbids its execution; as, to *countermand* orders.

2. To oppose; to contradict the orders of another. *Hooker.*

3. To prohibit. [*Little used.*] *Harvey.*

COUN'TERMAND, *n.* A contrary order; revocation of a former order or command. *Shak.*

COUNTERM'ANDED, *pp.* Revoked; annulled, as an order.

COUNTERM'ANDING, *ppr.* Revoking a former order; giving directions contrary to a former command.

COUNTERM'ARCH, *v. i.* [*counter* and *march.*] To march back.

COUN'TERMARCH, *n.* A marching back; a returning. *Collier.*

2. A change of the wings or face of a battalion, so as to bring the right to the left or the front into the rear. *Cyc.*

3. A change of measures; alteration of conduct. *Burnet.*

COUN'TERMARK, *n.* [*counter* and *mark.*] A second or third mark put on a bale of goods belonging to several merchants, that it may not be opened, but in the presence of all the owners.

2. The mark of the goldsmiths' company, to show the metal to be standard, added to that of the artificer.

3. An artificial cavity made in the teeth of horses, that have outgrown their natural mark, to disguise their age.

4. A mark added to a medal, a long time after it has been struck, by which its several changes of value may be known. *Chambers.*

COUNTERM'ARK, *v. t.* To mark the corner teeth of a horse by an artificial cavity, to disguise his age. *Farrier's Dict.*

COUN'TERMINE, *n.* [*counter* and *mine.*] In *military affairs*, a well and gallery sunk in the earth and running under ground, in search of the enemy's mine, or till it meets it, to defeat its effect. *Military Dict.*

2. Means of opposition or counteraction. *Sidney.*

3. A stratagem or project to frustrate any contrivance. *L' Estrange.*

COUNTERMI'NE, *v. t.* To sink a well and gallery in the earth, in search of an enemy's mine, to frustrate his designs.

2. To counterwork; to frustrate by secret and opposite measures.

COUN'TER-MOTION, *n.* [*counter* and *motion.*] An opposite motion; a motion counteracting another. *Digby. Collier.*

COUN'TER-MÖVEMENT, *n.* A movement in opposition to another.

COUN'TERMURE, *n.* [Fr. *contremur*; *contre* and *mur*, L. *murus*, a wall.] A wall raised behind another, to supply its place, when a breach is made.

COUN'TERMURE, *n.* To fortify with a wall behind another.

COUNTER-NATURAL, *a.* [*counter* and *natural.*] Contrary to nature. *Harvey.*

COUNTER-NEGOTIA'TION, *n.* [*counter* and *negotiation.*] Negotiation in opposition to other negotiation.

COUN'TERNOISE, *n.* [*counter* and *noise.*] A noise or sound by which another noise or sound is overpowered. *Calamy.*

COUNTER-O'PENING, *n.* [*counter* and *opening.*] An aperture or vent on the opposite side, or in a different place. *Sharp.*

COUN'TERPACE, *n.* [*counter* and *pace.*] A step or measure in opposition to another; contrary measure or attempt. *Swift.*

COUN'TERPALED, *a.* [*counter* and *pale.*] In *heraldry*, is when the escutcheon is divided into twelve pales parted perfesse, the two colors being counterchanged; so that the upper and lower are of different colors. *Encyc.*

COUN'TERPANE, *n.* A particular kind of coverlet for a bed. [See *Counterpoint.*]

2. One part of an indenture. *Obs.* *B. Jonson.*

COUN'TERPART, *n.* [*counter* and *part.*] The correspondent part; the part that answers to another, as the two papers of a contract or indentures; a copy; a duplicate. Also, the part which fits another, as the key of a cipher. *Addison. Johnson.*

2. In *music*, the part to be applied to another; as, the base is the *counterpart* to the treble. *Bailey. Encyc.*

COUNTERPAS'SANT, *a.* [*counter* and *passant.*] In *heraldry*, is when two lions in a coat of arms are represented as going contrary ways. *Bailey. Encyc.*

COUNTER-PETI''TION, *n.* A petition in opposition to another. *Clarendon.*

ȻOUN'TERPLEA, *n.* [*counter* and *plea.*] In *law*, a replication to a plea, or request. *Cowel.*

ȻOUNTERPLOT', *v. t.* [*counter* and *plot.*] To oppose one plot to another; to attempt to frustrate stratagem by stratagem.

ȻOUN'TERPLOT, *n.* A plot or artifice opposed to another. *L'Estrange.*

ȻOUN'TERPLOTTING, *n.* A plotting in opposition to a stratagem.

ȻOUN'TERPOINT, *n.* [Fr. *contrepointe;* Arm. *contrepoentenn; contre* and *point.*]

1. A coverlet; a cover for a bed, stitched or woven in squares; written corruptly *counterpane.*
2. In *music*, counterpoint is when the musical characters by which the notes in each part are signified, are placed in such a manner, each with respect to each, as to show how the parts answer one to another. Hence counterpoint in composition is the art of combining and modulating consonant sounds. *Encyc. Busby.*
3. An opposite point. *Sandys.*

ȻOUN'TERPOISE, *v. t. s* as *z.* [Fr. *contrepeser;* It. *contrappesare;* Sp. *contrapesar; contre, contra,* and *peser, pesar,* to weigh. See *Poise.*]

1. To counterbalance; to weigh against with equal weight; to be equiponderant to; to equal in weight.

The force and distance of weights *counterpoising* each other, ought to be reciprocal. *Digby.*

The heaviness of bodies must be *counterpoised* by a plummet fastened about the pulley to the axis. *Wilkins.*

2. To act against with equal power or effect; to balance. The wisdom of the senate may be able to *counterpoise* the rash impetuosity of a democratic house.

ȻOUN'TERPOISE, *n.* [Fr. *contrepoids;* It. *contrappeso;* Sp. *contrapeso.*]

1. Equal weight acting in opposition to something; equiponderance; a weight sufficient to balance another in the opposite scale; equal balance. *Milton.*
2. Equal power or force acting in opposition; a force sufficient to balance another force; equipollence.

The second nobles are a *counterpoise* to the higher nobility. *Bacon.*

3. In *the manege*, a position of the rider in which his body is duly balanced in his seat, not inclined more to one side than the other. *Encyc.*

ȻOUN'TERPOISED, *pp.* Balanced by an equivalent opposing weight, or by equal power.

ȻOUN'TERPOISING, *ppr.* Balancing by equal weight in the opposite scale, or by equal power.

ȻOUN'TERPOISON, *n. s* as *z.* [*counter* and *poison.*] One poison that destroys the effect of another; an antidote; a medicine that obviates the effects of poison. *Arbuthnot.*

ȻOUNTERPRAC'TICE, *n.* Practice in opposition to another.

ȻOUNTERPRESS'URE, *n.* [*counter* and *pressure.*] Opposing pressure; a force or pressure that acts in a contrary direction. *Blackmore.*

ȻOUN'TERPROJEȻT, *n.* [*counter* and *project.*]

A project, scheme or proposal, of one party, given in opposition to another, before given by the other party; as in the negotiation of a treaty. *Swift.*

ȻOUN'TERPROOF, *n.* [*counter* and *proof.*] In *rolling-press printing*, a print taken off from another fresh printed, which, by being passed through the press, gives the figure of the former, but inverted. *Encyc.*

ȻOUN'TERPRÖVE, *v. t.* [*counter* and *prove.*]

To take off a design in black lead or red chalk, by passing it through a rolling-press with another piece of paper, both being moistened with a spunge. *Chambers.*

ȻOUNTER-REVOLU'TION, *n.* A revolution opposed to a former one, and restoring a former state of things.

ȻOUNTER-REVOLU'TIONARY, *a.* Pertaining to a counter-revolution.

ȻOUNTER-REVOLU'TIONIST, *n.* One engaged in or befriending a counter-revolution.

ȻOUN'TERROLL, *n.* [*counter* and *roll.*] In *law*, a counterpart or copy of the rolls, relating to appeals, inquests, &c. *Bailey.*

2. As a verb, this word is contracted into *control*, which see.

ȻOUNTERRO'LMENT, *n.* A counter account. [See *Control.*]

ȻOUNTER-SA'LIANT, *a.* [Fr. *contre* and *saillir*, to leap.]

In *heraldry*, is when two beasts are borne in a coat leaping from each other. *Bailey.*

ȻOUN'TERSȻARP, *n.* [Fr. *contrescarpe;* It. *contrascarpa;* Sp. *contraescarpa; contre* and *escarpe, scarpa, escarpa,* a slope, from the root of *carve.*]

In *fortification*, the exterior talus or slope of the ditch, or the talus that supports the earth of the covered way; but it often signifies the whole covered way, with its parapet and glacis; as when it is said, the enemy have lodged themselves on the *counterscarp.* *Harris. Encyc.*

ȻOUN'TERSȻUFFLE, *n.* Opposite scuffle; contest.

ȻOUN'TERSEAL, *v. t.* To seal with another. *Shak.*

ȻOUNTER-SEȻU'RE, *v. t.* [*counter* and *secure.*] To secure one who has given security.

ȻOUNTER-SEȻU'RITY, *n.* Security given to one who has entered into bonds or become surety for another. *Bailey.*

ȻOUN'TERSENSE, *n.* Opposite meaning. *Howell.*

ȻOUN'TERSIGN, *v. t.* [*counter* and *sign.*] Literally, to sign on the opposite side of an instrument or writing; hence, to sign, as secretary or other subordinate officer, a writing signed by a principal or superior, to attest the authenticity of the writing. Thus charters signed by a king are *countersigned* by a secretary. Bank notes signed by the president are *countersigned* by the cashier.

ȻOUN'TERSIGN, *n.* A private signal, word or phrase, given to soldiers on guard, with orders to let no man pass unless he first names that sign; a military watchword. Advance and give the *countersign.*

ȻOUN'TERSIGNAL, *n.* A signal to answer or correspond to another; *a naval term.*

ȻOUNTER-SIG'NATURE, *n.* The name of a secretary or other subordinate officer, countersigned to a writing.

Below the Imperial name is commonly a *countersignature* of one of the cabinet ministers. *Tooke.*

ȻOUN'TERSIGNED, *pp.* Signed by a secretary or other subordinate officer.

ȻOUN'TERSIGNING, *ppr.* Attesting by the signature of a subordinate officer.

ȻOUNTERSTAT'UTE, *n.* A contrary statute, or ordinance. *Milton.*

ȻOUN'TERSTROKE, *n.* A contrary stroke; a stroke returned. *Spenser.*

ȻOUNTER-SU'RETY, *n.* A counterbond, or a surety to secure one that has given security.

ȻOUN'TERSWAY, *n.* Contrary sway; opposite influence. *Milton.*

ȻOUN'TERTALLY, *n.* A tally corresponding to another.

ȻOUN'TERTASTE, *n.* [*counter* and *taste.*] Opposite or false taste. *Shenstone.*

ȻOUNTERTEN'OR, ȻOUN'TER, } *n.* [*counter* and *tenor.*] In *music*, one of the middle parts, between the tenor and the treble; high tenor.

ȻOUN'TERTIDE, *n.* [*counter* and *tide.*] Contrary tide. *Dryden.*

ȻOUN'TERTIME, *n.* [*counter* and *time.*] In *the manege*, the defense or resistance of a horse that interrupts his cadence and the measure of his manege, occasioned by a bad horseman or the bad temper of the horse. *Encyc.*

2. Resistance; opposition. *Dryden.*

ȻOUN'TERTURN, *n.* The highth of a play, which puts an end to expectation. *Dryden.*

ȻOUNTERVA'IL, *v. t.* [*counter* and L. *valeo*, to avail or be strong.]

To act against with equal force, or power; to equal; to act with equivalent effect against any thing; to balance; to compensate.

The profit will hardly *countervail* the inconveniences.

Although the enemy could not *countervail* the king's damage. Esth. vii.

ȻOUN'TERVAIL, *n.* Equal weight or strength; power or value sufficient to obviate any effect; equal weight or value; compensation; requital. *Spenser. South.*

ȻOUNTERVA'ILED, *pp.* Acted against with equal force or power; balanced; compensated.

ȻOUNTERVA'ILING, *ppr.* Opposing with equal strength or value; balancing; obviating an effect.

ȻOUN'TERVIEW, *n.* [*counter* and *view.*] An opposite or opposing view; opposition; a posture in which two persons front each other. *Milton.*

2. Contrast; a position in which two dissimilar things illustrate each other by opposition. *Swift.*

ȻOUN'TERVOTE, *v. t.* To vote in opposition; to outvote. *Scott.*

ȻOUN'TERWEIGH, *v. t.* [See *Weigh.*] To weigh against; to counterbalance. *Ascham.*

ȻOUN'TERWHEEL, *v. t.* To cause to wheel in an opposite direction.

ȻOUN'TERWIND, *n.* Contrary wind.

ȻOUNTERWORK'. [See *Work.*] To work

in opposition to; to counteract; to hinder any effect by contrary operations.

That *counterworks* each folly and caprice. *Pope.*

COUNTERWROUGHT, *pp.* *counterraut′.* Counteracted; opposed by contrary action.

COUNT′ESS, *n.* [Fr. *comtesse;* It. *contessa;* Sp. *condesa.* See *Count.*] The consort of an earl or count.

COUNT′ING-HOUSE, } *n.* [See *Count*, the
COUNT′ING-ROOM, } verb.]
The house or room appropriated by merchants, traders and manufacturers to the business of keeping their books, accounts, letters and papers.

COUNT′LESS, *a.* [*count* and *less.*] That cannot be counted; not having the number ascertained, nor ascertainable; innumerable. The sands of the sea-shore are *countless.*

COUN′TRY, *n.* *kun′try.* [The correct orthography would be *contry*, Fr. *contrée*, It. *contrada*, contracted from L. *conterra*, *con* and *terra*, land adjacent to a city. Hence the citizen says, let us go into the *country.* The Latin has *conterraneus*, a countryman.]

1. Properly, the land lying about or near a city; the territory situated in the vicinity of a city. Our friend has a seat in the *country*, a few miles from town. See Mark v. Luke viii. Hence,

2. The whole territory of a kingdom or state, as opposed to city. We say, the gentleman has a seat in the *country*, at any distance from town indefinitely. Hence,

3. Any tract of land, or inhabited land; any region, as distinguished from other regions; a kingdom, state or lesser district. We speak of all the *countries* of Europe or Asia.

And they came into the *country* of Moab. Ruth i.

4. The kingdom, state or territory in which one is born; the land of nativity; or the particular district indefinitely in which one is born. America is my *country*, or Connecticut is my *country.*

Laban said, it must not be so done in our *country.* Gen. xxix.

5. The region in which one resides.

He sojourned in the land of promise, as in a strange *country.* Heb. xi.

6. Land, as opposed to water; or inhabited territory.

The shipmen deemed that they drew near to some *country.* Acts xxvii.

5. The inhabitants of a region.

All the *country* wept with a loud voice. 2 Sam. xv.

8. A place of residence; a region of permanent habitation.

They declare plainly that they seek a *country.* Heb. xi.

They desire a better *country*, a heavenly. Heb. xi.

9. In *law*, a jury or jurors; as, trial by the *country*, per pais.

COUN′TRY, *a.* Pertaining to the country or territory at a distance from a city; rural; rustic; as a *country* town; a *country* seat; a *country* squire; a *country* life; the *country* party, as opposed to *city* party.

2. Pertaining or peculiar to one's own country.

He spoke in his *country* language. *Maccabees.*

3. Rude; ignorant. *Dryden.*

Country-dance, an erroneous orthography. [See *Contra-dance.*]

COUN′TRYMAN, *n.* One born in the same country with another. This man is my *countryman.* [See 2 Cor. xi. 26.]

2. One who dwells in the country, as opposed to a citizen; a rustic; a farmer or husbandman; a man of plain unpolished manners.

3. An inhabitant or native of a region. What *countryman* is he?

COUN′TY, *n.* [Fr. *comté;* Sp. *condado;* It. *contéa;* L. *comitatus.* See *Count.*]

1. Originally, an earldom; the district or territory of a count or earl. Now, a circuit or particular portion of a state or kingdom, separated from the rest of the territory, for certain purposes in the administration of justice. It is called also a *shire.* [See *Shire.*] Each county has its sheriff and its court, with other officers employed in the administration of justice and the execution of the laws. In England there are fifty two counties, and in each is a Lord Lieutenant, who has command of the militia. The several states of America are divided by law into counties, in each of which is a county court of inferior jurisdiction; and in each, the supreme court of the state holds stated sessions.

2. A count; an earl or lord. *Obs.* *Shak.*

County court, the court whose jurisdiction is limited to a county, whose powers, in America, depend on statutes. In England, it is incident to the jurisdiction of the sheriff.

County palatine, in England, is a county distinguished by particular privileges; so called *a palatio*, the palace, because the owner had originally royal powers, or the same powers in the administration of justice, as the king had in his palace; but their powers are now abridged. The counties palatine, in England, are Lancaster, Chester and Durham.

County corporate, is a county invested with particular privileges by charter or royal grant; as London, York, Bristol, &c.

COUN′TY, *a.* Pertaining to a county; as *county* court.

COUPEE′, *n.* [Fr. *couper*, to cut.] A motion in dancing, when one leg is a little bent and suspended from the ground, and with the other a motion is made forward. *Chambers.*

COUP′LE, *n.* *kup′pl.* [Fr. *couple;* L. *copula;* It. Sp. *id.;* Arm. *couble;* D. *koppel;* G. *kuppel;* Sw. *koppel;* Dan. *kobbel;* Heb. כפל; Ch. id. and קפל to double or fold; Syr. id.; Sam. to shut.]

1. Two of the same species or kind, and near in place, or considered together; as a *couple* of men; a *couple* of oranges. I have planted a *couple* of cherry trees. We cannot call a horse and an ox a *couple*, unless we add a generic term. Of a horse and ox feeding in a pasture, we should say, a *couple of animals.* Among huntsmen and soldiers, *brace* is used for couple; as a *brace* of ducks; a *brace* of pistols. *Couple* differs from *pair*, which implies strictly, not only things of the same kind, but likeness, equality or customary association. A *pair* is a *couple;* but a *couple* may or may not be a *pair.*

2. Two things of any kind connected or linked together.

3. A male and a female connected by marriage, betrothed or allied; as a married *couple;* a young *couple.*

4. That which links or connects two things together; a chain.

COUP′LE, *v. t.* [Fr. *coupler;* L. *copulo;* Sp. *copular;* It. *copulare.*]

1. To link, chain or connect one thing with another; to sew or fasten together.

Thou shalt *couple* the curtains with taches. Ex. xxvi.

2. To marry; to wed; to unite, as husband and wife. *Swift.*

COUP′LE, *v. i.* To embrace, as the sexes. *Dryden.*

COUP′LED, *pp.* United, as two things; linked; married.

COUP′LEMENT, *n.* Union. *Spenser.*

COUP′LET, *n.* *cup′plet.* [Fr.] Two verses; a pair of rhymes.

2. A division of a hymn or ode in which an equal number or equal measure of verses is found in each part, called a *strophe.*

3. A pair; as a *couplet* of doves. [*Not used.*] *Shak.*

COUP′LING, *ppr.* Uniting in couples; fastening or connecting together; embracing.

COUP′LING, *n.* That which couples or connects. 2 Chron. xxxiv.

2. The act of coupling.

COUR′AGE, *n.* *kur′rage.* [Fr. from *cœur*, L. *cor*, the heart; Arm. *couraich;* Sp. *corage;* Port. *coragem;* It. *coraggio.*]

Bravery; intrepidity; that quality of mind which enables men to encounter danger and difficulties with firmness, or without fear or depression of spirits; valor; boldness; resolution. It is a constituent part of *fortitude;* but fortitude implies patience to bear continued suffering.

Courage that grows from constitution, often forsakes a man when he has occasion for it; *courage* which arises from a sense of duty, acts in a uniform manner. *Addison.*

Be strong, and of good *courage.* Deut. xxxi.

COURA′GEOUS, *a.* Brave; bold; daring; intrepid; hardy to encounter difficulties and dangers; adventurous; enterprising.

Be thou strong and *courageous.* Josh. i.

COURA′GEOUSLY, *adv.* With courage; bravely; boldly; stoutly.

COURA′GEOUSNESS, *n.* Courage; boldness; bravery; intrepidity; spirit; valor.

COURANT′, } *n.* [Fr. *courante*, running.]
COURAN′TO, } A piece of music in triple time; also, a kind of dance, consisting of a time, a step, a balance and a coupee. *Encyc.*

2. The title of a newspaper.

COURAP′, *n.* A distemper in the East Indies; a kind of herpes or itch in the arm-pits, groin, breast and face. *Encyc.*

COURB, *v. i.* [Fr. *courber.*] To bend. [*Not in use.*]

COURB, *a.* Crooked. [*Not in use.*]

COURBARIL, *n.* Gum anime, which flows from the Hymenæa, a tree of South America; used for varnishing. *Fourcroy.*

COUR′IER, *n.* [Fr. *courier*, from *courir*, to run, L. *curro.*]

A messenger sent express, for conveying letters or dispatches on public business.

COURSE, *n.* [Fr. *course*; Sp. *curso*; It. *corso*; Ir. *cursa*; from L. *cursus*, from *curro*, to run, W. *gyru*, Eng. *hurry*. See Class Gr. No. 7. 15. 32. 34.]

1. In *its general sense*, a passing; a moving, or motion forward, in a direct or curving line; applicable to any body or substance, solid or fluid.

Applied to animals, a running, or walking; a race; a career; a passing, or passage, with any degree of swiftness indefinitely.

Applied to fluids, a flowing, as in a stream in any direction; as a straight *course*, or winding *course*. It is applied to water or other liquids, to air or wind, and to light, in the sense of motion or passing.

Applied to solid bodies, it signifies motion or passing; as the *course* of a rolling stone; the *course* of a carriage; the *course* of the earth in its orbit.

Applied to navigation, it signifies a passing or motion on water, or in balloons in air; a voyage.

2. The direction of motion; line of advancing; point of compass, in which motion is directed; as, what *course* shall the pilot steer? In technical language, the angle contained between the nearest meridian and that point of compass on which a ship sails in any direction. *Mar. Dict.*
3. Ground on which a race is run.
4. A passing or process; the progress of any thing; as the *course* of an argument, or of a debate; a *course* of thought or reflexion.
5. Order of proceeding or of passing from an ancestor to an heir; as the *course* of descent in inheritance.
6. Order; turn; class; succession of one to another in office, or duty.

The chief fathers of every *course*. 1 Chron. xxvii.

Solomon appointed the *courses* of the priests. 2 Chron. viii.

7. Stated and orderly method of proceeding; usual manner. He obtained redress in due *course* of law. Leave nature to her *course*.
8. Series of successive and methodical procedure; a train of acts, or applications; as a *course* of medicine administered.
9. A methodical series, *applied to the arts or sciences*; a systemized order of principles in arts or sciences, for illustration or instruction. We say, the author has completed a *course* of principles or of lectures in philosophy. Also, the order pursued by a student; as, he has completed a *course* of studies in law or physics.
10. Manner of proceeding; way of life or conduct; deportment; series of actions.

That I might finish my *course* with joy. Acts xx.

Their *course* is evil. Jer. xxiii.

11. Line of conduct; manner of proceeding; as, we know not what *course* to pursue.
12. Natural bent; propensity; uncontrolled will. Let not a perverse child take his own *course*.
13. Tilt; act of running in the lists.
14. Orderly structure; system.

The tongue setteth on fire the *course* of nature. James iii.

15. Any regular series. In *architecture*, a continued range of stones, level or of the same highth, throughout the whole length of the building, and not interrupted by any aperture. A laying of bricks, &c.
16. The dishes set on table at one time; service of meat.
17. Regularity; order; regular succession; as, let the classes follow in *course*.
18. Empty form; as, compliments are often words of *course*.

Of course, by consequence; in regular or natural order; in the common manner of proceeding; without special direction or provision. This effect will follow *of course*. If the defendant resides not in the state, the cause is continued *of course*.

COURSES, *n. plu.* In a ship, the principal sails, as the main sail, fore sail, and mizen; sometimes the name is given to the stay sails on the lower masts; also to the main stay sails of all brigs and schooners. *Mar. Dict.*

2. Catamenia; menstrual flux.

COURSE, *v. t.* To hunt; to pursue; to chase.

We *coursed* him at the heels. *Shak.*

2. To cause to run; to force to move with speed. *May.*
3. To run through or over.

The blood *courses* the winding arteries.
The bounding steed *courses* the dusty plain.

COURSE, *v. i.* To run; to move with speed; to run or move about; as, the blood *courses*. *Shak.*

The grayhounds *coursed* through the fields.

COURSED, *pp.* Hunted; chased; pursued; caused to run.

COURSER, *n.* A swift horse; a runner; a war-horse; *a word used chiefly in poetry.* *Dryden. Pope.*

2. One who hunts; one who pursues the sport of coursing hares. *Johnson.*
3. A disputant. [*Not in use.*] *Wood.*

COURSEY, *n.* Part of the hatches in a galley. *Sherwood.*

COURSING, *ppr.* Hunting; chasing; running; flowing; compelling to run.

COURSING, *n.* The act or sport of chasing and hunting hares, foxes or deer.

COURT, *n.* [Sax. *curt*; Fr. *cour*; Arm. *court*; It. *corte*; Sp. *corte*; Port. *corte*; L. *curia*; Ir. *cuirt*. The primary sense and application are not perfectly obvious. Most probably the word is from a verb which signifies to go round, to collect. W. *cwr*, a circle; Ar. كَرَ to go round, to collect, to bind. Hence applied to a *yard* or inclosure. See Class Gr. No. 32. 34. It may possibly be allied to *yard*, Goth. *gards*; or it may be derived from a verb signifying to cut off or separate, and primarily signify the fence that *cuts off* or excludes access. The former is most probable.]

1. A place in front of a house, inclosed by a wall or fence; in popular language, a court-yard. *Bacon. Dryden.*
2. A space inclosed by houses, broader than a street; or a space forming a kind of recess from a public street.
3. A palace; the place of residence of a king or sovereign prince. *Europe.*
4. The hall, chamber or place where justice is administered.

St. Paul was brought into the highest *court* in Athens. *Atterbury.*

5. Persons who compose the retinue or council of a king or emperor. *Temple.*
6. The persons or judges assembled for hearing and deciding causes, civil, criminal, military, naval or ecclesiastical; as a *court* of law; a *court* of chancery; a *court* martial; a *court* of admiralty; an ecclesiastical *court*; *court* baron; &c. Hence,
7. Any jurisdiction, civil, military or ecclesiastical.
8. The art of pleasing; the art of insinuation; civility; flattery; address to gain favor. Hence the phrase, to *make court*, to attempt to please by flattery and address.
9. In *scripture*, an inclosed part of the entrance into a palace or house. The tabernacle had one *court*; the temple, three. The first was the court of the Gentiles; the second, the court of Israel, in which the people worshiped; the third was the court of the priests, where the priests and Levites exercised their ministry. Hence places of public worship are called the *courts of the Lord*.
10. In *the U. States*, a legislature consisting of two houses; as the *General Court* of Massachusetts. The original constitution of Connecticut established a *General Court* in 1639. *B. Trumbull.*
11. A session of the legislature.

COURT, *v. t.* In a general sense, to flatter; to endeavor to please by civilities and address; *a use of the word derived from the manners of a court.*

2. To woo; to solicit for marriage.

A thousand *court* you, though they *court* in vain. *Pope.*

3. To attempt to gain by address; to solicit; to seek; as, to *court* commendation or applause.

COURT-BAR'ON, *n.* A baron's court; a court incident to a manor. *Blackstone.*

COURT-BRED, *a.* [See *Breed.*] Bred at court. *Churchill.*

COURT-BREEDING, *n.* Education at a court. *Milton.*

COURT-BUBBLE, *n.* The trifle of a court. *Beaum.*

COURT-CHAPLAIN, *n.* A chaplain to a king or prince.

COURT-CUP'BOARD, *n.* The sideboard of ancient days. *Shak.*

COURT-DAY, *n.* A day in which a court sits to administer justice.

COURT-DRESS, *n.* A dress suitable for an appearance at court or levee.

COURT-DRESSER, *n.* A flatterer. *Locke.*

COURT-FASHION, *n.* The fashion of a court. *Fuller.*

COURT-FÄVOR, *n.* A favor or benefit bestowed by a court or prince. *L'Estrange.*

COURT-HAND, *n.* The hand or manner of writing used in records and judicial proceedings. *Shak.*

COURT-HOUSE, *n.* A house in which established courts are held, or a house appropriated to courts and public meetings. *America.*

COURT-LADY, *n.* A lady who attends or is conversant in court.

COURT-LEET, *n.* A court of record held once a year, in a particular hundred, lordship or manor, before the steward of the leet. *Blackstone.*

COURT-M'ARTIAL, *n.* A court consisting of military or naval officers, for the trial of offences of a military character.

COURTED, *pp.* Flattered; wooed; solicited in marriage; sought.

COURT'EOUS, *a. kurt'eous.* [from *court;* Fr. *courtois;* It. *cortese;* Sp. *cortes.*]

1. Polite; wellbred; being of elegant manners; civil; obliging; condescending; *applied to persons.*

2. Polite; civil; graceful; elegant; complaisant; *applied to manners,* &c.

COURT'EOUSLY, *adv.* In a courteous manner; with obliging civility and condescension; complaisantly.

COURT'EOUSNESS, *n.* Civility of manners; obliging condescension; complaisance.

COURTER, *n.* One who courts; one who solicits in marriage. *Sherwood.*

COURT'ESAN, *n. kurt'ezan.* [Fr. *courtisane;* Sp. *cortesana;* from *court.*]

A prostitute; a woman who prostitutes herself for hire, especially to men of rank.

COURT'ESY, *n. kurt'esy.* [Fr. *courtoisie;* Sp. It. *cortesia;* Port. *cortezia;* from Fr. *courtois,* Sp. *cortes,* courteous, from *court.*]

1. Elegance or politeness of manners; especially, politeness connected with kindness; civility; complaisance; as, the gentleman shows great *courtesy* to strangers; he treats his friends with great *courtesy.*

2. An act of civility or respect; an act of kindness or favor performed with politeness. *Shak. Bacon.*

3. The act of civility, respect or reverence, performed by a woman; a fall or inclination of the body, corresponding in design to the bow of a gentleman. *Dryden.*

4. A favor; as, to hold upon *courtesy,* that is, not of right, but by indulgence.

Tenure by courtesy or *curtesy,* is where a man marries a woman seized of an estate of inheritance, and has by her issue born alive, which was capable of inheriting her estate; in this case, on the death of his wife, he holds the lands for his life, as tenant by curtesy. *Blackstone.*

COURT'ESY, *v. i.* To perform an act of civility, respect or reverence, as a woman. Note. This word was formerly applied to the other sex; but is now used only of the acts of reverence or civility, performed by women.

COURT'ESY, *v. t.* To treat with civility. [*Not in use.*]

COURTIER, *n. ko'rtyur.* [from *court.*] A man who attends or frequents the courts of princes. *Bacon. Dryden.*

2. One who courts or solicits the favor of another; one who flatters to please; one who possesses the art of gaining favor by address and complaisance.

There was not among all our princes a greater *courtier* of the people than Richard III. *Suckling.*

COURTIERY, *n.* The manners of a courtier. [*Not used.*] *B. Jonson.*

COURTING, *ppr.* Flattering; attempting to gain by address; wooing; soliciting in marriage.

COURTLIKE, *a.* Polite; elegant. *Camden.*

COURTLINESS, *n.* [See *Courtly.*] Elegance of manners; grace of mien; civility; complaisance with dignity. *Digby.*

COURTLING, *n.* A courtier; a retainer to a court. *B. Jonson.*

COURTLY, *a.* [*court* and *like.*] Relating to a court; elegant; polite with dignity; *applied to men* and *manners;* flattering, *applied to language.* *Pope.*

COURTLY, *adv.* In the manner of courts; elegantly; in a flattering manner.

COURTSHIP, *n.* The act of soliciting favor. *Swift.*

2. The act of wooing in love; solicitation of a woman to marriage. *Dryden.*

3. Civility; elegance of manners. *Obs.* *Donne.*

COUSIN, *n. kuz'n.* [Fr. *cousin.* Qu. contracted from L. *consobrinus* or *consanguineus,* or is it allied to the Persian خويش related, kindred.]

1. In a general sense, one collaterally related more remotely than a brother or sister. But,

2. *Appropriately,* the son or daughter of an uncle or aunt; the children of brothers and sisters being usually denominated *cousins* or *cousin-germans.* In the second generation, they are called *second cousins.*

3. A title given by a king to a nobleman, particularly to those of the council. *Johnson.*

COUSIN, *a. kuz'n.* Allied. *Obs.* *Chaucer.*

COVE, *n.* [Sax. *cof, cofe,* an inner room, a den. Qu. Obs. L. *covum.* The Spanish has the word with the Arabic prefix, *alcoba,* an *alcove;* Port. *alcova;* It. *alcovo.* It may be allied to *cubby,* W. *cwb,* a hollow place, a cote or kennel; or to *cave,* Ar. قَبَّ to arch, or قَابَ to make hollow.]

A small inlet, creek or bay; a recess in the sea shore, where vessels and boats may sometimes be sheltered from the winds and waves.

COVE, *v. t.* To arch over; as a *coved* ceiling. *Swinburne.*

CO'VENABLE, *a.* [Old Fr.] Fit; suitable. *Obs.* *Wickliffe.*

COV'ENANT, *n.* [Fr. *convenant,* the participle of *convenir,* to agree, L. *convenio, con* and *venio,* to come; Norm. *conevence,* a covenant; It. *convenzione,* from L. *conventio.* Literally, a coming together; a meeting or agreement of minds.]

1. A mutual consent or agreement of two or more persons, to do or to forbear some act or thing; a contract; stipulation. A covenant is created by deed in writing, sealed and executed; or it may be implied in the contract. *Encyc. Blackstone.*

2. A writing containing the terms of agreement or contract between parties; or the clause of agreement in a deed containing the covenant.

3. In *theology,* the *covenant of works,* is that implied in the commands, prohibitions, and promises of God; the promise of God to man, that man's perfect obedience should entitle him to happiness. *This do, and live; that do, and die.*

The *covenant of redemption,* is the mutual agreement between the Father and Son, respecting the redemption of sinners by Christ.

The *covenant of grace,* is that by which God engages to bestow salvation on man, upon the condition that man shall believe in Christ and yield obedience to the terms of the gospel. *Cruden. Encyc.*

4. In *church affairs,* a solemn agreement between the members of a church, that they will walk together according to the precepts of the gospel, in brotherly affection.

COV'ENANT, *v. i.* To enter into a formal agreement; to stipulate; to bind one's self by contract. A *covenants with* B to convey to him a certain estate. When the terms are expressed, it has *for* before the thing or price.

They *covenanted with* him *for* thirty pieces of silver. Matth. xxvi.

COV'ENANT, *v. t.* To grant or promise by covenant.

COV'ENANTED, *pp.* Pledged or promised by covenant.

COVENANTEE', *n.* The person to whom a covenant is made. *Blackstone.*

COV'ENANTING, *ppr.* Making a covenant; stipulating.

COV'ENANTER, *n.* He who makes a covenant. *Blackstone.*

CO'VENOUS, } *a.* [See *Covin.*] Collusive;
CO'VINOUS, } fraudulent; deceitful; as a *covenous* lease of lands. *Bacon.*

COV'ER, *v. t.* [Fr. *couvrir;* Sp. Port. *cubrir;* It. *coprire;* Norm. *coverer* and *converer;* from L. *cooperio.*]

1. To overspread the surface of a thing with another substance; to lay or set over; as, to *cover* a table with a cloth, or a floor with a carpet.

The valleys are *covered* with corn. Ps. lxv.

The locusts shall *cover* the face of the earth. Ex. x.

2. To hide; to conceal by something overspread.

If I say, surely the darkness shall *cover* me— Ps. cxxxix.

3. To conceal by some intervening object; as, the enemy was *covered* from our sight by a forest.

4. To clothe; as, to *cover* with a robe or mantle; to *cover* nakedness. 1 Sam. xxviii. 14. Ex. xxviii. 42.

5. To overwhelm.

The waters *covered* the chariots and horsemen. Ex. xiv.

Let them be *covered* with reproach. Ps. lxxi.

6. To conceal from notice or punishment.

Charity shall *cover* the multitude of sins. 1 Pet. iv.

7. To conceal; to refrain from disclosing or confessing.

He that *covereth* his sin shall not prosper. Prov. xxviii.

8. To pardon or remit.

Blessed is he whose sin is *covered.* Ps. xxxii.

9. To vail, *applied to women.* 1 Cor. xi.

To wear a hat, *applied to men.* Be *covered,* sir.

10. To wrap, infold or envelop; as, to *cover* a package of goods.

11. To shelter; to protect; to defend. A squadron of horse *covered* the troops on the retreat.

And the soft wings of peace *cover* him around. *Cowley.*

12. To brood; to incubate; as, a hen *covering* her eggs. *Addison.*

13. To copulate with a female.
14. To equal, or be of equal extent; to be equivalent to; as, the receipts do not *cover* the expenses; *a mercantile use of the word.*
15. To disguise; to conceal hypocritically.
16. To include, embrace or comprehend. This land was *covered* by a mortgage. *Johnson's Rep.*

COV'ER, *n.* Any thing which is laid, set or spread over another thing; as the *cover* of a vessel; the *cover* of a bed.
2. Any thing which vails or conceals; a screen; disguise; superficial appearance. Affected gravity may serve as a *cover* for a deceitful heart.
3. Shelter; defense; protection. The troops fought under *cover* of the batteries.
4. Concealment and protection. The army advanced under *cover* of the night.
5. Shelter; retreat; in *hunting.*

COV'ERCHIEF, *n.* A covering for the head. *Obs.* *Chaucer.*

COV'ERCLE, *n.* [Fr.] A small cover; a lid.

COV'ERED, *pp.* Spread over; hid; concealed; clothed; vailed; having a hat on; wrapped; inclosed; sheltered; protected; disguised.

COV'ERING, *ppr.* Spreading over; laying over; concealing; vailing; clothing; wrapping; inclosing; protecting; disguising.

COV'ERING, *n.* That which covers, any thing spread or laid over another, whether for security or concealment.

Noah removed the *covering* of the ark. Gen. viii.

He spread a cloud for a *covering.* Ps. cv.

Destruction hath no *covering.* Job xxvi.

2. A cover; a lid.

Every open vessel that hath no *covering.* Numb. xix.

3. Clothing; raiment; garments; dress.

They cause the naked to lodge without clothing, that they have no *covering* in the cold. Job xxiv.

COV'ERLET, *n.* [*cover*, and Fr. *lit*, a bed.] The cover of a bed; a piece of furniture designed to be spread over all the other covering of a bed. *Dryden.*

COV'ER-SHAME, *n.* Something used to conceal infamy. *Dryden.*

COV'ERT, *a.* [Fr. *couvert*, participle of *couvrir*, to cover.]
1. Covered; hid; private; secret; concealed.

Whether of open war, or *covert* guile. *Milton.*

2. Disguised; insidious.
3. Sheltered; not open or exposed; as a *covert* alley, or place. *Bacon. Pope.*
4. Under cover, authority or protection; as a *feme-covert*, a married woman who is considered as being under the influence and protection of her husband.

COV'ERT, *n.* A covering, or covering place; a place which covers and shelters; a shelter; a defense.

A tabernacle—for a *covert* from storm and rain. Isa. iv.

I will trust in the *covert* of thy wings. Ps. lxi.

2. A thicket; a shady place, or a hiding place. 1 Sam. xxv. Job xxxviii.

COV'ERTLY, *adv.* Secretly; closely; in private; insidiously.

Among the poets, Persius *covertly* strikes at Nero. *Dryden.*

COV'ERTNESS, *n.* Secrecy; privacy.

COV'ERTURE, *n.* Covering; shelter; defense. *Milton. Bacon.*
2. In *law*, the state of a married woman, who is considered as under *cover*, or the power of her husband, and therefore called a *feme-covert*, or *femme-couvert.* The coverture of a woman disables her from making contracts to the prejudice of herself or husband, without his allowance or confirmation.

COV'ERT-WAY, *n.* In *fortification*, a space of ground level with the field, on the edge of the ditch, three or four fathoms broad, ranging quite round the half moons or other works, towards the country. It has a parapet raised on a level, together with its banquets and glacis. It is called also the corridor, and sometimes the counterscarp, because it is on the edge of the scarp. *Harris. Encyc.*

COV'ET, *v. t.* [Fr. *convoiter*, to covet; Norm. *coveitant*, covetous; *covetise*, greediness; W. *cybyz*, a covetous man; *cybyzu*, to covet. The Welsh word is pronounced *cybythu;* and *cy* has the power of *con*, and may be a contraction of it. The last constituent part of the word coincides in elements with the Latin *peto*, and more nearly with the Gr. ποθεω, to desire.]
1. To desire or wish for, with eagerness; to desire earnestly to obtain or possess; *in a good sense.*

Covet earnestly the best gifts. 1 Cor. xii.

2. To desire inordinately; to desire that which it is unlawful to obtain or possess; *in a bad sense.*

Thou shalt not *covet* thy neighbor's house, wife or servant. Ex. xx.

COV'ET, *v. i.* To have an earnest desire. 1 Tim. vi.

COV'ETABLE, *a.* That may be coveted.

COV'ETED, *pp.* Earnestly desired; greatly wished or longed for.

COV'ETING, *ppr.* Earnestly desiring or wishing for; desiring inordinately to obtain or possess.

COV'ETING, *n.* Inordinate desire. *Shak.*

COV'ETISE, *n.* Avarice. [*Not in use.*] *Spenser.*

COV'ETOUS, *a.* [Fr. *convoiteux.*] Very desirous; eager to obtain; *in a good sense;* as *covetous* of wisdom, virtue or learning. *Taylor. Shak.*
2. Inordinately desirous; excessively eager to obtain and possess; *directed to money or goods*, avaricious.

A bishop then must not be *covetous.* 1 Tim. iii.

COV'ETOUSLY, *adv.* With a strong or inordinate desire to obtain and possess; eagerly; avariciously.

COV'ETOUSNESS, *n.* A strong or inordinate desire of obtaining and possessing some supposed good; *usually in a bad sense, and applied to an inordinate desire of wealth or avarice.*

Out of the heart proceedeth *covetousness.* Mark vii.

Mortify your members—and *covetousness* which is idolatry. Col. iii.

2. Strong desire; eagerness. *Shak.*

COV'EY, *n.* [Fr. *couvée*, a brood; *couver*, to sit on or brood, to lurk or lie hid; It. *covare;* Sp. *cobijar*, to brood, to cover; L. *cubo, incubo.* See Class Gb. No. 14. 25. 31. 36. 88.]
1. A brood or hatch of birds; an old fowl with her brood of young. Hence, a small flock or number of fowls together; as a *covey* of partridges. *Addison.*
2. A company; a set.

CO'VIN, *n.* [Qu. Ar. غبن gabana, to defraud. More probably this word belongs to some verb in Gb. signifying to conceal, or to agree. In Norm. Fr. *covyne* is a secret place or meeting.]
In *law*, a collusive or deceitful agreement between two or more to prejudice a third person. *Encyc. Cowel.*

CO'VING, *n.* [See *Cove.*] In *building*, a term denoting an arch or arched projecture, as when houses are built so as to project over the ground-plot, and the turned projecture arched with timber, lathed and plastered. *Harris. Johnson.*

CO'VINOUS, *a.* Deceitful; collusive; fraudulent.

COW, *n.* plu. *cows;* old plu. *kine.* [Sax. *cu;* D. *koe;* G. *kuh;* Sw. *ko;* Dan. *koe;* L. *ceva;* Hindoo *gaj*, or *gou;* Pers. *koh;* Pahlavi, *gao;* Sans. *go*, a cow, and *gau*, an ox; *godama*, a cowherd.]
The female of the bovine genus of animals; a quadruped with cloven hoofs, whose milk furnishes an abundance of food and profit to the farmer.
Sea-cow, the Manatus, a species of the Trichechus. [See *Sea-cow.*]

COW, *v. t.* [Qu. Ice. *kufwa*, or *kuga*, to depress.] To depress with fear; to sink the spirits or courage; to oppress with habitual timidity. *Shak.*

COW'-BANE, *n.* [*cow* and *bane.*] A popular name of the *Æthusa cynapium.*

COW'HAGE, COW-ITCH, *n.* A leguminous plant of the genus *Dolichos*, a native of warm climates. It has a fibrous root and an herbaceous climbing stalk, with red papilionaceous flowers, and leguminous, coriaceous pods, crooked and covered with sharp hairs, which penetrate the skin, and cause an itching. *Encyc.*

COW'HERD, *n.* [See *Herd.*] One whose occupation is to tend cows.

COW'-HOUSE, *n.* A house or building in which cows are kept or stabled. *Mortimer.*

COW'-KEEPER, *n.* One whose business is to keep cows. *Broome.*

COW'-LEECH, *n.* [See *Leech.*] One who professes to heal the diseases of cows.

COW'-LEECHING, *n.* The act or art of healing the distempers of cows. *Mortimer.*

COW'-LICK, *n.* A tuft of hair that appears as if licked by a cow.

COW'-PARSNEP, *n.* A plant of the genus Heracleum.

COW'-PEN, *n.* A pen for cows.

COW'-POX, *n.* The vaccine disease.

COW'-QUAKES, *n.* Quaking grass, the Briza, a genus of plants.

COWSLIP, COW'S-LIP, *n.* A plant of the genus Primula, or primrose, of several varieties. The American cowslip belongs to the genus Dodecatheon; the Jerusalem and mountain cowslip, to the genus Pulmonaria.

COW'S'-LUNGWORT, *n.* A plant of the genus Verbascum.

COW'-WEED, *n.* A plant of the genus Chærophyllum, or chervil.

COW'-WHEAT, *n.* A plant of the genus Melampyrum.

COW'ARD, *n.* [Fr. *couard;* Arm. *couhard;* Sp. and Port. *cobarde.* The original French orthography was *culvert,* and it has been supposed to be from *culum vertere,* to turn the tail. This suggestion receives countenance from the corresponding word in Italian, *codardo, codardia,* which would seem to be from *coda,* the tail; and it derives confirmation from the use of the word in heraldry. In Welsh, it is *caçan, caçgi,* from the same root as L. *caco.*]

1. A person who wants courage to meet danger; a poltroon; a timid or pusillanimous man.

A *coward* does not always escape with disgrace, but sometimes loses his life. *South.*

2. In *heraldry,* a term given to a lion borne in the escutcheon with his tail doubled between his legs. *Encyc.*

COW'ARD, *a.* Destitute of courage; timid; base; as a *coward* wretch.

2. Proceeding from or expressive of fear, or timidity; as *coward* cry; *coward* joy. *Shak. Prior.*

COW'ARDICE, *n.* [Fr. *couardise;* Sp. *cobardia.*] Want of courage to face danger; timidity; pusillanimity; fear of exposing one's person to danger.

Cowardice alone is loss of fame. *Dryden.*

Did *cowardice;* did injustice ever save a sinking state. *Ames.*

COW'ARDLIKE, *a.* Resembling a coward; mean.

COW'ARDLINESS, *n.* Want of courage; timidity; cowardice.

COW'ARDLY, *a.* Wanting courage to face danger; timid; timorous; fearful; pusillanimous. *Bacon.*

2. Mean; base; befitting a coward; as a *cowardly* action.

3. Proceeding from fear of danger; as *cowardly* silence. *South.*

COW'ARDLY, *adv.* In the manner of a coward; meanly; basely. *Knolles.*

COW'ARDOUS, *a.* Cowardly. [*Not used.*] *Barret.*

COW'ARDSHIP, *n.* Cowardice. [*Not used.*] *Shak.*

COW'ER, *v. i.* [W. *cwrian,* to squat, or cower; *cwr,* a circle; G. *kauern.* See Class Gr. No. 32. 34. 37.]

To sink by bending the knees; to crouch; to squat; to stoop or sink downwards.

Our dame sits *cowering* o'er a kitchen fire. *Dryden.*

COW'ER, *v. t.* To cherish with care. [*Not used.*] *Spenser.*

COW'ISH, *a.* Timorous; fearful; cowardly. [*Little used.*] *Shak.*

COWL, *n.* [contracted from Sax. *cugle, cugele;* L. *cucullus;* Ir. *cochal;* Sp. *cogulla;* Port. *cogula, cucula.*]

1. A monk's hood, or habit, worn by the Bernardines and Benedictines. It is either white or black.

What differ more, you cry, than crown and *cowl?* *Pope.*

2. A vessel to be carried on a pole betwixt two persons, for the conveyance of water. *Johnson.*

COWL'-STAFF, *n.* A staff or pole on which a vessel is supported between two persons. *Suckling.*

COWL'ED, *a.* Wearing a cowl; hooded; in shape of a cowl, as a *cowled* leaf.

COW'LIKE, *a.* Resembling a cow. *Pope.*

CO-WŎRK'ER, *n.* One that works with another; a co-operator.

COW'RY, *n.* A small shell, the *Cypræa moneta,* used for coin in Africa and the East Indies.

COX'COMB, *n.* [*cock's comb.*] The top of the head. *Shak.*

2. The comb resembling that of a cock, which licensed fools wore formerly in their caps. *Shak.*

3. A fop; a vain showy fellow; a superficial pretender to knowledge or accomplishments. *Dryden. Pope.*

4. A kind of red flower; a name given to a species of Celosia, and some other plants.

COX'COMBLY, *a.* Like a coxcomb. [*Not used.*] *Beaum.*

COXCOM'ICAL, *a.* Foppish; vain; conceited; *a low word.*

COY, *a.* [Fr. *coi,* or *coy,* quiet, still, contracted probably from the L. *quietus* or its root, or from *cautus.*]

Modest; silent; reserved; not accessible; shy; not easily condescending to familiarity.

Like Daphne she, as lovely and as *coy.* *Waller.*

COY, *v. i.* To behave with reserve; to be silent or distant; to refrain from speech or free intercourse. *Dryden.*

2. To make difficulty; to be backward or unwilling; not freely to condescend. *Shak.*

3. To smooth or stroke. *Shak.*

COY, for *decoy,* to allure. [*Not in use.*] *Shak.*

COY'ISH, *a.* Somewhat coy, or reserved.

COY'LY, *adv.* With reserve; with disinclination to familiarity. *Chapman.*

COY'NESS, *n.* Reserve; unwillingness to become familiar; disposition to avoid free intercourse, by silence or retirement.

When the kind nymph would *coyness* feign,
And hides but to be found again. *Dryden.*

COYS'TREL, *n.* A species of degenerate hawk. *Dryden.*

COZ. A contraction of *cousin.* *Shak.*

CŎZ'EN, *v. t.* cuz'n. [Qu. Arm. *couçzyein, couchiein, concheza,* to cheat, or to waste and fritter away. In Russ. *koznodei* is a cheat. Qu. *chouse* and *cheat.*]

1. To cheat; to defraud.

He that suffers a government to be abused by carelessness and neglect, does the same thing with him that corruptly sets himself to *cozen* it. *L'Estrange.*

2. To deceive; to beguile.

Children may be *cozened* into a knowledge of the letters. *Locke.*

CŎZ'ENAĠE, *n.* Cheat; trick; fraud; deceit; artifice; the practice of cheating. *Dryden. Swift.*

CŎZ'ENED, *pp.* Cheated; defrauded; beguiled.

CŎZ'ENER, *n.* One who cheats, or defrauds.

CŎZ'ENING, *ppr.* Cheating; defrauding; beguiling.

CRAB, *n.* [Sax. *crabba* and *hrefen;* Sw. *krabba;* Dan. *krabbe, kræbs;* D. *krab, kreeft;* G. *krabbe, krebs;* Fr. *ecrevisse;* W. *crav,* claws; *cravanc,* a crab; *cravu,* to scratch; Gr. *καραβος;* L. *carabus.* It may be allied to the Ch. כרב kerabh, to plow, Eng. to *grave, engrave,* L. *scribo,* Gr. *γραφω,* literally, to *scrape* or scratch. See Class Rb. No. 30. 18. &c.]

1. A crustaceous fish, the cray-fish, Cancer, a genus containing numerous species. They have usually ten feet, two of which are furnished with claws; two eyes, pedunculated, elongated and movable. To this genus belong the lobster, the shrimp, &c.

2. A wild apple, or the tree producing it; so named from its rough taste.

3. A peevish morose person. *Johnson.*

4. A wooden engine with three claws for lanching ships and heaving them into the dock. *Phillips.*

5. A pillar used sometimes for the same purpose as a capstan. *Mar. Dict.*

6. Cancer, a sign in the zodiac.

Crab's claws, in the materia medica, the tips of the claws of the common crab; used as absorbents. *Encyc.*

Crab's eyes, in pharmacy, concretions formed in the stomach of the cray-fish. They are rounded on one side, and depressed and sinuated on the other, considerably heavy, moderately hard, and without smell. They are absorbent, discussive and diuretic. *Encyc.*

Crab-lice, small insects that stick fast to the skin.

CRAB, *a.* Sour; rough; austere. [Qu. *crab,* supra, or L. *acerbus.*]

CRAB'-APPLE, *n.* A wild apple. [See *Crab,* No. 2.]

CRAB'-GRASS, *n.* A genus of plants, the Digitaria. *Muhlenberg.*

CRAB'-TREE, *n.* The tree that bears crabs. *Shak.*

CRAB'-YAWS, *n.* The name of a disease in the West Indies, being a kind of ulcer on the soles of the feet, with hard callous lips. *Encyc.*

CRAB'BED, *a.* [from *crab.*] Rough; harsh; austere; sour; peevish; morose; cynical; *applied to the temper.* *Shak.*

2. Rough; harsh; *applied to things.*

3. Difficult; perplexing; as a *crabbed* author or subject. *Dryden.*

CRAB'BEDLY, *adv.* Peevishly; roughly; morosely; with perplexity. *Johnson.*

CRAB'BEDNESS, *n.* Roughness; harshness.

2. Sourness; peevishness; asperity.

3. Difficulty; perplexity.

CRAB'BY, *a.* Difficult. *Moxon.*

CRAB'ER, *n.* The water-rat. *Walton.*

CRACK, *v. t.* [Fr. *craquer;* D. *kraaken;* G. *krachen;* Dan. *krakker;* It. *croccare;* W. *rhecain;* Sp. *rajar;* Port. *rachar;* probably from the root of *break, wreck,* and coinciding with the Gr. *ερειχω, ρηγνυω;* also with Eng. *creak, croak.* The W. has also *crig,* a crack, from *rhig,* a notch. *Owen.* See Class Rg. No. 34.]

1. To rend, break, or burst into chinks; to break partially; to divide the parts a little from each other; as, to *crack* a board or a rock: or to break without an entire severance of the parts; as, to *crack* glass, or ice.

2. To break in pieces; as, to *crack* nuts.

3. To break with grief; to affect deeply; to pain; to torture; as, to *crack* the heart. We now use *break,* or *rend.* *Shak.*

4. To open and drink; as, to *crack* a bottle of wine. [*Low.*]

5. To thrust out, or cast with smartness; as, to *crack* a joke.
6. To snap; to make a sharp sudden noise; as, to *crack* a whip.
7. To break or destroy.
8. To impair the regular exercise of the intellectual faculties; to disorder; to make crazy; as, to *crack* the brain.

CRACK, *v. i.* To burst; to open in chinks; as, the earth *cracks* by frost: or to be marred without an opening; as, glass *cracks* by a sudden application of heat.
2. To fall to ruin, or to be impaired.

> The credit of the exchequer *cracks*, when little comes in and much goes out. [*Not elegant.*] *Dryden.*

3. To utter a loud or sharp sudden sound; as, the clouds *crack;* the whip *cracks.* *Shak.*
4. To boast; to brag; that is, to utter vain, pompous, blustering words; with *of.*

> The Ethiops *of* their sweet complexion *crack.* [*Not elegant.*] *Shak.*

CRACK, *n.* [Gr. ραγας.] A disruption; a chinkor fissure; a narrow breach; a crevice; a partial separation of the parts of a substance, with or without an opening; as a *crack* in timber, in a wall, or in glass.
2. A burst of sound; a sharp or loud sound, uttered suddenly or with vehemence; the sound of any thing suddenly rent; a violent report; as the *crack* of a falling house; the *crack* of a whip.
3. Change of voice in puberty. *Shak.*
4. Craziness of intellect; or a crazy person. *Addison.*
5. A boast, or boaster. [*Low.*]
6. Breach of chastity; and a prostitute. [*Low.*]
7. A lad; an instant. [*Not used.*]

CRACK'-BRAINED, *a.* Having intellects impaired; crazy.

CRACK'ED, *pp.* Burst or split; rent; broken; partially severed.
2. Impaired; crazy.

CRACK'ER, *n.* A noisy boasting fellow. *Shak.*
2. A rocket; a quantity of gunpowder confined so as to explode with noise.
3. A hard biscuit. *America.*
4. That which cracks any thing.

CRACK'-HEMP, } *n.* A wretch fated to the
CRACK'-ROPE, } gallows; one who deserves to be hanged. *Shak.*

CRACK'ING, *ppr.* Breaking or dividing partially; opening; impairing; snapping; uttering a sudden sharp or loud sound; boasting; casting jokes.

CRACK'LE, *v. i.* [dim. of *crack.*] To make slight cracks; to make small abrupt noises, rapidly or frequently repeated; to decrepitate; as, burning thorns *crackle.*

CRACK'LING, *ppr.* Making slight cracks, or abrupt noises.

CRACK'LING, *n.* The making of small abrupt cracks or reports, frequently repeated.

> The *crackling* of thorns under a pot. Eccles. vii.

CRACK'NEL, *n.* A hard brittle cake or biscuit. 1 Kings xiv. 3.

CRA'DLE, *n.* [Sax. *cradel;* W. *cryd*, a rocking or shaking, a cradle; *crydu*, to shake, or tremble; *crydian, crydiaw*, id.; from *rhyd*, a moving; Ir. *creatham*, to shake; Gr. χραδαω, id. and to swing; Heb. חרד, to tremble or shake, to palpitate; Syr. in Ethp., to rub or scrape. Without the first letter, W. *rhyd*, Heb. Ch. Eth. רעד to tremble, to shake. In Ar. رعد raada, to thunder, to impress terror, to tremble; and راد to run hither and thither, to move one way and the other, to tremble or shake. The Arabic رعد to thunder, coincides with the Latin *rudo*, to roar, and the W. *grydiaw*, to utter a rough sound, to shout, whoop or scream, *grydwst*, a murmur, from *gryd*, a shout or whoop, and this from *rhyd;* so that *crydiaw* and *grydiaw* are from the same root, and from this we have *cry*, and *cry* implies roughness, coinciding with the Syriac, supra, to scrape, whence *grate, gride*, &c. See Owen's Welsh Dictionary, and Castle's Heptaglot.]
1. A movable machine of various constructions, placed on circular pieces of board, for rocking children or infirm persons to sleep, for alleviating pain, or giving moderate exercise.

> Me let the tender office long engage,
> To rock the *cradle* of reposing age. *Pope.*

2. Infancy. *From the cradle*, is from the state of infancy; *in the cradle*, in a state of infancy.
3. That part of the stock of a cross-bow, where the bullet is put. *Encyc.*
4. In *surgery*, a case in which a broken leg is laid, after being set. *Encyc.*
5. In *ship-building*, a frame placed under the bottom of a ship for lanching. It supports the ship and slides down the timbers or passage called the *ways.* *Encyc.*
6. A standing bedstead for wounded seamen. *Mar. Dict.*
7. In *engraving*, an instrument, formed of steel, and resembling a chisel, with one sloping side, used in scraping mezzotintos, and preparing the plate. *Encyc.*
8. In *husbandry*, a frame of wood, with long bending teeth, to which is fastened a sythe, for cutting and laying oats and other grain in a swath.

CRA'DLE, *v. t.* To lay in a cradle; to rock in a cradle; to compose, or quiet.

> It *cradles* their fears to sleep. *D. A. Clark.*

2. To nurse in infancy. *D. Webster.*
3. To cut and lay with a cradle, as grain.

CRA'DLE, *v. i.* To lie or lodge in a cradle. *Shak.*

CRA'DLE-CLOTHES, *n.* The clothes used for covering one in a cradle.

CRA'DLED, *pp.* Laid or rocked in a cradle; cut and laid with a cradle, as grain.

CRA'DLING, *ppr.* Laying or rocking in a cradle; cutting and laying with a cradle, as grain.

CR'AFT, *n.* [Sax. *cræft*, art, cunning, power, force; G. Sw. Dan. *kraft*, power, faculty; W. *crev, cryv*, strong; *crevu*, to cry, to scream, to *crave; cryvau*, to strengthen, to wax strong; *craf*, a clasp; *crafu*, to hold, to comprehend, to perceive; *crafus*, of quick perception. The primary sense is to strain or stretch. Hence, strength, skill, a crying out, holding, &c.]
1. Art; ability; dexterity; skill.

> Poesy is the poet's skill or *craft* of making— *B. Jonson.*

2. Cunning, art or skill, in a bad sense, or applied to bad purposes; artifice; guile; skill or dexterity employed to effect purposes by deceit.

> The chief priests and scribes sought how they might take him by *craft*, and put him to death. Mark xiv.

3. Art; skill; dexterity in a particular manual occupation; hence, the occupation or employment itself; manual art; trade.

> Ye know that by this *craft* we have our wealth. Acts xix.

4. All sorts of vessels employed in loading or unloading ships, as lighters, hoys, barges, scows, &c.

Small craft is a term given to small vessels of all hinds, as sloops, schooners, cutters, &c.

CR'AFT, *v. i.* To play tricks. [*Not in use.*] *Shak.*

CR'AFTILY, *adv.* [See *Crafty.*] With craft, cunning or guile; artfully; cunningly; with more art than honesty.

CR'AFTINESS, *n.* Artfulness; dexterity in devising and effecting a purpose; cunning; artifice; stratagem.

> He taketh the wise in their own *craftiness.* Job v.
>
> Not walking in *craftiness*, nor handling the word of God deceitfully. 2 Cor. iv.

CR'AFTSMAN, *n.* An artificer; a mechanic; one skilled in a manual occupation.

CR'AFTSMASTER, *n.* One skilled in his craft or trade.

CR'AFTY, *a.* Cunning; artful; skilful in devising and pursuing a scheme, by deceiving others, or by taking advantage of their ignorance; wily; sly; fraudulent.

> He disappointeth the devices of the *crafty.* Job v.

2. Artful; cunning; in a good sense, or in a laudable pursuit.

> Being *crafty*, I caught you with guile. 2 Cor. xii.

CRAG, *n.* [W. Scot. Ir. *craig;* Gaelic, *creag;* Corn. *karak;* Arm. *garrecq;* probably Gr. ραχια, ραχις, from the root of ρηγνυω, to break, like *rupes*, in Latin, from the root of *rumpo, rupi*, and *crepido*, from *crepo.* See *Crack.* The name is taken from *breaking*, L. *frango*, for *frago;* and *fragosus*, and *craggy*, are the same word with different prefixes; Eng. *ragged.* The Κραγος in Cilicia, mentioned by Strabo and Pliny, retains the Celtic orthography.]
A steep rugged rock; a rough broken rock, or point of a rock.

CRAG, *n.* [Sax. *hracca*, the neck; Scot. *crag*, or *craig;* Gr. ραχις. The same word probably as the preceding, from its roughness, or break. We now call it *rack.*]
The neck, formerly applied to the neck of a human being, as in Spenser. We now apply it to the neck or neck-piece of mutton, and call it a *rack* of mutton.

CRAG'GED, *a.* Full of crags or broken rocks; rough; rugged; abounding with prominences, points and inequalities.

CRAG'GEDNESS, *n.* The state of abounding with crags, or broken, pointed rocks.

CRAG'GINESS, *n.* The state of being craggy.

CRAG'GY, *a.* Full of crags; abounding with broken rocks; rugged with projecting points of rocks; as the *craggy* side of a mountain; a *craggy* cliff.

ƇRAKE, *n.* A boast. [See *Crack.*] *Spenser.*

ƇRAKE, *n.* [Qu. Gr. κρεξ, from κρεκω.] The corn-crake, a migratory fowl, is a species of the rail, *Rallus*, found among grass, corn, broom or furze. Its cry is very singular, *crek, crek*, and is imitated by rubbing the blade of a knife on an indented bone, by which it may be decoyed into a net. *Encyc.*

ƇRA'KE-BERRY, *n.* A species of Empetrum or berry-bearing heath.

ƇRAM, *v. t.* [Sax. *crammian*; Sw. *krama*; coinciding in sense and probably in origin with *ram.*]

1. To press or drive, particularly in filling or thrusting one thing into another; to stuff; to crowd; to fill to superfluity; as, to *cram* any thing into a basket or bag; to *cram* a room with people; to *cram* victuals down the throat.

2. To fill with food beyond satiety; to stuff.

Children would be more free from diseases, if they were not *crammed* so much by fond mothers. *Locke.*

3. To thrust in by force; to crowd.

Fate has *crammed* us all into one lease. *Dryden.*

ƇRAM, *v. i.* To eat greedily or beyond satiety; to stuff. *Pope.*

ƇRAM'BO, *n.* A rhyme; a play in which one person gives a word to which another finds a rhyme. *Swift.*

ƇRAM'MED, *pp.* Stuffed; crowded; thrust in; filled with food.

ƇRAM'MING, *ppr.* Driving in; stuffing; crowding; eating beyond satiety or sufficiency.

ƇRAMP, *n.* [Sax. *hramma*; D. *kramp*; G. Dan. Sw. *krampe*; It. *rampone*, a cramp-iron. Qu. Ir. *crampa*, a knot. If *m* is radical, this word may accord with the Celtic *crom*, G. *krumm*, crooked, from shrinking, contracting. But if *p* is radical, this word accords with the W. *craf*, a clasp, a cramp-iron, *crafu*, to secure hold of, to comprehend, Ir. *crapadh*, to shrink or contract. The sense is to strain or stretch.]

1. Spasm; the contraction of a limb, or some muscle of the body, attended with pain, and sometimes with convulsions, or numbness.

2. Restraint; confinement; that which hinders from motion or expansion.

A narrow fortune is a *cramp* to a great mind. *L'Estrange.*

3. A piece of iron bent at the ends, serving to hold together pieces of timber, stones, &c.; a cramp-iron. [Fr. *crampon*; It. *rampone.*]

ƇRAMP, *v. t.* To pain or affect with spasms.

2. To confine; to restrain; to hinder from action or expansion; as, to *cramp* the exertions of a nation; to *cramp* the genius.

3. To fasten, confine or hold with a cramp or cramp-iron.

ƇRAMP, *a.* Difficult; knotty. [*Little used.*] *Goodman.*

ƇRAMP'ED, *pp.* Affected with spasm; convulsed; confined; restrained.

ƇRAMP'-FISH, *n.* The torpedo, or electric ray, the touch of which affects a person like electricity, causing a slight shock and producing numbness, tremor, and sickness of the stomach.

ƇRAMP'ING, *ppr.* Affecting with cramp; confining.

ƇRAMP'-IRON, *n.* An iron used for fastening things together; a cramp, which see.

ƇRA'NAGE, *n.* [from *crane*. Low L. *cranagium.*]

The liberty of using a crane at a wharf for raising wares from a vessel; also, the money or price paid for the use of a crane. *Cowel. Encyc.*

ƇRAN'BERRY, *n.* [*crane* and *berry.*] A species of Vaccinium; a berry that grows on a slender, bending stalk. Its botanical name is *oxycoccus*, [sour berry,] and it is also called moss-berry, or moor-berry, as it grows only on peat-bogs or swampy land. The berry when ripe is red, and of the size of a small cherry or of the hawthorn berry. These berries form a sauce of exquisite flavor, and are used for tarts. The cranberry of the United States is a distinct species, the *V. macrocarpon.* [The common pronunciation, *cramberry*, is erroneous.]

ƇRANE, *n.* [Sax. *cran*; G. *krahn*; D. *kraan*; Sw. *kran*, or *trana*; Dan. *krane*, or *trane*; W. *garan*; Corn. *krana*; Arm. *garan*; Gr. γερανος, whence *geranium*, the plant, crane's-bill. The word in Welsh signifies a shank or shaft, a *crane* or *heron.* This fowl then may be named from its long legs. Qu. קרן to shoot.]

1. A migratory fowl of the genus Ardea, belonging to the grallic order. The bill is straight, sharp and long, with a furrow from the nostrils towards the point; the nostrils are linear, and the feet have four toes. These fowls have long legs, and a long neck, being destined to wade and seek their food among grass and reeds in marshy grounds. The common crane is about four feet in length, of a slender body, with ash-coloured feathers.

2. A machine for raising great weights, consisting of a horizontal arm, or piece of timber, projecting from a post, and furnished with a tackle or pulley.

3. A siphon, or crooked pipe for drawing liquors out of a cask.

ƇRA'NE'S-BILL, *n.* The plant *Geranium*, of many species; so named from an appendage of the seed-vessel, which resembles the beak of a crane or stork. Some of the species have beautiful flowers and a fragrant scent, and several of them are valued for their astringent properties. [See *Crane.*] *Encyc.*

2. A pair of pinchers used by surgeons.

ƇRA'NE-FLY, *n.* An insect of the genus Tipula, of many species. The mouth is a prolongation of the head; the upper jaw is arched; the palpi are two, curved and longer than the head; the proboscis is short. *Encyc.*

ƇRANIOG'NOMY, *n.* [Gr. κρανιον, the skull, and γνωμα, knowledge.]

The knowledge of the cranium or skull; the science of the expression of human temper, disposition and talents. *Good.*

ƇRANIOLOG'ICAL, *a.* Pertaining to craniology.

ƇRANIOL'OGIST, *n.* One who treats of craniology, or one who is versed in the science of the cranium.

ƇRANIOL'OGY, *n.* [Gr. κρανιον, the skull, and λογος, discourse.]

A discourse or treatise on the craninm or skull; or the science which investigates the structure and uses of the skulls in various animals, particularly in relation to their specific character and intellectual powers. *Ed. Encyc.*

ƇRANIOM'ETER, *n.* [κρανιον, the skull, and μετρον, measure.]

An instrument for measuring the skulls of animals.

ƇRANIOMET'RICAL, *a.* Pertaining to craniometry.

ƇRANIOM'ETRY, *n.* The art of measuring the cranium, or skulls, of animals, for discovering their specific differences.

ƇRANIOS'COPY, *n.* [κρανιον, supra, and σκοπεω, to view.]

The science of the eminences produced in the cranium by the brain, intended to discover the particular part of the brain in which reside the organs which influence particular passions or faculties. *Ed. Encyc.*

ƇRA'NIUM, *n.* [L. from Gr. κρανιον.] The skull of an animal; the assemblage of bones which inclose the brain.

ƇRANK, *n.* [This word probably belongs to the root of *cringe*, *krinkle*, to bend. D. *krinkel*, a curl; *kronkel*, a bend or winding; and *krank*, weak, is probably from bending; Ir. *freanc*, to make crooked. Qu. ברע, or the root of *crook.*]

1. Literally, a bend or turn. Hence, an iron axis with the end bent like an elbow, for moving a piston, the saw in a saw-mill, &c., and causing it to rise and fall at every turn.

2. Any bend, turn or winding. *Shak.*

3. A twisting or turning in speech; a conceit which consists in a change of the form or meaning of a word.

Quips and *cranks*, and wanton wiles. *Milton.*

4. An iron brace for various purposes. *Mar. Dict.*

ƇRANK, *a.* [D. *krank*; G. *id.*, weak; Sw. *kråncka*, to afflict; Dan. *krænker*, id., or *krænger*, to careen a ship.]

In *seamen's language*, liable to be overset, as a ship when she is too narrow, or has not sufficient ballast to carry full sail.

2. Stout; bold; erect; as a cock crowing *crank.* *Spenser.*

ƇRANK, } *v. i.* [See *Crank*, *n.*, and *Crin-*
ƇRANK'LE, } *kle.*] To run in a winding course; to bend, wind and turn.

See how this river comes me *crankling* in. *Shak.*

ƇRANK'LE, *v. t.* To break into bends, turns or angles; to crinkle.

Old Vaga's stream——
Crankling her banks. *Philips.*

ƇRANK'LE, *n.* A bend or turn; a crinkle.

ƇRANK'NESS, *n.* Liability to be overset, as a ship.

2. Stoutness; erectness.

ƇRAN'NIED, *a.* [See *Cranny.*] Having rents, chinks or fissures; as a *crannied* wall. *Brown. Shak.*

ƇRAN'NY, *n.* [Fr. *cran*; Arm. *cran*, a notch; L. *crena*; from the root of *rend*, Sax. *hrendan* or *rendan*; Arm. *ran-*

na, to split; *crenna*, to cut off; W. *rhanu*, to divide; *rhan*, a piece; Ir. *roinnim*, or *ruinnim*, to divide; Gr. χρινω; L. *cerno*. See Class Rn. No. 4. 13. 16.]

1. Properly, a rent; but commonly, any small narrow opening, fissure, crevice or chink, as in a wall, or other substance.

In a firm building, the cavities ought to be filled with brick or stone, fitted to the *crannies*. *Dryden.*

2. A hole; a secret retired place.

He peeped into every *cranny*. *Arbuthnot.*

3. In *glass-making*, an iron instrument for forming the necks of glasses. *Encyc.*

CRANTS, *n.* [G. *kranz.*] Garlands carried before the bier of a maiden and hung over her grave. *Shak.*

CRAPE, *n.* [Fr. *crêpe*, and *crêper*, to curl, to *crisp*, to frizzle; Arm. *crep;* Sp. *crespon*, crape; *crespo*, crisp, curled; *crespar*, to crisp or curl; Port. *crespam*. *Crape* is contracted from *cresp*, *crisp*. [D. *krip*, G. *krepp*, Dan. *krep*.] See *Crisp*.]

A thin transparent stuff, made of raw silk gummed and twisted on the mill, woven without crossing, and much used in mourning. Crape is also used for gowns and the dress of the clergy.

A saint in *crape* is twice a saint in lawn. *Pope.*

CRAPE, *v. t.* To curl; to form into ringlets; as, to *crape* the hair.

CRAP'LE, *n.* [W. *crav.*] A claw. *Spenser.*

CRAP'NEL, *n.* A hook or drag. Qu. *grapnel*.

CRAP'ULENCE, *n.* [L. *crapula*, a surfeit. See *Crop*.]

Cropsickness; drunkenness; a surfeit, or the sickness occasioned by intemperance. *Dict.*

CRAP'ULOUS, *a.* Drunk; surcharged with liquor; sick by intemperance. *Dict.*

CRASH, *v. t.* [Fr. *ecraser*, to crush. *Crash* seems to be allied to *crush* and to *rush*, Sax. *hreosan*.]

To break; to bruise. *Shak.*

CRASH, *v. i.* To make the loud, clattering, multifarious sound of many things falling and breaking at once.

When convulsions cleave the lab'ring earth,
Before the dismal yawn appears, the ground
Trembles and heaves, the nodding houses
crash. *Smith.*

CRASH, *n.* The loud mingled sound of many things falling and breaking at once; as the sound of a large tree falling and its branches breaking, or the sound of a falling house.

CRASH'ING, *n.* The sound of many things falling and breaking at once.

There shall be a great *crashing* from the hills. Zeph. i.

CRA'SIS, *n.* [Gr. χρασις, from χεραννυμι, or χεραω, to mix, to temper.]

1. The temper or healthy constitution of the blood in an animal body; the temperament which forms a particular constitution of the blood. *Coxe.*

2. In *grammar*, a figure by which two different letters are contracted into one long letter or into a diphthong; as αληθεα into αληθη; τυχεος into τυχους.

CRASS, *a.* [L. *crassus*, the same as *gross*, which see.] Gross; thick; coarse; not thin, nor fine; *applied to fluids and solids;* as, *crass* and fumid exhalations. [*Little used.*] *Brown.*

CRASS'AMENT, *n.* The thick red part of the blood, as distinct from the serum, or aqueous part; the clot.

CRASS'ITUDE, *n.* [L. *crassitudo.*] Grossness; coarseness; thickness; *applied to liquids or solids.* *Bacon. Woodward.*

CRASS'NESS, *n.* Grossness. *Glanville.*

CRATCH, *n.* [Fr. *creche.*] A rack; a grated crib or manger.

[*I believe not used in New England.*]

CRATCH. [See *Scratch.*]

CRATCH'ES, *n. plu.* [G. *krätze*, the itch, cratches; *kratzen*, to scratch.]

In *the manege*, a swelling on the pastern, under the fetlock, and sometimes under the hoof of a horse.

CRATE, *n.* [L. *crates.*] A kind of basket or hamper of wicker-work, used for the transportation of china, crockery and similar wares.

CRA'TER, *n.* [L. *crater*, Gr. χρατηρ, a great cup.]

1. The aperture or mouth of a volcano.

2. A constellation of the southern hemisphere, said to contain 31 stars.

CR'AUNCH, *v. t.* [D. *schranssen;* Vulgar *scraunch.*]

To crush with the teeth; to chew with violence and noise.

CR'AUNCHING, *ppr.* Crushing with the teeth with violence.

CRAVAT', *n.* [Fr. *cravate;* It. *cravatta;* Sp. *corbata;* Port. *caravata*. In Dan. *krage*, and *krave*, is a collar, a cape, the neck of a shirt, &c.]

A neck-cloth; a piece of fine muslin or other cloth worn by men about the neck.

CRAVE, *v. t.* [Sax. *crafian*, to crave, ask, implore; W. *crevu*, to cry, to cry for, to crave; *crev*, a cry, a scream; Sw. *kräfia;* Dan. *kræver;* Ice. *krefa*. See Class Rb. No. 2. 4. Syr. So also D. *roepen*, Sax. *hreopen*, Goth. *hropyan*, to cry out, as our vulgar phrase is, to *rip* out. The primary sense is to cry out, or call.]

1. To ask with earnestness or importunity; to beseech; to implore; to ask with submission or humility, as a dependent; to beg; to entreat.

As for my nobler friends, I *crave* their pardons. *Shak.*

Joseph—went in boldly to Pilate, and *craved* the body of Jesus. Mark xv.

2. To call for, as a gratification; to long for; to require or demand, as a passion or appetite; as, the stomach or appetite *craves* food.

3. Sometimes intransitively, with *for* before the thing sought; as, I *crave for* mercy.

CRA'VED, *pp.* Asked for with earnestness; implored; entreated; longed for; required.

CRA'VEN, **CRA'VENT**, **CRA'VANT**, *n.* [Qu. from *crave*, that is, one who begs for his life, when vanquished.]

1. A word of obloquy, used formerly by one vanquished in trial by battle, and yielding to the conqueror. Hence, a recreant; a coward; a weak-hearted spiritless fellow. *Shak.*

2. A vanquished, dispirited cock. *Shak.*

CRA'VEN, *v. t.* To make recreant, weak or cowardly. *Shak.*

CRA'VER, *n.* One who craves or begs.

CRA'VING, *ppr.* Asking with importunity; urging for earnestly; begging; entreating.

2. Calling for with urgency; requiring; demanding gratification; as an appetite *craving* food.

CRA'VING, *n.* Vehement or urgent desire, or calling for; a longing for.

CRAW, *n.* [Dan. *kroe;* Sw. *kråfva*. This word coincides in elements with *crop;* W. *cropa;* Sax. *crop;* D. *krop;* G. *kropf*. The Danish *kroe* signifies the *craw*, and a victualling house, tavern or alehouse. It seems to be named from gathering.]

The crop or first stomach of fowls. *Ray.*

CRAW-FISH, **CRAY-FISH**, *n.* [*Craw* is contracted from *crab*, or from the Welsh *crag*, a shell; *pysgod cragen*, shell-fish. See *Crab*. Qu. is not *fish*, in these words, from the last syllable of the French *ecrevisse?*]

A species of Cancer or crab, a crustaceous fish, found in streams. It resembles the lobster, but is smaller, and is esteemed very delicate food.

CRAWL, *v. i.* [D. *krielen;* Scot. *crowl;* Dan. *kravler*, to crawl up, to climb; Sw. *kråla*, to crawl, to swarm; D. *grielen*, to swarm; *grillen*, to shiver or shudder; Fr. *grouiller*, to stir about, to crawl with insects; It. *grillare*, to simmer. Qu. Dan. *kriller*, to itch.]

1. To creep; to move slowly by thrusting or drawing the body along the ground, as a worm; or to move slowly on the hands and knees or feet, as a human being. A worm *crawls* on the earth; a boy *crawls* into a cavern, or up a tree.

2. To move or walk weakly, slowly, or timorously.

He was hardly able to *crawl* about the room. *Arbuthnot.*

3. To creep; to advance slowly and slyly; to insinuate one's self; as, to *crawl* into favor. [*This use is vulgar.*]

4. To move about; to move in any direction; used in contempt.

Absurd opinions *crawl* about the world. *South.*

5. To have the sensation of insects creeping about the body; as, the flesh *crawls*.

CRAWL, *n.* [Qu. D. *kraal.*] A pen or inclosure of stakes and hurdles on the sea coast for containing fish. *Mar. Dict.*

CRAWL'ER, *n.* He or that which crawls; a creeper; a reptile.

CRAWL'ING, *ppr.* Creeping; moving slowly along the ground, or other substance; moving or walking slowly, weakly or timorously; insinuating.

CRAY or **CRA'YER**, *n.* A small sea vessel. [*Not in use.*]

CRAY-FISH, *n.* The river lobster. [See *Craw-fish.*]

CRA'YON, *n.* [Fr. from *craie*, chalk, from L. *creta*, Sp. *greda.*]

1. A general name for all colored stones, earths, or other minerals and substances, used in designing or painting in pastel or paste, whether they have been beaten and reduced to paste, or are used in their primitive consistence. Red crayons are made of blood-stone or red chalk; black ones, of charcoal or black lead. *Encyc.*

2. A kind of pencil, or roll of paste, to draw lines with. *Dryden.*

3. A drawing or design done with a pencil or crayon. *Johnson.*

CRA'YON, *v. t.* To sketch with a crayon. Hence,

2. To sketch; to plan; to commit to paper one's first thoughts. *Bolingbroke.*

CRA'YON-PAINTING, *n.* The act or art of drawing with crayons.

CRAZE, *v. t.* [Fr. *ecraser;* Sw. *krossa;* to break or bruise, to *crush.* See *Crush.*]

1. To break; to weaken; to break or impair the natural force or energy of.

> Till length of years,
> And sedentary numbness, *craze* my limbs. *Milton.*

2. To crush in pieces; to grind to powder; as, to *craze* tin.

3. To crack the brain; to shatter; to impair the intellect; as, to be *crazed* with love or grief. *Shak.*

CRA'ZED, *pp.* Broken; bruised; crushed; impaired; deranged in intellect; decrepit.

CRA'ZEDNESS, *n.* A broken state; decrepitude; an impaired state of the intellect. *Hooker.*

CRA'ZE-MILL, CRA'ZING-MILL, *n.* A mill resembling a grist mill, used for grinding tin. *Encyc.*

CRA'ZILY, *adv.* [See *Crazy.*] In a broken or crazy manner.

CRA'ZINESS, *n.* [See *Crazy.*] The state of being broken or weakened; as the *craziness* of a ship or of the limbs.

2. The state of being broken in mind; imbecility or weakness of intellect; derangement.

CRA'ZY, *a.* [Fr. *ecrasé.*] Broken; decrepit; weak; feeble; *applied to the body, or constitution, or any structure;* as a *crazy* body; a *crazy* constitution; a *crazy* ship.

2. Broken, weakened, or disordered in intellect; deranged, weakened, or shattered in mind. We say, the man is *crazy.*

CREAGHT, *n.* [Irish.] Herds of cattle. [*Not used.*] *Davies.*

CREAGHT, *v. i.* To graze on lands. [*Not used.*] *Davies.*

CREAK, *v. i.* [W. *crecian,* to scream, to crash; *crec,* a scream, a shriek; connected with *creg, cryg,* rough, hoarse, harsh, from *rhyg,* Eng. *rye,* but the sense of which is *rough, rugged.* Indeed this is radically the same word as *rough,* L. *raucus.* The L. *rugio* is probably from the same root, and perhaps *rugo.* The Sax. *cearcian,* to creak, may be the same word, the letters transposed; as may the Sp. *cruxir,* to rustle, Gr. *χρεχω,* to comb, scrape, *rake,* and Russ. *crik,* a cry, *krichu,* to cry. On this word are formed *shriek* and *screech.*]

To make a sharp harsh grating sound, of some continuance, as by the friction of hard substances. Thus, the hinge of a door *creaks* in turning; a tight firm shoe *creaks* in walking, by the friction of the leather.

CRE'AKING, *ppr.* Making a harsh grating sound; as *creaking* hinges or shoes.

CRE'AKING, *n.* A harsh grating sound.

CREAM, *n.* [Fr. *crême;* L. *cremor;* G. *rahm;* Sax. *ream;* Ice. *riome;* D. *room;* Sp. *crema.* Class Rm.]

1. In a general sense, any part of a liquor that separates from the rest, rises and collects on the surface. More particularly, the oily part of milk, which, when the milk stands unagitated in a cool place, rises and forms a scum on the surface, as it is specifically lighter than the other part of the liquor. This by agitation forms butter.

2. The best part of a thing; as the *cream* of a jest or story.

Cream of lime, the scum of lime water; or that part of lime which, after being dissolved in its caustic state, separates from the water in the mild state of chalk or limestone. *Encyc.*

Cream of tartar, the scum of a boiling solution of tartar. *Coxe.*

The purified and crystalized supertartrate of potash. *Chim.*

CREAM, *v. t.* To skim; to take off cream by skimming.

2. To take off the quintessence or best part of a thing.

CREAM, *v. i.* To gather cream; to flower or mantle.

2. To grow stiff, or formal. *Shak.*

CRE'AM-BOWL, *n.* A bowl for holding cream.

CRE'AM-FACED, *a.* White; pale; having a coward look. *Shak.*

CRE'AM-POT, *n.* A vessel for holding cream.

CRE'AMY, *a.* Full of cream; like cream; having the nature of cream; luscious.

CRE'ANCE, *n.* [Fr. from L. *credo, credens.*] In *falconry,* a fine small line, fastened to a hawk's leash, when she is first lured. *Bailey.*

CREASE, *n.* [Qu. G. *kräusen,* Sw. *krusa,* Dan. *kruser,* Scot. *creis,* to curl, to crisp, Class Rd. No. 73. 83.; or Fr. *creuser,* to make hollow, from *creux,* hollow, Class Rg. See *Crisp.*]

A line or mark made by folding or doubling any thing; a hollow streak, like a groove.

CREASE, *v. t.* To make a crease or mark in a thing by folding or doubling.

CRE'AT, *n.* [Fr.] In *the manege,* an usher to a riding master. *Encyc.*

CREA'TE, *v. t.* [Fr. *creer;* It. *creare;* Sp. and Port. *criar;* L. *creo;* Arm. *croui;* Corn. *gurei.* In W. *crëu* signifies to *create,* and *creu,* to *cry,* to crave, to caw, to beg. W. *creth* and *crez,* constitution, temper; also, a trembling or shivering with cold. Ir. *croth* or *cruth,* form, shape; *cruthaighim,* to create, to prove, assert, maintain. From the Celtic then it appears that the L. *creo* is contracted by the loss of a *d* or *th.* The Welsh has also *cri,* a cry, and *criaw,* to cry, both deduced by Owen from *cre;* but *cre* is a contraction of *crevu,* to cry, or of *gryd,* a crying or whooping, or *cryd,* a shaking. In Welsh also *cri* signifies rough, *raw, crude;* all which unite in the root of *cry, cradle,* L. *rudo,* to bray. The primary sense of *create* and of *cry* is the same, to throw or drive out, to produce, to bring forth, precisely as in the Shemitic ברא. But the Welsh *crëu* and *creu* may perhaps be from different roots, both however with the same primary sense.]

1. To produce; to bring into being from nothing; to cause to exist.

> In the beginning, God *created* the heaven and the earth. Gen. i.

2. To make or form, by investing with a new character; as, to *create* one a peer or baron; to *create* a manor.

> I *create* you
> Companions to our person. *Shak.*

3. To produce; to cause; to be the occasion of.

> Your eye in Scotland
> Would *create* soldiers, and make women fight. *Shak.*

> Long abstinence *creates* uneasiness in the stomach; confusion is *created* by hurry.

4. To beget; to generate; to bring forth.

> The people which shall be *created,* shall praise the Lord. Ps. cii.

5. To make or produce, by new combinations of matter already created, and by investing these combinations with new forms, constitutions and qualities; to shape and organize.

> God *created* man in his own image. Gen. i.

6. To form anew; to change the state or character; to renew.

> *Create* in me a clean heart. Ps. li.
> We are his workmanship, *created* in Christ Jesus. Eph. ii.

CREA'TED, *pp.* Formed from nothing; caused to exist; produced; generated; invested with a new character; formed into new combinations, with a peculiar shape, constitution and properties; renewed.

CREA'TING, *ppr.* Forming from nothing; originating; producing; giving a new character; constituting new beings from matter by shaping, organizing and investing with new properties; forming anew.

CREA'TION, *n.* The act of creating; the act of causing to exist; and especially, the act of bringing this world into existence. Rom. i.

2. The act of making, by new combinations of matter, invested with new forms and properties, and of subjecting to different laws; the act of shaping and organizing; as the *creation* of man and other animals, of plants, minerals, &c.

3. The act of investing with a new character; as the *creation* of peers in England.

4. The act of producing.

5. The things created; creatures; the world; the universe.

> As subjects then the whole *creation* came. *Denham.*

6. Any part of the things created.

> Before the low *creation* swarmed with men. *Parnel.*

7. Any thing produced or caused to exist.

> A false *creation,*
> Proceeding from the heat-oppressed brain. *Shak.*

CREA'TIVE, *a.* Having the power to create, or exerting the act of creation; as *creative* fancy; *creative* power.

CREA'TOR, *n.* [L.] The being or person that creates.

> Remember thy *creator* in the days of thy youth. Eccles. xii.

2. The thing that creates, produces or causes.

CREA'TRESS, *n.* A female that creates any thing. *Spenser.*

CRE'ATURE, *n.* [Fr.] That which is created; every being besides the Creator, or every thing not self-existent. The sun, moon and stars; the earth, animals, plants, light, darkness, air, water, &c., are the *creatures* of God.

2. In a restricted sense, an animal of any kind; a living being; a beast. In a more restricted sense, man. Thus we say, he was in trouble and no *creature* was present to aid him.

3. A human being, in contempt; as an idle

creature; a poor *creature*; what a *creature!*

4. With words of endearment, it denotes a human being beloved; as a pretty *creature*; a sweet *creature*.
5. That which is produced, formed or imagined; as a *creature* of the imagination.
6. A person who owes his rise and fortune to another; one who is made to be what he is.

Great princes thus, when favorites they raise,
To justify their grace, their *creatures* praise. *Dryden.*

7. A dependent; a person who is subject to the will or influence of another.

CRE'ATURELY, *a.* Having the qualities of a creature. [*Little used.*] *Cheyne.*

CRE'ATURESHIP, *n.* The state of a creature. [*Little used.*] *Cave.*

CRE'DENCE, *n.* [It. *credenza*; Fr. *creance*; from L. *credens*, from *credo*, to believe. See *Creed.*]

1. Belief; credit; reliance of the mind on evidence of facts derived from other sources than personal knowledge, as from the testimony of others. We give *credence* to a historian of unsuspected integrity, or to a story which is related by a man of known veracity.
2. That which gives a claim to credit, belief or confidence; as a *letter of credence*, which is intended to commend the bearer to the confidence of a third person.

CREDEN'DA, *n.* [L. See *Creed.*]

In *theology*, things to be believed; articles of faith; distinguished from *agenda*, or practical duties. *Johnson.*

CRE'DENT, *a.* Believing; giving credit; easy of belief. *Shak.*

2. Having credit; not to be questioned. *Shak.*

[*This word is rarely used, and in the latter sense is improper.*]

CREDEN'TIALS, *n. plu.* [*Rarely or never used in the singular.*]

That which gives credit; that which gives a title or claim to confidence; the warrant on which belief, credit or authority is claimed, among strangers; as the letters of commendation and power given by a government to an embassador or envoy, which give him credit at a foreign court. So the power of working miracles given to the apostles may be considered as their *credentials*, authorizing them to propagate the gospel, and entitling them to credit.

CREDIBIL'ITY, *n.* [Fr. *credibilité*, from L. *credibilis.*]

Credibleness; the quality or state of a thing which renders it possible to be believed, or which admits belief, on rational principles; the quality or state of a thing which involves no contradiction, or absurdity. Credibility is less than certainty, and greater than possibility; indeed it is less than probability, but is nearly allied to it. [See *Credible.*]

CRED'IBLE, *a.* [L. *credibilis.*] That may be believed; worthy of credit. A thing is *credible*, when it is known to be possible, or when it involves no contradiction or absurdity; it is *more credible*, when it is known to come within the ordinary laws or operations of nature. With regard to the Divine Being and his operations, every thing is *credible* which is consistent with his perfections, and supported by evidence or unimpeachable testimony, for his power is unlimited. With regard to human affairs, we do not apply the word to things barely *possible*, but to things which come within the usual course of human conduct, and the general rules of evidence.

2. Worthy of belief; having a claim to credit; *applied to persons.* A *credible* person is one of known veracity and integrity, or whose veracity may be fairly deduced from circumstances. We believe the history of Aristides and Themistocles, on the authority of *credible* historians.

CRED'IBLENESS, *n.* Credibility; worthiness of belief; just claim to credit. [See *Credibility.*]

CRED'IBLY, *adv.* In a manner that deserves belief; with good authority to support belief.

CRED'IT, *n.* [Fr. *credit*; It. *credito*; Sp. *id.*; L. *creditum.* See *Creed.*]

1. Belief; faith; a reliance or resting of the mind on the truth of something said or done. We give *credit* to a man's declaration, when the mind rests on the truth of it, without doubt or suspicion, which is attended with wavering. We give *credit* to testimony or to a report, when we rely on its truth and certainty.
2. Reputation derived from the confidence of others. Esteem; estimation; good opinion founded on a belief of a man's veracity, integrity, abilities and virtue; as a physician in high *credit* with his brethren. Hence,
3. Honor; reputation; estimation; *applied to men or things.* A man gains no *credit* by profaneness; and a poem may lose no *credit* by criticism. The *credit* of a man depends on his virtues; the *credit* of his writings, on their worth.
4. That which procures or is entitled to belief; testimony; authority derived from one's character, or from the confidence of others. We believe a story on the *credit* of the narrator. We believe in miracles on the *credit* of inspired men. We trust to the *credit* of an assertion, made by a man of known veracity.
5. Influence derived from the reputation of veracity or integrity, or from the good opinion or confidence of others; interest; power derived from weight of character, from friendship, fidelity or other cause. A minister may have great *credit* with a prince. He may employ his *credit* to good or evil purposes. A man uses his *credit* with a friend; a servant, with his master.
6. In *commerce*, trust; transfer of goods in confidence of future payment. When the merchant gives a *credit*, he sells his wares on an expressed or implied promise that the purchaser will pay for them at a future time. The seller *believes* in the solvability and probity of the purchaser, and delivers his goods on that belief or trust; or he delivers them on the *credit* or reputation of the purchaser. The purchaser takes what is sold, on *credit*. In like manner, money is loaned on the *credit* of the borrower.
7. The capacity of being trusted; or the reputation of solvency and probity which entitles a man to be trusted. A customer has good *credit* or no *credit* with a merchant.
8. In *book-keeping*, the side of an account in which payment is entered; opposed to *debit*. This article is carried to one's *credit*, and that to his *debit*. We speak of the *credit* side of an account.
9. *Public credit*, the confidence which men entertain in the ability and disposition of a nation, to make good its engagements with its creditors; or the estimation in which individuals hold the public promises of payment, whether such promises are expressed or implied. The term is also applied to the general credit of individuals in a nation; when merchants and others are wealthy, and punctual in fulfilling engagements; or when they transact business with honor and fidelity; or when transfers of property are made with ease for ready payment. So we speak of the *credit* of a bank, when general confidence is placed in its ability to redeem its notes; and the *credit* of a mercantile house rests on its supposed ability and probity, which induce men to *trust* to its engagements.

Cherish *public credit*. *Washington.*

When the *public credit* is questionable, it raises the premium on loans.

10. The notes or bills which are issued by the public or by corporations or individuals, which circulate on the confidence of men in the ability and disposition in those who issue them, to redeem them. They are sometimes called *bills of credit*.
11. The time given for payment for lands or goods sold on trust; as a long *credit*, or a short *credit*.
12. A sum of money due to any person; any thing valuable standing on the creditor side of an account. A has a *credit* on the books of B. The *credits* are more than balanced by the debits.

[*In this sense the word has the plural number.*]

CRED'IT, *v. t.* [from the Noun.] To believe; to confide in the truth of; as, to *credit* a report, or the man who tells it.

2. To trust; to sell or loan in confidence of future payment; as, to *credit* goods or money.
3. To procure credit or honor; to do credit; to give reputation or honor.

May here her monument stand so,
To *credit* this rude age. *Waller.*

4. To enter upon the credit side of an account; as, to *credit* the amount paid.
5. To set to the credit of; as, to *credit* to a man the interest paid on a bond.

CRED'ITABLE, *a.* Reputable; that may be enjoyed or exercised with reputation or esteem; estimable. A man pursues a *creditable* occupation, or way of living. *Arbuthnot.*

CRED'ITABLENESS, *n.* Reputation; estimation. *Johnson.*

CRED'ITABLY, *adv.* Reputably; with credit; without disgrace.

CRED'ITED, *pp.* Believed; trusted; passed to the credit, or entered on the credit side of an account.

CRED'ITING, *ppr.* Believing; trusting; entering to the credit in account.

CRED'ITOR, *n.* [L. See *Creed.*] A person to whom a sum of money or other thing is due, by obligation, promise or in law; properly, one who gives credit in commerce; but in a general sense, one who has a just claim for money; correlative to *debtor.* In a figurative sense, one who has a just claim to services. *Addison.*

Creditors have better memories than debtors. *Franklin.*

2. One who believes. [*Not used.*] *Shak.*

CRED'ITRIX, *n.* A female creditor.

CREDU'LITY, *n.* [Fr. *credulité,* L. *credulitas,* from *credo,* to believe. See *Creed* and *Credulous.*]

Easiness of belief; a weakness of mind by which a person is disposed to believe, or yield his assent to a declaration or proposition, without sufficient evidence of the truth of what is said or proposed; a disposition to believe on slight evidence or no evidence at all.

CRED'ULOUS, *a.* [L. *credulus,* from *credo.* See *Creed.*]

Apt to believe without sufficient evidence; unsuspecting; easily deceived.

CRED'ULOUSNESS, *n.* Credulity; easiness of belief; readiness to believe without sufficient evidence.

Beyond all credulity is the *credulousness* of atheists, who believe that chance could make the world, when it cannot build a house. *S. Clarke.*

CREED, *n.* [W. *credo;* Sax. *creda;* It. and Sp. *credo.* This word seems to have been introduced by the use of the Latin *credo, I believe,* at the beginning of the Apostles' creed, or brief system of christian faith. L. *credo;* W. *credu;* Corn. *credzhi;* Arm. *cridi;* Ir. *creidim;* It. *credere;* Sp. *creer;* Port. *crer;* Fr. *croire;* Norm. *crere, cruer.* The primary sense is probably to throw, or to throw on; or to set, to rest on. See *Creed.* Class Rd.]

1. A brief summary of the articles of christian faith; a symbol; as the Apostolic *creed.*

2. That which is believed; any system of principles which are believed or professed; as a political *creed.*

CREEK, *v. t.* To make a harsh sharp noise. [See *Creak.*] *Shak.*

CREEK, *n. krik.* [Sax. *crecea;* D. *kreek;* Fr. *crique;* W. *crig,* a crack; *crigyll,* a creek; *rhig,* a notch or groove. See *Crack.*]

1. A small inlet, bay or cove; a recess in the shore of the sea, or of a river.

They discovered a certain *creek* with a shore. Acts xxvii.

2. Any turn or winding. *Shak.*

3. A prominence or jut in a winding coast. [*This sense is probably not legitimate.*] *Davies.*

4. In some of the *American States,* a small river. This sense is not justified by etymology, but as streams often enter into creeks and small bays or form them, the name has been extended to small streams in general.

CREEKY, *a. krik'y.* Containing creeks; full of creeks; winding. *Spenser.*

CREEP, *v. i.* pret. and pp. *crept.* [Sax. *creopan, crypan;* W. *crepian, cropian;* D. *kruipen;* Sw. *krypa;* to creep; Dan. *kryben,* a creeping; Ir. *dreapam;* Sp. and Port. *trepar;* L. *repo;* Gr. ἑρπω. The sense is to catch, to *grapple;* and the latter is from the same root, Welsh *crapiaw,* allied to L. *rapio,* and to W. *cripian,* to scrape or scratch. Class. Rb.]

1. To move with the belly on the ground, or the surface of any other body, as a worm or serpent without legs, or as many insects with feet and very short legs; to crawl.

2. To move along the ground, or on the surface of any other body, in growth, as a vine; to grow along.

3. To move slowly, feebly or timorously; as an old or infirm man, who *creeps* about his chamber.

4. To move slowly and insensibly, as time.

To morrow, and to morrow, and to morrow,
Creeps in this petty pace from day to day. *Shak.*

5. To move secretly; to move so as to escape detection, or prevent suspicion.

Of this sort are they who *creep* into houses, and lead captive silly women. 2 Tim. iii.

6. To steal in; to move forward unheard and unseen; to come or enter unexpectedly or unobserved; as, some error has *crept* into the copy of a history.

7. To move or behave with servility; to fawn. *Shak.*

CREE'PER, *n.* One who creeps; that which creeps; a reptile; also, a creeping plant, which moves along the surface of the earth or attaches itself to some other body, as ivy.

2. An iron used to slide along the grate in kitchens. *Johnson.*

3. A kind of patten or clog worn by women. *Johnson.*

4. Creeper or creepers, an instrument of iron with hooks or claws, for drawing up things from the bottom of a well, river or harbor.

5. A genus of birds, the *Certhia,* or ox-eye, of many species. These birds run along the body or branch of a tree, and when they observe a person near, they run to the side opposite, so as to keep out of sight. *Encyc.*

CREE'PHOLE, *n.* A hole into which an animal may creep to escape notice or danger; also, a subterfuge; an excuse. *Johnson.*

CREE'PING, *ppr.* Moving on the belly, or close to the surface of the earth or other body; moving slowly, secretly, or silently; moving insensibly; stealing along.

CREE'PINGLY, *adv.* By creeping; slowly; in the manner of a reptile. *Sidney.*

CREE'PLE. [*Not used.*] [See *Cripple.*]

CREESE, *n.* A Malay dagger.

CREMA'TION, *n.* [L. *crematio,* from *cremo,* to burn.]

A burning; particularly, the burning of the dead, according to the custom of many ancient nations. *Encyc.*

CRE'MOR, *n.* [L. See *Cream.*] Cream; any expressed juice of grain; yeast; scum; a substance resembling cream. *Coxe.*

CRE'NATE, CRE'NATED, *a.* [L. *crena,* a notch, whence *crenatus,* notched. See *Cranny.*]

Notched; indented; scolloped. In *botany,* a *crenate* leaf has its edge, as it were, cut with angular or circular incisures, not inclining towards either extremity. When the scallops are segments of small circles, it is said to be *obtusely crenated;* when the larger segments have smaller ones upon them, a leaf is said to be *doubly crenate.* *Martyn.*

CREN'ATURE, *n.* A scollop, like a notch, in a leaf, or in the style of a plant. *Bigelow.*

CRENKLE, CRENGLE, [See *Cringle.*]

CREN'ULATE, *a.* [dim. used by *Linne.*] Having the edge, as it were, cut into very small scollops. *Martyn.*

CRE'OLE, *n.* In *the West Indies* and *Spanish America,* a native of those countries descended from European ancestors.

CREP'ANCE, CREP'ANE, *n.* [L. *crepo,* to burst.] A chop or cratch in a horse's leg, caused by the shoe of one hind foot crossing and striking the other hind foot. It sometimes degenerates into an ulcer. *Encyc.*

CREP'ITATE, *v. i.* [L. *crepito,* to crackle, from *crepo,* to crack, to burst with a sharp sound; It. *crepitare, crepare;* Fr. *crever;* Sax. *hreopan;* Goth. *hropyan;* D. *roepen;* allied to Eng. *rip,* and probably from the root of *rumpo, rupi,* &c. See חרפ and خرق garafa. Class Rb. No 27. and No. 18. 26. 30.]

To crackle; to snap; to burst with a small sharp abrupt sound, rapidly repeated; as salt in fire, or during calcination. It differs from *detonate,* which signifies, to burst with a single loud report.

CREP'ITATING, *ppr.* Crackling; snapping.

CREPITA'TION, *n.* The act of bursting with a frequent repetition of sharp sounds; the noise of some salts in calcination; crackling. *Coxe. Encyc.*

2. The noise of fractured bones, when moved by a surgeon to ascertain a fracture. *Encyc.*

CREPT, *pret.* and *pp.* of *creep.*

CREPUS'CLE, CREPUSC'ULE, *n.* [L. *crepusculum,* from *crepo* or its root, a little burst or break of light, or broken light. *Creperus* is from the same root.]

Twilight; the light of the morning from the first dawn to sunrise, and of the evening from sunset to darkness. It is occasioned by the refraction of the sun's rays.

CREPUSC'ULAR, CREPUSC'ULOUS, *a.* Pertaining to twilight; glimmering; noting the imperfect light of the morning and evening; hence, imperfectly clear or luminous. *Brown. Glanville.*

CREPUSC'ULINE, *a.* Crepuscular. [*Not used.*]

CRES'CENT, *a.* [L. *crescens,* from *cresco,* to grow; Fr. *croissant.* See *Grow.*]

Increasing; growing; as *crescent* horns. *Milton.*

CRES'CENT, *n.* The increasing or new moon, which, when receding from the sun, shows a curving rim of light, terminating in points or horns. It is applied to the old or decreasing moon, in a like state, but less properly. *Dryden.*

2. The figure or likeness of the new moon; as that borne in the Turkish flag or national standard. The standard itself, and figuratively, the Turkish power. *Gibbon.*

3. In *heraldry,* a bearing in the form of a half moon.

4. The name of a military order, instituted by Renatus of Anjou, king of Sicily; so called from its symbol or badge, a crescent of gold enameled. *Encyc.*

ЄRES'CENT, *v. t.* To form into a crescent. *Seward.*

ЄRES'CENT-SHAPED, *a.* In *botany*, lunate; lunated; shaped like a crescent; as a leaf. *Martyn.*

ЄRES'CIVE, *a.* [L. *cresco*, to grow.] Increasing; growing. *Shak.*

ЄRESS, *n.* [Fr. *cresson*; It. *crescione*; Arm. *creçzon*; D. *kers*; G. *kresse*; Sax. *cœrse* or *cressen*. Qu. its alliance to *grass*, or to L. *cresco*.]
The name of several species of plants, most of them of the class *tetradynamia*. Water-cresses, of the genus Sisymbrium, are used as a salad, and are valued in medicine for their antiscorbutic qualities. The leaves have a moderately pungent taste. They grow on the brinks of rivulets and in other moist grounds. The word is generally used in the plural.

ЄRESS'ET, *n.* [Fr. *croisette*, dim. of *croix*, cross, because beacons formerly had *crosses* on their tops. See *Cross.*]
A great light set on a beacon, lighthouse, or watch tower. *Johnson. Shak.*
2. A lamp or torch. *Milton. Holinshed.*

ЄREST, *n.* [Fr. *crête*; L. *crista*; It. *cresta*; Sp. *creston*. This is probably, a growing or shooting up, from the root of *cresco*, Fr. *croître*; Norm. *crest*, it rises, it accrues; Russ. *rastu* or *rostu*, to grow; *rost*, growth, size, tallness.]
1. The plume of feathers or other material on the top of the ancient helmet; the helmet itself. *Shak.*
2. The ornament of the helmet in heraldry. *Encyc.*
3. The comb of a cock; also, a tuft of feathers on the head of other fowls.
4. Any tuft or ornament worn on the head. *Dryden.*
5. Loftiness; pride; courage; spirit; a lofty mien. *Shak.*

ЄREST, *v. t.* To furnish with a crest; to serve as a crest for. *Shak.*
2. To mark with long streaks.

ЄREST'ED, *a.* [from *crest.*] Wearing a crest; adorned with a crest or plume; having a comb; as a *crested* helmet; a *crested* cock.
2. In *natural history*, having a tuft like a crest.

ЄREST'-FALLEN, *a.* Dejected; sunk; bowed; dispirited; heartless; spiritless. *Shak. Howell.*
2. Having the upper part of the neck hanging on one side, as a horse. *Encyc.*

ЄREST'LESS, *a.* Without a crest; not dignified with coat-armor; not of an eminent family; of low birth. *Shak.*

ЄRETA'CEOUS, *a.* [L. *cretaceus*, from *creta*, chalk. Sp. It. *id.*; Fr. *craie*; D. *kryt*; G. *kreide*; Sw. *krita.*]
Chalky; having the qualities of chalk; like chalk; abounding with chalk.

ЄRE'TIЄ, *n.* [Gr, κρητικος.] A poetic foot of three syllables, one short between two long syllables. *Bentley.*

ЄRE'TIN, *n.* A name given to certain deformed and helpless idiots in the Alps.

ЄREV'ICE, *n.* [Fr. *crevasse*, from *crever*, to burst, to crack; It. *crepatura*; L. *crepo*, to burst. See *Crepitate* and *Rip.*]
A crack; a cleft; a fissure; a rent; an opening; as a *crevice* in a wall. *Addison.*

ЄREV'ICE, *v. t.* To crack; to flaw. *Wotton.*

ЄREV'IS, *n.* The craw-fish. [*Little used.*]

ЄREW, *n.* [contracted from Sax. *cread*, or *cruth*, a *crowd*; D. *rot*; G. *rotte*; Sw. *rote*; Eng. *rout*, an assembly, a collection, from gathering or pressing. Class Rd.]
1. A company of people associated; as a noble *crew*; a gallant *crew*. *Spenser. Chevy-Chase.*
2. A company, *in a low or bad sense, which is now most usual*; a herd; as a rebel *crew*. *Milton.*

So we say, a miserable *crew*.

3. The company of seamen who man a ship, vessel or boat; the company belonging to a vessel. Also, the company or gang of a carpenter, gunner, boatswain, &c. It is appropriated to the common sailors.

ЄREW, *pret.* of *crow*, but the regular preterit and participle, *crowed*, is now most commonly used.

ЄREW'EL, *n.* [Qu. D. *klewel.*] Yarn twisted and wound on a knot or ball, or two-threaded worsted. *Johnson. Bailey.*

ЄREWET. [See *Cruet.*]

ЄRIB, *n.* [Sax. *crybb*; D. *krib*; Sw. *krubba*; Dan. *krybbe*; Ir. *grib*. Qu. the root of *grapple*, to catch.]
1. The manger of a stable, in which oxen and cows feed. In America, it it distinguished from a rack for horses.

Where no oxen are, the *crib* is clean. Prov. xiv.

The manger for other beasts.

The ass knoweth his master's *crib*. Is. i.

2. A small habitation or cottage. *Shak.*
3. A stall for oxen.
4. A case or box in salt works. *Encyc.*
5. A small building, raised on posts, for storing Indian corn. *U. States.*

ЄRIB, *v. t.* To shut or confine in a narrow habitation; to cage. *Shak.*

ЄRIB'BAĠE, *n.* A game at cards.

ЄRIB'BED, *pp.* Shut up; confined; caged.

ЄRIB'BLE, *n.* [L. *cribellum*, from *cribrum*, and this from *cribro*, to sift; Sp. *criba*, *cribar*; Port. *crivo*; It. *cribro*, *cribrare*, and *crivello*, *crivellare*; Fr. *crible*, *cribler*; W. *cribaw*, to comb or card; Arm. *kribat*; Ir. *riobhar*, a sieve; allied to Eng. *garble*. See Ch. כרבל, Ar. غربل, Ch. רבל, to sift or riddle. Class Rb. No. 30. 34. 46.]
1. A corn-sieve or riddle.
2. Coarse flour or meal. [*Not used in the U. States.*]

ЄRIB'BLE, *v. t.* To sift; to cause to pass through a sieve or riddle.

ЄRIBRA'TION, *n.* [See *Cribble.*] The act of sifting or riddling; used in pharmacy.

ЄRIB'RIFORM, *a.* [L. *cribrum*, a sieve, and *forma*, form.]
Resembling a sieve or riddle; a term applied to the lamen of the ethmoid bone, through which the fibers of the olfactory nerve pass to the nose. *Anat.*

ЄRICH'TONITE, *n.* A mineral so called from Dr. Crichton, physician to the Emperor of Russia. It has a velvet black color, and crystalizes in very acute small rhomboids. It occurs in primitive rocks with octahedrite. *Ure.*

ЄRICK, *n.* [See *Creak.*] The creaking of a door. [*Not used.*]
2. A spasmodic affection of some part of the body, as of the neck or back; local spasm or cramp.

ЄRICK'ET, *n.* [D. *krekel*, from the root of *creak*; W. *cricell*, cricket, and *cricellu*, to chirp or chatter; *crig*, a *crack.*]
An insect of the genus Gryllus, belonging to the order of Hemipters. There are several species, so named probably on account of their *creaking* or chirping voice.

The *cricket* chirping in the hearth. *Goldsmith.*

ЄRICK'ET, *n.* [Qu. Sax. *cricc*, a stick.] A play or exercise with bats and ball. *Pope.*
2. A low stool. [British *kriget*, a little elevation. *Whitaker.* Qu. Sw. *krycka*, stilts or crutches.]

ЄRICK'ETER, *n.* One who plays at cricket. *Duncombe.*

ЄRICK'ET-MATCH, *n.* A match at cricket. *Duncombe.*

ЄRI'ED, *pret.* and *part.* of *cry*.

ЄRI'ER, } *n.* [See *Cry.*] One who cries;
ЄRY'ER, } one who makes proclamation. The crier of a court is an officer whose duty is to proclaim the orders or commands of the court, to open or adjourn the court, keep silence, &c. A crier is also employed to give notice of auctions, and for other purposes.

ЄRIME, *n.* [L. *crimen*; Gr. κριμα; It *crime*; Port. *id.*; Sp. *crimen*; Fr. *crime*; Arm. *crim*; Norm. *crisme*. This word is from the root of Gr. κρινω, L. *cerno*, to separate, to judge, to decree, to condemn. But this verb seems to be composed of two distinct roots, for in Latin, the pret. is *crevi*, which cannot be formed from *cerno*; and in Greek, the derivatives, κριθω, κρισις, κριτης, cannot be regularly formed from κρινω. The Gr. κριμα is undoubtedly a contraction, for in Norman the word is *crisme*. The root then of these derivatives is the same as of the Ir. *criathar*, a seive, W. *rhidyll*, Eng. *riddle*; W. *rhidiaw*, to secrete, to separate. We have *screen*, a riddle, from the root of κρινω, and *riddle*, from the Celtic root of κρισις, κριτης. To judge is to decide, to separate or cut off, hence to condemn; a *crime* is that which is condemned.]
1. An act which violates a law, divine or human; an act which violates a rule of moral duty; an offense against the laws of right, prescribed by God or man, or against any rule of duty plainly implied in those laws. A crime may consist in *omission* or neglect, as well as in *commission*, or positive transgression. The commander of a fortress who suffers the enemy to take possession by neglect, is as really criminal, as one who voluntarily opens the gates without resistance.

But in a more common and restricted sense, a crime denotes an offense, or violation of public law, of a deeper and more atrocious nature; a public wrong; or a violation of the commands of God, and the offenses against the laws made to preserve the public rights; as treason, murder, robbery, theft, arson, &c. The minor wrongs committed against individuals or private rights, are denominated *trespasses*, and the minor wrongs against public rights are called *misdemeanors.* Crimes and misdemeanors are punishable by indictment, information or public prosecution; trespasses or private injuries, at the suit of the individuals injured. But in many cases an act is considered both as a public offense and a trespass, and is punishable both by the public and the individual injured.

2. Any great wickedness; iniquity; wrong.

No *crime* was thine, if 'tis no *crime* to love. *Pope*

Capital crime, a crime punishable with death.

CRI'MEFUL, *a.* Criminal; wicked; partaking of wrong; contrary to law, right or duty. *Shak.*

CRI'MELESS, *a.* Free from crime; innocent. *Shak.*

CRIM'INAL, *a.* Guilty of a crime; *applied to persons.*

2. Partaking of a crime; involving a crime; that violates public law, divine or human; as, theft is a *criminal* act.

3. That violates moral obligation; wicked.

4. Relating to crimes; opposed to *civil;* as a *criminal* code; *criminal* law.

CRIM'INAL, *n.* A person who has committed an offense against public law; a violater of law, divine or human. More particularly, a person indicted or charged with a public offense, and one who is found guilty, by verdict, confession or proof.

Criminal conversation, the illegal commerce of the sexes; adultery.

CRIMINAL'ITY, CRIM'INALNESS, *n.* The quality of being criminal, or a violation of law; guiltiness; the quality of being guilty of a crime.

This is by no means the only criterion of *criminality.* *Blackstone,* iv. ch. 17. *Panoplist. Encyc.*

CRIM'INALLY, *adv.* In violation of public law; in violation of divine law; wickedly; in a wrong or iniquitous manner.

CRIM'INATE, *v. t.* [L. *criminor, criminatus.*]

To accuse; to charge with a crime; to alledge to be guilty of a crime, offense or wrong.

Our municipal laws do not require the offender to plead guilty or *criminate* himself. *Scott on Lev.* vi. *Beloe's Herod. Christ. Obs.*

CRIM'INATED, *pp.* Accused; charged with a crime.

CRIM'INATING, *ppr.* Accusing; alledging to be guilty.

CRIMINA'TION, *n.* [L. *criminatio.*] The act of accusing; accusation; charge of having been guilty of a criminal act, offense or wrong. *Johnson.*

CRIM'INATORY, *a.* Relating to accusation; accusing.

CRIM'INOUS, *a.* Very wicked; hainous; involving great crime. [*Not used.*] *Hammond.*

CRIM'INOUSLY, *adv.* Criminally; hainously; enormously. [*Not used.*]

CRIM'INOUSNESS, *n.* Wickedness; guilt; criminality. [*Not used.*] *King Charles.*

CRIM'OSIN. [See *Crimson.*]

CRIMP, *a.* [Sax. *acrymman,* to crumble; D. *kruim,* a crum; *kruimelen,* to crumble. See *Crumble.*]

1. Easily crumbled; friable; brittle. [*Little used.*]

The fowler—treads the *crimp* earth. *Philips.*

2. Not consistent. [Qu. Dan. *krum,* crooked, or supra, easily broken.] [*Not used.*] *Arbuthnot.*

CRIMP, *v. t.* [W. *crimpiaw,* to pinch, to form into a ridge or *rim.*]

To catch; to seize; to pinch and hold. [See *Crimple.*]

CRIMP, *v. t.* [Sax. *gecrympt.*] To curl or frizzle; as, to *crimp* the hair. This is evidently the same word as the foregoing.

CRIMP, *n.* In *England,* an agent for coal-merchants, and for persons concerned in shipping. *Bailey.*

2. One who decoys another into the naval or military service.

3. A game at cards. *Obs.*

CRIMP'LE, *v. t.* [D. *krimpen;* G. *id.;* Sw. *krimpa;* Dan. *krymper;* Scot. *crimp;* W. *crimpiaw,* to shrink, to pinch; *crwm, crom,* curving, bending, shrinking; *crymu,* to bend. See *Crumple* and *Rumple,* from the same root, W. *rhimp, rim,* a rim.]

To contract or draw together; to shrink; to cause to shrink; to curl. *Wiseman.*

CRIMP'LED, *pp.* Contracted; shrunk; curled.

CRIMP'LING, *ppr.* Contracting; shrinking; curling; hobbling. *Ash.*

CRIM'SON, *n.* *krim'zn.* [It. *cremisi, cremisino;* Fr. *cramoisi;* Sp. *carmesi;* Arm. *carmoasy;* D. *karmozyn;* G. *karmosin;* Sw. *karmesin;* Dan. *karmesie;* from Ar. قرمز kirmizon, kermes, the cochineal insect or berry.]

A deep red color; a red tinged with blue; also, a red color in general; as the virgin *crimson* of modesty. *Shak.*

He made the vail of blue, and purple, and *crimson.* 2 Chron. iii.

CRIM'SON, *a.* Of a beautiful deep red; as the *crimson* blush of modesty; a *crimson* stream of blood.

CRIM'SON, *v. t.* To dye with crimson; to dye of a deep red color; to make red.

CRIM'SON, *v. i.* To become of a deep red color; to be tinged with red; to blush.

Her cheeks *crimsoned* at the entrance of her lover.

CRIM'SONED, *pp.* Dyed or tinged with a deep red.

CRIM'SONING, *ppr.* Dyeing or tinging with a deep red.

CRINC'UM, *n.* A cramp; a contraction; a turn or bend; a whim. [*A vulgar word.*] *Hudibras.*

CRINGE, *v. t.* *crinj.* [probably from the root of *crank, crinkle,* Heb. and Ch. כרע; or from the root of *crook,* with a nasal sound of the last consonant; G. *kriechen;* W. *cryçu,* to curl.]

Properly, to shrink; to contract; to draw together; a popular use of the word. [Vulgarly, *scringe.*]

You see him *cringe* his face. *Shak.*

CRINGE, *v. i.* *crinj.* To bow; to bend with servility; to fawn; to make court by mean compliances.

Flatterers are always bowing and *cringing.* *Arbuthnot.*

CRINGE, *n.* *crinj.* A bow; servile civility. *Philips.*

CRIN'GER, *n.* One who cringes, or bows and flatters with servility.

CRIN'GING, *ppr.* Shrinking; bowing servilely.

CRIN'GLE, *n.* *cring'gl.* [D. *kring, krinkel, kronkel,* a bend, turn, *ring,* or twist. See *Crank* and *Cringe.*]

1. A withe for fastening a gate. [*Local.*]

2. In *marine language,* a hole in the bolt-rope of a sail, formed by intertwisting the division of a rope, called a strand, alternately round itself, and through the strand of the bolt-rope, till it becomes three-fold, and takes the shape of a ring. Its use is to receive the ends of the ropes by which the sail is drawn up to its yard, or to extend the leech by the bow-line-bridles.

Iron-cringles or hanks, are open rings running on the stays, to which the heads of the stay sails are made fast. *Mar. Dict.*

CRINIG'EROUS, *a.* [L. *criniger; crinis,* hair, and *gero,* to wear.] Hairy; overgrown with hair. *Dict.*

CRI'NITE, *a.* [L. *crinitus,* from *crinis,* hair. Qu. W. *crinaw,* to parch, to frizzle.] Having the appearance of a tuft of hair.

CRINK'LE, *v. i.* *crink'l.* [D. *krinkelen,* to wind or twist. Qu. *crank,* and *ring,* Sax. *hring.*]

To turn or wind; to bend; to wrinkle; to run in and out in little or short bends or turns; as, the lightning *crinkles.*

CRINK'LE, *v. t.* To form with short turns or wrinkles; to mold into inequalities.

CRINK'LE, *n.* A wrinkle; a winding or turn; sinuosity.

CRI'NOSE, *a.* Hairy. [See *Crinite.*] [*Little used.*]

CRINOS'ITY, *n.* Hairiness. [*Little used.*]

CRIP'PLE, *n.* *crip'l.* [D. *kreupel;* G. *krüppel;* Dan. *krypling, kröppel,* and *kröbling,* from *kröb,* a creeping animal; Ice. *crypen,* to move crooked. It would seem that this is from the root of *creep.*]

A lame person; primarily, one who creeps, halts or limps; one who has lost, or never enjoyed the use of his limbs. Acts xiv.

The word may signify one who is partially or totally disabled from using his limbs.

See the blind beggar dance, the *cripple* sing. *Pope.*

CRIP'PLE, *a.* Lame. *Shak.*

CRIP'PLE, *v. t.* To lame; to deprive of the use of the limbs, particularly of the legs and feet.

2. To disable; to deprive of the power of exertion. We say, a fleet was *crippled* in the engagement.

CRIP'PLED, *pp.* Lamed; rendered impotent in the limbs; disabled.

CRIP'PLENESS, *n.* Lameness.

CRIP'PLING, *ppr.* Laming; depriving of the use of the limbs; disabling.

CRI'SIS, *n.* plu. *cri'ses.* [Gr. κρισις, L. *crisis,* from the root of κρινω, to separate, to determine, to decide. See *Crime.*]

1. In *medical science,* the change of a disease which indicates its event; that change which indicates recovery or death. It is sometimes used to designate the excretion of something noxious from the body, or of the noxious fluids in a fever. *Encyc. Parr.*

2. The decisive state of things, or the point

of time when an affair is arrived to its highth, and must soon terminate or suffer a material change.

This hour's the very *crisis* of your fate. *Dryden.*

CRISP, *a.* [L. *crispus*; It. *crespo*; G. *kraus.* See the Verb.]
1. Curled; formed into curls or ringlets.
2. Indented; winding; as *crisp* channels. *Shak.*
3. Brittle; friable; easily broken or crumbled. *Bacon.*

CRISP, *v. t.* [L. *crispo*; It. *crespare*; Sp. *crespar*; Fr. *crêper*; Dan. *kruser*; Sw. *krusa*; W. *cris*, a crust; *crisb*, a crisp coating; *crisbin*, crisp, friable; from *rhis*, broken into points, mince; allied to *cresu*, *crasu*, to roast or parch. From the Gothic dialects, we observe that *p* is not radical. Class Rd. No. 20. 73. Ar.]
1. To curl; to twist; to contract or form into ringlets, as the hair; to wreathe or interweave, as the branches of trees. *B. Jonson. Milton.*
2. To indent. *Johnson.* To twist or eddy. *Mason.*

But the sense is, to curl; to wrinkle in little undulations, as a fretted surface.

From that sapphire fount the *crisped* brooks,
Rolling on orient pearl and sands of gold,
Ran nectar, visiting each plant. *Milton.*

CRISPA'TION, *n.* The act of curling, or state of being curled. *Bacon.*

CRISP'ATURE, *n.* A curling; the state of being curled. *Lee. Botany.*

CRISP'ED, *pp.* Curled; twisted; frizzled.

CRISP'ING, *ppr.* Curling; frizzling.

CRISP'ING-PIN, *n.* A curling-iron. *Isaiah.*

CRISP'NESS, *n.* A state of being curled; also, brittleness.

CRISP'Y, *a.* Curled; formed into ringlets; as *crispy* locks. *Shak.*
2. Brittle; dried so as to break short; as a *crispy* cake.

CRIST'ATE, } *a.* [L. *cristatus*, from *crista*, a crest.]
CRIST'ATED, }
In *botany*, crested; tufted; having an appendage like a crest or tuft, as some anthers and flowers. *Martyn.*

CRITE'RION, *n.* plu. *criteria.* [Gr. κριτηριον, from the root of κρινω, to judge. See *Crime.*]
A standard of judging; any established law, rule, principle or fact, by which facts, propositions and opinions are compared, in order to discover their truth or falsehood, or by which a correct judgment may be formed.

CRITH'OMANCY, *n.* [Gr. κριθη, barley, and μαντεια, divination.]
A kind of divination by means of the dough of cakes, and the meal strewed over the victims, in ancient sacrifices. *Encyc.*

CRIT'IC, *n.* [Gr. κριτικος, from κριτης, a judge or discerner, from the root of κρινω, to judge, to separate, to distinguish. See *Crime.*]
1. A person skilled in judging of the merit of literary works; one who is able to discern and distinguish the beauties and faults of writing. In a more general sense, a person skilled in judging with propriety of any combination of objects, or of any work of art; and particularly of what are denominated the *Fine Arts.* A critic is one who, from experience, knowledge, habit or taste, can perceive the difference between propriety and impropriety, in objects or works presented to his view; between the natural and unnatural; the high and the low, or lofty and mean; the congruous and incongruous; the correct and incorrect, according to the established rules of the art.
2. An examiner; a judge.

And make each day a *critic* on the last. *Pope.*

3. One who judges with severity; one who censures or finds fault. *Pope. Watts. Swift.*

CRIT'IC, *a.* Critical; relating to criticism, or the art of judging of the merit of a literary performance or discourse, or of any work in the fine arts. [See *Critical.*]

CRIT'IC, *v. i.* To criticise; to play the critic. [*Little used.*] *Temple.*

CRIT'ICAL, *a.* [L. *criticus*; Gr. κριτικος. See *Critic.*]
1. Relating to criticism; nicely exact; as a *critical* dissertation on Homer.
2. Having the skill or power nicely to distinguish beauties from blemishes; as a *critical* judge; a *critical* auditor; a *critical* ear; *critical* taste.
3. Making nice distinctions; accurate; as *critical* rules.
4. Capable of judging with accuracy; discerning beauties and faults; nicely judicious in matters of literature and the fine arts; as, Virgil was a *critical* poet.
5. Capable of judging with accuracy; conforming to exact rules of propriety; exact; particular; as, to be *critical* in rites and ceremonies, or in the selection of books.
6. Inclined to find fault, or to judge with severity.
7. [See *Crisis.*] Pertaining to a crisis; marking the time or state of a disease which indicates its termination in the death or recovery of the patient; as *critical* days, or *critical* symptoms.
8. Producing a crisis or change in a disease; indicating a crisis; as a *critical* sweat.
9. Decisive; noting a time or state on which the issue of things depends; important, as regards the consequences; as a *critical* time or moment; a *critical* juncture.
10. Formed or situated to determine or decide, or having the crisis at command; important or essential for determining; as a *critical* post. *Mitford.*

CRIT'ICALLY, *adv.* In a critical manner; with nice discernment of truth or falsehood, propriety or impropriety; with nice scrutiny; accurately; exactly; as, to examine evidence *critically*; to observe *critically.*
2. At the crisis; at the exact time.
3. In a critical situation, place or condition, so as to command the crisis; as a town *critically* situated. *Mitford.*

CRIT'ICALNESS, *n.* The state of being critical; incidence at a particular point of time.
2. Exactness; accuracy; nicety; minute care in examination.

CRIT'ICISE, *v. i.* *s* as *z.* To examine and judge critically; to judge with attention to beauties and faults; as, to *criticise* on a literary work, on an argument or discourse.
2. To write remarks on the merit of a performance; to notice beauties and faults.

Cavil you may, but never *criticise.* *Pope.*

3. To animadvert upon as faulty; to utter censure; as, to *criticise* on a man's manners, or his expenses. *Locke.*

CRIT'ICISE, *v. t.* To notice beauties and blemishes or faults in; to utter or write remarks on the merit of a performance; as, to *criticise* the writings of Milton.
2. To pass judgment on with respect to merit or blame; as, to *criticise* an author; to *criticise* the conduct.

CRIT'ICISED, *pp.* Examined and judged with respect to beauties and faults.

CRIT'ICISING, *ppr.* Examining and judging with regard to beauties and faults; remarking on; animadverting on.

CRIT'ICISM, *n.* The art of judging with propriety of the beauties and faults of a literary performance, or of any production in the fine arts; as the rules of *criticism.*
2. The act of judging on the merit of a performance; animadversion; remark on beauties and faults; critical observation, verbal or written. We say, the author's *criticisms* are candid, or they are severe.

CRITÏQUE, } *n.* [Fr. *critique.*] A *critical*
CRIT'IC, } examination of the merits of a performance; remarks or animadversions on beauties and faults.

Addison wrote a *critique* on PARADISE LOST.

2. Science of criticism; standard or rules of judging of the merit of performances.

If ideas and words were distinctly weighed, and duly considered, they would afford us another sort of logic and *critic.* *Locke.*

CRIZ'ZEL, } *n.* [See *Crisp.*] A kind
CRIZ'ZELING, } of roughness on the surface of glass, which clouds its transparency. *Encyc.*

CROAK, *v. i.* [Sax. *cracettan*; Goth. *hrukyan*; L. *crocio*, *crocito*; Sp. *croaxar*; It. *crocciare*; Fr. *croasser*; Arm. *crozal*; G. *krächzen*; D. *kraaijen*, to crow, and *kruchgen*, to groan; Ir. *grag*, *gragam*; coinciding in elements with W. *creg*, *cryg*, hoarse, *crygu*, to make *rough* or hoarse; Sax. *hreog*, rough, and *hreowian*, to rue: Gr. κρωζω, κρωγμος, and κραζω, κραγεις. These all appear to be of one family, and from the root of *rough*, and *creak*, W. *rhyg.* See *Crow.*]
1. To make a low, hoarse noise in the throat, as a frog or other animal.
2. To caw; to cry as a raven or crow.
3. To make any low, muttering sound, resembling that of a frog or raven; as, their bellies *croak.* *Locke.*
4. In contempt, to speak with a low, hollow voice.

CRŌAK, *n.* The low, harsh sound uttered by a frog or a raven, or a like sound.

CRŌAKER, *n.* One that croaks, murmurs or grumbles; one who complains unreasonably.

CRŌAKING, *ppr.* Uttering a low, harsh sound from the throat, or other similar sound.

CRŌAKING, *n.* A low, harsh sound, as of a frog, or the bowels.

CRO'ATS, *n.* Troops, natives of Croatia.

CRO'CALITE, *n.* [from *crocus*, saffron.] A mineral, a variety of zeolite, of an orange or brick red color. It is sometimes found in reniform or globular masses, with a radiated texture. *Cleaveland.*

CRO'CEOUS, *a.* [L. *croceus*, from *crocus*, saffron.]

Like saffron; yellow; consisting of saffron.

CRO'CHES, *n.* Little buds or knobs about the tops of a deer's horn. *Bailey.*

CROCITA'TION, *n.* [L. *crocito.*] A croaking.

CROCK, *n.* [Sax. *cruce, crocca*; D. *kruik*; G. *krug*; D. *krukke*; Sw. *kruka*; Fr. *cruche*; W. *cregen*, an earthern vessel; *crocan*, a pot.]

An earthern vessel; a pot or pitcher; a cup. *Obs.*

CROCK, *n.* [Qu. from *crock*, supra, or from Ch. חרך, Ar. حرق charaka, to burn.]

Soot, or the black matter collected from combustion on pots and kettles, or in a chimney. *Ray.*

CROCK, *v. t.* or *i.* To black with soot, or other matter collected from combustion; or to black with the coloring matter of cloth. *New England.*

CROCK'ERY, *n.* [W. *crocan*, a boiler or pot; *crocenu*, to make earthern vessels; *crocenyz*, a potter. See *Crock.*]

Earthern ware; vessels formed of clay, glazed and baked. The term is applied to the coarser kinds of ware; the finer kinds being usually called *china* or *porcelain.*

CROC'ODILE, *n.* [Gr. χροκοδειλος; [qu. χροκος, saffron, and δειλος, fearing;] L. *crocodilus*; It. *coccodrillo*; Sp. *cocodrilo.*]

An amphibious animal of the genus Lacerta or lizard, of the largest kind. It has a naked body, with four feet and a tail; it has five toes on the fore feet, and four on the hind feet. It grows to the length of sixteen or eighteen feet, runs swiftly on land, but does not easily turn itself. It inhabits the large rivers in Africa and Asia, and lays its eggs, resembling those of a goose, in the sand, to be hatched by the heat of the sun. [See *Alligator.*] *Encyc.*

2. In *rhetoric*, a captious and sophistical argument contrived to draw one into a snare.

CROC'ODILE, *a.* Pertaining to or like a crocodile; as *crocodile* tears, that is, false or affected tears, hypocritical sorrow.

CRO'CUS, *n.* [Gr. χροκος, from the Shemitic ירק, and its yellow color.]

1. Saffron, a genus of plants.

2. In *chimistry*, a yellow powder; any metal calcined to a red or deep yellow color. *Encyc.*

CROFT, *n.* [Sax. *croft*; allied probably to L. *crypta*, Gr. κρυπτω, to conceal.]

A little close adjoining or near to a dwelling-house, and used for pasture, tillage or other purposes. *Encyc.*

CROISA'DE, *n.* [Fr. from *croix*, a cross.] A holy war; an expedition of christians against the infidels, for the conquest of Palestine. [See the more common word, *Crusade.*]

CROIS'ES, *n.* [See *Cross.*] Soldiers enrolled under the banners of the cross. *Burke.*

2. Pilgrims who carry the cross.

CRO'KER, *n.* A fowl that inhabits the Chesapeak and the large rivers in Virginia; sometimes of three feet in length. *Pennant.*

CROM'LECH, *n.* [W. *cromleç*; *crom*, bent, concave, and *llec*, a flat stone.]

Huge flat stones resting on other stones, set on end for that purpose; supposed to be the remains of druidical altars. *Rowland, Mon. Antiq.*

CRONE, *n.* [Ir. *criona*, old; *crion*, withered; *crionaim*, to wither, fade, decay; W. *crinaw*, to wither, to become brittle; Gr. γερων, old.]

1. An old woman. *Shak. Dryden.*

2. An old ewe. *Tusser.*

CRO'NET, *n.* [*coronet.*] The hair which grows over the top of a horse's hoof. *Johnson.*

2. The iron at the end of a tilting spade. *Bailey.*

CRONICAL, CRONYCAL. [See *Acronical.*]

CRO'NY, *n.* [See *Crone.* But this word seems to carry the sense of *fellowship*, and is precisely the Ar. قرن karana, to join, to associate; whence its derivative, an associate.]

An intimate companion; an associate; a familiar friend.

> To oblige your *crony* Swift,
> Bring our dame a new year's gift. *Swift.*

Hence an *old crony* is an intimate friend of long standing.

CROOK, *n.* [Sw. *krok*; Dan. *krog*; Fr. *croc*, *crochet*; Arm. *crocq*; Ir. *cruca*; W. *crug*, *crwca, croca*; Goth. *hrugg*, a shepherd's *crook*, which in Italian is *rocco*; W. *crug*, a heap, a *rick*; Sax. *hric*; Eng. a *ridge*; G. *rücken*, the back, or ridge of an animal. These words appear to be connected with L. *ruga*, a wrinkle, Russ. *kryg*, *okrug*, a circle. Wrinkling forms roughness, and this is the radical sense of hoarseness, It. *roco*, hoarse, L. *raucus*, Eng. *rough*, W. *cryg*, rough, hoarse. The radical sense of *crook* is to strain or draw; hence, to bend.]

1. Any bend, turn or curve; or a bent or curving instrument. We speak of a *crook* in a stick of timber, or in a river; and any hook is a *crook.*

2. A shepherd staff, curving at the end; a pastoral staff. When used by a bishop or abbot, it is called a *crosier.*

> He left his *crook*, he left his flocks. *Prior.*

3. A gibbet.

4. An artifice; a trick. *Cranmer.*

CROOK, *v. t.* [Fr. *crochuer*; Sw. *kröka*; Dan. *kröger*; W. *crwcau, crocau.*]

1. To bend; to turn from a straight line; to make a curve or hook.

2. To turn from rectitude; to pervert. *Bacon.*

3. To thwart. [*Little used.*]

CROOK, *v. i.* To bend or be bent; to be turned from a right line; to curve; to wind. *Camden.*

CROOK'-BACK, *n.* A crooked back; one who has a crooked back or round shoulders. *Shak.*

CROOK'-BACKED, *a.* Having a round back, or shoulders. *Dryden.*

CROOK'ED, *pp.* or *a.* Bent; curved; curving; winding.

2. Winding in moral conduct; devious; froward; perverse; going out of the path of rectitude; given to obliquity or wandering from duty.

> They are a perverse and *crooked* generation. Deut. xxxii.

CROOK'EDLY, *adv.* In a winding manner.

2. Untowardly; not compliantly.

CROOK'EDNESS, *n.* A winding, bending or turning; curvity; curvature; inflection. *Hooker.*

2. Perverseness; untowardness; deviation from rectitude; iniquity; obliquity of conduct.

3. Deformity of a gibbous body. *Johnson. Taylor.*

CROOK'EN, *v. t.* To make crooked. [*Not in use.*]

CROOK'ING, *ppr.* Bending; winding.

CROOK'-KNEED, *a.* Having crooked knees. *Shak.*

CROOK'-SHOULDERED, *a.* Having bent shoulders.

CROOP, CRÖUP, *n.* [Scot. *croup, crope, crupe, crowp*, to croak, to cry or speak with a hoarse voice; Goth. *hropyan*; Sax. *hreopan*, to call out.]

The disease called technically *cynanche trachealis*, an affection of the throat accompanied with a hoarse difficult respiration. It is vulgarly called *rattles.*

CROP, *n.* [Sax. *crop, cropp*, the crop of a fowl, a cluster, ears of corn, grapes, grains of corn; D. *krop*; G. *kropf*; W. *crop*, the crop or craw; *cropiad*, a gathering into a heap, a *creeping*; *cropian*, to creep. Here we see that *crop* is a gathering, and that it is connected with *creep*, whose radical sense is to catch or take hold. Hence *crop* coincides with L. *carpo, carpus*, and perhaps with *reap, rapio*, as it does with *grapple.* Hence we see how the *crop* of a fowl, and a *crop* of grain or hay, are consistently the same word.]

1. The first stomach of a fowl; the *craw.*

2. The top or highest part of a thing; the end. [*Not in use.*] *Chaucer.*

3. That which is gathered; the corn, or fruits of the earth collected; harvest. The word includes every species of fruit or produce, gathered for man or beast.

4. Corn and other cultivated plants while growing; *a popular use of the word.*

5. Any thing cut off or gathered.

6. Hair cut close or short.

CROP, *v. t.* To cut off the ends of any thing; to eat off; to pull off; to pluck; to mow; to reap; as, to *crop* flowers, trees, or grass. Man *crops* trees or plants with an instrument, or with his fingers; a beast *crops* with his teeth.

2. To cut off prematurely; to gather before it falls.

> While force our youth, like fruits, untimely *crops.* *Denham.*

CROP, *v. i.* To yield harvest. [*Not in use.*] *Shak.*

CROP'-EAR, *n.* [*crop* and *ear.*] A horse whose ears are cropped. *Shak.*

CROP'-EARED, *a.* Having the ears cropped. *B. Jonson.*

CROP'FUL, *a.* Having a full crop or belly; satiated. *Milton.*

CROP'PED, CROPT, *pp.* Cut off; plucked; eaten off; reaped, or mowed.

CROP'PER, *n.* A pigeon with a large crop. *Johnson. Walton.*

CROP'PING, *ppr.* Cutting off; pulling off; eating off; reaping, or mowing.

CROP'PING, *n.* The act of cutting off.

2. The raising of crops.

CROP'-SICK, *a.* Sick or indisposed from a surcharged stomach; sick with excess in eating or drinking. *Tate.*

CROP'-SICKNESS, *n.* Sickness from repletion of the stomach. L. *crapula.*

CRO'SIER, *n. kro'zhur.* [Fr. *crosse*, a *crosier*, a bat or gaff-stick; *crosser*, to play at cricket; Arm. *croçz*; from the root of *cross.*]

1. A bishop's crook or pastoral staff, a symbol of pastoral authority and care. It consists of a gold or silver staff, crooked at the top, and is carried occasionally before bishops and abbots, and held in the hand when they give solemn benedictions. The use of crosiers is ancient. Originally a crosier was a staff with a cross on the top, in form of a crutch or T. *Encyc.*

2. In *astronomy*, four stars in the southern hemisphere, in the form of a cross. *Encyc.*

CROS'LET, *n.* [See *Cross.*] A small cross. In *heraldry*, a cross crossed at a small distance from the ends. *Encyc.*

CROSS, *n. craus.* [W. *croes*; Arm. *croaz*; G. *kreuz*; Sw. *kors*; Dan. *kryds* and *kors*; Russ. *krest.* Class Rd. But the English *cross* would seem to be from the L. *crux*, through the Fr. *croix*, *croiser*; It. *croce*; Sp. *cruz*; W. *crôg*, coinciding with the Ir. *regh*, *riagh*. Qu. the identity of these words. The Irish has *cros*, a cross; *crosadh*, *crosaim*, to cross, to hinder. If the last radical is *g* or *c*, this word belongs to the root of *crook.* Chaucer uses *crouche* for *cross.*]

1. A gibbet consisting of two pieces of timber placed across each other, either in form of a T or of an X. That on which our Savior suffered, is represented on coins and other monuments, to have been of the former kind. *Encyc.*

2. The ensign of the christian religion; and hence figuratively, the religion itself. *Rowe.*

3. A monument with a cross upon it to excite devotion, such as were anciently set in market places. *Johnson. Shak.*

4. Any thing in the form of a cross or gibbet.

5. A line drawn through another. *Johnson.*

6. Any thing that thwarts, obstructs, or perplexes; hindrance; vexation; misfortune; opposition; trial of patience.

> Heaven prepares good men with *crosses.* *B. Jonson.*

7. Money or coin stamped with the figure of a cross. *Dryden.*

8. The right side or face of a coin, stamped with a cross. *Encyc.*

9. The mark of a cross, instead of a signature, on a deed, formerly impressed by those who could not write. *Encyc.*

10. Church lands in Ireland. *Davies.*

11. In *theology*, the sufferings of Christ by crucifixion.

> That he might reconcile both to God in one body by the *cross.* Eph. ii.

12. The doctrine of Christ's sufferings and of the atonement, or of salvation by Christ.

> The preaching of the *cross* is to them that perish, foolishness. 1 Cor. i. Gal. v.

To take up the cross, is to submit to troubles and afflictions from love to Christ.

13. In *mining*, two nicks cut in the surface of the earth, thus +.

Cross and pile, a play with money, at which it is put to chance whether a coin shall fall with that side up, which bears the cross, or the other which is called *pile* or reverse.

CROSS, *a. craus.* Transverse; oblique; passing from side to side; falling athwart; as a *cross* beam.

> The *cross* refraction of a second prism. *Newton.*

2. Adverse; opposite; obstructing; sometimes with *to*; as an event *cross to* our inclinations.

3. Perverse; untractable; as the *cross* circumstances of a man's temper. *South.*

4. Peevish; fretful; ill-humored; *applied to persons or things*; as a *cross* woman or husband; a *cross* answer.

5. Contrary; contradictory; perplexing.

> Contradictions that seem to lie *cross* and uncouth. *South.*

6. Adverse; unfortunate.

> Behold the *cross* and unlucky issue of my design. *Glanville.*

7. Interchanged; as a *cross* marriage, when a brother and sister intermarry with two persons who have the same relation to each other. *Bailey.*

8. Noting what belongs to an adverse party; as a *cross* interrogatory. *Kent.*

CROSS, *prep.* Athwart; transversely; over; from side to side; so as to intersect.

> And *cross* their limits cut a sloping way. *Dryden.*

This is admissible in poetry, as an abbreviation of *across.*

CROSS, *v. t.* To draw or run a line, or lay a body across another; as, to *cross* a word in writing; to *cross* the arms.

2. To erase; to cancel; as, to *cross* an account.

3. To make the sign of the cross, as catholics in devotion.

4. To pass from side to side; to pass or move over; as, to *cross* a road; to *cross* a river, or the ocean. I *crossed* the English channel, from Dieppe to Brighton, in a steam-boat, Sept. 18, 1824. *W.*

5. To thwart; to obstruct; to hinder; to embarrass; as, to *cross* a purpose or design.

6. To counteract; to clash or interfere with; to be inconsistent with; as, natural appetites may *cross* our principles.

7. To counteract or contravene; to hinder by authority; to stop. [See No. 5.]

8. To contradict. *Bacon. Hooker.*

9. To debar or preclude. *Shak.*

To cross the breed of an animal, is to produce young from different varieties of the species.

CROSS, *v. i.* To lie or be athwart.

2. To move or pass laterally, or from one side towards the other, or from place to place, either at right angles or obliquely; as, to *cross* from Nantucket to New Bedford.

3. To be inconsistent; as, men's actions do not always *cross* with reason. [*Not used.*] *Sidney.*

CROSS'-ARMED, *a.* With arms across. In *botany*, brachiate; decussated; having branches in pairs, each at right angles with the next. *Martyn.*

CROSS'-BARRED, *a.* Secured by transverse bars. *Milton.*

CROSS'-BAR-SHOT, *n.* A bullet with an iron bar passing through it, and standing out a few inches on each side; used in naval actions for cutting the enemy's rigging. *Encyc.*

CROSS'-BEARER, *n.* In *the Romish church*, the chaplain of an archbishop or primate, who bears a cross before him on solemn occasions. Also, a certain officer in the inquisition, who makes a vow before the inquisitors to defend the Catholic faith, though with the loss of fortune and life. *Encyc.*

CROSS'-BILL, *n.* In *chancery*, an original bill by which the defendant prays relief against the plaintiff. *Blackstone.*

CROSS'-BILL, *n.* A species of bird, the *Loxia curvirostra*, the mandibles of whose bill curve opposite ways and cross each other. *Encyc.*

CROSS'-BITE, *n.* A deception; a cheat. *L'Estrange.*

CROSS'-BITE, *v. t.* To thwart or contravene by deception. *Collier.*

CROSS'-BOW, *n.* In *archery*, a missive weapon formed by placing a bow athwart a stock. *Bailey.*

CROSS'-BOWER, *n.* One who shoots with a cross-bow. *Raleigh.*

CROSS'CUT, *v. t.* To cut across.

CROSS'CUT-SAW, *n.* A saw managed by two men, one at each end.

CROSS'ED, *pp.* Having a line drawn over; canceled; erased; passed over; thwarted; opposed; obstructed; counteracted.

CROSS-EXAMINA'TION, *n.* The examination or interrogation of a witness called by one party, by the opposite party or his counsel.

CROSS-EXAM'INE, *v. t.* To examine a witness by the opposite party or his counsel, as the witness for the plaintiff by the defendant, and vice versa.

> The opportunity to *cross-examine* the witnesses has been expressly waived. *Kent.*

CROSS-EXAM'INED, *pp.* Examined or interrogated by the opposite party.

CROSS'-FLOW, *v. i.* To flow across. *Milton.*

CROSS'-GRAINED, *a.* Having the grain or fibers across or irregular; as in timber, where a branch shoots from the trunk, there is a curling of the grain.

2. Perverse; untractable; not condescending.

CROSS'ING, *ppr.* Drawing; running or passing a line over; erasing; canceling; thwarting; opposing; counteracting; passing over.

CROSS'ING, *n.* A thwarting; impediment; vexation. *Shak.*

CROSS'-JACK, *n. cro-jeck.* A sail extended on the lower yard of the mizen mast; but seldom used. *Encyc.*

CROSS'-LEGGED, *a.* Having the legs across.

CROSS'LY, *adv.* Athwart; so as to intersect something else.

2. Adversely; in opposition; unfortunately.

3. Peevishly; fretfully.

CROSS'NESS, *n.* Peevishness; fretfulness; ill humor; perverseness.

CROSS-PIECE, *n.* A rail of timber extending over the windlass of a ship, furnished with pins with which to fasten the rigging, as occasion requires. *Encyc.*

CROSS′-PURPOSE, *n.* A contrary purpose; contradictory system; also, a conversation in which one person does or pretends to misunderstand another's meaning. An enigma; a riddle. *Mason.*

CROSS′-QUESTION, *v. t.* To cross examine. *Killingbeck.*

CROSS′-RÖW, *n.* The alphabet, so named because a cross is placed at the beginning, to show that the end of learning is piety. *Johnson. Shak.*

2. A row that crosses others.

CROSS′-SEA, *n.* Waves running across others; a swell running in different directions.

CROSS′-STAFF, *n.* An instrument to take the altitude of the sun or stars.

CROSS′-STONE, *n.* A mineral called also harmotome, and staurolite. It is almost always in crystals. Its single crystals are rectangular four-sided prisms, broad or compressed, and terminated by four-sided pyramids, with rhombic faces, which stand on the lateral edges. But this mineral is generally found in double crystals, composed of two of the preceding crystals, so intersecting each other, that the two broader planes of one prism are perpendicular to the broader planes of the other, throughout their whole length. Its color is a grayish white or milk white, sometimes with a shade of yellow or red. *Cleaveland.*

CROSS′-TINING, *n.* In *husbandry*, a harrowing by drawing the harrow or drag back and forth on the same ground. *Encyc.*

CROSS′-TREES, *n.* In *ships*, certain pieces of timber, supported by the cheeks and trestle-trees, at the upper ends of the lower masts, to sustain the frame of the top, and on the top masts, to extend the top-gallant shrouds. *Mar. Dict.*

CROSS′-WAY, **CROSS′-RÖAD**, *n.* A way or road that crosses another road or the chief road; an obscure path intersecting the main road. *Johnson. Shak.*

CROSS′-WIND, *n.* A side wind; an unfavorable wind. *Boyle.*

CROSS′-WISE, *adv.* Across; in the form of a cross.

CROSS′-WŎRT, *n.* A plant of the genus Valantia.

CROTCH, *n.* [Fr. *croc*, a hook. See *Crook* and *Crutch.*]

1. A fork or forking; the parting of two legs or branches; as the *crotch* of a tree.

2. In *ships*, a crooked timber placed on the keel, in the fore and aft parts of a ship.

3. A piece of wood or iron, opening on the top and extending two horns or arms, like a half moon, used for supporting a boom, a spare topmast, yards, &c. *Mar. Dict.*

CROTCH′ED, *a.* Having a crotch; forked.

CROTCH′ET, *n.* [Fr. *crochet, croche*, from *croc.* See *Crook.*]

1. In *printing*, a hook including words, a sentence or a passage distinguished from the rest, thus [ ].

2. In *music*, a note or character, equal in time to half a minim, and the double of a quaver, thus ♩

3. A piece of wood resembling a fork, used as a support in building.

4. A peculiar turn of the mind; a whim, or fancy; a perverse conceit.

All the devices and *crotchets* of new inventions. *Howell.*

CROTCH′ETED, *a.* Marked with crotchets.

CROUCH, *v. i.* [G. *kriechen, kroch, kröche*, to creep, to stoop, to cringe, probably allied to *crook*, Fr. *crochu*, as *cringe* to *crank.* Class Rg. Vulgarly, *crooch, scrooch.*]

1. To bend down; to stoop low; to lie close to the ground; as an animal. A dog *crouches* to his master; a lion *crouches* in the thicket.

2. To bend servilely; to stoop meanly; to fawn; to cringe.

Every one that is left in thine house shall come and *crouch* to him for a piece of bread. 1 Sam. ii.

CROUCH, *v. t.* [See *Cross.*] To sign with the cross; to bless. [*Not in use.*] *Chaucer.*

CROUCH′ING, *ppr.* Bending; stooping; cringing.

CRÖUP, **CROOP**, *n.* [Fr. *croupe*, a ridge, top, buttocks; Sp. *grupa*; Port. *garupa*; It. *groppa*; W. *crib*; Russ. *krivei*, crooked; *krivlyu*, to bend.]

1. The rump of a fowl; the buttocks of a horse, or extremity of the reins above the hips.

2. [Scot. *croup.* See *Croop.*] The cynanche trachealis, a disease of the throat.

CRÖUPA′DE, **CROOPA′DE**, *n.* [from *croup*, or its root.] In *the manege*, a leap in which the horse pulls up his hind legs, as if he drew them up to his belly. *Encyc.*

CROUT, **KROUT**, *n.* [G. *kraut*, cabbage, an herb; D. *kruid.*] Sour crout is made by laying minced or chopped cabbage in layers in a barrel, with a handful of salt and caraway seeds between the layers; then ramming down the whole, covering it, pressing it with a heavy weight, and suffering it to stand, till it has gone through fermentation. It is an efficacious preservative against scurvy in long voyages. *Encyc.*

CRŌW, *n.* [Sax. *crawe*; Dan. *krage*; Sw. *kråka*; D. *kraai*; G. *krähe*; so named from its cry, G. *krähen*, D. *kraaijen*, Goth. *hruk*, a *croaking*, *hrukyan*, to *croak* or *crow*, L. *crocio*, Gr. κραζω, κραξω, κεκραγα. It has no connection with L. *corvus*, but *rook* is of the same family.]

1. A large black fowl, of the genus Corvus; the beak is convex and cultrated, the nostrils are covered with bristly feathers, the tongue is forked and cartilaginous. This is a voracious fowl, feeding on carrion and grain, particularly maiz, which it pulls up, just after it appears above ground.

To pluck or *pull a crow*, is to be industrious or contentious about a trifle, or thing of no value. *Johnson.*

2. A bar of iron with a beak, crook or two claws, used in raising and moving heavy weights. *Moxon.*

3. The voice of the cock. [See the Verb.]

CRŌW, *v. i.* pret. and pp. *crowed*; formerly, pret. *crew.* [Sax. *crawan*; D. *kraaijen*; G. *krähen*; Gr. κραζω. See the Noun.]

1. To cry or make a noise as a cock, in joy, gayety or defiance.

2. To boast in triumph; to vaunt; to vapor; to swagger. [*A popular, but not an elegant use of the word.*] *Grandison.*

CRŌW-BAR, *n.* A bar of iron sharpened at one end, used as a lever for raising weights.

CRŌW-BERRY, *n.* A plant of the genus Empetrum, or berry-bearing heath. One species bears the crow-crake berries. *Encyc.*

CRŌW'S-BILL, *n.* In *surgery*, a kind of forceps for extracting bullets and other things from wounds. *Encyc.*

CRŌW'S-FEET, *n.* The wrinkles under the eyes, which are the effects of age. *Obs.* *Chaucer.*

CRŌW-FLOWER, *n.* A kind of campion.

CRŌW-FOOT, *n.* On *board of ships*, a complication of small cords spreading out from a long block; used to suspend the awnings, or to keep the top sails from striking and fretting against the tops. *Encyc.*

2. In *botany*, the Ranunculus, a genus of plants.

CRŌW'S-FOOT, *n.* In *the military art*, a machine of iron, with four points, so formed that in whatever way it falls, there is one point upwards, and intended to stop or embarrass the approach or march of the enemy's cavalry; a caltrop. *Encyc.*

CRŌWING, *ppr.* Uttering a particular voice, as a cock; boasting in triumph; vaunting; bragging.

CRŌW-KEEPER, *n.* A scarecrow. [*Not used.*] *Shak.*

CRŌW-NET, *n.* In England, a net for catching wild fowls; the net used in New England for catching wild pigeons.

CRŌW-SILK, *n.* A plant, the Conferva rivalis. *Fam. of Plants.*

CRŌW-TOE, *n.* A plant; as the tufted *crow-toe.* *Milton.*

CROWD, **CROWTH**, *n.* [Ir. *cruit*; W. *crwth*, a swelling or bulging, a musical instrument.]

An instrument of music with six strings; a kind of violin.

CROWD, *n.* [Sax. *cruth, cread.* See *Crew.*]

1. Properly, a collection; a number of things collected, or closely pressed together.

2. A number of persons congregated and pressed together, or collected into a close body without order; a throng. Hence,

3. A multitude; a great number collected.

4. A number of things near together; a number promiscuously assembled or lying near each other; as a *crowd* of isles in the Egean Sea.

5. The lower orders of people; the populace; the vulgar. *Dryden.*

CROWD, *v. t.* To press; to urge; to drive together.

2. To fill by pressing numbers together without order; as, to *crowd* a room with people; to *crowd* the memory with ideas.

3. To fill to excess.

Volumes of reports *crowd* a lawyer's library.

4. To encumber by multitudes. *Shak.*

5. To urge; to press by solicitation; to dun.

6. In seamanship, to *crowd sail*, is to carry an extraordinary force of sail, with a view to accelerate the course of a ship, as in chasing or escaping from an enemy; to carry a press of sail.

CROWD, *v. i.* To press in numbers; as, the

multitude *crowded* through the gate or into the room.

2. To press; to urge forward; as, the man *crowded* into the room.

3. To swarm or be numerous.

CROWD'ED, *pp.* Collected and pressed; pressed together; urged; driven; filled by a promiscuous multitude.

CROWD'ER, *n.* A fiddler; one who plays on a crowd.

CROWD'ING, *ppr.* Pressing together; pushing; thrusting; driving; assembling in a promiscuous multitude; filling; urging.

CROWN, *n.* [Fr. *couronne;* Arm. *curun;* W. *coron;* D. *kroon;* G. *krone;* Sw. *krona;* Dan. *krone;* Ir. *coroin;* L. *corona;* Sp. It. *id.;* Gr. χορωνη. The radical letters appear to be Cr, as *corolla,* without *n,* indicates. Qu. a top or roundness. See *Chorus.*]

1. An ornament worn on the head by kings and sovereign princes, as a badge of imperial or regal power and dignity. Figuratively, regal power; royalty; kingly government, or executive authority.

2. A wreath or garland.

3. Honorary distinction; reward.

They do it to obtain a corruptible *crown;* we, an incorruptible. 1 Cor. ix.

4. Honor; splendor; dignity.

The *crown* has fallen from our heads. Lam. v. Phil. iv.

A virtuous woman is a *crown* to her husband. Prov. xii.

5. The top of the head; the top of a mountain or other elevated object. The end of an anchor, or the point from which the arms proceed.

6. The part of a hat which covers the top of the head.

7. A coin anciently stamped with the figure of a crown. The English crown is five shillings sterling. The French crown is a hundred and nine cents. Other coins bear the same name.

8. Completion; accomplishment.

9. Clerical tonsure in a circular form; a little circle shaved on the top of the head, as a mark of ecclesiastical office or distinction.

10. Among jewelers, the upper work of a rose diamond.

11. In *botany,* an appendage to the top of a seed, which serves to bear it in the wind.

CROWN, *v. t.* To invest with a crown or regal ornament. Hence, to invest with regal dignity and power.

2. To cover, as with a crown; to cover the top.

And peaceful olives *crowned* his hoary head. *Dryden.*

3. To honor; to dignify; to adorn.

Thou hast *crowned* him with glory and honor. Ps. viii.

4. To reward; to bestow an honorary reward or distinction on; as the victor *crowned* with laurel.

5. To reward; to recompense.

She'll *crown* a grateful and a constant flame. *Roscommon.*

6. To terminate or finish; to complete; to perfect.

7. To terminate and reward; as, our efforts were *crowned* with success.

CROWN'ED, *pp.* Invested with a crown, or with regal power and dignity; honored; dignified; rewarded with a crown, wreath, garland or distinction; recompensed; terminated; completed; perfected.

CROWN'ER, *n.* He or that which crowns or completes.

CROWN'ET, *n.* A coronet, which see. Shakspeare has used it for chief end or last purpose; but this sense is singular.

CROWN'-GLASS, *n.* The finest sort of English window-glass.

CROWN-IMPE'RIAL, *n.* A plant of the genus Fritillaria, having a beautiful flower.

CROWN'ING, *ppr.* Investing with a crown, or with royalty or supreme power; honoring with a wreath or with distinction; adorning; rewarding; finishing; perfecting.

CROWN'ING, *n.* In *architecture,* the finishing of a member or any ornamental work.

2. In *marine language,* the finishing part of a knot, or interweaving of the strands.

CROWN'-OFFICE, *n.* In *England,* an office belonging to the court of King's Bench, of which the king's coroner or attorney is commonly master, and in which the attorney general and clerk exhibit informations for crimes and misdemeanors.

CROWN'-POST, *n.* In *building,* a post which stands upright in the middle, between two principal rafters. *Bailey.*

CROWN'-SCAB, *n.* A scab formed round the corners of a horse's hoof, a cancerous and painful sore. *Farrier's Dict.*

CROWN'-THISTLE, *n.* A flower.

CROWN'-WHEEL, *n.* In a watch, the upper wheel next the balance, which drives the balance, and in royal pendulums, is called the swing-wheel.

CROWN'-WORK, *n.* In *fortification,* an outwork running into the field, consisting of two demi-bastions at the extremes and an entire bastion in the middle, with curtains. It is designed to gain some hill or advantageous post, and cover the other works. *Dict.*

CROYL'STONE, *n.* Crystalized cauk, in which the crystals are small. *Woodward. Johnson.*

CRU'CIAL, *a.* [Fr. *cruciale,* from L. *crux,* a cross.]

In *surgery,* transverse; passing across; intersecting; in form of a cross; as *crucial* incision. *Sharp.*

CRU'CIAN, *n.* A short, thick, broad fish, of a deep yellow color. *Dict. of Nat. Hist.*

CRU'CIATE, *v. t.* [L. *crucio,* to torture, from *crux,* a cross.]

To torture; to torment; to afflict with extreme pain or distress; *but the verb is seldom used.* [See *Excruciate.*]

CRU'CIATE, *a.* Tormented. [*Little used.*]

CRUCIA'TION, *n.* The act of torturing; torment. [*Little used.*] *Hall.*

CRU'CIBLE, *n.* [It. *crogiuolo,* and *crociuolo;* Sp. *crisol;* Port. *chrysol* or *crisol;* Fr. *creuset;* D. *kroes, smelt-kroes.* It is from *crux,* a cross, as Lunier supposes, from the figure of the cross, formerly attached to it. But qu.]

1. A chimical vessel or melting pot, made of earth, and so tempered and baked, as to endure extreme heat without melting. It is used for melting ores, metals, &c.

2. A hollow place at the bottom of a chimical furnace. *Fourcroy.*

CRUCIF'EROUS, *a.* [L. *crucifer;* *crux,* a cross, and *fero,* to bear.] Bearing the cross. *Dict.*

CRU'CIFIER, *n.* [See *Crucify.*] A person who crucifies; one who puts another to death on a cross.

CRU'CIFIX, *n.* [L. *crucifixus,* from *crucifigo,* to fix to a cross; *crux* and *figo,* to fix.]

1. A cross on which the body of Christ is fastened in effigy. *Encyc.*

2. A representation, in painting or statuary, of our Lord fastened to the cross. *Johnson.*

3. Figuratively, the religion of Christ. [*Little used.*] *Taylor.*

CRUCIFIX'ION, *n.* [See *Crucifix.*] The nailing or fastening of a person to a cross, for the purpose of putting him to death; the act or punishment of putting a criminal to death by nailing him to a cross. *Addison.*

CRU'CIFORM, *a.* [L. *crux,* a cross, and *forma,* form.] Cross-shaped.

In *botany,* consisting of four equal petals, disposed in the form of a cross. *Martyn.*

CRU'CIFȲ, *v. t.* [L. *crucifigo;* *crux,* cross, and *figo,* to fix; Fr. *crucifier;* It. *crocifiggere;* Sp. *crucificar.*]

1. To nail to a cross; to put to death by nailing the hands and feet to a cross or gibbet, sometimes anciently, by fastening a criminal to a tree, with cords. *Encyc.*

But they cried, *crucify* him, crucify him. Luke xxiii.

2. In *scriptural language,* to subdue; to mortify; to destroy the power or ruling influence of.

They that are Christ's have *crucified* the flesh, with the affections and lusts. Gal. v.

3. To reject and despise.

They *crucify* to themselves the Son of God afresh. Heb. vi.

To be crucified with Christ, is to become dead to the law and to sin, and to have indwelling corruption subdued. Gal. ii. and vi.

4. To vex or torment. [*Not used.*] *Burton.*

CRU'CIFȲING, *ppr.* Putting to death on a cross or gibbet; subduing; destroying the life and power of.

CRUD, *n.* Curd. [See *Curd,* the usual orthography.]

CRUDE, *a.* [L. *crudus;* Fr. *crud, cru;* Sp. It. *crudo;* Port. *cru;* Arm. *criz;* W. *cri;* D. *raauw;* Sax. *hreaw;* G. *roh;* Eng. *raw;* either from the root of *cry,* from roughness, [W. *cri,* a cry and crude;] or from the Ar. أرض to eat, to corrode, to rankle, to become raw, L. *rodo, rosi.* Class Rd. No. 35.]

1. Raw; not cooked or prepared by fire or heat; in its natural state; undressed; as *crude* flesh; *crude* meat. In this sense, *raw* is more generally used.

2. Not changed from its natural state; not altered or prepared by any artificial process; as *crude* salt; *crude* alum.

3. Rough; harsh; unripe; not mellowed by air or other means; as *crude* juice.

4. Unconcocted; not well digested in the stomach. *Bacon.*

5. Not brought to perfection; unfinished; immature; as the *crude* materials of the earth. *Milton.*

CRU
CRU

6. Having indigested notions. *Milton.*
7. Indigested; not matured; not well formed, arranged, or prepared in the intellect; as, *crude* notions; a *crude* plan; a *crude* theory. *Milton.*

CRU'DELY, *adv.* Without due preparation; without form or arrangement; without maturity or digestion.

CRU'DENESS, *n.* Rawness; unripeness; an undigested or unprepared state; as the *crudeness* of flesh or plants, or of any body in its natural state.
2. A state of being unformed, or indigested; immatureness; as the *crudeness* of a theory.

CRU'DITY, *n.* [L. *cruditas.*] Rawness; crudeness. Among *physicians*, undigested substances in the stomach; or unconcocted humors, not well prepared for expulsion; excrements. In the latter senses, it admits of the plural. *Coxe. Encyc.*

CRUD'LE, *v. t.* To coagulate. But this word is generally written *curdle*, which see.

CRUD'Y, *a.* Concreted; coagulated. [*Not in use.* See *Curd.*] *Spenser.*
2. Raw; chill. [*Not used.* See *Crude.*] *Shak.*

CRU'EL, *a.* [Fr. *cruel*; L. *crudelis*; It. *crudele.* See *Crude* and *Rude.*]
1. Disposed to give pain to others, in body or mind; willing or pleased to torment, vex or afflict; inhuman; destitute of pity, compassion or kindness; fierce; ferocious; savage; barbarous; hardhearted; *applied to persons or their dispositions.*

They are *cruel*, and have no mercy. Jer. vi.

2. Inhuman; barbarous; savage; causing pain, grief or distress; exerted in tormenting, vexing or afflicting.

Cursed be their wrath, for it was *cruel.* Gen. xlix.

The tender mercies of the wicked are *cruel.* Prov. xii.

Others had trials of *cruel* mockings. Heb. xi.

CRU'ELLY, *adv.* In a cruel manner; with cruelty; inhumanly; barbarously.

Because he *cruelly* oppressed, he shall die in his iniquity. Ezek. xviii.

2. Painfully; with severe pain, or torture; as, an instrument may cut the flesh most *cruelly.*

CRU'ELNESS, *n.* Inhumanity; cruelty. *Spenser.*

CRU'ELTY, *n.* [L. *crudelitas*; Fr. *cruauté.*]
1. Inhumanity; a savage or barbarous disposition or temper, which is gratified in giving unnecessary pain or distress to others; barbarity; *applied to persons*; as the *cruelty* of savages; the *cruelty* and envy of the people. *Shak.*
2. Barbarous deed; any act of a human being which inflicts unnecessary pain; any act intended to torment, vex or afflict, or which actually torments or afflicts, without necessity; wrong; injustice; oppression.

With force and with *cruelty* have ye ruled them. Ezek. xxxiv.

CRU'ENTATE, *a.* [L. *cruentatus.*] Smeared with blood. [*Little used.*] *Glanville.*

CRU'ET, *n.* [Qu. Fr. *creux*, hollow, or *cruchette*, from *cruche.* See *Cruse.*]
A vial or small glass bottle, for holding vinegar, oil, &c.

CRUISE, *n.* [See *Cruse.*]

CRUISE, *v. i.* *s* as *z.* [D. *kruissen*, from *kruis*, a cross; G. *kreuzen*; Dan. *krydser*; Fr. *croiser.* See *Cross.*]
To sail back and forth, or to rove on the ocean in search of an enemy's ships for capture, or for protecting commerce; or to rove for plunder as a pirate. The admiral *cruised* between the Bahama isles and Cuba. We *cruised* off Cape Finisterre. A pirate was *cruising* in the gulf of Mexico.

CRUISE, *n.* A voyage made in *crossing* courses; a sailing to and fro in search of an enemy's ships, or by a pirate in search of plunder.

CRUISER, *n.* A person or a ship that cruises; usually, an armed ship that sails to and fro for capturing an enemy's ships, for protecting the commerce of the country, or for plunder.

CRUISING, *ppr.* Sailing for the capture of an enemy's ships, or for protecting commerce, or for plunder as a pirate.

CRUM, *n.* [Sax *cruma*; D. *kruim*; G. *krume*; Heb. Ch. גרם to gnaw, or break. Class Rm. No. 14. 16. 19. 25. 26.]
A small fragment or piece; usually, a small piece of bread or other food, broken or cut off.

Lazarus, desiring to be fed with the *crums* which fell from the rich man's table. Luke xvi.

CRUM, *v. t.* To break or cut into small pieces; as, to *crum* bread into milk.

CRUM'BLE, *v. t.* [D. *kruimelen*; G. *krümeln.*]
To break into small pieces; to divide into minute parts.

CRUM'BLE, *v. i.* To fall into small pieces; to break or part into small fragments.

I a stone is brittle, it will *crumble* into gravel. *Arbuthnot.*

2. To fall to decay; to perish; as, our flesh shall *crumble* into dust.

CRUM'BLED, *pp.* Broken or parted into small pieces.

CRUM'BLING, *ppr.* Breaking into small fragments; falling into small pieces; decaying.

CRU'MENAL, *n.* [L. *crumena.*] A purse. [*Not used.*] *Spenser.*

CRUM'MY, *a.* Full of crums; soft.

CRUMP, *a.* [Sax. *crump*; D. *krom*; G. *krumm*; Dan. *krum*; W. *crom*, *crwm*, crooked; Ir. *crom*, whence *cromaim*, to bend, *croman*, the hip-bone, the *rump.* *Crump*, *rump*, *rumple*, *crumple*, *crimple*, are doubtless of one family.]
Crooked; as *crump*-shouldered.

CRUMP'ET, *n.* A soft cake.

CRUMP'LE, *v. t.* [from *crump.* See *Rumple*, the same word without a prefix.]
To draw or press into wrinkles or folds; to rumple. *Addison.*

CRUMP'LE, *v. i.* To contract; to shrink. *Smith.*

CRUMP'LED, *pp.* Drawn or pressed into wrinkles.

CRUMP'LING, *ppr.* Drawing or pressing into wrinkles.

CRUMP'LING, *n.* A small degenerate apple. *Johnson.*

CRUNK, **CRUN'KLE**, } *v. i.* To cry like a crane. [*Not used.*]

CRU'OR, *n.* [L.] Gore; coagulated blood. *Greenhill.*

CRUP or **CROUP**, *n.* The buttocks.

CRUP, *a.* Short; brittle. [*Not in use.*]

CRUP'PER, *n.* [Fr. *croupiere*; It. *groppiera*; Sp. *grupera*; from *croupe*, *groppa*, *grupa*, a ridge, the buttocks of a horse. See *Croup.*]
1. In *the manege*, the buttocks of a horse; the rump.
2. A strap of leather which is buckled to a saddle, and passing under a horse's tail, prevents the saddle from being cast forward on to the horse's neck.

CRUP'PER, *v. t.* To put a crupper on; as, to *crupper* a horse.

CRU'RAL, *a.* [L. *cruralis*, from *crus*, *cruris*, the leg.]
Belonging to the leg; as the *crural* artery, which conveys blood to the legs, and the *crural* vein, which returns it. *Encyc.*

CRUSA'DE, *n.* [Fr. *croisade*; It. *crociata*; Sp. *cruzada*; from L. *crux*, Fr. *croix*, Sp. *cruz*, It. *croce*, a cross. Class Rg.]
A military expedition undertaken by christians, for the recovery of the Holy Land, the scene of our Savior's life and sufferings, from the power of infidels or Mohammedans. Several of these expeditions were carried on from Europe, under the banner of the *cross*, from which the name originated.

CRUSA'DE, *n.* A Portuguese coin, stamped with a cross.

CRUSA'DER, *n.* A person engaged in a crusade. *Robertson.*

CRUSE, *n.* [D. *kroes.* See *Crucible.*] A small cup.

Take with thee a *cruse* of honey. 1 Kings xiv.

In New England, it is used chiefly or wholly for a small bottle or vial for vinegar, called a *vinegar-cruse.*

CRU'SET, *n.* [Fr. *creuset*, formerly *croiset.* See *Crucible.*]
A goldsmith's crucible or melting pot. *Phillips.*

CRUSH, *v. t.* [Fr. *ecraser*; Ir. *scriosam.* In Sw. *krossa*, in Dan. *kryster* signifies, to squeeze. In It. *croscio* is a crushing; and *crosciare*, to throw, strike, pour, or rain hard. There are many words in the Shemitic languages which coincide with *crush* in elements and signification. Ch. Heb. Syr. גרם to break in pieces; Ar. جرس id.; Eth. ሐረጸ to grind, whence *grist*; Heb. and Ch. חרץ, and Ch. Syr. Heb. רצץ to break, to crush; Ar. رضّ the same. So *crash*, in English, and Fr. *briser*, Arm. *freusa*, to bruise. See Class Rd. No. 16. 20. 22. 41. 48. and Syr. No. 36. See *Rush.*]
1. To press and bruise between two hard bodies; to squeeze, so as to force a thing out of its natural shape; to bruise by pressure.

The ass—*crushed* Balaam's foot against the wall. Numb. xxii.

To *crush* grapes or apples, is to squeeze them till *bruised* and broken, so that the juice escapes. Hence, to *crush out*, is to force out by pressure.

2. To press with violence; to force together into a mass.

3. To overwhelm by pressure; to beat or force down, by an incumbent weight, with breaking or bruising; as, the man was *crushed* by the fall of a tree.

To *crush* the pillars which the pile sustain. *Dryden.*

Who are *crushed* before the moth. Job iv.

4. To overwhelm by power; to subdue; to conquer beyond resistance; as, to *crush* one's enemies; to *crush* a rebellion.

5. To oppress grievously.

Thou shalt be only oppressed and *crushed* always. Deut. xxviii.

6. To bruise and break into fine particles by beating or grinding; to comminute.

ЄRUSH, *v. i.* To be pressed into a smaller compass by external weight or force.

ЄRUSH, *n.* A violent collision, or rushing together, which breaks or bruises the bodies; or a fall that breaks or bruises into a confused mass; as the *crush* of a large tree, or of a building.

The wrecks of matter, and the *crush* of worlds. *Addison.*

ЄRUSH'ED, *pp.* Pressed or squeezed so as to break or bruise; overwhelmed or subdued by power; broken or bruised by a fall; grievously oppressed; broken or bruised to powder; comminuted.

ЄRUSH'ING, *ppr.* Pressing or squeezing into a mass, or until broken or bruised; overwhelming; subduing by force; oppressing; comminuting.

ЄRUST, *n.* [L. *crusta*; Fr. *croûte*; It. *crosta*; D. *korst*; G. *kruste*; W. *crest*, from *cresu*, to parch or scorch, *cres*, a hardening by heat. But the primary sense is probably to shrink, contract, harden, whether by cold or heat, and it is probably allied to *crystal*, *freeze*, *crisp*, &c. See Class Rd. No. 19. 33. 73. 76. 83. 85. 88.]

1. An external coat or covering of a thing, which is hard or harder than the internal substance; as the *crust* of bread; the *crust* of snow; the *crust* of dross; the *crust* of a pie.

2. A piece of crust; a waste piece of bread. *Dryden. L'Estrange.*

3. A shell, as the hard covering of a crab and some other animals.

4. A scab.

5. The superficial substances of the earth are, in geology, called its *crust*.

ЄRUST, *v. t.* To cover with a hard case or coat; to spread over the surface a substance harder than the matter covered; to incrust; as, to *crust* a thing with clay; to *crust* cake with sugar; *crusted* with bark. *Addison.*

2. To cover with concretions. *Swift.*

ЄRUST, *v. i.* To gather or contract into a hard covering; to concrete or freeze, as superficial matter.

ЄRUSTACEOLOĠY. [See *Crustalogy.*]

ЄRUSTA'CEOUS, *a.* [Fr. *crustacée*, from L. *crusta.*]

Pertaining to crust; like crust; of the nature of crust or shell. *Crustaceous* animals, or *Crustacea*, have a crust or shell composed of several jointed pieces, and in their external form have a great resemblance to insects; but in their internal structure and economy, they are quite different. They were arranged by Linne, in the same class with the insects, but now form a class by themselves. They include the crab, lobster, shrimp, &c. *Ed. Encyc.*

ЄRUSTA'CEOUSNESS, *n.* The quality of having a soft and jointed shell.

ЄRUSTALOĠ'IЄAL, *a.* [See *Crustalogy.*] Pertaining to crustalogy.

ЄRUSTAL'OĠIST, *n.* One who describes, or is versed in the science of crustaceous animals.

ЄRUSTAL'OĠY, *n.* [L. *crusta*, a shell, and Gr. λογος, discourse.]

That part of zoology which treats of *crustaceous* animals, arranging them in orders, tribes and families, and describing their forms and habits.

[*Crustaceology*, the word sometimes used, is ill-formed, and its derivatives inconveniently long. Who can endure such words as *crustaceological?*]

ЄRUST'ATED, *a.* Covered with a crust; as *crustated* basalt. *Encyc.*

ЄRUSTA'TION, *n.* An adherent crust; incrustation.

ЄRUST'ED, *pp.* Covered with a crust.

ЄRUST'ILY, *adv.* [from *crusty.*] Peevishly; harshly; morosely.

ЄRUST'INESS, *n.* The quality of crust; hardness.

2. Peevishness; moroseness; surliness.

ЄRUST'ING, *ppr.* Covering with crust.

ЄRUST'Y, *a.* Like crust; of the nature of crust; pertaining to a hard covering; hard; as a *crusty* coat; a *crusty* surface or substance.

2. Peevish; snappish; morose; surly; *a word used in familiar discourse, but not deemed elegant.*

ЄRUTCH, *n.* [It. *croccia*, or *gruccia*; D. *kruk*; G. *krücke*; S. *krycka*; Dan. *krykke*; radically the same as *crotch* and *crook.*]

1. A staff with a curving cross piece at the head, to be placed under the arm or shoulder, to support the lame in walking.

2. Figuratively, old age. *Shak.*

ЄRUTCH, *v. t.* To support on crutches; to prop or sustain, with miserable helps, that which is feeble.

Two fools that *crutch* their feeble sense on verse. *Dryden.*

ЄRUX, *n.* [L. *crux*, a cross.] Any thing that puzzles and vexes. [*Little used.*] *Dr. Sheridan.*

ЄRU'YSHAĠE, *n.* A fish of the shark kind, having a triangular head and mouth. *Dict. Nat. Hist.*

ЄRȲ, *v. i.* pret. and pp. *cried.* It ought to be *cryed.* [Fr. *crier.* The Welsh has *cri*, a cry, and rough, raw, *criaw*, to cry, clamor or weep; and *crevu*, to cry, to *crave*; both deduced by Owen from *cre*, a combining cause, a principle, beginning or first motion; also, what pervades or penetrates, a *cry.* This is the root of *create*, or from the same root. *Cre*, Owen deduces from *rhe*, with the prefix *cy*; and *rhe*, he renders a run or swift motion. This is certainly contracted from *rhed*, a race, the root of *ride*; Owen to the contrary notwithstanding. All the senses of these words unite in that of shooting forth, driving forward or producing. There is a class of words a little different from the foregoing, which exactly give the sense of *cry.* It. *gridare*; Sp. and Port. *gritar*; Sax. *grædan*; Sw. *gråta*; Dan. *græder*; D. *kryten*; W. *grydiaw*, to utter a rough sound, from *rhyd*, the Welsh root of *crydu*, to shake or tremble, whence *cradle.* [W. *creth*, a trembling or shivering with cold, from *cre*; also, constitution, disposition.] The latter root *rhyd*, *crydu*, would give *cri*, rough, raw, *crude.* *Cry* is a contracted word; but whether from the former or latter class of roots, may be less obvious—possibly all are from one source. If not, I think *cry* is from the French *crier*, and this from *gridare*, *gritar.*]

1. To utter a loud voice; to speak, call or exclaim with vehemence; *in a very general sense.*

2. To call importunately; to utter a loud voice, by way of earnest request or prayer.

The people *cried* to Pharoah for bread. Gen. xli.

The people *cried* to Moses, and he prayed. Numb. xi.

3. To utter a loud voice in weeping; to utter the voice of sorrow; to lament.

But ye shall *cry* for sorrow of heart. Is. lxv.

Esau *cried* with a great and bitter cry. Gen. xxvii.

Also, to weep or shed tears in silence; *a popular use of the word.*

4. To utter a loud sound in distress; as, Heshbon shall *cry.* Is. xv.

He giveth food to the young ravens which *cry.* Ps. cxlvii.

5. To exclaim; to utter a loud voice; with *out.*

And, lo, a spirit taketh him, and he suddenly *crieth out.* Luke ix.

6. To proclaim; to utter a loud voice, in giving public notice.

Go, and *cry* in the ears of Jerusalem. Jer. ii.

The voice of him that *crieth* in the wilderness. Is. xl.

7. To bawl; to squall; as a child.

8. To yelp, as a dog. It may be used for the uttering of a loud voice by other animals.

To cry against, to exclaim, or utter a loud voice, by way of reproof, threatening or censure.

Arise, go to Nineveh, and *cry against* it. Jonah i.

To cry out, to exclaim; to vociferate; to scream; to clamor.

2. To complain loudly.

To cry out against, to complain loudly, with a view to censure; to blame; to utter censure.

To cry to, to call on in prayer; to implore.

ЄRȲ, *v. t.* To proclaim; to name loudly and publicly for giving notice; as, to *cry* goods; to *cry* a lost child.

To cry down, to decry; to depreciate by words or in writing; to dispraise; to condemn.

Men of dissolute lives *cry down* religion, because they would not be under the restraints of it. *Tillotson.*

2. To overbear.

Cry down this fellow's insolence. *Shak.*

To cry up, to praise; to applaud; to extol; as, to *cry up* a man's talents or patriotism, or a woman's beauty; to *cry up* the administration.

2. To raise the price by proclamation; as, to *cry up* certain coins. [*Not in use.*] *Temple.*

To cry off, in *the vulgar dialect*, is to publish intentions of marriage.

ЄRȲ, *n.* plu. *cries.* In *a general sense*, a lound sound uttered by the mouth of an animal; applicable to the voice of man or beast, and articulate or inarticulate.

2. A loud or vehement sound, uttered in weeping, or lamentation; it may be a shriek or scream.

And there shall be a great *cry* in all the land of Egypt. Ex. xi.

3. Clamor; outcry; as, war, war, is the public *cry*.

And there arose a great *cry*. Acts xxiii.

4. Exclamation of triumph, of wonder, or of other passion.

5. Proclamation; public notice.

At midnight there was a *cry* made. Matt. xxv.

6. The notices of hawkers of wares to be sold in the street are called *cries*; as the *cries of London*.

7. Acclamation; expression of popular favor.

The *cry* went once for thee. *Shak.*

8. A loud voice in distress, prayer or request; importunate call.

He forgetteth not the *cry* of the humble. Ps. ix.

There was a great *cry* in Egypt. Ex. xii.

9. Public reports or complaints; noise; fame.

Because the *cry* of Sodom and Gomorrah is great—I will go down, and see whether they have done altogether according to the *cry* of it. Gen. xviii.

10. Bitter complaints of oppression and injustice.

He looked for righteousness, and behold a *cry*. Is. v.

11. The sound or voice of irrational animals; expression of joy, fright, alarm, or want; as the *cries* of fowls, the yell or yelping of dogs, &c.

12. A pack of dogs. *Shak.*

CRY'AL, *n.* [W. *cregyr*, a screamer.] The heron. *Ainsworth.*

CRY'ER, *n.* A crier, which see.

CRY'ER, *n.* A kind of hawk, called the falcon gentle, an enemy to pigeons, and very swift. *Ainsworth.*

CRY'ING, *ppr.* Uttering a loud voice; proclaiming; &c.

CRY'ING, *a.* Notorious; common; great; as a *crying* sin or abuse. *Addison.*

CRY'ING, *n.* Importunate call; clamor; outcry.

CRY'OLITE, *n.* [Gr. κρυος, cold, and λιθος, stone, ice-stone.]

A fluate of soda and alumin, found in Greenland, of a pale grayish white, snow white, or yellowish brown. It occurs in masses of a foliated structure. It has a glistening, vitreous luster. *Jameson. Cleaveland.*

CRYOPH'ORUS, *n.* [Gr. κρυος, frost, and φορεω, to bear.]

Frost-bearer; an instrument for showing the relation between evaporation at low temperatures and the production of cold. *Wollaston.*

CRYPT, *n.* [Gr. κρυπτω, to hide.] A subterranean cell or cave, especially under a church for the interment of persons; also, a subterranean chapel or oratory, and the grave of a martyr.

CRYP'TIC, **CRYP'TICAL**, } *a.* [supra.] Hidden; secret; occult. *Watts.*

CRYP'TICALLY, *adv.* Secretly.

CRYP'TOGAM, *n.* [See *Cryptogamy.*] In *botany*, a plant whose stamens and pistils are not distinctly visible.

CRYPTOGAM'IAN, *a.* Pertaining to plants of the class *Cryptogamia*, including ferns, mosses, sea-weeds, mushrooms, &c.

CRYPTOG'AMY, *n.* [Gr. κρυπτος, concealed, and γαμος, marriage.]

Concealed marriage; a term applied to plants whose stamens and pistils are not well ascertained, or too small to be numbered with certainty. *Smith. Ed. Encyc.*

CRYPTOG'RAPHER, *n.* One who writes in secret characters.

CRYPTOGRAPH'ICAL, *a.* Written in secret characters or in cipher, or with sympathetic ink.

CRYPTOG'RAPHY, *n.* [Gr. κρυπτος, hidden, and γραφω, to write.]

The act or art of writing in secret characters; also, secret characters or cypher.

CRYPTOL'OGY, *n.* [Gr. κρυπτος, secret, and λογος, discourse.] Secret or enigmatical language.

CRYS'TAL, *n.* [L. *crystallus*; Gr. κρυςαλλος; Fr. *cristal*; Sp. *cristal*; It. *cristallo*; D. *kristal*; G. *krystall*; W. *crisial*, from *cris*, it is said, a hard *crust*. It is from the same root as *crisp*, and W. *cresu*, to parch, *crest*, a crust, *crasu*, to roast. The Greek, from which we have the word, is composed of the root of κρυος, frost, a contracted word, probably from the root of the Welsh words, supra, and ςελλω, to set. The primary sense of the Welsh words is to shrink, draw, contract; a sense equally applicable to the effects of heat and cold.

Qu. Ar. قَرَسَ karasa, Ch. קרש kerash, to congeal. Class Rd. No. 83. 85.]

1. In *chimistry* and *mineralogy*, an inorganic body, which, by the operation of affinity, has assumed the form of a regular solid, terminated by a certain number of plane and smooth surfaces. *Cleaveland.*

2. A factitious body, cast in glass houses, called crystal glass; a species of glass, more perfect in its composition and manufacture, than common glass. The best kind is the Venice crystal. It is called also factitious crystal or paste. *Encyc. Nicholson.*

3. A substance of any kind having the form of a crystal.

4. The glass of a watch-case.

Rock crystal, or mountain crystal, a general name for all the transparent crystals of quartz, particularly of limpid or colorless quartz.

Iceland crystal, a variety of calcarious spar, or crystalized carbonate of lime, brought from Iceland. It occurs in laminated masses, easily divisible into rhombs, and is remarkable for its double refraction. *Cleaveland.*

CRYS'TAL, *a.* Consisting of crystal, or like crystal; clear; transparent; lucid; pellucid.

By *crystal* streams that murmur through the meads. *Dryden.*

CRYS'TAL-FORM, *a.* Having the form of crystal. *Encyc.*

CRYS'TALINE, *a.* [L. *crystallinus*; Gr. κρυςαλλινος.]

1. Consistiug of crystal; as a *crystaline* palace. *Shak.*

2. Resembling crystal; pure; clear; transparent; pellucid; as a *crystaline* sky. *Milton.*

Crystaline heavens, in ancient astronomy, two spheres imagined between the primum mobile and the firmament, in the Ptolemaic system, which supposed the heavens to be solid and only susceptible of a single motion. *Encyc.*

Crystaline humor, *Crystaline lens*, } a lentiform pellucid body, composed of a very white, transparent, firm substance, inclosed in a membranous capsule, and situated in a depression in the anterior part of the vitreous humor of the eye. It is somewhat convex, and serves to transmit and refract the rays of light to the vitreous humor. *Encyc. Hooper.*

CRYS'TALIZABLE, *a.* [from *crystalize.*] That may be crystalized; that may form or be formed into crystals. *Clavigero. Lavoisier.*

CRYSTALIZA'TION, *n.* [from *crystalize.*] The act or process by which the parts of a solid body, separated by the intervention of a fluid or by fusion, again coalesce or unite, and form a solid body. If the process is slow and undisturbed, the particles assume a regular arrangement, each substance taking a determinate and regular form, according to its natural laws; but if the process is rapid or disturbed, the substance takes an irregular form. This process is the effect of refrigeration or evaporation. *Lavoisier. Kirwan.*

2. The mass or body formed by the process of crystalizing. *Woodward.*

CRYS'TALIZE, *v. t.* To cause to form crystals.

Common salt is *crystalized* by the evaporation of sea water.

CRYS'TALIZE, *v. i.* To be converted into a crystal; to unite, as the separate particles of a substance, and form a determinate and regular solid.

Each species of salt *crystalizes* in a peculiar form. *Lavoisier.*

CRYS'TALIZED, *pp.* Formed into crystals.

CRYS'TALIZING, *ppr.* Causing to crystalize; forming or uniting in crystals.

CRYS'TALLITE, *n.* A name given to whinstone, cooled slowly after fusion. *Hall. Thomson.*

CRYSTALOG'RAPHER, *n.* [infra.] One who describes crystals, or the manner of their formation.

CRYSTALOGRAPH'IC, **CRYSTALOGRAPH'ICAL**, } *a.* Pertaining to crystalography.

CRYSTALOGRAPH'ICALLY, *adv.* In the manner of crystalography.

CRYSTALOG'RAPHY, *n.* [*crystal*, as above, and γραφη, description.]

1. The doctrine or science of crystalization, teaching the principles of the process, and the forms and structure of crystals.

2. A discourse or treatise on crystalization.

CUB, *n.* [allied perhaps to Ir. *caobh*, a branch, a shoot. But the origin of the word is uncertain.]

1. The young of certain quadrupeds, as of the bear and the fox; a puppy; a whelp. Waller uses the word for the young of the whale.

2. A young boy or girl, in *contempt*. *Shak. Congreve.*

CUB, *n.* A stall for cattle. [*Not in use.*]

CUB, *v. t.* To bring forth a cub, or cubs. In

contempt, to bring forth young, as a woman. *Dryden.*

CUB, *v. t.* To shut up or confine. [*Not in use.*] *Burton.*

CUBA′TION, *n.* [L. *cubatio*, from *cubo*, to lie down.]
The act of lying down; a reclining. *Dict.*

CU′BATORY, *a.* Lying down; reclining; incumbent. *Dict.*

CU′BATURE, *n.* [from *cube.*] The finding exactly the solid or cubic contents of a body. *Harris.*

CUBE, *n.* [Gr. κυβος; L. *cubus*, a die or cube; Fr. *cube;* It. *cubo;* Sp. *cubo;* Port. *cubo*. In the two latter languages, it signifies also a pail or tub, and in Port. the nave of a wheel. W. *cub*, a bundle, *heap* or aggregate, a *cube;* Ch. עקב to square, to form into a cube; קוביא the game of dice, Gr. κυβεια. It seems to be allied to L. *cubo*, to set or throw down, and to signify that which is set or laid, a solid mass.]
1. In *geometry*, a regular solid body, with six equal sides, and containing equal angles.
2. In *arithmetic*, the product of a number multiplied into itself, and that product multiplied into the same number; or it is formed by multiplying any number twice by itself; as, $4\times4=16$, and $16\times4=64$, the cube of 4.

The law of the planets is, that the squares of the times of their revolutions are in proportion to the *cubes* of their mean distances.

Cube root, is the number or quantity, which, multiplied into itself, and then into the product, produces the cube; or which, twice multiplied into itself, produces the number of which it is the root; thus, 3 is the cube root or side of 27, for $3\times3=9$, and $3\times9=27$.

CUBE-ORE, *n.* Hexahedral olivenite, or arseniate of iron, a mineral of a greenish color. *Ure.*

CU′BEB, *n.* [Ar. كبابة. Class Gb. No. 45. Sp. *cubeba.*]
The small spicy berry of the *Piper cubeba*, from Java and the other E. India isles. It was formerly called, from its short stems, *Piper caudatum*, or tailed pepper. It resembles a grain of pepper, but is somewhat longer. In aromatic warmth and pungency, it is far inferior to pepper. *Coxe. Encyc.*

CU′BIC, } *a.* [L. *cubicus*, from *cubus*.
CU′BICAL, } See *Cube.*]
Having the form or properties of a cube; that may be or is contained within a cube. A *cubic* foot of water is the water that may be contained within six equal sides, each a foot square.
Cubic number, is a number produced by multiplying a number into itself, and that product by the same number; or it is the number arising from the multiplication of a square number by its root. [See *Cube.*]

CU′BICALNESS, *n.* The state or quality of being cubical.

CUBIC′ULAR, *a.* [L. *cubiculum.*] Belonging to a chamber.

CUBIC′ULARY, *a.* [L. *cubiculum*, a bedroom.]
Fitted for the posture of lying down. [*Little used.*] *Brown.*

CU′BIFORM, *a.* Having the form of a cube. *Coxe.*

CU′BIT, *n.* [L. *cubitus*, the elbow; Gr. κυβιτον; probably allied to L. *cubo*, and signifying a turn or corner.]
1. In *anatomy*, the fore arm; the ulna, a bone of the arm from the elbow to the wrist. *Coxe. Encyc.*
2. In *mensuration*, the length of a man's arm from the elbow to the extremity of the middle finger. The cubit among the ancients was of a different length among different nations. Dr. Arbuthnot states the Roman cubit at seventeen inches and four tenths; the cubit of the scriptures at a little less than 22 inches; and the English cubit at 18 inches. *Encyc.*

CU′BITAL, *a.* Of the length or measure of a cubit. *Brown.*
2. Pertaining to the cubit or ulna; as the *cubital* nerve; *cubital* artery; *cubital* muscle. *Hooper. Coxe.*

CU′BITED, *a.* Having the measure of a cubit. *Sheldon.*

CUBO-DODECAHE′DRAL, *a.* Presenting the two forms, a cube and a dodecahedron. *Cleaveland.*

CU′BOID, *a.* Having the form of a cube, or differing little from it.

CUBOID′AL, *a.* [Gr. κυβος, cube, and ειδος, form.]
Cubiform; in the shape of a cube; as the *cuboidal* bone of the foot. *Walsh.*

CUBO-OCTAHE′DRAL, *a.* [*cube* and *octahedral.*]
Presenting a combination of the two forms, a cube and an octahedron. *Cleaveland.*

CUCK′INGSTOOL, *n.* [Qu. from *choke.*] An engine for punishing scolds and refractory women; also brewers and bakers; called also a *tumbrel* and a *trebuchet*. The culprit was seated on the stool and thus immersed in water. *Old Eng. Law.*

CUCK′OLD, *n.* [Chaucer, *cokewold*. The first syllable is Fr. *cocu*, which seems to be the first syllable of *coucou*, cuckow; W. *cog;* Sw. *gök;* Dan. *giög*. The Dutch call a cuckold, *hoorndraager*, a *horn-wearer;* and the Germans, *hahnrei*, from *hahn*, a *cock;* the Spaniards and Portuguese, *cornudo*, Ital. *cornuto*, horned; Fr. *cornard*, obs. See Spelman's Glossary, voc. *Arga.*]
A man whose wife is false to his bed; the husband of an adulteress. *Swift.*

CUCK′OLD, *v. t.* To make a man a cuckold by criminal conversation with his wife; *applied to the seducer.* *Shak.*
2. To make a husband a cuckold by criminal conversation with another man; *applied to the wife.* *Dryden.*

CUCK′OLDDOM, *n.* The act of adultery; the state of a cuckold. *Johnson. Dryden.*

CUCK′OLDLY, *a.* Having the qualities of a cuckold; mean; sneaking. *Shak.*

CUCK′OLD-MAKER, *n.* One who has criminal conversation with another man's wife; one who makes a cuckold. *Dryden.*

CUCK′OO, *n.* [L. *cuculus;* Gr. κοκκυξ; Fr. *coucou;* Arm. *coucouq;* Sax. *geac;* Dan. *giög;* Sw. *gök;* W. *cog;* D. *koekoek;* G. *kuckuck;* Sp. *cuco* or *cuclillo;* It. *cuculo*. See *Gawk.*]
A bird of the genus Cuculus, whose name is supposed to be called from its note. The note is a call to love, and continued only during the amorous season. It is said the cuckoo lays its eggs in a nest formed by another bird, by which they are hatched.

CUCK′OO-FLOWER, } *n.* A plant, a species of Cardamine.
CUCK′OO-BUD, }

CUCK′OO-PINT, *n.* A plant, of the genus Arum.

CUCK′OO-SPIT, } *n.* A dew or exudation found on
CUCK′OO-SPITTLE, } plants, especially about the joints of lavender and rosemary. *Brown.*
Or a froth or spume found on the leaves of certain plants, as on white field-lychnis or catch-fly, called sometimes *spatling poppy.* *Encyc.*

CUC′QUEAN, *n.* [Fr. *coquine.*] A vile lewd woman. [*Not in use.*] *B. Jonson.*

CU′CULLATE, } *a.* [L. *cucullatus*, from
CU′CULLATED, } *cucullus*, a hood, a *cowl.*]
1. Hooded; cowled; covered as with a hood.
2. Having the shape or resemblance of a hood; or wide at the top and drawn to a point below, in shape of a conical roll of paper; as a *cucullate* leaf.

CU′CUMBER, *n.* [Fr. *coucombre*, or *concombre*, from L. *cucumer* or *cucumis;* Sp. *cohombro;* D. *komkommer;* Ir. *cucamhar.*]
The name of a plant and its fruit, of the genus *Cucumis*. The flower is yellow and bell-shaped; and the stalks are long, slender and trailing on the ground, or climbing by their claspers.

CU′CURBIT, *n.* [L. *cucurbita*, a gourd; It. *id.;* Fr. *cucurbite;* from L. *curvitas.*]
A chimical vessel in the shape of a gourd; but some of them are shallow, with a wide mouth. It may be made of copper, glass, tin or stone ware, and is used in distillation. This vessel, with its head or cover, constitutes the alembic.

CUCURBITA′CEOUS, *a.* Resembling a gourd; as *cucurbitaceous* plants, such as the melon and pumpkin or pompion. *Milne. Martyn.*

CUD, *n.* [As this word is often vulgarly pronounced *quid*, I suspect it to be a corruption of the D. *kaauwd*, *gekaauwd*, chewed, from *kaauwen*, to chew, Arm. *chaguein*, Sax. *ceowan*. See *Chew* and *Jaw.*]
1. The food which ruminating animals chew at leisure, when not grazing or eating; or that portion of it which is brought from the first stomach and chewed at once.
2. A portion of tobacco held in the mouth and chewed.
3. The inside of the mouth or throat of a beast that chews the cud. *Encyc.*

CUD′DEN, } *n.* A clown; a low rustic; a
CUD′DY, } dolt. [*Not used.*] *Dryden.*

CUD′DLE, *v. i.* [Arm. *cuddyo;* W. *cuziaw*, to hide, to lurk, to cover or keep out of sight; Sax. *cudele*, the *cuttle-fish*. Qu. *hide* and *cheat*. See Class Gd. No. 26. 30. 31. 38.]
To retire from sight; to lie close or snug; to squat. *Prior.*

CUD′DY, *n.* In *ships*, an apartment; a cabin under the poop, or a cook-room. It is applied to different apartments, in different kinds of ships.
2. The cole-fish.

CUD′GEL, *n.* [W. *cogel*, from *côg*, a mass, lump, or short piece of wood. The Scot.

cud, Teut. *kodde, kudse,* is a different word; *dg* in English being generally from *g*, as in *pledge, bridge, alledge,* &c.]

A short thick stick of wood, such as may be used by the hand in beating. It differs strictly from a club, which is larger at one end than the other. It is shorter than a pole, and thicker than a rod. *Dryden. Locke.*

To cross the cudgels, to forbear the contest; a phrase borrowed from the practice of cudgel-players, who lay one cudgel over another. *Johnson.*

CUD'GEL, *v. t.* To beat with a cudgel, or thick stick. *Swift.*

2. To beat in general. *Shak.*

CUD'GELLER, *n.* One who beats with a cudgel.

CUD'GEL-PROOF, *a.* Able to resist a cudgel; not to be hurt by beating. *Hudibras.*

CUD'LE, *n.* [Qu. Scot. *cuddie.*] A small sea fish. *Carew.*

CUD'WEED, *n.* A plant of the genus Gnaphalium, goldy-locks or eternal flower, of many species. The flowers are remarkable for retaining their beauty for years, if gathered in dry weather. *Encyc.*

CUE, *n.* [Fr. *queue;* L. *cauda;* It. Sp. *coda.*] The tail; the end of a thing; as the long curl of a wig, or a long roll of hair.

2. The last words of a speech, which a player, who is to answer, catches and regards as an intimation to begin. A hint given to an actor on the stage, what or when to speak. *Johnson. Encyc.*

3. A hint; an intimation; a short direction. *Swift.*

4. The part which any man is to play in his turn.

Were it my *cue* to fight. *Shak.*

5. Humor; turn or temper of mind. [*Vulgar.*]

6. A farthing, or farthing's worth. *Beaum.*

7. The straight rod, used in playing billiards.

CUER'PO, *n.* [Sp. *cuerpo,* L. *corpus,* body.] *To be in cuerpo,* or *to walk in cuerpo,* are Spanish phrases for being without a cloke or upper garment, or without the formalities of a full dress, so that the shape of the body is exposed. *Encyc.*

CUFF, *n.* [Pers. قفا kafa, a blow; Ch. נקף id.; Ar. نقف nakafa, to strike; Heb. נקף, to strike off, to sever by striking, to kill. The French *coup* coincides with *cuff* in elements, but it is supposed to be contracted from It. *colpo,* L. *colaphus.* *Cuff* however agrees with the Gr. *κοπτω.*]

1. A blow with the fist; a stroke; a box. *Shak. Swift.*

2. It is used of fowls that fight with their talons. *Johnson.*

To be at fisty-cuffs, to fight with blows of the fist.

CUFF, *v. t.* To strike with the fist, as a man; or with talons or wings, as a fowl. *Congreve. Dryden.*

CUFF, *v. i.* To fight; to scuffle. *Dryden.*

CUFF, *n.* [This word probably signifies a fold or doubling; Ar. كف to double the border and sew together; Ch. כוף to bend; Heb. כפף; Gr. *κυπτω;* Low L. *cippus.* Class Gb. No. 65. 68. 75.]

The fold at the end of a sleeve; the part of a sleeve turned back from the hand. *Arbuthnot.*

CUIN'AGE, *n.* The making up of tin into pigs, &c., for carriage. *Bailey. Cowel.*

CUIRASS', *n. kweras'.* [Fr. *cuirasse;* It. *corazza;* Sp. *coraza;* Port. *couraça;* W. *curas.* Qu. from *cor,* the heart.]

A breast-plate; a piece of defensive armor, made of iron plate, well hammered, and covering the body from the neck to the girdle. *Encyc.*

CUIRASSIE'R, *n. kwerassee'r.* A soldier armed with a cuirass, or breast-plate. *Milton.*

CUISH, *n. kwis.* [Fr. *cuisse,* the thigh or leg; W. *coes;* Ir. *cos.*]

Defensive armor for the thighs. *Shak. Dryden.*

CUL'DEE, *n.* [L. *cultores dei,* worshipers of God.]

A monkish priest, remarkable for religious duties. The Culdees formerly inhabited Scotland, Ireland and Wales. *Encyc.*

CU'LERAGE, *n.* [Fr. *cul.*] Another name of the arse-smart.

CU'LICIFORM, *a.* [L. *culex,* a gnat or flea, and *forma,* form.]

Of the form or shape of a flea; resembling a flea. *Encyc.*

CU'LINARY, *a.* [L. *culinarius,* from *culina,* a kitchen, W. *cyl.* See *Kiln.*]

Relating to the kitchen, or to the art of cookery; used in kitchens; as a *culinary* fire; a *culinary* vessel; *culinary* herbs. *Newton.*

CULL, *v. t.* [Qu. Fr. *cueillir,* It. *cogliere,* to gather; Norm. *culhir;* It. *scegliere.* To *cull,* is rather to separate, or to take.]

To pick out; to separate one or more things from others; to select from many; as, to *cull* flowers; to *cull* hoops and staves for market. *Pope. Prior. Laws of Conn.*

CULL'ED, *pp.* Picked out; selected from many.

CULL'ER, *n.* One who who picks or chooses from many.

2. An inspector who selects merchantable hoops and staves for market. *Laws of Mass. and Conn.*

CULLIBIL'ITY, *n.* [from *cully.*] Credulity; easiness of belief. [*Not elegant nor used.*] *Swift.*

CULL'ING, *ppr.* Selecting; choosing from many.

CULL'ION, *n. cul'yon.* [It. *coglione.*] A mean wretch. If from *cully,* one easily deceived; a dupe. *Dryden.*

2. A round or bulbous root; orchis. L. *coleus.*

CULL'IONLY, *a.* Mean; base. [*A bad word, and not used.*] *Shak.*

CUL'LIS, *n.* [Fr. *coulis,* from *couler,* to strain.]

1. Broth of boiled meat strained. *Beaum.*

2. A kind of jelly. *Marston.*

CUL'LY, *n.* [*See the Verb.*] A person who is meanly deceived, tricked or imposed on, as by a sharper, jilt, or strumpet; a mean dupe. *Hudibras.*

CUL'LY, *v. t.* [D. *kullen,* to cheat, to *gull.*] To deceive; to trick, cheat or impose on; to jilt.

CUL'LYISM, *n.* The state of a cully. [*Cully* and its derivatives are not elegant words.]

CULM, *n.* [L. *culmus;* Ir. *colbh;* W. *colov;* a stalk or stem; L. *caulis;* D. *kool.* See *Quill* and *Haulm.*]

1. In *botany,* the stalk or stem of corn and grasses, usually jointed and hollow, and supporting the leaves and fructification. *Martyn.*

2. The straw or dry stalks of corn and grasses.

3. A species of fossil coal, found in small masses, not adhering when heated, difficult to be ignited, and burning with little flame, but yielding a disagreeable smell. *Nicholson. Journ. of Science.*

CULMIF'EROUS, *a.* [L. *culmus,* a stalk, and *fero,* to bear.]

Producing stalks. *Culmiferous* plants have a smooth jointed stalk, usually hollow, and wrapped about at each joint with single, narrow, sharp-pointed leaves, and their seeds contained in chaffy husks, as wheat, rye, oats and barley. *Milne. Quincy.*

CUL'MINATE, *v. i.* [L. *culmen,* a top or ridge.]

To be vertical; to come or be in the meridian; to be in the highest point of altitude; as a planet. *Milton.*

CULMINA'TION, *n.* The transit of a planet over the meridian, or highest point of altitude for the day. *Encyc.*

2. Top; crown.

CULPABIL'ITY, *n.* [See *Culpable.*] Blamableness; culpableness.

CUL'PABLE, *a.* [Low L. *culpabilis;* Fr. *coupable;* It. *colpabile;* from L. *culpa,* a fault; W. *cwl,* a fault, a flagging, a drooping, like *fault,* from *fail.*]

1. Blamable; deserving censure; as the person who has done wrong, or the act, conduct or negligence of the person. We say, the man is *culpable,* or voluntary ignorance is *culpable.*

2. Sinful; criminal; immoral; faulty. But generally, *culpable* is applied to acts less atrocious than crimes.

3. Guilty of; as *culpable* of a crime. [*Not used.*] *Spenser.*

CUL'PABLENESS, *n.* Blamableness; guilt; the quality of deserving blame.

CUL'PABLY, *adv.* Blamably; in a faulty manner; in a manner to merit censure.

CUL'PRIT, *n.* [supposed to be formed from *cul,* for *culpable,* and *prit,* ready; certain abbreviations used by the clerks in noting the arraignment of criminals; the prisoner is guilty, and the king is ready to prove him so. *Blackstone.*]

1. A person arraigned in court for a crime. *Dryden.*

2. Any person convicted of a crime; a criminal.

CUL'TER, *n.* [L.] A colter, which see.

CUL'TIVABLE, *a.* [See *Cultivate.*] Capable of being tilled or cultivated. *Med. Repos. Edwards, W. Ind.*

CUL'TIVATE, *v. t.* [Fr. *cultiver;* Sp. Port. *cultivar;* It. *coltivare;* from L. *colo, cultus,* to till, to dwell.]

1. To till; to prepare for crops; to manure, plow, dress, sow and reap; to labor on,

manage and improve in husbandry; as, to *cultivate* land; to *cultivate* a farm. *Sinclair.*

2. To improve by labor or study; to advance the growth of; to refine and improve by correction of faults, and enlargement of powers or good qualities; as, to *cultivate* talents; to *cultivate* a taste for poetry.

3. To study; to labor to improve or advance; as, to *cultivate* philosophy; to *cultivate* the mind.

4. To cherish; to foster; to labor to promote and increase; as, to *cultivate* the love of excellence; to *cultivate* gracious affections.

5. To improve; to meliorate, or to labor to make better; to correct; to civilize; as, to *cultivate* the wild savage.

6. To raise or produce by tillage; as, to *cultivate* corn or grass. *Sinclair.*

CUL'TIVATED, *pp.* Tilled; improved in excellence or condition; corrected and enlarged; cherished; meliorated; civilized; produced by tillage.

CUL'TIVATING, *ppr.* Tilling; preparing for crops; improving in worth or good qualities; meliorating; enlarging; correcting; fostering; civilizing; producing by tillage.

CULTIVA'TION, *n.* The art or practice of tilling and preparing for crops; husbandry; the management of land. Land is often made better by *cultivation.* Ten acres under good *cultivation* will produce more than twenty when badly tilled.

2. Study, care and practice directed to improvement, correction, enlargement or increase; the application of the means of improvement; as, men may grow wiser by the *cultivation* of talents; they may grow better by the *cultivation* of the mind, of virtue, and of piety.

3. The producing by tillage; as the *cultivation* of corn or grass.

CUL'TIVATOR, *n.* One who tills, or prepares land for crops; one who manages a farm, or carries on the operations of husbandry in general; a farmer; a husbandman; an agriculturist.

2. One who studies or labors to improve, to promote and advance in good qualities, or in growth.

CUL'TRATED, *a.* [L. *cultratus,* from *culter,* a knife.]

Sharp-edged and pointed; formed like a knife; as, the beak of a bird is convex and *cultrated.* *Encyc. art. Corvus.*

CUL'TURE, *n.* [L. *cultura,* from *colo.* See *Cultivate.*]

1. The act of tilling and preparing the earth for crops; cultivation; the application of labor or other means of improvement.

> We ought to blame the *culture,* not the soil. *Pope.*

2. The application of labor or other means to improve good qualities in, or growth; as the *culture* of the mind; the *culture* of virtue.

3. The application of labor or other means in producing; as the *culture* of corn, or grass.

4. Any labor or means employed for improvement, correction or growth.

CUL'TURE, *v. t.* To cultivate. *Thomson.*

CUL'VER, *n.* [Sax. *culfer, culfra;* Arm. *çolm;* L. *columba.*]

A pigeon, or wood pigeon. *Thomson.*

CUL'VER-HOUSE, *n.* A dove-cote. *Harmar.*

CUL'VERIN, *n.* [Fr. *couleuvrine;* It. *colubrina;* Sp. *culebrina;* from L. *colubrinus,* from *coluber,* a serpent.]

A long slender piece of ordnance or artillery, serving to carry a ball to a great distance. *Encyc.*

CUL'VERKEY, *n.* A plant or flower. *Walton.*

CUL'VERT, *n.* A passage under a road or canal, covered with a bridge; an arched drain for the passage of water. *Cyc.*

CUL'VERTAIL, *n.* [*culver* and *tail.*] Dovetail, in joinery and carpentry.

CUL'VERTAILED, *a.* United or fastened, as pieces of timber by a dove-tailed joint; *a term used by shipwrights.* *Encyc.*

CUM'BENT, *a.* [L. *cumbo.*] Lying down.

CUM'BER, *v. t.* [Dan. *kummer,* distress, incumbrance, grief; D. *kommeren;* G. *kümmern,* to arrest, to concern, to trouble, to grieve; Fr. *encombrer,* to encumber.]

1. To load, or crowd.

> A variety of frivolous arguments *cumbers* the memory to no purpose. *Locke.*

2. To check, stop or retard, as by a load or weight; to make motion difficult; to obstruct.

> Why asks he what avails him not in fight,
> And would but *cumber* and retard his flight. *Dryden.*

3. To perplex or embarrass; to distract or trouble.

> Martha was *cumbered* about much serving. Luke x.

4. To trouble; to be troublesome to; to cause trouble or obstruction in, as any thing useless. Thus, brambles *cumber* a garden or field. [See *Encumber,* which is more generally used.]

CUM'BER, *n.* Hinderance; obstruction; burdensomeness; embarrassment; disturbance; distress.

> Thus fade thy helps, and thus thy *cumbers* spring. *Spenser.*

[*This word is now scarcely used.*]

CUM'BERSŌME, *a.* Troublesome; burdensome; embarrassing; vexatious; as *cumbersome* obedience. *Sidney.*

2. Unwieldy; unmanageable not easily borne or managed; as a *cumbersome* load; a *cumbersome* machine.

CUM'BERSŌMELY, *adv.* In a manner to encumber. *Sherwood.*

CUM'BERSŌMENESS, *n.* Burdensomeness; the quality of being cumbersome and troublesome.

CUM'BRANCE, *n.* That which obstructs, retards, or renders motion or action difficult and toilsome; burden; encumbrance; hinderance; oppressive load; embarrassment. *Milton.*

CUM'BROUS, *a.* Burdensome; troublesome; rendering action difficult or toilsome; oppressive; as a *cumbrous* weight or charge. *Milton. Dryden.*

2. Giving trouble; vexatious; as a cloud of *cumbrous* gnats. *Spenser.*

3. Confused; jumbled; obstructing each other; as the *cumbrous* elements. *Milton.*

CUM'BROUSLY, *adv.* In a cumbrous manner.

CUM'FREY, *n.* A genus of plants, the Symphytum; sometimes written *comfrey, comfry,* and *comphry.*

CUM'IN, *n.* [L. *cuminum;* Gr. κυμινον; Oriental כמון kamon. The verb with which this word seems to be connected, signifies, in Ar. Ch. Syr. and Sam., to retire from sight, to lie concealed.]

An annual plant of one species, whose seeds have a bitterish warm taste, with an aromatic flavor. *Encyc.*

CU'MULATE, *v. t.* [L. *cumulo;* Russ. *kom,* a mass or lump; L. *cumulus,* a heap; Fr. *combler,cumuler;* Sp. *cumular;* It. *cumulare.*]

To gather or throw into a heap; to form a heap; to heap together. *Woodward.*

[*Accumulate* is more generally used.]

CUMULA'TION, *n.* The act of heaping together; a heap. [See *Accumulation.*]

CU'MULATIVE, *a.* Composed of parts in a heap; forming a mass. *Bacon.*

2. That augments by addition; that is added to something else. In *law,* that augments, as evidence, facts or arguments of the same kind.

CUN, *v. t.* To know. [*Not used.*] [See *Con.*]

2. To direct the course of a ship. [See *Cond,* the true orthography.]

CUNCTA'TION, *n.* [L. *cunctor,* to delay.] Delay. [*Not much used.*]

CUNCTA'TOR, *n.* One who delays or lingers. [*Little used.*] *Hammond.*

CUND, *v. t.* To give notice. [See *Cond.*]

CU'NEAL, *a.* [L. *cuneus,* a wedge. See *Coin.*] Having the form of a wedge.

CU'NEATE, CU'NEATED, } *a.* Wedge-shaped.

CU'NEIFORM, CU'NIFORM, } *a.* [L. *cuneus,* a wedge, and *forma,* form.] Having the shape or form of a wedge.

CUN'NER, *n.* [*lepas.*] A kind of fish, less than an oyster, that sticks close to the rocks. *Ainsworth.*

CUN'NING, *a.* [Sax. *cunnan, connan;* Goth. *kunnan,* to know; Sw. *kunna,* to be able, to know; *kunnig,* known; also, knowing, skilful, *cunning;* D. *kunnen,* can, to be able, to hold, contain, understand, or know; G. *können.* See *Can.*]

1. Knowing; skilful; experienced; well-instructed. It is applied to all kinds of knowledge, but generally and appropriately, to the skill and dexterity of artificers, or the knowledge acquired by experience.

> Esau was a *cunning* hunter. Gen. xxiii.
> I will take away the *cunning* artificer. Is. iii.
> A *cunning* workman. Ex. xxxviii.

2. Wrought with skill; curious; ingenious.

> With cherubs of *cunning* work shalt thou make them. Ex. xxvi.

[*The foregoing senses occur frequently in our version of the scriptures, but are nearly or quite obsolete.*]

3. Artful; shrewd; sly; crafty; astute; designing; as a *cunning* fellow.

> They are resolved to be *cunning;* let others run the hazard of being sincere. *South.*

In this sense, the purpose or final end of the person may not be illaudable; but *cunning* implies the use of artifice to accomplish the purpose, rather than open, candid, or direct means. Hence,

4. Deceitful; trickish; employing stratagems for a bad purpose.
5. Assumed with subtilty; artful.

Accounting his integrity to be but a *cunning* face of falsehood. *Sidney.*

CUN'NING, *n.* Knowledge; art; skill; dexterity. *Obs.*

Let my right hand forget her *cunning.* Ps. cxxxvii.

2. Art; artifice; artfulness; craft; shrewdness; the faculty or act of using stratagem to accomplish a purpose. Hence in *a bad sense*, deceitfulness or deceit; fraudulent skill or dexterity.

Discourage *cunning* in a child; *cunning* is the ape of wisdom. *Locke.*

CUN'NINGLY, *adv.* Artfully; craftily; with subtilty; with fraudulent contrivance.

We have not followed *cunningly* devised fables. 2 Pet i.

CUN'NINGMAN, *n.* A man who pretends to tell fortunes, or teach how to recover stolen or lost goods. *Butler.*

CUN'NINGNESS, *n.* Cunning; craft; deceitfulness.

CUP, *n.* [Sax. *cop*, or *cupp*; D. *kop*; Dan. *id.*; Sw. *kopp*; Fr. *coupe*; Arm. *coupen*; It. *coppa*; Sp. *copa*; Ir. *capa*, or *capan*; W. *cwb*, *cwpan*; L. *cupa*, *cuppa*, whence *cupella*, a *cupel*, a little cup; Ch. כוב; Ar. كوب. Class Gb. No. 48. See also No. 6. The primary sense may be, hollow, bending, Russ. *kopayu*, or containing. See No. 50. 52. 68. and *Coop.*]

1. A small vessel of capacity, used commonly to drink out of. It is usually made of metal; as a silver *cup;* a tin *cup.* But the name is also given to vessels of like shape used for other purposes. It is usually more deep than wide; but tea-cups and coffee-cups are often exceptions.
2. The contents of a cup; the liquor contained in a cup, or that it may contain; as a *cup* of beer. See 1 Cor. xi.
3. In *a scriptural sense*, sufferings and afflictions; that which is to be received or endured.

O my father, if it be possible, let this *cup* pass from me. Math. xxvi.

4. Good received; blessings and favors.

My *cup* runneth over. Ps. xxiii.

Take the cup of salvation, that is, receive the blessings of deliverance and redemption with joy and thanksgiving. *Cruden. Brown.*

5. Any thing hollow like a cup; as the *cup* of an acorn. The bell of a flower, and a calyx is called a *flower-cup*.
6. A glass cup or vessel used for drawing blood in scarification.

Cup and can, familiar companions; the *can* being the large vessel out of which the *cup* is filled, and thus the two being constantly associated. *Swift.*

Cups, in the plural, social entertainment in drinking; merry bout.

Thence from *cups* to civil broils. *Milton.*

CUP, *v. i.* In *surgery*, to apply a cupping-glass to procure a discharge of blood from a scarified part of the body. *Encyc.*

2. To supply with cups. *Obs.* *Shak.*

CUP'BEARER, *n.* An attendant of a prince or at a feast, who conveys wine or other liquors to the guests; an officer of the king's household. Neh. 1.

CUP'BOARD, *n.* [*cup* and *board.*] Originally, a board or shelf for cups to stand on. In modern houses, a small case or inclosure in a room with shelves destined to receive cups, plates, dishes and the like. *Bacon. Dryden.*

CUP'BOARD, *v. t.* To collect into a cupboard; to hoard. [*Not used.*] *Shak.*

CUP'GALL, *n.* A singular kind of gall found on the leaves of oak, &c. It contains the worm of a small fly. *Encyc.*

CUP'-ROSE, *n.* The poppy.

CU'PEL, *n.* [L. *cupella*, a little cup.] A small cup or vessel used in refining metals. It retains them while in a metallic state, but when changed by fire into a fluid scoria, it absorbs them. Thus when a mixture of lead with gold or silver is heated in a strong fire, the lead is oxydated and vitrified, and sinks into the substance of the cupel, while the gold or silver remains pure. This kind of vessel is made usually of phosphate of lime, or the residue of burnt bones, rammed into a mold, which gives it its figure. *Encyc. Lavoisier. Nicholson.*

CUPELLA'TION, *n.* The refining of gold or silver by a cupel or by scorification. *Lavoisier. Nicholson. Encyc.*

CUPID'ITY, *n.* [L. *cupiditas*, from *cupidus*, from *cupio*, to desire, to covet. See class Gb. No. 22. 24.]

An eager desire to possess something; an ardent wishing or longing; inordinate or unlawful desire of wealth or power. It is not used, I believe, for the animal appetite, like lust or concupiscence, but for desire of the mind.

No property is secure when it becomes large enough to tempt the *cupidity* of indigent power. *Burke.*

CU'POLA, *n.* [It. *cupola*; Sp. *cupula*; from the root of *cup*, or rather from W. *cop*, a top or summit.]

In *architecture*, a spherical vault on the top of an edifice; a dome, or the round top of a dome. *Encyc.*

CU'POLAID, *a.* Having a cupola. [*Not used.*] *Herbert.*

CUP'PER, *n.* [from *cup.*] One who applies a cupping-glass; a scarifier.

CUP'PING, *ppr.* Applying a cupping-glass, with scarification; a drawing blood with a cupping-glass.

CUP'PING-GLASS, *n.* A glass vessel like a cup, to be applied to the skin, before and after scarification, for drawing blood.

CU'PREOUS, *a.* [L. *cupreus*, from *cuprum*, copper.]

Coppery; consisting of copper; resembling copper, or partaking of its qualities. *Encyc. Boyle.*

CUPRIF'EROUS, *a.* [L. *cuprum*, copper, and *fero*, to bear.]

Producing or affording copper; as *cupriferous* silver. *Tooke, Russ.*

CUR, *n.* [Qu. Lapponic *coira*; Basque *chaurra*; Ir. *gyr*, *gaier*, a dog.]

A degenerate dog; and in reproach, a worthless man. *Addison. Shak. Dryden.*

CU'RABLE, *a.* [See *Cure.*] That may be healed or cured; admitting a remedy; as a *curable* wound or disease; a *curable* evil. *Dryden.*

CU'RABLENESS, *n.* Possibility of being cured, healed or remedied.

CU'RACY, **CU'RATESHIP**, *n.* [See *Cure* and *Curate.*] The office or employment of a curate; the employment of a clergyman who represents the incumbent or beneficiary of a church, parson or vicar, and officiates in his stead. *Swift.*

2. A benefice held by license from the bishop.

CU'RATE, *n.* [L. *curator*, or *curatus*, from *cura*, care. See *Cure.*]

A clergyman in the church of England, who is employed to perform divine service in the place of the incumbent, parson or vicar. He must be licenced by the bishop or ordinary, and having no fixed estate in the curacy, he may be removed at pleasure. But some curates are perpetual. *Encyc.*

2. One employed to perform the duties of another. *Dryden.*

CU'RATIVE, *a.* Relating to the cure of diseases; tending to cure. *Arbuthnot.*

CURA'TOR, *n.* [L. See *Cure.*] One who has the care and superintendence of any thing. *Swift.*

2. A guardian appointed by law. *Ayliffe.*
3. Among *the Romans*, a trustee of the affairs and interests of a person emancipated or interdicted. Also, one appointed to regulate the price of merchandize in the cities, and to superintend the customs and tributes. *Encyc.*
4. In *the United Provinces*, or *Holland*, the Curator of a University superintends the affairs of the institution, the administration of the revenues, the conduct of the professors, &c. *Encyc.*

CURB, *n.* [Fr. *courber*, to bend; Russ. *koroblyu*, to bend, to draw in, to straiten.]

1. In *the manege*, a chain of iron made fast to the upper part of the branches of the bridle, in a hole called the *eye*, and running over the beard of the horse. It consists of three parts; the hook, fixed to the eye of the branch; the chain or links; and the two rings or mails. *Encyc.*
2. Restraint; check; hinderance.

Religion should operate as an effectual *curb* to the passions.

3. A frame or a wall round the mouth of a well.
4. [Fr. *courbe*; It. *corba*, a disease and a basket.] A hard and callous swelling on the hind part of the hock of a horse's leg, attended with stiffness, and sometimes pain and lameness. *Encyc.*

A tumor on the inside of a horse's hoof. *Johnson.*

A swelling beneath the elbow of a horse's hoof. *Bailey.*

CURB, *v. t.* To restrain; to guide and manage; as a horse. *Milton.*

2. To restrain; to check; to hold back; to confine; to keep in subjection; as, to *curb* the passions.

And wisely learn to *curb* thy sorrows wild. *Milton.*

3. To furnish or surround with a curb, as a well.
4. To bend. [*Not used.*]

CURB'ED, *pp.* Restrained; checked; kept in subjection; furnished with a curb.

CURB'ING, *ppr.* Holding back; checking; restraining.

CURB'ING, *n.* A check.

€URB'-STONE, *n.* A stone placed at the edge of a pavement, to hold the work together. It is written sometimes *kerb* or *kirb.*

€URD, *n.* [Ir. *cruth*; Scot. *cruds.* Sometimes in English, *crud.* The primary sense is to congeal or coagulate. See *Crystal.*]
The coagulated or thickened part of milk, which is formed into cheese, or, in some countries, eaten as common food. The word may sometimes perhaps be used for the coagulated part of any liquor. *Bacon.*

€URD, *v. t.* To cause to coagulate; to turn to curd. *Shak.*

€URD'LE, *v. i.* [sometimes written *crudle.* See *Curd.*]
1. To coagulate or concrete; to thicken, or change into curd. Milk *curdles* by a mixture of runnet.
2. To thicken; to congeal; as, the blood *curdles* in the veins.

€URD'LE, *v. t.* To change into curd; to cause to thicken, coagulate, or concrete. Runnet or brandy *curdles* milk.

At Florence they *curdle* their milk with artichoke flowers. *Encyc.*

2. To congeal or thicken. The recital *curdled* my blood.

€URD'LED, *pp.* Coagulated; congealed.

€URD'LING, *ppr.* Concreting; coagulating.

€URD'Y, *a.* Like curd; full of curd; coagulated. *Arbuthnot.*

€URE, *n.* [L. *cura*; Fr. *cure*; L. *curo*, to *cure*, to take *care*, to prepare; W. *cûr*, care, a blow or stroke, affliction; *curaw*, to beat, throb, strike; *curiaw*, to trouble, to vex, to pine or waste away; Fr. *curer*, to cleanse; "*se curer les dents*," to pick the teeth; It. *cura*, care, diligence; *curare*, to cure, attend, protect; also, to value or esteem; Sp. *cura*, cure, remedy, guardianship; *curar*, to administer medicines; to salt, as meat; to season, as timber; to bleach thread or linen; to take care; to recover from sickness; *curioso*, curious, neat, clean, handsome, fine, careful. The radical sense of this word is, to strain, stretch, extend, which gives the sense of healing, that is, making strong, and of *care*, superintendence. But the Welsh has the sense of *driving*, a modified application of extending, and this gives the sense of separation and purification. In its application to hay, timber, provisions, &c., the sense may be to *make right*, as in other cases; but of this I am not confident.]
1. A healing; the act of healing; restoration to health from disease, and to soundness from a wound. We say, a medicine will effect a *cure.*
2. Remedy for disease; restorative; that which heals.

Colds, hunger, prisons, ills without a *cure.* *Dryden.*

3. The employment of a curate; the *care* of souls; spiritual charge.

€URE, *v. t.* [L. *curo.* See the Noun.] To heal, as a person diseased or a wounded limb; to restore to health, as the body, or to soundness, as a limb.

The child was *cured* from that very hour. Math. xvii.

2. To subdue, remove, destroy or put an end to; to heal, as a disease.

Christ gave his disciples power to *cure* diseases. Luke ix.

When the person and the disease are both mentioned, *cure* is followed by *of* before the disease. The physician *cured* the man *of* his fever.

3. To remedy; to remove an evil, and restore to a good state.

Patience will alleviate calamities, which it cannot *cure.*

4. To dry; to prepare for preservation; as, to *cure* hay: or to prepare by salt, or in any manner, so as to prevent speedy putrefaction; as, to *cure* fish or beef.

€U'RED, *pp.* Healed; restored to health or soundness; removed, as a disease; remedied; dried, smoked, or otherwise prepared for preservation.

€U'RELESS, *a.* That cannot be cured or healed; incurable; not admitting of a remedy; as a *cureless* disorder; a *cureless* ill. *Dryden.*

€U'RER, *n.* A healer; a physician; one who heals. *Harvey.*

€UR'FEW, *n.* [Fr. *couvre-feu*, cover-fire.] The ringing of a bell or bells at night, as a signal to the inhabitants to rake up their fires and retire to rest. This practice originated in England from an order of William the conqueror, who directed that at the ringing of the bell, at eight o'clock, every one should put out his light and go to bed. This word is not used in America; although the practice of ringing a bell, at nine o'clock, continues in many places, and is considered in New England, as a signal for people to retire from company to their own abodes; and in general, the signal is obeyed.
2. A cover for a fire; a fire-plate. [*Not used.*] *Bacon.*

€URIAL'ITY, *n.* [L. *curialis*, from *curia*, a court.]
The privileges, prerogatives, or retinue of a court. [*Not used.*] *Bacon.*

€U'RING, *ppr.* Healing; restoring to health or soundness; removing, as an evil; preparing for preservation.

€U'RING-HOUSE, *n.* A building in which sugar is drained and dried. *Edwards, W. Ind.*

€URIOLOǴI€, *a.* [Gr. κυριολογια, propriety of speaking.]
Designating a rude kind of hieroglyphics, in which a thing is represented by its picture. *Warburton.*

€URIOS'ITY, *n.* [L. *curiositas.* See *Curious.*]
1. A strong desire to see something novel, or to discover something unknown, either by research or inquiry; a desire to gratify the senses with a sight of what is new or unusual, or to gratify the mind with new discoveries; inquisitiveness. A man's *curiosity* leads him to view the ruins of Balbec, to investigate the origin of Homer, to discover the component parts of a mineral, or the motives of another's actions.
2. Nicety; delicacy. *Shak.*
3. Accuracy; exactness; nice performance; curiousness; as the *curiosity* of workmanship. *Ray.*
4. A nice experiment; a thing unusual or worthy of curiosity.

There hath been practiced a *curiosity*, to set a tree on the north side of a wall, and at a little height, to draw it through the wall, &c. *Bacon.*

5. An object of curiosity; that which excites a desire of seeing, or deserves to be seen, as novel and extraordinary.

We took a ramble together to see the *curiosities* of this great town. *Addison.*

[*The first and the last senses are chiefly used.*]

€URIO'SO, *n.* [It.] A curious person; a virtuoso.

€U'RIOUS, *a.* [L. *curiosus*, from *cura*, care. See *Cure.*]
1. Strongly desirous to see what is novel, or to discover what is unknown; solicitous to see or to know; inquisitive.

Be not *curious* in unnecessary matters, nor to pry into the concerns of your neighbors.

2. Habitually inquisitive; addicted to research or enquiry; as a man of a *curious* turn of mind: sometimes followed by *after*, and sometimes by *of.*

Curious after things elegant and beautiful; *curious of* antiquities. *Woodward. Dryden.*

3. Accurate; careful not to mistake; solicitous to be correct.

Men were not *curious* what syllables or particles they used. *Hooker.*

4. Careful; nice; solicitous in selection; difficult to please.

A temperate man is not *curious of* delicacies. *Taylor.*

5. Nice; exact; subtile; made with care.

Both these senses embrace their objects—with a more *curious* discrimination. *Holder.*

6. Artful; nicely diligent.

Each ornament about her seemly lies,
By *curious* chance, or careless art, composed. *Fairfax.*

7. Wrought with care and art; elegant; neat; finished; as a *curious* girdle; *curious* work. Ex. xxviii. xxx.
8. Requiring care and nicety; as *curious* arts. Acts xix.
9. Rigid; severe; particular. [*Little used.*] *Shak.*
10. Rare; singular; as a *curious* fact.

€U'RIOUSLY, *adv.* With nice inspection; inquisitively; attentively.

I saw nothing at first, but observing it more *curiously*, the spots appeared. *Newton.*

2. With nice care and art; exactly; neatly; elegantly. Ps. cxxxix.
3. In a singular manner; unusually.

€U'RIOUSNESS, *n.* Fitness to excite curiosity; exactness of workmanship.
2. Singularity of contrivance.
3. Curiosity.

€URL, *v. t.* [D. *krullen*; Dan. *kröller*; to *curl*, to crisp; Corn. *krillia.*]
1. To turn, bend or form into ringlets; to crisp; as the hair.
2. To writhe; to twist; to coil; as a serpent.
3. To dress with curls.

The snaky locks
That *curled* Megæra. *Milton.*

4. To raise in waves or undulations; to ripple.

Seas would be pools, without the brushing air
To *curl* the waves. *Dryden.*

€URL, *v. i.* To bend in contraction; to shrink into ringlets. *Boyle.*
2. To rise in waves or undulations; to ripple; and particularly, to roll over at the summit; as a *curling* wave.

3. To rise in a winding current, and to roll over at the ends; as *curling* smoke.

4. To writhe; to twist itself.

> Then round her slender waist he *curled*. *Dryden.*

5. To shrink; to shrink back; to bend and sink. He *curled* down into a corner.

CURL, *n.* A ringlet of hair, or any thing of a like form.

2. Undulation; a waving; sinuosity; flexure. *Newton.*

3. A winding in the grain of wood.

CURL'ED, *pp.* Turned or formed into ringlets; crisped; twisted; undulated.

CUR'LEW, *n.* [Fr. *courlis* or *corlieu.*] An aquatic fowl of the genus Scolopax and the grallic order. It has a long bill; its color is diversified with ash and black; and the largest species spread more than three feet of wing. It frequents the sea shore in winter, and in summer, retires to the mountains.

2. A fowl, larger than a partridge, with longer legs, which frequents the corn-fields in Spain. *Trevour.*

CURL'INESS, *n.* A state of being curly.

CURL'ING, *ppr.* Bending; twisting; forming into ringlets.

CURL'ING-IRONS, } *n.* An instrument for curling the hair.
CURL'ING-TONGS, }

CURL'Y, *a.* Having curls; tending to curl; full of ripples.

CURMUD'GEON, *n.* [Fr. *cœur*, heart, and *mechant*, evil. *Nares.* Qu.]

An avaricious churlish fellow; a miser; a niggard; a churl. *Hudibras.*

CURMUD'GEONLY, *a.* Avaricious; covetous; niggardly; churlish. *L'Estrange.*

CUR'RANT, *n.* [from *Corinth.*] The fruit of a well known shrub belonging to the genus Ribes, of which Grossularia is now considered a species; the grossberry or gooseberry and the currant falling under the same genus. Currants are of various species and varieties; as the common red and white currants, and the black currant.

2. A small kind of dried grape, imported from the Levant, chiefly from Zante and Cephalonia; used in cookery.

CUR'RENCY, *n.* [See *Current.*] Literally, a flowing, running or passing; a continued or uninterrupted course, like that of a stream; as the *currency* of time. *Ayliffe.*

2. A continued course in public opinion, belief or reception; a passing from person to person, or from age to age; as, a report has had a long or general *currency.* *Johnson.*

3. A continual passing from hand to hand, as coin or bills of credit; circulation; as the *currency* of cents, or of English crowns; the *currency* of bank bills or treasury notes.

4. Fluency; readiness of utterance: but in this sense we generally use *fluency.*

5. General estimation; the rate at which any thing is generally valued.

> He takes greatness of kingdoms according to their bulk and *currency*, and not after intrinsic value. *Bacon.*

6. That which is current or in circulation, as a medium of trade. The word may be applied to coins, or to bills issued by authority. It is often applied to bank notes, and to notes issued by government. *Crawford.*

CUR'RENT, *a.* [L. *currens*, from *curro*, to flow or run; Fr. *courir*, whence *courier*, and *discourir*, to *discourse*, *concourir*, to *concur*, &c.; It. *correre*; Sp. Port. *correr*, to run; W. *gyru*, to drive, or run; Eng. *hurry.* It seems to be connected with the root of *car*, *cart*, *chariot*, like *currus.* See Ar. كر and جري. Class Gr. No. 7. 32. 15.]

1. Literally, flowing, running, passing. Hence, passing from person to person, or from hand to hand; circulating; as *current* opinions; *current* coin. Hence, common, general or fashionable; generally received; popular; as the *current* notions of the day or age; *current* folly. *Watts. Swift. Pope.*

2. Established by common estimation; generally received; as the *current* value of coin.

3. Passable; that may be allowed or admitted. *Shak.*

4. Now passing; present in its course; as the *current* month or year.

CUR'RENT, *n.* A flowing or passing; a stream; *applied to fluids;* as a *current* of water, or of air. The gulf stream is a remarkable *current* in the Atlantic. A *current* sets into the Mediterranean.

2. Course; progressive motion, or movement; continuation; as the *current* of time.

3. A connected series; successive course; as the *current* of events.

4. General or main course; as the *current* of opinion.

CUR'RENTLY, *a.* In constant motion; with continued progression. Hence, commonly; generally; popularly; with general reception; as, the story is *currently* reported and believed.

CUR'RENTNESS, *n.* Currency; circulation; general reception.

2. Fluency; easiness of pronunciation. [*Not much used.*]

CUR'RICLE, *n.* [L. *curriculum*, from *curro*, to run.]

1. A chaise or carriage, with two wheels, drawn by two horses abreast.

2. A chariot. [*Not in use.*]

3. A course. [*Not in use.*]

CUR'RIED, *pp.* [See *Curry.*] Dressed by currying; dressed as leather; cleaned; prepared.

CUR'RIER, *n.* [L. *coriarius;* Fr. *corroyeur.* See *Curry.*]

A man who dresses and colors leather, after it is tanned.

CUR'RISH, *a.* [See *Cur.*] Like a cur; having the qualities of a cur; brutal; malignant; snappish; snarling; churlish; intractable; quarrelsome. *Sidney. Fairfax. Shak.*

CUR'RISHLY, *adv.* Like a cur; in a brutal manner.

CUR'RISHNESS, *n.* Moroseness; churlishness. *Feltham.*

CUR'RY, *v. t.* [Fr. *corroyer;* Arm. *courreza;* Sp. *curtir;* Port. *cortir.* The French and Armoric word seems to be compounded of L. *corium*, a hide, and the root of *rado*, to scrape, or of a word of like signification. The Sp. and Port. word seems to be allied to *cortex*, bark, from stripping; or to L. *curtus*, short, from cutting. But the L. *corium* is probably from a root signifying to scrape, or to peel. See Class Gr. No. 5 and 8.]

1. To dress leather, after it is tanned; to soak, pare or scrape, cleanse, beat and color tanned hides, and prepare them for use.

2. To rub and clean with a comb; as, to *curry* a horse.

3. To scratch or claw; to tear, in quarrels.

> By setting brother against brother,
> To claw and *curry* one another. *Butler.*

4. To rub or stroke; to make smooth; to tickle by flattery; to humor. But generally used in the phrase,

To curry favor, to seek or gain favor by flattery, caresses, kindness, or officious civilities. [*Not elegant.*] *Hooker.*

CUR'RY-COMB, *n.* [See *Comb.*] An iron instrument or comb, for rubbing and cleaning horses.

CUR'RYING, *ppr.* Scraping and dressing; cleaning; scratching.

CURSE, *v. t.* pret. and pp. *cursed* or *curst.* [Sax. *cursian*, *corsian;* Arm. *argarzi.* Qu. Ar. كرط.]

1. To utter a wish of evil against one; to imprecate evil upon; to call for mischief or injury to fall upon; to execrate.

> Thou shalt not *curse* the ruler of thy people. Ex. xxii.
>
> Bless and *curse* not. Rom. xii.
>
> *Curse* me this people, for they are too mighty for me. Num. xxii.

2. To injure; to subject to evil; to vex, harass or torment with great calamities.

> On impious realms and barbarous kings impose
> Thy plagues, and *curse* 'em with such sons as those. *Pope.*

3. To devote to evil.

CURSE, *v. i.* To utter imprecations; to affirm or deny with imprecations of divine vengeance.

> Then began he to *curse* and to swear. Math. xxvi.

CURSE, *n.* Malediction; the expression of a wish of evil to another.

> Shimei—who *cursed* me with a grievous *curse.* 1 Kings ii.

2. Imprecation of evil.

> They entered into a *curse*, and into an oath. Neh. x.

3. Affliction; torment; great vexation.

> I will make this city a *curse* to all nations. Jer. xxvi.

4. Condemnation; sentence of divine vengeance on sinners.

> Christ hath redeemed us from the *curse* of the law. Gal. iii.

5. Denunciation of evil.

> The priest shall write all these *curses* in a book. Num. v.

CURS'ED, *pp.* Execrated; afflicted; vexed; tormented; blasted by a curse.

2. Devoted to destruction.

> Thou art *cursed* from the earth. Gen. iv.

3. *a.* Deserving a curse; execrable; hateful; detestable; abominable.

4. *a.* Vexatious; as a *cursed* quarrel; *cursed* thorns. *Dryden. Prior.*

CURS'EDLY, *adv.* In a cursed manner;

enormously; miserably; in a manner to be cursed or detested. [*A low word.*]

CURS'EDNESS, *n.* The state of being under a curse, or of being doomed to execration or to evil.

CURS'ER, *n.* One who curses, or utters a curse.

CUR'SHIP, *n.* [See *Cur.*] Dogship; meanness; ill-nature. *Hudibras.*

CURS'ING, *ppr.* Execrating; imprecating evil on; denouncing evil; dooming to evil, misery, or vexation.

CURS'ING, *n.* Execration; the uttering of a curse; a dooming to vexation or misery.

CUR'SITOR, *n.* [from the L. *curso, cursito,* to run.]

In *England,* a clerk in the court of chancery, whose business is to make out original writs. In the statute 18 Edward III. the cursitors are called *clerks of course.* They are twenty four in number, and are a corporation among themselves. To each are assigned certain counties, to which he issues writs. *Encyc.*

CUR'SIVE, *a.* [It. *corsivo,* running. See *Course* and *Current.*]

Running; flowing. *Cursive* hand is a running hand. *Fry.*

CUR'SORARY, *a.* Cursory; hasty. [*Not in use.*] *Shak.*

CUR'SORILY, *a.* [See *Cursory.*] In a running or hasty manner; slightly; hastily; without attention; as, I read the paper *cursorily.*

CUR'SORINESS, *n.* Slight view or attention.

CUR'SORY, *a.* [L. *cursorius,* from *cursus.* See *Course.*]

1. Running; hasty; slight; superficial; careless; not with close attention; as a *cursory* reading; a *cursory* view.

2. Running about; not stationary.

CURST, *pp.* of *curse.* [See *Cursed.*]

CURST, *a.* Hateful; detestable; froward; tormenting; vexatious; peevish; malignant; mischievous; malicious; snarling; a word however which can be hardly said to have a definite signification. It is applied to any thing vexatious. In some of its applications in old authors, it appears to be the Dutch *korst,* crust, and to signify *crusty,* crabbed, surly.

CURST'NESS, *n.* Peevishness; malignity; frowardness; crabbedness; surliness.

CURT, *a.* [L. *curtus.*] Short. [*Rarely used and not elegant.*] *Brown.*

CURTA'IL, *v. t.* [composed of L. *curtus,* Fr. *court,* short, and *tailler,* to cut; *taille,* edge.]

To shorten; to cut off the end or a part; as, to *curtail* words. Hence in a more general sense, to shorten in any manner; to abridge; to diminish; as, to *curtail* our privileges. It is followed by *of* before the thing shortened. His name was *curtailed of* three letters. We are *curtailed of* our rights.

CUR'TAIL-DOG, *n.* A dog whose tail is cut off, according to the forest laws, and therefore hindered from coursing. *Shak.*

CURTA'ILED, *pp.* Cut short or shorter; abridged.

CURTA'ILING, *ppr.* Cutting short or shorter; abridging.

CURTA'ILING, *n.* Abridgment; abbreviation. *Swift.*

CUR'TAIN, *n.* *kur'tin.* [It. *cortina;* Low L. Sp. Port. *id.;* D. *gordyn;* Fr. *courtine,* in fortification. This word may be from the root of *court,* and from the sense of separating. I think it is not a contraction of the It. *copertina.*]

1. A cloth hanging round a bed, or at a window, which may be contracted, spread or drawn aside at pleasure; intended for ornament, or for use. Also, the hangings about the ark, among the Israelites.

2. A cloth-hanging used in theaters, to conceal the stage from the spectators. This is raised or let down by cords. Hence the phrases, to *drop the curtain,* to close the scene, to end; to *raise the curtain* or *the curtain will rise,* to denote the opening of the play. And to *draw the curtain,* is to close it, to shut out the light or to conceal an object; or to open it and disclose the object. *Behind the curtain,* in concealment, in secret.

3. In *fortification,* that part of the rampart which is between the flanks of two bastions, bordered with a parapet five feet high, behind which the soldiers stand to fire on the covered way and into the moat. *Encyc.*

4. In *scripture,* tents; dwellings. Hab. iii. 7.

CUR'TAIN, *v. t.* To inclose with curtains; to furnish with curtains. *Shak.*

CUR'TAIN-LECTURE, *n.* Reproof given in bed by a wife to her husband. *Addison.*

CURT'AL, *n.* A horse with a docked tail. *B. Jonson.*

CURT'AL, *a.* Short; abridged; brief. *Milton.*

CURT'ATE, *a.* [L. *curtatus,* from *curto,* to shorten.]

The *curtate distance,* in astronomy, is the distance of a planet from the sun to that point, where a perpendicular let fall from the planet meets with the ecliptic. *Encyc.*

Or the interval between the sun or earth, and that point where a perpendicular, let fall from the planet, meets the ecliptic. *Cyc.*

CURTA'TION, *n.* [See *Curtate.*] The interval between a planet's distance from the sun and the curtate distance. *Chambers.*

CURT'ILAGE, *n.* In *law,* a yard, garden, inclosure or field near and belonging to a messuage. [This is probably from *court* or the same radix.]

CURT'LY, *adv.* Briefly. [*Not in use.*]

CU'RULE, *a.* [L. *curulis,* from *currus,* a chariot.]

Belonging to a chariot. The *curule* chair or seat, among the Romans, was a stool without a back, covered with leather, and so made as to be folded. It was conveyed in a chariot, and used by public officers.

CURV'ATED, *a.* [See *Curve.*] Curved; bent in a regular form.

CURV'ATURE, *n.* [L. *curvatura.* See *Curve.*]

A bending in a regular form; crookedness, or the manner of bending; flexure by which a curve is formed. *Encyc.*

CURVE, *a.* *curv.* [L. *curvus,* bent, crooked; *curvo,* to bend, turn or wind; Fr. *courbe, courber;* It. *curvo, curvare;* Sp. *curvo, corvar.* If *b* is not radical, this word belongs to Class Gr, W. *côr,* a circle; but qu., for in Russ. it is *krivei.*]

Bending; crooked; inflected in a regular form, and forming part of a circle; as a *curve* line, which may be cut by a right line in more points than one. *Encyc.*

A *curve* line is that which is neither a straight line, nor composed of straight lines. *Cyc.*

CURVE, *n.* A bending in a regular form, or without angles; that which is bent; a flexure; part of a circle. In *geometry,* a line which may be cut by a right line in more points than one. *Encyc.*

CURVE, *v. t.* [L. *curvo;* Fr. *courber;* Russ. *krivlyu.*] To bend; to crook; to inflect.

CURV'ED, *pp.* Bent; regularly inflected.

CURV'ET, *n.* [It. *corvetta;* Fr. *courbette;* Sp. *corveta.* See *Curve.*]

1. In *the manege,* a particular leap of a horse, when he raises both his fore legs at once, equally advanced, and as his fore legs are falling, he raises his hind legs, so that all his legs are raised at once. *Encyc.*

2. A prank; a frolic.

CURV'ET, *v. i.* [It. *corvettare;* Fr. *courbetter;* Sp. *corvetear.*]

1. To leap; to bound: to spring and form a curvet.

2. To leap and frisk.

CURVILIN'EAR, CURVILIN'EAL, } *a.* [L. *curvus,* bent, and *linea,* a line.]

Having a curve line; consisting of curve lines; bounded by curve lines; as a *curvilinear* figure.

CURVILINEAR'ITY, *n.* The state of being curvilinear, or of consisting in curve lines. *Guth. Quinctilian. Pref.*

CURV'ING, *ppr.* Bending in a regular form; crooked.

CURV'ITY, *n.* [L. *curvitas.*] A bending in a regular form; crookedness. *Holder.*

CUSH'AT, *n.* The ring-dove or wood-pigeon. *Scott.*

CUSH'ION, *n.* *cush'in.* [Fr. *coussin;* It. *cuscino;* D. *kussen;* G. *küssen;* Sp. *coxin;* Port. *coxim;* Arm. *couçzin.* Qu. Ar. كساء, Ch. כסי keesi, a little cushion for the elbow.]

1. A pillow for a seat; a soft pad to be placed on a chair; a bag, stuffed with wool, hair or other soft material.

2. A bag of leather filled with sand, used by engravers to support the plate.

3. In *gilding,* a stuffing of fine tow or wool, covered by leather, on a board; used for receiving the leaves of gold from the paper, in order to its being cut into proper sizes and figures. *Encyc.*

Lady's cushion, a plant, a species of Saxifraga. *Lee.*

Sea cushion, sea pink or thrift, a species of Statice. *Lee.*

CUSH'ION, *v. t.* To seat on a cushion.

CUSH'IONED, *a.* Seated on a cushion; supported by cushions. *Johnson.*

CUSH'IONET, *n.* A little cushion. *Beaum.*

CUSK'IN, *n.* A kind of ivory cup. [*Not in use.*] *Bailey.*

CUSP, *n.* [L. *cuspis,* a point.] The point or horn of the moon or other luminary. *Encyc.*

ƇUSP'ATED, *a.* [L. *cuspis*, a point.] Pointed; ending in a point.

ƇUSP'IDAL, *a.* Ending in a point. *More.*

ƇUSP'IDATE, ƇUSP'IDATED, *a.* [L. *cuspidatus*, from *cuspis*, a point.]
Having a sharp end, like the point of a spear; terminating in a bristly point; as a *cuspidate* leaf. *Martyn.*

ƇUS'TARD, *n.* [Cymbric *cwstard*. *Junius.* I suspect the first syllable to be W. *caws*, curd, cheese.]
A composition of milk and eggs, sweetened and baked or boiled, forming an agreeable kind of food.

ƇUS'TARD-APPLE, *n.* A plant, a species of Annona, growing in the West Indies, whose fruit is of the size of a tennis ball, of an orange color, containing a yellowish pulp, of the consistence of custard. *Encyc.*

ƇUSTO'DIAL, *a.* [from *custody*.] Relating to custody or guardianship.

ƇUS'TODY, *n.* [L. *custodia*; It. and Sp. *id.*; from L. *custos*, a watchman, a keeper. This word has the elements of *castle*, W. *cas*, the primary sense of which is to separate, to drive off; hence, to defend, to hold. See *Chaste.*]

1. A keeping; a guarding; care, watch, inspection, for keeping, preservation or security.

Uuder the *custody* and charge of the sons of Merari shall be the boards of the tabernacle. Num. iii.

The prisoner was committed to the *custody* of the sheriff. Hence,

2. Imprisonment; confinement; restraint of liberty.

3. Defense from a foe; preservation; security.

There was prepared a fleet of thirty ships for the *custody* of the narrow seas. *Bacon.*

ƇUS'TOM, *n.* [Fr. *coutume*, for *coustume*; It. *costuma*, *costume*; Sp. *costumbre*; Port. *costume*; Arm. *custum*. Qu. L. *consuetus*.]

1. Frequent or common use, or practice; a frequent repetition of the same act; hence, way; established manner; habitual practice.

The priest's *custom* with the people was—1 Sam. ii.

We have no such *custom*. 1 Cor. xi.

The *customs* of the people are vain. Jer. x.

2. A buying of goods; practice of frequenting a shop and purchasing or procuring to be done.

Let him have your *custom*, but not your votes. *Addison.*

The shopkeeper has extensive *custom*, or a good run of *custom*. A mill or a manufacturer has extensive *custom*, or little *custom*.

3. In *law*, long established practice, or usage, which constitutes the unwritten law, and long consent to which gives it authority. Customs are general, which extend over a state or kingdom, and particular, which are limited to a city or district. *Encyc.*

ƇUS'TOM, *v. t.* To make familiar. [See *Accustom*, which is the word used.]

2. To give custom to. *Bacon.*

ƇUS'TOM, *n.* [Fr. *coutume*, from *coûter*, for *couster*, to cost.]
Tribute, toll or tax; that is, *cost* or charge paid to the public.

Render *custom* to whom *custom* is due. Rom. xiii.

Customs, in the plural, the duties imposed by law on merchandize imported or exported. *In Great Britain and the U. States, this word is limited to these species of duties.*

ƇUS'TOM-HOUSE, *n.* The house where vessels enter and clear, and where the customs are paid or secured to be paid.

ƇUS'TOMABLE, *a.* Common; habitual; frequent. *Johnson.*

2. Subject to the payment of the duties called *customs*. *Law of Massachusetts.*

ƇUS'TOMABLENESS, *n.* Frequency; conformity to custom. [*Little used.*]

ƇUS'TOMABLY, *adv.* According to custom; in a customary manner. *Hayward.*

ƇUS'TOMARILY, *adv.* [See *Customary.*] Habitually; commonly. *Ray.*

ƇUS'TOMARINESS, *n.* Frequency; commonness; habitual use or practice.

ƇUS'TOMARY, *a.* [Fr. *coutumier.*] According to custom, or to established or common usage; as a *customary* dress; *customary* compliments.

2. Habitual; in common practice; as *customary* vices.

3. Holding by custom; as *customary* tenants, who are copyholders.

4. Held by custom; as a *customary* freehold.

ƇUS'TOMARY, *n.* [Fr. *coutumier*, *coustumier.*] A book containg laws and usages, or customs; as the *customary* of the Normans. *Cowel.*

ƇUS'TOMED, *a.* Usual; common; to which we are accustomed. [See *Accustomed.*] *Shak.*

2. Furnished with customers. *Bacon.*

ƇUS'TOMER, *n.* One who frequents any place of sale for the sake of purchasing goods; one who purchases goods or wares.

2. One who frequents or visits any place for procuring what he wants. We say, a mill has many *customers*. Hence a person who receives supplies is called a *customer*; the smith, the shoemaker and the tailor have their *customers*; and the coffee-house has its *customers*.

3. A toll-gatherer. *Obs.*

ƇUS'TOS, *n.* [L.] A keeper; as *custos brevium*, the principal clerk of the common pleas; *custos rotulorum*, keeper of the rolls and records of the sessions of the peace. *England.*

CUS'TREL, *n.* [Qu. Old Fr. *coustillier*, from L. *scutum.*]
A buckler-bearer. Also, a vessel for holding wine. [*Not in use.*]

ƇUT, *v. t.* pret. and pp. *cut.* [Norm. *cotu*, cut. This word coincides in elements with the W. *cat*, a piece, *cateia*, to cut, *cwta*, short, *cwtau*, to shorten, and with *ysgythru*, to cut off, to lop, to shred, to carve, which Owen deduces from *ysgwth*, a push, from *gwth*, a push or thrust, *gwthiaw*, to push, thrust, press. Whether *cut* is derived to us from the Welsh or not may be a question; but I have not found the word in any of the Gothic or Teutonic languages. It is obviously from a common root with the L. *cædo* and *cudo*, and the primary sense is to thrust, to drive, to strike; and to *cut off* is primarily to *strike off*. We have proof of this in our own language; for a stroke with a whip is called a *cut*, and our common people, when they urge a person to ride or run with haste, cry out, *cut on, cut on*. The fact is the same with many other words which now signify, to separate with an edged tool. See Class Gd. No. 2. 4. 8. 43. 49. 56. 59. and in a different dialect, Class Gs. No. 5. 6. 28. 32. 40. 41. 42. 67.]

1. To separate the parts of any body by an edged instrument, either by striking, as with an ax, or by sawing or rubbing; to make a gash, incision or notch, which separates the external part of a body, as to *cut* the flesh. It signifies also, to cut into pieces; to sever or divide; as, to *cut* timber in the forest. But when an entire separation of the body is intended, it is usually followed by *off*, *down*, *asunder*, *in two*, *in pieces*, or other word denoting such severance.

"Ye shall not *cut* yourselves," that is, ye shall not gash your flesh. Deut. xiv.

2. To hew.

Thy servants can skill to *cut* timber. 2 Chron. ii.

3. To carve, as meat; to carve or engrave in sculpture. *Addison.*

4. To divide; to cleave, by passing through; as, a ship *cuts* the briny deep.

5. To penetrate; to pierce; to affect deeply; as, a sarcasm *cuts* to the quick.

6. To divide, as a pack of cards; as, to *cut* and shuffle.

7. To intersect; to cross. One line *cuts* another at right angles. The ecliptic *cuts* the equator.

8. To castrate.

To cut across, to pass by a shorter course, so as to cut off an angle or distance.

To cut asunder, to cut into pieces; to divide; to sever.

He hath *cut asunder* the cords of the wicked. Ps. cxxix.

To cut down, to fell; to cause to fall by severing.

Ye shall *cut down* their groves. Ex. xxxiv.

Hence, to depress; to abash; to humble; to shame; to silence; as, his eloquence *cuts down* the finest orator. *Addison.*

[*This phrase is not elegant, but is in popular use.*]

To cut off, to separate one part from another; as, to *cut off* a finger, or an arm; to *cut off* the right hand figure; to *cut off* a letter or syllable.

2. To destroy; to extirpate; to put to death untimely.

Jezebel *cut off* the prophets of the Lord 1 Kings xviii.

Evil doers shall be *cut off*. Ps. xxxvii.

3. To separate; to remove to a distance, or to prevent all intercourse. A man in another country or in prison is *cut off* from his country or his friends.

4. To interrupt; as, to *cut off* communication.

5. To separate; to remove; to take away; as, to *cut off* ten years of life.

6. To intercept; to hinder from return, or union. The troops were *cut off* from the ships.

7. To end; to finish; as, to *cut off* all controversy.

8. To prevent or preclude; as, to *cut off* all occasion of blame.

9. To preclude or shut out. The sinner *cuts* himself *off* from the benefits of christianity.
10. To stop, interrupt or silence.
The judge *cut off* the counsel very short. *Bacon.*
To cut on, to hasten; to run or ride with the utmost speed; *a vulgar phrase.*
2. To urge or drive in striking; to quicken blows; to hasten.
To cut out, to remove a part by cutting or carving; as, to *cut out* a piece from a board; to *cut out* the tongue. Hence,
2. To shape or form by cutting; as, to *cut out* a garment; to *cut out* an image; to *cut out* a wood into walks. Hence,
3. To scheme; to contrive; to prepare; as, to *cut out* work for another day. So we say, to *strike out.*
4. To shape; to adapt. He is not *cut out* for an author. [*Not elegant.*]
5. To debar. [*Not common.*] *Pope.*
6. To take the preference or precedence of; as, to *cut out* a prior judgment creditor. *Kent.*
7. To step in and take the place of, as in courting and dancing. [*A vulgar phrase.*]
8. To interfere as a horse, when the shoe of one foot beats off the skin of the pastern joint of another.
To cut short, to hinder from proceeding by sudden interruption.
Achilles *cut* him *short.* *Dryden.*
2. To shorten; to abridge; as, to *cut short* of provisions or pay; to *cut* the matter *short.*
To cut up, to cut in pieces; as, to *cut up* beef.
2. To eradicate; to cut off; as, to *cut up* shrubs.
CUT, *v. i.* To pass into or through and sever; to enter and divide the parts; as, an instrument *cuts* well.
2. To be severed by a cutting instrument; as, this fruit *cuts* easy or smooth.
3. To divide by passing.
The teeth are ready to *cut.* *Arbuthnot.*
4. To perform a surgical operation by cutting, especially in lithotomy.
He saved lives by *cutting* for the stone. *Pope.*
5. To interfere, as a horse.
To cut in, to divide, or turn a card, for determining who are to play.
CUT, *pp.* Gashed; divided; hewn; carved; intersected; pierced; deeply affected; castrated.
Cut and dry, prepared for use; *a metaphor from hewn timber.*
CUT, *n.* The action of an edged instrument; a stroke or blow, as with an ax or sword.
2. A cleft; a gash; a notch; a wound; the opening made by an edged instrument, distinguished by its length from that made by perforation with a pointed instrument.
3. A stroke or blow with a whip.
4. A channel made by cutting or digging; a ditch; a groove; a furrow; a canal.
5. A part cut off from the rest; as a good *cut* of beef; a *cut* of timber. Also, any small piece or shred.
6. A lot made by cutting a stick; as, to draw *cuts.* *Sidney.*
7. A near passage, by which an angle is cut off; as a *shorter cut.*
8. A picture cut or carved on wood or metal, and impressed from it. *Brown.*
9. The stamp on which a picture is carved, and by which it is impressed.
10. The act of dividing a pack of cards. Also, the right to divide; as, whose *cut* is it?
11. Manner in which a thing is cut; form; shape; fashion; as the *cut* of a garment; the *cut* of his beard. *Stillingfleet.*
12. A fool; a cully; a gelding. [*Not in use.*]
Cut and long tail, men of all kinds; *a proverbial expression borrowed from dogs.*
CUTA'NEOUS, *a.* [See *Cuticle.*] Belonging to the skin, or cutis; existing on, or affecting the skin; as a *cutaneous* disease; *cutaneous* eruption.
CUTH, in Saxon, signifies known, or famous. Hence, *Cuthwin*, a famous conqueror; *Cuthred*, a famous or knowing counselor; *Cuthbert*, known bright, or famous for skill. *Gibson.*
CU'TICLE, *n.* [L. *cuticula*, dim. of *cutis*, skin, the same as *hide*, which see.]
1. The scarf-skin; the thin exterior coat of the skin, which rises in a blister; a thin pellucid membrane covering the true skin.
2. The thin external covering of the bark of a plant. *Darwin.*
3. A thin skin formed on the surface of liquor. *Newton.*
CUTIC'ULAR, *a.* Pertaining to the cuticle or external coat of the skin.
CUT'LAS, *n.* [Fr. *coutelas*; Arm. *contelaçzen*; It. *coltellaccio*; Port. *cutelo.* This word seems to be from the L. *cultellus*, at least the Italian and French are so; and *n* in the Armoric is casual, as in other words in that dialect. The *curteleaxe* or *curtelax* of some authors, and *curtax*, seem to be corrupted, or they are from Sp. *cortar*, L. *curto*, to cut. *Cutlas* is the more correct orthography.]
A broad curving sword; a hanger; used by soldiers in the cavalry, by seamen, &c.
CUT'LER, *n.* [Fr. *coutelier*; Norm. *coteller*; Arm. *conteller* or *coutellour*; Port. *cutileiro*; It. *coltellinaio*; from L. *culter*, a knife.]
One whose occupation is to make knives and other cutting instruments.
CUT'LERY, *n.* The business of making knives; or more generally, knives and other edged instruments in general.
CUT'LET, *n.* [Fr. *côtelette*, a little side or rib; *côté*, side.]
A small piece of meat for cooking; as a veal *cutlet.*
CUT'PURSE, *n.* [*cut* and *purse.*] One who cuts purses for stealing them or their contents; a practice said to have been common when men wore purses at their girdles. One who steals from the person; a thief; a robber. *Shak. Bentley.*
CUT'TER, *n.* One who cuts or hews.
2. An instrument that cuts; as a *straw-cutter.*
3. A fore tooth, that cuts meat, as distinguished from a grinder.
4. A small boat used by ships of war. Also, a vessel with one mast and a straight running bowsprit, which may be run in upon deck; rigged nearly like a sloop. *Mar. Dict.*
5. An officer in the exchequer that provides wood for the tallies.
6. A ruffian; a bravo; a destroyer. *Obs.*
CUT'-THRŎAT, *n.* A murderer; an assassin; a ruffian. *South. Dryden.*
CUT'-THRŎAT, *a.* Murderous; cruel; barbarous. *Carew.*
CUT'TING, *ppr.* [See *Cut.*] Dividing by an edged instrument; cleaving by the stroke or motion of an edged instrument, as by a knife, ax, or saw; hewing; carving; intersecting; piercing.
2. *a.* Piercing the heart; wounding the feelings; deeply affecting with shame or remorse; pungent; piquant; satirical; as a *cutting* reflection.
CUT'TING, *n.* A separation or division; a piece cut off; a slip; as the *cuttings* of vines.
2. The operation of removing a stone from the bladder.
CUT'TLE, } *n.* [Sax. *cudele*, from the
CUT'TLE-FISH, } sense of withdrawing or *hiding*, allied to *cuddle*, W. *cuziaw*, to hide, Arm. *cutaff*, or *cuddyo*, to hide.]
1. A genus of *mollusca*, called Sepia. They have small arms, with serrated cups, by which they lay fast hold of any thing. They have also two tentacula longer than the arms; the mouth is in the center of the arms, and is horny, and hooked like the bill of a hawk. They feed on sprats, lobsters and other shell-fish. They have a little bladder under the throat, [near the liver, *Cuvier*,] from which, when pursued, they throw out a black liquor that darkens the water, by which means they escape. Hence *cuttle* is used for a foul-mouthed fellow; one who blackens the character of another. *Encyc. Shak.*
2. A knife. [*Not in use.*] *Shak.*
CUT'-WATER, *n.* The fore part of a ship's prow, or knee of the head, which cuts the water. Also, a water-fowl, a species of gull; or rather, the Rynchops, or razor-bill.
CUT'-WŎRK, *n.* Embroidery. [*Not in use.*] *B. Jonson.*
CY'ANITE, *n.* [Gr. κυανος, sky-colored.] A mineral of a Berlin blue color, passing into gray and green; called by Haüy, disthene.
CYAN'OĠEN, *n.* [Gr. κυανος, blue, and γενναω, to beget.]
Carbureted azote, or carburet of nitrogen, the compound base of Prussic acid; otherwise called Prussine. *Ure.*
CYATH'IFORM, *a.* [L. *cyathus*, a cup; Gr. κυαθος.]
In the form of a cup, or drinking glass, a little widened at the top. *Lee.*
CYC'LADES, *n. plu.* [Gr. κυκλος, a circle.] A number of isles arranged round the isle of Delos, in the Grecian Sea, in the form of a circle.
CYC'LE, *n.* [Gr. κυκλος, L. *cyclus*, an orb or circle; Ir. *ciogal.* Qu. Eng. *gig*; Ch. Heb. חוג. Class Gk. No. 13. 16.]
1. In *chronology*, a period or series of numbers, which regularly proceed from first to last, and then return to the first, in a perpetual circle. Hence,
2. The *cycle of the moon*, or golden number, or Metonic cycle, so called from its inventor Meton, is a period of nineteen years,

which being completed, the new and full moons return on the same days of the month.

3. The *cycle of the sun*, is a period of twenty eight years, which having elapsed, the dominical or Sunday letters return to their former place, and proceed in the former order, according to the Julian calendar.

4. *Cycle of indiction*, a period of fifteen years, at the end of which the Roman emperors imposed an extraordinary tax, to pay the soldiers who were obliged to serve in the army for that period and no longer.

5. A round of years, or period of time, in which the same course begins again; a periodical space of time. *Holder.*

6. An imaginary orb or circle in the heavens. *Milton.*

CYC'LOGRAPH, *n.* [κυκλος, circle, and γραφω, to describe.]

An instrument for describing the arcs of circles.

CYC'LOID, *n.* [κυκλος, circle, and ειδος form.] A geometrical curve on which depends the doctrine of pendulums; a figure made by the upper end of the diameter of a circle, turning about a right line. *Bailey.*

The genesis of a cycloid may be conceived by imagining a nail in the circumference of a wheel; the line which the nail describes in the air, while the wheel revolves in a right line, is the cycloid. *Johnson.*

CYCLOID'AL, *a.* Pertaining or relating to a cycloid; as, the *cycloidal* space is the space contained between the cycloid and its substance. *Chambers.*

Or the space contained between the curve or crooked line and the subtense of the figure. *Bailey.*

CYC'LOLITE, *n.* A name given to Madrepores. *Dict. Nat. Hist.*

CYCLOM'ETRY, *n.* [Gr. κυκλος, circle, and μετρεω, to measure.] The art of measuring cycles or circles. *Wallis.*

CYCLOPE'AN, *a.* [from *Cyclops.*] Pertaining to the Cyclops; vast; terrific. *Hall.*

CYCLOPE'DIA, } *n.* [Gr. κυκλος, circle, and
CY'CLOPEDE, } παιδεια, discipline, erudition.]

The circle or compass of the arts and sciences; circle of human knowledge. Hence, the book or books that contain treatises on every branch of the arts and sciences, arranged under proper heads, in alphabetical order. [See *Encyclopedia.*]

CYCLOP'IC, *a.* Pertaining to the Cyclops; gigantic; savage. *Bryant.*

CY'CLOPS, *n.* [Gr. κυκλωψ; κυκλος, a circle, and ωψ, an eye.]

In *fabulous history*, certain giants, the sons of Neptune and Amphitrite, who had but one circular eye in the midst of the forehead. They inhabited Sicily, and assisted Vulcan in making thunderbolts for Jupiter. *Lempriere.*

CYDER. [See *Cider.*]

CYG'NET, *n.* [L. *cygnus, cycnus*, a swan; Gr. κυκνος.] A young swan. *Shak.*

CYL'INDER, *n.* [Gr. κυλινδρος, from κυλινδω, to roll, from κυλιω, id.; L. *cylindrus*; Sp. *cilindro*; It. *id.*; Fr. *cylindre*; Heb. Ch. גלל, Ar. جَال to roll.]

In *geometry*, a solid body supposed to be generated by the rotation of a parallelogram round one of its sides; or a long circular body of uniform diameter, and its extremities forming equal parallel circles. *Encyc. Bailey.*

CYLINDRA'CEOUS, *a.* Cylindrical. [*Little used.*] *Lee. Bot.*

CYLIN'DRIC, } *a.* Having the form of
CYLIN'DRICAL, } a cylinder; or partaking of its properties.

CYLIN'DRIFORM, *a.* [*cylinder* and *form.*] Having the form of a cylinder.

CYL'INDROID, *n.* [*cylinder* and ειδος, form.] A solid body, approaching to the figure of a cylinder, but differing in some respects, as having the bases elliptical, but parallel and equal. *Encyc.*

CYMAR', *n.* A slight covering; a scarf; properly, *simar.*

CYMA'TIUM, } *n.* [L.; Gr. κυματιον, a lit-
CY'MA, } tle wave, from κυμα, a wave.]

In *architecture*, a member or molding of the cornice, the profile of which is waving, that is, concave at the top and convex at bottom.

CYM'BAL, *n.* [L. *cymbalum*; Gr. κυμβαλον; It. *cembalo.*]

1. A musical instrument used by the ancients, hollow and made of brass, somewhat like a kettle-drum; but the precise form is not ascertained.

2. A mean instrument used by gypsies and vagrants, made of a steel wire, in a triangular form, on which are passed five rings, which are touched and shifted along the triangle with an iron rod held in the left hand, while it is supported in the right by a ring, to give it free motion. *Encyc.*

CYM'BIFORM, *a.* [L. *cymba*, a boat, and *forma*, form.] Shaped like a boat. *Martyn.*

CY'ME, } *n.* [Gr. κυμα, fetus, from κυω, to
CY'MA, } swell.] Literally, a sprout, particularly of the cabbage. Technically, an aggregate flower composed of several florets sitting on a receptacle, producing all the primary peduncles from the same point, but having the partial peduncles scattered and irregular; all fastigiate, or forming a flat surface at the top. It is naked or with bractes. *Martyn.*

CYM'LING, *n.* A squash. *Virginia.*

CYM'OPHANE, *n.* [Gr. κυμα, a wave, and φαινω, to appear.]

A mineral, called also chrysoberyl. Its color is green of different shades; its fracture conchoidal or undulated, and in hardness it ranks next to the sapphire. *Haüy. Cleaveland.*

CYMOPH'ANOUS, *a.* Having a wavy floating light; opalescent; chatoyant.

CY'MOSE, } *a.* Containing a cyme; in the
CY'MOUS, } form of a cyme. *Martyn.*

CYNAN'CHE, *n.* [Gr. κυναγχη, a dog-collar, angina; κυων, a dog, and αγχω, to press or bind, to suffocate.]

A disease of the throat, attended with inflammation, swelling, and difficulty of breathing and swallowing. It is of several kinds and comprehends the quinsy, croop and malignant sore throat.

CYNAN'THROPY, *n.* [Gr. κυων, a dog, and ανθρωπος, man.]

A kind of madness in which men have the qualities of dogs.

CYNARCTOM'ACHY, *n.* [Gr. κυων, a dog, αρκτος, a bear, and μαχη, a fight.]

Bear-baiting with a dog. [*A barbarous word.*] *Hudibras.*

CYN'IC, } *a.* [Gr. κυνικος, canine, from
CYN'ICAL, } κυων, a dog.] Having the qualities of a surly dog; snarling; captious; surly; currish; austere.

Cynic spasm, a kind of convulsion, in which the patient imitates the howling of dogs. *Encyc.*

CYN'IC, *n.* A man of a canine temper; a surly or snarling man or philosopher; a follower of Diogenes; a misanthrope. *Shak.*

CYN'ICALLY, *adv.* In a snarling, captious or morose manner. *Bacon.*

CYN'ICALNESS, *n.* Moroseness; contempt of riches and amusements.

CYN'ICS, *n.* In *ancient history*, a sect of philosophers, who valued themselves on their contempt of riches, of arts, sciences and amusements. They are said to owe their origin to Antisthenes of Athens. *Encyc.*

CYN'OSURE, *n.* [Gr. κυνοσουρα, the tail of the dog, ursa minor, the little bear.]

The constellation near the north pole, consisting of seven stars, four of which are disposed like the four wheels of a chariot, and three lengthwise, like the beam; hence called the chariot or Charles's wain. As seamen are accustomed to steer by this constellation, it is sometimes taken for that which directs or attracts attention. *Encyc. Milton.*

CYON. [See *Cion.*]

CYPHER. [See *Cipher.*]

CY'PRESS, *n.* [L. *cupressus*; Gr. κυπαρισσος.] A genus of plants or trees. The most remarkable are the sempervirens or common cypress, the evergreen American cypress or white cedar, and the disticha or deciduous American cypress. The wood of these trees is remarkable for its durability. The coffins in which the Athenian heroes and the mummies of Egypt were deposited, are said to have been made of the first species. *Encyc.*

2. The emblem of mourning for the dead, cypress branches having been anciently used at funerals.

> Had success attended the Americans, the death of Warren would have been sufficient to damp the joys of victory, and the *cypress* would have been united with the laurel. *Eliot's Biog.*

CYP'RIN, *a.* Pertaining to the fish of the genus Cyprinus.

CY'PRUS, *n.* A thin transparent black stuff. *Shak.*

CYRIOLOG'IC, *a.* [Gr. κυριος, chief, and λογος, discourse.] Relating or pertaining to capital letters. *Encyc.*

CYST, *n.* [Gr. κυςις, a bladder.] A bag or tunic which includes morbid matter in animal bodies. *Encyc.*

CYST'IC, *a.* Pertaining to a cyst, or contained in a cyst. The *cystic* duct is the membranous canal that conveys the bile from the hepatic duct into the gall-bladder. The *cystic* artery is a branch of the hepatic. *Hooper.*

Cystic oxyd, a name given to a peculiar substance, supposed to be generated in the bladder or rather in the kidneys. *Ure.*

CYS'TOCELE, *n.* [Gr. κυςις, a bladder, and κηλη, a tumor.]

A hernia or rupture formed by the protrusion of the urinary bladder. *Hooper.*

CYSTOT'OMY, *n.* [Gr. κυςις, a bladder, and τεμνω, to cut.]

The act or practice of opening encysted tumors, for the discharge of morbid matter.

CYT'ISUS, *n.* A shrub or tree. Also, a genus of trees; tree-trefoil.

CZ'AR, *n.* A king; a chief; a title of the emperor of Russia; pronounced *tzar*, and so written by good authors.

CZARI'NA, *n.* A title of the empress of Russia.

CZ'ARISH, *a.* Pertaining to the czar of Russia.

D.

D, in the English alphabet, is the fourth letter and the third articulation. It holds the same place in the English, as in the Chaldee, Syriac, Hebrew, Samaritan, Greek and Latin alphabets. In the Arabic, it is the eighth; in the Russian, the fifth; and in the Ethiopic, the nineteenth letter.

D is a dental articulation, formed by placing the end of the tongue against the gum just above the upper teeth. It is nearly allied to T, but is not so close a letter, or rather it does not interrupt the voice so suddenly as T, and in forming the articulation, there is a lingual and nasal sound, which has induced some writers to rank D among the lingual letters. It has but one sound, as in *do, din, bad;* and is never quiescent in English words, except in a rapid utterance of such words as *handkerchief.*

As a numeral, D represents *five hundred*, and when a dash or stroke is placed over it, thus D̄, it denotes *five thousand.*

As an abbreviation, D stands for Doctor; as M. D. Doctor of Medicine; D. T. Doctor of Theology, or S. T. D. Doctor of Sacred Theology; D. D. Doctor of Divinity, or dono dedit; D. D. D. dat, dicat, dedicat; and D. D. D. D. dignum Deo donum dedit.

Da Capo. [It. from the head.] In *music*, these words signify that the first part of the tune is to be repeated from the beginning.

DAB, *v. t.* [Fr. *dauber*, or from the same root. It has the elements of *dip, dub* and *tap*, Gr. τυπτω, and of *daub.* Class Db. No. 3. 21. 28. 58.]

1. To strike gently with the hand; to slap; to box. *Bailey.*

2. To strike gently with some soft or moist substance; as, to *dab* a sore with lint. *Sharp.*

DAB, *n.* A gentle blow with the hand.

2. A small lump or mass of any thing soft or moist.

3. Something moist or slimy thrown on one.

4. In *law language*, an expert man. [See *Dabster.*]

5. A small flat fish, of the genus Pleuronectes, of a dark brown color.

DAB'CHICK, *n.* [*dab* or *dip* and *chick.*] A small water-fowl.

DAB'BLE, *v. t.* [Heb. טבל tabal, or from the root of *dip*, Goth. *daupyan*, Belgic *dabben* or *dabbelen.* See *Dip.*]

Literally, to dip a little or often; hence, to wet; to moisten; to spatter; to wet by little dips or strokes; to sprinkle. *Swift. Wiseman.*

DAB'BLE, *v. i.* To play in water; to dip the hands, throw water and splash about; to play in mud and water.

2. To do any thing in a slight or superficial manner; to tamper; to touch here and there.

> You have, I think, been *dabbling* with the text. *Atterbury.*

3. To meddle; to dip into a concern.

DAB'BLER, *n.* One who plays in water or mud.

2. One who dips slightly into any thing; one who meddles, without going to the bottom; a superficial meddler; as a *dabbler* in politics.

DAB'BLING, *ppr.* Dipping superficially or often; playing in water, or in mud; meddling.

DAB'STER, *n.* [Qu. from *adept*, with *ster*, Sax. *steoran*, to steer.]

One who is skilled; one who is expert; a master of his business. [*Not an elegant word.* See *Dapper.*]

DACE, *n.* [D. *daas.* Qu. Fr. *vendoise.*] A fish, the *Cyprinus leuciscus*; a small river fish, resembling the roach. *Walton.*

DAC'TYL, *n.* [Gr. δακτυλος, a finger; L. *dactylus*; probably a shoot. See *Digit.*]

A poetical foot consisting of three syllables, the first long, and the others short, like the joints of a finger; as, *tĕgmĭnĕ, cārmĭnĕ.*

DAC'TYLET, *n.* A dactyl. *Bp. Hall.*

DAC'TYLIC, *a.* Pertaining to or consisting of dactyls; as *dactylic* verses; a *dactylic* flute, a flute consisting of unequal intervals. *Encyc.*

DAC'TYLIST, *n.* [from *dactyl.*] One who writes flowing verse. *Warton.*

DACTYLOL'OGY, *n.* [δακτυλος, finger, and λογος, discourse.]

The act or the art of communicating ideas or thoughts by the fingers. Deaf and dumb persons acquire a wonderful dexterity in this art.

DAD, DAD'DY, } *n.* [W. *tad*; Ir. *taid*; Arm. *tad*; Corn. *tad* or *taz*; ancient L. *tata*; Port. *taita*; Gypsey, *dad, dada*; Sans. *tada*; Hindoo, *dada*; Russ. *tiatia*; Finn. *taat.*]

Father; *a word used by infants*, from whom it is taken. The first articulations of infants or young children are *dental* or *labial*; dental, in *tad, dad*, and labial, in *mamma, papa.*

DAD'DLE, *v. i.* To walk with tottering, like a child or an old man. [*Little used.*]

DADE, *v. t.* To hold up by leading strings. [*Little used.*] *Drayton.*

D'ADO, *n.* [Ital. a die.] The plain part of a column between the base and the cornice; the die. *Dict.*

Or a cubical base of a column. *Thomson.*

DÆ'DAL, *a.* [L. *Dædalus*, Gr. Δαιδαλος, an ingenious artist.]

1. Various; variegated. *Spenser.*

2. Skilful.

DÆDALIAN. [See *Dedalian.*]

DAFF, DAFFE, } *n.* [Ice. *dauf*, allied to *deaf.*] A stupid blockish fellow. *Obs.* *Chaucer.*

DAFF, *v. t.* To daunt. [*Local.*] *Grose.*

DAFF, *v. t.* To toss aside; to put off. [See *Doff.*] *Shak.*

DAF'FODIL, *n.* [D. *affodille*; G. *doppelte narcisse*, double narcissus; It. *asfodillo*; Fr. *asphodele*; L. *asphodelus*; Gr. ασφοδελος.]

A plant of the genus Narcissus, of several species. These have a bulbous root, and beautiful flowers of various colors, white, yellow and purple. *Encyc.*

DAG, *n.* [Fr. *dague*, from thrusting.] A dagger; a hand-gun; a pistol. [*Not in use.*] *Burton.*

DAG, *n.* Dew. [*Not in use.*]

DAG, *n.* [Sax. *dag.*] A loose end, as of locks of wool; called also *dag-locks.* *Bailey.*

2. A leathern latchet.

DAG, *v. t.* To daggle. [*Not in use.*]

2. To cut into slips. *Obs.* *Chaucer.*

DAG'GER, *n.* [Fr. *dague*; D. *dagge*; Arm. *dager*; Sp. *daga*; Port. *adaga*; It. *daga*; Ir. *daigear.* In G. and D. *degen* is a sword.]

1. A short sword; a poniard. *Sidney.*

2. In *fencing schools*, a blunt blade of iron with a basket hilt, used for defense.

3. With *printers*, an obelisk, or obelus, a mark of reference in the form of a dagger; thus †.

DAG'GER, *v. t.* To pierce with a dagger; to stab.

DAG'GERS-DRAWING, *n.* The act of drawing daggers; approach to open attack or to violence; a quarrel. *Swift.*

DAG'GLE, *v. t.* [probably from *dag*, dew, or its root.]

To trail in mud or wet grass; to befoul; to dirty, as the lower end of a garment.

DAG'GLE, *v. i.* To run through mud and water.

DAG'GLED, *pp.* Dipped or trailed in mud or foul water; befouled.

DAG'GLE-TAIL, *a.* Having the lower ends of garments defiled with mud.

DAG'GLING, *ppr.* Drawing along in mud or foul water.

DAG'-SWAIN, *n.* [*dag*, a shred.] A kind of carpet. *Harrison.*

DAG'-TAILED, *a.* The same as *daggle-tail*; trailed in mud.

DA'ILY, *a.* [Sax. *dæglic*, from *dag*, day.] Happening or being every day; done day by day; bestowed or enjoyed every day; as *daily* labor; a *daily* allowance.

Give us this day our *daily* bread. *Lord's Prayer.*

DA'ILY, *adv.* Every day; day by day; as, a thing happens *daily*.

DA'INTILY, *adv.* [from *dainty*.] Nicely; elegantly; as a hat *daintily* made. [*Not legitimate, nor in use.*] *Bacon.*

2. Nicely; fastidiously; with nice regard to what is well tasted; as, to eat *daintily*.

3. Deliciously; as, to fare *daintily*.

4. Ceremoniously; scrupulously.

DA'INTINESS, *n.* Delicacy; softness; elegance; nicety; as the *daintiness* of the limbs. *Obs.* *B. Jonson.*

2. Delicacy; deliciousness; *applied to food*; as the *daintiness* of provisions.

3. Nicety in taste; squeamishness; fastidiousness; as the *daintiness* of the taste. *Wotton.*

4. Ceremoniousness; scrupulousness; nice attention to manners. *Obs.*

DA'INTREL, *n.* A delicacy. [*Not in use.*]

DA'INTY, *a.* [W. *deintiaiz*; Scot. *dainty*; from *dant*, *daint*, the teeth, L. *dens*, Gr. οδους, Sans. *danta*.]

1. Nice; pleasing to the palate; of exquisite taste; delicious; as *dainty* food.

His soul abhorreth *dainty* meat. Job xxxiii.

2. Delicate; of acute sensibility; nice in selecting what is tender and good; squeamish; soft; luxurious; as a *dainty* taste or palate; a *dainty* people.

3. Scrupulous in manners; ceremonious. *Shak.*

4. Elegant; tender; soft; pure; neat; effeminately beautiful; as *dainty* hands or limbs. *Milton. Shak.*

5. Nice; affectedly fine; as a *dainty* speaker. *Prior.*

DA'INTY, *n.* Something nice and delicate to the taste; that which is exquisitely delicious; a delicacy.

Be not desirous of *dainties*, for they are deceitful meat. Prov. xxiii.

2. A term of fondness. [*Not much used.*]

Why, that's my *dainty*. *Shak.*

DA'IRY, *n.* [This word I have not found in any other language. In Russ. *doyu* signifies to milk, and Junius mentions *dey*, an old word for milk, and Icelandic *deggia*, to milk. It may be, and probably is, a contracted word.]

1. Milk, and all that concerns it, on a farm; or the business of managing milk, and of making butter and cheese. The whole establishment respecting milk, in a family, or on a farm.

Grounds were turned much in England either to feeding or *dairy*; and this advanced the trade of English butter. *Temple.*

2. The place, room or house, where milk is set for cream, managed, and converted into butter or cheese. *Dryden.*

3. Milk-farm. *Bacon.*

DA'IRYHOUSE, } *n.* A house or room appropriated to the management of milk.
DA'IRYROOM, }

DA'IRYMAID, *n.* A female servant whose business is to manage milk. *Addison.*

DA'ISIED, *a.* [See *Daisy*.] Full of daisies; adorned with daisies. *Shak.*

DA'ISY, *n.* *s* as *z*. [Sax. *dæges-ege*, day's eye.].

A plant of the genus Bellis, of several varieties. The blue daisy belongs to the genus Globularia, as does the globe daisy; the greater or ox-eye daisy belongs to the genus Chrysanthemum; and the middle daisy, to the Doronicum. *Fam. of Plants.*

DA'KER-HEN, *n.* A fowl of the gallinaceous kind, somewhat like a patridge or quail. *Dict. Nat. Hist.*

The corn-crake or land-rail, a bird of the grallic order of Linne. *Ed. Encyc.*

DA'KIR, *n.* In English statutes, ten hides, or the twentieth part of a last of hides. *Encyc.*

DALE, *n.* [Goth. *dalei*; Dan. and Sw. *dal*; G. *thal*; D. *dal*; W. *dôl*; Russ. *dol*, *udol*, and *doline*; allied perhaps to *dell*. The Welsh *dôl* signifies a winding, bend or meander, and a *dale* through which a river runs; a band, a ring, &c. In D. *daalen* signifies to descend, to sink.]

A low place between hills; a vale or valley; *a poetic word.*

DAL'LIANCE, *n.* [See *Dally*.] Literally, delay; a lingering; appropriately, acts of fondness; interchange of caresses; toying, as males and females; as youthful *dalliance*. *Milton.*

2. Conjugal embraces; commerce of the sexes. *Milton.*

3. Delay. *Obs.* *Shak.*

DAL'LIER, *n.* One who fondles; a trifler; as a *dallier* with pleasant words. *Ascham.*

DAL'LY, *v. i.* [W. *dàl* or *dala*, to hold, bear, keep, stop; Arm. *dalea*, to stop or retard; Ir. *dail*, delay; Russ. *dlyu*. The sense of holding is often connected with that of extending, drawing out in time; Ar. طال to prolong, to delay. Class Dl. No. 20. See also No. 24. 29.]

1. Literally, to delay; to linger; to wait. Hence,

2. To trifle; to lose time in idleness and trifles; to amuse one's self with idle play.

It is madness to *dally* any longer. *Calamy.*

3. To toy and wanton, as man and woman; to interchange caresses; to fondle. *Shak.*

4. To sport; to play.

She *dallies* with the wind. *Shak.*

DAL'LY, *v. t.* To delay; to defer; to put off; to amuse till a proper opportunity; as, to *dally* off the time. [*Not much used.*] *Knolles.*

DAL'LYING, *ppr.* Delaying; procrastinating; trifling; wasting time in idle amusement; toying; fondling.

DAM, *n.* [supposed to be from *dame*, which see.]

1. A female parent; used of beasts, particularly of quadrupeds.

2. A human mother, in contempt. *Shak.*

3. [Fr. *dame*, the queen; Sp. *dama*.] A crowned man in the game of draughts.

DAM, *n.* [D. *dam*; G. *damm*; Sw. *id.*; Dan. *dam*, a pond. See the Verb.]

A mole, bank or mound of earth, or any wall, or a frame of wood, raised to obstruct a current of water, and to raise it, for the purpose of driving millwheels, or for other purposes. Any work that stops and confines water in a pond or bason, or causes it to rise.

DAM, *v. t.* [Sax. *demman*; G. *dämmen*; D. *dammen*; Dan. *dæmmer*; Ch. טום to stop, to shut; Heb. Ch. אטם, Ar. أطم to stop or shut. Qu. Ch. כטם, Ar. سطم id. This is the root of *dumb*. See Class Dm. No. 17. 18. 23. 39.]

1. To make a dam, or to stop a stream of water by a bank of earth, or by any other work; to confine or shut in water. It is common to use, after the verb, *in*, *up*, or *out*; as, to *dam in*, or to *dam up*, the water, and to *dam out* is to prevent water from entering.

2. To confine or restrain from escaping; to shut in; *used by Shakespeare of fire, and by Milton of light.*

DAM'AĠE, *n.* [Fr. *dommage*; Arm. *doumaich*; Norm. *domage*; Sax. *dem*; L. *damnum*; Sp. *daño*; Port. *dano*; It. *danno*; Ir. *damaiste*. This word seems to be allied to the Greek ζημια, a fine or mulct, Ch. זמה or זמי to impose a fine. But qu. See *Damn*.]

1. Any hurt, injury or harm to one's estate; any loss of property sustained; any hinderance to the increase of property; or any obstruction to the success of an enterprise. A man suffers *damage* by the destruction of his corn, by the burning of his house, by the detention of a ship which defeats a profitable voyage, or by the failure of a profitable undertaking. *Damage* then is any actual loss, or the prevention of profit. It is usually and properly applied to property, but sometimes to reputation and other things which are valuable. But in the latter case, *injury* is more correctly used.

2. The value of what is lost; the estimated equivalent for detriment or injury sustained; that which is given or adjudged to repair a loss. This is the legal signification of the word. It is the province of a jury to assess *damages* in trespass. In this sense, the word is generally used in the plural.

DAM'AĠE, *v. t.* [It. *danneggiare*; but Norm. *damager* is to oppress.]

To hurt or harm; to injure; to impair; to lessen the soundness, goodness or value of. Rain may *damage* corn or hay; a storm may *damage* a ship; a house is often *damaged* by fire, when it is not destroyed; heavy rains *damage* roads.

DAM'AGE, *v. i.* To receive harm; to be injured or impaired in soundness, or value; as, green corn will *damage* in a mow or stack.

DAMAGE-FEASANT, *a.* *dam'age-fez'ant.* [Fr. *faisant*, from *faire.*]
Doing injury; trespassing, as cattle. *Blackstone.*

DAM'AGEABLE, *a.* That may be injured or impaired; susceptible of damage; as *damageable* goods.
2. Hurtful; pernicious. [*Rare.*]

DAM'AGED, *pp.* Hurt; impaired; injured.

DAM'AGING, *ppr.* Injuring; impairing.

DAM'ASCENE, *n.* [L. *damascenus*, from *Damascus.*]
1. A particular kind of plum, now pronounced *damson*, which see.
2. It may be locally applied to other species of plums.

DAM'ASK, *n.* [It. *dommasco*; Fr. *damas*; Sp. *damasco*; from *Damascus*, in Syria.]
1. A silk stuff, having some parts raised above the ground, representing flowers and other figures; originally from Damascus.
2. A kind of wrought linen, made in Flanders, in imitation of damask silks.
3. Red color, from the damask-rose. *Fairfax.*

Damask steel, is a fine steel from the Levant, chiefly from Damascus, used for sword and cutlas blades.

DAM'ASK, *v. t.* To form flowers on stuffs; also, to variegate; to diversify; as, a bank *damasked* with flowers. *Milton.*
2. To adorn steel-work with figures. [See *Damaskeen.*]

DAM'ASK-PLUM, *n.* A small black plum.

DAM'ASK-ROSE, *n.* A species of rose which is red, and another which is white.

DAM'ASKEN, DAMASKEE'N, *v. t.* [Fr. *damasquiner.* See *Damask.*]
To make incisions in iron, steel, &c., and fill them with gold or silver wire, for ornament; used chiefly for adorning sword-blades, guards, locks of pistols, &c. *Chambers.*

DAMASKEE'NED, *pp.* Carved into figures and inlaid with gold or silver wire.

DAMASKEE'NING, *ppr* Engraving and adorning with gold or silver wire inlaid.

DAMASKEE'NING, *n.* The act or art of beautifying iron or steel, by engraving and inlaying it with gold or silver wire. This art partakes of the mosaic, of engraving, and of carving. Like the mosaic, it has inlaid work; like engraving, it cuts the metal into figures; and as in chasing, gold and silver is wrought in relievo. *Encyc.*

DAM'ASKIN, *n.* A saber, so called from the manufacture of Damascus.

DAME, *n.* [Fr. *dame*; Sp. Port. It. *dama*; from L. *domina*, a mistress or governess, from *domo*, Gr. δαμαω, to subdue, Eng. to *tame.* Class Dm. No. 3. 4. 23. 24.]
Literally, a mistress; hence, a lady; a title of honor to a woman. It is now generally applied to the mistress of a family in the common ranks of life; as is its compound, *madam.* In poetry, it is applied to a woman of rank. In short, it is applied with propriety to any woman who is or has been the mistress of a family, and it sometimes comprehends women in general.

DAME'S-VIOLET, DAME-WORT, *n.* A plant of the genus Hesperis; called also queen's gilliflower, or rocket. It is remarkable for its fragrant odor, and ladies are fond of having it in their apartments.

DA'MIANISTS, in *church history*, a sect who denied any distinction in the Godhead; believing in one single nature, yet calling God, the Father, Son, and Holy Spirit. *Encyc.*

DAMN, *v. t. dam.* [L. *damno*; Fr. *damner*; Arm. *dauna*; It. *dannare*; Sp. *dañar*; Port. *danar.* The Portuguese word is rendered to hurt, to damnify, to corrupt or spoil, to undo or ruin, to bend, to crook, to make mad. The latter sense would seem to be from the L. *demens*, and *damnum* is by Varro referred to *demendo, demo*, which is supposed to be a compound of *de* and *emo.* But qu., for *damno* and *condemno* coincide with the English *doom.*]
1. To sentence to eternal torments in a future state; to punish in hell.

He that believeth not shall be *damned.* Mark xvi.

2. To condemn; to decide to be wrong or worthy of punishment; to censure; to reprobate.

He that doubteth is *damned* if he eat. Rom. xiv.

3. To condemn; to explode; to decide to be bad, mean, or displeasing, by hissing or any mark of disapprobation; as, to *damn* a play, or a mean author.
4. A word used in profaneness; a term of execration.

DAM'NABLE, *a.* That may be damned or condemned; deserving damnation; worthy of eternal punishment. More generally, that which subjects or renders liable to damnation; as *damnable* heresies. 2 Pet. ii.
2. In *a low* or *ludicrous sense*, odious, detestable, or pernicious. *Shak.*

DAM'NABLENESS, *n.* The state or quality of deserving damnation.

DAM'NABLY, *adv.* In a manner to incur eternal punishment, or so as to exclude mercy. *South.*
2. In *a low sense*, odiously; detestably; sometimes, excessively.

DAMNA'TION, *n.* [L. *damnatio.*] Sentence or condemnation to everlasting punishment in the future state; or the state of eternal torments.

How can ye escape the *damnation* of hell. Matt. xxiii.

2. Condemnation. *Taylor.*

DAM'NATORY, *a.* Containing a sentence of condemnation. *Waterland.*

DAM'NED, *pp.* Sentenced to everlasting punishment in a future state; condemned.
2. *a.* Hateful; detestable; abominable; *a word chiefly used in profaneness by persons of vulgar manners.*

DAMNIF'IC, *a.* [See *Damnify.*] Procuring loss; mischievous.

DAM'NIFIED, *pp.* [See *Damnify.*] Injured; endamaged.

DAM'NIFY, *v. t.* [L. *damnifico*; *damnum* and *facio*; It. *dannificare.*]
1. To cause loss or damage to; to hurt in estate or interest; to injure; to endamage; as, to *damnify* a man in his goods or estate.
2. To hurt; to injure; to impair; *applied to the person.* *Spenser.*

DAM'NIFYING, *ppr.* Hurting; injuring; impairing.

DAM'NING, *ppr.* Dooming to endless punishment; condemning.
2. *a.* That condemns or exposes to damnation; as a *damning* sin.

DAM'NINGNESS, *n.* Tendency to bring damnation. *Hammond.*

DAMP, *a.* [G. *dampf*; D. *damp*; Sw. *damb*; Dan. *damp*, steam, vapor, fog, smoke; perhaps *steam* is from the same root, from wasting; Sans. *dhuma.* See Class Dm. No. 33.]
Moist; humid; being in a state between dry and wet; as a *damp* cloth; *damp* air: sometimes, foggy; as, the atmosphere is *damp*; but it may be *damp* without visible vapor.
2. Dejected; sunk; depressed; chilled. [*Unusual.*] *Milton.*

DAMP, *n.* Moist air; humidity; moisture; fog. *Milton.*
2. Dejection; depression of spirits; chill. We say, to strike a *damp*, or to cast a *damp*, on the spirits. *Milton.*
3. Damps. *plu.* Noxious exhalations issuing from the earth, and deleterious or fatal to animal life. These are often known to exist in wells, which continue long covered and not used, and in mines and coal-pits; and sometimes they issue from the old lavas of volcanoes. These damps are usually the carbonic acid gas, vulgarly called *choke-damp*, which instantly suffocates; or some inflammable gas, called *fire-damp.*

DAMP, *v. t.* To moisten; to make humid, or moderately wet.
2. To chill; to deaden; to depress or deject; to abate; as, to *damp* the spirits; to *damp* the ardor of passion. *Swift.*
3. To weaken; to make dull; as, to *damp* sound. *Bacon.*
4. To check or restrain, as action or vigor; to make languid; to discourage; as, to *damp* industry. *Bacon.*

DAMP'ED, *pp.* Chilled; depressed; abated; weakened; checked; discouraged.

DAMP'ER, *n.* That which damps or checks; a valve or sliding plate in a furnace to stop or lessen the quantity of air admitted, and thus to regulate the heat or extinguish the fire. *Edwards, W. Ind.* *Rumford.*
2. A part of a piano-forte, by which the sound is deadened.

DAMP'ING, *ppr.* Chilling; deadening; dejecting; abating; checking; weakening.

DAMP'ISH, *a.* Moderately damp, or moist.

DAMP'ISHNESS, *n.* A moderate degree of dampness, or moistness; slight humidity.

DAMP'NESS, *n.* Moisture; fogginess; moistness; moderate humidity; as the *dampness* of the air, of the ground, or of a cloth.

DAMPS, *n.* [See *Damp.*]

DAMP'Y. *a.* Dejected; gloomy. [*Little used.*] *Hayward.*

DAM'SEL, *n.* *s* as *z.* [Fr. *damoiselle* and *demoiselle*, a gentlewoman, and *damoiseau*, a spark or beau; Norm. *damoisells*, or *demicelles*, nobles, sons of kings, princes, knights, lords, ladies of quality, and *damoyseles*, damsels, female infants; Sp. *damisola*, a young gentlewoman, any girl not of the lower class. The Arm. *ma-mesell*, *va-mesell*, or *man-mesell*, a woman or madam, seems to indicate that the first syllable is a prefix, and *mesell*, Eng. *miss*, a distinct word. But *damoiselle*, Norm. *demicelle*, from which we have *damsel*, is doubtless from the Italian *damigella*, a diminutive formed from *dama*, like the L. *domicilium*, from *domus*, and *penicillus*, from the root of *penna*. The Italian *damigello*, in the masculine gender, shows the propriety of the ancient application of *damsel* to males.]

A young woman. Formerly, a young man or woman of noble or genteel extraction; as *Damsel* Pepin; *Damsel* Richard, prince of Wales. It is now used only of young women, and is applied to any class of young unmarried women, unless to the most vulgar, and sometimes to country girls.

With her train of *damsels* she was gone. *Dryden.*

Then Boaz said, whose *damsel* is this? Ruth ii.

This word is rarely used in conversation, or even in prose writings of the present day; but it occurs frequently in the scriptures, and in poetry.

DAM'SON, *n.* *dam'zn.* [contracted from *damascene*, the Damascus plum.]

The fruit of a variety of the Prunus domestica; a small black plum.

DAN, *n.* [Sp. *don.* Qu. from *dominus*, or Ar. دَانَ to be chief, to judge, Heb. Ch. Syr. Eth. דין. Class Dn. No. 2. 4.]

A title of honor equivalent to *master*; used by Shakspeare, Prior, &c., but now obsolete.

D'ANCE, *v. i.* *dans.* [Fr. *danser*; Sp. *danzar*; Port. *dançar*; Arm. *danczal*; It. *danzare*; G. *tanzen*; Sw. *dansa*; Dan. *dandser*; D. *danssen*; Basque *dantza*; Russ. *tantzyu*. Qu. the radical letters, and the Oriental דין, with a casual *n.*]

1. Primarily, to leap or spring; hence, to leap or move with measured steps, regulated by a tune, sung or played on a musical instrument; to leap or step with graceful motions of the body, corresponding with the sound of the voice or of an instrument.

There is a time to mourn, and a time to *dance.* Eccles. iii.

2. To leap and frisk about; to move nimbly or up and down.

To dance attendance, to wait with obsequiousness; to strive to please and gain favor by assiduous attentions and officious civilities; as, to *dance attendance* at court.

D'ANCE, *v. t.* To make to dance; to move up and down, or back and forth; to dandle; as, to *dance* a child on the knee. *Bacon.*

D'ANCE, *n.* In a general sense, a leaping and frisking about. Appropriately, a leaping or stepping with motions of the body adjusted to the measure of a tune, particularly by two or more in concert. A lively brisk exercise or amusement, in which the movements of the persons are regulated by art, in figure, and by the sound of instruments, in measure.

2. A tune by which dancing is regulated, as the minuet, the waltz, the cotillon, &c.

D'ANCER, *n.* One who practices dancing, or is skilful in the performance.

D'ANCING, *ppr.* Leaping and stepping to the sound of the voice or of an instrument; moving in measured steps; frisking about.

D'ANCING-MASTER, *n.* One who teaches the art of dancing.

D'ANCING-SCHOOL, *n.* A school in which the art of dancing is taught.

DAN'DELION, *n.* [Fr. *dent de lion*, lion's tooth.]

A well known plant of the genus *Leontodon*, having a naked stalk, with one large flower.

DAN'DIPRAT, *n.* [Fr. *dandin*, a ninny; It. *dondolone*, a loiterer; *dondolo*, any thing swinging; *dondolare*, to swing, to loiter. The Sp. and Port. *tonto*, a dolt, may be of the same family. Qu. *prat.*]

A little fellow; an urchin; *a word of fondness or contempt.* *Johnson.*

DAN'DLE, *v. t.* [G. *tändeln*, to toy, to trifle, to lounge, to dandle; Fr. *dandiner*, to jog; It. *dondolare*, to swing, to loiter; Sp. and Port. *tontear*, to dote, to talk nonsense; Scot. *dandill*, *dander*. These words seem to be allied.]

1. To shake or jolt on the knee, as an infant; to move up and down in the hand; literally, to amuse by play.

Ye shall be *dandled* on her knees. Is. lxvi.

2. To fondle; to amuse; to treat as a child; to toy with.

I am ashamed to be *dandled* thus. *Addison.*

3. To delay; to protract by trifles. *Obs.* *Spenser.*

DAN'DLED, *pp.* Danced on the knee, or in the arms; fondled; amused by trifles or play.

DAN'DLER, *n.* One who dandles or fondles children.

DAN'DLING, *ppr.* Shaking and jolting on the knee; moving about in play or for amusement, as an infant.

DANDRUFF, *n.* [Qu. Sax. *tan*, a scab, tetter, and *drof*, sordid; or Fr. *teigne*, Arm. *tign*, or *taign.*]

A scurf which forms on the head, and comes off in small scales or particles.

DAN'DY, *n.* [Qu. Scot. *dandie.* See *Dandiprat.*]

In *modern usage*, a male of the human species, who dresses himself like a doll, and who carries his character on his back.

DAN'DYISM, *n.* The manners and dress of a dandy.

DANE, *n.* A native of Denmark.

DA'NEGELT, *n.* [*Dane* and *gelt*, *geld*, money.]

In *England*, an annual tax formerly laid on the English nation, for maintaining forces to oppose the Danes, or to furnish tribute to procure peace. It was at first one shilling, and afterwards two, for every hide of land, except such as belonged to the church. *Encyc.*

DA'NEWŎRT, *n.* A plant of the genus Sambucus; a species of elder, called dwarf-elder or wall-wort.

DĀNǴER, *n.* [Fr. Arm. Scot. *danger*; Norm. *daungerous*, dubious. This word in Scottish, according to Jamieson, signifies peril, power, or dominion, doubt, hesitation. In Chaucer, it signifies peril, and coyness, sparingness or custody. In old English laws, it denotes a payment in money by forest tenants, to their lord, for permission to plow and sow in the time of pannage or mast-feeding. The primary sense is not obvious. Spenser has the following couplet.

Valiant he should be as fire,
Showing *danger* more than ire.]

Peril; risk; hazard; exposure to injury, loss, pain or other evil.

Our craft is in *danger* to be set at nought. Acts xix.

It is easy to boast of despising death, when there is no *danger.*

DĀNǴER, *v. t.* To put in hazard; to expose to loss or injury. *Shak.* But rarely used. [See *Endanger*, which is generally used.]

DĀNǴERLESS, *a.* Free from danger; without risk. [*Little used.*] *Sidney.*

DĀNǴEROUS, *a.* Perilous; hazardous; exposing to loss; unsafe; full of risk; as a *dangerous* voyage; a *dangerous* experiment.

2. Creating danger; causing risk of evil; as a *dangerous* man; a *dangerous* conspiracy.

DĀNǴEROUSLY, *adv.* With danger; with risk of evil; with exposure to injury or ruin; hazardously; perilously; as, to be *dangerously* sick; *dangerously* situated.

DĀNǴEROUSNESS, *n.* Danger; hazard; peril; a state of being exposed to evil; as the *dangerousness* of condition, or disease.

DAN'GLE, *v. i.* [Dan. *dingler*, to swing to and fro. Qu. *dandle* or Ch. Syr. חקל.]

1. To hang loose, flowing, shaking or waving; to hang and swing.

He'd rather on a gibbet *dangle.* *Hudibras.*

2. To hang on any one; to be a humble, officious follower; with *after* or *about*; as, to *dangle about* a woman; to *dangle after* a minister for favors.

DAN'GLER, *n.* One who dangles or hangs about.

DAN'GLING, *ppr.* Hanging loosely; busily or officiously adhering to.

DA'NISH, *a.* Belonging to the Danes or Denmark.

DA'NISH, *n.* The language of the Danes.

DANK, *a.* [Qu. G. *tunken*, to dip.] Damp; moist; humid; wet.

DANK, *n.* Moisture; humidity. *Milton. Shak.*

DANK'ISH, *a.* Somewhat damp.

DANK'ISHNESS, *n.* Dampness; humidity.

DA'ÖURITE, *n.* A mineral, called rubellite, resembling shorl, but differing from it in chimical characters. Its color is red of various shades. *Cleaveland.*

DAP, *v. i.* [Goth. *daupyan*, to dip.] To drop or let fall into the water; *a word used by anglers.* *Walton.*

DAPH'NATE, *n.* A compound of the bitter principle of the Daphne Alpina with a base.

DAPH'NIN, *n.* The bitter principle of the Daphne Alpina, discovered by Vauquelin. It is obtained in small crystals, hard, transparent, of a grayish color and a bitter taste.

DAP'IFER, *n.* [L. *dapes*, feast, and *fero*, to bear.]

One who brings meat to the table. Formerly, the title or office of the grand-master of a king's household. It still subsists in Germany. *Encyc.*

DAP'PER, *a.* [D. *dapper*, brave, valiant;

Sw. and Dan. *tapper;* *G. tapfer.* See Class Db. No. 13. 28.]
Active; nimble; brisk; or little and active; neat; tight; as a *dapper* fellow; a *dapper* spark. *L'Estrange.*

DAP'PERLING, *n.* A dwarf; a dandiprat.

DAP'PLE, *a.* [most probably allied to *tabby*, and from dipping, or to W. *davnu*, to drop. The word signifies *spotted*, and spots are often from dropping or sprinkling.]
Marked with spots; spotted; variegated with spots of different colors or shades of color, as a *dapple-bay* or *dapple-gray;* applied to a horse or other beast. It may sometimes express *streaked*, but this is not its true signification.

DAP'PLE, *v. t.* To spot; to variegate with spots.

> The gentle day
> *Dapples* the drowsy east with *spots* of gray. *Shak.*
> The *dappled* pink, and blushing rose. *Prior.*

DAP'PLED, *pp.* Spotted; variegated with spots of different colors or shades of color.

DAP'PLING, *ppr.* Variegating with spots.

DAR, } *n.* A fish found in the Severn.
DART, } *Bailey.*

DARE. *v. i.* pret. *durst.* [Sax. *dearran, durran;* D. *darren, durven;* G. *dürfen;* Sw. *dierf*, bold; *dierfvas*, to dare, and *töras*, to dare; Dan. *tör*, to dare, and *tör*, dry, torrid, L. *torreo;* Dan. *törhed*, dryness, barrenness; *törstig*, thirsty. The German *dürfen*, compounded, *bedürfen*, signifies, to want, to need, to lack, and this in Dutch is *derven.* The Sw. *dåre*, rash, mad, sottish, *dåra*, to infatuate, Dan. *daarer*, may be of the same family. The Gr. θαρρεω, and Russ. *derzayu*, to dare, are evidently the same word. Ar. ذار to be bold, audacious; to be angry, or averse; to be terrified, to flee. So in Sw. *darra*, to tremble. The sense of boldness, daring, is sometimes from the sense of advancing; but some of the senses of these words indicate the sense of receding.]
To have courage for any purpose; to have strength of mind or hardihood to undertake any thing; to be bold enough; not to be afraid; to venture; to be adventurous.

> I *dare* do all that may become a man. *Shak.*
> *Dare* any of you go to law before the unjust? 1 Cor. vi.
> None of his disciples *durst* ask him, who art thou. John xxi.

In this intransitive sense, *dare* is not generally followed by the sign *to* before another verb in the infinitive; though *to* may be used with propriety. In German, the verb is numbered among the auxiliaries. In the transitive form, it is regular: thus,

DARE, *v. t.* pret. and pp. *dared.* To challenge; to provoke; to defy; as, to *dare* a man to fight.

> Time, I *dare* thee to discover
> Such a youth, and such a lover. *Dryden.*

To dare larks, to catch them by means of a looking glass, or by keeping a bird of prey hovering aloft, which keeps them in amaze till caught; to terrify or amaze. *Johnson. Dryden.*

DARE, *n.* Defiance; challenge. [*Not used.*] *Shak.*

DARE, *n.* A small fish, the same as the *dace.* *Encyc. Johnson.*

DA'RED, *pp.* Challenged; defied.

DA'REFUL, *a.* Full of defiance. [*Not used.*] *Shak.*

DA'RER, *n.* One who dares or defies.

DAR'IC, *n.* A gold coin of Darius the Mede, value about 556 cents.

DA'RING, *ppr.* Having courage sufficient for a purpose; challenging; defying.
2. *a.* Bold; courageous; intrepid; fearless; adventurous; brave; stout.

> Grieve not, O *daring* prince, that noble heart. *Pope.*

3. Audacious; impudently bold and defying; as in *heaven-daring*, defying Almighty power.

DA'RINGLY, *adv.* Boldly; courageously; fearlessly; impudently.

> The principles of our holy religion are *daringly* attacked from the press. *Anon.*

DA'RINGNESS, *n.* Boldness; courageousness; audaciousness.

D'ARK, *a.* [Sax. *deorc;* Ir. *dorcha;* Pers. تیره tirah, dark; تاریک tarik, dark, darkness. See Class Dr. No. 15.]
1. Destitute of light; obscure. A *dark* atmosphere is one which prevents vision.
2. Wholly or partially black; having the quality opposite to white; as a *dark* color or substance.
3. Gloomy; disheartening; having unfavorable prospects; as a *dark* time in political affairs.

> There is in every true woman's heart a spark of heavenly fire, which beams and blazes in the *dark* hour of adversity. *Irving.*

4. Obscure; not easily understood or explained; as a *dark* passage in an author; a *dark* saying.
5. Mysterious; as, the ways of Providence are often *dark* to human reason.
6. Not enlightened with knowledge; destitute of learning and science; rude; ignorant; as a *dark* age.
7. Not vivid; partially black. Lev. xiii.
8. Blind. [*Not in use.*] *Dryden.*
9. Gloomy; not cheerful; as a *dark* temper. *Addison.*
10. Obscure; concealed; secret; not understood; as a *dark* design.
11. Unclean; foul. *Milton.*
12. Opake. But *dark* and *opake* are not synonymous. Chalk is *opake*, but not *dark.*
13. Keeping designs concealed.

> The *dark* unrelenting Tiberius. *Gibbon.*

D'ARK, *n.* [Sans. *tareki.*] Darkness; obscurity; the absence of light. We say, we can hear in the *dark.*

> Shall thy wonders be known in the *dark?* Ps. lxxxviii.

2. Obscurity; secrecy; a state unknown; as, things done in the *dark.*
3. Obscurity; a state of ignorance; as, we are all in the *dark.*

D'ARK, *v. t.* To darken; to obscure. *Obs.*

D'ARK-BROWED, *a.* Stern of aspect; frowning; as *dark-browed* Hotspur. *Percy's Masque.*

D'ARKEN, *v. t.* dàrkn. [Sax. *adeorcian.*]
1. To make dark; to deprive of light; as, close the shutters and *darken* the room.
2. To obscure; to cloud.

> His confidence seldom *darkened* his foresight. *Bacon.*

3. To make black.

> The locusts *darkened* the land. Ex. x.

4. To make dim; to deprive of vision.

> Let their eyes be *darkened.* Rom. xi.

5. To render gloomy; as, all joy is *darkened.* Is. xxiv.
6. To deprive of intellectual vision; to render ignorant or stupid.

> Their foolish heart was *darkened.* Rom. i.
> Having the understanding *darkened.* Eph. iv.

7. To obscure; to perplex; to render less clear or intelligible.

> Who is this that *darkeneth* counsel by words without knowledge? Job xxxviii.

8. To render less white or clear; to tan; as, a burning sun *darkens* the complexion.
9. To sully; to make foul. *Tillotson.*

D'ARKEN, *v. i.* To grow dark or darker; also, to grow less white or clear.

D'ARKENED, *pp.* Deprived of light; obscured; rendered dim; made black; made ignorant.

D'ARKENING, *ppr.* Depriving of light; obscuring; making black or less white or clear; clouding.

D'ARK-HOUSE, *n.* An old word for a mad-house. *Shak.*

D'ARKISH, *a.* Dusky; somewhat dark.

D'ARKLING, *a.* Being in the dark, or without light; *a poetical word.* *Milton. Shak.*

D'ARKLY, *adv.* Obscurely; dimly; blindly; uncertainly; with imperfect light, clearness or knowledge.

> They learn only what tradition has *darkly* conveyed to them. *Anon.*

D'ARKNESS, *n.* Absence of light.

> And *darkness* was on the face of the deep. Gen. i.

2. Obscurity; want of clearness or perspicuity; that quality or state which renders any thing difficult to be understood; as the *darkness* of counsels.
3. A state of being intellectually clouded; ignorance.

> Men loved *darkness* rather than light. John iii.

4. A private place; secrecy; privacy.

> What I tell you in *darkness*, that speak ye in light. Matt. x.

5. Infernal gloom; hell; as utter *darkness.* Matt. xxii.
6. Great trouble and distress; calamities; perplexities.

> A day of clouds and thick *darkness.* Joel ii. Is. viii.

7. Empire of Satan.

> Who hath delivered us from the power of *darkness.* Col. i.

8. Opakeness.
Land of darkness, the grave. Job x.

D'ARKSŎME, *a.* Dark; gloomy; obscure; as a *darksome* house; a *darksome* cloud. *Milton. Dryden.*

D'ARK-WŎRKING, *a.* Working in darkness or in secrecy. *Shak.*

D'ARLING, *a.* [Sax. *deorling;* *deor*, dear, and *ling*, which primarily denotes likeness, and in some words, is a diminutive. So in G. *liebling*, loveling, D. *lieveling.* See *Dear.*]
Dearly beloved; favorite; regarded with great kindness and tenderness; as a *darling* child; a *darling* science. *Watts.*

D'ARLING, *n.* One much beloved; a favorite; as, that son was the *darling* of his father.

D'ARN, *v. t.* [W. *darn;* Arm. *darn;* Fr. *darne;* a piece or patch.]
To mend a rent or hole, by imitating the texture of the cloth or stuff with yarn or thread and a needle; to sew together with yarn or thread. It is used particularly of stockings. *Gay. Swift.*
D'ARN, *n.* A place mended by darning.
D'ARNEL, *n.* A plant of the genus *Lolium*, a kind of grass; the most remarkable species are the red darnel or rye-grass, and the white darnel.
D'ARNER, *n.* One who mends by darning.
D'ARNING, *ppr.* Mending in imitation of the original texture; sewing together; as a torn stocking, or cloth.
D'ARNING, *n.* The act of mending, as a hole in a garment.
DAR'RAIN, *v. t.* [Norm. *dareigner, derener, dereigner, deraigner*, to prove, to testify, to clear himself, to institute; noun, *darrein*, or *derene*, or *d'reigne*, proof; also, *derreiner*, to endeavor. In Chaucer, the word is interpreted to *contest*.

But for thou art a worthy gentil knight,
And wilnest to *darraine* hire by bataille.

The word is probably compound. But neither the origin nor the signification is obvious.]
To prepare, or to order; or to try; to endeavor; to prove; to apply to the contest. *Obs.* *Carew. Spenser. Shak.*
D'ART, *n.* [Fr. *dard;* Arm. *dared* or *dard;* It. Sp. Port. *dardo;* Russ. *drot.* In Sw. *dart* is a dagger. The word is from some verb signifying to throw or thrust. In Gr. δορυ is a spear or lance.]
1. A pointed missile weapon to be thrown by the hand; a short lance. *Dryden.*
2. Any missile weapon; that which pierces and wounds.

And from about her shot *darts* of desire.

D'ART, *v. t.* To throw a pointed instrument with a sudden thrust; as, to *dart* a javelin. *Dryden.*
2. To throw suddenly or rapidly; to send; to emit; to shoot; *applied to small objects, which pass with velocity;* as, the sun *darts* his beams on the earth.

Or what ill eyes malignant glances *dart*. *Pope.*

D'ART, *v. i.* To fly or shoot, as a dart; to fly rapidly.
2. To spring and run with velocity; to start suddenly and run; as, the deer *darted* from the thicket.
D'ARTED, *pp.* Thrown or hurled as a pointed instrument; sent with velocity.
D'ARTER, *n.* One who throws a dart.
D'ARTING, *ppr.* Throwing, as a dart; hurling darts; flying rapidly.
DASH, *v. t.* [In Dan. *dask* signifies a blow; in Sw. *daska*, to strike; in Scot. *dusch*, to rush. In Persic تَازْ is an assault on an enemy. See Class Ds. No. 3. 4. 5. 14. 22. 30. 31. 40.]
1. To strike suddenly or violently, whether throwing or falling; as, to *dash* one stone against another. *Bacon.*

Lest thou *dash* thy foot against a stone. Matt. iv.

2. To strike and bruise or break; to break by collision; but usually with the words, *in pieces.*

Thou shalt *dash* them *in pieces*, as a potter's vessel. Ps. ii.

3. To throw water suddenly, in separate portions; as, to *dash* water on the head.
4. To bespatter; to sprinkle; as, to *dash* a garment. *Shak.*
5. To strike and break or disperse.

At once the brushing oars and brazen prow
Dash up the sandy waves, and ope the depth below. *Dryden.*

6. To mix and reduce or adulterate by throwing in another subtance; as, to *dash* wine with water; the story is *dashed* with fables.
7. To form or sketch out in haste, carelessly. [*Unusual.*] *Pope.*
8. To erase at a stroke; to strike out; to blot out or obliterate; as, to *dash* out a line or word. *Pope.*
9. To break; to destroy; to frustrate; as, to *dash* all their schemes and hopes.
10. To confound; to confuse; to put to shame; to abash; to depress by shame or fear; as, he was *dashed* at the appearance of the judge.

Dash the proud gamester in his gilded car. *Pope.*

DASH, *v. i.* To strike, break, scatter and fly off; as, agitate water and it will *dash* over the sides of a vessel; the waves *dashed* over the side of the ship.
2. To rush, strike and break or scatter; as, the waters *dash* down the precipice.
3. To rush with violence, and break through; as, he *dashed* into the enemy's ranks; or he *dashed* through thick and thin.
DASH, *n.* Collision; a violent striking of two bodies; as the *dash* of clouds. *Thomson.*
2. Infusion; admixture; something thrown into another substance; as, the wine has a *dash* of water.

Innocence, with a *dash* of folly. *Addison.*

3. Admixture; as, red with a *dash* of purple.
4. A rushing, or onset with violence; as, to make a *dash* upon the enemy.
5. A sudden stroke; a blow; an act.

She takes upon her bravely at first *dash*. *Shak.*

6. A flourish; blustering parade; as, the young fop made a *dash*. [*Vulgar.*]
7. A mark or line in writing or printing, noting a break or stop in the sentence; as in Virgil, quos ego —: or a pause; or the division of the sentence.
DASH'ED, *pp.* Struck violently; driven against; bruised, broken or scattered by collision; besprinkled; mixed or adulterated; erased, blotted out; broken; cast down; confounded; abashed.
DASH'ING, *ppr.* Driving and striking against; striking suddenly or violently; breaking or scattering by collision; infusing; mixing; confounding; blotting out; rushing.
2. *a.* Rushing; driving; blustering; as a *dashing* fellow.
3. *a.* Precipitate; rushing carelessly on. *Burke.*
DAS'TARD, *n.* [In Sax. *adastrigan* is to frighten, to deter.]
A coward; a poltroon; one who meanly shrinks from danger. *Dryden.*
DAS'TARD, *a.* Cowardly; meanly shrinking from danger.

Curse on their *dastard* souls. *Addison.*

DAS'TARD, *v. t.* To make cowardly; to intimidate; to dispirit. *Dryden.*
DAS'TARDIZE, *v. t.* To make cowardly. *Howell.*
DAS'TARDLINESS, *n.* [from *dastardly.*] Cowardliness. *Barrett.*
DAS'TARDLY, *a.* Cowardly; meanly timid; base; sneaking. *Herbert.*
DAS'TARDNESS, *n.* Cowardliness; mean timorousness.
DAS'TARDY, *n.* Cowardliness; base timidity.
DA'TA, *n. plu.* [L. *data*, given.] Things given, or admitted; quantities, principles or facts given, known, or admitted, by which to find things or results unknown.
DA'TARY, *n.* An officer of the chancery of Rome, who affixes the *datum Romæ* to the pope's bulls.
2. The employment of a datary.
DATE, *n.* [Fr. *date;* It. Sp. *data;* L. *datum*, given, from *do*, to give, Sans. *da, datu.*]
1. That addition to a writing which specifies the year, month and day when it was given or executed. In letters, it notes the time when they are written or sent; in deeds, contracts, wills and other papers, it specifies the time of execution, and usually the time from which they are to take effect and operate on the rights of persons. To the date is usually added the name of the place where a writing is executed, and this is sometimes included in the term *date.*
2. The time when any event happened, when any thing was transacted, or when any thing is to be done; as the *date* of a battle; the *date* of Cesar's arrival in Britain.
3. End; conclusion. [*Unusual.*]

What time would spare, from steel receives its *date.* *Pope*

4. Duration; continuance; as, ages of endless *date.* *Milton.*
DATE, *v. t.* To write or note the time when a letter is written, or a writing executed; to express, in an instrument, the year, month and day of its execution, and usually the place; as, to *date* a letter, a bond, a deed, or a charter.
2. To note or fix the time of an event or transaction. Historians *date* the fulfillment of a prophecy at different periods.
3. To note the time when something begins; as, to *date* a disease or calamity from a certain cause.
DATE, *v. i.* To reckon.
2. To begin; to have origin.

The Batavian republic *dates* from the successes of the French arms. *E. Everett.*

DATE, *n.* [Fr. *datte*, for *dacte;* It. *dattero;* Sp. *datil;* L. *dactylus;* Gr. δακτυλος.]
The fruit of the great palm-tree, or date-tree, the Phœnix dactylifera. This fruit is somewhat in the shape of an acorn, composed of a thin light glossy membrane, somewhat pellucid and yellowish, containing a soft pulpy fruit, firm and sweet, esculent and wholesome, and in this is inclosed a hard kernel. *Encyc.*
DA'TE-TREE, *n.* The tree that bears dates; the great palm-tree.
DA'TED, *pp.* Having the time of writing or execution specified; having the time of happening noted.

DA'TELESS, *a.* Having no date; having no fixed term. *Shak.*

DA'TER, *n.* One that dates.

DA'TING, *ppr.* Expressing the time of writing or of executing a paper or instrument; noting the time of happening, or originating.

DA'TIVE, *a.* [L. *dativus*, from *do*, to give.] In *grammar*, the epithet of the case of nouns, which usually follows verbs that express giving, or some act directed *to* an object. Thus, datur tibi, it is given *to* you; missum est illi, it was sent *to* him; fecit mihi, he made or did *to* or *for* me; loquebatur illis, he spoke *to* them. It also follows other words expressing something to be given to a person or for his benefit; as, utilis vobis, useful *to* you. In English, this relation is expressed by *to* or *for*.

Dative Executor, in law, one appointed by the judge of probate; an administrator.

DAT'OLITE, DATH'OLITE, *n.* The siliceous borate of lime, a mineral of two subspecies, the common and the botryoidal. The common is of a white color, of various shades, and greenish gray. It occurs in granular distinct concretions, and crystalized. The botryoidal occurs in mammillary concretions, or in botryoidal masses, white and earthy. It is named from its want of transparency. *Ure. Phillips.*

DA'TUM, *n.* [L.] Something given or admitted. [See *Data*.]

DATU'RA, *n.* A vegeto-alkali obtained from Datura stramonium.

DAUB, *v. t.* [W. *dwbiaw*, to daub; *dwb*, mortar; Ir. *dobhaimh*, to daub; *doib*, plaster; allied probably to Fr. *dauber*, to strike, that is, to throw or put on, and the root of this word probably occurs contracted in the L. *induo*.]

1. To smear with soft adhesive matter; to plaster; to cover with mud, slime, or other soft substance.

She took for him an ark of bulrushes, and *daubed* it with slime and with pitch. Ex. ii.

I will break down the wall ye have *daubed* with untempered mortar. Ezek. xiii.

2. To paint coarsely.

If a picture is *daubed* with many bright colors, the vulgar admire it. *Watts.*

3. To cover with something gross or specious; to disguise with an artificial covering.

So smooth he *daubed* his vice with show of virtue. *Shak.*

4. To lay or put on without taste; to deck awkwardly or ostentatiously, or to load with affected finery.

Let him be *daubed* with lace— *Dryden.*

5. To flatter grossly.

Conscience will not *daub* nor flatter. *South.*

DAUB, *v. i.* To practice gross flattery; to play the hypocrite. *Shak.*

DAUB'ED, *pp.* Smeared with soft adhesive matter; plastered; painted coarsely; disguised; loaded with ill chosen finery.

DAUB'ER, *n.* One who daubs; a coarse painter; a low and gross flatterer.

DAUB'ING, *ppr.* Plastering; painting coarsely; disguising clumsily; decking ostentatiously; flattering grossly.

DAUB'ING, *n.* Plastering; coarse painting; gross flattery.

DAUB'RY, DAUB'ERY, *n.* A daubing; any thing artful. *Shak.*

DAUB'Y, *a.* Viscous; glutinous; slimy; adhesive. *Dryden.*

DAUGHTER, *n.* *daw'ter.* [Sax. *dohter*; D. *dogter*; G. *tochter*; Sw. and Dan. *dotter*; Gr. θυγατηρ; Goth. *dauhtar*; Russ. *doch*; Pers. دُخْتَر dochtar, a daughter; also دخت docht, daughter, and a virgin; also, strength, power; Sans. *dugida*. The latter words coincide with the Sax. *dugan*, to avail, to be good; *dugoth*, strength, grace, L. *decus*. See *Decency*.]

1. The female offspring of a man or woman; a female child of any age.

2. A daughter in law; a son's wife. Ruth iii.

3. A woman; *plu.* female inhabitants.

Dinah went out to see the *daughters* of the land. Gen. xxxiv.

4. A female descendant; lineage of females. Luke i.

5. The female penitent of a confessor. *Shak.*

This word is used in scripture for the inhabitants of a city or country, male and female. Is. xvi. 2. Matt. xxi. Also as a term of affection or kindness.

Daughter, be of good comfort. Matt. ix.

DAUGH'TERLINESS, *n.* The state of a daughter. *More.*

2. The conduct becoming a daughter.

DAUGH'TERLY, *a.* Becoming a daughter; dutiful. *Cavendish.*

D'AUNT, *v. t.* [In Scot. *dant, danton*, signify to subdue. In Dan. *daaner*, Sw. *dåna*, signifies to faint or swoon. Qu. L. *domito*, Fr. *dompter*, contracted.]

To repress or subdue courage; to intimidate; to dishearten; to check by fear of danger. It expresses less than *fright* and *terrify*.

Some presences *daunt* and discourage us. *Glanville.*

D'AUNTED, *pp.* Checked by fear; intimidated.

D'AUNTING, *ppr.* Repressing courage; intimidating; disheartening.

D'AUNTLESS, *a.* Bold; fearless; intrepid; not timid; not discouraged; as a *dauntless* hero; a *dauntless* spirit.

D'AUNTLESSNESS, *n.* Fearlessness; intrepidity.

DAU'PHIN, *n.* [Fr. *dauphin*, a dolphin; L. *delphin, delphinus*; Gr. δελφιν; It. *delfino*; Sp. *delfin*.]

The eldest son of the king of France, and presumptive heir of the crown.

DAU'PHINESS, *n.* The wife or lady of the dauphin.

DAVINA, *n.* A new Vesuvian mineral of a hexahedral form and laminar texture; so called in honor of Sir H. Davy. *Journ. of Science.*

DAV'IT, *n.* A beam used on board of ships, as a crane to hoist the flukes of the anchor to the top of the bow, without injuring the sides of the ship; an operation called *fishing the anchor*.

DAW, *n.* A word that is found in the compound names of many species of birds; as the *jackdaw*; the *blue daw*; the *purple daw*.

DAW, *v. i.* To dawn. [*Not in use.* See *Dawn*.]

DAW'DLE, *v. i.* To waste time; to trifle. *Obs.*

DAW'DLER, *n.* A trifler. *Obs.*

DAWK, *n.* A hollow, rupture or incision in timber. [*Local.*] *Moxon.*

DAWK, *v. t.* To cut or mark with an incision.

[*I know not that this word is used in America.*]

DAWN, *v. i.* [Sax. *dagian*; G. *tagen*; D. *daagen*; Sw. *dagas*; from the root of *day*, which see. The primary sense is to shoot, as rays; hence, to open or expand, to shine. We observe in this word, the *n* of the Saxon infinitive is retained.]

1. To begin to grow light in the morning; to grow light; as, the day *dawns*; the morning *dawns*.

It began to *dawn* towards the first day of the week. Matt. xxviii.

2. To begin to open or expand; to begin to show intellectual light, or knowledge; as, the genius of the youth begins to *dawn*.

When life awakes and *dawns* at every line. *Pope.*

3. To glimmer obscurely. *Locke.*

4. To begin to open or appear. *Dryden.*

DAWN, *n.* The break of day; the first appearance of light, in the morning.

They arose about the *dawn* of the day. Josh. vi.

The word may express the whole time from the first appearance of light to sunrise.

2. First opening or expansion; first appearance of intellectual light; as the *dawn* of genius, intellect, or mental powers.

3. Beginning; rise; first appearance; as the *dawn* of time. *Shak.*

4. A feeble or incipient light; first beams.

These tender circumstances diffuse a *dawn* of serenity over the soul. *Pope.*

DAWN'ING, *ppr.* Growing light; first appearing luminous; opening; as the *dawning* day.

2. Opening; expanding; beginning to show intellectual light; beginning.

DAWN'ING, *n.* The first appearance of light in the morning.

2. The first opening or appearance of the intellectual powers; beginning; as the first *dawning* of notions in the understanding. *Locke.*

DAY, *n.* [Sax. *dæg, deg, dag*; Goth. *dags*; D. *dag*; G. *tag*; Sw. *dag*; Dan. *dag*. See *Dawn*.]

1. That part of the time of the earth's revolution on its axis, in which its surface is presented to the sun; the part of the twenty four hours when it is light; or the space of time between the rising and setting of the sun; called the *artificial* day.

And God called the light *day*. Gen. i.

2. The whole time or period of one revolution of the earth on its axis, or twenty four hours; called the *natural* day.

And the evening and the morning were the first *day*. Gen. i.

In this sense, the day may commence at any period of the revolution. The Babylonians began the day at sun-rising; the Jews, at sun-setting; the Egyptians, at midnight, as do several nations in modern times, the British, French, Spanish, American, &c. This day, in reference to civil transactions, is called the *civil* day. Thus with us the day when a legal instrument is dated, begins and ends at midnight.

3. Light; sunshine.

Let us walk honestly as in the *day*. Rom. xiii.

4. Time specified; any period of time distinguished from other time; age; time, with reference to the existence of a person or thing.

He was a useful man in his *day*.

In the *day* thou eatest thereof thou shalt surely die. Gen. ii.

In this sense, the plural is often used; as, from the *days* of the judges; in the *days* of our fathers. In this sense also, the word is often equivalent to life, or earthly existence.

5. The contest of a day; battle; or day of combat.

The *day* is his own.

He won the *day*, that is, he gained the victory.

6. An appointed or fixed time.

If my debtors do not keep their *day*. *Dryden.*

7. Time of commemorating an event; anniversary; the same day of the month, in any future year. We celebrate the *day* of our Savior's birth.

Day by day, daily; every day; each day in succession; continually; without intermission of a day.

Day by day, we magnify thee. *Common Prayer.*

But or *only from day to day*, without certainty of continuance; temporarily. *Shak.*

To-day, *adv.* [Sax. *to-dæg.*] On the present day; this day; or at the present time.

Days of grace, in *theology*, the time when mercy is offered to sinners.

To-day, if ye will hear his voice, harden not your hearts. Ps. xcv.

Days of grace, in *law*, are days granted by the court for delay, at the prayer of the plaintiff or defendant. *Encyc.*

Three days, beyond the day named in the writ, in which the person summoned may appear and answer. *Blackstone.*

Days of grace, in *commerce*, a customary number of days, in Great Britain and America, *three*, allowed for the payment of a note or bill of exchange, after it becomes due. A note *due* on the *seventh* of the month is *payable* on the *tenth*.

The days of grace are different in different countries. In France, they are *ten*; at Naples, *eight*; at Venice, Amsterdam and Antwerp, *six*; at Hamburg, *twelve*; in Spain, *fourteen*; in Genoa, *thirty*. *Encyc.*

Days in bank, in England, days of appearance in the court of common bench. *Blackstone.*

DA'YBED, *n.* A bed used for idleness, indulgence, or rest during the day. *Shak.*

DA'YBOOK, *n.* A journal of accounts; a book in which are recorded the debts and credits or accounts of the day.

DA'YBREAK, *n.* The dawn or first appearance of light in the morning.

DA'YCOAL, *n.* A name given by miners to the upper stratum of coal. *Encyc.*

DA'YDREAM, *n.* A vision to the waking senses. *Mason.*

DA'YFLOWER, *n.* A genus of plants, the Commelina. *Muhlenberg.*

DA'YFLY, *n.* A genus of insects that live one day only, or a very short time, called Ephemera. The species are numerous, some of which live scarcely an hour, others, several days. *Encyc.*

DA'YLABOR, *n.* Labor hired or performed by the day.

DAYLĀBORER, *n.* One who works by the day.

DA'YLIGHT, *n.* The light of the day; the light of the sun, as opposed to that of the moon or of a lamp or candle.

DA'Y-LILY, *n.* The same with asphodel. *Johnson.*

A species of Hemerocallis. *Bot.*

DA'YLY, *a.* The more regular orthography of *daily*.

DA'YSMAN, *n.* An umpire or arbiter; a mediator.

Neither is there any *daysman* betwixt us. Job ix.

DA'YSPRING, *n*, The dawn; the beginning of the day, or first appearance of light.

Whereby the *dayspring* from on high hath visited us. Luke i.

DA'YSTAR, *n.* The morning star, Lucifer, Venus; the star which precedes the morning light. *Milton.*

DA'YTIME, *n.* The time of the sun's light on the earth; opposed to *night*.

DA'YWEARIED, *a.* Wearied with the labor of the day. *Shak.*

DA'YWŎRK, *n.* Work by the day; daylabor.

DA'Y'S-WŎRK, *n.* The work of one day. Among seamen, the account or reckoning of a ship's course for 24 hours, from noon to noon. *Encyc.*

DAZE, *v. t.* [Qu. Sax. *dwæs, dysi, dysig*, Eng. *dizzy*. See *Dazzle*.]

To overpower with light; to dim or blind by too strong a light, or to render the sight unsteady. [*Not now used, unless in poetry.*] *Dryden.*

DAZE, *n.* Among *miners*, a glittering stone.

DAZ'ZLE, *v. t.* [In Sax. *dwæs* is dull, stupid, foolish; *dwæscan*, to extinguish; *dysi* or *dysig*, dizzy.]

1. To overpower with light; to hinder distinct vision by intense light; or to cause to shake; to render unsteady, as the sight. We say, the brightness of the sun *dazzles* the eyes or the sight.

2. To strike or surprise with a bright or intense light; to dim or blind by a glare of light, or by splendor, in a literal or figurative sense; as, to be *dazzled* by resplendent glory, or by a brilliant expression.

DA'ZZLE, *v. i.* To be overpowered by light; to shake or be unsteady; to waver, as the sight.

I dare not trust these eyes;
They dance in mists, and *dazzle* with surprise. *Dryden.*

DAZ'ZLED, *pp.* Made wavering, as the sight; overpowered or dimmed by a too strong light.

DAZ'ZLEMENT, *n.* The act or power of dazzling. [*Not used.*] *Donne.*

DAZ'ZLING, *ppr.* Rendering unsteady or wavering, as the sight; overpowering by a strong light; striking with splendor.

DAZ'ZLINGLY, *adv.* In a dazzling manner.

DE, a Latin prefix, denotes a moving from, separation; as in *debark, decline, decease, deduct, decamp.* Hence it often expresses a negative; as in *derange.* Sometimes it augments the sense, as in *deprave, despoil.* It coincides nearly in sense with the French *des* and L. *dis.*

DE'ACON, *n. de'kn.* [L. *diaconus*, from Gr. διακονος, a minister or servant; δια, by, and κονεω, to serve; Fr. *diacre*; Arm. *diagon*; It. Sp. *diacono*; D. *diaken.*]

A person in the lowest degree of holy orders. The office of deacon was instituted by the apostles, Acts 6, and seven persons were chosen at first, to serve at the feasts of christians and distribute bread and wine to the communicants, and to minister to the wants of the poor.

In *the Romish Church*, the office of the deacons is to incense the officiating priest; to lay the corporal on the altar; to receive the cup from the subdeacon and present it to the person officiating; to incense the choir; to receive the pax from the officiating prelate, and carry it to the subdeacon; and at the pontifical mass, to put the miter on the bishop's head. *Encyc.*

In *the church of England*, the office of deacons is declared to be to assist the priest in administering the holy commmunion; and their office in presbyterian and independent churches is to distribute the bread and wine to the communicants. In the latter, they are elected by the members of the church.

2. In *Scotland*, an overseer of the poor, and the master of an incorporated company.

DE'ACONESS, *n. de'kness.* A female deacon in the primitive church. *Encyc.*

DE'ACONRY, } *n.* The office, dignity or
DE'ACONSHIP, } ministry of a deacon or deaconess. *Encyc.*

DEAD, *a. ded.* [Sax. *dead*, probably contracted from *deged*; D. *dood*; G. *todt*; Sw. *död*; Dan. *död.* See *Die.*]

1. Deprived or destitute of life; that state of a being, animal or vegetable, in which the organs of motion and life have ceased to perform their functions, and have become incapable of performing them, or of being restored to a state of activity.

The men are *dead* who sought thy life. Ex. iv.

It is sometimes followed by *of* before the cause of death; as, *dead of* hunger, or *of* a fever.

2. Having never had life, or having been deprived of vital action before birth; as, the child was born *dead*.

3. Without life; inanimate.

All, all but truth, drops *dead*-born from the press. *Pope.*

4. Without vegetable life; as a *dead* tree.

5. Imitating death; deep or sound; as a *dead* sleep.

6. Perfectly still; motionless as death; as a *dead* calm; a *dead* weight.

7. Empty; vacant; not enlivened by variety; as a *dead* void space; a *dead* plain. *Dryden.*

We say also, a *dead* level, for a perfectly level surface.

8. Unemployed; useless; unprofitable. A man's faculties may lie *dead*, or his goods remain *dead* on his hands. So *dead* capital or stock is that which produces no profit.

9. Dull; inactive; as a *dead* sale of commodities.

10. Dull; gloomy; still; not enlivened; as a *dead* winter; a *dead* season. *Addison.*
11. Still; deep; obscure; as the *dead* darkness of the night.
12. Dull; not lively; not resembling life; as the *dead* coloring of a piece; a *dead* eye.
13. Dull; heavy; as a *dead* sound. *Boyle.*
14. Dull; frigid; lifeless; cold; not animated; not affecting; *used of prayer.* *Addison.*
15. Tasteless; vapid; spiritless; *used of liquors.*
16. Uninhabited; as *dead* walls. *Arbuthnot.*
17. Dull; without natural force or efficacy; not lively or brisk; as a *dead* fire.
18. In a state of spiritual death; void of grace; lying under the power of sin.
19. Impotent; unable to procreate. Rom. iv.
20. Decayed in grace.

Thou hast a name that thou livest, and art *dead.* Rev. iii.

21. Not proceeding from spiritual life; not producing good works; as, faith without works is *dead.* James ii.
22. Proceeding from corrupt nature, not from spiritual life or a gracious principle; as *dead* works. Heb. ix. 14.
23. In *law*, cut off from the rights of a citizen: deprived of the power of enjoying the rights of property; as one banished or becoming a monk is civilly *dead.* *Blackstone.*

Dead language, a language which is no longer spoken or in common use by a people, and known only in writings; as the Hebrew, Greek and Latin.

Dead rising or *rising line*, the parts of a ship's floor or bottom throughout her length, where the floor timber is terminated on the lower futtock. *Mar. Dict.*

DEAD, *n. ded.* *The dead* signifies dead men.

Ye shall not make cuttings for *the dead.* Lev. xix.

2. The state of the dead; or death.

This is John the Baptist; he is risen from *the dead.* Matt. xiv.

This may be understood thus, he is risen from among the *dead.*

DEAD, *n. ded.* The time when there is a remarkable stillness or gloom; depth; as in the midst of winter or of night. The *dead* of winter, the *dead* of night, are familiar expressions.

DEAD, *v. i. ded.* To lose life or force. [*Obs.*] *Bacon.*

DEAD, *v. t. ded.* To deprive of life, force or vigor. [*Obs.*] *Bacon.*

DEAD′-DOING, *a.* Destructive; killing. [*Obs.*] *Spenser.*

DEAD-DRUNK, *a.* So drunk as to be incaple of helping one's self.

DEAD′EN, *v. t. ded′n.* [D. *dooden*; G. *tödten.*]

1. To deprive of a portion of vigor, force or sensation; to abate vigor or action; as, to *deaden* the force of a ball; to *deaden* the natural powers or feelings.
2. To blunt; to render less susceptible or feeling; as, to *deaden* the senses.
3. To retard; to lessen velocity or motion; as, to *deaden* the motion of a ship or of the wind.
4. To diminish spirit; to make vapid or spiritless; as, to *deaden* wine or beer.

DEAD′-EYE, *n. ded′-eye.* [*dead-man's eye.*] Among *seamen*, a round flattish wooden block, encircled by a rope, or an iron band, and pierced with holes, to receive the laniard, used to extend the shrouds and stays, and for other purposes.

DEAD′-HEARTED, *a.* Having a dull, faint heart. *Hall.*

DEAD-HEARTEDNESS, *n.* Pusillanimity.

DEAD′-LIFT, *n.* A heavy weight; a hopeless exigency. *Hudibras.*

DEAD′-LIGHT, *n. ded′-light.* A strong wooden port, made to suit a cabin window, in which it is fixed, to prevent the water from entering a ship in a storm.

DEAD′LIHOOD, *n.* The state of the dead. *Pearson.*

DEAD′LINESS, *n. ded′liness.* The quality of being deadly.

DEAD′LY, *a. ded′ly.* That may occasion death; mortal; fatal; destructive; as a *deadly* blow or wound.

2. Mortal; implacable; aiming to kill or destroy; as a *deadly* enemy; *deadly* malice; a *deadly* feud.

DEAD′LY, *adv. ded′ly.* In a manner resembling death; as *deadly* pale or wan. *Shak.*

2. Mortally.

With groanings of a *deadly* wounded man. Ezek. xxx.

3. Implacably; destructively.
4. In *a vulgar* or *ludicrous sense*, very; extremely; as a *deadly* cunning man. *Arbuthnot.*

DEADLY-CARROT, *n.* A plant of the genus Thapsia.

DEADLY-NIGHTSHADE, *n.* A plant of the genus Atropa.

DEAD′NESS, *n. ded′ness.* Want of natural life or vital power, in an animal or plant; as the *deadness* of a limb, of a body, or of a tree.

2. Want of animation; dullness; languor; as the *deadness* of the eye.
3. Want of warmth or ardor; coldness; frigidity; as the *deadness* of the affections.
3. Vapidness; want of spirit; as the *deadness* of liquors.
4. State of being incapable of conception, according to the ordinary laws of nature. Rom. iv. 19.
5. Indifference; mortification of the natural desires; alienation of heart from temporal pleasures; as *deadness* to the world.

DEAD′NETTLE, *n.* A plant of the genus Lamium, and another of the genus Galeopsis.

DEAD′PLEDGE, *n.* A mortgage or pawning of things, or thing pawned. *Bailey.*

DEAD-RECKONING, *n.* In *navigation*, the judgment or estimation of the place of a ship, without any observation of the heavenly bodies; or an account of the distance she has run by the log, and of the course steered by the compass, and this rectified by due allowances for drift, lee-way, &c. *Mar. Dict.*

DEAD′STRUCK, *a.* Confounded; struck with horror. *Hall.*

DEAD′WATER, *n.* The eddy water closing in with a ship's stern, as she passes through the water.

DEAD′WOOD, *n.* Blocks of timber laid on the keel of a ship, particularly at the extremities.

DEAD′WORKS, *n.* The parts of a ship which are above the surface of the water, when she is balanced for a voyage. *Mar. Dict.*

DEAF, *n. deef.* [Sax. *deaf*; Ice. *dauf*; D. *doof*; G. *taub*; Dan. *döv*; Sw. *döf*; D. *dooven*, to quench or stifle; Dan. *döver*, to deafen; coinciding with Ch. טפא, to extinguish, L. *stipo*, Fr. *etouffer*, to *stuff.* Hence we say, *thick of hearing.* The true English pronunciation of this word is *deef*, as appears from the poetry of Chaucer, who uniformly makes it rhyme with *leaf*; and this proof is confirmed by poetry in the works of Sir W. Temple. Such was the pronunciation which our ancestors brought from England. The word is in analogy with *leaf, sheaf*, and the long sound of the vowels naturally precedes the semi-vowel *f*. *Def*, from the Danish and Swedish pronunciation, is an anomaly in English of a singular kind, there being not another word like it in the language. See Chaucer's Wife of Bath's Prologue.]

1. Not perceiving sounds; not receiving impressions from sonorous bodies through the air; as a *deaf* ear.
2. Wanting the sense of hearing; having organs which do not perceive sounds; as a *deaf* man. It is followed by *to* before that which ought to be heard; as *deaf to* the voice of the orator.
3. In *a metaphorical sense*, not listening; not regarding; not moved, persuaded or convinced; rejecting; as *deaf* to reason or arguments. Men are *deaf* to the calls of the gospel.
4. Without the ability or will to regard spiritual things; unconcerned; as, hear, ye *deaf.* Is. xlii.
5. Deprived of the power of hearing; deafened; as *deaf* with clamor.
6. Stifled; imperfect; obscurely heard; as a *deaf* noise or murmur. *Dryden.*

DEAF, *v. t.* to deafen, is used by Dryden, but is obsolete, unless perhaps in poetry.

DE′AFEN, *v. t. dee′fn.* To make deaf; to deprive of the power of hearing; to impair the organs of hearing, so as to render them unimpressible to sounds.

2. To stun; to render incapable of perceiving sounds distinctly; as *deafened* with clamor or tumult.

DE′AFLY, *adv. dee′fly.* Without sense of sounds; obscurely heard.

DE′AFNESS, *n. dee′fness.* Incapacity of perceiving sounds; the state of the organs which prevents the impressions which constitute hearing; as the *deafness* of the ears: hence, *applied to persons*, want of the sense of hearing.

2. Unwillingness to hear and regard; voluntary rejection of what is addressed to the ear and to the understanding. *King Charles.*

DEAL, *v. t.* pret. and pp. *dealt*, pron. *delt.* [Sax. *dælan, bedælan, gedælan*; Goth. *dailyan*; Sw. *dela*; Dan. *deeler*; G. *theilen*; D. *deelen, bedeelen*; Russ. *delyu*; W. *dydoli*, to separate; *dy* and *tawl*, separation, a throwing off, *tawlu*, to throw off, to separate; Ir. and Gael. *dailim*, to give; *dail*, a part, Eng. *dole*; Heb. and Ch. בדל to separate, or divide; Ar. بدل badala, to exchange, or give in exchange; بذل badhala, to give, to yield. [Qu. W. *gozoli*, to endow.] There is a remarkable coincidence between the Shemitic word and the Sax. and Dutch, *bedælan*, *bedeelen*. The Welsh *tawlu* gives the true original sense.]

To divide; to part; to separate; hence, to divide in portions; to distribute; often followed by *out*.

Is it not to *deal* thy bread to the hungry? Is. lviii.

And Rome *deals out* her blessings and her gold. *Tickel.*

2. To scatter; to throw about; as, to *deal* out feathered deaths. *Dryden.*

3. To throw out in succession; to give one after another; as, to *deal* out blows.

4. To distribute the cards of a pack to the players.

DEAL, *v. i.* To traffick; to trade; to negotiate.

They buy and sell, they *deal* and traffick. *South.*

2. To act between man and man; to intervene; to transact or negotiate between men.

He that *deals* between man and man, raiseth his own credit with both. *Bacon.*

3. To behave well or ill; to act; to conduct one's self in relation to others.

Thou shalt not steal, nor *deal* falsely, nor lie. Lev. xix.

4. To distribute cards.

To deal by, to treat, either well or ill; as, to *deal* well *by* domestics.

Such an one *deals* not fairly *by* his own mind. *Locke.*

To deal in, to have to do with; to be engaged in; to practice.

They *deal in* political matters; they *deal in* low humor.

2. To trade in; as, to *deal in* silks, or in cutlery.

To deal with, to treat in any manner; to use well or ill.

Now will we *deal* worse *with* thee. Gen. xix.

Return—and I will *deal* well *with* thee. Gen. xxxii.

2. To contend with; to treat with, by way of opposition, check or correction; as, he has turbulent passions to *deal with*.

3. To treat with by way of discipline, in ecclesiastical affairs; to admonish.

DEAL, *n.* [Sax. *dæl*, *dal*, *gedal*; Ir. *dal*; D. *deel*; G. *theil*; Dan. *deel*; Sw. *del*; Russ. *dolia*. See the Verb.]

1. Literally, a division; a part or portion; hence, an indefinite quantity, degree or extent; as a *deal* of time and trouble; a *deal* of cold; a *deal* of space. Formerly it was limited by *some*, as *some deal*; but this is now obsolete or vulgar. In general, we now qualify the word with *great*, as a *great deal* of labor; a *great deal* of time and pains; a *great deal* of land. In the phrases, it is a *great deal* better or worse, the words, *great deal*, serve as modifiers of the sense of better and worse. The true construction is, it is, *by* a great deal, better; it is better *by* a great deal, that is, by a great part or difference.

2. The division or distribution of cards; the art or practice of dealing cards.

The *deal*, the shuffle, and the cut. *Swift.*

3. The division of a piece of timber made by sawing; a board or plank; *a sense much more used in England than in the U. States.*

DEAL'BATE, *v. t.* [L. *dealbo*; *de* and *albus*, white.] To whiten. [*Little used.*]

DEALBA'TION, *n.* The act of bleaching; a whitening.

DE'ALER, *n.* One who deals; one who has to do with any thing, or has concern with; as a *dealer* in wit and learning *Swift.*

2. A trader; a trafficker; a shopkeeper; a broker; a merchant; a word of very extensive use; as a *dealer* in dry goods; a *dealer* in hardware; a *dealer* in stocks; a *dealer* in leather; a *dealer* in lumber; a *dealer* in linens or woolens; a small *dealer* in groceries; a money-*dealer*.

3. One who distributes cards to the players.

DE'ALING, *ppr.* Dividing; distributing; throwing out.

2. Trading; trafficking; negotiating.

3. Treating; behaving.

DE'ALING, *n.* Practice; action; conduct; behavior; as, observe the *dealings* of the men who administer the government. But it is now more generally used of the actions of men in private life.

2. Conduct in relation to others; treatment; as the *dealings* of a father with his children. God's *dealings* with men are the dispensations of his providence, or moral government.

3. Intercourse in buying and selling; traffick; business; negotiation. American merchants have extensive *dealings* with the merchants of Liverpool.

4. Intercourse of business or friendship; concern.

The Jews have no *dealings* with the Samaritans. John iv.

DEAM'BULATE. *v. i.* [L. *deambulo.*] To walk abroad. [*Not used.*]

DEAMBULA'TION, *n.* The act of walking abroad. *Elyot.*

DEAM'BULATORY, *a.* Pertaining to walks.

DEAM'BULATORY, *n.* A place to walk in.

DEAN, *n.* [Fr. *doyen*, the eldest of a corporation; Arm. *dean*; Sp. *dean*, *decano*; Port, *deam*, *decano*; It. *decano*; from L. *decanus*, the leader of a file ten deep, the head of a college, from *decem*, Gr. δεκα, W. *deg*, ten; so named because originally he was set over ten canons or prebendaries. *Ayliffe.*]

1. In *England*, an ecclesiastical dignitary in cathedral and collegiate churches, and the head of a chapter; the second dignitary of a diocese. Ancient deans are elected by the chapter in virtue of a conge d'elire from the king and letters missive of recommendation; but in the chapters founded by Henry VIII., out of the spoils of dissolved monasteries, the deanery is donative, and the installation merely by the king's letters patent. *Encyc.*

2. An officer in each college of the universities in England. *Warton.*

3. In *the U. States*, an officer in a medical school.

DE'ANERY, *n.* The office or the revenue of a dean. *Clarendon. Swift.*

2. The house of a dean. *Shak.*

3. The jurisdiction of a dean.

Each archdeaconry is divided into rural *deaneries*, and each *deanery* is divided into parishes. *Blackstone.*

Rural dean, or arch-presbyter, had originally jurisdiction over ten churches; but afterwards he became only the bishop's substitute, to grant letters of administration, probate of wills, &c. His office is now lost in that of the archdeacon and chancellor. *Encyc.*

Dean of a Monastery, a superior established under the abbot, to ease him in taking care of ten monks. Hence his name. *Encyc.*

Dean and Chapter, are the bishop's council, to aid him with their advice in affairs of religion, and in the temporal concerns of his see. *Encyc.*

DEAN'SHIP, *n.* The office of a dean.

DEAR, *a.* [Sax. *deor*; G. *theuer*, dear, rare; *theure* or *theurung*, dearness, scarcity, dearth; D. *duur*, dear; *duurte*, dearth; Sw. *dyr*, dear; *dyrhet*, dearth; Dan. *dyre*, *dyrtid*, id. It seems that the primary sense is scarce, rare, or close, narrow; this is obvious from *dearth*. So in L. *carus*, *caritas*.] Class Dr. No. 7. 8. 19. and Class Sr. No. 4. 34. 47.]

1. Scarce; not plentiful. *Obs.* *Shak.*

2. Bearing a high price in comparison of the usual price; more costly than usual; of a higher price than the customary one. Wheat is *dear* at a dollar a bushel, when the usual price is seventy five cents. This sense results from the former, as *dearness* is the effect of scarcity and demand.

3. Of a high value in estimation; greatly valued; beloved; precious.

And the last joy was *dearer* than the rest. *Pope.*

Be ye followers of God, as *dear* children. Eph. v.

DEAR, *a.* [Sax. *derian*, to hurt; Scot. *dere* or *deir*, to annoy, and *dere*, to fear.] Hurtful; grievous; hateful. *Obs.* *Shak.*

DEAR, *v. t.* To make dear. [*Not used.*] *Shelton.*

DEAR, *n.* A darling; a word denoting tender affection or endearment; as, *my dear*.

DE'ARBOUGHT, *a.* [See *Bought.*] Purchased at a high price; as *dearbought* experience; *dearbought* blessings.

DE'ARLING. [See *Darling.*]

DE'ARLŎVED, *a.* Greatly beloved. *Shak.*

DE'ARLY, *adv.* At a high price; as, he pays *dearly* for his rashness.

2. With great fondness; as, we love our children *dearly*; *dearly* beloved.

DEARN, *a.* [Sax. *deorn.*] Lonely; solitary; melancholy. *Obs.* *Shak.*

DE'ARNESS, *n.* Scarcity; high price, or a higher price than the customary one; as the *dearness* of corn.

2. Fondness; nearness to the heart or affections; great value in estimation; preciousness; tender love; as the *dearness* of friendship.

DEARNLY, *adv.* Secretly; privately. *Obs.* [See *Dernly.*]

DEARTH, *n.* *derth.* [See *Dear.*] Scarcity; as a *dearth* of corn.

2. Want; need; famine. *Shak.*

3. Barrenness; sterility; as a *dearth* of plot. *Dryden.*

DEARTIC'ULATE, *v. t.* To disjoint. [*Not used.*]

DEATH, *n.* *deth.* [Sax. *death*; D. *dood*; G. *tod*; Sw. *död*; Dan. *död*. See *Die* and *Dead.*]

1. That state of a being, animal or vegetable, but more particularly of an animal, in which there is a total and permanent cessation of all the vital functions, when the organs

have not only ceased to act, but have lost the susceptibility of renewed action. Thus the cessation of respiration and circulation in an animal may not be death, for during hybernation some animals become entirely torpid, and some animals and vegetables may be subjected to a fixed state by frost, but being capable of revived activity, they are not dead.

2. The state of the dead; as the gates of *death*. Job xxxviii.

3. The manner of dying.

Thou shalt die the *deaths* of them that are slain in the midst of the seas. Ezek. xxviii.

Let me die the *death* of the righteous. Numb. xxiii.

4. The image of mortality represented by a skeleton; as a *death's* head. *Shak.*

5. Murder; as a man of *death*. *Bacon.*

6. Cause of death.

O thou man of God, there is *death* in the pot. 2 Kings iv.

We say, he caught his *death*.

7. Destroyer or agent of death; as, he will be the *death* of his poor father.

8. In *poetry*, the means or instrument of death; as an arrow is called the feathered *death*; a ball, a leaden *death*.

Deaths invisible come winged with fire. *Dryden.*

9. In *theology*, perpetual separation from God, and eternal torments; called the *second death*. Rev. ii.

10. Separation or alienation of the soul from God; a being under the dominion of sin, and destitute of grace or divine life; called *spiritual death*.

We know that we have passed from *death* to life, because we love the brethren. 1 John iii. Luke i.

Civil death, is the separation of a man from civil society, or from the enjoyment of civil rights; as by banishment, abjuration of the realm, entering into a monastery, &c. *Blackstone.*

DEATH'-BED, *n.* *deth'-bed.* The bed on which a person dies or is confined in his last sickness.

DEATH'-BODING, *a.* Portending death. *Shak.*

DEATH'-DARTING, *a.* Darting or inflicting death. *Shak.*

DEATH'S-DOOR, *n.* A near approach to death; the gates of death. *Taylor.*

DEATH'FUL, *a.* Full of slaughter; murderous; destructive.

These eyes behold
The *deathful* scene. *Pope.*

DEATH'FULNESS, *n.* Appearance of death. *Taylor.*

DEATH'LESS, *a.* Immortal; not subject to death, destruction or extinction; as *deathless* beings; *deathless* fame.

DEATH'LIKE, *a.* Resembling death; gloomy; still; calm; quiet; peaceful; motionless; like death in horror or in stillness; as *deathlike* slumbers.

2. Resembling death; cadaverous.

DEATH'S-MAN, *n.* An executioner; a hangman. *Shak.*

DEATH'-SHADOWED, *a.* Surrounded by the shades of death. *More.*

DEATH'-TOKEN, *n.* That which indicates approaching death. *Shak.*

DEATH'WARD, *adv.* Toward death. *Beaum.*

DEATH'-WATCH, *n.* A small insect whose ticking is weakly supposed, by superstitious and ignorant people, to prognosticate death. *Gay.*

DEAU'RATE, *v. t.* [L. *deauro.*] To gild. [*Little used.*]

DEAU'RATE, *a.* Gilded.

DEBAC'LE, *n.* [Fr.] A breaking or bursting forth. *Buckland.*

The geological deluge, which is supposed to have swept the surface of the earth, and to have conveyed the fragments of rocks, and the remains of animals and vegetables, to a distance from their native localities. *Ed. Encyc.*

DEB'AR, *v. t.* [*de* and *bar.*] To cut off from entrance; to preclude; to hinder from approach, entry or enjoyment; to shut out or exclude; as, we are not *debarred* from any rational enjoyment; religion *debars* us from no real pleasure.

DEB'ARK, *v. t.* [Fr. *debarquer; de* and *barque*, a boat or vessel.]
To land from a ship or boat; to remove from on board any water-craft, and place on land; to disembark; as, to *debark* artillery. [It is less used, especially in a transitive sense, than *disembark.*]

DEB'ARK, *v. i.* To leave a ship or boat and pass to the land; as, the troops *debarked* at four o'clock.

DEBARKA'TION, *n.* The act of disembarking.

DEB'ARKED, *pp.* Removed to land from on board a ship or boat.

DEB'ARKING, *ppr.* Removing from a ship to the land; going from on board a vessel.

DEB'ARRED, *pp.* [from *debar.*] Hindered from approach, entrance or possession.

DEB'ARRING, *ppr.* Preventing from approach, entrance or enjoyment.

DEBA'SE, *v. t.* [*de* and *base.*] To reduce from a higher to a lower state or rank, in estimation.

The drunkard *debases* himself and his character.

Intemperance and debauchery *debase* men almost to a level with beasts.

2. To reduce or lower in quality, purity, or value; to adulterate; as, to *debase* gold or silver by alloy.

3. To lower or degrade; to make mean or despicable. Religion should not be *debased* by frivolous disputes. Vicious habits *debase* the mind, as well as the character.

4. To sink in purity or elegance; to vitiate by meanness; as, to *debase* style by the use of vulgar words.

DEBA'SED, *pp.* Reduced in estimated rank; lowered in estimation; reduced in purity, fineness, quality or value; adulterated; degraded; rendered mean.

DEBA'SEMENT, *n.* The act of debasing; degradation; reduction of purity, fineness, quality or value; adulteration; a state of being debased; as *debasement* of character, of our faculties, of the coin, of style, &c.

DEBA'SER, *n.* One who debases or lowers in estimation, or in value; one who degrades or renders mean; that which debases.

DEBA'SING, *ppr.* Reducing in estimation or worth; adulterating; reducing in purity or elegance; degrading; rendering mean.

2. *a.* Lowering; tending to debase or degrade; as *debasing* vices.

DEBA'TABLE, *a.* [See *Debate.*] That may be debated; disputable; subject to controversy or contention; as a *debatable* question.

DEBATE, *n.* [Fr. *debat;* Sp. *debate;* Port. *id.; de* and *battre*, to *beat.*]

1. Contention in words or arguments; discussion for elucidating truth; strife in argument or reasoning, between persons of different opinions, each endeavoring to prove his own opinion right, and that of his opposer wrong; dispute; controversy; as the *debates* in parliament or in congress.

2. Strife; contention.

Behold, ye fast for strife and *debate*. Is. lviii.

3. The power of being disputed; as, this question is settled beyond *debate;* the story is true beyond *debate*.

4. *Debate* or *debates*, the published report of arguments for and against a measure; as, the *debates* in the convention are printed.

DEBA'TE, *v. t.* [Fr. *debattre;* Sp. *debatir;* Port. *debater.* See *Beat* and *Abate.*]
To contend for in words or arguments; to strive to maintain a cause by reasoning; to dispute; to discuss; to argue; to contest, as opposing parties; as, the question was *debated* till a late hour.

Debate thy cause with thy neighbor himself. Prov. xxv.

DEBA'TE, *v. i.* To *debate on* or *in*, to deliberate; to discuss or examine different arguments in the mind. *Shak.*

2. To dispute. *Tatler.*

3. To engage in combat. [*Not in use.*]

DEBA'TED, *pp.* Disputed; argued; discussed.

DEBA'TEFUL, *a.* Of *things*, contested; occasioning contention. *Spenser.*

2. Of *persons*, quarrelsome; contentious. [*Little used.*]

DEBA'TEFULLY, *adv.* With contention. *Sherwood.*

DEBA'TEMENT, *n.* Controversy; deliberation. [*Little used.*] *Shak.*

DEBA'TER, *n.* One who debates; a disputant; a controvertist.

DEBA'TING, *ppr.* Disputing; discussing; contending by arguments.

DEBAUCH', *v. t.* [Fr. *debaucher;* Arm. *dibaucha.* This is said by Lunier, to be compounded of *de* and an old French word, signifying a shop, [*bauche,*] and that its primary sense is to draw or entice one from his shop or work, and in this sense it is still used. Hence *embaucher* is to help a journeyman to employment, and to enlist as a soldier. The general sense then of *debauch*, in English, is to lead astray, like *seduce.*]

1. To corrupt or vitiate; as, to *debauch* a prince or a youth; to *debauch* good principles.

2. To corrupt with lewdness; as, to *debauch* a woman.

3. To seduce from duty or allegiance; as, to *debauch* an army.

DEBAUCH', *n.* [Fr. *debauche;* Arm. *dibauch.*]
Excess in eating or drinking; intemperance; drunkenness; gluttony; lewdness.

DEBAUCH'ED, *pp.* Corrupted; vitiated in morals or purity of character.

DEBAUCH'EDLY, *adv.* In a profligate manner. *Cowley.*

DEBAUCH'EDNESS, *n.* Intemperance. *Bp. Hall.*

DEBAUCHEE', *n.* A man given to intemperance, or bacchanalian excesses. But chiefly, a man habitually lewd.

DEBAUCH'ER, *n.* One who debauches or corrupts others; a seducer to lewdness, or to any dereliction of duty.

DEBAUCH'ERY, *n.* Excess in the pleasures of the table; gluttony; intemperance. But chiefly, habitual lewdness; excessive unlawful indulgence of lust.

2. Corruption of fidelity; seduction from duty or allegiance.

The republic of Paris will endeavor to complete the *debauchery* of the army. *Burke.*

DEBAUCH'MENT, *n.* The act of debauching or corrupting; the act of seducing from virtue or duty. *Taylor.*

DEBEL'LATE, *v. t.* [L. *debello.*] To subdue. [*Not used.*] *Bacon.*

DEBELLA'TION, *n.* The act of conquering or subduing. [*Not used.*] *More.*

DEBEN'TURE, *n.* [Fr. from L. *debeo*, to owe. Class Db.]

1. A writing acknowledging a debt; a writing or certificate signed by a public officer, as evidence of a debt due to some person. This paper, given by an officer of the customs, entitles a merchant exporting goods, to the receipt of a bounty, or a drawback of duties. When issued by a treasurer, it entitles the holder to a sum of money from the state.

2. In *the customs*, a certificate of drawback; a writing which states that a person is entitled to a certain sum from the government, on the exportation of specified goods, the duties on which had been paid.

DEBEN'TURED, *a.* *Debentured* goods are those for which a debenture has been given, as being entitled to drawback.

DEB'ILE, *a.* [L. *debilis*; Fr. *debile*; It. *debile*; Sp. *debil.* See Class Db. No. 1. 2. 3. 5. 7. 15. 47. 51.]

Relaxed; weak; feeble; languid; faint; without strength. *Shak.*

DEBIL'ITATE, *v. t.* [L. *debilito*, from *debilis.*]

To weaken; to impair the strength of; to enfeeble; to make faint or languid. Intemperance *debilitates* the organs of digestion. Excessive indulgence *debilitates* the system.

DEBIL'ITATED, *pp.* Weakened; enfeebled; relaxed.

DEBIL'ITATING, *ppr.* Weakening; enfeebling; impairing strength.

DEBILITA'TION, *n.* The act of weakening; relaxation.

DEBIL'ITY, *n.* [L. *debilitas*, from *debilis.*] Relaxation of the solids; weakness; feebleness; languor of body; faintness; imbecility; as, morbid sweats induce *debility.* [*It may be applied to the mind, but this is less common.*]

DEB'IT, *n.* [L. *debitum*, from *debeo*, to owe, Fr. *devoir*, Sp. *deber*, It. *dovere.* See *Duty.* The sense is probably to press or bind; Gr. δεω.]

Debt. It is usually written *debt.* But it is used in mercantile language, as the *debit* side of an account.

DEB'IT, *v. t.* To charge with debt; as, to *debit* a purchaser the amount of goods sold.

2. To enter an account on the debtor side of a book; as, to *debit* the sum or amount of goods sold.

DEB'ITED, *pp.* Charged in debt; made debtor on account.

2. Charged to one's debt, as money or goods.

DEB'ITING, *ppr.* Making debtor on account, as a person.

2. Charging to the debt of a person, as goods.

DEB'ITOR, *n.* A debtor. *Shak.*

DEBOISE, DEBOISH, for *debauch.* [*Not in use.*]

DEBONNA'IR, *a.* [Fr.] Civil; wellbred; complaisant; elegant. *Milton.*

DEBÖUCH, *v. i.* [Fr. *deboucher*; *de* and *bouche*, mouth.]

To issue or march out of a narrow place, or from defiles, as troops.

DEBRIS, *n. debree'.* [Fr.] Fragments; rubbish; ruins; applied particularly to the fragments of rocks. *Buckland.*

DEBT, *n. det.* [L. *debitum*, contracted; Fr. *dette*; Sp. It. *debito.* See *Debit.*]

1. That which is due from one person to another, whether money, goods, or services; that which one person is bound to pay or perform to another; as the *debts* of a bankrupt; the *debts* of a nobleman. It is a common misfortune or vice to be in *debt.*

When you run in *debt*, you give to another power over your liberty. *Franklin.*

2. That which any one is obliged to do or to suffer.

Your son, my lord, has paid a soldier's *debt.* *Shak.*

Hence death is called the *debt* of nature.

3. In *law*, an action to recover a debt. This is a customary ellipsis. He brought *debt*, instead of an action of *debt.*

4. In *scripture*, sin; trespass; guilt; crime; that which renders liable to punishment.

Forgive us our *debts.* *Lord's Prayer.*

DEBT'ED, *pp. det'ted.* Indebted; obliged to. [*Not used.*] *Shak.*

DEBTEE', *n. dettee'.* A creditor; one to whom a debt is due. *Blackstone.*

DEBT'LESS, *a. det'less.* Free from debt. *Chaucer.*

DEBT'OR, *n. det'tor.* [L. *debitor.*] The person who owes another either money, goods or services.

In Athens an insolvent *debtor* became slave to his creditor. *Mitford.*

2. One who is under obligation to do something.

I am *debtor* to the Greeks and barbarians. Rom. i.

He is a *debtor* to do the whole law. Gal. v.

3. The side of an account in which debts are charged. [See *Debit.*]

DEC'ACHORD, DECACHORD'ON, *n.* [Gr. δεκα, ten, and χορδη, string.]

1. A musical instrument of ten strings.

2. Something consisting of ten parts. *Watson.*

DEC'ADAL, *a.* Pertaining to ten; consisting of tens.

DEC'ADE, *n.* [L. *decas*, *decadis*; Fr. *decade*; Sp. *decada*; from Gr. δεκα, ten. See *Ten.*]

The sum or number of ten; an aggregate consisting of ten; as a *decade* of years; the *decades* of Livy.

DECA'DENCE, DECA'DENCY, *n.* Decay. [See *Decay.*]

DEC'AGON, *n.* [Gr. δεκα, ten, and γωνια, a corner.]

In *geometry*, a plane figure having ten sides and ten angles.

DEC'AGRAM, *n.* [Gr. δεκα, ten, and *gram*, a weight.]

A French weight of ten grams, or 154 grains, 44 decimals, equal to 6 penny weights, 10 grains, 44 decimals, equal to 5 drams, 65 decimals, avoirdupoise.

DEC'AGYN, *n.* [Gr. δεκα, ten, and γυνη, a female.] In *botany*, a plant having ten pistils.

DECAGYN'IAN, *a.* Having ten pistils.

DECAHE'DRAL, *a.* Having ten sides.

DECAHE'DRON, *n.* [Gr. δεκα, ten, and εδρα, a base.] In *geometry*, a figure or body having ten sides.

DEC'ALITER, *n.* [Gr. δεκα, ten, and *liter.*] A French measure of capacity, containing ten liters, or 610.28 cubic inches, equal to two gallons and 64.44231 cubic inches.

DECAL'OGIST, *n.* [See *Decalogue.*] One who explains the decalogue. *Gregory.*

DEC'ALOGUE, *n. dec'alog.* [Gr. δεκα, ten, and λογος, speech.]

The ten commandments or precepts given by God to Moses at mount Sinai, and originally written on two tables of stone.

DECAM'ETER, *n.* [Gr. δεκα, ten, and μετρον, measure.]

A French measure of length, consisting of ten meters, and equal to 393 English inches, and 71 decimals.

DECAMP', *v. i.* [Fr. *decamper*; Sp. *decampar*; *de* and *camp.*]

To remove or depart from a camp; to march off; as, the army *decamped* at six o'clock.

DECAMP'MENT, *n.* Departure from a camp; a marching off.

DEC'ANAL, *a.* [See *Dean.*] Pertaining to a deanery.

DECAN'DER, *n.* [Gr. δεκα, ten, and ανηρ, a male.] In *botany*, a plant having ten stamens.

DECAN'DRIAN, *a.* Having ten stamens.

DECAN'GULAR, *a.* [Gr. δεκα, ten, and *angular.*] Having ten angles. *Lee.*

DECANT', *v. t.* [L. *decanto*; *de* and *canto*, to sing; literally, to throw; Fr. *decanter*, to pour off; Sp. *decantar*; It. *decantare.* See *Cant.*]

To pour off gently, as liquor from its sediment; or to pour from one vessel into another; as, to *decant* wine.

DECANTA'TION, *n.* The act of pouring liquor gently from its lees or sediment, or from one vessel into another.

DECANT'ED, *pp.* Poured off, or from one vessel into another.

DECANT'ER, *n.* A vessel used to decant liquors, or for receiving decanted liquors. A glass vessel or bottle used for holding wine or other liquors, for filling the drinking glasses.

2. One who decants liquors.

DECANT'ING, *ppr.* Pouring off, as liquor from its lees, or from one vessel to another.

DECAP'ITATE, *v. t.* [L. *decapito*; *de* and *caput*, head.] To behead; to cut off the head.

DECAPITA'TION, *n.* The act of beheading.

DECAPH'YLLOUS, *a.* [Gr. δεκα, ten, and φυλλον, a leaf.] Having ten leaves. *Martyn.*

DEC'ARBONIZE, *v. t.* [*de* and *carbonize*.] To deprive of carbon; as, to *decarbonize* steel. *Chimistry.*

DEC'ARBONIZED, *pp.* Deprived of carbon.

DEC'ARBONIZING, *ppr.* Depriving of carbon.

DEC'ASTICH, *n.* [Gr. δεκα, ten, and ςιχος, a verse.] A poem consisting of ten lines.

DEC'ASTYLE, *n.* [Gr. δεκα, ten, and ςυλος, a column.]

A building with an ordnance of ten columns in front. *Encyc.*

DECA'Y, *v. i.* [Fr. *dechoir*, from L. *de* and *cado*, to fall, or *decedo*; It. *scadere*; Sp. *decaer*; Port. *descahir*.]

1. To pass gradually from a sound, prosperous, or perfect state, to a less perfect state, or towards destruction; to fail; to decline; to be gradually impaired. Our bodies *decay* in old age; a tree *decays*; buildings *decay*; fortunes *decay*.

2. To become weaker; to fail; as, our strength *decays*, or hopes *decay*.

DECA'Y, *v. t.* To cause to fail; to impair; to bring to a worse state.

Infirmity, that *decays* the wise, doth ever make better the fool. *Shak.*

[The transitive sense of the verb is now rarely used.]

DECA'Y, *n.* Gradual failure of health, strength, soundness, prosperity, or any species of excellence or perfection; decline to a worse or less perfect state; tendency towards dissolution or extinction; a state of depravation or diminution. Old men feel the *decay* of the body. We perceive the *decay* of the faculties in age. We lament the *decay* of virtue and patriotism in the state. The northern nations invaded the Roman Empire, when in a state of *decay*.

2. Declension from prosperity; decline of fortune.

If thy brother be waxen poor, and fallen in *decay*. Lev. xxv.

3. Cause of decay. [*Not usual.*]

He that plots to be the only figure among ciphers, is the *decay* of the whole age. *Bacon.*

DECA'YED, *pp.* Having fallen from a good or sound state; impaired; weakened; diminished.

DECA'YEDNESS, *n.* A state of being impaired; decayed state.

DECA'YER, *n.* That which causes decay. *Shak.*

DECA'YING, *ppr.* Failing; declining; passing from a good, prosperous or sound state, to a worse condition; perishing.

DECA'YING, *n.* Decay; decline.

DECE'ASE, *n.* [L. *decessus*, from *decedo*, to depart; *de* and *cedo*, to withdraw; Fr. *decès*.]

Literally, departure; hence, departure from this life; death; *applied to human beings only*.

Moses and Elias, who appeared in glory, and spoke of his *decease*, which he should accomplish at Jerusalem. Luke ix.

DECE'ASE, *v. i.* To depart from this life; to die.

Gen. Washington *deceased*, December 14, 1799, in the 68th year of his age.

DECE'ASED, *pp.* or *a.* Departed from life. This is used as a passive participle. He *is* deceased, for he *has* deceased; he *was* deceased, for he *had* deceased. This use of the participle of an intransitive verb is not infrequent, but the word omitted is really *has*. He *has* deceased. It is properly an adjective, like *dead*.

DECE'ASING, *ppr.* Departing from life; dying.

DECE'DENT, *n.* [L. *decedens*.] A deceased person. *Laws of Penn.*

DECE'IT, *n.* [Norm. *deceut*, contracted from L. *deceptio*. See *Deceive*.]

1. Literally, a catching or ensnaring. Hence, the misleading of a person; the leading of another person to believe what is false, or not to believe what is true, and thus to ensnare him; fraud; fallacy; cheat; any declaration, artifice or practice, which misleads another, or causes him to believe what is false.

My lips shall not speak wickedness, nor my tongue utter *deceit*. Job xxvii.

2. Stratagem; artifice; device intended to mislead.

They imagine *deceits* all the day long. Ps. xxxviii.

3. In *scripture*, that which is obtained by guile, fraud or oppression.

Their houses are full of *deceit*. Jer. v. Zeph. i.

4. In *law*, any trick, device, craft, collusion, shift, covin, or underhand practice, used to defraud another. *Cowel.*

DECE'ITFUL, *a.* Tending to mislead, deceive or ensnare; as *deceitful* words; *deceitful* practices.

Favor is *deceitful*. Prov. xxxi.

2. Full of deceit; trickish; fraudulent; cheating; as a *deceitful* man.

DECE'ITFULLY, *adv.* In a deceitful manner; fraudulently; with deceit; in a manner or with a view to deceive.

The sons of Jacob answered Shechem and Hamor his father *deceitfully*. Gen. xxxiv.

DECE'ITFULNESS, *n.* Tendency to mislead or deceive; as the *deceitfulness* of sin.

2. The quality of being fraudulent; as the *deceitfulness* of a man's practices.

3. The disposition to deceive; as, a man's *deceitfulness* may be habitual.

DECE'ITLESS, *a.* Free from deceit. *Hall.*

DECE'IVABLE, *a.* [See *Deceive*.] Subject to deceit or imposition; capable of being misled or entrapped; exposed to imposture; as, young persons are very *deceivable*.

2. Subject or apt to produce error or deception; deceitful.

Fair promises often prove *deceivable*. *Milton. Hayward.*

[*The latter use of the word is incorrect, and I believe, not now used.*]

DECE'IVABLENESS, *n.* Liableness to be deceived.

2. Liableness to deceive.

The *deceivableness* of unrighteousness. 2 Thess. ii.

DECE'IVE, *v. t.* [L. *decipio*, to take aside, to ensnare; *de* and *capio*; Fr. *decevoir*; Arm. *decevi*. See *Capable*.]

1. To mislead the mind; to cause to err; to cause to believe what is false, or disbelieve what is true; to impose on; to delude.

Take heed that no man *deceive* you. Matt. xxiv.

If we say we have no sin, we *deceive* ourselves. 1 John i.

2. To beguile; to cheat.

Your father hath *deceived* me, and changed my wages ten times. Gen. xxxi.

3. To cut off from expectation; to frustrate or disappoint; as, his hopes were *deceived*. *Dryden.*

4. To take from; to rob.

Plant fruit trees in large borders, and set therein fine flowers, but thin and sparingly, lest they *deceive* the trees. [*The literal sense, but not now used.*] *Bacon.*

DECE'IVED, *pp.* Misled; led into error; beguiled; cheated; deluded.

DECE'IVER, *n.* One who deceives; one who leads into error; a cheat; an impostor.

I shall seem to my father as a *deceiver*. Gen. xxvii.

DECE'IVING, *ppr.* Misleading; ensnaring; beguiling; cheating.

DECEM'BER, *n.* [L. *december*, from *decem*, ten; this being the tenth month among the early Romans, who began the year in March.]

The last month in the year, in which the sun enters the tropic of Capricorn, and makes the winter solstice.

DECEMDEN'TATE, *a.* [L. *decem*, ten, and *dentatus*, toothed.] Having ten points or teeth.

DEC'EMFID, *a.* [L. *decem*, ten, and *fido*, to divide.]

Ten-cleft; divided into ten parts; having ten divisions. *Martyn.*

DECEMLOC'ULAR, *a.* [L. *decem*, ten, and *loculus*, a little bag or cell.] Having ten cells for seeds. *Martyn.*

DEC'EMPEDAL, *a.* [L. *decem*, ten, and *pes*, a foot.] Ten feet in length.

DEC'EMVIR, *n.* [L. *decem*, ten, and *vir*, a man.]

One of ten magistrates, who had absolute authority in ancient Rome.

DECEM'VIRAL, *a.* Pertaining to the decemvirs in Rome. *Encyc.*

DECEM'VIRATE, *n.* [L. *decemviratus*. See *Decemvir*.]

1. The office or term of office of the decemvirs or ten magistrates in Rome, who had absolute authority for two years.

2. A body of ten men in authority.

DE'CENCY, *n.* [Fr. *decence*; L. *decentia*, from *decens*, *deceo*, to be fit or becoming; Sp. *decencia*; It. *decenza*. The L. *deceo* coincides in elements with the G. *taugen*, to be good, or fit for; D. *deugen*, to be good or virtuous; Sax. *dugan*, to avail, to be strong, to be worth; *duguth*, virtue, valor; *dohtig*, doughty; *dohter*, daughter; W. *tygiaw*, to prosper, to befit, to succeed. The Teutonic and Welsh words have for their radical sense, to advance or proceed, to stretch forward. In Welsh also, *têg* signifies clear, fair, smooth, beautiful; *tegu*, to make smooth, fair, beautiful, which would seem to be allied to *deceo*, whence *decus*, *decoro*. See Class Dg. No. 18. 25.]

1. That which is fit, suitable or becoming, in words or behavior; propriety of form, in social intercourse, in actions or discourse; proper formality; becoming ceremony. It has a special reference to behavior; as *decency* of conduct; *decency* of worship.

But it is used also in reference to speech; as, he discoursed with *decency*.

> Those thousand *decencies*, that daily flow
> From all her words and actions. *Milton.*

2. Suitableness to character; propriety.
3. Propriety in speech; modesty; opposed to ribaldry, or obscenity.

> Want of *decency* is want of sense. *Pope.*

It may be also used for propriety of speech, opposed to rudeness, or disrespectful language; and for propriety in dress, opposed to raggedness, exposure of nakedness, filthiness, &c.

DEC'ENNARY, *n.* [L. *decennis, decennium*, from *decem*, ten, and *annus*, a year.]
1. A period of ten years.
2. A tithing consisting of ten freeholders and their families. *Blackstone.*

DECEN'NIAL, *a.* [L. *decennalis*, as above.] Continuing for ten years; consisting of ten years; or happening every ten years; as a *decennial* period; *decennial* games.

DEC'ENNOVAL, **DECEN'NOVARY**, *a.* [L. *decem*, ten, and *novem*, nine.] Pertaining to the number nineteen; designating a period or circle of nineteen years. [*Little used.*] *Holder.*

DE'CENT, *a.* [L. *decens*; Fr. *decent*. See *Decency*.]
1. Becoming; fit; suitable, in words, behavior, dress and ceremony; as *decent* language; *decent* conduct or actions; *decent* ornaments or dress.
2. Comely; not gaudy or ostentatious.

> A sable stole of Cyprus lawn
> O'er the *decent* shoulders drawn. *Milton.*

3. Not immodest.
4. In *popular language*, moderate, but competent; not large; as a *decent* fortune. So a *decent* person is one not highly accomplished, nor offensively rude.

DE'CENTLY, *adv.* In a decent or becoming manner; with propriety of behavior or speech.
2. Without immodesty.

> Past hope of safety, 'twas his latest care,
> Like falling Cæsar, *decently* to die. *Dryden.*

DE'CENTNESS, *n.* Decency.

DECEPTIBIL'ITY, *n.* The quality or state of being capable or liable to be deceived. *Glanville.*

DECEP'TIBLE, *a.* That may be deceived. *Brown.*

DECEP'TION, *n.* [L. *deceptio*, from *decipio*. See *Deceive*.]
1. The act of deceiving or misleading.

> All *deception* is a misapplication of the established signs used to communicate thoughts. *Anon.*

2. The state of being deceived or misled. Incautious and inexperienced youth is peculiarly exposed to *deception*.
3. Artifice practiced; cheat; as, a scheme is all a *deception*.

DECEP'TIOUS, *a.* Tending to deceive; deceitful. *Shak.*

DECEP'TIVE, *a.* Tending to deceive; having power to mislead, or impress false opinions; as a *deceptive* countenance or appearance.

DECEP'TORY, *a.* Tending to deceive; containing qualities or means adapted to mislead.

DECERPT', *a.* [L. *decerptus*.] Cropped. [*Not used.*]

DECERP'TION, *n.* [L. *decerpo*, to pluck off; *de* and *carpo*.] A pulling or plucking off; a cropping. *Glanville.*

DECERTA'TION, *n.* [L. *decertatio*; *de* and *certo*, to strive.] Strife; contest for mastery. [*Little used.*] *Brown.*

DECES'SION, *n.* [L. *decessio*; *de* and *cedo*, to pass.] Departure. [*Little used.*]

DECH'ARM, *v. t.* [Fr. *decharmer*. See *Charm*.] To remove a spell or enchantment; to disenchant. *Harvey.*

DECH'ARMED, *pp.* Disenchanted.

DECH'ARMING, *ppr.* Removing a spell.

DECHRIS'TIANIZE, *v. t.* [*de* and *christianize*.] To turn from christianity; to banish christian belief and principles from. *J. P. Smith.*

DECI'DABLE, *a.* That may be decided. *Jones.*

DECI'DE, *v. t.* [L. *decido*; *de* and *cædo*, to strike, to cut.] Literally, to cut off, and thus to end. Hence,
1. To end; to determine, as a controversy, by verdict of a jury, or by a judgment of court. We say, the court or the jury *decided* the cause in favor of the plaintiff, or of the defendant.
2. To end or determine, as a dispute or quarrel.
3. To end or determine a combat or battle; as, a body of reserve, brought to the charge, *decided* the contest.
4. To determine; to fix the event of.

> The fate of the bill is *decided*.

5. In *general*, to end; to terminate.

DECI'DE, *v. i.* To determine; to form a definite opinion; to come to a conclusion.

> We cannot *decide* how far resistance is lawful or practicable.
> The court *decided* in favor of the defendant.

DECI'DED, *pp.* Determined; ended; concluded.

DECI'DED, *a.* That implies decision; clear; unequivocal; that puts an end to doubt.

> I find much cause to reproach myself, that I have lived so long, and have given no *decided* and public proofs of my being a christian. *P. Henry, Wirt's Sketches.*

DECI'DEDLY, *adv.* In a decided or determined manner; clearly; indisputably; in a manner to preclude doubt.

DECI'DENCE, *n.* [L. *decidens*.] A falling off. [*Not in use.*] *Brown.*

DECI'DER, *n.* One who determines a cause or contest.

DECI'DING, *ppr.* Determining; ending; concluding.

DECID'UOUS, *a.* [L. *deciduus*, *decido*; *de* and *cado*, to fall.] Falling; not perennial or permanent. In botany, a *deciduous* leaf is one which falls in autumn; a *deciduous* calyx, is that which falls after the corol opens; distinguished from *permanent*. *Martyn.*

DECID'UOUSNESS, *n.* The quality of falling once a year.

DEC'IGRAM, *n.* A French weight of one tenth of a gram.

DE'CIL, *n.* An aspect or position of two planets, when they are distant from each other a tenth part of the zodiac. *Encyc.*

DEC'ILITER, *n.* A French measure of capacity equal to one tenth of a liter.

DEC'IMAL, *a.* [L. *decimus*, tenth, from *decem*, ten; Gr. δεκα; Goth. *tig*, ten, Sax. *a tie*.]
1. Numbered by ten; as *decimal* progression. *Locke.*
2. Increasing or diminishing by ten; as *decimal* numbers; *decimal* arithmetic; *decimal* fractions.
3. Tenth; as a *decimal* part.

DEC'IMAL, *n.* A tenth.

DEC'IMALLY, *adv.* By tens; by means of decimals.

DEC'IMATE, *v. t.* [L. *decimo*, from *decem*, ten.]
1. To tithe; to take the tenth part.
2. To select by lot and punish with death every tenth man; a practice in armies, for punishing mutinous or unfaithful troops.
3. To take every tenth. *Mitford.*

DECIMA'TION, *n.* A tithing; a selection of every tenth by lot.
2. The selecting by lot for punishment every tenth man, in a company or regiment, &c.

DEC'IMATOR, *n.* One who selects every tenth man for punishment. *South.*

DECIM'ETER, *n.* A French measure of length equal to the tenth part of a meter, or 3 inches and 93710 decimals.

DECIMO-SEXTO, *n.* [L.] A book is in *decimo-sexto*, when a sheet is folded into sixteen leaves. *Taylor.*

DECI'PHER, *v. t.* [Fr. *dechiffrer*; *de* and *chiffre*, a *cipher*; It. *deciferare*; Sp. *descifrar*; Port. *decifrar*. See *Cipher*.]
1. To find the alphabet of a cipher; to explain what is written in ciphers, by finding what letter each character or mark represents; as, to *decipher* a letter written in ciphers.
2. To unfold; to unravel what is intricate; to explain what is obscure or difficult to be understood; as, to *decipher* an ambiguous speech, or an ancient manuscript or inscription.
3. To write out; to mark down in characters. [*This use is now uncommon, and perhaps improper.*] *Locke.*
4. To stamp; to mark; to characterize. [*Unusual.*] *Shak.*

DECI'PHERED, *pp.* Explained; unravelled; marked.

DECI'PHERER, *n.* One who explains what is written in ciphers.

DECI'PHERING, *ppr.* Explaining; detecting the letters represented by ciphers; unfolding; marking.

DECIS'ION, *n.* *s* as *z*. [L. *decisio*. See *Decide*.]
1. Determination, as of a question or doubt; final judgment or opinion, in a case which has been under deliberation or discussion; as the *decision* of the Supreme Court. He has considered the circumstances of the case and come to a *decision*.
2. Determination of a contest or event; end of a struggle; as the *decision* of a battle by arms.
3. In *Scotland*, a narrative or report of the proceedings of the Court of Sessions. *Johnson.*
4. Report of the opinions and determinations

of any tribunal. We say, read the *decisions* of the Court of King's Bench.

5. Act of separation; division. [*Not used.*]

DECI'SIVE, *a.* Having the power or quality of determining a question, doubt, or any subject of deliberation; final; conclusive; putting an end to controversy; as, the opinion of the court is *decisive* of the question.

2. Having the power of determining a contest or event; as, the victory of the allies was *decisive*.

DECI'SIVELY, *adv.* In a conclusive manner; in a manner to end deliberation, controversy, doubt or contest. *Chesterfield.*

DECI'SIVENESS, *n.* The power of an argument or of evidence to terminate a difference or doubt; conclusiveness.

2. The power of an event to put an end to a contest.

DECI'SORY, *a.* Able to decide or determine. *Sherwood.*

DECK, *v. t.* [D. *dekken*; G. *decken*; Sw. *täckia*; Dan. *tækker*; Sax. *gedecan*, and *thecan* and *theccan*; L. *tego*, to cover, whence *tectum*, a roof, Fr. *toit*. The Gr. has τεγος, a roof, but the verb has a prefix, ςεγω, to cover. Hence L. *tegula*, a *tile*. The Ir. *teach*, a house, contracted in Welsh to *ty*, may be of the same family. In Ger. *dach* is a roof, and *thatch* may be also of this family. Class Dg. No. 2. 3. 10. The primary sense is to put on, to throw over, or to press and make close.]

1. Primarily, to cover; to overspread; to put on. Hence,

2. To clothe; to dress the person; but usually, to clothe with more than ordinary elegance; to array; to adorn; to embellish.

The dew with spangles *decked* the ground. *Dryden.*

3. To furnish with a deck, as a vessel.

DECK, *n.* The covering of a ship, which constitutes a floor, made of timbers and planks. Small vessels have only one deck; larger ships have two or three decks. A *flush deck* is a continued floor from stem to stern, on one line.

2. A pack of cards piled regularly on each other. *Grew.*

DECK'ED, *pp.* Covered; adorned; furnished with a deck.

DECK'ER, *n.* One who decks or adorns; a coverer; as a *table-decker*.

2. Of a ship, we say, she is a *two-decker* or a *three-decker*, that is, she has two decks or three decks.

DECK'ING, *ppr.* Covering; arraying; adorning.

DECK'ING, *n.* Ornament; embellishment. *Homilies.*

DECLA'IM, *v. i.* [L. *declamo*; *de* and *clamo*, to cry out. See *Claim* and *Clamor.*]

1. To speak a set oration in public; to speak rhetorically; to make a formal speech, or oration; as, the students *declaim* twice a week.

2. To harangue; to speak loudly or earnestly, to a public body or assembly, with a view to convince their minds or move their passions.

DECLA'IM, *v. t.* To speak in public.

2. To speak in favor of; to advocate. [*Not in use.*]

DECLA'IMANT, } *n.* One who declaims; **DECLA'IMER**, } a speaker in public; one who attempts to convince by a harangue.

2. One who speaks clamorously.

DECLA'IMING, *ppr.* Speaking rhetorically; haranguing.

DECLA'IMING, *n.* A harangue. *Bp. Taylor.*

DECLAMA'TION, *n.* [L. *declamatio.*] A speech made in public, in the tone and manner of an oration; a discourse addressed to the reason or to the passions; a set speech; a harangue. This word is applied especially to the public speaking and speeches of students in colleges, practiced for exercises in oratory. It is applied also to public speaking in the legislature, and in the pulpit. Very often it is used for a noisy harangue, without solid sense or argument; as, *mere declamation; empty declamation.*

2. A piece spoken in public, or intended for the public.

DECLAMA'TOR, *n.* A declaimer. [*Not used.*] *Taylor.*

DECLAM'ATORY, *a.* [L. *declamatorius.*]

1. Relating to the practice of declaiming; pertaining to declamation; treated in the manner of a rhetorician; as a *declamatory* theme. *Wotton.*

2. Appealing to the passions; noisy; rhetorical without solid sense or argument; as a *declamatory* way or style.

DECLA'RABLE, *a.* [See *Declare.*] That may be declared, or proved.

DECLARA'TION, *n.* [L. *declaratio.*] An affirmation; an open expression of facts or opinions; verbal utterance; as, he declared his sentiments, and I rely on his *declaration.*

2. Expression of facts, opinions, promises, predictions, &c., in writings; records or reports of what has been declared or uttered.

The scriptures abound in *declarations* of mercy to penitent sinners.

3. Publication; manifestation; as the *declaration* of the greatness of Mordecai. Esth. x.

5. A public annunciation; proclamation; as the *Declaration* of Independence, July 4, 1776.

5. In *law*, that part of the process or pleadings in which the plaintiff sets forth at large his cause of complaint; the narration or count.

DECLAR'ATIVE, *a.* Making declaration; explanatory; making show or manifestation; as, the name of a thing may be *declarative* of its form or nature. *Grew.*

2. Making proclamation, or publication.

DECLAR'ATORILY, *adv.* By declaration, or exhibition.

DECLAR'ATORY, *a.* Making declaration, clear manifestation, or exhibition; expressive; as, this clause is *declaratory* of the will of the legislature. The *declaratory* part of a law, is that which sets forth and defines what is right and what is wrong. A *declaratory* act, is an act or statute which sets forth more clearly and explains the intention of the legislature in a former act.

DECLA'RE, *v. t.* [L. *declaro*; *de* and *claro*, to make *clear*; Ir. *gluair*, or *gleair*; W. *eglur*, clear, bright; *egluraw*, to make clear or plain, to manifest, to explain. Fr. *declarer*; Sp. *declarar*; It. *dichiarare*. See *Clear* and *Glory*. The sense is to open, to separate, or to spread.]

1. To clear; to free from obscurity; to make plain. *Boyle.*

[*In this literal sense, the word is no longer in use.*]

2. To make known; to tell explicitly; to manifest or communicate plainly to others by words.

I will *declare* what he hath done for my soul. Ps. lxvi.

3. To make known; to show to the eye or to the understanding; to exhibit; to manifest by other means than words.

The heavens *declare* the glory of God. Ps. xix.

4. To publish; to proclaim.

Declare his glory among the heathen. 1 Chron. xvi.

Declaring the conversion of the Gentiles. Acts xv.

5. To assert; to affirm; as, he *declares* the story to be false.

To declare one's self, to throw off reserve and avow one's opinion; to show openly what one thinks, or which side he espouses.

DECLA'RE, *v. i.* To make a declaration; to proclaim or avow some opinion or resolution in favor or in opposition; to make known explicitly some determination; with *for* or *against*; as, the prince *declared for* the allies; the allied powers *declared against* France.

Like fawning courtiers, for success they wait;
And then come smiling, and *declare* for fate. *Dryden.*

2. In *law*, to recite the causes of complaint against the defendant; as, the plaintiff *declares* in debt or trespass.

3. To show or manifest the issue or event; to decide in favor of; as, victory had not *declared* for either party.

DECLA'RED, *pp.* Made known; told explicitly; avowed; exhibited; manifested; published; proclaimed; recited.

DECLA'REDLY, *adv.* Avowedly; explicitly.

DECLA'RER, *n.* One who makes known or publishes; that which exhibits.

DECLA'RING, *ppr.* Making known by words or by other means; manifesting; publishing; affirming; reciting the cause of complaint.

DECLA'RING, *n.* Declaration; proclamation.

DECLEN'SION, *n.* [L. *declinatio*, from *declino*. See *Decline.*]

1. Literally, a leaning back or down; hence, a falling or declining towards a worse state; a tendency towards a less degree of excellence or perfection. The *declension* of a state is manifested by corruption of morals. We speak of the *declension* of virtue, of manners, of taste, of the sciences, of the fine arts, and sometimes of life or years; but in the latter application, *decline* is more generally used.

2. Declination; a declining; descent; slope; as the *declension* of the shore towards the sea. *Burnet.*

3. In *grammar*, inflection of nouns, adjectives and pronouns; the declining, deviation or leaning of the termination of a word from the termination of the nominative case; change of termination to form the oblique cases. Thus from *rex* in the nominative case, are formed *regis* in the genitive, *regi* in the dative, *regem* in the accusative, and *rege* in the ablative.

DEƇLI'NABLE, *a.* That may be declined; changing its termination in the oblique cases; as a *declinable* noun.

DEƇ'LINATE, *a.* [L. *declinatus.*] In *botany*, bending or bent downwards, in a curve; declining. *Martyn.*

DEƇLINA'TION, *n.* A leaning; the act of bending down; as a *declination* of the head.

2. A declining, or falling into a worse state; change from a better to a worse condition; decay; deterioration; gradual failure or diminution of strength, soundness, vigor or excellence.

3. A deviation from a right line, in a literal sense; oblique motion; as the *declination* of a descending body. *Bentley.*

4. Deviation from rectitude in behavior or morals; obliquity of conduct; as a *declination* from the path of integrity.

5. In *astronomy*, a variation from a fixed point or line. The distance of any celestial object from the equinoctial line, or equator, either northward or southward. *Encyc.*

6. *Declination of the compass or needle*, is the variation of the needle from the true meridian of a place. *Encyc.*

7. In *dialing*, the declination of a wall or plane, is an arch of the horizon, contained between the plane and the prime vertical circle, if reckoned from the east or west, or between the meridian and the plane, if you reckon from the north or south. *Bailey.*

8. In *grammar*, declension; or the inflection of a noun through its various terminations. *Johnson.*

DEƇLINA'TOR, } *n.* An instrument for DEƇLIN'ATORY, } taking the declination, or inclination of a plane; an instrument in dialling. *Encyc. Chambers.*

Declinatory plea, in law, a plea before trial or conviction, intended to show that the party was not liable to the penalty of the law, or was specially exempted from the jurisdiction of the court. The plea of benefit of clergy is a *declinatory* plea. *Blackstone.*

DEƇLI'NE, *v. i.* [L. *declino*; *de* and *clino*, to *lean*. See *Lean.*]

1. To lean downward; as, the head *declines* towards the earth.

2. To lean from a right line; to deviate; *in a literal sense.*

3. To lean or deviate from rectitude, *in a moral sense*; to leave the path of truth or justice, or the course prescribed.

> Yet do I not *decline* from thy testimonies. Ps. cxix. 157.

4. To fall; to tend or draw towards the close; as, the day *declines.*

5. To avoid or shun; to refuse; not to comply; not to do; as, he *declined* to take any part in the concern.

6. To fall; to fail; to sink; to decay; to be impaired; to tend to a less perfect state; as, the vigor of youth *declines* in age; health *declines*; virtue *declines*; religion *declines*; national credit and prosperity *decline*, under a corrupt administration.

7. To sink; to diminish; to fall in value; as, the prices of land and goods *decline* at the close of a war.

DEƇLI'NE, *v. t.* To bend downward; to bring down.

> In melancholy deep, with head *declined.* *Thomson.*

2. To bend to one side; to move from a fixed point or right line.

3. To shun or avoid; to refuse; not to engage in; to be cautious not to do or interfere; not to accept or comply with; as, he *declined* the contest; he *declined* the offer; he *declined* the business or pursuit.

4. To inflect; to change the termination of a word, for forming the oblique cases; as, *Dominus, Domini, Domino, Dominum, Domine.*

DEƇLI'NE, *n.* Literally, a leaning from; hence, a falling off; a tendency to a worse state; diminution or decay; deterioration; as the *decline* of life; the *decline* of strength; the *decline* of virtue and religion; the *decline* of revenues; the *decline* of agriculture, commerce or manufactures; the *decline* of learning.

DEƇLI'NED, *pp.* Bent downward or from; inflected.

DEƇLI'NING, *ppr.* Leaning; deviating; falling; failing; decaying; tending to a worse state; avoiding; refusing; inflecting.

DEƇLIV'ITY, *n.* [L. *declivitas*, from *declivis*, sloping; *de* and *clivus.* See *Cliff.*]

Declination from a horizontal line; descent of land; inclination downward; a slope; a gradual descent of the earth, of a rock or other thing: chiefly used of the earth, and opposed to *acclivity*, or ascent; the same slope, considered as *descending*, being a *declivity*, and considered as *ascending*, an *acclivity.*

DEƇLI'VOUS, } *a.* Gradually descend- DEƇLIV'ITOUS, } ing; not precipitous; sloping.

DEƇOƇT', *v. t.* [L. *decoquo*, *decoctum*; *de* and *coquo*, to *cook*, to boil.]

1. To prepare by boiling; to digest in hot or boiling water. *Bacon.*

2. To digest by the heat of the stomach; to prepare as food for nourishing the body. *Davies.*

3. To boil in water, for extracting the principles or virtues of a substance. *Bacon.*

4. To boil up to a consistence; to invigorate. *Shak.*

[*This verb is little used, and in its last sense, is hardly proper.*]

DEƇOƇT'IBLE, *a.* That may be boiled or digested.

DEƇOƇ'TION, *n.* [Fr. *decoction*; It. *decozione.* See *Decoct.*]

1. The act of boiling a substance in water, for extracting its virtues.

2. The liquor in which a substance has been boiled; water impregnated with the principles of any animal or vegetable substance boiled in it; as a weak or a strong *decoction* of Peruvian bark.

DEƇOƇT'IVE, *a.* That may be easily decocted.

DEƇOƇT'URE, *n.* A substance drawn by decoction.

DE'ƇOLLATE, *v. t.* [L. *decollo.*] To behead. *Burke.*

DE'ƇOLLATED, *pp.* Beheaded.

DEƇOLLA'TION, *n.* [L. *decollatio*, from *decollo*, to behead; *de* and *collum*, the neck.]

The act of beheading; the act of cutting off the neck of an animal, and severing the head from the body. It is especially used of St. John the Baptist, and of a painting which represents his beheading.

DEƇŎLORA'TION, *n.* [L. *decoloratio.*] Absence of color. *Ferrand.*

DE'ƇOMPLEX, *a.* [*de* and *complex.*] Compounded of complex ideas. *Gregory. Locke.*

DEƇOMPO'SABLE, *a.* *s* as *z.* [See *Decompose.*]

That may be decomposed; capable of being resolved into its constituent elements. *Davy.*

DEƇOMPO'SE, *v. t.* *s* as *z.* [Fr. *decomposer*; *de* and *composer*, to *compose*, from L. *compono*, *compositus.*]

To separate the constituent parts of a body or substance; to disunite elementary particles combined by affinity or chimical attraction; to resolve into original elements.

DEƇOMPO'SED, *pp.* Separated or resolved into the constituent parts.

DEƇOMPO'SING, *ppr.* Separating into constituent parts.

DEƇOMPOS'ITE, *a.* *decompoz'it.* [L. *de* and *compositus.* See *Compose.*]

Compounded a second time; compounded with things already composite. *Bacon.*

DEƇOMPOSI''TION, *n.* Analysis; the act of separating the constituent parts of a substance, which are chimically combined. Decomposition differs from mechanical division, as the latter effects no change in the properties of the body divided, whereas the parts chimically decomposed have properties very different from those of the substance itself.

2. A second composition. [*In this sense, not now used.*] *Boyle.*

DEƇOMPOUND', *v. t.* [*de* and *compound.*] To compound a second time; to compound or mix with that which is already compound; to form by a second composition. *Boyle. Locke. Newton.*

2. To decompose. [*Little used, or not at all.*]

DEƇOMPOUND', *a.* Composed of things or words already compounded; compounded a second time. *Boyle.*

2. A *decompound leaf*, in botany, is when the primary petiole is so divided that each part forms a compound leaf. A *decompound flower* is formed of compound flowers, or containing, within a common calyx, smaller calyxes, common to several flowers. *Martyn.*

DEƇOMPOUND'ABLE, *a.* That may be decompounded.

DEƇOMPOUND'ED, *pp.* Compounded a second time; composed of things already compounded.

DEƇOMPOUND'ING, *ppr.* Compounding a second time.

DEƇ'ORATE, *v. t.* [L. *decoro*, from *decus*, *decor*, comeliness, grace. See *Decency.*]

1. To adorn; to beautify; to embellish; used of external ornaments or apparel; as, to *decorate* the person; to *decorate* an edifice; to *decorate* a lawn with flowers.

2. To adorn with internal grace or beauty; to render lovely; as, to *decorate* the mind with virtue.

3. To adorn or beautify with any thing agreeable; to embellish; as, to *decorate* a hero with honors, or a lady with accomplishments.

DEC'ORATED, *pp.* Adorned; beautified; embellished.

DEC'ORATING, *ppr.* Adorning; embellishing; rendering beautiful to the eye, or lovely to the mind.

DECORA'TION, *n.* Ornament; embellishment; any thing added which renders more agreeable to the eye or to the intellectual view.

2. In *architecture*, any thing which adorns and enriches an edifice, as vases, paintings, figures, festoons, &c.

3. In *theaters*, the scenes, which are changed as occasion requires.

DEC'ORATOR, *n.* One who adorns or embellishes.

DECO'ROUS, *a.* [L. *decorus.* See *Decency.*] Decent; suitable to a character, or to the time, place and occasion; becoming; proper; befitting; as a *decorous* speech; *decorous* behavior; a *decorous* dress for a judge.

DEC'OROUSLY, *adv.* In a becoming manner.

DECOR'TICATE, *v. t.* [L. *decortico; de* and *cortex*, bark.]
To strip off bark; to peel; to husk; to take off the exterior coat; as, to *decorticate* barley. *Arbuthnot.*

DECOR'TICATED, *pp.* Stripped of bark; peeled; husked.

DECOR'TICATING, *ppr.* Stripping off bark or the external coat; peeling.

DECORTICA'TION, *n.* The act of stripping off bark or husk.

DECO'RUM, *n.* [L. from *deceo*, to become. See *Decency.*]

1. Propriety of speech or behavior; suitableness of speech and behavior, to one's own character, and to the characters present, or to the place and occasion; seemliness; decency; opposed to rudeness, licentiousness, or levity.

To speak and behave with *decorum* is essential to good breeding.

2. In *architecture*, the suitableness of a building, and of its parts and ornaments, to its place and uses.

DECOY', *v. t.* [D. *kooi*, a cabin, birth, bed, fold, cage, decoy; *kooijen*, to lie, to bed.]
To lead or lure by artifice into a snare, with a view to catch; to draw into any situation to be taken by a foe; to entrap by any means which deceive. The fowler *decoys* ducks into a net. Troops may be *decoyed* into an ambush. One ship *decoys* another within reach of her shot.

DECOY', *n.* Any thing intended to lead into a snare; any lure or allurement that deceives and misleads into evil, danger or the power of an enemy.

2. A place for catching wild fowls.

DECOY'-DUCK, *n.* A duck employed to draw others into a net or situation to be taken.

DECOY'ED, *pp.* Lured or drawn into a snare or net; allured into danger by deception.

DECOY'ING, *ppr.* Luring into a snare or net by deception; leading into evil or danger.

DECOY'-MAN, *n.* A man employed in decoying and catching fowls.

DECRE'ASE, *v. i.* [L. *decresco; de* and *cresco*, to grow; Fr. *decroitre;* It. *decrescere;* Sp. *decrecer;* Arm. *digrisgi.* See *Grow.*]
To become less; to be diminished gradually, in extent, bulk, quantity, or amount, or in strength, quality, or excellence; as, the days *decrease* in length from June to December.

He must increase, but I must *decrease.* John iii.

DECRE'ASE, *v. t.* To lessen; to make smaller in dimensions, amount, quality or excellence, &c.; to diminish gradually or by small deductions; as, extravagance *decreases* the means of charity; every payment *decreases* a debt; intemperance *decreases* the strength and powers of life.

DECRE'ASE, *n.* A becoming less; gradual diminution; decay; as a *decrease* of revenue; a *decrease* of strength.

2. The wane of the moon; the gradual diminution of the visible face of the moon from the full to the change.

DECRE'ASED, *pp.* Lessened; diminished.

DECRE'ASING, *ppr.* Becoming less; diminishing; waning.

DECREE', *n.* [L. *decretum*, from *decerno*, to judge; *de* and *cerno*, to judge, to divide; Fr. *decret;* It. and Sp. *decreto.*]

1. Judicial decision, or determination of a litigated cause; as a *decree* of the court of chancery. The decision of a court of equity is called a *decree;* that of a court of law, a *judgment.*

2. In *the civil law*, a determination or judgment of the emperor on a suit between parties. *Encyc.*

3. An edict or law made by a council for regulating any business within their jurisdiction; as the *decrees* of ecclesiastical councils. *Encyc.*

4. In *general*, an order, edict or law made by a superior as a rule to govern inferiors.

There went a *decree* from Cesar Augustus, that all the world should be taxed. Luke ii.

5. Established law, or rule.

He made a *decree* for the rain. Job xxviii.

6. In *theology*, predetermined purpose of God; the purpose or determination of an immutable Being, whose plan of operations is, like himself, unchangeable.

DECREE', *v. t.* To determine judicially; to resolve by sentence; as, the court *decreed* that the property should be restored; or they *decreed* a restoration of the property.

2. To determine or resolve legislatively; to fix or appoint; to set or constitute by edict or in purpose.

Thou shalt *decree* a thing, and it shall be established. Job xxii.

Let us not be solicitous to know what God has *decreed* concerning us. *Anon.*

DECREE'D, *pp.* Determined judicially; resolved; appointed; established in purpose.

DECREE'ING, *ppr.* Determining; resolving; appointing; ordering.

DEC'REMENT, *n.* [L. *decrementum*, from *decresco.* See *Decrease.*]

1. Decrease; waste; the state of becoming less gradually.

Rocks and mountains suffer a continual *decrement.* *Woodward.*

2. The quantity lost by gradual diminution, or waste.

3. In *heraldry*, the wane of the moon.

4. In *crystalography*, a successive diminution of the lamens of molecules, applied to the faces of the primitive form, by which the secondary forms are supposed to be produced. *Haüy.*

DECREP'IT, *a.* [L. *decrepitus*, from *de* and *crepo*, to break.]
Broken down with age; wasted or worn by the infirmities of old age; being in the last stage of decay; weakened by age. *Milton. Pope.*

DECREP'ITATE, *v. t.* [L. *decrepo*, to break or burst, to crackle; *de* and *crepo.*]
To roast or calcine in a strong heat, with a continual bursting or crackling of the substance; as, to *decrepitate* salt.

DECREP'ITATE, *v. i.* To crackle, as salts when roasting.

DECREP'ITATED, *pp.* Roasted with a crackling noise.

DECREP'ITATING, *ppr.* Crackling; roasting with a crackling noise; suddenly bursting when exposed to heat.

DECREPITA'TION, *n.* The act of roasting with a continual crackling; or the separation of parts with a crackling noise, occasioned by heat.

DECREP'ITNESS, } *n.* [See *Decrepit.*] The
DECREP'ITUDE, } broken, crazy state of the body, produced by decay and the infirmities of age.

DECRES'CENT, *a.* [L. *decrescens.* See *Decrease.*]
Decreasing; becoming less by gradual diminution; as a *decrescent* moon.

DECRE'TAL, *a.* [See *Decree.*] Appertaining to a decree; containing a decree; as a *decretal* epistle. *Ayliffe.*

DECRE'TAL, *n.* A letter of the pope, determining some point or question in ecclesiastical law. The *decretals* form the second part of the canon law. *Encyc.*

2. A book of decrees, or edicts; a body of laws. *Spenser.*

3. A collection of the pope's decrees. *Howell.*

DECRE'TION, *n.* [See *Decrease.*] A decreasing. [*Not used.*] *Pearson.*

DECRE'TIST, *n.* One who studies or professes the knowledge of the decretals.

DEC'RETORILY, *adv.* In a definitive manner. *Goodman.*

DEC'RETORY, *a.* Judicial; definitive; established by a decree.

The *decretory* rigors of a condemning sentence. *South.*

2. Critical; determining; in which there is some definitive event; as, critical or *decretory* days. *Brown.*

DECREW', *v. i.* To decrease. [*Not in use.*]

DECRI'AL, *n.* [See *Decry.*] A crying down; a clamorous censure; condemnation by censure.

DECRI'ED, *pp.* Cried down; discredited; brought into disrepute.

DECRI'ER, *n.* One who decries.

DECROWN', *v. t.* [*de* and *crown.*] To deprive of a crown. [*Little used.*] *Overbury.*

DECRY', *v. t.* [Fr. *decrier; de* and *crier*, to cry.] To cry down; to censure as faulty, mean or worthless; to clamor against; to discredit by finding fault; as, to *decry* a poem.

2. To cry down, as improper or unnecessary; to rail or clamor against; to bring in-

to disrepute; as, to *decry* the measures of administration.

DECUBA'TION, *n.* [L. *decumbo.*] The act of lying down. *Evelyn.*

DECUM'BENCE, } *n.* [L. *decumbens*, from DECUM'BENCY, } *decumbo*, to lie down; *de* and *cumbo*, to lie down.]

The act of lying down; the posture of lying down. *Brown.*

DECUM'BENT, *a.* In *botany*, declined or bending down; having the stamens and pistils bending down to the lower side; as a *decumbent* flower. *Martyn.*

DECUM'BITURE, *n.* The time at which a person takes to his bed in a disease.

2. In *astrology*, the scheme or aspect of the heavens, by which the prognostics of recovery or death are discovered.

DEC'UPLE, *a.* [L. *decuplus*; Gr. δεκαπλους, from δεκα, ten.] Tenfold; containing ten times as many.

DEC'UPLE, *n.* A number ten times repeated.

DECU'RION, *n.* [L. *decurio*, from *decem*, Gr. δεκα, ten.]

An officer in the Roman army, who commanded a *decuria*, or ten soldiers, which was a third part of the turma, and a thirtieth of the legion of cavalry. *Encyc. Temple.*

DECUR'RENT, *a.* [L. *decurrens*, from *decurro*, to run down; *de* and *curro*, to run.]

Extending downwards. A *decurrent* leaf is a sessile leaf having its base extending downwards along the stem. *Martyn.*

DECUR'SION, *n.* [L. *decursio*, from *decurro*; *de* and *curro*, to run.]

The act of running down, as a stream. *Hale.*

DECUR'SIVE, *a.* Running down.

Decursively pinnate, in botany, applied to a leaf, having the leaflets decurrent or running along the petiole.

DECURT', *v. t.* [L. *decurto.*] To shorten by cutting off. [*Not in use.*]

DECURTA'TION, *n.* [L. *decurto*, to shorten; *de* and *curto.*] The act of shortening, or cutting short.

DEC'URY, *n.* [L. *decuria*, from *decem*, Gr. δεκα, ten.] A set of ten men under an officer called *decurio*.

DE'CUSSATE, *v. t.* [L. *decusso*, to cut or strike across.]

To intersect at acute angles, thus X; or in general, to intersect; to cross; as lines, rays, or nerves in the body. *Encyc.*

DE'CUSSATE, } *a.* Crossed; intersected. DE'CUSSATED, } In botany, *decussated* leaves and branches, are such as grow in pairs which alternately cross each other at right angles, or in a regular manner. *Martyn. Lee.*

In rhetoric, a *decussated* period is one that consists of two rising and two falling clauses, placed in alternate opposition to each other. For example, "If impudence could effect as much in courts of justice, as insolence sometimes does in the country, Cæsina would now yield to the impudence of Ebutius, as he then yielded to his insolent assault." *J. Q. Adams, Lect.*

DE'CUSSATING, *ppr.* Intersecting at acute angles; crossing.

DECUSSA'TION, *n.* The act of crossing at unequal angles; the crossing of two lines, rays or nerves, which meet in a point and then proceed and diverge. *Encyc.*

DEDA'LIAN, *a.* [from *Dædalus*, the Athenian, who invented sails or wings.] Various; variegated; intricate; complex; expert.

DED'ALOUS, *a.* [from *Dædalus.*] Having a margin with various windings and turnings; of a beautiful and delicate texture; *a term applied to the leaves of plants.* *Martyn. Lee.*

DEDEC'ORATE, *v. t.* [L. *dedecoro.*] To disgrace. [*Not used.*]

DEDECORA'TION, *n.* A disgracing. [*Not used.*]

DEDENTI''TION, *n.* [*de* and *dentition.*] The shedding of teeth. *Brown.*

DED'ICATE, *v. t.* [L. *dedico*; *de* and *dico*, *dicare*, to vow, promise, devote, dedicate. See Class Dg. No. 12. 15. 45. The sense is to send, to throw; hence, to set, to appoint.]

1. To set apart and consecrate to a divine Being, or to a sacred purpose; to devote to a sacred use, by a solemn act, or by religious ceremonies; as, to *dedicate* vessels, treasures, a temple, an altar, or a church, to God or to a religious use.

> Vessels of silver, of gold, and of brass, which king David did *dedicate* to the Lord. 2 Sam. viii.

2. To appropriate solemnly to any person or purpose; to give wholly or chiefly to. The ministers of the gospel *dedicate* themselves, their time and their studies, to the service of Christ. A soldier *dedicates* himself to the profession of arms.

3. To inscribe or address to a patron; as, to *dedicate* a book.

DED'ICATE, *a.* Consecrated; devoted; appropriated. *Shak.*

DED'ICATED, *pp.* Devoted to a divine Being, or to a sacred use; consecrated; appropriated; given wholly to.

DED'ICATING, *ppr.* Devoting to a divine Being, or to a sacred purpose; consecrating; appropriating; giving wholly to.

DEDICA'TION, *n.* The act of consecrating to a divine Being, or to a sacred use, often with religious solemnities; solemn appropriation; as the *dedication* of Solomon's temple.

2. The act of devoting or giving to.

3. An address to a patron, prefixed to a book, testifying respect and recommending the work to his protection and favor. *Pope.*

DED'ICATOR, *n.* One who dedicates; one who inscribes a book to the favor of a patron. *Pope.*

DED'ICATORY, *a.* Composing a dedication; as an epistle *dedicatory.*

DEDI''TION, *n.* [L. *deditio*, from *dedo*, to yield.]

The act of yielding any thing; surrendry. *Hale.*

DED'OLENT, *a.* [L. *dedoleo.*] Feeling no compunction. [*Not used.*]

DEDU'CE, *v. t.* [L. *deduco*; *de* and *duco*, to lead, bring or draw. The L. *duco* is the Sax. *teogan*, *teon*, Eng. to *tug*, to *tow*, G. *ziehen*; hence L. *dux*, Eng. *duke*. See *Duke*. Class Dg. No. 5. 12. 15. 37. 62. 64.]

1. To draw from; to bring from.

> O goddess, say, shall I *deduce* my rhymes
> From the dire nation in its early times? *Pope.*

2. To draw from, in reasoning; to gather a truth, opinion or proposition from premises; to infer something from what precedes.

> Reasoning is nothing but the faculty of *deducing* unknown truths from principles already known. *Locke.*

3. To deduct. [*Not in use.*] *B. Jonson.*

4. To transplant. [*Not in use.*] *Selden.*

DEDU'CED, *pp.* Drawn from; inferred; as a consequence from principles or premises.

DEDU'CEMENT, *n.* The thing drawn from or deduced; inference; that which is collected from premises. *Dryden.*

DEDU'CIBLE, *a.* That may be deduced; inferable; collectible by reason from premises; consequential.

> The properties of a triangle are *deducible* from the complex idea of three lines including a space. *Locke.*

DEDU'CING, *ppr.* Drawing from; inferring; collecting from principles or facts already established or known.

DEDU'CIVE, *a.* Performing the act of deduction. [*Little used.*]

DEDUCT', *v. t.* [L. *deduco*, *deductum*. See *Deduce.*]

To take from; to subtract; to separate or remove, in numbering, estimating or calculating. Thus we say, from the sum of two numbers, *deduct* the lesser number; from the amount of profits, *deduct* the charges of freight.

DEDUCT'ED, *pp.* Taken from; subtracted.

DEDUCT'ING, *ppr.* Taking from; subtracting.

DEDUC'TION, *n.* [L. *deductio.*] The act of deducting.

2. That which is deducted; sum or amount taken from another; defalcation; abatement; as, this sum is a *deduction* from the yearly rent.

3. That which is drawn from premises; fact, opinion, or hypothesis, collected from principles or facts stated, or established data; inference; consequence drawn; conclusion; as, this opinion is a fair *deduction* from the principles you have advanced.

DEDUCT'IVE, *a.* Deducible; that is or may be deduced from premises.

> All knowledge is *deductive.* *Glanville.*

DEDUCT'IVELY, *adv.* By regular deduction; by way of inference; by consequence. *Brown.*

DEED, *n.* [Sax. *dæd*; D. *daad*; G. *that*; Dan *daad*; the participle of Sax. *don*, Goth. *tauyan*, G. *thun*, D. *doen*, to do; probably a contracted word.]

1. That which is done, acted or effected; an act; a fact; a word of extensive application, including whatever is done, good or bad, great or small.

> And Joseph said to them, what *deed* is this which ye have done? Gen. xliv.
>
> We receive the due reward of our *deeds.* Luke xxv.

2. Exploit; achievement; illustrious act.

> Whose *deeds* some nobler poem shall adorn. *Dryden.*

3. Power of action; agency.

> With will and *deed* created free. *Milton.*

4. A writing containing some contract or agreement, and the evidence of its execu-

tion; particularly, an instrument on paper or parchment, conveying real estate to a purchaser or donee. This instrument must be executed, and the execution attested, in the manner prescribed by law.

Indeed, in fact; in reality. These words are united and called an adverb. But sometimes they are separated by *very, in very deed;* a more emphatical expression. Ex. ix.

DEED, *v. t.* To convey or transfer by deed; *a popular use of the word in America;* as, he *deeded* all his estate to his eldest son.

DEED-ACHIE'VING, *a.* That accomplishes great deeds.

DEE'DLESS, *a.* Inactive; not performing or having performed deeds or exploits. *Pope.*

DEED-POLL, *n.* A deed not indented, that is, shaved or even, made by one party only. *Blackstone.*

DEEM, *v. t.* [Sax. *deman;* D. *doemen;* Sw. *dôma;* Dan. *dömmer;* whence *doom.* Russ. *dumayu*, to think, reflect, reckon, believe; *duma*, a thought or idea, a privy council; *dumnoi*, a privy counselor. See Class Dm. No. 5. 36. 39. and Class Sm. No. 5.]

1. To think; to judge; to be of opinion; to conclude on consideration; as, he *deems* it prudent to be silent.

For never can I *deem* him less than god. *Dryden.*

The shipmen *deemed* that they drew near to some country. Acts xxvii.

2. To estimate. [*Obs.*] *Spenser.*

DEEM, *n.* Opinion; judgment; surmise. [*Obs.*] *Shak.*

DEE'MED, *pp.* Thought; judged; supposed.

DEE'MING, *ppr.* Thinking; judging; believing.

DEE'MSTER, *n.* [*deem* and *ster.* See *Steer.*] A judge in the Isle of Man and in Jersey. *Johnson.*

DEEP, *a.* [Sax. *deop, dypa;* D. *diep;* G. *tief;* Sw. *diup;* Dan. *dyb.* It seems to be allied to *dip* and *dive*, whose radical sense is to thrust or plunge. Qu. W. *dwvyn.*]

1. Extending or being far below the surface; descending far downward; profound; opposed to *shallow;* as *deep* water; a *deep* pit or well.

2. Low in situation; being or descending far below the adjacent land; as a *deep* valley.

3. Entering far; piercing a great way. A tree in a good soil takes *deep* root. A spear struck *deep* into the flesh.

4. Far from the outer part; secreted.

A spider *deep* ambushed in her den. *Dryden.*

5. Not superficial or obvious; hidden; secret.

He discovereth *deep* things out of darkness. Job xii.

6. Remote from comprehension.

O Lord, thy thoughts are very *deep.* Ps. xcii.

7. Sagacious; penetrating; having the power to enter far into a subject; as a man of *deep* thought; a *deep* divine.

8. Artful; contriving; concealing artifice; insidious; designing; as a friend, *deep*, hollow, treacherous.

9. Grave in sound; low; as the *deep* tones of an organ.

10. Very still; solemn; profound; as *deep* silence.

11. Thick; black; not to be penetrated by the sight.

Now *deeper* darkness brooded on the ground. *Hoole.*

12. Still; sound; not easily broken or disturbed.

The Lord God caused a *deep* sleep to fall on Adam. Gen. ii.

13. Depressed; sunk low, metaphorically; as *deep* poverty.

14. Dark; intense; strongly colored; as a *deep* brown; a *deep* crimson; a *deep* blue.

15. Unknown; unintelligible.

A people of *deeper* speech than thou canst perceive. Is. xxxiii.

16. Heart-felt; penetrating; affecting; as a *deep* sense of guilt.

17. Intricate; not easily understood or unraveled; as a *deep* plot or intrigue.

This word often qualifies a verb, like an adverb.

Drink *deep*, or taste not the Pierian spring. *Pope.*

DEEP, *n.* The sea; the abyss of waters; the ocean.

He maketh the *deep* to boil like a pot. Job xli.

2. A lake; a great collection of water.

Lanch out into the *deep*, and let down your nets. Luke v.

3. That which is profound, not easily fathomed, or incomprehensible.

Thy judgments are a great *deep.* Ps. xxxvi.

4. The most still or solemn part; the midst; as, in *deep* of night. *Shak. Philips.*

DEE'P-DRAWING, *a.* Sinking deep into the water. *Shak.*

DEE'PEN, *v. t.* dee'pn. To make deep or deeper; to sink lower; as, to *deepen* the channel of a river or harbor; to *deepen* a well.

2. To make dark or darker; to make more thick or gloomy; as, to *deepen* the shades of night; to *deepen* gloom.

3. To give a darker hue, or a stronger color; as, to *deepen* a color; to *deepen* a red, blue or crimson color.

4. To make more poignant or distressing; as, to *deepen* grief or sorrow.

5. To make more frightful; as, to *deepen* the horrors of the scene.

6. To make more sad or gloomy; as, to *deepen* the murmurs of the flood.

7. To make more grave; as, to *deepen* the tones of an organ.

DEE'PEN, *v. i.* To become more deep; as, the water *deepens* at every cast of the lead.

DEE'PENED, *pp.* Made more deep.

DEE'PENING, *ppr.* Sinking lower; making more deep.

DEE'PLY, *adv.* At or to a great depth; far below the surface; as a passion *deeply* rooted in our nature; precepts *deeply* engraven on the heart.

2. Profoundly; thoroughly; as *deeply* skilled in ethics or anatomy.

3. To or from the inmost recesses of the heart; with great sorrow; most feelingly.

He sighed *deeply* in his spirit. Mark viii.

He was *deeply* affected at the sight. *Anon.*

4. To a great degree; as, he has *deeply* offended.

They have *deeply* corrupted themselves. Hos. ix.

5. With a dark hue, or strong color; as a *deeply* red liquor; *deeply* colored.

6. Gravely; as a *deeply* toned instrument.

7. With profound skill; with art or intricacy; as a *deeply* laid plot or intrigue.

This word cannot easily be defined in all its various applications. In general it gives emphasis or intensity to the word which it qualifies.

DEE'P-MOUTHED, *a.* Having a hoarse, loud, hollow voice; as a *deep-mouthed* dog. *Shak.*

DEE'P-MUSING, *a.* Contemplative; thinking closely or profoundly. *Pope.*

DEE'PNESS, *n.* Depth; remoteness from the surface in a descending line; interior distance from the surface; profundity.

And forthwith they sprung up, because they had no *deepness* of earth. Matt. xiii.

2. Craft; insidiousness. [*Unusual.*]

DEE'P-READ, *a.* Having fully read; profoundly versed. *L'Estrange.*

DEEP-REVOLV'ING, *a.* Profoundly revolving or meditating. *Shak.*

DEE'P-THROATED, *a.* With deep throats. *Milton.*

DEE'P-TONED, *a.* Having a very low or grave tone.

DEE'P-VAULTED, *a.* Formed like a deep vault or arch. *Milton.*

DEE'P-WAISTED, *a.* Having a deep waist, as a ship when the quarter deck and forecastle are raised from four to six feet above the level of the main deck. *Mar. Dict.*

DEER, *n. sing.* and *plu.* [Sax. *deor;* D. *dier;* G. *thier;* Sw. *diur;* Dan. *dyr;* Polish *zwiers;* Gr. θηρ, a wild beast. The primary sense is simply roving, wild, untamed; hence, a wild beast.]

A quadruped of the genus *Cervus*, of several species, as the stag, the fallow deer, the roe-buck, the rane or rane-deer, &c. These animals are wild and hunted in the forest, or kept in parks. Their flesh called venison, is deemed excellent food.

DEE'R-STEALER, *n.* One who steals deer.

DEE'R-STEALING, *n.* The act or crime of stealing deer.

DE'ESS, *n.* [Fr. *deesse.*] A goddess. [*Not in use.*] *Croft.*

DEFA'CE, *v. t.* [Arm. *difaçza;* *de* and L. *facio;* Fr. *defaire*, to undo or unmake.]

1. To destroy or mar the face or surface of a thing; to injure the superficies or beauty; to disfigure; as, to *deface* a monument; to *deface* an edifice.

2. To injure any thing; to destroy, spoil or mar; to erase or obliterate; as, to *deface* letters or writing; to *deface* a note, deed or bond; to *deface* a record.

3. To injure the appearance; to disfigure.

DEFA'CED, *pp.* Injured on the surface; disfigured; marred; erased.

DEFA'CEMENT, *n.* Injury to the surface or beauty; rasure; obliteration; that which mars beauty or disfigures.

DEFA'CER, *n.* He or that which defaces; one who injures, mars or disfigures.

DEFA'CING, *ppr.* Injuring the face or surface; marring; disfiguring; erasing.

De facto. [L.] actually; in fact; existing; as a king *de facto*, distinguished from a king *de jure*, or by right.

DEFA'ILANCE, *n.* [Fr. See *Fail.*] Failure; miscarriage. *Obs.* *Taylor.*

DEFAL'CATE, *v. t.* [Fr. *defalquer;* It. *defalcare;* Sp. *desfalcar;* Port. *desfalcar;* from L. *defalco; de* and *falco*, from *falx*, a sickle.]

To cut off; to take away or deduct a part; used chiefly of money, accounts, rents, income, &c.

DEFALCA'TION, *n.* The act of cutting off, or deducting a part; deduction; diminution; abatement; as, let him have the amount of his rent without *defalcation.*

2. That which is cut off; as, this loss is a *defalcation* from the revenue.

DEFALK, *v. t.* To defalcate. [*Not in use.*] *Bp. Hall.*

DEFAMA'TION, *n.* [See *Defame.*] The uttering of slanderous words with a view to injure another's reputation; the malicious uttering of falsehood respecting another which tends to destroy or impair his good name, character or occupation; slander; calumny. To constitute defamation in law, the words must be false and spoken maliciously. Defamatory words written and published are called a *libel.* *Blackstone.*

DEFAM'ATORY, *a.* Calumnious; slanderous; containing defamation; false and injurious to reputation; as *defamatory* words; *defamatory* reports or writings.

DEFA'ME, *v. t.* [Fr. *diffamer;* It. *diffamare;* Sp. *disfamar;* from L. *diffamo; de* or *dis* and *fama*, fame.]

1. To slander; falsely and maliciously to utter words respecting another which tend to injure his reputation or occupation; as to say, a judge is corrupt; a man is perjured; a trader is a knave.

2. To speak evil of; to dishonor by false reports; to calumniate; to libel; to impair reputation by acts or words.

Being *defamed*, we entreat. 1 Cor. iv.

DEFA'MED, *pp.* Slandered; dishonored or injured by evil reports.

DEFA'MER, *n.* A slanderer; a detractor; a calumniator.

DEFA'MING, *ppr.* Slandering; injuring the character by false reports.

DEFA'MING, *n.* Defamation; slander. *Jeremiah.*

DEFAT'IGABLE, *a.* Liable to be wearied. [*Not much used.*] *Glanville.*

DEFAT'IGATE, *v. t.* [L. *defatigo; de* and *fatigo*, to tire. See *Fatigue.*] To weary or tire. [*Little used.*] *Herbert.*

DEFATIGA'TION, *n.* Weariness. [*Little used.*] *Bacon.*

DEFAULT', *n.* [Fr. *defaut*, for *default*, from *defaillir*, to fail; *de* and *faillir*, to fail. See *Fail* and *Fault.*]

1. A failing, or failure; an omission of that which ought to be done; neglect to do what duty or law requires; as, this evil has happened through the governor's *default.* A *default* or *fault*, may be a crime, a vice, or a mere defect, according to the nature of the duty omitted.

2. Defect; want; failure.

Cooks could make artificial birds, in *default* of real ones. *Arbuthnot.*

3. In *law*, a failure of appearance in court at a day assigned, particularly of the defendant in a suit when called to make answer. It may be applied to jurors, witnesses, &c.; but a plaintiff's failing to appear by himself or attorney, is usually called a *non-appearance.*

To suffer a default, is to permit an action to be called without appearing or answering; *applied to a defendant.*

DEFAULT, *v. i.* To fail in performing a contract or agreement. *Johnson.*

DEFAULT', *v. t.* In *law*, to call out a defendant, [according to the common expression.] To call a defendant officially, to appear and answer in court, and on his failing to answer, to declare him in default, and enter judgment against him; as, let the defendant be *defaulted.*

No costs are to be awarded for such town, if *defaulted.* *Mass. Laws.*

2. To call out a cause, in which the defendant does not appear, and enter judgment on the default; as, the cause was *defaulted.*

3. To fail in performance. *Milton.*

DEFAULT, *v. t.* To offend. *Obs.*

DEFAULT'ED, *pp.* Called out of court, as a defendant or his cause.

2. *a.* Having defect.

DEFAULT'ER, *n.* One who makes default; one who fails to appear in court when called.

2. One who fails to perform a public duty; particularly, one who fails to account for public money entrusted to his care; a delinquent.

DEFAULT'ING, *ppr.* Failing to fulfil a contract; delinquent.

2. Failing to perform a duty or legal requirement; as a *defaulting* creditor. *Walsh.*

3. Calling out of court, and entering judgment against for non-appearance, as a defendant.

DEFE'ASANCE, *n. s* as *z.* [Norm. *defesance;* Fr. *defesant*, from *defaire*, to undo; *de* and *faire*, L. *facio.*]

1. Literally, a defeating; a rendering null; the preventing of the operation of an instrument.

2. In *law*, a condition, relating to a deed, which being performed, the deed is defeated or rendered void; or a collateral deed, made at the same time with a feoffment or other conveyance, containing conditions, on the performance of which the estate then created may be *defeated.* A *defeasance*, on a bond, or a recognizance, or a judgment recovered, is a condition which, when performed, *defeats* it. A *defeasance* differs from the common condition of a bond, in being a separate deed, whereas a common condition is inserted in the bond itself. *Blackstone.*

3. The writing containing a defeasance.

4. Defeat. *Obs.* *Spenser.*

DEFE'ASIBLE, *a. s* as *z.* That may be defeated, or annulled; as a *defeasible* title; a *defeasible* estate.

DEFE'ASIBLENESS, *n.* The quality of being defeasible.

DEFE'AT, *n.* [Fr. *defaite*, from *defaire*, to undo; *de* and *faire.*]

1. Overthrow; loss of battle; the check, rout, or destruction of an army by the victory of an enemy.

2. Successful resistance; as the *defeat* of an attack.

3. Frustration; a rendering null and void; as the *defeat* of a title.

4. Frustration; prevention of success; as the *defeat* of a plan or design.

DEFE'AT, *v. t.* To overcome or vanquish, as an army; to check, disperse or ruin by victory; to overthrow; *applied to an army, or a division of troops; to a fleet, or to a commander.*

The English army *defeated* the French on the plains of Abraham. Gen. Wolf *defeated* Montcalm. The French *defeated* the Austrians at Marengo.

2. To frustrate; to prevent the success of; to disappoint.

Then mayest thou for me *defeat* the counsel of Ahithophel. 2 Sam. xv. and xvii.

We say, our dearest hopes are often *defeated.*

3. To render null and void; as, to *defeat* a title or an estate.

4. To resist with success; as, to *defeat* an attempt or assault.

DEFE'ATED, *pp.* Vanquished; effectually resisted; overthrown; frustrated; disappointed; rendered null or inoperative.

DEFE'ATING, *ppr.* Vanquishing; subduing; opposing successfully; overthrowing; frustrating; disappointing; rendering null and void.

DEFE'ATURE, *n.* Change of feature. *Shak.*

2. Overthrow; defeat. *Obs.* *Beaum.*

DEF'ECATE, *v. t.* [L. *defæco; de* and *fæx*, dregs.]

1. To purify; to refine; to clear from dregs or impurities; to clarify; as, to *defecate* liquor.

2. To purify from admixture; to clear; to purge of extraneous matter.

DEF'ECATED, *pp.* Purified; clarified; refined.

DEF'ECATING, *ppr.* Purifying; purging of lees or impurities.

DEFECA'TION, *n.* The act of separating from lees or dregs; purification from impurities or foreign matter.

DEFECT', *n.* [L. *defectus;* It. *difetto;* Sp. *defecto;* from L. *deficio*, to fail; *de* and *facio*, to make or do.]

1. Want or absence of something necessary or useful towards perfection; fault; imperfection.

Errors have been corrected, and *defects* supplied. *Davies.*

We say, there are numerous *defects* in the plan, or in the work, or in the execution.

2. Failing; fault; mistake; imperfection in moral conduct, or in judgment.

A deep conviction of the *defects* of our lives tends to make us humble.

Trust not yourself; but, your *defects* to know,
Make use of every friend and every foe. *Pope.*

3. Any want, or imperfection, in natural objects; the absence of any thing necessary to perfection; any thing unnatural or misplaced; blemish; deformity. We speak of a *defect* in the organs of seeing or hearing, or in a limb; a *defect* in timber; a *defect* in an instrument, &c.

DEFECT', *v. i.* To be deficient. [*Not in use.*] *Brown.*

DEFECTIBIL'ITY, *n.* Deficiency; imperfection. [*Little used.*] *Digby. Hale.*

DEFECT'IBLE, *a.* Imperfect; deficient; wanting. [*Little used.*] *Hale.*

DEFEC'TION, *n.* [L. *defectio.* See *Defect.*]

1. Want or failure of duty; particularly, a falling away; apostasy; the act of aban-

doning a person or cause to which one is bound by allegiance or duty, or to which one has attached himself. Our *defection* from God is proof of our depravity. The cause of the king was rendered desperate by the *defection* of the nobles.

2. Revolt; *used of nations or states.*

DEFEC'TIVE, *a.* [L. *defectivus.* See *Defect.*]

1. Wanting either in substance, quantity or quality, or in any thing necessary; imperfect; as a *defective* limb; *defective* timber; a *defective* copy or book; a *defective* account. *Defective* articulation, in speaking, renders utterance indistinct.

2. Wanting in moral qualities; faulty; blamable; not conforming to rectitude or rule; as a *defective* character.

3. In *grammar*, a *defective* noun is one which wants a whole number or a particular case; an indeclinable noun.

4. A *defective* verb, is one which wants some of the tenses.

DEFEC'TIVELY, *adv.* In a defective manner; imperfectly.

DEFEC'TIVENESS, *n.* Want; the state of being imperfect; faultiness.

DEFECTUOS'ITY, *n.* Defectiveness; faultiness. [*Not used.*] *Montagu.*

DEFEC'TUOUS, *a.* Full of defects. [*Little used.*] *Worthington.*

DEFEDA'TION, *n.* Pollution. [*Not in use.*] *Bentley.*

DEFEND', *v. t.* [L. *defendo*; *de* and obs. *fendo*; Fr. *defendre*; It. *difendere*; Sp. *defender*; Port. *id.*; Arm. *difenn* or *divenn*; W. *difyn*; Norm. *fendu*, struck; *defender*, to oppose, to prohibit. The primary sense is to strike, thrust or drive off; to repel.]

1. To drive from; to thrust back; hence, to deny; to repel a demand, charge, or accusation; to oppose; to resist; the effect of which is to maintain one's own claims.

2. To forbid; to prohibit; that is, to drive from, or back. Milton calls the forbidden fruit, the *defended* fruit.

> The use of wine in some places is *defended* by customs or laws. *Temple.*

[*This application is nearly obsolete.*]

3. To drive back a foe or danger; to repel from any thing that which assails or annoys; to protect by opposition or resistance; to support or maintain; to prevent from being injured, or destroyed.

> There arose, to *defend* Israel, Tola the son of Puah. Judges x.

4. To vindicate; to assert; to uphold; to maintain uninjured, by force or by argument; as, to *defend* our cause; to *defend* rights and privileges; to *defend* reputation.

5. To secure against attacks or evil; to fortify against danger or violence; to set obstacles to the approach of any thing that can annoy. A garden may be *defended* by a grove. A camp may be *defended* by a wall, a hill or a river.

DEFEND', *v. i.* To make opposition; as, the party comes into court, *defends* and says.

DEFEND'ABLE, *a.* That may be *defended.*

DEFEND'ANT, *a.* [French participle of *defendre.*] Defensive; proper for defense. *Shak.*

2. Making defense; being in the character of a defendant. *Wheaton's Rep.*

DEFEND'ANT, *n.* He that defends against an assailant, or against the approach of evil or danger.

2. In *law*, the party that opposes a complaint, demand or charge; he that is summoned into court, and *defends*, denies or opposes the demand or charge, and maintains his own right. It is applied to any party of whom a demand is made in court, whether the party denies and *defends*, or admits the claim and suffers a default.

DEFEND'ED, *pp.* Opposed; denied; prohibited; maintained by resistance; vindicated; preserved uninjured; secured.

DEFEND'ER, *n.* One who defends by opposition; one who maintains, supports, protects or vindicates; an assertor; a vindicator, either by arms or by arguments; a champion or an advocate.

DEFEND'ING, *ppr.* Denying; opposing; resisting; forbidding; maintaining uninjured by force or by reason; securing from evil.

DEFENS'ATIVE, *n.* Guard; defense; a bandage, plaster, or the like, to secure a wound from external injury. *Johnson.*

DEFENSE, *n. defens'.* [L. *defensio.*] Any thing that opposes attack, violence, danger or injury; any thing that secures the person, the rights or the possessions of men; fortification; guard; protection; security. A wall, a parapet, a ditch, or a garrison, is the *defense* of a city or fortress. The Almighty is the *defense* of the righteous. Ps. lix.

2. Vindication; justification; apology; that which repels or disproves a charge or accusation.

> Men, brethren, fathers, hear ye my *defense.* Acts xxii.

3. In *law*, the defendant's reply to the plaintiff's declaration, demands or charges.

4. Prohibition. *Obs.* *Temple.*

5. Resistance; opposition. *Shak.*

6. The science of defending against enemies; military skill.

7. In *fortification*, a work that flanks another.

DEFENSE, *v. t. defens'.* To defend by fortification. *Obs.* *Fairfax.*

DEFENS'ED, *pp.* Fortified.

DEFENSELESS, *a. defens'less.* Being without defense, or without means of repelling assault or injury; *applied to a town*, it denotes unfortified or ungarrisoned; open to an enemy; *applied to a person*, it denotes naked; unarmed; unprotected; unprepared to resist attack; weak; unable to oppose; uncovered; unsheltered.

DEFENSELESSNESS, *n. defens'lessness.* The state of being unguarded or unprotected.

DEFENS'IBLE, *a.* That may be defended; as a *defensible* city.

2. That may be vindicated, maintained or justified; as a *defensible* cause.

DEFENS'IVE, *a.* [Fr. *defensif.*] That serves to defend; proper for defense; as *defensive* armor, which repels attacks or blows, opposed to *offensive* arms, which are used in attack.

2. Carried on in resisting attack or aggression; as *defensive* war, in distinction from *offensive* war, which is aggressive.

3. In a state or posture to defend. *Milton.*

DEFENS'IVE, *n.* Safeguard; that which defends.

> Wars preventive, upon just fears, are true *defensives.* *Bacon.*

To be on the defensive, or *to stand on the defensive*, is to be or stand in a state or posture of defense or resistance, in opposition to aggression or attack.

DEFENS'IVELY, *adv.* In a defensive manner; on the defensive; in defense.

DEFER', *v. t.* [L. *differo*; *dis*, from, and *fero*, to bear.]

1. To delay; to put off; to postpone to a future time; as, to *defer* the execution of a design.

> When thou vowest a vow, *defer* not to pay it. Eccles. v.

> Hope *deferred* maketh the heart sick. Prov. xiii.

2. To refer; to leave to another's judgment and determination. *Bacon.*

[In this sense, *refer* is now used.]

DEFER', *v. i.* To yield to another's opinion; to submit in opinion; as, he *defers* to the opinion of his father.

DEF'ERENCE, *n.* A yielding in opinion; submission of judgment to the opinion or judgment of another. Hence, regard; respect. We often decline acting in opposition to those for whose wisdom we have a great *deference.*

2. Complaisance; condescension. *Locke.*

3. Submission. *Addison.*

DEF'ERENT, *a.* Bearing; carrying; conveying. [*Little used.*] *Bacon.*

DEF'ERENT, *n.* That which carries or conveys. The *deferent* of a planet, is an imaginary circle or orb in the Ptolemaic system, that is supposed to carry about the body of the planet. *Bailey.*

2. A vessel in the human body for the conveyance of fluids. *Chambers.*

DEFEREN'TIAL, *a.* Expressing deference.

DEFER'MENT, *n.* Delay. *Suckling.*

DEFER'RER, *n.* One who delays or puts off. *B. Jonson.*

DEFER'RING, *ppr.* Delaying; postponing.

DEFI'ANCE, *n.* [French, in a different sense. See *Defy.*]

1. A daring; a challenge to fight; invitation to combat; a call to an adversary to encounter, if he dare. Goliath bid *defiance* to the army of Israel.

2. A challenge to meet in any contest; a call upon one to make good any assertion or charge; an invitation to maintain any cause or point.

3. Contempt of opposition or danger; a daring or resistance that implies the contempt of an adversary, or of any opposing power. Men often transgress the law and act in *defiance* of authority.

DEFI'ATORY, *a.* Bidding or bearing defiance. *Shelford.*

DEFI''CIENCY, } *n.* [L. *deficiens*, from *deficio*, to fail; *de* and *facio*, to do.]
DEFI''CIENCE, }

1. A failing; a falling short; imperfection; as a *deficiency* in moral duties.

2. Want; defect; something less than is necessary; as a *deficiency* of means; a *deficiency* of revenue; a *deficiency* of blood.

DEFI''CIENT, *a.* Wanting; defective; imperfect; not sufficient or adequate; as *deficient* estate; *deficient* strength.

2. Wanting; not having a full or adequate supply; as, the country may be *deficient* in the means of carrying on war.

Deficient numbers, in arithmetic, are those numbers, whose parts, added together, make less than the integer, whose parts they are. *Johnson.*

DEF'ICIT, *n.* Want; deficiency; as a *deficit* in the taxes or revenue.

DEFI'ER, *n.* [See *Defy.*] A challenger; one who dares to combat or encounter; one who braves; one who acts in contempt of opposition, law or authority; as a *defier* of the laws.

DEFIGURA'TION, *n.* A disfiguring. [*Not in use.*] *Hall.*

DEFIG'URE, *v. t.* To delineate. [*Not in use.*] *Weever.*

DEFI'LE, *v. t.* [Sax. *afylan, befylan, gefylan, afulan*, from *ful, fula*, foul. See *Foul.* The Syr. ܛܦܠ is almost precisely the English word. Cast. 1553.]

1. To make unclean; to render foul or dirty; *in a general sense.*
2. To make impure; to render turbid; as, the water or liquor is *defiled.*
3. To soil or sully; to tarnish; as reputation, &c.

He is among the greatest prelates of the age, however his character may be *defiled* by dirty hands. *Swift.*

They shall *defile* thy brightness. Ezek. xxviii.

4. To pollute; to make ceremonially unclean.

That which dieth of itself, he shall not eat, to *defile* himself therewith. Lev. xxii.

5. To corrupt chastity; to debauch; to violate; to tarnish the purity of character by lewdness.

Schechem *defiled* Dinah. Gen. xxxiv.

6. To taint, *in a moral sense;* to corrupt; to vitiate; to render impure with sin.

Defile not yourselves with the idols of Egypt. Ezek. xx.

He hath *defiled* the sanctuary of the Lord. Numb. xix.

DEFI'LE, *v. i.* [Fr. *defiler; de* and *file*, a row or line, from L. *filum*, a thread.]

To march off in a line, or file by file; to file off. *Roscoe.*

DEFI'LE, *n.* [Fr. *defilé*, from *fil, file*, a thread, a line.]

A narrow passage or way, in which troops may march only in a file, or with a narrow front; a long narrow pass, as between hills, &c.

DEFI'LED, *pp.* Made dirty, or foul; polluted; soiled; corrupted; violated; vitiated.

DEFI'LEMENT, *n.* The act of defiling, or state of being defiled; foulness; dirtiness; uncleanness.

2. Corruption of morals, principles or character; impurity; pollution by sin.

The chaste cannot rake into such filth without danger of *defilement.* *Addison.*

DEFI'LER, *n.* One who defiles; one who corrupts or violates; that which pollutes.

DEFI'LING, *ppr.* Polluting; making impure.

2. Marching in a file, or with a narrow front.

DEFI'NABLE, *a.* [See *Define.*] Literally, that may be limited, or have its limits ascertained. Hence, capable of having its extent ascertained with precision; capable of being fixed and determined. The extent of the Russian empire is hardly *definable.* The limits are hardly *definable.*

2. That may be defined or described; capable of having its signification rendered certain, or expressed with certainty or precision; as *definable* words.
3. That may be fixed, determined or ascertained; as, the time or period is not *definable.*

DEFI'NE, *v. t.* [L. *definio; de* and *finio*, to end, to limit, from *finis*, end; Fr. *definir;* Sp. *definir;* It. *definire.*]

1. To determine or describe the end or limit; as, to *define* the extent of a kingdom or country.
2. To determine with precision; to ascertain; as, to *define* the limits of a kingdom.
3. To mark the limit; to circumscribe; to bound.
4. To determine or ascertain the extent of the meaning of a word; to ascertain the signification of a term; to explain what a word is understood to express; as, to *define* the words, *virtue, courage, belief*, or *charity.*
5. To describe; to ascertain or explain the distinctive properties or circumstances of a thing; as, to *define* a line or an angle.

DEFI'NE, *v. i.* To determine; to decide. [*Not used.*] *Bacon.*

DEFI'NED, *pp.* Determined; having the extent ascertained; having the signification determined.

2. Having the precise limit marked, or having a determinate limit; as, the shadow of a body is well *defined.*

DEFI'NER, *n.* He who defines; he who ascertains or marks the limits; he who determines or explains the signification of a word, or describes the distinctive properties of a thing.

DEFI'NING, *ppr.* Determining the limits; ascertaining the extent; explaining the meaning; describing the properties.

DEF'INITE, *a.* [L. *definitus.*] Having certain limits; bounded with precision; determinate; as a *definite* extent of land; *definite* dimensions; *definite* measure.

2. Having certain limits in signification; determinate; certain; precise; as a *definite* word, term or expression.
3. Fixed; determinate; exact; precise; as a *definite* time or period.
4. Defining; limiting; determining the extent; as a *definite* word.

DEF'INITE, *n.* Thing defined. *Ayliffe.*

DEF'INITENESS, *n.* Certainty of extent; certainty of signification; determinateness.

DEFINI"TION, *n.* [L. *definitio.* See *Define.*]

1. A brief description of a thing by its properties; as a *definition* of wit or of a circle.
2. In *logic*, the explication of the essence of a thing by its kind and difference.
3. In *lexicography*, an explanation of the signification of a word or term, or of what a word is understood to express.

DEFIN'ITIVE, *a.* [L. *definitivus.*] Limiting the extent; determinate; positive; express; as a *definitive* term.

2. Limiting; ending; determining; final; opposed to *conditional, provisional*, or *interlocutory;* as a *definitive* sentence or decree.

DEFIN'ITIVE, *n.* In *grammar*, an adjective used to define or limit the extent of the signification of an appellative or common noun. Such are the Greek ο, η, το; the Latin *hic, ille, ipse;* *the, this* and *that*, in English; *le, la, les*, in French; *il, la, lo*, in Italian. Thus *tree* is an appellative or common noun; *the* tree, *this* tree, *that* tree, designate a particular tree, determinate or known. *Homo* signifies man; *hic* homo, *ille* homo, a particular man, &c. But in some languages, the definitives have lost their original use, in a great degree; as in the Greek and French. Thus "La force de la vertu," must be rendered in English, *the force of virtue*, not the force of *the* virtue. The first *la* is a definitive; the last has no definitive effect.

DEFIN'ITIVELY, *adv.* Determinately; positively; expressly.

2. Finally; conclusively; unconditionally; as, the points between the parties are *definitively* settled.

DEFIN'ITIVENESS, *n.* Determinateness; decisiveness; conclusiveness.

DEFIX', *v. t.* [L. *defigo.*] To fix; to fasten. [*Not used.*] *Herbert.*

DEFLAGRABIL'ITY, *n.* [See *Deflagrate.*] Combustibility; the quality of taking fire and burning away, as a metallic wire; *a chimical term.* *Boyle.*

DEFLA'GRABLE, *a.* Combustible; having the quality of taking fire and burning, as alcohol, oils, &c. *Boyle.*

DEF'LAGRATE, *v. t.* [L. *deflagro; de* and *flagro*, to burn.]

To set fire to; to burn; to consume; as, to *deflagrate* oil or spirit.

DEFLAGRA'TION, *n.* A kindling or setting fire to a substance; burning; combustion.

The strength of spirit is proved by *deflagration.* *Encyc.*

A rapid combustion of a mixture, attended with much evolution of flame and vapor, as of niter and charcoal. *Cyc.*

This term is also applied to the rapid combustion of metals by galvanism.

DEF'LAGRATOR, *n.* A galvanic instrument for producing combustion, particularly the combustion of metallic substances. *Hare.*

DEFLECT', *v. i.* [L. *deflecto; de* and *flecto*, to turn or bend.]

To turn from or aside; to deviate from a true course or right line; to swerve.

The needle *deflects* from the meridian. *Brown.*

DEFLECT', *v. t.* To turn aside; to turn or bend from a right line or regular course.

DEFLECT'ED, *pp.* Turned aside, or from a direct line or course. In *botany*, bending downward archwise.

DEFLECT'ING, *ppr.* Turning aside; turning from a right line or regular course.

DEFLEC'TION, *n.* Deviation; the act of turning aside; a turning from a true line or the regular course.

2. The departure of a ship from its true course.
3. A deviation of the rays of light towards the surface of an opake body; inflection. *Hooke.*

DEFLEX'URE, *n.* A bending down; a turning aside; deviation.

DEF'LORATE, *a.* [L. *defloratus*, from *defloro*, to deflour; *de* and *floreo, flos.* See *Flower.*]

In *botany*, having cast its farin, pollen, or fecundating dust. *Martyn.*

DEFLORA'TION, *n.* [Fr. See *Deflour.*]

1. The act of deflouring; the act of depri-

ving of the flower or prime beauties; particularly, the act of taking away a woman's virginity.

2. A selection of the flower, or of that which is most valuable.

The laws of Normandy are, in a great measure, the *defloration* of the English laws. *Hale.*

DEFLOUR', *v. t.* [L. *defloro; de* and *floreo*, or *flos*, a flower; Fr. *deflorer;* It. *deflorare*, or *desiorare;* Sp. *desflorar.* See *Flower.*]

1. To deprive a woman of her virginity, either by force or with consent. When by force, it may be equivalent to *ravish* or *violate.*

2. To take away the prime beauty and grace of any thing.

The sweetness of his soul was *deflowred.* *Taylor.*

3. To deprive of flowers. *Montagu.*

DEFLOUR'ED, *pp.* Deprived of maidenhood; ravished; robbed of prime beauty.

DEFLOUR'ER, *n.* One who deprives a woman of her virginity.

DEFLOUR'ING, *ppr.* Depriving of virginity or maidenhood; robbing of prime beauties.

DEFLOW, *v. i.* [L. *defluo.*] To flow down. [*Not in use.*] *Brown.*

DEF'LUOUS, *a.* [L. *defluus; de* and *fluo*, to flow.] Flowing down; falling off. [*Little used.*]

DEFLUX', *n.* [L. *defluxus; de* and *fluo*, *fluxus.* See *Flow.*]

A flowing down; a running downward; as a *deflux* of humors. [See *Defluxion.*] *Bacon.*

DEFLUX'ION, *n.* [L. *defluxio*, from *defluo*, to flow down; *de* and *fluo*, to flow. See *Flow.*]

1. A flowing, running or falling of humors or fluid matter, from a superior to an inferior part of the body; properly, an inflammation of a part, attended with increased secretion.

2. A discharge or flowing off of humors; as a *defluxion* from the nose or head in catarrh.

DEF'LY, *adv.* Dextrously; skilfully. *Obs.* [See *Deft.*] *Spenser.*

DEFOLIA'TION, *n.* [L. *de* and *foliatio*, foliage, from *folium*, a leaf, or *folior.* See *Folio.*]

Literally, the fall of the leaf or shedding of leaves; but technically, the time or season of shedding leaves in autumn; *applied to trees and shrubs.* *Linne.*

DEFO'RCE, *v. t.* [*de* and *force.*] To disseize and keep out of lawful possession of an estate; to withhold the possession of an estate from the rightful owner; applied to any possessor whose entry was originally lawful, but whose detainer is become unlawful. *Blackstone.*

DEFO'RCED, *pp.* Kept out of lawful possession.

DEFO'RCEMENT, *n.* The holding of lands or tenements to which another person has a right; a general term including abatement, intrusion, disseisin, discontinuance, or any other species of wrong, by which he that hath a right to the freehold is kept out of possession. *Blackstone.*

2. In *Scotland*, a resisting of an officer in the execution of law.

DEFOR'CIANT, *n.* He that keeps out of possession the rightful owner of an estate; he against whom a fictitious action is brought in fine and recovery. *Blackstone.*

DEFO'RCING, *ppr.* Keeping out of lawful possession.

DEFORM', *v. t.* [L. *deformo ; de* and *forma*, form; Sp. *desformar;* It. *deformare.*]

1. To mar or injure the form; to alter that form or disposition of parts which is natural and esteemed beautiful, and thus to render it displeasing to the eye; to disfigure; as, a hump on the back *deforms* the body.

2. To render ugly or displeasing, by exterior applications or appendages; as, to *deform* the face by paint, or the person by unbecoming dress.

3. To render displeasing.

Wintry blasts *deform* the year. *Thomson.*

4. To injure and render displeasing or disgusting; to disgrace; to disfigure moral beauty; as, all vices *deform* the character of rational beings.

5. To dishonor; to make ungraceful. *Dryden.*

DEFORM', *a.* [L. *deformis.*] Disfigured; being of an unnatural, distorted, or disproportioned form; displeasing to the eye. *Spenser.*

Sight so *deform* what heart of rock could long
Dry-eyed behold? *Milton.*

DEFORMA'TION, *n.* A disfiguring or defacing.

DEFORM'ED, *pp.* Injured in the form; disfigured; distorted; ugly; wanting natural beauty, or symmetry.

2. Base; disgraceful. *B. Jonson.*

DEFORM'EDLY, *adv.* In an ugly manner.

DEFORM'EDNESS, *n.* Ugliness; a disagreeable or unnatural form.

DEFORM'ER, *n.* One who deforms.

DEFORM'ING, *ppr.* Marring the natural form or figure; rendering ugly or displeasing; destroying beauty.

DEFORM'ITY, *n.* [L. *deformitas.*] Any unnatural state of the shape or form; want of that uniformity or symmetry which constitutes beauty; distortion; irregularity of shape or features; disproportion of limbs; defect; crookedness, &c. Hence, ugliness; as bodily *deformity.*

2. Any thing that destroys beauty, grace or propriety; irregularity; absurdity; gross deviation from order, or the established laws of propriety. Thus we speak of *deformity* in an edifice, or *deformity* of character.

DEFO'RSER, *n.* [from *force.*] One that casts out by force. [*Ill formed and not in use.*] *Blount.*

DEFRAUD', *v. t.* [L. *defraudo ; de* and *fraudo*, to cheat, *fraus*, fraud; It. *defraudare ;* Sp. *defraudar.*]

1. To deprive of right, either by obtaining something by deception or artifice, or by taking something wrongfully without the knowledge or consent of the owner; to cheat; to cozen; followed by *of* before the thing taken; as, to *defraud* a man *of* his right.

We have corrupted no man, we have *defrauded* no man. 2 Cor. vii.

The agent who embezzles public property, *defrauds* the state.

The man who by deception obtains a price for a commodity above its value, *defrauds* the purchaser.

2. To withhold wrongfully from another what is due to him. *Defraud* not the hireling *of* his wages.

3. To prevent one wrongfully from obtaining what he may justly claim.

A man of fortune who permits his son to consume the season of education in hunting, shooting, or in frequenting horse-races, assemblies, &c., *defrauds* the community of a benefactor, and bequeaths them a nuisance. *Paley.*

4. To defeat or frustrate wrongfully.

By the duties deserted—by the claims *defrauded.* *Paley.*

DEFRAUD'ED, *pp.* Deprived of property or right by trick, artifice or deception; injured by the withholding of what is due.

DEFRAUD'ER, *n.* One who defrauds; one who takes from another his right by deception, or withholds what is his due; a cheat; a cozener; an embezzler; a peculator.

DEFRAUD'ING, *ppr.* Depriving another of his property or right by deception or artifice; injuring by withholding wrongfully what is due.

DEFRAUD'MENT, *n.* The act of defrauding. *Milton.*

DEFRA'Y, *v. t.* [Fr. *defrayer; de* and *frais*, *fraix*, expense; Arm. *defraei.*]

1. To pay; to discharge, as cost or expense; to bear, as charge, cost or expense. It is followed chiefly by *expense, charge* or *cost.* The acquisitions of war seldom *defray* the expenses. The profits of a voyage will not always *defray* the charges, or even the cost of the first outfits.

2. To satisfy; as, to *defray* anger. *Obs.* *Spenser.*

3. To fill; as, to *defray* a bottle. *Obs.* *Spenser.*

DEFRA'YED, *pp.* Paid; discharged; as expense, or cost.

DEFRA'YER, *n.* One who pays or discharges expenses.

DEFRA'YING, *ppr.* Paying; discharging.

DEFRA'YMENT, *n.* Payment. *Shelton.*

DEFT, *a.* [Sax. *dæft.*] Neat; handsome; spruce; ready; dextrous; fit; convenient. *Obs.* *Shak.* *Dryden.*

DEFT'LY, *adv.* Neatly; dextrously; in a skilful manner. *Obs.* *Shak.* *Gray.*

DEFT'NESS, *n.* Neatness; beauty. *Obs.* *Drayton.*

DEFUNCT', *a.* [L. *defunctus*, from *defungor*, to perform and discharge; *de* and *fungor*, id.] Having finished the course of life; dead; deceased. *Shak.*

DEFUNCT', *n.* A dead person; one deceased. *Shak.*

DEFUNC'TION, *n.* Death. [*Not used.*] *Shak.*

DEFY', *v. t.* [Fr. *defier; de*, *des*, from, and *fier*, to trust; It. *sfidare ;* Sp. *desafiar; des* and *fiar ;* Port. *id.;* Arm. *difyal ;* Low L. *diffidare*, and *diffiduciare*, from *fido*, to trust. See *Faith.* The word *diffidare* seems originally to have signified, to dissolve the bond of allegiance, as between the lord and his vassal; opposed to *affidare. Spelman, ad voc.* Hence it came to be used for the denunciation of enmity and of war. Hence, to challenge. If we understand *defier* to signify to *distrust*, then to *defy* is to call in question the courage of another, according to the popular phrase, "you dare not fight me."]

1. To dare; to provoke to combat or strife, by appealing to the courage of another; to invite one to contest; to challenge; as, Goliath *defied* the armies of Israel.

2. To dare; to brave; to offer to hazard a conflict by manifesting a contempt of opposition, attack or hostile force; as, to *defy* the arguments of an opponent; to *defy* the power of the magistrate.

Were we to abolish the common law, it would rise triumphant above its own ruins, deriding and *defying* its impotent enemies. *Duponceau.*

3. To challenge to say or do any thing.

DEFY′, *n.* A challenge. [*Not used.*] *Dryden.*

DEFY′ER. [See *Defier.*]

DEG′ARNISH, *v. t.* [Fr. *degarnir; de* and *garnir*, to furnish. See *Garnish.*]

1. To unfurnish; to strip of furniture, ornaments or apparatus.

2. To deprive of a garrison, or troops necessary for defense; as, to *degarnish* a city or fort. *Washington's Letter. Nov.* 11. 1778.

DEG′ARNISHED, *pp.* Stripped of furniture or apparatus; deprived of troops for defense.

DEG′ARNISHING, *ppr.* Stripping of furniture, dress, apparatus or a garrison.

DEG′ARNISHMENT, *n.* The act of depriving of furniture, apparatus or a garrison.

DEĠEN′DER, *v. i.* To degenerate. [*Not in use.*] *Spenser.*

DEĠEN′ERACY, *n.* [See *Degenerate*, the Verb.]

1. A growing worse or inferior; a decline in good qualities; or a state of being less valuable; as the *degeneracy* of a plant.

2. In *morals*, decay of virtue; a growing worse; departure from the virtues of ancestors; desertion of that which is good. We speak of the *degeneracy* of men in modern times, or of the *degeneracy* of manners, of the age, of virtue, &c., sometimes without reason.

3. Poorness; meanness; as a *degeneracy* of spirit.

DEĠEN′ERATE, *v. i.* [L. *degenero*, from *degener*, grown worse, ignoble, base; *de* and *gener, genus;* Fr. *degenerer;* Sp. *degenerar.*]

1. To become worse; to decay in good qualities; to pass from a good to a bad or worse state; to lose or suffer a diminution of valuable qualities, either in the natural or moral world. In the natural world, plants and animals *degenerate* when they grow to a less size than usual, or lose a part of the valuable qualities which belong to the species. In the moral world, men *degenerate* when they decline in virtue, or other good qualities. Manners *degenerate* when they become corrupt. Wit may *degenerate* into indecency or impiety.

DEĠEN′ERATE, *a.* Having fallen from a perfect or good state into a less excellent or worse state; having lost something of the good qualities possessed; having declined in natural or moral worth.

The *degenerate* plant of a strange vine. Jer. ii.

2. Low; base; mean; corrupt; fallen from primitive or natural excellence; having lost the good qualities of the species. Man is considered a *degenerate* being. A coward is a man of *degenerate* spirit.

DEĠEN′ERATELY, *adv.* In a degenerate or base manner. *Milton.*

DEĠEN′ERATENESS, *n.* A degenerate state; a state in which the natural good qualities of the species are decayed or lost.

DEĠENERA′TION, *n.* A growing worse, or losing of good qualities; a decline from the virtue and worth of ancestors; a decay of the natural good qualities of the species; a falling from a more excellent state to one of less worth, either in the natural or moral world.

2. The thing degenerated. *Brown.*

DEĠEN′EROUS, *a.* Degenerated; fallen from a state of excellence, or from the virtue and merit of ancestors. Hence,

2. Low; base; mean; unworthy; as a *degenerous* passion. *Dryden.*

DEĠEN′EROUSLY, *adv.* In a degenerous manner; basely; meanly.

DEGLU′TINATE, *v. t.* [L. *deglutino; de* and *glutino*, to glue. See *Glue.*]

To unglue; to loosen or separate substances glued together. *Scott.*

DEGLUTI′′TION, *n.* [L. *deglutio*, to swallow; *de* and *glutio.* See *Glutton.*]

1. The act of swallowing; as, *deglutition* is difficult.

2. The power of swallowing; as, *deglutition* is lost.

DEGRADA′TION, *n.* [Fr. See *Degrade.*]

1. A reducing in rank; the act of depriving one of a degree of honor, of dignity, or of rank; also, deposition; removal or dismission from office; as the *degradation* of a peer, of a knight, or of a bishop, in England.

2. The state of being reduced from an elevated or more honorable station, to one that is low in fact or in estimation; baseness; degeneracy.

Deplorable is the *degradation* of our nature. *South.*

3. Diminution or reduction of strength, efficacy or value.

4. In *painting*, a lessening and obscuring of the appearance of distant objects in a landscape, that they may appear as they would do to an eye placed at a distance. *Johnson. Encyc.*

5. Diminution; reduction of altitude or magnitude. *Journ. of Science.*

DEGRA′DE, *v. t.* [Fr. *degrader;* Sp. Port. *degradar;* It. *degradare;* L. *de* and *gradus*, a step, a degree. See *Grade.*]

1. To reduce from a higher to a lower rank or degree; to deprive one of any office or dignity, by which he loses rank in society; to strip of honors; as, to *degrade* a nobleman, an archbishop or a general officer.

2. To reduce in estimation; to lessen the value of; to lower; to sink. Vice *degrades* a man in the view of others; often in his own view. Drunkenness *degrades* a man to the level of a beast.

3. To reduce in altitude or magnitude.

Although the ridge is still there, the ridge itself has been *degraded.* *Journ. of Science.*

DEGRA′DED, *pp.* Reduced in rank; deprived of an office or dignity; lowered; sunk; reduced in estimation or value.

DEGRA′DEMENT, *n.* Deprivation of rank or office. *Milton.*

DEGRA′DING, *ppr.* Reducing in rank; depriving of honors or offices; reducing in value or estimation; lowering.

2. *a.* Dishonoring; disgracing the character; as *degrading* obsequiousness.

The inordinate love of money and of fame are base and *degrading* passions. *Wirt.*

DEGRA′DINGLY, *adv.* In a degrading manner, or in a way to depreciate.

DEGREE′, *n.* [Fr. *degré;* Norm. *degret;* from L. *gradus*, Sp. and It. *grado*, W. *rhaz*, Syr. ‌ܪܕܐ radah, to go. See *Grade* and *Degrade.*]

1. A step; a distinct portion of space of indefinite extent; a space in progression; as, the army gained the hill by *degrees;* a balloon rises or descends by slow *degrees;* and figuratively, we advance in knowledge by slow *degrees.* Men are yet in the first *degree* of improvement. It should be their aim to attain to the furthest *degree*, or the highest *degree.* There are *degrees* of vice and virtue.

2. A step or portion of progression, in elevation, quality, dignity or rank; as a man of great *degree.* *Spenser.*

We speak of men of high *degree*, or of low *degree;* of superior or inferior *degree.* It is supposed there are different *degrees* or orders of angels.

They purchase to themselves a good *degree.* 1 Tim. iii.

3. In *genealogy*, a certain distance or remove in the line of descent, determining the proximity of blood; as a relation in the third or fourth *degree.*

4. Measure; extent. The light is intense to a *degree* that is intolerable. We suffer an extreme *degree* of heat or cold.

5. In *geometry*, a division of a circle, including a three hundred and sixtieth part of its circumference. Hence a *degree of latitude* is the 360th part of the earth's surface north or south of the equator, and a *degree of longitude*, the same part of the surface east or west of any given meridian.

6. In *music*, an interval of sound, marked by a line on the scale. *Rousseau. Busby.*

7. In *arithmetic*, a degree consists of three figures; thus, 270, 360, compose two degrees.

8. A division, space or interval, marked on a mathematical or other instrument; as on a thermometer, or barometer.

9. In *colleges* and *universities*, a mark of distinction conferred on students, as a testimony of their proficiency in arts and sciences; giving them a kind of rank, and entitling them to certain privileges. This is usually evidenced by a diploma. Degrees are conferred *pro meritis* on the alumni of a college; or they are honorary tokens of respect, conferred on strangers of distinguished reputation. The *first degree* is that of *Bachelor of Arts;* the *second*, that of *Master of Arts.* Honorary degrees are those of *Doctor of Divinity, Doctor of Laws*, &c. Physicians also receive the degree of *Doctor of Medicine.*

By degrees, step by step; gradually; by little and little; by moderate advances. Frequent drinking forms *by degrees* a confirmed habit of intemperance.

DEGUSTA′TION, *n.* [L. *degusto.*] A tasting. *Bp. Hall.*

DEHIS'CENCE, *n.* [L. *dehiscens*, *dehisco*, to gape; *de* and *hisco*, id.]
A gaping. In *botany*, the opening of capsules; the season when capsules open. *Martyn.*

DEHIS'CENT, *a.* Opening, as the capsule of a plant. *Eaton.*

DEHORT', *v. t.* [L. *dehortor*, to dissuade; *de* and *hortor*, to advise.]
To dissuade; to advise to the contrary; to counsel not to do nor to undertake. *Wilkins. Ward.*

DEHORTA'TION, *n.* Dissuasion; advice or counsel against something.

DEHORT'ATORY, *a.* Dissuading; belonging to dissuasion.

DEHORT'ER, *n.* A dissuader; an adviser to the contrary.

DEHORT'ING, *ppr.* Dissuading.

DE'ICIDE, *n.* [It. *deicidio*; L. *deus*, God, and *cædo*, to slay.]
1. The act of putting to death Jesus Christ, our Savior. *Prior.*
2. One concerned in putting Christ to death.

DEIF'IC, *a.* [L. *deus*, god, and *facio*, to make.] Divine; pertaining to the gods. *Trans. of Pausanias.*
2. Making divine.

DEIFICA'TION, *n.* [See *Deify*.] The act of deifying; the act of exalting to the rank of, or enrolling among the heathen deities.

DE'IFIED, *pp.* Exalted or ranked among the gods; regarded or praised as divine.

DE'IFIER, *n.* One that deifies.

DE'IFORM, *a.* [L. *deus*, a god, and *forma*, form.] Like a god; of a godlike form.
These souls exhibit a *deiform* power. *Trans. of Pausanias.*

DE'IFY, *v. t.* [L. *deus*, a god, and *facio*, to make.]
1. To make a god; to exalt to the rank of a heathen deity; to enroll among the deities; as, Julius Cesar was *deified*.
2. To exalt into an object of worship; to treat as an object of supreme regard; as, a covetous man *deifies* his treasures. *Prior.*
3. To exalt to a deity in estimation; to reverence or praise as a deity.
The pope was formerly extolled and *deified* by his votaries.

DE'IFYING, *ppr.* Exalting to the rank of a deity; treating as divine.

DEIGN, *v. i. dane.* [Fr. *daigner*; It. *degnare*; Sp. *dignarse*; Port. *id.*; L. *dignor*, from *dignus*, worthy.]
To think worthy; to vouchsafe; to condescend.
O *deign* to visit our forsaken seats. *Pope.*

DEIGN, *v. t. dane.* To grant or allow; to condescend to give to.
Nor would we *deign* him burial of his men. *Shak.*

DEIGNING, *ppr. da'ning.* Vouchsafing; thinking worthy.

DEIN'TEGRATE, *v. t.* To disintegrate. [*Not used.* See *Disintegrate.*]

DEIP'AROUS, *a.* [L. *deiparus.*] Bearing or bringing forth a god; *an epithet applied to the Virgin Mary.*

DEIPNOSOPH'IST, *n.* [Gr. δειπνον, a feast, and σοφιςης, a sophist.]
One of an ancient sect of philosophers, who were famous for their learned conversation at meals. *Ash. Observer.*

DE'ISM, *n.* [Fr. *deisme*; Sp. *deismo*; It. *id.*; from L. *deus*, God.]
The doctrine or creed of a deist; the belief or system of religious opinions of those who acknowledge the existence of one God, but deny revelation: or deism is the belief in natural religion only, or those truths, in doctrine and practice, which man is to discover by the light of reason, independent and exclusive of any revelation from God. Hence deism implies infidelity or a disbelief in the divine origin of the scriptures.
The view which the rising greatness of our country presents to my eyes, is greatly tarnished by the general prevalence of *deism*, which, with me, is but another name for vice and depravity. *P. Henry, Wirt's Sketches.*

DE'IST, *n.* [Fr. *deiste*; It. *deista.*] One who believes in the existence of a God, but denies revealed religion; one who professes no form of religion, but follows the light of nature and reason, as his only guides in doctrine and practice; a freethinker.

DEIST'IC, **DEIST'ICAL**, } *a.* Pertaining to deism or to deists; embracing deism, as a *deistical* writer; or containing deism, as a *deistical* book.

DE'ITY, *n.* [Fr. *déité*; It. *deità*; Sp. *deidad*; L. *deitas*, from *deus*, Gr. θεος, God; W. *duw*; Ir. *dia*; Arm. *doue*; Fr. *dieu*; It. *dio*, *iddio*; Sp. *dios*; Port. *deos*; Gypsey, *dewe*, *dewel*; Sans. *deva*. The latter orthography coincides with the Gr. διος, ζευς, Jupiter, and L. *divus*, a god, and *dium*, the open air, or light. So in W. *dyw*, is day; Hindoo, *diw*; Gypsey *diwes*, day. Qu. Chinese *Ti*. The word is probably contracted from *dg*, and may coincide with *day*, Sax. *dæg*, the primary sense of which is to open, expand, or to shoot forth, as the morning light. But the precise primary meaning is not certain.]
1. Godhead; divinity; the nature and essence of the Supreme Being; as, the *deity* of the Supreme Being is manifest in his works.
2. God; the Supreme Being, or infinite self-existing Spirit.
3. A fabulous god or goddess; a superior being supposed, by heathen nations, to exist, and to preside over particular departments of nature; as *Jupiter*, *Juno*, *Apollo*, *Diana*, &c.
4. The supposed divinity or divine qualities of a pagan god. *Spenser. Raleigh.*

DEJECT', *v. t.* [L. *dejicio*; *de* and *jacio*, to throw.]
1. To cast down; usually, to cast down the countenance; to cause to fall with grief; to make to look sad or grieved, or to express discouragement.
But gloomy were his eyes, *dejected* was his face. *Dryden.*
2. To depress the spirits; to sink; to dispirit; to discourage; to dishearten.
Nor think to die *dejects* my lofty mind. *Pope.*

DEJECT', *a.* [L. *dejectus*, from *dejicio.*] Cast down; low-spirited. *Shak.*

DEJECT'ED, *pp.* Cast down; depressed; grieved; discouraged.

DEJECT'EDLY, *adv.* In a dejected manner; sadly; heavily. *Bacon.*

DEJECT'EDNESS, *n.* The state being cast down; lowness of spirits.

DEJECT'ING, *ppr.* Casting down; depressing; dispiriting.

DEJEC'TION, *n.* A casting down; depression of mind; melancholy; lowness of spirits, occasioned by grief or misfortune. *Milton.*
2. Weakness; as *dejection* of appetite. [*Unusual.*] *Arbuthnot.*
3. The act of voiding the excrements; or the matter ejected. *Ray.*

DEJECT'LY, *adv.* In a downcast manner.

DEJECT'ORY, *a.* Having power or tending to cast down, or to promote evacuations by stool. *Ferrand.*

DEJECT'URE, *n.* That which is ejected; excrements. *Arbuthnot.*

DELACRYMA'TION, *n.* [L. *delacrymatio*; *de* and *lacrymatio*, a weeping.]
A preternatural discharge of watery humors from the eyes; waterishness of the eyes. *Dict.*

DELACTA'TION, *n.* [L. *delactatio.*] A weaning. [*Not used.*] *Dict.*

DELAPSA'TION, *n.* A falling down. *Ray.*

DELAPSE, *v. i. delaps'.* [L. *delabor*, *delapsus*; *de* and *labor*, to slide.] To fall or slide down.

DELAP'SION, *n.* A falling down of the uterus, anus, &c.

DELAPS'ED, *pp.* Fallen down.

DELA'TE, *v. t.* [L. *delatus*; *de* and *latus*, part. of *fero*, to bear.]
1. To carry; to convey. [*Little used.*] *Bacon.*
2. To accuse; to inform against; that is, to bear a charge against. *B. Jonson.*

DELA'TION, *n.* Carriage; conveyance; as the *delation* of sound. [*Little used.*] *Bacon.*
2. Accusation; act of charging with a crime; *a term of the civil law.*

DELA'TOR, *n.* [L.] An accuser; an informer. *Sandys.*

DELA'Y, *v. t.* [Fr. *delai*, delay; Sp. *dilatar*, Port. *id.*, to delay; It. *dilata*, delay; *dilatare*, to dilate, to spread; from L. *dilatus*, *differo*. We see that *delay* is from spreading, extending. See *Dilate.*]
1. To prolong the time of acting, or proceeding; to put off; to defer.
My lord delayeth his coming. Matt. xxiv.
2. To retard; to stop, detain or hinder for a time; to restrain motion, or render it slow; as, the mail is *delayed* by bad roads.
Thyrsis, whose artful strains have oft *delayed*
The huddling brook to hear his madrigal. *Milton.*
3. To allay. [*Not in use, nor proper.*] *Spenser.*

DELA'Y, *v. i.* To linger; to move slow; or to stop for a time.
There are certain bounds to the quickness and slowness of the succession of ideas, beyond which they can neither *delay* nor hasten. *Locke.*

DELA'Y, *n.* A lingering; stay; stop.
2. A putting off or deferring; procrastination; as, the *delay* of trial is not to be imputed to the plaintiff.
3. Hinderance for a time.

DELA'YED, *pp.* Deferred; detained; hindered for a time; retarded.

DELA'YER, *n.* One who defers; one who lingers.

DELA'YING, *ppr.* Putting off; deferring; procrastinating; retarding; detaining.

DELA'YMENT, *n.* Hinderance. *Gower.*

DE'LE, *v. t.* [L. imperative of *deleo.*] Blot out; erase.

DEL'EBLE, *a.* [L. *delebilis.*] That can be blotted out. *More.*

DELEC'TABLE, *a.* [L. *delectabilis*, from *delector*, to delight. See *Delight.*]
Delightful; highly pleasing; that gives great joy or pleasure; as a *delectable* garden. *Milton.*

DELEC'TABLENESS, *n.* Delightfulness. *Barret.*

DELEC'TABLY, *adv.* Delightfully.

DELECTA'TION, *n.* Great pleasure; delight. *More.*

DEL'EGACY, *n.* A number of persons delegated. *Laud.*
[We now use *delegation.*]

DEL'EGATE, *v. t.* [L. *delego; de* and *lego*, to send. See *Legate.*]
1. To send away; appropriately, to send on an embassy; to send with power to transact business, as a representative. The President *delegated* three commissioners to the court of St. Cloud.
2. To entrust; to commit; to deliver to another's care and exercise; as, to *delegate* authority or power to an envoy, representative or judge.

DEL'EGATE, *n.* A person appointed and sent by another with powers to transact business as his representative; a deputy; a commissioner; a vicar. In *the United States*, a person elected or appointed to represent a state or a district, in the Congress, or in a Convention for forming or altering a constitution.
2. In *Great Britain*, a commissioner appointed by the king, under the great seal, to hear and determine appeals from the ecclesiastical court. Hence the *Court of Delegates* is the great court of appeal in all ecclesiastical causes. It is used also for the court of appeals from that of the admiralty. *Blackstone.*
3. A layman appointed to attend an ecclesiastical council.

DEL'EGATE, *a.* Deputed; sent to act for or represent another; as a *delegate* judge. *Taylor.*

DEL'EGATED, *pp.* Deputed; sent with a trust or commission to act for another; appointed a judge; committed, as authority.

DEL'EGATING, *ppr.* Deputing; sending with a commission to act for another; appointing; committing; entrusting.

DELEGA'TION, *n.* A sending away; the act of putting in commission, or investing with authority to act for another; the appointment of a delegate. *Burke.*

> The duties of religion cannot be performed by *delegation.* *S. Miller.*

2. The persons deputed to act for another, or for others. Thus, the representatives of Massachusetts in Congress are called the *delegation*, or *whole delegation.*
3. In *the civil law*, the assignment of a debt to another, as when a debtor appoints his debtor to answer to the creditor in his place.

DELE'TE, *v. t.* [L. *deleo.*] To blot out. [*Not used.*] *Fuller.*

DELETE'RIOUS, *a.* [L. *deleterius*, from *deleo*, to blot out or destroy, W. *dilëaw*, *dilëu.* Qu. Ir. *dallaim*, to blind.]
1. Having the quality of destroying, or extinguishing life; destructive; poisonous; as a *deleterious* plant or quality.
2. Injurious; pernicious.

DEL'ETERY, *a.* Destructive; poisonous. *Hudibras.*

DELE'TION, *n.* [L. *deletio*, from *deleo*, to blot out.]
1. The act of blotting out or erasing.
2. Destruction. [*Little used.*] *Hale.*

DEL'ETORY, *n.* That which blots out. *Taylor.*

DELF, *n.* [Sax. *delfan*, to delve, to dig.] A mine; a quarry; a pit dug. [*Rarely used.*] *Ray.*
2. Earthern ware, covered with enamel or white glazing in imitation of China ware or porcelain, made at Delft in Holland; properly, *Delft-ware.*

DEL'IBATE, *v. t.* [L. *delibo; de* and *libo*, to taste.] To taste; to take a sip. [*Little used.*]

DELIBA'TION, *n.* A taste; an essay. [*Little used.*] *Berkeley.*

DELIB'ERATE, *v. i.* [L. *delibero; de* and *libro*, to weigh, It. *librare.* See *Librate.*]
To weigh in the mind; to consider and examine the reasons for and against a measure; to estimate the weight or force of arguments, or the probable consequences of a measure, in order to a choice or decision; to pause and consider. A wise prince will *deliberate* before he wages war.

> The woman that *deliberates* is lost. *Addison.*

DELIB'ERATE, *v. t.* To balance in the mind; to weigh; to consider. *Laud.*

DELIB'ERATE, *a.* Weighing facts and arguments with a view to a choice or decision; carefully considering the probable consequences of a step; circumspect; slow in determining; *applied to persons;* as a *deliberate* judge or counselor.
2. Formed with deliberation; well advised or considered; not sudden or rash; as a *deliberate* opinion; a *deliberate* measure, or result.
3. Slow; as a *deliberate* death or echo. [*Hardly legitimate.*] *Bacon.*

DELIB'ERATELY, *adv.* With careful consideration, or deliberation; circumspectly; not hastily or rashly; slowly. This purpose was *deliberately* formed. *Dryden. Goldsmith.*

DELIB'ERATENESS, *n.* Calm consideration; circumspection; due attention to the arguments for and against a measure; caution. *K. Charles.*

DELIBERA'TION, [L. *deliberatio.*] The act of deliberating; the act of weighing and examining the reasons for and against a choice or measure; consideration. We say, a measure has been taken with *deliberation.*
2. Mutual discussion and examination of the reasons for and against a measure; as the *deliberations* of a legislative body or council.

DELIB'ERATIVE, *a.* Pertaining to deliberation; proceeding or acting by deliberation, or by mutual discussion and examination; as, the legislature is a *deliberative* body.
2. Having a right or power to deliberate or discuss.

> In councils, the bishops have a *deliberative* voice. *Encyc.*

3. Apt or disposed to consider. *Bp. Barlow.*

DELIB'ERATIVE, *n.* A discourse in which a question is discussed or weighed and examined. A kind of rhetoric employed in proving a thing and convincing others of its truth, in order to persuade them to adopt it. *Encyc.*

DELIB'ERATIVELY, *adv.* By deliberation. *Burke.*

DEL'ICACY, *n.* [Fr. *delicatesse;* Sp. *delicadeza;* It. *delicatezza;* but more directly from *delicate*, which see.]
In *a general sense*, that which delights or pleases. Hence,
1. Fineness of texture; smoothness; softness; tenderness; as the *delicacy* of the skin; and nearly in the same sense, applicable to food; as the *delicacy* of flesh, meat or vegetables. Hence,
2. Daintiness; pleasantness to the taste.
3. Elegant or feminine beauty; as *delicacy* of form.
4. Nicety; minute accuracy; as the *delicacy* of coloring in painting.
5. Neatness in dress; elegance proceeding from a nice selection and adjustment of the several parts of dress. *Spectator.*
6. Softness of manners; civility or politeness proceeding from a nice observance of propriety, and a desire to please; as *delicacy* of behavior.
7. Indulgence; gentle treatment; as *delicacy* of education.
8. Tenderness; scrupulousness; the quality manifested in nice attention to right, and care to avoid wrong, or offense. *Bp. Taylor.*
9. Acute or nice perception of what is pleasing to the sense of tasting; hence figuratively, a nice perception of beauty and deformity, or the faculty of such nice perception.

> *Delicacy* of taste tends to invigorate the social affections, and moderate those that are selfish. *Kames.*

10. That which delights the senses, particularly the taste; *applied to eatables;* as, the peach is a great *delicacy.*
11. Tenderness of constitution; weakness; that quality or state of the animal body which renders it very impressible to injury; as *delicacy* of constitution or frame.
12. Smallness; fineness; slenderness; tenuity; as the *delicacy* of a thread, or fiber.
13. Tenderness; nice susceptibility of impression; as *delicacy* of feeling.

DEL'ICATE, *a.* [Fr. *delicat;* Sp. *delicado;* It. *delicato;* L. *delicatus*, connected with *deliciæ*, delight, *delecto*, to delight; probably a compound of *de*, with the root of *like.* See *Delight* and *Like.*]
1. Of a fine texture; fine; soft; smooth; clear, or fair; as a *delicate* skin.
2. Nice; pleasing to the taste; of an agreeable flavor; as *delicate* food; a *delicate* dish.
3. Nice in perception of what is agreeable; dainty; as a *delicate* taste; and figuratively, nice and discriminating in beauty and deformity.
4. Nice; accurate; fine; soft to the eye; as a *delicate* color.
5. Nice in forms; regulated by minute observance of propriety, or by condescension

and attention to the wishes and feelings of others; as *delicate* behavior or manners; a *delicate* address.

6. Pleasing to the senses; as a *delicate* flavor.

7. Fine; slender; minute; as a *delicate* thread.

8. That cannot be handled without injury or danger; that must be touched with care; as a *delicate* point or topic; a *delicate* question.

9. Composed of fine threads, or nicely interwoven; as *delicate* texture; hence, soft and smooth to the touch; as *delicate* silk.

10. Tender; effeminate; not able to endure hardship; very impressible to injury; as a *delicate* frame or constitution.

11. Feeble; not sound or robust; as *delicate* health.

DEL'ICATE, *n.* Any thing nice; a nicety. *Obs.* Jer. li. 34. *Dryden.*

DEL'ICATELY, *adv.* In a delicate manner; with nice regard to propriety and the feelings of others.

2. Daintily; luxuriously.

They that live *delicately* are in kings' courts. Luke vii.

3. With soft elegance; as an expression *delicately* turned.

4. Tenderly; with indulgence in ease, elegance and luxury. Prov. xxix.

DEL'ICATENESS, *n.* The state of being delicate; tenderness; softness; effeminacy. Deut. xxviii.

DELI''CIOUS, *a.* [Fr. *delicieux;* L. *delicatus, deliciæ;* Sp. *delicioso;* It. *delizioso.*]

1. Highly pleasing to the taste; most sweet or grateful to the senses; affording exquisite pleasure; as a *delicious* viand; *delicious* fruit or wine.

2. Most pleasing to the mind; very grateful; yielding exquisite delight; as, this poem affords a *delicious* entertainment.

DELI''CIOUSLY, *adv.* In a delicious manner; in a manner to please the taste or gratify the mind; sweetly; pleasantly; delightfully; as, to feed *deliciously;* to be *deliciously* entertained.

DELI''CIOUSNESS, *n.* The quality of being delicious, or very grateful to the taste or mind; as the *deliciousness* of a repast.

2. Delight; great pleasure.

DELIGA'TION, *n.* [L. *deligatio, deligo; de* and *ligo*, to bind.] In *surgery*, a binding up; a bandaging.

DELI'GHT, *n.* *deli'te.* [Fr. *delice;* Sp. *delicia;* It. *delizia;* L. *deliciæ*, connected with *delector;* probably allied to Eng. *like.*]

1. A high degree of pleasure, or satisfaction of mind; joy.

His *delight* is in the law of the Lord. Ps. i.

2. That which gives great pleasure; that which affords delight.

Titus was the *delight* of human kind. *Dryden.*

I was daily his *delight.* Prov. viii.

Delight is a more permanent pleasure than *joy*, and not dependent on sudden excitement.

DELI'GHT, *v. t.* [Sp. *deleytar;* Port. *deleitar;* L. *delector;* Fr. *delecter.* See *Delight* and *Like.*]

1. To affect with great pleasure; to please highly; to give or afford high satisfaction or joy; as, a beautiful landscape *delights* the eye; harmony *delights* the ear; the good conduct of children, and especially their piety, *delights* their parents.

I will *delight* myself in thy statutes. Ps. cxix.

2. To receive great pleasure in.

I *delight* to do thy will. Ps. xl.

DELI'GHT, *v. i.* To have or take great pleasure; to be greatly pleased or rejoiced; followed by *in.*

I *delight in* the law of God after the inward man. Rom. vii.

DELI'GHTED, *pp.* Greatly pleased; rejoiced; followed by *with.*

That ye may be *delighted with* the abundance of her glory. Is. lxvi.

2. *a.* Full of delight. *Shak.*

DELI'GHTER, *n.* One who takes delight. *Barrow.*

DELI'GHTFUL, *a.* Highly pleasing; affording great pleasure and satisfaction; as a *delightful* thought; a *delightful* prospect.

DELI'GHTFULLY, *adv.* In a manner to receive great pleasure; very agreeably; as, we were *delightfully* employed, or entertained.

2. In a delightful manner; charmingly; in a manner to afford great pleasure; as, the lady sings and plays *delightfully.*

DELI'GHTFULNESS, *n.* The quality of being delightful, or of affording great pleasure; as the *delightfulness* of a prospect, or of scenery.

2. Great pleasure; delight. [*Less proper.*]

DELI'GHTLESS, *a.* Affording no pleasure or delight. *Thomson.*

DELI'GHTSOME, *a.* Very pleasing; delightful. *Grew.*

DELI'GHTSOMELY, *adv.* Very pleasantly; in a delightful manner.

DELI'GHTSOMENESS, *n.* Delightfulness; pleasantness in a high degree.

DELIN'EAMENT, *n.* [infra.] Representation by delineation. *Selden.*

DELIN'EATE, *v. t.* [L. *delineo; de* and *lineo*, from *linea*, a line.]

1. To draw the lines which exhibit the form of a thing; to mark out with lines; to make a draught; to sketch or design; as, to *delineate* the form of the earth, or a diagram.

2. To paint; to represent in picture; to draw a likeness of; as, to *delineate* Nestor like Adonis, or time with Absalom's head. *Brown.*

3. *Figuratively*, to describe; to represent to the mind or understanding; to exhibit a likeness in words; as, to *delineate* the character of Newton, or the virtue of Aristides.

DELIN'EATED, *pp.* Drawn; marked with lines exhibiting the form or figure; sketched; designed; painted; described.

DELIN'EATING, *ppr.* Drawing the form; sketching; painting; describing.

DELINEA'TION, *n.* [L. *delineatio.*] First draught of a thing; outline; representation of a form or figure by lines; sketch; design.

2. Representation in words; description; as the *delineation* of a character.

DELIN'EATURE, *n.* Delineation. [*Not in use.*]

DELIN'IMENT, *n.* [L. *delinimentum.*] Mitigation. [*Not used.*]

DELIN'QUENCY, *n.* [L. *delinquo*, to fail or omit duty; *de* and *linquo*, to leave.]

Failure or omission of duty; a fault; a misdeed; and positively, an offense; a crime. It is particularly, but not exclusively applied to neglect of duty in officers of public trust.

DELIN'QUENT, *a.* Failing in duty; offending by neglect of duty.

DELIN'QUENT, *n.* One who fails to perform his duty, particularly a public officer who neglects his duty; an offender; one who commits a fault or crime.

A *delinquent* ought to be cited in the place or jurisdiction where the *delinquency* was committed. *Ayliffe.*

DEL'IQUATE, *v. t.* or *i.* [L. *deliqueo*, to melt.] To melt or be dissolved. [See *Deliquesce* and *Deliquiate.*]

DELIQUA'TION, *n.* A melting. [See *Deliquescence* and *Deliquiation.*]

DELIQUESCE, *v. i.* *deliques'.* [L. *deliquesco*, to melt; *de* and *liquesco*, from *liqueo*, to melt or become soft. See *Liquid.*]

To melt gradually and become liquid by attracting and absorbing moisture from the air; as certain salts, acids and alkalies.

DELIQUES'CENCE, *n.* Spontaneous liquefaction in the air; a gradual melting or becoming liquid by absorption of water from the atmosphere. *Fourcroy.*

DELIQUES'CENT, *a.* Liquefying in the air; capable of attracting moisture from the atmosphere and becoming liquid; as *deliquescent* salts. *Fourcroy.*

DELIQ'UIATE, *v. i.* [See *Deliquate.*] To melt and become liquid by imbibing water from the air. [See *Deliquesce.*] *Fourcroy.*

DELIQUIA'TION, *n.* A melting by attracting water from the air.

DELIQ'UIUM, *n.* [L.] In *chimistry*, a melting or dissolution in the air, or in a moist place. *Encyc.*

2. A liquid state; as, a salt falls into a *deliquium.* *Fourcroy.*

3. In *medicine*, a swooning or fainting; called also *syncope.* *Encyc. Coxe.*

DELIR'AMENT, *n.* A wandering of the mind; foolish fancy. [*Little used.*]

DELIR'IOUS, *a.* [L. *delirus.* See *Delirium.*] Roving in mind; light-headed; disordered in intellect; having ideas that are wild, irregular and unconnected.

DELIR'IOUSNESS, *n.* The state of being delirious; delirium. *Johnson.*

DELIR'IUM, *n.* [L. from *deliro*, to wander in mind, to rave; *de* and *liro*, to make balks in plowing, that is, to err, wander, miss.]

A state in which the ideas of a person are wild, irregular and unconnected, or do not correspond with the truth or with external objects; a roving or wandering of the mind; disorder of the intellect. Fevers often produce *delirium.*

An alienation of mind connected with fever. *Cyc.*

Symptomatic derangement, or that which is dependent on some other disease, in distinction from idiopathic derangement or *mania.*

DELITES'CENCE, *n.* [L. *delitescentia; de* and *lateo.*] Retirement; obscurity. *Johnson.*

DELIV'ER, *v. t.* [Fr. *delivrer; de* and *livrer*, to deliver; Sp. *librar;* Port. *livrar;* L. *liber*, free, disengaged; *delibro*, to free, to peel; Arm. *delivra*. See *Liberal, Library, Librate*.]

1. To free; to release, as from restraint; to set at liberty; as, to *deliver* one from captivity.

2. To rescue, or save.

Deliver me, O my God, from the hand of the wicked. Ps. lxxi.

3. To give, or transfer; to put into another's hand or power; to commit; to pass from one to another.

Thou shalt *deliver* Pharaoh's cup into his hand. Gen. xl.

So we say, to *deliver* goods to a carrier; to *deliver* a letter; to *deliver* possession of an estate.

4. To surrender; to yield; to give up; to resign; as, to *deliver* a fortress to an enemy. It is often followed by *up;* as, to *deliver up* the city; to *deliver up* stolen goods.

Th' exalted mind
All sense of woe *delivers* to the wind. *Pope.*

5. To disburden of a child.

6. To utter; to pronounce; to speak; to send forth in words; as, to *deliver* a sermon, an address, or an oration.

7. To exert in motion. [*Not in use.*]

To deliver to the wind, to cast away; to reject.

To deliver over, to transfer; to give or pass from one to another; as, to *deliver over* goods to another.

2. To surrender or resign; to put into another's power; to commit to the discretion of; to abandon to.

Deliver me not *over* to the will of my enemies. Ps. xxvii.

To deliver up, to give up; to surrender.

DELIV'ER, *a.* [L. *liber.*] Free; nimble. *Obs.* *Chaucer.*

DELIV'ERABLE, *a.* That may be or is to be delivered.

A bill of lading may state that the goods are *deliverable* to a particular person therein named. *Mer. Usage. Amer. Review.*

DELIV'ERANCE, *n.* [Fr. *delivrance.*] Release from captivity, slavery, oppression, or any restraint.

He hath sent me to heal the broken-hearted, to preach *deliverance* to the captives. Luke iv.

2. Rescue from danger or any evil.

God sent me to save your lives by a great *deliverance.* Gen. xlv.

3. The act of bringing forth children. *Bacon.*

4. The act of giving or transferring from one to another.

5. The act of speaking or pronouncing; utterance. *Shak.*

[In the three last senses, *delivery* is now used.]

6. Acquittal of a prisoner, by the verdict of a jury. God send you a good *deliverance.*

DELIV'ERED, *pp.* Freed; released; transferred or transmitted; passed from one to another; committed; yielded; surrendered; rescued; uttered; pronounced.

DELIV'ERER, *n.* One who delivers; one who releases or rescues; a preserver.

The Lord raised up a *deliverer* to Israel. Judges iii.

2. One who relates, or communicates. *Boyle.*

DELIV'ERING, *ppr.* Releasing; setting free; rescuing; saving; surrendering; giving over; yielding; resigning.

DELIV'ERY, *n.* The act of delivering.

2. Release; rescue; as from slavery, restraint, oppression or danger.

3. Surrender; a giving up.

4. A giving or passing from one to another; as the *delivery* of goods, or of a deed.

5. Utterance; pronunciation; or manner of speaking. He has a good *delivery.* I was charmed with his graceful *delivery.*

6. Childbirth. Is. xxvi.

7. Free motion or use of the limbs. [*Obs.*] *Sidney. Wotton.*

DELL, *n.* [Qu. *dale*, or W. *dell*, a cleft or rift; or is it contracted from Sax. *degle?*] A pit, or a hollow place; a cavity or narrow opening. *Spenser. Milton.*

DELPH. [See *Delf.* No. 2.]

DELPH'IA, DELPHIN'IA, *n.* A vegetable alkali lately discovered in the Delphinium staphysagria. It is crystaline when wet, but it becomes opake when exposed to air. Its taste is bitter and acrid. When heated it melts, but on cooling becomes hard and brittle like resin. *Ure. Webster's Manual.*

DELPH'IAN, DELPH'IC, *a.* [from *Delphi*, a town of Phocis in Greece.] Relating to Delphi, and to the celebrated oracle of that place.

DELPH'INE, *a.* [L. *delphinus.*] Pertaining to the dolphin, a genus of fishes.

2. Pertaining to the dauphin of France; as the *delphine* edition of the classics.

DELPH'INITE, *n.* A mineral called also pistacite and epidote. *Ure.*

DEL'TOID, *n.* [Gr. δελτα, the letter Δ, and ειδος, form.]

1. Resembling the Gr. Δ; triangular; an epithet applied to a muscle of the shoulder which moves the arm forwards, upwards and backwards. *Coxe.*

2. In *botany*, shaped somewhat like a delta or rhomb, having four angles, of which the lateral ones are less distant from the base than the others; as a *deltoid* leaf. *Linne. Martyn.*

Trowel-shaped, having three angles, of which the terminal one is much further from the base than the lateral ones. *Smith.*

DELU'DABLE, *a.* [See *Delude.*] That may be deluded or deceived; liable to be imposed on. *Brown.*

DELU'DE, *v. t.* [L. *deludo*; *de* and *ludo*, to play, to mock; Ch. and Heb. לוץ. Class Ls. No. 3. 5. 30. 46.]

1. To deceive; to impose on; to lead from truth or into error; to mislead the mind or judgment; to beguile. *Cheat* is generally applied to deception in bargains; *delude*, to deception in opinion. An artful man *deludes* his followers. We are often *deluded* by false appearances.

2. To frustrate or disappoint.

DELU'DED, *pp.* Deceived; misled; led into error.

DELU'DER, *n.* One who deceives; a deceiver; an imposter; one who holds out false pretenses.

DELU'DING, *ppr.* Deceiving; leading astray; misleading the opinion or judgment.

DELU'DING, *n.* The act of deceiving; falsehood. *Prideaux.*

DEL'UGE, *n.* [Fr. *deluge;* Arm. *diluich;* Sp. *diluvio;* It. *id.;* L. *diluvies, diluvium,* from *diluo, diluvio; di* and *luo, lavo*, to wash. If *deluge* and *diluvium* are the same word, of which there can be little doubt, the fact proves that *luo, lavo*, is contracted or changed from *lugo*, and that the primitive word was *lugo;* and it is certain that the radix of *fluo* is *flugo.* See *Flow.*]

1. Any overflowing of water; an inundation; a flood; a swell of water over the natural banks of a river or shore of the ocean, spreading over the adjacent land. But appropriately, the great flood or overflowing of the earth by water, in the days of Noah; according to the common chronology, Anno Mundi, 1656. Gen. vi.

2. A sweeping or overwhelming calamity.

DEL'UGE, *v. t.* To overflow with water; to inundate; to drown. The waters *deluged* the earth and destroyed the old world.

2. To overwhelm; to cover with any flowing or moving, spreading body. The Northern nations *deluged* the Roman empire with their armies.

3. To overwhelm; to cause to sink under the weight of a general or spreading calamity; as, the land is *deluged* with corruption.

DEL'UGED, *pp.* Overflowed; inundated: overwhelmed.

DEL'UGING, *ppr.* Overflowing; inundating; overwhelming.

DELU'SION, *n. s* as *z*. [L. *delusio.* See *Delude.*] The act of deluding; deception; a misleading of the mind. We are all liable to the *delusions* of artifice.

2. False representation; illusion; error or mistake proceeding from false views.

And fondly mourn'd the dear *delusion* gone. *Prior.*

DELU'SIVE, *a.* Apt to deceive; tending to mislead the mind; deceptive; beguiling; as *delusive* arts; *delusive* appearances.

DELU'SIVENESS, *n.* The quality of being delusive; tendency to deceive.

DELU'SORY, *a.* Apt to deceive; deceptive. *Glanville.*

DELVE, *v. t.* *delv.* [Sax. *delfan;* D. *delven;* Russ. *dolblyu;* to dig. Qu. Arm. *toulla*, to dig or make a hole, W. *twll*, a hole, and L. *talpa*, a mole, perhaps the *delver.*]

1. To dig; to open the ground with a spade.

Delve of convenient depth your thrashing floor. *Dryden.*

2. To fathom; to sound; to penetrate. [*Not used.*]

I cannot *delve* him to the root. *Shak.*

DELVE, *n.* *delv.* A place dug: a pit; a pitfall; a ditch; a den; a cave. [*Not now used.*] *Spenser.*

Delve of coals, a quantity of fossil coals dug. [*Not used or local.*]

DELV'ER, *n.* One who digs, as with a spade.

DELV'ING, *ppr.* Digging.

DEM'AGOGUE, *n.* *dem'agog.* [Gr. δημαγωγος, from δημος, the populace, and αγω, to lead.]

1. A leader of the people; an orator who pleases the populace and influences them to adhere to him.

2. Any leader of the populace; any factious man who has great influence with the great body of people in a city or community.

DEMA'IN, *n.* [Norm. *demainer.* This might be from L. *dominium,* Fr. *domaine.* But in old law books it is written *demesne,* as if derived from *meisan, maison,* house. In Norman, it is written also *demaygne, demeigne,* as well as *demeine.*]

1. A manor-house and the land adjacent or near, which a lord keeps in his own hands or immediate occupation, for the use of his family, as distinguished from his tenemental lands, distributed among his tenants, called book-land, or charter-land, and folk-land, or estates held in villenage, from which sprung copyhold estates. *Blackstone.*

2. Estate in lands. *Shak.*

DEM'AND, *v. t.* [Fr. *demander;* Sp. Port. *demandar;* It. *domandare* or *dimandare;* Arm. *mennat; de* and L. *mando,* to command. The L. *mando* signifies to send; hence, to commit or entrust. To *ask* is to *press* or *urge.* Sw. *mana,* Dan. *maner,* to put in mind, to urge, press, dun; to admonish, L. *moneo.* It appears that *mando, moneo* and *mens, mind,* are all of one family; as also Ir. *muinim,* to teach; W. *mynu,* to will, to seek or procure, to insist, to obtain or have; Sax. *manian;* G. *mahnen.* See Class Mn. No. 7. 9.]

1. To ask or call for, as one who has a claim or right to receive what is sought; to claim or seek as due by right. The creditor *demands* principal and interest of his debt. Here the claim is derived from law or justice.

2. To ask by authority; to require; to seek or claim an answer by virtue of a right or supposed right in the interrogator, derived from his office, station, power or authority.

The officers of the children of Israel—were beaten, and *demanded,* wherefore have ye not fulfilled your task in making brick. Ex. v.

3. To require as necessary or useful; as, the execution of this work *demands* great industry and care.

4. To ask; to question; to inquire.

The soldiers also *demanded* of him, saying, what shall we do? Luke iii.

5. To ask or require, as a seller of goods; as, what price do you *demand?*

6. To sue for; to seek to obtain by legal process; as, the plaintiff, in his action, *demands* unreasonable damages.

In French, *demander* generally signifies simply to ask, request, or petition, when the answer or thing asked for, is a matter of grace or courtesy. But in English, *demand* is now seldom used in that sense, and rarely indeed can the French *demander* be rendered correctly in English by *demand,* except in the case of the seller of goods, who *demands,* [asks, requires,] a certain price for his wares. The common expression, "a king sent to *demand* another king's daughter in marriage," is improper.

DEM'AND, *n.* An asking for or claim made by virtue of a right or supposed right to the thing sought; an asking with authority; a challenging as due; as, the *demand* of the creditor was reasonable; the note is payable on *demand.*

He that has confidence to turn his wishes into *demands,* will be but a little way from thinking he ought to obtain them. *Locke.*

2. The asking or requiring of a price for goods offered for sale; as, I cannot agree to his *demand.*

3. That which is or may be claimed as due; debt; as, what are your *demands* on the estate?

4. The calling for in order to purchase; desire to possess; as, the *demand* for the Bible has been great and extensive; copies are in great *demand.*

5. A desire or a seeking to obtain. We say, the company of a gentleman is in great *demand;* the lady is in great *demand* or request.

6. In *law,* the asking or seeking for what is due or claimed as due, either expressly by words, or by implication, as by seizure of goods, or entry into lands.

DEM'ANDABLE, *a.* That may be demanded, claimed, asked for, or required; as, payment is *demandable* at the expiration of the credit.

DEM'ANDANT, *n.* One who demands; the plaintiff in a real action; any plaintiff.

DEM'ANDED, *pp.* Called for; claimed; challenged as due; requested; required; interrogated.

DEM'ANDER, *n.* One who demands; one who requires with authority; one who claims as due; one who asks; one who seeks to obtain.

DEM'ANDING, *ppr.* Claiming or calling for as due, or by authority; requiring; asking; pursuing a claim by legal process; interrogating.

DEM'ANDRESS, *n.* A female demandant.

DEM'ARCH, *n.* [Fr. *demarche.*] March; walk; gait. *Obs.*

DEMARKA'TION, *n.* [Sp. *demarcacion,* from *demarcar; de* and *marcar,* to mark, *marca,* a mark; Port. *demarcar.* See *Mark.*]

1. The act of marking, or of ascertaining and setting a limit.

2. A limit or bound ascertained and fixed; line of separation marked or determined.

The speculative line of *demarkation,* where obedience ought to end and resistance begin, is faint, obscure, and not easily definable. *Burke.*

DEME'AN, *v. t.* [Fr. *demener;* Norm. *demesner, demener,* to lead, to manage, to govern, to stir; It. *menare;* Sp. *menear.*]

1. To behave; to carry; to conduct; *with the reciprocal pronoun;* as, it is our duty to *demean ourselves* with humility.

2. To treat. *Spenser.*

DEME'AN, *v. t.* [*de* and *mean.*] To debase; to undervalue. [*Not used.*] *Shak.*

DEME'AN, *n.* Behavior; carriage; demeanor. *Obs.* *Spenser.*

2. Mien. *Obs.* *Ibm.*

DEME'ANOR, *n.* Behavior; carriage; deportment; as decent *demeanor;* sad *demeanor.* *Milton.*

DEME'ANURE, *n.* Behavior. [*Not in use.*]

DE'MENCY, *n.* [L. *dementia.*] Madness. [*Not in use.*] *Skelton.*

DEMEN'TATE, *a.* Mad; infatuated. *Hammond.*

DEMEN'TATE, *v. t.* [L. *demento; de* and *mens.*] To make mad. *Burton.*

DEMENTA'TION, *n.* The act of making frantic. *Whitlock.*

DEMEPHITIZA'TION, *n.* [See *Demephitize.*]

The act of purifying from mephitic or foul air. *Med. Repository.*

DEMEPH'ITIZE, *v. t.* [*de* and *mephitis,* foul air, or ill smell.] To purify from foul unwholesome air.

DEMEPH'ITIZED, *pp.* Purified; freed from foul air.

DEMEPH'ITIZING, *ppr.* Purifying from foul air.

DEMER'IT, *n.* [Fr. *demerite; de* and *merite,* merit, L. *meritum,* from *mereo,* to earn or deserve. The Latin *demereo* is used in a good sense. See *Merit.*]

1. That which deserves punishment, the opposite of *merit;* an ill-deserving; that which is blamable or punishable in moral conduct; vice or crime.

Mine is the merit, the *demerit* thine. *Dryden.*

2. Anciently, merit; desert; *in a good sense.* *Shak.*

DEMER'IT, *v. t.* To deserve blame or punishment. [*I believe not in use.*]

DEMERS'ED, *a.* [L. *demersus.*] Plunged; situated or growing under water.

DEMER'SION, *n.* [L. *demersio,* from *demergo,* to plunge or drown.]

1. A plunging into a fluid; a drowning. *Trans. of Pausanias.*

2. The state of being overwhelmed in water or earth. *Ray.*

3. The putting of a medicine in a dissolving liquor. *Dict.*

DEMESNE. [See *Demain.*]

DEM'I, a prefix, Fr. *demi,* from the L. *dimidium,* signifies *half.* It is used only in composition.

DEMI-BRIGA'DE, *n.* A half-brigade.

DEM'I-CADENCE, *n.* In *music,* an imperfect cadence, or one that falls on any other than the key note. *Busby.*

DEM'I-CANNON, *n.* A cannon of different sizes; the *lowest* carries a ball of thirty pounds weight, and six inches diameter; the *ordinary* is twelve feet long, and carries a shot of six inches and one-sixth diameter, and thirty two pounds weight; that of the greatest size is twelve feet long, and carries a ball of six inches and five eighths diameter, and thirty six pounds weight. *Dict.*

DEM'I-CROSS, *n.* An instrument for taking the altitude of the sun and stars.

DEMI-CUL'VERIN, *n.* A large gun, or piece of ordnance; the least is ten feet long, and carries a ball of nine pounds weight and four inches diameter; that of ordinary size carries a ball of four inches and two eighths diameter, and ten pounds eleven ounces in weight; the largest size is ten feet and a third in length, and carries a ball four inches and a half in diameter, and of twelve pounds eleven ounces in weight. *Johnson. Encyc.*

DEM'I-DEVIL, *n.* Half a devil. *Shak.*

DEM'I-DISTANCE, *n.* In *fortification,* the distance between the outward polygons and the flank.

DEM'I-DITONE, *n.* In *music,* a minor third. *Busby.*

DEM'I-GOD, *n.* Half a god; one partaking of the divine nature; a fabulous hero, produced by the cohabitation of a deity with a mortal. *Milton. Pope.*

DEM'I-GORGE, *n.* In *fortification,* that part of the polygon which remains after the flank is raised, and goes from the curtain to the angle of the polygon. It is half of the vacant space or entrance into a bastion. *Encyc.*

DEM'I-GROAT, *n.* A half-groat. *Shenstone.*

DEM'I-LANCE, *n.* A light lance; a short spear; a half-pike. *Dryden.*

DEM'I-LUNE, *n.* A half-moon.

DEM'I-MAN, *n.* Half a man; *a term of reproach.* *Knolles.*

DEM'I-NATURED, *a.* Having half the nature of another animal. *Shak.*

DEMI-PREM'ISES, *n. plu.* Half-premises. *Hooker.*

DEM'I-QUAVER, *n.* A note in music, of half the length of the quaver.

DEM'IREP, *n.* A woman of suspicious chastity. [Demi-reputation.]

DEMI-SEMI-QUAVER, *n.* The shortest note in music, two of which are equal to a semi-quaver.

DEM'I-TONE, *n.* In *music*, an interval of half a tone; a semi-tone.

DEM'I-VILL, *n.* A half-vill, consisting of five freemen or frank pledges. *Spelman. Blackstone.*

DEM'I-VOLT, *n.* [*demi* and *volt, vault.*] One of the seven artificial motions of a horse, in which he raises his fore legs in a particular manner.

DEM'I-WÖLF, *n.* Half a wolf; a mongrel dog between a dog and a wolf; lycisca. *Shak.*

DEMIGRATE, DEMIGRATION. [*Not used.* See *Migrate.*]

DEMI'SABLE, *a.* *s* as *z.* [See *Demise.*] That may be leased; as an estate *demisable* by copy of court roll. *Blackstone.*

DEMI'SE, *n.* *s* as *z.* [Fr. *demis, demise,* from *demettre,* L. *demitto, demissio; de* and *mitto,* Fr. *mettre.* Literally, a laying down, or sending from; a removing.]

1. In *England,* a laying down or removal, applied to the crown or royal authority. The *demise* of the crown, is a transfer of the crown, royal authority or kingdom to a successor. Thus when Edward fourth was driven from his throne for a few months by the house of Lancaster, this temporary transfer of his dignity was called a *demise.* Hence the natural death of a king or queen came to be denominated a *demise,* as by that event, the crown is transferred to a successor. *Blackstone.*

2. A conveyance or transfer of an estate, by lease or will.

Demise and redemise, a conveyance where there are mutual leases made from one to another of the same land, or something out of it. *Encyc.*

DEMI'SE, *v. t.* *s* as *z.* To transfer or convey; to lease.

2. To bequeath; to grant by will. *Swift.*

DEMIS'SION, *n.* A lowering; degradation; depression. *L'Estrange.*

DEMISS'IVE, DEMISS', *a.* Humble. [*Little used.*] *Shenstone.*

DEMISS'LY, *adv.* In a humble manner. [*Not used.*] *Sherwood.*

DEMIT', *v. t.* [L. *demitto.*] To let fall; to depress; to submit. [*Not used.*]

DEM'IURGE, *n.* [Gr. δημιουγρος; δημιος, a public servant, and εργον, work.]

In *the mythology of Eastern Philosophers,* an eon employed in the creation of the world; a subordinate workman. *Encyc.*

DEMIUR'GIC, *a.* Pertaining to a demiurge, or to creative power. *Trans. of Pausanias.*

DEMOC'RACY, *n.* [Gr. δημοκρατια; δημος, people, and κρατεω, to possess, to govern.] Government by the people; a form of government, in which the supreme power is lodged in the hands of the people collectively, or in which the people exercise the powers of legislation. Such was the government of Athens.

DEM'OCRAT, *n.* One who adheres to a government by the people, or favors the extension of the right of suffrage to all classes of men.

DEMOCRAT'IC, DEMOCRAT'ICAL, *a.* Popular; pertaining to democracy or government by the people; as a *democratical* form of government.

DEMOCRAT'ICALLY, *adv.* In a democratical manner. *Sidney.*

DEMOL'ISH, *v. t.* [Fr. *demolir, demolissant;* Sp. *demoler;* It. *demolire;* L. *demolior; de* and *molior,* to build. Class Ml. No. 12. 15.]

To throw or pull down; to raze; to destroy, as a heap or structure; to separate any collected mass, or the connected parts of a thing; to ruin; as, to *demolish* an edifice, or a mound; to *demolish* a wall or fortification.

DEMOL'ISHED, *pp.* Pulled down; thrown down; razed; destroyed, as a fabric or structure.

DEMOL'ISHER, *n.* One who pulls or throws down; one who destroys or lays waste; as a *demolisher* of towns.

DEMOL'ISHING, *ppr.* Pulling or throwing down; destroying.

DEMOL'ISHMENT, *n.* Ruin; overthrow. *Beaum.*

DEMOLI''TION, *n.* The act of overthrowing, pulling down or destroying a pile or structure; ruin; destruction; as the *demolition* of a house, or of military works.

DE'MON, *n.* [L. *dæmon;* Gr. δαιμων; Sp. It. *demonio;* Fr. *demon;* Ir. *deamal* or *deamon.* The origin and primary sense of this word I have not been able to ascertain. Qu. Ar. دهم dahima, daima, to fall suddenly, to rush, to overwhelm, to obscure, to blacken; whence misfortune, black, blackness, evil, a monster: or is it a compound of *dea, dia, deus,* and *mon,* a word signifying evil, from the Persian? I place little confidence in these conjectures.]

A spirit, or immaterial being, holding a middle place between men and the celestial deities of the Pagans. The ancients believed that there were good and evil demons, which had influence over the minds of men, and that these beings carried on an intercourse between men and gods, conveying the addresses of men to the gods, and divine benefits to men. Hence demons became the objects of worship. It was suppossd also that human spirits, after their departure from the body, became demons, and that the souls of virtuous men, if highly purified, were exalted from demons into gods. In *the scriptures,* the English word is not used, but the Greek δαιμων is rendered *devil,* and sometimes at least improperly; for nothing is more certain than that different beings are intended by διαβολος and δαιμων. The demons of the New Testament were supposed to be spiritual beings which vexed and tormented men. And in general, the word, in modern use, signifies an evil spirit or genius, which influences the conduct or directs the fortunes of mankind. [See *Campbell's Dissert.*]

DE'MONESS, *n.* A female demon. *Mede.*

DEMO'NIAC, DEMONI'ACAL, DEMO'NIAN, *a.* Pertaining to demons or evil spirits.

From thy *demoniac* holds. *Milton.*

2. Influenced by demons; produced by demons or evil spirits.

Demoniac phrensy. *Milton.*

DEMO'NIAC, *n.* A human being possessed by a demon; one whose volition and other mental faculties are overpowered, restrained, or disturbed, in their regular operation, by an evil spirit, or by a created spiritual being of superior power. *Encyc.*

DEMO'NIACS, *n.* In *church history,* a branch of the Anabaptists, whose distinguishing tenet is, that at the end of the world the devil will be saved. *Encyc.*

DEMONOC'RACY, *n.* [Gr. δαιμων, demon, and κρατεω, to hold.] The power or government of demons.

DEMONOL'ATRY, *n.* [Gr. δαιμων, demon, and λατρεια, worship.] The worship of demons, or of evil spirits.

DEMONOL'OGY, *n.* [Gr. δαιμων, demon, and λογος, discourse.]

A discourse on demons; a treatise on evil spirits. So King James entitled his book concerning witches.

DEMON'OMIST, *n.* [Gr. δαιμων, demon, and νομος, law.]

One that lives in subjection to the devil, or to evil spirits. *Herbert.*

DEMON'OMY, *n.* [supra.] The dominion of demons, or of evil spirits. *Herbert.*

DE'MONSHIP, *n.* The state of a demon. *Mede.*

DEMON'STRABLE, *a.* [See *Demonstrate.*]

That may be demonstrated; that may be proved beyond doubt or contradiction; capable of being shown by certain evidence, or by evidence that admits of no doubt; as, the principles of geometry are *demonstrable.*

DEMON'STRABLENESS, *n.* The quality of being demonstrable.

DEMON'STRABLY, *adv.* In a manner to preclude doubt; beyond the possibility of contradiction.

DEM'ONSTRATE, *v. t.* [L. *demonstro; de* and *monstro,* to show; Fr. *demontrer;* Sp. Port. *demostrar;* It. *dimostrare.* See *Muster.*]

1. To show or prove to be certain; to prove beyond the possibility of doubt; to prove in such a manner as to reduce the contrary position to evident absurdity. We *demonstrate* a problem in geometry, or a proposition in ethics, by showing that the contrary is absurd or impossible.

2. In *anatomy,* to exhibit the parts when dissected.

DEM'ONSTRATED, *pp.* Proved beyond the possibility of doubt; rendered certain to the mind.

DEM'ONSTRATING, *ppr.* Proving to be certain; evincing beyond the possibility of doubt.

DEMONSTRA'TION, *n.* The act of demonstrating, or of exhibiting certain proof.

2. The highest degree of evidence; certain proof exhibited, or such proof as establishes a fact or proposition beyond a possibility of doubt, or as shows the contrary position to be absurd or impossible.

3. Indubitable evidence of the senses, or of reason; evidence which satisfies the mind of the certainty of a fact or proposition. Thus we hold that the works of nature exhibit *demonstration* of the existence of a God.

4. In *logic*, a series of syllogisms, all whose premises are either definitions, self-evident truths, or propositions already established. *Encyc.*

5. Show; exhibition. *Milford.*

6. In *anatomy*, the exhibition of parts dissected.

DEMON'STRATIVE, *a.* Showing or proving by certain evidence; having the power of demonstration; invincibly conclusive; as a *demonstrative* argument, or *demonstrative* reasoning.

2. Having the power of showing with clearness and certainty; as a *demonstrative* figure in painting. *Dryden.*

DEMON'STRATIVELY, *adv.* With certain evidence; with proof which cannot be questioned; certainly; clearly; convincingly.

DEM'ONSTRATOR, *n.* One who demonstrates; one who proves any thing with certainty, or with indubitable evidence.

2. In *anatomy*, one who exhibits the parts when dissected.

DEMON'STRATORY, *a.* Tending to demonstrate; having a tendency to prove beyond a possibility of doubt.

DEMORALIZA'TION, *n.* [See *Demoralize.*] The act of subverting or corrupting morals; destruction of moral principles.

DEMOR'ALIZE, *v. t.* [*de* and *moralize* or *moral.*] To corrupt or undermine the morals of; to destroy or lessen the effect of moral principles on; to render corrupt in morals.

The effect would be to *demoralize* mankind. *Grattan on Catholic Petition.*

The native vigor of the soul must wholly disappear, under the steady influence and the *demoralizing* example of profligate power and prosperous crime. *Walsh, Letters on France.*

DEMOR'ALIZED, *pp.* Corrupted in morals.

DEMOR'ALIZING, *ppr.* Corrupting or destroying morals or moral principles.

2. *a.* Tending to destroy morals or moral principles.

DEMULCE, *v. t. demuls'.* [L. *demulceo.*] To sooth; to soften or pacify. [*Not used.*]

DEMUL'CENT, *a.* [L. *demulcens, demulceo*; *de* and *mulceo*, to stroke, to soften; allied perhaps to *mollis, mellow.*] Softening; mollifying; lenient; as, oil is *demulcent.*

DEMUL'CENT, *n.* Any medicine which lessens acrimony, or the effects of stimulus on the solids; that which softens or mollifies; as gums, roots of marsh-mallows, and other mucilaginous substances. *Coxe. Encyc. Hooper.*

DEMUR', *v. i.* [Fr. *demeurer*; Sp. *demorar*; Port. *demorar*; It. *dimorare*; L. *demoror*; *de* and *moror*, to stay or delay, *mora*, delay; Arm. *miret*, to hold; Sax. *merran, myrran*, to hinder; allied to L. *miror*, and Eng. to *moor*, Sp. *amarrar.*]

1. To stop; to pause; to hesitate; to suspend proceeding; to delay determination or conclusion.

On receiving this information, the minister *demurred*, till he could obtain further instructions.

2. In *law*, to stop at any point in the pleadings, and rest or abide on that point in law for a decision of the cause. Thus, the defendant may *demur* to the plaintiff's declaration, alledging it to be insufficient in law; the plaintiff may *demur* to the defendant's plea, for a like reason.

DEMUR', *v. t.* To doubt of. [*Not legitimate.*] *Milton.*

DEMUR', *n.* Stop; pause; hesitation as to the propriety of proceeding; suspense of proceeding or decision.

All my *demurs* but double his attacks. *Pope.*

DEMU'RE, *a.* [perhaps from *demur*, that is, set, fixed, stayed, silent.] Sober; grave; modest; downcast; as a *demure* countenance; a *demure* abasing of the eye. *Bacon.*

DEMU'RE, *v. i.* To look with a grave countenance. [*Not used.*] *Shak.*

DEMU'RELY, *adv.* With a grave, solemn countenance; with a fixed look; with a solemn gravity.

Esop's damsel sat *demurely* at the board's end. *Bacon.*

DEMU'RENESS, *n.* Gravity of countenance; soberness; a modest look. *Sidney.*

DEMUR'RAGE, *n.* [See *Demur.*] An allowance made to the master of a trading vessel, for delay or detention in port beyond the appointed time of departure. This expense is paid by the merchant who causes the detention.

DEMUR'RER, *n.* One who demurs.

2. In *law*, a stop at some point in the pleadings, and a resting of the decision of the cause on that point; an issue on matter of law. A demurrer confesses the fact or facts to be true, but denies the sufficiency of the facts in point of law to support the claim or defense. A demurrer may be tendered to the declaration, to the plea, to the replication, to the rejoinder, &c. *Blackstone.*

DEMUR'RING, *ppr.* Stopping; pausing; suspending proceedings or decision; resting or abiding on a point in law.

DEMY', *n.* [Fr. *demi*, half.] A particular size of paper; a kind of paper of small size.

2. A half fellow at Magdalen college, Oxford.

DEN, *n.* [Sax. *den, dene, denn*, a valley; It. *tana*; Fr. *taniere*; Ir. *tuinnedhe.*]

1. A cave or hollow place in the earth; usually applied to a cave, pit, or subterraneous recess, used for concealment, shelter, protection or security; as a lion's *den*; a *den* of robbers or thieves.

The beasts go into *dens*. The children of Israel made themselves *dens*. Job xxxvii. Judges vi.

2. As a termination, in names of places, it denotes the place to be in a valley or near a wood.

DEN, *v. i.* To dwell as in a den.

DEN'ARCOTIZE, *v. t.* [*de* and *narcotic.*] To deprive of narcotine; to depurate from the principle called narcotine. *Journ. of Science.*

DEN'ARY, *a.* [L. *denarius.*] Containing ten.

DEN'ARY, *n.* The number ten. *Digby.*

DENA'TIONALIZE, *v. t.* [*de* and *nation.*] To divest of national character or rights, by transferrence to the service of another nation. A ship built and registered in the United States, is *denationalized* by being employed in the service of another nation and bearing its flag. *French Decrees. Dec. of the Prince Regent.*

DENA'Y, *n.* Denial; refusal. *Obs.* *Shak.*

DENA'Y, *v. t.* To deny. *Obs.* *Spenser.*

DEN'DRACHATE, *n.* [Gr. δενδρον, a tree, and αχατης, agate.] Arborescent agate; agate containing the figures of shrubs or parts of plants. *Encyc.*

DEN'DRITE, *n.* [Gr. δενδριτις, from δενδρον, a tree.] A stone or mineral on or in which are the figures of shrubs or trees; an arborescent mineral. *Fourcroy.*

DENDRIT'IC, DENDRIT'ICAL, *a.* Containing the figures of shrubs or trees.

DEN'DROID, *a.* [Gr. δενδρον, a tree, and ειδος, form.] Resembling a shrub.

DEN'DROIT, *n.* A fossil which has some resemblance in form to the branch of a tree. *Dict. of Nat. Hist.*

DEN'DROLITE, *n.* [Gr. δενδρον, a tree, and λιθος, a stone.] A petrified or fossil shrub, plant, or part of a plant. *Dict. of Nat. Hist.*

DENDROL'OGY, *n.* [Gr. δενδρον, a tree, and λογος, a discourse.] A discourse or treatise on trees; the natural history of trees. *Dict.*

DENDROM'ETER, *n.* [Gr. δενδρον, tree, and μετρεω, to measure.] An instrument to measure the highth and diameter of trees. *Encyc.*

DEN'EGATE, *v. t.* [L. *denego.*] To deny. [*Not used.*]

DENEGA'TION, *n.* Denial. [*Not in use.*]

DENI'ABLE, *a.* [See *Deny.*] That may be denied, or contradicted. *Brown.*

DENI'AL, *n.* [See *Deny.*] An affirmation to the contrary; an assertion that a declaration or fact stated is not true; negation; contradiction. It is often expressed by *no* or *not*, simply.

2. Refusal to grant; the negation of a request or petition; the contrary to *grant, allowance* or *concession*; as, his request or application met with a direct *denial.*

3. A rejection, or refusing to acknowledge; a disowning; as a *denial* of God: or a refusing to receive or embrace; as a *denial* of the faith or the truth.

4. A *denial of one's self*, is a declining of some gratification; restraint of one's appetites or propensities.

DENI'ER, *n.* One who denies, or contradicts; one who refuses, or rejects; a disowner; one who does not own, avow or acknowledge; as a *denier* of a fact, or of the faith, or of Christ.

DENIE'R, *n.* [Fr. from L. *denarius*; It. *danaio, danaro*; Sp. *dinero.*] A small denomination of French money, the twelfth part of a sol; a small copper coin.

DEN'IGRATE, *v. t.* [L. *denigro*; *de* and *nigro*, from *niger*, black.] To blacken; to make black. *Boyle.*

DENIGRA'TION, *n.* The act of making black; a blackening.

DENITRA'TION, *n.* A disengaging of nitric acid. *Obs.*

DENIZA'TION, *n.* [See *Denizen.*] The act of making one a denizen, subject or citizen. This in England is done by the king's letters patent.

DEN'IZEN, *n.* *den'izn.* [In W. *dinaswr* is

a citizen, from *dinas*, *din*, a fortress or fortified town, a city. But in *denizen*, the last syllable seems to be the same as in *citizen*.]

1. In *England*, an alien who is made a subject by the king's letters patent, holding a middle state between an alien and a natural born subject. He may take land by purchase or devise, which an alien cannot; but he cannot take by inheritance. *Encyc. English Law.*

2. A stranger admitted to residence and certain rights in a foreign country.

Ye gods,
Natives, or *denizens*, of blest abodes. *Dryden.*

3. A citizen.

DEN'IZEN, *v. t.* To make a denizen; to admit to residence with certain rights and privileges; to infranchise.

DENOM'INABLE, *a.* [See *Denominate.*] That may be denominated, or named. *Brown.*

DENOM'INATE, *v, t.* [L. *denomino; de* and *nomino*, to name. See *Name.*] To name; to give a name or epithet to; as, a race of intelligent beings *denominated* MAN. Actions are *denominated* virtuous, or vicious, according to their character.

DENOM'INATED, *pp.* Named; called.

DENOM'INATING, *ppr.* Naming.

DENOMINA'TION, *n.* The act of naming.

2. A name or appellation; a vocal sound, customarily used to express a thing or a quality, in discourse; as, all men fall under the *denomination* of sinners; actions fall under the *denomination* of good or bad.

3. A class, society or collection of individuals, called by the same name; as a *denomination* of christians.

DENOM'INATIVE, *a.* That gives a name; that confers a distinct appellation.

DENOM'INATOR, *n.* He that gives a name.

2. In *arithmetic*, that number placed below the line in vulgar fractions, which shows into how many parts the integer is divided. Thus in $\frac{3}{5}$, 5 is the *denominator*, showing that the integer is divided into five parts; and the numerator 3 shows how many parts are taken, that is, *three fifths*.

DENO'TABLE, *a.* That may be denoted, or marked. *Brown.*

DENOTA'TION, *n.* [L. *denotatio.* See *Denote.*] The act of denoting. *Hammond.*

DENO'TATIVE, *a.* Having power to denote.

DENO'TE, *v. t.* [L. *denoto; de* and *noto*, to note or mark; Fr. *denoter;* Sp. *denotar;* It. *denotare.*]

1. To mark; to signify by a visible sign; to indicate; to express. The character × *denotes* multiplication. *Day's Algebra.*

2. To show; to betoken; to indicate; as, a quick pulse *denotes* fever.

DENO'TED, *pp.* Marked; signified, indicated.

DENO'TEMENT, *n.* Sign; indication. *Shak.*

DENO'TING, *ppr.* Marking; expressing; indicating.

DENOUEMENT, *n.* [Fr. from *denouer*, to untie; *de* and *nouer*, to tie, L. *nodo.*] The unraveling or discovery of a plot. [*Not English.*] *Warton.*

DENOUNCE, *v. t. denouns'.* [Fr. *denoncer;* Sp. *denunciar;* It. *denunziare;* L. *denuncio; de* and *nuncio*, to tell, or declare, from *nomen* or its root.]

1. To declare solemnly; to proclaim in a threatening manner; to announce or declare, as a threat.

I *denounce* to you this day, that ye shall surely perish. Deut. xxx.

So we say, to *denounce* war; to *denounce* wrath.

2. To threaten by some outward sign, or expression.

His look *denounced* revenge. *Milton.*

3. To inform against; to accuse; as, to *denounce* one for neglect of duty.

DENOUN'CED, *pp.* Threatened by open declaration; as, punishment is *denounced* against the ungodly.

2. Accused; proclaimed; as, he was *denounced* as an enemy.

DENOUNCEMENT, *n. denouns'ment.* The declaration of a menace, or of evil; denunciation. *Brown.*

DENOUN'CER, *n.* One who denounces, or declares a menace.

Here comes the sad *denouncer* of my fate. *Dryden.*

DENOUN'CING, *ppr.* Declaring, as a threat; threatening; accusing.

DENSE, *a. dens.* [L. *densus;* Fr. *dense;* Sp. It. *denso.* Qu. Gr. δασυς, *n* being casual.]

1. Close; compact; having its constituent parts closely united; applied to solids or fluids; as a *dense* body; *dense* air.

2. Thick; as a *dense* cloud, or fog.

DENSENESS, *n. dens'ness.* The same as *density.*

DENS'ITY, *n.* [L. *densitas.*] Closeness of constituent parts; compactness. *Density* is opposed to *rarity;* and in philosophy, the *density* of a body indicates the quantity of matter contained in it, under a given bulk. If a body of equal bulk with another is of double the density, it contains double the quantity of matter.

2. Thickness; as the *density* of fog.

DENT, *n.* [Arm. *danta*, to gap or notch. It seems to be from *dant*, a tooth; Fr. *dent;* L. *dens;* Gr. οδους; W. *dant;* It. *dente;* Sp. *diente*, whence *dentar*, *endentar*, to tooth; Port. *dente;* Pers. دندان dandan; Gypsey and Hindoo, *dant*, *danda.* Hence Fr. *denteler*, to dent or indent, to jag or notch.]

1. Literally, a tooth or projecting point. But it is used to express a gap or notch, or rather a depression or small hollow in a solid body; a hollow made by the pressure of a harder body on a softer; indentation. In this sense, it is in customary use in the United States.

2. A stroke. *Spenser.*

DENT, *v. t.* To make a dent or small hollow. [See *Indent.*]

DEN'TAL, *a.* [L. *dentalis.*] Pertaining to the teeth. In *grammar*, formed or pronounced by the teeth, with the aid of the tongue; as, D and T are *dental* letters.

DEN'TAL, *n.* An articulation or letter formed by placing the end of the tongue against the upper teeth, or against the gum that covers the root of the upper teeth, as D, T, and Th.

2. A genus of shell-fish, Dentalium, of several species. The shell consists of one tubulous straight valve, open at both ends. *Encyc.*

DEN'TALITE, *n.* A fossil shell of the genus Dentalium.

DEN'TATE, } *a.* [L. *dentatus*, from *dens.*]
DEN'TATED, } Toothed; notched.

In botany, a *dentated* root is one that consists of a concatenation of joints, resembling a necklace.

A *dentate* leaf is one that has horizontal points, with a space between each, or points in the plane of the disk, or having points like teeth on the margin. *Martyn.*

DENTATO-SIN'UATE, *a.* Having points like teeth with hollows about the edge.

DEN'TED, *a.* Indented; impressed with little hollows.

DENTEL'LI, *n.* [It. *dentello.* See *Dentil.*] Modillions. *Spectator.*

DEN'TICLE, *n.* [L. *denticulus.*] A small tooth or projecting point. *Lee.*

DENTIC'ULATE, } *a.* [L. *denticulatus*,
DENTIC'ULATED, } from *dens*, a tooth.]

Having small teeth or notches; as a *denticulate* leaf, calyx or seed. *Botany.*

DENTICULA'TION, *n.* The state of being set with small teeth, or prominences or points, resembling the teeth of a saw. *Grew.*

DEN'TIFORM, *a.* [L. *dens*, a tooth, and *forma*, form.] Having the form of a tooth. *Kirwan.*

DEN'TIFRICE, *n.* [Fr. from L. *dens*, a tooth, and *frico*, to rub.] A powder or other substance to be used in cleaning the teeth. Burnt shells and charcoal pulverized make an excellent *dentifrice.*

DEN'TIL, *n.* [L. *dens*, a tooth.] In *architecture*, an ornament in cornices bearing some resemblance to teeth; used particularly in the Ionic and Corinthian order.

DEN'TIST, *n.* One whose occupation is to clean and extract teeth, or repair the loss of them.

DENTI''TION, *n.* [L. *dentitio*, from *dentio*, to breed teeth, from *dens.*]

1. The breeding or cutting of teeth in infancy.

2. The time of breeding teeth.

DEN'TIZE, *v. t.* To renew the teeth, or have them renewed. *Bacon.*

DEN'TOID, *a.* [L. *dens*, a tooth, and Gr. ειδος, form.] Having the form of teeth. *Barton.*

DENU'DATE, } *v. t.* [L. *denudo; de* and
DENU'DE, } *nudo*, to make bare; *nudus*, naked.]

To strip; to divest of all covering; to make bare or naked. *Ray. Sharp.*

DENUDA'TION, *n.* The act of stripping off covering; a making bare.

2. In *geology*, the act of washing away the surface of the earth by the deluge or other flood. *Buckland.*

DENU'DED, *pp.* Stripped; divested of covering; laid bare.

DENU'DING, *ppr.* Stripping of covering; making bare.

DENUN'CIATE, *v. t.* [L. *denuncio.*] To denounce, *which see.*

DENUNCIA'TION, *n.* [L. *denunciatio*, from *denuncio.* See *Denounce.*]

1. Publication; proclamation; annunciation;

preaching; as a faithful *denunciation* of the gospel. *Milner.*

2. Solemn or formal declaration, accompanied with a menace; or the declaration of intended evil; proclamation of a threat; a public menace; as a *denunciation* of war, or of wrath.

DENUNCIA'TOR, *n.* He that denounces; one who publishes or proclaims, especially intended evil; one who threatens.

2. An accuser; one who informs against another. *Ayliffe.*

DENY', *v. t.* [Fr. *denier*; L. *denego*; *de* and *nego*, to deny, Sw. *neka*, W. *nacu*. Hence *nay*, Dan. *nej*. The sense is to thrust from.]

1. To contradict; to gainsay; to declare a statement or position not to be true. We *deny* what another says, or we *deny* a proposition. We *deny* the truth of an assertion, or the assertion itself. The sense of this verb is often expressed by *no* or *nay*.

2. To refuse to grant; as, we asked for bread, and the man *denied* us.

3. Not to afford; to withhold.

Who finds not Providence all good and wise,
Alike in what it gives, and what *denies*? *Pope.*

4. To disown; to refuse or neglect to acknowledge; not to confess.

He that *denieth* me before men, shall be *denied* before the angels of God. Luke xii.

5. To reject; to disown; not to receive or embrace.

He hath *denied* the faith, and is worse than an infidel. 1 Tim. v.

Denying ungodliness and worldly lusts. Tit. ii.

6. Not to afford or yield. *Kirwan.*

To deny one's self, is to decline the gratification of appetites or desires; to refrain from; to abstain. The temperate man *denies himself* the free use of spirituous liquors. I *denied myself* the pleasure of your company.

"God cannot *deny himself*." He cannot act in contradiction to his character and promises. He cannot be unfaithful. 2 Tim. ii.

DEOBSTRUCT', *v. t.* [L. *de* and *obstruo*, to stop; *ob* and *struo*, to pile.]

To remove obstructions, or impediments to a passage; to clear from any thing that hinders the passage of fluids in the proper ducts of the body; as, to *deobstruct* the pores or lacteals.

DEOBSTRUCT'ED, *pp.* Cleared of obstructions; opened.

DEOBSTRUCT'ING, *ppr.* Removing impediments to a passage.

DEOB'STRUENT, *a.* Removing obstructions; having power to clear or open the natural ducts of the fluids and secretions of the body; resolving viscidities; aperient. *Coxe. Encyc.*

DEOB'STRUENT, *n.* Any medicine which removes obstructions and opens the natural passages of the fluids of the body, as the pores and lacteal vessels; an aperient. Calomel is a powerful *deobstruent*.

DE'ODAND, *n.* [L. *Deo dandus*, to be given to God.]

In *England*, a personal chattel which is the immediate occasion of the death of a rational creature, and for that reason, *given to God*, that is, forfeited to the king, to be applied to pious uses, and distributed in alms by his high almoner. Thus, if a cart runs over a man and kills him, the cart is forfeited as a *deodand*. *Blackstone. Eng. Law.*

DEON'ERATE, *v. t.* [L. *deonero*; *de* and *onus*.] To unload. [*Not used.*]

DEOP'PILATE, *v. t.* [L. *de* and *oppilo*.] To free from obstructions; to clear a passage. [*Little used.*]

DEOPPILA'TION, *n.* The removal of obstructions. [*Little used.*] *Brown.*

DEOP'PILATIVE, *a.* Deobstruent; aperient. *Harvey.*

DEORDINA'TION, *n.* [L. *de* and *ordinatio*.] Disorder. [*Not in use.*] *Rawley.*

DEOS'CULATE, *v. t.* [L. *deosculor*.] To kiss. [*Not in use.*]

DEOSCULA'TION, *n.* A kissing. [*Not in use.*] *Stillingfleet.*

DEOX'YDATE, *v. t.* [*de* and *oxydate*, from Gr. οξυς, acid.]

To deprive of oxygen, or reduce from the state of an oxyd. *Chimistry.*

DEOX'YDATED, *pp.* Reduced from the state of an oxyd.

DEOX'YDATING, *ppr.* Reducing from the state of an oxyd.

DEOXYDA'TION, *n.* The act or process of reducing from the state of an oxyd.

DEOXYDIZA'TION, *n.* Deoxydation.

DEOX'YDIZE, *v. t.* To deoxydate.

DEOX'YDIZED, *pp.* Deoxydated.

DEOX'YDIZING, *ppr.* Deoxydating.

NOTE. *Deoxydate* and *deoxydize* are synonymous; but the former is preferable, on account of the length of the word *deoxydization*.

DEOX'YGENATE, *v. t.* [*de* and *oxygenate*.] To deprive of oxygen. *Davy. Med. Rep.*

DEOX'YGENATED, *v. t.* Deprived of oxygen.

DEOX'YGENATING, *ppr.* Depriving of oxygen.

DEOXYGENA'TION, *n.* The act or operation of depriving of oxygen.

DEPA'INT, *v. t.* [Fr. *depeindre*, *depeint*; *de* and *peindre*, L. *pingo*, to paint.]

1. To paint; to picture; to represent in colors, as by painting the resemblance of. *Spenser.*

2. To describe in words. *Gay.*

DEPA'INTED, *pp.* Painted; represented in colors; described.

DEPA'INTER, *n.* A painter. *Douglas.*

DEPA'INTING, *ppr.* Painting; representing in colors; describing.

DEP'ART, *v. i.* [Fr. *departir*; *de* and *partir*, to separate; Sp. *departir*. See *Part*.]

1. To go or move from.

Depart from me, ye cursed, into everlasting fire. Matt. xxv.

It is followed by *from*, or *from* is implied before the place left.

"I will *depart* to my own land," that is, I will depart *from* this place *to* my own land. Num. x.

2. To go from; to leave; to desist, as from a practice. Jehu *departed* not from the sins of Jeroboam. Jehoshaphat *departed* not from the way of Asa his father.

3. To leave; to deviate from; to forsake; not to adhere to or follow; as, we cannot *depart* from our rules.

I have not *departed* from thy judgments. Ps. cxix.

4. To desist; to leave; to abandon; as, he would not *depart* from his purpose, resolution, or demand.

5. To be lost; to perish; to vanish; as, his glory has *departed*.

6. To die; to decease; to leave this world.

Lord, now lettest thou thy servant *depart* in peace, according to thy word. Luke ii.

To depart this life is elliptical, *from* being understood.

7. To leave; to forsake; to abandon; as, to *depart* from evil.

8. To cease.

The prey *departeth* not. Nah. iii.

9. To deviate; to vary from.

If the plan of the convention be found to *depart* from republican principles— *Madison.*

10. To vary; to deviate from the title or defense in pleading. *Blackstone.*

11. To part with. [*Not in use.*] *Shak.*

To depart from God, is to forsake his service and live in sin; to apostatize; to revolt; to desert his government and laws.

God departs from men, when he abandons them to their own sinful inclinations, or ceases to bestow on them his favor. Hosea ix.

DEP'ART, *v. t.* To divide or separate; to part. [*Not used.*] *Shak. Spenser.*

DEP'ART, *n.* The act of going away; death. [*Not used.*] *Shak.*

2. Division; separation. [*Not used.*] *Bacon.*

DEP'ARTER, *n.* One who refines metals by separation. [*Not used.*]

DEP'ARTING, *ppr.* Going from; leaving; desisting; forsaking; vanishing; dying.

DEP'ARTING, *n.* A going away; separation. *Shak.*

DEP'ARTMENT, *n.* [Fr. *departement*; Sp. *departimiento*.]

1. Literally, a separation or division; hence, a separate part, or portion; a division of territory; as the *departments* of France.

2. A separate allotment or part of business; a distinct province, in which a class of duties are allotted to a particular person; as the *department* of state, assigned to the secretary of state; the treasury *department*; the *department* of war.

3. A separate station; as, the admirals had their respective *departments*. Nearly in this sense, during war, were used in America, the terms, Northern and Southern *departments*.

DEPARTMENT'AL, *a.* Pertaining to a department, or division.

DEP'ARTURE, *n.* The act of going away; a moving from or leaving a place; as a *departure* from London.

2. Death; decease; removal from the present life.

The time of my *departure* is at hand. 2 Tim. iv.

3. A forsaking; abandonment; as a *departure* from evil.

4. A desisting; as a *departure* from a purpose.

5. Ruin; destruction. Ezek. xxvi.

6. A deviation from the title or defense in pleading. *Blackstone.*

7. In *navigation*, the distance of two places on the same parallel, counted in miles of the equator. *Mar. Dict.*

DEPAS'CENT, *a.* [L. *depascens*, *depascor*; *de* and *pascor*, to feed.] Feeding.

DEP'ASTURE, *v. t.* [L. *depascor*, supra.] To eat up; to consume. *Spenser.*

DEP'ASTURE, *v. i.* To feed; to graze.

If a man takes in a horse, or other cattle, to graze and *depasture* in his grounds, which the law calls agistment— *Blackstone.*

DEP'ASTURING, *ppr.* Feeding; grazing; eating up.

DEPAU'PERATE, *v. t.* [L. *depaupero; de* and *paupero*, to beggar, from *pauper*, poor; Sp. *empobrecer.*]

To make poor; to impoverish; to deprive of fertility or richness; as, to *depauperate* the soil or the blood. *Mortimer. Arbuthnot.*

DEPAU'PERATED, *pp.* Impoverished; made poor.

DEPAU'PERATING, *ppr.* Impoverishing; making poor.

DEPEC'TIBLE, *a.* [L. *depecto*, to comb.] Tough; thick. [*Not used.*]

DEPEINCT', *v. t.* [L. *depingo.*] To paint. [*Not used.*] *Spenser.*

DEPEND', *v. i.* [L. *dependeo; de* and *pendeo*, to hang; Sp. *depender;* It. *dipendere;* Fr. *dependre;* Arm. *depanta.*]

1. To hang; to be sustained by being fastened or attached to something above; followed by *from.*

From the frozen beard
Long icicles *depend.* *Dryden.*

2. To be connected with any thing, as the cause of its existence or of its operation and effects; to rely on; to have such connection with any thing as a cause, that without it, the effect would not be produced; followed by *on* or *upon.* We *depend on* God for existence; we *depend on* air for respiration; vegetation *depends on* heat and moisture; the infant *depends on* its parents for support; the peace of society *depends on* good laws and a faithful administration.

3. To adhere; to hold to; to be retained. [See *Dependent.*] *Shak.*

4. To be in suspense; to be undetermined; as, the cause still *depends.* But the verb is seldom used in this sense. We use the participle; as, the suit is still *depending* in court. [See *Pending.*]

5. To rely; to rest with confidence; to trust; to confide; to have full confidence or belief. We *depend on* the word or assurance of our friends. We *depend on* the arrival of the mail at the usual hour. *Depend on* it, the knave will deceive us.

To depend on or *upon*, to rely; to trust in, with confidence.

DEPEND'ABLE, *a.* That may be depended on; as *dependable* friendships. [*Not in use.*] *Pope.*

DEPEND'ENCE, } *n.* A state of hanging
DEPEND'ENCY, } down from a supporter.

2. Any thing hanging down; a series of things hanging to another.

And made a long *dependence* from the bough. *Dryden.*

3. Concatenation; connection by which one thing is sustained by another, in its place, operations or effects, or is affected by it.

But of this frame the bearings and the ties,
The strong connections, nice *dependencies*— *Pope.*

4. A state of being at the disposal of another; a state of being subject to the will of an intelligent cause, or to the power and operation of any other cause; inability to sustain itself without the aid of.

We ought to feel our *dependence* on God for life and support. The child should be sensible of his *dependence* on his parents. In the natural and moral world, we observe the *dependence* of one thing on another.

5. Reliance; confidence; trust; a resting on; as, we may have a firm *dependence* on the promises of God.

6. Accident; that of which the existence presupposes the existence of something else; that which pertains to something else; as *modes* which are considered as *dependencies* or affections of substances. *Locke.*

7. That which is attached to, but subordinate to something else; as this earth and its *dependencies.* *Burnet.*

8. A territory remote from the kingdom or state to which it belongs, but subject to its dominion; as distant isles or countries. Great Britain has its *dependencies*, in Asia, Africa and America.

DEPEND'ENT, *a.* Hanging down; as a *dependent* leaf.

The furs in the tails were *dependent.* *Peacham.*

2. Subject to the power of; at the disposal of; not able to exist or sustain itself without the will or power of. Thus, we are *dependent* on God and his providence; an effect may be *dependent* on some unknown cause.

3. Relying on for support or favor; unable to subsist or to perform any thing, without the aid of.

Children are *dependent* on their parents for food and clothing. The pupil is *dependent* on his preceptor for instruction.

DEPEND'ENT, *n.* One who is at the disposal of another; one who is sustained by another, or who relies on another for support or favor; a retainer; as, the prince was followed by a numerous train of *dependents.*

DEPEND'ER, *n.* One who depends; a dependent. *Shak.*

DEPEND'ING, *ppr.* Hanging down; relying.

2. *a.* Pending; undecided; as a suit or question.

DEPER'DIT, *a.* [L. *deperditus.*] That which is lost or destroyed. *Paley.*

DEPERDI''TION, *n.* Loss; destruction. [See *Perdition.*] *Brown.*

DEPHLEG'MATE, *v. t.* [*de* and Gr. φλεγμα, phlegm, from φλεγω, to burn.]

To deprive of superabundant water, as by evaporation or distillation, used of spirit and acids; to clear spirit or acids of aqueous matter; to rectify. *Coxe. Encyc.*

[*Dephlegm* is used by Boyle.]

DEPHLEGMA'TION, *n.* The operation of separating water from spirits and acids, by evaporation or repeated distillation; called also *concentration*, particularly when acids are the subject. *Encyc.*

DEPHLEG'MEDNESS, *n.* A state of being freed from water. [*Not used.*] *Boyle.*

DEPHLOGIS'TICATE, *v. t.* [*de* and Gr. φλογιςος, burnt, inflammable, from φλογιζω, to burn. See *Phlogiston.*]

To deprive of phlogiston, or the supposed principle of inflammability. *Priestley.*

DEPHLOGIS'TICATED, *pp.* Deprived of phlogiston. *Dephlogisticated air*, is an elastic fluid capable of supporting animal life and flame much longer than common air. It is now called *oxygen, oxygen gas*, or *vital air.*

DEPICT', *v. t.* [L. *depingo, depictum; de* and *pingo*, to paint.]

To paint; to portray; to form a likeness in colors; as, to *depict* a lion on a shield. *Taylor.*

2. To describe; to represent in words; as, the poet *depicts* the virtues of his hero in glowing language.

DEPICT'ED, *pp.* Painted; represented in colors; described.

DEPICT'ING, *ppr.* Painting; representing in colors, or in words.

DEPIC'TURE, *v. t.* [*de* and *picture.*] To paint; to picture; to represent in colors. [See *Depict.*] *Weever.*

DEP'ILATE, *v. t.* [L. *depilo; de* and *pilus*, hair.] To strip of hair.

DEPILA'TION, *n.* The act of pulling off the hair. *Dryden.*

DEPIL'ATORY, *a.* Having the quality or power to take off hair and make bald.

DEPIL'ATORY, *n.* Any application which is used to take off the hair of an animal body; such as lime and orpiment. *Encyc.*

DEP'ILOUS, *a.* Without hair. [*Not used.*] *Brown.*

DEPLANTA'TION, *n.* [L. *deplanto.*] The act of taking up plants from beds.

DEPLE'TION, *n.* [L. *depleo; de* and *pleo*, to fill.]

The act of emptying; particularly, in the medical art, the act of diminishing the quantity of blood in the vessels by venesection; bloodletting.

DEPLO'RABLE, *a.* [See *Deplore.*] That may be deplored or lamented; lamentable; that demands or causes lamentation; hence, sad; calamitous; grievous; miserable; wretched; as, the evils of life are *deplorable;* the Pagan world is in a *deplorable* condition.

Deplorate, in a like sense, is not used.

2. In *popular use*, low; contemptible; pitiable; as *deplorable* stupidity.

DEPLO'RABLENESS, *n.* The state of being deplorable; misery; wretchedness; a miserable state.

DEPLO'RABLY, *adv.* In a manner to be deplored; lamentably; miserably; as, manners are *deplorably* corrupt.

DEPLORA'TION, *n.* The act of lamenting. In *music*, a dirge or mournful strain.

DEPLO'RE, *v. t.* [L. *deploro; de* and *ploro*, to howl, to wail; Fr. *deplorer;* It. *deplorare;* Sp. *deplorar, llorar.*]

To lament; to bewail; to mourn; to feel or express deep and poignant grief for. We *deplored* the death of Washington.

DEPLO'RED, *pp.* Lamented; bewailed; deeply regretted.

DEPLO'REDLY, *adv.* Lamentably. [*Not used.*] *Taylor.*

DEPLO'RER, *n.* One who deplores, or deeply laments; a deep mourner.

DEPLO'RING, *ppr.* Bewailing; deeply lamenting.

DEPLOY', *v. t.* [Fr. *deployer; de* and *ployer*, or *plier*, to fold; L. *plico;* Gr. πλεκω; Arm. *plega;* Sp. *plegar;* It. *piegare;* W. *plygu.* Hence Sp. *desplegar*, to *display;* It. *spiegare. Deploy* is only a different orthography of *deplier*, Sp. *desplegar*, to *display.*]

To display; to open; to extend; *a military term.*

DEPLOY′, *v. i.* To open; to extend; to form a more extended front or line.

DEPLOY′ING, *ppr.* Opening; extending; displaying.

DEPLUMA′TION, *n.* [See *Deplume.*] The stripping or falling off of plumes or feathers.

2. A tumor of the eye-lids with loss of hair. *Coxe.*

DEPLU′ME, *v. t.* [L. *deplumo; de* and *pluma*, a feather; Sp. *desplumar;* It. *spiumare.*]

To strip or pluck off feathers; to deprive of plumage. *Hayward.*

DEPLU′MED, *pp.* Stripped of feathers or plumes.

DEPLU′MING, *ppr.* Stripping off plumes or feathers.

DEPO′LARIZE, *v. t.* To deprive of polarity. [See *Polarity.*] *Ure.*

DEPO′NE, *v. t.* [L. *depono.*] To lay down as a pledge; to wage. [*Not in use.*] *Hudibras.*

DEPO′NENT, *a.* [L. *deponens, depono; de* and *pono*, to lay.] Laying down.

2. A *deponent verb*, in the Latin Grammar, is a verb which has a passive termination, with an active signification, and wants one of the passive participles; as, *loquor*, to speak.

DEPO′NENT, *n.* One who deposes, or gives a deposition under oath; one who gives written testimony to be used as evidence in a court of justice. With us in New-England, this word is never used, I believe, for a witness who gives oral testimony in court. In England, a *deponent* is one who gives answers under oath to interrogatories exhibited in chancery.

2. A deponent verb.

DEPOP′ULATE *v. t.* [L. *depopulor; de* and *populor*, to ravage or lay waste, from *populus*, people; Sp. *despoblar;* It. *spopolare;* Fr. *depeupler.*]

To dispeople; to unpeople; to deprive of inhabitants, whether by death, or by expulsion. It is not synonymous with laying waste or destroying, being limited to the loss of inhabitants; as, an army or a famine may *depopulate* a country. It rarely expresses an entire loss of inhabitants, but often a great diminution of their numbers. The deluge nearly *depopulated* the earth.

DEPOP′ULATE, *v. i.* To become dispeopled.

DEPOP′ULATED, *pp.* Dispeopled; deprived of inhabitants.

DEPOP′ULATING, *ppr.* Dispeopling; depriving of inhabitants.

DEPOPULA′TION, *n.* The act of dispeopling; destruction or expulsion of inhabitants.

DEPOP′ULATOR, *n.* One who depopulates; one who destroys or expels the inhabitants of a city, town or country; a dispeopler.

DEPO′RT, *v. t.* [Fr. *deporter;* Sp. *deportar;* L. *deporto; de* and *porto*, to carry.]

1. With *the reciprocal pronoun*, to carry; to demean; to behave.

Let an embassador *deport himself* in the most graceful manner before a prince. *Pope.*

2. To transport; to carry away, or from one country to another.

He told us, he had been *deported* to Spain, with a hundred others like himself. *Walsh.*

DEPO′RT, *n.* Behavior; carriage; demeanor; deportment; as goddess-like *deport.* [*A poetic word.*] *Milton.*

DEPORTA′TION, *n.* Transportation; a carrying away; a removal from one country to another, or to a distant place; exile; banishment. *Ayliffe.*

DEPO′RTED, *pp.* Carried away; transported; banished.

DEPO′RTING, *ppr.* Carrying away; removing to a distant place or country; transporting; banishing.

DEPO′RTMENT, *n.* [Fr. *deportement.*] Carriage; manner of acting in relation to the duties of life; behavior; demeanor; conduct; management. *Swift.*

DEPO′SABLE, *a.* That may be deposed, or deprived of office. *Howell.*

DEPO′SAL, *n.* The act of deposing, or divesting of office. *Fox.*

DEPO′SE, *v. t.* *s* as *z.* [Fr. *deposer;* L. *depono, depositum; de* and *pono*, to lay or *put;* Sp. *deponer;* It. *deporre.*]

1. To lay down; to throw; to let fall; as, the flood *deposed* fine particles of earth on the bank of the river. In this sense, we now use *deposit.* *Woodward.*

2. To reduce from a throne or other high station; to dethrone; to degrade; to divest of office; as, to *depose* a king or a pope.

3. To give testimony on oath, especially to give testimony which is committed to writing; to give answers to interrogatories, intended as evidence in a court.

4. To lay aside. *Barrow.*

5. To take away; to strip; to divest. [*Not in use.*] *Shak.*

6. To examine on oath. [*Not in use.*] *Shak.*

DEPO′SE, *v. i.* To bear witness. *Sidney.*

DEPO′SED, *pp.* Dethroned; degraded; testified.

DEPO′SER, *n.* One who deposes or degrades from office.

DEPO′SING, *ppr.* Dethroning; degrading; bearing witness.

DEPO′SING, *n.* The act of dethroning. *Selden.*

DEPOS′IT, *v. t.* *s* as *z.* [L. *depositum*, from *depono.*]

1. To lay down; to lay; to throw down. A crocodile *deposits* her eggs in the sand. A bird *deposits* eggs in a nest. An inundation *deposits* particles of earth on a meadow.

2. To lay up; to lay in a place for preservation. We *deposit* the produce of the earth in barns, cellars or storehouses. We *deposit* goods in a warehouse, and books in a library.

3. To lodge in the hands of a person for safe-keeping or other purpose; to commit to the care of; to entrust; to commit to one as a pledge. We say, the bond is *deposited* in the hands of an attorney; money is *deposited* as a pledge, or security.

4. To lay aside. [*Little used.*]

DEPOS′IT, *n.* That which is laid or thrown down; any matter laid or thrown down, or lodged.

The *deposit* already formed affording to the succeeding portions of the charged fluid, a basis. *Kirwan.*

2. Any thing entrusted to the care of another; a pledge; a pawn; a thing given as security, or for preservation; as, these papers are committed to you as a sacred *deposit;* he has a *deposit* of money in his hands.

3. A place where things are deposited; a depository.

4. A city or town where goods are lodged for safe-keeping or for reshipment. [Fr. *depôt.*]

In deposit, in a state of pledge, or for safe keeping.

DEPOS′ITARY, *n.* [Fr. *depositaire;* Low L. *depositarius.*]

A person with whom any thing is left or lodged in trust; one to whom a thing is committed for safe keeping, or to be used for the benefit of the owner; a trustee; a guardian. The Jews were the *depositaries* of the sacred writings.

DEPOS′ITING, *ppr.* Laying down; pledging; repositing.

DEPOSI″TION, *n.* [L. *depositio.*] The act of laying or throwing down; as, soil is formed by the *deposition* of fine particles, during a flood.

2. That which is thrown down; that which is lodged: as, banks are sometimes *depositions* of alluvial matter.

3. The act of giving testimony under oath.

4. The attested written testimony of a witness: an affidavit.

5. The act of dethroning a king, or the degrading of a person from an office or station; a divesting of sovereignty, or of office and dignity; a depriving of clerical orders. A *deposition* differs from *abdication;* an abdication being *voluntary*, and a deposition, *compulsory.*

DEPOS′ITORY, *n.* A place where any thing is lodged for safe-keeping. A warehouse is a *depository* for goods; a clerk's office, for records.

DEPOS′ITUM, *n.* A deposit. [*Not English, nor in use.*]

DEPOT. [A French word. See *Deposit.*]

DEPRAVA′TION, *n.* [L. *depravatio.* See *Deprave.*]

1. The act of making bad or worse; the act of corrupting.

2. The state of being made bad or worse; degeneracy; a state in which good qualities are lost, or impaired. We speak of the *depravation* of morals, manners or government; of the heart or mind; of nature, taste, &c.

3. Censure; defamation. [*Not used.*] *Shak.*

DEPRA′VE *v. t.* [L. *depravo; de* and *pravus*, crooked, perverse, wicked.]

1. To make bad or worse; to impair good qualities; to make bad qualities worse; to vitiate; to corrupt; as, to *deprave* manners, morals, government, laws; to *deprave* the heart, mind, will, understanding, taste, principles, &c.

2. To defame; to vilify. [*Not now used.*] *Shak.* *Spenser.*

DEPRA′VED, *pp.* Made bad or worse; vitiated; tainted; corrupted.

2. *a.* Corrupt; wicked; destitute of holiness or good principles.

DEPRA′VEDLY, *adv.* In a corrupt manner.

DEPRA′VEDNESS, *n.* Corruption; taint; a vitiated state. *Hammond.*

DEPRA'VEMENT, *n.* A vitiated state. *Brown.*

DEPRA'VER, *n.* A corrupter; he who vitiates; a vilifier.

DEPRA'VING, *ppr.* Making bad; corrupting.

DEPRA'VING, *n.* A traducing. *Obs.*

DEPRAV'ITY, *n.* Corruption; a vitiated state; as the *depravity* of manners and morals. *Burke.*

2. A vitiated state of the heart; wickedness; corruption of moral principles; destitution of holiness or good principles.

DEP'RECATE, *v. t.* [L. *deprecor; de* and *precor*, to pray. See *Pray* and *Preach.*]

1. To pray against; to pray or intreat that a present evil may be removed, or an expected one averted.

> The judgments we would *deprecate* are not removed. *Smallridge.*
>
> We should all *deprecate* the return of war.

2. *More generally*, to regret; to have or to express deep sorrow at a present evil, or at one that may occur. This word is seldom used to express actual prayer: but it expresses deep regret that an evil exists or may exist, which implies a strong desire that it may be removed or averted.

2. To implore mercy of. [*Improper.*] *Prior.*

DEP'RECATED, *pp.* Prayed against; deeply regretted.

DEP'RECATING, *ppr.* Praying against; regretting.

DEPRECA'TION, *n.* A praying against; a praying that an evil may be removed or prevented. *Milton.*

2. Intreaty; petitioning; an excusing; a begging pardon for. *Johnson.*

DEP'RECATOR, *n.* One who deprecates.

DEP'RECATORY, DEP'RECATIVE, *a.* That serves to deprecate; tending to remove or avert evil by prayer; as *deprecatory* letters. *Bacon.*

2. Having the form of prayer.

DEPRE'CIATE, *v. t.* [Low L. *depretio; de* and *pretium*, price; Fr. *depriser.* See *Price.*]

1. To lessen the price of a thing; to cry down the price or value.

2. To undervalue; to represent as of little value or merit, or of less value than is commonly supposed; as, one author is apt to *depreciate* the works of another, or to *depreciate* their worth.

3. To lower the value. The issue of a superabundance of notes *depreciates* them, or *depreciates* their value.

DEPRE'CIATE, *v. i.* To fall in value; to become of less worth. A paper currency will *depreciate*, unless it is convertible into specie. Estates are apt to *depreciate* in the hands of tenants on short leases. Continental bills of credit, issued by the congress, during the revolution, *depreciated* to the one hundredth part of their nominal value.

DEPRE'CIATED, *pp.* Lessened in value or price; undervalued.

DEPRE'CIATING, *ppr.* Lessening the price or worth; undervaluing.

2. Falling in value.

DEPRECIA'TION, *n.* The act of lessening or crying down price or value.

2. The falling of value; reduction of worth; as the *depreciation* of bills of credit.

DEP'REDATE, *v. t.* [L. *deprædor; de* and *prædor*, to plunder, *præda*, prey.]

1. To plunder; to rob; to pillage; to take the property of an enemy or of a foreign country by force; as, the army *depredated* the enemy's country.

> That kind of war which *depredates* and distresses individuals. *Marshall.*

2. To prey upon; to waste; to spoil. *Bacon.*

3. To devour; to destroy by eating; as, wild animals *depredate* the corn.

DEP'REDATE, *v. i.* To take plunder or prey; to commit waste; as, the troops *depredated* on the country.

DEP'REDATED, *pp.* Spoiled; plundered; wasted; pillaged.

DEP'REDATING, *ppr.* Plundering; robbing; pillaging.

DEPREDA'TION, *n.* The act of plundering; a robbing; a pillaging.

2. Waste; consumption; a taking away by any act of violence. The sea often makes *depredations* on the land. Intemperance commits *depredations* on the constitution.

DEP'REDATOR, *n.* One who plunders, or pillages; a spoiler; a waster.

DEP'REDATORY, *a.* Plundering; spoiling; consisting in pillaging. *Encyc.*

DEPREHEND', *v. t.* [L. *deprehendo; de* and *prehendo*, to take or seize.]

1. To catch; to take unawares or by surprise; to seize, as a person committing an unlawful act. *More. Hooker.*

2. To detect; to discover; to obtain the knowledge of. *Bacon.*

DEPREHEND'ED, *pp.* Taken by surprise; caught; seized; discovered.

DEPREHEND'ING, *ppr.* Taking unawares; catching; seizing; discovering.

DEPREHEN'SIBLE, *a.* That may be caught, or discovered.

DEPREHEN'SIBLENESS, *n.* Capableness of being caught or discovered.

DEPREHEN'SION, *n.* A catching or seizing; a discovery.

[*Deprehend* and its derivatives are little used.]

DEPRESS', *v. t.* [L. *depressus, deprimo; de* and *pressus, premo*, to press.]

1. To press down; to press to a lower state or position; as, to *depress* the end of a tube, or the muzzle of a gun.

2. To let fall; to bring down; as, to *depress* the eye.

3. To render dull or languid; to limit or diminish; as, to *depress* commerce.

4. To sink; to lower; to deject; to make sad; as, to *depress* the spirits or the mind.

5. To humble; to abase; as, to *depress* pride.

6. To sink in altitude; to cause to appear lower or nearer the horizon; as, a man sailing towards the equator *depresses* the pole.

7. To impoverish; to lower in temporal estate; as, misfortunes and losses have *depressed* the merchants.

8. To lower in value; as, to *depress* the price of stock.

DEPRESS'ED, *pp.* Pressed or forced down; lowered; dejected; dispirited; sad; humbled; sunk; rendered languid.

2. In *botany*, a *depressed* leaf is hollow in the middle, or having the disk more depressed than the sides; *used of succulent leaves, and opposed to convex.* *Martyn.*

DEPRESS'ING, *ppr.* Pressing down; lowering in place; letting fall; sinking; dejecting; abasing; impoverishing; rendering languid.

DEPRES'SION, *n.* The act of pressing down; or the state of being pressed down; a low state.

2. A hollow; a sinking or falling in of a surface; or a forcing inwards; as roughness consisting in little protuberances and *depressions;* the *depression* of the skull.

3. The act of humbling; abasement; as the *depression* of pride; the *depression* of the nobility.

4. A sinking of the spirits; dejection; a state of sadness; want of courage or animation; as *depression* of the mind.

5. A low state of strength; a state of body succeeding debility in the formation of disease. *Coxe.*

6. A low state of business or of property.

7. The sinking of the polar star towards the horizon, as a person recedes from the pole towards the equator. Also, the distance of a star from the horizon below, which is measured by an arch of the vertical circle or azimuth, passing through the star, intercepted between the star and the horizon. *Bailey. Encyc.*

8. In *algebra*, the *depression of an equation*, is the bringing of it into lower and more simple terms by division. *Bailey.*

DEPRESS'IVE, *a.* Able or tending to depress or cast down.

DEPRESS'OR, *n.* He that presses down; an oppressor.

2. In *anatomy*, a muscle that *depresses* or draws down the part to which it is attached; as the *depressor* of the lower jaw, or of the eyeball. It is called also *depriment* or *deprimens.*

DEPRI'VABLE, *a.* [See *Deprive.*] That may be deprived.

> A chaplain shall be *deprivable* by the founder, not by the bishop. *Encyc.*

[See *Deprive*, No. 4.]

DEPRIVA'TION, *n.* [See *Deprive.*] The act of depriving; a taking away.

2. A state of being deprived; loss; want; bereavement by loss of friends or of goods.

3. In *law*, the act of divesting a bishop or other clergyman of his spiritual promotion or dignity; the taking away of a preferment; deposition. This is of two kinds; *a beneficio*, and *ab officio.* The former is the deprivation of a minister of his living or preferment; the latter, of his order, and otherwise called *deposition* or *degradation.* *Encyc.*

DEPRI'VE, *v. t.* [L. *de* and *privo*, to take away, Sp. *privar*, It. *privare*, Fr. *priver.* See *Private.*]

1. To take from; to bereave of something possessed or enjoyed; followed by *of;* as, to *deprive* a man *of* sight; to *deprive* one *of* strength, of reason, or of property. This has a general signification, applicable to a lawful or unlawful taking.

> God hath *deprived* her of wisdom. Job xxxix.

2. To hinder from possessing or enjoying; to debar.

> From his face I shall be hid, *deprived*
> Of his blessed countenance. *Milton.*

[*This use of the word is not legitimate, but common.*]

3. To free or release from. *Spenser.*

4. To divest of an ecclesiastical preferment, dignity or office; to divest of orders; as a bishop, prebend or vicar.

DEPRI'VED, *pp.* Bereft; divested; hindered; stripped of office or dignity; deposed; degraded.

DEPRI'VEMENT, *n.* The state of losing or being deprived.

DEPRI'VER, *n.* He or that which deprives or bereaves.

DEPRI'VING, *ppr.* Bereaving; taking away what is possessed; divesting; hindering from enjoying; deposing.

DEPTH, *n.* [from *deep.*] Deepness; the distance or measure of a thing from the surface to the bottom, or to the extreme part downwards or inwards. The *depth* of a river may be ten feet. The *depth* of the ocean is unfathomable. The *depth* of a wound may be an inch. In a vertical direction, *depth* is opposed to *highth.*

2. A deep place.

3. The sea, the ocean.

The *depth* closed me round about. Jonah ii.

4. The abyss; a gulf of infinite profundity.

When he set a compass on the face of the *depth.* Prov. viii.

5. The middle or highth of a season, as the *depth* of winter; or the middle, the darkest or stillest part, as the *depth* of night; or the inner part, a part remote from the border, as the *depth* of a wood or forest.

6. Abstruseness; obscurity; that which is not easily explored; as the *depth* of a science.

7. Unsearchableness; infinity.

O the *depth* of the riches both of the wisdom and knowledge of God. Rom. xi.

8. The *breadth* and *depth* of the love of Christ, are its vast extent.

9. Profoundness; extent of penetration, or of the capacity of penetrating; as *depth* of understanding; *depth* of skill.

10. The *depth* of a squadron or battalion, is the number of men in a file, which forms the extent from the front to the rear; as a *depth* of three men or six men.

11. *Depth of a sail*, the extent of the square sails from the head-rope to the foot-rope, or the length of the after-leech of a stay-sail or boom-sail. *Mar. Dict.*

DEPUL'SION, *n.* [L. *depulsio*; *de* and *pello*, to drive.]

A driving or thrusting away. [See *Repulsion.*]

DEPUL'SORY, *a.* Driving or thrusting away; averting.

DEP'URATE, *v. t.* [Fr. *depurer*; It. *depurare*; Sp. *depurar*; from *de* and *pus, puris.*]

To purify; to free from impurities, heterogeneous matter or feculence; *a chemical term.*

DEP'URATED, *pp.* Purified from heterogeneous matter, or from impurities. *E. Stiles.*

DEP'URATING, *ppr.* Purifying; freeing from impurities.

DEPURA'TION, *n.* The act of purifying or freeing fluids from heterogeneous matter. This is done by decantation, when the feculent matter is deposited on the bottom of the vessel; or by despumation, effected by boiling or fermentation, and skimming; or by filtration; or by fining or clarification. *Parr.*

2. The cleansing of a wound from impure matter.

DEP'URATORY, *a.* Cleansing; purifying; or tending to purify. A *depuratory* fever, is a fever that expels morbid matter by a free perspiration. *Sydenham.*

DEPU'RE, *v. t.* To depurate. [*Not used.*]

DEPUTA'TION, *n.* [Fr. *id.*; It. *deputazione*; Sp. *diputacion.* See *Depute.*]

1. The act of appointing a substitute or representative to act for another; the act of appointing and sending a deputy or substitute to transact business for another, as his agent, either with a special commission and authority, or with general powers. This word may be used for the election of representatives to a legislature; but more generally it is employed to express the appointment of a special agent or commissioner, by an individual or public body, to transact a particular business.

2. A special commission or authority to act as the substitute of another; as, this man acts by *deputation* from the sheriff.

3. The person deputed; the person or persons authorized and sent to transact business for another; as, the General sent a *deputation* to the enemy to offer terms of peace.

DEPU'TE, *v. t.* [Fr. *deputer*; It. *deputare*; Port. *deputar*; Sp. *diputar*; L. *deputo*, but differently applied; *de* and *puto.* The primary sense of *puto* is to thrust, throw, send; but it has various applications. See Class Bd. No. 13. 19.]

To appoint as a substitute or agent to act for another; to appoint and send with a special commission or authority to transact business in another's name. The sheriff *deputes* a man to serve a writ.

There is no man *deputed* by the king to hear. 2 Sam. xv.

The bishop may *depute* a priest to administer the sacrament. *Ayliffe.*

DEPU'TED, *pp.* Appointed as a substitute; appointed and sent with special authority to act for another.

DEPU'TING, *ppr.* Appointing as a substitute; appointing and sending with a special commission to transact business for another.

DEP'UTIZE, *v. t.* To appoint a deputy; to empower to act for another, as a sheriff.

DEP'UTY, *n.* [Fr. *deputé.*] A person appointed or elected to act for another, especially a person sent with a special commission to act in the place of another; a lieutenant; a viceroy. A prince sends a *deputy* to a diet or council, to represent him and his dominions. A sheriff appoints a *deputy* to execute the duties of his office. The towns in New England send *deputies* to the legislature. In the latter sense, a *deputy* has general powers, and it is more common to use the word *representative.*

2. In *law*, one that exercises an office in another's right, and the forfeiture or misdemeanor of such deputy shall cause the person he represents to lose his office. *Phillips.*

DEPUTY-COLLECTOR, *n.* A person appointed to perform the duties of a collector of the customs, in place of the collector.

DEPUTY-M'ARSHAL, *n.* One appointed to act in the place of the marshal.

DEPUTY-POST-MASTER, *n.* A person who is appointed to act as post-master, in subordination to the Post-Master General.

DEPUTY-SHERIFF, *n.* A person deputed or authorized to perform the duties of the sheriff, as his substitute. In like manner, we use *deputy-commissary*, *deputy-paymaster*, &c.

DER, prefixed to names of places, may be from Sax. *deor*, a wild beast, or from *dur*, water.

DERAC'INATE, *v. t.* [Fr. *deraciner*; *de* and *racine*, a root.]

To pluck up by the roots; to extirpate. [*Little used.*] *Shak.*

DERAC'INATED, *pp.* Plucked up by the roots; extirpated.

DERAC'INATING, *ppr.* Tearing up by the roots; extirpating.

DERA'IGN, } *v. t.* [Norm. *derener*, *dereigner*, *deraigner*, or *derainer.*]
DERA'IN, }

To prove; to justify; to vindicate, as an assertion; to clear one's self. [*An old law term, now disused.*]

DERA'IGNMENT, } *n.* The act of deraining; proof; justification.
DERA'INMENT, }

A like word was formerly used in the sense of disordering, derangement, a discharge from a profession, or departure from a religious order. [Fr. *deranger*; *de* and *ranger.*]

DERANGE, *v. t.* [Fr. *deranger*; *de* and *ranger*, to set in order, from *rang*, rank; Arm. *direncqa.*]

1. To put out of order; to disturb the regular order of; to throw into confusion; as, to *derange* the plans of a commander, or the affairs of a nation.

I had long supposed that nothing could *derange* or interrupt the course of putrefaction. *Lavoisier, Tran.*

2. To embarrass; to disorder; as, his private affairs are *deranged.*

3. To disorder the intellect; to disturb the regular operations of reason.

4. To remove from place or office, as the personal staff of a principal military officer. Thus when a general officer resigns or is removed from office, the personal staff appointed by himself are said to be *deranged.* *W. H. Sumner.*

DERANGED, *pp.* Put out of order; disturbed; embarrassed; confused; disordered in mind; delirious; distracted.

DERANGEMENT, *n.* A putting out of order; disturbance of regularity or regular course; embarrassment. *Washington.*

2. Disorder of the intellect or reason; delirium; insanity; as a *derangement* of the mental organs. *Paley.*

DERANGING, *ppr.* Putting out of order; disturbing regularity or regular course; embarrassment; confusion. *Hamilton.*

2. Disordering the rational powers.

DERA'Y, *v. t.* [from the French.] Tumult; disorder; merriment. [*Not in use.*] *Douglas.*

DERE, *v. t.* [Sax. *derian.*] To hurt. *Obs.*

DER'ELICT, *a.* [L. *derelictus*, *derelinquo*; *de* and *relinquo*, to leave, *re* and *linquo*, id. Class Lg.] Left; abandoned.

DER'ELICT, *n.* In *law*, an article of goods,

or any commodity, thrown away, relinquished or abandoned by the owner.
2. A tract of land left dry by the sea, and fit for cultivation or use.

DERELIC'TION, *n.* [L. *derelictio.*] The act of leaving with an intention not to reclaim; an utter forsaking; abandonment.
2. The state of being left or abandoned. *Hooker.*
3. A leaving or receding from; as the *dereliction* of the sea. *Blackstone.*

DERI'DE, *v. t.* [L. *derideo; de* and *rideo*, to laugh; It. *deridere*. In Fr. *derider* is to unwrinkle, from *ride*, a wrinkle. Probably the primary sense of L. *rideo* is to wrinkle, to grin.]
To laugh at in contempt; to turn to ridicule or make sport of; to mock; to treat with scorn by laughter.

The Pharisees also—*derided* him. Luke xvi.

Some, who adore Newton for his fluxions, *deride* him for his religion. *Berkeley.*

DERI'DED, *pp.* Laughed at in contempt; mocked; ridiculed.

DERI'DER, *n.* One who laughs at another in contempt; a mocker; a scoffer. *Hooker.*
2. A droll or buffoon.

DERI'DING, *ppr.* Laughing at with contempt; mocking; ridiculing.

DERI'DINGLY, *adv.* By way of derision or mockery.

DERI'SION, *n. s* as *z*. [L. *derisio*. See *Deride*.]
1. The act of laughing at in contempt.
2. Contempt manifested by laughter; scorn.

I am in *derision* daily. Jer. xx.

3. An object of derision or contempt; a laughing-stock.

I was a *derision* to all my people. Lam. iii.

DERI'SIVE, *a.* Containing derision; mocking; ridiculing.

Derisive taunts. *Pope.*

DERI'SIVELY, *adv.* With mockery or contempt. *Herbert.*

DERI'SORY, *a.* Mocking; ridiculing. *Shaftesbury.*

DERI'VABLE, *a.* [See *Derive*.] That may be derived; that may be drawn, or received, as from a source. Income is *derivable* from land, money or stocks.
2. That may be received from ancestors; as an estate *derivable* from an ancestor.
3. That may be drawn, as from premises; deducible; as an argument *derivable* from facts or preceding propositions.
4. That may be drawn from a radical word; as a word *derivable* from an Oriental root.

DER'IVATE, *n.* [L. *derivatus.*] A word derived from another. *Stuart.*

DERIVA'TION, *n.* [L. *derivatio.*] The act of deriving, drawing or receiving from a source; as the *derivation* of an estate from ancestors, or of profits from capital, or of truth or facts from antiquity.
2. In *grammar*, the drawing or tracing of a word from its root or original; as, *derivation* is from the L. *derivo*, and the latter from *rivus*, a stream.
3. A drawing from, or turning aside from, a natural course or channel; as the *derivation* of water from its channel by lateral drains.
4. A drawing of humors from one part of the body to another; as the *derivation* of humors from the eye, by a blister on the neck.
5. The thing derived or deduced. *Glanville.*

DERIV'ATIVE, *a.* Derived; taken or having proceeded from another or something preceding; secondary; as a *derivative* perfection; a *derivative* conveyance, as a release. *Blackstone.*
2. A *derivative* chord, in music, is one derived from a fundamental chord.

DERIV'ATIVE, *n.* That which is derived; a word which takes its origin in another word, or is formed from it. Thus, *depravity* is a *derivative* from the L. *depravo*, and *acknowledge*, from *knowledge*, and this from *know*, the primitive word.
2. In *music*, a chord not fundamental.

DERIV'ATIVELY, *adv.* In a derivative manner; by derivation.

DERI'VE, *v. t.* [L. *derivo; de* and *rivus*, a stream; Fr. *deriver;* Sp. *derivar;* It. *derivare.*]
1. To draw from, as in a regular course or channel; to receive from a source by a regular conveyance. The heir *derives* an estate from his ancestors. We *derive* from Adam mortal bodies and natures prone to sin.
2. To draw or receive, as from a source or origin. We *derive* ideas from the senses, and instruction from good books.
3. To deduce or draw, as from a root, or primitive word. A hundred words are often *derived* from a single monosyllabic root, and sometimes a much greater number.
4. To turn from its natural course; to divert; as, to *derive* water from the main channel or current into lateral rivulets.
5. To communicate from one to another by descent.

An excellent disposition is *derived to* your lordship from your parents. *Felton.*

6. To spread in various directions; to cause to flow.

The streams of justice were *derived* into every part of the kingdom. *Davies.*

DERI'VE, *v. i.* To come or proceed from. [*Not common.*]

Power from heaven *derives*. *Prior.*

DERI'VED, *pp.* Drawn, as from a source; deduced; received; regularly conveyed; descended; communicated; transmitted.

DERI'VER, *n.* One who derives, or draws from a source. *South.*

DERI'VING, *ppr.* Drawing; receiving; deducing; communicating; diverting or turning into another channel.

DERM'AL, *a.* [Gr. δερμα, skin.] Pertaining to skin; consisting of skin. *Fleming.*

DERM'OID, *a.* [Gr. δερμα, and ειδος.] Pertaining to the skin; *a medical term.*

DERN, *a.* [Sax. *dearn.*] Solitary; sad; cruel. *Obs.* *More.*

DERN'FUL, *a.* Sad; mournful. *Obs.*

DERNIE'R, *a.* [Fr.] Last; final; ultimate; as the *dernier* resort. [*I know not that it is used in any other phrase.*]

DERN'LY, *adv.* Sadly; mournfully. *Obs.* *More.*

DER'OGATE, *v. t.* [L. *derogo; de* and *roga*, to ask, to propose. In ancient Rome, *rogo* was used in proposing new laws, and *derogo*, in repealing some section of a law. Hence the sense is to take from or annul a part. Class Rg.]
1. To repeal, annul or destroy the force and effect of some part of a law or established rule; to lessen the extent of a law; distinguished from *abrogate*.

By several contrary customs, many of the civil and canon laws are controlled and *derogated*. *Hale.*

2. To lessen the worth of a person or thing; to disparage.

[*In the foregoing senses, the word is now seldom used.*]

DER'OGATE, *v. i.* To take away; to detract; to lessen by taking away a part; as, say nothing to *derogate* from the merit or reputation of a brave man. [*The word is generally used in this sense.*]
2. To act beneath one's rank, place or birth. [*Unusual.*] *Shak.*

DER'OGATED, *pp.* Diminished in value; degraded; damaged. [Shakspeare uses *derogate* in this sense.]

DER'OGATELY, *adv.* In a manner to lessen or take from. *Shak.*

DER'OGATING, *ppr.* Annulling a part; lessening by taking from.

DEROGA'TION, *n.* The act of annulling or revoking a law, or some part of it. More generally, the act of taking away or destroying the value or effect of any thing, or of limiting its extent, or of restraining its operation; as, an act of parliament is passed in *derogation* of the king's prerogative; we cannot do any thing in *derogation* of the moral law.
2. The act of taking something from merit, reputation or honor; a lessening of value or estimation; detraction; disparagement; with *from* or *of;* as, I say not this in *derogation of* Virgil; let nothing be said in *derogation from* his merit.

DEROG'ATIVE, *a.* Derogatory. [*The latter is mostly used.*]

DEROG'ATORILY, *adv.* In a detracting manner.

DEROG'ATORINESS, *n.* The quality of being derogatory.

DEROG'ATORY, *a.* Detracting or tending to lessen by taking something from; that lessens the extent, effect or value; with *to*. Let us entertain no opinions *derogatory to* the honor of God, or his moral government. Let us say nothing *derogatory to* the merit of our neighbor.
2. A *derogatory* clause in a testament, is a sentence or secret character inserted by the testator, of which he reserves the knowledge to himself, with a condition that no will he may make hereafter shall be valid, unless this clause is inserted word for word; a precaution to guard against later wills extorted by violence or obtained by suggestion. *Encyc.*

DER'RING, *a.* Daring. [*Not in use.*] *Spenser.*

DER'VIS, *n.* [Persian.] A Turkish priest or monk, who professes extreme poverty, and leads an austere life. *Encyc.*

DES'CANT, *n.* [Sp. *discante*, *discantar; dis* and L. *canto*, to sing. See *Cant*. The Fr. *dechanter* has a different sense.]
1. A song or tune composed in parts.
2. A song or tune with various modulations.

The wakeful nightingale
All night long her amorous *descant* sung. *Milton.*

3. A discourse; discussion; disputation;

animadversion, comment, or a series of comments.

4. The art of composing music in several parts. Descant is *plain*, *figurative* and *double*.

Plain descant is the ground-work of musical compositions, consisting in the orderly disposition of concords, answering to simple counterpoint.

Figurative or *florid descant*, is that part of an air in which some discords are concerned.

Double descant, is when the parts are so contrived, that the treble may be made the base, and the base the treble. *Bailey. Encyc.*

DESCANT′, *v. i.* To run a division or variety with the voice, on a musical ground in true measure; to sing. *Bailey. Johnson.*

2. To discourse; to comment; to make a variety of remarks; to animadvert freely.

A virtuous man should be pleased to find people *descanting* on his actions. *Addison.*

DESCANT′ING, *ppr.* Singing in parts or with various modulations; discoursing freely; commenting.

DESCANT′ING, *n.* Remark; conjecture. *Burnet.*

DESCEND′, *v. i.* [L. *descendo; de* and *scando*, to climb; W. *discynu*, from *cynu*, to rise, *cwn*, top; It. *discendere;* Fr. *descendre;* Sp. *descender;* Arm. *disgenn.* The root *cwn* is from extending, shooting, thrusting, as *gin* in *begin.*]

1. To move or pass from a higher to a lower place; to move, come or go downwards; to fall; to sink; to run or flow down; *applicable to any kind of motion or of body.* We *descend* on the feet, on wheels, or by falling. A torrent *descends* from a mountain.

The rains *descended*, and the floods came. Matt. vii.

2. To go down, or to enter.

He shall *descend* into battle and perish. 1 Sam. xxvi.

3. To come suddenly; to fall violently.

And on the suitors let thy wrath *descend.* *Pope.*

4. To go in; to enter.

He, with honest meditations fed,
Into himself *descended.* *Milton.*

5. To rush; to invade, as an enemy.

The Grecian fleet *descending* on the town. *Dryden.*

6. To proceed from a source or original; to be derived. The beggar may *descend* from a prince, and the prince, from a beggar.

7. To proceed, as from father to son; to pass from a preceding possessor, in the order of lineage, or according to the laws of succession or inheritance. Thus, an inheritance *descends* to the son or next of kin; a crown *descends* to the heir.

8. To pass from general to particular considerations; as, having explained the general subject, we will *descend* to particulars.

9. To come down from an elevated or honorable station; *in a figurative sense.* Flavius is an honorable man; he cannot *descend* to acts of meanness.

10. In *music*, to fall in sound; to pass from any note to another less acute or shrill, or from sharp to flat. *Rousseau.*

DESCEND′, *v. t.* To walk, move or pass downwards on a declivity; as, to *descend* a hill; to *descend* an inclined plain. [But this may be considered as elliptical; *on* or *along* being understood.]

DESCEND′ANT, *n.* [Fr. *descendant;* L. *descendens.*]

Any person proceeding from an ancestor in any degree; issue; offspring, in the line of generation, *ad infinitum.* We are all the *descendants* of Adam and Eve.

DESCEND′ENT, *a.* Descending; falling; sinking.

2. Proceeding from an original or ancestor. *Pope.*

DESCENDIBIL′ITY, *n.* The quality of being descendible, or capable of being transmitted from ancestors; as the *descendibility* of an estate or of a crown. *Blackstone.*

DESCEND′IBLE, *a.* That may be descended, or passed down; as, the hill is *descendible.*

2. That may descend from an ancestor to an heir; as a *descendible* estate.

DESCEN′SION, *n.* [L. *descensio.*] The act of going downwards; descent; a falling or sinking; declension; degradation.

2. In *astronomy, right descension* is an arch of the equinoctial, intercepted between the next equinoctial point and the intersection of the meridian, passing through the center of the object, at its setting, in a right sphere. *Encyc.*

Oblique descension, is an arch of the equinoctial, intercepted between the next equinoctial point and the horizon, passing through the center of the object, at its setting, in an oblique sphere. *Encyc.*

Oblique descension, is an arch of the equator which descends with the sun below the horizon of an oblique sphere. *Bailey.*

Descension of a sign, is an arch of the equator, which sets with such a sign or part of the zodiac, or any planet in it. *Bailey.*

Right descension of a sign, is an arch of the equator, which descends with the sign below the horizon of a right sphere; or the time the sign is setting in a right sphere. *Bailey.*

DESCEN′SIONAL, *a.* Pertaining to descent.

DESCENS′IVE, *a.* Tending downwards; having power to descend. *Sherwood.*

DESCENT′, *n.* [Fr. *descente;* L. *descensus.*]

1. The act of descending; the act of passing from a higher to a lower place, by any form of motion, as by walking, riding, rolling, sliding, sinking or falling.

2. Inclination downward; obliquity; slope; declivity; as the *descent* of a hill, or a roof.

3. Progress downward; as the *descent* from higher to lower orders of beings. *Locke.*

4. Fall from a higher to a lower state or station. *Milton.*

5. A landing from ships; invasion of troops from the sea; as, to make a *descent* on Cuba.

6. A passing from an ancestor to an heir; transmission by succession or inheritance; as the *descent* of an estate or a title from the father to the son. Descent is *lineal*, when it proceeds directly from the father to the son, and from the son to the grandson; *collateral*, when it proceeds from a man to his brother, nephew or other collateral representative.

7. A proceeding from an original or progenitor. The Jews boast of their *descent* from Abraham. Hence,

8. Birth; extraction; lineage; as a noble *descent.*

9. A generation; a single degree in the scale of genealogy; distance from the common ancestor.

No man is a thousand *descents* from Adam. *Hooker.*

10. Offspring; issue; descendants.

The care of our *descent* perplexes most. *Milton.*

11. A rank in the scale of subordination. *Milton.*

12. Lowest place. *Shak.*

13. In *music*, a passing from a note or sound to one more grave or less acute.

DESCRI′BABLE, *a.* That may be described; capable of description.

DESCRI′BE, *v. t.* [L. *describo; de* and *scribo*, to write; Sp. *describir;* It. *descrivere;* Fr. *decrire;* Arm. *discriva.* See *Scribe.*]

1. To delineate or mark the form or figure; as, to *describe* a circle by the compasses.

2. To make or exhibit a figure by motion; as, a star *describes* a circle or an ellipsis in the heavens.

3. To show or represent to others in words; to communicate the resemblance of a thing, by naming its nature, form or properties. The poet *describes* the Trojan horse. The historian *describes* the battle of Pharsalia. The moralist *describes* the effects of corrupt manners. The geographer *describes* countries and cities.

4. To represent by signs. A deaf and dumb man may *describe* a distant object. Our passions may be *described* by external motions.

5. To draw a plan; to represent by lines and other marks on paper, or other material; as, to *describe* the surface of the earth by a map or chart.

6. To define laxly. *Gray.*

DESCRI′BED, *pp.* Represented in form by marks or figures; delineated; represented by words or signs.

DESCRI′BER, *n.* One who describes by marks, words or signs.

DESCRI′BING, *ppr.* Representing the form or figure of, by lines or marks; communicating a view of, by words or signs, or by naming the nature and properties.

DESCRI′ED, *pp.* [See *Descry.*] Espied; discovered; seen.

DESCRI′ER, *n.* [See *Descry.*] One who espies, or discovers; a discoverer; a detecter. *Crashaw.*

DESCRIP′TION, *n.* [L. *descriptio.*] The act of delineating, or representing the figure of any thing by a plan, to be presented to the eye.

2. The figure or appearance of any thing delineated, or represented by visible lines, marks, colors, &c.; as the *description* of a country, or of Solomon's temple.

3. The act of representing a thing by words or by signs, or the passage containing such representation; a representation of names, nature or properties, that gives to another a view of the thing. Homer abounds with beautiful and striking *descriptions.* Hence,

4. A definition. All definitions must be less perfect *descriptions* of a material thing, than a visible figure or delineation.

5. The qualities expressed in a representation; as, a man of this *description*. *Burke.*

Hence,

6. The persons having the qualities expressed; a class of persons to whom a description is applicable, or who are in a similar condition.

The secretary proceeds to examine, whether a difference ought to be permitted to remain between them and another *description* of public creditors. *Hamilton.*

Persons of different *descriptions*. *Scott.*

DESCRIP'TIVE, *a.* Containing description; tending to describe; having the quality of representing; as a *descriptive* figure; a *descriptive* narration; a story *descriptive* of the age.

DESCRY', *v. t.* [Norm. *descrier* or *discriver*, and *discever*, to discover.]

1. To espy; to explore; to examine by observation.

The house of Joseph sent to *descry* Bethel. Judges i.

2. To detect; to find out; to discover any thing concealed.

3. To see; to behold; to have a sight of from a distance; as, the seamen *descried* land.

4. To give notice of something suddenly discovered. [*Not in use.*] *Hall.*

DESCRY', *n.* Discovery; thing discovered. [*Unusual.*] *Shak.*

DESCRY'ING, *ppr.* Discovering; espying.

DES'ECRATE, *v. t.* [L. *desecro; de* and *sacro*, to consecrate, from *sacer*, sacred.]

1. To divert from a sacred purpose or appropriation; opposed to *consecrate;* as, to *desecrate* a donation to a church.

2. To divest of a sacred character or office.

The clergy—cannot suffer corporal punishment, without being previously *desecrated*. *Tooke's Russia.*

DES'ECRATED, *pp.* Diverted from a sacred purpose or appropriation; divested of a sacred character or office.

DES'ECRATING, *ppr.* Diverting from a purpose to which a thing is consecrated; divested of a sacred character or office.

DESECRA'TION, *n.* The act of diverting from a sacred purpose or use to which a thing had been devoted; the act of diverting from a sacred character or office.

DES'ERT, *a.* s as z. [L. *desertus, desero; de* and *sero*, to sow, plant or scatter; Fr. *desert;* Sp. *desierto.*]

1. Literally, forsaken; hence, uninhabited; as a *desert* isle. Hence, wild; untilled; waste; uncultivated; as a *desert* land or country.

2. Void; empty; unoccupied.

Full many a flower is born to blush unseen,
And waste its sweetness on the *desert* air. *Gray.*

DES'ERT, *n.* [L. *desertum.*] An uninhabited tract of land; a region in its natural state; a wilderness; a solitude; particularly, a vast sandy plain, as the *deserts* of Arabia and Africa. But the word may be applied to an uninhabited country covered with wood.

DESERT', *v. t.* [Fr. *deserter*, from the adjective, and this from the L. *desertus, desero*, to forsake.]

1. To forsake; to leave utterly; to abandon; to quit with a view not to return to; as, to *desert* a friend; to *desert* our country; to *desert* a cause.

2. To leave, without permission, a military band, or a ship, in which one is enlisted; to forsake the service in which one is engaged, in violation of duty; as, to *desert* the army; to *desert* one's colors; to *desert* a ship.

DESERT', *v. i.* To run away; to quit a service without permission; as, to *desert* from the army.

DESERT', *n.* [from *deserve.*] A deserving; that which gives a right to reward or demands, or which renders liable to punishment; merit or demerit; that which entitles to a recompense of equal value, or demands a punishment equal to the offense; good conferred, or evil done, which merits an equivalent return. A wise legislature will reward or punish men according to their *deserts.*

2. That which is deserved; reward or punishment merited. In a future life, every man will receive his *desert.*

DESERT'ED, *pp.* Wholly forsaken; abandoned; left.

DESERT'ER, *n.* A person who forsakes his cause, his post, or his party or friend; particularly, a soldier or seaman who quits the service without permission, and in violation of his engagement.

DESERT'FUL, *a.* High in desert; meritorious. *Beaum.*

DESERT'ING, *ppr.* Forsaking utterly; abandoning.

DESER'TION, *n.* The act of forsaking or abandoning, as a party, a friend, a country, an army or military band, or a ship; the act of quitting, with an intention not to return.

2. The state of being forsaken by God; spiritual despondency.

The agonies of a soul under *desertion*. *South.*

DESERT'LESS, *a.* Without merit or claim to favor or reward. *Dryden.*

DESERT'LESSLY, *adv.* Undeservedly. *Beaum.*

DESERT'RICE, } *n.* A female who deserts.
DESERT'RIX, } *Milton.*

DESERVE, *v. t. dezerv'.* [L. *deservio; de* and *servio*, to serve. The Fr. *deservir* is not used.]

1. To merit; to be worthy of; *applied to good or evil.*

2. To merit by labor or services; to have a just claim to an equivalent for good conferred. The laborer *deserves* his wages; he *deserves* the value of his services.

3. To merit by good actions or qualities in general; to be worthy of, on account of excellence. The virtuous man *deserves* esteem and commendation. A work of value *deserves* praise.

4. To be worthy of, *in a bad sense;* to merit by an evil act; as, to *deserve* blame or punishment.

God exacteth of thee less than thine iniquity *deserveth.* Job xi.

DESERVE, *v. i. dezerv'.* To merit; to be worthy of or deserving; as, he *deserves* well or ill of his neighbor.

DESERV'ED, *pp.* Merited; worthy of.

DESERV'EDLY, *adv.* Justly; according to desert, whether of good or evil. A man may be *deservedly* praised, blamed or punished.

DESERV'ER, *n.* He who deserves or merits; one who is worthy of; *used generally in a good sense.* *Dryden.*

DESERV'ING, *ppr.* Meriting; having a just claim to reward; justly meriting punishment.

2. *a.* Worthy of reward or praise; meritorious; possessed of good qualities that entitle to approbation; as a *deserving* officer.

DESERV'ING, *n.* The act of meriting; desert; merit.

If ye have done to him according to the *deserving* of his hands. Judges ix.

DESERV'INGLY, *adv.* Meritoriously; with just desert.

DESHABILLE, } *n. deshabil'.* [Fr. from *de* and *habiller*,
DESHABIL, } to clothe. I have restored the true orthography.]

An undress; a loose morning dress; hence, any home dress; as, the lady is in *deshabille.* [*It would be well to anglicize the orthography.*]

DESIC'CANT, *a.* [See *Desiccate.*] Drying.

DESIC'CANT, *n.* A medicine or application that dries a sore. *Wiseman.*

DES'ICCATE, *v. t.* [L. *desicco; de* and *sicco*, to dry.]

To dry; to exhaust of moisture; to exhale or remove moisture from.

DES'ICCATE, *v. i.* To become dry. *Bacon. Hale.*

DES'ICCATED, *pp.* Dried.

DES'ICCATING, *ppr.* Drying; exhausting moisture.

DESICCA'TION, *n.* The act of making dry; the state of being dried. *Bacon.*

DESIC'CATIVE, *a.* Drying; tending to dry; that has the power to dry.

DESID'ERATE, *v. t.* [from the L.] To want; to miss. [*Not in use.*]

DESIDERA'TUM, *n.* plu. *desiderata.* [L. *desideratus—um*, from *desidero*, to desire.]

That which is desired; that which is not possessed, but which is desirable; any perfection or improvement which is wanted. The longitude is a *desideratum* in navigation. A tribunal to settle national disputes without war is a great *desideratum.*

DESI'GN, *v. t. desi'ne.* [L. *designo; de* and *signo*, to seal or stamp, that is, to set or throw; Sp. *designar, diseñar;* It. *designare, disegnare;* Fr. *designer, dessiner.*]

1. To delineate a form or figure by drawing the outline; to sketch; as in painting and other works of art.

2. To plan; to form an outline or representation of any thing. Hence,

3. To project; to form in idea, as a scheme. Hence,

4. To purpose or intend; as, a man *designs* to write an essay, or to study law.

5. To mark out by tokens. [*Not used.*] *Locke.*

6. To intend to apply or appropriate; with *for;* as, we *design* this ground *for* a garden, and that *for* a park. The word *design* may include an adapting or planning a thing for a purpose, or mere intention or scheme of the mind, which implies a plan. The father *designs* his son *for* the profession of the law, or *for* the ministry. It was formerly followed by *to*, but this use is now uncommon.

DESI'GN, *n.* [Fr. *dessein.*] A plan or representation of a thing by an outline; sketch;

general view; first idea represented by visible lines; as in painting or architecture.
2. A scheme or plan in the mind. A wise man is distinguished by the judiciousness of his *designs*.
3. Purpose; intention; aim; implying a scheme or plan in the mind. It is my *design* to educate my son for the bar.
4. The idea or scheme intended to be expressed by an artist; as the *designs* of medals. *Addison.*
5. In *manufactories*, the figures with which workmen enrich their stuffs, copied from painting or draughts. *Encyc.*
6. In *music*, the invention and conduct of the subject; the disposition of every part, and the general order of the whole. *Rousseau.*

DESI'GNABLE, *a.* Capable of being designed or marked out.
2. Distinguishable. *Digby.*

DES'IGNATE, *v. t.* [L. *designo, designatum.*]
1. To mark out or show, so as to make known; to indicate by visible lines, marks, description or something known and determinate; as, to *designate* the limits of a country; the limits are *designated* on the map; *designate* the spot where a star appears in the heavens; *designate* the place where our ancestors first landed.
2. To point out, to distinguish from others by indication; as, to be able to *designate* every individual who was concerned in a riot.
3. To appoint; to select or distinguish for a particular purpose; to assign; with *for*, as to *designate* an officer *for* the command of a station; or with *to*, as this captain was *designated to* that station.

DES'IGNATE, *a.* Appointed; marked out. [*Little used.*]

DES'IGNATED, *pp.* Marked out; indicated; shown; pointed out; appointed.

DES'IGNATING, *ppr.* Marking out; indicating; pointing out; appointing.

DESIGNA'TION, *n.* The act of pointing or marking out by signs or objects; as the *designation* of an estate by boundaries.
2. Indication; a showing or pointing; a distinguishing from others.
3. Appointment; direction; as, a claim to a throne grounded on the *designation* of a predecessor.
4. Appointment; a selecting and appointing; assignment; as the *designation* of an officer to a particular command.
5. Import; distinct application.

Finite and infinite are primarily attributed in their first *designation* to things which have parts. *Locke.*

DES'IGNATIVE, *a.* Serving to designate or indicate. *Pritchard.*

DES'IGNATOR, *n.* A Roman officer who assigned to each person his rank and place in public shows and ceremonies.

DESI'GNED, *pp.* Marked out; delineated; planned; intended.

DESI'GNEDLY, *adv.* By design; purposely; intentionally; opposed to *accidentally*, *ignorantly*, or *inadvertently*.

DESI'GNER, *n.* One who designs, marks out or plans; one who frames a scheme or project; a contriver.
2. One who plots; one who lays a scheme; *in an ill sense*.

DESI'GNFULNESS, *n.* Abundance of design. [*Not used.*] *Barrow.*

DESI'GNING, *ppr.* Forming a design; planning; delineating the outline; drawing figures on a plane.
2. *a.* In *an ill sense*, artful; insidious; intriguing; contriving schemes of mischief; hence, deceitful. *Designing* men are always liable to suspicion.

DESI'GNING, *n.* The art of delineating objects. *Berkeley.*

DESI'GNLESS, *a.* Without design or intention; inadvertent.

DESI'GNLESSLY, *adv.* Without design; inadvertently; ignorantly.

DESI'GNMENT, *n.* Design; sketch; delineation. *Dryden.*
2. Design; purpose; aim; intent; scheme. *Glanville. Shak.*
[*This word is now little used.*]

DES'INENCE, *n.* [L. *desino.*] End; close. *Bp. Hall.*

DES'INENT, *a.* Ending; extreme; lowermost. *B. Jonson.*

DESIP'IENT, *a.* [L. *desipiens, desipio*, to dote; *de* and *sapio*, to be wise.] Trifling; foolish; playful.

DESI'RABLE, *a. s* as *z.* [See *Desire.*] Worthy of desire; that is to be wished for with sincerity or earnestness. An easy address is a *desirable* accomplishment; real virtue is still more *desirable*.
2. Pleasing; agreeable.

All of them *desirable* young men. Ezek. xxiii.

DESI'RABLENESS, *n.* The quality of being desirable. *Goodman.*

DESI'RE, *n. s* as *z.* [Fr. *desir*; It. *desio*; Sp. *deseo*; Port. *desejo*; Arm. *desir.* Qu. W. *dais.*]
1. An emotion or excitement of the mind, directed to the attainment or possession of an object from which pleasure, sensual, intellectual or spiritual, is expected; a passion excited by the love of an object, or uneasiness at the want of it, and directed to its attainment or possession. *Desire* is a wish to possess some gratification or source of happiness which is supposed to be *obtainable*. A *wish* may exist for something that is or is not *obtainable*. Desire, when directed solely to sensual enjoyment, differs little from appetite. In other languages, desire is expressed by longing or reaching towards, [Gr. ορεγω, L. *appeto*,] and when it is ardent or intense, it approaches to longing, but the word in English usually expresses less than longing.

We endeavored—to see your face with great *desire*. 1 Thess. ii.

Thou satisfiest the *desires* of every living thing. Ps. cxlv.

Desire is that internal act, which, by influencing the will, makes us proceed to action. *El. of Criticism.*

2. A prayer or request to obtain:

He will fulfill the *desire* of them that fear him. Ps. cxlv.

3. The object of desire; that which is desired.

The *desire* of all nations shall come. Hag. ii.

4. Love; affection.

His *desire* is towards me. Cant. vii.

5. Appetite; lust.

Fulfilling the *desires* of the flesh. Eph. ii.

DESI'RE, *v. t.* [Fr. *desirer*; Arm. *desira*; It. *desiare*, or *desirare*; Sp. *desear*; Port. *desejar*: supposed to be contracted from L. *desidero*; but qu. for the Spanish *deseo*, It. *desio*, Port. *desejo*, appear to be the W. *dais*, supra.]
1. To wish for the possession or enjoyment of, with a greater or less degree of earnestness; to covet. It expresses less strength of affection than *longing*.

Neither shall any man *desire* thy land. Ex. xxxiv.

Follow after charity, and *desire* spiritual gifts. 1 Cor. xiv.

2. To express a wish to obtain; to ask; to request; to petition.

Then she said, did I *desire* a son of my Lord? 2 Kings iv.

3. To require. [*Not in use.*] *Spenser.*

DESI'RED, *pp.* Wished for; coveted; requested; entreated.

DESI'RELESS, *a.* Free from desire. *Donne.*

DESI'RER, *n.* One who desires or asks; one who wishes.

DESI'RING, *ppr.* Wishing for; coveting; asking; expressing a wish; soliciting.

DESI'ROUS, *a.* Wishing for; wishing to obtain; coveting; solicitous to possess and enjoy.

Be not *desirous* of his dainties. Prov. xxiii.

Jesus knew they were *desirous* to ask him. John xvi.

DESI'ROUSLY, *adv.* With desire; with earnest wishes.

DESI'ROUSNESS, *n.* The state or affection of being desirous.

DESIST', *v. i.* [L. *desisto*; *de* and *sisto*, to stand.]
To stop; to cease to act or proceed; to forbear; with *from*; as, he *desisted from* his purpose; let us *desist*.

DESIST'ANCE, *n.* A ceasing to act or proceed; a stopping. *Boyle.*

DESIST'ING, *ppr.* Ceasing to act or proceed.

DES'ITIVE, *a.* [L. *desitus.*] Final; conclusive. *Obs.* *Watts.*

DESK, *n.* [D. *disch*, a table, a dish; Sax. *disc*; G. *tisch*; Dan. Sw. *disk*; Russ. *doska*; L. *discus*; Gr. δισκος. See *Dish.*]
1. An inclining table for the use of writers and readers; usually made with a box or drawer underneath, and sometimes with a book-case above. *Pope.*
2. The pulpit in a church, and figuratively the clerical profession. The man appears well in the *desk*. He intends one son for the bar, and another for the *desk*.

DESK, *v. t.* To shut up in a desk; to treasure. *J. Hall.*

DES'MINE, *n.* A mineral that crystalizes in little silken tufts, which accompany spinellane in the lava of extinct volcanoes on the banks of the Rhine. *Lucas.*

DES'OLATE, *a.* [L. *desolatus.* See the Verb.]
1. Destitute or deprived of inhabitants; desert; uninhabited; denoting either stripped of inhabitants, or never having been inhabited; as a *desolate* isle; a *desolate* wilderness.

I will make the cities of Judah *desolate*, without an inhabitant. Jer ix.

2. Laid waste; in a ruinous condition; neglected; destroyed; as *desolate* altars; *desolate* towers. Ezek. Zeph.

3. Solitary; without a companion; afflicted.
Tamar remained *desolate* in Absalom's house. 2 Sam. xiii.
Have mercy on me, for I am *desolate.* Ps. xxv.
4. Deserted of God; deprived of comfort.
My heart within me is *desolate.* Ps. cxliii.

DES'OLATE, *v. t.* [L. *desolo, desolatus; de* and *solo*, to lay waste, *solus*, alone; Sp. *desolar;* Fr. *desoler;* It. *desolare.*]
1. To deprive of inhabitants; to make desert. The earth was nearly *desolated* by the flood.
2. To lay waste; to ruin; to ravage; to destroy improvements or works of art. An inundation *desolates* fields. Whole countries have been *desolated* by armies.

DES'OLATED, *pp.* Deprived of inhabitants; wasted; ruined.

DES'OLATELY, *adv.* In a desolate manner.

DES'OLATER, *n.* One who lays waste or desolates; that which desolates.

DES'OLATING, *ppr.* Depriving of inhabitants; wasting; ravaging.

DES'OLATION, *n.* The act of desolating; destruction or expulsion of inhabitants; destruction; ruin; waste.
Every kingdom divided against itself is brought to *desolation.* Matt. xii.
2. A place deprived of inhabitants, or otherwise wasted, ravaged and ruined.
How is Babylon become a *desolation* among the nations. Jer. l.
3. A desolate state; gloominess; sadness; destitution. *Shak. Thomson.*
The abomination of desolation, Roman armies which ravaged and destroyed Jerusalem. Matt. xxiv.

DES'OLATORY, *a.* Causing desolation.

DESPA'IR, *n.* [Fr. *desespoir.* See the Verb.]
1. Hopelessness; a hopeless state; a destitution of hope or expectation.
We are perplexed, but not in *despair.* 2 Cor. iv.
All safety in *despair* of safety placed. *Denham.*
2. That which causes despair; that of which there is no hope.
The mere *despair* of surgery, he cures. *Shak.*
3. Loss of hope in the mercy of God. *Sprat.*

DESPA'IR, *v. i.* [Fr. *desesperer; des* and *esperer*, to hope; It. *disperare;* Sp. *desesperar;* Arm. *disesperi;* from L. *despero; de* and *spero*, to hope.]
To be without hope; to give up all hope or expectation; followed by *of.*
We *despaired* even *of* life. 2 Cor. i.
Never *despair of* God's blessings here, or *of* his reward hereafter. *Wake.*

DESPA'IRER, *n.* One without hope. *Dryden.*

DESPA'IRFUL, *a.* Hopeless. *Sidney.*

DESPA'IRING, *ppr.* Giving up all hope or expectation.

DESPA'IRINGLY, *adv.* In a despairing manner; in a manner indicating hopelessness; as, he speaks *despairingly* of the sick man's recovery.

DESPATCH. [See *Dispatch.*]

DESPEC'TION, *n.* [L. *despectio.*] A looking down; a despising. [*Little used.*]

DESPERA'DO, *n.* [from *desperate.*] A desperate fellow; a furious man; a madman; a person urged by furious passions; one fearless, or regardless of safety.

DES'PERATE, *a.* [L. *desperatus*, from *despero*, to despair.] Without hope.
I am *desperate* of obtaining her. *Shak.*
2. Without care of safety; rash; fearless of danger; as a *desperate* man. Hence,
3. Furious, as a man in despair.
4. Hopeless; despaired of; lost beyond hope of recovery; irretrievable; irrecoverable; forlorn. We speak of a *desperate* case of disease, *desperate* fortunes, a *desperate* situation or condition.
5. In *a popular sense*, great in the extreme; as a *desperate* sot or fool. *Pope.*

DES'PERATELY, *adv.* In a desperate manner; as in despair; hence, furiously; with rage; madly; without regard to danger or safety; as, the troops fought *desperately.*
2. In *a popular sense*, greatly; extremely; violently.
She fell *desperately* in love with him. *Addison.*

DES'PERATENESS, *n.* Madness; fury; rash precipitance.

DESPERA'TION, *n.* A despairing; a giving up of hope; as *desperation* of success. *Hammond.*
2. Hopelessness; despair; as, the men were in a state of *desperation.* Hence,
3. Fury; rage; disregard of safety or danger; as, the men fought with *desperation;* they were urged to *desperation.*

DES'PICABLE, *a.* [Low L. *despicabilis*, from *despicio*, to look down, to despise; *de* and *specio*, to look.]
That may be or deserves to be despised; contemptible; mean; vile; worthless; *applicable equally to persons and things;* as a *despicable* man; *despicable* company; a *despicable* gift.

DES'PICABLENESS, *n.* The quality or state of being despicable; meanness; vileness; worthlessness.

DES'PICABLY, *adv.* Meanly; vilely; contemptibly; as *despicably* poor.

DESPI''CIENCY, *n.* [L. *despicio.*] A looking down; a despising. [*Little used.*] *Mede.*

DESPI'SABLE, *a.* Despicable; contemptible.

DESPI'SAL, *n.* Contempt. *Obs.*

DESPI'SE, *v. t. despi'ze.* [I doubt whether this word is formed from the L. *despicio.* In Sp. and Port. *pisar* is to tread down, and to *despise.* It appears to be of different origin from *despite*, and to be formed on the root of the Spanish word. We probably see its affinities in Sp. *pison*, a rammer, and the L. *piso*, to stamp, whence *pistillum*, Eng. *pestle, piston*, &c. The primary sense then is to thrust, drive, and hence to cast off or tread down, to despise.]
1. To contemn; to scorn; to disdain; to have the lowest opinion of.
Fools *despise* wisdom and instruction. Prov. i.
Else he will hold to the one, and *despise* the other. Matt. vi.
2. To abhor. *Shak.*

DESPI'SED, *pp.* Contemned; disdained; abhorred.

DESPI'SEDNESS, *n.* The state of being despised.

DESPI'SER, *n.* A contemner; a scorner.

DESPI'SING, *ppr.* Contemning; scorning; disdaining.

DESPI'SING, *n.* Contempt.

DESPI'SINGLY, *adv.* With contempt.

DESPI'TE, *n.* [Fr. *depit;* Norm. *despite;* Arm. *desped;* It. *despetto*, spite, malice. Qu. from L. *despectus, despicio.* See *Spite.*]
1. Extreme malice; violent hatred; malignity; malice irritated or enraged; active malignity; angry hatred.
With all thy *despite* against the land of Israel. Ezek. xxv.
Thou wretch! *despite* o'erwhelm thee. *Shak.*
2. Defiance with contempt, or contempt of opposition. [See *Spite.*]
He will rise to fame in *despite* of his enemies.
3. An act of malice or contempt; as a *despite* to the Most High. *Milton.*

DESPI'TE, *v. t.* To vex; to offend; to tease. *Raleigh.*

DESPI'TEFUL, *a.* Full of spite; malicious; malignant; as a *despiteful* enemy. *King Charles.*
Haters of God, *despiteful*, proud, boasters. Rom. i.

DESPI'TEFULLY, *adv.* With despite; maliciously; contemptuously.
Pray for them that *despitefully* use you. Matt. v.

DESPI'TEFULNESS, *n.* Malice; extreme hatred; malignity.

DESPIT'EOUS, *a.* Malicious. *Obs. Milton.*

DESPIT'EOUSLY, *adv.* Furiously. *Obs. Spenser.*

DESPOIL', *v. t.* [L. *despolio; de* and *spolio*, to spoil; Fr. *depouiller;* It. *spogliare;* Sp. *despojar;* Port. *id.* See *Spoil.*]
1. To strip; to take from by force; to rob; to deprive; followed by *of;* as, to *despoil* one *of* arms; to *despoil of* honors; to *despoil of* innocence.
2. To strip or divest by any means. *Woodward.*

DESPOIL'ED, *pp.* Stripped; robbed; bereaved; deprived.

DESPOIL'ER, *n.* One who strips by force; a plunderer.

DESPOIL'ING, *ppr.* Depriving; stripping; robbing.

DESPOLIA'TION, *n.* The act of despoiling; a stripping.

DESPOND', *v. i.* [L. *despondeo; de* and *spondeo*, to promise; literally, to throw to or forward.]
1. To be cast down; to be depressed or dejected in mind; to fail in spirits.
I should despair, or at least *despond.* *Scott's Letters.*
2. To lose all courage, spirit or resolution; to sink by loss of hope.
Others depress their own minds, and *despond* at the first difficulty. *Locke.*
Note. The distinction between *despair* and *despond* is well marked in the foregoing passage from Scott. But although *despair* implies a total loss of hope, which *despond* does not, at least in every case, yet *despondency* is followed by the abandonment of effort, or cessation of action, and *despair* sometimes impels to violent action, even to rage.

DESPOND'ENCY, *n.* A sinking or dejection of spirits at the loss of hope; loss of courage at the failure of hope, or in deep affliction, or at the prospect of insurmountable difficulties.

DESPOND'ENT, *a.* Losing courage at the

loss of hope; sinking into dejection; depressed and inactive in despair. *Bentley. Thomson.*

DESPOND'ER, *n.* One destitute of hope.

DESPOND'ING, *ppr.* Losing courage to act, in consequence of loss of hope, or of deep calamity, or of difficulties deemed insurmountable; sinking into dejection; despairing, with depression of spirits.

DESPOND'INGLY, *adv.* In a desponding manner; with dejection of spirits; despairingly.

DESPONS'ATE, *v. t.* [L. *desponso.*] To betroth. [*Not in use.*]

DESPONSA'TION, *n.* A betrothing. [*Not in use.*]

DES'POT, *n.* [Gr. δεσποτης, a master or lord; It *despoto;* Fr. *despote;* Sp. *despoto.*]
An emperor, king or prince invested with absolute power, or ruling without any control from men, constitution or laws. Hence in a general sense, a tyrant. *Burke.*

DESPOT'IC, DESPOT'ICAL, *a.* Absolute in power; independent of control from men, constitution or laws; arbitrary in the exercise of power; as a *despotic* prince.
2. Unlimited or unrestrained by constitution, laws or men; absolute; arbitrary; as *despotic* authority or power. *Addison. Swift.*
3. Tyrannical.

DESPOT'ICALLY, *adv.* With unlimited power; arbitrarily; in a despotic manner. *Blackstone.*

DESPOT'ICALNESS, *n.* Absolute or arbitrary authority.

DES'POTISM, *n.* [Sp. *despotismo;* Fr. *despotisme.*]
1. Absolute power; authority unlimited and uncontrolled by men, constitution or laws, and depending alone on the will of the prince; as the *despotism* of a Turkish sultan.
2. An arbitrary government, as that of Turkey and Persia.

DES'PUMATE, *v. i.* [L. *despumo; de* and *spuma,* froth or scum.]
To foam; to froth; to form froth or scum.

DESPUMA'TION, *n.* The act of throwing off excrementitious matter and forming a froth or scum on the surface of liquor; clarification; scumming. *Coxe.*

DESQUAMA'TION, *n.* [L. *desquamo; de* and *squama,* a scale.]
A scaling or exfoliation of bone; the separation of the cuticle in small scales. *Coxe.*

DESS, for *desk.* [*Not in use.*] *Chaucer. Spenser.*

DESSERT', *n. dezzert'.* [Fr. *dessert,* from *desservir,* to clear the table; *de* and *servir,* to serve.]
A service of fruits and sweetmeats, at the close of an entertainment; the last course at the table, after the meat is removed. *Dryden.*

DES'TINATE, *v. t.* [L. *destino, destinatus.*] To design or appoint. [*Seldom used.* See *Destine.*]

DES'TINATE, *a.* Appointed; destined; determined. *Morton.*

DESTINA'TION, *n.* [L. *destinatio.*] The act of destining, or appointing.
2. The purpose for which any thing is intended or appointed; end or ultimate design. Every animal is fitted for its *destination.*
3. The place to which a thing is appointed, as the ship left her *destination;* but it is more usual to say, the place of her *destination.*

DES'TINE, *v. t.* [L. *destino;* probably *de* and *stino* or *stano.* There seems to have been a root of this orthography, different from L. *sto,* which we find in *obstinate, obstino, præstino,* and in Russ. *stanovlyu* is to set or place, *stan* is stature, and we have *stanchion,* and *stone,* Sax. *stan,* perhaps from the same root. The words beginning with *st,* as *stable, steady, stage, stand,* signify to *set,* but the difference of final articulation seems to indicate a difference of roots—*stab, stad, stag, stan.*]
1. To set, ordain or appoint to a use, purpose, state or place. We *destine* a son *to* the ministerial office; a house *for* a place of worship; a ship *for* the London trade or *to* Lisbon; and we are all *destined to* a future state of happines or misery.
2. To fix unalterably, as by a divine decree; as the *destined* hour of death.
3. To doom; to devote; to appoint unalterably. *Prior.*

DES'TINED, *pp.* Ordained; appointed by previous determination; devoted; fixed unalterably.

DES'TINING, *ppr.* Ordaining; appointing.

DES'TINY, *n.* [Fr. *destin;* It. *destino;* Sp. *id.*] State or condition appointed or predetermined; ultimate fate; as, men are solicitous to know their future *destiny,* which is however happily concealed from them.
2. Invincible necessity; fate; a necessity or fixed order of things established by a divine decree, or by an indissoluble connection of causes and effects.

But who can turn the stream of *destiny?* *Spenser.*

Destinies, the fates, or supposed powers which preside over human life, spin it out, and determine it; called by the Latins, *parcæ.*

DES'TITUTE, *a.* [L. *destitutus, destituo; de* and *statuo,* to set. Literally, set from or away.]
1. Not having or possessing; wanting; as *destitute* of virtue, or of piety; *destitute* of food and clothing. It differs from *deprived,* as it does not necessarily imply previous possession.
2. Needy; abject; comfortless; friendless.

He will regard the prayer of the *destitute.* Ps. cii.

DES'TITUTE, *n.* One who is without friends or comfort.

DES'TITUTE, *v. t.* To forsake. [*Not used.*] *Fotherby.*
2. To deprive. [*Not used.*] *Bacon.*

DESTITU'TION, *n.* Want; absence of a thing; a state in which something is wanted or not possessed; poverty. *Hooker. Taylor.*

DESTROY', *v. t.* [L. *destruo; de* and *struo,* to pile, to build; Fr. *detruire;* It. *distruggere;* Sp. Port. *destruir.* See *Structure.*]
1. To demolish; to pull down; to separate the parts of an edifice, the union of which is necessary to constitute the thing; as, to *destroy* a house or temple; to *destroy* a fortification.
2. To ruin; to annihilate a thing by demolishing or by burning; as, to *destroy* a city.
3. To ruin; to bring to naught; to annihilate; as, to *destroy* a theory or scheme; to *destroy* a government; to *destroy* influence.
4. To lay waste; to make desolate.

Go up against this land, and *destroy* it. Is. xxxvi.

5. To kill; to slay; to extirpate; *applied to men or other animals.*

Ye shall *destroy* all this people. Num. xxxii.
All the wicked will he *destroy.* Ps. cxlv.

6. To take away; to cause to cease; to put an end to; as, pain *destroys* happiness.

That the body of sin might be *destroyed.* Rom. vi.

7. To kill; to eat; to devour; to consume. Birds *destroy* insects. Hawks *destroy* chickens.
8. In *general,* to put an end to; to annihilate a thing or the form in which it exists. An army is *destroyed* by slaughter, capture or dispersion; a forest, by the ax, or by fire; towns, by fire or inundation, &c.
9. In *chimistry,* to resolve a body into its parts or elements.

DESTROY'ABLE, *a.* That may be destroyed.

Plants scarcely *destroyable* by the weather. [*Little used.*] *Derham.*

DESTROY'ED, *pp.* Demolished; pulled down; ruined; annihilated; devoured; swept away; &c.

DESTROY'ER, *n.* One who destroys, or lays waste; one who kills a man, or an animal, or who ruins a country, cities, &c.

DESTROY'ING, *ppr.* Demolishing; laying waste; killing; annihilating; putting an end to.

DESTROY'ING, *n.* Destruction. *Milton.*

DESTRUCT, for *destroy,* is not used.

DESTRUCTIBIL'ITY, *n.* The quality of being capable of destruction.

DESTRUC'TIBLE, *a.* [L. *destruo, destructum.*] Liable to destruction; capable of being destroyed.

DESTRUC'TION, *n.* [L. *destructio.* See *Destroy.*]
1. The act of destroying; demolition; a pulling down; subversion; ruin, by whatever means; as the *destruction* of buildings, or of towns. Destruction consists in the annihilation of the form of any thing; that form of parts which constitutes it what it is; as the *destruction* of grass or herbage by eating; of a forest, by cutting down the trees: or it denotes a total annihilation; as the *destruction* of a particular government; the *destruction* of happiness.
2. Death; murder; slaughter; massacre.

There was a deadly *destruction* throughout all the city. 1 Sam. v.

3. Ruin.

Destruction and misery are in their ways. Rom. 3.

4. Eternal death.

Broad is the way that leadeth to *destruction.* Matt. vii.

5. Cause of destruction; a consuming plague; a destroyer.

The *destruction* that wasteth at noon-day. Ps. xci.

DESTRUC'TIVE, *a.* Causing destruction; having the quality of destroying; ruinous; mischievous; pernicious; with *of* or *to;* as a *destructive* fire or famine. Intemperance is *destructive of* health; evil examples are *destructive to* the morals of youth.

DESTRUC'TIVELY, *adv.* With destruction; ruinously; mischievously; with power to destroy; as *destructively* lewd or intemperate.

DESTRUC'TIVENESS, *n.* The quality of destroying or ruining.

DESTRUC'TOR, *n.* A destroyer; a consumer. [*Not used.*] *Boyle.*

DESUDA'TION, *n.* [L. *desudo; de* and *sudo*, to sweat.]
A sweating; a profuse or morbid sweating, succeeded by an eruption of pustules, called heat-pimples. *Coxe. Encyc.*

DES'UETUDE, *n.* [L. *desuetudo*, from *desuesco; de* and *suesco*, to accustom one's-self.]
The cessation of use; disuse; discontinuance of practice, custom or fashion. Habit is contracted by practice, and lost by *desuetude.* Words in every language are lost by *desuetude.*

DESUL'PHURATE, *v. t.* [*de* and *sulphurate* or *sulphur.*] To deprive of sulphur. *Chimistry.*

DESUL'PHURATED, *pp.* Deprived of sulphur.

DESUL'PHURATING, *ppr.* Depriving of sulphur.

DESULPHURA'TION, *n.* The act or operation of depriving of sulphur.

DES'ULTORILY, *adv.* [See *Desultory.*] In a desultory manner; without method; loosely.

DES'ULTORINESS, *n.* A desultory manner; unconnectedness; a passing from one thing to another without order or method.

DES'ULTORY, *a.* [L. *desultorius*, from *desilio; de* and *salio*, to leap.]
1. Leaping; passing from one thing or subject to another, without order or natural connection; unconnected; immethodical; as a *desultory* conversation.
2. Coming suddenly; started at the moment; not proceeding from natural order or connection with what precedes; as a *desultory* thought.

DESU'ME, *v. t.* [L. *desumo.*] To take from; to borrow. [*Not in use.*] *Hale.*

DETACH', *v. t.* [Fr. *detacher*; Arm. *distaga*; Sp. Port. *destacar*; It. *staccare; de* and the root of Eng. *tack.* See *Attach.*]
1. To separate or disunite; to disengage; to part from; as, to *detach* the coats of a bulbous root from each other; to *detach* a man from the interest of the minister, or from a party.
2. To separate men from their companies or regiments; to draw from companies or regiments, as a party of men, and send them on a particular service.
3. To select ships from a fleet and send them on a separate service.

DETACH'ED, *pp.* Separated; parted from; disunited; drawn and sent on a separate service.
2. *a.* Separate; as *detached* parcels or portions.

DETACH'ING, *ppr.* Separating; parting from; drawing and sending on a separate employment.

DETACH'MENT, *n.* The act of detaching or separating.
2. A body of troops, selected or taken from the main army, and employed on some special service or expedition.
3. A number of ships, taken from a fleet, and sent on a separate service.

DETA'IL, *v. t.* [Fr. *detailler*, to cut in pieces; *de* and *tailler*, to cut, Sp. *tallar*, It. *tagliare.*]
1. To relate, report or narrate in particulars; to recite the particulars of; to particularize; to relate minutely and distinctly; as, he *detailed* all the facts in due order.
2. To select, as an officer or soldier from a division, brigade, regiment or battalion. *Law of Massachusetts.*

DETA'IL, *n.* [Fr.] A narration or report of particulars; a minute and particular account. He related the story in *detail.* He gave a *detail* of all the transactions.
2. A selecting of officers or soldiers from the rosters.

DETA'ILED, *pp.* Related in particulars; minutely recited; selected.

DETA'ILER, *n.* One who details.

DETA'ILING, *ppr.* Relating minutely; telling the particulars.
2. Selecting from the rosters.

DETA'IN, *v. t.* [L. *detineo; de* and *teneo*, to hold; Fr. *detenir; Sp. detener.* See *Tenant.*]
1. To keep back or from; to withhold; to keep what belongs to another. *Detain* not the wages of the hireling. *Taylor.*
2. To keep or restrain from proceeding, either going or coming; to stay or stop. We were *detained* by the rain.

> Let us *detain* thee, till we have made ready a kid. Judges xiii.

3. To hold in custody. *Blackstone.*

DETA'INDER, *n.* A writ. [See *Detinue.*]

DETA'INED, *pp.* Withheld; kept back; prevented from going or coming; held; restrained.

DETA'INER, *n.* One who withholds what belongs to another; one who detains, stops or prevents from going.
2. In *law*, a holding or keeping possession of what belongs to another; detention of what is another's, though the original taking may be lawful. *Blackstone.*

DETA'INING, *ppr.* Withholding what belongs to another; holding back; restraining from going or coming; holding in custody.

DETA'INMENT, *n.* The act of detaining; detention. *Blackstone.*

DETECT', *v. t.* [L. *detego, detectus; de* and *tego*, to cover, W. *toi*, Eng. to *deck*, which see.]
Literally, to uncover; hence, to discover; to find out; to bring to light; as, to *detect* the ramifications and inosculations of the fine vessels. But this word is especially applied to the discovery of secret crimes and artifices. We *detect* a thief, or the crime of stealing. We *detect* the artifices of the man, or the man himself. We *detect* what is concealed, especially what is concealed by design.

DETECT'ED, *pp.* Discovered; found out; laid open; brought to light.

DETECT'ER, *n.* A discoverer; one who finds out what another attempts to conceal.

DETECT'ING, *ppr.* Discovering; finding out.

DETEC'TION, *n.* The act of detecting; discovery of a person or thing attempted to be concealed; as the *detection* of a thief or burglarian; the *detection* of fraud or forgery; the *detection* of artifice, device or a plot.
2. Discovery of any thing before hidden, or unknown.

> The sea and rivers are instrumental to the *detection* of amber and other fossils, by washing away the earth that concealed them. *Woodward.*

DETEN'EBRATE, *v. t.* [L. *de* and *tenebræ.*] To remove darkness. [*Not in use.*] *Brown.*

DETENT', *n.* [L. *detentus;* Fr. *detente.*] A stop in a clock, which by being lifted up or let down, locks and unlocks the clock in striking. *Encyc.*

DETEN'TION, *n.* [See *Detain.*] The act of detaining; a withholding from another his right; a keeping what belongs to another, and ought to be restored. *Blackstone.*
2. Confinement; restraint; as *detention* in custody.
3. Delay from necessity; a detaining; as the *detention* of the mail by bad roads.

DETER', *v. t.* [L. *deterreo; de* and *terreo*, to frighten.]
1. To discourage and stop by fear; to stop or prevent from acting or proceeding, by danger, difficulty or other consideration which disheartens, or countervails the motive for an act. We are often *deterred* from our duty by trivial difficulties. The state of the road or a cloudy sky may *deter* a man from undertaking a journey.

> A million of frustrated hopes will not *deter* us from new experiments. *J. M. Mason.*

2. To prevent by prohibition or danger. *Mitford.*

DETERGE, *v. t.* *deterj'.* [L. *detergo; de* and *tergo*, to wipe or scour.]
To cleanse; to purge away foul or offending matter, from the body, or from an ulcer. *Wiseman.*

DETER'GED, *pp.* Cleansed; purged.

DETER'GENT, *a.* Cleansing; purging.

DETER'GENT, *n.* A medicine that has the power of cleansing the vessels or skin from offending matter.

DETER'GING, *ppr.* Cleansing; carrying off obstructions or foul matter.

DETE'RIORATE, *v. i.* [Fr. *deteriorer;* It. *deteriorare;* Sp. *deteriorar*, from *deterior*, worse, L. *deterior.*]
To grow worse; to be impaired in quality; to degenerate; opposed to *meliorate.*

DETE'RIORATE, *v. t.* To make worse; to reduce in quality; as, to *deteriorate* a race of men or their condition. *Hayley. Paley.*

DETE'RIORATED, *pp.* Made worse; impaired in quality.

DETE'RIORATING, *ppr.* Becoming worse or inferior in quality.

DETERIORA'TION, *n.* A growing or making worse; the state of growing worse.

DETERIOR'ITY, *n.* Worse state or quality; as *deteriority* of diet. *Ray.*

DETER'MENT, *n.* [See *Deter.*] The act of deterring; the cause of deterring; that which deters. *Boyle.*

DETERM'INABLE, *a.* [See *Determine.*]
1. That may be decided with certainty. *Boyle.*
2. That may end or be determined.

DETERM'INATE, *a.* [L. *determinatus.*]
1. Limited; fixed; definite; as a *determinate* quantity of matter.

2. Established; settled; positive; as a *determinate* rule or order.

The *determinate* counsel of God. Acts ii.

3. Decisive; conclusive; as a *determinate* resolution or judgment.

4. Resolved on. *Shak.*

5. Fixed; resolute. *Sidney.*

DETERM'INATE, *v. t.* To limit. [*Not used.* See *Determine.*]

DETERM'INATELY, *adv.* With certainty.

The principles of religion are *determinately* true or false. *Tillotson.*

2. Resolutely; with fixed resolve. [*Unusual.*] *Sidney.*

DETERM'INATENESS, *n.* The state of being determinate, certain, or precise.

DETERMINA'TION, *n.* The act of determining or deciding.

2. Decision of a question in the mind; firm resolution; settled purpose; as, they have acquainted me with their *determination.*

3. Judicial decision; the ending of a controversy or suit by the judgment of a court. Justice is promoted by a speedy *determination* of causes, civil and criminal.

4. Absolute direction to a certain end.

Remissness can by no means consist with a constant *determination* of the will to the greatest apparent good. *Locke.*

5. An ending; a putting an end to; as the *determination* of a will. *Blackstone.*

DETERM'INATIVE, *a.* That uncontrollably directs to a certain end.

The *determinative* power of a just cause. *Bramhall.*

2. Limiting; that limits or bounds; as, a word may be *determinative* and limit the subject. *Watts.*

DETERM'INATOR, *n.* One who determines. *Brown.*

DETERM'INE, *v. t.* [L. *determino; de* and *termino,* to bound; *terminus,* a boundary or limit; W. *tervyn,* an extremity, or limit; *terv,* outward, extreme; *tervynu,* to fix a bound, to limit, to determine; *term,* a term, extreme point; *termiaw,* to limit; Ir. *teora,* a border or limit; Gr. τερμα, τερμων. See *Term.*]

1. To end; particularly, to end by the decision or conclusion of a cause, or of a doubtful or controverted point; applicable to the decisions of the mind, or to judicial decisions. We say, I had *determined* this question in my own mind; the court has *determined* the cause.

2. To end and fix; to settle ultimately; as, this event *determined* his fate.

3. To fix on; to settle or establish; as, to *determine* the proper season for planting seeds.

God—hath *determined* the times before appointed. Acts xvii.

4. To end; to limit; to bound; to confine. Yonder hill *determines* our view. Knowledge is *determined* by the sight. *Bacon.*

5. To give a direction to; to influence the choice; that is, to limit to a particular purpose or direction; as, this circumstance *determined* him to the study of law. Also, to give a direction to material bodies in their course; as, impulse may *determine* a moving body to this or that point.

6. To resolve, that is, to end or settle a point in the mind, as in Definition first.

I *determined* this with myself. 2 Cor. ii.

Paul had *determined* to sail by Ephesus. Acts xx.

7. To destroy. [*Not used.*] *Shak.*

8. To put an end to; as, to *determine* a will. *Blackstone.*

9. To settle or ascertain, as something uncertain.

The character of the soul is *determined* by the character of its God. *J. Edwards.*

DETERM'INE, *v. i.* To resolve; to conclude; to come to a decision.

He shall pay as the judges *determine.* Ex. xxi.

It is indifferent how the learned shall *determine* concerning this matter. *Anon.*

2. To end; to terminate. The danger *determined* by the death of the conspirators. Revolutions often *determine* in setting up tyranny at home, or in conquest from abroad.

Some estates may *determine,* on future contingencies. *Blackstone.*

DETERM'INED, *pp.* Ended; concluded; decided; limited; fixed; settled; resolved; directed.

2. *a.* Having a firm or fixed purpose, as a *determined* man; or manifesting a firm resolution, as a *determined* countenance.

DETERM'INING, *ppr.* Ending; deciding; fixing; settling; resolving; limiting; directing.

DETERRA'TION, *n.* [L. *de* and *terra,* earth.] The uncovering of any thing which is buried or covered with earth; a taking from out of the earth. *Woodward.*

DETER'RED, *pp.* [See *Deter.*] Discouraged or prevented from proceeding or acting, by fear, difficulty or danger.

DETER'RING, *ppr.* Discouraging or influencing not to proceed or act, by fear, difficulty, danger, or prospect of evil.

2. *a.* Discouraging; frightening. *Ash.*

DETER'SION, *n.* [L. *detersus, detergo.* See *Deterge.*] The act of cleansing, as a sore. *Wiseman.*

DETER'SIVE, *a.* [It. *detersivo;* Fr. *detersif.* See *Deterge.*]

Cleansing; having power to cleanse from offending matter.

DETER'SIVE, *n.* A medicine which has the power of cleansing ulcers, or carrying off foul matter.

DETEST', *v. t.* [L. *detestor; de* and *testor,* to affirm or bear witness; It. *detestare;* Sp. *detestar;* Fr. *detester.* The primary sense of *testor* is to set, throw or thrust. To *detest* is to thrust away.]

To abhor; to abominate; to hate extremely; as, to *detest* crimes or meanness.

DETEST'ABLE, *a.* Extremely hateful; abominable; very odious; deserving abhorrence.

Thou hast defiled my sanctuary with all thy *detestable* things. Ezek. v.

DETEST'ABLENESS, *n.* Extreme hatefulness.

DETEST'ABLY, *adv.* Very hatefully; abominably.

DETESTA'TION, *n.* Extreme hatred; abhorrence; with *of.* The good man entertains uniformly a *detestation of* sin.

DETEST'ED, *pp.* Hated extremely; abhorred.

DETEST'ER, *n.* One who abhors.

DETEST'ING, *ppr.* Hating extremely; abhorring; abominating.

DETHRO'NE, *v. t.* [Fr. *detrôner;* Sp. *destronar;* It. *stronare; de* and *throne,* L. *thronus.*]

1. To remove or drive from a throne; to depose; to divest of royal authority and dignity.

2. To divest of rule or power, or of supreme power.

The protector was *dethroned.* *Hume.*

DETHRO'NED, *pp.* Removed from a throne; deposed.

DETHRO'NEMENT, *n.* Removal from a throne; deposition of a king, emperor or prince.

DETHRO'NER, *n.* One who dethrones.

DETHRO'NING, *ppr.* Driving from a throne; depriving of regal power.

DET'INUE, *n.* [Fr. *detenu,* detained; *detenir,* to detain.]

In *law,* a writ of *detinue* is one that lies against him who wrongfully *detains* goods or chattels delivered to him, or in his possession. This writ lies for a thing certain and valuable, as for a horse, cow, sheep, plate, cloth, &c., to recover the thing itself or damages for the detainer. *Blackstone.*

DET'ONATE, *v. t.* [L. *detono; de* and *tono,* to thunder.]

In *chimistry,* to cause to explode; to burn or inflame with a sudden report.

DET'ONATE, *v. i.* To explode; to burn with a sudden report. Niter *detonates* with sulphur.

DET'ONATED, *pp.* Exploded; burnt with explosion.

DET'ONATING, *ppr.* Exploding; inflaming with a sudden report.

DETONA'TION, *n.* An explosion or sudden report made by the inflammation of certain combustible bodies, as fulminating gold. *Detonation* is not *decrepitation.*

DETONIZA'TION, *n.* The act of exploding, as certain combustible bodies.

DET'ONIZE, *v. t.* [See *Detonate.*] To cause to explode; to burn with an explosion; to calcine with detonation.

DET'ONIZE, *v. i.* To explode; to burn with a sudden report.

This precipitate—*detonizes* with a considerable noise. *Fourcroy.*

DET'ONIZED, *pp.* Exploded, as a combustible body.

DET'ONIZING, *ppr.* Exploding with a sudden report.

DETOR'SION, *n.* A turning or wresting; perversion.

DETORT', *v. t.* [L. *detortus,* of *detorqueo; de* and *torqueo,* to twist.]

To twist; to wrest; to pervert; to turn from the original or plain meaning. *Dryden.*

DETORT'ED, *pp.* Twisted; wrested; perverted.

DETORT'ING, *ppr.* Wresting; perverting.

DETÖUR', *n.* [Fr.] A turning; a circuitous way.

DETRACT', *v. t.* [L. *detractum; detrecto; detraho; de* and *traho,* to draw; Sp. *detractar;* It. *detrarre;* Fr. *detracter.* See *Draw* and *Drag.*]

1. Literally, to draw from. Hence, to take away from reputation or merit, through envy, malice or other motive; hence, to *detract from,* is to lessen or depreciate reputation or worth; to derogate from.

Never circulate reports that *detract from* the reputation or honor of your neighbor, without obvious necessity to justify the act. *Anon.*

2. To take away; to withdraw, *in a literal sense.* *Wotton. Boyle.*

DETRAC'TION, *n.* [L. *detractio.*] The act of taking something from the reputation or worth of another, with the view to lessen him in estimation; censure; a lessening of worth; the act of depreciating another, from envy or malice. Detraction may consist in representing merit, as less than it really is; or in the imputation of faults, vices or crimes, which impair reputation; and if such imputation is false, it is slander or defamation.

DETRAC'TIOUS, *a.* Containing detraction; lessening reputation. [*Not in use.*]

DETRACT'IVE, *a.* Having the quality or tendency to lessen the worth or estimation.

DETRACT'OR, *n.* One who takes away or impairs the reputation of another injuriously; one who attempts to lessen the worth or honor of another.

DETRACT'ORY, *a.* Derogatory; defamatory by denial of desert; with *from.* *Johnson. Boyle.*

DETRACT'RESS, *n.* A female detractor; a censorious woman.

DETRECT', *v. t.* [L. *detrecto.*] To refuse. [*Not in use.*] *Fotherby.*

DET'RIMENT, *n.* [L. *detrimentum.* Qu. *deter*, worse, or *detero, detritum*, worn off.]
Loss; damage; injury; mischief; harm; diminution. We speak of *detriment* to interest, property, religion, morals, reputation, and to land or buildings. *It is a word of very general application.*

DETRIMENT'AL, *a.* Injurious; hurtful; causing loss or damage.

A spirit of speculation may be *detrimental* to regular commerce. *Anon.*

DETRI''TION, *n.* [L. *detero.*] A wearing off. *Stevens.*

DETRI'TUS, *n.* [L. *detritus*, worn; *detero*, to wear.]
In *geology*, a mass of substances worn off or detached from solid bodies by attrition; as diluvial *detritus.* *Buckland.*

DETRU'DE, *v. t.* [L. *detrudo; de* and *trudo*, to thrust.] To thrust down; to push down with force. *Locke. Thomson.*

DETRU'DED, *pp.* Thrust or forced down.

DETRU'DING, *ppr.* Thrusting or forcing down.

DETRUNC'ATE, *v. t.* [L. *detrunco; de* and *trunco*, to cut shorter; *truncus*, cut short; Fr. *trancher*; Arm. *troucha*, or *traincha.* See *Trench.*] To cut off; to lop; to shorten by cutting.

DETRUNCA'TION, *n.* The act of cutting off.

DETRU'SION, *n. s* as *z.* [See *Detrude.*] The act of thrusting or driving down.

DETURP'ATE, *v. t.* [L. *deturpo.*] To defile. [*Little used.*] *Taylor.*

DEUCE, *n.* [Fr. *deux*, two.] Two; a card with two spots; a die with two spots; *a term used in gaming.*

DEUCE, *n.* A demon. [See *Duse.*]

DEUTEROG'AMIST, *n.* [infra.] One who marries the second time. *Goldsmith.*

DEUTEROG'AMY, *n.* [Gr. δευτερος, second, and γαμος, marriage.]
A second marriage after the death of the first husband or wife. *Goldsmith.*

DEUTERON'OMY, *n.* [Gr. δευτερος, second, and νομος, law.]
The second law, or second giving of the law by Moses; the name given to the fifth book of the Pentateuch.

DEUTOX'YD, *n.* [Gr. δευτερος, second, and *oxyd*; strictly, *deuteroxyd.*]
In *chimistry*, a substance oxydized in the second degree.

DEVAPORA'TION, *n.* [*de* and L. *vaporatio.*] The change of vapor into water, as in the generation of rain. *Darwin.*

DEV'AST, *v. t.* [L. *devasto.*] To lay waste; to plunder. [*Not in use.*] *Sandys.*

DEV'ASTATE, *v. t.* [L. *devasto; de* and *vasto*, to waste; Fr. *devaster*; Sp. *devastar*; It. *devastare.* See *Waste.*]
To lay waste; to waste; to ravage; to desolate; to destroy improvements.

DEV'ASTATED, *pp.* Laid waste; ravaged.

DEV'ASTATING, *ppr.* Laying waste; desolating.

DEVASTA'TION, *n.* [L. *devastatio.*] Waste; ravage; desolation; destruction of works of art and natural productions which are necessary or useful to man; havock; as by armies, fire, flood, &c.

2. In *law*, waste of the goods of the deceased by an executor, or administrator. *Blackstone.*

DEVEL'OP, *v. t.* [Fr. *developper*; It. *sviluppare*, to unfold, to display; *viluppo*, a packet or bundle, intricacy.]

1. To uncover; to unfold; to lay open; to disclose or make known something concealed or withheld from notice.

The General began to *develop* the plan of his operations.

These serve to *develop* its tenets. *Milner.*

2. To unravel; to unfold what is intricate; as, to *develop* a plot.

DEVEL'OPED, *pp.* Unfolded; laid open; unraveled.

DEVEL'OPING, *ppr.* Unfolding; disclosing; unraveling.

DEVEL'OPMENT, *n.* An unfolding; the discovering of something secret or withheld from the knowledge of others; disclosure; full exhibition.

2. The unraveling of a plot.

DEVEST', *v. t.* [Fr. *devêtir*; *de* and *vêtir*, to clothe, L. *vestio*, id., *vestis*, a vest, a garment. Generally written *divest.*]

1. To strip; to deprive of clothing or arms; to take off. *Denham.*

2. To deprive; to take away; as, to *devest* a man or nation of rights. [See *Divest.*]

3. To free from; to disengage.

4. In *law*, to alienate, as title or right.

DEVEST', *v. i.* In *law*, to be lost or alienated, as a title or an estate.

[This word is generally written *divest*, except in the latter and legal sense.]

DEVEST'ED, *pp.* Stripped of clothes; deprived; freed from; alienated or lost, as title.

DEVEST'ING, *ppr.* Stripping of clothes; depriving; freeing from; alienating.

DEVEX', *a.* [L. *devexus.*] Bending down. [*Not in use.*]

DEVEX'ITY, *n.* [L. *devexitas*, from *de* and *veho*, to carry.]
A bending downward; a sloping; incurvation downward. *Davies.*

DE'VIATE, *v. i.* [It. *deviare*; Sp. *desviarse*; L. *devius*; *de*, from, and *via*, way.]

1. To turn aside or wander from the common or right way, course or line, either in a literal or figurative sense; as, to *deviate* from the common track or path, or from a true course.

There nature *deviates*, and here wanders will. *Pope.*

2. To stray from the path of duty; to wander, in a moral sense; to err; to sin.

DEVIA'TION, *n.* A wandering or turning aside from the right way, course or line.

2. Variation from a common or established rule, or from analogy.

3. A wandering from the path of duty; want of conformity to the rules prescribed by God; error; sin; obliquity of conduct.

4. In *commerce*, the voluntary departure of a ship, without necessity, from the regular and usual course of the specific voyage insured. This discharges the underwriters from their responsibility. *Park.*

DEVI'CE, *n.* [Fr. *devis, devise*; It. *divisa*; from L. *divisus, divido.*]

1. That which is formed by design, or invented; scheme; artificial contrivance; stratagem; project; *sometimes in a good sense; more generally in a bad sense, as artifices are usually employed for bad purposes.*

In *a good sense:*

His *device* is against Babylon, to destroy it. Jer. li.

In *a bad sense:*

He disappointeth the *devices* of the crafty. Job v.

They imagined a mischievous *device.* Ps. xxi.

2. An emblem intended to represent a family, person, action or quality, with a suitable motto; used in painting, sculpture and heraldry. It consists in a metaphorical similitude between the things representing and represented, as the figure of a plow representing agriculture.

Knights-errant used to distinguish themselves by *devices* on their shields. *Addison.*

3. Invention; genius; faculty of devising; as a man of noble *device.* *Shak.*

4. A spectacle or show. *Obs.* *Beaum.*

DEVI'CEFUL, *a.* Full of devices; inventive. *Spenser.*

DEVI'CEFULLY, *adv.* In a manner curiously contrived. *Donne.*

DEV'IL, *n.* dev'l. [Sax. *diafol*; D. *duivel*; G. *teufel*; Sw. *diefvul*; Dan. *diævel*; Russ. *diavol*; Tartar, *diof*; L. *diabolus*; Gr. διαβολος, said to be from διαβαλλω, to calumniate; Fr. *diable*; Sp. *diablo*; Port. *diabo*; It. *diavolo.* The Armoric is *diaul*; W. *diawl*, which Owen supposes to be compounded of *di*, a negative, and *awl*, light—one without light, [prince of darkness.] The Irish is *diabhail*, which, according to O'Brien, is composed of *dia*, deity, and *bhal*, air, [god of the air.] If these Celtic words are justly explained, they are not connected with *diabolus*, or the latter is erroneously deduced.]

1. In *the christian theology*, an evil spirit or being; a fallen angel, expelled from heaven for rebellion against God; the chief of the apostate angels; the implacable enemy and tempter of the human race. In the New Testament, the word is frequently and erroneously used for *demon.*

2. A very wicked person, and in ludicrous

language, any great evil. In profane language, it is an expletive expressing wonder, vexation, &c.

3. An idol, or false god. Lev. xvii. 2 Chron. xi.

DEV'ILING, *n.* A young devil. [*Not in use.*] *Beaum.*

DEV'ILISH, *a.* Partaking of the qualities of the devil; diabolical; very evil and mischievous; malicious; as a *devilish* scheme; *devilish* wickedness. *Sidney.*

2. Having communication with the devil; pertaining to the devil. *Shak.*

3. Excessive; enormous; *in a vulgar and ludicrous sense;* as a *devilish* cheat. *Addison.*

DEV'ILISHLY, *adv.* In a manner suiting the devil; diabolically; wickedly. *South.*

2. Greatly; excessively; *in a vulgar sense.*

DEV'ILISHNESS, *n.* The qualities of the devil.

DEV'ILISM, *n.* The state of devils. [*Not used.*] *Bp. Hall.*

DEV'ILIZE, *v. t.* To place among devils. [*Not used.*] *Bp. Hall.*

DEV'ILKIN, *n.* A little devil. *Clarissa.*

DEV'ILSHIP, *n.* The character of a devil.

DE'VIOUS, *a.* [L. *devius; de* and *via*, way.] Out of the common way or track; as a *devious* course.

2. Wandering; roving; rambling.

> To bless the wildly *devious* morning walk. *Thomson.*

3. Erring; going astray from rectitude or the divine precepts.

> One *devious* step at first may lead into a course of habitual vice. *Anon.*

DEVIR'GINATE, *v. t.* [Low L. *devirgino.*] To deflour. *Sandys.*

DEVI'SABLE, *a.* *s* as *z.* [See the Verb.]

1. That may be bequeathed or given by will. *Blackstone.*

2. That can be invented or contrived. *Sadler.*

DEVI'SE, *v. t.* *s* as *z.* [Fr. *deviser*, to talk or interchange thoughts; It. *divisare*, to think, divide or share; from L. *divisus, divido.*]

1. To invent; to contrive; to form in the mind by new combinations of ideas, new applications of principles, or new arrangement of parts; to excogitate; to strike out by thought; to plan; to scheme; to project; as, to *devise* an engine or machine; to *devise* a new mode of writing; to *devise* a plan of defense; to *devise* arguments.

> To *devise* curious works in gold and silver. Ex. xxxv.

> In *a bad sense:*

> *Devise* not evil against thy neighbor. Prov. iii.

2. To give or bequeath by will, as land or other real estate. *Blackstone.*

DEVI'SE, *v. i.* To consider; to contrive; to lay a plan; to form a scheme.

> *Devise* how you will use him, when he comes. *Shak.*

Formerly followed by *of;* as, let us *devise of* ease. *Spenser.*

DEVI'SE, *n.* Primarily, a dividing or division; hence, the act of bequeathing by will; the act of giving or distributing real estate by a testator. *Blackstone.*

2. A will or testament.

3. A share of estate bequeathed.

DEVI'SE, *n.* Contrivance; scheme invented. *Obs.* *Hooker.*

DEVI'SED, *pp.* Given by will; bequeathed; contrived.

DEVISEE', *n.* The person to whom a devise is made; one to whom real estate is bequeathed.

DEVI'SER, *n.* One who contrives or invents; a contriver; an inventor. *Grew.*

DEVI'SING, *ppr.* Contriving; inventing; forming a scheme or plan.

2. Giving by will; bequeathing.

DEVI'SOR, *n.* One who gives by will; one who bequeaths lands or tenements. *Blackstone.*

DEV'ITABLE, *a.* Avoidable. } [*Not in use.*]
DEVITA'TION, *n.* An escaping. }

DEVOCA'TION, *n.* [L. *devocatio.*] A calling away; seduction. [*Not in use.*] *Hallywell.*

DEVOID', *a.* [*de* and *void*, Fr. *vuide, vide.* See *Void.*]

1. Void; empty; vacant; *applied to place.* *Spenser.*

2. Destitute; not possessing; as *devoid* of understanding.

3. Free from; as *devoid* of fear or shame.

DEVOIR', *n.* [Fr. *devoir;* It. *dovere;* from L. *debeo*, to owe.]

Primarily, service or duty. Hence, an act of civility or respect; respectful notice due to another; as, we paid our *devoirs* to the queen, or to the ladies.

DEVOLU'TION, *n.* [L. *devolutio.*] The act of rolling down; as the *devolution* of earth into a valley. *Woodward.*

2. Removal from one person to another; a passing or falling upon a successor. *Hale.*

DEVOLVE, *v. t.* *devolv'.* [L. *devolvo; de* and *volvo*, to roll, Eng. to *wallow.*]

1. To roll down; to pour or flow with windings.

> Through splendid kingdoms he *devolves* his maze. *Thomson.*

2. To move from one person to another; to deliver over, or from one possessor to a successor.

> The king *devolved* the care and disposition of affairs on the duke of Ormond. *Temple. Gibbon.*

DEVOLVE, *v. i.* *devolv'.* Literally, to roll down; hence, to pass from one to another; to fall by succession from one possessor to his successor. In the absence of the commander in chief, the command *devolved* on the next officer in rank. On the death of the prince, the crown *devolved* on his eldest son.

DEVOLV'ED, *pp.* Rolled down; passed over to another.

DEVOLV'ING, *ppr.* Rolling down; falling to a successor.

DEVO'TARY, *n.* A votary. [*Not in use.*] *Gregory.*

DEVO'TE, *v. t.* [L. *devoveo, devotus; de* and *voveo*, to vow; Fr. *devouer.*]

1. To appropriate by vow; to set apart or dedicate by a solemn act; to consecrate.

> No *devoted* thing that a man shall *devote* to the Lord—shall be sold or redeemed. Every *devoted* thing is most holy to the Lord. Lev. xxvii.

2. To give up wholly; to addict; to direct the attention wholly or chiefly; to attach; as, to *devote* one's self to science; to *devote* ourselves to our friends, or to their interest or pleasure.

3. To give up; to resign; as, aliens were *devoted* to rapine; the city was *devoted* to the flames.

4. To doom; to consign over; as, to *devote* one to destruction.

5. To execrate; to doom to evil. *Rowe.*

DEVO'TE, *a.* Devoted. *Milton.*

DEVO'TE, *n.* A devotee. *Sandys.*

DEVO'TED, *pp.* Appropriated by vow; solemnly set apart or dedicated; consecrated; addicted; given up; doomed; consigned.

DEVO'TEDNESS, *n.* The state of being devoted or given; addictedness; as *devotedness* to religion. *Grew. Milner.*

DEVOTEE', *n.* [Fr. *devot.*] One who is wholly devoted; particularly, one given wholly to religion; one who is superstitiously given to religious duties and ceremonies; a bigot.

DEVO'TEMENT, *n.* Devotedness; devotion. *Mem. of Buchanan.*

2. Vowed dedication. *Mason.*

DEVO'TER, *n.* One that devotes; also, a worshiper.

DEVO'TING, *ppr.* Giving or appropriating by vow; solemnly setting apart or dedicating; consecrating; giving wholly; addicting; dooming; consigning.

DEVO'TION, *n.* The state of being dedicated, consecrated, or solemnly set apart for a particular purpose.

2. A solemn attention to the Supreme Being in worship; a yielding of the heart and affections to God, with reverence, faith and piety, in religious duties, particularly in prayer and meditation; devoutness.

3. External worship; acts of religion; performance of religious duties.

> As I passed by and beheld your *devotions.* Acts xvii.

4. Prayer to the Supreme Being. A christian will be regular in his morning and evening *devotions.*

5. An act of reverence, respect or ceremony. *Shak.*

6. Ardent love or affection; attachment manifested by constant attention; as, the duke was distinguished by his *devotion* to the king, and to the interest of the nation. *Clarendon.*

7. Earnestness; ardor; eagerness.

> He seeks their hate with greater *devotion* than they can render it him. *Shak.*

8. Disposal; power of disposing of; state of dependence.

> Arundel castle would keep that rich corner of the country at his majesty's *devotion.* *Clarendon.*

DEVO'TIONAL, *a.* Pertaining to devotion; used in devotion; as a *devotional* posture; *devotional* exercises.

2. Suited to devotion; as a *devotional* frame of mind.

DEVO'TIONALIST, } *n.* A person given to devotion; or one superstitiously or formally devout. *Spectator.*
DEVO'TIONIST, }

DEVO'TO, *n.* [It.] A devotee. [*Not in use.*] *Spenser.*

DEVO'TOR, *n.* One who reverences or worships. *Obs.* *Beaum.*

DEVOUR', *v. t.* [L. *devoro; de* and *voro*, to eat; It. *vorare, divorare;* Sp. *devorar;* Fr. *devorer;* Arm. *devori;* W. *pori*, to feed; Gr. βορα, pasture; Heb. Ch. בער, to consume. Class Br. No. 6.]

1. To eat up; to eat with greediness; to eat

ravenously, as a beast of prey, or as a hungry man.

We will say, some evil beast hath *devoured* him. Gen. xxxvii.

In the morning he shall *devour* the prey. Gen. xlix.

2. To destroy; to consume with rapidity and violence.

I will send a fire into the house of Hazael, which shall *devour* the palaces of Ben-Hadad. Amos i.

Famine and pestilence shall *devour* him. Ez. vii.

3. To destroy; to annihilate; to consume.

He seemed in swiftness to *devour* the way. *Shak.*

4. To waste; to consume; to spend in dissipation and riot.

As soon as this thy son had come, who hath *devoured* thy living with harlots. Luke xv.

5. To consume wealth and substance by fraud, oppression, or illegal exactions.

Ye *devour* widows' houses. Matt. xxiii.

6. To destroy spiritually; to ruin the soul.

Your adversary, the devil, as a roaring lion, walketh about, seeking whom he may *devour*. 1 Pet. v.

7. To slay.

The sword shall *devour* the young lions. Nah. ii.

8. To enjoy with avidity.

Longing they look, and gaping at the sight,
Devour her o'er and o'er with vast delight. *Dryden.*

DEVOUR'ED, *pp.* Eaten; swallowed with greediness; consumed; destroyed; wasted; slain.

DEVOUR'ER, *n.* One who devours; he or that which eats, consumes or destroys; he that preys on.

DEVOUR'ING, *ppr.* Eating greedily; consuming; wasting; destroying; annihilating.

DEVOUR'INGLY, *adv.* In a devouring manner.

DEVOUT', *a.* [It. *devoto;* Fr. *devot;* L. *devotus.* See *Devote.*]

1. Yielding a solemn and reverential attention to God in religious exercises, particularly in prayer.

We must be constant and *devout* in the worship of God. *Rogers.*

2. Pious; devoted to religion; religious.

Simeon was a just man and *devout.* Luke ii.

Devout men carried Stephen to his burial. Acts viii.

3. Expressing devotion or piety; as, with eyes *devout.* *Milton.*

4. Sincere; solemn; earnest; as, you have my *devout* wishes for your safety.

DEVOUT', *n.* A devotee. [*Not used.*] *Sheldon.*

DEVOUT'LESS, *a.* Destitute of devotion.

DEVOUT'LESSNESS, *n.* Want of devotion. *Bp. of Chichester.*

DEVOUT'LY, *adv.* With solemn attention and reverence to God; with ardent devotion.

He was *devoutly* engaged in prayer. *Anon.*

2. Piously; religiously; with pious thoughts; as, he viewed the cross *devoutly.*

3. Sincerely; solemnly; earnestly; as, a consummation *devoutly* to be wished.

DEVOUT'NESS, *n.* The quality or state of being devout. *Glanville.*

DEVOW', *v. t.* To give up. [*Not in use.*] *B. Jonson.*

DEW, *n.* [Sax. *deaw;* D. *dauw;* G. *thau;* Sw. *dagg;* Dan. *dugg.* See Class Dg. No. 24. 60. 62. 63. It is probably from the same primary root as *thaw;* G. *thau,* dew, *thauen,* to thaw.]

The water or moisture collected or deposited on or near the surface of the earth, during the night, by the escape of the heat which held the water in solution.

DEW, *v. t.* To wet with dew; to moisten. *Milton. Dryden.*

DEW'BENT, *a.* Bent by the dew. *Thomson.*

DEW'-BERRY, *n.* The fruit of a species of brier or bramble, that creeps along the ground, of the genus Rubus.

DEW-BESPAN'GLED, *a.* Spangled with dew-drops. *Gray.*

DEW-BESPRENT', *a.* Sprinkled with dew. *Obs.* *Milton.*

DEW-BESPRINK'LED, *a.* Sprinkled with dew. *Shenstone.*

DEW'-DROP, *n.* A drop of dew, which sparkles at sunrise; a spangle of dew. *Milton.*

DEW'-DROPPING, *a.* Wetting as with dew. *Thomson.*

DEW'ED, *pp.* Moistened with dew.

DEW-IMPEARL'ED, *a.* [See *Pearl.*] Covered with dew-drops, like pearls. *Drayton.*

DEW'ING, *ppr.* Wetting or moistening with dew.

DEW'-LAP, *n.* [*dew* and *lap,* to lick.] The flesh that hangs from the throat of oxen, which laps or licks the dew in grazing. *Addison.*

2. In *Shakspeare,* a lip flaccid with age.

DEW'-LAPT, *a.* Furnished with a dew-lap.

DEW'-WORM, *n.* A worm, called otherwise earth-worm, a species of Lumbricus, which lives just under the surface of the ground. It is of a pale red color, and does no injury to plants.

DEW'Y, *a.* Partaking of dew; like dew; as *dewy* mist.

2. Moist with dew; as *dewy* fields.

His *dewy* locks distilled
Ambrosia. *Milton.*

DEX'TER, *a.* [L. *dexter;* Gr. δεξιος; Ir. *deas.*] Right, as opposed to left; a term used in heraldry, to denote the right side of a shield or coat of arms; as, *bend-dexter;* *dexter-point.* *Encyc.*

DEXTER'ITY, *n.* [L. *dexteritas,* from *dexter,* right, fit, prompt.]

1. Readiness of limbs; adroitness; activity; expertness; skill; that readiness in performing an action, which proceeds from experience or practice, united with activity or quick motion. We say, a man handles an instrument, or eludes a thrust, with *dexterity.*

2. Readiness of mind or mental faculties, as in contrivance, or inventing means to accomplish a purpose; promptness in devising expedients; quickness and skill in managing or conducting a scheme of operations. We say, a negotiation is conducted with *dexterity.* *Gibbon.*

DEX'TRAL, *a.* Right, as opposed to left. *Brown.*

DEXTRAL'ITY, *n.* The state of being on the right side.

DEXTROR'SAL, *a.* [*dexter* and *vorsus, versus,* from *verto,* to turn.] Rising from right to left, as a spiral line or helix. *Henry.*

DEX'TROUS, *a.* Ready and expert in the use of the body and limbs; skilful and active in manual employment; adroit; as a *dextrous* hand; a *dextrous* workman.

2. Ready in the use of the mental faculties; prompt in contrivance and management; expert; quick at inventing expedients; as a *dextrous* manager.

3. Skilful; artful; done with dexterity; as *dextrous* management.

DEX'TROUSLY, *adv.* With dexterity; expertly; skilfully; artfully; adroitly; promptly.

DEX'TROUSNESS, *n.* Dexterity; adroitness.

DEY, *n.* The title of the governor or sovereign of Algiers, under the protection of the Grand Seignior. *Encyc.*

DI, a prefix, a contraction of *dis,* denotes *from, separation* or *negation,* or *two.*

DIA, Greek, a prefix, denotes *through.*

DI'ABASE, *n.* Another name of greenstone. *Cleaveland.*

DIABATE'RIAL, *a.* [Gr. διαβαινω.] Border-passing. *Milford.*

DIABE'TES, *n.* [Gr. διαβητης, from διαβαινω, to pass through; δια and βαινω, to go or pass.]

A long continued increased quantity of urine; an excessive and morbid discharge of urine. *Coxe. Encyc.*

DIABET'IC, *a.* Pertaining to diabetes.

DIABOL'IC, DIABOL'ICAL, *a.* [L. *diabolus,* the devil.] Devilish; pertaining to the devil; hence, extremely malicious; impious; atrocious; nefarious; outrageously wicked; partaking of any quality ascribed to the devil; as a *diabolical* temper; a *diabolical* scheme or action.

DIABOL'ICALLY, *adv.* In a diabolical manner; very wickedly; nefariously.

DIABOL'ICALNESS, *n.* The qualities of the devil.

DIAB'OLISM, *n.* The actions of the devil.

2. Possession by the devil. *Warburton.*

DIACAUS'TIC, *a.* [Gr. διακαιω, to burn or inflame.]

Belonging to curves formed by refraction. *Bailey.*

DIACH'YLON, *n.* [Gr. δια and χυλος.] An emollient plaster.

DIAC'ONAL, *a.* [L. *diaconus.*] Pertaining to a deacon.

DIACOUS'TIC, *a.* [Gr. διακουω, to hear; δια and ακουω, to hear.]

Pertaining to the science or doctrine of refracted sounds.

DIACOUS'TICS, *n.* The science or doctrine of refracted sounds; the consideration of the properties of sound refracted by passing through different mediums; called also *diaphonics.* *Encyc.*

DIACRIT'ICAL, *a.* [Gr. διακριτικος; διακρινω, to separate; δια and κρινω, to separate.]

That separates or distinguishes; distinctive; as a *diacritical* point or mark.

The short vowel is never signified by any *diacritical* mark. *Encyc.*

DI'ADELPH, *n.* [Gr. δις, δι, twice, and αδελφος, a brother.]

In *botany,* a plant whose stamens are united into two bodies or bundles by their filaments.

DIADELPH'IAN, *a.* Having its stamens united into two bodies by their filaments.

DI'ADEM, *n.* [Gr. διαδημα, from διαδεω, to gird; δια and δεω, to bind; L. *diadema.*]

1. Anciently, a head-band or fillet worn by kings as a badge of royalty. It was made of silk, linen or wool, and tied round the temples and forehead, the ends being tied behind and let fall on the neck. It was usually white and plain; sometimes embroidered with gold, or set with pearls and precious stones.

2. In *modern usage*, the mark or badge of royalty, worn on the head; a crown; and *figuratively*, empire; supreme power. *Gibbon.*

3. A distinguished or principal ornament.

A *diadem* of beauty. Is. xxviii.

DI'ADEMED, *a.* Adorned with a diadem; crowned; ornamented. *Pope.*

DI'ADROM, *n.* [Gr. διαδρομη, a running about; διαδρομεω; δια and δρεμω, to run.]

A course or passing; a vibration; the time in which the vibration of a pendulum is performed. *Locke.*

DIAGNOS'TIC, *a.* [Gr. διαγνωςιχος; διαγινωσχω; δια and γινωσχω, to know.]

Distinguishing; characteristic; indicating the nature of a disease.

DIAGNOS'TIC, *n.* The sign or symptom by which a disease is known or distinguished from others. *Diagnostics* are of two kinds; the *adjunct*, or such as are common to several diseases; and the *pathognomonic*, which always attend the disease, and distinguish it from all others. *Encyc.*

DIAG'ONAL, *a.* [Gr. διαγωνιος; δια and γωνια, a corner.]

1. In *geometry*, extending from one angle to another of a quadrilateral figure, and dividing it into two equal parts.

2. Being in an angular direction.

DIAG'ONAL, *n.* A right line drawn from angle to angle of a quadrilateral figure, as a square or parallelogram, and dividing it into two equal parts. It is sometimes called the *diameter*, and sometimes the *diametral.* *Encyc.*

DIAG'ONALLY, *adv.* In a diagonal direction.

DI'AGRAM, *n.* [Gr. διαγραμμα; δια and γραφω, to write.]

In *geometry*, a figure, draught or scheme delineated for the purpose of demonstrating the properties of any figure, as a square, triangle, circle, &c. Anciently, a musical scale.

DIAGRAPH'IC, DIAGRAPH'ICAL, } *a.* [Gr. δια and γραφω, to describe.] Descriptive.

DI'AL, *n.* [Ir. *diail*; probably from *day, dies.*]

An instrument for measuring time, by the aid of the sun; being a plate or plain surface, on which lines are drawn in such a manner, that the shadow of a wire, or of the upper edge of another plane, erected perpendicularly on the former, may show the true time of the day. The edge of the plane, which shows the time, is called the *stile* of the dial, and this must be parallel to the axis of the earth. The line on which this plane is erected, is called the *substile*; and the angle included between the *substile* and *stile*, is called the elevation or highth of the stile. A dial may be horizontal, vertical, or inclining. *Encyc.*

DI'AL-PLATE, *n.* The plate of a dial on which the lines are drawn, to show the hour or time of the day.

DI'ALECT, *n.* [Gr. διαλεχτος; δια and λεγω, to speak; It. *dialetto*; Fr. *dialecte*; Sp. *dialecto.*]

1. The form or idiom of a language, peculiar to a province, or to a kingdom or state; consisting chiefly in differences of orthography or pronunciation. The Greek language is remarkable for four dialects, the Attic, Ionic, Doric and Eolic. A dialect is the branch of a parent language, with such local alterations as time, accident and revolutions may have introduced among descendants of the same stock or family, living in separate or remote situations. But in regard to a large portion of words, many languages, which are considered as distinct, are really dialects of one common language.

2. Language; speech, or manner of speaking. *South.*

DIALEC'TICAL, *a.* Pertaining to a dialect, or dialects; not radical.

2. Logical; argumental. *Boyle.*

DIALEC'TICALLY, *adv.* In the manner of dialect.

DIALECTI''CIAN, *n.* A logician; a reasoner.

DIALEC'TICS, *n.* That branch of logic which teaches the rules and modes of reasoning. *Encyc.*

DI'ALING, *n.* The art of constructing dials, or of drawing dials on a plane. The sciateric science, or knowledge of showing the time by shadows. *Johnson. Encyc.*

DI'ALIST, *n.* A constructer of dials; one skilled in dialing.

DI'ALLAGE, *n.* [Gr. διαλλαγη, difference, alluding to the difference of luster between its natural joints.]

A mineral, the smaragdite of Saussure, of a lamellar or foliated structure. Its subspecies are green diallage, metalloidal diallage and bronzite. *Cleaveland.*

The metalloidal subspecies is called schillerstein, or shiller spar.

DIAL'OGISM, *n.* A feigned speech between two or more. *Fulke.*

DIAL'OGIST, *n.* [See *Dialogue.*] A speaker in a dialogue; also, a writer of dialogues. *Johnson.*

DIALOGIST'IC, *a.* Having the form of a dialogue.

DIALOGIST'ICALLY, *adv.* In the manner of dialogue.

DIAL'OGIZE, *v. i.* [See *Dialogue.*] To discourse in dialogue. *Fotherby.*

DI'ALOGUE, *n.* *di'alog.* [Fr. *dialogue*; It. *dialogo*; Sp. *id.*; from Gr. διαλογος, from διαλεγομαι, to dispute; δια and λεγω, to speak.]

1. A conversation or conference between two or more persons; particularly, a formal conversation in theatrical performances; also, an exercise in colleges and schools, in which two or more persons carry on a discourse.

2. A written conversation, or a composition in which two or more persons are represented as conversing on some topic; as the *dialogues* of Cicero de Oratore, and de Natura Deorum.

DI'ALOGUE, *v. i.* To discourse together; to confer. [*Not used.*] *Shak.*

DI'ALOGUE-WRITER, *n.* A writer of dialogues or feigned conversations.

DIAL'YSIS, *n.* [Gr. διαλυσις; διαλυω, to dissolve; δια and λυω, to dissolve.]

A mark in writing or printing, consisting of two points placed over one of two vowels, to dissolve a diphthong, or to show that the two vowels are to be separated in pronunciation; as, *aër, mosaïc.*

2. In *medicine*, debility; also, a solution of continuity. *Parr.*

DIAMAN'TINE, for *adamantine.* [*Not in use.*]

DIAM'ETER, *n.* [Gr. διαμετρος, δια and μετρον, measure through.]

1. A right line passing through the center of a circle or other curvilinear figure, terminated by the circumference, and dividing the figure into two equal parts.

2. A right line passing through the center of a piece of timber, a rock or other object, from one side to the other; as the *diameter* of a tree, or of a stone.

DIAM'ETRAL, *a.* Diametrical, which see.

DIAM'ETRALLY, *adv.* Diametrically.

DIAMET'RICAL, *a.* Describing a diameter.

2. Observing the direction of a diameter; direct; as *diametrical* opposition.

DIAMET'RICALLY, *adv.* In a diametrical direction; directly; as *diametrically* opposite.

DIAMOND, *n.* *di'mond.* [Fr. *diamant*; It. and Sp. *diamante*; G. and D. *diamant*; L. *adamas*; Gr. αδαμας, αδαμαντος, whence *adamant*, from the Celtic; W. *ehedvaen*, moving stone; *ehed*, to fly or move, and *maen*, stone; a name first given to the loadstone. See *Adamant.*]

1. A mineral, gem or precious stone, of the most valuable kind, remarkable for its hardness, as it scratches all other minerals. When pure, the diamond is usually clear and transparent, but it is sometimes colored. In its rough state, it is commonly in the form of a roundish pebble, or of octahedral crystals. It consists of carbon, and when heated to 14° Wedgewood, and exposed to a current of air, it is gradually, but completely combustible. When pure and transparent, it is said to be of the first water. *Encyc. Kirwan. Cleaveland.*

2. A very small printing letter.

3. A figure, otherwise called a rhombus.

DIAMOND, *a.* Resembling a diamond, as a *diamond* color; or consisting of diamonds, as a *diamond* chain.

DIAMONDED, *a.* Having the figure of an oblique angled parallelogram, or rhombus. *Fuller.*

DIAMOND-MINE, *n.* A mine in which diamonds are found.

DIAN'DER, *n.* [Gr. δις, δι, twice, and ανηρ, a male.] In *botany*, a plant having two stamens.

DIAN'DRIAN, *a.* Having two stamens.

DI'APASM, *n.* [Gr. διαπασσω, to sprinkle.] A perfume. *Obs.* *B. Jonson.*

DIAPA'SON, DI'APASE, } *n.* [Gr. δια πασων, through all.] In *music*, the octave or interval which includes all the tones.

2. Among *musical instrument-makers*, a rule or scale by which they adjust the pipes of organs, the holes of flutes, &c., in due proportion for expressing the several tones and semitones. *Busby.*

Diapáson-diapen'te, a compound consonance in a triple ratio, as 3 to 9, consisting of 9 tones and a semitone, or 19 semitones; a twelfth. *Encyc. Busby.*

Diapáson-diates'saron, a compound concord, founded on the proportion of 8 to 3, consisting of eight tones and a semitone.

Diapáson-ditone, a compound concord, whose terms are as 10 to 4, or 5 to 2.

Diapáson-semiditone, a compound concord, whose terms are in the proportion of 12 to 5. *Encyc.*

DIAPEN'TE, *n.* [Gr. δια and πεντε, five.]

1. A fifth; an interval making the second of the concords, and with the diatessaron, an octave. *Encyc.*

2. In *medicine*, a composition of five ingredients. *Coxe.*

DI'APER, *n.* [Fr. *diapré*, diapered; said to be from Ypres, in the Netherlands. *Anderson.*]

Figured linen cloth; a cloth wove in flowers or figures; much used for towels or napkins. Hence, a towel or napkin.

DI'APER, *v. t.* To variegate or diversify, as cloth, with figures; to flower. *Spenser. Howel.*

DI'APER, *v. i.* To draw flowers or figures, as upon cloth.

If you *diaper* on folds. *Peacham.*

DI'APHANED, *a.* Transparent. [*Little used.*]

DIAPHANE'ITY, *n.* [Gr. διαφανεια; διαφαινω, to shine through; δια and φαινω, to shine.]

The power of transmitting light; transparency; pellucidness. *Ray.*

DIAPHAN'IC, *a.* [Gr. διαφανης. See supra.] Having power to transmit light; transparent. *Raleigh.*

DIAPH'ANOUS, *a.* [See supra.] Having power to transmit rays of light, as glass; pellucid; transparent; clear.

DIAPHORE'SIS, *n.* [Gr. διαφορησις; διαφορεω, to carry through; δια and φορεω, to carry.]

Augmented perspiration; or an elimination of the humors of the body through the pores of the skin. *Coxe. Encyc.*

DIAPHORET'IC, *a.* [supra.] Having the power to increase perspiration; sudorific; sweating.

DIAPHORET'IC, *n.* A medicine which promotes perspiration; a sudorific. *Coxe. Encyc.*

Diaphoretics differ from sudorifics; the former only increase the insensible perspiration; the latter excite the sensible discharge called *sweat.* *Parr.*

DI'APHRAGM, *n.* *di'afram.* [Gr. διαφραγμα; δια and φρασσω, to break off, to defend.]

1. In *anatomy*, the midriff, a muscle separating the chest or thorax from the abdomen or lower belly. *Coxe. Encyc.*

2. A partition or dividing substance. *Woodward.*

DIAPOR'ESIS, *n.* [Gr. διαπορησις; διαπορεω, to doubt.] In *rhetoric*, doubt; hesitation. *Bailey.*

DIAR'ESIS, } *n.* [Gr. διαιρεσις, a division;
DIAR'ESY, } διαιρεω; δια and αιρεω, to take away.]

The dissolution of a diphthong; the mark ¨ placed over one of two vowels, denoting that they are to be pronounced separately, as distinct letters; as *aër.*

DIA'RIAN, *a.* [See *Diary.*] Pertaining to a diary; daily.

DI'ARIST, *n.* One who keeps a diary.

DIARRHE'A, *n.* [Gr. διαρροια; διαρρεω, to flow through; δια and ρεω, to flow.]

Purging or flux; a frequent and copious evacuation of excrement by stool. *Encyc.*

DIARRHET'IC, *a.* Promoting evacuation by stool; purgative.

DI'ARY, *n.* [L. *diarium*, from *dies*, a day.] An account of daily events or transactions; a journal; a register of daily occurrences or observations; as a *diary* of the weather.

A *diary fever* is a fever of one day.

DI'ASCHISM, *n.* [Gr. διασχισμα, a piece cut off; διασχιζω; δια and σχιζω, to cut off.]

In *music*, the difference between the comma and enharmonic diesis, commonly called the *lesser comma.* *Encyc.*

DI'ASPORE, *n.* [Gr. διασπειρω, to disperse.] A mineral occurring in lamellar concretions, of a pearly gray color, and infusible. A small fragment, placed in the flame of a candle, almost instantly decrepitates, and is dispersed; whence its name. It is a mineral little known. *Haüy. Brongniart. Cleaveland.*

DIASTAL'TIC, *a.* [Gr. διαςαλτικος, dilating.] Dilated; noble; bold; an epithet given by the Greeks to certain intervals in music, as the major third, major sixth and major seventh. *Busby.*

DI'ASTEM, *n.* [Gr. διαςημα.] In *music*, a simple interval.

DIAS'TOLE, } *n.* [Gr. διαςολη; δια and
DIAS'TOLY, } ςελλω, to set or send from.]

1. Among *physicians*, a dilatation of the heart, auricles and arteries; opposed to *systole* or contraction. *Encyc.*

2. In *grammar*, the extension of a syllable; or a figure by which a syllable naturally short is made long.

DI'ASTYLE, *n.* [Gr. δια and ςυλος.] An edifice in which three diameters of the columns are allowed for intercolumniations. *Harris.*

DIATES'SARON, *n.* [Gr. δια and τεσσαρα, four.]

Among *musicians*, a concord or harmonic interval, composed of a greater tone, a lesser tone, and one greater semitone. Its proportion is as 4 to 3, and it is called a perfect fourth. *Harris.*

DIATON'IC, *a.* [Gr. δια, by or through, and τονος, sound.]

Ascending or descending, as in sound, or from sound to sound. This epithet is given to a scale or gammut, to intervals of a certain kind, or to music composed of these intervals; as a *diatonic* series; a *diatonic* interval; *diatonic* melody or harmony. It is applied to ordinary music, containing only the two greater and lesser tones, and the greater semitone. *Encyc. Harris.*

DI'ATRIBE, *n.* [Gr. διατριβη.] A continued discourse or disputation. *Bailey.*

DIAZEU'TIC, *a.* [Gr. διαζευγνυμι, to disjoin.] A *diazeutic* tone, in ancient Greek music, disjoined two fourths, one on each side of it, and which, being joined to either, made a fifth. This is, in our music, from A to B. *Harris.*

DIB'BLE, *n.* [probably from the root of *top, tip*, a point, and denoting a little sharp point; or allied to *dip*, to thrust in.]

A pointed instrument, used in gardening and agriculture, to make holes for planting seeds, &c.

DIB'BLE, *v. t.* To plant with a dibble; or to make holes for planting seeds, &c.

DIB'BLE, *v. i.* To dibble or dip; *a term in angling.*

DIB'STONE, *n.* A little stone which children throw at another stone. *Locke.*

DICAC'ITY, *n.* [L. *dicacitas.*] Pertness. [*Little used.*] *Graves.*

DI'CAST, *n.* [Gr. δικαςης, from δικαζω, to judge, from δικη, justice.]

In *ancient Greece*, an officer answering nearly to our juryman. *Mitford.*

DICE, *n. plu.* of *die;* also, a game with dice.

DICE, *v. i.* To play with dice. *Shak.*

DI'CE-BOX, *n.* A box from which dice are thrown in gaming. *Addison.*

DI'CE-MAKER, *n.* A maker of dice.

DI'CER, *n.* A player at dice.

DICHOT'OMIZE, *v. t.* [See the next word.] To cut into two parts; to divide into pairs.

DICHOT'OMOUS, *a.* [Gr. διχα, doubly, by pairs, and τεμνω, to cut.]

In *botany*, regularly dividing by pairs from top to bottom; as a *dichotomous* stem. *Martyn.*

DICHOT'OMOUS-CORYMBED, *a.* Composed of corymbs, in which the pedicles divide and subdivide by pairs. *Martyn.*

DICHOT'OMY, *n.* [Gr. διχοτομια, a division into two parts; διχα and τεμνω, to cut.]

1. Division or distribution of ideas by pairs. [*Little used.*] *Watts.*

2. In *astronomy*, that phase of the moon in which it appears bisected, or shows only half its disk, as at the quadratures. *Encyc.*

DICH'ROIT, *n.* [See *Iolite.*]

DI'CING-HOUSE, *n.* A house where dice is played; a gaming house. [*Little used.*]

DICK'ER, *n.* [probably from Gr. δεκα, ten, W. *deg*, L. *decem.*]

In old authors, the number or quantity of ten, particularly ten hides or skins; but applied to other things, as a *dicker* of gloves, &c. [*I believe not used in America.*]

DICOC'COUS, *a.* [Gr. δις and κοκκος, L. *coccus*, a grain.] Two-grained; consisting of two cohering grains or cells, with one seed in each; as a *dicoccous* capsule. *Martyn.*

DICOTYL'EDON, *n.* [Gr. δις, two, and κοτυληδων, a cavity.]

A plant whose seeds divide into two lobes in germinating. *Martyn.*

DICOTYLED'ONOUS, *a.* Having two lobes. A *dicotyledonous* plant is one whose seeds have two lobes, and consequently rise with two seminal leaves. *Milne.*

DIC'TATE, *v. t.* [L. *dicto*, from *dico*, to speak; Sp. *dictar;* It. *dettare;* Fr. *dicter;* Ir. *deachtaim.* Class Dg.]

1. To tell with authority; to deliver, as an order, command, or direction; as, what God has *dictated*, it is our duty to believe.

2. To order or instruct what is to be said or

written; as, a general *dictates* orders to his troops.

3. To suggest; to admonish; to direct by impulse on the mind. We say, the spirit of God *dictated* the messages of the prophets to Israel. Conscience often *dictates* to men the rules by which they are to govern their conduct.

DIC'TATE, *n.* An order delivered; a command.

2. A rule, maxim or precept, delivered with authority.

> I credit what the Grecian *dictates* say. *Prior.*

3. Suggestion; rule or direction suggested to the mind; as the *dictates* of reason or conscience.

DIC'TATED, *pp.* Delivered with authority; ordered; directed; suggested.

DIC'TATING, *ppr.* Uttering or delivering with authority; instructing what to say or write; ordering; suggesting to the mind.

DICTA'TION, *n.* The act of dictating; the act or practice of prescribing.

> It affords security against the *dictation* of laws. *Paley.*

DICTA'TOR, *n.* [L.] One who dictates; one who prescribes rules and maxims for the direction of others.

2. One invested with absolute authority. In ancient Rome, a magistrate, created in times of exigence and distress, and invested with unlimited power. He remained in office six months.

DICTATO'RIAL, *a.* Pertaining to a dictator; absolute; unlimited; uncontrollable.

2. Imperious; dogmatical; overbearing; as, the officer assumed a *dictatorial* tone.

DICTA'TORSHIP, *n.* The office of a dictator; the term of a dictator's office.

2. Authority; imperiousness; dogmatism. *Dryden.*

DIC'TATORY, *a.* Overbearing; dogmatical. *Milton.*

DIC'TATURE, *n.* The office of a dictator; dictatorship.

2. Absolute authority; the power that dictates. *Tooke.*

DIC'TION, *n.* [L. *dictio*, from *dico*, to speak. Class Dg.]

Expression of ideas by words; style; manner of expression. *Dryden.*

DIC'TIONARY, *n.* [Fr. *dictionnaire*; It. *dizionario*; Sp. *diccionario*; from L. *dictio*, a word, or a speaking.]

A book containing the words of a language arranged in alphabetical order, with explanations of their meanings; a lexicon. *Johnson.*

DID, *pret.* of *do*, contracted from *doed*. I did, thou didst, he did; we did, you or ye did, they did.

> Have ye not read what David *did* when he was hungry? Matt. xii.

The proper signification is, made, executed, performed; but it is used also to express the state of health.

> And Mordecai walked every day before the court of the women's house, to know how Esther *did*. Esth. ii.

Did is used as the sign of the past tense of verbs, particularly in interrogative and negative sentences; as, *did* he command you to go? He *did* not command me. It is also used to express emphasis; as, I *did* love him beyond measure.

DIDAC'TIC, **DIDAC'TICAL**, *a.* [Gr. διδακτικος, from διδασκω, to teach.]

Adapted to teach; preceptive; containing doctrines, precepts, principles or rules; intended to instruct; as a *didactic* poem or essay.

DIDAC'TICALLY, *adv.* In a didactic manner; in a form to teach.

DI'DAPPER, *n.* [from *dip.*] A bird that dives into the water, a species of Colymbus.

DIDAS'CALIC, *a.* [Gr. διδασκαλικος, from διδασκω, to teach.]

Didactic; preceptive; giving precepts. [*Little used.*] *Prior.*

DID'DER, *v. i.* [Teut. *diddern*; qu. *titter*, *totter.*] To shiver with cold. [*Not used.*] *Sherwood.*

DID'DLE, *v. i.* To totter, as a child in walking.

DIDECAHE'DRAL, *a.* [*di* and *decahedral.*] In *crystalography*, having the form of a decahedral prism with pentahedral summits. *Cleaveland.*

DIDODECAHE'DRAL, *a.* [*di* and *dodecahedral.*] In *crystalography*, having the form of a dodecahedral prism with hexahedral summits. *Cleaveland.*

DIDRACH'MA, *n.* [Gr.] A piece of money, the fourth of an ounce of silver.

DIDUC'TION, *n.* [L. *diductio*; *di* and *duco*, to draw.]

Separation by withdrawing one part from the other. *Boyle.*

DID'YNAM, *n.* [Gr. δι, δις, and δυναμις, power.]

In *botany*, a plant of four stamens, disposed in two pairs, one being shorter than the other.

DIDYNAM'IAN, *a.* Containing four stamens, disposed in pairs, one shorter than the other.

DIE, *v. i.* [Sw. *dö*; Dan. *döer*. This appears to be a contracted word, and the radical letter lost is not obvious. The word *dye*, to tinge, is contracted from Dg, and the Arabic root signifies not only to *tinge*, but to *perish*; which circumstance would lead one to infer that they are radically one word, and that the primary sense is to plunge, fall or sink. The Saxon *deadian* is evidently a derivative of the participle *dead*. See *Dye.*]

1. To be deprived of respiration, of the circulation of blood, and other bodily functions, and rendered incapable of resuscitation, as animals, either by natural decay, by disease, or by violence; to cease to live; to expire; to decease; to perish; and with respect to man, to depart from this world.

> All the first born in the land of Egypt shall *die*. Ex. xi.
>
> The fish that is in the river shall *die*. Ex. vii.

This word is followed by *of* or *by*. Men *die of* disease; *of* a fever; *of* sickness; *of* a fall; *of* grief. They die *by* the sword; *by* famine; *by* pestilence; *by* violence; *by* sickness; *by* disease. In some cases, custom has established the use of the one, to the exclusion of the other; but in many cases, either *by* or *of* may be used at the pleasure of the writer or speaker. The use of *for*, he died *for* thirst, is not elegant nor common.

2. To be punished with death; to lose life for a crime, or for the sake of another.

> I will relieve my master, if I *die* for it.
> Christ *died* for the ungodly. Rom. v.
> Christ *died* for our sins. 1 Cor. xv.

3. To come to an end; to cease; to be lost; to perish or come to nothing; as, let the secret *die* in your own breast.

4. To sink; to faint.

> His heart *died* within him, and he became as a stone. 1 Sam. xxv.

5. To languish with pleasure or tenderness; followed by *away.*

> To sounds of heavenly harps she *dies away*. *Pope.*

6. To languish with affection.

> The young men acknowledged that they *died* for Rebecca. *Tatler.*

7. To recede as sound, and become less distinct; to become less and less; or to vanish from the sight, or disappear gradually. Sound or color *dies away.*

8. To lose vegetable life; to wither; to perish; as plants or seeds. Plants *die* for want of water. Some plants *die* annually.

9. To become vapid or spiritless, as liquors; mostly used in the participle; as the cider or beer is *dead.*

10. In *theology*, to perish everlastingly; to suffer divine wrath and punishment in the future world.

11. To become indifferent to, or to cease to be under the power of; as, to *die* to sin.

12. To endure great danger and distress.

> I *die* daily. 1 Cor. xv.

To die away, to decrease gradually; to cease to blow; as, the wind *dies away.*

DIE, *n.* plu. *dice.* [Fr. *dé*; It. *dado*; Sp. Port. *id.*; Arm. *diçz*; Ir. *disle.*]

1. A small cube, marked on its faces with numbers from one to six, used in gaming, by being thrown from a box.

> He ventured his all on the cast of a *die.*

2. Any cubic body; a flat tablet. *Watts.*

3. Hazard; chance.

> Such is the *die* of war. *Spenser.*

DIE, *n.* plu. *dies.* A stamp used in coining money, in founderies, &c.

DIE'CIAN, *n.* [Gr. δις, two, and οικος, house.] In *botany*, one of a class of plants, whose male and female flowers are on different plants of the same species.

DIER. [See *Dyer.*]

DI'ESIS, *n.* [Gr. διεσις, a division.] In *music*, the division of a tone, less than a semitone; or an interval consisting of a less or imperfect semitone. *Encyc.*

DI'ET, *n.* [L. *diæta*; Gr. διαιτα, manner of living, mode of life prescribed by a physician, food, a room, parlor or bed room; Sp. *dieta*; Fr. *diète*; It. *dieta*. In the middle ages, this word was used to denote the provision or food for one day, and for a journey of one day. *Spelman.* Hence it seems to be from *dies*, day, or its root; and hence the word may have come to signify a meal or supper, and the room occupied for eating.]

1. Food or victuals; as, milk is a wholesome *diet*; flesh is nourishing *diet.*

2. Food regulated by a physician, or by medical rules; food prescribed for the prevention or cure of disease, and limited in kind or quantity. I restrained myself to a regular *diet* of flesh once a day.

3. Allowance of provision.

> For his diet there was a continual *diet* given him by the king. Jer. lii.

4. Board, or boarding; as, to pay a certain sum for *diet*, washing and lodging.

DI'ET, *n.* [D. *ryksdag;* G. *reichstag;* Sw. *riksdag;* Dan. *rigsdag;* empire's day, imperial diet. These words prove that *diet* is from *dies*, day. So in Scots law, *diet* of appearance.]

An assembly of the states or circles of the empire of Germany and of Poland; a convention of princes, electors, ecclesiastical dignitaries, and representatives of free cities, to deliberate on the affairs of the empire. There are also diets of states and cantons. *Encyc.*

DI'ET, *v. t.* To feed; to board; to furnish provisions for; as, the master *diets* his apprentice.

2. To take food by rules prescribed; as, an invalid should carefully *diet* himself.

3. To feed; to furnish aliment; as, to *diet* revenge. *Shak.*

DI'ET, *v. i.* To eat according to rules prescribed.

2. To eat; to feed; as, the students *diet* in commons.

DI'ETARY, *a.* Pertaining to diet or the rules of diet.

DI'ET-DRINK, *n.* Medicated liquors; drink prepared with medicinal ingredients.

DI'ETED, *pp.* Fed; boarded; fed by prescribed rules.

DI'ETER, *n.* One who diets; one who prescribes rules for eating; one who prepares food by rules.

DIETET'IC, DIETET'ICAL, *a.* [Gr. διαιτητικη,] Pertaining to diet, or to the rules for regulating the kind and quantity of food to be eaten.

DI'ETINE, *n.* A subordinate or local diet; a cantonal convention.

DI'ETING, *ppr.* Taking food; prescribing rules for eating; taking food according to prescribed rules.

DIFFARREA'TION, *n.* [L. *dis* and *farreatio.*] The parting of a cake; a ceremony among the Romans, at the divorce of man and wife. *Encyc.*

DIF'FER, *v. i.* [L. *differo, dis* and *fero*, to bear or move apart; It. *differire;* Fr. *differer.* See *Bear.*]

1. Literally, to be separate. Hence, to be unlike, dissimilar, distinct or various, in nature, condition, form or qualities; followed by *from.* Men *differ from* brutes; a statue *differs from* a picture; wisdom *differs from* folly.

> One star *differeth* from another star in glory. 1 Cor. xv.

2. To disagree; not to accord; to be of a contrary opinion. We are all free to *differ* in opinion, and sometimes our sentiments *differ* less than we at first suppose.

3. To contend; to be at variance; to strive or debate in words; to dispute; to quarrel.

> We'll never *differ* with a crowded pit. *Rowe.*

DIF'FER, *v. t.* To cause to be different or various. A different dialect and pronunciation *differs* persons of divers countries. *Derham.*

[*This transitive use of the verb is not common, nor to be commended.*]

DIF'FERENCE, *n.* The state of being unlike or distinct; distinction; disagreement; want of sameness; variation; dissimilarity. *Difference* may be total or partial, and exist in the nature and essence of things, in the form, the qualities or degrees. There is a *difference* in nature between animals and plants; a *difference* in form between the genera and species of animals; a *difference* of quality in paper; and a *difference* in degrees of heat, or of light.

2. The quality which distinguishes one thing from another.

3. Dispute; debate; contention; quarrel; controversy.

> What was the *difference?* It was a contention in public. *Shak.*

4. The point in dispute; ground of controversy. *Shak.*

5. A logical distinction.

6. Evidences or marks of distinction.

> The marks and *differences* of sovereignty. *Davies.*

7. Distinction.

> There is no *difference* between the Jew and the Greek. Rom. x.

8. In *mathematics*, the remainder of a sum or quantity, after a lesser sum or quantity is subtracted.

9. In *logic*, an essential attribute, belonging to some species, and not found in the genus; being the idea that defines the species. *Encyc.*

10. In *heraldry*, a certain figure added to a coat of arms, serving to distinguish one family from another, or to show how distant a younger branch is from the elder or principal branch.

DIF'FERENCE, *v. t.* To cause a difference or distinction. A regular administration of justice according to fixed laws *differences* a civilized from a savage state.

DIF'FERENT, *a.* Distinct; separate; not the same; as, we belong to *different* churches or nations.

2. Various or contrary; of various or contrary natures, forms or qualities; unlike; dissimilar; as *different* kinds of food or drink; *different* states of health; *different* shapes; *different* degrees of excellence.

DIFFEREN'TIAL, *a.* An epithet applied to an infinitely small quantity, so small as to be less than any assignable quantity. This is called a *differential* quantity. The *differential* method is applied to the doctrine of infinitesimals, or infinitely small quantities, called the arithmetic of fluxions. It consists in descending from whole quantities to their infinitely small differences, and comparing them. Hence it is called the *differential calculus*, or analysis of infinitesimals. *Encyc. Harris.*

DIF'FERENTLY, *adv.* In a different manner; variously. Men are *differently* affected with the same eloquence.

DIF'FERING, *ppr.* Being unlike or distinct; disagreeing; contending.

DIF'FICILE, *a.* [L. *difficilis.*] Difficult; hard; scrupulous. [*Not used.*] *Bacon.*

DIF'FICILENESS, *n.* Difficulty to be persuaded. [*Not used.*] *Bacon.*

DIF'FICULT, *a.* [L. *difficilis; dis* and *facilis*, easy to be made or done, from *facio*, to make or do; Sp. *dificultoso;* It. *difficoltoso.*]

1. Hard to be made, done or performed; not easy; attended with labor and pains; as, our task is *difficult.* It is *difficult* to persuade men to abandon vice. It is *difficult* to ascend a steep hill, or travel a bad road.

2. Hard to be pleased; not easily wrought upon; not readily yielding; not compliant; unaccommodating; rigid; austere; not easily managed or persuaded; as a *difficult* man; a person of a *difficult* temper.

3. Hard to be ascended as a hill, traveled as a road, or crossed as a river, &c. We say, a *difficult* ascent; a *difficult* road; a *difficult* river to cross; &c.

DIF'FICULTY, *n.* [Fr. *difficulté;* It. *difficoltà;* Sp. *dificultad;* L. *difficultas.*]

1. Hardness to be done or accomplished; the state of any thing which renders its performance laborious or perplexing; opposed to *easiness* or *facility;* as the *difficulty* of a task or enterprise; a work of labor and *difficulty.*

2. That which is hard to be performed or surmounted. We often mistake *difficulties* for impossibilities. To overcome *difficulties* is an evidence of a great mind.

3. Perplexity; embarrassment of affairs; trouble; whatever renders progress or execution of designs laborious. We lie under many *difficulties*, by reason of bad markets, or a low state of trade.

4. Objection; obstacle to belief; that which cannot be easily understood, explained or believed. Men often raise *difficulties* concerning miracles and mysteries in religion, which candid research will remove.

5. In *a popular sense*, bodily complaints; indisposition.

DIFFI'DE, *v. i.* [L. *diffido; dis* and *fido*, to trust.]

To distrust; to have no confidence in. [*Little used.*] *Dryden.*

DIF'FIDENCE, *n.* [It. *diffidanza;* Sp. *difidencia;* from L. *diffidens, diffido; dis* and *fido*, to trust. See *Faith.*]

1. Distrust; want of confidence; any doubt of the power, ability or disposition of others. It is said there was a general *diffidence* of the strength and resources of the nation, and of the sincerity of the king.

2. More generally, distrust of one's self; want of confidence in our own power, competency, correctness or wisdom; a doubt respecting some personal qualification. We speak or write with *diffidence*, when we doubt our ability to speak or write correctly or to the satisfaction of others. The effect of diffidence is some degree of reserve, modesty, timidity or bashfulness. Hence,

3. Modest reserve; a moderate degree of timidity or bashfulness; as, he addressed the audience or the prince with *diffidence.*

DIF'FIDENT, *a.* Distrustful; wanting confidence; doubting of another's power, disposition, sincerity or intention.

> Be not *diffident* of wisdom. *Milton.*
> Be *diffident* in dealing with strangers. *Anon.*

2. Distrustful of one's self; not confident; doubtful of one's own power or competency.

> Distress makes the humble heart *diffident.* *Clarissa.*

3. Reserved; modest; timid; as a *diffident* youth.

DIF'FIDENTLY, *adv.* With distrust; in a distrusting manner; modestly.

DIF'FLUENCE, } *n.* [L. *diffluo.*] A flowing
DIF'FLUENCY, } or falling away on all sides. *Brown.*

DIF'FLUENT, *a.* Flowing away on all sides; not fixed.

DIF'FORM, *a.* [L. *dis* and *forma.* But it appears to have been adopted from the French or Italian, *difforme,* which we write *deform.*]

1. Irregular in form; not uniform; anomalous; as a *difform* flower or corol, the parts of which do not correspond in size or proportion; so *difform* leaves. *Martyn.*

2. Unlike; dissimilar.

The unequal refractions of *difform* rays. *Newton.*

DIFFORM'ITY, *n.* Irregularity of form; want of uniformity. *Brown.*

DIFFRAN'CHISE. } [See *Disfranchise,* which is
DIFFRAN'CHISEMENT. } the word in use.]

DIFFU'SE, *v. t. diffu'ze.* [L. *diffusus; diffundo; dis* and *fundo,* to pour, to spread. If *n* is casual, as it probably is, the root belongs to Class Bd or Bs.]

1. To pour out and spread, as a fluid; to cause to flow and spread.

The river rose and *diffused* its waters over the adjacent plain.

2. To spread; to send out or extend in all directions; to disperse. Flowers *diffuse* their odors. The fame of Washington is *diffused* over Europe. The knowledge of the true God will be *diffused* over the earth.

DIFFU'SE, *a.* Widely spread; dispersed.

2. Copious; prolix; using many words; giving full descriptions; as, Livy is a *diffuse* writer.

3. Copious; verbose; containing full or particular accounts; not concise; as a *diffuse* style.

DIFFU'SED, *pp. diffu'zed.* Spread; dispersed.

2. Loose; flowing; wild. *Shak.*

DIFFU'SEDLY, *adv. diffu'zedly.* In a diffused manner; with wide dispersion.

DIFFU'SEDNESS, *n. diffu'zedness.* The state of being widely spread. *Sherwood.*

DIFFU'SELY, *adv.* Widely; extensively.

2. Copiously; with many words; fully.

DIFFUSIBIL'ITY, *n. diffuzibil'ity.* The quality of being diffusible, or capable of being spread; as the *diffusibility* of clay in water. *Kirwan.*

DIFFU'SIBLE, *a. diffu'zible.* That may flow or be spread in all directions; that may be dispersed; as *diffusible* stimuli. *Brown.*

DIFFU'SIBLENESS, *n. s* as *z.* Diffusibility.

DIFFU'SION, *n. s* as *z.* A spreading or flowing of a liquid substance or fluid, in a lateral as well as a lineal direction; as the *diffusion* of water; the *diffusion* of air or light.

2. A spreading or scattering; dispersion; as a *diffusion* of dust or of seeds.

3. A spreading; extension; propagation; as the *diffusion* of knowledge, or of good principles.

4. Copiousness; exuberance, as of style. [*Little used.*]

DIFFU'SIVE, *a.* Having the quality of diffusing, or spreading by flowing, as liquid substances or fluids; or of dispersing, as minute particles. Water, air and light; dust, smoke and odors, are *diffusive* substances.

2. Extended; spread widely; extending in all directions; extensive; as *diffusive* charity or benevolence.

DIFFU'SIVELY, *adv.* Widely; extensively; every way.

DIFFU'SIVENESS, *n.* The power of diffusing, or state of being diffused; dispersion.

2. Extension, or extensiveness; as the *diffusiveness* of benevolence.

3. The quality or state of being diffuse, as an author or his style; verboseness; copiousness of words or expression. *Addison.*

DIG, *v. t.* pret. *digged* or *dug;* pp. *digged* or *dug.* [Sw. *dika;* Dan. *diger,* to dig, to *ditch;* Sw. *dike,* a ditch, Dan. *dige;* D. *dyk,* a *dike;* G. *deich,* Sax. *dic,* id.; Sax. *dician,* to ditch; Eth. ደሐየ, dachi. Class Dg. No. 14. The Irish, *tochlaim, tachlaim,* to dig, may be from the same root.]

1. To open and break or turn up the earth with a spade or other sharp instrument.

Be first to *dig* the ground. *Dryden.*

2. To excavate; to form an opening in the earth by digging and removing the loose earth; as, to *dig* a well, a pit or a mine.

3. To pierce or open with a snout or by other means, as swine or moles.

4. To pierce with a pointed instrument; to thrust in.

Still for the growing liver *digged* his breast. *Dryden.*

To dig down, is to undermine and cause to fall by digging; as, to *dig down* a wall.

To dig out, or *to dig from,* is to obtain by digging; as, to *dig* coals *from* a mine; to *dig out* fossils. But the preposition is often omitted, and it is said, the men are *digging* coals, or *digging* iron ore. In such phrases, some word is understood: They are *digging out* ore, or *digging for* coals, or *digging* ore *from* the earth.

To dig up, is to obtain something from the earth by opening it, or uncovering the thing with a spade or other instrument, or to force out from the earth by a bar; as, to *dig up* a stone.

DIG, *v. i.* To work with a spade or other piercing instrument; to do servile work.

I cannot *dig;* I am ashamed to beg. Luke xvi.

2. To work in search of; to search.

They *dig* for it, more than for hid treasures. Job iii.

To dig in, is to pierce with a spade or other pointed instrument.

Son of man, *dig* now *in* the wall. Ezek. viii.

To dig through, to open a passage through; to make an opening from one side to the other.

DIGAM'MA, *n.* [Gr. δις and γαμμα, double gamma.]

The name of F, most absurdly given to that letter, when first invented or used by the Eolians, on account of its figure. A letter should be named from its sound, and not from its shape. The letter is *ef.*

DIG'AMY, *n.* Second marriage. [*Not in use.*] *Herbert.*

DIGAS'TRIC, *a.* [Gr. δις and γαστηρ, belly.] Having a double belly; an epithet given to a muscle of the lower jaw. *Bailey.*

DIG'ERENT, *a.* [L. *digerens.*] Digesting. [*Not in use.*]

DI'GEST, *n.* [L. *digestus,* put in order.] A collection or body of Roman laws, digested or arranged under proper titles by order of the Emperor Justinian. A pandect.

2. Any collection, compilation, abridgment or summary of laws, disposed under proper heads or titles; as the *digest* of Comyns.

DIGEST', *v. t.* [L. *digestum,* from *digero,* to distribute, or to dissolve; *di* or *dis* and *gero,* to bear, carry, or wear; Fr. *digerer;* It. *digerire;* Sp. *digerir.*]

1. To distribute into suitable classes, or under proper heads or titles; to arrange in convenient order; to dispose in due method; as, to *digest* the Roman laws or the common law.

2. To arrange methodically in the mind; to form with due arrangement of parts; as, to *digest* a plan or scheme.

3. To separate or dissolve in the stomach, as food; to reduce to minute parts fit to enter the lacteals and circulate; to concoct; to convert into chyme. *Coxe. Encyc.*

4. In *chimistry,* to soften and prepare by heat; to expose to a gentle heat in a boiler or matrass, as a preparation for chimical operations.

5. To bear with patience; to brook; to receive without resentment; not to reject; as, say what you will, he will *digest* it. *Shak.*

6. To prepare in the mind; to dispose in a manner that shall improve the understanding and heart; to prepare for nourishing practical duties; as, to *digest* a discourse or sermon.

7. To dispose an ulcer or wound to suppurate.

8. To dissolve and prepare for manure, as plants and other substances.

DIGEST', *v. i.* To be prepared by heat.

2. To suppurate; to generate laudable pus; as an ulcer or wound.

3. To dissolve and be prepared for manure, as substances in compost.

DIGEST'ED, *pp.* Reduced to method; arranged in due order; concocted or prepared in the stomach or by a gentle heat; received without rejection; borne; disposed for use.

DIGEST'ER, *n.* He that digests or disposes in order.

2. One who digests his food.

3. A medicine or article of food that aids digestion, or strengthens the digestive power of the stomach.

4. A strong vessel contrived by Papin, in which to boil bony substances with a strong heat, and reduce them to a fluid state, or in general, to increase the solvent power of water.

DIGEST'IBLE, *a.* Capable of being digested. *Bacon.*

DIGEST'ING, *ppr.* Arranging in due order, or under proper heads; dissolving and preparing for circulation in the stomach; softening and preparing by heat; disposing for practice; disposing to generate pus; brooking; reducing by heat to a fluid state.

DIGES'TION, *n.* [L. *digestio.*] The conversion of food into chyme, or the process of dissolving aliment in the stomach and preparing it for circulation and nourishment. A good *digestion* is essential to health.

2. In *chimistry*, the operation of exposing bodies to a gentle heat, to prepare them for some action on each other; or the slow action of a solvent on any substance.

3. The act of methodizing and reducing to order; the maturation of a design. *Temple.*

4. The process of maturing an ulcer or wound, and disposing it to generate pus; or the generation of matter.

5. The process of dissolution and preparation of substances for manure, as in compost.

DIGEST'IVE, *a.* Having the power to cause digestion in the stomach; as a *digestive* preparation or medicine.

2. Capable of softening and preparing by heat.

3. Methodizing; reducing to order; as *digestive* thought. *Dryden.*

4. Causing maturation in wounds or ulcers.

5. Dissolving.

DIGEST'IVE, *n.* In *medicine*, any preparation or medicine which increases the tone of the stomach, and aids digestion; a stomachic; a corroborant.

2. In *surgery*, an application which ripens an ulcer or wound, or disposes it to suppurate.

Digestive salt, the muriate of potash.

DIGEST'URE, *n.* Concoction; digestion. [*Little used.*] *Harvey.*

DIG'GED, *pret.* and *pp.* of *dig.*

DIG'GER, *n.* One who digs; one who opens, throws up and breaks the earth; one who opens a well, pit, trench or ditch.

DIGHT, *v. t. dite.* [Sax. *diht*, disposition, order, command; *dihtan*, to set, establish, prepare, instruct, dictate. This seems to be from the same source as the L. *dico, dicto.*]

To prepare; to put in order; hence, to dress, or put on; to array; to adorn. [*Obsolete, or used only in poetry.*] *Milton.*

DIG'IT, *n.* [L. *digitus*, a finger, that is, a shoot; Gr. δακτυλος.]

1. The measure of a finger's breadth, or three fourths of an inch. *Boyle.*

2. The twelfth part of the diameter of the sun or moon; a term used to express the quantity of an eclipse; as, an eclipse of six *digits* is one which hides one half of the disk.

3. In *arithmetic*, any integer under 10; so called from counting on the fingers. Thus, 1. 2. 3. 4. 5. 6. 7. 8. 9. are called digits.

DIG'ITAL, *a.* [L. *digitalis.*] Pertaining to the fingers, or to digits.

DIG'ITATE, } *a.* In *botany*, a *digitate* leaf
DIG'ITATED, } is one which branches into several distinct leaflets like fingers; or when a simple, undivided petiole connects several leaflets at the end of it. *Martyn.*

DIGLA'DIATE, *v. t.* [L. *digladior.*] To fence; to quarrel. [*Little used.*]

DIGLADIA'TION, *n.* A combat with swords; a quarrel. *B. Jonson.*

DIGNIFICA'TION, *n.* [See *Dignify.*] The act of dignifying; exaltation; promotion. *Walton.*

DIG'NIFIED, *pp.* [See *Dignify.*] Exalted; honored; invested with dignity; as the *dignified* clergy.

2. *a.* Marked with dignity; noble; as *dignified* conduct, or manner.

To the great astonishment of the Jews, the manners of Jesus are familiar, yet *dignified.* *Buckminster.*

DIG'NIFY, *v. t.* [Sp. *dignificar*; L. *dignus*, worthy, and *facio*, to make.]

1. To invest with honor or dignity; to exalt in rank; to promote; to elevate to a high office.

2. To honor; to make illustrious; to distinguish by some excellence, or that which gives celebrity.

Your worth will *dignify* our feast. *B. Jonson.*

DIG'NITARY, *n.* An ecclesiastic who holds a dignity, or a benefice which gives him some pre-eminence over mere priests and canons, as a bishop, dean, archdeacon, prebendary, &c. *Encyc. Swift.*

DIG'NITY, *n.* [L. *dignitas*, from *dignus*, worthy; Sp. *digno*; It. *degno*; Fr. *digne*; Arm. *dign* or *din.* Qu. its relation to Sax. *dugan*, to be good, to avail, to be worth, to be profitable. It is probable that *g* and *n* are not both radical; but it is uncertain which.]

1. True honor; nobleness or elevation of mind, consisting in a high sense of propriety, truth and justice, with an abhorrence of mean and sinful actions; opposed to *meanness.* In this sense, we speak of the *dignity* of mind, and *dignity* of sentiments. This dignity is based on moral rectitude; all vice is incompatible with true *dignity* of mind. The man who deliberately injures another, whether male or female, has no true *dignity* of soul.

2. Elevation; honorable place or rank of elevation; degree of excellence, either in estimation, or in the order of nature. Man is superior in *dignity* to brutes.

3. Elevation of aspect; grandeur of mein; as a man of native *dignity.*

4. Elevation of deportment; as *dignity* of manners or behavior.

5. An elevated office, civil or ecclesiastical, giving a high rank in society; advancement; preferment, or the rank attached to it. We say, a man enjoys his *dignity* with moderation, or without haughtiness. Among ecclesiastics, *dignity* is office or preferment joined with power or jurisdiction. *Bailey. Johnson.*

6. The rank or title of a nobleman. *Encyc.*

7. In *oratory*, one of the three parts of elocution, consisting in the right use of tropes and figures. *Encyc.*

8. In *astrology*, an advantage which a planet has on account of its being in some particular place of the zodiac, or in a particular station in respect to other planets. *Bailey.*

9. A general maxim, or principle. [*Not used.*] *Brown.*

DIGNO'TION, *n.* [L. *dignosco.*] Distinguishing mark; distinction. [*Not in use.*] *Brown.*

DIG'ONOUS, *a.* [Gr. δις and γωνια, an angle.] In *botany*, having two angles, as a stem. *Lee.*

DIGRAPH, *n.* [Gr. δις and γραφω, to write.] A union of two vowels, of which one only is pronounced, as in *head, breath.* *Sheridan.*

DIGRESS', *v. i.* [L. *digressus*, *digredior*; *di* or *dis* and *gradior*, to step. See *Grade.*]

1. Literally, to step or go from the way or road; hence, to depart or wander from the main subject, design or tenor of a discourse, argument or narration; *used only of speaking or writing.*

In the pursuit of an argument there is hardly room to *digress* into a particular definition, as often as a man varies the signification of any term. *Locke.*

2. To go out of the right way or common track; to deviate; *in a literal sense.* [*Not now in use.*] *Shak.*

DIGRESS'ING, *ppr.* Departing from the main subject.

DIGRES'SION, *n.* [L. *digressio.*] The act of digressing; a departure from the main subject under consideration; an excursion of speech or writing.

2. The part or passage of a discourse, argument or narration, which deviates from the main subject, tenor or design, but which may have some relation to it, or be of use to it.

3. Deviation from a regular course; as, the *digression* of the sun is not equal. [*Little used.*] *Brown.*

DIGRES'SIONAL, *a.* Pertaining to or consisting in digression; departing from the main purpose or subject. *Warton. Adams' Lect.*

DIGRESS'IVE, *a.* Departing from the main subject; partaking of the nature of digression. *J. Q. Adams.*

DIGRESS'IVELY, *adv.* By way of digression.

DIGYN, *n.* [Gr. δις, two, and γυνη, a female.] In *botany*, a plant having two pistils.

DIGYN'IAN, *a.* Having two pistils.

DIHE'DRAL, *a.* [Gr. δις, supra, and εδρα, a seat or face.] Having two sides, as a figure.

DIHE'DRON, *n.* [supra.] A figure with two sides or surfaces.

DIHEXAHE'DRAL, *a.* [*di* and *hexahedral.*] In *crystalography*, having the form of a hexahedral prism with trihedral summits. *Cleaveland.*

DIJU'DICATE, *v. t.* [L. *dijudico.*] To judge or determine by censure. *Hales.*

DIJUDICA'TION, *n.* Judicial distinction.

DIKE, *n.* [Sax. *dic*; Sw. *dike*; Dan. *dige*; D. *dyk*; G. *deich*; Ir. *diog*; Scot. *dike*, *dyk*; Fr. *digue*; Sp. *dique*; from *digging.* See *Dig.* It is radically the same word as *ditch*, and this is its primary sense; but by an easy transition, it came to signify also the bank formed by digging and throwing up earth. *Intrenchment* is sometimes used both for a ditch and a rampart.]

1. A ditch; an excavation made in the earth by digging, of greater length than breadth, intended as a reservoir of water, a drain, or for other purpose. *Dryden. Pope.*

2. A mound of earth, of stones, or of other materials, intended to prevent low lands from being inundated by the sea or a river. The low countries of Holland are thus defended by *dikes.*

3. A vein of basalt, greenstone or other stony substance. *Cleaveland.*

DIKE, *v. t.* To surround with a dike; to secure by a bank.

DIKE, *v. i.* To dig. [*Not in use.*]

DILAC'ERATE, *v. t.* [L. *dilacero; di* and *lacero*, to tear.]

To tear; to rend asunder; to separate by force. *Brown.*

DILAC'ERATED, *pp.* Torn; rent asunder.

DILAC'ERATING, *ppr.* Tearing; rending in two.

DILACERA'TION, *n.* The act of rending asunder; a tearing, or rending. [In lieu of these words, *lacerate, laceration*, are generally used.]

DILA'NIATE, *v. t.* [L. *dilanio; di* and *lanio*, to rend in pieces.]

To tear; to rend in pieces; to mangle. [*Little used.*] *Howell.*

DILANIA'TION, *n.* A tearing in pieces.

DILAP'IDATE, *v. i.* [L. *dilapido; di* and *lapido*, to stone, from *lapis*, a stone. It seems originally to have signified to pull down stone-work, or to suffer such work to fall to pieces.]

To go to ruin; to fall by decay.

DILAP'IDATE, *v. t.* To pull down; to waste or destroy; to suffer to go to ruin.

If the bishop, parson, or vicar, &c., *dilapidates* the buildings, or cuts down the timber of the patrimony of the church— *Blackstone.*

2. To waste; to squander.

DILAP'IDATED, *pp.* Wasted; ruined; pulled down; suffered to go to ruin.

DILAP'IDATING, *ppr.* Wasting; pulling down; suffering to go to ruin.

DILAPIDA'TION, *n.* Ecclesiastical waste; a voluntary wasting or suffering to go to decay any building in possession of an incumbent. Dilapidation is *voluntary* or active, when an incumbent pulls down a building; *permissive* or passive, when he suffers it to decay and neglects to repair it. Dilapidation extends to the waste or destruction of wood, and other property of the church. *Blackstone.*

2. Destruction; demolition; decay; ruin. *Bryant.*

3. Peculation. *Stephens.*

DILAP'IDATOR, *n.* One who causes dilapidation.

DILATABIL'ITY, *n.* [See *Dilate.*] The quality of admitting expansion by the elastic force of the body itself, or of another elastic substance acting upon it; opposed to *contractibility.*

DILA'TABLE, *a.* Capable of expansion; possessing elasticity; elastic. A bladder is *dilatable* by the force of air; air is *dilatable* by heat. It is opposed to *contractible.*

DILATA'TION, *n.* The act of expanding; expansion; a spreading or extending in all directions; the state of being expanded; opposed to *contraction. Dilatation* differs from *extension*, as the latter is applied to lines and surfaces; the former to bodies that spread, open or enlarge in all directions. A line or a plain is *extended;* a bladder, an artery, a balloon is *dilated.*

DILA'TE, *v. t.* [L. *dilato; di* and *latus*, wide; Fr. *dilater;* It. *dilatare;* Sp. *dilatar.* See *Delay.*]

1. To expand; to distend; to enlarge or extend in all directions; opposed to *contract.* The air *dilates* the lungs; air is *dilated* by rarefaction.

2. To enlarge; to relate at large; to tell copiously or diffusely; as, to *dilate* upon the policy of a measure. In this sense, it is generally used intransitively. Spenser and Shakspeare have used it in a transitive sense; as, to *dilate* a theme.

DILA'TE, *v. i.* To widen; to expand; to swell or extend in all directions.

His heart *dilates* and glories in his strength. *Addison.*

2. To speak largely and copiously; to dwell on in narration.

An advocate may weaken his argument by *dilating* on trivial circumstances.

DILA'TE, *a.* Expanded; expansive.

DILA'TED, *pp.* Expanded; distended; enlarged so as to occupy a greater space.

DILA'TER, *n.* One who enlarges; that which expands.

DILA'TING, *ppr.* Expanding; enlarging; speaking largely.

DILA'TOR, *n.* That which widens or expands; a muscle that dilates.

DIL'ATORILY, *adv.* With delay; tardily.

DIL'ATORINESS, *n.* [from *dilatory.*] The quality of being dilatory or late; lateness; slowness in motion; delay in proceeding; tardiness.

DIL'ATORY, *a.* [Fr. *dilatoire;* It. *dilatorio;* Low L. *dilatorius*, from *differo, dilatus.* See *Delay* and *Dilate.*]

1. Literally, drawing out or extending in time; hence, slow; late; tardy; *applied to things;* as *dilatory* councils or measures.

2. Given to procrastination; not proceeding with diligence; making delay; slow; late; *applied to persons;* as a *dilatory* messenger. A man is *dilatory*, when he delays attendance, or performance of business, beyond the proper time.

3. In *law*, intended to make delay; tending to delay; as a *dilatory* plea, which is designed or which tends to delay the trial of a cause. *Blackstone.*

DILEC'TION, *n.* [L. *dilectio.*] A loving. *Martin.*

DILEM'MA, *n.* [Gr. διλημμα, a syllogism which strikes on each side; δις and λημμα, an assumption, from λαμβανω, to take.]

1. In *logic*, an argument equally conclusive by contrary suppositions. A young rhetorician said to an old sophist: "Instruct me in pleading, and I will pay you, when I gain a cause." The master sued for the reward, and the scholar endeavored to elude the claim by a *dilemma.* "If I gain my cause, I shall withhold your pay, because the award of the judge will be against you. If I lose it, I may withhold it, because I shall not yet have gained a cause." The master replied: "If you gain your cause, you must pay me, because you are to pay me, when you gain a cause; if you lose it, you must pay me, because the judge will award it." *Johnson.*

2. A difficult or doubtful choice; a state of things in which evils or obstacles present themselves on every side, and it is difficult to determine what course to pursue.

A strong *dilemma* in a desperate case!
To act with infamy, or quit the place. *Swift.*

DILETTAN'TE, *n.* [It.] One who delights in promoting science or the fine arts. *Burke.*

DIL'IGENCE, *n.* [L. *diligentia*, from *diligo*, to love earnestly; *di* and *lego*, to choose.]

1. Steady application in business of any kind; constant effort to accomplish what is undertaken; exertion of body or mind without unnecessary delay or sloth; due attention; industry; assiduity.

Diligence is the philosopher's stone that turns every thing to gold.

Brethren, give *diligence* to make your calling and election sure. 2 Pet. i.

2. Care; heed; heedfulness.

Keep thy heart with all *diligence.* Prov. iv.

3. The name of a stage-coach, used in France.

DIL'IGENT, *a.* [L. *diligens.*] Steady in application to business; constant in effort or exertion to accomplish what is undertaken; assiduous; attentive; industrious; not idle or negligent; *applied to persons.*

Seest thou a man *diligent* in his business? he shall stand before kings. Prov. xxii.

2. Steadily applied; prosecuted with care and constant effort; careful; assiduous; as, make *diligent* search.

The judges shall make *diligent* inquisition. Judges xix.

DIL'IGENTLY, *adv.* With steady application and care; with industry or assiduity; not carelessly; not negligently.

Ye shall *diligently* keep the commandments of the Lord your God. Deut. vi.

DILL, *n.* [Sax. *dil, dile;* Sw. *dill;* Dan. *dild;* D. *dille;* G. *dill.*]

An annual plant of the genus Anethum, the seeds of which are moderately warming, pungent and aromatic.

DILU'CID, *a.* [L. *dilucidus.*] Clear. [*Not in use.*]

DILU'CIDATE, *v. t.* To make clear. [*Not in use.* See *Elucidate.*]

DIL'UENT, *a.* [L. *diluens.* See *Dilute.*] Making liquid or more fluid; making thin; attenuating.

2. Weakening the strength of, by mixture with water.

DIL'UENT, *n.* That which thins or attenuates; that which makes more liquid.

2. That which weakens the strength of; as water, which, mixed with wine or spirit, reduces the strength of it.

DILU'TE, *v. t.* [L. *diluo, dilutus; di, dis*, and *lavo, luo*, to wash, contracted from *lago* or *lugo.* See *Deluge.*]

1. Literally, to wash; but appropriately, to render liquid, or more liquid; to make thin, or more fluid. Thus sirup or melasses is made thin or more liquid by an admixture with water; and the water is said to *dilute* it. Hence,

2. To weaken, as spirit or an acid, by an admixture of water, which renders the spirit or acid less concentrated. Thus, we *dilute* spirit, wine or a decoction by adding to it water.

3. To make weak or weaker, as color, by mixture. *Newton.*

4. To weaken; to reduce the strength or standard of; as, to *dilute* virtue. *Milner.*

DILU'TE, *a.* Thin; attenuated; reduced in strength, as spirit or color. *Newton.*

DILU'TED, *pp.* Made liquid; rendered more fluid; weakened, made thin, as liquids.

DILU'TER, *n.* That which makes thin, or more liquid.

DILU'TING, *ppr.* Making thin or more liquid; weakening.

DILU'TION, *n.* The act of making thin, weak, or more liquid. Opposite to *dilution* is coagulation or thickening. *Arbuthnot.*

DILU'VIAL, } *a.* [L. *diluvium*, a deluge,
DILU'VIAN, } from *diluo*. See *Dilute*.]

1. Pertaining to a flood or deluge, more especially to the deluge in Noah's days.
2. Effected or produced by a deluge, particularly by the great flood in the days of Noah. *Buckland.*

DILU'VIATE, *v. i.* To run as a flood. [*Not much used.*] *Sandys.*

DILU'VIUM, *n.* [L.] In *geology*, a deposit of superficial loam, sand, gravel, &c., caused by the deluge. *Buckland.*

DIM, *a.* [Sax. *dim*; Dan. *dum*, dark, obscure, dim, and dumb; *dummer*, to dim; *dummes*, to grow dim or dull, to stupify, Eng. *dumps*, *dumpish*; Sw. *dimba*, fog, mist, a cloud; Ir. *deimhe*, darkness; Russ. *tuman*, fog; *temnei*, dark, obscure; Sans. *tama*, black, Finn. *tumma*. It seems to be allied to *damp*, vapor, Russ. *dim* or *deim*. See *Damp*. If *dim* and *dumb* are of the same family, the sense is *close*, *thick*.]

1. Not seeing clearly; having the vision obscured and indistinct.

   When Isaac was old, and his eyes were *dim*. Gen. xxvii.

2. Not clearly seen; obscure; imperfectly seen or discovered; as a *dim* prospect.
3. Somewhat dark; dusky; not luminous; as a *dim* shade. *Spenser.*
4. Dull of apprehension; having obscure conceptions.

   The understanding is *dim*. *Rogers.*

5. Having its luster obscured; sullied; tarnished.

   How is the gold become *dim*? Lam. iv.

DIM, *v. t.* To cloud; to impair the powers of vision; as, to *dim* the eyes.

2. To obscure; as, to *dim* the sight; to *dim* the prospect.
3. To render dull the powers of conception.
4. To make less bright; to obscure.

   Each passion *dimmed* his face. *Milton.*

5. To render less bright; to tarnish or sully; as, to *dim* gold.

DIM'BLE, *n.* A bower; a cell or retreat. [*Not in use.*] *B. Jonson.*

DIME, *n.* [Fr. contracted from *dixieme* or *disme*, Norm. *dieme*, tenth.]

A silver coin of the United States, of the value of ten cents; the tenth of a dollar.

DIMEN'SION, *n.* [L. *dimensio*, from *dimetior*, to measure; *di* or *dis* and *metior*, to *mete*; Gr. *μετρεω*. See *Mete* and *Measure*.]

In *geometry*, the extent of a body, or length, breadth and thickness or depth. A line has one dimension, or length; a superficies has two dimensions, length and breadth; and a solid has three dimensions, length, breadth and thickness or depth. The word is generally used in the plural, and denotes the whole space occupied by a body, or its capacity, size, measure; as the *dimensions* of a room, or of a ship; the *dimensions* of a farm, of a kingdom, &c.

DIMEN'SIONLESS, *a.* Without any definite measure or extent; boundless. *Milton.*

DIMEN'SITY, *n.* Extent; capacity. *Howell.*

DIMEN'SIVE, *a.* That marks the boundaries or outlines.

   Who can draw the soul's *dimensive* lines? *Davies.*

DIM'ETER, *a.* [L.] Having two poetical measures. *Tyrwhitt.*

DIM'ETER, *n.* A verse of two measures.

DIMID'IATE, *v. t.* [L. *dimidio*.] To divide into two equal parts.

DIMID'IATED, *a.* [L. *dimidiatus*; *di* and *medius*, middle.] Divided into two equal parts; halved.

DIMIDIA'TION, *n.* The act of halving; division into two equal parts.

DIMIN'ISH, *v. t.* [L. *diminuo*; *di* and *minuo*, to lessen; *minor*, less; It. *diminuire*; Fr. *diminuer*; Sp. *diminuir*; Ir. *min*, fine; *mion*, small; W. *main*, *meinw*, small, slender; Russ. *menshe*, less; *umenshayu*, to diminish; Ar. مَنَّ manna, to cut off, to weaken, to diminish. Class Mn. No. 5.]

1. To lessen; to make less or smaller, by any means; opposed to *increase* and *augment*; as, to *diminish* the size of a thing by contraction, or by cutting off a part; to *diminish* a number by subtraction; to *diminish* the revenue by limiting commerce, or reducing the customs; to *diminish* strength or safety; to *diminish* the heat of a room. It is particularly applied to bulk and quantity, as *shorten* is to length.
2. To lessen; to impair; to degrade.

   I will *diminish* them, that they shall no more rule over the nations. Ezek. xxix.

3. In *music*, to take from a note by a sharp, flat or natural.

To diminish from, to take away something. *Obs.*

   Neither shall you *diminish* aught *from* it. Deut. iv.

DIMIN'ISH, *v. i.* To lessen; to become or appear less or smaller. The size of an object *diminishes*, as we recede from it.

DIMIN'ISHED, *pp.* Lessened; made smaller; reduced in size; contracted; degraded.

DIMIN'ISHING, *ppr.* Lessening; contracting; degrading.

DIMIN'ISHINGLY, *adv.* In a manner to lessen reputation. *Locke.*

DIMIN'UENT, *a.* Lessening. [*Little used.*] *Sanderson.*

DIM'INUTE, *a.* Small. [*Not in use.*] *Gorges.*

DIMINU'TION, *n.* [L. *diminutio*.] The act of lessening; a making smaller; opposed to *augmentation*; as the *diminution* of size, of wealth, of power, of safety.

2. The state of becoming or appearing less; opposed to *increase*; as the *diminution* of the apparent diameter of a receding body.
3. Discredit; loss of dignity; degradation. *Philips.*
4. Deprivation of dignity; a lessening of estimation. *Addison.*
5. In *architecture*, the contraction of the upper part of a column, by which its diameter is made less than that of the lower part.
6. In *music*, the imitation of or reply to a subject in notes of half the length or value of those of the subject itself. *Busby.*

DIMIN'UTIVE, *a.* [Fr. *diminutif*; It. *diminuitivo*; Sp. *diminutivo*.]

Small; little; narrow; contracted; as a *diminutive* race of men or other animals; a *diminutive* thought.

DIMIN'UTIVE, *n.* In *grammar*, a word formed from another word, usually an appellative or generic term, to express a little thing of the kind; as, in Latin, *lapillus*, a little stone, from *lapis*; *cellula*, a little cell, from *cella*, a cell; in French, *maisonnette*, a little house, from *maison*, a house; in English, *manikin*, a little man, from *man*.

DIMIN'UTIVELY, *adv.* In a diminutive manner; in a manner to lessen; as, to speak *diminutively* of another.

DIMIN'UTIVENESS, *n.* Smallness; littleness; want of bulk; want of dignity.

DIM'ISH, *a.* [from *dim*.] Somewhat dim, or obscure.

DIM'ISSORY, *a.* [L. *dimissorius*. See *Dismiss*.]

1. Sending away; dismissing to another jurisdiction. A *letter dimissory*, is one given by a bishop to a candidate for holy orders, having a title in his diocese, directed to some other bishop, and giving leave for the bearer to be ordained by him. *Encyc.*
2. Granting leave to depart. *Prideaux.*

DIMIT', *v. t.* [L. *dimitto*.] To permit to go; to grant to farm; to let. [*Not in use.*]

DIM'ITY, *n.* [D. *diemit*.] A kind of white cotton cloth, ribbed or figured.

DIM'LY, *adv.* [See *Dim*.] In a dim or obscure manner; with imperfect sight.

2. Not brightly, or clearly; with a faint light.

DIM'MING, *ppr.* Obscuring.

DIM'MING, *n.* Obscurity. *Shak.*

DIM'NESS, *n.* Dullness of sight; as the *dimness* of the eyes.

2. Obscurity of vision; imperfect sight; as the *dimness* of a view.
3. Faintness; imperfection; as the *dimness* of a color.
4. Want of brightness; as the *dimness* of gold or silver.
5. Want of clear apprehension; stupidity; as the *dimness* of perception.

DIM'PLE, *n.* [Qu. G. *taumeln*, to reel, to indent.]

A small natural cavity or depression in the cheek or other part of the face. *Prior.*

DIM'PLE, *v. i.* To form dimples; to sink into depressions or little inequalities.

   And smiling eddies *dimpled* on the main. *Dryden.*

DIM'PLED, *a.* Set with dimples; as a *dimpled* cheek.

DIM'PLY, *a.* Full of dimples, or small depressions; as the *dimply* flood. *Warton.*

DIM'-SIGHTED, *a.* Having dim or obscure vision. *Addison.*

DIN, *n.* [Sax. *dyn*, noise; *dyna*, to sound; Ice. *dyna*, to thunder; L. *tinnio*, *tonus*, *tono*. This word probably belongs to the root of *tone* and *thunder*, and denotes a rumbling or rattling noise. Sax. *eorth-dyne*, an earthquake.]

Noise; a loud sound; particularly, a rattling,

clattering or rumbling sound, long continued; as the *din* of arms; the *din* of war.

DIN, *v. t.* To strike with continued or confused sound; to stun with noise; to harass with clamor; as, to *din* the ears with cries; to *din* with clamor.

DINE, *v. i.* [Sax. *dynan*, to dine. The Fr. *diner*, is supposed to be contracted from It. *desinare*, to dine, L. *desino*, to cease; in which case, *dinner* must have been so named from the intermission of business. The Saxon and the French, in this case, are probably from different sources. The Gr. has δαινυμαι, and θοιναω, to feast.]

To eat the chief meal of the day. This meal seems originally to have been taken about the middle of the day, at least in northern climates, as it still is by laboring people. Among people in the higher walks of life, and in commercial towns, the time of dining is from two to five or six o'clock in the afternoon.

DINE, *v. t.* To give a dinner to; to furnish with the principal meal; to feed; as, the landlord *dined* a hundred men.

DINET'ICAL, *a.* [Gr. δινητικος.] Whirling round. [*Not used.*] *Brown.*

DING, *v. t.* pret. *dung* or *dinged.* [Sax. *dencgan*, to beat; Scot. *ding*, to drive or strike.]

To thrust or dash with violence. [*Little used.*] *Nash. Marston.*

DING, *v. i.* To bluster; to bounce. [*A low word.*] *Arbuthnot.*

DING-DONG. Words used to express the sound of bells. *Shak.*

DIN'GINESS, *n.* [See *Dingy.*] A dusky or dark hue; brownness.

DIN'GLE, *n.* A narrow dale or valley between hills. *Milton.*

DINGLE-DANGLE. Hanging loosely, or something dangling. *Warton.*

DIN'GY, *a.* Soiled; sullied; of a dark color; brown; dusky; dun.

DI'NING, *ppr.* Eating the principal meal in the day.

DI'NING-ROOM, *n.* A room for a family or for company to dine in; a room for entertainments.

DIN'NER, *n.* [Fr. *diner*; Ir. *dinner.* See *Dine.*]

1. The meal taken about the middle of the day; or the principal meal of the day, eaten between noon and evening.
2. An entertainment; a feast.

> Behold, I have prepared my *dinner.* Matt. xxii.

DIN'NER-TIME, *n.* The usual time of dining. *Pope.*

DINT, *n.* [Sax. *dynt*, a blow or striking. It may be connected with *din* and *ding.*]

1. A blow; a stroke. *Milton.*
2. Force; violence; power exerted; as, to win by *dint* of arms, by *dint* of war, by *dint* of argument or importunity.
3. The mark made by a blow; a cavity or impression made by a blow or by pressure on a substance; often pronounced *dent.*

> His hands had made a *dint.* *Dryden.*

DINT, *v. t.* To make a mark or cavity on a substance by a blow or by pressure. [See *Indent.*] *Donne.*

DINT'ED, *pp.* Marked by a blow or by pressure; as *deep-dinted* furrows. *Spenser.*

DINT'ING, *ppr.* Impressing marks or cavities.

DINUMERA'TION, *n.* The act of numbering singly. [*Little used.*]

DI'OCESAN, *a.* [See *Diocese.* The accent on the first and on the third syllable is nearly equal. The accent given to this word in the English books is wrong, almost to ridiculousness.] Pertaining to a diocese.

DI'OCESAN, *n.* A bishop; one in possession of a diocese, and having the ecclesiastical jurisdiction over it.

DI'OCESE, *n.* [Gr. διοικησις, administration, a province or jurisdiction; δια and οικησις, residence; οικεω, to dwell; οικος, a house. *Diocess* is a very erroneous orthography.]

The circuit or extent of a bishop's jurisdiction; an ecclesiastical division of a kingdom or state, subject to the authority of a bishop. In England there are two provinces or circuits of archbishop's jurisdiction, Canterbury and York. The province of Canterbury contains twenty-one *dioceses*, and that of York three, besides the isle of Man. Every diocese is divided into archdeaconries, of which there are sixty; and each archdeaconry, into rural deaneries; and every deanery, into parishes. *Blackstone.*

A diocese was originally a division of the Roman empire for the purpose of civil government, a prefecture. But the term is now exclusively appropriated to ecclesiastical jurisdiction. *Encyc.*

DIOCTAHE'DRAL, *a.* [*dis* and *octahedral.*] In *crystalography*, having the form of an octahedral prism with tetrahedral summits. *Cleaveland.*

DI'ODON, *n.* The sun-fish; a genus of fishes of a singular form, appearing like the fore part of the body of a deep fish amputated in the middle. *Dict. Nat. Hist.*

DI'OMEDE, *n.* An aquatic fowl of the webfooted kind, about the size of a common domestic hen, but its neck and legs much longer. *Dict. Nat. Hist.*

DIOP'SIDE, *n.* [Gr. διοψις.] A rare mineral, regarded by Haüy as a variety of augite, and called by Jameson a subspecies of oblique-edged augite, occurring in prismatic crystals, of a vitreous luster, and of a pale green, or a greenish or yellowish white. The variety with four-sided prisms has been called Mussite, from Mussa in Piedmont. It resembles the Sahlite. *Cleaveland.*

DIOP'TASE, *n.* Emerald copper ore, a translucent mineral, occurring crystalized in six-sided prisms. *Cyc.*

DIOP'TRIC, } *a.* [Gr. διοπτρικος, from
DIOP'TRICAL, } διοπτομαι, to see through; δια and οπτομαι, to see.]

1. Affording a medium for the sight; assisting the sight in the view of distant objects; as a *dioptric* glass. *Boyle.*
2. Pertaining to dioptrics, or the science of refracted light.

DIOP'TRICS, *n.* That part of optics which treats of the refractions of light passing through different mediums, as through air, water or glass. *Harris.*

DI'ORISM, *n.* [Gr. διορισμα.] Definition. [*Rarely used.*] *More.*

DIORIS'TIC, *a.* Distinguishing; defining. [*Rarely used.*]

DIORIS'TICALLY, *adv.* In a distinguishing manner. [*Rarely used.*]

DIP, *v. t.* pret. and pp. *dipped* or *dipt.* [Sax. *dippan*; Goth. *daupyan*; D. *doopen*; G. *tupfen*; Sw. *dôpa*, *doppa*; Dan. *dypper*; It. *tuffare*; Russ. *toplyu*; Gr. δυπτω; allied probably to *dive*, Heb. Ch. טבע. The primary sense is to thrust or drive, for the same word in Syr. and Ar. signifies to stamp or impress a mark, Gr. τυπτοω, whence *type*; and τυπτω, to strike, Eng. *tap*, seem to be of the same family. Class Db. No. 28.]

1. To plunge or immerse, for a moment or short time, in water or other liquid substance; to put into a fluid and withdraw.

> The priest shall *dip* his finger in the blood. Lev. iv.
>
> Let him *dip* his foot in oil. Deut. xxxiii.
>
> One *dip* the pencil, and one string the lyre. *Pope.*

2. To take with a ladle or other vessel by immersing it in a fluid, as to *dip* water from a boiler; often with *out*, as to *dip out* water.
3. To engage; to take concern; *used intransitively, but the passive participle is used.*

> He was a little *dipt* in the rebellion of the commons. *Dryden.*

4. To engage as a pledge; to mortgage. [*Little used.*] *Dryden.*
5. To moisten; to wet. [*Unusual.*] *Milton.*
6. To baptize by immersion.

DIP, *v. i.* To sink; to immerge in a liquid. *L'Estrange.*

2. To enter; to pierce. *Granville.*
3. To engage; to take a concern; as, to *dip* into the funds.
4. To enter slightly; to look cursorily, or here and there; as, to *dip* into a volume of history. *Pope.*
5. To choose by chance; to thrust and take. *Dryden.*
6. To incline downward; as, the magnetic needle *dips.* [See *Dipping.*]

DIP, *n.* Inclination downward; a sloping; a direction below a horizontal line; depression; as the *dip* of the needle.

The *dip of a stratum*, in geology, is its greatest inclination to the horizon, or that on a line perpendicular to its direction or course; called also the *pitch.* *Cyc.*

DIP-CHICK, *n.* A small bird that dives.

DIPET'ALOUS, *a.* [Gr. δις and πεταλον, a leaf or *petal.*]

Having two flower-leaves or petals; two-petaled. *Martyn.*

DIPH'THONG, *n.* [Gr. διφθογγος; δις and φθογγος, sound; L. *diphthongus.*]

A coalition or union of two vowels pronounced in one syllable. In uttering a diphthong, both vowels are pronounced; the sound is not simple, but the two sounds are so blended as to be considered as forming one syllable, as in *joy, noise, bound, out.* [The pronunciation *dipthong* is vulgar.]

DIPHTHONG'AL, *a.* Belonging to a diphthong; consisting of two vowel sounds pronounced in one syllable.

DIPH'YLLOUS, *a.* [Gr. δις and φυλλον, a leaf.] In *botany*, having two leaves, as a calyx, &c.

DIP'LOE, *n.* [Gr. διπλους, double.] The

soft meditullium, medullary substance, or porous part, between the plates of the skull. *Coxe. Encyc.*

DIPLO'MA, *n.* [Gr. διπλωμα, from διπλοω, to *double* or fold. Anciently, a letter or other composition written on paper or parchment and folded; afterwards, any letter, literary monument, or public document.]

A letter or writing conferring some power, authority, privilege or honor. Diplomas are given to graduates of colleges on their receiving the usual degrees; to clergymen who are licensed to exercise the ministerial functions; to physicians who are licensed to practice their profession; and to agents who are authorized to transact business for their principals. A diploma then is a writing or instrument, usually under seal and signed by the proper person or officer, conferring merely honor, as in the case of graduates, or authority, as in the case of physicians, agents, &c.

DIPLO'MACY, *n.* [This word, like *supremacy*, retains the accent of its original.]

1. The customs, rules and privileges of embassadors, envoys and other representatives of princes and states at foreign courts; forms of negotiation.
2. A diplomatic body; the whole body of ministers at a foreign court.
3. The agency or management of ministers at a foreign court. *Cevallos.*

DIP'LOMATED, *a.* Made by diplomas. *Kennet.*

DIPLOMAT'IC, *a.* Pertaining to diplomas; privileged.

2. Furnished with a diploma; authorized by letters or credentials to transact business for a sovereign at a foreign court. Ministers at a court are denominated a *diplomatic* body.
3. Pertaining to ministers at a foreign court, or to men authorized by diploma; as a *diplomatic* character; *diplomatic* management.

DIPLOMAT'IC, *n.* A minister, official agent or envoy to a foreign court.

DIPLOMAT'ICS, *n.* The science of diplomas, or of ancient writings, literary and public documents, letters, decrees, charters, codicils, &c., which has for its object to decipher old writings, to ascertain their authenticity, their date, signatures, &c. *Encyc. Lunier.*

DIP'PER, *n.* One that dips; he or that which dips.

2. A vessel used to dip water or other liquor; a ladle.

DIP'PING, *ppr.* Plunging or immersing into a liquid and speedily withdrawing, as to ascertain the temperature of water by *dipping* the finger in it; baptizing by immersion.

2. Engaging or taking a concern in.
3. Looking into here and there; examining in a cursory, slight or hasty manner.
4. Inclining downward, as the magnetic needle.
5. Breaking; inclining; as a vein of ore.

DIP'PING, *n.* The act of plunging or immersing.

2. The act of inclining towards the earth; inclination downwards; as the *dipping* of the needle.
3. The interruption of a vein of ore, or stratum of a fossil, in a mine; or a sloping downwards.
4. The act of baptizing by the immersion of the whole body in water.

DIP'PING-NEEDLE, *n.* A needle that dips; a magnetic needle which dips or inclines to the earth; an instrument which shows the inclination of the magnet, at the different points of the earth's surface. In the equatorial regions, the needle takes a horizontal position; but as we recede from the equator towards either pole, it dips or inclines one end to the earth, the north end, as we proceed northward, and the south end, as we proceed southward, and the farther north or south we proceed, the greater is the dip or inclination. This is on the supposition that the poles of the earth and the magnetic poles coincide, which is not the case. The above statement is strictly true, only of the magnetic equator and its poles. *Cavallo. Cyc.*

DIPRISMAT'IC, *a.* [*di* and *prismatic.*] Doubly prismatic. *Jameson.*

DIP'SAS, *n.* [Gr. διψας, dry, thirsty; διψαω, to thirst.]

A serpent whose bite produces a mortal thirst. See Deut. viii.

DIP'TER, **DIP'TERA**, *n.* [Gr. δις and πτερον, a wing.]

The *dipters* are an order of insects having only two wings, and two poisers, as the fly. *Encyc.*

DIP'TERAL, *a.* Having two wings only.

DIP'TOTE, *n.* [Gr. from δις and πιπτω, to fall.]

In *grammar*, a noun which has only two cases; as, *suppetiæ, suppetias.* *Encyc.*

DIP'TYCH, *n.* [Gr. διπτυχος; δις and πτυσσω, πτυξω, to fold.]

A public register of the names of consuls and other magistrates among pagans; and of bishops, martyrs and others, among christians; so called because it consisted of two leaves folded, but it sometimes contained three or more leaves. The sacred diptych was a double catalogue, in one of which were registered the names of the living, and in the other the names of the dead, which were to be rehearsed during the office. *Encyc.*

DIPY'RE, *n.* A mineral occurring in minute prisms, either single or adhering to each other in fascicular groups. Before the blowpipe, it melts with ebullition or intumescence, and its powder on hot coals phosphoresces with a feeble light. Its name, from Gr. δυο, two, and πυρ, fire, indicates the double effect of fire, in producing fusion and phosphorescence. *Cleaveland.*

DIRE, *a.* [L. *dirus.* If the primary sense is terrible, this word may belong to the root of *terreo.* But it may be great, wonderful, Syr. ܬܗܪ ther, to wonder; or it may be raging, furious, as in L. *diræ.*]

Dreadful; dismal; horrible; terrible; evil in a great degree.

> *Dire* was the tossing, deep the groans. *Milton.*

DIRECT', *a.* [L. *directus*, from *dirigo*; *di* and *rego*, *rectus*, to make straight. See *Right.*]

1. Straight; right; as, to pass in a *direct* line from one body or place to another. It is opposed to *crooked, winding, oblique.* It is also opposed to *refracted;* as a *direct* ray of light.
2. In *astronomy*, appearing to move forward in the zodiac, in the direction of the signs; opposed to *retrograde;* as, the motion of a planet is *direct.*
3. In the line of father and son; opposed to *collateral;* as a descendant in the *direct* line.
4. Leading or tending to an end, as by a straight line or course; not circuitous. Thus we speak of *direct* means to effect an object; a *direct* course; a *direct* way.
5. Open; not ambiguous or doubtful. *Bacon.*
6. Plain; express; not ambiguous; as, he said this in *direct* words; he made a *direct* acknowledgment.
7. In *music*, a *direct* interval is that which forms any kind of harmony on the fundamental sound which produces it; as the fifth, major third and octave. *Rousseau.*

Direct tax, is a tax assessed on real estate, as houses and lands.

DIRECT', *v. t.* [L. *directum, directus*, from *dirigo.*]

1. To point or aim in a straight line, towards a place or object; as, to *direct* an arrow or a piece of ordnance; to *direct* the eye; to *direct* a course or flight.
2. To point; to show the right road or course; as, he *directed* me to the left hand road.
3. To regulate; to guide or lead; to govern; to cause to proceed in a particular manner; as, to *direct* the affairs of a nation.

> Wisdom is profitable to *direct.* Eccles. x.

4. To prescribe a course; to mark out a way. Job xxxvii.
5. To order; to instruct; to point out a course of proceeding, with authority; to command. But *direct* is a softer term than *command.*

DIRECT', *n.* In *music*, a character placed at the end of a stave to direct the performer to the first note of the next stave. *Busby.*

DIRECT'ED, *pp.* Aimed; pointed; guided; regulated; governed; ordered; instructed.

DIRECT'ER, *n.* A director, which see.

DIRECT'ING, *ppr.* Aiming; pointing; guiding; regulating; governing; ordering.

DIREC'TION, *n.* [L. *directio.*] Aim at a certain point; a pointing towards, in a straight line or course; as, the *direction* of good works to a good end. *Smalridge.*

2. The line in which a body moves by impulse; course. Matter or body cannot alter the *direction* of its own motion.
3. A straight line or course. A star appeared in the *direction* of a certain tower. The ship sailed in a south-easterly *direction.*
4. The act of governing; administration; management; guidance; superintendence; as the *direction* of public affairs; *direction* of domestic concerns; the *direction* of a bank.
5. Regularity; adjustment.

> All chance, *direction* which thou canst not see. *Pope.*

6. Order; prescription, either verbal or written; instruction in what manner to proceed. The employer gives *directions* to his workmen; the physician, to his patient.
7. The superscription of a letter, including the name, title and place of abode of the person for whom it is intended.

8. A body or board of directors.

DIRE€T'IVE, *a.* Having the power of direction; as a *directive* rule. *Hooker.*

2. Informing; instructing; shewing the way.

DIRE€T'LY, *adv.* In a straight line or course; rectilineally; not in a winding course. Aim *directly* to the object. Gravity tends *directly* to the center of the earth. As a direct line is the shortest course, hence

2. Immediately; soon; without delay; as, he will be with us *directly.*

3. Openly; expressly; without circumlocution or ambiguity, or without a train of inferences.

No man hath been so impious, as *directly* to condemn prayer. *Hooker.*

DIRE€T'NESS, *n.* Straightness; a straight course; nearness of way. *Bentley.*

DIRE€T'OR, *n.* One who directs; one who superintends, governs or manages; one who prescribes to others, by virtue of authority; an instructor; a counselor.

2. That which directs; a rule; an ordinance.

3. One appointed to transact the affairs of a company; as the *director* of a bank, or of the India Company.

4. That which directs or controls by influence.

Safety from external danger is the most powerful *director* of national conduct. *Federalist, Hamilton.*

5. In *surgery,* a grooved probe, intended to direct the edge of the knife or scissors in opening sinuses or fistulæ; a guide for an incision-knife. *Encyc. Coxe.*

DIRE€TO'RIAL, *a.* Pertaining to directors or direction; containing direction or command.

DIRE€T'ORY, *a.* Containing directions; enjoining; instructing.

DIRE€T'ORY, *n.* A guide; a rule to direct; particularly, a book containing directions for public worship, or religious services. The Bible is our best *directory,* in faith and practice.

2. A book containing an alphabetical list of the inhabitants of a city, with their places of abode.

3. The supreme council of France, in the late revolution.

4. A board of directors.

DIRE€T'RESS, *n.* A female who directs or manages.

DIRE€T'RIX, *n.* A female who governs or directs.

DI'REFUL, *a.* [See *Dire.*] Dire; dreadful; terrible; calamitous; as *direful* fiend; a *direful* misfortune. *Spenser. Dryden. Pope.*

DI'REFULLY, *adv.* Dreadfully; terribly; wofully.

DIREMP'TION, *n.* [L. *diremptio.*] A separation. *Bp. Hall.*

DI'RENESS, *n.* Terribleness; horror; dismalness. *Shak.*

DIREP'TION, *n.* [L. *direptio.*] The act of plundering.

DIRĠE, *n. durj.* [Usually supposed to be a contraction of L. *dirige,* a word used in the funeral service. In Sw. *dyrka,* Dan. *dyrker,* signifies to worship, honor, reverence.]

A song or tune intended to express grief, sorrow and mourning; as a funeral *dirge.*

DIR'IĠENT, } *n.* DIRE€T'RIX, } [See *Direct.*] In *geometry,* the line of motion along which the describent line or surface is carried in the generation of any plane or solid figure. *Encyc.*

DIRK, *n. durk.* [Scot. *durk.*] A kind of dagger or poniard.

DIRK, *a. durk.* Dark. *Obs.* *Spenser.*

DIRK, *v. t. durk.* To darken. *Obs.* *Spenser.*

2. To poniard; to stab.

DIRT, *n. durt.* [Sax. *gedritan;* D. *dryten;* Ice. *drit,* cacare.]

1. Any foul or filthy substance; excrement; earth; mud; mire; dust; whatever adhering to any thing, renders it foul or unclean.

The fat closed, and the *dirt* came out. Judges iii.

Whose waters cast up mire and *dirt.* Is. lvii.

2. Meanness; sordidness. [*Not in use.*]

DIRT, *v. t. durt.* To make foul or filthy; to soil; to bedaub; to pollute; to defile. *Swift.*

DIRT'ILY, *adv. durt'ily.* [from *dirty.*] In a dirty manner; foully; nastily; filthily.

2. Meanly; sordidly; by low means.

DIRT'INESS, *n. durt'iness.* Filthiness; foulness; nastiness.

2. Meanness; baseness; sordidness.

DIRT'Y, *a. durt'y.* Foul; nasty; filthy; not clean; as *dirty* hands.

2. Not clean; not pure; turbid; as *dirty* water.

3. Cloudy; dark; dusky; as a *dirty* white.

4. Mean; base; low; despicable; groveling; as a *dirty* fellow; a *dirty* employment.

DIRT'Y, *v. t. durt'y.* To foul; to make filthy; to soil; as, to *dirty* the clothes or hands.

2. To tarnish; to sully; to scandalize; *applied to reputation.*

DIRUP'TION, *n.* [L. *diruptio; dirumpo,* to burst.] A bursting or rending asunder. [See *Disruption.*]

DIS, a prefix or inseparable preposition, from the Latin, whence Fr. *des,* Sp. *dis,* and *de* may in some instances be the same word contracted. *Dis* denotes separation, a parting from; hence it has the force of a privative and negative, as in *disarm, disoblige, disagree.* In some cases, it still signifies separation, as in *distribute, disconnect.*

DISABIL'ITY, *n.* [from *disable.*] Want of competent natural or bodily power, strength or ability; weakness; impotence; as *disability* arising from infirmity or broken limbs.

2. Want of competent intellectual power or strength of mind; incapacity; as the *disability* of a deranged person to reason or to make contracts.

3. Want of competent means or instruments. [In this sense, *inability* is generally used.]

4. Want of legal qualifications; incapacity; as a *disability* to inherit an estate, when the ancestor has been attainted. [*In this sense, it has a plural.*] *Blackstone.*

Disability differs from *inability,* in denoting *deprivation* of ability; whereas *inability* denotes *destitution* of ability, either by deprivation or otherwise.

DISA'BLE, *v. t.* [*dis* and *able.*] To render unable; to deprive of competent natural strength or power. A man is *disabled* to walk by a broken or paralytic leg, by sickness, &c.

2. To deprive of mental power, as by destroying or weakening the understanding.

3. To deprive of adequate means, instruments or resources. A nation may be *disabled* to carry on war by want of money. The loss of a ship may *disable* a man to prosecute commerce, or to pay his debts.

4. To destroy the strength; or to weaken and impair so as to render incapable of action, service or resistance. A fleet is *disabled* by a storm, or by a battle. A ship is *disabled* by the loss of her masts or spars.

5. To destroy or impair and weaken the means which render any thing active, efficacious or useful; to destroy or diminish any competent means.

6. To deprive of legal qualifications, or competent power; to incapacitate; to render incapable.

An attainder of the ancestor corrupts the blood and *disables* his children to inherit. *Eng. Law.*

DISA'BLED, *pp.* Deprived of competent power, corporeal or intellectual; rendered incapable; deprived of means.

DISA'BLEMENT, *n.* Weakness; disability; legal impediment. *Bacon.*

DISA'BLING, *ppr.* Rendering unable or incapable; depriving of adequate power or capacity, or of legal qualifications.

DISABU'SE, *v. t. disabu'ze.* [Fr. *desabuser.* See *Abuse.*]

To free from mistake; to undeceive; to disengage from fallacy or deception; to set right. It is our duty to *disabuse* ourselves of false notions and prejudices.

If men are now sufficiently enlightened to *disabuse* themselves of artifice, hypocrisy and superstition, they will consider this event as an era in their history. *J. Adams.*

DISABU'SED, *pp. disabu'zed.* Undeceived.

DISABU'SING, *ppr. disabu'zing.* Undeceiving.

DISA€€OM'MODATE, *v. t.* [*dis* and *accommodate.*] To put to inconvenience.

DISA€€OMMODA'TION, *n.* [*dis* and *accommodation.*]

A state of being unaccommodated; a state of being unprepared. *Hale.*

DISA€€ORD', *v. i.* [*dis* and *accord.*] To refuse assent. [*Not used.*] *Spenser.*

DISA€€US'TOM, *v. t.* [*dis* and *accustom.*] To neglect familiar or customary practice; to destroy the force of habit by disuse.

DISA€€US'TOMED, *pp.* Disused; having neglected practice or familiar use. *Tooke.*

DISA€KNOWL'EDĠE, *v. t.* [*dis* and *acknowledge.*] To deny; to disown. *South.*

DISA€KNOWL'EDĠED, *pp.* Denied; disowned.

DISA€KNOWL'EDĠING, *ppr.* Denying; disowning.

DISA€QUA'INT, *v. t.* [See *Acquaint.*] To dissolve acquaintance. [*Little used.*]

DISA€QUA'INTANCE, *n.* Neglect or disuse of familiarity, or familiar knowledge of. *South.*

DISADORN', *v. t.* To deprive of ornaments. *Congreve.*

DISADV'ANCE, *v. t.* or *i.* To check; to halt. [*Not in use.*] *Spenser.*

DISADV'ANTAGE, *n.* [Fr. *desavantage.*] That which prevents success, or renders it difficult; a state not favorable to successful operation. The army commenced an attack on the enemy, notwithstanding the *disadvantage* of its position.

2. Any unfavorable state; a state in which some loss or injury may be sustained. Hence,

3. Loss; injury; prejudice to interest, fame, credit, profit or other good; as, to sell goods to *disadvantage.*

DISADV'ANTAGE, *v. t.* To injure in interest; to prejudice.

DISADV'ANTAGEABLE, *a.* Not advantageous. [*Not in use.*] *Bacon.*

DISADVANTA'GEOUS, *a.* Unfavorable to success or prosperity; inconvenient; not adapted to promote interest, reputation or other good; as, the situation of an army is *disadvantageous* for attack or defense. We are apt to view characters in the most *disadvantageous* lights.

DISADVANTA'GEOUSLY, *adv.* In a manner not favorable to success, or to interest, profit or reputation; with loss or inconvenience.

DISADVANTA'GEOUSNESS, *n.* Unfavorableness to success; inconvenience; loss.

DISADVENT'URE, *n.* Misfortune. [*Not used.*] *Raleigh.*

DISADVENT'UROUS, *a.* Unprosperous. [*Not used.*] *Spenser.*

DISAFFECT', *v. t.* [*dis* and *affect.*] To alienate affection; to make less friendly to; to make less faithful to a person, party or cause, or less zealous to support it; to make discontented or unfriendly; as, an attempt was made to *disaffect* the army.

2. To disdain, or dislike. *Hall.*

3. To throw into disorder. *Hammond.*

DISAFFECT'ED, *pp.* or *a.* Having the affections alienated; indisposed to favor or support; unfriendly; followed by *with* or *to;* as, these men are *disaffected with* the government, or *disaffected to* the king, or *to* the administration.

DISAFFECT'EDLY, *adv.* In a disaffected manner.

DISAFFECT'EDNESS, *n.* The quality of being disaffected.

DISAFFECT'ING, *ppr.* Alienating the affections; making less friendly.

DISAFFEC'TION, *n.* Alienation of affection, attachment or good will; want of affection; or more generally, positive enmity, dislike or unfriendliness; disloyalty. It generally signifies more than indifference; as the *disaffection* of people to their prince or government; the *disaffection* of allies; *disaffection* to religion.

2. Disorder; bad constitution; *in a physical sense.* [*Little used.*] *Wiseman.*

DISAFFEC'TIONATE, *a.* Not well disposed; not friendly. *Blount.*

DISAFFIRM', *v. t. disafferm'.* [*dis* and *affirm.*] To deny; to contradict. *Davies.*

2. To overthrow or annul, as a judicial decision, by a contrary judgment of a superior tribunal.

DISAFFIRM'ANCE, *n.* Denial; negation; disproof; confutation. *Hale.*

2. Overthrow or annulment, by the decision of a superior tribunal; as *disaffirmance* of judgment.

DISAFFIRM'ED, *pp.* Denied; contradicted; overthrown.

DISAFFIRM'ING, *ppr.* Denying; contradicting; annulling.

DISAFFOR'EST, *v. t.* [*dis* and *afforest.*] To reduce from the privileges of a forest to the state of common ground; to strip of forest laws and their oppressive privileges.

> By Charter 9. Hen. III. many forests were *disafforested.* *Blackstone.*

DISAFFOR'ESTED, *pp.* Stripped of forest privileges.

DISAFFOR'ESTING, *ppr.* Depriving of forest privileges.

DISAG'GREGATE, *v. t.* [*dis* and *aggregate.*] To separate an aggregate mass into its component parts. *Dispensatory.*

DISAG'GREGATED, *pp.* Separated, as an aggregate mass.

DISAG'GREGATING, *ppr.* Separating, as the parts of an aggregate body.

DISAGGREGA'TION, *n.* The act or operation of separating an aggregate body into its component parts.

DISAGREE', *v. i.* [*dis* and *agree.*] To differ; to be not accordant or coincident; to be not the same; to be not exactly similar. Two ideas *disagree,* when they are not the same, or when they are not exactly alike. The histories of the same fact often *disagree.*

2. To differ, as in opinion; as, the best judges sometimes *disagree.*

> Who shall decide when doctors *disagree?* *Pope.*

3. To be unsuitable. Medicine sometimes *disagrees with* the patient; food often *disagrees with* the stomach or the taste.

4. To differ; to be in opposition.

> Men often reject the plainest sense of scripture, because it *disagrees* with their reason or preconceived opinions. *Anon.*

It is usually followed by *with.* But we say, I *disagree to* your proposal. The use of *from* after *disagree* is not common.

DISAGREE'ABLE, *a.* Contrary; unsuitable; not conformable; not congruous. [*Little used.*]

> This conduct was *disagreeable* to her natural sincerity. *Broome.*

2. Unpleasing; offensive to the mind, or to the senses; but expressing less than *disgusting* and *odious.* Behavior may be *disagreeable* to our minds; food may be *disagreeable* to the taste; many things are *disagreeable* to the sight; sounds may be *disagreeable* to the ear, and odors to the smell. Whatever is *disagreeable* gives some pain or uneasiness.

DISAGREE'ABLENESS, *n.* Unsuitableness; contrariety.

2. Unpleasantness; offensiveness to the mind, or to the senses; as the *disagreeableness* of another's manners; the *disagreeableness* of a taste, sound or smell.

DISAGREE'ABLY, *adv.* Unsuitably; unpleasantly; offensively.

DISAGREE'ING, *ppr.* Differing; not according or coinciding.

DISAGREE'MENT, *n.* Difference, either in form or essence; dissimilitude; diversity; as the *disagreement* of two ideas, of two pictures, of two stories or narrations.

2. Difference of opinion or sentiments. *Hooker.*

3. Unsuitableness.

DISALLIE'GE, *v. t.* To alienate from allegiance. [*Not in use.*] *Milton.*

DISALLOW', *v. t.* [*dis* and *allow.*] To refuse permission, or not to permit; not to grant; not to make or suppose lawful; not to authorize; to disapprove. God *disallows* that christians should conform to the immoral practices of the world. A good man *disallows* every kind of profaneness.

2. To testify dislike or disapprobation; to refuse assent.

> But if her father shall *disallow* her in the day that he heareth, not any of her vows or her bonds—shall stand. Num. xxx.

3. Not to approve; not to receive; to reject.

> To whom coming, as to a living stone, *disallowed* indeed of men, but chosen of God, and precious. 1 Pet. ii.

4. Not to allow or admit as just; to reject; as, to *disallow* an account or charge.

DISALLOW'ABLE, *a.* Not allowable; not to be suffered.

DISALLOW'ANCE, *n.* Disapprobation; refusal to admit or permit; prohibition; rejection.

DISALLOW'ED, *pp.* Not granted, permitted or admitted; disapproved; rejected.

DISALLOW'ING, *ppr.* Not permitting; not admitting; disapproving; rejecting.

DISALLY', *v. t.* [*dis* and *ally.*] To form an improper alliance. *Milton.*

DISAN'CHOR, *v. t.* [*dis* and *anchor.*] To force from its anchors, as a ship.

DISANGEL'ICAL, *a.* Not angelical. [*Not used.*] *Coventry.*

DISAN'IMATE, *v. t.* [*dis* and *animate.*] To deprive of life. [*Not used.*]

2. To deprive of spirit or courage; to discourage; to dishearten; to deject. *Boyle.*

DISAN'IMATED, *pp.* Discouraged; dispirited.

DISAN'IMATING, *ppr.* Discouraging; disheartening.

DISANIMA'TION, *n.* The act of discouraging; depression of spirits.

2. Privation of life. [*Not used.*] *Brown.*

DISANNUL', *v. t.* [*dis* and *annul.* In this instance, the prefix *dis* is improperly used, and of no effect. But its use is well established.] To annul; to make void; to deprive of authority or force; to nullify; to abolish; as, to *disannul* a law or an ordinance.

> Wilt thou also *disannul* my judgment? Job xl. Gal. iii. xv.

DISANNUL'LED, *pp.* Annulled; vacated; made void.

DISANNUL'LING, *ppr.* Making void; depriving of authority or binding force.

DISANNUL'MENT, *n.* The act of making void; as the *disannulment* of a law or decree.

Disannul differs from *repeal,* as the genus from the species. A *repeal* makes a law void by the same power that enacted it. *Annulment* or *disannulment* destroys its force and authority by repeal or by other means.

DISANOINT', *v. t.* To render consecration invalid. *Milton.*

DISAPPAR'EL, *v. t.* To disrobe; to strip of raiment. *Junius.*

DISAPPE'AR, *v. i.* [*dis* and *appear.*] To vanish from the sight; to recede from the view; to become invisible by vanishing or departing, or by being enveloped in any thing that conceals, or by the interposition of an object. Darkness *disappears* at the access of light, and light *disappears* at the approach of darkness. A ship *disappears* by departure to a distance; the sun *disappears* in a fog, or behind a cloud, or in setting.

2. To cease; as, the epidemic has *disappeared.*

3. To withdraw from observation. The debtor *disappears* when he absconds.

DISAPPE'ARANCE, *n.* Cessation of appearance; a removal from sight.

DISAPPE'ARING, *ppr.* Vanishing; receding from the sight; becoming invisible.

DISAPPE'ARING, *n.* A vanishing or removal from sight.

DISAPPOINT', *v. t.* [*dis* and *appoint*; properly, to unfix or unsettle.]

1. To defeat of expectation, wish, hope, desire or intention; to frustrate; to balk; to hinder from the possession or enjoyment of that which was intended, desired, hoped or expected. We say, a man is *disappointed of* his hopes or expectations, or his hopes, desires, intentions or expectations are *disappointed.* A bad season *disappoints* the farmer *of* his crops; a defeat *disappoints* an enemy *of* his spoil. The man promised me a visit, but he *disappointed* me.

> Without counsel purposes are *disappointed.* Prov. xv.

2. To frustrate; to prevent an effect intended.

> The retiring foe
> Shrinks from the wound, and *disappoints* the blow. *Addison.*

DISAPPOINT'ED, *pp.* Defeated of expectation, hope, desire or design; frustrated.

DISAPPOINT'ING, *ppr.* Defeating of expectation, hope, desire or purpose; frustrating.

DISAPPOINT'MENT, *n.* Defeat or failure of expectation, hope, wish, desire or intention; miscarriage of design or plan.

> We are apt to complain of the *disappointment* of our hopes and schemes, but *disappointments* often prove blessings and save us from calamity or ruin. *Anon.*

DISAPPRE'CIATE, *v. t.* [*dis* and *appreciate.*] To undervalue; not to esteem.

DISAPPROBA'TION, *n.* [*dis* and *approbation.*] A disapproving; dislike; the act of the mind which condemns what is supposed to be wrong, whether the act is expressed or not. We often *disapprove*, when we do not express *disapprobation.*

DISAP'PROBATORY, *a.* Containing disapprobation; tending to disapprove.

DISAPPRO'PRIATE, *a.* [*dis* and *appropriate.*] Not appropriated, or not having appropriated church property; a *disappropriate* church is one from which the appropriated parsonage, glebe and tithes are severed.

> The appropriation may be severed and the church become *disappropriate*, two ways. *Blackstone.*

DISAPPRO'PRIATE, *v. t.* To sever or separate, as an appropriation; to withdraw from an appropriate use.

> The appropriations of the several parsonages would have been, by the rules of the common law, *disappropriated.* *Blackstone.*

2. To deprive of appropriated property, as a church.

DISAPPRÖVAL, *n.* Disapprobation; dislike.

DISAPPRÖVE, *v. t.* [Fr. *desapprouver*; *dis* and *approve.*]

1. To dislike; to condemn in opinion or judgment; to censure as wrong. We often *disapprove* the conduct of others, or public measures, whether we express an opinion or not. It is often followed by *of*; as, to *disapprove of* behavior. But modern usage inclines to omit *of.*

2. To manifest dislike or disapprobation; to reject, as disliked, what is proposed for sanction.

> The sentence of the court-martial was *disapproved* by the commander in chief.

DISAPPRÖVED, *pp.* Disliked; condemned; rejected.

DISAPPRÖVING, *ppr.* Disliking; condemning; rejecting from dislike.

DIS'ARD, *n.* [Sax. *dysig*, foolish.] A prattler; a boasting talker. *Obs.*

DIS'ARM, *v. t.* *s* as *z.* [Fr. *desarmer*; Sp. Port. *desarmar*; *dis* and *arm.*]

1. To deprive of arms; to take the arms or weapons from, usually by force or authority; as, he *disarmed* his foes; the prince gave orders to *disarm* his subjects. With *of* before the thing taken away; as, to *disarm* one *of* his weapons.

2. To deprive of means of attack or defense; as, to *disarm* a venomous serpent.

3. To deprive of force, strength, or means of annoyance; to render harmless; to quell; as, to *disarm* rage or passion.

4. To strip; to divest of any thing injurious or threatening; as, piety *disarms* death *of* its terrors.

DIS'ARMED, *pp.* Deprived of arms; stripped of the means of defense or annoyance; rendered harmless; subdued.

DIS'ARMING, *ppr.* Stripping of arms or weapons; subduing; rendering harmless.

DISARRANGE, *v. t.* [*dis* and *arrange.*] To put out of order; to unsettle or disturb the order or due arrangement of parts. [See *Derange*, which is more generally used.] *Warton.*

DISARRANGEMENT, *n.* The act of disturbing order or method; disorder. *Baxter.*

DISARRA'Y, *v. t.* [*dis* and *array.*] To undress; to divest of clothes. *Spenser.*

2. To throw into disorder; to rout, as troops. *Milton.*

DISARRA'Y, *n.* Disorder; confusion; loss or want of array or regular order. *Dryden.*

2. Undress. *Spenser.*

DISARRA'YED, *pp.* Divested of clothes or array; disordered.

DISARRA'YING, *ppr.* Divesting of clothes; throwing into disorder.

DISASSIDU'ITY, *n.* Want of assiduity or care. [*Not used.*] *Wotton.*

DISASSO'CIATE, *v. t.* To disunite; to disconnect things associated.

DIS'ASTER, *n.* *diz'aster.* [Fr. *desastre*; Sp. Port. *id.*; It. *disastro*; *dis* and *astre*, Gr. ἀστηρ, a star; a word of astrological origin.]

1. A blast or stroke of an unfavorable planet. *Obs.* *Shak.*

2. Misfortune; mishap; calamity; any unfortunate event, especially a sudden misfortune; as, we met with many *disasters* on the road.

DIS'ASTER, *v. t.* To blast by the stroke of an unlucky planet; also, to injure; to afflict. *Shak.* *Thomson.*

DIS'ASTERED, *pp.* Blasted; injured; afflicted.

DIS'ASTROUS, *a.* Unlucky; unfortunate; calamitous; occasioning loss or injury; as, the day was *disastrous*; the battle proved *disastrous*; their fate was *disastrous.*

> Fly the pursuit of my *disastrous* love. *Dryden.*

2. Gloomy; dismal; threatening disaster.

> The moon,
> In dim eclipse, *disastrous* twilight sheds. *Milton.*

DIS'ASTROUSLY, *adv.* Unfortunately; in a dismal manner.

DIS'ASTROUSNESS, *n.* Unfortunateness; calamitousness.

DISAU'THORIZE, *v. t.* [*dis* and *authorize.*] To deprive of credit or authority. [*Little used.*] *Wotton.*

DISAVOUCH', *v. t.* [*dis* and *avouch.* See *Vow.*] To retract profession; to deny; to disown. [*Little used.*] *Davies.*

DISAVOW', *v. t.* [*dis* and *avow.* See *Vow.*] To deny; to disown; to deny to be true, as a fact or charge respecting one's self; as, he was charged with embezzlement, but he *disavows* the fact. A man may *disavow* his name or signature; he may *disavow* a knowledge of a fact, or his concern in a transaction. Opposed to *own* or *acknowledge.*

2. To deny; to disown; to reject.

3. To dissent from; not to admit as true or justifiable; not to vindicate.

> The Envoy *disavowed* some parts of the President's proclamation.

DISAVOW'AL, *n.* Denial; a disowning.

> A *disavowal* of fear often proceeds from fear. *Clarissa.*

2. Rejection; a declining to vindicate.

DISAVOW'ED, *pp.* Denied; disowned.

DISAVOW'ING, *ppr.* Denying; disowning; rejecting as something not to be maintained or vindicated.

DISAVOW'MENT, *n.* Denial; a disowning. *Wotton.*

DISBAND', *v. t.* [*dis* and *band*; Fr. *debander.*] To dismiss from military service; to break up a band, or body of men enlisted; as, to *disband* an army or a regiment; to *disband* troops.

2. To scatter; to disperse. *Woodward.*

DISBAND', *v. i.* To retire from military service; to separate; to break up; as, the army, at the close of the war, *disbands.*

2. To separate; to dissolve connection.

> Human society may *disband.* [*Improper.*] *Tillotson.*

3. To be dissolved. [*Not used.*]

> When both rocks and all things shall *disband.* *Herbert.*

DISBAND'ED, *pp.* Dismissed from military service; separated.

DISBAND'ING, *ppr.* Dismissing from military service; separating; dissolving connection.

DISB'ARK, *v. t.* [Fr. *debarquer*, or *dis* and *bark*; a word not well formed, and little used. We now use *debark* and *disembark.*] To land from a ship; to put on shore. *Pope.*

DISBELIE'F, *n.* [*dis* and *belief.*] Refusal of credit or faith; denial of belief.

Our belief or *disbelief* of a thing does not alter the nature of the thing. *Tillotson.*

DISBELIE'VE, *v. t.* [*dis* and *believe.*] Not to believe; to hold not to be true or not to exist; to refuse to credit. Some men *disbelieve* the inspiration of the scriptures, and the immortality of the soul.

DISBELIE'VED, *pp.* Not believed; discredited.

DISBELIE'VER, *n.* One who refuses belief; one who denies to be true or real. *Watts.*

DISBELIE'VING, *ppr.* Withholding belief; discrediting.

DISBENCH', *v. t.* [*dis* and *bench.*] To drive from a bench or seat. *Shak.*

DISBLA'ME, *v. t.* To clear from blame. [*Not used.*] *Chaucer.*

DISBOD'IED, *a.* Disembodied, *which is the word now used.*

DISBOW'EL, *v. t.* [*dis* and *bowel.*] To take out the intestines. *Spenser.*

DISBR'ANCH, *v. t.* [*dis* and *branch.*] To cut off or separate, as the branch of a tree. [*Little used.*]

2. To deprive of branches. [*Little used.*] *Evelyn.*

DISBUD', *v. t.* To deprive of buds or shoots. *Gardeners.*

DISBURD'EN, *v. t.* [*dis* and *burden.* See *Burden.*] To remove a burden from; to unload; to discharge. *Milton.*

2. To throw off a burden; to disencumber; to clear of any thing weighty, troublesome or cumbersome; as, to *disburden* one's self of grief or care; to *disburden* of superfluous ornaments.

DISBURD'EN, *v. i.* To ease the mind; to be relieved. *Milton.*

DISBURD'ENED, *pp.* Eased of a burden; unloaded; disencumbered.

DISBURD'ENING, *ppr.* Unloading; discharging; throwing off a burden; disencumbering.

DISBURSE, *v. t.* *disburs'.* [Fr. *debourser*; *de* or *dis* and *bourse*, a purse.]

To pay out, as money; to spend or lay out; primarily, to pay money from a public chest or treasury, but applicable to a private purse.

DISBURS'ED, *pp.* Paid out; expended.

DISBURSEMENT, *n.* *disburs'ment.* [Fr. *deboursement.*]

1. The act of paying out, as money from a public or private chest.

2. The money or sum paid out; as, the annual *disbursements* exceed the income.

DISBURS'ER, *n.* One who pays out or disburses money.

DISBURS'ING, *ppr.* Paying out, or expending.

DISC, *n.* [L. *discus.* See *Disk.*] The face or breadth of the sun or moon; also, the width of the aperture of a telescope glass.

DISCAL'CEATE, *v. t.* [L. *discalceatus*; *dis* and *calceus*, a shoe.] To pull off the shoes or sandals.

DISCAL'CEATED, *pp.* Stripped of shoes.

DISCALCEA'TION, *n.* The act of pulling off the shoes or sandals. *Brown.*

DISCAN'DY, *v. i.* [*dis* and *candy.*] To melt; to dissolve. *Shak.*

DISC'ARD, *v. t.* [Sp. *descartar*; Port. *id.*; *dis* and *card.*]

1. To throw out of the hand such cards as are useless.

2. To dismiss from service or employment, or from society; to cast off; as, to *discard* spies and informers; to *discard* an old servant; to *discard* an associate.

3. To thrust away; to reject; as, to *discard* prejudices.

DISC'ARDED, *pp.* Thrown out; dismissed from service; rejected.

DISC'ARDING, *ppr.* Throwing out; dismissing from employment; rejecting.

DISC'ARNATE, *a.* [*dis* and L. *caro*, flesh.] Stripped of flesh. *Glanville.*

DISCA'SE, *v. t.* [*dis* and *case.*] To take off a covering from; to strip; to undress. *Shak.*

DISCEPTA'TOR, *n.* [L.] One who arbitrates or decides. [*Not used.*]

DISCERN', *v. t.* *s* as *z.* [L. *discerno*; *dis* and *cerno*, to separate or distinguish, Gr. κρινω; It. *discernere*; Sp. *discernir*; Fr. *discerner*; Eng. *screen.* The sense is to separate.]

1. To separate by the eye, or by the understanding. Hence,

2. To distinguish; to see the difference between two or more things; to discriminate; as, to *discern* the blossom-buds from the leaf-buds of plants. *Boyle.*

Discern thou what is thine— Gen. xxxi.

3. To make the difference. *Obs.*

For nothing else *discerns* the virtue or the vice. *B. Jonson.*

4. To discover; to see; to distinguish by the eye.

I *discerned* among the youths, a young man void of understanding. Prov. vii.

5. To discover by the intellect; to distinguish; hence, to have knowledge of; to judge.

So is my lord the king to *discern* good and bad. 2 Sam. xiv.

A wise man's heart *discerneth* time and judgment. Eccles. viii.

DISCERN', *v. i.* To see or understand the difference; to make distinction; as, to *discern* between good and evil, truth and falsehood.

2. To have judicial cognizance. *Obs.* *Bacon.*

DISCERN'ED, *pp.* Distinguished; seen; discovered.

DISCERN'ER, *n.* One who sees, discovers or distinguishes; an observer.

2. One who knows and judges; one who has the power of distinguishing.

He was a great observer and *discerner* of men's natures and humors. *Clarendon.*

3. That which distinguishes; or that which causes to understand.

The word of God is quick and powerful—a *discerner* of the thoughts and intents of the heart. Heb. iv.

DISCERN'IBLE, *a.* That may be seen distinctly; discoverable by the eye or the understanding; distinguishable. A star is *discernible* by the eye; the identity or difference of ideas is *discernible* by the understanding.

DISCERN'IBLENESS, *n.* Visibleness.

DISCERN'IBLY, *adv.* In a manner to be discerned, seen or discovered; visibly. *Hammond.*

DISCERN'ING, *ppr.* Distinguishing; seeing; discovering; knowing; judging.

2. *a.* Having power to discern; capable of seeing, discriminating, knowing and judging; sharp-sighted; penetrating; acute; as a *discerning* man or mind.

DISCERN'ING, *n.* The act of discerning; discernment. *Spectator.*

DISCERN'INGLY, *adv.* With discernment; acutely; with judgment; skilfully. *Garth.*

DISCERN'MENT, *n.* The act of discerning; also, the power or faculty of the mind, by which it distinguishes one thing from another, as truth from falsehood, virtue from vice; acuteness of judgment; power of perceiving differences of things or ideas, and their relations and tendencies. The errors of youth often proceed from the want of *discernment.*

DISCERP', *v. t.* [L. *discerpo.*] To tear in pieces; to separate. [*Not used.*]

DISCERPIBIL'ITY, *n.* Capability or liableness to be torn asunder or disunited.

DISCERP'IBLE, *a.* [L. *discerpo*; *dis* and *carpo*, to seize, to tear. In some dictionaries it is written *discerptible*, on the authority of Glanville and More; an error indeed, but of little consequence, as the word is rarely or never used.]

That may be torn asunder; separable; capable of being disunited by violence.

DISCERP'TION, *n.* The act of pulling to pieces, or of separating the parts.

DISCES'SION, *n.* [L. *discessio.*] Departure. [*Not used.*] *Hall.*

DISCH'ARGE, *v. t.* [Fr. *decharger*; Sp. *descargar*; It. *scaricare*; *dis* and *charge* or *cargo*, from *car*, a cart or vehicle.]

1. To unload, as a ship; to take out, as a cargo; *applied both to the ship and the loading.* We say, to *discharge* a ship; but more generally, to *discharge* a cargo or the lading of the ship.

2. To free from any load or burden; to throw off or exonerate; as, *discharged* of business. *Dryden.*

3. To throw off a load or charge; to let fly; to shoot; *applied to fire-arms*; as, to *discharge* a pistol or a cannon; or to *discharge* a ball or grape-shot.

4. To pay; as, to *discharge* a debt, a bond, a note.

5. To send away, as a creditor by payment of what is due to him. He *discharged* his creditors.

6. To free from claim or demand; to give an acquittance to, or a receipt in full, as to a debtor. The creditor *discharged* his debtor.

7. To free from an obligation; as, to *discharge* a man from further duty or service; to *discharge* a surety.

8. To clear from an accusation or crime; to acquit; to absolve; to set free; with *of*; as, to *discharge* a man *of* all blame. *Hooker.*

9. To throw off or out; to let fly; to give vent to; as, to *discharge* a horrible oath; to *discharge* fury or vengeance. *Shak. Pope.*

10. To perform or execute, as a duty or office considered as a charge. One man *discharges* the office of a sheriff; another that of a priest. We are all bound to *dis-*

charge the duties of piety, of benevolence and charity.

11. To divest of an office or employment; to dismiss from service; as, to *discharge* a steward or a servant; to *discharge* a soldier or seaman; to *discharge* a jury.

12. To dismiss; to release; to send away from any business or appointment.

Discharge your powers to their several counties. *Shak.*

13. To emit or send out; as, an ulcer *discharges* pus; a pipe *discharges* water.

14. To release; to liberate from confinement; as, to *discharge* a prisoner.

15. To put away; to remove; to clear from; to destroy. In general, to throw off any load or incumbrance; to free or clear.

DISCH'ARGE, *v. i.* To break up.

The cloud, if it were oily or fatty, would not *discharge.* *Bacon.*

DISCH'ARGE, *n.* An unloading, as of a ship; as the *discharge* of a cargo.

2. A throwing out; vent; emission: *applied to a fluid,* a flowing or issuing out, or a throwing out; as the *discharge* of water from a spring, or from a spout: *applied to fire-arms,* an explosion; as a *discharge* of cannon.

3. That which is thrown out; matter emitted; as a thin serous *discharge;* a purulent *discharge.*

4. Dismission from office or service; or the writing which evidences the dismission. The general, the soldier, obtains a *discharge.*

5. Release from obligation, debt or penalty; or the writing which is evidence of it; an acquittance; as, the debtor has a *discharge.*

6. Absolution from a crime or accusation; acquittance. *South.*

7. Ransom; liberation; price paid for deliverance. *Milton.*

8. Performance; execution; *applied to an office, trust or duty.* A good man is faithful in the *discharge* of his duties, public and private.

9. Liberation; release from imprisonment or other confinement.

10. Exemption; escape.

There is no *discharge* in that war. Eccles. viii.

11. Payment, as of a debt.

DISCH'ARGED, *pp.* Unloaded; let off; shot; thrown out; dismissed from service; paid; released; acquitted; freed from debt or penalty; liberated; performed; executed.

DISCH'ARGER, *n.* He that discharges in any manner.

2. One who fires a gun.

3. In *electricity,* an instrument for discharging a Leyden phial, jar, &c., by opening a communication between the two surfaces. *Cyc.*

DISCH'ARGING, *ppr.* Unlading; letting fly; shooting; throwing out; emitting; dismissing from service; paying; releasing from debt, obligation or claim; acquitting; liberating; performing; executing.

DISCHURCH', *v. t.* To deprive of the rank of a church. *Hall.*

DISCI'DE, *v. t.* To divide; to cut in pieces. [*Not used.*]

DISCINCT', *a.* Ungirded.

DISCIND', *v. t.* To cut in two. [*Not used.*] *Boyle.*

DISCI'PLE, *n.* [L. *discipulus,* from *disco,* to learn.]

1. A learner; a scholar; one who receives or professes to receive instruction from another; as the *disciples* of Plato.

2. A follower; an adherent to the doctrines of another. Hence the constant attendants of Christ were called his *disciples;* and hence all christians are called his *disciples,* as they profess to learn and receive his doctrines and precepts.

DISCI'PLE, *v. t.* To teach; to train, or bring up. *Shak.*

2. To make disciples of; to convert to doctrines or principles.

This authority he employed in sending missionaries to *disciple* all nations. *E. D. Griffin.*

3. To punish; to discipline. [*Not in use.*] *Spenser.*

DISCI'PLED, *pp.* Taught; trained; brought up; made a disciple.

DISCI'PLE-LIKE, *a.* Becoming a disciple. *Milton.*

DISCI'PLESHIP, *n.* The state of a disciple or follower in doctrines and precepts. *Hammond.*

DISCIPLINABLE, *a.* [See *Discipline.*]

1. Capable of instruction, and improvement in learning.

2. That may be subjected to discipline; as a *disciplinable* offense, in church government.

3. Subject or liable to discipline, as the member of a church.

DISCIPLINABLENESS, *n.* Capacity of receiving instruction by education. *Hale.*

2. The state of being subject to discipline.

DIS'CIPLINANT, *n.* One of a religious order, so called from their practice of scourging themselves, or other rigid discipline. *Smollett.*

DISCIPLINA'RIAN, *a.* Pertaining to discipline. *Glanville.*

DISCIPLINA'RIAN, *n.* One who disciplines; one versed in rules, principles and practice, and who teaches them with precision; particularly, one who instructs in military and naval tactics and maneuvers. It is chiefly used in the latter sense, and especially for one who is well versed in, or teaches with exactness, military exercises and evolutions.

2. A puritan or presbyterian; so called from his rigid adherence to religious discipline. [*I believe not now used.*] *Sanderson.*

DIS'CIPLINARY, *a.* Pertaining to discipline; intended for discipline or government; promoting discipline; as, certain canons of the church are *disciplinary.*

2. Relating to a regular course of education; intended for instruction. *Milton.*

The evils of life, pain, sickness, losses, sorrows, dangers and disappointments, are *disciplinary* and remedial. *Buckminster.*

DIS'CIPLINE, *n.* [L. *disciplina,* from *disco,* to learn.]

1. Education; instruction; cultivation and improvement, comprehending instruction in arts, sciences, correct sentiments, morals and manners, and due subordination to authority.

2. Instruction and government, comprehending the communication of knowledge and the regulation of practice; as military *discipline,* which includes instruction in manual exercise, evolutions and subordination.

3. Rule of government; method of regulating principles and practice; as the *discipline* prescribed for the church.

4. Subjection to laws, rules, order, precepts or regulations; as, the troops are under excellent *discipline;* the passions should be kept under strict *discipline.*

5. Correction; chastisement; punishment intended to correct crimes or errors; as the *discipline* of the strap. *Addison.*

6. In *ecclesiastical affairs,* the execution of the laws by which the church is governed, and infliction of the penalties enjoined against offenders, who profess the religion of Jesus Christ. *Encyc.*

7. Chastisement or bodily punishment inflicted on a delinquent in the Romish Church; or that chastisement or external mortification which a religious person inflicts on himself. *Taylor. Encyc.*

DIS'CIPLINE, *v. t.* To instruct or educate; to inform the mind; to prepare by instructing in correct principles and habits; as, to *discipline* youth for a profession, or for future usefulness.

2. To instruct and govern; to teach rules and practice, and accustom to order and subordination; as, to *discipline* troops or an army.

3. To correct; to chastise; to punish.

4. To execute the laws of the church on offenders, with a view to bring them to repentance and reformation of life.

5. To advance and prepare by instruction. *Milton.*

DIS'CIPLINED, *pp.* Instructed; educated; subjected to rules and regulations; corrected; chastised; punished; admonished.

DIS'CIPLINING, *ppr.* Instructing; educating; subjecting to order and subordination; correcting; chastising; admonishing; punishing.

DISCLA'IM, *v. t.* [*dis* and *claim.*] To disown; to disavow; to deny the possession of; to reject as not belonging to one's self. A man *disclaims* all knowledge of a particular transaction; he *disclaims* every pretension to eloquence; he *disclaims* any right to interfere in the affairs of his neighbor; he *disclaims* all pretensions to military skill. It is opposed to *claim* or *challenge.*

2. To renounce; to reject; as, to *disclaim* the authority of the pope.

3. To deny all claim. A tenant may *disclaim* to hold of his lord. *Eng. Law.*

DISCLA'IM, *v. i.* To disavow all part or share. [*Unusual.*]

Nature *disclaims* in thee. *Shak.*

DISCLAIMA'TION, *n.* The act of disclaiming; a disavowing. [*Not used.*] *Scott.*

DISCLA'IMED, *pp.* Disowned; disavowed; rejected; denied.

DISCLA'IMER, *n.* A person who disclaims, disowns or renounces.

2. In *law,* an express or implied denial by a tenant that he holds an estate of his lord; a denial of tenure, by plea or otherwise. *Blackstone.*

DISCLA'IMING, *ppr.* Disowning; disavowing; denying; renouncing.

DISCLO'SE, *v. t.* *disclo'ze.* [*dis* and *close;* Fr. *declorre, declos;* L. *discludo.* See *Close.*]

1. To uncover; to open; to remove a cover from, and lay open to the view.

The shells being broken, the stone included in them is *disclosed.* *Woodward.*

2. To discover; to lay open to the view; to bring to light. Events have *disclosed* the designs of the ministry.

3. To reveal by words; to tell; to utter; as, to *disclose* the secret thoughts of the heart.

4. To make known; to show in any manner. A blush may *disclose* a secret passion in the breast.

5. To open; to hatch. [*Not used.*]

The ostrich layeth her eggs under sand, where the heat of the sun *discloseth* them. *Bacon.*

DISCLO'SE, *n.* Discovery. *Young.*

DISCLO'SED, *pp.* Uncovered; opened to view; made known; revealed; told; uttered.

DISCLO'SER, *n.* One who discloses or reveals.

DISCLO'SING, *ppr.* Uncovering; opening to view; revealing; making known; telling.

DISCLO'SURE, *n.* *disclo'zhur.* The act of disclosing; an uncovering and opening to view; discovery. *Bacon.*

2. The act of revealing; utterance of what was secret; a telling.

3. The act of making known what was concealed.

4. That which is disclosed or made known.

DISCLU'SION, *n.* *disclu'zhun.* [L. *disclusus, discludo; dis* and *claudo.*]

An emission; a throwing out. [*Little used.*] *More.*

DISCOAST, *v. i.* To depart from; to quit the coast. [*Not used.*]

DISCOHE'RENT, *a.* Incoherent. *The latter is generally used.*

DIS'COID, *n.* [*discus* and εἰδος.] Something in form of a discus or disk.

DIS'COID, DISCOID'AL, *a.* Having the form of a disk.

Discoid or *discous flowers,* are compound flowers, not radiated, but the florets all tubular, as the tansy, southern-wood, &c. *Cyc. Smith.*

DISCŎL'OR, *v. t.* [L. *discoloro; dis* and *coloro,* from *color.*]

1. To alter the natural hue or color of; to stain; to tinge. A drop of wine will *discolor* a glass of water; silver is *discolored* by sea-water.

2. To change any color, natural or artificial; to alter a color partially. It differs from *color* and *dye,* in denoting a partial alteration, rather than an entire change of color.

3. *Figuratively,* to alter the complexion; to change the appearance; as, to *discolor* ideas. *Watts.*

DISCŎLORA'TION, *n.* The act of altering the color; a staining.

2. Alteration of color; stain; as spots and *discolorations* of the skin.

3. Alteration of complexion or appearance.

DISCŎL'ORED, *pp.* Altered in color; stained.

2. *a.* Variegated; being of divers colors. *Spenser.*

DISCŎL'ORING, *ppr.* Altering the color or hue; staining; changing the complexion.

DISCŎM'FIT, *v. t.* [Fr. *deconfire, deconfit;* It. *sconfiggere, sconfitta;* from *dis* and the L. *configo,* to fasten, to nail; *con* and *figo,* to fix.]

To rout; to defeat; to scatter in fight; to cause to flee; to vanquish.

Joshua *discomfited* Amalek and his people with the edge of the sword. Ex. xvii.

He, fugitive, declined superior strength,
Discomfited, pursued. *Philips.*

DISCŎM'FIT, *n.* Rout; dispersion; defeat; overthrow.

DISCŎM'FITED, *pp.* Routed; defeated; overthrown.

DISCŎM'FITING, *ppr.* Routing; defeating.

DISCŎM'FITURE, *n.* Rout; defeat in battle; dispersion; overthrow.

Every man's sword was against his fellow, and there was a very great *discomfiture.* 1 Sam. xiv.

2. Defeat; frustration; disappointment.

DISCŎM'FORT, *n.* [*dis* and *comfort.*] Uneasiness; disturbance of peace; pain; grief; inquietude. *Shak. South.*

DISCŎM'FORT, *v. t.* To disturb peace or happiness; to make uneasy; to pain; to grieve; to sadden; to deject. *Sidney.*

DISCŎM'FORTABLE, *a.* Causing uneasiness; unpleasant; giving pain; making sad. [*Little used.*] *Sidney.*

2. Uneasy; melancholy; refusing comfort. [*Not used.*] *Shak.*

[Instead of this word, *uncomfortable* is used.]

DISCŎM'FORTED, *pp.* Made uneasy; disturbed; pained; grieved.

DISCŎM'FORTING, *ppr.* Disturbing peace and happiness; making uneasy; grieving.

DISCOMMEND', *v. t.* [*dis* and *commend.*] To blame; to censure; to mention with disapprobation.

I do not *discommend* the lofty style in tragedy. *Dryden.*

DISCOMMEND'ABLE, *a.* Blamable; censurable; deserving disapprobation. *Ayliffe.*

DISCOMMEND'ABLENESS, *n.* Blamableness; the quality of being worthy of disapprobation.

DISCOMMENDA'TION, *n.* Blame; censure; reproach. *Ayliffe.*

DISCOMMEND'ER, *n.* One who discommends; a dispraiser. *Johnson.*

DISCOMMEND'ING, *ppr.* Blaming; censuring.

DISCOMMO'DE, *v. t.* [*dis* and *commode,* Fr.]

To put to inconvenience; to incommode; to molest; to trouble. [*Discommodate* is not used.]

DISCOMMO'DED, *pp.* Put to inconvenience; molested; incommoded.

DISCOMMO'DING, *ppr.* Putting to inconvenience; giving trouble to.

DISCOMMO'DIOUS, *a.* Inconvenient; troublesome. *Spenser.*

DISCOMMOD'ITY, *n.* Inconvenience; trouble; hurt; disadvantage. *Bacon.*

DISCOM'MON, *v. t.* [*dis* and *common.*] To appropriate common land; to separate and inclose common. *Cowel.*

2. To deprive of the privileges of a place. *Warton.*

DISCOMPLEX'ION, *v. t.* To change the complexion or color. [*Not used.*] *Beaum.*

DISCOMPO'SE, *v. t.* *discompo'ze.* [*dis* and *compose.*]

1. To unsettle; to disorder; to disturb; *applied to things.*

2. To disturb peace and quietness; to agitate; to ruffle; *applied to the temper or mind;* expressing less agitation than *fret* and *vex,* or expressing vexation with decorum. *Swift.*

3. To displace; to discard. [*Not in use.*] *Bacon.*

DISCOMPO'SED, *pp.* Unsettled; disordered; ruffled; agitated; disturbed.

DISCOMPO'SING, *ppr.* Unsettling; putting out of order; ruffling; agitating; disturbing tranquility.

DISCOMPOSI''TION, *n.* Inconsistency. [*Not used.*]

DISCOMPO'SURE, *n.* *discompo'zhur.* Disorder; agitation; disturbance; perturbation; as *discomposure* of mind. *Clarendon.*

DISCONCERT', *v. t.* [*dis* and *concert.*] To break or interrupt any order, plan or harmonious scheme; to defeat; to frustrate. The emperor *disconcerted* the plans of his enemy. Their schemes were *disconcerted.*

2. To unsettle the mind; to discompose; to disturb; to confuse. An unexpected question may *disconcert* the ablest advocate in his argument.

DISCONCERT'ED, *pp.* Broken; interrupted; disordered; defeated; unsettled; discomposed; confused.

DISCONCERT'ING, *ppr.* Disordering; defeating; discomposing; disturbing.

DISCONCER'TION, *n.* The act of disconcerting. *Federalist, Hamilton.*

DISCONFORM'ITY, *n.* [*dis* and *conformity.*] Want of agreement or conformity; inconsistency. *Hakewill.*

DISCONGRU'ITY, *n.* [*dis* and *congruity.*] Want of congruity; incongruity; disagreement; inconsistency. *Hale.*

DISCONNECT', *v. t.* [*dis* and *connect.*] To separate; to disunite; to dissolve connection.

The commonwealth would, in a few generations, crumble away, be *disconnected* into the dust and powder of individuality— *Burke.*

This restriction *disconnects* bank paper and the precious metals. *Walsh.*

DISCONNECT'ED, *pp.* Separated; disunited. This word is not synonymous with *unconnected,* though often confounded with it. *Disconnected* implies a previous connection; *unconnected* does not necessarily imply any previous union.

DISCONNECT'ING, *ppr.* Separating; disuniting.

DISCONNEC'TION, *n.* The act of separating, or state of being disunited; separation; want of union.

Nothing was therefore to be left in all the subordinate members, but weakness, *disconnection* and confusion. *Burke.*

DISCONSENT', *v. i.* [*dis* and *consent.*] To differ; to disagree; not to consent. *Milton.*

DISCON'SOLATE, *a.* [*dis* and L. *consolatus.* See *Console.*]

1. Destitute of comfort or consolation; sorrowful; hopeless or not expecting comfort; sad; dejected; melancholy; as a parent, bereaved of an only child and *disconsŏlate.*
2. Not affording comfort; cheerless; as the *disconsolate* darkness of a winter's night. *Ray.*

DISCON'SOLATELY, *adv.* In a disconsolate manner; without comfort.

DISCON'SOLATENESS, *n.* The state of being disconsolate or comfortless.

DISCONSOLA'TION, *n.* Want of comfort. *Jackson.*

DISCONTENT', *n.* [*dis* and *content.*] Want of content; uneasiness or inquietude of mind; dissatisfaction at any present state of things.

DISCONTENT', *a.* Uneasy; dissatisfied. *Hayward.*

DISCONTENT', *v. t.* To make uneasy at the present state; to dissatisfy.

DISCONTENT'ED, *pp.* or *a.* Uneasy in mind; dissatisfied; unquiet; as, *discontented* citizens make bad subjects.

DISCONTENT'EDLY, *adv.* In a discontented manner or mood.

DISCONTENT'EDNESS, *n.* Uneasiness of mind; inquietude; dissatisfaction. *Addison.*

DISCONTENT'ING, *a.* Giving uneasiness.

DISCONTENT'MENT, *n.* The state of being uneasy in mind; uneasiness; inquietude; discontent. *Hooker. Bacon.*

DISCONTIN'UANCE, *n.* [See *Discontinue.*]
1. Want of continuance; cessation; intermission; interruption of continuance; as a *discontinuance* of conversation or intercourse. *Atterbury.*
2. Want of continued connection or cohesion of parts; want of union; disruption. *Bacon.*
3. In *law,* a breaking off or interruption of possession, as where a tenant in tail makes a feoffment in fee-simple, or for the life of the feoffee, or in tail, which he has not power to do; in this case, the entry of the feoffee is lawful, during the life of the feoffor; but if he retains possession after the death of the feoffor, it is an injury which is termed a *discontinuance,* the legal estate of the heir in tail being *discontinued,* till a recovery can be had in law. *Blackstone.*
4. *Discontinuance of a suit,* is when a plaintiff leaves a chasm in the proceedings in his cause, as by not continuing the process regularly from day to day; in which case the defendant is not bound to attend. Formerly the demise of the king caused a *discontinuance* of all suits; but this is remedied by statute 1. Ed. VI. *Blackstone.*

DISCONTINUA'TION, *n.* Breach or interruption of continuity; disruption of parts; separation of parts which form a connected series. *Newton.*

DISCONTIN'UE, *v. t.* [*dis* and *continue.*]
1. To leave off; to cause to cease, as a practice or habit; to stop; to put an end to; as, to *discontinue* the intemperate use of spirits. Inveterate customs are not *discontinued* without inconvenience.

> The depredations on our commerce were not to be *discontinued.* *T. Pickering.*

2. To break off; to interrupt.
3. To cease to take or receive; as, to *discontinue* a daily paper.

DISCONTIN'UE, *v. i.* To cease; to leave the possession, or lose an established or long enjoyed right.

> Thyself shalt *discontinue* from thine heritage. Jer. xvii.

2. To lose the cohesion of parts; to suffer disruption or separation of substance. [*Little used.*] *Bacon.*

DISCONTIN'UED, *pp.* Left off; interrupted; broken off.

DISCONTIN'UER, *n.* One who discontinues a rule or practice.

DISCONTIN'UING, *ppr.* Ceasing; interrupting; breaking off.

DISCONTINU'ITY, *n.* Disunion of parts; want of cohesion. *Newton.*

DISCONTIN'UOUS, *a.* Broken off; interrupted.
2. Separated; wide; gaping. *Milton.*

DISCONVE'NIENCE, *n.* [*dis* and *convenience.*] Incongruity; disagreement. [*Little used.*] *Bramhall.*

DISCONVE'NIENT, *a.* Incongruous. *Reynolds.*

DIS'CORD, *n.* [L. *discordia;* Fr. *discorde;* from L. *discors; dis* and *cor.*]
1. Disagreement among persons or things. Between persons, difference of opinions; variance; opposition; contention; strife; any disagreement which produces angry passions, contest, disputes, litigation or war. *Discord* may exist between families, parties and nations.
2. Disagreement; want of order; a clashing.

> All *discord,* harmony not understood. *Pope.*

3. In *music,* disagreement of sounds; dissonance; a union of sounds which is inharmonious, grating and disagreeable to the ear; or an interval whose extremes do not coalesce. Thus the second and the seventh, when sounded together, make a *discord.* The term *discord* is applied to each of the two sounds which form the dissonance, and to the interval; but more properly to the mixed sound of dissonant tones. It is opposed to *concord* and *harmony.*

DISCORD', *v. i.* To disagree; to jar; to clash; not to suit; not to be coincident. [*Not in use.*] *Bacon.*

DISCORD'ANCE, } *n.* [L. *discordans.*] Disagreement; opposition; inconsistency; as a *discordance* of opinions, or of sounds.
DISCORD'ANCY, }

DISCORD'ANT, *a.* [L. *discordans.*] Disagreeing; incongruous; contradictory; being at variance; as *discordant* opinions; *discordant* rules or principles.
2. Opposite; contrarious; not coincident; as the *discordant* attractions of comets, or of different planets. *Cheyne.*
3. Dissonant; not in unison; not harmonious; not accordant; harsh; jarring; as *discordant* notes or sounds.

DISCORD'ANTLY, *adv.* Dissonantly; in a discordant manner; inconsistently; in a manner to jar or clash; in disagreement with another, or with itself.

DISCORD'FUL, *a.* Quarrelsome; contentious. *Spenser.*

DISCOUN'SEL, *v. t.* To dissuade. [*Not in use.*] *Spenser.*

DIS'COUNT, *n.* [Fr. *deconte* or *decompte; de* or *dis* and *compte;* It. *sconto;* Sp. *descuento;* Arm. *discount* or *digont.* See *Count.* Literally, a counting back or from.]
1. A sum deducted for prompt or advanced payment; an allowance or deduction from a sum due, or from a credit; a certain rate per cent deducted from the credit price of goods sold, on account of prompt payment; or any deduction from the customary price, or from a sum due or to be due at a future time. Thus the merchant who gives a credit of three months will deduct a certain rate per cent for payment in hand, and the holder of a note or bill of exchange will deduct a certain rate per cent of the amount of the note or bill for advanced payment, which deduction is called a *discount.*
2. Among *bankers,* the deduction of a sum for advanced payment; particularly, the deduction of the interest on a sum lent, at the time of lending. The discounts at banking institutions are usually the amount of legal interest paid by the borrower, and deducted from the sum borrowed, at the commencement of the credit. *Hamilton's Report.*
3. The sum deducted or refunded; as, the *discount* was five per cent.
4. The act of discounting. A note is lodged in the bank for *discount.* The banks have suspended *discounts.*

DIS'COUNT, *v. t.* [Sp. *descontar;* Port. *id.;* Fr. *decompter;* Arm. *discounta, digontein;* It. *scontare.* In British books, the accent is laid on the last syllable. But in America, the accent is usually or always on the first.]
1. To deduct a certain sum or rate per cent from the principal sum. Merchants *discount* five or six per cent, for prompt or for advanced payment.
2. To lend or advance the amount of, deducting the interest or other rate per cent from the principal, at the time of the loan or advance. The banks *discount* notes and bills of exchange, on good security.

> The first rule—to *discount* only unexceptionable paper. *Walsh.*

DIS'COUNT, *v. i.* To lend or make a practice of lending money, deducting the interest at the time of the loan. The banks *discount* for sixty or ninety days, sometimes for longer terms.

DISCOUNT'ABLE, *a.* That may be discounted. Certain forms are necessary to render notes *discountable* at a bank. A bill may be *discountable* for more than sixty days.

DIS'COUNT-DAY, *n.* The day of the week on which a bank discounts notes and bills.

DIS'COUNTED, *pp.* Deducted from a principal sum; paid back; refunded or allowed; as, the sum of five per cent was *discounted.*
2. Having the amount lent on discount or deduction of a sum in advance; as, the bill was *discounted* for sixty days.

DISCOUN'TENANCE, *v. t.* [*dis* and *countenance.*] To abash; to ruffle or discompose the countenance; to put to shame: to put out of countenance. [*Not used.*]

> How would one look from his majestic brow——
> *Discountenance* her despised. *Milton.*

2. To discourage; to check; to restrain by frowns, censure, arguments, opposition, or cold treatment. The good citizen will *discountenance* vice by every lawful means.

DISCOUN'TENANCE, *n.* Cold treatment; unfavorable aspect; unfriendly regard; disapprobation; whatever tends to check or discourage.

He thought a little *discountenance* on those persons would suppress that spirit. *Clarendon.*

DISCOUN'TENANCED, *pp.* Abashed; discouraged; checked; frowned on.

DISCOUN'TENANCER, *n.* One who discourages by cold treatment, frowns, censure or expression of disapprobation; one who checks or depresses by unfriendly regards.

DISCOUN'TENANCING, *ppr.* Abashing; discouraging; checking by disapprobation or unfriendly regards.

DIS'COUNTER, *n.* One who advances money on discounts. *Burke.*

DIS'COUNTING, *ppr.* Deducting a sum for prompt or advanced payment.

2. Lending on discount.

DIS'COUNTING, *n.* The act or practice of lending money on discounts.

The profitable business of a bank consists in *discounting.* *Hamilton.*

DISCOUR'AGE, *v. t.* *discur'age.* [*dis* and *courage;* Fr. *decourager;* Arm. *digouragi;* It. *scoraggiare.* The Italian is from *ex* and *coraggio.* See *Courage.*]

1. To extinguish the courage of; to dishearten; to depress the spirits; to deject; to deprive of confidence.

Fathers, provoke not your children, lest they be *discouraged.* Col. iii.

2. To deter from any thing; with *from.*

Why *discourage* ye the hearts of the children of Israel *from* going over into the land which the Lord hath given them? Num. xxxii.

3. To attempt to repress or prevent; to dissuade from; as, to *discourage* an effort.

DISCOUR'AGED, *pp.* *discur'aged.* Disheartened; deprived of courage or confidence; depressed in spirits; dejected; checked.

DISCOUR'AGEMENT, *n.* *discur'agement.* The act of disheartening, or depriving of courage; the act of deterring or dissuading from an undertaking; the act of depressing confidence.

2. That which destroys or abates courage; that which depresses confidence or hope; that which deters or tends to deter from an undertaking, or from the prosecution of any thing. Evil examples are great *discouragements* to virtue. The revolution was commenced under every possible *discouragement.*

DISCOUR'AGER, *n.* *discur'ager.* One who discourages; one who disheartens, or depresses the courage; one who impresses diffidence or fear of success; one who dissuades from an undertaking.

DISCOUR'AGING, *ppr.* *discur'aging.* Disheartening; depressing courage.

2. *a.* Tending to dishearten, or to depress the courage; as *discouraging* prospects.

DISCOURSE, *n.* *discōrs.* [Fr. *discours;* L. *discursus,* from *discurro,* to ramble; *dis* and *curro,* to run; It. *discorso.*]

1. The act of the understanding, by which it passes from premises to consequences; the act which connects propositions, and deduces conclusions from them. *Johnson. Glanville.*

[*This sense is now obsolete.*]

2. Literally, a running over a subject in speech; hence, a communication of thoughts by words, either to individuals, to companies, or to public assemblies. *Discourse* to an individual or to a small company is called *conversation* or *talk;* mutual interchange of thoughts; mutual intercourse of language. It is applied to the familiar communication of thoughts by an individual, or to the mutual communication of two or more. We say, I was pleased with *his discourse,* and he heard *our discourse.*

The vanquished party with the victors joined,
Nor wanted sweet *discourse,* the banquet of the mind. *Dryden.*

3. Effusion of language; speech. *Locke.*

4. A written treatise; a formal dissertation; as the *discourse* of Plutarch on garrulity; of Cicero on old age.

5. A sermon, uttered or written. We say, an extemporaneous *discourse,* or a written *discourse.*

DISCOURSE, *v. i.* To talk; to converse; but it expresses rather more formality than *talk.* He *discoursed* with us an hour on the events of the war. We *discoursed* together on our mutual concerns.

2. To communicate thoughts or ideas in a formal manner; to treat upon in a solemn, set manner; as, to *discourse* on the properties of the circle; the preacher *discoursed* on the nature and effects of faith.

3. To reason; to pass from premises to consequences. *Davies.*

DISCOURSE, *v. t.* To treat of; to talk over; to discuss. [*Not used.*]

Let us *discourse* our fortunes. *Shak.*

DISCOURSER, *n.* One who discourses; a speaker; a haranguer.

2. The writer of a treatise or dissertation. *Swift.*

DISCOURSING, *ppr.* Talking; conversing; preaching; discussing; treating at some length or in a formal manner.

DISCOURSIVE, *a.* Reasoning; passing from premises to consequences. *Milton.*

2. Containing dialogue or conversation; interlocutory.

The epic is interlaced with dialogue or *discoursive* scenes. *Dryden.*

DISCOUR'TEOUS, *a.* *discur'teous.* [*dis* and *courteous.*] Uncivil; rude; uncomplaisant; wanting in good manners; as *discourteous* knight.

DISCOUR'TEOUSLY, *adv.* *discur'teously.* In a rude or uncivil manner; with incivility.

DISCOUR'TESY, *n.* *discur'tesy.* [*dis* and *courtesy.*] Incivility; rudeness of behavior or language; ill manners; act of disrespect.

Be calm in arguing; for fierceness makes
Error a fault, and truth *discourtesy.* *Herbert.*

DISCOURTSHIP, *n.* Want of respect. *Obs.* *B. Jonson.*

DISC'OUS, *a.* [from L. *discus.*] Broad; flat; wide; used of the middle plain and flat part of some flowers. *Quincy.*

DISCOV'ER, *v. t.* [Fr. *decouvrir; de,* for *des* or *dis,* and *couvrir,* to cover; Sp. *descubrir;* Port. *descobrir;* It. *scoprire.* See *Cover.*]

1. Literally, to uncover; to remove a covering. Is. xxii.

2. To lay open to the view; to disclose; to show; to make visible; to expose to view something before unseen or concealed.

Go, draw aside the curtains and *discover*
The several caskets to this noble prince. *Shak.*

He *discovereth* deep things out of darkness. Job xii.

Law can *discover* sin, but not remove. *Milton.*

3. To reveal; to make known.

We will *discover* ourselves to them. 1 Sam. xiv.

Discover not a secret to another. Prov. xxv.

4. To espy; to have the first sight of; as, a man at mast-head *discovered* land.

When we had *discovered* Cyprus, we left it on the left hand. Acts xxi.

5. To find out; to obtain the first knowledge of; to come to the knowledge of something sought or before unknown. Columbus *discovered* the variation of the magnetic needle. We often *discover* our mistakes, when too late to prevent their evil effects.

6. To detect; as, we *discovered* the artifice; the thief, finding himself *discovered,* attempted to escape.

Discover differs from *invent.* We *discover* what before existed, though to us unknown; we *invent* what did not before exist.

DISCOV'ERABLE, *a.* That may be discovered; that may be brought to light, or exposed to view.

2. That may be seen; as, many minute animals are *discoverable* only by the help of the microscope.

3. That may be found out, or made known; as, the scriptures reveal many things not *discoverable* by the light of reason.

4. Apparent; visible; exposed to view.

Nothing *discoverable* in the lunar surface is ever covered. *Bentley.*

DISCOV'ERED, *pp.* Uncovered; disclosed to view; laid open; revealed; espied or first seen; found out; detected.

DISCOV'ERER, *n.* One who discovers; one who first sees or espies; one who finds out, or first comes to the knowledge of something.

2. A scout; an explorer. *Shak.*

DISCOV'ERING, *ppr.* Uncovering; disclosing to view; laying open; revealing; making known; espying; finding out; detecting.

DISCOV'ERTURE, *n.* [Fr. *decouvert,* uncovered.]

A state of being released from coverture; freedom of a woman from the coverture of a husband.

DISCOV'ERY, *n.* The action of disclosing to view, or bringing to light; as, by the *discovery* of a plot, the public peace is preserved.

2. Disclosure; a making known; as, a bankrupt is bound to make a full *discovery* of his estate and effects.

3. The action of finding something hidden; as the *discovery* of lead or silver in the earth.

4. The act of finding out, or coming to the

knowledge of; as the *discovery* of truth; the *discovery* of magnetism.

5. The act of espying; first sight of; as the *discovery* of America by Columbus, or of the Continent by Cabot.

6. That which is discovered, found out or revealed; that which is first brought to light, seen or known. The properties of the magnet were an important *discovery.* Redemption from sin was a *discovery* beyond the power of human philosophy.

7. In *dramatic poetry,* the unraveling of a plot, or the manner of unfolding the plot or fable of a comedy or tragedy.

DISCRED'IT, *n.* [Fr. *discredit;* Sp. *descredito;* It. *scredito.* See the Verb.]

1. Want of credit or good reputation; some degree of disgrace or reproach; disesteem; *applied to persons or things.* Frauds in manufactures bring them into *discredit.*

> It is the duty of every christian to be concerned for the reputation or *discredit* his life may bring on his profession. *Rogers.*

2. Want of belief, trust or confidence; disbelief; as, later accounts have brought the story into *discredit.*

DISCRED'IT, *v. t.* [Fr. *decrediter; de, des, dis,* and *credit.*]

1. To disbelieve; to give no credit to; not to credit or believe; as, the report is *discredited.*

2. To deprive of credit or good reputation; to make less reputable or honorable; to bring into disesteem; to bring into some degree of disgrace, or into disrepute.

> He least *discredits* his travels, who returns the same man he went. *Wotton.*
>
> Our virtues will be often *discredited* with the appearance of evil. *Rogers.*

3. To deprive of credibility. *Shak.*

DISCRED'ITABLE, *a.* Tending to injure credit; injurious to reputation; disgraceful; disreputable. *Blair.*

DISCRED'ITED, *pp.* Disbelieved; brought into disrepute; disgraced.

DISCRED'ITING, *ppr.* Disbelieving; not trusting to; depriving of credit; disgracing.

DISCREE'T, *a.* [Fr. *discret;* Sp. *discreto;* It. *id;* L. *discretus,* the participle assigned to *discerno, dis* and *cerno,* but probably from the root of *riddle,* W. *rhidyll,* from *rhidiaw,* to secrete, as *screen* is from the root of *secerno,* or *excerno,* Gr. *χρινω,* L. *cerno;* Gr. *διαχρισις.* Class Rd. It is sometimes written *discrete;* the distinction between *discreet* and *discrete* is arbitrary, but perhaps not entirely useless. The literal sense is, separate, reserved, wary, hence discerning.]

1. Prudent; wise in avoiding errors or evil, and in selecting the best means to accomplish a purpose; circumspect; cautious; wary; not rash.

> It is the *discreet* man, not the witty, nor the learned, nor the brave, who guides the conversation, and gives measures to society. *Addison.*
>
> Let Pharaoh look out a man *discreet* and wise. Gen. xli.

DISCREE'TLY, *adv.* Prudently; circumspectly; cautiously; with nice judgment of what is best to be done or omitted.

DISCREE'TNESS, *n.* The quality of being discreet; discretion.

DISCREP'ANCE, } *n.* [L. *discrepantia, dis-*
DISCREP'ANCY, } *crepans,* from *discrepo,* to give a different sound, to vary, to jar; *dis* and *crepo,* to creak. See *Crepitate.*]

Difference; disagreement; contrariety; *applicable to facts or opinions.*

> There is no real *discrepancy* between these two genealogies. *Faber.*

DISCREP'ANT, *a.* Different; disagreeing; contrary.

DISCRE'TE, *a,* [L. *discretus.* See *Discreet.*]

1. Separate; distinct; disjunct. *Discrete proportion* is when the ratio of two or more pairs of numbers or quantities is the same, but there is not the same proportion between all the numbers; as 3 : 6 :: 8 : 16, 3 bearing the same proportion to 6, as 8 does to 16. But 3 is not to 6 as 6 to 8. It is thus opposed to continued or continual proportion, as 3 : 6 :: 12 : 24. *Harris*

2. Disjunctive; as, I resign my life, but not my honor, is a *discrete* proposition. *Johnson.*

DISCRE'TE, *v. t.* To separate; to discontinue. [*Not used.*] *Brown.*

DISCRE''TION, *n.* [Fr. *discretion;* It. *discrezione;* Sp. *discrecion;* from the L. *discretio,* a separating; *discretus, discerno.* See *Discreet.*]

1. Prudence, or knowledge and prudence; that discernment which enables a person to judge critically of what is correct and proper, united with caution; nice discernment and judgment, directed by circumspection, and primarily regarding one's own conduct.

> A good man—will guide his affairs with *discretion.* Ps. cxii.
>
> My son, keep sound wisdom and *discretion.* Prov. iii.

2. Liberty or power of acting without other control than one's own judgment; as, the management of affairs was left to the *discretion* of the prince; he is left to his own *discretion.* Hence,

To surrender at discretion, is to surrender without stipulation or terms, and commit one's self entirely to the power of the conqueror.

3. Disjunction; separation. [*Not much used.*] *Mede.*

DISCRE''TIONARY, } *a.* Left to discre-
DISCRE''TIONAL, } tion; unrestrained except by discretion or judgment; that is to be directed or managed by discretion only. Thus, the President of the U. States is, in certain cases, invested with *discretionary* powers, to act according to circumstances.

DISCRE''TIONARILY, } *adv.* At discre-
DISCRE''TIONALLY, } tion; according to discretion.

DISCRE'TIVE, *a.* [See *Discreet* and *Discrete.*] Disjunctive; noting separation or opposition. In *logic,* a *discretive* proposition expresses some distinction, opposition or variety, by means of *but, though, yet,* &c.; as, travelers change their climate, *but* not their temper; Job was patient, *though* his grief was great.

2. In *grammar, discretive* distinctions are such as imply opposition or difference; as, not a man, *but* a beast. *Johnson.*

3. Separate; distinct.

DISCRE'TIVELY, *adv.* In a discretive manner.

DISCRIM'INABLE, *a.* That may be discriminated.

DISCRIM'INATE, *v. t.* [L. *discrimino,* from *discrimen,* difference, distinction; *dis* and *crimen,* differently applied; coinciding with the sense of Gr. *διαχρινω, χρινω,* L. *cerno.*]

1. To distinguish; to observe the difference between; as, we may usually *discriminate* true from false modesty.

2. To separate; to select from others; to make a distinction between; as, in the last judgment, the righteous will be *discriminated* from the wicked.

3. To mark with notes of difference; to distinguish by some note or mark. We *discriminate* animals by names, as nature has *discriminated* them by different shapes and habits.

DISCRIM'INATE, *v. i.* To make a difference or distinction; as, in the application of law, and the punishment of crimes, the judge should *discriminate* between degrees of guilt.

2. To observe or note a difference; to distinguish; as, in judging of evidence, we should be careful to *discriminate* between probability and slight presumption.

DISCRIM'INATE, *a.* Distinguished; having the difference marked. *Bacon.*

DISCRIM'INATED, *pp.* Separated; distinguished.

DISCRIM'INATELY, *adv.* Distinctly; with minute distinction; particularly. *Johnson.*

DISCRIM'INATENESS, *n.* Distinctness; marked difference. *Dict.*

DISCRIM'INATING, *ppr.* Separating; distinguishing; marking with notes of difference.

2. *a.* Distinguishing; peculiar; characterized by peculiar differences; as the *discriminating* doctrines of the gospel.

3. *a.* That discriminates; able to make nice distinctions; as a *discriminating* mind. *Journ. of Science.*

DISCRIMINA'TION, *n.* The act of distinguishing; the act of making or observing a difference; distinction; as the *discrimination* between right and wrong.

2. The state of being distinguished. *Stillingfleet.*

3. Mark of distinction. *K. Charles.*

DISCRIM'INATIVE, *a.* That makes the mark of distinction; that constitutes the mark of difference; characteristic; as the *discriminative* features of men.

2. That observes distinction; as *discriminative* providence. *More.*

DISCRIM'INATIVELY, *adv.* With discrimination or distinction. *Foster.*

DISCRIM'INOUS, *a.* Hazardous. [*Not used.*] *Harvey.*

DISCU'BITORY, *a.* [L. *discubitorius; discumbo; dis* and *cubo,* to lie down or lean.] Leaning; inclining; or fitted to a leaning posture. *Brown.*

DISCULP'ATE, *v. t.* [Fr. *disculper;* Sp. *disculpar; dis* and L. *culpa,* a fault.]

To free from blame or fault; to exculpate; to excuse.

> Neither does this effect of the independence of nations *disculpate* the author of an unjust war. *Trans. of Vattel. Hist. of California.*

DISCULP'ATED, *pp.* Cleared from blame; exculpated.

DISCULP'ATING, *ppr.* Freeing from blame; excusing.

DISCUM'BENCY, *n.* [L. *discumbens.* See *Discubitory.*]
The act of leaning at meat, according to the manner of the ancients. *Brown.*

DISCUM'BER, *v. t.* [*dis* and *cumber.*] To unburden; to throw off any thing cumbersome; to disengage from any troublesome weight, or impediment; to disencumber. [*The latter is generally used.*] *Pope.*

DISCU'RE, *v. t.* To discover; to reveal. [*Not used.*] *Spenser.*

DISCUR'RENT, *a.* Not current. [*Not used.*] *Sandys.*

DISCUR'SION, *n.* [L. *discurro; dis* and *curro,* to run.] A running or rambling about. *Bailey.*

DISCURS'IST, *n.* [See *Discourse.*] A disputer. [*Not in use.*] *L. Addison.*

DISCURS'IVE, *a.* [Sp. *discursivo,* from L. *discurro,* supra.] Moving or roving about; desultory. *Bacon.*

2. Argumentative; reasoning; proceeding regularly from premises to consequences; sometimes written *discoursive.* Whether brutes have a kind of *discursive* faculty. *Hale.*

DISCURS'IVELY, *adv.* Argumentatively; in the form of reasoning or argument. *Hale.*

DISCURS'IVENESS, *n.* Range or gradation of argument.

DISCURS'ORY, *a.* Argumental; rational. *Johnson.*

DISC'US, *n.* [L. See Eng. *Dish* and *Disk.*]

1. A quoit; a piece of iron, copper or stone, to be thrown in play; *used by the ancients.*

2. In *botany,* the middle plain part of a radiated compound flower, generally consisting of small florets, with a hollow regular petal, as in the marigold and daisy. *Bailey. Encyc.*

3. The face or surface of the sun or moon. [See *Disk.*]

DISCUSS', *v. t.* [L. *discutio, discussum; dis* and *quatio;* Fr. *discuter;* Sp. *discutir. Quatio* may be allied to *quasso,* and to *cudo* and *cædo,* to strike. See Class Gs. No. 17. 28. 68. 79. and Class Gd. No. 38. 40. 76.]
Literally, to drive; to beat or to shake in pieces; to separate by beating or shaking.

1. To disperse; to scatter; to dissolve; to repel; as, to *discuss* a tumor; *a medical use of the word.*

2. To debate; to agitate by argument; to clear of objections and difficulties, with a view to find or illustrate truth; to sift; to examine by disputation; to ventilate; to reason on, for the purpose of separating truth from falsehood. We *discuss* a subject, a point, a problem, a question, the propriety, expedience or justice of a measure, &c.

3. To break in pieces. [*The primary sense, but not used.*] *Brown.*

4. To shake off. [*Not in use.*] *Spenser.*

DISCUSS'ED, *pp.* Dispersed; dissipated; debated; agitated; argued.

DISCUSS'ER, *n.* One who discusses; one who sifts or examines.

DISCUSS'ING, *ppr.* Dispersing; resolving; scattering; debating; agitating; examining by argument.

DISCUSS'ING, *n.* Discussion; examination.

DISCUS'SION, *n.* In *surgery,* resolution; the dispersion of a tumor or any coagulated matter. *Coxe. Wiseman.*

2. Debate; disquisition; the agitation of a point or subject with a view to elicit truth; the treating of a subject by argument, to clear it of difficulties, and separate truth from falsehood.

DISCUSS'IVE, *a.* Having the power to discuss, resolve or disperse tumors or coagulated matter.

DISCUSS'IVE, *n.* A medicine that discusses; a discutient.

DISCU'TIENT, *a.* [L. *discutiens.*] Discussing; dispersing morbid matter.

DISCU'TIENT, *n.* A medicine or application which disperses a tumor or any coagulated fluid in the body; sometimes it is equivalent to *carminative.* *Coxe.*

DISDA'IN, *v. t.* [Fr. *dedaigner;* Sp. *desdeñar;* It. *sdegnare;* Port. *desdenhar;* L. *dedignor; de, dis,* and *dignor,* to think worthy; *dignus,* worthy. See *Dignity.*]
To think unworthy; to deem worthless; to consider to be unworthy of notice, care, regard, esteem, or unworthy of one's character; to scorn; to contemn. The man of elevated mind *disdains* a mean action; he *disdains* the society of profligate, worthless men; he *disdains* to corrupt the innocent, or insult the weak. Goliath *disdained* David.

> Whose fathers I would have *disdained* to set with the dogs of my flock. Job xxx.

DISDA'IN, *n.* Contempt; scorn; a passion excited in noble minds, by the hatred or detestation of what is mean and dishonorable, and implying a consciousness of superiority of mind, or a supposed superiority. In ignoble minds, *disdain* may spring from unwarrantable pride or haughtiness, and be directed toward objects of worth. It implies hatred, and sometimes anger.

> How my soul is moved with just *disdain.* *Pope.*

DISDA'INED, *pp.* Despised; contemned; scorned.

DISDA'INFUL, *a.* Full of disdain; as *disdainful* soul.

2. Expressing disdain; as a *disdainful* look.

3. Contemptuous; scornful; haughty; indignant. *Hooker. Dryden.*

DISDA'INFULLY, *adv.* Contemptuously; with scorn; in a haughty manner. *South.*

DISDA'INFULNESS, *n.* Contempt; contemptuousness; haughty scorn. *Sidney.*

DISDA'INING, *ppr.* Contemning; scorning.

DISDA'INING, *n.* Contempt; scorn.

DISDIACLAS'TIC, *a.* An epithet given by Bartholine and others to a substance supposed to be crystal, but which is a fine pellucid spar, called also Iceland crystal, and by Dr. Hill, from its shape, *parallelopipedum.* *Encyc.*

DISDIAPA'SON, BISDIAPA'SON, *n.* [See *Diapason.*]
In *music,* a compound concord in the quadruple ratio of 4 : 1 or 8 : 2.
Disdiapason diapente, a concord in a sextuple ratio of 1 : 6.
Disdiapason semi-diapente, a compound concord in the proportion of 16 : 3.
Disdiapason ditone, a compound consonance in the proportion of 10 : 2.
Disdiapason semi-ditone, a compound concord in the proportion of 24 : 5. *Encyc.*

DISE'ASE, *n. dize'ze.* [*dis* and *ease.*] In *its primary sense,* pain, uneasiness, distress, and so used by Spenser; but in this sense, obsolete.

2. The cause of pain or uneasiness; distemper; malady; sickness; disorder; any state of a living body in which the natural functions of the organs are interrupted or disturbed, either by defective or preternatural action, without a disrupture of parts by violence, which is called a *wound.* The first effect of disease is uneasiness or pain, and the ultimate effect is death. A disease may affect the whole body, or a particular limb or part of the body. We say, a *diseased* limb; a *disease* in the head or stomach; and such partial affection of the body is called a *local* or *topical disease.* The word is also applied to the disorders of other animals, as well as to those of man; and to any derangement of the vegetative functions of plants.

> The shafts of *disease* shoot across our path in such a variety of courses, that the atmosphere of human life is darkened by their number, and the escape of an individual becomes almost miraculous. *Buckminster.*

3. A disordered state of the mind or intellect, by which the reason is impaired.

4. In *society,* vice; corrupt state of morals. Vices are called *moral diseases.*

> A wise man converses with the wicked, as a physician with the sick, not to catch the *disease,* but to cure it. *Maxim of Antisthenes.*

5. Political or civil disorder, or vices in a state; any practice which tends to disturb the peace of society, or impede or prevent the regular administration of government.

> The instability, injustice and confusion introduced into the public councils have, in truth, been the mortal *diseases* under which popular governments have every where perished. *Federalist, Madison.*

DISE'ASE, *v. t. dize'ze.* To interrupt or impair any or all the natural and regular functions of the several organs of a living body; to afflict with pain or sickness; to make morbid; used chiefly in the passive participle, as a *diseased* body, a *diseased* stomach; but *diseased* may here be considered as an adjective.

2. To interrupt or render imperfect the regular functions of the brain, or of the intellect; to disorder; to derange.

3. To infect; to communicate disease to, by contagion.

4. To pain; to make uneasy. *Locke.*

DISE'ASED, *pp.* or *a. dize'zed.* Disordered; distempered; sick.

DISE'ASEDNESS, *n. dize'zedness.* The state of being diseased; a morbid state; sickness. *Burnet.*

DISE'ASEFUL, *a. dize'zeful.* Abounding with disease; producing diseases; as a *diseaseful* climate.

2. Occasioning uneasiness.

DISE'ASEMENT, *n. dize'zement.* Uneasiness; inconvenience. *Bacon.*

DISEDG'ED, *a.* [*dis* and *edge.*] Blunted; made dull. *Shak.*

DISEMB'ARK, *v. t.* [*Dis* and *embark;* Fr. *desembarquer.*]
To land; to debark; to remove from on

board a ship to the land; to put on shore; applied particularly to the landing of troops and military apparatus; as, the general *disembarked* the troops at sun-rise.

DISEMB'ARK, *v. i.* To land; to debark; to quit a ship for residence or action on shore; as, the light infantry and cavalry *disembarked*, and marched to meet the enemy.

DISEMB'ARKED, *pp.* Landed; put on shore.

DISEMB'ARKING, *ppr.* Landing; removing from on board a ship to land.

DISEMB'ARKMENT, *n.* The act of disembarking.

DISEMBAR'RASS, *v. t.* [*dis* and *embarrass.*] To free from embarrassment or perplexity; to clear; to extricate. *Mason.*

DISEMBAR'RASSED, *pp.* Freed from embarrassment; extricated from difficulty.

DISEMBAR'RASSING, *ppr.* Freeing from embarrassment or perplexity; extricating.

DISEMBAR'RASSMENT, *n.* The act of extricating from perplexity.

DISEMBA'Y, *v. t.* To clear from a bay. *Sherburne.*

DISEMBIT'TER, *v. t.* [*dis* and *embitter.*] To free from bitterness; to clear from acrimony; to render sweet or pleasant. *Addison*

DISEMBOD'IED, *a.* [*dis* and *embodied.*] Divested of the body; as *disembodied* spirits or souls.

2. Separated; discharged from keeping in a body. *Militia Act. Geo. III.*

DISEMBOD'Y, *v. t.* To divest of body; to free from flesh.

2. To discharge from military array.

DISEMBO'GUE, *v. t. disembōg.* [*dis* and the root of Fr. *bouche*, mouth. The French has *emboucher* and *debouquer*. Sp. *boca*, mouth, Port. *id.*, It. *bocca*. See *Voice.*]

To pour out or discharge at the mouth, as a stream; to vent; to discharge into the ocean or a lake.

> Rolling down, the steep Timavus raves,
> And through nine channels *disembogues* his waves. *Addison.*

DISEMBO'GUE, *v. i.* To flow out at the mouth, as a river; to discharge waters into the ocean, or into a lake. Innumerable rivers *disembogue* into the ocean.

2. To pass out of a gulf or bay.

DISEMBO'GUEMENT, *n.* Discharge of waters into the ocean or a lake. *Mease.*

DISEMBŌSOM, *v. t.* To separate from the bosom. *Young.*

DISEMBOW'EL, *v. t.* [*dis* and *embowel.*] To take out the bowels; to take or draw from the bowels, as the web of a spider.

DISEMBOW'ELED, *pp.* Taken or drawn from the bowels.

> *Disemboweled* web. *Philips.*

DISEMBOW'ELING *ppr.* Taking or drawing from the bowels.

DISEMBRAN'GLE, *v. t.* To free from litigation. [*Not used.*]

DISEMBROIL', *v. t.* [*dis* and *embroil.*] To disentangle; to free from perplexity; to extricate from confusion. *Dryden. Addison.*

DISEMBROIL'ED, *pp.* Disentangled; cleared from perplexity or confusion.

DISEMBROIL'ING, *ppr.* Disentangling; freeing from confusion.

DISENA'BLE, *v. t.* [*dis* and *enable.*] To deprive of power, natural or moral; to disable; to deprive of ability or means. A man may be *disenabled* to walk by lameness; and by poverty he is *disenabled* to support his family.

DISENA'BLED, *pp.* Deprived of power, ability or means.

DISENA'BLING, *ppr.* Depriving of power, ability or means.

DISENCH'ANT, *v. t.* [*dis* and *enchant.*] To free from enchantment; to deliver from the power of charms or spells.

> Haste to thy work; a noble stroke or two
> Ends all the charms, and *disenchants* the grove. *Dryden.*

DISENCH'ANTED, *pp.* Delivered from enchantment, or the power of charms.

DISENCH'ANTING, *ppr.* Freeing from enchantment, or the influence of charms.

DISENCUM'BER, *v. t.* [*dis* and *encumber.*] To free from encumbrance; to deliver from clogs and impediments; to disburden; as, to *disencumber* troops of their baggage; to *disencumber* the soul of its body of clay; to *disencumber* the mind of its cares and griefs.

2. To free from any obstruction; to free from any thing heavy or unnecessary; as a *disencumbered* building. *Addison.*

DISENCUM'BERED, *pp.* Freed from incumbrance.

DISENCUM'BERING, *ppr.* Freeing from incumbrance.

DISENCUM'BRANCE, *n.* Freedom or deliverance from incumbrance, or any thing burdensome or troublesome. *Spectator.*

DISENGA'GE, *v. t.* [*dis* and *engage.*] To separate, as a substance from any thing with which it is in union; to free; to loose; to liberate; as, to *disengage* a metal from extraneous substances.

> Caloric and light must be *disengaged* during the process. *Lavoisier.*

2. To separate from that to which one adheres, or is attached; as, to *disengage* a man from a party.

3. To disentangle; to extricate; to clear from impediments, difficulties or perplexities; as, to *disengage* one from broils or controversies.

4. To detach; to withdraw; to wean; as, to *disengage* the heart or affections from earthly pursuits.

5. To free from any thing that commands the mind, or employs the attention; as, to *disengage* the mind from study; to *disengage* one's self from business.

6. To release or liberate from a promise or obligation; to set free by dissolving an engagement; as, the men, who were enlisted, are now *disengaged*; the lady, who had promised to give her hand in marriage, is *disengaged.*

Let it be observed that *disengaged* properly implies previous engagement; and is not to be confounded with *unengaged*, which does not always imply prior engagement. This distinction is sometimes carelessly overlooked.

DISENGA'GED, *pp.* Separated; detached; set free; released; disjoined; disentangled.

2. *a.* Vacant; being at leisure; not particularly occupied; not having the attention confined to a particular object. [This word is thus used by mistake for *unengaged, not engaged.*]

DISENGA'GEDNESS, *n.* The quality or state of being disengaged; freedom from connection; disjunction.

2. Vacuity of attention.

DISENGA'GEMENT, *n.* A setting free; separation; extrication.

> It is easy to render this *disengagement* of caloric and light evident to the senses. *Lavoisier.*

2. The act of separating or detaching.

3. Liberation or release from obligation.

4. Freedom from attention; vacancy; leisure.

DISENGA'GING, *ppr.* Separating; loosing; setting free; detaching; liberating; releasing from obligation.

DISENNO'BLE, *v. t.* To deprive of title, or of that which ennobles. *Guardian.*

DISENRŌLL, *v. i.* To erase from a roll or list. *Donne.*

DISENSLA'VE, *v. t.* To free from bondage. *South.*

DISENTAN'GLE, *v. t.* [*dis* and *entangle.*]

1. To unravel; to unfold; to untwist; to loose, separate or disconnect things which are interwoven, or united without order; as, to *disentangle* net-work; to *disentangle* a skain of yarn.

2. To free; to extricate from perplexity; to disengage from complicated concerns; to set free from impediments or difficulties; as, to *disentangle* one's self from business, from political affairs, or from the cares and temptations of life.

3. To disengage; to separate.

DISENTAN'GLED, *pp.* Freed from entanglement; extricated.

DISENTAN'GLING, *ppr.* Freeing from entanglement; extricating.

DISENTER'. [See *Disinter.*]

DISENTHRO'NE, *v. t.* [*dis* and *enthrone.*] To dethrone; to depose from sovereign authority; as, to *disenthrone* a king. *Milton.*

DISENTHRO'NED, *pp.* Deposed; deprived of sovereign power.

DISENTHRO'NING, *ppr.* Deposing; depriving of royal authority.

DISENTI'TLE, *v. t.* To deprive of title. *South.*

DISENTR'ANCE, *v. t.* [*dis* and *entrance.*] To awaken from a trance, or from deep sleep; to arouse from a reverie. *Hudibras.*

DISENTR'ANCED, *pp.* Awakened from a trance, sleep or reverie.

DISENTR'ANCING, *ppr.* Arousing from a trance, sleep or reverie.

DISESPOUSE, *v. t. disespouz'.* [*dis* and *espouse.*]

To separate after espousal or plighted faith; to divorce. *Milton.*

DISESPOUS'ED, *pp.* Separated after espousal; released from obligation to marry.

DISESPOUS'ING, *ppr.* Separating after plighted faith.

DISESTEE'M, *n.* [*dis* and *esteem.*] Want of esteem; slight dislike; disregard. It expresses less than *hatred* or *contempt.* *Locke.*

DISESTEE'M, *v. t.* To dislike in a moderate degree; to consider with disregard, disapprobation, dislike or slight contempt; to slight.

But if this sacred gift you *disesteem*. *Denham.*

DISESTEE'MED, *pp.* Disliked; slighted.

DISESTEE'MING, *ppr.* Disliking; slighting.

DISESTIMA'TION, *n.* Disesteem; bad repute.

DISEX'ERCISE, *v. t.* To deprive of exercise. [*A bad word.*] *Milton.*

DISFAN'CY, *v. t.* To dislike. [*Not used.*] *Hammond.*

DISFA'VOR, *n.* [*dis* and *favor.*] Dislike; slight displeasure; discountenance; unfavorable regard; disesteem; as, the conduct of the minister incurred the *disfavor* of his sovereign.

2. A state of unacceptableness; a state in which one is not esteemed or favored, or not patronized, promoted or befriended; as, to be in *disfavor* at court.

3. An ill or disobliging act; as, no generous man will do a *disfavor* to the meanest of his species.

DISFA'VOR, *v. t.* To discountenance; to withdraw or withhold from one, kindness, friendship or support; to check or oppose by disapprobation; as, let the man be countenanced or *disfavored*, according to his merits.

DISFA'VORED, *pp.* Discountenanced; not favored.

DISFA'VORER, *n.* One who discountenances. *Bacon.*

DISFA'VORING, *ppr.* Discountenancing.

DISFIGURA'TION, *n.* [See *Disfigure.*] The act of disfiguring, or marring external form.

2. The state of being disfigured; some degree of deformity.

DISFIG'URE, *v. t.* [*dis* and *figure.*] To change to a worse form; to mar external figure; to impair shape or form and render it less perfect and beautiful; as, the loss of a limb *disfigures* the body.

2. To mar; to impair; to injure beauty, symmetry or excellence.

DISFIG'URED, *pp.* Changed to a worse form; impaired in form or appearance.

DISFIG'UREMENT, *n.* Change of external form to the worse; defacement of beauty. *Milton. Suckling.*

DISFIG'URER, *n.* One who disfigures.

DISFIG'URING, *ppr.* Injuring the form or shape; impairing the beauty of form.

DISFOREST. [See *Disafforest.*]

DISFRAN'CHISE, *v. t.* [*dis* and *franchise.*] To deprive of the rights and privileges of a free citizen; to deprive of chartered rights and immunities; to deprive of any franchise, as of the right of voting in elections, &c. *Blackstone.*

DISFRAN'CHISED, *pp.* Deprived of the rights and privileges of a free citizen, or of some particular franchise.

DISFRAN'CHISEMENT, *n.* The act of disfranchising, or depriving of the privileges of a free citizen, or of some particular immunity.

DISFRAN'CHISING, *ppr.* Depriving of the privileges of a free citizen, or of some particular immunity.

DISFRI'AR, *v. t.* [*dis* and *friar.*] To deprive of the state of a friar. [*Not used.*] *Sandys.*

DISFUR'NISH, *v. t.* [*dis* and *furnish.*] To deprive of furniture; to strip of apparatus, habiliments or equipage. *Shak. Knolles.*

DISFUR'NISHED, *pp.* Deprived of furniture; stripped of apparatus.

DISFUR'NISHING, *ppr.* Depriving of furniture or apparatus.

DISGAL'LANT, *v. t.* To deprive of gallantry. [*Not used.*] *B. Jonson.*

DISG'ARNISH, *v. t.* [*dis* and *garnish.*] To divest of garniture or ornaments.

2. To deprive of a garrison, guns and military apparatus; to degarnish.

DISGAR'RISON, *v. t.* To deprive of a garrison. *Hewyt.*

DISGAV'EL, *v. t.* [See *Gavelkind.*] To take away the tenure of gavelkind. *Blackstone.*

DISGAV'ELED, *pp.* Deprived of the tenure by gavelkind.

DISGAV'ELING, *ppr.* Taking away tenure by gavelkind. *Blackstone.*

DISGLO'RIFY, *v. t.* [*dis* and *glorify.*] To deprive of glory; to treat with indignity. The participle *disglorified* is used by Milton; but the word is little used.

DISGORGE, *v. t.* *disgorj'.* [Fr. *degorger; de, dis,* and *gorge*, the throat.]

1. To eject or discharge from the stomach, throat or mouth; to vomit.

2. To throw out with violence; to discharge violently or in great quantities from a confined place. Thus, volcanoes are said to *disgorge* streams of burning lava, ashes and stones. Milton's infernal rivers *disgorge* their streams into a burning lake.

DISGORG'ED, *pp.* Ejected; discharged from the stomach or mouth; thrown out with violence and in great quantities.

DISGORGEMENT, *n.* *disgorj'ment.* The act of disgorging; a vomiting. *Hall.*

DISGORG'ING, *ppr.* Discharging from the throat or mouth; vomiting; ejecting with violence and in great quantities.

DISGOS'PEL, *v. i.* [*dis* and *gospel.*] To differ from the precepts of the gospel. [*Not used.*] *Milton.*

DISGRA'CE, *n.* [*dis* and *grace.*] A state of being out of favor; disfavor; disesteem; as, the minister retired from court in *disgrace.*

2. State of ignominy; dishonor; shame.

3. Cause of shame; as, to turn the back to the enemy is a foul *disgrace;* every vice is a *disgrace* to a rational being.

4. Act of unkindness. [*Not used.*] *Sidney.*

DISGRA'CE, *v. t.* To put out of favor; as, the minister was *disgraced.*

2. To bring a reproach on; to dishonor; as *an agent.* Men are apt to take pleasure in *disgracing* an enemy and his performances.

3. To bring to shame; to dishonor; to sink in estimation; as *a cause;* as, men often boast of actions which *disgrace* them.

DISGRA'CED, *pp.* Put out of favor; brought under reproach; dishonored.

DISGRA'CEFUL, *a.* Shameful; reproachful; dishonorable; procuring shame; sinking reputation. Cowardice is *disgraceful* to a soldier. Intemperance and profaneness are *disgraceful* to a man, but more *disgraceful* to a woman.

DISGRA'CEFULLY, *adv.* With disgrace.

The senate have cast you forth *disgracefully.* *B. Jonson.*

2. Shamefully; reproachfully; ignominiously; in a disgraceful manner; as, the troops fled *disgracefully.*

DISGRA'CEFULNESS, *n.* Ignominy; shamefulness.

DISGRA'CER, *n.* One who disgraces; one who exposes to disgrace; one who brings into disgrace, shame or contempt.

DISGRA'CING, *ppr.* Bringing reproach on: dishonoring.

DISGRA'CIOUS, *a.* [*dis* and *gracious.*] Ungracious; unpleasing. *Shak.*

DIS'GREGATE, *v. t.* To separate; to disperse. [*Little used.*] *More.*

DISGUI'SE, *v. t.* *disgi'ze.* [Fr. *deguiser; de, dis,* and *guise*, manner.]

1. To conceal by an unusual habit, or mask. Men sometimes *disguise* themselves for the purpose of committing crimes without danger of detection. They *disguise* their faces in a masquerade.

2. To hide by a counterfeit appearance; to cloke by a false show, by false language, or an artificial manner; as, to *disguise* anger, sentiments or intentions.

3. To disfigure; to alter the form, and exhibit an unusual appearance.

They saw the faces, which too well they knew,
Though then *disguised* in death. *Dryden.*

4. To disfigure or deform by liquor; to intoxicate. *Spectator.*

DISGUI'SE, *n.* A counterfeit habit; a dress intended to conceal the person who wears it.

By the laws of England, persons doing unlawful acts in *disguise* are subjected to heavy penalties, and in some cases, declared felons.

2. A false appearance; a counterfeit show; an artificial or assumed appearance intended to deceive the beholder.

A treacherous design is often concealed under the *disguise* of great candor.

3. Change of manner by drink; intoxication. *Shak.*

DISGUI'SED, *pp.* Concealed by a counterfeit habit or appearance; intoxicated.

DISGUI'SEMENT, *n.* Dress of concealment; false appearance.

DISGUI'SER, *n.* One who disguises himself or another.

2. He or that which disfigures.

DISGUI'SING, *ppr.* Concealing by a counterfeit dress, or by a false show; intoxicating.

DISGUI'SING, *n.* The act of giving a false appearance.

2. Theatrical mummery or masking.

DISGUST', *n.* [Fr. *degoût; de, dis,* and *goût*, taste, L. *gustus.*]

1. Disrelish; distaste; aversion to the taste of food or drink; an unpleasant sensation excited in the organs of taste by something disagreeable, and when extreme, producing loathing or nausea.

2. Dislike; aversion; an unpleasant sensation in the mind excited by something offensive in the manners, conduct, language or opinions of others. Thus, obscenity in language and clownishness in behavior excite *disgust.*

DISGUST', *v. t.* To excite aversion in the stomach; to offend the taste.

2. To displease; to offend the mind or moral taste; with *at* or *with;* as, to be *disgusted at* foppery, or *with* vulgar manners. To *disgust from* is unusual and hardly legitimate.

DISGUST'ED, *pp.* Displeased; offended.

DISGUST'FUL, *a.* Offensive to the taste; nauseous; exciting aversion in the natural or moral taste.

DISGUST'ING, *ppr.* Provoking aversion; offending the taste.

2. *a.* Provoking dislike; odious; hateful; as *disgusting* servility.

DISGUST'INGLY, *adv.* In a manner to give disgust. *Swinburne.*

DISH, *n.* [Sax. *disc*, a dish, and *dixas*, dishes; L. *discus*; Gr. δισχος; Fr. *disque*; Arm. *disg*; W. *dysgyl*; Sp. It. *disco.* It is the same word as *disk* and *desk*, and seems to signify something flat, plain or extended.]

1. A broad open vessel, made of various materials, used for serving up meat and various kinds of food at the table. It is sometimes used for a deep hollow vessel for liquors. *Addison. Milton.*

2. The meat or provisions served in a dish. Hence, any particular kind of food.

I have here a *dish* of doves. *Shak.*

We say, a *dish* of veal or venison; a cold *dish*; a warm *dish*; a delicious *dish*.

3. Among *miners*, a trough in which ore is measured, about 28 inches long, 4 deep and 6 wide. *Encyc.*

DISH, *v. t.* To put in a dish; as, the meat is all *dished*, and ready for the table.

DISH'-CLOTH, } *n.* A cloth used for washing and wiping dishes. *Swift.*
DISH'-CLOUT,

DISH'-WASHER, *n.* The name of a bird, the mergus. *Johnson.*

DISH'-WATER, *n.* Water in which dishes are washed.

DISHABILLE, } *n.* [Fr. *deshabillé*; *des* and *habiller*, to dress. See *Habit.*]
DISHABIL',

An undress; a loose negligent dress for the morning. But see *Deshabille*, the French and more correct orthography.

Dryden uses the word as a participle. "Queens are not to be too negligently dressed or *dishabille*." In this use, he is not followed.

DISHAB'IT, *v. t.* To drive from a habitation. [*Not in use.*] *Shak.*

DISHARMO'NIOUS, *a.* Incongruous. [See *Unharmonious.*] *Hallywell.*

DISHAR'MONY, *n.* [*dis* and *harmony.*] Want of harmony; discord; incongruity. [*Not used.*]

DISHEARTEN, *v. t.* *dishart'n.* [*dis* and *heart.*]

To discourage; to deprive of courage; to depress the spirits; to deject; to impress with fear; as, it is weakness to be *disheartened* by small obstacles.

DISHEARTENED, *pp.* *dishart'ned.* Discouraged; depressed in spirits; cast down.

DISHEARTENING, *ppr.* *dishart'ning.* Discouraging; depressing the spirits.

DISH'ED, *pp.* Put in a dish or dishes.

DISHEIR, *v. t.* *diza're.* To debar from inheriting. [*Not in use.*] *Dryden.*

DISHER'ISON, *n.* [See *Disherit.*] The act of disinheriting, or cutting off from inheritance. *Bp. Hall.*

DISHER'IT, *v. t.* [Fr. *desheriter*; *des*, *dis*, and *heriter*; Arm. *diserita*; It. *diseredare*; Sp. *desheredar.* See *Heir.*]

To disinherit; to cut off from the possession or enjoyment of an inheritance. [See *Disinherit*, which is more generally used.]

DISHER'ITANCE, *n.* The state of disheriting or of being disinherited. *Beaum.*

DISHER'ITED, *pp.* Cut off from an inheritance or hereditary succession.

DISHER'ITING, *ppr.* Cutting off from an inheritance. *Spenser.*

DISHEV'EL, *v. t.* [Fr. *decheveler*; *de*, *dis*, and *cheveu*, hair, *chevelu*, hairy, L. *capillus.* Class Gb.]

To spread the hair loosely; to suffer the hair of the head to hang negligently, and to flow without confinement; *used chiefly in the passive participle.*

DISHEV'EL, *v. i.* To spread in disorder. *Herbert.*

DISHEV'ELED, *pp.* or *a.* Hanging loosely and negligently without confinement; flowing in disorder; as *disheveled* locks.

DISHEV'ELING, *ppr.* Spreading loosely.

DISH'ING, *ppr.* [See *Dish.*] Putting in a dish or dishes.

2. *a.* Concave; having the hollow form of a dish. *Mortimer.*

DISHON'EST, *a.* *dizon'est.* [*dis* and *honest.*]

1. Void of honesty; destitute of probity, integrity or good faith; faithless; fraudulent; knavish; having or exercising a disposition to deceive, cheat and defraud; *applied to persons*; as a *dishonest* man.

2. Proceeding from fraud or marked by it; fraudulent; knavish; as a *dishonest* transaction.

3. Disgraced; dishonored; *from the sense in Latin.*

Dishonest with lopped arms the youth appears. *Dryden.*

4. Disgraceful; ignominious; *from the Latin sense.*

Inglorious triumphs, and *dishonest* scars. *Pope.*

5. Unchaste; lewd. *Shak.*

DISHON'ESTLY, *adv.* *dizon'estly.* In a dishonest manner; without good faith, probity or integrity; with fraudulent views; knavishly. *Shak.*

2. Lewdly; unchastely. *Ecclesiasticus.*

DISHON'ESTY, *n.* *dizon'esty.* Want of probity, or integrity in principle; faithlessness; a disposition to cheat or defraud, or to deceive and betray; *applied to persons.*

2. Violation of trust or of justice; fraud; treachery; any deviation from probity or integrity; *applied to acts.*

3. Unchastity; incontinence; lewdness. *Shak.*

4. Deceit; wickedness; shame. 2 Cor. iv.

DISHON'OR, *n.* *dizon'or.* [*dis* and *honor.*] Reproach; disgrace; ignominy; shame; whatever constitutes a stain or blemish in the reputation.

It was not meet for us to see the king's *dishonor.* Ezra iv.

It may express less than *ignominy* and *infamy.*

DISHON'OR, *v. t.* To disgrace; to bring reproach or shame on; to stain the character of; to lessen reputation. The duelist *dishonors* himself to maintain his honor.

The impunity of the crimes of great men *dishonors* the administration of the laws.

2. To treat with indignity. *Dryden.*

3. To violate the chasity of; to debauch. *Dryden.*

DISHON'ORABLE, *a.* Shameful; reproachful; base; vile; bringing shame on; staining the character, and lessening reputation. Every act of meanness, and every vice is *dishonorable.*

2. Destitute of honor; as a *dishonorable* man.

3. In a state of neglect or disesteem.

He that is *dishonorable* in riches, how much more in poverty? *Ecclesiasticus.*

DISHON'ORABLY, *adv.* Reproachfully; in a dishonorable manner.

DISHON'ORARY, *a.* *dizon'orary.* Bringing dishonor on; tending to disgrace; lessening reputation. *Holmes.*

DISHON'ORED, *pp.* Disgraced; brought into disrepute.

DISHON'ORER, *n.* One who dishonors or disgraces; one who treats another with indignity. *Milton.*

DISHON'ORING, *ppr.* Disgracing; bringing into disrepute; treating with indignity.

DISHORN', *v. t.* [*dis* and *horn.*] To deprive of horns. *Shak.*

DISHORN'ED, *pp.* Stripped of horns.

DISHU'MOR, *n.* [*dis* and *humor.*] Peevishness; ill humor. [*Little used.*] *Spectator.*

DISIMPARK', *v. t.* [*dis*, *in* and *park.*] To free from the barriers of a park; to free from restraints or seclusion. [*Little used.*] *Spectator.*

DISIMPRÖVEMENT, *n.* [*dis* and *improvement.*]

Reduction from a better to a worse state; the contrary to *improvement* or *melioration*; as the *disimprovement* of the earth. [*Little used.*] *Norris. Swift.*

DISINC'ARCERATE, *v. t.* [*dis* and *incarcerate.*]

To liberate from prison; to set free from confinement. [*Not much used.*] *Harvey.*

DISINCLINA'TION, *n.* [*dis* and *inclination.*]

Want of inclination; want of propensity, desire or affection; slight dislike; aversion; expressing less than hate.

Disappointment gave him a *disinclination* to the fair sex. *Arbuthnot.*

DISINCLI'NE, *v. t.* [*dis* and *incline.*] To excite dislike or slight aversion; to make disaffected; to alienate from. His timidity *disinclined* him from such an arduous enterprise.

DISINCLI'NED, *pp.* Not inclined; averse.

DISINCLI'NING, *ppr.* Exciting dislike or slight aversion.

DISINCORP'ORATE, *v. t.* To deprive of corporate powers; to disunite a corporate body, or an established society. *Hume.*

2. To detach or separate from a corporation or society. *Bacon.*

DISINCORPORA'TION, *n.* Deprivation of the rights and privileges of a corporation. *Warton.*

DISINFECT', *v. t.* [*dis* and *infect.*] To cleanse from infection; to purify from contagious matter.

DISINFECT'ED, *pp.* Cleansed from infection.

DISINFECT'ING, *ppr.* Purifying from infection.

DISINFEC'TION, *n.* Purification from infecting matter. *Med. Repos.*

DISINGENU'ITY, *n.* [*dis* and *ingenuity.*] Meanness of artifice; unfairness; disingenuousness; want of candor. *Clarendon.*

[This word is little used, or not at all, in the sense here explained. See *Ingenuity.* We now use in lieu of it *disingenuousness.*]

DISINGEN'UOUS, *a.* [*dis* and *ingenuous.*] Unfair; not open, frank and candid; meanly artful; illiberal; *applied to persons.*

2. Unfair; meanly artful; unbecoming true honor and dignity; as *disingenuous* conduct; *disingenuous* schemes.

DISINGEN'UOUSLY, *adv.* In a disingenuous manner; unfairly; not openly and candidly; with secret management.

DISINGEN'UOUSNESS, *n.* Unfairness; want of candor; low craft; as the *disingenuousness* of a man, or of his mind.

2. Characterized by unfairness, as conduct or practices.

DISINHER'ISON, *n.* [*dis* and *inherit.*] The act of cutting off from hereditary succession; the act of disinheriting. *Bacon. Clarendon.*

2. The state of being disinherited. *Taylor.*

DISINHER'IT, *v. t.* [*dis* and *inherit.*] To cut off from hereditary right; to deprive of an inheritance; to prevent as an heir from coming into possession of any property or right, which, by law or custom, would devolve on him in the course of descent. A father sometimes *disinherits* his children by will. In England, the crown is descendible to the eldest son, who cannot be *disinherited* by the will of his father.

DISINHER'ITED, *pp.* Cut off from an inheritance.

DISINHER'ITING, *ppr.* Depriving of an hereditary estate or right.

DISIN'TEGRABLE, *a.* [*dis* and *integer.*] That may be separated into integrant parts; capable of disintegration.

Argillo-calcite is readily *disintegrable* by exposure to the atmosphere. *Kirwan.*

DISIN'TEGRATE, *v. t.* [*dis* and *integer.*] To separate the integrant parts of.

Marlites are not *disintegrated* by exposure to the atmosphere, at least in six years. *Kirwan.*

DISIN'TEGRATED, *pp.* Separated into integrant parts without chimical action.

DISINTEGRA'TION, *n.* The act of separating *integrant* parts of a substance, as distinguished from decomposition or the separation of *constituent* parts. *Kirwan.*

DISINTER', *v. t.* [*dis* and *inter.*] To take out of a grave, or out of the earth; as, to *disinter* a dead body that is buried.

2. To take out as from a grave; to bring from obscurity into view.

The philosopher—may be concealed in a plebeian, which a proper education might have *disinterred.* [*Unusual.*] *Addison.*

DISINTERESSED. } [See *Disinterest-*
DISINTERESSMENT. } *ed,* &c.]

DISIN'TEREST, *n.* [*dis* and *interest.*] What is contrary to the interest or advantage; disadvantage; injury. [*Little used or not at all.*] *Glanville.*

2. Indifference to profit; want of regard to private advantage. *Johnson.*

DISIN'TEREST, *v. t.* To disengage from private interest or personal advantage. [*Little used.*] *Feltham.*

DISIN'TERESTED, *a.* Uninterested; indifferent; free from self-interest; having no personal interest or private advantage in a question or affair. It is important that a judge should be perfectly *disinterested.*

2. Not influenced or dictated by private advantage; as a *disinterested* decision.

[This word is more generally used than *uninterested.*]

DISIN'TERESTEDLY, *adv.* In a disinterested manner.

DISIN'TERESTEDNESS, *n.* The state or quality of having no personal interest or private advantage in a question or event; freedom from bias or prejudice, on account of private interest; indifference. *Brown.*

DISIN'TERESTING, *a.* Uninteresting. [*The latter is the word now used.*]

DISINTER'MENT, *n.* The act of disinterring, or taking out of the earth.

DISINTER'RED, *pp.* Taken out of the earth or grave.

DISINTER'RING, *ppr.* Taking out of the earth, or out of a grave.

DISINTHRALL', *v. t.* [*dis* and *enthrall.*] To liberate from slavery, bondage or servitude; to free or rescue from oppression. *South.*

DISINTHRALL'ED, *pp.* Set free from bondage.

DISINTHRALL'ING, *ppr.* Delivering from slavery or servitude.

DISINTHRALL'MENT, *n.* Liberation from bondage; emancipation from slavery. *E. Nott.*

DISINU'RE, *v. t.* [*dis* and *inure.*] To deprive of familiarity or custom. *Milton.*

DISINVI'TE, *v. t.* To recall an invitation. *Finett.*

DISINVOLVE, *v. t.* *disinvolv'.* [*dis* and *involve.*] To uncover; to unfold or unroll; to disentangle. *More.*

DISJOIN', *v. t.* [*dis* and *join.*] To part; to disunite; to separate; to sunder.

DISJOIN'ED, *pp.* Disunited; separated.

DISJOIN'ING, *ppr.* Disuniting; severing.

DISJOINT', *v. t.* [*dis* and *joint.*] To separate a joint; to separate parts united by joints; as, to *disjoint* the limbs; to *disjoint* bones; to *disjoint* a fowl in carving.

2. To put out of joint; to force out of its socket; to dislocate.

3. To separate at junctures; to break at the part where things are united by cement; as *disjointed* columns.

4. To break in pieces; to separate united parts; as, to *disjoint* an edifice; the *disjointed* parts of a ship.

5. To break the natural order and relations of a thing; to make incoherent; as a *disjointed* speech.

DISJOINT', *v. i.* To fall in pieces. *Shak.*

DISJOINT', *a.* Disjointed. *Shak.*

DISJOINT'ED, *pp.* Separated at the joints; parted limb from limb; carved; put out of joint; not coherent.

DISJOINT'ING, *ppr.* Separating joints; disjoining limb from limb; breaking at the seams or junctures; rendering incoherent.

DISJOINT'LY, *adv.* In a divided state. *Sandys.*

DISJUDICA'TION, *n.* [L. *dijudicatio.*] Judgment; determination. [*Not used.*] *Boyle.*

DISJUNCT', *a.* [L. *disjunctus, disjungo*; *dis* and *jungo*, to join.] Disjoined; separated.

DISJUNC'TION, *n.* [L. *disjunctio.*] The act of disjoining; disunion; separation; a parting; as the *disjunction* of soul and body.

DISJUNC'TIVE, *a.* Separating; disjoining.

2. Incapable of union. [*Unusual.*] *Grew.*

3. In *grammar*, a *disjunctive* conjunction or connective, is a word which unites sentences or the parts of discourse in construction, but *disjoins* the sense, noting an alternative or opposition; as, I love him, *or* I fear him; I neither love him, *nor* fear him.

4. In *logic*, a *disjunctive proposition*, is one in which the parts are opposed to each other, by means of disjunctives; as, *it is either day or night.*

A *disjunctive syllogism*, is when the major proposition is *disjunctive*; as, *the earth moves in a circle, or an ellipsis*; but it does not move in a circle, therefore it moves in an ellipsis. *Watts.*

DISJUNC'TIVE, *n.* A word that disjoins, as *or, nor, neither.*

DISJUNC'TIVELY, *adv.* In a disjunctive manner; separately.

DISK, *n.* [L. *discus.* See *Dish* and *Desk.*] The body and face of the sun, moon or a planet, as it appears to us on the earth; or the body and face of the earth, as it appears to a spectator in the moon. *Newton. Dryden.*

2. A quoit; a piece of stone, iron or copper, inclining to an oval figure, which the ancients hurled by the help of a leathern thong tied round the person's hand, and put through a hole in the middle.

Some whirl the *disk*, and some the jav'lin dart. *Pope.*

3. In *botany*, the whole surface of a leaf; the central part of a radiate compound flower. *Martyn.*

DISKI'NDNESS, *n.* [*dis* and *kindness.*] Want of kindness; unkindness; want of affection.

2. Ill turn; injury; detriment. *Woodward.*

DISLI'KE, *n.* [*dis* and *like.*] Disapprobation; disinclination; displeasure; aversion; a moderate degree of hatred. A man shows his *dislike* to measures which he disapproves, to a proposal which he is disinclined to accept, and to food which he does not relish. All wise and good men manifest their *dislike* to folly.

2. Discord; disagreement. [*Not in use.*] *Fairfax.*

DISLI'KE, *v. t.* To disapprove; to regard with some aversion or displeasure. We *dislike* proceedings which we deem wrong; we *dislike* persons of evil habits; we *dislike* whatever gives us pain.

2. To disrelish; to regard with some disgust; as, to *dislike* particular kinds of food.

DISLI'KED, *pp.* Disapproved; disrelished.

DISLI'KEFUL, *a.* Disliking; disaffected. [*Not used.*] *Spenser.*

DISLI'KEN, *v. t.* To make unlike. *Shak.*

DISLI'KENESS, *n.* [*dis* and *likeness.*] Unlikeness; want of resemblance; dissimilitude. *Locke.*

DISLI'KER, *n.* One who disapproves, or disrelishes.

DISLI'KING, *ppr.* Disapproving; disrelishing.

DISLIMB', *v. t. dislim'.* To tear the limbs from. *Dict.*

DISLIMN', *v. t. dislim'.* To strike out of a picture. [*Not in use.*] *Shak.*

DIS'LOCATE, *v. t.* [*dis* and *locate*, L. *locus*, place; Fr. *disloquer*; It. *dislocare.*]

To displace; to put out of its proper place; particularly, to put out of joint; to disjoint; to move a bone from its socket, cavity or place of articulation.

DIS'LOCATED, *pp.* Removed from its proper place; put out of joint.

DIS'LOCATING, *ppr.* Putting out of its proper place or out of joint.

DISLOCA'TION, *n.* The act of moving from its proper place; particularly, the act of removing or forcing a bone from its socket; luxation. *Encyc.*

2. The state of being displaced. *Burnet.*

3. A joint displaced.

4. In *geology*, the displacement of parts of rocks, or portions of strata, from the situations which they originally occupied. *Cyc.*

DISLODGE, *v. t. dislodj'.* [*dis* and *lodge.*] To remove or drive from a lodge or place of rest; to drive from the place where a thing naturally rests or inhabits. Shells resting in the sea at a considerable depth, are not *dislodged* by storms.

2. To drive from a place of retirement or retreat; as, to *dislodge* a coney or a deer.

3. To drive from any place of rest or habitation, or from any station; as, to *dislodge* the enemy from their quarters, from a hill or wall.

4. To remove an army to other quarters. *Shak.*

DISLODGE, *v. i.* To go from a place of rest. *Milton.*

DISLODG'ED, *pp.* Driven from a lodge or place of rest; removed from a place of habitation, or from any station.

DISLODG'ING, *ppr.* Driving from a lodge, from a place of rest or retreat, or from any station.

DISLOY'AL, *a.* [*dis* and *loyal*; Fr. *deloyal*; Sp. *desleal.*]

1. Not true to allegiance; false to a sovereign; faithless; as a *disloyal* subject.

2. False; perfidious; treacherous; as a *disloyal* knave. *Shak.*

3. Not true to the marriage-bed. *Shak.*

4. False in love; not constant. *Johnson.*

DISLOY'ALLY, *adv.* In a disloyal manner; with violation of faith or duty to a sovereign; faithlessly; perfidiously.

DISLOY'ALTY, *n.* Want of fidelity to a sovereign; violation of allegiance, or duty to a prince or sovereign authority.

2. Want of fidelity in love. *Shak.*

DIS'MAL, *a.* s as z. [I am not satisfied with the etymologies of this word which I have seen.] Dark; gloomy; as a *dismal* shade.

2. Sorrowful; dire; horrid; melancholy; calamitous; unfortunate; as a *dismal* accident; *dismal* effects. *Milton.*

2. Frightful; horrible; as a *dismal* scream.

DIS'MALLY, *adv.* Gloomily; horribly; sorrowfully; uncomfortably.

DIS'MALNESS, *n.* Gloominess; horror.

DISMAN'TLE, *v. t.* [*dis* and *mantle*; Fr. *demanteler.*]

1. To deprive of dress; to strip; to divest. *South.*

2. To loose; to throw open. *Shak.*

3. More generally, to deprive or strip of apparatus, or furniture; to unrig; as, to *dismantle* a ship.

4. To deprive or strip of military furniture; as, to *dismantle* a fortress.

5. To deprive of outworks or forts; as, to *dismantle* a town.

6. To break down; as, his nose *dismantled.* *Dryden.*

DISMAN'TLED, *pp.* Divested; stripped of furniture; unrigged.

DISMAN'TLING, *ppr.* Stripping of dress; depriving of apparatus or furniture.

DISM'ASK, *v. t.* [*dis* and *mask*; Fr. *demasquer.*]

To strip off a mask; to uncover; to remove that which conceals. *Shak. Wotton.*

DISM'ASKED, *pp.* Divested of a mask; stripped of covering or disguise; uncovered.

DISM'ASKING, *ppr.* Stripping of a mask or covering.

DISM'AST, *v. t.* [*dis* and *mast*; Fr. *demâter.*]

To deprive of a mast or masts; to break and carry away the masts from; as, a storm *dismasted* the ship.

DISM'ASTED, *pp.* Deprived of a mast or masts.

DISM'ASTING, *ppr.* Stripping of masts.

DISM'ASTMENT, *n.* The act of dismasting; the state of being dismasted. *Marshall.*

DISMA'Y, *v. t.* [Sp. *desmayar*; Port. *desmaiar*; probably formed by *des* and the Teutonic *magan*, to be strong or able. The sense then is to deprive of strength. Sp. *desmayarse*, to faint; It. *smagarsi*, to despond.]

To deprive of that strength or firmness of mind which constitutes courage; to discourage; to dishearten; to sink or depress the spirits or resolution; hence, to affright or terrify.

> Be strong, and of a good courage; be not afraid, neither be thou *dismayed.* Josh. i.

DISMA'Y, *n.* [Sp. *desmayo*, Port. *desmaio*, a swoon or fainting fit.]

Fall or loss of courage; a sinking of the spirits; depression; dejection; a yielding to fear; that loss of firmness which is effected by fear or terror; fear impressed; terror felt.

> And each
> In other's countenance read his own *dismay.* *Milton.*

DISMA'YED, *pp.* Disheartened; deprived of courage.

DISMA'YEDNESS, *n.* A state of being dismayed; dejection of courage; dispiritedness. [*A useless word, and not used.*] *Sidney.*

DISMA'YING, *ppr.* Depriving of courage.

DISME, } *n.* [French.] A tenth part; a
DIME, } tithe. *Ayliffe.*

DISMEM'BER, *v. t.* [*dis* and *member.*] To divide limb from limb; to separate a member from the body; to tear or cut in pieces; to dilacerate; to mutilate.

> Fowls obscene *dismembered* his remains. *Pope.*

2. To separate a part from the main body; to divide; to sever; as, to *dismember* an empire, kingdom or republic. Poland was *dismembered* by the neighboring powers.

DISMEM'BERED, *pp.* Divided member from member; torn or cut in pieces; divided by the separation of a part from the main body.

DISMEM'BERING, *ppr.* Separating a limb or limbs from the body; dividing by taking a part or parts from the body.

DISMEM'BERING, *n.* Mutilation. *Blackstone.*

DISMEM'BERMENT, *n.* The act of severing a limb or limbs from the body; the act of tearing or cutting in pieces; mutilation; the act of severing a part from the main body; division; separation.

> He pointed out the danger of a *dismemberment* of the republic. *Hist. of Poland. Encyc.*

DISMET'TLED, *a.* Destitute of fire or spirit. [*Not much used.*] *Llewellyn.*

DISMISS', *v. t.* [L. *dimissus*, *dimitto*; *di*, *dis*, and *mitto*, to send; Fr. *demettre.*]

1. To send away; properly, to give leave of departure; to permit to depart; implying authority in a person to retain or keep. The town clerk *dismissed* the assembly. *Acts.*

2. To discard; to remove from office, service or employment. The king *dismisses* his ministers; the master *dismisses* his servant; and the employer, his workmen. Officers are *dismissed* from service, and students from college.

3. To send; to dispatch.

> He *dismissed* embassadors from Pekin to Tooshoo Loomboo. [*Improper.*] *Encyc.*

4. To send or remove from a docket; to discontinue; as, to *dismiss* a bill in chancery.

DISMISS', *n.* Discharge; dismission. [*Not used.*]

DISMISS'AL, *n.* Dismission.

DISMISS'ED, *pp.* Sent away; permitted to depart; removed from office or employment.

DISMISS'ING, *ppr.* Sending away; giving leave to depart; removing from office or service.

DISMIS'SION, *n.* [L. *dimissio.*] The act of sending away; leave to depart; as the *dismission* of the grand jury.

2. Removal from office or employment; discharge, either with honor or disgrace.

3. An act requiring departure. [*Not usual.*] *Shak.*

4. Removal of a suit in equity.

DISMISS'IVE, *a.* Giving dismission.

DISMORT'GAGE, *v. t. dismor'gage.* To redeem from mortgage. *Howell.*

DISMOUNT', *v. i.* [*dis* and *mount*; Fr. *demonter*; Sp. *desmontar*; It. *smontare.*]

1. To alight from a horse; to descend or get off, as a rider from a beast; as, the officer ordered his troops to *dismount.*

2. To descend from an elevation. *Spenser.*

DISMOUNT', *v. t.* To throw or remove from a horse; to unhorse; as, the soldier *dismounted* his adversary.

2. To throw or bring down from any elevation. *Sackville.*

3. To throw or remove cannon or other artillery from their carriages; or to break the carriages or wheels, and render guns useless.

DISMOUNT'ED, *pp.* Thrown from a horse, or from an elevation; unhorsed, or removed from horses by order; as *dismounted* troops. Applied to horses, it signifies unfit for service.

2. Thrown or removed from carriages.

DISMOUNT'ING, *ppr.* Throwing from a horse; unhorsing; removing from an elevation; throwing or removing from carriages.

DISNAT'URALIZE, *v. t.* To make alien; to deprive of the privileges of birth.

DISNA'TURED, *a.* Deprived or destitute of natural feelings; unnatural. *Shak.*

DISOBE'DIENCE, *n.* [*dis* and *obedience.*] Neglect or refusal to obey; violation of a command or prohibition; the omission of that which is commanded to be done, or the doing of that which is forbid; breach of duty prescribed by authority.

By one man's *disobedience,* many were made sinners. Rom. v.

2. Non-compliance.

This *disobedience* of the moon. *Blackmore.*

DISOBE'DIENT, *a.* Neglecting or refusing to obey; omitting to do what is commanded, or doing what is prohibited; refractory; not observant of duty or rules prescribed by authority; as children *disobedient* to parents; citizens *disobedient* to the laws.

I was not *disobedient* to the heavenly vision. Acts xxvi.

2. Not yielding to exciting force or power.

Medicines used unnecessarily contribute to shorten life, by sooner rendering peculiar parts of the system *disobedient* to stimuli. *Darwin.*

DISOBEY', *v. t.* [*dis* and *obey.*] To neglect or refuse to obey; to omit or refuse to do what is commanded, or to do what is forbid; to transgress or violate an order or injunction. Refractory children *disobey* their parents; men *disobey* their maker and the laws; and we all *disobey* the precepts of the gospel. [*The word is applicable both to the command and to the person commanding.*]

DISOBEY'ED, *pp.* Not obeyed; neglected; transgressed.

DISOBEY'ING, *ppr.* Omitting or refusing to obey; violating; transgressing, as authority or law.

DISOBLIGA'TION, *n.* [*dis* and *obligation.*] The act of disobliging; an offense; cause of disgust. *Clarendon.*

DISOB'LIGATORY, *a.* Releasing obligation. *K. Charles.*

DISOBLI'GE, *v. t.* [*dis* and *oblige.*] To do an act which contravenes the will or desires of another; to offend by an act of unkindness or incivility; to injure in a slight degree; *a term by which offense is tenderly expressed.*

My plan has given offense to some gentlemen, whom it would not be very safe to *disoblige.* *Addison.*

2. To release from obligation. [*Not used.*] *Bp. Hall.*

DISOBLI'GED, *pp.* Offended; slightly injured.

DISOBLI'GER, *n.* One who disobliges.

DISOBLI'GING, *ppr.* Offending; contravening the wishes of; injuring slightly.

2. *a.* Not obliging; not disposed to gratify the wishes of another; not disposed to please; unkind; offensive; unpleasing; unaccommodating; as a *disobliging* coachman.

DISOBLI'GINGLY, *adv.* In a disobliging manner; offensively.

DISOBLI'GINGNESS, *n.* Offensiveness; disposition to displease, or want of readiness to please.

DISOPIN'ION, *n.* Difference of opinion. [*A bad word and not used.*] *Bp. Reynolds.*

DISORB'ED, *a.* [*dis* and *orb.*] Thrown out of the proper orbit; as a star *disorbed.* *Shak.*

DISOR'DER, *n.* [*dis* and *order;* Fr. *desordre;* Sp. *desorden;* It. *disordine.*]

1. Want of order or regular disposition; irregularity; immethodical distribution; confusion; *a word of general application;* as, the troops were thrown into *disorder;* the papers are in *disorder.*

2. Tumult; disturbance of the peace of society; as, the city is sometimes troubled with the *disorders* of its citizens.

3. Neglect of rule; irregularity.

From vulgar bounds with brave *disorder* part,
And snatch a grace beyond the reach of art. *Pope.*

4. Breach of laws; violation of standing rules, or institutions.

5. Irregularity, disturbance or interruption of the functions of the animal economy; disease; distemper; sickness. [See *Disease.*] *Disorder* however is more frequently used to express a slight disease.

6. Discomposure of the mind; turbulence of passions.

7. Irregularity in the functions of the brain; derangement of the intellect or reason.

DISOR'DER, *v. t.* To break order; to derange; to disturb any regular disposition or arrangement of things; to put out of method; to throw into confusion; to confuse; *applicable to every thing susceptible of order.*

2. To disturb or interrupt the natural functions of the animal economy; to produce sickness or indisposition; as, to *disorder* the head or stomach.

3. To discompose or disturb the mind; to ruffle.

4. To disturb the regular operations of reason; to derange; as, the man's reason is *disordered.*

5. To depose from holy orders. [*Unusual.*] *Dryden.*

DISOR'DERED, *pp.* Put out of order; deranged; disturbed; discomposed; confused; sick; indisposed.

DISOR'DERED, *a.* Disorderly; irregular; vicious; loose; unrestrained in behavior. *Shak.*

DISOR'DEREDNESS, *n.* A state of disorder or irregularity; confusion.

DISOR'DERLY, *a.* Confused; immethodical; irregular; being without proper order or disposition; as, the books and papers are in a *disorderly* state.

2. Tumultuous; irregular; as the *disorderly* motions of the spirits.

3. Lawless; contrary to law; violating or disposed to violate law and good order; as *disorderly* people; *disorderly* assemblies.

4. Inclined to break loose ftom restraint; unruly; as *disorderly* cattle.

DISOR'DERLY, *adv.* Without order, rule or method; irregularly; confusedly; in a disorderly manner.

Savages fighting *disorderly* with stones. *Raleigh.*

2. In a manner violating law and good order; in a manner contrary to rules or established institutions.

Withdraw from every brother that walketh *disorderly.* 2 Thess. iii.

DISOR'DINATE, *a.* Disorderly; living irregularly. *Milton.*

DISOR'DINATELY, *adv.* Inordinately; irregularly; viciously.

DISORGANIZA'TION, *n.* [See *Disorganize.*] The act of disorganizing; the act of destroying organic structure, or connected system; the act of destroying order.

2. The state of being disorganized. We speak of the *disorganization* of the body, or of government, or of society, or of an army.

DISOR'GANIZE, *v. t.* [*dis* and *organize.* See *Organ.*] To break or destroy organic structure or connected system; to dissolve regular system or union of parts; as, to *disorganize* a government or society; to *disorganize* an army.

Every account of the settlement of Plymouth mentions the conduct of Lyford, who attempted to *disorganize* the church. *Eliot's Biog. Dict.*

DISOR'GANIZED, *pp.* Reduced to disorder; being in a confused state.

DISOR'GANIZER, *n.* One who disorganizes; one who destroys or attempts to interrupt regular order or system; one who introduces disorder and confusion.

DISOR'GANIZING, *ppr.* Destroying regular and connected system; throwing into confusion.

2. *a.* Disposed or tending to disorganize; as a *disorganizing* spirit.

DISOWN, *v. t.* [*dis* and *own.*] To deny; not to own; to refuse to acknowledge as belonging to one's self. A parent can hardly *disown* his child. An author will sometimes *disown* his writings.

2. To deny; not to allow.

To *disown* a brother's better claim. *Dryden.*

DISOWNED, *pp.* Not owned; not acknowledged as one's own; denied; disallowed.

DISOWNING, *ppr.* Not owning; denying; disallowing.

DISOX'YDATE, *v. t.* [*dis* and *oxydate.*] To reduce from oxydation; to reduce from the state of an oxyd, by disengaging oxygen from a substance; as, to *disoxydate* iron or copper.

DISOX'YDATED, *pp.* Reduced from the state of an oxyd.

DISOX'YDATING, *ppr.* Reducing from the state of an oxyd.

DISOXYDA'TION, *n.* The act or process of freeing from oxygen and reducing from the state of an oxyd. *Med. Repos.*

[*This word seems to be preferable to* deoxydate.]

DISOX'YGENATE, *v. t.* [*dis* and *oxygenate.*] To deprive of oxygen.

DISOX'YGENATED, *pp.* Freed from oxygen.

DISOX'YGENATING, *ppr.* Freeing from oxygen.

DISOXYGENA'TION, *n.* The act or process of separating oxygen from any substance containing it.

DISPA'CE, *v. i.* [*dis* and *spatior*, L.] To range about. *Obs.* *Spenser.*

DISPA'IR, *v. t.* [*dis* and *pair.*] To separate a pair or couple. *Beaum.*

DISPAND', *v. t.* [L. *dispando.*] To display. [*Not in use.*] *Dict.*

DISPAN'SION, *n.* The act of spreading or displaying. [*Not in use.*]

DISPAR'ADISED, *a.* [*dis* and *paradise.*] Removed from paradise.

DISPAR'AGE, *v. t.* [Norm. *desperager; des, dis*, and *parage*, from *peer, par*, equal.]

1. To marry one to another of inferior condition or rank; to dishonor by an unequal match or marriage, against the rules of decency.
2. To match unequally; to injure or dishonor by union with something of inferior excellence. *Johnson.*
3. To injure or dishonor by a comparison with something of less value or excellence.
4. To treat with contempt; to undervalue; to lower in rank or estimation; to vilify; to bring reproach on; to reproach; to debase by words or actions; to dishonor.

> Thou durst not thus *disparage* glorious arms. *Milton.*

DISPAR'AGED, *pp.* Married to one beneath his or her condition; unequally matched; dishonored or injured by comparison with something inferior; undervalued; vilified; debased; reproached.

DISPAR'AGEMENT, *n.* The matching of a man or woman to one of inferior rank or condition, and against the rules of decency. *Encyc. Cowel.*

2. Injury by union or comparison with something of inferior excellence. *Johnson.*
3. Diminution of value or excellence; reproach; disgrace; indignity; dishonor; followed by *to.*

> It ought to be no *disparagement to* a star that it is not the sun. *South.*

> To be a humble christian is no *disparagement to* a prince, or a nobleman. *Anon.*

DISPAR'AGER, *n.* One who disparages or dishonors; one who vilifies or disgraces.

DISPAR'AGING, *ppr.* Marrying one to another of inferior condition; dishonoring by an unequal union or comparison; disgracing; dishonoring.

DISPAR'AGINGLY, *adv.* In a manner to disparage or dishonor.

DIS'PARATE, *a.* [L. *disparata*, things unlike; *dispar; dis* and *par*, equal.] Unequal; unlike; dissimilar. *Robison.*

DIS'PARATES, *n. plu.* Things so unequal or unlike that they cannot be compared with each other. *Johnson.*

DISPAR'ITY, *n.* [Fr. *disparité*; Sp. *disparidad;* It. *disparità;* from L. *dispar*, unequal; *dis* and *par*, equal.]

1. Irregularity; difference in degree, in age, rank, condition or excellence; as a *disparity* of years or of age; *disparity* of condition or circumstances: followed by *of* or *in.* We say, disparity *in* or *of* years.
2. Dissimilitude; unlikeness.

DISP'ARK, *v. t.* [*dis* and *park.*] To throw open a park; to lay open. *Shak.*

2. To set at large; to release from inclosure or confinement. *Waller.*

DISP'ART, *v. t.* [*dis* and *part;* Fr. *departir;* L. *dispartior.* See *Part. Dis* and *part* both imply *separation.*]

To part asunder; to divide; to separate; to sever; to burst; to rend; to rive or split; as *disparted* air; *disparted* towers; *disparted* chaos. [*An elegant poetic word.*] *Milton.*

DISP'ART, *v. i.* To separate; to open; to cleave.

DISP'ART, *n.* In *gunnery*, the thickness of the metal of a piece of ordnance at the mouth and britch. *Bailey.*

DISP'ART, *v. t.* In *gunnery*, to set a mark on the muzzle-ring of a piece of ordnance, so that a sight-line from the top of the base-ring to the mark on or near the muzzle may be parallel to the axis of the bore or hollow cylinder. *Encyc.*

DISP'ARTED, *pp.* Divided; separated; parted; rent asunder.

DISP'ARTING, *ppr.* Severing; dividing; bursting; cleaving.

DISPAS'SION, *n.* [*dis* and *passion.*] Freedom from passion; an undisturbed state of the mind; apathy. *Temple.*

DISPAS'SIONATE, *a.* Free from passion; calm; composed; impartial; moderate; temperate; unmoved by feelings; *applied to persons;* as *dispassionate* men or judges.

2. Not dictated by passion; not proceeding from temper or bias; impartial; *applied to things;* as *dispassionate* proceedings.

DISPAS'SIONATELY, *adv.* Without passion; calmly; coolly.

DISPATCH', *v. t.* [Fr. *depêcher;* Sp. *despachar;* Port. *id.;* It. *dispacciare;* Arm. *dibech, disbachat.* In It. *spacciare* signifies to sell, put off, speed, dispatch; *spaccio*, sale, vent, dispatch, expedition. This word belongs to Class Bg, and the primary sense is to send, throw, thrust, drive, and this is the sense of *pack*, L. *pango, pactus.* Hence our vulgar phrases, *to pack off*, and *to budge.* The same word occurs in *impeach.*]

1. To send or send away; particularly applied to the sending of messengers, agents and letters on special business, and often implying haste. The king *dispatched* an envoy to the court of Madrid. He *dispatched* a messenger to his envoy in France. He *dispatched* orders or letters to the commander of the forces in Spain. The president *dispatched* a special envoy to the court of St. James in 1794.
2. To send out of the world; to put to death.

> The company shall stone them with stones, and *dispatch* them with their swords. Ezek. xxiii.

3. To perform; to execute speedily; to finish; as, the business was *dispatched* in due time.

DISPATCH', *v. i.* To conclude an affair with another; to transact and finish. [*Not now used.*]

> They have *dispatched* with Pompey. *Shak.*

DISPATCH', *n.* Speedy performance; execution or transaction of business with due diligence. *Bacon.*

2. Speed; haste; expedition; due diligence; as, the business was done with *dispatch;* go, but make *dispatch.*
3. Conduct; management. [*Not used.*] *Shak.*
4. A letter sent or to be sent with expedition, by a messenger express; or a letter on some affair of state, or of public concern; or a packet of letters, sent by some public officer, on public business. It is often used in the plural. A vessel or a messenger has arrived with *dispatches* for the American minister. A *dispatch* was immediately sent to the admiral. The secretary was preparing his *dispatches.*

DISPATCH'ED, *pp.* Sent with haste or by a courier express; sent out of the world; put to death; performed; finished.

DISPATCH'ER, *n.* One that dispatches; one that kills.

2. One that sends on a special errand.

DISPATCH'FUL, *a.* Bent on haste; indicating haste; intent on speedy execution of business; as *dispatchful* looks. *Milton.*

DISPATCH'ING, *ppr.* Sending away in haste; putting to death; executing; finishing.

DISPAU'PER, *v. t.* [*dis* and *pauper.*] To deprive of the claim of a pauper to public support, or of the capacity of suing in *forma pauperis;* to reduce back from the state of a pauper.

> A man is *dispaupered*, when he has lands fallen to him or property given him. *Encyc.*

DISPEL', *v. t.* [L. *dispello; dis* and *pello*, to drive, Gr. βαλλω. See *Appeal, Peal, Pulse* and *Bawl.*]

To scatter by driving or force; to disperse; to dissipate; to banish; as, to *dispel* vapors; to *dispel* darkness or gloom; to *dispel* fears; to *dispel* cares or sorrows; to *dispel* doubts.

DISPEL'LED, *pp.* Driven away; scattered; dissipated.

DISPEL'LING, *ppr.* Driving away; dispersing; scattering.

DISPEND', *v. t.* [L. *dispendo; dis* and *pendo*, to weigh.]

To spend; to lay out; to consume. [See *Expend*, which is generally used.] *Spenser.*

DISPEND'ER, *n.* One that distributes.

DISPENS'ABLE, *a.* That may be dispensed with. *More.*

DISPENS'ABLENESS, *n.* The capability of being dispensed with. *Hammond.*

DISPENS'ARY, *n.* A house, place or store, in which medicines are dispensed to the poor, and medical advice given, gratis.

DISPENSA'TION, *n.* [L. *dispensatio.* See *Dispense.*]

1. Distribution; the act of dealing out to different persons or places; as the *dispensation* of water indifferently to all parts of the earth. *Woodward.*
2. The dealing of God to his creatures; the distribution of good and evil, natural or moral, in the divine government.

> Neither are God's methods or intentions different in his *dispensations* to each private man. *Rogers.*

3. The granting of a license, or the license itself, to do what is forbidden by laws or canons, or to omit something which is

commanded; that is, the dispensing with a law or canon, or the exemption of a particular person from the obligation to comply with its injunctions. The pope has power to dispense with the canons of the church, but has no right to grant *dispensations* to the injury of a third person.

A *dispensation* was obtained to enable Dr. Barrow to marry. *Ward.*

4. That which is dispensed or bestowed; a system of principles and rites enjoined; as the *Mosaic dispensation*; the *gospel dispensation*; including, the former the Levitical law and rites; the latter the scheme of redemption by Christ.

DISPENS'ATIVE, *a.* Granting dispensation.

DISPENS'ATIVELY, *adv.* By dispensation. *Wotton.*

DISPENSA'TOR, *n.* [L.] One whose employment is to deal out or distribute; a distributor; a dispenser: *the latter word is generally used.*

DISPENS'ATORY, *a.* Having power to grant dispensations.

DISPENS'ATORY, *n.* A book containing the method of preparing the various kinds of medicines used in pharmacy, or containing directions for the composition of medicines, with the proportions of the ingredients, and the methods of preparing them.

DISPENSE, *v. t. dispens'.* [Fr. *dispenser*; Sp. *dispensar*; It. *dispensare*; from L. *dispenso*; *dis* and *penso*, from *pendo*, to weigh, primarily to move; and perhaps the original idea of expending was to weigh off, or to distribute by weight.]

1. To deal or divide out in parts or portions; to distribute. The steward *dispenses* provisions to every man, according to his directions. The society *dispenses* medicines to the poor gratuitously or at first cost. God *dispenses* his favors according to his good pleasure.

2. To administer; to apply, as laws to particular cases; to distribute justice.

While you *dispense* the laws and guide the state. *Dryden.*

To dispense with, to permit not to take effect; to neglect or pass by; to suspend the operation or application of something required, established or customary; as, to *dispense with* the law, in favor of a friend; I cannot *dispense with* the conditions of the covenant. So we say, to *dispense with* oaths; to *dispense with* forms and ceremonies.

2. To excuse from; to give leave not to do or observe what is required or commanded. The court will *dispense with* your attendance, or *with* your compliance.

3. To permit the want of a thing which is useful or convenient; or in the vulgar phrase, to do without. I can *dispense with* your services. I can *dispense with* my cloke. In this application, the phrase has an allusion to the requisitions of law or necessity; the thing dispensed with being supposed, in some degree, necessary or required.

I could not *dispense with* myself from making a voyage to Caprea. [*Not to be imitated.*] *Addison.*

Canst thou *dispense with* heaven for such an oath? [*Not legitimate.*] *Shak.*

DISPENSE, *n. dispens'.* Dispensation. [*Not used.*] *Milton.*

2. Expense; profusion. [*Not in use.*] *Spenser.*

DISPENS'ED, *pp.* Distributed; administered.

DISPENS'ER, *n.* One who dispenses; one who distributes; one who administers; as a *dispenser* of favors or of the laws.

DISPENS'ING, *ppr.* Distributing; administering.

2. *a.* That may dispense with; granting dispensation; that may grant license to omit what is required by law, or to do what the law forbids; as a *dispensing* power.

DISPEOPLE, *v. t.* [*dis* and *people.*] To depopulate; to empty of inhabitants, as by destruction, expulsion or other means. *Milton. Pope.*

DISPEOPLED, *pp.* Depopulated; deprived of inhabitants.

DISPEOPLER, *n.* One who depopulates; a depopulator; that which deprives of inhabitants.

DISPEOPLING, *ppr.* Depopulating.

DISPERGE, *v. t. disperj'.* [L. *dispergo.*] To sprinkle. [*Not in use.*]

DISPERM'OUS, *a.* [Gr. δι, δις, and σπερμα, seed.] In *botany*, two-seeded; containing two seeds only; as, umbellate and stellate plants are *dispermous*.

DISPERS'E, *v. t. dispers'.* [L. *dispersus*, from *dispergo*; *di*, *dis*, and *spargo*, to scatter; Fr. *disperser.*]

1. To scatter; to drive asunder; to cause to separate into different parts; as, the Jews are *dispersed* among all nations.

2. To diffuse; to spread.

The lips of the wise *disperse* knowledge. Prov. xv.

3. To dissipate; as, the fog or the cloud is *dispersed*.

4. To distribute. *Bacon.*

DISPERSE, *v. i. dispers'.* To be scattered; to separate; to go or move into different parts; as, the company *dispersed* at ten o'clock.

2. To be scattered; to vanish; as fog or vapors.

DISPERS'ED, *pp.* Scattered; driven apart; diffused; dissipated.

DISPERS'EDLY, *adv.* In a dispersed manner; separately. *Hooker.*

DISPERS'EDNESS, *n.* The state of being dispersed or scattered.

DISPERSENESS, *n. dispers'ness.* Thinness; a scattered state. [*Little used.*] *Brerewood.*

DISPERS'ER, *n.* One who disperses; as the disperser of *libels*. *Spectator.*

DISPERS'ING, *ppr.* Scattering; dissipating.

DISPER'SION, *n.* The act of scattering.

2. The state of being scattered, or separated into remote parts; as, the Jews, in their *dispersion*, retain their rites and ceremonies.

3. *By way of eminence*, the scattering or separation of the human family, at the building of Babel.

4. In *optics*, the divergency of the rays of light, or rather the separation of the different colored rays, in refraction, arising from their different refrangibilities.

The point of *dispersion*, is the point where refracted rays begin to diverge.

5. In *medicine* and *surgery*, the removing of inflammation from a part, and restoring it to its natural state.

DISPERS'IVE, *a.* Tending to scatter or dissipate. *Green.*

DISPIR'IT, *v. t.* [*dis* and *spirit.*] To depress the spirits; to deprive of courage; to discourage; to dishearten; to deject; to cast down. We may be *dispirited* by afflictions, by obstacles to success, by poverty, and by fear. When fear is the cause, *dispirit* is nearly equivalent to *intimidate* or *terrify*.

2. To exhaust the spirits or vigor of the body. [*Not usual.*] *Collier.*

DISPIR'ITED, *pp.* Discouraged; depressed in spirits; dejected; intimidated.

DISPIR'ITEDNESS, *n.* Want of courage; depression of spirits.

DISPIR'ITING, *ppr.* Discouraging; disheartening; dejecting; intimidating.

DISPIT'EOUS, *a.* Having no pity; cruel; furious. [*Not used.*] *Spenser.*

DISPLA'CE, *v. t.* [*dis* and *place*; Fr. *deplacer*; Arm. *diblaçza.*]

1. To put out of the usual or proper place; to remove from its place; as, the books in the library are all *displaced*.

2. To remove from any state, condition, office or dignity; as, to *displace* an officer of the revenue.

3. To disorder.

You have *displaced* the mirth. *Shak.*

DISPLA'CED, *pp.* Removed from the proper place; deranged; disordered; removed from an office or state.

DISPLA'CEMENT, *n.* [Fr. *deplacement.*] The act of displacing; the act of removing from the usual or proper place, or from a state, condition or office.

The *displacement* of the centers of the circles. *Asiat. Researches.* v. 185.

Unnecessary *displacement* of funds. *Hamilton's Rep.* ii.

DISPLA'CENCY, *n.* [L. *displicentia*, from *displiceo*, to displease; *dis* and *placeo*, to please.]

Incivility; that which displeases or disobliges. *Decay of Piety.*

DISPLA'CING, *ppr.* Putting out of the usual or proper place; removing from an office, state or condition.

DISPLANT', *v. t.* [*dis* and *plant.*] To pluck up or to remove a plant.

2. To drive away or remove from the usual place of residence; as, to *displant* the people of a country. *Bacon.*

3. To strip of inhabitants; as, to *displant* a country. *Spenser.*

DISPLANTA'TION, *n.* The removal of a plant.

2. The removal of inhabitants or resident people. *Raleigh.*

DISPLANT'ED, *pp.* Removed from the place where it grew, as a plant.

2. Removed from the place of residence; *applied to persons.*

3. Deprived of inhabitants; *applied to a country.*

DISPLANT'ING, *ppr.* Removing, as a plant.

DISPLANT'ING, *n.* Removal from a fixed place.

DISPLAT', *v. t.* [*dis* and *plat.*] To untwist; to uncurl. *Hakewill.*

DISPLA'Y, *v. t.* [Fr. *deployer*, and *deploy* is the same word. It is a different orthography of *deplier*, to unfold; Arm. *displega*; Sp. *desplegar*; It. *spiegare*; *dis* and Fr. *plier*, Sp. *plegar*, It. *piegare*, to fold; L. *plico*, W. *plygu*, Gr. πλεκω; and απλοος, απλοω, to unfold, may be from the same root.]

1. Literally, to unfold; hence, to open; to spread wide; to expand.

The northern wind his wings did broad *display*. *Spenser.*

2. To spread before the view; to show; to exhibit to the eyes, or to the mind; to make manifest. The works of nature *display* the power and wisdom of the Supreme Being. Christian charity *displays* the effects of true piety. A dress, simple and elegant, *displays* female taste and beauty to advantage.

3. To carve; to dissect and open.

He carves, *displays*, and cuts up to a wonder. *Spectator.*

4. To set to view ostentatiously. *Shak.*

5. To discover. [*Not in use.*] *Spenser.*

6. To open; to unlock. [*Not used.*] *B. Jonson.*

DISPLA'Y, *v. i.* To talk without restraint; to make a great show of words. *Shak.*

DISPLA'Y, *n.* An opening or unfolding; an exhibition of any thing to the view.

2. Show; exhibition; as, they make a great *display* of troops; a great *display* of magnificence.

DISPLA'YED, *pp.* Unfolded; opened; spread; expanded; exhibited to view; manifested.

DISPLA'YER, *n.* He or that which displays.

DISPLA'YING, *ppr.* Unfolding; spreading; exhibiting; manifesting.

DISPLE'ASANCE, *n.* [Fr. *deplaisance.*] Anger; discontent. [*Not used.*] *Spenser.*

DISPLEAS'ANT, *a.* *displez'ant.* [See *Displease.*]
Unpleasing; offensive; unpleasant. [*The latter word is generally used.*]

DISPLE'ASE, *v. t.* *disple'ze.* [*dis* and *please.*]

1. To offend; to make angry, sometimes in a slight degree. It usually expresses less than *anger*, *vex*, *irritate* and *provoke*. Applied to the Almighty in scripture, it may be considered as equivalent to *anger*.

God was *displeased* with this thing; therefore he smote Israel. 1 Chron. xxi.

2. To disgust; to excite aversion in; as, acrid and rancid substances *displease* the taste.

3. To offend; to be disagreeable to. A distorted figure *displeases* the eye.

DISPLE'ASED, *pp.* Offended; disgusted.

DISPLE'ASEDNESS, *n.* Displeasure; uneasiness. *Mountague.*

DISPLE'ASING, *ppr* or *a.* Offensive to the eye, to the mind, to the smell, or to the taste; disgusting; disagreeable.

DISPLE'ASINGNESS, *n.* Offensiveness; the quality of giving some degree of disgust.

DISPLEAS'URE, *n.* *displezh'ur.* Some irritation or uneasiness of the mind, occasioned by any thing that counteracts desire or command, or which opposes justice and a sense of propriety. A man incurs the *displeasure* of another by thwarting his views or schemes; a servant incurs the *displeasure* of his master by neglect or disobedience; we experience *displeasure* at any violation of right or decorum. *Displeasure* is anger, but it may be slight anger. It implies disapprobation or hatred, and usually expresses less than *vexation* and *indignation*. Thus, slighter offenses give *displeasure*, although they may not excite a violent passion.

2. Offense; cause of irritation.

Now shall I be more blameless than the Philistines, though I do them a *displeasure*. Judges xv.

3. State of disgrace or disfavor.

He went into Poland, being in *displeasure* with the pope for overmuch familiarity. *Peacham.*

DISPLEAS'URE, *v. t.* To displease. [*An unnecessary word, and not used.*] *Bacon.*

DIS'PLICENCE, *n.* [L. *displicentia.*] Dislike. [*Not in use.*] *Mountague.*

DISPLO'DE, *v. t.* [L. *displodo*; *dis* and *plaudo*, to break forth.]
To vent, discharge or burst with a violent sound.

In posture to *displode* their second tire
Of thunder. *Milton.*

DISPLO'DE, *v. i.* To burst with a loud report; to explode; as, a meteor *disploded* with a tremendous sound.

DISPLO'DED, *pp.* Discharged with a loud report.

DISPLO'DING, *ppr.* Discharging or bursting with a loud report.

DISPLO'SION, *n.* *s* as *z.* The act of disploding; a sudden bursting with a loud report; an explosion.

DISPLO'SIVE, *a.* Noting displosion.

DISPLU'ME, *v. t.* [*dis* and *plume.*] To strip or deprive of plumes or feathers; to strip of badges of honor. *Burke.*

DISPLU'MED, *pp.* Stripped of plumes.

DISPLU'MING, *ppr.* Depriving of plumes.

DISPON'DEE, *n.* In *Greek* and *Latin poetry*, a double spondee, consisting of four long syllables. *Encyc.*

DISPO'RT, *n.* [*dis* and *sport.*] Play; sport; pastime; diversion; amusement; merriment. *Milton. Hayward.*

DISPO'RT, *v. i.* To play; to wanton; to move lightly and without restraint; to move in gayety; as lambs *disporting* on the mead.

Where light *disports* in ever mingling dyes. *Pope.*

DISPO'RT, *v. t.* To divert or amuse; as, he *disports* himself. *Shak.*

DISPO'RTING, *ppr.* Playing; wantoning.

DISPO'SABLE, *a.* [See *Dispose.*] Subject to disposal; not previously engaged or employed; free to be used or employed as occasion may require.

The whole *disposable* force consisted in a regiment of light infantry, and a troop of cavalry.

DISPO'SAL, *n.* [See *Dispose.*] The act of disposing; a setting or arranging.

This object was effected by the *disposal* of the troops in two lines.

2. Regulation, order or arrangement of things, in the moral government of God; dispensation.

Tax not divine *disposal*. *Milton.*

3. Power of ordering, arranging or distributing; government; management; as, an agent is appointed, and every thing is left to his *disposal*. The effects in my hands are entirely at my *disposal*.

4. Power or right of bestowing. Certain offices are at the *disposal* of the president. The father has the *disposal* of his daughter in marriage.

5. The passing into a new state or into new hands.

DISPO'SE, *v. t.* *dispo'ze.* [Fr. *disposer*; *dis* and *poser*, to place; Arm. *disposi*; L. *dispositus*, *dispono*. But the Latin *posui*, *positus*, is probably from a different root from *pono*, and coinciding with Eng. *put*, with a dialectical change of the last articulation. *Pono* belongs to Class Bn, and *posui*, to Class Bs or Bd. The literal sense is to *set apart.*]

1. To set; to place or distribute; to arrange; *used with reference to order.* The ships were *disposed* in the form of a crescent. The general *disposed* his troops in three lines. The trees are *disposed* in the form of a quincunx.

2. To regulate; to adjust; to set in right order. Job xxxiv. and xxxvii.

The knightly forms of combat to *dispose*. *Dryden.*

3. To apply to a particular purpose; to give; to place; to bestow; as, you have *disposed* much in works of public piety. In this sense, *to dispose of* is more generally used.

4. To set, place or turn to a particular end or consequence.

Endure and conquer; Jove will soon *dispose*
To future good our past and present woes. *Dryden.*

5. To adapt; to form for any purpose.

Then must thou thee *dispose* another way. *Hubberd's Tale.*

6. To set the mind in a particular frame; to incline. Avarice *disposes* men to fraud and oppression.

Suspicions *dispose* kings to tyranny, husbands to jealousy, and wise men to irresolution and melancholy. *Bacon.*

He was *disposed* to pass into Achaia. Acts xviii. 1 Cor. x. 27.

To dispose of, to part with; to alienate; as, the man has *disposed of* his house, and removed.

2. To part with to another; to put into another's hand or power; to bestow; as, the father has *disposed of* his daughter to a man of great worth.

3. To give away or transfer by authority.

A rural judge *disposed of* beauty's prize. *Waller.*

4. To direct the course of a thing. Prov. xvi.

5. To place in any condition; as, how will you *dispose of* your son?

6. To direct what to do or what course to pursue; as, they know not how to *dispose of* themselves.

7. To use or employ; as, they know not how to *dispose of* their time.

8. To put away. The stream supplies more water than can be *disposed of*.

DISPO'SE, *v. i.* To bargain; to make terms. *Obs.* *Shak.*

DISPO'SE, *n.* Disposal; power of disposing; management. *Obs.* *Shak.*

2. Dispensation; act of government. *Obs.* *Milton.*

3. Disposition; cast of behavior. *Obs.* *Shak.*

4. Disposition; cast of mind; inclination. *Obs.* *Shak.*

DISPO'SED, *pp.* Set in order; arranged; placed; adjusted; applied; bestowed; inclined.

DISPO'SER, *n.* One who disposes; a distributor; a bestower; as a *disposer* of gifts.

2. A director; a regulator.

The Supreme Being is the rightful *disposer* of all events, and of all creatures.

3. That which disposes. *Prior.*

DISPO'SING, *ppr.* Setting in order; arranging; distributing; bestowing; regulating; adjusting; governing.

DISPO'SING, *n.* The act of arranging; regulation; direction. Prov. xvi. 33.

DISPOSI''TION, *n.* [L. *dispositio.*] The act of disposing, or state of being disposed.

2. Manner in which things or the parts of a complex body are placed or arranged; order; method; distribution; arrangement. We speak of the *disposition* of the infantry and cavalry of an army; the *disposition* of the trees in an orchard; the *disposition* of the several parts of an edifice, of the parts of a discourse, or of the figures in painting.

3. Natural fitness or tendency. The refrangibility of the rays of light is their *disposition* to be refracted. So we say, a *disposition* in plants to grow in a direction upwards; a *disposition* in bodies to putrefaction.

4. Temper or natural constitution of the mind; as an amiable or an irritable *disposition.*

5. Inclination; propensity; the temper or frame of mind, as directed to particular objects. We speak of the *disposition* of a person to undertake a particular work; the *dispositions* of men towards each other; a *disposition* friendly to any design.

6. Disposal; alienation; distribution; a giving away or giving over to another; as, he has made *disposition* of his effects; he has satisfied his friends by the judicious *disposition* of his property.

DISPOS'ITIVE, *a.* That implies disposal. [*Not used.*] *Ayliffe.*

DISPOS'ITIVELY, *adv.* In a dispositive manner; distributively. [*Not used.*] *Brown.*

DISPOS'ITOR, *n.* A disposer; in *astrology,* the planet which is lord of the sign where another planet is. [*Not used.*]

DISPOSSESS', *v. t.* [*dis* and *possess.*] To put out of possession, by any means; to deprive of the actual occupancy of a thing, particularly of land or real estate; to disseize.

Ye shall *dispossess* the inhabitants of the land, and dwell therein. Num. xxxiii.

Usually followed by *of,* before the thing taken away; as, to *dispossess* a king *of* his crown.

DISPOSSESS'ED, *pp.* Deprived of possession or occupancy.

DISPOSSESS'ING, *ppr.* Depriving of possession; disseizing.

DISPOSSES'SION, *n.* The act of putting out of possession. *Hall.*

DISPO'SURE, *n. dispo'zhur.* [See *Dispose.*] Disposal; the power of disposing; management; direction. *Sandys.*

[The use of this word is superseded by that of *disposal.*]

2. State; posture; disposition. [*Not used.*] *Wotton.*

DISPRA'ISE, *n. dispra'ze.* [*dis* and *praise.*] Blame; censure. Be cautious not to speak in *dispraise* of a competitor.

2. Reproach; dishonor.

The general has seen Moors with as bad faces; no *dispraise* to Bertran's. *Dryden.*

DISPRA'ISE, *v. t.* To blame; to censure; to mention with disapprobation, or some degree of reproach.

I *dispraised* him before the wicked. *Shak.*

DISPRA'ISED, *pp.* Blamed; censured.

DISPRA'ISER, *n.* One who blames or dispraises.

DISPRA'ISING, *ppr.* Blaming; censuring.

DISPRA'ISINGLY, *adv.* By way of dispraise; with blame or some degree of reproach.

DISPREAD, *v. t. dispred'.* [*dis* and *spread.* See *Spread.*]

To spread in different ways; to extend or flow in different directions. *Spenser. Pope.*

DISPREAD', *v. i.* To expand or be extended. *Thomson.*

DISPREAD'ER, *n.* A publisher; a divulger. *Milton.*

DISPRI'ZE, *v. t.* To undervalue. *Cotton.*

DISPROFESS', *v. i.* To renounce the profession of. *Spenser.*

DISPROF'IT, *n.* [*dis* and *profit.*] Loss; detriment; damage. [*Little used.*]

DISPROOF', *n.* [*dis* and *proof.*] Confutation; refutation; a proving to be false or erroneous; as, to offer evidence in *disproof* of a fact, argument, principle or allegation.

DISPROP'ERTY, *v. t.* To deprive of property; to dispossess. [*Not used.*] *Shak.*

DISPROPO'RTION, *n.* [*dis* and *proportion.*]

1. Want of proportion of one thing to another, or between the parts of a thing; want of symmetry. We speak of the *disproportion* of a man's arms to his body; of the *disproportion* of the length of an edifice to its highth.

2. Want of proper quantity, according to rules prescribed; as, the *disproportion* of the ingredients in a compound.

3. Want of suitableness or adequacy; disparity; inequality; unsuitableness; as the *disproportion* of strength or means to an object.

DISPROPO'RTION, *v. t.* To make unsuitable in form, size, length or quantity; to violate symmetry in; to mismatch; to join unfitly.

To shape my legs of an unequal size,
To *disproportion* me in every part. *Shak.*

DISPROPO'RTIONABLE, *a.* Disproportional; not in proportion; unsuitable in form, size or quantity to something else; inadequate. [Note. The sense in which this word is used is generally anomalous. In its true sense, *that may be made disproportional,* it is rarely or never used. The regular word which ought to be used is *disproportional,* as used by Locke.]

DISPROPO'RTIONABLENESS, *n.* Want of proportion or symmetry; unsuitableness to something else.

DISPROPO'RTIONABLY, *adv.* With want of proportion or symmetry; unsuitably to something else. *Tillotson.*

DISPROPO'RTIONAL, *a.* Not having due proportion to something else; not having proportion or symmetry of parts; unsuitable in form or quantity; unequal; inadequate. A *disproportional* limb constitutes deformity in the body. The studies of youth should not be *disproportional* to their capacities. [This is the word which ought to be used for *disproportionable.*]

DISPROPORTIONAL'ITY, *n.* The state of being disproportional.

DISPROPO'RTIONALLY, *adv.* Unsuitably with respect to form, quantity or value; inadequately; unequally.

DISPROPO'RTIONATE, *a.* Not proportioned; unsymmetrical; unsuitable to something else, in bulk, form or value; inadequate. In a perfect form of the body, none of the limbs are *disproportionate.* It is wisdom not to undertake a work with *disproportionate* means.

DISPROPO'RTIONATELY, *adv.* In a disproportionate degree; unsuitably; inadequately.

DISPROPO'RTIONATENESS, *n.* Unsuitableness in form, bulk or value; inadequacy.

DISPRO'PRIATE, *v. t.* To destroy appropriation; to withdraw from an appropriate use. *Anderson.*

[See *Disappropriate,* which is more regularly formed, and more generally used.]

DISPRÖV'ABLE, *a.* Capable of being disproved or refuted. *Boyle.*

DISPRÖVE, *v. t.* [*dis* and *prove.*] To prove to be false or erroneous; to confute; as, to *disprove* an assertion, a statement, an argument, a proposition.

2. To convict of the practice of error. [*Not in use.*] *Hooker.*

3. To disallow or disapprove. [*Not in use.*] *Hooker.*

DISPRÖV'ED, *pp.* Proved to be false or erroneous; refuted.

DISPRÖV'ER, *n.* One that disproves or confutes.

DISPRÖV'ING, *ppr.* Proving to be false or erroneous; confuting; refuting.

DISPUNGE, *v. t.* [*dis* and *spunge.*] To expunge; to erase; also, to discharge as from a spunge. [*Ill formed and little used.*] *Wotton. Shak.*

DISPUN'ISHABLE, *a.* [*dis* and *punishable.*] Without penal restraint; not punishable. *Swift.*

DISPURSE, for *disburse.* [*Not in use.*] *Shak.*

DISPURVEY, *v. t.* To unprovide. [*Not in use.*]

DISPURVEYANCE, *n.* Want of provisions. [*Not in use.*] *Spenser.*

DIS'PUTABLE, *a.* [See *Dispute.*] That may be disputed; liable to be called in question, controverted or contested; controvertible; of doubtful certainty. We speak of *disputable* opinions, statements, propositions, arguments, points, cases, questions, &c.

DIS'PUTANT, *n.* One who disputes; one who argues in opposition to another; a controvertist; a reasoner in opposition.

DIS'PUTANT, *a.* Disputing; engaged in controversy. *Milton.*

DISPUTA'TION, *n.* [L. *disputatio.*] The act of disputing; a reasoning or argumentation in opposition to something, or on opposite sides; controversy in words; verbal contest, respecting the truth of some fact, opinion, proposition or argument.

2. An exercise in colleges, in which parties reason in opposition to each other, on some question proposed.

DISPUTA'TIOUS, *a.* Inclined to dispute; apt to cavil or controvert; as a *disputatious* person or temper.

> The christian doctrine of a future life was no recommendation of the new religion to the wits and philosophers of that *disputatious* period. *Buckminster.*

DISPU'TATIVE, *a.* Disposed to dispute; inclined to cavil or to reason in opposition; as a *disputative* temper. *Watts.*

DISPU'TE, *v. i.* [L. *disputo; dis* and *puto.* The primary sense of *puto* is to throw, cast, strike or drive, as we see by *imputo*, to impute, to throw on, to charge, to ascribe. *Amputo*, to prune, is to strike off, to throw off from all sides; *computo*, to *compute*, is to throw together, to cast. *Dispute* then is radically very similar to *debate* and *discuss*, both of which are from beating, driving, agitation.]

1. To contend in argument; to reason or argue in opposition; to debate; to altercate; and to *dispute violently* is to wrangle. Paul *disputed* with the Jews in the synagogue. The disciples of Christ *disputed* among themselves who should be the greatest. Men often *dispute* about trifles.

2. To strive or contend in opposition to a competitor; as, we *disputed* for the prize.

DISPU'TE, *v. t.* To attempt to disprove by arguments or statements; to attempt to prove to be false, unfounded or erroneous; to controvert; to attempt to overthrow by reasoning. We *dispute* assertions, opinions, arguments or statements, when we endeavor to prove them false or unfounded. We *dispute* the validity of a title or claim. Hence to *dispute* a cause or case with another, is to endeavor to maintain one's own opinions or claims, and to overthrow those of his opponent.

2. To strive or contend for, either by words or actions; as, to *dispute* the honor of the day; to *dispute* a prize. But this phrase is elliptical, being used for *dispute for*, and primarily the verb is intransitive. See the Intransitive Verb, No. 2.

3. To call in question the propriety of; to oppose by reasoning. An officer is never to *dispute* the orders of his superior.

4. To strive to maintain; as, to *dispute* every inch of ground.

DISPU'TE, *n.* Strife or contest in words or by arguments; an attempt to prove and maintain one's own opinions or claims, by arguments or statements, in opposition to the opinions, arguments or claims of another; controversy in words. They had a *dispute* on the lawfulness of slavery, a subject which, one would think, could admit of no *dispute.*

Dispute is usually applied to verbal contest; *controversy* may be in words or writing. *Dispute* is between individuals; *debate* and *discussion* are applicable to public bodies.

2. The possibility of being controverted; as in the phrase, this is a fact, *beyond all dispute.*

DISPU'TED, *pp.* Contested; opposed by words or arguments; litigated.

DISPU'TELESS, *a.* Admitting no dispute; incontrovertible.

DISPU'TER, *n.* One who disputes, or who is given to disputes; a controvertist.

> Where is the *disputer* of this world. 1 Cor. i.

DISPU'TING, *ppr.* Contending by words or arguments; controverting.

DISPU'TING, *n.* The act of contending by words or arguments; controversy; altercation.

> Do all things without murmurings or *disputings.* Phil. ii.

DISQUALIFICA'TION, *n.* [See *Disqualify.*] The act of disqualifying; or that which disqualifies; that which renders unfit, unsuitable or inadequate; as, sickness is a *disqualification* for labor or study.

2. The act of depriving of legal power or capacity; that which renders incapable; that which incapacitates in law; disability. Conviction of a crime is a *disqualification* for office.

3. Want of qualification. It is used in this sense, though improperly. In strictness, *disqualification* implies a previous qualification; but careless writers use it for the want of qualification, where no previous qualification is supposed. Thus, I must still retain the consciousness of those *disqualifications*, which you have been pleased to overlook. *Sir John Shore, Asiat. Res.* 4. 175.

DISQUAL'IFIED, *pp.* Deprived of qualifications; rendered unfit.

DISQUAL'IFY, *v. t.* [*dis* and *qualify.*] To make unfit; to deprive of natural power, or the qualities or properties necessary for any purpose; with *for.* Indisposition *disqualifies* the body *for* labor, and the mind *for* study. Piety *disqualifies* a person *for* no lawful employment.

2. To deprive of legal capacity, power or right; to disable. A conviction of perjury *disqualifies* a man for a witness. A direct interest in a suit *disqualifies* a person to be a juror in the cause.

DISQUAL'IFYING, *ppr.* Rendering unfit; disabling.

DISQUAN'TITY, *v. t.* To diminish. [*Not in use.*] *Shak.*

DISQUI'ET, *a.* [*dis* and *quiet.*] Unquiet; restless; uneasy. [*Seldom used.*] *Shak.*

DISQUI'ET, *n.* Want of quiet; uneasiness; restlessness; want of tranquility in body or mind; disturbance; anxiety. *Swift. Tillotson.*

DISQUI'ET, *v. t.* To disturb; to deprive of peace, rest or tranquility; to make uneasy or restless; to harass the body; to fret or vex the mind.

> That he may *disquiet* the inhabitants of Babylon. Jer. l.
>
> Why hast thou *disquieted* me. 1 Sam. xxviii.
>
> O my soul, why art thou *disquieted* within me? Ps. xlii.

DISQUI'ETED, *pp.* Made uneasy or restless; disturbed; harassed.

DISQUI'ETER, *n.* One who disquiets; he or that which makes uneasy.

DISQUI'ETFUL, *a.* Producing inquietude. *Barrow.*

DISQUI'ETING, *ppr.* Disturbing: making uneasy; depriving of rest or peace.

2. *a.* Tending to disturb the mind; as *disquieting* apprehensions.

DISQUI'ETLY, *adv.* Without quiet or rest; in an uneasy state; uneasily; anxiously; as, he rested *disquietly* that night. [*Unusual.*] *Wiseman.*

DISQUI'ETNESS, *n.* Uneasiness; restlessness; disturbance of peace in body or mind. *Hooker.*

DISQUI'ETOUS, *a.* Causing uneasiness. [*Not used.*] *Milton.*

DISQUI'ETUDE, *n.* Want of peace or tranquility; uneasiness; disturbance; agitation; anxiety. It is, I believe, most frequently used of the mind.

> Religion is our best security from the *disquietudes* that embitter life.

DISQUISI''TION, *n.* [L. *disquisitio; disquiro; dis* and *quæro*, to seek.]

A formal or systematic inquiry into any subject, by arguments, or discussion of the facts and circumstances that may elucidate truth; as a *disquisition* on government or morals; a *disquisition* concerning the antediluvian earth. *Woodward.*

[*It is usually applied to a written treatise.*]

DISRANK', *v. t.* To degrade from rank. [*Not used.*]

2. To throw out of rank or into confusion. *Decker.*

DISREG'ARD, *n.* [*dis* and *regard.*] Neglect; omission of notice; slight; implying indifference or some degree of contempt; as, to pass one with *disregard.*

DISREG'ARD, *v. t.* To omit to take notice of; to neglect to observe; to slight as unworthy of regard or notice.

> Studious of good, man *disregarded* fame. *Blackmore.*
>
> We are never to *disregard* the wants of the poor, nor the admonitions of conscience.

DISREG'ARDED, *pp.* Neglected; slighted; unnoticed.

DISREG'ARDFUL, *a.* Neglectful; negligent; heedless.

DISREG'ARDFULLY, *adv.* Negligently; heedlessly.

DISREL'ISH, *n.* [*dis* and *relish.*] Distaste; dislike of the palate; some degree of disgust. Men generally have a *disrelish* for tobacco, till the taste is reconciled to it by custom.

2. Bad taste; nauseousness. *Milton.*

3. Distaste or dislike, in a *figurative sense;* dislike of the mind, or of the faculty by which beauty and excellence are perceived.

DISREL'ISH, *v. t.* To dislike the taste of; as, to *disrelish* a particular kind of food.

2. To make nauseous or disgusting; to infect with a bad taste. [*In this sense, I believe, the word is little used.*] *Milton.*

3. To dislike; to feel some disgust at; as, to *disrelish* vulgar jests.

DISREL'ISHED, *pp.* Not relished; disliked; made nauseous.

DISREL'ISHING, *ppr.* Disliking the taste of; experiencing disgust at: rendering nauseous.

DISREP'UTABLE, *a.* [*dis* and *reputable.*]
1. Not reputable; not in esteem; not honorable; low; mean; as *disreputable* company.
2. Dishonorable; disgracing the reputation; tending to impair the good name, and bring into disesteem. It is *disreputable* to associate familiarly with the mean, the lewd and the profane.

DISREPUTA'TION, *n.* [*dis* and *reputation.*] Loss or want of reputation or good name; disrepute; disesteem; dishonor; disgrace; discredit. Ill success often brings an enterprising man, as well as his project, into *disreputation.*

DISREPU'TE, *n.* [*dis* and *repute.*] Loss or want of reputation; disesteem; discredit; dishonor. The alchimist and his books have sunk into *disrepute.*

DISRESPECT', *n.* [*dis* and *respect.*] Want of respect or reverence; disesteem. *Disrespect* often leads a man to treat another with neglect or a degree of contempt.
2. *As an act,* incivility; irreverence; rudeness.

DISRESPECT'FUL, *a.* Wanting in respect; irreverent; as a *disrespectful* thought or opinion.
2. Manifesting disesteem or want of respect; uncivil; as *disrespectful* behavior.

DISRESPECT'FULLY, *adv.* In a disrespectful manner; irreverently; uncivilly.

DISRO'BE, *v. t.* [*dis* and *robe.*] To divest of a robe; to divest of garments; to undress.
2. To strip of covering; to divest of any surrounding appendage. Autumn *disrobes* the fields of verdure.

These two peers were *disrobed* of their glory. *Wotton.*

DISRO'BED, *pp.* Divested of clothing; stripped of covering.

DISRO'BER, *n.* One that strips of robes or clothing.

DISRO'BING, *ppr.* Divesting of garments; stripping of any kind of covering.

DISROOT', *v. t.* [*dis* and *root.*] To tear up the roots, or by the roots.
2. To tear from a foundation; to loosen or undermine.

A piece of ground *disrooted* from its situation by subterraneous inundations. *Goldsmith.*

DISROOT'ED, *pp.* Torn up by the roots; undermined.

DISROOT'ING, *ppr.* Tearing up by the roots; undermining.

DISRUPT', *a.* [L. *disruptus; dis* and *rumpo,* to burst.]
Rent from; torn asunder; severed by rending or breaking.

DISRUP'TION, *n.* [L. *disruptio,* from *disrumpo.*]
1. The act of rending asunder; the act of bursting and separating.
2. Breach; rent; dilaceration; as the *disruption* of rocks in an earthquake; the *disruption* of a stratum of earth; *disruption* of the flesh.

DISRUP'TURE, *v. t.* [*dis* and *rupture.*] To rend; to sever by tearing, breaking or bursting. [*Unnecessary, as it is synonymous with* rupture.]

DISRUP'TURED, *pp.* Rent asunder; severed by breaking. *Med. Repos.*

DISRUP'TURING, *ppr.* Rending asunder; severing.

DISSATISFAC'TION, *n.* [*dis* and *satisfaction.*] The state of being dissatisfied; discontent; uneasiness proceeding from the want of gratification, or from disappointed wishes and expectations.

The ambitious man is subject to uneasiness and *dissatisfaction.* *Addison.*

DISSATISFAC'TORINESS, *n.* Inability to satisfy or give content; a failing to give content.

DISSATISFAC'TORY, *a.* Unable to give content. *Johnson.*
Rather, giving discontent; displeasing.

To have reduced the different qualifications, in the different states, to one uniform rule, would probably have been as *dissatisfactory* to some of the states, as difficult for the convention. *Hamilton. Mitford.*

DISSAT'ISFIED, *pp.* Made discontented; displeased.
2. *a.* Discontented; not satisfied; not pleased; offended. *Locke.*

DISSAT'ISFY, *v. t.* To render discontented; to displease; to excite uneasiness by frustrating wishes or expectations.

DISSAT'ISFYING, *ppr.* Exciting uneasiness or discontent.

DISSE'AT, *v. t.* To remove from a seat. *Shak.*

DISSECT', *v. t.* [L. *disseco, dissectus; dis* and *seco,* to cut; Fr. *dissequer.*]
1. To cut in pieces; to divide an animal body, with a cutting instrument, by separating the joints; as, to *dissect* a fowl. Hence appropriately,
2. To cut in pieces, as an animal or vegetable, for the purpose of examining the structure and use of its several parts; to anatomize. Also, to open any part of a body to observe its morbid appearances, or to ascertain the cause of death or the seat of a disease.
3. To divide into its constituent parts, for the purpose of examination; as, *dissect* your mind; *dissect* a paragraph. *Roscommon. Pope.*

DISSECT'ED, *pp.* Cut in pieces; separated by parting the joints; divided into its constituent parts; opened and examined.

DISSECT'ING, *ppr.* Cutting in pieces; dividing the parts; separating constituent parts for minute examination.

DISSEC'TION, *n.* [L. *dissectio.*] The act of cutting in pieces an animal or vegetable, for the purpose of examining the structure and uses of its parts; anatomy.

Dissection was held sacrilege till the time of Francis I. *Encyc.*
2. The act of separating into constituent parts, for the purpose of critical examination.

DISSECT'OR, *n.* One who dissects; an anatomist.

DISSE'IZE, *v. t.* [*dis* and *seize;* Fr. *dessaisir.*] In *law,* to dispossess wrongfully; to deprive of actual seizin or possession; followed by *of;* as, to *disseize* a tenant *of* his freehold.

A man may suppose himself *disseized,* when he is not so. *Blackstone.*

DISSE'IZED, *pp.* Put out of possession wrongfully or by force; deprived of actual possession.

DISSEIZEE', *n.* A person put out of possession of an estate unlawfully.

DISSE'IZIN, *n.* The act of disseizing; an unlawful dispossessing of a person of his lands, tenements, or incorporeal hereditaments; a deprivation of actual seizin. *Blackstone.*

DISSE'IZING, *ppr.* Depriving of actual seizin or possession; putting out of possession.

DISSE'IZOR, *n.* One who puts another out of possession wrongfully; he that dispossesses another. *Blackstone.*

DISSEM'BLANCE, *n.* [*dis* and *semblance.*] Want of resemblance. [*Little used.*] *Osborne.*

DISSEM'BLE, *v. t.* [L. *dissimulo; dis* and *simulo,* from *similis,* like; Fr. *dissimuler;* It. *dissimulare;* Sp. *disimular;* Arm. *diçzumula.*]
1. To hide under a false appearance; to conceal; to disguise; to pretend that not to be which really is; as, I will not *dissemble* the truth; I cannot *dissemble* my real sentiments. [*This is the proper sense of this word.*]
2. To pretend that to be which is not; to make a false appearance of. This is the sense of *simulate.*

Your son Lucentio
Doth love my daughter, and she loveth him,
Or both *dissemble* deeply their affections. *Shak.*

DISSEM'BLE, *v. i.* To be hypocritical; to assume a false appearance; to conceal the real fact, motives, intention or sentiments under some pretense.

Ye have stolen and *dissembled* also. Josh. vii.

He that hateth, *dissembleth* with his lips. Prov. xxvi.

DISSEM'BLED, *pp.* Concealed under a false appearance; disguised.

DISSEM'BLER, *n.* One who dissembles; a hypocrite; one who conceals his opinions or dispositions under a false appearance.

DISSEM'BLING, *ppr.* Hiding under a false appearance; acting the hypocrite.

DISSEM'BLINGLY, *adv.* With dissimulation; hypocritically; falsely. *Knolles.*

DISSEM'INATE, *v. t.* [L. *dissemino; dis* and *semino,* to sow, from *semen,* seed.]
1. Literally, to sow; to scatter seed; but seldom or never used in its literal sense. But hence,
2. To scatter for growth and propagation, like seed; to spread. Thus, principles, opinions and errors are *disseminated,* when they are spread and propagated. To *disseminate* truth or the gospel is highly laudable.
3. To spread; to diffuse.

A uniform heat *disseminated* through the body of the earth. *Woodward.*
4. To spread; to disperse.

The Jews are *disseminated* through all the trading parts of the world. *Addison.*

[The second is the most proper application of the word, as it should always include the idea of growth or taking root. The fourth sense is hardly vindicable.]

DISSEM'INATED, *pp.* Scattered, as seed; propagated; spread.
2. In *mineralogy,* occurring in portions less than a hazel nut; being scattered.

DISSEM'INATING, *ppr.* Scattering and propagating; spreading.

DISSEMINA'TION, *n.* The act of scattering and propagating, like seed; the act of spreading for growth and permanence. We trust the world is to be reformed by the *dissemination* of evangelical doctrines.

DISSEM'INATOR, *n.* One who disseminates; one who spreads and propagates.

DISSEN'SION, *n.* [L. *dissensio; dis* and *sentio*, to think; Fr. *dissension.*]
Disagreement in opinion, usually a disagreement which is violent, producing warm debates or angry words; contention in words; strife; discord; quarrel; breach of friendship and union.

Debates, *dissensions*, uproars are thy joy. *Dryden.*

Paul and Barnabas had no small *dissension* with them. Acts xv.

We see *dissensions* in church and state, in towns, parishes, and families, and the word is sometimes applied to differences which produce war; as the *dissensions* between the houses of York and Lancaster in England.

DISSEN'SIOUS, *a.* Disposed to discord; quarrelsome; contentious; factious. [*Little used.*] *Shak. Ascham.*

DISSENT', *v. i.* [L. *dissensio; dis* and *sentio*, to think.]
1. To disagree in opinion; to differ; to think in a different or contrary manner; with *from*. There are many opinions in which men *dissent from* us, as they *dissent from* each other.
2. To differ from an established church, in regard to doctrines, rites or government.
3. To differ; to be of a contrary nature. [*Less proper.*] *Hooker.*

DISSENT', *n.* Difference of opinion; disagreement.
2. Declaration of disagreement in opinion; as, they entered their *dissent* on the journals of the house.
3. Contrariety of nature; opposite quality. [*Not in use.*] *Bacon.*

DISSENTA'NEOUS, *a.* Disagreeable; contrary.

DIS'SENTANY, *a.* Dissentaneous; inconsistent. [*Not used.*] *Milton.*

DISSENT'ER, *n.* One who dissents; one who differs in opinion, or one who declares his disagreement.
2. One who separates from the service and worship of any established church. The word is in England particularly applied to those who separate from, or who do not unite with, the church of England.

DISSEN'TIENT, *a.* Disagreeing; declaring dissent.

DISSEN'TIENT, *n.* One who disagrees and declares his dissent.

DISSENT'ING, *ppr.* Disagreeing in opinion; separating from the communion of an established church. It is used as an adjective; as a *dissenting* minister or congregation.

DISSEN'TIOUS, *a.* Disposed to disagreement or discord.

DISSEP'IMENT, *n.* [L. *dissepimentum; dissepio*, to separate; *dis* and *sepio*, to inclose or guard.]
In *botany*, a partition in dry seed-vessels, as in capsules and pods, which separates the fruit into cells. *Encyc.*

DISSERT', *v. i.* [L. *dissero, diserto.*] To discourse or dispute. [*Little in use.*]

DISSERTA'TION, *n.* [L. *dissertatio*, from *disserto*, to discourse, from *dissero*, id.; *dis* and *sero*, to sow, that is, to throw. *Dissero* is to throw out, to cast abroad.]
1. A discourse, or rather a formal discourse, intended to illustrate a subject.
2. A written essay, treatise or disquisition; as Plutarch's *dissertation* on the poets; Newton's *dissertations* on the prophecies.

DIS'SERTATOR, *n.* One who writes a dissertation; one who debates. *Boyle.*

DISSERVE, *v. t.* *disserv'.* [*dis* and *serve.*] To injure; to hurt; to harm; to do injury or mischief to.

He took the first opportunity to *disserve* him. *Clarendon.*

Too much zeal often *disserves* a good cause. *Anon.*

DISSERV'ED, *pp.* Injured.

DISSERV'ICE, *n.* Injury; harm; mischief; as, violent remedies often do a *disservice.*

DISSERV'ICEABLE, *a.* Injurious; hurtful.

DISSERV'ICEABLENESS, *n.* The quality of being injurious; tendency to harm. *Norris.*

DISSET'TLE, *v. t.* To unsettle. [*Not used.*] *More.*

DISSEV'ER, *v. t.* [*dis* and *sever.* In this word, *dis*, as in *dispart*, can have no effect, unless to augment the signification, as *dis* and *sever* both denote separation.]
To dispart; to part in two; to divide asunder; to separate; to disunite, either by violence or not. When with force, it is equivalent to *rend* and *burst.* It may denote either to *cut* or to *tear* asunder. In beheading, the head is *dissevered* from the body. The lightning may *dissever* a branch from the stem of a tree. Jealousy *dissevers* the bonds of friendship. The reformation *dissevered* the catholic church; it *dissevered* protestants from catholics.

DISSEV'ERANCE, *n.* The act of dissevering; separation.

DISSEV'ERED, *pp.* Disparted; disjoined; separated.

DISSEV'ERING, *ppr.* Dividing asunder; separating; tearing or cutting asunder.

DISSEV'ERING, *n.* The act of separating; separation.

DIS'SIDENCE, *n.* [infra.] Discord.

DIS'SIDENT, *a.* [L. *dissideo*, to disagree; *dis* and *sedeo*, to sit.] Not agreeing.

DIS'SIDENT, *n.* A dissenter; one who separates from the established religion; a word applied to the members of the Lutheran, Calvinistic and Greek churches in Poland. *Encyc.*

DISSIL'IENCE, *n.* [L. *dissilio; dis* and *salio*, to leap.] The act of leaping or starting asunder.

DISSIL'IENT, *a.* Starting asunder; bursting and opening with an elastic force, as the dry pod or capsule of a plant; as a *dissilient* pericarp. *Martyn.*

DISSILI''TION, *n.* The act of bursting open; the act of starting or springing different ways. *Boyle.*

DISSIM'ILAR, *a.* [*dis* and *similar.*] Unlike, either in nature, properties or external form; not similar; not having the resemblance of; heterogeneous. Newton denominates *dissimilar*, the rays of light of different refrangibility. The tempers of men are as *dissimilar* as their features.

DISSIMILAR'ITY, *n.* Unlikeness; want of resemblance; dissimilitude; as the *dissimilarity* of human faces and forms.

DISSIM'ILE, *n.* *dissim'ily.* Comparison or illustration by contraries. [*Little used.*]

DISSIMIL'ITUDE, *n.* [L. *dissimilitudo.*] Unlikeness; want of resemblance; as a *dissimilitude* of form or character.

DISSIMULA'TION, *n.* [L. *dissimulatio; dis* and *simulatio*, from *simulo*, to make like, *similis*, like.]
The act of dissembling; a hiding under a false appearance; a feigning; false pretension; hypocrisy. Dissimulation may be simply concealment of the opinions, sentiments or purpose; but it includes also the assuming of a false or counterfeit appearance which conceals the real opinions or purpose. *Dissimulation* among statesmen is sometimes regarded as a necessary vice, or as no vice at all.

Let love be without *dissimulation.* Rom. xii.

DISSIM'ULE, *v. t.* To dissemble. [*Not in use.*] *Elyot.*

DIS'SIPABLE, *a.* [See *Dissipate.*] Liable to be dissipated; that may be scattered or dispersed.

The heat of those plants is very *dissipable.* *Bacon.*

DIS'SIPATE, *v. t.* [L. *dissipatus, dissipo; dis* and an obsolete verb, *sipo*, to throw. We perhaps see its derivatives in *siphon, prosapia* and *sept*, and *sepio*, to inclose, may be primarily to repel and thus to guard.]
1. To scatter; to disperse; to drive asunder. Wind *dissipates* fog; the heat of the sun *dissipates* vapor; mirth *dissipates* care and anxiety; the cares of life tend to *dissipate* serious reflections.

Scatter, disperse and *dissipate* are in many cases synonymous; but *dissipate* is used appropriately to denote the dispersion of things that vanish, or are not afterwards collected; as, to *dissipate* fog, vapor or clouds. We say, an army is *scattered* or *dispersed*, but not *dissipated.* Trees are *scattered* or *dispersed* over a field, but not *dissipated.*

2. To expend; to squander; to scatter property in wasteful extravagance; to waste; to consume; as, a man has *dissipated* his fortune in the pursuit of pleasure.
3. To scatter the attention.

DIS'SIPATE, *v. i.* To scatter; to disperse; to separate into parts and disappear; to waste away; to vanish.

A fog or cloud gradually *dissipates*, before the rays or heat of the sun. The heat of a body *dissipates;* the fluids *dissipate.*

DIS'SIPATED, *pp.* Scattered; dispersed; wasted; consumed; squandered.
2. *a.* Loose; irregular; given to extravagance in the expenditure of property; devoted to pleasure and vice; as a *dissipated* man; a *dissipated* life.

DIS'SIPATING, *ppr.* Scattering; dispersing; wasting; consuming; squandering; vanishing.

DISSIPA'TION, *n.* The act of scattering; dispersion; the state of being dispersed; as the *dissipation* of vapor or heat.
2. In *physics*, the insensible loss or waste of the minute parts of a body, which fly off,

by which means the body is diminished or consumed.

3. Scattered attention; or that which diverts and calls off the mind from any subject. *Swift.*

4. A dissolute, irregular course of life; a wandering from object to object in pursuit of pleasure; a course of life usually attended with careless and exorbitant expenditures of money, and indulgence in vices, which impair or ruin both health and fortune.

What! is it proposed then to reclaim the spendthrift from his *dissipation* and extravagance, by filling his pockets with money? *P. Henry, Wirt's Sketches.*

DISSO'CIABLE, *a.* [See *Dissociate.*] Not well associated, united or assorted.

They came in two and two, though matched in the most *dissociable* manner. *Spectator.* No. 4.

DISSO'CIAL, *a.* [*dis* and *social.*] Unfriendly to society; contracted; selfish; as a *dissocial* passion. *Kames.*

DISSO'CIATE, *v. t.* [L. *dissociatus, dissocio; dis* and *socio*, to unite, *socius*, a companion.]

To separate; to disunite; to part; as, to *dissociate* the particles of a concrete substance. *Boyle.*

DISSO'CIATED, *pp.* Separated; disunited.

DISSO'CIATING, *ppr.* Separating; disuniting.

DISSOCIA'TION, *n.* The act of disuniting; a state of separation; disunion.

It will add to the *dissociation*, distraction and confusion of these confederate republics. *Burke.*

DISSOLUBIL'ITY, *n.* Capacity of being dissolved by heat or moisture, and converted into a fluid.

DIS'SOLUBLE, *a.* [L. *dissolubilis.* See *Dissolve.*]

2. Capable of being dissolved; that may be melted; having its parts separable by heat or moisture; convertible into a fluid. *Woodward.*

2. That may be disunited.

DIS'SOLUTE, *a.* [L. *dissolutus*, from *dissolvo.*]

1. Loose in behavior and morals; given to vice and dissipation; wanton; lewd; luxurious; debauched; not under the restraints of law; as a *dissolute* man; *dissolute* company.

2. Vicious; wanton; devoted to pleasure and dissipation; as a *dissolute* life.

DIS'SOLUTELY, *adv.* Loosely; wantonly; in dissipation or debauchery; without restraint; as, to live *dissolutely.*

DIS'SOLUTENESS, *n.* Looseness of manners and morals; vicious indulgences in pleasure, as in intemperance and debauchery; dissipation; as *dissoluteness* of life or manners.

DISSOLU'TION, *n.* [L. *dissolutio*, from *dissolvo.*]

In *a general sense*, the separation of the parts of a body which, in the natural structure, are united; or the reduction of concrete bodies into their smallest parts, without regard to solidity or fluidity. Thus we speak of the *dissolution* of salts in water, of metals in nitro-muriatic acid, and of ice or butter by heat; in which cases, the dissolution is effected by a menstruum or particular agent. We speak also of the *dissolution* of flesh or animal bodies, when the parts separate by putrefaction. Dissolution then is,

1. The act of liquefying or changing from a solid to a fluid state by heat; a melting; a thawing; as the *dissolution* of snow and ice, which converts them into water.

2. The reduction of a body into its smallest parts, or into very minute parts, by a dissolvent or menstruum, as of a metal by nitro-muriatic acid, or of salts in water.

3. The separation of the parts of a body by putrefaction, or the analysis of the natural structure of mixed bodies, as of animal or vegetable substances; decomposition.

4. The substance formed by dissolving a body in a menstruum. [This is now called a *solution.*] *Bacon.*

5. Death; the separation of the soul and body. *Milton.*

6. Destruction; the separation of the parts which compose a connected system, or body; as the *dissolution* of the world, or of nature; the *dissolution* of government.

7. The breaking up of an assembly, or the putting an end to its existence.

Dissolution is the civil death of parliament. *Blackstone.*

8. Looseness of manners; dissipation. *Taylor. South.*

In this latter sense the word is obsolete, *dissoluteness* being substituted.

9. *Dissolution of the blood*, in medicine, that state of the blood, in which it does not readily coagulate, on its cooling out of the body, as in malignant fevers. *Cyc.*

DISSOLV'ABLE, *a. dizzolv'able.* [See *Dissolve.*] That may be dissolved; capable of being melted; that may be converted into a fluid. Sugar and ice are *dissolvable* bodies.

DISSOLVE, *v. t. dizzolv'.* [L. *dissolvo; dis* and *solvo*, to loose, to free.]

1. To melt; to liquefy; to convert from a solid or fixed state to a fluid state, by means of heat or moisture.

To dissolve by heat, is to loosen the parts of a solid body and render them fluid or easily movable. Thus ice is converted into water by dissolution.

To dissolve in a liquid, is to separate the parts of a solid substance, and cause them to mix with the fluid; or to reduce a solid substance into minute parts which may be sustained in that fluid. Thus water *dissolves* salt and sugar.

2. To disunite; to break; to separate.

Seeing then that all these things shall be *dissolved*, what manner of persons ought ye to be in all holy conversation and godliness? 2 Pet. iii.

3. To loose; to disunite.

Down fell the duke, his joints *dissolved.* *Fairfax.*

4. To loose the ties or bonds of any thing; to destroy any connected system; as, to *dissolve* a government; to *dissolve* a corporation.

5. To loose; to break; as, to *dissolve* a league; to *dissolve* the bonds of friendship.

6. To break up; to cause to separate; to put an end to; as, to *dissolve* the parliament; to *dissolve* an assembly.

7. To clear; to solve; to remove; to dissipate, or to explain; as, to *dissolve* doubts. We usually say, to *solve* doubts and difficulties.

8. To break; to destroy; as, to *dissolve* a charm, spell or enchantment. *Milton.*

9. To loosen or relax; to make languid; as *dissolved* in pleasure.

10. To waste away; to consume; to cause to vanish or perish.

Thou *dissolvest* my substance. Job xxx.

11. To annul; to rescind; as, to *dissolve* an injunction. *Johnson's Rep.*

DISSOLVE, *v. i. dizzolv'.* To be melted; to be converted from a solid to a fluid state; as, sugar *dissolves* in water.

2. To sink away; to lose strength and firmness. *Shak.*

3. To melt away in pleasure; to become soft or languid.

4. To fall asunder; to crumble; to be broken. A government may *dissolve* by its own weight or extent.

5. To waste away; to perish; to be decomposed. Flesh *dissolves* by putrefaction.

6. To come to an end by a separation of parts.

DISSOLV'ED, *pp.* Melted; liquefied; disunited; parted; loosed; relaxed; wasted away; ended.

Dissolved blood, is that which does not readily coagulate.

DISSOLV'ENT, *a.* Having power to melt or dissolve; as the *dissolvent* juices of the stomach. *Ray.*

DISSOLV'ENT, *n.* Any thing which has the power or quality of melting, or converting a solid substance into a fluid, or of separating the parts of a fixed body so that they mix with a liquid; as, water is a *dissolvent* of salts and earths. It is otherwise called a *menstruum.*

2. In *medicine*, a remedy supposed capable of dissolving concretions in the body, such as calculi, tubercles, &c. *Parr.*

DISSOLV'ER, *n.* That which dissolves or has the power of dissolving. Heat is the most powerful *dissolver* of substances.

DISSOLV'ING, *ppr.* Melting; making or becoming liquid.

DIS'SONANCE, *n.* [Fr. *dissonance*, from L. *dissonans, dissono*, to be discordant; *dis* and *sono*, to sound.]

1. Discord; a mixture or union of harsh, unharmonious sounds, which are grating or unpleasing to the ear; as the *dissonance* of notes, sounds or numbers.

2. Disagreement.

DIS'SONANT, *a.* Discordant; harsh; jarring; unharmonious; unpleasant to the ear; as *dissonant* notes or intervals.

2. Disagreeing; incongruous; usually with *from*; as, he advanced propositions very *dissonant from* truth.

DISSUA'DE, *v. t.* [L. *dissuadeo; dis* and *suadeo*, to advise or incite to any thing.]

1. To advise or exhort against; to attempt to draw or divert from a measure, by reason or offering motives to; as, the minister *dissuaded* the prince from adopting the measure; he *dissuaded* him from his purpose.

2. To represent as unfit, improper or dangerous.

War therefore, open or concealed, alike
My voice *dissuades.* *Milton.*

This phraseology is probably elliptical,

and merely poetical; *from* being understood.

DISSUA'DED, *pp.* Advised against; counseled or induced by advice not to do something; diverted from a purpose.

DISSUA'DER, *n.* He that dissuades; a dehorter.

DISSUA'DING, *ppr.* Exhorting against; attempting, by advice, to divert from a purpose.

DISSUA'SION, *n. disua'zhun.* Advice or exhortation in opposition to something; the act of attempting, by reason or motives offered, to divert from a purpose or measure; dehortation. *Boyle.*

DISSUA'SIVE, *a.* Tending to dissuade, or divert from a measure or purpose; dehortatory.

DISSUA'SIVE, *n.* Reason, argument, or counsel, employed to deter one from a measure or purpose; that which is used or which tends to divert the mind from any purpose or pursuit. The consequences of intemperance are powerful *dissuasives* from indulging in that vice.

DISSUN'DER, *v. t.* [*dis* and *sunder.*] To separate; to rend. *Chapman.*

DISSWEE'TEN, *v. t.* To deprive of sweetness. [*Not used.*] *Bp. Richardson.*

DISSYLLAB'IC, *a.* Consisting of two syllables only; as a *dissyllabic* foot in poetry.

DISSYL'LABLE, *n.* [Gr. δισσυλλαβος; δις, two or twice, and συλλαβος, a syllable.]

A word consisting of two syllables only; as, *paper, whiteness, virtue.*

DIS'TAFF, *n.* [The English books refer this word to the Saxon *distæf;* but I have not found the word in the Saxon Dictionary.]

1. The staff of a spinning-wheel, to which a bunch of flax or tow is tied, and from which the thread is drawn.

> She layeth her hands to the spindle, and her hands hold the *distaff.* Prov. xxxi.

2. Figuratively, a woman, or the female sex.

> His crown usurped, a *distaff* on the throne. *Dryden.*

DIS'TAFF-THISTLE, *n.* A species of thistle; a name of the *Atractylis,* and of the *Carthamus,* or false saffron.

DISTA'IN, *v. t.* [*dis* and *stain.* This seems to be from the French *deteindre,* from the L. *tingo;* but see *Stain.*]

1. To stain; to tinge with any different color from the natural or proper one; to discolor. We speak of a sword *distained* with blood; a garment *distained* with gore. It has precisely the signification of *stain,* but is used chiefly or appropriately in poetry and the higher kinds of prose.

2. To blot; to sully; to defile; to tarnish.

> She *distained* her honorable blood. *Spenser.*

> The worthiness of praise *distains* his worth. *Shak.*

DISTA'INED, *pp.* Stained; tinged; discolored; blotted; sullied.

DISTA'INING, *ppr.* Staining; discoloring; blotting; tarnishing.

DIS'TANCE, *n.* [Fr. *distance;* Sp. *distancia;* It. *distanza;* L. *distantia,* from *disto,* to stand apart; *dis* and *sto,* to stand.]

1. An interval or space between two objects; the length of the shortest line which intervenes between two things that are separate; as a great or small *distance. Distance* may be a line, an inch, a mile, or any indefinite length; as the *distance* between the sun and saturn.

2. Preceded by *at,* remoteness of place.

> He waits *at distance* till he hears from Cato. *Addison.*

3. Preceded by *thy, his, your, her, their,* a suitable space, or such remoteness as is common or becoming; as, let him keep *his distance;* keep *your distance.* [See No. 8.]

4. A space marked on the course where horses run.

> This horse ran the whole field out of *distance.* *L'Estrange.*

5. Space of time; any indefinite length of time, past or future, intervening between two periods or events; as the *distance* of an hour, of a year, of an age.

6. Ideal space or separation.

> Qualities that affect our senses are, in the things themselves, so united and blended, that there is no *distance* between them. *Locke.*

7. Contrariety; opposition.

> Banquo was your enemy,
> So he is mine, and in such bloody *distance*— *Shak.*

8. The remoteness which respect requires; hence, respect.

> I hope your modesty
> Will know what *distance* to the crown is due. *Dryden.*

> 'Tis by respect and *distance* that authority is uphold. *Atterbury.*

[See No. 3.]

9. Reserve; coldness; alienation of heart.

> On the part of heaven
> Now alienated, *distance* and distaste. *Milton.*

10. Remoteness in succession or relation; as the *distance* between a descendant and his ancestor.

11. In *music,* the interval between two notes; as the *distance* of a fourth or seventh.

DIS'TANCE, *v. t.* To place remote; to throw off from the view. *Dryden.*

2. To leave behind in a race; to win the race by a great superiority.

3. To leave at a great distance behind.

> He *distanced* the most skilful of his cotemporaries. *Milner.*

DIS'TANCED, *pp.* Left far behind; cast out of the race.

DIS'TANT, *a.* [L. *distans,* standing apart.]

1. Separate; having an intervening space of any indefinite extent. One point may be less than a line or a hair's breadth *distant* from another. Saturn is supposed to be nearly nine hundred million miles *distant* from the sun.

2. Remote in place; as, a *distant* object appears under a small angle.

3. Remote in time, past or future; as a *distant* age or period of the world.

4. Remote in the line of succession or descent, indefinitely; as a *distant* descendant; a *distant* ancestor; *distant* posterity.

5. Remote in natural connection or consanguinity; as a *distant* relation; *distant* kindred; a *distant* collateral line.

6. Remote in nature; not allied; not agreeing with or in conformity to; as practice very *distant* from principles or profession.

7. Remote in view; slight; faint; not very likely to be realized; as, we have a *distant* hope or prospect of seeing better times.

8. Remote in connection; slight; faint; indirect; not easily seen or understood; as a *distant* hint or allusion to a person or subject. So also we say, a *distant* idea; a *distant* thought; a *distant* resemblance.

9. Reserved; shy; implying haughtiness, coldness of affection, indifference, or disrespect; as, the manners of a person are *distant.*

DIS'TANTLY, *adv.* Remotely; at a distance; with reserve.

DISTA'STE, *n.* [*dis* and *taste.*] Aversion of the taste; dislike of food or drink; disrelish; disgust, or a slight degree of it. *Distaste* for a particular kind of food may be constitutional, or the effect of a diseased stomach.

2. Dislike; uneasiness.

> Prosperity is not without many fears and *distastes,* and adversity is not without comfort and hopes. *Bacon.*

3. Dislike; displeasure; alienation of affection. *Milton. Pope.*

DISTA'STE, *v. t.* To disrelish; to dislike; to lothe; as, to *distaste* drugs or poisons.

2. To offend; to disgust.

> He thought it no policy to *distaste* the English or Irish, but sought to please them. *Davies.*

3. To vex; to displease; to sour. *Pope.*

[*The two latter significations are rare.*]

DISTA'STED, *pp.* Disrelished; disliked; offended; displeased.

DISTA'STEFUL, *a.* Nauseous; unpleasant or disgusting to the taste.

2. Offensive; displeasing; as a *distasteful* truth. *Dryden.*

3. Malevolent; as *distasteful* looks. *Shak.*

DISTA'STEFULNESS, *n.* Disagreeableness; dislike. *Whitlock.*

DISTA'STING, *ppr.* Disrelishing; disliking; offending; displeasing.

DISTA'STIVE, *n.* That which gives disrelish or aversion. *Whitlock.*

DISTEM'PER, *n.* [*dis* and *temper.*] Literally, an undue or unnatural temper, or disproportionate mixture of parts. Hence,

2. Disease; malady; indisposition; any morbid state of an animal body, or of any part of it; a state in which the animal economy is deranged or imperfectly carried on. [See *Disease.*] It is used of the slighter diseases, but not exclusively. In general, it is synonymous with *disease,* and is particularly applied to the diseases of brutes.

3. Want of due temperature, applied to climate; *the literal sense of the word, but not now used.*

> Countries under the tropic of a *distemper* uninhabitable. *Raleigh.*

4. Bad constitution of the mind; undue predominance of a passion or appetite. *Shak.*

5. Want of due balance of parts or opposite qualities and principles; as, the temper and *distemper* of an empire consist of contraries. [*Not now used.*] *Bacon.*

6. Ill humor of mind; depravity of inclination. [*Not used.*] *King Charles.*

7. Political disorder; tumult. *Waller.*

8. Uneasiness; ill humor or bad temper.

> There is a sickness,
> Which puts some of us in *distemper.* *Shak.*

9. In *painting,* the mixing of colors with something besides oil and water. When colors are mixed with size, whites of eggs, or other unctuous or glutinous matter, and

not with oil, it is said to be done *in distemper*. *Encyc.*

DISTEM'PER, *v. t.* To disease; to disorder; to derange the functions of the body or mind. *Shak. Boyle.*

2. To disturb; to ruffle. *Dryden.*

3. To deprive of temper or moderation. *Dryden.*

4. To make disaffected, ill humored or malignant. *Shak.*

This verb is seldom used, except in the participles.

DISTEM'PERANCE, *n.* Distemperature.

DISTEM'PERATE, *a.* Immoderate. [*Little used.*] *Raleigh.*

DISTEM'PERATURE, *n.* Bad temperature; intemperateness; excess of heat or cold, or of other qualities; a noxious state; as the *distemperature* of the air or climate.

2. Violent tumultuousness; outrageousness. *Johnson.*

3. Perturbation of mind. *Shak.*

4. Confusion; commixture of contrarieties; loss of regularity; disorder. *Shak.*

5. Slight illness; indisposition. *Brewer.*

DISTEM'PERED, *pp.* or *a.* Diseased in body, or disordered in mind. We speak of a *distempered* body, a *distempered* limb, a *distempered* head or brain.

2. Disturbed; ruffled; as *distempered* passions.

3. Deprived of temper or moderation; immoderate; as *distempered* zeal. *Dryden.*

4. Disordered; biased; prejudiced; perverted; as minds *distempered* by interest or passion.

> The imagination, when completely *distempered*, is the most incurable of all disordered faculties. *Buckminster.*

5. Disaffected; made malevolent.

> *Distempered* lords. *Shak.*

DISTEM'PERING, *ppr.* Affecting with disease or disorder; disturbing; depriving of moderation.

DISTEND', *v. t.* [L. *distendo*; *dis* and *tendo*, to tend, to stretch, from the root of *teneo*, to hold, Gr. τεινω, to stretch. Class Dn.]

1. To stretch or spread in all directions; to dilate; to enlarge; to expand; to swell; as, to *distend* a bladder; to *distend* the bowels; to *distend* the lungs. [*This is the appropriate sense of the word.*]

2. To spread apart; to divaricate; as, to *distend* the legs. We seldom say, to *distend* a plate of metal, and never, I believe, to *distend* a line; *extend* being used in both cases. We use *distend* chiefly to denote the stretching, spreading or expansion of any thing, by means of a substance inclosed within it, or by the elastic force of something inclosed. In this case the body distended swells or spreads in all directions, and usually in a spherical form. A bladder is *distended* by inflation, or by the expansion of rarefied air within it. The skin is *distended* in boils and abscesses, by matter generated within them. This appropriation of the word has not always been observed.

DISTEND'ED, *pp.* Spread; expanded; dilated by an inclosed substance or force.

DISTEND'ING, *ppr.* Stretching in all directions; dilating; expanding.

DISTENSIBIL'ITY, *n.* The quality or capacity of being distensible.

DISTEN'SIBLE, *a.* Capable of being distended or dilated.

DISTENT', *a.* Spread. [*Not in use.*] *Spenser.*

DISTENT', *n.* Breadth. [*Not used.*] *Wotton.*

DISTEN'TION, *n.* [L. *distentio.*] The act of distending; the act of stretching in breadth or in all directions; the state of being distended; as the *distention* of the lungs or bowels.

2. Breadth; extent or space occupied by the thing distended.

3. An opening, spreading or divarication; as the *distention* of the legs.

DISTERM'INATE, *a.* [L. *disterminatus.*] Separated by bounds. *Obs.* *Hale.*

DISTERMINA'TION, *n.* Separation. *Obs.* *Hammond.*

DIS'THENE, *n.* [Gr. δις, two, and σθενος, force.]

A mineral so called by Haüy, because its crystals have the property of being electrified both positively and negatively. It is the sappare of Saussure, and the cyanite or kyanite of Werner. *Lunier. Cleaveland.*

DISTHRO'NIZE, *v. t.* To dethrone. [*Not used.*] *Spenser.*

DIS'TICH, *n.* [L. *distichon*; Gr. δις and ϛιχος, a verse.]

A couplet; a couple of verses or poetic lines, making complete sense; an epigram of two verses. *Johnson. Encyc.*

DIS'TICHOUS, } *a.* Having two rows, or
DIS'TICH, } disposed in two rows. *Lee.*

A *distichous* spike has all the flowers pointing two ways. *Martyn.*

DISTILL', *v. i.* [L. *distillo*; *dis* and *stillo*, to drop, *stilla*, a drop; Fr. *distiller*; It. *distillare*; Sp. *destilar*; Gr. ϛαλαω.] To drop; to fall in drops.

> Soft showers *distill'd*, and suns grew warm in vain. *Pope.*

2. To flow gently, or in a small stream.

> The Euphrates *distilleth* out of the mountains of Armenia. *Raleigh.*

3. To use a still; to practice distillation. *Shak.*

DISTILL', *v. t.* To let fall in drops; to throw down in drops. The clouds *distill* water on the earth.

> The dew, which on the tender grass
> The evening had *distilled*. *Drayton.*

2. To extract by heat; to separate spirit or essential oils from liquor by heat or evaporation, and convert that vapor into a liquid by condensation in a refrigeratory; to separate the volatile parts of a substance by heat; to rectify; as, to *distill* brandy from wine, or spirit from melasses.

3. To extract spirit from, by evaporation and condensation; as, to *distill* cyder or melasses; to *distill* wine.

4. To extract the pure part of a fluid; as, to *distill* water.

5. To dissolve or melt. [*Unusual.*]

> Swords by the lightning's subtle force *distilled*. *Addison.*

DISTIL'LABLE, *a.* That may be distilled; fit for distillation. *Sherwood.*

DISTILLA'TION, *n.* The act of falling in drops, or the act of pouring or throwing down in drops.

2. The vaporization and subsequent condensation of a liquid by means of an alembic, or still and refrigeratory, or of a retort and receiver; the operation of extracting spirit from a substance by evaporation and condensation; rectification.

3. The substance extracted by distilling. *Shak.*

4. That which falls in drops. *Johnson.*

DISTIL'LATORY, *a.* Belonging to distillation; used for distilling; as *distillatory* vessels. *Hooper.*

DISTIL'LED, *pp.* Let fall or thrown down in drops; subjected to the process of distillation; extracted by evaporation.

DISTIL'LER, *n.* One who distills; one whose occupation is to extract spirit by evaporation and condensation.

DISTIL'LERY, *n.* The act or art of distilling.

2. The building and works where distilling is carried on.

DISTIL'LING, *ppr.* Dropping; letting fall in drops; extracting by distillation.

DISTILL'MENT, *n.* That which is drawn by distillation. *Shak.*

DISTINCT', *a.* [L. *distinctus*, from *distinguo*. See *Distinguish.*]

1. Literally, having the difference marked; separated by a visible sign, or by a note or mark; as a place *distinct* by name. *Milton.*

2. Different; separate; not the same in number or kind; as, he holds two *distinct* offices; he is known by *distinct* titles.

3. Separate in place; not conjunct; as, the two regiments marched together, but had *distinct* encampments.

4. So separated as not to be confounded with any other thing; clear; not confused. To reason correctly we must have *distinct* ideas. We have a *distinct* or indistinct view of a prospect.

5. Spotted; variegated.

> Tempestuous fell
> His arrows from the fourfold-visag'd four,
> *Distinct* with eyes. *Milton.*

DISTINCT', *v. t.* To distinguish. [*Not in use.*] *Chaucer.*

DISTINC'TION, *n.* [L. *distinctio.*] The act of separating or distinguishing.

2. A note or mark of difference. [*Seldom used.*]

3. Difference made; a separation or disagreement in kind or qualities, by which one thing is known from another. We observe a *distinction* between matter and spirit; a *distinction* between the animal and vegetable kingdoms; a *distinction* between good and evil, right and wrong; between sound reasoning and sophistry.

3. Difference regarded; separation; preference; as in the phrase, *without distinction*, which denotes promiscuously, all together, alike.

> Maids, women, wives, *without distinction* fall. *Dryden.*

4. Separation; division; as the *distinction* of tragedy into acts. *Dryden.*

[In this sense, *division* would be preferable.]

5. Notation of difference; discrimination; as a *distinction* between real and apparent good.

> In classing the qualities of actions, it is necessary to make accurate *distinctions*. *Anon.*

6. Eminence; superiority; elevation of rank in society, or elevation of character; honorable estimation. Men who hold a high rank by birth or office, and men who are eminent for their talents, services or worth, are called men of *distinction*, as being raised above others by positive institutions or by reputation. So we say, a man of *note*.
7. That which confers eminence or superiority; office, rank or public favor.
8. Discernment; judgment. *Johnson.*

DISTINCT′IVE, *a.* That marks distinction or difference; as *distinctive* names or titles.
2. Having the power to distinguish and discern. [*Less proper.*] *Brown.*

DISTINCT′IVELY, *adv.* With distinction; plainly.

DISTINCT′LY, *adv.* Separately; with distinctness; not confusedly; without the blending of one part or thing with another; as a proposition *distinctly* understood; a figure *distinctly* defined. Hence,
2. Clearly; plainly; as, to view an object *distinctly.*

DISTINCT′NESS, *n.* The quality or state of being distinct; a separation or difference that prevents confusion of parts or things; as the *distinctness* of two ideas, or of distant objects.
2. Nice discrimination; whence, clearness; precision; as, he stated his arguments with great *distinctness.*

DISTIN′GUISH, *v. t.* [L. *distinguo*; *dis* and *stingo* or *stinguo*, *n* not radical. This seems to be Gr. ϛιζω, ϛιξω, for the second future is ϛιγω, and the derivatives prove the primary elements to be *stg*, as in ϛιγευς, ϛιγμα, ϛικτος. Hence also L. *stigo*, whence *instigo*, to *instigate*. The primary sense is, to prick, to pierce with a sharp point, to thrust in or on; and we retain the precise word in the verb, to *stick*, which see. The practice of making marks by puncturing, or sticking, gave rise to the applications of this word, as such marks were used to note and ascertain different things, to *distinguish* them. See *Extinguish*, and Class Dg. No. 31.]
1. To ascertain and indicate difference by some external mark. The farmer *distinguishes* his sheep by marking their ears. The manufacturer *distinguishes* pieces of cloth by some mark or impression.
2. To separate one thing from another by some mark or quality; to know or ascertain difference.

First, by sight; as, to *distinguish* one's own children from others by their features.

Secondly, by feeling. A blind man *distinguishes* an egg from an orange, but rarely *distinguishes* colors.

Thirdly, by smell; as, it is easy to *distinguish* the smell of a peach from that of an apple.

Fourthly, by taste; as, to *distinguish* a plum from a pear.

Fifthly, by hearing; as, to *distinguish* the sound of a drum from that of a violin.

Sixthly, by the understanding; as, to *distinguish* vice from virtue, truth from falsehood.

3. To separate or divide by any mark or quality which constitutes difference. We *distinguish* sounds into high and low, soft and harsh, lively and grave. We *distinguish* causes into direct and indirect, immediate and mediate.
4. To discern critically; to judge.

> Nor more can you *distinguish* of a man,
> Than of his outward show. *Shak.*

5. To separate from others by some mark of honor or preference. Homer and Virgil are *distinguished* as poets; Demosthenes and Cicero, as orators.
6. To make eminent or known. *Johnson.*

DISTIN′GUISH, *v. i.* To make a distinction; to find or show the difference. It is the province of a judge to *distinguish* between cases apparently similar, but differing in principle.

DISTIN′GUISHABLE, *a.* Capable of being distinguished; that may be separated, known or made known, by notes of diversity, or by any difference. A tree at a distance is *distinguishable* from a shrub. A simple idea is not *distinguishable* into different ideas.
2. Worthy of note or special regard. *Swift.*

DISTIN′GUISHED, *pp.* Separated or known by a mark of difference, or by different qualities.
2. *a.* Separated from others by superior or extraordinary qualities; whence, eminent; extraordinary; transcendent; noted; famous; celebrated. Thus, we admire *distinguished* men, *distinguished* talents or virtues, and *distinguished* services.

DISTIN′GUISHER, *n.* He or that which distinguishes, or that separates one thing from another by marks of diversity. *Brown.*
2. One who discerns accurately the difference of things; a nice or judicious observer. *Dryden.*

DISTIN′GUISHING, *ppr.* Separating from others by a note of diversity; ascertaining difference by a mark.
2. Ascertaining, knowing or perceiving a difference.
3. *a.* Constituting difference, or distinction from every thing else; peculiar; as the *distinguishing* doctrines of christianity.

DISTIN′GUISHINGLY, *adv.* With distinction; with some mark of preference. *Pope.*

DISTIN′GUISHMENT, *n.* Distinction; observation of difference. *Graunt.*

DISTI′TLE, *v. t.* To deprive of right. *B. Jonson.*

DISTORT′, *v. t.* [L. *distortus*, *distorqueo*; *dis* and *torqueo*, to twist, Fr. *tordre*, Sp. *torcer.*]
1. To twist out of natural or regular shape; as, to *distort* the neck, the limbs or the body; to *distort* the features.
2. To force or put out of the true posture or direction.

> Wrath and malice, envy and revenge *distort* the understanding. *Tillotson.*

3. To wrest from the true meaning; to pervert; as, to *distort* passages of scripture, or their meaning.

DISTORT′, *a.* Distorted. *Spenser.*

DISTORT′ED, *pp.* Twisted out of natural or regular shape; wrested; perverted.

DISTORT′ING, *ppr.* Twisting out of shape; wresting; perverting.

DISTOR′TION, *n.* [L. *distortio.*] The act of distorting or wresting; a twisting out of regular shape; a twisting or writhing motion; as the *distortions* of the face or body.
2. The state of being twisted out of shape; deviation from natural shape or position; crookedness; grimace.
3. A perversion of the true meaning of words.

DISTRACT′, *v. t.* [L. *distractus*, *distraho*; *dis* and *traho*, to draw. See *Draw* and *Drag*. The old participle *distraught* is obsolete.]
1. Literally, to draw apart; to pull in different directions, and separate. Hence, to divide; to separate; and hence, to throw into confusion. Sometimes in a literal sense. Contradictory or mistaken orders may *distract* an army.
2. To turn or draw from any object; to divert from any point, towards another point or toward various other objects; as, to *distract* the eye or the attention.

> If he cannot avoid the eye of the observer, he hopes to *distract* it by a multiplicity of the object. *South.*

3. To draw towards different objects; to fill with different considerations; to perplex; to confound; to harass; as, to *distract* the mind with cares; you *distract* me with your clamor.

> While I suffer thy terrors, I am *distracted.* Ps. lxxxviii.

4. To disorder the reason; to derange the regular operations of intellect; to render raving or furious; most frequently used in the participle *distracted.*

DISTRACT′, *a.* Mad. [*Not in use.*]

DISTRACT′ED, *pp.* Drawn apart; drawn in different directions; diverted from its object; perplexed; harassed; confounded.
2. *a.* Deranged; disordered in intellect; raving; furious; mad; frantic. *Locke.*

DISTRACT′EDLY, *adv.* Madly; furiously; wildly. *Shak.*

DISTRACT′EDNESS, *n.* A state of being mad; madness. *Bp. Hall.*

DISTRACT′ER, *n.* One who distracts. *More.*

DISTRACT′ING, *ppr.* Drawing apart; separating; diverting from an object; perplexing; harassing; disordering the intellect.

DISTRAC′TION, *n.* [L. *distractio.*] The act of distracting; a drawing apart; separation.
2. Confusion from a multiplicity of objects crowding on the mind and calling the attention different ways; perturbation of mind; perplexity; as, the family was in a state of *distraction*. [See 1 Cor. vii.]
3. Confusion of affairs; tumult; disorder; as political *distractions.*

> Never was known a night of such *distraction.* *Dryden.*

4. Madness; a state of disordered reason; franticness; furiousness. [*We usually apply this word to a state of derangement which produces raving and violence in the patient.*]
5. Folly in the extreme, or amounting to insanity.

> On the supposition of the truth of the birth, death and resurrection of Jesus Christ, irreligion is nothing better than *distraction.* *Buckminster.*

DISTRACT′IVE, *a.* Causing perplexity; as *distractive* cares. *Dryden.*

DISTRA′IN, *v. t.* [L. *distringo*; *dis* and

stringo. See *Strain*. Blackstone writes *distrein*.]

1. To seize for debt; to take a personal chattel from the possession of a wrong-doer into the possession of the injured party, to satisfy a demand, or compel the performance of a duty; as, to *distrain* goods for rent, or for an amercement.

2. To rend; to tear. *Obs.* *Spenser.*

DISTRA'IN, *v. i.* To make seizure of goods.

On whom I cannot *distrain* for debt. *Camden.*

For neglecting to do suit to the lord's court, or other personal service, the lord may *distrain* of common right. *Blackstone.*

[In this phrase however some word seems to be understood; as, to *distrain goods*.]

DISTRA'INABLE; *a.* That is liable to be taken for distress. *Blackstone.*

DISTRA'INED, *pp.* Seized for debt or to compel the performance of duty.

DISTRA'INING, *ppr.* Seizing for debt, or for neglect of suit and service.

DISTRA'INOR, *n.* He who seizes goods for debt or service. *Blackstone.*

DISTRAUGHT'. *Obs.* [See *Distract*.]

DISTRE'AM, *v. i.* [*dis* and *stream*.] To spread or flow over.

Yet o'er that virtuous blush *distreams* a tear. *Shenstone.*

DISTRESS', *n.* [Fr. *detresse*; Norm. *id.*; from the Celtic, W. *trais*, violence, *treisiaw*, to strain or force. See *Stress*.]

1. The act of distraining; the taking of any personal chattel from a wrong-doer, to answer a demand, or procure satisfaction for a wrong committed. *Blackstone.*

2. The thing taken by distraining; that which is seized to procure satisfaction.

A *distress* of household goods shall be impounded under cover. If the lessor does not find sufficient *distress* on the premises, &c. *Blackstone.*

3. Extreme pain; anguish of body or mind; as, to suffer great *distress* from the gout, or from the loss of near friends.

4. Affliction; calamity; misery.

On earth *distress* of nations. Luke xxi.

5. A state of danger; as a ship in *distress*, from leaking, loss of spars, or want of provisions or water, &c.

DISTRESS', *v. t.* To pain; to afflict with pain or anguish; *applied to the body or the mind*. [Literally, to press or strain.]

2. To afflict greatly; to harass; to oppress with calamity; to make miserable.

Distress not the Moabites. Deut. ii.

We are troubled on every side, but not *distressed*. 2 Cor. iv.

3. To compel by pain or suffering.

There are men who can neither be *distressed* nor won into a sacrifice of duty. *Federalist, Hamilton.*

DISTRESS'ED, *pp.* Suffering great pain or torture; severely afflicted; harassed; oppressed with calamity or misfortune.

DISTRESS'EDNESS, *n.* A state of being greatly pained. *Scott.*

DISTRESS'FUL, *a.* Inflicting or bringing distress; as a *distressful* stroke. *Shak.*

2. Indicating distress; proceeding from pain or anguish; as *distressful* cries. *Pope.*

3. Calamitous; as a *distressful* event. *Watts.*

4. Attended with poverty; as *distressful* bread. *Shak.*

DISTRESS'ING, *ppr.* Giving severe pain; oppressing with affliction.

2. *a.* Very afflicting; affecting with severe pain; as a *distressing* sickness.

DISTRIB'UTABLE, *a.* [See *Distribute*.] That may be distributed; that may be assigned in portions. *Ramsay.*

DISTRIB'UTE, *v. t.* [L. *distribuo*; *dis* and *tribuo*, to give or divide.]

1. To divide among two or more; to deal; to give or bestow in parts or portions. Moses *distributed* lands to the tribes of Israel. Christ *distributed* the loaves to his disciples.

2. To dispense; to administer; as, to *distribute* justice.

3. To divide or separate, as into classes, orders, kinds or species.

4. To give in charity.

Distributing to the necessities of the saints. Rom. xii.

5. In *printing*, to separate types, and place them in their proper cells in the cases.

DISTRIB'UTED, *pp.* Divided among a number; dealt out; assigned in portions; separated; bestowed.

DISTRIB'UTER, *n.* One who divides or deals out in parts; one who bestows in portions; a dispenser.

DISTRIB'UTING, *ppr.* Dividing among a number; dealing out; dispensing.

DISTRIBU'TION, *n.* [L. *distributio*.] The act of dividing among a number; a dealing in parts or portions; as the *distribution* of an estate among heirs or children.

2. The act of giving in charity; a bestowing in parts. *Bacon. Atterbury.*

3. Dispensation; administration to numbers; a rendering to individuals; as the *distribution* of justice.

4. The act of separating into distinct parts or classes; as the *distribution* of plants into genera and species.

5. In *architecture*, the dividing and disposing of the several parts of the building, according to some plan, or to the rules of the art.

6. In *rhetoric*, a division and enumeration of the several qualities of a subject.

7. In *general*, the division and disposition of the parts of any thing.

8. In *printing*, the taking a form apart; the separating of the types, and placing each letter in its proper cell in the cases.

DISTRIB'UTIVE, *a.* That distributes; that divides and assigns in portions; that deals to each his proper share; as *distributive* justice.

2. That assigns the various species of a general term.

3. That separates or divides; as a *distributive* adjective.

DISTRIB'UTIVE, *n.* In *grammar*, a word that divides or distributes, as *each* and *every*, which represent the individuals of a collective number as separate.

DISTRIB'UTIVELY, *adv.* By distribution; singly; not collectively. *Hooker. Watts.*

DISTRIB'UTIVENESS, *n.* Desire of distributing. [*Little used.*] *Fell.*

DIS'TRICT, *n.* [L. *districtus*, from *distringo*, to press hard, to bind; It. *distretto*. See *Distrain*.]

1. Properly, a limited extent of country; a circuit within which power, right or authority may be exercised, and to which it is restrained; a word applicable to any portion of land or country, or to any part of a city or town, which is defined by law or agreement. A governor, a prefect, or a judge may have his *district*. Some of the states are divided into *districts* for the choice of senators, representatives or electors. Cities and towns are divided into *districts* for various purposes, as for schools, &c. The United States are divided into *districts* for the collection of the revenue.

2. A region; a territory within given lines; as the *district* of the earth which lies between the tropics, or that which is north of a polar circle.

3. A region; a country; a portion of territory without very definite limits; as the *districts* of Russia covered by forest.

DIS'TRICT, *v. t.* To divide into districts or limited portions of territory. Legislatures *district* states for the choice of senators. In New England, towns are *districted* for the purpose of establishing and managing schools.

DIS'TRICT-COURT, *n.* A court which has cognizance of certain causes within a district defined by law. The district-courts of the United States are courts of subordinate jurisdiction.

DIS'TRICT-JUDGE, *n.* The judge of a district-court. *U. States.*

DIS'TRICT-SCHOOL, *n.* A school within a certain district of a town. *N. England.*

DIS'TRICTED, *pp.* Divided into districts or definite portions.

DIS'TRICTING, *ppr.* Dividing into limited or definite portions.

DISTRIC'TION, *n.* Sudden display. [*Unusual.*] *Collier.*

DISTRIN'GAS, *n.* In *law*, a writ commanding the sheriff to distrain a person for debt, or for his appearance at a certain day.

DISTRUST', *v. t.* [*dis* and *trust*. The Danes have *miströster*; the Swedes, *misstrôsta*. See *Mistrust*.]

1. To doubt or suspect the truth, fidelity, firmness or sincerity of; not to confide in or rely on. We *distrust* a man, when we question his veracity, &c. We may often *distrust* our own firmness.

2. To doubt; to suspect not to be real, true, sincere or firm. We *distrust* a man's courage, friendship, veracity, declarations, intentions or promises, when we question their reality or sincerity. We cannot *distrust* the declarations of God. We often have reason to *distrust* our own resolutions.

DISTRUST', *n.* Doubt or suspicion of reality or sincerity; want of confidence, faith or reliance. Sycophants should be heard with *distrust*. *Distrust* mars the pleasures of friendship and social intercourse.

2. Discredit; loss of confidence. *Milton.*

DISTRUST'ED, *pp.* Doubted; suspected.

DISTRUST'FUL, *a.* Apt to distrust; suspicious. *Boyle.*

2. Not confident; diffident; as *distrustful* of ourselves.

3. Diffident; modest. *Pope.*

DISTRUST'FULLY, *adv.* In a distrustful manner; with doubt or suspicion. *Milton.*

DISTRUST'FULNESS, *n.* The state of being distrustful; want of confidence.

DISTRUST'ING, *ppr.* Doubting the reality or sincerity of; suspecting; not relying on or confiding in.

DISTRUST'LESS, *a.* Free from distrust or suspicion. *Shenstone.*

DISTU'NE, *v. t.* To put out of tune. [*Not used.*] *Wotton.*

DISTURB', *v. t.* [Sp *disturbar*; It. *disturbare*; L. *disturbo*; *dis* and *turbo*, to trouble, disorder, discompose; *turba*, a crowd, a tumult; Gr. τυρβη or συρβη, a tumult; θορυβος, id. The primary sense seems to be to stir, or to turn or whirl round. The word *trouble* is probably from the L. *turbo*, by transposition. If *tr* are the primary elements, as I suppose, the word coincides in origin with *tour* and *turn*. If *t* is a prefix, the word belongs to Class Rb, coinciding with the Swedish *rubba*, to remove, to trouble. See Class Rb. No. 3. 4. 34. and Class Dr. No. 3. 25. 27.]

1. To stir; to move; to discompose; to excite from a state of rest or tranquillity. We say, the man is asleep, do not *disturb* him. Let the vessel stand, do not move the liquor, you will *disturb* the sediment. *Disturb* not the public peace.

2. To move or agitate; to disquiet; to excite uneasiness or a slight degree of anger in the mind; to move the passions; to ruffle. The mind may be *disturbed* by an offense given, by misfortune, surprise, contention, discord, jealousy, envy, &c.

3. To move from any regular course or operation; to interrupt regular order; to make irregular. It has been supposed that the approach of a comet may *disturb* the motions of the planets in their orbits. An unexpected cause may *disturb* a chimical operation, or the operation of medicine.

4. To interrupt; to hinder; to incommode. Care *disturbs* study. Let no person *disturb* my franchise.

5. To turn off from any direction; with *from*. [*Unusual.*]

> ——And *disturb*
> His inmost counsels *from* their destin'd aim. *Milton.*

DISTURB', *n.* Confusion; disorder. [*Not used.*] *Milton.*

DISTURB'ANCE, *n.* A stirring or excitement; any disquiet or interruption of peace; as, to enter the church without making *disturbance*.

2. Interruption of a settled state of things; disorder; tumult. We have read much at times of *disturbances* in Spain, England and Ireland.

3. Emotion of the mind; agitation; excitement of passion; perturbation. The merchant received the news of his losses without apparent *disturbance*.

4. Disorder of thoughts; confusion.

> They can survey a variety of complicated ideas, without fatigue or *disturbance*. *Watts.*

5. In *law*, the hindering or disquieting of a person in the lawful and peaceable enjoyment of his right; the interruption of a right; as the *disturbance* of a franchise, of common, of ways, of tenure, of patronage. *Blackstone.*

DISTURB'ED, *pp.* Stirred; moved; excited; discomposed; disquieted; agitated; uneasy.

DISTURB'ER, *n.* One who disturbs or disquiets; a violator of peace; one who causes tumults or disorders.

2. He or that which excites passion or agitation; he or that which causes perturbation. *Shak.*

3. In *law*, one that interrupts or incommodes another in the peaceable enjoyment of his right.

DISTURB'ING, *ppr.* Moving; exciting; rendering uneasy; making a tumult; interrupting peace; incommoding the quiet enjoyment of.

DISTURN', *v. t.* [*dis* and *turn.*] To turn aside. [*Not in use.*] *Daniel.*

DISU'NIFORM, *a.* *disyu'niform.* Not uniform. [*Not in use.*] *Coventry.*

DISU'NION, *n.* *disyu'nion.* [*dis* and *union.*] Separation; disjunction; or a state of not being united. It sometimes denotes a breach of concord, and its effect, contention.

DISUNI'TE, *v. t.* *disyuni'te.* [*dis* and *unite.*] To separate; to disjoin; to part; as, to *disunite* two allied countries; to *disunite* particles of matter; to *disunite* friends.

DISUNI'TE, *v. i.* To part; to fall asunder; to become separate. Particles of matter may spontaneously *disunite*.

DISUNI'TED, *pp.* Separated; disjoined.

DISUNI'TER, *n.* He or that which disjoins.

DISUNI'TING, *ppr.* Separating; parting.

DISU'NITY, *n.* *disyu'nity.* A state of separation. *More.*

DISU'SAGE, *n.* *disyu'zage.* [*dis* and *usage.*] Gradual cessation of use or custom; neglect of use, exercise or practice. We lose words by *disusage*.

DISU'SE, *n.* *disyu'se.* [*dis* and *use.*] Cessation of use, practice or exercise; as, the limbs lose their strength and pliability by *disuse*; language is altered by the *disuse* of words.

2. Cessation of custom; desuetude.

DISU'SE, *v. t.* *disyu'ze.* [*dis* and *use.*] To cease to use; to neglect or omit to practice.

2. To disaccustom; with *from*, *in* or *to*; as *disused to* toils; *disused from* pain.

DISU'SED, *pp.* *disyu'zed.* No longer used; obsolete, as words, &c.

> Priam in arms *disused*. *Dryden.*

2. Disaccustomed.

DISU'SING, *ppr.* *disyu'zing.* Ceasing to use; disaccustoming.

DISVALUA'TION, *n.* [See *Disvalue.*] Disesteem; disreputation.

DISVAL'UE, *v. t.* [*dis* and *value.*] To undervalue; to disesteem. *Shak.*

DISVAL'UE, *n.* Disesteem; disregard. *B. Jonson.*

DISVOUCH', *v. t.* [*dis* and *vouch.*] To discredit; to contradict. *Shak.*

DISWARN', *v. t.* [*dis* and *warn.*] To direct by previous notice. [*Not used.*]

DISWIT'TED, *a.* Deprived of wits or understanding. *Drayton.*

DISWŎNT', *v. t.* [*dis* and *wont.*] To wean; to deprive of wonted usage. *Bp. Hall.*

DISWŎR'SHIP, *n.* [*dis* and *worship.*] Cause of disgrace. *Barret.*

DIT, *n.* A ditty. [*Not used.*] *Spenser.*

DIT, *v. t.* [Sax. *dyttan.*] To close up. [*Not used.*] *More.*

DITA'TION, *n.* [L. *ditatus.*] The act of making rich. [*Not used.*] *Bp. Hall.*

DITCH, *n.* [Sax. *dic*, a *ditch*; D. *dyk*, a *dike*; G. *deich*, a *dike*; *deicher*, a *ditcher*; D. *dige*, a *ditch*, a *dike*; Sw. *dike*; Fr. *digue*; Eth. ደሐየ dachi, to *dig*. Class Dg. No 14. The *primary sense* is a digging or place dug. After the practice of embanking commenced, the word was used for the bank made by digging, the *dike*.]

1. A trench in the earth made by digging, particularly a trench for draining wet land, or for making a fence to guard inclosures, or for preventing an enemy from approaching a town or fortress. In the latter sense, it is called also a *foss* or *moat*, and is dug round the rampart or wall between the scarp and counterscarp. *Encyc.*

2. Any long, hollow receptacle of water.

DITCH, *v. i.* To dig or make a ditch or ditches.

DITCH, *v. t.* To dig a ditch or ditches in; to drain by a ditch; as, to *ditch* moist land.

2. To surround with a ditch. *Barret.*

DITCH-DELIV'ERED, *a.* Brought forth in a ditch. *Shak.*

DITCH'ER, *n.* One who digs ditches.

DITCH'ING, *ppr.* Digging ditches; also, draining by a ditch or ditches; as *ditching* a swamp.

DITETRAHE'DRAL, *a.* [*dis* and *tetrahedral.*] In *crystalography*, having the form of a tetrahedral prism with dihedral summits. *Cleaveland.*

DITH'YRAMB, **DITHYRAMB'US**, *n.* [Gr. διθυραμβος, a title of Bacchus, the signification of which is not settled. See Heder. Lex. and Bochart De Phœn. Col. Lib. 1. Ca. 18.]

In *ancient poetry*, a hymn in honor of Bacchus, full of transport and poetical rage. Of this species of writing we have no remains. *Encyc.*

DITHYRAMB'IC, *n.* A song in honor of Bacchus, in which the wildness of intoxication is imitated. *Johnson.*

2. Any poem written in wild enthusiastic strains. *Walsh.*

DITHYRAMB'IC, *a.* Wild; enthusiastic. *Cowley.*

DI''TION, *n.* [L. *ditio.*] Rule; power; government; dominion. *Evelyn.*

DI'TONE, *n.* [Gr. δις and τονος, tone.] In *music*, an interval comprehending two tones. The proportion of the sounds that form the ditone is 4:5, and that of the semiditone, 5:6. *Encyc.*

DITRIHE'DRIA, *n.* [Gr. δις, τρεις and εδρα, twice three sides.]

In *mineralogy*, a genus of spars with six sides or planes; being formed of two trigonal pyramids joined base to base, without an intermediate column. *Encyc.*

DITTAN'DER, *n.* Pepper-wort, Lepidium, a genus of plants of many species. The common dittander has a hot biting taste, and is sometimes used in lieu of pepper. *Encyc.*

DIV
DIV

DIT'TANY, *n.* [L. *dictamnus*; Gr. δικταμνος, or δικταμον.]
The *white dittany* is a plant of the genus Dictamnus. Its leaves are covered with a white down; in smell, they resemble lemon-thyme, but are more aromatic. When fresh, they yield an essential oil.
The *dittany of Crete* is a species of Origanum, and the *bastard dittany* is a species of Marrubium. *Encyc. Fam. of Plants.*

DIT'TIED, *a.* [See *Ditty.*] Sung; adapted to music.

> He, with his soft pipe, and smooth *dittied* song. *Milton.*

DIT'TO, contracted into *do*, in books of accounts, is the Italian *detto*, from L. *dictum, dictus*, said. It denotes said, aforesaid, or the same thing; an abbreviation used to save repetition.

DIT'TY, *n.* [supposed to be from the D. *dicht*, a poem, Sax. *diht, dihtan*. If so, it coincides in origin with the L. *dico, dictum.*]
A song; a sonnet or a little poem to be sung.

> And to the warbling lute soft *ditties* sing. *Sandys.*

DIT'TY, *v. i.* To sing; to warble a little tune. *Herbert.*

DIURET'IC, *a.* [Gr. διουρητικος, from διουρεω, δια and ουρεω, urinam reddo, ουρον, urine.]
Having the power to provoke urine; tending to produce discharges of urine. *Coxe.*

DIURET'IC, *n.* A medicine that provokes urine, or increases its discharges.

DIURN'AL, *a.* [L. *diurnus*, daily; W. *diwrnod*, a day. The word is a compound of *diw, dies*, day, and a word which I do not understand.]
1. Relating to a day; pertaining to the daytime; as *diurnal* heat; *diurnal* hours.
2. Daily; happening every day; performed in a day; as a *diurnal* task.
3. Performed in 24 hours; as the *diurnal* revolution of the earth.
4. In *medicine*, an epithet of diseases whose exacerbations are in the day time; as a *diurnal* fever. *Parr.*

DIURN'AL, *n.* A day-book; a journal. [See *Journal*, which is mostly used.]

DIURN'ALIST, *n.* A journalist. [*Not in use.*] *Hall.*

DIURN'ALLY, *adv.* Daily; every day.

DIUTURN'AL, *a.* Lasting; being of long continuance. *Milton.*

DIUTURN'ITY, *n.* [L. *diuturnitas*, from *diuturnus*, of long continuance, from *diu, dies.*] Length of time; long duration. *Brown.*

DIVAN', *n.* [Ar. Pers. دِیوان diwan. The Arabic verb دان is rendered, to be low, mean, vile, contemptible, [qu. *down*,] and also, to write on a white table. Hence *divan* is a register or table of names or accounts, and hence it came to signify a court or council assembled, as we use *board* and *exchequer.*]
1. Among the Turks and other orientals, a court of justice, or a council.
2. A council-chamber; a hall; a court.
3. Any council assembled. *Pope. Milton.*

DIVAR'ICATE, *v. i.* [L. *divaricatus, divarico; di, dis*, and *varico*, to straddle.] To open; to fork; to part into two branches. *Woodward.*

DIVAR'ICATE, *v. t.* To divide into two branches. *Grew.*

DIVAR'ICATE, *a.* In *botany*, standing out wide. A *divaricate* branch forms an obtuse angle with the stem. It is applied also to panicles, peduncles and petioles. *Martyn.*

DIVAR'ICATED, *pp.* Parted into two branches.

DIVAR'ICATING, *ppr.* Parting into two branches.

DIVARICA'TION, *n.* A parting; a forking; a separation into two branches.
2. A crossing or intersection of fibers at different angles. *Coxe.*

DIVE, *v. i.* [Sax. *dyfan, ge-dufian*; Gr. δυπτω; It. *tuffare*; coinciding with *dip*, Heb. Ch. טבע. The same word in Syr. and Ar. signifies to stamp, strike, print, impress. Class Db. No 28. The sense then is, to thrust or drive.]
1. To descend or plunge into water, as an animal head first; to thrust the body into water or other liquor, or if already in water, to plunge deeper. In the pearl fishery men are employed to *dive* for shells.
2. To go deep into any subject; as, to *dive* into the nature of things, into arts or science. *Dryden.*
3. To plunge into any business or condition, so as to be thoroughly engaged in it. *Shak.*
4. To sink; to penetrate.

> *Dive*, thoughts, down to my soul. *Shak.*

DIVE, *v. t.* To explore by diving. [*Rare.*]

> The Curtii bravely *dived* the gulf of fame. *Denham.*

DI'VEL, *n.* A large cartilaginous fish, with a bifurcated snout; the sea *duvvil* of Nieuhoff. *Pennant.*

DIVEL'LENT, *a.* [L. *divellens, divello; dis* and *vello*, to pull.] Drawing asunder; separating.

DIVEL'LICATE, *v. t.* To pull in pieces.

DI'VER, *n.* One who dives; one who plunges head first into water; one who sinks by effort; as a *diver* in the pearl fishery.
2. One who goes deep into a subject, or enters deep into study.
3. A fowl, so called from diving. The name is given to several species of the genus Colymbus.

DI'VERB, *n.* A proverb. [*Not in use.*] *Burton.*

DIVERGE, *v. i. diverj'.* [L. *divergo; di, dis*, and *vergo*, to incline.]
To tend from one point and recede from each other; to shoot, extend or proceed from a point in different directions, or not in parallel lines. Rays of light proceed from the sun and continually *diverge*. It is opposed to *converge.*

DIVERG'ENCE, *n.* A receding from each other; a going farther apart; as the *divergence* of lines, or the angle of *divergence.* *Gregory.*

DIVERG'ENT, *a.* Departing or receding from each other, as lines which proceed from the same point; opposed to *convergent.*

DIVERG'ING, *ppr.* Receding from each other, as they proceed.

DIVERG'INGLY, *adv.* In a diverging manner.

DI'VERS, *a. s* as *z.* [Fr. *divers*; L. *diversus*, from *diverto; di, dis*, and *verto*, to turn.]
1. Different; various.

> Thou shalt not sow thy fields with *divers* seeds. Deut. xxii.
>
> Nor let thy cattle gender with *divers* kinds. Lev. xix.

[This is now generally written *diverse.*]
2. Several; sundry; more than one, but not a great number. We have *divers* examples of this kind.
[This word is not obsolete even in common discourse, and is much used in law-proceedings.]

DI'VERS-COLORED, *a.* Having various colors. *Shak.*

DI'VERSE, *a.* [L. *diversus.*] Different; differing.

> Four great beasts came up from the sea, *diverse* one from another. Dan. vii.

2. Different from itself; various; multiform.

> Eloquence is a *diverse* thing. *B. Jonson.*

3. In different directions.

> And with tendrils creep *diverse.* *Philips.*

DIVERSE, *v. i. divers'.* To turn aside. [*Not used.*] *Spenser.*

DIVERSIFICA'TION, *n.* [See *Diversify.*]
1. The act of changing forms or qualities, or of making various. *Boyle.*
2. Variation; variegation.
3. Variety of forms. *Hale.*
4. Change; alteration.

DIVERS'IFIED, *pp.* Made various in form or qualities; variegated; altered.
2. *a.* Distinguished by various forms, or by a variety of objects; as *diversified* scenery; a *diversified* landscape.

DIVERS'IFORM, *a.* [*diversus* and *forma.*] Of a different form; of various forms. *Dict.*

DIVERS'IFY, *v. t.* [Fr. *diversifier*; Sp. *diversificar*; L. *diversus* and *facio.*]
1. To make different or various in form or qualities; to give variety to; to variegate; as, to *diversify* the colors of a robe; to *diversify* a landscape with mountains, plains, trees and lakes.
2. To give diversity to; to distinguish by different things; as a council *diversified* by different characters.
3. In *oratory*, to vary a subject, by enlarging on what has been briefly stated, by brief recapitulation, by adding new ideas, by transposing words or periods, &c.

DIVERS'IFYING, *ppr.* Making various in form or qualities; giving variety to; variegating.

DIVER'SION, *n.* [Fr. from L. *diverto*, to *divert.*]
1. The act of turning aside from any course; as the *diversion* of a stream from its usual channel; the *diversion* of a purpose to another object; the *diversion* of the mind from business or study.
2. That which diverts; that which turns or draws the mind from care, business or study, and thus relaxes and amuses; sport; play; pastime; whatever unbends the mind; as the *diversions* of youth. Works of wit and humor furnish an agreeable *diversion* to the studious.
3. In *war*, the act of drawing the attention and force of an enemy from the point where the principal attack is to be made, as by an attack or alarm on one wing of an army, when the other wing or center

is intended for the principal attack. The enemy, if deceived, is thus induced to withdraw a part of his force from the part where his foe intends to make the main impression.

DIVERS'ITY, *n.* [L. *diversitas*; Fr. *diversité*; from L. *diversus*, *diverto*.]

1. Difference; dissimilitude; unlikeness. There may be *diversity* without contrariety. There is a great *diversity* in human constitutions.
2. Variety; as a *diversity* of ceremonies in churches.
3. Distinct being, as opposed to identity. *Locke.*
4. Variegation.

Blushing in bright *diversities* of day. *Pope.*

DI'VERSLY, *adv.* [from *diverse.*] In different ways; differently; variously; as, a passage of scripture *diversly* interpreted or understood.

2. In different directions; to different points.

On life's vast ocean *diversly* we sail. *Pope.*

DIVERT', *v. t.* [L. *diverto*; *di*, *dis*, and *verto*, to turn; Fr. *divertir*; Sp. *id.*; It. *divertire.*]

1. To turn off from any course, direction or intended application; to turn aside; as, to *divert* a river from its usual channel; to *divert* commerce from its usual course; to *divert* appropriated money to other objects; to *divert* a man from his purpose.
2. To turn the mind from business or study, hence, to please; to amuse; to entertain; to exhilarate. Children are *diverted* with sports; men are *diverted* with works of wit and humor; low minds are *diverted* with buffoonery in stage-playing.
3. To draw the forces of an enemy to a different point. *Davies.*
4. To subvert. [*Not in use.*] *Shak.*

DIVERT'ED, *pp.* Turned aside; turned or drawn from any course, or from the usual or intended direction; pleased; amused; entertained.

DIVERT'ER, *n.* He or that which diverts, turns off, or pleases.

DIVERT'ICLE, *n.* [L. *diverticulum.*] A turning; a by-way. [*Not used.*] *Hale.*

DIVERT'ING, *ppr.* Turning off from any course; pleasing; entertaining.

2. *a.* Pleasing; amusing; entertaining; as a *diverting* scene or sport.

DIVERTI'SE, *v. t.* *s* as *z.* [Fr. *divertir*, *divertissant.*] To divert; to please. [*Not used.*] *Dryden.*

DIVER'TISEMENT, *n.* Diversion. [*Little used.*] Originally, a certain air or dance between the acts of the French opera, or a musical composition.

DIVERT'IVE, *a.* Tending to divert; amusing. *Rogers.*

DIVEST', *v. t.* [Fr. *devêtir*; *de* and *vêtir*, to clothe, L. *vestio*. It is the same word as *devest*, but the latter is appropriately used as a technical term in law.]

1. To strip of clothes, arms or equipage; opposed to *invest.*
2. To deprive; as, to *divest* one of his rights or privileges; to *divest* one of title or property.
3. To deprive or strip of any thing that covers, surrounds or attends; as, to *divest* one of his glory; to *divest* a subject of deceptive appearances, or false ornaments.

DIVEST'ED, *pp.* Stripped; undressed; deprived.

DIVEST'ING, *ppr.* Stripping; putting off; depriving.

DIVEST'ITURE, } *n.* The act of stripping,
DIVEST'URE, } putting off, or depriving. *Boyle. Encyc.*

DIVI'DABLE, *a.* [See *Divide.*] That may be divided.

2. Separate; parted. [*Not used nor proper.*] *Shak.*

DIVI'DE, *v. t.* [L. *divido*; *di* or *dis* and *iduo*, that is, *viduo*, to part. The Greek, *ιδιος*, *ιδιωμα*, *ιδιωτης*, are from the same root, as is the L. *individuus*, *viduus*, *vidua*, Eng. *widow*, and *wide* and *void*. See the latter words.]

1. To part or separate an entire thing; to part a thing into two or more pieces.

Divide the living child in two. 1 Kings iii.

2. To cause to be separate; to keep apart by a partition or by an imaginary line or limit. A wall *divides* two houses. The equator *divides* the earth into two hemispheres.

Let the firmament *divide* the waters from the waters. Gen. i.

3. To make partition of, among a number.

Ye shall *divide* the land by lot. Num. xxxiii.

4. To open; to cleave.

Thou didst *divide* the sea. Neh. ix.

5. To disunite in opinion or interest; to make discordant.

There shall be five in one house *divided*, three against two— Luke xii.

6. To distribute; to separate and bestow in parts or shares.

And he *divided* to them his living. Luke xv.

7. To make dividends; to apportion the interest or profits of stock among proprietors; as, the bank *divides* six per cent.
8. To separate into two parts, for ascertaining opinions for and against a measure; as, to *divide* a legislative house, in voting.

DIVI'DE, *v. i.* To part; to open; to cleave.

2. To break friendship; as, brothers *divide.* *Shak.*
3. To vote by the division of a legislative house into two parts.

The emperors sat, voted and *divided* with their equals. *Gibbon.*

DIVI'DED, *pp.* Parted; disunited; distributed.

DIVI'DEDLY, *adv.* Separately. *Knatchbull.*

DIV'IDEND, *n.* A part or share; particularly, the share of the interest or profit of stock in trade or other employment, which belongs to each proprietor according to his proportion of the stock or capital.

2. In *arithmetic*, the number to be divided into equal parts.

DIVI'DER, *n.* He or that which divides; that which separates into parts.

2. A distributor; one who deals out to each his share.

Who made me a judge or *divider* over you. Luke xii.

3. He or that which disunites. *Swift.*
4. A kind of compasses.

DIVI'DING, *ppr.* Parting; separating; distributing; disuniting; apportioning to each his share.

2. *a.* That indicates separation or difference; as a *dividing* line.

DIVI'DING, *n.* Separation.

DIVID'UAL, *a.* [L. *dividuus*, from *divido.*] Divided, shared or participated in common with others. [*Little used.*] *Milton.*

DIVINA'TION, *n.* [L. *divinatio*, from *divino*, to foretell, from *divinus*. See *Divine.*]

1. The act of divining; a foretelling future events, or discovering things secret or obscure, by the aid of superior beings, or by other than human means. The ancient heathen philosophers divided divination into two kinds, *natural* and *artificial*. *Natural* divination was supposed to be effected by a kind of inspiration or divine afflatus; *artificial* divination was effected by certain rites, experiments or observations, as by sacrifices, cakes, flour, wine, observation of entrails, flight of birds, lots, verses, omens, position of the stars, &c. *Encyc.*
2. Conjectural presage; prediction. *Shak.*

DIV'INATOR, *n.* One who pretends to divination.

DIVIN'ATORY, *a.* Professing divination.

DIVI'NE, *a.* [L. *divinus*, from *divus*, a god, coinciding in origin with *deus*, *θεος*.]

1. Pertaining to the true God; as the *divine* nature; *divine* perfections.
2. Pertaining to a heathen deity, or to false gods.
3. Partaking of the nature of God.

Half human, half *divine.* *Dryden.*

4. Proceeding from God; as *divine* judgments.
5. Godlike; heavenly; excellent in the highest degree; extraordinary; apparently above what is human. In this application the word admits of comparison; as a *divine* invention; a *divine* genius; the *divinest* mind. *Davies.*

A *divine* sentence is in the lips of the king. Prov. xvi.

6. Presageful; foreboding; prescient. [*Not used.*] *Milton.*
7. Appropriated to God, or celebrating his praise; as *divine* service; *divine* songs; *divine* worship.

DIVI'NE, *n.* A minister of the gospel; a priest; a clergyman. *Swift.*

The first *divines* of New England were surpassed by none in extensive erudition, personal sanctity, and diligence in the pastoral office. *J. Woodbridge.*

2. A man skilled in divinity; a theologian; as a great *divine.*

DIVI'NE, *v. t.* [L. *divino.*] To foreknow; to foretell; to presage.

Dar'st thou *divine* his downfall? *Shak.*

2. To deify. [*Not in use.*] *Spenser.*

DIVI'NE, *v. i.* To use or practice divination.

2. To utter presages or prognostications.

The prophets thereof *divine* for money. Micah iii.

3. To have presages or forebodings.

Suggest but truth to my *divining* thoughts— *Shak.*

4. To guess or conjecture.

Could you *divine* what lovers bear. *Granville.*

DIVI'NELY, *adv.* In a divine or godlike manner; in a manner resembling deity.

2. By the agency or influence of God; as a prophet *divinely* inspired; *divinely* taught.
3. Excellently; in the supreme degree; as *divinely* fair; *divinely* brave.

DIVI'NENESS, *n.* Divinity; participation of the divine nature; as the *divineness* of the scriptures. [*Little used.*]

2. Excellence in the supreme degree. *Shak.*

DIVI'NER, *n.* One who professes divination; one who pretends to predict events, or to reveal occult things, by the aid of superior beings, or of supernatural means.

These nations hearkened to *diviners*. Deut. xviii.

2. One who guesses; a conjecturer. *Locke.*

DIVI'NERESS, *n.* A female diviner; a woman professing divination. *Dryden.*

DI'VING, *ppr.* [See *Dive.*] Plunging or sinking into water or other liquid; applied to animals only.

2. Going deep into a subject.

DI'VING-BELL, *n.* A hollow vessel in form of a truncated cone or pyramid, with the smaller base close, and the larger one open, in which a person may descend into deep water and remain, till the inclosed air ceases to be respirable.

DIVIN'ITY, *n.* [L. *divinitas*; Fr. *divinité*; It. *divinità*; Sp. *divinidad*; from *divinus*, *divus.*]

1. The state of being divine; Deity; Godhead; the nature or essence of God. Christians ascribe *divinity* to one Supreme Being only.
2. God; the Deity; the Supreme Being.

'Tis the *Divinity* that stirs within us. *Addison.*

3. A false God; a pretended deity of pagans.

Beastly *divinities*, and droves of gods. *Prior.*

4. A celestial being, inferior to the Supreme God, but superior to man. Many nations believe in these inferior *divinities*.
5. Something supernatural.

They say there is *divinity* in odd numbers. *Shak.*

6. The science of divine things; the science which unfolds the character of God, his laws and moral government, the duties of man, and the way of salvation; theology; as the study of *divinity*; a system of *divinity*.

DIVISIBIL'ITY, *n.* [Fr. *divisibilité*, from L. *divisibilis*. See *Divide.*]

The quality of being divisible; the property of bodies by which their parts or component particles are capable of separation. *Locke.*

DIVIS'IBLE, *a.* *s* as *z*. [L. *divisibilis*, from *divido*. See *Divide.*]

Capable of division; that may be separated or disunited; separable. Matter is *divisible* indefinitely.

DIVIS'IBLENESS, *n.* Divisibility; capacity of being separated.

DIVI''SION, *n.* *s* as *z*. [L. *divisio*, from *divido*, *divisi*. See *Divide.*]

1. The act of dividing or separating into parts, any entire body.
2. The state of being divided.
3. That which divides or separates; that which keeps apart; partition.
4. The part separated from the rest by a partition or line, real or imaginary; as the *divisions* of a field.
5. A separate body of men; as, communities and *divisions* of men. *Addison.*
6. A part or distinct portion; as the *divisions* of a discourse.
7. A part of an army or militia; a body consisting of a certain number of brigades, usually two, and commanded by a major-general. But the term is often applied to other bodies or portions of an army, as to a brigade, a squadron or a platoon.
8. A part of a fleet, or a select number of ships under a commander, and distinguished by a particular flag or pendant.
9. Disunion; discord; variance; difference.

There was a *division* among the people. John vii.

10. Space between the notes of music, or the dividing of the tones. *Johnson. Bailey.*
11. Distinction.

I will put a *division* between my people and thy people. Ex. viii.

12. The separation of voters in a legislative house.
13. In *arithmetic*, the dividing of a number or quantity into any parts assigned; or the rule by which is found how many times one number is contained in another.

DIVI''SIONAL, **DIVI''SIONARY**, *a.* Pertaining to division; noting or making division; as a *divisional* line.

DIVI''SIONER, *n.* One who divides. [*Not used.*] *Sheldon.*

DIVI'SIVE, *a.* Forming division or distribution. *Mede.*

2. Creating division or discord. *Burnet.*

DIVI'SOR, *n.* In *arithmetic*, the number by which the dividend is divided.

DIVŌRCE, *n.* [Fr. *divorce*; Sp. *divorcio*; It. *divorzio*; L. *divortium*, from *divorto*, a different orthography of *diverto*, to turn away. See *Divert.*]

1. A legal dissolution of the bonds of matrimony, or the separation of husband and wife by a judicial sentence. This is properly a divorce, and called technically, divorce *a vinculo matrimonii*.
2. The separation of a married woman from the bed and board of her husband, *a mensa et thoro*.
3. Separation; disunion of things closely united.
4. The sentence or writing by which marriage is dissolved.
5. The cause of any penal separation.

The long *divorce* of steel falls on me. *Shak.*

DIVŌRCE, *v. t.* To dissolve the marriage contract, and thus to separate husband and wife.

2. To separate, as a married woman from the bed and board of her husband.
3. To separate or disunite things closely connected; to force asunder. *Hooker. Shak.*
4. To take away; to put away. *Blackmore.*

DIVŌRCED, *pp.* Separated by a dissolution of the marriage contract; separated from bed and board; parted; forced asunder.

DIVŌRCEMENT, *n.* Divorce; dissolution of the marriage tie.

Let him write her a bill of *divorcement*. Deut. xxiv.

DIVŌRCER, *n.* The person or cause that produces divorce. *Drummond.*

2. One of a sect called *divorcers*, said to have sprung from Milton.

DIVŌRCING, *ppr.* Dissolving the marriage contract; separating from bed and board; disuniting.

DIVŌRCIVE, *a.* Having power to divorce. *Milton.*

DIVUL'GATE, *a.* Published. [*Little used.*]

DIVULGA'TION, *n.* The act of divulging or publishing.

DIVULGE, *v. t.* *divulj'*. [L. *divulgo*; *di* or *dis* and *vulgo*, to make public, from *vulgus*, the common people, as *publish*, *public*, from L. *populus*, people.]

1. To make public; to tell or make known something before private or secret; to reveal; to disclose; as, to *divulge* the secret sentiments of a friend; to *divulge* the proceedings of the cabinet. *Divulge* is more generally applied to verbal disclosures, and *publish* to printed accounts. But they may be used synonymously. We may *publish* by words, and *divulge* by the press.
2. To declare by a public act; to proclaim. [*Unusual.*] *Milton.*

DIVULG'ED, *pp.* Made public; revealed; disclosed; published.

DIVULG'ER, *n.* One who divulges or reveals.

DIVULG'ING, *ppr.* Disclosing; publishing; revealing.

DIVUL'SION, *n.* [L. *divulsio*, from *divellor*; *di*, *dis*, and *vello*, to pull.]

The act of pulling or plucking away; a rending asunder.

And dire *divulsions* shook the changing world. *J. Barlow.*

DIVUL'SIVE, *a.* That pulls asunder; that rends. *Kirwan.*

DIZ'EN, *v. t.* *diz'n*. To dress gayly; to deck. *Swift.*

This word is not esteemed elegant, and is nearly obsolete. Its compound *bedizen* is used in burlesque.

DIZZ, *v. t.* [See *Dizzy.*] To astonish; to puzzle; to make dizzy. [*Not used.*] *Gayton.*

DIZ'ZARD, *n.* [See *Dizzy.*] A blockhead. [*Not used.*]

DIZ'ZINESS, *n.* [See *Dizzy.*] Giddiness; a whirling in the head; vertigo.

DIZ'ZY, *a.* [Sax. *dysi* or *dysig*, foolish; *dysignesse*, folly; *dysian*, to be foolish; *gedisigan*, to err; G. *dusel*, dizziness; *duselig*, dizzy; D. *deuzig*, stupid; *dyzig*, misty, hazy; Dan. *taasse*, a foolish person; qu. *döser*, to make sleepy.]

1. Giddy; having a sensation of whirling in the head, with instability or proneness to fall; vertiginous.
2. Causing giddiness; as a *dizzy* highth.
3. Giddy; thoughtless; heedless; as the *dizzy* multitude. *Milton.*

DIZ'ZY, *v. t.* To whirl round; to make giddy; to confuse. *Shak.*

DŌ, *v. t.* or *auxiliary*; pret. *did*; pp. *done*, pronounced *dun*. This verb, when transitive, is formed in the indicative, present tense, thus, I do, thou doest, he does or doth; when auxiliary, the second person is, thou *dost*. [Sax. *don*; D. *doen*; G. *thun*; Goth. *tauyan*; Russ. *deyu* or *dayu*. This is probably a contracted word, for in Sax. *dohte* signifies *made* or *did*, as if the pret. of this verb. If the elements are *dg*, it coincides in elements with Sax. *dugan*, to be able, and with *teagan*, to taw, as leather.]

1. To perform; to execute; to carry into effect; to exert labor or power for bringing any thing to the state desired, or to completion; or to bring any thing to pass. We say, this man *does* his work well; he

does more in one day than some men will *do* in two days.

In six days thou shalt *do* all thy work. Ex. xx.

I will teach you what ye shall *do*. Ex. iv.

I the Lord *do* all these things. Is. xlv.

2. To practice; to perform; as, to *do* good or evil.

3. To perform for the benefit or injury of another; with *for* or *to*; *for*, when the thing is beneficial; *to*, in either case.

Till I know what God will *do for* me. 1 Sam. xxii.

Do to him neither good nor evil. But *to* is more generally omitted. *Do* him neither good nor harm.

4. To execute; to discharge; to convey; as, *do* a message to the king.

5. To perform; to practice; to observe.

We lie and *do* not the truth. 1 John i.

6. To exert.

Do thy diligence to come shortly to me. 2 Tim. iv.

7. To transact; as, to *do* business with another.

8. To finish; to execute or transact and bring to a conclusion. The sense of completion is often implied in this verb; as, we will *do* the business and adjourn; we *did* the business and dined.

9. To perform in an exigency; to have recourse to, as a consequential or last effort; to take a step or measure; as, in this crisis, we knew not what to *do*.

What will ye *do* in the day of visitation. Is. x.

10. To make or cause.

Nothing but death can *do* me to respire. *Obs.* *Spenser.*

11. To put. *Obs.*

Who should *do* the duke to death? *Shak.*

12. To answer the purpose.

I'll make the songs of Durfey *do*.

To have to do, to have concern with.

What *have I to do* with you? 2 Sam. xvi.

What *have I to do* any more with idols? Hos. xiv.

To do with, to dispose of; to make use of; to employ. Commerce is dull; we know not what to *do with* our ships. Idle men know not what to *do with* their time or *with* themselves.

Also, to gain; to effect by influence.

A jest with a sad brow will *do with* a fellow who never had the ache in his shoulders. *Shak.*

I can *do* nothing *with* this obstinate fellow. *Anon.*

Also, to have concern with; to have business; to deal. [See No. 12.]

To do away, to remove; to destroy; as, to *do away* imperfections; to *do away* prejudices.

DŌ, *v. i.* To act or behave, in any manner, well or ill; to conduct one's self.

They fear not the Lord, neither *do* they after the law and commandment. 2 Kings xvii.

2. To fare; to be in a state with regard to sickness or health.

How *dost thou?* *Shak.*

We asked him how he *did*. How do you *do*, or how *do* you?

3. To succeed; to accomplish a purpose. We shall *do* without him. Will this plan *do?* *Addison.*

Also, to fit; to be adapted; to answer the design; with *for*; as, this piece of timber will *do for* the corner post; this tenon will *do for* the mortise; the road is repaired and will *do for* the present.

To have to do with, to have concern or business with; to deal with. *Have* little to *do with* jealous men.

Also, to have carnal commerce with.

Do is used for a verb to save the repetition of it. I shall probably come, but if I *do* not, you must not wait; that is, if I *do* not *come*, if I *come* not.

Do is also used in the imperative, to express an urgent request or command; as, *do* come; help me, *do*; make haste, *do*. In this case, *do* is uttered with emphasis.

As an auxiliary, *do* is used in asking questions. *Do* you intend to go? *Does* he wish me to come?

Do is also used to express emphasis. She is coquetish, but still I *do* love her.

Do is sometimes a mere expletive.

This just reproach their virtue *does* excite. *Dryden.*

Expletives their feeble aid *do* join. *Pope.*

[The latter use of *do* is nearly obsolete.]

Do is sometimes used by way of opposition; as, I *did* love him, but he has lost my affections.

DOAT. [See *Dote.*]

DO'CIBLE, *a.* [See *Docile.*] Teachable; docile; tractable; easily taught or managed. *Milton.*

DOCIBIL'ITY, DO'CIBLENESS, *n.* Teachableness; docility; readiness to learn. *Walton.*

DO'CILE, *a.* [L. *docilis*, from *doceo*, to teach. *Doceo* and *teach* are the same word. See *Teach.*]

Teachable; easily instructed; ready to learn; tractable; easily managed. Some children are far more *docile* than others. Dogs are more *docile* than many other animals.

DOCIL'ITY, *n.* Teachableness; readiness to learn; aptness to be taught. The *docility* of elephants is remarkable.

DO'CIMACY, *n.* [Gr. δοκιμασια. See the next word.]

The art or practice of assaying metals; metallurgy. *Med. Repos.*

DOCIMAS'TIC, *a.* [Gr. δοκιμαςικος, from δοκιμαζω, to try, essay, examine, from δοκιμος, proved, from δοκεω, to prove. Ch. דוק. Class Dg. No. 9.]

Properly, essaying, proving by experiments, or relating to the assaying of metals. The docimastic art is otherwise called metallurgy. It is the art of assaying metals, or the art of separating them from foreign matters, and determining the nature and quantity of metallic substance contained in any ore or mineral. *Lavoisier.*

DOCK, *n.* [Sax. *docce*; L. *daucus*; Gr. δαυκος; from Ar. Syr. Class Dg. No. 9.]

A genus of plants, the Rumex, of several species. Its root resembles a carrot.

DOCK, *v. t.* [W. *tociaw*, and *twciaw*, to clip, to cut off; whence *docket* and *ticket*. Class Dg. No. 19. 47.]

1. To cut off, as the end of a thing; to curtail; to cut short; to clip; as, to *dock* the tail of a horse.

2. To cut off a part; to shorten; to deduct from; as, to *dock* an account.

3. To cut off, destroy or defeat; to bar; as, to *dock* an entail.

4. To bring, draw or place a ship in a dock.

DOCK, *n.* The tail of a beast cut short or clipped; the stump of a tail; the solid part of the tail.

2. A case of leather to cover a horse's dock. *Encyc.*

DOCK, *n.* A broad deep trench on the side of a harbor, or bank of a river, in which ships are built or repaired. A *dry dock* has flood-gates to admit the tide, and to prevent the influx, as occasion may require. *Wet docks* have no flood-gates, but ships may be repaired in them during the recess of the tide. *Wet docks* are also constructed with gates to keep the water in at ebb tide, so that vessels may lie constantly afloat in them. *Mar. Dict.* *Cyc.*

In America, the spaces between wharves are called *docks*.

DOCK'-YARD, *n.* A yard or magazine near a harbor, for containing all kinds of naval stores and timber.

DOCK'ET, *n.* [W. *tociaw*, to cut off, to clip, to *dock*; hence *docket* is a piece.]

1. A small piece of paper or parchment, containing the heads of a writing. Also, a subscription at the foot of letters patent, by the clerk of the dockets. *Bailey.*

2. A bill, tied to goods, containing some direction, as the name of the owner, or the place to which they are to be sent. [See *Ticket.*] *Bailey.*

3. An alphabetical list of cases in a court, or a catalogue of the names of the parties who have suits depending in a court. In some of the states, this is the principal or only use of the word.

DOCK'ET, *v. t.* To make an abstract or summary of the heads of a writing or writings; to abstract and enter in a book; as, judgments regularly *docketed*. *Blackstone.*

2. To enter in a docket; to mark the contents of papers on the back of them.

3. To mark with a docket. *Chesterfield.*

DOCK'ING, *ppr.* Clipping; cutting off the end; placing in a dock.

DOCK'ING, *n.* The act of drawing, as a ship, into a dock. *Mar. Dict.*

DOC'TOR, *n.* [L. from *doceo*, to teach.] A teacher.

There stood up one in the council, a Pharisee, named Gamaliel, a *doctor* of the law. Acts v.

2. One who has passed all the degrees of a faculty, and is empowered to practice and teach it, as a *doctor* in divinity, in physic, in law; or according to modern usage, a person who has received the highest degree in a faculty. The degree of *doctor* is conferred by universities and colleges, as an honorary mark of literary distinction. It is also conferred on physicians, as a professional degree.

3. A learned man; a man skilled in a profession; a man of erudition. *Dryden.* *Digby.*

4. A physician; one whose occupation is to cure diseases.

5. The title, *doctor*, is given to certain fathers of the church whose opinions are received as authorities, and in the Greek church, it is given to a particular officer who interprets the scriptures. *Encyc.*

Doctors' Commons, the college of civilians in London.

DOC'TOR, *v. t.* To apply medicines for the cure of diseases. [*A popular use of this word, but not elegant.*]

DOC'TOR, *v. i.* To practice physic. [*Not elegant.*]

DOC'TORAL, *a.* Relating to the degree of a doctor. *Johnson.*

DOC'TORALLY, *adv.* In the manner of a doctor. *Hakewill.*

DOC'TORATE, *n.* The degree of a doctor. *Encyc.*

DOC'TORATE, *v. t.* To make a doctor by conferring a degree. *Warton.*

DOC'TORLY, *a.* Like a learned man. *Bp. Hall.*

DOC'TORSHIP, *n.* The degree or rank of a doctor. *Clarendon.*

[*Doctorate* is now generally used.]

DOC'TRESS, } DOC'TORESS, } *n.* A female physician.

DOC'TRINAL, *a.* [See *Doctrine.*] Pertaining to doctrine; containing a doctrine or something taught; as a *doctrinal* observation; a *doctrinal* proposition.

2. Pertaining to the act or means of teaching.

The word of God serveth no otherwise, than in the nature of a *doctrinal* instrument. *Hooker.*

DOC'TRINAL, *n.* Something that is a part of doctrine. *South.*

DOC'TRINALLY, *adv.* In the form of doctrine or instruction; by way of teaching or positive direction. *Ray.*

DOC'TRINE, *n.* [L. *doctrina*, from *doceo*, to teach.]

1. In *a general sense*, whatever is taught. Hence, a principle or position in any science; whatever is laid down as true by an instructor or master. The *doctrines* of the gospel are the principles or truths taught by Christ and his apostles. The *doctrines* of Plato are the principles which he taught. Hence a *doctrine* may be true or false; it may be a mere tenet or opinion.

2. The act of teaching.

He taught them many things by parables, and said to them in his *doctrine*. Mark iv.

3. Learning; knowledge.

Whom shall he make to understand *doctrine?* Is. xxviii.

4. The truths of the gospel in general.

That they may adorn the *doctrine* of God our Savior in all things. Tit. ii.

5. Instruction and confirmation in the truths of the gospel. 2 Tim. iii.

DOC'UMENT, *n.* [L. *documentum*, from *doceo*, to teach.]

1. Precept; instruction; direction. *Bacon. Watts.*

2. Dogmatical precept; authoritative dogma.

3. *More generally, in present usage*, written instruction, evidence or proof; any official or authoritative paper containing instructions or proof, for information and the establishment of facts. Thus, the president laid before congress the report of the secretary, accompanied with all the *documents.*

DOC'UMENT, *v. t.* To furnish with documents; to furnish with instructions and proofs, or with papers necessary to establish facts. A ship should be *documented* according to the directions of law.

2. To teach; to instruct; to direct. *Dryden.*

DOCUMENT'AL, *a.* Pertaining to instruction or to documents; consisting in or derived from documents; as *documental* testimony.

Court Martial on Gen. Wilkinson.

DOCUMENT'ARY, *a.* Pertaining to written evidence; consisting in documents.

DOD'DER, *n.* [G. *dotter.*] A plant of the genus Cuscuta, one species of which is called hell-weed. It is almost destitute of leaves, parasitical, creeping and fixing itself to some other plant, as to hops, flax and particularly to the nettle. It decays at the root, and is nourished by the plant that supports it, by means of little vesicles or papillæ, which attach themselves to the stalk. *Hill. Encyc.*

DOD'DERED, *a.* Overgrown with dodder; covered with supercrescent plants. *Johnson. Dryden.*

DODEC'AGON, *n.* [Gr. δωδεκα, twelve, and γωνια, an angle.] A regular figure or polygon, consisting of twelve equal sides and angles. *Encyc.*

DODEC'AGYN, *n.* [Gr. δωδεκα, twelve, and γυνη, a female.] In *botany*, a plant having twelve pistils.

DODECAGYN'IAN, *a.* Having twelve pistils.

DODECAHE'DRAL, *a.* [infra.] Pertaining to a dodecahedron; consisting of twelve equal sides.

DODECAHE'DRON, *n.* [Gr. δωδεκα, twelve, and εδρα, a base.] A regular solid contained under twelve equal and regular pentagons, or having twelve equal bases. *Chambers.*

DODECAN'DER, *n.* [Gr. δωδεκα, twelve, and ανηρ, a male.] In *botany*, a plant having twelve stamens; one of the class dodecandria. But this class includes all plants that have any number of stamens from twelve to nineteen inclusive. *Linne.*

DODECAN'DRIAN, *a.* Pertaining to the plants or class of plants that have twelve stamens, or from twelve to nineteen. *Lee.*

DODECATEMO'RION, *n.* [Gr. composed of δωδεκατος, twelfth, and μοριον, part.] A twelfth part. [*Little used.*] *Creech.*

DODECATEM'ORY, *n.* A denomination sometimes given to each of the twelve signs of the zodiac. *Burton.*

DODGE, *v. i. doj.* [from some root signifying to shoot, dart or start.]

1. To start suddenly aside; to shift place by a sudden start. *Milton.*

2. To play tricks; to be evasive; to use tergiversation; to play fast and loose; to raise expectations and disappoint them; to quibble. *Hale. Addison.*

DODGE, *v. t.* To evade by a sudden shift of place; to escape by starting aside; as, to *dodge* a blow aimed; to *dodge* a cannon ball.

[*This is a common word, very expressive and useful, but not admissable in solemn discourse or elegant composition.*]

DODG'ER, *n.* One who dodges or evades.

DODG'ING, *ppr.* Starting aside; evading.

DOD'KIN, *n.* [*doit*, D *duit*, and *kin.*] A little doit; a small coin.

DOD'MAN, *n.* A fish that casts its shell, like the lobster and crab. *Bacon.*

DO'DO, *n.* The Didus, a genus of fowls of the gallinaceous order. The hooded dodo is larger than a swan, with a strong hooked bill. The general color of the plumage is cinereous; the belly and thighs whitish. The head is large, and seems as if covered with a hood. The solitary dodo is a large fowl, and is said to weigh sometimes forty five pounds. The plumage is gray and brown mixed. *Encyc.*

DOE, *n. do.* [Sax. *da*; Dan. *daa.*] A she deer; the female of the fallow-deer. The male is called a *buck.*

DOE, *n.* A feat. [*Not used.*] *Hudibras.*

DÖER, *n.* [from *do.*] One who does; one who performs or executes; an actor; an agent.

2. One who performs what is required; one who observes, keeps or obeys, in practice.

The *doers* of the law shall be justified. Rom. ii.

DOES, the third person of the verb *do*, indicative mode, present tense, contracted from *doeth.*

DOFF, *v. t.* [Qu. *do-off.* Rather D. *doffen*, to push, to thrust. Class Db. No 17. 18.]

1. To put off, as dress.

And made us *doff* our easy robes of peace. *Shak.*

2. To strip or divest; as, he *doffs* himself. *Crashaw.*

3. To put or thrust away; to get rid of.

To *doff* their dire distresses. *Shak.*

4. To put off; to shift off; with a view to delay.

Every day thou *doff'st* me with some device. *Shak.*

[*This word is, I believe, entirely obsolete in discourse, at least in the U. States, but is retained in poetry.*]

DOG, *n.* [Fr. *dogue*, a bull dog or mastiff; *se doguer*, to butt; Arm. *dog* or *dogues*; D. *dog*; probably, the runner or starter.]

1. A species of quadrupeds, belonging to the genus Canis, of many varieties, as the mastiff, the hound, the spaniel, the shepherd's dog, the terrier, the harrier, the bloodhound, &c.

2. It is used for *male*, when applied to several other animals; as a *dog-fox*; a *dog-otter*; *dog-ape.* *Dryden.*

It is prefixed to other words, denoting what is mean, degenerate or worthless; as *dog-rose.* *Johnson.*

3. An andiron, so named from the figure of a dog's head on the top. [Russ. *tagan.*]

4. A term of reproach or contempt given to a man.

5. A constellation called Sirius or Canicula. [See *Dog-day.*]

6. An iron hook or bar with a sharp fang, used by seamen. *Mar. Dict.*

7. An iron used by sawyers to fasten a log of timber in a saw-pit.

8. A gay young man; a buck. [*Not in use.*] *Johnson.*

To give or *throw to the dogs*, is to throw away, as useless.

To go to the dogs, is to be ruined.

DOG, *v. t.* To hunt; to follow insidiously or indefatigably; to follow close; to urge; to worry with importunity.

I have been pursued, *dogged* and way-laid. *Pope.*

DO'GATE, *n.* [See *Doge.*] The office or dignity of a doge. *Encyc.*

DOG'BERRY, *n.* The berry of the dog-wood.

DOG'BERRY-TREE, *n.* The dogwood.

DOG'BRIER, *n.* The brier that bears the hip; the cynosbaton. *Johnson.*

DOG'-CABBAGE, *n.* A plant growing in the south of Europe, the cynocrambe, constituting the genus Theligonum. *Encyc.*

DOG'CHEAP, *a.* Cheap as dog's meat, or offal; very cheap. *Johnson.*

DOG'DAY, *n.* One of the days when Sirius or the dogstar rises and sets with the sun. The dogdays commence the latter part of July, and end the beginning of September.

DOG'DRAW, *n.* A manifest deprehension of an offender against the venison in the forest, when he is found drawing after the deer by the scent of a hound led by the hand. *Eng. Law. Cowel.*

DOGE, *n.* [It.; L. *dux;* Eng. *duke;* from L. *duco,* to lead; Sax. *toga, teoche.*] The chief magistrate of Venice and Genoa.

DOG'FIGHT, *n.* A battle between two dogs.

DOG'FISH, *n.* A name given to several species of shark, as the spotted shark or greater dogfish, the piked dogfish, &c. *Encyc. Cyc.*

DOG'FLY, *n.* A voracious, biting fly. *Chapman.*

DOG'GED, *pp.* Pursued closely; urged frequently and importunately.

2. *a.* Sullen; sour; morose; surly; severe. *Shak. Hudibras.*

DOG'GEDLY, *adv.* Sullenly; gloomily; sourly; morosely; severely.

DOG'GEDNESS, *n.* Sullenness; moroseness.

DOG'GER, *n.* A Dutch fishing vessel used in the German ocean, particularly in the herring fishery. It is equipped with two masts, a main-mast and a mizen-mast, somewhat resembling a ketch. *Encyc.*

DOG'GEREL, *a.* An epithet given to a kind of loose, irregular measure in burlesque poetry, like that of Hudibras; as *doggerel* verse or rhyme. *Dryden. Addison.*

DOG'GEREL, *n.* A loose, irregular kind of poetry; *used in burlesque.* *Dryden. Swift.*

DOG'GERMAN, *n.* A sailor belonging to a dogger.

DOG'GERS, *n.* In *English alum works,* a sort of stone found in the mines with the true alum-rock, containing some alum. *Encyc.*

DOG'GING, *ppr.* [from *dog.*] Hunting; pursuing incessantly or importunately.

DOG'GISH, *a.* Like a dog; churlish; growling; snappish; brutal.

DOG'HEARTED, *a.* Cruel; pitiless; malicious. *Shak.*

DOG'HOLE, *n.* A place fit only for dogs; a vile, mean habitation. *Dryden. Pope.*

DOG'HOUSE, *n.* A kennel for dogs. *Overbury.*

DOG'KENNEL, *n.* A kennel or hut for dogs. *Dryden.*

DOG'LEACH, *n.* A dog-doctor. *Beaum.*

DOG'LOUSE, *n.* An insect that is found on dogs.

DOG'LY, *a.* Like a dog. [*Not in use.*]

DOG'-MAD, *a.* Mad as a dog.

DOG'MA, *n.* [Gr. δογμα, from δοκεω, to think; L. *dogma.*]

A settled opinion; a principle, maxim or tenet; a doctrinal notion, particularly in matters of faith and philosophy; as the *dogmas* of the church; the *dogmas* of Plato.

> Compliment *my dogma,* and I will compliment *yours.* *J. M. Mason.*

DOGMAT'IC, } *a.* Pertaining to a dog-
DOGMAT'ICAL, } ma, or to settled opinion.

2. Positive; magisterial; asserting or disposed to assert with authority or with overbearing and arrogance; *applied to persons;* as a *dogmatic* schoolman or philosopher. *Boyle.*

3. Positive; asserted with authority; authoritative; as a *dogmatical* opinion.

4. Arrogant; overbearing in asserting and maintaining opinions.

DOGMAT'ICALLY, *adv.* Positively; in a magisterial manner; arrogantly.

DOGMAT'ICALNESS, *n.* The quality of being dogmatical; positiveness.

DOG'MATISM, *n.* Positive assertion; arrogance; positiveness in opinion.

DOG'MATIST, *n.* A positive asserter; a magisterial teacher; a bold or arrogant advancer of principles. *Watts.*

DOG'MATIZE, *v. i.* To assert positively; to teach with bold and undue confidence; to advance with arrogance.

> Men often *dogmatize* most, when they are least supported by reason. *Anon.*

DOG'MATIZER, *n.* One who dogmatizes; a bold assertor; a magisterial teacher. *Hammond.*

DOG'MATIZING, *ppr.* Asserting with excess of confidence.

DOG'ROSE, *n.* The flower of the hip. *Derham.*

DOG'S'-BANE, *n.* [Gr. αποκυνον.] A genus of plants, the Apocynum, of several species; also, the Asclepias.

DOG'S'-EAR, *n.* The corner of a leaf in a book turned down like a dog's ear. *Gray.*

DOG'SICK, *a.* Sick as a dog.

DOG'SKIN, *a.* Made of the skin of a dog. *Tatler.*

DOG'SLEEP, *n.* Pretended sleep. *Addison.*

DOG'S'-MEAT, *n.* Refuse; offal; meat for dogs. *Dryden.*

DOG'S'-RUE, *n.* A plant, a species of Scrophularia.

DOG'STAR, *n.* Sirius, a star of the first magnitude, whose rising and setting with the sun gives name to the dogdays.

DOG'STONES, *n.* A plant, the Orchis or fool-stones.

DOG'TOOTH, *n.* plu. *dogteeth.* A sharp-pointed human tooth growing between the foreteeth and grinders, and resembling a dog's tooth. It is called also an eye tooth.

DOG'TOOTH-VIOLET, *n.* A plant, the Erythronium.

DOG'TRICK, *n.* A currish trick; brutal treatment. *Dryden.*

DOG'TROT, *n.* A gentle trot like that of a dog.

DOG'VANE, *n.* Among *seamen,* a small vane composed of thread, cork and feathers, fastened to a half pike and placed on the weather gun-wale, to assist in steering a ship on the wind. *Mar. Dict.*

DOG'WATCH, *n.* Among *seamen,* a watch of two hours. The dogwatches are two reliefs between 4 and 8 o'clock, P. M.

DOG'WEARY, *a.* Quite tired; much fatigued.

DOG'WOOD, *n.* A common name of different species of the Cornus or cornelian cherry.

DOG'WOOD-TREE, *n.* The Piscidia erythrina, a tree growing in Jamaica. *Encyc.*

DOI'LY, *n.* A species of woolen stuff, said to be so called from the first maker. *Congreve.*

2. Linen made into a small napkin. *Mason.*

DÖING, *ppr.* [See *Do.*] Performing; executing.

DÖINGS, *n. plu.* Things done; transactions; feats; actions, good or bad.

2. Behavior; conduct.

3. Stir; bustle.

DOIT, *n.* [D. *duit;* G. *deut.* Qu. Fr. *doigt,* a finger, a point, L. *digitus.*]

1. A small piece of money. *Pope.*

2. A trifle. Hence our vulgar phrase, I care not a *doit.* It is used adverbially and commonly pronounced *dite.*

DOLAB'RIFORM, *a.* [L. *dolabra,* an ax, and *forma,* form.]

Having the form of an ax or hatchet. *Martyn.*

DOLE, *n.* [Sax. *dal;* Russ. *dolia,* a part or portion; Ir. *dail;* from the root of *deal.* See *Deal.*]

1. The act of dealing or distributing; as the power of *dole* and donative. [*Not in use.*] *Bacon.*

2. That which is dealt or distributed; a part, share or portion. *Shak.*

3. That which is given in charity; gratuity. *Dryden.*

4. Blows dealt out. *Milton.*

5. Boundary. [*Not in use.*]

6. A void space left in tillage. [*Local.*]

DOLE, *n.* [L. *dolor,* pain, grief.] Grief; sorrow. *Obs.* *Milton.*

DOLE, *v. t.* To deal; to distribute. [*Not used.*]

DO'LEFUL, *a.* [*dole* and *full.*] Sorrowful; expressing grief; as a *doleful* whine; a *doleful* cry.

2. Melancholy; sad; afflicted; as a *doleful* sire. *Sidney.*

3. Dismal; impressing sorrow; gloomy; as *doleful* shades. *Milton.*

DO'LEFULLY, *adv.* In a doleful manner; sorrowfully; dismally; sadly.

DO'LEFULNESS, *n.* Sorrow; melancholy; querulousness; gloominess; dismalness.

DO'LENT, *a.* [L. *dolens.*] Sorrowful. [*Not in use.*]

DO'LESOME, *a.* Gloomy; dismal; sorrowful; doleful.

> The *dolesome* passage to th' infernal sky. *Pope.*

DO'LESOMENESS, *n.* Gloom; dismalness.

DOLL, *n.* [W. *delw,* form, image, resemblance, an idol, a false god; *dull,* form, figure; Arm. *dailh,* or *tailh,* which seems to be the L. *talis.* Also Ir. *dealbh,* an image. But qu. Gr. ειδωλον, an *idol,* from ειδω, to see.]

A puppet or baby for a child; a small image in the human form, for the amusement of little girls.

DOL'LAR, *n.* [G. *thaler*; D. *daalder*; Dan. and Sw. *daler*; Sp. *dalera*; Russ. *taler*; said to be from *Dale*, the town where it was first coined.]

A silver coin of Spain and of the United States, of the value of one hundred cents, or four shillings and sixpence sterling. The dollar seems to have been originally a German coin, and in different parts of Germany, the name is given to coins of different values.

DOL'OMITE, *n.* A variety of magnesian carbonate of lime, so called from the French geologist Dolomieu. Its structure is granular. *Cyc.*

DO'LOR, *n.* [L.] Pain; grief; lamentation. *Sidney. Shak.*

DOLORIF'EROUS, *a.* [L. *dolor*, pain, and *fero*, to produce.] Producing pain. *Whitaker.*

DOLORIF'IC, *a.* [L. *dolorificus*; *dolor* and *facio*.]

1. That causes pain or grief.
2. Expressing pain or grief.

DOL'OROUS, *a.* [L. *dolor*, pain, grief.] Sorrowful; doleful; dismal; impressing sorrow or grief; as a *dolorous* object; a *dolorous* region. *Hooker. Milton.*

2. Painful; giving pain.

Their dispatch is quick, and less *dolorous* than the paw of the bear. *More.*

3. Expressing pain or grief; as *dolorous* sighs.

DOL'OROUSLY, *adv.* Sorrowfully; in a manner to express pain.

DOL'PHIN, *n.* [L. *delphin* or *delphinus*; Gr. δελφιν; Ir. *deilf*; Fr. *dauphin*; Sp. *delfin*; It. *delfino*; Arm. *daofin*, *dolfin*; W. *dolfyn*, from *dolf*, a curve or winding.]

1. A genus of cetaceous fish, with teeth in both jaws, and a pipe in the head, comprehending the dolphin, the porpess, the grampus and the beluga. But the fish to which seamen give this name, is the Coryphæna hippuris of *Linne*. It has a flat roundish snout and a tapering body, with a fin running along the back from the head to the tail, consisting of a coriaceous membrane with soft spines. *Dict. of Nat. Hist.*

2. In ancient Greece, a machine suspended over the sea, to be dropped on any vessel passing under it. *Mitford.*

DOL'PHINET, *n.* A female dolphin. *Spenser.*

DOLT, *n.* [G. *tölpel*; Sax. *dol*; W. *dol*. Qu. *dull*. The Gothic has *dwala*, foolish, stupid; Sax. *dwolian*, to wander. The Sw. has *dvala*, to sleep or be drowsy; Dan. *dvale*, sound sleep; D. *doolen*, and *dwaalen*, to wander.]

A heavy, stupid fellow; a blockhead; a thick-skull. *Sidney. Swift.*

DOLT, *v. i.* To waste time foolishly; to behave foolishly.

DOLTISH, *a.* Dull in intellect; stupid; blockish; as a *doltish* clown. *Sidney.*

DOLTISHNESS, *n.* Stupidity.

DOM, used as a termination, denotes jurisdiction, or property and jurisdiction; primarily, *doom*, judgment; as in *kingdom*, *earldom*. Hence it is used to denote state, condition or quality, as in *wisdom*, *freedom*.

DOMA'IN, *n.* [Fr. *domaine*; Arm. *domany*. This would seem to be from L. *dominium*. Qu. is it the same word as *demain*, which is from the Old French *demesne*. The latter cannot be regularly deduced from *dominium*, *domino*. The Norman French has *demesner*, to rule, to *demean*; and the phrase, "de son demainer," in his demain, would seem to be from a different source. *Mainor*, in Norman, is tenancy or occupation, from *main*, the hand. *Domain* seems to be the L. *dominium*, and to have been confounded with *demain*, *demesne*.]

1. Dominion; empire; territory governed, or under the government of a sovereign; as the vast *domains* of the Russian emperor; the *domains* of the British king.
2. Possession; estate; as a portion of the king's *domains*. *Dryden.*
3. The land about the mansion house of a lord, and in his immediate occupancy. In this sense, the word coincides with *demain*, *demesne*. *Shenstone.*

DO'MAL, *a.* [L. *domus*.] Pertaining to house in astrology. *Addison.*

DOME, *n.* [Fr. *dôme*; Arm. *dom*; L. *domus*; Gr. δομος; Ir. *dom*; Russ. *dom*; supposed to be from δεμω, to build. The Greek has also δωμα, a house, a plain roof. Qu. Sax. *timbrian*, Goth. *timbryan*, to build.]

1. A building; a house; a fabric; *used in poetry*. *Pope.*
2. A cathedral. *Burnet.*
3. In *architecture*, a spherical roof, raised over the middle of a building; a cupola. *Encyc.*
4. In *chimistry*, the upper part of a furnace, resembling a hollow hemisphere or small dome. This form serves to reflect or reverberate a part of the flame; hence these furnaces are called *reverberating* furnaces. *Encyc.*

DOMESDAY. [See *Doomsday*.]

DO'MESMAN, *n.* [See *Doom*.] A judge; an umpire. *Obs.*

DOMES'TIC, *a.* [L. *domesticus*, from *domus*, a house.]

1. Belonging to the house, or home; pertaining to one's place of residence, and to the family; as *domestic* concerns; *domestic* life; *domestic* duties; *domestic* affairs; *domestic* contentions; *domestic* happiness; *domestic* worship.
2. Remaining much at home; living in retirement; as a *domestic* man or woman.
3. Living near the habitations of man; tame; not wild; as *domestic* animals.
4. Pertaining to a nation considered as a family, or to one's own country; intestine: not foreign; as *domestic* troubles; *domestic* dissensions.
5. Made in one's own house, nation or country; as *domestic* manufactures.

DOMES'TIC, *n.* One who lives in the family of another, as a chaplain or secretary. Also, a servant or hired laborer, residing with a family.

DOMES'TICALLY, *adv.* In relation to domestic affairs.

DOMES'TICATE, *v. t.* To make domestic; to retire from the public; to accustom to remain much at home; as, to *domesticate* *one's self*.

2. To make familiar, as if at home. *Chesterfield.*
3. To accustom to live near the habitations of man; to tame; as, to *domesticate* wild animals.

DOMESTICA'TION, *n.* The act of withdrawing from the public notice and living much at home.

2. The act of taming or reclaiming wild animals.

DOM'ICIL, *n.* [L. *domicilium*, a mansion.] An abode or mansion; a place of permanent residence, either of an individual or family; a residence, *animo manendi*. *Story. Hopkinson.*

DOM'ICIL, **DOMICIL'IATE**, } *v. t.* To establish a fixed residence, or a residence that constitutes habitancy. *Kent.*

DOM'ICILED, **DOMICIL'IATED**, } *pp.* Having gained a permanent residence or inhabitancy.

DOMICIL'IARY, *a.* Pertaining to an abode, or the residence of a person or family. A *domiciliary* visit is a visit to a private dwelling, particularly for the purpose of searching it, under authority.

DOMICILIA'TION, *n.* Permanent residence; inhabitancy.

DOM'ICILING, **DOMICIL'IATING**, } *ppr.* Gaining or taking a permanent residence.

DOM'IFY, *v. t.* [L. *domus*, a house, and *facio*, to make.]

1. In *astrology*, to divide the heavens into twelve houses, in order to erect a theme or horoscope, by means of six great circles, called circles of position. *Obs.* *Encyc.*
2. To tame. [*Not in use and improper*.]

DOM'INANT, *a.* [L. *dominans*, from *dominor*, to rule; *dominus*, lord, master; either from *domus*, a house, or from *domo*, δαμαω, to overcome, to *tame*, to subdue, W. *dovi*. Both roots unite in the sense, to set, to press, to fix. See Class Dm. No. 1. 3.]

1. Ruling; prevailing; governing; predominant; as the *dominant* party, or faction. *Reid. Tooke.*
2. In *music*, the *dominant* or sensible chord is that which is practiced on the dominant of the tone, and which introduces a perfect cadence. Every perfect major chord becomes a dominant chord, as soon as the seventh minor is added to it. *Rousseau. Encyc.*

DOM'INANT, *n.* In *music*, of the three notes essential to the tone, the dominant is that which is a fifth from the tonic. *Ibm.*

DOM'INATE, *v. t.* [L. *dominatus*, *dominor*. See *Dominant*.]

To rule; to govern; to prevail; to predominate over.

We every where meet with Slavonian nations either dominant or *dominated*. *Tooke, Russ.*

DOM'INATE, *v. i.* To predominate. [*Little used*.]

DOM'INATED, *pp.* Ruled; governed.

DOM'INATING, *ppr.* Ruling; prevailing; predominating.

DOMINA'TION, *n.* [L. *dominatio*.] The exercise of power in ruling; dominion; government. *Shak.*

2. Arbitrary authority; tyranny.
3. One highly exalted in power; or the fourth order of angelic beings.

Thrones, *dominations*, princedoms, virtues, powers. *Milton.*

DOM'INATIVE, *a.* Governing; also, imperious. *Sandys.*

DOM'INATOR, *n.* A ruler or ruling power; the presiding or predominant power.

Jupiter and Mars are *dominators* for this northwest part of the world. *Camden.*

2. An absolute governor.

DOMINEE'R, *v. i.* [L. *dominor;* Fr. *dominer;* Sp. *dominar;* It. *dominare.* See *Dominant.*]

1. To rule over with insolence or arbitrary sway.

To *domineer* over subjects or servants is evidence of a low mind. *Anon.*

2. To bluster; to hector; to swell with conscious superiority, or haughtiness.

Go to the feast, revel and *domineer.* *Shak.*

DOMINEE'RING, *ppr.* Ruling over with insolence; blustering; manifesting haughty superiority.

2. *a.* Overbearing.

DOMIN'ICAL, *a.* [Low L. *dominicalis*, from *dominicus*, from *dominus*, lord.]

1. That notes the Lord's day or Sabbath. The *Dominical* letter is the letter which, in almanacks, denotes the sabbath, or *dies domini*, the Lord's day. The first seven letters of the alphabet are used for this purpose.

2. Noting the prayer of our Lord. *Howell.*

DOMIN'ICAL, *n.* [infra.] The Lord's day. *Hammond.*

DOMIN'ICAN, *a.* or *n.* [from *Dominic*, the founder.]

The *Dominicans*, or Dominican Friars, are an order of religious or monks, called also *Jacobins*, or Predicants, preaching friars; an order founded about the year 1215. *Encyc.*

DOMIN'ION, *n.* [L. *dominium.* See *Dominant.*]

1. Sovereign or supreme authority; the power of governing and controlling.

The *dominion* of the Most High is an everlasting *dominion.* Dan. iv.

2. Power to direct, control, use and dispose of at pleasure; right of possession and use without being accountable; as the private *dominion* of individuals. *Locke.*

3. Territory under a government; region; country; district governed, or within the limits of the authority of a prince or state; as the British *dominions.*

4. Government; right of governing. Jamaica is under the *dominion* of Great Britain.

5. Predominance; ascendant. *Dryden.*

6. An order of angels.

Whether they be thrones, or *dominions*, or principalities, or powers. Col. i.

7. Persons governed.

Judah was his sanctuary; Israel his *dominion.* Ps. cxiv.

DOM'INO, *n.* A kind of hood; a long dress; a masquerade dress.

DO'MITE, *n.* A mineral named from Dome in Auvergne, in France, of a white or grayish white color, having the aspect and gritty feel of a sandy chalk. *Phillips.*

DON. A title in Spain, formerly given to noblemen and gentlemen only, but now common to all classes. It is commonly supposed to be contracted from *dominus*, *dom*, and the Portuguese *dono*, the master or owner of any thing, gives some countenance to the opinion. It coincides nearly with the Heb. דין, and אדון, a judge, ruler, or lord. It was formerly used in England, and written by Chaucer *Dan.* [See *Spelman.*]

Dona, or *dueña*, the feminine of *don*, is the title of a lady, in Spain and Portugal.

DON, *v. t.* [To *do on;* opposed to *doff.*] To put on; to invest with. *Obs.* *Shak.* *Fairfax.*

DO'NACITE, *n.* A petrified shell of the genus Donax. *Jameson.*

DO'NARY, *n.* [L. *donarium*, from *dono*, to give.]

A thing given to a sacred use. [*Little used.*] *Johnson.*

DONA'TION, *n.* [L. *donatio*, from *dono*, to give, Fr. *donner.*]

1. The act of giving or bestowing; a grant.

That right we hold by his *donation.* *Milton.*

2. In *law*, the act or contract by which a thing or the use of it is transferred to a person, or corporation, as a free gift. To be valid, a *donation* supposes capacity both in the donor to give, and donee to take, and requires consent, acceptance and delivery.

3. That which is given or bestowed; that which is transferred to another gratuitously, or without a valuable consideration; a gift; a grant. *Donation* is usually applied to things of more value than *present.*

Mr. Boudinot made a *donation* of ten thousand dollars to the American Bible Society.

DO'NATISM, *n.* The doctrines of the Donatists.

DO'NATIST, *n.* One of the sect founded by Donatus. They held that theirs was the only pure church, and that baptism and ordination, unless by their church, were invalid. *Encyc.*

DONATIS'TIC, *a.* Pertaining to Donatism.

DO'NATIVE, *n.* [Sp. Ital. *donativo;* L. *donativum*, from *dono*, to give.]

1. A gift; a largess; a gratuity; a present; a dole.

The Romans were entertained with shows and *donatives.* *Dryden.*

2. In *the canon law*, a benefice given and collated to a person, by the founder or patron, without either presentation, institution or induction by the ordinary. *Encyc.*

DO'NATIVE, *a.* Vested or vesting by donation; as a *donative* advowson. *Blackstone.*

DŎNE, *pp.* dun. [See *Do.*] Performed; executed; finished.

2. A word by which agreement to a proposal is expressed; as in laying a wager, an offer being made, the person accepting or agreeing says, *done;* that is, it is agreed, I agree, I accept.

DONEE', *n.* [from L. *dono*, to give.] The person to whom a gift or donation is made.

2. The person to whom lands or tenements are given or granted; as a *donee* in fee-simple, or fee-tail. *Blackstone.*

DONJON or DONGEON. [See *Dungeon.*]

DON'NAT, *n.* [*do* and *naught.*] An idle fellow. [*Not in use.*] *Granger.*

DO'NOR, *n.* [from L. *dono*, to give.] One who gives or bestows; one who confers any thing gratuitously; a benefactor.

2. One who grants an estate; as, a conditional fee may revert to the *donor*, if the *donee* has no heirs of his body.

DON'SHIP, *n.* [See *Don.*] The quality or rank of a gentleman or knight. *Hudibras.*

DON'ZEL, *n.* [It.] A young attendant; a page. *Butler.*

DOO'DLE, *n.* A trifler; a simple fellow. [Qu. *dote*, Fr. *radoter;* Port. *doudo*, mad, foolish.]

DOOLE, [See *Dole.*]

DOOM, *v. t.* [Sax. *dom*, judgment; *deman*, to *deem;* *gedeman*, to judge; D. *doemen*, to *doom*, to *condemn;* Dan. *dömmer;* Sw. *dōma.* *Doom* is from the root of *deem*, which seems to coincide also with L. *estimo*, to *esteem*, and perhaps with the root of *condemn.* See *Deem.*]

1. To judge. [*Unusual.*]

Thou didst not *doom* so strictly. *Milton.*

2. To condemn to any punishment; to consign by a decree or sentence; as, the criminal is *doomed* to chains.

3. To pronounce sentence or judgment on.

Absolves the just, and *dooms* the guilty souls. *Dryden.*

4. To command authoritatively.

Have I a tongue to *doom* my brother's death. *Shak.*

5. To destine; to fix irrevocably the fate or direction of; as, we are *doomed* to suffer for our sins and errors.

6. To condemn, or to punish by a penalty.

DOOM, *n.* [Sax. *dom;* D. *doem;* Dan. Sw. *dom.*] Judgment; judicial sentence.

To Satan, first in sin, his *doom* applied. *Milton.*

Hence the *final doom* is the last judgment.

2. Condemnation; sentence; decree; determination affecting the fate or future state of another; usually a determination to inflict evil, sometimes otherwise.

Revoke that *doom* of mercy. *Shak.*

3. The state to which one is doomed, or destined. To suffer misery is the *doom* of sinners. To toil for subsistence is the *doom* of most men.

4. Ruin; destruction.

From the same foes, at last, both felt their *doom.* *Pope.*

5. Discrimination. [*Not used.*]

DOOM'AGE, *n.* A penalty or fine for neglect. *N. Hampshire.*

DOOM'ED, *pp.* Adjudged; sentenced; condemned; destined; fated.

DOOM'FUL, *a.* Full of destruction. *Drayton.*

DOOM'ING, *ppr.* Judging; sentencing; condemning; destining.

DOOMS'DAY, *n.* [*doom* and *day.*] The day of the final judgment; the great day when all men are to be judged and consigned to endless happiness or misery. *Shak.* *Dryden.*

2. The day of sentence or condemnation. *Shak.*

DOOMSDAY-BOOK, } *n.*
DOMESDAY-BOOK, }

A book compiled by order of William the Conqueror, containing a survey of all the lands in England. It consists of two volumes; a large folio, and a quarto. The folio contains 382 double pages of vellum, written in a small but plain character. The quarto contains 450 double pages of vellum, written in a large fair character. *Encyc.*

DŎOR, *n.* [Sax. *dora, dur, dure*; G. *thür*; D. *deur*; Sw. *dör*; Dan. *dör*; Gr. θυρα; W. *dôr*; Ir. *doras*; Arm. *dor*; Basque, *dorrea*; Russ. *dver*; Persic دَرْ dar; Sans. *dura*; Armenian, *turu*; Ch. תרע or תרעא; Syr. ܬܪܥܐ; Ar. تُرْعَةٌ. It is also in the Slavonic languages, Polish, Bohemian, Carinthian, &c. The verb תרע, ܬܪܥ, in Ch. and Syr. signifies to *tear* or cut open, to open or break open; in Syr. also, to pray, to supplicate, to burst, to crack; in Ar. to rush headlong, to drive, to crowd, to fill. In Dutch, *door* is *through*, G. *durch*. In Tartar, *thurne* is a door. Class Dr. No. 42. The Hebrew שער, a gate, seems to be the same word dialectically varied, and the verb coincides in sense with the Arabic, supra, to rush. The primary sense of the verb is to pass, to drive, to rush. Hence a door is a passage, or break.]

1. An opening or passage into a house, or other building, or into any room, apartment or closet, by which persons enter. Such a passage is seldom or never called a *gate*.
2. The frame of boards, or any piece of board or plank that shuts the opening of a house or closes the entrance into an apartment or any inclosure, and usually turning on hinges.
3. In *familiar language*, a house; often in the plural, *doors*. My house is the first *door* from the corner. We have also the phrases, *within doors*, in the house; *without doors*, out of the house, abroad.
4. Entrance; as the *door* of life. *Dryden.*
5. Avenue; passage; means of approach or access. An unforgiving temper shuts the *door* against reconciliation, or the *door* of reconciliation.

I am the *door*; by me if any man enter in, he shall be saved. John x.

A *door* was opened to me of the Lord. 2 Cor. ii.

To lie at the door, in a figurative sense, is to be imputable or chargeable to one. If the thing is wrong, the fault *lies at my door.*

Next door to, near to; bordering on.

A riot unpunished is but *next door to* a tumult. *L'Estrange.*

Out of door or *doors*, quite gone; no more to be found. [*Not now used.*] *Dryden.*

In doors, within the house; at home.

DŎOR-CASE, *n.* The frame which incloses a door.

DŎORING, *n.* A door-case. [*Not used.*] *Milton.*

DŎOR-KEEPER, *n.* A porter; one who guards the entrance of a house or apartment.

DŎOR-NAIL, *n.* The nail on which the knocker formerly struck.

DŎOR-POST, *n.* The post of a door.

DŎOR-STEAD, *n.* Entrance or place of a door. *Warburton.*

DOQ'UET, *n. dok'et.* A warrant; a paper granting license. [See *Docket.*] *Bacon.*

DOR, } *n.* [Qu. Ir. *dord*, humming, buz-
DORR, } zing, also rough.] The name of the black-beetle, or the hedge-chafer, a species of Scarabæus. We usually say, the *dor-beetle.*

DORA'DO, *n.* [Sp. *dorado*, gilt, from *dorar*, to gild.]

1. A southern constellation, containing six stars, called also *xiphias*; not visible in our latitude. *Encyc.*
2. A large fish resembling the dolphin. *Dict. of Nat. Hist.*

DOREE', *n.* A fish of the genus Zeus. It is called also faber, and gallus marinus. The body is oval and greatly compressed on the sides; the head is large and the snout long.

DO'RIAN, *a.* Pertaining to Doris in Greece. [See *Doric.*]

DOR'IC, *a.* [from *Doris* in Greece.] In *general*, pertaining to Doris, or the Dorians, in Greece, who dwelt near Parnassus.

In *architecture*, noting the second order of columns, between the Tuscan and Ionic. The Doric order is distinguished for simplicity and strength. It is used in the gates of cities and citadels, on the outside of churches, &c.

The *Doric* dialect of the Greek language was the dialect of the Dorians, and little different from that of Lacedemon. *Encyc.*

The *Doric* mode, in music, was the first of the authentic modes of the ancients. Its character is to be severe, tempered with gravity and joy. *Encyc.*

DOR'ICISM, } *n.* A phrase of the Doric
DO'RISM, } dialect.

DOR'MANCY, *n.* [infra.] Quiescence. *Horsley.*

DOR'MANT, *a.* [Fr. from *dormir*, L. *dormio*, to sleep.]

1. Sleeping; hence, at rest; not in action; as *dormant* passions.
2. Being in a sleeping posture; as the lion *dormant*, in heraldry.
3. Neglected; not used; as a *dormant* title; *dormant* privileges.
4. Concealed; not divulged; private. [*Unusual.*] *Bacon.*
5. Leaning; inclining; not perpendicular; as a *dormant* window, supposed to be so called from a beam of that name. This is now written *dormer* or *dormar.*

DOR'MANT, *n.* A beam; a sleeper.

DORMAR, *n.* A beam; a sleeper.

DOR'MAR, } *n.* A window in
DOR'MAR-WINDOW, } the roof of a house, or above the entablature, being raised upon the rafters. *Encyc.*

DOR'MITIVE, *n.* [L. *dormio*, to sleep.] A medicine to promote sleep; an opiate. *Arbuthnot.*

DOR'MITORY, *n.* [L. *dormitorium*, from *dormio*, to sleep.]

1. A place, building or room to sleep in.
2. A gallery in convents divided into several cells, where the religious sleep. *Encyc.*
3. A burial place. *Ayliffe.*

DOR'MOUSE, *n.* plu. *dormice.* [L. *dormio*, to sleep, and *mouse.*]

An animal of the mouse kind, which makes a bed of moss or dry leaves, in a hollow tree or under shrubs, lays in a store of nuts or other food, and on the approach of cold weather, rolls itself in a ball and sleeps the greatest part of the winter. *Dict. of Nat. Hist.*

DORN, *n.* [G. *dorn*, a thorn.] A fish. *Carew.*

DO'RON, *n.* [Gr. δωρον, a gift; δωρεω, Russ. *dariyu*, to give.] A gift; a present. [*Not in use.*]

2. A measure of three inches. *Ash.*

DORP, *n.* [G. *dorf*; D. *dorp*; Sw. Dan. *torp*; W. *trev.* See *Tribe.*] A small village.

DORR. [See *Dor.*]

DORR, *v. t.* To deafen with noise. [*Not in use.*]

DOR'RER, *n.* A drone. [*Not in use.*]

DOR'SAL, *a.* [from L. *dorsum*, the back.] Pertaining to the back; as the *dorsal* fin of a fish; *dorsal* awn, in botany.

DORSE, *n.* A canopy. *Sutton.*

DOR'SEL, *n.* [See *Dosser.*]

DORSIF'EROUS, } *a.* [L. *dorsum*, the back,
DORSIP'AROUS, } and *fero* or *pario*, to bear.]

In *botany*, bearing or producing seeds on the back of their leaves; an epithet given to ferns or plants of the capillary kind without stalks. *Encyc.*

DOR'SUM, *n.* [L.] The ridge of a hill. *Walton.*

DOR'TURE, *n.* [contraction of *dormiture.*] A dormitory. [*Not in use.*] *Bacon.*

DOSE, *n.* [Fr. *dose*; It. *dosa*; Gr. δοσις, that which is given, from διδωμι, to give; W. *dodi*, to give.]

1. The quantity of medicine given or prescribed to be taken at one time. *Quincy.*
2. Any thing given to be swallowed; any thing nauseous, that one is obliged to take. *South.*
3. A quantity; a portion. *Granville.*
4. As much as a man can swallow. *Johnson.*

DOSE, *v. t.* [Fr. *doser.*] To proportion a medicine properly to the patient or disease; to form into suitable doses. *Derham.*

2. To give in doses; to give medicine or physic.
3. To give any thing nauseous.

DOS'SER, *n.* [Fr. *dos*, the back; *dossier*, a bundle.]

A pannier, or basket, to be carried on the shoulders of men. *Encyc.*

DOS'SIL, *n.* In *surgery*, a pledget or portion of lint made into a cylindric form, or the shape of a date. *Encyc.*

DOST, the second person of *do*, used in the solemn style; thou *dost.*

DOT, *n.* [I know not the origin and affinities of this word. It would be naturally deduced from a verb signifying to set, or to prick, like *punctum, point.* It coincides in elements with *tatoo*, and with W. *dodi*, to give, that is, to thrust or cause to pass.]

A small point or spot, made with a pen or other pointed instrument; a speck; used in marking a writing or other thing.

DOT, *v. t.* To mark with dots.

2. To mark or diversify with small detached objects; as a landscape *dotted* with cottages, or clumps of trees.

DOT, *v. i.* To make dots or spots.

DO'TAGE, *n.* [from *dote.*] Feebleness or imbecility of understanding or mind, particularly in old age; childishness of old age; as a venerable man now in his *dotage.*

2. A doting; excessive fondness. *Dryden.*
3. Deliriousness. [See the verb, to *dote*.]

DO'TAL, *a.* [Fr. from L. *dotalis*, from *dos*, dower.]
Pertaining to dower, or a woman's marriage portion; constituting dower or comprised in it; as a *dotal* town. *Garth.*

DO'TARD, *n.* [*dote* and *ard*, kind.] A man whose intellect is impaired by age; one in his second childhood.

The sickly *dotard* wants a wife. *Prior.*

2. A doting fellow; one foolishly fond.

DO'TARDLY, *a.* Like a dotard; weak. *More.*

DOTA'TION, *n.* [L. *dotatio*, from *dos*, dower, *doto*, to endow.]
1. The act of endowing, or of bestowing a marriage portion on a woman.
2. Endowment; establishment of funds for support; as of a hospital or eleemosynary corporation. *Blackstone.*

DOTE, *v. i.* [D. *dutten*, to dote, to doze; W. *dotiaw*, to put out, to cause to mistake, to err, to dote; *dotian*, to be confused; Fr. *radoter*, to rave, to talk idly or extravagantly. The French word is rendered in Armoric, *rambreal*, which seems to be our *ramble*.]
1. To be delirious; to have the intellect impaired by age, so that the mind wanders or wavors; to be silly.

Time has made you *dote*, and vainly tell
Of arms imagined in your lonely cell. *Dryden.*

2. To be excessively in love; usually with *on* or *upon*: to *dote on*, is to love to excess or extravagance.

What dust we *dote on*, when 'tis man we love. *Pope.*

Aholah *doted on* her lovers, the Assyrians. Ezek. xxiii.

3. To decay. *Howson.*

DO'TER, *n.* One who dotes; a man whose understanding is enfeebled by age; a dotard. *Burton.*
2. One who is excessively fond, or weakly in love. *Boyle.*

DO'TING, *ppr.* Regarding with excessive fondness.

DO'TINGLY, *adv.* By excessive fondness. *Dryden.*

DOT'TARD, *n.* A tree kept low by cutting. *Bacon.*

DOT'TED, *pp.* Marked with dots or small spots; diversified with small detached objects.
2. In *botany*, sprinkled with hollow dots or points. *Martyn.*

DOT'TEREL, *n.* The name of different species of fowls, of the genus Charadrius and the grallic order; as the Alexandrine dotterel, the ringed dotterel, and the Morinellus; also, the turnstone or sea dotterel, a species of the genus Tringa. *Encyc. Ed. Encyc.*

DOT'TING, *ppr.* Marking with dots or spots; diversifying with small detached objects.

DÖUANIE'R, *n.* [Fr.] An officer of the customs. *Gray.*

DOUB'LE, *a. dub'l.* [Fr. *double*; Arm. *doubl*; Sp. *doble*; Port. *dobre*; It. *doppio*; W. *dyblyg*; D. *dubbel*; G. *doppelt*; Dan. *dobbelt*; Sw. *dubbel*; L. *duplus*, *duplex*; Gr. διπλοος; compounded of *duo*, two, and *plico*, to fold, *plexus*, a fold. See *Two*.]
1. Two of a sort together; one corresponding to the other; being in pairs; as *double* chickens in the same egg; *double* leaves connected by one petiole.
2. Twice as much; containing the same quantity or length repeated.

Take *double* money in your hand. Gen. xliii.

Let a *double* portion of thy spirit be on me. 2 Kings ii.

With *to*; as, the amount is *double to* what I expected.

3. Having one added to another; as a *double* chin.
4. Twofold; also, of two kinds.

Darkness and tempest make a *double* night. *Dryden.*

5. Two in number; as *double* sight or sound. [See No. 1.] *Davies.*
6. Deceitful; acting two parts, one openly, the other in secret.

And with a *double* heart do they speak. Ps. xii.

DOUB'LE, *adv. dub'l.* Twice.

I was *double* their age. *Swift.*

DOUBLE, in composition, denotes, two ways, or twice the number or quantity.

DOUBLE-BANKED, *a.* In *seamanship*, having two opposite oars managed by rowers on the same bench, or having two men to the same oar. *Mar. Dict.*

DOUBLE-BITING, *a.* Biting or cutting on either side; as a *double-biting* ax. *Dryden.*

DOUBLE-BUTTONED, *a.* Having two rows of buttons. *Gay.*

DOUBLE-CHARGE, *v. t.* To charge or intrust with a double portion. *Shak.*

DOUBLE-DEALER, *n.* One who acts two different parts, in the same business, or at the same time; a deceitful, trickish person; one who says one thing and thinks or intends another; one guilty of duplicity. *L'Estrange.*

DOUBLE-DEALING, *n.* Artifice; duplicity; deceitful practice; the profession of one thing and the practice of another. *Shak. Broome.*

DOUBLE-DYE, *v. t.* To dye twice over. *Dryden.*

DOUBLE-EDGED, *a.* Having two edges.

DOUBLE-ENTENDRE, *n.* [Fr.] Double meaning of a word or expression.

DOUBLE-EYED, *a.* Having a deceitful countenance. *Spenser.*

DOUBLE-FACE, *n.* Duplicity; the acting of different parts in the same concern.

DOUBLE-FACED, *a.* Deceitful; hypocritical; showing two faces. *Milton.*

DOUBLE-FORMED, *a.* Of a mixed form. *Milton.*

DOUBLE-FORTIFIED, *a.* Twice fortified; doubly strengthened.

DOUBLE-FOUNTED, *a.* Having two sources. *Milton.*

DOUBLE-GILD, *v. t.* To gild with double coloring. *Shak.*

DOUBLE-HANDED, *a.* Having two hands; deceitful. *Glanville.*

DOUBLE-HEADED, *a.* Having two heads.
2. Having the flowers growing one to another. *Mortimer.*

DOUBLE-HEARTED, *a.* Having a false heart; deceitful; treacherous.

DOUBLE-LOCK, *v. t.* To shoot the bolt twice; to fasten with double security. *Tatler.*

DOUBLE-MANNED, *a.* Furnished with twice the complement of men, or with two men instead of one.

DOUBLE-MEANING, *a.* Having two meanings.

DOUBLE-MINDED, *a.* Having different minds at different times; unsettled; wavering; unstable; undetermined. James i.

DOUBLE-MOUTHED, *a.* Having two mouths. *Milton.*

DOUBLE-NATURED, *a.* Having a twofold nature. *Young.*

DOUBLE-OCTAVE, *n.* In *music*, an interval composed of two octaves or fifteen notes in diatonic progression; a fifteenth. *Encyc.*

DOUBLE-PLEA, *n.* In *law*, a plea in which the defendant alledges two different matters in bar of the action. *Cowel.*

DOUBLE-QUARREL, *n.* A complaint of a clerk to the archbishop against an inferior ordinary, for delay of justice. *Cowel.*

DOUBLE-SHADE, *v. t.* To double the natural darkness of a place. *Milton.*

DOUBLE-SHINING, *a.* Shining with double luster. *Sidney.*

DOUBLE-THREADED, *a.* Consisting of two threads twisted together.

DOUBLE-TONGUED, *a.* Making contrary declarations on the same subject at different times; deceitful.

The deacons must be grave, not *double-tongued*. 1 Tim. iii.

DOUB'LE, *v. t. dub'l.* [Fr. *doubler*; Arm. *doubla*; Sp. *doblar*; Port. *dobrar*; It. *doppiare*; D. *dubbelen*; G. *doppeln*; Dan. *doblerer*; Sw. *dublera*; Ir. *dublaighim*; W. *dyblygu*; L. *duplico*; Gr. διπλοω.]
1. To fold; as, to *double* the leaf of a book; to *double* down a corner. *Prior.*
2. To increase or extend by adding an equal sum, value, quantity or length; as, to *double* a sum of money; to *double* the amount; to *double* the quantity or size of a thing; to *double* the length; to *double* dishonor.
3. To contain twice the sum, quantity or length, or twice as much; as, the enemy *doubles* our army in numbers.
4. To repeat; to add; as, to *double* blow on blow. *Dryden.*
5. To add one to another in the same order.

Thou shalt *double* the sixth curtain in the fore-front of the tabernacle. Ex. xxvi.

6. In *navigation*, to *double* a cape or point, is to sail round it, so that the cape or point shall be between the ship and her former situation. *Mar. Dict.*
7. In *military affairs*, to unite two ranks or files in one.

To double and twist, is to add one thread to another and twist them together.

To double upon, in tactics, is to inclose between two fires.

DOUB'LE, *v. i.* To increase to twice the sum, number, value, quantity or length; to increase or grow to twice as much. A sum of money *doubles* by compound interest in a little more than eleven years. The inhabitants of the United States *double* in about twenty five years.
2. To enlarge a wager to twice the sum laid.

I am resolved to *double* till I win. *Dryden.*

3. To turn back or wind in running.

Doubling and turning like a hunted hare. *Dryden.*

4. To play tricks; to use sleights. *Johnson.*

DOUB'LE, *n.* Twice as much; twice the number, sum, value, quantity or length.

If the thief be found, let him pay *double.* Ex. xxii.

2. A turn in running to escape pursuers. *Blackmore.*

3. A trick; a shift; an artifice to deceive. *Addison.*

DOUB'LED, *pp.* Folded; increased by adding an equal quantity, sum or value; repeated; turned or passed round.

DOUB'LENESS, *n.* The state of being doubled. *Shak.*

2. Duplicity.

DOUB'LER, *n.* He that doubles.

2. An instrument for augmenting a very small quantity of electricity, so as to render it manifest by sparks or the electrometer. *Cyc.*

DOUB'LET, *n.* [Ir. *duiblead;* Fr. *doublet.*]

1. The inner garment of a man; a waistcoat or vest.

2. Two; a pair. *Grew.*

3. Among *lapidaries*, a counterfeit stone composed of two pieces of crystal, with a color between them, so that they have the same appearance as if the whole substance of the crystal were colored. *Encyc.*

DOUB'LETS, *n.* A game on dice within tables.

2. The same number on both dice. *Encyc.*

3. A double meaning. *Mason.*

DOUB'LING, *ppr.* Making twice the sum, number or quantity; repeating; passing round; turning to escape.

DOUB'LING, *n.* The act of making double; also, a fold; a plait; also, an artifice; a shift.

DOUBLOON', *n.* [Fr. *doublon;* Sp. *doblon;* It. *dobblone.*]

A Spanish and Portuguese coin, being double the value of the pistole. *Encyc.*

DOUB'LY, *adv.* In twice the quantity; to twice the degree; as *doubly* wise or good; to be *doubly* sensible of an obligation. *Dryden.*

DOUBT, *v. i.* *dout.* [Fr. *douter;* L. *dubito;* It. *dubitare;* Sp. *dudar;* Arm. *doueti.* According to Ainsworth, this is composed of *duo* and *bito*, to go. It is evidently from the root of *dubius*, and of *two;* but the manner of formation is not clear. So D. *twyffelen*, to doubt, G. *zweifeln*, Sw. *tvifla*, D. *twivler*, are from *two.*]

1. To waver or fluctuate in opinion; to hesitate; to be in suspense; to be in uncertainty, respecting the truth or fact; to be undetermined.

Even in matters divine, concerning some things, we may lawfully *doubt* and suspend our judgment. *Hooker.*

So we say, I *doubt* whether it is proper; I *doubt* whether I shall go; sometimes with *of*, as we *doubt of* a fact.

2. To fear; to be apprehensive; to suspect.

I *doubt* there's deep resentment in his mind. *Otway.*

DOUBT, *v. t.* *dout.* To question, or hold questionable; to withhold assent from; to hesitate to believe; as, I have heard the story, but I *doubt* the truth of it.

2. To fear; to suspect.

If they turn not back perverse;
But that I *doubt.* *Milton.*

3. To distrust; to withhold confidence from; as, to *doubt* our ability to execute an office.

T'admire superior sense, and *doubt* their own. *Pope.*

4. To fill with fear. *Obs.* *Beaum.*

DOUBT, *n.* *dout.* A fluctuation of mind respecting truth or propriety, arising from defect of knowledge or evidence; uncertainty of mind; suspense; unsettled state of opinion; as, to have *doubts* respecting the theory of the tides.

Joseph is without *doubt* rent in pieces. Gen. xxxvii.

2. Uncertainty of condition.

Thy life shall hang in *doubt* before thee. Deut. xxviii.

3. Suspicion; fear; apprehension.

I stand in *doubt* of you. Gal. iv.

4. Difficulty objected.

To every *doubt* your answer is the same. *Blackmore.*

5. Dread; horror and danger. *Obs.*

DOUBT'ABLE, *a.* That may be doubted. *Sherwood.*

DOUBT'ED, *pp.* Scrupled; questioned; not certain or settled.

DOUBT'ER, *n.* One who doubts; one whose opinion is unsettled; one who scruples.

DOUBT'FUL, *a.* Dubious; not settled in opinion; undetermined; wavering; hesitating; *applied to persons;* as, we are *doubtful* of a fact, or of the propriety of a measure.

2. Dubious; ambiguous; not clear in its meaning; as a *doubtful* expression.

3. Admitting of doubt; not obvious, clear or certain; questionable; not decided; as a *doubtful* case; a *doubtful* proposition; it is *doubtful* what will be the event of the war.

4. Of uncertain issue.

We have sustained one day in *doubtful* fight. *Milton.*

5. Not secure; suspicious; as, we cast a *doubtful* eye. *Hooker.*

6. Not confident; not without fear; indicating doubt.

With *doubtful* feet, and wavering resolution. *Milton.*

7. Not certain or defined; as a *doubtful* hue. *Milton.*

DOUBT'FULLY, *adv.* In a doubtful manner; dubiously. *Spenser.*

2. With doubt; irresolutely.

3. Ambiguously; with uncertainty of meaning.

Nor did the goddess *doubtfully* declare. *Dryden.*

4. In a state of dread. *Obs.* *Spenser.*

DOUBT'FULNESS, *n.* A state of doubt or uncertainty of mind; dubiousness; suspense; instability of opinion. *Watts.*

2. Ambiguity; uncertainty of meaning. *Locke.*

3. Uncertainty of event or issue; uncertainty of condition. *Johnson.*

DOUBT'ING, *ppr.* Wavering in mind; calling in question; hesitating.

DOUBT'INGLY, *adv.* In a doubting manner; dubiously; without confidence.

DOUBT'LESS, *a.* Free from fear of danger; secure. *Obs.*

Pretty child, sleep *doubtless* and secure. *Shak.*

DOUBT'LESS, *adv.* Without doubt or question; unquestionably.

The histories of Christ by the evangelists are *doubtless* authentic.

DOUBT'LESSLY, *adv.* Unquestionably. *Beaum.*

DÖUCED, *n.* [from Fr. *douce.*] A musical instrument. [*Not in use.*] *Chaucer.*

DÖUCET, *n.* [Fr.] A custard. [*Not in use.*]

DÖUCEUR, *n.* [Fr. from *doux*, sweet, L. *dulcis.*] A present or gift; a bribe.

DÖUCINE, *n.* [Fr.] A molding concave above and convex below, serving as a cymatium to a delicate cornice; a gula. *Encyc.*

DOUCK'ER, *n.* [See *Duck.*] A fowl that dips or dives in water. *Ray.*

DŌUGH, *n.* *do.* [Sax. *dah;* D. *deeg;* Sw. *deg;* Dan. *dej;* G. *teig.* Probably a soft mass, and perhaps allied to *thick.* See Class Dg. No. 8. 17. 21. 22. 36.]

Paste of bread; a mass composed of flour or meal moistened and kneaded, but not baked.

My cake is dough, that is, my undertaking has not come to maturity. *Shak.*

DŌUGH-BAKED, *a.* Unfinished; not hardened to perfection; soft. *Donne.*

DŌUGH-KNEADED, *a.* Soft; like dough. *Milton.*

DŌUGH-NUT, *n.* [*dough* and *nut.*] A small roundish cake, made of flour, eggs and sugar, moistened with milk and boiled in lard.

DOUGHTINESS, *n.* *dou'tiness.* [See *Doughty.*] Valor; bravery.

DOUGHTY, *a.* *dou'ty.* [Sax. *dohtig*, brave, noble; Dan. *dygtig*, able, fit; Sax. *dugan*, to be able or strong, to be good; D. *deugen;* G. *taugen;* Sw. *duga;* Dan. *duer;* hence Sax. *dugoth*, valor, strength or virtue; Ir. *deagh*, *diagh*, good; allied propably to L. *deceo.* See *Decent.*]

Brave; valiant; eminent; noble; illustrious; as a *doughty* hero. *Pope.*

It is now seldom used except in irony or burlesque.

DŌUGHY, *a.* *dōy.* Like dough; soft; yielding to pressure; pale. *Shak.*

DOUSE, *v. t.* [This word seems to accord with *dowse*, or rather with the Gr. δυω, δυσις.]

1. To thrust or plunge into water.

2. In *seamen's language*, to strike or lower in haste; to slacken suddenly. *Douse* the top-sail. *Mar. Dict.*

DOUSE, *v. i.* To fall suddenly into water. *Hudibras.*

DOUT, *v. t.* [Qu. *do out.*] To put out; to extinguish. *Shak.*

DOUT'ER, *n.* An extinguisher for candles.

DÖUZEAVE, *n.* *doo'zeve.* [Fr. *douze*, twelve.] In *music*, a scale of twelve degrees. *A. M. Fisher.*

DŎVE, *n.* [Sax. *duua;* Goth. *dubo;* D. *duif;* G. *taube;* Dan. *due;* Sw. *dufva;* Ice. *dufa;* Gypsey, *tovadei;* Hindoo, *tubbeter;* Scot. *dow;* probably from cooing, Heb. דבב to murmur, or Ar. هتف hatafa, to coo, as a dove.]

1. The œnas, or domestic pigeon, a species of Columba. Its color is a deep bluish ash color; the breast is dashed with a fine changeable green and purple; the sides of the neck, with a copper color. In a wild state, it builds its nest in holes of rocks or in hollow trees, but it is easily domesti-

cated, and forms one of the luxuries of the table.

2. A word of endearment, or an emblem of innocence. Cant. ii. 14.

DŎVE-COT, *n.* A small building or box in which domestic pigeons breed.

DŎVE'S-FOOT, *n.* A plant, a species of Geranium.

DŎVE-HOUSE, *n.* A house or shelter for doves.

DŎVELIKE, *a.* Resembling a dove. *Milton.*

DŎVESHIP, *n.* The qualities of a dove. *Hall.*

DŎVE-TAIL, *n.* In *carpentry*, the manner of fastening boards and timbers together by letting one piece into another in the form of a dove's tail spread, or wedge reversed, so that it cannot be drawn out. This is the strongest of all the fastenings or jointings.

DŎVE-TAIL, *v. t.* To unite by a tenon in form of a pigeon's tail spread, let into a board or timber.

DŎVE-TAILED, *pp.* United by a tenon in form of a dove's tail.

DŎVE-TAILING, *ppr.* Uniting by a dove-tail.

DŎVISH, *a.* Like a dove; innocent. [*Not in use.*]

DOW'ABLE, *a.* [See *Dower.*] That may be endowed; entitled to dower. *Blackstone.*

DOW'AGER, *n.* [Fr. *douairiere*, from *douaire*, dower.]

A widow with a jointure; a title particularly given to the widows of princes and persons of rank. The widow of a king is called *queen dowager.*

DOW'CETS, *n.* The testicles of a hart or stag. *B. Jonson.*

DOW'DY, *n.* [Scot. *dawdie*, perhaps from *daw*, a sluggard, or its root. *Jamieson.*]

An awkward, ill-dressed, inelegant woman. *Shak. Dryden.*

DOW'DY, *a.* Awkward. *Gay.*

DOW'ER, *n.* [W. *dawd*, a gift; *dawni*, to endow; Fr. *douaire*, from *douer*, to endow. Supposed to be from L. *dos, dotis, dotatio*; Gr. δως, a gift, from διδωμι, to give, W. *dodi*, L. *do.* It is written in the Latin of the middle ages, *dodarium, dotarium, douarium.* Spelman. In Ir. *diobhadth* is dower.]

1. That portion of the lands or tenements of a man which his widow enjoys during her life, after the death of her husband. [*This is the usual present signification of the word.*] *Blackstone.*

2. The property which a woman brings to her husband in marriage. *Dryden.*

3. The gift of a husband for a wife.

> Ask me never so much *dowry* and gift. Gen. xxxiv.

4. Endowment; gift.

> How great, how plentiful, how rich a *dower.* *Davies.*

DOW'ERED, *a.* Furnished with dower, or a portion. *Shak.*

DOW'ERLESS, *a.* Destitute of dower; having no portion or fortune. *Shak.*

DOW'ERY. } A different spelling of *dower*,
DOW'RY. } but little used, and they may well be neglected.

DOW'LAS, *n.* A kind of coarse linen cloth. *Shak.*

DOWLE, *n.* A feather. [*Not in use.*] *Shak.*

DOWN, *n.* [Sw. *dun*; D. *dons*; Dan. *duun*; Ice. *id.* In Sw. *dyna* is a feather-bed, or cushion; Dan. *dyne.* Arm. *dum*, down. Qu. Class Dn. No. 25. But the primitive orthography and signification are uncertain.]

1. The fine soft feathers of fowls, particularly of the duck kind. The eider duck yields the best kind. Also, fine hair; as the *down* of the chin.

2. The pubescence of plants, a fine hairy substance.

3. The pappus or little crown of certain seeds of plants; a fine feathery or hairy substance by which seeds are conveyed to a distance by the wind; as in dandelion and thistle.

4. Any thing that soothes or mollifies.

> Thou bosom softness; *down* of all my cares. *Southern.*

DOWN, *n.* [Sax. *dun*; D. *duin*, a sandy hill; G. *düne*; Fr. *dune*, plu. *dunes*; Arm. *dunenn*, or *tunenn.* In French *dunette* is the highest part of the poop of a ship, and as this appears to be a diminutive of *dune*, it proves that the primary sense is a hill or elevation.]

1. A bank or elevation of sand, thrown up by the sea. *Encyc.*

2. A large open plain, primarily on elevated land. Sheep feeding on the *downs.* *Milton.*

DOWN, *prep.* [Sax. *dun, adun.* In W. *dwvyn* is deep, Corn. *doun*, Arm. *doun*, Ir. *domhain*; and in Welsh, *dan* is under, beneath. In Russ. *tonu* is to sink.]

1. Along a descent; from a higher to a lower place; as, to run *down* a hill; to fall *down* a precipice; to go *down* the stairs.

2. Toward the mouth of a river, or toward the place where water is discharged into the ocean or a lake. We sail or swim *down* a stream; we sail *down* the sound from New York to New London. Hence figuratively, we pass *down* the current of life or of time.

Down the sound, in the direction of the ebb-tide towards the sea.

Down the country, towards the sea, or towards the part where rivers discharge their waters into the ocean.

DOWN, *adv.* In a descending direction; tending from a higher to a lower place; as, he is going *down.*

2. On the ground, or at the bottom; as, he is *down*; hold him *down.*

3. Below the horizon; as, the sun is *down.*

4. In the direction from a higher to a lower condition; as, his reputation is going *down.*

5. Into disrepute or disgrace. A man may sometimes preach *down* error; he may write *down* himself or his character, or run *down* his rival; but he can neither preach nor write *down* folly, vice or fashion.

6. Into subjection; into a due consistence; as, to boil *down*, in decoctions and culinary processes.

7. At length; extended or prostrate, on the ground or on any flat surface; as, to lie *down*; he is lying *down.*

Up and down, here and there; in a rambling course.

It is sometimes used without a verb, as *down, down*; in which cases, the sense is known by the construction.

Down with a building, is a command to pull it down, to demolish it.

Down with him, signifies, throw him.

Down, down, may signify, come down, or go down, or take down, lower.

It is often used by seamen, *down* with the fore sail, &c.

Locke uses it for *go down*, or be received; as, any kind of food will *down*: but the use is not elegant, nor legitimate.

Sidney uses it as a verb, "To *down* proud hearts," to subdue or conquer them; but the use is not legitimate.

DOWN'-BED, *n.* A bed of down.

DOWN'CAST, *a.* Cast downward; directed to the ground; as a *downcast* eye or look, indicating bashfulness, modesty or dejection of mind.

DOWN'CAST, *n.* Sadness; melancholy look. *Obs.* *Beaum.*

DOWN'ED, *a.* Covered or stuffed with down. *Young.*

DOWN'FALL, *n.* A falling, or body of things falling; as the *downfall* of a flood. *Dryden.*

2. Ruin; destruction; a sudden fall, or ruin by violence, in distinction from slow decay or declension; as the *downfall* of the Roman empire, occasioned by the conquests of the Northern nations; the *downfall* of a city.

3. The sudden fall, depression or ruin of reputation or estate. We speak of the *downfall* of pride or glory, and of distinguished characters.

DOWN'FALLEN, *a.* Fallen; ruined. *Carew.*

DOWN'GYVED, *a.* Hanging down like the loose cincture of fetters. *Steevens.*

DOWN'-HAUL, *n.* In *seaman's language*, a rope passing along a stay, through the cringles of the stay-sail or jib, and made fast to the upper corner of the sail, to haul it down. *Mar. Dict.*

DOWN'HEARTED, *a.* Dejected in spirits.

DOWN'HILL, *n.* Declivity; descent; slope.

> And though 'tis *downhill* all. *Dryden.*

DOWN'HILL, *a.* Declivous; descending; sloping.

> A *downhill* greensward. *Congreve.*

DOWN'LOOKED, *a.* Having a downcast countenance; dejected; gloomy; sullen; as jealousy *downlooked.* *Dryden.*

DOWN'LYING, *n.* The time of retiring to rest; time of repose. *Cavendish.*

DOWN'LYING, *a.* About to be in travel of childbirth. *Johnson.*

DOWN'RIGHT, *adv.* Right down; straight down; perpendicularly.

> A giant cleft *downright.* *Hudibras.*

2. In plain terms; without ceremony or circumlocution.

> We shall chide *downright.* *Shak.*

3. Completely; without stopping short; as, she fell *downright* into a fit. *Arbuthnot.*

DOWN'RIGHT, *a.* Directly to the point; plain; open; artless; undisguised; as *downright* madness; *downright* nonsense; *downright* wisdom; *downright* falsehood; *downright* atheism.

2. Plain; artless; unceremonious; blunt; as, he spoke in his *downright* way.

DOWN'RIGHTLY, *adv.* Plainly; in plain terms; bluntly. *Barrow.*

DOWN'-SITTING, *n.* The act of sitting down; repose; a resting.

Thou knowest my *down-sitting* and my uprising. Ps. cxxxix.

DOWN'TROD, } *a.* Trodden down;
DOWN'TRODDEN, } trampled down. *Shak.*

DOWN'WARD, } *adv.* [Sax. *duneweard.*
DOWN'WARDS, } See *Ward.*]

1. From a higher place to a lower; in a descending course, whether directly toward the center of the earth, or not; as, to tend *downward*; to move or roll *downwards*; to look *downward*; to take root *downwards*.
2. In a course or direction from a head, spring, origin or source. Water flows *downward* toward the sea; we sailed *downward* on the stream.
3. In a course of lineal descent from an ancestor, considered as a head; as, to trace successive generations *downward* from Adam or Abraham.
4. In the course of falling or descending from elevation or distinction.

DOWN'WARD, *a.* Moving or extending from a higher to a lower place, as on a slope or declivity, or in the open air; tending towards the earth or its center; as a *downward* course; he took his way with *downward* force. *Dryden.*
2. Declivous; bending; as the *downward* heaven. *Dryden.*
3. Descending from a head, origin or source.
4. Tending to a lower condition or state; depressed; dejected; as *downward* thoughts. *Sidney.*

DOWN'WEED, *n.* Cottonweed, a downy plant. *Barret.*

DOWN'Y, *a.* [See *Down.*] Covered with down or nap; as a *downy* feather; *downy* wings.
2. Covered with pubescence or soft hairs, as a plant.
3. Made of down or soft feathers; as a *downy* pillow.
4. Soft, calm, soothing; as *downy* sleep.
5. Resembling down.

DOW'RY, *n.* [See *Dower.* This word differs not from *dower.* It is the same word differently written, and the distinction made between them is arbitrary.]
1. The money, goods or estate which a woman brings to her husband in marriage; the portion given with a wife. *Shak. Dryden.*
2. The reward paid for a wife. *Cowley.*
3. A gift; a fortune given. *Johnson.*

DOWSE, *v. t.* [Sw. *daska.*] To strike on the face. [*Not in use.*] *Bailey.*

DOWST, *n.* A stroke. [*Not in use.*] *Beaum.*

DOXOLOG'ICAL, *a.* Pertaining to doxology; giving praise to God. *Howell.*

DOXOL'OGY, *n.* [Gr. δοξολογια; δοξα, praise, glory, and λεγω, to speak.]
In *christian worship*, a hymn in praise of the Almighty; a particular form of giving glory to God.

DOX'Y, *n.* [Qu. Sw. *docka*, a baby, doll or plaything.] A prostitute. *Shak.*

DOZE, *v. i.* [Dan. *döser*, to stifle, suppress or quiet; to make heavy, sleepy or drowsy; *dysser*, to lull to sleep. The Saxon has *dwæs*, *dwes*, dull, stupid, foolish, D. *dwaas.* The Saxon *dysig* is rendered foolish or *dizzy.* See *Dote*, and Class Ds. No. 1. 3.]
1. To slumber; to sleep lightly.

If he happened to *doze* a little, the jolly cobler waked him. *L'Estrange.*

2. To live in a state of drowsiness; to be dull or half asleep; as, to *doze* away the time; to *doze* over a work. *Dryden. Pope.*

DOZE, *v. t.* To make dull; to stupify. Dryden uses the participle *dozed*, "*Dozed* with his fumes;" but the transitive verb is seldom or never used.

DOZ'EN, *a.* *duz'n.* [Fr. *douzaine*; Arm. *douçzenn*; from Fr. *douze*, twelve; Norm. Fr. *dudzime*, a dozen; Sp. *doce*, twelve; *docena*, a dozen; Port. *duzia*, dozen; It. *dozzina*, id.; D. *dozyn*; G. *duzend*, or *dutzend*; Sw. *dussin*; Dan. *dusin.* Qu. *two* and *ten*, G. *zehn.* The composition of the word is not obvious.]
Twelve in number, applied to things of the same kind, but rarely or never to that number in the abstract. We say, a *dozen* men; a *dozen* pair of gloves. It is a word much used in common discourse and in light compositions; rarely in the grave or elevated style.

DOZ'EN, *n.* The number twelve of things of a like kind; as a *dozen* of eggs; twelve *dozen* of gloves; a *dozen* of wine.

DO'ZER, *n.* One that dozes or slumbers.

DO'ZINESS, *n.* [from *dozy.*] Drowsiness; heaviness; inclination to sleep. *Locke.*

DO'ZING, *ppr.* Slumbering.

DO'ZING, *n.* A slumbering; sluggishness. *Chesterfield.*

DO'ZY, *a.* [See *Doze.*] Drowsy; heavy; inclined to sleep; sleepy; sluggish; as a *dozy* head. *Dryden.*

DRAB, *n.* [Sax. *drabbe*, lees, dregs; D. *drabbe*, dregs. This seems to be the Dan. *draabe*, a *drop.*]
1. A strumpet; a prostitute. *Shak. Pope.*
2. A low, sluttish woman. [*This seems to be the sense in which it is generally used in New England.*]
3. A kind of wooden box, used in salt works for holding the salt when taken out of the boiling pans. Its bottom is shelving or inclining that the water may drain off. *Encyc.*

DRAB, *n.* [Fr. *drap*, cloth; It. *drappo*; Sp. *trapo*, and without the prefix *t*, *ropa*, cloth, Port. *roupa*, whence *robe.* From the French we have *draper*, *drapery*, as the Spanish have *ropage*, for drapery. This word seems allied to the L. *trabea.*] A kind of thick woolen cloth.

DRAB, *a.* Being of a dun color, like the cloth so called.

DRAB, *v. i.* To associate with strumpets. *Beaum.*

DRAB'BING, *ppr.* Keeping company with lewd women.

DRAB'BING, *n.* An associating with strumpets. *Beaum.*

DRAB'BLE, *v. t.* To draggle; to make dirty by drawing in mud and water; to wet and befoul; as, to *drabble* a gown or cloke. *N. England.*

In Scottish, this word signifies to dirty by slabbering, as if it were allied to *dribble*, *drivel*, from the root of *drip*, which coincides with *drop.*

DRAB'BLE, *v. i.* To fish for barbels with a long line and rod. *Encyc.*

DRAB'BLING, *a.* Drawing in mud or water; angling for barbels.

DRAB'BLING, *n.* A method of angling for barbels with a rod and a long line passed through a piece of lead. *Encyc.*

DRAB'LER, *n.* In *seaman's language*, a small additional sail, sometimes laced to the bottom of a bonnet on a square sail, in sloops and schooners. It is the same to a bonnet, as a bonnet is to a course. *Encyc. Mar. Dict.*

DRACH'MA, *n.* [L. from Gr. δραχμη; Fr. *dragme*; It. *dramma*, by contraction, Eng. *dram.*]
1. A Grecian coin, of the value of seven pence, three farthings, sterling, or nearly fourteen cents.
2. The eighth part of an ounce, or sixty grains, or three scruples; a weight used by apothecaries, but usually written *dram.*

DRA'CO, *n.* [See *Dragon.*] In *astronomy*, a constellation of the northern hemisphere, containing, according to Flamstead, eighty stars.
2. A luminous exhalation from marshy grounds. *Encyc.*
3. A genus of animals of two species. [See *Dragon.*]

DRACON'TIC, *a.* [L. *draco.*] In *astronomy*, belonging to that space of time in which the moon performs one entire revolution. *Bailey.*

DRACUN'CULUS, *n.* [from L. *draco*, dragon.] In *botany*, a plant, a species of Arum, with a long stalk, spotted like a serpent's belly.
2. In *medicine*, a long slender worm, bred in the muscular parts of the arms and legs, called *Guinea worm.* These are troublesome in tropical climates, and are usually extirpated by the point of a needle. *Encyc.*

DRAD, *a.* Terrible. *Obs.* [See *Dread.*] This was also the old pret. of *dread.*

DR'AFF, *n.* [D. *draf*, *droef*, dregs, grains. Shakespear wrote *draugh*, and the French have *drague*, grains. The latter coincides in elements with *draw*, *drag.*]
Refuse; lees; dregs; the wash given to swine, or grains to cows; waste matter. *Milton. Dryden.*

DR'AFFISH, *a.* Worthless.

DR'AFFY, *a.* Dreggy; waste; worthless.

DR'AFT, *n.* [corrupted from *draught*, from *drag*, *draw*, but authorized by respectable use.] A drawing; as, this horse is good for *draft.* In this sense, *draught* is perhaps most common.
2. A drawing of men from a military band; a selecting or detaching of soldiers from an army, or any part of it, or from a military post. Sometimes a drawing of men from other companies or societies.

Several of the States had supplied the deficiency by *drafts* to serve for the year. *Marshall.*

These important posts, in consequence of *heavy drafts*, were left weakly defended.

3. An order from one man to another directing the payment of money; a bill of exchange.

I thought it most prudent to defer the *drafts*, till advice was received of the progress of the loan. *Hamilton.*

4. A drawing of lines for a plan; a figure described on paper; delineation; sketch; plan delineated. [See *Draught.*]
5. Depth of water necessary to float a ship. [See *Draught.*]
6. A writing composed.

DR'AFT, *v. t.* To draw the outline; to delineate.

2. To compose and write; as, to *draft* a memorial or a lease.

3. To draw men from a military band or post; to select; to detach.

4. To draw men from any company, collection or society.

This Cohen-Caph-El was some royal seminary in Upper Egypt, from whence they *drafted* novices to supply their colleges and temples. *Holwell's Dict.*

DR'AFT-HORSE, *n.* A horse employed in drawing, particularly in drawing heavy loads or in plowing.

DR'AFT-OX, *n.* An ox employed in drawing.

DR'AFTED, *pp.* Drawn; delineated; detached.

DR'AFTING, *ppr.* Drawing; delineating; detaching.

DR'AFTS, *n.* A game played on checkers.

DRAG, *v. t.* [Sax. *dragan*; W. *dragiaw*; D. *draagen*; Sw. *draga*; Dan. *drager*; G. *tragen*; also Dan. *trekker*; D. *trekken*; Sax. *dreogan*; L. *traho*; Fr. *traire*; Malayan, *tarek*; It. *treggia*, a sled or *drag*; Sp. *trago*, a draught; *tragar*, to swallow, Eng. to *drink*. See *Drink* and *Drench*. The Russ. has *dergayu*, and *torgayu*, to draw, as *truck* is written *torguyu*. See Class Rg. No. 27. 37. 56.]

1. To pull; to haul; to draw along the ground by main force; applied particularly to drawing heavy things with labor, along the ground or other surface; as, to *drag* stone or timber; to *drag* a net in fishing. John xxi. 8.

2. To break land by drawing a drag or harrow over it; to harrow; *a common use of this word in New England.*

3. To draw along slowly or heavily; to draw any thing burdensome; as, to *drag* a lingering life. *Dryden.*

4. To draw along in contempt, as unworthy to be carried.

He *drags* me at his chariot-wheels. *Stillingfleet.*

To *drag* one in chains. *Milton.*

5. To pull or haul about roughly and forcibly. *Dryden.*

In *seamen's language*, to *drag* an anchor, is to draw or trail it along the bottom when loosened, or when the anchor will not hold the ship.

DRAG, *v. i.* To hang so low as to trail on the ground.

2. To fish with a drag; as, they have been *dragging* for fish all day, with little success.

3. To be drawn along; as, the anchor *drags*.

4. To be moved slowly; to proceed heavily; as, this business *drags*.

5. To hang or grate on the floor, as a door.

DRAG, *n.* Something to be drawn along the ground, as a net or a hook.

2. A particular kind of harrow.

3. A car; a low cart.

4. In *sea-language*, a machine consisting of a sharp square frame of iron, encircled with a net, used to take the wheel off from the platform or bottom of the decks. *Mar. Dict. Encyc.*

5. Whatever is drawn; a boat in tow; whatever serves to retard a ship's way. *Encyc.*

DRAG'GED, *pp.* Drawn on the ground; drawn with labor or force; drawn along slowly and heavily; raked with a drag or harrow.

DRAG'GING, *ppr.* Drawing on the ground; drawing with labor or by force; drawing slowly or heavily; raking with a drag.

DRAG'GLE, *v. t.* [dim. of *drag*.] To wet and dirty by drawing on the ground or mud, or on wet grass; to drabble. *Gray.*

DRAG'GLE, *v. i.* To be drawn on the ground; to become wet or dirty by being drawn on the mud or wet grass.

DRAG'GLE-TAIL, *n.* A slut. *Sherwood.*

DRAG'GLED, *pp.* Drawn on the ground; wet or dirtied by being drawn on the ground or mire.

DRAG'GLING, *ppr.* Drawing on the ground; making dirty by drawing on the ground or wet grass.

DRAG'MAN, *n.* A fisherman that uses a dragnet. *Hale.*

DRAG'NET, *n.* A net to be drawn on the bottom of a river or pond for taking fish. *Dryden. Watts.*

DRAG'OMAN, DRO'GMAN, *n.* [It. *dragomanno*; Fr. *trucheman*; Sp. *trujaman*; Ch. תורגמן, Ar. تَرجمان, from תרגם, Ch. Ar. Syr. Eth. to interpret.]

An interpretor; a term in general use in the Levant and other parts of the East.

DRAG'ON, *n.* [L. *draco*; Gr. δρακων; It. *dragone*; Fr. *dragon*; D. *draak*; G. *drache*; Ir. *draic* or *draig*; W. *draig*; Sw. *drake*; Dan. *drage*. The origin of this word is not obvious. In Ir. *drag* is fire; in W. *dragon* is a leader, chief or sovereign, from *dragiaw*, to draw. In Scotch, the word signifies a paper kite, as also in Danish; probably from the notion of flying or shooting along, like a fiery meteor. In Welsh, *draig* is rendered by Owen a procreator or generating principle, a fiery serpent, a dragon, and the Supreme; and the plural *dreigiau*, silent lightnings, *dreigiaw*, to lighten silently. Hence I infer that the word originally signified a shooting meteor in the atmosphere, a fiery meteor, and hence a fiery or flying serpent, from a root which signified to shoot or draw out.]

1. A kind of winged serpent, much celebrated in the romances of the middle ages. *Johnson.*

2. A fiery, shooting meteor, or imaginary serpent.

Swift, swift, ye *dragons* of the night! that dawning
May bear the raven's eye. *Shak.*

3. A fierce, violent person, male or female; as, this man or woman is a *dragon*.

4. A constellation of the northern hemisphere. [See *Draco*.]

In scripture, *dragon* seems sometimes to signify a large marine fish or serpent, Is. xxvii. where the leviathan is also mentioned; also Ps. lxxiv.

Sometimes it seems to signify a venomous land serpent. Ps. xci. The *dragon* shalt thou trample under foot.

It is often used for the devil, who is called the old serpent. Rev. xx. 2.

DRAG'ON, *n.* A genus of animals, the Draco. They have four legs, a cylindrical tail, and membranaceous wings, radiated like the fins of a flying-fish. *Encyc.*

DRAG'ONET, *n.* A little dragon. *Spenser.*

2. A fish with a slender round body, colored with yellow, blue and white; the head is large and depressed at the top and has two orifices, through which it breathes and ejects water, like the cetaceous tribe.

DRAG'ON-FISH, *n.* A species of Trachinus, called the weaver. This fish is about twelve inches in length; it has two or three longitudinal lines of a dirty yellow on the sides, and the belly of a silvery hue. The wounds of its spines occasion inflammation. It buries itself in the sand, except its nose. *Dict. of Nat. Hist.*

DRAG'ON-FLY, *n.* A genus of insects, the Libella or Libellula, having four extended wings; they are furnished with jaws; the antennæ are shorter than the thorax; and the tail of the male is terminated by a kind of hooked forceps. There are many species, with a great diversity of colors. *Dict. of Nat. Hist.*

DRAG'ONISH, *a.* In the form of a dragon; dragonlike. *Shak.*

DRAG'ONLIKE, *a.* Like a dragon; fiery; furious. *Shak.*

DRAG'ONS, *n.* A genus of plants, the Dracontium, of several species, natives of the Indies.

DRAG'ON'S-BLŎOD, *n.* [Sax. *dracan-blod*.] A resinous substance, or red juice, extracted from the *Dracæna draco*, and other trees of a similar nature. It comes from the East Indies, in small flat cakes or round balls, or in oval drops, wrapped in leaves, and knotted like a chaplet. It has no sensible smell or taste. It has been considered as an astringent medicine, but is now little used for medicinal purposes. A solution of it in spirit of wine is used for staining marble, to which it gives a red tinge. *Fourcroy. Encyc.*

DRAG'ON'S-HEAD, *n.* A genus of plants, the Dracocephalum, of many species, most of them herbaceous, annual or perennial plants. *Encyc.*

Dragon's Head and Tail, in astronomy, are the nodes of the planets, or the two points in which the orbits of the planets intersect the ecliptic. *Encyc.*

DRAG'ON-SHELL, *n.* A species of concamerated patella or limpet. The top is much curved, and of an ash-color on the outside, but internally, of a bright flesh color. It is found adhering to larger shells, or to the back of the tortoise, as common limpets do to the sides of rocks.

DRAG'ON'S-WATER, *n.* A plant, the Calla or African Arum. *Fam. of Plants.*

DRAG'ON'S-WŎRT, *n.* A plant, a species of Artemisia. *Fam. of Plants.*

DRAG'ON-TREE, *n.* A species of palm. *Johnson.*

DRAGOON', *n.* [Fr. *dragon*; Sp. *id.*; Port. *dragam*, a dragon and *dragoon*; It. *dragone*; G. *dragoner*; D. *dragonder*; Dan. *dragon*; Sw. *id.*; L. *draconarius*, an ensign bearer, from *draco*, dragon; an appellation given to horsemen, perhaps for their rapidity or fierceness.]

A soldier or musketeer who serves on horseback or on foot, as occasion may require. Their arms are a sword, a musket and a bayonet. *Encyc.*

DRAGOON′, *v. t.* To persecute by abandoning a place to the rage of soldiers. *Johnson.*

2. To enslave or reduce to subjection by soldiers.

3. To harass; to persecute; to compel to submit by violent measures; to force. [*This is the more usual sense.*]

The colonies may be influenced to any thing, but they can be *dragooned* to nothing. *Price.*

DRAGOONA′DE, *n.* The abandoning of a place to the rage of soldiers. *Burnet.*

DRAGOON′ED, *pp.* Abandoned to the violence of soldiers; persecuted; harassed.

DRAGOON′ING, *ppr.* Abandoning to the rage of soldiers; persecuting; harassing; vexing.

DRAIL, *v. t.* To trail. [*Not in use.*] *More.*

DRAIL, *v. i.* To draggle. [*Not in use.*] *South.*

DRA′IN, *v. t.* [Sax. *drehnigean*, to drain, to strain. This may be a derivative from the root of *draw.* Qu. Sax. *drygan*, to dry.]

1. To filter; to cause to pass through some porous substance.

Salt water, *drained* through twenty vessels of earth, hath become fresh. *Bacon.*

2. To empty or clear of liquor, by causing the liquor to drop or run off slowly; as, to *drain* a vessel or its contents.

3. To make dry; to exhaust of water or other liquor, by causing it to flow off in channels, or through porous substances; as, to *drain* land; to *drain* a swamp or marsh.

4. To empty; to exhaust; to draw off gradually; as, a foreign war *drains* a country of specie.

DRAIN, *v. i.* To flow off gradually; as, let the water of low ground *drain* off.

2. To be emptied of liquor, by flowing or dropping; as, let the vessel stand and *drain;* let the cloth hang and *drain.*

DRAIN, *n.* A channel through which water or other liquid flows off; particularly, a trench or ditch to convey water from wet land; a watercourse; a sewer; a sink.

DRA′INABLE, *a.* Capable of being drained. *Sherwood.*

DRA′INAGE, *n.* A draining; a gradual flowing off of any liquid.

DRA′INED, *pp.* Emptied of water or other liquor by a gradual discharge, flowing or dropping; exhausted; drawn off.

DRA′INING, *ppr.* Emptying of water or other liquor by filtration or flowing in small channels.

DRAKE, *n.* [G. *enterich;* Dan. *andrik;* Sw. *andrak.* It is compounded of *ente, and,* Sax. *ened,* L. *anas,* a duck, and a word which I do not understand.]

1. The male of the duck kind.

2. [L. *draco,* dragon.] A small piece of artillery. *Clarendon.*

3. The drake-fly.

DRAM, *n.* [contracted from *drachma,* which see.]

1. Among druggists and physicians, a weight of the eighth part of an ounce, or sixty grains In avoirdupois weight, the sixteenth part of an ounce.

2. A small quantity; as no *dram* of judgment. *Dryden.*

3. As much spirituous liquor as is drank at once; as a *dram* of brandy. *Drams* are the slow poison of life. *Swift.*

4. Spirit; distilled liquor. *Pope.*

DRAM, *v. i.* To drink drams; to indulge in the use of ardent spirit. [*A low word expressing a low practice.*]

DRAM′-DRINKER, *n.* One who habitually drinks spirits.

DR′AMA, *n.* [Gr δραμα, from δραω, to make.]

A poem or composition representing a picture of human life, and accommodated to action. The principal species of the drama are tragedy and comedy; inferior species are tragi-comedy, opera, &c. *Encyc.*

DRAMAT′IC, } *a.* Pertaining to the drama; represented by action; theatrical; not narrative. *Bentley.*
DRAMAT′ICAL, }

DRAMAT′ICALLY, *a.* By representation; in the manner of the drama. *Dryden.*

DRAM′ATIST, *n.* The author of a dramatic composition; a writer of plays. *Burnet.*

DRAM′ATIZE, *v. t.* To compose in the form of the drama; or to give to a composition the form of a play.

At Riga in 1204 was acted a prophetic play, that is, a *dramatized* extract from the history of the Old and New Testaments. *Tooke's Russia.*

DRANK, *pret.* and *pp.* of *drink.*

DRANK, *n.* A term for wild oats. *Encyc.*

DRAPE, *v. t.* [Fr. *draper.*] To make cloth; also, to banter. *Obs.*

DRA′PER, *n.* [Fr. *drapier; draper,* to make cloth; from *drap,* cloth.]

One who sells cloths; a dealer in cloths; as a *linen-draper* or *woolen-draper.*

DRA′PERY, *n.* [Fr. *draperie;* It. *drapperia;* from *drap, drappo;* Sp. *ropage,* from *ropa,* cloth.]

1. Clothwork; the trade of making cloth. *Bacon.*

2. Cloth; stuffs of wool. *Arbuthnot.*

3. In *sculpture* and *painting,* the representation of the clothing or dress of human figures; also, tapestry, hangings, curtains, &c. *Encyc.*

DRA′PET, *n.* Cloth; coverlet. [*Not in use.*]

DRAS′TIC, *a.* [Gr. δραςικος, from δραω, to make.]

Powerful; acting with strength or violence; efficacious; as a *drastic* cathartic.

DRAUGH. [See *Draff.*]

DRAUGHT, *n. draft.* [from *draw, drag.*]

1. The act of drawing; as a horse or ox fit for *draught.*

2. The quality of being drawn; as a cart or plow of easy *draught.*

3. The drawing of liquor into the mouth and throat; the act of drinking.

4. The quantity of liquor drank at once.

5. The act of delineating, or that which is delineated; a representation by lines, as the figure of a house, a machine, a fort, &c., described on paper. [Qu. Ir. *dreach,* W. *dryç.*] *Encyc.*

6. Representation by picture; figure painted, or drawn by the pencil. *Dryden.*

7. The act of drawing a net; a sweeping for fish.

8. That which is taken by sweeping with a net; as a *draught* of fishes. Luke v.

9. The drawing or bending of a bow; the act of shooting with a bow and arrow. *Camden.*

10. The act of drawing men from a military band, army or post; also, the forces drawn; a detachment. [See *Draft,* which is more generally used.]

11. A sink or drain. Matt. xv.

12. An order for the payment of money; a bill of exchange. [See *Draft.*]

13. The depth of water necessary to float a ship, or the depth a ship sinks in water, especially when laden; as a ship of twelve feet *draught.*

14. In *England,* a small allowance on weighable goods, made by the king to the importer, or by the seller to the buyer, to insure full weight. *Encyc.*

15. A sudden attack or drawing on an enemy. [Query.] *Spenser.*

16. A writing composed.

17. *Draughts,* a kind of game resembling chess.

DRAUGHT, *v. t.* To draw out; to call forth. [See *Draft.*] *Addison.*

DRAUGHT′-HOOKS, *n.* Large hooks of iron fixed on the cheeks of a cannon carriage, two on each side, one near the trunnion hole, and the other at the train; used in drawing the gun backwards and forwards by means of draught ropes. *Encyc.*

DRAUGHT′-HORSE, *n.* A horse used in drawing a plow, cart or other carriage, as distinguished from a saddle horse.

DRAUGHT′-HOUSE, *n.* A house for the reception of filth or waste matter.

DRAUGHTS′MAN, *n.* A man who draws writings or designs, or one who is skilled in such drawings.

2. One who drinks drams; a tippler. *Tatler.*

DRAVE, the old participle of *drive.* We now use *drove.*

DRAW, *v. t.* pret. *drew;* pp. *drawn.* [Sax. *dragan;* L. *traho.* It is only a dialectical spelling of *drag,* which see.]

1. To pull along; to haul; to cause to move forward by force applied in advance of the thing moved or at the fore-end, as by a rope or chain. It differs from *drag* only in this, that *drag* is more generally applied to things moved along the ground by sliding, or moved with greater toil or difficulty, and *draw* is applied to all bodies moved by force in advance, whatever may be the degree of force. *Draw* is the more general or generic term, and *drag,* more specific. We say, the horses *draw* a coach or wagon, but they *drag* it through mire; yet *draw* is properly used in both cases.

2. To pull out, as to *draw* a sword or dagger from its sheath; to unsheathe. Hence, to *draw the sword,* is to wage war.

3. To bring by compulsion; to cause to come.

Do not rich men oppress you, and *draw* you before the judgment seat? James ii.

4. To pull up or out; to raise from any depth; as, to *draw* water from a well.

5. To suck; as, to *draw* the breasts.

6. To attract; to cause to move or tend towards itself; as a magnet or other attracting body is said to *draw* it.

7. To attract; to cause to turn towards itself; to engage; as, a beauty or a popular speaker *draws* the eyes of an assembly, or *draws* their attention.

8. To inhale; to take air into the lungs; as, there I first *drew* air; I *draw* the sultry air. *Milton. Addison.*
9. To pull or take from a spit, as a piece of meat. *Dryden.*
10. To take from a cask or vat; to cause or to suffer a liquid to run out; as, to *draw* wine or cider.
11. To take a liquid from the body; to let out; as, to *draw* blood or water.
12. To take from an oven; as, to *draw* bread.
13. To cause to slide, as a curtain, either in closing or unclosing; to open or unclose and discover, or to close and conceal. To *draw the curtain* is used in both senses. *Dryden. Sidney.*
14. To extract; as, to *draw* spirit from grain or juice.
15. To produce; to bring, as an agent or efficient cause; usually followed by a modifying word; as, piety *draws down* blessings; crimes *draw down* vengeance; vice *draws on* us many temporal evils; war *draws after* it a train of calamities.
16. To move gradually or slowly; to extend.

They *drew* themselves more westerly. *Raleigh.*

17. To lengthen; to extend in length.

How long her face is *drawn*. *Shak.*

In some similes, men *draw* their comparisons into minute particulars of no importance. *Felton.*

18. To utter in a lingering manner; as, to *draw* a groan. *Dryden.*
19. To run or extend, by marking or forming; as, to *draw* a line on paper, or a line of circumvallation. Hence,
20. To represent by lines drawn on a plain surface; to form a picture or image; as, to *draw* the figure of a man; to *draw* the face. Hence,
21. To describe; to represent by words; as, the orator *drew* an admirable picture of human misery.
22. To represent in fancy; to image in the mind. *Shak.*
23. To derive; to have or receive from some source, cause or donor; as, to *draw* the rudiments of science from a civilized nation; to *draw* consolation from divine promises.
24. To deduce; as, to *draw* arguments from facts, or inferences from circumstantial evidence.
25. To allure; to entice; to lead by persuasion or moral influence; to excite to motion.

Draw me; we will run after thee. Cant. i.

Men shall arise, speaking perverse things, to *draw* away disciples after them. Acts xx.

26. To lead, as a motive; to induce to move.

My purposes do *draw* me much about. *Shak.*

27. To induce; to persuade; to attract towards; *in a very general sense.*
28. To win; to gain; *a metaphor from gaming.* *Shak.*
29. To receive or take, as from a fund; as, to *draw* money from a bank or from stock in trade.
30. To bear; to produce; as, a bond or note *draws* interest from its date.
31. To extort; to force out; as, his eloquence *drew* tears from the audience; to *draw* sighs or groans.
32. To wrest; to distort; as, to *draw* the scriptures to one's fancy. *Whitgift.*
33. To compose; to write in due form; to form in writing; as, to *draw* a bill of exchange; to *draw* a deed or will.
34. To take out of a box or wheel, as tickets in a lottery. We say, to *draw* a lottery, or to *draw* a number in the lottery.
35. To receive or gain by drawing; as, to *draw* a prize. We say also, a number *draws* a prize or a blank, when it is drawn at the same time.
36. To extend; to stretch; as, to *draw* wire; to *draw* a piece of metal by beating, &c.
37. To sink into the water; or to require a certain depth of water for floating; as, a ship *draws* fifteen feet of water.
38. To bend; as, to *draw* the bow. Is. lxvi.
39. To eviscerate; to pull out the bowels; as, to *draw* poultry. *King.*
40. To withdraw. [*Not used.*] *Shak.*

To draw back, to receive back, as duties on goods for exportation.

To draw in, to collect; to apply to any purpose by violence.

A dispute, in which every thing is *drawn in*, to give color to the argument. *Locke.*

2. To contract; to pull to a smaller compass; to pull back; as, to *draw in* the reins. *Gay.*
3. To entice, allure or inveigle; as, to *draw in* others to support a measure.

To draw off, to draw from or away; also, to withdraw; to abstract; as, to *draw off* the mind from vain amusements.

2. To draw or take from; to cause to flow from; as, to *draw off* wine or cider from a vessel.
3. To extract by distillation. *Addison.*

To draw on, to allure; to entice; to persuade or cause to follow.

The reluctant may be *drawn on* by kindness or caresses.

2. To occasion; to invite; to bring on; to cause.

Under color of war, which either his negligence *drew on*, or his practices procured, he levied a subsidy. *Hayward.*

To draw over, to raise, or cause to come over, as in a still.

2. To persuade or induce to revolt from an opposing party, and to join one's own party. Some men may be *drawn over* by interest; others by fear.

To draw out, to lengthen; to stretch by force; to extend.

2. To beat or hammer out; to extend or spread by beating, as a metal.
3. To lengthen in time: to protract; to cause to continue.

Thy unkindness shall his death *draw out*
To lingering sufferance. *Shak.*

Wilt thou *draw out* thine anger to all generations? Ps. lxxxiv.

4. To cause to issue forth; to draw off; as liquor from a cask.
5. To extract, as the spirit of a substance.
6. To bring forth; to pump out, by questioning or address; to cause to be declared, or brought to light; as, to *draw out* facts from a witness.
7. To induce by motive; to call forth.

This was an artifice to *draw out* from us an accusation. *Anon.*

8. To detach; to separate from the main body; as, to *draw out* a file or party of men.
9. To range in battle; to array in a line.

To draw together, to collect or be collected.

To draw up, to raise; to lift; to elevate.

2. To form in order of battle; to array. *Dryden.*
3. To compose in due form, as a writing; to form in writing; as, to *draw up* a deed; to *draw up* a paper. *Swift.*

In this use, it is often more elegant to omit the modifying word. [See No. 33.]

DRAW, *v. i.* To pull; to exert strength in drawing. We say, a horse or an ox *draws* well.

2. To act as a weight.

Watch the bias of the mind, that it may not *draw* too much. *Addison.*

3. To shrink; to contract into a smaller compass. *Bacon.*
4. To move; to advance. The day *draws* towards evening.
5. To be filled or inflated with wind, so as to press on and advance a ship in her course; as, the sails *draw.*
6. To unsheathe a sword. His love *drew* to defend him. In this phrase, *sword* is understood.
7. To use or practice the art of delineating figures; as, he *draws* with exactness.
8. To collect the matter of an ulcer or abscess; to cause to suppurate; to excite to inflammation, maturation and discharge; as, an epispastic *draws* well.

To draw back, to retire; to move back; to withdraw.

2. To renounce the faith; to apostatize. Heb. x.

To draw near or *nigh*, to approach; to come near.

To draw off, to retire; to retreat; as, the company *drew off* by degrees.

To draw on, to advance; to approach; as, the day *draws on.* *Dryden.*

2. To gain on; to approach in pursuit; as, the ship *drew on* the chase.
3. To demand payment by an order or bill, called a *draught.*

He *drew on* his factor for the amount of the shipment.

You may *draw on* me for the expenses of your journey. *Jay.*

To draw up, to form in regular order; as, the troops *drew up* in front of the palace; the fleet *drew up* in a semicircle.

Draw, in most of its uses, retains some shade of its original sense, to pull, to move forward by the application of force in advance, or to extend in length. And Johnson justly observes, that it expresses an action gradual or continuous, and leisurely. We *pour* liquor quick, but we *draw* it in a continued stream. We *force* compliance by threats, but we *draw* it by gradual prevalence. We write a letter with haste, but we *draw* a bill with slow caution, and regard to a precise form. We *draw* a bar of metal by continued beating.

DRAW, *n.* The act of drawing.

2. The lot or chance drawn.

DRAW′ABLE, *a.* That may be drawn. *More.*

DRAW′BACK, *n.* Money or an amount paid back. Usually, a certain amount of duties or customs, paid or bonded by an importer, paid back or remitted to him on the exportation of the goods; or a certain amount of excise paid back or allowed on the exportation of home manufactures.

2. In *a popular sense*, any loss of advantage, or deduction from profit.

DRAW′-BRIDGE, *n.* A bridge which may be drawn up or let down to admit or hinder communication, as before the gate of a town or castle, or in a bridge over a navigable river. In the latter, the draw-bridge usually consists of two movable platforms, which may be raised to let a vessel pass through.

DRAW′-NET, *n.* A net for catching the larger sorts of fowls, made of pack-thread, with wide meshes.

DRAW′-WELL, *n.* A deep well, from which water is drawn by a long cord or pole. *Grew.*

DRAW′EE, *n.* The person on whom an order or bill of exchange is drawn; the payer of a bill of exchange.

DRAW′ER, *n.* One who draws or pulls; one who takes water from a well; one who draws liquors from a cask.

2. That which draws or attracts, or has the power of attraction. *Swift.*

3. He who draws a bill of exchange or an order for the payment of money.

4. A sliding box in a case or table, which is drawn at pleasure.

5. *Drawers*, *in the plural*, a close under garment worn on the lower limbs.

DRAW′ING, *ppr.* Pulling; hauling; attracting; delineating.

DRAW′ING, *n.* The act of pulling, hauling or attracting.

2. The act of representing the appearance or figures of objects on a plain surface, by means of lines and shades, as with a pencil, crayon, pen, compasses, &c.; delineation.

DRAW′ING-MASTER, *n.* One who teaches the art of drawing.

DRAW′ING-ROOM, *n.* A room appropriated for the reception of company; a room in which distinguished personages hold levees, or private persons receive parties. It is written by Coxe, *withdrawing-room*, a room to which company *withdraws* from the dining-room.

2. The company assembled in a drawing-room.

DRAWL, *v. t.* [D. *draalen*, to linger.] To utter words in a slow lengthened tone.

DRAWL, *v. i.* To speak with slow utterance.

DRAWL, *n.* A lengthened utterance of the voice.

DRAWL′ING, *ppr.* Uttering words slowly.

DRAWN, *pp.* [See *Draw.*] Pulled; hauled; allured; attracted; delineated; extended; extracted; derived; deduced; written.

2. Equal, where each party takes his own stake; as a *drawn* game.

3. Having equal advantage, and neither party a victory; as a *drawn* battle.

4. With a sword drawn. *Shak.*

5. Moved aside, as a curtain; unclosed, or closed.

6. Eviscerated; as a *drawn* fox. *Shak.*

7. Induced, as by a motive; as, men are *drawn* together by similar views, or by motives of interest.

Drawn and quartered, drawn on a sled, and cut into quarters.

DRAY, *n.* [Sax. *dræge*, L. *trahea*, from *draw*, *traho.*]

1. A low cart or carriage on wheels, drawn by a horse. *Addison.*

2. A sled. *Encyc.*

DRA′Y-CART, *n.* A dray.

DRA′Y-HORSE, *n.* A horse used for drawing a dray. *Tatler.*

DRA′Y-MAN, *n.* A man who attends a dray. *South.*

DRA′Y-PLOW, *n.* A particular kind of plow. *Mortimer.*

DRAZ′EL, *n.* *draz′l.* A dirty woman; a slut. [This is a vulgar word; in New-England pronounced *droz′l*, and I believe always applied to a female.]

DREAD, *n.* *dred.* [Sax. *dræd.* Qu. from the root of the L. *terreo*, or that of Sw. *rådd*, fearful, *rådas*, to dread, Dan. *ræd*, fearful, Sp. *arredrar*, to terrify, or Ir. *cratham*, to tremble. If *d* is a prefix, see Class Rd. No. 14. 19. 22. 25. 60. 78. The primary sense is probably to tremble, or to shrink.]

1. Great fear, or apprehension of evil or danger. It expresses more than fear, and less than terror or fright. It is an uneasiness or alarm excited by expected pain, loss or other evil. We speak of the *dread* of evil; the *dread* of suffering; the *dread* of the divine displeasure. It differs from terror also in being less sudden or more continued.

2. Awe; fear united with respect.

3. Terror.

> Shall not his *dread* fall on you. Job xiii.

4. The cause of fear; the person or the thing dreaded.

> Let him be your *dread.* Is. viii.

DREAD, *a.* Exciting great fear or apprehension. *Shak.*

2. Terrible; frightful. *Shak.*

3. Awful; venerable in the highest degree; as *dread* sovereign; *dread* majesty; *dread* tribunal.

DREAD, *v. t.* To fear in a great degree; as, to *dread* the approach of a storm.

DREAD, *v. i.* To be in great fear.

> *Dread* not, neither be afraid of them. Deut. i.

DREAD′ABLE, *a.* That is to be dreaded. [*Not used.*]

DREAD′ED, *pp.* Feared.

DREAD′ER, *n.* One that fears, or lives in fear. *Swift.*

DREAD′FUL, *a.* Impressing great fear; terrible; formidable; as a *dreadful* storm, or *dreadful* night.

> The great and *dreadful* day of the Lord. Mal. iv.

2. Awful; venerable.

> How *dreadful* is this place. Gen. xlviii.

DREAD′FULLY, *adv.* Terribly; in a manner to be dreaded. *Dryden.*

DREAD′FULNESS, *n.* Terribleness; the quality of being dreadful; frightfulness.

DREAD′LESS, *a.* Fearless; bold; not intimidated; undaunted; free from fear or terror; intrepid. *Milton.*

DREAD′LESSNESS, *n.* Fearlessness; undauntedness; freedom from fear or terror; boldness. *Sidney.*

DREAM, *n.* [D. *droom*; G. *traum*; Sw. *dröm*; Dan. *drøm.* In Russ. *dremlyu* is to sleep. But I take the primary sense to be, to rove, and the word to be allied to Gr. δρομη, a running, which seems to be from the root of *roam*, *ramble.* If not, it may signify to form images and be allied to *frame.*]

1. The thought or series of thoughts of a person in sleep. We apply *dream*, in the singular, to a series of thoughts, which occupy the mind of a sleeping person, in which he imagines he has a view of real things or transactions. A *dream* is a series of thoughts not under the command of reason, and hence wild and irregular. *Stewart.*

2. In scripture, *dreams* were sometimes impressions on the minds of sleeping persons, made by divine agency. God came to Abimelech in a *dream.* Joseph was warned by God in a *dream.* Gen. xx. Math. ii.

3. A vain fancy; a wild conceit; an unfounded suspicion.

DREAM, *v. i.* pret. *dreamed* or *dreamt.* [D. *droomen*; G. *träumen*; Sw. *drömma*; Dan. *drömmer.*]

1. To have ideas or images in the mind, in the state of sleep; with *of* before a noun; as, to *dream of* a battle; to *dream of* an absent friend.

2. To think; to imagine; as, he little *dreamed* of his approaching fate.

3. To think idly.

> They *dream* on in a course of reading, without digesting. *Locke.*

4. To be sluggish; to waste time in vain thoughts; as, to *dream* away life.

DREAM, *v. t.* To see in a dream.

> And *dreamt* the future fight. *Dryden.*

It is followed by a noun of the like signification; as, to *dream* a *dream.*

DRE′AMER, *n.* One who dreams.

2. A fanciful man; a visionary; one who forms or entertains vain schemes; as a political *dreamer.* *Marshall.*

3. A man lost in wild imagination; a mope; a sluggard.

DRE′AMFUL, *a.* Full of dreams. *Johnson.*

DRE′AMING, *ppr.* Having thoughts or ideas in sleep.

DRE′AMLESS, *a.* Free from dreams. *Camden.*

DREAMT, *pp.* *dremt.* From *dream.*

DREAR, *n.* Dread; dismalness. *Obs.* *Spenser.*

DREAR, *a.* [Sax. *dreorig*, dreary.] Dismal; gloomy with solitude.

> A *drear* and dying sound. *Milton.*

DRE′ARIHEAD, *n.* Dismalness; gloominess. [*Not in use.*] *Spenser.*

DRE′ARILY, *adv.* Gloomily; dismally. *Spenser.*

DRE′ARIMENT, *n.* Dismalness; terror. *Obs.*

DRE′ARINESS, *n.* Dismalness; gloomy solitude.

DRE′ARY, *a.* [Sax. *dreorig.*] Dismal; gloomy; as a *dreary* waste; *dreary* shades. This word implies both solitude and gloom.

2. Sorrowful; distressing; as *dreary* shrieks. *Spenser.*

DREDGE, *n.* [Fr. *drege*; Arm. *drag*, as in English.]

1. A dragnet for taking oysters, &c. *Carew.*

2. A mixture of oats and barley sown together.

DREDGE, *v. t.* To take, catch or gather with a dredge. *Carew.*

DREDGE, *v. t.* [This seems to be connected with the Fr. *drague*, grains, *dragée*, sugar plums, small shot, meslin.] To sprinkle flour on roast meat.

DREDG'ER, *n.* One who fishes with a dredge; also, an utensil for scattering flour on meat while roasting.

DREDG'ING-BOX, *n.* A box used for dredging meat.

DREDG'ING-MACHINE, *n.* An engine used to take up mud or gravel from the bottom of rivers, docks, &c. *Cyc.*

DREE, *v. t.* [Sax. *dreah.*] To suffer. [*Not used.*] *Ray.*

DREG'GINESS, *n.* [from *dreggy.*] Fullness of dregs or lees; foulness; feculence.

DREG'GISH, *a.* Full of dregs; foul with lees; feculent. *Harvey.*

DREG'GY, *a.* [See *Dregs.*] Containing dregs or lees; consisting of dregs; foul; muddy; feculent. *Boyle.*

DREGS, *n. plu.* [Sw. *drägg*; Dan. *drank*; Gr. τρυξ, τρυγια. That which is drained or thrown off, or that which subsides. See Class Rg. No. 8. 28. 58.]

1. The sediment of liquors; lees; grounds; feculence; any foreign matter of liquors that subsides to the bottom of a vessel.
2. Waste or worthless matter; dross; sweepings; refuse. Hence, the most vile and despicable part of men; as the *dregs* of society.

Dreg, in the singular, is found in Spenser, but is not now used.

DREIN. [See *Drain.*]

DRENCH, *v. t.* [Sax. *drencean*, to drench, to soak, to inebriate, and *drencan*, to *drink*, to give drink; *drenc*, drench, and drink; D. *drenken*; G. *tränken*, to water, to soak; Sw. *dränckia*, to plunge, to soak; Scot. *drouk*; W. *troci.* *Drench*, *drink*, *drown*, and probably *drag*, are from the same root. See *Drink* and *Drag*.]

1. To wet thoroughly; to soak; to fill or cover with water or other liquid; as garments *drenched* in rain or in the sea; the flood has *drenched* the earth; swords *drenched* in blood.
2. To saturate with drink. *Shak.*
3. To purge violently. *Mortimer.*

DRENCH, *n.* A draught; a swill; also, a portion of medicine to purge a beast, particularly a horse. Hence, a violent dose of physic to be forced down the throat.

DRENCH'ED, *pp.* Soaked; thoroughly wet; purged with a dose.

DRENCH'ER, *n.* One who wets or steeps; one who gives a drench to a beast.

DRENCH'ING, *ppr.* Wetting thoroughly; soaking; purging.

DRENT, *pp.* Drenched. [*Not in use.*] *Spenser.*

DRESS, *v. t.* pret. and pp. *dressed* or *drest.* [Fr. *dresser*, to make straight, to set up, to erect; Arm. *dreçza*, *dreçzein*; It. *rizzare*, to erect, to make straight; *dirizzare*, to direct, to address; Sp. *enderezar*, Port. *endereçar*, to direct; Norm. *adrescer*, to redress. The primary sense is, to make straight, to strain or stretch to straightness. The It. *rizzare* is supposed to be formed from *ritto*, straight, upright, L. *erectus*, *rectus*, from *erigo*, *rego.*]

1. To make straight or a straight line; to adjust to a right line. We have the primary sense in the military phrase, *dress* your ranks. Hence the sense, to put in order.
2. To adjust; to put in good order; as, to *dress* the beds of a garden. Sometimes, to till or cultivate. Gen. ii. Deut. xxviii.
3. To put in good order, as a wounded limb; to cleanse a wound, and to apply medicaments. The surgeon *dresses* the limb or the wound.
4. To prepare, *in a general sense*; to put in the condition desired; to make suitable or fit; as, to *dress* meat; to *dress* leather or cloth; to *dress* a lamp: but we, in the latter case, generally use *trim.* To *dress* hemp or flax, is to break and clean it.
5. To curry, rub and comb; as, to *dress* a horse: or to break or tame and prepare for service, as used by Dryden; *but this is unusual.*
6. To put the body in order, or in a suitable condition; to put on clothes; as, he *dressed* himself for breakfast.
7. To put on rich garments; to adorn; to deck; to embellish; as, the lady *dressed* herself for a ball.

To dress up, is to clothe pompously or elegantly; as, to *dress up* with tinsel.

The sense of *dress* depends on its application. To *dress* the body, to *dress* meat, and to *dress* leather, are very different senses, but all uniting in the sense of preparing or fitting for use.

DRESS, *v. i.* To arrange in a line; as, look to the right and *dress.*

2. To pay particular regard to dress or raiment. *Bramston.*

DRESS, *n.* That which is used as the covering or ornament of the body; clothes; garments; habit; as, the *dress* of a lady is modest and becoming; a gaudy *dress* is evidence of a false taste.

2. A suit of clothes; as, the lady has purchased an elegant *dress.*
3. Splendid clothes; habit of ceremony; as a full *dress.*
4. Skill in adjusting dress, or the practice of wearing elegant clothing; as men of *dress.* *Pope.*

DRESS'ED, *pp.* Adjusted; made straight; put in order; prepared; trimmed; tilled; clothed; adorned; attired.

DRESS'ER, *n.* One who dresses; one who is employed in putting on clothes and adorning another; one who is employed in preparing, trimming or adjusting any thing.

2. [Fr. *dressoir.*] A side-board; a table or bench on which meat and other things are dressed or prepared for use.

DRESS'ING, *ppr.* Adjusting to a line; putting in order; preparing; clothing; embellishing; cultivating.

DRESS'ING, *n.* Raiment; attire. *B. Jonson.*

2. That which is used as an application to a wound or sore.
3. That which is used in preparing land for a crop; manure spread over land. When it remains on the surface, it is called a *top-dressing.*
4. In *popular language*, correction; a flogging, or beating.

DRESS'ING-ROOM, *n.* An apartment appropriated for dressing the person.

DRESS'-MAKER, *n.* A maker of gowns, or similar garments; a mantuamaker.

DRESS'Y, *a.* Showy in dress; wearing rich or showy dresses.

DREST, *pp.* of *dress.*

DREUL, *v. i.* [Qu. *drivel*, or Ar. رال to slaver.]

To emit saliva; to suffer saliva to issue and flow down from the mouth.

DRIB, *v. t.* [Qu. from *dribble*, but the word is not elegant, nor much used.] To crop or cut off; to defalcate. *Dryden.*

DRIB, *n.* A drop. [*Not used.*] *Swift.*

DRIB'BLE, *v. i.* [A diminutive from *drip*, and properly *dripple.*]

1. To fall in drops or small drops, or in a quick succession of drops; as, water *dribbles* from the eaves.
2. To slaver as a child or an idiot.
3. To fall weakly and slowly; as the *dribling* dart of love. *Shak.*

DRIB'BLE, *v. t.* To throw down in drops. *Swift.*

DRIB'BLET, *n.* [W. *rhib.*] A small piece or part; a small sum; odd money in a sum; as, the money was paid in *dribblets.*

DRIB'BLING, *ppr.* Falling in drops or small drops.

DRIB'BLING, *n.* A falling in drops.

DRI'ED, *pp.* of *dry.* Free from moisture or sap.

DRI'ER, *n.* [from *dry.*] That which has the quality of drying; that which may expel or absorb moisture; a desiccative. The sun and a northwesterly wind are great *driers* of the earth.

DRIFT, *n.* [Dan. *drift*; from *drive.*] That which is driven by wind or water, as *drift* seems to be primarily a participle. Hence,

2. A heap of any matter driven together; as a *drift* of snow, called also a *snow-drift*; a *drift* of sand.
3. A driving; a force impelling or urging forward; impulse; overbearing power or influence; as the *drift* of a passion.
4. Course of any thing; tendency; aim; main force; as the *drift* of reasoning or argument; the *drift* of a discourse.
5. Any thing driven by force, as a *drift* of dust; a log or a raft driven by a stream of water, without guidance. *Dryden.*
6. A shower; a number of things driven at once; as a *drift* of bullets. *Shak.*
7. In *mining*, a passage cut between shaft and shaft; a passage within the earth. *Encyc. Fourcroy.*
8. In *navigation*, the angle which the line of a ship's motion makes with the nearest meridian, when she drives with her side to the wind and waves, and is not governed by the helm. Also, the distance which the ship drives on that line. *Encyc.*
9. The *drift* of a current, is its angle and velocity. *Mar. Dict.*

DRIFT, *v. i.* To accumulate in heaps by the force of wind; to be driven into heaps; as, snow or sand *drifts.*

2. To float or be driven along by a current of water; as, the ship *drifted* astern; a raft *drifted* ashore.

DRIFT, *v. t.* To drive into heaps; as, a current of wind *drifts* snow or sand.

DRIFT'ED, *pp.* Driven along; driven into heaps.

DRIFT'ING, *ppr.* Driving by force; driving into heaps.

DRIFT'-SAIL, *n.* In *navigation*, a sail used under water, veered out right ahead by sheets. *Encyc.*

DRIFT'-WAY, *n.* A common way for driving cattle in. *Cowel.*

DRIFT'-WIND, *n.* A driving wind; a wind that drives things into heaps. *Beaum.*

DRILL, *v. t.* [Sax. *thirlian*; G. and D. *drillen*; Dan. *driller*; Sw. *drilla*; to turn, wind or twist; W. *rhill*, a row or drill; *rhilliaw*, to drill, to trench; *truliaw*, to drill, as a hole; *troel*, a whirl; *troelli*, to turn or whirl. The latter is evidently connected with *roll*. Class Rl. No. 4.]

1. To pierce with a drill; to perforate by turning a sharp pointed instrument of a particular form; to bore and make a hole by turning an instrument. We say, to *drill* a hole through a piece of metal, or to *drill* a cannon.

2. To draw on; to entice; to amuse and put off.

She *drilled* him on to five and fifty. [*Not elegant.*] *Addison.*

3. To draw on from step to step. [*Not elegant.*] *South.*

4. To draw through; to drain; as, waters *drilled* through a sandy stratum. *Thomson.*

5. In *a military sense*, to teach and train raw soldiers to their duty, by frequent exercise; *a common and appropriate use of the word.*

6. In *husbandry*, to sow grain in rows, drills or channels.

DRILL, *v. t.* To sow in drills.

2. To flow gently.

3. To muster, for exercise. *Beaum.*

DRILL, *n.* A pointed instrument, used for boring holes, particularly in metals and other hard substances. *Moxon.*

2. An ape or baboon. *Locke.*

3. The act of training soldiers to their duty.

4. A small stream; now called a *rill*. *Sandys.*

[Drill is formed on the root of *rill*, G. *rille*, a channel.]

5. In *husbandry*, a row of grain, sowed by a drill-plow.

DRILL'ED, *pp.* Bored or perforated with a drill; exercised; sown in rows.

DRILL'ING, *ppr.* Boring with a drill; training to military duty; sowing in drills.

DRILL-PLOW, *n.* A plow for sowing grain in drills.

DRINK, *v. i.* pret. and pp. *drank*. Old pret. and pp. *drunk*; pp. *drunken*. [Sax. *drincan*, *drican*, *drycian*; Goth. *dragyan*, to give drink; D. *drinken*; G. *trinken*; Sw. *dricka*; Dan. *drikker*, to drink; Sp. *tragar*, Port. *id.*, to swallow; *trago*, a draught. The latter, and probably *drink*, is from *drawing*, or the latter may be more nearly allied to W. *trochi*, or *troçi*, to plunge, bathe, immerse. *Drink* and *drench* are radically the same word, and probably *drown*. We observe that *n* is not radical.]

1. To swallow liquor, for quenching thirst or other purpose; as, to *drink* of the brook.

Ye shall indeed *drink* of my cup. Matt. xx.

2. To take spirituous liquors to excess; to be intemperate in the use of spirituous liquors; to be a habitual drunkard. *Pope.*

3. To feast; to be entertained with liquors. *Shak.*

To drink to, to salute in drinking; to invite to drink by drinking first; as, I *drink to* your grace. *Shak.*

2. To wish well to, in the act of taking the cup. *Shak.*

DRINK, *v. t.* To swallow, as liquids; to receive, as a fluid, into the stomach; as, to *drink* water or wine.

2. To suck in; to absorb; to imbibe.

And let the purple violets *drink* the stream. *Dryden.*

3. To take in by any inlet; to hear; to see; as, to *drink* words or the voice. *Shak. Pope.*

I *drink* delicious poison from thy eye. *Pope.*

4. To take in air; to inhale.

To drink down, is to act on by drinking; to reduce or subdue; as, to *drink down* unkindness. *Shak.*

To drink off, to drink the whole at a draught; as, to *drink off* a cup of cordial.

To drink in, to absorb; to take or receive into any inlet.

To drink up, to drink the whole.

To drink health, or *to the health*, a customary civility in which a person at taking a glass or cup, expresses his respect or kind wishes for another.

DRINK, *n.* Liquor to be swallowed; any fluid to be taken into the stomach, for quenching thirst, or for medicinal purposes; as water, wine, beer, cider, decoctions, &c.

DRINK'ABLE, *a.* That may be drank; fit or suitable for drink; potable.

DRINK'ABLE, *n.* A liquor that may be drank. *Steele.*

DRINK'ER, *n.* One who drinks, particularly one who practices drinking spirituous liquors to excess; a drunkard; a tipler.

DRINK'ING, *ppr.* Swallowing liquor; sucking in; absorbing.

DRINK'ING, *n.* The act of swallowing liquors, or of absorbing.

2. The practice of drinking to excess. We say, a man is given to *drinking*.

DRINK'ING-HORN, *n.* A horn cup, such as our rude ancestors used.

DRINK'ING-HOUSE, *n.* A house frequented by tiplers; an alehouse.

DRINK'LESS, *a.* Destitute of drink. *Chaucer.*

DRINK'-MŎNEY, *n.* Money given to buy liquor for drink.

DRIP, *v. i.* [Sax. *drypan*, *driopan*, *dropian*, to drip, to drop; D. *druipen*; G. *triefen*; Sw. *drypa*; Dan. *drypper*. This seems to be of the same family as *drop*. Hence *dribble*, *dripple*, *drivel*. The Ar. has the precise word ذَرَفَ tharafa, to drop or distil. Qu. רעף Heb. and Ar. to drop. The Persic has تِرَابِيدَن tirabidan, to exude: See Class Rb. No. 11. 35.]

1. To fall in drops; as, water *drips* from eaves.

2. To have any liquid falling from it in drops; as, a wet garment *drips*.

DRIP, *v. t.* To let fall in drops.

The thatch *drips* fast a shower of rain. *Swift.*

So we say, roasting flesh *drips* fat.

DRIP, *n.* A falling in drops, or that which falls in drops.

In building, avoid the *drip* of your neighbor's house.

2. The edge of a roof; the eaves; a large flat member of the cornice. *Bailey. Chambers.*

DRIP'PING, *ppr.* Falling or letting fall in drops.

DRIP'PING, *n.* The fat which falls from meat in roasting; that which falls in drops.

DRIP'PING-PAN, *n.* A pan for receiving the fat which drips from meat in roasting.

DRIP'PLE, *a.* Weak or rare. [*Not in use.*]

DRIVE, *v. t.* pret. *drove*, [formerly *drave*;] pp. *driven*. [Sax. *drifan*; Goth. *dreiban*; D. *dryven*; G. *treiben*; Sw. *drifva*; Dan. *driver*; also Sax. *dryfan*, to vex; *adrifan*, to drive. From the German we have *thrive*. See Ar. طَرَقَ tarafa, to drive, Class Rb. No. 29. and Heb. Syr. Ar. רוב id. No. 4.]

1. To impel or urge forward by force; to force; to move by physical force. We *drive* a nail into wood with a hammer; the wind or a current *drives* a ship on the ocean.

2. To compel or urge forward by other means than absolute physical force, or by means that compel the will; as, to *drive* cattle to market. A smoke *drives* company from the room. A man may be *driven* by the necessities of the times, to abandon his country.

Drive thy business; let not thy business *drive* thee. *Franklin.*

3. To chase; to hunt.

To *drive* the deer with hound and horn. *Chevy Chase.*

4. To impel a team of horses or oxen to move forward, and to direct their course; hence, to guide or regulate the course of the carriage drawn by them. We say, to *drive* a team, or to *drive* a carriage drawn by a team.

5. To impel to greater speed.

6. To clear any place by forcing away what is in it.

To *drive* the country, force the swains away. *Dryden.*

7. To force; to compel; in a general sense.

8. To hurry on inconsiderately; often with *on*. In this sense it is more generally intransitive.

9. To distress; to straighten; as desperate men far *driven*. *Spenser.*

10. To impel by the influence of passion. Anger and lust often *drive* men into gross crimes.

11. To urge; to press; as, to *drive* an argument.

12. To impel by moral influence; to compel; as, the reasoning of his opponent *drove* him to acknowledge his error.

13. To carry on; to prosecute; to keep in motion; as, to *drive* a trade; to *drive* business.

14. To make light by motion or agitation; as, to *drive* feathers.

His thrice *driven* bed of down. *Shak.*

The sense is probably to *beat;* but I do not recollect this application of the word in America.

To drive away, to force to remove to a distance; to expel; to dispel; to scatter.

To drive off, to compel to remove from a place; to expel; to drive to a distance.

To drive out, to expel.

DRIVE, *v. i.* To be forced along; to be impelled; to be moved by any physical force or agent; as, a ship *drives* before the wind.

2. To rush and press with violence; as, a storm *drives* against the house.

> Fierce Boreas *drove* against his flying sails. *Dryden.*

3. To pass in a carriage; as, he *drove* to London. This phrase is elliptical. He *drove* his horses or carriage to London.

4. To aim at or tend to; to urge towards a point; to make an effort to reach or obtain; as, we know the end the author is *driving* at.

5. To aim a blow; to strike at with force.

> Four rogues in buckram let *drive* at me. *Shak.*

Drive, in all its senses, implies forcible or violent action. It is opposed to *lead.* To *drive* a body is to move it by applying a force behind; to *lead* is to cause to move by applying the force before, or forward of the body.

DRIVE, *n.* Passage in a carriage. *Boswell.*

DRIV'EL, *v. i.* *driv'l.* [from the root of *drip.*]

1. To slaver; to let spittle drop or flow from the mouth, like a child, idiot or dotard. *Sidney. Grew.*

2. To be weak or foolish; to dote; as a *driveling* hero; *driveling* love. *Shak. Dryden.*

DRIV'EL, *n.* Slaver; saliva flowing from the mouth. *Dryden.*

2. A driveller; a fool; an idiot. [*Not used.*] *Sidney.*

DRIV'ELER, *n.* A slaverer; a slabberer; an ideot; a fool. *Swift.*

DRIV'ELING, *ppr.* Slavering; foolish.

DRIV'EN, *pp.* *driv'n.* [from *drive.*] Urged forward by force; impelled to move; constrained by necessity.

DRI'VER, *n.* One who drives; the person or thing that urges or compels any thing else to move.

2. The person who drives beasts.

3. The person who drives a carriage; one who conducts a team.

4. A large sail occasionally set on the mizen-yard or gaff, the foot being extended over the stern by a boom. *Mar. Dict.*

DRI'VING, *ppr.* Urging forward by force; impelling.

DRI'VING, *n.* The act of impelling.

2. Tendency.

DRIZ'ZLE, *v. i.* [G. *rieseln.* The sense is probably to sprinkle, or to scatter. Qu. L. *ros,* dew, and Fr. *arroser.* See Heb. Ch. רסס, Ar. رسّ. Class Rs. No. 16. 28.]

To rain in small drops; to fall as water from the clouds in very fine particles. We say, it *drizzles; drizzling* drops; *drizzling* rain; *drizzling* tears. *Addison.*

DRIZ'ZLE, *v. t.* To shed in small drops or particles.

> The air doth *drizzle* dew. *Shak.*
> Winter's *drizzled* snow. *Shak.*

DRIZ'ZLED, *pp.* Shed or thrown down in small drops or particles.

DRIZ'ZLING, *ppr.* Falling in fine drops or particles; shedding in small drops or particles.

DRIZ'ZLING, *n.* The falling of rain or snow in small drops.

DRIZ'ZLY, *a.* Shedding small rain, or small particles of snow.

> The winter's *drizzly* reign. *Dryden.*

DROGMAN. [See *Dragoman.*]

DROIL, *v. i.* [D. *druilen,* to mope.] To work sluggishly or slowly; to plod. [*Not much used.*] *Spenser.*

DROIL, *n.* A mope; a drone; a sluggard; a drudge. [*Little used.*]

DRÔLL, *a.* [Fr. *drôle;* G. *drollig;* D. *id.;* Sw. *troll,* a satyr; *trolla,* to use magic arts, to enchant. Qu. its alliance to *roll, troll.*]

Odd; merry; facetious; comical; as a *droll* fellow.

DRÔLL, *n.* One whose occupation or practice is to raise mirth by odd tricks; a jester; a buffoon. *Prior.*

2. A farce; something exhibited to raise mirth or sport. *Swift.*

DRÔLL, *v. i.* To jest; to play the buffoon. *South.*

DRÔLL, *v. t.* To cheat. *L'Estrange.*

DRÔLLER, *n.* A jester; a buffoon. *Glanville.*

DRÔLLERY, *n.* Sportive tricks; buffoonery; comical stories; gestures, manners or tales adapted to raise mirth.

2. A puppet-show. *Shak.*

DRÔLLING, *n.* Low wit; buffoonery.

DRÔLLINGLY, *adv.* In a jesting manner.

DRÔLLISH, *a.* Somewhat droll.

DROM'EDARY, *n.* [Fr. *dromadaire;* Sp. *dromedario;* Port. It. *id.;* Ir. *droman;* Gr. δρομας; perhaps from swiftness, running, Gr. δρομος, εδραμον, δρεμω. This explanation supposes the word to be of Greek origin.]

A species of camel, called also the Arabian camel, with one bunch or protuberance on the back, in distinction from the Bactrian camel, which has two bunches. It has four callous protuberances on the fore legs, and two on the hind ones. It is a common beast of burden in Egypt, Syria, and the neighboring countries. *Encyc.*

DRONE, *n.* [Sax. *drane, dræn;* G. *drohne,* whence *dröhnen,* to tinkle, to shake, to tingle. See Ar. No. 4. and 7. Class Rn.]

1. The male of the honey bee. It is smaller than the queen bee, but larger than the working bee. The drones make no honey, but after living a few weeks, they are killed or driven from the hive. *Encyc.*

Hence,

2. An idler; a sluggard; one who earns nothing by industry. *Addison.*

3. A humming or low sound, or the instrument of humming. *Milton.*

4. The largest tube of the bag-pipe, which emits a continued deep note.

DRONE, *v. i.* To live in idleness; as a *droning* king. *Dryden.*

2. To give a low, heavy, dull sound; as the cymbal's *droning* sound. *Dryden.*

DRO'NE-FLY, *n.* A two-winged insect, resembling the drone-bee. *Encyc.*

DRO'NING, *ppr.* Living in idleness; giving a dull sound.

DRO'NISH, *a.* Idle; sluggish; lazy; indolent; inactive; slow. *Rowe.*

DROOP, *v. i.* [Sax. *drepan;* Ice. *driupa.* This word is probably from the root of the L. *torpeo,* the letters being transposed; or from the root of *drop,* D. *druipen,* to drip, drop or droop. Indeed all may be of one family.]

1. To sink or hang down; to lean downwards, as a body that is weak or languishing. Plants *droop* for want of moisture; the human body *droops* in old age or infirmity.

2. To languish from grief or other cause. *Sandys.*

3. To fail or sink; to decline; as, the courage or the spirits *droop.*

4. To faint; to grow weak; to be dispirited; as, the soldiers *droop* from fatigue.

DROOP'ING, *ppr.* Sinking; hanging or leaning downward; declining; languishing; failing.

DROP, *n.* [Sax. *dropa,* a drop; *dropian,* to drop; G. *tropfen;* D. *drop;* Sw. *droppe;* Dan. *draabe.* Heb. רעף, Ar. رعف and ذرف to drop. Class Rb. No. 11. Heb. ערף id.]

1. A small portion of any fluid in a spherical form, which falls at once from any body, or a globule of any fluid which is pendent, as if about to fall; a small portion of water falling in rain; as a *drop* of water; a *drop* of blood; a *drop* of laudanum.

2. A diamond hanging from the ear; an earring; something hanging in the form of a drop.

3. A very small quantity of liquor; as, he had not drank a *drop.*

4. The part of a gallows which sustains the criminal before he is executed, and which is suddenly dropped.

DROPS, *n. plu.* In *medicine,* a liquid remedy, the dose of which is regulated by a certain number of drops. *Encyc.*

DROP, *v. t.* [Sax. *dropian;* D. *druipen;* G. *träufen* or *tropfen;* Sw. *drypa;* Dan. *drypper;* Russ. *krapayu.*]

1. To pour or let fall in small portions or globules, as a fluid; to distill.

> The heavens shall *drop* down dew. Deut. xxxiii.

2. To let fall as any substance; as, to *drop* the anchor; to *drop* a stone.

3. To let go; to dismiss; to lay aside; to quit; to leave; to permit to subside; as, to *drop* an affair; to *drop* a controversy; to *drop* a pursuit.

4. To utter slightly, briefly or casually; as, to *drop* a word in favor of a friend.

5. To insert indirectly, incidentally, or by way of digression; as, to *drop* a word of instruction in a letter.

6. To lay aside; to dismiss from possession; as, to *drop* these frail bodies.

7. To leave; as, to *drop* a letter at the post-office.

8. To set down and leave; as, the coach *dropped* a passenger at the inn.

9. To quit; to suffer to cease; as, to *drop* an acquaintance.
10. To let go; to dismiss from association; as, to *drop* a companion.
11. To suffer to end or come to nothing; as, to *drop* a fashion.
12. To bedrop; to speckle; to variegate, as if by sprinkling with drops; as a coat *dropped* with gold. *Milton.*
13. To lower; as, to *drop* the muzzle of a gun.

DROP, *v. i.* To distill; to fall in small portions, globules or drops, as a liquid. Water *drops* from the clouds or from the eaves.
2. To let drops fall; to discharge itself in drops.

The heavens *dropped* at the presence of God. Ps. lxviii.

3. To fall; to descend suddenly or abruptly.
4. To fall spontaneously; as, ripe fruit *drops* from a tree.
5. To die, or to die suddenly. We see one friend after another *dropping* round us. They *drop* into the grave.
6. To come to an end; to cease; to be neglected and come to nothing; as, the affair *dropped.*
7. To come unexpectedly; with *in* or *into;* as, my old friend *dropped in,* a moment.
8. To fall short of a mark. [*Not usual.*]

Often it *drops* or overshoots. *Collier.*

9. To fall lower; as, the point of the spear *dropped* a little.
10. To be deep in extent.

Her main top-sail *drops* seventeen yards. *Mar. Dict.*

To drop astern, in seamen's language, is to pass or move towards the stern; to move back; or to slacken the velocity of a vessel to let another pass beyond her.

To drop down, in seamen's language, is to sail, row or move down a river, or toward the sea.

DROP-SERE'NE, *n.* [*gutta serena.*] A disease of the eye; amaurosis, or blindness from a diseased retina. *Milton. Coxe.*

DROP'-STONE, *n.* Spar in the shape of drops. *Woodward.*

DROP'-WŎRT, *n.* The name of a plant, the *Spiræa filipendula.*

The hemlock drop-wort, and the water drop-wort, are species of Œnanthe.

DROP'LET, *n.* A little drop. *Shak.*

DROP'PED, *pp.* Let fall; distilled; laid aside; dismissed; let go; suffered to subside; sprinkled or variegated.

DROP'PING, *ppr.* Falling in globules; distilling; falling; laying aside; dismissing; quitting; suffering to rest or subside; variegating with ornaments like drops.

DROP'PING, *n.* The act of dropping; a distilling; a falling.
2. That which drops.

DROP'SICAL, *a.* [See *Dropsy.*] Diseased with dropsy; hydropical; inclined to the dropsy; *applied to persons.*
2. Partaking of the nature of the dropsy; *applied to disease.*

DROP'SIED, *a.* Diseased with dropsy. *Shak.*

DROP'SY, *n.* [L. *hydrops;* Gr. ὑδρωψ, from ὑδωρ, water, and ωψ, the face. Formerly written *hydropisy;* whence by contraction, *dropsy.*] In *medicine,* an unnatural collection of water, in any part of the body, proceeding from a greater effusion of serum by the exhalant arteries, than the absorbents take up. It occurs most frequently in persons of lax habits, or in bodies debilitated by disease. The dropsy takes different names, according to the part affected; as *ascites,* or dropsy of the abdomen; *hydrocephalus,* or water in the head; *anasarca,* or a wattery swelling over the whole body; &c. *Encyc.*

DROSS, *n.* [Sax. *dros;* D. *droes,* G. *druse,* strangles, glanders; D. *droessem,* G. *drusen,* dregs; perhaps from rejecting or throwing off.]
1. The recrement or despumation of metals; the scum or extraneous matter of metals, thrown off in the process of melting.
2. Rust; crust of metals; an incrustation formed on metals by oxydation. *Addison.*
3. Waste matter; refuse; any worthless matter separated from the better part; impure matter.

The world's glory is but *dross* unclean. *Spenser.*

DROSS'INESS, *n.* Foulness; rust; impurity; a state of being drossy. *Boyle.*

DROSS'Y, *a.* Like dross; pertaining to dross.
2. Full of dross; abounding with scorious or recrementitious matter; as *drossy* gold.
3. Worthless; foul; impure. *Donne.*

DROTCH'EL, *n.* An idle wench; a sluggard. [*Not in use.*]

DROUGHT. [See *Drouth.*]

DROUGHT'INESS, *n.* Drouthiness.

DROUGHT'Y, *a.* Drouthy.

DROUM'Y, *a.* Troubled; dirty. *Obs. Bacon.* Chaucer has *drovy.*

DROUTH, *n.* [contracted from Sax. *drugothe,* D. *droogte,* from *drigan* or *drygan,* to dry. See *Dry.* This is usually written *drought,* after the Belgic dialect; but improperly. The word generally used is now, as it was written by Bacon, *drouth* or *drowth;* its regular termination is *th.*]
1. Dryness; want of rain or of water; particularly, dryness of the weather, which affects the earth, and prevents the growth of plants; aridness; aridity. *Temple. Bacon.*
2. Dryness of the throat and mouth; thirst; want of drink. *Milton.*

DROUTH'INESS, *n.* A state of dryness of the weather; want of rain.

DROUTH'Y, *a.* Dry, as the weather: arid; wanting rain.
2. Thirsty; dry; wanting drink.

DROVE, *pret.* of *drive.*

DROVE, *n.* [Sax. *draf;* from *drive.*] A collection of cattle driven; a number of animals, as oxen, sheep or swine, driven in a body. We speak of a *herd* of cattle, and a *flock* of sheep, when a number is collected; but properly a *drove* is a herd or flock *driven.* It is applicable to any species of brutes. Hence,
2. Any collection of irrational animals, moving or driving forward; as a finny *drove.* *Milton.*
3. A crowd of people in motion.

Where *droves,* as at a city gate, may pass. *Dryden.*

4. A road for driving cattle. [*English.*]

DRO'VER, *n.* One who drives cattle or sheep to market. Usually in New England, a man who makes it his business to purchase fat cattle and drive them to market.
2. A boat driven by the tide. *Spenser.*

DROWN, *v. t.* [Dan. *drugner;* Sw. *drånckia;* Sax. *adrencan,* to drown, to *drench;* from the root of *drench* and *drink.*]
1. Literally, to overwhelm in water; and appropriately, to extinguish life by immersion in water or other fluid; *applied to animals:* also, to suspend animation by submersion.
2. To overwhelm in water; as, to *drown* weeds.
3. To overflow; to deluge; to inundate; as, to *drown* land.
4. To immerse; to plunge and lose; to overwhelm; as, to *drown* one's self in sensual pleasure.
5. To overwhelm; to overpower.

My private voice is *drowned* amid the senate. *Addison.*

DROWN, *v. i.* To be suffocated in water or other fluid; to perish in water.

Methought what pain it was to *drown.* *Shak.*

DROWN'ED, *pp.* Deprived of life by immersion in a fluid; overflowed; inundated; overwhelmed.

DROWN'ER, *n.* He or that which drowns.

DROWN'ING, *ppr.* Destroying life by submersion in a liquid; overflowing; overwhelming.

DROWSE, *v. i. drowz.* [Old Belgic, *droosen.*]
1. To sleep imperfectly or unsoundly; to slumber; to be heavy with sleepiness. *Milton.*
2. To look heavy; to be heavy or dull.

DROWSE, *v. t.* To make heavy with sleep; to make dull or stupid. *Milton.*

DROW'SIHED, *n.* Sleepiness. *Obs. Spenser.*

DROW'SILY, *adv.* Sleepily; heavily; in a dull sleepy manner. *Dryden.*
2. Sluggishly; idly; slothfully; lazily. *Raleigh.*

DROW'SINESS, *n.* Sleepiness; heaviness with sleep; disposition to sleep. *Milton. Locke.*
2. Sluggishness; sloth; idleness; inactivity. *Bacon.*

DROW'SY, *a.* Inclined to sleep; sleepy; heavy with sleepiness; lethargic; comatose. *Bacon. Dryden.*
2. Dull; sluggish; stupid. *Atterbury.*
3. Disposing to sleep; lulling; as a *drowsy* couch.

DROW'SY-HEADED, *a.* Heavy; having a sluggish disposition. *Fotherby.*

DRUB, *v. t.* [Sw. *drabba,* to touch, hit, beat; *trăffa,* to hit, touch, reach, find; Dan. *dræber,* to kill; *treffer,* to hit; G. D. *treffen;* Gr. τριβω, to beat; Sax. *tribulan, trifelan;* It. *trebbiare;* L. *tribula.* These words seem to be from the same root as the Fr. *trouver,* to find, that is, to hit, to strike on, and *attraper* and *frapper,* Eng. to *rap.* But perhaps there may be two different roots. See Class Rb. No. 4. 28. 29. 37. 39. *Drubbing* is a particular form of *driving.*]
To beat with a stick; to thrash; to cudgel.

The little thief had been soundly *drubbed* with a cudgel. *L'Estrange.*

DRUB, *n.* A blow with a stick or cudgel; a thump; a knock. *Addison.*

DRUB'BED, *pp.* Beat with a cudgel; beat soundly.

DRUB'BING, *ppr.* Beating with a cudgel; beating soundly.

DRUB'BING, *n.* A cudgeling; a sound beating.

DRUDGE, *v. i. druj.* [Scot. *drug*, to *drag*, to tug, to pull with force; whence *drug-gare*, drudging; Ice. *droogur*, a drawer or carrier; Ir. *drugaire*, a drudge or slave. This seems to be a dialectical form of *drag*, *draw.*]

To work hard; to labor in mean offices; to labor with toil and fatigue.

In merriment did *drudge* and labor. *Hudibras.*

DRUDGE, *n.* One who works hard, or labors with toil and fatigue; one who labors hard in servile employments; a slave. *Milton.*

DRUDG'ER, *n.* A drudge.

2. A drudging-box. [See *Dredging-box.*]

DRUDG'ERY, *n.* Hard labor; toilsome work; ignoble toil; hard work in servile occupations.

Paradise was a place of bliss—without *drudgery* or sorrow. *Locke.*

DRUDG'ING, *ppr.* Laboring hard; toiling.

DRUDG'ING-BOX. [See *Dredging-box.*]

DRUDG'INGLY, *adv.* With labor and fatigue; laboriously.

DRUG, *n.* [Fr. *drogue*; Arm. *droguerezou*; Sp. Port. It. *droga*. In Dutch, *droogery* is a *drug* and a drying place, so that *drug* is a *dry* substance, and from the root of *dry*. Junius supposes it to have signified, originally, spices or aromatic plants. See the verb, to *dry.*]

1. The general name of substances used in medicine, sold by the druggist, and compounded by apothecaries and physicians; any substance, vegetable, animal or mineral, which is used in the composition or preparation of medicines. It is also applied to dyeing materials.

2. Any commodity that lies on hand, or is not salable; an article of slow sale, or in no demand in market.

3. A *mortal drug*, or a *deadly drug*, is poison.

4. A drudge. [Scot. *drug.*] *Shak.*

DRUG, *v. i.* To prescribe or administer drugs or medicines. *B. Jonson.*

DRUG, *v. t.* To season with drugs or ingredients. *Shak.*

2. To tincture with something offensive. *Milton.*

DRUG'GER, *n.* A druggist. [*Not used.*] *Burton.*

DRUG'GET, *n.* [Fr. *droguet*; Sp. *droguete*; It. *droghetto.*]

A cloth or thin stuff of wool, or of wool and thread, corded or plain, usually plain. *Encyc.*

DRUG'GIST, *n.* [Fr. *droguiste*; Sp. *droguero*; It. *droghiere*; from *drug.*]

One who deals in drugs; properly, one whose occupation is merely to buy and sell drugs, without compounding or preparation. In America, the same person often carries on the business of the druggist and the apothecary.

DRUG'STER, *n.* A druggist. [*Not used.*] *Boyle.*

DRU'ID, *n.* [Ir. *draoi*, formerly *drui*, a magician, a druid; plu. *draoithe*; Sax. *dry*, a magician; W. *derwyz*, [*derwyth*,] which Owen supposes to be a compound of *dar*, *derw*, an oak, and *gwyz*, knowledge, presence. The Welsh derivation accords with that of Pliny, who supposes the druids were so called, because they frequented or instructed in the forest, or sacrificed under an oak. But some uncertainty rests on this subject.]

A priest or minister of religion, among the ancient Celtic nations in Gaul, Britain and Germany. The Druids possessed some knowledge of geometry, natural philosophy, &c., superintended the affairs of religion and morality, and performed the office of judges. *Owen. Encyc.*

DRUID'IC, } *a.* Pertaining to the Druids.
DRUID'ICAL, }

DRU'IDISM, *n.* The system of religion, philosophy and instruction taught by the Druids, or their doctrines, rites and ceremonies. *Whitaker. Christ. Observer.*

DRUM, *n.* [D. *trom*, *trommel*; G. *trommel*; Sw. *trumma*; Dan. *tromme*; Ir. *druma*; probably from its sound, and the root of *rumble*, Gr. βρεμω, L. *fremo*. See Class Rm. No. 10. 11.]

1. A martial instrument of music, in form of a hollow cylinder, and covered at the ends with vellum, which is stretched or slackened at pleasure.

2. In *machinery*, a short cylinder revolving on an axis, generally for the purpose of turning several small wheels, by means of straps passing round its periphery. *Cyc.*

3. The *drum of the ear*, the tympanum, or barrel of the ear; the hollow part of the ear, behind the membrane of the tympanum. The latter is a tense membrane, which closes the external passage of the ear, and receives the vibrations of the air. *Hooper.*

DRUM, *v. i.* To beat a drum with sticks; to beat or play a tune on a drum.

2. To beat with the fingers, as with drumsticks; to beat with a rapid succession of strokes; as, to *drum* on the table.

3. To beat as the heart. *Dryden.*

DRUM, *v. t.* To expel with beat of drum. *Military phrase.*

DRUM'BLE, *v. i.* To drone; to be sluggish. [*Not in use.*] *Shak.*

DRUM'-FISH, *n.* A fish, found on the coast of N. America.

DRUM'LY, *a.* [W. *trom*, heavy.] Thick; stagnant; muddy. [*Not in use.*]

DRUM-MAJOR, *n.* The chief or first drummer of a regiment.

DRUM'-MAKER, *n.* One who makes drums.

DRUM'MER, *n.* One whose office is to beat the drum, in military exercises and marching; one who drums.

DRUM'-STICK, *n.* The stick with which a drum is beaten, or shaped for the purpose of beating a drum.

DRUNK, *a.* [from *drunken*. See *Drink.*]

1. Intoxicated; inebriated; overwhelmed or overpowered by spirituous liquor; stupified or inflamed by the action of spirit on the stomach and brain. It is brutish to be *drunk.*

Be not *drunk* with wine, wherein is excess. *St. Paul.*

2. Drenched, or saturated with moisture or liquor.

I will make my arrows *drunk* with blood. Deut. xxxii.

[Note. *Drunk* was formerly used as the participle of *drink*; as, he had *drunk* wine. But in modern usage, *drank* has taken its place; and *drunk* is now used chiefly as an adjective.]

DRUNK'ARD, *n.* One given to ebriety or an excessive use of strong liquor; a person who habitually or frequently is drunk.

A *drunkard* and a glutton shall come to poverty. Prov. xxiii.

DRUNK'EN, *a. drunk'n.* [participle of *drink*, but now used chiefly as an adjective, and often contracted to *drunk.*]

1. Intoxicated; inebriated with strong liquor.

2. Given to drunkenness; as a *drunken* butler.

3. Saturated with liquor or moisture; drenched.

Let the earth be *drunken* with our blood. *Shak.*

4. Proceeding from intoxication; done in a state of drunkenness; as a *drunken* quarrel. *Swift.*

A *drunken* slaughter. *Shak.*

DRUNK'ENLY, *adv.* In a drunken manner. [*Little used.*] *Shak.*

DRUNK'ENNESS, *n.* Intoxication; inebriation; a state in which a person is overwhelmed or overpowered with spirituous liquors, so that his reason is disordered, and he reels or staggers in walking. Drunkenness renders some persons stupid, others gay, others sullen, others furious.

Let us walk honestly as in the day; not in rioting and *drunkenness*. *St. Paul.*

2. Habitual ebriety or intoxication. *Watts.*

3. Disorder of the faculties resembling intoxication by liquors; inflammation; frenzy; rage.

Passion is the *drunkenness* of the mind. *Spenser.*

DRUPE, *n.* [L. *drupæ*, Gr. δρυπετης, olives ready to fall; Gr. δρυς, a tree, and πιπτω, to fall.]

In *botany*, a pulpy pericarp or fruit without valves, containing a nut or stone with a kernel; as the plum, cherry, apricot, peach, almond, olive, &c. *Martyn.*

DRUPA'CEOUS, *a.* Producing drupes; as *drupaceous* trees.

2. Pertaining to drupes; or consisting of drupes; as *drupaceous* fruit; *drupaceous* follicles. *Asiat. Researches.*

DRUSE, *n.* [G. *druse*, a gland, glanders.] Among *miners*, a cavity in a rock having its interior surface studded with crystals, or filled with water.

DRU'SY, *a. s* as *z.* Abounding with very minute crystals; as a *drusy* surface. *Kirwan.*

DRȲ, *a.* [Sax. *dri*, *drig*, or *dryg*; D. *droog*; G. *trocken*. See the Verb.]

1. Destitute of moisture; free from water or wetness; arid; not moist; as *dry* land; *dry* clothes.

2. Not rainy; free from rain or mist; as *dry* weather; a *dry* March or April.

3. Not juicy; free from juice, sap or aqueous matter; not green; as *dry* wood; *dry* stubble; *dry* hay; *dry* leaves.

4. Without tears; as *dry* eyes; *dry* mourning. *Dryden.*

5. Not giving milk; as, the cow is *dry.*

6. Thirsty; craving drink.
7. Barren; jejune; plain; unembellished; destitute of pathos, or of that which amuses and interests; as a *dry* style; a *dry* subject; a *dry* discussion.
8. Severe; sarcastic; wiping; as a *dry* remark or repartee; a *dry* rub. *Goodman.*
9. Severe; wiping; as a *dry* blow: a *dry* basting. See the Verb, which signifies properly to wipe, rub, scour. *Bacon.*
10. *Dry goods*, in commerce, cloths, stuffs, silks, laces, ribins, &c., in distinction from groceries.

DRȲ, *v. t.* [Sax. *drigan, adrigan*, or *drygan, adrygan, adrugan, gedrigan*; D. *droogen*; G. *trocknen*, to dry, to wipe; Gr. *φρυγεω*; L. *tergo, tergeo*; Fr. *torcher*; Sw. *torcka.* The German has also *dürr*, Sw. *torr*, Dan. *tör*, but these seem to be connected with L. *torreo*, Russ. *obterayu* or *oterayu.* Class Dr. Whether *drigan* and *dry* are derivatives of that root, or belong to Class Rg, the root of *rake*, is not certain. See *Dry*, Class Rg. The primary sense is to *wipe, rub, scour.*]
1. To free from water, or from moisture of any kind, and by any means; originally by wiping, as to *dry* the eyes; to exsiccate.
2. To deprive of moisture by evaporation or exhalation; as, the sun *dries* a cloth; wind *dries* the earth.
3. To deprive of moisture by exposure to the sun or open air. We *dry* cloth in the sun.
4. To deprive of natural juice, sap or greenness; as, to *dry* hay or plants.
5. To scorch or parch with thirst; with *up*.

> Their honorable men are famished, and their multitude *dried up* with thirst. Isa. v.

6. To deprive of water by draining; to drain; to exhaust; as, to *dry* a meadow.
To dry up, to deprive wholly of water.

DRȲ, *v. i.* To grow dry; to lose moisture; to become free from moisture or juice. The road *dries* fast in a clear windy day. Hay will *dry* sufficiently in two days.
2. To evaporate wholly; to be exhaled; sometimes with *up*; as, the stream *dries* or *dries up*.

DRY'AD, *n.* [L. *dryades*, plu. from Gr. *δρυς*, a tree.]
In *mythology*, a deity or nymph of the woods; a nymph supposed to preside over woods.

DRY'ED, *pp.* of *dry*. [See *Dried.*]

DRY'ER, *n.* He or that which dries; that which exhausts of moisture or greenness.

DRY'EYED, *a.* Not having tears in the eyes.

DRY'FAT, *n.* A dry vat or basket.

DRY'FOOT, *n.* A dog that pursues game by the scent of the foot. *Shak.*

DRY'ING, *ppr.* Expelling or losing moisture, sap or greenness.

DRY'ING, *n.* The act or process of depriving of moisture or greenness.

DRY'ITE, *n.* [Gr. *δρυς*, an oak.] Fragments of petrified or fossil wood in which the structure of the wood is recognized. *Dict.*

DRY'LY, *adv.* Without moisture.
2. Coldly; frigidly; without affection. *Bacon.*
3. Severely; sarcastically.
4. Barrenly; without embellishment; without any thing to enliven, enrich or entertain. *Pope.*

DRY'NESS, *n.* Destitution of moisture; want of water or other fluid; siccity; aridity; aridness; as the *dryness* of a soil; *dryness* of the road.
2. Want of rain; as *dryness* of weather.
3. Want of juice or succulence; as *dryness* of the bones or fibers. *Arbuthnot.*
4. Want of succulence or greenness; as the *dryness* of hay or corn.
5. Barrenness; jejuneness; want of ornament or pathos; want of that which enlivens and entertains; as the *dryness* of style or expression; the *dryness* of a subject.
6. Want of feeling or sensibility in devotion; want of ardor; as *dryness* of spirit. *Taylor.*

DRY'NURSE, *n.* A nurse who attends and feeds a child without the breast.
2. One who attends another in sickness.

DRY'NURSE, *v. t.* To feed, attend and bring up without the breast. *Hudibras.*

DRY'RUB, *v. t.* To rub and cleanse without wetting. *Dodsley's Poems.*

DRYSALT'ER, *n.* A dealer in salted or dry meats, pickles, sauces, &c. *Fordyce.*

DRY'SHOD, *a.* Without wetting the feet. Is. xi. 15.

DU'AL, *a.* [L. *dualis*, from *duo*, two.] Expressing the number two; as the *dual* number in Greek.

DUALIS'TIC, *a.* Consisting of two. The *dualistic* system of Anaxagoras and Plato taught that there are two principles in nature, one active, the other passive. *Enfield.*

DUAL'ITY, *n.* That which expresses two in number. *Hales.*
2. Division; separation. *Davies.*
3. The state or quality of being two. *Hayley.*

DUB, *v. t.* [Sax. *dubban*; coinciding with Gr. *τυπτω*, and Eng. *tap.* Class Db.] Literally, to strike. Hence,
1. To strike a blow with a sword, and make a knight.

> Se cyng—*dubbade* his sunu Henric to ridere.
> The King *dubbed* his son Henry a knight.
> *Sax. Chron.* An. 1085.

2. To confer any dignity or new character.

> A man of wealth is *dubb'd* a man of worth. *Pope.*

DUB, *v. i.* To make a quick noise. *Beaum.*

DUB, *n.* A blow. [*Little used.*] *Hudibras.*
2. In *Irish*, a puddle.

DUB'BED, *pp.* Struck; made a knight.

DUB'BING, *ppr.* Striking; making a knight.

DUBI'ETY, *n.* [See *Doubt.*] Doubtfulness. [*Little used.*] *Richardson.*

DU'BIOUS, *a.* [L. *dubius.* See *Doubt.* The primary sense is probably to turn or to waver.]
1. Doubtful; wavering or fluctuating in opinion; not settled; not determined; as, the mind is in a *dubious* state.
2. Uncertain; that of which the truth is not ascertained or known; as a *dubious* question.
3. Not clear; not plain; as *dubious* light. *Milton.*
4. Of uncertain event or issue.

> In *dubious* battle. *Milton.*

DU'BIOUSLY, *adv.* Doubtfully; uncertainly; without any determination. *Swift.*

DU'BIOUSNESS, *n.* Doubtfulness; a state of wavering and indecision of mind; as, he speaks with *dubiousness.*
2. Uncertainty; as the *dubiousness* of the question.

DU'BITABLE, *a.* [L. *dubito.* See *Doubt.*] Doubtful; uncertain. [*Little used.*] But the derivative *indubitable* is often used.

DU'BITANCY, *n.* Doubt; uncertainty. [*Little used.*]

DUBITA'TION, *n.* [L. *dubitatio*, from *dubito*, to *doubt.*] The act of doubting; doubt. [*Little used.*] *Brown. Grew.*

DU'CAL, *a.* [Fr. Sp. Port. from *duke.*] Pertaining to a duke; as a *ducal* coronet. *Johnson.*

DUC'AT, *n.* [from *duke.*] A coin of several countries in Europe, struck in the dominions of a duke. It is of silver or gold. The silver ducat is generally of the value of four shillings and sixpence sterling, equal to an American dollar, or to a French crown, and the gold ducat of twice the value. *Encyc.*

DUCATOON', *n.* [Fr. *ducaton*; Sp. *id*; from *ducat.*]
A silver coin, struck chiefly in Italy, of the value of about four shillings and eight pence sterling, or nearly 104 cents. The gold ducatoon of Holland is worth twenty florins. *Encyc.*

DUCH'ESS, *n.* [Fr. *duchesse*, from *duc*, duke.]
The consort or widow of a duke. Also, a lady who has the sovereignty of a duchy.

DUCH'Y, *n.* [Fr. *duché.*] The territory or dominions of a duke; a dukedom; as the *duchy* of Lancaster. *Blackstone.*

DUCH'Y-COURT, *n.* The court of the duchy of Lancaster in England.

DUCK, *n.* [Sw. *duk*, a cloth; Dan. *duug*; G. *tuch*; D. *doek*; allied perhaps to L. *toga*, and to *tego*, to cover, or *texo*, to weave.]
A species of coarse cloth or canvas, used for sails, sacking of beds, &c.

DUCK, *n.* [from the verb, to *duck.*] A water fowl, so called from its plunging. There are many species or varieties of the duck, some wild, others tame.
2. An inclination of the head, resembling the motion of a duck in water. *Milton.*
3. A stone thrown obliquely on the water, so as to rebound; as in *duck* and drake. *Johnson.*

DUCK, *n.* [Dan. *dukke*, a baby or puppet.] A word of endearment or fondness. *Shak.*

DUCK, *v. t.* [G. *ducken*, and *tauchen*; D. *duiken*, pret. *dook*, to stoop, dive, plunge. Qu. Sax. *theachan*, to wash, and its alliance to *tingo* and *dye.* Class Dg.]
1. To dip or plunge in water and suddenly withdraw; as, to *duck* a seaman. It differs from *dive*, which signifies to plunge one's self, without immediately emerging.
2. To plunge the head in water and immediately withdraw it; as, *duck* the boy.
3. To bow, stoop or nod.

DUCK, *v. i.* To plunge into water and immediately withdraw; to dip; to plunge the head in water or other liquid.

> In Tiber *ducking* thrice by break of day. *Dryden.*

2. To drop the head suddenly; to bow; to cringe.

> *Duck* with French nods. *Shak.*

DUCK'ED, *pp.* Plunged; dipped in water.

DUCK'ER, *n.* A plunger; a diver; a cringer.

DUCK'ING, *ppr.* Plunging; thrusting suddenly into water and withdrawing; dipping.

DUCK'ING, *n.* The act of plunging or putting in water and withdrawing. Ducking is a punishment of offenders in France, and among English seamen, it is a penalty to which sailors are subject on passing, for the first time, the equator or tropic.

DUCK'ING-STOOL, *n.* A stool or chair in which common scolds were formerly tied and plunged into water. *Blackstone.*

DUCK'-LEGGED, *a.* Having short legs, like a duck. *Dryden.*

DUCK'LING, *n.* A young duck. *Ray.*

DUCK'-MEAT, DUCK'S-MEAT, *n.* A plant, the Lemna, growing in ditches and shallow water, and serving for food for ducks and geese. *Encyc.*

The starry duck's-meat is the Callitriche. *Fam. of Plants.*

DUCKOY. [See *Decoy.*]

DUCK'S-FOOT, *n.* A plant, the Podophyllum; called also May-apple. *Fam. of Plants.*

DUCK'-WEED, *n.* The same as *duck-meat.*

DUCT, *n.* [L. *ductus*, from *duco*, to lead. See *Duke.*]

1. Any tube or canal by which a fluid or other substance is conducted or conveyed. It is particularly used to denote the vessels of an animal body, by which the blood, chyle, lymph, &c., are carried from one part to another, and the vessels of plants in which the sap is conveyed.

2. Guidance; direction. [*Little used.*] *Hammond.*

DUC'TILE, *a.* [L. *ductilis*, from *duco*, to lead.]

1. That may be led; easy to be led or drawn; tractable; complying; obsequious; yielding to motives, persuasion or instruction; as the *ductile* minds of youth; a *ductile* people. *Philips. Addison.*

2. Flexible; pliable.

> The *ductile* rind and leaves of radiant gold. *Dryden.*

3. That may be drawn out into wire or threads. Gold is the most *ductile* of the metals.

4. That may be extended by beating.

DUC'TILENESS, *n.* The quality of suffering extension by drawing or percussion; ductility. *Donne.*

DUCTIL'ITY, *n.* The property of solid bodies, particularly metals, which renders them capable of being extended by drawing without breaking; as the *ductility* of gold, iron or brass.

2. Flexibility; obsequiousness; a disposition of mind that easily yields to motives or influence; ready compliance. *Roscoe.*

DUC'TURE, *n.* [L. *duco.*] Guidance. [*Not in use.*] *South.*

DUDG'EON, *n.* [G. *degen.*] A small dagger. *Hudibras.*

DUDG'EON, *n.* [W. *dygen.*] Anger; resentment; malice; ill will; discord. *L'Estrange. Hudibras.*

DUDS, *n.* [Scot. *dud*, a rag; *duds*, clothes, or old worn clothes.]

Old clothes; tattered garments. [*A vulgar word.*]

DUE, *a. du.* [Fr. *dû*, pp. of *devoir*, L. *debeo*, Sp. *deber*, It. *dovere*. Qu. Gr. δεω, to bind. Class Db. It has no connection with *owe.*]

1. Owed; that ought to be paid or done to another. That is *due* from me to another which contract, justice or propriety requires me to pay, and which he may justly claim as his right. Reverence is *due* to the creator; civility is *due* from one man to another. Money is *due* at the expiration of the credit given, or at the period promised.

2. Proper; fit; appropriate; suitable; becoming; required by the circumstances; as, the event was celebrated with *due* solemnities. Men seldom have a *due* sense of their depravity.

3. Seasonable; as, he will come in *due* time.

4. Exact; proper; as, the musicians keep *due* time.

5. Owing to; occasioned by. [*Little used.*] *Boyle.*

6. That ought to have arrived, or to be present, before the time specified; as, two mails are now *due.*

DUE, *adv.* Directly; exactly; as a *due* east course.

DUE, *n.* That which is owed; that which one contracts to pay, do or perform to another; that which law or justice requires to be paid or done. The money that I contract to pay to another is his *due;* the service which I covenant to perform to another is his *due;* reverence to the creator is his *due.*

2. That which office, rank, station, social relations, or established rules of right or decorum, require to be given, paid or done. Respect and obedience to parents and magistrates are their *due.*

3. That which law or custom requires; as toll, tribute, fees of office, or other legal perquisites. *Addison.*

4. Right; just title.

> The key of this infernal pit by *due*—
> I keep. *Milton.*

DUE, *v. t.* To pay as due. [*Not used.*] *Shak.*

DU'EL, *n.* [L. *duellum;* Fr. *duel;* It. *duello;* Port. *id.;* Sp. *duelo.* In Armoric, the word is *dufell*, or *duvell*, and Gregoire supposes the word to be compounded of *dou*, two, and *bell*, bellum, war, combat. So in Dutch, *tweegevegt*, two-fight; in G. *zweikampf*, id.]

1. Single combat; a premeditated combat between two persons, for the purpose of deciding some private difference or quarrel. A sudden fight, not premeditated, is called a *rencounter.* A duel is fought with deadly weapons and with a purpose to take life.

2. Any contention or contest. *Milton.*

DU'EL, *v. i.* To fight in single combat. *South.*

DU'EL, *v. t.* To attack or fight singly. *Milton.*

DU'ELER, *n.* A combatant in single fight.

DU'ELING, *ppr.* Fighting in single combat.

DU'ELING, *n.* The act or practice of fighting in single combat.

DU'ELIST, *n.* One who fights in single combat. *Dryden.*

> The *duelist* values his *honor* above the life of his antagonist, his own life, and the happiness of his family.

2. One who professes to study the rules of honor.

DUEL'LO, *n.* Duel; or rule of dueling. [*Not used.*] *Shak.*

DU'ENESS, *n. du'ness.* [See *Due.*] Fitness; propriety; due quality.

DUEN'NA, *n.* [Sp. *dueña*, fem. of *dueño;* Fr. *duegne;* the same as *dona*, the feminine of *don.* Qu. W. *dyn*, Ir. *duine*, man, a person. See *Don.*]

An old woman who is kept to guard a younger; a governess. *Arbuthnot.*

DUET', DUET'TO, *n.* [Ital. *duetto*, from *duo*, two.] A song or air in two parts.

DUG, *n.* [Ice. *deggia.* This word corresponds with the root of L. *digitus*, Eng. *toe*, Norm. *doy*, a finger, signifying a shoot or point.]

The pap or nipple of a cow or other beast. It is applied to a human female in contempt, but seems to have been used formerly of the human breast without reproach.

> From tender *dug* of common nurse. *Spenser.*

DUG, *pret.* and *pp.* of *dig;* as, they *dug* a ditch; a ditch was *dug.*

DUKE, *n.* [Fr. *duc;* Sp. Port. *duque;* It. *duca;* Arm. *dug* or *doug;* Sax. *teoche*, and in composition, *toga, toge*, as in *heretoga*, an army leader, a general; D. *hertog;* G. *herzog;* Dan. *hertug;* Sw. *hertig;* Venetian, *doge;* L. *dux*, from *duco*, to lead, as in Saxon, *tiogan, teon*, to draw, to *tug;* Gr. ταγος; Thessalian, *tagus.* Class Dg. No. 5. 14.]

1. In *Great Britain*, one of the highest order of nobility; a title of honor or nobility next below the princes; as the *Duke* of Bedford or of Cornwall.

3. In some countries on the Continent, a sovereign prince, without the title of king; as the *Duke* of Holstein, of Savoy, of Parma, &c.

2. A chief; a prince; as the *dukes* of Edom. Gen. xxxvi.

DU'KEDOM, *n.* The seignory or possessions of a duke; the territory of a duke. *Shak.*

2. The title or quality of a duke. *Ibid.*

DUL'BRAINED, *a.* [*dull* and *brain.*] Stupid; doltish; of dull intellects. [See *Dull-brained.*] *Shak.*

DUL'CET, *a.* [L. *dulcis*, sweet.] Sweet to the taste; luscious.

> She tempers *dulcet* creams. *Milton.*

2. Sweet to the ear; melodious; harmonious; as *dulcet* sounds; *dulcet* symphonies. *Milton.*

DULCIFICA'TION, *n.* [See *Dulcify.*] The act of sweetening; the act of freeing from acidity, saltness or acrimony. *Boyle.*

DUL'CIFIED, *pp.* Sweetened; purified from salts.

Dulcified spirits, a term formerly applied to the different ethers; as *dulcified spirits* of niter and vitriol, nitric and sulphuric ethers. *Dispensatory.*

DULCIFY, *v. t.* [Fr. *dulcifier*, from L. *dulcis*, sweet, and *facio*, to make.]

To sweeten; to free from acidity, saltness or acrimony. *Wiseman.*

DUL'CIMER, *n.* [It. *dolcimello*, from *dolce*, sweet. *Skinner.*]

An instrument of music played by striking brass wires with little sticks. Daniel iii. 5. *Johnson.*

DUL'CINESS, *n.* [L. *dulcis.*] Softness; easiness of temper. [*Not used.*] *Bacon.*

DUL'CORATE, *v. t.* [L. *dulcis*, sweet; Low L. *dulco*, to sweeten.] To sweeten. *Bacon.*

2. To make less acrimonious. *Johnson. Wiseman.*

DULCORA'TION, *n.* The act of sweetening. *Bacon.*

DU'LIA, *n.* [Gr. δουλεια, service.] An inferior kind of worship or adoration. [Not an English word.] *Stillingfleet.*

DULL, *a.* [W. *dol*, *dwl*; Sax. *dol*, a wandering; also *dull*, foolish, stupid; D. *dol*, mad; G. *toll*, and *tölpel*, a dolt; Sax. *dwolian*, to wander, to rave. Qu. Dan. *dvæler*, to loiter; Sw. *dvălias*, id., or *dvala*, a trance.]

1. Stupid; doltish; blockish; slow of understanding; as a lad of *dull* genius.
2. Heavy; sluggish; without life or spirit; as, a surfeit leaves a man very *dull*.
3. Slow of motion; sluggish; as a *dull* stream.
4. Slow of hearing or seeing; as *dull* of hearing; *dull* of seeing.
5. Slow to learn or comprehend; unready; awkward; as a *dull* scholar.
6. Sleepy; drowsy.
7. Sad; melancholy.
8. Gross; cloggy; insensible; as the *dull* earth.
9. Not pleasing or delightful; not exhilarating; cheerless; as, to make dictionaries is *dull* work. *Johnson.*
10. Not bright or clear; clouded; tarnished; as, the mirror is *dull*.
11. Not bright; not briskly burning; as a *dull* fire.
12. Dim; obscure; not vivid; as a *dull* light.
13. Blunt; obtuse; having a thick edge; as a *dull* knife or ax.
13. Cloudy; overcast; not clear; not enlivening; as *dull* weather.
15. With *seamen*, being without wind; as, a ship has a *dull* time.
16. Not lively or animated; as a *dull* eye.

DULL, *v. t.* To make dull; to stupify; as, to *dull* the senses. *Shak.*

2. To blunt; as, to *dull* a sword or an ax.
3. To make sad or melancholy.
4. To hebetate; to make insensible or slow to perceive; as, to *dull* the ears; to *dull* the wits. *Spenser. Ascham.*
5. To damp; to render lifeless; as, to *dull* the attention. *Hooker.*
6. To make heavy or slow of motion; as, to *dull* industry. *Bacon.*
7. To sully; to tarnish or cloud; as, the breath *dulls* a mirror.

DULL, *v. i.* To become dull or blunt; to become stupid.

DULL'-BRAINED, *a.* Stupid; of dull intellect.

DULL'-BROWED, *a.* Having a gloomy look. *Quarles.*

DULL-DISPO'SED, *a.* Inclined to dullness or sadness. *B. Jonson.*

DULL'-EYED, *a.* Having a downcast look. *Shak.*

DULL'-HEAD, *n.* A person of dull understanding; a dolt; a blockhead.

DULL'-SIGHTED, *a.* Having imperfect sight; purblind.

DULL'-WITTED, *a.* Having a dull intellect; heavy.

DULL'ARD, *a.* Doltish; stupid. *Hall.*

DULL'ARD, *n.* A stupid person; a dolt; a blockhead; a dunce. *Shak.*

DULL'ED, *pp.* Made dull; blunted.

DULL'ER, *n.* That which makes dull.

DULL'ING, *ppr.* Making dull.

DULL'NESS, *n.* Stupidity; slowness of comprehension; weakness of intellect; indocility; as the *dullness* of a student. *South.*

2. Want of quick perception or eager desire.
3. Heaviness; drowsiness; inclination to sleep.
4. Heaviness; disinclination to motion.
5. Sluggishness; slowness.
6. Dimness; want of clearness or luster.
7. Bluntness; want of edge.
8. Want of brightness or vividness; as *dullness* of color.

DUL'LY, *adv.* Stupidly; slowly; sluggishly; without life or spirit.

DU'LY, *adv.* [from *due.*] Properly; fitly; in a suitable or becoming manner; as, let the subject be *duly* considered.

2. Regularly; at the proper time; as, a man *duly* attended church with his family.

DUMB, *a. dum.* [Sax. *dumb*; Goth. *dumbs*, *dumba*; G. *dumm*; D. *dom*; Sw. *dumm* or *dumbe*; Dan. *dum*; Heb. Ch. דום, to be silent; Ar. دَامَ to continue or be permanent, to appease, to quiet. Class Dm. No. 3. In this word, *b* is improperly added.]

1. Mute; silent; not speaking.
   I was *dumb* with silence; I held my peace. Ps. xxxix.
2. Destitute of the power of speech; unable to utter articulate sounds; as the *dumb* brutes. The asylum at Hartford in Connecticut was the first institution in America for teaching the deaf and *dumb* to read and write.
3. Mute; not using or accompanied with speech; as a *dumb* show; *dumb* signs.

To strike dumb, is to confound; to astonish; to render silent by astonishment; or it may be, to deprive of the power of speech.

DUMB, *v. t.* To silence. *Shak.*

DUMB'LY, *adv. dum'ly.* Mutely; silently; without words or speech.

DUMB'NESS, *n. dum'ness.* Muteness; silence or holding the peace; omission of speech. *This is voluntary dumbness.*

2. Incapacity to speak; inability to articulate sounds. *This is involuntary dumbness.*

DUM'FOUND, *v. t.* To strike dumb; to confuse. [*A low word.*] *Spectator.*

DUM'MERER, *n.* One who feigns dumbness. [*Not in use.*]

DUMP, *n.* [from the root of *dumb*; D. *dom*; G. *dumm.*]

1. A dull gloomy state of the mind; sadness; melancholy; sorrow; heaviness of heart.
   In doleful *dumps*. *Gay.*
2. Absence of mind; reverie. *Locke.*
3. A melancholy tune or air. *Shak.*

[This is not an elegant word, and in America, I believe, is always used in the plural; as, the woman is in the *dumps.*]

DUMP'ISH, *a.* Dull; stupid; sad; melancholy; depressed in spirits; as, he lives a *dumpish* life.

DUMP'ISHLY, *adv.* In a moping manner.

DUMP'ISHNESS, *n.* A state of being dull, heavy and moping.

DUMP'LING, *n.* [from *dump.*] A kind of pudding or mass of paste in cookery; usually, a cover of paste inclosing an apple and boiled, called *apple-dumpling*.

DUMP'Y, *a.* Short and thick.

DUN, *a.* [Sax. *dunn*; W. *dwn*; Ir. *donn*; qu. *tan*, *tawny*. See Class Dn. No. 3. 24. 28. 35.]

1. Of a dark color; of a color partaking of a brown and black; of a dull brown color; swarthy.
2. Dark; gloomy.
   In the *dun* air sublime. *Milton.*

DUN, *v. t.* To cure, as fish, in a manner to give them a dun color. [See *Dunning.*]

DUN, *v. t.* [Sax. *dynan*, to clamor, to *din*. See *Din*. Qu. Gr. δονεω.]

1. Literally, to clamor for payment of a debt. Hence, to urge for payment; to demand a debt in a pressing manner; to urge for payment with importunity. But in common usage, *dun* is often used in a milder sense, and signifies to call for, or ask for payment.
2. To urge importunately, *in a general sense, but not an elegant word.*

DUN, *n.* An importunate creditor who urges for payment. *Philips. Arbuthnot.*

2. An urgent request or demand of payment in writing; as, he sent his debtor a *dun*.
3. An eminence or mound. [See *Down* and *Town.*]

DUNCE, *n. duns.* [G. *duns*. Qu. Pers. دُنْس a stupid man.]

A person of weak intellects; a dullard; a dolt; a thickskull.

I never knew this town without *dunces* of figure. *Swift.*

DUN'CERY, *n.* Dullness; stupidity. *Smith.*

DUN'CIFY, *v. t.* To make stupid in intellect. [*Not used.*] *Warburton.*

DUN'DER, *n.* [Sp. *redundar*, to overflow; L. *redundo.*]

Lees; dregs; a word used in Jamaica.

The use of *dunder* in the making of rum answers the purpose of yeast in the fermentation of flour. *Edwards, W. Ind.*

DUNE, *n.* A hill. [See *Down.*]

DUN'-FISH, *n.* Codfish cured in a particular manner. [See *Dunning.*]

DUNG, *n.* [Sax. *dung*, or *dincg*, or *dinig*; G. *dung*, *dünger*; Dan. *dynd*; Sw. *dynga.*] The excrement of animals. *Bacon.*

DUNG, *v. t.* To manure with dung. *Dryden.*

DUNG, *v. i.* To void excrement.

DUNG'ED, *pp.* Manured with dung.

DUN'GEON, *n.* [Fr. *dongeon*, or *donjon*, a tower or platform in the midst of a castle, a turret or closet on the top of a house. In one Armoric dialect it is *domjou*, and Gregoire suggests that it is compounded of *dom*, lord or chief, and *jou*, Jupiter, Jove, an elevated or chief tower consecrated to Jupiter. In Scottish, it is written *doungeoun*, and denotes the keep or strongest tower of a fortress, or an inner tower surrounded by a ditch. *Jamieson.* It was used for confining prisoners, and hence its application to prisons of eminent strength.]

1. A close prison; or a deep, dark place of confinement.

And in a *dungeon* deep. *Spenser.*

They brought Joseph hastily out of the *dungeon.* Gen. xli.

2. A subterraneous place of close confinement. *Jeremiah.*

DUN'GEON, *v.t.* To confine in a dungeon. *Hall.*

DUNG'FORK, *n.* A fork used to throw dung from a stable or into a cart, or to spread it over land.

DUNG'HILL, *n.* A heap of dung.

2. A mean or vile abode. *Dryden.*

3. Any mean situation or condition.

He lifteth the beggar from the *dunghill.* 1 Sam. ii.

4. A term of reproach for a man meanly born. [*Not used.*] *Shak.*

DUNG'HILL, *a.* Sprung from the dunghill; mean; low; base; vile. *Shak.*

DUNG'Y, *a.* Full of dung; filthy; vile. *Shak.*

DUNG'YARD, *n.* A yard or inclosure where dung is collected. *Mortimer.*

DUN'LIN, *n.* A fowl, a species of sandpiper. *Pennant.*

DUN'NAGE, *n.* Faggots, boughs or loose wood laid on the bottom of a ship to raise heavy goods above the bottom. *Mar. Dict.*

DUN'NED, *pp.* [from *dun.*] Importuned to pay a debt; urged.

DUN'NER, *n.* [from *dun.*] One employed in soliciting the payment of debts. *Spectator.*

DUN'NING, *ppr.* [from *dun.*] Urging for payment of a debt, or for the grant of some favor, or for the obtaining any request; importuning.

DUN'NING, *ppr.* or *n.* [from *dun,* a color.] The operation of curing codfish, in such a manner as to give it a particular color and quality. Fish for dunning are caught early in spring, and often in February. At the Isles of Shoals, off Portsmouth, in New Hampshire, the cod are taken in deep water, split and slack-salted; then laid in a pile for two or three months, in a dark store, covered, for the greatest part of the time, with salt-hay or eel-grass, and pressed with some weight. In April or May, they are opened and piled again as close as possible in the same dark store, till July or August, when they are fit for use. *J. Haven.*

DUN'NISH, *a.* Inclined to a dun color; somewhat dun. *Ray.*

DUN'NY, *a.* Deaf; dull of apprehension. [*Local.*] *Grose.*

DU'O, *n.* [L. two.] A song in two parts.

DUODECAHE'DRAL. } [See *Dodecahedral, Dodecahedron.*]
DUODECAHE'DRON. }

DUODEC'IMFID, *a.* [L. *duodecim,* twelve, and *findo,* to cleave.] Divided into twelve parts.

DUODEC'IMO, *a.* [L. *duodecim,* twelve.] Having or consisting of twelve leaves to a sheet; as a book of *duodecimo* form or size.

DUODEC'IMO, *n.* A book in which a sheet is folded into twelve leaves.

DUODEC'UPLE, *a.* [L. *duo,* two, and *decuplus,* tenfold.] Consisting of twelves. *Arbuthnot.*

DUOD'ENUM, *n.* [L.] The first of the small intestines.

DUOLIT'ERAL, *a.* [L. *duo,* two, and *litera,* a letter.] Consisting of two letters only; biliteral. *Stuart.*

DUPE, *n.* [Fr. *dupe.* See the Verb.] A person who is deceived; or one easily led astray by his credulity; as the *dupe* of a party.

DUPE, *v. t.* [Fr. *duper;* Sw. *tubba.* Qu. Sp. and Port. *estafar.*]

To deceive; to trick; to mislead by imposing on one's credulity; as, to be *duped* by flattery.

DU'PION, *n.* A double cocoon, formed by two or more silk-worms. *Encyc.*

DU'PLE, *a.* [L. *duplus.*] Double. *Duple* ratio is that of 2 to 1, 8 to 4, &c. *Sub-duple* ratio is the reverse, or as 1 to 2, 4 to 8, &c.

DU'PLICATE, *a.* [L. *duplicatus,* from *duplico,* to double, from *duplex,* double, twofold; *duo,* two, and *plico,* to fold. See *Double.*] Double; twofold.

Duplicate proportion or *ratio,* is the proportion or ratio of squares. Thus in geometrical proportion, the first term to the third is said to be in a *duplicate* ratio of the first to the second, or as its square is to the square of the second. Thus in 2. 4. 8. 16, the ratio of 2 to 8 is a *duplicate* of that of 2 to 4, or as the square of 2 is to the square of 4.

DU'PLICATE, *n.* Another corresponding to the first; or a second thing of the same kind.

2. A copy; a transcript. Thus a second letter or bill of exchange exactly like the first is called a *duplicate.*

DU'PLICATE, *v. t.* [L. *duplico.*] To double; to fold.

DUPLICA'TION, *n.* The act of doubling; the multiplication of a number by 2.

2. A folding; a doubling; also, a fold; as the *duplication* of a membrane.

DU'PLICATURE, *n.* A doubling; a fold. In *anatomy,* the fold of a membrane or vessel. *Encyc.*

DUPLIC'ITY, *n.* [Fr. *duplicité;* Sp. *duplicidad;* It. *duplicità;* from L. *duplex,* double.]

1. Doubleness; the number two. *Watts.*

2. Doubleness of heart or speech; the act or practice of exhibiting a different or contrary conduct, or uttering different or contrary sentiments, at different times, in relation to the same thing; or the act of dissembling one's real opinions for the purpose of concealing them and misleading persons in the conversation and intercourse of life; double-dealing; dissimulation; deceit.

3. In *law,* duplicity is the pleading of two or more distinct matters or single pleas. *Blackstone.*

DURABIL'ITY, *n.* [See *Durable.*] The power of lasting or continuing, in any given state, without perishing; as the *durability* of cedar or oak timber; the *durability* of animal and vegetable life is very limited.

DU'RABLE, *a.* [L. *durabilis,* from *duro,* to last, *durus,* hard; W. *dur,* steel; *duraw,* to harden.]

Having the quality of lasting or continuing long in being, without perishing or wearing out; as *durable* timber; *durable* cloth; *durable* happiness.

DU'RABLENESS, *n.* Power of lasting; durability; as the *durableness* of honest fame.

DU'RABLY, *adv.* In a lasting manner; with long continuance.

DU'RANCE, *n.* [from Fr. *dur, durer,* L. *duro.*]

1. Imprisonment; restraint of the person; custody of the jailer. *Shak.*

2. Continuance; duration. [See *Endurance.*] *Dryden.*

DURANT', *n.* A glazed woolen stuff; called by some *everlasting.*

DURA'TION, *n.* Continuance in time; length or extension of existence, indefinitely; as the *duration* of life; the *duration* of a partnership; the *duration* of any given period of time; everlasting *duration.* This holding on or continuance of time is divided by us arbitrarily into certain portions, as minutes, hours and days; or it is measured by a succession of events, as by the diurnal and annual revolutions of the earth, or any other succession; and the interval between two events is called a part of *duration.* This interval may be of any indefinite length, a minute or a century.

2. Power of continuance. *Rogers.*

DURE, *v. i.* [L. *duro;* Fr. *durer;* Sp. *durar;* It. *durare.* See *Durable.*]

To last, to hold on in time or being; to continue; to endure. [This word is obsolete; *endure* being substituted.]

DU'REFUL, *a.* Lasting. *Obs.* *Spenser.*

DU'RELESS, *a.* Not lasting; fading. *Raleigh.*

DURESS', *n.* [Norm. *duresse, durette,* from *dur,* hard, grievous; L. *durities, durus.* See *Durable.*]

1. Literally, hardship; hence, constraint. Technically, duress, in law, is of two kinds; *duress of imprisonment,* which is imprisonment or restraint of personal liberty; and *duress by menaces or threats* [per minas,] when a person is threatened with loss of life or limb. Fear of battery is no duress. Duress then is imprisonment or threats intended to compel a person to do a legal act, as to execute a deed; or to commit an offense; in which cases the act is voidable or excusable. *Blackstone.*

2. Imprisonment; restraint of liberty.

DU'RING, *ppr.* of *dure.* Continuing; lasting; holding on; as *during* life, that is, life continuing; *during* our earthly pilgrimage; *during* the space of a year; *during* this or that. These phrases are the case absolute, or independent clauses; *durante vita, durante hoc.*

DU'RITY, *n.* [Fr. *dureté,* from *dur,* L. *durus, duro.*]

1. Hardness; firmness.

2. Hardness of mind; harshness. [*Little used.*]

DU'ROUS, *a.* Hard. [*Not used.*] *Smith.*

DUR'RA, *n.* A kind of millet, cultivated in N. Africa.

DURST, *pret.* of *dare.* [D. *darst.*]

DUSE, *n.* A demon or evil spirit. "Quosdam dæmones quos *dusios* Galli nuncupant." August. De Civ. Dei, 15. 23. What the *duse* is the matter? The *duse* is in you. [*Vulgar.*]

DUSK, *a.* [D. *duister;* G. *düster;* Russ.

tusk, tarnish; *tusknu*, to tarnish, to become dull or obscure. Qu. Gr. δασυς.]

1. Tending to darkness, or moderately dark.
2. Tending to a dark or black color; moderately black. *Milton.*

DUSK, *n.* A tending to darkness; incipient or imperfect obscurity; a middle degree between light and darkness; twilight; as the *dusk* of the evening.

2. Tendency to a black color; darkness of color.

Whose *dusk* set off the whiteness of the skin. *Dryden.*

DUSK, *v. t.* To make dusky. [*Little used.*]

DUSK, *v. i.* To begin to lose light or whiteness; to grow dark. [*Little used.*]

DUSK'ILY, *adv.* With partial darkness; with a tendency to blackness or darkness. *Sherwood.*

DUSK'INESS, *n.* Incipient or partial darkness; a slight or moderate degree of darkness or blackness.

DUSK'ISH, *a.* Moderately dusky; partially obscure; slightly dark or black; as *duskish* smoke. *Spenser.*

Duskish tincture. *Wotton.*

DUSK'ISHLY, *adv.* Cloudily; darkly. *Bacon.*

DUSK'ISHNESS, *n.* Duskiness; approach to darkness. *More.*

DUSK'Y, *a.* Partially dark or obscure; not luminous; as a *dusky* valley. *Dryden.*

A *dusky* torch. *Shak.*

2. Tending to blackness in color; partially black; dark-colored; not bright; as a *dusky* brown. *Bacon.*

Dusky clouds. *Dryden.*

3. Gloomy; sad.

This *dusky* scene of horror. *Bentley.*

4. Intellectually clouded; as a *dusky* sprite. *Pope.*

DUST, *n.* [Sax. *dust, dyst*; Scot. *dust*; Teut. *doest, duyst*, dust, fine flour.]

1. Fine dry particles of earth or other matter, so attenuated that it may be raised and wafted by the wind; powder; as clouds of *dust* and seas of blood.
2. Fine dry particles of earth; fine earth.

The peacock warmeth her eggs in the *dust*. Job xxxix.

3. Earth; unorganized earthy matter.

Dust thou art, and to *dust* shalt thou return. Gen. iii.

4. The grave.

For now shall I sleep in the *dust*. Job vii.

5. A low condition.

God raiseth the poor out of the *dust*. 1 Sam. ii.

DUST, *v. t.* To free from dust; to brush, wipe or sweep away dust; as, to *dust* a table or a floor.

2. To sprinkle with dust.
3. To levigate. *Sprat.*

DUST'-BRUSH, *n.* A brush for cleaning rooms and furniture.

DUST'ER, *n.* An utensil to clear from dust; also, a sieve.

DUST'INESS, *n.* The state of being dusty.

DUST'-MAN, *n.* One whose employment is to carry away dirt and filth. *Gay.*

DUST'Y, *a.* Filled, covered or sprinkled with dust; clouded with dust. *Dryden.*

2. Like dust; of the color of dust; as a *dusty* white; a *dusty* red.

DUTCH, *n.* The people of Holland; also, their language.

DUTCH, *a.* Pertaining to Holland, or to its inhabitants.

DU'TEOUS, *a.* [from *duty.*] Performing that which is due, or that which law, justice or propriety requires; obedient; respectful to those who have natural or legal authority to require service or duty; as a *duteous* child or subject.

2. Obedient; obsequious; *in a good or bad sense.*

Duteous to the vices of thy mistress. *Shak.*

3. Enjoined by duty, or by the relation of one to another; as *duteous* ties. [*Little used.*] *Shak.*

DU'TIABLE, *a.* [See *Duty.*] Subject to the imposition of duty or customs; as *dutiable* goods. *Supreme Court, U. S.*

DU'TIED, *a.* Subjected to duties or customs. *Ames.*

DU'TIFUL, *a.* Performing the duties or obligations required by law, justice or propriety; obedient; submissive to natural or legal superiors; respectful; as a *dutiful* son or daughter; a *dutiful* ward or servant; a *dutiful* subject.

2. Expressive of respect or a sense of duty; respectful; reverential; required by duty; as *dutiful* reverence; *dutiful* attentions.

DU'TIFULLY, *adv.* In a dutiful manner; with a regard to duty; obediently; submissively; reverently; respectfully. *Swift.*

DU'TIFULNESS, *n.* Obedience; submission to just authority; habitual performance of duty; as *dutifulness* to parents. *Dryden.*

2. Reverence; respect. *Taylor.*

DU'TY, *n.* [from *due*, Fr. *dû.*] That which a person owes to another; that which a person is bound, by any natural, moral or legal obligation, to pay, do or perform. Obedience to princes, magistrates and the laws is the *duty* of every citizen and subject; obedience, respect and kindness to parents are *duties* of children; fidelity to friends is a *duty*; reverence, obedience and prayer to God are indispensable *duties*; the government and religious instruction of children are *duties* of parents which they cannot neglect without guilt.

2. Forbearance of that which is forbid by morality, law, justice or propriety. It is our *duty* to refrain from lewdness, intemperance, profaneness and injustice.
3. Obedience; submission.
4. Act of reverence or respect.

They both did *duty* to their lady. *Spenser.*

5. The business of a soldier or marine on guard; as, the company is on *duty*. It is applied also to other services or labor.
6. The business of war; military service; as, the regiment did *duty* in Flanders.
7. Tax, toll, impost, or customs; excise; any sum of money required by government to be paid on the importation, exportation, or consumption of goods. An impost on land or other real estate, and on the stock of farmers, is not called a *duty*, but a *direct tax*. *U. States.*

DU'UMVIR, *n.* [L. *duo*, two and *vir*, man.] One of two Roman officers or magistrates united in the same public functions.

DUUM'VIRAL, *a.* Pertaining to the duumvirs or duumvirate of Rome.

DUUM'VIRATE, *n.* The union of two men in the same office; or the office, dignity or government of two men thus associated; as in ancient Rome.

DWALE, *n.* In *heraldry*, a sable or black color.

2. The deadly nightshade, a plant or a sleepy potion. *Chaucer.*

DWARF, *n.* [Sax. *dwerg, dweorg*; D. *dwerg*; Sw. *id.*; Dan. *dværg.*]

1. A general name for an animal or plant which is much below the ordinary size of the species or kind. A man that never grows beyond two or three feet in highth, is a *dwarf*. This word when used alone usually refers to the human species, but sometimes to other animals. When it is applied to plants, it is more generally used in composition; as a *dwarf-tree*; *dwarf-elder*.
2. An attendant on a lady or knight in romances. *Spenser.*

DWARF, *v. t.* To hinder from growing to the natural size; to lessen; to make or keep small. *Addison.*

DWARF'ISH, *a.* Like a dwarf; below the common stature or size; very small; low; petty; despicable; as a *dwarfish* animal; a *dwarfish* shrub. *Dryden.*

DWARF'ISHLY, *adv.* Like a dwarf.

DWARF'ISHNESS, *n.* Smallness of stature; littleness of size.

DWAUL, *v. i.* [Sax. *dwelian, dwolian*, to wander.] To be delirious. *Obs. Junius.*

DWELL, *v. i.* pret. *dwelled*, usually contracted into *dwelt*. [Dan. *dvæler*, to stay, wait, loiter, delay; Sw. *dvala*, a trance; *dvålias*, to delay, abide, remain or linger. Teut. *dualla*; Ice. *duelia*; Scot. *duel, dwell.* Qu. W. *attal, dal*, to hold, stop, stay, and Ir. *tuilim*, to sleep. This word coincides nearly with *dally*, in its primitive signification, and may be of the same family. Its radical sense is probably to *draw out in time*; hence, to hold, rest, remain. We see like senses united in many words, as in *teneo*, τεινω, *continue*. See *Dally* and Class Dl. No. 3. 5. 6. 21.]

1. To abide as a permanent resident, or to inhabit for a time; to live in a place; to have a habitation for some time or permanence.

God shall enlarge Japheth, and he shall *dwell* in the tents of Shem. Gen. ix.

Dwell imports a residence of some continuance. We use *abide* for the resting of a night or an hour; but we never say, he *dwelt* in a place a day or a night. *Dwell* may signify a residence for life or for a much shorter period, but not for a day. In scripture, it denotes a residence of seven days during the feast of tabernacles.

Ye shall *dwell* in booths seven days. Lev. xxiii.

The word was made flesh, and *dwelt* among us. John i.

2. To be in any state or condition; to continue.

To *dwell* in doubtful joy. *Shak.*

3. To continue; to be fixed in attention; to hang upon with fondness.

The attentive queen
Dwelt on his accents. *Smith.*

They stand at a distance, *dwelling* on his looks and language, fixed in amazement. *Buckminster.*

4. To continue long; as, to *dwell* on a subject, in speaking, debate or writing; to *dwell* on a note in music.

Dwell, as a verb transitive, is not used. We who *dwell* this wild, in Milton, is not a legitimate phrase.

DWELL'ER, *n.* An inhabitant; a resident of some continuance in a place. *Dryden.*

DWELL'ING, *ppr.* Inhabiting; residing; sojourning; continuing with fixed attention.

DWELL'ING, *n.* Habitation; place of residence; abode.

Hazor shall be a *dwelling* for dragons. Jer. xlix.

2. Continuance; residence; state of life.

Thy *dwelling* shall be with the beasts of the field. Dan. iv.

DWELL'ING-HOUSE, *n.* The house in which one lives.

DWELL'ING-PLACE, *n.* The place of residence.

DWIN'DLE, *v. i.* [Sax. *dwinan*, to pine, to vanish; Sw. *tvina*; G. *schwinden*. I suppose, formed on the root of *vain, vanish.*]

1. To diminish; to become less; to shrink; to waste or consume away. The body *dwindles* by pining or consumption; an estate *dwindles* by waste, by want of industry or economy; an object *dwindles* in size, as it recedes from view; an army *dwindles* by death or desertion.

Our drooping days have *dwindled* down to naught. *Thomson.*

2. To degenerate; to sink; to fall away.

Religious societies may *dwindle* into factious clubs. *Swift.*

DWIN'DLE, *v. t.* To make less; to bring low. *Thomson.*

2. To break; to disperse. *Clarendon.*

DWIN'DLED, *a.* Shrunk; diminished in size.

DWIN'DLING, *ppr.* Falling away; becoming less; pining; consuming; moldering away.

DYE, *v. t.* [Sax. *deagan*; L. *tingo*, for *tigo*; Gr. τεγγω; Fr. *teindre*, whence *tint, taint, attaint*; Sp. *teñir*; Port. *tingir*; It. *tignere*; Ar. طاخ taicha, to *dye* and to *die*. Class Dg. No. 40. The primary sense is to throw down, to dip, to plunge.]

To stain; to color; to give a new and permanent color to; applied particularly to cloth or the materials of cloth, as wool, cotton, silk and linen; also to hats, leather, &c. It usually expresses more or a deeper color than *tinge*.

DY'ED, *pp.* Stained; colored.

DY'EING, *ppr.* Staining; giving a new and permanent color.

DY'EING, *n.* The art or practice of giving new and permanent colors; the art of coloring cloth, hats, &c.

DY'ER, *n.* One whose occupation is to dye cloth and the like.

DY'ING, *ppr.* [from *die.*] Losing life; perishing; expiring; fading away; languishing.

2. *a.* Mortal; destined to death; as *dying* bodies.

DYNAM'ETER, *n.* [Gr. δυναμις, strength, and μετρεω, to measure.]

An instrument for determining the magnifying power of telescopes. *Ramsden.*

DYNAMET'RICAL. *a.* Pertaining to a dynameter.

DYNAM'ICAL, *a.* [Gr. δυναμις, power.] Pertaining to strength or power.

DYNAMOM'ETER, *n.* [See *Dynameter.*] An instrument for measuring the relative strength of men and other animals. *Ed. Encyc.*

DY'NAST, *n.* [See *Dynasty.*] A ruler; a governor; a prince; a government.

DYNAST'IC, *a.* Relating to a dynasty or line of kings.

DY'NASTY, *n.* [Gr. δυναςεια, power, sovereignty, from δυναςης, a lord or chief, from δυναμαι, to be able or strong, to prevail; Ir. *tanaiste*. The W. *dyn*, man, is probably from the same root. Class Dn.]

Government; sovereignty; or rather a race or succession of kings of the same line or family, who govern a particular country; as the *dynasties* of Egypt or Persia. *Encyc.*

The obligation of treaties and contracts is allowed to survive the change of *dynasties*. *E. Everett.*

DYS'CRASY, *n.* [Gr. δυσκρασια; δυς, evil, and κρασις, habit.]

In *medicine*, an ill habit or state of the humors; distemperature of the juices. *Coxe. Encyc.*

DYSENTER'IC, *a.* Pertaining to dysentery; accompanied with dysentery; proceeding from dysentery.

2. Afflicted with dysentery; as a *dysenteric* patient.

DYS'ENTERY, *n.* [L. *dysenteria*; Gr. δυσεντερια; δυς, bad, and εντερον, intestines.]

A flux in which the stools consist chiefly of blood and mucus or other morbid matter, accompanied with griping of the bowels, and followed by tenesmus. *Encyc.*

DYS'ODILE, *n.* A species of coal of a greenish or yellowish gray color, in masses composed of thin layers. When burning, it emits a very fetid odor. *Haüy. Cleaveland.*

DYS'OREXY, *n.* [Gr. δυς, bad and ορεξις, appetite.] A bad or depraved appetite; a want of appetite. *Coxe.*

DYSPEP'SY, *n.* [Gr. δυσπεψια; δυς, bad, and πεπτω, to concoct.] Bad digestion; indigestion, or difficulty of digestion. *Encyc. Coxe.*

DYSPEP'TIC, *a.* Afflicted with indigestion; as a *dyspeptic* person.

2. Pertaining to or consisting in dyspepsy; as a *dyspeptic* complaint.

DYS'PHONY, *n.* [Gr. δυσφωνια; δυς, bad, hard, and φωνη, voice.]

A difficulty of speaking, occasioned by an ill disposition of the organs of speech. *Dict.*

DYSPNOE'A, *n.* [Gr. δυσπνοια.] A difficulty of breathing. *Coxe.*

DYS'URY, *n.* [Gr. δυσουρια; δυς and ουρον, urine.]

Difficulty in discharging the urine, attended with pain and a sensation of heat. *Encyc.*

E.

E, the second vowel and the fifth letter of the English Alphabet, seems to be the ancient Phenician and Hebrew ﬧ inverted, corresponding nearly with the Chaldaic and later Hebrew ה. Its long and natural sound in English coincides with the sound of *i* in the Italian and French languages, and is formed by a narrower opening of the glottis than that of *a*. It has a long sound, as in *here, mere, me*; a short sound, as in *met, men*; and the sound of *a* open or long, in *there, prey, vein*. As a final letter, it is generally quiescent; but it serves to lengthen the sound of the preceding vowel, or at least to indicate that the preceding vowel is to have its long sound, as in *mane, cane, plume*, which, without the final *e*, would be pronounced *man, can, plum*. After *c* and *g*, the final *e* serves to change these letters from hard to soft, or to indicate that *c* is to be pronounced as *s*, and *g*, as *j*. Thus without the final *e*, in *mace* [mase,] this word would be pronounced *mac* [mak,] and *rage* [raj] would be pronounced *rag*. In a numerous class of words, indeed in almost every word, except a few from the Greek, the final *e* is silent, serving no purpose whatever, unless to show from what language we have received the words, and in many cases, it does not answer this purpose. In words ending in *ive*, as *active*; in *ile*, as *futile*; in *ine*, as in *sanguine, examine*; in *ite* as in *definite*; *e* is, for the most part, silent. In some of these words, the use of *e* is borrowed from the French; in most or all cases, it is not authorized by the Latin originals; it is worse than useless, as it leads to a wrong pronunciation; and the retaining of it in such words is, beyond measure, absurd.

When two of this vowel occur together, the sound is the same as that of the single *e* long, as in *deem, esteem, need*; and it occurs often with *a* and *i*, as in *mean, hear, siege, deceive*, in which cases, when one vowel only has a sound, the combination I call a digraph [*double written.*] In these combinations, the sound is usually that of *e* long, but sometimes the short sound of *e*, as in *lĕad*, a metal, *rĕad*, pret. of *rēad*, and sometimes the sound of *a* long, as in *rein, feign*, pronounced *rane, fane*. Irregularities of this kind are not reducible to rules.

As a numeral, E stands for 250. In the calendar, it is the fifth of the dominical letters. As an abbreviation, it stands for *East*, as in charts; E. by S., East by South.

EACH, *a.* [Scot. *eik*. This word is either a contraction of the Sax. *ælc, elc*, D. *elk*, or the Ir. *ceach*, or *gach*, Basque, *gucia*, Fr. *chaque*, with the loss of the first articulation. With the Celtic corresponds the Russ. *kajdei*, each. I am inclined to believe both the English and Scottish words to be contractions of the Celtic *ceach*.]

Every one of any number separately considered or treated.

To all of them he gave *each* man changes of raiment. Gen. xlv.

And the princes of Israel, being twelve men, *each* one was for the house of his fathers. Num. i.

Simeon and Levi took *each* man his sword. Gen. xxxiv.

The emperor distributed to *each* soldier in his army a liberal donative.

To *each* corresponds *other*. Let *each* esteem *other* better than himself. It is our duty to assist *each other*; that is, it is our duty to assist, *each* to assist the *other*.

E'ACHWHERE, *adv.* Every where. *Obs.*

EAD, ED, in names, is a Saxon word signifying happy, fortunate; as in *Edward*, happy preserver; *Edgar*, happy power; *Edwin*, happy conqueror; *Eadulph*, happy assistance; like *Macarius* and *Eupolemus* in Greek, and *Fausta*, *Fortunatus*, *Felicianus*, in Latin. *Gibson.*

E'AGER, *a.* [Er. *aigre*; Arm. *egr*; W. *egyr*; It. *agro*; Sp. *agrio*; L. *acer*, fierce, brisk, sharp, sour. If *r* is radical, this word belongs to Class Gr. Ir. *gear*, *geire*, sharp; Ger. *gier*. Otherwise, it coincides with L. *acus*, Eng. *edge*, Sax. *ecg*.]

1. Excited by ardent desire in the pursuit of any object; ardent to pursue, perform or obtain; inflamed by desire; ardently wishing or longing. The soldiers were *eager* to engage the enemy. Men are *eager* in the pursuit of wealth. The lover is *eager* to possess the object of his affections.
2. Ardent; vehement; impetuous; as *eager* spirits; *eager* zeal; *eager* clamors.
3. Sharp; sour; acid; as *eager* droppings into milk. [*Little used.*] *Shak.*
4. Sharp; keen; biting; severe; as *eager* air; *eager* cold. [*Little used.*] *Shak. Bacon.*
5. Brittle; inflexible; not ductile; as, the gold is too *eager*. [*Local.*] *Locke.*

E'AGERLY, *adv.* With great ardor of desire; ardently; earnestly; warmly; with prompt zeal; as, he *eagerly* flew to the assistance of his friend.

2. Hastily; impetuously.
3. Keenly; sharply.

E'AGERNESS, *n.* Ardent desire to do, pursue or obtain any thing; animated zeal; vehement longing; ardor of inclination. Men pursue honor with *eagerness*. Detraction is often received with *eagerness*. With *eagerness* the soldier rushes to battle. The lover's *eagerness* often disappoints his hopes.

2. Tartness; sourness. *Obs.*

E'AGLE, *n.* [Fr. *aigle*; Sp. *aguila*; It. *aquila*; L. *aquila*. Qu. from his beak, Ch. Heb. עקל to be crooked, [see *Buxtorf*,] or Pers. اجل.]

1. A rapacious fowl of the genus Falco. The beak is crooked and furnished with a cere at the base, and the tongue is cloven or bifid. There are several species, as the bald or white-headed eagle, the sea eagle or ossifrage, the golden eagle, &c.

The eagle is one of the largest species of fowls, has a keen sight, and preys on small animals, fish, &c. He lives to a great age; and it is said that one died at Vienna, after a confinement of a hundred and four years. On account of the elevation and rapidity of his flight, and of his great strength, he is called the king of birds. Hence the figure of an eagle was made the standard of the Romans, and a spread eagle is a principal figure in the arms of the United States of America. Hence also in heraldry, it is one of the most noble bearings in armory.

2. A gold coin of the United States, of the value of ten dollars, or forty-five shillings sterling.
3. A constellation in the northern hemisphere, having its right wing contiguous to the equinoctial. *Encyc.*

E'AGLE-EYED, *a.* Sharpsighted as an eagle; having an acute sight. *Dryden.*

2. Discerning; having acute intellectual vision.

E'AGLE-SIGHTED, *a.* Having acute sight. *Shak.*

E'AGLE-SPEED, *n.* Swiftness like that of an eagle. *Pope.*

E'AGLESS, *n.* A female or hen eagle.

E'AGLE-STONE, *n.* Etite, a variety of argillaceous oxyd of iron, occurring in masses varying from the size of a walnut to that of a man's head. Their form is spherical, oval or nearly reniform, or sometimes like a parallelopiped with rounded edges and angles. They have a rough surface, and are essentially composed of concentric layers. These nodules often embrace at the center a kernel or nucleus, sometimes movable, and always differing from the exterior in color, density and fracture. To these hollow nodules the ancients gave the name of *eagle-stones*, from an opinion that the eagle transported them to her nest to facilitate the laying of her eggs. *Cleaveland.*

E'AGLET, *n.* A young eagle or a diminutive eagle.

E'AGLE-WINGED, *a.* Having the wings of an eagle; swift as an eagle. *Milton.*

EA'GRE, *n.* A tide swelling above another tide, as in the Severn. *Dryden.*

EALDERMAN. [See *Alderman*.]

EAME, *n.* [Sax. *eam*.] Uncle. *Obs.* *Spenser.*

EAN, *v. t.* or *i.* To yean. [See *Yean*.]

E'ANLING, *n.* A lamb just brought forth. [*Not used.*]

E'AR, *n.* [Sax. *ear*, *eare*; D. *oor*; Sw. *öra*; Dan. *öre*; G. *ohr* or *öhr*; L. *auris*, whence *auricula*, Fr. *oreille*, Sp. *oreja*, Port. *orelha*, It. *orecchio*. The sense is probably a shoot or limb. It may be connected with *hear*, as the L. *audio* is with the Gr. ους, ωτος.]

1. The organ of hearing; the organ by which sound is perceived; and in general, both the external and internal part is understood by the term. The external ear is a cartilaginous funnel, attached, by ligaments and muscles, to the temporal bone. *Encyc.*
2. The sense of hearing, or rather the power of distinguishing sounds and judging of harmony; the power of nice perception of the differences of sound, or of consonances and dissonances. She has a delicate *ear* for music, or a good *ear*.
3. In *the plural*, the head or person.

It is better to pass over an affront from one scoundrel, than to draw a herd about one's *ears*. *L'Estrange.*

4. The top, or highest part.

The cavalier was up to the *ears* in love. [*Low.*] *L'Estrange.*

5. A favorable hearing; attention; heed; regard. Give no *ear* to flattery.

I cried to God—and he gave *ear* to me. Ps. lxxvii.

He could not gain the prince's *ear*.

6. Disposition to like or dislike what is heard; opinion; judgment; taste.

He laid his sense closer—according to the style and *ear* of those times. *Denham.*

7. Any part of a thing resembling an ear; a projecting part from the side of any thing; as the *ears* of a vessel used as handles.
8. The spike of corn; that part of certain plants which contains the flowers and seeds; as an *ear* of wheat or maiz.

To be by the ears,
To fall together by the ears, } to fight or scuffle; to quarrel.
To go together by the ears,

To set by the ears, to make strife; to cause to quarrel.

EAR, *v. i.* To shoot, as an ear; to form ears, as corn.

EAR, *v. t.* [L. *aro.*] To plow or till. *Obs.*

E'ARABLE, *a.* Used to be tilled. *Obs.* *Barret.*

E'ARACHE, *n.* [See *Ache*.] Pain in the ear.

E'ARAL, *a.* Receiving by the ear. [*Not used.*] *Hewyt.*

E'AR-BORED, *a.* Having the ear perforated. *Hall.*

E'AR-DEAFENING, *a.* Stunning the ear with noise. *Shak.*

E'ARED, *pp.* Having ears; having spikes formed, as corn.

EAR-ERECT'ING, *a.* Setting up the ears. *Cowper.*

E'ARING, *n.* In *seamen's language*, a small rope employed to fasten the upper corner of a sail to its yard.

E'ARING, *n.* A plowing of land. Gen. xliv.

E'ARLAP, *n.* The tip of the ear.

E'ARLOCK, *n.* [Sax. *ear-loca*.] A lock or curl of hair, near the ear.

E'ARMARK, *n.* A mark on the ear, by which a sheep is known.

E'ARMARK, *v. t.* To mark, as sheep by cropping or slitting the ear.

E'ARPICK, *n.* An instrument for cleansing the ear.

E'AR-PIERCING, *a.* Piercing the ear, as a shrill or sharp sound. *Shak.*

E'ARRING, *n.* A pendant; an ornament, sometimes set with diamonds, pearls or other jewels, worn at the ear, by means of a ring passing through the lobe.

E'ARSHOT, *n.* Reach of the ear; the distance at which words may be heard. *Dryden.*

E'ARWAX, *n.* The cerumen; a thick viscous substance, secreted by the glands of the ear into the outer passage. *Encyc.*

E'ARWIG, *n.* [Sax. *ear-wigga*, *ear-wicga*; ear and worm or grub.]

A genus of insects of the order of Coleopters. The antennæ are bristly; the elytra dimidiated; the wings covered; and the tail forked. This animal is called in Latin *forficula*, from the forceps at the end of the abdomen. The English name was given to it from an ill founded notion that the animal creeps into the ear and causes injury.

In New England, this name is vulgarly given to a species of centiped.

E'AR-WITNESS, *n.* One who is able to give testimony to a fact from his own hearing. *Watts.*

EARL, *n. erl.* [Sax. *eorl;* Ir. *iarla*, an earl; *earlamh*, noble. This word is said to have been received from the Danes, although not now used in Denmark. Formerly this title among the Danes was equivalent to the English *alderman*. *Spelman.*]

A British title of nobility, or a nobleman, the third in rank, being next below a marquis, and next above a viscount. The title answers to *count* [*compte*] in France, and *graaf* in Germany. The earl formerly had the government of a *shire*, and was called *shireman*. After the conquest earls were called counts, and from them shires have taken the name of *counties*. *Earl* is now a mere title, unconnected with territorial jurisdiction. *Spelman. Encyc.*

EARLDOM, *n. erl'dom.* The seignory, jurisdiction or dignity of an earl.

EARL-M'ARSHAL, *n.* An officer in Great Britain, who has the superintendence of military solemnities. He is the eighth great officer of state. The office was originally conferred by grant of the king, but is now hereditary in the family of the Howards. *Encyc.*

EARLES-PENNY, *n.* Money given in part payment. [Qu. L. *arrha.*] [*Not in use.*]

E'ARLESS, *a.* Destitute of ears; disinclined to hear or listen.

EARLINESS, *n. er'liness.* [See *Early* and *Ere.*]

A state of advance or forwardness; a state of being before any thing, or at the beginning; as the *earliness* of rising in the morning is a rising at the dawn of the morning, or before the usual time of rising. So we speak of the *earliness* of spring, or the *earliness* of plants, to express a state somewhat in advance of the usual time of spring, or growth of plants.

EARLY, *a. er'ly.* [from Sax. *ær, er*, before in time, Eng. *ere*, which indicates the root of the word to signify, to advance, to pass along or shoot up. It is probably connected with the D. *eer*, G. *ehre*, Sw. *åhra*, Dan. *ære*, honor, denoting the highest point.]

1. In advance of something else; prior in time; forward; as *early* fruit, that is, fruit that comes to maturity before other fruit; *early* growth; *early* manhood; *early* old age or decrepitude, that is, premature old age. So an *early* spring; an *early* harvest.
2. First; being at the beginning; as *early* dawn.
3. Being in good season; as, the court met at an *early* hour.

EARLY, *adv. er'ly.* Soon; in good season; betimes; as, rise *early;* come *early;* begin *early* to instill into children principles of piety.

Those who seek me *early* shall find me. Prov. viii.

EARN, *v. t. ern.* [Sax. *earnian, ærnian, gearnian*, to earn, to merit. It is connected in origin with *earnest* and *yearn*, which see. The primary sense is to strive or urge, implying an effort to advance or stretch forward.]

1. To merit or deserve by labor, or by any performance; to do that which entitles to a reward, whether the reward is received or not. Men often *earn* money or honor which they never receive.

   Earn money before you spend it, and spend less than you *earn.*

2. To gain by labor, service or performance; to deserve and receive as compensation; as, to *earn* a dollar a day; to *earn* a good living; to *earn* honors or laurels.

EARNED, *pp. ern'ed.* Merited by labor or performance; gained.

EARNEST, *a. ern'est.* [Sax. *eornest*, or *geornest*, from *georn*, desirous, studious, diligent, assiduous, whence *geornian, gyrnan*, to desire, to *yearn;* Dan. *gierne*, willingly, freely, gladly, cheerfully; *gierning*, a deed, act, exploit; Ger. *ernst;* D. *ernst;* W. *ern*, earnest-money. The radical sense is to strive to advance, to reach forward, to urge, to strain.]

1. Ardent in the pursuit of an object; eager to obtain; having a longing desire; warmly engaged or incited.

   They are never more *earnest* to disturb us, than when they see us most *earnest* in this duty. *Duppa.*

2. Ardent; warm; eager; zealous; animated; importunate; as *earnest* in love; *earnest* in prayer.
3. Intent; fixed.

   On that prospect strange
   Their *earnest* eyes were fixed. *Milton.*

4. Serious; important; that is, really intent or engaged; whence the phrase, *in earnest*. To *be in earnest*, is to be really urging or stretching towards an object; intent on a pursuit. Hence, from fixed attention, comes the sense of *seriousness* in the pursuit, as opposed to trifling or jest. Are you *in earnest* or *in jest?*

EARNEST, *n. ern'est.* Seriousness; a reality; a real event; as opposed to jesting or feigned appearance.

Take heed that this jest do not one day turn to *earnest.* *Sidney.*

And given *in earnest* what I begg'd in jest. *Shak.*

2. First fruits; that which is in advance, and gives promise of something to come. Early fruit may be an *earnest* of fruit to follow. The first success in arms may be an *earnest* of future success. The christian's peace of mind in this life is an *earnest* of future peace and happiness. Hence *earnest* or *earnest-money* is a first payment or deposit giving promise or assurance of full payment. Hence the practice of giving an *earnest* to ratify a bargain.

This sense of the word is primary, denoting that which goes before, or in advance. Thus the *earnest* of the spirit is given to saints, as a pledge or assurance of their future enjoyment of God's presence and favor.

EARNESTLY, *adv. ern'estly.* Warmly; zealously; importunately; eagerly; with real desire.

Being in an agony, he prayed more *earnestly.* Luke xxii.

That ye should *earnestly* contend for the faith once delivered to the saints. Jude 3.

2. With fixed attention; with eagerness.

   A certain maid looked *earnestly* upon him. Luke xxii.

EARNESTNESS, *n. ern'estness.* Ardor or zeal in the pursuit of any thing; eagerness; animated desire; as, to seek or ask with *earnestness;* to engage in a work with *earnestness.*

2. Anxious care; solicitude; intenseness of desire. *Dryden.*
3. Fixed desire or attention; seriousness; as, the charge was maintained with a show of gravity and *earnestness.*

EARNFUL, *a. ern'ful:* Full of anxiety. [*Not used.*] *Fletcher.*

EARNING, *ppr. ern'ing.* Meriting by services; gaining by labor or performance.

EARNING, *n. ern'ing.* plu. *earnings.* That which is earned; that which is gained or merited by labor, services or performance; wages; reward. The folly of young men is to spend their *earnings* in dissipation or extravagance. It is wise for the poor to invest their *earnings* in a productive fund.

EARSH, *n.* [See *Ear*, to plow.] A plowed field. [*Not in use.*] *May.*

EARTH, *n. erth.* [Sax. *eard, eorth, yrth;* D. *aarde;* G. *erde;* Sw. *iord, jord;* Dan. *iord;* Scot. *erd, yerd, yerth;* Turk. *jerda;* Tartaric, *yirda*. It coincides with the Heb. ארץ. The Ar. أَرْضٌ aratza, from which the Arabic and Hebrew words corresponding to the Teutonic above, are derived, signifies to eat, gnaw or corrode as a worm, or the teredo. It is obvious then that the primary sense of *earth* is fine particles, like *mold*. The verb may be from רצץ to break or bruise. The Ch. and Syr. ארעא earth, may be contracted from the same word. See *Corrode*. It is by no means improbable that *aro*, to plow, may be contracted from the same root.]

1. Earth, in its primary sense, signifies the particles which compose the mass of the globe, but more particularly the particles which form the fine mold on the surface of the globe; or it denotes any indefinite mass or portion of that matter. We throw up *earth* with a spade or plow; we fill a pit or ditch with *earth;* we form a rampart with *earth*. This substance being considered, by ancient philosophers, as simple, was called an element; and in popular language, we still hear of the four elements, *fire, air, earth* and *water.*
2. In *chimistry*, the term earth was, till lately, employed to denote a simple elementary body or substance, tasteless, inodorous, uninflammable and infusible. But it has also been applied to substances which have a very sensible alkaline taste, as lime. The primitive earths are reckoned ten in number, viz., *silex, alumin, lime, magnesia, baryte, strontian, zircon, glucin, yttria* and *thorina*. Recent experiments prove that most or all of them are compounds of oxygen with bases, some of which appear to possess the properties of metals. In this case the earths are to be considered as metallic oxyds. *Davy. Silliman. Phillips.*

3. The terraqueous globe which we inhabit. The earth is nearly spherical, but a little flatted at the poles, and hence its figure is called an *oblate spheroid*. It is one of the primary planets, revolving round the sun in an orbit which is between those of Venus and Mars. It is nearly eight thousand miles in diameter, and twenty five thousand miles in circumference. Its distance from the sun is about ninety five millions of miles, and its annual revolution constitutes the year of 365 days, 5 hours, and nearly 49 minutes.

4. The world, as opposed to other scenes of existence. *Shak.*

5. The inhabitants of the globe.

The whole *earth* was of one language. Gen. xi.

6. Dry land, opposed to the sea.

God called the dry land *earth*. Gen. i.

7. Country; region; a distinct part of the globe. *Dryden.*

In this sense, *land* or *soil* is more generally used.

In scripture, *earth* is used for a part of the world. Ezra i. 2.

8. The ground; the surface of the earth. He fell to the *earth*. The ark was lifted above the *earth*.

In the second month—was the *earth* dried. Gen. viii.

9. In scripture, *things on the earth*, are carnal, sensual, temporary things; opposed to heavenly, spiritual or divine things.

10. Figuratively, a low condition. Rev. xii.

11. [from *ear*, Sax. *erian*, L. *aro*, to plow.] The act of turning up the ground in tillage. [*Not used.*] *Tusser.*

EARTH, *v. t.* To hide in the earth.

The fox is *earthed*. *Dryden.*

2. To cover with earth or mold. *Evelyn.*

EARTH, *v. i.* To retire under ground; to burrow. Here foxes *earthed.*

EARTH'BAG, *n.* A bag filled with earth, used for defense in war.

EARTH'BANK, *n.* A bank or mound of earth.

EARTH'BŌARD, *n.* The board of a plow that turns over the earth; the mold-board.

EARTH'BORN, *a.* Born of the earth; terrigenous; springing originally from the earth; as the fabled *earthborn* giants.

2. Earthly; terrestrial.

All *earthborn* cares are wrong. *Goldsmith.*

EARTH'BOUND, *a.* Fastened by the pressure of the earth. *Shak.*

EARTH'BRED, *a.* Low; abject; groveling.

EARTH-CREA'TED, *a.* Formed of earth. *Young.*

EARTH'EN, *a.* erth'n. Made of earth; made of clay; as an *earthen* vessel; *earthen* ware.

EARTH'FED, *a.* Low; abject. *B. Jonson.*

EARTH'FLAX, *n.* Amianth; a fibrous, flexile, elastic mineral substance, consisting of short interwoven, or long parallel filaments. *Encyc.*

EARTH'INESS, *n.* The quality of being earthy, or of containing earth; grossness. *Johnson.*

EARTH'LINESS, *n.* [from *earthly.*] The quality of being earthly; grossness.

2. Worldliness; strong attachment to worldly things.

EARTH'LING, *n.* An inhabitant of the earth; a mortal; a frail creature. *Drummond.*

EARTH'LY, *a.* Pertaining to the earth, or to this world.

Our *earthly* house of this tabernacle. 2 Cor. v.

2. Not heavenly; vile; mean.

This *earthly* load
Of death called life. *Milton.*

3. Belonging to our present state; as *earthly* objects; *earthly* residence.

4. Belonging to the earth or world; carnal; vile; as opposed to spiritual or heavenly.

Whose glory is in their shame, who mind *earthly* things. Phil. iii.

5. Corporeal; not mental. *Spenser.*

EARTHLY-MINDED, *a.* Having a mind devoted to earthly things.

EARTHLY-MINDEDNESS, *n.* Grossness; sensuality; extreme devotedness to earthly objects. *Gregory.*

EARTH'NUT, *n.* The groundnut, or root of the Arachis; a small round bulb or knob, like a nut. This root or bulb is formed from the germen, which becomes a pod and is thrust into the ground by a natural motion of the stalk. *Encyc.*

It is properly the fruit of the plant, and differs from other fruit only in the circumstance of ripening in the earth.

EARTH'NUT, *n.* The pignut, or *bunium*; a globular root, somewhat resembling in taste a chesnut, whence it is called *bulbocastanum.* *Encyc.*

EARTH'QUAKE, *n.* A shaking, trembling or concussion of the earth; sometimes a slight tremor; at other times a violent shaking or convulsion; at other times a rocking or heaving of the earth. Earthquakes are usually preceded by a rattling sound in the air, or by a subterraneous rumbling noise. Hence the name, *earthdin*, formerly given to an earthquake.

EARTH'SHAKING, *a.* Shaking the earth; having power to shake the earth. *Milton.*

EARTH'WŌRM, *n.* The dew worm, a species of Lumbricus; a worm that lives under ground. *Encyc.*

2. A mean sordid wretch.

EARTH'Y, *a.* Consisting of earth; as *earthy* matter.

2. Resembling earth; as an *earthy* taste or smell.

3. Partaking of earth; terrene. *Milton.*

4. Inhabiting the earth; terrestrial; as *earthy* spirits. *Dryden.*

5. Relating to earth; as an *earthy* sign. *Dryden.*

6. Gross; not refined; as an *earthy* conceit. *Shak.*

7. *Earthy fracture*, in mineralogy, is when the fracture of a mineral is rough, with minute elevations and depressions. *Cleaveland.*

EASE, *n.* *s* as *z.* [Fr. *aise*; Arm. *aez*; W. *hawz*; Corn. *hedh*; Sax. *æth* or *eath*, easy; L. *otium*; It. *agio*; Ir. *easgaidh.*]

1. Rest; an undisturbed state. *Applied to the body*, freedom from pain, disturbance, excitement or annoyance. He sits at his *ease*. He takes his *ease*.

2. *Applied to the mind*, a quiet state; tranquillity; freedom from pain, concern, anxiety, solicitude, or any thing that frets or ruffles the mind.

His soul shall dwell at *ease*. Ps. xxv.

Wo to them that are at *ease* in Zion. Amos vi.

3. Rest from labor.

4. Facility; freedom from difficulty or great labor. One man will perform this service with *ease*. This author writes with *ease*.

5. Freedom from stiffness, harshness, forced expressions, or unnatural arrangement; as the *ease* of style.

6. Freedom from constraint or formality; unaffectedness; as *ease* of behavior.

At ease, in an undisturbed state; free from pain or anxiety.

EASE, *v. t.* To free from pain or any disquiet or annoyance, *as the body;* to relieve; to give rest to; as, the medicine has *eased* the patient.

2. To free from anxiety, care or disturbance, *as the mind;* as, the late news has *eased* my mind.

3. To remove a burden from, either of body or mind; to relieve; with *of.* *Ease* me *of* this load; *ease* them *of* their burdens.

4. To mitigate; to alleviate; to assuage; to abate or remove in part any burden, pain, grief, anxiety or disturbance.

Ease thou somewhat the grievous servitude of thy father. 2 Chron. x.

5. To quiet; to allay; to destroy; as, to *ease* pain.

To ease off or *ease away*, in seamen's language, is to slacken a rope gradually.

To ease a ship, is to put the helm hard alee, to prevent her pitching, when close hauled. *Mar. Dict.*

E'ASEFŲL, *a.* Quiet; peaceful; fit for rest. *Shak.*

E'ASEFŲLLY, *adv.* With ease or quiet. *Sherwood.*

E'ASEL, *n.* The frame on which painters place their canvas.

Easel-pieces, among painters, are the smaller pieces, either portraits or landscapes, which are painted on the easel, as distinguished from those which are drawn on walls, ceilings, &c. *Encyc.* *Chalmers.*

E'ASEMENT, *n.* Convenience; accommodation; that which gives ease, relief or assistance.

He has the advantage of a free lodging, and some other *easements*. *Swift.*

2. In *law*, any privilege or convenience which one man has of another, either by prescription or charter, without profit; as a way through his land, &c. *Encyc.* *Cowel.*

E'ASILY, *adv.* [from *easy.*] Without difficulty or great labor; without great exertion, or sacrifice of labor or expense; as, this task may be *easily* performed; that event might have been *easily* foreseen.

2. Without pain, anxiety or disturbance; in tranquillity; as, to pass life well and *easily*. *Temple.*

3. Readily; without the pain of reluctance.

Not soon provoked, she *easily* forgives. *Prior.*

4. Smoothly; quietly; gently; without tumult or discord.

5. Without violent shaking or jolting; as, a carriage moves *easily.*

E'ASINESS, *n.* Freedom from difficulty; ease.

Easiness and difficulty are relative terms. *Tillotson.*

2. Flexibility; readiness to comply; prompt

compliance; a yielding or disposition to yield without opposition or reluctance.

Give to him, and he shall but laugh at your *easiness*. *South.*

So we say, a man's *easiness* of temper is remarkable.

3. Freedom from stiffness, constraint, effort or formality; *applied to manners or to the style of writing.* *Roscommon.*
4. Rest; tranquillity; ease; freedom from pain. *Ray.*
5. Freedom from shaking or jolting, as of a moving vehicle.
6. Softness; as the *easiness* of a seat.

EAST, *n.* [Sax. *east*; D. *oost, oosten*; G. *ost*; Sw. *ost, osten*; Dan. *öst, östen*; Fr. *est.* If the radical sense coincides with that of the L. *oriens*, this word may belong to the root of *hoise, hoist.*]

1. The point in the heavens, where the sun is seen to rise at the equinox, or when it is in the equinoctial, or the corresponding point on the earth; one of the four cardinal points. The east and the west are the points where the equator intersects the horizon. But to persons under the equinoctial line, that line constitutes east and west.
2. The eastern parts of the earth; the regions or countries which lie east of Europe, or other country. In this indefinite sense, the word is applied to Asia Minor, Syria, Chaldea, Persia, India, China, &c. We speak of the riches of the *east*, the diamonds and pearls of the *east*, the kings of the *east.*

The gorgeous *east*, with richest hand,
Pours on her kings barbaric, pearl and gold. *Milton.*

EAST, *a.* Towards the rising sun; or towards the point where the sun rises, when in the equinoctial; as the *east* gate; the *east* border; the *east* side. The *east* wind is a wind that blows from the east.

E'ASTER, *n.* [Sax. *easter*; G. *ostern*; supposed to be from *Eostre*, the goddess of love or Venus of the north, in honor of whom a festival was celebrated by our pagan ancestors, in April; whence this month was called *Eostermonath.* *Eoster* is supposed by Beda and others to be the *Astarte* of the Sidonians. See Beda, Cluver, and the authorities cited by Cluver, and by Jamieson, under *Paysyad.* But query.]

A festival of the christian church observed in commemoration of our Savior's resurrection. It answers to the pascha or passover of the Hebrews, and most nations still give it this name, *pascha, pask, paque.*

E'ASTERLING, *n.* A native of some country eastward of another. *Spenser.*

2. A species of waterfowl. *Johnson.*

E'ASTERLY, *a.* Coming from the eastward; as an *easterly* wind.

2. Situated towards the east; as the *easterly* side of a lake or country.
3. Towards the east; as, to move in an *easterly* direction.
4. Looking towards the east; as an *easterly* exposure.

E'ASTERLY, *adv.* On the east; in the direction of east.

E'ASTERN, *a.* [Sax. *eastern.*] Oriental; being or dwelling in the east; as *eastern* kings; *eastern* countries; *eastern* nations.

2. Situated towards the east; on the east part; as the *eastern* side of a town or church; the *eastern* gate.
3. Going towards the east, or in the direction of east; as an *eastern* voyage.

E'ASTWARD, *adv.* [*east* and *ward.*] Toward the east; in the direction of east from some point or place. New Haven lies *eastward* from New York. Turn your eyes *eastward.*

E'ASY, *a.* *s* as *z.* [See *Ease.*] Quiet; being at rest; free from pain, disturbance or annoyance. The patient has slept well and is *easy.*

2. Free from anxiety, care, solicitude or peevishness; quiet; tranquil; as an *easy* mind.
3. Giving no pain or disturbance; as an *easy* posture; an *easy* carriage.
4. Not difficult; that gives or requires no great labor or exertion; that presents no great obstacles; as an *easy* task. It is often more *easy* to resolve, than to execute.

Knowledge is *easy* to him that understandeth. Prov. xiv.

5. Not causing labor or difficulty. An *easy* ascent or slope, is a slope rising with a small angle.
6. Smooth; not uneven; not rough or very hilly; that may be traveled with ease; as an *easy* road.
7. Gentle; moderate; not pressing; as a ship under *easy* sail.
8. Yielding with little or no resistance; complying; credulous.

With such deceits he gained their *easy* hearts. *Dryden.*

9. Ready; not unwilling; as *easy* to forgive. *Dryden.*
10. Contented; satisfied. Allow hired men wages that will make them *easy.*
11. Giving ease; freeing from labor, care or the fatigue of business; furnishing abundance without toil; affluent; as *easy* circumstances; an *easy* fortune.
12. Not constrained; not stiff or formal; as *easy* manners; an *easy* address; *easy* movements in dancing.
13. Smooth; flowing; not harsh; as an *easy* style.
14. Not jolting; as, the horse has an *easy* gait.
15. Not heavy or burdensome.

My yoke is *easy*, and my burden light. Matt. xi.

EAT, *v. t.* pret. *ate*; pp. *eat* or *eaten.* [Sax. *hitan, eatan, ytan* and *etan*; Goth. *itan*; Dan. *æder*; Sw. *äta*; D. *eeten*, pp. *gegeeten*; G. *essen*, pp. *gegessen*; Russ. *ida, iada*, the act of eating; L. *edo, esse, esum*; Gr. *εδω*; W. *ysu*; Ir. *ithim, itheadh*; Sans. *ada.* The Dutch and German, with the prefix *ge*, form the pass. part. *gegeeten, gegessen*, which indicates that the original was *geeten, gessen.* Class Gd or Gs, in which there are several roots from which this word may be deduced. *Etch* is from the same root.]

1. To bite or chew and swallow, as food. Men *eat* flesh and vegetables.

They shall make thee to *eat* grass as oxen. Dan. iv.

2. To corrode; to wear away; to separate parts of a thing gradually, as an animal by gnawing. We say a cancer *eats* the flesh.
3. To consume; to waste.

When goods increase, they are increased that *eat* them. Ecc. v.

4. To enjoy.

If ye be willing and obedient, ye shall *eat* the good of the land. Is. i.

5. To consume; to oppress.

Who *eat* up my people as they eat bread. Ps. xiv.

6. To feast.

Let us *eat* and drink, for to-morrow we shall die. Is. xxii.

In scripture, to *eat* the flesh of Christ, is to believe on him and be nourished by faith.

To eat one's words, is to swallow back; to take back what has been uttered; to retract. *Hudibras.*

EAT, *v. i.* To take food; to feed; to take a meal, or to board.

He did *eat* continually at the king's table. 2 Sam.

Why *eateth* your master with publicans and sinners. Matt. ix.

2. To take food; to be maintained in food.

To eat, or *to eat in* or *into*, is to make way by corrosion; to gnaw; to enter by gradually wearing or separating the parts of a substance. A cancer *eats into* the flesh.

Their word will *eat* as doth a canker. 2 Tim. ii.

To eat out, to consume.

Their word will *eat out* the vitals of religion, corrupt and destroy it. *Anon.*

E'ATABLE, *a.* That may be eaten; fit to be eaten; proper for food; esculent.

E'ATABLE, *n.* Any thing that may be eaten; that which is fit for food; that which is used as food.

E'ATEN, *pp.* *ee'tn.* Chewed and swallowed; consumed; corroded.

E'ATER, *n.* One who eats; that which eats or corrodes; a corrosive.

EATH, *a.* easy, and *adv.* easily. *Obs.*

E'ATING, *ppr*, Chewing and swallowing; consuming; corroding.

E'ATING-HOUSE, *n.* A house where provisions are sold ready dressed.

EAVES, *n. plu.* [Sax. *efese.* In English the word has a plural ending; but not in Saxon.]

The edge or lower border of the roof of a building, which overhangs the walls, and casts off the water that falls on the roof.

E'AVES-DROP, *v. i.* [*eaves* and *drop.*] To stand under the eaves or near the windows of a house, to listen and learn what is said within doors. *Milton.*

E'AVES-DROPPER, *n.* One who stands under the eaves or near the window or door of a house, to listen and hear what is said within doors, whether from curiosity, or for the purpose of tattling and making mischief. *Shak.*

EBB, *n.* [Sax. *ebbe, ebba*; G. and D. *ebbe*; Dan. *id.*; Sw. *ebb.*]

The reflux of the tide; the return of tide-water towards the sea; opposed to *flood* or flowing.

2. Decline; decay; a falling from a better to a worse state; as the *ebb* of life; the *ebb* of prosperity.

EBB, *v. i.* [Sax. *ebban*; D. *ebben*; W. *eb*, to go from.]

To flow back; to return as the water of a tide towards the ocean; opposed to *flow*. The tide *ebbs* and flows twice in twenty four hours.

2. To decay; to decline; to return or fall back from a better to a worse state. *Shak. Halifax.*

EBB'ING, *ppr.* Flowing back; declining; decaying.

EBB'ING, *n.* The reflux of the tide.

EBB'TIDE, *n.* The reflux of tide-water; the retiring tide.

EB'IONITE, *n.* The Ebionites were heretics who denied the divinity of Christ and rejected many parts of the scriptures.

EB'ON, *a.* [See *Ebony.*] Consisting of ebony; like ebony; black.

EB'ONIZE, *v. t.* [See *Ebony.*] To make black or tawny; to tinge with the color of ebony; as, to *ebonize* the fairest complexion. *Walsh.*

EB'ONY, *n.* [L. *ebenus*; Gr. εϐενος or εϐελος; Fr. *ebene*; It. and Sp. *ebano*; D. *ebbenhout*; G. *ebenholz*.]

A species of hard, heavy and durable wood, which admits of a fine polish or gloss; said to be brought from Madagascar. The most usual color is black, red or green. The best is a jet black, free from veins and rind, very heavy, astringent and of an acrid pungent taste. On burning coals it yields an agreeable perfume, and when green it readily takes fire from its abundance of fat. It is wrought into toys, and used for mosaic and inlaid work. *Encyc.*

EB'ONY-TREE, *n.* The Ebenus, a small tree constituting a genus, growing in Crete and other isles of the Archipelago. *Encyc.*

EBRAC'TEATE, *a.* [*e* priv. and *bractea.*] In *botany*, without a bractea or floral leaf. *Martyn.*

EBRI'ETY, *n.* [L. *ebrietas*, from *ebrius*, intoxicated. It appears by the Spanish *embriagar*, and the It. *imbriacarsi*, that *ebrius* is contracted by the loss of a palatal, and hence it is obvious that this word is from the Gr. βρεχω, to moisten, to drench. So *drunk* is from the root of *drench.*]

Drunkenness; intoxication by spirituous liquors. *Brown.*

EBRIL'LADE, *n.* [Fr.] A check given to a horse, by a sudden jerk of one rein, when he refuses to turn.

EBRIOS'ITY, *n.* [L. *ebriositas.*] Habitual drunkenness. *Brown.*

EBUL'LIENCY, *n.* [See *Ebullition.*] A boiling over. *Cudworth.*

EBUL'LIENT, *a.* Boiling over, as a liquor. *Young.*

EBULLI''TION, *n.* [L. *ebullitio*, from *ebullio, bullio*, Eng. to *boil*, which see.]

1. The operation of boiling; the agitation of a liquor by heat, which throws it up in bubbles; or more properly, the agitation produced in a fluid by the escape of a portion of it, converted into an aeriform state by heat. Ebullition is produced by the heat of fire directly applied, or by the heat or caloric evolved by any substance in mixture. Thus, in slaking lime, the caloric set at liberty by the absorption of water, produces ebullition.

2. Effervescence, which is occasioned by fermentation, or by any other process which causes the extrication of an aeriform fluid, as in the mixture of an acid with a carbonated alkali.

ECAU'DATE, *a.* [*e* priv. and L. *cauda*, a tail.] In *botany*, without a tail or spur.

ECCEN'TRIC, ECCEN'TRICAL, } *a.* [L. *eccentricus*; *ex*, from, and *centrum*, center.]

1. Deviating or departing from the center.

2. In *geometry*, not having the same center; a term applied to circles and spheres which have not the same center, and consequently are not parallel; in opposition to *concentric*, having a common center. *Encyc.*

3. Not terminating in the same point, nor directed by the same principle. *Bacon.*

4. Deviating from stated methods, usual practice or established forms or laws; irregular; anomalous; departing from the usual course; as *eccentric* conduct; *eccentric* virtue; an *eccentric* genius.

ECCEN'TRIC, *n.* A circle not having the same center as another. *Bacon.*

2. That which is irregular or anomalous. *Hammond.*

ECCENTRIC'ITY, *n.* Deviation from a center.

2. The state of having a center different from that of another circle. *Johnson.*

3. In *astronomy*, the distance of the center of a planet's orbit from the center of the sun; that is, the distance between the center of an ellipsis and its focus. *Encyc.*

4. Departure or deviation from that which is stated, regular or usual; as the *eccentricity* of a man's genius or conduct.

5. Excursion from the proper sphere. *Wotton.*

ECCHYM'OSIS, *n.* [Gr. εκχυμωσις.] In *medicine*, an appearance of livid spots on the skin, occasioned by extravasated blood. *Wiseman.*

ECCLESIAS'TES, *n.* [Gr.] A canonical book of the old testament.

ECCLESIAS'TIC, ECCLESIAS'TICAL, } *a.* [L.; Gr. εκκλησιαςικος, from εκκλησια, an assembly or meeting, whence a church, from εκκαλεω, to call forth or convoke; εκ and καλεω, to call.]

Pertaining or relating to the church; as *ecclesiastical* discipline or government; *ecclesiastical* affairs, history or polity; *ecclesiastical* courts.

Ecclesiastical State, is the body of the clergy.

ECCLESIAS'TIC, *n.* A person in orders, or consecrated to the service of the church and the ministry of religion.

ECCLESIAS'TICUS, *n.* A book of the apocrypha.

ECCOPROT'IC, *a.* [Gr. εκ, εξ, out or from, and κοπρος, stercus.]

Having the quality of promoting alvine discharges; laxative; loosening; gently cathartic. *Coxe. Encyc.*

ECCOPROT'IC, *n.* A medicine which purges gently, or which tends to promote evacuations by stool; a mild cathartic. *Coxe. Encyc.*

EСHELON', *n.* [French, from *echelle*, a ladder, a *scale.*]

In *military tactics*, the position of an army in the form of steps, or with one division more advanced than another. *Wellington.*

ECH'INATE, ECH'INATED, } *a.* [L. *echinus*, a hedgehog.] Set with prickles; prickly, like a hedgehog; having sharp points; bristled; as an *echinated* pericarp. *Martyn.*

Echinated pyrites, in mineralogy. *Woodward.*

ECH'INITE, *n.* [See *Echinus.*] A fossil found in chalk pits, called *centronia*; a petrified shell set with prickles or points; a calcarious petrifaction of the echinus or sea-hedgehog. *Encyc. Ure.*

ECH'INUS, *n.* [L. from Gr. εχινος.] A hedgehog.

2. A shell-fish set with prickles or spines. The Echinus, in natural history, forms a genus of Mollusca. The body is roundish, covered with a bony crust, and often beset with movable prickles. There are several species and some of them eatable. *Encyc.*

3. With *botanists*, a prickly head or top of a plant; an echinated pericarp.

4. In *architecture*, a member or ornament near the bottom of Ionic, Corinthian or Composite capitals, so named from its roughness, resembling, in some measure, the spiny coat of a hedgehog. *Johnson. Encyc.*

ECH'O, *n.* [L. *echo*; Gr. ηχω, from ηχος, sound, ηχεω, to sound.]

1. A sound reflected or reverberated from a solid body; sound returned; repercussion of sound; as an *echo* from a distant hill.

The sound must seem an *echo* to the sense. *Pope.*

2. In *fabulous history*, a nymph, the daughter of the Air and Tellus, who pined into a sound, for love of Narcissus. *Lempriere. Johnson.*

3. In *architecture*, a vault or arch for redoubling sounds. *Encyc.*

ECH'O, *v. i.* To resound; to reflect sound. The hall *echoed* with acclamations.

2. To be sounded back; as *echoing* noise. *Blackmore.*

ECH'O, *v. t.* To reverberate or send back sound; to return what has been uttered.

Those peals are *echoed* by the Trojan throng. *Dryden.*

ECH'OED, *pp.* Reverberated, as sound.

ECH'OING, *ppr.* Sending back sound; as *echoing* hills.

ECHOM'ETER, *n.* [Gr. ηχος, sound, and μετρον, measure.]

Among *musicians*, a scale or rule, with several lines thereon, serving to measure the duration of sounds, and to find their intervals and ratios. *Encyc.*

ECHOM'ETRY, *n.* The art or act of measuring the duration of sounds.

2. The art of constructing vaults to produce echoes.

ECLA'IRCISE, *v. t.* [Fr. *eclaircir*, from *clair*, clear. See *Clear.*]

To make clear; to explain; to clear up what is not understood or misunderstood.

ECLA'IRCISSEMENT, *n.* [Fr.] Explanation; the clearing up of any thing not before understood. *Clarendon.*

ECLAMP'SY, *n.* [Gr. εκλαμψις, a shining; εκλαμπω, to shine.]

A flashing of light, a symptom of epilepsy. Hence, epilepsy itself. *Med. Repos.*

ECLAT, *n.* eclà. [French. The word signifies a bursting forth, a crack, and brightness, splendor; *eclater*, to split, to crack, to break forth, to shine.]

1. Primarily, a burst of applause; acclamation. Hence, applause; approbation; renown.
2. Splendor; show; pomp. *Pope.*

E€LE€'TI€, *a.* [Gr. εκλεκτικος; εξ and λεγω, to choose.]

Selecting; choosing; an epithet given to certain philosophers of antiquity, who did not attach themselves to any particular sect, but selected from the opinions and principles of each, what they thought solid and good. Hence we say, an *eclectic* philosopher; the *eclectic* sect. *Encyc.*

E€LE€'TI€, *n.* A philosopher who selected from the various systems such opinions and principles as he judged to be sound and rational. *Enfield.*

2. A christian who adhered to the doctrines of the Eclectics. Also, one of a sect of physicians.

E€LE€'TI€ALLY, *adv.* By way of choosing or selecting; in the manner of the eclectical philosophers. *Enfield.*

E€LEGM', *n.* [Gr. εκ and λειχω.] A medicine made by the incorporation of oils with syrups. *Quincy.*

E€LIPSE, *n. eclips'.* [L. *eclipsis*; Gr. εκλειψις, defect, from εκλειπω, to fail; εξ and λειπω, to *leave*.]

1. Literally, a defect or failure; hence in *astronomy*, an interception or obscuration of the light of the sun, moon or other luminous body. An *eclipse* of the sun is caused by the intervention of the moon, which totally or partially hides the sun's disk; an *eclipse* of the moon is occasioned by the shadow of the earth, which falls on it and obscures it in whole or in part, but does not entirely conceal it.
2. Darkness; obscuration. We say, his glory has suffered an *eclipse*.

All the posterity of our first parents suffered a perpetual *eclipse* of spiritual life. *Raleigh.*

E€LIPSE, *v. t. eclips'.* To hide a luminous body in whole or in part and intercept its rays; as, to *eclipse* the sun or a star.

2. To obscure; to darken, by intercepting the rays of light which render luminous; as, to *eclipse* the moon.
3. To cloud; to darken; to obscure; as, to *eclipse* the glory of a hero. Hence,
4. To disgrace. *Milton.*
5. To extinguish.

Born to *eclipse* thy life. *Shak.*

E€LIPSE, *v. i. eclips'.* To suffer an eclipse. *Milton.*

E€LIPS'ED, *pp.* Concealed; darkened; obscured; disgraced.

E€LIPS'ING, *ppr.* Concealing; obscuring; darkening; clouding.

E€LIP'TI€, *n.* [Gr. εκλειπτικος, from εκλειπω, to fail or be defective; L. *eclipticus*, linea ecliptica, the ecliptic line, or line in which eclipses are suffered.]

1. A great circle of the sphere supposed to be drawn through the middle of the zodiac, making an angle with the equinoctial of 23° 30′, which is the sun's greatest declination. The ecliptic is the apparent path of the sun, but as in reality it is the earth which moves, the ecliptic is the path or way among the fixed stars which the earth in its orbit appears to describe, to an eye placed in the sun. *Harris. Encyc.*
2. In *geography*, a great circle on the terrestrial globe, answering to and falling within the plane of the celestial ecliptic. *Encyc.*

E€LIP'TI€, *a.* Pertaining to or described by the ecliptic. *Blackmore.*

2. Suffering an eclipse. *Herbert.*

E€'LOGUE, *n. ec'log.* [Gr. εκλογη, choice; εκλεγω, to select.]

Literally, a select piece. Hence, in poetry, a pastoral composition, in which shepherds are introduced conversing with each other, as the *eclogues* of Virgil; or it is a little elegant composition in a simple natural style and manner. An eclogue differs from an idyllion, in being appropriated to pieces in which shepherds are introduced. *Encyc.*

E€ONOM'I€, } *a.* [See *Economy.*] Pertaining to the regulation of household concerns; as the *economic* art. *Davies.*
E€ONOM'I€AL,

2. Managing domestic or public pecuniary concerns with frugality; as an *economical* housekeeper; an *economical* minister or administration.
3. Frugal; regulated by frugality; not wasteful or extravagant; as an *economical* use of money.

E€ONOM'I€ALLY, *adv.* With economy; with frugality.

E€ON'OMIST, *n.* One who manages domestic or other concerns with frugality; one who expends money, time or labor judiciously, and without waste.

2. One who writes on economy; the writer of a treatise on economy.

E€ON'OMIZE, *v. i.* To manage pecuniary concerns with frugality; to make a prudent use of money, or of the means of saving or acquiring property. It is our duty to *economize*, in the use of public money, as well as of our own.

E€ON'OMIZE, *v. t.* To use with prudence; to expend with frugality; as, to *economize* one's income.

To manage and *economize* the use of circulating medium. *Walsh.*

E€ON'OMIZED, *pp.* Used with frugality.

E€ONOMIZING, *ppr.* Using with frugality.

E€ON'OMY, *n.* [L. *œconomia*; Gr. οικονομια; οικος, house, and νομος, law, rule.]

1. Primarily, the management, regulation and government of a family or the concerns of a household. *Taylor.*
2. The management of pecuniary concerns or the expenditure of money. Hence,
3. A frugal and judicious use of money; that management which expends money to advantage, and incurs no waste; frugality in the necessary expenditure of money. It differs from *parsimony*, which implies an improper saving of expense. Economy includes also a prudent management of all the means by which property is saved or accumulated; a judicious application of time, of labor, and of the instruments of labor.
4. The disposition or arrangement of any work; as the *economy* of a poem. *Dryden. B. Jonson.*
5. A system of rules, regulations, rites and ceremonies; as the Jewish *economy*.

The Jews already had a sabbath, which, as citizens and subjects of that *economy*, they were obliged to keep, and did keep. *Paley.*

6. The regular operations of nature in the generation, nutrition and preservation of animals or plants; as animal *economy*; vegetable *economy*.
7. Distribution or due order of things. *Blackmore.*
8. Judicious and frugal management of public affairs; as political *economy*.
9. System of management; general regulation and disposition of the affairs of a state or nation, or of any department of government.

E€PHRA€'TI€, *a.* [Gr. εκ and φραττω.] In *medicine*, deobstruent; attenuating.

E€PHRA€'TI€, *n.* A medicine which dissolves or attenuates viscid matter, and removes obstructions. *Coxe. Quincy.*

E€'STASIED, *a.* [See *Ecstasy.*] Enraptured; ravished; transported; delighted. *Norris.*

E€'STASY, *n.* [Gr. εκςασις, from εξιςημι; εξ and ιςημι, to stand.]

1. Primarily, a fixed state; a trance; a state in which the mind is arrested and fixed, or as we say, lost; a state in which the functions of the senses are suspended by the contemplation of some extraordinary or supernatural object.

Whether what we call *ecstasy* be not dreaming with our eyes open, I leave to be examined. *Locke.*

2. Excessive joy; rapture; a degree of delight that arrests the whole mind; as a pleasing *ecstasy*; the *ecstasy* of love; joy may rise to *ecstasy*.
3. Enthusiasm; excessive elevation and absorption of mind; extreme delight.

He on the tender grass
Would sit and hearken even to *ecstasy*. *Milton.*

4. Excessive grief or anxiety. [*Not used.*] *Shak.*
5. Madness; distraction. [*Not used.*] *Shak.*
6. In *medicine*, a species of catalepsy, when the person remembers, after the paroxysm is over, the ideas he had during the fit. *Encyc.*

E€'STASY, *v. t.* To fill with rapture or enthusiasm.

E€STAT'I€, } *a.* Arresting the mind; suspending the senses; entrancing.
E€STAT'I€AL,

In pensive trance, and anguish, and *ecstatic* fit. *Milton.*

2. Rapturous; transporting; ravishing; delightful beyond measure; as *ecstatic* bliss or joy.
3. Tending to external objects. [*Not used.*] *Norris.*

E€'TYPAL, *a.* [infra.] Taken from the original. *Ellis.*

E€'TYPE, *n.* [Gr. εκτυπος.] A copy. [*Not used.*] *Locke.*

E€UMEN'I€, } *a.* [Gr. οικουμενικος, from οικουμενη, the habitable world.]
E€UMEN'I€AL,

General; universal; as an *ecumenical* council.

E€'URIE, *n.* [Fr.] A stable; a covered place for horses.

EDA'CIOUS, *a.* [L. *edax*, from *edo*, to eat.] Eating; given to eating; greedy; voracious.

EDAC′ITY, *n.* [L. *edacitas*, from *edax*, *edo*, to eat.]

Greediness; voracity; ravenousness; rapacity. *Bacon.*

ED′DER, *n.* [Qu. Sax. *eder*, a hedge.] In *husbandry*, such wood as is worked into the top of hedge-stakes to bind them together. *Mason.*

ED′DER, *v. t.* To bind or make tight by edder; to fasten the tops of hedge-stakes, by interweaving edder. *England.*

ED′DISH, } *n.* The latter pasture or grass
E′ADISH, } that comes after mowing or reaping; called also *eagrass*, *earsh*, *etch.* [Not used, I believe, in America.] *Encyc.*

ED′DOES, } *n.* A name given to a variety
ED′DERS, } of the Arum esculentum, an esculent root. *Mease. Encyc.*

ED′DY, *n.* [I find this word in no other language. It is usually considered as a compound of Sax. *ed*, backward, and *ea*, water.]

1. A current of water running back, or in a direction contrary to the main stream. Thus a point of land extending into a river, checks the water near the shore, and turns it back or gives it a circular course. The word is applied also to the air or wind moving in a circular direction.

2. A whirlpool; a current of water or air in a circular direction.

And smiling *eddies* dimpled on the main. *Dryden.*

Wheel through the air, in circling *eddies* play. *Addison.*

ED′DY, *v. i.* To move circularly, or as an eddy.

ED′DY, *a.* Whirling; moving circularly. *Dryden.*

ED′DY-WATER, *n.* Among seamen, the water which falls back on the rudder of a ship under sail, called *dead-water.* *Encyc.*

ED′DY-WIND, *n.* The wind returned or beat back from a sail, a mountain or any thing that hinders its passage. *Encyc.*

ED′ELITE, *n.* A siliceous stone of a light gray color. *Kirwan.*

EDEM′ATOUS, *a.* [Gr. οιδημα, a tumor; οιδεω, to swell.]

Swelling with a serous humor; dropsical. An *edematous* tumor is white, soft and insensible. *Quincy.*

E′DEN, *n.* [Heb. Ch. עדן pleasure, delight.]

The country and garden in which Adam and Eve were placed by God himself.

E′DENIZED, *a.* Admitted into paradise. *Davies.*

EDEN′TATED, *a.* [L. *edentatus*, *e* and *dens.*] Destitute or deprived of teeth. *Dict.*

EDǴE, *n.* [Sax. *ecg*; Dan. *eg*; Sw. *egg*; G. *ecke*, *ege*; L. *acies*, *acus*; Fr. *aigu*, whence *aiguille*, a needle; Gr. *αχη*; W. *awç*, *awg*, edge.]

1. In *a general sense*, the extreme border or point of any thing; as the *edge* of the table; the *edge* of a book; the *edge* of cloth. It coincides nearly with border, brink, margin. It is particularly applied to the sharp border, the thin cutting extremity of an instrument, as the *edge* of an ax, razor, knife or sythe; also, to the point of an instrument, as the *edge* of a sword.

2. Figuratively, that which cuts or penetrates; that which wounds or injures; as the *edge* of slander. *Shak.*

3. A narrow part rising from a broader.

Some harrow their gronnd over, and then plow it upon an *edge.* *Mortimer.*

4. Sharpness of mind or appetite; keenness; intenseness of desire; fitness for action or operation; as the *edge* of appetite or hunger.

Silence and solitude set an *edge* on the genius. *Dryden.*

5. Keenness; sharpness; acrimony.

Abate the *edge* of traitors. *Shak.*

To set the teeth on edge, to cause a tingling or grating sensation in the teeth. *Bacon.*

EDǴE, *v. t.* [W. *hogi*; Sax. *eggian*; Dan. *egger.*]

1. To sharpen.

To *edge* her champion's sword. *Dryden.*

2. To furnish with an edge.

A sword *edged* with flint. *Dryden.*

3. To border; to fringe.

A long descending train,
With rubies *edged.* *Dryden.*

4. To border; to furnish with an ornamental border; as, to *edge* a flower-bed with box.

5. To sharpen; to exasperate; to embitter.

By such reasonings, the simple were blinded, and the malicious *edged.* *Hayward.*

6. To incite; to provoke; to urge on; to instigate; that is, to push on as with a sharp point; to goad. Ardor or passion will *edge* a man forward, when arguments fail.

[This, by a strange mistake, has been sometimes written *egg*, from the Sax. *eggian*, Dan. *egger*, to incite; the writers not knowing that this verb is from the noun *ecg*, *eg*, an edge. The verb ought certainly to follow the noun, and the popular use is correct.]

7. To move sideways; to move by little and little; as, *edge* your chair along.

EDǴE, *v. i.* To move sideways; to move gradually. *Edge* along this way.

2. To sail close to the wind. *Dryden.*

To edge away, in sailing, is to decline gradually from the shore or from the line of the course. *Mar. Dict.*

To edge in with, to draw near to, as a ship in chasing. *Cyc.*

EDǴ′ED, *pp.* Furnished with an edge or border.

2. Incited; instigated.

3. *a.* Sharp; keen.

EDǴELESS, *a.* Not sharp; blunt; obtuse; unfit to cut or penetrate; as an *edgeless* sword or weapon. *Shak.*

EDǴETOOL, *n.* An instrument having a sharp edge. *Moxon.*

EDǴEWISE, *adv.* [*edge* and *wise.*] With the edge turned forward, or towards a particular point; in the direction of the edge.

2. Sideways; with the side foremost.

EDǴ′ING, *ppr.* Giving an edge; furnishing with an edge.

2. Inciting; urging on; goading; stimulating; instigating.

3. Moving gradually or sideways.

4. Furnishing with a border.

EDǴ′ING, *n.* That which is added on the border, or which forms the edge; as lace, fringe, trimming, added to a garment for ornament.

Bordered with a rosy *edging.* *Dryden.*

2. A narrow lace.

3. In *gardening*, a row of small plants set along the border of a flower-bed; as an *edging* of box. *Encyc.*

ED′IBLE, *a.* [from L. *edo*, to eat.] Eatable; fit to be eaten as food; esculent.

Some flesh is not *edible.* *Bacon.*

E′DICT, *n.* [L. *edictum*, from *edico*, to utter or proclaim; *e* and *dico*, to speak.]

That which is uttered or proclaimed by authority as a rule of action; an order issued by a prince to his subjects, as a rule or law requiring obedience; a proclamation of command or prohibition. An edict is an order or ordinance of a sovereign prince, intended as a permanent law, or to erect a new office, to establish new duties, or other temporary regulation; as the *edicts* of the Roman emperors; the *edicts* of the French monarch.

ED′IFICANT, *a.* [infra.] Building. [*Little used.*]

EDIFICA′TION, *n.* [L. *ædificatio.* See *Edify.*]

1. A building up, in a moral and religious sense; instruction; improvement and progress of the mind, in knowledge, in morals, or in faith and holiness.

He that prophesieth, speaketh to men to *edification.* 1 Cor. xiv.

2. Instruction; improvement of the mind in any species of useful knowledge. *Addison.*

ED′IFICATORY, *a.* Tending to edification. *Hall.*

ED′IFICE, *n.* [L. *ædificium.* See *Edify.*]

A building; a structure; a fabric; but appropriately, a large or splendid building. The word is not applied to a mean building, but to temples, churches or elegant mansion-houses, and to other great structures. *Milton. Addison.*

EDIFI″CIAL, *a.* Pertaining to edifices or to structure.

ED′IFIED, *pp.* Instructed; improved in literary, moral or religious knowledge.

ED′IFIER, *n.* One that improves another by instructing him.

ED′IFȲ, *v. t.* [L. *ædifico*; Fr. *edifier*; Sp. *edificar*; It. *edificare*; from L. *ædes*, a house, and *facio*, to make.]

1. To build, in a literal sense. [*Not now used.*] *Spenser.*

2. To instruct and improve the mind in knowledge generally, and particularly in moral and religious knowledge, in faith and holiness.

Edify one another. 1 Thess. v.

3. To teach or persuade. [*Not used.*] *Bacon.*

ED′IFȲING, *ppr.* Building up in christian knowledge; instructing; improving the mind.

ED′IFȲINGLY, *adv.* In an edifying manner.

E′DILE, *n.* [L. *ædilis*, from *ædes*, a building.]

A Roman magistrate whose chief business was to superintend buildings of all kinds, more especially public edifices, temples, bridges, aqueducts, &c. The ediles had also the care of the highways, public places, weights and measures, &c. *Encyc.*

E′DILESHIP, *n.* The office of Edile in ancient Rome. *Gray.*

ED′IT, *v. t.* [from L. *edo*, to publish; *e* and *do*, to give.]

1. Properly, to publish; more usually, to superintend a publication; to prepare a book or paper for the public eye, by writing, correcting or selecting the matter.

Those who know how volumes of the fathers are generally *edited*. *Christ. Observer.*

2. To publish.

Abelard wrote many philosophical treatises which have never been *edited*. *Enfield.*

ED'ITED, *pp.* Published; corrected; prepared and published.

ED'ITING, *ppr.* Publishing; preparing for publication.

EDI''TION, *n.* [L. *editio*, from *edo*, to publish.]

1. The publication of any book or writing; as the first *edition* of a new work.
2. Republication, sometimes with revision and correction; as the second *edition* of a work.
3. Any publication of a book before published; also, one impression or the whole number of copies published at once; as the tenth *edition*.

ED'ITOR, *n.* [L. from *edo*, to publish.] A publisher; particularly, a person who superintends an impression of a book; the person who revises, corrects and prepares a book for publication; as Erasmus, Scaliger, &c.

2. One who superintends the publication of a newspaper.

EDITO'RIAL, *a.* Pertaining to an editor, as *editorial* labors; written by an editor, as *editorial* remarks.

ED'ITORSHIP, *n.* The business of an editor; the care and superintendence of a publication. *Walsh.*

EDIT'UATE, *v. t.* [Low L. *œdituor*, from *œdes*, a temple or house.]

To defend or govern the house or temple. [*Not in use.*] *Gregory.*

ED'UCATE, *v. t.* [L. *educo*, *educare*; *e* and *duco*, to lead; It. *educare*; Sp. *educar.*]

To bring up, as a child; to instruct; to inform and enlighten the understanding; to instill into the mind principles of arts, science, morals, religion and behavior. To *educate* children well is one of the most important duties of parents and guardians.

ED'UCATED, *pp.* Brought up; instructed; furnished with knowledge or principles; trained; disciplined.

ED'UCATING, *ppr.* Instructing; enlightening the understanding, and forming the manners.

EDUCA'TION, *n.* [L. *educatio.*] The bringing up, as of a child; instruction; formation of manners. Education comprehends all that series of instruction and discipline which is intended to enlighten the understanding, correct the temper, and form the manners and habits of youth, and fit them for usefulness in their future stations. To give children a good *education* in manners, arts and science, is important; to give them a religious *education* is indispensable; and an immense responsibility rests on parents and guardians who neglect these duties.

EDUCA'TIONAL, *a.* Pertaining to education; derived from education; as *educational* habits. *Smith.*

ED'UCATOR, *n.* One who educates. *Beddoes.*

EDU'CE, *v. t.* [L. *educo*, *eduxi*; *e* and *duco*, to lead.]

To bring or draw out; to extract; to produce from a state of occultation.

Th' eternal art *educing* good from ill. *Pope.*

EDU'CED, *pp.* Drawn forth; extracted; produced.

EDU'CING, *ppr.* Drawing forth; producing.

E'DUCT, *n.* [L. *eductum*, from *educo.*] Extracted matter; that which is educed; that which is brought to light, by separation, analysis or decomposition.

We must consider the *educts* of its analysis by Bergman, &c. *Kirwan.*

EDUC'TION, *n.* The act of drawing out or bringing into view.

EDUC'TOR, *n.* That which brings forth, elicits or extracts.

Stimulus must be called an *eductor* of vital ether. *Darwin.*

EDUL'CORATE, *v. t.* [Low L. *edulco*, from *dulcis*, sweet; Fr. *edulcorer.*]

1. To purify; to sweeten. In *chimistry*, to render substances more mild, by freeing them from acids and salts or other soluble impurities, by washing. *Encyc.*
2. To sweeten by adding sugar, sirup, &c. *Encyc.*

EDUL'CORATED, *pp.* Sweetened; purified from acid or saline substances, and rendered more mild.

EDUL'CORATING, *ppr.* Sweetening; rendering more mild.

EDULCORA'TION, *n.* The act of sweetening or rendering more mild, by freeing from acid or saline substances, or from any soluble impurities.

2. The act of sweetening by admixture of some saccharine substance.

EDUL'CORATIVE, *a.* Having the quality of sweetening.

EEK. [See *Eke.*]

EEL, *n.* [Sax. *æl*; G. *aal*; D. *aal*; Dan. *id.*; Sw. *ål*; Gypsey, *alo*; Turk. *ilan.* The word, in Saxon, is written precisely like *awl.*]

A species of Muræna, a genus of fishes belonging to the order of apodes. The head is smooth; there are ten rays in the membrane of the gills; the eyes are covered with a common skin; the body is cylindrical and slimy. Eels, in some respects, resemble reptiles, particularly in their manner of moving by a serpentine winding of the body; and they often creep upon land and wander about at night in search of snails or other food. In winter, they lie buried in mud, being very impatient of cold. They grow to the weight of 15 or 20 pounds; and the conger eel is said to grow to a hundred pounds in weight, and to 10 feet in length. They are esteemed good food. *Encyc.*

EE'L-FISHING, *n.* The act or art of catching eels.

EE'LPOT, *n.* A kind of basket used for catching eels.

EE'LPOUT, *n.* A species of Gadus, somewhat resembling an eel, but shorter in proportion, seldom exceeding a foot in length. It is a delicate fish. *Encyc. Dict. Nat. Hist.*

EE'LSKIN, *n.* The skin of an eel.

EE'LSPEAR, *n.* A forked instrument used for stabbing eels.

E'EN, contracted from *even*, which see.

I have *e'en* done with you. *L'Estrange.*

EFF, *n.* A lizard.

EF'FABLE, *a.* [L. *effabilis*, from *effor*; *ex* and *for*, to speak.]

Utterable; that may be uttered or spoken. [This word is not used; but *ineffable* is in common use.]

EFFA'CE, *v. t.* [Fr. *effacer*, from the L. *ex* and *facio* or *facies.*]

1. To destroy a figure on the surface of any thing, whether painted or carved, so as to render it invisible or not distinguishable; as, to *efface* the letters on a monument.
2. To blot out; to erase, strike or scratch out, so as to destroy or render illegible; as, to *efface* a writing; to *efface* a name.
3. To destroy any impression on the mind; to wear away; as, to *efface* the image of a person in the mind; to *efface* ideas or thoughts; to *efface* gratitude. *Dryden.*

To *deface* is to injure or impair a figure; to *efface* is to rub out or destroy, so as to render invisible.

EFFA'CED, *pp.* Rubbed or worn out; destroyed, as a figure or impression.

EFFA'CING, *ppr.* Destroying a figure, character or impression, on any thing.

EFFECT', *n.* [L. *effectus*, from *efficio*; *ex* and *facio*, to make; It. *effetto*; Fr. *effet.*]

1. That which is produced by an agent or cause; as the *effect* of luxury; the *effect* of intemperance.

Poverty, disease and disgrace are the natural *effects* of dissipation.

2. Consequence; event.

To say that a composition is imperfect, is *in effect* to say the author is a man. *Anon.*

3. Purpose; general intent.

They spoke to her to that *effect.* 2 Chron. xxxiv.

4. Consequence intended; utility; profit; advantage.

Christ is become of no *effect* to you. Gal. v.

5. Force; validity. The obligation is void and of no *effect.*
6. Completion; perfection.

Not so worthily to be brought to heroical *effect* by fortune or necessity. *Sidney.*

7. Reality; not mere appearance; fact.

No other in *effect* than what it seems. *Denham.*

8. In the plural, *effects* are goods; movables; personal estate. The people escaped from the town with their *effects.*

EFFECT', *v. t.* [from the Noun.] To produce, as a cause or agent; to cause to be. The revolution in France *effected* a great change of property.

2. To bring to pass; to achieve; to accomplish; as, to *effect* an object or purpose.

EFFECT'ED, *pp.* Done; performed; accomplished.

EFFECT'IBLE, *a.* That may be done or achieved; practicable; feasible. *Brown.*

EFFECT'ING, *ppr.* Producing; performing; accomplishing.

EFFECT'IVE, *a.* Having the power to cause or produce; efficacious.

They are not *effective* of any thing. *Bacon.*

2. Operative; active; having the quality of producing effects.

Time is not *effective*, nor are bodies destroyed by it. *Brown.*

3. Efficient; causing to be; as an *effective* cause. *Taylor.*
4. Having the power of active operation; able; as *effective* men in an army; an *effective* force.

EFFECT'IVELY, *adv.* With effect; powerfully; with real operation.

This *effectively* resists the devil. *Taylor.*

[In this sense, *effectually* is generally used.]

EFFECT'LESS, *a.* Without effect; without advantage; useless. *Shak.*

EFFECT'OR, *n.* One who effects; one who produces or causes; a maker or creator. *Derham.*

EFFECT'UAL, *a.* Producing an effect, or the effect desired or intended; or having adequate power or force to produce the effect. The means employed were *effectual.*

According to the gift of the grace of God given me by the *effectual* working of his power. Eph. iii.

2. Veracious; expressive of facts. [*Not used.*] *Shak.*

3. *Effectual* assassin, in Mitford, is unusual and not well authorized.

EFFECT'UALLY, *adv.* With effect; efficaciously; in a manner to produce the intended effect; thoroughly. The weeds on land for grain must be *effectually* subdued. The city is *effectually* guarded.

EFFECT'UATE, *v. t.* [Fr. *effectuer.* See *Effect.*]

To bring to pass; to achieve; to accomplish; to fulfil; as, to *effectuate* a purpose or desire. *Sidney.*

EFFECT'UATED, *pp.* Accomplished.

EFFECT'UATING, *ppr.* Achieving; performing to effect.

EFFEM'INACY, *n.* [from *effeminate.*] The softness, delicacy and weakness in men, which are characteristic of the female sex, but which in males are deemed a reproach; unmanly delicacy; womanish softness or weakness. *Milton.*

2. Voluptuousness; indulgence in unmanly pleasures; lasciviousness. *Taylor.*

EFFEM'INATE, *a.* [L. *effœminatus*, from *effœminor*, to grow or make womanish, from *fœmina*, a woman. See *Woman.*]

1. Having the qualities of the female sex; soft or delicate to an unmanly degree; tender; womanish; voluptuous.

The king, by his voluptuous life and mean marriage, became *effeminate*, and less sensible of honor. *Bacon.*

2. Womanish; weak; resembling the practice or qualities of the sex; as an *effeminate* peace; an *effeminate* life.

3. Womanlike, tender, in a sense not reproachful. *Shak.*

EFFEM'INATE, *v. t.* To make womanish; to unman; to weaken; as, to *effeminate* children. *Locke.*

EFFEM'INATE, *v. i.* To grow womanish or weak; to melt into weakness.

In a slothful peace courage will *effeminate.* *Pope.*

EFFEM'INATELY, *adv.* In a womanish manner; weakly; softly.

2. By means of a woman; as *effeminately* vanquished. *Milton.*

EFFEM'INATENESS, *n.* Unmanlike softness.

EFFEMINA'TION, *n.* The state of one grown womanish; the state of being weak or unmanly. [*Little used.*] *Bacon.*

EFFERVESCE, *v. i.* *efferves'.* [L. *effervesco*, from *ferveo*, to be hot, to rage. See *Fervent.*]

To be in natural commotion, like liquor when gently boiling; to bubble and hiss, as fermenting liquors, or any fluid, when some part escapes in an elastic form; to work, as new wine.

EFFERVES'CENCE, *n.* A kind of natural ebullition; that commotion of a fluid, which takes place, when some part of the mass flies off in an elastic form, producing innumerable small bubbles; as the *effervescence* or working of new wine, cider or beer; the *effervescence* of a carbonate with nitric acid.

EFFERVES'CENT, *a.* Gently boiling or bubbling, by means of the disengagement of an elastic fluid. *Encyc.*

EFFERVES'CIBLE, *a.* That has the quality of effervescing; capable of producing effervescence.

A small quantity of *effervescible* matter. *Kirwan.*

EFFERVES'CING, *ppr.* Boiling; bubbling, by means of an elastic fluid extricated in the dissolution of bodies.

EFFE'TE, *a.* [L. *effœtus, effetus*; *ex* and *fœtus*, embryo.]

1. Barren; not capable of producing young, as an animal, or fruit, as the earth. An animal becomes *effete* by losing the power of conception. The earth may be rendered *effete*, by drouth, or by exhaustion of fertility. *Ray. Bentley.*

2. Worn out with age; as *effete* sensuality. *South.*

EFFICA'CIOUS, *a.* [L. *efficax*, from *efficio.* See *Effect.*]

Effectual; productive of effects; producing the effect intended; having power adequate to the purpose intended; powerful; as an *efficacious* remedy for disease.

EFFICA'CIOUSLY, *adv.* Effectually; in such a manner as to produce the effect desired. We say, a remedy has been *efficaciously* applied.

EFFICA'CIOUSNESS, *n.* The quality of being efficacious. *Ash.*

EF'FICACY, *n.* [Sp. It. *efficacia*; Fr. *efficace*; from L. *efficax.*]

Power to produce effects; production of the effect intended; as the *efficacy* of the gospel in converting men from sin; the *efficacy* of prayer; the *efficacy* of medicine in counteracting disease; the *efficacy* of manure in fertilizing land.

EFFI''CIENCE, EFFI''CIENCY, *n.* [L. *efficiens*, from *efficio.* See *Effect.*]

1. The act of producing effects; a causing to be or exist; effectual agency.

The manner of this divine *efficiency* is far above us. *Hooker.*

Gravity does not proceed from the *efficiency* of any contingent or unstable agent. *Woodward.*

2. Power of producing the effect intended; active competent power.

EFFI''CIENT, *a.* Causing effects; producing; that causes any thing to be what it is. The *efficient* cause is that which produces; the final cause is that for which it is produced.

EFFI''CIENT, *n.* The agent or cause which produces or causes to exist.

2. He that makes.

EFFI''CIENTLY, *adv.* With effect; effectively.

EFFIERCE, *v. t.* *effers'.* To make fierce or furious. [*Not used.*] *Spenser.*

EF'FIGY, *n.* [L. *effigies*, from *effingo*, to fashion; *ex* and *fingo*, to form or devise; Sp. It. Fr. *effigie.* See *Feign.*]

1. The image or likeness of a person; resemblance; representation; any substance fashioned into the shape of a person.

2. Portrait; likeness; figure, in sculpture or painting.

3. On *coins*, the print or impression representing the head of the prince who struck the coin.

To burn or *hang in effigy*, is to burn or hang an image or picture of the person intended to be executed, disgraced or degraded. In France, when a criminal cannot be apprehended, his picture is hung on a gallows or gibbet, at the bottom of which is written his sentence of condemnation. *Encyc.*

EFFLA'TE, *v. t.* [L. *efflo.*] To fill with breath or air. [*Little used.*]

EFFLORESCE, *v. t.* *effloresʹ.* [L. *effloresco*, from *floresco, floreo*, to blossom, *flos*, a flower. See *Flower.*]

1. In *chimistry*, to form a mealy powder on the surface; to become pulverulent or dusty on the surface. Substances *effloresce* by losing their water of crystalization.

Those salts whose crystals *effloresce*, belong to the class which is most soluble, and crystalizes by cooling. *Fourcroy.*

2. To form saline vegetation on the surface; or rather to shoot out minute spicular crystals; as the *efflorescencc* of salts on plaster.

EFFLORES'CENCE, *n.* In *botany*, the time of flowering; the season when a plant shows its first blossoms. *Martyn.*

2. Among *physicians*, a redness of the skin; eruptions; as in rash, measles, small pox, scarlatina, &c.

3. In *chimistry*, the formation of small white threads, resembling the sublimated matter called flowers, on the surface of certain bodies, as salts. This is properly a shooting out of minute spicular crystals, called sometimes a saline vegetation, as that of the sulphate of magnesia on the deserts of Siberia, and of natron in Egypt. In butter much salted, the salt shoots in spiculæ, and an efflorescence is often seen on walls formed with plaster. In some species of salts, as in sulphate and carbonate of soda, the efflorescence consists of a fine white dust. This kind of efflorescence is the contrary of deliquescence. In the latter, the saline crystals decompose the air, or rather abstract moisture from it; in the former, the atmosphere decomposes the saline crystals, and the water of crystalization is abstracted from the salts.

Fourcroy. Encyc. Dict. Nat. Hist.

EFFLORES'CENT, *a.* Shooting into white threads or spiculæ; forming a white dust on the surface. *Fourcroy.*

EF'FLUENCE, *n.* [L. *effluens*, *effluo*; *ex* and *fluo*, to flow. See *Flow.*]

A flowing out; that which flows or issues from any body or substance.

Bright *effluence* of bright essence increate. *Milton.*

EFFLU'VIUM, *n.* plu. *effluvia.* [L. from *effluo*, to flow out. See *Flow.*]

The minute and often invisible particles which exhale from most, if not all terrestrial bodies, such as the odor or smell of plants, and the noxious exhalations from diseased bodies or putrefying animal or vegetable substances.

EF'FLUX, *n.* [L. *effluxus*, from *effluo*, to flow out.]

1. The act of flowing out, or issuing in a stream; as an *efflux* of matter from an ulcer. *Harvey.*
2. Effusion; flow; as the first *efflux* of men's piety. *Hammond.*
3. That which flows out; emanation.

Light—*efflux* divine. *Thomson.*

EFFLUX', *v. i.* To run or flow away. [*Not used.*] *Boyle.*

EFFLUX'ION, *n.* [L. *effluxum*, from *effluo.*]

1. The act of flowing out. *Brown.*
2. That which flows out; effluvium; emanation. *Bacon.*

EFFO'RCE, *v. t.* [Fr. *efforcer*, from *force.*]

1. To force; to break through by violence. *Spenser.*
2. To force; to ravish. *Spenser.*
3. To strain; to exert with effort. *Spenser.*

[This word is now rarely used; perhaps never, except in poetry. We now use *force.*]

EFFORM', *v. t.* [from *form.*] To fashion; to shape. *Taylor.*

[For this we now use *form.*]

EFFORMA'TION, *n.* The act of giving shape or form. *Ray.*

[We now use *formation.*]

EF'FORT, *n.* [Fr. *effort*; It. *sforzo*; from *fort*, strong, L. *fortis*. See *Force.*]

A straining; an exertion of strength; endeavor; strenuous exertion to accomplish an object; *applicable to physical or intellectual power.* The army, by great *efforts*, scaled the walls. Distinction in science is gained by continued *efforts* of the mind.

EFFOS'SION, *n.* [L. *effossus*, from *effodio*, to dig out.]

The act of digging out of the earth; as the *effossion* of coins. *Arbuthnot.*

EFFRA'Y, *v. t.* [Fr. *effrayer.*] To frighten. [*Not in use.*] *Spenser.*

EFFRA'YABLE, *a.* Frightful; dreadful. [*Not in use.*] *Harvey.*

EFFRENA'TION, *n.* [L. *effrænatio*, from *frænum*, a rein.]

Unbridled rashness or licence; unruliness. [*Not in use.*]

EFFRONT'ERY, *n.* [Fr. *effronterie*, from *front.*] Impudence; assurance; shameless boldness; sauciness; boldness transgressing the bounds of modesty and decorum. *Effrontery* is a sure mark of ill-breeding.

EFFULĠE, *v. i.* *effulj'.* [L. *effulgeo*; *ex* and *fulgeo*, to shine.]

To send forth a flood of light; to shine with splendor.

EFFUL'ĠENCE, *n.* A flood of light; great luster or brightness; splendor; as the *effulgence* of divine glory. It is a word of superlative signification, and applied, with peculiar propriety, to the sun and to the Supreme Being.

EFFUL'ĠENT, *a.* Shining; bright; splendid; diffusing a flood of light; as the *effulgent* sun.

EFFUL'ĠING, *ppr.* Sending out a flood of light. *Savage.*

EFFUMABIL'ITY, *n.* The quality of flying off in fumes or vapor. *Boyle.*

EFFU'ME, *v. t.* To breathe out. [*Not used.*] *Spenser.*

EFFU'SE, *v. t.* *effu'ze.* [L. *effusus*, from *effundo*; *ex* and *fundo*, to pour.]

To pour out as a fluid; to spill; to shed.

With gushing blood *effused.* *Milton.*

EFFU'SE, *a.* Dissipated; profuse. [*Not in use.*] *Richardson.*

EFFU'SED, *pp.* *effu'zed.* Poured out; shed.

EFFU'SING, *ppr.* *effu'zing.* Pouring out; shedding.

EFFU'SION, *n.* *effu'zhon.* The act of pouring out as a liquid.

2. The act of pouring out; a shedding or spilling; waste; as the *effusion* of blood.
3. The pouring out of words. *Hooker.*
4. The act of pouring out or bestowing divine influence; as the *effusions* of the Holy Spirit; *effusions* of grace.
5. That which is poured out.

Wash me with that precious *effusion*, and I shall be whiter than snow. *King Charles.*

6. Liberal donation. [*Not used.*] *Hammond.*

EFFU'SIVE, *a.* Pouring out; that pours forth largely.

Th' *effusive* south. *Thomson.*

EFT, *n.* [Sax. *efeta.*] A newt; an evet; the common lizard. *Encyc.*

EFT, *adv.* [Sax.] After; again; soon; quickly. *Obs.* *Spenser.*

EFTSOONS', *adv.* [Sax. *eft*, after, and *sona*, *sones*, soon.] Soon afterwards; in a short time. *Obs.* *Spenser.*

E. G. [*exempli gratia.*] For the sake of an example; for instance.

EGAD', *exclam.* Qu. Ch. אגד a lucky star, good fortune, as we say, *my stars!*

E'GER or **E'AGRE**, *n.* An impetuous flood; an irregular tide. *Brown.*

E'GERAN, *n.* [from *Eger*, in Bohemia.] A subspecies of pyramidical garnet, of a reddish brown color. It occurs massive or crystalized. *Ure.*

EĠERM'INATE. [*Not used.* See *Germinate.*]

EĠEST', *v. t.* [L. *egestum*, from *egero.*] To cast or throw out; to void, as excrement. *Bacon.*

EĠES'TION, *n.* [L. *egestio.*] The act of voiding digested matter at the natural vent. *Hale.*

EGG, *n.* [Sax. *æg*; G. and D. *ei*; Sw. *ägg*; Dan. *eg.* Qu. L. *ovum*, by a change of *g* into *v*. W. *wy*; Arm. *oy*; Ir. *ugh*; Russ. *ikra*, eggs, and the fat or calf of the leg.]

A body formed in the females of fowls and certain other animals, containing an embryo or fetus of the same species, or the substance from which a like animal is produced. The eggs of fowls when laid are covered with a shell, and within is the white or albumen, which incloses the yelk or yellow substance. The eggs of fish and some other animals are united by a viscous substance, and called spawn. Most insects are oviparous.

Egg, to incite, is a mere blunder. [See *Edge.*]

EGG'BIRD, *n.* A fowl, a species of tern. *Cook's Voyages.*

EĠILOP'ICAL, *a.* Affected with the egilops.

E'ĠILOPS, *n.* [Gr. αιγιλωψ.] Goat's eye; an abscess in the inner canthus of the eye; fistula lachrymalis. *Coxe.*

EGLAND'ULOUS, *a.* [*e* neg. and *glandulous*. See *Gland.*] Destitute of glands.

EG'LANTINE, *n.* [Fr. *eglantier*; D. *egelantier.*] A species of rose; the sweet brier; a plant bearing an odoriferous flower.

E'GOIST, *n.* [from L. *ego*, I.] A name given to certain followers of Des Cartes, who held the opinion that they were uncertain of every thing except their own existence and the operations and ideas of their own minds. *Reid.*

EGO'ITY, *n.* Personality. [*Not authorized.*] *Swift.*

E'GOTISM, *n.* [Fr. *egoisme*; Sp. *egoismo*; from L. *ego*, I.]

Primarily, the practice of too frequently using the word *I*. Hence, a speaking or writing much of one's self; self-praise; self-commendation; the act or practice of magnifying one's self, or making one's self of importance. *Spectator.*

A deplorable *egotism* of character. *Dwight on Dueling.*

E'GOTIST, *n.* One who repeats the word *I* very often in conversation or writing; one who speaks much of himself, or magnifies his own achievements; one who makes himself the hero of every tale.

EGOTIST'IC, *a.* Addicted to egotism.

2. Containing egotism.

E'GOTIZE, *v. i.* To talk or write much of one's self; to make pretensions to self-importance.

EGRE'ĠIOUS, *a.* [L. *egregius*, supposed to be from *e* or *ex grege*, from or out of or beyond the herd, select, choice.]

1. Eminent; remarkable; extraordinary; distinguished; as *egregious* exploits; an *egregious* prince. But in this sense it is seldom applied to persons.
2. In *a bad sense*, great; extraordinary; remarkable; enormous; as an *egregious* mistake; *egregious* contempt. In this sense it is often applied to persons; as an *egregious* rascal; an *egregious* murderer.

EGRE'ĠIOUSLY, *adv.* Greatly; enormously; shamefully; *usually in a bad sense*; as, he is *egregiously* mistaken; they were *egregiously* cheated.

EGRE'ĠIOUSNESS, *n.* The state of being great or extraordinary.

E'GRESS, *n.* [L. *egressus*, from *egredior*; *e* and *gradior*, to step, Sw. *resa*, Dan. *rejser.*]

The act of going or issuing out, or the power of departing from any inclosed or confined place.

Gates of burning adamant,
Barr'd over us, prohibit all *egress.* *Milton.*

EGRES'SION, *n.* [L. *egressio.*] The act of going out from any inclosure or place of confinement. *Pope.*

E'GRET, *n.* [Fr. *aigrette.*] The lesser white heron, a fowl of the genus Ardea; an elegant fowl with a white body and a crest on the head. *Encyc.*

2. In *botany*, the flying feathery or hairy crown of seeds, as the down of the thistle.

E'GRIOT, *n.* [Fr. *aigre*, sour.] A kind of sour cherry. *Bacon.*

EĠYP'TIAN, *a.* [from *Egypt*, Gr. Αιγυπτος; supposed to be so called from the name *Coptos*, a principal town, from *gupta*, guarded, fortified. Asiat. Res. iii. 304. 335.

So *Mesr*, *Mazor*, Heb. מצור, whence *Misraim*, signifies a fortress, from צר to bind or inclose.] Pertaining to Egypt in Africa.

EGYP'TIAN, *n.* A native of Egypt; also, a gypsey. *Blackstone.*

EI'DER, *n.* [G. Sw. *eider.*] A species of duck.

EI'DER-DOWN, *n.* Down or soft feathers of the eider duck.

EIGH, *exclam.* An expression of sudden delight.

EIGHT, *a. ait.* [Sax. *æhta*, *eahta* or *ehta*; G. *acht*; D. *agt*; Sw. *otta*; Dan. *otte*; Goth. *ahtau*; L. *octo*; Gr. οκτω; It. *otto*; Sp. *ocho*; Port. *oito*; Fr. *huit*; Arm. *eih* or *eiz*; Ir. *ocht*; W. *wyth* or *wyth*; Corn. *eath*; Gypsey, *ochto*; Hindoo, *aute.*]

Twice four; expressing the number twice four. Four and four make *eight.*

EIGHTEEN, *a. áteen.* Eight and ten united.

EIGHTEENTH, *a. áteenth.* The next in order after the seventeenth.

EIGHTFOLD, *a. átefóld.* Eight times the number or quantity.

EIGHTH, *a. aitth.* Noting the number eight; the number next after seven; the ordinal of eight.

EIGHTH, *n.* In *music*, an interval composed of five tones and two semitones. *Encyc.*

EIGHTHLY, *adv. aitthly.* In the eighth place.

EIGHTIETH, *a. átieth.* [from *eighty.*] The next in order to the seventy ninth; the eighth tenth.

EIGHTSCORE, *a.* or *n. átescore.* [*eight* and *score*; score is a notch noting twenty.] Eight times twenty; a hundred and sixty.

EIGHTY, *a. áty.* Eight times ten; fourscore.

EIGNE, *a.* [Norm. *aisne.*] Eldest; an epithet used in law to denote the eldest son; as bastard *eigne.* *Blackstone.*

2. Unalienable; entailed; belonging to the eldest son. [*Not used.*] *Bacon.*

E'ISEL, *n.* [Sax.] Vinegar. [*Not in use.*] *More.*

EI'SENRAHM, *n.* [G. iron-cream.] The red and brown eisenrahm, the scaly red and brown hematite. *Cleaveland.*

E'ITHER, *a.* or *pron.* [Sax. *ægther*, *egther*; D. *yder*; G. *jeder*; Ir. *ceachtar.* This word seems to be compound, and the first syllable to be the same as *each.* So Sax. *æghwær*, *each where*, every where. Sax. Chron. An. 1114. 1118.]

1. One or another of any number. Here are ten oranges; take *either* orange of the whole number, or take *either* of them. In the last phrase, *either* stands as a pronoun or substitute.

2. One of two. This sense is included in the foregoing.

> Lepidus flatters both,
> Of both is flattered; but he neither loves,
> Nor *either* cares for him. *Shak.*

3. Each; every one separately considered.

> On *either* side of the river. Rev. xxii.

4. This word, when applied to sentences or propositions, is called a distributive or a conjunction. It precedes the first of two or more alternatives, and is answered by *or* before the second, or succeeding alternatives.

> *Either* he is talking, *or* he is pursuing, *or* he is on a journey, or perhaps he sleepeth. 1 Kings xviii.

In this sentence, *either* refers to each of the succeeding clauses of the sentence.

EJAC'ULATE, *v. t.* [L. *ejaculor*, from *jaculor*, to throw or dart, *jaculum*, a dart, from *jacio*, to throw.]

To throw out; to cast; to shoot; to dart; as rays of light *ejaculated.* *Blackmore.*

It is now seldom used, except to express the utterance of a short prayer; as, he *ejaculated* a few words.

EJACULA'TION, *n.* The act of throwing or darting out with a sudden force and rapid flight; as the *ejaculation* of light. *Bacon.*

[*This sense is nearly obsolete.*]

2. The uttering of a short prayer; or a short occasional prayer uttered. *Taylor.*

EJAC'ULATORY, *a.* Suddenly darted out; uttered in short sentences; as an *ejaculatory* prayer or petition.

2. Sudden; hasty; as *ejaculatory* repentance. *L'Estrange.*

3. Casting; throwing out.

EJECT', *v. t.* [L. *ejicio*, *ejectum*; *e* and *jacio*, to throw, Fr. *jeter*, L. *jacto.*]

1. To throw out; to cast forth; to thrust out, as from a place inclosed or confined. *Sandys. South.*

2. To discharge through the natural passages or emunctories; to evacuate. *Encyc.*

3. To throw out or expel from an office; to dismiss from an office; to turn out; as, to *eject* a clergyman.

4. To dispossess of land or estate.

5. To drive away; to expel; to dismiss with hatred. *Shak.*

6. To cast away; to reject; to banish; as, to *eject* words from a language. *Swift.*

EJECT'ED, *pp.* Thrown out; thrust out; discharged; evacuated; expelled; dismissed; dispossessed; rejected.

EJECT'ING, *ppr.* Casting out; discharging; evacuating; expelling; dispossessing; rejecting.

EJEC'TION, *n.* [L. *ejectio.*] The act of casting out; expulsion.

2. Dismission from office.

3. Dispossession; a turning out from possession by force or authority.

4. The discharge of any excrementitious matter through the pores or other emunctories; evacuation; vomiting.

5. Rejection.

EJECT'MENT, *n.* Literally, a casting out; a dispossession.

2. In *law*, a writ or action which lies for the recovery of possession of land from which the owner has been ejected, and for trial of title. Ejectment may be brought by the lessor against the lessee for rent in arrear, or for holding over his term; also by the lessee for years, who has been ejected before the expiration of his term. *Encyc.*

EJECT'OR, *n.* One who ejects or dispossesses another of his land. *Blackstone.*

EJULA'TION, *n.* [L. *ejulatio*, from *ejulo*, to cry, to yell, to wail. Perhaps *j* represents *g*, and this word may be radically one with *yell*, Sax. *giellan*, *gyllan.*]

Outcry; a wailing; a loud cry expressive of grief or pain; mourning; lamentation. *Philips.*

EKE, *v. t.* [Sax. *eacan*; Sw. *öka*; Dan. *øger.* The primary sense is to add, or to stretch, extend, increase. Qu. L. *augeo.* The latter seems to be the Eng. to *wax.*]

1. To increase; to enlarge; as, to *eke* a store of provisions. *Spenser.*

2. To add to; to supply what is wanted; to enlarge by addition; sometimes with *out*; as, to *eke* or *eke out* a piece of cloth; to *eke out* a performance. *Pope.*

3. To lengthen; to prolong; as, to *eke out* the time. *Shak.*

EKE, *adv.* [Sax. *eac*; D. *ook*; G. *auch*; Sw. *och*; Dan. *og*; W. *ac*; L. *ac*, and, also. This seems to be the same word as the verb, and to denote, add, join, or addition. Ch. אחה to join.]

Also; likewise; in addition.

> 'Twill be prodigious hard to prove,
> That this is *eke* the throne of love. *Prior.*

[This word is nearly obsolete, being used only in poetry of the familiar and ludicrous kind.]

EKEBERG'ITE, *n.* [from *Ekeberg.*] A mineral, supposed to be a variety of scapolite. *Cleaveland.*

E'KED, *pp.* Increased; lengthened.

E'KING, *ppr.* Increasing; augmenting; lengthening.

E'KING, *n.* Increase or addition.

ELAB'ORATE, *v. t.* [L. *elaboro*, from *laboro*, *labor.* See *Labor.*]

1. To produce with labor.

> They in full joy *elaborate* a sigh. *Young.*

2. To improve or refine by successive operations. The heat of the sun *elaborates* the juices of plants and renders the fruit more perfect.

ELAB'ORATE, *a.* [L. *elaboratus.*] Wrought with labor; finished with great diligence; studied; executed with exactness; as an *elaborate* discourse; an *elaborate* performance.

> Drawn to the life in each *elaborate* page. *Waller.*

ELAB'ORATED, *pp.* Produced with labor or study; improved.

ELAB'ORATELY, *adv.* With great labor or study; with nice regard to exactness.

ELAB'ORATENESS, *n.* The quality of being elaborate or wrought with great labor. *Johnson.*

ELAB'ORATING, *ppr.* Producing with labor; improving; refining by successive operations.

ELABORA'TION, *n.* Improvement or refinement by successive operations. *Ray.*

ELA'IN, *n.* [Gr. ελαινος, oily.] The oily or liquid principle of oils and fats. *Chevreul.*

ELAMP'ING, *a.* [See *Lamp.*] Shining. [*Not in use.*]

EL'ANCE, *v. t.* [Fr. *elancer*, *lancer*, from *lance* or its root.] To throw or shoot; to hurl; to dart.

> While thy unerring hand *elanced*—a dart. *Prior.*

E'LAND, *n.* A species of heavy, clumsy antelope in Africa. *Barrow.*

ELA'OLITE, *n.* [Gr. ελαια, an olive.] A mineral, called also *fettstein* [fat-stone] from its greasy appearance. It has a crystaline structure, more or less distinctly foliated in directions parallel to the sides of a rhombic prism, and also in the direction of the shorter diagonals of the bases. Its fracture is uneven, and sometimes imperfectly conchoidal. Some varieties are slightly chatoyant. It is fusible by the blow-pipe into a white enamel. Its colors are greenish or bluish gray, greenish blue and flesh red, and it is more or less translucent. *Cleaveland.*

ELAPSE, *v. i.* *elaps'.* [L. *elapsus*, from *elabor, labor*, to slide.]
To slide away; to slip or glide away; to pass away silently, as time; *applied chiefly or wholly to time.*

[Instead of *elapse*, the noun, we use *lapse.*]

ELAPS'ED, *pp.* Slid or passed away, as time.

ELAPS'ING, *ppr.* Sliding away; gliding or passing away silently, as time.

ELAS'TIC, ELAS'TICAL, *a.* [from the Gr. ελαςρεω, to impel, or ελαω, or ελαυνω, to drive; Fr. *elastique;* It. Sp. *elastico.*]
Springing back; having the power of returning to the form from which it is bent, extended, pressed or distorted; having the inherent property of recovering its former figure, after any external pressure, which has altered that figure, is removed; rebounding; flying back. Thus a bow is *elastic*, and when the force which bends it is removed, it instantly returns to its former shape. The air is *elastic;* vapors are *elastic;* and when the force compressing them is removed, they instantly expand or dilate, and recover their former state.

ELAS'TICALLY, *adv.* In an elastic manner; by an elastic power; with a spring. *Lee.*

ELASTIC'ITY, *n.* The inherent property in bodies by which they recover their former figure or state, after external pressure, tension or distortion. Thus *elastic* gum, extended, will contract to its natural dimensions, when the force is removed. Air, when compressed, will, on the removal of the compressing force, instantly dilate and fill its former space.

ELA'TE, *a.* [L. *elatus.*] Raised; elevated in mind; flushed, as with success. Whence, lofty; haughty; as *elate* with victory. [*It is used chiefly in poetry.*]

ELA'TE, *v. t.* To raise or swell, as the mind or spirits; to elevate with success; to puff up; to make proud.
2. To raise; to exalt. [*Unusual.*] *Thomson.*

ELA'TED, *pp.* Elevated in mind or spirits; puffed up, as with honor, success or prosperity. We say, *elated* with success; *elated* with pride. [*This is used in prose.*]

ELA'TEDLY, *adv.* With elation.

ELATE'RIUM, *n.* A substance deposited from the very acrid juice of the Momordica elaterium, wild cucumber. It is in thin cakes of a greenish color and bitter taste, and is a powerful cathartic. *Webster's Manual.*

EL'ATERY, *n.* [Gr. ελατειρα.] Acting force or elasticity; as the *elatery* of the air. [*Unusual.*] *Ray.*

EL'ATIN, *n.* The active principle of the elaterium, from which the latter is supposed to derive its cathartic power. *Webster's Manual.*

ELA'TION, *n.* An inflation or elevation of mind proceding from self-approbation; self-esteem, vanity or pride, resulting from success. Hence, haughtiness; pride of prosperity. *Atterbury.*

EL'BOW, *n.* [Sax. *elnboga*, or *elneboga; ulna*, the arm, the ell, and *boga*, bow; contracted into *elboga*, elbow; G. *elbogen;* D. *elleboog;* Scot. *elbock, elbuck.*]
1. The outer angle made by the bend of the arm. *Encyc.*

> The wings that waft our riches out of sight
> Grow on the gamester's *elbows.* *Cowper.*

2. Any flexure or angle; the obtuse angle of a wall, building or road. *Encyc.*
To be at the elbow, is to be very near; to be by the side; to be at hand.

EL'BOW, *v. t.* To push with the elbow. *Dryden.*
2. To push or drive to a distance; to encroach on.

> He'll *elbow* out his neighbors. *Dryden.*

EL'BOW, *v. i.* To jut into an angle; to project; to bend.

EL'BOW-CHAIR, *n.* A chair with arms to support the elbows; an arm-chair. *Gay.*

EL'BOW-ROOM, *n.* Room to extend the elbows on each side; hence, in its usual acceptation, perfect freedom from confinement; ample room for motion or action. *South. Shak.*

ELD, *n.* [Sax. *eld*, or *æld*, old age. See *Old.*] Old age; decrepitude. *Obs.* *Spenser.*
2. Old people; persons worn out with age. *Chapman.*

[*This word is entirely obsolete. But its derivative* elder *is in use.*]

ELD'ER, *a.* [Sax. *ealdor*, the comparative degree of *eld*, now written *old.* See *Old.*]
1. Older; senior; having lived a longer time; born, produced or formed before something else; opposed to *younger.*

> The *elder* shall serve the younger. Gen. xxv.
> His *elder* son was in the field. Luke xv.

2. Prior in origin; preceding in the date of a commission; as an *elder* officer or magistrate. In this sense, we generally use *senior.*

ELD'ER, *n.* One who is older than another or others.
2. An ancestor.

> Carry your head as your *elders* have done before you. *L'Estrange.*

3. A person advanced in life, and who, on account of his age, experience and wisdom, is selected for office. Among rude nations, elderly men are rulers, judges, magistrates or counselors. Among the Jews, the seventy men associated with Moses in the government of the people, were *elders.* In the first christian churches, *elders* were persons who enjoyed offices or ecclesiastical functions, and the word includes apostles, pastors, teachers, presbyters, bishops or overseers. Peter and John call themselves *elders.* The first councils of christians were called presbyteria, councils of *elders.*

In the modern presbyterian churches, *elders* are officers who, with the pastors or ministers and deacons, compose the consistories or kirk-sessions, with authority to inspect and regulate matters of religion and discipline.

In the first churches of New England, the pastors or ministers were called elders or teaching elders.

ELD'ER, *n.* [Sax. *ellarn;* Sw. *hyll* or *hylletrå;* Dan. *hyld* or *hylde-træ;* G. *holder* or *hohlunder.* It seems to be named from *hollowness.*]
A tree or genus of trees, the Sambucus, of several species. The common elder of America bears black berries. Some species bear red berries. The stem and branches contain a soft pith.

ELD'ERLY, *a.* Somewhat old; advanced beyond middle age; bordering on old age; as *elderly* people.

ELD'ERSHIP, *n.* Seniority; the state of being older. *Dryden.*
2. The office of an elder. *Eliot.*
3. Presbytery; order of elders. *Hooker.*

ELD'EST, *a.* [Sax. *ealdest*, superlative of *eld*, old.]
Oldest; most advanced in age; that was born before others; as the *eldest* son or daughter. It seems to be always applied to persons or at least to animals, and not to things. If ever applied to things, it must signify, that was first formed or produced, that has existed the longest time. But applied to things we use *oldest.*

ELD'ING, *n.* [Sax. *ælan*, to burn.] Fuel. [*Local.*] *Grose.*

ELEAT'IC, *a.* An epithet given to a certain sect of philosophers, so called from Elea, or Velia, a town of the Lucani; as the *Eleatic* sect or philosophy. *Encyc.*

ELECAMPA'NE, *n.* [D. *alant;* G. *alant* or *alantwurzel;* L. *helenium*, from Gr. ελενιον, which signifies this plant and a feast in honor of Helen. Pliny informs us that this plant was so called because it was said to have sprung from the tears of Helen. The last part of the word is from the Latin *campana;* inula campana.]
A genus of plants, the Inula, of many species. The common elecampane has a perennial, thick, branching root, of a strong odor, and is used in medicine. It is sometimes called yellow star-wort. The Germans are said to candy the root, like ginger, calling it German spice. *Encyc. Hill.*

ELECT', *v. t.* [L. *electus*, from *eligo; e* or *ex* and *lego*, Gr. λεγω, to choose; Fr. *elire*, from *eligere;* It. *eleggere;* Sp. *elegir;* Port. *eleger.*]
1. Properly, to pick out; to select from among two or more, that which is preferred. Hence,
2. To select or take for an office or employment; to choose from among a number; to select or manifest preference by vote or designation; as, to *elect* a representative by ballot or viva voce; to *elect* a president or governor.
3. In *theology*, to designate, choose or select as an object of mercy or favor.
4. To choose; to prefer; to determine in favor of.

ELECT', *a.* Chosen; taken by preference from among two or more. Hence,
2. In *theology*, chosen as the object of mercy; chosen, selected or designated to eternal life; predestinated in the divine counsels.
3. Chosen, but not inaugurated, consecrated or invested with office; as bishop *elect;* emperor *elect;* governor or mayor

elect. But in the scriptures, and in theology, this word is generally used as a noun.

ELECT', *n*. One chosen or set apart; *applied to Christ*.

Behold my servant, whom I uphold; mine *elect*, in whom my soul delighteth. Is. xlii.

2. Chosen or designated by God to salvation; predestinated to glory as the end, and to sanctification as the means; usually with a plural signification, *the elect*.

Shall not God avenge his own *elect?* Luke xviii.

If it were possible, they shall deceive the very *elect*. Matt. xxiv.

He shall send his angels—and they shall gather his *elect* from the four winds. Matt. xxiv.

3. Chosen; selected; set apart as a peculiar church and people; *applied to the Israelites*. Is. xlv.

ELECT'ED, *pp*. Chosen; preferred; designated to office by some act of the constituents, as by vote; chosen or predestinated to eternal life.

ELECT'ING, *ppr*. Choosing; selecting from a number; preferring; designating to office by choice or preference; designating or predestinating to eternal salvation.

ELEC'TION, *n*. [L. *electio*.] The act of choosing; choice; the act of selecting one or more from others. Hence appropriately,

2. The act of choosing a person to fill an office or employment, by any manifestation of preference, as by ballot, uplifted hands or viva voce; as the *election* of a king, of a president, or a mayor.

Corruption in *elections* is the great enemy of freedom. *J. Adams*.

3. Choice; voluntary preference; free will; liberty to act or not. It is at his *election* to accept or refuse.

4. Power of choosing or selecting. *Davies*.

5. Discernment; discrimination; distinction.

To use men with much difference and *election* is good. *Bacon*.

6. In *theology*, divine choice; predetermination of God, by which persons are distinguished as objects of mercy, become subjects of grace, are sanctified and prepared for heaven.

There is a remnant according to the *election* of grace. Rom. xi.

7. The public choice of officers.

8. The day of a public choice of officers.

9. Those who are elected.

The *election* hath obtained it. Rom. xi.

ELECTIONEE'R, *v. i.* To make interest for a candidate at an election; to use arts for securing the election of a candidate.

ELECTIONEE'RING, *ppr*. Using influence to procure the election of a person.

ELECTIONEE'RING, *n*. The arts or practices used for securing the choice of one to office.

ELECT'IVE, *a*. Dependent on choice, as an *elective* monarchy, in which the king is raised to the throne by election; opposed to *hereditary*.

2. Bestowed or passing by election; as an office is *elective*.

3. Pertaining to or consisting in choice or right of choosing; as *elective* franchise.

4. Exerting the power of choice; as an *elective* act.

5. Selecting for combination; as *elective* attraction, which is a tendency in bodies to unite with certain kinds of matter in preference to others.

ELECT'IVELY, *adv*. By choice; with preference of one to another.

ELECT'OR, *n*. One who elects, or one who has the right of choice; a person who has, by law or constitution, the right of voting for an officer. In free governments, the people or such of them as possess certain qualifications of age, character and property, are the electors of their representatives, &c., in parliament, assembly, or other legislative body. In the United States, certain persons are appointed or chosen to be *electors* of the president or chief magistrate. In Germany, certain princes were formerly *electors* of the emperor, and elector was one of their titles, as the *elector* of Saxony.

ELECT'ORAL, *a*. Pertaining to election or electors. The *electoral college* in Germany consisted of all the electors of the empire, being nine in number, six secular princes and three archbishops.

ELECTORAL'ITY, for *electorate*, is not used.

ELECT'ORATE, *n*. The dignity of an elector in the German empire.

2. The territory of an elector in the German empire.

ELEC'TRE, *n*. [L. *electrum*.] Amber. [Bacon used this word for a compound or mixed metal. But the word is not now used.]

ELECT'RESS, *n*. The wife or widow of an elector in the German empire. *Chesterfield*.

ELEC'TRIC, } *a* [Fr. *electrique*; It. *elettrico*; Sp. *electrico*;
ELEC'TRICAL, }
from L. *electrum*, Gr. ηλεκτρον, amber.]

1. Containing electricity, or capable of exhibiting it when excited by friction; as an *electric* body, such as amber and glass; an *electric* substance.

2. In *general*, pertaining to electricity; as *electric* power or virtue; *electric* attraction or repulsion; *electric* fluid.

3. Derived from or produced by electricity; as *electrical* effects; *electric* vapor; *electric* shock.

4. Communicating a shock like electricity; as the *electric* eel or fish.

ELEC'TRIC, *n*. Any body or substance capable of exhibiting electricity by means of friction or otherwise, and of resisting the passage of it from one body to another. Hence an *electric* is called a *non-conductor*, an *electric per se*. Such are amber, glass, rosin, wax, gum-lac, sulphur, &c.

ELEC'TRICALLY, *adv*. In the manner of electricity, or by means of it.

ELECTRI''CIAN, *n*. A person who studies electricity, and investigates its properties, by observation and experiments; one versed in the science of electricity.

ELECTRIC'ITY, *n*. The operations of a very subtil fluid, which appears to be diffused through most bodies, remarkable for the rapidity of its motion, and one of the most powerful agents in nature. The name is given to the operations of this fluid, and to the fluid itself. As it exists in bodies, it is denominated a property of those bodies, though it may be a distinct substance, invisible, intangible and imponderable. When an electric body is rubbed with a soft dry substance, as with woolen cloth, silk or fur, it attracts or repels light substances, at a greater or less distance, according to the strength of the electric virtue; and the friction may be continued, or increased, till the electric body will emit sparks or flashes resembling fire, accompanied with a sharp sound. When the electric fluid passes from cloud to cloud, from the clouds to the earth, or from the earth to the clouds, it is called *lightning*, and produces thunder. Bodies which, when rubbed, exhibit this property, are called *electrics* or *non-conductors*. Bodies, which, when excited, do not exhibit this property, as water and metals, are called *non-electrics* or *conductors*, as they readily convey electricity from one body to another, at any distance, and such is the rapidity of the electric fluid in motion, that no perceptible space of time is required for its passage to any known distance. *Cavallo. Encyc.*

It is doubted by modern philosophers whether electricity is a fluid or material substance. Electricity, according to Professor Silliman, is a power which causes repulsion and attraction between the *masses* of bodies under its influence; a power which causes the *heterogeneous particles* of bodies to separate, thus producing chimical decomposition; one of the causes of magnetism.

ELEC'TRIFIABLE, *a*. [from *electrify*.] Capable of receiving electricity, or of being charged with it; that may become electric. *Fourcroy*.

2. Capable of receiving and transmitting the electrical fluid.

ELECTRIFICA'TION, *n*. The act of electrifying, or state of being charged with electricity. *Encyc*, art. *Bell*.

ELEC'TRIFIED, *pp*. Charged with electricity. *Encyc*.

ELEC'TRIFY, *v. t.* To communicate electricity to; to charge with electricity. *Encyc. Cavallo*.

2. To cause electricity to pass through; to affect by electricity; to give an electric shock to.

3. To excite suddenly; to give a sudden shock; as, the whole assembly was *electrified*.

ELECTRIFY, *v. i.* To become electric.

ELEC'TRIFYING, *ppr*. Charging with electricity; affecting with electricity; giving a sudden shock.

ELECTRIZA'TION, *n*. The act of electrizing. *Ure*.

ELEC'TRIZE, *v. t.* [Fr. *electriser*.] To electrify: *a word in popular use*.

ELECTRO-CHIM'ISTRY, *n*. That science which treats of the agency of electricity and galvanism in effecting chimical changes.

ELECTRO-MAGNET'IC, *a*. Designating what pertains to magnetism, as connected with electricity, or affected by it. *Electro-magnetic* phenomena. *Henry*.

ELECTRO-MAG'NETISM, *n*. That science which treats of the agency of electricity and galvanism in communicating magnetic properties.

ELECTROM'ETER, *n.* [L. *electrum*, Gr. ηλεκτρον, amber, and μετρεω, to measure.] An instrument for measuring the quantity or intensity of electricity, or its quality; or an instrument for discharging it from a jar. *Encyc. Henry. Ure.*

ELECTROMET'RICAL, *a.* Pertaining to an electrometer; made by an electrometer; as an *electrometrical* experiment.

ELECTRO-MO'TION, *n.* The motion of electricity or galvanism, or the passing of it from one metal to another, by the attraction or influence of one metal plate in contact with another. *Volta.*

ELECTRO-MO'TIVE, *a.* Producing electro-motion; as *electro-motive* power. *Henry.*

ELEC'TROMOTOR, *n.* [*electrum* and *motor.*] A mover of the electric fluid; an instrument or apparatus so called. *Volta.*

ELEC'TRON, *n.* Amber; also, a mixture of gold with a fifth part of silver. *Coxe.*

ELECTRO-NEG'ATIVE, *a.* Repelled by bodies negatively electrified, and attracted by those positively electrified. *Henry.*

ELEC'TROPHOR, } *n.* [*electrum* and
ELECTROPH'ORUS, } φορεω, to bear.] An instrument for preserving electricity a long time. *Dict. Nat. Hist.*

ELECTRO-POS'ITIVE, *a.* Attracted by bodies negatively electrified, or by the negative pole of the galvanic arrangement. *Henry.*

ELEC'TRUM, *n.* [L. amber.] In *mineralogy*, an argentiferous gold ore, or native alloy, of a pale brass yellow color. *Dict.*

ELEC'TUARY, *n.* [Low L. *electarium, electuarium*; Gr. εκλειγμα, or εκλεικτον, from λειχω, to lick. *Vossius.*]

In *pharmacy*, a form of medicine composed of powders, or other ingredients, incorporated with some conserve, honey or sirup, and made into due consistence, to be taken in doses, like boluses. *Quincy. Encyc.*

ELEEMOS'YNARY, *a.* [Gr. ελεημοσυνη, alms, from ελεεω, to pity, ελεος, compassion; W. *elus*, charitable; *elusen*, alms, benevolence. See *Alms.* It would be well to omit one *e* in this word.]

1. Given in charity; given or appropriated to support the poor; as *eleemosynary* rents or taxes. *Encyc.*

2. Relating to charitable donations; intended for the distribution of alms, or for the use and management of donations, whether for the subsistence of the poor or for the support and promotion of learning; as an *eleemosynary* corporation. A hospital founded by charity is an *eleemosynary* institution for the support of the poor, sick and impotent; a college founded by donations is an *eleemosynary* institution for the promotion of learning. The corporation entrusted with the care of such institutions is *eleemosynary.*

ELEEMOS'YNARY, *n.* One who subsists on charity. *South.*

EL'EGANCE, } *n.* [L. *elegantia*; Fr. *ele-*
EL'EGANCY, } *gance*; It. *eleganza.* Probably from L. *eligo*, to choose, though irregularly formed.]

In its primary sense, this word signifies that which is choice or select, as distinguished from what is common.

1. "The beauty of propriety, not of greatness," says Johnson.

Applied to manners or behavior, elegance is that fine polish, politeness or grace, which is acquired by a genteel education, and an association with wellbred company.

Applied to language, elegance respects the manner of speaking or of writing. *Elegance of speaking* is the propriety of diction and utterance, and the gracefulness of action or gesture; comprehending correct, appropriate and rich expressions, delivered in an agreeable manner. *Elegance of composition* consists in correct, appropriate and rich expressions, or well chosen words, arranged in a happy manner. Elegance implies neatness, purity, and correct, perspicuous arrangement, and is calculated to please a delicate taste, rather than to excite admiration or strong feeling. Elegance is applied also to form. Elegance in *architecture*, consists in the due symmetry and distribution of the parts of an edifice, or in regular proportions and arrangement. And in a similar sense, the word is applied to the person or human body. It is applied also to penmanship, denoting that form of letters which is most agreeable to the eye. In short, in a looser sense, it is applied to many works of art or nature remarkable for their beauty; as *elegance* of dress or furniture.

2. That which pleases by its nicety, symmetry, purity or beauty. In this sense it has a plural; as the nicer *elegancies* of art. *Spectator.*

EL'EGANT, *a.* [L. *elegans.*] Polished; polite; refined; graceful; pleasing to good taste; as *elegant* manners.

2. Polished; neat; pure; rich in expressions; correct in arrangement; as an *elegant* style or composition.

3. Uttering or delivering elegant language with propriety and grace; as an *elegant* speaker.

4. Symmetrical; regular; well formed in its parts, proportions and distribution; as an *elegant* structure.

5. Nice; sensible to beauty; discriminating beauty from deformity or imperfection; as an *elegant* taste. [This is a loose application of the word; *elegant* being used for *delicate.*]

6. Beautiful in form and colors; pleasing; as an *elegant* flower.

7. Rich; costly and ornamental; as *elegant* furniture or equipage.

EL'EGANTLY, *adv.* In a manner to please; with elegance; with beauty; with pleasing propriety; as a composition *elegantly* written.

2. With due symmetry; with well formed and duly proportioned parts; as a house *elegantly* built.

3. Richly; with rich or handsome materials well disposed; as a room *elegantly* furnished; a woman *elegantly* dressed.

ELE'GIAC, *a.* [Low L. *elegiacus.* See *Elegy.*] Belonging to elegy; plaintive; expressing sorrow or lamentation; as an *elegiac* lay; *elegiac* strains. *Gay.*

2. Used in elegies. Pentameter verse is *elegiac.* *Roscommon.*

EL'EGIST, *n.* A writer of elegies. *Goldsmith.*

ELE'GIT, *n.* [L. *eligo, elegi*, to choose.] A writ of execution, by which a defendant's goods are apprized, and delivered to the plaintiff, and if not sufficient to satisfy the debt, one moiety of his lands are delivered, to be held till the debt is paid by the rents and profits.

2. The title to estate by elegit. *Blackstone.*

EL'EGY, *n.* [L. *elegia*; Gr. ελεγειον, ελεγος, supposed to be from λεγω, to speak or utter. Qu. the root of the L. *lugeo.* The verbs may have a common origin, for to speak and to cry out in wailing are only modifications of the same act, to throw out the voice with more or less vehemence.]

1. A mournful or plaintive poem, or a funeral song; a poem or a song expressive of sorrow and lamentation. *Shak. Dryden.*

2. A short poem without points or affected elegancies. *Johnson.*

EL'EMENT, *n.* [L. *elementum*; Fr. *element*; It. and Sp. *elemento*; Arm. *elfenn*; W. *elven*, or *elvyz.* This word Owen refers to *elv* or *el*, a moving principle, that which has in itself the power of motion; and *el* is also a spirit or angel, which seems to be the Sax. *ælf*, an *elf.* Vossius assigns *elementum* to *eleo*, for *oleo*, to grow. See *Elf.*]

1. The first or constituent principle or minutest part of any thing; as the *elements* of earth, water, salt, or wood; the *elements* of the world; the *elements* of animal or vegetable bodies. So letters are called the *elements* of language.

2. An ingredient; a constituent part of any composition.

3. In *a chemical sense*, an atom; the minutest particle of a substance; that which cannot be divided by chemical analysis, and therefore considered as a simple substance, as oxygen, hydrogen, nitrogen, &c.

An *element* is strictly the last result of chemical analysis; that which cannot be decomposed by any means now employed. An *atom* is the last result of mechanical division; that which cannot be any farther divided, without decomposition: hence there may be both *elementary* and *compound* atoms.

4. In *the plural*, the first rules or principles of an art or science; rudiments; as the *elements* of geometry; the *elements* of music; the *elements* of painting; the *elements* of a theory.

5. In *popular language*, fire, air, earth and water, are called the four *elements*, as formerly it was supposed that these are simple bodies, of which the world is composed. Later discoveries prove air, earth and water to be compound bodies, and fire to be only the extrication of light and heat during *combustion.*

6. Element, in the singular, is sometimes used for the air. *Shak.*

7. The substance which forms the natural or most suitable habitation of an animal. Water is the proper *element* of fishes; air, of man. Hence,

8. The proper state or sphere of any thing; the state of things suited to one's temper

or habits. Faction is the *element* of a demagogue.

9. The matter or substances which compose the world.

The *elements* shall melt with fervent heat. 2 Pet. iii.

10. The outline or sketch; as the *elements* of a plan.

11. Moving cause or principle; that which excites action.

Passions, the *elements* of life. *Pope.*

EL'EMENT, *v, t.* To compound of elements or first principles. *Boyle.*

2. To constitute; to make as a first principle. *Donne.*

[*This word is rarely or never used.*]

ELEMENT'AL, *a.* Pertaining to elements.

2. Produced by some of the four supposed elements; as *elemental* war. *Dryden.*

3. Produced by elements; as *elemental* strife. *Pope.*

4. Arising from first principles. *Brown.*

ELEMENTAL'ITY, *n.* Composition of principles or ingredients. *Whitlock.*

ELEMENT'ALLY, *adv.* According to elements; literally; as the words, "Take, eat; this is my body," *elementally* understood. *Milton.*

ELEMENTAR'ITY, } *n.* The state of
ELEMENT'ARINESS, } being elementary; the simplicity of nature; uncompounded state. *Brown.*

ELEMENT'ARY, *a.* Primary; simple; uncompounded; uncombined; having only one principle or constituent part; as an *elementary* substance. *Elementary* particles are those into which a body is resolved by decomposition.

2. Initial; rudimental; containing, teaching or discussing first principles, rules or rudiments; as an *elementary* treatise or disquisition. *Reid. Blackstone.*

3. Treating of elements; collecting, digesting or explaining principles; as an *elementary* writer.

EL'EMI, *n.* The gum elemi, so called; but said to be a resinous substance, the produce of the *Amyris elemifera*, a small tree or shrub of South America. It is of a whitish color tinged with green or yellow.

ELENCH', *n.* [L. *elenchus*; Gr. ελεγχος, from ελεγχω, to argue, to refute.]

1. A vicious or fallacious argument, which is apt to deceive under the appearance of truth; a sophism. [*Little used.*] *Brown.*

2. In *antiquity*, a kind of earring set with pearls. *Encyc.*

ELENCH'ICAL, *a.* Pertaining to an elench.

ELENCH'ICALLY, *adv.* By means of an elench. [*Not in use.*] *Brown.*

ELENCH'IZE, *v. i.* To dispute. [*Not in use.*] *B. Jonson.*

EL'EPHANT, *n.* [Sax. *elp, ylp*; Gr. ελεφας; L. *elephas, elephantus*; probably from the Heb. אלף, a leader or chief, the chief or great animal.]

1. The largest of all quadrupeds, belonging to the order of Bruta. This animal has no foreteeth in either jaw; the canine-teeth are very long; and he has a long proboscis or trunk, by which he conveys food and drink to his mouth. The largest of these animals is about 16 feet long and 14 feet high; but smaller varieties are not more than seven feet high. The eyes are small and the feet short, round, clumsy, and distinguishable only by the toes. The trunk is a cartilaginous and muscular tube, extending from the upper jaw, and is seven or eight feet in length. The general shape of his body resembles that of swine. His skin is rugged, and his hair thin. The two large tusks are of a yellowish color, and extremely hard. The bony substance of these is called *ivory*. The elephant is 30 years in coming to his full growth, and he lives to 150 or 200 years of age. Elephants are natives of the warm climates of Africa and Asia, where they are employed as beasts of burden. They were formerly used in war. *Encyc.*

2. Ivory; the tusk of the elephant. *Dryden.*

EL'EPHANT-BEETLE, *n.* A large species of Scarabæus, or beetle, found in South America. It is of a black color; the body covered with a hard shell, as thick as that of a crab. It is nearly four inches long. The feelers are horny, and the proboscis an inch and a quarter in length. *Encyc.*

ELEPHANT'S-FOOT, *n.* A plant, the Elephantopus. *Muhlenberg.*

ELEPHANTI'ASIS, *n.* [L. and Gr. from ελεφας, elephant.]

A species of leprosy, so called from covering the skin with incrustations, like those of an elephant. It is a chronic and contagious disease, marked by a thickening and greasiness of the legs, with loss of hair and feeling, a swelling of the face, and a hoarse nasal voice. It affects the whole body; the bones, as well as the skin, are covered with spots and tumors, at first red, but afterwards black. *Coxe. Encyc.*

ELEPHANT'INE, *a.* Pertaining to the elephant; huge; resembling an elephant: or perhaps white, like ivory.

2. In *antiquity*, an appellation given to certain books in which the Romans registered the transactions of the senate, magistrates, emperors and generals; so called perhaps, as being made of ivory.

ELEUSIN'IAN, *a.* Relating to Eleusis in Greece; as *Eleusinian* mysteries or festivals, the festivals and mysteries of Ceres.

EL'EVATE, *v. t.* [L. *elevo*; *e* and *levo*, to raise; Fr. *elever*; Sp. *elevar*; It. *elevare*; Eng. to *lift*. See *Lift*.]

1. To raise, in a literal and general sense; to raise from a low or deep place to a higher.

2. To exalt; to raise to higher state or station; as, to *elevate* a man to an office.

3. To improve, refine or dignify; to raise from or above low conceptions; as, to *elevate* the mind.

4. To raise from a low or common state; to exalt; as, to *elevate* the character; to *elevate* a nation.

5. To elate with pride. *Milton.*

6. To excite; to cheer; to animate; as, to *elevate* the spirits.

7. To take from; to detract; to lessen by detraction. [*Not used.*] *Hooker.*

8. To raise from any tone to one more acute; as, to *elevate* the voice.

9. To augment or swell; to make louder, as sound.

EL'EVATE, *a.* [L. *elevatus.*] Elevated; raised aloft. *Milton.*

EL'EVATED, *pp.* Raised; exalted; dignified; elated; excited; made more acute or more loud, as sound.

EL'EVATING, *ppr.* Raising; exalting; dignifying; elating; cheering.

ELEVA'TION, *n.* [L. *elevatio.*] The act of raising or conveying from a lower or deeper place to a higher.

2. The act of exalting in rank, degree or condition; as the *elevation* of a man to a throne.

3. Exaltation; an elevated state; dignity.

Angels, in their several degrees of *elevation* above us, may be endowed with more comprehensive faculties. *Locke.*

4. Exaltation of mind by more noble conceptions; as *elevation* of mind, of thoughts, of ideas. *Norris.*

5. Exaltation of style; lofty expressions; words and phrases expressive of lofty conceptions. *Wotton*

6. Exaltation of character or manners.

7. Attention to objects above us; a raising of the mind to superior objects. *Hooker.*

8. An elevated place or station.

9. Elevated ground; a rising ground; a hill or mountain.

10. A passing of the voice from any note to one more acute; also, a swelling or augmentation of voice.

11. In *astronomy*, altitude; the distance of a heavenly body above the horizon, or the arc of a vertical circle intercepted between it and the horizon.

12. In *gunnery*, the angle which the chace of a cannon or mortar, or the axis of the hollow cylinder, makes with the plane of the horizon. *Bailey.*

13. In *dialling*, the angle which the style makes with the substylar line. *Bailey.*

Elevation of the Host, in Catholic countries, that part of the mass in which the priest raises the host above his head for the people to adore. *Encyc.*

EL'EVATOR, *n.* One who raises, lifts or exalts.

2. In *anatomy*, a muscle which serves to raise a part of the body, as the lip or the eye.

3. A surgical instrument for raising a depressed portion of a bone. *Coxe.*

EL'EVATORY, *n.* An instrument used in trepanning, for raising a depressed or fractured part of the skull. *Coxe. Encyc.*

ELE'VE, *n.* [Fr.] One brought up or protected by another. *Chesterfield.*

ELEV'EN, *a.* elev'n. [Sax. *endlefene, endleof, endlufa*; Sw. *elfva*; Dan. *elleve*; G. and D. *elf*; Isl. *ellefu*. Qu. *one left* after ten.] Ten and one added; as *eleven* men.

ELEV'ENTH, *a.* [Sax. *endlyfta, endlefta*; Sw. *elfte*; Dan. *ellevte*; D. *elfde*; G. *elfte*.] The next in order to the tenth; as the *eleventh* chapter.

ELF, *n.* plu. *elves.* [Sax. *ælf*, or *elfenne*, a spirit, the night-mar; a ghost, hag or witch; Sw. *älfver*. In W. *el* is a moving principle, a spirit; *elv* is the same; *elu* is to move onward, to go; *elven* is an operative cause, a constituent part, an *element*; and *elf* is what moves in a simple or pure state, a spirit or demon. From these facts, it would seem that *elf* is from a verb signifying to move, to flow; and *älf* or *elf* in Swedish, *elv* in Danish, is a river, whence *Elbe*. So *spirit* is from blowing, a flowing of air. In Saxon *æl* is *oil* and an *eel*, and *ælan* is to kindle; all perhaps from the sense of moving, flowing or shooting along. The *elf* seems to correspond to the *demon* of the Greeks.]

1. A wandering spirit; a fairy; a hobgoblin; an imaginary being which our rude ancestors supposed to inhabit unfrequented places, and in various ways to affect mankind. Hence in Scottish, *elf-shot* is an elf-arrow; an arrow-head of flint, supposed to be shot by elfs; and it signifies also a disease supposed to be produced by the agency of spirits.

Every *elf*, and fairy sprite,
Hop as light as bird from brier. *Shak.*

2. An evil spirit; a devil. *Dryden.*
3. A diminutive person. *Shenstone.*

ELF, *v. t.* To entangle hair in so intricate a manner, that it cannot be disentangled. This work was formerly ascribed to *elves.* *Johnson. Shak.*

ELF′-ARROW, *n.* A name given to flints in the shape of arrow-heads, vulgarly supposed to be shot by fairies. *Encyc.*

ELF′-LOCK, *n.* A knot of hair twisted by elves. *Shak.*

ELF′IN, *a.* Relating or pertaining to elves. *Spenser.*

ELF′IN, *n.* A little urchin. *Shenstone.*

ELF′ISH, *a.* Resembling elves; clad in disguise. *Mason.*

ELIC′IT, *v. t.* [L. *elicio; e* or *ex* and *lacio*, to allure, D. *lokken*, G. *locken*, Sw. *locka*, Dan. *lokker*. Class Lg.]

1. To draw out; to bring to light; to deduce by reason or argument; as, to *elicit* truth by discussion.
2. To strike out; as, to *elicit* sparks of fire by collision.

ELIC′IT, *a.* Brought into act; brought from possibility into real existence. [*Little used.*] *Johnson.*

ELICITA′TION, *n.* The act of eliciting; the act of drawing out. *Bramhall.*

ELIC′ITED, *pp.* Brought or drawn out; struck out.

ELIC′ITING, *ppr.* Drawing out; bringing to light; striking out.

ELI′DE, *v. t.* [L. *elido; e* and *lædo.*] To break or dash in pieces; to crush. [*Not used.*] *Hooker.*

2. To cut off a syllable. *Brit. Crit.*

ELIĠIBIL′ITY, *n.* [from *eligible.*] Worthiness or fitness to be chosen; the state or quality of a thing which renders it preferable to another, or desirable.

2. The state of being capable of being chosen to an office. *U. States.*

EL′IĠIBLE, *a.* [Fr. from L. *eligo*, to choose or select; *e* and *lego.*]

1. Fit to be chosen; worthy of choice; preferable.

In deep distress, certainty is more *eligible* than suspense. *Clarissa.*

2. Suitable; proper; desirable; as, the house stands in an *eligible* situation.
3. Legally qualified to be chosen; as, a man is or is not *eligible* to an office.

EL′IĠIBLENESS, *n.* Fitness to be chosen in preference to another; suitableness; desirableness.

EL′IĠIBLY, *adv.* In a manner to be worthy of choice; suitably.

ELIM′INATE, *v. t.* [L. *elimino; e* or *ex* and *limen*, threshhold.]

1. To thrust out of doors. *Lovelace.*
2. To expel; to thrust out; to discharge, or throw off; to set at liberty.

This detains secretions which nature finds it necessary to *eliminate.* *Med. Repos.*

ELIM′INATED, *pp.* Expelled; thrown off; discharged.

ELIM′INATING, *ppr.* Expelling; discharging; throwing off.

ELIMINA′TION, *n.* The act of expelling or throwing off; the act of discharging, or secreting by the pores.

ELIQUA′TION, *n.* [L. *eliquo*, to melt; *e* and *liquo.*]

In *chimistry*, the operation by which a more fusible substance is separated from one that is less so, by means of a degree of heat sufficient to melt the one and not the other; as an alloy of copper and lead. *Encyc. Ure.*

ELI″SION, *n.* *s* as *z.* [L. *elisio*, from *elido*, to strike off; *e* and *lædo.*]

1. In *grammar*, the cutting off or suppression of a vowel at the end of a word, for the sake of sound or measure, when the next word begins with a vowel; as, th' embattled plain; th' empyreal sphere.
2. Division; separation. [*Not used.*] *Bacon.*

ELI′SOR, *n.* *s* as *z.* [Norm. *eliser*, to chuse; Fr. *elire, elisant.*]

In *law*, a sheriff's substitute for returning a jury. When the sheriff is not an indifferent person, as when he is a party to a suit, or related by blood or affinity to either of the parties, the *venire* is issued to the coroners; or if any exception lies to the coroners, the *venire* shall be directed to two clerks of the court, or to two persons of the county, named by the court, and sworn; and these, who are called *elisors* or electors, shall return the jury. *Blackstone.*

ELIX′ATE, *v. t.* [L. *elixo.*] To extract by boiling.

ELIXA′TION, *n.* [L. *elixus*, from *elixio*, to boil, to moisten or macerate, from *lixo, lix.*]

1. The act of boiling or stewing; also, concoction in the stomach; digestion. *Brown.*
2. In *pharmacy*, the extraction of the virtues of ingredients by boiling or stewing; also, lixiviation. *Bailey. Encyc.*

ELIX′IR, *n.* [Fr. Sp. Port. *elixir; It. elisire;* from L. *elixus, elixio, lixo, lix*, or as others alledge, it is from the Arabic *al-ecsir*, chimistry.]

1. In *medicine*, a compound tincture, extracted from two or more ingredients. A tincture is drawn from one ingredient; an elixir from several. But tincture is also applied to a composition of many ingredients. An elixir is a liquid medicine made by a strong infusion, where the ingredients are almost dissolved in the menstruum, and give it a thicker consistence than that of a tincture. *Encyc. Quincy.*
2. A liquor for transmuting metals into gold. *Donne.*
3. Quintessence; refined spirit. *South.*
4. Any cordial; that substance which invigorates. *Milton.*

ELK, *n.* [Sax. *elch;* Sw. *elg;* L. *alce, alces;* Dan. *els-dyr.* This animal is described by Cesar and Pausanias.]

A quadruped of the Cervine genus, with palmated horns, and a fleshy protuberance on the throat. The neck is short, with a short, thick, upright mane; the eyes are small; the ears long, broad and slouching; and the upper lip hangs over the under lip. It is the largest of the deer kind, being seventeen hands high and weighing twelve hundred pounds. It is found in the northern regions of Europe, Asia and America. In the latter country it is usually called *Moose*, from the Indian name *musu.*

ELK-NUT, *n.* A plant, the Hamiltonia, called also oil-nut. *Muhlenberg.*

ELL, *n.* [Sax. *elne;* Sw. *aln;* D. *ell, elle;* G. *elle;* Fr. *aune;* Arm. *goalen;* L. *ulna;* Gr. *ωλενη;* W. *elin*, an elbow, and *glin*, the knee. Qu.]

A measure of different lengths in different countries, used chiefly for measuring cloth. The ells chiefly used in Great Britain are the English and Flemish. The English ell is three feet and nine inches, or a yard and a quarter. The Flemish ell is 27 inches, or three quarters of a yard. The English is to the Flemish as five to three. In Scotland, an ell is 37 $\frac{2}{10}$ English inches. *Encyc.*

ELLIPSE, *n.* *ellips′.* An ellipsis.

ELLIP′SIS, *n.* plu. *ellip′ses.* [Gr. *ελλειψις*, an omission or defect, from *ελλειπω*, to leave or pass by, *λειπω*, to *leave.*]

1. In *geometry*, an oval figure generated from the section of a cone, by a plane cutting both sides of it, but not parallel to the base. *Bailey. Encyc. Harris.*
2. In *grammar*, defect; omission; a figure of syntax, by which one or more words are omitted, which the hearer or reader may supply; as, the heroic virtues I admire, for the heroic virtues *which* I admire.

ELLIPS′OID, *n.* [*ellipsis* and Gr. *ειδος*, form.]

In *conics*, a solid or figure formed by the revolution of an ellipse about its axis; an elliptic conoid; a spheroid. *Edin. Encyc.*

ELLIPSOID′AL, *a.* Pertaining to an ellipsoid; having the form of an ellipsoid.

ELLIP′TIC, ELLIP′TICAL, } *a.* Pertaining to an ellipsis; having the form of an ellipse; oval.

The planets move in *elliptical* orbits, having the sun in one focus, and by a radius from the sun, they describe equal areas in equal times. *Cheyne.*

2. Defective; as an *elliptical* phrase.

ELLIPTICALLY, *adv.* According to the figure called an ellipsis.

2. Defectively.

ELM, *n.* [Sax. *elm*, or *ulm-treou;* D. *olm;* G. *ulme;* Sw. *alm*, or *alm-trâ*, elm-tree; Dan. *alm;* L. *ulmus;* Sp. *olmo*, and *alamo;* Corn. *elau;* Russ. *ilema, ilma*, or *ilina.* Qu. W. *llwyv*, a platform, a frame, an *elm*, from extending.]

A tree of the genus Ulmus. The common elm is one of the largest and most majestic trees of the forest, and is cultivated for shade and ornament. Another species, the fulva, is called slippery elm, from the quality of its inner bark. One species seems to have been used to support vines.

The treaty which William Penn made with the natives in 1682 was negotiated under a large *Elm* which grew on the spot now called Kensington, just above Philadelphia. It was pros-trated by a storm in 1810, at which time its stem measured 24 feet in circumference.

Memoirs of Hist. Soc. Penn.

ELM'Y, *a.* Abounding with elms. *Warton.*

ELOCA'TION, *n.* [L. *eloco.*] A removal from the usual place of residence. *Bp. Hall.*

2. Departure from the usual method; an ecstasy. *Fotherby.*

ELOCU'TION, *n.* [L. *elocutio*, from *eloquor*; *e* and *loquor*, to speak, Gr. ληκεω, λακεω.]

1. Pronunciation; the utterance or delivery of words, particularly in public discourses and arguments. We say of *elocution*, it is good or bad; clear, fluent or melodious.

Elocution, which anciently embraced style and the whole art of rhetoric, now signifies manner of delivery. *E. Porter.*

2. In *rhetoric, elocution* consists of elegance, composition and dignity; and Dryden uses the word as nearly synonymous with *eloquence*, the act of expressing thoughts with elegance or beauty.

3. Speech; the power of speaking.

Whose taste—gave *elocution* to the mute. *Milton.*

4. In *ancient treatises on oratory*, the wording of a discourse; the choice and order of words; composition; the act of framing a writing or discourse. *Cicero. Quinctilian.*

ELOCU'TIVE, *a.* Having the power of eloquent speaking.

EL'OGIST, *n.* An eulogist. [*Not used.*]

EL'OGY, **ELO'GIUM**, *n.* [Fr. *eloge*; L. *elogium*; Gr. λογος. See *Eulogy.*] The praise bestowed on a person or thing; panegyric. [But we generally use *eulogy.*] *Wotton. Holder.*

ELOIN', *v. t.* [Fr. *eloigner*, to remove far off.]

1. To separate and remove to a distance. *Spenser. Donne.*

2. To convey to a distance, and withhold from sight.

The sheriff may return that the goods or beasts are *eloined.* *Blackstone.*

ELOIN'ATE, *v. t.* To remove. *Howell.*

ELOIN'ED, *pp.* Removed to a distance; carried far off.

ELOIN'ING, *ppr.* Removing to a distance from another, or to a place unknown.

ELOIN'MENT, *n.* Removal to a distance; distance.

ELONG', *v. t.* [Low L. *elongo.*] To put far off; to retard. *Obs.* *Shenstone.*

ELON'GATE, *v. t.* [Low L. *elongo*, from *longus.* See *Long.*]

1. To lengthen; to extend.

2. To remove farther off. *Brown.*

ELON'GATE, *v. i.* To depart from; to recede; to move to a greater distance; particularly, to recede apparently from the sun, as a planet in its orbit.

ELON'GATED, *pp.* Lengthened; removed to a distance.

ELON'GATING, *ppr.* Lengthening; extending.

2. Receding to a greater distance, particularly as a planet from the sun in its orbit.

ELONGA'TION, *n.* The act of stretching or lengthening; as the *elongation* of a fiber. *Arbuthnot.*

2. The state of being extended.

3. Distance; space which separates one thing from another. *Glanville.*

4. Departure; removal; recession.

5. Extension; continuation.

May not the mountains of Westmoreland and Cumberland be considered as *elongations* of these two chains. *Pinkerton.*

6. In *astronomy*, the recess of a planet from the sun, as it appears to the eye of a spectator on the earth; apparent departure of a planet from the sun in its orbit; as the *elongation* of Venus or Mercury.

7. In *surgery*, an imperfect luxation, occasioned by the stretching or lengthening of the ligaments; or the extension of a part beyond its natural dimensions. *Encyc. Coxe.*

ELO'PE, *v. i.* [D. *loopen, wegloopen*; G. *laufen, entlaufen*; Sw. *lôpa*; Dan. *löber*; Sax. *hleapan*; Eng. to *leap.* In all the dialects, except the English, *leap* signifies to run. Qu. Heb. חלף. Class Lb. No. 30.]

1. To run away; to depart from one's proper place or station privately or without permission; to quit, without permission or right, the station in which one is placed by law or duty. Particularly and appropriately, to run away or depart from a husband, and live with an adulterer, as a married woman; or to quit a father's house, privately or without permission, and marry or live with a gallant, as an unmarried woman.

2. To run away; to escape privately; to depart, without permission, as a son from a father's house, or an apprentice from his master's service.

ELO'PEMENT, *n.* Private or unlicensed departure from the place or station to which one is assigned by duty or law; as the *elopement* of a wife from her husband, or of a daughter from her father's house, usually with a lover or gallant. It is sometimes applied to the departure of a son or an apprentice, in like manner.

ELO'PING, *ppr.* Running away; departing privately, or without permission, from a husband, father or master.

E'LOPS, *n.* [Gr. ελλοψ.] A fish, inhabiting the seas of America and the West Indies, with a long body, smooth head, one dorsal fin, and a deeply furcated tail, with a horizontal lanceolated spine, above and below, at its base. *Pennant.*

2. The sea-serpent. *Dict. Nat. Hist.*

EL'OQUENCE, *n.* [L. *eloquentia*, from *eloquor, loquor*, to speak; Gr. ληκεω, λακω, to crack, to sound, to speak. The primary sense is probably to burst with a sound, for the Gr. has λακις, a fissure, from the same root; whence λακιζω, to open or split; whence L. *lacero*, to tear; and hence perhaps Eng. a *leak.* Qu. the root of *clack.* See Class Lg. No. 51. 27.]

1. Oratory; the act or the art of speaking well, or with fluency and elegance. Eloquence comprehends a good elocution or utterance; correct, appropriate and rich expressions, with fluency, animation and suitable action. Hence *eloquence* is adapted to please, affect and persuade. Demosthenes in Greece, Cicero in Rome, lord Chatham and Burke in Great Britain, were distinguished for their *eloquence* in declamation, debate or argument.

2. The power of speaking with fluency and elegance.

3. Elegant language, uttered with fluency and animation.

She uttereth piercing *eloquence.* *Shak.*

4. It is sometimes applied to written language.

EL'OQUENT, *a.* Having the power of oratory; speaking with fluency, propriety, elegance and animation; as an *eloquent* orator; an *eloquent* preacher.

2. Composed with elegance and spirit; elegant and animated; adapted to please, affect and persuade; as an *eloquent* address; an *eloquent* petition or remonstrance; an *eloquent* history.

EL'OQUENTLY, *adv.* With eloquence; in an eloquent manner; in a manner to please, affect and persuade.

ELSE, *a.* or *pron. els.* [Sax. *elles*; Dan. *ellers*, from *eller*, or; L. *alius, alias.* See *Alien.*] Other; one or something beside. Who *else* is coming? What *else* shall I give? Do you expect any thing *else?* [This word, if considered to be an adjective or pronoun, never precedes its noun, but always follows it.]

ELSE, *adv. els.* Otherwise; in the other case; if the fact were different. Thou desirest not sacrifice, *else* would I give it; that is, *if* thou didst desire sacrifice, I would give it. Ps. v. 16. Repent, or *else* I will come to thee quickly; that is, repent, or if thou shouldst not repent, if the case or fact should be different, I will come to thee quickly. Rev. ii. 5.

2. Beside; except that mentioned; as, no where *else.*

ELSEWHERE, *adv.* In any other place; as, these trees are not to be found *elsewhere.*

2. In some other place; in other places indefinitely. It is reported in town and *elsewhere.*

ELU'CIDATE, *v. t.* [Low L. *elucido*, from *eluceo, luceo*, to shine, or from *lucidus*, clear, bright. See *Light.*] To make clear or manifest; to explain; to remove obscurity from, and render intelligible; to illustrate. An example will *elucidate* the subject. An argument may *elucidate* an obscure question. A fact related by one historian may *elucidate* an obscure passage in another's writings.

ELU'CIDATED, *pp.* Explained; made plain, clear or intelligible.

ELU'CIDATING, *ppr.* Explaining; making clear or intelligible.

ELUCIDA'TION, *n.* The act of explaining or throwing light on any obscure subject; explanation; exposition; illustration; as, one example may serve for an *elucidation* of the subject.

ELU'CIDATOR, *n.* One who explains; an expositor.

ELU'DE, *v. t.* [L. *eludo*; *e* and *ludo*, to play; Sp. *eludir*; It. *eludere*; Fr. *eluder.* The Latin verb forms *lusi, lusum*; and this may be the Heb. Ch. Ar. לוץ to deride. Class Ls. No. 5.]

1. To escape; to evade; to avoid by artifice, stratagem, wiles, deceit, or dexterity; as, to *elude* an enemy; to *elude* the sight; to *elude* an officer; to *elude* detection; to *elude* vigilance; to *elude* the force of an argument; to *elude* a blow or stroke.

2. To mock by an unexpected escape.

> Me gentle Delia beckons from the plain,
> Then, hid in shades, *eludes* her eager swain. *Pope.*

3. To escape being seen; to remain unseen or undiscovered. The cause of magnetism has hitherto *eluded* the researches of philosophers.

ELU'DIBLE, *a.* That may be eluded or escaped. *Swift.*

ELU'SION, *n. s* as *z.* [L. *elusio.* See *Elude.*] An escape by artifice or deception; evasion. *Brown.*

ELU'SIVE, *a.* Practising elusion; using arts to escape.

> *Elusive* of the bridal day, she gives
> Fond hopes to all, and all with hopes deceives. *Pope.*

ELU'SORINESS, *n.* The state of being elusory.

ELU'SORY, *a.* Tending to elude; tending to deceive; evasive; fraudulent; fallacious; deceitful. *Brown.*

ELU'TE, *v. t.* [L. *eluo, elutum;* qu. *e* and *lavo.* See *Elutriate.*] To wash off; to cleanse. *Arbuthnot.*

ELU'TRIATE, *v. t.* [L. *elutrio;* Sw. *lutra, luttra,* to cleanse, to defecate; Dan. *lutter,* pure; Sax. *lutter,* pure; *ladian,* to purify; G. *lauter;* D. *louter,* pure; Ir. *gleith.* Qu. Class Ls. No. 30.]

To purify by washing; to cleanse by separating foul matter, and decanting or straining off the liquor. In *chimistry,* to pulverize and mix a solid substance with water, and decant the extraneous lighter matter that may rise or be suspended in the water. *Coxe. Encyc.*

ELU'TRIATED, *pp.* Cleansed by washing and decantation.

ELU'TRIATING, *ppr.* Purifying by washing and decanting.

ELUTRIA'TION, *n.* The operation of pulverizing a solid substance, mixing it with water, and pouring off the liquid, while the foul or extraneous substances are floating, or after the coarser particles have subsided, and while the finer parts are suspended in the liquor.

ELUX'ATE, *v. t.* [L. *eluxatus.*] To dislocate. [See *Luxate.*]

ELUXA'TION, *n.* The dislocation of a bone. [See *Luxation.*]

ELVELOCKS. [See *Elf-lock.*]

ELV'ERS, *n.* Young eels; young congers or sea-eels.

ELVES, *plu.* of *elf.*

ELV'ISH, *a.* More properly *elfish,* which see.

ELYS'IAN, *a. elyzh'un.* [L. *elysius.*] Pertaining to elysium or the seat of delight; yielding the highest pleasures; deliciously soothing; exceedingly delightful; as *elysian* fields.

ELYS'IUM, *n. elyzh'um.* [L. *elysium;* Gr. *ηλυσιον.*]

In *ancient mythology,* a place assigned to happy souls after death; a place in the lower regions, furnished with rich fields, groves, shades, streams, &c., the seat of future happiness. Hence, any delightful place. *Encyc. Shak.*

'EM, A contraction of *them.*

> They took 'em. *Hudibras.*

EMAC'ERATE, *v. t.* To make lean. [*Not in use.*]

EMA'CIATE, *v. i.* [L. *emacio,* from *maceo,* or *macer,* lean; Gr. *μικκος, μικρος,* small; Fr. *maigre;* Eng. *meager, meek;* It. Sp. Port. *magro;* D. Sw. Dan. G. *mager;* Ch. מאן, to be thin. Class Mg. No. 2. 9. 13.]

To lose flesh gradually; to become lean by pining with sorrow, or by loss of appetite or other cause; to waste away, as flesh; to decay in flesh.

EMA'CIATE, *v. t.* To cause to lose flesh gradually; to waste the flesh and reduce to leanness.

> Sorrow, anxiety, want of appetite, and disease, often *emaciate* the most robust bodies.

EMA'CIATE, *a.* Thin; wasted. *Shenstone.*

EMA'CIATED, *pp.* Reduced to leanness by a gradual loss of flesh; thin; lean.

EMA'CIATING, *ppr.* Wasting the flesh gradually; making lean.

EMACIA'TION, *n.* The act of making lean or thin in flesh; or a becoming lean by a gradual waste of flesh.

2. The state of being reduced to leanness.

EMAC'ULATE, *v. t.* [infra.] To take spots from. [*Little used.*]

EMACULA'TION, *n.* [L. *emaculo,* from *e* and *macula,* a spot.]

The act or operation of freeing from spots. [*Little used.*]

EM'ANANT, *a.* [L. *emanans.* See *Emanate.*] Issuing or flowing from. *Hale.*

EM'ANATE, *v. i.* [L. *emano; e* and *mano,* to flow; Sp. *emanar;* Fr. *emaner;* It. *emanare.* Class Mn. No. 11. 9.]

1. To issue from a source; to flow from; *applied to fluids;* as, light *emanates* from the sun; perspirable matter, from animal bodies.

2. To proceed from a source or fountain; as, the powers of government in republics *emanate* from the people.

EM'ANATING, *ppr.* Issuing or flowing from a fountain.

EMANA'TION, *n.* The act of flowing or proceeding from a fountain-head or origin.

2. That which issues, flows or proceeds from any source, substance or body; efflux; effluvium. Light is an *emanation* from the sun; wisdom, from God; the authority of laws, from the supreme power.

EM'ANATIVE, *a.* Issuing from another.

EMAN'CIPATE, *v. t.* [L. *emancipo,* from *e* and *mancipium,* a slave; *manus,* hand, and *capio,* to take, as slaves were anciently prisoners taken in war.]

1. To set free from servitude or slavery, by the voluntary act of the proprietor; to liberate; to restore from bondage to freedom; as, to *emancipate* a slave.

2. To set free or restore to liberty; *in a general sense.*

3. To free from bondage or restraint of any kind; to liberate from subjection, controlling power or influence; as, to *emancipate* one from prejudices or error.

4. In *ancient Rome,* to set a son free from subjection to his father, and give him the capacity of managing his affairs, as if he was of age. *Encyc.*

EMAN'CIPATE, *a.* Set at liberty. *Cowper.*

EMAN'CIPATED, *pp.* Set free from bondage, slavery, servitude, subjection or dependence; liberated.

EMAN'CIPATING, *ppr.* Setting free from bondage, servitude or dependence; liberating.

EMANCIPA'TION, *n.* The act of setting free from slavery, servitude, subjection or dependence; deliverance from bondage or controlling influence; liberation; as the *emancipation* of slaves by their proprietors; the *emancipation* of a son among the Romans; the *emancipation* of a person from prejudices, or from a servile subjection to authority.

EMAN'CIPATOR, *n.* One who emancipates or liberates from bondage or restraint.

EMA'NE, *v. i.* [L. *emano.*] To issue or flow from. *Enfield.*

But this is not an elegant word. [See *Emanate.*]

EM'ARGINATE, } *a.* [Fr. *marge;* L. *margo,* whence *emargino.*]
EM'ARGINATED,

1. In *botany,* notched at the end; *applied to the leaf, corol or stigma.* *Martyn.*

2. In *mineralogy,* having all the edges of the primitive form truncated, each by one face. *Cleaveland.*

EM'ARGINATELY, *adv.* In the form of notches. *Eaton.*

EM'ASCULATE, *v. t.* [Low L. *emasculo,* from *e* and *masculus,* a male. See *Male.*]

1. To castrate; to deprive a male of certain parts which characterize the sex; to geld; to deprive of virility.

2. To deprive of masculine strength or vigor; to weaken; to render effeminate; to vitiate by unmanly softness.

> Women *emasculate* a monarch's reign. *Dryden.*
>
> To *emasculate* the spirits. *Collier.*

EM'ASCULATE, *a.* Unmanned; deprived of vigor. *Hammond.*

EM'ASCULATED, *pp.* Castrated; weakened.

EM'ASCULATING, *ppr.* Castrating; gelding; depriving of vigor.

EMASCULA'TION, *n.* The act of depriving a male of the parts which characterize the sex; castration.

2. The act of depriving of vigor or strength; effeminacy; unmanly weakness.

EMBA'LE, *v. t.* [Fr. *emballer;* Sp. *embalar;* It. *imballare; em, im,* for *en* or *in,* and *balla, balle,* bale.]

1. To make up into a bundle, bale or package; to pack.

2. To bind; to inclose. *Spenser.*

EMB'ALM, *v. t. emb'am.* [Fr. *embaumer,* from *baume,* balm, from *balsam;* It. *imbalsamare;* Sp. *embalsamar.*]

1. To open a dead body, take out the intestines, and fill their place with odoriferous and desiccative spices and drugs, to prevent its putrefaction.

> Joseph commanded his servants, the physicians, to embalm his father: and the physicians *embalmed* Israel. Gen. l.

2. To fill with sweet scent. *Milton.*

3. To preserve, with care and affection, from loss or decay.

> The memory of my beloved daughter is *embalmed* in my heart. *N. W.*
>
> Virtue alone, with lasting grace,
> *Embalms* the beauties of the face. *Trumbull.*

EMB'ALMED, *pp.* Filled with aromatic

plants for preservation; preserved from loss or destruction.

EMB'ALMER, *n.* One who embalms bodies for preservation.

EMB'ALMING, *ppr.* Filling a dead body with spices for preservation; preserving with care from loss, decay or destruction.

EMB'AR, *v. t.* [*en* and *bar.*] To shut, close or fasten with a bar; to make fast.

2. To inclose so as to hinder egress or escape.

Where fast *embarr'd* in mighty brazen wall. *Spenser.*

3. To stop; to shut from entering; to hinder; to block up.

He *embarred* all further trade. *Bacon.*

EMBARCA'TION, *n.* Embarkation, which see.

EMB'ARGO, *n.* [Sp. *embargo;* Port. Fr. *id.* This is a modern word from the Spanish and Portuguese. In Portuguese, *embaraçàr*, which the Spanish write *embarazar*, is to *embarrass*, entangle, stop, hinder; Port. *embaraço*, impediment, embarrassment, stop, hinderance. The palatal being changed into *z* and *s*, we have *embarrass* from this word; but *embargo* retains the palatal letter.]

In *commerce*, a restraint on ships, or prohibition of sailing, either out of port, or into port, or both; which prohibition is by public authority, for a limited time. Most generally it is a prohibition of ships to leave a port.

EMB'ARGO, *v. t.* [Sp. Port. *embargar.*] To hinder or prevent ships from sailing out of port, or into port, or both, by some law or edict of sovereign authority, for a limited time. Our ships were for a time *embargoed* by a law of congress.

2. To stop; to hinder from being prosecuted by the departure or entrance of ships. The commerce of the United States has been *embargoed.*

EMB'ARGOED, *pp.* Stopped; hindered from sailing; hindered by public authority, as ships or commerce.

EMB'ARGOING, *ppr.* Restraining from sailing by public authority; hindering.

EMB'ARK, *v. t.* [Sp. *embarcar;* Port. *id.;* It. *imbarcare;* Fr. *embarquer; en* and *barco*, a boat, a barge, a bark.]

1. To put or cause to enter on board a ship or other vessel or boat. The general *embarked* his troops and their baggage.

2. To engage a person in any affair. This projector *embarked* his friends in the design or expedition.

EMB'ARK, *v. i.* To go on board of a ship, boat or vessel; as, the troops *embarked* for Lisbon.

2. To engage in any business; to undertake in; to take a share in. The young man *embarked* rashly in speculation, and was ruined.

EMBARKA'TION, *n.* The act of putting on board of a ship or other vessel, or the act of going aboard.

2. That which is embarked; as an *embarkation* of Jesuits. *Smollett.*

3. [Sp. *embarcacion.*] A small vessel, or boat. [*Unusual.*] *Anson's Voyage.*

EMB'ARKED, *pp.* Put on shipboard; engaged in any affair.

EMB'ARKING, *ppr.* Putting on board of a ship or boat; going on shipboard.

EMBAR'RASS, *v. t.* [Fr. *embarrasser;* Port. *embaraçar;* Sp. *embarazar;* from Sp. *embarazo*, Port. *embaraço*, Fr. *embarras*, perplexity, intricacy, hinderance, impediment. In Spanish, formerly *embargo* signified embarrassment, and *embarrar* is to perplex.]

1. To perplex; to render intricate; to entangle. We say, public affairs are *embarrassed;* the state of our accounts is *embarrassed;* want of order tends to *embarrass* business.

2. To perplex, as the mind or intellectual faculties; to confuse. Our ideas are sometimes *embarrassed.*

3. To perplex, as with debts, or demands, beyond the means of payment; *applied to a person or his affairs.* In mercantile language, a man or his business is *embarrassed*, when he cannot meet his pecuniary engagements.

4. To perplex; to confuse; to disconcert; to abash. An abrupt address may *embarrass* a young lady. A young man may be too much *embarrassed* to utter a word.

EMBAR'RASSED, *pp.* Perplexed; rendered intricate; confused; confounded.

EMBAR'RASSING, *ppr.* Perplexing; entangling; confusing; confounding; abashing.

EMBAR'RASSMENT, *n.* Perplexity; intricacy; entanglement.

2. Confusion of mind.

3. Perplexity arising from insolvency, or from temporary inability to discharge debts.

4. Confusion; abashment.

EMBA'SE, *v. t.* [*en* and *base.*] To lower in value; to vitiate; to deprave; to impair.

The virtue—of a tree *embased* by the ground. *Bacon.*

I have no ignoble end—that may *embase* my poor judgment. *Wotton.*

2. To degrade; to vilify. *Spenser.*

[*This word is seldom used.*]

EMBA'SEMENT, *n.* Act of depraving; depravation; deterioration. *South.*

EM'BASSADE, *n.* An embassy. *Obs.* *Spenser.*

EMBAS'SADOR, *n.* [Sp. *embaxador;* Port. *id.;* Fr. *ambassadeur;* It. *ambasciadore;* Arm. *ambaçzador;* Norm. *ambaxeur.* Spelman refers this word to the G. *ambact*, which Cesar calls *ambactus*, a client or retainer, among the Gauls. Cluver. *Ant. Ger.* l. 8. favors this opinion, and mentions that, in the laws of Burgundy, *ambascia* was equivalent to the Ger. *ambact*, service, now contracted to *amt*, D. *ampt*, Dan. *ambt*, Sw. *embete*, office, duty, function, employment, province. The Dutch has *ambagt*, trade, handicraft, a manor, a lordship, and *ambagtsman*, a journeyman or mechanic, which is evidently the Sw. *embetesman.* The Danish has also *embede*, office, employment. In Sax. *embeht, ymbeht*, is office, duty, employment; *embehtan*, to serve; *embehtman*, a servant; also *ambeht*, collation; *ambyht*, a message or legation, an embassy; *ambyhtsecga*, a legate or envoy [*a message-sayer.*] The word in Gothic is *andbahts*, a servant; *andbahtyan*, to serve. The German has *amtsbote*, a messenger. The first syllable *em* is from *emb*, *ymb*, αμφι, about, and the root of *ambact* is Bg. See *Pack* and *Dispatch.*]

1. A minister of the highest rank, employed by one prince or state, at the court of another, to manage the public concerns of his own prince or state, and representing the power and dignity of his sovereign. Embassadors are *ordinary*, when they reside permanently at a foreign court; or *extraordinary*, when they are sent on a special occasion. They are also called ministers. Envoys are ministers employed on special occasions, and are of less dignity. *Johnson. Encyc.*

2. In *ludicrous language*, a messenger. *Ash.*

EMBAS'SADRESS, *n.* The consort of an embassador. *Chesterfield.*

2. A woman sent on a public message.

EM'BASSAGE, an embassy, is not used.

EM'BASSY, *n.* [Sp. Port. *embaxada;* Fr. *ambassade.*]

1. The message or public function of an embassador; the charge or employment of a public minister, whether ambassador or envoy; the word signifies the message or commission itself, and the person or persons sent to convey or to execute it. We say the king sent an *embassy*, meaning an envoy, minister, or ministers; or the king sent a person on an *embassy.* The *embassy* consisted of three envoys. The *embassy* was instructed to inquire concerning the king's disposition. *Mitford.*

2. A solemn message. *Taylor.*

Eighteen centuries ago, the gospel went forth from Jerusalem on an *embassy* of mingled authority and love. *B. Dickenson.*

3. Ironically, an errand. *Sidney.*

[The old orthography, *ambassade, ambassage*, being obsolete, and *embassy* established, I have rendered the orthography of *embassador* conformable to it in the initial letter.]

EMBAT'TLE, *v. t.* [*en* and *battle.*] To arrange in order of battle; to array troops for battle.

On their *embattled* ranks the waves return. *Milton.*

2. To furnish with battlements. *Cyc.*

EMBAT'TLE, *v. i.* To be ranged in order of battle. *Shak.*

EMBAT'TLED, *pp.* Arrayed in order of battle.

2. Furnished with battlements; and in *heraldry*, having the outline resembling a battlement, as an ordinary. *Cyc. Bailey.*

2. *a.* Having been the place of battle; as an *embattled* plain or field.

EMBAT'TLING, *ppr.* Ranging in battle array.

EMBA'Y, *v. t.* [*en, in*, and *bay.*] To inclose in a bay or inlet; to land-lock; to inclose between capes or promontories. *Mar. Dict.*

2. [Fr. *baigner.*] To bathe; to wash. [*Not used.*] *Spenser.*

EMBA'YED, *pp.* Inclosed in a bay, or between points of land, as a ship.

EMBED', *v. t.* [*en, in*, and *bed.*] To lay as in a bed; to lay in surrounding matter; as, to *embed* a thing in clay or in sand.

EMBED'DED, *pp.* Laid as in a bed; deposited or inclosed in surrounding matter; as ore *embedded* in sand.

EMBED'DING, *ppr.* Laying, depositing or forming, as in a bed.

EMBEL'LISH, *v. t.* [Fr. *embellir*, from *belle*, L. *bellus*, pretty.]

1. To adorn; to beautify; to decorate; to make beautiful or elegant by ornaments; *applied to persons or things.* We *embellish* the person with rich apparel, a garden with shrubs and flowers, and style with metaphors.
2. To make graceful or elegant; as, to *embellish* manners.

EMBEL'LISHED, *pp.* Adorned; decorated; beautified.

EMBEL'LISHING, *ppr.* Adorning; decorating; adding grace, ornament or elegance to a person or thing.

EMBEL'LISHMENT, *n.* The act of adorning.
2. Ornament; decoration; any thing that adds beauty or elegance; that which renders any thing pleasing to the eye, or agreeable to the taste, in dress, furniture, manners, or in the fine arts. Rich dresses are *embellishments* of the person. Virtue is an *embellishment* of the mind, and liberal arts, the *embellishments* of society.

EMBER, in *ember-days, ember-weeks,* is the Saxon *emb-ren,* or *ymb-ryne,* a circle, circuit or revolution, from *ymb,* αμφι, around, and *ren,* or *ryne,* course, from the root of *run.* Ember-days are the Wednesday, Friday and Saturday, after Quadragesima Sunday, after Whitsunday, after Holy-rood day in September, and after St. Lucia's day in December. *Ember-days* are days returning at certain seasons; *Ember-weeks,* the weeks in which these days fall; and formerly, our ancestors used the words *Ember-fast* and *Ember-tide* or season.
Lye. Encyc. LL. Alfred. Sect. 39.

EM'BER-GOOSE, *n.* A fowl of the genus Colymbus and order of ansers. It is larger than the common goose; the head is dusky; the back, coverts of the wings and tail, clouded with lighter and darker shades of the same; the primaries and tail are black; the breast and belly silvery. It inhabits the northern regions, about Iceland and the Orkneys. *Encyc.*

EM'BERING, *n.* The ember-days, supra. [*Obs.*] *Tusser.*

EM'BERS, *n. plu.* [Sax. *æmyrian;* Scot. *ameris, aumers;* Ice. *einmyria.*]
Small coals of fire with ashes; the residuum of wood, coal or other combustibles not extinguished; cinders.

> He rakes hot *embers,* and renews the fires. *Dryden.*

It is used by Colebrooke in the singular.

> He takes a lighted *ember* out of the covered vessel. *Asiat. Res.* vii. 234.

EMBER-WEEK. [See *Ember,* supra.]

EMBEZ'ZLE, *v t.* [Norm. *embeasiler,* to filch; *beseler,* id. The primary sense is not quite obvious. If the sense is to strip, to peel, it coincides with the Ar. بَصَلَ to strip, or Heb. Ch. Syr. פצל. In Heb. Ch. Syr. Sam. בזז or בזה signifies to plunder. See Class Bs. No. 2. 21. 22. Perhaps the sense is to cut off. No. 21. 54.]
1. To appropriate fraudulently to one's own use what is entrusted to one's care and management. It differs from stealing and robbery in this, that the latter imply a wrongful taking of another's goods, but embezzlement denotes the wrongful appropriation and use of what came into possession by right. It is not uncommon for men entrusted with public money to *embezzle* it.
2. To waste; to dissipate in extravagance.

> When thou hast *embezzled* all thy store. *Dryden.*

EMBEZ'ZLED, *pp.* Appropriated wrongfully to one's own use.

EMBEZ'ZLEMENT, *n.* The act of fraudulently appropriating to one's own use, the money or goods entrusted to one's care and management. An accurate account of the *embezzlements* of public money would form a curious history.
2. The thing appropriated.

EMBEZ'ZLER, *n.* One who embezzles.

EMBEZ'ZLING, *ppr.* Fraudulently applying to one's own use what is entrusted to one's care and employment.

EMBLA'ZE, *v. t.* [Fr. *blasonner;* Sp. *blasonar;* Port. *blazonar, brazonar;* allied to G. *blasen,* D. *blaazen,* to blow, and Fr. *blaser,* to burn, Eng. *blaze.* The sense is to swell, to enlarge, to make showy.]
1. To adorn with glittering embellishments.

> No weeping orphan saw his father's stores
> Our shrines irradiate, or *emblaze* the floors. *Pope.*

2. To blazon; to paint or adorn with figures armorial.

> The imperial ensign, streaming to the wind,
> With gems and golden luster rich *emblazed.* *Milton.*

EMBLA'ZED, *pp.* Adorned with shining ornaments, or with figures armorial.

EMBLA'ZING, *ppr.* Embellishing with glittering ornaments, or with figures armorial.

EMBLA'ZON, *v. t.* *embla'zn.* [Fr. *blasonner.* See *Emblaze.*]
1. To adorn with figures of heraldry or ensigns armorial. *Johnson.*
2. To deck in glaring colors; to display pompously.

> We find Augustus—*emblazoned* by the poets. *Hakewill.*

EMBLA'ZONED, *pp.* Adorned with figures or ensigns armorial; set out pompously.

EMBLA'ZONER, *n.* A blazoner; one that emblazons; a herald.
2. One that publishes and displays with pomp.

EMBLA'ZONING, *ppr.* Adorning with ensigns or figures armorial; displaying with pomp.

EMBLA'ZONMENT, *n.* An emblazoning. *Roscoe.*

EMBLA'ZONRY, *n.* Pictures on shields; display of figures. *Milton.*

EM'BLEM, *n.* [Gr. εμβλημα, from εμβαλλω, to cast in, to insert.]
1. Properly, inlay; inlayed or mosaic work; something inserted in the body of another.
2. A picture representing one thing to the eye, and another to the understanding; a painted enigma, or a figure representing some obvious history, instructing us in some moral truth. Such is the image of Scævola holding his hand in the fire, with these words, "*agere et pati fortiter Romanum est,*" to do and to suffer with fortitude is Roman. *Encyc.*
3. A painting or representation, intended to hold forth some moral or political instruction; an allusive picture; a typical designation. A balance is an *emblem* of justice; a crown is the *emblem* of royalty; a scepter, of power or sovereignty.
4. That which represents another thing in its predominant qualities. A white robe in scripture is an *emblem* of purity or righteousness; baptism, of purification.

EM'BLEM, *v. t.* To represent by similar qualities. *Feltham.*

EMBLEMAT'IC, EMBLEMAT'ICAL, } *a.* Pertaining to or comprising an emblem.
2. Representing by some allusion or customary connection; as, a crown is *emblematic* of royalty, a crown being worn by kings.
3. Representing by similar qualities; as, whiteness is *emblematic* of purity.
4. Using emblems; as *emblematic* worship.

EMBLEMAT'ICALLY, *adv.* By way or means of emblems; in the manner of emblems; by way of allusive representation. *Swift.*

EMBLEM'ATIST, *n.* A writer or inventor of emblems. *Brown.*

EM'BLEMENT, *n.* used mostly in the plural. [Norm. *emblear,* emblements; *embleer,* to sow; Fr. *emblaver;* Norm. *bleer,* to sow with corn, from *blé, bled,* corn.]
The produce or fruits of land sown or planted. This word is used for the produce of land sown or planted by a tenant for life or years, whose estate is determined suddenly after the land is sown or planted and before harvest. In this case the tenant's executors shall have the emblements. *Emblements* comprehend not only corn, but the produce of any annual plant. But the produce of grass and perennial plants belongs to the lord, or proprietor of the land. *Blackstone.*

EM'BLEMIZE, *v. t.* To represent by an emblem.

EM'BLEMIZED, *pp.* Represented by an emblem.

EM'BLEMIZING, *ppr.* Representing by an emblem.

EMBLOOM', *v. t.* To cover or enrich with bloom. *Good.*

EMBOD'IED, *pp.* [See *Embody.*] Collected or formed into a body.

EMBOD'Y, *v. t.* [*en, in,* and *body.*] To form or collect into a body or united mass; to collect into a whole; to incorporate; to concentrate; as, to *embody* troops; to *embody* detached sentiments.

EMBOD'YING, *ppr.* Collecting or forming into a body.

EMBO'GUING, *n.* The mouth of a river or place where its waters are discharged into the sea. [*An ill formed word.*]

EMBÖLDEN, *v. t.* [*en* and *bold.*] To give boldness or courage; to encourage. 1 Cor. viii.

EMBÖLDENED, *pp.* Encouraged.

EMBÖLDENING, *ppr.* Giving courage or boldness.

EM'BOLISM, *n.* [Gr. εμβολισμος, from εμβαλλω, to throw in, to insert.]
1. Intercalation; the insertion of days, months or years, in an account of time, to produce regularity. The Greeks made use of the lunar year of 354 days, and to adjust it to the solar year of 365, they ad-

ded a lunar month every second or third year, which additional month they called *embolimæus*. *Encyc.*

2. Intercalated time.

EMBOLIS'MAL, *a.* Pertaining to intercalation; intercalated; inserted.

The *embolismal* months are either natural or civil. *Encyc.*

EMBOLIS'MIC, *a.* Intercalated; inserted.

Twelve lunations form a common year; and thirteen, the *embolismic* year. *Grosier's China.*

EM'BOLUS, *n.* [Gr. εμβολος, from εμβαλλω, to thrust in.]

Something inserted or acting in another; that which thrusts or drives; a piston. *Arbuthnot.*

EMBOR'DER, *v. t.* [Old Fr. *emborder.*] To adorn with a border.

EMBOSS', *v. t.* [*en, in*, and *boss.*] In *architecture* and *sculpture*, to form bosses or protuberances; to fashion in relievo or raised work; to cut or form with prominent figures.

2. To form with bosses; to cover with protuberances. *Milton.*

3. To drive hard in hunting, till a deer foams, or a dog's knees swell. *Hanmer.*

EMBOSS', *v. t.* [Fr. *emboîter*, for *emboister*, from *boîte, boiste*, a box.]

To inclose as in a box; to include; to cover. [*Not used.*] *Spenser.*

EMBOSS', *v. t.* [It. *imboscare*, from *bosco*, a wood.]

To inclose in a wood; to conceal in a thicket. [*Not used.*] *Milton.*

EMBOSS'ED, *pp.* Formed with bosses or raised figures.

EMBOSS'ING, *ppr.* Forming with figures in relievo. *Bacon.*

EMBOSS'MENT, *n.* A prominence, like a boss; a jut.

2. Relief; figures in relievo; raised work. *Addison.*

EMBOT'TLE, *v. t.* [*en, in*, and *bottle.*] To put in a bottle; to bottle; to include or confine in a bottle.

EMBOT'TLED, *pp.* Put in or included in bottles. *Philips.*

EMBOW, *v. t.* To form like a bow; to arch; to vault. *Spenser.*

EMBOW'EL, *v. t.* [*en, in*, and *bowel.*] To take out the entrails of an animal body; to eviscerate. *Shak.*

2. To take out the internal parts.

Fossils and minerals that the *emboweled* earth
Displays. *Philips.*

3. To sink or inclose in another substance. *Spenser.*

EMBOW'ELED, *pp.* Deprived of intestines; eviscerated; buried.

EMBOW'ELER, *n.* One that takes out the bowels.

EMBOW'ELING, *ppr.* Depriving of entrails; eviscerating; burying.

EMBOW'ER, *v. i.* [from *bower.*] To lodge or rest in a bower. *Spenser.*

EMBRA'CE, *v. t.* [Fr. *embrasser*, from *en* and *bras*, the arm; Sp. *abrazar*, from *brazo*, the arm; It. *abbracciare, imbracciare*, from *braccio*, the arm; Ir. *umbracaim*, from *brac*, the arm. See *Brace.*]

1. To take, clasp or inclose in the arms; to press to the bosom, in token of affection.

Paul called to him the disciples and *embraced* them. Acts xx.

2. To seize eagerly; to lay hold on; to receive or take with willingness that which is offered; as, to *embrace* the christian religion; to *embrace* the opportunity of doing a favor.

3. To comprehend; to include or take in; as, natural philosophy *embraces* many sciences. *Johnson.*

4. To comprise; to inclose; to encompass; to contain; to encircle.

Low at his feet a spacious plain is placed,
Between the mountain and the stream *embraced.* *Denham.*

5. To receive; to admit.

What is there that he may not *embrace* for truth? *Locke.*

6. To find; to take; to accept.

Fleance—must *embrace* the fate
Of that dark hour. *Shak.*

7. To have carnal intercourse with.

8. To put on. *Spenser.*

9. To attempt to influence a jury corruptly. *Blackstone.*

EMBRA'CE, *v. i.* To join in an embrace. *Shak.*

EMBRA'CE, *n.* Inclosure or clasp with the arms; pressure to the bosom with the arms.

2. Reception of one thing into another.

3. Sexual intercourse; conjugal endearment.

EMBRA'CED, *pp.* Inclosed in the arms; clasped to the bosom; seized; laid hold on; received; comprehended; included; contained; accepted.

2. Influenced corruptly; biassed; as a juror. *Blackstone.*

EMBRA'CEMENT, *n.* A clasp in the arms; a hug; embrace. *Sidney.*

2. Hostile hug; grapple. [*Little used.*] *Sidney.*

3. Comprehension; state of being contained; inclosure. [*Little used.*] *Bacon.*

4. Conjugal endearment; sexual commerce. *Shak.*

5. Willing acceptance. [*Little used.*]

EMBRA'CER, *n.* The person who embraces. *Howel.*

2. One who attempts to influence a jury corruptly.

EMBRA'CERY, *n.* In *law*, an attempt to influence a jury corruptly to one side, by promises, persuasions, entreaties, money, entertainments, or the like. *Blackstone.*

EMBRA'CING, *ppr.* Clasping in the arms; pressing to the bosom; seizing and holding; comprehending; including; receiving; accepting; having conjugal intercourse.

2. Attempting to influence a jury corruptly. *Blackstone.*

EMBRA'ID, *v. t.* To upbraid. [*Not in use.*] *Elyot.*

EMBRASU'RE, *n. s* as *z.* [Fr. from *ebraser*, to widen. *Lunier.* If Lunier is right, this coincides with the Sp. *abrasar*, Port. *abrazar*, to burn, Sp. to squander or dissipate.]

1. An opening in a wall or parapet, through which cannon are pointed and discharged.

2. In *architecture*, the enlargement of the aperture of a door or window, on the inside of the wall, for giving greater play for the opening of the door or casement, or for admitting more light. *Encyc.*

EMBRA'VE, *v. t.* [See *Brave.*] To embellish; to make showy. *Obs.* *Spenser.*

2. To inspire with bravery; to make bold. *Beaum.*

EM'BROCATE, *v. t.* [Gr. εμβρεχω, βρεχω, to moisten, to rain; It. *embroccare.*]

In *surgery* and *medicine*, to moisten and rub a diseased part of the body, with a liquid substance, as with spirit, oil, &c., by means of a cloth or spunge. *Coxe. Encyc.*

EM'BROCATED, *pp.* Moistened and rubbed with a wet cloth or spunge.

EM'BROCATING, *ppr.* Moistening and rubbing a diseased part with a wet cloth or spunge.

EMBROCA'TION, *n.* The act of moistening and rubbing a diseased part, with a cloth or spunge, dipped in some liquid substance, as spirit, oil, &c. *Coxe. Encyc.*

2. The liquid or lotion with which an affected part is rubbed or washed.

EMBROID'ER, *v. t.* [Fr. *broder*; Sp. Port. *bordar*; W. *brodiaw*, to embroider, to make compact, to darn. Qu. *border.*]

To border with ornamental needle-work, or figures; to adorn with raised figures of needle-work; as cloth, stuffs or muslin.

Thou shalt *embroider* the coat of fine linen. Ex. xxviii.

EMBROID'ERED, *pp.* Adorned with figures of needle-work.

EMBROID'ERER, *n.* One who embroiders.

EMBROID'ERING, *ppr.* Ornamenting with figured needle-work.

EMBROID'ERY, *n.* Work in gold, silver or silk thread, formed by the needle on cloth, stuffs and muslin, into various figures; variegated needle-work. *Pope. Encyc.*

2. Variegation or diversity of figures and colors; as the natural *embroidery* of meadows. *Spectator.*

EMBROIL', *v. t.* [Fr. *embrouiller, brouiller*; It. *imbrogliare, brogliare*; Sp. *embrollar*; Port. *embrulhar*; properly to turn, to stir or agitate, to mix, to twist. See *Broil.*]

1. To perplex or entangle; to intermix in confusion.

The christian antiquities at Rome—are *embroiled* with fable and legend. *Addison.*

2. To involve in troubles or perplexities; to disturb or distract by connection with something else; to throw into confusion or commotion; to perplex.

The royal house *embroiled* in civil war. *Dryden.*

EMBROIL'ED, *pp.* Perplexed; entangled; intermixed and confused; involved in trouble.

EMBROIL'ING, *ppr.* Perplexing; entangling; involving in trouble.

EMBROIL'MENT, *n.* Confusion; disturbance. *Maundrell.*

EMBROTH'EL, *v. t.* [See *Brothel.*] To inclose in a brothel. *Donne.*

EM'BRYO, EM'BRYON, *n.* [Gr. εμβρυον; L. *embryon*; from Gr. εν and βρυω, to shoot, bud, germinate. The Greek word is contracted probably from βρυδω, for it gives βρυσις; and if so, it coincides in elements with Eng. *brood* and *breed.*]

In *physiology*, the first rudiments of an animal in the womb, before the several members are distinctly formed; after which it is called a fetus. *Encyc.*

2. The rudiments of a plant.

3. The beginning or first state of any thing not fit for production; the rudiments of any thing yet imperfectly formed.

The company little suspected what a noble work I had then in *embryo*. *Swift.*

EM'BRYO, } **EM'BRYON,** } *a.* Pertaining to or noting any thing in its first rudiments or unfinished state; as an *embryon* bud. *Darwin.*

EMBRYOT'OMY, *n.* [*embryo* and Gr. τομη, a cutting, from τεμνω, to cut.]

A cutting or forcible separation of the fetus in utero. *Coxe.*

EMBUSY, *v. t.* To employ. [*Not used.*]

EMEND', *v. t.* To amend. [*Not used.*]

EMEND'ABLE, *a.* [L. *emendabilis*, from *emendo*, to correct; *e* and *menda*, a spot or blemish.] Capable of being amended or corrected. [See *Amendable.*]

EMENDA'TION, *n.* [L. *emendatio.*] The act of altering for the better, or correcting what is erroneous or faulty; correction; *applied particularly to the correction of errors in writings.* When we speak of life and manners, we use *amend*, *amendment*, the French orthography.

2. An alteration for the better; correction of an error or fault.

The last edition of the book contains many *emendations.*

EMENDA'TOR, *n.* A corrector of errors or faults in writings; one who corrects or improves.

EMEND'ATORY, *a.* Contributing to emendation or correction. *Warton.*

EM'ERALD, *n.* [Sp. *esmeralda*; Port. *id.*; It. *smeraldo*; Fr. *emeraude*; Arm. *emeraudenn*; G. D. Dan. *smaragd*; L. *smaragdus*; Gr. μαραγδος and σμαραγδος; Ch. זמרגד; Syr. ܙܡܪܓܕܐ; Ar. زمرد. It is probable that the European words are from the oriental, though much altered. The verb זמר signifies to sing, to call, to amputate, &c.; but the meaning of emerald is not obvious.]

A mineral and a precious stone, whose colors are a pure, lively green, varying to a pale, yellowish, bluish, or grass green. It is always crystalized, and almost always appears in regular, hexahedral prisms, more or less perfect, and sometimes slightly modified by truncations on the edges, or on the solid angles. It is a little harder than quartz, becomes electric by friction, is often transparent, sometimes only translucent, and before the blowpipe is fusible into a whitish enamel or glass. The finest emeralds have been found in Peru.

The subspecies of emerald are the precious emerald and the beryl. *Kirwan. Cleaveland.*

EMERGE, *v. i.* emerj'. [L. *emergo*; *e*, *ex*, and *mergo*, to plunge.]

1. To rise out of a fluid or other covering or surrounding substance; as, to *emerge* from the water or from the ocean.

Thetis—*emerging* from the deep. *Dryden.*

We say, a planet *emerges* from the sun's light; a star *emerging* from chaos. It is opposed to *immerge.*

2. To issue; to proceed from. *Newton.*

3. To reappear, after being eclipsed; to leave the sphere of the obscuring object. The sun is said to *emerge*, when the moon ceases to obscure its light; the satellites of Jupiter *emerge*, when they appear beyond the limb of the planet.

4. To rise out of a state of depression or obscurity; to rise into view; as, to *emerge* from poverty or obscurity; to *emerge* from the gloom of despondency.

EMERG'ENCE, } **EMERG'ENCY,** } *n.* The act of rising out of a fluid or other covering or surrounding matter.

2. The act of rising or starting into view; the act of issuing from or quitting.

The white color of all refracted light, at its first *emergence*—is compounded of various colors. *Newton.*

3. That which comes suddenly; a sudden occasion; an unexpected event.

Most of our rarities have been found out by casual *emergency*. *Glanville.*

4. Exigence; any event or occasional combination of circumstances which calls for immediate action or remedy; pressing necessity.

In case of *emergency*, [or in an *emergency*] he would employ the whole wealth of his empire. *Addison.*

EMERG'ENT, *a.* Rising out of a fluid or any thing that covers or surrounds.

The mountains huge appear *emergent*. *Milton.*

2. Issuing or proceeding from. *South.*

3. Rising out of a depressed state or from obscurity.

4. Coming suddenly; sudden; casual; unexpected; hence, calling for immediate action or remedy; urgent; pressing; as an *emergent* occasion. *Clarendon.*

EMER'ITED, *a.* [L. *emeritus.*] Allowed to have done sufficient public service. *Evelyn.*

EM'ERODS, *n.* with a plural termination. [Corrupted from *hemorrhoids*, Gr. αιμορροιδες, from αιμορροεω, to labor under a flowing of blood; αιμα, blood, and ρεω, to flow.]

Hemorrhoids; piles; a dilatation of the veins about the rectum, with a discharge of blood.

The Lord will smite thee—with the *emerods*. Deut. xxviii.

EMER'SION, *n.* [from L. *emergo*. See *Emerge.*]

1. The act of rising out of a fluid or other covering or surrounding substance; opposed to *immersion.*

2. In *astronomy*, the reappearance of a heavenly body after an eclipse; as the *emersion* of the moon from the shadow of the earth: also, the time of reappearance.

3. The reappearance of a star, which has been hid by the effulgence of the sun's light.

4. Extrication. *Black.*

EM'ERY, *n.* [Fr. *emeril*, *emeri*; Sp. *esmeril*; D. *ameril*; G. *schmergel*; Gr. and L. *smiris.*]

A mineral, said to be a compact variety of corundum, being equal to it in hardness. It is always amorphous; its structure finely granular; its color varying from a deep gray to a bluish or blackish gray, sometimes brownish. This is almost indispensable in polishing metals and hard stones. The lapidaries cut ordinary gems on their wheels, by sprinkling them with the moistened powder of emery; but it will not cut the diamond. *Hill. Cleaveland.*

EMET'IC, *a.* [It. Sp. *emetico*; Fr. *emetique*; from Gr. εμεω, to vomit.]

Inducing to vomit; exciting the stomach to discharge its contents by the œsophagus and mouth.

EMET'IC, *n.* A medicine that provokes vomiting.

EMET'ICALLY, *adv.* In such a manner as to excite vomiting. *Boyle.*

EM'ETIN, *n.* [See *Emetic.*] A substance obtained from the root of ipecacuana, half a grain of which is a powerful emetic. *Ure.*

E'MEW, *n.* A name of the Cassowary.

EMICA'TION, *n.* [L. *emicatio*, *emico*, from *e* and *mico*, to sparkle, that is, to dart.]

A sparkling; a flying off in small particles, as from heated iron or fermenting liquors.

EMIC'TION, *n.* [L. *mingo*, *mictum.*] The discharging of urine; urine; what is voided by the urinary passages. *Harvey.*

EM'IGRANT, *a.* [See *Emigrate.*] Removing from one place or country to another distant place with a view to reside.

EM'IGRANT, *n.* One who removes his habitation, or quits one country or region to settle in another.

EM'IGRATE, *v. i.* [L. *emigro*; *e* and *migro*, to *migrate.*]

To quit one country, state or region and settle in another; to remove from one country or state to another for the purpose of residence. Germans, Swiss, Irish and Scotch, *emigrate*, in great numbers, to America. Inhabitants of New England *emigrate* to the Western States.

EM'IGRATING, *ppr.* Removing from one country or state to another for residence.

EMIGRA'TION, *n.* Removal of inhabitants from one country or state to another, for the purpose of residence, as from Europe to America, or in America, from the Atlantic States to the Western.

The removal of persons from house to house in the same town, state or kingdom is not called *emigration*, but simply *removal.*

EM'INENCE, } **EM'INENCY,** } *n.* [L. *eminentia*, from *eminens*, *emineo*, to stand or show itself above; *e* and *minor*, to threaten, that is, to stand or push forward. See Class Mn. No. 9. 11.]

1. Elevation, highth, in a literal sense; but usually, a rising ground; a hill of moderate elevation above the adjacent ground.

The temple of honor ought to be seated on an *eminence*. *Burke.*

2. Summit; highest part. *Ray.*

3. A part rising or projecting beyond the rest, or above the surface. We speak of *eminences* on any plain or smooth surface.

4. An elevated situation among men; a place or station above men in general, either in rank, office or celebrity. Merit may place a man on an *eminence*, and make him conspicuous. *Eminence* is always exposed to envy.

5. Exaltation; high rank; distinction; celebrity; fame; preferment; conspicuousness.

Office, rank and great talents give *eminence* to men in society.

Where men cannot arrive at *eminence*, religion may make compensation, by teaching content. *Tillotson.*

6. Supreme degree. *Milton.*
7. Notice; distinction. *Shak.*
8. A title of honor given to cardinals and others. *Encyc.*

EM'INENT, *a.* [L. *eminens*, from *emineo.*]

1. High; lofty; as an *eminent* place. Ezek. xvi.
2. Exalted in rank; high in office; dignified; distinguished. Princes hold *eminent* stations in society, as do ministers, judges and legislators.
3. High in public estimation; conspicuous; distinguished above others; remarkable; as an *eminent* historian or poet; an *eminent* scholar. Burke was an *eminent* orator; Watts and Cowper were *eminent* for their piety.

EM'INENTLY, *adv.* In a high degree; in a degree to attract observation; in a degree to be conspicuous and distinguished from others; as, to be *eminently* learned or useful.

E'MIR, *n.* [Ar. أَمِير Emir, a commander, from أَمَرَ to command, Heb. אמר to speak, Ch. Syr. Sam. id.]

A title of dignity among the Turks, denoting a prince; a title at first given to the Caliphs, but when they assumed the title of Sultan, that of Emir remained to their children. At length it was attributed to all who were judged to descend from Mohammed, by his daughter Fatimah. *Encyc.*

EM'ISSARY, *n.* [L. *emissarius*, from *emitto*; *e* and *mitto*, to send; Fr. *emissaire*; Sp. *emisario*; It. *emissario.*]

A person sent on a mission; a missionary employed to preach and propagate the gospel.

If one of the four gospels be genuine, we have, in that one, strong reason to believe, that we possess the accounts which the original *emissaries* of the religion delivered. *Paley, Evid. Christ.*

[*This sense is now unusual.*]

2. A person sent on a private message or business; a secret agent, employed to sound or ascertain the opinions of others, and to spread reports or propagate opinions favorable to his employer, or designed to defeat the measures or schemes of his opposers or foes; a spy; but an *emissary* may differ from a *spy*. A *spy* in war is one who enters an enemy's camp or territories to learn the condition of the enemy; an *emissary* may be a secret agent employed not only to detect the schemes of an opposing party, but to influence their councils. A spy in war must be concealed, or he suffers death; an *emissary* may in some cases be known as the agent of an adversary, without incurring similar hazard. *Bacon. Swift.*
3. That which sends out or emits. [*Not used.*] *Arbuthnot.*

Emissary vessels, in anatomy, the same as *excretory.*

EM'ISSARY, *a.* Exploring; spying. *B. Jonson.*

EMIS'SION, *n.* [L. *emissio*, from *emitto*, to send out.] The act of sending or throwing out; as the *emission* of light from the sun or other luminous body; the *emission* of odors from plants; the *emission* of heat from a fire.

2. The act of sending abroad or into circulation notes of a state or of a private corporation; as the *emission* of state notes, or bills of credit, or treasury notes.
3. That which is sent out or issued at one time; an impression or a number of notes issued by one act of government. We say, notes or bills of various *emissions* were in circulation.

EMIT', *v. t.* [L. *emitto*; *e* and *mitto*, to send.]

1. To send forth; to throw or give out; as, fire *emits* heat and smoke; boiling water *emits* steam; the sun and moon *emit* light; animal bodies *emit* perspirable matter; putrescent substances *emit* offensive or noxious exhalations.
2. To let fly; to discharge; to dart or shoot; as, to *emit* an arrow. [*Unusual.*] *Prior.*
3. To issue forth, as an order or decree. [*Unusual.*] *Ayliffe.*
4. To issue, as notes or bills of credit; to print, and send into circulation. The United States have once *emitted* treasury notes.

No state shall *emit* bills of credit. *Const. United States.*

EMMEN'AGOGUE, *n.* [Gr. εμμηνος, menstruous, or εν, in, and μην, month, and αγω, to lead.]

A medicine that promotes the menstrual discharge. *Encyc.*

EM'MET, *n.* [Sax. *æmet*, *æmette*; G. *ameise.*] An ant or pismire.

EMMEW', *v. t.* [See *Mew.*] To mew; to coop up; to confine in a coop or cage. *Shak.*

EMMÖVE, *v. t.* To move; to rouse; to excite. [*Not used.*] *Spenser.*

EMOLLES'CENCE, *n.* [L. *emollescens*, softening. See *Emolliate.*]

In *metallurgy*, that degree of softness in a fusible body which alters its shape; the first or lowest degree of fusibility. *Kirwan.*

EMOL'LIATE, *v. t.* [L. *emollio*, *mollio*, to soften; *mollis*, soft; Eng. *mellow*, *mild*; Russ. *miluyu*, to pity; *umiliayus*, to repent. See *Mellow.*]

To soften; to render effeminate.

Emolliated by four centuries of Roman domination, the Belgic colonies had forgotten their pristine valor. *Pinkerton, Geog.*

[This is a new word, though well formed and applied; but what connection is there between *softening* and *forgetting*? *Lost* is here the proper word for *forgotten.*]

EMOL'LIATED, *pp.* Softened; rendered effeminate.

EMOL'LIATING, *ppr.* Softening; rendering effeminate.

EMOL'LIENT, *a.* Softening; making supple; relaxing the solids.

Barley is *emollient.* *Arbuthnot.*

EMOL'LIENT, *n.* A medicine which softens and relaxes, or sheaths the solids; that which softens or removes the asperities of the humors. *Quincy. Coxe.*

EMOLLI''TION, *n.* The act of softening or relaxing. *Bacon.*

EMOL'UMENT, *n.* [L. *emolumentum*, from *emolo*, *molo*, to grind. Originally, toll taken for grinding. See *Mill.*]

1. The profit arising from office or employment; that which is received as a compensation for services, or which is annexed to the possession of office, as salary, fees and perquisites.
2. Profit; advantage; gains in general.

EMOLUMENT'AL, *a.* Producing profit; useful; profitable; advantageous. *Evelyn.*

Emongst, for *among*, in Spenser, is a mistake.

EMO'TION, *n.* [Fr. from L. *emotio*; *emoveo*, to move from; It. *emozione.*]

1. Literally, a moving of the mind or soul; hence, any agitation of mind or excitement of sensibility.
2. In *a philosophical sense*, an internal motion or agitation of the mind which passes away without desire; when desire follows, the motion or agitation is called a *passion*. *Kames' El. of Criticism.*
3. *Passion* is the *sensible effect*, the *feeling* to which the mind is subjected, when an object of importance suddenly and imperiously demands its attention. The state of absolute passiveness, in consequence of any sudden percussion of mind, is of short duration. The strong impression, or vivid sensation, immediately produces a reaction correspondent to its nature, either to appropriate and enjoy, or avoid and repel the exciting cause. This reaction is very properly distinguished by the term *emotion.*

Emotions therefore, according to the genuine signification of the word, are principally and primarily applicable to the sensible changes and visible effects, which particular *passions* produce on the frame, in consequence of this reaction, or particular agitation of mind. *Cogan on the Passions.*

EMPA'IR, *v. t.* To impair. *Obs.* [See *Impair.*]

EMPA'LE, *v. t.* [Port. *empalar*; Sp. *id.*; It. *impalare*; Fr. *empaler*; *en*, *in*, and L. *palus*, It. Sp. *palo*, a stake, a *pale.*]

1. To fence or fortify with stakes; to set a line of stakes or posts for defense.

All that dwell near enemies *empale* villages, to save themselves from surprise. *Raleigh.*

[We now use *stockade*, in a like sense.]

2. To inclose; to surround.

Round about her work she did *empale*,
With a fair border wrought of sundry flowers. *Spenser.*

3. To inclose; to shut in.

Impenetrable, *empal'd* with circling fire. *Milton.*

4. To thrust a stake up the fundament, and thus put to death; to put to death by fixing on a stake; a punishment formerly practiced in Rome, and still used in Turkey. *Addison. Encyc.*

EMPA'LED, *pp.* Fenced or fortified with stakes; inclosed; shut in; fixed on a stake.

EMPA'LEMENT, *n.* A fencing, fortifying or inclosing with stakes; a putting to death by thrusting a stake into the body.

2. In *botany*, the calyx or flower-cup of a

plant, which surrounds the fructification, like a fence of pales. *Martyn.*

3. In *heraldry*, a conjunction of coats of arms, pale-wise. *Warton.*

EMPA'LING, *ppr.* Fortifying with pales or stakes; inclosing; putting to death on a stake.

EMPAN'NEL, *n.* [Fr. *panneau*; Eng. *pane*, a square. See *Pane* and *Pannel.*]

A list of jurors; a small piece of paper or parchment containing the names of the jurors summoned by the sheriff. It is now written *pannel*, which see.

EMPAN'NEL, *v. t.* To form a list of jurors. It is now written *impannel*, which see.

EMP'ARK, *v. t.* [*in* and *park.*] To inclose as with a fence. *King.*

EMPAR'LANCE, *n.* [See *Imparlance.*]

EMPASM, *n.* empazm'. [Gr. εμπασσω, to sprinkle.]

A powder used to prevent the bad scent of the body. *Johnson.*

EMPAS'SION, *v. t.* To move with passion; to affect strongly. [See *Impassion.*] *Milton.*

EMPEACH. [See *Impeach.*]

EMPE'OPLE, *v. t.* empee'pl. To form into a people or community. [*Little used.*] *Spenser.*

EM'PERESS. [See *Empress.*]

EMPER'ISHED, *a.* [See *Perish.*] Decayed. [*Not in use.*] *Spenser.*

EM'PEROR, *n.* [Fr. *empereur*; Sp. *emperador*; It. *imperadore*; L. *imperator*, from *impero*, to command, W. *peri*, to command, to cause.]

Literally, the commander of an army. In modern times, the sovereign or supreme monarch of an empire; a title of dignity superior to that of king; as the *emperor* of Germany or of Russia.

EM'PERY, *n.* Empire. *Obs.* *Shak.*

EM'PHASIS, *n.* [Gr. εμφασις; εν and φασις.] In *rhetoric*, a particular stress of utterance, or force of voice, given to the words or parts of a discourse, whose signification the speaker intends to impress specially upon his audience; or a distinctive utterance of words, specially significant, with a degree and kind of stress suited to convey their meaning in the best manner. *Encyc. E. Porter.*

The province of *emphasis* is so much more important than accent, that the customary seat of the latter is changed, when the claims of *emphasis* require it. *E. Porter.*

EMPHAT'IC, } *a.* Forcible; strong; impressive; as an *emphatic* voice, tone or pronunciation; *emphatical* reasoning.
EMPHAT'ICAL, }

2. Requiring emphasis; as an *emphatical* word.

3. Uttered with emphasis. We remonstrated in *emphatical* terms.

4. Striking to the eye; as *emphatic* colors. *Boyle.*

EMPHAT'ICALLY, *adv.* With emphasis; strongly; forcibly; in a striking manner.

2. According to appearance. [*Not used.*] *Brown.*

EMPHYSE'MA, } *n.* [Gr. εμφυσημα, from εμφυσαω, to inflate.]
EM'PHYSEM, }

In *surgery*, a puffy tumor, easily yielding to pressure, but returning to its former state, as soon as that pressure is removed. A swelling of the integuments, from the admission of air into the cellular membrane. *Wiseman. Coxe.*

EMPHYSEM'ATOUS, *a.* Pertaining to emphysema; swelled, bloated, but yielding easily to pressure.

EMPHYTEU'TIC, *a.* [Gr. εμ, εν, and φυτευσις, a planting, φυτευω, to plant.]

Taken on hire; that for which rent is to be paid; as *emphyteutic* lands. *Blackstone.*

EMPIERCE, *v. t.* empers'. [*em*, *in*, and *pierce.*] To pierce into; to penetrate. [*Not used.*] *Spenser.*

EMPIGHT, *a.* [from *pight*, to fix.] Fixed. *Obs.* *Spenser.*

EM'PIRE, *n.* [Fr. from L. *imperium*; Sp. It. *imperio.* See *Emperor.*]

1. Supreme power in governing; supreme dominion; sovereignty; imperial power. No nation can rightfully claim the *empire* of the ocean.

2. The territory, region or countries under the jurisdiction and dominion of an emperor. An empire is usually a territory of greater extent than a kingdom, which may be and often is a territory of small extent. Thus we say, the Russian *empire*; the Austrian *empire*; the sovereigns of which are denominated *emperors.* The British dominions are called an *empire*, and since the union of Ireland, the parliament is denominated the *imperial* parliament, but the sovereign is called *king.* By custom in Europe, the *empire* means the German empire; and in juridical acts, it is called the *holy Roman empire.* Hence we say, the *diet of the empire*; the *circles of the empire*; &c. But the German empire no longer exists; the states of Germany now form a confederacy.

3. Supreme control; governing influence; rule; sway; as the *empire* of reason, or of truth.

4. Any region, land or water, over which dominion is extended; as the *empire* of the sea. *Shak.*

EM'PIRIC, *n.* [Gr. εμπειρικος; εν and πειραω, to attempt; L. *empiricus*; Fr. *empirique*; Sp. It. *empirico.* See *Peril* and *Pirate.*]

Literally, one who makes experiments. Hence its appropriate signification is, a physician who enters on practice without a regular professional education, and relies on the success of his own experience. Hence the word is used also for a quack, an ignorant pretender to medical skill, a charlatan. *Encyc.*

EMPIR'IC, } *a.* Pertaining to experiments or experience.
EMPIR'ICAL, }

2. Versed in experiments; as an *empiric* alchimist.

3. Known only by experience; derived from experiment; used and applied without science; as *empiric* skill; *empiric* remedies. *Dryden.*

I have avoided that *empirical* morality that cures one vice by means of another. *Rambler.*

EMPIR'ICALLY, *adv.* By experiment; according to experience; without science; in the manner of quacks. *Brown.*

EMPIR'ICISM, *n.* Dependence of a physician on his experience in practice, without the aid of a regular medical education.

2. The practice of medicine without a medical education. Hence, quackery; the pretensions of an ignorant man to medical skill.

Shudder to destroy life, either by the naked knife, or by the surer and safer medium of *empiricism.* *Dwight.*

EMPL'ASTER, *n.* [Gr. εμπλαςρον, a *plaster.*] [See *Plaster*, which is now used.]

EMPL'ASTER, *v. t.* To cover with a plaster. *Mortimer.*

EMPL'ASTIC, *a.* [Gr. εμπλαςικος. See *Plaster, Plastic.*]

Viscous; glutinous; adhesive; fit to be applied as a plaster; as *emplastic* applications. *Arbuthnot.*

EMPLE'AD, *v. t.* [*em* and *plead.*] To charge with a crime; to accuse. But it is now written *implead*, which see.

EMPLOY', *v. t.* [Fr. *employer*; Arm. *impligea* or *impligein*; Sp. *emplear*; Port. *empregar*; It. *impiegare*; *em* or *en* and *ployer*, *plier*; W. *plygu*; L. *plico*; Gr. πλεκω; D. *pleegen.* See *Apply*, *Display*, *Deploy.*]

1. To occupy the time, attention and labor of; to keep busy, or at work; to use. We *employ* our hands in labor; we *employ* our heads or faculties in study or thought; the attention is *employed*, when the mind is fixed or occupied upon an object; we *employ* time, when we devote it to an object. A portion of time should be daily *employed* in reading the scriptures, meditation and prayer; a great portion of life is *employed* to little profit or to very bad purposes.

2. To use as an instrument or means. We *employ* pens in writing, and arithmetic in keeping accounts. We *employ* medicines in curing diseases.

3. To use as materials in forming any thing. We *employ* timber, stones or bricks, in building; we *employ* wool, linen and cotton, in making cloth.

4. To engage in one's service; to use as an agent or substitute in transacting business; to commission and entrust with the management of one's affairs. The president *employed* an envoy to negotiate a treaty. Kings and States *employ* embassadors at foreign courts.

5. To occupy; to use; to apply or devote to an object; to pass in business; as, to *employ* time; to *employ* an hour, a day or a week; to *employ* one's life.

To employ one's self, is to apply or devote one's time and attention; to busy one's self.

EMPLOY', *n.* That which engages the mind, or occupies the time and labor of a person; business; object of study or industry; employment.

Present to grasp, and future still to find,
The whole *employ* of body and of mind. *Pope.*

2. Occupation, as art, mystery, trade, profession.

3. Public office; agency; service for another.

EMPLOY'ABLE, *a.* That may be employed; capable of being used; fit or proper for use. *Boyle.*

EMPLOY'ED, *pp.* Occupied; fixed or engaged; applied in business; used in agency.

EMPLOY'ER, *n.* One who employs; one

who uses; one who engages or keeps in service.

EMPLOY'ING, *ppr.* Occupying; using; keeping busy.

EMPLOY'MENT, *n.* The act of employing or using.

2. Occupation; business; that which engages the head or hands; as agricultural *employments*; mechanical *employments*. Men, whose *employment* is to make sport and amusement for others, are always despised.

3. Office; public business or trust; agency or service for another or for the public. The secretary of the treasury has a laborious and responsible *employment*. He is in the *employment* of government.

EMPLUNGE. [See *Plunge*.]

EMPOIS'ON, *v. t.* *s* as *z*. [Fr. *empoisonner*. See *Poison*.]

1. To poison; to administer poison to; to destroy or endanger life by giving or causing to be taken into the stomach any noxious drug or preparation. [In this sense, *poison* is generally used; but *empoison* may be used, especially in poetry.] *Sidney. Bacon.*

2. To taint with poison or venom; to render noxions or deleterious by an admixture of poisonous substance. [This may be used, especially in poetry.]

3. To embitter; to deprive of sweetness; as, to *empoison* the joys and pleasures of life.

EMPOIS'ONED, *pp.* Poisoned; tainted with venom; embittered.

EMPOIS'ONER, *n.* One who poisons; one who administers a deleterious drug; he or that which embitters.

EMPOIS'ONING, *ppr.* Poisoning; embittering.

EMPOIS'ONMENT, *n.* The act of administering poison, or causing it to be taken; the act of destroying life by a deleterious drug.

EMPO'RIUM, *n.* [L. from the Gr. εμποριον, from εμπορευομαι, to buy; εν and πορευομαι, to pass or go, Sax. *faran*.]

1. A place of merchandize; a town or city of trade; particularly, a city or town of extensive commerce, or in which the commerce of an extensive country centers, or to which sellers and buyers resort from different countries. Such are London, Amsterdam and Hamburg. New York will be an *emporium*.

2. In *medicine*, the common sensory in the brain. *Coxe.*

EMPOV'ERISH. [See *Impoverish*.]

EMPOW'ER, *v. t.* [from *en* or *in* and *power*.]

1. To give legal or moral power or authority to; to authorize, either by law, commission, letter of attorney, natural right, or by verbal license. The supreme court is *empowered* to try and decide all cases, civil or criminal. The attorney is *empowered* to sign an acquittance and discharge the debtor.

2. To give physical power or force; to enable. [*In this sense the use is not frequent, and perhaps not used at all*.]

EMPOW'ERED, *pp.* Authorized; having legal or moral right.

EMPOW'ERING, *ppr.* Authorizing; giving power.

EM'PRESS, *n.* [contracted from *emperess*. See *Emperor*.] The consort or spouse of an emperor.

2. A female who governs an empire; a female invested with imperial power or sovereignty.

EMPRI'SE, *n.* *s* as *z*. [Norm.; *em*, *en*, and *prise*, from *prendre*, to take.]

An undertaking; an enterprise. *Spenser. Pope.*

[*This word is now rarely or never used, except in poetry*.]

EMP'TIER, *n.* One that empties or exhausts.

EMP'TINESS, *n.* [from *empty*.] A state of being empty; a state of containing nothing except air; destitution; absence of matter; as the *emptiness* of a vessel.

2. Void space; vacuity; vacuum. *Dryden.*

3. Want of solidity or substance; as the *emptiness* of light and shade. *Dryden.*

4. Unsatisfactoriness; inability to satisfy desire; as the *emptiness* of earthly things.

5. Vacuity of head; want of intellect or knowledge. *Pope.*

EMP'TION, *n.* [L. *emptio*, from *emo*, to buy.] The act of buying; a purchasing. [*Not much used*.] *Arbuthnot.*

EMP'TY, *a.* [Sax. *æmtig* or *æmti*, from *æmtian*, to be idle, to be vacant, to evacuate, *æmta*, ease, leisure, quiet.]

1. Containing nothing, or nothing but air; as an *empty* chest; *empty* space; an *empty* purse is a serious evil.

2. Evacuated; not filled; as *empty* shackles. *Spenser.*

3. Unfurnished; as an *empty* room.

4. Void; devoid.

> In civility thou seemest so *empty*. *Shak.*

5. Void; destitute of solid matter; as *empty* air.

6. Destitute of force or effect; as *empty* words.

7. Unsubstantial; unsatisfactory; not able to fill the mind or the desires. The pleasures of life are *empty* and unsatisfying.

> Pleased with *empty* praise. *Pope.*

8. Not supplied; having nothing to carry.

> They beat him, and sent him away *empty*. Mark xii.

9. Hungry.

> My falcon now is sharp and passing *empty*. *Shak.*

10. Unfurnished with intellect or knowledge; vacant of head; ignorant; as an *empty* coxcomb.

11. Unfruitful; producing nothing.

> Israel is an *empty* vine. Hosea x.
>
> Seven *empty* ears blasted with the east wind. Gen. xli.

12. Wanting substance; wanting solidity; as *empty* dreams.

13. Destitute; waste; desolate.

> Nineveh is *empty*. Nah. ii.

14. Without effect.

> The sword of Saul returned not *empty*. 2 Sam. i.

15. Without a cargo; in ballast; as, the ship returned *empty*.

EMP'TY, *v. t.* To exhaust; to make void or destitute; to deprive of the contents; as, to *empty* a vessel; to *empty* a well or a cistern.

2. To pour out the contents.

> The clouds *empty* themselves on the earth. Eccles. xi.
>
> Rivers *empty* themselves into the ocean.

3. To waste; to make desolate. Jer. li.

EMP'TY, *v. i.* To pour out or discharge its contents.

> The Connecticut *empties* into the Sound.

2. To become empty.

EMP'TYING, *ppr.* Pouring out the contents; making void.

EMP'TYINGS, *n.* The lees of beer, cider, &c.

EMPUR'PLE, *v. t.* [from *purple*.] To tinge or dye of a purple color; to discolor with purple.

> The deep *empurpled* ran. *Philips.*

EMPUR'PLED, *pp.* Stained with a purple color.

EMPUR'PLING, *ppr.* Tinging or dyeing of a purple color.

EMPU'SE, *n.* [Gr. εμπουσα.] A phantom or specter. [*Not used*.] *Bp. Taylor.*

EMPUZ'ZLE. [See *Puzzle*.]

EMPYR'EAL, *a.* [Fr. *empyrée*; Sp. It. *empireo*; L. *empyræus*; from Gr. εμπυρος; εν and πυρ, fire.]

1. Formed of pure fire or light; refined beyond aerial substance; pertaining to the highest and purest region of heaven.

> Go, soar with Plato to the *empyreal* sphere. *Pope.*

2. Pure; vital; dephlogisticated; an epithet given to the air, or rather gas, now called *oxygen*. *Higgins.*

EMPYRE'AN, *a.* Empyreal. *Akenside.*

EMPYRE'AN, *n.* [See *Empyreal*.] The highest heaven, where the pure element of fire has been supposed to subsist.

> The *empyrean* rung
> With halleluiahs. *Milton.*

EMPYREU'MA, *n.* [Gr. from εν and πυρ, fire.]

In *chimistry*, a disagreeable smell produced from burnt oils, in distillations of animal and vegetable substances. *Nicholson. Encyc.*

EMPYREUMAT'IC, **EMPYREUMAT'ICAL**, } *a.* Having the taste or smell of burnt oil, or of burning animal and vegetable substances.

EMPYR'ICAL, *a.* Containing the combustible principle of coal. *Kirwan.*

EMPYRO'SIS, *n.* [Gr. εμπυροω, to burn.] A general fire; a conflagration. [*Little used*.] *Hale.*

EMRODS. [See *Emerods*.]

E'MU, *n.* A large fowl of S. America, with wings unfit for flight.

This name properly belongs to the Cassowary, but has been erroneously applied, by the Brazilians, to the Rhea or S. American ostrich. *Cuvier.*

EM'ULATE, *v. t.* [L. *æmulor*; Sp. *emular*; It. *emulare*. Qu. Gr. αμιλλα, strife, contest.]

1. To strive to equal or excel, in qualities or actions; to imitate, with a view to equal or excel; to vie with; to rival. Learn early to *emulate* the good and the great. *Emulate* the virtues and shun the vices of distinguished men.

2. To be equal to.

> Thy eye would *emulate* the diamond. *Shak.*

3. To imitate; to resemble. [*Unusual*.]

> Convulsion *emulating* the motion of laughter. *Arbuthnot.*

EM'ULATE, *a.* Ambitious. [*Little used*.] *Shak.*

EM'ULATED, *pp.* Rivaled; imitated.

EM'ULATING, *ppr.* Rivaling; attempting to equal or excel; imitating; resembling.

EMULA'TION, *n.* The act of attempting to equal or excel in qualities or actions; rivalry; desire of superiority, attended with effort to attain to it; generally in a good sense, or an attempt to equal or excel others in that which is praise-worthy, without the desire of depressing others. Rom. xi. In a bad sense, a striving to equal or do more than others to obtain carnal favors or honors. Gal. v.

2. An ardor kindled by the praise-worthy examples of others, inciting to imitate them, or to equal or excel them.

A noble *emulation* heats your breast. *Dryden.*

3. Contest; contention; strife; competition; rivalry accompanied with a desire of depressing another.

Such factious *emulations* shall arise. *Shak.*

EM'ULATIVE, *a.* Inclined to emulation; rivaling; disposed to competition.

EM'ULATOR, *n.* One who emulates; a rival; a competitor.

EM'ULATRESS, *n.* A female who emulates another.

EMU'LE, *v. t.* To emulate. [*Not used.*]

EMULG'ENT, *a.* [L. *emulgeo*; *e* and *mulgeo*, to milk out.]

Milking or draining out. In *anatomy*, the *emulgent* or renal arteries are those which supply the kidneys with blood, being sometimes single, sometimes double. The *emulgent* veins return the blood, after the urine is secreted. This the ancients considered as a *milking* or straining of the serum, whence the name.

Encyc. Harris. Quincy. Parr.

EMULG'ENT, *n.* An emulgent vessel.

EM'ULOUS, *a.* [L. *æmulus.*] Desirous or eager to imitate, equal or excel another; desirous of like excellence with another; with *of*; as *emulous of* another's example or virtues.

2. Rivaling; engaged in competition; as *emulous* Carthage. *B. Jonson.*

3. Factious; contentious. *Shak.*

EM'ULOUSLY, *adv.* With desire of equaling or excelling another. *Granville.*

EMUL'SION, *n.* [Fr. from L. *emulsus*, *emulgeo*, to milk out.]

A soft liquid remedy of a color and consistence resembling milk; any milk-like mixture prepared by uniting oil and water, by means of another substance, saccharine or mucilaginous. *Encyc. Ure.*

EMUL'SIVE, *a.* Softening; milk-like.

2. Producing or yielding a milk-like substance; as *emulsive* acids. *Fourcroy.*

EMUNC'TORY, *n.* [L. *emunctorium*, from *emunctus*, *emungo*, to wipe, to cleanse.]

In *anatomy*, any part of the body which serves to carry off excrementitious matter; a secretory gland; an excretory duct.

Encyc. Coxe.

The kidneys and skin are called the *common emunctories.* *Cyc.*

EMUSCA'TION, *n.* [L. *emuscor.*] A freeing from moss. [*Not much used.*] *Evelyn.*

EN, a prefix to many English words, chiefly borrowed from the French. It coincides with the Latin, *in*, Gr. εν, and some English words are written indifferently with *en* or *in*. For the ease of pronunciation, it is changed to *em*, particularly before a labial, as in *employ, empower.*

En was formerly a plural termination of nouns and of verbs, as in *housen, escapen.* It is retained in *oxen* and *children.* It is also still used as the termination of some verbs, as in *hearken*, from the Saxon infinitive.

ENA'BLE, *v. t.* [Norm. *enhabler*; *en* and *hable*, able. See *Able.*]

1. To make able; to supply with power, physical or moral; to furnish with sufficient power or ability. By strength a man is *enabled* to work. Learning and industry *enable* men to investigate the laws of nature. Fortitude *enables* us to bear pain without murmuring.

2. To supply with means. Wealth *enables* men to be charitable, or to live in luxury.

3. To furnish with legal ability or competency; to authorize. The law *enables* us to dispose of our property by will.

4. To furnish with competent knowledge or skill, and in general, with adequate means.

ENA'BLED, *pp.* Supplied with sufficient power, physical, moral or legal.

ENA'BLEMENT, *n.* The act of enabling; ability. *Bacon.*

ENA'BLING, *ppr.* Giving power to; supplying with sufficient power, ability or means; authorizing.

ENACT', *v. t.* [*en* and *act.*] To make, as a law; to pass, as a bill into a law; to perform the last act of a legislature to a bill, giving it validity as a law; to give legislative sanction to a bill.

Shall this bill pass to be *enacted?* *T. Bigelow.*

2. To decree; to establish as the will of the supreme power.

3. To act; to perform; to effect. [*Not used.*] *Spenser.*

4. To represent in action. [*Not used.*] *Shak.*

ENACT'ED, *pp.* Passed into a law; sanctioned as a law, by legislative authority.

ENACT'ING, *ppr.* Passing into a law; giving legislative sanction to a bill, and establishing it as a law.

2. *a.* Giving legislative forms and sanction; as the *enacting* clause of a bill.

ENACT'MENT, *n.* The passing of a bill into a law; the act of voting, decreeing and giving validity to a law.

Christian Observer. Walsh.

ENACT'OR, *n.* One who enacts or passes a law; one who decrees or establishes, as a law. *Atterbury.*

2. One who performs any thing. [*Not used.*] *Shak.*

ENAC'TURE, *n.* Purpose. [*Not in use.*] *Shak.*

ENAL'LAGE, *n.* *enal'lajy.* [Gr. εναλλαγη, change; εναλλαττω, to change; εν and αλλαττω.]

A figure, in *grammar*, by which some change is made in the common mode of speech, or when one word is substituted for another; as *exercitus victor*, for *victoriosus*; *scelus*, for *scelestus.* *Encyc.*

ENAM'BUSH, *v. t.* [*en* and *ambush.*] To hide in ambush.

2. To ambush. *Chapman.*

ENAM'BUSHED, *pp.* Concealed in ambush, or with hostile intention; ambushed.

ENAM'EL, *n.* [*en* and Fr. *email*, Sp. *esmalte*, It. *smalto*, G. *schmelz*, from the root of *melt.*]

1. In *mineralogy*, a substance imperfectly vitrified, or matter in which the granular appearance is destroyed, and having a vitreous gloss.

In *the arts*, a substance of the nature of glass, differing from it by a greater degree of fusibility or opacity. *Ed. Encyc.*

Enamels have for their basis a pure crystal glass or frit, ground with a fine oxyd of lead and tin. These baked together are the matter of enamels, and the color is varied by adding other substances. Oxyd of gold gives a red color; that of copper, a green; manganese, a violet; cobalt, a blue; and iron, a fine black.

Encyc. Nicholson.

2. That which is enameled; a smooth, glossy surface of various colors, resembling enamel.

3. In *anatomy*, the smooth hard substance which covers the crown of a tooth. *Cyc.*

ENAM'EL, *v. t.* To lay enamel on a metal, as on gold, silver, copper, &c.

2. To paint in enamel. *Encyc.*

3. To form a glossy surface like enamel.

ENAM'ELAR, *a.* Consisting of enamel; resembling enamel; smooth; glossy.

ENAM'ELED, *pp.* Overlaid with enamel; adorned with any thing resembling enamel.

ENAM'ELER, *n.* One who enamels; one whose occupation is to lay enamels, or inlay colors.

ENAM'ELING, *ppr.* Laying enamel.

ENAM'ELING, *n.* The act or art of laying enamels.

ENAM'OR, *v. t.* [from the French *amour*, L. *amor*, love.]

To inflame with love; to charm; to captivate; with *of* before the person or thing; as, to be *enamored of* a lady; to be *enamored of* books or science.

[*But it is now followed by* with.]

ENAMORA'DO, *n.* One deeply in love. *Herbert.*

ENAM'ORED, *pp.* Inflamed with love; charmed; delighted.

ENAM'ORING, *ppr.* Inflaming with love; charming; captivating.

EN'ARMED, *a.* In *heraldry*, having arms, that is, horns, hoofs, &c. of a different color from that of the body.

ENARRA'TION, *n.* [L. *enarro*, *narro*, to relate.]

Recital; relation; account; exposition. [*Little used.*]

ENARTHRO'SIS, *n.* [Gr. εναρθρωσις; εν and αρθρον, a joint.]

In *anatomy*, that species of articulation which consists in the insertion of the round end of a bone in the cup-like cavity of another, forming a movable joint; the ball and socket. *Quincy.*

ENA'TE, *a.* [L. *enatus.*] Growing out. *Smith.*

ENAUN'TER, *adv.* Lest that. *Obs.* *Spenser.*

ENCA'GE, *v. t.* [from *cage.*] To shut up or confine in a cage; to coop. *Shak. Donne.*

ENCA'GED, *pp.* Shut up or confined in a cage.

ENCA'GING, *ppr.* Cooping; confining in a cage.

ENCAMP', *v. i.* [from *camp.*] To pitch tents or form huts, as an army; to halt on a march, spread tents and remain for a night or for a longer time, as an army or company.

They *encamped* in Etham. Ex. xiii.

The Levites shall *encamp* about the tabernacle. Num. i.

2. To pitch tents for the purpose of a siege; to besiege.

Encamp against the city and take it. 2 Sam. xii.

ENCAMP', *v. t.* To form into a camp; to place a marching army or company in a temporary habitation or quarters.

ENCAMP'ED, *pp.* Settled in tents or huts for lodging or temporary habitation.

ENCAMP'ING, *ppr.* Pitching tents or forming huts, for a temporary lodging or rest.

ENCAMP'MENT, *n.* The act of pitching tents or forming huts, as an army or traveling company, for temporary lodging or rest.

2. The place where an army or company is encamped; a camp; a regular order of tents or huts for the accommodation of an army or troop.

ENCANK'ER, *v. t.* To corrode; to canker. *Shelton.*

ENCA'SE, *v. t.* To inclose or confine in a case or cover. *Beaum.*

ENCAUS'TIC, *a.* [Gr. εν and καυστικος, caustic, from καιω, to burn.]
Pertaining to the art of enameling, and to painting in burnt wax. *Encaustic* painting, is a method in which wax is employed to give a gloss to colors. *Encyc.*

ENCAUS'TIC, *n.* Enamel or enameling.

2. The method of painting in burnt wax. *Encyc.*

ENCA'VE, *v. t.* [from *cave.*] To hide in a cave or recess. *Shak.*

ENCE'INT, *n.* [Fr. from *enceindre; en* and *ceindre,* L. *cingo,* to gird.]
In *fortification,* inclosure; the wall or rampart which surrounds a place, sometimes composed of bastions and curtains. It is sometimes only flanked by round or square towers, which is called a Roman wall. *Encyc.*

ENCE'INT, *a.* In *law,* pregnant; with child. *Blackstone.*

ENCHA'FE, *v. t.* [*en* and *chafe,* Fr. *chauffer.*]
To chafe or fret; to provoke; to enrage; to irritate. [See *Chafe.*] *Shak.*

ENCHA'FED, *pp.* Chafed; irritated; enraged.

ENCHA'FING, *ppr.* Chafing; fretting; enraging.

ENCHA'IN, *v. t.* [Fr. *enchainer.* See *Chain.*]

1. To fasten with a chain; to bind or hold in chains; to hold in bondage.

2. To hold fast; to restrain; to confine. *Dryden.*

3. To link together; to connect. *Howell.*

ENCHA'INED, *pp.* Fastened with a chain; held in bondage; held fast; restrained; confined.

ENCHA'INING, *ppr.* Making fast with a chain; binding; holding in chains; confining.

ENCH'ANT, *v. t.* [Fr. *enchanter; en* and *chanter,* to sing; L. *incanto; in* and *canto,* to sing. See *Chant* and *Cant.*]

1. To practice sorcery or witchcraft on any thing; to give efficacy to any thing by songs of sorcery, or fascination.

And now about the cauldron sing,
Like elves and fairies in a ring,
Enchanting all that you put in. *Shak.*

2. To subdue by charms or spells. *Sidney.*

3. To delight to the highest degree; to charm; to ravish with pleasure; as, the description *enchants* me; we were *enchanted* with the music.

ENCH'ANTED, *pp.* Affected by sorcery; fascinated; subdued by charms; delighted beyond measure.

2. Inhabited or possessed by elves, witches, or other imaginary mischievous spirits; as an *enchanted castle.*

ENCH'ANTER, *n.* One who enchants; a sorcerer or magician; one who has spirits or demons at his command; one who practices enchantment, or pretends to perform surprising things by the agency of demons.

2. One who charms or delights.

Enchanter's nightshade, a genus of plants, the Circæa.

ENCH'ANTING, *ppr.* Affecting with sorcery, charms or spells.

2. Delighting highly; ravishing with delight; charming.

3. *a.* Charming; delighting; ravishing; as an *enchanting* voice; an *enchanting* face.

Simplicity in manners has an *enchanting* effect. *Kames.*

ENCH'ANTINGLY, *adv.* With the power of enchantment; in a manner to delight or charm; as, the lady sings *enchantingly.*

ENCH'ANTMENT, *n.* The act of producing certain wonderful effects by the invocation or aid of demons, or the agency of certain supposed spirits; the use of magic arts, spells or charms; incantation.

The magicians of Egypt did so with their *enchantments.* Ex. vii.

2. Irresistible influence; overpowering influence of delight.

The warmth of fancy—which holds the heart of a reader under the strongest *enchantment.* *Pope.*

ENCH'ANTRESS, *n.* A sorceress; a woman who pretends to effect wonderful things by the aid of demons; one who pretends to practice magic. *Tatler.*

2. A woman whose beauty or excellencies give irresistible influence.

From this *enchantress* all these ills are come. *Dryden.*

ENCH'ARGE, *v. t.* To give in charge or trust. [*Not in use.*] *Bp. Hall.*

ENCHA'SE, *v. t.* [Fr. *enchasser;* Sp. *engastar,* or *encaxar,* from *caxa,* a box, a chest; Port. *encastoar, encaxar;* It. *incastonare;* Fr. *chassis,* a frame; Eng. a *case.*]

1. To infix or inclose in another body so as to be held fast, but not concealed. *Johnson.*

2. *Technically,* to adorn by embossed work; to enrich or beautify any work in metal, by some design or figure in low relief, as a watch case. *Encyc.*

3. To adorn by being fixed on it.

To drink in bowls which glittering gems *enchase.* *Dryden.*

4. To mark by incision. *Fairfax.*

5. To delineate. *Spenser.*

ENCHA'SED, *pp.* Enclosed as in a frame or in another body; adorned with embossed work.

ENCHA'SING, *ppr.* Inclosing in another body; adorning with embossed work.

ENCHE'ASON, *n.* [Old Fr.] Cause; occasion. *Obs.* *Spenser.*

ENCHIRID'ION, *n.* [Gr. εν and χειρ, the hand.]
A manual; a book to be carried in the hand. [*Not used.*]

ENCIN'DERED, *a.* Burnt to cinders. *Cockeram.*

ENCIR'CLE, *v. t.* *ensur'cl.* [from *circle.*]

1. To inclose or surround with a circle or ring, or with any thing in a circular form. Luminous rings *encircle* Saturn.

2. To encompass; to surround; to environ.

3. To embrace; as, to *encircle* one in the arms.

ENCIR'CLED, *pp.* Surrounded with a circle; encompassed; environed; embraced.

ENCIR'CLET, *n.* A circle; a ring. *Sidney.*

ENCIR'CLING, *ppr.* Surrounding with a circle or ring; encompassing; embracing.

ENCLIT'IC, *a.* [Gr. εγκλιτικος, inclined; εγκλινω, to incline.]

1. Leaning; inclining, or inclined. In *grammar,* an *enclitic* particle or word, is one which is so closely united to another as to seem to be a part of it; as *que, ne,* and *ve,* in *virumque, nonne, aliusve.*

2. Throwing back the accent upon the foregoing syllable. *Harris.*

ENCLIT'IC, *n.* A word which is joined to the end of another, as *que,* in *virumque,* which may vary the accent.

2. A particle or word that throws the accent or emphasis back upon the former syllable. *Harris.*

ENCLIT'ICALLY, *adv.* In an enclitic manner; by throwing the accent back. *Walker.*

ENCLIT'ICS, *a.* In *grammar,* the art of declining and conjugating words.

ENCLOSE. [See *Inclose.*]

ENCLOUD'ED, *a.* [from *cloud.*] Covered with clouds. *Spenser.*

ENCOACH, *v. t.* To carry in a coach. *Davies.*

ENCOF'FIN, *v. t.* To put in a coffin.

ENCOF'FINED, *pp.* Inclosed in a coffin. *Spenser.*

ENCOM'BER. [See *Encumber.*]

ENCOM'BERMENT, *n.* Molestation. [*Not used.*] *Spenser.*

ENCO'MIAST, *n.* [Gr. εγκωμιαςης.] One who praises another; a panegyrist; one who utters or writes commendations.

ENCOMIAS'TIC, ENCOMIAS'TICAL, *a.* Bestowing praise; praising; commending; laudatory; as an *encomiastic* address or discourse.

ENCOMIAS'TIC, *n.* A panegyric.

ENCO'MIUM, *n.* plu. *encomiums.* [L. from Gr. εγκωμιον.]
Praise; panegyric; commendation. Men are quite as willing to receive as to bestow *encomiums.*

ENCOM'PASS, *v. t.* [from *compass.*] To encircle; to surround; as, a ring *encompasses* the finger.

2. To environ; to inclose; to surround; to shut in. A besieging army *encompassed* the city of Jerusalem.

3. To go or sail round; as, Drake *encompassed* the globe.

ENCŌM′PASSED, *pp.* Encircled; surrounded; inclosed; shut in.

ENCŌM′PASSING, *ppr.* Encircling; surrounding; confining.

ENCŌM′PASSMENT, *n.* A surrounding.

2. A going round; circumlocution in speaking. *Shak.*

ENCO′RE, a French word, pronounced nearly *ongkore*, and signifying, again, once more; used by the auditors and spectators of plays and other sports, when they call for a repetition of a particular part.

ENCO′RE, *v. t.* To call for a repetition of a particular part of an entertainment.

ENCOUNT′ER, *n.* [Fr. *encontre*, *en* and *contre*, L. *contra*, against, or rather *rencontre*; Sp. *encuentro*; Port. *encontro*; It. *incontro*.]

1. A meeting, particularly a sudden or accidental meeting of two or more persons.

To shun th' *encounter* of the vulgar crowd. *Pope.*

2. A meeting in contest; a single combat, on a sudden meeting of parties; sometimes less properly, a duel.

3. A fight; a conflict; a skirmish; a battle; but more generally, a fight between a small number of men, or an accidental meeting and fighting of detachments, rather than a set battle or general engagement.

4. Eager and warm conversation, either in love or anger. *Shak.*

5. A sudden or unexpected address or accosting. *Shak.*

6. Occasion; casual incident. [*Unusual.*] *Pope.*

ENCOUNT′ER, *v. t.* [Sp. Port. *encontrar*; It. *incontrare*; Fr. *rencontrer.*]

1. To meet face to face; particularly, to meet suddenly or unexpectedly.

[This sense is now uncommon, but still in use.]

2. To meet in opposition, or in a hostile manner; to rush against in conflict; to engage with in battle; as, two armies *encounter* each other.

3. To meet and strive to remove or surmount; as, to *encounter* obstacles, impediments or difficulties.

4. To meet and oppose; to resist; to attack and attempt to confute; as, to *encounter* the arguments of opponents. Acts xvii. 18.

5. To meet as an obstacle. Which ever way the infidel turns, he *encounters* clear evidence of the divine origin of the scriptures.

6. To oppose; to oppugn. *Hale.*

7. To meet in mutual kindness. [*Little used.*] *Shak.*

ENCOUNT′ER, *v. i.* To meet face to face; to meet unexpectedly. [*Little used.*]

2. To rush together in combat; to fight; to conflict. Three armies *encountered* at Waterloo.

When applied to one party, it is sometimes followed by *with*; as, the christian army *encountered with* the Saracens.

3. To meet in opposition or debate.

ENCOUNT′ERED, *pp.* Met face to face; met in opposition or hostility; opposed.

ENCOUNT′ERER, *n.* One who encounters; an opponent; an antagonist. *Atterbury.*

ENCOUNT′ERING, *ppr.* Meeting; meeting in opposition, or in battle; opposing; resisting.

ENCOUR′AGE, *v. t.* *enkur′rage.* [Fr. *encourager*; *en* and *courage*, from *cœur*, the heart; It. *incoraggiare.*]

To give courage to; to give or increase confidence of success; to inspire with courage, spirit, or strength of mind; to embolden; to animate; to incite; to inspirit.

But charge Joshua, and *encourage* him. Deut. iii.

ENCOUR′AGED, *pp.* Emboldened; inspirited; animated; incited.

ENCOUR′AGEMENT, *n.* The act of giving courage, or confidence of success; incitement to action or to practice; incentive. We ought never to neglect the *encouragement* of youth in generous deeds. The praise of good men serves as an *encouragement* to virtue and heroism.

2. That which serves to incite, support, promote or advance, as favor, countenance, rewards, profit. A young man attempted the practice of law, but found little *encouragement*. The fine arts find little *encouragement* among a rude people.

ENCOUR′AGER, *n.* One who encourages, incites or stimulates to action; one who supplies incitements, either by counsel, reward or means of execution.

The pope is a master of polite learning and a great *encourager* of arts. *Addison.*

ENCOUR′AGING, *ppr.* Inspiring with hope and confidence; exciting courage.

2. *a.* Furnishing ground to hope for success; as an *encouraging* prospect.

ENCOUR′AGINGLY, *adv.* In a manner to give courage, or hope of success.

ENCRA′DLE, *v. t.* [*en* and *cradle.*] To lay in a cradle. *Spenser.*

ENCRIM′SON, *v. t.* *s* as *z.* To cover with a crimson color.

ENCRIM′SONED, *pp.* Covered with a crimson color.

EN′CRINITE, *n.* [Gr. κρινον, a lily.] Stone-lily; a fossil zoophyte, formed of many joints, all perforated by some starry form. *Edin. Encyc.*

ENCRISP′ED, *a.* [from *crisp*; Sp. *encrespar.*] Curled; formed in curls. *Skelton.*

ENCRŌACH, *v. i.* [Fr. *accrocher*, to catch, to grapple, from *croc*, a hook, W. *crôg*, Eng. *crook.*] Primarily, to catch as with a hook. Hence,

1. To enter on the rights and possessions of another; to intrude; to take possession of what belongs to another, by gradual advances into his limits or jurisdiction, and usurping a part of his rights or prerogatives; with *on*. The farmer who runs a fence on his neighbor's land, and incloses a piece with his own, *encroaches on* his neighbor's property. Men often *encroach*, in this manner, *on* the highway. The sea is said to *encroach on* the land, when it wears it away gradually; and the land *encroaches on* the sea, when it is extended into it by alluvion. It is important to prevent one branch of government from *encroaching on* the jurisdiction of another.

2. To creep on gradually without right.

Superstition—a creeping and *encroaching* evil. *Hooker.*

3. To pass the proper bounds, and enter on another's rights.

Exclude th' *encroaching* cattle from thy ground. *Dryden.*

ENCRŌACHER, *n.* One who enters on and takes possession of what is not his own, by gradual steps. *Swift.*

2. One who makes gradual advances beyond his rights. *Clarissa.*

ENCRŌACHING, *ppr.* Entering on and taking possession of what belongs to another.

ENCRŌACHING, *a.* Tending or apt to encroach.

The *encroaching* spirit of power. *Madison.*

ENCRŌACHINGLY, *adv.* By way of encroachment. *Bailey.*

ENCRŌACHMENT, *n.* The entering gradually on the rights or possessions of another, and taking possession; unlawful intrusion; advance into the territories or jurisdiction of another, by silent means, or without right. *Milton. Atterbury. Addison.*

2. That which is taken by encroaching on another.

3. In *law*, if a tenant owes two shillings rent-service to the lord, and the lord takes three, it is an *encroachment.* *Cowel.*

ENCRUST′, *v. t.* To cover with a crust. It is written also *incrust.*

ENCUM′BER, *v. t.* [Fr. *encombrer.* See *Incumber.*]

1. To load; to clog; to impede motion with a load, burden or any thing inconvenient to the limbs; to render motion or operation difficult or laborious.

2. To embarrass; to perplex; to obstruct.

3. To load with debts; as, an estate is *encumbered* with mortgages, or with a widow's dower.

ENCUM′BERED, *pp.* Loaded; impeded in motion or operation, by a burden or difficulties; loaded with debts.

ENCUM′BERING, *ppr.* Loading; clogging; rendering motion or operation difficult; loading with debts.

ENCUM′BRANCE, *n.* A load; any thing that impedes motion, or renders it difficult and laborious; clog; impediment.

2. Useless addition or load.

Strip from the branching Alps their piny load,
The huge *encumbrance* of horrific wood. *Thomson.*

3. Load or burden on an estate; a legal claim on an estate, for the discharge of which the estate is liable.

ENCYC′LICAL, *a.* [Gr. εγκυκλικος; εν and κυκλος, a circle.]

Circular; sent to many persons or places; intended for many, or for a whole order of men. [This word is not used. We now use *circular.*] *Stillingfleet.*

ENCYCLOPE′DIA, ENCYCLOPE′DY, *n.* [Gr. εν, in, κυκλος, a circle, and παιδεια, instruction; instruction in a circle, or circle of instruction.]

The circle of sciences; a general system of instruction or knowledge. More particularly, a collection of the principal facts, principles and discoveries, in all branches of science and the arts, digested under proper titles and arranged in alphabetical order; as the French *Encyclopedia*; the *Encyclopedia* Brittannica.

ENCYCLOPE′DIAN, *a.* Embracing the whole circle of learning.

ENCYCLOPE'DIST, *n.* The compiler of an Encyclopedia, or one who assists in such compilation.

ENCYST'ED, *a.* [from *cyst.*] Inclosed in a bag, bladder or vesicle; as an *encysted* tumor. *Sharp.*

END, *n.* [Sax. *end*, *ende*, or *ænde*; G. *ende*; D. *eind*; Sw. *ände*; Dan. *ende*; Goth. *andei*; Basque, *ondoa*; Sans. *anda* or *anta*; Per. اندان andan.]

1. The extreme point of a line, or of any thing that has more length than breadth; as the *end* of a house; the *end* of a table; the *end* of a finger; the *end* of a chain or rope. When bodies or figures have equal dimensions, or equal length and breadth, the extremities are called *sides*.
2. The extremity or last part, in general; the close or conclusion, applied to time.
   At the *end* of two months, she returned. Judges xi.
3. The conclusion or cessation of an action.
   Of the increase of his government there shall be no *end*. Is. ix.
4. The close or conclusion; as the *end* of a chapter.
5. Ultimate state or condition; final doom.
   Mark the perfect man, and behold the upright, for the *end* of that man is peace. Ps. xxxvii.
6. The point beyond which no progression can be made.
   They reel to and fro, and stagger like a drunken man, and are at their wit's *end*. Ps. cvii.
7. Final determination; conclusion of debate or deliberation.
   My guilt be on my head and there's an *end!* *Shak.*
8. Close of life; death; decease.
   Unblamed through life, lamented in thy *end*. *Pope.*
9. Cessation; period; close of a particular state of things; as the *end* of the world.
10. Limit; termination.
   There is no *end* of the store. Nahum ii.
11. Destruction. Amos viii.
   The *end* of all flesh is come. Gen. vi.
12. Cause of death; a destroyer.
   And award
   Either of you to be the other's *end*. *Shak.*
13. Consequence; issue; result; conclusive event; conclusion.
   The *end* of these things is death. Rom. vi.
14. A fragment or broken piece.
   Old odd *ends*. *Shak.*
15. The ultimate point or thing at which one aims or directs his views; the object intended to be reached or accomplished by any action or scheme; purpose intended; scope; aim; drift; as private *ends*; public *ends*.
   Two things I shall propound to you, as *ends*. *Suckling.*
   The *end* of the commandments is charity. 1 Tim. i.
   A right to the *end*, implies a right to the means necessary for attaining it. *Law.*
16. *An end*, for *on end*, upright; erect; as, his hair stands *an end*.
17. *The ends of the earth*, in scripture, are the remotest parts of the earth, or the inhabitants of those parts.

END, *v. t.* To finish; to close; to conclude; to terminate; as, to *end* a controversy; to *end* a war.
   On the seventh day God *ended* his work. Gen. ii.
2. To destroy; to put to death.
   King Harry, thy sword hath *ended* him. *Shak.*

END, *v. i.* To come to the ultimate point; to be finished; as, a voyage *ends* by the return of a ship.
2. To terminate; to close; to conclude. The discourse *ends* with impressive words.
3. To cease; to come to a close. Winter *ends* in March, and summer in September. A good life *ends* in peace.

END'-ALL, *n.* Final close. [*Not used.*] *Shak.*

ENDAM'AGE, *v. t.* [from *damage.*] To bring loss or damage to; to harm; to injure; to mischief; to prejudice.
   The trial hath *endamaged* thee no way. *Milton.*
   So thou shalt *endamage* the revenue of the kings. Ezra iv.

ENDAM'AGED, *pp.* Harmed; injured.

ENDAM'AGEMENT, *n.* Damage; loss; injury. *Shak.*

ENDAM'AGING, *ppr.* Harming; injuring.

ENDAN'GER, *v. t.* [from *danger.*] To put in hazard; to bring into danger or peril; to expose to loss or injury. We dread any thing that *endangers* our life, our peace or our happiness.
2. To incur the hazard of. [*Unusual.*] *Bacon.*

ENDAN'GERED, *pp.* Exposed to loss or injury.

ENDAN'GERING, *ppr.* Putting in hazard; exposing to loss or injury.

ENDAN'GERING, *n.* Injury; damage. *Milton.*

ENDAN'GERMENT, *n.* Hazard; danger. *Spenser.*

ENDE'AR, *v. t.* [from *dear.*] To make dear; to make more beloved. The distress of a friend *endears* him to us, by exciting our sympathy.
2. To raise the price. [*Not in use.*]

ENDE'ARED, *pp.* Rendered dear, beloved, or more beloved.

ENDE'ARING, *ppr.* Making dear or more beloved.

ENDE'ARMENT, *n.* The cause of love; that which excites or increases affection, particularly that which excites tenderness of affection.
   Her first *endearments* twining round the soul. *Thomson.*
2. The state of being beloved; tender affection. *South.*

ENDEAV'OR, *n.* *endev'or.* [Norm. *devoyer*, endeavor; *endevera*, he ought; *endeyvent*, they ought. It seems to be from Fr. [*endevoir*] *devoir*, to owe or be indebted, and hence it primarily signifies duty, from the sense of binding, pressure, urgency. Hence our popular phrase, I will do my *endeavor*. In Ir. *dibhirce* is *endeavor.*]

An effort; an essay; an attempt; an exertion of physical strength, or the intellectual powers, towards the attainment of an object.
   The bold and sufficient pursue their game with more passion, *endeavor* and application, and therefore often succeed. *Temple.*
   Imitation is the *endeavor* of a later poet to write like one who has written before him on the same subject. *Dryden.*
   Labor is a continued *endeavor*, or a succession of *endeavors*. *Anon.*

ENDEAV'OR, *v. i.* *endev'or.* To exert physical strength or intellectual power, for the accomplishment of an object; to try; to essay; to attempt. In a race, each man *endeavors* to outstrip his antagonist. A poet may *endeavor* to rival Homer, but without success. It is followed by *after* before a noun; as, the christian *endeavors after* more strict conformity to the example of Christ.
2. *v. t.* To attempt to gain; to try to effect.
   It is our duty to *endeavor* the recovery of these beneficial subjects. *Chatham.*

ENDEAV'ORED, *pp.* Essayed; attempted.

ENDEAV'ORER, *n.* One who makes an effort or attempt.

ENDEAV'ORING, *ppr.* Making an effort or efforts; striving; essaying; attempting.

ENDEC'AGON, *n.* [Gr. ἑν, δεκα and γωνια.] A plain figure of eleven sides and angles. *Bailey. Johnson.*

ENDEI'CTIC, *a.* [Gr. ενδεικνυμι, to show.] Showing; exhibiting. An *endeictic* dialogue, in the Platonic philosophy, is one which exhibits a specimen of skill. *Enfield.*

ENDEM'IC, **ENDEM'ICAL**, **ENDE'MIAL**, } *a.* [Gr. ενδημιος; εν and δημος, people.] Peculiar to a people or nation. An *endemic* disease, is one to which the inhabitants of a particular country are peculiarly subject, and which, for that reason, may be supposed to proceed from local causes, as bad air or water. The epithet is also applied to a disease which prevails in a particular season, chiefly or wholly in a particular place.

ENDEN'IZE, *v. t.* [from *denizen*, or its root.] To make free; to naturalize; to admit to the privileges of a denizen. [*Little used.*] *Camden.*

ENDEN'IZEN, *v. t.* [from *denizen.*] To naturalize. *B. Jonson.*

ENDICT, **ENDICTMENT.** [See *Indict*, *Indictment.*]

END'ING, *ppr.* [from *end.*] Terminating; closing; concluding.

END'ING, *n.* Termination; conclusion.
2. In *grammar*, the terminating syllable or letter of a word.

ENDITE. [See *Indite.*]

EN'DIVE, *n.* [Fr. *endive*; It. *endivia*; Sp. *endibia*; L. *intybum*; Ar. هندب hindabon.]

A species of plant, of the genus Cichorium or succory; used as a salad.

END'LESS, *a.* [See *End.*] Without end; having no end or conclusion; applied to length, and to duration; as an *endless* line; *endless* progression; *endless* duration; *endless* bliss.
2. Perpetual; incessant; continual; as *endless* praise; *endless* clamor.

END'LESSLY, *adv.* Without end or termination; as, to extend a line *endlessly*.
2. Incessantly; perpetually; continually.

END'LESSNESS, *n.* Extension without end or limit.
2. Perpetuity; endless duration.

END'LONG, *adv.* In a line; with the end forward. [*Little used.*] *Dryden.*

ENDOC'TRINE, *v. t.* To teach; to indoctrinate. [See the latter word.] *Donne.*

ENDORSE, ENDORSEMENT. [See *Indorse, Indorsement.*]

ENDOSS', *v. t.* [Fr. *endosser.*] To engrave or carve. *Spenser.*

ENDOW', *v. t.* [Norm. *endouer;* Fr. *douer.* Qu. from L. *dos, doto,* or a different Celtic root, for in Ir. *diobhadh* is *dower.* The sense is to set or put on.]

1. To furnish with a portion of goods or estate, called *dower;* to settle a dower on, as on a married woman or widow.

A wife is by law entitled to be *endowed* of all lands and tenements, of which her husband was seized in fee simple or fee tail during the coverture. *Blackstone.*

2. To settle on, as a permanent provision; to furnish with a permanent fund of property; as, to *endow* a church; to *endow* a college with a fund to support a professor.

3. To enrich or furnish with any gift, quality or faculty; to indue. Man is *endowed* by his maker with reason.

ENDOW'ED, *pp.* Furnished with a portion of estate; having dower settled on; supplied with a permanent fund; indued.

ENDOW'ING, *ppr.* Settling a dower on; furnishing with a permanent fund; induing.

ENDOW'MENT, *n.* The act of settling dower on a woman, or of settling a fund or permanent provision for the support of a parson or vicar, or of a professor, &c.

2. That which is bestowed or settled on; property, fund or revenue permanently appropriated to any object; as the *endowments* of a church, of a hospital, or of a college.

3. That which is given or bestowed on the person or mind by the creator; gift of nature; any quality or faculty bestowed by the creator. Natural activity of limbs is an *endowment* of the body; natural vigor of intellect is an *endowment* of the mind. Chatham and Burke, in Great Britain, and Jay, Ellsworth and Hamilton, in America, possessed uncommon *endowments* of mind.

ENDRUDGE, *v. t. endruj'.* To make a drudge or slave. [*Not used.*] *Hall.*

ENDU'E, *v. t.* [Fr. *enduire;* L. *induo.*] To indue, which see.

ENDU'RABLE, *a.* That can be borne or suffered.

ENDU'RANCE, *n.* [See *Endure.*] Continuance; a state of lasting or duration; lastingness. *Spenser.*

2. A bearing or suffering; a continuing under pain or distress without resistance, or without sinking or yielding to the pressure; sufferance; patience.

Their fortitude was most admirable in their presence and *endurance* of all evils, of pain, and of death. *Temple.*

3. Delay; a waiting for. [*Not used.*] *Shak.*

ENDU'RE, *v. i.* [Fr. *endurer; en* and *durer,* to last, from *dur,* L. *durus, duro;* Sp. *endurar.* The primary sense of *durus,* hard, is set, fixed. See *Durable.*]

1. To last; to continue in the same state without perishing; to remain; to abide.

The Lord shall *endure* forever. Ps. ix.

He shall hold it [his house] fast, but it shall not *endure.* Job viii.

2. To bear; to brook; to suffer without resistance, or without yielding.

How can I *endure* to see the evil that shall come to my people? Esther viii.

Can thy heart *endure,* or thy hands be strong? Ezek. xxii.

ENDU'RE, *v. t.* To bear; to sustain; to support without breaking or yielding to force or pressure. Metals *endure* a certain degree of heat without melting.

Both were of shining steel, and wrought so pure,
As might the strokes of two such arms *endure.* *Dryden.*

2. To bear with patience; to bear without opposition or sinking under the pressure.

Therefore I *endure* all things for the elect's sake. 2 Tim. ii.

If ye *endure* chastening, God dealeth with you as with sons. Heb. xii.

3. To undergo; to sustain.

I wish to die, yet dare not death *endure.* *Dryden.*

4. To continue in. [*Not used.*] *Brown.*

ENDU'RED, *pp.* Borne; suffered; sustained.

ENDU'RER, *n.* One who bears, suffers or sustains.

2. He or that which continues long.

ENDU'RING, *ppr.* Lasting; continuing without perishing; bearing; sustaining; supporting with patience, or without opposition or yielding.

2. *a.* Lasting long; permanent.

END'WISE, *adv.* On the end; erectly; in an upright position.

2. With the end forward.

EN'ECATE, *v. t.* [L. *eneco.*] To kill. [*Not in use.*] *Harvey.*

E'NEID, *n.* [L. *Æneis.*] A heroic poem, written by Virgil, in which Æneas is the hero.

EN'EMY, *n.* [Fr. *ennemi;* Sp. *enemigo;* It. *nemico;* Ir. *namha;* from L. *inimicus;* *in* neg. and *amicus,* friend.]

1. A foe; an adversary. A *private enemy* is one who hates another and wishes him injury, or attempts to do him injury to gratify his own malice or ill will. A *public enemy* or foe, is one who belongs to a nation or party, at war with another.

I say to you, love your *enemies.* Matt. v.

Enemies in war; in peace friends. *Declaration of Independence.*

2. One who hates or dislikes; as an *enemy* to truth or falsehood.

3. In *theology,* and by way of eminence, *the enemy* is the Devil; the archfiend.

4. In *military affairs,* the opposing army or naval force in war, is called the *enemy.*

ENERGET'IC, ENERGET'ICAL, *a.* [Gr. ενεργητικος, from ενεργης, ενεργεω; εν and εργον, work. See *Energy.*]

1. Operating with force, vigor and effect; forcible; powerful; efficacious. We say, the public safety required *energetic* measures. The vicious inclinations of men can be restrained only by *energetic* laws. [*Energic* is not used.]

2. Moving; working; active; operative. We must conceive of God as a Being eternally *energetic.*

ENERGET'ICALLY, *adv.* With force and vigor; with energy and effect.

EN'ERGIZE, *v. i.* [from *energy.*] To act with force; to operate with vigor; to act in producing an effect. *Harris. Trans. of Pausanias.*

EN'ERGIZE, *v. t.* To give strength or force to; to give active vigor to.

EN'ERGIZED, *pp.* Invigorated.

EN'ERGIZER, *n.* He or that which gives energy; he or that which acts in producing an effect.

EN'ERGIZING, *ppr.* Giving energy, force or vigor; acting with force.

EN'ERGY, *n.* [Gr. ενεργεια; εν and εργον, work.]

1. Internal or inherent power; the power of operating, whether exerted or not; as, men possessing *energies* sometimes suffer them to lie inactive. Danger will rouse the dormant *energies* of our natures into action.

2. Power exerted; vigorous operation; force; vigor. God, by his Almighty *energy,* called the universe into existence. The administration of the laws requires *energy* in the magistrate.

3. Effectual operation; efficacy; strength or force producing the effect.

Beg the blessed Jesus to give an *energy* to your imperfect prayers, by his most powerful intercession. *Smalridge.*

4. Strength of expression; force of utterance; life; spirit; emphasis. The language of Lord Chatham is remarkable for its *energy.*

ENERV'ATE, *a.* [infra.] Weakened; weak; without strength or force. *Johnson. Pope.*

EN'ERVATE, *v. t.* [L. *enervo; e* and *nervus,* nerve.]

1. To deprive of nerve, force or strength; to weaken; to render feeble. Idleness and voluptuous indulgences *enervate* the body. Vices and luxury *enervate* the strength of states.

2. To cut the nerves; as, to *enervate* a horse. *Encyc.*

EN'ERVATED, *pp.* Weakened; enfeebled; emasculated.

EN'ERVATING, *ppr.* Depriving of strength, force or vigor; weakening; enfeebling.

ENERVA'TION, *n.* The act of weakening, or reducing strength.

2. The state of being weakened; effeminacy.

ENERVE, *v. t. enerv'.* To weaken; the same as *enervate.*

ENFAM'ISH, *v. t.* To famish. [See *Famish.*]

ENFEE'BLE, *v. t.* [from *feeble.*] To deprive of strength; to reduce the strength or force of; to weaken; to debilitate; to enervate. Intemperance *enfeebles* the body, and induces premature infirmity. Excessive grief and melancholy *enfeeble* the mind. Long wars *enfeeble* a state.

ENFEE'BLED, *pp.* Weakened; deprived of strength or vigor.

ENFEE'BLEMENT, *n.* The act of weakening; enervation. *Spectator.*

ENFEE'BLING, *ppr.* Weakening; debilitating; enervating.

ENFEL'ONED, *a.* [See *Felon.*] Fierce; cruel. *Spenser.*

ENFEOFF, *v. t. enfeff'.* [Law L. *feoffo, feoffare,* from *fief,* which see.]

1. To give one a feud; hence, to invest with a fee; to give to another any corporeal hereditament, in fee simple or fee tail, by livery of seizin. *Cowel. Blackstone.*

2. To surrender or give up. [*Not used.*] *Shak.*

ENFEOFF'ED, *pp.* Invested with the fee of any corporeal hereditament.

ENFEOFF'ING, *ppr.* Giving to one the fee simple of any corporeal hereditament.

ENFEOFF'MENT, *n.* The act of giving the fee simple of an estate.

2. The instrument or deed by which one is invested with the fee of an estate.

ENFET'TER, *v. t.* To fetter; to bind in fetters. *Shak.*

ENFE'VER, *v. t.* To excite fever in. *Seward.*

ENFIERCE, *v. t. enfers'.* To make fierce. [*Not in use.*] *Spenser.*

ENFILA'DE, *n.* [Fr. a row, from *en* and *fil*, a thread, L. *filum*, Sp. *hilo.*]

A line or straight passage; or the situation of a place which may be seen or scoured with shot all the length of a line, or in the direction of a line. *Johnson. Bailey.*

ENFILA'DE, *v. t.* [from the noun; Sp. *enfilar.*]

To pierce, scour or rake with shot, in the direction of a line, or through the whole length of a line.

In conducting approaches at a siege, care should be taken that the trenches be not *enfiladed.* *Encyc.*

In a position to *enfilade* the works at Fort Isle. *Washington.*

ENFILA'DED, *pp.* Pierced or raked in a line.

ENFILA'DING, *ppr.* Piercing or sweeping in a line.

ENFI'RE, *v. t.* To inflame; to set on fire. [*Not used.*] *Spenser.*

ENFO'RCE, *v. t.* [Fr. *enforcir; en* and *force.*]

1. To give strength to; to strengthen; to invigorate. [See Def. 5.]

2. To make or gain by force; to force; as, to *enforce* a passage.

3. To put in act by violence; to drive.

Stones *enforced* from the old Assyrian slings. *Shak.*

4. To instigate; to urge on; to animate. *Shak.*

5. To urge with energy; to give force to; to impress on the mind; as, to *enforce* remarks or arguments.

6. To compel; to constrain; to force. *Davies.*

7. To put in execution; to cause to take effect; as, to *enforce* the laws.

8. To press with a charge. *Shak.*

9. To prove; to evince. [*Little used.*] *Hooker.*

ENFO'RCE, *v. i.* To attempt by force. [*Not used.*]

ENFO'RCE, *n.* Force; strength; power. [*Not used.*] *Milton.*

ENFO'RCEABLE, *a.* That may be enforced.

ENFO'RCED, *pp.* Strengthened; gained by force; driven; compelled; urged; carried into effect.

ENFO'RCEDLY, *adv.* By violence; not by choice. *Shak.*

ENFO'RCEMENT, *n.* The act of enforcing; compulsion; force applied. *Raleigh.*

2. That which gives force energy or effect; sanction. The penalties of law are *enforcements.* *Locke.*

3. Motive of conviction; urgent evidence. *Hammond.*

4. Pressing exigence; that which urges or constrains. *Shak.*

5. In a general sense, any thing which compels or constrains; any thing which urges either the body or the mind.

6. A putting in execution; as the *enforcement* of law.

ENFO'RCER, *n.* One who compels, constrains or urges; one who effects by violence; one who carries into effect.

ENFO'RCING, *ppr.* Giving force or strength; compelling; urging; constraining; putting in execution.

ENFORM', *v. t.* To form; to fashion. [See *Form.*]

ENFOUL'DERED, *a.* [Fr. *foudroyer.*] Mixed with lightning. [*Not in use.*] *Spenser.*

ENFRAN'CHISE, *v. t. s* as z. [from *franchise.*] To set free; to liberate from slavery. *Bacon.*

2. To make free of a city, corporation or state; to admit to the privileges of a freeman. The English colonies were *enfranchised* by special charters. *Davies. Hale.*

3. To free or release from custody. *Shak.*

4. To naturalize; to denizen; to receive as denizens; as, to *enfranchise* foreign words. *Watts.*

ENFRAN'CHISED, *pp.* Set free; released from bondage.

2. Admitted to the rights and privileges of freemen.

ENFRAN'CHISEMENT, *n.* Release from slavery or custody. *Shak.*

2. The admission of persons to the freedom of a corporation or state; investiture with the privileges of free citizens; the incorporating of a person into any society or body politic.

ENFRAN'CHISER, *n.* One who enfranchises.

ENFRAN'CHISING, *ppr.* Setting free from slavery or custody; admitting to the rights and privileges of denizens or free citizens in a state, or to the privileges of a freeman in a corporation. *Cowel.*

ENFRO'WARD, *v. t.* To make froward or perverse. [*Not used.*] *Sandys.*

ENFRO'ZEN, *a.* Frozen; congealed. [*Not used.*] *Spenser.*

ENGA'ĠE, *v. t.* [Fr. *engager; en* and *gager*, to lay, to bet, to hire; Arm. *ingagi.* See *Gage* and *Wage.*]

1. To make liable for a debt to a creditor; to bind one's self as surety. *Shak.*

2. To pawn; to stake as a pledge. *Hudibras.*

3. To enlist; to bring into a party; as, to *engage* men for service; to *engage* friends to aid in a cause.

4. To embark in an affair; as, be not hasty to *engage* yourself in party disputes.

5. To gain; to win and attach; to draw to. Good nature *engages* every one to its possessor.

To every duty he could minds *engage.* *Waller.*

6. To unite and bind by contract or promise. Nations *engage* themselves to each other by treaty. The young often *engage* themselves to their sorrow.

7. To attract and fix; as, to *engage* the attention.

8. To occupy; to employ assiduously. We were *engaged* in conversation. The nation is *engaged* in war.

9. To attack in contest; to encounter. The army *engaged* the enemy at ten o'clock. The captain *engaged* the ship, at point blank distance.

ENGA'ĠE, *v. i.* To encounter; to begin to fight; to attack in conflict. The armies *engaged* at Marengo, in a general battle.

2. To embark in any business; to take a concern in; to undertake. Be cautious not to *engage* in controversy, without indispensable necessity.

3. To promise or pledge one's word; to bind one's self; as, a friend has *engaged* to supply the necessary funds.

ENGA'ĠED, *pp.* or *a.* Pledged; promised; enlisted; gained and attached; attracted and fixed; embarked; earnestly employed; zealous.

ENGA'ĠEDLY, *adv.* With earnestness; with attachment.

ENGA'ĠEDNESS, *n.* The state of being seriously and earnestly occupied; zeal; animation. *Flint's Massillon. Panoplist.*

ENGA'ĠEMENT, *n.* The act of pawning, pledging or making liable for debt.

2. Obligation by agreement or contract. Men are often more ready to make *engagements* than to fulfil them.

3. Adherence to a party or cause; partiality. *Swift.*

4. Occupation; employment of the attention.

Play, by too long or constant *engagement*, becomes like an employment or profession. *Rogers.*

6. Employment in fighting; the conflict of armies or fleets; battle; a general action; appropriately the conflict of whole armies or fleets, but applied to actions between small squadrons or single ships, rarely to a fight between detachments of land forces.

6. Obligation; motive; that which engages. *Hammond.*

ENGA'ĠER, *n.* One that enters into an engagement or agreement.

ENGA'ĠING, *ppr.* Pawning; making liable for debt; enlisting; bringing into a party or cause; promising; binding; winning and attaching; encountering; embarking.

2. *a.* Winning; attractive; tending to draw the attention or the affections; pleasing; as *engaging* manners or address.

ENGA'ĠINGLY, *adv.* In a manner to win the affections.

ENGAL'LANT, *v. t.* To make a gallant of. [*Not used.*] *B. Jonson.*

ENĠAOL, *v. t. enja'le.* To imprison. [*Not used.*] *Shak.*

ENG'ARBOIL, *v. t.* To disorder. [*Not in use.*]

ENG'ARLAND, *v. t.* To encircle with a garland. *Sidney.*

ENGAR'RISON, *v. t.* To furnish with a garrison; to defend or protect by a garrison. *Bp. Hall.*

ENGAS'TRIMUTH, *n.* [Gr. εν, γαςηρ and μυθος.] A ventriloquist. [*Not in use.*]

ENĠEN'DER, *v. t.* [Fr. *engendrer;* Arm. *enguehenta;* Sp. *engendrar;* from the L. *gener, genero, geno, gigno.* See *Generate.*]

2. To beget between the different sexes; to form in embryo.
3. To produce; to cause to exist; to cause to bring forth. Meteors are *engendered* in the atmosphere; worms are sometimes *engendered* in the stomach; intemperance *engenders* fatal maladies; angry words *engender* strife.

ENĠEN'DER, *v. i.* To be caused or produced.

Thick clouds are spread, and storms *engender* there. *Dryden.*

ENĠEN'DERED, *pp.* Begotten; caused; produced.

ENĠEN'DERER, *n.* He or that which engenders.

ENĠEN'DERING, *ppr.* Begetting; causing to be; producing.

ENGILD', *v. t.* To gild; to brighten. *Shak.*

EN'ĠINE, *n.* [Fr. *engin*; Sp. *ingenio*; Port. *engenho*; Arm. *ingin*; from L. *ingenium*; so called from contrivance.]
1. In *mechanics*, a compound machine, or artificial instrument, composed of different parts, and intended to produce some effect by the help of the mechanical powers; as a pump, a windlas, a capstan, a fire engine, a steam engine.
2. A military machine; as a battering ram, &c.
3. Any instrument; that by which any effect is produced. An arrow, a sword, a musket is an *engine* of death.
4. A machine for throwing water to extinguish fire.
5. Means; any thing used to effect a purpose.
6. An agent for another; *usually in an ill sense.*

ENĠINEE'R, *n.* [Fr. *ingenieur.*] In *the military art*, a person skilled in mathematics and mechanics, who forms plans of works for offense or defense, and marks out the ground for fortifications. Engineers are also employed in delineating plans and superintending the construction of other public works, as aqueducts and canals. The latter are called *civil engineers.*
2. One who manages engines or artillery. *Philips.*

EN'ĠINERY, *n.* *en'ginry.* The act of managing engines or artillery. *Milton.*
2. Engines in general; artillery; instruments of war. *Milton.*
3. Machination. *Shenstone.*

ENGIRD'. *v. t.* [See *Gird.*] To surround; to encircle; to encompass. *Shak.*

ENGIRD'ED, } *pp.* Surrounded; encompassed.
ENGIRT', }

ENGIRD'ING, *ppr.* Encircling; surrounding.

ENGLAD', *v. t.* To make glad; to cause to rejoice. *Skelton.*

ENGLA'IMED, *a.* Furred; clammy. [*Not used.*]

ENGLAND, *n.* [See *English.*]

ENGLISH, *a.* *ing'glish.* [Sax. *Englisc*, from *Engles*, *Angles*, a tribe of Germans who settled in Britain, and gave it the name of *England.* The name seems to be derived from *eng*, *ing*, a meadow or plain, a level country; Sax. *ing*; Ice. *einge*; Dan. *eng*; Goth. *winga*; all which seem to be the same word as the Sax. *wang*, *wong*, a plain, and to coincide with the G. *enge*, D. *eng*, W. *ing*, strait, narrow, L. *ango*, from the sense of pressing, depression, laying, which gives the sense of level. The English are the descendants of the *Ingævones* of Tacitus, De Mor. Germ. 2; this name being composed of *ing*, a plain, and G. *wohnen*, D. *woonen*, to dwell. The Ingævones were inhabitants of the level country.] Belonging to England, or to its inhabitants.

ENGLISH, *n.* The people of England.
2. The language of England or of the English nation, and of their descendants in India, America and other countries.

ENGLISH, *v. t.* To translate into the English language. *Bacon.*

ENGLISHED, *pp.* Rendered into English.

ENGLISHRY, *n.* The state or privilege of being an Englishman. [*Not used.*] *Cowel.*

ENGLUT', *v. t.* [Fr. *engloutir*; L. *glutio.*]
1. To swallow. *Shak.*
2. To fill; to glut. *Spenser. Ascham.*
[This word is little used. See *Glut.*]

ENGO'RE, *v. t.* To pierce; to gore. [See *Gore.*] *Spenser.*

ENGORĠE, *v. t.* *engorj'.* [Fr. *engorger*, from *gorge*, the throat.]
To swallow; to devour; to gorge; properly, to swallow with greediness, or in large quantities. *Spenser.*

ENGORĠE, *v. i.* *engorj'.* To devour; to feed with eagerness or voracity. *Milton.*

ENGORĠ'ED, *pp.* Swallowed with greediness, or in large draughts.

ENGORĠEMENT, *n.* *engorj'ment.* The act of swallowing greedily; a devouring with voracity.

ENGORĠ'ING, *ppr.* Swallowing with voracity.

ENGR'AFT, *v. t.* To ingraft, which see.

ENGRA'IL, *v. t.* [Fr. *engrêler*, from *grêle*, *gresle*, hail.]
In *heraldry*, to variegate; to spot as with hail; to indent or make ragged at the edges, as if broken with hail; to indent in curve lines. *Johnson. Chapman. Encyc.*

ENGRA'ILED, *pp.* Variegated; spotted.

ENGRA'IN, *v. t.* [from *grain.*] To dye in grain, or in the raw material; to dye deep.

ENGRA'INED, *pp.* Dyed in the grain; as *engrained* carpets.

ENGRA'INING, *ppr.* Dyeing in the grain.

ENGRAP'PLE, *v. t.* [from *grapple.*] To grapple; to seize and hold; to close in and hold fast. [See *Grapple*, which is generally used.]

ENGR'ASP, *v. t.* [from *grasp.*] To seize with a clasping hold; to hold fast by inclosing or embracing; to gripe. [See *Grasp*, which is generally used.]

ENGRA'VE, *v. t.* pret. *engraved*; pp. *engraved* or *engraven.* [Fr. *graver*; Sp. *grabar*; It. *graffiare*; W. *cravu*; G. *graben*; D. *graaven*; Gr. γραφω. See *Grave.*] Literally, to scratch or scrape. Hence,
1. To cut, as metals, stones or other hard substances, with a chisel or graver; to cut figures, letters or devices, on stone or metal; to mark by incisions.

Thou shalt *engrave* the two stones with the names of the children of Israel. Ex. 28.

2. To picture or represent by incisions.
3. To imprint; to impress deeply; to infix. Let the laws of God and the principles of morality be *engraved* on the mind in early years.
4. To bury; to deposit in the grave; to inter; to inhume. [*Not now used.*] *Spenser.*

ENGRA'VED, } *pp.* Cut or marked, as with a chisel or graver; imprinted; deeply impressed.
ENGRA'VEN, }

ENGRA'VEMENT, *n.* Engraved work; act of engraving.

ENGRA'VER, *n.* One who engraves; a cutter of letters, figures or devices, on stone, metal or wood; a sculptor; a carver.

ENGRA'VERY, *n.* The work of an engraver. [*Little used.*]

ENGRA'VING, *ppr.* Cutting or marking stones or metals, with a chisel or graver; imprinting.

ENGRA'VING, *n.* The act or art of cutting stones, metals and other hard substances, and representing thereon figures, letters, characters and devices; a branch of sculpture.

ENGRIE'VE, *v. t.* To grieve; to pain. [See *Grieve.*] *Spenser.*

ENGRO'SS, *v. t.* [from *gross*, or Fr. *grossir*, *engrossir*, *grossoyer*; Sp. *engrosar.* See *Gross.*]
1. Primarily, to make thick or gross; to thicken. [*Not now used.*] *Spenser.*
2. To make larger; to increase in bulk. [*Not used.*] *Wotton.*
3. To seize in the gross; to take the whole; as, worldly cares *engross* the attention of most men, but neither business nor amusement should *engross* our whole time.
4. To purchase, with a view to sell again, either the whole or large quantities of commodities in market, for the purpose of making a profit by enhancing the price. *Engrossing* does not necessarily imply the purchase of the whole of any commodity, but such quantities as to raise the price, by diminishing the supplies in open market, and taking advantage of an increased demand.
5. To copy in a large hand; to write a fair, correct copy, in large or distinct, legible characters, for preservation or duration; as records of public acts, on paper or parchment.
6. To take or assume in undue quantities or degrees; as, to *engross* power.

ENGRO'SSED, *pp.* Made thick; taken in the whole; purchased in large quantities for sale; written in large fair characters.

ENGRO'SSER, *n.* He or that which takes the whole; a person who purchases the whole or such quantities of articles in a market as to raise the price.
2. One who copies a writing in large, fair characters.

ENGRO'SSING, *ppr.* Taking the whole; buying commodities in such quantities as to raise the price in market.
2. Writing correct copies in large, fair characters.

ENGRO'SSMENT, *n.* The act of engrossing; the act of taking the whole.
2. The appropriation of things in the gross, or in exorbitant quantities; exorbitant acquisition. *Swift.*

ENGU'ARD, *v. t.* [See *Guard.*] To guard; to defend. *Shak.*

ENGULF′, *v. t.* To throw or to absorb in a gulf.

ENGULF′ED, *pp.* Absorbed in a whirlpool, or in a deep abyss or gulf.

ENGULF′MENT, *n.* An absorption in a gulf, or deep cavern, or vortex.

ENH‵ANCE, *v. t.* *enh‵ans.* [Norm. *enhauncer*, from *hauncer*, to raise. Qu. Norm. *enhauce, hauz, haulz*, high.]

1. To raise; to lift; *applied to material things by Spenser, but this application is entirely obsolete.*
2. To raise; to advance; to highthen; *applied to price or value.* War *enhances* the price of provisions; it *enhances* rents, and the value of lands.
3. To raise; *applied to qualities, quantity, pleasures, enjoyments*, &c. Pleasure is *enhanced* by the difficulty of obtaining it.
4. To increase; to aggravate. The guilt of a crime may be *enhanced* by circumstances.

ENH‵ANCE, *v. i.* *enh‵ans.* To be raised; to swell; to grow larger. A debt *enhances* rapidly by compound interest.

ENH‵ANCED, *pp.* Raised; advanced; highthened; increased.

ENH‵ANCEMENT, *n.* Rise; increase; augmentation; as the *enhancement* of value, price, enjoyment, pleasure, beauty.

2. Increase; aggravation; as the *enhancement* of evil, grief, punishment, guilt or crime.

ENH‵ANCER, *n.* One who enhances; he or that which raises price, &c.

ENH‵ANCING, *ppr.* Raising; increasing; augmenting; aggravating.

ENH‵ARBOR, *v. i.* To dwell in or inhabit. *Browne.*

ENH‵ARDEN, *v. t.* To harden; to encourage. *Howell.*

ENHARMON′IC, *a.* [from *harmonic, harmony.*]

In *music*, an epithet applied to such species of composition, as proceed on very small intervals, or smaller intervals than the diatonic and chromatic. An *enharmonic* interval is the eighth of a tone. *Encyc.*

ENIG′MA, *n.* [L. *ænigma*; Gr. αινιγμα, from αινισσομαι, to hint.]

A dark saying, in which some known thing is concealed under obscure language; an obscure question; a riddle. A question, saying or painting, containing a hidden meaning, which is proposed to be guessed. *Johnson. Encyc.*

ENIGMAT′IC, ENIGMAT′ICAL, *a.* Relating to or containing a riddle; obscure; darkly expressed; ambiguous.

2. Obscurely conceived or apprehended.

ENIGMAT′ICALLY, *adv.* In an obscure manner; in a sense different from that which the words in common acceptation imply.

ENIG′MATIST, *n.* A maker or dealer in enigmas and riddles. *Addison.*

ENIG′MATIZE, *v. i.* To utter or form enigmas; to deal in riddles.

ENIGMATOG′RAPHY, ENIGMATOL′OGY, *n.* [Gr. αινιγμα, and γραφω, or λογος.]

The art of making riddles; or the art of solving them.

ENJOIN′, *v. t.* [Fr. *enjoindre*; *en* and *joindre*, to join; It. *ingiugnere*; L. *injungo*; *in* and *jungo.* See *Join.* We observe that the primary sense of *join* is to set, extend or lay to, to throw to or on; otherwise the sense of order or command could not spring from it. To *enjoin* is to *set* or *lay to* or *on.*]

1. To order or direct with urgency; to admonish or instruct with authority; to command. Says Johnson, "this word is more authoritative than *direct*, and less imperious than *command.*" It has the force of pressing admonition with authority; as, a parent *enjoins* on his children the duty of obedience. But it has also the sense of *command*; as the duties *enjoined* by God in the moral law.
2. In *law*, to forbid judicially; to issue or direct a legal injunction to stop proceedings.

This is a suit to *enjoin* the defendants from disturbing the plaintiffs. *Kent.*

ENJOIN′ED, *pp.* Ordered; directed; admonished with authority; commanded.

ENJOIN′ER, *n.* One who enjoins.

ENJOIN′ING, *ppr.* Ordering; directing. *Brown.*

ENJOIN′MENT, *n.* Direction; command; authoritative admonition.

ENJOY′, *v. t.* [Fr. *jouir*; Arm. *jouiçza*; It. *gioire.* See *Joy.*]

1. To feel or perceive with pleasure; to take pleasure or satisfaction in the possession or experience of. We *enjoy* the dainties of a feast, the conversation of friends, and our own meditations.

I could *enjoy* the pangs of death,
And smile in agony. *Addison.*

2. To possess with satisfaction; to take pleasure or delight in the possession of.

Thou shalt beget sons, but thou shalt not *enjoy* them. Deut. xxviii.

3. To have, possess and use with satisfaction; to have, hold or occupy, as a good or profitable thing, or as something desirable. We *enjoy* a free constitution and inestimable privileges.

That the children of Israel may *enjoy* every man the inheritance of his fathers. Num. xxxvi.

The land shall *enjoy* her sabbaths. Lev. xxvi.

To enjoy one's self, is to feel pleasure or satisfaction in one's own mind, or to relish the pleasures in which one partakes; to be happy.

ENJOY′, *v. i.* To live in happiness. [*Unusual.*] *Milton.*

ENJOY′ABLE, *a.* Capable of being enjoyed. *Pope.*

ENJOY′ED, *pp.* Perceived with pleasure or satisfaction; possessed or used with pleasure; occupied with content.

ENJOY′ER, *n.* One who enjoys.

ENJOY′ING, *ppr.* Feeling with pleasure; possessing with satisfaction.

ENJOY′MENT, *n.* Pleasure; satisfaction; agreeable sensations; fruition.

2. Possession with satisfaction; occupancy of any thing good or desirable; as the *enjoyment* of an estate; the *enjoyment* of civil and religious privileges.

ENKIN′DLE, *v. t.* [from *kindle.*] To kindle; to set on fire; to inflame; as, to *enkindle* sparks into a flame. In this literal sense, *kindle* is generally used.

2. To excite; to rouse into action; to inflame; as, to *enkindle* the passions into a flame; to *enkindle* zeal; to *enkindle* war or discord, or the flames of war.

ENKIN′DLED, *pp.* Set on fire; inflamed; roused into action; excited.

ENKIN′DLING, *ppr.* Setting on fire; inflaming; rousing; exciting.

ENL′ARD, *v. t.* To cover with lard or grease; to baste. *Shak.*

ENL‵ARGE, *v. t.* *enl‵arj.* [from *large.*] To make greater in quantity or dimensions; to extend in limits, breadth or size; to expand in bulk. Every man desires to *enlarge* his possessions; the prince, his dominions; and the landholder, his farm. The body is *enlarged* by nutrition, and a good man rejoices to *enlarge* the sphere of his benevolence.

God shall *enlarge* Japhet. Gen. ix.

2. To dilate; to expand; as with joy or love.

O ye, Corinthians, our mouth is open to you, our heart is *enlarged.* *St. Paul.*

3. To expand; to make more comprehensive. Science *enlarges* the mind.
4. To increase in appearance; to magnify to the eye; as by a glass.
5. To set at liberty; to release from confinement or pressure. *Shak.*
6. To extend in a discourse; to diffuse in eloquence.

They *enlarged* themselves on this subject. *Clarendon.*

In this application, the word is generally intransitive.

7. To augment; to increase; to make large or larger, *in a general sense; a word of general application.*

To enlarge the heart, may signify to open and expand in good will; to make free, liberal and charitable.

ENL‵ARGE, *v. i.* *enl‵arj.* To grow large or larger; to extend; to dilate; to expand. A plant *enlarges* by growth; an estate *enlarges* by good management; a volume of air *enlarges* by rarefaction.

2. To be diffuse in speaking or writing; to expatiate. I might *enlarge* on this topic.
3. To exaggerate. *Swift.*

ENL‵ARGED, *pp.* Increased in bulk; extended in dimensions; expanded; dilated; augmented; released from confinement or straits.

ENL‵ARGEDLY, *adv.* With enlargement. *Mountagu.*

ENL‵ARGEMENT, *n.* Increase of size or bulk, real or apparent; extension of dimensions or limits; augmentation; dilatation; expansion. The *enlargement* of bulk may be by accretion or addition; of dimensions, by spreading, or by additions to length and breadth; of a sum or amount, by addition, collection or accumulation.

2. Expansion or extension, applied to the mind, to knowledge, or to the intellectual powers, by which the mind comprehends a wider range of ideas or thought.
3. Expansion of the heart, by which it becomes more benevolent and charitable.
4. Release from confinement, servitude, distress or straits. Esther iv. *Shak.*
5. Diffusiveness of speech or writing; an expatiating on a particular subject; a wide range of discourse or argument. *Clarendon.*

ENL‵ARGER, *n.* He or that which enlarges, increases, extends or expands; an amplifier. *Brown.*

ENL‵ARGING, *ppr.* Increasing in bulk; extending in dimensions; expanding; making free or liberal; speaking diffusively.

ENL'ARGING, *n.* Enlargement.

ENLI'GHT, *v. t.* *enli'te.* To illuminate; to enlighten. *Pope.*

[See *Enlighten. Enlight* is rarely used.]

ENLI'GHTEN, *v. t.* *enli'tn.* [from *light*; Sax. *enlihtan, onlihtan.*]

1. To make light; to shed light on; to supply with light; to illuminate; as, the sun *enlightens* the earth.

His lightnings *enlightened* the world. Ps. xcvii.

2. To quicken in the faculty of vision; to enable to see more clearly.

Jonathan's—eyes were *enlightened.* 1 Sam. xiv.

3. To give light to; to give clearer views; to illuminate; to instruct; to enable to see or comprehend truth; as, to *enlighten* the mind or understanding.

4. To illuminate with divine knowledge, or a knowledge of the truth.

Those who were once *enlightened.* Heb. vi.

ENLI'GHTENED, *pp.* Rendered light; illuminated; instructed; informed; furnished with clear views.

ENLI'GHTENER, *n.* One who illuminates; he or that which communicates light to the eye, or clear views to the mind. *Milton.*

ENLI'GHTENING, *ppr.* Illuminating; giving light to; instructing.

ENLINK', *v. t.* [from *link.*[To chain to; to connect. *Shak.*

ENLIST', *v. t.* [See *List.*] To enroll; to register; to enter a name on a list.

2. To engage in public service, by entering the name in a register; as, an officer *enlists* men.

ENLIST', *v. i.* To engage in public service, by subscribing articles, or enrolling one's name.

ENLIST'MENT, *n.* The act of enlisting; the writing by which a soldier is bound.

ENLI'VEN, *v. t.* *enli'vn.* [from *life, live.*] Literally, to give life. Hence,

1. To give action or motion to; to make vigorous or active; to excite; as, fresh fuel *enlivens* a fire.

2. To give spirit or vivacity to; to animate; to make sprightly. Social mirth and good humor *enliven* company; they *enliven* the dull and gloomy.

3. To make cheerful, gay or joyous.

ENLI'VENED, *pp.* Made more active; excited; animated; made cheerful or gay.

ENLI'VENER, *n.* He or that which enlivens or animates; he or that which invigorates.

ENLI'VENING, *ppr.* Giving life, spirit or animation; inspiriting; invigorating; making vivacious, sprightly or cheerful.

ENLU'MINE, *v. t.* To illumine; to enlighten. [See the latter words.]

ENMAR'BLE, *v. t.* To make hard as marble; to harden. *Spenser.*

ENMESH', *v. t.* [from *mesh.*] To net; to entangle; to entrap. *Shak.*

EN'MITY, *n.* [Fr. *inimitié; in* and *amitié,* friendship, amity. See *Enemy.*]

1. The quality of being an enemy; the opposite of friendship; ill will; hatred; unfriendly dispositions; malevolence. It expresses more than *aversion* and less than *malice,* and differs from *displeasure* in denoting a fixed or rooted hatred, whereas *displeasure* is more transient.

I will put *enmity* between thee and the woman. Gen. iii.

The carnal mind is *enmity* against God. Rom. viii.

2. A state of opposition.

The friendship of the world is *enmity* with God. James iv.

ENNEACONTAHE'DRAL, *a.* [Gr. εννενηκοντα and εδρα.] Having ninety faces. *Cleaveland.*

EN'NEAGON, *n.* [Gr. εννεα, nine, and γωνια, an angle.] In *geometry,* a polygon or figure with nine sides or nine angles.

ENNEAN'DER, *n.* [Gr. εννεα, nine, and ανηρ, a male.] In *botany,* a plant having nine stamens.

ENNEAN'DRIAN, *a.* Having nine stamens.

ENNEAPET'ALOUS, *a.* [Gr. εννεα, nine, and πεταλον, a leaf.] Having nine petals or flower-leaves.

ENNEAT'ICAL, *a.* [Gr. εννεα, nine.] *Enneatical days,* are every ninth day of a disease. *Enneatical years,* are every ninth year of a man's life. *Johnson.*

ENNEW', *v. t.* To make new. [*Not in use.*] *Skelton.*

ENNO'BLE, *v. t.* [Fr. *ennoblir.* See *Noble.*]

1. To make noble; to raise to nobility; as, to *ennoble* a commonor.

2. To dignify; to exalt; to aggrandize; to elevate in degree, qualities or excellence.

What can *ennoble* sots, or slaves, or cowards? *Pope.*

3. To make famous or illustrious. *Bacon.*

ENNO'BLED, *pp.* Raised to the rank of nobility; dignified; exalted in rank, excellence or value.

ENNO'BLEMENT, *n.* The act of advancing to nobility. *Bacon.*

2. Exaltation; elevation in degree or excellence. *Glanville.*

ENNO'BLING, *ppr.* Advancing to the rank of a nobleman; exalting; dignifying.

ENNUI, *n.* [Fr. weariness; It. *noia,* whence *noiare, annoiare,* to tire, to vex, Fr. *ennuyer.* Class Ng.] Weariness; heaviness; lassitude of fastidiousness.

ENODA'TION, *n.* [L. *enodatio,* from *enodo,* to clear from knots; *e* and *nodus,* a knot.]

1. The act or operation of clearing of knots, or of untying.

2. Solution of a difficulty. [*Little used.*]

ENO'DE, *a.* [L. *enodis; e* and *nodus,* knot.] In *botany,* destitute of knots or joints; knotless.

ENOM'OTARCH, *n.* The commander of an enomoty. *Mitford.*

ENOM'OTY, *n.* [Gr. ενωμοτια; εν and ομνυμι, to swear.] In Lacedæmon, anciently, a body of soldiers, supposed to be thirty two; but the precise number is uncertain. *Mitford.*

ENORM', *a.* [*Not used.* See *Enormous.*]

ENOR'MITY, *n.* [L. *enormitas.* See *Enormous.*]

1. Literally, the transgression of a rule, or deviation from right. Hence, any wrong, irregular, vicious or sinful act, either in government or morals.

We shall speak of the *enormities* of the government. *Spenser.*

This law will not restrain the *enormity.* *Hooker.*

2. Atrocious crime; flagitious villainy; a crime which exceeds the common measure. *Swift.*

3. Atrociousness; excessive degree of crime or guilt. Punishment should be proportioned to the *enormity* of the crime.

ENOR'MOUS, *a.* [L. *enormis; e* and *norma,* a rule.]

1. Going beyond the usual measure or rule.

Enormous in their gait. *Milton.*

2. Excursive; beyond the limits of a regular figure.

The *enormous* part of the light in the circumference of every lucid point. *Newton.*

3. Great beyond the common measure; excessive; as *enormous* crime or guilt.

4. Exceeding, in bulk or highth, the common measure; as an *enormous* form; a man of *enormous* size.

5. Irregular; confused; disordered; unusual. *Shak.*

ENOR'MOUSLY, *adv.* Excessively; beyond measure; as an opinion *enormously* absurd.

ENOR'MOUSNESS, *n.* The state of being enormous or excessive; greatness beyond measure.

ENOUGH', *a.* *enuf'.* [Sax. *genog, genoh;* Goth. *ganah;* G. *genug, gnug;* D. *genoeg;* Sw. *nog;* Dan. *nok;* Sax. *genogan,* to multiply; G. *genügen,* to satisfy; D. *genoegen,* to satisfy, please, content. The Swedes and Danes drop the prefix, as the Danes do in *nogger,* to gnaw. This word may be the Heb. Ch. Syr. Sam. Eth. נוח to rest, to be quiet or satisfied. Class Ng. No. 14.] That satisfies desire, or gives content; that may answer the purpose; that is adequate to the wants.

She said, we have straw and provender *enough.* Gen. xxiv.

How many hired servants of my father have bread *enough,* and to spare. Luke xv.

[Note. This word, in vulgar language, is sometimes placed before its noun, like most other adjectives. But in elegant discourse or composition, it always follows the noun, to which it refers; as, bread *enough;* money *enough.*]

ENOUGH', *n.* *enuf'.* A sufficiency; a quantity of a thing which satisfies desire, or is adequate to the wants. We have *enough* of this sort of cloth.

And Esau said, I have *enough,* my brother. Gen. xxxiii.

Israel said, it is *enough;* Joseph is yet alive. Gen. xlv.

2. That which is equal to the powers or abilities. He had *enough* to do to take care of himself.

ENOUGH', *adv.* *enuf'.* Sufficiently; in a quantity or degree that satisfies, or is equal to the desires or wants.

The land, behold, it is large *enough* for them. Gen. xxxiv.

Ye have dwelt long *enough* in this mount. Deut. i.

2. Fully; quite; denoting a slight augmentation of the positive degree. He is ready *enough* to embrace the offer. It is pleasant *enough* to consider the different notions of different men respecting the same thing.

3. Sometimes it denotes diminution, delicately expressing rather less than is desired; such a quantity or degree as commands acquiescence, rather than full satisfaction. The song or the performance is well *enough.*

4. An exclamation denoting sufficiency.
Enough, enough, I'll hear no more.

ENOUNCE, *v. t. enouns'.* [Fr. *enoncer;* L. *enuncio; e* and *nuncio,* to declare.]
To utter; to pronounce; to declare. [*Little used.*]

ENOUN'CED, *pp.* Uttered; pronounced.

ENOUN'CING, *ppr.* Uttering; pronouncing.

ENOW, the old plural of *enough,* is nearly obsolete.

En passant. [Fr.] In passing; by the way.

ENQUICK'EN, *v. t.* To quicken; to make alive. [*Not used.*]

ENQUIRE, usually written *inquire,* which see and its derivatives.

ENRA'CE, *v. t.* To implant. [*Not used.*] *Spenser.*

ENRA'GE, *v. t.* [Fr. *enrager.* See *Rage.*] To excite rage in; to exasperate; to provoke to fury or madness; to make furious.

ENRA'GED, *pp.* Made furious; exasperated; provoked to madness.

ENRA'GING, *ppr.* Exasperating; provoking to madness.

ENRA'NGE, *v. t.* To put in order; to rove over. [*Not in use.*] *Spenser.*

ENRANK', *v. t.* To place in ranks or order. *Shak.*

ENRAP'TURE, *v. t.* [from *rapture.*] To transport with pleasure; to delight beyond measure. *Enrapt,* in a like sense, is little used, and is hardly legitimate.

ENRAP'TURED, *pp.* Transported with pleasure; highly delighted.

ENRAP'TURING, *ppr.* Transporting with pleasure; highly delighting.

ENRAV'ISH, *v. t.* [from *ravish.*] To throw into ecstasy; to transport with delight; to enrapture. *Spenser.*

ENRAV'ISHED, *pp.* Transported with delight or pleasure; enraptured.

ENRAV'ISHING, *ppr.* Throwing into ecstasy; highly delighting.

ENRAV'ISHMENT, *n.* Ecstasy of delight; rapture. *Glanville.*

ENREG'ISTER, *v. t.* [Fr. *enregistrer.*] To register; to enroll or record. *Spenser.*

ENRHEUM, *v. i.* [Fr. *enrhumer.*] To have rheum through cold.

ENRICH', *v. t.* [Fr. *enrichir,* from *riche,* rich.]

1. To make rich, wealthy or opulent; to supply with abundant property. Agriculture, commerce and manufactures *enrich* a nation. War and plunder seldom *enrich,* more generally they impoverish a country.
2. To fertilize; to supply with the nutriment of plants and render productive; as, to *enrich* land by manures or irrigation.
3. To store; to supply with an abundance of any thing desirable; as, to *enrich* the mind with knowledge, science or useful observations.
4. To supply with any thing splendid or ornamental; as, to *enrich* a painting with elegant drapery; to *enrich* a poem or oration with striking metaphors or images; to *enrich* a garden with flowers or shrubbery.

ENRICH'ED, *pp.* Made rich or wealthy; fertilized; supplied with that which is desirable, useful or ornamental.

ENRICH'ER, *n.* One that enriches.

ENRICH'ING, *ppr.* Making opulent; fertilizing; supplying with what is splendid, useful or ornamental.

ENRICH'MENT, *n.* Augmentation of wealth; amplification; improvement; the addition of fertility or ornament.

ENRIDGE, *v. t. enrij'.* To form into ridges. *Shak.*

ENRING', *v. t.* To encircle; to bind. *Shak.*

ENRI'PEN, *v. t.* To ripen; to bring to perfection. *Donne.*

ENRI'VE, *v. t.* To rive; to cleave. *Spenser.*

ENRO'BE, *v. t.* [from *robe.*] To clothe with rich attire; to attire; to invest. *Shak.*

ENRO'BED, *pp.* Attired; invested.

ENRO'BING, *ppr.* Investing; attiring.

ENRÔLL, *v. t.* [Fr. *enrôler,* from *rôle, rolle,* a roll or register.]

1. To write in a roll or register; to insert a name or enter in a list or catalogue; as, men are *enrolled* for service.
2. To record; to insert in records; to leave in writing. *Milton. Shak.*
3. To wrap; to involve. [*Not now used.*] *Spenser.*

ENRÔLLED, *pp.* Inserted in a roll or register; recorded.

ENRÔLLER, *n.* He that enrolls or registers.

ENRÔLLING, *ppr.* Inserting in a register; recording.

ENRÔLLMENT, *n.* A register; a record; a writing in which any thing is recorded.
2. The act of enrolling.

ENROOT', *v. t.* [from *root.*] To fix by the root; to fix fast; to implant deep. *Shak.*

ENROOT'ED, *pp.* Fixed by the root; planted or fixed deep.

ENROOT'ING, *ppr.* Fixing by the root; planting deep.

ENROUND', *v. t.* To environ; to surround; to inclose. [*Not used.*] *Shak.*

ENS, *n.* [L. *ens,* part. present of *esse,* to be.] Entity; being; existence. Among the old chimists, the power, virtue or efficacy, which certain substances exert on our bodies; or the things which are supposed to contain all the qualities or virtues of the ingredients they are drawn from, in little room. [*Little used.*] *Encyc. Johnson.*

ENSAM'PLE, *n.* [Irregularly formed from *example* or *sample,* It. *esempio,* L. *exemplum.*]
An example; a pattern or model for imitation.
Being *ensamples* to the flock. 1 Pet. v.

ENSAM'PLE, *v. t.* To exemplify; to shew by example. This word is seldom used, either as a noun or a verb. [See *Example.*]

ENSAN'GUINE, *v. t.* [L. *sanguis,* blood; Eng. *sanguine.*]
To stain or cover with blood; to smear with gore; as an *ensanguined* field. *Milton.*

ENSAN'GUINED, *pp.* Suffused or stained with blood.

EN'SATE, *a.* [L. *ensis,* a sword.] Having sword-shaped leaves.

ENSCHED'ULE, *v. t.* To insert in a schedule. [See *Schedule.*] *Shak.*

ENSCONCE, *v. t. enscons'.* [from *sconce.*] To cover, or shelter, as with a sconce or fort; to protect; to secure.
I will *ensconce* me behind the arras. *Shak.*

ENSCON'CED, *pp.* Covered, or sheltered, as by a sconce or fort; protected; secured.

ENSCON'CING, *ppr.* Covering, or sheltering, as by a fort.

ENSE'AL, *v. t.* [from *seal.*] To seal; to fix a seal on; to impress.

ENSE'ALED, *pp.* Impressed with a seal.

ENSE'ALING, *ppr.* Sealing; affixing a seal to.

ENSE'ALING, *n.* The act of affixing a seal to.

ENSE'AM, *v. t.* [from *seam.*] To sew up; to inclose by a seam or juncture of needlework. *Camden.*

ENSE'AMED, *a.* Greasy. [*Not in use.*] *Shak.*

ENSE'AR, *v. t.* [from *sear.*] To sear; to cauterize; to close or stop by burning to hardness. *Shak.*

ENSEARCH', *v. i. enserch'.* To search for; to try to find. [*Not used.*] *Elyot.*

ENSEM'BLE, *n.* [Fr.] One with another; on an average.

ENSHIE'LD, *v. t.* [from *shield.*] To shield; to cover; to protect. *Shak.*

ENSHRI'NE, *v. t.* [from *shrine.*] To inclose in a shrine or chest; to deposit for safe-keeping in a cabinet. *Milton.*

ENSHRI'NED, *pp.* Inclosed or preserved in a shrine or chest.
2. Inclosed; placed as in a shrine.
Wisdom *enshrined* in beauty. *Percival.*

ENSHRI'NING, *ppr.* Inclosing in a shrine or cabinet.

ENSIF'EROUS, *a.* [L. *ensis,* sword, and *fero,* to bear.] Bearing or carrying a sword.

EN'SIFORM, *a.* [L. *ensiformis; ensis,* sword, and *forma,* form.]
Having the shape of a sword; as the *ensiform* or xiphoid cartilage; an *ensiform* leaf. *Quincy. Martyn.*

EN'SIGN, *n. en'sine.* [Fr. *enseigne;* L. *insigne, insignia,* from *signum,* a mark impressed, a *sign.*]

1. The flag or banner of a military band; a banner of colors; a standard; a figured cloth or piece of silk, attached to a staff, and usually with figures, colors or arms thereon, borne by an officer at the head of a company, troop or other band.
2. Any signal to assemble or to give notice.
He will lift up an *ensign* to the nations. Is. v.
Ye shall be left as an *ensign* on a hill. Is. xxx.
3. A badge; a mark of distinction, rank or office; as *ensigns* of power or virtue. *Waller. Dryden.*
4. The officer who carries the flag or colors, being the lowest commissioned officer in a company of infantry.
5. *Naval ensign,* is a large banner hoisted on a staff and carried over the poop or stern of a ship; used to distinguish ships of different nations, or to characterize different squadrons of the same navy. *Mar. Dict.*

EN'SIGN-BEARER, *n.* He that carries the flag; an ensign.

EN'SIGNCY, *n.* The rank, office or commission of an ensign.

ENSKI'ED, *a.* Placed in heaven; made immortal. [*Not in use.*] *Shak.*

ENSLA'VE, *v. t.* [from *slave.*] To reduce to slavery or bondage; to deprive of liberty and subject to the will of a master. Barbarous nations *enslave* their prisoners of war, but civilized men barbarously and wickedly purchase men to *enslave* them.

2. To reduce to servitude or subjection. Men often suffer their passions and appetites to *enslave* them. They are *enslaved* to lust, to anger, to intemperance, to avarice.

ENSLA'VED, *pp.* Reduced to slavery or subjection.

ENSLA'VEMENT, *n.* The state of being enslaved; slavery; bondage; servitude. *South.*

ENSLA'VER, *n.* He who reduces another to bondage. *Swift.*

ENSLA'VING, *ppr.* Reducing to bondage; depriving of liberty.

ENSNARE. [See *Insnare.*]

ENSO'BER, *v. t.* [from *sober.*] To make sober. *Taylor.*

ENSPHE'RE, *v. t.* [from *sphere.*] To place in a sphere. *Hall.*

2. To make into a sphere. *Carew.*

ENSTAMP', *v. t.* [from *stamp.*] To impress as with a stamp; to impress deeply.

God *enstamped* his image on man. *Enfield.*

ENSTAMP'ED, *pp.* Impressed deeply.

ENSTAMP'ING, *ppr.* Impressing deeply.

ENSTY'LE, *v. t.* To style; to name; to call. [*Little used.*] *Drayton.*

ENSU'E, *v. t.* [Fr. *ensuivre;* Norm. *ensuer;* Sp. *seguir;* It. *seguire;* L. *sequor*, to follow. See *Seek.*]

To follow; to pursue.

Seek peace, and *ensue* it. 1 Pet. iii.

[*In this sense, it is obsolete.*]

ENSU'E, *v. i.* To follow as a consequence of premises; as, from these facts or this evidence, the argument will *ensue.*

2. To follow in a train of events or course of time; to succeed; to come after. He spoke and silence *ensued.* We say, the *ensuing* age or years; the *ensuing* events.

ENSU'ING, *ppr.* Following as a consequence; succeeding.

ENSURE, and its derivatives. [See *Insure.*]

ENSWEE'P, *v. t.* To sweep over; to pass over rapidly. *Thomson.*

ENTAB'LATURE, } *n.* [Sp. *entablamento;*
ENTAB'LEMENT, } Fr. *entablement;* Sp. *entablar*, to cover with boards, from L. *tabula*, a board or table.]

In *architecture*, that part of the order of a column, which is over the capital, including the architrave, frieze and cornice, being the extremity of the flooring. *Encyc. Harris.*

ENTACK'LE, *v. t.* To supply with tackle. [*Not used.*] *Skelton.*

ENTA'IL, *n.* [Fr. *entailler*, to cut, from *tailler*, It. *tagliare*, id. *Feudum talliatum*, a fee entailed, abridged, curtailed, limited.]

1. An estate or fee entailed, or limited in descent to a particular heir or heirs. Estates-tail are *general*, as when lands and tenements are given to one and the heirs of his body begotten; or *special*, as when lands and tenements are given to one and the heirs of his body by a particular wife. *Blackstone.*

2. Rule of descent settled for an estate.

3. Engraver's work; inlay. *Obs. Spenser.*

ENTA'IL, *v. t.* To settle the descent of lands and tenements, by gift to a man and to certain heirs specified, so that neither the donee nor any subsequent possessor can alienate or bequeath it; as, to *entail* a manor to AB and to his eldest son, or to his heirs of his body begotten, or to his heirs by a particular wife.

2. To fix unalienably on a person or thing, or on a person and his descendants. By the apostasy misery is supposed to be *entailed* on mankind. The intemperate often *entail* infirmities, diseases and ruin on their children.

3. [from the French verb.] To cut; to carve for ornament. [*Obs.*] *Spenser.*

ENTA'ILED, *pp.* Settled on a man and certain heirs specified.

2. Settled on a person and his descendants.

ENTA'ILING, *ppr.* Settling the descent of an estate; giving, as lands and tenements, and prescribing the mode of descent; settling unalienably on a person or thing.

ENTA'ILMENT, *n.* The act of giving, as an estate, and directing the mode of descent, or of limiting the descent to a particular heir or heirs.

2. The act of settling unalienably on a man and his heirs.

ENTA'ME, *v. t.* [from *tame.*] To tame; to subdue. *Gower.*

ENTAN'GLE, *v. t.* [from *tangle.*] To twist or interweave in such a manner as not to be easily separated; to make confused or disordered; as, thread, yarn or ropes may be *entangled;* to *entangle* the hair.

2. To involve in any thing complicated, and from which it is difficult to extricate one's self; as, to *entangle* the feet in a net, or in briers.

3. To lose in numerous or complicated involutions, as in a labyrinth.

4. To involve in difficulties; to perplex; to embarrass; as, to *entangle* a nation in alliances.

5. To puzzle; to bewilder; as, to *entangle* the understanding. *Locke.*

6. To insnare by captious questions; to catch; to perplex; to involve in contradictions.

The Pharisees took counsel how they might *entangle* him in his talk. Matt. xxii.

7. To perplex or distract, as with cares.

No man that warreth *entangleth* himself with the affairs of this life. 2 Tim. ii.

8. To multiply intricacies and difficulties.

ENTAN'GLED, *pp.* or *a.* Twisted together; interwoven in a confused manner; intricate; perplexed; involved; embarrassed; insnared.

ENTAN'GLEMENT, *n.* Involution; a confused or disordered state; intricacy; perplexity. *Locke.*

ENTAN'GLER, *n.* One who entangles.

ENTAN'GLING, *ppr.* Involving; interweaving or interlocking in confusion; perplexing; insnaring.

ENTEN'DER, *v. t.* To treat with tenderness or kindness. *Young.*

EN'TER, *v. t.* [Fr. *entrer*, from *entre*, between, L. *inter, intra*, whence *intro*, to enter; It. *entrare;* Sp. *entrar.* The L. *inter* seems to be *in*, with the termination *ter*, as in *subter*, from *sub.*]

1. To move or pass into a place, in any manner whatever; to come or go in; to walk or ride in; to flow in; to pierce or penetrate. A man *enters* a house; an army *enters* a city or a camp; a river *enters* the sea; a sword *enters* the body; the air *enters* a room at every crevice.

2. To advance into, in the progress of life; as, a youth has *entered* his tenth year.

3. To begin in a business, employment or service; to enlist or engage in; as, the soldier *entered* the service at eighteen years of age.

4. To become a member of; as, to *enter* college; to *enter* a society.

5. To admit or introduce; as, the youth was *entered* a member of College.

6. To set down in writing; to set an account in a book or register; as, the clerk *entered* the account or charge in the journal; he *entered* debt and credit at the time.

7. To set down, as a name; to enroll; as, to *enter* a name in the enlistment.

8. To lodge a manifest of goods at the custom-house, and gain admittance or permission to land; as, to *enter* goods. We say also, to *enter* a ship at the custom-house.

EN'TER, *v. i.* To go or come in; to pass into; as, to *enter* into a country.

2. To flow in; as, water *enters* into a ship.

3. To pierce; to penetrate; as, a ball or an arrow *enters* into the body.

4. To penetrate mentally; as, to *enter* into the principles of action.

5. To engage in; as, to *enter* into business or service; to *enter* into visionary projects.

6. To be initiated in; as, to *enter* into a taste of pleasure or magnificence. *Addison.*

7. To be an ingredient; to form a constituent part. Lead *enters* into the composition of pewter.

EN'TERDEAL, *n.* Mutual dealings. [*Not in use.*] *Spenser.*

EN'TERED, *pp.* Moved in; come in; pierced; penetrated; admitted; introduced; set down in writing.

EN'TERING, *ppr.* Coming or going in; flowing in; piercing; penetrating; setting down in writing; enlisting; engaging.

EN'TERING, *n.* Entrance; a passing in. 1 Thes. i.

ENTERLACE. [See *Interlace.*]

EN'TEROCELE, *n.* [Gr. εντερον, intestine, and κηλη, tumor.]

In *surgery*, intestinal hernia; a rupture of the intestines. *Coxe.*

ENTEROL'OGY, *n.* [Gr. εντερον, intestine, and λογος, discourse.]

A treatise or discourse on the bowels or internal parts of the body, usually including the contents of the head, breast and belly. *Quincy.*

ENTEROM'PHALOS, *n.* [Gr. εντερον, intestine, and ομφαλος, navel.] Navel rupture; umbilical rupture.

ENTERP'ARLANCE, *n.* [Fr. *entre*, between, and *parler*, to speak.]

Parley; mutual talk or conversation; conference. *Hayward.*

ENTERPLEAD. [See *Interplead.*]

EN'TERPRISE, *n.* *s* as z. [Fr. from *entreprendre*, to undertake; *entre*, in or between, and *prendre*, to take, *prise*, a taking.]

That which is undertaken, or attempted to be performed; an attempt; a project attempted; particularly, a bold, arduous or hazardous undertaking, either physical or moral. The attack on Stoney-Point was a bold, but successful *enterprise.* The attempts to evangelize the heathen are noble *enterprises*.

Their hands cannot perform their *enterprise*. Job v.

EN'TERPRISE, *v. t.* To undertake; to begin and attempt to perform.

The business must be *enterprised* this night. *Dryden.*

EN'TERPRISED, *pp.* Undertaken; attempted; essayed.

EN'TERPRISER, *n.* An adventurer; one who undertakes any projected scheme, especially a bold or hazardous one; a person who engages in important or dangerous designs. *Hayward.*

EN'TERPRISING, *ppr.* Undertaking, especially a bold design.

2. *a.* Bold or forward to undertake; resolute, active, or prompt to attempt great or untried schemes. *Enterprising* men often succeed beyond all human probability.

ENTERTA'IN, *v. t.* [Fr. *entretenir; entre*, in or between, and *tenir*, to hold, L. *teneo.*]

1. To receive into the house and treat with hospitality, either at the table only, or with lodging also.

Be not forgetful to *entertain* strangers; for thereby some have *entertained* angels unawares. Heb. xiii.

2. To treat with conversation; to amuse or instruct by discourse; properly, to engage the attention and retain the company of one, by agreeable conversation, discourse or argument. The advocate *entertained* his audience an hour, with sound argument and brilliant displays of eloquence.

3. To keep in one's service; to maintain. He *entertained* ten domestics.

You, sir, I *entertain* for one of my hundred. *Shak.*

[This original and French sense is obsolete or little used.]

4. To keep, hold or maintain in the mind with favor; to reserve in the mind; to harbor; to cherish. Let us *entertain* the most exalted views of the Divine character. It is our duty to *entertain* charitable sentiments towards our fellow men.

5. To maintain; to support; as, to *entertain* a hospital. *Obs.*

6. To please; to amuse; to divert. David *entertained* himself with the meditation of God's law. Idle men *entertain* themselves with trifles.

7. To treat; to supply with provisions and liquors, or with provisions and lodging, for reward. The innkeeper *entertains* a great deal of company.

ENTERTA'IN, *n.* Entertainment. [*Not in use.*] *Spenser.*

ENTERTA'INED, *pp.* Received with hospitality, as a guest; amused; pleased and engaged; kept in the mind; retained.

ENTERTA'INER, *n.* He who entertains; he who receives company with hospitality, or for reward.

2. He who retains others in his service.

3. He that amuses, pleases or diverts.

ENTERTA'INING, *ppr.* Receiving with hospitality; receiving and treating with provisions and accommodations, for reward; keeping or cherishing with favor; engaging the attention; amusing.

2. *a.* Pleasing; amusing; diverting; as an *entertaining* discourse; an *entertaining* friend.

ENTERTA'ININGLY, *adv.* In an amusing manner. *Warton.*

ENTERTA'INMENT, *n.* The receiving and accommodating of guests, either with or without reward. The hospitable man delights in the *entertainment* of his friends.

2. Provisions of the table; hence also, a feast; a superb dinner or supper.

3. The amusement, pleasure or instruction, derived from conversation, discourse, argument, oratory, music, dramatic performances, &c.; the pleasure which the mind receives from any thing interesting, and which holds or arrests the attention. We often have rich *entertainment*, in the conversation of a learned friend.

4. Reception; admission. *Tillotson.*

5. The state of being in pay or service. [*Not used.*] *Shak.*

6. Payment of those retained in service. *Obs.* *Davies.*

7. That which entertains; that which serves for amusement; the lower comedy; farce. *Gay.*

ENTERTIS'SUED, *a.* [Fr. *entre* and *tissu.*] Interwoven; having various colors intermixed. *Shak.*

ENTHEAS'TIC, *a.* [Gr. εν and θεος, God.] Having the energy of God.

ENTHEAS'TICALLY, *adv.* According to deific energy. *Trans. of Pausanias.*

EN'THEAT, *a.* [Gr. ενθεος.] Enthusiastic. [*Not in use.*]

ENTHRALL', *v. t.* To enslave. [See *Inthrall.*]

ENTHRILL', *v. t.* To pierce. [See *Thrill.*]

ENTHRO'NE, *v. t.* [from *throne.*] To place on a throne; to exalt to the seat of royalty.

Beneath a sculptured arch he sits *enthroned.* *Pope.*

2. To exalt to an elevated place or seat. *Shak.*

3. To invest with sovereign authority. *Ayliffe.*

ENTHRO'NED, *pp.* Seated on a throne; exalted to an elevated place.

ENTHRO'NING, *ppr.* Seating on a throne; raising to an exalted seat.

ENTHUN'DER, *v. i.* To make a loud noise, like thunder.

ENTHU'SIASM, *n.* *enthu'ziazm.* [Gr. ενθουσιασμος, from ενθουσιαζω, to infuse a divine spirit, from ενθους, ενθεος, inspired, divine; εν and θεος, God.]

1. A belief or conceit of private revelation; the vain confidence or opinion of a person, that he has special divine communications from the Supreme Being, or familiar intercourse with him.

Enthusiasm is founded neither on reason nor divine revelation, but rises from the conceits of a warmed or overweening imagination. *Locke.*

2. Heat of imagination; violent passion or excitement of the mind, in pursuit of some object, inspiring extravagant hope and confidence of success. Hence the same heat of imagination, chastised by reason or experience, becomes a noble passion, an elevated fancy, a warm imagination, an ardent zeal, that forms sublime ideas, and prompts to the ardent pursuit of laudable objects. Such is the *enthusiasm* of the poet, the orator, the painter and the sculptor. Such is the *enthusiasm* of the patriot, the hero and the christian.

Faction and *enthusiasm* are the instruments by which popular governments are destroyed. *Ames.*

ENTHU'SIAST, *n.* *enthu'ziast.* [Gr. ενθουσιαςης.]

1. One who imagines he has special or supernatural converse with God, or special communications from him.

2. One whose imagination is warmed; one whose mind is highly excited with the love or in the pursuit of an object; a person of ardent zeal; as an *enthusiast* in poetry or music.

3. One of elevated fancy or exalted ideas. *Dryden.*

ENTHUSIAS'TIC, ENTHUSIAS'TICAL, *a.* Filled with enthusiasm, or the conceit of special intercourse with God or revelations from him.

2. Highly excited; warm and ardent; zealous in pursuit of an object; heated to animation. Our author was an *enthusiastic* lover of poetry and admirer of Homer.

3. Elevated; warm; tinctured with enthusiasm. The speaker addressed the audience in *enthusiastic* strains.

ENTHUSIAS'TICALLY, *adv.* With enthusiasm.

ENTHYMEMAT'ICAL, *a.* Pertaining to an enthymeme; including an enthymeme. *Encyc.*

EN'THYMEME, *n.* [Gr. ενθυμημα, from ενθυμεομαι, to think or conceive; εν and θυμος, mind.]

In *rhetoric*, an argument consisting of only two propositions, an antecedent and a consequent deduced from it; as, we are dependent, therefore we should be humble. Here the major proposition is suppressed; the complete syllogism would be, dependent creatures should be humble; we are dependent creatures; therefore we should be humble.

ENTI'CE, *v. t.* [This word seems to be the Sp. *atizar*, Port. *atiçar*, Fr. *attiser*, Arm. *attisa*, from Sp. *tizon*, It. *tizzone*, Fr. *tison*, L. *titio*, a firebrand. The sense, in these languages, is to lay the firebrands together, or to stir the fire; to provoke; to incense. The sense in English is a little varied. If it is not the same word, I know not its origin.]

1. To incite or instigate, by exciting hope or desire; *usually in a bad sense;* as, to *entice* one to evil. Hence, to seduce; to lead astray; to induce to sin, by promises or persuasions.

My son, if sinners *entice* thee, consent thou not. Prov. i.

2. To tempt; to incite; to urge or lead astray.

Every man is tempted, when he is drawn away by his own lust, and *enticed.* James i.

3. To incite; to allure; *in a good sense.* *Enfield.*

ENTI'CED, *pp.* Incited; instigated to evil; seduced by promises or persuasions; persuaded; allured.

ENTI'CEMENT, *n.* The act or practice of inciting to evil; instigation; as the *enticements* of evil companions.

2. Means of inciting to evil; that which seduces by exciting the passions. Flattery often operates as an *enticement* to sin.

3. Allurement.

ENTI'CER, *n.* One who entices; one who incites or instigates to evil; one who seduces.

ENTI'CING, *ppr.* Inciting to evil; urging to sin by motives, flattery or persuasion; alluring.

2. *a.* Having the qualities that entice or allure.

ENTI'CINGLY, *adv.* Charmingly; in a winning manner.

She sings most *enticingly*. *Addison.*

ENTI'RE, *a.* [Fr. *entier;* Sp. *entero;* Port. *inteiro;* It. *intero;* Arm. *anterin;* L. *integer*, said to be *in* neg. and *tango*, to touch. *Qu.*]

1. Whole; undivided; unbroken; complete in its parts.
2. Whole; complete; not participated with others. This man has the *entire* control of the business.
3. Full; complete; comprising all requisites in itself.

An action is *entire*, when it is complete in all its parts. *Spectator.*

4. Sincere; hearty.

He run a course more *entire* with the king of Arragon. *Bacon.*

5. Firm; solid; sure; fixed; complete; undisputed.

Entire and sure the monarch's rule must prove,
Who founds her greatness on her subjects' love. *Prior.*

6. Unmingled; unalloyed.

In thy presence joy *entire*. *Milton.*

7. Wholly devoted; firmly adherent; faithful.

No man had a heart more *entire* to the king. *Clarendon.*

8. In full strength; unbroken. *Spenser.*
9. In *botany*, an *entire* stem is one without branches; an *entire* leaf is without any opening in the edge, not divided. *Martyn.*

ENTI'RELY, *adv.* Wholly; completely; fully; as, the money is *entirely* lost.

2. In the whole; without division.

Euphrates—falls not *entirely* into the Persian sea. *Raleigh.*

3. With firm adherence or devotion; faithfully. *Spenser.*

ENTI'RENESS, *n.* Completeness; fullness; totality; unbroken form or state; as the *entireness* of an arch or a bridge.

2. Integrity; wholeness of heart; honesty.

ENTI'RETY, *n.* Wholeness; completeness; as *entirety* of interest. *Blackstone.*

2. The whole. *Bacon.*

EN'TITATIVE, *a.* [from *entity.*] Considered by itself. [This word, and *entitatively*, rarely or never used.]

ENTI'TLE, *v. t.* [Fr. *intituler;* Sp. *intitular;* It. *intitolare;* from L. *titulus*, a title.]

1. To give a title to; to give or prefix a name or appellation; as, to *entitle* a book, Commentaries on the laws of England.
2. To superscribe or prefix as a title. Hence as titles are evidences of claim or property, to give a claim to; to give a right to demand or receive. The labor of the servant *entitles* him to his wages. Milton is *entitled* to fame. Our best services do not *entitle* us to heaven.
3. To assign or appropriate by giving a title.
4. To qualify; to give a claim by the possession of suitable qualifications; as, an officer's talents *entitle* him to command.
5. To dignify by a title or honorable appellation. In this sense, *title* is often used.
6. To ascribe. *Obs.* *Burnet.*

ENTI'TLED, *pp.* Dignified or distinguished by a title; having a claim; as, every good man is *entitled* to respect.

ENTI'TLING, *ppr.* Dignifying or distinguishing by a title; giving a title; giving a claim.

EN'TITY, *n.* [Low L. *entitas;* Fr. *entité;* Sp. *entidad;* It. *entità;* from *ens, esse*, to be.] Being; existence.

Fortune is no real *entity*. *Bentley.*

2. A real being, or species of being.

ENTOIL', *v. t.* [See *Toil.*] To take with toils; to ensnare; to entangle. *Bacon.*

ENTÖMB, *v. t. entoom'.* [from *tomb.*] To deposit in a tomb, as a dead body. *Hooker.*

2. To bury in a grave; to inter.

ENTÖMBED, *pp.* Deposited in a tomb; buried; interred.

ENTÖMBING, *ppr.* Depositing in a tomb; burying; interring.

ENTÖMBMENT, *n.* Burial. *Barrow.*

EN'TOMOLITE, *n.* [Gr. εντομα, insect, and λιθος, stone.]

A fossil substance bearing the figure of an insect, or a petrified insect. *Ed. Encyc.*

ENTOMOLOĠ'ICAL, *a.* Pertaining to the science of insects.

ENTOMOL'OĠIST, *n.* One versed in the science of insects.

ENTOMOL'OĠY, *n.* [Gr. εντομα, insect, from τεμνω, to cut, and λογος, discourse.]

That part of zoology which treats of insects; the science or history and description of insects.

ENTORTILA'TION, *n.* [Fr. *entortillement.*] A turning into a circle. *Donne.*

EN'TRAIL, EN'TRAILS, } *n.* [Fr. *entrailles;* Arm. *entrailhou;* Gr. εντερα. See *Enter.*]

1. The internal parts of animal bodies; particularly, the guts or intestines; the bowels; used chiefly in the plural.
2. The internal parts; as the *entrails* of the earth.

The dark *entrails* of America. *Locke.*

ENTRA'IL, *v. t.* [It. *intralciare;* Fr. *treillis, treillisser.*] To interweave; to diversify. [*Not in use.*] *Spenser.*

ENTRAM'MELED, *a.* [from *trammel.*] Curled; frizzed. [*Not used.*]

EN'TRANCE, *n.* [L. *intrans, intro;* or from Fr. *entrant.* See *Enter.*]

1. The act of entering into a place; as the *entrance* of a person into a house or an apartment.
2. The power of entering. Let the porter give no *entrance* to strangers.

Where diligence opens the door of the understanding, and impartiality keeps it, truth is sure to find an *entrance* and a welcome too. *South.*

3. The door, gate, passage or avenue, by which a place may be entered.

They said, show us the *entrance* into the city. Judges i.

4. Commencement; initiation; beginning. A youth at his *entrance* on a difficult science, is apt to be discouraged.
5. The act of taking possession, as of land; as the *entrance* of an heir or a disseizor into lands and tenements.
6. The act of taking possession, as of an office. Magistrates at their *entrance* into office, usually take an oath.
7. The act of entering a ship or goods at the custom-house.
8. The beginning of any thing.

St. Augustine, in the *entrance* of one of his discourses, makes a kind of apology. *Hakewill.*

ENTR'ANSE, *v. t.* or *i.* [from *transe*, Fr. *transe*, Arm. *treand.* Qu. L. *transeo.* The Armoric is from *trè*, across, and *antren*, to enter, or It. *andare*, to go.]

1. To put in a transe; to withdraw the soul, and leave the body in a kind of dead sleep or insensibility; to make insensible to present objects. The verb is seldom used, but the participle, *entransed*, is common.
2. To put in an ecstasy; to ravish the soul with delight or wonder.

And I so ravish'd with her heavenly note,
I stood *entransed*, and had no room for thought. *Dryden.*

ENTR'ANSED, *pp.* Put in a transe; having the soul withdrawn, and the body left in a state of insensibility; enraptured; ravished.

ENTR'ANSING, *ppr.* Carrying away the soul; enrapturing; ravishing.

ENTRAP', *v. t.* [Fr. *attraper;* It. *attrappare.* See *Trap.*]

To catch as in a trap; to insnare; *used chiefly or wholly in a figurative sense.* To catch by artifices; to involve in difficulties or distresses; to entangle; to catch or involve in contradictions; in short, to involve in any difficulties from which an escape is not easy or possible. We are *entrapped* by the devices of evil men. We are sometimes *entrapped* in our own words.

ENTRAP'PED, *pp.* Ensnared; entangled.

ENTRAP'PING, *ppr.* Ensnaring; involving in difficulties.

ENTRE'AT, *v. t.* [Fr. *en* and *traiter*, It. *trattare*, Sp. Port. *tratar*, from L. *tracto*, to handle, feel, treat, use, manage.]

1. To ask earnestly; to beseech; to petition or pray with urgency; to supplicate; to solicit pressingly; to importune.

Isaac *entreated* Jehovah for his wife. Gen. xxv.

2. To prevail on by prayer or solicitation. Hence in the passive form, to be prevailed on; to yield to entreaty.

It were a fruitless attempt to appease a power, whom no prayers could *entreat*. *Rogers.*

3. To treat, in any manner; properly, to use or manage; but I believe, *entreat* is always applied to *persons*, as *treat* is to *persons* or *things*. Applied to *persons*, to *entreat* is to use, or to deal with; to manifest to others any particular deportment, good or ill.

I will cause the enemy to *entreat* thee well. Jer. xv.

The Egyptians evil-*entreated* us. Deut. xxvi.

[In this application, the prefix *en* is now dropped, and *treat* is used.]

4. To entertain; to amuse. *Obs.* *Shak.*
5. To entertain; to receive. *Obs.* *Spenser.*

ENTRE'AT, *v. i.* To make an earnest petition or request.

The Janizaries *entreated* for them, as valiant men. *Knowles.*

2. To offer a treaty. [*Not used.*] *Maccabees.*

3. To treat; to discourse. [*Not used.*] *Hakewill.*

ENTRE'ATANCE, *n.* Entreaty; solicitation. *Obs.* *Fairfax.*

ENTRE'ATED, *pp.* Earnestly supplicated, besought or solicited; importuned; urgently requested.

2. Prevailed on by urgent solicitation; consenting to grant what is desired.

3. Used; managed. *Obs.*

ENTRE'ATER, *n.* One that entreats, or asks earnestly.

ENTRE'ATING, *ppr.* Earnestly asking; pressing with request or prayer; importuning.

2. Treating; using. *Obs.*

ENTRE'ATIVE, *a.* Pleading; treating. *Brewer.*

ENTRE'ATY, *n.* Urgent prayer; earnest petition; pressing solicitation; supplication.

The poor useth *entreaties;* but the rich answereth roughly. Prov. xviii.

Praying with much *entreaty.* 2 Cor. viii.

ENTREMETS, *n.* [Fr. *entre* and *mets,* or L. *intromissum,* It. *tramesso.*]

Small plates set between the principal dishes at table, or dainty dishes. *Mortimer.* *Fr. Dict.*

ENTREPOT, *n.* [Fr. *entre* and *pôt,* for *post, positum.*]

A warehouse, staple or magazine, for the deposit of goods.

ENTRICK', *v. t.* [from *trick.*] To trick; to deceive; to entangle. *Obs.* *Chaucer.*

EN'TROCHITE, *n.* [Gr. τροχος, a wheel.] A kind of extraneous fossil, usually about an inch in length, and made up of round joints, which, when separated, are called *trochites.* These seem to be composed of the same kind of substance as the fossil shells of the echini. They are striated from the center to the circumference and have a cavity in the middle. They appear to be the petrified arms of the sea-star, called *stella arborescens.* *Nicholson.* *Encyc.*

EN'TRY, *n.* [Fr. *entrée.* See *Enter.*] The passage by which persons enter a house or other building.

2. The act of entering; entrance; ingress; as the *entry* of a person into a house or city; the *entry* of a river into the sea or a lake; the *entry* of air into the blood; the *entry* of a spear into the flesh.

3. The act of entering and taking possession of lands or other estate.

4. The act of committing to writing, or of recording in a book. Make an *entry* of every sale, of every debt and credit.

5. The exhibition or depositing of a ship's papers at the custom house, to procure license to land goods; or the giving an account of a ship's cargo to the officer of the customs, and obtaining his permission to land the goods.

ENTU'NE, *v. t.* [from *tune.*] To tune. *Chaucer.*

ENTWINE, *v. t.* [from *twine.*] To twine; to twist round.

ENTWIST', *v. t.* [from *twist.*] To twist or wreath round.

ENU'BILATE, *v. t.* [L. *e* and *nubila,* mist, clouds.]

To clear from mist, clouds or obscurity. [*Not in use.*] *Dict.*

ENU'BILOUS, *a.* Clear from fog, mist or clouds.

ENU'€LEATE, *v. t.* [L. *enucleo; e* and *nucleus,* a kernel.] Properly, to take out the kernel. Hence,

1. To clear from knots or lumps; to clear from intricacy; to disentangle. *Tooke.*

2. To open as a nucleus; hence, to explain; to clear from obscurity; to make manifest. *Good.*

ENU'€LEATED, *pp.* Cleared from knots; disclosed; explained.

ENU'€LEATING, *ppr.* Clearing from knots; explaining.

ENU€LEA'TION, *n.* The act of clearing from knots; a disentangling.

Neither air, nor water, nor food seem directly to contribute any thing to the *enucleation* of this disease [the *plica Polonica.*] *Tooke.*

2. Explanation; full exposition.

ENU'MERATE, *v. t.* [L. *enumero; e* and *numero, numerus,* number.]

To count or tell, number by number; to reckon or mention a number of things, each separately; as, to *enumerate* the stars in a constellation; to *enumerate* particular acts of kindness; we cannot *enumerate* our daily mercies.

ENU'MERATED, *pp.* Counted or told, number by number; reckoned or mentioned by distinct particulars.

ENU'MERATING, *ppr.* Counting or reckoning any number, by the particulars which compose it.

ENUMERA'TION, *n.* [L. *enumeratio.*] The act of counting or telling a number, by naming each particular.

2. An account of a number of things, in which mention is made of every particular article.

3. In *rhetoric,* a part of a peroration, in which the orator recapitulates the principal points or heads of the discourse or argument.

ENU'MERATIVE, *a.* Counting; reckoning up. *Bp. Taylor.*

ENUN'CIATE, *v. t.* [L. *enuncio; e* and *nuncio,* to tell.]

To utter; to declare; to proclaim; to relate. *Bp. Barlow.*

ENUN'CIATED, *pp.* Uttered; declared; pronounced; proclaimed.

ENUN'CIATING, *ppr.* Uttering; declaring; pronouncing.

ENUNCIA'TION, *n.* The act of uttering or pronouncing; expression; manner of utterance. In a public discourse, it is important that the *enunciation* should be clear and distinct.

2. Declaration; open proclamation; public attestation. *Taylor.*

3. Intelligence; information. *Hale.*

ENUN'CIATIVE, *a.* Declarative; expressive. *Ayliffe.*

ENUN'CIATIVELY, *adv.* Declaratively.

ENUN'CIATORY, *a.* Containing utterance or sound. *Wilson's Heb. Gram.*

ENVAS'SAL, *v. t.* [from *vassal.*] To reduce to vassalage.

2. To make over to another as a slave. *More.*

ENVEL'OP, *v. t.* [Fr. *envelopper;* It. *inviluppare, avviluppare,* to wrap; *viluppo,* a bundle, intricacy.]

1. To cover by wrapping or folding; to inwrap; to invest with a covering. Animal bodies are usually *enveloped* with skin; the merchant *envelops* goods with canvas; a letter is *enveloped* with paper.

2. To surround entirely; to cover on all sides; to hide. A ship was *enveloped* in fog; the troops were *enveloped* in dust.

3. To line; to cover on the inside.

His iron coat—*enveloped* with gold. *Spenser.*

ENVEL'OP, *n.* A wrapper; an inclosing cover; an integument; as the *envelop* of a letter, or of the heart.

2. In *fortification,* a work of earth, in form of a parapet or of a small rampart with a parapet. *Encyc.*

ENVEL'OPED, *pp.* Inwrapped; covered on all sides; surrounded on all sides; inclosed.

ENVEL'OPING, *ppr.* Inwrapping; folding around; covering or surrounding on all sides, as a case or integument.

ENVEL'OPMENT, *n.* A wrapping; an inclosing or covering on all sides.

ENVEN'OM, *v. t.* [from *venom.*] To poison; to taint or impregnate with venom, or any substance noxious to life; *never applied, in this sense, to persons, but to meat, drink or weapons;* as an *envenomed* arrow or shaft; an *envenomed* potion.

2. To taint with bitterness or malice; as the *envenomed* tongue of slander.

3. To make odious.

O what a world is this, when what is comely *Envenoms* him that bears it! *Shak.*

4. To enrage; to exasperate. *Dryden.*

ENVEN'OMED, *pp.* Tainted or impregnated with venom or poison; embittered; exasperated.

ENVEN'OMING, *ppr.* Tainting with venom; poisoning; embittering; enraging.

ENVER'MEIL, *v. t.* [Fr. *vermeil.*] To dye red. *Milton.*

EN'VIABLE, *a.* [See *Envy.*] That may excite envy; capable of awakening ardent desire of possession. The situation of men in office is not always *enviable.*

EN'VIED, *pp.* [See *Envy,* the verb.] Subjected to envy.

EN'VIER, *n.* One who envies another; one who desires what another possesses, and hates him because his condition is better than his own, or wishes his downfall.

EN'VIOUS, *a.* [Fr. *envieux.* See *Envy.*] Feeling or harboring envy; repining or feeling uneasiness, at a view of the excellence, prosperity or happiness of another; pained by the desire of possessing some superior good which another possesses, and usually disposed to deprive him of that good, to lessen it or to depreciate it in common estimation. Sometimes followed by *against,* but generally and properly by *at,* before the person envied.

Neither be thou *envious at* the wicked. Prov. xxiv.

It is followed by *of* before the thing. Be not *envious of* the blessings or prosperity of others.

2. Tinctured with envy; as an *envious* disposition.

3. Excited or directed by envy; as an *envious* attack.

EN'VIOUSLY, *adv.* With envy; with malignity excited by the excellence or prosperity of another.

How *enviously* the ladies look,
When they surprise me at my book. *Swift.*

ENVI'RON, *v. t.* [Fr. *environner*, from *environ*, thereabout; *en* and *viron*, from *virer*, to turn, Sp. *birar*, Eng. to *veer*. Class Br.]

1. To surround; to encompass; to encircle; as a plain *environed* with mountains.
2. To involve; to envelop; as, to *environ* with darkness, or with difficulties.
3. To besiege; as a city *environed* with troops.
4. To inclose; to invest.

That soldier, that man of iron,
Whom ribs of horror all *environ*. *Cleaveland.*

ENVI'RONED, *pp.* Surrounded; encompassed; besieged; involved; invested.

ENVI'RONING, *ppr.* Surrounding; encircling; besieging; inclosing; involving; investing. The appropriation of different parts of the globe to some particular species of stone *environing* it.

ENVI'RONS, *n. plu.* The parts or places which surround another place, or lie in its neighborhood, on different sides; as the *environs* of a city or town. *Chesterfield.*

EN'VOY, *n.* [Fr. *envoyé*, an envoy, from *envoyer*, to send. The corresponding Italian word is *inviato*, an envoy, that is, sent; and the verb, *inviare*, to send. The Spanish is *enviado;* and the verb, *enviar*, to send. Port. *id.* Hence *envoy* is from the root of L. *via*, Eng. *way*, contracted from *viag*, *vag*, or *wag;* It. *viaggiare*, to travel; Sp. *viage*, way, voyage. Class Bg.]

1. A person deputed by a prince or government, to negotiate a treaty, or transact other business, with a foreign prince or government. We usually apply the word to a public minister sent on a special occasion, or for one particular purpose; hence an *envoy* is distinguished from an embassador or permanent resident at a foreign court, and is of inferior rank. But envoys are *ordinary* and *extraordinary*, and the word may sometimes be applied to resident ministers.
2. A common messenger. [*Not in use.*] *Blackmore.*
3. Formerly, a postscript sent with compositions, to enforce them. [Fr. *envoi.*] *Warton.*

EN'VOYSHIP, *n.* The office of an envoy. *Coventry.*

EN'VY, *v. t.* [Fr. *envier;* Arm. *avia;* from L. *invideo*, *in* and *video*, to see against, that is, to look with enmity.]

1. To feel uneasiness, mortification or discontent, at the sight of superior excellence, reputation or happiness enjoyed by another; to repine at another's prosperity; to fret or grieve one's self at the real or supposed superiority of another, and to hate him on that account.

Envy not thou the oppressor. Prov. iii.
Whoever *envies* another, confesses his superiority. *Rambler.*

2. To grudge; to withhold maliciously. *Dryden.*

To envy at, used by authors formerly, is now obsolete.

Who would *envy at* the prosperity of the wicked? *Taylor.*

EN'VY, *n.* Pain, uneasiness, mortification or discontent excited by the sight of another's superiority or success, accompanied with some degree of hatred or malignity, and often or usually with a desire or an effort to depreciate the person, and with pleasure in seeing him depressed. Envy springs from pride, ambition or love, mortified that another has obtained what one has a strong desire to possess.

Envy and admiration are the Scylla and Charybdis of authors. *Pope.*

All human virtue, to its latest breath,
Finds *envy* never conquered, but by death. *Pope.*

Emulation differs from *envy*, in not being accompanied with hatred and a desire to depress a more fortunate person.

Envy, to which th' ignoble mind's a slave,
Is *emulation* in the learn'd or brave. *Pope.*

It is followed by *of* or *to.* They did this in *envy of* Cesar, or in *envy to* his genius. The former seems to be preferable.

2. Rivalry; competition. [*Little used.*] *Dryden.*
3. Malice; malignity.

You turn the good we offer into *envy.* *Shak.*

4. Public odium; ill repute; invidiousness.

To discharge the king of the *envy* of that opinion. *Bacon.*

EN'VYING, *ppr.* Feeling uneasiness at the superior condition and happiness of another.

EN'VYING, *n.* Mortification experienced at the supposed prosperity and happiness of another.

2. Ill will at others, on account of some supposed superiority. Gal. v. 21.

ENWAL'LOWED, *a.* [from *wallow.*] Being wallowed or wallowing. *Spenser.*

ENWHEE'L, *v. t.* [from *wheel.*] To encircle. *Shak.*

ENWI'DEN, *v. t.* [from *wide.*] To make wider. [*Not used.*]

ENWÖMB, *v. t.* *enwoom'.* [from *womb.*] To make pregnant. [*Not used.*] *Spenser.*

2. To bury; to hide as in a gulf, pit or cavern. *Donne.*

ENWÖMBED, *pp.* Impregnated; buried in a deep gulf or cavern.

ENWRAP', *v. t.* *enrap'.* To envelop. [See *Inwrap.*]

ENWRAP'MENT, *n.* A covering; a wrapping or wrapper.

EO'LIAN, EOL'IC, } *a.* Pertaining to Æolia or Æolis, in Asia Minor, inhabited by Greeks.

The *Eolic* dialect of the Greek language, was the dialect used by the inhabitants of that country.

Eolian lyre or *harp*, is a simple stringed instrument that sounds by the impulse of air, from *Æolus*, the deity of the winds.

EOL'IPILE, *n.* [*Æolus*, the deity of the winds, and *pila*, a ball.]

A hollow ball of metal, with a pipe or slender neck, used in hydraulic experiments. The ball being filled with water, is heated, till the vapor issues from the pipe with great violence and noise, exhibiting the elastic power of steam. *Encyc.*

E'ON, *n.* [Gr. αιων, age, duration.] In *the Platonic philosophy*, a virtue, attribute or perfection. The Platonists represented the Deity as an assemblage of eons. The Gnostics considered *eons* as certain substantial powers or divine natures emanating from the Supreme Deity, and performing various parts in the operations of the universe. *Encyc. Enfield.*

EP, EPI, Gr. επι, in composition, usually signifies *on.*

E'PACT, *n.* [Gr. επακτος, adscititious, from επαγω, to adduce or bring; επι and αγω, to drive.]

In *chronology*, the excess of the solar month above the lunar synodical month, and of the solar year above the lunar year of twelve synodical months. The epacts then are *annual* or *menstrual.* Suppose the new moon to be on the first of January; the month of January containing 31 days, and the lunar month only 29 days, 12h. 44′ 3″, the difference, or 1 day, 11h. 15′ 57″, is the menstrual epact. The annual epact is nearly eleven days; the solar year being 365 days, and the lunar year 354. *Encyc.*

EP'ARCH, *n.* [Gr. επαρχος; επι and αρχη, dominion.] The governor or prefect of a province. *Ash.*

EP'ARCHY, *n.* [Gr. επαρχια, a province; επι and αρχη, government.]

A province, prefecture or territory under the jurisdiction of an *eparch* or governor. *Tooke.*

EP'AULET, *n.* [Fr. *epaulette*, from *epaule*, the shoulder, It. *spalla*, Sp. *espalda.*]

A shoulder-piece; an ornamental badge worn on the shoulder by military men. Officers, military and naval, wear *epaulets* on one shoulder, or on both, according to their rank.

EPAUL'MENT, *n.* [from Fr. *epaule*, a shoulder.]

In *fortification*, a side-work or work to cover sidewise, made of gabions, fascines or bags of earth. It sometimes denotes a semi-bastion and a square orillon, or mass of earth faced and lined with a wall, designed to cover the cannon of the casemate. *Harris.*

EPENET'IC, *a.* [Gr. επαινητικος.] Laudatory; bestowing praise. *Phillips.*

EPEN'THESIS, EPEN'THESY, } *n.* [Gr. επενθεσις; επι, εν, and τιθημι, to put.] The insertion of a letter or syllable in the middle of a word, as *alituum* for *alitum.* *Encyc.*

EPENTHET'IC, *a.* Inserted in the middle of a word. *M. Stuart.*

E'PHA, *n.* [Heb. אפה, or איפה, properly a baking.]

A Hebrew measure of three pecks and three pints, or according to others, of seven gallons and four pints, or about 15 solid inches. *Johnson. Encyc.*

EPHEM'ERA, *n.* [L. from Gr. εφημερος, daily; επι and ημερα, a day.] A fever of one day's continuance only.

2. The Day-fly: strictly, a fly that lives one day only; but the word is applied also to insects that are very short-lived, whether they live several days or an hour only. There are several species.

EPHEM'ERAL, EPHEM'ERIC, } *a.* Diurnal; beginning and ending in a day; continuing or existing one day only.

2. Short-lived; existing or continuing for a short time only. [*Ephemeral* is generally

used. *Ephemerous* is not analogically formed.]

EPHEM'ERIS, *n.* plu. *ephemer'ides.* [Gr. εφημερις.]

1. A journal or account of daily transactions; a diary.
2. In *astronomy*, an account of the daily state or positions of the planets or heavenly orbs; a table, or collection of tables, exhibiting the places of all the planets every day at noon. From these tables are calculated eclipses, conjunctions and other aspects of the planets. *Encyc.*

EPHEM'ERIST, *n.* One who studies the daily motions and positions of the planets; an astrologer. *Howell.*

EPHEM'ERON-WORM, *n.* [See *Ephemera.*] A worm that lives one day only. *Derham.*

EPHE'SIAN, *a.* *s* as *z.* Pertaining to Ephesus, in Asia Minor. As a noun, a native of Ephesus.

EPHIAL'TES, *n.* [Gr.] The night-mar.

EPH'OD, *n.* [Heb. אפוד, from אפד to bind.] In *Jewish antiquity*, a part of the sacerdotal habit, being a kind of girdle, which was brought from behind the neck over the two shoulders, and hanging down before, was put across the stomach, then carried round the waist and used as a girdle to the tunic. There were two sorts; one of plain linen, the other embroidered for the high priest. On the part in front were two precious stones, on which were engraven the names of the twelve tribes of Israel. Before the breast was a square piece or breastplate. *Encyc. Calmet.*

EPH'OR, *n.* [Gr. εφορος, from εφοραω, to inspect.]

In *ancient Sparta*, a magistrate chosen by the people. The ephors were five, and they were intended as a check on the regal power, or according to some writers, on the senate. *Encyc. Mitford.*

EPH'ORALTY, *n.* The office or term of office of an ephor. *Mitford.*

EP'IC, *a.* [L. *epicus*, Gr. επικος, from επος, a song, or επω, ειπω, to speak.]

Narrative; containing narration; rehearsing. An *epic* poem, otherwise called *heroic*, is a poem which narrates a story, real or fictitious or both, representing, in an elevated style, some signal action or series of actions and events, usually the achievements of some distinguished hero, and intended to form the morals and affect the mind with the love of virtue. The *matter* of the poem includes the action of the fable, the incidents, episodes, characters, morals and machinery. The *form* includes the manner of narration, the discourses introduced, descriptions, sentiments, style, versification, figures and other ornaments. The *end* is to improve the morals, and inspire a love of virtue, bravery and illustrious actions. *Encyc.*

EP'ICEDE, *n.* [Gr. επικηδιος.] A funeral song or discourse.

EPICE'DIAN, *a.* Elegiac; mournful.

EPICE'DIUM, *n.* An elegy.

EP'ICENE, *a.* [Gr. επικοινος; επι and κοινος, common.] Common to both sexes; of both kinds.

EPICTE'TIAN, *a.* Pertaining to Epictetus, the Grecian writer. *Arbuthnot.*

EP'ICURE, *n.* [L. *epicurus*, a voluptuary, from *Epicurus.*]

Properly, a follower of Epicurus; a man devoted to sensual enjoyments; hence, one who indulges in the luxuries of the table. [*The word is now used only or chiefly in the latter sense.*]

EPICU'REAN, EPICURE'AN, } *a.* [L. *epicureus.*] Pertaining to Epicurus; as the *Epicurean* philosophy or tenets. *Reid.*

2. Luxurious; given to luxury; contributing to the luxuries of the table.

EPICU'REAN, EPICURE'AN, } *n.* A follower of Epicurus. *Encyc. Shaftesbury.*

EPICU'REANISM, *n.* Attachment to the doctrines of Epicurus. *Harris.*

EP'ICURISM, *n.* Luxury; sensual enjoyments; indulgence in gross pleasure; voluptuousness. *Shak.*

2. The doctrines of Epicurus. *Warton. Bailey.*

EP'ICURIZE, *v. i.* To feed or indulge like an epicure; to riot; to feast. *Fuller.*

2. To profess the doctrines of Epicurus. *Cudworth.*

EP'ICYCLE, *n.* [Gr. επι and κυκλος, a circle.] A little circle, whose center is in the circumference of a greater circle; or a small orb, which, being fixed in the deferent of a planet, is carried along with it, and yet by its own peculiar motion, carries the body of the planet fastened to it round its proper center. *Harris.*

EPICYC'LOID, *n.* [Gr. επικυκλοειδης; επι, κυκλος, and ειδος, form.]

In *geometry*, a curve generated by the revolution of the periphery of a circle along the convex or concave side of the periphery of another circle. *Encyc. Harris.*

A curve generated by any point in the plane of a movable circle which rolls on the inside or outside of the circumference of a fixed circle. *Ed. Encyc.*

EPICYCLOID'AL, *a.* Pertaining to the epicycloid, or having its properties. *Encyc.*

EPIDEM'IC, EPIDEM'ICAL, } *a.* [Gr. επι and δημος, people.] Common to many people. An *epidemic* disease is one which seizes a great number of people, at the same time, or in the same season. Thus we speak of *epidemic* measles; *epidemic* fever; *epidemic* catarrh. It is used in distinction from *endemic* or *local.* Intemperate persons have every thing to fear from an *epidemic* influenza.

2. Generally prevailing; affecting great numbers; as *epidemic* rage; an *epidemic* evil.

EPIDEM'IC, *n.* A popular disease: a disease generally prevailing. The influenza of October and November 1789, that of March and April 1790, that of the winter 1824—5, and that of 1825—6, were very severe *epidemics.*

EPIDERM'IC, EPIDERM'IDAL, } *a.* Pertaining to the cuticle; covering the skin.

The *epidermic* texture. *Kirwan.*

EPIDERM'IS, *n.* [Gr. επιδερμις; επι and δερμα, skin.]

In *anatomy*, the cuticle or scarf-skin of the body; a thin membrane covering the skin of animals, or the bark of plants. *Encyc. Martyn.*

EP'IDOTE, *n.* [from Gr. επιδιδωμι; so named from the apparent *enlargement* of the base of the prism in one direction. It is called by Werner, *pistazit*, and by Hausmann, *thallit.*]

A mineral occurring in lamellar, granular or compact masses, in loose grains, or in prismatic crystals of six or eight sides, and sometimes ten or twelve. Its color is commonly some shade of green, yellowish, bluish or blackish green. It has two varieties, zoisite and arenaceous or granular epidote. *Jameson. Cleaveland.*

Epidote is granular or manganesian. *Phillips.*

EPIGAS'TRIC, *a.* [Gr. επι and γαςηρ, belly.] Pertaining to the upper part of the abdomen; as the *epigastric* region; the *epigastric* arteries and veins. *Quincy.*

EPIGEE or EPIGEUM. [See *Perigee.*]

EP'IGLOT, EPIGLOT'TIS, } *n.* [Gr. επιγλωττις; επι and γλωττα, the tongue.] In *anatomy*, one of the cartilages of the larynx, whose use is to cover the glottis, when food or drink is passing into the stomach, to prevent it from entering the larynx and obstructing the breath. *Quincy.*

EP'IGRAM, *n.* [Gr. επιγραμμα, inscription; επι and γραμμα, a writing.]

A short poem treating only of one thing, and ending with some lively, ingenious and natural thought. Conciseness and point form the beauty of *epigrams.*

Epigrams were originally inscriptions on tombs, statues, temples, triumphal arches, &c. *Encyc.*

EPIGRAMMAT'IC, EPIGRAMMAT'ICAL, } *a.* Writing epigrams; dealing in epigrams; as an *epigrammatic* poet.

2. Suitable to epigrams; belonging to epigrams; like an epigram; concise; pointed; poignant; as *epigrammatic* style or wit.

EPIGRAM'MATIST, *n.* One who composes epigrams, or deals in them. Martial was a noted *epigrammatist.*

EP'IGRAPH, *n.* [Gr. επιγραφη; επι and γραφω, to write.]

Among *antiquaries*, an inscription on a building, pointing out the time of its erection, the builders, its uses, &c. *Encyc.*

EP'ILEPSY, *n.* [Gr. επιληψια, from επιλαμβανω, to seize.]

The falling sickness, so called because the patient falls suddenly to the ground; a disease accompanied with spasms or convulsions and loss of sense. *Quincy.*

EPILEP'TIC, *a.* Pertaining to the falling sickness; affected with epilepsy; consisting of epilepsy.

EPILEP'TIC, *n.* One affected with epilepsy.

EP'ILOGISM, *n.* [Gr. επιλογισμος.] Computation; enumeration. *Gregory.*

EPILOGIS'TIC, *a.* Pertaining to epilogue; of the nature of an epilogue.

EP'ILOGUE, *n.* ep'ilog. [L. *epilogus*, from Gr. επιλογος, conclusion; επιλεγω, to conclude; επι and λεγω, to speak.]

1. In *oratory*, a conclusion; the closing part of a discourse, in which the principal matters are recapitulated. *Encyc.*
2. In *the drama*, a speech or short poem addressed to the spectators by one of the actors, after the conclusion of the play.

EP'ILOGUIZE, } *v. i.* To pronounce an ep-
EP'ILOGIZE, } ilogue.

EP'ILOGUIZE, *v. t.* To add to, in the manner of an epilogue.

EPINI''CION, *n.* [Gr. επινικιον; επι and νικαω, to conquer.] A song of triumph. [*Not in use.*] *Warton.*

EPIPH'ANY, *n.* [Gr. επιφανεια, appearance; επιφαινω, to appear; επι and φαινω.]

A christian festival celebrated on the sixth day of January, the twelfth day after Christmas, in commemoration of the appearance of our Savior to the magians or philosophers of the East, who came to adore him with presents; or as others maintain, to commemorate the appearance of the star to the magians, or the manifestation of Christ to the Gentiles. Jerome and Chrysostom take the epiphany to be the day of our Savior's baptism, when a voice from heaven declared, "This is my beloved son, in whom I am well pleased." The Greek fathers use the word for the appearance of Christ in the world, the sense in which Paul uses the word, 2 Tim. i. 10. *Encyc.*

EPIPH'ONEM, } *n.* [Gr. επιφωνημα, excla-
EPIPHONE'MA, } mation; επιφωνεω, to cry out; επι and φωνεω.]

In *oratory*, an exclamation; an ecphonesis; a vehement utterance of the voice to express strong passion, in a sentence not closely connected with the general strain of the discourse; as, O mournful day! Miserable fate! Admirable clemency! *Johnson. Encyc.*

EPIPH'ORA, *n.* [Gr. επι and φερω, to bear.] The watery eye; a disease in which the tears, from increased secretion, or an obstruction in the lachrymal duct, accumulate in front of the eye and trickle over the cheek. *Cyc. Parr.*

EPIPHYLLOSPERM'OUS, *a.* [Gr. επι, φυλλον, a leaf, and σπερμα, seed.]

In *botany*, bearing their seeds on the back of the leaves, as ferns. *Harris.*

EPIPH'YSIS, } *n.* [Gr. επιφυσις; επι and φυω,
EPIPH'YSY, } to grow.] Accretion; the growing of one bone to another by simple contiguity, without a proper articulation. *Quincy.*

The spongy extremity of a bone; any portion of a bone growing on another, but separated from it by a cartilage. *Coxe.*

Epiphyses are appendixes of the long bones, for the purpose of articulation, formed from a distinct center of ossification, and in the young subject connected with the larger bones by an intervening cartilage, which in the adult is obliterated. *Parr.*

EPIP'LOCE, } *n.* [Gr. επιπλοκη, implica-
EPIP'LOCY, } tion; επι and πλεκω, to fold.]

A figure of rhetoric, by which one aggravation, or striking circumstance, is added in due gradation to another; as, "He not only spared his enemies, but continued them in employment; not only continued them, but advanced them." *Johnson.*

EPIP'LOCELE, *n.* [Gr. επιπλοκηλη; επιπλοον, the caul, and κηλη, a tumor.] A rupture of the caul or omentum. *Coxe.*

EPIP'LOIC, *a.* [Gr. επιπλοον, the caul.] Pertaining to the caul or omentum.

EPIP'LOON, *n.* [Gr. επιπλοον; επι and πλεω.] The caul or omentum.

EPIS'COPACY, *n.* [L. *episcopatus*; Sp. *obispado*; Port. *bispado*; It. *episcopato*; from the Gr. επισκοπεω, to inspect; επι and σκοπεω, to see. See *Bishop.*]

Government of the church by bishops; that form of ecclesiastical government, in which diocesan bishops are established, as distinct from and superior to priests or presbyters. *Encyc.*

EPIS'COPAL, *a.* Belonging to or vested in bishops or prelates; as *episcopal* jurisdiction; *episcopal* authority.

2. Governed by bishops; as the *episcopal* church.

EPISCOPA'LIAN, *a.* Pertaining to bishops or government by bishops; episcopal.

EPISCOPA'LIAN, *n.* One who belongs to an episcopal church, or adheres to the episcopal form of church government and discipline.

EPIS'COPALLY, *adv.* By episcopal authority; in an episcopal manner.

EPIS'COPATE, *n.* A bishopric; the office and dignity of a bishop.

2. The order of bishops.

EPIS'COPATE, *v. i.* To act as a bishop; to fill the office of a prelate. *Harris. Milner.*

EPIS'COPY, *n.* Survey; superintendence; search. *Milton.*

EP'ISODE, *n.* [from the Gr.] In *poetry*, a separate incident, story or action, introduced for the purpose of giving a greater variety to the events related in the poem; an incidental narrative, or digression, separable from the main subject, but naturally arising from it. *Johnson. Encyc.*

EPISOD'IC, } *a.* Pertaining to an epi-
EPISOD'ICAL, } sode; contained in an episode or digression. *Dryden.*

EPISPAS'TIC, *a.* [Gr. επισπαστικα, from επισπαω, to draw.]

In *medicine*, drawing; attracting the humors to the skin; exciting action in the skin; blistering.

EPISPAS'TIC, *n.* A topical remedy, applied to the external part of the body, for the purpose of drawing the humors to the part, or exciting action in the skin; a blister. *Encyc. Coxe.*

EPISTIL'BITE, *n.* A mineral, said to be the same as the *heulandite*. *Journ. of Science.*

EPIS'TLE, *n. epis'l.* [L. *epistola*, Gr. επιστολη, from επιστελλω, to send to; επι and στελλω, to send, G. *stellen*, to set.]

A writing, directed or sent, communicating intelligence to a distant person; a letter; a letter missive. It is rarely used in familiar conversation or writings, but chiefly in solemn or formal transactions. It is used particularly in speaking of the letters of the Apostles, as the *epistles* of Paul; and of other letters written by the ancients, as the *epistles* of Pliny or of Cicero.

EPIS'TLER, *n.* A writer of epistles. [*Little used.*]

2. Formerly, one who attended the communion table and read the epistles.

EPIS'TOLARY, *a.* Pertaining to epistles or letters; suitable to letters and correspondence; familiar; as an *epistolary* style.

2. Contained in letters; carried on by letters; as an *epistolary* correspondence.

EPISTOL'IC, } *a.* Pertaining to letters
EPISTOL'ICAL, } or epistles.

2. Designating the method of representing ideas by letters and words. *Warburton.*

EPIS'TOLIZE, *v. i.* To write epistles or letters. *Howell.*

EPIS'TOLIZER, *n.* A writer of epistles. *Howell.*

EPISTOLOGRAPH'IC, *a.* Pertaining to the writing of letters.

EPISTOLOG'RAPHY, *n.* [Gr. επιστολη, a letter, and γραφω, to write.]

The art or practice of writing letters. *Encyc.*

EPIS'TROPHE, } *n.* [Gr. επιστροφη; επι and
EPIS'TROPHY, } στροφη, a return.]

A figure, in *rhetoric*, in which several successive sentences end with the same word or affirmation. *Bailey. Ash.*

EP'ISTYLE, *n.* [Gr. επι and στυλος, a column.]

In *ancient architecture*, a term used by the Greeks for what is now called the *architrave*, a massive piece of stone or wood laid immediately over the capital of a column or pillar. *Encyc.*

EP'ITAPH, *n.* [Gr. επι and ταφος, a sepulcher.]

1. An inscription on a monument, in honor or memory of the dead.

> The *epitaphs* of the present day are crammed with fulsome compliments never merited. *Encyc.*

> Can you look forward to the honor of a decorated coffin, a splendid funeral, a towering monument—it may be a lying *epitaph*. *W. B. Sprague.*

2. An eulogy, in prose or verse, composed without any intent to be engraven on a monument, as that on Alexander:

> "Sufficit huic tumulus, cui non sufficeret orbis." *Encyc.*

EPITAPH'IAN, *a.* Pertaining to an epitaph. *Milton.*

EPITHALA'MIUM, } *n.* [Gr. επιθαλαμιον;
EPITHAL'AMY, } επι and θαλαμος, a bed-chamber.]

A nuptial song or poem, in praise of the bride and bridegoom, and praying for their prosperity.

> The forty fifth Psalm is an *epithalamium* to Christ and the church. *Burnet.*

EP'ITHEM, *n.* [Gr. επιθημα; επι and τιθημι, to place.]

In *pharmacy*, a kind of fomentation or poultice, to be applied externally to strengthen the part. *Encyc.*

Any external application, or topical medicine. The term has been restricted to liquids in which cloths are dipped, to be applied to a part. *Parr. Turner.*

EP'ITHET, *n.* [Gr. επιθετον, a name added, from επι and τιθημι, to place.]

An adjective expressing some real quality of the thing to which it is applied, or an attributive expressing some quality ascribed to it; as a *verdant* lawn; a *brilliant* appearance; a *just* man; an *accurate* description.

It is sometimes used for title, name, phrase or expression; but improperly.

EP'ITHET, *v. t.* To entitle; to describe by epithets. *Wotton.*

EPITHET'IC, *a.* Pertaining to an epithet or epithets.

2. Abounding with epithets. A style or composition may be too *epithetic.*

EPITHUMET'IC, EPITHUMET'ICAL, *a.* [Gr. επιθυμητικος.] Inclined to lust; pertaining to the animal passion. *Brown.*

EPIT'OME, EPIT'OMY, *n.* [Gr. επιτομη, from επι and τεμνω, to cut, τομη, a cutting, a section.]

An abridgment; a brief summary or abstract of any book or writing; a compendium containing the substance or principal matters of a book.

Epitomes are helpful to the memory. *Wotton.*

EPIT'OMIST, *n.* An epitomizer.

EPIT'OMIZE, *v. t.* To shorten or abridge, as a writing or discourse; to abstract, in a summary, the principal matters of a book; to contract into a narrower compass. Xiphilin *epitomized* Dion's Roman History.

2. To diminish; to curtail. [*Less proper.*]

EPIT'OMIZED, *pp.* Abridged; shortened; contracted into a smaller compass, as a book or writing.

EPIT'OMIZER, *n.* One who abridges; a writer of an epitome.

EPIT'OMIZING, *ppr.* Abridging; shortening; making a summary.

EP'ITRITE, *n.* [Gr. επιτριτος; επι and τριτος, third.]

In *prosody*, a foot consisting of three long syllables and one short one; as sălūtāntēs, cōncĭtātī, incāntārĕ. *Encyc.*

EPIT'ROPE, EPIT'ROPY, *n.* [Gr. επιτροπη, from επιτρεπω, to permit.]

In *rhetoric*, concession; a figure by which one thing is granted, with a view to obtain an advantage; as, I admit all this may be true, but what is this to the purpose? I concede the fact, but it overthrows your own argument. *Encyc.*

EPIZOOT'IC, *a.* [Gr. επι and ζωον, animal.]

In *geology*, an epithet given to such mountains as contain animal remains in their natural or in a petrified state, or the impressions of animal substances.

Epizootic mountains are of secondary formation. *Kirwan.*

EPIZO'OTY, *n.* [supra.] A murrain or pestilence among irrational animals. *Ed. Encyc.*

E'POCH, *n.* [L. *epocha*; Gr. εποχη, retention, delay, stop, from επεχω, to inhibit; επι and εχω, to hold.]

1. In *chronology*, a fixed point of time, from which succeeding years are numbered; a point from which computation of years begins. The Exodus of the Israelites from Egypt, and the Babylonish captivity, are remarkable *epochs* in their history.

2. Any fixed time or period; the period when any thing begins or is remarkably prevalent; as the *epoch* of falsehood; the *epoch* of woe. *Donne. Prior.*

The fifteenth century was the unhappy *epoch* of military establishments in time of peace. *Madison.*

EP'ODE, *n.* [Gr. επωδη; επι and ωδη, ode.] In *lyric poetry*, the third or last part of the ode; that which follows the strophe and antistrophe; the ancient ode being divided into strophe, antistrophe and epode. The word is now used as the name of any little verse or verses, that follow one or more great ones. Thus a pentameter after a hexameter is an epode. *Encyc.*

EPOPEE', *n.* [Gr. επος, a song, and ποιεω, to make.]

An epic poem. More properly, the history, action or fable, which makes the subject of an epic poem. *Encyc.*

E'POS, *n.* [Gr. επος.] An epic poem, or its fable or subject.

Epsom salt, the sulphate of magnesia, a cathartic.

EP'ULARY, *a.* [L. *epularis*, from *epulum*, a feast.] Pertaining to a feast or banquet. *Bailey.*

EPULA'TION, *n.* [L. *epulatio*, from *epulor*, to feast.] A feasting or feast. *Brown.*

EPULOT'IC, *a.* [Gr. επουλωτικα, from επουλοω, to heal, to cicatrize; επι and ουλη, a cicatrix, ουλω, to be sound, ουλος, whole.] Healing; cicatrizing.

EPULOT'IC, *n.* A medicament or application which tends to dry, cicatrize and heal wounds or ulcers, to repress fungous flesh and dispose the parts to recover soundness. *Coxe. Quincy.*

EQUABIL'ITY, *n.* [See *Equable.*] Equality in motion; continued equality, at all times, in velocity or movement; uniformity; as the *equability* of the motion of a heavenly body, or of the blood in the arteries and veins.

2. Continued equality; evenness or uniformity; as the *equability* of the temperature of the air; the *equability* of the mind.

E'QUABLE, *a.* [L. *æquabilis*, from *æquus*, equal, even, *æquo*, to equal, to level.]

1. Equal and uniform at all times, as motion. An *equable* motion continues the same in degree of velocity, neither accelerated nor retarded.

2. Even; smooth; having a uniform surface or form; as an *equable* globe or plain. *Bentley.*

E'QUABLY, *adv.* With an equal or uniform motion; with continued uniformity; evenly; as, bodies moving *equably* in concentric circles. *Cheyne.*

E'QUAL, *a.* [L. *æqualis*, from *æquus*, equal, even, *æquo*, to equal, perhaps Gr. εικος, similar; Fr. *egal*; Sp. *igual*; Port. *id.*; It. *eguale.*]

1. Having the same magnitude or dimensions; being of the same bulk or extent; as an *equal* quantity of land; a house of *equal* size; two persons of *equal* bulk; an *equal* line or angle.

2. Having the same value; as two commodities of *equal* price or worth.

3. Having the same qualities or condition; as two men of *equal* rank or excellence; two bodies of *equal* hardness or softness.

4. Having the same degree; as two motions of *equal* velocity.

5. Even; uniform; not variable; as an *equal* temper or mind.

Ye say, the way of the Lord is not *equal*. Ezek. xvi.

6. Being in just proportion; as, my commendation is not *equal* to his merit.

7. Impartial; neutral; not biased.

Equal and unconcerned, I look on all. *Dryden.*

8. Indifferent; of the same interest or concern. He may receive them or not, it is *equal* to me.

9. Just; equitable; giving the same or similar rights or advantages. The terms and conditions of the contract are *equal*.

10. Being on the same terms; enjoying the same or similar benefits.

They made the married, orphans, widows, yea and the aged also, *equal* in spoils with themselves. *Maccabees.*

11. Adequate; having competent power, ability or means. The ship is not *equal* to her antagonist. The army was not *equal* to the contest. We are not *equal* to the undertaking.

E'QUAL, *n.* One not inferior or superior to another; having the same or a similar age, rank, station, office, talents, strength, &c.

Those who were once his *equals*, envy and defame him. *Addison.*

It was thou, a man my *equal*, my guide. Ps. lv. Gal. i.

E'QUAL, *v. t.* To make equal; to make one thing of the same quantity, dimensions or quality as another.

2. To rise to the same state, rank or estimation with another; to become equal to. Few officers can expect to *equal* Washington in fame.

3. To be equal to.

One whose all not *equals* Edward's moiety. *Shak.*

4. To make equivalent to; to recompense fully; to answer in full proportion.

He answer'd all her cares, and *equal'd* all her love. *Dryden.*

5. To be of like excellence or beauty.

The gold and the crystal cannot *equal* it. Job xxviii.

EQUAL'ITY, *n.* [L. *æqualitas.*] An agreement of things in dimensions, quantity or quality; likeness; similarity in regard to two things compared. We speak of the *equality* of two or more tracts of land, of two bodies in length, breadth or thickness, of virtues or vices.

2. The same degree of dignity or claims; as the *equality* of men in the scale of being; the *equality* of nobles of the same rank; an *equality* of rights.

3. Evenness; uniformity; sameness in state or continued course; as an *equality* of temper or constitution.

4. Evenness; plainness; uniformity; as an *equality* of surface.

EQUALIZA'TION, *n.* The act of equalizing, or state of being equalized.

E'QUALIZE, *v. t.* To make equal; as, to *equalize* accounts; to *equalize* burdens or taxes.

E'QUALIZED, *pp.* Made equal; reduced to equality.

E'QUALIZING, *ppr.* Making equal.

E'QUALLY, *adv.* In the same degree with another; alike; as, to be *equally* taxed; to be *equally* virtuous or vicious; to be *equally* impatient, hungry, thirsty, swift or slow; to be *equally* furnished.

2. In equal shares or proportions. The estate is to be *equally* divided among the heirs.

3. Impartially; with equal justice. *Shak.*

E'QUALNESS, *n.* Equality; a state of being equal. *Shak.*

2. Evenness; uniformity; as the *equalness* of a surface.

EQUAN'GULAR, *a.* [L. *æquus* and *angulus.*] Consisting of equal angles. [See *Equiangular*, which is generally used.]

EQUANIM'ITY, *n.* [L. *æquanimitas*; *æquus* and *animus*, an equal mind.]

Evenness of mind; that calm temper or

firmness of mind which is not easily elated or depressed, which sustains prosperity without excessive joy, and adversity without violent agitation of the passions or depression of spirits. The great man bears misfortunes with *equanimity*.

EQUAN'IMOUS, *a.* Of an even, composed frame of mind; of a steady temper; not easily elated or depressed.

EQUA'TION, *n.* [L. *æquatio*, from *æquo*, to make equal or level.]

1. Literally, a making equal, or an equal division.

2. In *algebra*, a proposition asserting the equality of two quantities, and expressed by the sign = between them; or an expression of the same quantity in two dissimilar terms, but of equal value, as 3s=36d, or $x=b+m-r$. In the latter case, x is equal to b added to m, with r subtracted, and the quantities on the right hand of the sign of equation are said to be the value of x on the left hand. *Encyc. Johnson.*

3. In *astronomy*, the reduction of the apparent time or motion of the sun to equable, mean or true time. *Encyc.*

4. The reduction of any extremes to a mean proportion. *Harris.*

EQUA'TOR, *n.* [L. from *æquo*, to make equal.]

In *astronomy* and *geography*, a great circle of the sphere, equally distant from the two poles of the world, or having the same poles as the world. It is called *equator*, because when the sun is in it, the days and nights are of *equal* length; hence it is called also the *equinoctial*, and when drawn on maps, globes and planispheres, it is called the *equinoctial line*, or simply the *line*. Every point in the equator is 90 degrees or a quadrant's distance from the poles; hence it divides the globe or sphere into two equal hemispheres, the northern and southern. At the meridian, the equator rises as much above the horizon as is the complement of the latitude of the place. *Encyc. Harris.*

EQUATO'RIAL, *a.* Pertaining to the equator; as *equatorial* climates. The *equatorial* diameter of the earth is longer than the polar diameter.

E'QUERY, *n.* [Fr. *ecuyer*, for *escuyer*; It. *scudiere*; Low L. *scutarius*, from *scutum*, a shield. See *Esquire*.]

1. An officer of princes, who has the care and management of his horses.

2. A stable or lodge for horses.

EQUES'TRIAN, *a.* [L. *equester*, *equestris*, from *eques*, a horseman, from *equus*, a horse.]

1. Pertaining to horses or horsemanship; performed with horses; as *equestrian* feats.

2. Being on horseback; as an *equestrian* lady. *Spectator.*

3. Skilled in horsemanship.

4. Representing a person on horseback; as an *equestrian* statue.

5. Celebrated by horse-races; as *equestrian* games, sports or amusements.

6. Belonging to knights. Among the Romans, the *equestrian order* was the order of knights, *equites*; also their troopers or horsemen in the field. In *civil life*, the *knights* stood contra-distinguished from the *senators*; in the *field*, from the *infantry*. *Encyc.*

EQUIAN'GULAR, *a.* [L. *æquus*, equal, and *angulus*, an angle.]

In *geometry*, consisting of or having equal angles; an epithet given to figures whose angles are all equal, such as a square, an equilateral triangle, a parallelogram, &c.

EQUIBAL'ANCE, *n.* [L. *æquus* and *bilanx*.] Equal weight.

EQUIBAL'ANCE, *v. t.* To have equal weight with something. *Ch. Relig. Appeal.*

EQUICRU'RAL, *a.* [L. *æquus*, equal, and *crus*, a leg.] Having legs of equal length.

2. Having equal legs, but longer than the base; isosceles; as an *equicrural* triangle. *Johnson.*

EQUIDIF'FERENT, *a.* Having equal differences; arithmetically proportional.

In *crystalography*, having a different number of faces presented by the prism and by each summit; and these three numbers form a series in arithmetical progression, as 6.4.2. *Cleaveland.*

EQUIDIS'TANCE, *n.* Equal distance. *Hall.*

EQUIDIS'TANT, *a.* [L. *æquus*, equal, and *distans*, distant.]

Being at an equal distance from some point or place.

EQUIDIS'TANTLY, *adv.* At the same or an equal distance. *Brown.*

EQUIFORM'ITY, *n.* [L. *æquus*, equal, and *forma*, form.] Uniform equality. *Brown.*

EQUILAT'ERAL, *a.* [L. *æquus*, equal, and *lateralis*, from *latus*, side.]

Having all the sides equal; as an *equilateral* triangle. A square must necessarily be *equilateral*.

EQUILAT'ERAL, *n.* A side exactly corresponding to others. *Herbert.*

EQUILI'BRATE, *v. t.* [L. *æquus* and *libro*, to poise.]

To balance equally two scales, sides or ends; to keep even with equal weight on each side.

The bodies of fishes are *equilibrated* with the water. *Arbuthnot.*

EQUILI'BRATED, *pp.* Balanced equally on both sides or ends.

EQUILI'BRATING, *ppr.* Balancing equally on both sides or ends.

EQUILIBRA'TION, *n.* Equipoise; the act of keeping the balance even, or the state of being equally balanced.

Nature's laws of *equilibration*. *Derham.*

EQUILIB'RIOUS, *a.* Equally poised.

EQUILIB'RIOUSLY, *adv.* In equal poise.

EQUIL'IBRIST, *n.* One that balances equally.

EQUILIB'RITY, *n.* [L. *æquilibritas*.] The state of being equally balanced; equal balance on both sides; equilibrium; as the theory of *equilibrity*. *Gregory.*

EQUILIB'RIUM, *n.* [L.] In *mechanics*, equipose; equality of weight; the state of the two ends of a lever or balance, when both are charged with equal weight, and they maintain an even or level position, parallel to the horizon. *Encyc.*

2. Equality of powers.

Health consists in the *equilibrium* between those two powers. *Arbuthnot.*

3. Equal balancing of the mind between motives or reasons; a state of indifference or of doubt, when the mind is suspended in indecision, between different motives, or the different forces of evidence.

EQUIMUL'TIPLE, *a.* [L. *æquus* and *multiplico* or *multiplex*.] Multiplied by the same number or quantity.

EQUIMUL'TIPLE, *n.* In *arithmetic* and *geometry*, a number multiplied by the same number or quantity. Hence *equimultiples* are always in the same ratio to each other, as the simple numbers or quantities before multiplication. If 6 and 9 are multiplied by 4, the multiples, 24 and 36, will be to each other as 6 to 9. *Encyc.*

E'QUINE, *a.* [L. *equinus*, from *equus*, a horse.] Pertaining to a horse or to the genus.

The shoulders, body, thighs and mane are *equine*; the head completely bovine. *Barrow's Travels.*

EQUINEC'ESSARY, *a.* [L. *æquus* and *necessary*.]

Necessary or needful in the same degree. *Hudibras.*

EQUINOC'TIAL, *a.* [L. *æquus*, equal, and *nox*, night.]

1. Pertaining to the equinoxes; designating an equal length of day and night; as the *equinoctial* line.

2. Pertaining to the regions or climate of the equinoctial line or equator; in or near that line; as *equinoctial* heat; an *equinoctial* sun; *equinoctial* wind.

3. Pertaining to the time when the sun enters the equinoctial points; as an *equinoctial* gale or storm, which happens at or near the equinox, in any part of the world.

4. *Equinoctial flowers*, flowers that open at a regular, stated hour. *Martyn.*

EQUINOC'TIAL, *n.* [for *equinoctial line*.] In *astronomy*, a great circle of the sphere, under which the equator moves in its diurnal course. This should not be confounded with the equator, as there is a difference between them; the equator being movable, and the equinoctial immovable; the equator being drawn about the convex surface of the sphere, and the equinoctial on the concave surface of the magnus orbis. These words however are often confounded. When the sun, in its course through the ecliptic, comes to this circle, it makes equal days and nights in all parts of the globe. The equinoctial then is the circle which the sun describes, or appears to describe, at the time the days and nights are of equal length, viz. about the 21st of March and 23d of September. *Encyc.*

Equinoctial points, are the two points wherein the equator and ecliptic intersect each other; the one, being in the first point of Aries, is called the *vernal* point or equinox; the other, in the first point of Libra, the *autumnal* point or equinox. *Encyc.*

Equinoctial dial, is that whose plane lies parallel to the equinoctial. *Encyc.*

EQUINOC'TIALLY, *adv.* In the direction of the equinox. *Brown.*

E'QUINOX, *n.* [L. *æquus*, equal, and *nox*, night.]

The precise time when the sun enters one of the equinoctial points, or the first point of Aries, about the 21st of March, and the first point of Libra, about the 23d of September, making the day and the night of equal length. These are called the *vernal* and *autumnal* equinoxes. These points are found to be moving backward or westward, at the rate of 50″ of a degree in a year. This is called the *precession* of the equinoxes. *Encyc.*

EQUINU′MERANT, *a.* [L. *æquus*, equal, and *numerus*, number.]
Having or consisting of the same number. [*Little used.*] *Arbuthnot.*

EQUIP′, *v. t.* [Fr. *equiper*; Arm. *aqipa*, *aqipein*; Sp. *equipar*; Ch. יקף, Aphel אקיף to surround, to gird; perhaps the same root as Eth. ሐቀፈ [חקף] to embrace.]
1. Properly, to dress; to habit. Hence, to furnish with arms, or a complete suit of arms, for military service. Thus we say, to *equip* men or troops for war; to *equip* a body of infantry or cavalry. But the word seems to include not only arms, but clothing, baggage, utensils, tents, and all the apparatus of an army, particularly when applied to a body of troops. Hence, to furnish with arms and warlike apparatus; as, to *equip* a regiment.
2. To furnish with men, artillery and munitions of war, as a ship. Hence, in common language, to fit for sea; to furnish with whatever is necessary for a voyage.

EQ′UIPAĠE, *n.* The furniture of a military man, particularly arms and their appendages.
2. The furniture of an army or body of troops, infantry or cavalry; including arms, artillery, utensils, provisions, and whatever is necessary for a military expedition. *Camp equipage* includes tents, and every thing necessary for accommodation in camp. *Field equipage* consists of arms, artillery, wagons, tumbrils, &c.
3. The furniture of an armed ship, or the necessary preparations for a voyage; including cordage, spars, provisions, &c.
4. Attendance, retinue, as persons, horses, carriages, &c.; as the *equipage* of a prince.
5. Carriage of state; vehicle; as celestial *equipage*. *Milton.*
6. Accouterments; habiliments; ornamental furniture. *Prior.*

EQ′UIPAĠED, *a.* Furnished with equipage; attended with a splendid retinue. *Cowper. Spenser.*

EQUIPEN′DENCY, *n.* [L. *æquus*, equal, and *pendeo*, to hang.]
The act of hanging in equipoise; a being not inclined or determined either way. *South.*

EQUIP′MENT, *n.* The act of equipping, or fitting for a voyage or expedition.
2. Any thing that is used in equipping; furniture; habiliments; warlike apparatus; necessaries for an expedition, or for a voyage; as the *equipments* of a ship or an army.

E′QUIPOISE, *n.* *s* as *z*. [L. *æquus*, equal, and Fr. *poids*, or rather W. *pwys*, weight. See *Poise*.]
Equality of weight or force; hence, equilibrium; a state in which the two ends or sides of a thing are balanced. Hold the scales in *equipoise*. The mind may be in a state of *equipoise*, when motives are of equal weight.

EQUIPOL′LENCE, **EQUIPOL′LENCY**, *n.* [L. *æquus* and *pollentia*, power, *polleo*, to be able.]
1. Equality of power or force.
2. In *logic*, an equivalence between two or more propositions; that is, when two propositions signify the same thing, though differently expressed. *Encyc.*

EQUIPOL′LENT, *a.* [supra.] Having equal power or force; equivalent. In *logic*, having equivalent signification. *Bacon.*

EQUIPON′DERANCE, *n.* [L. *æquus*, equal, and *pondus*, weight.] Equality of weight; equipoise.

EQUIPON′DERANT, *a.* [supra.] Being of the same weight. *Locke.*

EQUIPON′DERATE, *v. i.* [L. *æquus*, equal, and *pondero*, to weigh.]
To be equal in weight; to weigh as much as another thing. *Wilkins.*

EQUIPON′DIOUS, *a.* Having equal weight on both sides. *Glanville.*

EQUIP′PED, *pp.* Furnished with habiliments, arms, and whatever is necessary for a military expedition, or for a voyage or cruise.

EQUIP′PING, *ppr.* Furnishing with habiliments or warlike apparatus; supplying with things necessary for a voyage.

EQUISO′NANCE, *n.* An equal sounding; a name by which the Greeks distinguished the consonances of the octave and double octave. *Busby.*

EQ′UITABLE, *n.* [Fr. *equitable*, from L. *æquitas*, from *æquus*, equal.]
1. Equal in regard to the rights of persons; distributing equal justice; giving each his due; assigning to one or more what law or justice demands; just; impartial. The judge does justice by an *equitable* decision. The court will make an *equitable* distribution of the estate.
2. Having the disposition to do justice, or doing justice; impartial; as an *equitable* judge.
3. Held or exercised in equity, or with chancery powers; as the *equitable* jurisdiction of a court. *Kent.*

EQ′UITABLENESS, *n.* The quality of being just and impartial; as the *equitableness* of a judge.
2. Equity; the state of doing justice, or distributing to each according to his legal or just claims; as the *equitableness* of a decision or distribution of property.

EQ′UITABLY, *adv.* In an equitable manner; justly; impartially. The laws should be *equitably* administered.

EQ′UITANT, *a.* [L. *equitans*, *equito*, to ride, from *eques*, a horseman, or *equus*, a horse.]
In *botany*, riding, as *equitant* leaves: a term of leafing or foliation, when two opposite leaves converge so with their edges, that one incloses the other; or when the inner leaves are inclosed by the outer ones. *Martyn.*

EQUITA′TION, *n.* A riding on horseback. *Barrow.*

EQ′UITY, *n.* [L. *æquitas*, from *æquus*, equal, even, level; Fr. *equité*; It. *equità*.]
1. Justice; right. In practice, equity is the impartial distribution of justice, or the doing that to another which the laws of God and man, and of reason, give him a right to claim. It is the treating of a person according to justice and reason.

> The Lord shall judge the people with *equity*. Ps. xcviii.
>
> With righteousness shall he judge the poor, and *reprove* with *equity*. Is. xi.

2. Justice; impartiality; a just regard to right or claim; as, we must, in *equity*, allow this claim.
3. In *law*, an equitable claim. "I consider the wife's *equity* to be too well settled to be shaken." *Kent.*
4. In *jurisprudence*, the correction or qualification of law, when too severe or defective; or the extension of the words of the law to cases not expressed, yet coming within the reason of the law. Hence a court of equity or chancery, is a court which corrects the operation of the literal text of the law, and supplies its defects, by reasonable construction, and by rules of proceeding and deciding, which are not admissible in a court of law. Equity then is the law of reason, exercised by the chancellor or judge, giving remedy in cases to which the courts of law are not competent. *Blackstone.*
5. *Equity of redemption*, in law, the advantage, allowed to a mortgager, of a reasonable time to redeem lands mortgaged, when the estate is of greater value than the sum for which it was mortgaged. *Blackstone.*

EQUIV′ALENCE, *n.* [L. *æquus*, equal, and *valens*, from *valeo*, to be worth.]
1. Equality of value; equal value or worth. Take the goods and give an *equivalence* in corn.
2. Equal power or force. [To *equivalence*, a verb, used by Brown, has not gained currency.]

EQUIV′ALENT, *a.* Equal in value or worth. In barter, the goods given are supposed to be *equivalent* to the goods received. *Equivalent* in *value* or *worth*, is tautological.
2. Equal in force, power or effect. A steam engine may have force or power *equivalent* to that of thirty horses.
3. Equal in moral force, cogency or effect on the mind. Circumstantial evidence may be almost *equivalent* to full proof.
4. Of the same import or meaning. Friendship and amity are *equivalent* terms.

> For now to serve and to minister, servile and ministerial, are terms *equivalent*. *South.*

Equivalent propositions in logic are called also *equipollent*.
5. Equal in excellence or moral worth. *Milton.*

EQUIV′ALENT, *n.* That which is equal in value, weight, dignity or force, with something else. The debtor cannot pay his creditor in money, but he will pay him an *equivalent*. Damages in money cannot be an *equivalent* for the loss of a limb.
2. In *chimistry*, equivalent is the particular weight or quantity of any substance which is necessary to saturate any other with which it can combine. It is ascertained that chemical combinations are definite, that is, the same body always enters into combination in the same weight, or if it can combine with a particular body in more

than one proportion, the higher proportion is always a multiple of the lower. *Silliman.*

EQUIV'ALENTLY, *adv.* In an equal manner.

EQUIV'OCACY, *n.* Equivocalness. [*Not used.*] *Brown.*

EQUIV'OCAL, *a.* [Low L. *æquivocus; æquus*, equal, and *vox*, a word; Fr. *equivoque;* It. *equivocale.* See *Vocal.*]

1. Being of doubtful signification; that may be understood in different senses; capable of a double interpretation; ambiguous; as *equivocal* words, terms or senses. Men may be misled in their opinions by the use of *equivocal* terms.

2. Doubtful; ambiguous; susceptible of different constructions; not decided. The character of the man is somewhat *equivocal.* His conduct is *equivocal.*

3. Uncertain; proceeding from some unknown cause, or not from the usual cause. *Equivocal* generation is the production of animals without the intercourse of the sexes, and of plants without seed. This doctrine is now exploded.

EQUIV'OCAL, *n.* A word or term of doubtful meaning, or capable of different meanings. *Dennis.*

EQUIV'OCALLY, *adv.* Ambiguously; in a doubtful sense; in terms susceptible of different senses. He answered the question *equivocally.*

2. By uncertain birth; by equivocal generation. *Bentley.*

EQUIV'OCALNESS, *n.* Ambiguity; double meaning. *Norris.*

EQUIV'OCATE, *v. i.* [It. *equivocare;* Fr. *equivoquer.* See *Equivocal.*]

To use words of a doubtful signification; to express one's opinions in terms which admit of different senses; to use ambiguous expressions. To *equivocate* is the dishonorable work of duplicity. The upright man will not *equivocate* in his intercourse with his fellow men.

EQUIV'OCATING, *ppr.* Using ambiguous words or phrases.

EQUIVOCA'TION, *n.* Ambiguity of speech; the use of words or expressions that are susceptible of a double signification. Hypocrites are often guilty of *equivocation*, and by this means lose the confidence of their fellow men. *Equivocation* is incompatible with the christian character and profession.

EQUIV'OCATOR, *n.* One who equivocates; one who uses language which is ambiguous and may be interpreted in different ways; one who uses mental reservation.

E'QUIVOKE, *n.* [Fr. *equivoque.*] An ambiguous term; a word susceptible of different significations.

2. Equivocation.

EQUIV'OROUS, *a.* [L. *equus*, horse, and *voro*, to eat.]

Feeding or subsisting on horse flesh.

Equivorous Tartars. *Quart. Rev.*

ER, the termination of many English words, is the Teutonic form of the Latin *or;* the one contracted from *wer*, the other from *vir*, a man. It denotes an agent, originally of the masculine gender, but now applied to men or things indifferently; as in *hater, farmer, heater, grater.* At the end of names of places, *er* signifies a man of the place; *Londoner* is the same as *Londonman.*

There is a passage in Herodotus, Melpomene, 110, in which the word *wer, vir*, a man, is mentioned as used by the Scythians; a fact proving the affinity of the Scythian and the Teutonic nations. Τας δε Αμαζονας καλεουσι Σκυθαι Οιορπατα. Δυναται δε το ουνομα τουτο κατ' Ελλαδα γλωσσαν ανδροκτονοι. Οιορ γαρ καλεουσι τον ανδρα, το δε πατα, κτεινειν. "The Scythians call the Amazons *Oiorpata*, a word which may be rendered, in Greek, *menkillers;* for *oior* is the name they give to *man*, *pata* signifies to kill." *Pata*, in the Burman language, signifies to *kill;* but it is probable that this is really the English *beat.*

E'RA, *n.* [L. *æra;* Fr. *ere;* Sp. *era.* The origin of the term is not obvious.]

1. In *chronology*, a fixed point of time, from which any number of years is begun to be counted; as the Christian *Era.* It differs from *epoch* in this; *era* is a point of time fixed by some nation or denomination of men; *epoch* is a point fixed by historians and chronologists. The christian *era* began at the *epoch* of the birth of Christ. *Encyc.*

2. A succession of years proceeding from a fixed point, or comprehended between two fixed points. The *era* of the Seleucides ended with the reign of Antiochus. *Rollin.*

ERA'DIATE, *v. i.* [L. *e* and *radio*, to beam.] To shoot as rays of light; to beam.

ERADIA'TION, *n.* Emission of rays or beams of light; emission of light or splendor. *King Charles.*

ERAD'ICATE, *v. t.* [L. *eradico*, from *radix*, root.]

1. To pull up the roots, or by the roots. Hence, to destroy any thing that grows; to extirpate; to destroy the roots, so that the plant will not be reproduced; as, to *eradicate* weeds.

2. To destroy thoroughly; to extirpate; as, to *eradicate* errors, or false principles, or vice, or disease.

ERAD'ICATED, *pp.* Plucked up by the roots; extirpated; destroyed.

ERAD'ICATING, *ppr.* Pulling up the roots of any thing; extirpating.

ERADICA'TION, *n.* The act of plucking up by the roots; extirpation; excision; total destruction.

2. The state of being plucked up by the roots.

ERAD'ICATIVE, *a.* That extirpates; that cures or destroys thoroughly.

ERAD'ICATIVE, *n.* A medicine that effects a radical cure. *Whitlock.*

ERA'SABLE, *a.* That may or can be erased.

ERA'SE, *v. t.* [L. *erado, erasi; e* and *rado*, to scrape, Fr. *raser*, Sp. *raer*, It. *raschiare*, Arm. *raza.* See Ar. أرض to corrode, Ch. גרד to scrape, Heb. חרט a graving tool, Syr. and Ar. خرط garata, to scrape. Class Rd. No 35. 38 and 58.]

1. To rub or scrape out, as letters or characters written, engraved or painted; to efface; as, to *erase* a word or a name.

2. To obliterate; to expunge; to blot out; as with pen and ink.

3. To efface; to destroy; as ideas in the mind or memory.

4. To destroy to the foundation. [See *Raze.*]

ERA'SED, *pp.* Rubbed or scratched out; obliterated; effaced.

ERA'SEMENT, *n.* The act of erasing; a rubbing out; expunction; obliteration; destruction.

ERA'SING, *ppr.* Rubbing or scraping out; obliterating; destroying.

ERA'SION, *n.* *s* as *z.* The act of erasing; a rubbing out; obliteration. *Black, Chim.*

ERAS'TIAN, *n.* A follower of one Erastus, the leader of a religious sect, who denied the power of the church to discipline its members. *Chambers.*

ERAS'TIANISM, *n.* The principles of the Erastians. *Leslie.*

ERA'SURE, *n.* *era'zhur.* The act of erasing; a scratching out; obliteration.

2. The place where a word or letter has been erased or obliterated.

ERE, *adv.* [Sax. *ær;* G. *eher;* D. *eer;* Goth. *air.* This is the root of *early*, and *ær*, in Saxon, signifies the morning. Before *ever*, we use *or*, "or ever." Let it be observed, that *ere* is not to be confounded with *e'er*, for *ever.*]

Before; sooner than.

Ere sails were spread new oceans to explore. *Dryden.*

The nobleman saith to him, Sir, come down *ere* my child die. John iv.

In these passages, *ere* is really a preposition, followed by a sentence, instead of a single word, as below.

ERE, *prep.* Before.

Our fruitful Nile
Flow'd *ere* the wonted season. *Dryden.*

E'RELONG, *adv.* [*ere* and *long.*] Before a long time *had elapsed.* [*Obs.* or *little used.*]

He mounted the horse, and following the stag, *erelong* slew him. *Spenser.*

2. Before a long time *shall elapse;* before long. *Erelong* you will repent of your folly.

The world *erelong* a world of tears must weep. *Milton.*

E'RENOW, *adv.* [*ere* and *now.*] Before this time. *Dryden.*

E'REWHILE, **E'REWHILES**, *adv.* [*ere* and *while.*] Some time ago; before a little while. *Obs.*

I am as fair now as I was *erewhile.* *Shak.*

ER'EBUS, *n.* [L. *erebus;* Gr. ερεβος; Oriental ערב evening, the decline of the sun, whence darkness, blackness.]

In *mythology*, darkness; hence, the region of the dead; a deep and gloomy place; hell. *Shak. Milton.*

EREC'T', *a.* [L. *erectus*, from *erigo*, to set upright; *e* and *rego*, to stretch or make straight, *right, rectus;* It. *eretto.* See *Right.*]

1. Upright, or in a perpendicular posture; as, he stood *erect.*

2. Directed upward.

And suppliant hands, to heaven *erect.* *Philips.*

3. Upright and firm; bold; unshaken.

> Let no vain fear thy generous ardor tame;
> But stand *erect*. *Granville.*

4. Raised; stretched; intent; vigorous; as a vigilant and *erect* attention of mind in prayer. *Hooker.*
5. Stretched; extended.
6. In *botany*, an *erect* stem is one which is without support from twining, or nearly perpendicular; an *erect* leaf is one which grows close to the stem; an *erect* flower has its aperture directed upwards. *Martyn.*

ERE€T′, *v. t.* To raise and set in an upright or perpendicular direction, or nearly such; as, to *erect* a pole or flag-staff.

To erect a perpendicular, is to set or form one line on another at right angles.

2. To raise, as a building; to set up; to build; as, to *erect* a house or temple; to *erect* a fort.
3. To set up or establish anew; to found; to form; as, to *erect* a kingdom or commonwealth; to *erect* a new system or theory.
4. To elevate; to exalt.

> I am far from pretending to infallibility: that would be to *erect* myself into an apostle. *Locke.*

5. To raise; to excite; to animate; to encourage.

> Why should not hope
> As much *erect* our thoughts, as fear deject them? *Denham.*

6. To raise a consequence from premises. [*Little used.*]

> Malebranche *erects* this proposition. *Locke.*

7. To extend; to distend.

ERE€T′, *v. i.* To rise upright. *Bacon.*

ERE€T′ABLE, *a.* That can be erected; as an *erectable* feather. *Montagu.*

ERE€T′ED, *pp.* Set in a straight and perpendicular direction; set upright; raised; built; established; elevated; animated; extended and distended.

ERE€T′ER, *n.* One that erects; one that raises or builds.

ERE€T′ING, *ppr.* Raising and setting upright; building; founding; establishing; elevating; inciting; extending and distending.

ERE€′TION, *n.* The act of raising and setting perpendicular to the plane of the horizon; a setting upright.

2. The act of raising or building, as an edifice or fortification; as the *erection* of a wall, or of a house.
3. The state of being raised, built or elevated.
4. Establishment; settlement; formation; as the *erection* of a commonwealth, or of a new system; the *erection* of a bishoprick or an earldom.
5. Elevation; exaltation of sentiments.

> Her peerless height my mind to high *erection* draws up. *Sidney.*

6. Act of rousing; excitement; as the *erection* of the spirits. *Bacon.*
7. Any thing erected; a building of any kind. *O. Wolcott.*
8. Distension and extension.

ERE€T′IVE, *a.* Setting upright; raising.

ERE€T′LY, *adv.* In an erect posture. *Brown.*

ERE€T′NESS, *n.* Uprightness of posture or form.

ERE€T′OR, *n.* A muscle that erects; one that raises.

ER′EMITAĠE, *n.* [See *Hermitage.*]

ER′EMITE, *n.* [L. *eremita;* Gr. ερημιτης, from ερημος, a desert.]

One who lives in a wilderness, or in retirement, secluded from an intercourse with men. It is generally written *hermit*, which see. *Raleigh. Milton.*

EREMIT′I€AL, *a.* Living in solitude, or in seclusion from the world.

EREP′TION, *n.* [L. *ereptio.*] A taking or snatching away by force.

ER′GAT, *v. i.* [L. *ergo.*] To infer; to draw conclusions. [*Not used.*] *Hewyt.*

ER′GO, *adv.* [L.] Therefore.

ER′GOT, *n.* [Fr. a spur.] In *farriery*, a stub, like a piece of soft horn, about the bigness of a chestnut, situated behind and below the pastern joint, and commonly hid under the tuft of the fetlock.

2. A morbid excrescence in grain; a dark-colored shoot, often an inch long, from the ears of grain, particularly of rye.

ER′GOTISM, *n.* [L. *ergo.*] A logical inference; a conclusion. *Brown.*

ER′IA€H, *n.* [Irish.] A pecuniary fine. *Spenser.*

ER′IĠIBLE, *a.* That may be erected. [*Ill formed and not used.*] *Shaw's Zool.*

ERINGO. [See *Eryngo.*]

ERIST′I€, ERIST′I€AL, *a.* [Gr. ερις, contention; εριςικος, contentious.]

Pertaining to disputes; controversial. [*Not in use.*]

ERKE, *n.* [Gr. αεργος.] Idle; slothful. [*Not in use.*] *Chaucer.*

ERMELIN. [See *Ermin.*]

ER′MIN, ER′MINE, *n.* [Fr. *hermine;* It. *armellino;* Sp. *armiño;* Port. *arminho;* Arm. *erminicq;* D. *hermelyn;* G. Dan. Sw. *hermelin.*]

1. An animal of the genus Mustela, an inhabitant of northern climates, in Europe and America. It nearly resembles the martin in shape, but the weasel, in food and manners. In winter, the fur is entirely white; in summer, the upper part of the body is of a pale tawny brown color, but the tail is tipped with black. The fur is much valued.
2. The fur of the ermin.

ER′MINED, *a.* Clothed with ermin; adorned with the fur of the ermin; as *ermined* pride; *ermined* pomp. *Pope.*

ERNE, or ÆRNE, a Saxon word, signifying a place or receptacle, forms the termination of some English words, as well as Latin; as in *barn, lantern, tavern, taberna.*

ERO′DE, *v. t.* [L. *erodo; e* and *rodo*, to gnaw, Sp. *roer*, It. *rodere*, Ar. ارض to gnaw. Class Rd. No. 35.]

To eat in or away; to corrode; as, canker *erodes* the flesh.

> The blood, being too sharp or thin, *erodes* the vessels. *Wiseman.*

ERO′DED, *pp.* Eaten; gnawed; corroded.

ERO′DING, *ppr.* Eating into; eating away; corroding.

ER′OGATE, *v. t.* [L. *erogo.*] To lay out; to give; to bestow upon. [*Not used.*] *Elyot.*

EROGA′TION, *n.* The act of conferring. [*Not used.*] *Elyot.*

ERO′SE, *a.* [L. *erosus.*] In *botany*, an erose leaf has small sinuses in the margin, as if gnawed. *Martyn.*

ERO′SION, *n. s* as *z.* [L. *erosio.*] The act or operation of eating away.

2. The state of being eaten away; corrosion; canker.

EROT′I€, EROT′I€AL, *a.* [Gr. ερως, love.] Pertaining to love; treating of love. *Encyc.*

EROT′I€, *n.* An amorous composition or poem. *Encyc.*

ERPETOL′OĠIST, *n.* [Gr. ερπετος, reptile, and λογος, discourse.]

One who writes on the subject of reptiles, or is versed in the natural history of reptiles. *Ch. Observer.*

ERPETOL′OĠY, *n.* [supra.] That part of natural history which treats of reptiles. *Dict. of Nat. Hist.*

ERR, *v. i.* [L. *erro;* Fr. *errer;* Sp. *errar;* It. *errare;* G. *irren;* Sw. *irra;* Dan. *irrer.*]

1. To wander from the right way; to deviate from the true course or purpose.

> But *errs* not nature from this gracious end,
> From burning suns when livid deaths descend? *Pope.*

2. To miss the right way, in morals or religion; to deviate from the path or line of duty; to stray by design or mistake.

> We have *erred* and strayed like lost sheep. *Com. Prayer.*

3. To mistake; to commit error; to do wrong from ignorance or inattention. Men *err* in judgment from ignorance, from want of attention to facts, or from previous bias of mind.
4. To wander; to ramble.

> A storm of strokes, well meant, with fury flies,
> And *errs* about their temples, ears, and eyes. *Dryden.*

ER′RABLE, *a.* Liable to mistake; fallible. [*Little used.*]

ER′RABLENESS, *n.* Liableness to mistake or error.

> We may infer from the *errableness* of our nature, the reasonableness of compassion to the seduced. *Decay of piety.*

ER′RAND, *n.* [Sax. *ærend*, a message, mandate, legation, business, narration; *ærendian*, to tell or relate; Sw. *årende;* Dan. *ærinde.*]

1. A verbal message; a mandate or order; something to be told or done; a communication to be made to some person at a distance. The servant was sent on an *errand;* he told his *errand;* he has done the *errand.* These are the most common modes of using this word.

> I have a secret *errand* to thee, O King. Judges iii.

2. Any special business to be transacted by a messenger.

ER′RANT, *a.* [Fr. *errant;* L. *errans*, from *erro*, to err.]

1. Wandering; roving; rambling; applied particularly to knights, who, in the middle ages, wandered about to seek adventures and display their heroism and generosity, called *knights errant.*
2. Deviating from a certain course. *Shak.*
3. Itinerant. *Obs.*

Errant, for *arrant*, a false orthography. [See *Arrant.*]

ER′RANTRY, *n.* A wandering; a roving or rambling about. *Addison.*

2. The employment of a knight errant.

ERRAT'IC, *a.* [L. *erraticus*, from *erro*, to wander.] Wandering; having no certain course; roving about without a fixed destination. *Pope.*

2. Moving; not fixed or stationary; *applied to the planets, as distinguished from the fixed stars.*

3. Irregular; mutable. *Harvey.*

ERRAT'ICALLY, *adv.* Without rule, order or established method; irregularly. *Brown.*

ERRA'TION, *n.* A wandering. [*Not used.*]

ERRA'TUM, *n.* plu. *errata.* [See *Err.*] An error or mistake in writing or printing. A list of the *errata* of a book is usually printed at the beginning or end, with references to the pages and lines in which they occur.

ER'RHINE, *a. er'rine.* [Gr. ερρινον; εν and ριν, the nose.]

Affecting the nose, or to be snuffed into the nose; occasioning discharges from the nose.

ER'RHINE, *n. er'rine.* A medicine to be snuffed up the nose, to promote discharges of mucus. *Coxe. Encyc.*

ER'RING, *ppr.* Wandering from the truth or the right way; mistaking; irregular.

ERRO'NEOUS, *a.* [L. *erroneus*, from *erro*, to err.]

1. Wandering; roving; unsettled.

> They roam
> *Erroneous* and disconsolate. *Philips.*

2. Deviating; devious; irregular; wandering from the right course.

> *Erroneous* circulation of blood. *Arbuthnot.*

[*The foregoing applications of the word are less common.*]

3. Mistaking; misled; deviating, by mistake, from the truth. Destroy not the *erroneous* with the malicious.

4. Wrong; false; mistaken; not conformable to truth; erring from truth or justice; as an *erroneous* opinion or judgment.

ERRO'NEOUSLY, *adv.* By mistake; not rightly; falsely.

ERRO'NEOUSNESS, *n.* The state of being erroneous, wrong or false; deviation from right; inconformity to truth; as the *erroneousness* of a judgment or proposition.

ER'ROR, *n.* [L. *error*, from *erro*, to wander.] A wandering or deviation from the truth; a mistake in judgment, by which men assent to or believe what is not true. *Error* may be *voluntary*, or *involuntary*. *Voluntary*, when men neglect or pervert the proper means to inform the mind; *involuntary*, when the means of judging correctly are not in their power. An error committed through carelessness or haste is a *blunder*.

> Charge home upon *error* its most tremendous consequences. *J. M. Mason.*

2. A mistake made in writing or other performance. It is no easy task to correct the *errors* of the press. Authors sometimes charge their own *errors* to the printer.

3. A wandering; excursion; irregular course.

> Driv'n by the winds and *errors* of the sea. *Dryden.*

[*This sense is unusual and hardly legitimate.*]

4. Deviation from law, justice or right; oversight; mistake in conduct.

> Say not, it was an *error*. Eccles. v.

5. In *scripture and theology*, sin; iniquity; transgression.

> Who can understand his *errors?* cleanse thou me from secret faults. Ps. xix.

6. In *law*, a mistake in pleading or in judgment. A *writ of error*, is a writ founded on an alledged error in judgment, which carries the suit to another tribunal for redress. Hence the following verb,

ER'ROR, *v. t.* To determine a judgment of court to be erroneous.

[*The use of this verb is not well authorized.*]

ERSE, *n.* The language of the descendants of the Gaels or Celts, in the highlands of Scotland.

ERST, *adv.* [Sax. *ærest*, superlative of *ær.* See *Ere.*]

1. First; at first; at the beginning.
2. Once; formerly; long ago.
3. Before; till then or now; hitherto.

[*This word is obsolete, except in poetry.*]

ERSTWHILE, *adv.* Till then or now; formerly. *Obs.* *Glanville.*

ERUBES'CENCE, *n.* [L. *erubescens*, *erubesco*, from *rubeo*, to be red.]

A becoming red; redness of the skin or surface of any thing; a blushing.

ERUBES'CENT, *a.* Red, or reddish; blushing.

ERUCT', **ERUCT'ATE**, } *v. t.* [L. *eructo*, *ructor*, coinciding in elements with Ch. רוק Heb. ירק to spit. Qu. *yerk.*]

To belch; to eject from the stomach, as wind. [*Little used.*] *Howell.*

ERUCTA'TION, *n.* [L. *eructatio.*] The act of belching wind from the stomach; a belch.

2. A violent bursting forth or ejection of wind or other matter from the earth. *Woodward.*

ER'UDITE, *a.* [L. *eruditus*, from *erudio*, to instruct. Qu. *e* and *rudis*, rude. Rather Ch. Syr. Sam. רדה redah, to teach. Class Rd. No. 2.] Instructed; taught; learned. *Chesterfield.*

ERUDI''TION, *n.* Learning; knowledge gained by study, or from books and instruction; particularly, learning in literature, as distinct from the sciences, as in history, antiquity and languages. The Scaligers were men of deep *erudition.*

> The most useful *erudition* for republicans is that which exposes the causes of discords. *J. Adams.*

ERU'GINOUS, *a.* [L. *æruginosus*, from *ærugo*, rust.]

Partaking of the substance or nature of copper or the rust of copper; resembling rust.

ERUPT', *v. i.* To burst forth. [*Not used.*]

ERUP'TION, *n.* [L. *eruptio*, from *erumpo*, *erupi*; *e* and *rumpo*, for *rupo*; Sp. *romper*; Fr. *rompre.* See Class Rb. No. 26. 27. 29.]

1. The act of breaking or bursting forth from inclosure or confinement; a violent emission of any thing, particularly of flames and lava from a volcano. The *eruptions* of Hecla in 1783, were extraordinary for the quantity of lava discharged.

2. A sudden or violent rushing forth of men or troops for invasion; sudden excursion.

> Incensed at such *eruption* bold. *Milton.*

3. A burst of voice; violent exclamation. [*Little used.*] *South.*

4. In *medical science*, a breaking out of humors; a copious excretion of humors on the skin, in pustules; also, an efflorescence or redness on the skin, as in scarlatina; exanthemata; petechiæ; vibices; as in small pox, measles and fevers.

ERUP'TIVE, *a.* Bursting forth.

> The sudden glance
> Appears far south *eruptive* through the cloud. *Thomson.*

2. Attended with eruptions or efflorescence, or producing it; as an *eruptive* fever.

ERYN'GO, *n.* [Gr. ηρυγγιον.] The sea-holly, *Eryngium*, a genus of plants of several species. The flowers are collected in a round head; the receptacle is paleaceous or chaffy. The young shoots are esculent. *Encyc.*

ERYSIP'ELAS, *n.* [Gr. ερυσιπελας.] A disease called St. Anthony's fire; a diffused inflammation with fever of two or three days, generally with coma or delirium; an eruption of a fiery acrid humor, on some part of the body, but chiefly on the face. One species of erysipelas is called shingles, or eruption with small vesicles. *Coxe. Encyc. Quincy.*

ERYSIPEL'ATOUS, *a.* Eruptive; resembling erysipelas, or partaking of its nature.

ESCALA'DE, *n.* [Fr. *id.*; Sp. *escalada*; It. *scalata*; from Sp. *escala*, It. *scala*, L. *scala*, a ladder, Fr. *echelle.* See *Scale.*]

In *the military art*, a furious attack made by troops on a fortified place, in which ladders are used to pass a ditch or mount a rampart.

> Sin enters, not by *escalade*, but by cunning or treachery. *Buckminster.*

ESCALA'DE, *v. t.* To scale; to mount and pass or enter by means of ladders; as, to *escalade* a wall. *Life of Wellington.*

ESCAL'OP, *n. skal'lup.* [D. *schulp*, a shell.] A family of bivalvular shell-fish, whose shell is regularly indented. In the center of the top of the shell is a trigonal sinus with an elastic cartilage for its hinge.

2. A regular curving indenture in the margin of any thing. [See *Scallop* and *Scollop.*]

ESCAPA'DE, *n.* [Fr. See *Escape.*] The fling of a horse. In Spanish, flight, escape.

ESCA'PE, *v. t.* [Fr. *echapper*; Norm. *echever*; Arm. *achap*; It. *scappare*; Sp. Port. *escapar*; probably from L. *capio*, with a negative prefix, or from a word of the same family.]

1. To flee from and avoid; to get out of the way; to shun; to obtain security from; to pass without harm; as, to *escape* danger.

> A small number, that *escape* the sword, shall return. Jer. xliv.

> Having *escaped* the corruption that is in the world through lust. 2 Pet. i.

2. To pass unobserved; to evade; as, the fact *escaped* my notice or observation.

3. To avoid the danger of; as, to *escape* the sea. Acts xxviii.

Note. This verb is properly intransitive, and in strictness should be followed by *from*; but usage sanctions the omission of it.

ESCA'PE, *v. i.* To flee, shun and be secure from danger; to avoid an evil.

Escape for thy life to the mountains. Gen. xix.

2. To be passed without harm. The balls whistled by me, my comrades fell, but I *escaped*.

ESCA'PE, *n.* Flight to shun danger or injury; the act of fleeing from danger.

I would hasten my *escape* from the windy storm. Ps. lv.

2. A being passed without receiving injury, as when danger comes near a person, but passes by, and the person is passive. Every soldier who survives a battle has had such an *escape*.

3. Excuse; subterfuge; evasion. *Raleigh.*

4. In *law*, an evasion of legal restraint or the custody of the sheriff, without due course of law. Escapes are *voluntary* or *involuntary*; *voluntary*, when an officer permits an offender or debtor to quit his custody, without warrant; and *involuntary*, or negligent, when an arrested person quits the custody of the officer against his will, and is not pursued forthwith and retaken before the pursuer hath lost sight of him.

5. Sally; flight; irregularity. [*Little used.*] *Shak.*

6. Oversight; mistake. [*Little used, or improper.*]

ESCA'PEMENT, *n.* That part of a clock or watch, which regulates its movements, and prevents their acceleration. *Ed. Encyc.*

ESCA'PING, *ppr.* Fleeing from and avoiding danger or evil; being passed unobserved or unhurt; shunning; evading; securing safety; quitting the custody of the law, without warrant.

ESCA'PING, *n.* Avoidance of danger. Ezra ix.

ESC'ARGATOIRE, *n.* [Fr. from *escargot*, a snail.] A nursery of snails. *Addison.*

ESC'ARP, *v. t.* [Fr. *escarper*, to cut to a slope; It. *scarpa*, a slope. See *Carve.*]

To slope; to form a slope; *a military term.* *Carleton.*

ESC'ARPMENT, *n.* A slope; a steep descent or declivity. *Buckland.*

ESCHALOT, *n.* shallo'te. [Fr. *echalote.*] A species of small onion or garlic, belonging to the genus Allium; the *ascalonicum.* *Encyc.*

ES'CHAR, *n.* [Gr. εσχαρα.] In *surgery*, the crust or scab occasioned by burns or caustic applications. *Encyc.*

2. A species of Coralline, resembling a net or woven cloth.

ESCHAROT'IC, *a.* Caustic; having the power of searing or destroying the flesh. *Coxe. Encyc.*

ESCHAROT'IC, *n.* A caustic application; a medicine which sears or destroys flesh. *Coxe.*

ESCHE'AT, *n.* [Fr. *echeoir, echoir, choir*; Norm. *eschier, eschire, eschever*, to fall, to happen to, to escheat. The Fr. *echoir*, seems to be the Sp. *caer*, which is contracted from the L. *cado, cadere.*]

1. Any land or tenements which casually fall or revert to the lord within his manor, through failure of heirs. It is the determination of the tenure or dissolution of the mutual bond between the lord and tenant, from the extinction of the blood of the tenant, by death or natural means, or by civil means, as forfeiture or corruption of blood. *Blackstone.*

2. In *the U. States*, the falling or passing of lands and tenements to the state, through failure of heirs or forfeiture, or in cases where no owner is found. *Stat. of Mass. and Connecticut.*

3. The place or circuit within which the king or lord is entitled to escheats. *England.*

4. A writ to recover escheats from the person in possession. *Blackstone. Cowel. Encyc.*

5. The lands which fall to the lord or state by escheat.

6. In *Scots law*, the forfeiture incurred by a man's being denounced a rebel.

ESCHE'AT, *v. i.* In *England*, to revert, as land, to the lord of a manor, by means of the extinction of the blood of the tenant.

2. In *America*, to fall or come, as land, to the state, through failure of heirs or owners, or by forfeiture for treason. In the feudal sense, no *escheat* can exist in the United States; but the word is used in statutes confiscating the estates of those who abandoned their country, during the revolution, and in statutes giving to the state the lands for which no owner can be found.

ESCHE'AT, *v. t.* To forfeit. [*Not used.*] *Bp. Hall.*

ESCHE'ATABLE, *a.* Liable to escheat.

ESCHE'ATAGE, *n.* The right of succeding to an escheat. *Sherwood.*

ESCHE'ATED, *pp.* Having fallen to the lord through want of heirs, or to the state for want of an owner, or by forfeiture.

ESCHE'ATING, *ppr.* Reverting to the lord through failure of heirs, or to the state for want of an owner, or by forfeiture.

ESCHE'ATOR, *n.* An officer who observes the escheats of the king in the county whereof he is escheator, and certifies them into the treasury. *Camden.*

ESCHEW', *v. t.* [Norm. *eschever*; Old Fr. *escheoir*; G. *scheuen*; It. *schivare*; Fr. *esquiver*; Dan. *skyer*; to shun. The G. *scheu*, Dan. *sky*, It. *schifo*, is the Eng. *shy.* In Sw. the corresponding words are *skygg* and *skyggia*, which leads to the opinion that the radical letters are Kg or Skg; and if so, these words correspond with the G. *scheuchen*, to frighten, to drive away, which we retain in the word *shoo*, used to scare away fowls.]

To flee from; to shun; to avoid.

He who obeys, destruction shall *eschew*. *Sandys.*

Job—feared God and *eschewed* evil. Job 1.

ESCHEW'ED, *pp.* Shunned; avoided.

ESCHEW'ING, *ppr.* Shunning; avoiding. [*This word is nearly obsolete, or at least little used.*]

ESCO'CHEON, *n.* [Fr.] The shield of the family. *Warton.*

ES'CORT, *n.* [Fr. *escorte*; It. *scorta*, a guard, and *scortare*, to escort, to abridge, to *shorten.* From this Italian word, we may infer that *escort* is from the root of *short*, which signifies curtailed, cut off; hence the sense is a detachment or small party, or a cutting off, a defense. The Sp. and Port. word is *escolta*, *r* being changed into *l.* See *Short.*]

A guard; a body of armed men which attends an officer, or baggage, provisions or munitions conveyed by land from place to place, to protect them from an enemy, or in general, for security. [This word is rarely, and never properly used for *naval* protection or protectors; the latter we call a *convoy.* I have found it applied to naval protection, but it is unusual.]

ESCORT', *v. t.* To attend and guard on a journey by land; to attend and guard any thing conveyed by land. General Washington arrived at Boston, *escorted* by a detachment of dragoons. The guards *escorted* Lord Wellington to London.

ESCORT'ED, *pp.* Attended and guarded by land.

ESCORT'ING, *ppr.* Attending and guarding by land.

ESCOT. [See *Scot.*]

ESCOUADE. [See *Squad.*]

ESCOUT. [See *Scout.*]

ESCRITO'IR, *n.* [Sp. *escritorio*; It. *scrittoio*; Fr. *ecritoire*, from *ecrire*, *ecrit*, to write, from the root of L. *scribo*, Eng. to *scrape.*]

A box with instruments and conveniences for writing; sometimes, a desk or chest of drawers with an apartment for the instruments of writing. It is often pronounced *scrutoir.*

ES'CROW, *n.* [Fr. *ecrou*, Norm. *escrover*, *escrowe*, a scroll, a contraction of *scroll*, or otherwise from the root of *ecrire*, *ecrivons*, to write.]

In *law*, a deed of lands or tenements delivered to a third person, to hold till some condition is performed by the grantee, and which is not to take effect till the condition is performed. It is then to be delivered to the grantee. *Blackstone.*

ES'CUAGE, *n.* [from Fr. *ecu*, for *escu*, L. *scutum*, a shield.]

In *feudal law*, service of the shield, called also *scutage*; a species of tenure by knight service, by which a tenant was bound to follow his lord to war; afterwards exchanged for a pecuniary satisfaction. *Blackstone.*

ESCULA'PIAN, *a.* [from *Æsculapius*, the physician.]

Medical; pertaining to the healing art. *Young.*

ES'CULENT, *a.* [L. *esculentus*, from *esca*, food.]

Eatable; that is or may be used by man for food; as *esculent* plants; *esculent* fish.

ES'CULENT, *n.* Something that is eatable; that which is or may be safely eaten by man.

ESCU'RIAL, *n.* The palace or residence of the King of Spain, about 15 miles North West of Madrid. This is the largest and most superb structure in the kingdom, and one of the most splendid in Europe. It is built in a dry barren spot, and the name itself is said to signify *a place full of rocks.* *Encyc.*

The Escurial is a famous monastery built by Philip II. in the shape of a gridiron, in honor of St. Laurence. It takes its name from a village near Madrid. It contains the king's palace, St. Laurence's church, the monastery of Jeronomites, and the free schools. *Port. Dict.*

ESCUTCH'EON, *n.* [Fr. *ecusson*, for *escusson*, from L. *scutum*, a shield, It. *scudo*, Sp. *escudo*, Arm. *scoeda.*]
The shield on which a coat of arms is represented; the shield of a family; the picture of ensigns armorial. *Encyc. Johnson.*

ESCUTCH'EONED, *a.* Having a coat of arms or ensign. *Young.*

ESLOIN', *v. t.* [Fr. *eloigner.*] To remove. [*Not in use.*]

ESOPHAGOT'OMY, *n.* [*esophagus* and τομη, a cutting.]
In *surgery*, the operation of making an incision into the esophagus, for the purpose of removing any foreign substance that obstructs the passage. *Journ. of Science.*

ESOPH'AGUS, *n.* [Gr. οισοφαγος.] The gullet; the canal through which food and drink pass to the stomach.

ESO'PIAN, *a.* [from *Æsop.*] Pertaining to Æsop; composed by him or in his manner. *Warton.*

ESOT'ERIC, *a.* [Gr. εσωτερος, interior, from εσω, within.]
Private; an epithet applied to the private instructions and doctrines of Pythagoras; opposed to *exoteric*, or public. *Enfield.*

ESOT'ERY, *n.* Mystery; secrecy. [*Little used.*]

ESPAL'IER, *n.* [Fr. *espalier*; Sp. *espalera*; It. *spalliera*; from L. *palus*, a stake or *pole.*]
A row of trees planted about a garden or in hedges, so as to inclose quarters or separate parts, and trained up to a lattice of wood-work, or fastened to stakes, forming a close hedge or shelter to protect plants against injuries from wind or weather. *Encyc.*

ESPAL'IER, *v. t.* To form an espalier, or to protect by an espalier.

ESPAR'CET, *n.* A kind of sainfoin. *Mortimer.*

ESPE''CIAL, *a.* [Fr. *special*; L. *specialis*, from *specio*, to see, *species*, kind.]
Principal; chief; particular; as, in an *especial* manner or degree.

ESPE''CIALLY, *adv.* Principally; chiefly; particularly; in an uncommon degree; in reference to one person or thing in particular.

ESPE''CIALNESS, *n.* The state of being especial.

ES'PERANCE, *n.* [Fr. from L. *spero*, to hope.] Hope. [*Not English.*] *Shak.*

ESPI'AL, *n.* [See *Spy.*] A spy; the act of espying. *Elyot.*

ES'PINEL, *n.* A kind of ruby. [See *Spinel.*]

ES'PIONAGE, *n.* [Fr. from *espionner*, to spy, *espion*, a spy.]
The practice or employment of spies; the practice of watching the words and conduct of others and attempting to make discoveries, as spies or secret emissaries; the practice of watching others without being suspected, and giving intelligence of discoveries made.

ESPLANA'DE, *n.* [Fr. *id.*; Sp. *esplanada*; It. *spianata*; from L. *planus*, plain.]
1. In *fortification*, the glacis of the counterscarp, or the sloping of the parapet of the covered-way towards the country; or the void space between the glacis of a citadel, and the first houses of the town. *Encyc. Bailey.*
2. In *gardening*, a grass-plat.

ESPOUS'AL, *a.* *espouz'al.* [See *Espouse.*] Used in or relating to the act of espousing or betrothing. *Bacon.*

ESPOUS'AL, *n.* The act of espousing or betrothing.
2. Adoption; protection. *Ld. Orford.*

ESPOUS'ALS, *n. plu.* The act of contracting or affiancing a man and woman to each other; a contract or mutual promise of marriage.

> I remember thee, the kindness of thy youth, the love of thine *espousals.* Jer. ii.

ESPOUSE, *v. t.* *espouz'.* [Fr. *epouser*; It. *sposare*; Port. *desposar*; Sp. *desposar*, to marry; *desposarse*, to be betrothed. If this word is the same radically as the L. *spondeo, sponsus*, the letter *n*, in the latter, must be casual, or the modern languages have lost the letter. The former is most probable; in which case, *spondeo* was primarily *spodeo, sposus.*]
1. To betroth.

> When as his mother Mary was *espoused* to Joseph. Matt. i.

2. To betroth; to promise or engage in marriage, by contract in writing, or by some pledge; as, the king *espoused* his daughter to a foreign prince. Usually and properly followed by *to*, rather than *with.*
3. To marry; to wed. *Shak. Milton.*
4. To unite intimately or indissolubly.

> I have *espoused* you to one husband, that I may present you as a chaste virgin to Christ. 2 Cor. xi.

5. To embrace; to take to one's self, with a view to maintain; as, to *espouse* the quarrel of another; to *espouse* a cause. *Dryden.*

ESPOUS'ED, *pp.* Betrothed; affianced; promised in marriage by contract; married; united intimately; embraced.

ESPOUS'ER, *n.* One who espouses; one who defends the cause of another.

ESPOUS'ING, *ppr.* Betrothing; promising in marriage by covenant; marrying; uniting indissolubly; taking part in.

ESPY', *v. t.* [Fr. *epier, espier*; Sp. *espiar*; It. *spiare*; D. *bespieden*, from *spiede*, a spy; G. *spähen*, to spy; Sw. *speia*; Dan. *speider*; W. *yspiaw*, and *yspeithiaw*, from *yspaith, paith.* See *Spy.* The radical letters seem to be *Pd*; if not, the word is a contraction from the root of L. *specio.*]
1. To see at a distance; to have the first sight of a thing remote. Seamen *espy* land as they approach it.
2. To see or discover something intended to be hid, or in a degree concealed and not very visible; as, to *espy* a man in a crowd, or a thief in a wood.
3. To discover unexpectedly.

> As one of them opened his sack, he *espied* his money. Gen. xlii.

4. To inspect narrowly; to examine and make discoveries.

> Moses sent me to *espy* out the land, and I brought him word again. Josh. xiv.

ESPY', *v. i.* To look narrowly; to look about; to watch.

> Stand by the way and *espy.* Jer. xlviii.

[This word is often pronounced *spy*, which see.]

ESPY', *n.* A spy; a scout.

ESQUI'RE, *n.* [Fr. *ecuyer*; It. *scudiere*; Sp. *escudero*; Port. *escudeiro*; from L. *scutum*, a shield, from Gr. σκυτος, a hide, of which shields were anciently made, or from the root of that word, Sax. *sceadan.* See *Shade.*]
Properly, a shield-bearer or armor-bearer, *scutifer*; an attendant on a knight. Hence in modern times, a title of dignity next in degree below a knight. In England, this title is given to the younger sons of noblemen, to officers of the king's courts and of the household, to counselors at law, justices of the peace, while in commission, sheriffs, and other gentlemen. In the United States, the title is given to public officers of all degrees, from governors down to justices and attorneys. Indeed the title, in addressing letters, is bestowed on any person at pleasure, and contains no definite description. It is merely an expression of respect.

ESQUI'RE, *v. t.* To attend; to wait on.

ESSA'Y, *v. t.* [Fr. *essayer*; Norm. *essoyer*; Arm. *æczaca*; D. *zoeken*, to seek; *bezoeken*, *verzoeken*, to essay; G. *suchen*, to seek; *versuchen*, to essay; Dan. *forsöger*; Sw. *försökia*; Sp. *ensayar*; Port. *ensaiar*; It. *saggiare, assaggiare.* The primary word is *seek*, the same as L. *sequor.* See *Seek.* The radical sense is to press, drive, urge, strain, strive, Ch. אסק. Class Sg. No. 46.]
1. To try; to attempt; to endeavor; to exert one's power or faculties, or to make an effort to perform any thing.

> While I this unexampled task *essay.* *Blackmore.*

2. To make experiment of.
3. To try the value and purity of metals. In this application, the word is now more generally written *assay*, which see.

ES'SAY, *n.* A trial; attempt; endeavor; an effort made, or exertion of body or mind, for the performance of any thing. We say, to make an *essay.*

> Fruitless our hopes, though pious our *essays.* *Smith.*

2. In *literature*, a composition intended to prove or illustrate a particular subject; usually shorter and less methodical and finished than a system; as an *essay* on the life and writings of Homer; an *essay* on fossils; an *essay* on commerce.
3. A trial or experiment; as, this is the first *essay.*
4. Trial or experiment to prove the qualities of a metal. [In this sense, see *Assay.*]
5. First taste of any thing. *Dryden.*

ESSA'YED, *pp.* Attempted; tried.

ESSA'YER, *n.* One who writes essays. *Addison.*

ESSA'YING, *ppr.* Trying; making an effort; attempting.

ESSA'YIST, *n.* A writer of an essay, or of essays. *Butler.*

ES'SENCE, *n.* [L. *essentia*; Fr. *essence*; It. *essenza*; Sp. *esencia*; from L. *esse*, to be; Sw. *våsende*; Goth. *wisands*, from *wisan*, Sax. *wesan*, to be, whence *was.* The sense of the verb is, to set, to fix, to be permanent.]
1. That which constitutes the particular nature of a being or substance, or of a genus, and which distinguishes it from all others.

Mr. Locke makes a distinction between *nominal* essence and *real* essence. The *nominal* essence, for example, of gold, is that complex idea expressed by *gold;* the *real* essence is the constitution of its insensible parts, on which its properties depend, which is unknown to us.

The *essence* of God bears no relation to place. *E. D. Griffin.*

2. Formal existence; that which makes any thing to be what it is; or rather, the peculiar nature of a thing; the very substance; as the *essence* of christianity.
3. Existence; the quality of being.

I could have resigned my very *essence.* *Sidney.*

4. A being; an existent person; as heavenly *essences.* *Milton.*
5. Species of being. *Bacon.*
6. Constituent substance; as the pure *essence* of a spirit. [Locke's *real* essence, supra.] *Milton.*
7. The predominant qualities or virtues of any plant or drug, extracted, refined or rectified from grosser matter; or more strictly, a volatile essential oil; as the *essence* of mint.
8. Perfume, odor, scent; or the volatile matter constituting perfume.

Nor let th' imprisoned *essences* exhale. *Pope.*

ES'SENCE, *v. t.* To perfume; to scent.

ES'SENCED, *pp.* Perfumed; as *essenced* fops. *Addison.*

ESSE'NES, *n.* Among the Jews, a sect remarkable for their strictness and abstinence.

ESSEN'TIAL, *a.* [L. *essentialis.*] Necessary to the constitution or existence of a thing. Piety and good works are *essential* to the christian character. Figure and extension are *essential* properties of bodies.

And if each system in gradation roll,
Alike *essential* to the amazing whole— *Pope.*

2. Important in the highest degree.

Judgment is more *essential* to a general than courage. *Denham.*

3. Pure; highly rectified. *Essential* oils are such as are drawn from plants by distillation in an alembic with water, as distinguished from *empyreumatic oils,* which are raised by a naked fire without water. *Encyc.*

ESSEN'TIAL, *n.* Existence; being. [*Little used.*] *Milton.*

2. First or constituent principles; as the *essentials* of religion.
3. The chief point; that which is most important.

ESSENTIAL'ITY, *n.* The quality of being essential; first or constituent principles. *Swift.*

ESSEN'TIALLY, *adv.* By the constitution of nature; in essence; as, minerals and plants are *essentially* different.

2. In an important degree; in effect. The two statements differ, but not *essentially.*

ESSEN'TIATE, *v. i.* To become of the same essence. *B. Jonson.*

ESSEN'TIATE, *v. t.* To form or constitute the essence or being of. *Boyle.*

ESSOIN', *n.* [Norm. *exon,* excuse; Law L. *exonia, sonium;* Old Fr. *exonier, essonier,* to excuse. *Spelman* deduces the word from *ex* and *soing,* care. But qu.]

1. An excuse; the alledging of an excuse for him who is summoned to appear in court and answer, and who neglects to appear at the day. In England, the three first days of a term are called *essoin-days,* as three days are allowed for the appearance of suitors. *Blackstone. Cowel. Spelman.*
2. Excuse; exemption. *Spenser.*
3. He that is excused for non-appearance in court, at the day appointed. *Johnson.*

ESSOIN', *v. t.* To allow an excuse for non-appearance in court; to excuse for absence. *Cowel.*

ESSOIN'ER, *n.* An attorney who sufficiently excuses the absence of another.

ESTAB'LISH, *v. t.* [Fr. *etablir;* Sp. *establecer;* Port. *estabelecer;* It. *stabilire;* L. *stabilio;* Heb. יצב or נצב; Ch. Syr. id.; Ar. نَصَبَ to set, fix, establish. Class Sb. No. 37. and see No. 35. See also Ar. وَتَبَ Ch. יתב to settle, to place, to dwell. Class Db. No. 53. 54.]

1. To set and fix firmly or unalterably; to settle permanently.

I will *establish* my covenant with him for an everlasting covenant. Gen. xvii.

2. To found permanently; to erect and fix or settle; as, to *establish* a colony or an empire.
3. To enact or decree by authority and for permanence; to ordain; to appoint; as, to *establish* laws, regulations, institutions, rules, ordinances, &c.
4. To settle or fix; to confirm; as, to *establish* a person, society or corporation, in possessions or privileges.
5. To make firm; to confirm; to ratify what has been previously set or made.

Do we then make void the law through faith? God forbid: yea, we *establish* the law. Rom. iii.

6. To settle or fix what is wavering, doubtful or weak; to confirm.

So were the churches *established* in the faith. Acts xvi.

To the end he may *establish* your hearts unblamable in holiness. 1 Thess. iii.

7. To confirm; to fulfill; to make good.

Establish thy word to thy servant. Ps. cxix.

8. To set up in the place of another and confirm.

Who go about to *establish* their own righteousness. Rom. x.

ESTAB'LISHED, *pp.* Set; fixed firmly; founded; ordained; enacted; ratified; confirmed.

ESTAB'LISHER, *n.* He who establishes, ordains or confirms.

ESTAB'LISHING, *ppr.* Fixing; settling permanently; founding; ratifying; confirming; ordaining.

ESTAB'LISHMENT, *n.* [Fr. *etablissement.*] The act of establishing, founding, ratifying or ordaining.

2. Settlement; fixed state. *Spenser.*
3. Confirmation; ratification of what has been settled or made. *Bacon.*
4. Settled regulation; form; ordinance; system of laws; constitution of government.

Bring in that *establishment* by which all men should be contained in duty. *Spenser.*

5. Fixed or stated allowance for subsistence; income; salary.

His excellency—might gradually lessen your *establishment.* *Swift.*

6. That which is fixed or established; as a permanent military force, a fixed garrison, a local government, an agency, a factory, &c. The king has *establishments* to support, in the four quarters of the globe. *G. Britain.*
7. The episcopal form of religion, so called in England.
8. Settlement or final rest.

We set up our hopes and *establishment* here. *Wake.*

ESTAFET', *n.* [Sp. *estafeta.*] A military courier. [See *Staff.*]

ESTA'TE, *n.* [Fr. *etat,* for *estat;* D. *staat;* G. *staat;* Arm. *stad;* It. *stato;* Sp. *estado;* L. *status,* from *sto,* to stand. The roots *stb, std* and *stg,* have nearly the same signification, to set, to fix. It is probable that the L. *sto* is contracted from *stad,* as it forms *steti.* See Ar. وَصَدَ Class Sd. No. 46. and Class Dd. No. 22. 23. 24.]

1. In a general sense, fixedness; a fixed condition; now generally written and pronounced *state.*

She cast us headlong from our high *estate.* *Dryden.*

2. Condition or circumstances of any person or thing, whether high or low. Luke i.
3. Rank; quality.

Who hath not heard of the greatness of your *estate?* *Sidney.*

4. In *law,* the interest, or quantity of interest, a man has in lands, tenements, or other effects. *Estates* are *real* or *personal.* *Real* estate consists in lands or freeholds, which descend to heirs; *personal* estate consists in chattels or movables, which go to executors and administrators. There are also *estates* for life, for years, at will, &c.
5. Fortune; possessions; property in general. He is a man of a great *estate.* He left his *estate* unincumbered.
6. The general business or interest of government; hence, a political body; a commonwealth; a republic. But in this sense, we now use *State.*

Estates, in the plural, dominions; possessions of a prince.

2. Orders or classes of men in society or government. Herod made a supper for his chief *estates.* Mark vi.

In Great Britain, the *estates* of the realm are the king, lords and commons; or rather the lords and commons.

ESTA'TE, *v. t.* To settle as a fortune. [*Little used.*] *Shak.*

2. To establish. [*Little used.*]

ESTA'TED, *pp.* or *a.* Possessing an estate. *Swift.*

ESTEE'M, *v. t.* [Fr. *estimer;* It. *estimare;* Sp. Port. *estimar;* Arm. *istimout, istimein;* L. *æstimo;* Gr. ἐιςιμαομαι; εις and τιμαω, to honor or esteem. See Class Dm. No. 28.]

1. To set a value on, whether high or low; to estimate; to value.

Then he forsook God who made him, and lightly *esteemed* the rock of his salvation. Deut. xxxii.

They that despise me shall be lightly *esteemed.* 1 Sam. ii.

2. To prize; to set a high value on; to re-

gard with reverence, respect or friendship. When our minds are not biased, we always *esteem* the industrious, the generous, the brave, the virtuous, and the learned.

Will he *esteem* thy riches? Job xxxvi.

3. To hold in opinion; to repute; to think.

One man *esteemeth* one day above another: another *esteemeth* every day alike. Rom. xiv.

4. To compare in value; to estimate by proportion. [*Little used.*] *Davies.*

ESTEE'M, *n.* Estimation; opinion or judgment of merit or demerit. This man is of no worth in my *esteem.*

2. High value or estimation; great regard; favorable opinion, founded on supposed worth.

Both those poets lived in much *esteem* with good and holy men in orders. *Dryden.*

ESTEE'MABLE, *a.* Worthy of esteem; estimable.

ESTEE'MED, *pp.* Valued; estimated; highly valued or prized on account of worth; thought; held in opinion.

ESTEE'MER, *n.* One who esteems; one who sets a high value on any thing.

A proud *esteemer* of his own parts. *Locke.*

ESTEE'MING, *ppr.* Valuing; estimating; valuing highly; prizing; thinking; deeming.

ES'TIMABLE, *a.* [Fr.; It. *estimevole.*]

1. That is capable of being estimated or valued; as *estimable* damage. *Paley.*

2. Valuable; worth a great price.

A pound of man's flesh, taken from a man,
Is not so *estimable* or profitable. *Shak.*

3. Worthy of esteem or respect; deserving our good opinion or regard.

A lady said of her two companions, that one was more amiable, the other more *estimable.* *Temple.*

ES'TIMABLE, *n.* That which is worthy of regard. *Brown.*

ES'TIMABLENESS, *n.* The quality of deserving esteem or regard. *R. Newton.*

ES'TIMATE, *v. t.* [L. *æstimo.* See *Esteem.*]

1. To judge and form an opinion of the value of; to rate by judgment or opinion, without weighing or measuring either value, degree, extent or quantity. We *estimate* the value of cloth by inspection, or the extent of a piece of land, or the distance of a mountain. We *estimate* the worth of a friend by his known qualities. We *estimate* the merits or talents of two different men by judgment. We *estimate* profits, loss and damage. Hence,

2. To compute; to calculate; to reckon.

ES'TIMATE, *n.* A valuing or rating in the mind; a judgment or opinion of the value, degree, extent or quantity of any thing, without ascertaining it. We form *estimates* of the expenses of a war, of the probable outfits of a voyage, of the comparative strength or merits of two men, of the extent of a kingdom or its population. Hence *estimate* may be equivalent to calculation, computation, without measuring or weighing.

2. Value. *Shak.*

ES'TIMATED, *pp.* Valued; rated in opinion or judgment.

ES'TIMATING, *ppr.* Valuing; rating; forming an opinion or judgment of the value, extent, quantity, or degree of worth of any object; calculating; computing.

ESTIMA'TION, *n.* [L. *æstimatio.*] The act of estimating.

2. Calculation; computation; an opinion or judgment of the worth, extent or quantity of any thing, formed without using precise data. We may differ in our *estimations* of distance, magnitude or amount, and no less in our *estimation* of moral qualities.

3. Esteem; regard; favorable opinion; honor.

I shall have *estimation* among the multitude, and honor with the elders. *Wisdom.*

ES'TIMATIVE, *a.* Having the power of comparing and adjusting the worth or preference. [*Little used.*] *Hale. Boyle.*

2. Imaginative.

ES'TIMATOR, *n.* One who estimates or values.

ES'TIVAL, *a.* [L. *æstivus,* from *æstas,* summer. See *Heat.*]

Pertaining to summer, or continuing for the summer.

ES'TIVATE, *v. i.* To pass the summer.

ESTIVA'TION, *n.* [L. *æstivatio,* from *æstas,* summer, *æstivo,* to pass the summer.]

1. The act of passing the summer. *Bacon.*

2. In *botany,* the disposition of the petals within the floral gem or bud; 1. *convolute,* when the petals are rolled together like a scroll; 2. *imbricate,* when they lie over each other like tiles on a roof; 3. *conduplicate,* when they are doubled together at the midrib; 4. *valvate,* when as they are about to expand they are placed like the glumes in grasses. *Martyn.*

ESTOP', *v. t.* [Fr. *etouper,* to *stop.* See *Stop.*] In *law,* to impede or bar, by one's own act.

A man shall always be *estopped* by his own deed, or not permitted to aver or prove any thing in contradiction to what he has once solemnly avowed. *Blackstone.*

ESTOP'PED, *pp.* Hindered; barred; precluded by one's own act.

ESTOP'PING, *ppr.* Impeding; barring by one's own act.

ESTOP'PEL, *n.* In *law,* a stop; a plea in bar, grounded on a man's own act or deed, which *estops* or precludes him from averring any thing to the contrary.

If a tenant for years levies a fine to another person, it shall work as an *estoppel* to the cognizor. *Blackstone.*

ESTO'VERS, *n.* [Norm. *estoffer,* to store, stock, furnish; *estuffeures,* stores; Fr. *etoffer,* to *stuff.* See *Stuff.*]

In *law,* necessaries, or supplies; a reasonable allowance out of lands or goods for the use of a tenant; such as sustenance of a felon in prison, and for his family, during his imprisonment; alimony for a woman divorced, out of her husband's estate. *Common of estovers* is the liberty of taking the necessary wood for the use or furniture of a house or farm, from another's estate. In Saxon, it is expressed by *bote,* which signifies more or supply, as *house-bote, plow-bote, fire-bote, cart-bote,* &c. *Blackstone.*

ESTRA'DE, *n.* [Fr.] An even or level place. *Dict.*

ESTRANGE, *v. t.* [Fr. *etranger.* See *Strange.*]

1. To keep at a distance; to withdraw; to cease to frequent and be familiar with.

Had we *estranged* ourselves from them in things indifferent. *Hooker.*

I thus *estrange* my person from her bed. *Dryden.*

2. To alienate; to divert from its original use or possessor; to apply to a purpose foreign from its original or customary one.

They have *estranged* this place, and burnt incense in it to other gods. Jer. xix.

3. To alienate, as the affections; to turn from kindness to indifference or malevolence.

I do not know, to this hour, what it is that has *estranged* him from me. *Pope.*

4. To withdraw; to withhold.

We must *estrange* our belief from what is not clearly evidenced. *Glanville.*

ESTRANGED, *pp.* Withdrawn; withheld; alienated.

ESTRANGEMENT, *n.* Alienation; a keeping at a distance; removal; voluntary abstraction; as an *estrangement* of affection.

An *estrangement* of desires from better things. *South.*

ESTRANGING, *ppr.* Alienating; withdrawing; keeping at or removing to a distance.

ESTRAPA'DE, *n.* [Fr. strappado.] The defense of a horse that will not obey, and which, to get rid of his rider, rises before and yerks furiously with his hind legs. *Farrier's Dict.*

ESTRA'Y, *v. i.* To stray. [See *Stray.*]

ESTRA'Y, *n.* [Norm. *estrayer,* probably allied to *straggle,* and perhaps from the root of W. *trag,* beyond.]

A tame beast, as a horse, ox or sheep, which is found wandering or without an owner; a beast supposed to have strayed from the power or inclosure of its owner. It is usually written *stray.* *Blackstone.*

ESTRE'AT, *n.* [Norm. *estraite* or *estreite,* from L. *extractum, extraho,* to draw out.]

In *law,* a true copy or duplicate of an original writing, especially of amercements or penalties set down in the rolls of court to be levied by the bailiff or other officer, on every offender. *Cowel. Encyc.*

ESTRE'AT, *v. i.* To extract; to copy. *Blackstone.*

ESTRE'ATED, *pp.* Extracted; copied.

ESTRE'PEMENT, *n.* [Norm. *estreper, estripper,* to waste; Eng. to *strip.*]

In *law,* spoil; waste; a *stripping* of land by a tenant, to the prejudice of the owner. *Blackstone. Cowel.*

ES'TRICH, *n.* The ostrich, which see.

ES'TUANCE, *n.* [L. *æstus.*] Heat. [*Not in use.*] *Brown.*

ES'TUARY, *n.* [L. *æstuarium,* from *æstuo,* to boil or foam, *æstus,* heat, fury, storm.]

1. An arm of the sea; a frith; a narrow passage, or the mouth of a river or lake, where the tide meets the current, or flows and ebbs.

2. A vapor-bath.

ES'TUATE, *v. i.* [L. *æstuo,* to boil.] To boil; to swell and rage; to be agitated.

ESTUA'TION, *n.* A boiling; agitation; commotion of a fluid. *Brown. Norris.*

ES'TURE, *n.* [L. *æstuo.*] Violence; commotion. [*Not used.*] *Chapman.*

ESU'RIENT, *a.* [L. *esuriens, esurio.*] Inclined to eat; hungry. *Dict.*

ES'URINE, *a.* Eating; corroding. [*Little used.*] *Wiseman.*

ET CÆTERA, and the contraction *etc.,* denote the rest, or others of the kind; and so on; and so forth.

ETCH, *v. t.* [G. *etzen*, D. *etsen*, to *eat*. See *Eat.*]

1. To make prints on copper-plate by means of lines or strokes first drawn, and then eaten or corroded by nitric acid. The plate is first covered with a proper varnish or ground, which is capable of resisting the acid, and the ground is then scored or scratched by a needle or similar instrument, in the places where the hatchings or engravings are intended to be; the plate is then covered with nitric acid, which corrodes or eats the metal in the lines thus laid bare. *Encyc.*
2. To sketch; to delineate. [*Not in use.*] *Locke.*

ETCH'ED, *pp.* Marked and corroded by nitric acid.

ETCH'ING, *ppr.* Marking or making prints with nitric acid.

ETCH'ING, *n.* The impression taken from an etched copper-plate.

ETEOS'TIC, *n.* [Gr. ετεος, true, and στιχος, a verse.]

A chronogrammatical composition. *B. Jonson.*

ETERN', *a.* Eternal; perpetual; endless. [*Not used.*] *Shak.*

ETER'NAL, *a.* [Fr. *eternel*; L. *æternus*, composed of *ævum* and *ternus*, *æviternus*. *Varro.* The origin of the last component part of the word is not obvious. It occurs in *diuturnus*, and seems to denote continuance.]

1. Without beginning or end of existence.

   The *eternal* God is thy refuge. Deut. xxxiii.

2. Without beginning of existence.

   To know whether there is any real being, whose duration has been *eternal*. *Locke.*

3. Without end of existence or duration; everlasting; endless; immortal.

   That they may obtain the salvation which is in Christ Jesus with *eternal* glory. 2 Tim. ii.

   What shall I do, that I may have *eternal* life? Matt. xix.

   Suffering the vengeance of *eternal* fire. Jude 7.

4. Perpetual; ceaseless; continued without intermission.

   And fires *eternal* in thy temple shine. *Dryden.*

5. Unchangeable; existing at all times without change; as *eternal* truth.

ETER'NAL, *n.* An appellation of God. *Hooker. Milton.*

ETER'NALIST, *n.* One who holds the past existence of the world to be infinite. *Burnet.*

ETER'NALIZE, *v. t.* To make eternal; to give endless duration to. [We now use *eternize.*]

ETER'NALLY, *adv.* Without beginning or end of duration, or without end only.

2. Unchangeably; invariably; at all times.

   That which is morally good must be *eternally* and unchangeably so. *South.*

3. Perpetually; without intermission; at all times.

   Where western gales *eternally* reside. *Addison.*

ETER'NITY, *n.* [L. *æternitas.*] Duration or continuance without beginning or end.

By repeating the idea of any length of duration, with the endless addition of number, we come by the idea of *eternity*. *Locke.*

The high and lofty one who inhabiteth *eternity*. Is. lvii.

We speak of eternal duration preceding the present time. God has existed from *eternity*. We also speak of endless or everlasting duration in future, and dating from present time or the present state of things. Some men doubt the *eternity* of future punishment, though they have less difficulty in admitting the *eternity* of future rewards.

ETER'NIZE, *v. t.* [Fr. *eterniser*; Sp. *eternizar*; It. *eternare*; Low L. *æterno.*]

1. To make endless.
2. To continue the existence or duration of indefinitely; to perpetuate; as, to *eternize* woe. *Milton.*

   So we say, to *eternize* fame or glory.

3. To make forever famous; to immortalize; as, to *eternize* a name; to *eternize* exploits.

ETER'NIZED, *pp.* Made endless; immortalized.

ETER'NIZING, *ppr.* Giving endless duration to; immortalizing.

ETE'SIAN, *a. ete'zhan.* [L. *etesius*; Gr. ετησιος, from ετος, a year. Qu. Eth. ዐወደ owed, awed, a circuit or circle, and the verb, to go round.]

Stated; blowing at stated times of the year; periodical. *Etesian* winds are yearly or anniversary winds, answering to the monsoons of the East Indies. The word is applied, in Greek and Roman writers, to the periodical winds in the Mediterranean, from whatever quarter they blow. *Encyc.*

ETHE, *a.* Easy. *Obs.* *Chaucer.*

E'THEL, *a.* Noble. *Obs.*

E'THER, *n.* [L. *æther*; Gr. αιθηρ, αιθω, to burn, to shine; Eng. *weather*; Sax. *wæder*, the air; D. *weder*; G. *wetter*; Sw. *våder.*]

1. A thin, subtil matter, much finer and rarer than air, which, some philosophers suppose, begins from the limits of the atmosphere and occupies the heavenly space. *Newton.*

   There fields of light and liquid *ether* flow. *Dryden.*

2. In *chimistry*, a very light, volatile and inflammable fluid, produced by the distillation of alcohol or rectified spirit of wine, with an acid. It is lighter than alcohol, of a strong sweet smell, susceptible of great expansion, and of a pungent taste. It is so volatile, that when shaken it is dissipated in an instant. *Encyc. Fourcroy.*

ETHE'REAL, *a.* Formed of ether; containing or filled with ether; as *ethereal* space; *ethereal* regions.

2. Heavenly; celestial; as *ethereal* messenger.
3. Consisting of ether or spirit.

   Vast chain of being, which from God began,
   Natures *ethereal*, human, angel, man. *Pope.*

ETHE'REOUS, *a.* Formed of ether; heavenly. *Milton.*

E'THERIZE, *v. t.* To convert into ether. *Med. Repos.*

E'THERIZED, *pp.* Converted into ether.

E'THERIZING, *ppr.* Converting into ether.

ETH'IC, ETH'ICAL, *a.* [L. *ethicus*; Gr. ηθικος, from ηθος, manners.]

Relating to manners or morals; treating of morality; delivering precepts of morality; as *ethic* discourses or epistles.

ETH'ICALLY, *adv.* According to the doctrines of morality.

ETH'ICS, *n.* The doctrines of morality or social manners; the science of moral philosophy, which teaches men their duty and the reasons of it. *Paley. Encyc.*

2. A system of moral principles; a system of rules for regulating the actions and manners of men in society.

Ethiops martial, black oxyd of iron; iron in the form of a very fine powder, and in the first stage of calcination.

Ethiops mineral, a combination of mercury and sulphur, of a black color; black sulphuret of mercury. *Thomson. Nicholson.*

ETH'MOID, ETHMOID'AL, *a.* [Gr. ηθμος, a sieve, and ειδος, form.] Resembling a sieve.

ETH'MOID, *n.* A bone at the top of the root of the nose.

ETH'NIC, ETH'NICAL, *a.* [L. *ethnicus*; Gr. εθνικος, from εθνος, nation, from the root of G. *heide*, heath, woods, whence *heathen*. See *Heathen.*]

Heathen; pagan; pertaining to the gentiles or nations not converted to christianity; opposed to *Jewish* and *Christian*.

ETH'NIC, *n.* A heathen; a pagan.

ETH'NICISM, *n.* Heathenism; paganism; idolatry. *B. Jonson.*

ETHNOL'OGY, *n.* [Gr. εθνος, nation, and λογος, discourse.] A treatise on nations.

ETHOLOG'ICAL, *a.* [See *Ethology.*] Treating of ethics or morality.

ETHOL'OGIST, *n.* One who writes on the subject of manners and morality.

ETHOL'OGY, *n.* [Gr. εθος, or ηθος, manners, morals, and λογος, discourse.]

A treatise on morality or the science of ethics. *Owen. Lunier.*

E'TIOLATE, *v. i.* [Gr. αιθω, to shine.] To become white or whiter; to be whitened by excluding the light of the sun, as plants.

E'TIOLATE, *v. t.* To blanch; to whiten by excluding the sun's rays.

E'TIOLATED, *pp.* Blanched; whitened by excluding the sun's rays.

E'TIOLATING, *ppr.* Blanching; whitening by excluding the sun's rays.

ETIOLA'TION, *n.* The operation of being whitened or of becoming white by excluding the light of the sun. *Fourcroy. Darwin.*

In *gardening*, the rendering plants white, crisp and tender, by excluding the action of light from them. *Cyc.*

ETIOLOG'ICAL, *a.* Pertaining to etiology. *Arbuthnot.*

ETIOL'OGY, *n.* [Gr. αιτια, cause, and λογος, discourse.]

An account of the causes of any thing, particularly of diseases. *Quincy.*

ETIQUET', *n. etiket'.* [Fr. *etiquette*, a ticket; W. *tocyn*, a little piece or slip, from *tociaw*, to cut off, Eng. to *dock*. Originally, a little piece of paper, or a mark or title, affixed to a bag or bundle, expressing its contents.]

Primarily, an account of ceremonies. Hence in present usage, forms of ceremony or decorum; the forms which are observed towards particular persons, or in particular places, especially in courts, levees, and on public occasions. From the original sense of the word, it may be inferred that it was formerly the custom to deliver cards containing orders for regulating ceremonies on public occasions.

E'TITE, *n.* [Gr. αετος, an eagle.] Eagle-stone, a variety of bog iron. [See *Eagle-stone.*]

ETNE'AN, *a.* [from *Ætna.*] Pertaining to Etna, a volcanic mountain in Sicily.

ET'TIN, *n.* A giant. *Obs.* *Beaum.*

ET'TLE, *v. t.* To earn. [*Not in use.*] *Boucher.*

ETUI, ETWEE', ETWEE'-CASE, } *n.* [Fr. *etui*, a case.] A case for pocket instruments.

ETYMOL'OĠER, *n.* An etymologist. [*Not in use.*] *Griffith.*

ETYMOLOĠ'ICAL, *a.* [See *Etymology.*] Pertaining to etymology or the derivation of words; according to or by means of etymology. *Locke.*

ETYMOLOĠ'ICALLY, *adv.* According to etymology.

ETYMOL'OĠIST, *n.* One versed in etymology or the deduction of words from their originals; one who searches into the original of words.

ETYMOL'OĠIZE, *v. i.* To search into the origin of words; to deduce words from their simple roots. *Encyc.*

ETYMOL'OĠY, *n.* [Gr. ετυμος, true, and λογος, discourse.]

1. That part of philology which explains the origin and derivation of words, with a view to ascertain their radical or primary signification.

In *grammar*, etymology comprehends the various inflections and modifications of words, and shows how they are formed from their simple roots.

2. The deduction of words from their originals; the analysis of compound words into their primitives.

ET'YMON, *n.* [Gr. ετυμον, from ετυμος, true.] An original root, or primitive word.

EU'CHARIST, *n.* [Gr. ευχαριστια, a giving of thanks; ευ, well, and χαρις, favor.]

1. The sacrament of the Lord's supper; the solemn act or ceremony of commemorating the death of our Redeemer, in the use of bread and wine, as emblems of his flesh and blood, accompanied with appropriate prayers and hymns.

2. The act of giving thanks.

EUCHARIS'TIC, EUCHARIS'TICAL, } *a.* Containing expressions of thanks. *Brown.*

2. Pertaining to the Lord's supper.

Euchloric gas, the same as *euchlorine.* *Davy.*

EUCHLO'RINE, *n.* [See *Chlorine.*] In *chimistry*, protoxyd of chlorine. *Davy. Ure.*

EUCHOL'OĠY, *n.* [Gr. ευχολογιον; ευχη, prayer or vow, and λογος, discourse.]

A formulary of prayers; the Greek ritual, in which are prescribed the order of ceremonies, sacraments and ordinances. *Encyc.*

EU'CHYMY, *n.* [Gr. ευχυμια.] A good state of the blood and other fluids of the body.

EUCHYSID'ERITE, *n.* A mineral, considered as a variety of augite. *Phillips.*

EU'CLASE, *n.* [Gr. ευ and κλαω, to break; easily broken.]

A mineral, a species of emerald, prismatic emerald, of a greenish white, apple or mountain green, bluish green, or dark sky blue color. It is a rare mineral, and remarkably brittle, whence its name. *Cleaveland. Jameson.*

EU'CRASY, *n.* [Gr. ευ, well, and κρασις, temperament.]

In *medicine*, such a due or well proportioned mixture of qualities in bodies, as to constitute health or soundness. *Quincy. Encyc.*

EU'DIALYTE, *n.* A mineral of a brownish red color. *Jameson.*

EUDIOM'ETER, *n.* [Gr. ευδιος, serene, ευ and διος, Jove, air, and μετρον, measure.]

An instrument for ascertaining the purity of the air, or the quantity of oxygen it contains. *Encyc. Ure.*

EUDIOMET'RIC, EUDIOMET'RICAL, } *a.* Pertaining to an eudiometer; performed or ascertained by an eudiometer; as *eudiometrical* experiments or results.

EUDIOM'ETRY, *n.* The art or practice of ascertaining the purity of the air by the eudiometer.

EU'ĠE, *n.* Applause. [*Not used.*] *Hammond.*

EUGH, a tree. [See *Yew.*]

EUHARMON'IC, *a.* [Gr. ευ, well, and *harmonic.*]

Producing harmony or concordant sounds; as the *euharmonic* organ. *Liston.*

EUK'AIRITE, *n.* [Gr. ευκαιρος, opportune.] Cupreous seleniuret of silver, a mineral of a shining lead gray color and granular structure. *Cleaveland.*

EULOĠ'IC, EULOĠ'ICAL, } *a.* [See *Eulogy.*] Containing praise; commendatory.

EU'LOĠIST, *n.* [See *Eulogy.*] One who praises and commends another; one who writes or speaks in commendation of another, on account of his excellent qualities, exploits or performances.

EULO'ĠIUM, *n.* An eulogy.

EU'LOĠIZE, *v. t.* [See *Eulogy.*] To praise; to speak or write in commendation of another; to extol in speech or writing.

EU'LOĠIZED, *pp.* Praised; commended.

EU'LOĠIZING, *ppr.* Commending; writing or speaking in praise of.

EU'LOĠY, *n.* [Gr. ευλογια; ευ and λογος.] Praise; encomium; panegyric; a speech or writing in commendation of a person, on account of his valuable qualities, or services.

EU'NOMY, *n.* [Gr. ευνομια; ευ and νομος, law.]

Equal law, or a well adjusted constitution of government. *Mitford.*

EU'NUCH, *n.* [Gr. ευνουχος; ευνη, a bed, and εχω, to keep.] A male of the human species castrated.

EU'NUCHATE, *v. t.* To make a eunuch; to castrate.

EU'NUCHISM, *n.* The state of being an eunuch.

EU'PATHY, *n.* [Gr. ευπαθεια.] Right feeling. *Harris.*

EU'PATORY, *n.* [L. *eupatorium*; Gr. ευπατοριον.] The plant hemp agrimony.

EUPEP'SY, *n.* [Gr. ευπεψια; ευ and πεψις, concoction.]

Good concoction in the stomach; good digestion.

EUPEP'TIC, *a.* Having good digestion.

EU'PHEMISM, *n.* [Gr. ευφημισμος; ευ, well, and φημι, to speak.]

A representation of good qualities; particularly in *rhetoric*, a figure in which a harsh or indelicate word or expression is softened, or rather by which a delicate word or expression is substituted for one which is offensive to good manners or to delicate ears. *Ash. Campbell.*

EUPHON'IC, EUPHON'ICAL, } *a.* [See *Euphony.*] Agreeable in sound; pleasing to the ear; as *euphonical* orthography. *Colebrooke.*

The Greeks adopted many changes in the combination of syllables to render their language *euphonic*, by avoiding such collisions. *E. Porter.*

EU'PHONY, *n.* [Gr. ευφωνια; ευ and φωνη, voice.]

An agreeable sound; an easy, smooth enunciation of sounds; a pronunciation of letters and syllables which is pleasing to the ear.

EUPHOR'BIA, *n.* [Gr. ευφορβια, with a different signification.]

In *botany*, spurge, or bastard spurge, a genus of plants of many species, mostly shrubby herbaceous succulents, some of them armed with thorns. *Encyc.*

EUPHOR'BIUM, *n.* [L. from Gr. ευφορβιον, Ar. فربيون forbion.]

In *the materia medica*, a gummi-resinous substance, exuding from an oriental tree. It has a sharp biting taste, and is vehemently acrimonious, inflaming and ulcerating the fauces. *Encyc.*

EU'PHOTIDE, *n.* A name given by the French to the aggregate of diallage and saussurite. *Cleaveland.*

EU'PHRASY, *n.* [According to De Theis, this word is contracted from *euphrosyne*, ευφροσυνη, joy, pleasure; a name given to the plant on account of its wonderful effects in curing disorders of the eyes.]

Eyebright, a genus of plants, Euphrasia, called in French *casse-lunette.*

EU'RIPUS, *n.* [Gr. ευριπος; L. *Euripus.*]

A strait; a narrow tract of water, where the tide or a current flows and reflows, as that in Greece, between Eubœa and Attica, or Eubœa and Bœotia. It is sometimes used for a strait or frith much agitated. *Burke.*

EU'RITE, *n.* The white stone [weiss stein] of Werner; a very small-grained granite, with the parts intimately blended, and hence often apparently compact. It is gray, red, &c., according to the color of the felspar, of which it is principally composed. *Geol. Primer.*

Whitestone is a finely granular felspar, containing grains of quartz and scales of mica. *Cleaveland.*

EUROC'LYDON, *n.* [Gr. ευρος, wind, and κλυδων, a wave.]

A tempestuous wind, which drove ashore, on Malta, the ship in which Paul was sailing to Italy. It is supposed to have blown from an easterly point. Acts xxvii. *Encyc.*

EU'ROPE, *n.* [Bochart supposes this word to be composed of חור אפא white face, the land of white people, as distinguished from the Ethiopians, black-faced people, or tawny inhabitants of Asia and Africa.]

The great quarter of the earth that lies between the Atlantic ocean and Asia, and between the Mediterranean sea and the North sea.

EUROPE'AN, *a.* Pertaining to Europe.

EUROPE'AN, *n.* A native of Europe.

EU'RUS, *n.* [L.] The east wind.

EU'RYTHMY, *n.* [Gr. ευ and ρυθμος, *rythmus*, number or proportion.]

In *architecture*, *painting* and *sculpture*, ease, majesty and elegance of the parts of a body, arising from just proportions in the composition. *Encyc.*

EUSE'BIAN, *n.* An Arian, so called from one Eusebius.

EU'STȲLE, *n.* [Gr. ευ and ϛυλος, a column.] In *architecture*, a sort of building in which the columns are placed at the most convenient distances from each other, the intercolumniations being just two diameters and a quarter of the column, except those in the middle of the face, before and behind, which are three diameters distant. *Encyc.*

EU'THANASY, *n.* [Gr. ευθανασια; ευ and θανατος, death.] An easy death. *Arbuthnot.*

EUTYCH'IAN, *n.* A follower of Eutychius, who denied the two natures of Christ.

EUTYCH'IANISM, *n.* The doctrines of Eutychius, who denied the two natures of Christ.

EVA'CATE, *v. t.* [L. *vaco.*] To empty. [*Not in use.*] *Harvey.*

EVAC'UANT, *a.* [L. *evacuans.*] Emptying; freeing from.

EVAC'UANT, *n.* A medicine which procures evacuations, or promotes the natural secretions and excretions.

EVAC'UATE, *v. t.* [L. *evacuo; e* and *vacuus*, from *vaco*, to empty. See *Vacant.*]

1. To make empty; to free from any thing contained; as, to *evacuate* the church. *Hooker.*

2. To throw out; to eject; to void; to discharge; as, to *evacuate* dark-colored matter from the bowels. Hence,

3. To empty; to free from contents, or to diminish the quantity contained; as, to *evacuate* the bowels; to *evacuate* the vessels by bleeding.

4. To quit; to withdraw from a place. The British army *evacuated* the city of New-York, November 25, 1783.

5. To make void; to nullify; as, to *evacuate* a marriage or any contract. [In this sense, *vacate* is now generally used.]

EVAC'UATED, *pp.* Emptied; cleared; freed from the contents; quitted, as by an army or garrison; ejected; discharged; vacated.

EVAC'UATING, *ppr.* Emptying; making void or vacant; withdrawing from.

EVACUA'TION, *n.* The act of emptying or clearing of the contents; the act of withdrawing from, as an army or garrison.

2. Discharges by stool or other natural means; a diminution of the fluids of an animal body by cathartics, venesection, or other means. *Quincy.*

3. Abolition; nullification.

EVAC'UATIVE, *a.* That evacuates.

EVAC'UATOR, *n.* One that makes void. *Hammond.*

EVA'DE, *v. t.* [L. *evado; e* and *vado*, to go; Sp. *evadir;* Fr. *evader.*]

1. To avoid by dexterity. The man *evaded* the blow aimed at his head.

2. To avoid or escape by artifice or stratagem; to slip away; to elude. The thief *evaded* his pursuers.

3. To elude by subterfuge, sophistry, address or ingenuity. The advocate *evades* an argument or the force of an argument.

4. To escape as imperceptible or not to be reached or seized. *South.*

EVA'DE, *v. i.* To escape; to slip away; formerly and properly with *from;* as, to *evade from* perils. But *from* is now seldom used.

2. To attempt to escape; to practice artifice or sophistry for the purpose of eluding.

The ministers of God are not to *evade* and take refuge in any such ways. *South.*

EVA'DED, *pp.* Avoided; eluded.

EVA'DING, *ppr.* Escaping; avoiding; eluding; slipping away from danger, pursuit or attack.

EVAGA'TION, *n.* [L. *evagatio, evagor; e* and *vagor*, to wander.]

The act of wandering; excursion; a roving or rambling. *Ray.*

E'VAL, *a.* [L. *ævum.*] Relating to time or duration. [*Not in use.*]

EVANES'CENCE, *n.* [L. *evanescens*, from *evanesco; e* and *vanesco*, to vanish, from *vanus*, vain, empty. See *Vain.*]

1. A vanishing; a gradual departure from sight or possession, either by removal to a distance, or by dissipation, as vapor.

2. The state of being liable to vanish and escape possession.

EVANES'CENT, *a.* Vanishing; subject to vanishing; fleeting; passing away; liable to dissipation, like vapor, or to become imperceptible. The pleasures and joys of life are *evanescent.*

EVAN'GEL, *n.* [L. *evangelium.*] The gospel. [*Not in use.*] *Chaucer.*

EVANGE'LIAN, *a.* Rendering thanks for favors. *Mitford.*

EVANGEL'IC, EVANGEL'ICAL, *a.* [Low L. *evangelicus*, from *evangelium*, the gospel; Gr. ευαγγελικος, from ευαγγελιον; ευ, well, good, and αγγελλω, to announce, Ir. *agalla*, to tell, to speak, Ar. قال to tell, Class Gl. No. 49, or Ch. כלא, אכלי, to call, No. 36.]

1. According to the gospel; consonant to the doctrines and precepts of the gospel, published by Christ and his apostles; as *evangelical* righteousness, obedience or piety.

2. Contained in the gospel; as an *evangelical* doctrine.

3. Sound in the doctrines of the gospel; orthodox; as an *evangelical* preacher.

EVANGEL'ICALLY, *adv.* In a manner according to the gospel.

EVAN'GELISM, *n.* The promulgation of the gospel. *Bacon.*

EVAN'GELIST, *n.* A writer of the history, or doctrines, precepts, actions, life and death of our blessed Savior, Jesus Christ; as the four *evangelists*, Matthew, Mark, Luke and John.

2. A preacher or publisher of the gospel of Jesus Christ, licensed to preach, but not having charge of a particular church.

EVAN'GELISTARY, *n.* A selection of passages from the gospels, as a lesson in divine service. *Gregory.*

EVANGELIZA'TION, *n.* The act of evangelizing.

EVAN'GELIZE, *v. t.* [Low L. *evangelizo.*] To instruct in the gospel; to preach the gospel to, and convert to a belief of the gospel; as, to *evangelize* heathen nations; to *evangelize* the world. *Milner. Buchanan.*

EVAN'GELIZE, *v. i.* To preach the gospel.

EVAN'GELIZED, *pp.* Instructed in the gospel; converted to a belief of the gospel, or to christianity.

EVAN'GELIZING, *ppr.* Instructing in the doctrines and precepts of the gospel; converting to christianity.

EVAN'GELY, *n.* Good tidings; the gospel. [*Not in use.*] *Spenser.*

EVAN'ID, *a.* [L. *evanidus.* See *Vain.*] Faint; weak; evanescent; liable to vanish or disappear; as an *evanid* color or smell. *Bacon. Encyc.*

EVAN'ISH, *v. i.* [L. *evanesco.* See *Vain.*] To vanish; to disappear; to escape from sight or perception. [*Vanish* is more generally used.]

EVAN'ISHMENT, *n.* A vanishing; disappearance. *Barton.*

EVAP'ORABLE, *a.* [See *Evaporate.*] That may be converted into vapor and pass off in fumes; that may be dissipated by evaporation. *Grew.*

EVAP'ORATE, *v. i.* [L. *evaporo; e* and *vaporo*, from *vapor*, which see.]

1. To pass off in vapor, as a fluid; to escape and be dissipated, either in visible vapor, or in particles too minute to be visible. Fluids when heated often *evaporate* in visible steam; but water, on the surface of the earth, generally *evaporates* in an imperceptible manner.

2. To escape or pass off without effect; to be dissipated; to be wasted. Arguments *evaporate* in words. The spirit of a writer often *evaporates* in translating.

EVAP'ORATE, *v. t.* To convert or resolve a fluid into vapor, which is specifically lighter than the air; to dissipate in fumes, steam, or minute particles. Heat *evaporates* water at every point of temperature, from 32° to 212°, the boiling point, of Fahrenheit. A north west wind, in New England, *evaporates* water and dries the earth more rapidly, than the heat alone of a summer's day.

2. To give vent to; to pour out in words or sound. *Wotton.*

EVAP'ORATE, *a.* Dispersed in vapors.

EVAP'ORATED, *pp.* Converted into vapor or steam and dissipated; dissipated in insensible particles, as a fluid.

EVAP'ORATING, *ppr.* Resolving into vapor; dissipating, as a fluid.

EVAPORA'TION, *n.* The conversion of a fluid into vapor specifically lighter than the atmospheric air. *Evaporation* is increased by heat and is followed by cold. It is now generally considered as a solution in the atmosphere.

2. The act of flying off in fumes; vent; discharge.

3. In *pharmacy*, the operation of drawing off a portion of a fluid in steam, that the remainder may be of a greater consistence, or more concentrated.

EVAPOROM'ETER, *n.* [L. *evaporo*, and Gr. μετρον, measure.]

An instrument for ascertaining the quantity of a fluid evaporated in a given time; an atmometer. *Journ. of Science.*

EVA'SION, *n.* *s* as *z.* [L. *evasio*, from *evado*, *evasi.* See *Evade.*]

The act of eluding or avoiding, or of escaping, particularly from the pressure of an argument, from an accusation or charge, from an interrogatory and the like; excuse; subterfuge; equivocation; artifice to elude; shift. *Evasion* of a direct answer weakens the testimony of a witness.

Thou by *evasions* thy crime uncover'st more. *Milton.*

EVA'SIVE, *a.* Using evasion or artifice to avoid; elusive; shuffling; equivocating.

He—answered *evasive* of the sly request. *Pope.*

2. Containing evasion; artfully contrived to elude a question, charge or argument; as an *evasive* answer; an *evasive* argument or reasoning.

EVA'SIVELY, *adv.* By evasion or subterfuge; elusively; in a manner to avoid a direct reply or a charge.

EVA'SIVENESS, *n.* The quality or state of being evasive.

EVE, *n.* The consort of Adam, and mother of the human race; so called by Adam, because she was the mother of all living. In this case, the word would properly belong to the Heb. חיה. But the Hebrew name is חוה havah or chavah, coinciding with the verb, to shew, to discover, and Parkhurst hence denominates Eve, the manifester. In the Septuagint, *Eve*, in Gen. iii. 20, is rendered Ζωη, life; but in Gen. iv. 1, it is rendered Ευαν, *Euan* or *Evan*. The reason of this variation is not obvious, as the Hebrew is the same in both passages. In Russ. Eve is *Evva*. In the Chickasaw language of America, a wife is called *awah*, says Adair.

EVEC'TION, *n.* [L. *eveho*, to carry away.] A carrying out or away; also, a lifting or extolling; exaltation. *Pearson.*

E'VEN, } *n.* *e'vn.* [Sax. *æfen*, *efen*; D. *avond*;
EVE, } G. *abend*; Sw. *afton*; Dan. *aften*; Ice. *afftan*. Qu. Ch. פניא, from פנה fanah, to turn, to decline. The evening is the decline of the day, or fall of the sun.]

1. The decline of the sun; the latter part or close of the day, and beginning of the night. *Eve* is used chiefly in poetry. In prose, we generally use *evening*.

Winter, oft at *eve*, resumes the breeze. *Thomson.*

They, like so many Alexanders,
Have in these parts from morn till *even* fought. *Shak.*

2. Eve is used also for the fast or the evening before a holiday; as Christmas *Eve*. *Johnson.*

E'VEN-SONG, *n.* A song for the evening; a form of worship for the evening. *Milton.*

2. The evening, or close of the day. *Dryden.*

E'VEN-TIDE, *n.* [*even* and Sax. *tid*, time.] Literally, the time of evening; that is, evening.

Isaac went out to meditate in the field at the *even-tide*. Gen. xxiv.

This word is nearly obsolete; *tide* being a useless addition to *even*.

E'VEN, *a.* *e'vn.* [Sax. *efen*; D. *even*; G. *eben*; Sw. *efven*; Pers. هون hovan. The sense is laid or pressed down, level.]

1. Level; smooth; of an equal surface; flat; not rough or waving; as an *even* tract of land; an *even* country; an *even* surface.

2. Uniform; equal; calm; not easily ruffled or disturbed, elevated or depressed; as an *even* temper.

3. Level with; parallel to.

And shall lay thee *even* with the ground. Luke xix.

4. Not leaning.

He could not carry his honors *even*. *Shak.*

5. Equally favorable; on a level in advantage; fair. He met the enemy on *even* ground. The advocates meet on *even* ground in argument.

6. Owing nothing on either side; having accounts balanced. We have settled accounts and now are *even*.

7. Settled; balanced; as, our accounts are *even*.

8. Equal; as *even* numbers.

9. Capable of being divided into equal parts, without a remainder; opposed to *odd*. 4. 6. 8. 10. are *even* numbers.

Let him tell me whether the number of the stars is *even* or odd. *Taylor.*

E'VEN, *v. t.* *e'vn.* To make even or level; to level; to lay smooth.

This will *even* all inequalities. *Evelyn.*
This temple Xerxes *evened* with the soil. *Raleigh.*

2. To place in an equal state, as to obligation, or in a state in which nothing is due on either side; to balance accounts. *Shak.*

E'VEN, *v. i.* To be equal to. [*Not used.*] *Carew.*

E'VEN, *adv.* *e'vn.* Noting a level or equality, or emphatically, a like manner or degree. As it has been done to you, *even* so shall it be done to others. Thou art a soldier *even* to Cato's wishes, that is, your qualities, as a soldier, are equal to his wishes.

2. Noting equality or sameness of time; hence emphatically, the very time. I knew the facts, *even* when I wrote to you.

3. Noting, emphatically, identity of person.

And behold I, *even* I, do bring a flood of waters on the earth. Gen. vi.

4. Likewise; in like manner.

Here all their rage, and *ev'n* their murmurs cease. *Pope.*

5. So much as. We are not *even* sensible of the change.

6. Noting the application of something to that which is less probably included in the phrase; or bringing something within a description, which is unexpected. The common people are addicted to this vice, and *even* the great are not free from it. He made several discoveries which are new, *even* to the learned.

Here also we see the sense of equality, or bringing to a level. So in these phrases, I shall *even* let it pass, I shall *even* do more, we observe the sense of bringing the mind or will to a level with what is to be done.

EVE'NE, *v. i.* [L. *evenio.*] To happen. [*Not in use.*] *Hewyt.*

E'VENED, *pp.* Made even or level.

E'VENER, *n.* One that makes even.

E'VENHAND, *n.* Equality. *Bacon.*

E'VENHANDED, *a.* Impartial; equitable; just. *Shak.*

E'VENING, *n.* [See *Eve*, *Even.*] The latter part and close of the day, and the beginning of darkness or night; properly, the decline or fall of the day, or of the sun.

The *evening* and the morning were the first day. Gen. i.

The precise time when *evening* begins, or when it ends, is not ascertained by usage. The word often includes a part at least of the afternoon, and indeed the whole afternoon; as in the phrase, "The morning and *evening* service of the sabbath." In strictness, *evening* commences at the setting of the sun, and continues during twilight, and *night* commences with total darkness. But in customary language, the *evening* extends to bed-time, whatever that time may be. Hence we say, to spend an *evening* with a friend; an *evening* visit.

2. The decline or latter part of life. We say, the *evening* of life, or of one's days.

3. The decline of any thing; as the *evening* of glory.

E'VENING, *a.* Being at the close of day; as the *evening* sacrifice.

E'VENING HYMN, } *n.* A hymn or song
E'VENING SONG, } to be sung at evening.

E'VENING-STAR, *n.* Hesperus or Vesper; Venus, when visible in the evening.

E'VENLY, *adv.* *e'vnly.* With an even, level or smooth surface; without roughness, elevations and depressions; as things *evenly* spread.

2. Equally; uniformly; in an equipoise; as *evenly* balanced.

3. In a level position; horizontally.

The surface of the sea is *evenly* distant from the center of the earth. *Brerewood.*

4. Impartially; without bias from favor or enmity. *Bacon.*

E'VENNESS, *n.* The state of being even, level or smooth; equality of surface.

2. Uniformity; regularity; as *evenness* of motion.

3. Freedom from inclination to either side; equal distance from either extreme. *Hale.*

4. Horizontal position; levelness of surface; as the *evenness* of a fluid at rest.

5. Impartiality between parties; equal respect.

6. Calmness; equality of temper; freedom from perturbation; a state of mind not subject to elevation or depression; equanimity. *Atterbury.*

EVENT', *n.* [L. *eventus*, *evenio*; *e* and *venio*, to come; Fr. *evenement*; It. and Sp. *evento*; Ar. فان. Class Bn. No. 21.]

1. That which comes, arrives or happens; that which falls out; any incident good or bad.

There is one *event* to the righteous and to the wicked. Eccles. ix.

2. The consequence of any thing; the issue; conclusion; end; that in which an action, operation, or series of operations terminates. The *event* of the campaign was to bring about a negotiation for peace.

EVENT', *v. i.* To break forth. [*Not used.*]

EVENT'ERATE, *v. t.* [Fr. *eventrer*, from the L. *e* and *venter*, the belly.]
To open the bowels; to rip open; to disembowel. *Brown.*

EVENT'ERATED, *pp.* Having the bowels opened.

EVENT'ERATING, *ppr.* Opening the bowels.

EVENT'FUL, *a.* [from *event.*] Full of events or incidents; producing numerous or great changes, either in public or private affairs; as an *eventful* period of history; an *eventful* period of life.

EVEN'TILATE, *v. t.* To winnow; to fan; to discuss. [See *Ventilate.*]

EVENTILA'TION, *n.* A fanning; discussion.

EVENT'UAL, *a.* [from *event.*] Coming or happening as a consequence or result of any thing; consequential.

2. Final; terminating; ultimate. *Burke.*

Eventual provision for the payment of the public securities. *Hamilton.*

EVENT'UALLY, *adv.* In the event; in the final result or issue.

EVENT'UATE, *v. i.* To issue; to come to an end; to close; to terminate. *J. Lloyd.*

EVENT'UATING, *ppr.* Issuing; terminating.

EV'ER, *adv.* [Sax. *æfre, efre.*] At any time; at any period or point of time, past or future. Have you *ever* seen the city of Paris, or shall you *ever* see it?

No man *ever* yet hated his own flesh. Eph. v.

2. At all times; always; continually.

He shall *ever* love, and always be
The subject of my scorn and cruelty. *Dryden.*

He will *ever* be mindful of his covenant. Ps. cxi.

Ever learning, and never able to come to the knowledge of the truth. 2 Tim. iii.

3. *Forever*, eternally; to perpetuity; during everlasting continuance.

This is my name *forever.* Ex. iii.

In a more lax sense, this word signifies continually, for an indefinite period.

His master shall bore his ear through with an awl, and he shall serve him *forever.* Ex. xxi.

These words are sometimes repeated, for the sake of emphasis; *forever* and *ever*, or *forever* and *forever.* *Pope. Shak.*

4. *Ever and anon*, at one time and another; now and then. *Dryden.*

5. In any degree. No man is *ever* the richer or happier for injustice.

Let no man fear that creature *ever* the less, because he sees the apostle safe from his poison. *Hall.*

In modern usage, this word is used for *never*, but very improperly.

And all the question, wrangle e'er so long,
Is only this, if God has placed him wrong. *Pope.*

This ought to be, *ne'er* so long, as the phrase is always used in the Anglo-Saxon, and in our version of the scriptures, that is, so long as *never*, so long as *never* before, to any length of time indefinitely. Ask me *never* so much dowry. Charmers, charming *never* so wisely. These are the genuine English phrases. Let them charm so wisely as *never* before.

6. A word of enforcement or emphasis; thus, as soon as *ever* he had done it; as like him as *ever* he can look.

They broke all their bones in pieces or *ever* they came to the bottom of the den. Dan. vi.

The latter phrase is however anomalous; *or-ever* being equivalent to *before*, and *or* may be a mistake for *ere*.

7. In poetry, and sometimes in prose, *ever* is contracted into *e'er.*

Ever in composition signifies always or continually, without intermission, or to eternity.

EVERBUB'BLING, *a.* [*ever* and *bubbling.*] Continually boiling or bubbling. *Crashaw.*

EVERBURN'ING, *a.* [*ever* and *burning.*] Burning continually or without intermission; never extinct; as an *everburning* lamp; *everburning* sulphur. *Milton.*

EVERDU'RING, *a.* [*ever* and *during.*] Enduring forever; continuing without end; as *everduring* glory. *Raleigh.*

EV'ERGREEN, *a.* [*ever* and *green.*] Always green; verdant throughout the year. The pine is an *evergreen* tree.

EV'ERGREEN, *n.* A plant that retains its verdure through all the seasons; as a garden furnished with *evergreens.*

EVERHON'ORED, *a.* [*ever* and *honored.*] Always honored; ever held in esteem; as an *everhonored* name. *Pope.*

EVERL'ASTING, *a.* [*ever* and *lasting.*] Lasting or enduring for ever; eternal; existing or continuing without end; immortal.

The *everlasting* God, or Jehovah. Gen. xxi.
Everlasting fire; *everlasting* punishment. Matt. xviii. xxv.

2. Perpetual; continuing indefinitely, or during the present state of things.

I will give thee, and thy seed after thee, the land of Canaan, for an *everlasting* possession. Gen. xvii.

The *everlasting* hills or mountains. *Genesis. Habakkuk.*

3. In *popular usage*, endless; continual; unintermitted; as, the family is disturbed with *everlasting* disputes.

EVERL'ASTING, *n.* Eternity; eternal duration, past and future.

From *everlasting* to *everlasting*, thou art God. Ps. xc.

2. A plant, the Gnaphalium; also, the Xeranthemum. *Fam. of Plants.*

EVERL'ASTINGLY, *adv.* Eternally; perpetually; continually. *Swift.*

EVERL'ASTINGNESS, *n.* Eternity; endless duration; indefinite duration. [*Little used.*] *Donne.*

EVERL'ASTING-PEA, *n.* A plant, the *Lathyrus latifolia.*

EVERLIV'ING, *a.* [*ever* and *living.*] Living without end; eternal; immortal; having eternal existence; as the *everliving* God.

2. Continual; incessant; unintermitted.

EVERMO'RE, *adv.* [*ever* and *more.*] Always; eternally.

Religion prefers the pleasures which flow from the presence of God for *evermore.* *Tillotson.*

2. Always; at all times; as *evermore* guided by truth.

EVERO'PEN, *a.* [*ever* and *open.*] Always open; never closed. *Taylor.*

EVERPLE'ASING, *a.* [*ever* and *pleasing.*] Always pleasing; ever giving delight.

The *everpleasing* Pamela. *Sidney.*

EVERSE, *v. t.* *evers'.* [L. *eversus.*] To overthrow or subvert. [*Not used.*] *Glanville.*

EVER'SION, *n.* [L. *eversio.*] An overthrowing; destruction. *Taylor.*

Eversion of the eye-lids, ectropium, a disease in which the eye-lids are turned outward, so as to expose the red internal tunic. *Good.*

EVERT', *v. t.* [L. *everto*; *e* and *verto*, to turn.]
To overturn; to overthrow; to destroy. [*Little used.*] *Ayliffe.*

EVERWA'KING, *a.* [*ever* and *waking.*] Always awake.

EVERWATCH'FUL, *a.* [*ever* and *watchful.*] Always watching or vigilant; as *everwatchful* eyes. *Pope.*

EV'ERY, *a.* [Old Eng. *everich.* *Chaucer.* It is formed from *ever.* The Scots write *everich* and *everilk*; the latter is the Sax. *æfre* and *ælc*, each. The former may be *eac, eaca*, addition, or the common termination *ich, ig*, like.]
Each individual of a whole collection or aggregate number. The word includes the whole number, but each separately stated or considered.

Every man at his best state is altogether vanity. Ps. xxxix.

EV'ERYDAY, *a.* [*every* and *day.*] Used or being every day; common; usual; as *everyday* wit; an *everyday* suit of clothes.

EV'ERYWHERE, *adv.* [See *Where*, which signifies *place.*] In every place; in all places.

EVERYOUNG, *a.* [*ever* and *young.*] Always young or fresh; not subject to old age or decay; undecaying.

Joys *everyoung*, unmixed with pain or fear. *Pope.*

E'VES-DROP. [See *Eaves-drop*, the usual spelling.]

E'VES-DROPPER, *n.* One who stands under the eaves or at a window or door, to listen privately to what is said in the house. [See *Eaves-dropper.*]

EVES'TIGATE, *v. t.* [*Not in use.*] [See *Investigate.*]

EVI'BRATE, [*Not in use.*] [See *Vibrate.*]

EVICT', *v. t.* [L. *evinco, evictum*; *e* and *vinco*, to conquer.]

1. To dispossess by a judicial process, or course of legal proceedings; to recover lands or tenements by law.

If either party be *evicted* for defect of the other's title. *Blackstone.*

2. To take away by sentence of law. *King Charles.*

3. To evince; to prove. [*Not used.*] *Cheyne.*

EVICT'ED, *pp.* Dispossessed by sentence of law; *applied to persons.* Recovered by legal process; *applied to things.*

EVICT'ING, *ppr.* Dispossessing by course of law.

EVIC'TION, *n.* Dispossession by judicial sentence; the recovery of lands or tenements from another's possession, by due course of law.

2. Proof; conclusive evidence. *L'Estrange.*

EV'IDENCE, *n.* [Fr. from L. *evidentia*, from *video*, to see. Class Bd.]

1. That which elucidates and enables the mind to see truth; proof arising from our own perceptions by the senses, or from the testimony of others, or from inductions of reason. Our senses furnish *evidence*

of the existence of matter, of solidity, of color, of heat and cold, of a difference in the qualities of bodies, of figure, &c. The declarations of a witness furnish *evidence* of facts to a court and jury; and reasoning, or the deductions of the mind from facts or arguments, furnish *evidence* of truth or falsehood.

2\. Any instrument or writing which contains proof.

I delivered the *evidence* of the purchase to Baruch. Jer. xxxii.

I subscribed the *evidence* and sealed it. Jer. xxxii.

3\. A witness; one who testifies to a fact. This sense is improper and inelegant, though common, and found even in Johnson's writings.

EV'IDENCE, *v. t.* To elucidate; to prove; to make clear to the mind; to show in such a manner that the mind can apprehend the truth, or in a manner to convince it. The testimony of two witnesses is usually sufficient to *evidence* the guilt of an offender. The works of creation clearly *evidence* the existence of an infinite first cause.

EV'IDENCED, *pp.* Made clear to the mind; proved.

EV'IDENCING, *ppr.* Proving clearly; manifesting.

EV'IDENT, *a.* Plain; open to be seen; clear to the mental eye; apparent; manifest. The figures and colors of bodies are *evident* to the senses; their qualities may be made *evident.* The guilt of an offender cannot always be made *evident.*

EVIDEN'TIAL, *a.* Affording evidence; clearly proving. *Scott.*

EV'IDENTLY, *adv.* Clearly; obviously; plainly; in a manner to be seen and understood; in a manner to convince the mind; certainly; manifestly. The evil of sin may be *evidently* proved by its mischievous effects.

EVIĠILA'TION, *n.* [L. *evigilatio.*] A waking or watching. [*Little used.*]

E'VIL, *a.* *e'vl.* [Sax. *efel, yfel,* or *hyfel*; D. *euvel*; G. *übel*; Arm. *fall, goall.* Qu. W. *gwael,* vile; Ir. *feal.* The Irish word is connected with *feallaim,* to fail, which may be allied to *fall.* Perhaps this is from a different root. Qu. Heb. Ch. Syr. עול to be unjust or injurious, to defraud, Ar. عَالَ to decline, and غَالَ to fall on or invade suddenly.]

1\. Having bad qualities of a natural kind; mischievous; having qualities which tend to injury, or to produce mischief.

Some *evil* beast hath devoured him. Gen. xxxvii.

2\. Having bad qualities of a moral kind; wicked; corrupt; perverse; wrong; as *evil* thoughts; *evil* deeds; *evil* speaking; an *evil* generation. *Scripture.*

3\. Unfortunate; unhappy; producing sorrow, distress, injury or calamity; as *evil* tidings; *evil* arrows; *evil* days. *Scripture.*

E'VIL, *n. Evil* is *natural* or *moral. Natural evil* is any thing which produces pain, distress, loss or calamity, or which in any way disturbs the peace, impairs the happiness, or destroys the perfection of natural beings.

Moral evil is any deviation of a moral agent from the rules of conduct prescribed to him by God, or by legitimate human authority; or it is any violation of the plain principles of justice and rectitude.

There are also *evils* called *civil,* which affect injuriously the peace or prosperity of a city or state; and *political* evils, which injure a nation, in its public capacity.

All wickedness, all crimes, all violations of law and right are *moral evils.* Diseases are *natural evils,* but they often proceed from *moral evils.*

2\. Misfortune; mischief; injury.

There shall no *evil* befall thee. Ps. xci.

A prudent man foreseeth the *evil,* and hideth himself. Prov. xxii.

3\. Depravity; corruption of heart, or disposition to commit wickedness; malignity.

The heart of the sons of men is full of *evil.* Eccles. ix.

4\. Malady; as the *king's evil* or scrophula.

E'VIL, *adv.* [generally contracted to *ill.*]

1\. Not well; not with justice or propriety; unsuitably.

Evil it beseems thee. *Shak.*

2\. Not virtuously; not innocently.

3\. Not happily; unfortunately.

It went *evil* with his house. *Deut.*

4\. Injuriously; not kindly.

The Egyptians *evil* entreated us, and afflicted us. *Deut.*

In composition, *evil,* denoting something bad or wrong, is often contracted to *ill.*

EVIL-AFFECTED, *a.* Not well disposed; unkind; now *ill-affected.*

EVILDÖ'ER, *n.* [*evil* and *doer,* from *do.*] One who does evil; one who commits sin, crime, or any moral wrong.

They speak evil against you as *evildoers.* 1 Pet. ii.

E'VILEYED, *a.* [*evil* and *eye.*] Looking with an evil eye, or with envy, jealousy or bad design.

EVIL-FA'VORED, *a.* [*evil* and *favor.*] Having a bad countenance or external appearance; ill-favored. *Bacon.*

EVIL-FA'VOREDNESS, *n.* Deformity. *Deut.*

E'VILLY, *adv.* Not well. [*Little used.*] *Bp. Taylor.*

EVIL-MINDED, *a.* [*evil* and *mind.*] Having evil dispositions or intentions; disposed to mischief or sin; malicious; malignant; wicked. Slanderous reports are propagated by *evil-minded* persons. [*This word is in common use.*]

E'VILNESS, *n.* Badness; viciousness; malignity; as *evilness* of heart; the *evilness* of sin.

EVILSPE'AKING, *n.* [*evil* and *speak.*] Slander; defamation; calumny; censoriousness. 1 Pet. ii.

EVILWISH'ING, *a.* [*evil* and *wish.*] Wishing harm to; as an *evilwishing* mind. *Sidney.*

EVILWÖRK'ER, *n.* [*evil* and *work.*] One who does wickedness. Phil. iii.

EVINCE, *v. t. evins'.* [L. *evinco,* to vanquish, to prove or show; *e* and *vinco,* to conquer.]

1\. To show in a clear manner; to prove beyond any reasonable doubt; to manifest; to make evident. Nothing *evinces* the depravity of man more fully than his unwillingness to believe himself depraved.

2\. To conquer. [*Not in use.*]

EVIN'CED, *pp.* Made evident; proved.

EVIN'CIBLE, *a.* Capable of proof; demonstrable. *Hale.*

EVIN'CIBLY, *adv.* In a manner to demonstrate, or force conviction.

EVIN'CIVE, *a.* Tending to prove; having the power to demonstrate.

E'VIRATE, *v. t.* [L. *vir, eviratus.*] To emasculate. [*Not in use.*] *Bp. Hall.*

EVIS'CERATE, *v. t.* [L. *eviscero*; *e* and *viscera,* the bowels.]

To embowel or disembowel; to take out the entrails; to search the bowels. *Johnson. Griffith.*

EVIS'CERATED, *pp.* Deprived of the bowels.

EVIS'CERATING, *ppr.* Disemboweling.

EV'ITABLE, *a.* [L. *evitabilis.* See *Evitate.*] That may be shunned; avoidable. [*Little used.*] *Hooker.*

EV'ITATE, *v. t.* [L. *evito*; *e* and *vito,* from the root of *void, wide.*]

To shun; to avoid; to escape. [*Little used.*] *Shak.*

EVITA'TION, *n.* An avoiding; a shunning. [*Little used.*] *Bacon.*

EVI'TE, *v. t.* [L. *evito.*] To shun. [*Not used.*] *Drayton.*

EV'OCATE, } *v. t.* [L. *evoco*; *e* and *voco,* to
EVO'KE, } call.] To call forth.

Neptune is a deity who *evocates* things into progression. *Paus. Trans.*

2\. To call from one tribunal to another; to remove.

The cause was *evoked* to Rome. *Hume.*

[*Evoke* is the preferable word.]

EVOCA'TION, *n.* A calling forth; a calling or bringing from concealment. *Brown.*

2\. A calling from one tribunal to another.

3\. Among *the Romans,* a calling on the gods of a besieged city to forsake it and come over to the besiegers; a religious ceremony of besieging armies. *Encyc.*

EVOLA'TION, *n.* [L. *evolo*; *e* and *volo,* to fly.] The act of flying away. *Bp. Hall.*

EV'OLUTE, *n.* An original curve from which another curve is described; the origin of the evolvent. *Ash.*

EVOLU'TION, *n.* [L. *evolutio.*] The act of unfolding or unrolling. *Boyle.*

2\. A series of things unrolled or unfolded; as the *evolution* of ages. *Moore.*

3\. In *geometry,* the unfolding or opening of a curve, and making it describe an evolvent. The equable evolution of the periphery of a circle, or other curve, is such a gradual approach of the circumference to rectitude, as that its parts do all concur, and equally evolve or unbend; so that the same line becomes successively a less arc of a reciprocally greater circle, till at last they change into a straight line. *Harris.*

4\. In *algebra,* evolution is the extraction of roots from powers; the reverse of involution. *Harris. Encyc.*

5\. In *military tactics,* the doubling of ranks or files, wheeling, countermarching or other motion by which the disposition of troops is changed, in order to attack or defend with more advantage, or to occupy a different post. *Encyc.*

EVOLVE, *v. t. evolv'.* [L. *evolvo*; *e* and *volvo,* to roll, Eng. to *wallow.*]

1\. To unfold; to open and expand.

The animal soul sooner *evolves* itself to its full orb and extent than the human soul. *Hale.*

2. To throw out; to emit. *Prior.*

EVOLVE, *v. i.* To open itself; to disclose itself. *Prior.*

EVOLV'ED, *pp.* Unfolded; opened; expanded; emitted.

EVOLV'ENT, *n.* In *geometry*, a curve formed by the evolution of another curve; the curve described from the evolute. *Ash.*

EVOLV'ING, *ppr.* Unfolding; expanding; emitting.

EVOMI''TION, *n.* A vomiting. *Swift.*

EVULGA'TION, *n.* A divulging. [*Not in use.*]

EVUL'SION, *n.* [L. *evulsio*, from *evello*; *e* and *vello*, to pluck.]

The act of plucking or pulling out by force. *Brown.*

EWE, *n. yu.* [Sax. *eowa, eowe*; D. *ooi*; Ir. *ai* or *oi*; Sp. *oveja*. It seems to be the L. *ovis*.]

A female sheep; the female of the ovine race of animals.

EW'ER, *n. yu're.* [Sax. *huer* or *hwer*.] A kind of pitcher with a wide spout, used to bring water for washing the hands. *Shak. Pope.*

EW'RY, *n. yu'ry.* [from *ewer*.] In *England*, an office in the king's household, where they take care of the linen for the king's table, lay the cloth, and serve up water in ewers after dinner. *Dict.*

EX. A Latin preposition or prefix, Gr. εξ or εx, signifying *out of, out, proceeding from*. Hence in composition, it signifies sometimes *out of*, as in *exhale, exclude*; sometimes *off, from* or *out*, as in L. *excindo*, to cut off or out; sometimes *beyond*, as in *excess, exceed, excel*. In some words it is merely emphatical; in others it has little effect on the signification.

EXACERB'ATE, *v. t.* [L. *exacerbo*, to irritate; *ex* and *acerbo*, from *acerbus*, severe, bitter, harsh, sour, G. *herbe*. See *Harvest*.]

1. To irritate; to exasperate; to inflame angry passions; to imbitter; to increase malignant qualities.

2. To increase the violence of a disease. *Med. Repos.*

EXACERBA'TION, *n.* The act of exasperating; the irritation of angry or malignant passions or qualities; increase of malignity.

2. Among *physicians*, the increased violence of a disease; hence, a paroxysm, as in the return of an intermitting fever.

This term is more generally restricted to the periodical increase of remittent and continued fevers, where there is no absolute cessation of the fever. *Cyc.*

3. Increased severity; as violent *exacerbations* of punishment. [*Unusual.*] *Paley.*

EXACERBES'CENCE, *n.* [L. *exacerbesco*.] Increase of irritation or violence, particularly the increase of a fever or disease. *Darwin.*

EXAET', *a. egzact'.* [L. *exactus*, from *exigo*, to drive; *ex* and *ago*, Gr. αγω, to drive, urge or press.]

1. Closely correct or regular; nice; accurate; conformed to rule; as a man *exact* in his dealings.

All this, *exact* to rule, were brought about. *Pope.*

2. Precise; not different in the least. This is the *exact* sum or amount, or the *exact* time. We have an *exact* model for imitation.

3. Methodical; careful; not negligent; correct; observing strict method, rule or order. This man is very *exact* in keeping his accounts.

4. Punctual. Every man should be *exact* in paying his debts when due; he should be *exact* in attendance on appointments.

5. Strict. We should be *exact* in the performance of duties.

The *exactest* vigilance cannot maintain a single day of unmingled innocence. *Rambler.*

EXAET', *v. t. egzact'.* [L. *exigo, exactum*; Sp. *exigir*; It. *esigere*; Fr. *exiger*. See the Adjective.]

1. To force or compel to pay or yield; to demand or require authoritatively; to extort by means of authority or without pity or justice. It is an offense for an officer to *exact* illegal or unreasonable fees. It is customary for conquerors to *exact* tribute or contributions from conquered countries.

2. To demand of right. Princes *exact* obedience of their subjects. The laws of God *exact* obedience from all men.

3. To demand of necessity; to enforce a yielding or compliance; or to enjoin with pressing urgency.

Duty,
And justice to my father's soul, *exact*
This cruel piety. *Denham.*

EXAET', *v. i.* To practice extortion.

The enemy shall not *exact* upon him. Ps. lxxxix.

EXAET'ED, *pp.* Demanded or required by authority; extorted.

EXAET'ING, *ppr.* Demanding and compelling to pay or yield under color of authority; requiring authoritatively; demanding without pity or justice; extorting; compelling by necessity.

EXAE'TION, *n.* The act of demanding with authority, and compelling to pay or yield; authoritative demand; a levying or drawing from by force; a driving to compliance; as the *exaction* of tribute or of obedience.

2. Extortion; a wresting from one unjustly; the taking advantage of one's necessities, to compel him to pay illegal or exorbitant tribute, fees or rewards.

Take away your *exactions* from my people. Ezek. xlv.

3. That which is exacted; tribute, fees, rewards or contributions demanded or levied with severity or injustice. Kings may be enriched by *exactions*, but their power is weakened by the consequent disaffection of their subjects.

EXAET'ITUDE, *n.* Exactness. [*Little used.*]

EXAET'LY, *adv.* Precisely according to rule or measure; nicely; accurately. A tenon should be *exactly* fitted to the mortise.

2. Precisely according to fact. The story *exactly* accords with the fact or event.

3. Precisely according to principle, justice or right.

EXAET'NESS, *n.* Accuracy; nicety; precision; as, to make experiments with *exactness.*

2. Regularity; careful conformity to law or rules of propriety; as *exactness* of deportment.

3. Careful observance of method and conformity to truth; as *exactness* in accounts or business.

EXAET'OR, *n.* One who exacts; an officer who collects tribute, taxes or customs.

I will make thine officers peace, and thine *exactors* righteousness. Isa. lx.

2. An extortioner; one who compels another to pay more than is legal or reasonable; one who demands something without pity or regard to justice. *Bacon.*

3. He that demands by authority; as an *exactor* of oaths. *Bacon.*

4. One who is unreasonably severe in his injunctions or demands. *Tillotson.*

EXAET'RESS, *n.* A female who exacts or is severe in her injunctions. *B. Jonson.*

EXAE'UATE, *v. t.* [L. *exacuo*.] To whet or sharpen. [*Not in use.*] *B. Jonson.*

EXAĠ'ĠERATE, *v. t.* [L. *exaggero*; *ex* and *aggero*, to heap, from *agger*, a heap.]

1. To heap on; to accumulate. *In this literal sense, it is seldom used; perhaps never.*

2. To highthen; to enlarge beyond the truth; to amplify; to represent as greater than strict truth will warrant. A friend *exaggerates* a man's virtues; an enemy *exaggerates* his vices or faults.

3. In *painting*, to highthen in coloring or design. *Encyc.*

EXAĠ'ĠERATED, *pp.* Enlarged beyond the truth.

EXAĠ'ĠERATING, *ppr.* Enlarging or amplifying beyond the truth.

EXAĠĠERA'TION, *n.* A heaping together; heap; accumulation. [*Little used.*] *Hale.*

2. In *rhetoric*, amplification; a representation of things beyond the truth; hyperbolical representation, whether of good or evil.

3. In *painting*, a method of giving a representation of things too strong for the life.

EXAĠ'ĠERATORY, *a.* Containing exaggeration.

EXAĠ'ITATE, *v. t.* [L. *exagito*.] To shake; to agitate; to reproach. [*Little used or obs.*] *Arbuthnot.*

EXALT', *v. t. egzolt'.* [Fr. *exalter*; Sp. *exaltar*; It. *esaltare*; Low L. *exalto*; *ex* and *altus*, high.]

1. To raise high; to elevate.

2. To elevate in power, wealth, rank or dignity; as, to *exalt* one to a throne, to the chief magistracy, to a bishopric.

3. To elevate with joy or confidence: as, to be *exalted* with success or victory. [We now use *elate*.]

4. To raise with pride; to make undue pretensions to power, rank or estimation; to elevate too high or above others.

He that *exalteth* himself shall be abased. Luke xiv. Matt. xxiii.

5. To elevate in estimation and praise; to magnify; to praise; to extol.

He is my father's God, and I will *exalt* him. Ex. xv.

6. To raise, as the voice; to raise in opposition. 2 Kings xix.

7. To elevate in diction or sentiment; to make sublime; as *exalted* strains.

8. In *physics*, to elevate; to purify; to sub-

tilize; to refine; as, to *exalt* the juices or the qualities of bodies.

EXALTA'TION, *n.* The act of raising high.

2. Elevation to power, office, rank, dignity or excellence.

3. Elevated state; state of greatness or dignity.

I wondered at my flight, and change
To this high *exaltation.* *Milton.*

4. In *pharmacy*, the refinement or subtilization of bodies or their qualities and virtues, or the increase of their strength.

5. In *astrology*, the dignity of a planet in which its powers are increased. *Johnson.*

EXALT'ED, *pp.* Raised to a lofty highth; elevated; honored with office or rank; extolled; magnified; refined; dignified; sublime.

Time never fails to bring every *exalted* reputation to a strict scrutiny. *Ames.*

EXALT'EDNESS, *n.* The state of being elevated.

2. Conceited dignity or greatness.

EXALT'ER, *n.* One who exalts or raises to dignity.

EXALT'ING, *ppr.* Elevating; raising to an eminent station; praising; extolling; magnifying; refining.

EXA'MEN, *n.* egza'men. [L. *examen*, the tongue, needle or beam of a balance. It signifies also a swarm of bees. Sp. *enxambre*, a swarm of bees, a crowd; Port. *enxame;* It. *sciamo;* Fr. *essaim.* From its use in a balance, it came to signify *examination.*]

Examination; disquisition; enquiry. [*Little used.*] *Brown.*

EXAM'INABLE, *a.* [See *Examine.*] That may be examined; proper for judicial examination or inquiry. *S. Court, U. States.*

EXAM'INANT, *n.* One who is to be examined. [*Not legitimate.*] *Prideaux.*

EXAM'INATE, *n.* The person examined. *Bacon.*

EXAMINA'TION, *n.* [L. *examinatio.* See *Examen.*]

1. The act of examining; a careful search or inquiry, with a view to discover truth or the real state of things; careful and accurate inspection of a thing and its parts; as an *examination* of a house or a ship.

2. Mental inquiry; disquisition; careful consideration of the circumstances or facts which relate to a subject or question; a view of qualities and relations, and an estimate of their nature and importance.

3. Trial by a rule or law.

4. In *judicial proceedings*, a careful inquiry into facts by testimony; an attempt to ascertain truth by inquiries and interrogatories; as the *examination* of a witness or the merits of a cause.

5. In *seminaries of learning*, an inquiry into the acquisitions of the students, by questioning them in literature and the sciences, and by hearing their recitals.

6. In *chimistry* and *other sciences*, a searching for the nature and qualities of substances, by experiments; the practice or application of the docimastic art.

EXAM'INATOR, *n.* An examiner. [*Not used.*] *Brown.*

EXAM'INE, *v. t.* egzam'in. [L. *examino*, from *examen.*]

1. To inspect carefully, with a view to discover truth or the real state of a thing; as, to *examine* a ship to know whether she is sea-worthy, or a house to know whether repairs are wanted.

2. To search or inquire into facts and circumstances by interrogating; as, to *examine* a witness.

3. To look into the state of a subject; to view in all its aspects; to weigh arguments and compare facts, with a view to form a correct opinion or judgment. Let us *examine* this proposition; let us *examine* this subject in all its relations and bearings; let us *examine* into the state of this question.

4. To inquire into the improvements or qualifications of students, by interrogatories, proposing problems, or by hearing their recitals; as, to *examine* the classes in college; to *examine* the candidates for a degree, or for a license to preach or to practice in a profession.

5. To try or assay by experiments; as, to *examine* minerals.

6. To try by a rule or law.

Examine yourselves whether ye are in the faith. 2 Cor. xiii.

7. In general, to search; to scrutinize; to explore, with a view to discover truth; as, to *examine* ourselves; to *examine* the extent of human knowledge.

EXAM'INED, *pp.* Inquired into; searched; inspected; interrogated; tried by experiment.

EXAM'INER, *n.* One who examines, tries or inspects; one who interrogates a witness or an offender.

2. In *chancery*, in *Great Britain*, the Examiners are two officers of that court, who examine, on oath, the witnesses for the parties. *Encyc.*

EXAM'INING, *ppr.* Inspecting carefully; searching or inquiring into; interrogating; trying or assaying by experiment.

EX'AMPLARY, *a.* [from *example.*] Serving for example or pattern; proposed for imitation. [It is now written *exemplary.*] *Hooker.*

EXAM'PLE, *n.* egzam'pl. [L. *exemplum;* Fr. *exemple;* It. *esempio;* Sp. *exemplo.* Qu. from *ex* and the root of *similis*, Gr. ομαλος.]

1. A pattern; a copy; a model; that which is proposed to be imitated. This word, when applied to material things, is now generally written *sample*, as a *sample* of cloth; but *example* is sometimes used. *Raleigh.*

2. A pattern, in morals or manners; a copy, or model; that which is proposed or is proper to be imitated.

I have given you an *example*, that you should do as I have done to you. John xiii.

Example is our preceptor before we can reason. *Kollock.*

3. Precedent; a former instance. Buonaparte furnished many *examples* of successful bravery.

4. Precedent or former instance, in a bad sense, intended for caution.

Lest any man fall after the same *example* of unbelief. Heb. iv.

Sodom and Gomorrah—are set forth for an *example*, suffering the vengeance of eternal fire. Jude 7.

5. A person fit to be proposed for a pattern; one whose conduct is worthy of imitation.

Be thou an *example* of the believers. 1 Tim. iv.

6. Precedent which disposes to imitation. *Example* has more effect than precept.

7. Instance serving for illustration of a rule or precept; or a particular case or proposition illustrating a general rule, position or truth. The principles of trigonometry and the rules of grammar are illustrated by *examples.*

8. In *logic*, or *rhetoric*, the conclusion of one singular point from another; an induction of what may happen from what has happened. If civil war has produced calamities of a particular kind in one instance, it is inferred that it will produce like consequences in other cases. This is an *example.* *Bailey. Encyc.*

EXAM'PLE, *v. t.* To exemplify; to set an example. [*Not used.*] *Shak.*

EXAM'PLELESS, *a.* Having no example. [*Not used.*] *B. Jonson.*

EXAM'PLER, *n.* A pattern; now *sample* or *sampler.*

EXAN'GUIOUS, *a.* Having no blood. [*Not used.* See *Exsanguious.*]

EXAN'IMATE, *a.* egzan'imate. [L. *exanimatus, exanimo; ex* and *anima*, life.]

Lifeless; spiritless; disheartened; depressed in spirits. *Thomson.*

EXAN'IMATE, *v. t.* To dishearten; to discourage. *Coles.*

EXANIMA'TION, *n.* Deprivation of life or of spirits. [*Little used.*]

EXAN'IMOUS, *a.* [L. *exanimis; ex* and *anima*, life.] Lifeless; dead. [*Little used.*]

EXAN'THEMA, *n.* plu. *exanthem'ata.* [Gr. from εξανθεω, to blossom; εξ and ανθος, a flower.]

Among *physicians*, eruption; a breaking out; pustules, petechiæ, or vibices; any efflorescence on the skin, as in measles, small pox, scarlatina, &c.

This term is now limited by systematic nosologists, to such eruptions as are accompanied with fever. *Good.*

EXANTHEMAT'IC, } *a.* Eruptive; efflorescent; noting morbid redness of the skin. The measles is an *exanthematous* disease. Tooke uses *exanthematic.*
EXANTHEM'ATOUS, }

EXANT'LATE, *v. t.* [L. *exantlo.*] To draw out; to exhaust. [*Not used.*] *Boyle.*

EXANTLA'TION, *n.* The act of drawing out; exhaustion. [*Not used.*] *Brown.*

EXARA'TION, *n.* [L. *exaro; ex* and *aro.*] The act of writing. [*Not used.*] *Dict.*

EX'ARCH, *n.* [Gr. from αρχος, a chief.] A prefect or governor under the eastern emperors. Also, a deputy or legate in the Greek church.

EX'ARCHATE, *n.* The office, dignity or administration of an exarch. *Taylor.*

EXARTICULA'TION, *n.* [*ex* and *articulation.*] Luxation; the dislocation of a joint. *Quincy.*

EX'ASPERATE, *v. t.* [L. *exaspero*, to irritate; *ex* and *aspero*, from *asper*, rough, harsh.]

1. To anger; to irritate to a high degree; to provoke to rage; to enrage; to excite anger, or to inflame it to an extreme degree. We say, to *exasperate* a person, or to *exasperate* the passion of anger or resentment.

2. To aggravate; to embitter; as, to *exasperate* enmity.
3. To augment violence; to increase malignity; to exacerbate; as, to *exasperate* pain or a part inflamed. *Bacon.*

EX'ASPERATE, *a.* Provoked; embittered; inflamed. *Shak.*

EX'ASPERATED, *pp.* Highly angered or irritated; provoked; enraged; embittered; increased in violence.

EX'ASPERATER, *n.* One who exasperates or inflames anger, enmity or violence.

EX'ASPERATING, *ppr.* Exciting keen resentment; inflaming anger; irritating; increasing violence.

EXASPERA'TION, *n.* Irritation; the act of exciting violent anger; provocation.
2. Extreme degree of anger; violent passion.
3. Increase of violence or malignity; exacerbation.

EXAUC'TORATE, EXAU'THORATE, *v. t.* [L. *exauctoro*; *ex* and *auctoro*, to hire or bind, from *auctor*, author.]
To dismiss from service; to deprive of a benefice. *Ayliffe.*

EXAUCTORA'TION, EXAUTHORA'TION, *n.* Dismission from service; deprivation; degradation; the removal of a person from an office or dignity in the church. *Ayliffe.*

EXAU'THORIZE, *v. t.* To deprive of authority. *Selden.*

EXCAL'CEATED, *a.* [L. *excalceo*, to pull off the shoes; *ex* and *calceus*, a shoe.] Deprived of shoes; unshod; barefooted.

EXCANDES'CENCE, *n.* [L. *excandescentia*, *excandesco*; *ex* and *candesco*, *candeo*, to glow or be hot, from *caneo*, to be white, to shine.]
1. A growing hot; or a white heat; glowing heat.
2. Heat of passion; violent anger; or a growing angry.

EXCANDES'CENT, *a.* White with heat.

EXCANTA'TION, *n.* [L. *excanto*, but with an opposite signification.]
Disenchantment by a countercharm. [*Little used.*] *Bailey.*

EXC'ARNATE, *v. t.* [L. *ex* and *caro*, flesh.] To deprive or clear of flesh. *Grew.*

EXCARNIFICA'TION, *n.* [L. *excarnifico*, to cut in pieces, from *caro*, flesh.]
The act of cutting off flesh, or of depriving of flesh. *Johnson.*

EX'CAVATE, *v. t.* [L. *excavo*; *ex* and *cavo*, to hollow, *cavus*, hollow. See *Cave*.]
To hollow; to cut, scoop, dig or wear out the inner part of any thing and make it hollow; as, to *excavate* a ball; to *excavate* the earth; to *excavate* the trunk of a tree and form a canoe.

EX'CAVATED, *pp.* Hollowed; made hollow.

EX'CAVATING, *ppr.* Making hollow.

EXCAVA'TION, *n.* The act of making hollow, by cutting, wearing or scooping out the interior substance or part of a thing.
2. A hollow or a cavity formed by removing the interior substance. Many animals burrow in *excavations* of their own forming.

EX'CAVATOR, *n.* One who excavates.

EX'CECATE, *v. t.* [L. *excæco.*] To make blind. [*Not used.*]

EXCECA'TION, *n.* The act of making blind. *Richardson.*

EXCE'DENT, *n.* Excess. [*Not authorized.*]

EXCEE'D, *v. t.* [L. *excedo*; *ex* and *cedo*, to pass.]
1. To pass or go beyond; to proceed beyond any given or supposed limit, measure or quantity, or beyond any thing else; used equally in a physical or moral sense. One piece of cloth *exceeds* the customary length or breadth; one man *exceeds* another in bulk, stature or weight; one offender *exceeds* another in villainy.
2. To surpass; to excel. Homer *exceeded* all men in epic poetry. Demosthenes and Cicero *exceeded* their cotemporaries in oratory.

> King Solomon *exceeded* all the kings of the earth for riches and for wisdom. 1 Kings x.

EXCEE'D, *v. i.* To go too far; to pass the proper bounds; to go over any given limit, number or measure.

> Forty stripes may he give him, and not *exceed.* Deut. xxv.

2. To bear the greater proportion; to be more or larger. *Dryden.*
[*This verb is intransitive only by ellipsis.*]

EXCEE'DABLE, *a.* That may surmount or exceed. [*Ill.*] *Sherwood.*

EXCEE'DED, *pp.* Excelled; surpassed; outdone.

EXCEE'DER, *n.* One who exceeds or passes the bounds of fitness. *Mountagu.*

EXCEE'DING, *ppr.* Going beyond; surpassing; excelling; outdoing.
2. *a.* Great in extent, quantity or duration; very extensive.

> Cities were built an *exceeding* space of time before the flood. [*This sense is unusual.*] *Raleigh.*

3. *adv.* In a very great degree; unusually; as *exceeding* rich.

> The Genoese were *exceeding* powerful by sea. *Raleigh.*
> I am thy shield, and thy *exceeding* great reward. Gen. xv.

EXCEE'DING, *n.* Excess; superfluity. *Smollett.*

EXCEE'DINGLY, *adv.* To a very great degree; in a degree beyond what is usual; greatly; very much.

> Isaac trembled *exceedingly.* Gen. xxvii.

EXCEE'DINGNESS, *n.* Greatness in quantity, extent or duration. [*Not used.*]

EXCEL', *v. t.* [L. *excello*, the root of which, *cello*, is not in use. In Ar. قَالَ signifies to lift, raise, excel; also, to speak, to strike, to beat. So we use *beat* in the sense of *surpass.* See Class Gl. No. 31. and 49.]
1. To go beyond; to exceed; to surpass in good qualities or laudable deeds; to outdo.

> *Excelling* others, these were great;
> Thou greater still, must these *excel.* *Prior.*
> Many daughters have done virtuously, but thou *excellest* them all. Prov. xxxi.

2. To exceed or go beyond in bad qualities or deeds.
3. To exceed; to surpass.

EXCEL', *v. i.* To have good qualities, or to perform meritorious actions, in an unusual degree; to be eminent, illustrious or distinguished.

> Bless the Lord, ye his angels, that *excel* in strength. Ps. ciii.

We say, to *excel* in mathematics; to *excel* in painting; to *excel* in heroic achievements.

EXCEL'LED, *pp.* Surpassed; outdone; exceeded in good qualities or laudable achievements.

EX'CELLENCE, EX'CELLENCY, *n.* [Fr. from L. *excellentia.*] The state of possessing good qualities in an unusual or eminent degree; the state of excelling in any thing.
2. Any valuable quality; any thing highly laudable, meritorious or virtuous, in persons, or valuable and esteemed, in things. Purity of heart, uprightness of mind, sincerity, virtue, piety, are *excellencies* of character; symmetry of parts, strength and beauty are *excellencies* of body; an accurate knowledge of an art is an *excellence* in the artisan; soundness and durability are *excellencies* in timber; fertility, in land; elegance, in writing. In short, whatever contributes to exalt man, or to render him esteemed and happy, or to bless society, is in him an *excellence.*
3. Dignity; high rank in the scale of beings. Angels are beings of more *excellence* than men; men are beings of more *excellence* than brutes.
4. A title of honor formerly given to kings and emperors, now given to embassadors, governors, and other persons, below the rank of kings, but elevated above the common classes of men.

EX'CELLENT, *a.* Being of great virtue or worth; eminent or distinguished for what is amiable, valuable or laudable; as an *excellent* man or citizen; an *excellent* judge or magistrate.
2. Being of great value or use, applied to things; remarkable for good properties; as *excellent* timber; an *excellent* farm; an *excellent* horse; *excellent* fruit.
3. Distinguished for superior attainments; as an *excellent* artist.
4. Consummate; complete; *in an ill sense.*

> Elizabeth was an *excellent* hypocrite. *Hume.*

EX'CELLENTLY, *adv.* In an excellent manner; well in a high degree; in an eminent degree; in a manner to please or command esteem, or to be useful.

EXCEPT', *v. t.* [Fr. *excepter*; It. *eccettare*; from L. *excipio*; *ex* and *capio*, to take. See *Caption, Capture.*]
1. To take or leave out of any number specified; to exclude; as, of the thirty persons present and concerned in a riot, we must *except* two.
2. To take or leave out any particular or particulars, from a general description.

> When he saith, all things are put under him, it is manifest that he is *excepted* who did put all things under him. 1 Cor. xv.

EXCEPT', *v. i.* To object; to make an objection or objections; usually followed by *to*; sometimes by *against.* I *except to* a witness, or *to* his testimony, on account of his interest or partiality.

EXCEPT', *pp.* contracted from *excepted.* Taken out; not included. All were involved in this affair, *except* one; that is, *one excepted*, the case absolute or independent clause. *Except* ye repent, ye shall all likewise perish; that is, except this fact, that ye repent, or this fact being excepted, removed, taken away, ye shall all likewise perish. Or *except* may be considered as the imperative mode. *Except*, thou or ye, this fact, ye shall all likewise perish. Hence *except* is equivalent to *without, unless*, and denotes exclusion.

EXCEPT'ED, *pp.* [See *Except*.]

EXCEPT'ING, *ppr.* Taking or leaving out; excluding.

2. This word is also used in the sense of *except*, as above explained. The prisoners were all condemned, *excepting* three. This is an anomalous use of the word, unless, in some cases, it may be referred to a pronoun. *Excepted* would be better: three excepted; three being excepted.

EXCEP'TION, *n.* The act of excepting, or excluding from a number designated, or from a description; exclusion. All the representatives voted for the bill, with the *exception* of five. All the land is in tillage, with an *exception* of two acres.

2. Exclusion from what is comprehended in a general rule or proposition.

3. That which is excepted, excluded, or separated from others in a general description; the person or thing specified as distinct or not included. Almost every general rule has its *exceptions*.

4. An objection; that which is or may be offered in opposition to a rule, proposition, statement or allegation; with *to*; sometimes with *against*. He made some *exceptions to* the argument.

5. Objection with dislike; offense; slight anger or resentment; with *at, to* or *against*, and commonly used with *take*; as, to take *exception at* a severe remark; to take *exception to* what was said.

Roderigo, thou hast taken *against* me an *exception*. *Shak.*

But it is more generally followed by *at*.

6. In *law*, the denial of what is alledged and considered as valid by the other party, either in point of law or in pleading; or an allegation against the sufficiency of an answer. In law, it is a stop or stay to an action, and it is either *dilatory* or *peremptory*. *Blackstone.*

7. A saving clause in a writing.

Bill of exceptions, in *law*, is a statement of exceptions to evidence, filed by the party, and which the judge must sign or seal.

EXCEP'TIONABLE, *a.* Liable to objection.

This passage I look upon to be the most *exceptionable* in the whole poem. *Addison.*

EXCEP'TIOUS, *a.* Peevish; disposed or apt to cavil, or take exceptions. [*Little used.*] *South.*

EXCEP'TIOUSNESS, *n.* Disposition to cavil. *Barrow.*

EXCEPT'IVE, *a.* Including an exception; as an *exceptive* preposition. *Watts.*

2. Making or being an exception. *Milton.*

EXCEPT'LESS, *a.* Omitting all exception. [*Not in use.*] *Shak.*

EXCEPT'OR, *n.* One who objects, or makes exceptions. *Burnet.*

EXCERN', *v. t.* [L. *excerno*; *ex* and *cerno*, Gr. κρινω, to separate.]

To separate and emit through the pores, or through small passages of the body; to strain out; to excrete; as, fluids are *excerned* in perspiration. *Bacon.*

EXCERN'ED, *pp.* Separated; excreted; emitted through the capillary vessels of the body.

EXCERN'ING, *ppr.* Emitting through the small passages; excreting.

EXCERP', *v. t.* [L. *excerpo.*] To pick out. [*Little used.*] *Hales.*

EXCERPT', *v. t.* [L. *excerpo*; *ex* and *carpo*, to take.] To select. [*Not used.*] *Barnard.*

EXCERP'TION, *n.* [L. *excerptio.*] A picking out; a gleaning; selection. [*Little used.*]

2. That which is selected or gleaned. [*Little used.*] *Raleigh.*

EXCERP'TOR, *n.* A picker; a culler. *Barnard.*

EXCERPTS', *n.* Extracts from authors. [*A bad word.*]

EXCESS', *n.* [L. *excessus*, from *excedo*. See *Exceed*.]

1. Literally, that which *exceeds* any measure or limit, or which *exceeds* something else, or a going beyond a just line or point. Hence, superfluity; that which is beyond necessity or wants; as an *excess* of provisions; *excess* of light.

2. That which is beyond the common measure, proportion, or due quantity; as the *excess* of a limb; the *excess* of bile in the system.

3. Superabundance of any thing. *Newton.*

4. Any transgression of due limits. *Atterbury.*

5. In *morals*, any indulgence of appetite, passion or exertion, beyond the rules of God's word, or beyond any rule of propriety; intemperance in gratifications; as *excess* in eating or drinking; *excess* of joy; *excess* of grief; *excess* of love, or of anger; *excess* of labor.

6. In *arithmetic* and *geometry*, the difference between any two unequal numbers or quantities; that which remains when the lesser number or quantity is taken from the greater.

EXCESS'IVE, *a.* Beyond any given degree, measure or limit, or beyond the common measure or proportion; as the *excessive* bulk of a man; *excessive* labor; *excessive* wages.

2. Beyond the established laws of morality and religion, or beyond the bounds of justice, fitness, propriety, expedience or utility; as *excessive* indulgence of any kind.

Excessive bail shall not be required. *Bill of Rights.*

3. Extravagant; unreasonable. His expenditures of money were *excessive*.

4. Vehement; violent; as *excessive* passion.

EXCESS'IVELY, *adv.* In an extreme degree; beyond measure; exceedingly; as *excessively* impatient; *excessively* grieved.

2. Vehemently; violently; as, the wind blew *excessively*.

EXCESS'IVENESS, *n.* The state or quality of being excessive; excess.

EXCHANĠE, *v. t.* [Fr. *echanger*; Arm. *eceinch*; from *changer, ceinch*, to change.]

1. In *commerce*, to give one thing or commodity for another; to alienate or transfer the property of a thing and receive in compensation for it something of supposed equal value; to barter; and in vulgar language, to swap; to truck. It differs from *sell*, only in the kind of compensation. To *sell* is to alienate for *money*; to *exchange* is to alienate one commodity for another; as, to *exchange* horses; to *exchange* oxen for corn.

2. To lay aside, quit or resign one thing, state or condition, and take another in the place of it; as, to *exchange* a crown for a cowl; to *exchange* a throne for a cell or a hermitage; to *exchange* a life of ease for a life of toil.

3. To give and receive reciprocally; to give and receive in compensation the same thing.

Exchange forgiveness with me, noble Hamlet. *Shak.*

4. To give and receive the like thing; as, to *exchange* thoughts; to *exchange* work; to *exchange* blows; to *exchange* prisoners.

It has *with* before the person receiving the thing given, and *for* before the equivalent. Will you *exchange* horses *with* me? Will you *exchange* your horse *for* mine?

EXCHANĠE, *n.* In *commerce*, the act of giving one thing or commodity for another; barter; traffick by permutation, in which the thing received is supposed to be equivalent to the thing given.

Joseph gave them bread in *exchange* for horses. Gen. xlvii.

2. The act of giving up or resigning one thing or state for another, without contract.

3. The act of giving and receiving reciprocally; as an *exchange* of thoughts; an *exchange* of civilities.

4. The contract by which one commodity is transferred to another for an equivalent commodity.

5. The thing given in return for something received; or the thing received in return for what is given.

There's my *exchange*. *Shak.*

In ordinary business, this is called *change*.

6. The form of exchanging one debt or credit for another; or the receiving or paying of money in one place, for an equal sum in another, by order, draft or bill of exchange. *A* in London is creditor to *B* in New York, and *C* in London owes *D* in New York a like sum. *A* in London draws a bill of exchange on *B* in New York; *C* in London purchases the bill, by which *A* receives his debt due from *B* in New York. *C* transmits the bill to *D* in New York, who receives the amount from *B*.

Bills of exchange, drawn on persons in a foreign country, are called *foreign bills* of exchange; the like bills, drawn on persons in different parts or cities of the same country, are called *inland bills* of exchange.

A bill of exchange is a mercantile contract in which four persons are primarily concerned.

7. In mercantile language, a bill drawn for money is called *exchange*, instead of a *bill of exchange*.

8. The course of exchange, is the current price between two places, which is above or below par, or at par. Exchange is *at par*, when a bill in New York for the payment of one hundred pounds sterling in London, can be purchased for one hundred pounds. If it can be purchased for less,

exchange is *under par*. If the purchaser is obliged to give more, exchange is *above par*.

9. In *law*, a mutual grant of equal interests, the one in consideration of the other. Estates exchanged must be equal in quantity, as fee simple for fee simple. *Blackstone.*

10. The place where the merchants, brokers and bankers of a city meet to transact business, at certain hours; often contracted into *change*.

EXCHANGEABIL'ITY, *n.* The quality or state of being exchangeable.

Though the law ought not to be contravened by an express article admitting the *exchangeability* of such persons. *Washington.*

EXCHANGEABLE, *a.* That may be exchanged; capable of being exchanged; fit or proper to be exchanged.

The officers captured with Burgoyne were *exchangeable* within the powers of Gen. Howe. *Marshall.*

Bank bills *exchangeable* for gold or silver. *Ramsay.*

EXCHANGED, *pp.* Given or received for something else; bartered.

EXCHANGER, *n.* One who exchanges; one who practices exchange. Matt. xxv.

EXCHANGING, *ppr.* Giving and receiving one commodity for another; giving and receiving mutually; laying aside or relinquishing one thing or state for another.

EXCHEQ'UER, *n.* *exchek'er.* [Fr. *echiquier*, checker-work, a chess-board. See *Chess* and *Checker*.]

In *England*, an ancient court of record, intended principally to collect and superintend the king's debts and duties or revenues, and so called from *scaccharium*, or from the same root, denoting a checkered cloth, which covers the table. It consists of two divisions: the receipt of the exchequer, which manages the royal revenue; and the judicial part, which is divided into a court of law and a court of equity. The court of equity is held in the exchequer chamber, before the lord treasurer, the chancellor of the exchequer, the chief baron and three inferior barons. The common law court is held before the barons, without the treasurer or chancellor. *Blackstone.*

Exchequer-bills, in *England*, bills for money, or promissory bills, issued from the exchequer; a species of paper currency emitted under the authority of the government and bearing interest.

EXCHEQ'UER, *v. t.* To institute a process against a person in the court of exchequer. *Pegge.*

EXCI'SABLE, *a.* *s* as *z.* Liable or subject to excise; as, coffee is an *excisable* commodity.

EXCI'SE, *n.* *s* as *z.* [L. *excisum*, cut off, from *excido*; D. *accys*; G. *accise*.]

An inland duty or impost, laid on commodities consumed, or on the retail, which is the last stage before consumption; as an *excise* on coffee, soap, candles, which a person consumes in his family. But many articles are excised at the manufactories, as spirit at the distillery, printed silks and linens at the printer's, &c. *Encyc.*

EXCI'SE, *v. t.* *s* as *z.* To lay or impose a duty on articles consumed, or in the hands of merchants, manufacturers and retailers; to levy an excise on.

EXCI'SED, *pp.* Charged with the duty of excise.

EXCI'SEMAN, *n.* An officer who inspects commodities and rates the excise duty on them. *Johnson.*

EXCI'SING, *ppr.* Imposing the duty of excise.

EXCIS'ION, *n.* *s* as *z.* [L. *excisio.*] In *surgery*, a cutting out or cutting off any part of the body; extirpation; amputation.

2. The cutting off of a person from his people; extirpation; destruction.

The rabbins reckon three kinds of *excision*. *Encyc.*

EXCITABIL'ITY, *n.* [from *excite.*] The quality of being capable of excitement; susceptibility of increased vital action by the force of stimulants. *Brown.*

EXCI'TABLE, *a.* Having the quality of being susceptible of excitement; capable of increased action by the force of stimulants.

2. Capable of being excited, or roused into action.

EXCI'TANT, *n.* That which produces or may produce increased action in a living body; a stimulant.

EX'CITATE, *v. t.* To excite. [*Not in use.*] *Bacon.*

EXCITA'TION, *n.* The act of exciting or putting in motion; the act of rousing or awakening. *Bacon. Watts.*

EXCI'TATIVE, *a.* Having power to excite. *Barrow.*

EXCI'TATORY, *a.* Tending to excite; containing excitement. *Miller.*

EXCI'TE, *v. t.* [L. *excito*; *ex* and *cito*, to *cite*, to call or provoke.]

1. To rouse; to call into action; to animate; to stir up; to cause to act that which is dormant, stupid or inactive; as, to *excite* the spirits or courage.

2. To stimulate; to give new or increased action to; as, to *excite* the human system; to *excite* the bowels.

3. To raise; to create; to put in motion; as, to *excite* a mutiny or insurrection.

4. To rouse; to inflame; as, to *excite* the passions.

EXCI'TED, *pp.* Roused; awakened; animated; put in motion; stimulated; inflamed.

EXCI'TEMENT, *n.* The act of exciting; stimulation.

2. The state of being roused into action, or of having increased action. Stimulants are intended to produce *excitement* in the animal system.

3. Agitation; a state of being roused into action; as an *excitement* of the people.

4. That which excites or rouses; that which moves, stirs, or induces action; a motive. *Shak.*

EXCI'TER, *n.* He or that which excites; he that puts in motion, or the cause which awakens and moves.

2. In *medicine*, a stimulant.

EXCI'TING, *ppr.* Calling or rousing into action; stimulating.

Exciting causes, in *medicine*, are those which immediately produce disease, or those which excite the action of predisponent causes. *Parr.*

EXCI'TING, *n.* Excitation. *Herbert.*

EXCLA'IM, *v. i.* [L. *exclamo*; *ex* and *clamo*, to cry out. See *Claim, Clamor.*]

1. To utter the voice with vehemence; to cry out; to make a loud outcry in words; as, to *exclaim* against oppression; to *exclaim* with wonder or astonishment; to *exclaim* with joy.

2. To declare with loud vociferation.

—That thus you do *exclaim* you'll go with him. *Shak.*

EXCLA'IMER, *n.* One who cries out with vehemence; one who speaks with heat, passion or much noise; as an *exclaimer* against tyranny. *Atterbury.*

EXCLA'IMING, *ppr.* Crying out; vociferating; speaking with heat or passion.

EXCLAMA'TION, *n.* Outcry; noisy talk; clamor; as *exclamations* against abuses in government.

2. Vehement vociferation.

Thus will I drown your *exclamations*. *Shak.*

3. Emphatical utterance; a vehement extension or elevation of voice; ecphonesis; as, O dismal night!

4. A note by which emphatical utterance or outcry is marked: thus !

5. In *grammar*, a word expressing outcry; an interjection; a word expressing some passion, as wonder, fear or grief.

EXCLAM'ATORY, *a.* Using exclamation; as an *exclamatory* speaker.

2. Containing or expressing exclamation; as an *exclamatory* phrase.

EXCLU'DE, *v. t.* [L. *excludo*; *ex* and *claudo*, to shut, Gr. κλειδοω, κλειω.] Properly, to thrust out or eject; but used as synonymous with *preclude*.

1. To thrust out; to eject; as, to *exclude* young animals from the womb or from eggs.

2. To hinder from entering or admission; to shut out; as, one body *excludes* another from occupying the same space. The church ought to *exclude* immoral men from the communion.

3. To debar; to hinder from participation or enjoyment. European nations, in time of peace, *exclude* our merchants from the commerce of their colonies. In some of the states, no man who pays taxes is *excluded* from the privilege of voting for representatives.

4. To except; not to comprehend or include in a privilege, grant, proposition, argument, description, order, species, genus, &c. in a general sense.

EXCLU'DED, *pp.* Thrust out; shut out; hindered or prohibited from entrance or admission; debarred; not included or comprehended.

EXCLU'DING, *ppr.* Ejecting; hindering from entering; debarring; not comprehending.

EXCLU'SION, *n.* *s* as *z.* The act of excluding, or of thrusting out; ejection: as the *exclusion* of a fetus.

2. The act of denying entrance or admission; a shutting out.

3. The act of debarring from participation in a privilege, benefit, use or enjoyment. *Burnet.*

4. Rejection; non-reception or admission, in a general sense. *Addison.*

5. Exception. *Bacon.*

6. Ejection; that which is emitted or thrown out. *Brown.*

EXCLU'SIONIST, *n.* One who would preclude another from some privilege. *Fox.*

EXCLU'SIVE, *a.* Having the power of preventing entrance; as *exclusive* bars. *Milton.*

2. Debarring from participation; possessed and enjoyed to the exclusion of others; as an *exclusive* privilege.

3. Not taking into the account; not including or comprehending; as, the general had five thousand troops, *exclusive* of artillery and cavalry. He sent me all the numbers from 78 to 94 *exclusive;* that is, all the numbers between 78 and 94, but these numbers, the first and last, are excepted or not included.

EXCLU'SIVELY, *adv.* Without admission of others to participation; with the exclusion of all others; as, to enjoy a privilege *exclusively.*

2. Without comprehension in an account or number; not inclusively.

EXCLU'SORY, *a.* Exclusive; excluding; able to exclude. [*Little used.*] *Walsh.*

EXCOCT', *v. t.* [L. *excoctus.*] To boil. [*Not in use.*] *Bacon.*

EXCOG'ITATE, *v. t.* [L. *excogito; ex* and *cogito,* to think.]

To invent; to strike out by thinking; to contrive. *More. Hale.*

EXCOGITA'TION, *n.* Invention; contrivance; the act of devising in the thoughts.

EX-COM'MISSARY, *n.* [*ex* and *commissary.*] A commissary dismissed from office; one formerly a commissary.

EXCOMMU'NE, *v. t.* To exclude. [*Not used.*] *Gayton.*

EXCOMMU'NICABLE, *a.* [See *Excommunicate.*] Liable or deserving to be excommunicated. *Hooker.*

EXCOMMU'NICATE, *v. t.* [L. *ex* and *communico.*]

To expel from communion; to eject from the communion of the church, by an ecclesiastical sentence, and deprive of spiritual advantages; as, to *excommunicate* notorious offenders.

EXCOMMU'NICATED, *pp.* Expelled or separated from communion with a church, and a participation of its ordinances, rights and privileges.

EXCOMMU'NICATING, *ppr.* Expelling from the communion of a church, and depriving of spiritual advantages, by an ecclesiastical sentence or decree.

EXCOMMUNICA'TION, *n.* The act of ejecting from a church; expulsion from the communion of a church, and deprivation of its rights, privileges and advantages; an ecclesiastical penalty or punishment inflicted on offenders. Excommunication is an ecclesiastical interdict, of two kinds, the *lesser* and the *greater;* the *lesser* excommunication is a separation or suspension of the offender from partaking of the eucharist; the *greater,* is an absolute separation and exclusion of the offender from the church and all its rites and advantages. *Encyc.*

EXCO'RIATE, *v. t.* [Low L. *excorio; ex* and *corium,* skin, hide.]

To flay; to strip or wear off the skin; to abrade; to gall; to break and remove the cuticle in any manner, as by rubbing, beating, or by the action of acrid substances.

EXCO'RIATED, *pp.* Flayed; galled; stripped of skin or the cuticle; abraded.

EXCO'RIATING, *ppr.* Flaying; galling; stripping of the cuticle.

EXCORIA'TION, *n.* The act of flaying, or the operation of wearing off the skin or cuticle; a galling; abrasion; the state of being galled or stripped of skin.

2. Plunder; the act of stripping of possessions. [*Little used.*] *Howell.*

EXCORTICA'TION, *n.* [L. *ex* and *cortex,* bark.] The act of stripping off bark. *Coxe.*

EX'CREABLE, *a.* That may be discharged by spitting. [*Little used.*]

EX'CREATE, *v. t.* [L. *excreo, exscreo,* to hawk and spit.]

To hawk and spit; to discharge from the throat by hawking and spitting.

EXCREA'TION, *n.* A spitting out.

EX'CREMENT, *n.* [L. *excrementum,* from *excerno, excretus; ex* and *cerno,* to separate, Gr. *κρινω.*]

Matter excreted and ejected; that which is discharged from the animal body after digestion; alvine discharges.

EXCREMENT'AL, *a.* Excreted or ejected by the natural passages of the body.

EXCREMENTI''TIAL, *a.* Pertaining to or consisting in excrement. *Fourcroy.*

EXCREMENTI''TIOUS, *a.* Pertaining to excrement; containing excrement; consisting in matter evacuated or proper to be evacuated from the animal body. *Bacon. Harvey.*

EXCRES'CENCE, *n.* [L. *excrescens,* from *excresco; ex* and *cresco,* to grow.]

In *surgery,* a preternatural protuberance growing on any part of the body, as a wart or a tubercle; a superfluous part. *Encyc.*

2. Any preternatural enlargement of a plant, like a wart or tumor; or something growing out from a plant. *Bentley.*

3. A preternatural production. *Tatler.*

EXCRES'CENT, *a.* Growing out of something else, in a preternatural manner; superfluous; as a wart or tumor.

Expunge the whole or lop the *excrescent* parts. *Pope.*

EXCRE'TE, *v. t.* [L. *excretus,* infra.] To separate and throw off; to discharge; as, to *excrete* urine.

EXCRE'TION, *n.* [L. *excretio,* from *excerno,* to separate.]

1. A separation of some fluid from the blood, by means of the glands; a throwing off or discharge of animal fluids from the body.

2. That which is excreted; fluids separated from the body by the glands and called *excrement.* *Bacon. Quincy.*

The term *excretion* is more usually applied to those *secretions* which are directly discharged from the body. It is also applied to the discharges from the bowels, which are called *alvine excretions.* *Cyc.*

EX'CRETIVE, *a.* Having the power of separating and ejecting fluid matter from the body.

Excretive faculty. *Harvey.*

EX'CRETORY, *a.* Having the quality of excreting or throwing off excrementitious matter by the glands.

EX'CRETORY, *n.* A little duct or vessel, destined to receive secreted fluids, and to excrete them; also, a secretory vessel.

The *excretories* are nothing but slender slips of the arteries, deriving an appropriated juice from the blood. *Cheyne.*

EXCRU'CIABLE, *a.* [infra.] Liable to torment. [*Little used.*]

EXCRU'CIATE, *v. t.* [L. *excrucio; ex* and *crucio,* to torment, from *crux,* a cross.]

To torture; to torment; to inflict most severe pain on; as, to *excruciate* the heart or the body. *Chapman.*

EXCRU'CIATED, *pp.* Tortured; racked; tormented.

EXCRU'CIATING, *ppr.* Torturing; tormenting; putting to most severe pain.

2. *a.* Extremely painful; distressing; as *excruciating* fears.

EXCUBA'TION, *n.* The act of watching all night. [*Little used.*] *Dict.*

EXCUL'PATE, *v. t.* [It. *scolpare;* L. *ex* and *culpo,* to blame, *culpa,* fault.]

To clear by words from a charge or imputation of fault or guilt; to excuse. How naturally are we inclined to *exculpate* ourselves and throw the blame on others. Eve endeavored to *exculpate* herself for eating the forbidden fruit, and throw the blame on the serpent; Adam attempted to *exculpate* himself and throw the blame on Eve.

EXCUL'PATED, *pp.* Cleared by words from the imputation of fault or guilt.

EXCUL'PATING, *ppr.* Clearing by words from the charge of fault or crime.

EXCULPA'TION, *n.* The act of vindicating from a charge of fault or crime; excuse.

EXCUL'PATORY, *a.* Able to clear from the charge of fault or guilt; excusing; containing excuse. *Johnson.*

EXCUR'SION, *n.* [L. *excursio, excurso,* from *cursus,* from *curro,* to run.]

1. A rambling; a deviating from a stated or settled path.

She in low numbers short *excursions* tries. *Pope.*

2. Progression beyond fixed limits; as, the *excursions* of the seasons into the extremes of heat and cold. *Arbuthnot.*

3. Digression; a wandering from a subject or main design. *Atterbury.*

4. An expedition or journey into a distant part; any rambling from a point or place, and return to the same point or place.

EXCUR'SIVE, *a.* Rambling; wandering; deviating; as an *excursive* fancy or imagination.

EXCUR'SIVELY, *adv.* In a wandering manner. *Boswell.*

EXCUR'SIVENESS, *n.* The act of wandering or of passing usual limits.

EXCU'SABLE, *a.* *s* as *z.* [See *Excuse.*] That may be excused; pardonable; as, the man is *excusable.*

2. Admitting of excuse or justification; as an *excusable* action.

EXCU'SABLENESS, *n.* *s* as *z.* The state of being excusable; pardonableness; the quality of admitting of excuse. *Boyle.*

EXCUSA'TION, *n.* *s* as *z.* Excuse; apology. [*Little used.*] *Bacon.*

EXCUSA'TOR, *n.* *s* as *z.* One who makes or is authorized to make an excuse or carry an apology. *Hume.*

EXCU'SATORY, *a.* *s* as *z.* Making excuse;

containing excuse or apology; apologetical; as an *excusatory* plea.

EX€U'SE, *v. t. s* as *z.* [L. *excuso; ex* and *causor*, to blame. See *Cause.*]

1. To pardon; to free from the imputation of fault or blame; to acquit of guilt. We *excuse* a person in our own minds, when we acquit him of guilt or blame; or we *excuse* him by a declaration of that acquittal.

2. To pardon, as a fault; to forgive entirely, or to admit to be little censurable, and to overlook. We *excuse* a fault, which admits of apology or extenuation; and we *excuse* irregular conduct, when extraordinary circumstances appear to justify it.

3. To free from an obligation or duty.

I pray thee have me *excused.* Luke xiv.

4. To remit; not to exact; as, to *excuse* a forfeiture. *Johnson.*

5. To pardon; to admit an apology for.

Excuse some courtly strains. *Pope.*

6. To throw off an imputation by apology.

Think you that we *excuse* ourselves to you? 2 Cor. xii.

7. To justify; to vindicate.

Their thoughts accusing or else *excusing* one another. Rom. ii.

EX€U'SE, *n.* A plea offered in extenuation of a fault or irregular deportment; apology. Every man has an *excuse* to offer for his neglect of duty; the debtor makes *excuses* for delay of payment.

2. The act of excusing or apologizing.

3. That which excuses; that which extenuates or justifies a fault. His inability to comply with the request must be his *excuse.*

EX€U'SELESS, *a.* Having no excuse; that for which no excuse or apology can be offered. [*Little used.*]

EX€U'SER, *n. s* as *z.* One who offers excuses or pleads for another.

2. One who excuses or forgives another.

EX€U'SING, *ppr. s* as *z.* Acquitting of guilt or fault; forgiving; overlooking.

EX€USS', *v. t.* [L. *excussus.*] To shake off; also, to seize and detain by law. [*Not used.*]

EX€US'SION, *n.* A seizing by law. [*Not used.*] *Ayliffe.*

EX-DIRE€T'OR, *n.* One who has been a director, but is displaced.

EX'E€RABLE, *a.* [L. *execrabilis.* See *Execrate.*]

Deserving to be cursed; very hateful; detestable; abominable; as an *execrable* wretch.

EX'E€RABLY, *adv.* Cursedly; detestably.

EX'E€RATE, *v. t.* [L. *execror*, from *ex* and *sacer*, the primary sense of which is to separate. See *Sacred.*]

Literally, to curse; to denounce evil against, or to imprecate evil on; hence, to detest utterly; to abhor; to abominate. *Temple.*

EXE€RA'TION, *n.* The act of cursing; a curse pronounced; imprecation of evil; utter detestation expressed. *Milton.*

Cease, gentle queen, these *execrations:* *Shak.*

EX'E€RATORY, *n.* A formulary of execration. *L. Addison.*

EXE€T', *v. t.* [L. *execo*, for *exseco.*] To cut off or out; to cut away. [*Little used.*] *Harvey.*

EXE€'TION, *n.* A cutting off or out. [*Little used.*]

EX'E€UTE, *v. t.* [Fr. *executer;* It. *eseguire;* Sp. *executar;* L. *exequor*, for *exsequor; ex* and *sequor*, to follow. See *Seek.*]

1. Literally, to follow out or through. Hence, to perform; to do; to effect; to carry into complete effect; to complete; to finish. We *execute* a purpose, a plan, design or scheme; we *execute* a work undertaken, that is, we pursue it to the end.

2. To perform; to inflict; as, to *execute* judgment or vengeance. *Scripture.*

3. To carry into effect; as, to *execute* law or justice.

4. To carry into effect the law, or the judgment or sentence on a person; to inflict capital punishment on; to put to death; as, to *execute* a traitor.

5. To kill. *Shak.*

6. To complete, as a legal instrument; to perform what is required to give validity to a writing, as by signing and sealing; as, to *execute* a deed or lease.

EX'E€UTE, *v. i.* To perform the proper office; to produce an effect.

EX'E€UTED, *pp.* Done; performed; accomplished; carried into effect; put to death.

EX'E€UTER, *n.* One who performs or carries into effect. [See *Executor.*]

EX'E€UTING, *ppr.* Doing; performing; finishing; accomplishing; inflicting; carrying into effect.

EXE€U'TION, *n.* Performance; the act of completing or accomplishing.

The excellence of the subject contributed much to the happiness of the *execution.* *Dryden.*

2. In *law*, the carrying into effect a sentence or judgment of court; the last act of the law in completing the process by which justice is to be done, by which the possession of land or debt, damages or cost, is obtained, or by which judicial punishment is inflicted.

3. The instrument, warrant or official order, by which an officer is empowered to carry a judgment into effect. An *execution* issues from the clerk of a court, and is levied by a sheriff, his deputy or a constable, on the estate, goods or body of the debtor.

4. The act of signing and sealing a legal instrument, or giving it the forms required to render it a valid act; as the *execution* of a deed.

5. The last act of the law in the punishment of criminals; capital punishment; death inflicted according to the forms of law.

6. Effect; something done or accomplished. Every shot did *execution.*

7. Destruction; slaughter. *Shak.*

It is used after *do*, to *do* execution; never after *make.*

8. Performance, as in music or other art.

EXE€U'TIONER, *n.* One who executes; one who carries into effect a judgment of death; one who inflicts a capital punishment in pursuance of a legal warrant. *It is chiefly used in this sense.*

2. He that kills; he that murders. *Shak.*

3. The instrument by which any thing is performed. *Crashaw.*

EXE€'UTIVE, *a. egzec'utive.* Having the quality of executing or performing; as *executive* power or authority; an *executive* officer. Hence, in government, *executive* is used in distinction from *legislative* and *judicial.* The body that deliberates and enacts laws, is *legislative;* the body that judges, or applies the laws to particular cases, is *judicial;* the body or person who carries the laws into effect, or superintends the enforcement of them, is *executive.*

It is of the nature of war to increase the *executive*, at the expense of the legislative authority. *Federalist, Hamilton.*

EXE€'UTIVE, *n.* The officer, whether king, president or other chief magistrate, who superintends the execution of the laws; the person who administers the government; executive power or authority in government.

Men most desirous of places in the executive gift, will not expect to be gratified, except by their support of the *executive.* *J. Quincy.*

EXE€'UTOR, *n.* The person appointed by a testator to execute his will, or to see it carried into effect.

EXE€UTO'RIAL, *a.* Pertaining to an executor; executive. *Blackstone.*

EXE€'UTORSHIP, *n.* The office of an executor.

EXE€'UTORY, *a.* Performing official duties. *Burke.*

2. In *law*, to be executed or carried into effect in future; to take effect on a future contingency; as an *executory* devise or remainder. *Blackstone.*

EXE€'UTRESS, } *n.* A female executor; a
EXE€'UTRIX, } woman appointed by a testator to execute his will. [*The latter word is generally used.*]

EXEĠE'SIS, *n.* [Gr. ἐξηγησις, from ἐξηγεομαι, to explain, from ἐξ and ἡγεομαι, to lead.]

1. Exposition; explanation; interpretation.

2. A discourse intended to explain or illustrate a subject. *Encyc.*

EXEĠET'I€AL, *a.* Explanatory; tending to unfold or illustrate; expository. *Walker.*

EXEĠET'I€ALLY, *adv.* By way of explanation.

EXEM'PLAR, *n. egzem'plar.* [L. See *Example.*]

1. A model, original or pattern, to be copied or imitated.

2. The idea or image of a thing, formed in the mind of an artist, by which he conducts his work; the ideal model which he attempts to imitate. *Encyc.*

EX'EMPLARILY, *adv.* In a manner to deserve imitation; in a worthy or excellent manner.

She is *exemplarily* loyal. *Howell.*

2. In a manner that may warn others, by way of terror; in such a manner that others may be cautioned to avoid an evil; or in a manner intended to warn others.

Some he punished *exemplarly* in this world. *Hakewill.*

EX'EMPLARINESS, *n.* The state or quality of being a pattern for imitation.

EX'EMPLARY, *a.* [from *exemplar.*] Serving for a pattern or model for imitation; worthy of imitation. The christian should be *exemplary* in his life, as well as correct in his doctrines.

2. Such as may serve for a warning to others; such as may deter from crimes or vi-

ces; as *exemplary* justice; *exemplary* punishment.

3. Such as may attract notice and imitation.

When any duty has fallen into general neglect, the most visible and *exemplary* performance is required. *Rogers.*

4. Illustrating. *Fuller.*

EXEMPLIFICA'TION, *n.* [from *exemplify.*]

1. The act of exemplifying; a showing or illustrating by example.

2. A copy; a transcript; an attested copy; as an *exemplification* of a deed, or of letters patent.

EXEM'PLIFIED, *pp.* Illustrated by example or copy.

EXEM'PLIFIER, *n.* One that exemplifies by following a pattern.

EXEM'PLIFY, *v. t.* *egzem'plify.* [from *exemplar; Low L. exemplo; It. esemplificare; Sp. exemplificar.*]

1. To show or illustrate by example. The life and conversation of our Savior *exemplified* his doctrines and precepts.

2. To copy; to transcribe; to take an attested copy.

3. To prove or show by an attested copy.

EXEM'PLIFYING, *ppr.* Illustrating by example; transcribing; taking an attested copy; proving by an attested copy.

EXEMPT', *v. t.* *egzemt'.* [Fr. *exempter;* Sp. *exentar;* It. *esentare;* from L. *eximo, exemptus; ex* and *emo*, to take.]

Literally, to take out or from; hence, to free, or permit to be free, from any charge, burden, restraint, duty, evil or requisition, to which others are subject; to privilege; to grant immunity from. Officers and students of colleges are *exempted* from military duty. No man is *exempted* from pain and suffering. The laws of God *exempt* no man from the obligation to obedience.

Certain abbeys claimed to be *exempted* from the jurisdiction of their bishops. *Henry, Hist. Brit.*

EXEMPT', *a.* Free from any service, charge, burden, tax, duty, evil or requisition, to which others are subject; not subject; not liable to; as, to be *exempt* from military duty, or from a poll tax; to be *exempt* from pain or fear. Peers in G. Britain are *exempt* from serving on inquests.

2. Free by privilege; as *exempt* from the jurisdiction of a lord or of a court.

3. Free; clear; not included.

4. Cut off from. [*Not used.*] *Shak.*

EXEMPT', *n.* One who is exempted or freed from duty; one not subject.

EXEMPT'ED, *pp.* Freed from charge, duty, tax or evils, to which others are subject; privileged; not subjected.

EXEMPT'IBLE, *a.* Free; privileged. [*Not in use.*]

EXEMPT'ING, *ppr.* Freeing from charge, duty, tax or evil; granting immunity to.

EXEMP'TION, *n.* The act of exempting; the state of being exempt.

2. Freedom from any service, charge, burden, tax, evil or requisition, to which others are subject; immunity; privilege. Many cities of Europe purchased or obtained *exemptions* from feudal servitude. No man can claim an *exemption* from pain, sorrow or death.

EXEMPTI''TIOUS, *a.* Separable; that may be taken from. [*Not used.*] *More.*

EXEN'TERATE, *v. t.* [L. *exentero; ex* and Gr. εντερον, entrails.]

To take out the bowels or entrails; to embowel. *Brown.*

EXENTERA'TION, *n.* The act of taking out the bowels.

EXEQUA'TUR, *n.* [L.] A written recognition of a person in the character of consul or commercial agent, issued by the government, and authorizing him to exercise his powers in the country.

EXE'QUIAL, *a.* [L. *exequialis.*] Pertaining to funerals. *Pope.*

EX'EQUIES, *n. plu.* [L. *exequiæ*, from *exequor*, that is, *exsequor*, to follow.]

Funeral rites; the ceremonies of burial; funeral procession. *Dryden.*

EXER'CENT, *a.* [L. *exercens.* See *Exercise.*]

Using; practising; following; as a calling or profession. [*Little used.*] *Ayliffe.*

EX'ERCISABLE, *a.* *s* as *z.* That may be exercised, used, employed or exerted. *Z. Swift.*

EX'ERCISE, *n.* *s* as *z.* [L. *exercitium*, from *exerceo; ex* and the root of Gr. εργον, Eng. *work;* Fr. *exercice;* Sp. *exercicio;* It. *esercizio.*] In a general sense, any kind of work, labor or exertion of body. Hence,

1. Use; practice; the exertions and movements customary in the performance of business; as the *exercise* of an art, trade, occupation, or profession.

2. Practice; performance; as the *exercise* of religion.

3. Use; employment; exertion; as the *exercise* of the eyes or of the senses, or of any power of body or mind.

4. Exertion of the body, as conducive to health; action; motion, by labor, walking, riding, or other exertion.

The wise for cure on *exercise* depend. *Dryden.*

5. Exertion of the body for amusement, or for instruction; the habitual use of the limbs for acquiring an art, dexterity, or grace, as in fencing, dancing, riding; or the exertion of the muscles for invigorating the body.

6. Exertion of the body and mind or faculties for improvement, as in oratory, in painting or statuary.

7. Use or practice to acquire skill; preparatory practice. Military *exercises* consist in using arms, in motions, marches and evolutions. Naval *exercise* consists in the use or management of artillery, and in the evolutions of fleets.

8. Exertion of the mind; application of the mental powers.

9. Task; that which is appointed for one to perform. *Milton.*

10. Act of divine worship. *Shak.*

11. A lesson or example for practice.

EX'ERCISE, *v. t.* [L. *exerceo;* Fr. *exercer;* It. *esercere;* Sp. *exercer.* See the Noun.]

1. In a general sense, to move; to exert; to cause to act, in any manner; as, to *exercise* the body or the hands; to *exercise* the mind, the powers of the mind, the reason or judgment.

2. To use; to exert; as, to *exercise* authority or power.

3. To use for improvement in skill; as, to *exercise* arms.

4. To exert one's powers or strength; to practice habitually; as, to *exercise* one's self in speaking or music.

5. To practice; to perform the duties of; as, to *exercise* an office.

6. To train to use; to discipline; to cause to perform certain acts, as preparatory to service; as, to *exercise* troops.

7. To task; to keep employed; to use efforts.

Herein do I *exercise* myself, to have always a conscience void of offense towards God and men. Acts xxiv.

8. To use; to employ.

9. To busy; to keep busy in action, exertion or employment.

10. To pain or afflict; to give anxiety to; to make uneasy.

EX'ERCISE, *v. i.* To use action or exertion; as, to *exercise* for health or amusement. [*Elliptical.*]

EX'ERCISED, *pp.* Exerted; used; trained; disciplined; accustomed; made skilful by use; employed; practiced; pained; afflicted; rendered uneasy.

EX'ERCISER, *n.* One who exercises.

EX'ERCISING, *ppr.* Exerting; using; employing; training; practicing.

EXERCITA'TION, *n.* [L. *exercitatio*, from *exerceo.* See *Exercise.*] Exercise; practice; use. *Brown. Felton.*

EXER'GUE, *n.* [Gr. εξ and εργον, work.]

A little space around or without the figures of a medal, left for the inscription, cipher, device, date, &c. *Encyc.*

EXERT', *v. t.* *egzert'.* [L. *exero*, for *exsero; ex* and *sero*, to throw, to thrust, for this is the radical sense of *sero.*]

1. Literally, to thrust forth; to emit; to push out. *Dryden.*

Before the gems *exert*
Their feeble heads. *Philips.*

[*An unusual application.*]

2. To bring out; to cause to come forth; to produce. But more generally,

3. To put or thrust forth, as strength, force or ability; to strain; to put in action; to bring into active operation; as, to *exert* the strength of the body or limbs; to *exert* efforts; to *exert* powers or faculties; to *exert* the mind.

4. To put forth; to do or perform.

When the will has *exerted* an act of command on any faculty of the soul. *South.*

To exert one's self, is to use efforts; to strive.

EXERT'ED, *pp.* Thrust or pushed forth; put in action.

EXERT'ING, *ppr.* Putting forth; putting in action.

EXER'TION, *n.* The act of exerting or straining; the act of putting into motion or action; effort; a striving or struggling; as an *exertion* of strength or power; an *exertion* of the limbs, of the mind or faculties. The ship was saved by great *exertions* of the crew. No *exertions* will suppress a vice which great men countenance.

EXE'SION, *n.* *s* as *z.* [L. *exesus, exedo; ex* and *edo*, to eat.]

The act of eating out or through. [*Little used.*] *Brown.*

EXESTUA'TION, *n.* [L. *exæstuatio; ex* and *æstuo*, to boil.]

A boiling; ebullition; agitation caused by heat; effervescence. *Boyle.*

EXFO'LIATE, *v. i.* [L. *exfolio; ex* and *folium*, a leaf.]
In *surgery* and *mineralogy*, to separate and come off in scales, as pieces of carious bone; to scale off, as the lamins of a mineral.

EXFO'LIATED, *pp.* Separated in thin scales, as a carious bone.

EXFO'LIATING, *ppr.* Separating and coming off in scales.

EXFOLIA'TION, *n.* The scaling of a bone; the process of separating, as pieces of unsound bone from the sound part; desquamation. *Coxe.*

EXFO'LIATIVE, *a.* That has the power of causing exfoliation or the desquamation of a bone.

EXFO'LIATIVE, *n.* That which has the power or quality of procuring exfoliation. *Wiseman.*

EXHA'LABLE, *a.* [See *Exhale.*] That may be exhaled or evaporated. *Boyle.*

EXHALA'TION, *n.* [L. *exhalatio.* See *Exhale.*]
1. The act or process of exhaling, or sending forth fluids in the form of steam or vapor; evaporation.
2. That which is exhaled; that which is emitted, or which rises in the form of vapor; fume or steam; effluvia. *Exhalations* are visible or invisible. The earth is often dried by evaporation, without visible *exhalations.* The smell of fragrant plants is caused by invisible *exhalations.*

EXHA'LE, *v. t. egzha'le.* [L. *exhalo; ex* and *halo*, to breathe, to send forth vapor; Ir. *gal, gail*, vapor; *gailim*, to evaporate.]
1. To send out; to emit; as vapor, or minute particles of a fluid or other substance. The rose *exhales* a fragrant odor. The earth *exhales* vapor. Marshes *exhale* noxious effluvia.
2. To draw out; to cause to be emitted in vapor or minute particles; to evaporate. The sun *exhales* the moisture of the earth.

EXHA'LED, *pp.* Sent out; emitted, as vapor; evaporated.

EXHA'LEMENT, *n.* Matter exhaled; vapor. *Brown.*

EXHA'LING, *ppr.* Sending or drawing out in vapor or effluvia.

EXHAUST', *v. t. egzhaust'.* [L. *exhaurio, exhaustum; ex* and *haurio*, to draw, Gr. αρυω.]
1. To draw out or drain off the whole of any thing; to draw out, till nothing of the matter drawn is left. We *exhaust* the water in a well, by drawing or pumping; the water of a marsh is *exhausted* by draining; the moisture of the earth is *exhausted* by evaporation.
2. To empty by drawing out the contents. Venesection may *exhaust* the veins and arteries.
3. To draw out or to use and expend the whole; to consume. The treasures of the prince were *exhausted;* his means or his resources were *exhausted.* The strength or fertility of land may be *exhausted.*
4. To use or expend the whole by exertion; as, to *exhaust* the strength or spirits; to *exhaust* one's patience. Hence this phrase is equivalent to tire, weary, fatigue.

EXHAUST', *a.* Drained; exhausted. [*Little used.*] *Burton.*

EXHAUST'ED, *pp.* Drawn out; drained off; emptied by drawing, draining or evaporation; wholly used or expended; consumed.

EXHAUST'ER, *n.* He or that which exhausts or draws out.

EXHAUST'IBLE, *a.* That may be exhausted or drained off.

EXHAUST'ING, *ppr.* Drawing out; draining off; emptying; using or expending the whole; consuming.
2. *a.* Tending to exhaust; as *exhausting* labor.

EXHAUST'ION, *n.* The act of drawing out or draining off; the act of emptying completely of the contents.
2. The state of being exhausted or emptied; the state of being deprived of strength or spirits.
3. In *mathematics*, a method of proving the equality of two magnitudes by a *reductio ad absurdum*, or showing that if one is supposed either greater or less than the other, there will arise a contradiction. *Encyc.*

EXHAUST'LESS, *a.* Not to be exhausted; not to be wholly drawn off or emptied; inexhaustible; as an *exhaustless* fund or store.

EXHAUST'MENT, *n.* Exhaustion; drain.

EXHER'EDATE, *v. t.* [infra.] To disinherit.

EXHEREDA'TION, *n.* [L. *exhæredatio, exhæredo; ex* and *hæres*, an heir.]
In *the civil law*, a disinheriting; a father's excluding a child from inheriting any part of his estate. *Encyc.*

EXHIB'IT, *v. t. egzhib'it.* [L. *exhibeo; ex* and *habeo*, to have or hold, as we say, to *hold out* or *forth.*]
1. To offer or present to view; to present for inspection; to show; as, to *exhibit* paintings or other specimens of art; to *exhibit* papers or documents in court.
2. To show; to display; to manifest publicly; as, to *exhibit* a noble example of bravery or generosity.
3. To present; to offer publicly or officially; as, to *exhibit* a charge of high treason.

EXHIB'IT, *n.* Any paper produced or presented to a court or to auditors, referees or arbitrators, as a voucher, or in proof of facts; a voucher or document produced.
2. In *chancery*, a deed or writing produced in court, sworn to by a witness, and a certificate of the oath indorsed on it by the examiner or commissioner. *Encyc.*

EXHIB'ITED, *pp.* Offered to view; presented for inspection; shown; displayed.

EXHIB'ITER, *n.* One who exhibits; one who presents a petition or charge. *Shak.*

EXHIB'ITING, *ppr.* Offering to view; presenting; showing; displaying.

EXHIBI''TION, *n.* [L. *exhibitio.*] The act of exhibiting for inspection; a showing or presenting to view; display.
2. The offering, producing or showing of titles, authorities or papers of any kind before a tribunal, in proof of facts.
3. Public show; representation of feats or actions in public; display of oratory in public; any public show.
4. Allowance of meat and drink; pension; salary; benefaction settled for the maintenance of scholars in universities, not depending on the foundation. *Swift. Bacon. Encyc.*
5. Payment; recompense. *Shak.*

EXHIBI''TIONER, *n.* In *English universities*, one who has a pension or allowance, granted for the encouragement of learning.

EXHIB'ITIVE, *a.* Serving for exhibition; representative. *Norris.*

EXHIB'ITIVELY, *adv.* By representation. *Waterland.*

EXHIB'ITORY, *a.* Exhibiting; showing; displaying.

EXHIL'ARATE, *v. t. egzhil'arate.* [L. *exhilaro; ex* and *hilaro*, to make merry, *hilaris*, merry, jovial, Gr. ιλαρος.]
To make cheerful or merry; to enliven; to make glad or joyous; to gladden; to cheer. Good news *exhilarates* the mind, as good wine *exhilarates* the animal spirits.

EXHIL'ARATE, *v. i.* To become cheerful or joyous. *Bacon.*

EXHIL'ARATED, *pp.* Enlivened; animated; cheered; gladdened; made joyous or jovial.

EXHIL'ARATING, *ppr.* Enlivening; giving life and vigor to the spirits; cheering; gladdening.

EXHILARA'TION, *n.* The act of enlivening the spirits; the act of making glad or cheerful.
2. The state of being enlivened or cheerful. *Exhilaration* usually expresses less than *joy* or *mirth*, but it may be used to express both.

EXHORT', *v. t. egzhort'.* [L. *exhortor; ex* and *hortor*, to encourage, to embolden, to cheer, to advise; It. *esortàre;* Fr. *exhorter;* Sp. *exhortar.* The primary sense sèems to be to excite or to give strength, spirit or courage.]
1. To incite by words or advice; to animate or urge by arguments to a good deed or to any laudable conduct or course of action.

> I *exhort* you to be of good cheer. Acts xxvii.
>
> Young men also *exhort* to be sober minded. *Exhort* servants to be obedient to their masters. Tit. ii.

2. To advise; to warn; to caution.
3. To incite or stimulate to exertion. *Goldsmith.*

EXHORT', *v. i.* To deliver exhortation; to use words or arguments to incite to good deeds.

> And with many other words did he testify and *exhort.* Acts ii.

EXHORTA'TION, *n.* The act or practice of exhorting; the act of inciting to laudable deeds; incitement to that which is good or commendable.
2. The form of words intended to incite and encourage.
3. Advice; counsel.

EXHORT'ATIVE, *a.* Containing exhortation.

EXHORT'ATORY, *a.* Tending to exhort; serving for exhortation.

EXHORT'ED, *pp.* Incited by words to good deeds; animated to a laudable course of conduct; advised.

EXHORT'ER, *n.* One who exhorts or encourages.

EXHORT'ING, *ppr.* Inciting to good deeds by words or arguments; encouraging; counseling.

EXHUMA'TION, *n.* [Fr. from *exhumer*, to dig out of the ground; Sp. *exhumar*; L. *ex* and *humus*, ground.]
1. The digging up of a dead body interred; the disinterring of a corpse.
2. The digging up of any thing buried. *Goldsmith.*

EXICCATE, EXICCATION. [See *Exsiccate.*]

EX'IGENCE, EX'IGENCY, *n.* [L. *exigens* from *exigo*, to exact; *ex* and *ago*, to drive.]
1. Demand; urgency; urgent need or want. We speak of the *exigence* of the case; the *exigence* of the times, or of business.
2. Pressing necessity; distress; any case which demands immediate action, supply or remedy. A wise man adapts his measures to his *exigencies*. In the present *exigency*, no time is to be lost.

EX'IGENT, *n.* Pressing business; occasion that calls for immediate help. [*Not used.*] [See *Exigence.*] *Hooker.*
2. In *law*, a writ which lies where the defendant is not to be found, or after a return of *non est inventus* on former writs; the *exigent* or *exigi facias* then issues, which requires the sheriff to cause the defendant to be proclaimed or *exacted*, in five county courts successively, to render himself; and if he does not, he is outlawed. *Blackstone.*
3. End; extremity. [*Not used.*] *Shak.*

EX'IGENTER, *n.* An officer in the court of Common Pleas in England who makes out exigents and proclamations, in cases of outlawry. *Encyc.*

EX'IGIBLE, *a.* [See *Exigence.*] That may be exacted; demandable; requirable.

EXIGU'ITY, *n.* [L. *exiguitas.*] Smallness; slenderness. [*Little used.*] *Boyle.*

EXIG'UOUS, *a.* [L. *exiguus.*] Small; slender; minute; diminutive. [*Little used.*] *Harvey.*

EX'ILE, *n. eg'zile.* [L. *exilium*, *exul*; Fr. *exil*; It. *esilio*. The word is probably compounded of *ex* and a root in *Sl*, signifying to depart, or to cut off, to separate, or to thrust away, perhaps L. *salio.*]
1. Banishment; the state of being expelled from one's native country or place of residence by authority, and forbid to return, either for a limited time or for perpetuity.
2. An abandonment of one's country, or removal to a foreign country for residence, through fear, disgust or resentment, or for any cause distinct from business, is called a *voluntary exile*, as is also a separation from one's country and friends by distress or necessity.
3. The person banished, or expelled from his country by authority; also, one who abandons his country and resides in another; or one who is separated from his country and friends by necessity.

EX'ILE, *v. t.* To banish, as a person from his country or from a particular jurisdiction by authority, with a prohibition of return; to drive away, expel or transport from one's country.
2. To drive from one's country by misfortune, necessity or distress.

To exile one's self, is to quit one's country with a view not to return.

EX'ILE, *a. eg'zil.* [L. *exilis.*] Slender; thin; fine. *Bacon.*

EX'ILED, *pp.* Banished; expelled from one's country by authority.

EX'ILEMENT, *n.* Banishment.

EX'ILING, *ppr.* Banishing; expelling from one's country by law, edict or sentence; voluntarily departing from one's country, and residing in another.

EXILI''TION, *n.* [L. *exilio*, for *exsalio*, to leap out.]
A sudden springing or leaping out. [*Little used.*] *Brown.*

EXIL'ITY, *n.* [L. *exilitas.*] Slenderness; fineness; thinness.

EXIM'IOUS, *a.* [L. *eximius.*] Excellent. [*Little used.*] *Bacon.*

EXIN'ANITE, *v. t.* [L. *exinanio.*] To make empty; to weaken. [*Not used.*] *Pearson.*

EXINANI'TION, *n.* [L. *exinanitio*, from *exinanio*, to empty or evacuate; *ex* and *inanio*, to empty, *inanis*, empty, void.]
An emptying or evacuation; hence, privation; loss; destitution. [*Little used.*]

EXIST', *v. i. egzist'.* [L. *existo*; *ex* and *sisto*, or more directly from Gr. ιϛω, ιϛημι, to set, place or fix, or ϛαω, L. *sto*, to stand, Sp. Port. *estar*, It. *stare*, G. *stehen*, D. *staan*, Russ. *stoyu*. The primary sense is to set, fix or be fixed, whence the sense of permanence, continuance.]
1. To be; to have an essence or real being; *applicable to matter or body, and to spiritual substances.* A supreme being and first cause of all other beings must have *existed* from eternity, for no being can have created himself.
2. To live; to have life or animation. Men cannot *exist* in water, nor fishes on land.
3. To remain; to endure; to continue in being. How long shall national enmities *exist?*

EXIST'ENCE, *n.* The state of being or having essence; as the *existence* of body and of soul in union; the separate *existence* of the soul; immortal *existence*; temporal *existence*.
2. Life; animation.
3. Continued being; duration; continuation. We speak of the *existence* of troubles or calamities, or of happiness. During the *existence* of national calamities, our pious ancestors always had recourse to prayer for divine aid.

EXIST'ENT, *a.* Being; having being, essence or existence.

> The eyes and mind are fastened on objects which have no real being, as if they were truly *existent*. *Dryden.*

EXISTEN'TIAL, *a.* Having existence. *Bp. Barlow.*

EX'IT, *n.* [L. the 3d person of *exeo*, to go out.] Literally, he goes out or departs. Hence,
1. The departure of a player from the stage, when he has performed his part. This is also a term set in a play, to mark the time of an actor's quitting the stage.
2. Any departure; the act of quitting the stage of action or of life; death; decease. *Swift.*
3. A way of departure; passage out of a place. *Woodward.*
4. A going out; departure. *Glanville.*

EXI''TIAL, EXI''TIOUS, *a.* [L. *exitialis.*] Destructive to life. *Homilies.*

EX-LEG'ISLATOR, *n.* One who has been a legislator, but is not at present.

EX-MIN'ISTER, *n.* One who has been minister, but is not in office.

EX'ODE, *n.* [Gr. εξοδιον. See *Exodus.*] In *the Greek drama*, the concluding part of a play, or the part which comprehends all that is said after the last interlude. *Anacharsis.*

EX'ODUS, EX'ODY, *n.* [Gr. εξοδος; εξ and οδος, way.] Departure from a place; particularly, the departure of the Israelites from Egypt under the conduct of Moses.
2. The second book of the Old Testament, which gives a history of the departure of the Israelites from Egypt.

Ex officio, [L.] By virtue of office, and without special authority. A justice of the peace may *ex officio* take sureties of the peace.

EX'OGLOSS, *n.* [Gr. εξω and γλωσσα, tongue.]
A genus of fishes found in the American seas, whose lower jaw is trilobed, and the middle lobe protruded performs the office of a tongue.

EXOLE'TE, *a.* [L. *exoletus.*] Obsolete. [*Not in use.*]

EXOLU'TION, *n.* Laxation of the nerves. [*Not in use.*] *Brown.*

EXOLVE, *v. t.* To loose. [*Not in use.*]

EXOM'PHALOS, *n.* [Gr. εξ and ομφαλος.] A navel rupture.

EXON'ERATE, *v. t. egzon'erate.* [L. *exonero*; *ex* and *onero*, to load, *onus*, a load.]
1. To unload; to disburden.

> The vessels *exonerate* themselves into a common duct. *Ray.*

But more generally, in a figurative sense,
2. To cast off, as a charge or as blame resting on one; to clear of something that lies upon the character as an imputation; as, to *exonerate* one's self from blame, or from the charge of avarice.
3. To cast off, as an obligation, debt or duty; to discharge of responsibility or liability; as, a surety *exonerates* himself by producing a man in court.

EXON'ERATED, *pp.* Unloaded; disburdened; freed from a charge, imputation or responsibility.

EXON'ERATING, *ppr.* Unloading; disburdening; freeing from any charge or imputation.

EXONERA'TION, *n.* The act of disburdening or discharging; the act of freeing from a charge or imputation.

EXON'ERATIVE, *a.* Freeing from a burden or obligation.

EX'ORABLE, *a.* [L. *exorabilis*, from *exoro*; *ex* and *oro*, to pray.]
That may be moved or persuaded by entreaty. *Harrington.*

EXORB'ITANCE, EXORB'ITANCY, *n. egzorb'itance.* [L. *exorbitans*, from *ex* and *orbita*, the track of a wheel, *orbis*, an *orb.*]
Literally, a going beyond or without the track or usual limit. Hence, enormity; extravagance; a deviation from rule or the ordinary limits of right or propriety; as the *exorbitances* of the tongue, or of deportment.

The reverence of my presence may be a curb to your *exorbitancies*. *Dryden.*

EXORB'ITANT, *a.* [L. *exorbitans.*] Literally, departing from an orbit or usual track. Hence, deviating from the usual course; going beyond the appointed rules or established limits of right or propriety; hence, excessive; extravagant; enormous. We speak of *exorbitant* appetites and passions; *exorbitant* demands or claims; *exorbitant* taxes.

2. Anomalous; not comprehended in a settled rule or method.

The Jews were inured with causes *exorbitant*. *Hooker.*

EXORB'ITANTLY, *adv.* Enormously; excessively.

EXORB'ITATE, *v. i.* To go beyond the usual track or orbit; to deviate from the usual limit. *Bentley.*

EX'ORCISE, *v. i.* *s* as *z.* [Gr. εξορκιζω, to adjure, from ορκιζω, to bind by oath, from ορκος, an oath.]

1. To adjure by some holy name; but chiefly, to expel evil spirits by conjurations, prayers and ceremonies. To *exorcise* a person, is to expel from him the evil spirit supposed to possess him. To *exorcise* a demon or evil spirit, is to cast him out or drive him from a person, by prayers or other ceremonies. *Encyc.*

2. To purify from unclean spirits by adjurations and ceremonies; to deliver from the influence of malignant spirits or demons; as, to *exorcise* a bed or a house.

EX'ORCISED, *pp.* Expelled from a person or place by conjurations and prayers; freed from demons in like manner.

EX'ORCISER, *n.* One who pretends to cast out evil spirits by adjurations and conjuration.

EX'ORCISING, *ppr.* Expelling evil spirits by prayers and ceremonies.

EX'ORCISM, *n.* [L. *exorcismus;* Gr. εξορκισμος.]

The expulsion of evil spirits from persons or places by certain adjurations and ceremonies. *Exorcism* was common among the Jews, and still makes a part of the superstitions of some churches. *Encyc.*

EX'ORCIST, *n.* One who pretends to expel evil spirits by conjuration, prayers and ceremonies. Acts xix.

EXORD'IAL, *a.* [infra.] Pertaining to the exordium of a discourse; introductory. *Brown.*

EXORD'IUM, *n.* plu. *exordiums.* [L. from *exordior; ex* and *ordior*, to begin. See *Order.*]

In *oratory*, the beginning; the introductory part of a discourse, which prepares the audience for the main subject; the preface or proemial part of a composition. The *exordium* may be formal and deliberate, or abrupt and vehement, according to the nature of the subject and occasion.

EXORNA'TION, *n.* [L. *exornatio*, from *exorno; ex* and *orno*, to adorn.] Ornament; decoration; embellishment. *Hale. Hooker.*

EXORT'IVE, *a.* [L. *exortivus; ex* and *ortus*, a rising.] Rising; relating to the east.

EXOS'SATED, *a.* [infra.] Deprived of bones.

EXOS'SEOUS, *a.* [L. *ex* and *ossa*, bones.] Without bones; destitute of bones; as *exosseous* animals. *Brown.*

EXOT'ERIC, *a.* [Gr. εξωτερος, exterior.] External; public; opposed to *esoteric* or secret. The *exoteric* doctrines of the ancient philosophers were those which were openly professed and taught. The *esoteric* were secret, or taught only to a few chosen disciples. *Enfield. Encyc.*

EX'OTERY, *n.* What is obvious or common. *Search.*

EXOT'IC, *a.* [Gr. εξωτικος, from εξω, without.] Foreign; pertaining to or produced in a foreign country; not native; extraneous; as an *exotic* plant; an *exotic* term or word.

EXOT'IC, *n.* A plant, shrub or tree not native; a plant produced in a foreign country. *Addison.*

2. A word of foreign origin.

EXPAND', *v. t.* [L. *expando; ex* and *pando*, to open, or spread; It. *spandere*, to pour out; coinciding with Eng. *span*, D. *span, spannen*, Sw. *spånna*, Dan. *spænder.* See Ar. بَانَ Class Bn. No. 3. The primary sense is to strain or stretch, and this seems to be the sense of *bend*, L. *pandus.*]

1. To open; to spread; as, a flower *expands* its leaves.

2. To spread; to enlarge a surface; to diffuse; as, a stream *expands* its waters over a plain.

3. To dilate; to enlarge in bulk; to distend; as, to *expand* the chest by inspiration; heat *expands* all bodies; air is *expanded* by rarefaction.

4. To enlarge; to extend; as, to *expand* the sphere of benevolence; to *expand* the heart or affections.

EXPAND', *v. i.* To open; to spread. Flowers *expand* in spring.

2. To dilate; to extend in bulk or surface. Metals *expand* by heat. A lake *expands*, when swelled by rains.

3. To enlarge; as, the heart *expands* with joy.

EXPAND'ED, *pp.* Opened; spread; extended; dilated; enlarged; diffused.

EXPAND'ING, *ppr.* Opening; spreading; extending; dilating; diffusing.

EXPANSE, *n.* *expans'.* [L. *expansum.*] A spreading; extent; a wide extent of space or body; as the *expanse* of heaven.

The smooth *expanse* of crystal lakes. *Pope.*

EXPANSIBIL'ITY, *n.* [from *expansible.*] The capacity of being expanded; capacity of extension in surface or bulk; as the *expansibility* of air.

EXPANS'IBLE, *a.* [Fr. from *expand.*] Capable of being expanded or spread; capable of being extended, dilated or diffused.

Bodies are not *expansible* in proportion to their weight. *Grew.*

EXPANS'ILE, *a.* Capable of expanding, or of being dilated.

EXPAN'SION, *n.* [L. *expansio.*] The act of expanding or spreading out.

2. The state of being expanded; the enlargement of surface or bulk; dilatation. We apply *expansion* to surface, as the *expansion* of a sheet or of a lake, and to bulk, as the *expansion* of fluids or metals by heat; but not to a line or length without breadth.

3. Extent; space to which any thing is enlarged; also, pure space or distance between remote bodies.

4. Enlargement; as the *expansion* of the heart or affections.

EXPANS'IVE, *a.* [Fr.] Having the power to expand, to spread, or to dilate; as the *expansive* force of heat or fire. *Gregory.*

2. Having the capacity of being expanded; as the *expansive* quality of air; the *expansive* atmosphere. *Thomson.*

3. Widely extended; as *expansive* benevolence.

EXPANS'IVENESS, *n.* The quality of being expansive.

Ex parte, [L.] On one part; as a hearing or a council *ex parte*, on one side only.

EXPA'TIATE, *v. i.* [L. *expatior; ex* and *spatior*, to wander, to enlarge in discourse, *spatium*, space, probably allied to *pateo*, to open. Class Bd.]

1. To move at large; to rove without prescribed limits; to wander in space without restraint.

He bids his soul *expatiate* in the skies. *Pope.*

Expatiate free o'er all this scene of man *Pope.*

2. To enlarge in discourse or writing; to be copious in argument or discussion. On important topics the orator thinks himself at liberty to *expatiate.*

EXPA'TIATING, *ppr.* Roving at large; moving in space without certain limits or restraint; enlarging in discourse or writing.

EXPA'TIATOR, *n.* One who enlarges or amplifies in language.

EXPAT'RIATE, *v. t.* [Fr. *expatrier;* It. *spatriare;* from L. *ex* and *patria*, country.]

In a general sense, to banish.

To expatriate one's self, is to quit one's country, renouncing citizenship and allegiance in that country, to take residence and become a citizen in another country. The right to *expatriate one's self* is denied in feudal countries, and much controverted in the U. States.

EXPAT'RIATED, *pp.* Banished; removed from one's native country, with renunciation of citizenship and allegiance.

EXPAT'RIATING, *ppr.* Banishing; abandoning one's country, with renunciation of allegiance.

EXPATRIA'TION, *n.* Banishment. More generally, the forsaking one's own country, with a renunciation of allegiance, and with the view of becoming a permanent resident and citizen in another country.

EXPECT', *v. t.* [L. *expecto; ex* and *specto*, to look, that is, to reach forward, or to fix the eyes.]

1. To wait for.

The guards,
By me encamp'd on yonder hill, *expect*
Their motion. *Milton.*

[This sense, though often used by Gibbon, seems to be obsolescent.]

2. To look for; to have a previous apprehension of something future, whether good or evil; to entertain at least a slight belief that an event will happen. We *expect* a visit that has been promised. We *expect* money will be paid at the time it is due, though we are often disappointed. *Expect*, in its legitimate sense, always re-

fers to a *future* event. The common phrase, *I expect it was*, is as vulgar as it is improper.

EXPE€T'ABLE, *a.* To be expected; that may be expected.

EXPE€T'ANCE, } *n.* The act or state of
EXPE€T'ANCY, } expecting; expectation. *Milton. Shak.*

2. Something expected. *Shak.*
3. Hope; a looking for with pleasure. *Shak.*

EXPE€T'ANCY, *n.* In *law*, a state of waiting or suspension. An *estate in expectancy* is one which is to take effect or commence after the determination of another estate. Estates of this kind are *remainders* and *reversions.* A remainder, or estate in remainder, is one which is limited to take effect and be enjoyed after another estate is determined. Thus when a grant of land is made to A for twenty years, and after the determination of that term, to B and his heirs forever; A is tenant for years, remainder to B in fee. In this case, the estate of B is in *expectancy*, that is, waiting for the determination of the estate for years. A reversion is the residue of an estate left in the grantor, to commence in possession after the determination of a particular estate granted out by him. As when A leases an estate to B for twenty years; after the determination of that period, the estate *reverts* to the lessor, but during the term the estate of the lessor is in *expectancy.* *Blackstone.*

EXPE€T'ANT, *a.* Waiting; looking for. *Swift.*

2. An *expectant* estate, is one which is suspended till the determination of a particular estate. *Blackstone.*

EXPE€T'ANT, *n.* One who expects; one who waits in expectation; one held in dependence by his belief or hope of receiving some good. Those who have the gift of offices are usually surrounded by *expectants.*

EXPE€TA'TION, *n.* [L. *expectatio.*] The act of expecting or looking forward to a future event with at least some reason to believe the event will happen. *Expectation* differs from *hope. Hope* originates in desire, and may exist with little or no ground of belief that the desired event will arrive. *Expectation* is founded on some reasons which render the event probable. *Hope* is directed to some good; *expectation* is directed to good or evil.

> The same weakness of mind which indulges absurd *expectations*, produces petulance in disappointment. *Irving.*

2. The state of expecting, either with hope or fear.
3. Prospect of good to come.

> My soul, wait thou only on God, for my *expectation* is from him. Ps. lxii.

4. The object of expectation; the expected Messiah. *Milton.*
5. A state or qualities in a person which excite expectations in others of some future excellence; as a youth of *expectation.* *Sidney. Otway.*

We now more generally say, a youth of *promise.*

6. In chances, *expectation* is applied to contingent events, and is reducible to computation. A sum of money in expectation, when an event happens, has a determinate value before that event happens. If the chances of receiving or not receiving a hundred dollars, when an event arrives, are equal; then, before the arrival of the event, the expectation is worth half the money. *Encyc.*

EXPE€T'ATIVE, *n.* That which is expected. [*Not used.*]

EXPE€T'ER, *n.* One who expects; one who waits for something, or for another person. *Swift. Shak.*

EXPE€T'ING, *ppr.* Waiting or looking for the arrival of.

EXPE€'TORANT, *a.* [See *Expectorate.*] Having the quality of promoting discharges from the lungs.

EXPE€'TORANT, *n.* A medicine which promotes discharges from the lungs.

EXPE€'TORATE, *v. t.* [L. *expectoro;* Sp. *expectorar;* Fr. *expectorer;* from L. *ex* and *pectus*, the breast.]

To eject from the trachea or lungs; to discharge phlegm or other matter, by coughing, hawking and spitting. *Coxe.*

EXPE€'TORATED, *pp.* Discharged from the lungs.

EXPE€'TORATING, *ppr.* Throwing from the lungs by hawking and spitting.

EXPE€TORA'TION, *n.* The act of discharging phlegm or mucus from the lungs, by coughing, hawking and spitting. *Encyc.*

EXPE€'TORATIVE, *a.* Having the quality of promoting expectoration.

EXPE'DIATE, *v. t.* To expedite. [*Not in use.*]

EXPE'DIENCE, } *n.* [See *Speed, Expedient*
EXPE'DIENCY, } and *Expedite.*]

1. Fitness or suitableness to effect some good end or the purpose intended; propriety under the particular circumstances of a case. The practicability of a measure is often obvious, when the *expedience* of it is questionable.
2. Expedition; adventure. [*Not now used.*] *Shak.*
3. Expedition; haste; dispatch. [*Not now used.*] *Shak.*

EXPE'DIENT, *a.* [L. *expediens; expedio*, to hasten; Eng. *speed;* Gr. σπευδω.]

1. Literally, hastening; urging forward. Hence, tending to promote the object proposed; fit or suitable for the purpose; proper under the circumstances. Many things may be lawful, which are not *expedient.*
2. Useful; profitable.
3. Quick; expeditious. [*Not used.*] *Shak.*

EXPE'DIENT, *n.* That which serves to promote or advance; any means which may be employed to accomplish an end. Let every *expedient* be employed to effect an important object, nor let exertions cease till all *expedients* fail of producing the effect.

2. Shift; means devised or employed in an exigency. *Dryden.*

EXPE'DIENTLY, *adv.* Fitly; suitably; conveniently.

2. Hastily; quickly. [*Obs.*] *Shak.*

EXPED'ITATE, *v. t.* [L. *ex* and *pes*, foot.] In *the forest laws of England*, to cut out the balls or claws of a dog's fore feet, for the preservation of the king's game.

EXPEDITA'TION, *n.* The act of cutting out the balls or claws of a dog's fore feet. *Encyc.*

EX'PEDITE, *v. t.* [L. *expedio;* Sp. *expedir;* Fr. *expedier;* It. *spedire;* Ar. أفد to hasten, or وفد to send, to move hastily, to be suitable; Eng. *speed. Expedio* is compound. We see the same root in *impedio*, to hinder, to send against, to move in opposition.]

1. To hasten; to quicken; to accelerate motion or progress. The general sent orders to *expedite* the march of the army. Artificial heat may *expedite* the growth of plants.
2. To dispatch; to send from.

> Such charters are *expedited* of course. *Bacon.*

3. To hasten by rendering easy. See No. 1.

EX'PEDITE, *a.* [L. *expeditus.*] Quick; speedy; expeditious; as *expedite* execution. [*Little used.*] *Sandys.*

2. Easy; clear of impediments; unencumbered; as, to make a way plain and *expedite.* [*Unusual.*] *Hooker.*
3. Active; nimble; ready; prompt.

> The more *expedite* will be the soul in its operations. [*Unusual.*] *Tillotson.*

4. Light-armed. [*Not used.*] *Bacon.*

EX'PEDITELY, *adv.* Readily; hastily; speedily; promptly. *Grew.*

EXPEDI''TION, *n.* [L. *expeditio.*] Haste; speed; quickness; dispatch. The mail is conveyed with *expedition.*

2. The march of an army, or the voyage of a fleet, to a distant place, for hostile purposes; as the *expedition* of the French to Egypt; the *expedition* of Xerxes into Greece.
3. Any enterprize, undertaking or attempt by a number of persons; or the collective body which undertakes. We say, our government sent an *expedition* to the Pacific; the *expedition* has arrived.

EXPEDI''TIOUS, *a.* Quick; hasty; speedy; as an *expeditious* march.

2. Nimble; active; swift; acting with celerity; as an *expeditious* messenger or runner.

EXPEDI''TIOUSLY, *adv.* Speedily; hastily; with celerity or dispatch.

EXPED'ITIVE, *a.* Performing with speed. *Bacon.*

EXPEL', *v. t.* [L. *expello; ex* and *pello*, to drive, Gr. βαλλω; It. *espellare;* W. *yspeliaw;* and from the L. participle, Fr. *expulser.* Class Bl.]

1. To drive or force out from any inclosed place; as, to *expel* wind from the stomach, or air from a bellows. [*The word is applicable to any force, physical or moral.*]
2. To drive out; to force to leave; as, to *expel* the inhabitants of a country; to *expel* wild beasts from a forest.
3. To eject; to throw out. *Dryden.*
4. To banish; to exile. *Pope.*
5. To reject; to refuse. [*Little used.*]

> And would you not poor fellowship *expel?* *Hub. Tale.*

6. To exclude; to keep out or off. *Shak.*
7. In *college government*, to command to leave; to dissolve the connection of a stu-

dent; to interdict him from further connection.

EXPEL'LABLE, *a.* That may be expelled or driven out.

Acid *expellable* by heat. *Kirwan.*

EXPEL'LED, *pp.* Driven out or away; forced to leave; banished; exiled; excluded.

EXPEL'LER, *n.* He or that which drives out or away.

EXPEL'LING, *ppr.* Driving out; forcing away; compelling to quit or depart; banishing; excluding.

EXPEND', *v. t.* [L. *expendo; ex* and *pendo*, to weigh; Sp. *expender;* Fr. *depenser*, from L. *dispendo;* It. *spendere;* properly, to weigh off; hence, to lay out.]

1. To lay out; to disburse; to spend; to deliver or distribute, either in payment or in donations. We *expend* money for food, drink and clothing. We *expend* a little in charity, and a great deal in idle amusements.

2. To lay out; to use; to employ; to consume; as, to *expend* time and labor. I hope the time, labor and money *expended* on this book will not be wholly misemployed.

3. To use and consume; as, to *expend* hay in feeding cattle.

4. To consume; to dissipate; to waste; as, the oil of a lamp is *expended* in burning; water is *expended* in mechanical operations.

EXPEND', *v. i.* To be laid out, used or consumed.

EXPEND'ED, *pp.* Laid out; spent; disbursed; used; consumed.

EXPEND'ING, *ppr.* Spending; using; employing; wasting.

EXPEND'ITURE, *n.* The act of expending; a laying out, as of money; disbursement. A corrupt administration is known by extravagant *expenditures* of public money.

National income and *expenditure.* *Price.*

2. Money expended; expense.

The receipts and *expenditures* of this extensive country. *Hamilton.*

EXPENSE, *n. expens'.* [L. *expensum.*] A laying out or expending; the disbursing of money, or the employment and consumption, as of time or labor. Great enterprises are accomplished only by a great *expense* of money, time and labor.

2. Money expended; cost; charge; that which is disbursed in payment or in charity. A prudent man limits his *expenses* by his income. The *expenses* of war are rarely or never reimbursed by the acquisition either of goods or territory.

3. That which is used, employed, laid out or consumed; as the *expense* of time or labor.

EXPENSEFUL, *a. expens'ful.* Costly; expensive. [*Little used.*] *Wotton.*

EXPENSELESS, *a. expens'less.* Without cost or expense. *Milton.*

EXPENS'IVE, *a.* Costly; requiring much expense; as an *expensive* dress or equipage; an *expensive* family. Vices are usually more *expensive* than virtues.

2. Given to expense; free in the use of money; extravagant; lavish; *applied to persons.* Of men, some are frugal and industrious; others, idle and *expensive.* *Temple.*

3. Liberal; generous in the distribution of property.

This requires an active, *expensive*, indefatigable goodness. *Spratt.*

EXPENS'IVELY, *adv.* With great expense; at great cost or charge. *Swift.*

EXPENS'IVENESS, *n.* Costliness; the quality of incurring or requiring great expenditures of money. The *expensiveness* of war is not its greatest evil.

2. Addictedness to expense; extravagance; *applied to persons.*

EXPE'RIENCE, *n.* [L. *experientia*, from *experior*, to try; *ex* and ant. *perior;* Gr. πειραω, to attempt, whence *pirate;* G. *erfahren*, from *fahren*, to move, to go, to drive, to *ferry;* D. *ervaaren*, from *vaaren*, to go, to move, to sail; Sw. *förfara, fara;* Dan. *forfarer, farer;* Sax. and Goth. *faran;* Eng. to *fare.* The L. *periculum*, Eng. *peril*, are from the same root. We see the root of these words is to go, to *fare*, to drive, urge or press, to strain or stretch forward. See Class Br. No. 3. Ar. No. 4. 19. 23.]

1. Trial, or a series of trials or experiments; active effort or attempt to do or to prove something, or repeated efforts. A man attempts to raise wheat on moist or clayey ground; his attempt fails of success; *experience* proves that wheat will not flourish on such a soil. He repeats the trial, and his *experience* proves the same fact. A single trial is usually denominated an *experiment; experience* may be a series of trials, or the result of such trials.

2. Observation of a fact or of the same facts or events happening under like circumstances.

3. Trial from suffering or enjoyment; suffering itself; the use of the senses; as the *experience* we have of pain or sickness. We know the effect of light, of smell or of taste by *experience.* We learn the instability of human affairs by observation or by *experience.* We learn the value of integrity by *experience.* Hence,

4. Knowledge derived from trials, use, practice, or from a series of observations.

EXPE'RIENCE, *v. t.* To try by use, by suffering or by enjoyment. Thus we all *experience* pain, sorrow and pleasure; we *experience* good and evil; we often *experience* a change of sentiments and views.

2. To know by practice or trial; to gain knowledge or skill by practice or by a series of observations.

EXPE'RIENCED, *pp.* Tried; used; practiced.

2. *a.* Taught by practice or by repeated observations; skilful or wise by means of trials, use or observation; as an *experienced* artist; an *experienced* physician.

EXPE'RIENCER, *n.* One who makes trials or experiments.

EXPE'RIENCING, *ppr.* Making trial; suffering or enjoying.

EXPER'IMENT, *n.* [L. *experimentum*, from *experior*, as in *experience*, which see.]

A trial; an act or operation designed to discover some unknown truth, principle or effect, or to establish it when discovered. *Experiments* in chimistry disclose the qualities of natural bodies. A series of *experiments* proves the uniformity of the laws of matter. It is not always safe to trust to a single *experiment.* It is not expedient to try many *experiments* in legislation.

A political *experiment* cannot be made in a laboratory, nor determined in a few hours. *J. Adams.*

EXPER'IMENT, *v. i.* To make trial; to make an experiment; to operate on a body in such a manner as to discover some unknown fact, or to establish it when known. Philosophers *experiment* on natural bodies for the discovery of their qualities and combinations.

2. To try; to search by trial.

3. To experience. [*Not used.*] *Locke.*

EXPER'IMENT, *v. t.* To try; to know by trial. [*Little used.*] *Herbert.*

EXPERIMENT'AL, *a.* Pertaining to experiment.

2. Known by experiment or trial; derived from experiment. *Experimental* knowledge is the most valuable, because it is most certain, and most safely to be trusted.

3. Built on experiments; founded on trial and observations, or on a series of results, the effects of operations; as *experimental* philosophy.

4. Taught by experience; having personal experience.

Admit to the holy communion such only as profess and appear to be regenerated, and *experimental* christians. *H. Humphreys.*

5. Known by experience; derived from experience; as *experimental* religion.

EXPERIMENT'ALIST, *n.* One who makes experiments. *Burgess.*

EXPERIMENT'ALLY, *adv.* By experiment; by trial; by operation and observation of results.

2. By experience; by suffering or enjoyment. We are all *experimentally* acquainted with pain and pleasure.

EXPER'IMENTER, *n.* One who makes experiments; one skilled in experiments.

EXPER'IMENTING, *ppr.* Making experiments or trials.

EXPERT', *a.* [L. *expertus*, from *experior*, to try. See *Experience.*]

1. Properly, experienced; taught by use, practice or experience; hence, skilful; well instructed; having familiar knowledge of; as an *expert* philosopher.

2. Dextrous; adroit; ready; prompt; having a facility of operation or performance from practice; as an *expert* operator in surgery. It is usually followed by *in;* as *expert in* surgery; *expert in* performance on a musical instrument. Pope uses *expert of* arms, but improperly.

EXPERT'LY, *adv.* In a skilful or dextrous manner; adroitly; with readiness and accuracy.

EXPERT'NESS, *n.* Skill derived from practice; readiness; dexterity; adroitness; as *expertness* in musical performance; *expertness* in war or in seamanship; *expertness* in reasoning.

EXPE'TIBLE, *a.* [L. *expetibilis.*] That may be wished for; desirable. [*Not used.*]

EX'PIABLE, *a.* [L. *expiabilis.* See *Expiate.*]

That may be expiated; that may be atoned for and done away; as an *expiable* offense; *expiable* guilt.

EX'PIATE, *v. t.* [L. *expio; ex* and *pio*, to worship, to atone; *pius*, pious, mild. The primary sense is probably to *appease*, to pacify, to allay resentment, which is the usual sense of *atone* in most languages which I have examined. *Pio* is probably contracted from *pico*, and from the root of *paco*, the radical sense of which is to lay, set or fix; the primary sense of peace, *pax*. Hence the sense of *mild* in *pius*. But this opinion is offered only as probable.]

1. To atone for; to make satisfaction for; to extinguish the guilt of a crime by subsequent acts of piety or worship, by which the obligation to punish the crime is canceled. To *expiate* guilt or a crime, is to perform some act which is supposed to purify the person guilty; or some act which is accepted by the offended party as satisfaction for the injury; that is, some act by which his wrath is appeased, and his forgiveness procured.
2. To make reparation for; as, to *expiate* an injury. *Clarendon.*
3. To avert the threats of prodigies. *Johnson.*

EX'PIATED, *pp.* Atoned for; done away by satisfaction offered and accepted.

EX'PIATING, *ppr.* Making atonement or satisfaction for; destroying or removing guilt, and canceling the obligation to punish.

EXPIA'TION, *n.* [L. *expiatio.*] The act of atoning for a crime; the act of making satisfaction for an offense, by which the guilt is done away, and the obligation of the offended person to punish the crime is canceled; atonement; satisfaction. Among pagans and Jews, *expiation* was made chiefly by sacrifices, or washings and purification. Among christians, *expiation* for the sins of men is usually considered as made only by the obedience and sufferings of Christ.

2. The means by which atonement for crimes is made; atonement; as sacrifices and purification among heathens, and the obedience and death of Christ among christians.
3. Among ancient heathens, an act by which the threats of prodigies were averted. *Hayward.*

EX'PIATORY, *a.* Having the power to make atonement or expiation; as an *expiatory* sacrifice. *Hooker.*

EXPILA'TION, *n.* [L. *expilatio*, from *expilo*, to strip; *ex* and *pilo*, to *peel.*]

A stripping; the act of committing waste on land; waste. [*Little used.*]

EXPI'RABLE, *a.* [from *expire.*] That may expire; that may come to an end.

EXPIRA'TION, *n.* [L. *expiratio*, from *expiro.* See *Expire.*]

1. The act of breathing out, or forcing the air from the lungs. Respiration consists of *expiration* and *inspiration.*
2. The last emission of breath; death. *Rambler.*
3. The emission of volatile matter from any substance; evaporation; exhalation; as the *expiration* of warm air from the earth.
4. Matter expired; exhalation; vapor; fume. *Bacon.*
5. Cessation; close; end; conclusion; termination of a limited time; as the *expiration* of a month or year; the *expiration* of a term of years; the *expiration* of a lease; the *expiration* of a contract or agreement.

EXPI'RE, *v. t.* [L. *expiro*, for *exspiro*; *ex* and *spiro*, to breathe.]

1. To breathe out; to throw out the breath from the lungs; opposed to *inspire.* We *expire* air at every breath.
2. To exhale; to emit in minute particles, as a fluid or volatile matter. The earth *expires* a damp or warm vapor; the body *expires* fluid matter from the pores; plants *expire* odors.
3. To conclude. *Obs.*

EXPI'RE, *v. i.* To emit the last breath, as an animal; to die; to breathe the last.

2. To perish; to end; to fail or be destroyed; to come to nothing; to be frustrated. With the loss of battle all his hopes of empire *expired.*
3. To fly out; to be thrown out with force. [*Unusual.*]

The ponderous ball *expires.* *Dryden.*

4. To come to an end; to cease; to terminate; to close or conclude, as a given period. A lease will *expire* on the first of May. The year *expires* on Monday. The contract will *expire* at Michaelmas. The days had not *expired.*

When forty years had *expired.* Acts vii.

EXPI'RING, *ppr.* Breathing out air from the lungs; emitting fluid or volatile matter; exhaling; breathing the last breath; dying; ending; terminating.

2. *a.* Pertaining to or uttered at the time of dying; as *expiring* words; *expiring* groans. *J. Lathrop.*

EXPLA'IN, *v. t.* [L. *explano*; *ex* and *planus*, plain, open, smooth; Sp. *explanar*; It. *spianare.* See *Plain.*]

To make plain, manifest or intelligible; to clear of obscurity; to expound; to illustrate by discourse, or by notes. The first business of a preacher is to *explain* his text. Notes and comments are intended to *explain* the scriptures.

EXPLA'IN, *v. i.* To give explanations.

EXPLA'INABLE, *a.* That may be cleared of obscurity; capable of being made plain to the understanding; capable of being interpreted. *Brown.*

EXPLA'INED, *pp.* Made clear or obvious to the understanding; cleared of doubt, ambiguity or obscurity; expounded; illustrated.

EXPLA'INER, *n.* One who explains; an expositor; a commentator; an interpreter. *Harris.*

EXPLA'INING, *ppr.* Expounding; illustrating; interpreting; opening to the understanding; clearing of obscurity.

EXPLANA'TION, *n.* [L. *explanatio.*] The act of explaining, expounding or interpreting; exposition; illustration; interpretation; the act of clearing from obscurity and making intelligible; as the *explanation* of a passage in scripture, or of a contract or treaty.

2. The sense given by an expounder or interpreter.
3. A mutual exposition of terms, meaning or motives, with a view to adjust a misunderstanding and reconcile differences. Hence, reconciliation, agreement or good understanding of parties who have been at variance. The parties have come to an *explanation.*

EXPLAN'ATORY, *a.* Serving to explain; containing explanation; as *explanatory* notes.

EXPLE'TION, *n.* [L. *expletio.*] Accomplishment; fulfilment. [*Little used.*] *Killingbeck.*

EX'PLETIVE, *a.* [Fr. *expletif*, from L. *expleo*, to fill.] Filling; added for supply or ornament.

EX'PLETIVE, *n.* In *language*, a word or syllable inserted to fill a vacancy, or for ornament. The Greek language abounds with *expletives.*

EX'PLICABLE, *a.* [L. *explicabilis.* See *Explicate.*]

1. Explainable; that may be unfolded to the mind; that may be made intelligible. Many difficulties in old authors are not *explicable.*
2. That may be accounted for. The conduct and measures of the administration are not *explicable*, by the usual rules of judging.

EX'PLICATE, *v. t.* [L. *explico*, to unfold; *ex* and *plico*, to fold; Fr. *expliquer*; Sp. *explicar*; It. *spiegare.*]

1. To unfold; to expand; to open. "They *explicate* the leaves." [*In this sense, the word is not common, and hardly admissible.*] *Blackmore.*
2. To unfold the meaning or sense; to explain; to clear of difficulties or obscurity; to interpret.

The last verse of his last satyr is not yet sufficiently *explicated.* *Dryden.*

EX'PLICATED, *pp.* Unfolded; explained.

EX'PLICATING, *ppr.* Unfolding; explaining; interpreting.

EXPLICA'TION, *n.* The act of opening or unfolding.

2. The act of explaining; explanation; exposition; interpretation; as the *explication* of the parables of our Savior.
3. The sense given by an expositor or interpreter. *Johnson.*

EX'PLICATIVE, } *a.* Serving to unfold or explain; tending to lay open to the understanding. *Watts.*
EX'PLICATORY, }

EX'PLICATOR, *n.* One who unfolds or explains; an expounder.

EXPLIC'IT, *a.* [L. *explicitus*, part. of *explico*, to unfold.]

1. Literally, unfolded. Hence, plain in language; open to the understanding; clear, not obscure or ambiguous; express, not merely implied. An *explicit* proposition or declaration is that in which the words, in their common acceptation, express the true meaning of the person who utters them, and in which there is no ambiguity or disguise.
2. Plain; open; clear; unreserved; having no disguised meaning or reservation; *applied to persons.* He was *explicit* in his terms.

EXPLIC'ITLY, *adv.* Plainly; expressly; without duplicity; without disguise or reservation of meaning; not by inference or implication. He *explicitly* avows his intention.

EXPLIC'ITNESS, *n.* Plainness of language or expression; clearness; direct expression of ideas or intention, without reserve or ambiguity.

EXPLO'DE, *v. i.* [L. *explodo*; *ex* and *plaudo*, to utter a burst of sound, from the root of *loud.*]

Properly, to burst forth, as sound; to utter a report with sudden violence. Hence, to burst and expand with force and a violent report, as an elastic fluid. We say, gun powder *explodes*, on the application of fire; a volcano *explodes;* a meteor *explodes.*

EXPLO'DE, *v. t.* To decry or reject with noise; to express disapprobation of, with noise or marks of contempt; as, to *explode* a play on the stage. Hence,

2. To reject with any marks of disapprobation or disdain; to treat with contempt, and drive from notice; to drive into dispute; or in general, to condemn; to reject; to cry down. Astrology is now *exploded.*

3. To drive out with violence and noise. [*Little used.*]

The kindled powder *exploded* the ball. *Blackmore.*

EXPLO'DED, *pp.* Driven away by hisses or noise; rejected with disapprobation or contempt; condemned; cried down.

EXPLO'DER, *n.* One who explodes; a hisser; one who rejects.

EXPLO'DING, *ppr.* Bursting and expanding with force and a violent report; rejecting with marks of disapprobation or contempt; rejecting; condemning.

EXPLOIT', *n.* [Fr. *exploit;* Norm. *exploit, esploit*, dispatch; *expleiter*, to be dispatched, exercised or employed; *ploit*, dispatch; Arm. *espled, espledi, explet.*]

1. A deed or act; more especially, a heroic act; a deed of renown; a great or noble achievement; as the *exploits* of Alexander, of Cesar, of Washington. [*Exploiture*, in a like sense, is not in use.]

2. In a *ludicrous sense*, a great act of wickedness.

EXPLOIT', *v. t.* To achieve. [*Not in use.*] *Camden.*

EXPLO'RATE, *v. t.* To explore. [*Not used.* See *Explore.*]

EXPLORA'TION, *n.* [See *Explore.*] The act of exploring; close search; strict or careful examination. *Boyle.*

EXPLORA'TOR, *n.* One who explores; one who searches or examines closely.

EXPLO'RATORY, *a.* Serving to explore; searching; examining.

EXPLO'RE, *v. t.* [L. *exploro; ex* and *ploro*, to cry out, to wail, to bawl. The compound appears to convey a very different sense from the simple verb *ploro;* but the primary sense is to stretch, strain, drive; applied to the *voice*, it is to strain or press out sounds or words; applied to the *eyes*, it is to stretch or reach, as in prying curiosity.]

1. To search for making discovery; to view with care; to examine closely by the eye. Moses sent spies to *explore* the land of Canaan.

2. To search by any means; to try; as, to *explore* the deep by a plummet or lead.

3. To search or pry into; to scrutinize; to inquire with care; to examine closely with a view to discover truth; as, to *explore* the depths of science.

EXPLO'RED, *pp.* Searched; viewed; examined closely.

EXPLO'REMENT, *n.* Search; trial. [*Little used.*] *Brown.*

EXPLO'RING, *ppr.* Searching; viewing; examining with care.

EXPLO'SION, *n.* s as z. [from *explode.*]

1. A bursting with noise; a bursting or sudden expansion of any elastic fluid, with force and a loud report; as the *explosion* of powder.

2. The discharge of a piece of ordnance with a loud report.

3. The sudden burst of sound in a volcano, &c.

EXPLO'SIVE, *a.* Driving or bursting out with violence and noise; causing explosion; as the *explosive* force of gun-powder. *Woodward.*

EXPOLIA'TION, *n.* [L. *expoliatio.*] A spoiling; a wasting. [See *Spoliation.*]

EXPOLISH, for *polish*, a *useless word.*

EXPO'NENT, *n.* [L. *exponens; expono*, to expose or set forth; *ex* and *pono*, to place.]

1. In *algebra*, the number or figure which, placed above a root at the right hand, denotes how often that root is repeated, or how many multiplications are necessary to produce the power. Thus, a^2 denotes the second power of the root *a*, or *aa:* a^4 denotes the fourth power. The figure is the exponent or index of the power. *Day's Algebra.*

2. The exponent of the ratio or proportion between two numbers or quantities, is the quotient arising when the antecedent is divided by the consequent. Thus *six* is the *exponent* of the ratio of *thirty* to *five.* *Bailey. Harris. Encyc.*

EXPONEN'TIAL, *a.* *Exponential* curves are such as partake both of the nature of algebraic and transcendental ones. They partake of the former, because they consist of a finite number of terms, though these terms themselves are indeterminate; and they are in some measure transcendental, because they cannot be algebraically constructed. *Harris.*

EXPO'RT, *v. t.* [L. *exporto; ex* and *porto*, to carry. *Porto* seems allied to *fero*, and Eng. *bear.* Class Br.]

To carry out; but appropriately, and perhaps exclusively, to convey or transport, in traffick, produce and goods from one country to another, or from one state or jurisdiction to another, either by water or land. We *export* wares and merchandize from the United States to Europe. The Northern States *export* manufactures to South Carolina and Georgia. Goods are *exported* from Persia to Syria and Egypt on camels.

EX'PORT, *n.* A commodity actually conveyed from one country or state to another in traffick, or a commodity which may be exported; used chiefly in the plural, *exports.* We apply the word to goods or produce actually carried abroad, or to such as are usually exported in commerce.

EXPO'RTABLE, *a.* That may be exported.

EXPORTA'TION, *n.* The act of exporting; the act of conveying goods and productions from one country or state to another in the course of commerce. A country is benefited or enriched by the *exportation* of its surplus productions.

2. The act of carrying out.

EXPO'RTED, *pp.* Carried out of a country or state in traffick.

EXPO'RTER, *n.* The person who exports; the person who ships goods, wares and merchandize of any kind to a foreign country, or who sends them to market in a distant country or state; opposed to *importer.*

EXPO'RTING, *ppr.* Conveying to a foreign country or to another state, as goods, produce or manufactures.

EX'PORT-TRADE, *n.* The trade which consists in the exportation of commodities.

EXPO'SAL, *n.* Exposure. [*Not in use.*] *Swift.*

EXPO'SE, *v. t.* s as z. [Fr. *exposer;* L. *expositum*, from *expono; ex* and *pono*, to place; It. *esporre*, for *exponere.* The radical sense of *pono* is to set or place, or rather to throw or thrust down. To *expose* is to set or throw open, or to thrust forth.]

1. To lay open; to set to public view; to disclose; to uncover or draw from concealment; as, to *expose* the secret artifices of a court; to *expose* a plan or design.

2. To make bare; to uncover; to remove from any thing that which guards or protects; as, to *expose* the head or the breast to the air.

3. To remove from shelter; to place in a situation to be affected or acted on; as, to *expose* one's self to violent heat.

4. To lay open to attack, by any means; as, to *expose* an army or garrison.

5. To make liable; to subject; as, to *expose* one's self to pain, grief or toil; to *expose* one's self to insult.

6. To put in the power of; as, to *expose* one's self to the seas.

7. To lay open to censure, ridicule or contempt.

A fool might once himself alone *expose.* *Pope.*

8. To lay open, in almost any manner; as, to *expose* one's self to examination or scrutiny.

9. To put in danger. The good soldier never shrinks from *exposing* himself, when duty requires it.

10. To cast out to chance; to place abroad, or in a situation unprotected. Some nations *expose* their children.

11. To lay open; to make public. Be careful not unnecessarily to *expose* the faults of a neighbor.

12. To offer; to place in a situation to invite purchasers; as, to *expose* goods to sale.

13. To offer to inspection; as, to *expose* paintings in a gallery.

EXPO'SED, *pp.* Laid open; laid bare; uncovered; unprotected; made liable to attack; offered for sale; disclosed; made public; offered to view.

EXPO'SEDNESS, *n.* A state of being exposed, open to attack, or unprotected; as an *exposedness* to sin or temptation. *Edwards.*

EXPO'SER, *n.* One who exposes.

EXPO'SING, *ppr.* Lying or laying open; making bare; putting in danger; disclosing; placing in any situation without protection; offering to inspection or to sale.

EXPOSI''TION, *n.* A laying open; a setting to public view.

2. A situation in which a thing is exposed or laid open, or in which it has an unobstructed view, or in which a free passage to it is open; as, a house has an easterly *exposition*, an *exposition* to the south or to a southern prospect. The *exposition* gives

a free access to the air or to the sun's rays. *Arbuthnot.*

3. Explanation; interpretation; a laying open the sense or meaning of an author, or of any passage in a writing. *Dryden.*

EXPOS'ITIVE, *a.* Explanatory; laying open. *Pearson.*

EXPOS'ITOR, *n.* [L.] One who expounds or explains; an interpreter. *South.*

2. A dictionary or vocabulary which explains words. *Encyc.*

EXPOS'ITORY, *a.* Serving to explain; tending to illustrate. *Johnson.*

Ex post facto. [L.] In law, done after another thing. An estate granted may be made good by matter *ex post facto*, which was not good at first.

An *ex post facto* law, in criminal cases, consists in declaring an act penal or criminal, which was innocent when done; or in raising the grade of an offense, making it greater than it was when committed, or increasing the punishment after the commission of the offense; or in altering the rules of evidence, so as to allow different or less evidence to convict the offender, than was required when the offense was committed. *Sergeant.*

An *ex post facto* law is one that renders an act punishable in a manner in which it was not punishable at the time it was committed. *Cranch, Reports.*

This definition is distinguished for its comprehensive brevity and precision. *Kent's Commentaries.*

In a free government, no person can be subjected to punishment by an *ex post facto* law.

EXPOS'TULATE, *v. i.* [L. *expostulo; ex* and *postulo*, to require, probably from the root of *posco.*]

To reason earnestly with a person, on some impropriety of his conduct, representing the wrong he has done or intends, and urging him to desist, or to make redress; followed by *with.*

The emperor's embassador *expostulated* with the king, that he had broken the league with the emperor. *Hayward.*

EXPOS'TULATE, *v. t.* To discuss; to examine. [*Not used.*]

EXPOS'TULATING, *ppr.* Reasoning or urging arguments against any improper conduct.

EXPOSTULA'TION, *n.* Reasoning with a person in opposition to his conduct; the act of pressing on a person reasons or arguments against the impropriety of his conduct, and in some cases, demanding redress or urging reformation.

2. In *rhetoric*, an address containing expostulation. *Encyc.*

EXPOS'TULATOR, *n.* One who expostulates.

EXPOS'TULATORY, *a.* Containing expostulation; as an *expostulatory* address or debate.

EXPO'SURE, *n. s* as z. [from *expose.*] The act of exposing or laying open.

2. The state of being laid open to view, to danger or to any inconvenience; as *exposure* to observation; *exposure* to cold, or to the air; *exposure* to censure.

3. The situation of a place in regard to points of compass, or to a free access of air or light. We say, a building or a garden or a wall has a northern or a southern *exposure.* We speak of its *exposure* or exposition to a free current of air, or to the access of light.

EXPOUND', *v. t.* [L. *expono; ex* and *pono*, to set.]

1. To explain; to lay open the meaning; to clear of obscurity; to interpret; as, to *expound* a text of scripture; to *expound* a law.

2. To lay open; to examine; as, to *expound* the pocket. [*Not used.*] *Hudibras.*

EXPOUND'ED, *pp.* Explained; laid open; interpreted.

EXPOUND'ER, *n.* An explainer; one who interprets or explains the meaning.

EXPOUND'ING, *ppr.* Explaining; laying open; making clear to the understanding; interpreting.

EX-PRE'FECT, *n.* A prefect out of office; one who has been a prefect and is displaced.

EX-PRES'IDENT, *n.* One who has been president, but is no longer in the office.

EXPRESS', *v. t.* [Sp. *expresar;* Port. *expressar;* L. *expressum, exprimo; ex* and *premo*, to press. See *Press.*]

1. To press or squeeze out; to force out by pressure; as, to *express* the juice of grapes or of apples.

2. To utter; to declare in words; to speak. He *expressed* his ideas or his meaning with precision. His views were *expressed* in very intelligible terms.

3. To write or engrave; to represent in written words or language. The covenants in the deed are well *expressed.*

4. To represent; to exhibit by copy or resemblance.

So kids and whelps their sires and dams *express.* *Dryden.*

5. To represent or show by imitation or the imitative arts; to form a likeness; as in painting or sculpture.

Each skilful artist shall *express* thy form. *Smith.*

6. To show or make known; to indicate. A downcast eye or look may *express* humility, shame or guilt.

7. To denote; to designate.

Moses and Aaron took these men, who are *expressed* by their names. Num. i.

8. To extort; to elicit. [*Little used.*] *B. Jonson.*

EXPRESS', *a.* Plain; clear; expressed; direct; not ambiguous. We are informed in *express* terms or words. The terms of the contract are *express.*

2. Given in direct terms; not implied or left to inference. This is the *express* covenant or agreement. We have his *express* consent. We have an *express* law on the subject. *Express* warranty; *express* malice.

3. Copied; resembling; bearing an exact representation.

His face *express.* *Milton.*

4. Intended or sent for a particular purpose, or on a particular errand; as, to send a messenger *express.*

EXPRESS', *n.* A messenger sent on a particular errand or occasion; usually, a courier sent to communicate information of an important event, or to deliver important dispatches. It is applied also to boats or vessels sent to convey important information. *Clarendon. Dryden.*

2. A message sent. *King Charles.*

3. A declaration in plain terms. [*Not in use.*] *Norris.*

EXPRESS'ED, *pp.* Squeezed or forced out, as juice or liquor; uttered in words; set down in writing or letters; declared; represented; shown.

EXPRESS'IBLE, *a.* That may be expressed; that may be uttered, declared, shown or represented.

2. That may be squeezed out.

EXPRESS'ING, *ppr.* Forcing out by pressure; uttering; declaring; showing; representing.

EXPRES'SION, *n.* The act of expressing; the act of forcing out by pressure, as juices and oils from plants.

2. The act of uttering, declaring or representing; utterance; declaration; representation; as an *expression* of the public will.

3. A phrase, or mode of speech; as an old *expression;* an odd *expression.*

4. In *rhetoric*, elocution; diction; the peculiar manner of utterance, suited to the subject and sentiment.

No adequate description can be given of the nameless and ever varying shades of *expression* which real pathos gives to the voice. *Porter's Analysis.*

5. In *painting*, a natural and lively representation of the subject; as the expression of the eye, of the countenance, or of a particular action or passion.

6. In *music*, the tone, grace or modulation of voice or sound suited to any particular subject; that manner which gives life and reality to ideas and sentiments.

7. *Theatrical expression*, is a distinct, sonorous and pleasing pronunciation, accompanied with action suited to the subject.

EXPRESS'IVE, *a.* Serving to express; serving to utter or represent; followed by *of.* He sent a letter couched in terms *expressive of* his gratitude.

Each verse so swells *expressive of* her woes. *Tickel.*

2. Representing with force; emphatical. These words are very *expressive.*

3. Showing; representing; as an *expressive* sign.

EXPRESS'IVELY, *adv.* In an expressive manner; clearly; fully; with a clear representation.

EXPRESS'IVENESS, *n.* The quality of being expressive; the power of expression or representation by words.

2. The power or force of representation; the quality of presenting a subject strongly to the senses or to the mind; as the *expressiveness* of the eye, or of the features, or of sounds.

EXPRESS'LY, *adv.* In direct terms; plainly.

EXPRESS'URE, *n.* Expression; utterance; representation; mark; impression. [*Little used.*] *Shak.*

EX'PROBRATE, *v. t.* [L. *exprobro; ex* and *probrum*, deformity, a shameful act.]

To upbraid; to censure as reproachful; to blame; to condemn. *Brown.*

EXPROBRA'TION, *n.* The act of charging or censuring reproachfully; reproachful accusation; the act of upbraiding.

No need such boasts, or *exprobrations* false
Of cowardice. *Philips.*

EXPROBRA'TIVE, *a.* Upbraiding; expressing reproach. *Sherley.*

EXPRO'PRIATE, *v. t.* [L. *ex* and *proprius*, own.]
To disengage from appropriation; to hold no longer as one's own; to give up a claim to exclusive property. *Boyle.*

EXPROPRIA'TION, *n.* The act of discarding appropriation, or declining to hold as one's own; the surrender of a claim to exclusive property. *Walsh.*

EXPU'GN, *v. t.* *expu'ne.* [L. *expugno*; *ex* and *pugno*, to fight.] To conquer; to take by assault. *Johnson.*

EXPU'GNABLE, *a.* That may be forced.

EXPUGNA'TION, *n.* Conquest; the act of taking by assault. *Sandys.*

EXPU'GNER, *n.* One who subdues. *Sherwood.*

EXPULSE, *v. t.* *expuls'.* [Fr. *expulser*, from L. *expulsus*, *expello*; *ex* and *pello*, to drive.]
To drive out; to expel. [*Little used.*] *Shak. Bacon.*

EXPUL'SION, *n.* The act of driving out or expelling; a driving away by violence; as the *expulsion* of the thirty tyrants from Athens, or of Adam from paradise.
2. The state of being driven out or away.

EXPUL'SIVE, *a.* Having the power of driving out or away; serving to expel. *Wiseman.*

EXPUNC'TION, *n.* [See *Expunge.*] The act of expunging; the act of blotting out or erasing. *Milton.*

EXPUNGE, *v. t.* *expunj'.* [L. *expungo*; *ex* and *pungo*, to thrust, to prick.]
1. To blot out, as with a pen; to rub out; to efface, as words; to obliterate. We *expunge* single words or whole lines or sentences.
2. To efface; to strike out; to wipe out or destroy; to annihilate; as, to *expunge* an offense. *Sandys.*

Expunge the whole, or lop the excrescent parts. *Pope.*

EXPUN'GED, *pp.* Blotted out; obliterated; destroyed.

EXPUN'GING, *ppr.* Blotting out; erasing; effacing; destroying.

EX'PURGATE, *v. t.* [L. *expurgo*; *ex* and *purgo*, to cleanse.]
To purge; to cleanse; to purify from any thing noxious, offensive or erroneous. *Faber.*

EX'PURGATED, *pp.* Purged; cleansed; purified.

EX'PURGATING, *ppr.* Purging; cleansing; purifying.

EXPURGA'TION, *n.* The act of purging or cleansing; evacuation. *Wiseman.*
2. A cleansing; purification from any thing noxious, offensive, sinful or erroneous. *Brown.*

EX'PURGATOR, *n.* One who expurgates or purifies.

EXPURG'ATORY, *a.* Cleansing; purifying; serving to purify from any thing noxious or erroneous; as the *expurgatory* index of the Romanists, which directs the expunction of passages of authors contrary to their creed or principles.

Expurgatory animadversions. *Brown.*

EXPURGE, *v. t.* *expurj'.* [L. *expurgo.*] To purge away. [*Not in use.*] *Milton.*

EXQUI'RE, *v. t.* [L. *exquiro.*] To search into or out. [*Not in use.*] *Sandys.*

EX'QUISITE, *a.* *s* as *z.* [L. *exquisitus*, from *exquiro*; *ex* and *quæro*, to seek.] Literally, sought out or searched for with care; whence, choice; select. Hence,
1. Nice; exact; very excellent; complete; as a vase of *exquisite* workmanship.
2. Nice; accurate; capable of nice perception; as *exquisite* sensibility.
3. Nice; accurate; capable of nice discrimination; as *exquisite* judgment, taste or discernment.
4. Being in the highest degree; extreme; as, to relish pleasure in an *exquisite* degree. So we say, *exquisite* pleasure or pain.

The most *exquisite* of human satisfactions flows from an approving conscience. *J. M. Mason.*

5. Very sensibly felt; as a painful and *exquisite* impression on the nerves. *Cheyne.*

EX'QUISITELY, *adv.* Nicely; accurately; with great perfection; as a work *exquisitely* finished; *exquisitely* written.
2. With keen sensation or with nice perception. We feel pain more *exquisitely* when nothing diverts our attention from it.

We see more *exquisitely* with one eye shut. *Bacon.*

EX'QUISITENESS, *n.* Nicety; exactness; accuracy; completeness; perfection; as the *exquisiteness* of workmanship.
2. Keenness; sharpness; extremity; as the *exquisiteness* of pain or grief.

EXQUIS'ITIVE, *a.* Curious; eager to discover. [*Not in use.*]

EXQUIS'ITIVELY, *adv.* Curiously; minutely. [*Not in use.*] *Sidney.*

EX-REPRESENT'ATIVE, *n.* One who has been formerly a representative, but is no longer one.

EXSAN'GUIOUS, *a.* [L. *exsanguis*; *ex* and *sanguis*, blood.]
Destitute of blood, or rather of red blood, as an animal. *Encyc.*

EXSCIND', *v. t.* [L. *exscindo.*] To cut off. [*Little used.*]

EXSCRI'BE, *v. t.* [L. *exscribo.*] To copy; to transcribe. [*Not in use.*] *B. Jonson.*

EX'SCRIPT, *n.* A copy; a transcript. [*Not used.*]

EX-SEC'RETARY, *n.* One who has been secretary, but is no longer in office.

EXSEC'TION, *n.* [L. *exsectio.*] A cutting off, or a cutting out. *Darwin.*

EX-SEN'ATOR, *n.* One who has been a senator, but is no longer one.

EXSERT', EXSERT'ED, } *a.* [L. *exsero*; *ex* and *sero.* See *Exert.*] Standing out; protruded from the corol; as stamens *exsert.* *Eaton.*

A small portion of the basal edge of the shell *exserted.* *Barnes.*

EXSERT'ILE, *a.* That may be thrust out or protruded. *Fleming.*

EXSIC'CANT, *a.* [See *Exsiccate.*] Drying; evaporating moisture; having the quality of drying.

EX'SICCATE, *v. t.* [L. *exsicco*; *ex* and *sicco*, to dry.]
To dry; to exhaust or evaporate moisture. *Brown. Mortimer.*

EX'SICCATED, *pp.* Dried.

EX'SICCATING, *ppr.* Drying; evaporating moisture.

EXSICCA'TION, *n.* The act or operation of drying; evaporation of moisture; dryness. *Brown.*

EXSPUI''TION, EXPUI''TION, } *n.* [L. *expuo* for *exspuo.*] A discharge of saliva by spitting. *Darwin.*

EXSTIP'ULATE, *a.* [L. *ex* and *stipula*, straw.] In *botany*, having no stipules. *Martyn.*

EXSUC'COUS, *a.* [L. *exsuccus*; *ex* and *succus*, juice.] Destitute of juice; dry. *Brown.*

EXSUC'TION, *n.* [L. *exugo*, *exsugo*, to suck out; *sugo*, to suck.] The act of sucking out. *Boyle.*

EXSUDA'TION, *n.* [L. *exudo*, for *exsudo.*] A sweating; a discharge of humors or moisture from animal bodies by sweat or extillation through the pores.
2. The discharge of the juices of a plant, moisture from the earth, &c.

EXSU'DE, *v. t.* [supra.] To discharge the moisture or juices of a living body through the pores; also, to discharge the liquid matter of a plant by incisions.

Our forests *exude* turpentine in the greatest abundance. *Dwight.*

EXSU'DE, *v. i.* To flow from a living body through the pores or by a natural discharge, as juice.

EXSU'DED, *pp.* Emitted, as juice.

EXSU'DING, *ppr.* Discharging, as juice.

EXSUFFLA'TION, *n.* [L. *ex* and *sufflo*, to blow.]
1. A blowing or blast from beneath. [*Little used.*] *Bacon.*
2. A kind of exorcism. *Fulke.*

EXSUF'FOLATE, *a.* Contemptible. [*Not in use.*] *Shak.*

EXSUS'CITATE, *v. t.* [L. *exsuscito.*] To rouse; to excite. [*Not used.*]

EXSUSCITA'TION, *n.* A stirring up; a rousing. [*Not used.*] *Hallywell.*

EX'TANCE, *n.* [L. *extans.*] Outward existence. [*Not used.*] *Brown.*

EX'TANCY, *n.* [L. *exstans*, *extans*, standing out, from *exsto*; *ex* and *sto*, to stand.]
1. The state of rising above others.
2. Parts rising above the rest; opposed to *depression.* [*Little used.*] *Boyle.*

EX'TANT, *a.* [L. *exstans*, *extans*, supra.] Standing out or above any surface; protruded.

That part of the teeth which is *extant* above the gums. *Ray.*

A body partly immersed in a fluid and partly *extant.* *Bentley.*

2. In being; now subsisting; not suppressed, destroyed, or lost. A part only of the history of Livy, and of the writings of Cicero, is now *extant.* Socrates wrote much, but none of his writings are *extant.* The *extant* works of orators and philosophers. *Mitford.*

EXTASY, EXTATIC. [See *Ecstasy*, *Ecstatic.*]

EXTEM'PORAL, *a.* [L. *extemporalis*; *ex* and *tempus*, time.] Made or uttered at the moment, without premeditation; as an *extemporal* discourse. *Hooker. Wotton.*
2. Speaking without premeditation. *B. Jonson.*
Instead of this word, *extemporaneous* and *extemporary* are now used.

EXTEM'PORALLY, *adv.* Without premeditation. *Shak.*

EXTEMPORA'NEAN, *a.* [*Not used.* See *Extemporaneous.*]

EXTEMPORA'NEOUS, *a.* [L. *extemporaneus; ex* and *tempus*, time.]
Composed, performed or uttered at the time the subject occurs, without previous study; unpremeditated; as an *extemporaneous* address; an *extemporaneous* production; an *extemporaneous* prescription.

EXTEMPORA'NEOUSLY, *adv.* Without previous study.

EXTEM'PORARILY, *adv.* Without previous study.

EXTEM'PORARY, *a.* [L. *ex* and *temporarius*, from *tempus*, time.]
Composed, performed or uttered without previous study or preparation. [See *Extemporaneous.*]

EXTEM'PORE, *adv. extem'pory.* [L. abl.]
1. Without previous study or meditation; without preparation; suddenly; as, to write or speak *extempore*.
2. It is used as an adjective, improperly, at least without necessity; as an *extempore* dissertation. *Addison.*

EXTEM'PORINESS, *n.* The state of being unpremeditated; the state of being composed, performed or uttered without previous study. *Johnson.*

EXTEM'PORIZE, *v. i.* To speak extempore; to speak without previous study or preparation. To *extemporize* well requires a ready mind well furnished with knowledge.
2. To discourse without notes or written composition.

EXTEM'PORIZER, *n.* One who speaks without previous study, or without written composition.

EXTEM'PORIZING, *ppr.* Speaking without previous study, or preparation by writing.

The *extemporizing* faculty is never more out of its element than in the pulpit. *South.*

EXTEND', *v. t.* [L. *extendo; ex* and *tendo*, from Gr. τεινω, L. *teneo*; Fr. *etendre*; It. *stendere*; Sp. *extender*; Arm. *astenna*; W. *estyn*, from *tynu*, to pull, or *tyn*, a pull, a stretch.]
1. To stretch in any direction; to carry forward, or continue in length, as a line; to spread in breadth; to expand or dilate in size. The word is particularly applied to length and breadth. We *extend* lines in surveying; we *extend* roads, limits, bounds; we *extend* metal plates by hammering.
2. To stretch; to reach forth; as, to *extend* the arm or hand.
3. To spread; to expand; to enlarge; to widen; as, to *extend* the capacities, or intellectual powers; to *extend* the sphere of usefulness; to *extend* commerce.
4. To continue; to prolong; as, to *extend* the time of payment; to *extend* the season of trial.
5. To communicate; to bestow on; to use or exercise towards.

He hath *extended* mercy to me before the king. Ezra vii.

6. To impart; to yield or give.

I will *extend* peace to her like a river. Is. lxvi.

7. In *law*, to value lands taken by a writ of extent in satisfaction of a debt; or to levy on lands, as an execution.

The execution was delivered to the sheriff, who *extended* the same on certain real estate. *Mass. Rep.*

EXTEND', *v. i.* To stretch; to reach; to be continued in length or breadth. The state of Massachusetts *extends* west to the border of the state of New York. Connecticut river *extends* from Canada to the sound. How far will your argument or proposition *extend?* Let our charities *extend* to the heathen.

EXTEND'ED, *pp.* Stretched; spread; expanded; enlarged; bestowed on; communicated; valued under a writ of *extendi facias*; levied.

EXTEND'ER, *n.* He or that which extends or stretches.

EXTEND'IBLE, *a.* Capable of being extended; that may be stretched, extended, enlarged, widened or expanded.
2. That may be taken by a writ of extent and valued.

EXTEND'ING, *ppr.* Stretching; reaching; continuing in length; spreading; enlarging; valuing.

EXTEND'LESSNESS, *n.* Unlimited extension. [*Not used.*] *Hale.*

EXTENS'IBILITY, *n.* [from *extensible.*] The capacity of being extended, or of suffering extension; as the *extensibility* of a fiber, or of a plate of metal. *Grew.*

EXTENS'IBLE, *a.* [from L. *extensus.*] That may be extended; capable of being stretched in length or breadth; susceptible of enlargement. *Holder.*

EXTENS'IBLENESS, *n.* Extensibility, which see.

EXTENS'ILE, *a.* Capable of being extended.

EXTEN'SION, *n.* [L. *extensio.*] The act of extending; a stretching.
2. The state of being extended; enlargement in breadth, or continuation of length.
3. In *philosophy*, that property of a body by which it occupies a portion of space.

EXTEN'SIONAL, *a.* Having great extent. [*Not used.*] *More.*

EXTENS'IVE, *a.* Wide; large; having great enlargement or extent; as an *extensive* farm; an *extensive* field; an *extensive* lake; an *extensive* sphere of operations; *extensive* benevolence.
2. That may be extended. [*Not used.*] *Boyle.*

EXTENS'IVELY, *adv.* Widely; largely; to a great extent; as, a story is *extensively* circulated.

EXTENS'IVENESS, *n.* Wideness; largeness; extent; as the *extensiveness* of the ocean.
2. Extent; diffusiveness; as the *extensiveness* of a man's charities or benevolence.
3. Capacity of being extended. [*Little used.*] *Ray.*

EXTENS'OR, *n.* In *anatomy*, a muscle which serves to extend or straighten any part of the body, as an arm or a finger; opposed to *flexor*. *Coxe. Cyc.*

EXTENT', *a.* Extended. *Spenser.*

EXTENT', *n.* [L. *extentus.* It is frequently accented on the first syllable.]
1. Space or degree to which a thing is extended; hence, compass; bulk; size; as a great *extent* of country, or of body.
2. Length; as an *extent* of line.
3. Communication; distribution.

The *extent* of equal justice. *Shak.*

4. In *law*, a writ of execution or *extendi facias*, commanding a sheriff to value the lands of a debtor; or *extent* is the act of the sheriff or commissioner in making the valuation. *Encyc.*

EXTEN'UATE, *v. t.* [L. *extenuo; ex* and *tenuo*, to make *thin*; Sp. *extenuar*; It. *stenuare.* See *Thin.*]
1. To make thin, lean or slender. Sickness *extenuates* the body. *Encyc.*
2. To lessen; to diminish; as a crime or guilt.

But fortune there *extenuates* the crime. *Dryden.*

3. To lessen in representation; to palliate; opposed to *aggravate*.
4. To lessen or diminish in honor. [*Little used.*] *Milton.*
5. To make thin or rare; opposed to *condense*. [*Little used.*] *Bacon.*

EXTEN'UATE, *a.* Thin; slender. [*Not used.*]

EXTEN'UATED, *pp.* Made thin, lean or slender; made smaller; lessened; diminished; palliated; made rare.

EXTEN'UATING, *ppr.* Making thin or slender; lessening; diminishing; palliating; making rare.

EXTENUA'TION, *n.* The act of making thin; the process of growing thin or lean; the losing of flesh.
2. The act representing any thing less wrong, faulty or criminal than it is in fact; palliation; opposed to *aggravation*; as the *extenuation* of faults, injuries or crimes.
3. Mitigation; alleviation; as the *extenuation* of punishment. [*Not common.*] *Atterbury.*

EXTE'RIOR, *a.* [L. from *exterus*, foreign; Fr. *exterieur*; It. *esteriore.*]
1. External; outward; applied to the outside or outer surface of a body, and opposed to *interior*. We speak of the *exterior* and interior surfaces of a concavo-convex lens.
2. External; on the outside, with reference to a person; extrinsic. We speak of an object *exterior* to a man, as opposed to that which is within or in his mind.
3. Foreign; relating to foreign nations; as the *exterior* relations of a state or kingdom.

EXTE'RIOR, *n.* The outward surface; that which is external.
2. Outward or visible deportment; appearance.

EXTE'RIORLY, *adv.* Outwardly; externally. [*An ill formed word.*] *Shak.*

EXTE'RIORS, *n. plu.* The outward parts of a thing. *Shak.*
2. Outward or external deportment, or forms and ceremonies; visible acts; as the *exteriors* of religion.

EXTERM'INATE, *v. t.* [L. *extermino; ex* and *terminus*, limit.] Literally, to drive from within the limits or borders. Hence,
1. To destroy utterly; to drive away; to extirpate; as, to *exterminate* a colony, a tribe or a nation; to *exterminate* inhabitants or a race of men.
2. To eradicate; to root out; to extirpate; as, to *exterminate* error, heresy, infidelity or atheism; to *exterminate* vice.

3. To root out, as plants; to extirpate; as, to *exterminate* weeds.
4. In *algebra*, to take away; as, to *exterminate* surds or unknown quantities.

EXTERM'INATED, *pp.* Utterly driven away or destroyed; eradicated; extirpated.

EXTERM'INATING, *ppr.* Driving away or totally destroying; eradicating; extirpating.

EXTERMINA'TION, *n.* The act of exterminating; total expulsion or destruction; eradication; extirpation; excision; as the *extermination* of inhabitants or tribes, of error or vice, or of weeds from a field.
2. In *algebra*, a taking away.

EXTERM'INATOR, *n.* He or that which exterminates.

EXTERM'INATORY, *a.* Serving or tending to exterminate. *Burke.*

EXTERM'INE, *v. t.* To exterminate. [*Not used.*] *Shak.*

EXTERN', *a.* [L. *externus.*] External; outward; visible. *Shak.*
2. Without itself; not inherent; not intrinsic. [*Little used.*] *Digby.*

EXTERN'AL, *a.* [L. *externus*; It. *esterno*; Sp. *externo.*]
1. Outward; exterior; as the *external* surface of a body; opposed to *internal.*
2. Outward; not intrinsic; not being within; as *external* objects; *external* causes or effects.
3. Exterior; visible; apparent; as *external* deportment.
4. Foreign; relating to or connected with foreign nations; as *external* trade or commerce; the *external* relations of a state or kingdom.

External taxes, are duties or imposts laid on goods imported into a country. *Federalist.*

EXTERNAL'ITY, *n.* External perception. *A. Smith.*

EXTERN'ALLY, *adv.* Outwardly; on the outside.
2. In appearance; visibly.

EXTERN'ALS, *n. plu.* The outward parts; exterior form.

> Adam was no less glorious in his *externals*: he had a beautiful body, as well as an immortal soul. *South.*

2. Outward rites and ceremonies; visible forms; as the *externals* of religion.

EXTERRA'NEOUS, *a.* [L. *exterraneus*; *ex* and *terra*, a land.]
Foreign; belonging to or coming from abroad.

EXTER'SION, *n.* [L. *extersio*, from *extergeo*; *ex* and *tergeo*, to wipe.] The act of wiping or rubbing out.

EXTILL', *v. i.* [L. *extillo*; *ex* and *stillo*, to drop.] To drop or distil from.

EXTILLA'TION, *n.* The act of distilling from, or falling from in drops.

EXTIMULATE. [*Not in use.*] [See *Stimulate.*]

EXTIMULATION. [See *Stimulation.*]

EXTINCT', *a.* [L. *extinctus.* See *Extinguish.*]
1. Extinguished; put out; quenched; as, fire, light or a lamp is *extinct.*
2. Being at an end; having no survivor; as, a family or race is *extinct.*
3. Being at an end; having ceased. The enmity between the families is *extinct.*

> My days are *extinct.* Job xvii.

4. Being at an end, by abolition or disuse; having no force; as, the law is *extinct.*

EXTINC'TION, *n.* [L. *extinctio.* See *Extinguish.*]
1. The act of putting out or destroying light or fire, by quenching, suffocation or otherwise.
2. The state of being extinguished, quenched or suffocated; as the *extinction* of fire or of a candle.
3. Destruction; excision; as the *extinction* of nations.
4. Destruction; suppression; a putting an end to; as the *extinction* of life, or of a family; the *extinction* of feuds, jealousies or enmity; the *extinction* of a claim.

EXTIN'GUISH, *v. t.* [L. *extinguo*; *ex* and *stingo*, *stinguo*, or the latter may be a contraction; Gr. ϛιζω for ϛιγω, to prick, that is, to thrust; or more directly from *tingo*, to dip, to stain; both probably allied to *tango*, for *tago*, to touch. Fr. *eteindre*; It. *estinguere*; Sp. *extinguir.* See Class Dg. No 19. 31. 40.]
1. To put out; to quench; to suffocate; to destroy; as, to *extinguish* fire or flame.
2. To destroy; to put an end to; as, to *extinguish* love or hatred in the breast; to *extinguish* desire or hope; to *extinguish* a claim or title.
3. To cloud or obscure by superior splendor. *Shak.*
4. To put an end to, by union or consolidation. [See *Extinguishment.*]

EXTIN'GUISHABLE, *a.* That may be quenched, destroyed or suppressed.

EXTIN'GUISHED, *pp.* Put out; quenched; stifled; suppressed; destroyed.

EXTIN'GUISHER, *n.* He or that which extinguishes.
2. A hollow conical utensil to be put on a candle to extinguish it.

EXTIN'GUISHING, *ppr.* Putting out; quenching; suppressing; destroying.

EXTIN'GUISHMENT, *n.* The act of putting out or quenching; extinction; suppression; destruction; as the *extinguishment* of fire or flame; of discord, enmity or jealousy; or of love or affection.
2. Abolition; nullification.

> Divine laws of christian church polity may not be altered by *extinguishment.* *Hooker.*

3. Extinction; a putting an end to, or a coming to an end; termination; as the *extinguishment* of a race or tribe.
4. The putting an end to a right or estate, by consolidation or union.

> If my tenant for life makes a lease to *A* for life, remainder to *B* and his heirs, and I release to *A*; this release operates as an *extinguishment* of my right to the reversion. *Blackstone.*

EXTIRP', *v. t.* To extirpate. [*Not used.*] *Spenser.*

EXTIRP'ABLE, *a.* That may be eradicated. *Evelyn.*

EX'TIRPATE, *v. t.* [L. *extirpo*; *ex* and *stirps*, root; It. *estirpare.*]
1. To pull or pluck up by the roots; to root out; to eradicate; to destroy totally; as, to *extirpate* weeds or noxious plants from a field.
2. To eradicate; to root out; to destroy wholly; as, to *extirpate* error or heresy; to *extirpate* a sect.
3. In *surgery*, to cut out; to cut off; to eat out; to remove; as, to *extirpate* a wen.

EX'TIRPATED, *pp.* Plucked up by the roots; rooted out; eradicated; totally destroyed.

EX'TIRPATING, *ppr.* Pulling up or out by the roots; eradicating; totally destroying.

EXTIRPA'TION, *n.* The act of rooting out; eradication; excision; total destruction; as the *extirpation* of weeds from land; the *extirpation* of evil principles from the heart; the *extirpation* of a race of men; the *extirpation* of heresy.

EX'TIRPATOR, *n.* One who roots out; a destroyer.

EXTOL', *v. t.* [L. *extollo*; *ex* and *tollo*, to raise, Ch. דול, or Heb. and Ch. נטל. Class Dl. No. 3. 18. 28.]
To raise in words or eulogy; to praise; to exalt in commendation; to magnify. We *extol* virtues, noble exploits, and heroism. Men are too much disposed to *extol* the rich and despise the poor.

> *Extol* him that rideth upon the heavens by his name Jah. Ps. lxviii.

EXTOL'LED, *ppr.* Exalted in commendation; praised; magnified.

EXTOL'LER, *n.* One who praises or magnifies; a praiser or magnifier.

EXTOL'LING, *ppr.* Praising; exalting by praise or commendation; magnifying.

EXTORS'IVE, *a.* [See *Extort.*] Serving to extort; tending to draw from by compulsion.

EXTORS'IVELY, *adv.* In an extorsive manner; by extortion.

EXTORT', *v. t.* [L. *extortus*, from *extorqueo*, to wrest from; *ex* and *torqueo*, to twist; Fr. *extorquer.*]
1. To draw from by force or compulsion; to wrest or wring from by physical force, by menace, duress, violence, authority, or by any illegal means. Conquerors *extort* contributions from the vanquished; tyrannical princes *extort* money from their subjects; officers often *extort* illegal fees; confessions of guilt are *extorted* by the rack. A promise *extorted* by duress is not binding.
2. To gain by violence or oppression. *Spenser.*

EXTORT', *v. i.* To practice extortion. *Spenser. Davies.*

EXTORT'ED, *pp.* Drawn from by compulsion; wrested from.

EXTORT'ER, *n.* One who extorts, or practices extortion. *Camden.*

EXTORT'ING, *ppr.* Wresting from by force or undue exercise of power.

EXTOR'TION, *n.* The act of extorting; the act or practice of wresting any thing from a person by force, duress, menaces, authority, or by any undue exercise of power; illegal exaction; illegal compulsion to pay money, or to do some other act. *Extortion* is an offense punishable at common law.
2. Force or illegal compulsion by which any thing is taken from a person. *King Charles.*

EXTOR'TIONER, *n.* One who practices extortion.

> *Extortioners* shall not inherit the kingdom of God. 1 Cor. vi.

EXTOR'TIOUS, *a.* Oppressive; violent; unjust.

EXTRA, a Latin preposition, denoting beyond or excess; as *extra-work*, *extra-pay*, work or pay beyond what is usual or agreed on.

EXTRACT', *v. t.* [L. *extractus*, from *extraho; ex* and *traho*, to draw. See *Draw* and *Drag*. Sp. *extraer;* It. *estrarre;* Fr. *extraire*.]

1. To draw out; as, to *extract* a tooth.
2. To draw out, as the juices or essence of a substance, by distillation, solution or other means; as, to *extract* spirit from the juice of the cane; to *extract* salts from ashes.
3. To take out; to take from.

Woman is her name, of man *Extracted*. *Milton.*

4. To take out or select a part; to take a passage or passages from a book or writing.

I have *extracted* from the pamphlet a few notorious falsehoods. *Swift.*

5. In a general sense, to draw from by any means or operation.

EX'TRACT, *n.* That which is extracted or drawn from something.

1. In *literature*, a passage taken from a book or writing. *Camden.*
2. In *pharmacy*, any thing drawn from a substance, as essences, tinctures, &c.; or a solution of the purer parts of a mixed body inspissated by distillation or evaporation, nearly to the consistence of honey. *Encyc. Quincy.*

Any substance obtained by digesting vegetable substances in water, and evaporating them to a solid consistence. *Webster's Manual.*

3. In *chimistry*, a peculiar principle, supposed to form the basis of all vegetable extracts; called also the *extractive principle*. *Webster's Manual.*
4. Extraction; descent. [*Not now used.*] *South.*

EXTRACT'ED, *pp.* Drawn or taken out.

EXTRACT'ING, *ppr.* Drawing or taking out.

EXTRAC'TION, *n.* [L. *extractio.*] The act of drawing out; as the *extraction* of a tooth; the *extraction* of a bone or an arrow from the body; the *extraction* of a fetus or child in midwifery.

2. Descent; lineage; birth; derivation of persons from a stock or family. Hence, the stock or family from which one has descended. We say, a man is of a noble *extraction*.
3. In *pharmacy*, the operation of drawing essences, tinctures, &c. from a substance. *Encyc.*
4. In *arithmetic* and *algebra*, the extraction of roots is the operation of finding the root of a given number or quantity; also, the method or rule by which the operation is performed.

EXTRACT'IVE, *a.* That may be extracted. *Kirwan.*

EXTRACT'IVE, *n.* The proximate principle of vegetable extracts. *Parr.*

EXTRACT'OR, *n.* In *midwifery*, a forceps or instrument for extracting children.

EXTRADIC'TIONARY, *a.* [L. *extra* and *dictio.*] Consisting not in words, but in realities. [*Not used.*] *Brown.*

EXTRAFOLIA'CEOUS, *a.* [L. *extra*, on the outside, and *folium*, a leaf.]

In *botany*, growing on the outside of a leaf; as *extrafoliaceous* stipules. *Martyn.*

EXTRAGE'NEOUS, *a.* [L. *extra* and *genus*, kind.] Belonging to another kind.

EXTRAJUDI''CIAL, *a.* [*extra*, without, and *judicial.*]

Out of the proper court, or the ordinary course of legal procedure. *Encyc.*

EXTRAJUDI''CIALLY, *adv.* In a manner out of the ordinary course of legal proceedings. *Ayliffe.*

EXTRALIM'ITARY, *a.* [*extra* and *limit.*] Being beyond the limit or bounds; as *extralimitary* land. *Mitford.*

EXTRAMIS'SION, *n.* [L. *extra* and *mitto*, to send.] A sending out; emission. *Brown.*

EXTRAMUN'DANE, *a.* [L. *extra* and *mundus*, the world.] Beyond the limit of the material world. *Glanville.*

EXTRA'NEOUS, *a.* [L. *extraneus.*] Foreign; not belonging to a thing; existing without; not intrinsic; as, to separate gold from *extraneous* matter.

Relation is not contained in the real existence of things, but is *extraneous* and superinduced. *Locke.*

Extraneous fossils, organic remains; exuviæ of organized beings, imbedded in the strata of the earth. *Cyc.*

EXTRAOR'DINARIES, *n. plu.* Things which exceed the usual order, kind or method. Rarely used in the singular.

EXTRAOR'DINARILY, *adv. extror'dinarily.* [See *Extraordinary.*]

In a manner out of the ordinary or usual method; beyond the common course, limits or order; in an uncommon degree; remarkably; particularly; eminently.

The temple of Solomon was *extraordinarily* magnificent. *Wilkins.*

EXTRAOR'DINARINESS, *n.* Uncommonness; remarkableness.

EXTRAOR'DINARY, *a. extror'dinary.* [L. *extraordinarius; extra* and *ordinarius*, usual, from *ordo*, order.]

1. Beyond or out of the common order or method; not in the usual, customary or regular course; not ordinary. *Extraordinary* evils require *extraordinary* remedies.
2. Exceeding the common degree or measure; hence, remarkable; uncommon; rare; wonderful; as the *extraordinary* talents of Shakspeare; the *extraordinary* powers of Newton; an edifice of *extraordinary* grandeur.
3. Special; particular; sent for a special purpose, or on a particular occasion; as an *extraordinary* courier or messenger; an embassador *extraordinary;* a gazette *extraordinary*.

EXTRAPARO'CHIAL, *a.* [*extra* and *parochial.*] Not within the limits of any parish. *Blackstone.*

EXTRAPROFES'SIONAL, *a.* [*extra* and *professional.*]

Foreign to a profession; not within the ordinary limits of professional duty or business.

Molina was an ecclesiastic, and these studies were *extraprofessional*. *Med. Repos.*

EXTRAPROVIN'CIAL, *a.* [*extra* and *provincial.*] Not within the same province; not within the jurisdiction of the same archbishop. *Ayliffe.*

EXTRAREG'ULAR, *a.* [*extra* and *regular.*] Not comprehended within a rule or rules. *Taylor.*

EXTRATERRITO'RIAL, *a.* Being beyond or without the limits of a territory or particular jurisdiction. *Hunter, Wheaton's Rep.*

EXTRAUGHT, old *pp.* of *extract*. *Obs.*

EXTRAV'AGANCE, } *a.* [L. *extra* and *vagans; vagor*, to
EXTRAV'AGANCY, } wander. See *Vague.*]

1. Literally, a wandering beyond a limit; an excursion or sally from the usual way, course or limit. *Hammond.*
2. In *writing* or *discourse*, a going beyond the limits of strict truth, or probability; as *extravagance* of expression or description.
3. Excess of affection, passion or appetite; as *extravagance* of love, anger, hatred or hunger.
4. Excess in expenditures of property; the expending of money without necessity, or beyond what is reasonable or proper; dissipation.

The income of three dukes was not enough to supply her *extravagance*. *Arbuthnot.*

5. In general, any excess or wandering from prescribed limits; irregularity; wildness; as the *extravagance* of imagination; *extravagance* of claims or demands.

EXTRAV'AGANT, *a.* Literally, wandering beyond limits. *Shak.*

2. Excessive; exceeding due bounds; unreasonable. The wishes, demands, desires and passions of men are often *extravagant*.
3. Irregular; wild; not within ordinary limits of truth or probability, or other usual bounds; as *extravagant* flights of fancy.

There is something nobly wild and *extravagant* in great geniuses. *Addison.*

4. Exceeding necessity or propriety; wasteful; prodigal; as *extravagant* expenses; an *extravagant* mode of living.
5. Prodigal; profuse in expenses; as an *extravagant* man.

He that is *extravagant* will quickly become poor, and poverty will enforce dependence, and invite corruption. *Rambler.*

EXTRAV'AGANT, *n.* One who is confined to no general rule. *L'Estrange.*

EXTRAV'AGANTLY, *adv.* In an extravagant manner; wildly; not within the limits of truth or probability. Men often write and talk *extravagantly*.

2. Unreasonably; excessively. It is prudent not to praise or censure *extravagantly*.
3. In a manner to use property without necessity or propriety, or to no good purpose; expensively, or profusely to an unjustifiable degree; as, to live, eat. drink, or dress *extravagantly*.

EXTRAV'AGANTNESS, *n.* Excess; extravagance. [*Little used.*]

EXTRAV'AGANTS, *n.* In *church history*, certain decretal epistles, or constitutions of the popes, which were published after the Clementines, and not at first arranged and digested with the other papal constitutions. They were afterward inserted in the body of the canon law. *Encyc.*

EXTRAV'AGATE, *v. i.* To wander beyond the limits. [*Not used.*] *Warburton.*

EXTRAVAGA'TION, *n.* Excess; a wandering beyond limits. *Smollet.*

EXTRAV'ASATED, *a.* [L. *extra* and *vasa*, vessels.] Forced or let out of its proper vessels; as *extravasated* blood. *Arbuthnot.*

EXTRAVASA'TION, *n.* The act of forcing or letting out of its proper vessels or ducts, as a fluid; the state of being forced or let out of its containing vessels; effusion; as an *extravasation* of blood after a rupture of the vessels.

EXTRAVE'NATE, *a.* [L. *extra* and *vena*, vein.] Let out of the veins. [*Not in use.*] *Glanville.*

EXTRAVER'SION, *n.* [L. *extra* and *versio*, a turning.] The act of throwing out; the state of being turned or thrown out. [*Little used.*] *Boyle.*

EXTRE'AT, *n.* Extraction. *Obs.* *Spenser.*

EXTRE'ME, *a.* [L. *extremus*, last.] Outermost; utmost; farthest; at the utmost point, edge or border; as the *extreme* verge or point of a thing.

2. Greatest; most violent; utmost; as *extreme* pain, grief, or suffering; *extreme* joy or pleasure.

3. Last; beyond which there is none; as an *extreme* remedy.

4. Utmost; worst or best that can exist or be supposed; as an *extreme* case.

5. Most pressing; as *extreme* necessity.

Extreme unction, among the Romanists, is the anointing of a sick person with oil, when decrepit with age or affected with some mortal disease, and usually just before death. It is applied to the eyes, ears, nostrils, mouth, hands, feet and reins of penitents, and is supposed to represent the grace of God poured into the soul. *Encyc.*

Extreme and mean proportion, in geometry, is when a line is so divided, that the whole line is to the greater segment, as that segment is to the less; or when a line is so divided, that the rectangle under the whole line and the lesser segment is equal to the square of the greater segment. *Euclid.*

EXTRE'ME, *n.* The utmost point or verge of a thing; that part which terminates a body; extremity.

2. Utmost point; furthest degree; as the *extremes* of heat and cold; the *extremes* of virtue and vice. Avoid *extremes*. *Extremes* naturally beget each other.

> There is a natural progression from the *extreme* of anarchy to the *extreme* of tyranny. *Washington.*

3. In *logic*, the *extremes* or extreme terms of a syllogism are the predicate and subject. Thus, "Man is an animal: Peter is a man, therefore Peter is an animal;" the word animal is the greater extreme, Peter the less extreme, and man the medium. *Encyc.*

4. In *mathematics*, the *extremes* are the first and last terms of a proportion; as, when three magnitudes are proportional, the rectangle contained by the *extremes* is equal to the square of the mean. *Euclid.*

EXTRE'MELY, *adv.* In the utmost degree; to the utmost point. It is *extremely* hot or cold; it is *extremely* painful.

2. In familiar language, very much; greatly.

EXTREM'ITY, *n.* [L. *extremitas.*] The utmost point or side; the verge; the point or border that terminates a thing; as the *extremities* of a country.

2. The utmost parts. The *extremities* of the body, in *painting* and *sculpture*, are the head, hands and feet; but in *anatomy*, the term is applied to the limbs only. *Encyc. Cyc.*

3. The utmost point; the highest or furthest degree; as the *extremity* of pain or suffering; the *extremity* of cruelty. Even charity and forbearance may be carried to *extremity*.

4. Extreme or utmost distress, straits or difficulties; as a city besieged and reduced to *extremity*.

5. The utmost rigor or violence. The Greeks have endured oppression in its utmost *extremity*.

6. The most aggravated state.

> The world is running after farce, the *extremity* of bad poetry. *Dryden.*

EX'TRICABLE, *a.* [infra.] That can be extricated.

EX'TRICATE, *v. t.* [L. *extrico.* The primary verb *trico* is not in the Latin. We probably see its affinities in the Gr. θριξ, τριχος, hair, or a bush of hair, from interweaving, entangling. I suspect that τρεις and *three* are contracted from this root; *three* for *threg*, folded, or a plexus. The same word occurs in *intricate* and *intrigue*; Fr. *tricher*, to cheat; *tricoter*, to weave; Eng. *trick*; It. *treccia*, a lock of hair. Class Rg. No. 25.]

1. Properly, to disentangle; hence, to free from difficulties or perplexities; to disembarrass; as, to *extricate* one from complicated business, from troublesome alliances or other connections; to *extricate* one's self from debt.

2. To send out; to cause to be emitted or evolved.

EX'TRICATED, *pp.* Disentangled; freed from difficulties and perplexities; disembarrassed; evolved.

EX'TRICATING, *ppr.* Disentangling; disembarrassing; evolving.

EXTRICA'TION, *n*, The act of disentangling; a freeing from perplexities; disentanglement.

2. The act of sending out or evolving; as the *extrication* of heat or moisture from a substance.

EXTRIN'SIC, } *a.* [L. *extrinsecus.*] External; outward; not contained in or belonging to a body. Mere matter cannot move without the impulse of an *extrinsic* agent. It is opposed to *intrinsic*.
EXTRIN'SICAL, }

EXTRIN'SICALLY, *adv.* From without; externally.

EXTRUCT', *v. t.* [L. *extruo, extructus.*] To build; to construct. [*Not in use.*]

EXTRUC'TION, *n.* A building. [*Not used.*]

EXTRUCT'IVE, *a.* Forming into a structure. *Fulke.*

EXTRUCT'OR, *n.* A builder; a fabricator; a contriver. [*Not used.*]

EXTRU'DE, *v. t.* [L. *extrudo*; *ex* and *trudo*, to *thrust*. Class Rd.]

1. To thrust out; to urge, force or press out; to expel; as, to *extrude* a fetus.

2. To drive away; to drive off. *Woodward.*

EXTRU'DED, *pp.* Thrust out; driven out or away; expelled.

EXTRU'DING, *ppr.* Thrusting out; driving out; expelling.

EXTRU'SION, *n.* *s* as *z*. The act of thrusting or throwing out; a driving out; expulsion.

EXTU'BERANCE, } *n.* [L. *extuberans*, *ex-tubero*; *ev* and *tuber*, a puff.]
EXTU'BERANCY, }

1. In *medicine*, a swelling or rising of the flesh; a protuberant part. *Encyc.*

2. A knob or swelling part of a body. *Moxon.*

EXTU'BERANT, *a.* Swelled; standing out.

EXTU'BERATE, *v. i.* [L. *extubero.*] To swell. [*Not in use.*]

EXTUMES'CENCE, *n.* [L. *extumescens*, *extumesco*; *ex* and *tumesco*, *tumeo*, to swell.] A swelling or rising. [*Little used.*]

EXU'BERANCE, } *n.* [L. *exuberans*, *exubero*; *ex* and *ubero*, to fatten; *uber*, a pap or breast, that is, a swelling or mass.]
EXU'BERANCY, }

1. An abundance; an overflowing quantity; richness; as an *exuberance* of fertility or fancy.

2. Superfluous abundance; luxuriance.

3. Overgrowth; superfluous shoots, as of trees.

EXU'BERANT, *a.* Abundant; plenteous; rich; as *exuberant* fertility; *exuberant* goodness.

2. Over-abundant; superfluous; luxuriant.

3. Pouring forth abundance; producing in plenty; as *exuberant* spring. *Thomson.*

EXU'BERANTLY, *adv.* Abundantly; very copiously; in great plenty; to a superfluous degree. The earth has produced *exuberantly*.

EXU'BERATE, *v. i.* [L. *exubero.*] To abound; to be in great abundance. [*Little used.*] *Boyle.*

EX'UDATE, } *v. t.* and *i.* [See *Exsude*, the preferable orthography.]
EXU'DE, }

EXUDA'TION *n.* [See *Exsudation.*]

EXU'DED, *pp.* [See *Exsuded.*]

EXU'DING, *ppr.* [See *Exsuding.*]

EXUL'CERATE, *v. t.* [L. *exulcero*; *ex* and *ulcero*, to ulcerate, *ulcus*, an *ulcer.*]

1. To cause or produce an ulcer or ulcers. *Arbuthnot. Encyc.*

2. To afflict; to corrode; to fret or anger. *Milton.*

EXUL'CERATE, *v. i.* To become an ulcer or ulcerous. *Bacon.*

EXUL'CERATED, *pp.* Affected with ulcers; having become ulcerous.

EXUL'CERATING, *ppr.* Producing ulcers on; fretting; becoming ulcerous.

EXULCERA'TION, *n.* The act of causing ulcers on a body, or the process of becoming ulcerous; the beginning erosion which wears away the substance and forms an ulcer. *Encyc. Quincy.*

2. A fretting; exacerbation; corrosion. *Hooker.*

EXUL'CERATORY, *a.* Having a tendency to form ulcers.

EXULT', *v. i.* *egzult'.* [L. *exulto*; *ex* and *salto*, *salio*, to leap; It. *esultare.*]

Properly, to leap for joy; hence, to rejoice in triumph; to rejoice exceedingly, at success or victory; to be glad above measure; to triumph. It is natural to man to *exult* at the success of his schemes, and to *exult* over a fallen adversary.

EXULT'ANCE, } *n.* Exultation. [*Not used.*]
EXULT'ANCY, } *Hammond.*

EXULT'ANT, *a.* Rejoicing triumphantly. *More.*

EXULTA'TION, *n.* The act of exulting; lively joy at success or victory, or at any advantage gained; great gladness; rapturous delight; triumph. *Exultation* usually springs from the gratification of our desire of some good; particularly of distinction or superiority, or of that which confers distinction. It often springs from the gratification of pride or ambition. But *exultation* may be a lively joy springing from laudable causes.

EXULT'ING, *ppr.* Rejoicing greatly or in triumph.

EXUN'DATE, *v. i.* To overflow. [*Not used.*]

EXUNDA'TION, *n.* [L. *exundatio*, from *exundo*, to overflow; *ex* and *undo*, to rise in waves, *unda*, a wave.]

An overflowing abundance. [*Little used.*] *Ray.*

EXU'PERATE, *v. t.* To excel; to surmount. [*Not used, nor its derivatives.*]

EXUS'TION, *n.* [L. *exustus.*] The act or operation of burning up.

EXU'VIÆ, *n. plu.* [L.] Cast skins, shells or coverings of animals; any parts of animals which are shed or cast off, as the skins of serpents and caterpillars, the shells of lobsters, &c. *Encyc.*

2. The spoils or remains of animals found in the earth, supposed to be deposited there at the deluge, or in some great convulsion or change which the earth has undergone, in past periods. *Cuvier.*

EY, in old writers, Sax. *ig*, signifies an isle.

EY'AS, *n.* [Fr. *niais*, silly.] A young hawk just taken from the nest, not able to prey for itself. *Hanmer. Shak.*

EY'AS, *a.* Unfledged. [*Not used.*] *Spenser.*

EY'AS-MUSKET, *n.* A young unfledged male hawk of the musket kind or sparrow hawk. *Hanmer. Shak.*

EYE, *n.* pronounced as I. [Sax. *eag, eah*; Goth. *auga*; D. *oog*; G. *auge*; Sw. *öga*; Dan. *öye*; Russ. *oko*; Sans. *akshi*; L. *oculus*, a diminutive, whence Fr. *œil*, Sp. *ojo*, It. *occhio*, Port. *olho*. The original word must have been *ag, eg*, or *hag* or *heg*, coinciding with *egg*. The old English plural was *eyen*, or *eyne.*]

1. The organ of sight or vision; properly, the globe or ball movable in the orbit. The eye is nearly of a spherical figure, and composed of coats or tunics. But in the term *eye*, we often or usually include the ball and the parts adjacent.

2. Sight; view; ocular knowledge; as, I have a man now in my *eye*. In this sense, the plural is more generally used.

> Before whose *eyes* Jesus Christ hath been evidently set forth, crucified among you. Gal. iii.

3. Look; countenance.

> I'll say yon gray is not the morning's *eye*. *Shak.*

4. Front; face.

> Her shall you hear disproved to your *eyes*. *Shak.*

5. Direct opposition; as, to sail in the wind's *eye*.

6. Aspect; regard; respect; view.

> Booksellers mention with respect the authors they have printed, and consequently have an *eye* to their own advantage. *Addison.*

7. Notice; observation; vigilance; watch.

> After this jealousy, he kept a strict *eye* upon him. *L'Estrange.*

8. View of the mind; opinion formed by observation or contemplation.

> It hath, in their *eye*, no great affinity with the form of the church of Rome. *Hooker.*

9. Sight; view, either in a literal or figurative sense.

10. Something resembling the eye in form; as the *eye* of a peacock's feather. *Newton.*

11. A small hole or aperture; a perforation; as the *eye* of a needle.

12. A small catch for a hook; as we say, hooks and *eyes*. In nearly the same sense, the word is applied to certain fastenings in the cordage of ships.

13. The bud of a plant; a shoot. *Encyc.*

14. A small shade of color. [*Little used.*]

> Red with an *eye* of blue makes a purple. *Boyle.*

15. The power of perception.

> The *eyes* of your understanding being enlightened. Eph. i.

16. Oversight; inspection.

> The *eye* of the master will do more work than both his hands. *Franklin.*

The *eyes of a ship*, are the parts which lie near the hawse-holes, particularly in the lower apartments. *Mar. Dict.*

To set the eyes on, is to see; to have a sight of.

To find favor in the eyes, is to be graciously received and treated.

EYE, *n.* A brood; as an *eye* of pheasants.

EYE, *v. t.* To fix the eye on; to look on; to view; to observe; particularly, to observe or watch narrowly, or with fixed attention.

> *Eye* nature's walks, shoot folly as it flies. *Pope.*

EYE, *v. i.* To appear; to have an appearance. *Shak.*

EY'EBALL, *n.* The ball, globe or apple of the eye.

EY'EBEAM, *n.* A glance of the eye. *Shak.*

EY'EBOLT, *n.* In *ships*, a bar of iron or bolt, with an eye, formed to be driven into the deck or sides, for the purpose of hooking tackles to. *Mar. Dict.*

EY'EBRIGHT, *n.* A genus of plants, the Euphrasia, of several species.

EY'E-BRIGHTENING, *n.* A clearing of the sight. *Milton.*

EY'EBROW, *n.* The brow or hairy arch above the eye.

EY'ED, *pp.* Viewed; observed; watched.

2. *a.* Having eyes; used in composition, as a *dull-eyed* man, *ox-eyed* Juno.

EY'EDROP, *n.* A tear. *Shak.*

EY'EGLANCE, *n.* A glance of the eye; a rapid look. *Spenser.*

EY'EGLASS, *n.* A glass to assist the sight; spectacles. *Shak.*

In *telescopes*, the glass next the eye; and where there are several, all except the object glass are called *eye-glasses*. *Cyc.*

EY'E-GLUTTNIG, *n.* A feasting of the eyes. [*Not in use.*] *Spenser.*

EY'ELASH, *n.* The line of hair that edges the eyelid. *Johnson.*

EY'ELESS, *a.* Wanting eyes; destitute of sight. *Milton. Addison.*

EY'ELET, *n.* [Fr. *œillet*, a little eye, from *œil*, eye.]

A small hole or perforation, to receive a lace or small rope or cord. We usually say, *eyelet-hole.*

EY'ELIAD, *n.* [Fr. *œillade.*] A glance of the eye. *Shak.*

EY'ELID, *n.* The cover of the eye; that portion of movable skin with which an animal covers the eyeball, or uncovers it, at pleasure.

EYE-OFFEND'ING, *a.* That hurts the eyes. *Shak.*

EY'E-PLEASING, *a.* Pleasing the eye. *Davies.*

EY'ER, *n.* One who eyes another. *Gayton.*

EY'E-SALVE, *n.* Ointment for the eye. *Revelation.*

EY'E-SERVANT, *n.* A servant who attends to his duty only when watched, or under the eye of his master or employer.

EY'E-SERVICE, *n.* Service performed only under inspection or the eye of an employer.

> Not with *eye-service*, as men-pleasers; but in singleness of heart, fearing God. Col. iii.

EY'ESHOT, *n.* Sight; view; glance of the eye. *Dryden.*

EY'ESIGHT, *n.* The sight of the eye; view; observation. Ps. xviii.

> Josephus sets this down from his own *eyesight*. *Wilkins.*

2. The sense of seeing. His *eyesight* fails.

EY'ESORE, *n.* Something offensive to the eye or sight.

> Mordecai was an *eyesore* to Haman. *L'Estrange.*

EY'ESPLICE, *n.* In *seaman's language*, a sort of eye or circle at the end of a rope. *Mar. Dict.*

EY'ESPOTTED, *a.* Marked with spots like eyes. *Spenser.*

EY'ESTRING, *n.* The tendon by which the eye is moved. *Shak.*

EY'ETOOTH, *n.* A tooth under the eye; a pointed tooth in the upper jaw next to the grinders, called also a canine tooth; a fang. *Ray.*

EY'EWINK, *n.* A wink, or motion of the eyelid; a hint or token. *Shak.*

EY'E-WITNESS, *n.* One who sees a thing done; one who has ocular view of any thing.

> We were *eye-witnesses* of his majesty. 2 Pet. i.

EY'OT, *n.* A little isle. *Blackstone.*

EYRE, *n.* *ire.* [Old Fr. from L. *iter.*] Literally, a journey or circuit. In England, the justices in *eyre* were itinerant judges, who rode the circuit to hold courts in the different counties.

2. A court of itinerant justices. *Blackstone.*

EY'RY, *n.* The place where birds of prey construct their nests and hatch. It is written also *eyrie*. [See *Aerie.*]

> The eagle and the stork
> On cliffs and cedar-tops their *eyries* build. *Milton.*

F.

F, the sixth letter of the English Alphabet, is a labial articulation, formed by placing the upper teeth on the under lip, and accompanied with an emission of breath. Its kindred letter is *v*, which is chiefly distinguished from *f* by being more vocal, or accompanied with more sound, as may be perceived by pronouncing *ef*, *ev*. This letter may be derived from the Oriental ו *vau*, or from פ *pe* or *phe*; most probably the former. The Latins received the letter from the Eolians in Greece, who wrote it in the form of a double *g*, F, Ⅎ; whence it has been called most absurdly digamma. It corresponds in power to the Greek φ phi, and its proper name is *ef*.

As a Latin numeral, it signifies 40, and with a dash over the top F̅, forty thousand.

In the civil law, two of these letters together *ff*, signify the pandects.

In English criminal law, this letter is branded on felons, when admitted to the benefit of clergy; by Stat. 4. H. VII. c. 13.

In *medical prescriptions*, F stands for *fiat*, let it be made; F. S. A. *fiat secundum artem*.

F stands also for *Fellow*; F. R. S. Fellow of the Royal Society.

F or *fa*, in *music*, is the fourth note rising in this order in the gamut, *ut*, *re*, *mi*, *fa*. It denotes also one of the Greek keys in music, destined for the base.

F in English has one uniform sound, as in *father*, *after*.

FABA'CEOUS, *a.* [Low L. *fabaceus*, from *faba*, a bean.]

Having the nature of a bean; like a bean. [*Little used.*]

FA'BIAN, *a.* Delaying; dilatory; avoiding battle, in imitation of Q. Fabius Maximus, a Roman general who conducted military operations against Hannibal, by declining to risk a battle in the open field, but harassing the enemy by marches, countermarches and ambuscades.

FA'BLE, *n.* [L. *fabula*; Fr. *fable*; It. *favola*; Ir. *fabhal*; Sp. *fabula*, from the Latin, but the native Spanish word is *habla*, speech. Qu. W. *hebu*, to speak; Gr. επω. The radical sense is that which is spoken or told.]

1. A feigned story or tale, intended to instruct or amuse; a fictitious narration intended to enforce some useful truth or precept.

 Jotham's *fable* of the trees is the oldest extant, and as beautiful as any made since. *Addison.*

2. Fiction in general; as, the story is all a *fable*.

3. An idle story; vicious or vulgar fictions.

 But refuse profane and old wives' *fables*. 1 Tim. iv.

4. The plot, or connected series of events, in an epic or dramatic poem.

 The moral is the first business of the poet; this being formed, he contrives such a design or *fable* as may be most suitable to the moral. *Dryden.*

5. Falsehood; a softer term for a lie. *Addison.*

FA'BLE, *v. i.* To feign; to write fiction.

 Vain now the tales which *fabling* poets tell. *Prior.*

2. To tell falsehoods; as, he *fables* not. *Shak.*

FA'BLE, *v. t.* To feign; to invent; to devise and speak of, as true or real.

 The hell thou *fablest*. *Milton.*

FA'BLED, *pp.* Feigned; invented, as stories.

2. *a.* Told or celebrated in fables.

 Hail, *fabled* grotto. *Tickel.*

FA'BLER, *n.* A writer of fables or fictions; a dealer in feigned stories. *Johnson.*

FA'BLING, *ppr.* Feigning; devising, as stories; writing or uttering false stories.

FAB'RIC, *n.* [L. *fabrica*, a frame, from *faber*, a workman; Fr. *fabrique*.]

1. The structure of any thing; the manner in which the parts of a thing are united by art and labor; workmanship; texture. This is cloth of a beautiful *fabric*.

2. The frame or structure of a building; construction. More generally, the building itself; an edifice; a house; a temple; a church; a bridge, &c. The word is usually applied to a large building.

3. Any system composed of connected parts; as the *fabric* of the universe.

4. Cloth manufactured.

 Silks and other fine *fabrics* of the east. *Henry.*

FAB'RIC, *v. t.* To frame; to build; to construct. [*Little used.*] *Philips.*

FAB'RICATE, *v. t.* [L. *fabrico*, to frame, from *faber*, supra.]

1. To frame; to build; to construct; to form a whole by connecting its parts; as, to *fabricate* a bridge or a ship.

2. To form by art and labor; to manufacture; as, to *fabricate* woolens.

3. To invent and form; to forge; to devise falsely; as, to *fabricate* a lie or story.

 Our books were not *fabricated* with an accommodation to prevailing usages. *Paley.*

4. To coin; as, to *fabricate* money. [*Unusual.*] *Henry, Hist.*

FAB'RICATED, *pp.* Framed; constructed; built; manufactured; invented; devised falsely; forged.

FAB'RICATING, *ppr.* Framing; constructing; manufacturing; devising falsely; forging.

FABRICA'TION, *n.* The act of framing or constructing; construction; as the *fabrication* of a bridge or of a church.

2. The act of manufacturing.

3. The act of devising falsely; forgery.

4. That which is fabricated; a falsehood. The story is doubtless a *fabrication*.

FAB'RICATOR, *n.* One that constructs or makes.

FAB'RILE, *a.* [L. *fabrilis*.] Pertaining to handicrafts. [*Not used.*]

FAB'ULIST, *n.* [from *fable*.] The inventor or writer of fables. *Garrick.*

FAB'ULIZE, *v. t.* To invent, compose or relate fables. *Faber.*

FABULOS'ITY, *n.* Fabulousness; fullness of fables. [*Little used.*] *Abbot.*

FAB'ULOUS, *a.* Feigned, as a story; devised; fictitious; as a *fabulous* story; a *fabulous* description.

2. Related in fable; described or celebrated in fables; invented; not real; as a *fabulous* hero; the *fabulous* exploits of Hercules.

3. The *fabulous* age of Greece and Rome, was the early age of those countries, the accounts of which are mostly *fabulous*, or in which the *fabulous* achievments of their heroes were performed; called also the *heroic* age.

FAB'ULOUSLY, *adv.* In fable or fiction; in a fabulous manner. *Brown.*

FAB'ULOUSNESS, *n.* The quality of being fabulous or feigned.

FACADE, *n.* *fassa'de.* [Fr.] Front. *Warton.*

FACE, *n.* [Fr. *face*; It. *faccia*; Sp. *faz*, or *haz*; Arm. *façz*; L. *facies*, from *facio*, to make.]

1. In *a general sense*, the surface of a thing, or the side which presents itself to the view of a spectator; as the *face* of the earth; the *face* of the waters.

2. A part of the surface of a thing; or the plane surface of a solid. Thus, a cube or die has six *faces*; an octahedron has eight *faces*.

3. The surface of the fore part of an animal's head, particularly of the human head; the visage.

 In the sweat of thy *face* shalt thou eat bread. Gen. iii.

 Joseph bowed himself with his *face* to the earth. Gen. xlviii.

4. Countenance; cast of features; look; air of the face.

 We set the best *face* on it we could. *Dryden.*

5. The front of a thing; the forepart; the flat surface that presents itself first to view; as the *face* of a house. Ezek. xli.

6. Visible state; appearance.

 This would produce a new *face* of things in Europe. *Addison.*

7. Appearance; look.

 Nor heaven, nor sea, their former *face* retained. *Waller.*

 His dialogue has the *face* of probability. *Baker.*

8. State of confrontation. The witnesses were presented *face* to *face*.

9. Confidence; boldness; impudence; a bold front.

 He has the *face* to charge others with false citations. *Tillotson.*

10. Presence; sight; as in the phrases, *be-*

fore the face, *in the face*, *to the face*, *from the face*.

11. The person.

I had not thought to see thy *face*. Gen. xlviii.

12. In *scripture*, *face* is used for anger or favor.

Hide us from the *face* of him that sitteth on the throne. Rev. vi.

Make thy *face* to shine on thy servant. Ps. xxxi.

How long wilt thou hide thy *face* from me? Ps. xiii.

Hence, *to seek the face*, that is, to pray to, to seek the favor of.

To set the face against, is to oppose.

To accept one's face, is to show him favor or grant his request. So, *to entreat the face*, is to ask favor; but these phrases are nearly obsolete.

13. A distorted form of the face; as in the phrase, to make *faces*, or to make wry *faces*.

Face to face, when both parties are present; as, to have accusers *face to face*. Acts xxv.

2. Nakedly; without the interposition of any other body.

Now we see through a glass, darkly; but then *face to face*. 1 Cor. xiii.

FACE, *v. t.* To meet in front; to oppose with firmness; to resist, or to meet for the purpose of stopping or opposing; as, to *face* an enemy in the field of battle.

I'll *face*
This tempest, and deserve the name of king. *Dryden.*

2. To stand opposite to; to stand with the face or front towards. The colleges in New Haven *face* the public square.

3. To cover with additional superficies; to cover in front; as a fortification *faced* with marble; to *face* a garment with silk.

To face down, to oppose boldly or impudently.

FACE, *v. i.* To carry a false appearance; to play the hypocrite.

To lie, to *face*, to forge. *Hubberd's Tale.*

2. To turn the face; as, to *face* to the right or left.

FA'CE€LOTH, *n.* [*face* and *cloth*.] A cloth laid over the face of a corpse. *Brand.*

FA'CED, *pp.* Covered in front. In composition, denoting the kind of face; as *full-faced*. *Bailey.*

FA'CELESS, *a.* Without a face.

FA'CEPAINTER, *n.* A painter of portraits; one who draws the likeness of the face.

FA'CEPAINTING, *n.* The act or art of painting portraits. *Dryden.*

FAC'ET, *n.* [Fr. *facette*, from *face*; Sp. *faceta*.]

A little face; a small surface; as the *facets* of a diamond.

FACE'TE, *a.* [L. *facetus*.] Gay; cheerful. [*Not in use.*] *Burton.*

FACE'TENESS, *n.* Wit; pleasant representation. [*Not used.*] *Hales.*

FACE'TIOUS, *a.* [Fr. *facetieux*; Sp. *facecioso*; It. *faceto*; L. *facetus*; *facetia*, or plu. Qu. Ar. فكه to be merry.]

1. Merry; sportive; jocular; sprightly with wit and good humor; as a *facetious* companion.

2. Witty; full of pleasantry playful; exciting laughter; as a *facetious* story; a *facetious* reply.

FACE'TIOUSLY, *adv.* Merrily; gayly; wittily; with pleasantry.

FACE'TIOUSNESS, *n.* Sportive humor; pleasantry; the quality of exciting laughter or good humor.

FA''CIAL, *a.* [L. *facies*, face.] Pertaining to the face; as the *facial* artery, vein or nerve.

Facial angle, in anatomy, is the angle contained by a line drawn horizontally from the middle of the external entrance of the ear to the edge of the nostrils, and another from this latter point to the superciliary ridge of the frontal bone; serving to measure the elevation of the forehead. *Ed. Encyc.*

FAC'ILE, *a.* [Fr. *facile*; Sp. *facil*; L. *facilis*, from *facio*, to make.]

1. Properly, easy to be done or performed; easy; not difficult; performable or attainable with little labor.

Order—will render the work *facile* and delightful. *Evelyn.*

2. Easy to be surmounted or removed; easily conquerable.

The *facile* gates of hell too slightly barred. *Milton.*

3. Easy of access or converse; mild; courteous; not haughty, austere or distant.

I mean she should be courteous, *facile*, sweet. *B. Jonson.*

4. Pliant; flexible; easily persuaded to good or bad; yielding; ductile to a fault.

Since Adam, and his *facile* consort Eve,
Lost Paradise, deceived by me. *Milton.*

FAC'ILELY, *adv.* Easily. [*Little used.*] *Herbert.*

FAC'ILENESS, *n.* Easiness to be persuaded. *Beaum.*

FACIL'ITATE, *v. t.* [Fr. *faciliter*, from *facilité*, L. *facilitas*, from *facilis*, easy.]

To make easy or less difficult; to free from difficulty or impediment, or to diminish it; to lessen the labor of. Machinery *facilitates* manual labor and operations. Pioneers may *facilitate* the march of an army.

FACIL'ITATED, *pp.* Made easy or easier.

FACIL'ITATING, *ppr.* Rendering easy or easier.

FACILITA'TION, *n.* The act of making easy. *Johnson.*

FACIL'ITY, *n.* [Fr. *facilité*; L. *facilitas*, from *facilis*, easy.]

1. Easiness to be performed; freedom from difficulty; ease. He performed the work or operation with great *facility*.

Though *facility* and hope of success might invite some other choice. *Bacon.*

2. Ease of performance; readiness proceeding from skill or use; dexterity. Practice gives a wonderful *facility* in executing works of art.

3. Pliancy; ductility; easiness to be persuaded; readiness of compliance, usually in a bad sense, implying a disposition to yield to solicitations to evil.

It is a great error to take *facility* for good nature: tenderness without discretion, is no better than a more pardonable folly. *L'Estrange.*

4. Easiness of access; complaisance; condescension; affability.

He offers himself to the visits of a friend with *facility*. *South.*

FACIL'ITIES, *n. plu.* The means by which the performance of any thing is rendered easy; convenient opportunities or advantages.

FA'CING, *ppr.* [from *face*.] Fronting; having the face towards; opposite.

2. Covering the fore part.

3. Turning the face.

FA'CING, *n.* A covering in front for ornament or defense; as the *facing* of a fortification or of a garment.

FACIN'OROUS, *a.* [L. *facinus*.] Atrociously wicked. [*Little used.*] *Shak.*

FACIN'OROUSNESS, *n.* Extreme or atrocious wickedness.

FA€SIM'ILE, *n.* [L. *facio*, to make, and *similis*, like. See *Simile*.]

An exact copy or likeness, as of handwriting.

FA€T, *n.* [L. *factum*, from *facio*, to make or do; Fr. *fait*; It. *fatto*; Sp. *hecho*.]

1. Any thing done, or that comes to pass; an act; a deed; an effect produced or achieved; an event. Witnesses are introduced into court to prove a *fact*. *Facts* are stubborn things. To deny a *fact* knowingly is to lie.

2. Reality; truth; as, *in fact*. So we say, *indeed*.

FA€'TION, *n.* [Fr. from L. *factio*, from *facio*, to make or do.]

1. A party, in political society, combined or acting in union, in opposition to the prince, government or state; usually applied to a minority, but it may be applied to a majority. Sometimes a state is divided into *factions* nearly equal. Rome was almost always disturbed by *factions*. Republics are proverbial for *factions*, and *factions* in monarchies have often effected revolutions.

A feeble government produces more *factions* than an oppressive one. *Ames.*

By a *faction*, I understand a number of citizens, whether amounting to a majority or minority of the whole, who are united and actuated by some common impulse of passion, or of interest, adverse to the rights of other citizens, or to the permanent and aggregate interests of the community. *Federalist, Madison.*

2. Tumult; discord; dissension. *Clarendon.*

FA€'TIONARY, *n.* A party man; one of a faction. [*Little used.*] *Shak.*

FA€'TIONER, *n.* One of a faction. [*Not in use.*] *Bancroft.*

FA€'TIONIST, *n.* One who promotes faction. *Mountagu.*

FA€'TIOUS, *a.* [Fr. *factieux*; L. *factiosus*.]

1. Given to faction; addicted to form parties and raise dissensions, in opposition to government; turbulent; prone to clamor against public measures or men. No state is free from *factious* citizens.

2. Pertaining to faction; proceeding from faction; as *factious* tumults; *factious* quarrels. *Dryden.*

FA€'TIOUSLY, *adv.* In a factious manner; by means of faction; in a turbulent or disorderly manner.

FA€'TIOUSNESS, *n.* Inclination to form parties in opposition to the government, or to the public interest; disposition to clamor and raise opposition; clamorousness for a party.

FA€TI''TIOUS, *a.* [L. *factitius*, from *facio*.] Made by art, in distinction from what is produced by nature; artificial; as *facti-*

tious cinnabar; *factitious* stones; *factitious* air.

FAC'TIVE, *a.* Making; having power to make. [*Not used.*] *Bacon.*

FAC'TOR, *n.* [L. *factor;* Fr. *facteur;* It. *fattore;* from L. *facio.*]

1. In *commerce,* an agent employed by merchants, residing in other places, to buy and sell, and to negotiate bills of exchange, or to transact other business on their account.

2. An agent; a substitute.

3. In *arithmetic,* the multiplier and multiplicand, from the multiplication of which proceeds the product.

FAC'TORAGE, *n.* The allowance given to a factor by his employer, as a compensation for his services; called also a *commission.* This is sometimes a certain sum or rate by the cask or package; more generally it is a certain rate per cent. of the value of the goods, purchased or sold.

FAC'TORSHIP, *n.* A factory; or the business of a factor. *Sherwood.*

FAC'TORY, *n.* A house or place where factors reside, to transact business for their employers. The English merchants have factories in the East Indies, Turkey, Portugal, Hamburg, &c.

2. The body of factors in any place; as a chaplain to a British *factory.* *Guthrie.*

3. Contracted from *manufactory,* a building or collection of buildings, appropriated to the manufacture of goods; the place where workmen are employed in fabricating goods, wares or utensils.

FACTO'TUM, *n.* [L. do every thing.] A servant employed to do all kinds of work. *B. Jonson.*

FAC'TURE, *n.* [Fr.] The art or manner of making. *Bacon.*

FAC'ULTY, *n.* [Fr. *faculté;* L. *facultas,* from *facio,* to make.]

1. That power of the mind or intellect which enables it to receive, revive or modify perceptions; as the *faculty* of seeing, of hearing, of imagining, of remembering, &c.: or in general, the faculties may be called the powers or capacities of the mind.

2. The power of doing any thing; ability. There is no *faculty* or power in creatures, which can rightly perform its functions, without the perpetual aid of the Supreme Being. *Hooker.*

3. The power of performing any action, natural, vital or animal.

> The vital *faculty* is that by which life is preserved. *Quincy.*

4. Facility of performance; the peculiar skill derived from practice, or practice aided by nature; habitual skill or ability; dexterity; adroitness; knack. One man has a remarkable *faculty* of telling a story; another, of inventing excuses for misconduct; a third, of reasoning; a fourth, of preaching.

5. Personal quality; disposition or habit, good or ill. *Shak.*

6. Power; authority.

> This Duncan
> Hath borne his *faculties* so meek. *Shak.*

[*Hardly legitimate.*]

7. Mechanical power; as the *faculty* of the wedge. [*Not used, nor legitimate.*] *Wilkins.*

8. Natural virtue; efficacy; as the *faculty* of simples. [*Not used, nor legitimate.*] *Milton.*

9. Privilege; a right or power granted to a person by favor or indulgence, to do what by law he may not do; as the *faculty* of marrying without the bans being first published, or of ordaining a deacon under age. The archbishop of Canterbury has a court of *faculties,* for granting such privileges or dispensations. *Encyc.*

10. In *colleges,* the masters and professors of the several sciences. *Johnson.*

One of the members or departments of a university. In most universities there are four *faculties;* of arts, including humanity and philosophy; of theology; of medicine; and of law. *Encyc.*

In *America,* the *faculty* of a college or university consists of the president, professors and tutors.

The *faculty of advocates,* in Scotland, is a respectable body of lawyers who plead in all causes before the Courts of Session, Justiciary and Exchequer. *Encyc.*

FAC'UND, *a.* [L. *facundus,* supposed to be from the root of *for, fari,* to speak. If so, the original word was *faco,* or *facor.*] Eloquent. [*Little used.*]

FACUND'ITY, *n.* [L. *facunditas.*] Eloquence; readiness of speech.

FAD'DLE, *v. i.* To trifle; to toy; to play. [*A low word.*]

FADE, *a.* [Fr.] Weak; slight; faint. [*Not in use.*] *Berkeley.*

FADE, *v. i.* [Fr. *fade,* insipid, tasteless. Qu. L. *vado,* or Ar. نفد nafeeda, to vanish, Syr. to fail, to err. See Class Bd. No. 48. and 39. 44.]

1. To lose color; to tend from a stronger or brighter color to a more faint shade of the same color, or to lose a color entirely. A green leaf *fades* and becomes less green or yellow. Those colors are deemed the best, which are least apt to *fade.*

2. To wither, as a plant; to decay.

> Ye shall be as an oak, whose leaf *fadeth.* Is. i.

3. To lose strength gradually; to vanish.

> When the memory is weak, ideas in the mind quickly *fade.* *Locke.*

4. To lose luster; to grow dim.

> The stars shall *fade* away. *Addison.*

5. To decay; to perish gradually.

> We all do *fade* as a leaf. Is. lxiv.
> An inheritance that *fadeth* not away. 1 Pet. i.

6. To decay; to decline; to become poor and miserable.

> The rich man shall *fade* away in his ways. James i.

7. To lose strength, health or vigor; to decline; to grow weaker. *South.*

8. To disappear gradually; to vanish.

FADE, *v. t.* To cause to wither; to wear away; to deprive of freshness or vigor.

> No winter could his laurels *fade.* *Dryden.*
> This is a man, old, wrinkled, *faded,* withered. *Shak.*

FA'DED, *pp.* Become less vivid, as color; withered; decayed; vanished.

FADGE, *v. i. faj.* [Sax. *fægen, gefegen,* to unite, to fit together; G. *fügen;* D. *voegen;* Sw. *foga;* Dan. *fuge,* a seam or joint; W. *fag,* a meeting in a point. It coincides with L. *pango, pegi, pepegi,* Gr. πηγω, πηγνυω, L. *figo.* See דבק Class Bg. No. 33. See also No. 34. 35. Of this word *fay* is a contraction.]

1. To suit; to fit; to come close, as the parts of things united. Hence, to have one part consistent with another. *Shak.*

2. To agree; to live in amity. [*Ludicrous.*] *Hudibras.*

3. To succeed; to hit. *L'Estrange.*

[This word is now vulgar, and improper in elegant writing.]

FA'DING, *ppr.* [See *Fade.*] Losing color; becoming less vivid; decaying; declining; withering.

2. *a.* Subject to decay; liable to lose freshness and vigor; liable to perish; not durable; transient; as a *fading* flower.

FA'DING, *n.* Decay; loss of color, freshness or vigor. *Sherwood.*

FA'DINGNESS, *n.* Decay; liableness to decay. *Mountagu.*

FA'DY, *a.* Wearing away; losing color or strength. *Shenstone.*

FÆCAL, *a.* [See *Fecal.*]

FÆ'CES, *n.* [L.] Excrement; also, settlings; sediment after infusion or distillation. *Quincy.*

FAF'FEL, *v. i.* To stammer. [*Not in use.*] *Barret.*

FAG, *v. t.* To beat. [*Not in use.*]

FAG, *n.* A slave; one who works hard. [*Not in use.*]

FAG, *v. i.* [Scot. *faik.* Qu. Heb. Ch. Syr. פוג to fail, to languish. See Class Bg. No. 44. 60. 76.]

To become weary; to fail in strength; to be faint with weariness.

> The Italian began to *fag.* *Mackenzie.*

[*A vulgar word.*]

FAG, *n.* A knot in cloth. [*Not in use.*]

FAGEND', *n.* [*fag* and *end.* See *Fag, v. i.* supra.]

1. The end of a web of cloth, generally of coarser materials. *Johnson.*

2. The refuse or meaner part of any thing. *Collier.*

3. Among *seamen,* the untwisted end of a rope; hence, to *fag out,* is to become untwisted and loose. *Mar. Dict.*

We observe that the use of this word among seamen leads to the true sense of the verb, as well as the noun. The sense is, to open by receding, or to yield and become lax, and hence weak.

FAG'OT, *n.* [W. *fagod;* Gr. φακελλος; connected with W. *fag,* that which unites or meets; *fagiad,* a gathering round a point; Scot. *faik,* to fold, to grasp; *fake,* in seamen's language, a coil; allied to Sax. *fægan, gefegan,* to unite. See *Fadge.* The sense is a bundle or collection, like *pack.*]

1. A bundle of sticks, twigs or small branches of trees, used for fuel, or for raising batteries, filling ditches, and other purposes in fortification. The French use *fascine,* from the L. *fascis,* a bundle; *a term now adopted in English.*

2. A person hired to appear at musters in a company not full and hide the deficiency. *Encyc.*

FAG'OT, *v. t.* To tie together; to bind in a bundle; to collect promiscuously. *Dryden.*

F'AHLERZ, *n.* Gray copper, or gray copper ore, called by Jameson tetrahedral copper pyrite. This mineral is easily broken, and its fracture usually uneven, but sometimes a little conchoidal. It is found amorphous and in regular crystals. *Cleaveland.*

F'AHLUNITE, *n.* [from *Fahlun*, in Sweden.]

Automalite, a subspecies of octahedral corundum. *Ure.*

FAIL, *v. i.* [Fr. *faillir*; W. *faelu*, or *pallu* and *aballu*; Scot. *failye*; It. *fallire*; Sp. *falir*, *faltar*; Port. *falhar*; L. *fallo*; Ir. *feallam*; Gr. φηλεω, φηλοω, whence σφαλλω; D. *feilen*, *faalen*; G. *fehlen*; Sw. *fela*; Dan. *fejler*; Arm. *fallaat*, *fellel*, whence *falloni*, wickedness, Eng. *felony*. It seems to be allied to *fall*, *fallow*, *pale*, and many other words. See Class Bl. No. 6. 7. 8. 13. 18. 21. 28.]

1. To become deficient; to be insufficient; to cease to be abundant for supply; or to be entirely wanting. We say, in a dry season, the springs and streams *fail*, or are *failing*, before they are entirely exhausted. We say also, the springs *failed*, when they entirely ceased to flow. Crops *fail* wholly or partially.
2. To decay; to decline; to sink; to be diminished. We say of a sick person, his strength *fails* daily.
3. To decline; to decay; to sink; to become weaker; as, the patient *fails* every hour.
4. To be extinct; to cease; to be entirely wanting; to be no longer produced.

   Help, Lord, for the godly man ceaseth; for the faithful *fail* from among the children of men. Ps. xii.

5. To be entirely exhausted; to be wanting; to cease from supply.

   Money *failed* in the land of Egypt. Gen. xlvii.

6. To cease; to perish; to be lost.

   Lest the remembrance of his grief should *fail*. *Addison.*

7. To die.

   They shall all *fail* together. Isaiah xxxi.

8. To decay; to decline; as, the sight *fails* in old age.
9. To become deficient or wanting; as, the heart or the courage *fails*.
10. To miss; not to produce the effect. The experiment was made with care, but *failed*, or *failed* to produce the effect, or *failed* of the effect.
11. To be deficient in duty; to omit or neglect. The debtor *failed* to fulfil his promise.
12. To miss; to miscarry; to be frustrated or disappointed. The enemy attacked the fort, but *failed* in his design, or *failed* of success.
13. To be neglected; to fall short; not to be executed. The promises of a man of probity seldom *fail*.

    The soul or the spirit *fails*, when a person is discouraged. The eyes *fail*, when the desires and expectations are long delayed, and the person is disappointed.

14. To become insolvent or bankrupt. When merchants and traders *fail*, they are said to become bankrupt. When other men *fail*, they are said to become insolvent.

FAIL, *v. t.* To desert; to disappoint; to cease or to neglect or omit to afford aid, supply or strength. It is said, fortune never *fails* the brave. Our friends sometimes *fail* us, when we most need them. The aged attempt to walk, when their limbs *fail* them. In bold enterprises, courage should never *fail* the hero.

2. To omit; not to perform.

   The inventive God, who never *fails* his part. *Dryden.*

3. To be wanting to.

   There shall never *fail* thee a man on the throne. 1 Kings ii.

[In the transitive use of this verb, there is really an ellipsis of *from* or *to*, or other word. In strictness, the verb is not transitive, and the passive participle is, I believe, never used.]

FAIL, *n.* Omission; non-performance.

   He will without *fail* drive out from before you the Canaanites. Josh. iii.

2. Miscarriage; failure; deficience; want; death. [*In these senses little used.*]

FA'ILANCE, *n.* Fault; failure. *Obs.*

FA'ILING, *ppr.* Becoming deficient or insufficient; becoming weaker; decaying; declining; omitting; not executing or performing; miscarrying; neglecting; wanting; becoming bankrupt or insolvent.

FA'ILING, *n.* The act of failing; deficiency; imperfection; lapse; fault. *Failings*, in a moral sense, are minor faults, proceeding rather from weakness of intellect or from carelessness, than from bad motives. But the word is often abusively applied to vices of a grosser kind.

2. The act of failing or becoming insolvent.

FA'ILURE, *n.* *fa'ilyur.* A failing; deficience; cessation of supply, or total defect; as the *failure* of springs or streams; *failure* of rain; *failure* of crops.

2. Omission; non-performance; as the *failure* of a promise; a man's *failure* in the execution of a trust.
3. Decay, or defect from decay; as the *failure* of memory or of sight.
4. A breaking, or becoming insolvent. At the close of a war, the prices of commodities fall, and innumerable *failures* succeed.
5. A failing; a slight fault. [*Little used.*]

FAIN, *a.* [Sax. *fagen*, *fægan*, glad; *fagnian*, Goth. *faginon*, to rejoice; Sw. *fägen*. Class Bg. No. 3. 43. 77.]

1. Glad; pleased; rejoiced. But the appropriate sense of the word is, glad or pleased to do something under some kind of necessity; that is, glad to evade evil or secure good. Thus, says Locke, "The learned Castalio was *fain* to make trenches at Basil, to keep himself from starving." This appropriation of the word, which is modern, led Dr. Johnson into a mistake in defining the word. The proper signification is glad, joyful.

FAIN, *adv.* Gladly; with joy or pleasure.

   He would *fain* flee out of his hand. Job xxvii.

   He would *fain* have filled his belly with husks. Luke xv.

FAIN, *v. i.* To wish or desire. [*Not used.*]

FA'INING, *ppr.* Wishing; desiring fondly.

   In his *faining* eye. *Spenser.*

FAINT, *a.* [Ir. *faine*, a weakening; *fann*, weak; *fanntais*, weakness, inclination to faint; *anbhfaine*, fainting; Fr. *faineant*, idle, sluggish. This word is perhaps allied to Fr. *faner*, to fade, wither, decay, to make hay, *foin*, L. *fœnum*; and to *vain*, L. *vanus*, whence to *vanish*, Ar. فني fani, to vanish, to fail, Eng. to *wane*, Sax. *fynig*, musty. Class Bn. No. 25.]

1. Weak; languid; inclined to swoon; as, to be rendered *faint* by excessive evacuations.
2. Weak; feeble; languid; exhausted; as *faint* with fatigue, hunger or thirst.
3. Weak, as color; not bright or vivid; not strong; as a *faint* color; a *faint* red or blue; a *faint* light.
4. Feeble; weak, as sound; not loud; as a *faint* sound; a *faint* voice.
5. Imperfect; feeble; not striking; as a *faint* resemblance or image.
6. Cowardly; timorous. A *faint* heart never wins a fair lady.
7. Feeble; not vigorous; not active; as a *faint* resistance; a *faint* exertion.
8. Dejected; depressed; dispirited.

   My heart is *faint*. Lam. i.

FAINT, *v. i.* To lose the animal functions; to lose strength and color, and become senseless and motionless; to swoon; sometimes with *away*. He *fainted* for loss of blood.

   On hearing the honor intended her, she *fainted away*. *Guardian.*

2. To become feeble; to decline or fail in strength and vigor; to be weak.

   If I send them away fasting to their own houses, they will *faint* by the way. Mark viii.

3. To sink into dejection; to lose courage or spirit.

   Let not your hearts *faint*. Deut. xx.

   If thou *faint* in the day of adversity, thy strength is small. Prov. xxiv.

4. To decay; to disappear; to vanish.

   Gilded clouds, while we gaze on them, *faint* before the eye. *Pope.*

FAINT, *v. t.* To deject; to depress; to weaken. [*Unusual.*] *Shak.*

FAINTHEARTED, *a.* Cowardly; timorous; dejected; easily depressed, or yielding to fear.

   Fear not, neither be *fainthearted*. Is. vii.

FAINTHEARTEDLY, *adv.* In a cowardly manner.

FAINTHEARTEDNESS, *n.* Cowardice; timorousness; want of courage.

FA'INTING, *ppr.* Falling into a swoon; failing; losing strength or courage; becoming feeble or timid.

FA'INTING, *n.* A temporary loss of strength, color and respiration; syncope; deliquium; leipothymy; a swoon. *Wiseman.*

FA'INTISH, *a.* Slightly faint.

FA'INTISHNESS, *n.* A slight degree of faintness. *Arbuthnot.*

FA'INTLING, *a.* Timorous; feeble-minded. [*Not used.*] *Arbuthnot.*

FA'INTLY, *adv.* In a feeble, languid manner; without vigor or activity; as, to attack or defend *faintly*.

2. With a feeble flame; as, a torch burns *faintly*.
3. With a feeble light; as, the candle burns *faintly*.
4. With little force; as, to breathe *faintly*.
5. Without force of representation; imperfectly; as, to describe *faintly* what we have seen.

6. In a low tone; with a feeble voice; as, to speak *faintly*.
7. Without spirit or courage; timorously.

He *faintly* now declines the fatal strife. *Denham.*

FA'INTNESS, *n.* The state of being faint; loss of strength, color and respiration.
2. Feebleness; languor; want of strength. *Hooker.*
3. Inactivity; want of vigor. *Spenser.*
4. Feebleness, as of color or light.
5. Feebleness of representation; as *faintness* of description.
6. Feebleness of mind; timorousness; dejection; irresolution.

I will send a *faintness* into their hearts. Lev. xxvi.

FAINTS, *n. plu.* The gross fetid oil remaining after distillation, or a weak spirituous liquor that runs from the still in rectifying the low wines after the proof spirit is drawn off; also, the last runnings of all spirits distilled by the alembic. *Encyc. Edwards, W. Ind.*

FA'INTY, *a.* Weak; feeble; languid. *Dryden.*

FAIR, *a.* [Sax. *fæger*; Sw. *fager*; Dan. *faver*. If the sense is primarily to open, to clear, to separate, this word may belong to the root of Sw. *fäja*, Dan. *fejer*, D. *veegen*, G. *fegen*, to sweep, scour, furbish.]
1. Clear; free from spots; free from a dark hue; white; as a *fair* skin; a *fair* complexion. Hence,
2. Beautiful; handsome; properly, having a handsome face.

Thou art a *fair* woman to look upon. Gen. xii. Hence,

3. Pleasing to the eye; handsome or beautiful in general.

Thus was he *fair* in his greatness, in the length of his branches. Ezek. xxxi.

4. Clear; pure; free from feculence or extraneous matter; as *fair* water.
5. Clear; not cloudy or overcast; as *fair* weather; a *fair* sky.
6. Favorable; prosperous; blowing in a direction towards the place of destination; as a *fair* wind at sea.
7. Open; direct, as a way or passage. You are in a *fair* way to promotion. Hence, likely to succeed. He stands as *fair* to succeed as any man.
8. Open to attack or access; unobstructed; as a *fair* mark; a *fair* butt; *fair* in sight; in *fair* sight; a *fair* view.
9. Open; frank; honest; hence, equal; just; equitable. My friend is a *fair* man; his offer is *fair*; his propositions are *fair* and honorable.
10. Not effected by insidious or unlawful methods; not foul.

He died a *fair* and natural death. *Temple.*

11. Frank; candid; not sophistical or insidious; as a *fair* disputant.
12. Honest; honorable; mild; opposed to insidious and compulsory; as, to accomplish a thing by *fair* means.
13. Frank; civil; pleasing; not harsh.

When *fair* words and good counsel will not prevail on us, we must be frighted into our duty. *L'Estrange.*

14. Equitable; just; merited.

His doom is *fair*,
That dust I am, and shall to dust return. *Milton.*

15. Liberal; not narrow; as a *fair* livelihood. *Carew.*
16. Plain; legible; as, the letter is written in a *fair* hand.
17. Free from stain or blemish; unspotted; untarnished; as a *fair* character or fame.

FAIR, *adv.* Openly; frankly; civilly; complaisantly.

One of the company spoke him *fair*. *L'Estrange.*

2. Candidly; honestly; equitably. He promised *fair*.
3. Happily; successfully.

Now *fair* befall thee. *Shak.*

4. On good terms; as, to keep *fair* with the world; to stand *fair* with one's companions.

To bid fair, is to be likely, or to have a fair prospect.

Fair and square, just dealing; honesty.

FAIR, *n.* *Elliptically*, a fair woman; a handsome female. *The fair*, the female sex.
2. Fairness; *applied to things or persons.* [*Not in use.*]

FAIR, *n.* [Fr. *foire*; W. *fair*; Arm. *foar*, *foer*, *feur*, or *for*; L. *forum*, or *feriæ*. The It. *fiera*, and Sp. *feria*, a fair, are the L. *feriæ*, a holiday, a day exempt from labor; G. *feier*, whence *feiern*, to rest from labor. If *fair* is from *forum*, it may coincide in origin with Gr. πορευω, εμπορευομαι, to trade, whence εμποριον, *emporium*, the primary sense of which is to pass. In Norman French we find *fair* and *feire*. If *fair* is from *feriæ*, it is so called from being held in places where the wakes or feasts at the dedication of churches were held, or from the feasts themselves. It is a fact that Sundays were formerly market-days.]

A stated market in a particular town or city; a stated meeting of buyers and sellers for trade. A fair is annual or more frequent. The privilege of holding fairs is granted by the king or supreme power. Among the most celebrated *fairs* in Europe are those of Francfort and Leipsic in Germany; of Novi in the Milanese; of Riga and Archangel in Russia; of Lyons and St. Germain in France. In Great Britain many towns enjoy this privilege. *Encyc.*

FA'IR-HAND, *a.* Having a fair appearance. *Shak.*

FA'IRING, *n.* A present given at a fair. *Gay.*

FA'IRLY, *adv.* Beautifully; handsomely. [*Little used.*]
2. Commodiously; conveniently; as a town *fairly* situated for foreign trade.
3. Frankly; honestly; justly; equitably; without disguise, fraud or prevarication. The question was *fairly* stated and argued. Let us deal *fairly* with all men.
4. Openly; ingenuously; plainly. Let us deal *fairly* with ourselves or our own hearts.
5. Candidly.

I interpret *fairly* your design. *Dryden.*

6. Without perversion or violence; as, an inference may be *fairly* deduced from the premises.
7. Without blots; in plain letters; plainly; legibly; as an instrument or record *fairly* written.
8. Completely; without deficience. His antagonist fought till he was *fairly* defeated.
9. Softly; gently. *Milton.*

FA'IRNESS, *n.* Clearness; freedom from spots or blemishes; whiteness; as the *fairness* of skin or complexion.
2. Clearness; purity; as the *fairness* of water.
3. Freedom from stain or blemish; as the *fairness* of character or reputation.
4. Beauty; elegance; as the *fairness* of form.
5. Frankness; candor; hence, honesty; ingenuousness; as *fairness* in trade.
6. Openness; candor; freedom from disguise, insidiousness or prevarication; as the *fairness* of an argument.
7. Equality of terms; equity; as the *fairness* of a contract.
8. Distinctness; freedom from blots or obscurity; as the *fairness* of hand-writing; the *fairness* of a copy.

FA'IR-SPOKEN, *a.* Using fair speech; bland; civil; courteous; plausible.

Arius, a *fair-spoken* man. *Hooker.*

FA'IRY, *n.* [G. *fee*; Fr. *fée*, whence *féer*, to enchant, *féerie*, a *fairy* land; It. *fata*. The origin of this word is not obvious, and the radical letters are uncertain. The conjectures of Baxter, Jamieson and others throw no satisfactory light on the subject.]
1. A *fay*; an imaginary being or spirit, supposed to assume a human form, dance in meadows, steal infants and play a variety of pranks. [See *Elf* and *Demon.*] *Locke. Pope.*
2. An enchantress. *Shak.*

Fairy of the mine, an imaginary being supposed to inhabit mines, wandering about in the drifts and chambers, always employed in cutting ore, turning the windlass, &c., yet effecting nothing. The Germans believe in two species; one fierce and malevolent; the other gentle. [See *Cobalt.*] *Encyc.*

Fairy ring or *circle*, a phenomenon observed in fields, vulgarly supposed to be caused by fairies in their dances. This circle is of two kinds; one about seven yards in diameter, containing a round bare path, a foot broad, with green grass in the middle; the other of different size, encompassed with grass. *Encyc.*

FA'IRY, *a.* Belonging to fairies; as *fairy* land. *Shak.*
2. Given by fairies; as *fairy* money or favors. *Dryden. Locke.*

FA'IRYLIKE, *a.* Imitating the manner of fairies. *Shak.*

FA'IRYSTONE, *n.* A stone found in gravel pits. *Johnson.*

The fossil echinite, abundant in chalk pits. *Cyc.*

FAITH, *n.* [W. *fyz*; Arm, *feiz*; L. *fides*; It. *fede*; Port. and Sp. *fe*; Fr. *foi*; Gr. πιςις; L. *fido*, to trust; Gr. πειθω, to persuade, to draw towards any thing, to conciliate; πειθομαι, to believe, to obey. In the Greek Lexicon of Hederic it is said, the primitive signification of the verb is to bind and draw or lead, as πεισα signifies a rope or cable, as does πεισμα. But this remark is a little incorrect. The sense of the verb, from which that of rope and binding is derived, is to strain, to draw, and thus to bind or make fast. A rope or cable is that which makes fast. Qu. Heb. Ch. Syr. Sam. בטח. Class Bd. No. 16.]

1. Belief; the assent of the mind to the truth of what is declared by another, resting on his authority and veracity, without other evidence; the judgment that what another states or testifies is the truth. I have strong *faith* or no *faith* in the testimony of a witness, or in what a historian narrates.

2. The assent of the mind to the truth of a proposition advanced by another; belief, on probable evidence of any kind.

3. In *theology*, the assent of the mind or understanding to the truth of what God has revealed. Simple belief of the scriptures, of the being and perfections of God, and of the existence, character and doctrines of Christ, founded on the testimony of the sacred writers, is called *historical* or *speculative faith*; a faith little distinguished from the belief of the existence and achievments of Alexander or of Cesar.

4. *Evangelical*, *justifying*, or *saving faith*, is the assent of the mind to the truth of divine revelation, on the authority of God's testimony, accompanied with a cordial assent of the will or approbation of the heart; an entire confidence or trust in God's character and declarations, and in the character and doctrines of Christ, with an unreserved surrender of the will to his guidance, and dependence on his merits for salvation. In other words, that firm belief of God's testimony, and of the truth of the gospel, which influences the will, and leads to an entire reliance on Christ for salvation.

Being justified by *faith*. Rom. v.

Without *faith* it is impossible to please God. Heb. xi.

For we walk by *faith*, and not by sight. 2 Cor. v.

With the *heart* man believeth to righteousness. Rom. x.

The *faith* of the gospel is that emotion of the mind, which is called trust or confidence, exercised towards the moral character of God, and particularly of the Savior. *Dwight.*

Faith is an affectionate practical confidence in the testimony of God. *J. Hawes.*

Faith is a firm, cordial belief in the veracity of God, in all the declarations of his word; or a full and affectionate confidence in the certainty of those things which God has declared, and because he has declared them. *L. Woods.*

5. The object of belief; a doctrine or system of doctrines believed; a system of revealed truths received by christians.

They heard only, that he who persecuted us in times past, now preacheth the *faith* which once he destroyed. Gal. i.

6. The promises of God, or his truth and faithfulness.

Shall their unbelief make the *faith* of God without effect? Rom. iii.

7. An open profession of gospel truth.

Your *faith* is spoken of throughout the whole world. Rom. i.

8. A persuasion or belief of the lawfulness of things indifferent.

Hast thou *faith*? Have it to thyself before God. Rom. xiv.

9. Faithfulness; fidelity; a strict adherence to duty and fulfillment of promises.

Her failing, while her *faith* to me remains,
I would conceal. *Milton.*

Children in whom is no *faith*. Deut. xxxii.

10. Word or honor pledged; promise given; fidelity. He violated his plighted *faith*.

For you alone
I broke my *faith* with injured Palamon. *Dryden.*

11. Sincerity; honesty; veracity; faithfulness. We ought, in good *faith*, to fulfill all our engagements.

12. Credibility or truth. [*Unusual.*]

The *faith* of the foregoing narrative. *Mitford.*

FA'ITH-BREACH, *n.* Breach of fidelity; disloyalty; perfidy. *Shak.*

FA'ITHED, *a.* Honest; sincere. [*Not used.*] *Shak.*

FA'ITHFUL, *a.* Firm in adherence to the truth and to the duties of religion.

Be thou *faithful* unto death, and I will give thee a crown of life. Rev. ii.

2. Firmly adhering to duty; of true fidelity; loyal; true to allegiance; as a *faithful* subject.

3. Constant in the performance of duties or services; exact in attending to commands; as a *faithful* servant.

4. Observant of compact, treaties, contracts, vows or other engagements; true to one's word. A government should be *faithful* to its treaties; individuals, to their word.

5. True; exact; in conformity to the letter and spirit; as a *faithful* execution of a will.

6. True to the marriage covenant; as a *faithful* wife or husband.

7. Conformable to truth; as a *faithful* narrative or representation.

8. Constant; not fickle; as a *faithful* lover or friend.

9. True; worthy of belief. 2. Tim. ii.

FA'ITHFULLY, *adv.* In a faithful manner; with good faith.

2. With strict adherence to allegiance and duty; *applied to subjects.*

3. With strict observance of promises, vows, covenants or duties; without failure of performance; honestly; exactly. The treaty or contract was *faithfully* executed.

4. Sincerely; with strong assurances; he *faithfully* promised.

5. Honestly; truly; without defect, fraud, trick or ambiguity. The battle was *faithfully* described or represented.

They suppose the nature of things to be *faithfully* signified by their names. *South.*

6. Confidently; steadily. *Shak.*

FA'ITHFULNESS, *n.* Fidelity; loyalty; firm adherence to allegiance and duty; as the *faithfulness* of a subject.

2. Truth; veracity; as the *faithfulness* of God.

3. Strict adherence to injunctions, and to the duties of a station; as the *faithfulness* of servants or ministers.

4. Strict performance of promises, vows or covenants; constancy in affection; as the *faithfulness* of a husband or wife.

FA'ITHLESS, *a.* Without belief in the revealed truths of religion; unbelieving.

O *faithless* generation. Matt. xvii.

2. Not believing; not giving credit to.

3. Not adhering to allegiance or duty; disloyal; perfidious; treacherous; as a *faithless* subject.

4. Not true to a master or employer; neglectful; as a *faithless* servant.

5. Not true to the marriage covenant; false; as a *faithless* husband or wife.

6. Not observant of promises.

7. Deceptive.

Yonder *faithless* phantom. *Goldsmith.*

FA'ITHLESSNESS, *n.* Unbelief, as to revealed religion.

2. Perfidy; treachery; disloyalty; as in subjects.

3. Violation of promises or covenants; inconstancy; as of husband or wife.

FA'ITOUR, *n.* [Norm. from L. *factor.*] An evildoer; a scoundrel; a mean fellow. *Obs.* *Spenser.*

FAKE, *n.* [Scot. *faik*, to fold, a fold, a layer or stratum; perhaps Sw. *vika*, *vickla*, to fold or involve. The sense of *fold* may be to lay, to fall, or to set or throw together, and this word may belong to Sax. *fægan*, *fegan*, to unite, to suit, to fadge, that is, to set or lay together.]

One of the circles or windings of a cable or hawser, as it lies in a coil; a single turn or coil. *Mar. Dict.*

FA'KIR, **FA'QUIR**, *n.* [This word signifies in Arabic, a poor man; in Ethiopic, an interpreter.]

A monk in India. The fakirs subject themselves to severe austerities and mortifications. Some of them condemn themselves to a standing posture all their lives, supported only by a stick or rope under their arm-pits. Some mangle their bodies with scourges or knives. Others wander about in companies, telling fortunes, and these are said to be arrant villains. *Encyc.*

FALCA'DE, *n.* [L. *falx*, a sickle or sythe.] A horse is said to make a *falcade*, when he throws himself on his haunches two or three times, as in very quick curvets; that is, a *falcade* is a bending very low. *Harris.*

FAL'CATE, **FAL'CATED**, *a.* [L. *falcatus*, from *falx*, a sickle, sythe or reaping-hook.]

Hooked; bent like a sickle or sythe; an epithet applied to the new moon. *Bailey.*

FALCA'TION, *n.* Crookedness; a bending in the form of a sickle. *Brown.*

FAL'CHION, *n.* *fal'chun.* *a* is pronounced as in fall. [Fr. *fauchon*, from L. *falx*, a reaping-hook.]

A short crooked sword; a cimiter. *Dryden.*

FAL'CIFORM, *a.* [L. *falx*, a reaping-hook, and *form.*]

In the shape of a sickle; resembling a reaping-hook.

FAL'CON, *n.* sometimes pron. *fawcon.* [Fr. *faucon*; It. *falcone*; L. *falco*, a hawk; W. *gwalç*, a crested one, a hero, a hawk, that which rises or towers. The falcon is probably so named from its curving beak or talons.]

1. A hawk; but appropriately, a hawk trained to sport, as in *falconry*, which see. It is said that this name is, by sportsmen, given to the female alone; for the male is smaller, weaker and less courageous, and is therefore called *tircelet* or tarsel. *Encyc.*

This term, in ornithology, is applied to a division of the genus Falco, with a short hooked beak and very long wings, the strongest armed and most courageous species, and therefore used in falconry. *Cuvier. Ed. Encyc.*

2. A sort of cannon, whose diameter at the bore is five inches and a quarter, and carrying shot of two pounds and a half. *Harris.*

FAL'€ONER, *n.* [Fr. *fauconnier.*] A person who breeds and trains hawks for taking wild fowls; one who follows the sport of fowling with hawks. *Johnson.*

FAL'€ONET, *n.* [Fr. *falconette.*] A small cannon or piece of ordnance, whose diameter at the bore is four inches and a quarter, and carrying shot of one pound and a quarter. *Harris.*

FAL'€ONRY, *n.* [Fr. *fauconnerie*, from L. *falco*, a hawk.]

1. The art of training hawks to the exercise of hawking.

2. The practice of taking wild fowls by means of hawks.

FALD'AĠE, *n.* *a* as in *all.* [W. *fald*, a fold; Goth. *faldan*; Sax. *fealdan*, to fold; Law L. *faldagium.*]

In *England*, a privilege which anciently several lords reserved to themselves of setting up folds for sheep, in any fields within their manors, the better to manure them. *Harris.*

FALD'FEE, *n.* A fee or composition paid anciently by tenants for the privilege of faldage. *Dict.*

FALD'ING, *n.* A kind of coarse cloth. *Obs. Chaucer.*

FALD'STOOL, *n.* [*fald* or *fold* and stool.] A kind of stool placed at the south side of the altar, at which the kings of England kneel at their coronation. *Johnson.*

2. The chair of a bishop inclosed by the railing of the altar.

3. An arm-chair or folding chair. *Ashmole.*

FALL, *v. i.* pret. *fell*; pp. *fallen.* [Sax. *feallan*; G. *fallen*; D. *vallen*; Sw. *falla*; Dan. *falder*; allied probably to L. *fallo*, to *fail*, to deceive, Gr. σφαλλω; Sp. *hallar*, to find, to fall on; Fr. *affaler*, to lower. See Class Bl. No. 18. 28. 43. 49. 52. *Fall* coincides exactly with the Shemitic נפל Heb. Ch. Syr. and Sam. to *fall.* *Fail* agrees better with the Heb. נבל, and הבל, but these words may have had one primitive root, the sense of which was to move, to recede, to pass. As these words are unquestionably the same in the Shemitic and Japhetic languages, they afford decisive evidence that the נ or first letter of the Shemitic words is a prefix. The Chaldee sense of נבל is to defile, to make *foul.* See *Foul.* The same verb in Ar. نبل signifies to shoot, to drive or throw an arrow, Gr. βαλλω.]

1. To drop from a higher place; to descend by the power of gravity alone. Rain *falls* from the clouds; a man *falls* from his horse; ripe fruits *fall* from trees; an ox *falls* into a pit.

I beheld Satan as lightning *fall* from heaven. Luke x.

2. To drop from an erect posture.

I *fell* at his feet to worship him. Rev. xix.

3. To disembogue; to pass at the outlet; to flow out of its channel into a pond, lake or sea, as a river. The Rhone *falls* into the Mediterranean sea. The Danube *falls* into the Euxine. The Mississippi *falls* into the gulf of Mexico.

4. To depart from the faith, or from rectitude; to apostatize. Adam *fell* by eating the forbidden fruit.

Labor to enter into that rest, lest any man *fall* after the same example of unbelief. Heb. iv.

5. To die, particularly by violence.

Ye shall chase your enemies, and they shall *fall* before you by the sword. Lev. xxvi.

A thousand shall *fall* at thy side. Ps. xci.

6. To come to an end suddenly; to vanish; to perish.

The greatness of these Irish lords suddenly *fell* and vanished. *Davies.*

7. To be degraded; to sink into disrepute or disgrace; to be plunged into misery; as, to *fall* from an elevated station, or from a prosperous state.

8. To decline in power, wealth or glory; to sink into weakness; to be overthrown or ruined. This is the renowned Tyre; but oh, how *fallen.*

Heaven and earth will witness,
If Rome must *fall*, that we are innocent. *Addison.*

9. To pass into a worse state than the former; to come; as, to *fall* into difficulties; to *fall* under censure or imputation; to *fall* into error or absurdity; to *fall* into a snare. In these and similar phrases, the sense of suddenness, accident or ignorance is often implied; but not always.

10. To sink; to be lowered. The mercury in a thermometer rises and *falls* with the increase and diminution of heat. The water of a river rises and *falls.* The tide *falls.*

11. To decrease; to be diminished in weight or value. The price of goods *falls* with plenty and rises with scarcity. Pliny tells us, the as *fell* from a pound to two ounces in the first Punic war. *Arbuthnot.*

12. To sink; not to amount to the full.

The greatness of finances and revenue doth *fall* under computation. *Bacon.*

13. To be rejected; to sink into disrepute.

This book must stand or *fall* with thee. *Locke.*

14. To decline from violence to calmness, from intensity to remission. The wind *falls* and a calm succeeds.

At length her fury *fell.* *Dryden.*

15. To pass into a new state of body or mind; to become; as, to *fall* asleep; to *fall* distracted; to *fall* sick; to *fall* into rage or passion; to *fall* in love; to *fall* into temptation.

16. To sink into an air of dejection, discontent, anger, sorrow or shame; applied to the countenance or look.

Cain was very wroth, and his countenance *fell.* Gen. iv.

I have observed of late thy looks are *fallen.* *Addison.*

17. To happen; to befall; to come.

Since this fortune *falls* to you. *Shak.*

18. To light on; to come by chance.

The Romans *fell* on this model by chance. *Swift.*

19. To come; to rush on; to assail.

Fear and dread shall *fall* on them. Ex. xv.

And fear *fell* on them all. Acts xix.

20. To come; to arrive.

The vernal equinox, which at the Nicene council *fell* on the 21st of March, *falls* now about ten days sooner. *Holder.*

21. To come unexpectedly.

It happened this evening that we *fell* into a pleasing walk. *Addison.*

22. To begin with haste, ardor or vehemence; to rush or hurry to. They *fell* to blows.

The mixt multitude *fell* to lusting. Num. xi.

23. To pass or be transferred by chance, lot, distribution, inheritance or otherwise, as possession or property. The estate or the province *fell* to his brother. The kingdom *fell* into the hands of his rival. A large estate *fell* to his heirs.

24. To become the property of; to belong or appertain to.

If to her share some female errors *fall*,
Look in her face, and you'll forget them all. *Pope.*

25. To be dropped or uttered carelessly. Some expressions *fell* from him. An unguarded expression *fell* from his lips. Not a word *fell* from him on the subject.

26. To sink; to languish; to become feeble or faint. Our hopes and fears rise and *fall* with good or ill success.

27. To be brought forth. Take care of lambs when they first *fall.* *Mortimer.*

28. To issue; to terminate.

Sit still, my daughter, till thou knowest how the matter will *fall.* Ruth iii.

To fall aboard of, to strike against another ship.

To fall astern, to move or be driven backward; or to remain behind. A ship *falls* astern by the force of a current, or when outsailed by another.

To fall away, to lose flesh; to become lean or emaciated; to pine.

2. To renounce or desert allegiance; to revolt or rebel.

3. To renounce or desert the faith; to apostatize; to sink into wickedness.

These for awhile believe, and in time of temptation *fall away.* Luke viii.

4. To perish; to be ruined; to be lost.

How can the soul—*fall away* into nothing. *Addison.*

5. To decline gradually; to fade; to languish, or become faint.

One color *falls away* by just degrees, and another rises insensibly. *Addison.*

To fall back, to recede; to give way.

2. To fail of performing a promise or purpose; not to fulfill.

To fall calm, to cease to blow; to become calm.

To fall down, to prostrate one's self in worship.

All nations shall *fall down* before him. Ps. lxxii.

2. To sink; to come to the ground.

Down fell the beauteous youth. *Dryden.*

3. To bend or bow as a suppliant. Isaiah xlv.

4. To sail or pass towards the mouth of a river, or other outlet.

To fall foul, to attack; to make an assault.

To fall from, to recede from; to depart; not to adhere; as, to *fall from* an agreement or engagement.

2. To depart from allegiance or duty; to revolt.

To fall in, to concur; to agree with. The measure *falls in* with popular opinion.

2. To comply; to yield to.

You will find it difficult to persuade learned men to *fall in* with your projects. *Addison.*

3. To come in; to join; to enter. *Fall into* the ranks; *fall in* on the right.

To fall in with, to meet, as a ship; also, to discover or come near, as land.

To fall off, to withdraw; to separate; to be broken or detached. Friends *fall off* in adversity.

Love cools, friendship *falls off*, brothers divide. *Shak.*

2. To perish; to die away. Words *fall off* by disuse.

3. To apostatize; to forsake; to withdraw from the faith, or from allegiance or duty.

Those captive tribes *fell off*
From God to worship calves. *Milton.*

4. To forsake; to abandon. His subscribers *fell off.*

5. To drop. Fruits *fall off* when ripe.

6. To depreciate; to depart from former excellence; to become less valuable or interesting. The magazine or the review *falls off;* it has *fallen off.*

7. To deviate or depart from the course directed, or to which the head of the ship was before directed; to fall to leeward.

To fall on, to begin suddenly and eagerly.

Fall on, and try thy appetite to eat. *Dryden.*

2. To begin an attack; to assault; to assail.

Fall on, fall on, and hear him not. *Dryden.*

3. To drop on; to descend on.

To fall out, to quarrel; to begin to contend.

A soul exasperated in ills, *falls out*
With every thing, its friend, itself—
Addison.

2. To happen; to befall; to chance.

There *fell out* a bloody quarrel betwixt the frogs and the mice. *L'Estrange.*

To fall over, to revolt; to desert from one side to another.

2. To fall beyond. *Shak.*

To fall short, to be deficient. The corn *falls short.* We all *fall short* in duty.

To fall to, to begin hastily and eagerly.

Fall to, with eager joy, on homely food.
Dryden.

2. To apply one's self to. He will never after *fall to* labor.

They *fell to* raising money, under pretense of the relief of Ireland. *Clarendon.*

To fall under, to come under, or within the limits of; to be subjected to. They *fell under* the jurisdiction of the emperor.

2. To come under; to become the subject of. This point did not *fall under* the cognizance or deliberations of the court. These things do not *fall under* human sight or observation.

3. To come within; to be ranged or reckoned with. These substances *fall under* a different class or order.

To fall upon, to attack. [See to *fall on.*]

2. To attempt.

I do not intend to *fall upon* nice disquisitions. *Holder.*

3. To rush against.

Fall primarily denotes descending motion, either in a perpendicular or inclined direction, and in most of its applications, implies literally or figuratively velocity, haste, suddenness or violence. Its use is so various and so much diversified by modifying words, that it is not easy to enumerate its senses in all its applications.

FALL, *v. t.* To let fall; to drop. And *fall* thy edgeless sword. I am willing to *fall* this argument. *Shak. Dryden.*

[*This application is obsolete.*]

2. To sink; to depress; as, to raise or *fall* the voice.

3. To diminish; to lessen or lower; as, to *fall* the price of commodities. [*Little used.*]

4. To bring forth; as, to *fall* lambs. [*Little used.*] *Shak.*

5. To fell; to cut down; as, to *fall* a tree. [This use is now common in America, and *fell* and *fall* are probably from a common root.]

FALL, *n.* The act of dropping or descending from a higher to a lower place by gravity; descent; as a *fall* from a horse or from the yard of a ship.

2. The act of dropping or tumbling from an erect posture. He was walking on ice and had a *fall.*

3. Death; destruction; overthrow.

Our fathers had a great *fall* before our enemies. *Judith.*

4. Ruin; destruction.

They conspire thy *fall.* *Denham.*

5. Downfall; degradation; loss of greatness or office; as the *fall* of cardinal Wolsey.

Behold thee glorious only in thy *fall.* *Pope.*

6. Declension of greatness, power or dominion; ruin; as the *fall* of the Roman empire.

7. Diminution; decrease of price or value; depreciation; as the *fall* of prices; the *fall* of rents; the *fall* of interest.

8. Declination of sound; a sinking of tone; cadence; as the *fall* of the voice at the close of a sentence.

9. Declivity; the descent of land or a hill; a slope. *Bacon.*

10. Descent of water; a cascade; a cataract; a rush of water down a steep place; usually in the plural; sometimes in the singular; as the *falls* of Niagara, or the Mohawk; the *fall* of the Hoosatonuc at Canaan. *Fall* is applied to a perpendicular descent, or to one that is very steep. When the descent is moderate, we name it *rapids.* Custom however sometimes deviates from this rule, and the *rapids* of rivers are called *falls.*

11. The outlet or discharge of a river or current of water into the ocean, or into a lake or pond; as the *fall* of the Po into the gulf of Venice. *Addison.*

12. Extent of descent; the distance which any thing falls; as, the water of a pond has a *fall* of five feet.

13. The fall of the leaf; the season when leaves *fall* from trees; autumn.

14. That which falls; a falling; as a *fall* of rain or snow.

15. The act of felling or cutting down; as the *fall* of timber.

16. *Fall*, or *the fall*, by way of distinction, the apostasy; the act of our first parents in eating the forbidden fruit; also, the apostasy of the rebellious angels.

17. Formerly, a kind of vail. *B. Jonson.*

18. In *seamen's language*, the loose end of a tackle. *Mar. Dict.*

19. In *Great Britain*, a term applied to several measures, linear, superficial and solid. *Cyc.*

FALLA'CIOUS, *a.* [Fr. *fallacieux;* L. *fallax*, from *fallo*, to deceive. See *Fail.*]

1. Deceptive; deceiving; deceitful; wearing a false appearance; misleading; producing error or mistake; sophistical; *applied to things only;* as a *fallacious* argument or proposition; a *fallacious* appearance.

2. Deceitful; false; not well founded; producing disappointment; mocking expectation; as a *fallacious* hope.

FALLA'CIOUSLY, *adv.* In a fallacious manner; deceitfully; sophistically; with purpose or in a manner to deceive.

We have seen how *fallaciously* the author has stated the cause. *Addison.*

FALLA'CIOUSNESS, *n.* Tendency to deceive or mislead; inconclusiveness; as the *fallaciousness* of an argument, or of appearances.

FAL'LACY, *n.* [L. *fallacia.*] Deceptive or false appearance; deceitfulness; that which misleads the eye or the mind. Detect the *fallacy* of the argument.

2. Deception; mistake. This appearance may be all a *fallacy.*

I'll entertain the favored *fallacy.* *Shak.*

FALL'EN, *pp.* or *a.* Dropped; descended; degraded; decreased; ruined.

FAL'LENCY, *n.* Mistake. *Obs.*

FALL'ER, *n.* One that falls.

FALLIBIL'ITY, *n.* [It. *fallibilità.* See *Fallible.*]

1. Liableness to deceive; the quality of being fallible; uncertainty; possibility of being erroneous, or of leading to mistake; as the *fallibility* of an argument, of reasoning or of testimony.

2. Liableness to err or to be deceived in one's own judgment; as the *fallibility* of men.

FAL'LIBLE, *a.* [It. *fallibile;* Sp. *falible;* from L. *fallo*, to deceive.]

1. Liable to fail or mistake; that may err or be deceived in judgment. All men are *fallible.*

2. Liable to error; that may deceive. Our judgments, our faculties, our opinions are *fallible;* our hopes are *fallible.*

FALL'ING, *ppr.* Descending; dropping; disemboguing; apostatizing; declining; decreasing; sinking; coming.

FALL'ING, } *n.* An indenting or hol-
FALL'ING IN, } low; opposed to rising or prominence. *Addison.*

Falling away, apostasy.

Falling off, departure from the line or course; declension.

FALL'ING-SICKNESS, *n.* The epilepsy; a disease in which the patient suddenly loses his senses and falls.

FALL'ING-STAR, *n.* A luminous meteor, suddenly appearing and darting through the air.

FALL'ING-STONE, *n.* A stone falling from the atmosphere; a meteorite; an aerolite. *Cyc.*

FAL'LOW, *a.* [Sax. *falewe, falu* or *fealo;* D. *vaal;* G. *falb, fahl;* Fr. *fauve*, for *falve;* L. *fulvus;* qu. *helvus*, for *felvus.* This word may be from the root of *fail*, *fallo;* so called from the fading color of autumnal leaves, or from failure, withering. Hence also the sense of unoccupied, applied to land, which in Spanish is *baldio.*]

1. Pale red, or pale yellow; as a *fallow* deer.

2. Unsowed; not tilled; left to rest after a

year or more of tillage; as *fallow* ground; a *fallow* field.

Break up your *fallow* ground. Jer. iv.

3. Left unsowed after plowing. The word is applied to the land after plowing.
4. Unplowed; uncultivated. *Tooke. Shak.*
5. Unoccupied; neglected. [*Not in use.*]

Let the cause lie *fallow*. *Hudibras.*

FAL'LOW, *n.* Land that has lain a year or more untilled or unseeded. It is also called *fallow* when plowed without being sowed.

The plowing of *fallows* is a benefit to land. *Mortimer.*

2. The plowing or tilling of land, without sowing it, for a season. Summer *fallow*, properly conducted, has ever been found a sure method of destroying weeds.

By a complete summer *fallow*, land is rendered tender and mellow. The *fallow* gives it a better tilth, than can be given by a *fallow* crop. *Sinclair.*

A *green fallow*, in England, is that where land is rendered mellow and clean from weeds, by means of some green crop, as turneps, potatoes, &c. *Cyc.*

FAL'LOW, *v. i.* To fade; to become yellow. *Obs.*

FAL'LOW, *v. t.* To plow, harrow and break land without seeding it, for the purpose of destroying weeds and insects, and rendering it mellow. It is found for the interest of the farmer to *fallow* cold, strong, clayey land.

FAL'LOW-CROP, *n.* The crop taken from fallowed ground. *Sinclair.*

FAL'LOWED, *pp.* Plowed and harrowed for a season, without being sown.

FAL'LOW-FINCH, *n.* A small bird, the œnanthe or wheat-ear.

FAL'LOWING, *ppr.* Plowing and harrowing land without sowing it.

FAL'LOWING, *n.* The operation of plowing and harrowing land without sowing it. *Fallowing* is found to contribute to the destruction of snails and other vermin. *Sinclair.*

FAL'LOWIST, *n.* One who favors the practice of fallowing land.

On this subject, a controversy has arisen between two sects, the *fallowists* and the anti-fallowists. [*Unusual.*] *Sinclair.*

FAL'LOWNESS, *n.* A fallow state; barrenness; exemption from bearing fruit. *Donne.*

FALS'ARY, *n.* [See *False.*] A falsifier of evidence. [*Not in use.*] *Sheldon.*

FALSE, *a.* [L. *falsus*, from *fallo*, to deceive; Sp. *falso*; It. *id.*; Fr. *faux, fausse*; Sax. *false*; D. *valsch*; G. *falsch*; Sw. and Dan. *falsk*; W. *fals*; Ir. *falsa*. See *Fall* and *Fail.*]

1. Not true; not conformable to fact; expressing what is contrary to that which exists, is done, said or thought. A *false* report communicates what is not done or said. A *false* accusation imputes to a person what he has not done or said. A *false* witness testifies what is not true. A *false* opinion is not according to truth or fact. The word is applicable to any subject, physical or moral.
2. Not well founded; as a *false* claim.
3. Not true; not according to the lawful standard; as a *false* weight or measure.
4. Substituted for another; succedaneous; supposititious; as a *false* bottom.
5. Counterfeit; forged; not genuine; as *false* coin; a *false* bill or note.
6. Not solid or sound; deceiving expectations; as a *false* foundation.

False and slippery ground. *Dryden.*

7. Not agreeable to rule or propriety; as *false* construction in language.
8. Not honest or just; not fair; as *false* play.
9. Not faithful or loyal; treacherous; perfidious; deceitful. The king's subjects may prove *false* to him. So we say, a *false* heart.
10. Unfaithful; inconstant; as a *false* friend; a *false* lover; *false* to promises and vows. The husband and wife proved *false* to each other.
11. Deceitful; treacherous; betraying secrets.
12. Counterfeit; not genuine or real; as a *false* diamond.
13. Hypocritical; feigned; made or assumed for the purpose of deception; as *false* tears; *false* modesty. The man appears in *false* colors. The advocate gave the subject a *false* coloring.

False fire, a blue flame, made by the burning of certain combustibles, in a wooden tube; used as a signal during the night. *Mar. Dict.*

False imprisonment, the arrest and imprisonment of a person without warrant or cause, or contrary to law; or the unlawful detaining of a person in custody.

FALSE, *adv.* Not truly; not honestly; falsely. *Shak.*

FALSE, *v. t.* To violate by failure of veracity; to deceive. *Obs.* *Spenser.*

2. To defeat; to balk; to evade. *Obs.* *Spenser.*

FALSE-HEART, } *a.* Hollow; treacherous; deceitful; perfidious. [*The former is not used.*] *Bacon.*
FALSE-HEARTED, }

FALSE-HEARTEDNESS, *n.* Perfidiousness; treachery. *Stillingfleet.*

FALSEHOOD, *n.* *fols'hood.* [*false* and *hood.*]

1. Contrariety or inconformity to fact or truth; as the *falsehood* of a report.
2. Want of truth or veracity; a lie; an untrue assertion.
3. Want of honesty; treachery; deceitfulness; perfidy. *Milton.*

But *falsehood* is properly applied to things only. [See *Falseness.*]

4. Counterfeit; false appearance; imposture. *Milton.*

FALSELY, *adv.* *fols'ly.* In a manner contrary to truth and fact; not truly; as, to speak or swear *falsely*; to testify *falsely*.

2. Treacherously; perfidiously.

Swear to me—that thou wilt not deal *falsely* with me. Gen. xxi.

3. Erroneously; by mistake. *Smallridge.*

FALSENESS, *n.* *fols'ness.* Want of integrity and veracity, either in principle or in act; as the *falseness* of a man's heart, or his *falseness* to his word.

2. Duplicity; deceit; double-dealing. *Hammond.*
3. Unfaithfulness; treachery; perfidy; traitorousness.

The prince is in no danger of being betrayed by the *falseness*, or cheated by the avarice of such a servant. *Rogers.*

FALS'ER, *n.* A deceiver. *Spenser.*

FALSET'TO, *n.* [It.] A feigned voice. *Burke.*

FALS'IFIABLE, *a.* [from *falsify.*] That may be falsified, counterfeited or corrupted. *Johnson.*

FALSIFICA'TION, *n.* [Fr. from *falsifier.*]

1. The act of making false; a counterfeiting; the giving to a thing an appearance of something which it is not; as the *falsification* of words. *Hooker.*
2. Confutation. *Broome.*

FALSIFICA'TOR, *n.* A falsifier. *Bp. Morton.*

FALS'IFIED, *pp.* Counterfeited.

FALS'IFIER, *n.* One who counterfeits, or gives to a thing a deceptive appearance; or one who makes false coin. *Boyle.*

2. One who invents falsehood; a liar. *L'Estrange.*
3. One who proves a thing to be false.

FALS'IFY, *v. t.* [Fr. *falsifier*, from *false.*]

1. To counterfeit; to forge; to make something false, or in imitation of that which is true; as, to *falsify* coin.

The Irish bards use to *falsify* every thing. *Spenser.*

2. To disprove; to prove to be false; as, to *falsify* a record.
3. To violate; to break by falsehood; as, to *falsify* one's faith or word. *Sidney.*
4. To show to be unsound, insufficient or not proof. [*Not in use.*]

His ample shield is *falsified*. *Dryden.*

FALS'IFY, *v. i.* To tell lies; to violate the truth.

It is universally unlawful to lie and *falsify*. *South.*

FALS'IFYING, *ppr.* Counterfeiting; forging; lying; proving to be false; violating.

FALS'ITY, *n.* [L. *falsitas.*] Contrariety or inconformity to truth; the quality of being false.

Probability does not make any alteration, either in the truth or *falsity* of things. *South.*

2. Falsehood; a lie; a false assertion. [This sense is less proper.] *Glanville.*

FAL'TER, *v. i.* [Sp. *faltar*, to be deficient, from *falta*, fault, defect, failing, from *falir*, to fail, *falla*, fault, defect; Port. *faltar*, to want, to miss; from L. *fallo*, the primary sense of which is to fall short, or to err, to miss, to deviate.]

1. To hesitate, fail or break in the utterance of words; to speak with a broken or trembling utterance; to stammer. His tongue *falters*. He speaks with a *faltering* tongue. He *falters* at the question.
2. To fail, tremble or yield in exertion; not to be firm and steady. His legs *falter*. *Wiseman.*
3. To fail in the regular exercise of the understanding. We observe ideots to *falter*. *Locke.*

FAL'TER, *v. t.* To sift. [*Not in use.*] *Mortimer.*

FAL'TERING, *ppr.* Hesitating; speaking with a feeble, broken, trembling utterance; failing.

FAL'TERING, *n.* Feebleness; deficiency. *Killingbeck.*

FAL'TERINGLY, *adv.* With hesitation;

with a trembling, broken voice; with difficulty or feebleness.

FAME, *n.* [L. *fama;* Fr. *fame;* Sp. It. *fama;* Gr. φαμα, φημη, from φαω, to speak. I suspect this root to be contracted from φαγω, or φαχω, Class Bg. See No. 48. 62. and *Facund.*]

1. Public report or rumor.

The *fame* thereof was heard in Pharaoh's house, saying, Joseph's brethren are come. Gen. xlv.

2. Favorable report; report of good or great actions; report that exalts the character; celebrity; renown; as the *fame* of Howard or of Washington; the *fame* of Solomon.

And the *fame* of Jesus went throughout all Syria. Matt. iv.

FAME, *v. t.* To make famous. *B. Jonson.*

2. To report. *Buck.*

FA'MED, *a.* Much talked of; renowned; celebrated; distinguished and exalted by favorable reports. Aristides was *famed* for learning and wisdom, and Cicero for eloquence.

He is *famed* for mildness, peace and prayer. *Shak.*

FA'ME-GIVING, *a.* Bestowing fame.

FA'MELESS, *a.* Without renown. *Beaum.*

FAMIL'IAR, *a.* *famil'yar.* [L. *familiaris;* Fr. *familier;* Sp. *familiar;* from L. *familia,* family, which see.]

1. Pertaining to a family; domestic. *Pope.*

2. Accustomed by frequent converse; well acquainted with; intimate; close; as a *familiar* friend or companion.

3. Affable; not formal or distant; easy in conversation.

Be thou *familiar,* but by no means vulgar. *Shak.*

4. Well acquainted with; knowing by frequent use. Be *familiar* with the scriptures.

5. Well known; learnt or well understood by frequent use. Let the scriptures be *familiar* to us.

6 Unceremonious; free; unconstrained; easy. The emperor conversed with the gentleman in the most *familiar* manner.

7. Common; frequent and intimate. By *familiar* intercourse, strong attachments are soon formed.

8. Easy; unconstrained; not formal. His letters are written in a *familiar* style.

He sports in loose *familiar* strains. *Addison.*

9. Intimate in an unlawful degree.

A poor man found a priest *familiar* with his wife. *Camden.*

FAMIL'IAR, *n.* An intimate; a close companion; one long acquainted; one accustomed to another by free, unreserved converse.

All my *familiars* watched for my halting. Jer. xx.

2. A demon or evil spirit supposed to attend at a call. But in general we say, a *familiar* spirit. *Shak.*

3. In the court of Inquisition, a person who assists in apprehending and imprisoning the accused. *Encyc.*

FAMILIAR'ITY, *n.* Intimate and frequent converse, or association in company. The gentlemen lived in remarkable *familiarity.* Hence,

2. Easiness of conversation; affability; freedom from ceremony.

3. Intimacy; intimate acquaintance; unconstrained intercourse.

FAMIL'IARIZE, *v. t.* To make familiar or intimate; to habituate; to accustom; to make well known, by practice or converse; as, to *familiarize* one's self to scenes of distress.

2. To make easy by practice or customary use, or by intercourse.

3. To bring down from a state of distant superiority.

The genius smiled on me with a look of compassion and affability that *familiarized* him to my imagination. *Addison.*

FAMIL'IARIZED, *pp.* Accustomed; habituated; made easy by practice, custom or use.

FAMIL'IARIZING, *ppr.* Accustoming; rendering easy by practice, custom or use.

FAMIL'IARLY, *adv.* In a familiar manner; unceremoniously; without constraint; without formality.

2. Commonly; frequently; with the ease and unconcern that arises from long custom or acquaintance.

FAM'ILISM, *n.* The tenets of the familists.

FAM'ILIST, *n.* [from *family.*] One of the religious sect called the family of love.

FAM'ILY, *n.* [L. Sp. *familia;* Fr. *famille;* It. *famiglia.* This word is said to have originally signified servants, from the Celtic *famul;* but qu.]

1. The collective body of persons who live in one house and under one head or manager; a household, including parents, children and servants, and as the case may be, lodgers or boarders.

2. Those who descend from one common progenitor; a tribe or race; kindred; lineage. Thus the Israelites were a branch of the *family* of Abraham; and the descendants of Reuben, of Manasseh, &c., were called their *families.* The whole human race are the *family* of Adam, the human *family.*

3. Course of descent; genealogy; line of ancestors.

Go and complain thy *family* is young. *Pope.*

4. Honorable descent; noble or respectable stock. He is a man of *family.*

5. A collection or union of nations or states.

The states of Europe were, by the prevailing maxims of its policy, closely united in one *family.* *E. Everett.*

6. In *popular language,* an order, class or genus of animals or of other natural productions, having something in common, by which they are distinguished from others; as, quadrupeds constitute a *family* of animals, and we speak of the *family* or *families* of plants.

FAM'INE, *n.* [Fr. *famine,* from *faim;* L. *fames;* It. *fame;* Sp. *fame* or *hambre;* Port. *fome.*]

1. Scarcity of food; dearth; a general want of provisions sufficient for the inhabitants of a country or besieged place.

There was a *famine* in the land. Gen. xxvi.

Famines are less frequent than formerly. A due attention to agriculture tends to prevent *famine,* and commerce secures a country from its destructive effects.

2. Want; destitution; as a *famine* of the word of life.

FAM'ISH, *v. t.* [Fr. *affamer,* from *faim,* hunger, L. *fames;* It. *affamire, affamare;* Sp. *hambrear.*]

1. To starve; to kill or destroy with hunger. *Shak.*

2. To exhaust the strength of, by hunger or thirst; to distress with hunger.

The pains of *famished* Tantalus he'll feel. *Dryden.*

3. To kill by deprivation or denial of any thing necessary for life. *Milton.*

FAM'ISH, *v. i.* To die of hunger. More generally,

2. To suffer extreme hunger or thirst; to be exhausted in strength, or to come near to perish, for want of food or drink.

You are all resolved rather to die, than to *famish.* *Shak.*

3. To be distressed with want; to come near to perish by destitution.

The Lord will not suffer the righteous to *famish.* Prov. x.

FAM'ISHED, *pp.* Starved; exhausted by want of sustenance.

FAM'ISHING, *ppr.* Starving; killing; perishing by want of food.

FAM'ISHMENT, *n.* The pain of extreme hunger or thirst; extreme want of sustenance. *Hakewill.*

FA'MOUS, *a.* [L. *famosus;* Fr. *fameux.* See *Fame.*]

1. Celebrated in fame or public report; renowned; much talked of and praised; distinguished in story.

Two hundred and fifty princes of the assembly, *famous* in the congregation. Num. xvi.

It is followed by *for.* One man is *famous for* erudition; another, *for* eloquence; and another, *for* military skill.

2. Sometimes in a bad sense; as a *famous* counterfeiter; a *famous* pirate.

FA'MOUSED, *a.* Renowned. [*An ill formed word.*] *Shak.*

FA'MOUSLY, *adv.* With great renown or celebration.

Then this land was *famously* enriched
With politic grave counsel. *Shak.*

FA'MOUSNESS, *n.* Renown; great fame; celebrity. *Boyle.*

FAN, *n.* [Sax. *fann;* Sw. *vanna;* D. *wan;* G. *wanne;* L. *vannus;* Fr. *van;* Sp. Port. *abano.* The word, in German and Swedish, signifies a *fan* and a tub, as if from opening or spreading; if so, it seems to be allied to *pane, pannel.* Class Bn.]

1. An instrument used by ladies to agitate the air and cool the face in warm weather. It is made of feathers, or of thin skin, paper or taffety mounted on sticks, &c.

2. Something in the form of a woman's fan when spread, as a peacock's tail, a window, &c.

3. An instrument for winnowing grain, by moving which the grain is thrown up and agitated, and the chaff is separated and blown away.

4. Something by which the air is moved; a wing. *Dryden.*

5. An instrument to raise the fire or flame; as a *fan* to inflame love. *Hooker.*

FAN-LIGHT, *n.* A window in form of an open fan.

FAN, *v. t.* To cool and refresh, by moving the air with a fan; to blow the air on the face with a fan.

2. To ventilate; to blow on; to affect by air put in motion.

The *fanning* wind upon her bosom blows;
To meet the *fanning* wind the bosom rose. *Dryden.*

Calm as the breath which *fans* our eastern groves. *Dryden.*

3. To move as with a fan.

The air—*fanned* with plumes. *Milton.*

4. To winnow; to ventilate; to separate chaff from grain and drive it away by a current of air; as, to *fan* wheat.

FANAT'IC, } FANAT'ICAL, } *a.* [L. *fanaticus, phanaticus*, from G. φαινομαι, to appear; literally, seeing visions.]

Wild and extravagant in opinions, particularly in religious opinions; excessively enthusiastic; possessed by a kind of frenzy. Hence we say, *fanatic* zeal; *fanatic* notions or opinions.

FANAT'IC, } FANAT'ICAL, } *n.* A person affected by excessive enthusiasm, particularly on religious subjects; one who indulges wild and extravagant notions of religion, and sometimes exhibits strange motions and postures, and vehement vociferation in religious worship. Fanatics sometimes affect to be inspired or to have intercourse with superior beings.

FANAT'ICALLY, *adv.* With wild enthusiasm.

FANAT'ICALNESS, *n.* Fanaticism.

FANAT'ICISM, *n.* Excessive enthusiasm; wild and extravagant notions of religion; religious frenzy. *Rogers.*

FANAT'ICIZE, *v. t.* To make fanatic.

FAN'CIED, *pp.* [See *Fancy.*] Imagined; conceived; liked. *Stephens.*

FAN'CIFUL, *a.* [See *Fancy.*] Guided by the imagination, rather than by reason and experience; subject to the influence of fancy; whimsical; *applied to persons.* A *fanciful* man forms visionary projects.

2. Dictated by the imagination; full of wild images; chimerical; whimsical; ideal; visionary; *applied to things;* as a *fanciful* scheme; a *fanciful* theory.

FAN'CIFULLY, *adv.* In a fanciful manner; wildly; whimsically.

2. According to fancy.

FAN'CIFULNESS, *n.* The quality of being fanciful, or influenced by the imagination, rather than by reason and experience; the habit of following fancy; *applied to persons.*

2. The quality of being dictated by imagination; *applied to things.*

FAN'CY, *n.* [contracted from *fantasy*, L. *phantasia*, Gr. φαντασια, from φανταζω, to cause to appear, to seem, to imagine, from φαινω, to show, to appear, to shine. The primary sense seems to be to open, or to shoot forth. Ar. بَانَ to open, to appear; or فَعَنَ to open or expand. Class Bn. No. 3. 28.]

1. The faculty by which the mind forms images or representations of things at pleasure. It is often used as synonymous with *imagination;* but imagination is rather the power of combining and modifying our conceptions. *Stewart.*

2. An opinion or notion.

I have always had a *fancy*, that learning might be made a play and recreation to children. *Locke.*

3. Taste; conception.

The little chapel called the salutation is very neat, and built with a pretty *fancy.* *Addison.*

4. Image; conception; thought.

How now, my lord, why do you keep alone;
Of sorriest *fancies* your companions making? *Shak.*

5. Inclination; liking. Take that which suits your *fancy.* How does this strike your *fancy?*

His *fancy* lay to travelling. *L'Estrange.*

6. Love.

Tell me where is *fancy* bred. *Shak.*

7. Caprice; humor; whim; as an odd or strange *fancy.*

True worth shall gain me, that it may be said,
Desert, not *fancy*, once a woman led. *Dryden.*

8. False notion. *Bacon.*

9. Something that pleases or entertains without real use or value.

London-pride is a pretty *fancy* for borders. *Mortimer.*

FAN'CY, *v. i.* To imagine; to figure to one's self; to believe or suppose without proof. All may not be our enemies whom we *fancy* to be so.

If our search has reached no farther than simile and metaphor, we rather *fancy* than know. *Locke.*

FAN'CY, *v. t.* To form a conception of; to portray in the mind; to imagine.

He whom I *fancy*, but can ne'er express. *Dryden.*

2. To like; to be pleased with, particularly on account of external appearance or manners. We *fancy* a person for beauty and accomplishment. We sometimes *fancy* a lady at first sight, whom, on acquaintance, we cannot esteem.

FAN'CYFRAMED, *a.* Created by the fancy. *Crashaw.*

FAN'CYFREE, *a.* Free from the power of love. *Shak.*

FAN'CYING, *ppr.* Imagining; conceiving; liking.

FAN'CYMONGER, *n.* One who deals in tricks of imagination. *Shak.*

FAN'CYSICK, *a.* One whose imagination is unsound, or whose distemper is in his own mind. *L'Estrange.*

FAND, old *pret.* of *find. Obs.* *Spenser.*

FANDAN'GO, *n.* [Spanish.] A lively dance. *Sp. Dict.*

FANE, *n.* [L. *fanum.*] A temple; a place consecrated to religion; a church; *used in poetry.*

From men their cities, and from gods their *fanes.* *Pope.*

FAN'FARE, *n.* [Fr.] A coming into the lists with sound of trumpets; a flourish of trumpets.

FAN'FARON, *n.* [Fr. *fanfaron;* Sp. *fanfarron;* Port. *fanfarram.*]

A bully; a hector; a swaggerer; an empty boaster; a vain pretender. *Dryden.*

FANFARONA'DE, *n.* A swaggering; vain boasting; ostentation; a bluster. *Swift.*

FANG, *v. t.* [Sax. *fengan*, to catch, seize or take, to begin; D. *vangen;* G. *fangen;* Dan. *fanger;* Sw. *fånga.* See *Finger.*]

To catch; to seize; to lay hold; to gripe; to clutch. *Obs.* *Shak.*

FANG, *n.* [Sax. *fang;* D. *vang;* G. *fang*, a seizing.]

1. The tusk of a boar or other animal by which the prey is seized and held; a pointed tooth. *Bacon.*

2. A claw or talon.

3. Any shoot or other thing by which hold is taken.

The protuberant *fangs* of the Yuca. *Evelyn.*

FANG'ED, *a.* Furnished with fangs, tusks, or something long and pointed; as a *fanged adder.* *Shak.*

Chariots *fanged* with sythes. *Philips.*

FAN'GLE, *n. fang'gl.* [from Sax. *fengan*, to begin.]

A new attempt; a trifling scheme. [*Not used.*]

FAN'GLED, *a.* Properly, begun, new made; hence, gawdy; showy; vainly decorated. [Seldom used, except with *new.* See *New-fangled.*] *Shak.*

FANG'LESS, *a.* Having no fangs or tusks; toothless; as a *fangless* lion.

FAN'GOT, *n.* A quantity of wares, as raw silk, &c., from one to two hundred weight and three quarters. *Dict.*

FAN'ION, *n. fan'yon.* [Fr. from Goth. *fana*, L. *pannus*, G. *fahne*, a cloth, a flag, a banner.]

In *armies*, a small flag carried with the baggage. *Encyc.*

FAN'NED, *pp.* Blown with a fan; winnowed; ventilated.

FAN'NEL, } FAN'ON, } *n.* [Fr. *fanon;* Goth. *fana*, supra.] A sort of ornament like a scarf, worn about the left arm of a mass-priest, when he officiates. *Dict.*

FAN'NER, *n.* One who fans. *Jeremiah.*

FAN'NING, *ppr.* Blowing; ventilating.

FAN'TASIED, *a.* [from *fantasy*, fancy.] Filled with fancies or imaginations; whimsical. [*Not used.*] *Shak.*

FAN'TASM, *n.* [Gr. φαντασμα, from φαινω, to appear. Usually written *phantasm.*]

That which appears to the imagination; a phantom; something not real.

FANTAS'TIC, } FANTAS'TICAL, } *a.* [Fr. *fantastique;* It. *fantastico;* from Gr. φαντασια, vision, fancy, from φαινω, to appear.]

1. Fanciful; produced or existing only in imagination; imaginary; not real; chimerical. *South.*

2. Having the nature of a phantom; apparent only. *Shak.*

3. Unsteady; irregular. *Prior.*

4. Whimsical; capricious; fanciful; indulging the vagaries of imagination; as *fantastic* minds; a *fantastic* mistress.

5. Whimsical; odd.

FANTAS'TICALLY, *adv.* By the power of imagination.

2. In a fantastic manner; capriciously; unsteadily.

Her scepter so *fantastically* borne. *Shak.*

3. Whimsically; in compliance with fancy. *Grew.*

FANTAS'TICALNESS, *n.* Compliance with fancy; humorousness; whimsicalness; unreasonableness; caprice. *Johnson.*

FAN'TASY, *n.* Now written *fancy*, which see.

Is not this something more than *fantasy?* *Shak.*

FAN'TOM, *n.* [Fr. *fantôme*, probably contracted from L. *phantasma*, from the Greek. See *Fancy.*]

Something that appears to the imagination; also, a specter; a ghost; an apparition. It is generally written *phantom*, which see.

FAP, *a.* Fuddled. [*Not in use.*] *Shak.*

FAQUIR, [See *Fakir.*]

F'AR, *a.* [Sax. *feor, fior* or *fyr*; D. *ver, verre*; G. *fern*, and in composition, *ver*; Sw. *fierran*; Dan. *fiern*; L. *porro*; Gr. πορρω; connected with πορος, a way, a passing, πορευω, πορευομαι, to pass or go, Sax. and Goth. *faran*, G. *fahren*, D. *vaaren*, Dan. *farer*, Sw. *fara*, Eng. to *fare*. See *Fare.*]

1. Distant, in any direction; separated by a wide space from the place where one is, or from any given place remote.

They said, we are come from a *far* country. Josh. ix.

The kingdom of heaven is as a man travelling into a *far* country. Matt. xxv.

The nations *far* and near contend in choice. *Dryden.*

2. *Figuratively*, remote from purpose; contrary to design or wishes; as, *far* be it from me to justify cruelty.

3. Remote in affection or obedience; at enmity with; alienated; *in a spiritual sense.*

They that are *far* from thee shall perish. Ps. lxxiii.

4. More or most distant of the two; as the *far* side of a horse. But the drivers of teams in New England generally use *off*; as the *off* side, or *off* horse or ox.

F'AR, *adv.* To a great extent or distance of space; as the *far* extended ocean; we are separated *far* from each other.

Only ye shall not go very *far* away. Ex. viii.

2. *Figuratively*, distantly in time from any point; remotely. He pushed his researches very *far* into antiquity.

3. In *interrogatories*, to what distance or extent. How *far* will such reasoning lead us?

4. In great part; as, the day is *far* spent.

5. In a great proportion; by many degrees; very much.

Who can find a virtuous woman? for her price is *far* above rubies. Prov. xxxi.

For I am in a strait betwixt two, having a desire to depart, and to be with Christ, which is *far* better. Phil. i.

6. To a certain point, degree or distance. This argument is sound and logical, as *far* as it goes.

Answer them
How *far* forth you do like their articles. *Shak.*

From far, from a great distance; from a remote place.

Far from, at a great distance; as *far from* home; *far from* hope.

Far off, at a great distance.

They tarried in a place that was *far off*. 2 Sam. xv.

2. To a great distance.

Lo then would I wander *far off*, and remain in the wilderness. Ps. lv.

3. In *a spiritual sense*, alienated; at enmity; in a state of ignorance and alienation.

Ye, who were sometime *far off*, are made nigh by the blood of Christ. Eph. ii.

Far other, very different. *Pope.*

FAR-ABOUT', *n.* A going out of the way. [*Not in use.*] *Fuller.*

F'AR-FAMED, *a.* Widely celebrated. *Pope.*

F'AR-FETCH, *n.* A deep laid stratagem. [*Little used.*] *Hudibras.*

F'AR-FETCHED, *a.* Brought from a remote place.

Whose pains have earned the *far-fetched* spoil. *Milton.*

2. Studiously sought; not easily or naturally deduced or introduced; forced; strained.

York with all his *far-fetched* policy. *Shak.*

So we say, *far-fetched* arguments; *far-fetched* rhymes; *far-fetched* analogy. [*Far-fet*, the same, is not used.]

FAR-PIER'CING, *a.* Striking or penetrating a great way; as a *far-piercing* eye. *Pope.*

FAR-SHOOT'ING, *a.* Shooting to a great distance.

Great Jove, he said, and the *far-shooting* god. *Dryden.*

F'AR, *n.* [Sax. *færh, fearh.* See *Farrow.*] The young of swine; or a litter of pigs. [*Local.*] *Tusser.*

F'ARCE, *v. t.* *fàrs.* [L. *farcio*, Fr. *farcir*, to stuff, Arm. *farsa.*]

1. To stuff; to fill with mingled ingredients. [*Little used.*]

The first principles of religion should not be *farced* with school points and private tenets. *Sanderson.*

2. To extend; to swell out; as the *farced* title. [*Little used.*] *Shak.*

F'ARCE, *n.* *fàrs.* [Fr. *farce*; It. *farsa*; Sp. *id.*; from *farcio*, to stuff. Literally, seasoning, stuffing or mixture, like the stuffing of a roasted fowl; *force-meat.*]

A dramatic composition, originally exhibited by charlatans or buffoons, in the open street, for the amusement of the crowd, but now introduced upon the stage. It is written without regularity, and filled with ludicrous conceits. The dialogue is usually low, the persons of inferior rank, and the fable or action trivial or ridiculous. *Encyc.*

Farce is that in poetry which grotesque is in a picture: the persons and actions of a *farce* are all unnatural, and the manners false. *Dryden.*

F'ARCICAL, *a.* Belonging to a farce; appropriated to farce.

They deny the characters to be *farcical*, because they are actually in nature. *Gay.*

2. Droll; ludicrous; ridiculous.

3. Illusory; deceptive.

F'ARCICALLY, *adv.* In a manner suited to farce; hence, ludicrously.

F'ARCILITE, *n.* [from *farce.*] Pudding-stone. The calcarious *farcilite*, called amenla, is formed of rounded calcarious pebbles, agglutinated by a calcarious cement. *Kirwan, Geol.*

F'ARCIN, } *n.* A disease of horses, sometimes of oxen, of the nature
F'ARCY, } of a scabies or mange. *Encyc.*

F'ARCING, *n.* Stuffing composed of mixed ingredients. *Carew.*

F'ARCTATE, *a.* [L. *farctus*, stuffed, from *farcio.*]

In *botany*, stuffed; crammed, or full; without vacuities; in opposition to tubular or hollow; as a *farctate* leaf, stem or pericarp. *Martyn.*

F'ARD, *v. t.* [Fr.] To paint. [*Not used.*] *Shenstone.*

F'ARDEL, *n.* [It. *fardello*; Fr. *fardeau*; Sp. *fardel, fardo*; Arm. *fardell*; probably from the root of L. *fero*, to bear, or of *farcio*, to stuff.] A bundle or little pack. *Shak.*

F'ARDEL, *v. t.* To make up in bundles. *Fuller.*

FARE, *v. i.* [Sax. and Goth. *faran*, to go; D. *vaaren*; G. *fahren*; Sw. *fara*; Dan. *farer.* This word may be connected in origin with the Heb. Ch. Syr. Sam. עבר, Ar. عبر abara, to go, to pass; or with افر afara, to pass, or pass over, which seems to be radically the same word as نفر nafara, to flee. This coincides with the Eth. ወፈረ wafar, to go, to pass, Gr. πορευω, Ir. *bara.* Class Br. No. 23. 37. 41.]

1. To go; to pass; to move forward; to travel.

So on he *fares*, and to the border comes
Of Eden. *Milton.*

[*In this literal sense the word is not in common use.*]

2. To be in any state, good or bad; to be attended with any circumstances or train of events, fortunate or unfortunate.

So *fares* the stag among th' enraged hounds *Denham.*

So *fared* the knight between two foes. *Hudibras.*

He *fared* very well; he *fared* very ill. Go further and *fare* worse. The sense is taken from *going*, having a certain course; hence, being subjected to a certain train of incidents. The rich man *fared* sumptuously every day. He enjoyed all the pleasure which wealth and luxury could afford. Luke xvi.

3. To feed; to be entertained. We *fared* well; we had a good table, and courteous treatment.

4. To proceed in a train of consequences, good or bad.

So *fares* it when with truth falsehood contends. *Milton.*

5. To happen well or ill; with *it* impersonally. We shall see how *it* will *fare* with him.

FARE, *n.* The price of passage or going; the sum paid or due, for conveying a person by land or water; as the *fare* for crossing a river, called also *ferriage*; the *fare* for conveyance in a coach; stage-*fare*. The price of conveyance over the ocean is now usually called the *passage*, or *passage money*. *Fare* is never used for the price of conveying goods; this is called *freight* or *transportation*.

2. Food; provisions of the table. We lived on coarse *fare*, or we had delicious *fare*.

3. The person conveyed in a vehicle. [*Not in use in U. States.*] *Drummond.*

FA'REWELL, a compound of *fare*, in the imperative, and *well.* *Go well*; originally applied to a person departing, but by custom now applied both to those who depart and those who remain. It expresses a kind wish, a wish of happiness to those who leave or those who are left.

The verb and adverb are often separated by the pronoun; *fare you well*; I wish you a happy departure; may you be well in your absence.

It is sometimes an expression of separation only. *Farewell* the year; *farewell* ye sweet groves; that is, I take my leave of you.

FA'REWELL, *n.* A wish of happiness or welfare at parting; the parting compliment; adieu.

2. Leave; act of departure.

And takes her *farewell* of the glorious sun. *Shak.*

Before I take my *farewell* of the subject. *Addison.*

FAR'IN, FARI'NA, } *n.* [L. *farina*, meal.] In *botany*, the pollen, fine dust or powder, contained in the anthers of plants, and which is supposed to fall on the stigma, and fructify the plant.

2. In *chimistry*, starch or fecula, one of the proximate principles of vegetables.

Fossil farina, a variety of carbonate of lime, in thin white crusts, light as cotton, and easily reducible to powder. *Cleaveland.*

FARINA'CEOUS, *a.* [from L. *farina*, meal.]

1. Consisting or made of meal or flour; as a *farinaceous* diet, which consists of the meal or flour of the various species of corn or grain.

2. Containing meal; as *farinaceous* seeds.

3. Like meal; mealy; pertaining to meal; as a *farinaceous* taste or smell.

F'ARM, *n.* [Sax. *farma*, *fearm*, or *feorm*, food, provisions, board, a meal, a dinner or supper, hospitality, substance, goods, use, fruit. Hence, *feormian*, to supply provisions, to entertain; also, to purge or purify, to expiate, to avail, to profit. Arm. *ferm*, or *feurm*; in ancient laws, *firma*; Fr. *ferme*, a farm, or letting to farm, whence *affermer*, to hire or lease. The sense of *feorm* seems to be corn or provisions, in which formerly rents were paid. The radical sense of *feorm*, provisions, is probably produce, issues, from one of the verbs in Br; produce and purification both implying separation, a throwing off or out.]

1. A tract of land leased on rent reserved; ground let to a tenant on condition of his paying a certain sum annually or otherwise for the use of it. A farm is usually such a portion of land as is cultivated by one man, and includes the buildings and fences. Rents were formerly paid in provisions, or the produce of land; but now they are generally paid in money.

This is the signification of *farm* in Great Britain, where most of the land is leased to cultivators.

2. In the United States, a portion or tract of land, consisting usually of grass land, meadow, pasture, tillage and woodland, cultivated by one man and usually owned by him in fee. A like tract of land under lease is called a *farm*; but most cultivators are proprietors of the land, and called *farmers*.

A tract of new land, covered with forest, if intended to be cultivated by one man as owner, is also called a *farm*. A man goes into the new States, or into the unsettled country, to buy a *farm*, that is, land for a farm.

3. The state of land leased on rent reserved; a lease.

It is great wilfulness in landlords to make any longer *farms* to their tenants. *Spenser.*

F'ARM, *v. t.* To lease, as land, on rent reserved; to let to a tenant on condition of paying rent.

We are enforced to *farm* our royal realm. *Shak.*

[*In this sense, I believe, the word is not used in America.*]

2. To take at a certain rent or rate. [*Not used in America.*]

3. To lease or let, as taxes, impost or other duties, at a certain sum or rate per cent. It is customary in many countries for the prince or government to *farm* the revenues, the taxes or rents, the imposts and excise, to individuals, who are to collect and pay them to the government at a certain percentage or rate per cent.

4. To take or hire for a certain rate per cent.

5. To cultivate land.

To farm let, or *let to farm*, is to lease on rent.

F'ARMHOUSE, *n.* A house attached to a farm, and for the residence of a farmer.

F'ARM-OFFICE, *n.* *Farm-offices*, are the out buildings pertaining to a farm.

F'ARMYARD, *n.* The yard or inclosure attached to a barn; or the inclosure surrounded by the farm buildings.

F'ARMABLE, *a.* That may be farmed. *Sherwood.*

F'ARMED, *pp.* Leased on rent; let out at a certain rate or price.

F'ARMER, *n.* In Great Britain, a tenant; a lessee; one who hires and cultivates a farm; a cultivator of leased ground. *Shak.*

2. One who takes taxes, customs, excise or other duties, to collect for a certain rate per cent; as a *farmer* of the revenues.

3. One who cultivates a farm; a husbandman; whether a tenant or the proprietor. *United States.*

4. In *mining*, the lord of the field, or one who farms the lot and cope of the king. *Encyc.*

F'ARMING, *ppr.* Letting or leasing land on rent reserved, or duties and imposts at a certain rate per cent.

2. Taking on lease.

3. Cultivating land; carrying on the business of agriculture.

F'ARMING, *n.* The business of cultivating land.

F'ARMOST, *a.* [*far* and *most.*] Most distant or remote. *Dryden.*

F'ARNESS, *n.* [from *far.*] Distance; remoteness. *Carew.*

FARRAG'INOUS, *a.* [L. *farrago*, a mixture, from *far*, meal.]

Formed of various materials; mixed; as a *farraginous* mountain. *Kirwan.*

FARRA'GO, *n.* [L. from *far*, meal.] A mass composed of various materials confusedly mixed; a medley.

FARREATION. [See *Confarreation.*]

FAR'RIER, *n.* [Fr. *ferrant*; It. *ferraio*; Sp. *herrador*; L. *ferrarius*, from *ferrum*, iron. Fr. *ferrer*; It. *ferrare*, to bind with iron; "ferrare un cavallo", to shoe a horse. *Ferrum* is probably from hardness; W. *fer*, dense, solid; *feru*, to harden, or congeal; *feris*, steel. A *farrier* is literally a worker in iron.]

1. A shoer of horses; a smith who shoes horses.

2. One who professes to cure the diseases of horses.

FAR'RIER, *v. i.* To practice as a farrier.

FAR'RIERY, *n.* The art of preventing, curing or mitigating the diseases of horses. *Encyc.*

This is now called the *veterinary* art.

FAR'ROW, *n.* [Sax. *fearh*, *færh*; D. *varken*; G. *ferkel.*] A litter of pigs. *Shak.*

FAR'ROW, *v. t.* To bring forth pigs. [*Used of swine only.*] *Tusser.*

FAR'ROW, *a.* [D. *vaare*; "een vaare koe," a dry cow; Scot. *ferry* cow. Qu. the root of *bare*, *barren.*]

Not producing young in a particular season or year; *applied to cows only.* If a cow has had a calf, but fails in a subsequent year, she is said to be *farrow*, or to go *farrow*. Such a cow may give milk through the year. *New England.*

F'ARTHER, *a.* comp. [Sax. *forther*, from *feor*, far, or rather from *forth*, from the root of *faran*, to go; D. *verder.*]

1. More remote; more distant than something else.

Let me add a *farther* truth. *Dryden.*

2. Longer; tending to a greater distance.

Before our *farther* way the fates allow. *Dryden.*

F'ARTHER, *adv.* At or to a greater distance; more remotely; beyond. Let us rest with what we have, without looking *farther*.

2. Moreover; by way of progression in a subject. *Farther*, let us consider the probable event.

F'ARTHER, *v. t.* To promote; to advance; to help forward. [*Little used.*]

F'ARTHERANCE, *n.* A helping forward; promotion. [*Not used.*]

F'ARTHERMORE, *adv.* Besides; moreover. [*Little used.*]

Instead of the last three words, we now use *furtherance*, *furthermore*, *further*; which see.

F'ARTHEST, *a.* superl. [Sax. *feorrest*; D. *verst.* See *Furthest.*]

Most distant or remote; as the *farthest* degree.

F'ARTHEST, *adv.* At or to the greatest distance. [See *Furthest.*]

F'ARTHING, *n.* [Sax. *feorthung*, from *feorth*, fourth, from *feower*, four.]

1. The *fourth* of a penny; a small copper coin of Great Britain, being the fourth of a penny in value. In America we have no coin of this kind. We however use the word to denote the fourth part of a penny in value, but the *penny* is of different value from the English penny, and different in different states. It is becoming obsolete, with the old denominations of money.

2. *Farthings*, in the plural, copper coin. *Gay.*

3. Very small price or value. It is not worth a *farthing*, that is, it is of very little worth, or worth nothing.

4. A division of land. [*Not now used.*]

Thirty acres make a *farthing*-land; nine *farthings* a Cornish acre; and four Cornish acres a knight's fee. *Carew.*

F'ARTHINGALE, *n.* [This is a compound word, but it is not easy to analyze it. The French has *vertugadin*; the Sp. *verdugado*; Port. *verdugada*; which do not well correspond with the English word. The Italian has *guardinfante*, infant-guard; and it has been said that the hoop petticoat was first worn by pregnant women.]

A hoop petticoat; or circles of hoops, formed of whalebone, used to extend the petticoat.

F'ARTHINGSWORTH, *n.* As much as is sold for a farthing. *Arbuthnot.*

FAS'CES, *n. plu.* [L. *fascis*, W. *fasg*, a bundle; *fascia*, a band. See Class Bz. No. 24. 35. 60.]

In *Roman antiquity*, an ax tied up with a bundle of rods, and borne before the Roman magistrates as a badge of their authority. *Dryden.*

FAS'CIA, *n. fash'ia.* [L. a band or sash.]

1. A band, sash or fillet. In *architecture*, any flat member with a small projecture, as the band of an architrave. Also, in brick buildings, the jutting of the bricks beyond the windows in the several stories except the highest. *Encyc.*

2. In *astronomy*, the belt of a planet.

3. In *surgery*, a bandage, roller or ligature. *Parr.*

4. In *anatomy*, a tendinous expansion or aponeurosis; a thin tendinous covering which surrounds the muscles of the limbs, and binds them in their places. *Parr. Cyc.*

FAS'CIAL, *a. fash'ial.* Belonging to the fasces.

FAS'CIATED, *a. fash'iated.* Bound with a fillet, sash or bandage.

FASCIA'TION, *n. fashia'tion.* The act or manner of binding up diseased parts; bandage. *Wiseman.*

FAS'CICLE, *n.* [L. *fasciculus*, from *fascis*, a bundle.]

In *botany*, a bundle, or little bundle; a species of inflorescence, or manner of flowering, in which several upright, parallel, fastigiate, approximating flowers are collected together. *Martyn.*

FASCIC'ULAR, *a.* [L. *fascicularis.*] United in a bundle; as a *fascicular* root, a root of the tuberous kind, with the knobs collected in bundles, as in Pæonia. *Martyn.*

FASCIC'ULARLY, *adv.* In the form of bundles. *Kirwan.*

FASCIC'ULATE, FASCIC'ULATED, FAS'CICLED, *a.* [from *fasciculus*, supra.]

Growing in bundles or bunches from the same point, as the leaves of the Larix or larch. *Martyn.*

FASCIC'ULITE, *n.* [supra.] A variety of fibrous hornblend, of a fascicular structure. *Hitchcock.*

FAS'CINATE, *v. t.* [L. *fascino*; Gr. βασκαινω.]

1. To bewitch; to enchant; to operate on by some powerful or irresistible influence; to influence the passions or affections in an incontrollable manner.

None of the affections have been noted to *fascinate* and bewitch, but love and envy. *Bacon.*

2. To charm; to captivate; to excite and allure irresistibly or powerfully. The young are *fascinated* by love; female beauty *fascinates* the unguarded youth; gaming is a *fascinating* vice.

FAS'CINATED, *pp.* Bewitched; enchanted; charmed.

FAS'CINATING, *ppr.* Bewitching; enchanting; charming; captivating.

FASCINA'TION, *n.* The act of bewitching or enchanting; enchantment; witchcraft; a powerful or irresistible influence on the affections or passions; unseen inexplicable influence. The ancients speak of two kinds of fascination; one by the look or eye; the other by words.

The Turks hang old rags on their fairest horses, to secure them against *fascination.* *Waller.*

FAS'CINE, *n.* [Fr. from L. *fascis*, a bundle.] In *fortification*, a fagot, a bundle of rods or small sticks of wood, bound at both ends and in the middle; used in raising batteries, in filling ditches, in strengthening ramparts, and making parapets. Sometimes being dipped in melted pitch or tar, they are used to set fire to the enemy's lodgments or other works. *Encyc.*

FAS'CINOUS, *a.* Caused or acting by witchcraft. [*Not used.*] *Harvey.*

FASH'ION, *n. fash'on.* [Fr. *façon*; Arm. *facczoun*; Norm. *facion*; from *faire*, to make; L. *facio, facies.*]

1. The make or form of any thing; the state of any thing with regard to its external appearance; shape; as the *fashion* of the ark, or of the tabernacle.

Or let me lose the *fashion* of a man. *Shak.*

The *fashion* of his countenance was altered. Luke ix.

2. Form; model to be imitated; pattern.

King Ahaz sent to Urijah the priest the *fashion* of the altar. 2 Kings xvi.

3. The form of a garment; the cut or shape of clothes; as the *fashion* of a coat or of a bonnet. Hence,

4. The prevailing mode of dress or ornament. We import *fashions* from England, as the English often import them from France. What so changeable as *fashion*!

5. Manner; sort; way; mode; *applied to actions or behavior.*

Pluck Casca by the sleeve,
And he will, after his sour *fashion*, tell you
What hath proceeded. *Shak.*

6. Custom; prevailing mode or practice. *Fashion* is an inexorable tyrant, and most of the world its willing slaves.

It was the *fashion* of the age to call every thing in question. *Tillotson.*

Few enterprises are so hopeless as a contest with *fashion.* *Rambler.*

7. Genteel life or good breeding; as men of *fashion.*

8. Any thing worn. [*Not used.*] *Shak.*

9. Genteel company.

10. Workmanship. *Overbury.*

FASH'ION, *v. t. fash'on.* [Fr. *façonner.*] To form; to give shape or figure to; to mold.

Here the loud hammer *fashions* female toys. *Gay.*

Aaron *fashioned* the calf with a graving tool. Ex. xxxii.

Shall the clay say to him that *fashioneth* it, what makest thou? Is. xlv.

2. To fit; to adapt; to accommodate; with *to.*

Laws ought to be *fashioned to* the manners and conditions of the people. *Spenser.*

3. To make according to the rule prescribed by custom.

Fashioned plate sells for more than its weight. *Locke.*

4. To forge or counterfeit. [*Not used.*] *Shak.*

FASH'IONABLE, *a.* Made according to the prevailing form or mode; as a *fashionable* dress.

2. Established by custom or use; current; prevailing at a particular time; as the *fashionable* philosophy; *fashionable* opinions.

3. Observant of the fashion or customary mode; dressing or behaving according to the prevailing fashion; as a *fashionable* man. Hence,

4. Genteel; well bred; as *fashionable* company or society.

FASH'IONABLENESS, *n.* The state of being fashionable; modish elegance; such appearance as is according to the prevailing custom. *Locke.*

FASH'IONABLY, *adv.* In a manner according to fashion, custom or prevailing practice; with modish elegance; as, to dress *fashionably.*

FASH'IONED, *pp.* Made; formed; shaped; fitted; adapted.

FASH'IONER, *n.* One who forms or gives shape to.

FASH'IONING, *ppr.* Forming; giving shape to; fitting; adapting.

FASH'ION-MONGER, *n.* One who studies the fashion; a fop.

Fashion-pieces, in ships, the hindmost timbers which terminate the breadth, and form the shape of the stern. *Mar. Dict.*

FAS'SAITE, *n.* A mineral, a variety of augite, found in the valley of Fassa, in the Tyrol.

F'AST, *a.* [Sax. *fæst, fest*; G. *fest*; D. *vast*; Sw. and Dan. *fast*; from pressing, binding. Qu. Pers. بستن bastan, to bind, to make close or fast, to shut, to stop; Ir. *fosadh*, or *fos*, a stop. See Class Bz. No. 24. 35. 41. 60. 66. 86.]

1. Literally, set, stopped, fixed, or pressed close. Hence, close; tight; as, make *fast* the door; take *fast* hold.

2. Firm; immovable.

Who, by his strength, setteth *fast* the mountains. Ps. lxv.

3. Close; strong.

Robbers and outlaws—lurking in woods and *fast* places. *Spenser.*

4. Firmly fixed; closely adhering; as, to stick *fast* in mire; to make *fast* a rope.

5. Close, as sleep; deep; sound; as a *fast* sleep. *Shak.*

6. Firm in adherence; as a *fast* friend.

Fast and loose, variable; inconstant; as, to play *fast and loose.*

F'AST, *adv.* Firmly; immovably.

We will bind thee *fast*, and deliver thee into their hand. Judges xv.

Fast by, or *fast beside*, close or near to.

Fast by the throne obsequious fame resides. *Pope.*

F'AST, *a.* [W. *fêst*, fast, quick; *festu*, to hasten; L. *festino.* If *f* is not written for *h*, as in *haste*, see Class Bz. No. 44. 45. 46. The sense is to press, drive, urge, and it may be from the same root as the preceding word, with a different application.]

Swift; moving rapidly; quick in motion; as a *fast* horse.

F'AST, *adv.* Swiftly; rapidly; with quick steps or progression; as, to run *fast*; to move *fast* through the water, as a ship; the work goes on *fast.*

F'AST, *v. i.* [Sax. *fæstan;* Goth. *fastan*, to fast, to keep, to observe, to hold; G. *fasten;* D. *vast*, firm; *vasten*, to fast; Sw. *fasta;* from the same root as *fast*, firm. The sense is to hold or stop.]

1. To abstain from food, beyond the usual time; to omit to take the usual meals, for a time; as, to *fast* a day or a week.
2. To abstain from food voluntarily, for the mortification of the body or appetites, or as a token of grief, sorrow and affliction.
   Thou didst *fast* and weep for the child. 2 Sam. xii.
   When ye *fast*, be not, as the hypocrites, of a sad countenance. Matt. vi.
3. To abstain from food partially, or from particular kinds of food; as, the Catholics *fast* in Lent.

F'AST, *n.* Abstinence from food; properly a total abstinence, but it is used also for an abstinence from particular kinds of food, for a certain time.
   Happy were our forefathers, who broke their *fasts* with herbs. *Taylor.*
2. Voluntary abstinence from food, as a religious mortification or humiliation; either total or partial abstinence from customary food, with a view to mortify the appetites, or to express grief and affliction on account of some calamity, or to deprecate an expected evil.
3. The time of fasting, whether a day, week or longer time. An annual *fast* is kept in New England, usually one day in the spring.
   The *fast* was now already past. Acts xxvii.

F'AST, *n.* That which fastens or holds.

F'AST-DAY, *n.* The day on which fasting is observed.

F'ASTEN, *v. t.* *f'asn.* [Sax. *fæstnian;* Sw. *fastna;* D. *vesten;* Dan. *fæster;* Ir. *fostugadh, fostughim.*]

1. To fix firmly; to make fast or close; as, to *fasten* a chain to the feet, or to *fasten* the feet with fetters.
2. To lock, bolt or bar; to secure; as, to *fasten* a door or window.
3. To hold together; to cement or to link; to unite closely in any manner and by any means, as by cement, hooks, pins, nails, cords, &c.
4. To affix or conjoin.
   The words Whig and Tory have been pressed to the service of many successions of parties, with different ideas *fastened* to them. [*Not common.*] *Swift.*
5. To fix; to impress.
   Thinking, by this face,
   To *fasten* in our thoughts that they have courage. *Shak.*
6. To lay on with strength.
   Could he *fasten* a blow, or make a thrust, when not suffered to approach? *Dryden.*

F'ASTEN, *v. i.* *To fasten on*, is to fix one's self; to seize and hold on; to clinch.
   The leech will hardly *fasten on* a fish. *Brown.*

F'ASTENED, *pp.* Made firm or fast; fixed firmly; impressed.

F'ASTENER, *n.* One that makes fast or firm.

F'ASTENING, *ppr.* Making fast.

F'ASTENING, *n.* Any thing that binds and makes fast; or that which is intended for that purpose.

F'ASTER, *n.* One who abstains from food.

F'AST-HANDED, *a.* Closehanded; covetous; closefisted; avaricious. *Bacon.*

FASTIDIOS'ITY, *n.* Fastidiousness. [*Not used.*] *Swift.*

FASTID'IOUS, *a.* [L. *fastidiosus*, from *fastidio*, to disdain, from *fastus*, haughtiness. See Heb. בז. Class Bz. No. 2. 3. and 10. 30.]

1. Disdainful; squeamish; delicate to a fault; over nice; difficult to please; as a *fastidious* mind or taste.
2. Squeamish; rejecting what is common or not very nice; suited with difficulty; as a *fastidious* appetite.

FASTID'IOUSLY, *adv.* Disdainfully; squeamishly; contemptuously. They look *fastidiously* and speak disdainfully.

FASTID'IOUSNESS, *n.* Disdainfulness; contemptuousness; squeamishness of mind, taste or appetite.

FASTIG'IATE, FASTIG'IATED, *a.* [L. *fastigiatus*, pointed, from *fastigio*, to point, *fastigium*, a top or peak.]

1. In *botany*, a *fastigiate* stem is one whose branches are of an equal highth. Peduncles are *fastigiate*, when they elevate the fructifications in a bunch, so as to be equally high, or when they form an even surface at the top. *Martyn.*
2. Roofed; narrowed to the top.

F'ASTING, *ppr.* Abstaining from food.

F'ASTING, *n.* The act of abstaining from food.

F'ASTING-DAY, *n.* A day of fasting; a fast-day; a day of religious mortification and humiliation.

F'ASTNESS, *n.* [Sax. *fæstenesse*, from *fast.*]

1. The state of being fast and firm; firm adherence.
2. Strength; security.
   The places of *fastness* are laid open. *Davies.*
3. A strong hold; a fortress or fort; a place fortified; a castle. The enemy retired to their *fastnesses.*
4. Closeness; conciseness of style. [*Not used.*] *Ascham.*

FAS'TUOUS, *a.* [L. *fastuosus*, from *fastus*, haughtiness.]
Proud; haughty; disdainful. *Barrow.*

FAT, *a.* [Sax. *fæt, fett;* G. *fett;* D. *vet;* Sw. *fet;* Dan. *feed;* Basque, *betea.*]

1. Fleshy; plump; corpulent; abounding with an oily concrete substance, as an animal body; the contrary to *lean;* as a *fat* man; a *fat* ox.
2. Coarse; gross.
   Nay, added *fat* pollutions of our own. *Dryden.*
3. Dull; heavy; stupid; unteachable.
   Make the heart of this people *fat.* Is. vi.
4. Rich; wealthy; affluent.
   These are terrible alarms to persons grown *fat* and wealthy. *South.*
5. Rich; producing a large income; as a *fat* benefice.
6. Rich; fertile; as a *fat* soil: or rich; nourishing; as *fat* pasture.
7. Abounding in spiritual grace and comfort.
   They (the righteous) shall be *fat* and flourishing. Ps. xcii.

FAT, *n.* An oily concrete substance, deposited in the cells of the adipose or cellular membrane of animal bodies. In most parts of the body, the fat lies immediately under the skin. Fat is of various degrees of consistence, as in tallow, lard and oil. It has been recently ascertained to consist of two substances, stearine and elaine, the former of which is solid, the latter liquid, at common temperatures, and on the different proportions of which its degree of consistence depends. *Encyc. Webster's Manual.*
2. The best or richest part of a thing.
   Abel brought of the *fat* of his flock. Gen. iv.

FAT, *v. t.* To make fat; to fatten; to make plump and fleshy with abundant food; as, to *fat* fowls or sheep. *Locke. Shak.*

FAT, *v. i.* To grow fat, plump and fleshy.
   An old ox *fats* as well, and is as good, as a young one. *Mortimer.*

FAT, VAT, *n.* [Sax. *fæt, fat, fet;* D. *vat;* G. *fass;* Sw. *fat;* Dan. *fad.* It seems to be connected with D. *vatten*, G. *fassen*, Sw. *fatta*, Dan. *fatter*, to hold. Qu. Gr. πιθος.]
A large tub, cistern or vessel used for various purposes, as by brewers to run their wort in, by tanners for holding their bark and hides, &c. It is also a wooden vessel containing a quarter or eight bushels of grain, and a pan for containing water in salt-works, a vessel for wine, &c.
   The *fats* shall overflow with wine and oil. Joel ii.

FAT, *n.* A measure of capacity, but indefinite.

FA'TAL, *a.* [L. *fatalis.* See *Fate.*] Proceeding from fate or destiny; necessary; inevitable.
   These things are *fatal* and necessary. *Tillotson.*
2. Appointed by fate or destiny.
   It was *fatal* to the king to fight for his money. *Bacon.*
In the foregoing senses the word is now little used.
3. Causing death or destruction; deadly; mortal; as a *fatal* wound; a *fatal* disease.
4. Destructive; calamitous; as a *fatal* day; a *fatal* event.

FA'TALISM, *n.* The doctrine that all things are subject to fate, or that they take place by inevitable necessity. *Rush.*

FA'TALIST, *n.* One who maintains that all things happen by inevitable necessity. *Watts.*

FATAL'ITY, *n.* [Fr. *fatalité*, from *fate.*]

1. A fixed unalterable course of things, independent of God or any controlling cause; an invincible necessity existing in things themselves; a doctrine of the Stoics. *South.*
2. Decree of fate. *King Charles.*
3. Tendency to danger, or to some great or hazardous event. *Brown.*
4. Mortality. *Med. Repos.*

FA'TALLY, *adv.* By a decree of fate or destiny; by inevitable necessity or determination. *Bentley.*
2. Mortally; destructively; in death or ruin. This encounter ended *fatally.* The prince was *fatally* deceived.

FA'TALNESS, *n.* Invincible necessity.

FAT'BRAINED, *a.* Dull of apprehension. *Shak.*

FATE, *n.* [L. *fatum*, from *for, fari*, to speak, whence *fatus.*]

1. Primarily, a decree or word pronounced by God; or a fixed sentence by which the order of things is prescribed. Hence, inevitable necessity; destiny depending on

a superior cause and uncontrollable. According to the Stoics, every event is determined by *fate.*

Necessity or chance
Approach not me; and what I will is *fate.* — *Milton.*

2. Event predetermined; lot; destiny. It is our *fate* to meet with disappointments. It is the *fate* of mortals.

Tell me what *fates* attend the duke of Suffolk? — *Shak.*

3. Final event; death; destruction.

Yet still he chose the longest way to *fate.* — *Dryden.*

The whizzing arrow sings,
And bears thy *fate,* Antinous, on its wings. — *Pope.*

4. Cause of death. Dryden calls an arrow a feathered *fate.*

Divine fate, the order or determination of God; providence. *Encyc.*

FA'TED, *a.* Decreed by fate; doomed; destined. He was *fated* to rule over a factious people.

2. Modelled or regulated by fate.

Her awkward love indeed was oddly *fated.* — *Prior.*

3. Endued with any quality by fate. *Dryden.*

4. Invested with the power of fatal determination.

The *fated* sky
Gives us free scope. — *Shak.*

The two last senses are hardly legitimate.

FA'TEFUL, *a.* Bearing fatal power; producing fatal events.

The *fateful* steel. — *J. Barlow.*

FATES, *n. plu.* In *mythology,* the destinies or *parcæ;* goddesses supposed to preside over the birth and life of men. They were three in number, Clotho, Lachesis and Atropos. *Lempriere.*

F'ATHER, *n.* [Sax. *fæder, feder;* G. *vater;* D. *vader;* Ice. Sw. and Dan. *fader;* Gr. πατηρ; L. *pater;* Sp. *padre;* It. *padre;* Port. *pai,* or *pay;* Fr. *père,* by contraction; Pers. پدر padar; Russ. *batia;* Sans. and Bali, *pita;* Zend, *fedre;* Syr. ܒܛܪܐ batara. This word signifies the begetter, from the verb, Sw. *föda,* Dan. *föder,* to beget, to *feed;* Goth. *fodyan;* Sax. *fedan;* D. *voeden,* to feed; whence *fodder,* G. *futter, füttern.* The primary sense is obvious. See Class Bd. No. 54. 55. The Goth. *atta,* Ir. *aithir* or *athair,* Basque *aita,* must be from a different root, unless the first letter has been lost.]

1. He who begets a child; in L. *genitor* or *generator.*

The *father* of a fool hath no joy. Prov. xvii.
A wise son maketh a glad *father.* Prov. x.

2. The first ancestor; the progenitor of a race or family. Adam was the *father* of the human race. Abraham was the *father* of the Israelites.

3. The appellation of an old man, and a term of respect.

The king of Israel said to Elisha, my *father,* shall I smite them? 2 Kings vi.

The servants of Naaman call him *father.* Ibm. v. Elderly men are called *fathers;* as the *fathers* of a town or city. In *the church,* men venerable for age, learning and piety are called *fathers,* or reverend *fathers.*

4. The grandfather, or more remote ancestor. Nebuchadnezzar is called the *father* of Belshazzar, though he was his grandfather. Dan. v.

5. One who feeds and supports, or exercises paternal care over another. God is called the *father* of the fatherless. Ps. lxviii.

I was a *father* to the poor. Job xxix.

6. He who creates, invents, makes or composes any thing; the author, former or contriver; a founder, director or instructor. God as creator is the *father* of all men. John viii. Jabal was the *father* of such as dwell in tents; and Jubal of musicians. Gen. iv. God is the *father* of spirits and of lights. Homer is considered as the *father* of epic poetry. Washington, as a defender and an affectionate and wise counselor, is called the *father* of his country. And see I Chron. ii. 51.—iv. 14.—ix. 35. Satan is called the *father* of lies; he introduced sin, and instigates men to sin. John viii. Abraham is called the *father* of believers. He was an early believer, and a pattern of faith and obedience. Rom. iv.

7. *Fathers,* in the plural, ancestors.

David slept with his *fathers.* 1 Kings ii.

8. A father in law. So Heli is called the *father* of Joseph. Luke iii.

9. The appellation of the first person in the adorable Trinity.

Go ye, therefore, and teach all nations, baptizing them in the name of the *Father,* and of the Son, and of the Holy Spirit. Matt. xxviii.

10. The title given to dignitaries of the church, superiors of convents, and to popish confessors.

11. The appellation of the ecclesiastical writers of the first centuries, as Polycarp, Jerome, &c.

12. The title of a senator in ancient Rome; as conscript *fathers.*

Adoptive father, he who adopts the children of another, and acknowledges them as his own.

Natural father, the father of illegitimate children.

Putative father, one who is only reputed to be the father; the supposed father.

F'ATHER-IN-LAW, *n.* The father of one's husband or wife; and a man who marries a woman who has children by a former husband is called the *father in law* or step-father of those children.

F'ATHER, *v. t.* To adopt; to take the child of another as one's own. *Shak.*

2. To adopt any thing as one's own; to profess to be the author.

Men of wit
Often *father'd* what he writ. — *Swift.*

3. To ascribe or charge to one as his offspring or production; with *on.*

My name was made use of by several persons, one of whom was pleased to *father on* me a new set of productions. — *Swift.*

F'ATHERED, *pp.* Adopted; taken as one's own; ascribed to one as the author.

2. Having had a father of particular qualities.

I am no stronger than my sex,
Being so *father'd* and so husbanded. [*Unusual.*] — *Shak.*

F'ATHERHOOD, *n.* The state of being a father, or the character or authority of a father.

We might have had an entire notion of this *fatherhood,* or fatherly authority. — *Locke.*

F'ATHERING, *ppr.* Adopting; taking or acknowledging as one's own; ascribing to the father or author.

F'ATHERLASHER, *n.* A fish of the genus Cottus or bull-head, called *scorpius* or *scolping.* The head is large and its spines formidable. It is found on the rocky coasts of Britain, and near Newfoundland and Greenland. In the latter country it is a great article of food. *Encyc. Pennant.*

F'ATHERLESS, *a.* Destitute of a living father; as a *fatherless* child.

2. Without a known author.

F'ATHERLESSNESS, *n.* The state of being without a father.

F'ATHERLINESS, *n.* [See *Fatherly.*] The qualities of a father; parental kindness, care and tenderness.

F'ATHERLY, *a.* [*father* and *like.*] Like a father in affection and care; tender; paternal; protecting; careful; as *fatherly* care or affection.

2. Pertaining to a father.

F'ATHERLY, *adv.* In the manner of a father.

Thus Adam, *fatherly* displeased. [*Not proper.*] — *Milton.*

FATH'OM, *n.* [Sax. *fæthem;* Ir. *fead;* G. *faden;* D. *vadem.* Qu. Dan. *favn.* The German word signifies a thread, a fathom, and probably thread or line is the real signification.]

1. A measure of length containing six feet, the space to which a man may extend his arms; used chiefly at sea for measuring cables, cordage, and the depth of the sea in sounding by a line and lead.

2. Reach; penetration; depth of thought or contrivance. *Shak.*

FATH'OM, *v. t.* To encompass with the arms extended or encircling.

2. To reach; to master; to comprehend.

Leave to *fathom* such high points as these. — *Dryden.*

3. To reach in depth; to sound; to try the depth.

Our depths who *fathoms.* — *Pope.*

4. To penetrate; to find the bottom or extent. I cannot *fathom* his design.

FATH'OMED, *pp.* Encompassed with the arms; reached; comprehended.

FATH'OMER, *n.* One who fathoms.

FATH'OMING, *ppr.* Encompassing with the arms; reaching; comprehending; sounding; penetrating.

FATH'OMLESS, *a.* That of which no bottom can be found; bottomless.

2. That cannot be embraced, or encompassed with the arms. *Shak.*

3. Not to be penetrated or comprehended.

FATID'ICAL, *a.* [L. *fatidicus; fatum* and *dico.*] Having power to foretell future events; prophetic. *Howell.*

FATIF'EROUS, *a.* [L. *fatifer; fatum* and *fero.*] Deadly; mortal; destructive. *Dict.*

FAT'IGABLE, *a.* [See *Fatigue.*] That may be wearied; easily tired.

FAT'IGATE, *v. t.* [L. *fatigo.*] To weary; to tire. [*Little used.*]

FAT'IGATE, *a.* Wearied; tired. [*Little used.*] *Elyot.*

FATIGA'TION, *n.* Weariness. *W. Mount.*

FATĬGUE, *n. fatee'g.* [Fr. *id.*; Arm. *faticq*; It. *fatica*; Sp. *fatiga*; from L. *fatigo*. It seems to be allied to L. *fatisco*; if so, the sense is a yielding or relaxing.]

1. Weariness with bodily labor or mental exertion; lassitude or exhaustion of strength. We suffer *fatigue* of the mind as well as of the body.
2. The cause of weariness; labor; toil; as the *fatigues* of war.
3. The labors of military men, distinct from the use of arms; as a party of men on *fatigue.*

FATĬGUE, *v. t. fatee'g.* [L. *fatigo*; It. *faticare*; Sp. *fatigar.*]

1. To tire; to weary with labor or any bodily or mental exertion; to harass with toil; to exhaust the strength by severe or long continued exertion.
2. To weary by importunity; to harass.

FATĬGUED, *pp. fatee'ged.* Wearied; tired; harassed.

FATĬGUING, *ppr. fatee'ging.* Tiring; wearying; harassing.

2. *a.* Inducing weariness or lassitude; as *fatiguing* services or labors.

FATIS'CENCE, *n.* [L. *fatisco*, to open, to gape.] A gaping or opening; a state of being chinky. *Dict. Kirwan.*

FATKID'NEYED, *n.* [*fat* and *kidney.*] Fat; gross; *a word used in contempt.* *Shak.*

FAT'LING, *n.* [from *fat.*] A lamb, kid or other young animal fattened for slaughter; a fat animal; *applied to quadrupeds whose flesh is used for food.*

David sacrificed oxen and *fatlings.* 2 Sam. vi.

FAT'LY, *adv.* Grossly; greasily.

FAT'NER, *n.* That which fattens; that which gives fatness or richness and fertility. *Arbuthnot.*

FAT'NESS, *n.* [from *fat.*] The quality of being fat, plump, or full fed; corpulency; fullness of flesh.

Their eyes stand out with *fatness.* Ps. lxxiii.

2. Unctuous or greasy matter. *Bacon.*
3. Unctuousness; sliminess; *applied to earth:* hence richness; fertility; fruitfulness.

God give thee of the dew of heaven, and the *fatness* of the earth, and plenty of corn and wine. Gen. xxvii.

4. That which gives fertility.

Thy paths drop *fatness.* Ps. lxv.
The clouds drop *fatness.* *Philips.*

5. The privileges and pleasures of religion; abundant blessings.

Let your soul delight itself in *fatness.* Is. lv.

FAT'TEN, *v. t. fat'n.* To make fat; to feed for slaughter; to make fleshy, or plump with fat.

2. To make fertile and fruitful; to enrich; as, to *fatten* land; to *fatten* fields with blood. *Dryden.*
3. To feed grossly; to fill. *Dryden.*

FAT'TEN, *v. i. fat'n.* To grow fat or corpulent; to grow plump, thick or fleshy; to be pampered.

And villains *fatten* with the brave man's labor. *Otway.*

Tigers and wolves shall in the ocean breed,
The whale and dolphin *fatten* on the mead. *Glanville.*

FAT'TENED, *pp. fat'nd.* Made fat, plump or fleshy.

FAT'TENER, *n.* [See *Fatner.*]

FAT'TENING, *ppr. fat'ning.* Making fat; growing fat; making or growing rich and fruitful.

FAT'TINESS, *n.* [from *fatty.*] The state of being fat; grossness; greasiness. *Sherwood.*

FAT'TISH, *a.* Somewhat fat. *Sherwood.*

FAT'TY, *a.* Having the qualities of fat; greasy; as a *fatty* substance. *Arbuthnot.*

FATU'ITY, *n.* [Fr. *fatuité*; L. *fatuitas.*] Weakness or imbecility of mind; feebleness of intellect; foolishness. *Arbuthnot.*

FAT'UOUS, *a.* [L. *fatuus.* Class Bd. No. 2. 6. 63.]

1. Feeble in mind; weak; silly; stupid; foolish. *Glanville.*
2. Impotent; without force or fire; illusory; alluding to the *ignis fatuus.*

Thence *fatuous* fires and meteors take their birth. *Denham.*

FAT'WITTED, *a.* [*fat* and *wit.*] Heavy; dull; stupid. *Shak.*

FAU'CET, *n.* [Fr. *fausset*, probably contracted from *falset.*] A pipe to be inserted in a cask for drawing liquor, and stopped with a peg or spiggot. These are called *tap* and *faucet.*

FAUCHION. [See *Falchion.*]

FAU'FEL, *n.* [said to be Sanscrit.] The fruit of a species of the palm-tree.

FAULT, *n.* [Fr. *faute*, for *faulte*; Sp. *falta*; Port. *id.*; It. *fallo*; from *fail.* See *Fail.*]

1. Properly, an erring or missing; a failing; hence, an error or mistake; a blunder; a defect; a blemish; whatever impairs excellence; *applied to things.*
2. In *morals* or *deportment*, any error or defect; an imperfection; any deviation from propriety; a slight offense; a neglect of duty or propriety, resulting from inattention or want of prudence, rather than from design to injure or offend, but liable to censure or objection.

I do remember my *faults* this day. Gen. xli.

If a man be overtaken in a *fault*, ye, who are spiritual, restore such an one in the spirit of meekness. Gal. vi.

Fault implies wrong, and often some degree of criminality.

3. Defect; want; absence. [*Not now used.* See *Default.*]

I could tell to thee, as to one it pleases me, for *fault* of a better, to call my friend. *Shak.*

4. Puzzle; difficulty.

Among sportsmen, when dogs lose the scent, they are said to be *at fault.* Hence the phrase, the inquirer is *at fault.*

5. In *mining*, a fissure in strata, causing a dislocation of the same, and thus interrupting the course of veins. *Cyc.*

To find fault, to express blame; to complain.

Thou wilt say then, why doth he yet *find fault?* Rom. ix.

To find fault with, to blame; to censure; as, to *find fault with* the times, or with a neighbor's conduct.

FAULT, *v. i.* To fail; to be wrong. [*Not used.*] *Spenser.*

FAULT, *v. t.* To charge with a fault; to accuse.

For that I will not *fault* thee. *Old Song.*

FAULT'ED, *pp.* Charged with a fault; accused.

FAULT'ER, *n.* An offender; one who commits a fault. *Fairfax.*

FAULT'-FINDER, *n.* One who censures or objects.

FAULT'FUL, *a.* Full of faults or sins. *Shak.*

FAULT'ILY, *adv.* [from *faulty.*] Defectively; erroneously; imperfectly; improperly; wrongly.

FAULT'INESS, *n.* [from *faulty.*] The state of being faulty, defective or erroneous; defect.

2. Badness; vitiousness; evil disposition; as the *faultiness* of a person.
3. Delinquency; actual offenses. *Hooker.*

FAULT'ING, *ppr.* Accusing.

FAULT'LESS, *a.* Without fault; not defective or imperfect; free from blemish; free from incorrectness; perfect; as a *faultless* poem or picture.

2. Free from vice or imperfection; as a *faultless* man.

FAULT'LESSNESS, *n.* Freedom from faults or defects.

FAULT'Y, *a.* Containing faults, blemishes or defects; defective; imperfect; as a *faulty* composition or book; a *faulty* plan or design; a *faulty* picture.

2. Guilty of a fault or of faults; hence, blamable; worthy of censure.

The king doth speak this thing as one who is *faulty.* 2 Sam. xiv.

3. Wrong; erroneous; as a *faulty* polity. *Hooker.*
4. Defective; imperfect; bad; as a *faulty* helmet. *Bacon.*

FAUN, *n.* [L. *faunus.*] Among *the Romans*, a kind of demigod, or rural deity, called also *sylvan*, and differing little from satyr. The fauns are represented as half goat and half man. *Encyc.*

FAUN'IST, *n.* One who attends to rural disquisitions; a naturalist. *White.*

FAU'SEN, *n.* A large eel. *Chapman.*

FAU'TOR, *n.* [L. See *Favor.*] A favorer; a patron; one who gives countenance or support. [*Little used.*] *B. Jonson.*

FAU'TRESS, *n.* A female favorer; a patroness. *Chapman.*

FAVIL'LOUS, *a.* [L. *favilla*, ashes.] Consisting of or pertaining to ashes. *Brown.*

2. Resembling ashes.

FA'VOR, *n.* [L. *favor*; Fr. *faveur*; Arm. *faver*; Sp. *favor*; It. *favore*; from L. *faveo*; Ir. *fabhar*, favor; *fabhraim*, to favor.]

1. Kind regard; kindness; countenance; propitious aspect; friendly disposition.

His dreadful navy, and his lovely mind,
Gave him the fear and *favor* of mankind. *Waller.*

The king's *favor* is as dew on the grass. Prov. xix.

God gave Joseph *favor* and wisdom in the sight of Pharaoh. Acts vii.

Favor is deceitful, and beauty is vain. Prov. xxxi.

2. Support; defense; vindication; or disposition to aid, befriend, support, promote or justify. To be *in favor of* a measure, is to have a disposition or inclination to support it or carry it into effect. To be *in favor of* a party, is to be disposed or inclined to support it, to justify its proceedings, and to promote its interests.
3. A kind act or office; kindness done or granted; benevolence shown by word or deed; any act of grace or good will, as distinguished from acts of justice or re-

muneration. To pardon the guilty is a *favor;* to punish them is an act of justice.
4. Lenity; mildness or mitigation of punishment.
I could not discover the lenity and *favor* of this sentence. *Swift.*
5. Leave; good will; a yielding or concession to another; pardon.
But, with your *favor*, I will treat it here. *Dryden.*
6. The object of kind regard; the person or thing favored.
All these his wondrous works, but chiefly man
His chief delight and *favor*. *Milton.*
7. A gift or present; something bestowed as an evidence of good will; a token of love; a knot of ribins; something worn as a token of affection. *Bacon. Spectator. Shak.*
8. A feature; countenance. [*Not used.*] *Shak.*
9. Advantage; convenience afforded for success. The enemy approached under *favor* of the night.
10. Partiality; bias. A *challenge to the favor*, in law, is the challenge of a juror on account of some supposed partiality, by reason of favor or malice, interest or connection.

FA'VOR, *v. t.* To regard with kindness; to support; to aid or have the disposition to aid, or to wish success to; to be propitious to; to countenance; to befriend; to encourage. To *favor* the cause of a party, may be merely to wish success to it, or it may signify to give it aid, by counsel, or by active exertions. Sometimes men professedly *favor* one party and secretly *favor* another.
The lords *favor* thee not. 1 Sam. xxix.
Thou shalt arise, and have mercy on Zion; for the time to *favor* her, yea, the set time is come. Ps. cii.
O happy youth! and *favored* of the skies. *Pope.*
2. To afford advantages for success; to facilitate. A weak place in the fort *favored* the entrance of the enemy; the darkness of the night *favored* his approach. A fair wind *favors* a voyage.
3. To resemble in features. The child *favors* his father.
4. To ease; to spare. A man in walking *favors* a lame leg.

FA'VORABLE, *a.* [L. *favorabilis;* Fr. *favorable;* Sp. *id.;* It. *favorabile*, or *favorevole.*]
1. Kind; propitious; friendly; affectionate.
Lend *favorable* ear to our request. *Shak.*
Lord, thou hast been *favorable* to thy land. Ps. lxxxv.
2. Palliative; tender; averse to censure.
None can have the *favorable* thought
That to obey a tyrant's will they fought. *Dryden.*
3. Conducive to; contributing to; tending to promote. A salubrious climate and plenty of food are *favorable* to population.
4. Convenient; advantageous; affording means to facilitate, or affording facilities. The low price of labor and provisions is *favorable* to the success of manufactures. The army was drawn up on *favorable* ground. The ship took a station *favorable* for attack.
The place was *favorable* for making levies of men. *Clarendon.*
5. Beautiful; well favored. *Obs.* *Spenser.*

FA'VORABLENESS, *n.* Kindness; kind disposition or regard.
2. Convenience; suitableness; that state which affords advantages for success; conduciveness; as the *favorableness* of a season for crops; the *favorableness* of the times for the cultivation of the sciences.

FA'VORABLY, *adv.* Kindly; with friendly dispositions; with regard or affection; with an inclination to favor; as, to judge or think *favorably* of a measure; to think *favorably* of those we love.

FA'VORED, *pp.* Countenanced; supported; aided; supplied with advantages; eased; spared.
2. *a.* Regarded with kindness; as a *favored* friend.
3. With *well* or *ill* prefixed, featured.
Well-favored is well-looking, having a good countenance or appearance, fleshy, plump, handsome.
Ill-favored, is ill-looking, having an ugly appearance, lean. See Gen. xxxix. xli. &c.
Well-favoredly, with a good appearance. [*Little used.*]
Ill-favoredly, with a bad appearance. [*Little used.*]

FA'VOREDNESS, *n.* Appearance. *Deut.*

FA'VORER, *n.* One who favors; one who regards with kindness or friendship; a wellwisher; one who assists or promotes success or prosperity. *Hooker. Shak.*

FA'VORING, *ppr.* Regarding with friendly dispositions; countenancing; wishing well to; contributing to success; facilitating.

FA'VORITE, *n.* [Fr. *favori, favorite;* It. *favorito.*]
A person or thing regarded with peculiar favor, preference and affection; one greatly beloved. Select *favorites* from among the discrete and the virtuous. Princes are often misled, and sometimes ruined by *favorites.* Gaveston and the Spensers, the *favorites* of Edward II., fell a sacrifice to public indignation.

FA'VORITE, *a.* Regarded with particular kindness, affection, esteem or preference; as a *favorite* walk; a *favorite* author; a *favorite* child.

FA'VORITISM, *n.* The act or practice of favoring, or giving a preference to one over another.
2. The disposition to favor, aid and promote the interest of a favorite, or of one person or family, or of one class of men, to the neglect of others having equal claims.
It has been suggested that the proceeds of the foreign bills—were calculated merely to indulge a spirit of *favoritism* to the bank of the United States. *Hamilton.*
Which consideration imposes such a necessity on the crown, as hath, in a great measure, subdued the influence of *favoritism.* *Paley.*
3. Exercise of power by favorites. *Burke.*

FA'VORLESS, *a.* Unfavored; not regarded with favor; having no patronage or countenance.
2. Not favoring; unpropitious. *Spenser.*

FAV'OSITE, *n.* [L. *favus*, a honey-comb.] A genus of fossil zoophytes.

FAWN, *n.* [Fr. *faon*, fawn. Qu. W. *fynu*, to produce.]
A young deer; a buck or doe of the first year. *Bacon. Pope.*

FAWN, *v. i.* [Fr. *faonner.*] To bring forth a fawn.

FAWN, *v. i.* [Sax. *fægenian.* See *Fain.*]
1. To court favor, or show attachment to, by frisking about one; as, a dog *fawns* on his master.
2. To soothe; to flatter meanly; to blandish; to court servilely; to cringe and bow to gain favor; as a *fawning* favorite or minion.
My love, forbear to *fawn* upon their frowns. *Shak.*

FAWN, *n.* A servile cringe or bow; mean flattery.

FAWN'ER, *n.* One who fawns; one who cringes and flatters meanly.

FAWN'ING, *ppr.* Courting servilely; flattering by cringing and meanness; bringing forth a fawn.

FAWN'ING, *n.* Gross flattery. *Shak.*

FAWN'INGLY, *adv.* In a cringing servile way; with mean flattery.

FAX'ED, *a.* [Sax. *feax*, hair.] Hairy. [*Not in use.*] *Camden.*

FAY, *n.* [Fr. *fée.*] A fairy; an elf. *Milton. Pope.*

FAY, *v. i.* [Sax. *fægan;* Sw. *foga;* D. *voegen.* See *Fadge.*]
To fit; to suit; to unite closely with. [This is a contraction of the Teutonic word, and the same as *fadge*, which see. It is not an elegant word.]

FEAGUE, *v. t. feeg.* [G. *fegen.*] To beat or whip. [*Not in use.*] *Buckingham.*

FE'AL, *a.* Faithful. [Infra.]

FE'ALTY, *n.* [Fr. *feal*, trusty, contracted from L. *fidelis;* It. *fedeltà;* Fr. *fidelité;* Sp. *fe*, faith, contracted from *fides;* hence, *fiel*, faithful; *fieldad*, fidelity.]
Fidelity to a lord; faithful adherence of a tenant or vassal to the superior of whom he holds his lands; loyalty. Under the feudal system of tenures, every vassal or tenant was bound to be true and faithful to his lord, and to defend him against all his enemies. This obligation was called his *fidelity* or fealty, and an oath of *fealty* was required to be taken by all tenants to their landlords. The tenant was called a *liege* man; the land, a *liege* fee; and the superior, *liege* lord. [See *Liege.*]

FEAR, *n.* [See the Verb.] A painful emotion or passion excited by an expectation of evil, or the apprehension of impending danger. *Fear* expresses less apprehension than *dread*, and dread less than *terror* and *fright.* The force of this passion, beginning with the most moderate degree, may be thus expressed, *fear, dread, terror, fright. Fear* is accompanied with a desire to avoid or ward off the expected evil. *Fear* is an uneasiness of mind, upon the thought of future evil likely to *befall* us. *Watts.*
Fear is the passion of our nature which excites us to provide for our security, on the approach of evil. *Rogers.*
2. Anxiety; solicitude.
The principal *fear* was for the holy temple. *Maccabees.*
3. The cause of fear.
Thy angel becomes a *fear.* *Shak.*
4. The object of fear.
Except the God of Abraham, and the *fear* of Isaac, had been with me. Gen. xxxi.

5. Something set or hung up to terrify wild animals, by its color or noise. Is. xxiv. Jer. xlviii.

6. In scripture, *fear* is used to express a *filial* or a *slavish* passion. In good men, the *fear* of God is a holy awe or reverence of God and his laws, which springs from a just view and real love of the divine character, leading the subjects of it to hate and shun every thing that can offend such a holy being, and inclining them to aim at perfect obedience. This is *filial* fear.

I will put my *fear* in their hearts. Jer. xxxii.

Slavish fear is the effect or consequence of guilt; it is the painful apprehension of merited punishment. Rom. viii.

The love of God casteth out *fear*. 1 John iv.

7. The worship of God.

I will teach you the *fear* of the Lord. Ps. xxxiv.

8. The law and word of God.

The *fear* of the Lord is clean, enduring for ever. Ps. xix.

9. Reverence; respect; due regard.

Render to all their dues; *fear* to whom *fear*. Rom. xiii.

FEAR, *v. t.* [Sax. *færan*, *afæran*, to impress fear, to terrify; D. *vaaren*, to put in fear, to disorder, to derange; L. *vereor*. In Saxon and Dutch, the verb coincides in elements with *fare*, to go or depart, and the sense seems to be to scare or drive away. Qu. Syr. and Ar. نفر nafara, to flee or be fearful. See Class Br. No 46. and 33.]

1. To feel a painful apprehension of some impending evil; to be afraid of; to consider or expect with emotions of alarm or solicitude. We *fear* the approach of an enemy or of a storm. We have reason to *fear* the punishment of our sins.

I will *fear* no evil, for thou art with me. Ps. xxiii.

2. To reverence; to have a reverential awe; to venerate.

This do, and live: for I *fear* God. Gen. xlii.

3. To affright; to terrify; to drive away or prevent approach by fear, or by a scarecrow. [This seems to be the primary meaning, but now obsolete.]

We must not make a scarecrow of the law,
Setting it up to *fear* the birds of prey. *Shak.*

FEAR, *v. i.* To be in apprehension of evil; to be afraid; to feel anxiety on account of some expected evil.

But I *fear*, lest by any means, as the serpent beguiled Eve through his subtilty, so your minds should be corrupted from the simplicity that is in Christ. 2 Cor. xi.

Fear not, Abram: I am thy shield, and thy exceeding great reward. Gen. xv.

FEAR, *n.* [Sax. *fera*, *gefera*.] A companion. [*Not in use.* See *Peer.*] *Spenser.*

FE'ARED, *pp.* Apprehended or expected with painful solicitude; reverenced.

FE'ARFUL, *a.* Affected by fear; feeling pain in expectation of evil; apprehensive with solicitude; afraid. I am *fearful* of the consequences of rash conduct. Hence,

2. Timid; timorous; wanting courage.

What man is there that is *fearful* and faint-hearted? Deut. xx.

3. Terrible; impressing fear; frightful; dreadful.

It is a *fearful* thing to fall into the hands of the living God. Heb. x.

4. Awful; to be reverenced.

O Lord, who is like thee, glorious in holiness, *fearful* in praises? Ex. xv.

That thou mayest fear this glorious and *fearful* name, Jehovah, thy God. Deut. xxviii.

FE'ARFULLY, *adv.* Timorously; in fear.

In such a night
Did Thisbe *fearfully* o'ertrip the dew. *Shak.*

2. Terribly; dreadfully; in a manner to impress terror.

There is a cliff, whose high and bending head
Looks *fearfully* on the confined deep. *Shak.*

3. In a manner to impress admiration and astonishment.

I am *fearfully* and wonderfully made. Ps. cxxxix.

FE'ARFULNESS, *n.* Timorousness; timidity.

2. State of being afraid; awe; dread.

A third thing that makes a government despised, is *fearfulness* of, and mean compliances with, bold popular offenders. *South.*

3. Terror; alarm; apprehension of evil.

Fearfulness hath surprised the hypocrites. Is. xxxiii.

FE'ARLESS, *a.* Free from fear; as *fearless* of death; *fearless* of consequences.

2. Bold; courageous; intrepid; undaunted; as a *fearless* hero; a *fearless* foe.

FE'ARLESSLY, *adv.* Without fear; in a bold or courageous manner; intrepidly. Brave men *fearlessly* expose themselves to the most formidable dangers.

FE'ARLESSNESS, *n.* Freedom from fear; courage; boldness; intrepidity.

He gave instances of an invincible courage and *fearlessness* in danger. *Clarendon.*

FEASIBIL'ITY, *n.* *s* as *z.* [See *Feasible.*] The quality of being capable of execution; practicability. Before we adopt a plan, let us consider its *feasibility*.

FE'ASIBLE, *a.* *s* as *z.* [Fr. *faisable*, from *faire*, to make, L. *facere*; It. *fattibile*; Sp. *factible*.]

That may be done, performed, executed or effected; practicable. We say a thing is *feasible*, when it can be effected by human means or agency. A thing may be possible, but not *feasible*.

2. That may be used or tilled, as land. *B. Trumbull.*

FE'ASIBLE, *n.* That which is practicable; that which can be performed by human means.

FE'ASIBLENESS, *n.* Feasibility; practicability. *Bp. Hall.*

FE'ASIBLY, *adv.* Practicably.

FEAST, *n.* [L. *festum*; Fr. *fête*; Sp. *fiesta*; It. *festa*; Ir. *feasda*; D. *feest*; G. *fest.*]

1. A sumptuous repast or entertainment, of which a number of guests partake; particularly, a rich or splendid public entertainment.

On Pharaoh's birth day, he made a *feast* to all his servants. Gen. xl.

2. A rich or delicious repast or meal; something delicious to the palate.

3. A ceremony of feasting; joy and thanksgiving on stated days, in commemoration of some great event, or in honor of some distinguished personage; an anniversary, periodical or stated celebration of some event; a festival; as on occasion of the games in Greece, and the *feast* of the passover, the *feast* of Pentecost, and the *feast* of tabernacles among the Jews.

4. Something delicious and entertaining to the mind or soul; as the dispensation of the gospel is called a *feast* of fat things. Is. xxv.

5. That which delights and entertains.

He that is of a merry heart hath a continual *feast*. Prov. xv.

In the English church, feasts are *immovable* or *movable: immovable*, when they occur on the same day of the year, as Christmas-day, &c.; and *movable*, when they are not confined to the same day of the year, as Easter, which regulates many others.

FEAST, *v. i.* To eat sumptuously; to dine or sup on rich provisions; particularly in large companies, and on public festivals.

And his sons went and *feasted* in their houses. Job i.

2. To be highly gratified or delighted.

FEAST, *v. t.* To entertain with sumptuous provisions; to treat at the table magnificently; as, he was *feasted* by the king. *Hayward.*

2. To delight; to pamper; to gratify luxuriously; as, to *feast* the soul.

Whose taste or smell can bless the *feasted* sense. *Dryden.*

FE'ASTED, *pp.* Entertained sumptuously; delighted.

FE'ASTER, *n.* One who fares deliciously. *Taylor.*

2. One who entertains magnificently. *Johnson.*

FE'ASTFUL, *a.* Festive; joyful; as a *feastful* day or friend. *Milton.*

2. Sumptuous; luxurious; as *feastful* rites. *Pope.*

FE'ASTING, *ppr.* Eating luxuriously; faring sumptuously.

2. Delighting; gratifying.

3. Entertaining with a sumptuous table.

FE'ASTING, *n.* An entertainment.

FE'ASTRITE, *n.* Custom observed in entertainments. *Philips.*

FEAT, *n.* [Fr. *fait*; It. *fatto*; L. *factum*, from *facio*, to perform.]

1. An act; a deed; an exploit; as a bold *feat*; a noble *feat*; *feats* of prowess.

2. In *a subordinate sense*, any extraordinary act of strength, skill or cunning, as *feats* of horsemanship, or of dexterity; a trick.

FEAT, *a.* Ready; skilful; ingenious.

Never master had a page—so *feat*. *Obs. Shak.*

FEAT, *v. t.* To form; to fashion. *Obs. Shak.*

FE'ATEOUS, *a.* Neat; dextrous.

FE'ATEOUSLY, *adv.* Neatly; dextrously. *Obs. Spenser.*

FEATH'ER, } *n.* [Sax. *fether*; G. *feder*; D.
FETH'ER, } *veder*; Dan. *fiær*; Sw. *fieder*; allied probably to πτερον, and πεταλον, from πεταω, to open or expand. The most correct orthography is *fether.*]

1. A plume; a general name of the covering of fowls. The smaller fethers are used for the filling of beds; the larger ones, called quills, are used for ornaments of the head, for writing pens, &c. The fether consists of a shaft or stem, corneous, round, strong and hollow at the lower part, and at the upper part, filled with pith. On each side of the shaft are the vanes, broad on one side and narrow on

the other, consisting of thin lamins. The fethers which cover the body are called the *plumage*; the fethers of the wings are adapted to flight.

2. Kind; nature; species; from the proverbial phrase, "Birds of a *fether*," that is, of the same species. [*Unusual.*]

I am not of that *feather* to shake off
My friend, when he most needs me. *Shak.*

3. An ornament; an empty title.

4. On a horse, a sort of natural frizzling of the hair, which, in some places, rises above the lying hair, and there makes a figure resembling the tip of an ear of wheat. *Far. Dict.*

A fether in the cap, is an honor, or mark of distinction.

FEATH'ER, FETH'ER, *v. t.* To dress in fethers; to fit with fethers, or to cover with fethers.

2. To tread as a cock. *Dryden.*

3. To enrich; to adorn; to exalt.

The king cared not to plume his nobility and people, to *feather* himself. *Bacon.*

To fether one's nest, to collect wealth, particularly from emoluments derived from agencies for others; a proverb taken from birds which collect fethers for their nests.

FEATH'ER-BED, FETH'ER-BED, *n.* A bed filled with fethers; a soft bed.

FEATH'ER-DRIVER, FETH'ER-DRIVER, *n.* One who beats fethers to make them light or loose. *Derham.*

FEATH'ERED, FETH'ERED, *pp.* Covered with fethers; enriched.

2. *a.* Clothed or covered with fethers. A fowl or bird is a *fethered* animal.

Rise from the ground like *feathered* Mercury. *Shak.*

3. Fitted or furnished with fethers; as a *fethered* arrow.

4. Smoothed, like down or fethers. *Scott.*

5. Covered with things growing from the substance; as land *fethered* with trees. *Coxe.*

FEATH'EREDGE, FETH'EREDGE, *n.* An edge like a fether.

A board that has one edge thinner than the other, is called *featheredge* stuff. *Moxon.*

FEATH'EREDGED, FETH'EREDGED, *a.* Having a thin edge.

FEATH'ER-FEW, a corruption of *feverfew*.

FEATH'ER-GRASS, FETH'ER-GRASS, *n.* A plant, gramen plumosum. *Johnson.*

FEATH'ERLESS, FETH'ERLESS, *a.* Destitute of fethers; unfledged. *Howel.*

FEATH'ERLY, FETH'ERLY, *a.* Resembling fethers. [*Not used.*] *Brown.*

FEATH'ER-SELLER, FETH'ER-SELLER, *n.* One who sells fethers for beds.

FEATH'ERY, FETH'ERY, *a.* Clothed or covered with fethers. *Milton.*

2. Resembling fethers.

FE'ATLY, *adv.* [from *feat.*] Neatly; dextrously; adroitly. [*Little used.*] *Shak. Dryden.*

FE'ATNESS, *n.* [from *feat.*] Dexterity; adroitness; skilfulness. [*Little used.*]

FE'ATURE, *n.* [Norm. *faiture*; L. *factura*, a making, from *facio*, to make; It. *fattura.*]

1. The make, form or cast of any part of the face; any single lineament. We speak of large *features* or small *features*. We see a resemblance in the *features* of a parent and of a child.

2. The make or cast of the face.

Report the *feature* of Octavia, her years. *Shak.*

3. The fashion; the make; the whole turn or cast of the body.

4. The make or form of any part of the surface of a thing, as of a country or landscape.

5. Lineament; outline; prominent parts; as the *features* of a treaty.

FE'ATURED, *a.* Having features or good features; resembling in features. *Shak.*

FEAZE, *v. t.* To untwist the end of a rope. *Ainsworth.*

FEB'RIFACIENT, *a.* [L. *febris*, a fever, and *facio*, to make.] Causing fever. *Beddoes.*

FEB'RIFACIENT, *n.* That which produces fever. *Beddoes.*

FEBRIF'IC, *a.* [L. *febris*, fever, and *facio*, to make.] Producing fever; feverish.

FEB'RIFUGE, *n.* [L. *febris*, fever, and *fugo*, to drive away.]

Any medicine that mitigates or removes fever. *Encyc.*

FEB'RIFUGE, *a.* Having the quality of mitigating or subduing fever; antifebrile. *Arbuthnot.*

FE'BRILE, *a.* [Fr. from L. *febrilis*, from *febris*, fever.]

Pertaining to fever; indicating fever, or derived from it; as *febrile* symptoms; *febrile* action.

FEB'RUARY, *n.* [L. *Februarius*; Fr. *Fevrier*; It. *Febbraio*; Sp. *Febrero*; Arm. *Fevrer*; Port. *Fevereiro*; Ir. *Feabhra*; Russ. *Phebral*. The Latin word is said to be named from *februo*, to purify by sacrifice, and thus to signify the month of purification, as the people were, in this month, purified by sacrifices and oblations. The word *februo* is said to be a Sabine word, connected with *ferveo*, *ferbeo*, to boil, as boiling was used in purifications. *Varro. Ovid.*

This practice bears a resemblance to that of making atonement among the Jews; but the connection between *ferveo* and *February* is doubtful. The W. *çwevral*, February, Arm. *heuvrer*, Corn. *huevral*, is from W. *çwevyr*, violence; the severe month.]

The name of the second month in the year, introduced into the Roman calendar by Numa. In common years, this month contains 28 days; in the bissextile or leap year, 29 days.

FEBRUA'TION, *n.* Purification. [See *February.*] *Spenser.*

FE'CAL, *a.* [See *Fæces.*] Containing or consisting of dregs, lees, sediment or excrement.

FE'CES, *n. plu.* [L. *fæces.*] Dregs; lees; sediment; the matter which subsides in casks of liquor.

2. Excrement. *Arbuthnot.*

FE'CIAL, *a.* [L. *fecialis.*] Pertaining to heralds and the denunciation of war to an enemy; as *fecial* law. *Kent.*

FEC'ULA, *n.* The green matter of plants; chlorophyl. *Ure.*

2. Starch or farina; called also *amylaceous fecula*.

This term is applied to any pulverulent matter obtained from plants by simply breaking down the texture, washing with water, and subsidence. Hence its application to starch and the green fecula, though entirely different in chimical properties. *Cyc.*

FEC'ULENCE, FEC'ULENCY, *n.* [L. *fæculentia*, from *fæcula*, *fæces*, *fæx*, dregs.]

1. Muddiness; foulness; the quality of being foul with extraneous matter or lees.

2. Lees; sediment; dregs; or rather the substances mixed with liquor, or floating in it, which, when separated and lying at the bottom, are called lees, dregs or sediment. The refining or fining of liquor is the separation of it from its *feculencies*.

FEC'ULENT, *a.* Foul with extraneous or impure substances; muddy; thick; turbid; abounding with sediment or excrementitious matter.

FEC'ULUM, *n.* [from *fæces*, supra.] A dry, dusty, tasteless substance obtained from plants. *Fourcroy, Trans.*

[This should be *fecula*.]

FE'CUND, *a.* [L. *fæcundus*, from the root of *fœtus*.] Fruitful in children; prolific. *Graunt.*

FE'CUNDATE, *v. t.* To make fruitful or prolific.

2. To impregnate; as, the pollen of flowers *fecundates* the stigma. *Anacharsis, Trans.*

FE'CUNDATED, *pp.* Rendered prolific or fruitful; impregnated.

FE'CUNDATING, *ppr.* Rendering fruitful; impregnating.

FECUNDA'TION, *n.* The act of making fruitful or prolific; impregnation.

FECUND'IFY, *v. t.* To make fruitful; to fecundate. [*Little used.*]

FECUND'ITY, *n.* [L. *fæcunditas.*] Fruitfulness; the quality of producing fruit; particularly, the quality in female animals of producing young in great numbers.

2. The power of producing or bringing forth. It is said that the seeds of some plants retain their *fecundity* forty years. *Ray.*

3. Fertility; the power of bringing forth in abundance; richness of invention.

FED, *pret.* and *pp.* of *feed*, which see.

FED'ERAL, *a.* [from L. *fœdus*, a league, allied perhaps to Eng. *wed*, Sax. *weddian*, L. *vas*, *vadis*, *vador*, *vadimonium*. See Heb. Ch. Syr. עבט to pledge, Class Bd. No. 25.]

1. Pertaining to a league or contract; derived from an agreement or covenant between parties, particularly between nations.

The Romans, contrary to *federal* right, compelled them to part with Sardinia. *Grew.*

2. Consisting in a compact between parties, particularly and chiefly between states or nations; founded on alliance by contract or mutual agreement; as a *federal* government, such as that of the United States.

3. Friendly to the constitution of the United States. [See the Noun.]

FED'ERAL, FED'ERALIST, *n.* An appellation in America, given to the friends of the constitution of the United States, at its formation and adoption, and to the political party which favored the administration of President Washington.

FED'ERARY, } *n.* A partner; a confederate; an accomplice.
FED'ARY, }
[*Not used.*] *Shak.*

FED'ERATE, *a.* [L. *fœderatus.*] Leagued; united by compact, as sovereignties, states or nations; joined in confederacy; as *federate* nations or powers.

FEDERA'TION, *n.* The act of uniting in a league.

2. A league; a confederacy. *Burke.*

FED'ERATIVE, *a.* Uniting; joining in a league; forming a confederacy.

FE'DITY, *n.* [L. *fœditas.*] Turpitude; vileness. [*Not in use.*] *Hall.*

FEE, *n.* [Sax. *feo, feoh*; D. *vee*; G. *vieh*; Sw. *fä*; Dan. *fœ*; Scot. *fee, fey*, or *fie*, cattle; L. *pecu, pecus.* From the use of cattle in transferring property, or from barter and payments in cattle, the word came to signify money; it signified also goods, substance in general. The word belongs to Class Bg, but the primary sense is not obvious.]

1. A reward or compensation for services; recompense, either gratuitous, or established by law and claimed of right. It is applied particularly to the reward of professional services; as the *fees* of lawyers and physicians; the *fees* of office; clerk's *fees*; sheriff's *fees*; marriage *fees*, &c. Many of these are fixed by law; but gratuities to professional men are also called *fees*.

FEE, *n.* [This word is usually deduced from Sax. *feoh*, cattle, property, and *fee*, a reward. This is a mistake. *Fee*, in land, is a contraction of *feud* or *fief*, or from the same source; It. *fede*, Sp. *fe*, faith, trust. *Fee*, a reward, from *feoh*, is a Teutonic word; but *fee, feud, fief*, are words wholly unknown to the Teutonic nations, who use, as synonymous with them, the word, which, in English, is *loan.* This word, *fee*, in land, or an estate in trust, originated among the descendants of the northern conquerors of Italy, but it originated in the south of Europe. See *Feud.*]

Primarily, a loan of land, an estate in trust, granted by a prince or lord, to be held by the grantee on condition of personal service, or other condition; and if the grantee or tenant failed to perform the conditions, the land reverted to the lord or donor, called the *landlord*, or *lend-lord*, the lord of the loan. A fee then is any land or tenement held of a superior on certain conditions. It is synonymous with *fief* and *feud.* All the land in England, except the crown land, is of this kind. Fees are absolute or limited. An *absolute fee* or *fee-simple* is land which a man holds to himself and his heirs forever, who are called *tenants in fee simple.* Hence in modern times, the term *fee* or *fee simple* denotes an estate of inheritance; and in America, where lands are not generally held of a superior, a *fee* or *fee-simple* is an estate in which the owner has the whole property without any condition annexed to the tenure. A *limited fee* is an estate limited or clogged with certain conditions; as a *qualified* or *base fee*, which ceases with the existence of certain conditions; and a *conditional fee*, which is limited to particular heirs. *Blackstone. Encyc.*

In the U. States, an estate in *fee* or *fee-simple* is what is called in English law an allodial estate, an estate held by a person in his own right, and descendible to the heirs in general.

FEE'-FARM, *n.* [*fee* and *farm.*] A kind of tenure of estates without homage, fealty or other service, except that mentioned in the feoffment, which is usually the full rent. The nature of this tenure is, that if the rent is in arrear or unpaid for two years, the feoffor and his heirs may have an action for the recovery of the lands. *Encyc.*

FEE'-TAIL, *n.* An estate entailed; a conditional fee.

FEE, *v. t.* To pay a fee to; to reward. Hence,

2. To engage in one's service by advancing a fee or sum of money to; as, to *fee* a lawyer.

3. To hire; to bribe. *Shak.*

4. To keep in hire. *Shak.*

FEE'BLE, *a.* [Fr. *foible*; Sp. *feble*; Norm. *id.*; It. *fievole.* I know not the origin of the first syllable.]

1. Weak; destitute of much physical strength; as, infants are *feeble* at their birth.

2. Infirm; sickly; debilitated by disease.

3. Debilitated by age or decline of life.

4. Not full or loud; as a *feeble* voice or sound.

5. Wanting force or vigor; as *feeble* efforts.

6. Not bright or strong; faint; imperfect; as *feeble* light; *feeble* colors.

7. Not strong or vigorous; as *feeble* powers of mind.

8. Not vehement or rapid; slow; as *feeble* motion.

FEE'BLE, *v. t.* To weaken. [*Not used.* See *Enfeeble.*]

FEE'BLE-MINDED, *a.* Weak in mind; wanting firmness or constancy; irresolute.

Comfort the *feeble-minded.* 1 Thess. v.

FEE'BLENESS, *n.* Weakness of body or mind, from any cause; imbecility; infirmity; want of strength, physical or intellectual; as *feebleness* of the body or limbs; *feebleness* of the mind or understanding.

2. Want of fullness or loudness; as *feebleness* of voice.

3. Want of vigor or force; as *feebleness* of exertion, or of operation.

4. Defect of brightness; as *feebleness* of light or color.

FEE'BLY, *adv.* Weakly; without strength; as, to move *feebly.*

Thy gentle numbers *feebly* creep. *Dryden.*

FEED, *v. t.* pret. and pp. *fed.* [Sax. *fedan*; Dan. *föder*, Sw. *föda*, to feed and to beget; Goth. *fodyan*; D. *voeden*, to feed; G. *futter*, fodder; *füttern*, to feed; Norm. *foder*, to feed and to dig, uniting with *feed* the L. *fodio*; Ar. فطأ fata, to feed, and congressus fuit cum fæmina, sæpius concubuit. Class Bd. No. 14. See *Father.* In Russ. *petayu*, is to nourish; and in W. *buyd* is food, and *bwyta*, to eat; Arm. *boeta*; Ir. *fiadh*, food.]

1. To give food to; as, to *feed* an infant; to *feed* horses and oxen.

2. To supply with provisions. We have flour and meat enough to *feed* the army a month.

3. To supply; to furnish with any thing of which there is constant consumption, waste or use. Springs *feed* ponds, lakes and rivers; ponds and streams *feed* canals. Mills are *fed* from hoppers.

4. To graze; to cause to be cropped by feeding, as herbage by cattle. If grain is too forward in autumn, *feed* it with sheep.

Once in three years *feed* your mowing lands. *Mortimer.*

5. To nourish; to cherish; to supply with nutriment; as, to *feed* hope or expectation; to *feed* vanity.

6. To keep in hope or expectation; as, to *feed* one with hope.

7. To supply fuel; as, to *feed* a fire.

8. To delight; to supply with something desirable; to entertain; as, to *feed* the eye with the beauties of a landscape.

9. To give food or fodder for fattening; to fatten. The county of Hampshire, in Massachusetts, *feeds* a great number of cattle for slaughter.

10. To supply with food, and to lead, guard and protect; *a scriptural sense.*

He shall *feed* his flock like a shepherd. Is. xl.

FEED, *v. i.* To take food; to eat. *Shak.*

2. To subsist by eating; to prey. Some birds *feed* on seeds and berries, others on flesh.

3. To pasture; to graze; to place cattle to feed. Ex. xxii.

4. To grow fat. *Johnson.*

FEED, *n.* Food; that which is eaten; pasture; fodder; *applied to that which is eaten by beasts, not to the food of men.* The hills of our country furnish the best *feed* for sheep.

2. Meal, or act of eating.

For such pleasure till that hour
At *feed* or fountain never had I found. *Milton.*

FEE'DER, *n.* One that gives food, or supplies nourishment.

2. One who furnishes incentives; an encourager.

The *feeder* of my riots. *Shak.*

3. One that eats or subsists; as, small birds are *feeders* on grain or seeds.

4. One that fattens cattle for slaughter. *U. States.*

5. A fountain, stream or channel that supplies a main canal with water.

Feeder of a vein, in mining, a short cross vein. *Cyc.*

FEE'DING, *ppr.* Giving food or nutriment; furnishing provisions; eating; taking food or nourishment; grazing; supplying water or that which is constantly consumed; nourishing; supplying fuel or incentives.

FEE'DING, *n.* Rich pasture. *Drayton.*

FEEL, *v. t.* pret. and pp. *felt.* [Sax. *felan, fœlan, gefelan*; G. *fühlen*; D. *voelen*; allied probably to L. *palpo.* Qu. W. *pwyllaw*, to impel. The primary sense is to touch, to pat, to strike gently, or to press, as is evident from the L. *palpito*, and other derivatives of *palpo.* If so, the word seems to be allied to L. *pello.* See Class Bl. No. 8.]

1. To perceive by the touch; to have sensation excited by contact of a thing with the body or limbs.

Suffer me that I may *feel* the pillars. Judges xvi.

Come near, I pray thee, that I may *feel* thee, my son. Gen. xxvii.

2. To have the sense of; to suffer or enjoy; as, to *feel* pain; to *feel* pleasure.

3. To experience; to suffer.

Whoso keepeth the commandments shall *feel* no evil thing. Eccles. viii.

3. To be affected by; to perceive mentally; as, to *feel* grief or woe.

Would I had never trod this English earth,
Or *felt* the flatteries that grow upon it. *Shak.*

5. To know; to be acquainted with; to have a real and just view of.

For then, and not till then, he *felt* himself. *Shak.*

6. To touch; to handle; with or without *of*. *Feel* this piece of silk, or *feel of* it.

To feel, or *to feel out*, is to try; to sound; to search for; to explore; as, to *feel* or *feel out* one's opinions or designs.

To feel after, to search for; to seek to find; to seek as a person groping in the dark.

If haply they might *feel after* him, and find him. Acts xvii.

FEEL, *v. i.* To have perception by the touch, or by the contact of any substance with the body.

2. To have the sensibility or the passions moved or excited. The good man *feels* for the woes of others.

Man, who *feels* for all mankind. *Pope.*

3. To give perception; to excite sensation.

Blind men say black *feels* rough, and white *feels* smooth. *Dryden.*

So we say, a thing *feels* soft or hard, or it *feels* hot or cold.

4. To have perception mentally; as, to *feel* hurt; to *feel* grieved; to *feel* unwilling.

FEEL, *n.* The sense of feeling, or the perception caused by the touch. The difference of tumors may be ascertained by the *feel*. Argillaceous stones may sometimes be known by the *feel*. [In America, *feeling* is more generally used; but the use of *feel* is not uncommon.]

FEE'LER, *n.* One who feels.

2. One of the *palpi* of insects. The feelers of insects are usually four or six, and situated near the mouth. They are filiform and resemble articulated, movable antennæ. They are distinguished from antennæ or horns, by being short, naked and placed near the mouth. They are used in searching for food. *Encyc.*

This term is also applied to the *antennæ* or horns of insects. *Paley.*

FEE'LING, *ppr.* Perceiving by the touch; having perception.

2. *a.* Expressive of great sensibility; affecting; tending to excite the passions. He made a *feeling* representation of his wrongs. He spoke with *feeling* eloquence.

3. Possessing great sensibility; easily affected or moved; as a *feeling* man; a *feeling* heart.

4. Sensibly or deeply affected; as, I had a *feeling* sense of his favors. [*This use is not analogical, but common.*]

FEE'LING, *n.* The sense of touch; the sense by which we perceive external objects which come in contact with the body, and obtain ideas of their tangible qualities; one of the five senses. It is by *feeling* we know that a body is hard or soft, hot or cold, wet or dry, rough or smooth.

2. Sensation; the effect of perception.

The apprehension of the good
Gives but the greater *feeling* to the worse. *Shak.*

3. Faculty or power of perception; sensibility.

Their king, out of a princely *feeling*, was sparing and compassionate towards his subjects. *Bacon.*

4. Nice sensibility; as a man of *feeling*.

5. Excitement; emotion.

FEE'LINGLY, *adv.* With expression of great sensibility; tenderly; as, to speak *feelingly*.

2. So as to be sensibly felt.

These are counselors,
That *feelingly* persuade me what I am. *Shak.*

FEESE, *n.* A race. [*Not in use.*] *Barret.*

FEET, *n. plu.* of *foot.* [See *Foot.*]

FEE'TLESS, *a.* Destitute of feet; as *feetless* birds. *Camden.*

FEIGN, *v. t. fane.* [Fr. *feindre*; Sp. *fingir*; It. *fingere*, or *fignere*; L. *fingo*; D. *veinzen*; Arm. *feinta*, *fincha*. The Latin forms *fictum*, *fictus*, whence *figura*, *figure*. Hence it agrees with W. *fugiaw*, to feign or dissemble; *fug*, feint, disguise; also L. *fucus*.]

1. To invent or imagine; to form an idea or conception of something not real.

There are no such things done as thou sayest, but thou *feignest* them out of thine own heart. Neh. vi.

2. To make a show of; to pretend; to assume a false appearance; to counterfeit.

I pray thee, *feign* thyself to be a mourner. 2 Sam. xiv.

She *feigns* a laugh. *Pope.*

3. To represent falsely; to pretend; to form and relate a fictitious tale.

The poet
Did *feign* that Orpheus drew trees, stones, and floods. *Shak.*

4. To dissemble; to conceal. *Obs.* *Spenser.*

FEIGNED, *pp.* Invented; devised; imagined; assumed.

FEIGNEDLY, *adv.* In fiction; in pretense; not really. *Bacon.*

FEIGNEDNESS, *n.* Fiction; pretense; deceit. *Harmar.*

FEIGNER, *n.* One who feigns; an inventor; a deviser of fiction. *B. Jonson.*

FEIGNING, *ppr.* Imagining; inventing; pretending; making a false show.

FEIGNING, *n.* A false appearance; artful contrivance. *B. Jonson.*

FEIGNINGLY, *adv.* With false appearance.

FEINT, *n.* [Fr. *feinte*, from *feindre*.] An assumed or false appearance; a pretense of doing something not intended to be done.

Courtley's letter is but a *feint* to get off. *Spectator.*

2. A mock attack; an appearance of aiming at one part when another is intended to be struck. In fencing, a show of making a thrust at one part, to deceive an antagonist, when the intention is to strike another part. *Prior. Encyc.*

FEINT, *a.* or *pp.* Counterfeit; seeming. [*Not used.*] *Locke.*

FE'LANDERS, *n.* [See *Filanders.*] *Ainsworth.*

FELD'SPAR, FEL'SPAR, FELD'SPATH, FEL'SPATH, *n.* [G. *feld*, field, and *spar*. It is written by some authors *felspar*, which is *rock-spar*, or *fel* is a contraction of *feld*. *Spath* in German signifies *spar*.]

A mineral widely distributed and usually of a foliated structure. When in crystals or crystaline masses, it is very susceptible of mechanical division at natural joints. Its hardness is a little inferior to that of quartz. There are several varieties, as common feldspar, the adularia, the siliceous, the glassy, the ice-spar, the opalescent, aventurine feldspar, petuntze, the granular, and the compact. *Cleaveland.*

FELDSPATH'IC, *a.* Pertaining to feldspar, or consisting of it. *Journ. of Science.*

FELIC'ITATE, *v. t.* [Fr. *feliciter*; Sp. *felicitar*; It. *felicitare*; L. *felicito*, from *felix*, happy.]

1. To make very happy.

What a glorious entertainment and pleasure would fill and *felicitate* his spirit, if he could grasp all in a single survey. *Watts.*

More generally,

2. To congratulate; to express joy or pleasure to. We *felicitate* our friends on the acquisition of good, or an escape from evil.

FELIC'ITATE, *a.* Made very happy. *Shak.*

FELIC'ITATED, *pp.* Made very happy; congratulated.

FELIC'ITATING, *ppr.* Making very happy; congratulating.

FELICITA'TION, *n.* Congratulation. *Dict.*

FELIC'ITOUS, *a.* Very happy; prosperous; delightful. *Dict.*

FELIC'ITOUSLY, *adv.* Happily. *Dict.*

FELIC'ITY, *n.* [L. *felicitas*, from *felix*, happy.]

1. Happiness, or rather great happiness; blessedness; blissfulness; appropriately, the joys of heaven.

2. Prosperity; blessing; enjoyment of good.

The *felicities* of her wonderful reign may be complete. *Atterbury.*

Females—who confer on life its finest *felicities*. *Rawle.*

FE'LINE, *a.* [L. *felinus*, from *felis*, a cat. Qu. *fell*, fierce.]

Pertaining to cats, or to their species; like a cat; noting the cat kind or the genus Felis. We say, the *feline* race; *feline* rapacity.

FELL, *pret.* of *fall.*

FELL, *a.* [Sax. *fell*; D. *fel.*] Cruel; barbarous; inhuman.

It seemed fury, discord, madness *fell*. *Fairfax.*

2. Fierce; savage; ravenous; bloody.

More *fell* than tigers on the Libyan plain. *Pope.*

FELL, *n.* [Sax. *fell*; G. *id.*; D. *vel*; L. *pellis*; Fr. *peau*; probably from *peeling*.]

A skin or hide of a beast; used chiefly in composition, as *wool-fell*.

FELL, *n.* [G. *fels.*] A barren or stony hill. [*Local.*] *Gray.*

FELL, *v. t.* [D. *vellen*; G. *fällen*; Sw. *fälla*; Dan. *fælder*; probably from the root of *fall.*]

To cause to fall; to prostrate; to bring to the ground, either by cutting, as to *fell* trees, or by striking, as to *fell* an ox.

FELL'ED, *pp.* Knocked or cut down.

FELL'ER, *n.* One who hews or knocks down. Is. xiv.

FELLIF'LUOUS, *a.* [L. *fel*, gall, and *fluo*, to flow.] Flowing with gall. *Dict.*

FELL'ING, *ppr.* Cutting or beating to the ground.

FELL'MŎNGER, *n.* [*fell* and *monger.*] A dealer in hides.

FELL'NESS, *n.* [See *Fell*, cruel.] Cruelty; fierce barbarity; rage. *Spenser.*

FELL'OE. [See *Felly.*]

FEL'LŌW, *n.* [Sax. *felaw*; Scot. *falow.* Qu. from *follow.* More probably, Heb. טפל Ch. חפל to tie or connect, to be joined or associated. Class Bl. No. 46. 53.]

1. A companion; an associate.

> In youth I had twelve *fellows*, like myself. *Ascham.*
>
> Each on his *fellow* for assistance calls. *Dryden.*

2. One of the same kind.

> A shepherd had one favorite dog: he fed him with his own hand, and took more care of him than of his *fellows.* *L'Estrange.*

3. An equal.

> Awake, O sword, against my shepherd, and against the man that is my *fellow*, saith Jehovah of hosts. Zech. xiii.

4. One of a pair, or of two things used together and suited to each other. Of a pair of gloves, we call one the *fellow* of the other.

5. One equal or like another. Of an artist we say, this man has not his *fellow*, that is, one of like skill.

6. An appellation of contempt; a man without good breeding or worth; an ignoble man; as a mean *fellow.*

> Worth makes the man, and want of it the *fellow.* *Pope.*

7. A member of a college that shares its revenues; or a member of any incorporated society. *Johnson.*

8. A member of a corporation; a trustee. *U. States.*

FEL'LŌW, *v. t.* To suit with; to pair with; to match. [*Little used.*] *Shak.*

In composition, *fellow* denotes community of nature, station or employment.

FELLŌW-CIT'IZEN, *n.* A citizen of the same state or nation. Eph. ii.

FELLŌW-ƇOM'MONER, *n.* One who has the same right of common.

2. In Cambridge, England, one who dines with the fellows.

FELLŌW-ƇOUN'SELOR, *n.* An associate in council. *Shak.*

FELLŌW-ƇRE'ATURE, *n.* One of the same race or kind. Thus men are all called *fellow-creatures.* Watts uses the word for one made by the same creator. "Reason by which we are raised above our *fellow-creatures*, the brutes." *But the word is not now used in this sense.*

FELLŌW-FEE'LING, *n.* Sympathy; a like feeling.

2. Joint interest. [*Not in use.*]

FELLŌW-HEIR, *n.* A co-heir, or joint-heir; one entitled to a share of the same inheritance.

> That the Gentiles should be *fellow-heirs.* Eph. iii.

FELLŌW-HELP'ER, *n.* A co-adjutor; one who concurs or aids in the same business. 3 John 8.

FELLŌW-LA'BORER, *n.* One who labors in the same business or design.

FEL'LŌWLIKE, *a.* Like a companion; companionable; on equal terms. *Carew.*

FELLŌW-MA'IDEN, *n.* A maiden who is an associate. *Shak.*

FELLŌW-MEM'BER, *n.* A member of the same body.

FELLŌW-MIN'ISTER, *n.* One who officiates in the same ministry or calling. *Shak.*

FELLŌW-PEE'R, *n.* One who has the like privileges of nobility. *Shak.*

FELLŌW-PRIS'ONER, *n.* One imprisoned in the same place. Rom. xvi.

FELLŌW-RA'KE, *n.* An associate in vice and profligacy. *Armstrong.*

FELLŌW-SƇHOL'AR, *n.* An associate in studies. *Shak.*

FELLŌW-SERV'ANT, *n.* One who has the same master. *Milton.*

FEL'LŌWSHIP, *n.* Companionship; society; consort; mutual association of persons on equal and friendly terms; familiar intercourse.

> Have no *fellowship* with the unfruitful works of darkness. Eph. v.
>
> Men are made for society and mutual *fellowship.* *Calamy.*

2. Association; confederacy; combination.

> Most of the other christian princes were drawn into the *fellowship* of that war. [*Unusual.*] *Knolles.*

3. Partnership; joint interest; as *fellowship* in pain. *Milton.*

4. Company; a state of being together.

> The great contention of the sea and skies
> Parted our *fellowship.* *Shak.*

5. Frequency of intercourse.

> In a great town friends are scattered, so that there is not that *fellowship* which is in less neighborhoods. *Bacon.*

6. Fitness and fondness for festive entertainments; with *good* prefixed.

> He had by his *good fellowship*—made himself popular, with all the officers of the army. *Clarendon.*

7. Communion; intimate familiarity. 1 John i.

8. In *arithmetic*, the rule of proportions, by which the accounts of partners in business are adjusted, so that each partner may have a share of gain or sustain a share of loss, in proportion to his part of the stock.

9. An establishment in colleges, for the maintenance of a fellow.

FELLŌW-SO'LDIER, *n.* One who fights under the same commander, or is engaged in the same service. Officers often address their companions in arms by this appellation.

FELLŌW-STRE'AM, *n.* A stream in the vicinity. *Shenstone.*

FELLŌW-STU'DENT, *n.* One who studies in the same company or class with another, or who belongs to the same school.

FELLŌW-SUB'JEƇT, *n.* One who is subject to the same government with another. *Swift.*

FELLŌW-SUF'FERER, *n.* One who shares in the same evil, or partakes of the same sufferings with another.

FELLŌW-TRAV'ELER, *n.* One who travels in company with another.

FELLŌW-WRI'TER, *n.* One who writes at the same time. *Addison.*

FELLŌW-WŎRK'ER, *n.* One employed in the same occupation.

FEL'LY, *adv.* [See *Fell*, cruel.] Cruelly; fiercely; barbarously. *Spenser.*

FEL'LY, *n.* [Sax. *fælge*; Dan. *id.*; D. *velge*; G. *felge.*]

The exterior part or rim of a wheel, supported by the spokes.

Felo de se, in *law*, one who commits felony by suicide, or deliberately destroys his own life.

FEL'ON, *n.* [Fr. *felon*; Low L. *felo*; Arm. *fellon*; It. *fello* or *fellone*, a thief. I accord with Spelman in deducing this word from the root of *fail*, the original signification being, a vassal who *failed* in his fidelity or allegiance to his lord, and committed an offense by which he forfeited his feud. Hence in French, *felon* is traitorous, rebellious. So the word is explained and deduced in Gregoire's Armoric Dictionary. The derivation from *fee* and *lon* in Spelman, copied by Blackstone, is unnatural.]

1. In *law*, a person who has committed felony. [See *Felony.*]

2. A whitlow; a painful swelling formed in the periosteum at the end of the finger. *Wiseman.*

FEL'ON, *a.* Malignant; fierce; malicious; proceeding from a depraved heart.

> Vain shows of love to vail his *felon* hate. *Pope.*

2. Traitorous; disloyal.

FELO'NIOUS, *a.* Malignant; malicious; indicating or proceeding from a depraved heart or evil purpose; villainous; traitorous; perfidious; as a *felonious* deed.

2. In *law*, proceeding from an evil heart or purpose; done with the deliberate purpose to commit a crime; as *felonious* homicide.

FELO'NIOUSLY, *adv.* In a felonious manner; with the deliberate intention to commit a crime. Indictments for capital offenses must state the fact to be done *feloniously.*

FEL'ON-WŎRT, *n.* A plant of the genus Solanum. *Fam. of plants.*

FEL'ONY, *n.* [See *Felon.*] In *common law*, any crime which incurs the forfeiture of lands or goods. Treason was formerly comprised under the name of *felony*, but is now distinguished from crimes thus denominated, although it is really a felony. All offenses punishable with death are felonies; and so are some crimes not thus punished, as suicide, homicide by chance-medley, or in self-defense, and petty larceny. Capital punishment therefore does not necessarily enter into the true idea or definition of felony; the true criterion of felony being forfeiture of lands or goods. But the idea of felony has been so generally connected with that of capital punishment, that law and usage now confirm that connection. Thus if a statute makes any new offense a felony, it is understood to mean a crime punishable with death. *Blackstone.*

FEL'SITE, *n.* [See *Feldspar.*] A species of compact feldspar, of an azure blue or green color, found amorphous associated with quartz and mica. *Kirwan.*

FELT, *pret.* of *feel.*

FELT, *n.* [Sax. *felt*; G. *filz*; D. *vilt*; Fr. *feutre*, for *feultre*; Arm. *feltr*, or *feultr*; It. *feltro*. This may be derived naturally from the root of *fill* or *full*, to stuff and make thick, or from the root of L. *pellis*, Eng. *fell*, a skin, from plucking or stripping, L. *vello*, *vellus*, Eng. *wool*. In Ir. *folt*, W. *gwallt*, is hair.]

1. A cloth or stuff made of wool, or wool and hair, fulled or wrought into a compact substance by rolling and pressure with lees or size. *Encyc.*
2. A hat made of wool.
3. Skin.

To know whether sheep are sound or not, see that the *felt* be loose. *Mortimer.*

FELT, *v. t.* To make cloth or stuff of wool, or wool and hair, by fulling. *Hale.*

FELT'ER, *v. t.* To clot or meet together like felt. *Fairfax.*

FELT'MAKER, *n.* One whose occupation is to make felt.

FELUC'CA, *n.* [It. *feluca*; Fr. *felouque*; Sp. *faluca*.]

A boat or vessel, with oars and lateen sails, used in the Mediterranean. It has this peculiarity, that the helm may be applied to the head or stern, as occasion requires. *Mar. Dict. Encyc.*

FEL'WÖRT, *n.* A plant, a species of Gentian.

FE'MALE, *n.* [Fr. *femelle*; L. *femella*; Arm. *femell*; Fr. *femme*, woman. See *Feminine*.]

1. Among *animals*, one of that sex which conceives and brings forth young.
2. Among *plants*, that which produces fruit; that which bears the pistil and receives the pollen of the male flowers.

FE'MALE, *a.* Noting the sex which produces young; not male; as a *female* bee.

2. Pertaining to females; as a *female* hand or heart; *female* tenderness.

To the generous decision of a *female* mind, we owe the discovery of America. *Belknap.*

3. Feminine; soft; delicate; weak.

Female rhymes, double rhymes, so called from the French, in which language they end in *e* feminine.

FEMALE-FLOWER, *n.* In *botany*, a flower which is furnished with the pistil, pointal, or female organs.

FEMALE-PLANT, *n.* A plant which produces female flowers.

FEMALE-SCREW, *n.* A screw with grooves or channels.

FEME-CÖVERT, / **FEMME-CÖVERT,** } *n.* [Fr.] A married woman, who is under covert of her baron or husband.

FEME-SOLE, / **FEMME-SOLE,** } *n.* An unmarried woman.

Femme-sole merchant, a woman who uses a trade alone, or without her husband.

FEMINAL'ITY, *n.* The female nature. *Brown.*

FEM'INATE, *a.* Feminine. [*Not in use.*] *Ford.*

FEM'ININE, *a.* [Fr. *feminin*; L. *femininus*, from *femina*, woman. The first syllable may be and probably is from *wemb* or *womb*, by the use of *f* for *w*; the *b* not being radical. The last part of the word is probably from *man*, quasi, *femman*, womb-man.]

1. Pertaining to a woman, or to women, or to females; as the *female* sex.
2. Soft; tender; delicate.

Her heavenly form
Angelic, but more soft and *feminine*. *Milton.*

3. Effeminate; destitute of manly qualities. *Raleigh.*
4. In *grammar*, denoting the gender or words which signify females, or the terminations of such words. Words are said to be of the *feminine* gender, when they denote females, or have the terminations proper to express females in any given language. Thus in L. *dominus*, a lord, is masculine; but *domina*, is mistress, a female.

Milton uses *feminine* as a noun, for *female*.

FEMIN'ITY, *n.* The quality of the female sex. [*Not used.*] *Spenser.*

FEM'INIZE, *v. t.* To make womanish. [*Not used.*] *More.*

FEM'ORAL, *a.* [L. *femoralis*, from *femur*, the thigh.]

Belonging to the thigh; as the *femoral* artery.

FEN, *n.* [Sax. *fen* or *fenn*; D. *veen*; Arm. *fenna*, to overflow; W. *fynu*, to abound, to produce; hence L. *fons*, Eng. *fountain*.]

Low land overflowed, or covered wholly or partially with water, but producing sedge, coarse grasses, or other aquatic plants; boggy land; a moor or marsh.

A long canal the muddy *fen* divides. *Addison.*

FEN'-BERRY, *n.* A kind of blackberry. *Skinner.*

FEN'-BORN, *a.* Born or produced in a fen. *Milton.*

FEN'-CRESS, *n.* [Sax. *fen-cerse*.] Cress growing in fens.

FEN'-CRICKET, *n.* [*Gryllotalpa*.] An insect that digs for itself a little hole in the ground. *Johnson.*

FEN'-DUCK, *n.* A species of wild duck.

FEN'-FOWL, *n.* Any fowl that frequents fens.

FEN'-LAND, *n.* Marshy land.

FEN'-SUCKED, *a.* Sucked out of marshes; as *fen-sucked* fogs. *Shak.*

FENCE, *n. fens.* [See *Fend*.] A wall, hedge, ditch, bank, or line of posts and rails, or of boards or pickets, intended to confine beasts from straying, and to guard a field from being entered by cattle, or from other encroachment. A good farmer has good *fences* about his farm; an insufficient *fence* is evidence of bad management. Broken windows and poor *fences* are evidences of idleness or poverty or of both.

2. A guard; any thing to restrain entrance; that which defends from attack, approach or injury; security; defense.

A *fence* betwixt us and the victor's wrath. *Addison.*

3. Fencing, or the art of fencing; defense. *Shak.*
4. Skill in fencing or defense. *Shak.*

FENCE, *v. t. fens.* To inclose with a hedge, wall, or any thing that prevents the escape or entrance of cattle; to secure by an inclosure. In *New England*, farmers, for the most part, *fence* their lands with posts and rails, or with stone walls. In *England*, lands are usually *fenced* with hedges and ditches.

He hath *fenced* my way that I cannot pass. Job xix.

2. To guard; to fortify.

So much of adder's wisdom I have learnt,
To *fence* my ear against thy sorceries. *Milton.*

FENCE, *v. i.* To practice the art of fencing; to use a sword or foil, for the purpose of learning the art of attack and defense. To *fence* well is deemed a useful accomplishment for military gentlemen.

2. To fight and defend by giving and avoiding blows or thrusts.

They *fence* and push, and, pushing, loudly roar,
Their dewlaps and their sides are bathed in gore. *Dryden.*

3. To raise a fence; to guard. It is difficult to *fence* against unruly cattle.

FEN'CED, *pp.* Inclosed with a fence; guarded; fortified.

FENCEFUL, *a. fens'ful.* Affording defense. *Congreve.*

FENCELESS, *a. fens'less.* Without a fence; uninclosed; unguarded.

2. Open; not inclosed; as the *fenceless* ocean. *Rowe.*

FENCE-MÖNTH, *n.* The month in which hunting in any forest is prohibited. *Bullokar.*

FEN'CER, *n.* One who fences; one who teaches or practices the art of fencing with sword or foil. *Digby.*

FEN'CIBLE, *a.* Capable of defense. *Spenser. Addison.*

2. *n.* A soldier for defense of the country; as a regiment of *fencibles*.

FEN'CING, *ppr.* Inclosing with fence; guarding; fortifying.

FEN'CING, *n.* The art of using skilfully a sword or foil in attack or defense; an art taught in schools.

2. The materials of fences for farms. *N. England.*

FEN'CING-MASTER, *n.* One who teaches the art of attack and defense with sword or foil.

FEN'CING-SCHOOL, *n.* A school in which the art of fencing is taught.

FEND, *v. t.* [The root of *defend* and *offend*. The primary sense is to fall on, or to strike, to repel.]

To keep off; to prevent from entering; to ward off; to shut out.

With fern beneath to *fend* the bitter cold. *Dryden.*

It is usually followed by *off*; as, to *fend off* blows.

To fend off a boat or *vessel*, is to prevent its running against another, or against a wharf, &c., with too much violence.

FEND, *v. i.* To act in opposition; to resist; to parry; to shift off. *Locke.*

FEND'ED, *pp.* Kept off; warded off; shut out.

FEND'ER, *n.* That which defends; an utensil employed to hinder coals of fire from rolling forward to the floor.

2. A piece of timber or other thing hung over the side of a vessel to prevent it from striking or rubbing against a wharf, also to preserve a small vessel from being injured by a large one.

FEND'ING, *ppr.* Keeping or warding off.

FEN'ERATE, *v. i.* [L. *fœnero*.] To put to use; to lend on interest. [*Not used.*]

FENERA'TION, *n.* The act of lending on

use; or the interest or gain of that which is lent.

FENES'TRAL, *a.* [L. *fenestralis*, from *fenestra*, a window.] Pertaining to a window. *Nicholson.*

FEN'NEL, *n.* [Sax. *fenol*; G. *fenchel*; D. *venkel*; Sw. *fenkål*; Dan. *fennikel*; W. *fenigyl*; Fr. *fenouil*; Sp. *hinojo*; It. *finocchio*; Ir. *feneul*; L. *fœniculum*, from *fœnum*, hay.]

A fragrant plant of the genus *Anethum*, cultivated in gardens.

FEN'NEL-FLOWER, *n.* A plant of the genus Nigella.

FEN'NEL-GIANT, *n.* A plant of the genus Ferula.

FEN'NY, *a.* [from *fen.*] Boggy; marshy; moorish. *Moxon.*

2. Growing in fens; as *fenny* brake. *Prior.*

3. Inhabiting marshy ground; as a *fenny* snake. *Shak.*

FENNYSTONES, *n.* A plant.

FEN'OWED, *a.* Corrupted; decayed. [*Not in use.*]

FEN'UGREEK, *n.* [L. *fœnum græcum.*] A plant of the genus Trigonella.

FE'OD, *n.* A feud. So written by Blackstone and other authors; but more generally, *feud*, which see.

FE'ODAL, *a.* Feudal, which see.

FEODAL'ITY, *n.* Feudal tenures; the feudal system. *Burke.*

FE'ODARY, *n.* One who holds lands of a superior, on condition of suit and service. [*Little used.*] [See *Feudatory.*]

FEODATORY. [See *Feudatory.*]

FEOFF, *v. t. feff.* [Norm. *feffre*; Fr. *fieffer*, from *fief*. The first syllable is the It. *fede*, Sp. *fe*, contracted from *fides*, faith; the last syllable I am not able to trace.]

To invest with a fee or feud; to give or grant to one any corporeal hereditament. The compound *infeoff* is more generally used.

FEOFF, a fief. [See *Fief.*]

FEOFFEE, *n. feffee'.* A person who is infeoffed, that is, invested with a fee or corporeal hereditament.

FEOFFER, FEOFFOR, } *n. feff'er.* One who infeoffs or grants a fee.

FEOFFMENT, *n. feff'ment.* [Law L. *feoffamentum.*] The gift or grant of a fee or corporeal hereditament, as land, castles, honors, or other immovable thing; a grant in fee simple, to a man and his heirs forever. When in writing, it is called a *deed of feoffment*. The primary sense is the grant of a feud or an estate in trust. [See *Feud.*]

FERA'CIOUS, *a.* [L. *ferax*, from *fero*, to bear.] Fruitful; producing abundantly. *Thomson.*

FERAC'ITY, *n.* [L. *feracitas.*] Fruitfulness. [*Little used.*]

FE'RAL, *a.* [L. *feralis.*] Funereal; pertaining to funerals; mournful. *Burton.*

FERE, *n.* [Sax. *fera*, or *gefera*, with a prefix.] A fellow; a mate; a *peer*. *Obs.* *Chaucer.*

FER'ETORY, *n.* [L. *feretrum*, a bier.] A place in a church for a bier.

FE'RIAL, *a.* [L. *ferialis.*] Pertaining to holidays, or to common days. *Gregory.*

FERIA'TION, *n.* [L. *feriatio*, from *feriæ*, vacant days, holidays; G. *feier*, whence *feiern*, to rest from labor, to keep holiday, D. *vieren.*]

The act of keeping holiday; cessation from work. *Brown.*

FE'RINE, *a.* [L. *ferinus*, from *ferus*, wild, probably from the root of Sax. *faran*, to go, to wander, or a verb of the same family.]

Wild; untamed; savage. Lions, tigers, wolves and bears are *ferine* beasts. *Hale.*

FE'RINENESS, *n.* Wildness; savageness. *Hale.*

FER'ITY, *n.* [L. *feritas*, from *ferus*, wild.] Wildness; savageness; cruelty. *Woodward.*

FERM, *n.* A farm or rent; a lodging-house. *Obs.* [See *Farm.*]

FER'MENT, *n.* [L. *fermentum*, from *ferveo*, to boil. See *Fervent.*]

1. A gentle boiling; or the internal motion of the constituent parts of a fluid.

[In this sense it is rarely used. See *Fermentation.*]

2. Intestine motion; heat; tumult; agitation; as, to put the passions in a *ferment*; the state or people are in a *ferment*.

Subdue and cool the *ferment* of desire. *Rogers.*

3. That which causes fermentation, as yeast, barm, or fermenting beer.

FERMENT', *v. t.* [L. *fermento*; Fr. *fermenter*; Sp. *fermentar*; It. *fermentare.*]

To set in motion; to excite internal motion; to heat; to raise by intestine motion.

While youth *ferments* the blood. *Pope.*

FERMENT', *v. i.* To work; to effervesce; to be in motion, or to be excited into sensible internal motion, as the constituent particles of an animal or vegetable fluid. To the vinous fermentation we apply the term, *work*. We say that new cider, beer or wine *ferments* or works. But *work* is not applied to the other kinds of fermentation.

FERMENT'ABLE, *a.* Capable of fermentation; thus, cider, beer of all kinds, wine, and other vegetable liquors, are *fermentable*.

FERMENTA'TION, *n.* [L. *fermentatio.*] The sensible internal motion of the constituent particles of animal and vegetable substances, occasioned by a certain degree of heat and moisture, and accompanied by an extrication of gas and heat. Fermentation is followed by a change of properties in the substances fermented, arising from new combinations of their principles. It may be defined, in its most general sense, any spontaneous change which takes place in animal or vegetable substances, after life has ceased. It is of three kinds, *vinous*, *acetous* and *putrefactive*. The term is also applied to other processes, as the *panary* fermentation, or the raising of bread; but it is limited, by some authors, to the vinous and acetous fermentations, which terminate in the production of alcohol or vinegar. Fermentation differs from effervescence. The former is confined to animal and vegetable substances; the latter is applicable to mineral substances. The former is spontaneous; the latter produced by the mixture of bodies. *Encyc. Parr. Thomson.*

FERMENT'ATIVE, *a.* Causing or having power to cause fermentation; as *fermentative* heat.

2. Consisting in fermentation; as *fermentative* process.

FERMENT'ATIVENESS, *n.* The state of being fermentative.

FERMENT'ED, *pp.* Worked; having undergone the process of fermentation.

FERMENT'ING, *ppr.* Working; effervescing.

FERN, *n.* [Sax. *fearn*; G. *farn-kraut*; D. *vaaren.*]

A plant of several species constituting the tribe or family of Filices, which have their fructification on the back of the fronds or leaves, or in which the flowers are borne on footstalks which overtop the leaves. The stem is the common footstalk or rather the middle rib of the leaves, so that most ferns want the stem altogether. The ferns constitute the first order of cryptogams, in the sexual system. *Milne. Encyc.*

FERN-OWL, *n.* The goatsucker.

FERN'Y, *a.* Abounding or overgrown with fern. *Barret.*

FERO'CIOUS, *a.* [Fr. *feroce*; Sp. *feroz*; It. *feroce*; L. *ferox*; allied to *ferus*, wild, *fera*, a wild animal.]

1. Fierce; savage; wild; indicating cruelty; as a *ferocious* look, countenance or features.

2. Ravenous; rapacious; as a *ferocious* lion.

3. Fierce; barbarous; cruel; as *ferocious* savages.

FERO'CIOUSLY, *adv.* Fiercely; with savage cruelty.

FERO'CIOUSNESS, *n.* Savage fierceness; cruelty; ferocity.

FEROC'ITY, *n.* [L. *ferocitas.*] Savage wildness or fierceness; fury; cruelty; as the *ferocity* of barbarians.

2. Fierceness indicating a savage heart; as *ferocity* of countenance.

FER'REOUS, *a.* [L. *ferreus*, from *ferrum*, iron, Fr. *fer*, Sp. *hierro*, from the Celtic; W. *fer*, solid; *feru*, to concrete.]

Partaking of iron; pertaining to iron; like iron; made of iron. *Brown.*

FER'RET, *n.* [D. *vret*; Fr. *furet*; G. *frett*, or *frettchen*, or *frettwiesel*; W. *fured*; Ir. *firead*; Sp. *huron*; It. *furetto*. *Fur* in W. is subtil, penetrating, cunning.]

1. An animal of the genus Mustela, or Weasel kind, about 14 inches in length, of a pale yellow color with red eyes. It is a native of Africa, but has been introduced into Europe. It cannot however bear cold, and cannot subsist even in France, except in a domestic state. Ferrets are used to catch rabbits. *Encyc.*

2. A kind of narrow woolen tape.

3. Among *glass makers*, the iron used to try the melted matter, to see if it is fit to work, and to make the rings at the mouths of bottles. *Encyc.*

FER'RET, *v. t.* To drive out of a lurking place, as a ferret does the coney. *Johnson. Heylin.*

FER'RETED, *pp.* Driven from a burrow or lurking place.

FER'RETER, *n.* One that hunts another in his private retreat.

FER'RETING, *ppr.* Driving from a lurking place.

FER'RIAGE, *n.* [See *Ferry.*] The price or fare to be paid at a ferry; the compensation established or paid for conveyance over a river or lake in a boat.

FER'RIC, *a.* Pertaining to or extracted from iron. *Ferric* acid is the acid of iron saturated with oxygen. *Lavoisier.*

FERRI-CAL'CITE, *n.* [L. *ferrum*, iron, and *calx*, lime.]
A species of calcarious earth or limestone combined with a large portion of iron, from 7 to 14 per cent. *Kirwan.*

FERRIF'EROUS, *a.* [L. *ferrum* and *fero.*] Producing or yielding iron. *Phillips.*

FER'RILITE, *n.* [L. *ferrum*, iron, and Gr. λιθος, a stone.]
Rowley ragg; a variety of trap, containing iron in the state of oxyd. *Kirwan.*

FERRO-CY'ANATE, *n.* A compound of the ferro-cyanic acid with a base.

FERRO-CYAN'IC, *a.* [L. *ferrum*, iron, and *cyanic*, which see.] The same as *ferro-prussic.*

FERRO-PRUS'SIATE, *n.* A compound of the ferro-prussic acid with a base.

FERRO-PRUS'SIC, *a.* [L. *ferrum*, iron, and *prussic.*] Designating a peculiar acid, formed of prussic acid and protoxyd of iron. *Coxe.*

FERRO-SIL'ICATE, *n.* A compound of ferro-silicic acid with a base, forming a substance analogous to a salt.

FERRO-SILIC'IC, *a.* [L. *ferrum*, iron, and *silex.*] Designating a compound of iron and silex.

FERRU'GINATED, *a.* [infra.] Having the color or properties of the rust of iron.

FERRU'GINOUS, *a.* [L. *ferrugo*, rust of iron, from *ferrum*, iron.]
1. Partaking of iron; containing particles of iron.
2. Of the color of the rust or oxyd of iron. [*Ferrugineous* is less used.]

FER'RULE, *n.* [Sp. *birola*, a ring or cap for a cane.]
A ring of metal put round a cane or other thing to strengthen it.

FER'RY, *v. t.* [Sax. *feran, ferian; G. führen;* Gr. φερω; L. *fero;* allied to *bear*, and more nearly to Sax. *faran*, to pass. See *Bear* and *Fare*, and Class Br. No. 33. 35.]
To carry or transport over a river, strait or other water, in a boat. We *ferry* men, horses, carriages, over rivers, for a moderate fee or price called *fare* or *ferriage.*

FER'RY, *v. i.* To pass over water in a boat. *Milton.*

FER'RY, *n.* A boat or small vessel in which passengers and goods are conveyed over rivers or other narrow waters; sometimes called a *wherry. This application of the word is, I believe, entirely obsolete, at least in America.*
2. The place or passage where boats pass over water to convey passengers.
3. The right of transporting passengers over a lake or stream. A. B. owns the *ferry* at Windsor. [*In New England, this word is used in the two latter senses.*]

FER'RYBOAT, *n.* A boat for conveying passengers over streams and other narrow waters.

FER'RYMAN, *n.* One who keeps a ferry, and transports passengers over a river.

FER'TILE, *a.* [Fr. *fertile;* Sp. *fertil;* It. *fertile;* L. *fertilis*, from *fero*, to bear.]
1. Fruitful; rich; producing fruit in abundance; as *fertile* land, ground, soil, fields or meadows. This word in America is rarely applied to trees, or to animals, but to land. It formerly had *of* before the thing produced; as *fertile of* all kinds of grain: but *in* is now used; *fertile in* grain.
2. Rich; having abundant resources; prolific; productive; inventive; able to produce abundantly; as a *fertile* genius, mind or imagination.

FER'TILENESS, *n.* [See *Fertility.*]

FERTIL'ITY, *n.* [L. *fertilitas.*] Fruitfulness; the quality of producing fruit in abundance; as the *fertility* of land, ground, soil, fields and meadows.
2. Richness; abundant resources; fertile invention; as the *fertility* of genius, of fancy or imagination.

FER'TILIZE, *v. t.* To enrich; to supply with the pabulum of plants; to make fruitful or productive; as, to *fertilize* land, soil, ground and meadows. [*Fertilitate* is not used.]

FER'TILIZED, *pp.* Enriched; rendered fruitful.

FER'TILIZING, *ppr.* Enriching; making fruitful or productive. The Connecticut overflows the adjacent meadows, *fertilizing* them by depositing fine particles of earth or vegetable substances.
2. *a.* Enriching; furnishing the nutriment of plants.

FERULA'CEOUS, *a.* [L. *ferula.*] Pertaining to reeds or canes; having a stalk like a reed; or resembling the Ferula, as *ferulaceous* plants. *Fourcroy.*

FER'ULE, *n.* [L. *ferula*, from *ferio*, to strike, or from the use of stalks of the Ferula.]
1. A little wooden pallet or slice, used to punish children in school, by striking them on the palm of the hand. [*Ferular* is not used.]
2. Under the Eastern empire, the *ferula* was the emperor's scepter. It was a long stem or shank, with a flat square head. *Encyc.*

FER'ULE, *v. t.* To punish with a ferule.

FERV'ENCY; *n.* [See *Fervent.*] Heat of mind; ardor; eagerness. *Shak.*
2. Pious ardor; animated zeal; warmth of devotion.

When you pray, let it be with attention, with *fervency*, and with perseverance. *Wake.*

FERV'ENT, *a.* [L. *fervens*, from *ferveo*, to be hot, to boil, to glow; Ar. فار to boil, to swell with heat, to ferment. Class Br. No. 30. *Ferveo* gives the Spanish *hervir*, to boil, to swarm as bees, whose motions resemble the boiling of water.]
1. Hot; boiling; as a *fervent* summer; *fervent* blood. *Spenser. Wotton.*
2. Hot in temper; vehement.

They are *fervent* to dispute. *Hooker.*

3. Ardent; very warm; earnest; excited; animated; glowing; as *fervent* zeal; *fervent* piety.

Fervent in spirit. Rom. xii.

FERV'ENTLY, *adv.* Earnestly; eagerly; vehemently; with great warmth.
2. With pious ardor; with earnest zeal; ardently.

Epaphras—saluteth you, laboring *fervently* for you in prayers. Col. iv.

FERV'ID, *a.* [L. *fervidus.*] Very hot; burning; boiling; as *fervid* heat.
2. Very warm in zeal; vehement; eager; earnest; as *fervid* zeal.

FERV'IDLY, *adv.* Very hotly; with glowing warmth.

FERV'IDNESS, *n.* Glowing heat; ardor of mind; warm zeal. *Bentley.*

FERV'OR, *n.* [L. *fervor.*] Heat or warmth; as the *fervor* of a summer's day.
2. Heat of mind; ardor; warm or animated zeal and earnestness in the duties of religion, particularly in prayer.

FES'CENNINE, *a.* Pertaining to Fescennium in Italy; licentious. *Kennet.*

FES'CENNINE, *n.* A nuptial song, or a licentious song. *Cartwright.*

FES'CUE, *n.* [Fr. *fétu*, for *festu*, a straw; L. *festuca*, a shoot or stalk of a tree, a rod.]
A small wire used to point out letters to children when learning to read. *Dryden. Holder.*

FES'CUE-GRASS, *n.* The Festuca, a genus of grasses. *Lee.*

FE'SELS, *n.* A kind of base grain. *May.*

FESSE, *n. fess.* [L. *fascia*, a band.] In *heraldry*, a band or girdle, possessing the third part of the escutcheon; one of the nine honorable ordinaries. *Peacham. Encyc.*

FESSE-POINT, *n.* The exact center of the escutcheon. *Encyc.*

FES'TAL, *a.* [L. *festus*, festive. See *Feast.*] Pertaining to a feast; joyous; gay; mirthful. *Chesterfield.*

FES'TER, *v. i.* [Qu. L. *pestis, pus*, or *pustula.*]
To rankle; to corrupt; to grow virulent. We say of a sore or wound, it *festers.*

Passion and unkindness may give a wound that shall bleed and smart; but it is treachery that makes it *fester.* *South.*

FES'TERING, *ppr.* Rankling; growing virulent.

FES'TINATE, *a.* [L. *festino, festinatus.*] Hasty; hurried. [*Not in use.*] *Shak.*

FESTINA'TION, *n.* Haste. [*Not used.*]

FES'TIVAL, *a.* [L. *festivus*, from *festus*, or *festum*, or *fasti.* See *Feast.*]
Pertaining to a feast; joyous; mirthful; as a *festival* entertainment. *Atterbury.*

FES'TIVAL, *n.* The time of feasting; an anniversary day of joy, civil or religious.

The morning trumpets *festival* proclaimed. *Milton.*

FES'TIVE, *a.* [L. *festivus.*] Pertaining to or becoming a feast; joyous; gay; mirthful.

The glad circle round them yield their souls
To *festive* mirth and wit that knows no gall. *Thomson.*

FESTIV'ITY, *n.* [L. *festivitas.*] Primarily, the mirth of a feast; hence, joyfulness; gayety; social joy or exhilaration of spirits at an entertainment. *Taylor.*
2. A festival. [*Not in use.*] *Brown.*

FESTOON', *n.* [Fr. *feston;* Sp. *id.;* It. *festone;* probably a tie, from the root of *fast*, W. *fest.*]
Something in imitation of a garland or wreath. In *architecture* and *sculpture*, an ornament of carved work in the form of a wreath of flowers, fruits and leaves intermixed or twisted together. It is in the form of a string or collar, somewhat largest in the middle, where it falls down in an arch, being suspended by the ends, the

extremities of which hang down perpendicularly. *Harris. Encyc.*

FES'TUCINE, *a.* [L. *festuca.*] Being of a straw-color. *Brown.*

FES'TUCOUS, *a.* Formed of straw. *Brown.*

FET, *n.* [Fr. *fait.*] A piece. [*Not used.*]

FET, *v. t.* or *i.* To fetch; to come to. [*Not used.*] *Tusser. Sackville.*

FE'TAL, *a.* [from *fetus.*] Pertaining to a fetus.

FETCH, *v. t.* [Sax. *feccan*, or *feccean.* I have not found this word in any other language. *Fet, fettan*, must be a different word or a corruption.]

1. To go and bring, or simply to bring, that is, to bear a thing *towards* or *to* a person.

We will take men to *fetch* victuals for the people. Judges xx.

Go to the flock, and *fetch* me from thence two kids of the goats. Gen. xxvii.

In the latter passage, *fetch* signifies only to *bring.*

2. To derive; to draw, as from a source.

——On you noblest English,
Whose blood is *fetched* from fathers of war-proof. *Shak.*

[*In this sense, the use is neither common nor elegant.*]

3. To strike at a distance. [*Not used.*]

The conditions and improvements of weapons are the *fetching* afar off. *Bacon.*

4. To bring back; to recall; to bring to any state. [*Not used or vulgar.*]

In smells we see their great and sudden effect in *fetching* men again, when they swoon. *Bacon.*

5. To bring or draw; as, to *fetch* a thing within a certain compass.

6. To make; to perform; as, to *fetch* a turn; to *fetch* a leap or bound. *Shak.*

Fetch a compass behind them. 2 Sam. v.

7. To draw; to heave; as, to *fetch* a sigh. *Addison.*

8. To reach; to attain or come to; to arrive at.

We *fetched* the syren's isle. *Chapman.*

9. To bring; to obtain as its price. Wheat *fetches* only 75 cents the bushel. A commodity is worth what it will *fetch.*

To fetch out, to bring or draw out; to cause to appear.

To fetch to, to restore; to revive, as from a swoon.

To fetch up, to bring up; to cause to come up or forth.

To fetch a pump, to pour water into it to make it draw water. *Mar. Dict.*

FETCH, *v. i.* To move or turn; as, to *fetch* about. *Shak.*

FETCH, *n.* A stratagem, by which a thing is indirectly brought to pass, or by which one thing seems intended and another is done; a trick; an artifice; as a *fetch* of wit. *Shak.*

Straight cast about to over-reach
Th' unwary conqueror with a *fetch.* *Hudibras.*

FETCH'ER, *n.* One that brings.

FETCH'ING, *ppr.* Bringing; going and bringing; deriving; drawing; making; reaching; obtaining as price.

FET'ICHISM, } *n.* The worship of idols
FET'ICISM, } among the negroes of Africa, among whom *fetich* is an idol, any tree, stone or other thing worshipped.

FET'ID, *a.* [L. *fœtidus*, from *fœteo*, to have an ill scent.]

Having an offensive smell; having a strong or rancid scent.

Most putrefactions smell either *fetid* or moldy. *Bacon.*

FET'IDNESS, *n.* The quality of smelling offensively; a fetid quality.

FETIF'EROUS, *a.* [L. *fœtifer; fœtus* and *fero*, to bear.] Producing young, as animals.

FET'LOCK, *n.* [*foot* or *feet* and *lock.*] A tuft of hair growing behind the pastern joint of many horses. Horses of low size have scarce any such tuft. *Far. Dict.*

FE'TOR, *n.* [L. *fœtor.*] Any strong offensive smell; stench. *Arbuthnot.*

FET'TER, *n.* [Sax. *fetor*, from *foot, feet*, as in L. *pedica;* G. *fessel.* Chiefly used in the plural, *fetters.*]

1. A chain for the feet; a chain by which an animal is confined by the foot, either made fast or fixed, as a prisoner, or impeded in motion and hindered from leaping, as a horse whose fore and hind feet are confined by a chain.

The Philistines bound Samson with *fetters* of brass. Judges xvi.

2. Any thing that confines or restrains from motion.

Passions too fierce to be in *fetters* bound. *Dryden.*

FET'TER, *v. t.* To put on fetters; to shackle or confine the feet with a chain.

2. To bind; to enchain; to confine; to restrain motion; to impose restraints on.

Fetter strong madness in a silken thread. *Shak.*

FET'TERED, *pp.* Bound or confined by fetters; enchained. *Marston.*

FET'TERING, *ppr.* Binding or fastening by the feet with a chain; confining; restraining motion.

FET'TERLESS, *a.* Free from fetters or restraint. *Marston.*

FETT'STEIN, *n.* [Ger. fat-stone.] A mineral of a greenish or bluish gray color or flesh red, called also elaolite. *Aikin. Jameson.*

FE'TUS, *n.* plu. *fetuses.* [L. *fœtus.*] The young of viviparous animals in the womb, and of oviparous animals in the egg, after it is perfectly formed; before which time it is called *embryo.* A young animal then is called a *fetus* from the time its parts are distinctly formed, till its birth. *Encyc.*

Feu de joie, fire of joy, a French phrase for a bonfire, or a firing of guns in token of joy.

FEUD, *n.* [Sax. *fæhth*, or *fægth*, from *figan, feon*, to hate. Hence also *fah*, a foe, and from the participle, *feond*, a fiend; D. *vyand*, G. *feind*, an enemy; G. *fehde*, war, quarrel; Sw. *fegd;* Dan. *fejde.* In Irish, *fuath* is hatred, abhorrence. Class Bg.]

1. Primarily, a deadly quarrel; hatred and contention that was to be terminated only by death. Among our rude ancestors, these quarrels, though originating in the murder of an individual, involved the whole tribe or family of the injured and of the aggressing parties. Hence in modern usage,

2. A contention or quarrel; particularly, an inveterate quarrel between families or parties in a state; the discord and animosities which prevail among the citizens of a state or city, sometimes accompanied with civil war. In the north of Great Britain, the word is still used in its original sense; denoting a combination of kindred to revenge the death of any of their blood, on the offender and all his race, or any other great enemy. We say, it is the policy of our enemies to raise and cherish intestine *feuds.*

The word is not strictly applicable to wars between different nations, but to intestine wars, and to quarrels and animosities between families or small tribes.

FEUD, *n.* [Usually supposed to be composed of the Teutonic *fee*, goods, reward, and *ead* or *odh*, W. *eizaw*, possession, property. But if feuds had been given as rewards for services, that consideration would have vested the *title* to the land in the donee. Yet *feud* is not a Teutonic or Gothic word, being found among none of the northern nations of Europe. This word originated in the south of Europe, whether in France, Spain or Italy, may perhaps be ascertained by writings of the middle ages, which I do not possess. It probably originated among the Franks, or in Lombardy or Italy, and certainly among men who studied the civil law. In Italian, a feoffee is called *fede-commessario*, a trust-commissary; *fede-commesso*, is a feoffment, a trust-estate; Sp. *fideicomiso*, a feoffment. These words are the *fidei-commissarius, fidei-commissum*, of the Digest and Codex. In Spanish *fiado* signifies security given for another or bail; *al fiado*, on trust; *fiador*, one who trusts; *feudo*, a fief, fee or feud; Port. *id.* In Norman, *fidz* de chevalers signifies knight's fees. *Feud*, then, and *fee*, which is a contraction of it, is a word formed from the L. *fides*, It. *fede*, Sp. *fe*, Norm. *fei*, faith, trust, with *had*, state, or *ead* or *odh*, estate; and a *feud* is an estate in trust, or on condition, which coincides nearly in sense with the northern word, G. *lehen*, D. *leen*, Sw. *lån*, Dan. *lehn*, Eng. *loan.* From the origin of this word, we see the peculiar propriety of calling the donee *fidelis*, and his obligation to his lord *fidelitas*, whence *fealty.*]

A fief; a fee; a right to lands or hereditaments held in trust, or on the terms of performing certain conditions; the right which a vassal or tenant has to the lands or other immovable thing of his lord, to use the same and take the profits thereof hereditarily, rendering to his superior such duties and services as belong to military tenure, &c., the property of the soil always remaining in the lord or superior.

From the foregoing explanation of the origin of the word, result very naturally the definition of the term, and the doctrine of forfeiture, upon non-performance of the conditions of the trust or loan.

FEU'DAL, *a.* [Sp. *feudal.*] Pertaining to feuds, fiefs or fees; as *feudal* rights or services; *feudal* tenures.

2. Consisting of feuds or fiefs; embracing tenures by military services; as the *feudal* system.

FEUDAL'ITY, *n.* The state or quality of being feudal; feudal form or constitution. *Burke.*

FEU'DALISM, *n.* The feudal system; the principles and constitution of feuds, or lands held by military services. *Whitaker.*

FEU'DARY, *a.* Holding land of a superior.

FEU'DATARY, *n.* A feudatory, which see.

FEU'DATORY, *n.* [Sp. *feudatorio;* Port. *feudatario.*]
A tenant or vassal who holds his lands of a superior, on condition of military service; the tenant of a feud or fief. *Blackstone. Encyc.*

FEU'DIST, *n.* A writer on feuds. *Spelman.*

FEUILLAGE, *n.* [Fr. foliage.] A bunch or row of leaves. *Jervas.*

FEUILLEMORT, *n.* [Fr. dead leaf.] The color of a faded leaf.

FEU'TER, *v. t.* To make ready. [*Not in use.*] *Spenser.*

FEU'TERER, *n.* A dog keeper. [*Not used.*] *Massenger.*

FE'VER, *n.* [Fr. *fievre;* Sp. *fiebre;* It. *febbre;* L. *febris*, supposed to be so written by transposition for *ferbis*, or *fervis*, from *ferbeo, ferveo*, to be hot, Ar. فار Class Br. No. 30.]
1. A disease, characterized by an accelerated pulse, with increase of heat, impaired functions, diminished strength, and often with preternatural thirst This order of diseases is called by Cullen *pyrexy*, Gr. *πυρεξια*. Fevers are often or generally preceded by chills or rigors, called the cold stage of the disease. Fevers are of various kinds; but the principal division of fevers is into *remitting* fevers, which subside or abate at intervals; *intermitting* fevers, which intermit or entirely cease at intervals; and *continued* or *continual* fevers, which neither remit nor intermit.
2. Heat; agitation; excitement by any thing that strongly affects the passions. This news has given me a *fever.* This quarrel has set my blood in a *fever.*

FE'VER, *v. t.* To put in a fever. *Dryden.*

FE'VER-COOLING, *a.* Allaying febrile heat. *Thomson.*

FE'VERET, *n.* A slight fever. [*Not used.*] *Ayliffe.*

FE'VERFEW, *n.* [Sax. *feferfuge;* L. *febris* and *fugo.*]
A plant, or rather a genus of plants, the Matricaria, so named from supposed febrifuge qualities. The common feverfew grows to the highth of two or three feet, with compound leaves and compound radiated white flowers, with a yellow disk.

FE'VERISH, *a.* Having a slight fever; as the patient is *feverish.*
2. Diseased with fever or heat; as *feverish* nature. *Creech.*
3. Uncertain; inconstant; fickle; now hot, now cold.

> We toss and turn about our *feverish* will. *Dryden.*

4. Hot; sultry; burning; as the *feverish* north. *Dryden.*

FE'VERISHNESS, *n.* The state of being feverish; a slight febrile affection.

FE'VEROUS, *a.* Affected with fever or ague. *Shak.*
2. Having the nature of fever.

> All *feverous* kinds. *Milton.*

3. Having a tendency to produce fever; as a *feverous* disposition of the year. [*This word is little used.*] *Bacon.*

FE'VER-ROOT, *n.* A plant of the genus Triosteum.

FE'VER-SICK, *a.* [Sax. *fefer-seoc.*] Diseased with fever. *Peele.*

FE'VER-WEAKENED, *a.* Debilitated by fever.

FE'VER-WEED, *n.* A plant of the genus Eryngium.

FE'VER-WORT, *n.* [See *Fever-root.*]

FE'VERY, *a.* Affected with fever. *B. Jonson.*

FEW, *a.* [Sax. *fea*, or *feawa;* Dan. *faye;* Fr. *peu;* Sp. and It. *poco;* L. *pauci.* The senses of *few* and *small* are often united. Class Bg.]
Not many; small in number. Party is the madness of many for the gain of a *few;* but *few* men, in times of party, regard the maxim.

FEW'EL, *n.* Combustible matter. [See *Fuel.*]

FEW'NESS, *n.* Smallness of number; paucity. *Dryden.*
2. Paucity of words; brevity. [*Not used.*] *Shak.*

FI'ANCE, *v. t.* To betroth. [See *Affiance.*]

FI'AT. [L. from *fio.*] Let it be done; a decree; a command to do something.

FIB, *n.* [See *Fable.* Ir. *meabhra.*] A lie or falsehood; a word used among children and the vulgar, as a softer expression than *lie.*

FIB, *v. i.* To lie; to speak falsely.

FIB'BER, *n.* One who tells lies or fibs.

FIB'BING, *ppr.* Telling fibs; as a noun, the telling of fibs.

FI'BER, *n.* [Fr. *fibre;* L. *fibra;* Sp. *hebra, fibra;* It. *fibra.*]
A thread; a fine, slender body which constitutes a part of the frame of animals. Of fibers, some are soft and flexible; others more hard and elastic. Those that are soft are hollow, or spungy and full of little cells, as the nervous and fleshy. Some are so small as scarcely to be visible; others are larger and appear to be composed of still smaller fibers. These fibers constitute the substance of the bones, cartilages, ligaments, membranes, nerves, veins, arteries, and muscles. *Quincy.*
2. A filament or slender thread in plants or minerals; the small slender root of a plant.
3. Any fine, slender thread.

FI'BRIL, *n.* [Fr. *fibrille.*] A small fiber; the branch of a fiber; a very slender thread. *Cheyne.*

FI'BRIN, *n.* [See *Fiber.*] A peculiar organic compound substance found in animals and vegetables. It is a soft solid, of a greasy appearance, which softens in air, becoming viscid, brown and semi-transparent, but is insoluble in water. It is the chief constituent of muscular flesh. *Ure.*

FIB'ROLITE, *n.* [from L. *fibra*, and Gr. *λιθος.*] A mineral that occurs with corundum, of a white or gray color, composed of minute fibres, some of which appear to be rhomboidal prisms. *Cleaveland.*

FI'BROUS, *a.* Composed or consisting of fibers; as a *fibrous* body or substance.
2. Containing fibers. In mineralogy, a *fibrous* fracture, is that which presents fine threads or slender lines, either straight or curved, parallel, diverging, or stellated, like the rays of a star. *Kirwan.*

FIB'ULA, *n.* [L.] The outer and lesser bone of the leg, much smaller than the tibia. *Quincy.*
2. A clasp or buckle.

FICK'LE, *a.* [Sax. *ficol;* but it seems to be connected with *wicelian*, Sw. *vackla*, to waver, from the root of *wag;* L. *vacillo;* Gr. *ποικιλος;* Heb. Ch. Syr. פוג to fail, or rather Heb. פוק, to stagger. Class Bg. No. 44. 60.]
1. Wavering; inconstant; unstable; of a changeable mind; irresolute; not firm in opinion or purpose; capricious.

> They know how *fickle* common lovers are. *Dryden.*

2. Not fixed or firm; liable to change or vicissitude; as a *fickle* state. *Milton.*

FICK'LENESS, *n.* A wavering; wavering disposition; inconstancy; instability; unsteadiness in opinion or purpose; as the *fickleness* of lovers.
2. Instability; changeableness; as the *fickleness* of fortune.

FICK'LY, *adv.* Without firmness or steadiness. *Southern.*

FI'CO, *n.* [It. a *fig.*] An act of contempt done with the fingers, expressing *a fig for you.* *Carew.*

FIC'TILE, *a.* [L *fictilis*, from *fictus, fingo*, to feign.]
Molded into form by art; manufactured by the potter.

> *Fictile* earth is more fragile than crude earth. *Bacon.*

FIC'TION, *n.* [L. *fictio*, from *fingo*, to feign.]
1. The act of feigning, inventing or imagining; as, by the mere *fiction* of the mind. *Stillingfleet.*
2. That which is feigned, invented or imagined. The story is a *fiction.*

> So also was the *fiction* of those golden apples kept by a dragon, taken from the serpent which tempted Eve. *Raleigh.*

FIC'TIOUS, for *fictitious*, not used.

FICTI''TIOUS, *a.* [L. *fictitius*, from *fingo*, to feign.]
1. Feigned; imaginary; not real.

> The human persons are as *fictitious* as the airy ones. *Pope.*

2. Counterfeit; false; not genuine; as *fictitious* fame. *Dryden.*

FICTI''TIOUSLY, *adv.* By fiction; falsely; counterfeitly.

FICTI''TIOUSNESS, *n.* Feigned representation. *Brown.*

FIC'TIVE, *a.* Feigned. [*Not used.*]

FID, *n.* A square bar of wood or iron, with a shoulder at one end, used to support the top-mast, when erected at the head of the lower mast. *Mar. Dict.*
2. A pin of hard wood or iron, tapering to a point, used to open the strands of a rope in splicing. *Mar. Dict.*

FID'DLE, *n.* [G. *fiedel;* D. *vedel;* L. *fides, fidicula.*] A stringed instrument of music; a violin.

FID'DLE, *v. i.* To play on a fiddle or violin.

> Themistocles said he could not *fiddle*, but he could make a small town a great city. *Bacon.*
>
> It is said that Nero *fiddled*, when Rome was in flames. *History.*

2. To trifle; to shift the hands often and do nothing, like a fellow that plays on a fiddle.

Good cooks cannot abide what they call *fiddling* work. *Swift.*

FID'DLE, *v. t.* To play a tune on a fiddle.

FID'DLE-FADDLE, *n.* Trifles. [*A low cant word.*] *Spectator.*

FID'DLE-FADDLE, *a.* Trifling; making a bustle about nothing. [*Vulgar.*]

FID'DLER, *n.* One who plays on a fiddle or violin.

FID'DLE-STICK, *n.* The bow and string with which a fiddler plays on a violin.

FID'DLE-STRING, *n.* The string of a fiddle, fastened at the ends and elevated in the middle by a bridge.

FID'DLE-WOOD, *n.* A plant of the genus Citharexylon.

FID'DLING, *ppr.* Playing on a fiddle.

FID'DLING, *n.* The act of playing on a fiddle. *Bacon.*

FI'DEJUSSOR, *n.* [L.] A surety; one bound for another. *Blackstone.*

FIDEL'ITY, *n.* [L. *fidelitas*, from *fides*, faith, *fido*, to trust. See *Faith.*]

1. Faithfulness; careful and exact observance of duty, or performance of obligations. We expect *fidelity* in a public minister, in an agent or trustee, in a domestic servant, in a friend.

The best security for the *fidelity* of men, is to make interest coincide with duty. *Federalist, Hamilton.*

2. Firm adherence to a person or party with which one is united, or to which one is bound; loyalty; as the *fidelity* of subjects to their king or government; the *fidelity* of a tenant or liege to his lord.

3. Observance of the marriage covenant; as the *fidelity* of a husband or wife.

4. Honesty; veracity; adherence to truth; as the *fidelity* of a witness.

FIDGE, } *v. i.* [allied probably to *fickle.*]
FIDG'ET, } To move one way and the other; to move irregularly or in fits and starts. [*A low word.*] *Swift.*

FIDG'ET, *n.* Irregular motion; restlessness. [*Vulgar.*]

FIDG'ETY, *a.* Restless; uneasy. [*Vulgar.*]

FIDU'CIAL, *a.* [from L. *fiducia*, from *fido*, to trust.]

1. Confident; undoubting; firm; as a *fiducial* reliance on the promises of the gospel.

2. Having the nature of a trust; as *fiducial* power. *Spelman.*

FIDU'CIALLY, *adv.* With confidence. *South.*

FIDU'CIARY, *a.* [L. *fiduciarius*, from *fido*, to trust.]

1. Confident; steady; undoubting; unwavering; firm. *Wake.*

2. Not to be doubted; as *fiduciary* obedience. *Howell.*

3. Held in trust. *Spelman.*

FIDU'CIARY, *n.* One who holds a thing in trust; a trustee.

2. One who depends on faith for salvation, without works; an antinomian. *Hammond.*

FIE, pronounced *fi*, an exclamation denoting contempt or dislike.

FIEF, *n.* [Fr. *fief*, probably a compound word, consisting of *fe*, faith, and a word I do not understand. See *Fee, Feoff* and *Feud.*]

A fee; a feud; an estate held of a superior on condition of military service.

FIELD, *n.* [Sax. *feld*; G. *feld*; D. *veld*; Sw. Dan. *felt*; probably level land, a plain, from D. *vellen*, to *fell*, to lay or throw down.]

1. A piece of land inclosed for tillage or pasture; any part of a farm, except the garden and appurtenances of the mansion; properly land not covered with wood, and more strictly applicable to tillage land than to mowing land, which is often called meadow. But we say, the master of the house is in the *field* with his laborers, when he is at a distance from his house on his farm. He is in the *field*, plowing, sowing, reaping or making hay.

2. Ground not inclosed. *Mortimer.*

3. The ground where a battle is fought. We say, the *field* of battle; these veterans are excellent soldiers in the *field.*

4. A battle; action in the field.

What though the *field* be lost. *Milton.*

5. To *keep the field*, is to keep the campaign open; to live in tents, or to be in a state of active operations. At the approach of cold weather, the troops, unable to *keep the field*, were ordered into winter quarters.

6. A wide expanse.

Ask of yonder argent *fields* above. *Pope.*

7. Open space for action or operation; compass; extent. This subject opens a wide *field* for contemplation.

8. A piece or tract of land.

The *field* I give thee and the cave that is therein. Gen. xxiii.

9. The ground or blank space on which figures are drawn; as the *field* or ground of a picture. *Dryden.*

10. In *heraldry*, the whole surface of the shield, or the continent. *Encyc.*

11. In *scripture*, *field* often signifies the open country, ground not inclosed, as it may in some countries in modern times.

12. A *field of ice*, a large body of floating ice.

FIE'LDED, *a.* Being in the field of battle; encamped. *Shak.*

FIE'LD-BASIL, *n.* A plant of several kinds.

FIE'LD-BED, *n.* A bed for the field. *Shak.*

FIE'LD-BOOK, *n.* A book used in surveying, in which are set down the angles, stations, distances, &c. *Encyc.*

FIE'LD-COLORS, *n. plu.* In war, small flags of about a foot and half square, carried along with the quarter-master general, for marking out the ground for the squadrons and battalions. *Encyc.*

FIE'LD-DUCK, *n.* A species of bustard, nearly as large as a pheasant; found chiefly in France. *Dict. Nat. Hist.*

FIE'LDFARE, *n.* [*field* and *fare*, wandering in the field. Sax. *faran*, to go.]

A bird of the genus Turdus or thrush, about ten inches in length, the head ash-colored, the back and greater coverts of the wings, of a fine deep chesnut, and the tail black. These birds pass the summer in the northern parts of Europe, but visit Great Britain in winter. *Encyc.*

FIELD-M'ARSHAL, *n.* The commander of an army; a military officer of high rank in France and Germany, and the highest military officer in England.

FIE'LDMOUSE, *n.* A species of mouse that lives in the field, burrowing in banks, &c. *Mortimer.*

FIE'LD-OFFICER, *n.* A military officer above the rank of captain, as a major or colonel.

FIE'LD-PIECE, *n.* A small cannon which is carried along with armies, and used in the field of battle.

FIE'LD-PREACHER, *n.* One who preaches in the open air. *Lavington.*

FIE'LD-PREACHING, *n.* A preaching in the field or open air. *Warburton.*

FIE'LDROOM, *n.* Open space. [*Not in use.*] *Drayton.*

FIE'LD-SPORTS, *n. plu.* Diversions of the field, as shooting and hunting. *Chesterfield.*

FIE'LD-STAFF, *n.* A weapon carried by gunners, about the length of a halbert, with a spear at the end; having on each side ears screwed on, like the cock of a match-lock, where the gunners screw in lighted matches, when they are on command. *Encyc.*

FIE'LD-WORKS, *n.* In *the military art*, works thrown up by an army in besieging a fortress, or by the besieged to defend the place. *Encyc.*

FIE'LDY, *a.* Open like a field. [*Not in use.*] *Wickliffe.*

FIEND, *n.* [Sax. *feond*, Goth. *fiands*, from *fian*, *feon*, *figan*, to hate; G. *feind*; D. *vyand*; Sw. Dan. *fiende*. See *Feud*, contention.]

An enemy in the worst sense; an implacable or malicious foe; the devil; an infernal being.

O woman! woman! when to ill thy mind
Is bent, all hell contains no fouler *fiend*. *Pope.*

FIE'NDFUL, *a.* Full of evil or malignant practices. *Marlowe.*

FIE'NDLIKE, *a.* Resembling a fiend; maliciously wicked; diabolical.

FIERCE, *n. fers.* [Fr. *fier*; It. *fiero*, *feroce*; Sp. *fiero*, *feroz*; from L. *ferus*, *ferox*, the primary sense of which is wild, running, rushing.]

1. Vehement; violent; furious; rushing; impetuous; as a *fierce* wind. *Watts.*

2. Savage; ravenous; easily enraged; as a *fierce* lion.

3. Vehement in rage; eager of mischief; as a *fierce* tyrant; a monster *fierce* for blood.

4. Violent; outrageous; not to be restrained.

Cursed be their anger, for it was *fierce*. Gen. xlix.

5. Passionate; angry; furious.

6. Wild; staring; ferocious; as a *fierce* countenance.

7. Very eager; ardent; vehement; as a man *fierce* for his party.

FIERCELY, *adv. fers'ly.* Violently; furiously; with rage; as, both sides *fiercely* fought.

2. With a wild aspect; as, to look *fiercely.*

FIERCE-MINDED, *a.* Vehement; of a furious temper. *Bp. Wilson.*

FIERCENESS, *n. fers'ness.* Ferocity; savageness.

The defect of heat which gives *fierceness* to our natures. *Swift.*

2. Eagerness for blood; fury; as the *fierceness* of a lion or bear.
3. Quickness to attack; keenness in anger and resentment.

The Greeks are strong, and skilful to their strength,
Fierce to their skill, and to their *fierceness* valiant. *Shak.*

4. Violence; outrageous passion.

His pride and brutal *fierceness* I abhor. *Dryden.*

5. Vehemence; fury; impetuosity; as the *fierceness* of a tempest.

FIERI FA'CIAS, *n.* [L.] In *law*, a judicial writ that lies for him who has recovered in debt or damages, commanding the sheriff to levy the same on the goods of him against whom the recovery was had. *Cowel.*

FI'ERINESS, *n.* [See *Fiery, Fire.*] The quality of being fiery; heat; acrimony; the quality of a substance that excites a sensation of heat. *Boyle.*

2. Heat of temper; irritability; as *fieriness* of temper. *Addison.*

FI'ERY, *a.* [from *fire.*] Consisting of fire; as the *fiery* gulf of Etna.

And *fiery* billows roll below. *Watts.*

2. Hot like fire; as a *fiery* heart. *Shak.*
3. Vehement; ardent; very active; impetuous; as a *fiery* spirit.
4. Passionate; easily provoked; irritable.

You know the *fiery* quality of the duke. *Shak.*

5. Unrestrained; fierce; as a *fiery* steed.
6. Heated by fire.

The sword which is made *fiery*. *Hooker.*

7. Like fire; bright; glaring; as a *fiery* appearance.

FIFE, *n.* [Fr. *fifre*; G. *pfeife*. It is radically the same as *pipe*, W. *pib*, Ir. *pib* or *pip*, D. *pyp*, Dan. *pibe*, Sw. *pipa*, coinciding with L. *pipio*, to *pip* or *peep*, as a chicken. The word may have received its name from a hollow stalk, or from its sound.]
A small pipe, used as a wind instrument, chiefly in martial music with drums.

FIFE, *v. i.* To play on a fife.

FI'FER, *n.* One who plays on a fife.

FIFTEE'N, *a.* [Sax. *fiftyn.*] Five and ten.

FIFTEE'NTH, *a.* [Sax. *fiftyntha.*] The ordinal of fifteen; the fifth after the tenth.

2. Containing one part in fifteen.

FIFTEE'NTH, *n.* A fifteenth part.

FIFTH, *a.* [Sax. *fifta.* See *Five.*] The ordinal of five; the next to the fourth.

2. Elliptically, a fifth part; or the word may be considered as a noun, as to give a *fifth* or two *fifths*.

FIFTH, *n.* In *music*, an interval consisting of three tones and a semitone. *Encyc.*

FIFTH'LY, *adv.* In the fifth place.

FIF'TIETH, *a.* [Sax. *fifteogetha*; *fif*, five, and *teogetha*, tenth.]
The ordinal of fifty; as the *fiftieth* part of a foot. This may be used elliptically, as a *fiftieth* of his goods, *part* being understood; or in this case, the word may be treated in grammars as a noun, admitting a plural, as two *fiftieths*.

FIF'TY, *a.* [Sax. *fiftig*; *fif*, five, and Goth. *tig*, ten.]
Five tens; five times ten; as *fifty* men. It may be used as a noun in the plural.

And they sat down by *fifties*. Mark vi.

FIG, *n.* [L. *ficus*; Sp. *figo* or *higo*; It. *fico*; Fr. *figue*; G. *feige*; D. *vyg*; Heb. פגי; Ch. פגה.]

1. The fruit of the fig-tree, which is of a round or oblong shape, and a dark purplish color, with a pulp of a sweet taste. But the varieties are numerous; some being blue, others red, and others of a dark brown color. *Encyc.*
2. The fig-tree. *Pope.*

FIG, *v. t.* To insult with ficoes or contemptuous motions of the fingers. [*Little used.*] *Shak.*

2. To put something useless into one's head. [*Not used.*] *L'Estrange.*

FIG'-APPLE, *n.* A species of apple. *Johnson.*

FIG'-GNAT, *n.* An insect of the fly kind. *Johnson.*

FIG'-LEAF, *n.* The leaf of a fig-tree; also, a thin covering, in allusion to the first covering of Adam and Eve.

FIG-MAR'IGOLD, *n.* The Mesembryanthemum, a succulent plant, resembling houseleek; the leaves grow opposite by pairs. *Fam. of Plants. Miller.*

FIG'-PECKER, *n.* [L. *ficedula.*] A bird.

FIG'-TREE, *n.* A tree of the genus Ficus, growing in warm climates. The receptacle is common, turbinated, carnous and connivent, inclosing the florets either in the same or in a distinct one. The male calyx is tripartite; no corol; three stamens. The female calyx is quinquepartite; no corol; one pistil; one seed. *Encyc.*

To dwell under our vine and fig-tree, is to live in peace and safety. 1 Kings iv.

FIG'-WŎRT, *n.* A plant of the genus Scrophularia.

Figary, for *vagary*, is not English.

FIGHT, *v. i.* pret. and pp. *fought*, pronounced *faut*. [Sax. *feahtan*, *feohtan*; G. *fechten*; D. *vegten*; Sw. *fäckta*; Dan. *fegter*; Ir. *fichim.*]

1. To strive or contend for victory, in battle or in single combat; to attempt to defeat, subdue or destroy an enemy, either by blows or weapons; to contend in arms.

Come and be our captain, that we may *fight* with the children of Ammon. Judges xi.

When two persons or parties contend in person, *fight* is usually followed by *with*. But when we speak of *carrying on war*, in any other form, we may say, to *fight against*.

Saul took the kingdom over Israel, and *fought against* all his enemies on every side. 1 Sam. xiv.

Hazael king of Syria went up, and *fought against* Gath. 2 Kings xii.

It is treason for a man to join an enemy to *fight against* his country. Hence, *To fight against*, is to act in opposition; to oppose; to strive to conquer or resist.

The stars in their courses *fought against* Sisera. Judges v.

2. To contend; to strive; to struggle to resist or check.
3. To act as a soldier. *Shak.*

FIGHT, *v. t.* To carry on contention; to maintain a struggle for victory over enemies.

I have *fought* a good fight. 2 Tim. iv.

2. To contend with in battle; to war against. They *fought* the enemy in two pitched battles. The captain *fought* the frigate seven glasses. [Elliptical; *with* being understood.]

FIGHT, *n.* A battle; an engagement; a contest in arms; a struggle for victory, either between individuals, or between armies, ships or navies. A duel is called a single *fight* or combat.

2. Something to screen the combatants in ships.

Up with your *fights* and your nettings prepare. *Dryden.*

FIGHTER, *n.* One that fights; a combatant; a warrior.

FIGHTING, *ppr.* Contending in battle; striving for victory or conquest.

2. *a.* Qualified for war; fit for battle.

A host of *fighting* men. 2 Chron. xxvi.

3. Occupied in war; being the scene of war; as a *fighting* field. *Pope.*

FIGHTING, *n.* Contention; strife; quarrel.

Without were *fightings*, within were fears. 2 Cor. vii.

FIG'MENT, *n.* [L. *figmentum*, from *fingo*, to feign.]
An invention; a fiction; something feigned or imagined. These assertions are the *figments* of idle brains. *Bp. Lloyd.*

FIG'ULATE, *a.* [L. *figulo*, to fashion, from *fingo*, or rather *figo*, which appears to be the root of *fingo.*]
Made of potter's clay; molded; shaped. [*Little used.*]

FIGURABIL'ITY, *n.* The quality of being capable of a certain fixed or stable form.

FIG'URABLE, *a.* [from *figure.*] Capable of being brought to a certain fixed form or shape. Thus lead is *figurable*, but water is not. *Bacon.*

FIG'URAL, *a.* Represented by figure or delineation; as *figural* resemblances. *Brown.*

Figural numbers, in geometry, such numbers as do or may represent some geometrical figure, in relation to which they are always considered, and are either lineary, superficial or solid. *Harris.*

FIG'URATE, *a.* [L. *figuratus.*] Of a certain determinate form.

Plants are all *figurate* and determinate, which inanimate bodies are not. *Bacon.*

2. Resembling any thing of a determinate form; as *figurate* stones, stones or fossils resembling shells.
3. Figurative. [*Not used.*]

Figurate counterpoint, in *music*, that wherein there is a mixture of discords with concords. *Harris.*

Figurate descant, that in which discords are concerned, though not so much as concords. It may be called the ornament or rhetorical part of music, containing all the varieties of points, figures, syncopes, and diversities of measure. *Harris.*

FIG'URATED, *a.* Having a determinate form. *Potter.*

FIGURA'TION, *n.* The act of giving figure or determinate form. *Bacon.*

2. Determination to a certain form. *Bacon.*
3. Mixture of concords and discords in music. *Gregory.*

FIG'URATIVE, *a.* [Fr. *figuratif*, from *figure.*]

1. Representing something else; representing by resemblance; typical.

This they will say, was *figurative*, and served by God's appointment but for a time, to shadow out the true glory of a more divine sanctity. *Hooker.*

2. Representing by resemblance; not literal or direct. A *figurative* expression, is one in which the words are used in a sense different from that in which they are ordinarily used; as,

Slander,
Whose edge is sharper than the sword. *Shak.*

3. Abounding with figures of speech; as a description highly *figurative.*

FIG'URATIVELY, *adv.* By a figure; in a manner to exhibit ideas by resemblance; in a sense different from that which words originally imply. Words are used *figuratively*, when they express something different from their usual meaning.

FIG'URE, *n. fig'ur.* [Fr. *figure;* L. *figura*, from *figo*, to fix or set; W. *fugyr*, from *fugiaw*, to feign. See Feign.]

1. The form of any thing as expressed by the outline or terminating extremities. Flowers have exquisite *figures.* A triangle is a *figure* of three sides. A square is a *figure* of four equal sides and equal angles.

2. Shape; form; person; as a lady of elegant *figure.*

A good *figure*, or person, in man or woman, gives credit at first sight to the choice of either. *Richardson.*

3. Distinguished appearance; eminence; distinction; remarkable character. Ames made a *figure* in Congress; Hamilton, in the cabinet.

4. Appearance of any kind; as an ill *figure;* a mean *figure.*

5. Magnificence; splendor; as, to live in *figure* and indulgence. *Law.*

6. A statue; an image; that which is formed in resemblance of something else; as the *figure* of a man in plaster.

7. Representation in painting; the lines and colors which represent an animal, particularly a person; as the principal *figures* of a picture; a subordinate *figure.*

8. In *manufactures*, a design or representation wrought on damask, velvet and other stuffs.

9. In *logic*, the order or disposition of the middle term in a syllogism with the parts of the question. *Watts.*

10. In *arithmetic*, a character denoting a number; as 2. 7. 9.

11. In *astrology*, the horoscope; the diagram of the aspects of the astrological houses. *Shak.*

12. In *theology*, type; representative.

Who was the *figure* of him that was to come. Rom. v.

13. In *rhetoric*, a mode of speaking or writing in which words are deflected from their ordinary signification, or a mode more beautiful and emphatical than the ordinary way of expressing the sense; the language of the imagination and passions; as, knowledge is the light of the mind; the soul mounts on the wings of faith; youth is the morning of life. In strictness, the change of a word is a *trope*, and any affection of a sentence a *figure;* but these terms are often confounded. *Locke.*

14. In *grammar*, any deviation from the rules of analogy or syntax.

15. In *dancing*, the several steps which the dancer makes in order and cadence, considered as they form certain figures on the floor.

FIG'URE, *v. t. fig'ur.* To form or mold into any determinate shape.

Accept this goblet, rough with *figured* gold. *Dryden.*

2. To show by a corporeal resemblance, as in picture or statuary.

3. To cover or adorn with figures or images; to mark with figures; to form figures in by art; as, to *figure* velvet or muslin.

4. To diversify; to variegate with adventitious forms of matter.

5. To represent by a typical or figurative resemblance.

The matter of the sacraments *figureth* their end. *Hooker.*

6. To imagine; to image in the mind. *Temple.*

7. To prefigure; to foreshow. *Shak.*

8. To form figuratively; to use in a sense not literal; as *figured* expressions. [*Little used.*] *Locke.*

9. To note by characters.

As through a crystal glass the *figured* hours are seen. *Dryden.*

10. In *music*, to pass several notes for one; to form runnings or variations. *Encyc.*

FIG'URE, *v. i.* To make a figure; to be distinguished. The envoy *figured* at the court of St. Cloud.

FIG'URE-CASTER, } *n.* A pretender to
FIG'URE-FLINGER, } astrology. *Obs.*

FIG'URE-STONE, *n.* A name of the agalmatolite, or bildstein.

FIG'URED, *pp.* Represented by resemblance; adorned with figures; formed into a determinate figure.

2. In *music*, free and florid.

FIG'URING, *ppr.* Forming into determinate shape; representing by types or resemblances; adorning with figures; making a distinguished appearance.

FILA'CEOUS, *a.* [L. *filum*, a thread; Fr. *file;* Sp. *hilo.*] Composed or consisting of threads. *Bacon.*

FIL'ACER, *n.* [Norm. *filicer*, from *file*, a thread, or file, L. *filum*, Sp. *hilo.*]

An officer in the English Court of Common Pleas, so called from filing the writs on which he makes process. There are fourteen of them in their several divisions and counties. They make out all original processes, real, personal and mixed. *Harris.*

FIL'AMENT, *n.* [Fr. from L. *filamenta*, threads, from *filum.*]

A thread; a fiber. In *anatomy* and *natural history*, a fine thread of which flesh, nerves, skin, plants, roots, &c., and also some minerals, are composed. So the spider's web is composed of *filaments.* The thread-like, part of the stamens of plants, is called the *filament.*

FILAMENT'OUS, *a.* Like a thread; consisting of fine filaments.

FIL'ANDERS, *n.* [Fr. *filandres*, from *filum*, a thread.]

A disease in hawks, consisting of filaments of coagulated blood; also, small worms wrapt in a thin skin or net, near the reins of a hawk. *Encyc.*

FIL'ATORY, *n.* [from L. *filum*, a thread.] A machine which forms or spins threads.

This manufactory has three *filatories*, each of 640 reels, which are moved by a water-wheel, and besides a small *filatory* turned by men. *Tooke.*

FIL'BERT, *n.* [L. *avellana*, with which the first syllable corresponds; *fil, vel.*]

The fruit of the Corylus or hazel; an egg-shaped nut, containing a kernel, that has a mild, farinaceous, oily taste, which is agreeable to the palate. The oil is said to be little inferior to the oil of almonds. *Encyc.*

FILCH, *v. t.* [This word, like *pilfer*, is probably from the root of *file* or *peel*, to strip or rub off. But I know not from what source we have received it. In Sp. *pellizcar* is to pilfer, as *filouter*, in French, is to pick the pocket.]

To steal something of little value; to pilfer; to steal; to pillage; to take wrongfully from another.

Fain would they *filch* that little food away. *Dryden.*

But he that *filches* from me my good name,
Robs me of that which not enriches him,
And makes me poor indeed. *Shak.*

FILCH'ED, *pp.* Stolen; taken wrongfully from another; pillaged; pilfered.

FILCH'ER, *n.* A thief; one who is guilty of petty theft.

FILCH'ING, *ppr.* Stealing; taking from another wrongfully; pilfering.

FILCH'INGLY, *adv.* By pilfering; in a thievish manner.

FILE, *n.* [Fr. *file*, a row; *filet*, a thread; L. *filum;* Sp. *hilo;* Port. *fila;* It. *fila, filo;* Russ. *biel*, a thread of flax. The primary sense is probably to draw out or extend, or to twist. W. *filliaw*, to twist.]

1. A thread, string or line; particularly, a line or wire on which papers are strung in due order for preservation, and for conveniently finding them when wanted. Documents are kept on *file.*

2. The whole number of papers strung on a line or wire; as a *file* of writs. A *file* is a record of court.

3. A bundle of papers tied together, with the title of each indorsed; *the mode of arranging and keeping papers being changed, without a change of names.*

4. A roll, list or catalogue. *Shak.*

5. A row of soldiers ranged one behind another, from front to rear; the number of men constituting the depth of the battalion or squadron.

FILE, *v. t.* To string; to fasten, as papers, on a line or wire for preservation. Declarations and affidavits must be *filed.* An original writ may be *filed* after judgment.

2. To arrange or insert in a bundle, as papers, indorsing the title on each paper. *This is now the more common mode of filing papers in public and private offices.*

3. To present or exhibit officially, or for trial; as, to *file* a bill in chancery.

FILE, *v. i.* To march in a file or line, as soldiers, not abreast, but one after another.

FILE, *n.* [Sax. *feol;* D. *vyl;* G. *feile;* Sw. and Dan. *fil*, a file; Russ. *pila*, a saw; perhaps connected in origin with *polish*, which see. Class Bl. No. 30. 32. 33. 45.]

An instrument used in smoothing and polishing metals, formed of iron or steel, and cut in little furrows.

FILE, *v. t.* [Russ. *opilevayu*, and *spilivayu*, to file.]

1. To rub and smooth with a file; to polish.
2. To cut as with a file; to wear off or away by friction; as, to *file* off a tooth.
3. [from *defile*.] To foul or defile. [*Not used.*] *Shak.*

FI'LE-CUTTER, *n.* A maker of files. *Moxon.*

FI'LED, *pp.* Placed on a line or wire; placed in a bundle and indorsed; smoothed or polished with a file.

FILE-LE'ADER, *n.* The soldier placed in the front of a file. *Cyc.*

FI'LEMOT, *n.* [Fr. *feuille-morte*, a dead leaf.] A yellowish brown color; the color of a faded leaf. *Swift.*

FI'LER, *n.* One who uses a file in smoothing and polishing.

FIL'IAL, *a. fil'yal.* [Fr. *filial*; It. *filiale*; Sp. *filial*; from L. *filius*, a son, *filia*, a daughter, Sp. *hijo*, Coptic *falu*, Sans. *bala* or *bali*. It agrees in elements with *foal* and *pullus*. The Welsh has *hiliaw* and *eppiliaw*, to bring forth; *hil* and *eppil*, progeny.]

1. Pertaining to a son or daughter; becoming a child in relation to his parents. *Filial* love is such an affection as a child naturally bears to his parents. *Filial* duty or obedience is such duty or obedience as the child owes to his parents.
2. Bearing the relation of a son.

> Sprigs of like leaf erect their *filial* heads. *Prior.*

FILIA'TION, *n.* [Fr. from L. *filius*, a son.]

1. The relation of a son or child to a father; correlative to *paternity*. *Hale.*
2. Adoption.

FIL'IFORM, *n.* [L. *filum*, a thread, and *form*.]

Having the form of a thread or filament; of equal thickness from top to bottom; as a *filiform* style or peduncle. *Martyn.*

FIL'IGRANE, *n.* sometimes written *filigree*. [L. *filum*, a thread, and *granum*, a grain.]

A kind of enrichment on gold and silver, wrought delicately in the manner of little threads or grains, or of both intermixed. *Encyc.*

FIL'IGRANED, or **FIL'IGREED**, *a.* Ornamented with filigrane. *Tatler.*

FI'LING, *ppr.* Placing on a string or wire, or in a bundle of papers; presenting for trial; marching in a file; smoothing with a file.

FI'LINGS, *n. plu.* Fragments or particles rubbed off by the act of filing; as *filings* of iron.

FILL, *v. t.* [Sax. *fyllan*, *gefillan*; D. *vullen*; G. *füllen*; Sw. *fylla*; Dan. *fylder*, to fill; Fr. *fouler*, to *full*, to tread, that is, to press, to crowd; *foule*, a crowd; Gr. πολυς, πολλοι; allied perhaps to *fold* and *felt*; Ir. *fillim*; Gr. πιλος; πιλοω, to stuff; L. *pilus*, *pileus*. We are told that the Gr. πελαω, to approach, signified originally to thrust or drive, L. *pello*, and contracted into πλαω, it is rendered to *fill*, and πλεος is full. If a vowel was originally used between π and λ, in these words, they coincide with *fill*; and the L. *pleo*, [for *peleo*,] in all its compounds, is the same word. In Russ. *polnei* is full; *polnyu*, to fill. See Class Bl. No. 9. 11. 12. 15. 22. 30. 45. 47.]

1. Properly, to press; to crowd; to stuff. Hence, to put or pour in, till the thing will hold no more; as, to *fill* a basket, a bottle, a vessel.

> *Fill* the water-pots with water: and they *filled* them to the brim. John ii.

2. To store; to supply with abundance.

> Be fruitful, and multiply, and *fill* the waters in the seas. Gen. i.

3. To cause to abound; to make universally prevalent.

> The earth was *filled* with violence. Gen. vi.

4. To satisfy; to content.

> Whence should we have so much bread in the wilderness, as to *fill* so great a multitude? Matt. xv.

5. To glut; to surfeit.

> Things that are sweet and fat are more *filling*. *Bacon.*

6. To make plump; as, in a good season the grain is well *filled*. In the summer of 1816, the driest and coldest which the oldest man remembered, the rye was so well *filled*, that the grain protruded beyond the husk, and a shock yielded a peck more than in common years.
7. To press and dilate on all sides or to the extremities; as, the sails were *filled*.
8. To supply with liquor; to pour into; as, to *fill* a glass for a guest.
9. To supply with an incumbent; as, to *fill* an office or vacancy. *Hamilton.*
10. To hold; to possess and perform the duties of; to officiate in, as an incumbent; as, a king *fills* a throne; the president *fills* the office of chief magistrate; the speaker of the house *fills* the chair.
11. In *seamanship*, to brace the sails so that the wind will bear upon them and dilate them.

To fill out, to extend or enlarge to the desired limit.

To fill up, to make full.

> It pours the bliss that *fills up* all the mind. *Pope.*

But in this and many other cases, the use of *up* weakens the force of the phrase.

2. To occupy; to fill. Seek to *fill up* life with useful employments.
3. To fill; to occupy the whole extent; as, to *fill up* a given space.
4. To engage or employ; as, to *fill up* time.
5. To complete; as, to *fill up* the measure of sin. Matt. xxiii.
6. To complete; to accomplish.

> —And *fill up* what is behind of the afflictions of Christ. Col. i.

FILL, *v. i.* To fill a cup or glass for drinking; to give to drink.

> In the cup which she hath filled, *fill* to her double. Rev. xviii.

2. To grow or become full. Corn *fills* well in a warm season. A mill-pond *fills* during the night.
3. To glut; to satiate.

To fill up, to grow or become full. The channel of the river *fills up* with sand, every spring.

FILL, *n.* Fullness; as much as supplies want; as much as gives complete satisfaction. Eat and drink to the *fill*. Take your *fill* of joy.

> The land shall yield her fruit, and ye shall eat your *fill*, and dwell therein in safety. Lev. xxv.

FILLAGREE. [See *Filigrane*.]

FILL'ED, *pp.* Made full; supplied with abundance.

FILL'ER, *n.* One who fills; one whose employment is to fill vessels.

> They have six diggers to four *fillers*, so as to keep the *fillers* always at work. *Mortimer.*

2. That which fills any space. *Dryden.*
3. One that supplies abundantly.

FIL'LET, *n.* [Fr. *filet*, a thread, from *file*, L. *filum*.]

1. A little band to tie about the hair of the head.

> A belt her waist, a *fillet* binds her hair. *Pope.*

2. The fleshy part of the thigh; *applied to veal*; as a *fillet* of veal.
3. Meat rolled together and tied round. *Swift.*
4. In *architecture*, a little square member or ornament used in divers places, but generally as a corona over a greater molding; called also *listel*.
5. In *heraldry*, a kind of orle or bordure, containing only the third or fourth part of the breadth of the common bordure. It runs quite round near the edge, as a lace over a cloke. *Encyc.*
6. Among *painters* and *gilders*, a little rule or reglet of leaf-gold, drawn over certain moldings, or on the edges of frames, panels, &c., especially when painted white, by way of enrichment. *Encyc.*
7. In *the manege*, the loins of a horse, beginning at the place where the hinder part of the saddle rests. *Encyc.*

FIL'LET, *v. t.* To bind with a fillet or little band.

2. To adorn with an astragal. Ex. xxxviii.

FIL'LIBEG, *n.* [Gael. *filleadh-beg*.] A little plaid; a dress reaching only to the knees, worn in the highlands of Scotland.

FILL'ING, *ppr.* Making full; supplying abundantly; growing full.

FILL'ING, *n.* A making full; supply.

2. The woof in weaving.

FIL'LIP, *v. t.* [probably from the root of L. *pello*, like *pelt*, W. *fil*. See *Filly*.]

To strike with the nail of the finger, first placed against the ball of the thumb, and forced from that position with some violence.

FIL'LIP, *n.* A jerk of the finger forced suddenly from the thumb.

FIL'LY, *n.* [W. *filawg*, from *fil*, a scud, a dart; coinciding with Fr. *fille*, L. *filia*, Eng. *foal*, a shoot, issue.]

1. A female or mare colt; a young mare.
2. A young horse. [*Not used.*] *Tusser.*
3. A wanton girl. *Beaum.*

FILM, *n.* [Sax. *film*. Qu. W. *fylliaw*, to shade or grow over, or It. *velame*, a vail, a *film*, L. *velamen*, or from L. *pellis*.]

A thin skin; a pellicle, as on the eye. In plants, it denotes the thin skin which separates the seeds in pods.

FILM, *v. t.* To cover with a thin skin or pellicle. *Shak.*

FILM'Y, *a.* Composed of thin membranes or pellicles.

> Whose *filmy* cord should bind the struggling fly. *Dryden.*

FIL'TER, *n.* [Fr. *filtre*, *feutre*; Sp. *filtro*; It. *feltro*; properly *felt*, fulled wool, lana coacta, this being used for straining liquors.]

A strainer; a piece of woolen cloth, paper

or other substance, through which liquors are passed for defecation. A filter may be made in the form of a hollow inverted cone, or by a twist of thread or yarn, being wetted and one end put in the liquor and the other suffered to hang out below the surface of the liquor. Porous stone is often used as a *filter*.

FIL'TER, *v. t.* To purify or defecate liquor, by passing it through a filter, or causing it to pass through a porous substance that retains any feculent matter.

FIL'TER, *v. i.* To percolate; to pass through a filter.

FIL'TER, *n.* [See *Philter.*]

FIL'TERED, *pp.* Strained; defecated by a filter.

FIL'TERING, *ppr.* Straining; defecating.

FILTH, *n.* [Sax. *fylth*, from *ful*, *fula*, foul; D. *vuilte.* See *Foul* and *Defile.*]

1. Dirt; any foul matter; any thing that soils or defiles; waste matter; nastiness.

2. Corruption; pollution; any thing that sullies or defiles the moral character.

> To purify the soul from the dross and *filth* of sensual delights. *Tillotson.*

FILTH'ILY, *adv.* In a filthy manner; foully; grossly.

FILTH'INESS, *n.* The state of being filthy.

2. Foulness; dirtiness; filth; nastiness.

> Carry forth the *filthiness* out of the holy place. 2 Chron. xxix.

3. Corruption; pollution; defilement by sin; impurity.

> Let us cleanse ourselves from all *filthiness* of the flesh and spirit, perfecting holiness in the fear of God. 2 Cor. vii.

FILTH'Y, *a.* Dirty; foul; unclean; nasty.

2. Polluted; defiled by sinful practices; morally impure.

> He that is *filthy*, let him be *filthy* still. Rev. xxii.

3. Obtained by base and dishonest means; as *filthy* lucre. Tit. i.

FIL'TRATE, *v. t.* [Sp. *filtrar;* It. *filtrare;* Fr. *filtrer.* See *Filter.*]

To filter; to defecate, as liquor, by straining or percolation.

FILTRA'TION, *n.* The act or process of filtering; defecation by passing liquors through woolen cloth, brown paper, or other porous substance, as certain kinds of stone, which permit the liquor to pass, but retain the foreign matter.

FIMBLE-HEMP, *n.* [*Female-hemp.*] Light summer hemp that bears no seed. *Mortimer.*

FIM'BRIATE, *a.* [L. *fimbria*, a border or fringe.]

In *botany*, fringed; having the edge surrounded by hairs or bristles. *Martyn.*

FIM'BRIATE, *v. t.* To hem; to fringe. *Fuller.*

FIM'BRIATED, *a.* In *heraldry*, ornamented, as an ordinary, with a narrow border or hem of another tincture. *Encyc.*

FIN, *n.* [Sax. *finn;* D. *vin;* Sw. *fena;* Dan. *finne;* L. *pinna* or *penna.* The sense is probably a shoot, or it is from diminishing. See *Fine.* Class Bn.]

The fin of a fish consists of a membrane supported by rays, or little bony or cartilaginous ossicles. The fins of fish serve to keep their bodies upright, and to prevent wavering or vacillation. The fins, except the caudal, do not assist in progressive motion; the tail being the instrument of swimming.

FIN, *v. t.* To carve or cut up a chub.

FI'NABLE, *a.* [See *Fine.*] That admits a fine.

2. Subject to a fine or penalty; as a *finable* person or offense.

FI'NAL, *a.* [Fr. Sp. *final;* L. *finalis;* It. *finale.* See *Fine.*]

1. Pertaining to the end or concluion; last; ultimate; as the *final* issue or event of things; *final* hope; *final* salvation.

2. Conclusive; decisive; ultimate; as a *final* judgment. The battle of Waterloo was *final* to the power of Buonaparte; it brought the contest to a *final* issue.

3. Respecting the end or object to be gained; respecting the purpose or ultimate end in view. The efficient cause is that which produces the event or effect; the *final* cause is that for which any thing is done.

FI'NALLY, *adv.* At the end or conclusion; ultimately; lastly. The cause is expensive, but we shall *finally* recover. The contest was long, but the Romans *finally* conquered.

2. Completely; beyond recovery.

> The enemy was *finally* exterminated. *Davies.*

FINANCE, *n.* *finans'.* [Fr. and Norm. *finance;* Arm. *financz*, fine, subsidy. *Finance* is from *fine*, in the sense of a sum of money paid by the subject to the king for the enjoyment of a privilege, a feudal sense. Hence *finance* was originally revenue arising from *fines.* See *Fine.*]

Revenue; income of a king or state. *Bacon.*

The United States, near the close of the revolution, appointed a superintendent of *finance.*

[*It is more generally used in the plural.*]

FINAN'CES, *n. plu.* Revenue; funds in the public treasury, or accruing to it; public resources of money. The *finances* of the king or government were in a low condition. The *finances* were exhausted.

2. The income or resources of individuals. [*But the word is most properly applicable to public revenue.*]

FINAN'CIAL, *a.* Pertaining to public revenue; as *financial* concerns or operations. *Anderson.*

FINAN'CIALLY, *adv.* In relation to finances or public revenue; in a manner to produce revenue.

> We should be careful not to consider as *financially* effective exports, all the goods and produce which have been sent abroad. *Walsh.*

FINANCIE'R, *n.* [In France, a receiver or farmer of the public revenues.]

1. An officer who receives and manages the public revenues; a treasurer.

2. One who is skilled in the principles or system of public revenue; one who understands the mode of raising money by imposts, excise or taxes, and the economical management and application of public money.

3. One who is entrusted with the collection and management of the revenues of a corporation.

4. One skilled in banking operations.

FI'NARY, *n.* [from *fine*, *refine.*] In iron works, the second forge at the iron-mill. [See *Finery.*] *Dict.*

FINCH, *n.* [Sax. *finc;* G. *fink;* D. *vink;* It. *pincione;* W. *pinc*, fine, gay, a *finch.*]

A bird. But *finch* is used chiefly in composition; as *chaffinch*, *goldfinch.* These belong to the genus Fringilla.

FIND, *v. t.* pret. and pp. *found.* [Sax. *findan;* G. *finden;* D. *vinden*, or *vynen;* Sw. *finna;* Dan. *finder.* This word coincides in origin with the L. *venio;* but in sense, with *invenio.* The primary sense is to come to, to rush, to fall on, to meet, to set on; and the Sw. *finna* is rendered not only by *invenire*, but by *offendere.* So in Sp. *venir*, to come, and to assault. It is probable therefore that *find* and *fend* are from one root. Ar. فَانَ to come. Class Bn. No. 21. See also No. 7.]

1. Literally, to come to; to meet; hence, to discover by the eye; to gain first sight or knowledge of something lost; to recover either by searching for it or by accident.

> Doth she not light a candle, and sweep the house, and seek diligently till she *find* it? and when she hath *found* it— Luke xv.

2. To meet; to discover something not before seen or known.

> He saith to him, we have *found* the Messiah. John i.

3. To obtain by seeking.

> Ask, and it shall be given you; seek, and ye shall *find.* Matt. vii.

4. To meet with.

> In woods and forests thou art *found.* *Cowley.*

5. To discover or know by experience.

> The torrid zone is now *found* habitable. *Cowley.*

6. To reach; to attain to; to arrive at.

> Strait is the gate, and narrow is the way, which leadeth to life, and few there be that *find* it. Matt. vii.

7. To discover by study, experiment or trial. Air and water are *found* to be compound substances. Alchimists long attempted to *find* the philosopher's stone, but it is not yet *found.*

8. To gain; to have; as, to *find* leisure for a visit.

9. To perceive; to observe; to learn. I *found* his opinions to accord with my own.

10. To catch; to detect.

> When first *found* in a lie, talk to him of it as a strange monstrous matter. *Locke.*

In this sense *find* is usually followed by out.

11. To meet.

> In ills their business and their glory *find.* *Cowley.*

12. To have; to experience; to enjoy.

> Behold, in the day of your fast ye *find* pleasure. Is. lviii.

13. To select; to choose; to designate.

> I have *found* David my servant. Ps. lxxxix.

14. To discover and declare the truth of disputed facts; to come to a conclusion and decide between parties, as a jury. The jury *find* a verdict for the plaintiff or defendant. They *find* the accused to be guilty.

15. To determine and declare by verdict. The jury have *found* a large sum in damages for the plaintiff.

16. To establish or pronounce charges alledged to be true. The grand jury have *found* a bill against the accused, or they *find* a true bill.

17. To supply; to furnish. Who will *find* the money or provisions for this expedition? We will *find* ourselves with provisions and clothing.

18. To discover or gain knowledge of by touching or by sounding. We first sounded and *found* bottom at the depth of ninety five fathoms on the Sole bank.

To find one's self, to be; to fare in regard to ease or pain, health or sickness. Pray, sir, how do you *find yourself* this morning.

To find in, to supply; to furnish; to provide. He *finds* his nephew *in* money, victuals and clothes.

To find out. To invent; to discover something before unknown.

> A man of Tyre, skilful to work in gold—and to *find out* every device. 2 Chron. ii.

2. To unriddle; to solve; as, to *find out* the meaning of a parable or an enigma.

3. To discover; to obtain knowledge of what is hidden; as, to *find out* a secret.

4. To understand; to comprehend.

> Canst thou by searching *find out* God? Job xi.

5. To detect; to discover; to bring to light; as, to *find out* a thief or a theft; to *find out* a trick

To find fault with, to blame; to censure.

FINDER, *n.* One who meets or falls on any thing; one that discovers what is lost or is unknown; one who discovers by searching, or by accident.

FINDFAULT, *n.* A censurer; a caviller. *Shak.*

FINDFAULT'ING, *a.* Apt to censure; captious. *Whitlock.*

FINDING, *ppr.* Discovering.

FINDING, *n.* Discovery; the act of discovering.

2. In *law*, the return of a jury to a bill; a verdict.

FIN'DY, *a.* [Sax. *findig*, heavy; *gefindig*, capacious; Dan. *fyndig*, strong, emphatical, nervous, weighty, from *fynd*, force, energy, emphasis, strength; probably from crowding, tension, stretching, from *find.*]

Full; heavy; or firm, solid, substantial. *Obs.*

> A cold May and a windy,
> Makes the barn fat and *findy*.
> *Old Prov. Junius.*

FINE, *a.* [Fr. *fin*, whence *finesse*; Sp. Port. *fino*, whence *fineza*; It. *fino*, whence *finezza*; Dan *fiin*; Sw. *fin*; G. *fein*; D. *fyn*; hence to *refine.* The Ir. has *fion*; and the W. *fain*, *feined*, signify rising to a point, as a cone. Ar. أفن afana, to diminish. Class Bn. No 29.]

1. Small; thin; slender; minute; of very small diameter; as a *fine* thread; *fine* silk; a *fine* hair. We say also, *fine* sand, *fine* particles.

2. Subtil; thin; tenuous; as, *fine* spirits evaporate; a *finer* medium opposed to a *grosser.* *Bacon.*

3. Thin; keen; smoothly sharp; as the *fine* edge of a razor.

4. Made of fine threads; not coarse; as *fine* linen or cambric.

5. Clear; pure; free from feculence or foreign matter; as *fine* gold or silver; wine is not good till *fine.*

6. Refined.

> Those things were too *fine* to be fortunate, and succeed in all parts. *Bacon.*

7. Nice; delicate; perceiving or discerning minute beauties or deformities; as a *fine* taste; a *fine* sense.

8. Subtil; artful; dextrous. [See *Finess.*] *Bacon.*

9. Subtil; sly; fraudulent. *Hubberd's Tale.*

10. Elegant; beautiful in thought.

> To call the trumpet by the name of the metal was *fine.* *Dryden.*

11. Very handsome; beautiful with dignity. The lady has a *fine* person, or a *fine* face.

12. Accomplished; elegant in manners. He was one of the *finest* gentlemen of his age.

13. Accomplished in learning; excellent; as a *fine* scholar.

14. Excellent; superior; brilliant or acute; as a man of *fine* genius.

15. Amiable; noble; ingenuous; excellent; as a man of a *fine* mind.

16. Showy; splendid; elegant; as a range of *fine* buildings; a *fine* house or garden; a *fine* view.

17. *Ironically*, worthy of contemptuous notice; eminent for bad qualities.

> That same knave, Ford, her husband, has the *finest* mad devil of jealousy in him, Master Brook, that ever governed frenzy. *Shak.*

Fine Arts, or polite arts, are the arts which depend chiefly on the labors of the mind or imagination, and whose object is pleasure; as poetry, music, painting and sculpture.

The uses of this word are so numerous and indefinite, as to preclude a particular definition of each. In general, *fine*, in popular language, expresses whatever is excellent, showy or magnificent.

FINE, *n.* [This word is the basis of *finance*, but I have not found it, in its simple form, in any modern language, except the English. Junius says that *ffin*, in Cimbric, is a mulct, and *ffinio*, to fine. The word seems to be the L. *finis*, and the application of it to pecuniary compensation seems to have proceeded from its feudal use, in the transfer of lands, in which a *final* agreement or concord was made between the lord and his vassal. See פנה fanah. Class Bn. No. 23.]

1. In *a feudal sense*, a final agreement between persons concerning lands or rents, or between the lord and his vassal, prescribing the conditions on which the latter should hold his lands. *Spelman.*

2. A sum of money paid to the lord by his tenant, for permission to alienate or transfer his lands to another. This in England was exacted only from the king's tenants *in capite.* *Blackstone.*

3. A sum of money paid to the king or state by way of penalty for an offense; a mulct; a pecuniary punishment. *Fines* are usually prescribed by statute, for the several violations of law; or the limit is prescribed, beyond which the judge cannot impose a *fine* for a particular offense.

In fine. [Fr. *enfin*; L. *in* and *finis.*] In the end or conclusion; to conclude; to sum up all.

FINE, *v. t.* [See *Fine*, the adjective.] To clarify; to refine; to purify; to defecate; to free from feculence or foreign matter; as, to *fine* wine.

[*This is the most general use of this word.*]

2. To purify, as a metal; as, to *fine* gold or silver. In this sense, we now generally use *refine*; but *fine* is proper. Job xxviii. Prov. xvii.

3. To make less coarse; as, to *fine* grass. [*Not used.*] *Mortimer.*

4. To decorate; to adorn. [*Not in use.*] *Shak.*

FINE, *v. t.* [See *Fine*, the noun.] To impose on one a pecuniary penalty, payable to the government, for a crime or breach of law; to set a fine on by judgment of a court; to punish by fine. The trespassers were *fined* ten dollars and imprisoned a month.

2. *v. i.* To pay a fine. [*Not used.*] *Oldham.*

FI'NEDRAW, *v. t.* [*fine* and *draw.*] To sew up a rent with so much nicety that it is not perceived. *Johnson.*

FI'NEDRAWER, *n.* One who finedraws.

FI'NEDRAWING, *n.* Rentering; a dextrous or nice sewing up the rents of cloths or stuffs. *Encyc.*

FI'NEFINGERED, *a.* Nice in workmanship; dextrous at fine work. *Johnson.*

FI'NESPOKEN, *a.* Using fine phrases. *Chesterfield.*

FI'NESPUN, *a.* Drawn to a fine thread; minute; subtle.

FI'NESTILL, *v. t.* To distill spirit from melasses, treacle or some preparation of saccharine matter. *Encyc.*

FI'NESTILLER, *n.* One who distills spirit from treacle or melasses. *Encyc.*

FI'NESTILLING, *n.* The operation of distilling spirit from melasses or treacle. *Encyc.*

FI'NED, *pp.* Refined; purified; defecated.

2. Subjected to a pecuniary penalty.

FI'NELESS, *a.* Endless; boundless. [*Not used.*] *Shak.*

FI'NELY, *adv.* In minute parts; as a substance *finely* pulverized.

2. To a thin or sharp edge; as an instrument *finely* sharpened.

3. Gaily; handsomely; beautifully; with elegance and taste. She was *finely* attired.

4. With elegance or beauty.

> Plutarch says very *finely*, that a man should not allow himself to hate even his enemies; for if you indulge this passion on some occasions, it will rise of itself in others. *Addison.*

5. With advantage; very favorably; as a house or garden *finely* situated.

6. Nicely; delicately; as a stuff *finely* wrought.

7. Purely; completely. *Clarendon.*

8. *By way of irony*, wretchedly; in a manner deserving of contemptuous notice. He is *finely* caught in his own snare.

FI'NENESS, *n.* [Fr. *finesse*; It. *finezza.*] Thinness; smallness; slenderness; as the *fineness* of a thread or silk. Hence,

2. Consisting of fine threads; as *fine* linen.

3. Smallness; minuteness; as the *fineness* of sand or particles; the *fineness* of soil or mold.

4. Clearness; purity; freedom from foreign matter; as the *fineness* of wine or other liquor; the *fineness* of gold.
5. Niceness; delicacy; as the *fineness* of taste.
6. Keenness; sharpness; thinness; as the *fineness* of an edge.
7. Elegance; beauty; as *fineness* of person.
8. Capacity for delicate or refined conceptions; as the *fineness* of genius.
9. Show; splendor; gayety of appearance; elegance; as the *fineness* of clothes or dress.
10. Clearness; as the *fineness* of complexion.
11. Subtilty; artfulness; ingenuity; as the *fineness* of wit.
12. Smoothness. *Drayton.*

FI'NER, *n.* One who refines or purifies. Prov. xxv. 4.
2. *a.* Comparative of *fine.*

FI'NERY, *n.* Show; splendor; gayety of colors or appearance; as the *finery* of a dress.
2. Showy articles of dress; gay clothes, jewels, trinkets, &c.
3. In iron-works, the second forge at the iron-mills. [See *Finary.*]

FINESS', **FINESSE**, *n.* [Fr. *finesse*; It. *finezza*; Sp. *fineza*; properly, *fineness.*]
Artifice; stratagem; subtilty of contrivance to gain a point.

FINESS', *v. i.* To use artifice or stratagem.

FINESS'ING, *ppr.* Practicing artifice to accomplish a purpose.

FIN'-FISH, *n.* A species of slender whale.

FIN-FOOTED, *a.* Having palmated feet, or feet with toes connected by a membrane. *Brown.*

FIN'GER, *n. fing'ger.* [Sax. *finger*, from *fengan*, to take or seize; G. Sw. Dan. *id*; D. *vinger*. But *n* is not radical, for the Goth. is *figgrs.*]
1. One of the extreme parts of the hand, a small member shooting to a point. The fingers have joints which peculiarly fit them to be the instruments of catching, seizing and holding. When we speak of the fingers generally, we include the thumb; as the *five* fingers. But we often make a distinction. The *fingers* and thumb consist of fifteen bones; three to each. The word is applied to some other animals as well as to man.
2. A certain measure. We say a *finger's* breadth, or the breadth of the four *fingers*, or of three *fingers.*
3. The hand. *Waller.*

Who teacheth my *fingers* to fight. Ps. cxliv.

4. The *finger* or *fingers of God*, in scripture, signify his power, strength or operation.

The magicians said to Pharaoh, this is the *finger* of God. Ex. viii.

5. In *music*, ability; skill in playing on a keyed instrument. She has a good *finger.* *Busby.*

FIN'GER, *v. t.* To handle with the fingers; to touch lightly; to toy. The covetous man delights to *finger* money.
2. To touch or take thievishly; to pilfer. *South.*
3. To touch an instrument of music; to play on an instrument. *Shak.*
4. To perform work with the fingers; to execute delicate work.
5. To handle without violence. *Bp. Hall.*

FIN'GER, *v. i.* To dispose the fingers aptly in playing on an instrument. *Busby.*

FIN'GER-BOARD, *n.* The board at the neck of a violin, guitar or the like, where the fingers act on the strings. *Wood.*

FIN'GERED, *pp.* Played on; handled; touched.
2. *a.* Having fingers. In *botany*, digitate; having leaflets like fingers.

FIN'GER-FERN, *n.* A plant, asplenium. *Johnson.*

FIN'GERING, *ppr.* Handling; touching lightly.

FIN'GERING, *n.* The act of touching lightly or handling. *Grew.*
2. The manner of touching an instrument of music. *Shak.*
3. Delicate work made with the fingers. *Spenser.*

FIN'GER-SHELL, *n.* A marine shell resembling a finger. *Dict. of Nat. Hist.*

FIN'GER-STONE, *n.* A fossil resembling an arrow. *Johnson.*

FIN'GLE-FANGLE, *n.* A trifle. [*Vulgar.*] *Hudibras.*

FIN'GRIGO, *n.* A plant, of the genus Pisonia. The fruit is a kind of berry or plum. *Lee. Ed. Encyc.*

FIN'ICAL, *a.* [from *fine.*] Nice; spruce; foppish; pretending to great nicety or superfluous elegance; as a *finical* fellow.
2. Affectedly nice or showy; as a *finical* dress.

FIN'ICALLY, *adv.* With great nicety or spruceness; foppishly.

FIN'ICALNESS, *n.* Extreme nicety in dress or manners; foppishness. *Warburton.*

FI'NING, *ppr.* [See *Fine*, the verb.] Clarifying; refining; purifying; defecating; separating from extraneous matter.
2. [See *Fine*, the noun.] Imposing a fine or pecuniary penalty.

FI'NING-POT, *n.* A vessel in which metals are refined.

FI'NIS, *n.* [L.] An end; conclusion.

FIN'ISH, *v. t.* [Arm. *finiçza*; Fr. *finir*; L. *finio*, from *finis*, an end, Ir. *fuin*, W. *fin.* Class Bn. No. 23.]
1. To arrive at the end of, in performance; to complete; as, to *finish* a house; to *finish* a journey.

Thus the heavens and the earth were *finished.* Gen. ii.

2. To make perfect.

Episodes, taken separately, *finish* nothing. *Broome.*

3. To bring to an end; to end; to put an end to.

Seventy weeks are determined on thy people, and on thy holy city, to *finish* the transgression, and make an end of sins. Dan. ix.

4. To perfect; to accomplish; to polish to the degree of excellence intended. In this sense it is frequently used in the participle of the perfect tense as an adjective. It is a *finished* performance. He is a *finished* scholar.

FIN'ISHED, *pp.* Completed; ended; done; perfected.
2. *a.* Complete; perfect; polished to the highest degree of excellence; as a *finished* poem; a *finished* education.

FIN'ISHER, *n.* One who finishes; one who completely performs. *Shak.*
2. One who puts an end to. *Hooker.*
3. One who completes or perfects.

Jesus, the author and *finisher* of our faith. Heb. xii.

FIN'ISHING, *ppr.* Completing; perfecting; bringing to an end.

FIN'ISHING or **FIN'ISH**, *n.* Completion; completeness; perfection; last polish. *Warburton.*

FI'NITE, *a.* [L. *finitus*, from *finio*, to finish, from *finis*, limit.]
Having a limit; limited; bounded; opposed to *infinite*, as *finite* number, *finite* existence; *applied to this life*, we say, a *finite* being, *finite* duration.

FI'NITELY, *adv.* Within limits; to a certain degree only. *Stillingfleet.*

FI'NITENESS, *n.* Limitation; confinement within certain boundaries; as the *finiteness* of our natural powers.

FIN'ITUDE, *n.* Limitation. [*Not used.*] *Cheyne.*

FIN'LESS, *a.* [from *fin.*] Destitute of fins; as *finless* fish. *Shak.*

FIN'LIKE, *a.* Resembling a fin; as a *finlike* oar. *Dryden.*

FINN, *n.* A native of Finland, in Europe.

FIN'NED, *a.* Having broad edges on either side; *applied to a plow.* *Mortimer.*

FIN'NIKIN, *n.* A sort of pigeon, with a crest somewhat resembling the mane of a horse. *Dict. of Nat. Hist.*

FIN'NY, *a.* Furnished with fins; as *finny* fish; *finny* tribes; *finny* prey. *Dryden. Pope.*

FIN'-TOED, *a.* [*fin* and *toe.*] Palmiped; palmated; having toes connected by a membrane, as aquatic fowls.

FINO'CHIO, *n.* [It. *finocchio.*] A variety of fennel.

FIN'SCALE, *n.* A river fish, called the rudd. *Chambers.*

FIP'PLE, *n.* [L. *fibula.*] A stopper. [*Not in use.*] *Bacon.*

FIR, *n.* [W. *pyr*, what shoots to a point, a fir-tree; Sax *furh-wudu*, fir-wood; G. *föhre*; Sw. *furu-trä*; Dan. *fyrre-træe.* The Dutch call it *sparre-boom*, spar-tree.]
The name of several species of the genus Pinus; as the Scotch fir, the silver fir, spruce fir, hemlock fir, and oriental fir.

FIR-TREE. [See *Fir.*]

FIRE, *n.* [Sax. *fyr*; G. *feuer*; D. *vuur*; Dan. Sw. *fyr*; Gr. πυρ. Qu. Coptic, *pira*, the sun; New Guinea, *for.* The radical sense of *fire* is usually, to rush, to rage, to be violently agitated; and if this is the sense of *fire*, it coincides with L. *furo.* It may be from shining or consuming. See Class Br. No. 2. 6. 9. 30.]
1. Heat and light emanating visibly, perceptibly and simultaneously from any body; caloric; the unknown cause of the sensation of heat and of the retrocession of the homogeneous particles of bodies from one another, producing expansion, and thus enlarging all their dimensions; one of the causes of magnetism, as evinced by Dr. Hare's calorimotor. *Silliman.*

In *the popular acceptation of the word*, fire is the effect of combustion. The combustible body ignited or heated to redness we call *fire*; and when ascending in a stream or body, we call it *flame*. A piece of charcoal in combustion, is of a red color and very hot. In this state it is said to be *on fire*, or to contain *fire*. When combustion ceases, it loses its redness and extreme heat, and we say, the *fire* is extinct.

2. The burning of fuel on a hearth, or in any other place. We kindle a *fire* in the morning, and at night we rake up the *fire*. Anthracite will maintain *fire* during the night.

3. The burning of a house or town; a conflagration. Newburyport and Savannah have suffered immense losses by *fire*. The great *fire* in Boston in 1711 consumed a large part of the town.

4. Light; luster; splendor.

Stars, hide your *fires!* — *Shak.*

5. Torture by burning. *Prior.*

6. The instrument of punishment; or the punishment of the impenitent in another state.

Who among us shall dwell with the devouring *fire?* Is. xxxiii.

7. That which inflames or irritates the passions.

What *fire* is in my ears? — *Shak.*

8. Ardor of temper; violence of passion.

He had *fire* in his temper. — *Atterbury.*

9. Liveliness of imagination; vigor of fancy; intellectual activity; animation; force of sentiment or expression.

And warm the critic with a poet's *fire*. — *Pope.*

10. The passion of love; ardent affection.

The God of love retires;
Dim are his torches, and extinct his *fires*. — *Pope.*

11. Ardor; heat; as the *fire* of zeal or of love.

12. Combustion; tumult; rage; contention.

13. Trouble; affliction.

When thou walkest through the *fire*, thou shalt not be burnt. Is. xliii.

To set on fire, to kindle; to inflame; to excite violent action.

St. Anthony's fire, a disease marked by an eruption on the skin, or a diffused inflammation, with fever; the Erysipelas.

Wild fire, an artificial or factitious fire, which burns even under water. It is made by a composition of sulphur, naphtha, pitch, gum and bitumen. It is called also Greek fire. *Encyc.*

FIRE, *v. t.* To set on fire; to kindle; as, to *fire* a house or chimney; to *fire* a pile. *Dryden.*

2. To inflame; to irritate the passions; as, to *fire* with anger or revenge.

3. To animate; to give life or spirit; as, to *fire* the genius.

4. To drive by fire. [*Little used.*] *Shak.*

5. To cause to explode; to discharge; as, to *fire* a musket or cannon.

6. To cauterize; *a term in farriery.*

FIRE, *v. i.* To take fire; to be kindled.

2. To be irritated or inflamed with passion.

3. To discharge artillery or firearms. They *fired* on the town.

FI'REARMS, *n. plu.* Arms or weapons which expel their charge by the combustion of powder, as pistols, muskets, &c.

FI'RE-ARRŌW, *n.* A small iron dart, furnished with a match impregnated with powder and sulphur, used to fire the sails of ships. *Encyc.*

FI'REBALL, *n.* A grenade; a ball filled with powder or other combustibles, intended to be thrown among enemies, and to injure by explosion.

2. A meteor which passes rapidly through the air and displodes.

FI'REBARE, *n.* In old writers, a beacon. *Cyc.*

FI'REBARREL, *n.* A hollow cylinder used in fireships, to convey the fire to the shrouds. *Encyc.*

FI'REBAVIN, *n.* A bundle of brush-wood, used in fireships. *Encyc.*

FI'REBL'AST, *n.* A disease in hops, chiefly towards the later periods of their growth. *Cyc.*

FI'REBOTE, *n.* An allowance of fuel, to which a tenant is entitled. *England.*

FI'REBRAND, *n.* A piece of wood kindled or on fire.

2. An incendiary; one who inflames factions, or causes contention and mischief. *Bacon.*

FI'REBRICK, *n.* A brick that will sustain intense heat without fusion.

FI'REBRUSH, *n.* A brush used to sweep the hearth. *Swift.*

FI'REBUCKET, *n.* A bucket to convey water to engines for extinguishing fire.

FI'RECLAY, *n.* A kind of clay that will sustain intense heat, used in making firebricks. *Cyc.*

FI'RECOCK, *n.* A cock or spout to let out water for extinguishing fire.

FI'RE-COMPANY, *n.* A company of men for managing an engine to extinguish fires.

FI'RECROSS, *n.* Something used in Scotland as a signal to take arms; the ends being burnt black, and in some parts smeared with blood. *Johnson.*

FI'RED, *pp.* Set on fire; inflamed; kindled; animated; irritated.

FI'REDAMP. [See *Damp.*]

FI'REDRAKE, *n.* A fiery serpent.

2. An ignis fatuus. *Beaum.*

FI'RE-ENGINE, *n.* An engine for throwing water to extinguish fire and save buildings.

FIRE-ESCA'PE, *n.* A machine for escaping from windows, when houses are on fire. *Cyc.*

FI'REFLAIR, *n.* A species of ray-fish or Raja.

FI'REFLŸ, *n.* A species of fly which has on its belly a spot which shines; and another species which emits light from under its wings, as it flies. *Encyc.*

FI'REHOOK, *n.* A large hook for pulling down buildings in conflagrations.

FI'RELOCK, *n.* A musket, or other gun, with a lock, which is discharged by striking fire with flint and steel.

FI'REMAN, *n.* A man whose business is to extinguish fires in towns.

2. A man of violent passions. [*Not used.*] *Tatler.*

FI'REM'ASTER, *n.* An officer of artillery who superintends the composition of fireworks.

FI'RENEW, *a.* Fresh from the forge; bright. *Addison.*

FI'RE-OFFICE, *n.* An office for making insurance against fire.

FIRE-ORDEAL, *n.* [See *Ordeal.*]

FI'REPAN, *n.* A pan for holding or conveying fire. Ex. xxvii.

FI'REPLACE, *n.* The part of a chimney appropriated to the fire; a hearth.

FI'REPLUG, *n.* A plug for drawing water from a pipe to extinguish fire.

FI'REPOT, *n.* A small earthern pot filled with combustibles, used in military operations.

FI'RER, *n.* One who sets fire to any thing; an incendiary.

FI'RESHIP, *n.* A vessel filled with combustibles and furnished with grappling irons to hook and set fire to an enemy's ships. *Encyc.*

FI'RESHŎVEL, *n.* A shovel or instrument for taking up or removing coals of fire.

FIRESIDE, *n.* A place near the fire or hearth; home; domestic life or retirement.

FI'RESTICK, *n.* A lighted stick or brand. *Digby.*

FI'RESTŎNE, *n.* A fossil, the pyrite. [See *Pyrite.*]

2. A kind of freestone which bears a high degree of heat. *Cyc.*

FIREWARD, / FIREWARDEN, *n.* An officer who has authority to direct others in the extinguishing of fires.

FI'REWOOD, *n.* Wood for fuel.

FI'REWŎRK, *n.* Usually in the plural, *fireworks.*

Preparations of gun-powder, sulphur and other inflammable materials, used for making explosions in the air, on occasions of public rejoicing; pyrotechnical exhibitions. This word is applied also to various combustible preparations used in war.

FI'REWŎRKER, *n.* An officer of artillery subordinate to the firemaster.

FI'RING, *ppr.* Setting fire to; kindling; animating; exciting; inflaming; discharging firearms.

FI'RING, *n.* The act of discharging firearms.

2. Fuel; firewood or coal. *Mortimer.*

FI'RING-IRON, *n.* An instrument used in farriery to discuss swellings and knots. *Encyc.*

FIRK, *v. t.* To beat; to whip; to chastise. [*Not used.*] *Hudibras.*

FIRKIN, *n. fur'kin.* [The first syllable is probably the Dan. *fire*, D. *vier*, four, and the latter, as in *kilderkin.*]

A measure of capacity, being the fourth part of a barrel. It is nine gallons of beer, or eight gallons of ale, soap or herrings. In *America*, the *firkin* is rarely used, except for butter or lard, and signifies a small vessel or cask of indeterminate size, or of different sizes, regulated by the statutes of the different states.

FIR'LOT, *n.* A dry measure used in Scotland. The oat firlot contains 21¼ pints of that country; the wheat firlot 224 cubic inches; the barley firlot 21 standard pints. *Encyc.*

FIRM, *a. ferm.* [L. *firmus;* Fr. *ferme;* Sp. *firme;* It. *fermo;* W. *fyrv.* This Welsh word may be from the Latin. The root of the word is probably Celtic; W. *fêr*, hard, solid; *fyr*, a solid; *feru*, to concrete or congeal, to fix, to freeze. This is the root of L. *ferrum*, iron.]

1. Properly, fixed; hence, applied to the matter of bodies, it signifies closely com-

pressed; compact; hard; solid; as *firm* flesh; *firm* muscles; some species of wood are more *firm* than others; a cloth of *firm* texture.

2. Fixed; steady; constant; stable; unshaken; not easily moved; as a *firm* believer; a *firm* friend; a *firm* adherent or supporter; a *firm* man, or a man of *firm* resolution.

3. Solid; not giving way; opposed to *fluid*; as *firm* land.

FIRM, *n. ferm.* A partnership or house; or the name or title under which a company transact business; as the *firm* of Hope & Co.

FIRM, *v. t. ferm.* [L. *firmo.*] To fix; to settle; to confirm; to establish.

And Jove has *firm'd* it with an awful nod. *Dryden.*

This word is rarely used, except in poetry. In prose, we use *confirm.*

FIRMAMENT, *n. ferm'ament.* [L. *firmamentum*, from *firmus, firmo.*]

The region of the air; the sky or heavens. In *scripture*, the word denotes an expanse, a wide extent; for such is the signification of the Hebrew word, coinciding with *regio, region*, and *reach.* The original therefore does not convey the sense of solidity, but of stretching, extension; the great arch or expanse over our heads, in which are placed the atmosphere and the clouds, and in which the stars *appear* to be placed, and are *really* seen.

And God said, Let there be a *firmament* in the midst of the waters, and let it divide the waters from the waters. Gen. i. 6.

And God said, Let there be lights in the *firmament.* Ibm. i. 14.

FIRMAMENT'AL, *a.* Pertaining to the firmament; celestial; being of the upper regions. *Dryden.*

FIR'MAN, *n.* An Asiatic word, denoting a passport, permit, license, or grant of privileges.

FIRMED, *pp. ferm'ed.* Established; confirmed.

FIRMING, *ppr. ferm'ing.* Settling; making firm and stable.

FIRMITUDE, *n. ferm'itude.* Strength; solidity. [*Not in use.*] *Bp. Hall.*

FIRMITY, *n. ferm'ity.* Strength; firmness. [*Not used.*] *Chillingworth.*

FIRMLESS, *a. ferm'less.* Detached from substance.

Does passion still the *firmless* mind control. *Pope.*

FIRMLY, *adv. ferm'ly.* Solidly; compactly; closely; as particles of matter *firmly* cohering.

2. Steadily; with constancy or fixedness; immovably; steadfastly. He *firmly* believes in the divine origin of the scriptures. His resolution is *firmly* fixed. He *firmly* adheres to his party.

FIRM'NESS, *n. ferm'ness.* Closeness or denseness of texture or structure; compactness; hardness; solidity; as the *firmness* of wood, stone, cloth or other substance.

2. Stability; strength; as the *firmness* of a union, or of a confederacy.

3. Steadfastness; constancy; fixedness; as the *firmness* of a purpose or resolution; the *firmness* of a man, or of his courage; *firmness* of mind or soul.

4. Certainty; soundness; as the *firmness* of notions or opinions.

FIRST, *a. furst.* [Sax. *first* or *fyrst*, Sw. *fórste*, Dan. *förste*, first; G. *fürst*, D. *vorst*, Dan. *fyrste*, a prince, that is, *first* man. It is the superlative of *fore, fyr*, before, advanced, that is, *forest, fyrest*, from Sax. *faran*, to go, or a root of the same family. See *Fare* and *For.*]

1. Advanced before or further than any other in progression; foremost in place; as the *first* man in a marching company or troop is the man that precedes all the rest. Hence,

2. Preceding all others in the order of time. Adam was the *first* man. Cain was the *first* murderer. Monday was the *first* day of January.

3. Preceding all others in numbers or a progressive series; the ordinal of one; as, 1 is the *first* number.

4. Preceding all others in rank, dignity or excellence. Demosthenes was the *first* orator of Greece. Burke was one of the *first* geniuses of his age. Give God the *first* place in your affections.

FIRST, *adv. furst.* Before any thing else in the order of time.

Adam was *first* formed, then Eve. 1 Tim. ii.

2. Before all others in place or progression. Let the officers enter the gate *first.*

3. Before any thing else in order of proceeding or consideration. *First*, let us attend to the examination of the witnesses.

4. Before all others in rank. He stands or ranks *first* in public estimation.

At first, at the first, at the beginning or origin.

First or last, at one time or another; at the beginning or end.

And all are fools and lovers *first or last.* *Dryden.*

FIRST-BEGOT'TEN, *a.* First produced; the eldest of children. *Milton.*

FIRST'-BORN, *a.* First brought forth; first in the order of nativity; eldest; as the *first-born* son.

2. Most excellent; most distinguished or exalted. Christ is called the *first-born* of every creature. Col. i.

FIRST'-BORN, *n.* The eldest child; the first in the order of birth.

The *first-born* of the poor are the most wretched. Is. xiv.

The *first-born* of death is the most terrible death. Job. xviii.

FIRST-CREA'TED, *a.* Created before any other. *Milton.*

FIRST-FRUIT, **FIRST-FRUITS**, *n.* The fruit or produce first matured and collected in any season. Of these the Jews made an oblation to God, as an acknowledgment of his sovereign dominion.

2. The first profits of any thing. In *the church of England*, the profits of every spiritual benefice for the first year. *Encyc.*

3. The first or earliest effect of any thing, in a good or bad sense; as the *first-fruits* of grace in the heart, or the *first-fruits* of vice.

FIRST'LING, *a.* First produced; as *firstling* males. Deut. xv.

FIRST'LING, *n.* The first produce or offspring; *applied to beasts*; as the *firstlings* of cattle.

2. The thing first thought or done. [*Not used.*]

The very *firstlings* of my heart shall be
The *firstlings* of my hand. *Shak.*

FIRST'-RATE, *a.* Of the highest excellence; preeminent; as a *first-rate* scholar or painter.

2. Being of the largest size; as a *first-rate* ship.

FISC, *n.* [L. *fiscus*; Fr. *fisc*; Sp. *fisco*; It. *id.* *Fiscus*, φισκος, signifies a basket or hanaper, probably from the twigs which composed the first baskets, Eng. *whisk.* The word coincides in elements with *basket*, and L. *fascia*, twigs being the primitive bands.]

The treasury of a prince or state; hence, to *confiscate* is to take the goods of a criminal and appropriate them to the public treasury.

FISC'AL, *a.* Pertaining to the public treasury or revenue.

The *fiscal* arrangements of government. *Hamilton.*

FISC'AL, *n.* Revenue; the income of a prince or state.

2. A treasurer. *Swinburne.*

FISH, *n.* [Sax. *fisc*; D. *visch*; G. *fisch*; Dan. and Sw. *fisk*; Sp. *pez*; It. *pesce*; Fr. *poisson*; verb, *pêcher, pescher*; Arm. *pesk*; W. *pysg*; L. *piscis*; Ir. *iasg.* This animal may be named from its rapid motion. In W. *fysg* is hasty, impetuous.]

An animal that lives in water. *Fish* is a general name for a class of animals subsisting in water, which were distributed by Linne into six orders. They breathe by means of gills, swim by the aid of fins, and are oviparous. Some of them have the skeleton bony, and others cartilaginous. Most of the former have the opening of the gills closed by a peculiar covering, called the gill-lid; many of the latter have no gill-lid, and are hence said to breathe through apertures. Cetaceous animals, as the whale and dolphin, are, in popular language, called fishes, and have been so classed by some naturalists; but they breathe by lungs, and are viviparous, like quadrupeds. The term *fish* has been also extended to other aquatic animals, such as shell-fish, lobsters, &c. We use *fish*, in the singular, for fishes in general or the whole race.

2. The flesh of fish, used as food. But we usually apply *flesh* to land animals.

FISH, *v. i.* To attempt to catch fish; to be employed in taking fish, by any means, as by angling or drawing nets.

2. To attempt or seek to obtain by artifice, or indirectly to seek to draw forth; as, to *fish* for compliments.

FISH, *v. t.* To search by raking or sweeping; as, to *fish* the jakes for papers. *Swift.*

2. In *seamanship*, to strengthen, as a mast or yard, with a piece of timber. *Mar. Dict.*

3. To catch; to draw out or up; as, to *fish up* a human body when sunk; to *fish* an anchor.

FISH, *n.* In *ships*, a machine to hoist and draw up the flukes of an anchor, towards the top of the bow.

2. A long piece of timber, used to strengthen a lower mast or a yard, when sprung or damaged.

FISH'ER, *n.* One who is employed in catching fish.

2. A species of weasel. *Pennant.*

FISH'ERBOAT, *n.* A boat employed in catching fish.

FISH'ERMAN, *n.* One whose occupation is to catch fish.

2. A ship or vessel employed in the business of taking fish, as in the cod and whale fishery.

FISH'ERTOWN, *n.* A town inhabited by fishermen. *Carew.*

FISH'ERY, *n.* The business of catching fish. *Addison.*

2. A place for catching fish with nets or hooks, as the banks of Newfoundland, the coast of England or Scotland, or on the banks of rivers.

FISH'FUL, *a.* Abounding with fish; as a *fishful* pond. *Carew.*

FISH'GIG, FIZ'GIG, *n.* An instrument used for striking fish at sea, consisting of a staff with barbed prongs, and a line fastened just above the prongs. *Mar. Dict.*

FISH'HOOK, *n.* A hook for catching fish.

FISH'ING, *ppr.* Attempting to catch fish; searching; seeking to draw forth by artifice or indirectly; adding a piece of timber to a mast or spar to strengthen it.

FISH'ING, *n.* The art or practice of catching fish.

2. A fishery. *Spenser.*

FISH'ING-FROG, *n.* The toad-fish, or Lophius, whose head is larger than the body. *Encyc.*

FISH'ING-PLACE, *n.* A place where fishes are caught with seines; a convenient place for fishing; a fishery.

FISH'KETTLE, *n.* A kettle made long for boiling fish whole.

FISH'LIKE, *a.* Resembling fish. *Shak.*

FISH'MARKET, *n.* A place where fish are exposed for sale.

FISH'MEAL, *n.* A meal of fish; diet on fish; abstemious diet.

FISH'MONGER, *n.* A seller of fish; a dealer in fish.

FISH'POND, *n.* A pond in which fishes are bred and kept.

FISH'ROOM, *n.* An apartment in a ship between the after-hold and the spirit room. *Mar. Dict.*

FISH'SPEAR, *n.* A spear for taking fish by stabbing them.

FISH'WIFE, *n.* A woman that cries fish for sale. *Beaum.*

FISH'WOMAN, *n.* A woman who sells fish.

FISH'Y, *a.* Consisting of fish.

2. Inhabited by fish; as the *fishy* flood. *Pope.*

3. Having the qualities of fish; like fish; as a *fishy* form; a *fishy* taste or smell.

FIS'SILE, *a.* [L. *fissilis*, from *fissus*, divided, from *findo*, to split.]

That may be split, cleft or divided in the direction of the grain, or of natural joints.

> This crystal is a pellucid *fissile* stone. *Newton.*

FISSIL'ITY, *n.* The quality of admitting to be cleft.

FIS'SIPED, *a.* [L. *fissus*, divided, and *pes*, foot.] Having separate toes.

FIS'SIPED, *n.* An animal whose toes are separate, or not connected by a membrane. *Brown.*

FIS'SURE, *n.* *fish'ure.* [Fr. from L. *fissura*, from *findo*, to split.]

1. A cleft; a narrow chasm made by the parting of any substance; a longitudinal opening; as the *fissure* of a rock.

2. In *surgery*, a crack or slit in a bone, either transversely or longitudinally, by means of external force. *Encyc.*

3. In *anatomy*, a deep, narrow sulcus, or depression, dividing the anterior and middle lobes of the cerebrum on each side. *Coxe.*

FIS'SURE, *v. t.* To cleave; to divide; to crack or fracture. *Wiseman.*

FIS'SURED, *pp.* Cleft; divided; cracked.

FIST, *n.* [Sax. *fyst*; D. *vuist*; G. *faust*; Russ. *piast*; Bohem. *bost*. Qu. is it from the root of *fast*?]

The hand clinched; the hand with the fingers doubled into the palm.

FIST, *v. t.* To strike with the fist. *Dryden.*

2. To gripe with the fist. [*Little used.*] *Shak.*

FIST'ICUFFS, *n.* [*fist* and *cuff*.] Blows or a combat with the fist; a boxing. *Swift.*

FIS'TULA, *n.* [L.; Eng. *whistle*.] Properly, a pipe; a wind instrument of music, originally a reed.

2. In *surgery*, a deep, narrow and callous ulcer, generally arising from abscesses. It differs from a sinus, in being callous.

Fistula lachrymalis, a fistula of the lachrymal sac, a disorder accompanied with a flowing of tears. *Coxe. Sharp.*

FIS'TULAR, *a.* Hollow, like a pipe or reed.

FIS'TULATE, *v. i.* To become a pipe or fistula.

FIS'TULATE, *v. t.* To make hollow like a pipe. [*Little used.*]

FIS'TULIFORM, *a.* [*fistula* and *form*.] Being in round hollow columns, as a mineral.

> Stalactite often occurs *fistuliform*. *Phillips.*

FIS'TULOUS, *a.* Having the form or nature of a fistula; as a *fistulous* ulcer. *Wiseman.*

FIT, *n.* [Qu. W. *fith*, a gliding or darting motion. The French express the sense of this word by *boutade*, from *bout*, the primary sense of which is to shoot or push out. It seems to be allied to L. *peto*, *impeto*, to assault, or to Eng. *pet*, and primarily to denote a rushing on or attack, or a start. See *Fit*, suitable.]

1. The invasion, exacerbation or paroxysm of a disease. We apply the word to the return of an ague, after intermission, as a cold *fit*. We apply it to the first attack, or to the return of other diseases, as a *fit* of the gout or stone; and in general, to a disease however continued, as a *fit* of sickness.

2. A sudden and violent attack of disorder, in which the body is often convulsed, and sometimes senseless; as a *fit* of apoplexy or epilepsy; hysteric *fits*.

3. Any short return after intermission; a turn; a period or interval. He moves by *fits* and starts.

> By *fits* my swelling grief appears. *Addison.*

4. A temporary affection or attack; as a *fit* of melancholy, or of grief; a *fit* of pleasure.

5. Disorder; distemperature. *Shak.*

6. [Sax. *fitt*, a song.] Anciently, a song, or part of a song; a strain; a canto. *Lye. Johnson.*

FIT, *a.* [Flemish, *vitten*; G. *pass*, fit, and a pace; *passen*, to be fit, suitable, right. This is from the root of Eng. *pass*; D. *pas*, time, season; *van pas*, fitting, fit, convenient; Eng. *pat*; Dan. *passer*, to be fit. In L. *competo*, whence *compatible*, signifies properly to meet or to fall on, hence to suit or be fit, from *peto*. This is probably the same word. The primary sense is to come to, to fall on, hence to meet, to extend to, to be close, to suit. To *come* or *fall*, is the primary sense of time or season, as in the Dutch. See Class Bd. No. 45. 64. and Class Bz. No. 52. 53. 70.]

1. Suitable; convenient; meet; becoming.

> Is it *fit* to say to a king, thou art wicked? Job xxxiv.
>
> Wives, submit yourselves to your husbands, as it is *fit* in the Lord. Col. iii.

2. Qualified; as men of valor *fit* for war.

> No man having put his hand to the plow, and looking back, is *fit* for the kingdom of God. Luke ix.

FIT, *v. t.* To adapt; to suit; to make suitable.

> The carpenter—marketh it out with a line, he *fitteth* it with planes. Is. xliv.

2. To accommodate a person with any thing; as, the tailor *fits* his customer with a coat. The original phrase is, he *fits* a coat *to* his customer. But the phrase implies also furnishing, providing a thing suitable for another.

3. To prepare; to put in order for; to furnish with things proper or necessary; as, to *fit* a ship *for* a long voyage. *Fit* yourself *for* action or defense.

4. To qualify; to prepare; as, to *fit* a student *for* college.

To fit out, to furnish; to equip; to supply with necessaries or means; as, to *fit out* a privateer.

To fit up, to prepare; to furnish with things suitable; to make proper for the reception or use of any person; as, to *fit up* a house for a guest.

FIT, *v. i.* To be proper or becoming.

> Nor *fits* it to prolong the feast. *Pope.*

2. To suit or be suitable; to be adapted. His coat *fits* very well. *But this is an elliptical phrase.*

FITCH, *n.* A chick-pea.

FITCH'ET, FITCH'EW, *n.* A polecat; a foumart. [W. *gwicyll* or *gwicyn*.]

FIT'FUL, *a.* Varied by paroxysms; full of fits. *Shak.*

FIT'LY, *adv.* Suitably; properly; with propriety. A maxim *fitly* applied.

2. Commodiously; conveniently.

FIT'MENT, *n.* Something adapted to a purpose. [*Not used.*] *Shak.*

FIT'NESS, *n.* Suitableness; adaptedness; adaptation; as the *fitness* of things to their use.

2. Propriety; meetness; justness; reasonableness; as the *fitness* of measures or laws.

3. Preparation; qualification; as a student's *fitness* for college.

4. Convenience; the state of being fit.

FIT'TED, *pp.* Made suitable; adapted; prepared; qualified.

FIT'TER, *n.* One who makes fit or suitable; one who adapts; one who prepares.

FIT'TING, *ppr.* Making suitable; adapting; preparing; qualifying; providing with.

FIT'TINGLY, *adv.* Suitably. *More.*

FITZ, Norm. *fites, fiuz*, or *fiz*, a son, is used in names, as in *Fitzherbert, Fitzroy, Carlovitz.*

FIVE, *a.* [Sax. *fif;* D. *vyf;* G. *fünf;* Sw. Dan. *fem;* W. *pum, pump;* Arm. *pemp.*]

Four and one added; the half of ten; as *five* men; *five* loaves. Like other adjectives, it is often used as a noun.

Five of them were wise, and *five* were foolish. Matt. xxv.

FI'VEBAR, } *a.* Having five bars; as
FI'VEBARRED, } a *fivebarred* gate.

FI'VECLEFT, *a.* Quinquefid; divided into five segments.

FI'VEFOLD, *a.* In fives; consisting of five in one; five-double; five times repeated.

FI'VELEAF, *n.* Cinquefoil. *Drayton.*

FI'VELEAFED, *a.* Having five leaves; as *fiveleafed* clover, or *cinquefoil.*

FI'VELOBED, *a.* Consisting of five lobes.

FI'VEPARTED, *a.* Divided into five parts.

FIVES, *n.* A kind of play with a ball.

FIVES or **VIVES**, *n.* A disease of horses, resembling the strangles. *Encyc.*

FI'VETOOTHED, *a.* Having five teeth.

FI'VEVALVED, *a.* Having five valves. *Botany.*

FIX, *v. t.* [Fr. *fixer;* Sp. *fixar;* It. *fissare;* L. *fixus, figo.* Class Bg.]

1. To make stable; to set or establish immovably. The universe is governed by *fixed* laws.
2. To set or place permanently; to establish. The prince *fixed* his residence at York. The seat of our government is *fixed* at Washington in the district of Columbia. Some men have no *fixed* opinions.
3. To make fast; to fasten; to attach firmly; as, to *fix* a cord or line to a hook.
4. To set or place steadily; to direct, as the eye, without moving it; to fasten. The gentleman *fixed* his eyes on the speaker, and addressed him with firmness.
5. To set or direct steadily, without wandering; as, to *fix* the attention. The preacher *fixes* the attention of his audience, or the hearers *fix* their attention on the preacher.
6. To set or make firm, so as to bear a high degree of heat without evaporating; to deprive of volatility. Gold, diamonds, silver, platina, are among the most *fixed* bodies.
7. To transfix; to pierce. [*Little used.*] *Sandys.*
8. To withhold from motion.
9. In *popular use*, to put in order; to prepare; to adjust; to set or place in the manner desired or most suitable; as, to *fix* clothes or dress; to *fix* the furniture of a room. This use is analogous to that of *set*, in the phrase, to *set* a razor.

FIX, *v. i.* To rest; to settle or remain permanently; to cease from wandering.

Your kindness banishes your fear,
Resolved to *fix* forever here. *Waller.*

2. To become firm, so as to resist volatilization.
3. To cease to flow or be fluid; to congeal; to become hard and malleable; as a metallic substance. *Bacon.*

To fix on, to settle the opinion or resolution on any thing; to determine on. The contracting parties have *fixed on* certain leading points. The legislature *fixed on* Wethersfield as the place for a State Prison.

FIX'ABLE, *a.* That may be fixed, established, or rendered firm.

FIXA'TION, *n.* The act of fixing.

2. Stability; firmness; steadiness; a state of being established; as *fixation* in matters of religion. *King Charles.*
3. Residence in a certain place; or a place of residence. [*Little used.*]

To light, created in the first day, God gave no certain place or *fixation.* *Raleigh.*

4. That firm state of a body which resists evaporation or volatilization by heat; as the *fixation* of gold or other metals. *Bacon. Encyc.*
5. The act or process of ceasing to be fluid and becoming firm; state of being fixed. *Glanville.*

FIX'ED, *pp.* Settled; established; firm; fast; stable.

Fixed air, an invisible and permanently elastic fluid, heavier than common air and fatal to animal life, produced from the combustion of carbonaceous bodies, as wood or charcoal, and by artificial processes; called also *aerial acid, cretaceous acid*, and more generally, *carbonic acid.*

Fixed bodies, are those which bear a high heat without evaporation or volatilization.

Fixed stars, are such stars as always retain the same apparent position and distance with respect to each other, and are thus distinguished from planets and comets, which are revolving bodies.

Fixed oils, such as are obtained by simple pressure, and are not readily volatilized; so called in distinction from *volatile* or *essential oils.*

FIX'EDLY, *adv.* Firmly; in a settled or established manner; steadfastly.

FIX'EDNESS, *n.* A state of being fixed; stability; firmness; steadfastness; as a *fixedness* in religion or politics; *fixedness* of opinion on any subject.

2. The state of a body which resists evaporation or volatilization by heat; as the *fixedness* of gold.
3. Firm coherence of parts; solidity. *Bentley.*

FIXID'ITY, *n.* Fixedness. [*Not used.*] *Boyle.*

FIX'ITY, *n.* Fixedness; coherence of parts; that property of bodies by which they resist dissipation by heat. *Newton.*

FIX'TURE, *n.* Position. *Shak.*

2. Fixedness; firm pressure; as the *fixture* of the foot. *Shak.*
3. Firmness; stable state.
4. That which is fixed to a building; any appendage or part of the furniture of a house which is fixed to it, as by nails, screws, &c., and which the tenant cannot legally take away, when he removes to another house.

FIX'URE, *n.* Position; stable pressure; firmness. [*Little used.*] *Shak.*

FIZ'GIG, *n.* A fishgig, which see.

2. A gadding flirting girl.
3. A fire-work, made of powder rolled up in a paper.

FIZZ, } *v. i.* To make a hissing sound.
FIZ'ZLE, }

FLAB'BINESS, *n.* [See *Flabby.*] A soft, flexible state of a substance, which renders it easily movable and yielding to pressure.

FLAB'BY, *a.* [W. *llib*, a soft, lank, limber state; *llibin*, flaccid, lank; *llipa*, flaccid, lank, *flapping;* *llipâu*, to become flabby, to droop; *llipanu*, to make *glib* or smooth. *Flabby, flap*, and *glib* appear to be from the same root.]

Soft; yielding to the touch and easily moved or shaken; easily bent; hanging loose by its own weight; as *flabby* flesh. *Swift.*

FLAC'CID, *a.* [L. *flaccidus*, from *flacceo*, to hang down, to *flag;* Sp. *floxo;* Port. *froxo;* Ir. *floch;* W. *llac*, and *llag*, slack, sluggish, lax; *llaciaw*, to slacken, to relax, to droop; *llaca*, slop, mud; *lleigiaw*, to flag, to lag, to skulk; *lleigus*, flagging, drooping, sluggish, slow. We see that *flaccid, flag, slack, sluggish, slow*, and *lag*, are all of this family. See Class Lg. No. 40. 41. 42. 43.]

Soft and weak; limber; lax; drooping; hanging down by its own weight; yielding to pressure for want of firmness and stiffness; as a *flaccid* muscle; *flaccid* flesh.

FLAC'CIDNESS, } *n.* Laxity; limberness; want of firmness or stiffness. *Wiseman.*
FLACCID'ITY, }

FLAG, *v. i.* [W. *llacâu*, or *llaciaw*, to relax, to droop; *llegu*, to flag; L. *flacceo;* Sp. *flaquear;* Port. *fraquear*, to flag; Ir. *lag*, weak. See *Flaccid.* The sense is primarily to bend, or rather to recede, to *lag.*]

1. To hang loose without stiffness; to bend down as flexible bodies; to be loose and yielding; as the *flagging* sails. *Dryden.*
2. To grow spiritless or dejected; to droop; to grow languid; as, the spirits *flag.*
3. To grow weak; to lose vigor; as, the strength *flags.*
4. To become dull or languid.

The pleasures of the town begin to *flag.* *Swift.*

FLAG, *v. t.* To let fall into feebleness; to suffer to drop; as, to *flag* the wings. *Prior.*

FLAG, *n.* [W. *llec;* Ir. *liag*, a broad flat stone; allied perhaps to *lay.*] A flat stone, or a pavement of flat stones.

FLAG, *v. t.* To lay with flat stones.

The sides and floor were all *flagged* with excellent marble. *Sandys.*

FLAG, *n.* [W. *llaç*, a blade.] An aquatic plant, with a bladed leaf, probably so called from its bending or yielding to the wind.

FLAG, *n.* [G. *flagge;* D. *vlag, vlagge;* Dan. *flag;* Sw. *flagg;* allied probably to the preceding word, in the sense of bending or spreading.]

An ensign or colors; a cloth on which are usually painted or wrought certain figures, and borne on a staff. In *the army*, a banner by which one regiment is distinguished from another. In *the marine*, a banner or standard by which the ships of one nation are distinguished from those of another, or by which an admiral is distinguished from other ships of his squadron. In the British navy, an admiral's *flag* is displayed at the main-top-gallant-mast-head, a vice-admiral's at the fore-top-gallant-mast-head, and a rear-admiral's at the mizen-top-gallant-mast-head.

To strike or *lower the flag*, is to pull it down upon the cap in token of respect or submission. To *strike the flag* in an engagement, is the sign of surrendering.

To hang out the white flag, is to ask quarter; or in some cases, to manifest a friendly design. The *red flag*, is a sign of defiance or battle.

To hang the flag half mast high, is a token or signal of mourning.

Flag-officer, an admiral; the commander of a squadron.

Flag-ship, the ship which bears the admiral, and in which his flag is displayed.

Flag-staff, the staff that elevates the flag. *Encyc. Mar. Dict.*

FLAG'BROOM, *n.* A broom for sweeping flags. *Johnson.*

FLAG'STONE, *n.* A flat stone for pavement.

FLAG'WŎRM, *n.* A worm or grub found among flags and sedge. *Walton.*

FLAĠ'ELET, *n.* [Fr. *flageolet*, from L. *flatus*, by corruption, or Gr. πλαγιαυλος, πλαγιος, oblique, and αυλος, a flute. *Lunier.*]

A little flute; a small wind instrument of music. *More.*

FLAĠ'ELLANT, *n.* [L. *flagellans*, from *flagello*, to *flog*.]

One who whips himself in religious discipline. The flagellants were a fanatical sect which arose in Italy, AD. 1260, who maintained that flagellation was of equal virtue with baptism and the sacrament. They walked in procession with shoulders bare, and whipped themselves till the blood ran down their bodies, to obtain the mercy of God, and appease his wrath against the vices of the age. *Encyc.*

FLAĠ'ELLATE, *v. t.* To whip; to scourge.

FLAĠELLA'TION, *n.* [L. *flagello*, to beat or whip, to *flog*, from *flagellum*, a whip, scourge or *flail*, D. *vlegel*, G. *flegel*, Fr. *fleau*. See *Flail* and *Flog*.]

A beating or whipping; a flogging; the discipline of the scourge. *Garth.*

FLAG'GED, *pp.* Laid with flat stones.

FLAG'GINESS, *n.* Laxity; limberness; want of tension.

FLAG'GING, *ppr.* Growing weak; drooping; laying with flat stones.

FLAG'GY, *a.* Weak; flexible; limber; not stiff. *Dryden.*

2. Weak in taste; insipid; as a *flaggy* apple. *Bacon.*

3. Abounding with flags, the plant.

FLAĠI''TIOUS, *a.* [L. *flagitium*, a scandalous crime, probably from the root of *flagrant*.]

1. Deeply criminal; grossly wicked; villainous; atrocious; scandalous; as a *flagitious* action or crime. *South.*

2. Guilty of enormous crimes; corrupt; wicked; as a *flagitious* person. *Pope.*

3. Marked or infected with scandalous crimes or vices; as *flagitious* times. *Pope.*

FLAĠI''TIOUSLY, *adv.* With extreme wickedness.

FLAĠI''TIOUSNESS, *n.* Extreme wickedness; villainy.

FLAG'ON, *n.* [L. *lagena*; Gr. λαγηνος; Ir. *clagun*; Fr. *flacon*; Sam. Castel. col. 3013.]

A vessel with a narrow mouth, used for holding and conveying liquors.

> Stay me with *flagons*, comfort me with apples; for I am sick of love. Cant. ii.

FLA'GRANCY, *n.* [See *Flagrant.*] A burning; great heat; inflammation. *Obs.*

> Lust causeth a *flagrancy* in the eyes. *Bacon.*

2. Excess; enormity; as the *flagrancy* of a crime.

FLA'GRANT, *a.* [L. *flagrans*, from *flagro*, to burn, Gr. φλεγω, φλογοω. In D. *flakkeren* is to blaze.]

1. Burning; ardent; eager; as *flagrant* desires. *Hooker.*

2. Glowing; red; flushed.

> See Sapho, at her toilet's greasy task,
> Then issuing *flagrant* to an evening mask. *Pope.*

3. Red; inflamed.

> The beadle's lash still *flagrant* on their back. *Prior.*

[*The foregoing senses are unusual.*]

4. Flaming in notice; glaring; notorious; enormous; as a *flagrant* crime.

FLA'GRANTLY, *adv.* Ardently; notoriously. *Warton.*

FLA'GRATE, *v. t.* To burn. [*Little used.*] *Greenhill.*

FLAGRA'TION, *n.* A burning. [*Little used.*]

FLA'IL, *n.* [D. *vlegel*; G. *flegel*; L. *flagellum*; Fr. *fleau*. We retain the original verb in *flog*, to strike, to *lay* on, L. *fligo*, whence *affligo*, to afflict; Gr. πληγη, L. *plaga*, a stroke, or perhaps from the same root as *lick* and *lay*. See *Lick.*]

An instrument for thrashing or beating corn from the ear.

FLAKE, *n.* [Sax. *flace*; D. *vlaak*, a hurdle for wool; *vlok*, a flock, a flake, a tuft; G. *flocke*, *fluge*, id.; Dan. *flok*, a herd, and *lok*, a *lock* or flock of wool; L. *floccus*; Gr. πλοκη, πλοκος; It. *flocco*; Ir. *flocas*. *Flake* and *flock* are doubtless the same word, varied in orthography, and connected perhaps with L. *plico*, Gr. πλεκω. The sense is a complication, a crowd, or a *lay*.]

1. A small collection of snow, as it falls from the clouds or from the air; a little bunch or cluster of snowy crystals, such as fall in still moderate weather. This is a *flake*, *lock* or *flock* of snow.

2. A platform of hurdles, or small sticks made fast or interwoven, supported by stanchions, on which cod-fish is dried. *Massachusetts.*

3. A layer or stratum; as a *flake* of flesh or tallow. Job xli.

4. A collection or little particle of fire, or of combustible matter on fire, separated and flying off.

5. Any scaly matter in layers; any mass cleaving off in scales.

> Little *flakes* of scurf. *Addison.*

6. A sort of carnations of two colors only, having large stripes going through the leaves. *Encyc.*

White-flake, in painting, is lead corroded by means of the pressing of grapes, or a ceruse prepared by the acid of grapes. It is brought from Italy, and of a quality superior to common white lead. It is used in oil and varnished painting, when a clean white is required. *Encyc.*

FLAKE, *v. t.* To form into flakes. *Pope.*

FLAKE, *v. i.* To break or separate in layers; to peel or scale off. We more usually say, to *flake off*.

FLAKE-WHITE, *n.* Oxyd of bismuth. *Ure.*

FLA'KY, *a.* Consisting of flakes or locks; consisting of small loose masses.

2. Lying in flakes; consisting of layers, or cleaving off in layers.

FLAM, *n.* [Ice. *flim*; W. *llam*, a leap.] A freak or whim; also, a falsehood; a lie; an illusory pretext; deception; delusion.

> Lies immortalized and consigned over as a perpetual abuse and *flam* upon posterity. *South.*

FLAM, *v. t.* To deceive with falsehood; to delude. *South.*

FLAM'BEAU, *n.* *flam'bo.* [Fr. from L. *flamma*, flame.]

A light or luminary made of thick wicks covered with wax, and used in the streets at night, at illuminations, and in processions. Flambeaus are made square, and usually consist of four wicks or branches, near an inch thick, and about three feet long, composed of coarse hempen yarn, half twisted. *Encyc.*

FLAME, *n.* [Fr. *flamme*; L. *flamma*; It. *flamma*; Sp. *llama*; D. *vlam*; G. *flamme.*]

1. A blaze; burning vapor; vapor in combustion; or according to modern chimistry, hydrogen or any inflammable gas, in a state of combustion, and naturally ascending in a stream from burning bodies, being specifically lighter than common air.

2. Fire in general. *Cowley.*

3. Heat of passion; tumult; combustion; blaze; violent contention. One jealous, tattling mischief-maker will set a whole village in a *flame*.

4. Ardor of temper or imagination; brightness of fancy; vigor of thought.

> Great are their faults, and glorious is their *flame*. *Waller.*

5. Ardor of inclination; warmth of affection.

> Smit with the love of kindred arts we came,
> And met congenial, mingling *flame* with *flame*. *Pope.*

6. The passion of love; ardent love.

> My heart's on *flame*. *Cowley.*

7. Rage; violence; as the *flames* of war.

FLAME, *v. t.* To inflame; to excite. *Spenser.*

FLAME, *v. i.* To blaze; to burn in vapor, or in a current; to burn as gas emitted from bodies in combustion.

2. To shine like burning gas.

> In *flaming* yellow bright. *Prior.*

3. To break out in violence of passion. *Beaum.*

FLA'MECŎLOR, *n.* Bright color, as that of flame. *B. Jonson.*

FLA'MECŎLORED, *a.* Of the color of flame; of a bright yellow color. *Shak.*

FLA'MEEYED, *a.* Having eyes like a flame.

FLA'MELESS, *a.* Destitute of flame; without incense.

FLA'MEN, *n.* [L.] In *ancient Rome*, a priest. Originally there were three priests so called; the *Flamen Dialis*, consecrated to Jupiter; *Flamen Martialis*, sacred to Mars; and *Flamen Quirinalis*, who superintended the rites of Quirinus or Romulus.

2. A priest. *Pope.*

FLA'MING, *ppr.* Burning in flame.

2. *a.* Bright; red. Also, violent; vehement; as a *flaming* harangue.

FLA'MING, *n.* A bursting out in a flame.

FLA'MINGLY, *adv.* Most brightly; with great show or vehemence.

FLAMIN'GO, *n.* [Sp. and Port. *flamenco*, from *flamma*, flame.]

A fowl constituting the genus Phœnicopterus, of the grallic order. The beak is naked, toothed, and bent as if broken; the feet palmated and four-toed. This fowl resembles the heron in shape, but is entirely red, except the quill-fethers. It is a native of Africa and America. *Encyc.*

FLAMIN'ICAL, *a.* Pertaining to a Roman flamen. *Milton.*

FLAMMABIL'ITY, *n.* The quality of admitting to be set on fire, or enkindled into a flame or blaze; inflammability. *Brown.*

FLAM'MABLE, *a.* Capable of being enkindled into flame.

FLAMMA'TION, *n.* The act of setting on flame. *Brown.*

The three last words are little used. Instead of them are used the compounds, *inflammable, inflammability, inflammation.*

FLAM'MEOUS, *a.* Consisting of flame; like flame. *Brown.*

FLAMMIF'EROUS, *a.* [L. *flamma* and *fero*, to bring.] Producing flame.

FLAMMIV'OMOUS, *a.* [L. *flamma* and *vomo*, to vomit.] Vomiting flames, as a volcano.

FLA'MY, *a.* [from *flame.*] Blazing; burning; as *flamy* breath. *Sidney.*

2. Having the nature of flame; as *flamy* matter. *Bacon.*

3. Having the color of flame. *Herbert.*

FLANK, *n.* [Fr. *flanc*; Sp. and Port. *flanco*; It. *fianco*; G. *flanke*; Sw. and Dan. *flank*; Gr. λαγων; probably connected with *lank*, W. *llac*, Eng. *flag*, Gr. λαγαρος, and so called from its laxity, or from breadth.]

1. The fleshy or muscular part of the side of an animal, between the ribs and the hip. Hence,

2. The side of an army, or of any division of an army, as of a brigade, regiment or battalion. To attack an enemy *in flank*, is to attack them on the side.

3. In *fortification*, that part of a bastion which reaches from the curtain to the face, and defends the opposite face, the flank and the curtain; or it is a line drawn from the extremity of the face towards the inside of the work. *Harris. Encyc.*

FLANK, *v. t.* [Fr. *flanquer*; Sp. *flanquear.*]

1. To attack the side or flank of an army or body of troops; or to place troops so as to command or attack the flank.

2. To post so as to overlook or command on the side; as, to *flank* a passage. *Dryden.*

3. To secure or guard on the side; as *flanked* with rocks. *Dryden.*

FLANK, *v. i.* To border; to touch. *Butler.*

2. To be posted on the side.

FLANK'ED, *pp.* Attacked on the side; covered or commanded on the flank.

FLANK'ER, *n.* A fortification projecting so as to command the side of an assailing body. *Knolles. Fairfax.*

FLANK'ER, *v. t.* To defend by lateral fortifications. *Herbert.*

2. To attack sideways. *Evelyn.*

FLAN'NEL, *n.* [Fr. *flanelle*; D. Dan. *flanel*; G. *flanell*; W. *gwlanen*, from *gwlan*, wool, L. *lana*, Fr. *laine*, Ir. *olann*, Arm. *gloan.*]

A soft nappy woolen cloth of loose texture.

FLAP, *n.* [G. *lappen* and *klappe*; D. *lap* or *klap*; Sw. *klapp* or *lapp*; Dan. *klap* or *lap*; Sax. *læppa*, a lap; W. *llab*, a stroke, a whipping; *llabiaw*, to *slap*; L. *alapa*, a slap. There is a numerous family of words in *Lb*, which spring from striking with something broad, or from a noun denoting something flat and broad. It seems difficult to separate *flap* from *clap*, *slap*, *flabby*, *lap*, &c.]

1. Any thing broad and limber that hangs loose, or is easily moved.

> A cartilaginous *flap* on the opening of the larynx. *Brown.*

We say, the *flap* of a garment, the *flap* of the ear, the *flap* of a hat.

2. The motion of any thing broad and loose, or a stroke with it.

3. The *flaps*, a disease in the lips of horses. *Farrier's Dict.*

FLAP, *v. t.* To beat with a flap.

> Yet let me *flap* this bug with gilded wings. *Pope.*

2. To move something broad; as, to *flap* the wings.

3. To let fall, as the brim of a hat. [This sense seems to indicate a connection with *lap.*]

FLAP, *v. i.* To move as wings, or as something broad or loose.

2. To fall, as the brim of a hat, or other broad thing.

FLAP'DRAGON, *n.* A play in which they catch raisins out of burning brandy, and extinguishing them by closing the mouth, eat them.

2. The thing eaten. *Johnson.*

FLAP'DRAGON, *v. t.* To swallow or devour. *Shak.*

FLAP'EARED, *a.* Having broad loose ears. *Shak.*

FLAP'JACK, *n.* An apple-puff. *Shak.*

FLAP'MOUTHED, *a.* Having loose hanging lips. *Shak.*

FLAP'PED, *pp.* Struck with something broad; let down; having the brim fallen, as a *flapped* hat.

FLAP'PER, *n.* One who flaps another. *Chesterfield.*

FLAP'PING, *ppr.* Striking; beating; moving something broad; as *flapping* wings. The ducks run *flapping* and fluttering. *L'Estrange.*

FLARE, *v. i.* [If this word is not contracted, it may be allied to *clear*, *glare*, *glory*, L. *floreo*, Eng. *floor*, the primary sense of which is to open, to spread, from parting, departing, or driving apart. But in Norm. *flair* is to blow, and possibly it may be from L. *flo*, or it may be contracted from G. *flackern.*]

1. To waver; to flutter; to burn with an unsteady light; as, the candle *flares*, that is, the light wanders from its natural course.

2. To flutter with splendid show; to be loose and waving as a showy thing.

> With ribbands pendant *flaring* 'bout her head. *Shak.*

3. To glitter with transient luster.

> —But speech alone
> Doth vanish like a *flaring* thing. *Herbert.*

4. To glitter with painful splendor.

> When the sun begins to fling
> His *flaring* beams— *Milton.*

5. To be exposed to too much light.

> I cannot stay
> *Flaring* in sunshine all the day. [Qu.] *Prior.*

6. To open or spread outward.

FLA'RING, *ppr.* or *a.* Burning with a wavering light; fluttering; glittering; showy.

2. Opening; widening outward; as a *flaring* fireplace.

FLASH, *n.* [Ir. *lasair*, *lasrach*, a flame, a *flash*; *lasadh*, *lasaim*, to burn, to kindle; *leos*, light; *leosam*, to give light; also, *loisgim*, *losgadh*, to burn; *loisi*, flame; Dan. *lys*, light; *lyser*, to shine, to *glisten* or *glister*; Sw. *lius*, *lysa*, id. Qu. G. *blitz*, a glance; *blitzen*, to lighten, to *flash*; Russ. *blesk*, *bleschu*, id. There is a numerous class of words in *Ls*, with different prefixes, that denote to *shine*, to throw light, as *gloss*, *glass*, *glisten*, *blush*, *flush*, *flash*, *luster*, &c.; but perhaps they are not all of one family. The Welsh has *llathru*, to make smooth and glossy, to polish, to glitter; *llethrid*, a gleam, a *flash*. See Class Ld. No. 5. and Ls. No. 25. and see *Flush.*]

1. A sudden burst of light; a flood of light instantaneously appearing and disappearing; as a *flash* of lightning.

2. A sudden burst of flame and light; an instantaneous blaze; as the *flash* of a gun.

3. A sudden burst, as of wit or merriment; as a *flash* of wit; a *flash* of joy or mirth.

> His companions recollect no instance of premature wit, no striking sentiment, no *flash* of fancy— *Wirt.*

4. A short, transient state.

> The Persians and Macedonians had it for a *flash*. *Bacon.*

5. A body of water driven by violence. [*Local.*] *Pegge.*

6. A little pool. Qu. *plash*. [*Local.*]

FLASH, *v. i.* To break forth, as a sudden flood of light; to burst or open instantly on the sight, as splendor. It differs from *glitter*, *glisten* and *gleam* in denoting a flood or wide extent of light. The latter words may express the issuing of light from a small object, or from a pencil of rays. A diamond may *glitter* or *glisten*, but it does not *flash*. *Flash* differs from other words also in denoting *suddenness* of appearance and disappearance.

2. To burst or break forth with a flood of flame and light; as, the powder *flashed* in the pan. *Flashing* differs from *exploding* or *disploding*, in not being accompanied with a loud report.

3. To burst out into any kind of violence.

> Every hour
> He *flashes* into one gross crime or other. *Shak.*

4. To break out, as a sudden expression of wit, merriment or bright thought. *Felton.*

FLASH, *v. t.* To strike up a body of water from the surface. *Carew.*

He rudely *flashed* the waves. *Spenser.*

[*In this sense I believe this word is not used in America.*]

2. To strike or to throw like a burst of light; as, to *flash* conviction on the mind.

FLASH'ER, *n.* A man of more appearance of wit than reality. *Dict.*

2. A rower. [*Not in use.*]

FLASH'ILY, *adv.* With empty show; with a sudden glare; without solidity of wit or thought.

FLASH'ING, *ppr.* Bursting forth as a flood of light, or of flame and light, or as wit, mirth or joy.

FLASH'Y, *a.* Showy, but empty; dazzling for a moment, but not solid; as *flashy* wit.

2. Showy; gay; as a *flashy* dress.

3. Insipid; vapid; without taste or spirit; as food or drink.

4. Washy; plashy. [See *Plash.*]

FL'ASK, *n.* [G. *flasche*; Sw. *flaska*; Dan. *flaske*; D. *fles*, *flesch*; Sax. *flaxa*; Sp. Port. *frasco*; It. *flasco*; W. *flasg*, a basket.]

1. A kind of bottle; as a *flask* of wine or oil.

2. A vessel for powder.

3. A bed in a gun-carriage. *Bailey.*

FL'ASKET, *n.* A vessel in which viands are served up. *Pope. Ray.*

2. A long shallow basket. *Spenser.*

FLAT, *a.* [D. *plat*; G. *platt*; Dan. *flad*; Sw. *flat*; Fr. *plat*; Arm. *blad*, or *pladt*; It. *piatto*; from extending or laying. Allied probably to W. *llez*, *llêd*, *llyd*; L. *latus*, broad; Gr. πλατυς; Eng. *blade.*]

1. Having an even surface, without risings or indentures, hills or valleys; as *flat* land.

2. Horizontal; level; without inclination; as a *flat* roof: or with a moderate inclination or slope; for we often apply the word to the roof of a house that is not steep, though inclined.

3. Prostrate; lying the whole length on the ground. He fell or lay *flat* on the ground.

4. Not elevated or erect; fallen.

Cease t'admire, and beauty's plumes
Fall *flat*. *Milton.*

5. Level with the ground; totally fallen.

What ruins kingdoms, and lays cities *flat*. *Milton.*

6. In *painting*, wanting relief or prominence of the figures.

7. Tasteless; stale; vapid; insipid; dead; as fruit *flat* to the taste. *Philips.*

8. Dull; unanimated; frigid; without point or spirit; applied to discourses and compositions. The sermon was very *flat*.

9. Depressed; spiritless; dejected.

I feel—my hopes all *flat*. *Milton.*

10. Unpleasing; not affording gratification. How *flat* and insipid are all the pleasures of this life!

11. Peremptory; absolute; positive; downright. He gave the petitioner a *flat* denial.

Thus repulsed, our final hope
Is *flat* despair. *Milton.*

12. Not sharp or shrill; not acute; as a *flat* sound. *Bacon.*

13. Low, as the prices of goods; or dull, as sales.

FLAT, *n.* A level or extended plain. In America, it is applied particularly to low ground or meadow that is level, but it denotes any land of even surface and of some extent.

2. A level ground lying at a small depth under the surface of water; a shoal; a shallow; a strand; a sand bank under water.

3. The broad side of a blade. *Dryden.*

4. Depression of thought or language. *Dryden.*

5. A surface without relief or prominences. *Bentley.*

6. In *music*, a mark of depression in sound. A *flat* denotes a fall or depression of half a tone.

7. A boat, broad and flat-bottomed. A *flat-bottomed* boat is constructed for conveying passengers or troops, horses, carriages and baggage.

FLAT, *v. t.* [Fr. *flatir*, *applatir.*] To level; to depress; to lay smooth or even; to make broad and smooth; to flatten. *Bacon.*

2. To make vapid or tasteless. *Bacon.*

3. To make dull or unanimated.

FLAT, *v. i.* To grow flat; to fall to an even surface. *Temple.*

2. To become insipid, or dull and unanimated. *King Charles.*

FLAT'-BOTTOMED, *a.* Having a flat bottom, as a boat, or a moat in fortification.

FLA'TIVE, *a.* [L. *flatus*, from *flo*, to blow.] Producing wind; flatulent. [*Not in use.*] *Brewer.*

FLAT'LONG, *adv.* With the flat side downward; not edgewise. *Shak.*

FLAT'LY, *adv.* Horizontally; without inclination.

2. Evenly; without elevations and depressions.

3. Without spirit; dully; frigidly.

4. Peremptorily; positively; downright.

He *flatly* refused his aid. *Sidney.*

FLAT'NESS, *n.* Evenness of surface; levelness; equality of surface.

2. Want of relief or prominence; as the *flatness* of a figure in sculpture. *Addison.*

3. Deadness; vapidness; insipidity; as the *flatness* of cider or beer. *Mortimer.*

4. Dejection of fortune; low state.

The *flatness* of my misery. *Shak.*

5. Dejection of mind; a low state of the spirits; depression; want of life. *Collier.*

6. Dullness; want of point; insipidity; frigidity.

Some of Homer's translators have swelled into fustian, and others sunk into *flatness*. *Pope.*

7. Gravity of sound, as opposed to sharpness, acuteness or shrillness.

Flatness of sound—joined with a harshness. *Bacon.*

FLAT'-NOSED, *a.* Having a flat nose. *Burton.*

FLAT'TED, *pp.* Made flat; rendered even on the surface; also, rendered vapid or insipid.

FLAT'TEN, *v. t.* *flat'n.* [Fr. *flatir*, from *flat.*]

1. To make flat; to reduce to an equal or even surface; to level.

2. To beat down to the ground; to lay flat. *Mortimer.*

3. To make vapid or insipid; to render stale.

4. To depress; to deject, as the spirits; to dispirit.

5. In *music*, to reduce, as sound; to render less acute or sharp.

FLAT'TEN, *v. i.* *flat'n.* To grow or become even on the surface.

2. To become dead, stale, vapid or tasteless.

3. To become dull or spiritless.

FLAT'TENING, *ppr.* Making flat.

FLAT'TER, *n.* The person or thing by which any thing is flattened.

FLAT'TER, *v. t.* [Fr. *flatter*; D. *vleijen*; Teut. *fletsen*; Ice. *fladra*; Dan. *flatterer*. In Ir. *bladaire* is a flatterer; *bleid*, a wheedling; *blaith* is plain, smooth; and *blath* is praise. *Flatter* may be from the root of *flat*, that is, to make smooth, to appease, to soothe; but the Ir. *blath* would seem to be connected with L. *plaudo*. Perhaps *flat* and *plaudo* are from one root, the radical sense of which must be to extend, strain, stretch.]

1. To soothe by praise; to gratify self-love by praise or obsequiousness; to please a person by applause or favorable notice, by respectful attention, or by any thing that exalts him in his own estimation, or confirms his good opinion of himself. We *flatter* a woman when we praise her children.

A man that *flattereth* his neighbor, spreadeth a net for his feet. Prov. xxix.

2. To please; to gratify; as, to *flatter* one's vanity or pride.

3. To praise falsely; to encourage by favorable notice; as, to *flatter* vices or crimes.

4. To encourage by favorable representations or indications; as, to *flatter* hopes. We are *flattered* with the prospect of peace.

5. To raise false hopes by representations not well founded; as, to *flatter* one with a prospect of success; to *flatter* a patient with the expectation of recovery when his case is desperate.

6. To please; to soothe.

A concert of voices—makes a harmony that *flatters* the ears. *Dryden.*

7. To wheedle; to coax; to attempt to win by blandishments, praise or enticements. How many young and credulous persons are *flattered* out of their innocence and their property, by seducing arts!

FLAT'TERED, *pp.* Soothed by praise; pleased by commendation; gratified with hopes, false or well founded; wheedled.

FLAT'TERER, *n.* One who flatters; a fawner; a wheedler; one who praises another, with a view to please him, to gain his favor, or to accomplish some purpose.

When I tell him he hates *flatterers*,
He says he does; being then most flattered. *Shak.*

The most abject *flatterers* degenerate into the greatest tyrants. *Addison.*

FLAT'TERING, *ppr.* Gratifying with praise; pleasing by applause; wheedling; coaxing.

2. *a.* Pleasing to pride or vanity; gratifying to self-love; as a *flattering* eulogy. The minister gives a *flattering* account of his reception at court.

3. Pleasing; favorable; encouraging hope. We have a *flattering* prospect of an abundant harvest. The symptoms of the disease are *flattering*.

4. Practicing adulation; uttering false praise; as a *flattering* tongue.

FLAT'TERINGLY, *adv.* In a flattering manner; in a manner to flatter.

2. In a manner to favor; with partiality. *Cumberland.*

FLAT'TERY, *n.* [Fr. *flatterie.*] False praise; commendation bestowed for the purpose of gaining favor and influence, or to accomplish some purpose. Direct *flattery* consists in praising a person himself; indirect *flattery* consists in praising a person through his works or his connections.

Simple pride for *flattery* makes demands. *Pope.*

Just praise is only a debt, but *flattery* is a present. *Rambler.*

2. Adulation; obsequiousness; wheedling. *Rowe.*

3. Just commendation which gratifies self-love.

FLAT'TISH, *a.* [from *flat.*] Somewhat flat; approaching to flatness. *Woodward.*

FLAT'ULENCE, FLAT'ULENCY, *n.* [See *Flatulent.*] Windiness in the stomach; air generated in a weak stomach and intestines by imperfect digestion, occasioning distension, uneasiness, pain, and often belchings. *Encyc.*

2. Airiness; emptiness; vanity. *Glanville.*

FLAT'ULENT, *a.* [L. *flatulentus, flatus,* from *flo,* to blow.]

1. Windy; affected with air generated in the stomach and intestines.

2. Turgid with air; windy; as a *flatulent* tumor. *Quincy.*

3. Generating or apt to generate wind in the stomach. Pease are a *flatulent* vegetable. *Arbuthnot.*

4. Empty; vain; big without substance or reality; puffy; as a *flatulent* writer; *flatulent* vanity. *Dryden. Glanville.*

FLATUOS'ITY, *n.* Windiness; fullness of air; flatulence. [*Not used.*] *Bacon.*

FLAT'UOUS, *a.* [L. *flatuosus.*] Windy; generating wind. [*Not used.*] *Bacon.*

FLA'TUS, *n.* [L. from *flo,* to blow.] A breath; a puff of wind. *Clarke.*

2. Wind generated in the stomach or other cavities of the body; flatulence. *Quincy.*

FLAT'WISE, *a.* or *adv.* [from *flat.*] With the flat side downward or next to another object; not edgewise. *Woodward.*

FL'AUNT, *v. i.* [I know not whence we have this word. It is doubtless of Celtic origin, from the root *Ln,* bearing the sense of throwing out, or spreading. Qu. Scot. *flanter,* to waver. See *Flounce.*]

To throw or spread out; to flutter; to display ostentatiously; as a *flaunting* show.

You *flaunt* about the streets in your new gilt chariot. *Arbuthnot.*

One *flaunts* in rags, one flutters in brocade. *Pope.*

[This correctly expresses the author's meaning, which is, that the proud often attempt to make a show and parade of their importance, even in poverty. Johnson's remark on the use of the word seems therefore to be unfounded.]

2. To carry a pert or saucy appearance. *Boyle.*

FL'AUNT, *n.* Any thing displayed for show. *Shak.*

FL'AUNTING, *ppr.* Making an ostentatious display.

FLA'VOR, *n.* [Qu. Fr. *flairer,* to smell; W. *fleiriaw.*]

The quality of a substance which affects the taste or smell, in any manner. We say, the wine has a fine *flavor,* or a disagreeable *flavor*; the fruit has a bad *flavor*; a rose has a sweet *flavor.* The word then signifies the quality which is tasted or smelt; taste, odor, fragrance, smell.

FLA'VOR, *v. t.* To communicate some quality to a thing, that may affect the taste or smell.

FLA'VORED, *a.* Having a quality that affects the sense of tasting or smelling; as *high-flavored* wine, having the quality in a high degree.

FLA'VORLESS, *a.* Without flavor; tasteless; having no smell or taste. *Encyc.*

FLA'VOROUS, *a.* Pleasant to the taste or smell. *Dryden.*

FLA'VOUS, *a.* [L. *flavus.*] Yellow. [*Not used.*] *Smith.*

FLAW, *n.* [W. *flaw,* a piece rent, a splinter, a ray, a dart, a *flaw*; *flau,* a spreading out, radiation; *fla,* a parting from; also *floçen,* a splinter; *floç,* a flying about; *floçi,* to dart suddenly; *flyçiaw,* to break out abruptly. The Gr. φλαω seems to be contracted from φλαδω or φλαθω.]

2. A breach; a crack; a defect made by breaking or splitting; a gap or fissure; as a *flaw* in a sythe, knife or razor; a *flaw* in a china dish, or in a glass; a *flaw* in a wall.

2. A defect; a fault; any defect made by violence, or occasioned by neglect; as a *flaw* in reputation; a *flaw* in a will, or in a deed, or in a statute.

3. A sudden burst of wind; a sudden gust or blast of short duration; *a word of common use among seamen.* [*This proves the primary sense to be, to burst or rush.*]

4. A sudden burst of noise and disorder; a tumult; uproar.

And deluges of armies from the town
Came pouring in; I heard the mighty *flaw.* *Dryden.*

[*In this sense, the word is not used in the United States.*]

5. A sudden commotion of mind. [*Not used.*] *Shak.*

FLAW, *v. t.* To break; to crack.

The brazen cauldrons with the frosts are *flawed.* *Dryden.*

2. To break; to violate; as, to *flaw* a league. [*Little used.*] *Shak.*

FLAW'ED, *pp.* Broken; cracked.

FLAW'ING, *ppr.* Breaking; cracking.

FLAW'LESS, *a.* Without cracks; without defect. *Boyle.*

FLAWN, *n.* [Sax. *flena*; Fr. *flan.*] A sort of custard or pie. [*Obs.*] *Tusser.*

FLAW'TER, *v. t.* To scrape or pare a skin. [*Not used.*] *Ainsworth.*

FLAW'Y, *a.* Full of flaws or cracks; broken; defective; faulty.

2. Subject to sudden gusts of wind.

FLAX, *n.* [Sax. *fleax, flex*; G. *flachs*; D. *vlas.* The elements are the same as in *flaccid.*]

1. A plant of the genus Linum, consisting of a single slender stalk, the skin or herl of which is used for making thread and cloth, called linen, cambric, lawn, lace, &c. The skin consists of fine fibers, which may be so separated as to be spun into threads as fine as silk.

2. The skin or fibrous part of the plant when broken and cleaned by hatcheling or combing.

FLAX'COMB, *n.* An instrument with teeth through which flax is drawn for separating from it the tow or coarser part and the shives. In America, we call it a *hatchel.*

FLAX'DRESSER, *n.* One who breaks and swingles flax.

FLAX'PLANT, *n.* The Phormium, a plant in New Zealand that serves the inhabitants for flax.

FLAX'RAISER, *n.* One who raises flax.

FLAX'SEED, *n.* The seed of flax.

FLAX'EN, *a.* Made of flax; as *flaxen* thread.

2. Resembling flax; of the color of flax; fair, long, and flowing; as *flaxen* hair.

FLAX'Y, *a.* Like flax; being of a light color; fair. *Sandys.*

FLAY, *v. t.* [Sax. *flean*; Dan. *flaaer*; Sw. *flå*: G. *flöhen*; Gr. φλοιω, φλοιζω, whence φλοιος, bark, rind; probably a contracted word.]

1. To skin; to strip off the skin of an animal; as, to *flay* an ox.

2. To take off the skin or surface of any thing. [*Not used.*] *Swift.*

FLA'YED, *pp.* Skinned; stripped of the skin.

FLA'YER, *n.* One who strips off the skin.

FLA'YING, *ppr.* Stripping off the skin.

FLEA, *n.* [Sax. *flea*; G. *floh*; D. *vloo*; Scot. *flech*; Ice. *floc*; from Sax. *fleogan,* to fly. See *Flee* and *Fly.*]

An insect of the genus Pulex. It has two eyes, and six feet; the feelers are like threads; the rostrum is inflected, setaceous, and armed with a sting. The flea is remarkable for its agility, leaping to a surprising distance, and its bite is very troublesome.

FLE'ABANE, *n.* A plant of the genus Conyza.

FLE'ABITE, FLE'ABITING, *n.* The bite of a flea, or the red spot caused by the bite.

2. A trifling wound or pain, like that of the bite of a flea. *Harvey.*

FLE'ABITTEN, *a.* Bitten or stung by a flea.

2. Mean; worthless; of low birth or station. *Cleaveland.*

FLE'AWŎRT, *n.* A plant.

FLEAK, a lock. [See *Flake.*]

FLEAM, *n.* [D. *vlym*; W. *flaim*; Arm. *flemm* or *flem,* the sting of a bee, a sharp point. In Welsh, *llem* and *llym* signify sharp, penetrating.]

In *surgery* and *farriery,* a sharp instrument used for opening veins for letting blood.

FLECK, FLECK'ER, *v. t.* [G. *fleck,* a spot; *flecken,* to spot; D. *vlek, vlak, vlakken*; Sw. *fläck, fläcka*; Dan. *flek, flekker.*]

To spot; to streak or stripe; to variegate; to dapple.

Both *flecked* with white, the true Arcadian strain. *Dryden.*

[These words are obsolete or used only in poetry.]

FLEC'TION, *n.* [L. *flectio.*] The act of bending, or state of being bent.

FLEC′TOR, *n.* A flexor, which see.

FLED, *pret.* and *pp.* of *flee*; as, truth has *fled.*

FLEDGE, *a. flej.* [G. *flügge*; D. *vlug*, fledged, quick, nimble; connected with G. *fliegen*, D. *vliegen*, Sax. *fleogan*, to fly.]

Fethered; furnished with fethers or wings; able to fly.

> His locks behind,
> Illustrious on his shoulders, *fledge* with wings,
> Lay waving round. *Milton.*

FLEDGE, *v. t.* To furnish with fethers; to supply with the fethers necessary for flight.

> The birds were not yet *fledged* enough to shift for themselves. *L'Estrange.*

FLEDG′ED, *pp.* Furnished with fethers for flight; covered with fethers.

FLEDG′ING, *ppr.* Furnishing with fethers for flight.

FLEE, *v. i.* [Sax. *flean*, *fleon*, *fleogan*; G. *fliehen.*]

1. To run with rapidity, as from danger; to attempt to escape; to hasten from danger or expected evil. The enemy *fled* at the first fire.

> Arise, take the young child and his mother, and *flee* into Egypt. Matt. ii.

2. To depart; to leave; to hasten away.

> Resist the devil, and he will *flee* from you. James iv.

3. To avoid; to keep at a distance from. *Flee* fornication; *flee* from idolatry. 1 Cor. vi. x.

To flee the question or *from the question*, in legislation, is said of a legislator who, when a question is to be put to the house, leaves his seat to avoid the dilemma of voting against his conscience, or giving an unpopular vote. In the phrases in which this verb appears to be transitive, there is really an ellipsis.

FLEECE, *n. flees.* [Sax. *fleos*, *flys*, *flese*; D. *vlies*; G. *fliess*; most probably from shearing or stripping, as in Dutch the word signifies a film or membrane, as well as a *fleece*. The verb to *fleece* seems to favor the sense of stripping. See Class Ls. No. 25. 28. 30. But Qu. L. *vellus*, from *vello*, to pluck or tear off. *Varro.* See Class Bl. In Russ. *volos* is hair or wool, written also *vlas*. It was probably the practice to pluck off wool, before it was to shear it.]

The coat of wool shorn from a sheep at one time.

FLEECE, *v. t.* To shear off a covering or growth of wool.

2. To strip of money or property; to take from, by severe exactions, under color of law or justice, or pretext of necessity, or by virtue of authority. Arbitrary princes *fleece* their subjects; and clients complain that they are sometimes *fleeced* by their lawyers.

This word is rarely or never used for plundering in war by a licentious soldiery; but is properly used to express a stripping by contributions levied on a conquered people.

3. To spread over as with wool; to make white. *Thomson.*

FLEE′CED, *pp.* Stripped by severe exactions.

FLEE′CED, *a.* Furnished with a fleece or with fleeces; as, a sheep is well *fleeced.*

FLEE′CER, *n.* One who strips or takes by severe exactions.

FLEE′CING, *ppr.* Stripping of money or property by severe demands of fees, taxes or contributions.

FLEE′CY, *a.* Covered with wool; woolly; as a *fleecy* flock. *Prior.*

2. Resembling wool or a fleece; soft; complicated; as *fleecy* snow; *fleecy* locks; *fleecy* hosiery.

FLEER, *v. i.* [Scot. *flyre*, or *fleyr*, to make wry faces, to leer, to look surly; Ice. *flyra.* In D. *gluuren* signifies to leer, to peep; Sw. *plira*; Dan. *plirende*, ogling, leering. This word seems to be *leer*, with a prefix, and *leer* presents probably the primary sense.]

1. To deride; to sneer; to mock; to gibe; to make a wry face in contempt, or to grin in scorn; as, to *fleer* and flout.

> Covered with an antic face,
> To *fleer* and scorn at our solemnity. *Shak.*

2. To leer; to grin with an air of civility. *Burton.*

FLEER, *v. t.* To mock; to flout at. *Beaum.*

FLEER, *n.* Derision or mockery, expressed by words or looks.

> And mark the *fleers*, the gibes, and notable scorns. *Shak.*

2. A grin of civility.

> A treacherous *fleer* on the face of deceivers. *South.*

FLEE′RER, *n.* A mocker; a fawner.

FLEE′RING, *ppr.* Deriding; mocking; counterfeiting an air of civility.

FLEET, in English names, [Sax. *fleot*,] denotes a *flood*, a creek or inlet, a bay or estuary, or a river; as in *Fleet-street*, *Northfleet*, *Fleet-prison.*

FLEET, *n.* [Sax. *flota*, *fliet*; G. *flotte*; D. *vloot*; Sw. *flotte*; Dan. *flode*; Fr. *flotte.* *Fleet* and *float* seem to be allied. But whether they are formed from the root of *flow*, or whether the last consonant is radical, is not obvious. See *Float.*]

A navy or squadron of ships; a number of ships in company, whether ships of war, or of commerce. It more generally signifies ships of war.

FLEET, *a.* [Ice. *fliotr*; Ir. *luath*, swift; Russ. *letayu*, to fly; Eng. to *flit*. If the last consonant is radical, this word seems to be allied to D. *vlieden*, to flee, to fly, and possibly to the Shemitic פלט; but from the Ethiopic it would appear that the latter word is our *split*, the sense being to divide or separate.]

1. Swift of pace; moving or able to move with rapidity; nimble; light and quick in motion, or moving with lightness and celerity; as a *fleet* horse or dog.

2. Moving with velocity; as *fleet* winds.

3. Light; superficially fruitful; or thin; not penetrating deep; as soil. *Mortimer.*

4. Skimming the surface. *Ibid.*

FLEET, *v. i.* To fly swiftly; to hasten; to flit as a light substance. To *fleet away* is to vanish.

> How all the other passions *fleet* to air. *Shak.*

2. To be in a transient state.

3. To float.

FLEET, *v. t.* To skim the surface; to pass over rapidly; as a ship that *fleets* the gulf. *Spenser.*

2. To pass lightly, or in mirth and joy; as, to *fleet* away time. [*Not used.*] *Shak.*

3. To skim milk. [*Local, in England.*]

The verb in the transitive form is rarely or never used in America.

FLEE′TFOOT, *a.* Swift of foot; running or able to run with rapidity. *Shak.*

FLEE′TING, *ppr.* Passing rapidly; flying with velocity.

2. *a.* Transient; not durable; as the *fleeting* hours or moments.

FLEE′TING-DISH, *n.* A skimming bowl. [*Local.*]

FLEE′TLY, *adv.* Rapidly; lightly and nimbly; swiftly.

FLEE′TNESS, *n.* Swiftness; rapidity; velocity; celerity; speed; as the *fleetness* of a horse or a deer.

FLEM′ING, *n.* A native of Flanders, or the Low Countries in Europe.

FLEM′ISH, *a.* Pertaining to Flanders.

FLESH, *n.* [Sax. *flæc*, *flec*, or *flæsc*; G. *fleisch*; D. *vleesch*; Dan. *flesk*. In Danish, the word signifies the flesh of swine. I know not the primary sense; it may be *soft.*]

A compound substance forming a large part of an animal, consisting of the softer solids, as distinguished from the bones and the fluids. Under the general appellation of *flesh*, we include the muscles, fat, glands &c., which invest the bones and are covered with the skin. It is sometimes restricted to the muscles.

2. Animal food, in distinction from vegetable.

> *Flesh* without being qualified with acids, is too alkalescent a diet. *Arbuthnot.*

3. The body of beasts and fowls used as food, distinct from *fish*. In Lent, the Catholics abstain from *flesh*, but eat fish.

4. The body, as distinguished from the soul.

> As if this *flesh*, which walls about our life,
> Were brass impregnable. *Shak.*

5. Animal nature; animals of all kinds.

> The end of all *flesh* is come before me. Gen. vi.

6. Men in general; mankind.

> My spirit shall not always strive with man, for that he also is *flesh*. Gen. vi.

7. Human nature.

> The word was made *flesh*, and dwelt among us. John i.

8. Carnality; corporeal appetites.

> Fasting serves to mortify the *flesh*. *Smalridge.*
>
> The *flesh* lusteth against the spirit. Gal. v.

9. A carnal state; a state of unrenewed nature.

> They that are in the *flesh* cannot please God. Rom. viii.

10. The corruptible body of man, or corrupt nature.

> *Flesh* and blood cannot inherit the kingdom of God. 1 Cor. xv.

11. The present life; the state of existence in this world.

> To abide in the *flesh* is more needful for you. Phil. i.

12. Legal righteousness, and ceremonial services.

> What shall we then say that Abraham, our father as pertaining to the *flesh*, hath found Rom. iv. Gal. iii.

13. Kindred; stock; family.

> He is our brother, and our *flesh*. Gen. xxxvii.

14. In *botany*, the soft pulpy substance of fruit; also, that part of a root, fruit, &c., which is fit to be eaten.

One flesh, denotes intimate relation. To *be one flesh* is to be closely united, as in marriage. Gen. ii. Eph. v.

After the flesh, according to outward appearances, John viii:

Or according to the common powers of nature. Gal. iv.:

Or according to sinful lusts and inclinations. Rom. viii.

An *arm of flesh*, human strength or aid.

FLESH, *v. t.* To initiate; a sportsman's use of the word, from the practice of training hawks and dogs by feeding them with the first game they take or other flesh.

2. To harden; to accustom; to establish in any practice, as dogs by often feeding on any thing. Men *fleshed* in cruelty; women *fleshed* in malice. *Sidney.*

3. To glut; to satiate.

> The wild dog
> Shall *flesh* his tooth on every innocent. *Shak.*

FLESH'BROTH, *n.* Broth made by boiling flesh in water.

FLESH'BRUSH, *n.* A brush for exciting action in the skin by friction.

FLESH'COLOR, *n.* The color of flesh; carnation.

FLESH'COLORED, *a.* Being of the color of flesh.

FLESH'DIET, *n.* Food consisting of flesh.

FLESH'ED, *pp.* Initiated; accustomed; glutted.

2. Fat; fleshy.

FLESH'FLY, *n.* A fly that feeds on flesh, and deposits her eggs in it. *Ray.*

FLESH'HOOK, *n.* A hook to draw flesh from a pot or caldron. 1 Sam. ii.

FLESH'INESS, *n.* [from *fleshy.*] Abundance of flesh or fat in animals; plumpness; corpulence; grossness.

FLESH'ING, *ppr.* Initiating; making familiar; glutting.

FLESH'LESS, *a.* Destitute of flesh; lean.

FLESH'LINESS, *n.* Carnal passions and appetites. *Spenser.*

FLESH'LY, *a.* Pertaining to the flesh; corporeal. *Denham.*

2. Carnal; worldly; lascivious.

> Abstain from *fleshly* lusts. 1 Pet. ii.

3. Animal; not vegetable. *Dryden.*

4. Human; not celestial; not spiritual or divine.

> Vain of *fleshly* arm. *Milton.*
> *Fleshly* wisdom. 2 Cor. i.

FLESH'MEAT, *n.* Animal food; the flesh of animals prepared or used for food. *Swift.*

FLESH'MENT, *n.* Eagerness gained by a successful initiation. *Shak.*

FLESH'MONGER, *n.* One who deals in flesh; a procurer; a pimp. [*Little used.*] *Shak.*

FLESH'POT, *n.* A vessel in which flesh is cooked; hence, plenty of provisions. Ex. xvi.

FLESH'QUAKE, *n.* A trembling of the flesh. [*Not used.*] *B. Jonson.*

FLESH'Y, *a.* Full of flesh; plump; musculous.

> The sole of his foot is *fleshy*. *Ray.*

2. Fat; gross; corpulent; as a *fleshy* man.

3. Corporeal. *Eccles.*

4. Full of pulp; pulpous; plump; as fruit. *Bacon.*

FLET, *pp.* of *fleet.* Skimmed. [*Not used.*] *Mortimer.*

FLETCH, *v. t.* [Fr. *fleche.*] To fether an arrow. *Warburton.*

FLETCH'ER, *n.* [Fr. *fleche*, an arrow.] An arrow-maker; a manufacturer of bows and arrows. Hence the name of *Fletcher.* But the use of the word as an appellative has ceased with the practice of archery.

FLETZ, *a.* [G. *flötz*, a layer.] In *geology*, the fletz formations, so called, consist of rocks which lie immediately over the transition rocks. These formations are so called because the rocks usually appear in beds more nearly horizontal than the transition class. These formations consist of sandstone, limestone, gypsum, calamine, chalk, coal and trap. They contain abundance of petrifactions, both of animal and vegetable origin. *Good.*

FLEW, *pret.* of *fly.*

> The people *flew* upon the spoil. 1 Sam. xiv.

FLEW, *n.* The large chaps of a deep-mouthed hound. *Hanmer.*

FLEW'ED, *a.* Chapped; mouthed; deep-mouthed. *Shak.*

FLEXAN'IMOUS, *a.* [from L.] Having power to change the mind. [*Not used.*] *Howell.*

FLEXIBIL'ITY, *n.* [See *Flexible.*] The quality of admitting to be bent; pliancy; flexibleness; as the *flexibility* of rays of light. *Newton.*

2. Easiness to be persuaded; the quality of yielding to arguments, persuasion or circumstances; ductility of mind; readiness to comply; facility; as *flexibility* of temper.

FLEX'IBLE, *a.* [L. *flexibilis*, from *flecto*, *flexi*, to bend, Fr. *flechir*, coinciding with G. *flechten*, to braid, D. *vlegten.* These words have the same elements as L. *plico.*]

1. That may be bent; capable of being turned or forced from a straight line or form without breaking; pliant; yielding to pressure; not stiff; as a *flexible* rod; a *flexible* plant.

2. Capable of yielding to intreaties, arguments or other moral force; that may be persuaded to compliance; not invincibly rigid or obstinate; not inexorable.

> Phocion was a man of great severity, and no ways *flexible* to the will of the people. *Bacon.*

It often denotes, easy or too easy to yield or comply; wavering; inconstant; not firm.

3. Ductile; manageable; tractable; as the tender and *flexible* minds of youth. *Flexible* years or time of life, the time when the mind is tractable.

4. That may be turned or accommodated.

> This was a principle more *flexible* to their purpose. *Rogers.*

FLEX'IBLENESS, *n.* Possibility to be bent or turned from a straight line or form without breaking; easiness to be bent; pliantness; pliancy; flexibility. *Boyle.*

2. Facility of mind; readiness to comply or yield; obsequiousness; as the *flexibleness* of a courtier.

3. Ductility; manageableness; tractableness; as the *flexibleness* of youth.

FLEX'ILE, *a.* [L. *flexilis.*] Pliant; pliable; easily bent; yielding to power, impulse or moral force. *Thomson.*

FLEX'ION, *n.* [L. *flexio.*] The act of bending.

2. A bending; a part bent; a fold. *Bacon.*

3. A turn; a cast; as a *flexion* of the eye. *Bacon.*

FLEX'OR, *n.* In *anatomy*, a muscle whose office is to bend the part to which it belongs, in opposition to the *extensors.*

FLEX'UOUS, *a.* [L. *flexuosus.*] Winding; having turns or windings; as a *flexuous* rivulet. *Digby.*

2. Bending; winding; wavering; not steady; as a *flexuous* flame. *Bacon.*

3. In *botany*, bending or bent; changing its direction in a curve, from joint to joint, from bud to bud, or from flower to flower. *Martyn.*

FLEX'URE, *n.* [L. *flexura.*] A winding or bending; the form of bending; as the *flexure* of a joint.

2. The act of bending. *Shak.*

3. The part bent; a joint. *Sandys.*

4. The bending of the body; obsequious or servile cringe. *Shak.*

FLICK'ER, *v. i.* [Sax. *flicerian*; Scot. *flecker*, to quiver; D. *flikkeren*, to twinkle; probably a diminutive from the root of *fly.*]

1. To flutter; to flap the wings without flying; to strike rapidly with the wings.

> And *flickering* on her nest made short essays to sing. *Dryden.*

2. To fluctuate. *Burton.*

FLICK'ERING, *ppr.* Fluttering; flapping the wings without flight.

2. *a.* With amorous motions of the eye.

> The fair Lavinia—looks a little *flickering* after Turnus. *Dryden.*

FLICK'ERING, *n.* A fluttering; short irregular movements.

FLICK'ERMOUSE, *n.* The bat. *B. Jonson.*

FLI'ER, *n.* [See *Fly.* It ought to be *flyer.*] One that flies or flees.

2. A runaway; a fugitive. *Shak.*

3. A part of a machine which, by moving rapidly, equalizes and regulates the motion of the whole; as the *flier* of a jack.

FLIGHT, *n. flite.* [Sax. *fliht*; G. *flug*, *flucht*; D. *vlugt*; Dan. *flugt*; Sw. *flycht.* See *Fly.*]

1. The act of fleeing; the act of running away, to escape danger or expected evil; hasty departure.

> Pray ye that your *flight* be not in winter. Matt. xxiv.

To *put to flight*, to *turn to flight*, is to compel to run away; to force to escape.

2. The act of flying; a passing through the air by the help of wings; volation; as the *flight* of birds and insects.

3. The manner of flying. Every fowl has its particular *flight*; the *flight* of the eagle is high; the *flight* of the swallow is rapid, with sudden turns.

4. Removal from place to place by flying.

5. A flock of birds flying in company; as a *flight* of pigeons or wild geese.

6. A number of beings flying or moving through the air together; as a *flight* of angels. *Milton.*

FLI
FLI

7. A number of things passing through the air together; a volley; as a *flight* of arrows.

8. A periodical flying of birds in flocks; as the spring *flight* or autumnal *flight* of ducks or pigeons.

9. In *England*, the birds produced in the same season.

10. The space passed by flying.

11. A mounting; a soaring; lofty elevation and excursion; as a *flight* of imagination or fancy; a *flight* of ambition.

12. Excursion; wandering; extravagant sally; as a *flight* of folly. *Tillotson.*

13. The power of flying. *Shak.*

14. In certain lead works, a substance that flies off in smoke. *Encyc.*

Flight of stairs, the series of stairs from the floor, or from one platform to another.

FLIGHTINESS, *n.* The state of being flighty; wildness; slight delirium.

FLIGHT-SHOT, *n.* The distance which an arrow flies.

FLIGHTY, *a.* Fleeting; swift.

The *flighty* purpose never is o'ertook. *Shak.*

2. Wild; indulging the sallies of imagination.

3. Disordered in mind; somewhat delirious.

FLIM'FLAM, *n.* [Ice. *flim.*] A freak; a trick. *Beaum.*

FLIM'SINESS, *n.* State or quality of being flimsy; thin, weak texture; weakness; want of substance or solidity.

FLIM'SY, *a.* *s* as *z.* [W. *llymsi*, having a fickle motion; *llymu*, to make sharp, quick, pungent. *Owen.* But Lluyd renders *llymsi*, vain, weak. The word is retained by the common people in New England in *limsy*, weak, limber, easily bending. See Class Lm. No. 2. 5. 6.]

1. Weak; feeble; slight; vain; without strength or solid substance; as a *flimsy* pretext; a *flimsy* excuse; *flimsy* objections. *Milner.*

2. Without strength or force; spiritless.

Proud of a vast extent of *flimsy* lines. *Pope.*

3. Thin; of loose texture; as *flimsy* cloth or stuff. [*Little used.*]

FLINCH, *v. i.* [I have not found this word in any other language; but the sense of it occurs in *blench*, and not improbably it is from the same root, with a different prefix.]

1. To shrink; to withdraw from any suffering or undertaking, from pain or danger; to fail of proceeding, or of performing any thing. Never *flinch* from duty. One of the parties *flinched* from the combat.

A child, by a constant course of kindness, may be accustomed to bear very rough usage without *flinching* or complaining. *Locke.*

2. To fail. *Shak.*

FLINCH'ER, *n.* One who flinches or fails.

FLINCH'ING, *ppr.* Failing to undertake, perform or proceed; shrinking; withdrawing.

FLIN'DER, *n.* [D. *flenter*, a splinter, a tatter.]

A small piece or splinter; a fragment. *New England.*

[*This seems to be* splinter, *without the prefix.*]

FLING, *v. t.* pret. and pp. *flung.* [Ir. *lingim*, to fling, to dart, to fly off, to skip. If *n* is not radical, as I suppose, this may be the W. *lluciaw*, to fling, to throw, to dart, and L. *lego, legare.*]

1. To cast, send or throw from the hand; to hurl; as, to *fling* a stone at a bird.

'Tis fate that *flings* the dice; and as she *flings*,
Of kings makes peasants, and of peasants, kings. *Dryden.*

2. To dart; to cast with violence; to send forth.

He—like Jove, his lightning *flung.* *Dryden.*

3. To send forth; to emit; to scatter.

Every beam new transient colors *flings.* *Pope.*

4. To throw; to drive by violence.

5. To throw to the ground; to prostrate. The wrestler *flung* his antagonist.

6. To baffle; to defeat; as, to *fling* a party in litigation.

To fling away, to reject; to discard.

Cromwell, I charge thee, *fling* away ambition. *Shak.*

To fling down, to demolish; to ruin.

2. To throw to the ground.

To fling off, to baffle in the chase; to defeat of prey. *Addison.*

To fling out, to utter; to speak; as, to *fling out* hard words against another.

To fling in, to throw in; to make an allowance or deduction, or not to charge in an account. In settling accounts, one party *flings in* a small sum, or a few days work.

To fling open, to throw open; to open suddenly or with violence; as, to *fling open* a door.

To fling up, to relinquish; to abandon; as, to *fling up* a design.

FLING, *v. i.* To flounce; to wince; to fly into violent and irregular motions. The horse began to kick and *fling.*

2. To cast in the teeth; to utter harsh language; to sneer; to upbraid. The scold began to flout and *fling.*

To fling out, to grow unruly or outrageous. *Shak.*

FLING, *n.* A throw; a cast from the hand.

2. A gibe; a sneer; a sarcasm; a severe or contemptuous remark.

I, who love to have a *fling*,
Both at senate house and king. *Swift.*

FLING'ER, *n.* One who flings; one who jeers.

FLING'ING, *ppr.* Throwing; casting; jeering.

FLINT, *n.* [Sax. *flint;* Sw. *flinta.* In Dan. *flint* is a light gun, and *flint* is called *flint-steen*, flint-stone. So also in German. The Dutch and Germans call it also *fire-stone.* It may be from the root of *splendor.*]

1. In *natural history*, a sub-species of quartz, of a yellowish or bluish gray, or grayish black color. It is amorphous, interspersed in other stones, or in nodules or rounded lumps. Its surface is generally uneven, and covered with a rind or crust, either calcarious or argillaceous. It is very hard, strikes fire with steel, and is an ingredient in glass. *Kirwan. Encyc.*

2. A piece of the above described stone used in firearms to strike fire.

3. Any thing proverbially hard; as a heart of *flint.* *Spenser.*

FLINT-HEART, } *a.* Having a hard,
FLINT-HEARTED, } unfeeling heart.

FLINT'Y, *a.* Consisting of flint; as a *flinty* rock.

2. Like flint; very hard; not impressible; as a *flinty* heart.

3. Cruel; unmerciful; inexorable. *Shak.*

4. Full of flint stones; as *flinty* ground. *Bacon.*

Flinty-slate, a mineral of two kinds, the common and the Lydian stone. *Ure.*

FLIP, *n.* A mixed liquor consisting of beer and spirit sweetened.

FLIP'DOG, *n.* An iron used, when heated, to warm flip.

FLIP'PANCY, *n.* [See *Flippant.*] Smoothness and rapidity of speech; volubility of tongue; fluency of speech.

FLIP'PANT, *a.* [W. *llipanu*, to make smooth or glib, from *llib*, *llipa*, flaccid, soft, limber; allied to *flabby*, and to *glib*, and probably to L. *labor*, to slide or slip, and to *liber*, free. Class Lb.]

1. Of smooth, fluent and rapid speech; speaking with ease and rapidity; having a voluble tongue; talkative.

2. Pert; petulant; waggish.

Away with *flippant* epilogues. *Thomson.*

FLIP'PANTLY, *adv.* Fluently; with ease and volubility of speech.

FLIP'PANTNESS, *n.* Fluency of speech; volubility of tongue; flippancy.

[This is not a low, vulgar word, but well authorized and peculiarly expressive.]

FLIRT, *v. t.* *flurt.* [This word evidently belongs to the root of L. *floreo*, or *ploro*, signifying to throw, and coinciding with *blurt.* Qu. Sax. *fleardian*, to trifle.]

1. To throw with a jerk or sudden effort or exertion. The boys *flirt* water in each other's faces. He *flirted* a glove or a handkerchief.

2. To toss or throw; to move suddenly; as, to *flirt* a fan.

FLIRT, *v. i.* To jeer or gibe; to throw harsh or sarcastic words; to utter contemptuous language, with an air of disdain.

2. To run and dart about; to be moving hastily from place to place; to be unsteady or fluttering. The girls *flirt* about the room or the street.

FLIRT, *n.* A sudden jerk; a quick throw or cast; a darting motion.

In unfurling the fan are several little *flirts* and vibrations. *Addison.*

2. A young girl who moves hastily or frequently from place to place; a pert girl.

Several young *flirts* about town had a design to cast us out of the fashionable world. *Addison.*

FLIRT, *a.* Pert; wanton. *Shak.*

FLIRTA'TION, *n.* A flirting; a quick sprightly motion.

2. Desire of attracting notice. [*A cant word.*] *Addison.*

FLIRT'ED, *pp.* Thrown with a sudden jerk.

FLIRT'ING, *ppr.* Throwing; jerking; tossing; darting about; rambling and changing place hastily.

FLIT, *v. i.* [D. *vlieden*, to fly or flee; Dan. *flyder*, Sw. *flyta*, to flow, to glide away; Dan. *flytter*, Sw. *flyttia*, to remove; Ice. *fliutur*, swift. This word coincides in elements with Heb. Ch. Syr. פלט. Class Ld. No. 43. It is undoubtedly from the same root as *fleet*, which see.]

1. To fly away with a rapid motion; to dart along; to move with celerity through the air. We say, a bird *flits* away, or *flits* in air; a cloud *flits* along.
2. To flutter; to rove on the wing. *Dryden.*
3. To remove; to migrate; to pass rapidly, as a light substance, from one place to another.

It became a received opinion, that the souls of men, departing this life, did *flit* out of one body into some other. *Hooker.*

4. In *Scotland*, to remove from one habitation to another.
5. To be unstable; to be easily or often moved.

And the free soul to *flitting* air resigned. *Dryden.*

FLIT, *a.* Nimble; quick; swift. *Obs.* [See *Fleet.*]

FLITCH, *n.* [Sax. *flicce*; Fr. *fleche*, an arrow, a coach-beam, a flitch of bacon.]
The side of a hog salted and cured. *Dryden. Swift.*

FLIT'TER, *v. i.* To flutter, which see. *Chaucer.*

FLIT'TER, *n.* A rag; a tatter. [See *Fritter.*]

FLIT'TERMOUSE, *n.* [*Flit, flitter* and *mouse.*]
A bat; an animal that has the fur of a mouse, and membranes which answer the purpose of wings, and enable the animal to sustain itself in a fluttering flight.

FLIT'TINESS, *n.* [from *flit.*] Unsteadiness; levity; lightness. *Bp. Hopkins.*

FLIT'TING, *ppr.* Flying rapidly; fluttering; moving swiftly.

FLIT'TING, *n.* A flying with lightness and celerity; a fluttering.

FLIT'TY, *a.* Unstable; fluttering. *More.*

FLIX, *n.* [Qu. from *flax.*] Down; fur. [*Not used.*] *Dryden.*

FLIX'WEED, *n.* The *Sisymbrium sophia*, a species of water-cresses, growing on walls and waste grounds. *Encyc.*

FLO, *n.* An arrow. [*Not in use.*] *Chaucer.*

FLOAT, *n.* [Sax. *flota*; G. *floss*; D. *vlot, vloot*; Dan. *flode*; Sw. *flotte*; Fr. *flotte*; Sp. *flota*; It. *flotta*; Russ. *plot.*]
1. That which swims or is borne on water; as a *float* of weeds and rushes. But particularly, a body or collection of timber, boards or planks fastened together and conveyed down a stream; a raft. [*The latter word is more generally used in the U. States.*]
2. The cork or quill used on an angling line, to support it and discover the bite of a fish. *Encyc. Walton.*
3. The act of flowing; flux; flood; *the primary sense, but obsolete.* *Hooker.*
4. A quantity of earth, eighteen feet square and one deep. *Mortimer.*
5. A wave. [French *flot*; Lat. *fluctus.*]

FLOAT, *v. i.* [Sax. *fleotan, flotan*; G. *flössen*; D. *vlooten, vlotten*; Fr. *flotter*; Dan. *flöder.* Either from the noun, or from the root of the L. *fluo*, to flow.]
1. To be borne or sustained on the surface of a fluid; to swim; to be buoyed up; not to sink; not to be aground. We say, the water is so shallow, the ship will not *float.*
2. To move or be conveyed on water; to swim. The raft *floats* down the river.

Three blustering nights, borne by the southern blast,
I *floated.* *Dryden.*

3. To be buoyed up and moved or conveyed in a fluid, as in air.

They stretch their plumes and *float* upon the wind. *Pope.*

4. To move with a light irregular course. Qu. *Locke.*

FLOAT, *v. t.* To cause to pass by swimming; to cause to be conveyed on water. The tide *floated* the ship into the harbor.
2. To flood; to inundate; to overflow; to cover with water.

Proud Pactolus *floats* the fruitful lands. *Dryden.*

FLO'ATAĠE, *n.* Any thing that floats on the water. *Encyc.*

FLO'AT-BOARD, *n.* A board of the water-wheel of undershot mills, which receives the impulse of the stream, by which the wheel is driven.

FLO'ATED, *pp.* Flooded; overflowed.
2. Borne on water.

FLO'ATER, *n.* One that floats or swims. *Eusden.*

FLO'ATING, *ppr.* Swimming; conveying on water; overflowing.
2. Lying flat on the surface of the water; as a *floating* leaf. *Martyn.*

FLOAT'ING-BRIDĠE, *n.* In the *U. States*, a bridge, consisting of logs or timber with a floor of plank, supported wholly by the water.
2. In *war*, a kind of double bridge, the upper one projecting beyond the lower one, and capable of being moved forward by pulleys, used for carrying troops over narrow moats in attacking the outworks of a fort.

FLO'ATSTONE, *n.* Swimming flint, spungiform quartz, a mineral of a spungy texture, of a whitish gray color, often with a tinge of yellow. It frequently contains a nucleus of common flint. *Cleaveland.*

FLO'ATY, *a.* Buoyant; swimming on the surface; light. *Raleigh.*

FLOC'CULENCE, *n.* [L. *flocculus, floccus.* See *Flock.*]
The state of being in locks or flocks; adhesion in small flakes. *Higgins Med. Rep.*

FLOC'CULENT, *a.* Coalescing and adhering in locks or flakes.

I say the liquor is broken to *flocculence*, when the particles of herbaceous matter, seized by those of the lime, and coalescing, appear large and *flocculent.* *Ibm.*

FLOCK, *n.* [Sax. *floce*; L. *floccus*; G. *flocke*; D. *vlok*; Dan. *flok*; Sw. *flock*, a crowd; *ulle-lock*, wool-lock; Gr. πλοκη, πλοκος; Russ. *klok.* It is the same radically as *flake*, and applied to wool or hair, we write it *lock.* See *Flake.*]
1. A company or collection; *applied to sheep and other small animals.* A *flock* of sheep answers to a *herd* of larger cattle. But the word may sometimes perhaps be applied to larger beasts, and in the plural, *flocks* may include all kinds of domesticated animals.
2. A company or collection of fowls of any kind, and when applied to birds on the wing, a flight; as a *flock* of wild-geese; a *flock* of ducks; a *flock* of blackbirds. In the U. States, *flocks* of wild-pigeons sometimes darken the air.
3. A body or crowd of people. [*Little used.* Qu. Gr. λοχος, a troop.]
4. A *lock* of wool or hair. Hence, a *flock*-bed.

FLOCK, *v. i.* To gather in companies or crowds; *applied to men or other animals.* People *flock* together. They *flock* to the play-house.

Friends daily *flock.* *Dryden.*

FLOCK'ING, *ppr.* Collecting or running together in a crowd.

FLOG, *v. t.* [L. *fligo*, to strike, that is, to lay on; L. *flagrum, flagellum*, Eng. *flail*; Goth. *bliggwan*, to strike; Gr. πλαγα, πληγη, L. *plaga*, a stroke, Eng. *plague.* We have *lick*, which is probably of the same family; as is D. *slag*, G. *schlag*, Eng. *slay.*]
To beat or strike with a rod or whip; to whip; to lash; to chastise with repeated blows; *a colloquial word, applied to whipping or beating for punishment*; as, to *flog* a schoolboy or a sailor.

FLOG'GED, *pp.* Whipped or scourged for punishment; chastised.

FLOG'GING, *ppr.* Whipping for punishment; chastising.

FLOG'GING, *n.* A whipping for punishment.

FLŎOD, *n. flud.* [Sax. *flod*; G. *fluth*; D. *vloed*; Sw. *flod*; Dan. *flod*; from *flow.*]
1. A great flow of water; a body of moving water; particularly, a body of water, rising, swelling and overflowing land not usually covered with water. Thus there is a *flood*, every spring, in the Connecticut, which inundates the adjacent meadows. There is an annual *flood* in the Nile, and in the Missisippi.
2. *The flood*, by way of eminence, the deluge; the great body of water which inundated the earth in the days of Noah. Before the *flood*, men lived to a great age.
3. A river; a sense chiefly poetical.
4. The flowing of the tide; the semi-diurnal swell or rise of water in the ocean; opposed to *ebb.* The ship entered the harbor on the *flood.* Hence *flood-tide*; young *flood*; high *flood.*
5. A great quantity; an inundation; an overflowing; abundance; superabundance; as a *flood* of bank notes; a *flood* of paper currency.
6. A great body or stream of any fluid substance; as a *flood* of light; a *flood* of lava. Hence, figuratively, a *flood* of vice.
7. Menstrual discharge. *Harvey.*

FLŎOD, *v. t.* To overflow; to inundate; to deluge; as, to *flood* a meadow. *Mortimer.*

FLŎOD'ED, *pp.* Overflowed; inundated.

FLŎOD'GATE, *n.* A gate to be opened for letting water flow through, or to be shut to prevent it.
2. An opening or passage; an avenue for a flood or great body.

FLŎOD'ING, *ppr.* Overflowing; inundating.

FLŎOD'ING, *n.* Any preternatural discharge of blood from the uterus. *Cyc.*

FLŎOD'-MARK, *n.* The mark or line to which the tide rises; high-water mark.

FLOOK. [See *Fluke*, the usual orthography.]

FLOOK'ING, *n.* In *mining*, an interruption or shifting of a load of ore, by a cross vein or fissure. *Encyc.*

FLOOR, *n. flore.* [Sax. *flor, flore*; D. *vloer*; W. *llawr*, and *clawr*, the earth or ground. an area, or ground plot, a floor; Ir. *lar*, and *urlar*; Basque, or Cantabrian, *lurra*; Arm. *leur*, flat land or *floor*; G. *flur*, a field, level ground or floor. In early ages, the inhabitants of Europe had no floor in their huts, but the ground. The sense of the word is probably that which is laid or spread.]

1. That part of a building or room on which we walk; the bottom or lower part, consisting, in modern houses, of boards, planks or pavement; as the *floor* of a house, room, barn, stable or outhouse.
2. A platform of boards or planks laid on timbers, as in a bridge; any similar platform.
3. A story in a building; as the first or second *floor*.
4. A floor or earthen floor is still used in some kinds of business, made of loam, or of lime, sand and iron dust, as in malting. *Encyc.*
5. The bottom of a ship, or that part which is nearly horizontal. *Mar. Dict.*

FLOOR, *v. t.* To lay a floor; to cover timbers with a floor; to furnish with a floor; as, to *floor* a house with pine boards.

FLOOR'ED, *pp.* Covered with boards, plank or pavement; furnished with a floor.

FLOOR'ING, *ppr.* Laying a floor; furnishing with a floor.

FLOOR'ING, *n.* A platform; the bottom of a room or building; pavement.

2. Materials for floors.

FLOOR-TIMBERS, *n.* The timbers on which a floor is laid.

FLOP, *v. t.* [A different spelling of *flap*.]

1. To clap or strike the wings.
2. To let down the brim of a hat.

FLO'RA, *n.* [See *Floral*.] In *antiquity*, the goddess of flowers.

2. In *modern usage*, a catalogue or account of flowers or plants.

FLO'RAL, *a.* [L. *floralis*, from *flos*, a flower, which see.]

1. Containing the flower, as a *floral* bud; immediately attending the flower, as a *floral* leaf. *Martyn.*
2. Pertaining to Flora or to flowers; as *floral* games; *floral* play. *Prior.*

FLOR'EN, **FLOR'ENCE**, } *n.* An ancient gold coin of Edward III. of six shillings sterling value, about 134 cents. *Camden.*

FLOR'ENCE, *n.* A kind of cloth.

2. A kind of wine from Florence in Italy.

FLOR'ENTINE, *n.* A native of Florence.

2. A kind of silk cloth, so called.

FLORES'CENCE, *n.* [L. *florescens, floresco*. See *Flower*.]

In *botany*, the season when plants expand their flowers. *Martyn.*

FLO'RET, *n.* [Fr. *fleurette*; It. *fioretto*.] A little flower; the partial or separate little flower of an aggregate flower. *Martyn.*

FLOR'ID, *a.* [L. *floridus*, from *floreo*, to flower.]

1. Literally, flowery; covered or abounding with flowers; but in this sense little used.
2. Bright in color; flushed with red; of a lively red color; as a *florid* countenance; a *florid* cheek.
3. Embellished with flowers of rhetoric; enriched with lively figures; splendid; brilliant; as a *florid* style; *florid* eloquence.

FLORID'ITY, *n.* Freshness or brightness of color; floridness. *Floyer.*

FLOR'IDNESS, *n.* Brightness or freshness of color or complexion.

2. Vigor; spirit. [*Unusual.*] *Feltham.*
3. Embellishment; brilliant ornaments; ambitious elegance; *applied to style.* *Boyle.*

FLORIF'EROUS, *a.* [L. *florifer*, from *flos*, a flower, and *fero*, to bear.] Producing flowers.

FLORIFICA'TION, *n.* The act, process or time of flowering. *Williams. Journ. of Science.*

FLOR'IN, *n.* [Fr. *florin*; It. *fiorino*.] A coin, originally made at Florence. The name is given to different coins of gold or silver, and of different values in different countries. It is also used as a money of account.

FLO'RIST, *n.* [Fr. *fleuriste*.] A cultivator of flowers; one skilled in flowers. *Thomson.*

2. One who writes a flora, or an account of plants. *Encyc.*

FLOR'ULENT, *a.* Flowery; blossoming. [*Not in use.*]

FLOS'CULAR, **FLOS'CULOUS**, } *a.* [infra.] In *botany*, a flosculous flower is a compound flower, composed entirely of florets with funnel-shaped petals, as in burdock, thistle and artichoke. This is the term used by Tournefort. For this Linne used *tubulous*. *Milne. Martyn.*

FLOS'CULE, *n.* [L. *flosculus*.] In *botany*, a partial or lesser floret of an aggregate flower. *Milne.*

FLOS FERRI, *n.* [L. flower of iron.] A mineral, a variety of arragonite, called by Jameson, after Haüy, coralloidal arragonite. It occurs in little cylinders, sometimes diverging and ending in a point, and sometimes branched, like coral. Its structure is fibrous, and the surface, which is smooth, or garnished with little crystaline points, is often very white, with a silken luster. It takes this name from its being often found in cavities in veins of sparry iron. *Cleaveland.*

FLOSS, *n.* [L. *flos*.] A downy or silky substance in the husks of certain plants. *Tooke.*

FLOSSIFICA'TION, *n.* A flowering; expansion of flowers. [*Novel.*] *Med. Repos.*

FLO'TA, *n.* [Sp. See *Fleet*.] A fleet; but appropriately a fleet of Spanish ships which formerly sailed every year from Cadiz to Vera Cruz, in Mexico, to transport to Spain the productions of Spanish America.

FLO'TAGE, *n.* [Fr. *flottage*.] That which floats on the sea, or on rivers. [*Little used.*] *Chambers.*

FLOTE, *v. t.* To skim. [*Not used or local.*] *Tusser.*

FLOTIL'LA, *n.* [dim. of *flota*.] A little fleet, or fleet of small vessels.

FLOT'SAM, **FLOT'SON**, } *n.* [from *float*.] Goods lost by shipwreck, and floating on the sea. When such goods are cast on shore or found, the owner being unknown, they belong to the king. *English Law. Blackstone.*

FLOT'TEN, *pp.* Skimmed. [*Not in use.*]

FLOUNCE, *v. i. flouns.* [D. *plonssen*. See *Flounder*.]

To throw the limbs and body one way and the other; to spring, turn or twist with sudden effort or violence; to struggle as a horse in mire.

> You neither fume, nor fret, nor *flounce*. *Swift.*

2. To move with jerks or agitation.

FLOUNCE, *v. t.* To deck with a flounce; as, to *flounce* a petticoat or frock. *Pope.*

FLOUNCE, *n.* A narrow piece of cloth sewed to a petticoat, frock or gown, with the lower border loose and spreading. The present is the age of *flounces*. 1827.

FLOUN'DER, *n.* [Sw. *flundra*; G. *flünder*.] A flat fish of the genus Pleuronectes.

FLOUN'DER, *v. i.* [This seems to be allied to *flaunt* and *flounce*.]

To fling the limbs and body, as in making efforts to move; to struggle as a horse in the mire; to roll, toss and tumble. *Pope.*

FLOUN'DERING, *ppr.* Making irregular motions; struggling with violence.

FLOUR, *n.* [originally *flower*; Fr. *fleur*; Sp. *flor*; It. *fiore*; L. *flos, floris*, from *floreo*, to flourish.]

The edible part of corn; meal. *Johnson.*

In the United States, the modern practice is to make a distinction between *flour* and *meal*; the word *flour* being more usually applied to the finer part of meal, separated from the bran, as wheat *flour*, rye *flour*. This is a just and useful distinction.

FLOUR, *v. t.* [Sp. *florear*.] To grind and bolt; to convert into flour. Wheat used formerly to be sent to market; but now great quantities of it are *floured* in the interior country.

2. To sprinkle with flour.

FLOUR'ED, *pp.* Converted into flour; sprinkled with flour.

FLOUR'ING, *ppr.* Converting into flour; sprinkling with flour.

FLOURISH, *v. i. flur'ish.* [L. *floresco*, from *floreo*; Fr. *fleurir, fleurissant*; Sp. *florear*; It. *fiorire*. The primary sense is to open, expand, enlarge, or to shoot out, as in *glory*, L. *ploro*, or in other words in *Lr*.]

1. To thrive; to grow luxuriantly; to increase and enlarge, as a healthy growing plant. The beech and the maple *flourish* best in a deep, rich and moist loam.
2. To be prosperous; to increase in wealth or honor.

> Bad men as frequently prosper and *flourish*, and that by the means of their wickedness. *Nelson.*
>
> When all the workers of iniquity do *flourish*. Ps. xcii.

3. To grow in grace and in good works; to abound in the consolations of religion.

> The righteous shall *flourish* like the palm-tree. Ps. xcii.

4. To be in a prosperous state; to grow or be augmented. We say agriculture *flourishes*, commerce *flourishes*, manufactures *flourish*.
5. To use florid language; to make a display of figures and lofty expressions; to be copious and flowery.

> They dilate and *flourish* long on little incidents. *Watts.*

6. To make bold strokes in writing; to make large and irregular lines; as, to *flourish* with the pen.
7. To move or play in bold and irregular figures.

> Impetuous spread
> The stream, and smoking, *flourished* o'er his head. *Pope.*

8. In *music*, to play with bold and irregular notes, or without settled form; as, to *flourish* on an organ or violin.
9. To boast; to vaunt; to brag.

FLOURISH, *v. t. flur'ish.* To adorn with flowers or beautiful figures, either natural or artificial; to ornament with any thing showy.
2. To spread out; to enlarge into figures. *Bacon.*
3. To move in bold or irregular figures; to move in circles or vibrations by way of show or triumph; to brandish; as, to *flourish* a sword.
4. To embellish with the flowers of diction; to adorn with rhetorical figures; to grace with ostentatious eloquence; to set off with a parade of words. *Collier.*
5. To adorn; to embellish. *Shak.*
6. To mark with a flourish or irregular stroke.

> The day book and inventory book shall be *flourished.* French Com. Code. *Walsh.*

FLOURISH, *n. flur'ish.* Beauty; showy splendor.

> The *flourish* of his sober youth. *Crashaw.*

2. Ostentatious embellishment; ambitious copiousness or amplification; parade of words and figures; show; as a *flourish* of rhetoric; a *flourish* of wit.

> He lards with *flourishes* his long harangue. *Dryden.*

3. Figures formed by bold, irregular lines, or fanciful strokes of the pen or graver; as the *flourishes* about a great letter. *More.*
4. A brandishing; the waving of a weapon or other thing; as the *flourish* of a sword.

FLOURISHED, *pp. flur'ished.* Embellished; adorned with bold and irregular figures or lines; brandished.

FLOURISHER, *n. flur'isher.* One who flourishes; one who thrives or prospers.
2. One who brandishes.
3. One who adorns with fanciful figures.

FLOURISHING, *ppr.* or *a. flur'ishing.* Thriving; prosperous; increasing; making a show.

FLOURISHINGLY, *adv. flur'ishingly.* With flourishes; ostentatiously.

FLOUT, *v. t.* [Scot. *flyte*, to scold or brawl; Sax. *flitan.*]
To mock or insult; to treat with contempt.

> Phillida *flouts* me. *Walton.*
> He *flouted* us downright. *Shak.*

FLOUT, *v. i.* To practice mocking; to sneer; to behave with contempt.

> Fleer and gibe, and laugh and *flout.* *Shak.*

FLOUT, *n.* A mock; an insult.

FLOUT'ED, *pp.* Mocked; treated with contempt.

FLOUT'ER, *n.* One who flouts and flings; a mocker.

FLOUT'ING, *ppr.* Mocking; insulting; fleering.

FLOUT'INGLY, *adv.* With flouting; insultingly.

FLOW, *v. i.* [Sax. *flowan*; D. *vloeijen.* If the last radical was originally a dental, this word coincides with the D. *vlieten*, G. *fliessen*, Sw. *flyta*, Dan. *flyder*, to flow. If *g* was the last radical, *flow* coincides with the L. *fluo*, contracted from *flugo*, for it forms *fluxi*, *fluctum.* In one case, the word would agree with the root of *blow*, L. *flo*; in the other, with the root of *fly.*]
1. To move along an inclined plane, or on descending ground, by the operation of gravity, and with a continual change of place among the particles or parts, as a fluid. A solid body descends or moves in mass, as a ball or a wheel; but in the *flowing* of liquid substances, and others consisting of very fine particles, there is a constant change of the relative position of some parts of the substance, as is the case with a stream of water, of quicksilver, and of sand. Particles at the bottom and sides of the stream, being somewhat checked by friction, move slower than those in the middle and near the surface of the current. Rivers *flow* from springs and lakes; tears *flow* from the eyes.
2. To melt; to become liquid.

> That the mountains might *flow* down at thy presence. Is. lxiv.

3. To proceed; to issue. Evils *flow* from different sources. Wealth *flows* from industry and economy. All our blessings *flow* from divine bounty.
4. To abound; to have in abundance.

> In that day the mountains shall drop down new wine, and the hills shall *flow* with milk. Joel iii.

5. To be full; to be copious; as *flowing* cups or goblets.
6. To glide along smoothly, without harshness or asperity; as a *flowing* period; *flowing* numbers.
7. To be smooth, as composition or utterance. The orator has a *flowing* tongue.

> Virgil is sweet and *flowing* in his hexameters. *Dryden.*

8. To hang loose and waving; as a *flowing* mantle; *flowing* locks.

> The imperial purple *flowing* in his train. *Federalist, Hamilton.*

9. To rise, as the tide; opposed to *ebb.* The tide *flows* twice in twenty four hours.
10. To move in the arteries and veins of the body; to circulate, as blood.
11. To issue, as rays or beams of light. Light *flows* from the sun.
12. To move in a stream, as air.

FLOW, *v. t.* To cover with water; to overflow; to inundate. The low grounds along the river are annually *flowed.*

FLOW, *n.* A stream of water or other fluid; a current; as a *flow* of water; a *flow* of blood.
2. A current of water with a swell or rise; as the *flow* and ebb of tides.
3. A stream of any thing; as a *flow* of wealth into the country.
4. Abundance; copiousness with action; as a *flow* of spirits.
5. A stream of diction, denoting abundance of words at command and facility of speaking; volubility.
6. Free expression or communication of generous feelings and sentiments.

> The feast of reason, and the *flow* of soul.

FLOWED, *pp.* Overflowed; inundated.

FLOW'ER, *n.* [Fr. *fleur*; Sp. *flor*; It. *fiore* Basque, *lora*; W. *flur*, bloom; *fluraw*, to bloom, to be bright; L. *flos*, *floris*, a flower; *floreo*, to blossom. See *Flourish.*]
1. In *botany*, that part of a plant which contains the organs of fructification, with their coverings. A flower, when complete, consists of a calyx, corol, stamen and pistil; but the essential parts are the anther and stigma, which are sufficient to constitute a flower, either together in hermaphrodite flowers, or separate in male and female flowers. *Martyn. Milne.*
2. In *vulgar acceptation*, a blossom or flower is the flower-bud of a plant, when the petals are expanded; open petals being considered as the principal thing in constituting a flower. But in *botany*, the petals are now considered as a finer sort of covering, and not at all necessary to constitute a flower. *Milne.*
3. The early part of life, or rather of manhood; the prime; youthful vigor; youth; as the *flower* of age or of life.
4. The best or finest part of a thing; the most valuable part. The most active and vigorous part of an army are called the *flower* of the troops. Young, vigorous and brave men are called the *flower* of a nation. *Addison.*
5. The finest part; the essence.

> The choice and *flower* of all things profitable the Psalms do more briefly contain. *Hooker.*

6. He or that which is most distinguished for any thing valuable. We say, the youth are the *flower* of the country.
7. The finest part of grain pulverized. In this sense, it is now always written *flour*, which see.

Flowers, in *chimistry*, fine particles of bodies, especially when raised by fire in sublimation, and adhering to the heads of vessels in the form of a powder or mealy substance; as the *flowers* of sulphur. *Encyc.*

A substance, somewhat similar, formed spontaneously, is called *efflorescence.*

2. In *rhetoric*, figures and ornaments of discourse or composition.
3. Menstrual discharges.

FLOW'ER, *v. i.* [from the Noun. The corresponding word in L. is *floreo*, Fr. *fleurir*, It. *fiorire*, Sp. Port. *florecer*, W. *fluraw.*]
1. To blossom; to bloom; to expand the petals, as a plant. In New England, peach-trees usually *flower* in April, and apple-trees in May.
2. To be in the prime and spring of life; to flourish; to be youthful, fresh and vigorous.

> When *flowered* my youthful spring. *Spenser.*

3. To froth; to ferment gently; to mantle, as new beer.

> The beer did *flower* a little. *Bacon.*

4. To come as cream from the surface. *Milton.*

FLOW'ER, *v. t.* To embellish with figures of flowers; to adorn with imitated flowers.

FLOW'ER-DE-LIS, *n.* [Fr. *fleur de lis*, flower of the lily.]
1. In *heraldry*, a bearing representing a lily, the hieroglyphic of royal majesty. *Encyc.*
2. In *botany*, the Iris, a genus of monogynian

triandera, called also flag-flower, and often written incorrectly *flower-de-luce*. The species are numerous.

FLOW'ERED, *pp.* Embellished with figures of flowers.

FLOW'ERET, *n.* [Fr. *fleurette.*] A small flower; a floret. *Shak. Milton. Dryden.*

[In botany, *floret* is solely used.]

FLOW'ER-FENCE, *n.* The name of certain plants. The *flower-fence of Barbadoes* is of the genus Poinciana. The *bastard flower-fence* is the Adenanthera. *Fam. of Plants.*

FLOW'ER-G'ARDEN, *n.* A garden in which flowers are chiefly cultivated.

FLOW'ER-GENTLE, *n.* A plant, the amaranth.

FLOW'ERINESS, *n.* [from *flowery.*] The state of being flowery, or of abounding with flowers.

2. Floridness of speech; abundance of figures.

FLOW'ERING, *ppr.* Blossoming; blooming; expanding the petals, as plants.

2. Adorning with artificial flowers, or figures of blossoms.

FLOW'ERING, *n.* The season when plants blossom.

2. The act of adorning with flowers.

FLOWER-INWO'VEN, *a.* Adorned with flowers. *Milton.*

FLOW'ER-KIRTLED, *a.* Dressed with garlands of flowers. *Milton.*

FLOW'ERLESS, *a.* Having no flower. *Chaucer.*

FLOW'ER-STALK, *n.* In *botany*, the peduncle of a plant, or the stem that supports the flower or fructification.

FLOW'ERY, *a.* Full of flowers; abounding with blossoms; as a *flowery* field. *Milton.*

2. Adorned with artificial flowers, or the figures of blossoms.

3. Richly embellished with figurative language; florid; as a *flowery* style.

FLOWING, *ppr.* Moving as a fluid; issuing; proceeding; abounding; smooth, as style; inundating.

FLOWING, *n.* The act of running or moving as a fluid; an issuing; an overflowing; rise of water.

FLOWINGLY, *adv.* With volubility; with abundance.

FLOWINGNESS, *n.* Smoothness of diction; stream of diction. *Nichols.*

FLOWK, } *n.* [Sax. *floc.*] A flounder.
FLUKE, } *Carew.*

FLOWN, had fled, in the following phrases, is not good English.

> *Was* reason *flown.* *Prior.*
> Sons of Belial, *flown* with insolence and wine. *Milton.*

In the former passage, *flown* is used as the participle of *fly* or *flee*, both intransitive verbs, and the phrase should have been, *had* reason *flown* or fled. In the latter passage, *flown* is used for *blown*, inflated, but most improperly. *Flown* is the participle of the perfect or past tense of *fly*, but cannot regularly be used in a passive sense.

FLU'ATE, *n.* [from *fluor*, which see.] In *chimistry*, a salt formed by the fluoric acid combined with a base; as *fluate* of alumin, or of soda.

FLUC'TUANT, *a.* [L. *fluctuans.* See *Fluctuate.*]

Moving like a wave; wavering; unsteady. *L'Estrange.*

FLUC'TUATE, *v. i.* [L. *fluctuo*, from *fluctus*, a wave, from *fluo*, to *flow.*]

1. To move as a wave; to roll hither and thither; to wave; as a *fluctuating* field of air. *Blackmore.*

2. To float backward and forward, as on waves.

3. To move now in one direction and now in another; to be wavering or unsteady. Public opinion often *fluctuates.* Men often *fluctuate* between different parties and opinions. Hence,

4. To be irresolute or undetermined.

5. To rise and fall; to be in an unsettled state; to experience sudden vicissitudes. The funds or the prices of stocks *fluctuate* with the events of the day.

FLUC'TUATING, *ppr.* Wavering; rolling as a wave; moving in this and that direction; rising and falling.

2. *a.* Unsteady; wavering; changeable. We have little confidence in *fluctuating* opinions.

FLUCTUA'TION, *n.* [L. *fluctuatio.*] A motion like that of waves; a moving in this and that direction; as the *fluctuations* of the sea.

2. A wavering; unsteadiness; as *fluctuations* of opinion.

3. A rising and falling suddenly; as *fluctuations* of prices or of the funds.

FLUD'ER, } *n.* An aquatic fowl of the di-
FLUD'DER, } ver kind, nearly as large as a goose. *Dict. of Nat. Hist.*

FLUE, *n.* [probably contracted from *flume*, L. *flumen*, from *fluo.*]

A passage for smoke in a chimney, leading from the fireplace to the top of the chimney, or into another passage; as a chimney with four *flues.*

FLUE, *n.* [G. *flaum*; L. *pluma.*] Soft down or fur; very fine hair. [*Local.*] *Tooke.*

FLUEL'LEN, *n.* The female speedwell, a plant of the genus Antirrhinum, or snapdragon.

FLUENCE, for *fluency*, is not used.

FLU'ENCY, *n.* [L. *fluens*, from *fluo*, to flow.]

1. The quality of flowing, *applied to speech or language*; smoothness; freedom from harshness; as *fluency* of numbers.

2. Readiness of utterance; facility of words; volubility; as *fluency* of speech; a speaker of remarkable *fluency.*

3. Affluence; abundance. *Obs.* *Sandys.*

FLU'ENT, *a.* [See *Fluency.*] Liquid; flowing. *Bacon.*

2. Flowing; passing.

> Motion being a *fluent* thing. *Ray.*

3. Ready in the use of words; voluble; copious; having words at command and uttering them with facility and smoothness; as a *fluent* speaker.

4. Flowing; voluble; smooth; as *fluent* speech.

FLU'ENT, *n.* A stream; a current of water. [*Little used.*] *Philips.*

2. The variable or flowing quantity in fluxions. *Berkeley.*

FLU'ENTLY, *adv.* With ready flow; volubly; without hesitation or obstruction; as, to speak *fluently.*

FLU'GELMAN, *n.* [G. from *flügel*, a wing.]

In German, the leader of a file. But with us, a soldier who stands on the wing of a body of men, and marks time for the motions.

FLU'ID, *a.* [L. *fluidus*, from *fluo*, to flow.] Having parts which easily move and change their relative position without separation, and which easily yield to pressure; that may flow; liquid. Water, spirit, air, are *fluid* substances. All bodies may be rendered *fluid* by heat or caloric.

FLU'ID, *n.* Any substance whose parts easily move and change their relative position without separation, and which yields to the slightest pressure; a substance which flows, or which moves spontaneously on a plane with the least inclination; a liquid; liquor; opposed to a *solid.* Water, blood, chyle, are *fluids.*

FLUID'ITY, *n.* The quality of being capable of flowing; that quality of bodies which renders them impressible to the slightest force, and by which the parts easily move or change their relative position without a separation of the mass; a liquid state; opposed to *solidity.* *Fluidity* is the effect of heat.

FLU'IDNESS, *n.* The state of being fluid; fluidity, which see.

FLUKE, *n.* [supposed to be D. *ploeg*, G. *pflug*, a plow.]

The part of an anchor which fastens in the ground.

FLUKE, } *n.* A flounder.
FLOWK, }

FLU'KE-WORM, *n.* The gourd-worm, a species of Fasciola.

FLUME, *n.* [Sax. *flum*, a stream; L. *flumen*, from *fluo*, to flow.]

Literally, a flowing; hence, the passage or channel for the water that drives a millwheel.

FLUM'MERY, *n.* [W. *llymry*, from *llymyr*, harsh, raw, crude, from *llym*, sharp, severe. In Welsh, a kind of food made of oatmeal steeped in water, until it has turned sour. See *Lumber.*]

1. A sort of jelly made of flour or meal; pap.

> Milk and *flummery* are very fit for children. *Locke.*

2. In *vulgar use*, any thing insipid or nothing to the purpose; flattery.

FLUNG, *pret.* and *pp.* of *fling.*

> Several statues the Romans themselves *flung* into the river. *Addison.*

FLUOBO'RATE, *n.* A compound of fluoboric acid with a base.

FLUOBO'RIC, *a.* The *fluoboric* acid or gas is a compound of fluorine and boron. *Davy.*

FLU'OR, *n.* [Low L. from *fluo*, to flow.]

1. A fluid state. *Newton.*

2. Menstrual flux. [*Little used in either sense.*]

3. In *mineralogy*, fluate of lime. *Fluor spar* is the foliated fluate of lime. This mineral, though sometimes massive, is almost always regularly crystalized. Its crystals present most frequently the form of a

cube, often perfect, sometimes truncated on all its edges by planes, which form with the sides of the cube an angle of 135°. The colors are very numerous and beautiful.

The fluate of lime, *fluor*, was so named from its use as a flux for certain ores. *Cleaveland.*

FLU'OR-ACID, *n.* The acid of fluor.

FLU'ORATED, *a.* Combined with fluoric acid.

FLUOR'IC, *a.* Pertaining to fluor; obtained from fluor; as *fluoric* acid.

FLU'ORIN, FLU'ORINE, *n.* The supposed basis of fluoric acid. *Davy.*

FLU'OROUS, *a.* The *fluorous* acid is the acid of fluor in its first degree of oxygenation. *Lavoisier.*

FLUOSIL'ICATE, *n.* [*fluor* and *silex* or *silica.*]
In *chimistry*, a compound of fluoric acid, containing silex, with some other substance. *Silliman.*

FLUOSILIC'IC, *a.* Composed of or containing fluoric acid with silex.

FLUR'RY, *n.* A sudden blast or gust, or a light temporary breeze; as a *flurry* of wind. *It is never with us applied to a storm of duration.*
2. A sudden shower of short duration; as a *flurry* of snow.
3. Agitation; commotion; bustle; hurry.

FLUR'RY, *v. t.* To put in agitation; to excite or alarm. *Swinburne.*

FLUSH, *v. i.* [G. *fliessen*, imperf. *floss*, to flow; D. *vlieten*, in a different dialect. It coincides in elements with *blush*, *blaze* and *flash.*]
1. To flow and spread suddenly; to rush; as, blood *flushes* into the face.
2. To come in haste; to start. *B. Jonson.*
3. To appear suddenly, as redness or a blush.

> A blush rose on their cheeks,
> *Flushing* and fading like the changeful play
> Of colors on a dolphin. *Percival.*

4. To become suddenly red; to glow; as, the cheeks *flush.*
5. To be gay, splendid or beautiful.

> At once, arrayed
> In all the colors of the *flushing* year,
> The garden glows. *Thomson.*

FLUSH, *v. t.* To redden suddenly; to cause the blood to rush suddenly into the face.

> Nor *flush* with shame the passing virgin's cheek. *Gay.*

2. To elate; to elevate; to excite the spirits; to animate with joy; as, to *flush* with victory.

FLUSH, *a.* Fresh; full of vigor; glowing; bright.

> *Flush* as May. *Shak.*

2. Affluent; abounding; well furnished.

> Lord Strut was not very *flush* in ready. *Arbuthnot.*

3. Free to spend; liberal; prodigal. He is very *flush* with his money. *This is a popular use of the word in America.*

A *flush deck*, in seamen's language, is a deck without a half-deck or forecastle. [Qu. Russ. *ploskei*, flat. The sense of spreading naturally results from that of flowing.]

FLUSH, *n.* A sudden flow of blood to the face; or more generally, the redness of face which proceeds from such an afflux of blood. Hectic constitutions are often known by a frequent *flush* in the cheeks.
2. Sudden impulse or excitement; sudden glow; as a *flush* of joy.
3. Bloom; growth; abundance. *Goldsmith.*
4. [Fr. Sp. *flux.*] A run of cards of the same suit.
5. A term for a number of ducks. *Spenser.*

FLUSH'ED, *pp.* Overspread or tinged with a red color from the flowing of blood to the face. We say, the skin, face or cheek is *flushed.*
2. Elated; excited; animated; as *flushed* with joy or success.

FLUSH'ER, *n.* The lesser butcher-bird. *Chambers.*

FLUSH'ING, *ppr.* Overspreading with red; glowing.

FLUSH'ING, *n.* A glow of red in the face.

FLUS'TER, *v. t.* To make hot and rosy, as with drinking; to heat; to hurry; to agitate; to confuse. *Swift.*

FLUS'TER, *v. i.* To be in a heat or bustle; to be agitated.

FLUS'TER, *n.* Heat; glow; agitation; confusion; disorder.

FLUS'TERED, *pp.* Heated with liquor; agitated; confused.

FLUTE, *n.* [Fr. *flûte*; Arm. *fleut*; D. *fluit*; G. *flöte*; Dan. *flöjte*; Sp. *flauta*; Port. *frauta*; It. *flauto*; L. *flo*, *flatus*, to blow, or L. *fluta*, a lamprey, with the same number of holes.]
1. A small wind instrument; a pipe with lateral holes or stops, played by blowing with the mouth, and by stopping and opening the holes with the fingers.
2. A channel in a column or pillar; a perpendicular furrow or cavity, cut along the shaft of a column or pilaster; so called from its resemblance to a flute. It is used chiefly in the Ionic order; sometimes in the Composite and Corinthian; rarely in the Doric and Tuscan. It is called also a *reed.* *Encyc.*
3. A long vessel or boat, with flat ribs or floor timbers, round behind, and swelled in the middle; a different orthography of *float*, *flota.* *Encyc.*

Armed in flute. An armed ship, with her guns of the lower tier and part of those of the upper tier removed, used as a transport, is said to be armed in flute. *Lunier.*

FLUTE, *v. i.* To play on a flute. *Chaucer.*

FLUTE, *v. t.* To form flutes or channels in a column.

FLU'TED, *pp.* or *a.* Channeled; furrowed; as a column.
2. In *music*, thin; fine; flutelike; as *fluted* notes. *Busby.*

FLU'TING, *ppr.* Channeling; cutting furrows; as in a column.

FLU'TING, *n.* A channel or furrow in a column; fluted work.

FLU'TIST, *n.* A performer on the flute. *Busby.*

FLUT'TER, *v. i.* [Sax. *floteran*; D. *flodderen*; G. *flattern.* Qu. Fr. *flotter*, to waver, from *flot*, a wave. It is possible that the word is contracted.]
1. To move or flap the wings rapidly, without flying, or with short flights; to hover.

> As an eagle stirreth up her nest, *fluttereth* over her young, spreadeth abroad her wings—Deut. xxxii.

2. To move about briskly, irregularly or with great bustle and show, without consequence.

> No rag, no scrap of all the beau or wit,
> That once so *fluttered*, and that once so writ. *Pope.*

3. To move with quick vibrations or undulations; as a *fluttering* fan; a *fluttering* sail. *Pope.*
4. To be in agitation; to move irregularly; to fluctuate; to be in uncertainty.

> How long we *fluttered* on the wings of doubtful success. *Howell.*
> His thoughts are very *fluttering* and wandering. *Watts.*

FLUT'TER, *v. t.* To drive in disorder. [*Little used.*] *Shak.*
2. To hurry the mind; to agitate.
3. To disorder; to throw into confusion.

FLUT'TER, *n.* Quick and irregular motion; vibration; undulation; as the *flutter* of a fan. *Addison.*
2. Hurry; tumult; agitation of the mind.
3. Confusion; disorder; irregularity in position.

FLUT'TERED, *pp.* Agitated; confused; disordered.

FLUT'TERING, *ppr.* Flapping the wings without flight or with short flights; hovering; fluctuating; agitating; throwing into confusion.

FLUT'TERING, *n.* The act of hovering, or flapping the wings without flight; a wavering; agitation.

FLUVIAT'IC, FLU'VIAL, *a.* [L. *fluviaticus*, from *fluvius*, a river; *fluo*, to flow.] Belonging to rivers; growing or living in streams or ponds; as a *fluviatic* plant.

FLU'VIATILE, *a.* [L. *fluviatilis.*] Belonging to rivers. *Kirwan.*
[*Fluviatic* is the preferable word.]

FLUX, *n.* [L. *fluxus*; Sp. *fluxo*; Fr. *flux*; It. *flusso*; from L. *fluo*, *fluxi.*]
1. The act of flowing; the motion or passing of a fluid.
2. The moving or passing of any thing in continued succession. Things in this life, are in a continual *flux.*
3. Any flow or issue of matter. In *medicine*, an extraordinary issue or evacuation from the bowels or other part; as the bloody *flux* or dysentery, hepatic *flux*, &c.
4. In *hydrography*, the flow of the tide. The ebb is called *reflux.*
5. In *metallurgy*, any substance or mixture used to promote the fusion of metals or minerals, as alkalies, borax, tartar and other saline matter, or in large operations limestone or fluor. Alkaline fluxes are either the crude, the white or the black flux. *Nicholson. Encyc.*
6. Fusion; a liquid state from the operation of heat. *Encyc.*
7. That which flows or is discharged.
8. Concourse; confluence. [*Little used.*] *Shak.*

FLUX, *a.* Flowing; moving; maintained by a constant succession of parts; inconstant; variable. [*Not well authorized.*]

FLUX, *v. t.* To melt; to fuse; to make fluid.

> One part of mineral alkali will *flux* two of siliceous earth with effervescence. *Kirwan.*

2. To salivate. [*Little used.*] *South.*

FLUXA'TION, *n.* A flowing or passing away, and giving place to others. *Leslie.*

FLUX'ED, *pp.* Melted; fused; reduced to a flowing state.

FLUXIBIL'ITY, *n.* The quality of admitting fusion.

FLUX'IBLE, *a.* [from Low L.] Capable of being melted or fused, as a mineral.

FLUXIL'ITY, *n.* [Low L. *fluxilis.*] The quality of admitting fusion; possibility of being fused or liquified. *Boyle.*

FLUX'ION, *n.* [L. *fluxio*, from *fluo*, to flow.]
1. The act of flowing.
2. The matter that flows. *Wiseman.*
3. *Fluxions*, in *mathematics*, the analysis of infinitely small variable quantities, or a method of finding an infinitely small quantity, which being taken an infinite number of times, becomes equal to a quantity given. *Harris.*

In *fluxions*, magnitudes are supposed to be generated by motion; a line by the motion of a point, a surface by the motion of of a line, and a solid by the motion of a surface. And some part of a figure is supposed to be generated by a uniform motion, in consequence of which the other parts may increase uniformly, or with an accelerated or retarded motion, or may decrease in any of these ways, and the computations are made by tracing the comparative velocities with which the parts flow. *Encyc.*

A *fluxion* is an infinitely small quantity, an increment; the infinitely small increase of the fluent or flowing quantity. *Bailey.*

FLUX'IONARY, *a.* Pertaining to mathematical fluxions.

FLUX'IONIST, *n.* One skilled in fluxions. *Berkeley.*

FLUX'IVE, *a.* Flowing; wanting solidity. [*Not used.*] *B. Jonson.*

FLUX'URE, *n.* A flowing or fluid matter. [*Not used.*] *Drayton.*

FLȲ, *v. i.* pret. *flew*; part. *flōwn.* [Sax. *fleogan*; G. *fliegen*; D. *vliegen*; Sw. *flyga*; Dan. *flyver.* In Saxon, the same verb signifies to *fly* and to *flee*; in German, different words are used.]
1. To move through air by the aid of wings, as fowls.
2. To pass or move in air, by the force of wind or other impulse; as, clouds and vapors *fly* before the wind. A ball *flies* from a cannon, an arrow from a bow.
3. To rise in air, as light substances, by means of a current of air or by having less specific gravity than air, as smoke.

Man is born to trouble, as the sparks *fly* upward. Job v.

4. To move or pass with velocity or celerity, either on land or water. He *flew* to the relief of his distressed friend. The ship *flies* upon the main.
5. To move rapidly, in any manner; as, a top *flies* about.
6. To pass away; to depart; with the idea of haste, swiftness or escape. The bird has *flown.*
7. To pass rapidly, as time. Swift *fly* the fleeting hours.
8. To part suddenly or with violence; to burst, as a bottle. *Swift.*
9. To spring by an elastic force.
10. To pass swiftly, as rumor or report.
11. To flee; to run away; to attempt to escape; to escape.

I'll *fly* from shepherds, flocks, and flowery plains. *Pope.*

12. To flutter; to vibrate or play; as a flag in the wind.

To fly at, to spring towards; to rush on; to fall on suddenly. A hen *flies at* a dog or cat; a dog *flies at* a man.

To fly in the face, to insult.
2. To assail; to resist; to set at defiance; to oppose with violence; to act in direct opposition.

To fly off, to separate or depart suddenly.
2. To revolt.

To fly open, to open suddenly or with violence; as, the doors *flew open.*

To fly out, to rush out; also, to burst into a passion.
2. To break out into licence.
3. To start or issue with violence from any direction.

To let fly, to discharge; to throw or drive with violence; as, to *let fly* a shower of darts.
2. In *seamanship*, to let go suddenly. *Let fly* the sheets.

FLȲ, *v. t.* [This is used for *flee*, and *from* is understood after *fly*, so that it can hardly be called a transitive verb.]
1. To shun; to avoid; to decline; as, to *fly* the sight of one we hate. That is, primarily, to *flee from.*

Sleep *flies* the wretch. *Dryden.*

2. To quit by flight.
3. To attack by a bird of prey. [*Not used.*] *Bacon.*
4. To cause to float in the air.

FLȲ, *n.* [Sax. *fleoge*; Sw. *fluga*; Dan. *flue*; G. *fliege*; D. *vlieg*; from the verb, *fleogan*, to fly.]
1. In *zoology*, a winged insect of various species, whose distinguishing characteristic is that the wings are transparent. By this flies are distinguished from beetles, butterflies, grasshoppers, &c. Of flies, some have two wings and others four. *Encyc.*

In common language, *fly* is the house fly, of the genus Musca.

2. In *mechanics*, a cross with leaden weights at the ends, or a heavy wheel at right angles with the axis of a windlass, jack or the like. The use of this is, to regulate and equalize the motion in all parts of the revolution of the machine. *Encyc.*
3. That part of a vane which points and shows which way the wind blows.
4. The extent of an ensign, flag or pendant from the staff to the end that flutters loose in the wind. *Mar. Dict.*

FLȲ'BANE, *n.* A plant called catch-fly, of the genus Silene.

FLȲBITTEN, *a.* Marked by the bite of flies. *Shak.*

FLȲBLOW, *v. t.* To deposit an egg in any thing, as a fly; to taint with the eggs which produce maggots.

Like a *flyblown* cake of tallow. *Swift.*

FLȲBLOW, *n.* The egg of a fly.

FLȲBOAT, *n.* A large flat-bottomed Dutch vessel, whose burden is from 600 to 1200 tons, with a stern remarkably high, resembling a Gothic turret, and very broad buttocks below. *Encyc.*

FLȲCATCHER, *n.* One that hunts flies.
2. In *zoology*, a genus of birds, the Muscicapa, with a bill flatted at the base, almost triangular, notched at the upper mandible, and beset with bristles. These birds are of the order of Passers, and the species are very numerous. *Encyc.*

FLȲER, *n.* One that flies or flees; usually written *flier.*
2. One that uses wings.
3. The fly of a jack.
4. In *architecture*, stairs that do not wind, but are made of an oblong square figure, and whose fore and back sides are parallel to each other, and so are their ends. The second of these *flyers* stands parallel behind the first, the third behind the second, and so are said to *fly off* from one another. *Moxon.*
5. A performer in Mexico, who flies round an elevated post.

FLȲFISH, *v. i.* To angle with flies for bait.

FLȲFISHING, *n.* Angling; the art or practice of angling for fish with flies, natural or artificial, for bait. *Walton.*

FLȲFLAP, *n.* Something to drive away flies. *Congreve.*

FLȲ-HŎNEYSUCKLE, *n.* A plant, the Lonicera. The *African fly-honeysuckle* is the Halleria. *Fam. of Plants.*

FLȲING, *ppr.* Moving in air by means of wings; passing rapidly; springing; bursting; avoiding.
2. *a.* Floating; waving; as *flying* colors.
3. *a.* Moving; light, and suited for prompt motion; as a *flying* camp.

Flying colors, a phrase expressing triumph.

FLȲING-BRIDGE, *n.* A bridge of pontoons; also, a bridge composed of two boats.

FLȲING-FISH, *n.* A small fish which flies by means of its pectoral fins. It is of the genus Exocœtus.

FLȲING-PARTY, *n.* In military affairs, a detachment of men employed to hover about an enemy.

FLȲING-PINION, *n.* The part of a clock, having a fly or fan, by which it gathers air, and checks the rapidity of the clock's motion, when the weight descends in the striking part. *Encyc.*

FLȲTRAP, *n.* In *botany*, a species of sensitive plant, called *Venus' Fly-trap*, the *Dionæa Muscipula*; a plant that has the power of seizing insects that light on it. *Encyc.*

FLȲTREE, *n.* A tree whose leaves are said to produce flies, from a little bag on the surface. *Encyc.*

FŌAL, *n.* [Sax. *fola*, *fole*; G. *füllen*; D. *veulen*; Dan. *föl*; Sw. *fåla*; Fr. *poulain*; Arm. *poull*, *pull* or *heubeul*; W. *ebawl*; Corn. *ebol*; L. *pullus*; Gr. *πωλος*; Ch. פולא; Ar. طفل to rise or to set as the sun, to bear young, and طفل pullus. The primary sense of the verb is to shoot, to cast or throw, to *fall.* The same verb in Heb. and Ch. signifies to unite, to fasten; in Syr. to *foul*, to *defile*; both senses from that of putting or throwing on. The verb belongs probably to the root of Eng. *fall* and *foul*, that is נפל with a different prefix. *Foal* is literally a shoot, issue, or that which is cast, or which falls.]

The young of the equine genus of quadrupeds, and of either sex; a colt; a filly.

FŌAL, *v. t.* To bring forth a colt or filly; to bring forth young, as a mare or a she-ass.

FŌAL, *v. i.* To bring forth young, as a mare and certain other beasts.

FŌALBIT, *n.* A plant.

FŌALFOOT, *n.* The colt's-foot, Tussilago.

FŌAM, *n.* [Sax. *fæm*, *fam*, G. *faum*, foam; L. *fumo*, to smoke, to foam.]

Froth; spume; the substance which is formed on the surface of liquors by fermentation or violent agitation, consisting of bubbles.

FŌAM, *v. i.* To froth; to gather foam. The billows *foam*. A horse *foams* at the mouth, when violently heated.

2. To be in a rage; to be violently agitated.

He *foameth*, and gnasheth with his teeth. Mark ix.

FŌAM, *v. t.* To throw out with rage or violence; with *out.*

Foaming out their own shame. Jude 13.

FŌAMING, *ppr.* Frothing; fuming.

FŌAMINGLY, *adv.* Frothily.

FŌAMY, *a.* Covered with foam; frothy.

Behold how high the *foamy* billows ride! *Dryden.*

FOB, *n.* [Qu. G. *fuppe*. I have not found the word.] A little pocket for a watch.

FOB, *v. t.* [G. *foppen*.] To cheat; to trick; to impose on.

To fob off, to shift off by an artifice; to put aside; to delude with a trick. [*A low word.*] *Shak.*

FOB'BED, *pp.* Cheated; imposed on.

FOB'BING, *ppr.* Cheating; imposing on.

FO'CAL, *a.* [from L. *focus*.] Belonging to a focus; as a *focal* point; *focal* distance.

FO'CIL, *n.* [Fr. *focile*.] The greater focil is the ulna or tibia, the greater bone of the fore-arm or leg. The lesser focil is the radius or fibula, the lesser bone of the fore-arm or leg. *Coxe. Wiseman.*

FO'CUS, *n.* plu. *focuses*, or *foci*. [L. *focus*, a fire, the hearth; Sp. *fuego*; Port. *fogo*; It. *fuoco*; Fr. *feu*; Arm. *fo*.]

1. In *optics*, a point in which any number of rays of light meet, after being reflected or refracted; as the *focus* of a lens. *Encyc. Newton.*

2. In *geometry* and *conic sections*, a certain point in the parabola, ellipsis and hyperbola, where rays reflected from all parts of these curves, concur or meet. *Encyc.*

The *focus of an ellipsis*, is a point towards each end of the longer axis, from which two right lines drawn to any point in the circumference, shall together be equal to the longer axis. *Harris.*

The *focus of a parabola*, is a point in the axis within the figure, and distant from the vertex by the fourth part of the parameter. *Harris.*

The *focus of a hyperbola*, is a point in the principal axis, within the opposite hyperbolas, from which if any two lines are drawn, meeting in either of the opposite hyperbolas, the difference will be equal to the principal axis. *Dict.*

3. A central point; point of concentration.

FOD'DER, *n.* [Sax. *foddor*, or *fother*; G. *futter*; D. *voeder*; Dan. *foeder*; Sw. *foder*; from the root of *feed*, the sense of which is to thrust in, to stuff. Hence in German, *futter* is a *lining* as well as *fodder*.]

1. Food or dry food for cattle, horses and sheep, as hay, straw and other kinds of vegetables. The word is never applied to pasture.

2. In *mining*, a measure containing 20 hundred, or 22½ hundred. *Encyc.*

FOD'DER, *v. t.* To feed with dry food, or cut grass, &c.; to furnish with hay, straw, oats, &c. Farmers *fodder* their cattle twice or thrice in a day.

FOD'DERED, *pp.* Fed with dry food, or cut grass, &c.; as, to *fodder* cows.

FOD'DERER, *n.* He who fodders cattle.

FOD'DERING, *ppr.* Feeding with dry food, &c.

FO'DIENT, *a.* [L. *fodio*, to dig.] Digging; throwing up with a spade. [*Little used.*]

FŌE, *n. fo.* [Sax. *fah*, from *fean*, *feon*, *figan*, to hate; the participle is used in the other Teutonic dialects. See *Fiend.*]

1. An enemy; one who entertains personal enmity, hatred, grudge or malice against another.

A man's *foes* shall be they of his own household. Matt. x.

2. An enemy in war; one of a nation at war with another, whether he entertains enmity against the opposing nation or not; an adversary.

Either three years famine, or three months to be destroyed before thy *foes*. 1 Chron. xxi.

3. *Foe*, like *enemy*, in the singular, is used to denote an opposing army, or nation at war.

4. An opponent; an enemy; one who opposes any thing in principle; an ill-wisher; as a *foe* to religion; a *foe* to virtue; a *foe* to the measures of the administration.

FŌE, *v. t.* To treat as an enemy. *Obs.* *Spenser.*

FŌEHOOD, *n.* Enmity. [*Not in use.*] *Bedell.*

FŌELIKE, *a.* Like an enemy. *Sandys.*

FŌEMAN, *n.* An enemy in war. *Obs.* *Spenser.*

FŒTUS. [See *Fetus.*]

FOG, *n.* [In Sp. *vaho* is steam; *vahar*, to exhale. In Italian, *sfogo* is exhalation; *sfogare*, to exhale. In Scot. *fog* is moss. In Italian, *affogare* is to suffocate, Sp. *ahocar*. The sense probably is thick or that which it exhaled.]

1. A dense watery vapor, exhaled from the earth, or from rivers and lakes, or generated in the atmosphere near the earth. It differs from *mist*, which is rain in very small drops.

2. A cloud of dust or smoke.

FOG, *n.* [W. *fwg*, long dry grass. Johnson quotes a forest law of Scotland, which mentions *fogagium*. It may be allied to Scot. *fog*, moss.]

After-grass; a second growth of grass; but it signifies also long grass that remains on land.

Dead grass, remaining on land during winter, is called in New England, the *old tore.*

FOG'BANK, *n.* At sea, an appearance in hazy weather sometimes resembling land at a distance, but which vanishes as it is approached. *Mar. Dict.*

FOG'GAGE, *n.* Rank grass not consumed or mowed in summer. *Encyc.*

FOG'GINESS, *n.* [from *foggy*.] The state of being foggy; a state of the air filled with watery exhalations.

FOG'GY, *a.* [from *fog*.] Filled or abounding with fog or watery exhalations; as a *foggy* atmosphere; a *foggy* morning.

2. Cloudy; misty; damp with humid vapors.

3. Producing frequent fogs; as a *foggy* climate.

4. Dull; stupid; clouded in understanding. *Johnson.*

FOH, an exclamation of abhorrence or contempt, the same as *poh* and *fy*.

FOI'BLE, *a.* Weak. [*Not used.*] *Herbert.*

FOI'BLE, *n.* [Fr. *foible*, weak. See *Feeble.*] A particular moral weakness; a failing. When we speak of a man's *foible*, in the singular, which is also called his *weak side*, we refer to a predominant failing. We use also the plural, *foibles*, to denote moral failings or defects. It is wise in every man to know his own *foibles*.

FOIL, *v. t.* [In Norm. *afolee* is rendered crippled; and *afoula*, damaged, wasted. If the primary or true literal sense is, to blunt, this word may be from the same root as *fool*; if, to render vain, it would naturally be allied to *fail*.]

1. To frustrate; to defeat; to render vain or nugatory, as an effort or attempt. The enemy attempted to pass the river, but was *foiled*. He *foiled* his adversaries.

And by a mortal man at length am *foiled*. *Dryden.*

2. To blunt; to dull.

When light wing'd toys
Of feathered Cupid *foil*— *Shak.*

3. To defeat; to interrupt, or to render imperceptible; as, to *foil* the scent in a chase. *Addison.*

FOIL, *n.* Defeat; frustration; the failure of success when on the point of being secured; miscarriage.

Death never won a stake with greater toil,
Nor e'er was fate so near a *foil*. *Dryden.*

FOIL, *n.* [W. *fwyl*, a driving, impulsion, a stroke, a *foil*.]

A blunt sword, or one that has a button at the end covered with leather; used in fencing.

Isocrates contended with a *foil*, against Demosthenes with a sword. *Mitford.*

FOIL, *n.* [Fr. *feuille*; It. *foglia*; Port. *folha*; Sp. *hoja*; L. *folium*; Gr. φυλλον.]

1. A leaf or thin plate of metal used in gilding.

2. Among jewelers, a thin leaf of metal placed under precious stones, to make them appear transparent, and to give them a particular color, as the stone appears to be of the color of the *foil*. Hence,

3. Any thing of another color, or of different qualities, which serves to adorn, or set off another thing to advantage.

Hector has a *foil* to set him off. *Broome.*

4. A thin coat of tin, with quicksilver, laid on the back of a looking glass, to cause reflection. *Encyc.*

FOIL'ED, *pp.* Frustrated; defeated.

FOIL'ER, *n.* One who frustrates another, and gains an advantage himself.

FOIL'ING, *ppr.* Defeating; frustrating; disappointing of success.

FOIL'ING, *n.* Among *hunters*, the slight mark of a passing deer on the grass. *Todd.*

FOIN, *v. t.* [Fr. *poindre*, to sting, to dawn;

L. *pungo*. The sense is to push, thrust, shoot.]

1. To push in fencing. *Spenser.*
2. To prick; to sting. [*Not in use.*]

FOIN, *n.* A push; a thrust. *Robinson.*

FOIN'ING, *ppr.* Pushing; thrusting.

FOIN'INGLY, *adv.* In a pushing manner.

FOIS'ON, *n.* [L. *fusio.*] Plenty; abundance. [*Not used.*] *Tusser.*

FOIST, *v. t.* [Usually supposed to be from Fr. *fausser*, to violate, literally, to falsify; Norm. *fauser*. This is doubtful.]

To insert surreptitiously, wrongfully, or without warrant.

> Lest negligence or partiality might admit or *foist* in abuses and corruption. *Carew.*

FOIST, *n.* A light and fast sailing ship. *Obs.* *Beaum.*

FOIST'ED, *pp.* Inserted wrongfully.

FOIST'ER, *n.* One who inserts without authority.

FOIST'IED, *a.* Mustied. [See *Fusty.*]

FOIST'INESS, *n.* Fustiness, which see.

FOIST'ING, *ppr.* Inserting surreptitiously or without authority.

FOIST'Y, *a.* Fusty, which see.

FŌLD, *n.* [Sax. *fald, falde*; W. *fald*; Ir. *fal*, a fold, a wall or hedge; Dan. *fold*. See the verb, to *fold*.]

1. A pen or inclosure for sheep; a place where a flock of sheep is kept, whether in the field or under shelter.
2. A flock of sheep. Hence in a *scriptural sense*, the church, the flock of the Shepherd of Israel.

> Other sheep I have, which are not of this *fold*. John x.

3. A limit. [*Not in use.*]

FŌLD, *n.* [Sax. *feald*; Sw. *fåll*; G. *falte*; Russ. *phalda*; but the same word as the preceding.]

1. The doubling of any flexible substance, as cloth; complication; a plait; one part turned or bent and laid on another; as a *fold* of linen.
2. In *composition*, the same quantity added; as *two fold, four fold, ten fold*, that is, twice as much, four times as much, ten times as much.

FŌLD, *v. t.* [Sax. *fealdan*; Goth. *faldan*; G. *falten*; Dan. *folder*; Sw. *fålla*. Qu. Heb. כפל Ch. קפל, to double. Class Bl. No. 47. 51. See also No. 22. The primary sense is to *fall*, or to lay, to set, throw or press together.]

1. To double; to lap or lay in plaits; as, to *fold* a piece of cloth.
2. To double and insert one part in another; as, to *fold* a letter.
3. To double or lay together, as the arms. He *folds* his arms in despair.
4. To confine sheep in a fold.

FŌLD, *v. i.* To close over another of the same kind; as, the leaves of the door *fold*.

FŌLDAĠE, *n.* The right of folding sheep.

FŌLDED, *pp.* Doubled; laid in plaits; complicated; kept in a fold.

FŌLDER, *n.* An instrument used in folding paper.

2. One that folds.

FŌLDING, *ppr.* Doubling; laying in plaits; keeping in a fold.

2. *a.* Doubling; that may close over another, or that consists of leaves which may close one over another; as a *folding* door.

FŌLDING, *n.* A fold; a doubling.

2. Among farmers, the keeping of sheep in inclosures on arable land, &c.

FOLIA'CEOUS, *a.* [L. *foliaceus*, from *folium*, a leaf. See *Foil.*]

1. Leafy; having leaves intermixed with flowers; as a *foliaceous* spike. *Foliaceous* glands are those situated on leaves.
2. Consisting of leaves or thin lamins; having the form of a leaf or plate; as *foliaceous* spar. *Woodward.*

FO'LIAĠE, *n.* [Fr. *feuillage*, from *feuille*, L. *folium*, a leaf; It. *fogliame*; Sp. *follage*. See *Foil.*]

1. Leaves in general; as a tree of beautiful *foliage*.
2. A cluster of leaves, flowers and branches; particularly, the representation of leaves, flowers and branches, in architecture, intended to ornament and enrich capitals, friezes, pediments, &c.

FO'LIAĠE, *v. t.* To work or to form into the representation of leaves. *Drummond.*

FO'LIAĠED, *a.* Furnished with foliage. *Shenstone.*

FO'LIATE, *v. t.* [L. *foliatus*, from *folium*, a leaf, Gr. φυλλον.]

1. To beat into a leaf, or thin plate or lamin. *Bacon.*
2. To spread over with a thin coat of tin and quicksilver, &c.; as, to *foliate* a looking-glass.

FO'LIATE, *a.* In *botany*, leafy, furnished with leaves; as a *foliate* stalk. *Martyn. Lee.*

FO'LIATED, *pp.* Spread or covered with a thin plate or foil.

2. In *mineralogy*, consisting of plates; resembling or in the form of a plate; lamellar; as a *foliated* fracture.

> Minerals that consist of grains, and are at the same time *foliated*, are called granularly *foliated*. *Kirwan.*

FO'LIATING, *ppr.* Covering with a leaf or foil.

FOLIA'TION, *n.* [L. *foliatio.*] In *botany*, the leafing of plants; vernation; the disposition of the nascent leaves within the bud. *Martyn.*

2. The act of beating a metal into a thin plate, leaf or foil.
3. The act or operation of spreading foil over the back side of a mirror or looking glass.

FO'LIATURE, *n.* The state of being beaten into foil.

FO'LIER, *n.* Goldsmith's foil.

FOLIF'EROUS, *a.* [L. *folium*, leaf, and *fero*, to bear.] Producing leaves.

FO'LIO, *n.* [L. *folium*, a leaf; *in folio.*] A book of the largest size, formed by once doubling a sheet of paper.

2. Among *merchants*, a page, or rather both the right and left hand pages of an account-book, expressed by the same figure. *Encyc.*

FO'LIOLE, *n.* [from L. *folium*, a leaf.] A leaflet; one of the single leaves, which together constitute a compound leaf. *Lee.*

FO'LIOMORT, *a.* [L. *folium mortuum.*] Of a dark yellow color, or that of a faded leaf; filemot. *Woodward.*

FO'LIOUS, *a.* Leafy; thin; unsubstantial. *Brown.*

2. In *botany*, having leaves intermixed with the flowers.

FŌLK, *n. foke.* [Sax. *folc*; D. *volk*; G. *volk*; Sw. *folck*; Dan. *folk*; L. *vulgus*. The sense is a crowd, from collecting or pressing, not from *following*, but from the same root, as to *follow* is to press toward. It may be allied to Sax. *fela*, G. *viel*, D. *veel*, Gr. πολυς and πολλοι. Originally and properly it had no plural, being a collective noun; but in modern use, in America, it has lost its singular number, and we hear it only in the plural. It is a colloquial word, not admissible into elegant style.]

1. People in general, or any part of them without distinction. What do *folks* say respecting the war? Men love to talk about the affairs of other *folks*.
2. Certain people, discriminated from others; as old *folks*, and young *folks*. Children sometimes call their parents, the old *folks*. So we say sick *folks*; poor *folks*; proud *folks*.
3. In *scripture*, the singular number is used; as a few sick *folk*; impotent *folk*. Mark vi. John v.
4. Animals.

> The coneys are but a feeble *folk*. Prov. xxx.

FŌLKLAND, *n.* [Sax. *folcland.*] In *English law*, copyhold land; land held by the common people, at the will of the lord. *Blackstone.*

FŌLKMOTE, *n.* [Sax. *folcmote*, folk-meeting.]

An assembly of the people, or of bishops, thanes, aldermen and freemen, to consult respecting public affairs; an annual convention of the people, answering in some measure, to a modern parliament; a word used in England before the Norman conquest, after which, the national Council was called a *parliament*. *Somner. Spelman.* But some authors alledge that the *folkmote* was an inferior meeting or court.

FOL'LICLE, *n.* [L. *folliculus*, from *follis*, a bag or bellows.]

1. In *botany*, a univalvular pericarp; a seed vessel opening on one side longitudinally, and having the seeds loose in it. *Martyn.*
2. An air bag; a vessel distended with air; as at the root in Utricularia, and on the leaves in Aldrovanda. *Martyn.*
3. A little bag, in animal bodies; a gland; a folding; a cavity. *Coxe.*

FOLLIC'ULOUS, *a.* Having or producing follicles.

FOL'LIFUL, *a.* Full of folly. [*Not used.*] *Shenstone.*

FOL'LOW, *v. t.* [Sax. *folgian, filian, fylgan*; D. *volgen*; G. *folgen*; Dan *fölger*; Sw. *följa*; Ir. *foilcanam*. The sense is, to urge forward, drive, press. Class Bl. No. 14. 46.]

1. To go after or behind; to walk, ride or move behind, but in the same direction. Soldiers will usually *follow* a brave officer.
2. To pursue; to chase; as an enemy, or as game.
3. To accompany; to attend in a journey.

> And Rebekah arose, and her damsels, and they rode on the camels, and *followed* the man. Gen. xxiv.

4. To accompany; to be of the same company; to attend, for any purpose. Luke v.
5. To succeed in order of time; to come after; as, a storm is *followed* by a calm.

> Signs *following* signs lead on the mighty year. *Pope.*

6. To be consequential; to result from, as

effect from a cause. Intemperance is often *followed* by disease or poverty, or by both.

7. To result from, as an inference or deduction. It *follows* from these facts that the accused is guilty.

8. To pursue with the eye; to keep the eyes fixed on a moving body. He *followed* or his eyes *followed* the ship, till it was beyond sight.

He *followed* with his eyes the fleeting shade. *Dryden.*

9. To imitate; to copy; as, to *follow* a pattern or model; to *follow* fashion.

10. To embrace; to adopt and maintain; to have or entertain like opinions; to think or believe like another; as, to *follow* the opinions and tenets of a philosophic sect; to *follow* Plato.

11. To obey; to observe; to practice; to act in conformity to. It is our duty to *follow* the commands of Christ. Good soldiers *follow* the orders of their general; good servants *follow* the directions of their master.

12. To pursue as an object of desire; to endeavor to obtain.

Follow peace with all men. Heb. xii.

13. To use; to practice; to make the chief business; as, to *follow* the trade of a carpenter; to *follow* the profession of law.

14. To adhere to; to side with.

The house of Judah *followed* David. 2 Sam. ii.

15. To adhere to; to honor; to worship; to serve.

If the Lord be God, *follow* him. 1 Kings xviii.

16. To be led or guided by.

Wo to the foolish prophets, who *follow* their own spirit, and have seen nothing. Ezek. xiii.

17. To move on in the same course or direction; to be guided by; as, to *follow* a track or course.

FOL'LOW, *v. i.* To come after another.

The famine—shall *follow* close after you. Jer. xlii.

2. To attend; to accompany. *Shak.*

3. To be posterior in time; as *following* ages.

4. To be consequential, as effect to cause. From such measures, great mischiefs must *follow*.

5. To result, as an inference. The facts may be admitted, but the inference drawn from them does not *follow*.

To follow on, to continue pursuit or endeavor; to persevere.

Then shall we know, if we *follow on* to know the Lord. Hosea vi.

FOL'LOWED, *pp.* Pursued; succeeded; accompanied; attended; imitated; obeyed; observed; practiced; adhered to.

FOL'LOWER, *n.* One who comes, goes or moves after another, in the same course.

2. One that takes another as his guide in doctrines, opinions or example; one who receives the opinions, and imitates the example of another; an adherent; an imitator.

That ye be not slothful, but *followers* of them who, through faith and patience, inherit the promises. Heb. vi.

3. One who obeys, worships and honors.

Be ye *followers* of God, as dear children. Eph. v.

4. An adherent; a disciple; one who embraces the same system; as a *follower* of Plato.

5. An attendant; a companion; an associate or a dependent. The warrior distributed the plunder among his *followers*.

No *follower*, but a friend. *Pope.*

6. One under the command of another. *Spenser. Dryden.*

7. One of the same faction or party.

FOL'LOWING, *ppr.* Coming or going after or behind; pursuing; attending; imitating; succeeding in time; resulting from, as an effect or an inference; adhering to; obeying, observing; using, practicing; proceeding in the same course.

FOL'LY, *n.* [Fr. *folie*, from *fol*, *fou*; Arm. *follez*; It. *follia*. See *Fool*.]

1. Weakness of intellect; imbecility of mind; want of understanding.

A fool layeth open his *folly*. Prov. xiii.

2. A weak or absurd act not highly criminal; an act which is inconsistent with the dictates of reason, or with the ordinary rules of prudence. In this sense it may be used in the singular, but is generally in the plural. Hence we speak of the *follies* of youth.

Whom folly pleases, or whose *follies* please. *Pope.*

3. An absurd act which is highly sinful; any conduct contrary to the laws of God or man; sin; scandalous crimes; that which violates moral precepts and dishonors the offender. Shechem wrought *folly* in Israel. Achan wrought *folly* in Israel. Gen. xxxiv. Josh. vii.

4. Criminal weakness; depravity of mind. *Johnson.*

FO'MAHANT, *n.* A star of the first magnitude, in the constellation Aquarius. *Encyc.*

FOMENT', *v. t.* [L. *fomento*, from *foveo*, to warm; Fr. *fomenter*; Sp. *fomentar*; It. *fomentare*.]

1. To apply warm lotions to; to bathe with warm medicated liquors, or with flannel dipped in warm water.

2. To cherish with heat; to encourage growth. [*Not usual.*] *Milton.*

3. To encourage; to abet; to cherish and promote by excitements; *in a bad sense*; as, to *foment* ill humors. *Locke.*

So we say, to *foment* troubles or disturbances; to *foment* intestine broils.

FOMENTA'TION, *n.* The act of applying warm liquors to a part of the body, by means of flannels dipped in hot water or medicated decoctions, for the purpose of easing pain, by relaxing the skin, or of discussing tumors. *Encyc. Quincy.*

2. The lotion applied, or to be applied to a diseased part. *Arbuthnot.*

3. Excitation; instigation; encouragement. *Wotton.*

FOMENT'ED, *pp.* Bathed with warm lotions; encouraged.

FOMENT'ER, *n.* One who foments; one who encourages or instigates; as a *fomenter* of sedition.

FOMENT'ING, *ppr.* Applying warm lotions.

2. Encouraging; abetting; promoting.

FON, *n.* [Chaucer, *fonne*, a fool; Ice. *faane*.] A fool; an idiot. *Obs.* *Spenser.*

FOND, *a.* [Chaucer, *fonne*, a fool; Scot. *fon*, to play the fool; *fone*, to fondle, to toy; Ir. *fonn*, delight, desire, a longing. Qu. Ar. أفن which signifies to diminish, to impair mental powers, to make foolish, to be destitute of reason; and فني is to fail. These are the most probable affinities I have been able to find.]

1. Foolish; silly; weak; indiscreet; imprudent.

Grant I may never prove so *fond*
To trust man on his oath or bond. *Shak.*
Fond thoughts may fall into some idle brain. *Davies.*

2. Foolishly tender and loving; doting; weakly indulgent; as a *fond* mother or wife. *Addison.*

3. Much pleased; loving ardently; delighted with. A child is *fond* of play; a gentleman is *fond* of his sports, or of his country seat. In present usage, *fond* does not always imply weakness or folly.

4. Relishing highly. The epicure is *fond* of high-seasoned food. Multitudes of men are too *fond* of strong drink.

5. Trifling; valued by folly. [*Little used.*] *Shak.*

FOND, *v. t.* To treat with great indulgence or tenderness; to caress; to cocker.

The Tyrian hugs and *fonds* thee on her breast. *Dryden.*

Fond is thus used by the poets only. We now use *fondle*.

FOND, *v. i.* To be fond of; to be in love with; to dote on. [*Little used.*] *Shak.*

FOND'LE, *v. t.* To treat with tenderness; to caress; as, a nurse *fondles* a child.

FOND'LED, *pp.* Treated with affection; caressed.

FOND'LER, *n.* One who fondles.

FOND'LING, *ppr.* Caressing; treating with tenderness.

FOND'LING, *n.* A person or thing fondled or caressed. *L'Estrange.*

FOND'LY, *adv.* Foolishly; weakly; imprudently; with indiscreet affection.

Fondly we think we merit honor then,
When we but praise ourselves in other men. *Pope.*

2. With great or extreme affection. We *fondly* embrace those who are dear to us.

FOND'NESS, *n.* Foolishness; weakness; want of sense or judgment. *Obs.* *Spenser.*

2. Foolish tenderness.

3. Tender passion; warm affection.

Her *fondness* for a certain earl
Began when I was but a girl. *Swift.*

4. Strong inclination or propensity; as a *fondness* for vice or sin. *Hammond.*

5. Strong appetite or relish; as *fondness* for ardent spirit, or for a particular kind of food.

[*It is now used chiefly in the three latter senses.*]

FONT, *n.* [Fr. *fonts*; Sp. *fuente*; It. *fonte*; L. *fons*; W. *fynnon*, a fountain, and *fyniaw*, to produce, to abound; allied to L. *fundo*, to pour out.]

A large bason or stone vessel in which water is contained for baptizing children or other persons in the church.

FONT, *n.* [Fr. *fonte*, from *fondre*, to melt or

cast; L. *fundo*, to pour out; Sp. *fundir*; It. *fondere*; properly, a casting.]

A complete assortment of printing types of one size, including a due proportion of all the letters in the alphabet, large and small, points, accents, and whatever else is necessary for printing with that letter.

FONT'AL, *a.* Pertaining to a fount, fountain, source or origin. *Trans. of Pausanias.*

FONT'ANEL, *n.* [from the Fr.] An issue for the discharge of humors from the body. *Hall.*

2. A vacancy in the infant cranium, between the frontal and parietal bones, and also between the parietal and occipital, at the two extremities of the sagittal suture. *Cyc. Parr.*

FONTANGE, *n.* *fontanj'.* [Fr. from the name of the first wearer.]

A knot of ribins on the top of a head-dress. *Addison.*

FOOD, *n.* [Sax. *fod*, *foda*; G. *futter*; D. *voedzel*; Dan. *foeder*; Sw. *föda*; from *feeding*. See *Feed*.]

1. In a general sense, whatever is eaten by animals for nourishment, and whatever supplies nutriment to plants.
2. Meat; aliment; flesh or vegetables eaten for sustaining human life; victuals; provisions; whatever is or may be eaten for nourishment.

   Feed me with *food* convenient for me. Prov. xxx.

3. Whatever supplies nourishment and growth to plants, as water, carbonic acid gas, &c. Manuring substances furnish plants with *food*.
4. Something that sustains, nourishes and augments. Flattery is the *food* of vanity.

FOOD, *v. t.* To feed. [*Not in use.*] *Barret.*

FOOD'FUL, *a.* Supplying food; full of food. *Dryden.*

FOOD'LESS, *a.* Without food; destitute of provisions; barren. *Sandys.*

FOOD'Y, *a.* Eatable; fit for food. [*Not used.*] *Chapman.*

FOOL, *n.* [Fr. *fol*, *fou*; It. *folle*, mad, foolish; Ice. *fol*; Arm. *foll*; W. *fol*, round, blunt, foolish, vain; *fwl*, a fool, a blunt one, a stupid one; Russ. *phalia*. It would seem from the Welsh that the primary sense of the adjective is thick, blunt, lumpish. Heb. חפל.]

1. One who is destitute of reason, or the common powers of understanding; an ideot. Some persons are born *fools*, and are called *natural fools*; others may become *fools* by some injury done to the brain.
2. In *common language*, a person who is somewhat deficient in intellect, but not an ideot; or a person who acts absurdly; one who does not exercise his reason; one who pursues a course contrary to the dictates of wisdom.

   Experience keeps a dear school, but *fools* will learn in no other. *Franklin.*

3. In *scripture*, *fool* is often used for a wicked or depraved person; one who acts contrary to sound wisdom in his moral deportment; one who follows his own inclinations, who prefers trifling and temporary pleasures to the service of God and eternal happiness.

   The *fool* hath said in his heart, there is no God. Ps. xiv.

4. A weak christian; a godly person who has much remaining sin and unbelief.

   O *fools*, and slow of heart to believe all the prophets have written. Luke xxiv.

   Also, one who is accounted or called a fool by ungodly men. 1 Cor. iv. 10.

5. A term of indignity and reproach.

   To be thought knowing, you must first put the *fool* upon all mankind. *Dryden.*

6. One who counterfeits folly; a buffoon; as a king's *fool*.

   I scorn, although their drudge, to be their *fool* or jester. *Milton.*

To play the fool, to act the buffoon; to jest; to make sport.

2. To act like one void of understanding.

To put the fool on, to impose on; to delude.

To make a fool of, to frustrate; to defeat; to disappoint.

FOOL, *v. i.* To trifle; to toy; to spend time in idleness, sport or mirth.

Is this a time for *fooling*? *Dryden.*

FOOL, *v. t.* To treat with contempt; to disappoint; to defeat; to frustrate; to deceive; to impose on.

When I consider life, 'tis all a cheat;
For *fooled* with hope, men favor the deceit. *Dryden.*

2. To infatuate; to make foolish. *Shak.*
3. To cheat; as, to *fool* one out of his money.

To fool away, to spend in trifles, idleness, folly, or without advantage; as, to *fool away* time.

2. To spend for things of no value or use; to expend improvidently; as, to *fool away* money.

FOOL, *n.* A liquid made of gooseberries scalded and pounded, with cream. *Shak.*

FOOL'BORN, *a.* Foolish from the birth. *Shak.*

FOOL'ED, *pp.* Disappointed; defeated; deceived; imposed on.

FOOL'ERY, *n.* The practice of folly; habitual folly; attention to trifles. *Shak.*

2. An act of folly or weakness. *Watts.*
3. Object of folly. *Raleigh.*

FOOL'HAPPY, *a.* Lucky without judgment or contrivance. *Spenser.*

FOOLH'ARDINESS, *n.* Courage without sense or judgment; mad rashness. *Dryden.*

FOOLH'ARDISE, *n.* Foolhardiness. [*Not in use.*] *Spenser.*

FOOLH'ARDY, *a.* [*fool* and *hardy*.] Daring without judgment; madly rash and adventurous; foolishly bold. *Howell.*

FOOL'ING, *ppr.* Defeating; disappointing; deceiving.

FOOL'ISH, *a.* Void of understanding or sound judgment; weak in intellect; *applied to general character.*

2. Unwise; imprudent; acting without judgment or discretion in particular things.
3. Proceeding from folly, or marked with folly; silly; vain; trifling.

   But *foolish* questions avoid. 2 Tim. ii.

4. Ridiculous; despicable.

   A *foolish* figure he must make. *Prior.*

5. In *scripture*, wicked; sinful; acting without regard to the divine law and glory, or to one's own eternal happiness.

   O *foolish* Galatians—Gal. iii.

6. Proceeding from depravity; sinful; as *foolish* lusts. 1 Tim. vi.

FOOL'ISHLY, *adv.* Weakly; without understanding or judgment; unwisely; indiscretely.

2. Wickedly; sinfully.

   I have done very *foolishly*. 2 Sam. xxiv.

FOOL'ISHNESS, *n.* Folly; want of understanding.

2. Foolish practice; want of wisdom or good judgment.
3. In *a scriptural sense*, absurdity; folly.

   The preaching of the cross is to them that perish *foolishness*. 1 Cor. i.

FOOLS'CAP, *n.* [Qu. *full* and L. *scapus*, or *folio* and *shape*.] A kind of paper of small size.

FOOL'S-P'ARSLEY, *n.* A plant, of the genus Æthusa.

FOOL'STONES, *n.* A plant, the Orchis.

FOOL'TRAP, *n.* A trap to catch fools; as a fly trap. *Dryden.*

FOOT, *n.* plu. *feet.* [Sax. *fot*, *fet*; D. *voet*; G. *fuss*; Sw. *fot*; Dan. *fod*; Gr. πους, ποδος; L. *pes*, *pedis*; Sanscrit, *pad*; Siam. *bat*; Fr. *pied*, *pie*; Sp. *pie*; Port. *pe*; It. *piede*, *piè*; Copt. *bat*, *fat*. Probably this word is allied to the Gr. πατεω, to walk, to tread; as the W. *troed*, foot, is to the Eng. verb, to *tread*.]

1. In *animal bodies*, the lower extremity of the leg; the part of the leg which treads the earth in standing or walking, and by which the animal is sustained and enabled to step.
2. That which bears some resemblance to an animal's foot in shape or office; the lower end of any thing that supports a body; as the *foot* of a table.
3. The lower part; the base; as the *foot* of a column or of a mountain.
4. The lower part; the bottom; as the *foot* of an account; the *foot* of a sail.
5. Foundation; condition; state. We are not on the same *foot* with our fellow citizens. In this sense, it is more common, in America, to use *footing*; and in this sense the plural is not used.
6. Plan of establishment; fundamental principles. Our constitution may hereafter be placed on a better *foot*. [*In this sense the plural is not used.*]
7. In *military language*, soldiers who march and fight on foot; infantry, as distinguished from cavalry. [*In this sense the plural is not used.*]
8. A measure consisting of twelve inches; supposed to be taken from the length of a man's foot. Geometricians divide the foot into 10 digits, and the digit into 10 lines. *Encyc.*
9. In *poetry*, a certain number of syllables, constituting part of a verse; as the iambus, the dactyl, and the spondee.
10. Step; pace. *L'Estrange.*
11. Level; par. *Obs.* *Bacon.*
12. The part of a stocking or boot which receives the foot.

By foot, or rather, *on foot*, by walking, as to go or pass *on foot*; or by fording, as to pass a stream *on foot*. See the next definition.

To set on foot, to originate; to begin; to put in motion; as, to *set on foot* a subscription. Hence, to be *on foot*, is to be in motion, action or process of execution.

FOOT, *v. i.* To dance; to tread to measure or music; to skip. *Dryden.*

2. To walk; opposed to *ride* or *fly*. In this sense, the word is commonly followed by *it.*

If you are for a merry jaunt, I'll try, for once, who can *foot it* farthest. *Dryden.*

FOOT, *v. t.* To kick; to strike with the foot; to spurn. *Shak.*

2. To settle; to begin to fix. [*Little used.*] *Shak.*

3. To tread; as, to *foot* the green. *Tickel.*

4. To add the numbers in a column, and set the sum at the foot; as, to *foot* an account.

5. To seize and hold with the foot. [*Not used.*] *Herbert.*

6. To add or make a foot; as, to *foot* a stocking or boot.

FOOT'BALL, *n.* A ball consisting of an inflated bladder, cased in lether, to be driven by the foot. *Waller.*

2. The sport or practice of kicking the football. *Arbuthnot.*

FOOT'BAND, *n.* A band of infantry.

FOOT'BOY, *n.* A menial; an attendant in livery. *Swift.*

FOOT'BREADTH, *n.* The breadth of the foot. Deut. ii.

FOOT'BRIDGE, *n.* A narrow bridge for foot passengers. *Sidney.*

FOOT'CLOTH, *n.* A sumpter cloth. *Shak.*

FOOT'ED, *pp.* Kicked; trod; summed up; furnished with a foot, as a stocking.

FOOT'ED, *a.* Shaped in the foot; as *footed* like a goat. *Grew.*

FOOT'FALL, *n.* A trip or stumble. *Shak.*

FOOT'FIGHT, *n.* A conflict by persons on foot, in opposition to a fight on horseback. *Sidney.*

FOOT'GUARDS, *n. plu.* Guards of infantry.

FOOT'HALT, *n.* A disease incident to sheep, and said to proceed from a worm, which enters between the claws. *Encyc.*

FOOT'HOLD, *n.* That which sustains the feet firmly and prevents them from slipping or moving; that on which one may tread or rest securely. *L'Estrange.*

FOOT'HOT, *adv.* Immediately; a word borrowed from hunting. *Gower.*

FOOT'ING, *ppr.* Dancing; treading; settling; adding a new foot.

FOOT'ING, *n.* Ground for the foot; that which sustains; firm foundation to stand on.

In ascents, every step gained is a *footing* and help to the next. *Holder.*

2. Support; root. *Dryden.*

3. Basis; foundation. *Locke.*

4. Place; stable position. *Dryden.*

5. Permanent settlement. Let not these evils gain *footing.*

6. Tread; step; walk. *Milton.*

7. Dance; tread to measure. *Shak.*

8. Steps; road; track. [*Little used.*] *Bacon.*

9. State; condition; settlement. Place both parties on an equal *footing.*

FOOT'LICKER, *n.* A mean flatterer; a sycophant; a fawner. *Shak.*

FOOT'MAN, *n.* A soldier who marches and fights on foot.

2. A menial servant; a runner; a servant in livery.

FOOT'MANSHIP, *n.* The art or faculty of a runner. *Hayward.*

FOOT'MANTLE, *n.* A garment to keep the gown clean in riding.

FOOT'PACE, *n.* A slow step, as in walking; a broad stair. *Johnson.*

FOOT'PAD, *n.* A highwayman or robber on foot.

FOOT'PATH, *n.* A narrow path or way for foot passengers only.

FOOT'PLOW, *n.* A kind of swing-plow.

FOOT'POST, *n.* A post or messenger that travels on foot. *Carew.*

FOOT'ROPE, *n.* The lower boltrope, to which the lower edge of a sail is sewed. Also, a horse or rope to support men when reefing, &c. *Mar. Dict.*

FOOT'ROT, *n.* An ulcer in the feet of sheep.

FOOT'SOLDIER, *n.* A soldier that serves on foot.

FOOT'STALL, *n.* A woman's stirrup. *Johnson.*

FOOT'STEP, *n.* A track; the mark or impression of the foot. *Locke.*

2. Token; mark; visible sign of a course pursued; as the *footsteps* of divine wisdom. *Bentley.*

Footsteps, plural, example; as, follow the *footsteps* of good men.

2. Way; course. Ps. lxxvii.

FOOT'STOOL, *n.* A stool for the feet; that which supports the feet of one when sitting.

To make enemies a footstool, is to reduce them to entire subjection. Ps. cx.

FOOT'-WALING, *n.* The whole inside planks or lining of a ship. *Cyc.*

FOP, *n.* [Sp. and Port. *guapo*, spruce, gay, affected, foppish, affectedly nice; also in Sp. stout, bold, from the root of *vapor*, *vapid;* Sp. *guapear*, to brag. The Latin *vappa*, a senseless fellow, is evidently from the same root, with the sense of emptiness or lightness.]

A vain man of weak understanding and much ostentation; one whose ambition is to gain admiration by showy dress and pertness; a gay trifling man; a coxcomb.

FOP'DOODLE, *n.* An insignificant fellow. [*Vulgar and not used.*] *Hudibras.*

FOP'LING, *n.* A petty fop. *Tickell.*

FOP'PERY, *n.* Affectation of show or importance; showy folly; as the *foppery* of dress or of manners.

2. Folly; impertinence.

Let not the sound of shallow *foppery* enter
My sober house. *Shak.*

3. Foolery; vain or idle practice; idle affectation. *Swift.*

FOP'PISH, *a.* Vain of dress; making an ostentatious display of gay clothing; dressing in the extreme of fashion.

2. Vain; trifling; affected in manners.

FOP'PISHLY, *adv.* With vain ostentation of dress; in a trifling or affected manner.

FOP'PISHNESS, *n.* Vanity and extravagance in dress; showy vanity.

FOR, *prep.* [Sax. *for* or *fore;* D. *voor*, for and before; G. *für* and *vor;* Sw. *för;* Dan. *for*, *för;* Ir. *far;* Fr. *pour;* Sp. Port. *por*, *para;* It. *per*, which unites *for* and L. *per*, and if this is the same word, so is the Fr. *par*. Indeed *far* seems to be radically the same word; for the Germans and Dutch use *ver*, far, in composition, in the same manner, and in the same words, as the English, Danes and Swedes use *for*. Thus, Ger. *verbieten*, D. *verbieden*, Dan. *forbyder*, Sw. *förbiuda*, are all the same word, Eng. to *forbid*. The French use *par*, as we use *for*, in *pardonner*, to pardon, to *forgive*, It. *perdonare*. Arm. *par* and *pour*, in composition; Hindoo, *para;* Pers. بَر bar or ber, and بَهر behr. *For* corresponds in sense with the L. *pro*, as *fore* does with *præ*, but *pro* and *præ* are probably contracted from *prod*, *præd*. The Latin *por*, in composition, as in *porrigo*, is probably contracted from *porro*, Gr. πορρω, which is the English *far*. The Gr. παρα, and probably, περα, περαν, are from the same root. The radical sense of *for* is to go, to pass, to advance, to reach or stretch; and it is probably allied to the Sax. *faran*, to *fare*, W. *for*, a pass, *foriaw*, to travel. Class Br. No 23. 37. 41. *To go towards*, to *meet* or *turn to*, is the primary sense of *for*, in two of its most common uses; one implying *opposition*, *against;* the other, a *favor* or *benefit:* or *for* may be from *fore*, hence opposite. To sell or exchange a hat *for* a guinea, is to set or pass one *against* the other; this is the primary sense of all prepositions which are placed before equivalents in sale and barter. *Benefit* or *favor* is expressed by *moving towards* a person, or by advancing him. This present is *for* my friend; this advice *for* his instruction. And in the Old Testament, the *face* or front is taken for *favor*. *For*, in some phrases, signifies *during*, that is, *passing*, continuing in time. I will lend a book *for* a day or a month. In composition, *for* is used to give a negative sense, as in *forbid*, which is *forebid*, to command *before*, that is *against*, and in *forgive*, to give back or away, to remit, to send back or to send away.]

1. Against; in the place of; as a substitute or equivalent, noting equal value or satisfactory compensation, either in barter and sale, in contract, or in punishment. "And Joseph gave them bread in exchange *for* horses, and *for* flocks, and *for* the cattle of the herds;" that is, according to the original, he gave them bread *against* horses, like the Gr. αντι and Fr. *contre*. Gen. xlvii. 17.

Buy us and our land *for* bread. Gen. xlvii. 19.

And if any mischief follow, then thou shalt give life *for* life, eye *for* eye, tooth *for* tooth, hand *for* hand, foot *for* foot. Ex. xxi.

As the son of man came not to be ministered unto, but to minister, and to give his life a ransom *for* many. Matt. xx. See also Mark viii. 37. Matt. xvi. 26.

2. In the place of; instead of; noting substitution of persons, or agency of one in the place of another with equivalent authority. An attorney is empowered to act *for* his principal. Will you take a letter and deliver it *for* me at the post office? that is, in my place, or for my benefit.

3. In exchange of; noting one thing taken or given in place of another; as, to quit the profession of law *for* that of a clergyman.

4. In the place of; instead of; as, to translate a poem line *for* line.

5. In the character of; noting resemblance; a sense derived from substitution or standing in the place of, like αντιθεος in Greek.

If a man can be fully assured of any thing *for* a truth, without having examined, what is there that he may not embrace *for* truth? *Locke.*

But let her go *for* an ungrateful woman. *Philips.*

I hear *for* certain, and do speak the truth. *Shak.*

He quivered with his feet and lay *for* dead. *Dryden.*

6. Towards; with the intention of going to.

We sailed from Peru *for* China and Japan. *Bacon.*

We sailed directly *for* Genoa, and had a fair wind. *Addison.*

So we say, a ship is bound *for* or *to* France.

7. In advantage of; for the sake of; on account of; that is, towards, noting use, benefit or purpose.

An ant is a wise creature *for* itself. *Bacon.*

Shall I think the world was made *for* one,
And men are born *for* kings, as beasts *for* men,
Not *for* protection, but to be devoured. *Dryden.*

8. Conducive to; beneficial to; in favor of.

It is *for* the general good of human society, and consequently of particular persons, to be true and just; and it is *for* men's health to be temperate. *Tillotson.*

9. Leading or inducing to, as a motive.

There is a natural, immutable, and eternal reason *for* that which we call virtue, and against that which we call vice. *Tillotson.*

10. Noting arrival, meeting, coming or possession. Wait patiently *for* an expected good. So in the phrases, *looking for*, *staying for*.

11. Towards the obtaining of; in order to the arrival at or possession of. After all our exertions, we depend on divine aid *for* success.

12. Against; in opposition to; with a tendency to resist and destroy; as a remedy *for* the head-ache or tooth-ache. Alkalies are good *for* the heart-burn. So we say, to provide clothes or stores *for* winter, or against winter.

13. Against or on account of; in prevention of.

She wrapped him close *for* catching cold. *Richardson.*

And, *for* the time shall not seem tedious— *Shak.*

This use is nearly obsolete. The sense however is derived from *meeting*, opposing, as in No. 12.

14. Because; on account of; by reason of. He cried out *for* anguish. I cannot go *for* want of time. *For* this cause, I cannot believe the report.

That which we *for* our unworthiness are afraid to crave, our prayer is, that God *for* the worthiness of his son would notwithstanding vouchsafe to grant. *Hooker.*

Edward and Richard,
With fiery eyes sparkling *for* very wrath,
Are at our backs. *Shak.*

How to choose dogs *for* scent or speed. *Waller.*

For as much as it is a fundamental law— *Bacon.*

15. With respect or regard to; on the part of.

It was young counsel *for* the persons, and violent counsel *for* the matters. *Bacon.*

Thus much *for* the beginning and progress of the deluge. *Burnet.*

So we say, *for* me, *for* myself, or as *for* me, I have no anxiety, but *for* you I have apprehensions; all implying *towards* or *on the side of.*

16. Through a certain space; during a certain time; as, to travel *for* three days; to sail *for* seven weeks; he holds his office *for* life; he traveled on sand *for* ten miles together. These senses seem to imply *passing*, the proper sense of *for*.

17. In quest of; in order to obtain; as, to search *for* arguments; to recur to antiquity *for* examples. See No. 11.

18. According to; as far as.

Chimists have not been able, *for* aught is vulgarly known, by fire alone to separate true sulphur from antimony. *Boyle.*

19. Noting meeting, coming together, or reception. I am ready *for* you; that is, I am ready to meet or receive you.

20. Towards; of tendency to; as an inclination *for* drink.

21. In favor of; on the part or side of; that is, towards or inclined to. One is *for* a free government; another is *for* a limited monarchy.

Aristotle is *for* poetical justice. *Dennis.*

22. With a view to obtain; in order to possess. He writes *for* money, or *for* fame; that is, towards meeting, or to have in return, as a reward.

23. Towards; with tendency to, or in favor of. It is *for* his honor to retire from office. It is *for* our quiet to have few intimate connections.

24. Notwithstanding; against; in opposition to. The fact may be so, *for* any thing that has yet appeared. The task is great, but *for* all that, I shall not be deterred from undertaking it. This is a different application of the sense of No. 1. 2. 3. 4. [*Hoc non obstante.*]

The writer will do what she pleases *for* all me. *Spect.* No. 79.

25. For the use of; to be used in; that is, towards, noting advantage.

The oak *for* nothing ill,
The osier good *for* twigs, the poplar *for* the mill. *Spenser.*

26. In recompense of; in return of.

Now, *for* so many glorious actions done,
For peace at home, and *for* the public wealth,
I mean to crown a bowl *for* Cesar's health. *Dryden.*

[See No. 1.]

27. In proportion to; or rather, looking towards, regarding. He is tall *for* one of his years, or tall *for* his age.

28. By means of.

Moral consideration can no way move the sensible appetite, were it not *for* the will. *Hale.*

29. By the want of.

The inhabitants suffered severely both *for* provisions and fuel. *Marshall.*

30. *For my life* or *heart*, though my life were to be given in exchange, or as the price of purchase. I cannot, *for my life*, understand the man. No. 1.

31. *For to*, denoting purpose. *For* was anciently placed before the infinitives of verbs, and the use is correct, but now obsolete except in vulgar language. I came *for* to see you; *pour vous voir.*

FOR, *con.* The word by which a reason is introduced of something before advanced. "That ye may be the children of your father who is in heaven; *for* he maketh his sun to rise on the evil and on the good." In such sentences, *for* has the sense of *because*, *by reason that*, as in No. 14; with this difference that in No. 14, the word precedes a single noun, and here it precedes a sentence or clause: but the phrase seems to be elliptical, *for this cause or reason, which follows*, he maketh his sun to rise, &c. In Romans, xiii. 6. we find the word in both its applications, "*For, for* this cause ye pay tribute also—;" the first *for* referring to the sentence following; the latter to the noun *cause.*

2. Because; on this account that; properly, *for that.*

For as much, compounded, *forasmuch*, is equivalent to, in regard to that, in consideration of. *Forasmuch* as the thirst is intolerable, the patient may be indulged in a little drink.

For why, Fr. *pour quoi*, [*per quod, pro quo*,] because; for this reason.

FOR'AĠE, *n.* [Fr. *fourrage*; Arm. *fouraich*; It. *foraggio*; Sp. *forrage*; Port. *forragem*; D. *voeraadge*. If this word signifies primarily food or fodder, it is connected with W. *pori*, to feed, and L. *voro*. But I take it to be from the root of Sax. *faran*, to go, and primarily to signify that which is collected in wandering, roving, excursion. In Port. *foragido* is a vagabond, and *forrejar* is to waste, to ravage.]

1. Food of any kind for horses and cattle, as grass, pasture, hay, corn and oats.

2. The act of providing forage.

Col. Mawhood completed his *forage* unmolested. *Marshall.*

If the *forage* is to be made at a distance from the camp— *Encyc.*

3. Search for provisions; the act of feeding abroad. *Milton.*

FOR'AĠE, *v. i.* To collect food for horses and cattle, by wandering about and feeding or stripping the country. *Marshall.*

2. To wander far; to rove. *Obs.* *Shak.*

3. To ravage; to feed on spoil. *Shak.*

FOR'AĠE, *v. t.* To strip of provisions for horses, &c. *Encyc.*

FOR'AĠER, *n.* One that goes in search of food for horses or cattle.

FOR'AĠING, *ppr.* or *a.* Collecting provisions for horses and cattle, or wandering in search of food; ravaging; stripping. The general sent out a *foraging* party, with a guard.

FOR'AĠING, *n.* An inroad or incursion for forage or plunder. *Bp. Hall.*

FORAM'INOUS, *a.* [L. *foramen*, a hole, from *foro*, to bore.]

Full of holes; perforated in many places; porous. [*Little used.*] *Bacon.*

FOR, as a prefix to verbs, has usually the force of a negative or privative, denoting *against*, that is, *before*, or *away*, *aside.*

FORBAD', *pret.* of *forbid.*

FORBA'THE, *v. t.* To bathe. [*Not in use.*] *Sackville.*

FORBEAR, *v. i.* pret. *forbore*; pp. *forborne.* [Sax. *forbæran*; *for* and *bear.*]

1. To stop; to cease; to hold from proceeding; as, *forbear* to repeat these reproachful words.

2. To pause; to delay; as, *forbear* a while.

3. To abstain; to omit; to hold one's self from motion or entering on an affair.

Shall I go against Ramoth Gilead to battle, or shall I *forbear*? 1 Kings xxii.

4. To refuse; to decline.

Whether they will hear, or whether they will *forbear*. Ezek. ii.

5. To be patient; to restrain from action or violence. Prov. xxv. 15.

FORBEAR, *v. t.* To avoid voluntarily; to decline.

Forbear his presence. *Shak.*

2. To abstain from; to omit; to avoid doing. Learn from the scriptures what you ought to do and what to *forbear*.

Have we not power to *forbear* working? 1 Cor. ix.

3. To spare; to treat with indulgence and patience.

Forbearing one another in love. Eph. iv.

4. To withhold.

Forbear thee from meddling with God, who is with me, that he destroy thee not. 2 Chron. xxxv.

FORBEARANCE, *n.* The act of avoiding, shunning or omitting; either the cessation or intermission of an act commenced, or a withholding from beginning an act. Liberty is the power of doing or forbearing an action, according as the doing or *forbearance* has a preference in the mind. The *forbearance* of sin is followed with satisfaction of mind.

2. Command of temper; restraint of passions.

Have a continent *forbearance*, till the speed of his rage goes slower. *Shak.*

3. The exercise of patience; long suffering; indulgence towards those who injure us; lenity; delay of resentment or punishment.

Or despisest thou the riches of his goodness, and *forbearance*, and long suffering? Rom. ii.

FORBEARER, *n.* One that intermits or intercepts. *Tusser.*

FORBEARING, *ppr.* Ceasing; pausing; withholding from action; exercising patience and indulgence.

2. *a.* Patient; long suffering.

FORBEARING, *n.* A ceasing or restraining from action; patience; long suffering.

FORBID′, *v. t.* pret. *forbad*; pp. *forbid*, *forbidden*. [Sax. *forbeodan*; D. *verbieden*; G. *verbieten*; Dan. *forbyder*; Sw. *förbiuda*; *for* and *bid*.] Literally, to bid or command against. Hence,

1. To prohibit; to interdict; to command to forbear or not to do. The laws of God *forbid* us to swear. Good manners also *forbid* us to use profane language. All servile labor and idle amusements on the sabbath are *forbidden*.

2. To command not to enter; as, I have *forbid* him my house or presence. This phrase seems to be elliptical; to forbid *from entering* or *approaching*.

3. To oppose; to hinder; to obstruct. An impassable river *forbids* the approach of the army.

A blaze of glory that *forbids* the sight. *Dryden.*

4. To accurse; to blast. *Obs.* *Shak.*

FORBID′, *v. i.* To utter a prohibition; but in the intransitive form, there is always an ellipsis. I would go, but my state of health *forbids*, that is, forbids me to go, or my going.

FORBID′, FORBID′DEN, *pp.* Prohibited; as the *forbidden* fruit.

2. Hindered; obstructed.

FORBID′DANCE, *n.* Prohibition; command or edict against a thing. [*Little used.*] *Shak.*

FORBID′DENLY, *adv.* In an unlawful manner. *Shak.*

FORBID′DENNESS, *n.* A state of being prohibited. [*Not used.*] *Boyle.*

FORBID′DER, *n.* He or that which forbids or enacts a prohibition.

FORBID′DING, *ppr.* Prohibiting; hindering.

2. *a.* Repelling approach; repulsive; raising abhorrence, aversion or dislike; disagreeable; as a *forbidding* aspect; a *forbidding* formality; a *forbidding* air.

FORBID′DING, *n.* Hindrance; opposition. *Shak.*

FORBO′RE, *pret.* of *forbear.*

FORBORNE, *pp.* of *forbear.*

Few ever repented of having *forborne* to speak. *Rambler.*

FORCE, *n.* [Fr. *force*; It. *forza*; Sp. *fuerza*; Port. *força*; from L. *fortis*. All words denoting force, power, strength, are from verbs which express straining, or driving, rushing, and this word has the elements of Sax. *faran*, and L. *vireo*.]

1. Strength; active power; vigor; might; energy that may be exerted; that physical property in a body which may produce action or motion in another body, or may counteract such action. By the *force* of the muscles we raise a weight, or resist an assault.

2. Momentum; the quantity of power produced by motion or the action of one body on another; as the *force* of a cannon ball.

3. That which causes an operation or moral effect; strength; energy; as the *force* of the mind, will or understanding.

4. Violence; power exerted against will or consent; compulsory power. Let conquerors consider that *force* alone can keep what *force* has obtained.

5. Strength; moral power to convince the mind. There is great *force* in an argument.

6. Virtue; efficacy. No presumption or hypothesis can be of *force* enough to overthrow constant experience.

7. Validity; power to bind or hold. If the conditions of a covenant are not fulfilled, the contract is of no *force*. A testament is of *force* after the testator is dead. Heb. ix. 17.

8. Strength or power for war; armament; troops; an army or navy; as a military or naval *force*: sometimes in the plural; as military *forces*.

9. Destiny; necessity; compulsion; any extraneous power to which men are subject; as the *force* of fate or of divine decrees.

10. Internal power; as the *force* of habit.

11. In *law*, any unlawful violence to person or property. This is *simple*, when no other crime attends it, as the entering into another's possession, without committing any other unlawful act. It is *compound*, when some other violence or unlawful act is committed. The law also implies force, as when a person enters a house or inclosure lawfully, but afterwards does an unlawful act. In this case, the law supposes the first entrance to be for that purpose, and therefore by force.

Physical force, is the force of material bodies.

Moral force, is the power of acting on the reason in judging and determining.

Mechanical force, is the power that belongs to bodies at rest or in motion. The pressure or tension of bodies at rest is called a *mechanical* force, and so is the power of a body in motion. There is also the *force* of gravity or attraction, centrifugal and centripetal *forces*, expansive *force*, &c.

FORCE, *v. t.* To compel; to constrain to do or to forbear, by the exertion of a power not resistible. Men are *forced* to submit to conquerors. Masters *force* their slaves to labor.

2. To overpower by strength.

I should have *forced* thee soon with other arms. *Milton.*

3. To impel; to press; to drive; to draw or push by main strength; a sense of very extensive use; as, to *force* along a wagon or a ship; to *force* away a man's arms; water *forces* its way through a narrow channel; a man may be *forced* out of his possessions.

4. To enforce; to urge; to press.

Forcing my strength, and gathering to the shore. *Dryden.*

5. To compel by strength of evidence; as, to *force* conviction on the mind; to *force* one to acknowledge the truth of a proposition.

6. To storm; to assault and take by violence; as, to *force* a town or fort.

7. To ravish; to violate by force, as a female.

8. To overstrain; to distort; as a *forced* conceit.

9. To cause to produce ripe fruit prematurely, as a tree; or to cause to ripen prematurely, as fruit.

10. To man; to strengthen by soldiers; to garrison. *Obs.* *Shak.* *Raleigh.*

To force from, to wrest from; to extort.

To force out, to drive out; to compel to issue out or to leave; also, to extort.

To force wine, is to fine it by a short process, or in a short time.

To force plants, is to urge the growth of plants by artificial heat.

To force meat, is to stuff it.

FORCE, *v. i.* To lay stress on. *Obs.* *Camden.*

2. To strive. *Obs.* *Spenser.*

3. To use violence. *Spenser.*

FORCED, *pp.* Compelled; impelled; driven by violence; urged; stormed; ravished.

2. *a.* Affected; overstrained; unnatural; as a *forced* style.

FORCEDLY, *adv.* Violently; constrainedly; unnaturally. [*Little used.*]

FORCEDNESS, *n.* The state of being forced; distortion.

FORCEFUL, *a.* Impelled by violence; driven with force; acting with power.

Against the steed he threw
His *forceful* spear. *Dryden.*

2. Violent; impetuous.

FORCEFULLY, *adv.* Violently; impetuously.

FORCELESS, *a.* Having little or no force; feeble; impotent. *Shak.*

FORCEMEAT, *n.* A kind of stuffing in cookery.

FOR′CEPS, *n.* [L.] Literally, a pair of pinchers or tongs.

In *surgery*, an instrument for extracting any thing from a wound, and for like purposes. *Quincy.*

A pair of scissors for cutting off or dividing the fleshy membranous parts of the body. *Encyc.*

FÖRCER, *n.* He or that which forces, drives or constrains.

2. The embolus of a pump; the instrument by which water is driven up a pump. *Wilkins.*

FÖRCIBLE, *a.* Powerful; strong; mighty; as a punishment *forcible* to bridle sin. *Hooker.*

2. Violent; impetuous; driving forward with force; as a *forcible* stream.

3. Efficacious; active; powerful.

Sweet smells are most *forcible* in dry substances, when broken. *Bacon.*

4. Powerful; acting with force; impressive; as *forcible* words or arguments.

5. Containing force; acting by violence; as *forcible* means.

6. Done by force; suffered by force. The abdication of James, his advocates hold to have been *forcible*. *Swift.*

7. Valid; binding; obligatory. [*Not used.*] *Johnson.*

8. In *law*, *forcible entry* is an actual violent entry into houses or lands.

Forcible detainer, is a violent withholding of the lands, &c. of another from his possession.

Forcible abduction, is the act of taking away wrongfully, as a child without the consent of the father, a ward without the consent of the guardian, or any person contrary to his or her will. *Blackstone.*

FÖRCIBLENESS, *n.* Force; violence.

FÖRCIBLY, *adv.* By violence or force.

2. Strongly; powerfully; with power or energy; impressively.

The gospel offers such considerations as are fit to work very *forcibly* on our hopes and fears. *Tillotson.*

3. Impetuously; violently; with great strength; as a stream rushing *forcibly* down a precipice.

FÖRCING, *ppr.* Compelling; impelling; driving; storming; ravishing.

2. Causing to ripen before the natural season, as fruit; or causing to produce ripe fruit prematurely, as a tree.

3. Fining wine by a speedy process.

FÖRCING, *n.* In *gardening*, the art of raising plants, flowers, and fruits, at an earlier season than the natural one, by artificial heat. *Cyc.*

2. The operation of fining wines by a speedy process.

FOR'CIPATED, *a.* [from *forceps.*] Formed like a pair of pinchers to open and inclose; as a *forcipated* mouth. *Derham.*

FÖRD, *n.* [Sax. *ford*, *fyrd*; G. *furt*; from the verb *faran*, to go or pass, or its root.]

1. A place in a river or other water, where it may be passed by man or beast on foot, or by wading.

2. A stream; a current.

Permit my ghost to pass the Stygian *ford*. *Dryden.*

FÖRD, *v. t.* To pass or cross a river or other water by treading or walking on the bottom; to pass through water by wading; to wade through.

FÖRDABLE, *a.* That may be waded or passed through on foot, as water.

FÖRDED, *pp.* Passed through on foot; waded.

FÖRDING, *ppr.* Wading; passing through on foot, as water.

FORDÖ', *v. t.* [Sax. *fordon*; *for* and *do.*] To destroy; to undo; to ruin; to weary. [*Not in use.*] *Chaucer.*

FORE, *a.* [Sax. *fore*, *foran*; G. *vor*; D. *voor*; Sw. *för*; Dan. *for*; Hindo, *para*; Ir. *for*. This is the same word in origin as *for*, from the root of Sax. *faran*, to go, to advance.]

1. Properly, advanced, or being in advance of something in motion or progression; as the *fore* end of a chain carried in measuring land; the *fore* oxen or horses in a team.

2. Advanced in time; coming in advance of something; coming first; anterior; preceding; prior; as the *fore* part of the last century; the *fore* part of the day, week or year.

3. Advanced in order or series; antecedent; as the *fore* part of a writing or bill.

4. Being in front or towards the face; opposed to *back* or *behind*; as the *fore* part of a garment.

5. Going first; usually preceding the other part; as the *fore* part of a ship, or of a coach.

FORE, *adv.* In the part that precedes or goes first.

In seamen's language, *fore and aft* signifies the whole length of the ship, or from end to end, from stem to stern. *Mar. Dict.*

Fore, in composition, denotes, for the most part, priority of time; sometimes, advance in place.

For the etymologies of the compounds of *fore*, see the principal word.

FOREADMON'ISH, *v. t.* To admonish beforehand, or before the act or event.

FOREADVI'SE, *v. t.* *s* as *z.* To advise or counsel before the time of action or before the event; to preadmonish. *Shak.*

FOREALLEDĠE, *v. t.* *foreallej'.* To alledge or cite before. *Fotherby.*

FOREAPPOINT', *v. t.* To set, order or appoint beforehand. *Sherwood.*

FOREAPPOINT'MENT, *n.* Previous appointment; preordination. *Sherwood.*

FORE'ARM, *v. t.* To arm or prepare for attack or resistance before the time of need. *South.*

FOREBO'DE, *v. t.* To foretell; to prognosticate.

2. To foreknow; to be prescient of; to feel a secret sense of something future; as, my heart *forebodes* a sad reverse.

FOREBO'DEMENT, *n.* A presaging; presagement.

FOREBO'DER, *n.* One who forebodes; a prognosticator; a soothsayer. *L'Estrange.*

2. A foreknower.

FOREBO'DING, *ppr.* Prognosticating; foretelling; foreknowing.

FOREBO'DING, *n.* Prognostication.

FOREBRACE, *n.* A rope applied to the fore yard-arm to change the position of the foresail. *Mar. Dict.*

FOREBY', *prep.* [*fore* and *by.*] Near; hard by; fast by. *Obs.* *Spenser.*

FOREC'AST, *v. t.* To foresee; to provide against.

It is wisdom to *forecast* consequences. *L'Estrange.*

2. To scheme; to plan before execution.

He shall *forecast* his devices against the strong holds. Dan. xi.

3. To adjust, contrive or appoint beforehand.

The time so well *forecast*. *Dryden.*

FOREC'AST, *v. i.* To form a scheme previously; to contrive beforehand.

Forecasting how his foe he might annoy. *Spenser.*

FO'REC'AST, *n.* Previous contrivance; foresight, or the antecedent determination proceeding from it; as a man of little *forecast*.

FOREC'ASTER, *n.* One who foresees or contrives beforehand.

FOREC'ASTING, *ppr.* Contriving previously.

FO'REC'ASTLE, *n.* A short deck in the forepart of a ship above the upper deck, usually terminated in ships of war with a breast-work; the foremost part forming the top of the beak-head, and the hind part reaching to the after part of the fore chains. *Mar. Dict.*

FORECHO'SEN, *a.* *forecho'zn.* Preelected; chosen beforehand.

FORECITED, *a.* Cited or quoted before or above. *Arbuthnot.*

FORECLO'SE, *v. t.* *s* as *z.* To shut up; to preclude; to stop; to prevent.

The embargo with Spain *foreclosed* this trade. *Carew.*

To foreclose a mortgager, in *law*, is to cut him off from his equity of redemption, or the power of redeeming the mortgaged premises, by a judgment of court. *Blackstone.*

[*To foreclose a mortgage* is not technically correct, but is often used.]

FORECLO'SURE, *n.* *s* as *z.* Prevention.

2. The act of foreclosing, or depriving a mortgager of the right of redeeming a mortgaged estate. *Blackstone.*

FORECONCEI'VE, *v. t.* To preconceive. *Bacon.*

FOREDA'TE, *v. t.* To date before the true time.

FOREDA'TED, *pp.* Dated before the true time. *Milton.*

FO'REDECK, *n.* The forepart of a deck, or of a ship.

FOREDESI'GN, *v. t.* To plan beforehand; to intend previously. *Cheyne.*

FORE-DETERM'INE, *v. t.* To decree beforehand. *Hopkins.*

FOREDOOM', *v. t.* To doom beforehand; to predestinate.

Thou art *foredoomed* to view the Stygian state. *Dryden.*

FOREDOOM', *n.* Previous doom or sentence.

FOREDOOR, *n.* The door in the front of a house.

FORE-END', *n.* The end which precedes; the anterior part. *Bacon.*

FOREF'ATHER, *n.* An ancestor; one who precedes another in the line of genealogy, in any degree; usually in a remote degree.

FOREFEND', *v. t.* To hinder; to fend off; to avert; to prevent approach; to forbid or prohibit. *Dryden.*

2. To defend; to guard; to secure. *Shak.*
This word, like the L. *arceo*, is applied to the thing assailing, and to the thing assailed. To drive back or resist that which assails, is to hinder its approach, to forbid or avert, and this act *defends* the thing threatened or assailed.

FOREFIN'GER, *n.* The finger next to the thumb; the index; called by our Saxon ancestors, the *shoot-finger*, from its use in archery.

FOREFLOW, *v. t.* To flow before. *Dryden.*

FOREFOOT, *n.* One of the anterior feet of a quadruped or multiped.
2. A hand, in contempt. *Shak.*
3. In *a ship*, a piece of timber which terminates the keel at the fore-end.

FOREFRONT', *n.* The foremost part. The *forefront* of the battle, is the part where the contest is most warm, and where a soldier is most exposed. 2 Sam. xi. 15.

FO'REGAME, *n.* A first game; first plan. *Whitlock.*

FOREGO', *v. t.* [See *Go.*] To forbear to possess or enjoy; voluntarily to avoid the enjoyment of good. Let us *forego* the pleasures of sense, to secure immortal bliss.
2. To give up; to renounce; to resign. *But this word is usually applied to things not possessed or enjoyed, and which cannot be resigned.*
3. To lose.
4. To go before; to precede. *Obs.* *Shak.*

FOREGO'ER, *n.* An ancestor; a progenitor. [*Not used.*] *Shak.*
2. One who goes before another. *Davies.*
3. One who forbears to enjoy.

FOREGO'ING, *ppr.* Forbearing to have, possess or enjoy.
2. *a.* Preceding; going before, in time or place; antecedent; as a *foregoing* period of time; a *foregoing* clause in a writing.

FOREGONE, *pp. foregawn'.* Forborne to be possessed or enjoyed. *Spenser.*
2. Gone before; past. *Obs.* *Shak.*

FO'REGROUND, *n.* The part of the field or expanse of a picture which seems to lie before the figures. *Dryden. Johnson.*

FOREGUESS', *v. t.* To conjecture. [*Bad.*] *Sherwood.*

FO'REHAND, *n.* The part of a horse which is before the rider.
2. The chief part. *Shak.*

FO'REHAND, *a.* Done sooner than is regular.

> And so extenuate the *forehand* sin. *Shak.*

FO'REHANDED, *a.* Early; timely; seasonable; as a *forehanded* care. *Taylor.*
2. In *America*, in good circumstances as to property; free from debt and possessed of property; as a *forehanded* farmer.
3. Formed in the foreparts.

> A substantial true-bred beast, bravely *forehanded.* *Dryden.*

FOREHEAD, *n. for'hed*, or rather *for'ed.* The part of the face which extends from the hair on the top of the head to the eyes.
2. Impudence; confidence; assurance; audaciousness. *Bp. Hall. Swift.*

FOR'HEAD-BALD, *a.* Bald above the forehead. Levit. xiii. 47.

FOREHE'AR, *v. i.* To be informed before.

FOREHEND', *v. t.* To seize. [*Not in use.*] *Spenser.*

FOREHEW', *v. t.* To hew or cut in front. *Sackville.*

FOREHOLDING, *n.* Predictions; ominous forebodings; superstitious prognostications. [*Not used.*] *L'Estrange.*

FO'REHOOK, *n.* In *ships*, a breast-hook; a piece of timber placed across the stem to unite the bows and strengthen the forepart of the ship. *Mar. Dict.*

FO'REHORSE, *n.* The horse in a team which goes foremost.

FOREIGN, *a. for'an.* [Fr. *forain;* Norm. *forein;* Sp. *foraneo;* from the root of Sax. *faran*, to go or depart; L. *foris, foras*, Fr. *hors*, abroad.]
1. Belonging to another nation or country; alien; not of the country in which one resides; extraneous. We call every country *foreign*, which is not within the jurisdiction of our own government. In this sense, Scotland before the union was *foreign* to England, and Canada is now *foreign* to the United States. More generally *foreign* is applied to countries more remote than an adjacent territory; as a *foreign* market; a *foreign* prince. In the United States, all transatlantic countries are *foreign.*
2. Produced in a distant country or jurisdiction; coming from another country; as *foreign* goods; goods of *foreign* manufacture; a *foreign* minister.
3. Remote; not belonging; not connected; with *to* or *from.* You dissemble; the sentiments you express are *foreign to* your heart. This design is *foreign from* my thoughts. [The use of *from* is preferable and best authorized.]
4. Impertinent; not pertaining; not to the purpose. The observation is *foreign* from the subject under consideration.
5. Excluded; not admitted; held at a distance. *Shak.*
6. Extraneous; adventitious; not native or natural.
7. In *law*, a *foreign attachment* is an attachment of the goods of a foreigner within a city or liberty, for the satisfaction of a debt due from the foreigner to a citizen; or an attachment of the money or goods of a debtor, in the hands of another person.

A *foreign bill of exchange*, is a bill drawn by a person in one country, on his correspondent or agent in another, as distinguished from an *inland bill*, which is drawn by one person on another in the same jurisdiction or country.

Foreign plea, a plea or objection to a judge as incompetent to try the question, on the ground that it is not within his jurisdiction. *Encyc.*

FOR'EIGNER, *n. for'aner.* A person born in a foreign country, or without the country or jurisdiction of which one speaks. A Spaniard is a *foreigner* in France and England. All men not born in the United States are to them *foreigners*, and they are aliens till naturalized. A naturalized person is a citizen; but we still call him a *foreigner by birth.*

FOR'EIGNNESS, *n. for'anness.* Remoteness; want of relation; as the *foreignness* of a subject from the main business.

FORE-IMAG'INE, *v. t.* To conceive or fancy before proof, or beforehand.

FOREJUDGE, *v. t. forejuj'.* To prejudge; to judge beforehand, or before hearing the facts and proof.
2. In *law*, to expel from a court, for malpractice or non-appearance. When an attorney is sued, and called to appear in court, if he declines, he is *forejudged*, and his name is struck from the rolls.

FOREJUDG'MENT, *n.* Judgment previously formed. *Spenser.*

FOREKNOW, *v. t.* [See *Know.*] To have previous knowledge of; to foresee.

> Who would the miseries of man *foreknow?* *Dryden.*
>
> For whom he did *foreknow*, he also did predestinate to be conformed to the image of his Son. Rom. viii.

FOREKNOWABLE, *a.* That may be foreknown. *More.*

FOREKNOWER, *n.* One that foreknows.

FOREKNOWL'EDGE, *n.* Knowledge of a thing before it happens; prescience.

> If I foreknew,
> *Foreknowledge* had no influence on their fault. *Milton.*

FOR'EL, *n.* A kind of parchment for the cover of books.

FO'RELAND, *n.* A promontory or cape; a point of land extending into the sea some distance from the line of the shore; a head land; as the North and South *Foreland* in Kent, in England.

FORELA'Y, *v. t.* To lay wait for; to entrap by ambush. *Dryden.*
2. To contrive antecedently. *Johnson.*

FORELE'ADER, *n.* One who leads others by his example.

FORELEND', *v. t.* To lend or give beforehand. *Spenser.*

FO'RELOCK, *n.* The lock or hair that grows from the forepart of the head.

> Take time by the *forelock.* *Swift.*

2. In *sea language*, a little flat pointed wedge of iron, used at the end of a bolt, to retain it firmly in its place. *Mar. Dict.*

FORELOOK', *v. t.* To look beforehand or forward. *Spenser.*

FO'REMAN, *n.* The first or chief man; particularly, the chief man of a jury, who acts as their speaker.
2. The chief man in a printing office or other establishment, who conducts the whole work.

FO'REMAST, *n.* The mast of a ship or other vessel which is placed in the forepart or forecastle, and carries the foresail and foretop-sail yards. *Encyc.*

Foremast-men, on board of ships, the men who take in the top-sails, sling the yards, furl the sails, &c. *Encyc.*

FOREMEANT', *a. forement'.* Intended beforehand. *Spenser.*

FOREMEN'TIONED, *a.* Mentioned before; recited or written in a former part of the same writing or discourse.

FO'REMOST, *a.* First in place; most advanced; as the *foremost* troops of an army.
2. First in dignity. In honor he held the *foremost* rank.

FO'REMOTHER, *n.* A female ancestor. *Prideaux.*

FO'RENAMED, *a.* Named or nominated before.
2. Mentioned before in the same writing or discourse.

FO'RENOON, *n.* The former part of the day, from the morning to meridian or noon. We usually call the first part of the day, from the dawn to the time of breakfast, or the hour of business, the *morning*, and from this period to noon, the *forenoon*. But the limits are not precisely defined by custom.

FORENO'TICE, *n.* Notice or information of an event before it happens. *Rymer.*

FOREN'SIC, *a.* [from L. *forensis*, from *forum*, a court.]
Belonging to courts of judicature; used in courts or legal proceedings; as a *forensic* term; *forensic* eloquence or disputes. *Locke. Watts.*

FOREORDA'IN, *v. t.* To ordain or appoint beforehand; to preordain; to predestinate; to predetermine. *Hooker.*

FOREORDINA'TION, *n.* Previous ordination or appointment; predetermination; predestination. *Jackson.*

FO'REPART, *n.* The part first in time; as the *forepart* of the day or week.
2. The part most advanced in place; the anterior part; as the *forepart* of any moving body.
3. The beginning; as the *forepart* of a series.

FO'REPAST, *a.* Past before a certain time; as *forepast* sins. [*Little used.*] *Hammond.*

FORE-POSSESS'ED, *a.* Holding formerly in possession; also, preoccupied; prepossessed; preengaged. *Sanderson.*

FOREPRI'ZE, *v. t.* To prize or rate beforehand. *Hooker.*

FOREPROM'ISED, *a.* Promised beforehand; preengaged.

FOREQUO'TED, *a.* Cited before; quoted in a foregoing part of the work.

FO'RERANK, *n.* The first rank; the front. *Shak.*

FORERE'ACH *upon*, *v. t.* In *navigation*, to gain or advance upon in progression or motion. *Mar. Dict.*

FORERE'AD, *v. t.* To signify by tokens. *Obs.* *Spenser.*

FORERE'ADING, *n.* Previous perusal. *Hales.*

FORERECI'TED, *a.* Named or recited before. *Shak.*

FOREREMEM'BERED, *a.* Called to mind previously. *Mountagu.*

FO'RERIGHT, *a.* Ready; forward; quick. *Massinger.*

FO'RERIGHT, *adv.* Right forward; onward. *Beaum.*

FORERUN', *v. t.* To advance before; to come before as an earnest of something to follow; to introduce as a harbinger.

> Heaviness *foreruns* the good event. *Shak.*

2. To precede; to have the start of. *Graunt.*

FORERUN'NER, *n.* A messenger sent before to give notice of the approach of others; a harbinger.

> My elder brothers, my *forerunners* came. *Dryden.*

2. An ancestor or predecessor. *Obs.*
3. A prognostic; a sign foreshowing something to follow. Certain pains in the head, back and limbs are the *forerunners* of a fever.

FO'RESAID, *a.* Spoken before. [See *Aforesaid.*]

FO'RESAIL, *n.* A sail extended on the foreyard, which is supported by the foremast.

FORESA'Y, *v. t.* To predict; to foretell. *Shak.*

FORESA'YING, *n.* A prediction. *Sherwood.*

FORESEE', *v. t.* To see beforehand; to see or know an event before it happens; to have prescience of; to foreknow.

> A prudent man *foreseeth* the evil and hideth himself. Prov. xxii.

FORESEE'ING, *ppr.* Seeing before the event.

FORESEE'N, *pp.* Seen beforehand.

FORESEE'R, *n.* One who foresees or foreknows.

FORESE'IZE, *v. t.* To seize beforehand.

FORESHAD'OW, *v. t.* To shadow or typify beforehand. *Dryden.*

FORESHA'ME, *v. t.* To shame; to bring reproach on. *Shak.*

FORESHEW. [See *Foreshow.*]

FO'RESHIP, *n.* The forepart of a ship. Acts xxvii.

FORESHORT'EN, *v. t.* In *painting*, to shorten figures for the sake of showing those behind. *Dryden.*

FORESHORT'ENING, *n.* In *painting*, the act of shortening figures for the sake of showing those behind. *Dryden.*
The art of conveying to the mind the impression of the entire length of an object, when represented as viewed in an oblique or receding position. *Cyc.*

FORESHOW, *v. t.* To show beforehand; to prognosticate.

> Next, like Aurora, Spenser rose,
> Whose purple blush the day *foreshows*. *Denham.*

2. To predict; to foretell.
3. To represent beforehand, or before it comes. *Hooker.*

FORESHOWER, *n.* One who predicts.

FORESHROUDS', *n.* The shrouds of a ship attached to the foremast.

FO'RESIDE, *n.* The front side; also, a specious outside. *Spenser.*

FO'RESIGHT, *n.* Prescience; foreknowledge; prognostication; the act of foreseeing. *Milton.*
2. Provident care of futurity; foreknowledge accompanied with prudence in guarding against evil. *Spenser.*

FORESIGHTFUL, *a.* Prescient; provident. [*Little used.*] *Sidney.*

FORESIG'NIFY, *v. t.* To signify beforehand; to betoken previously; to foreshow; to typify. *Hooker.*

FO'RESKIN, *n.* The skin that covers the glans penis; the prepuce.

FO'RESKIRT, *n.* The loose and pendulous part of a coat before. *Shak.*

FORESLACK', *v. t.* To neglect by idleness. [*Not used.*] *Spenser.*

FORESLOW, *v. t.* To delay; to hinder; to impede; to obstruct. [*Not used.*]

> No stream, no wood, no mountain could *foreslow*
> Their hasty pace. *Fairfax.*

2. To neglect; to omit. [*Not used.*] *Bacon.*

FORESLOW, *v. i.* To be dilatory; to loiter. [*Not used.*] *Shak.*

FORESPE'AK, *v. t.* To foresay; to foreshow; to foretell or predict. *Camden.*
2. To forbid. [*Not used.*] *Shak.*
3. To bewitch. [*Not used.*] *Drayton.*

FORESPE'AKING, *n.* A prediction; also, a preface. [*Not used.*]

FORESPEE'CH, *n.* A preface. [*Not used.*] *Sherwood.*

FORESPENT', *a.* Wasted in strength; tired; exhausted. *Shak.*
2. Past; as life *forespent*. [*Little used.*] *Spenser.*

FORESPUR'RER, *n.* One that rides before. [*Not used.*] *Shak.*

FOR'EST, *n.* [It. *foresta*; Fr. *forêt*; Arm. *forest*; G. *forst*; Ir. *foraois*, *foraighis*; Norm. *fores*; from the same root as L. *foris*, Fr. *hors*, and the Sax. *faran*, to go, to depart. Hence the It. *forestiere*, Sp. *forastero*, signifies strange, foreign; It. *foresto*, wild, savage; Port. *forasteiro*, a stranger. This enables us to understand the radical meaning of other words which signify *strange*, *wild*, *barbarous*, &c. They all express distance from cities and civilization, and are from roots expressing departure or wandering.]
1. An extensive wood, or a large tract of land covered with trees. In *America*, the word is usually applied to a wood of native growth, or a tract of woodland which has never been cultivated. It differs from wood or woods chiefly in extent. We read of the Hercynian *forest*, in Germany, and the *forest* of Ardennes, in France or Gaul.
2. In *law*, in Great Britain, a certain territory of woody grounds and pastures, privileged for wild beasts and fowls of forest, chase and warren, to rest and abide in, under the protection of the king, for his pleasure. *In this sense, the word has no application in America.*
Forest laws, laws for governing and regulating forests, and preserving game. *England.*

FOR'EST, *v. t.* To cover with trees or wood.

FO'REST'AFF, *n.* An instrument used at sea, for taking the altitudes of heavenly bodies; called also *cross-staff*. *Encyc.*

FOR'ESTAGE, *n.* An ancient service paid by foresters to the king; also, the right of foresters. *England.*

FORESTALL', *v. t.* [See *Stall.*] To anticipate; to take beforehand.

> Why need a man *forestall* his date of grief,
> And run to meet what he would most avoid? *Milton.*

2. To hinder by preoccupation or prevention.

> I will not *forestall* your judgment of the rest. *Pope.*

3. In *law*, to buy or bargain for corn, or provisions of any kind, before they arrive at the market or fair, with intent to sell them at higher prices. This is a penal offense. *Encyc.*
4. To deprive by something prior. [*Not in use.*] *Shak.*

FORESTALL'ED, *pp.* Anticipated; hindered; purchased before arrival in market.

FORESTALL'ER, *n.* One who forestalls; a person who purchases provisions before they come to the fair or market, with a view to raise the price. *Locke.*

FORESTALL'ING, *ppr.* Anticipating; hindering; buying provisions before they arrive in market, with intent to sell them at higher prices.

FORESTALL'ING, *n.* Anticipation; prevention; the act of buying provisions before they are offered in market, with intent to sell them at higher prices.

FORESTAY, *n.* In *a ship's rigging*, a large strong rope reaching from the foremast head towards the bowsprit end, to support the mast. *Mar. Dict.*

FOR'ESTED, *pp.* Covered with trees; wooded. *Tooke.*

FOR'ESTER, *n.* In *England*, an officer appointed to watch a forest, preserve the game, and institute suits for trespasses. *Encyc.*

2. An inhabitant of a forest. *Shak.*

3. A forest tree. *Evelyn.*

FO'RESWAT, *a.* [See *Sweat.*] Exhausted by heat. *Obs.* *Sidney.*

FORETACK'LE, *n.* The tackle on the foremast.

FO'RETASTE, *n.* A taste beforehand; anticipation. The pleasures of piety are a *foretaste* of heaven.

FORETA'STE, *v. t.* To taste before possession; to have previous enjoyment or experience of something; to anticipate.

2. To taste before another.

FORETA'STED, *pp.* Tasted beforehand or before another. *Milton.*

FORETA'STER, *n.* One that tastes beforehand or before another.

FORETA'STING, *ppr.* Tasting before.

FORETE'ACH, *v. t.* To teach beforehand. *Spenser.*

FORETELL', *v. t.* To predict; to tell before an event happens; to prophesy. *Milton. Pope.*

2. To foretoken; to foreshow. *Warton.*

FORETELL', *v. i.* To utter prediction or prophecy.

All the prophets from Samuel, and those that follow after, as many as have spoken, have likewise *foretold* of these days. Acts iii.

FORETELL'ER, *n.* One who predicts or prophesies; a foreshower. *Boyle.*

FORETELL'ING, *n.* Prediction.

FORETHINK', *v. t.* To think beforehand; to anticipate in the mind.

The soul of every man
Perpetually does *forethink* thy fall. *Shak.*

2. To contrive beforehand. *Bp. Hall.*

FORETHINK', *v. i.* To contrive beforehand. *Smith.*

FORETHOUGHT', *forethaut'. pret.* of *forethink.*

FO'RETHOUGHT, *n. fo'rethaut.* A thinking beforehand; anticipation; prescience; premeditation.

2. Provident care. *Blackstone.*

FORETO'KEN, *v. t.* To foreshew; to presignify; to prognosticate.

Whilst strange prodigious signs *foretoken* blood. *Daniel.*

FORETO'KEN, *n.* Prognostic; previous sign. *Sidney.*

FO'RETOOTH, *n.* plu. *foreteeth.* One of the teeth in the forepart of the mouth; an incisor.

FO'RETOP, *n.* The hair on the forepart of the head.

2. That part of a woman's headdress that is forward, or the top of a periwig.

3. In *ships*, the platform erected at the head of the foremast. *In this sense, the accent on the two syllables is nearly equal.*

FORETOP'-MAST, *n.* The mast erected at the head of the foremast, and at the head of which stands the foretop-gallant-mast.

FOREVOUCH'ED, *pp.* Affirmed before; formerly told. *Shak.*

FO'REWARD, *n.* The van; the front. 1 Maccabees.

FOREWARN', *v. t. forewaurn'.* To admonish beforehand.

I will *forewarn* you whom ye shall fear. Luke xii.

2. To inform previously; to give previous notice. *Milton.*

3. To caution beforehand. *Dryden.*

FOREWARN'ED, *pp.* Admonished, cautioned or informed beforehand.

FOREWARN'ING, *ppr.* Previously admonishing or informing.

FOREWARN'ING, *n.* Previous admonition, caution or notice.

FOREWEND', *v. t.* To go before. *Obs.* *Spenser.*

FOREWISH', *v. t.* To wish beforehand. *Knolles.*

FO'REWÖMAN, *n.* A woman who is chief; the head woman. *Tatler.*

FOREWÖRN, *pp.* [See *Wear.*] Worn out; wasted or obliterated by time or use. *Sidney.*

FOR'FEIT, *v. t. for'fit.* [Fr. *forfaire, forfait*; Low L. *forisfacere*, from L. *foris*, out or abroad, and *facio*, to make; Norm. *forface*, forfeit, and *forfist*, forfeited.]

To lose or render confiscable, by some fault, offense or crime; to lose the right to some species of property or that which belongs to one; to alienate the right to possess by some neglect or crime; as, to *forfeit* an estate by a breach of the condition of tenure or by treason. By the ancient laws of England, a man *forfeited* his estate by neglecting or refusing to fulfill the conditions on which it was granted to him, or by a breach of fealty. A man now *forfeits* his estate by committing treason. A man *forfeits* his honor or reputation by a breach of promise, and by any criminal or disgraceful act. Statutes declare that by certain acts a man shall *forfeit* a certain sum of money. Under the feudal system, the right to the land *forfeited*, vested in the lord or superior. In modern times, the right to things *forfeited* is generally regulated by statutes; it is vested in the state, in corporations, or in prosecutors or informers, or partly in the state or a corporation, and partly in an individual.

The duelist, to secure the reputation of bravery, *forfeits* the esteem of good men, and the favor of heaven.

FOR'FEIT, *n. for'fit.* [Fr. *forfait*; W. *forfed*; Low L. *forisfactura.* Originally, and still in French, a trespass, transgression or crime. But with us, the effect of some transgression or offense.]

1. That which is forfeited or lost, or the right to which is alienated by a crime, offense, neglect of duty, or breach of contract; hence, a fine; a mulct; a penalty. He that murders pays the *forfeit* of his life. When a statute creates a penalty for a transgression, either in money or in corporal punishment, the offender who, on conviction, pays the money or suffers the punishment, pays the *forfeit.*

2. One whose life is forfeited. [*Not used.*] *Shak.*

FOR'FEIT, *part. a.* used for *forfeited.* Lost or alienated for an offense or crime; liable to penal seizure.

And his long toils were *forfeit* for a look. *Dryden.*

FOR'FEITABLE, *a.* Liable to be forfeited; subject to forfeiture.

—For the future, uses shall be subject to the statutes of mortmain, and *forfeitable* like the lands themselves. *Blackstone.*

FOR'FEITED, *pp.* Lost or alienated by an offense, crime or breach of condition.

FOR'FEITING, *ppr.* Alienating or losing, as a right, by an offense, crime or breach of condition.

FOR'FEITURE, *n.* The act of forfeiting; the losing of some right, privilege, estate, honor, office or effects, by an offense, crime, breach of condition or other act. In regard to property, forfeiture is a loss of the right to possess, but not generally the actual possession, which is to be transferred by some subsequent process. In the feudal system, a forfeiture of lands gave him in reversion or remainder a right to enter.

2. That which is forfeited; an estate forfeited; a fine or mulct. The prince enriched his treasury by fines and *forfeitures.*

FOR'FEX, *n.* [L.] A pair of scissors. *Pope.*

FORGA'VE, *pret.* of *forgive*, which see.

FORĠE, *n.* [Fr. *forge*; Sp. Port. *forja*; probably from L. *ferrum*, iron; It. *ferriera*, a forge; Port. *ferragem*, iron-work.]

1. A furnace in which iron or other metal is heated and hammered into form. A larger forge is called with us *iron-works.* Smaller forges consisting of a bellows so placed as to cast a stream of air upon ignited coals, are of various forms and uses. Armies have travelling forges, for repairing gun-carriages, &c.

2. Any place where any thing is made or shaped. *Hooker.*

3. The act of beating or working iron or steel; the manufacture of metalline bodies.

In the greater bodies the *forge* was easy. *Bacon.*

FORĠE, *v. t.* To form by heating and hammering; to beat into any particular shape, as a metal.

2. To make by any means.

Names that the schools *forged*, and put into the mouths of scholars. *Locke.*

2. To make falsely; to falsify; to counterfeit; to make in the likeness of something else; as, to *forge* coin; to *forge* a bill of exchange or a receipt.

FORĠED, *pp.* Hammered; beaten into shape; made; counterfeited.

FORĠER, *n.* One that makes or forms.

2. One who counterfeits; a falsifier.

FORĠERY, *n.* The act of forging or working metal into shape. *In this sense, rarely or never now used.*

2. The act of falsifying; the crime of counterfeiting; as the *forgery* of coin, or of bank notes, or of a bond. *Forgery* may

consist in counterfeiting a writing, or in setting a false name to it, to the prejudice of another person.

3. That which is forged or counterfeited. Certain letters, purporting to be written by Gen. Washington, during the revolution, were *forgeries*.

FORGET′, *v. t.* pret. *forgot*, [*forgat*, obs.] pp. *forgot*, *forgotten*. [Sax. *forgetan*, *forgitan*, *forgytan*; G. *vergessen*; D. *vergeeten*; Sw. *förgäta*; Dan. *forgietter*; *for* and *get*.]

1. To lose the remembrance of; to let go from the memory.

Bless the Lord, O my soul, and *forget* not all his benefits. Ps. ciii.

2. To slight; to neglect.

Can a woman *forget* her sucking child—? Yea, they may *forget*, yet will I not *forget* thee. Is. xlix.

FORGET′FUL, *a.* Apt to forget; easily losing the remembrance of. A *forgetful* man should use helps to strengthen his memory.

2. Heedless; careless; neglectful; inattentive.

Be not *forgetful* to entertain strangers. Heb. xiii.

3. Causing to forget; inducing oblivion; oblivious; as *forgetful* draughts. *Dryden.*

FORGET′FULNESS, *n.* The quality of losing the remembrance or recollection of a thing; or rather, the quality of being apt to let any thing slip from the mind.

2. Loss of remembrance or recollection; a ceasing to remember; oblivion.

A sweet *forgetfulness* of human care. *Pope.*

3. Neglect; negligence; careless omission; inattention; as *forgetfulness* of duty. *Hooker.*

FORGET′TER, *n.* One that forgets; a heedless person.

FORGET′TING, *ppr.* Losing the remembrance of.

FORGET′TING, *n.* The act of forgetting; forgetfulness; inattention.

FORGET′TINGLY, *adv.* By forgetting or forgetfulness. *B. Jonson.*

FORGIV′ABLE, *a.* [See *Forgive.*] That may be pardoned. *Sherwood.*

FORGIVE, *v. t.* *forgiv′.* pret. *forgave*; pp. *forgiven*. [*for* and *give*; Sax. *forgifan*; Goth. *fragiban*; G. *vergeben*; D. *vergeeven*; Dan. *forgiver*; Sw. *tilgifva*. The sense is to give from, that is, away, as we see by the Gothic *fra*, from. The English *for*, and G. and D. *ver*, are the same word, or from the same root; *ver* is the Eng. *far*. The Swedish *til* signifies *to*, and in this compound, it signifies toward or back; so in L. *remitto*. See *Give.*]

1. To pardon; to remit, as an offense or debt; to overlook an offense, and treat the offender as not guilty. The original and proper phrase is to *forgive the offense*, to send it away, to reject it, that is, not to *impute it*, [put it to] the offender. But by an easy transition, we also use the phrase, to *forgive the person* offending.

Forgive us our debts. *Lord's Prayer.*

If ye *forgive* men their trespasses, your heavenly father will also *forgive* you. Matt. vi.

As savages never forget a favor, so they never *forgive* an injury. *N. Chipman.*

It is to be noted that *pardon*, like *forgive*, may be followed by the name or person, and by the offense; but *remit* can be followed by the offense only. We forgive or pardon the man, but we do not *remit* him.

2. To remit as a debt, fine or penalty.

FORGIV′EN, *pp.* Pardoned; remitted.

FORGIV′ENESS, *n.* *forgiv′ness.* The act of forgiving; the pardon of an offender, by which he is considered and treated as not guilty. The *forgiveness* of enemies is a christian duty.

2. The pardon or remission of an offense or crime; as the *forgiveness* of sin or of injuries.

3. Disposition to pardon; willingness to forgive.

And mild *forgiveness* intercede
To stop the coming blow. *Dryden.*

4. Remission of a debt, fine or penalty.

FORGIV′ER, *n.* One who pardons or remits.

FORGIV′ING, *ppr.* Pardoning; remitting.

2. *a.* Disposed to forgive; inclined to overlook offenses; mild; merciful; compassionate; as a *forgiving* temper.

FORGOT′, **FORGOT′TEN**, } *pp.* of *forget.*

FORHA′IL, *v. t.* To draw or distress. [*Not used.*] *Spenser.*

FORIN′SECAL, *a.* [L. *forinsecus.*] Foreign; alien. [*Little used.*]

FORISFAMIL′IATE, *v. t.* [L. *foris*, without, and *familia*, family.]

To renounce a legal title to a further share of paternal inheritance. *Literally, to put one's self out of the family.* *El. of Criticism.*

FORISFAMILIA′TION, *n.* When a child has received a portion of his father's estate, and renounces all title to a further share, his act is called *forisfamiliation*, and he is said to be *forisfamiliated*. *Encyc.*

FORK, *n.* [Sax. *forc*; D. *vork*; W. *forc*; Fr. *fourche*; Arm. *fork*; Sp. *horca*; Port. It. *forca*; L. *furca.*]

1. An instrument consisting of a handle, and a blade of metal, divided into two or more points or prongs, used for lifting or pitching any thing; as a *tablefork* for feeding; a *pitchfork*; a *dungfork*, &c. Forks are also made of ivory, wood or other material.

2. A point; as a thunderbolt with three *forks*. Shakspeare uses it for the point of an arrow.

3. *Forks*, in the plural, the point where a road parts into two; and the point where a river divides, or rather where two rivers meet and unite in one stream. Each branch is called a *fork*.

FORK′, *v. i.* To shoot into blades, as corn. *Mortimer.*

2. To divide into two; as, a road *forks*.

FORK, *v. t.* To raise or pitch with a fork, as hay.

2. To dig and break ground with a fork.

3. To make sharp; to point.

FORK′ED, *pp.* Raised, pitched or dug with a fork.

2. *a.* Opening into two or more parts, points or shoots; as a *forked* tongue; the *forked* lightning.

3. Having two or more meanings. [*Not in use.*] *B. Jonson.*

FORK′EDLY, *adv.* In a forked form.

FORK′EDNESS, *n.* The quality of opening into two or more parts.

FORK′HEAD, *n.* The point of an arrow. *Spenser.*

FORK′TAIL, *n.* A salmon, in his fourth year's growth. [*Local.*]

FORK′Y, *a.* Forked; furcated; opening into two or more parts, shoots or points; as a *forky* tongue. *Pope.*

FORLO′RE, *a.* Forlorn. [*Not in use.*]

FORLORN′, *a.* [Sax. *forloren*, from *forleoran*, to send away, to relinquish, to desert, to lose; *leoran*, to pass, to migrate; D. *verlooren*; Dan. *forloren*, from *forlorer*, Sw. *förlora*, to lose. Class Lr.]

1. Deserted; destitute; stripped or deprived; forsaken. Hence, lost; helpless; wretched; solitary.

Of fortune and of hope at once *forlorn*. *Hubberd.*

To live again in these wild woods *forlorn*. *Milton.*

For here *forlorn* and lost I tread. *Goldsmith.*

2. Taken away. *Obs.*

When as night hath us of light *forlorn*. *Spenser.*

3. Small; despicable; *in a ludicrous sense.* *Shak.*

Forlorn hope, properly, a desperate case; hence in military affairs, a detachment of men appointed to lead in an assault, to storm a counterscarp, enter a breach, or perform other service attended with uncommon peril.

FORLORN′, *n.* A lost, forsaken, solitary person. *Shak.*

FORLORN′NESS, *n.* Destitution; misery; a forsaken or wretched condition. *Boyle.*

FORLŸE, *v. i.* To lye before. [*Not used.*] *Spenser.*

FORM, *n.* [L. *forma*; Fr. *forme*; Sp. *forma*, *horma*; It. *forma*; Ir. *foirm*; D. *vorm*; G. *form*; Sw. and Dan. *form*. The root of this word is not certainly known. The primary sense is probably to set, to fix, to fit. The D. *vormen*, is rendered, to form, to shape, to mold, to *confirm*; and *form* may be allied to *firm*.]

1. The shape or external appearance of a body; the figure, as defined by lines and angles; that manner of being peculiar to each body, which exhibits it to the eye as distinct from every other body. Thus we speak of the *form* of a circle, the *form* of a square or triangle, a circular *form*, the *form* of the head or of the human body, a handsome *form*, an ugly *form*, a frightful *form*.

Matter is the basis or substratum of bodies; *form* is the particular disposition of matter in each body which distinguishes its appearance from that of every other body.

The *form* of his visage was changed. Dan. iii.

After that he appeared in another *form* to two of them, as they walked. Mark xvi.

2. Manner of arranging particulars; disposition of particular things; as a *form* of words or expressions.

3. Model; draught; pattern.

Hold fast the *form* of sound words, which thou hast heard of me. 2 Tim. i.

4. Beauty; elegance; splendor; dignity.

He hath no *form* nor comeliness. Isa. liii.

5. Regularity; method; order. This is a rough draught to be reduced to *form*.

6. External appearance without the essential qualities; empty show.

Having the *form* of godliness, but denying the power thereof. 2 Tim. iii.

7. Stated method; established practice; ritual or prescribed mode; as the *forms* of public worship; the *forms* of judicial proceeding; *forms* of civility.

8. Ceremony; as, it is a mere matter of *form*.

9. Determinate shape.

The earth was without *form*, and void. Gen. i.

10. Likeness; image.

Who, being in the *form* of God— Phil. ii.
He took on him the *form* of a servant. Ibm.

11. Manner; system; as a *form* of government; a monarchical or republican *form*.

12. Manner of arrangement; disposition of component parts; as the interior *form* or structure of the flesh or bones, or of other bodies.

13. A long seat; a bench without a back. *Watts.*

14. In *schools*, a class; a rank of students. *Dryden.*

15. The seat or bed of a hare. *Prior.*

16. A mold; something to give shape, or on which things are fashioned. *Encyc.*

17. In *printing*, an assemblage of types, composed and arranged in order, disposed into pages or columns, and inclosed and locked in a chase, to receive an impression.

18. *Essential form*, is that mode of existence which constitutes a thing what it is, and without which it could not exist. Thus water and light have each its particular *form* of existence, and the parts of water being decomposed, it ceases to be water. *Accidental form* is not necessary to the existence of a body. *Earth* is *earth* still, whatever may be its color.

FORM, *v. t.* [L. *formo.*] To make or cause to exist.

And the Lord God *formed* man of the dust of the ground. Gen. ii.

2. To shape; to mold or fashion into a particular shape or state; as, to *form* an image of stone or clay.

3. To plan; to scheme; to modify. *Dryden.*

4. To arrange; to combine in a particular manner; as, to *form* a line or square of troops.

5. To adjust; to settle.

Our differences with the Romanists are thus *formed* into an interest— *Decay of Piety.*

6. To contrive; to invent; as, to *form* a design or scheme.

7. To make up; to frame; to settle by deductions of reason; as, to *form* an opinion or judgment; to *form* an estimate.

8. To mold; to model by instruction and discipline; as, to *form* the mind to virtuous habits by education.

9. To combine; to unite individuals into a collective body; as, to *form* a society for missions.

10. To make; to establish. The subscribers are *formed* by law into a corporation. They have *formed* regulations for their government.

11. To compile; as, to *form* a body of laws or customs; to *form* a digest.

12. To constitute; to make. Duplicity *forms* no part of his character. These facts *form* a safe foundation for our conclusions. The senate and house of representatives *form* the legislative body.

13. In *grammar*, to make by derivation, or by affixes or prefixes. L. *do*, in the preterit, forms *dedi.*

14. To enact; to make; to ordain; as, to *form* a law or an edict.

FORM, *v. i.* To take a form.

FORM'AL, *a.* According to form; agreeable to established mode; regular; methodical.

2. Strictly ceremonious; precise; exact to affectation; as a man *formal* in his dress, his gait or deportment.

3. Done in due form, or with solemnity; express; according to regular method; not incidental, sudden or irregular. He gave his *formal* consent to the treaty.

4. Regular; methodical; as the *formal* stars. *Waller.*

5. Having the form or appearance without the substance or essence; external; as *formal* duty; *formal* worship.

6. Depending on customary forms.

Still in constraint your suffering sex remains,
Or bound in *formal* or in real chains. *Pope.*

7. Having the power of making a thing what it is; constituent; essential.

Of letters the material part is breath and voice; the *formal* is constituted by the motions and figure of the organs of speech. *Holder.*

8. Retaining its proper and essential characteristic; regular; proper.

To make of him a *formal* man again. *Shak.*

FORM'ALISM, *n.* Formality. [*The latter is generally used.*] *Burke.*

FORM'ALIST, *n.* One who observes forms, or practices external ceremonies. More generally,

2. One who regards appearances only, or observes the forms of worship, without possessing the life and spirit of religion; a hypocrite. A grave face and the regular practice of ceremonies have often gained to a *formalist* the reputation of piety.

FORMAL'ITY, *n.* The practice or observance of forms.

Formalities of extraordinary zeal and piety are never more studied and elaborate than in desperate designs. *K. Charles.*

2. Ceremony; mere conformity to customary modes.

Nor was his attendance on divine offices a matter of *formality* and custom, but of conscience. *Atterbury.*

3. Established order; rule of proceeding; mode; method; as the *formalities* of judicial process; *formalities* of law.

4. Order; decorum to be observed; customary mode of behavior. *L'Estrange.*

5. Customary mode of dress; habit; robe. *Swift.*

6. External appearance. *Glanville.*

7. Essence; the quality which constitutes a thing what it is.

The *formality* of the vow lies in the promise made to God. *Stillingfleet.*

8. In *the schools*, the manner in which a thing is conceived; or a manner in an object, importing a relation to the understanding, by which it may be distinguished from another object. Thus *animality* and *rationality* are *formalities*. *Encyc.*

FORM'ALIZE, *v. t.* To model. [*Not used.*] *Hooker.*

FORM'ALIZE, *v. i.* To affect formality. [*Little used.*] *Hales.*

FORM'ALLY, *adv.* According to established form, rule, order, rite or ceremony. A treaty was concluded and *formally* ratified by both parties.

2. Ceremoniously; stiffly; precisely; as, to be stiff and *formally* reserved.

3. In open appearance; in a visible and apparent state.

You and your followers do stand *formally* divided against the authorized guides of the church, and the rest of the people. *Hooker.*

4. Essentially; characteristically.

That which *formally* makes this [charity] a christian grace, is the spring from which it flows. *Smalridge.*

FORMA'TION, *n.* [Fr. from L. *formatio.*] The act of forming or making; the act of creating or causing to exist; or more generally, the operation of composing, by bringing materials together, or of shaping and giving form; as the *formation* of the earth; the *formation* of a state or constitution.

2. Generation; production; as the *formation* of ideas.

3. The manner in which a thing is formed. Examine the peculiar *formation* of the heart.

4. In *grammar*, the act or manner of forming one word from another, as *controller* from *control.*

5. In *geology*, formation may signify a single mass of one kind of rock, more or less extensive, or a collection of mineral substances, formed by the same agent, under the same or similar circumstances; or it may convey the idea, that certain masses or collections of minerals were formed not only by the same agent, but also at the same time. In this latter sense the term is almost always employed. *Cleaveland.*

FORM'ATIVE, *a.* Giving form; having the power of giving form; plastic.

The meanest plant cannot be raised without seeds, by any *formative* power residing in the soil. *Bentley.*

2. In *grammar*, serving to form; derivative; not radical; as a termination merely *formative.*

FORM'ED, *pp.* Made; shaped; molded; planned; arranged; combined; enacted; constituted.

FORM'EDON, *n.* [*forma doni.*] A writ for the recovery of lands by statute of Westminster. *Eng. Law.*

FORM'ER, *n.* He that forms; a maker; an author.

FOR'MER, *a.* comp. deg. [Sax. *form, forma*, but it is rendered *primus*, first. The Saxon word seems to be composed of *fore* and *ma*, more; but of this I am not confident.]

1. Before in time; preceding another or something else in order of time; opposed to *latter.*

Her *former* husband, who sent her away, may not take her again to be his wife, after that she is defiled. Deut. xxiv.
The *former* and the latter rain. Jer. 5.

2. Past, and frequently ancient, long past.

For inquire, I pray thee, of the *former* age. Job viii.

3. Near the beginning; preceding; as the *former* part of a discourse or argument.

4. Mentioned before another.

A bad author deserves better usage than a bad critic; a man may be the *former* merely through the misfortune of want of judgment; but he cannot be the latter without both that and an ill temper. *Pope.*

FOR'MERLY, *adv.* In time past, either in time immediately preceding, or at any indefinite distance; of old; heretofore. We *formerly* imported slaves from Africa. Nations *formerly* made slaves of prisoners taken in war.

FORM'FUL, *a.* Ready to form; creative; imaginative. *Thomson.*

FOR'MIATE, *n.* [from L. *formica*, an ant.] A neutral salt, composed of the formic acid and a base.

FOR'MIC, *a.* [L. *formica*, an ant.] Pertaining to ants; as the *formic* acid, the acid of ants.

FORMICA'TION, *n.* [L. *formicatio*, from *formico*, or *formica*, an ant.]
A sensation of the body resembling that made by the creeping of ants on the skin.

FORM'IDABLE, *a.* [L. *formidabilis*, from *formido*, fear.]
Exciting fear or apprehension; impressing dread; adapted to excite fear and deter from approach, encounter or undertaking. It expresses less than *terrible, terrific, tremendous, horrible*, and *frightful.*

They seemed to fear the *formidable* sight. *Dryden.*

I swell my preface into a volume, and make it *formidable*, when you see so many pages behind. *Dryden.*

FORM'IDABLENESS, *n.* The quality of being formidable, or adapted to excite dread.

FORM'IDABLY, *adv.* In a manner to impress fear.

FORM'LESS, *a.* [from *form.*] Shapeless; without a determinate form; wanting regularity of shape. *Shak.*

FORM'ULA, } *n.* [L.] A prescribed form; a
FORM'ULE, } rule or model.
2. In *medicine*, a prescription.
3. In *church affairs*, a confession of faith. *Encyc.*
4. In *mathematics*, a general expression for resolving certain cases or problems. *Cyc.*

FORM'ULARY, *n.* [Fr. *formulaire*, from L. *formula.*]
A book containing stated and prescribed forms, as of oaths, declarations, prayers and the like; a book of precedents. *Encyc.*
2. Prescribed form.

FORM'ULARY, *a.* Stated; prescribed; ritual. *Johnson.*

FORN'ICATE, } *a.* [L. *fornicatus*, from
FORN'ICATED, } *fornix*, an arch.]
Arched; vaulted like an oven or furnace. *Encyc.*

FORN'ICATE, *v. i.* [L. *fornicor*, from *fornix*, a brothel.]
To commit lewdness, as an unmarried man or woman, or as a married man with an unmarried woman.

If a brahmen *fornicate* with a Nayr woman, he shall not thereby lose his cast. *As. Researches.*

FORNICA'TION, *n.* [L. *fornicatio.*] The incontinence or lewdness of unmarried persons, male or female; also, the criminal conversation of a married man with an unmarried woman. *Laws of Connecticut.*
2. Adultery. Matt. v.
3. Incest. 1 Cor. v.
4. Idolatry; a forsaking of the true God, and worshipping of idols. 2 Chron. xxi. Rev. xix.
5. An arching; the forming of a vault.

FORN'ICATOR, *n.* An unmarried person, male or female, who has criminal conversation with the other sex; also, a married man who has sexual commerce with an unmarried woman. [See *Adultery.*]
2. A lewd person.
3. An idolater.

FORN'ICATRESS, *n.* An unmarried female guilty of lewdness. *Shak.*

FORPASS, *v. i.* To go by; to pass unnoticed. *Obs.* *Spenser.*

FORPI'NE, *v. i.* To pine or waste away. *Obs.* *Spenser.*

FORRA'Y, *v. t.* To ravage. *Obs.* *Spenser.* [Qu. *forage.*]

FORRA'Y, *n.* The act of ravaging. *Obs.*

FORSA'KE, *v. t.* pret. *forsook*; pp. *forsaken.* [Sax. *forsacan, forsæcan*; *for*, a negative, and *secan*, to *seek*. See *Seek*. Sw. *försaka*, Dan. *forsager*, G. *versagen*, D. *verzaaken*, to deny, to renounce. See *Seek* and *Say.*]
1. To quit or leave entirely; to desert; to abandon; to depart from. Friends and flatterers *forsake* us in adversity.

Forsake the foolish, and live. Prov. ix.

2. To abandon; to renounce; to reject.

If his children *forsake* my law, and walk not in my judgments— Ps. lxxxix.

Cease from anger, and *forsake* wrath. Ps. xxxvii.

3. To leave; to withdraw from; to fail. In anger, the color *forsakes* the cheeks. In severe trials, let not fortitude *forsake* you.
4. In *scripture*, God *forsakes* his people, when he withdraws his aid, or the light of his countenance. *Brown.*

FORSA'KER, *n.* One that forsakes or deserts.

FORSA'KEN, *pp.* Deserted; left; abandoned.

FORSA'KING, *ppr.* Leaving or deserting.

FORSA'KING, *n.* The act of deserting; dereliction.

FORSA'Y, *v. t.* To forbid; to renounce. *Obs.* *Spenser.*

FORSLACK', *v. t.* To delay. *Obs.* *Spenser.*

FORSOOTH', *adv.* [Sax. *forsothe*; *for* and *soth*, true.]
In truth; in fact; certainly; very well.

A fit man, *forsooth*, to govern a realm. *Hayward.*

It is generally used in an ironical or contemptuous sense.

FORS'TER, *n.* A forester. *Obs.* *Chaucer.*

FORSWEAR, *v. t.* pret. *forswore*; pp. *forsworn.* [Sax. *forswærian*; Dan. *forsværer*; Sw. *försvåra*; G. *verschwören, abschwören*; D. *afzweeren.* See *Swear* and *Answer.*]
1. To reject or renounce upon oath. *Shak.*
2. To deny upon oath.

Like innocence, and as serenely bold
As truth, how loudly he *forswears* thy gold. *Dryden.*

To forswear one's self, is to swear falsely; to perjure one's self.

Thou shalt not *forswear thyself.* Matt. v.

FORSWEAR, *v. i.* To swear falsely; to commit perjury. *Shak.*

FORSWEARER, *n.* One who rejects on oath; one who is perjured; one that swears a false oath.

FORSWEARING, *ppr.* Denying on oath; swearing falsely.

FORSWONK', *a.* [Sax. *swincan*, to labor.] Overlabored. *Obs.* *Spenser.*

FORSWORE, *pret.* of *forswear.*

FORSWORN, *pp.* of *forswear.* Renounced on oath; perjured.

FORSWORNNESS, *n.* The state of being forsworn. *Manning.*

FORT, *n.* [Fr. *fort*; It. Port. *forte*; Sp. *fuerte, fuerza*; L. *fortis*, strong.]
1. A fortified place; usually, a small fortified place; a place surrounded with a ditch, rampart, and parapet, or with palisades, stockades, or other means of defense; also, any building or place fortified for security against an enemy; a castle.
2. A strong side, opposed to weak side or foible.

FORTE, *adv.* [Ital.] A direction to sing with strength of voice.

FORTED, *a.* Furnished with forts; guarded by forts. *Shak.*

FORTH, *adv.* [Sax. *forth*; G. *fort*; D. *voort*; from *fore, for, faran*, to go, to advance.]
1. Forward; onward in time; in advance; as from that day *forth*; from that time *forth.*
2. Forward in place or order; as one, two, three, and so *forth.*
3. Out; abroad; noting progression or advance from a state of confinement; as, the plants in spring put *forth* leaves.

When winter past, and summer scarce begun,
Invites them *forth* to labor in the sun. *Dryden.*

4. Out; away; beyond the boundary of a place; as, send him *forth* of France. [*Little used.*]
5. Out into public view, or public character. Your country calls you *forth* into its service.
6. Thoroughly; from beginning to end. *Obs.* *Shak.*
7. On to the end. *Obs.*

FORTH, *prep.* Out of.

From *forth* the streets of Pomfret. *Shak.*
Some *forth* their cabins peep. *Donne.*

FORTH-COM'ING, *a.* [See *Come.*] Ready to appear; making appearance. Let the prisoner be *forth-coming.*

FORTHINK', *v. t.* To repent of. [*Not in use.*] *Spenser.*

FORTH-IS'SUING, *a.* [See *Issue.*] Issuing; coming out; coming forward as from a covert. *Pope.*

FORTHRIGHT, *adv.* [See *Right.*] Straight forward; in a straight direction. *Obs.* *Sidney.*

FORTHRIGHT, *n.* A straight path. *Obs.* *Shak.*

FORTHWARD, *adv.* Forward. *Bp. Fisher.*

FORTHWITH', *adv.* [*forth* and *with.*] Immediately; without delay; directly.

Immediately there fell from his eyes as it had been scales; and he received his sight *forthwith.* Acts ix.

FO'RTHY, *adv.* [Sax. *forthi.*] Therefore. [*Not used.*] *Spenser.*

FOR'TIETH, *a.* [See *Forty.*] The fourth tenth; noting the number next after the thirty ninth.

FOR'TIFIABLE, *a.* That may be fortified. [*Little used.*]

FORTIFICA'TION, *n.* [See *Fortify.*] The act of fortifying.

2. The art or science of fortifying places to defend them against an enemy, by means of moats, ramparts, parapets and other bulwarks. *Encyc.*

3. The works erected to defend a place against attack.

4. A fortified place; a fort; a castle.

5. Additional strength.

FOR'TIFIER, *n.* One who erects works for defense. *Carew.*

2. One who strengthens, supports and upholds; that which strengthens. *Sidney.*

FOR'TIFY, *v. t.* [Fr. *fortifier*; Sp. *fortificar*; It. *fortificare.*]

1. To surround with a wall, ditch, palisades or other works, with a view to defend against the attacks of an enemy; to strengthen and secure by forts, batteries and other works of art; as, to *fortify* a city, town or harbor.

2. To strengthen against any attack; as, to *fortify* the mind against sudden calamity.

3. To confirm; to add strength and firmness to; as, to *fortify* an opinion or resolution; to *fortify* hope or desire.

4. To furnish with strength or means of resisting force, violence or assault.

FOR'TIFY, *v. i.* To raise strong places. *Milton.*

FORTILAGE, *n.* A little fort; a block-house. [*Not used.*] *Spenser.*

FORTIN, *n.* [Fr.] A little fort; a field fort; a sconce. *Shak.*

FOR'TITUDE, *n.* [L. *fortitudo*, from *fortis*, strong.]

That strength or firmness of mind or soul which enables a person to encounter danger with coolness and courage, or to bear pain or adversity without murmuring, depression or despondency. Fortitude is the basis or source of genuine courage or intrepidity in danger, of patience in suffering, of forbearance under injuries, and of magnanimity in all conditions of life. We sometimes confound the effect with the cause, and use *fortitude* as synonymous with courage or patience; but *courage* is an active virtue or vice, and patience is the effect of *fortitude.*

> *Fortitude* is the guard and support of the other virtues. *Locke.*

FORTLET, *n.* A little fort.

FORT'NIGHT, *n. fort'nit.* [contracted from *fourteen nights*, our ancestors reckoning time by nights and winters; so also, *sevennights*, *sennight*, a week. Non dierum numerum, ut nos, sed noctium computant. *Tacitus.*] The space of fourteen days; two weeks.

FOR'TRESS, *n.* [Fr. *forteresse*; It. *fortezza*; from *fort*, *forte*, strong.]

1. Any fortified place; a fort; a castle; a strong hold; a place of defense or security. The English have a strong *fortress* on the rock of Gibraltar, or that rock is a *fortress.*

2. Defense; safety; security.

> The Lord is my rock, and my *fortress.* Ps. xviii.

FOR'TRESS, *v. t.* To furnish with fortresses; to guard; to fortify. *Shak.*

FOR'TRESSED, *a.* Defended by a fortress; protected; secured. *Spenser.*

FORTU'ITOUS, *a.* [L. *fortuitus*, from the root of *fors*, *forte*, *fortuna*; Fr. *fortuit*; It. Sp. *fortuito.* The primary sense is to come, to fall, to happen. See *Fare.*]

Accidental; casual; happening by chance; coming or occurring unexpectedly, or without any known cause. We speak of *fortuitous* events, when they occur without our foreseeing or expecting them, and of a *fortuitous* concourse of atoms, when we suppose the concourse not to result from the design and power of a controlling agent. But an event cannot be in fact *fortuitous.* [See *Accidental* and *Casual.*]

FORTU'ITOUSLY, *adv.* Accidentally; casually; by chance.

FORTU'ITOUSNESS, *n.* The quality of being accidental; accident; chance.

FOR'TUNATE, *a.* [L. *fortunatus.* See *Fortune.*]

Coming by good luck or favorable chance; bringing some unexpected good; as a *fortunate* event; a *fortunate* concurrence of circumstances; a *fortunate* ticket in a lottery.

2. Lucky; successful; receiving some unforeseen or unexpected good, or some good which was not dependent on one's own skill or efforts; as a *fortunate* adventurer in a lottery. I was most *fortunate* thus unexpectedly to meet my friend.

3. Successful; happy; prosperous; receiving or enjoying some good in consequence of efforts, but where the event was uncertain, and not absolutely in one's power. The brave man is usually *fortunate.* We say, a *fortunate* competitor for a fair lady, or for a crown.

FOR'TUNATELY, *adv.* Luckily; successfully; happily; by good fortune, or favorable chance or issue.

FOR'TUNATENESS, *n.* Good luck; success; happiness. *Sidney.*

FOR'TUNE, *n.* [Fr. from L. *fortuna*; Sp. and It. *fortuna*; Arm. *fortun*; from the root of Sax. *faran*, to go, or L. *fero* or *porto.* So in D. *gebeuren*, to happen, to fall, from the root of *bear*; *gebeurtenis*, an event. We find the same word in *opportunus*, [*ob-portunus*,] seasonable. The primary sense is an event, that which comes or befalls. So Fr. *heureux*, from *heure*, hour, that is, time, season, and L. *tempestivus.* See *Hour* and *Time.* The Russ. *pora*, time, season, is of this family, and *fortune* is closely allied to it.]

1. Properly, chance; accident; luck; the arrival of something in a sudden or unexpected manner. Hence the heathens deified chance, and consecrated temples and altars to the goddess. Hence the modern use of the word, for a power supposed to distribute the lots of life, according to her own humor.

> Though *fortune's* malice overthrow my state. *Shak.*

2. The good or ill that befalls man.

> In you the *fortune* of Great Britain lies. *Dryden.*

3. Success, good or bad; event.

> Our equal crimes shall equal *fortune* give. *Dryden.*

4. The chance of life; means of living; wealth.

> His father dying, he was driven to London to seek his *fortune.* *Swift.*

5. Estate; possessions; as a gentleman of small *fortune.*

6. A large estate; great wealth. This is often the sense of the word standing alone or unqualified; as a gentleman or lady of *fortune.* To the ladies we say, beware of *fortune*-hunters.

7. The portion of a man or woman; generally of a woman.

8. Futurity; future state or events; destiny. The young are anxious to have their *fortunes* told.

> You who men's *fortunes* in their faces read. *Cowley.*

FOR'TUNE, *v. t.* To make fortunate. [*Not used.*] *Chaucer.*

2. To dispose fortunately or not; also, to presage. *Obs.* *Dryden.*

FOR'TUNE, *v. i.* To befall; to fall out; to happen; to come casually to pass.

> It *fortuned* the same night that a christian serving a Turk in the camp, secretly gave the watchmen warning. *Knolles.*

FOR'TUNEBOOK, *n.* A book to be consulted to discover future events. *Crashaw.*

FOR'TUNED, *a.* Supplied by fortune. *Shak.*

FOR'TUNE-HUNTER, *n.* A man who seeks to marry a woman with a large portion, with a view to enrich himself. *Addison.*

FOR'TUNELESS, *a.* Luckless; also, destitute of a fortune or portion.

FOR'TUNETELL, *v. t.* To tell or pretend to tell the future events of one's life; to reveal futurity. *Shak.*

FOR'TUNETELLER, *n.* One who tells or pretends to foretell the events of one's life; an impostor who deceives people by pretending to a knowledge of future events.

FOR'TUNETELLING, *ppr.* Telling the future events of one's life.

FOR'TUNETELLING, *n.* The act or practice of foretelling the future fortune or events of one's life, which is a punishable crime.

FOR'TUNIZE, *v. t.* To regulate the fortune of. [*Not in use.*] *Spenser.*

FOR'TY, *a.* [Sax. *feowertig*; *feower*, four, and *tig*, ten. See *Four.*]

1. Four times ten.

2. An indefinite number; *a colloquial use.* A, B and C, and *forty* more. *Swift.*

FO'RUM, *n.* [L. See *Fair.*] In *Rome*, a public place, where causes were judicially tried, and orations delivered to the people; also, a market place. Hence,

2. A tribunal; a court; any assembly empowered to hear and decide causes; also, jurisdiction.

FORWANDER, *v. i.* To wander away; to rove wildly. [*Not used.*] *Spenser.*

FOR'WARD, *adv.* [Sax. *forweard*; *for*, *fore*, and *weard*, turned, L. *versus*; directed to the forepart. *Forwards* is also used, but it is a corruption.]

Toward a part or place before or in front; onward; progressively; opposed to *backward.* Go *forward*; move *forward.* He ran backward and *forward.*

In a ship, *forward* denotes toward the forepart.

FOR'WARD, *a.* Near or at the forepart; in advance of something else; as the *forward* gun in a ship, or the *forward* ship in a fleet; the *forward* horse in a team.

2. Ready; prompt; strongly inclined.

Only they would that we should remember the poor; the same which I also was *forward* to do. Gal. ii.

3. Ardent; eager; earnest; violent.

Or lead the *forward* youth to noble war. *Prior.*

4. Bold; confident; less reserved or modest than is proper; *in an ill sense;* as, the boy is too *forward* for his years.

5. Advanced beyond the usual degree; advanced for the season. The grass or the grain is *forward*, or *forward* for the season; we have a *forward* spring.

6. Quick; hasty; too ready. Be not *forward* to speak in public. Prudence directs that we be not too *forward* to believe current reports.

7. Anterior; fore.

Let us take the instant by the *forward* top. *Shak.*

8. Advanced; not behindhand. *Shak.*

FOR'WARD, *v. t.* To advance; to help onward; to promote; as, to *forward* a good design.

2. To accelerate; to quicken; to hasten; as, to *forward* the growth of a plant; to *forward* one in improvement.

3. To send forward; to send towards the place of destination; to transmit; as, to *forward* a letter or dispatches.

FOR'WARDED, *pp.* Advanced; promoted; aided in progress; quickened; sent onward; transmitted.

FOR'WARDER, *n.* He that promotes, or advances in progress.

FOR'WARDING, *ppr.* Advancing; promoting; aiding in progress; accelerating in growth; sending onwards; transmitting.

FOR'WARDLY, *adv.* Eagerly; hastily; quickly. *Atterbury.*

FOR'WARDNESS, *n.* Cheerful readiness; promptness. It expresses more than *willingness.* We admire the *forwardness* of christians in propagating the gospel.

2. Eagerness; ardor. It is sometimes difficult to restrain the *forwardness* of youth.

3. Boldness; confidence; assurance; want of due reserve or modesty.

In France it is usual to bring children into company, and cherish in them, from their infancy, a kind of *forwardness* and assurance. *Addison.*

4. A state of advance beyond the usual degree; as the *forwardness* of spring or of corn.

FORWA'STE, *v. t.* To waste; to desolate. [*Not in use.*] *Spenser.*

FORWE'ARY, *v. t.* To dispirit. [*Not in use.*] *Spenser.*

FORWEE'P, *v. i.* To weep much. *Chaucer.*

FOR'WŎRD, *n.* [*fore* and *word.*] A promise. [*Not in use.*] *Spenser.*

FOSS, *n.* [Fr. *fosse;* Sp. *fosa;* L. It. *fossa;* from *fossus, fodio,* to dig. Class Bd.]

1. A ditch or moat; *a word used in fortification.*

2. In *anatomy,* a kind of cavity in a bone, with a large aperture. *Encyc.*

FOS'SIL, *a.* [Fr. *fossile;* Sp. *fosil;* It. *fossile;* L. *fossilis,* from *fodio, fossus,* to dig.]

1. Dug out of the earth; as *fossil* coal; *fossil* salt. The term *fossil* is now usually appropriated to those inorganic substances, which have become penetrated by earthy or metallic particles. Thus we say, *fossil* shells, *fossil* bones, *fossil* wood. *Cleaveland.*

2. That may be taken from the earth by digging.

FOS'SIL, *n.* A substance dug from the earth, or penetrated with earthy or metallic particles.

Fossils are *native* or *extraneous.* *Native fossils* are minerals, properly so called, as earths, salts, combustibles and metallic bodies. *Extraneous fossils* are bodies of vegetable or animal origin accidentally buried in the earth, as plants, shells, bones and other substances, many of which are petrified. *Encyc.*

FOSSIL-COPAL, *n.* Highgate resin; a resinous substance found in perforating the bed of blue clay at Highgate, near London. It appears to be a true vegetable gum or resin, partly changed by remaining in the earth. *Cyc. Aikin.*

FOS'SILIST, *n.* One who studies the nature and properties of fossils; one who is versed in the science of fossils. *Black.*

FOSSILIZA'TION, *n.* The act or process of converting into a fossil or petrifaction. *Journ. of Science.*

FOS'SILIZE, *v. t.* To convert into a fossil; as, to *fossilize* bones or wood. *Ibm.*

FOS'SILIZE, *v. i.* To become or be changed into a fossil.

FOS'SILIZED, *pp.* Converted into a fossil.

FOS'SILIZING, *ppr.* Changing into a fossil.

FOSSIL'OGY, *n.* [*fossil,* and Gr. λογος, discourse.]

A discourse or treatise on fossils; also, the science of fossils.

FOSS'ROAD, } *n.* A Roman military way
FOSS'WAY, } in England, leading from Totness through Exeter to Barton on the Humber; so called from the ditches on each side. *Encyc.*

FOS'TER, *v. t.* [Sax. *fostrian,* from *foster,* a nurse or food; Sw. and Dan. *foster,* a child, one fed; Dan. *fostrer,* to nurse. I suspect this word to be from *food,* quasi, *foodster,* for this is the D. word, *voedster,* a nurse, from *voeden,* to feed; D. *voedsterheer,* a foster-father.]

1. To feed; to nourish; to support; to bring up.

Some say that ravens *foster* forlorn children. *Shak.*

3. To cherish; to forward; to promote growth. The genial warmth of spring *fosters* the plants.

3. To cherish; to encourage; to sustain and promote; as, to *foster* passion or genius.

FOS'TER, *v. i.* To be nourished or trained up together. *Spenser.*

FOS'TERAGE, *n.* The charge of nursing. *Raleigh.*

FOS'TER-BRŎTHER, *n.* A male nursed at the same breast, or fed by the same nurse.

FOS'TER-CHILD, *n.* A child nursed by a woman not the mother, or bred by a man not the father. *Addison.*

FOS'TER-DAM, *n.* A nurse; one that performs the office of a mother by giving food to a child. *Dryden.*

FOS'TER-EARTH, *n.* Earth by which a plant is nourished, though not its native soil. *Philips.*

FOS'TERED, *pp.* Nourished; cherished; promoted.

FOS'TERER, *n.* A nurse; one that feeds and nourishes in the place of parents. *Davies.*

FOS'TER-F'ATHER, *n.* One who takes the place of a father in feeding and educating a child. *Bacon.*

FOS'TERING, *ppr.* Nursing; cherishing; bringing up.

FOS'TERING, *n.* The act of nursing, nourishing and cherishing.

2. Nourishment. *Chaucer.*

FOS'TERLING, *n.* A fosterchild. *B. Jonson.*

FOS'TERMENT, *n.* Food; nourishment. [*Not used.*]

FOS'TER-MŎTHER, *n.* A nurse.

FOS'TER-NURSE, *n.* A nurse. [*Tautological.*]

FOS'TER-SISTER, *n.* A female nursed by the same person. *Swift.*

FOS'TER-SŎN, *n.* One fed and educated, like a son, though not a son by birth. *Dryden.*

FOS'TRESS, *n.* A female who feeds and cherishes; a nurse. *B. Jonson.*

FOTH'ER, *n.* [G. *fuder,* a tun or load; D. *voeder;* Sax. *fother,* food, fodder, and a mass of lead, from the sense of stuffing, crowding. See *Food.*]

A weight of lead containing eight pigs, and every pig twenty one stone and a half. But the *fother* is of different weights. With the plumbers in London it is nineteen hundred and a half, and at the mines, it is twenty two hundred and a half. *Encyc.*

FOTH'ER, *v. t.* [from stuffing. See the preceding word.]

To endeavor to stop a leak in the bottom of a ship, while afloat, by letting down a sail by the corners, and putting chopped yarn, oakum, wool, cotton, &c. between it and the ship's sides. These substances are sometimes sucked into the cracks and the leak stopped. *Mar. Dict.*

FOTH'ERING, *ppr.* Stopping leaks, as above.

FOTH'ERING, *n.* The operation of stopping leaks in a ship, as above.

FÖUG'ADE, *n.* [Fr. *fougade;* Sp. *fogada;* from L. *focus.*]

In *the art of war,* a little mine, in the form of a well, 8 or 10 feet wide, and 10 or 12 deep, dug under some work, fortification or post, charged with sacks of powder and covered with stones or earth, for destroying the works by explosion. *Encyc.*

FOUGHT, *pret.* and *pp.* of *fight;* pron. *faut.* [See *Fight.*]

FOUGHTEN, for *fought.* *Obs.*

FOUL, *a.* [Sax. *ful, faul;* D. *vuil;* G. *faul;* Dan. *fœl.* In Ch. with a prefix, נבל nabail, to defile. The Syr. with a different prefix, ܛܦܠ tafel, to *defile.* It coincides in elements with *full*, and probably the primary sense of both is to put or throw on, or to stuff, to crowd. See the signification of the word in seamen's language.]

1. Covered with or containing extraneous matter which is injurious, noxious or offensive; filthy; dirty; not clean; as a *foul* cloth; *foul* hands; a *foul* chimney.

My face is *foul* with weeping. Job xvi.

2. Turbid; thick; muddy; as *foul* water; a *foul* stream.
3. Impure; polluted; as a *foul* mouth. *Shak.*
4. Impure; scurrilous; obscene or profane; as *foul* words; *foul* language.
5. Cloudy and stormy; rainy or tempestuous; as *foul* weather.
6. Impure; defiling; as a *foul* disease.
7. Wicked; detestable; abominable; as a *foul* deed; a *foul* spirit.

Babylon—the hold of every *foul* spirit. Rev. xviii.

8. Unfair; not honest; not lawful or according to established rules or customs; as *foul* play.
9. Hateful; ugly; loathsome.

Hast thou forgot
The *foul* witch Sycorax. *Shak.*

10. Disgraceful; shameful; as a *foul* defeat.

Who first seduced them to that *foul* revolt? *Milton.*

11. Coarse; gross.

They are all for rank and *foul* feeding. *Felton.*

12. Full of gross humors or impurities.

You perceive the body of our kingdom,
How *foul* it is. *Shak.*

13. Full of weeds; as, the garden is very *foul*.
14. Among *seamen*, entangled; hindered from motion; opposed to *clear*; as, a rope is *foul*.
15. Covered with weeds or barnacles; as, the ship has a *foul* bottom.
16. Not fair; contrary; as a *foul* wind.
17. Not favorable or safe; dangerous; as a *foul* road or bay.

To fall foul, is to rush on with haste, rough force and unseasonable violence.

2. To run against; as, the ship fell *foul* of her consort.

These latter phrases show that this word is allied to the Fr. *fouler*, Eng. *full*, the sense of which is to press.

FOUL, *v. t.* [Sax. *fulian*, *gefylan*.] To make filthy; to defile; to daub; to dirty; to bemire; to soil; as, to *foul* the clothes; to *foul* the face or hands. Ezek. xxxiv. 18.

FOUL'DER, *v. i.* To emit great heat. [*Not used.*] *Spenser.*

FOUL'ED, *pp.* Defiled; dirtied.

FOUL'FACED, *a.* Having an ugly or hateful visage. *Shak.*

FOULFEE'DING, *a.* Gross; feeding grossly. *Hall.*

FOUL'ING, *ppr.* Making foul; defiling.

FOUL'LY, *adv.* Filthily; nastily; hatefully; scandalously; disgracefully; shamefully.

I *foully* wronged him; do, forgive me, do. *Gay.*

2. Unfairly; not honestly.

Thou play'dst most *foully* for it. Shak.

FOUL'MOUTHED, *a.* Using language scurrilous, opprobrious, obscene or profane; uttering abuse, or profane or obscene words; accustomed to use bad language.

So *foulmouthed* a witness never appeared in any cause. *Addison.*

FOUL'NESS, *n.* The quality of being foul or filthy; filthiness; defilement.

2. The quality or state of containing or being covered with any thing extraneous which is noxious or offensive; as the *foulness* of a cellar, or of a well; the *foulness* of a musket; the *foulness* of a ship's bottom.
3. Pollution; impurity.

There is not so chaste a nation as this, nor so free from all pollution or *foulness*. *Bacon.*

4. Hatefulness; atrociousness; as the *foulness* of a deed.
5. Ugliness; deformity.

The *foulness* of th' infernal form to hide. *Dryden.*

6. Unfairness; dishonesty; want of candor.

Piety is opposed to hypocrisy and insincerity, and all falseness or *foulness* of intentions. *Hammond.*

FOUL'SPOKEN, *a.* Slanderous. *Shak.*

2. Using profane, scurrilous or obscene language.

FOU'MART, *n.* [Scot. *foumarte*. Qu. *foulmartin*.] The polecat.

FOUND, *pret.* and *pp.* of *find*.

I am *found* of them that sought me not. Is. lxv.

FOUND, *v. t.* [L. *fundo*, *fundare*; Fr. *fonder*; It. *fondare*; Sp. *fundar*; Ir. *bun*, stump, bottom, stock, origin; *bunadhu*, *bunait*, foundation. If *n* is radical in *found*, as I suppose, it seems to be the Ar. بَنَى Heb. Ch. בנה to build, that is, to set, found, erect. Class Bn. No. 7.]

1. To lay the basis of any thing; to set, or place, as on something solid for support.

It fell not, for it was *founded* on a rock. Matt. vii.

2. To begin and build; to lay the foundation, and raise a superstructure; as, to *found* a city.
3. To set or place; to establish, as on something solid or durable; as, to *found* a government on principles of liberty.
4. To begin; to form or lay the basis; as, to *found* a college or a library. Sometimes to endow is equivalent to *found*.
5. To give birth to; to originate; as, to *found* an art or a family.
6. To set; to place; to establish on a basis. Christianity is *founded* on the rock of ages. Dominion is sometimes *founded* on conquest; sometimes on choice or voluntary consent.

Power, *founded* on contract, can descend only to him who has right by that contract. *Locke.*

7. To fix firmly.

I had else been perfect,
Whole as the marble, *founded* as the rock. *Shak.*

FOUND, *v. t.* [L. *fundo*, *fudi*, *fusum*; Fr. *fondre*; Sp. *fundir*, or *hundir*; It. *fondere*. The elements are probably *Fd*; *n* being adventitious.]

To cast; to form by melting a metal and pouring it into a mold. *Milton.*

[This verb is seldom used, but the derivative *foundery* is in common use. For *found* we use *cast*.]

FOUNDA'TION, *n.* [L. *fundatio*; Fr. *fondation*; from L. *fundo*.]

1. The basis of an edifice; that part of a building which lies on the ground; usually a wall of stone which supports the edifice.
2. The act of fixing the basis. *Tickel.*
3. The basis or ground-work, of any thing; that on which any thing stands, and by which it is supported. A free government has its *foundation* in the choice and consent of the people to be governed. Christ is the *foundation* of the church.

Behold, I lay in Zion for a *foundation*, a stone—a precious corner-stone. Is. xxviii.

Other *foundation* can no man lay than that which is laid, which is Jesus Christ. 1 Cor. iii.

4. Original; rise; as the *foundation* of the world.
5. Endowment; a donation or legacy appropriated to support an institution, and constituting a permanent fund, usually for a charitable purpose.
6. Establishment; settlement.

FOUNDA'TIONLESS, *a.* Having no foundation. *Hammond.*

FOUND'ED, *pp.* Set; fixed; established on a basis; begun and built.

FOUND'ER, *n.* One that founds, establishes and erects; one that lays a foundation; as the *founder* of a temple or city.

2. One who begins; an author; one from whom any thing originates; as the *founder* of a sect of philosophers; the *founder* of a family or race.
3. One who endows; one who furnishes a permanent fund for the support of an institution; as the *founder* of a college or hospital.
4. [Fr. *fondeur*.] A caster; one who casts metals in various forms; as a *founder* of cannon, bells, hardware, printing types, &c.

FOUND'ER, *v. i.* [Fr. *fondre*, to melt, to fall.]

1. In *seamen's language*, to fill or be filled and sink, as a ship.
2. To fail: to miscarry. *Shak.*
3. To trip; to fall. *Chaucer.*

FOUND'ER, *v. t.* To cause internal inflammation and great soreness in the feet of a horse, so as to disable or lame him. *Encyc.*

FOUND'ERED, *pp.* Made lame in the feet by inflammation and extreme tenderness.

FOUND'EROUS, *a.* Failing; liable to perish; ruinous. [*Not in use.*] *Burke.*

FOUND'ERY, *n.* [Fr. *fonderie*.] The art of casting metals into various forms for use; the casting of statues.

2. The house and works occupied in casting metals; as a *foundery* of bells, of hollow ware, of cannon, of types, &c.

FOUND'LING, *n.* [from *found*, *find*.] A deserted or exposed infant; a child found without a parent or owner. A hospital for such children is called a *foundling hospital*.

FOUND'RESS, *n.* A female founder; a woman who founds or establishes, or who endows with a fund.

FOUNT', **FOUNT'AIN**, *n.* [L. *fons*; Fr. *fontaine*; Sp. *fuente*; It. *fonte*, *fontana*; W. *fynnon*, a fountain or source; *fyniaw*, *fynu*, to produce, to generate, to abound; *fwn*, a source, breath, puff; *fwnt*, produce.]

1. A spring, or source of water; properly, a spring or issuing of water from the earth. This word accords in sense with *well*, in our mother tongue; but we now distinguish them, applying *fountain* to a natural spring of water, and *well* to an artificial pit of water, issuing from the interior of the earth.
2. A small basin of springing water. *Taylor.*
3. A jet; a spouting of water; an artificial spring. *Bacon.*
4. The head or source of a river. *Dryden.*
5. Original; first principle or cause; the source of any thing.

Almighty God, the *fountain* of all goodness. *Common Prayer.*

Fount of types. [See *Font.*]

FOUNT'AIN-HEAD, *n.* Primary source; original; first principle. *Young.*

FOUNT'AINLESS, *a.* Having no fountain; wanting a spring.

A barren desert *fountainless* and dry. *Milton.*

FOUNT'AIN-TREE, *n.* In the Canary isles, a tree which distills water from its leaves, in sufficient abundance for the inhabitants near it. *Encyc.*

FOUNT'FUL, *a.* Full of springs; as *fountful* Ida. *Chapman.*

FOUR, *a.* [Sax. *feower*; G. *vier*; D. *vier*; Sw. *fyra*; Dan. *fire*. I suspect this word to be contracted from Goth. *fidwor*, W. *pedwar*, Arm. *pevar*, *peder* or *petor*, *peoar*, from which L. *petoritum*, *petorritum*, a carriage with four wheels, *petor-rota*.]

Twice two; denoting the sum of two and two.

FÔURBE, *n.* [Fr.] A tricking fellow; a cheat. [*Not English.*] *Denham.*

FÔURFOLD, *a.* Four double; quadruple; four times told; as a *fourfold* division.

He shall restore the lamb *fourfold.* 2 Sam. xii.

FÔURFOLD, *n.* Four times as much.

FÔURFOOTED, *a.* Quadruped; having four feet; as the horse and the ox.

FÔURRIER, *n.* [Fr.] A harbinger. [*Not English.*] *Buck.*

FÔURSCORE, *a.* [See *Score.*] Four times twenty; eighty. It is used elliptically for fourscore years; as a man of *fourscore.* *Temple.*

FÔURSQUARE, *a.* Having four sides and four angles equal; quadrangular. *Raleigh.*

FÔURTEEN, *a.* [*four* and *ten*; Sax. *feowertyn.*] Four and ten; twice seven.

FÔURTEENTH, *a.* The ordinal of fourteen; the fourth after the tenth.

FÔURTH, *a.* The ordinal of four; the next after the third.

FÔURTH, *n.* In *music*, an interval composed of two tones and a semitone. Three full tones compose a triton, or fourth redundant.

FÔURTHLY, *adv.* In the fourth place.

FÔURWHEELED, *a.* Having or running on four wheels.

FOVIL'LA, *n.* [L. *foveo.*] A fine substance, imperceptible to the naked eye, emitted from the pollen of flowers. *Martyn.*

FOWL, *n.* [Sax. *fugel*, *fugl*; G. and D. *vogel*; Dan. *fugl*; Sw. *fogel*; from the root of the L. *fugio*, *fugo*, Gr. φευγω, and signifying the flying animal.]

A flying or winged animal; the generic name of certain animals that move through the air by the aid of wings. Fowls have two feet, are covered with fethers, and have wings for flight. *Bird* is a young fowl or chicken, and may well be applied to the smaller species of fowls. But it has usurped the place of *fowl*, and is used improperly as the generic term.

Fowl is used as a collective noun. We dined on fish and *fowl.*

Let them have dominion over the fish of the sea, and over the *fowl* of the air. Gen. i.

But this use in America is not frequent. We generally use the plural, *fowls.* The word is colloquially used for poultry, or rather, in a more limited sense, for barn-door fowls.

FOWL, *v. i.* To catch or kill wild fowls for game or food; as by means of bird-lime, decoys, nets and snares, or by pursuing them with hawks, or by shooting.

FOWL'ER, *n.* A sportsman who pursues wild fowls, or takes or kills them for food.

FOWL'ING, *ppr.* Pursuing or taking wild fowls.

FOWL'ING, *n.* The art or practice of catching or shooting fowls; also, falconry.

FOWL'INGPIECE, *n.* A light gun for shooting fowls.

FOX, *n.* [Sax. *fox*; G. *fuchs*; D. *vos.*] An animal of the genus Canis, with a straight tail, yellowish or straw-colored hair, and erect ears. This animal burrows in the earth, is remarkable for his cunning, and preys on lambs, geese, hens or other small animals.

2. A sly, cunning fellow.
3. In *seaman's language*, a seizing made by twisting several rope-yarns together.
4. Formerly, a cant expression for a sword. *Shak.*

FOX, *v. t.* To intoxicate; to stupify. [*Not used.*] *Boyle.*

FOX'CASE, *n.* The skin of a fox. [*Not used.*] *L'Estrange.*

FOX'CHASE, *n.* The pursuit of a fox with hounds. *Pope.*

FOX'ERY, *n.* Behavior like that of a fox. [*Not in use.*] *Chaucer.*

FOX'EVIL, *n.* A kind of disease in which the hair falls off. *Dict.*

FOX'GLOVE, *n.* The name of a plant, the Digitalis.

FOX'HOUND, *n.* A hound for chasing foxes. *Shenstone.*

FOX'HUNT, *n.* The chase or hunting of a fox.

FOX'HUNTER, *n.* One who hunts or pursues foxes with hounds.

FOX'ISH, } *a.* Resembling a fox in qualities; cunning.
FOX'LIKE, }

FOX'SHIP, *n.* The character or qualities of a fox; cunning. *Shak.*

FOX'TAIL, *n.* A species of grass, the Alopecurus.

FOX'TRAP, *n.* A trap, or a gin or snare to catch foxes.

FOX'Y, *a.* Pertaining to foxes; wily. [*Not used.*]

FOY, *n.* [Fr. *foi.*] Faith. [*Not used.*] *Spenser.*

FRA'CAS, *n.* [Fr.] An uproar; a noisy quarrel; a disturbance.

FRACT, *v. t.* To break. [*Not used.*]

FRAC'TION, *n.* [L. *fractio*; Fr. *fraction*; from L. *frango*, *fractus*, to *break.* See *Break.*]

1. The act of breaking or state of being broken, especially by violence. *Burnet.*
2. In *arithmetic* and *algebra*, a broken part of an integral or integer; any division of a whole number or unit, as $\frac{2}{5}$, two fifths, $\frac{1}{4}$, one fourth, which are called *vulgar fractions.* In these, the figure above the line is called the *numerator*, and the figure below the line the *denominator.* In *decimal fractions*, the denominator is a unit, or 1, with as many cyphers annexed, as the numerator has places. They are commonly expressed by writing the numerator only, with a point before it by which it is separated from the whole number; thus .5, which denotes five tenths, $\frac{5}{10}$, or half the whole number; .25, that is, $\frac{25}{100}$, or a fourth part of the whole number.

FRAC'TIONAL, *a.* Belonging to a broken number; comprising a part or the parts of a unit; as *fractional* numbers.

FRAC'TIOUS, *a.* Apt to break out into a passion; apt to quarrel; cross; snappish; as a *fractious* man.

FRAC'TIOUSLY, *adv.* Passionately; snappishly.

FRAC'TIOUSNESS, *n.* A cross or snappish temper.

FRAC'TURE, *n.* [L. *fractura.* See *Break.*] A breach in any body, especially a breach caused by violence; a rupture of a solid body.

2. In *surgery*, the rupture or disruption of a bone. A fracture is *simple* or *compound*; *simple*, when the bone only is divided; *compound*, when the bone is broken, with a laceration of the integuments.
3. In *mineralogy*, the manner in which a mineral breaks, and by which its texture is displayed; as a *compact fracture*; a *fibrous fracture*; *foliated*, *striated* or *conchoidal fracture*, &c. *Kirwan.*

FRAC'TURE, *v. t.* To break; to burst asunder; to crack; to separate continuous parts; as, to *fracture* a bone; to *fracture* the skull. *Wiseman.*

FRAC'TURED, *pp.* Broken; cracked.

FRAC'TURING, *ppr.* Breaking; bursting asunder; cracking.

FRAG'ILE, *a.* [L. *fragilis*, from *frango*, to break.]

1. Brittle; easily broken.

The stalk of ivy is tough, and not *fragile.* *Bacon.*

2. Weak; liable to fail; easily destroyed; as *fragile* arms. *Milton.*

FRAGIL'ITY, *n.* Brittleness; easiness to be broken. *Bacon.*

2. Weakness; liableness to fail. *Knolles.*
3. Frailty; liableness to fault. *Wotton.*

FRAG'MENT, *n.* [L. *fragmentum*, from *frango*, to break.]

1. A part broken off; a piece separated from any thing by breaking.

Gather up the *fragments* that remain, that nothing be lost. John vi.

2. A part separated from the rest; an imperfect part; as *fragments* of ancient writings.
3. A small detached portion; as *fragments* of time. *Franklin.*

FRAG'MENTARY, *a.* Composed of fragments. *Donne.*

FRA'GOR, *n.* [L. See *Break.*] A loud and sudden sound; the report of any thing bursting; a loud harsh sound; a crash.

2. A strong or sweet scent. *Obs.*

FRA'GRANCE, } *n.* [L. *fragrantia*, from
FRA'GRANCY, } *fragro*, to smell strong. Ar. أَرِجَ to emit or diffuse odor. The Arabic is without a prefix, and the word belongs probably to the great family of *reach, stretch.*]

Sweetness of smell; that quality of bodies which affects the olfactory nerves with an agreeable sensation; pleasing scent; grateful odor.

> Eve separate he spies,
> Vailed in a cloud of *fragrance*— *Milton.*
> The goblet crown'd,
> Breathed aromatic *fragrancies* around. *Pope.*

FRA'GRANT, *a.* Sweet of smell; odorous.

> *Fragrant* the fertile earth
> After soft showers. *Milton.*

FRA'GRANTLY, *adv.* With sweet scent. *Mortimer.*

FRAIL, *a.* [supposed to be from Fr. *frêle*, It. *frale.* Qu. L. *fragilis*, or from a different root.]

1. Weak; infirm; liable to fail and decay; subject to casualties; easily destroyed; perishable; not firm or durable.

> That I may know how *frail* I am. Ps. xxxix.

2. Weak in mind or resolution; liable to error or deception.

> Man is *frail*, and prone to evil. *Taylor.*

3. Weak; easily broken or overset; as a *frail* bark.

FRAIL, *n.* [Norm. *fraile.*] A basket made of rushes.

2. A rush for weaving baskets. *Johnson.*

3. A certain quantity of raisins, about 75 pounds. *Encyc.*

FRA'ILNESS, *n.* Weakness; infirmity; as the *frailness* of the body.

FRA'ILTY, *n.* Weakness of resolution; infirmity; liableness to be deceived or seduced.

> God knows our *frailty*, and pities our weakness. *Locke.*

2. Frailness; infirmity of body.

3. Fault proceeding from weakness; foible; sin of infirmity; in this sense it has a plural.

FRAISCHEUR, *n.* [Fr.] Freshness; coolness. [*Not English.*] *Dryden.*

FRAISE, *n.* [Fr. from It. *fregio*, ornament, frieze.]

1. In *fortification*, a defense consisting of pointed stakes driven into the retrenchments, parallel to the horizon. *Encyc.*

2. A pancake with bacon in it. *Obs.* *Johnson.*

FRAME, *v. t.* [Sax. *fremman*, to frame, to effect or perform; Arm. *framma*, to join; D. *raam*, a frame, G. *rahm*, a frame and cream; Dan. *rame*; Sw. *ram*; Russ. *rama.* Qu. Class Rm. No. 6. In Russ. *rama* is a *frame*, and *ramo*, the shoulder, L. *armus*, Eng. *arm.*]

1. To fit or prepare and unite several parts in a regular structure or entire thing; to fabricate by orderly construction and union of various parts; as, to *frame* a house or other building.

2. To fit one thing to another; to adjust; to make suitable. *Abbot.*

3. To make; to compose; as, to *frame* a law.

> For thou art *framed* of the firm truth of valor. *Shak.*

4. To regulate; to adjust; to shape; to conform; as, to *frame* our lives according to the rules of the gospel.

5. To form and digest by thought; as, to *frame* ideas in the mind.

> How many excellent reasonings are *framed* in the mind of a man of wisdom and study in a length of years! *Watts.*

6. To contrive; to plan; to devise; as, to *frame* a project or design.

7. To invent; to fabricate; *in a bad sense*; as, to *frame* a story or lie.

FRAME, *v. i.* To contrive. Judges xii. 6.

FRAME, *n.* The timbers of an edifice fitted and joined in the form proposed, for the purpose of supporting the covering; as the *frame* of a house, barn, bridge or ship.

2. Any fabric or structure composed of parts united; as the *frame* of an ox or horse. So we say, the *frame* of the heavenly arch; the *frame* of the world. *Hooker. Tillotson.*

3. Any kind of case or structure made for admitting, inclosing or supporting things; as the *frame* of a window, door, picture or looking glass.

4. Among *printers*, a stand to support the cases in which the types are distributed.

5. Among *founders*, a kind of ledge, inclosing a board, which being filled with wet sand, serves as a mold for castings. *Encyc.*

6. A sort of loom on which linen, silk, &c. is stretched for quilting or embroidering. *Encyc.*

7. Order; regularity; adjusted series or composition of parts. We say, a person is out of *frame*; the mind is not in a good *frame.*

> Your steady soul preserves her *frame.* *Swift.*

8. Form; scheme; structure; constitution; system; as a *frame* of government.

9. Contrivance; projection.

> John the bastard,
> Whose spirits toil in *frame* of villainies. *Shak.*

10. Shape; form; proportion. *Hudibras.*

FRA'MEWORK, *n.* Work done in a frame. *Milton.*

FRA'MED, *pp.* Fitted and united in due form; made; composed; devised; adjusted.

FRA'MER, *n.* One who frames; a maker; a contriver.

FRA'MING, *ppr.* Fitting and joining in due construction; making; fabricating; composing; adjusting; inventing; contriving.

FRAM'POLD, *a.* Peevish; rugged. [*Low and not in use.*] *Hacket.*

FRAN'CHISE, *n.* *fran'chiz.* [Fr. from *franc*, free; It. *franchezza*; Sp. Port. *franqueza.* See *Frank.*] Properly, liberty, freedom. Hence,

1. A particular privilege or right granted by a prince or sovereign to an individual, or to a number of persons; as the right to be a body corporate with perpetual succession; the right to hold a court leet or other court; to have waifs, wrecks, treasure-treve, or forfeitures. So the right to vote for governor, senators and representatives, is a *franchise* belonging to citizens, and not enjoyed by aliens. The right to establish a bank, is a *franchise.*

2. Exemption from a burden or duty to which others are subject.

3. The district or jurisdiction to which a particular privilege extends; the limits of an immunity. *Spenser.*

4. An asylum or sanctuary, where persons are secure from arrest.

> Churches and monasteries in Spain are *franchises* for criminals. *Encyc.*

FRAN'CHISE, *v. t.* To make free; but *enfranchise* is more generally used. *Shak.*

FRAN'CHISEMENT, *n.* Release from burden or restriction; freedom. *Spenser.*

FRAN'CIC, *a.* Pertaining to the Franks or French.

FRANCIS'CAN, *a.* Belonging to the order of St. Francis.

FRANCIS'CAN, *n.* One of the order of St. Francis; an order of monks founded by him in 1209. They are called also *Gray Friars.*

FRANGIBIL'ITY, *n.* The state or quality of being frangible.

FRAN'GIBLE, *a.* [from L. *frango*, to break.] That may be broken; brittle; fragile; easily broken. *Boyle.*

FRAN'ION, *n.* A paramour, or a boon companion. [*Not used.*] *Spenser.*

FRANK, *a.* [Fr. *franc*; It. Sp. *franco*; G. *frank*; D. *vrank.* Qu. Ar. فَرَغَ to free. Class Br. No. 36. or Class Brg. No. 5. 6. 7. 8. *Free* and *frank* may be from the same root or family, for *free* in Saxon is *frigan*, coinciding in elements with *break*, and the nasal sound of *g* would give *frank.* The French *franchir* gives the sense of *breaking out* or *over limits.*]

1. Open; ingenuous; candid; free in uttering real sentiments; not reserved; using no disguise. Young persons are usually *frank*; old persons are more reserved.

2. Open; ingenuous; as a *frank* disposition or heart.

3. Liberal; generous; not niggardly. [*This sense is now rare.*] *Bacon.*

4. Free; without conditions or compensation; as a *frank* gift.

5. Licentious; unrestrained. [*Not used.*] *Spenser.*

FRANK, } *n.* An ancient coin of France.
FRANC, } The value of the gold frank was something more than that of the gold crown. The silver franc was in value a third of the gold one. The gold coin is no longer in circulation. The present *franc* or frank, is a silver coin of the value nearly of nineteen cents, or ten pence sterling.

2. A letter which is exempted from postage; or the writing which renders it free.

3. A sty for swine. [*Not used.*] *Shak.*

FRANK, *n.* A name given by the Turks, Greeks and Arabs to any of the inhabitants of the western parts of Europe, English, French, Italians, &c.

2. The people of Franconia in Germany.

FRANK, *v. t.* To exempt, as a letter from the charge of postage.

2. To shut up in a sty or frank. [*Not used.*] *Shak.*

3. To feed high; to cram; to fatten. [*Not used.*]

FRANKALMOIGNE, *n.* *frankalmoin'.* [*frank* and Norm. *almoignes*, alms.]

Free alms; in English law, a tenure by which a religious corporation holds lands to them and their successors forever, on condition of praying for the souls of the donor. *Blackstone.*

FRANK'CHASE, *n.* A liberty of free chase, whereby persons having lands within the compass of the same, are prohibited to cut down any wood, &c. out of the view of the forester. *Cowel.*

Free chase, is the liberty of keeping beasts of chase or royal game therein, protected even from the owner of the land himself, with a power of hunting them thereon. *Blackstone.*

FRANK'ED, *pp.* Exempted from postage.

FRANK'FEE, *n.* Freehold; a holding of lands in fee simple. *Encyc.*

FRANKIN'CENSE, *n.* [*frank* and *incense.*] A dry resinous substance in pieces or drops, of a pale yellowish white color, of a bitterish acrid taste, and very inflammable; used as a perfume. *Hill. Encyc.*

FRANK'ING, *ppr.* Exempting from postage.

FRANK'LAW, *n.* Free or common law, or the benefit a person has by it. *Encyc.*

FRANK'LIN, *n.* A freeholder. *Obs.* *Spenser.*

FRANK'LINITE, *n.* A mineral compound of iron, zink and manganese, found in New Jersey, and named from Dr. Franklin. *Cleaveland.*

FRANK'LY, *adv.* Openly; freely; ingenuously; without reserve, constraint or disguise; as, to confess one's faults *frankly.*

2. Liberally; freely; readily. Luke vii.

FRANK'MARRIAGE, *n.* A tenure in tail special; or an estate of inheritance given to a person, together with a wife, and descendible to the heirs of their two bodies begotten. *Blackstone.*

FRANK'NESS, *n.* Plainness of speech; candor; freedom in communication; openness; ingenuousness. He told me his opinions with *frankness.*

2. Fairness; freedom from art or craft; as *frankness* of dealing.

3. Liberality; bounteousness. [*Little used.*]

FRANK'PLEDGE, *n.* A pledge or surety for the good behavior of freemen. Anciently in England, a number of neighbors who were bound for each other's good behavior. *Encyc.*

FRANKTEN'EMENT, *n.* An estate of freehold; the possession of the soil by a freeman. *Blackstone.*

FRAN'TIC, *a.* [L. *phreneticus*; Gr. φρενητικος, from φρενιτις, delirium or raving, from φρην, mind, the radical sense of which is to rush, to drive forward. So *animus* signifies mind, soul, courage, spirit; and *anima* signifies soul, wind, breath.]

1. Mad; raving; furious; outrageous; wild and disorderly; distracted; as a *frantic* person; *frantic* with fear or grief.

2. Characterized by violence, fury and disorder; noisy; mad; wild; irregular; as the *frantic* rites of Bacchus.

FRAN'TICLY, *adv.* Madly; distractedly; outrageously.

FRAN'TICNESS, *n.* Madness; fury of passion; distraction.

FRAP, *v. t.* In *seamen's language*, to cross and draw together the several parts of a tackle to increase the tension. *Mar. Dict.*

FRATERN'AL, *a.* [Fr. *fraternel*; L. *fraternus*, from *frater*, brother.]

Brotherly; pertaining to brethren; becoming brothers; as *fraternal* love or affection; a *fraternal* embrace.

FRATERN'ALLY, *adv.* In a brotherly manner.

FRATERN'ITY, *n.* [L. *fraternitas.*] The state or quality of a brother; brotherhood.

2. A body of men associated for their common interest or pleasure; a company; a brotherhood; a society; as the *fraternity* of free masons.

3. Men of the same class, profession, occupation or character.

> With what terms of respect knaves and sots will speak of their own *fraternity*. *South.*

FRATERNIZA'TION, *n.* The act of associating and holding fellowship as brethren. *Burke.*

FRATERN'IZE, *v. i.* To associate or hold fellowship as brothers, or as men of like occupation or character.

FRAT'RICIDE, *n.* [L. *fratricidium*; *frater*, brother, and *cædo*, to kill.]

1. The crime of murdering a brother.

2. One who murders or kills a brother. *L. Addison.*

FRAUD, *n.* [L. *fraus*; Fr. Sp. It. Port. *fraude*. This agrees in elements with Sax. *bræd*, *bred*, fraud, which is contracted from *brægden*, fraud, guile, disguise; and *bræg* coincides with *brigue*. But I know not that these words are connected with the Latin *fraus*.]

Deceit; deception; trick; artifice by which the right or interest of another is injured; a stratagem intended to obtain some undue advantage; an attempt to gain or the obtaining of an advantage over another by imposition or immoral means, particularly deception in contracts, or bargain and sale, either by stating falsehoods, or suppressing truth.

> If success a lover's toil attends,
> Who asks if force or *fraud* obtained his ends. *Pope.*

FRAUD'FUL, *a.* Deceitful in making bargains; trickish; treacherous; *applied to persons.* *Shak.*

2. Containing fraud or deceit; *applied to things.* *Dryden.*

FRAUD'FULLY, *adv.* Deceitfully; with intention to deceive and gain an undue advantage; trickishly; treacherously; by stratagem.

FRAUD'ULENCE, } *n.* Deceitfulness; trick-
FRAUD'ULENCY, } ishness in making bargains, or in social concerns. *Hooker.*

FRAUD'ULENT, *a.* Deceitful in making contracts; trickish; *applied to persons.*

2. Containing fraud; founded on fraud; proceeding from fraud; as a *fraudulent* bargain.

3. Deceitful; treacherous; obtained or performed by artifice. *Milton.*

FRAUD'ULENTLY, *adv.* By fraud; by deceit; by artifice or imposition.

FRAUGHT, *a.* *fraut.* [D. *vragt*; G. *fracht*; Dan. *fragt*; Sw. *fracht*. A different orthography of *freight*, which see.]

1. Laden; loaded; charged; as a vessel richly *fraught* with goods from India. This sense is used in poetry; but in common business, *freighted* only is used.

2. Filled; stored; full; as a scheme *fraught* with mischief; the scriptures are *fraught* with excellent precepts. *Hooker.*

FRAUGHT, *n.* A freight; a cargo. [*Not now used.*] *Dryden.*

FRAUGHT, *v. t.* To load; to fill; to crowd. *Obs.* *Shak.*

FRAUGHT'AGE, *n.* Loading; cargo. [*Not used.*] *Shak.*

FRAY, *n.* [Fr. *fracas*, It. *fracasso*, a great crash, havoc, ruin; Fr. *fracasser*, It. *fracassare*, to break; coinciding with L. *fractura*, from *frango*. Under *Affray*, this is referred to Fr. *effrayer*, to fright, but incorrectly, unless *fright* is from the same root. In the sense of rubbing, fretting, this is from the L. *frico*, Sp. *fregar*. But *break*, *fright* and *frico*, all have the same radicals.]

1. A broil, quarrel or violent riot, that puts men in fear. This is the vulgar word for *affray*, and the sense seems to refer the word to Fr. *effrayer*.

2. A combat; a battle; also, a single combat or duel. *Pope.*

3. A contest; contention. *Milton.*

4. A rub; a fret or chafe in cloth; a place injured by rubbing. *Tatler.*

FRAY, *v. t.* To fright; to terrify. *Obs.* *Spenser. Bacon.*

FRAY, *v. t.* [Fr. *frayer*, L. *frico*, to rub.] To rub; to fret, as cloth by wearing.

2. To rub; as, a deer *frays* his head.

FRA'YED, *pp.* Frightened; rubbed; worn.

FRA'YING, *ppr.* Frightening; terrifying; rubbing.

FRA'YING, *n.* Peel of a deer's horn. *B. Jonson.*

FREAK, *n.* [Ice. *freka*. Qu. G. *frech*, bold, saucy, petulant; Dan. *frek*, id.; Scot. *frack*, active. The English word does not accord perfectly with the Ger. Dan. and Scot. But it is probably from the root of *break*, denoting a sudden start.]

1. Literally, a sudden starting or change of place. Hence,

2. A sudden causeless change or turn of the mind; a whim or fancy; a capricious prank.

> She is restless and peevish, and sometimes in a *freak* will instantly change her habitation. *Spectator.*

FREAK, *v. t.* [from the same root as the preceding, to *break*; W. *bryc*, Ir. *breac*, speckled, party-colored; like *pard*, from the Heb. פרד to divide.]

To variegate; to checker.

> —*Freaked* with many a mingled hue. *Thomson.*

FRE'AKISH, *a.* Apt to change the mind suddenly; whimsical; capricious.

> It may be a question, whether the wife or the woman was the more *freakish* of the two. *L'Estrange.*

FRE'AKISHLY, *adv.* Capriciously; with sudden change of mind, without cause.

FRE'AKISHNESS, *n.* Capriciousness; whimsicalness.

FRECK'LE, *n.* [from the same root as *freak*; W. *bryc*, Ir. *breac*, spotted, freckled; W. *brycu*, to freckle; from *breaking*, unless by a change of letters, it has been corrupted from G. *fleck*, D. *vlak* or *vlek*, Sw. *fläck*, Dan. *flek*, a spot; which is not probable.]

1. A spot of a yellowish color in the skin, particularly on the face, neck and hands. Freckles may be natural or produced by the action of the sun on the skin, or from the jaundice.

2. Any small spot or discoloration. *Evelyn.*

FRECK'LED, *a.* Spotted; having small yellowish spots on the skin or surface; as a *freckled* face or neck.

2. Spotted; as a *freckled* cowslip. *Shak.*

FRECK'LEDNESS, *n.* The state of being freckled. *Sherwood.*

FRECK'LEFACED, *a.* Having a face full of freckles. *Beaum.*

FRECK'LY, *a.* Full of freckles; sprinkled with spots.

FRED, Sax. *frith*, Dan. *fred*, Sw. *frid*, G. *friede*, D. *vreede*, peace; as in *Frederic*, dominion of peace, or rich in peace; *Winfred*, victorious peace. Our ancestors called a sanctuary, *fredstole*, a seat of peace.

FREE, *a.* [Sax. *frig*, *freoh*, free; *frigan*, *freogan*, to free; G. *frei*; D. *vry*; Dan. *fri*; Sw. *fri*; all contracted from *frig*, which corresponds with Heb. and Ch. פרק, Syr. ܦܪܩ, Sam. ࠐࠓࠒ, Ar. فرق faraka, to *break*, to separate, to divide, to free, to redeem, &c. See *Frank*.]

1. Being at liberty; not being under necessity or restraint, physical or moral; a word of general application to the body, the will or mind, and to corporations.

2. In *government*, not enslaved; not in a state of vassalage or dependence; subject only to fixed laws, made by consent, and to a regular administration of such laws; not subject to the arbitrary will of a sovereign or lord; as a *free* state, nation or people.

3. Instituted by a free people, or by consent or choice of those who are to be subjects, and securing private rights and privileges by fixed laws and principles; not arbitrary or despotic; as a *free* constitution or government.

> There can be no *free* government without a democratical branch in the constitution. *J. Adams.*

4. Not imprisoned, confined or under arrest; as, the prisoner is set *free*.

5. Unconstrained; unrestrained; not under compulsion or control. A man is *free* to pursue his own choice; he enjoys *free* will.

6. Permitted; allowed; open; not appropriated; as, places of honor and confidence are *free* to all; we seldom hear of a commerce perfectly *free*.

7. Not obstructed; as, the water has a *free* passage or channel; the house is open to a *free* current of air.

8. Licentious; unrestrained. The reviewer is very *free* in his censures.

9. Open; candid; frank; ingenuous; unreserved; as, we had a *free* conversation together.

> Will you be *free* and candid to your friend? *Otway.*

10. Liberal in expenses; not parsimonious; as a *free* purse; a man is *free* to give to all useful institutions.

11. Gratuitous; not gained by importunity or purchase. He made him a *free* offer of his services. It is a *free* gift. The salvation of men is of *free* grace.

12. Clear of crime or offense; guiltless; innocent.

> My hands are guilty, but my heart is *free*. *Dryden.*

13. Not having feeling or suffering; clear; exempt; with *from*; as *free from* pain or disease; *free from* remorse.

14. Not encumbered with; as *free* from a burden.

15. Open to all, without restriction or without expense; as a *free* school.

16. Invested with franchises; enjoying certain immunities; with *of*; as a man *free of* the city of London.

17. Possessing without vassalage or slavish conditions; as *free* of his farm. *Dryden.*

18. Liberated from the government or control of parents, or of a guardian or master. A son or an apprentice, when of age, is *free*.

19. Ready; eager; not dull; acting without spurring or whipping; as a *free* horse.

20. Genteel; charming. [*Not in use.*] *Chaucer.*

FREE, *v. t.* To remove from a thing any encumbrance or obstruction; to disengage from; to rid; to strip; to clear; as, to *free* the body from clothes; to *free* the feet from fetters; to *free* a channel from sand.

2. To set at liberty; to rescue or release from slavery, captivity or confinement; to loose. The prisoner is *freed* from arrest.

3. To disentangle; to disengage.

4. To exempt.

> He that is dead is *freed* from sin. Rom. vi.

5. To manumit; to release from bondage; as, to *free* a slave.

6. To clear from water, as a ship by pumping.

7. To release from obligation or duty.

To free from or *free of*, is to rid of, by removing, in any manner.

FREEBENCH', *n.* A widow's dower in a copyhold. *Blackstone.*

FREE'BOOTER, *n.* [D. *vrybuiter*; G. *freibeuter*. See *Booty*.] One who wanders about for plunder; a robber; a pillager; a plunderer. *Bacon.*

FREE'BOOTING, *n.* Robbery; plunder; a pillaging. *Spenser.*

FREE'BORN, *a.* Born free; not in vassalage; inheriting liberty.

FREECHAP'EL, *n.* In *England*, a chapel founded by the king and not subject to the jurisdiction of the ordinary. The king may also grant license to a subject to found such a chapel. *Cowel.*

Free city, in *Germany*, an imperial city, not subject to a prince, but governed by its own magistrates. *Encyc.*

FREE'COST, *n.* Without expense; freedom from charges. *South.*

FREED, *pp.* Set at liberty; loosed; delivered from restraint; cleared of hinderance or obstruction.

FREEDEN'IZEN, *n.* A citizen. *Jackson.*

FREE'DMAN, *n.* A man who has been a slave and is manumitted.

FREE'DOM, *n.* A state of exemption from the power or control of another; liberty; exemption from slavery, servitude or confinement. *Freedom is personal, civil, political,* and *religious.* See *Liberty*.]

2. Particular privileges; franchise; immunity; as the *freedom* of a city.

3. Power of enjoying franchises. *Swift.*

4. Exemption from fate, necessity, or any constraint in consequence of predetermination or otherwise; as the *freedom* of the will.

5. Any exemption from constraint or control.

6. Ease or facility of doing any thing. He speaks or acts with *freedom*.

7. Frankness; boldness. He addressed his audience with *freedom*.

8. License; improper familiarity; violation of the rules of decorum; with a plural. Beware of what are called innocent *freedoms*.

FREEFISH'ERY, *n.* A royal franchise or exclusive privilege of fishing in a public river. *Encyc.*

FREE'FOOTED, *a.* Not restrained in marching. [*Not used.*] *Shak.*

FREEHEARTED, *a.* [See *Heart*.] Open; frank; unreserved.

2. Liberal; charitable; generous.

FREEHEARTEDNESS, *n.* Frankness; openness of heart; liberality. *Burnet.*

FREE'HOLD, *n.* That land or tenement which is held in fee-simple, fee-tail, or for term of life. It is of two kinds; in *deed*, and in *law*. The first is the real possession of such land or tenement; the last is the right a man has to such land or tenement, before his entry or seizure. *Eng. Law.*

Freehold is also extended to such offices as a man holds in fee or for life. It is also taken in opposition to *villenage*. *Encyc.*

In *the United States*, a *freehold* is an estate which a man holds in his own right, subject to no superior nor to conditions.

FREE'HOLDER, *n.* One who owns an estate in fee-simple, fee-tail or for life; the possessor of a freehold. Every juryman must be a *freeholder*.

FREE'ING, *ppr.* Delivering from restraint; releasing from confinement; removing incumbrances or hinderances from any thing; clearing.

FREE'LY, *adv.* At liberty; without vassalage, slavery or dependence.

2. Without restraint, constraint or compulsion; voluntarily. To render a moral agent accountable, he must act *freely*.

3. Plentifully; in abundance; as, to eat or drink *freely*.

4. Without scruple or reserve; as, to censure *freely*.

5. Without impediment or hinderance.

> Of every tree of the garden thou mayest *freely* eat. Gen. ii.

6. Without necessity, or compulsion from divine predetermination.

> *Freely* they stood who stood, and fell who fell. *Milton.*

7. Without obstruction; largely; copiously. The patient bled *freely*.

8. Spontaneously; without constraint or persuasion.

9. Liberally; generously; as, to give *freely* to the poor.

10. Gratuitously; of free will or grace, without purchase or consideration.

Freely ye have received, *freely* give. Matt. x.

FREE'MAN, *n.* [*free* and *man.*] One who enjoys liberty, or who is not subject to the will of another; one not a slave or vassal.
2. One who enjoys or is entitled to a franchise or peculiar privilege; as the *freemen* of a city or state.

FREE'MASON, *n.* One of the fraternity of masons.

FREE'MINDED, *a.* Not perplexed; free from care. *Bacon.*

FREE'NESS, *n.* The state or quality of being free, unconstrained, unconfined, unincumbered, or unobstructed.
2. Openness; unreservedness; frankness; ingenuousness; candor; as the *freeness* of a confession.
3. Liberality; generosity; as *freeness* in giving. *Spratt.*
4. Gratuitousness; as the *freeness* of divine grace.

FREE'SCHOOL, *n.* A school supported by funds, &c., in which pupils are taught without paying for tuition.
2. A school open to admit pupils without restriction.

FREE'SPOKEN, *a.* Accustomed to speak without reserve. *Bacon.*

FREE'STONE, *n.* Any species of stone composed of sand or grit, so called because it is easily cut or wrought.

FREE'THINKER, *n.* A softer name for a deist; an unbeliever; one who discards revelation.

FREE'THINKING, *n.* Unbelief. *Berkeley.*

FREE'TÖNGUED, *a.* Speaking without reserve. *Bp. Hall.*

FREEWAR'REN, *n.* A royal franchise or exclusive right of killing beasts and fowls of warren within certain limits. *Encyc.*

FREEWILL', *n.* The power of directing our own actions without restraint by necessity or fate. *Locke.*
2. Voluntariness; spontaneousness.

FREE'WÖMAN, *n.* A woman not a slave.

FREEZE, *v. i.* pret. *froze*; pp. *frozen*, or *froze.* [Sax. *frysan*; D. *vriezen*; Dan. *fryser*; Sw. *frysa.* It coincides in elements with D. *vrezen*, to fear, that is, to shrink, contract, tremble, shiver, Fr. *friser*, to curl, whence *frissoner*, to shiver, Sp. *frisar.* These are of one family, unless there has been a change of letters. The Italian has *fregio*, for frieze, and the Gr. φρισσω had for its radical letters φρξ. These may be of a different family. To *freeze* is to contract. See Class Rd. Rs. No. 14. 19. 25. Qu. Russ. *mroz*, frost.]
1. To be congealed by cold; to be changed from a liquid to a solid state by the abstraction of heat; to be hardened into ice or a like solid body. Water *freezes* at the temperature of 32° above zero by Fahrenheit's thermometer. Mercury *freezes* at 40° below zero.
2. To be of that degree of cold at which water congeals. *Shak.*
3. To chill; to stagnate, or to retire from the extreme vessels; as, the blood *freezes* in the veins.
4. To be chilled; to shiver with cold.
5. To die by means of cold. We say a man *freezes* to death.

FREEZE, *v. t.* To congeal; to harden into ice; to change from a fluid to a solid form by cold or abstraction of heat. This weather will *freeze* the rivers and lakes.
2. To kill by cold; but we often add the words *to death.* This air will *freeze* you, or *freeze* you *to death.*
3. To chill; to give the sensation of cold and shivering. This horrid tale *freezes* my blood.

FREEZE, in *architecture.* [See *Frieze.*]

FREIGHT, *n. frate.* [D. *vragt*; G. *fracht*; Sw. *fracht*; Dan. *fragt*; Fr. *fret*; Port. *frete*; Sp. *flete*; Arm. *fret.* See *Fraught.* Qu. from the root of L. *fero*; formed like *bright*, from the Ethiopic *barah.*]
1. The cargo, or any part of the cargo of a ship; lading; that which is carried by water. The *freight* of a ship consists of cotton; the ship has not a full *freight*; the owners have advertised for *freight*; *freight* will be paid for by the ton.
2. Transportation of goods. We paid four dollars a ton for the *freight* from London to Barcelona.
3. The hire of a ship, or money charged or paid for the transportation of goods. After paying *freight* and charges, the profit is trifling.

FREIGHT, *v. t.* To load with goods, as a ship or vessel of any kind, for transporting them from one place to another. We *freighted* the ship for Amsterdam; the ship was *freighted* with flour for Havanna.
2. To load as the burden. *Shak.*

FREIGHTED, *pp.* Loaded, as a ship or vessel.

FREIGHTER, *n.* One who loads a ship, or one who charters and loads a ship.

FREIGHTING, *ppr.* Loading, as a ship or vessel.

FREISLEBEN, *n.* A mineral of a blue or bluish gray color, brittle and soft to the touch. *Cleaveland.*

FREN, *n.* A stranger. [*Not used.*] *Spenser.*

FRENCH, *a.* Pertaining to France or its inhabitants.

French Chalk, scaly talck, a variety of indurated talck, in masses composed of small scales; its color is pearly white or grayish. *Cleaveland.*

FRENCH, *n.* The language spoken by the people of France.

FRENCH-HORN', *n.* A wind instrument of music made of metal.

FRENCH'IFY, *v. t.* To make French; to infect with the manner of the French. *Camden.*

FRENCH'LIKE, *a.* Resembling the French. *Bp. Hall.*

FRENET'IC, *a.* [See *Frantic* and *Phrenetic.*]

FREN'ZIED, *part. a.* Affected with madness.

FREN'ZY, *n.* [Fr. *frenesie*; It. *frenesia*; from L. *phrenitis*, Gr. φρενιτις, from φρην, mind, which is from moving, rushing. See *Frantic.*]
Madness; distraction; rage; or any violent agitation of the mind approaching to distraction.

All else is towering *frenzy* and distraction. *Addison.*

FRE'QUENCE, *n.* [Fr. from L. *frequentia.*] A crowd; a throng; a concourse; an assembly. [*Little used.*] *Shak. Milton.*

FRE'QUENCY, *n.* A return or occurrence of a thing often repeated at short intervals. The *frequency* of crimes abates our horror at the commission; the *frequency* of capital punishments tends to destroy their proper effect.
2. A crowd; a throng. [*Not used.*] *B. Jonson.*

FRE'QUENT, *a.* [Fr. from L. *frequens.*]
1. Often seen or done; often happening at short intervals; often repeated or occurring. We made *frequent* visits to the hospital.
2. Used often to practice any thing. He was *frequent* and loud in his declamations against the revolution.
3. Full; crowded; thronged. [*Not used.*] *Milton.*

FRE'QUENT, *v. t.* [L. *frequento*; Fr. *frequenter.*]
To visit often; to resort to often or habitually. The man who *frequents* a dram-shop, an ale house, or a gaming table, is in the road to poverty, disgrace and ruin.

He *frequented* the court of Augustus. *Dryden.*

FREQUENT'ABLE, *a.* Accessible. [*Not used.*] *Sidney.*

FREQUENTA'TION, *n.* The act of frequenting. *Chesterfield.*
2. The habit of visiting often.

FREQUENT'ATIVE, *a.* [It. *frequentativo*; Fr. *frequentatif.*]
In *grammar*, signifying the frequent repetition of an action; as a *frequentative* verb.

FRE'QUENTED, *pp.* Often visited.

FRE'QUENTER, *n.* One who often visits or resorts to customarily.

FRE'QUENTLY, *adv.* Often; many times; at short intervals; commonly.

FRE'QUENTNESS, *n.* The quality of being frequent or often repeated.

FRES'CO, *n.* [It. *fresco*, fresh.] Coolness; shade; a cool refreshing state of the air; duskiness. *Prior.*
2. A picture not drawn in glaring light, but in dusk. *Pope.*
3. A method of painting in relief on walls, performed with water-colors on fresh plaster, or on a wall laid with mortar not yet dry. The colors, incorporating with the mortar, and drying with it, become very durable. It is called *fresco*, either because it is done on *fresh* plaster, or because it is used on walls and buildings in the open air. *Encyc.*
4. A cool refreshing liquor.

FRESH, *a.* [Sax. *fersc*; D. *versch*; G. *frisch*; Dan. *fersk*, and *frisk*; Sw. *frisk*; It. *fresco*; Sp. Port. *id.*; Fr. *frais*, *fraiche*; Arm. *fresq*; W. *fres*, *fresg.* This is radically the same word as *frisk*, and it coincides also in elements with *brisk*, W. *brysg*, which is from *rhys*, a rushing, extreme ardency, Eng. *rush*, which gives the radical sense, though it may not be the same word.]
1. Moving with celerity; brisk; strong; somewhat vehement; as a *fresh* breeze; *fresh* wind; *the primary sense.*
2. Having the color and appearance of young thrifty plants; lively; not impaired or faded; as when we say, the fields look *fresh* and green.
3. Having the appearance of a healthy

youth; florid; ruddy; as a *fresh*-colored young man. *Harvey. Addison.*

4. New; recently grown; as *fresh* vegetables.

5. New; recently made or obtained. We have a *fresh* supply of goods from the manufactory, or from India; *fresh* tea; *fresh* raisins.

6. Not impaired by time; not forgotten or obliterated. The story is *fresh* in my mind; the ideas are *fresh* in my recollection.

7. Not salt; as *fresh* water; *fresh* meat.

8. Recently from the well or spring; pure and cool; not warm or vapid. Bring a glass of *fresh* water.

9. In a state like that of recent growth or recentness; as, to preserve flowers and fruit *fresh*.

> *Fresh* as April, sweet as May. *Carew.*

10. Repaired from loss or diminution; having new vigor. He rose *fresh* for the combat.

11. New; that has lately come or arrived; as *fresh* news; *fresh* dispatches.

12. Sweet; in a good state; not stale.

13. Unpracticed; unused; not before employed; as a *fresh* hand on board of a ship.

14. Moderately rapid; as, the ship makes *fresh* way.

FRESH, *n.* A freshet. *Beverly, Hist. Virginia.*

FRESH'EN, *v. t. fresh'n.* To make fresh; to dulcify; to separate, as water from saline particles; to take saltness from any thing; as, to *freshen* water, fish or flesh.

2. To refresh; to revive. [*Not used.*] *Spenser.*

3. In *seaman's language*, to apply new service to a cable; as, to *freshen* hawse.

FRESH'EN, *v. i.* To grow fresh; to lose salt or saltness.

2. To grow brisk or strong; as, the wind *freshens.*

FRESH'ENED, *pp.* Deprived of saltness; sweetened.

FRESH'ES, *n.* The mingling of fresh water with salt water in rivers or bays, or the increased current of an ebb tide by means of a flood of fresh water, flowing towards or into the sea, and discoloring the water. *Beverly. Encyc.*

2. A flood; an overflowing; an inundation; a freshet.

FRESH'ET, *n.* A flood or overflowing of a river, by means of heavy rains or melted snow; an inundation. *New England.*

2. A stream of fresh water. *Browne.*

FRESH'LY, *adv.* Newly; in the former state renewed; in a new or fresh state.

2. With a healthy look; ruddily. *Shak.*

3. Briskly; strongly.

4. Coolly.

FRESH'MAN, *n.* A novice; one in the rudiments of knowledge.

2. In *colleges*, one of the youngest class of students.

FRESH'MANSHIP, *n.* The state of a freshman.

FRESH'NESS, *n.* Newness; vigor; spirit; the contrary to vapidness; as the *freshness* of liquors or odors.

2. Vigor; liveliness; the contrary to a faded state; as the *freshness* of plants or of green fields.

3. Newness of strength; renewed vigor; opposed to weariness or fatigue.

> The Scots had the advantage both for number and *freshness* of men. *Hayward.*

4. Coolness; invigorating quality or state.

> And breathe the *freshness* of the open air. *Dryden.*

5. Color of youth and health; ruddiness.

> Her cheeks their *freshness* lose and wonted grace. *Granville.*

6. Freedom from saltness; as the *freshness* of water or flesh.

7. A new or recent state or quality; rawness.

8. Briskness, as of wind.

FRESH'NEW, *a.* Unpracticed. [*Not used.*] *Shak.*

FRESH'WATER, *a.* Accustomed to sail on freshwater only, or in the coasting trade; as a *freshwater* sailor.

2. Raw; unskilled. *Knolles.*

FRESH'WATERED, *a.* Newly watered; supplied with fresh water.

FRET, *v. t.* [Sw. *fräta*, to fret, to corrode; Fr. *frotter*, to rub; Arm. *frota.* This seems to be allied to Goth. and Sax. *fretan*, to eat, to gnaw, G. *fressen*, D. *vreeten*, which may be formed from the root of L. *rodo, rosi*, Sp. *rozar*, or of L. *rado*, to scrape. To *fret* or gnaw gives the sense of unevenness, roughness, in substances; the like appearance is given to fluids by agitation.]

1. To rub; to wear away a substance by friction; as, to *fret* cloth; to *fret* a piece of gold or other metal. *Newton.*

2. To corrode; to gnaw; to eat away; as, a worm *frets* the planks of a ship.

3. To impair; to wear away.

> By starts,
> His *fretted* fortunes give him hope and fear. *Shak.*

4. To form into raised work. *Milton.*

5. To variegate; to diversify.

> Yon gray lines
> That *fret* the clouds are messengers of day. *Shak.*

6. To agitate violently. *Shak.*

7. To agitate; to disturb; to make rough; to cause to ripple; as, to *fret* the surface of water.

8. To tease; to irritate; to vex; to make angry.

> *Fret* not thyself because of evil doers. Ps. xxxvii.

9. To wear away; to chafe; to gall. Let not a saddle or harness *fret* the skin of your horse.

FRET, *v. i.* To be worn away; to be corroded. Any substance will in time *fret* away by friction.

2. To eat or wear in; to make way by attrition or corrosion.

> Many wheals arose, and *fretted* one into another with great excoriation. *Wiseman.*

3. To be agitated; to be in violent commotion; as the rancor that *frets* in the malignant breast.

4. To be vexed; to be chafed or irritated; to be angry; to utter peevish expressions.

> He *frets*, he fumes, he stares, he stamps the ground. *Dryden.*

FRET, *n.* The agitation of the surface of a fluid by fermentation or other cause; a rippling on the surface of water; small undulations continually repeated. *Addison.*

2. Work raised in protuberances; or a kind of knot consisting of two lists or small fillets interlaced, used as an ornament in architecture.

3. Agitation of mind; commotion of temper; irritation; as, he keeps his mind in a continual *fret.*

> Yet then did Dennis rave in furious *fret.* *Pope.*

4. A short piece of wire fixed on the finger-board of a guitar, &c., which being pressed against the strings varies the tone. *Busby.*

5. In *heraldry*, a bearing composed of bars crossed and interlaced.

FRET, *v. t.* To furnish with frets, as an instrument of music. *As. Res.*

FRET, *n.* [L. *fretum.*] A frith, which see.

FRET'FUL, *a.* Disposed to fret; ill-humored; peevish; angry; in a state of vexation; as a *fretful* temper.

FRET'FULLY, *adv.* Peevishly; angrily.

FRET'FULNESS, *n.* Peevishness; ill-humor; disposition to fret and complain.

FRETT, *n.* With *miners*, the worn side of the bank of a river. *Encyc.*

FRET'TED, *pp.* Eaten; corroded; rubbed or worn away; agitated; vexed; made rough on the surface; variegated; ornamented with fretwork; furnished with frets.

FRET'TER, *n.* That which frets.

FRET'TING, *ppr.* Corroding; wearing away; agitating; vexing; making rough on the surface; variegating.

FRET'TING, *n.* Agitation; commotion.

FRET'TY, *a.* Adorned with fretwork.

FRE'TUM, *n.* [L.] An arm of the sea. *Ray.*

FRET'WORK, *n.* Raised work; work adorned with frets.

FRIABIL'ITY, } **FRI'ABLENESS**, } *n.* [See *Friable.*] The quality of being easily broken, crumbled and reduced to powder. *Locke.*

FRI'ABLE, *a.* [Fr. *friable*; L. *friabilis*, from *frio*, to break or crumble. *Frio* is probably a contracted word. Ch. פרך or Ch. Heb. פרק to break.]

Easily crumbled or pulverized; easily reduced to powder. Pumice and calcined stones are very *friable.*

FRI'AR, *n.* [Fr. *frère*, a brother, contracted from L. *frater.* See *Brother.*]

1. An appellation common to the monks of all orders; those who enter religious orders considering themselves as a fraternity or brotherhood. Friars are generally distinguished into four principal branches, viz.: 1. Minors, gray friars or Franciscans; 2. Augustines; 3. Dominicans or black friars; 4. White Friars or Carmelites.

2. In a restricted sense, a monk who is not a priest; those friars who are in orders being called *fathers.*

FRI'ARLIKE, *a.* Like a friar; monastic; unskilled in the world. *Knolles.*

FRI'ARLY, *a.* Like a friar; untaught in the affairs of life. *Bacon.*

FRI'AR'S-COWL, *n.* A plant, a species of Arum, with a flower resembling a cowl. *Johnson. Fam. of Plants.*

FRIAR'S-LAN'TERN, *n.* The ignis fatuus. *Milton.*

FRI'ARY, *n.* A monastery; a convent of friars. *Dugdale.*

FRI'ARY, *a.* Like a friar; pertaining to friars. *Camden.*

FRIB'BLE, *a.* [L. *frivolus*, Fr. *frivole*, from rubbing; from *rub*, if *b* is radical, or from *frico*, if the *b* represents a palatal letter. If *b* is radical, the word accords with Dan. *rips*, trifles, frivolousness.]

Frivolous; trifling; silly. *Brit. Crit.*

FRIB'BLE, *n.* A frivolous, trifling, contemptible fellow.

FRIB'BLE, *v. i.* To trifle; also, to totter. *Tatler.*

FRIB'BLER, *n.* A trifler. *Spectator.*

FRI'BORG, *n.* [*free* and *burg.*] The same as frankpledge. *Cowel.*

FRI€'ACE, *n.* [See *Fricassee.*] Meat sliced and dressed with strong sauce; also, an unguent prepared by frying things together. *Obs.* *B. Jonson.*

FRI€ASSEE', *n.* [Fr.; It. *frigasea*; Sp. *fricasea*; Port. *fricassé*; from Fr. *fricasser*, to fry, It. *friggere*, Port. *frigir*, Sp. *freir*, L. *frigo.*]

A dish of food made by cutting chickens, rabbits or other small animals into pieces, and dressing them in a frying pan, or a like utensil. *King.*

FRI€ASSEE', *v. t.* To dress in fricassee.

FRI€A'TION, *n.* [L. *fricatio*, from *frico*, to rub.]

The act of rubbing; friction. [*Little used.*] *Bacon.*

FRI€'TION, *n.* [L. *frictio*; Fr. *friction*; from L. *frico*, to rub, It. *fregare*, Sp. *fricar.*]

1. The act of rubbing the surface of one body against that of another; attrition. Many bodies by *friction* emit light, and *friction* generates or evolves heat.
2. In *mechanics*, the effect of rubbing, or the resistance which a moving body meets with from the surface on which it moves. *Encyc.*
3. In *medicine*, the rubbing of the body with the hand, or with a brush, flannel, &c.; or the rubbing of a diseased part with oil, unguent or other medicament. *Encyc.*

FRI'DAY, *n.* [Sax. *frig-dæg*; G. *freitag*; D. *vrydag*; from *Frigga*, the Venus of the north; D. *vrouw*, G. *frau*, Ir. *frag*, a woman.]

The sixth day of the week, formerly consecrated to Frigga.

FRIDGE, *v. t.* [Sax. *frician.*] To move hastily. [*Not in use.*] *Hallywell.*

FRID-STOLE. [See *Fred.*]

FRIEND, *n. frend.* [Sax. *freond*, the participle of *freon*, to free, to love, contracted from *frigan*, to free; G. *freund*; D. *vriend*; Dan. *frende*; Sw. *frände.* We see the radical sense is to free; hence, to be ready, willing, or cheerful, joyous, and allied perhaps to *frolick.*]

1. One who is attached to another by affection; one who entertains for another sentiments of esteem, respect and affection, which lead him to desire his company, and to seek to promote his happiness and prosperity; opposed to *foe* or *enemy.*

   A *friend* loveth at all times. Prov. xvii.

   There is a *friend* that sticketh closer than a brother. Prov. xviii.

2. One not hostile; *opposed to an enemy in war.* *Shak.*
3. One reconciled after enmity. Let us be *friends* again.
4. An attendant; a companion. *Dryden.*
5. A favorer; one who is propitious; as a *friend* to commerce; a *friend* to poetry; a *friend* to charitable institutions.
6. A favorite. Hushai was David's *friend.*
7. A term of salutation; a familiar compellation.

   Friend, how camest thou in hither? Matt. xxii.

   So Christ calls Judas his *friend*, though a traitor. Matt. xxvi.

8. Formerly, a paramour.
9. *A friend at court*, one who has sufficient interest to serve another. *Chaucer.*

FRIEND, *v. t. frend.* To favor; to countenance; to befriend; to support or aid. [But we now use *befriend.*] *Shak.*

FRIEND'ED, *pp. frend'ed.* Favored; befriended.

2. *a.* Inclined to love; well disposed. *Shak.*

FRIEND'LESS, *a. frend'less.* Destitute of friends; wanting countenance or support; forlorn. *Pope.*

FRIEND'LIKE, *a. frend'like.* Having the dispositions of a friend.

FRIEND'LINESS, *n. frend'liness.* A disposition to friendship; friendly disposition. *Sidney.*

2. Exertion of benevolence or kindness. *Taylor.*

FRIEND'LY, *a. frend'ly.* Having the temper and disposition of a friend; kind; favorable; disposed to promote the good of another.

   Thou to mankind
   Be good and *friendly* still, and oft return. *Milton.*

2. Disposed to peace. *Pope.*
3. Amicable. We are on *friendly* terms.
4. Not hostile; as a *friendly* power or state.
5. Favorable; propitious; salutary; promoting the good of; as a *friendly* breeze or gale. Excessive rains are not *friendly* to the ripening fruits. Temperance is *friendly* to longevity.

FRIEND'LY, *adv. frend'ly.* In the manner of friends; amicably. [*Not much used.*] *Shak.*

FRIEND'SHIP, *n. frend'ship.* An attachment to a person, proceeding from intimate acquaintance, and a reciprocation of kind offices, or from a favorable opinion of the amiable and respectable qualities of his mind. *Friendship* differs from *benevolence*, which is good will to mankind in general, and from that *love* which springs from animal appetite. *True* friendship is a noble and virtuous attachment, springing from a pure source, a respect for worth or amiable qualities. *False* friendship may subsist between bad men, as between thieves and pirates. This is a temporary attachment springing from interest, and may change in a moment to enmity and rancor.

   There can be no *friendship* without confidence, and no confidence without integrity. *Rambler.*

   There is little *friendship* in the world. *Bacon.*

   The first law of *friendship* is sincerity. *Anon.*

2. Mutual attachment; intimacy.

   If not in *friendship*, live at least in peace. *Dryden.*

3. Favor; personal kindness.

   His *friendships*, still to few confined,
   Were always of the middling kind. *Swift.*

4. Friendly aid; help; assistance. *Shak.*
5. Conformity; affinity; correspondence; aptness to unite.

   We know those colors which have a *friendship* with each other. *Dryden.*

   [*Not common and hardly legitimate.*]

FRIEZE, FRIZE, *n. freez.* [Sp. *frisa*, frieze; *frisar*, to raise a nap on cloth, to *frizzle*; Fr. *friser*, to curl or crisp, to shiver, to ruffle; Port. *frisar*; Arm. *frisa.* Qu. Sp. *rizar*, to crisp or curl, to frizzle; Gr. φρισσω, to shiver or tremble with fear, whose elements are *Frg* or *Frk*, as appears by φριξω, φρικτος, φριξ. If *frieze*, in architecture, is the same word, which seems to be the fact, we have evidence that the elements are *Frg*, for in Italian, frieze is *fregio.* The primary sense is probably to draw or contract.]

1. Properly, the nap on woolen cloth; hence, a kind of coarse woolen cloth or stuff, with a nap on one side.
2. In *architecture*, that part of the entablature of a column which is between the architrave and cornice. It is a flat member or face, usually enriched with figures of animals or other ornaments of sculpture, whence its name.

   Cornice or *frieze* with bossy sculptures graven. *Milton.*

FRIE'ZED, *a.* Napped; shaggy with nap or frieze.

FRIE'ZELIKE, *a.* Resembling frieze. *Addison.*

FRIG'ATE, *n.* [Fr. *fregate*; It. *fregata*; Sp. Port. *fragata*; Turkish, *forgata*; perhaps Gr. αφρακτος, L. *aphractum*, an open ship or vessel, for in Portuguese it signifies a boat as well as a frigate. The Greek word αφρακτος signifies not fortified; α and φρασσω. It was originally a vessel without decks used by the Rhodians. The frigate was originally a kind of vessel used in the Mediterranean, and propelled both by sails and by oars. *Lunier.*]

A ship of war, of a size larger than a sloop or brig, and less than a ship of the line; usually having two decks and carrying from thirty to forty four guns. But ships mounting a less number than thirty guns are sometimes called frigates; as are ships carrying a larger number.

2. Any small vessel on the water. [*Not used.*] *Spenser.*

FRIG'ATE-BUILT, *a.* Having a quarter deck and forecastle raised above the main deck.

FRIGATOON', *n.* A Venetian vessel with a square stern, without a foremast, having only a mainmast and mizenmast. *Encyc.*

FRIGEFA€'TION, *n.* [L. *frigus*, cold, and *facio*, to make.]

The act of making cold. [*Little used.*] *Dict.*

FRIGHT, *n. frite.* [Dan. *frygt*; Sw. *fruchtan*; Sax. *fyrhto, fyrhtu, fyrhtnis*, fright, and *firhted*, frighted, *frihtan*, to *frighten*; G. *furcht, fürchten*; D. *vrugten*, to fear; Fr. *effrayer.* Qu. Gr. φρισσω, φριξω, to fear, that is, to shrink or shiver. But *fright*, or the Sax. *fyrhto*, is precisely the Ethiopic participle ፍርሀት ferht, from ፈረሀ ferah, to fear, which seems to be allied to L. *vereor*. Class Br. No. 33.]

Sudden and violent fear; terror; a passion excited by the sudden appearance of danger. It expresses more than *fear*, and is distinguished from *fear* and *dread*, by its sudden invasion and temporary existence; *fright* being usually of short duration, whereas *fear* and *dread* may be long continued.

FRIGHT, FRIGHTEN, *v. t.* To terrify; to scare; to alarm suddenly with danger; to shock suddenly with the approach of evil; to daunt; to dismay.

Nor exile or danger can *fright* a brave spirit. *Dryden.*

FRIGHTED, FRIGHTENED, *pp.* Terrified; suddenly alarmed with danger.

FRIGHTFUL, *a.* Terrible; dreadful; exciting alarm; impressing terror; as a *frightful* chasm or precipice; a *frightful* tempest.

FRIGHTFULLY, *adv.* Terribly; dreadfully; in a manner to impress terror and alarm; horribly.

2. Very disagreeably; shockingly. She looks *frightfully* to day.

FRIGHTFULNESS, *n.* The quality of impressing terror.

FRIG'ID, *a.* [L. *frigidus*, from *frigeo*, to be or to grow cold; *rigeo*, to be stiff or frozen; Gr. ῥιγεω. If the radical sense is to be stiff, the root coincides nearly with that of *right, rectus*, or with that of *reach, region*, which is to stretch, that is, to draw or contract.]

1. Cold; wanting heat or warmth; as the *frigid* zone.
2. Wanting warmth of affection; unfeeling; as a *frigid* temper or constitution.
3. Wanting natural heat or vigor sufficient to excite the generative power; impotent.
4. Dull; jejune; unanimated; wanting the fire of genius or fancy; as a *frigid* style; *frigid* rhymes.
5. Stiff; formal; forbidding; as a *frigid* look or manner.
6. Wanting zeal; dull; formal; lifeless; as *frigid* services.

FRIGID'ITY, *n.* Coldness; want of warmth. *But not applied to the air or weather.*

2. Want of natural heat, life and vigor of body; impotency; imbecility; as the *frigidity* of old age.
3. Coldness of affection.
4. Dullness; want of animation or intellectual fire; as the *frigidity* of sentiments or style.

FRIG'IDLY, *adv.* Coldly; dully; without affection.

FRIG'IDNESS, *n.* Coldness; dullness; want of heat or vigor; want of affection. [See *Frigidity*.]

FRIGORIF'IC, *a.* [Fr. *frigorifique*; L. *frigorificus*; *frigus*, cold, and *facio*, to make.] Causing cold; producing or generating cold. *Encyc. Quincy.*

FRILL, *n.* [infra.] An edging of fine linen on the bosom of a shirt or other similar thing; a ruffle. *Mason.*

FRILL, *v. i.* [Fr. *frileux*, chilly. We have the word in *trill*, D. *trillen*, to shake, G. *trillern*; all with a different prefix. Class Rl.]

To shake; to quake; to shiver as with cold; as, the hawk *frills*. *Encyc.*

FRIM, *a.* [Sax. *freom.*] Flourishing. [*Not in use.*] *Drayton.*

FRINGE, *n. frinj.* [Fr. *frange*; It. *frangia*; Sp. Port. *franja*; Arm. *frainch*, or *flainch*; G. *franse*; D. *franje*; Dan. *frynse*. It seems to be from L. *frango*, to break, Sp. *frangir*.]

1. An ornamental appendage to the borders of garments or furniture, consisting of loose threads.

The golden *fringe* ev'n set the ground on flame. *Dryden.*

2. Something resembling fringe; an open broken border. *Mountagu.*

FRINGE, *v. t.* To adorn or border with fringe or a loose edging.

FRING'ED, *pp.* Bordered with fringe.

FRINGEMAKER, *n.* One who makes fringe.

FRING'ING, *ppr.* Bordering with fringe.

FRING'Y, *a.* Adorned with fringes. *Shak.*

FRIP'PERER, *n.* [See *Frippery*.] One who deals in old cloths.

FRIP'PERY, *n.* [Fr. *friperie*, from *friper*, to fumble, to ruffle, to wear out, to waste; Arm. *fripa*, or *flippa*; Sp. *roperia*, *ropavejeria*, from *ropa*, cloth, stuff, apparel, which seems to be the Eng. *robe*; Port. *roupa*, clothes, furniture; *farrapo*, a rag; perhaps from the root of Eng. *rub*, that is, to wear, to use, as we say wearing apparel, for to *wear* is to rub. See *Robe*.]

1. Old clothes; cast dresses; clothes thrown aside, after wearing. Hence, waste matter; useless things; trifles; as the *frippery* of wit. *B. Jonson.*
2. The place where old clothes are sold. *Shak.*
3. The trade or traffick in old clothes. *Encyc.*

FRISEU'R, *n.* [Fr. from *friser*, to curl.] A hair dresser. *Warton.*

FRISK, *v. i.* [Dan. *frisk*, fresh, new, green, *brisk*, lively, gay, vigorous; *frisker*, to freshen, to renew; *friskhed*, coolness, freshness, briskness; Sw. *frisk*; G. *frisch*, fresh, brisk. This is the same word as *fresh*, but from the Gothic. If it is radically the same as *brisk*, it is W. *brysg*, speedy, nimble, from *rhys*, a *rushing*. But this is doubtful. In some languages, *fresh* is written *fersc*, *versch*, as if from the root Br. But I think it cannot be the Ch. פרכס to be moved, to tremble.]

1. To leap; to skip; to spring suddenly one way and the other.

The fish fell a *frisking* in the net. *L'Estrange.*

2. To dance, skip and gambol in frolick and gayety.

The *frisking* satyrs on the summits danced. *Addison.*

In vain to *frisk* or climb he tries. *Swift.*

FRISK, *a.* Lively; brisk; blithe. *Hall.*

FRISK, *n.* A frolick; a fit of wanton gayety. *Johnson.*

FRISK'AL, *n.* A leap or caper. [*Not in use.*] *B. Jonson.*

FRISK'ER, *n.* One who leaps or dances in gayety; a wanton; an inconstant or unsettled person. *Camden.*

FRISK'ET, *n.* [Fr. *frisquette*. So named from the velocity or frequency of its motion. See *Frisk*.]

In *printing*, the light frame in which a sheet of paper is confined to be laid on the form for impression.

FRISK'FUL, *a.* Brisk; lively. *Thomson.*

FRISK'INESS, *n.* Briskness and frequency of motion; gayety; liveliness; a dancing or leaping in frolick.

FRISK'ING, *ppr.* Leaping; skipping; dancing about; moving with life and gayety.

FRISK'Y, *a.* Gay; lively.

FRIT, *n.* [Fr. *fritte*; Sp. *frita*; It. *fritto*, fried, from L. *frictus*, *frigo*, Eng. to *fry*.]

In the manufacture of glass, the matter of which glass is made after it has been calcined or baked in a furnace. It is a composition of silex and fixed alkali, occasionally with other ingredients.

FRITH, *n.* [L. *fretum*; Gr. πορθμος, from πειρω, to pass over, or πορευω, πορευομαι, to pass; properly, a passage, a narrow channel that is passable or passed.]

1. A narrow passage of the sea; a strait. It is used for the opening of a river into the sea; as the *frith* of Forth, or of Clyde.
2. A kind of wear for catching fish. *Carew.*

FRITH, *n.* [W. *frith* or *friz.*] A forest; a woody place. *Drayton.*

2. A small field taken out of a common. *Wynne.*

[*Not used in America.*]

FRITH'Y, *a.* Woody. [*Not in use.*] *Skelton.*

FRIT'ILLARY, *n.* [L. *fritillus*, a dice-box.] The crown imperial, a genus of plants, called in the Spanish dictionary checkered lily. *De Theis.*

FRIT'TER, *n.* [It. *frittella*; Sp. *fritillas*, plu.; from L. *frictus*, fried; Dan. *fritte*.]

1. A small pancake; also, a small piece of meat fried.
2. A fragment; a shred; a small piece.

And cut whole giants into *fritters*. *Hudibras.*

FRIT'TER, *v. t.* To cut meat into small pieces to be fried.

2. To break into small pieces or fragments.

Break all their nerves, and *fritter* all their sense. *Pope.*

To fritter away, is to diminish; to pare off; to reduce to nothing by taking away a little at a time.

FRIVOL'ITY, *n.* [See *Frivolousness*.]

FRIV'OLOUS, *a.* [L. *frivolus*, from the root of *frio*, to break into small pieces, to crumble; Fr. *frivole*; Sp. It. *frivolo*. We observe the same radical letters, *Rb*, *Rv*, in *trivial*, *trifle*, L. *tero*, *trivi*, to *rub* or wear out. Class Rb.]

Slight; trifling; trivial; of little weight, worth or importance; not worth notice; as a *frivolous* argument; a *frivolous* objection or pretext. *Swift.*

FRIV'OLOUSNESS, *n.* The quality of being trifling or of very little worth or importance; want of consequence.

FRIV'OLOUSLY, *adv.* In a trifling manner.

FRIZ, *v. t.* [Sp. *frisar;* Fr. *friser.* See *Frieze.*]

1. To curl; to crisp; to form into small curls with a crisping-pin.
2. To form the nap of cloth into little hard burs, prominences or knobs.

FRIZ'ED, *pp.* Curled; formed into little burs on cloth.

FRIZ'ING, *ppr.* Curling; forming little hard burs on cloth.

FRIZ'ZLE, *v. t.* To curl; to crisp; as hair. *Gay.*

FRIZ'ZLED, *pp.* Curled; crisped.

FRIZ'ZLER, *n.* One who makes short curls.

FRIZ'ZLING, *ppr.* Curling; crisping.

FRO, *adv.* [Sax. *fra;* Scot. *fra, frae;* Dan. *fra.* It denotes departure and distance, like *from*, of which it may be a contraction. In some languages it is a prefix, having the force of a negative. Thus in Danish, *frabringer*, to bring from, is to avert, to dispel; *frakalder*, to recall. In Goth. *bugyan* is to buy; *frabugyan* is to sell, that is, in literal English, *frombuy.*]

From; away; back or backward; as in the phrase, *to* and *fro*, that is, *to* and *from*, forward or toward and backward, hither and thither.

FROCK, *n.* [Fr. *froc;* Arm. *frocq;* G. *frack;* Scot. *frog.*]

An upper coat, or an outer garment. The word is now used for a loose garment or shirt worn by men over their other clothes, and for a kind of gown open behind, worn by females. The *frock* was formerly a garment worn by monks. *Ingulphus. Spelman.*

FROG, *n.* [Sax. *froga, frogga;* Dan. *fröe.* Qu. from the root of *break*, as L. *rana*, from the root of *rend*, from its broken shape, or from leaping, or its *fragor* or hoarse voice.]

1. An amphibious animal of the genus Rana, with four feet, a naked body, and without a tail. It is remarkable for swimming with rapidity, and for taking large leaps on land. Frogs lie torpid during winter. *Encyc.*
2. In *farriery.* [See *Frush.*]

FROG'BIT, *n.* A plant, the Hydrocharis.

FROG'FISH, *n.* An animal of Surinam, which is said to change from a fish to a frog and then to a fish again. It is cartilaginous, and exquisite food. *Edwards.*

2. The Lophius, or fishing-frog.

FROG'GRASS, *n.* A plant.

FROG'GY, *a.* Having frogs. *Sherwood.*

FROISE, *n.* [Fr. *froisser*, to bruise.] A kind of food made by frying bacon inclosed in a pancake. *Todd.*

FROL'ICK, *a.* [G. *fröhlich; froh*, glad, and *lich*, like; D. *vrolyk;* Dan. *fro*, glad; Sw. *frögdelig*, from *frögd*, joy, *frögda*, to exhilarate; Ar. فرح faracha, to be glad, to rejoice. Class Brg. No. 6. Probably allied to *free.*]

Gay; merry; full of levity; dancing, playing or frisking about; full of pranks.

> The *frolick* wind that breathes the spring. *Milton.*
>
> The gay, the *frolick*, and the loud. *Waller.*

[This adjective is seldom used except in poetry. As a noun and a verb, its use is common.]

FROL'ICK, *n.* A wild prank; a flight of levity, or gayety and mirth.

> He would be at his *frolick* once again. *Roscommon.*

2. A scene of gayety and mirth, as in dancing or play. [*This is a popular use of the word in America.*]

FROL'ICK, *v. i.* To play wild pranks; to play tricks of levity, mirth and gayety.

> The buzzing insects *frolick* in the air. *Anon.*

FROL'ICKLY, *adv.* With mirth and gayety. *Obs. Beaum.*

FROL'ICKSŎME, *a.* Full of gayety and mirth; given to pranks.

FROL'ICKSŎMENESS, *n.* Gayety; wild pranks.

FROM, *prep.* [Sax. *fram, from;* Goth. *fram.* In Swedish, it signifies before or forward, but its sense is, past or gone, for *fråmling* is a stranger, and *fråmgå* is to go out, to depart. Dan. *frem*, whence *fremmer*, to forward, to promote, *fremmed*, strange, *fremkommer*, to come forth or out; G. *fremd*, strange, foreign; D. *vreemd*, id. If *m* is radical, this word is probably from the root of *roam, ramble*, primarily to pass, to go.]

The sense of *from* may be expressed by the noun *distance*, or by the adjective *distant*, or by the participles, *departing*, removing to a distance. Thus it is one hundred miles *from* Boston to Hartford. He took his sword *from* his side. Light proceeds *from* the sun. Water issues *from* the earth in springs. Separate the coarse wool *from* the fine. Men have all sprung *from* Adam. Men often go *from* good to bad, and *from* bad to worse. The merit of an action depends on the principle *from* which it proceeds. Men judge of facts *from* personal knowledge, or *from* testimony. We should aim to judge *from* undeniable premises.

The sense of *from* is literal or figurative, but it is uniformly the same.

In certain phrases, generally or always elliptical, *from* is followed by certain adverbs, denoting place, region or position, indefinitely, no precise point being expressed; as,

From above, from the upper regions.

From afar, from a distance.

From beneath, from a place or region below.

From below, from a lower place.

From behind, from a place or position in the rear.

From far, from a distant place.

From high, from on high, from a high place, from an upper region, or from heaven.

From hence, from this place; but *from* is superfluous before *hence.* The phrase however is common.

From thence, from that place; *from* being superfluous.

From whence, from which place; *from* being superfluous.

From where, from which place.

From within, from the interior or inside.

From without, from the outside, from abroad.

From precedes another preposition, followed by its proper object or case.

From amidst, as *from amidst* the waves.

From among, as *from among* the trees.

From beneath, as *from beneath* my head.

From beyond, as *from beyond* the river.

From forth, as *from forth* his bridal bower. But this is an inverted order of the words; *forth from* his bower.

From off, as *from off* the mercy seat, that is, *from* the top or surface.

From out, as *from out* a window, that is, through an opening or from the inside.

From out of, is an ill combination of words and not to be used.

From under, as *from under* the bed, *from under* the ashes, that is, from beneath or the lower side.

From within, as *from within* the house, that is, from the inner part or interior.

FROM'WARD, *adv.* [Sax. *fram* and *weard.*] Away from; the contrary of *toward.*

FROND, *n.* [L. *frons, frondis.* The sense is a shoot or shooting forward, as in *frons, frontis.*]

In *botany*, a term which Linne applies to the peculiar leafing of palms and ferns. He defines it, a kind of stem which has the branch united with the leaf and frequently with the fructification. The term seems to import the union of a leaf and a branch. *Martyn. Milne.*

FRONDA'TION, *n.* A lopping of trees. *Evelyn.*

FRONDES'CENCE, *n.* [L. *frondesco*, from *frons.*]

In *botany*, the precise time of the year and month in which each species of plants unfolds its leaves. *Milne. Martyn.*

FRONDIF'EROUS, *a.* [L. *frons*, and *fero*, to bear.] Producing fronds.

FROND'OUS, *a.* A *frondous flower* is one which is leafy, one which produces branches charged with both leaves and flowers. Instances of this luxuriance sometimes occur in the rose and anemone. *Milne.*

FRŎNT, *n.* [L. *frons, frontis;* Fr. *front;* Sp. *frente, fronte;* It. *fronte;* from a root signifying, to shoot forward, to project, as in Gr. ῥιν, the nose, W. *trwyn* and *rhôn*, a pike. Class Rn.]

1. Properly, the forehead, or part of the face above the eyes; hence, the whole face.

> His *front* yet threatens, and his frowns command. *Prior.*

2. The forehead or face, as expressive of the temper or disposition; as a *bold front*, equivalent to boldness or impudence. So a *hardened front* is shamelessness.
3. The forepart of any thing; as the *front* of a house, the principal face or side.
4. The forepart or van of an army or a body of troops.
5. The part or place before the face, or opposed to it, or to the forepart of a thing. He stood in *front* of his troops. The road passes in *front* of his house.
6. The most conspicuous part or particular.
7. Impudence; as men of *front*. *Tatler.*

FRŎNT, *v. t.* To oppose face to face; to oppose directly.

> I shall *front* thee, like some staring ghost,
> With all my wrongs about me. *Dryden.*

2. To stand opposed or opposite, or over against any thing; as, his house *fronts* the church.

FRŎNT, *v. i.* To stand foremost. *Shak.*
2. To have the face or front towards any point of compass.

FRONT'AL, *n.* [L. *frontale;* Fr. *frontal;* from L. *frons.*]
1. In *medicine*, a medicament or preparation to be applied to the forehead. *Quincy.*
2. In *architecture*, a little pediment or front-piece, over a small door or window. *Encyc.*
3. In *Jewish ceremonies*, a frontlet or brow-band, consisting of four pieces of vellum, laid on lether, and tied round the fore-head in the synagogue; each piece containing some text of scripture. *Encyc.*

FRŎNT'BOX, *n.* The box in a playhouse before the rest. *Pope.*

FRŎNT'ED, *a.* Formed with a front. *Milton.*

FRONTIE'R, *n.* [Fr. *frontiere;* It. *frontiera;* Sp. *frontera.*]
The marches; the border, confine, or extreme part of a country, bordering on another country; that is, the part furthest advanced, or the part that fronts an enemy, or which an invading enemy meets in front, or which fronts another country.

FRONTIE'R, *a.* Lying on the exterior part; bordering; conterminous; as a *frontier* town.

FRONTIE'RED, *a.* Guarded on the frontiers. *Spenser.*

FRONTINAC', **FRONTINIAC'**, *n.* A species of French wine, named from the place in Languedoc where it is produced.

FRONT'ISPIECE, *n.* [L. *frontispicium; frons* and *specio*, to view.]
1. In *architecture*, the principal face of a building; the face that directly presents itself to the eye.
2. An ornamental figure or engraving fronting the first page of a book, or at the beginning.

FRŎNT'LESS, *a.* Wanting shame or modesty; not diffident; as *frontless* vice; *frontless* flattery. *Dryden. Pope.*

FRONT'LET, *n.* [from *front.*] A frontal or browband; a fillet or band worn on the forehead. Deut. vi.

FRŎNTROOM, *n.* A room or apartment in the forepart of a house. *Moxon.*

FROP'PISH, *a.* Peevish; froward. [*Not in use.*] *Clarendon.*

FRORE, *a.* [G. *fror, gefroren;* D. *vroor, bevrooren.*] Frozen. [*Not in use.*] *Milton.*

FRORNE, *a.* Frozen.

FRO'RY, *a.* Frozen. *Spenser.*
2. Covered with a froth resembling hoar-frost. [*Not in use.*] *Fairfax.*

FROST, *n. fraust.* [Sax. G. Sw. and Dan. *frost;* D. *vorst;* from *freeze, froze.* Qu. Slav. *mraz, mroz*, id.]
1. A fluid congealed by cold into ice or crystals; as hoar-*frost*, which is dew or vapor congealed.

> He scattereth the hoar-*frost* like ashes. Ps. cxlvii.

2. The act of freezing; congelation of fluids.

> The third day comes a *frost*, a killing *frost*. *Shak.*

3. In *physiology*, that state or temperature of the air which occasions freezing or the congelation of water. *Encyc.*
4. The appearance of plants sparkling with icy crystals. *Pope.*

FROST, *v. t.* In *cookery*, to cover or sprinkle with a composition of sugar, resembling hoar-frost; as, to *frost* cake.
2. To cover with any thing resembling hoar-frost.

FROST'BITTEN, *a.* Nipped, withered or affected by frost.

FROST'ED, *pp.* Covered with a composition like white frost.
2. *a.* Having hair changed to a gray or white color, as if covered with hoar-frost; as a head *frosted* by age.

FROST'ILY, *adv.* With frost or excessive cold.
2. Without warmth of affection; coldly.

FROST'INESS, *n.* The state or quality of being frosty; freezing cold.

FROST'ING, *ppr.* Covering with something resembling hoar-frost.

FROST'ING, *n.* The composition resembling hoar-frost, used to cover cake, &c.

FROST'LESS, *a.* Free from frost; as a *frostless* winter. *Swift.*

FROST'NAIL, *n.* A nail driven into a horse-shoe, to prevent the horse from slipping on ice. In some of the United States, the ends of the shoe are pointed for this purpose, and these points are called *calks.*

FROST'WŎRK, *n.* Work resembling hoar-frost on shrubs. *Blackmore.*

FROST'Y, *a.* Producing frost; having power to congeal water; as a *frosty* night; *frosty* weather.
2. Containing frost; as, the grass is *frosty.*
3. Chill in affection; without warmth of affection or courage. *Johnson.*
4. Resembling hoar-frost; white; gray-haired; as a *frosty* head. *Shak.*

FROTH, *n. frauth.* [Gr. αφρος; Sw. *fradga.* It is allied perhaps to G. *brausen*, to roar, fret, froth; Ir. *bruithim*, to boil; W. *brydiaw*, to heat.]
1. Spume; foam; the bubbles caused in liquors by fermentation or agitation. *Bacon. Milton.*
2. Any empty, senseless show of wit or eloquence. *Johnson.*
3. Light, unsubstantial matter. *Tusser.*

FROTH, *v. t.* To cause to foam. *Beaum.*

FROTH, *v. i.* To foam; to throw up spume; to throw out foam or bubbles. Beer *froths* in fermentation. The sea *froths* when violently agitated. A horse *froths* at the mouth when heated.

FROTH'ILY, *adv.* With foam or spume.
2. In an empty trifling manner.

FROTH'INESS, *n.* The state of being frothy; emptiness; senseless matter.

FROTH'Y, *a.* Full of foam or froth, or consisting of froth or light bubbles.
2. Soft; not firm or solid. *Bacon.*
3. Vain; light; empty; unsubstantial; as a vain *frothy* speaker; a *frothy* harangue.

FROUNCE, *n.* A distemper of hawks, in which white spittle gathers about the bill. [See the Verb.] *Skinner.*

FROUNCE, *v. t.* [Sp. *fruncir*, to plait or gather the edge of cloth into plaits, to frizzle, to wrinkle; Fr. *froncer*, to gather, to knit, to contract; Arm. *fronça.* See *Frown.*]
To curl or frizzle the hair about the face.

> Not tricked and *frounced* as she was wont. *Milton.*

FROUNCE, *n.* A wrinkle, plait or curl; an ornament of dress. *Beaum.*

FROUN'CED, *pp.* Curled; frizzled.

FROUN'CELESS, *a.* Having no plait or wrinkle. *Chaucer.*

FROUN'CING, *ppr.* Curling; crisping.

FROU'ZY, *a.* Fetid; musty; rank; dim; cloudy. *Swift.*

FROW, *n.* [G. *frau;* D. *vrouw;* Dan. *frue.*] A woman. [*Not used.*] *Beaum.*

FRO'WARD, *a.* [Sax. *framweard; fram* or *fra* and *weard*, L. *versus:* turned or looking from.]
Perverse, that is, turning from, with aversion or reluctance; not willing to yield or comply with what is required; unyielding; ungovernable; refractory; disobedient; peevish; as a *froward* child.

> They are a very *froward* generation, children in whom is no faith. Deut. xxxii.

FRO'WARDLY, *adv.* Perversely; in a peevish manner.

FRO'WARDNESS, *n.* Perverseness; reluctance to yield or comply; disobedience; peevishness. *South.*

FROW'ER, *n.* A sharp edged tool to cleave laths. *Tusser.*

FROWN, *v. i.* [Fr. *refrogner*, properly to knit the brows. *Frogner*, the primitive word, is not used. It is allied perhaps to *frounce*, from the root Rn.]
1. To express displeasure by contracting the brow, and looking grim or surly; to look stern; followed by *on* or *at;* as, to *frown on* a profligate man, or to *frown at* his vices.

> Heroes in animated marble *frown.* *Pope.*

2. To manifest displeasure in any manner. When providence *frowns* on our labors, let us be humble and submissive.
3. To lower; to look threatening.

FROWN, *v. t.* To repel by expressing displeasure; to rebuke. *Frown* the impudent fellow into silence.

FROWN, *n.* A wrinkled look, particularly expressing dislike; a sour, severe or stern look, expressive of displeasure.

> His front yet threatens and his *frowns* command. *Prior.*

2. Any expression of displeasure; as the *frowns* of providence; the *frowns* of fortune.

FROWN'ING, *ppr.* Knitting the brow in anger or displeasure; expressing displeasure by a surly, stern or angry look; lowering; threatening.

FROWN'INGLY, *adv.* Sternly; with a look of displeasure.

FROW'Y, *a.* [The same as *frouzy;* perhaps a contracted word.] Musty; rancid; rank; as *frowy* butter.

FRO'ZEN, *pp.* of *freeze.* Congealed by cold.
2. Cold; frosty; chill; as the *frozen* climates of the north.
3. Chill or cold in affection. *Sidney.*
4. Void of natural heat or vigor. *Pope.*

F. R. S. Fellow of the Royal Society.

FRUBISH, for *furbish*, is not used.

FRUC'TED, *a.* [L. *fructus*, fruit.] In *heraldry*, bearing fruit.

FRUCTES'CENCE, *n.* [from L. *fructus*, fruit. See *Fruit.*]
In *botany*, the precise time when the fruit of

a plant arrives at maturity, and its seeds are dispersed; the fruiting season. *Milne. Martyn. Encyc.*

FRUCTIF'EROUS, *a.* [L. *fructus*, fruit, and *fero*, to bear.] Bearing or producing fruit.

FRUCTIFICA'TION, *n.* [See *Fructify*.]
1. The act of fructifying, or rendering productive of fruit; fecundation.
2. In *botany*, the temporary part of a plant appropriated to generation, terminating the old vegetable and beginning the new. It consists of seven parts, the calyx, empalement or flower-cup, the corol or petals, the stamens, and the pistil, which belong to the flower, the pericarp and seed, which pertain to the fruit, and the receptacle or base, on which the other parts are seated. The receptacle belongs both to the flower and fruit. *Linne. Milne.*

FRUC'TIFY, *v. t.* [Low L. *fructifico*; Fr. *fructifier*; *fructus*, fruit, and *facio*, to make.]
To make fruitful; to render productive; to fertilize; as, to *fructify* the earth. *Howell.*

FRUC'TIFY, *v. i.* To bear fruit. [*Unusual.*] *Hooker.*

FRUCTUA'TION, *n.* Produce; fruit. [*Not used.*] *Pownall.*

FRUC'TUOUS, *a.* [Fr. *fructueux.*] Fruitful; fertile; also, impregnating with fertility. *Philips.*

FRUC'TURE, *n.* Use; fruition; enjoyment. [*Not used.*]

FRU'GAL, *a.* [L. *frugalis*; Fr. Sp. *frugal*; said to be from *fruges*, corn, grain of any kind. Most probably it is from the root of *fruor*, for *frugor*, to use, to take the profit of, which coincides in elements and sense with G. *brauchen*, Sax. *brucan*. See *Fruit*.]
Economical in the use or appropriation of money, goods or provisions of any kind; saving unnecessary expense, either of money or of any thing else which is to be used or consumed; sparing; not profuse, prodigal or lavish. We ought to be *frugal* not only in the expenditure of money and of goods, but in the employment of time. It is followed by *of*, before the thing saved; as *frugal of* time. It is not synonymous with *parsimonious*, nor with *thrifty*, as now used.

FRUGAL'ITY, *n.* Prudent economy; good husbandry or housewifery; a sparing use or appropriation of money or commodities; a judicious use of any thing to be expended or employed; that careful management of money or goods which expends nothing unnecessarily, and applies what is used to a profitable purpose; that use in which nothing is wasted. It is not equivalent to *parsimony*, the latter being an excess of frugality, and a fault. *Frugality* is always a virtue. Nor is it synonymous with *thrift*, in its proper sense; for *thrift* is the effect of frugality.

Without *frugality* none can become rich, and with it few would be poor. *Johnson.*

2. A prudent and sparing use or appropriation of any thing; as *frugality* of praise. *Dryden.*

FRU'GALLY, *adv.* With economy; with good management; in a saving manner. He seldom lives *frugally*, that lives by chance.

FRUGIF'EROUS, *a.* [L. *frugifer*; *fruges*, corn, and *fero*, to bear.] Producing fruit or corn.

FRUGIV'OROUS, *a.* [L. *fruges*, corn, and *voro*, to eat.]
Feeding on fruits, seeds or corn, as birds and other animals. *Nat. Hist.*

FRUIT, *n.* [Fr. *fruit*; It. *frutto*; Sp. *fruto*; from L. *fructus*; Arm. *frouczen*, or *froehen*; D. *vrught*; G. *frucht*; Dan. *frugt*; Sw. *frucht*. The Latin word is the participle of *fruor*, contracted from *frugor*, or *frucor*, to use, to take the profit of; allied perhaps to Sax. *brucan*, *brycean*, G. *brauchen*, to use, to enjoy. Class Brg. No. 6. 7.]
1. In a general sense, whatever the earth produces for the nourishment of animals, or for clothing or profit. Among the *fruits* of the earth are included not only corn of all kinds, but grass, cotton, flax, grapes and all cultivated plants. In this comprehensive sense, the word is generally used in the plural.
2. In a more limited sense, the produce of a tree or other plant; the last production for the propagation or multiplication of its kind; the seed of plants, or the part that contains the seeds; as wheat, rye, oats, apples, quinces, pears, cherries, acorns, melons, &c.
3. In *botany*, the seed of a plant, or the seed with the pericarp.
4. Production; that which is produced.

The *fruit* of the spirit is in all goodness, and righteousness, and truth. Eph. v.

5. The produce of animals; offspring; young; as the *fruit* of the womb, of the loins, of the body. *Scripture.*
6. Effect or consequence.

They shall eat the *fruit* of their doings. Is. iii.

7. Advantage; profit; good derived.

What *fruit* had ye then in those things whereof ye are now ashamed? Rom. vi.

8. Production, effect or consequence; *in an ill sense*; as the *fruits* of sin; the *fruits* of intemperance.

FRUIT, *v. i.* To produce fruit. [*Not well authorized.*] *Chesterfield.*

FRUITAGE, *n.* [Fr.] Fruit collectively; various fruits. *Milton.*

FRUITBEARER, *n.* That which produces fruit. *Mortimer.*

FRUITBEARING, *a.* Producing fruit; having the quality of bearing fruit. *Mortimer.*

FRUITERER, *n.* One who deals in fruit; a seller of fruits.

FRUITERY, *n.* [Fr. *fruiterie.*] Fruit collectively taken. *Philips.*
2. A fruitloft; a repository for fruit. *Johnson.*

FRUITFUL, *a.* Very productive; producing fruit in abundance; as *fruitful* soil; a *fruitful* tree; a *fruitful* season.
2. Prolific; bearing children; not barren.

Be *fruitful*, and multiply— Gen. i.

3. Plenteous; abounding in any thing. *Pope.*
4. Productive of any thing; fertile; as *fruitful* in expedients.
4. Producing in abundance; generating; as *fruitful* in crimes.

FRUITFULLY, *adv.* In such a manner as to be prolific. *Roscommon.*
2. Plenteously; abundantly *Shak.*

FRUITFULNESS, *n.* The quality of producing fruit in abundance; productiveness; fertility; as the *fruitfulness* of land.
2. Fecundity; the quality of being prolific, or producing many young; *applied to animals.*
3. Productiveness of the intellect; as the *fruitfulness* of the brain.
4. Exuberant abundance. *B. Jonson.*

FRUIT-GROVE, *n.* A grove or close plantation of fruit-trees.

FRUI''TION, *n.* [from L. *fruor*, to use or enjoy.]
Use, accompanied with pleasure, corporeal or intellectual; enjoyment; the pleasure derived from use or possession.

If the affliction is on his body, his appetites are weakened, and capacity of *fruition* destroyed. *Rogers.*

FRUITIVE, *a.* Enjoying. *Boyle.*

FRUITLESS, *a.* Not bearing fruit; barren; destitute of fruit; as a *fruitless* plant. *Raleigh.*
2. Productive of no advantage or good effect; vain; idle; useless; unprofitable; as a *fruitless* attempt; a *fruitless* controversy.
3. Having no offspring. *Shak.*

FRUITLESSLY, *a.* [from *fruitless.*] Without any valuable effect; idly; vainly; unprofitably. *Dryden.*

FRUITLESSNESS, *n.* The quality of being vain or unprofitable.

FRUIT-LOFT, *n.* A place for the preservation of fruit.

FRUIT-TIME, *n.* The time for gathering fruit.

FRUIT-TREE, *n.* A tree cultivated for its fruit, or a tree whose principal value consists in the fruit it produces, as the cherry-tree, apple-tree, pear-tree. The oak and beech produce valuable fruit, but the fruit is not their principal value.

FRUMENTA'CEOUS, *a.* [L. *frumentaceus.*]
1. Made of wheat, or like grain.
2. Resembling wheat, in respect to leaves, ears, fruit, and the like. *Encyc.*

FRUMENTA'RIOUS, *a.* [L. *frumentarius*, from *frumentum*, corn.] Pertaining to wheat or grain.

FRUMENTA'TION, *n.* [L. *frumentatio.*] Among the Romans, a largess of grain bestowed on the people to quiet them when uneasy or turbulent. *Encyc.*

FRU'MENTY, *n.* [L. *frumentum*, wheat or grain.] Food made of wheat boiled in milk.

FRUMP, *n.* A joke, jeer or flout. [*Not used.*] *Bp. Hall.*

FRUMP, *v. t.* To insult. [*Not in use.*] *Beaum.*

FRUSH, *v. t.* [Fr. *froisser.*] To bruise; to crush. *Obs.* *Shak.*

FRUSH, *n.* [G. *frosch*, a frog.] In *farriery*, a sort of tender horn that grows in the middle of the sole of a horse, at some distance from the toe, dividing into two branches, and running toward the heel in the form of a fork. *Farrier's Dict.*

FRUS'TRABLE, *a.* [See *Frustrate.*] That may be frustrated or defeated.

FRUSTRA'NEOUS, *a.* [See *Frustrate.*] Vain; useless; unprofitable. [*Little used.*] *More. South.*

FRUS'TRATE, *v. t.* [L. *frustro*; Fr. *frustrer*; Sp. *frustrar*; allied probably to Fr.

froisser, briser, Arm. *brousia, freuza*, to break. Class Rd or Rs.]
1. Literally, to break or interrupt; hence, to defeat; to disappoint; to balk; to bring to nothing; as, to *frustrate* a plan, design or attempt; to *frustrate* the will or purpose.
2. To disappoint; *applied to persons.*
3. To make null; to nullify; to render of no effect; as, to *frustrate* a conveyance or deed.

FRUS'TRATE, *part. a.* Vain; ineffectual; useless; unprofitable; null; void; of no effect. *Hooker. Dryden.*

FRUS'TRATED, *pp.* Defeated; disappointed; rendered vain or null.

FRUS'TRATING, *ppr.* Defeating; disappointing; making vain or of no effect.

FRUSTRA'TION, *n.* The act of frustrating; disappointment; defeat; as the *frustration* of one's attempt or design. *South.*

FRUS'TRATIVE, *a.* Tending to defeat; fallacious. *Dict.*

FRUS'TRATORY, *a.* That makes void; that vacates or renders null; as a *frustatory* appeal. *Ayliffe.*

FRUS'TUM, *n.* [L. See *Frustrate.*] A piece or part of a solid body separated from the rest. The *frustum* of a cone, is the part that remains after the top is cut off by a plane parallel to the base; called otherwise a *truncated cone.* *Encyc.*

FRUTES'CENT, *a.* [L. *frutex*, a shrub.] In *botany*, from herbaceous becoming shrubby; as a *frutescent* stem. *Martyn.*

FRU'TEX, *n.* [L.] In *botany*, a shrub; a plant having a woody, durable stem, but less than a tree. *Milne.*

FRU'TICANT, *a.* Full of shoots. *Evelyn.*

FRU'TICOUS, *a.* [L. *fruticosus.*] Shrubby; as a *fruticous* stem.

FRY, *v. t.* [L. *frigo*; Gr. φρυγω; Sp. *freir*; It. *friggere*; Port. *frigir*; Fr. *frire*; Ir. *friochtalaim.* The sense is nearly the same as in *boil* or *broil*, to agitate, to fret.]
To dress with fat by heating or roasting in a pan over a fire; to cook and prepare for eating in a fryingpan; as, to *fry* meat or vegetables.

FRY, *v. i.* To be heated and agitated; to suffer the action of fire or extreme heat.
2. To ferment, as in the stomach. *Bacon.*
3. To be agitated; to boil. *Dryden.*

FRY, *n.* [Fr. *frai*, from the verb.] A swarm or crowd of little fish; so called from their crowding, tumbling and agitation. [So Sp. *hervir*, to swarm or be crowded, from L. *ferveo*, and vulgarly *boiling* is used for a crowd.] *Milton.*
2. A dish of any thing fried.
3. A kind of sieve. [*Not used in America.*] *Mortimer.*

FRY'ING, *ppr.* Dressing in a fryingpan; heating; agitating.

FRY'INGPAN, *n.* A pan with a long handle, used for frying meat and vegetables.

FUB, *n.* A plump boy; a woman. [*Not in use.*] *Todd.*

FUB, *v. t.* To put off; to delay; to cheat. [See *Fob.*] *Shak.*

FU'CATE, } *a.* [L. *fucatus*, from *fuco*, to
FU'CATED, } stain.]
Painted; disguised with paint; also, disguised with false show. *Johnson.*

FU'CUS, *n.* [L. See *Feign.*] A paint; a dye; also, false show. *B. Jonson. Sandys.*
2. plu. *fucuses*, in botany, a genus of Algæ, or sea-weeds; the sea-wrack, &c. *Encyc.*

FUDDER *of lead.* [See *Fother.*]

FUD'DLE, *v. t.* To make drunk; to intoxicate. *Thomson.*

FUD'DLE, *v. i.* To drink to excess. *L'Estrange.*

FUD'DLED, *pp.* Drunk; intoxicated.

FUD'DLING, *ppr.* Intoxicating; drinking to excess.

FUDGE, a word of contempt.

FU'EL, *n.* [from Fr. *feu*, fire, contracted from Sp. *fuego*, It. *fuoco*, L. *focus.*]
1. Any matter which serves as aliment to fire; that which feeds fire; combustible matter, as wood, coal, peat, &c.
2. Any thing that serves to feed or increase flame, heat or excitement.

FU'EL, *v. t.* To feed with combustible matter.

> Never, alas! the dreadful name,
> That *fuels* the infernal flame. *Cowley.*

2. To store with fuel or firing. *Wotton.*

FU'ELED, *pp.* Fed with combustible matter; stored with firing.

FU'ELER, *n.* He or that which supplies fuel. *Donne.*

FU'ELING, *ppr.* Feeding with fuel; supplying with fuel.

FUGA'CIOUS, *a.* [L. *fugax*, from *fugo*, to chase, or *fugio*, to flee.] Flying or fleeing away; volatile.

FUGA'CIOUSNESS, *n.* The quality of flying away; volatility.

FUGAC'ITY, *n.* [L. *fugax*, supra.] Volatility; the quality of flying away; as the *fugacity* of spirits. *Boyle.*
2. Uncertainty; instability. *Johnson.*

FUGH, or **FOH**, an exclamation expressing abhorrence. *Dryden.*

FU'GITIVE, *a.* [Fr. *fugitif*; L. *fugitivus*, from *fugio*, to flee, Gr. φευγω.]
1. Volatile; apt to flee away; readily wafted by the wind.

> The more tender and *fugitive* parts— *Woodward.*

2. Not tenable; not to be held or detained; readily escaping; as a *fugitive* idea. *Locke.*
3. Unstable; unsteady; fleeting; not fixed or durable. *Johnson.*
4. Fleeing; running from danger or pursuit. *Milton.*
5. Fleeing from duty; eloping; escaping.

> Can a *fugitive* daughter enjoy herself, while her parents are in tears? *Clarissa.*

6. Wandering; vagabond; as a *fugitive* physician. *Wotton.*
7. In *literature*, fugitive compositions are such as are short and occasional, written in haste or at intervals, and considered to be fleeting and temporary.

FU'GITIVE, *n.* One who flees from his station or duty; a deserter; one who flees from danger. *Bacon. Milton.*
2. One who has fled or deserted and taken refuge under another power, or one who has fled from punishment. *Dryden.*
3. One hard to be caught or detained.

> Or catch that airy *fugitive*, called wit. *Harte.*

FU'GITIVENESS, *n.* Volatility; fugacity; an aptness to fly away. *Boyle.*
2. Instability; unsteadiness. *Johnson.*

FUGUE, *n. fug.* [Fr. *fugue*; L. Sp. It. *fuga.*] In *music*, a chase or succession in the parts; that which expresses the capital thought or sentiment of the piece, in causing it to pass successively and alternately from one part to another. *Encyc.*

FU'GUIST, *n.* A musician who composes fugues, or performs them extemporaneously. *Busby.*

FUL'CIMENT, *n.* [L. *fulcimentum*, from *fulcio*, to prop.]
A prop; a fulcrum; that on which a balance or lever rests. [*Little used.*] *Wilkins.*

FUL'CRATE, *a.* [from L. *fulcrum*, a prop.]
1. In *botany*, a *fulcrate* stem is one whose branches descend to the earth, as in Ficus. *Lee.*
2. Furnished with fulcres.

FUL'CRUM, } *n.* [L.] A prop or support.
FUL'CRE, }
2. In *mechanics*, that by which a lever is sustained.
3. In *botany*, the part of a plant which serves to support or defend it, or to facilitate some necessary secretion, as a stipule, a bracte, a tendril, a gland, &c. *Milne. Martyn.*

FULFILL', *v. t.* [A tautological compound of *full* and *fill.*]
1. To accomplish; to perform; to complete; to answer in execution or event what has been foretold or promised; as, to *fulfill* a prophecy or prediction; to *fulfill* a promise.
2. To accomplish what was intended; to answer a design by execution.

> Here nature seems *fulfilled* in all her ends. *Milton.*

3. To accomplish or perform what was desired; to answer any desire by compliance or gratification.

> He will *fulfill* the desire of them that fear him. Ps. cxlv.

4. To perform what is required; to answer a law by obedience.

> If ye *fulfill* the royal law according to the scripture, Thou shalt love thy neighbor as thyself, ye do well. James ii.

5. To complete in time.

> *Fulfill* her week. Gen. xxix.

6. In general, to accomplish; to complete; to carry into effect.

FULFILL'ED, *pp.* Accomplished; performed; completed; executed.

FULFILL'ER, *n.* One that fulfills or accomplishes.

FULFILL'ING, *ppr.* Accomplishing; performing; completing.

FULFILL'MENT, } *n.* Accomplishment;
FULFILL'ING, } completion; as the *fulfillment* of prophecy.
2. Execution; performance; as the *fulfillment* of a promise.

FUL'FRAUGHT, *a.* [*full* and *fraught.*] Full-stored. *Shak.*

FUL'GENCY, *n.* [L. *fulgens*, from *fulgeo*, to shine. See *Effulgence.*] Brightness; splendor; glitter. *Dict.*

FUL'GENT, *a.* Shining; dazzling; exquisitely bright. *Milton.*

FUL'GID, *a.* [L. *fulgidus*, from *fulgeo*, to shine.] Shining; glittering; dazzling. [*Not in use.*]

FUL'GOR, *n.* [L.] Splendor; dazzling brightness. [*Little used.*] *Brown. More.*

FUL'GURANT, *a.* Lightening. [*Not used.*]

FUL'GURATE, *v. i.* To flash as lightning. [*Not used.*] *Chambers.*

FULGURA'TION, *n.* [L. *fulguratio*, from *fulgur*, lightning.]
Lightning; the act of lightening. [*Little used or not at all.*]

FULIGINOS'ITY, *n.* [L. *fuligo*, soot, probably from the root of *foul.*]
Sootiness; matter deposited by smoke. *Kirwan, Geol.*

FULIG'INOUS, *a.* [L. *fuligineus, fuliginosus*, from *fuligo*, soot.]
1. Pertaining to soot; sooty; dark; dusky.
2. Pertaining to smoke; resembling smoke; dusky. *Shenstone.*

FULIG'INOUSLY, *a.* By being sooty.

FU'LIMART. [See *Foumart.*]

FULL, *a.* [Sax. Sw. *full*; G. *voll*; D. *vol*; Goth. *fulds*; Dan. *fuld*; W. *gwala*, fullness. Qu. It. *vole*, in composition, See *Fill* and to *Full.*]
1. Replete; having within its limits all that it can contain; as a vessel *full* of liquor.
2. Abounding with; having a large quantity or abundance; as a house *full* of furniture; life is *full* of cares and perplexities.
3. Supplied; not vacant.

Had the throne been *full*, their meeting would not have been regular. *Blackstone.*

4. Plump; fat; as a *full* body.
5. Saturated; sated.

I am *full* of the burnt offerings of rams. Is. i.

6. Crowded, with regard to the imagination or memory.

Every one is *full* of the miracles done by cold baths on decayed and weak constitutions. *Locke.*

7. Large; entire; not partial; that fills; as a *full* meal.
8. Complete; entire; not defective or partial; as the *full* accomplishment of a prophecy.
9. Complete; entire; without abatement.

It came to pass, at the end of two *full* years, that Pharaoh dreamed— Gen. xli.

10. Containing the whole matter; expressing the whole; as a *full* narration or description.
11. Strong; not faint or attenuated; loud; clear; distinct; as a *full* voice or sound.
12. Mature; perfect; as a person of *full* age.
13. Entire; complete; denoting the completion of a sentence; as a *full* stop or point.
14. Spread to view in all dimensions; as a head drawn with a *full* face. *Addison.*
15. Exhibiting the whole disk or surface illuminated; as the *full* moon.
16. Abundant; plenteous; sufficient. We have a *full* supply of provisions for the year.
17. Adequate; equal; as a *full* compensation or reward for labor.
18. Well fed.
19. Well supplied or furnished; abounding.
20. Copious; ample. The speaker or the writer was *full* upon that point. *Mitford.*

A *full* band, in music, is when all the voices and instruments are employed.

A *full* organ, is when all or most of the stops are out.

FULL, *n.* Complete measure; utmost extent. This instrument answers to the *full.*
2. The highest state or degree.

The swan's down feather,
That stands upon the swell at *full* of tide— *Shak.*

3. The whole; the total; in the phrase, *at full.* *Shak.*
4. The state of satiety; as fed to the *full.*

The *full* of the moon, is the time when it presents to the spectator its whole face illuminated, as it always does when in opposition to the sun.

FULL, *adv.* Quite; to the same degree; without abatement or diminution.

The pawn I proffer shall be *full* as good. *Dryden.*

2. With the whole effect.

The diapason closing *full* in man. *Dryden.*

3. Exactly.

Full in the center of the sacred wood. *Addison.*

4. Directly; as, he looked him *full* in the face.

It is placed before adjectives and adverbs to heighten or strengthen their signification; as *full* sad. *Milton.*

Full well ye reject the commandment of God, that ye may keep your own tradition. Mark vii.

Full is prefixed to other words, chiefly participles, to express utmost extent or degree.

FULL-ACORNED, *a.* Fed to the full with acorns. *Shak.*

FULL-BLOOMED, *a.* Having perfect bloom. *Crashaw.*

FULL-BLOWN, *a.* Fully expanded, as a blossom. *Denham.*
2. Fully distended with wind. *Dryden.*

FULL-BOTTOM, *n.* A wig with a large bottom.

FULL-BOTTOMED, *a.* Having a large bottom, as a wig.

FULL-BUTT, *adv.* Meeting directly and with violence. [*Vulgar.*] *L'Estrange.*

FULL-CHARGED, *a.* Charged to fullness. *Shak.*

FULL-CRAMMED, *a.* Crammed to fullness. *Marston.*

FULL-DRESSED, *a.* Dressed in form or costume.

FULL-DRIVE, *a.* Driving with full speed. *Chaucer.*

FULL-EARED, *a.* Having the ears or heads full of grain. *Denham.*

FULL-EYED, *a.* Having large prominent eyes.

FULL-FACED, *a.* Having a broad face.

FULL-FED, *a.* Fed to fullness; plump with fat.

FULL'-FRAUGHT, *a.* Laden or stored to fullness. *Shak.*

FULL-GORGED, *a.* Over fed; *a term of hawking.* *Shak.*

FULL-GROWN, *a.* Grown to full size. *Milton.*

FULL-HEARTED, *a.* Full of courage or confidence. *Shak.*

FULL-HOT, *a.* Heated to the utmost. *Shak.*
2. Quite as hot as it ought to be.

FULL-LADEN, *a.* Laden to the full.

FULL-MANNED, *a.* Completely furnished with men.

FULL-MOUTHED, *a.* Having a full or strong voice.

FULL-ORBED, *a.* Having the orb complete or fully illuminated, as the moon; like the full moon. *Addison. Mason.*

FULL-SPREAD, *a.* Extended to the utmost. *Dryden.*

FULL-STOMACHED, *a.* Having the stomach crammed.

FULL-STUFFED, *a.* Filled to the utmost extent. *Drayton.*

FULL-SUMMED, *a.* Complete in all its parts. *Howell.*

FULL-WINGED, *a.* Having complete wings or large strong wings. *Shak.*
2. Ready for flight; eager. *Beaum.*

FULL, *v. t.* [Sax. *fullian*; L. *fullo*; D. *vollen, vullen*; Fr. *fouler*, to tread, to press, to full; *foule*, a crowd; It. *folla*, and *folta*, a crowd; *folto*, dense; allied to Eng. *felt*, *filter*, It. *feltro*, from being thick or fulled. Sax. *feala*, many, Gr. *πολλοι*, that is, a crowd, a throng. *Foul* and *defile* are probably of the same family. As the French *fouler* signifies to tread and to full cloth, so *walker*, a fuller, is from the root of *walk.*]
To thicken cloth in a mill. *This is the primary sense:* but in practice, to *full* is to mill; to make compact; or to scour, cleanse and thicken in a mill.

FULL'AGE, *n.* Money paid for fulling cloth.

FULL'ED, *pp.* Cleansed; thickened; made dense and firm in a mill.

FULL'ER, *n.* One whose occupation is to full cloth.

FULL'ER'S-EARTH, *n.* A variety of clay, compact, but friable, unctuous to the touch, and of various colors, usually with a shade of green. It is useful in scouring and cleansing cloth, as it imbibes the grease and oil used in preparing wool. *Cleaveland. Encyc.*

FULL'ER'S-THISTLE, }
FULL'ER'S-WEED, } *n.* Teasel, a plant of the genus Dipsacus. The burs are used in dressing cloth.

FULL'ERY, *n.* The place or the works where the fulling of cloth is carried on.

FULL'ING, *ppr.* Thickening cloth in a mill; making compact.

FULL'ING, *n.* The art or practice of thickening cloth and making it compact and firm in a mill, at the same time the cloth is cleansed of oily matter.

FULL'INGMILL, *n.* A mill for fulling cloth by means of pestles or stampers, which beat and press it to a close or compact state and cleanse it.

FULL'NESS, *n.* [from *full.*] The state of being filled, so as to leave no part vacant.
2. The state of abounding or being in great plenty; abundance.
3. Completeness; the state of a thing in which nothing is wanted; perfection.

In thy presence is *fullness* of joy. Ps. xvi.

4. Repletion; satiety; as from intemperance. *Taylor.*
5. Repletion of vessels; as *fullness* of blood.
6. Plenty; wealth; affluence. *Shak.*
7. Struggling perturbation; swelling; as the *fullness* of the heart.
8. Largeness; extent.

There wanted the *fullness* of a plot, and variety of characters to form it as it ought. *Dryden.*

9. Loudness; force of sound, such as fills the ear. *Pope.*

FULL'SOME, *a.* [Sax. *ful*, foul or full.] Gross; disgusting by plainness, grossness or excess; as *fullsome* flattery or praise.

FULL'SOMELY, *adv.* Grossly; with disgusting plainness or excess.

FULL'SOMENESS, *n.* Offensive grossness, as of praise.

[These are the senses of this word and the only senses used in New England, as far as my knowledge extends.]

FUL'LY, *adv.* Completely; entirely; without lack or defect; in a manner to give satisfaction; to the extent desired; as, to be *fully* persuaded of the truth of a proposition.

2. Completely; perfectly. Things partially known in this life will be hereafter *fully* disclosed.

FUL'MAR, *n.* A fowl of the genus Procellaria, or petrel kind, larger than a gull, possessing the singular faculty of spouting from its bill a quantity of pure oil against its adversary. It is an inhabitant of the Hebrides; it feeds on the fat of whales, and when one of them is taken, will perch on it even when alive and pick out pieces of flesh. *Dict. of Nat. Hist.*

2. The foulemart or fulimart. [See *Foumart.*]

FUL'MINANT, *a.* [Fr. from L. *fulminans.*] Thundering.

FUL'MINATE, *v. i.* [L. *fulmino*, from *fulmen*, thunder, from a root in *Bl*, which signifies to throw or to burst forth.]

1. To thunder. *Davies.*

2. To make a loud sudden noise, or a sudden sharp crack; to detonate; as *fulminating* gold. *Boyle.*

3. To hurl papal thunder; to issue forth ecclesiastical censures, as the pope. *Herbert.*

FUL'MINATE, *v. t.* To utter or send out, as a denunciation or censure; to send out, as a menace or censure by ecclesiastical authority. *Warburton. Ayliffe.*

2. To cause to explode. *Sprat.*

FUL'MINATING, *ppr.* Thundering; crackling; exploding; detonating.

2. Hurling papal denunciations, menaces or censures.

Fulminating powder, a detonating compound of sulphur, carbonate of potash and niter.

FULMINA'TION, *n.* A thundering.

2. Denunciation of censure or threats, as by papal authority.

The *fulminations* from the Vatican were turned into ridicule. *Ayliffe.*

3. The explosion of certain chimical preparations; detonation. *Encyc.*

FUL'MINATORY, *a.* Thundering; striking terror. *Johnson.*

FUL'MINE, *v. t.* To thunder. [*Not in use.*] *Spenser. Milton.*

FULMIN'IC, *a.* *Fulminic* acid, in chimistry, is a peculiar acid contained in fulminating silver. *Henry.*

FUL'SOME, *a.* [Sax. *ful*, foul.] Nauseous; offensive.

He that brings *fulsome* objects to my view,
With nauseous images my fancy fills. *Roscommon.*

2. Rank; offensive to the smell; as a rank and *fulsome* smell. *Bacon.*

3. Lustful; as *fulsome* ewes. *Shak.*

4. Tending to obscenity; as a *fulsome* epigram. *Dryden.*

These are the English definitions of *fulsome*, but I have never witnessed such applications of the word in the United States. It seems then that *full* and *foul* are radically the same word, the primary sense of which is stuffed, crowded, from the sense of putting on or in. In the United States, the compound *fullsome* takes its signification from *full*, in the sense of cloying or satiating, and in England, *fulsome* takes its predominant sense from *foulness*.

FUL'SOMELY, *adv.* Rankly; nauseously; obscenely. *Eng.*

FUL'SOMENESS, *n.* Nauseousness; rank smell; obscenity. *Eng.*

FUL'VID, *a.* [See *Fulvous*, which is generally used.]

FUL'VOUS, *a.* [L. *fulvus.*] Yellow; tawny; saffron-colored. *Encyc.*

FUMA'DO, *n.* [L. *fumus*, smoke.] A smoked fish. *Carew.*

FU'MATORY, *n.* [L. *fumaria herba*; Fr. *fumeterre*; from *fumus*, smoke.]

A plant or genus of plants, called *Fumaria*, of several species. *Encyc.*

FUM'BLE, *v. i.* [D. *fommelen*; Dan. *famler*; Sw. *famla*; properly, to stop, stammer, falter, hesitate, to feel along, to grope.]

1. To feel or grope about; to attempt awkwardly. *Cudworth.*

2. To grope about in perplexity; to seek awkwardly; as, to *fumble* for an excuse. *Dryden.*

3. To handle much; to play childishly; to turn over and over.

I saw him *fumble* with the sheets, and play with flowers. *Shak.*

FUM'BLE, *v. t.* To manage awkwardly; to crowd or tumble together. *Shak.*

FUM'BLER, *n.* One who gropes or manages awkwardly.

FUM'BLING, *ppr.* Groping; managing awkwardly.

FUM'BLINGLY, *adv.* In an awkward manner.

FUME, *n.* [L. *fumus*, Fr. *fumée*, smoke.] Smoke; vapor from combustion, as from burning wood or tobacco. *Bacon.*

2. Vapor; volatile matter ascending in a dense body. *Woodward.*

3. Exhalation from the stomach; as the *fumes* of wine. *Dryden.*

4. Rage; heat; as the *fumes* of passion. *South.*

5. Any thing unsubstantial or fleeting. *Shak.*

6. Idle conceit; vain imagination. *Bacon.*

FUME, *v. i.* [L. *fumo*, Fr. *fumer*, Sp. *fumar*, It. *fumare*, to smoke.]

1. To smoke; to throw off vapor, as in combustion.

Where the golden altar *fumed*. *Milton.*

2. To yield vapor or visible exhalations.

Silenus lay,
Whose constant cups lay *fuming* to his brain. *Roscommon.*

3. To pass off in vapors.

Their parts are kept from *fuming* away by their fixity. *Cheyne.*

4. To be in a rage; to be hot with anger.

He frets, he *fumes*, he stares, he stamps the ground. *Dryden.*

FUME, *v. t.* To smoke; to dry in smoke. *Carew.*

2. To perfume.

She *fumed* the temples with an od'rous flame. *Dryden.*

3. To disperse or drive away in vapors.

The heat will *fume* away most of the scent. *Mortimer.*

FU'MET, *n.* The dung of deer. *B. Jonson.*

FU'MID, *a.* [L. *fumidus.*] Smoky; vaporous. *Brown.*

FU'MIGATE, *v. t.* [L. *fumigo*; Fr. *fumiger*; from *fumus*, smoke.]

1. To smoke; to perfume. *Dryden.*

2. To apply smoke to; to expose to smoke; as in chimistry, or in medicine by inhaling it, or in cleansing infected apartments.

FU'MIGATED, *pp.* Smoked; exposed to smoke.

FU'MIGATING, *ppr.* Smoking; applying smoke to.

FUMIGA'TION, *n.* [L. *fumigatio.*] The act of smoking or applying smoke, as in chimistry for softening a metal, or in the healing art by inhaling tbe smoke of certain substances. Expectoration is often assisted and sometimes ulcers of the lungs healed by *fumigation*. Fumigation is also used in cleansing infected rooms.

2. Vapors; scent raised by fire.

FU'MING, *ppr.* Smoking; emitting vapors; raging; fretting.

FU'MINGLY, *adv.* Angrily; in a rage. *Hooker.*

FU'MISH, *a.* Smoky; hot; choleric. [*Little used.*]

FU'MITER, *n.* A plant.

FU'MOUS, } *a.* Producing fume; full of vapor.
FU'MY, }

From dice and wine the youth retir'd to rest,
And puffed the *fumy* god from out his breast. *Dryden.*

FUN, *n.* Sport; vulgar merriment. *A low word.* [Qu. Eth. ወፈቦ wani, to play.]

FUNAM'BULATORY, *a.* Performing like a rope dancer; narrow like the walk of a rope dancer. *Brown. Chambers.*

FUNAM'BULIST, *n.* [L. *funis*, rope, and *ambulo*, to walk.] A rope walker or dancer.

FUNC'TION, *n.* [L. *functio*, from *fungor*, to perform.]

1. In a general sense, the doing, executing or performing of any thing; discharge; performance; as the *function* of a calling or office. More generally,

2. Office or employment, or any duty or business belonging to a particular station or character, or required of a person in that station or character. Thus we speak of the *functions* of a chancellor, judge or bishop; the *functions* of a parent or guardian.

3. Trade; occupation. [*Less proper.*]

4. The office of any particular part of animal bodies; the peculiar or appropriate action of a member or part of the body, by which the animal economy is carried on. Thus we speak of the *functions* of the brain and nerves, of the heart, of the liver, of the muscles, &c.

5. Power; faculty, animal or intellectual.

As the mind opens, and its *functions* spread. *Pope.*

6. In *mathematics*, the *function* of a variable quantity, is any algebraic expression into which that quantity enters, mixed with other quantities that have invariable values. *Cyc.*

FUNC'TIONALLY, *adv.* By means of the functions. *Lawrence, Lect.*

FUNC'TIONARY, *n.* One who holds an office or trust; as a public *functionary*; secular *functionaries*. *Walsh.*

FUND, *n.* [Fr. *fond*; Sp. *fondo*, *funda*; L. *fundus*, ground, bottom, foundation; connected with L. *fundo*, to found, the sense of which is to throw down, to set, to lay; Ir. *bon* or *bun*, bottom; Heb. Ch. Syr. בנה, Ar. بَنَى, to build. Class Bn. No. 7. The L. *funda*, a sling, a casting net or purse, It. *fonda*, is from the same source.]

1. A stock or capital; a sum of money appropriated as the foundation of some commercial or other operation, undertaken with a view to profit, and by means of which expenses and credit are supported. Thus the capital stock of a banking institution is called its *fund*; the joint stock of a commercial or manufacturing house constitutes its *fund* or *funds*; and hence the word is applied to the money which an individual may possess, or the means he can employ for carrying on any enterprise or operation. No prudent man undertakes an expensive business without *funds*.
2. Money lent to government, constituting a national debt; or the stock of a national debt. Thus we say, a man is interested in the *funds* or *public funds*, when he owns the stock or the evidences of the public debt; and the *funds* are said to rise or fall, when a given amount of that debt sells for more or less in the market.
3. Money or income destined to the payment of the interest of a debt.
4. A *sinking fund* is a sum of money appropriated to the purchase of the public stocks or the payment of the public debt.
5. A stock or capital to afford supplies of any kind; as a *fund* of wisdom or good sense; a *fund* of wit. Hence,
6. Abundance; ample stock or store.

FUND, *v. t.* To provide and appropriate a fund or permanent revenue for the payment of the interest of; to make permanent provision of resources for discharging the annual interest of; as, to *fund* exchequer bills or government notes; to *fund* a national debt. *Bolingbroke. Hamilton.*

2. To place money in a fund.

FUND'AMENT, *n.* [L. *fundamentum*, from *fundo*, to set.]

1. The seat; the lower part of the body or of the intestinum rectum. *Hume.*
2. Foundation. [*Not in use.*] *Chaucer.*

FUNDAMENT'AL, *a.* Pertaining to the foundation or basis; serving for the foundation. Hence, essential; important; as a *fundamental* truth or principle; a *fundamental* law; a *fundamental* sound or chord in music.

FUNDAMENT'AL, *n.* A leading or primary principle, rule, law or article, which serves as the ground work of a system; essential part; as the *fundamentals* of the christian faith.

FUNDAMENT'ALLY, *n.* Primarily; originally; essentially; at the foundation. All power is *fundamentally* in the citizens of a state.

FUND'ED, *pp.* Furnished with funds for regular payment of the interest of.

FUND'ING, *ppr.* Providing funds for the payment of the interest of.

FUNE'BRIAL, *a.* [L. *funebris.*] Pertaining to funerals. *Brown.*

FU'NERAL, *n.* [It. *funerale*; Fr. *funerailles*; from L. *funus*, from *funale*, a cord, a torch, from *funis*, a rope or cord, as torches were made of cords, and were used in burials among the Romans.]

1. Burial; the ceremony of burying a dead body; the solemnization of interment; obsequies.
2. The procession of persons attending the burial of the dead. *Pope.*
3. Burial; interment. *Denham.*

FU'NERAL, *a.* Pertaining to burial; used at the interment of the dead; as *funeral* rites, honors or ceremonies; a *funeral* torch; *funeral* feast or games; *funeral* oration. *Encyc. Dryden.*

FUNERA'TION, *n.* Solemnization of a funeral. [*Not used.*]

FUNE'REAL, *a.* Suiting a funeral; pertaining to burial. *Shak.*

2. Dark; dismal; mournful. *Taylor.*

FUN'GATE, *n.* [from *fungus.*] A compound of fungic acid and a base. *Coxe.*

FUN'GIC, *a.* Pertaining to or obtained from mushrooms; as *fungic* acid.

FUN'GIFORM, *a.* [*fungus* and *form.*] In *mineralogy*, having a termination similar to the head of a fungus. *Philips.*

FUN'GIN, *n.* The fleshy part of mushrooms, now considered as a peculiar vegetable principle. *Coxe.*

FUN'GITE, *n.* [from *fungus.*] A kind of fossil coral.

FUNGOS'ITY, *n.* Soft excrescence.

FUN'GOUS, *a.* [See *Fungus.*] Like fungus or a mushroom; excrescent; spungy; soft.

2. Growing suddenly, but not substantial or durable. *Harris.*

FUN'GUS, *n.* [L.] A mushroom, vulgarly called a toadstool. The Fungi constitute an order of plants of a peculiar organization and manner of growth. The word is also applied to excrescences on plants. *Encyc.*

2. A spungy excrescence in animal bodies, as proud flesh formed in wounds. *Coxe.* The term is particularly applied to any morbid excrescence, whether in wounds or arising spontaneously. *Cyc. Cooper.*

FU'NICLE, *n.* [L. *funiculus*, dim. of *funis*, a cord.] A small cord; a small ligature; a fiber. *Johnson.*

FUNIC'ULAR, *a.* Consisting of a small cord or fiber.

FUNK, *n.* [Qu. Arm. *fancq*, Fr. *fange*, mud, mire, matter.] An offensive smell. [*Vulgar.*]

FUN'NEL, *n.* [W. *fynel*, an air-hole, funnel or chimney, from *fwn*, breath, source, connected with *fount*, which see.]

1. A passage or avenue for a fluid or flowing substance, particularly the shaft or hollow channel of a chimney through which smoke ascends.
2. A vessel for conveying fluids into close vessels; a kind of hollow cone with a pipe; a tunnel. *Ray.*

FUN'NELFORM, FUN'NELSHAPED, } *a.* Having the form of a funnel or inverted hollow cone. *Fam. of Plants.*

FUN'NY, *a.* [from *fun.*] Droll; comical.

FUN'NY, *n.* A light boat.

FUR, *n.* [Fr. *fourrure*, from *fourrer*, to put on, to thrust in, to stuff; Sp. *aforrar*; Arm. *feura*. The sense seems to be, to stuff, to make thick, or to put on and thus make thick. In Welsh, *fer* is dense, solid.]

1. The short, fine, soft hair of certain animals, growing thick on the skin, and distinguished from the hair, which is longer and coarser. Fur is one of the most perfect non-conductors of heat, and serves to keep animals warm in cold climates.
2. The skins of certain wild animals with the fur; peltry; as a cargo of *furs*.
3. Strips of skin with fur, used on garments for lining or for ornament. Garments are lined or faced with *fur*.
4. Hair in general; *a loose application of the word*.
5. A coat of morbid matter collected on the tongue in persons affected with fever.

FUR, *v. t.* To line, face or cover with fur; as a *furred* robe.

2. To cover with morbid matter, as the tongue.
3. To line with a board, as in carpentry.

FUR'-WROUGHT, *a. fur'-raut.* Made of fur. *Gay.*

FURA'CIOUS, *a.* [L. *furax*, from *furor*, to steal.] Given to theft; inclined to steal; thievish. [*Little used.*]

FURAC'ITY, *n.* Thievishness. [*Little used.*]

FUR'BELOW, *n.* [Fr. It. Sp. *falbala.*] A piece of stuff plaited and puckered, on a gown or petticoat; a flounce; the plaited border of a petticoat or gown.

FUR'BELOW, *v. t.* To put on a furbelow; to furnish with an ornamental appendage of dress. *Prior.*

FUR'BISH, *v. t.* [It. *forbire*; Fr. *fourbir.*] To rub or scour to brightness; to polish; to burnish; as, to *furbish* a sword or spear; to *furbish* arms.

FUR'BISHED, *pp.* Scoured to brightness; polished; burnished.

FUR'BISHER, *n.* One who polishes or makes bright by rubbing; one who cleans.

FUR'BISHING, *ppr.* Rubbing to brightness; polishing.

FUR'CATE, *a.* [L. *furca*, a fork.] Forked; branching like the prongs of a fork. *Lee, Botany.*

FURCA'TION, *n.* A forking; a branching like the tines of a fork. *Brown.*

FUR'DLE, *v. t.* [Fr. *fardeau*, a bundle.] To draw up into a bundle. [*Not used.*] *Brown.*

FUR'FUR, *n.* [L.] Dandruff; scurf; scales like bran.

FURFURA'CEOUS, *a.* [L. *furfuraceus.*] Scaly; branny; scurfy; like bran.

FU'RIOUS, *a.* [L. *furiosus*; It. *furioso*; Fr. *furieux*. See *Fury.*]

1. Rushing with impetuosity; moving with violence; as a *furious* stream; a *furious* wind or storm.
2. Raging; violent; transported with passion; as a *furious* animal.

3. Mad; phrenetic.

FU'RIOUSLY, *adv.* With impetuous motion or agitation; violently; vehemently; as, to run *furiously*; to attack one *furiously.*

FU'RIOUSNESS, *n.* Impetuous motion or rushing; violent agitation.

2. Madness; phrensy; rage.

FURL, *v. t.* [Fr. *ferler*; Arm. *farlea*; Sp. *aferrar*, to grapple, to seize, to furl; Port. *ferrar.*]

To draw up; to contract; to wrap or roll a sail close to the yard, stay or mast, and fasten it by a gasket or cord. *Mar. Dict.*

FURL'ED, *pp.* Wrapped and fastened to a yard, &c.

FURL'ING, *ppr.* Wrapping or rolling and fastening to a yard, &c.

FUR'LONG, *n.* [Sax. *furlang*; *far* or *fur* and *long.*]

A measure of length; the eighth part of a mile; forty rods, poles or perches.

FUR'LOW, *n.* [D. *verlof*; G. *urlaub*; Dan. *orlov*; Sw. *orlof*; compounded of the root of *fare*, to go, and *leave*, permission. See *Fare* and *Leave.* The common orthography *furlough* is corrupt, as the last syllable exhibits false radical consonants. The true orthography is *furlow.*]

Leave of absence; a word used only in military affairs. Leave or license given by a commanding officer to an officer or soldier to be absent from service for a certain time.

FUR'LOW, *v. t.* To furnish with a furlow; to grant leave of absence to an officer or soldier.

FUR'MENTY, *n.* [See *Frumenty.*]

FUR'NACE, *n.* [Fr. *fournaise, fourneau*; It. *fornace*; Sp. *horno*; from L. *fornax, furnus*, either from *burning*, or the sense is an arch.]

1. A place where a vehement fire and heat may be made and maintained, for melting ores or metals, &c. A furnace for casting cannon and other large operations is inclosed with walls through which a current of air is blown from a large bellows. In smaller operations a vessel is constructed with a chamber or cavity, with a door and a grate.

2. In *scripture*, a place of cruel bondage and affliction. Deut. iv.

3. Grievous afflictions by which men are tried. Ezek. xxii.

4. A place of temporal torment. Dan. iii.

5. Hell; the place of endless torment. Matt. xiii.

FUR'NACE, *v. t.* To throw out sparks as a furnace *Shak.*

FUR'NIMENT, *n.* [Fr. *fourniment.*] Furniture. [*Not in use.*] *Spenser.*

FUR'NISH, *v. t.* [Fr. *fournir*; Arm. *fourniçza*; It. *fornire.* There is a close affinity, in sense and elements, between *furnish*, *garnish*, and the L. *orno*, which may have been *forno* or *horno*. We see in *furlow*, above, the *f* is lost in three of the languages, and it may be so in *orno*. The primary sense is to put on, or to set on.]

1. To supply with any thing wanted or necessary; as, to *furnish* a family with provisions; to *furnish* arms for defense; to *furnish* a table; to *furnish* a library; to *furnish* one with money or implements.

2. To supply; to store; as, to *furnish* the mind with ideas; to *furnish* one with knowledge or principles.

3. To fit up; to supply with the proper goods, vessels or ornamental appendages; as, to *furnish* a house or a room.

4. To equip; to fit for an expedition; to supply.

FUR'NISHED, *a.* Supplied; garnished; fitted with necessaries.

FUR'NISHER, *n.* One who supplies or fits out.

FUR'NISHING, *ppr.* Supplying; fitting; garnishing.

FUR'NITURE, *n.* [Fr. *fourniture*; It. *fornimento*; Arm. *fournimand.*]

1. Goods, vessels, utensils and other appendages necessary or convenient for housekeeping; whatever is added to the interior of a house or apartment, for use or convenience.

2. Appendages; that which is added for use or ornament; as the earth with all its *furniture.*

3. Equipage; ornaments; decorations; *in a very general sense.*

FUR'RED, *pp.* [See *Fur.*] Lined or ornamented with fur; thickened by the addition of a board.

FUR'RIER, *n.* A dealer in furs; one who makes or sells muffs, tippets, &c.

FUR'RIERY, *n.* Furs in general. *Tooke.*

FUR'RING, *ppr.* Lining or ornamenting with fur; lining with a board.

FUR'ROW, *n.* [Sax. *fur* or *furh*; G. *furche*; Dan. *furre*; Sw. *fora.* Qu. Gr. φαροω, to plow.] A trench in the earth made by a plow.

2. A long narrow trench or channel in wood or metal; a groove.

3. A hollow made by wrinkles in the face.

FUR'ROW, *v. t.* [Sax. *fyrian.*] To cut a furrow; to make furrows in; to plow.

2. To make long narrow channels or grooves in.

3. To cut; to make channels in; to plow; as, to *furrow* the deep.

4. To make hollows in by wrinkles. Sorrow *furrows* the brow.

FUR'ROWFACED, *a.* Having a wrinkled or furrowed face. *B. Jonson.*

FUR'ROWWEED, *n.* A weed growing on plowed land. *Shak.*

FUR'RY, *a.* [from *fur.*] Covered with fur; dressed in fur.

2. Consisting of fur or skins; as *furry* spoils. *Dryden.*

FUR'THER, *a.* [Sax. *further*, comparative of *forth*, from the root of *far*, *faran*, to go, to advance.]

1. More or most distant; as the *further* end of the field.

2. Additional. We have a *further* reason for this opinion. We have nothing *further* to suggest.

> What *further* need have we of witnesses? Matt. xxvi.

FUR'THER, *adv.* To a greater distance. He went *further.*

FUR'THER, *v. t.* [Sax. *fyrthrian*; G. *fördern*; D. *vorderen*; Sw. *befordra*; Dan. *befordrer.*]

To help forward; to promote; to advance onward; to forward; hence, to help or assist.

> This binds thee then to *further* my design. *Dryden.*

FUR'THERANCE, *n.* A helping forward; promotion; advancement.

> I know that I shall abide and continue with you all, for your *furtherance* and joy of faith. Phil. i.

FUR'THERED, *pp.* Promoted; advanced.

FUR'THERER, *n.* One who helps to advance; a promoter.

FUR'THERMORE, *adv.* Moreover; besides; in addition to what has been said.

FUR'THEST, *a.* Most distant either in time or place.

FUR'THEST, *adv.* At the greatest distance.

FUR'TIVE, *a.* [L. *furtivus*; Fr. *furtif*; from *fur*, a thief, *furor*, to steal.]

Stolen; obtained by theft. *Prior.*

FU'RUNCLE, *n.* [L. *furunculus*; Fr. *furoncle*; Sp. *hura*; from L. *furia, furo.*]

A small tumor or boil, with inflammation and pain, arising under the skin in the adipose membrane. *Encyc.*

FU'RY, *n.* [L. *furor, furia*; Fr. *fureur, furie*; Sp. *furia*; from L. *furo*, to rage; W. *fwyraw*, to drive. Class Br.]

1. A violent rushing; impetuous motion; as the *fury* of the winds.

2. Rage; a storm of anger; madness; turbulence.

> I do oppose my patience to his *fury.* *Shak.*

3. Enthusiasm; heat of the mind. *Dryden.*

4. In *mythology*, a deity, a goddess of vengeance; hence, a stormy, turbulent, violent woman. *Addison.*

FU'RYLIKE, *a.* Raging; furious; violent. *Thomson.*

FURZ, *n.* [Sax. *fyrs*; probably W. *ferz*, thick.]

Gorse; whin; a thorny plant of the genus Ulex. *Miller. Fam. of Plants.*

FURZ'Y, *a.* Overgrown with furz; full of gorse. *Gay.*

FUS'CITE, *n.* A mineral of a grayish or greenish black color, found in Norway. *Phillips.*

FUS'COUS, *a.* [L. *fuscus.*] Brown; of a dark color. *Ray.*

FUSE, *v. t.* *s* as *z.* [L. *fundo, fusum*, to pour out.]

To melt; to liquefy by heat; to render fluid; to dissolve. *Chimistry.*

FUSE, *v. i.* To be melted; to be reduced from a solid to a fluid state by heat.

FU'SED, *pp.* Melted; liquefied.

FUSEE', *n.* *s* as *z.* [Fr. *fusée, fuseau*; It. *fuso*; Sp. *huso*; Port. *fuso*; from L. *fusus*, a spindle, from *fundo, fudi, fusum.*]

The cone or conical part of a watch or clock, round which is wound the chain or cord. *Encyc. Johnson.*

FUSEE', *n.* *s* as *z.* [Fr. a squib.] A small neat musket or firelock. But we now use *fusil.*

2. *Fusee* or *fuse* of a bomb or granade, a small pipe filled with combustible matter by which fire is communicated to the powder in the bomb; but as the matter burns slowly, time is given before the charge takes fire, for the bomb to reach its destination.

3. The track of a buck.

FUSIBIL'ITY, *n.* [See *Fusible.*] The quality of being fusible, or of being convertible from a solid to a fluid state by heat.

FU'SIBLE, *a.* *s* as *z.* [Fr. from L. *fusus*, from *fundo.*]

That may be melted or liquefied. The earths are found to be *fusible.*

FU'SIFORM, *a.* [L. *fusus*, a spindle, and *form.*]
Shaped like a spindle. *Pennant.*

FU'SIL, *a. s* as *z.* [Fr. *fusile*; L. *fusilis*, from *fusus, fundo.*]
1. Capable of being melted or rendered fluid by heat.
2. Running; flowing, as a liquid. *Milton. Philips.*

FU'SIL, *n. s* as *z.* [Fr. from L. *fusus, fundo.*]
1. A light musket or firelock.
2. A bearing in heraldry of a rhomboidal figure, named from its shape, which resembles that of a spindle. *Encyc.*

FUSILEE'R, *n.* [from *fusil.*] Properly, a soldier armed with a fusil; but in modern times, a soldier armed like others of the infantry, and distinguished by wearing a cap like a grenadier, but somewhat shorter.

FU'SION, *n. s* as *z.* [L. *fusio*; Fr. *fusion*; from L. *fundo, fusum.*]
1. The act or operation of melting or rendering fluid by heat, without the aid of a solvent; as the *fusion* of ice or of metals.
2. The state of being melted or dissolved by heat; a state of fluidity or flowing in consequence of heat; as metals in *fusion.*
Watery fusion, the melting of certain crystals by heat in their own water of crystalization. *Chimistry.*

FUSS, *n.* [allied perhaps to Gr. φυσαω, to blow or puff.]
A tumult; a bustle; *but the word is vulgar.*

FUST, *n.* [Fr. *fût*; It. *fusta*; L. *fustis*, a staff.] The shaft of a column.

FUST, *n.* [Fr. *fût.*] A strong musty smell.

FUST, *v. i.* To become moldy; to smell ill. *Shak.*

FUST'ED, *a.* Moldy; ill smelling.

FUS'TET, *n.* [Fr.; Sp. Port. *fustete.*] The wood of the *Rhus cotinus*, which yields a fine orange color. *Ure.*

FUS'TIAN, *n.* [Fr. *futaine*; Arm. *fustenn*; Sp. *fustan*, the name of a place.]
1. A kind of cotton stuff, or stuff of cotton and linen.
2. An inflated style of writing; a kind of writing in which high sounding words are used, above the dignity of the thoughts or subject; a swelling style; bombast.

Fustian is thoughts and words ill sorted. *Dryden.*

FUS'TIAN, *a.* Made of fustian.
2. In *style*, swelling above the dignity of the thoughts or subject; too pompous; ridiculously tumid; bombastic. *Dryden.*

FUS'TIANIST, *n.* One who writes bombast. *Milton.*

FUS'TIC, *n.* [Sp. *fuste*, wood, timber; L. *fustis.*]
The wood of the *Morus tinctoria*, a tree growing in the West Indies, imported and used in dyeing yellow. *Encyc.*

FUSTIGA'TION, *n.* [L. *fustigatio*, from *fustigo*, to beat with a cudgel, from *fustis*, a stick or club.]
Among *the ancient Romans*, a punishment by beating with a stick or club, inflicted on freemen. *Encyc.*

FUST'INESS, *n.* A fusty state or quality; an ill smell from moldiness, or moldiness itself.

FUST'Y, *a.* [See *Fust.*] Moldy; musty; ill-smelling; rank; rancid. *Shak.*

FU'TILE, *a.* [Fr.; L. *futilis*, from *futio*, to pour out; *effutio*, to prate or babble; Heb. Ch. בטא to utter rashly or foolishly. Class Bd. No. 2. 6. 15.]
1. Talkative; loquacious; tatling. *Obs. Bacon.*
2. Trifling; of no weight or importance; answering no valuable purpose; worthless.
3. Of no effect.

FUTIL'ITY, *n.* Talkativeness; loquaciousness; loquacity. [In this sense, not now used.] *L'Estrange.*
2. Triflingness; unimportance; want of weight or effect; as, to expose the *futility* of arguments.
3. The quality of producing no valuable effect, or of coming to nothing; as the *futility* of measures or schemes.

FU'TILOUS, *a.* Worthless; trifling. [*Not used.*] *Howell.*

FUT'TOCK, *n.* [Qu. *foot-hook.* It is more probably corrupted from *foot-lock.*]
In *a ship*, the futtocks are the middle timbers, between the floor and the upper timbers, or the timbers raised over the keel which form the breadth of the ship.

FU'TURE, *a.* [L. *futurus*; Fr. *futur.*] That is to be or come hereafter; that will exist at any time after the present, indefinitely. The next moment is *future* to the present.
2. The *future tense*, in grammar, is the modification of a verb which expresses a future act or event.

FU'TURE, *n.* Time to come; a time subsequent to the present; as, the *future* shall be as the present; in *future*; for the *future.* In such phrases, time or season is implied.

FU'TURELY, *adv.* In time to come. [*Not used.*] *Raleigh.*

FUTURI''TION, *n.* The state of being to come or exist hereafter. *South. Stiles.*

FUTU'RITY, *n.* Future time; time to come.
2. Event to come.

All *futurities* are naked before the all-seeing eye. *South.*

3. The state of being yet to come, or to come hereafter.

FUZZ, *v. i.* To fly off in minute particles.

FUZZ, *n.* Fine, light particles; loose, volatile matter.

FUZZ'BALL, *n.* A kind of fungus or mushroom, which when pressed bursts and scatters a fine dust.
2. A puff.

FUZ'ZLE, *v. t.* To intoxicate. *Burton.*

FY, *exclam.* A word which expresses blame, dislike, disapprobation, abhorrence or contempt.

Fy, my lord, *fy!* a soldier, and afraid? *Shak.*

G.

G, the seventh letter and the fifth articulation of the English Alphabet, is derived to us, through the Latin and Greek, from the Assyrian languages; it being found in the Chaldee, Syriac, Hebrew, Samaritan, Phenician, Ethiopic and Arabic. In the latter language, it is called *giim* or *jim*; but in the others, *gimel, gomal* or *gamal*; that is, *camel*, from its shape, which resembles the neck of that animal, at least in the Chaldee and Hebrew. It is the third letter in the Chaldee, Syriac, Hebrew, Samaritan and Greek; the fifth in the Arabic, and the twentieth in the Ethiopic. The Greek Γ *gamma* is the Chaldaic ג inverted. The early Latins used C for the Greek *gamma*, and hence C came to hold the third place in the order of the Alphabet; the place which *gimel* holds in the oriental languages. The two letters are primarily palatals, and so nearly allied in sound that they are easily convertible; and they have been reciprocally used the one for the other. But in the Assyrian languages, *gimel* had two sounds; one hard or close, as we pronounce the letter in *gave, good*; the other soft, or rather compound, as the English *j* or as *ch* in *chase*. In the Arabic, this letter has the sound of the English *j* or *dzh*, and this sound it has in many English words, as in *genius, gem, ginger.* It retains its hard sound in all cases, before *a, o* and *u*; but before *e, i* and *y*, its sound is hard or soft, as custom has dictated, and its different sounds are not reducible to rules. It is silent in some words before *n*, as in *benign, condign, malign, campaign*; but it resumes its sound in *benignity* and *malignity.* G is mute before *n* in *gnash*; it is silent also in many words when united with *h*, as in *bright, might, night, nigh, high.* The Saxon *g* has in many words been softened or liquefied into *y* or *ow*; as Sax. *dæg, gear*, Eng. *day, year*; Sax. *bugan*, Eng. to *bow.*

The Celtic nations had a peculiar manner of beginning the sound of *u* or *w* with the articulation *g*, or rather prefixing this articulation to that vowel. Thus *guard* for *ward, gwain* for *wain, guerre* for *war, gwell* for *well.* Whether this *g* has been added by the Celtic races, or whether the Teutonic nations have lost it, is a question I have not examined with particular attention.

As a *numeral*, G was anciently used to denote 400, and with a dash over it $\bar{G}$, 40,000. As an *abbreviation*, it stands for *Gaius, Gellius*, &c. In *music*, it is the mark of the treble cliff, and from its being placed at the head or marking the first sound in Guido's scale, the whole scale took the name, *Gammut*, from the Greek name of the letter.

GA, in Gothic, is a prefix, answering to *ge* in Saxon and other Teutonic languages. It sometimes has the force of the Latin *cum* or *con*, as in *gawithan*, to conjoin. But in most words it appears to have no use, and in modern English it is entirely lost. *Y-cleped*, in which *ge* is changed into *y*, is the last word in which the English retained this prefix.

GAB, *n.* [Scot. *gab*, Dan. *gab*, the mouth, and a *gap* or gaping; Sw. *gap;* Russ. *guba*, a lip, a bay or gulf, the mouth of a river; Ir. *cab*, the mouth; connected probably with *gabble*, *giberish*, Sax. *gabban*, to mock, perhaps to make mouths. See *Gabble* and *Gape*.]

The mouth; as in the phrase, the gift of the *gab*, that is, loquaciousness. But the word is so vulgar as rarely to be used.

GAB'ARDINE, *n*, [Sp. *gabardina ; gaban*, a great coat with a hood and close sleeves; *gabacha*, a loose garment; Port. *gabam*, a frock; It. *gavardina ;* Fr. *gaban*.]

A coarse frock or loose upper garment; a mean dress. *Shak.*

GAB'BLE, *v. i.* [D. *gabberen*, to prate; Sax. *gabban*, to jeer or deride; Fr. *gaber*, id.; Eng. to *gibe*; Sw. *gabberi*, derision; It. *gabbare*, to deceive; *gabbo*, a jeering. These may all be from one root. See Class Gb. No. 7.]

1. To prate; to talk fast, or to talk without meaning.

> Such a rout, and such a rabble,
> Run to hear Jack Pudding *gabble*. *Swift.*

2. To utter inarticulate sounds with rapidity; as *gabbling* fowls. *Dryden.*

GAB'BLE, *n.* Loud or rapid talk without meaning. *Milton.*

2. Inarticulate sounds rapidly uttered, as of fowls. *Shak.*

GAB'BLER, *n.* A prater; a noisy talker; one that utters inarticulate sounds.

GAB'BLING, *ppr.* Prating; chattering; uttering unmeaning or inarticulate sounds.

GAB'BRO, *n.* In *mineralogy*, the name given by the Italians to the aggregate of diallage and saussurite. It is the *euphotide* of the French, and the *verde di Corsica duro* of artists. *Cleaveland.*

GA'BEL, *n.* [Fr. *gabelle ;* It. *gabella ;* Sp. *gabela* ; Sax. *gafel* or *gafol*.]

A tax, impost or duty; usually an excise.

GA'BELER, *n.* A collector of the gabel or of taxes. *Wright.*

GA'BION, *n.* [Fr. *id.;* It. *gabbione*, a large cage; *gabbia*, a cage; Sp. *gavion*, *gabion*, a basket. In Ir. *gabham* signifies to take or hold; W. *gavaelu*, id.]

In *fortification*, a large basket of wicker-work, of a cylindrical form; filled with earth, and serving to shelter men from an enemy's fire. *Encyc.*

GA'BLE, *n.* [W. *gavael*, a hold or grasp, the gable of a house; *gavaelu*, to grasp, hold, arrest, Ir. *gabham.* Qu. G. *gabel*, Ir. *gabhlan*, a fork.]

The triangular end of a house or other building, from the cornice or eaves to the top. In America, it is usually called the *gable-end.*

GA'BRIELITES, *n.* In *ecclesiastical history*, a sect of anabaptists in Pomerania, so called from one Gabriel Scherling.

GA'BRONITE, *n.* A mineral, supposed to be a variety of *fettstein*. It occurs in masses, whose structure is more or less foliated, or sometimes compact. Its colors are gray, bluish or greenish gray, and sometimes red. *Cleaveland.*

GAD, *n.* [Sax. *gad*, a goad and a wedge; Ir. *gadh*, a dart.]

1. A wedge or ingot of steel. *Moxon.*
2. A style or graver. *Shak.*
3. A punch of iron with a wooden handle, used by miners. *Encyc.*

GAD, *v. i.* [Ir. *gad*, a stealing, properly a roving, as *rob* is connected with *rove ; gadaim*, to steal. It coincides with the Russ. *chod*, a going or passing; *choju*, to go, to pass, to march. See Class Gd. No. 17. Eth. and No. 38.]

1. To walk about; to rove or ramble idly or without any fixed purpose.

> Give the water no passage, neither a wicked woman liberty to *gad* abroad. *Ecclus.*

2. To ramble in growth; as the *gadding* vine. *Milton.*

GAD'DER, *n.* A rambler; one that roves about idly.

GAD'DING, *ppr.* Rambling; roving; walking about.

GAD'FLY, *n.* [Sax. *gad*, a goad, and *fly*.] An insect of the genus Oestrus, which stings cattle, and deposits its eggs in their skin; called also the *breeze.*

GADO'LINITE, *n.* A mineral, so called from Professor Gadolin, usually in amorphous masses of a blackish color, and having the appearance of vitreous lava. It contains a new earth called yttria. *Dict. of Nat. Hist.*

GAD'WALL, *n.* A fowl of the genus Anas, inhabiting the north of Europe. *Pennant.*

GA'ELIC, } *a.* [from *Gael*, *Gaul*, *Gallia*.]
GA'LIC, } An epithet denoting what belongs to the *Gaels*, tribes of Celtic origin inhabiting the highlands of Scotland; as the *Gaelic* language.

GA'ELIC, *n.* The language of the highlanders of Scotland.

GAFF, *n.* [Ir. *gaf*, a hook; Sp. and Port. *gafa ;* Shemitic כפף, כפה to bend.]

1. A harpoon.
2. A sort of boom or pole, used in small ships, to extend the upper edge of the mizen, and of those sails whose foremost edge is joined to the mast by hoops or lacings, and which are extended by a boom below, as the main-sail of a sloop. [Qu. Sax. *geafle*, a pole.] *Mar. Dict.*

GAF'FER, *n.* [Qu. Chal. and Heb. גבר gebar, a man, *vir* ; or Sax. *gefere*, a companion, a *peer ;* or Sw. *gubbe*, an old man.]

A word of respect, which seems to have degenerated into a term of familiarity or contempt. [*Little used.*] *Gay.*

GAF'FLE, *n.* [Sax. *geaflas*, chops, spurs on cocks.]

1. An artificial spur put on cocks when they are set to fight.
2. A steel lever to bend cross-bows. *Ainsworth.*

GAG, *v. t.* [W. *cegiaw*, to choke, to strangle, from *cèg*, a choking. *Cég* signifies the mouth, an opening.]

1. To stop the mouth by thrusting something into the throat, so as to hinder speaking. *Johnson.*
2. To keck; to heave with nausea. [In Welsh, *gag* is an opening or cleft; *gagenu*, to open, chap or gape.]

GAG, *n.* Something thrust into the mouth and throat to hinder speaking.

GAĠE, *n.* [Fr. *gage*, a pledge, whence *gager*, to pledge; *engager*, to *engage ;* G. *wagen*, to *wage*, to hazard or risk; *wage*, a balance; D. *waagen*, to venture, Sw. *våga*, Eng. to *wage*. It seems to be allied to *wag*, *weigh*. The primary sense is to throw, to lay, or deposit. If the elements are *Bg*, *Wg*, the original French orthography was *guage*.]

1. A pledge or pawn; something laid down or given as a security for the performance of some act to be done by the person depositing the thing, and which is to be forfeited by non-performance. It is used of a movable thing; not of land or other immovable.

> There I throw my *gage*. *Shak.*

2. A challenge to combat; that is, a glove, a cap, a gauntlet, or the like, cast on the ground by the challenger, and taken up by the accepter of the challenge. *Encyc.*
3. A measure, or rule of measuring; a standard. [See *Gauge*.] *Young.*
4. The number of feet which a ship sinks in the water.
5. Among *letter-founders*, a piece of hard wood variously notched, used to adjust the dimensions, slopes, &c. of the various sorts of letters. *Encyc.*
6. An instrument in joinery made to strike a line parallel to the straight side of a board. *Encyc.*

A *sliding-gage*, a tool used by mathematical instrument makers for measuring and setting off distances. *Encyc.*

Sea-gage, an instrument for finding the depth of the sea. *Encyc.*

Tide-gage, an instrument for determining the highth of the tides. *Encyc.*

Wind-gage, an instrument for measuring the force of the wind on any given surface. *Encyc.*

Weather-gage, the windward side of a ship.

GAĠE, *v. t.* To pledge; to pawn; to give or deposit as a pledge or security for some other act; to wage or wager. *Obs.* *Shak.*

2. To bind by pledge, caution or security; to engage. *Shak.*
3. To measure; to take or ascertain the contents of a vessel, cask or ship; written also *gauge.*

GA'ĠED, *pp.* Pledged; measured.

GA'ĠER, *n.* One who gages or measures the contents.

GAG'GER, *n.* One that gags.

GAG'GLE, *v. i.* [D. *gaggelen ;* G. *gackern ;* coinciding with *cackle*.] To make a noise like a goose. *Bacon.*

GAG'GLING, *n.* The noise of geese.

GA'ĠING, *ppr.* Pledging; measuring the contents.

G'AHNITE, *n.* [from *Gahn*, the discoverer.] A mineral, called also automalite and octahedral corundum. It is always crystalized in regular octahedrons, or in tetrahedrons with truncated angles. *Cleaveland. Ure.*

GA'ILY, *adv.* [from *gay*, and better written *gayly.*]

1. Splendidly; with finery or showiness.
2. Joyfully; merrily.

GAIN, *v. t.* [Fr. *gagner*; Arm. *gounit*; Sw. *gagna*; Sax. *gynan*; Sp. *ganar*; Port. *ganhar*; Heb. Ch. Syr. קנה, Ar. قَنَا to gain, to possess. Class Gn. No. 49. 50. 51. The radical sense is to take, or rather to extend to, to reach.]

1. To obtain by industry or the employment of capital; to get as profit or advantage; to acquire. Any industrious person may *gain* a good living in America; but it is less difficult to *gain* property, than it is to use it with prudence. Money at interest may *gain* five, six, or seven per cent.

   What is a man profited, if he shall *gain* the whole world, and lose his own soul? Matt. xvi.

2. To win; to obtain by superiority or success; as, to *gain* a battle or a victory; to *gain* a prize; to *gain* a cause in law.
3. To obtain; to acquire; to procure; to receive; as, to *gain* favor; to *gain* reputation.

   For fame with toil we *gain*, but lose with ease *Pope.*

4. To obtain an increase of any thing; as, to *gain* time.
5. To obtain or receive any thing, good or bad; as, to *gain* harm and loss. Acts xxvii.
6. To draw into any interest or party; to win to one's side; to conciliate.

   To gratify the queen, and *gain* the court. *Dryden.*

   If he shall hear thee, thou hast *gained* thy brother. Matt. xviii.

7. To obtain as a suitor. *Milton.*
8. To reach; to attain to; to arrive at; as, to *gain* the top of a mountain; to *gain* a good harbor.

To gain into, to draw or persuade to join in.

He *gained* Lepidus *into* his measures. *Middleton.*

To gain over, to draw to another party or interest; to win over.

To gain ground, to advance in any undertaking; to prevail; to acquire strength or extent; to increase.

GAIN, *v. i.* To have advantage or profit; to grow rich; to advance in interest or happiness.

Thou hast greedily *gained* of thy neighbors by extortion. Ezek. xxii.

2. To encroach; to advance on; to come forward by degrees; with *on*; as, the ocean or river *gains on* the land.
3. To advance nearer; to gain ground on; with *on*; as, a fleet horse *gains on* his competitor.
4. To get ground; to prevail against or have the advantage.

   The English have not only *gained upon* the Venetians in the Levant, but have their cloth in Venice itself. *Addison.*

5. To obtain influence with.

   My good behavior had so far *gained on* the emperor, that I began to conceive hopes of liberty. *Swift.*

To gain the wind, in sea language, is to arrive on the windward side of another ship.

GAIN, *n.* [Fr. *gain.*] Profit; interest; something obtained as an advantage.

But what things were *gain* to me, those I counted loss for Christ. Phil. iii.

2. Unlawful advantage. 2 Cor. xii.
3. Overplus in computation; any thing opposed to loss.

GAIN, *n.* [W. *gàn*, a mortise; *ganu*, to contain.]

In *architecture*, a beveling shoulder; a lapping of timbers, or the cut that is made for receiving a timber. *Encyc.*

GAIN, *a.* Handy; dextrous. *Obs.*

GA'INABLE, *a.* That may be obtained or reached. *Sherwood.*

GA'INAĠE, *n.* In *old laws*, the same as *wainage*, that is, *guainage*; the horses, oxen and furniture of the wain, or the instruments for carrying on tillage, which, when a villain was amerced, were left free, that cultivation might not be interrupted. The word signifies also the land itself, or the profit made by cultivation. *Encyc.*

GA'INED, *pp.* Obtained as profit or advantage; won; drawn over to a party; reached.

GA'INER, *n.* One that gains or obtains profit, interest or advantage.

GA'INFUL, *a.* Producing profit or advantage; profitable; advantageous; advancing interest or happiness.

2. Lucrative; productive of money; adding to the wealth or estate.

GA'INFULLY, *adv.* With increase of wealth; profitably; advantageously.

GA'INFULNESS, *n.* Profit; advantage.

GA'INGIVING, *n.* [from the root of *again*, *against*, and *give*. See *Gainsay.*]

A misgiving; a giving against or away. [*Not used.*] *Shak.*

GA'INLESS, *a.* Not producing gain; unprofitable; not bringing advantage. *Hammond.*

GA'INLESSNESS, *n.* Unprofitableness; want of advantage. *Decay of Piety.*

GA'INLY, *adv.* Handily; readily; dextrously. *Obs.*

GAINSA'Y, *v. t.* [Sax. *gean*, or *ongean*, and *say*; Eng. *against*; Sw. *igen*; Dan. *gien*, *igien*. See *Again*, *Against.*]

To contradict; to oppose in words; to deny or declare not to be true what another says; to controvert; to dispute; applied to persons, or to propositions, declarations or facts.

I will give you a mouth and wisdom, which all your adversaries shall not be able to *gainsay* nor resist. Luke xxi.

GAINSA'YER, *n.* One who contradicts or denies what is alledged; an opposer. Tit. i.

GAINSA'YING, *ppr.* Contradicting; denying; opposing.

'GAINST. [See *Against.*]

GA'INSTAND, *v. t.* [Sax. *gean*, against, and *stand.*] To withstand; to oppose; to resist. *Obs.* *Sidney.*

GA'INSTRIVE, *v. i.* [Sax. *gean* and *strive.*] To make resistance. *Obs.* *Spenser.*

GA'INSTRIVE, *v. t.* To withstand. *Obs.*

GA'IRISH, *a.* [Qu. from the root of *gear*, Sax. *gearwian*, to prepare or dress; or Scot. *gair*, a stripe, whence *gaired*, *gairie*, striped, streaked. In Gr. γαυρος is proud, boasting.]

1. Gaudy; showy; fine; affectedly fine; tawdry.

   Monstrous hats and *gairish* colors. *Ascham.*

2. Extravagantly gay; flighty.

   Fame and glory transport a man out of himself; it makes the mind loose and *gairish.* *South.*

GA'IRISHNESS, *n.* Gaudiness; finery; affected or ostentatious show.

2. Flighty or extravagant joy, or ostentation. *Taylor.*

GAIT, *n.* [This word is probably connected with *go* or *gad.*]

1. A going; a walk; a march; a way. *Shak.* *Spenser.*
2. Manner of walking or stepping. Every man has his peculiar *gait.*

GA'ITER, *n.* A covering of cloth for the leg.

GA'LA, *n.* [Sp. *gala*, a court dress; It. *gala*, finery; Fr. *gala*, show, pomp.]

A gala day is a day of pomp, show or festivity, when persons appear in their best apparel.

GALAC'TITE, *n.* [Gr. γαλα, γαλακτος, milk.] A fossil substance resembling the morochthus or French chalk in many respects, but different in color. Immersed or triturated in water, it gives it the color of milk. *Encyc. Morin. Lunier.*

GALA'ĠE, *n.* [Sp. *galocha.* See *Galoche.*] A wooden shoe. *Obs.* *Spenser.*

GALAN'GA, *n.* A plant, a species of the Maranta or Indian Arrow-Root, so called because the root is used to extract the virus communicated by poisoned arrows. This plant has thick, knotty, creeping roots, crowned with long, broad, arundinaceous leaves, with stalks half a yard high, terminated by bunches of monopetalous, ringent flowers. *Encyc.*

GALAN'GAL, *n.* Zedoary, a species of Kæmpferia. It has tuberous, thick, oblong, fleshy roots, crowned with oval close-sitting leaves, by pairs, without footstalks. *Encyc.*

GALA'TIANS, *n.* Inhabitants of Galatia, in the Lesser Asia, said to be descendants of the Gauls. [See Paul's epistle to them.]

GAL'AXY, *n.* [Gr. γαλαξιας, from γαλα, milk; Ir. *geal*, white; W. *gâl*, clear, fair, whence *galaeth*, the milky way; Gr. καλος, fair.]

1. The milky way; that long, white, luminous track which seems to encompass the heavens like a girdle. This luminous appearance is found by the telescope to be occasioned by a multitude of stars, so small as not to be distinguished by the naked eye. *Encyc.*
2. An assemblage of splendid persons or things. *Bp. Hall.*

GAL'BAN, } *n.* [Heb. חלבנה, and in
GAL'BANUM, } Ch. and Syr. varied in orthography, from חלב to milk.]

The concrete gummy resinous juice of an umbelliferous plant, called *Ferula Africana*, &c., and by Linne, *Bubon galbanum*, which grows in Syria, the East Indies and Ethiopia. This gum comes in pale-colored, semitransparent, soft, tenacious masses, of different shades, from white to brown. It is rather resinous than gummy, and has a strong unpleasant smell, with a bitterish warm taste. It is unctuous to the touch, and softens between the fingers. When distilled with water or spirit, it yields an essential oil, and by distillation in a retort without mixture, it yields an empyreumatic oil of a fine blue color, but this is changed in the air to a purple. *Parr.*

GALE, *n.* [In Dan. *gal* is furious, and *kuler* is to blow strong, *kuling*, a gentle gale, from the root of *coal* and *cold*. In Ir. *gal* is a puff, a blast, and steam. The sense is obvious.]

A current of air; a strong wind. The sense of this word is very indefinite. The poets use it in the sense of a moderate breeze or current of air, as a *gentle gale*. A stronger wind is called a *fresh gale*.

In the language of seamen, the word *gale*, unaccompanied by an epithet, signifies a vehement wind, a storm or tempest. They say, the ship carried away her top-mast in a *gale*, or *gale* of wind; the ship rode out the *gale*. But the word is often qualified, as a *hard* or *strong gale*, a *violent gale*. A current of wind somewhat less violent is denominated a *stiff gale*. A less vehement wind is called a *fresh gale*, which is a wind not too strong for a ship to carry single reefed top-sails, when close hauled. When the wind is not so violent but that a ship will carry her top-sails a-trip or full spread, it is called a *loom-gale*. *Mar. Dict. Encyc.*

GALE, *v. i.* In *seamen's language*, to sail, or sail fast.

GA'LEA, *n.* [L. *galea*, a helmet.] A genus of sea hedge-hogs.

GAL'EAS, *n.* A Venetian ship, large, but low built, and moved both by oars and sails.

GA'LEATED, *a.* [L. *galeatus*, from *galea*, a helmet.]

1. Covered as with a helmet. *Woodward.*
2. In *botany*, having a flower like a helmet, as the monk's-hood.

GALEE'TO, *n.* A fish of the genus Blennius, of a greenish color, sometimes variegated with blue transverse lines, and like the eel, living many hours after being taken from the water.

GALE'NA, *n.* [Gr. γαληνη, tranquillity, so named from its supposed effects in mitigating the violence of disease.] Originally, the name of the theriaca. *Parr.*

2. Sulphuret of lead; its common color is that shining bluish gray, usually called lead gray; sometimes it is nearly steel gray. Its streak has a metallic luster, but its fine powder is nearly black. Its structure is commonly foliated, sometimes granular or compact, and sometimes striated or fibrous. It occurs in regular crystals, or more frequently massive. *Cleaveland.*

GALEN'IC, } *a.* Pertaining to or con-
GALEN'ICAL, } taining galena. *Encyc.*

2. [from *Galen*, the physician.] Relating to Galen or his principles and method of treating diseases. The *galenic* remedies consist of preparations of herbs and roots, by infusion, decoction, &c. The chimical remedies consist of preparations by means of calcination, digestion, fermentation, &c.

GA'LENISM, *n.* The doctrines of Galen.

GA'LENIST, *n.* A follower of Galen in the preparation of medicine and modes of treating diseases; opposed to the *chimists*.

GA'LERITE, *n.* [L. *galerus*, a hat or cap.] A genus of fossil shells.

GALILE'AN, *n.* A native or inhabitant of Galilee, in Judea. Also, one of a sect among the Jews, who opposed the payment of tribute to the Romans.

GALIMA'TIA, *n.* [Fr. *galimatias.*] Nonsense. *Addison.*

GAL'IOT, *n.* [Fr. *galiote*; Sp. *galeota*; It. *galeotta*; L. *galea.*]

1. A small galley, or sort of brigantine, built for chase. It is moved both by sails and oars, having one mast and sixteen or twenty seats for rowers. *Dict.*
2. *Galiot* or *galliott*, a Dutch vessel, carrying a main-mast and a mizen-mast, and a large gaff main-sail. *Mar. Dict.*

GAL'IPOT, *n.* [Sp.] A white resin or resinous juice which flows by incision from the pine tree, especially the maritime pine. *Sp. Dict. Fourcroy. Dict. Nat. Hist.*

Galipot encrusts the wounds of fir trees during winter. It consists of resin and oil. *Coxe.*

GALL, *n.* [Sax. *gealla*; G. *galle*; D. *gal*; Dan. *galde*; Sw. *galle*; Gr. χολη; probably from its color, Sax. *gealew*, yellow. See *Yellow* and *Gold.*]

1. In *the animal economy*, the bile, a bitter, yellowish green fluid, secreted in the glandular substance of the liver. It is glutinous or imperfectly fluid, like oil. *Encyc. Nicholson.*
2. Any thing extremely bitter. *Dryden.*
3. Rancor; malignity. *Spenser.*
4. Anger; bitterness of mind. *Prior.*

GALLBLADDER, *n.* A small membranous sack, shaped like a pear, which receives the bile from the liver by the cystic duct.

GALLSICKNESS, *n.* A remitting bilious fever in the Netherlands. *Parr.*

GALLSTONE, *n.* A concretion formed in the gallbladder.

GALL, *n.* [L. *galla*; Sax. *gealla*; Sp. *agalla*; It. *galla.*]

A hard round excrescence on the oak tree in certain warm climates, said to be the nest of an insect called *cynips*. It is formed from the tear issuing from a puncture made by the insect, and gradually increased by accessions of fresh matter, till it forms a covering to the eggs and succeeding insects. Galls are used in making ink; the best are from Aleppo. *Parr.*

GALL, *v. t.* [Fr. *galer*, to scratch or rub; *gale*, scab.]

1. To fret and wear away by friction; to excoriate; to hurt or break the skin by rubbing; as, a saddle *galls* the back of a horse, or a collar his breast.

   Tyrant, I well deserve thy *galling* chain. *Pope.*

2. To impair; to wear away; as, a stream *galls* the ground. *Ray.*
3. To tease; to fret; to vex; to chagrin; as, to be *galled* by sarcasm.
4. To wound; to break the surface of any thing by rubbing; as, to *gall* a mast or a cable.
5. To injure; to harass; to annoy. The troops were *galled* by the shot of the enemy.

   In our wars against the French of old, we used to *gall* them with our long bows, at a greater distance than they could shoot their arrows. *Addison.*

GALL, *v. i.* To fret; to be teased. *Shak.*

GALL, *n.* A wound in the skin by rubbing.

GAL'LANT, *a.* [Fr. *galant*; Sp. *galante*; It. *id.* This word is from the root of the W. *gallu*, to be able, to have power; Eng. *could*; L. *gallus*, a cock. See *Could*, *Call*, and *Gala*. The primary sense is to stretch, strain or reach forward.]

1. Gay; well dressed; showy; splendid; magnificent.

   Neither shall *gallant* ships pass thereby. Is. xxxiii.

   The gay, the wise, the *gallant*, and the grave. *Waller.*

   [*This sense is obsolete.*]

2. Brave; high-spirited; courageous; heroic; magnanimous; as a *gallant* youth; a *gallant* officer.
3. Fine; noble. *Shak.*
4. Courtly; civil; polite and attentive to ladies; courteous. *Clarendon.*

GALLANT', *n.* A gay, sprightly man; a courtly or fashionable man. *Shak.*

2. A man who is polite and attentive to ladies; one who attends upon ladies at parties, or to places of amusement.
3. A wooer; a lover; a suitor.
4. In *an ill sense*, one who caresses a woman for lewd purposes.

GALLANT', *v. t.* To attend or wait on, as a lady.

2. To handle with grace or in a modish manner; as, to *gallant* a fan. *Connoisseur.*

GAL'LANTLY, *adv.* Gaily; splendidly.

2. Bravely; nobly; heroically; generously; as, to fight *gallantly*; to defend a place *gallantly*.

GAL'LANTNESS, *n.* Elegance or completeness of an acquired qualification. *Howell.*

GAL'LANTRY, *n.* [Sp. *galanteria*; Fr. *galanterie.*]

1. Splendor of appearance; show; magnificence; ostentatious finery. [*Obsolete or obsolescent.*] *Waller.*
2. Bravery; courageousness; heroism; intrepidity. The troops entered the fort with great *gallantry*.
3. Nobleness; generosity. *Glanville.*
4. Civility or polite attentions to ladies.
5. Vicious love or pretensions to love; civilities paid to females for the purpose of wining favors; hence, lewdness; debauchery.

GAL'LATE, *n.* [from *gall.*] A neutral salt formed by the gallic acid combined with a base. *Lavoisier.*

GAL'LEASS. [See *Galeas.*]

GALL'ED, *pp.* [See *Gall*, the verb.] Having the skin or surface worn or torn by wearing or rubbing; fretted; teased; injured; vexed.

GAL'LEON, [Sp. *galeon*; Port. *galeam*; It. *galeone*. See *Galley.*]

A large ship formerly used by the Spaniards, in their commerce with South America, usually furnished with four decks. *Mar. Dict.*

GAL'LERY, *n.* [Fr. *galerie*; Sp. Port. *galeria*; It. *galleria*; Dan. *gallerie*; G. *id.*; D. *galdery*; Sw. *galler-verck*, and *gall-rad.* Lunier supposes this word to be from the root of G. *wallen*, to walk.]

1. In *architecture*, a covered part of a building, commonly in the wings, used as an ambulatory or place for walking. *Encyc.*
2. An ornamental walk or apartment in gardens, formed by trees. *Encyc.*
3. In *churches*, a floor elevated on columns and furnished with pews or seats; usually ranged on three sides of the edifice. A similar structure in a play-house.
4. In *fortification*, a covered walk across the ditch of a town, made of beams covered with planks and loaded with earth. *Encyc.*
5. In *a mine*, a narrow passage or branch of the mine carried under ground to a work designed to be blown up. *Encyc.*
6. In *a ship*, a frame like a balcony projecting from the stern or quarter of a ship of war or of a large merchantman. That part at the stern, is called the *stern-gallery*; that at the quarters, the *quarter-gallery.*

GAL'LETYLE, *n.* Gallipot. *Bacon.*

GAL'LEY, *n.* plu. *galleys.* [Sp. *galera*; It. *galera* or *galea*; Fr. *galère*; Port. *galé*; L. *galea.* The Latin word signifies a helmet, the top of a mast, and a galley; and the name of this vessel seems to have been derived from the head-piece, or kind of basket-work, at mast-head.]

1. A low flat-built vessel, with one deck, and navigated with sails and oars; used in the Mediterranean. The largest sort of galleys, employed by the Venetians, are 162 feet in length, or 133 feet keel. They have three masts and thirty two banks of oars; each bank containing two oars, and each oar managed by six or seven slaves. In the fore-part they carry three small batteries of cannon. *Encyc. Mar. Dict.*
2. A place of toil and misery. *South.*
3. An open boat used on the Thames by custom-house officers, press-gangs, and for pleasure. *Mar. Dict.*
4. The cook room or kitchen of a ship of war; answering to the caboose of a merchantman. *Mar. Dict.*
5. An oblong reverberatory furnace, with a row of retorts whose necks protrude through lateral openings. *Nicholson.*

GAL'LEYFOIST, *n.* A barge of state. *Hakewell.*

GAL'LEY-SLAVE, *n.* A person condemned for a crime to work at the oar on board of a galley.

GALL'FLȲ, *n.* The insect that punctures plants and occasions galls; the cynips. *Encyc.*

GAL'LIARD, *a.* [Fr. *gaillard*, from *gai*, gay.] Gay; brisk; active. *Obs.* *Chaucer.*

GAL'LIARD, *n.* A brisk, gay man; also, a lively dance. *Obs.* *Bacon.*

GAL'LIARDISE, *n.* Merriment; excessive gayety. *Obs.* *Brown.*

GAL'LIARDNESS, *n.* Gayety. *Obs.* *Gayton.*

GAL'LIC, *a.* [from *Gallia*, Gaul, now France.] Pertaining to Gaul or France.

GAL'LIC, *a.* [from *gall.*] Belonging to galls or oak apples; derived from galls; as the *gallic* acid.

GAL'LICAN, *a.* [L. *Gallicus*, from *Gallia*, Gaul.] Pertaining to Gaul or France; as the *Gallican* church or clergy.

GAL'LICISM, *n.* [Fr. *gallicisme*, from *Gallia*, Gaul.] A mode of speech peculiar to the French nation; an idiomatic manner of using words in the French language.

GALLIGAS'KINS, *n.* [Qu. *Caligæ Vasconum*, Gascon-hose.] Large open hose; *used only in ludicrous language.* *Philips.*

GAL'LIMAUFRY, *n.* [Fr. *galimafrée.*] A hash; a medley; a hodge-podge. [*Little used.*] *Spenser.*

2. Any inconsistent or ridiculous medley. *Dryden.*
3. A woman. [*Not in use.*] *Shak.*

GALLINA'CEOUS, *a.* [L. *gallinaceus*, from *gallina*, a hen, *gallus*, a cock, whose name is from crowing, W. *galw*, Eng. to *call.*]

1. Designating that order of fowls called *gallinæ*, including the domestic fowls or those of the pheasant kind.

Gallinaceus Lapis, a glossy substance produced by volcanic fires; the *lapis obsidianus* of the ancients. A kind of it brought from Peru is of a beautiful black, or crow-color, like the *gallinaço.* *Encyc.*

GALL'ING, *ppr.* [See *Gall*, the verb.]

1. Fretting the skin; excoriating.
2. *a.* Adapted to fret or chagrin; vexing.

GAL'LINULE, *n.* [L. *gallinula*, dim. of *gallina*, a hen.]

A tribe of fowls of the grallic order, included under the genus *Fulica*, with the coot.

GALLIOT, **GALLEOT**, } [See *Galiot.*]

GAL'LIPOT, *n.* [D. *gleye*, potter's clay, and *pot.*]

A small pot or vessel painted and glazed, used by druggists and apothecaries for containing medicines.

GALLIT'ZINITE, *n.* Rutile, an ore of titanium. *Ure.*

GAL'LIVAT, *n.* A small vessel used on the Malabar coast. *Todd.*

GALL'LESS, *a.* [from *gall.*] Free from gall or bitterness.

GAL'LON, *n.* [Sp. *galon*; Law L. *galona.* In French, *galon* is a grocer's box. See *Gill.*]

A measure of capacity for dry or liquid things, but usually for liquids, containing four quarts. But the gallon is not in all cases of uniform contents or dimensions. The gallon of wine contains 231 cubic inches, or eight pounds avordupois of pure water. The gallon of beer and ale contains 281 cubic inches, or ten pounds three ounces and a quarter avordupois of water; and the gallon of corn, meal, &c., 272¼ cubic inches, or nine pounds thirteen ounces of pure water. *Encyc.*

GALLOON', *n.* [Fr. *galon*; Sp. *galon*; It. *gallone*; Port. *galam.*]

A kind of close lace made of gold or silver, or of silk only. *Tatler.*

GAL'LOP, *v. i.* [Fr. *galoper*; Sp. *galopear*; Port. *id.*; It. *galoppare*; Arm. *galoupat* or *galompat*; G. *galoppiren.* If this word is from the elements *Gl*, I know not the origin or meaning of the last constituent part of the word. I suppose it to be formed with the prefix *ga* on *leap*, G. *laufen*, D. *loopen*, *geloopen.* See *Leap.*]

1. To move or run with leaps, as a horse to run or move with speed.

> But *gallop* lively down the western hill. *Donne.*

2. To ride with a galloping pace. We *galloped* towards the enemy.
3. To move very fast; to run over.

> Such superficial ideas he may collect in *galloping* over it. *Locke.*

GAL'LOP, *n.* The movement or pace of a quadruped, particularly of a horse, by springs, reaches or leaps. The animal lifts his fore feet nearly at the same time, and as these descend and are just ready to touch the ground, the hind feet are lifted at once. The gallop is the swiftest pace of a horse, but it is also a moderate pace, at the pleasure of a rider.

GAL'LOPER, *n.* A horse that gallops; also, a man that gallops or makes haste.

2. In *artillery*, a carriage which bears a gun of a pound and a half ball. It has shafts so as to be drawn without a limbon, and it may serve for light three and six pounders.

GAL'LOPIN, *n.* [Fr.] A servant for the kitchen. *Obs.*

GAL'LŌW, *v. t.* [Sax. *agælwan.*] To fright or terrify. *Obs.* *Shak.*

GAL'LOWAY, *n.* A horse or species of horses of a small size, bred in Galloway in Scotland. *Hawkesworth.*

GAL'LŌWGLASS, *n.* An ancient Irish foot soldier. *Spenser.*

GAL'LŌWS, *n.* singular. [Sax. *galg*, *gealga*; Goth. *galga*; G. *galgen*; D. *galg*; Sw. *galge*; Dan. *id.* *Gallows* is in the singular number and should be preceded by *a*, *a gallows.* The plural is *gallowses.*]

1. An instrument of punishment whereon criminals are executed by hanging. It consists of two posts and a cross beam on the top, to which the criminal is suspended by a rope fastened round his neck.
2. A wretch that deserves the gallows. [*Not used.*] *Shak.*

GAL'LŌWSFREE, *a.* Free from danger of the gallows. *Dryden.*

GAL'LŌWTREE, *n.* The tree of execution. *Spenser.*

GALL'Y, *a.* Like gall; bitter as gall. *Cranmer.*

GAL'LY, *n.* [Port. *galé*, a galley, and a printer's frame; Fr. *galée.*]

A printer's frame or oblong square board with a ledge on three sides, into which types are emptied from the composing stick. It has a groove to admit a false bottom, called a *gally-slice.* *Encyc.*

GAL'LY-WŌRM, *n.* An insect of the centiped kind, of several species.

GALO'CHE, *n.* [Fr. from Sp. *galocha*, a clog or wooden shoe.]

A patten, clog or wooden shoe, or a shoe to be worn over another shoe to keep the foot dry. It is written also *galoshe.*

GALSŌME, *a.* *gaul'som.* [from *gall.*] Angry; malignant. *Obs.* *Morton.*

GALVAN'IC, *a.* Pertaining to galvanism; containing or exhibiting it.

GAL'VANISM, *n.* [from *Galvani* of Bologna, the discoverer.]

Electrical phenomena in which the electricity is developed without the aid of friction, and in which a chemical action takes place between certain bodies. *Edin. Encyc.*

Galvanism is heat, light, electricity and magnetism, united in combination or in simultaneous action; sometimes one and sometimes another of them predominating, and thus producing more or less all the effects of each: usual means of excitement, contact of dissimilar bodies, especially of metals and fluids. *Hare. Silliman.*

GAL'VANIST, *n.* One who believes in galvanism; one versed in galvanism.

GAL'VANIZE, *v. t.* To affect with galvanism.

GALVANOL'OGIST, *n.* One who describes the phenomena of galvanism.

GALVANOL'OGY, *n.* [*galvanism*, and Gr. λογος, discourse.]
A treatise on galvanism, or a description of its phenomena.

GALVANOM'ETER, *n.* [*galvanism*, and Gr. μετρον, measure.]
An instrument or apparatus for measuring minute quantities of electricity, or the operations of galvanism. *Ure.*

GAMASH'ES, *n.* Short spatterdashes worn by plowmen. *Shelton.*

GAMBA'DOES, *n.* Spatterdashes. [It. *gamba*, the leg.]

GAM'BET, *n.* A bird of the size of the greenshank, found in the Arctic sea, and in Scandinavia and Iceland. *Pennant.*

GAM'BLE, *v. i.* [from *game.*] To play or game for money or other stake.

GAM'BLE, *v. t.* To *gamble away*, is to squander by gaming.

Bankrupts or sots who have *gambled* or slept *away* their estates. *Ames.*

GAM'BLER, *n.* One who games or plays for money or other stake. *Gamblers* often or usually become cheats and knaves.

GAM'BLING, *ppr.* Gaming for money.

GAMBO'GE, *n.* A concrete vegetable juice or gum-resin. It is brought in orbicular masses or cylindrical rolls, from *Cambaja, Cambodja*, or *Cambogia*, in the E. Indies, whence its name. It is of a dense, compact texture, and of a beautiful reddish yellow. It is used chiefly as a pigment. Taken internally, it is a strong and harsh cathartic and emetic. *Nicholson.*

GAM'BOL, *v. i.* [Fr. *gambiller*, to wag the leg or kick, from It. *gamba*, the leg, Fr. *jambe*, Sp. *gamba.*]
1. To dance and skip about in sport; to frisk; to leap; to play in frolick, like boys and lambs. *Milton. Dryden.*
2. To leap; to start. *Shak.*

GAM'BOL, *n.* A skipping or leaping about in frolick; a skip; a hop; a leap; a sportive prank. *Dryden.*

GAM'BOLING, *ppr.* Leaping; frisking; playing pranks.

GAM'BREL, *n.* [from It. *gamba*, the leg.] The hind leg of a horse. Hence, in America, a crooked stick used by butchers. A hipped roof is called a *gambrel-roof.*

GAM'BREL, *v. t.* To tie by the leg. *Beaum.*

GAME, *n.* [Ice. *gaman;* Sax. *gamen*, a jest, sport; *gamian*, to jest, to sport; It. *giambare*, to jest or jeer; W. *camp*, a feat, a game; *campiaw*, to contend in games. The latter seems to unite *game* with *camp*, which in Saxon and other northern dialects signifies a combat.]
1. Sport of any kind. *Shak.*
2. Jest; opposed to *earnest;* as, betwixt earnest and *game.* [*Not used.*] *Spenser.*
3. An exercise or play for amusement or winning a stake; as a *game* of cricket; a *game* of chess; a *game* of whist. Some *games* depend on skill; others on hazard.
4. A single match at play. *Addison.*
5. Advantage in play; as, to play the *game* into another's hand.
6. Scheme pursued; measures planned.

This seems to be the present *game* of that crown. *Temple.*

7. Field sports; the chase, falconry, &c. *Shak. Waller.*
8. Animals pursued or taken in the chase, or in the sports of the field; animals appropriated in England to legal sportsmen; as deer, hares, &c.
9. In *antiquity*, games were public diversions or contests exhibited as spectacles for the gratification of the people. These *games* consisted of running, leaping, wrestling, riding, &c. Such were the Olympic games, the Pythian, the Isthmian, the Nemean, &c. among the Greeks; and among the Romans, the Apollinarian, the Circensian, the Capitoline, &c. *Encyc.*
10. Mockery; sport; derision; as, to make *game* of a person.

GAME, *v. i.* [Sax. *gamian.*] To play at any sport or diversion.
2. To play for a stake or prize; to use cards, dice, billiards or other instruments, according to certain rules, with a view to win money or other thing waged upon the issue of the contest.
3. To practice gaming.

GA'MECOCK, *n.* A cock bred or used to fight; a cock kept for barbarous sport. *Locke.*

GA'ME-EGG, *n.* An egg from which a fighting cock is bred. *Garth.*

GA'MEKEEPER, *n.* One who has the care of game; one who is authorized to preserve beasts of the chase, or animals kept for sport. *Blackstone.*

GA'MESOME, *a.* Gay; sportive; playful; frolicksome.

This *gamesome* humor of children. *Locke.*

GA'MESOMENESS, *n.* Sportiveness; merriment.

GA'MESOMELY, *adv.* Merrily; playfully.

GA'MESTER, *n.* [*game*, and Sax. *steora*, a director.]
1. A person addicted to gaming; one who is accustomed to play for money or other stake, at cards, dice, billiards and the like; a gambler; one skilled in games. *Addison.*

It is as easy to be a scholar as a *gamester.* *Harris.*

2. One engaged at play. *Bacon.*
3. A merry, frolicksome person. [*Not used.*] *Shak.*
4. A prostitute. [*Not in use.*] *Shak.*

GA'MING, *ppr.* Playing; sporting; playing for money.

GA'MING, *n.* The act or art of playing any game in a contest for a victory, or for a prize or stake.
2. The practice of using cards, dice, billiards and the like, according to certain rules, for winning money, &c.

GA'MING-HOUSE, *n.* A house where gaming is practiced. *Blackstone.*

GA'MING-TABLE, *n.* A table appropriated to gaming.

GAM'MER, *n.* [Sw. *gammal*, Dan. *gammel*, old; Sw. *gumma*, an old woman.]
The compellation of an old woman, answering to *gaffer*, applied to an old man.

GAM'MON, *n.* [It. *gamba;* Fr. *jambe*, a leg; *jambon*, a leg of bacon.]
1. The buttock or thigh of a hog, pickled and smoked or dried; a smoked ham.
2. A game, called usually *back-gammon*, which see.

GAM'MON, *v. t.* To make bacon; to pickle and dry in smoke.
2. To fasten a bowsprit to the stem of a ship by several turns of a rope. *Mar. Dict.*

GAM'MON, *v. t.* In *the game of baek-gammon*, the party that, by fortunate throws of the dice or by superior skill in moving, withdraws all his men from the board, before his antagonist has been able to get his men home and withdraw any of them from his table, *gammons* his antagonist.

GAM'MUT, *n.* [Sp. *gamma;* Port. *id.;* Fr. *gamme;* from the Greek letter so named.]
1. A scale on which notes in music are written or printed, consisting of lines and spaces, which are named after the seven first letters of the alphabet.
2. The first or gravest note in Guido's scale of music, the modern scale.

GAN, a contraction of *began*, or rather the original simple word, Sax. *gynnan*, to begin.

GANCH, *v. t.* [It. *gancio*, a hook.] To drop from a high place on hooks, as the Turks do malefactors, by way of punishment.

GAN'DER, *n.* [Sax. *gandra, ganra;* Ir. *ganra.* In Ger. and D. *gans* is a goose; D. *ganserick*, a gander; Gr. χην, and probably L. *anser.* Pliny says, that in Germany the small white geese were called *ganzæ.* Lib. 10. 22.] The male of fowls of the goose kind.

GANG, *v. i.* [Sax. *gangan;* Goth. *gaggan.*] To go; to walk. [*Local, or used only in ludicrous language.*]

GANG, *n.* [Goth. *gagg*, a street.] Properly, a going; hence, a number going in company; hence, a company, or a number of persons associated for a particular purpose; as a *gang* of thieves.
2. In *seamen's language*, a select number of a ship's crew appointed on a particular service, under a suitable officer. *Mar. Dict.*

GANG'BOARD, *n.* A board or plank with cleats for steps, used for walking into or out of a boat.

GANG'DAYS, *n.* Days of perambulation.

GANG'HON, *n.* A flower. *Ainsworth.*

GANG'LION, *n.* [Gr. γαγγλιον.] In *anatomy*, a small circumscribed tumor, found in certain parts of the nervous system. *Wistar. Cyc.*
2. In *surgery*, a movable tumor formed on the tendons, generally about the wrist. *Parr.*

GAN'GRENATE, *v. t.* To produce a gangrene. *Brown.*

GAN'GRENE, *n.* [Fr. from L. *gangræna;* Gr. γαγγραινα; Syr. *gangar.*]

A mortification of living flesh, or of some part of a living animal body. It is particularly applied to the first stage of mortification, before the life of the part is completely extinct. When the part is completely dead, it is called *sphacelus*. *Encyc. Cyc.*

GAN'GRENE, *v. t.* To mortify, or to begin mortification in.

GAN'GRENE, *v. i.* To become mortified.

GANGRENES'CENT, *a.* Tending to mortification; beginning to corrupt or putrefy, as living flesh.

GAN'GRENOUS, *a.* Mortified; indicating mortification of living flesh.

GANGUE, *n. gang.* [See *Gang.*] In *mining*, the earthy, stony, saline, or combustible substance, which contains the ore of metals, or is only mingled with it without being chimically combined, is called the *gangue* or matrix of the ore. It differs from a *mineralizer*, in not being combined with the metal. *Cleaveland.*

GANG'WAY, *n.* A passage, way or avenue into or out of any inclosed place, especially a passage into or out of a ship, or from one part of a ship to another; also, a narrow platform of planks laid horizontally along the upper part of a ship's side, from the quarter deck to the forecastle.

To bring to the gangway, in the discipline of ships, is to punish a seaman by seizing him up and flogging him.

GANG'WEEK, *n.* Rogation week, when processions are made to lustrate or survey the bounds of parishes. *Dict.*

GAN'IL, *n.* A kind of brittle limestone. *Kirwan.*

GAN'NET, *n.* [Sax. *ganot.* See *Gander.*] The Solan Goose, a fowl of the genus Pelicanus, about seven pounds in weight, with a straight bill, six inches long, and palmated feet. These fowls frequent the isles of Scotland in summer, and feed chiefly on herrings. *Encyc.*

GANT'LET, } *n.* [Fr. *gantelet*, from *gant*,
GAUNT'LET, } a glove; It. *guanto*; D. *want*; Dan. and Sw. *vante*, a glove.]

A large iron glove with fingers covered with small plates, formerly worn by cavaliers, armed at all points.

To throw the gantlet, is to challenge; and

To take up the gantlet, is to accept the challenge.

GANT'LOPE, *n.* [The last syllable is from the Teutonic, D. *loopen*, to run. The first is probably from *gang*, a passage.]

A military punishment inflicted on criminals for some hainous offense. It is executed in this manner; soldiers are arranged in two rows, face to face, each armed with a switch or instrument of punishment; between these rows, the offender, stripped to his waist, is compelled to pass a certain number of times, and each man gives him a stroke. A similar punishment is used on board of ships. Hence this word is chiefly used in the phrase, *to run the gantlet* or *gantlope*. *Dryden. Mar. Dict.*

GAN'ZA, *n.* [Sp. *ganso*, a goose. See *Gander.*] A kind of wild goose, by a flock of which a virtuoso was fabled to be carried to the lunar world. *Johnson. Hudibras.*

GAÖL, *n.* [Fr. *geôle*; Arm. *geol* or *jol*; W. *geol*; Norm. *geaule, geole*; Sp. *jaula*, a cage, a cell; Port. *gaiola*. Qu. Class Gl. No. 11. 36. Ar. As the pronunciation *gole* accords with that of *goal*, a different word, it would be convenient to write and pronounce this word uniformly *jail.*]

A prison; a place for the confinement of debtors and criminals.

GAÖL, *v. t.* To imprison; to confine in prison. *Bacon.*

GAÖLDELIV'ERY, *n.* A judicial process for clearing jails of criminals, by trial and condemnation or acquittal.

GAÖLER, *n.* The keeper of a gaol or prisoner; a jailor.

GAP, *n.* [See *Gape* and *Gab.* Gipsey, *geb*, Hindoo, *gibah*, a hole.]

1. An opening in any thing made by breaking or parting; as a *gap* in a fence or wall.

2. A breach.

Manifold miseries ensued by the opening of that *gap* to all that side of christendom. *Knolles.*

3. Any avenue or passage; way of entrance or departure. *Dryden.*

4. A breach; a defect; a flaw; as a *gap* in honor or reputation. *Shak. More.*

5. An interstice; a vacuity.

A third can fill the *gap* with laughing. *Swift.*

6. A hiatus; a chasm; as a *gap* between words. *Pope.*

To stop a gap, to secure a weak point; to repair a defect.

To stand in the gap, to expose one's self for the protection of something; to make defense against any assailing danger. Ezek. xxii.

G'APE, *v. i.* [Sax. *geapan*; Sw. *gapa*; D. *gaapen*; G. *gaffen*; Dan. *gaber*; Ar. جَابَ jauba, to split, tear or cut open.]

1. To open the mouth wide, from sleepiness, drowsiness or dullness; to yawn. *Swift.*

2. To open the mouth for food, as young birds. *Dryden.*

3. To *gape for* or *after*, to desire earnestly; to crave; to look and long for; as, men often *gape after* court favor.

The hungry grave *for* her due tribute *gapes*. *Denham.*

To gape at, in a like sense, is hardly correct.

4. To open in fissures or crevices; as a *gaping* rock.

May that ground *gape*, and swallow me alive. *Shak.*

5. To have a hiatus; as one vowel *gaping* on another. *Dryden.*

6. To open the mouth in wonder or surprise; as the *gaping* fool; the *gaping* crowd.

7. To utter sound with open throat. *Roscommon.*

8. To open the mouth with hope or expectation. *Hudibras.*

9. To open the mouth with a desire to injure or devour.

They have *gaped* upon me with their mouth. Job xvi.

G'APE, *n.* A gaping. *Addison.*

G'APER, *n.* One who gapes; a yawner.

2. One who opens his mouth for wonder and stares foolishly.

3. One who longs or craves. *Carew.*

4. A fish with six or seven bands and tail undivided. *Pennant.*

G'APING, *ppr.* Opening the mouth wide from sleepiness, dullness, wonder or admiration; yawning; opening in fissures; craving.

GAP'TOOTHED, *a.* Having interstices between the teeth. *Dryden.*

G'AR, in Saxon, a dart, a weapon; as in *Edgar*, or *Eadgar*, a happy weapon; *Ethelgar*, noble weapon. *Gibson.*

This may be the Ch. גירא or גררא an arrow, a dart; Sam. an arrow.

GAR'AGAY, *n.* A rapacious fowl of Mexico, of the size of the kite. *Dict.*

G'ARB, *n.* [Fr. *garbe*, looks, countenance; It. Sp. *garbo*; Norm. *garbs*, clothes, dress; Russ. *gerb*, arms; from the root of *gear.*]

1. Dress; clothes; habit; as the *garb* of a clergyman or judge.

2. Fashion or mode of dress. *Denham.*

3. Exterior appearance; looks. *Shak.*

4. In *heraldry*, a sheaf of corn. [Fr. *gerbe*; Sp. *garba.*]

G'ARBAĠE, *n.* [I know not the component parts of this word.] The bowels of an animal; refuse parts of flesh; offal. *Shak. Dryden.*

G'ARBAĠED, *a.* Stripped of the bowels. *Sherwood.*

G'ARBEL, *n.* The plank next the keel of a ship. [See *Garboard-streak.*]

G'ARBLE, *v. t.* [Sp. *garbillar*; It. *cribrare, crivellare*; Fr. *cribler*; L. *cribro, cribello.* Qu. Ar. غربل or Ch. כרבל to sift, to bolt. Class Rb. No. 30. 34. 46.]

1. Properly, to sift or bolt; to separate the fine or valuable parts of a substance from the coarse and useless parts, or from dross or dirt; as, to *garble* spices.

2. To separate; to pick; to cull out. *Dryden. Locke.*

G'ARBLED, *pp.* Sifted; bolted; separated; culled out.

G'ARBLER, *n.* One who garbles, sifts or separates. A *garbler* of spices, is an officer of great antiquity in London.

2. One who picks out, culls or selects.

G'ARBLES, *n. plu.* The dust, soil or filth, severed from good spices, drugs, &c. *Cyc.*

G'ARBLING, *ppr.* Sifting; separating; sorting; culling.

G'ARBOARD, *n.* The *garboard plank*, in a ship, is the first plank fastened on the keel on the outside. *Bailey.*

Garboard-streak, in a ship, is the first range or streak of planks laid on a ship's bottom, next the keel. *Mar. Dict.*

G'ARBOIL, *n.* [Old Fr. *garbouil*; It. *garbuglio.*] Tumult; uproar. [*Not used.*]

GARD. [See *Guard* and *Ward.*]

G'ARDEN, *n.* [G. *garten*; W. *garth*; It. *giardino*; Sp. *jardin*; Fr. *id.*; Port. *jardim*; Arm. *jardd, jardin* or *gardd.* The first syllable is the Sax. *geard*, Goth. *gards*, Eng. *yard*, an inclosed place. The Saxon is *ortgeard*, Dan. *urtegaard*, Sw. *örtegård*, wortyard, an inclosure for herbs. The Irish is *gairdin* or *garrdha*; Hungarian, *korth*; L. *hortus*. In Slavonic, *gard*, Russ. *gorod*, signifies a town or city, and the derivative verb *goroju*, to inclose with a hedge. Hence *Stuttgard*, *Novogrod* or *Novogardia*. The primary sense of *gar-*

den is an inclosed place, and inclosures were originally made with hedges, stakes or palisades. It is probable that in the east, and in the pastoral state, men had little or no inclosed land except such as was fenced for the protection of herbs and fruits, and for villages. See Coxe's Russ. B. 4.]

1. A piece of ground appropriated to the cultivation of herbs, or plants, fruits and flowers; usually near a mansion-house. Land appropriated to the raising of culinary herbs and roots for domestic use, is called a *kitchen-garden;* that appropriated to flowers and shrubs is called a *flower-garden;* and that to fruits, is called a *fruit-garden.* But these uses are sometimes blended.

2. A rich, well cultivated spot or tract of country; a delightful spot. The intervals on the river Connecticut are all a *garden.* Lombardy is the *garden* of Italy.

Garden, in composition, is used adjectively, as *garden-mold,* a rich fine mold or soil; *garden-tillage,* the tillage used in cultivating gardens.

G'ARDEN, *v. i.* To lay out and to cultivate a garden; to prepare ground, to plant and till it, for the purpose of producing plants, shrubs, flowers and fruits.

G'ARDENER, *n.* One whose occupation is to make, tend and dress a garden.

G'ARDENING, *ppr.* Cultivating or tilling a garden.

G'ARDENING, *n.* The act of laying out and cultivating gardens; horticulture. *Encyc.*

G'ARDEN-PLOT, *n.* The plot or plantation of a garden. *Milton.*

G'ARDEN-STUFF, *n.* Plants growing in a garden; vegetables for the table. [*A word in popular use.*]

G'ARDEN-WARE, *n.* The produce of gardens. [*Not in use.*] *Mortimer.*

G'ARDON, *n.* A fish of the roach kind.

GARE, *n.* Coarse wool growing on the legs of sheep. *Dict.*

G'ARGARISM, *n.* [L. *gargarismus;* Gr. γαργαριζω, to wash the mouth; allied probably to *gorge,* the throat.]

A gargle; any liquid preparation used to wash the mouth and throat, to cure inflammations or ulcers, &c. *Encyc.*

G'ARGARIZE, *v. t.* [Fr. *gargariser;* L. *gargarizo;* Gr. γαργαριζω.]

To wash or rinse the mouth with any medicated liquor. *Bacon.*

G'ARGET, *n.* [See *Gorge.*] A distemper in cattle, consisting in a swelling of the throat and the neighboring parts. *Encyc.*

G'ARGIL, *n.* A distemper in geese, which stops the head and often proves fatal. *Encyc.*

G'ARGLE, *v. t.* [Fr. *gargouiller,* to paddle or dabble; It. *gargagliare,* to murmur; Eng. to *gurgle;* D. *gorgelen;* G. *gurgeln;* allied to *gorge, gurges.*]

1. To wash the throat and mouth with a liquid preparation, which is kept from descending into the stomach by a gentle expiration of air.

2. To warble; to play in the throat. [*Unusual.*] *Waller.*

G'ARGLE, *n.* Any liquid preparation for washing the mouth and throat. *Wiseman.*

G'ARGLION, *n.* An exsudation of nervous juice from a bruise, which indurates into a tumor. *Quincy.*

G'ARGOL, *n.* A distemper in swine. *Mortimer.*

GARISH. [See *Gairish.*]

G'ARLAND, *n.* [Fr. *guirlande;* It. *ghirlanda;* Sp. *guirnalda;* Port. *grinalda;* Arm. *garlantez.* This word has been referred to the L. *gyrus,* and it may be from the same root. It seems to denote something round or twisted, for in Spanish it is used for a wreath of cordage or puddening.]

1. A wreath or chaplet made of branches, flowers, fethers and sometimes of precious stones, to be worn on the head like a crown. *Pope. Encyc.*

2. An ornament of flowers, fruits and leaves intermixed, anciently used at the gates of temples where feasts and solemn rejoicings were held. *Encyc.*

3. The top; the principal thing, or thing most prized. *Shak.*

4. A collection of little printed pieces. *Percy.*

5. In *ships,* a sort of net used by sailors instead of a locker or cupboard. *Mar. Dict.*

G'ARLAND, *v. t.* To deck with a garland. *B. Jonson.*

G'ARLIC, *n.* [Sax. *garlec* or *garleac; gar,* a dart or lance, in Welsh, a shank, and *leac,* a leek; Ir. *gairliog;* W. *garlleg.* The Germans call it *knoblauch,* knobleek; D. *knoflook;* Gr. σκοροδον.]

A plant of the genus Allium, having a bulbous root, a very strong smell, and an acrid, pungent taste. Each root is composed of several lesser bulbs, called cloves of garlic, inclosed in a common membranous coat and easily separable. *Encyc.*

G'ARLICEATER, *n.* A low fellow. *Shak.*

G'ARLICPEAR-TREE, *n.* A tree in Jamaica, the Crateva, bearing a fruit which has a strong scent of garlic. *Miller.*

G'ARMENT, *n.* [Norm. *garnament;* Old Fr. *guarniment;* It. *guarnimento,* furniture, ornament; from the root of *garnish,* and denoting what is put on or furnished.]

Any article of clothing, as a coat, a gown, &c. *Garments,* in the plural, denotes clothing in general; dress.

> No man putteth a piece of new cloth to an old *garment.* Matt. ix.

G'ARNER, *n.* [Fr. *grenier;* Ir. *geirneal;* Norm. *guernier, garnier.* See *Grain.*]

A granary; a building or place where grain is stored for preservation.

G'ARNER, *v. t.* To store in a granary. *Shak.*

G'ARNET, *n.* [It. *granato;* Fr. *grenat;* Sp. *granate;* L. *granatus,* from *granum,* or *granatum,* the pomegranate.]

1. A mineral usually occurring in crystals more or less regular. The crystals have numerous sides, from twelve to sixty or even eighty four. Its prevailing color is red of various shades, but often brown, and sometimes green, yellow or black. It sometimes resembles the hyacinth, the leucite, and the idocrase. Of this gem there are several varieties, as the *precious* or *oriental,* the *pyrope,* the *topazolite,* the *succinite,* the *common garnet,* the *melanite,* the *pyreneite,* the *grossular,* the *allochroite,* and the *colophonite.* *Haüy. Cleaveland.*

2. In *ships,* a sort of tackle fixed to the main stay, and used to hoist in and out the cargo.

G'ARNISH, *v. t.* [Fr. *garnir;* Arm. *goarniça;* Sp. *guarnecer;* It. *guarnire, guernire;* Norm. *garner, garnisher,* to warn, to summon. The latter sense is still used in law language, and it would seem that *warn* and *garnish* are from the same root, for *warn,* written in the Celtic manner, would be *guarn.*]

1. To adorn; to decorate with appendages; to set off.

> All within with flowers was *garnished.* *Spenser.*

2. To fit with fetters; *a cant term.*

3. To furnish; to supply; as a fort *garnished* with troops.

4. In *law,* to warn; to give notice. [See *Garnishee.*]

G'ARNISH, *n.* Ornament; something added for embellishment; decoration.

> Matter and figure they produce;
> For *garnish* this, and that for use. *Prior.*

2. In *jails,* fetters; *a cant term.*

3. *Pensiuncula carceraria;* a fee; an acknowledgment in money when first a prisoner goes to jail. *Ainsworth.*

G'ARNISHED, *pp.* Adorned; decorated; embellished.

2. Furnished.

3. Warned; notified.

GARNISHEE', *n.* In *law,* one in whose hands the property of an absconding or absent debtor is attached, who is warned or notified of the demand or suit, and who may appear and defend in the suit, in the place of the principal. *Stat. of Connecticut.*

G'ARNISHING, *ppr.* Adorning; decorating; warning.

G'ARNISHMENT, *n.* Ornament; embellishment. *Wotton.*

2. Warning; legal notice to the agent or attorney of an absconding debtor.

3. A fee.

G'ARNITURE, *n.* Ornamental appendages; embellishment; furniture; dress. *Addison. Beattie. Gray.*

GA'ROUS, *a.* [L. *garum,* pickle.] Resembling pickle made of fish. *Brown.*

GAR'RAN, } *n.* [Ir. *garran;* Scot. *garron;*
GAR'RON, } G. *gurre.*]

A small horse; a highland horse; a hack; a jade; a galloway. [*Not used in America.*] *Temple.*

GAR'RET, *n.* [Scot. *garret,* a watch-tower, the top of a hill; *garritour,* a watchman on the battlements of a castle; Fr. *guerite,* a centinel-box; Sp. *guardilla;* Arm. *garid;* from the root of *ward, guard,* which see.]

1. That part of a house which is on the upper floor, immediately under the roof.

2. Rotten wood. [*Not in use.*] *Bacon.*

GAR'RETED, *a.* Protected by turrets. *Carew.*

GARRETEE'R, *n.* An inhabitant of a garret; a poor author.

GAR'RISON, *n.* [Fr. *garnison;* Arm. *goarnison;* Sp. *guarnicion*, a garrison, a flounce, furbelow or trimming, the setting of any thing in gold or silver, the guard of a sword, garniture, ornament; It. *guernigione;* Port. *guarniçam;* D. *waarison.* The French, English, Armoric, Spanish and Italian words are from *garnish;* the Dutch is from *waaren*, to keep, to *guard*, Eng. *warren*, and from this root we have *warrant* and *guaranty*, as well as *guard* and *regard*, all from one source. See *Warren.*]
1. A body of troops stationed in a fort or fortified town, to defend it against an enemy, or to keep the inhabitants in subjection.
2. A fort, castle or fortified town, furnished with troops to defend it. *Waller.*
3. The state of being placed in a fortification for its defense; as troops laid in *garrison.* *Spenser.*

GAR'RISON, *v. t.* To place troops in a fortress for its defense; to furnish with soldiers; as, to *garrison* a fort or town.
2. To secure or defend by fortresses manned with troops; as, to *garrison* a conquered territory.

GARRU'LITY, *n.* [L. *garrulitas*, from *garrio*, to prate; Gr. γαρυω, γηρυω; Ir. *gairim;* W. *gair*, a word. Class Gr. No. 2. 9. 15. 49.]
Talkativeness; loquacity; the practice or habit of talking much; a babbling or tattling. *Ray.*

GAR'RULOUS, *a.* Talkative; prating; as *garrulous* old age. *Thomson.*

G'ARTER, *n.* [Fr. *jarretiere*, from W. *gar*, Arm. *garr*, the leg, ham or shank.]
1. A string or band used to tie a stocking to the leg.
2. The badge of an order of knighthood in Great Britain, called the *order of the garter*, instituted by Edward III. This order is a college or corporation.
3. The principal king at arms. *Johnson.*
4. A term in heraldry, signifying the half of a bend. *Encyc.*

G'ARTER, *v. t.* To bind with a garter.
2. To invest with the order of the garter. *Warton.*

G'ARTERFISH, *n.* A fish having a long depressed body, like the blade of a sword; the Lepidopus. *Dict. Nat. Hist.*

GARTH, *n.* [W. *garz.* See *Garden.*]
1. A dam or wear for catching fish.
2. A close; a little backside; a yard; a croft; a garden. [*Not used.*]

GAS, *n.* [Sax. *gast*, G. *geist*, D. *geest*, spirit, *ghost.* The primary sense of air, wind, spirit, is to flow, to rush. Hence this word may be allied to Ir. *gaisim*, to flow; *gasaim*, to shoot forth, to *gush;* *gast*, a blast of wind. It may also be allied to *yeast*, which see.]
In *chimistry*, a permanently elastic aeriform fluid, or a substance reduced to the state of an aeriform fluid by its permanent combination with caloric. *Dict. Nat. Hist.*
Gases are invisible except when colored, which happens in two or three instances.

GAS'CON, *n.* A native of Gascony in France.

GAS'CONADE, *n.* [Fr. from *Gascon*, an inhabitant of Gascony, the people of which are noted for boasting.]
A boast or boasting; a vaunt; a bravado; a bragging. *Swift.*

GASCONA'DE, *v. i.* To boast; to brag; to vaunt; to bluster.

GAS'EOUS, *a.* In the form of gas or an aeriform fluid.

GASH, *n.* [I know not through what channel we have received this word. It may be allied to *chisel.* See Class Gs. No. 5. 6. 12. 28.]
A deep and long cut; an incision of considerable length, particularly in flesh. *Milton.*

GASH, *v. i.* To make a gash, or long, deep incision; applied chiefly to incisions in flesh.

GASH'ED, *pp.* Cut with a long, deep incision.

GASH'FUL, *a.* Full of gashes; hideous.

GASH'ING, *ppr.* Cutting long, deep incisions.

GASIFICA'TION, *n.* [See *Gasify.*] The act or process of converting into gas.

GAS'IFIED, *pp.* Converted into an aeriform fluid.

GAS'IFY, *v. t.* [*gas* and L. *facio*, to make.] To convert into gas or an aeriform fluid by combination with caloric.

GAS'IFYING, *ppr.* Converting into gas.

GAS'KET, *n.* [Sp. *caxeta.* See *Case.*] A plaited cord fastened to the sail-yard of a ship, and used to furl or tie the sail to the yard. *Mar. Dict.*

GAS'KINS, *n. plu.* Galligaskins; wide open hose. [See *Galligaskins.*] *Shak.*

GAS'LIGHT, *n.* Light produced by the combustion of carbureted hydrogen gas. Gaslights are now substituted for oil-lights, in illuminating streets and apartments in houses.

GASOM'ETER, *n.* [*gas* and μετρον.] In *chimistry*, an instrument or apparatus, intended to measure, collect, preserve or mix different gases. *Coxe.*
An instrument for measuring the quantity of gas employed in an experiment; also, the place where gas is prepared for lighting streets. *R. S. Jameson.*

GASOM'ETRY, *n.* The science, art or practice of measuring gases. It teaches also the nature and properties of these elastic fluids. *Coxe.*

G'ASP, *v. i.* [Sw. *gispa*, Dan. *gisper*, to gape, to yawn.]
1. To open the mouth wide in catching the breath or in laborious respiration; particularly in dying. *Addison.*
2. To long for. [*Not in use.*]

G'ASP, *v. t.* To emit breath by opening wide the mouth.

> And with short sobs he *gasps* away his breath. *Dryden.*

G'ASP, *n.* The act of opening the mouth to catch the breath.
2. The short catch of the breath in the agonies of death. *Addison.*

G'ASPING, *ppr.* Opening the mouth to catch the breath.

G'AST, **G'ASTER**, *v. t.* To make aghast; to frighten. [*Not used.*] *Shak.*

G'ASTNESS, *n.* Amazement; fright. [*Not used.*] *Shak.*

GAS'TRIC, *a.* [from Gr. γαςηρ, the belly or stomach.]
Belonging to the belly, or rather to the stomach. The *gastric* juice is a thin, pellucid liquor, separated by the capillary exhaling arteries of the stomach, which open upon its internal tunic. It is the principal agent in digestion. *Hooper.*

GASTRIL'OQUIST, *n.* [Gr. γαςηρ, belly, and L. *loquor*, to speak.]
Literally, one who speaks from his belly or stomach; hence, one who so modifies his voice that it seems to come from another person or place. *Reid.*

GAS'TROCELE, *n.* [Gr. γαςηρ, the stomach, and κηλη, a tumor.] A rupture of the stomach. *Quincy.*

GAS'TROMANCY, *n.* [Gr. γαςηρ, belly, and μαντεια, divination.]
A kind of divination among the ancients by means of words seeming to be uttered from the belly. *Encyc.*

GASTROR'APHY, *n.* [Gr. γαςηρ, belly, and ραφη, a sewing or suture.]
The operation of sewing up wounds of the abdomen. *Quincy.*

GASTROT'OMY, *n.* [Gr. γαςηρ, belly, and τεμνω, to cut.]
The operation of cutting into or opening the abdomen. *Encyc.*

GAT, *pret.* of *get.*

GATE, *n.* [Sax. *gate*, *geat;* Ir. *geata;* Scot. *gait.* The Goth. *gatwo*, Dan. *gade*, Sw. *gata*, G. *gasse*, Sans. *gaut*, is a way or street. In D. *gat* is a gap or channel. If the radical letters are *gd* or *gt*, it may be connected with *gad*, to go, as it signifies a passage.]
1. A large door which gives entrance into a walled city, a castle, a temple, palace or other large edifice. It differs from *door* chiefly in being larger. *Gate* signifies both the opening or passage, and the frame of boards, planks or timber which closes the passage.
2. A frame of timber which opens or closes a passage into any court, garden or other inclosed ground; also, the passage.
3. The frame which shuts or stops the passage of water through a dam into a flume.
4. An avenue; an opening; a way. *Knolles.*
In *scripture*, *figuratively*, power, dominion. "Thy seed shall possess the *gate* of his enemies;" that is, towns and fortresses. Gen. xxii.
The *gates of hell*, are the power and dominion of the devil and his instruments. Matt. xvi.
The *gates of death*, are the brink of the grave. Ps. ix.

GA'TED, *a.* Having gates. *Young.*

GA'TEVEIN, *n.* The vena portæ, a large vein which conveys the blood from the abdominal viscera into the liver. *Bacon. Hooper.*

GA'TEWAY, *n.* A way through the gate of some inclosure. *Mortimer.*
2. A building to be passed at the entrance of the area before a mansion. *Todd.*

GATH'ER, *v. t.* [Sax. *gaderian*, or *gatherian;* D. *gaderen.* I know not whether the first syllable is a prefix or not. The Ch. גדר signifies to inclose, and to *gather* dates. If the elements are primarily *Gd*, the word coincides with the Ger. *gattern*, Ch. אגד *to gather*, to bind.]

1. To bring together; to collect a number of separate things into one place or into one aggregate body.

Gather stones: and they took stones, and made a heap. Gen. xxxi.

2. To get in harvest; to reap or cut and bring into barns or stores. Levit. xxv. 20.
3. To pick up; to glean; to get in small parcels and bring together.

Gather out the stones. Is. lxii.

He must *gather* up money by degrees. *Locke.*

4. To pluck; to collect by cropping, picking or plucking.

Do men *gather* grapes of thorns, or figs of thistles? Matt. vii.

5. To assemble; to congregate; to bring persons into one place. Ezek. xxii. 19.
6. To collect in abundance; to accumulate; to amass.

I *gathered* me also silver and gold, and the peculiar treasure of kings. Eccles. ii.

7. To select and take; to separate from others and bring together.

Save us, O Lord our God, and *gather* us from among the heathen. Ps. cvi.

8. To sweep together.

The kingdom of heaven is like a net that was cast into the sea, and *gathered* of every kind. Matt. xiii.

9. To bring into one body or interest.

Yet will I *gather* others to him. Is. lvi.

10. To draw together from a state of expansion or diffusion; to contract.

Gathering his flowing robe he seemed to stand,
In act to speak, and graceful stretch'd his hand. *Pope.*

11. To gain.

He *gathers* ground upon her in the chase. *Dryden.*

12. To pucker; to plait.
13. To deduce by inference; to collect or learn by reasoning. From what I hear I *gather* that he was present.

After he had seen the vision, immediately we endeavored to go into Macedonia, assuredly *gathering* that the Lord had called us to preach the gospel to them. Acts xvi.

14. To coil as a serpent.

To gather breath, to have respite. *Obs.* *Spenser.*

GATH'ER, *v. i.* To collect; to unite; to increase; to be condensed. The clouds *gather* in the west.

2. To increase; to grow larger by accretion of like matter.

Their snow ball did not *gather* as it went. *Bacon.*

3. To assemble. The people *gather* fast.
4. To generate pus or matter. [See *Gathering.*]

GATH'ERABLE, *a.* That may be collected; that may be deduced. [*Unusual.*] *Godwin.*

GATH'ERED, *pp.* Collected; assembled; contracted; plaited; drawn by inference.

GATH'ERER, *n.* One who gathers or collects; one who gets in a crop.

GATH'ERING, *ppr.* Collecting; assembling; drawing together; plaiting; wrinkling.

GATH'ERING, *n.* The act of collecting or assembling.

2. Collection; a crowd; an assembly.
3. Charitable contribution. 1 Cor. xvi.
4. A tumor suppurated or maturated; a collection of pus; an abscess.

GATH'ERS, *n.* Plaits; folds; puckers; wrinkles in cloth. *Hudibras.*

GAT'TERTREE, *n.* A species of Cornus or Cornelian cherry. *Fam. of Plants.*

GAT-TOOTHED, *a.* Goat-toothed; having a lickerish tooth. *Obs.* *Chaucer.*

GAUD, *v. i.* [L. *gaudeo*, to rejoice.] To exult; to rejoice. *Obs.* *Shak.*

GAUD, *n.* [L. *gaudium.*] An ornament; something worn for adorning the person; a fine thing. *Obs.* *Shak.*

GAUD'ED, *a.* Adorned with trinkets; colored. *Obs.* *Chaucer.* *Shak.*

GAUD'ERY, *n.* Finery; fine things; ornaments. *Bacon.* *Dryden.*

GAUD'ILY, *adv.* Showily; with ostentation of fine dress. *Guthrie.*

GAUD'INESS, *n.* Showiness; tinsel appearance; ostentatious finery. *Whitlock.*

GAUD'Y, *a.* Showy; splendid; gay.

A goldfinch there I saw, with *gaudy* pride
Of painted plumes— *Dryden.*

2. Ostentatiously fine; gay beyond the simplicity of nature or good taste.

Costly thy habit as thy purse can buy,
But not express'd in fancy; rich, not *gaudy*. *Shak.*

GAUD'Y, *n.* A feast or festival; *a word in the university.* *Cheyne.*

GAUĠE, *v. t. gage.* [Fr. *jauger*, to gage; *jauge*, a measuring rod; Arm. *jauja*, or *jauchi*, to gage; *jauch*, a rod. It is supposed by J. Thomson, that this is contracted from *jaulge*, from *gaule*, a rod or pole. But qu.]

1. To measure or to ascertain the contents of a cask or vessel, as a pipe, puncheon, hogshead, barrel, tierce or keg.
2. To measure in respect to proportion.

The vanes nicely *gauged* on each side— *Derham.*

GAUĠE, *n. gage.* A measure; a standard of measure. *Moxon.*

2. Measure; dimensions. *Burke.*

GA'UĠED, *pp.* Measured.

GA'UĠER, *n.* One who gauges; an officer whose business is to ascertain the contents of casks.

GA'UĠING, *ppr.* Measuring a cask; ascertaining dimensions or proportions of quantity.

GA'UĠING, *n.* The art of measuring the contents or capacities of vessels of any form. *Ed. Encyc.*

GA'UĠING-ROD, *n.* An instrument to be used in measuring the contents of casks or vessels.

GAUL, *n.* [L. *Gallia.*] A name of ancient France; also, an inhabitant of Gaul.

GAUL'ISH, *a.* Pertaining to ancient France or Gaul.

GAUNT, } *a. gant.* [The origin is uncertain. Qu. Sax. *gewanian*, *wanian*, to wane. In W. *gwan* is weak, poor.]
GANT, }

Vacant; hollow; empty, as an animal after long fasting; hence, lean; meager; thin; slender. *Shak.* *Dryden.*

GAUNT'LY, *adv. gant'ly.* Leanly; meagerly.

GAUNT'LET, *n.* [See *Gantlet.*]

GAUZE, *n.* [Sp. *gasa*; Fr. *gaze*; Arm. *gazen.* Qu. L. *gausape*, or *gossipium.*]

A very thin, slight, transparent stuff, of silk or linen. *Encyc.*

GAUZELOOM, *n.* A loom in which gauze is wove.

GAUZ'Y, *a.* Like gauze; thin as gauze.

GAVE, *pret.* of *give.*

GAV'EL, *n.* In *law*, tribute; toll; custom. [See *Gabel.*]

GAV'EL, *n.* [Fr. *javelle*; Port. *gavela*, a sheaf; W. *gavael*, a hold or grasp.]

1. A small parcel of wheat, rye or other grain, laid together by reapers, consisting of two, three or more handfuls. *New England.*
2. In *England*, a provincial word for ground. *Eng. Dict.*

GAV'EL, for *gable* or *gable-end.* [See *Gable.*]

GAV'ELET, *n.* An ancient and special *cessavit* in Kent, in England, where the custom of gavelkind continues, by which the tenant, if he withdraws his rent and services due to his lord, forfeits his lands and tenements. *Encyc.*

2. In London, a writ used in the hustings, given to lords of rents in the city. *Encyc.*

GAV'ELKIND, *n.* [This word *gavel* is British. In W. *gavael* signifies a hold, a grasp, tenure; *gavael-cenedyl*, the hold or *tenure of a family*, [not the *kind* of tenure;] *gavaelu*, to hold, grasp, arrest. Ir. *gabhail*, *gabham*, to take; *gabhail-cine*, gavelkind. In Ir. *gabhal* is a fork, [G. *gabel*,] and the groin, and it expresses the collateral branches of a family; but the Welsh application is most probably the true one.]

A tenure in England, by which land descended from the father to all his sons in equal portions, and the land of a brother, dying without issue, descended equally to his brothers. This species of tenure prevailed in England before the Norman conquest, in many parts of the kingdom, perhaps in the whole realm; but particularly in Kent, where it still exists. *Selden.* *Cowel.* *Blackstone.* *Cyc.*

GAV'ELOCK, *n.* [Sax.] An iron crow.

GAV'ILAN, *n.* A species of hawk in the Philippine isles; the back and wings yellow; the belly white.

GAV'OT, *n.* [Fr. *gavotte*; It. *gavotta.*] A kind of dance, the air of which has two brisk and lively strains in common time, each of which is played twice over. The first has usually four or eight bars, and the second contains eight, twelve or more. *Encyc.*

GAW'BY, *n.* A dunce. [*Not in use.*]

GAWK, *n.* [Sax. *gæc*, *geac*, a cuckoo; G. *gauch*, a cuckoo, and a fool, an unfledged fop, a chough; Scot. *gaukie*, *gauky*, a fool; D. *gek*; Sw. *gắck*, a fool, a buffoon; Dan. *giek*, a jest, a *joke*. It seems that this word is radically one with *joke*, *juggle*, which see.]

1. A cuckoo.
2. A fool; a simpleton. [In both senses, it is retained in Scotland.]

GAWK'Y, *a.* Foolish; awkward; clumsy; clownish. [In this sense it is retained in vulgar use in America.]

[Is not this allied to the Fr. *gauche*, left, untoward, unhandy, Eng. *awk*, awkward; *gauchir*, to shrink back or turn aside, to use shifts, to double, to dodge. This verb well expresses the actions of a jester or buffoon.]

GAWK'Y, *n.* A stupid, ignorant, awkward fellow.

GAY, *a.* [Fr. *gai;* Arm. *gae;* It. *gaio*, gay. In Sp. *gaya* is a stripe of different colors on stuffs; *gaytero* is gaudy; and *gayo* is a jay. The W. has *gwyç*, gay, gaudy, brave. This is a contracted word, but whether from the root of *gaudy*, or not, is not obvious. In some of its applications, it seems allied to *joy.*]

1. Merry; airy; jovial; sportive; frolicksome. It denotes more life and animation than *cheerful.*

Belinda smiled, and all the world was *gay.* *Pope.*

2. Fine; showy; as a *gay* dress.

3. Inflamed or merry with liquor; intoxicated; *a vulgar use of the word in America.*

GAY, *n.* An ornament. [*Not used.*] *L'Estrange.*

GA'YETY, *n.* [Fr. *gaieté;* It. *gaiezza.*]

1. Merriment; mirth; airiness; as a company full of *gayety.*

2. Act of juvenile pleasure; the *gayeties* of youth. *Denham.*

3. Finery; show; as the *gayety* of dress.

GA'YLY, *adv.* Merrily; with mirth and frolick.

2. Finely; splendidly; pompously; as ladies *gayly* dressed; a flower *gayly* blooming. *Pope.*

GA'YNESS, *n.* Gayety; finery.

GA'YSŎME, *a.* Full of gayety. [*Little used.*]

GAZE, *v. i.* [Qu. Gr. αγαζομαι, to be astonished, and Heb. Ch. Syr. Sam. חזה chazah, to see or look, that is, to fix the eye or to reach with the eye.]

To fix the eyes and look steadily and earnestly; to look with eagerness or curiosity; as in admiration, astonishment, or in study.

A lover's eyes will *gaze* an eagle blind. *Shak.*

Ye men of Galilee, why stand ye *gazing* up into heaven? Acts i.

GAZE, *v. t.* To view with fixed attention.

And *gazed* awhile the ample sky. *Milton.*

[It is little used as a transitive verb.]

GAZE, *n.* A fixed look; a look of eagerness, wonder or admiration; a continued look of attention.

With secret *gaze*,
Or open admiration, him behold— *Milton.*

2. The object gazed on; that which causes one to gaze.

Made of my enemies the scorn and *gaze.* *Milton.*

GA'ZEFUL, *a.* Looking with a gaze; looking intently. *Spenser.*

GA'ZEHOUND, *n.* A hound that pursues by the sight rather than by the scent. *Encyc. Johnson.*

GAZ'EL, *n.* [Fr. *gazelle;* Sp. *gazela;* Port. *gazella;* from the Arabic. The verb under which this word is placed غزل is rendered to remove, withdraw, retire or be separate.]

An animal of Africa and India, of the genus Antilope. It partakes of the nature of the goat and the deer. Like the goat, the gazel has hollow permanent horns, and it feeds on shrubs; but in size and delicacy, and in the nature and color of its hair, it resembles the roe-buck. It has cylindrical horns, most frequently annulated at the base, and bunches of hair on its fore legs. It has a most brilliant, beautiful eye. *Goldsmith. Ed. Encyc.*

GA'ZEMENT, *n.* View. [*Not in use.*] *Spenser.*

GA'ZER, *n.* One who gazes; one who looks steadily and intently, from delight, admiration or study. *Pope.*

GAZETTE, *n.* *gazet'.* [It. *gazzetta;* Fr. *gazette. Gazetta* is said to have been a Venetian coin, which was the price of the first newspaper, and hence the name.]

A newspaper; a sheet or half sheet of paper containing an account of transactions and events of public or private concern, which are deemed important and interesting. The first gazette in England was published at Oxford in 1665. On the removal of the court to London, the title was changed to the *London Gazette.* It is now the official newspaper, and published on Tuesdays and Saturdays. *Encyc.*

GAZETTE, *v. t.* *gazet'.* To insert in a gazette; to announce or publish in a gazette.

GAZETT'ED, *pp.* Published in a gazette.

GAZETTEE'R, *n.* A writer of news, or an officer appointed to publish news by authority. *Johnson. Pope.*

2. The title of a newspaper.

3. A book containing a brief description of empires, kingdoms, cities, towns and rivers, in a country or in the whole world, alphabetically arranged; a book of topographical descriptions.

GA'ZING, *ppr.* [See *Gaze.*] Looking with fixed attention.

GA'ZINGSTOCK, *n.* A person gazed at with scorn or abhorrence; an object of curiosity or contempt. *Bp. Hall.*

GAZŎN, *n.* [Fr. turf.] In *fortification*, pieces of turf used to line parapets and the traverses of galleries. *Harris.*

ĠEAL, *v. i.* [Fr. *geler;* L. *gelo.*] To congeal. *Obs.*

GEAR, *n.* [Sax. *gearwian, gyrian*, to prepare; *gearw*, prepared, prompt; *gearwa*, habit, clothing, apparatus; G. *gar*, D. *gaar*, dressed, done, ready; perhaps Sw. *garfva*, to tan.]

1. Apparatus; whatever is prepared; hence, habit; dress; ornaments.

Array thyself in her most gorgeous *gear.* *Spenser.*

2. *More generally*, the harness or furniture of beasts; whatever is used in equipping horses or cattle for draught; tackle.

3. In *Scotland*, warlike accouterments; also, goods, riches. *Jamieson.*

4. Business; matters. *Obs.* *Spenser.*

5. By seamen pronounced *jears*, which see.

GEAR, *v. t.* To dress; to put on gear; to harness.

GE'ARED, *pp.* Dressed; harnessed.

GE'ARING, *ppr.* Dressing; harnessing.

GE'ASON, *n.* *s* as z. Rare; uncommon; wonderful. *Obs.* *Spenser.*

GEAT, *n.* [D. *gat.* See *Gate.*] The hole through which metal runs into a mold in castings. *Moxon.*

GECK, *n.* [G. *geck;* Sw. *gäck;* Dan. *giek.*] A dupe. *Obs.* *Shak.*

GECK, *v. t.* To cheat, trick or gull. *Obs.*

ĠEE. } A word used by teamsters, direct-
JEE. } ing their teams to pass further to the right, or from the driver, when on the near side; opposed to *hoi* or *haw.*

GEESE, *n.* plu. of *goose.*

GEEST, *n.* Alluvial matter on the surface of land, not of recent origin. *Jameson.*

GEHEN'NA, *n.* [Gr. γεεννα, from the Heb. ge-hinom, the valley of Hinom, in which was Tophet, where the Israelites sacrificed their children to Moloch. 2 Kings xxiii. 10.]

This word has been used by the Jews as equivalent to hell, place of fire or torment and punishment, and the Greek word is rendered by our translators by hell and hell-fire. Matt. xviii. 9. xxiii. 15.

GEHLENITE, *n.* [from *Gehlen*, the chimist.]

A mineral recently discovered, in the description of which authors are not perfectly agreed. According to the description and analysis of Fuchs, it appears to be a variety of idocrase; but according to the observations of Prof. Clarke, it is probably a new species. *Cleaveland.*

ĠEL'ABLE, *a.* [from L. *gelu*, frost, or *gelo*, to congeal.]

That may or can be congealed; capable of being converted into jelly.

ĠEL'ATIN, *n.* [It. Sp. *gelatina*, from L. *gelo*, to congeal, to freeze.]

A concrete animal substance, transparent, and soluble slowly in cold water, but rapidly in warm water. With tannin, a yellowish white precipitate is thrown down from a solution of gelatin, which forms an elastic adhesive mass, not unlike vegetable gluten, and is a compound of tannin and gelatin. *Parr.*

ĠEL'ATIN, } *a.* Of the nature and con-
ĠELAT'INOUS, } sistence of gelatin; resembling jelly; viscous; moderately stiff and cohesive.

ĠELAT'INATE, *v. i.* To be converted into gelatin or into a substance like jelly.

Lapis lazuli, if calcined, does not effervesce, but *gelatinates* with the mineral acids. *Kirwan.*

ĠELAT'INATE, *v. t.* To convert into gelatin or into a substance resembling jelly.

ĠELATINA'TION, *n.* The act or process of converting or being turned into gelatin, or into a substance like jelly. *Kirwan.*

ĠEL'ATINIZE, *v. i.* The same as *gelatinate.* *Fleming.*

GELD, *n.* [Sax. *gild;* Sw. *gäld;* Dan. *gield;* G. D. *geld.*]

Money; tribute; compensation. This word is obsolete in English, but it occurs in old laws and law books in composition; as in *Danegeld*, or *Danegelt*, a tax imposed by the Danes; *Weregeld*, compensation for the life of a man, &c.

GELD, *v t.* pret. *gelded* or *gelt;* pp. *gelded* or *gelt.* [G. *geilen, gelten;* Sw. *gälla;* Dan. *gilder*, to geld, and to cut off the *gills* of herrings; Ir. *caillim*, to geld, to lose, to destroy. Qu. W. *colli*, to lose, or Eth. ገለየ gali, to cut off.]

1. To castrate; to emasculate.

2. To deprive of any essential part. *Shak.*

3. To deprive of any thing immodest or exceptionable. *Dryden.*

GELD'ED, } *pp.* Castrated; emascula-
GELT, } ted.
GELD'ER, *n.* One who castrates.
GELD'ER-ROSE, [Qu. from *Guelderland.*] A plant, a species of Viburnum; also, a species of Spiræa.
GELD'ING, *ppr.* Castrating.
GELD'ING, *n.* A castrated animal, but chiefly a horse.
ĠEL'ID, *a.* [L. *gelidus*, from *gelo*, to freeze, Fr. *geler*. See *Cool, Cold.*]
Cold; very cold. *Thomson.*
ĠEL'IDNESS, *n.* Coldness.
ĠEL'LY, *n.* [Fr. *gelée*; Port. *gelea*; Sp. *jalea*; L. *gelo, gelatus*. It is now more generally written *jelly.*]
1. The inspissated juice of fruit boiled with sugar.
2. A viscous or glutinous substance; a gluey substance, soft, but cohesive. [See *Jelly.*]
GELT, *pp.* of *geld.*
GELT, *n.* for *gelding*. [*Not used.*]
GELT, for *gilt*. Tinsel, or gilt surface. [*Not used.*] *Spenser.*
ĠEM, *n.* [L. *gemma*; It. *id.*; Sp. *yema*; Port. *gomo*; Ir. *geam*; G. *keim*; D. *kiem*. The sense is probably a shoot. See Class Gm. No. 5. Ar.]
1. A bud. In *botany*, the bud or compendium of a plant, covered with scales to protect the rudiments from the cold of winter and other injuries; called the hybernacle or winter quarters of a plant. *Encyc.*
2. A precious stone of any kind, as the ruby, topaz, emerald, &c.
ĠEM, *v. t.* To adorn with gems, jewels or precious stones.
2. To bespangle; as foliage *gemmed* with dew drops.
3. To embellish with detached beauties.

England is studded and *gemmed* with castles and palaces. *Irving.*

ĠEM, *v. i.* To bud; to germinate. *Milton.*
GEMAR'A, *n.* [Ch. גמר to finish.] The second part of the Talmud or commentary on the Jewish laws.
GEMAR'IC, *a.* Pertaining to the Gemara. *Encyc.*
ĠEM'EL, *n.* [L. *gemellus.*] A pair; a term in heraldry. *Drayton.*
ĠEMELLIP'AROUS, *a.* [L. *gemellus* and *pario.*] Producing twins. *Dict.*
ĠEM'INATE, *v. t.* [L. *gemino.*] To double. [*Little used.*]
ĠEMINA'TION, *n.* A doubling; duplication; repetition. *Boyle.*
ĠEM'INI, *n. plu.* [L.] Twins. In *astronomy*, a constellation or sign of the zodiac, representing Castor and Pollux. In the Britannic catalogue, it contains 85 stars. *Encyc.*
ĠEM'INOUS, *a.* [L. *geminus.*] Double; in pairs. *Brown.*
ĠEM'INY, *n.* [supra.] Twins; a pair; a couple. *Shak.*
ĠEM'MARY, *a.* [from *gem.*] Pertaining to gems or jewels.
ĠEMMA'TION, *n.* [L. *gemmatio*, from *gemma.*]
In *botany*, budding; the state, form or construction of the bud of plants, of the leaves, stipules, petioles or scales. *Martyn.*
ĠEM'MEOUS, *a.* [L. *gemmeus.*] Pertaining to gems; of the nature of gems; resembling gems.

ĠEMMIP'AROUS, *a.* [L. *gemma*, a bud, and *pario*, to bear.] Producing buds or gems. *Martyn.*
ĠEM'MULE, *n.* A little gem or bud. *Eaton.*
ĠEM'MY, *a.* Bright; glittering; full of gems.
2. Neat; spruce; smart.
GEMO'TE, *n.* [Sax.] A meeting. *Obs.* [See *Meet.*]
ĠEMS'BOK, *n.* The name given to a variety of the antelope. *J. Barrow.*
ĠEND'ARM, *n.* In France, *gens d'armes* is the denomination given to a select body of troops, destined to watch over the interior public safety. In the singular, *gendarme*, as written by Lunier, is properly anglicized *gendarm.*
ĠEND'ARMERY, *n.* [supra.] The body of gendarms. *Hume.*
ĠEN'DER, *n.* [Fr. *genre*; Sp. *genero*; It. *genere*; from L. *genus*, from *geno, gigno*, Gr. γενναω, γινομαι, to beget, or to be born; Ir. *geinim*; W. *geni*, to be born; *gân*, a birth; *cenaw*, offspring; Gr. γενος, γονος; Eng. *kind*. From the same root, Gr. γυνη, a woman, a wife; Sans. *gena*, a wife, and *genaga*, a father. We have *begin* from the same root. See *Begin* and *Can.*]
1. Properly, kind; sort. *Obs.* *Shak.*
2. A sex, male or female. Hence,
3. In *grammar*, a difference in words to express distinction of sex; usually a difference of termination in nouns, adjectives and participles, to express the distinction of male and female. But although this was the orginal design of different terminations, yet in the progress of language, other words having no relation to one sex or the other, came to have genders assigned them by custom. Words expressing males are said to be of the *masculine gender*; those expressing females, of the *feminine gender*; and in some languages, words expressing things having no sex, are of the *neuter* or *neither gender.*
ĠEN'DER, *v. t.* To beget; but *engender* is more generally used.
ĠEN'DER, *v. i.* To copulate; to breed. Levit. xix.
ĠENEALOĠ'ICAL, *a.* [from *genealogy.*]
1. Pertaining to the descent of persons or families; exhibiting the succession of families from a progenitor; as a *genealogical* table.
2. According to the descent of a person or family from an ancestor; as *genealogical* order.
ĠENEAL'OĠIST, *n.* He who traces descents of persons or families.
ĠENEAL'OĠIZE, *v. i.* To relate the history of descents. *Trans. of Pausanias.*
ĠENEAL'OĠY, *n.* [L. *genealogia*; Gr. γενεαλογια; γενος, race, and λογος, discourse; Sax. *cyn, gecynd*; Eng. *kind.*]
1. An account or history of the descent of a person or family from an ancestor; enumeration of ancestors and their children in the natural order of succession.
2. Pedigree; lineage; regular descent of a person or family from a progenitor.
ĠEN'ERABLE, *a.* That may be engendered, begotten or produced. *Bentley.*

ĠEN'ERAL, *a.* [Fr. from L. *generalis*, from *genus*, a kind.]
1. Properly, relating to a whole genus or kind; and hence, relating to a whole class or order. Thus we speak of a *general* law of the animal or vegetable economy. This word, though from *genus*, kind, is used to express whatever is common to an order, class, kind, sort or species, or to any company or association of individuals.
2. Comprehending many species or individuals; not special or particular; as, it is not logical to draw a *general* inference or conclusion from a particular fact.
3. Lax in signification; not restrained or limited to a particular import; not specific; as a loose and *general* expression.
4. Public; common; relating to or comprehending the whole community; as the *general* interest or safety of a nation.

To all *general* purposes, we have uniformly been one people. *Federalist, Jay.*

5. Common to many or the greatest number; as a *general* opinion; a *general* custom.
6. Not directed to a single object.

If the same thing be peculiarly evil, that *general* aversion will be turned into a particular hatred against it. *Spratt.*

7. Having a relation to all; common to the whole. Adam, our *general* sire. *Milton.*
8. Extensive, though not universal; common; usual.
This word is prefixed or annexed to words, to express the extent of their application. Thus a *general assembly* is an assembly of a whole body, in fact or by representation. In *Scotland*, it is the whole church convened by its representatives. In *America*, a legislature is sometimes called a *general assembly.*
In logic, a *general* term is a term which is the sign of a *general* idea.
An *attorney general*, and a *solicitor general*, is an officer who conducts suits and prosecutions for the king or for a nation or state, and whose authority is *general* in the state or kingdom.
A *vicar general* has authority as vicar or substitute over a whole territory or jurisdiction.
An *adjutant general* assists the general of an army, distributes orders, receives returns, &c.
The word *general* thus annexed to a name of office, denotes chief or superior; as a *commissary general, quarter-master general.*
In the line, a *general* officer is one who commands an army, a division or a brigade.
ĠEN'ERAL, *n.* The whole; the total; that which comprehends all or the chief part; opposed to *particular.*

In particulars our knowledge begins, and so spreads itself by degrees to *generals.* *Locke.*

A history painter paints man in *general.* *Reynolds.*

2. *In general*, in the main; for the most part; not always or universally.

I have shown that he excels, *in general*, under each of these heads. *Addison.*

3. The chief commander of an army. But to distinguish this officer from other generals, he is often called *general in chief.* The officer second in rank is called *lieutenant general.*

4. The commander of a division of an army or militia, usually called a *major general.*
5. The commander of a brigade, called a *brigadier general.*
6. A particular beat of drum or march, being that which, in the morning, gives notice for the infantry to be in readiness to march. *Encyc.*
7. The chief of an order of monks, or of all the houses or congregations established under the same rule. *Encyc.*
8. The public; the interest of the whole; the vulgar. [*Not in use.*] *Shak.*

ĠENERALIS'SIMO, *n.* [It.] The chief commander of an army or military force.
2. The supreme commander; sometimes a title of honor; as Alexander *generalissimo* of Greece. *Brown.*

ĠENERAL'ITY, *n.* [Fr. *generalité;* It. *generalità.*]
1. The state of being general; the quality of including species or particulars. *Hooker.*
2. The main body; the bulk; the greatest part; as the *generality* of a nation or of mankind. *Addison.*

ĠENERALIZA'TION, *n.* The act of extending from particulars to generals; the act of making general.

ĠEN'ERALIZE, *v. t.* To extend from particulars or species to genera, or to whole kinds or classes; to make general, or common to a number.

Copernicus *generalized* the celestial motions, by merely referring them to the moon's motion. Newton *generalized* them still more, by referring this last to the motion of a stone through the air. *Nicholson.*

2. To reduce to a genus. *Reid.*

ĠEN'ERALLY, *adv.* In general; commonly; extensively, though not universally; most frequently, but not without exceptions. A hot summer *generally* follows a cold winter. Men are *generally* more disposed to censure than to praise, as they generally suppose it easier to depress excellence in others than to equal or surpass it by elevating themselves.
2. In the main; without detail; in the whole taken together.

Generally speaking, they live very quietly. *Addison.*

ĠEN'ERALNESS, *n.* Wide extent, though short of universality; frequency; commonness. *Sidney.*

ĠEN'ERALSHIP, *n.* The skill and conduct of a general officer; military skill in a commander, exhibited in the judicious arrangements of troops, or the operations of war.

ĠEN'ERALTY, *n.* The whole; the totality. [*Little used.*] *Hale.*

ĠEN'ERANT, *n.* [L. *generans.*] The power that generates; the power or principle that produces. *Glanville. Ray.*

ĠEN'ERATE, *v. t.* [L. *genero.* See *Gender.*]
1. To beget; to procreate; to propagate; to produce a being similar to the parent. Every animal *generates* his own species.
2. To produce; to cause to be; to bring into life; as great whales which the waters *generated.* *Milton.*
3. To cause; to produce; to form.

Sounds are *generated* where there is no air at all. *Bacon.*

Whatever *generates* a quantity of good chyle, must likewise *generate* milk. *Arbuthnot.*

In *music,* any given sound *generates* with itself its octave and two other sounds extremely sharp, viz. its twelfth above or the octave of its fifth, and the seventeenth above. *Encyc.*

ĠEN'ERATED, *pp.* Begotten; engendered; procreated; produced; formed.

ĠEN'ERATING, *ppr.* Begetting; procreating; producing; forming.

ĠENERA'TION, *n.* The act of begetting; procreation, as of animals.
2. Production; formation; as the *generation* of sounds or of curves or equations.
3. A single succession in natural descent, as the children of the same parents; hence, an age. Thus we say, the third, the fourth, or the tenth *generation.* Gen. xv. 16.
4. The people of the same period, or living at the same time.

O faithless and perverse *generation.* Luke ix.

5. Genealogy; a series of children or descendants from the same stock.

This is the book of the *generations* of Adam. Gen. v.

6. A family; a race. *Shak.*
7. Progeny; offspring. *Shak.*

ĠEN'ERATIVE, *a.* Having the power of generating or propagating its own species. *Raleigh.*
2. Having the power of producing. *Bentley.*
3. Prolific. *Bentley.*

ĠEN'ERATOR, *n.* He or that which begets, causes or produces.
2. In *music,* the principal sound or sounds by which others are produced. Thus the lowest C for the treble of the harpsichord, besides its octave, will strike an attentive ear with its twelfth above, or G in alt., and with its seventeenth above, or E in alt. Hence C is called their *generator,* the G and E its products or harmonics. *Encyc.*
3. A vessel in which steam is generated. *Perkins.*

ĠENER'IC, } *a.* [It. and Sp. *generico;*
ĠENER'ICAL, } Fr. *generique;* from L. *genus.*]
Pertaining to a genus or kind; comprehending the genus, as distinct from species, or from another genus. A *generic* description is a description of a genus; a *generic* difference is a difference in genus; a *generic* name is the denomination which comprehends all the species, as of animals, plants or fossils, which have certain essential and peculiar characters in common. Thus *Canis* is the *generic* name of animals of the dog kind; *Felis,* of the cat kind; *Cervus,* of the deer kind.

ĠENER'ICALLY, *adv.* With regard to genus; as an animal *generically* distinct from another, or two animals *generically* allied. *Woodward.*

GENEROS'ITY, *n.* [Fr. *generosité;* L. *generositas,* from *genus,* race, kind, with reference to birth, blood, family.]
1. The quality of being generous; liberality in principle; a disposition to give liberally or to bestow favors; a quality of the heart or mind opposed to meanness or parsimony.
2. Liberality in act; bounty.
3. Nobleness of soul; magnanimity. [*This is the primary sense, but is now little used.*]

ĠEN'EROUS, *a.* [L. *generosus;* Fr. *genereux;* from *genus,* birth, extraction, family. See *Gender.*]
1. Primarily, being of honorable birth or origin; hence, noble; honorable; magnanimous; *applied to persons;* as a *generous* foe; a *generous* critic.
2. Noble; honorable; *applied to things;* as a *generous* virtue; *generous* boldness. It is used also to denote like qualities in irrational animals; as a *generous* pack of hounds. *Addison.*
3. Liberal; bountiful; munificent; free to give; as a *generous* friend; a *generous* father.
4. Strong; full of spirit; as *generous* wine. *Boyle. Swift.*
5. Full; overflowing; abundant; as a *generous* cup; a *generous* table.
6. Sprightly; courageous; as a *generous* steed.

ĠEN'EROUSLY, *adv.* Honorably; not meanly.
2. Nobly; magnanimously. *Dryden.*
3. Liberally; munificently.

ĠEN'EROUSNESS, *n.* The quality of being generous; magnanimity; nobleness of mind.
2. Liberality; munificence; generosity.

ĠEN'ESIS, *n.* [Gr. γενεσις, from γενναω, γινομαι. See *Gender.*]
1. The first book of the sacred scriptures of the Old Testament, containing the history of the creation, of the apostasy of man, of the deluge, and of the first patriarchs, to the death of Joseph. In the original Hebrew, this book has no title; the present title was prefixed to it by those who translated it into Greek.
2. In *geometry,* the formation of a line, plane or solid, by the motion or flux of a point, line or surface. *Encyc.*

ĠEN'ET, *n.* [Fr.] A small-sized, well-proportioned Spanish horse. *Johnson.*
2. An animal of the weasel kind, less than the martin.

ĠENETHLI'ACAL, } *a.* [Gr. γενεθλιακος,
ĠENETH'LIAC, } from γινομαι, to be born.]
Pertaining to nativities as calculated by astrologers; showing the positions of the stars at the birth of any person. [*Little used.*] *Howell.*

ĠENETH'LIACS, *n.* The science of calculating nativities or predicting the future events of life from the stars which preside at the birth of persons. [*Little used.*] *Johnson.*

ĠENETHLIAT'IC, *n.* He who calculates nativities. [*Little used.*] *Drummond.*

ĠENE'VA, *n.* [Fr. *genevre* or *genievre,* a juniper-berry; It. *ginepra;* Arm. *genevra.* The Spanish word is *nebrina,* and the tree is called *enebro,* Port. *zimbro.*]
A spirit distilled from grain or malt, with the addition of juniper berries. But instead of these berries, the spirit is now flavored with the oil of turpentine. The word is usually contracted and pronounced *gin.* *Encyc.*

ĠENE'VANISM, *n.* [from *Geneva,* where Calvin resided.] Calvinism. *Mountagu.*

ĠENEVOIS, *n. plu. jeneva'y.* People of Geneva. *Addison.*

ĠE'NIAL, *a.* [L. *genialis*, from *geno*, *gigno*, Gr. γενναω, γινομαι.]

1. Contributing to propagation or production; that causes to produce.

Creator, Venus, *genial* power of love. *Dryden.*

2. Gay; merry. *Warton.*

3. Enlivening; contributing to life and cheerfulness; supporting life.

So much I feel my *genial* spirits droop. *Milton.*

4. Native; natural. [*Not usual.*] *Brown.*

The *genial gods*, in pagan antiquity, were supposed to preside over generation, as earth, air, fire and water.

ĠE'NIALLY, *adv.* By genius or nature; naturally. [*Little used.*] *Glanville.*

2. Gayly; cheerfully. *Johnson.*

ĠENIC'ULATED, *a.* [L. *geniculatus*, from *geniculum*, a knot or joint, from the root of *genu*, the knee. See *Knee.*]

Kneed; knee-jointed; having joints like the knee a little bent; as a *geniculated* stem or peduncle. *Martyn.*

ĠENICULA'TION, *n.* Knottiness; the state of having knots or joints like a knee. *Johnson.*

ĠE'NII, *n.* [L. plu.] A sort of imaginary intermediate beings between men and angels; some good and some bad. *Encyc.*

ĠE'NIO, *n.* [It. from L. *genius.*] A man of a particular turn of mind. *Tatler.*

ĠEN'ITAL, *a.* [L. *genitalis*, from the root of *gigno*, Gr. γενναω, to beget.]

Pertaining to generation or the act of begetting.

ĠEN'ITALS, *n. plu.* The parts of an animal which are the immediate instruments of generation.

ĠEN'ITING, *n.* [Fr. *janeton.*] A species of apple that ripens very early.

ĠEN'ITIVE, *a.* [L. *genitivus*, from the root of gender.]

In *grammar*, an epithet given to a case in the declension of nouns, expressing primarily the thing from which something else proceeds; as *filius patris*, the son of a father; *aqua fontis*, the water of a fountain. But by custom this case expresses other relations, particularly possession or ownership; as *animi magnitudo*, greatness of mind, greatness possessed by or inherent in the mind. This case often expresses also that which proceeds from something else; as *pater septem filiorum*, the father of seven sons.

ĠEN'ITOR, *n.* One who procreates; a sire; a father. *Sheldon.*

ĠEN'ITURE, *n.* Generation; procreation; birth. *Burton.*

ĠE'NIUS, *n.* [L. from the root of *gigno*, Gr. γενναω, to beget.]

1. Among the ancients, a good or evil spirit or demon supposed to preside over a man's destiny in life, that is, to direct his birth and actions and be his guard and guide; a tutelary deity; the ruling and protecting power of men, places or things. This seems to be merely a personification or deification of the particular structure or bent of mind which a man receives from nature, which is the primary signification of the word.

2. The peculiar structure of mind which is given by nature to an individual, or that disposition or bent of mind which is peculiar to every man, and which qualifies him for a particular employment; a particular natural talent or aptitude of mind for a particular study or course of life; as a *genius* for history, for poetry or painting.

3. Strength of mind; uncommon powers of intellect, particularly the power of invention. In this sense we say, Homer was a man of *genius.* Hence,

4. A man endowed with uncommon vigor of mind; a man of superior intellectual faculties. Shakespeare was a rare *genius.* *Addison.*

5. Mental powers or faculties. [See No. 2.]

6. Nature; disposition; peculiar character; as the *genius* of the times.

ĠENT, *a.* Elegant; pretty; gentle. [*Not in use.*] *Spenser.*

ĠENTEE'L, *a.* [Fr. *gentil*; It. *gentile*; Sp. *gentil*; L. *gentilis*, from *gens*, race, stock, family, and with the sense of noble or at least respectable birth, as we use *birth* and *family.*]

1. Polite; well bred; easy and graceful in manners or behavior; having the manners of well bred people; as *genteel* company; *genteel* guests.

2. Polite; easy and graceful; becoming well bred persons; as *genteel* manners or behavior; a *genteel* address.

3. Graceful in mein or form; elegant; as the lady has a *genteel* person.

4. Elegantly dressed. *Law.*

5. Decorous; refined; free from any thing low or vulgar; as *genteel* comedy. *Addison.*

ĠENTEE'LLY, *adv.* Politely; gracefully; elegantly; in the manner of well bred people.

ĠENTEE'LNESS, *n.* Gracefulness of manners or person; elegance; politeness. We speak of the *genteelness* of a person or of his deportment.

2. Qualities befitting a person of rank. *Johnson.*

ĠEN'TIAN, *n.* [L. *gentiana*; Fr. *gentiane*; Ar. كَنْطَا kanta.]

A genus of plants, of many species. The common gentian is a native of the mountainous parts of Germany. The root, the only part used, has a yellowish brown color and a very bitter taste, and is used as an ingredient in stomachic bitters. It is sometimes called *felwort.* *Encyc.*

ĠEN'TIL, *n.* A species of falcon or hawk.

ĠEN'TILE, *n.* [L. *gentilis*; Fr. *gentil*; Sp. *gentil*; from L. *gens*, nation, race; *applied to pagans.*]

In *the scriptures*, a pagan; a worshipper of false gods; any person not a Jew or a christian; a heathen. The Hebrews included in the term *goim* or nations, all the tribes of men who had not received the true faith, and were not circumcised. The christians translated *goim* by the L. *gentes*, and imitated the Jews in giving the name *gentiles* to all nations who were not Jews nor christians. In civil affairs, the denomination was given to all nations who were not Romans. *Encyc.*

ĠEN'TILE, *a.* Pertaining to pagans or heathens.

ĠENTILESSE, *n.* Complaisance. [*Not in use.*] *Hudibras.*

ĠEN'TILISH, *a.* Heathenish; pagan. *Milton.*

ĠEN'TILISM, *n.* Heathenism; paganism; the worship of false gods. *Stillingfleet.*

ĠENTILI''TIOUS, *a.* [L. *gentilitius*, from *gens.*]

1. Peculiar to a people or nation; national. *Brown.*

2. Hereditary; entailed on a family. *Arbuthnot.*

ĠENTIL'ITY, *n.* [Fr. *gentilité*, heathenism. So in Sp. and It. from the Latin; but we take the sense from *genteel.*]

1. Politeness of manners; easy, graceful behavior; the manners of well bred people; genteelness.

2. Good extraction; dignity of birth. *Edward.*

3. Gracefulness of mien. *Shak.*

4. Gentry. [*Not in use.*] *Davies.*

5. Paganism; heathenism. [*Not in use.*] *Hooker.*

ĠEN'TILIZE, *v. i.* To live like a heathen. *Milton.*

ĠEN'TLE, *a.* [See *Genteel.*] Well born; of a good family or respectable birth, though not noble; as the studies of noble and *gentle* youth; *gentle* blood. *Obs.* *Milton. Pope.*

2. Mild; meek; soft; bland; not rough, harsh or severe; as a *gentle* nature, temper or disposition; a *gentle* manner; a *gentle* address; a *gentle* voice. 1 Thess. xxvii. 2 Tim. ii.

3. Tame; peaceable; not wild, turbulent or refractory; as a *gentle* horse or beast.

4. Soothing; pacific. *Davies.*

5. Treating with mildness; not violent.

A *gentle* hand may lead the elephant with a hair. *Persian Rosary.*

ĠEN'TLE, *n.* A gentleman. *Obs.* *Shak.*

2. A kind of worm. *Walton.*

ĠEN'TLE, *v. t.* To make genteel; to raise from the vulgar. *Obs.* *Shak.*

ĠEN'TLEFOLK, *n.* [*gentle* and *folk.*] Persons of good breeding and family. It is now used only in the plural, *gentlefolks*, and this use is vulgar.

ĠEN'TLEMAN, *n.* [*gentle*, that is, *genteel*, and *man.* So in Fr. *gentilhomme*, It. *gentiluomo*, Sp. *gentilhombre.* See *Genteel.*]

1. In its most extensive sense, in *Great Britain*, every man above the rank of yeomen, comprehending noblemen. In a more limited sense, a man, who without a title, bears a coat of arms, or whose ancestors have been freemen. In this sense, *gentlemen* hold a middle rank between the nobility and yeomanry.

2. In *the United States*, where titles and distinctions of rank do not exist, the term is applied to men of education and of good breeding, of every occupation. Indeed this is also the popular practice in Great Britain. Hence,

3. A man of good breeding, politeness, and civil manners, as distinguished from the vulgar and clownish.

A plowman on his legs is higher than a *gentleman* on his knees. *Franklin.*

4. A term of complaisance. In *the plural*, the appellation by which men are addressed in popular assemblies, whatever may be their condition or character.

5. In *Great Britain*, the servant of a man of rank, who attends his person. *Camden.*

ǴEN'TLEMANLIKE, } *a.* Pertaining to or
ǴEN'TLEMANLY, } becoming a gentleman, or a man of good family and breeding; polite; complaisant; as *gentlemanly* manners.

3. Like a man of birth and good breeding; as a *gentlemanly* officer.

ǴEN'TLEMANLINESS, *n.* Behavior of a well bred man. *Sherwood.*

ǴEN'TLENESS, *n.* [See *Gentle.*] Dignity of birth. [*Little used.*]

2. Genteel behavior. *Obs.*

3. Softness of manners; mildness of temper; sweetness of disposition; meekness.

The fruit of the Spirit is love, joy, peace, long suffering, *gentleness*, goodness, faith. Gal. v.

4. Kindness; benevolence. *Obs. Shak.*

5. Tenderness; mild treatment.

ǴEN'TLESHIP, *n.* The deportment of a gentleman. *Obs. Ascham.*

ǴEN'TLEWÖMAN, *n.* [*gentle* and *woman.*] A woman of good family or of good breeding; a woman above the vulgar.

2. A woman who waits about the person of one of high rank.

3. A term of civility to a female, sometimes ironical. *Dryden.*

ǴEN'TLY, *adv.* Softly; meekly; mildly; with tenderness.

My mistress *gently* chides the fault I made. *Dryden.*

2. Without violence, roughness or asperity. *Shak.*

ǴENTOO', *n.* A native of India or Hindoostan; one who follows the religion of the Bramins. *Encyc.*

ǴEN'TRY, *n.* Birth; condition; rank by birth. *Shak.*

2. People of education and good breeding. In Great Britain, the classes of people between the nobility and the vulgar.

3. A term of civility; civility; complaisance. *Obs.*

ǴENUFLEC'TION, *n.* [L. *genu*, the knee, and *flectio*, a bending.]
The act of bending the knee, particularly in worship. *Stillingfleet.*

ǴEN'UINE, *a.* [L. *genuinus*, from *genus*, or its root. See *Gender.*]
Native; belonging to the original stock; hence, real; natural; true; pure; not spurious, false or adulterated. The Gaels are supposed to be *genuine* descendants of the Celts. Vices and crimes are the *genuine* effects of depravity, as virtue and piety are the *genuine* fruits of holiness. It is supposed we have the *genuine* text of Homer.

ǴEN'UINELY, *adv.* Without adulteration or foreign admixture; naturally. *Boyle.*

ǴEN'UINENESS, *n.* The state of being native, or of the true original; hence, freedom from adulteration or foreign admixture; freedom from any thing false or counterfeit; purity; reality; as the *genuineness* of Livy's history; the *genuineness* of faith or repentance.

ǴE'NUS, *n.* plu. *genuses* or *genera.* [L. *genus*, Gr. γενος, Ir. *gein*, offspring, race or family, Sans. *jana*; hence, kind, sort. See *Gender.*]

1. In *logic*, that which has several species under it; a class of a greater extent than species; a universal which is predicable of several things of different species. *Cyc.*

2. In *natural history*, an assemblage of *species* possessing certain characters in common, by which they are distinguished from all others. It is subordinate to *class* and *order*, and in some arrangements, to *tribe* and *family.* A single species, possessing certain peculiar characters, which belong to no other species, may also constitute a *genus*; as the camelopard, and the flamingo.

3. In *botany*, a genus is a subdivision containing plants of the same class and order, which agree in their parts of fructification. *Martyn.*

ǴEOCEN'TRI€, *a.* [Gr. γη, earth, and κεντρον, center.]
Having the earth for its center, or the same center with the earth. The word is applied to a planet or its orbit. *Harris. Encyc.*

ǴE'ODE, *n.* [Gr. γαιωδης, earthy, from γαια or γη, earth. Plin. *gæodes*, Lib. 36. 19.]
In *mineralogy*, a round or roundish lump of agate or other mineral, or a mere incrustation. Its interior is sometimes empty, and in this case the sides of its cavity are lined with crystals, as in agate balls. Sometimes it contains a solid movable nucleus; and sometimes it is filled with an earthy matter different from the envelop. *Cleaveland.*

ǴE'ODESY, *n.* [Gr. γεωδαισια; γεα, the earth, and δαιω, to divide.]
That part of geometry which respects the doctrine of measuring surfaces, and finding the contents of all plain figures. *Harris.*

ǴEODET'I€, } *a.* Pertaining to the art
ǴEODET'I€AL, } of measuring surfaces.

ǴE'OGNOST, *n.* [See *Geognosy.*] One versed in geognosy; a geologist.

ǴEOGNOS'TI€, *a.* Pertaining to a knowledge of the structure of the earth; geological.

ǴE'OGNOSY, *n.* [Gr. γη, the earth, and γνωσις, knowledge.]
That part of natural history which treats of the structure of the earth. It is the science of the substances which compose the earth or its crust, their structure, position, relative situation, and properties. *Cleaveland.*

[This word originated among the German mineralogists, and is nearly synonymous with *geology.* But some writers consider geognosy as only a branch of geology; including in the latter, hydrography, geogony, meteorology and even geography.]

ǴEOG'ONY, *n.* [Gr. γη, the earth, and γονη, generation.] The doctrine of the formation of the earth.

ǴEOG'RAPHER, *n.* [See *Geography.*] One who describes that part of this globe or earth, which is exhibited upon the surface, as the continents, isles, ocean, seas, lakes, rivers, mountains, countries, &c. One who is versed in geography, or one who compiles a treatise on the subject.

ǴEOGRAPH'I€, } *a.* Relating to or con-
ǴEOGRAPH'I€AL, } taining a description of the terraqueous globe; pertaining to geography.

ǴEOGRAPH'I€ALLY, *adv.* In a geographical manner; according to the usual practice of describing the surface of the earth.

ǴEOG'RAPHY, *n.* [Gr. γη, the earth, and γραφω, to write, to describe.]

1. Properly, a description of the earth or terrestrial globe, particularly of the divisions of its surface, natural and artificial, and of the position of the several countries, kingdoms, states, cities, &c. As a science, geography includes the doctrine or knowledge of the astronomical circles or divisions of the sphere, by which the relative position of places on the globe may be ascertained, and usually treatises of geography contain some account of the inhabitants of the earth, of their government, manners, &c., and an account of the principal animals, plants and minerals.

2. A book containing a description of the earth.

ǴEOLOǴ'I€AL, *a.* [See *Geology.*] Pertaining to geology; relating to the science of the earth or terraqueous globe.

ǴEOL'OǴIST, *n.* One versed in the science of geology.

ǴEOL'OǴY, *n.* [Gr. γη, the earth, and λογος, discourse.]
The doctrine or science of the structure of the earth or terraqueous globe, and of the substances which compose it; or the science of the compound minerals or aggregate substances which compose the earth, the relations which the several constituent masses bear to each other, their formation, structure, position and direction: it extends also to the various alterations and decompositions to which minerals are subject. *Dict. Nat. Hist. Cleaveland.*

ǴE'OMANCER, *n.* [See *Geomancy.*] One who foretells or divines, by means of lines, figures or points on the ground or on paper. *Encyc.*

ǴE'OMANCY, *n.* [Gr. γη, the earth, and μαντεια, divination.]
A kind of divination by means of figures or lines, formed by little dots or points, originally on the earth and afterwards on paper. *Encyc.*

ǴEOMAN'TI€, *a.* Pertaining to geomancy.

ǴEOM'ETER, *n.* [Gr. γεωμετρης. See *Geometry.*]
One skilled in geometry. [See *Geometrician*, which is generally used.] *Watts.*

ǴEOM'ETRAL, *a.* Pertaining to geometry.

ǴEOMET'RI€, } *a.* [Gr. γεωμετρικος.]
ǴEOMET'RI€AL, } Pertaining to geometry.

2. According to the rules or principles of geometry; done by geometry.

3. Disposed according to geometry.

Geometrical progression, is when the terms increase or decrease by equal ratios; as 2. 4. 8. 16. 32. or 32. 16. 8. 4. 2.

ǴEOMET'RI€ALLY, *adv.* According to the rules or laws of geometry.

ǴEOMETRI''CIAN, *n.* One skilled in geometry; a geometer. *Watts.*

ǴEOM'ETRIZE, *v. t.* To act according to the laws of geometry; to perform geometrically. *Boyle.*

ǴEOM'ETRY, *n.* [Gr. γεωμετρια; γη, the earth, and μετρον, measure.]

Originally and properly, the art of measuring the earth, or any distances or dimensions on it. But geometry now denotes the science of magnitude in general, comprehending the doctrine and relations of whatever is susceptible of augmentation and diminution; as the mensuration of lines, surfaces, solids, velocity, weight, &c. with their various relations. *Bailey. Encyc.*

ĠEOPON'IC, *a.* [Gr. γη, the earth, and πονος, labor.]
Pertaining to tillage of the earth, or agriculture. [*Now little used.*]

ĠEOPON'ICS, *n.* The art or science of cultivating the earth. *Evelyn.*

ĠE'ORAMA, *n.* [Gr. γη, the earth, and οραμα, view.]
An instrument or machine which exhibits a very complete view of the earth, lately invented in Paris. It is a hollow sphere of forty feet diameter, formed by thirty six bars of iron representing the parallels and meridians, and covered with a bluish cloth, intended to represent seas and lakes. The land, mountains and rivers are painted on paper and pasted on this cover. *Journ. of Science.*

ĠEORĠE, *n.* A figure of St. George on horseback, worn by knights of the garter. *Shak.*
2. A brown loaf. *Dryden.*

ĠEORĠE-NOBLE, *n.* A gold coin in the time of Henry VIII. of the value of 6s. 8d. sterling.

ĠEOR'ĠIC, *n.* [Gr. γεωργικος, rustic; γη and εργον, labor.]
A rural poem; a poetical composition on the subject of husbandry, containing rules for cultivating lands, in a poetical dress; as the *Georgics* of Virgil.

ĠEOR'ĠIC, *a.* Relating to the doctrine of agriculture and rural affairs.

ĠEORĠIUM SIDUS. [See *Herschel.*]

ĠEOS'COPY, *n.* [Gr. γη and σκοπεω.]
Knowledge of the earth, ground or soil, obtained by inspection. *Chambers.*

ĠERA'NIUM, *n.* [L. from Gr. γερανιον, from γερανος, a crane.]
Crane's-bill, a genus of plants, of numerous species, some of which are cultivated for their fragrance or the beauty of their flowers.

ĠE'RENT, *a.* [L. *gerens.*] Bearing; used in *Vicegerent.*

ĠERFALCON. [See *Gyrfalcon.*]

ĠERM, *n.* [L. *germen.*] In *botany*, the ovary or seed-bud of a plant, the rudiment of fruit yet in embryo. It is the base or lower part of the pistil, which, in the progress of vegetation, swells and becomes the seed-vessel. *Martyn. Milne.*
2. Origin; first principle; that from which any thing springs; as the *germ* of civil liberty, or of prosperity.

ĠER'MAN, *a.* [L. *germanus*, a brother; Fr. *germain.*]
1. Cousins *german*, are the sons or daughters of brothers or sisters; first cousins.
2. Related. *Obs.* *Shak.*

ĠER'MAN, *a.* Belonging to Germany.

ĠER'MAN, *n.* A native of Germany; and by ellipsis, the German language.

ĠERMAN'DER, *n*, A plant, or rather the name of several plants, as the *rock germander*, of the genus Veronica, and the *common* and *water germander*, of the genus Teucrium.

ĠERMAN'IC, *a.* Pertaining to Germany; as the *Germanic* body or confederacy.

ĠER'MANISM, *n.* An idiom of the German language. *Chesterfield.*

ĠERM'EN, *n.* plu. *germens.* Now contracted to *germ*, which see.

ĠERM'INAL, *a.* [from *germen.* See *Germ.*] Pertaining to a germ or seed-bud. *Med. Repos.*

ĠERM'INANT, *a.* Sprouting.

ĠERM'INATE, *v. i.* [L. *germino*, from *germen.*]
To sprout; to bud; to shoot; to begin to vegetate, as a plant or its seed. *Bacon.*

ĠERM'INATE, *v. t.* To cause to sprout. [*Unusual.*] *Price.*

ĠERMINA'TION, *n.* The act of sprouting; the first beginning of vegetation in a seed or plant.
2. The time in which seeds vegetate, after being planted or sown. *Martyn.*

ĠEROCOM'ICAL, *a.* Pertaining to gerocomy. [*Little used.*] *Smith.*

ĠEROC'OMY, *n.* [Gr. γερων and κομεω.] That part of medicine which treats of the proper regimen for old people.

ĠER'UND, *n.* [L. *gerundium*, from *gero*, to bear.]
In *the Latin grammar*, a kind of verbal noun, partaking of the nature of a participle. *Encyc.*

GESLING, for *gosling.* [*Not in use.*]

ĠEST, *n.* [L. *gestum*, from *gero*, to carry, to do.]
1. A deed, action or achievment. *Obs.* *Spenser.*
2. Show; representation. *Obs.*
3. [Fr. *gite*, for *giste*, from *gesir*, to lie.] A stage in travelling; so much of a journey as is made without resting; or properly, a rest; a stop. *Obs.* *Brown.*
4. A roll or journal of the several days and stages prefixed, in the journeys of the English kings, many of which are extant in the herald's office. *Hanmer.*

ĠESTA'TION, *n.* [L. *gestatio*, from *gero*, to carry.]
1. The act of carrying young in the womb from conception to delivery; pregnancy. *Ray. Coxe.*
2. The act of wearing, as clothes or ornaments. *Brown.*
3. The act of carrying sick persons in carriages, as a salutary exercise, by which fevers have often been cured. *Med. Repos.*

ĠES'TATORY, *a.* That may be carried or worn. *Brown.*

ĠES'TIC, *a.* Pertaining to deeds; legendary. *Goldsmith.*

ĠESTIC'ULATE, *v. i.* [L. *gesticulor*, from *gestum*, *gero*, to bear or carry, or *gestio.*]
To make gestures or motions, as in speaking; to use postures. *Herbert.*

ĠESTIC'ULATE, *v. t.* To imitate; to act. *B. Jonson.*

ĠESTICULA'TION, *n.* [L. *gesticulatio.*]
1. The act of making gestures, to express passion or enforce sentiments.
2. Gesture; a motion of the body or limbs in speaking, or in representing action or passion, and enforcing arguments and sentiments.
3. Antic tricks or motions.

ĠESTIC'ULATOR, *n.* One that shows postures, or makes gestures.

ĠESTIC'ULATORY, *a.* Representing in gestures. *Warton.*

ĠES'TURE, *n.* [L. *gestus*, from *gero*, to bear, to do; Fr. *geste.*]
1. A motion of the body or limbs, expressive of sentiment or passion; any action or posture intended to express an idea or a passion, or to enforce an argument or opinion. It consists chiefly in the actions or movements of the hands and face, and should be suited to the subject. *Encyc.*
2. Movement of the body or limbs.

> Grace was in all her steps, heaven in her eye,
> In every *gesture* dignity and love. *Milton.*

ĠES'TURE, *v. t.* To accompany with gesture or action. *Hooker. Wotton.*

GET, *v. t.* pret. *got*, [*gat*, obs.] pp. *got*, *gotten.* [Sax. *getan*, *gytan* or *geatan*, to get; *agytan*, to know or understand; *angitan*, *andgitan*, to find, to understand. The Danish has *forgietter*, to forget, but *gietter* signifies to *guess*, or to suppose, to think; the Swedish also has *förgåta*, to forget, to give to oblivion, *ex animo ejicere.* The simple verb *gietter*, *gåta*, coincides with the D. *gieten*, G. *giessen*, to *cast*, to pour out, to found, as vessels of metal, Sax. *geotan.* To *get*, then, is primarily, to throw, and with respect to acquisition, it is to rush on and seize. The Italian has *cattare*, to get; *raccattare*, to regain, to acquire. Qu. Sp. *rescatar*, Port. *resgatar*, to redeem, to ransom. See *Rescue.*]
1. To procure; to obtain; to gain possession of, by almost any means. We *get* favor by kindness; we *get* wealth by industry and economy; we *get* land by purchase; we *get* praise by good conduct; and we *get* blame by doing injustice. The merchant should *get* a profit on his goods; the laborer should *get* a due reward for his labor; most men *get* what they can for their goods or for their services. *Get* differs from *acquire*, as it does not always express permanence of possession, which is the appropriate sense of *acquire.* We *get* a book or a loaf of bread by borrowing, we do not *acquire* it; but we *get* or *acquire* an estate.
2. To have.

> Thou hast *got* the face of a man. *Herbert.*

This is a most common, but gross abuse of this word. We constantly hear it said, I have *got* no corn, I have *got* no money, she has *got* a fair complexion, when the person means only, I have no corn, I have no money, she has a fair complexion.
3. To beget; to procreate; to generate. *Locke.*
4. To learn; as, to *get* a lesson.
5. To prevail on; to induce; to persuade.

> Though the king could not *get* him to engage in a life of business. *Spectator.*

[*This is not elegant.*]
6. To procure to be. We could not *get* the work done. [*Not elegant.*]

To get off, to put off; to take or pull off; as, to *get off* a garment: also, to remove; as, to *get off* a ship from shoals.

2. To sell; to dispose of; as, to *get off* goods.

To get on, to put on; to draw or pull on; as, to *get on* a coat; to *get on* boots.

To get in, to collect and shelter; to bring under cover; as, to *get in* corn.

To get out, to draw forth; as, to *get out* a secret.

2. To draw out; to disengage.

To get the day, to win; to conquer; to gain the victory.

To get together, to collect; to amass.

To get over, to surmount; to conquer; to pass without being obstructed; as, to *get over* difficulties: also, to recover; as, to *get over* sickness.

To get above, to surmount; to surpass.

To get up, to prepare and introduce upon the stage; to bring forward.

With a pronoun following, it signifies to betake; to remove; to go; as, *get* you to bed; *get* thee out of the land. But this mode of expression can hardly be deemed elegant.

GET, *v. i.* To arrive at any place or state; followed by some modifying word, and sometimes implying difficulty or labor; as,

To get away or *away from*, to depart; to quit; to leave; or to disengage one's self from.

To get among, to arrive in the midst of; to become one of a number.

To get before, to arrive in front, or more forward.

To get behind, to fall in the rear; to lag.

To get back, to arrive at the place from which one departed; to return.

To get clear, to disengage one's self; to be released, as from confinement, obligation or burden; also, to be freed from danger or embarrassment.

To get down, to descend; to come from an elevation.

To get home, to arrive at one's dwelling.

To get in or *into*, to arrive within an inclosure, or a mixed body; to pass in; to insinuate one's self.

To get loose or *free*, to disengage one's self; to be released from confinement.

To get off, to escape; to depart; to get clear; also, to alight; to descend from.

To get out, to depart from an inclosed place or from confinement; to escape; to free one's self from embarrassment.

To get along, to proceed; to advance.

To get rid of, to disengage one's self from; also, to shift off; to remove.

To get together, to meet; to assemble; to convene.

To get up, to arise; to rise from a bed or a seat; also, to ascend; to climb.

To get through, to pass through and reach a point beyond any thing; also, to finish; to accomplish.

To get quit of, to get rid of; to shift off, or to disengage one's self from.

To get forward, to proceed; to advance; also, to prosper; to advance in wealth.

To get near, to approach within a small distance.

To get ahead, to advance; to prosper.

To get on, to proceed; to advance.

To get a mile or *other distance*, to pass over it in traveling.

To get at, to reach; to make way to.

To get asleep, to fall asleep.

To get drunk, to become intoxicated.

To get between, to arrive between.

To get to, to reach; to arrive.

GET'TER, *n.* One who gets, gains, obtains or acquires.

2. One who begets or procreates.

GET'TING, *ppr.* Obtaining; procuring; gaining; winning; begetting.

GET'TING, *n.* The act of obtaining, gaining or acquiring; acquisition.

> Get wisdom; and with all thy *getting*, get understanding. Prov. iv.

2. Gain; profit. *Swift.*

GEW'GAW, *n.* [Qu. Sax. *ge-gaf*, a trifle, or Fr. *joujou*, a plaything, or from the root of *gaud*, joy, jewel.]

A showy trifle; a pretty thing of little worth; a toy; a bauble; a splendid plaything.

> A heavy *gewgaw*, called a crown. *Dryden.*

GEW'GAW, *a.* Showy without value. *Law.*

GH'ASTFUL, *a.* [See *Ghastly.*] Dreary; dismal; fit for walking ghosts. *Obs.* *Spenser.*

GH'ASTFULLY, *adv.* Frightfully. *Pope.*

GH'ASTLINESS, *n.* [from *ghastly.*] Horror of countenance; a deathlike look; resemblance of a ghost; paleness.

GH'ASTLY, *a.* [Sax. *gastlic*, from *gast*, spirit, G. *geist*, D. *geest*. In Sax. *gast* is both a *ghost* and a *guest*, both from the same radical sense, to move, to rush; Ir. *gaisim*, to flow; Eng. *gush*, *gust.*]

1. Like a ghost in appearance; deathlike; pale; dismal; as a *ghastly* face; *ghastly* smiles. *Milton.*

2. Horrible; shocking; dreadful.

> Mangled with *ghastly* wounds. *Milton.*

GH'ASTNESS, *n.* Ghastliness. [*Not used.*] *Shak.*

GHER'KIN, *n.* [G. *gurke*, a cucumber.] A small pickled cucumber. *Skinner.*

GHESS, for *guess.* [*Not used.*]

GHŌST, *n.* [Sax. *gast*; G. *geist*; D. *geest*; Ir. *gasda*. See *Ghastly.*]

1. Spirit; the soul of man. *Shak.*

In this sense seldom used. But hence,

2. The soul of a deceased person; the soul or spirit separate from the body; an apparition.

> The mighty *ghosts* of our great Harrys rose. *Dryden.*

To give up the ghost, is to die; to yield up the breath or spirit; to expire. *Scripture.*

The *Holy Ghost*, is the third person in the adorable Trinity. *Scripture.*

GHŌST, *v. i.* To die; to expire. *Obs.* *Sidney.*

GHŌST, *v. t.* To haunt with an apparition. *Obs.* *Shak.*

GHŌSTLIKE, *a.* Withered; having sunken eyes; ghastly. *Sherwood.*

GHŌSTLINESS, *n.* Spiritual tendency. [*Little used.*] *Johnson.*

GHŌSTLY, *a.* Spiritual; relating to the soul; not carnal or secular.

> Save and defend us from our *ghostly* enemies. *Com. Prayer.*

2. Spiritual; having a character from religion; as a *ghostly* father. *Shak.*

3. Pertaining to apparitions. *Akenside.*

ĠIALLOLĪNO, *n.* [It. *giallo*; Eng. *yellow.*] A fine yellow pigment much used under the name of *Naples Yellow.* *Encyc.*

ĠIAM'BEAUX, *n.* [Fr. *jambe*, the leg.] Greaves; armor for the legs. *Obs.*

ĠI'ANT, *n.* [Fr. *geant*; Sp. *gigante*; It. *id.*; L. *gigas*; Gr. γιγας, probably from γη, the earth, and γαω or γινομαι. The word originally signified earth-born, *terrigena*. The ancients believed the first inhabitants of the earth to be produced from the ground and to be of enormous size.]

1. A man of extraordinary bulk and stature.

> *Giants* of mighty bone, and bold emprise. *Milton.*

2. A person of extraordinary strength or powers, bodily or intellectual. The judge is a *giant* in his profession.

Giants-causey, a vast collection of basaltic pillars in the county of Antrim, in Ireland. *Encyc.*

ĠI'ANT, *a.* Like a giant; extraordinary in size or strengh; as *giant* brothers; a *giant* son. *Dryden. Pope.*

ĠI'ANTESS, *n.* A female giant; a female of extraordinary size and stature. *Shak.*

ĠI'ANTIZE, *v. i.* To play the giant. *Sherwood.*

ĠI'ANT-KILLING, *a.* Killing or destroying giants. *Cowper.*

ĠI'ANTLIKE, } *a.* Of unusual size; resembling a giant in bulk or
ĠI'ANTLY, } stature; gigantic; huge. *South.*

[*Giantly* is not much used.]

ĠI'ANTRY, *n.* The race of giants. [*Little used.*]

ĠI'ANTSHIP, *n.* The state, quality or character of a giant.

> His *giantship* is gone somewhat crestfallen. *Milton.*

GIB, *n.* A cat. [*Not in use.*] *Skelton.*

GIB, *v. i.* To act like a cat. [*Not in use.*] *Beaum.*

GIBBE, *n.* An old worn-out animal. [*Not used.*] *Shak.*

GIB'BER, *v. i.* [See *Gabble.* It is probably allied to *gabble*, and to *jabber.*]

To speak rapidly and inarticulately. [*Not used.*] *Shak.*

GIB'BERISH, *n.* [from *gibber.*] Rapid and inarticulate talk; unintelligible language; unmeaning words.

GIB'BERISH, *a.* Unmeaning, as words. *Swift.*

ĠIB'BET, *n.* [Fr. *gibet*; Arm. *gibel.*] A gallows; a post or machine in form of a gallows, on which notorious malefactors are hanged in chains, and on which their bodies are suffered to remain, as spectacles *in terrorem.* *Swift.*

2. Any traverse beam. *Johnson.*

ĠIB'BET, *v. t.* To hang and expose on a gibbet or gallows.

2. To hang or expose on any thing going travers, as the beam of a gibbet. *Shak.*

ĠIB'BETED, *pp.* Hanged and exposed on a gibbet.

ĠIB'BETING, *ppr.* Hanging and exposing on a gibbet.

GIB'BIER, *n.* [Fr.] Wild fowl; game. [*Not used.*] *Addison.*

GIBBOS'ITY, *n.* [Fr. *gibbosité*, from L. *gibbosus*. See *Gibbous.*]

Protuberance; a round or swelling prominence; convexity. *Ray.*

GIB'BOUS, *a.* [L. *gibbus*; Fr. *gibbeux*; It. *gibboso*; Sp. *giboso*; Gr. κυφος, from κυπτω, to bend. Class Gb. No. 1. 2. 3. 4. 5.]

1. Swelling; protuberant; convex. The moon is *gibbous* between the quarters and the full moon; the enlightened part being then convex.

The bones will rise, and make a *gibbous* member. *Wiseman.*

2. Hunched; hump-backed; crook-backed. *Brown.*

GIB'BOUSLY, *adv.* In a gibbous or protuberant form. *Eaton.*

GIB'BOUSNESS, *n.* Protuberance; a round prominence; convexity. [This word is preferable to *gibbosity.*]

GIBBS'ITE, *n.* A mineral found at Richmond, in Massachusetts, and named in honor of George Gibbs, Esq. It occurs in irregular stalactical masses, which present an aggregation of elongated, tuberous branches, parallel and united. Its structure is fibrous, the fibers radiating from an axis. Its colors are a dirty white, greenish white and grayish. *Cleaveland.*

GIB'CAT, *n.* A he-cat, or an old worn-out cat. *Shak.*

GIBE, *v. i.* [Sax, *gabban*; Fr. *gaber*; It. *gabbare*. See *Gabble.* The sense is probably to throw or cast at, or make mouths. But see Class Gb. No. 67. 79.]

To cast reproaches and sneering expressions; to rail at; to utter taunting, sarcastic words; to flout; to fleer; to scoff.

Fleer and *gibe*, and laugh and flout. *Swift.*

GIBE, *v. t.* To reproach with contemptuous words; to deride; to scoff at; to treat with sarcastic reflections; to taunt.

Draw the beasts as I describe them,
From their features, while I *gibe* them. *Swift.*

GIBE, *n.* An expression of censure mingled with contempt; a scoff; a railing; an expression of sarcastic scorn.

Mark the fleers, the *gibes*, and the notable scorns,
That dwell in every region of his face. *Shak.*

GIB'ELINE, *n.* The Gibelines were a faction in Italy, that opposed another faction called *Guelfs*, in the 13th century. *J. Adams.*

GI'BER, *n.* One who utters reproachful, censorious and contemptuous expressions, or who casts cutting, sarcastic reflections; one who derides; a scoffer. *B. Jonson.*

GI'BING, *ppr.* Uttering reproachful, contemptuous and censorious words; scoffing.

GI'BINGLY, *adv.* With censorious, sarcastic and contemptuous expressions; scornfully. *Shak.*

GIB'LETS, *n.* [Qu. Fr. *gibier*, game, or Goth. *gibla*, a wing. See *Gip.*]

The entrails of a goose or other fowl, as the heart, liver, gizzard, &c.; a considerable article in cookery; as, to boil or stew *giblets*. It is used only in the plural, except in composition; as a *giblet-pie*.

GIB'STAFF, *n.* A staff to gauge water or to push a boat; formerly, a staff used in fighting beasts on the stage. *Dict.*

GID'DILY, *adv.* [See *Giddy.*] With the head seeming to turn or reel.

2. Inconstantly; unsteadily; with various turnings; as, to roam about *giddily*. *Donne.*

3. Carelessly; heedlessly; negligently. *Shak.*

GID'DINESS, *n.* The state of being giddy or vertiginous; vertigo; a sensation of reeling or whirling, when the body loses the power of preserving its balance or a steady attitude, or when objects at rest appear to reel, tremble or whirl; a swimming of the head.

2. Inconstancy; unsteadiness; mutability. *Bacon.*

3. Frolick; wantonness; levity. *Donne. South.*

GID'DY, *a.* [Sax. *gidig.* Class Gd.] Vertiginous; reeling; whirling; having in the head a sensation of a circular motion or swimming; or having lost the power of preserving the balance of the body, and therefore wavering and inclined to fall, as in the case of some diseases and of drunkenness. In walking on timber aloft, or looking down a precipice, we are apt to be *giddy*.

2. That renders giddy; that induces giddiness; as a *giddy* highth; a *giddy* precipice. *Prior.*

3. Rotary; whirling; running round with celerity.

The *giddy* motion of the whirling mill. *Pope.*

4. Inconstant; unstable; changeable.

You are as *giddy* and volatile as ever. *Swift.*

5. Heedless; thoughtless; wild; roving. *Rowe.*

6. Tottering; unfixed.

As we have paced along
Upon the *giddy* footing of the hatches. *Shak.*

7. Intoxicated; elated to thoughtlessness; rendered wild by excitement or joy.

Art thou not *giddy* with the fashion too? *Shak.*

GID'DY, *v. i.* To turn quick. *Chapman.*

GID'DY, *v. t.* To make reeling or unsteady. *Farindon.*

GID'DY-BRAINED, *a.* Careless; thoughtless; unsteady. *Otway.*

GID'DY-HEAD, *n.* A person without thought or judgment.

GID'DY-HEADED, *a.* Heedless; unsteady; volatile; incautious. *Donne.*

GID'DY-PACED, *a.* Moving irregularly. *Shak.*

GIE, a contraction of *guide.* [*Not in use.*] *Chaucer.*

GIE'R-EAGLE, *n.* [Qu. D. *gier*, a vulture.] A fowl of the eagle kind, mentioned in Leviticus ii.

GIE'SECKITE, *n.* A mineral of a rhomboidal form and compact texture, of a gray or brown color, and nearly as hard as calcarious spar. *Cleaveland.*

GIF, *v. t.* [from Sax. *gifan.*] The old but true spelling of *if.*

GIFT, *n.* [from *give.*] A present; any thing given or bestowed; any thing, the property of which is voluntarily transferred by one person to another without compensation; a donation. It is applicable to any thing movable or immovable.

2. The act of giving or conferring. *Milton.*

3. The right or power of giving or bestowing. The prince has the *gift* of many lucrative offices.

4. An offering or oblation.

If thou bring thy *gift* to the altar. Matt. v.

5. A reward.

Let thy *gifts* be to thyself. Dan. v.

6. A bribe; any thing given to corrupt the judgment.

Neither take a *gift*; for a *gift* doth blind the eyes of the wise. Deut. xvi.

7. Power; faculty; some quality or endowment conferred by the author of our nature; as the *gift* of wit; the *gift* of ridicule. *Addison.*

GIFT, *v. t.* To endow with any power or faculty.

GIFT'ED, *pp.* or *a.* Endowed by nature with any power or faculty; furnished with any particular talent.

GIFT'EDNESS, *n.* The state of being gifted. *Echard.*

GIFT'ING, *ppr.* Endowing with any power or faculty.

GIG, *v. t.* [L. *gigno.*] To engender. [*Not in use.*] *Dryden.*

2. To fish with a gig or fishgig.

GIG, *n.* [It. *giga*, a jig; Fr. *gigue*, a jig, a romp; Sw. *giga*, a jews-harp; Ice. *gigia*, a fiddle.]

1. Any little thing that is whirled round in play. *Locke.*

2. A light carriage with one pair of wheels, drawn by one horse; a chair or chaise.

3. A fiddle.

4. A dart or harpoon. [See *Fishgig.*]

5. A ship's boat.

6. A wanton girl.

GIGANTE'AN, *a.* [L. *giganteus.* See *Giant.*] Like a giant; mighty. *More.*

GIGAN'TIC, *a.* [L. *giganticus.*] Of extraordinary size; very large; huge; like a giant. A man of *gigantic* stature.

2. Enormous; very great or mighty; as *gigantic* deeds; *gigantic* wickedness.

Gigantical and *gigantine*, for *gigantic*, rarely or never used.

GIGANTOL'OGY, *n.* [Gr. γιγας, a giant, and λογος, discourse.] An account or description of giants.

GIG'GLE, *n.* [Sax. *geagl*; Scot. *geck.*] A kind of laugh, with short catches of the voice or breath.

GIG'GLE, *v. i.* [D. *gichgelen*; Sax. *geagl*, a laugh or sneer, and *gagol*, sportive, wanton; It. *ghignare*, to simper; *ghignazzare*, to laugh or grin. In Ir. *giglim* is to tickle; Gr. γιγγλισμος.]

To laugh with short catches of the breath or voice; to laugh in a silly, puerile manner; to titter; to grin with childish levity or mirth. *Garrick.*

GIG'GLER, *n.* One that giggles or titters.

GIG'LET, GIG'LOT, } *n.* [Sax. *geagl*, wanton; Fr. *giguer*, to romp, to frisk. See *Gig.*] A wanton; a lascivious girl. *Shak.*

GIG'LOT, *a.* Giddy; light; inconstant; wanton. *Shak.*

GIG'OT, *n.* [Fr.] The hip-joint; also, a slice. [*Not English.*]

GIL'BERTINE, *n.* One of a religious order, so named from Gilbert, lord of Sempringham, in Lincolnshire, England.

GIL'BERTINE, *a.* Belonging to the monastic order, mentioned above. *Weever.*

GILD, *v. t.* pret. and pp. *gilded* or *gilt.* [Sax. *gildan*, *gyldan*, *geldan*, to pay a debt, to *gild*, and *gild*, tribute, tax, toll; D. and G. *geld*, money; Dan. *gield*, a debt; Sw. *gäld.* To gild is to cover with *gold*; G. *vergolden*; D. *vergulden*; Dan. *forgylder*; Sw. *förgylla*; from *gold*, or its root, Dan.

guul, Sw. *gul*, Sax. *gealew*, yellow, connected with Ir. *geal*, W. *golau*, light, bright. Class Gl. No. 6. 7.]

2. To overlay with gold, either in leaf or powder, or in amalgam with quicksilver; to overspread with a thin covering of gold; as the *gilt* frame of a mirror. *Cyc.*

Her joy in *gilded* chariots when alive,
And love of ombre after death survive. *Pope.*

2. To cover with any yellow matter. *Shak.*

3. To adorn with luster; to render bright.

No more the rising sun shall *gild* the morn. *Pope.*

4. To illuminate; to brighten. *South.*

Let oft good humor, mild and gay,
Gild the calm evening of your day. *Trumbull.*

5. To give a fair and agreeable external appearance; to recommend to favor and reception by superficial decoration; as, to *gild* flattery or falsehood.

GILD'ED, *pp.* Overlaid with gold leaf or liquid; illuminated.

GILD'ER, *n.* One who gilds; one whose occupation is to overlay things with gold.

2. A Dutch coin of the value of 20 stivers, about 38 cents, or one shilling and ninepence sterling. It is usually written *guilder.*

GILD'ING, *ppr.* Overlaying with gold; giving a fair external appearance.

GILD'ING, *n.* The art or practice of overlaying things with gold leaf or liquid.

2. That which is laid on in overlaying with gold.

GILL, *n.* [Sw. *gel*; Sp. *agalla*, a gland in the throat, a gall-nut, a wind-gall on a horse, the beak of a shuttle, and the gill of a fish; Port. *guelra* or *guerra*. Hence it would seem that *gill* is a shoot or prominence, the fringe-like substance, not the aperture. In Danish, *gilder* signifies to geld, and to cut off the gills of herrings, and in Scot. *gil* or *gul* is a crack or fissure.]

1. The organ of respiration in fishes, consisting of a cartilaginous or bony arch, attached to the bones of the head, and furnished on the exterior convex side with a multitude of fleshy leaves, or fringed vascular fibrils, resembling plumes, and of a red color in a healthy state. The water is admitted by the gill-opening, and acts upon the blood as it circulates in the fibrils. Other animals also breathe by gills, as frogs in their tadpole state, lobsters, &c. *Ed. Encyc.*

Fishes perform respiration under water by the *gills.* *Ray.*

2. The flap that hangs below the beak of a fowl. *Bacon.*

3. The flesh under the chin. *Bacon. Swift.*

4. In *England*, a pair of wheels and a frame on which timber is conveyed. [*Local.*]

GILL-FLAP, *n.* A membrane attached to the posterior edge of the gill-lid, immediately closing the gill-opening.

GILL-LID, *n.* The covering of the gills.

GILL-ŌPENING, *n.* The aperture of a fish or other animal, by which water is admitted to the gills. *Ed. Encyc.*

ĠILL, *n.* [Low L. *gilla*, *gillo* or *gello*, a drinking glass, a gill. This word has the same elementary letters as Gr. *γαυλος*, a pail or bucket, and Eng. *gallon*, probably from one of the roots in *Gl*, which signify to hold or contain.]

1. A measure of capacity, containing the fourth part of a pint. It is said to be in some places in England, half a pint. *Encyc.*

2. A measure among miners, equal to a pint. *Carew.*

ĠILL, *n.* A plant, ground-ivy, of the genus Glechoma. *Fam. of Plants.*

2. Malt liquor medicated with ground-ivy.

ĠILL, *n.* [In Sw. *gilja* signifies to woo.]

1. In *ludicrous language*, a female; a wanton girl.

Each Jack with his *Gill.* *B. Jonson.*

2. A fissure in a hill; also, a place between steep banks and a rivulet flowing through it; a brook. *Ray. Grose.*

ĠILLHOUSE, *n.* A place where gill is sold. *Pope.*

ĠIL'LIAN, *n.* A wanton girl. *Obs.* *Beaum.*

ĠIL'LYFLOWER, *n.* [supposed to be a corruption of *July-flower.* But qu. is it not a corruption of Fr. *giroflée*, *giroflier.* The corresponding word in Arm. is *genofles* or *genoflen.*]

The name of certain plants. The *clove gillyflower* is of the genus Dianthus, or carnation pink; the *stock gillyflower* is the Cheiranthus; the *queen's gillyflower* is the Hesperis. *Fam. of Plants.*

GILSE, *n.* A young salmon.

GILT, *pp.* of *gild.* Overlaid with gold leaf, or washed with gold; illuminated; adorned.

GILT, *n.* Gold laid on the surface of a thing; gilding. *Shak.*

2. In *England*, a young female pig. *Cyc.*

GILT'HEAD, *n.* [*gilt* and *head.*] In *ichthyology*, a fish or a genus of fishes, the Sparus, of many species; so named from their color, or from a golden spot between the eyes. *Encyc.*

2. A bird. *Hakewill.*

GILTTAIL, *n.* A worm so called from its yellow tail. *Johnson.*

ĠIM, *a.* [contracted from *gemmy.*] Neat; spruce; well dressed.

GIM'BAL, *n.* A brass ring by which a sea compass is suspended in its box, by means of which the card is kept in a horizontal position, notwithstanding the rolling of the ship. *Mar. Dict.*

GIMB'LET, *n.* [Fr. *gibelet*; Arm. *guymeled.* *Gimblet* seems to be the same word as *wimble*, with the Celtic pronunciation, *guimble*, and if *m* is casual, and the primary word is *gibelet* or *guibelet*, the elements of the word coincide with *wabble*, *quibble*, and with the W. *gwib*, a serpentine motion, *gwibiaw*, to wander, to move in a circular direction, *gwiber*, a serpent, a *viper*, and the primary sense is to turn.]

A borer; a small instrument with a pointed screw at the end, for boring holes in wood by turning. It is applied only to small instruments; a large instrument of the like kind is called an *auger.*

GIMB'LET, *v. t.* In *seamen's language*, to turn round an anchor by the stock; a motion resembling that of the turning of a *gimblet.* *Mar. Dict.*

ĠIM'CRACK, *n.* A trivial mechanism; a device; a toy; a pretty thing. *Prior. Arbuthnot.*

GIM'MAL, *n.* Some device or machinery. *Shak.*

GIM'MAL, *a.* Consisting of links. *Shak.*

GIM'MER, *n.* Movement or machinery. *Obs.* *More.*

GIMP, *n.* [Fr. *guiper*, to cover or *whip* about with silk; Eng. to *whip.*] A kind of silk twist or edging.

ĠIMP, *a.* [W. *gwymp.*] Smart; spruce; trim; nice. [*Not in use.*]

ĠIN, *n.* A contraction of *Geneva*, a distilled spirit. [See *Geneva.*]

ĠIN, *n.* [A contraction of *engine.*] A machine or instrument by which the mechanical powers are employed in aid of human strength. The word is applied to various engines, as a machine for driving piles, another for raising weights, &c.; and a machine for separating the seeds from cotton, invented by E. Whitney, is called a *cotton-gin.* It is also the name given to an engine of torture, and to a pump moved by rotary sails.

2. A trap; a snare. *Milton. Shak.*

ĠIN, *v. t.* To clear cotton of its seeds by a machine which separates them with expedition. *Trans. of Society of Arts.*

2. To catch in a trap.

GIN, *v. i.* To begin. [Sax. *gynnan.*]

ĠIN'ĠER, *n.* [It. *gengiovo*; Sp. *gengibre*; Port. *gengivre*; Fr. *gingembre*; G. *ingber*; D. *gember*; Sw. *ingefära*; Dan. *ingefer*; L. *zinziber*; Gr. *ζιγγιβερις*; Arm. *zindibel* or *singebel*; Ar. Pers. and Turk. *zingibil* or *zinjibil*; Syr. Ch. nearly the same.]

A plant, or the root of a species of Amomum, a native of the East and West Indies. The roots are jointed, and the stalks rise two or three feet, with narrow leaves. The flower stems arise by the side of these, immediately from the root, naked and ending in an oblong scaly spike. The dried roots are used for various purposes, in the kitchen and in medicine. *Encyc.*

ĠIN'ĠERBREAD, *n.* [*ginger* and *bread.*] A kind of cake, composed of flour with an admixture of butter, pearlash and ginger, sweetened.

ĠIN'ĠERLY, *adv.* Nicely; cautiously. [*Not used.*] *Skelton.*

ĠIN'ĠERNESS, *n.* Niceness; tenderness. [*Not used.*]

GING'HAM, *n.* A kind of striped cotton cloth.

ĠIN'ĠING, *n.* In *mining*, the lining of a mine-shaft with stones or bricks for its support, called *steining* or *staining*, which I suppose is from Sax. *stan*, stone. *Cyc.*

ĠIN'ĠIVAL, *a.* [L. *gingiva*, the gum.] Pertaining to the gums. *Holder.*

ĠIN'GLE, } *v. i.* [In Pers. *zangl* is a little
JIN'GLE, } bell. In Ch. and Syr. זנג is the same. Qu. its alliance to *chink* and *jangle.*]

1. To make a sharp clattering sound; to ring as a little bell, or as small pieces of sonorous metal; as *gingling* halfpence. *Gay.*

2. To utter affected or chiming sounds in periods or cadence. *Johnson.*

ĠIN'GLE, *v. t.* To shake so as to make clattering sounds in quick succession; to ring, as a little bell, or as small coins.

The bells she *gingled*, and the whistle blew. *Pope.*

ĠIN'GLE, *n.* A shrill clattering sound, or a succession of sharp sounds, as those made by a little bell or by small coins.

2. Affectation in the sounds of periods in reading or speaking, or rather chiming sounds.

GIN'GLYMOID, *a.* [Gr. γιγγλυμος, a hinge, and ειδος, form.] Pertaining to or resembling a ginglymus.

GIN'GLYMUS, *n.* [Gr. γιγγλυμος.] In *anatomy*, a species of articulation resembling a hinge. That species of articulation in which each bone partly receives and is partly received by the other, so as to admit only of flexion and extension, is called *angular ginglymus*. *Parr.*

ĠIN'NET, *n.* A nag. [See *Jennet.*]

ĠIN'SENG, *n.* [This word is probably Chinese, and it is said by Grosier, to signify the resemblance of a man, or man's thigh. He observes also that the root in the language of the Iroquois is called *garentoquen*, which signifies *legs and thighs separated.* *Grosier's China.* i. 534.]

A plant, of the genus Panax, the root of which is in great demand among the Chinese. It is found in the Northern parts of Asia and America, and is an article of export from America to China. It has a jointed, fleshy, taper root, as large as a man's finger, which when dry is of a yellowish white color, with a mucilaginous sweetness in the taste, somewhat resembling that of liquorice, accompanied with a slight bitterness. *Encyc.*

ĠIP, *v. t.* To take out the entrails of herrings. *Bailey.*

ĠIP'SEY, *n.* The Gipseys are a race of vagabonds which infest Europe, Africa and Asia, strolling about and subsisting mostly by theft, robbery and fortune-telling. The name is supposed to be corrupted from *Egyptian*, as they were thought to have come from Egypt. But their language indicates that they originated in Hindoostan. *Grellman.*

2. A reproachful name for a dark complexion. *Shak.*

3. A name of slight reproach to a woman; sometimes implying artifice or cunning.

A slave I am to Clara's eyes:
The *gipsey* knows her power and flies. *Prior.*

ĠIP'SEY, *n.* The language of the gipseys.

ĠIP'SEYISM, *n.* The arts and practices of gipseys; deception; cheating; flattery. *Grellman.*

2. The state of a gipsey.

ĠIRAFF', *n.* [Sp. *girafa*; It. *giraffa*; Ar. زرافة so called from leaping or the extreme length of its neck, from زرف zarafa, to leap on, to hasten.]

The camelopard, a quadruped. [See *Camelopard.*]

ĠIR'ANDOLE, *n.* [It. *girandola*, from *giro*, a turn, and *andare*, to go.]

A chandelier; a large kind of branched candlestick.

ĠIR'ASOL, *n.* [Fr. Sp.; It. *girasole*; *giro*, L. *gyrus*, a turn, It. *girare*, to turn, and *sole*, L. *sol*, the sun.]

1. The turnsole, a plant of the genus Heliotropium.

2. A mineral usually milk white, bluish white or sky blue, but when turned towards the sun or any bright light, it constantly reflects a reddish color; hence its name. It sometimes strongly resembles a translucid jelly. *Cleaveland.*

GIRD, *n.* *gurd.* [Sax. *geard*, or *gyrd*, or *gyrda*, a twig, branch, rod, pole, Eng. a *yard*; G. *gurt*, a girth, a girdle; Dan. *gierde*, a hedge, a rail. This word signifies primarily a twig, shoot or branch; hence a pole or stick, used in measuring. In measuring land, among our Saxon ancestors, the *gyrd* seems to have been a certain measure like our rod, perch or pole, all of which signify the same thing, a branch or shoot, a little pole. We now apply the word *yard*, to a measure of three feet in length. In rude ages, *gyrds*, shoots of trees, were used for binding things together, whence the verb to *gird.* See *Withe.* *Gyrds* were also used for driving, or for punishment, as we now use whips; and our common people use *gird*, for a severe stroke of a stick or whip. See *Lye*, under *gyrd* and *weal-stylling.*]

1. A twitch or pang; a sudden spasm, which resembles the stroke of a rod or the pressure of a band.

2. In *popular language*, a severe stroke of a stick or whip.

GIRD, *v. t.* *gurd.* pret. and pp. *girded* or *girt.* [Sax. *gyrdan*; G. *gürten*; D. *gorden*; Sw. *giorda*, to gird or surround; Dan. *gierder*, to hedge, to inclose. See the Noun. It is probable, that *garden*, Ir. *gort*, is from the same root; originally an inclosed field, a piece of ground surrounded with poles, stakes and branches of trees. If the noun is the primary word, the sense of the root is to shoot, as a branch; if the verb is the root, the sense is to surround, or rather to bind or make fast. The former is the most probable.]

1. To bind by surrounding with any flexible substance, as with a twig, a cord, bandage or cloth; as, to *gird* the loins with sackcloth.

2. To make fast by binding; to put on; usually with *on*; as, to *gird on* a harness; to *gird on* a sword.

3. To invest; to surround.

The Son appeared,
Girt with omnipotence. *Milton.*

4. To clothe; to dress; to habit.

I *girded* thee about with fine linen. Ezek. xvi.

5. To furnish; to equip.

Girded with snaky wiles. *Milton.*

6. To surround; to encircle; to inclose; to encompass.

The Nyseian isle,
Girt with the river Triton. *Milton.*

7. To gibe; to reproach severely; to lash. *Shak.*

GIRD, *v. i.* To gibe; to sneer; to break a scornful jest; to utter severe sarcasms.

Men of all sorts take a pride to *gird* at me. *Shak.*

GIRD'ED, *pp.* Bound; surrounded; invested; put on.

GIRD'ER, *n.* In *architecture*, the principal piece of timber in a floor. Its end is usually fastened into the summers or breast summers, and the joists are framed into it at one end. In buildings entirely of timber, the *girder* is fastened by tenons into the posts.

2. A satirist. *Lilly.*

GIRD'ING, *ppr.* Binding; surrounding; investing.

GIRD'ING, *n.* A covering. Is. iii.

GIRD'LE, *n.* [Sax. *gyrdle*, *gyrdl*; Sw. *gördel*; G. *gürtel*; D. *gordel.*]

1. A band or belt; something drawn round the waist of a person, and tied or buckled; as a *girdle* of fine linen; a leathern *girdle.*

2. Inclosure; circumference.

Within the *girdle* of these walls. *Shak.*

3. The zodiac. *Bacon.*

4. A round iron plate for baking. *Pegge.* Qu. *griddle.*

5. Among *jewelers*, the line which encompasses the stone, parallel to the horizon. *Cyc.*

GIRD'LE, *v. t.* To bind with a belt or sash; to gird. *Shak.*

2. To inclose; to environ; to shut in. *Shak.*

3. In America, to make a circular incision, like a belt, through the bark and alburnum of a tree to kill it. *New England.* *Belknap.* *Dwight.*

GIRD'LE-BELT, *n.* A belt that encircles the waist. *Dryden.*

GIRD'LER, *n.* One who girdles; a maker of girdles. *Beaum.*

GIRD'LE-STEAD, *n.* The part of the body where the girdle is worn. *Mason.*

ĠIRE, *n.* [L. *gyrus.*] A circle, or circular motion. [See *Gyre.*]

GIRL, *n.* *gerl.* [Low L. *gerula*, a young woman employed in tending children and carrying them about, from *gero*, to carry; a word probably received from the Romans while in England.]

1. A female child, or young woman. In familiar language, any young unmarried woman. *Dryden.*

2. Among *sportsmen*, a roebuck of two years old.

GIRL'HOOD, *n.* The state of a girl. [*Little used.*] *Miss Seward.*

GIRL'ISH, *a.* Like a young woman or child; befitting a girl.

2. Pertaining to the youth of a female. *Carew.*

GIRL'ISHLY, *adv.* In the manner of a girl.

GIR'ROCK, *n.* A species of gar-fish, the *lacertus.* *Cyc.*

GIRT, *pret.* and *pp.* of *gird.*

GIRT, *v. t.* To gird; to surround. *Thomson.* *Tooke.*

[This verb, if derived from the noun, *girt*, may be proper.]

GIRT, } *n.* The band or strap by which a
GIRTH, } saddle or any burden on a horse's back is made fast, by passing under his belly.

2. A circular bandage. *Wiseman.*

3. The compass measured by a girth or inclosing bandage.

He's a lusty, jolly fellow, that lives well, at least three yards in the *girth.* *Addison.*

GIRTH, *v. t.* To bind with a girth.

GISE, *v. t.* To feed or pasture. [See *Agist.*]

GIS'LE, *n.* A pledge. [*Not in use.*]

ĠIST, *n.* [Fr. *gesir*, to lie; *gîte*, a lodging-place.]

In *law*, the main point of a question; the point on which an action rests.

GITH, *n.* Guinea pepper.

GIT′TERN, *n.* [L. *cithara.*] A guitar. [See *Guitar.*]

GIT′TERN, *v. i.* To play on a gittern. *Milton.*

GIVE, *v. t. giv.* pret. *gave*; pp. *given.* [Sax. *gifan, gyfan*; Goth. *giban*; G. *geben*; D. *geeven*; Sw. *gifva*; Dan. *giver.* Hence Sax. *gif*, Goth. *iabai* or *yabai*, now contracted into *if.* Chaucer wrote *yeve, yave.* Qu. Heb. Ch. Syr. Sam. יהב to give. See Class Gb. No. 3. 26. 43. The sense of *give* is generally to pass, or to transfer, that is, to send or throw.]

1. To bestow; to confer; to pass or transfer the title or property of a thing to another person without an equivalent or compensation.

For generous lords had rather *give* than pay. *Young.*

2. To transmit from himself to another by hand, speech or writing; to deliver.

The woman whom thou gavest to be with me, she *gave* me of the tree, and I did eat. Gen. iii.

3. To impart; to bestow.

Give us of your oil, for our lamps are gone out. Matt. xxv.

4. To communicate; as, to *give* an opinion; to *give* counsel or advice; to *give* notice.

5. To pass or deliver the property of a thing to another for an equivalent; to pay. We *give* the full value of all we purchase. A dollar is *given* for a day's labor.

What shall a man *give* in exchange for his soul? Matt. xvi.

6. To yield; to lend; in the phrase to *give ear*, which signifies to listen; to hear.

7. To quit; in the phrase to *give place*, which signifies to withdraw, or retire to make room for another.

8. To confer; to grant.

What wilt thou *give* me, seeing I go childless? Gen. xv.

9. To expose; to yield to the power of.

Give to the wanton winds their flowing hair. *Dryden.*

10. To grant; to allow; to permit.

It is *given* me once again to behold my friend. *Rowe.*

11. To afford; to supply; to furnish.

Thou must *give* us also sacrifices and burnt-offerings. Ex. x.

12. To empower; to license; to commission.

Then *give* thy friend to shed the sacred wine. *Pope.*

But this and similar phrases are probably elliptical; *give* for *give* power or license. So in the phrases, *give* me to understand, *give* me to know, *give* the flowers to blow, that is, to *give* power, to enable.

13. To pay or render; as, to *give* praise, applause or approbation.

14. To render; to pronounce; as, to *give* sentence or judgment; to *give* the word of command.

15. To utter; to vent; as, to *give* a shout.

16. To produce; to show; to exhibit as a product or result; as, the number of men divided by the number of ships, *gives* four hundred to each ship.

17. To cause to exist; to excite in another; as, to *give* offense or umbrage; to *give* pleasure.

18. To send forth; to emit; as, a stone *gives* sparks with steel.

19. To addict; to apply; to devote one's self, followed by the reciprocal pronoun. The soldiers *give* themselves to plunder. The passive participle is much used in this sense; as, the people are *given* to luxury and pleasure; the youth is *given* to study.

Give thyself wholly to them. 1 Tim. iv.

20. To resign; to yield up; often followed by *up.*

Who say, I care not, those I *give* for lost. *Herbert.*

21. To pledge; as, I *give* my word that the debt shall be paid.

22. To present for taking or acceptance; as, I *give* you my hand.

23. To allow or admit by way of supposition.

To give away, to alienate the title or property of a thing; to make over to another; to transfer.

Whatsoever we employ in charitable uses, during our lives, is *given away* from ourselves. *Atterbury.*

To give back, to return; to restore. *Atterbury.*

To give forth, to publish; to tell; to report publicly. *Hayward.*

To give the hand, to yield preeminence, as being subordinate or inferior. *Hooker.*

To give in, to allow by way of abatement or deduction from a claim; to yield what may be justly demanded.

To give over, to leave; to quit; to cease; to abandon; as, to *give over* a pursuit.

2. To addict; to attach to; to abandon.

When the Babylonians had *given* themselves *over* to all manner of vice. *Grew.*

3. To despair of recovery; to believe to be lost, or past recovery. The physician had *given over* the patient, or *given* the patient *over.* *Addison.*

4. To abandon. *Milton.*

To give out, to utter publicly; to report; to proclaim; to publish. It was *given out* that parliament would assemble in November.

2. To issue; to send forth; to publish.

The night was distinguished by the orders which he *gave out* to his army. *Addison.*

3. To show; to exhibit in false appearance. *Shak.*

4. To send out; to emit; as, a substance *gives out* steam or odors.

To give up, to resign; to quit; to yield as hopeless; as, to *give up* a cause; to *give up* the argument.

2. To surrender; as, to *give up* a fortress to an enemy.

3. To relinquish; to cede. In this treaty the Spaniards *gave up* Louisiana.

4. To abandon; as, to *give up* all hope. They are *given up* to believe a lie.

5. To deliver.

And Joab *gave up* the sum of the number of the people to the king. 2 Sam. xxiv.

To give one's self up, to despair of one's recovery; to conclude to be lost.

2. To resign or devote.

Let us *give ourselves* wholly *up* to Christ in heart and desire. *Taylor.*

3. To addict; to abandon. He *gave himself up* to intemperance.

To give way, to yield; to withdraw to make room for. Inferiors should *give way* to superiors.

2. To fail; to yield to force; to break or fall. The ice *gave way* and the horses were drowned. The scaffolding *gave way.* The wheels or axletree *gave way.*

3. To recede; to make room for.

4. In *seamen's language*, *give way* is an order to a boat's crew to row after ceasing, or to increase their exertions. *Mar. Dict.*

GIVE, *v. i. giv.* To yield to pressure. The earth *gives* under the feet.

2. To begin to melt; to thaw; to grow soft, so as to yield to pressure. *Bacon.*

3. To move; to recede.

Now back he *gives*, then rushes on amain. *Daniel's Civil War.*

To give in, to go back; to give way. [*Not in use.*]

To give into, to yield assent; to adopt.

This consideration may induce a translator to *give in* to those general phrases— *Pope.*

To give off, to cease; to forbear. [*Little used.*] *Locke.*

To give on, to rush; to fall on. [*Not in use.*]

To give out, to publish; to proclaim.

2. To cease from exertion; to yield; applied to persons. He labored hard, but *gave out* at last.

To give over, to cease; to act no more; to desert.

It would be well for all authors, if they knew when to *give over*, and to desist from any further pursuits after fame. *Addison.*

GIV′EN, *pp. giv'n.* Bestowed; granted; conferred; imparted; admitted or supposed.

GIV′ER, *n.* One who gives; a donor; a bestower; a grantor; one who imparts or distributes.

It is the *giver*, and not the gift, that engrosses the heart of the christian. *Kollock.*

ĠIVES, *n. plu.* [Ir. *geibhion*, from *geibhim*, to get or hold.]

Fetters or shackles for the feet. [See *Gyves.*]

GIV′ING, *ppr.* Bestowing; conferring; imparting; granting; delivering.

GIV′ING, *n.* The act of conferring. *Pope.*

2. An alledging of what is not real. *Shak.*

GIZ′ZARD, *n.* [Fr. *gesier.*] The strong muscular stomach of a fowl. *Ray. Dryden.*

To fret the gizzard, to harass; to vex one's self, or to be vexed. *Hudibras.*

GLA′BRIATE, *v. t.* [L. *glabro.*] To make smooth. [*Not used.*]

GLA′BRITY, *n.* Smoothness. [*Not used.*]

GLA′BROUS, *a.* [L. *glaber*, allied to Eng. *glib.* Class Lb. No. 10. 24. 27. 34. 37.]

Smooth; having an even surface.

GLA′CIAL, *a.* [Fr. *glacial*; L. *glacialis*, from *glacies*, ice.] Icy; consisting of ice; frozen.

GLA′CIATE, *v. i.* To turn to ice. *Dict.*

GLACIA′TION, *n.* [supra.] The act of freezing; ice formed. *Brown.*

GLA′CIER, *n.* [Fr. *glaciere*, an ice-house, from *glace*, It. *ghiaccio*, ice. See *Glacial.*]

A field or immense mass of ice, formed in deep but elevated valleys, or on the sides of the Alps or other mountains. These masses of ice extend many miles in length and breadth, and remain undissolved by the heat of summer. *Coxe.*

GLA'CIOUS, *a.* Like ice; icy. *Brown.*

GLA'CIS, *n.* [Fr.] In *building*, or *gardening*, an easy, insensible slope. *Encyc.*

2. In *fortification*, a sloping bank; that mass of earth which serves as a parapet to the covered way, having an easy slope or declivity towards the champaign or field. *Encyc.*

GLAD, *a.* [Sax. *glæd* or *glad*; Sw. *glad*; Dan. *glad*; perhaps L. *lætus*, without a prefix. See Class Ld. No. 2. Ar.]

1. Pleased; affected with pleasure or moderate joy; moderately happy.

A wise son maketh a *glad* father. Prov. x.

It is usually followed by *of*. I am *glad of* an opportunity to oblige my friend.

It is sometimes followed by *at*.

He that is *glad at* calamities shall not be unpunished. Prov. xvii.

It is sometimes followed by *with*.

The Trojan, *glad with* sight of hostile blood— *Dryden.*

With, after *glad*, is unusual, and in this passage *at* would have been preferable.

2. Cheerful; joyous.

They blessed the king, and went to their tents, joyful and *glad* of heart. 1 Kings viii.

3. Cheerful; wearing the appearance of joy; as a *glad* countenance.

4. Wearing a gay appearance; showy; bright.

The wilderness and the solitary place shall be *glad* for them. Is. xxxv.

Glad evening and *glad* morn crown'd the fourth day. *Milton.*

5. Pleasing; exhilarating.

Her conversation
More *glad* to me than to a miser money is. *Sidney.*

6. Expressing gladness or joy; exciting joy.

Hark! a *glad* voice the lonely desert cheers. *Pope.*

GLAD, *v. t.* [The pret. and pp. *gladed* is not used. See *Gladden.*]

To make glad; to affect with pleasure; to cheer; to gladden; to exhilarate.

Each drinks the juice that *glads* the heart of man. *Pope.*

GLAD'DEN, *v. t.* glad'n. [Sax. *gladian*; Dan. *glæder*; Sw. *glädia.*]

To make glad; to cheer; to please; to exhilarate. The news of peace *gladdens* our hearts.

Churches will every where *gladden* his eye, and hymns of praise vibrate upon his ear. *Dwight.*

GLAD'DEN, *v. i.* glad'n. To become glad; to rejoice.

So shall your country ever *gladden* at the sound of your voice. *Adams' Inaugural Oration.*

GLAD'DER, *n.* One that makes glad, or gives joy. *Dryden.*

GLAD'DING, *ppr.* Making glad; cheering; giving joy.

GLADE, *n.* [Ice. *hlad.* Qu.] An opening or passage made through a wood by lopping off the branches of the trees. Locally, in the U. States, a natural opening or open place in a forest.

There interspersed in lawns and opening *glades.* *Pope.*

2. In *New England*, an opening in the ice of rivers or lakes, or a place left unfrozen.

GLADE, *n.* [D. *glad*, G. *glatt*, smooth.] Smooth ice. *New England.*

GLA'DEN, GLA'DER, } *n.* [L. *gladius*, a sword.] Sword-grass; the general name of plants that rise with a broad blade like sedge. *Junius.*

GLAD'FUL, *a.* Full of gladness. *Obs.* *Spenser.*

GLAD'FULNESS, *n.* Joy; gladness. *Obs.* *Spenser.*

GLA'DIATE, *a.* [L. *gladius*, a sword.] Sword-shaped; resembling the form of a sword; as the legume of a plant. *Martyn.*

GLADIA'TOR, *n.* [L. from *gladius*, a sword.]

A sword-player; a prize-fighter. The gladiators, in Rome, were men who fought in the arena, for the entertainment of the people.

GLADIATO'RIAL, *a.* Pertaining to gladiators, or to combats for the entertainment of the Roman people. *Bp. Reynolds.*

GLA'DIATORY, *a.* Relating to gladiators. *Bp. Porteus.*

GLA'DIATURE, *n.* Sword-play; fencing. [*Not in use.*] *Gayton.*

GLAD'IOLE, *n.* [L. *gladiolus*, a dagger.] A plant, the sword-lily, of the genus Gladiolus. The *water gladiole* is of the genus Butomus or flowering rush, and also of the genus Lobelia or cardinal flower. *Cyc.* *Fam. of Plants.*

GLAD'LY, *adv.* [See *Glad.*] With pleasure; joyfully; cheerfully.

The common people heard him *gladly.* Mark xii.

GLAD'NESS, *n.* [See *Glad.*] Joy, or a moderate degree of joy and exhilaration; pleasure of mind; cheerfulness.

They—did eat their meat with *gladness* and singleness of heart. Acts ii.

[*Gladness* is rarely or never equivalent to *mirth*, *merriment*, *gayety* and *triumph*, and it usually expresses less than *delight.* It sometimes expresses great joy. Esther viii. ix.]

GLAD'SŎME, *a.* Pleased; joyful; cheerful. *Spenser.*

2. Causing joy, pleasure or cheerfulness; having the appearance of gayety; pleasing.

Of opening heaven they sung, and *gladsome* day. *Prior.*

GLAD'SŎMELY, *adv.* With joy; with pleasure of mind.

GLAD'SŎMENESS, *n.* Joy, or moderate joy; pleasure of mind.

2. Showiness. *Johnson.*

GLAD'WIN, *n.* A plant of the genus Iris. *Fam. of Plants.*

GLAIR, *n.* [Fr. *glaire.* In Sax. *glære* is amber, or any thing transparent. This coincides with W. *eglur*, Eng. *clear*, L. *clarus*, and with Eng. *glare*, and L. *gloria*; perhaps with L. *glarea*, gravel, or pieces of quartz.]

1. The white of an egg. It is used as a varnish for preserving paintings. *Encyc.*

2. Any viscous transparent substance, resembling the white of an egg.

3. A kind of halbert. *Dict.*

GLAIR, *v. t.* To smear with the white of an egg; to varnish.

GLA'IRY, *a.* Like glair, or partaking of its qualities. *Fleming.*

GL'ANCE, *n.* [G. *glanz*, a ray, a beam or shoot of light, splendor; D. *glans*; Dan. *glands*; Sw. *glans.* The primary sense is to shoot, to throw, to dart.]

1. A sudden shoot of light or splendor. *Milton.*

2. A shoot or darting of sight; a rapid or momentary view or cast; a snatch of sight; as a sudden *glance*; a *glance* of the eye. *Dryden.* *Watts.*

GL'ANCE, *v. i.* To shoot or dart a ray of light or splendor.

When through the gloom the *glancing* lightnings fly. *Rowe.*

2. To fly off in an oblique direction; to dart aside. The arrow struck the shield and *glanced.* So we say, a *glancing* ball or shot.

3. To look with a sudden, rapid cast of the eye; to snatch a momentary or hasty view.

Then sit again, and sigh and *glance.* *Suckling.*

4. To hint; to cast a word or reflection; as, to *glance* at a different subject.

5. To censure by oblique hints. *Shak.*

GL'ANCE, *v. t.* To shoot or dart suddenly or obliquely; to cast for a moment; as, to *glance* the eye. *Shak.*

GL'ANCE-COAL, *n.* Anthracite; a mineral composed chiefly of carbon. [See *Anthracite.*] *Cyc.*

GL'ANCING, *ppr.* Shooting; darting; casting suddenly; flying off obliquely.

GL'ANCINGLY, *adv.* By glancing; in a glancing manner; transiently. *Hakewill.*

GLAND, *n.* [L. *glans*, a nut; *glandula*, a gland; Fr. *glande.* Qu. Gr. βαλανος, with a different prefix.]

1. In *anatomy*, a distinct soft body, formed by the convolution of a great number of vessels, either constituting a part of the lymphatic system, or destined to secrete some fluid from the blood. Glands have been divided into *conglobate* and *conglomerate*, from their structure; but a more proper division is into *lymphatic* and *secretory.* The former are found in the course of the lymphatic vessels, and are conglobate. The latter are of various structure. They include the mucous follicles, the conglomerate glands, properly so called, such as the parotid glands and the pancreas, the liver, kidneys, &c. The term has also been applied to other bodies of a similar appearance, neither lymphatic nor secretory; such as the thymus and thyroid glands, whose use is not certainly known, certain portions of the brain, as the pineal and pituitary glands, &c. [See *Conglobate* and *Conglomerate.*] *Encyc.* *Parr.* *Coxe.*

2. In *botany*, a *gland* or *glandule* is an excretory or secretory duct or vessel in a plant. Glands are found on the leaves, petioles, peduncles and stipules. *Martyn.*

GLAND'ERED, *a.* Affected with glanders. *Berkley.*

GLAND'ERS, *n.* [from *gland.*] In *farriery*, the running of corrupt slimy matter from the nose of a horse. *Cyc.*

GLANDIF'EROUS, *a.* [L. *glandifer*; *glans*, an acorn, and *fero*, to bear.]

Bearing acorns or other nuts; producing

nuts or mast. The beech and the oak are *glandiferous* trees.

GLAND'IFORM, *a.* [L. *glans* and *forma*, form.]
In the shape of a gland or nut; resembling a gland.

GLAND'ULAR, *a.* Containing glands; consisting of glands; pertaining to glands.

GLANDULA'TION, *n.* In *botany*, the situation and structure of the secretory vessels in plants. *Martyn.*

Glandulation respects the secretory vessels, which are either glandules, follicles or utricles. *Lee.*

GLAND'ULE, *n.* [L. *glandula.*] A small gland or secreting vessel.

GLANDULIF'EROUS, *a.* [L. *glandula* and *fero*, to bear.] Bearing glands. *Lee.*

GLANDULOS'ITY, *n.* A collection of glands. [*Little used.*] *Brown.*

GLAND'ULOUS, *a.* [L. *glandulosus.*] Containing glands; consisting of glands; pertaining to glands; resembling glands.

GLARE, *n.* [Dan. *glar*, Ice. *gler*, glass. It coincides with *clear*, *glory*, *glair*, which see.]

1. A bright dazzling light; clear, brilliant luster or splendor, that dazzles the eyes.

The frame of burnished steel that cast a *glare*. *Dryden.*

2. A fierce, piercing look.

—About them round,
A lion now he stalks with fiery *glare*. *Milton.*

3. A viscous transparent substance. [See *Glair.*]

GLARE, *v. i.* To shine with a clear, bright, dazzling light; as *glaring* light.

The cavern *glares* with new admitted light. *Dryden.*

2. To look with fierce, piercing eyes.

They *glared*, like angry lions. *Dryden.*

3. To shine with excessive luster; to be ostentatiously splendid; as a *glaring* dress. *Milton.*

She *glares* in balls, front boxes and the ring. *Pope.*

GLARE, *v. t.* To shoot a dazzling light.

GLA'REOUS, *a.* [Fr. *glaireux.* See *Glair.*] Resembling the white of an egg; viscous and transparent or white.

GLA'RING, *ppr.* Emitting a clear and brilliant light; shining with dazzling luster.

2. *a.* Clear; notorious; open and bold; barefaced; as a *glaring* crime.

GLA'RINGLY, *adv.* Openly; clearly; notoriously.

GL'ASS, *n.* [Sax. *glæs*; Sw. Dan. G. and D. *glas*; so named from its color; W. *glâs*, from *llâs*, blue, azure, green, fresh, pale; *glasu*, to make blue, to become green or verdant, to grow pale, to dawn; *glaslys*, woad, L. *glastum*; *glesid*, blueness. Tacitus, De Mor. Ger. 45, mentions *glesum*, amber collected in the Baltic, probably the same word, and so named from its clearness. Greenness is usually named from vegetation or growing, as L. *viridis*, from *vireo.*]

1. A hard, brittle, transparent, factitious substance, formed by fusing sand with fixed alkalies. *Encyc.*

In *chimistry*, a substance or mixture, earthy, saline or metallic, brought by fusion to the state of a hard, brittle, transparent mass, whose fracture is conchoidal. *Aikin.*

2. A glass vessel of any kind; as a drinking-*glass.*

3. A mirror; a looking-*glass.*

4. A vessel to be filled with sand for measuring time; as an hour-*glass.*

5. The destined time of man's life. His *glass* is run.

6. The quantity of liquor that a glass vessel contains. Drink a *glass* of wine with me.

7. A vessel that shows the weight of the air. *Tatler.*

8. A perspective glass; as an optic *glass.* *Milton.*

9. The time which a glass runs, or in which it is exhausted of sand. The *seamen's watch-glass* is half an hour. We say, a ship fought three *glasses.*

10. *Glasses*, in the plural, spectacles.

GL'ASS, *a.* Made of glass; vitreous; as a *glass* bottle.

GL'ASS, *v. t.* To see as in a glass. [*Not used.*] *Sidney.*

2. To case in glass. [*Little used.*] *Shak.*

3. To cover with glass; to glaze. *Boyle.*

[In the latter sense, *glaze* is generally used.]

GL'ASSBLŎWER, *n.* One whose business is to blow and fashion glass.

GL'ASSFULL, *n.* As much as a glass holds.

GL'ASSFURNACE, *n.* A furnace in which the materials of glass are melted. *Cyc.*

GL'ASS GAZING, *a.* Addicted to viewing one's self in a glass or mirror; finical. *Shak.*

GL'ASSGRINDER, *n.* One whose occupation is to grind and polish glass. *Boyle.*

GL'ASSHOUSE, *n.* A house where glass is made. *Addison.*

GL'ASSINESS, *n.* The quality of being glassy or smooth; a vitreous appearance.

GL'ASSLIKE, *a.* Resembling glass.

GL'ASSMAN, *n.* One who sells glass. *Swift.*

GL'ASSMETAL, *n.* Glass in fusion. *Boyle.*

GL'ASSPOT, *n.* A vessel used for melting glass in manufactories. *Cyc.*

GL'ASSWŎRK, *n.* Manufacture of glass.

GL'ASSWŎRKS, *n. plu.* The place or buildings where glass is made.

GL'ASSWŎRT, *n.* A plant, the Salsola, of several species, all which may be used in the manufacture of glass. The Barilla of commerce, is the semifused ashes of the *Salsola soda*, which is largely cultivated on the Mediterranean in Spain. *Encyc. Webster's Manual.*

GL'ASSY, *a.* Made of glass; vitreous; as a *glassy* substance. *Bacon.*

2. Resembling glass in its properties, as in smoothness, brittleness, or transparency; as a *glassy* stream; a *glassy* surface; the *glassy* deep. *Shak. Dryden.*

GLAUB'ERITE, *n.* A mineral of a grayish white or yellowish color, consisting of dry sulphate of lime and dry sulphate of soda. *Ure.*

GLAUB'ER-SALT, *n.* Sulphate of soda, a well known cathartic.

GLAUCO'MA, *n.* [Gr.] A fault in the eye, in which the crystaline humor becomes gray, but without injury to the sight. *Quincy.*

A disease in the eye, in which the crystaline humor becomes of a bluish or greenish color, and its transparency is diminished. *Encyc.*

An opacity of the vitreous humor. *Hooper.*

According to Sharp, the *glaucoma* of the Greeks is the same as the cataract; and according to St. Yves and others, it is a cataract with amaurosis. *Parr.*

GLAUC'OUS, *a.* [L. *glaucus.*] Of a sea green color; of a light green.

GLAVE, *n.* [Fr. *glaive*; W. *glaiv*, a billhook, a crooked sword, a cimiter; Arm. *glaif.*]
A broad sword; a falchion. [*Not used.*] *Fairfax. Hudibras.*

GLAV'ER, *v. i.* [W. *glavru*, to flatter; *glav*, something smooth or shining; L. *glaber*, *lævis*, or *lubricus*; Eng. *glib.*]
To flatter; to wheedle. [*Little used and vulgar.*] *L'Estrange.*

GLAV'ERER, *n.* A flatterer. [supra.]

GLAZE, *v. t.* [from *glass.*] To furnish with windows of glass; as, to *glaze* a house.

2. To incrust with a vitreous substance, the basis of which is lead, but combined with silex, pearl-ashes and common salt; as, to *glaze* earthern ware.

3. To cover with any thing smooth and shining; or to render the exterior of a thing smooth, bright and showy.

Though with other ornaments he may *glaze* and brandish the weapons. *Grew.*

4. To give a glassy surface; to make glossy; as, to *glaze* cloth.

GLA'ZED, *pp.* Furnished with glass windows; incrusted with a substance resembling glass; rendered smooth and shining.

GLA'ZIER, *n. gla'zhur.* [from *glaze* or *glass.*] One whose business is to set window glass, or to fix panes of glass to the sashes of windows, to pictures, &c. *Moxon.*

GLA'ZING, *ppr.* Furnishing with window glass.

2. Crusting with a vitreous substance, as potter's ware.

3. Giving a smooth, glossy, shining surface, as to cloth.

GLA'ZING, *n.* The vitreous substance with which potter's ware is incrusted.

GLEAM, *n.* [Sax. *gleam* or *glæm*, properly a shoot of light, coinciding with *glimmer*, *glimpse*, Ir. *laom*, [perhaps L. *flamma.*] The radical sense is to throw, to shoot or dart, and it may be of the same family as *clamo*, *clamor*, a shoot of the voice, and W. *llam*, Ir. *leam*, a leap, Ar. لَمَحَ Class Lm. No. 8.]

1. A shoot of light; a beam; a ray; a small stream of light. A *gleam* of dawning light, metaphorically, a *gleam* of hope.

2. Brightness; splendor.

In the clear azure *gleam* the flocks are seen. *Pope.*

GLEAM, *v. i.* To shoot or dart, as rays of light. At the dawn light *gleams* in the east.

2. To shine; to cast light. *Thomson.*

3. To flash; to spread a flood of light. [*Less common.*]

4. Among *falconers*, to disgorge filth, as a hawk. *Encyc.*

GLE'AMING, *ppr.* Shooting as rays of light; shining.

GLE'AMING, *n.* A shoot or shooting of light.

GLE'AMY, *a.* Darting beams of light; casting light in rays.

> In brazen arms, that cast a *gleamy* ray,
> Swift through the town the warrior bends his way. *Pope.*

GLEAN, *v. t.* [Fr. *glaner*, to glean; *glane*, a handful or cluster. In W. *glân* is *clean.*]

1. To gather the stalks and ears of grain which reapers leave behind them.

> Let me now go to the field, and *glean* ears of corn— Ruth ii.

2. To collect things thinly scattered; to gather what is left in small parcels or numbers, or what is found in detached parcels; as, to *glean* a few passages from an author.

> They *gleaned* of them in the highways five thousand men. Judges xx.

GLEAN, *v. i.* To gather stalks or ears of grain left by reapers.

> And she went, and came and *gleaned* in the field after the reapers. Ruth ii.

GLEAN, *n.* A collection made by gleaning, or by gathering here and there a little.

> The *gleans* of yellow thyme distend his thighs. *Dryden.*

GLE'ANED, *pp.* Gathered after reapers; collected from small detached parcels; as grain *gleaned* from the field.

2. Cleared of what is left; as, the field is *gleaned.*

3. Having suffered a gleaning. The public prints have been *gleaned.*

GLE'ANER, *n.* One who gathers after reapers. *Thomson.*

2. One who collects detached parts or numbers, or who gathers slowly with labor. *Locke.*

GLE'ANING, *ppr.* Gathering what reapers leave; collecting in small detached parcels.

GLE'ANING, *n.* The act of gathering after reapers.

2. That which is collected by gleaning.

GLEBE, *n.* [L. *gleba*, a clod or lump of earth; Fr. *glebe*, land, ground; probably from collecting, as in *globe, club.*]

1. Turf; soil; ground.

> Till the glad summons of a genial ray
> Unbinds the *glebe*— *Garth.*

2. The land belonging to a parish church or ecclesiastical benefice. *Spelman. Encyc.*

3. A crystal. *Obs. Arbuthnot.*

4. Among *miners*, a piece of earth in which is contained some mineral ore. *Encyc.*

GLE'BOUS, *a.* Gleby; turfy. *Dict.*

GLE'BY, *a.* Turfy; cloddy.

GLEDE, *n.* [Sax. *glida*, from *glidan*, to glide; Sw. *glada.*]

A fowl of the rapacious kind, the kite, a species of Falco. The word is used in Deut. xiv. 13. but the same Hebrew word, Lev. xi. 14. is rendered a vulture.

GLEE, *n.* [Sax. *glie*, from *glig, gligg*, sport, music.]

1. Joy; merriment; mirth; gayety; particularly, the mirth enjoyed at a feast. *Spenser.*

2. A sort of catch or song sung in parts. *Mason. Busby.*

GLEED, *n.* [Sax. *gled.*] A glowing coal. *Obs. Chaucer.*

GLEE'FUL, *a.* Merry; gay; joyous. *Shak.*

GLEEK, *n.* [See *Glee.*] Music, or a musician. *Obs. Shak.*

2. A scoff; a game at cards. *Obs.*

GLEEK, *v. i.* To make sport of; to gibe; to sneer; to spend time idly. *Obs. Shak.*

GLEE'MAN, *n.* A musician. *Obs.*

GLEEN, *v. i.* [W. *glan*, clean, pure, holy, bright; *gleiniaw*, to purify, to brighten; Ir. *glan.*] To shine; to glisten. [*Not used.*] *Prior.*

GLEE'SŎME, *a.* Merry; joyous. *Obs.*

GLEET, *n.* [from Sax. *glidan*, to glide, or *hlyttrian*, to melt; Ice. *glat.*]

The flux of a thin humor from the urethra; a thin ichor running from a sore. *Encyc. Wiseman.*

GLEET, *v. i.* To flow in a thin limpid humor; to ooze. *Wiseman.*

2. To flow slowly, as water. *Cheyne.*

GLEET'Y, *a.* Ichorous; thin; limpid.

GLEN, *n.* [W. *glyn*, a valley in which a river flows, as if from *llyn*, liquor, water; Sax. *glen*; Ir. *glean.*]

A valley; a dale; a depression or space between hills.

GLENE, *n.* [Gr. γληνη.] In *anatomy*, the cavity or socket of the eye, and the pupil; any slight depression or cavity receiving a bone in articulation. *Parr. Cyc.*

GLEW. [See *Glue.*]

GLI'ADINE, *n.* [Gr. γλια, gluc.] One of the constituents of gluten, a slightly transparent, brittle substance, of a straw-yellow color, having a slight smell, similar to that of honeycomb. *Ure.*

GLIB, *a.* [D. *glibberen, glippen*, to slide; *glibberig*, glib, slippery; W. *llipyr*; L. *glaber*, smooth; *labor*, to slide. This word contains the elements of *slip*. Qu. L. *glubo*, Gr. γλυφω. Class Lb. No. 27. 37.]

1. Smooth; slippery; admitting a body to slide easily on the surface; as, ice is *glib.*

2. Smooth; voluble; easily moving; as a *glib* tongue.

GLIB, *n.* A thick curled bush of hair hanging down over the eyes. [*Not in use.*] *Spenser.*

GLIB, *v. t.* To castrate. [Qu. to make smooth, *glubo*, γλυφω.] *Shak.*

2. To make smooth. *Bp. Hall.*

GLIB'LY, *adv.* Smoothly; volubly; as, to slide *glibly*; to speak *glibly.*

GLIB'NESS, *n.* Smoothness; slipperiness; as a polished ice-like *glibness. Chapman.*

2. Volubility of the tongue. *Government of the Tongue.*

GLIDE, *v. i.* [Sax. *glidan*; G. *gleiten*; D. *glyden*; Dan. *glider*. Qu. Fr. *glisser*, in a different dialect. It has the elements of *slide*, as *glib* has of *slip.*]

1. To flow gently; to move without noise or violence; as a river.

> By east, among the dusty vallies *glide*
> The silver streams of Jordan's crystal flood. *Fairfax.*

2. To move silently and smoothly; to pass along without apparent effort; as a hawk or an eagle *gliding* through the air.

3. To move or pass rapidly and with apparent ease; as, a ship *glides* through the water.

4. In *a general sense*, to move or slip along with ease as on a smooth surface, or to pass along rapidly without apparent effort, and without obstruction.

GLIDE, *n.* The act or manner of moving smoothly, swiftly and without labor or obstruction. *Shak.*

GLI'DER, *n.* He or that which glides. *Spenser.*

GLI'DING, *ppr.* Passing along gently and smoothly; moving rapidly, or with ease.

GLIM'MER, *v. i.* [G. *glimmen, glimmern*, to gleam, to glimmer; D. *glimmen*; Sw. *glimma*; Dan. *glimrer*; Ir. *laom*, flame.]

1. To shoot feeble or scattered rays of light; as the *glimmering* dawn; a *glimmering* lamp.

> When rosy morning *glimmer'd* o'er the dales. *Pope.*
>
> The west yet *glimmers* with some streaks of day. *Shak.*

2. To shine faintly; to give a feeble light.

> Mild evening *glimmered* on the lawn. *Trumbull.*

GLIM'MER, *n.* A faint light; feeble scattered rays of light.

2. In *mineralogy*, mica, glist, muscovy-glass; a mineral resulting from crystalization, but rarely found in regular crystals. Usually it appears in thin, flexible, elastic lamins, which exhibit a high polish and strong luster. It is an essential ingredient in granite, gneiss, and mica slate. *Cleaveland.*

GLIM'MERING, *ppr.* Shining faintly; shooting feeble scattered rays of light.

GLIM'MERING, *n.* A faint beaming of light.

2. A faint view.

GLIMPSE, *n. glims.* [D. *glimp*, from *glimmen.*]

1. A weak faint light.

> Such vast room in Nature,
> Only to shine, yet scarce to contribute
> Each orb a *glimpse* of light. *Milton.*

2. A flash of light; as the lightning's *glimpse. Milton.*

3. Transient luster.

> One *glimpse* of glory to my issue give. *Dryden.*

4. A short transitory view. He saw at a *glimpse* the design of the enemy.

5. Short fleeting enjoyment; as a *glimpse* of delight. *Prior.*

6. Exhibition of a faint resemblance. *Shak.*

GLIMPSE, *v. i.* To appear by glimpses. *Drayton.*

GLIS'SA, *n.* A fish of the tunny kind, without scales. *Dict. Nat. Hist.*

GLIST, *n.* [from *glisten.*] Glimmer; mica. [See *Glimmer.*]

GLIS'TEN, *v. i. glis'n.* [Sax. *glisnian*; G. *gleissen*. This word and *glitter* are probably dialectical forms of the same word. In Irish *lasadh, lasaim*, is to burn, to light; Dan. *lyser*, Sw. *lysa*, to shine; Russ. *oblistayu*. In W. *llathru* is to make smooth and glossy, to polish, to glitter. Qu. Heb. גלש to shine, L. *glisco*, Eng. *gloss.*]

To shine; to sparkle with light; as the *glistening* stars.

> The ladies' eyes *glistened* with pleasure. *Richardson.*

GLIS'TENING, *ppr.* Shining; sparkling; emitting rays of light.

GLIS'TER, *v. i.* [See *Glisten.*] To shine; to be bright; to sparkle; to be brilliant.

> All that *glistens* is not gold. *Shak.*

GLISTER. [See *Clyster.*]

GLIS'TERING, *ppr.* Shining; sparkling with light.

GLIS'TERINGLY, *adv.* With shining luster.

GLIT'TER, *v. i.* [Sax. *glitenan*; Sw. *glittra.* See *Glisten.*]

1. To shine; to sparkle with light; to gleam; to be splendid; as a *glittering* sword.

> The field yet *glitters* with the pomp of war. *Dryden.*

2. To be showing, specious or striking, and hence attractive; as the *glittering* scenes of a court.

GLIT'TER, *n.* Brightness; brilliancy; splendor; luster; as the *glitter* of arms; the *glitter* of royal equipage; the *glitter* of dress.

GLIT'TERAND, *ppr.* or *a.* Sparkling. [*Not in use.*] *Chaucer.*

GLIT'TERING, *ppr.* Shining; splendid; brilliant.

GLIT'TERINGLY, *adv.* With sparkling luster.

GLŌAM, *v. i.* To be sullen. [See *Glum.*]

GLŌAR, *v. i.* [D. *gluuren*, to *leer.*] To squint; to stare. *Obs.*

GLŌAT, *v. i.* [Sw *glutta*, to peep.] To cast side glances; to stare with eagerness or admiration. *Obs.* *Rowe.*

GLO'BATE, } *a.* [L. *globatus.*] Having the
GLO'BATED, } form of a globe; spherical; spheroidal.

GLOBE, *n.* [L. *globus*; Fr. *globe*; Sp. It. *globo*; Sax. *cleow*, *cliwe* or *cliaw*; Eng. *clew.* See *Clew.* Russ. *klub*, a ball.]

1. A round or spherical solid body; a ball; a sphere; a body whose surface is in every part equidistant from the center.

2. The earth; the terraqueous ball; so called, though not perfectly spherical. *Locke.*

3. An artificial sphere of metal, paper or other matter, on whose convex surface is drawn a map or representation of the earth or of the heavens. That on which the several oceans, seas, continents, isles and countries of the earth are represented, is called a *terrestrial globe.* That which exhibits a delineation of the constellations in the heavens, is called a *celestial globe.*

4. A body of soldiers formed into a circle. *Milton.*

GLOBE, *v. t.* To gather round or into a circle. *Milton.*

GLOBE-AMARANTH, *n.* A plant of the genus Gomphrena. [See *Amaranth.*] *Fam. of Plants.*

GLOBE-ANIMAL, *n.* A species of animalcule of a globular form. *Encyc.*

GLOBE-DAISY, *n.* A plant or flower of the genus Globularia. *Fam. of Plants.*

GLO'BE-FISH, *n.* A fish of a globular shape, the Ostracion. *Johnson. Encyc.*

GLO'BE-FLOWER, *n.* A plant or flower of the genus Sphæranthus. *Fam. of Plants.*

GLOBE-RANUN'CULUS, *n.* A plant, the Trollius europæus. *Fam. of Plants. Lee.*

GLO'BE-THISTLE, *n.* A plant of the genus Echinops. *Fam. of Plants.*

GLOBO'SE, *a.* [L. *globosus*, from *globe.*] Round; spherical; globular. *Milton.*

GLOBOS'ITY, *n.* The quality of being round; sphericity. *Ray.*

GLO'BOUS, *a.* [L. *globosus.*] Round; spherical. *Milton.*

GLOB'ULAR, *a.* [from *globe.*] Round; spherical; having the form of a small ball or sphere; as *globular* atoms. *Grew.*

GLOBULA'RIA, *n.* A flosculous flower. *Miller.*

GLOB'ULE, *n.* [Fr. *globule*; L. *globulus*, dim. of *globus.*]

A little globe; a small particle of matter of a spherical form; a word particularly applied to the red particles of blood, which swim in a transparent serum, and may be discovered by the microscope. *Quincy. Arbuthnot. Encyc.*

> Hail stones have opake *globules* of snow in their center. *Newton.*

GLOB'ULOUS, *a.* Round; globular; having the form of a small sphere. *Boyle.*

GLO'BY, *a.* Round; orbicular. *Sherwood.*

GLODE, old *pret.* of *glide.* *Obs.*

GLOME, *n.* [L. *glomus*, a ball; Heb. Ch. גלם, Ar. لَمَّ lamma, to wind, convolve, or collect into a mass. Class Lm. No. 5. 11. Qu. its alliance to *lump*, *clump*, *plumbum.*]

In *botany*, a roundish head of flowers. *Martyn.*

GLOM'ERATE, *v. t.* [L. *glomero*, from *glomus*, supra.]

To gather or wind into a ball; to collect into a spherical form or mass, as threads.

GLOM'ERATED, *pp.* Gathered into a ball or round mass.

GLOM'ERATING, *ppr.* Collecting or winding into a ball or round mass.

GLOMERA'TION, *n.* [L. *glomeratio.*] The act of gathering, winding or forming into a ball or spherical body.

2. A body formed into a ball. *Bacon.*

GLOM'EROUS, *a.* [L. *glomerosus.*] Gathered or formed into a ball or round mass. [Qu. the use.]

GLOOM, *n.* [Scot. *gloum*, gloom, a frown. In D. *lommer* is a shade, and *loom* is slow, heavy, dull. In Sax. *glomung* is twilight.]

1. Obscurity; partial or total darkness; thick shade; as the *gloom* of a forest, or the *gloom* of midnight.

2. Cloudiness or heaviness of mind; melancholy; aspect of sorrow. We say, the mind is sunk into *gloom*; a *gloom* overspreads the mind.

3. Darkness of prospect or aspect.

4. Sullenness.

GLOOM, *v. i.* To shine obscurely or imperfectly. *Spenser.*

2. To be cloudy, dark or obscure.

3. To be melancholy or dejected. *Goldsmith.*

GLOOM, *v. t.* To obscure; to fill with gloom; to darken; to make dismal. *Young.*

GLOOM'ILY, *adv.* [from *gloomy.*] Obscurely; dimly; darkly; dismally.

2. With melancholy aspect; sullenly; not cheerfully. *Dryden. Thomson.*

GLOOM'INESS, *n.* Want of light; obscurity; darkness; dismalness.

2. Want of cheerfulness; cloudiness of look; heaviness of mind; melancholy; as, to involve the mind in *gloominess.* *Addison.*

GLOOM'Y, *a.* [from *gloom.*] Obscure; imperfectly illuminated; or dark; dismal; as the *gloomy* cells of a convent; the *gloomy* shades of night.

2. Wearing the aspect of sorrow; melancholy; clouded; dejected; depressed; heavy of heart; as a *gloomy* countenance or state of mind; a *gloomy* temper.

3. Of a dark complexion. [*Little used.*] *Milton.*

GLORIA'TION, *n.* [L. *gloriatio.*] Boast; a triumphing. [*Not used.*] *Richardson.*

GLO'RIED, *a.* [See *Glory.*] Illustrious; honorable. [*Not used.*] *Milton.*

GLORIFICA'TION, *n.* [See *Glorify.*] The act of giving glory or of ascribing honors to. *Taylor.*

2. Exaltation to honor and dignity; elevation to glory; as the *glorification* of Christ after his resurrection.

GLO'RIFIED, *pp.* Honored; dignified; exalted to glory.

GLO'RIFY, *v. t.* [Fr. *glorifier*; L. *gloria* and *facio*, to make.]

1. To praise; to magnify and honor in worship; to ascribe honor to, in thought or words. Ps. lxxxvi. 9.

> God is *glorified*, when such his excellency, above all things, is with due admiration acknowledged. *Hooker.*

2. To make glorious; to exalt to glory, or to celestial happiness.

> Whom he justified, them he also *glorified.* Rom. viii.

> The God of our fathers hath *glorified* his son Jesus. Acts iii.

3. To praise; to honor; to extol.

> Whomsoever they find to be most licentious of life—him they set up and *glorify.* *Spenser.*

4. To procure honor or praise to. *Shak.*

GLO'RIFȲING, *ppr.* Praising; honoring in worship; exalting to glory; honoring; extolling.

GLO'RIOUS, *a.* [Fr. *glorieux*; L. *gloriosus.* See *Glory.*]

1. Illustrious; of exalted excellence and splendor; resplendent in majesty and divine attributes; *applied to God.* Ex. xv. 11.

2. Noble; excellent; renowned; celebrated; illustrious; very honorable; *applied to men, their achievments, titles*, &c.

> Let us remember we are Cato's friends,
> And act like men who claim that *glorious* title. *Addison.*

3. Boastful; self-exulting; haughty; ostentatious. *Obs.* *Bacon.*

GLO'RIOUSLY, *adv.* Splendidly; illustriously; with great renown or dignity.

> Sing ye to the Lord, for he hath triumphed *gloriously.* Ex. xv.

GLO'RY, *n.* [L. *gloria*; Fr. *gloire*; Sp. and It. *gloria*; Ir. *gloir*, glory, and *glor*, clear; W. *eglur*, clear, bright; Arm. *gloar*, glory. It coincides with *clear*, and the primary sense seems to be to open, to expand, to enlarge. So *splendor* is from the Celtic *ysplan*, open, clear, plain, L. *planus*; hence, bright, shining. *Glory*, then, is brightness, splendor. The L. *floreo*, to blossom, to *flower*, to *flourish*, is probably of the same family.]

1. Brightness; luster; splendor.

> The moon, serene in *glory*, mounts the sky. *Pope.*

For he received from God the Father honor and glory, when there came such a voice to him from the excellent *glory*. 2 Pet. i.

In this passage of Peter, the latter word *glory* refers to the visible splendor or bright cloud that overshadowed Christ at his transfiguration. The former word *glory*, though the same in the original, is to be understood in a figurative sense.

2. Splendor; magnificence.

Solomon, in all his *glory*, was not arrayed like one of these. Matt. vi.

3. The circle of rays surrounding the head of a figure in painting.

4. Praise ascribed in adoration; honor.

Glory to God in the highest. Luke ii.

5. Honor; praise; fame; renown; celebrity. The hero pants for *glory* in the field. It was the *glory* of Howard to relieve the wretched.

6. The felicity of heaven prepared for the children of God; celestial bliss.

Thou shalt guide me with thy counsel, and afterwards receive me to *glory*. Ps. lxxiii.

7. In *scripture*, the divine presence; or the ark, the manifestation of it.

The *glory* is departed from Israel. 1 Sam. iv.

8. The divine perfections or excellence.

The heavens declare the *glory* of God. Ps. xix.

9. Honorable representation of God. 1 Cor. xi. viii.

10. Distinguished honor or ornament; that which honors or makes renowned; that of which one may boast.

Babylon, the *glory* of kingdoms. Is. xiii.

11. Pride; boastfulness; arrogance; as vain *glory*.

12. Generous pride. *Sidney.*

GLO'RY, *v. i.* [L. *glorior*, from *gloria*.] To exult with joy; to rejoice.

Glory ye in his holy name. Ps. cv. 1 Chron. xvi.

2. To boast; to be proud of.

No one should *glory* in his prosperity. *Richardson.*

GLO'RYING, *ppr.* Exulting with joy; boasting.

GLO'RYING, *n.* The act of exulting; exultation; boasting; display of pride.

Your *glorying* is not good. 1 Cor. v.

GLOSE, GLOSER. [See *Gloze*.]

GLOSS, *n.* [G. *glosse*, a gloss or comment; *glotzen*, to gleam, to glimmer. In Sax. *glesan* signifies to explain, to flatter, to *gloze*. From the Gr. γλωσσα, the tongue, and a strap, the L. has *glossa*, a tongue, and interpretation. In Heb. גלש signifies to shine, but from the sense of smoothness; Syr. ܓܠܦ to peel, to shave, to make bald. Whether these words are all of one family, let the reader judge. The radical sense appears to be, to open, to make clear, and the sense of *tongue* is probably to extend. If the first letter is a prefix, the other letters *Ls* are the elements of Ir. *leos*, light, L. *lustro*, Eng. *luster*; and it is remarkable that in Russ. *losk* is luster, polish, and *laskayu* is to flatter. The Gr. γλωττα, in the Attic dialect, is a tongue, and in Swedish and German, *glatt*, Dan. *glat*, D. *glad*, is smooth.]

1. Brightness or luster of a body proceeding from a smooth surface; as the *gloss* of silk; cloth is calendered to give it a *gloss*.

2. A specious appearance or representation; external show that may mislead opinion.

It is no part of my secret meaning to set on the face of this cause any fairer *gloss* than the naked truth doth afford. *Hooker.*

3. An interpretation artfully specious. *Sidney.*

4. Interpretation; comment; explanation; remark intended to illustrate a subject.

All this, without a *gloss* or comment,
He would unriddle in a moment. *Hudibras.*

Explaining the text in short *glosses*. *Baker.*

5. A literal translation. *Encyc.*

GLOSS, *v. t.* To give a superficial luster to; to make smooth and shining; as, to *gloss* cloth by the calender; to *gloss* mahogany.

2. To explain; to render clear and evident by comments; to illustrate.

3. To give a specious appearance to; to render specious and plausible; to palliate by specious representation.

You have the art to *gloss* the foulest cause. *Philips.*

GLOSS, *v. i.* To comment; to write or make explanatory remarks. *Dryden.*

2. To make sly remarks. *Prior.*

GLOSSA'RIAL, *a.* Containing explanation.

GLOSS'ARIST, *n.* A writer of glosses or comments. *Tyrwhitt.*

GLOSS'ARY, *n.* [Fr. *glossaire*; Low L. *glossarium*.]

A dictionary or vocabulary, explaining obscure or antiquated words found in old authors; such as Du Cange's Glossary; Spelman's Glossary.

GLOSSA'TOR, *n.* [Fr. *glossateur*.] A writer of comments; a commentator. [*Not used.*] *Ayliffe.*

GLOSS'ED, *pp.* Made smooth and shining; explained.

GLOSS'ER, *n.* A writer of glosses; a scholiast; a commentator.

2. A polisher; one who gives a luster.

GLOSS'INESS, *n.* [from *glossy*.] The luster or brightness of a smooth surface. *Boyle.*

GLOSS'ING, *ppr.* Giving luster to; polishing; explaining by comments; giving a specious appearance.

GLOSS'IST, *n.* A writer of comments. [*Not in use.*] *Wilton.*

GLOSSOG'RAPHER, *n.* [*gloss* and Gr. γραφω, to write.]

A writer of glosses; a commentator; a scholiast. *Hayward.*

GLOSSOG'RAPHY, *n.* The writing of comments for illustrating an author.

GLOSSOL'OGIST, *n.* [*gloss* and Gr. λογος.] One who writes glosses; a commentator.

GLOSSOL'OGY, *n.* [*gloss* and Gr. λογος, discourse.]

Glosses or commentaries; explanatory notes for illustrating an author.

GLOSS'Y, *a.* Smooth and shining; reflecting luster from a smooth surface; highly polished; as *glossy* silk; a *glossy* raven; a *glossy* plum. *Dryden.*

GLOT'TIS, *n.* [Gr. γλωττα, the tongue.]

The narrow opening at the upper part of the aspera arteria or windpipe, which, by its dilatation and contraction, contributes to the modulation of the voice. *Encyc. Parr.*

GLOUT, *v. i.* [Scot.] To pout; to look sullen. [*Not used.*] *Garth.*

GLOUT, *v. t.* To view attentively. [*Not in use.*]

GLŎVE, *n.* [Sax. *glof*. Qu. W. *golov*, a cover. The G. D. Sw. Dan. call it a *hand-shoe*.]

A cover for the hand, or for the hand and arm, with a separate sheath for each finger. The latter circumstance distinguishes the *glove* from the *mitten*.

To throw the glove, with our ancestors, was to challenge to single combat.

GLŎVE, *v. t.* To cover with a glove. *Shak.*

GLŎVER, *n.* One whose occupation is to make and sell gloves.

GLŌW, *v. i.* [Sax. *glowan*, G. *glühen*, D. *gloeijen*, Dan. *glöder*, to glow, to be red with heat; Dan. *glöd*, *gloe*, Sax. *gled*, D. *gloed*, G. *gluth*, Sw. *glöd*, W. *glo*, Corn. *glou*, Arm. *glaouen*, a live coal; W. *gla* or *glaw*, a shining; *gloyw*, bright; *gloywi*, to brighten or make clear.]

1. To shine with intense heat; or perhaps more correctly, to shine with a white heat; to exhibit incandescence. Hence, in a more general sense, to shine with a bright luster.

Glows in the stars, and blossoms in the trees. *Pope.*

2. To burn with vehement heat.

The scorching fire that in their entrails *glows*. *Addison.*

3. To feel great heat of body; to be hot.

Did not his temples *glow*
In the same sultry winds and scorching heats? *Addison.*

4. To exhibit a strong bright color; to be red.

Clad in a gown that *glows* with Tyrian rays. *Dryden.*

Fair ideas flow,
Strike in the sketch, or in the picture *glow*. *Pope.*

5. To be bright or red with heat or animation, or with blushes; as *glowing* cheeks.

6. To feel the heat of passion; to be ardent; to be animated, as by intense love, zeal, anger, &c.

We say, the heart *glows* with love or zeal; the *glowing* breast.

When real virtue fires the *glowing* bard. *Lewis.*

If you have never *glowed* with gratitude to the author of the christian revelation, you know nothing of christianity. *Buckminster.*

7. To burn with intense heat; to rage; as passion.

With pride it mounts, and with revenge it *glows*. *Dryden.*

GLŌW, *v. i.* To heat so as to shine. [*Not used.*] *Shak.*

GLŌW, *n.* Shining heat, or white heat.

2. Brightness of color; redness; as the *glow* of health in the cheeks.

A waving *glow* his bloomy beds display,
Blushing in bright diversities of day. *Pope.*

3. Vehemence of passion.

GLŌWING, *ppr.* Shining with intense heat; white with heat.

2. Burning with vehement heat.

3. Exhibiting a bright color; red; as a *glowing* color; *glowing* cheeks.

4. Ardent; vehement; animated; as *glowing* zeal.

5. Inflamed; as a *glowing* breast.

GLOWINGLY, *adv.* With great brightness; with ardent heat or passion.

GLOWWORM, *n.* The female of the *Lampyris noctiluca*, an insect of the order of Coleopters. It is without wings and resembles a caterpillar. It emits a shining green light from the extremity of the abdomen. The male is winged and flies about in the evening, when it is attracted by the light of the female. *Encyc.*

GLOZE, *v. i.* [Sax. *glesan.* See *Gloss.*] To flatter; to wheedle; to fawn; that is, to smooth, or to talk smoothly.

So *glozed* the tempter, and his proem tun'd. *Milton.*

A false *glozing* parasite. *South.*

GLOZE, *n.* Flattery; adulation. *Shak.*

2. Specious show; gloss. [*Not used.* See *Gloss.*] *Sidney.*

GLO'ZER, *n.* A flatterer. *Gifford.*

GLO'ZING, *ppr.* Flattering; wheedling.

GLO'ZING, *n.* Specious representation. *Mountagu.*

GLU'CIN, *n.* [Gr. γλυκυς.] A soft white earth or powder obtained from the beryl and emerald; so named from its forming, with acids, salts that are sweet to the taste. *Ure.*

Glucin is a compound, of which *glucinum* is the base. *Davy.*

GLUE, *n.* glu. [Fr. *glu*; W. *glyd*; Arm. *glud*; Ir. *glydh*, *gliu*, *gleten*; L. *gluten*; Gr. γλια; Russ. *klei.* See Class Ld. No. 8. 9. 10.]

Inspissated animal gluten; a tenacious, viscid matter, which serves as a cement to unite other substances. It is made of the skins, parings, &c. of animals, as of oxen, calves or sheep, by boiling them to a jelly. *Encyc. Parr.*

GLUE, *v. t.* [Fr. *gluer.*] To join with glue or a viscous substance. Cabinet makers *glue* together some parts of furniture.

2. To unite; to hold together. *Newton.*

[This word is now seldom used in a figurative sense. The phrases, to *glue* friends together, vices *glue* us to low pursuits or pleasures, found in writers of the last century, are not now used, or are deemed inelegant.]

GLU'EBOILER, *n.* [*glue* and *boil.*] One whose occupation is to make glue.

GLU'ED, *pp.* United or cemented with glue.

GLU'ER, *n.* One who cements with glue.

GLU'EY, *a.* Viscous; glutinous.

GLU'EYNESS, *n.* The quality of being gluey.

GLU'ING, *ppr.* Cementing with glue.

GLU'ISH, *a.* Having the nature of glue. *Sherwood.*

GLUM, *a.* [Scot. *gloum*, a frown.] Frowning; sullen. [*Little used.*]

GLUM, *n.* Sullenness; and, as a verb, to look sullen. [*Not in use.*]

GLUMA'CEOUS, *a.* Having glumes; consisting of glumes. *Barton.*

GLUME, *n.* [L. *gluma*, from *glubo*, to bark or peel, or Gr. γλυφω.]

In *botany*, the calyx or corol of corn and grasses, formed of valves embracing the seed, often terminated by the *arista* or beard; the husk or chaff. *Milne. Martyn.*

GLUM'MY, *a.* Dark; gloomy; dismal.

GLU'MOUS, *a.* A *glumous* flower is a kind of aggregate flower, having a filiform receptacle, with a common glume at the base. *Martyn.*

GLUT, *v. i.* [L. *glutio*; Fr. *engloutir*; Russ. *glotayu*, to swallow; W. *glwth*, a glutton; *glythu*, to gormandize; from *llwth*, a swallow, greediness; It. *ghiotto*, Low L. *gluto*, a glutton; Heb. Ch. לעט. [See Ar. غلط.] Class Ld. No. 17. The sense is to crowd, to stuff.]

1. To swallow, or to swallow greedily; to gorge. *Milton.*

2. To cloy; to fill beyond sufficiency; to sate; to disgust; as, to *glut* the appetites. *Denham.*

3. To feast or delight even to satiety.

His faithful heart, a bloody sacrifice,
Torn from his breast, to *glut* the tyrant's eyes. *Dryden.*

4. To fill or furnish beyond sufficiency; as, to *glut* the market.

5. To saturate. *Boyle.*

GLUT, *n.* That which is swallowed. *Milton.*

2. Plenty even to lothing.

He shall find himself miserable, even in the very *glut* of his delights. *L'Estrange.*

A *glut* of study and retirement. *Pope.*

3. More than enough; superabundance. *B. Jonson.*

4. Any thing that fills or obstructs the passage. *Woodward.*

5. A wooden wedge. *New England.*

GLU'TEAL, *a.* [Gr. γλουτος, nates.] The *gluteal artery*, is a branch of the hypogastric or internal iliac artery, which supplies the gluteal muscles. *Coxe. Hooper.*

The *gluteal muscles*, are three large muscles on each side, which make up the fleshy part of the buttocks. *Parr.*

GLUTEN, *n.* [L. See *Glue.*] A tough elastic substance, of a grayish color, which becomes brown and brittle by drying; found in the flour of wheat and other grain. It contributes much to the nutritive quality of flour, and gives tenacity to its paste. A similar substance is found in the juices of certain plants. *Webster's Manual.*

2. That part of the blood which gives firmness to its texture. *Parr.*

GLU'TINATE, *v. t.* To unite with glue; to cement. *Bailey.*

GLUTINA'TION, *n.* The act of uniting with glue. *Bailey.*

GLU'TINATIVE, *a.* Having the quality of cementing; tenacious.

GLUTINOS'ITY, *n.* The quality of being glutinous; viscousness.

GLU'TINOUS, *n.* [L. *glutinosus.*] Viscous; viscid; tenacious; having the quality of glue; resembling glue. Starch is *glutinous.*

2. In *botany*, besmeared with a slippery moisture; as a *glutinous* leaf. *Martyn.*

GLU'TINOUSNESS, *n.* Viscosity; viscidity; the quality of glue, tenacity. *Cheyne.*

GLUT'TON, *n.* glut'n. [Low L. *gluto*; Fr. *glouton.* See *Glut.*] One who indulges to excess in eating.

2. One eager of any thing to excess.

Gluttons in murder, wanton to destroy. *Granville.*

3. In *zoology*, an animal of the genus Ursus, found in the N. of Europe and Siberia. It grows to the length of three feet, but has short legs and moves slowly. It is a carnivorous animal, and in order to catch its prey, it climbs a tree and from that darts down upon a deer or other animal. It is named from its voracious appetite. *Dict. Nat. Hist.*

GLUT'TONIZE, *v. i.* To eat to excess; to eat voraciously; to indulge the appetite to excess; to be luxurious. *Trans. of Grellman.*

GLUT'TONOUS, *a.* Given to excessive eating; indulging the appetite for food to excess; as a *gluttonous* age. *Raleigh.*

2. Consisting in excessive eating; as *gluttonous* delight. *Milton.*

GLUT'TONOUSLY, *adv.* With the voracity of a glutton; with excessive eating.

GLUT'TONY, *n.* Excess in eating; extravagant indulgence of the appetite for food.

2. Luxury of the table.

Their sumptuous *gluttonies* and gorgeous feasts. *Milton.*

3. Voracity of appetite. *Encyc.*

GLYCO'NIAN, **GLYCON'IC**, } *a.* [Low L. *glyconium.*] Denoting a kind of verse in Greek and Latin poetry, consisting of three feet, a spondee, a choriamb, and a pyrrhich; as *Glyconic* measure. *Johnson.*

GLYN. [See *Glen.*]

GLYPH, *n.* [Gr. γλυφη, from γλυφω, to carve.]

In *sculpture* and *architecture*, a canal, channel or cavity intended as an ornament. *Chambers.*

GLYPH'IC, *n.* A picture or figure by which a word is implied. [See *Hieroglyphic.*]

GLYP'TIC, *n.* [supra.] The art of engraving figures on precious stones.

GLYPTOGRAPH'IC, *a.* [Gr. γλυπτος, and γραφω.]

Describing the methods of engraving on precious stones.

GLYPTOG'RAPHY, *n.* [supra.] A description of the art of engraving on precious stones. *British Critic.*

GN'AR, **GN'ARL**, } *v. i.* n'ar. n'arl. } [Sax. *gnyrran*, *gnornian*; Dan. *knurrer*; Sw. *knarra*; D. *gnorren*, *knorren*; G. *gnurren*, *knarren.*] To growl; to murmur; to snarl.

And wolves are *gnarling* which shall gnaw thee first. *Shak.*

[*Gnar* is nearly obsolete.]

GN'ARLED, *a.* n'arled. Knotty; full of knots; as the *gnarled* oak. *Shak.*

GNASH, *v. t.* nash. [Dan. *knasker*; Sw. *gnissla* and *knastra.* Qu. D. *knarzen*, G. *knirrschen*, to gnash, and It. *ganascia*, the jaw.]

To strike the teeth together, as in anger or pain; as, to *gnash* the teeth in rage. *Dryden.*

GNASH, *v. i.* nash. To grind the teeth.

He shall *gnash* with his teeth and melt away. Ps. cxii.

2. To rage even to collision with the teeth; to growl.

They *gnashed* on me with their teeth. Ps. xxxv.

GNASH'ING, *ppr.* nash'ing. Striking the teeth together, as in anger, rage or pain.

GNASH'ING, *n. nash'ing.* A grinding or striking of the teeth in rage or anguish.

There shall be weeping and *gnashing* of teeth. Matt. viii.

GNAT, *n. nat.* [Sax. *gnæt.* Qu. Gr. κωνωψ.] A small insect, or rather a genus of insects, the Culex, whose long cylindric body is composed of eight rings. They have six legs and their mouth is formed by a flexible sheath, inclosing bristles pointed like stings. The sting is a tube containing five or six spicula of exquisite fineness, dentated or edged. The most troublesome of this genus is the musketoe. *Encyc. Cyc.*

2. Any thing proverbially small.

Ye blind guides, who strain at a *gnat,* and swallow a camel. Matt. xxiii.

GNAT'FLOWER, *n.* A flower, called also bee-flower. *Johnson.*

GNAT'SNAPPER, *n.* A bird that catches gnats. *Hakewill.*

GNAT'WŎRM, *n.* A small water insect produced by a gnat, and which after its several changes is transformed into a gnat; the larva of a gnat. *Cyc.*

GNAW, *v. t. naw.* [Sax. *gnagan;* G. *nagen;* D. *knaagen;* Sw. *gnaga;* W. *cnoi;* Gr. κναω, to scrape; Ir. *cnagh, cnaoi,* consumption; *cnuigh,* a maggot; *cnaoidhim,* to gnaw, to consume.]

1. To bite off by little and little; to bite or scrape off with the fore teeth; to wear away by biting. The rats *gnaw* a board or plank; a worm *gnaws* the wood of a tree or the plank of a ship.

2. To eat by biting off small portions of food with the fore teeth.

3. To bite in agony or rage.

They *gnawed* their tongues for pain. Rev. xvi.

4. To waste; to fret; to corrode.

5. To pick with the teeth.

His bones clean picked; his very bones they *gnaw.* *Dryden.*

GNAW, *v. i. naw.* To use the teeth in biting.

I might well, like the spaniel, *gnaw* upon the chain that ties me. *Sidney.*

GNAW'ED, *pp. naw'ed.* Bit; corroded.

GNAW'ER, *n. naw'er.* He or that which gnaws or corrodes.

GNAW'ING, *ppr. naw'ing.* Biting off by little and little; corroding; eating by slow degrees.

GNE'ISS, *n. ne'is.* [Qu. Dan. *gnister,* Sw. *gnistas,* to sparkle.]

In *mineralogy,* a species of aggregated rock, composed of quartz, feldspar and mica, of a structure more or less distinctly slaty. The layers, whether straight or curved, are frequently thick, but often vary considerably in the same specimen. It passes on one side into granite, from which it differs in its slaty structure, and on the other into mica slate. It is rich in metallic ores. *Kirwan. Cleaveland.*

GNOFF, *n. nof.* A miser. [*Not in use.*]

GNOME, *n. nome.* [Gr. γνωμη.] An imaginary being, supposed by the cabalists, to inhabit the inner parts of the earth, and to be the guardian of mines, quarries, &c. *Encyc.*

2. A brief reflection or maxim. [*Not used.*]

GNO'MICAL, *a. nomical.* [Gr. γνωμη.] Sententious; containing maxims. [*Little used.*]

GNOMIOMET'RICAL, *a.* [Gr. γνωμων, an index, and μετρεω, to measure.]

The *gnomiometrical* telescope and microscope is an instrument for measuring the angles of crystals by reflection, and for ascertaining the inclination of strata, and the apparent magnitude of angles when the eye is not placed at the vertex. *Brewster.*

GNOMOLOG'IC, } *a.* Pertaining to gnomology.
GNOMOLOG'ICAL, }

GNOMOL'OGY, *n.* [Gr. γνωμη, a maxim or sentence, and λογος, discourse.]

A collection of maxims, grave sentences or reflections. [*Little used.*] *Milton.*

GNO'MON, *n. no'mon.* [Gr. γνωμων, an index, from the root of γινωσκω, to know.]

1. In *dialling,* the style or pin, which by its shadow shows the hour of the day. It represents the axis of the earth. *Encyc.*

2. In *astronomy,* a style erected perpendicular to the horizon, in order to find the altitude of the sun. *Encyc.*

3. The *gnomon* of a globe, is the index of the hour-circle. *Encyc.*

GNOMON'IC, } *a.* Pertaining to the art of dialling.
GNOMON'ICAL, } *Chambers.*

GNOMON'ICS, *n.* The art or science of dialling, or of constructing dials to show the hour of the day by the shadow of a gnomon.

GNOS'TIC, *n. nostic.* [L. *gnosticus;* Gr. γνωςικος, from γινωσκω, to know.]

The Gnostics were a sect of philosophers that arose in the first ages of christianity, who pretended they were the only men who had a true knowledge of the christian religion. They formed for themselves a system of theology, agreeable to the philosophy of Pythagoras and Plato, to which they accommodated their interpretations of scripture. They held that all natures, intelligible, intellectual and material, are derived by successive emanations from the infinite fountain of deity. These emanations they called *æons,* αιωνες. These doctrines were derived from the oriental philosophy. *Encyc. Enfield.*

GNOS'TIC, *a. nostic.* Pertaining to the Gnostics or their doctrines.

GNOS'TICISM, *n. nos'ticism.* The doctrines, principles or system of philosophy taught by the Gnostics. *Enfield.*

GNU, *n.* A species of Antelope, in Southern Africa, whose form partakes of that of the horse, the ox, and the deer.

GO, *v. i.* pret. *went;* pp. *gone.* *Went* belongs to the root, Sax. *wendan,* a different word. [Sax. *gan;* G. *gehen;* Dan. *gaaer;* Sw. *gå;* D. *gaan;* Basque, *gan.* This is probably a contracted word, but the original is obscure. In Goth. *gaggan,* to go, seems to be the Eng. *gang;* and *gad* may belong to a different family. The primary sense is to pass, and either to *go* or *come.* Sax. *ga forth,* go forth; *ga hither,* come hither; *her gœth,* he comes.]

1. In *a general sense,* to move; to pass; to proceed from one place, state or station to another; *opposed to resting.* A mill *goes* by water or by steam; a ship *goes* at the rate of five knots an hour; a clock *goes* fast or slow; a horse *goes* lame; a fowl or a ball *goes* with velocity through the air.

The mourners *go* about the streets. Eccles. xii.

2. To walk; to move on the feet or step by step. The child begins to *go* alone at a year old.

You know that love
Will creep in service where it cannot *go.* *Shak.*

3. To walk leisurely; not to run.

Thou must run to him; for thou hast staid so long that *going* will scarce serve the turn. *Shak.*

4. To travel; to journey by land or water. I must *go* to Boston. He has *gone* to Philadelphia. The minister is *going* to France.

5. To depart; to move from a place; opposed to *come.* The mail *goes* and comes every day, or twice a week.

I will let you *go,* that ye may sacrifice. Ex. viii.

6. To proceed; to pass.

And so the jest *goes* round. *Dryden.*

7. To move; to pass in any manner or to any end; as, to *go* to bed; to *go* to dinner; to *go* to war.

8. To move or pass customarily from place to place, denoting custom or practice. The child *goes* to school. A ship *goes* regularly to London. We *go* to church.

9. To proceed from one state or opinion to another; to change. He *goes* from one opinion to another. His estate is *going* to ruin.

10. To proceed in mental operations; to advance; to penetrate. We can *go* but a very little way in developing the causes of things.

11. To proceed or advance in accomplishing an end. This sum will not *go* far towards full payment of the debt.

12. To apply; to be applicable. The argument *goes* to this point only; it *goes* to prove too much.

13. To apply one's self.

Seeing himself confronted by so many, like a resolute orator, he *went* not to denial, but to justify his cruel falsehood. *Sidney.*

14. To have recourse to; as, to *go* to law.

15. To be about to do; as, I was *going* to say. I am *going* to begin harvest. [This use is chiefly confined to the participle.]

16. To pass; to be accounted in value. All this *goes* for nothing. This coin *goes* for a crown.

17. To circulate; to pass in report. The story *goes.*

18. To pass; to be received; to be accounted or understood to be.

And the man *went* among men for an old man in the days of Saul. 1 Sam. xvii.

19. To move, or be in motion; as a machine. [See No. 1.]

20. To move as a fluid; to flow.

The god I am, whose yellow water flows
Around these fields, and fattens as it *goes,*
Tiber my name. *Dryden.*

21. To have a tendency.

Against right reason all your counsels *go.* *Dryden.*

22. To be in compact or partnership.

They were to *go* equal shares in the booty. *L'Estrange.*

23. To be guided or regulated; to proceed by some principle or rule. We are to *go* by the rules of law, or according to the precepts of scripture.

We are to *go* by another measure. *Sprat.*

24. To be pregnant. The females of different animals *go* some a longer, some a shorter time.

25. To pass; to be alienated in payment or exchange. If our exports are of less value than our imports, our money must *go* to pay the balance.
26. To be loosed or released; to be freed from restraint. Let me *go;* let *go* the hand.
27. To be expended. His estate *goes* or has *gone* for spirituous liquors. [See No. 24.]
28. To extend; to reach. The line *goes* from one end to the other. His land *goes* to the bank of the Hudson.
29. To extend or lead in any direction. This road *goes* to Albany.
30. To proceed; to extend. This argument *goes* far towards proving the point. It *goes* a great way towards establishing the innocence of the accused.
31. To have effect; to extend in effect; to avail; to be of force or value. Money *goes* farther now than it did during the war.
32. To extend in meaning or purport.

His amorous expressions *go* no further than virtue may allow. *Dryden.*

[In the three last examples, the sense of *go* depends on *far, farther, further.*]

33. To have a currency or use, as custom, opinion or manners.

I think, as the world *goes,* he was a good sort of man enough. *Arbuthnot.*

34. To contribute; to conduce; to concur; to be an ingredient; with *to* or *into.* The substances which *go into* this composition. Many qualifications *go to* make up the well bred man.
35. To proceed; to be carried on. The business *goes* on well.
36. To proceed to final issue; to terminate; to succeed.

Whether the cause *goes* for me or against me, you must pay me the reward. *Watts.*

37. To proceed in a train, or in consequences.

How *goes* the night, boy? *Shak.*

38. To fare; to be in a good or ill state. How *goes* it, comrade?
39. To have a tendency or effect; to operate.

These cases *go* to show that the court will vary the construction of instruments. *Mass. Reports.*

To go about, to set one's self to a business; to attempt; to endeavor.

They never *go about* to hide or palliate their vices. *Swift.*

2. In *seaman's language,* to tack; to turn the head of a ship.

To go abroad, to walk out of a house.
2. To be uttered, disclosed or published.

To go against, to invade; to march to attack.
2. To be in opposition; to be disagreeable.

To go aside, to withdraw; to retire into a private situation.
2. To err; to deviate from the right way.

To go astray, to wander; to break from an inclosure; also, to leave the right course; to depart from law or rule; to sin; to transgress.

To go away, to depart; to go to a distance.

To go between, to interpose; to mediate; to attempt to reconcile or to adjust differences.

To go by, to pass near and beyond.
2. To pass away unnoticed; to omit.
3. To find or get in the conclusion.

In argument with men, a woman ever
Goes by the worse, whatever be her cause. *Milton.*

[A phrase now little used.]

To go down, to descend in any manner.
2. To fail; to come to nothing.
3. To be swallowed or received, not rejected. The doctrine of the divine right of kings will not *go down* in this period of the world.

To go forth, to issue or depart out of a place.

To go forward, to advance.

To go hard with, to be in danger of a fatal issue; to have difficulty to escape.

To go in, to enter.

To go in to, to have sexual commerce with. *Scripture.*

To go in and out, to do the business of life.
2. To go freely; to be at liberty. John x.

To go off, to depart to a distance; to leave a place or station.
2. To die; to decease.
3. To be discharged, as fire arms; to explode.

To go on, to proceed; to advance forward.
2. To be put on, as a garment. The coat will not *go on.*

To go out, to issue forth; to depart from.
2. To go on an expedition. *Shak.*
3. To become extinct, as light or life; to expire. A candle *goes out;* fire *goes out.*

And life itself *goes out* at thy displeasure. *Addison.*

4. To become public. This story *goes out* to the world.

To go over, to read; to peruse; to study.
2. To examine; to view or review; as, to *go over* an account.

If we *go over* the laws of christianity— *Tillotson.*

3. To think over; to proceed or pass in mental operation.
4. To change sides; to pass from one party to another.
5. To revolt.
6. To pass from one side to the other, as of a river.

To go through, to pass in a substance; as, to *go through* water.
2. To execute; to accomplish; to perform thoroughly; to finish; as, to *go through* an undertaking.
3. To suffer; to bear; to undergo; to sustain to the end; as, to *go through* a long sickness; to *go through* an operation.

To go through with, to execute effectually.

To go under, to be talked of or known, as by a title or name; as, to *go under* the name of reformers.

To go up, to ascend; to rise.

To go upon, to proceed as on a foundation; to take as a principle supposed or settled; as, to *go upon* a supposition.

To go with, to accompany; to pass with others.
2. To side with; to be in party or design with.

To go ill with, to have ill fortune; not to prosper.

To go well with, to have good fortune; to prosper.

To go without, to be or remain destitute.

Go to, come, move, begin; *a phrase of exhortation;* also a phrase of scornful exhortation.

GO′-BETWEEN, *n.* [*go* and *between.*] An interposer; one who transacts business between parties. *Shak.*

GO′-BY, [*go* and *by.*] Evasion; escape by artifice. *Collier.*
2. A passing without notice; a thrusting away; a shifting off.

GO′-CART, *n.* [*go* and *cart.*] A machine with wheels, in which children learn to walk without danger of falling.

GŌAD, *n.* [Sax. *gad,* a goad; Sw. *gadd,* a sting; Scot. *gad,* a goad, a rod, the point of a spear; Ir. *gath, goth,* a goad; W. *goth,* a push. The sense is a shoot, a point.]

A pointed instrument used to stimulate a beast to move faster.

GŌAD, *v. t.* To prick; to drive with a goad.
2. To incite; to stimulate; to instigate; to urge forward, or to rouse by any thing pungent, severe, irritating or inflaming. He was *goaded* by sarcastic remarks or by abuse; *goaded* by desire or other passion.

GŌADED, *pp.* Pricked; pushed on by a goad; instigated.

GŌADING, *ppr.* Pricking; driving with a goad; inciting; urging on; rousing.

GŌAL, *n.* [Fr. *gaule,* a long pole; W. *gwyal;* Arm. *goalenn,* a staff.]
1. The point set to bound a race, and to which they run; the mark.

Part curb their fiery steeds, or shun the *goal*
With rapid wheels. *Milton.*

2. Any starting post. *Milton.*
3. The end or final purpose; the end to which a design tends, or which a person aims to reach or accomplish.

Each individual seeks a several *goal.* *Pope.*

GŌAR, *n.* More usually *gore,* which see.

GŌARISH, *a.* Patched; mean. *Obs.* *Beaum.*

GŌAT, *n.* [Sax. *gæt;* D. *geit;* G. *geiss;* Sw. *get;* Dan. *gedebuk,* a he-goat; Russ. *koza.*]

An animal or quadruped of the genus Capra. The horns are hollow, turned upwards, erect and scabrous. Goats are nearly of the size of sheep, but stronger, less timid and more agile. They delight to frequent rocks and mountains, and subsist on scanty coarse food. The milk of the goat is sweet, nourishing and medicinal, and the flesh furnishes provisions to the inhabitants of countries where they abound.

GŌAT-CHAFFER, *n.* An insect, a kind of beetle. *Bailey.*

GŌATFISH, *n.* A fish of the Mediterranean.

GŌATHERD, *n.* One whose occupation is to tend goats. *Spenser.*

GŌATISH, *a.* Resembling a goat in any quality; of a rank smell. *More.*
2. Lustful. *Shak.*

GŌAT-MILKER, *n.* A kind of owl, so called from sucking goats. *Bailey.*

GŌAT'S-BEARD, *n.* In *botany,* a plant of the genus Tragopogon.

GŌATSKIN, *n.* The skin of a goat. *Pope.*

GŌAT'S-RUE, *n.* A plant of the genus Galega.

GŌAT'S-STONES, *n.* The *greater goat's stones* is the Satyrium; the *lesser,* the Orchis.

GŌAT'S-THORN, *n.* A plant of the genus Astragalus.

GŌAT-SUCKER, *n.* In *ornithology,* a fowl of the genus Caprimulgus, so called from the opinion that it would suck goats. It is called also the fern-owl. In Bailey, it is called a goat-milker.

GOB, *n.* [Fr. *gobe;* W. *gob*, a heap. Qu. Heb. גב a hill, a boss; Ch. גבא geba, to raise.]

A little mass or collection; a mouthful. [*A low word.*] *L'Estrange.*

GOB'BET, *n.* [Fr. *gobe*, supra.] A mouthful; a lump. *Shak. Addison.*

GOB'BET, *v. t.* To swallow in large masses or mouthfuls. [*A low word.*] *L'Estrange.*

GOB'BLE, *v. t.* [Fr. *gober*, to swallow.] To swallow in large pieces; to swallow hastily. *Prior. Swift.*

GOB'BLE, *v. i.* To make a noise in the throat, as a turkey. *Prior.*

GOB'BLER, *n.* One who swallows in haste; a greedy eater; a gormandizer.

2. A name sometimes given to the turkey cock.

GOB'LET, *n.* [Fr. *gobelet;* Arm. *gob* or *gobeled;* Heb. גביע.]

A kind of cup or drinking vessel without a handle.

We love not loaded boards, and *goblets* crown'd. *Denham.*

GOB'LIN, *n.* [Fr. *gobelin;* G. *kobold*, a goblin; D. *kabouter*, a boy, an elf; *kaboutermanneltje*, a goblin; Arm. *gobylin;* W. *coblyn*, a knocker, a thumper, a pecker, a fiend; *cobiaw*, to knock; from *cob*, a top, a thump.]

1. An evil spirit; a walking spirit; a frightful phantom.

To whom the *goblin*, full of wrath, replied. *Milton.*

2. A fairy; an elf. *Shak.*

GOD, *n.* [Sax. *god;* G. *gott;* D. *god;* Sw. and Dan. *gud;* Goth. *goth* or *guth;* Pers. خدا goda or choda; Hindoo, *khoda*, *codam*. As this word and *good* are written exactly alike in Saxon, it has been inferred that *God* was named from his *goodness*. But the corresponding words in most of the other languages, are not the same, and I believe no instance can be found of a name given to the Supreme Being from the attribute of goodness. It is probably an idea too remote from the rude conceptions of men in early ages. Except the word Jehovah, I have found the name of the Supreme Being to be usually taken from his supremacy or power, and to be equivalent to lord or ruler, from some root signifying to press or exert force. Now in the present case, we have evidence that this is the sense of this word, for in Persic *goda* is rendered *dominus, possessor, princeps*, as is a derivative of the same word. See Cast. Lex. Col. 231.]

1. The Supreme Being; Jehovah; the eternal and infinite spirit, the creator, and the sovereign of the universe.

God is a spirit; and they that worship him, must worship him in spirit and in truth. John iv.

2. A false god; a heathen deity; an idol.

Fear not the *gods* of the Amorites. Judges vi.

3. A prince; a ruler; a magistrate or judge; an angel. Thou shalt not revile the *gods*, nor curse the ruler of thy people. Ex. xxii. Ps. xcvii.

[*Gods* here is a bad translation.]

4. Any person or thing exalted too much in estimation, or deified and honored as the chief good.

Whose *god* is their belly. Phil. iii.

GOD, *v. t.* To deify. [*Not used.*] *Shak.*

GOD'CHILD, *n.* [*god* and *child.*] One for whom a person becomes sponsor at baptism, and promises to see educated as a christian.

GOD'DAUGHTER, *n.* [*god* and *daughter.*] A female for whom one becomes sponsor at baptism. [See *Godfather.*]

GOD'DESS, *n.* A female deity; a heathen deity of the female sex.

When the daughter of Jupiter presented herself among a crowd of *goddesses*, she was distinguished by her graceful stature and superior beauty. *Addison.*

2. In *the language of love*, a woman of superior charms or excellence.

GOD'DESSLIKE, *a.* Resembling a goddess. *Pope.*

GOD'FATHER, *n.* [Sax. *god* and *fæder.* The Saxons used also *godsibb*, good relation.]

The man who is sponsor for a child at baptism, who promises to answer for his future conduct and that he shall follow a life of piety, by this means laying himself under an indispensable obligation to instruct the child and watch over his conduct. This practice is of high antiquity in the christian church, and was probably intended to prevent children from being brought up in idolatry, in case the parents died before the children had arrived to years of discretion. In the catholic church the number of godfathers and godmothers is reduced to two; in the church of England, to three; but formerly the number was not limited. *Encyc.*

GOD'FATHER, *v. t.* To act as godfather; to take under one's fostering care. *Burke.*

GOD'HEAD, *n.* god'hed. [*god* and Sax. *hade*, state.]

1. Godship; deity; divinity; divine nature or essence; *applied to the true God, and to heathen deities.* *Milton. Prior.*

2. A deity in person; a god or goddess. *Dryden.*

GOD'LESS, *a.* Having no reverence for God; impious; ungodly; irreligious; wicked. *Hooker.*

2. Atheistical; having no belief in the existence of God. *Milton.*

GOD'LESSNESS, *n.* The state of being impious or irreligious. *Bp. Hall.*

GOD'LIKE, *a.* Resembling God; divine.

2. Resembling a deity, or heathen divinity.

3. Of superior excellence; as *godlike* virtue; a *godlike* prince.

GOD'LILY, *adv.* Piously; righteously. *H. Wharton.*

GOD'LINESS, *n.* [from *godly.*] Piety; belief in God, and reverence for his character and laws.

2. A religious life; a careful observance of the laws of God and performance of religious duties, proceeding from love and reverence for the divine character and commands; christian obedience.

Godliness is profitable unto all things. 1 Tim. iv.

3. Revelation; the system of christianity.

Without controversy, great is the mystery of *godliness;* God was manifest in the flesh. 1 Tim. iii.

GOD'LING, *n.* A little deity; a diminutive god; as a puny *godling.* *Dryden.*

GOD'LY, *a.* [*god-like.*] Pious; reverencing God, and his character and laws.

2. Living in obedience to God's commands, from a principle of love to him and reverence of his character and precepts; religious; righteous; as a *godly* person.

3. Pious; conformed to God's law; as a *godly* life.

GOD'LY, *adv.* Piously; righteously.

All that will live *godly* in Christ Jesus shall suffer persecution. 2 Tim. iii.

GOD'LYHEAD, *n.* [Sax. *god*, good, and *head.*] Goodness. *Obs.* *Spenser.*

GOD'MŎTHER, *n.* [*god* and *mother.*] A woman who becomes sponsor for a child in baptism.

GOD'SHIP, *n.* Deity; divinity; the rank or character of a god.

O'er hills and dales their *godships* came. *Prior*

GOD'SMITH, *n.* A maker of idols. *Dryden.*

GOD'SŎN, *n.* [Sax. *godsunu.*] One for whom another has been sponsor at the font.

GOD SPEED, *n.* Good speed, that is, success. 2 John 10.

GOD'S-PENNY, *n.* An earnest-penny. *Beaum.*

GOD'WARD. Toward God. [*An ill-formed word.*]

GOD'WIT, *n.* [Ice. *god*, and *veide.*] A fowl of the grallic order and genus Scolopax. It has a bill four inches long; the fethers on the head, neck and back are of a light reddish brown; those on the belly white, and the tail is regularly barred with black and white. This fowl frequents fens and the banks of rivers, and its flesh is esteemed a great delicacy. *Encyc.*

GOD'YELD, GOD'YIELD, } *adv.* [Supposed to be contracted from *good* or *god*, and *shield.*]

A term of thanks. *Obs.* *Shak.*

GO'EL, *a.* [Sax. *gealew.*] Yellow. *Obs.* *Tusser.*

GO'ER, *n.* [from *go.*] One that goes; a runner or walker; one that has a gait good or bad. *Wotton.*

2. One that transacts business between parties; *in an ill sense.* *Shak.*

3. A foot. *Chapman.*

4. A term applied to a horse; as a good *goer;* a safe *goer.* [*Unusual in the U. States.*] *Beaum.*

GO'ETY, *n.* [Gr. γοητεια.] Invocation of evil spirits. [*Not in use.*] *Hallywell.*

GOFF, *n.* [Qu. W. *gofol*, contracted, a word composed of *go* and *fŏl*, foolish; or Fr. *goffe;* or a contraction of D. *kolf*, a club.]

A foolish clown; also, a game. *Obs.* [See *Golf.*]

GOFF'ISH, *a.* Foolish; stupid. *Obs.* *Chaucer.*

GOG, *n.* [W. *gog*, activity, rapidity; probably allied to *gig*. See *Agog.*]

Haste; ardent desire to go. *Beaum.*

GOG'GLE, *v. i.* [W. *gogelu*, to shun; *go*, a prefix, and *gelu*, from *cêl*, a shelter, coinciding with L. *celo;* or from *gog.*]

To strain or roll the eyes.

And wink and *goggle* like an owl. *Hudibras.*

GOG'GLE, *a.* Having full eyes; staring. *B. Jonson.*

GOG'GLE, *n.* A strained or affected rolling of the eye.

GOG'GLED, *a.* Prominent; staring, as the eye. *Herbert.*

GOG'GLE-EȲE, *n.* A rolling or staring eye. *B. Jonson.*

GOG'GLE-EȲED, *a.* Having prominent, distorted or rolling eyes. *Ascham.*

GOG'GLES, *n. plu.* [W. *gogelu*, to shelter. See *Goggle*, the verb.]

1. In *surgery*, instruments used to cure squinting, or the distortion of the eyes which occasions it. *Encyc.*
2. Cylindrical tubes, in which are fixed glasses for defending the eyes from cold, dust, &c. and sometimes with colored glasses to abate the intensity of light.
3. Blinds for horses that are apt to take fright.

GO'ING, *ppr.* [from *go.*] Moving; walking; traveling; turning; rolling; flying; sailing, &c.

GO'ING, *n.* The act of moving in any manner.

2. The act of walking. *Shak.*
3. Departure. *Milton.*
4. Pregnancy. *Grew.*
5. Procedure; way; course of life; behavior; deportment; used chiefly in the plural.

His eyes are on the ways of man, and he seeeth all his *goings*. Job xxxiv.

6. Procedure; course of providential agency or government.

They have seen thy *goings*, O God; even the *goings* of my God, my King, in the sanctuary. Ps. lxviii.

Going out, } in *scripture*, utmost extremity
Goings out, } or limit; the point where an extended body terminates. Num. xxxiv. 5. 9.

2. Departure or journeying. Num. xxxiii.

GOIT'ER, *n.* [Fr. *goître.*] The bronchocele; a large tumor that forms gradually on the human throat between the trachea and the skin. *Encyc.*

The inhabitants of this part of the Valais are subject to *goiters*. *Coxe, Switz.*

GOIT'ROUS, *a.* [Fr. *goîtreux.*] Pertaining to the goiter; partaking of the nature of bronchocele.

2. Affected with bronchocele. *Journ. of Science.*

Let me not be understood as insinuating that the inhabitants in general are either *goitrous* or idiots. *Coxe, Switz.*

GO'LA, *n.* In *architecture*, the same as *cymatium.*

GŌLD, *n.* [Sax. G. *gold*; D. *goud*, a contracted word; Sw. and Dan. *guld*, from *gul*, *guul*, yellow. Hence the original pronunciation *goold*, still retained by some people. The Dan. *guul* is in Sax. *gealew*, whence our *yellow*, that is, primarily, *bright*, from the Celtic, W. *gawl*, *galau*, *gole*, light, splendor; Gaelic, *geal*, bright; Ar. جَلَا to be clear or bright. Class Gl. No. 7.]

1. A precious metal of a bright yellow color, and the most ductile and malleable of all the metals. It is the heaviest metal except platina; and being a very dense, fixed substance, and not liable to be injured by air, it is well fitted to be used as coin, or a representative of commodities in commerce. Its ductility and malleability render it the most suitable metal for gilding. It is often found native in solid masses, as in Hungary and Peru; though generally in combination with silver, copper or iron. *Encyc.*
2. Money.

For me, the *gold* of France did not seduce— *Shak.*

3. Something pleasing or valuable; as a heart of *gold*. *Shak.*
4. A bright yellow color; as a flower edged with *gold*.
5. Riches; wealth.

Gold of pleasure, a plant of the genus Myagrum.

GŌLD, *a.* Made of gold; consisting of gold; as a *gold* chain.

GŌLDBEATEN, *a.* Gilded. [*Little used.*]

GŌLDBEATER, *n.* One whose occupation is to beat or foliate gold for gilding. *Boyle.*

Goldbeater's skin, the intestinum rectum of an ox, which goldbeaters lay between the leaves of the metal while they beat it, whereby the membrane is reduced very thin, and made fit to be applied to cuts and fresh wounds. *Quincy.*

GŌLDBOUND, *a.* Encompassed with gold. *Shak.*

GŌLD COAST, *n.* In *geography*, the coast of Africa where gold is found; being a part of the coast of Guinea.

GŌLDEN, *a.* *gōldn.* Made of gold; consisting of gold.

2. Bright; shining; splendid; as the *golden* sun.

Reclining soft on many a *golden* cloud. *Rowe.*

3. Yellow; of a gold color; as a *golden* harvest; *golden* fruit.
4. Excellent; most valuable; as the *golden* rule. *Watts.*
5. Happy; pure; as the *golden* age, the age of simplicity and purity of manners.
6. Preeminently favorable or auspicious.

Let not slip the *golden* opportunity. *Hamilton.*

Golden number, in *chronology*, a number showing the year of the moon's cycle.

Golden rule, in *arithmetic*, the rule of three or rule of proportion.

GŌLDEN-CUPS, *n.* A plant, the Ranunculus.

GŌLDEN-LUNGWŌRT, *n.* A plant of the genus Hieracium.

GŌLDENLY, *adv.* Splendidly; delightfully. [*Not used.*] *Shak.*

GŌLDEN-MAIDENHAIR, *n.* A plant of the genus Polytrichum.

GŌLDEN-MOUSEEAR, *n.* A plant of the genus Hieracium.

GŌLDENROD, *n.* A plant, the Solidago.

GŌLDENROD-TREE, *n.* A plant, the Bosea.

GŌLDEN-SAM'PHIRE, *n.* A plant, the Inula crithmifolia. *Lee.*

GŌLDEN-SAX'IFRAGE, *n.* A plant, the Chrysosplenium.

GŌLDEN-THISTLE, *n.* A plant of the genus Scolymus.

GŌLDFINCH, *n.* [Sax. *goldfinc.*] The *Fringilla carduelis*, a bird so named from the color of its wings.

GŌLD-FINDER, *n.* One who finds gold; one who empties jakes. [*Not much used.*] *Swift.*

GŌLDFISH, } *n.* A fish of the genus Cy-
GŌLDENFISH, } prinus, of the size of a pilchard, so named from its bright color. These fishes are bred by the Chinese, in small ponds, in basons or porcelain vessels, and kept for ornament.

GŌLD-HAMMER, *n.* A kind of bird. *Dict.*

GŌLD-HILTED, *a.* Having a golden hilt.

GŌLDING, *n.* A sort of apple. *Dict.*

GŌLDLACE, *n.* A lace wrought with gold.

GŌLDLACED, *a.* Trimmed with gold lace.

GŌLDLEAF, *n.* Gold foliated or beaten into a thin leaf.

GŌLDNEY, *n.* A fish, the gilthead. *Dict.*

GŌLD-PLEASURE, for *gold of pleasure*, a plant of the genus Myagrum.

GŌLD-PROOF, *a.* Proof against bribery or temptation by money. *Beaum.*

GŌLD-SIZE, *n.* A size or glue for burnishing gilding. *Encyc.*

GŌLDSMITH, *n.* An artisan who manufactures vessels and ornaments of gold and silver.

2. A banker; one who manages the pecuniary concerns of others. [*Goldsmiths* were formerly bankers in England, but in America the practice does not exist, nor is the word used in this sense.]

GŌLDTHREAD, *n.* A thread formed of flatted gold laid over a thread of silk, by twisting it with a wheel and iron bobbins. *Encyc.*

2. A plant, the *Helleborus trifolius*; so called from its fibrous yellow roots. *U. States.*

GŌLDWIRE, *n.* An ingot of silver, superficially covered with gold and drawn through small round holes. *Encyc.*

GŌLDYLOCKS, *n.* A name given to certain plants of the genera Chrysocoma and Gnaphalium.

GOLF, *n.* [D. *kolf*, a club or bat; Dan. *kolv*, the butt end of a gun-stock.]

A game with ball and bat, in which he who drives the ball into a hole with the fewest strokes is the winner. *Strutt.*

GOLL, *n.* [Gr. *γυαλον*, a cavity, and the hollow of the hand. Qu. is this the Celtic form of *vola*?]

Hands; paws; claws. [*Not in use or local.*] *Sidney.*

GOLO'E-SHŌE, *n.* [Arm. *golo* or *golei*, to cover.]

An over-shoe; a shoe worn over another to keep the foot dry.

GOM, *n.* [Sax. *gum*; Goth. *guma.*] A man. *Obs.*

GON'DOLA, *n.* [It. *id.*; Fr. *gondole*; Arm. *gondolenn.*]

A flat-bottomed boat, very long and narrow, used at Venice in Italy on the canals. A gondola of middle size is about thirty feet long and four broad, terminating at each end in a sharp point or peak rising to the highth of a man. It is usually rowed by two men, called *gondoliers*, who propel the boat by pushing the oars. The gondola is also used in other parts of Italy for a passage boat. *Encyc.*

GONDOLIE'R, *n.* A man who rows a gondola.

GONE, *pp.* of *go*; pronounced nearly *gawn.*

1. Departed.

It was told Solomon that Shimei had *gone* from Jerusalem to Gath. 1 Kings ii.

2. Advanced; forward in progress; with *far*, *farther*, or *further*; as a man *far gone* in intemperance.

3. Ruined; undone. Exert yourselves, or we are *gone*.

4. Past; as, these happy days are *gone*; sometimes with *by*. Those times are *gone by*.

5. Lost.

When her masters saw that the hope of their gains was *gone*— Acts xvi.

6. Departed from life; deceased; dead.

GON'FALON, } *n.* [*gonfanon*, Chaucer;
GON'FANON, } Fr. *gonfalon*; Sax. *guth-fana*, war-flag, composed of *guth*, war, Ir. *cath* or *cad*, W. *cad*, and Sax. and Goth. *fana*, L. *pannus*, cloth; in Sax. a flag.]

An ensign or standard; colors. *Obs.* *Milton.*

GONFALONIE'R, *n.* A chief standard-bearer. *Obs.* *Bp. Wren.*

GONG, *n.* [Sax. *gang.*] A privy or jakes. *Obs.* *Chaucer.*

2. An instrument made of brass, of a circular form, which the Asiatics strike with a wooden mallet. *Todd.*

GONIOM'ETER, *n.* [Gr. *γωνια*, angle, and *μετρον*, measure.

An instrument for measuring solid angles, or the inclination of planes. *Cyc.*

GONIOMET'RICAL, *a.* Pertaining to a goniometer. *Goniometrical lines* are used for measuring the quantity of angles. *Chambers.*

GONORRHE'A, *n.* [Gr. *γονος*, semen, and *ρεω*, to flow.] A morbid discharge in venereal complaints.

GOOD, *a.* [Sax. *god* or *good*; Goth. *goda*, *gods*, *goth*; G. *gut*; D. *goed*; Sw. and Dan. *god*; Gr. *αγαθος*; Pers. جود. In Russ. *godnei*, fit, suitable, seems to be the same word. The primary sense is strong, from extending, advancing, whence free, large, abundant, fit, and particularly, strong, firm, valid, [like *valid*, from *valeo*; *worth*, *virtue*, from *vireo*; Sax. *duguth*, virtue, from *dugan*, to be strong.] In the phrase, a *good* deal, we observe the sense of extending; in the phrases, a *good* title, a medicine *good* for a disease, we observe the sense of strong, efficacious. Ar. جاد to be liberal or copious, to overflow, to be good, to become better or more firm. See also جدا to be useful, profitable or convenient. This word *good* has not the comparative and superlative degrees of comparison; but instead of them, *better* and *best*, from another root, are used. Class Gd. No. 3. and 8.]

1. Valid; legally firm; not weak or defective; having strength adequate to its support; as a *good* title; a *good* deed; a *good* claim.

2. Valid; sound; not weak, false or fallacious; as a *good* argument.

3. Complete or sufficiently perfect in its kind; having the physical qualities best adapted to its design and use; opposed to *bad*, *imperfect*, *corrupted*, *impaired*. We say, *good* timber, *good* cloth, a *good* soil, a *good* color.

And God saw every thing that he had made, and behold, it was very *good*. Gen. i.

4. Having moral qualities best adapted to its design and use, or the qualities which God's law requires; virtuous; pious; religious; applied to *persons*, and opposed to *bad*, *vitious*, *wicked*, *evil*.

Yet peradventure for a *good* man some would even dare to die. Rom. v.

5. Conformable to the moral law; virtuous; *applied to actions.*

In all things showing thyself a pattern of *good* works. Tit. ii.

6. Proper; fit; convenient; seasonable; well adapted to the end. It was a *good* time to commence operations. He arrived in *good* time.

7. Convenient; useful; expedient; conducive to happiness.

It is not *good* that the man should be alone. Gen. ii.

8. Sound; perfect; uncorrupted; undamaged. This fruit will keep *good* the whole year.

9. Suitable to the taste or to health; wholesome; salubrious; palatable; not disagreeable or noxious; as fruit *good* to eat; a tree *good* for food. Gen. ii.

10. Suited to produce a salutary effect; adapted to abate or cure; medicinal; salutary; beneficial; as, fresh vegetables are *good* for scorbutic diseases.

11. Suited to strengthen or assist the healthful functions; as, a little wine is *good* for a weak stomach.

12. Pleasant to the taste; as a *good* apple.

My son, eat thou honey, because it is *good*, and the honeycomb, which is sweet to thy taste. Prov. xxiv.

13. Full; complete.

The protestant subjects of the abbey make up a *good* third of its people. *Addison.*

14. Useful; valuable; having qualities or a tendency to produce a good effect.

All quality, that is *good* for any thing, is originally founded on merit. *Collier.*

15. Equal; adequate; competent. His security is *good* for the amount of the debt; applied to *persons* able to fulfill contracts.

Antonio is a *good* man. *Shak.*

16. Favorable; convenient for any purpose; as a *good* stand for business; a *good* station for a camp.

17. Convenient; suitable; safe; as a *good* harbor for ships.

18. Well qualified; able; skillful; or performing duties with skill and fidelity; as a *good* prince; a *good* commander; a *good* officer; a *good* physician.

19. Ready; dextrous.

Those are generally *good* at flattering who are *good* for nothing else. *South.*

20. Kind; benevolent; affectionate; as a *good* father; *good* will.

21. Kind; affectionate; faithful; as a *good* friend.

22. Promotive of happiness; pleasant; agreeable; cheering; gratifying.

Behold, how *good* and how pleasant it is for brethren to dwell together in unity. Ps. cxxxiii.

23. Pleasant or prosperous; as, *good* morrow, Sir; *good* morning.

24. Honorable; fair; unblemished; unimpeached; as a man of *good* fame or report.

A *good* name is better than precious ointment. Eccles. vii.

25. Cheerful; favorable to happiness. Be of *good* comfort.

26. Great or considerable; not small nor very great; as a *good* while ago; he is a *good* way off, or at a *good* distance; he has a *good* deal of leisure; I had a *good* share of the trouble. Here we see the primary sense of *extending*, *advancing*.

27. Elegant; polite; as *good* breeding.

28. Real; serious; not feigned.

Love not in *good* earnest. *Shak.*

29. Kind; favorable; benevolent; humane.

The men were very *good* to us. 1 Sam. xxv.

30. Benevolent; merciful; gracious.

Truly God is *good* to Israel, even to such as are of a clean heart. Ps. lxxiii.

31. Seasonable; commendable; proper.

Why trouble ye the woman, for she hath wrought a *good* work on me. Matt. xxvi.

32. Pleasant; cheerful; festive.

We come in a *good* day. 1 Sam. xxv.

33. Companionable; social; merry.

It is well known, that Sir Roger had been a *good* fellow in his youth. *Arbuthnot.*

34. Brave; *in familiar language.* You are a *good* fellow.

35. In the phrases, the *good* man, applied to the master of the house, and *good* woman, applied to the mistress, *good* sometimes expresses a moderate degree of respect, and sometimes slight contempt. Among the first settlers of New England, it was used as a title instead of Mr.; as *Goodman* Jones; *Goodman* Wells.

36. The phrase *good will* is equivalent to benevolence; but it signifies also an earnest desire, a hearty wish, entire willingness or fervent zeal; as, we entered into the service with a *good will*; he laid on stripes with a *good will.*

37. Comely; handsome; well formed; as a *good* person or shape.

38. Mild; pleasant; expressing benignity or other estimable qualities; as a *good* countenance.

39. Mild; calm; not irritable or fractious; as a *good* temper.

40. Kind; friendly; humane; as a *good* heart or disposition.

Good advice, wise and prudent counsel.

Good heed, great care; due caution.

In good sooth, in good truth; in reality. *Obs.*

To make good, to perform; to fulfill; as, to *make good* one's word or promise; that is, to make it entire or unbroken.

2. To confirm or establish; to prove; to verify; as, to *make good* a charge or accusation.

3. To supply deficiency; to make up a defect or loss. I will *make good* what is wanting.

4. To indemnify; to give an equivalent for damages. If you suffer loss, I will *make* it *good* to you.

5. To maintain; to carry into effect; as, to *make good* a retreat.

To stand good, to be firm or valid. His word or promise *stands good.*

To think good, to see good, is to be pleased or satisfied; to think to be expedient.

If ye *think good*, give me my price Zech. xi.

As good as, equally; no better than; the same as. We say, one is *as good as* dead. Heb. xi.

As good as his word, equaling in fulfillment what was promised; performing to the extent.

GOOD, *n.* That which contributes to diminish or remove pain, or to increase happiness or prosperity; benefit; advantage; opposed to *evil* or *misery*. The medicine will do neither *good* nor harm. It does my heart *good* to see you so happy.

There are many that say, who will show us any *good?* Ps. iv.

2. Welfare; prosperity; advancement of interest or happiness. He labored for the *good* of the state.

The *good* of the whole community can be promoted only by advancing the *good* of each of the members composing it. *Federalist, Jay.*

3. Spiritual advantage or improvement; as the *good* of souls.

4. Earnest; not jest.

The good woman never died after this, till she came to die for *good* and all. *L'Estrange.*

The phrase, for *good* and all, signifies, finally; to close the whole business; for the last time.

5. Moral works; actions which are just and in conformity to the moral law or divine precepts.

Depart from evil, and do *good.* Ps. xxxiv.

6. Moral qualities; virtue; righteousness. I find no *good* in this man.

7. The best fruits; richness; abundance.

I will give you the *good* of the land. Gen. xlv.

GOOD, *v. t.* To manure. [*Not in use.*] *Hall.*

GOOD, *adv.* *As good*, as well; with equal advantage. Had you not *as good* go with me? In America we use *goods*, the Gothic word. Had you not *as goods* go?

In replies, *good* signifies well; right; it is satisfactory; I am satisfied. I will be with you to morrow; answer, *good*, very *good.* So we use *well*, from the root of L. *valeo*, to be strong.

GOOD-BREE′DING, *n.* Polite manners, formed by a good education; a polite education.

GOOD-BY. [See *By.*]

GOOD-CONDI′′TIONED, *a.* Being in a good state; having good qualities or favorable symptoms. *Sharp.*

GOOD-FEL′LOW, *n.* A jolly companion. [*This is hardly to be admitted as a compound word.*]

GOOD-FEL′LOW, *v. t.* To make a jolly companion; to besot. [*Little used.*]

GOOD-FEL′LOWSHIP, *n.* Merry society.

GOOD-FRI′DAY, *n.* A fast of the christian church, in memory of our Savior's sufferings, kept in *passion week.*

GOOD-HU′MOR, *n.* A cheerful temper or state of mind.

GOOD-HU′MORED, *a.* Being of a cheerful temper.

GOOD-HU′MOREDLY, *adv.* With a cheerful temper; in a cheerful way.

GOOD-MAN′NERS, *n.* Propriety of behavior; politeness; decorum.

GOOD-NA′TURE, *n.* Natural mildness and kindness of disposition.

GOOD-NA′TURED, *a.* Naturally mild in temper; not easily provoked.

GOOD-NA′TUREDLY, *adv.* With mildness of temper.

GOOD-NOW. An exclamation of wonder or surprise. *Dryden.*

2. An exclamation of entreaty. [*Not used.*] *Shak.*

GOOD-SPEED, *n.* Good success; *an old form of wishing success.* [See *Speed.*]

GOOD-WIFE, *n.* The mistress of a family. *Burton.*

GOOD-WILL, *n.* Benevolence.

GOOD-WOMAN, *n.* The mistress of a family.

GOOD′LESS, *a.* Having no goods. *Obs.* *Chaucer.*

GOOD′LINESS, *n.* [from *goodly.*] Beauty of form; grace; elegance.

Her *goodliness* was full of harmony to his eyes. *Sidney.*

GOOD′LY, *adv.* Excellently. *Spenser.*

GOOD′LY, *a.* Being of a handsome form; beautiful; graceful; as a *goodly* person; *goodly* raiment; *goodly* houses. *Shak.*

2. Pleasant; agreeable; desirable; as *goodly* days. *Shak.*

3. Bulky; swelling; affectedly turgid. *Obs.* *Dryden.*

GOOD′LYHEAD, *n.* Goodness; grace. [*Not in use.*] *Spenser.*

GOOD′MAN, *n.* A familiar appellation of civility; sometimes used ironically.

With you, *goodman* boy, if you please. *Shak.*

2. A rustic term of compliment; as old *goodman* Dobson. *Swift.*

3. A familiar appellation of a husband; also, the master of a family. Prov. vii. Matt. xxiv.

GOOD′NESS, *n.* The state of being good; the physical qualities which constitute value, excellence or perfection; as the *goodness* of timber; the *goodness* of a soil.

2. The moral qualities which constitute christian excellence; moral virtue; religion.

The fruit of the Spirit is love, joy, peace, long-suffering, gentleness, *goodness*, faith. Gal. v.

3. Kindness; benevolence; benignity of heart; but more generally, acts of kindness; charity; humanity exercised. I shall remember his *goodness* to me with gratitude.

4. Kindness; benevolence of nature; mercy.

The Lord God—abundant in *goodness* and truth. Ex. xxxiv.

5. Kindness; favor shown; acts of benevolence, compassion or mercy.

Jethro rejoiced for all the *goodness* which Jehovah had done to Israel. Ex. xviii.

GOODS, *n. plu.* Movables; household furniture.

2. Personal or movable estate; as horses, cattle, utensils, &c.

3. Wares; merchandize; commodities bought and sold by merchants and traders.

GOOD′SHIP, *n.* Favor; grace. [*Not in use.*]

GOOD′Y, *n.* [Qu. *goodwife.*] A low term of civility; as *goody* Dobson. *Swift. Gay.*

GOOD′YSHIP, *n.* The state or quality of a goody. [*Ludicrous.*] *Hudibras.*

GOOG′INGS, } *n.* In *seamen's language*,
GOOD′INGS, } clamps of iron bolted on the stern-post of a ship, whereon to hang the rudder. *Mar. Dict.*

GOOM, *n.* [Sax. and Goth. *guma*, a man.] A man recently married, or who is attending his proposed spouse for the purpose of marriage; used in composition, as in *bridegoom.* It has been corrupted into *groom.*

GOOS′ANDER, *n.* A migratory fowl of the genus Mergus, the diver or plunger; called also *merganser.*

GOOSE, *n.* *goos.* plu. *geese.* [Sax. *gos*; Sw. *gås*; Dan. *gaas*; Arm. *goas*; W. *gwyz*; Russ. *gus*; Ir. *gedh* or *geadh*; Pers. قاز.

The G. and D. is *gans*, but whether the same word or not, let the reader judge. The Ch. אוז or אוזא, and the corresponding Arabic and Syriac words, may possibly be the same word, the Europeans prefixing *g* in the Celtic manner.]

1. A well known aquatic fowl of the genus Anas; but the domestic goose lives chiefly on land, and feeds on grass. The soft fethers are used for beds, and the quills for pens. The wild goose is migratory.

2. A tailor's smoothing iron, so called from its handle which resembles the neck of a goose.

GOOSEBERRY, *n.* *goos′berry.* [In Ger. *kräuselbeere*, from *kraus*, crisp; D. *kruisbes*, from *kruis*, a cross; L. *grossula*; W. *grwys*, from *rhwys*, luxuriant. The English word is undoubtedly corrupted from *crossberry*, *grossberry*, or *gorseberry*; a name taken from the roughness of the shrub. See *Cross* and *Gross.*]

The fruit of a shrub, and the shrub itself, the *Ribes grossularia.* The shrub is armed with spines. Of the fruit there are several varieties.

The *American gooseberry* belongs to the genus Melastoma, and the *West Indian gooseberry* to the genus Cactus. *Lee.*

GOOSECAP, *n.* *goos′cap.* A silly person. *Beaum. Johnson.*

GOOSEFOOT, *n.* *goos′foot.* A plant, the Chenopodium.

GOOSEGR′ASS, *n.* *goos′grass.* A plant of the genus Galium. Also, the name of certain plants of the genera Potentilla and Asperugo.

GOOSENECK, *n.* *goos′neck.* In *a ship*, a piece of iron fixed on one end of the tiller, to which the laniard of the whip-staff or wheel-rope comes, for steering the ship; also, an iron hook on the inner end of a boom. *Encyc. Mar. Dict.*

GOOSEQUILL, *n.* *goos′quill.* The large fether or quill of a goose; or a pen made with it.

GOOSETONGUE, *n.* *goos′tung.* A plant of the genus Achillea.

GOOSEWING, *n.* *goos′wing.* In *seamen's language*, a sail set on a boom on the lee side of a ship; also, the clues or lower corners of a ship's main-sail or fore-sail, when the middle part is furled. *Encyc. Mar. Dict.*

GOP′PISH, *a.* Proud; pettish. [*Not in use.*] *Ray.*

GOR′-BELLIED, *a.* Big-bellied. *Shak.*

GOR′-BELLY, *n.* [In W. *gor* signifies swelled, extreme, over.] A prominent belly. [*Not in use.*]

GOR′-COCK, *n.* The moor-cock, red-grouse, or red-game; a fowl of the gallinaceous kind. *Dict. Nat. Hist.*

GOR′-CROW, *n.* The carrion-crow. *Johnson.*

GORD, *n.* An instrument of gaming.

GORD'IAN, *a.* Intricate. [*See the next word.*]

Gordian knot, in antiquity, a knot in the lether or harness of Gordius, a king of Phrygia, so very intricate, that there was no finding where it began or ended. An oracle declared that he who should untie this knot should be master of Asia. Alexander, fearing that his inability to untie it should prove an ill augury, cut it asunder with his sword. Hence, in modern language, a *Gordian knot* is an inextricable difficulty; and to *cut the Gordian knot*, is to remove a difficulty by bold or unusual measures. *Encyc. Lempriere.*

GORE, *n.* [Sax. *gor*, gore, mud; W. *gor*; Ir. *cear*, blood, and red; Gr. ιχωρ; from issuing.]

1. Blood; but generally, thick or clotted blood; blood that after effusion becomes inspissated. *Milton.*

2. Dirt; mud. [*Unusual.*] *Bp. Fisher.*

GORE, *n.* [Scot. *gore* or *gair*; Ice. *geir*; D. *geer.*]

1. A wedge-shaped or triangular piece of cloth sewed into a garment to widen it in any part. *Chaucer.*

2. A slip or triangular piece of land. *Cowel.*

3. In *heraldry*, an abatement denoting a coward. It consists of two arch lines, meeting in an acute angle in the middle of the fess point. *Encyc.*

GORE, *v. t.* [W. *gyru*, to thrust; Gipsey, *goro*, a dagger. See Heb. כאר. Class Gr. No. 30. 35. 36. 53. 57. &c.]

1. To stab; to pierce; to penetrate with a pointed instrument, as a spear. *Dryden.*

2. To pierce with the point of a horn.

If an ox *gore* a man or a woman— Ex. xxi.

GO'RED, *pp.* Stabbed; pierced with a pointed instrument.

GORĠE, *n. gorj.* [Fr. *gorge*; It. *gorga, gorgia*; Sp. *gorja*, the throat, and *gorga*, a whirlpool; *gorgear*, to warble; G. *gurgel*, whence *gargle*; L. *gurges.*]

1. The throat; the gullet; the canal of the neck by which food passes to the stomach.

2. In *architecture*, the narrowest part of the Tuscan and Doric capitals, between the astragal, above the shaft of the column, and the annulets. *Encyc.*

3. In *fortification*, the entrance of the platform of any work. *Encyc.*

4. That which is gorged or swallowed, especially by a hawk or other fowl. *Shak.*

GORĠE, *v. t. gorj.* To swallow; especially, to swallow with greediness, or in large mouthfuls or quantities. Hence,

2. To glut; to fill the throat or stomach; to satiate.

The giant, *gorged* with flesh— *Addison.*

GORĠE, *v. i.* To feed. *Milton.*

GORĠ'ED, *pp.* Swallowed; glutted.

GORĠ'ED, *a.* Having a gorge or throat. *Shak.*

2. In *heraldry*, bearing a crown or the like about the neck. *Encyc.*

GOR'ĠEOUS, *a.* Showy; fine; splendid; glittering with gay colors.

With *gorgeous* wings, the marks of sovereign sway. *Dryden.*

A *gorgeous* robe. Luke xxiii.

GOR'ĠEOUSLY, *adv.* With showy magnificence; splendidly; finely. The prince was *gorgeously* arrayed.

GOR'ĠEOUSNESS, *n.* Show of dress or ornament; splendor of raiment.

GORĠ'ET, *n.* [Fr. *gorgette*, from *gorge.*] A piece of armor for defending the throat or neck; a kind of breast-plate like a half-moon; also, a small convex ornament worn by officers on the breast. *Encyc. Todd.*

2. Formerly, a ruff worn by females.

3. In *surgery, gorget*, or *gorgeret*, is a cutting instrument used in lithotomy; also, a concave or cannulated conductor, called a *blunt gorget*. *Cyc. Encyc.*

GORĠ'ING, *ppr.* Swallowing; eating greedily; glutting.

GORG'ON, *n.* [Gr.] A fabled monster of terrific aspect, the sight of which turned the beholder to stone. The poets represent the Gorgons as three sisters, *Stheno, Euryale* and *Medusa*; but authors are not agreed in the description of them.

2. Any thing very ugly or horrid. *Milton.*

GORG'ON, *a.* Like a gorgon; very ugly or terrific; as a *gorgon* face. *Dryden.*

GORGO'NEAN, } *a.* Like a gorgon; pertaining to gorgons. *Milton.*
GORGO'NIAN, }

Gorgonia nobilis, in *natural history*, red coral. *Ure.*

GOR'-HEN, *n.* The female of the gor-cock.

GO'RING, *ppr.* [from *gore.*] Stabbing; piercing.

GO'RING, *n.* A pricking; puncture. *Dryden.*

GOR'MAND, } *n.* [Fr. *gourmand*, from W. *gormant*, plenitude, exuberance; *gor*, extreme; *gormoz*, excess.] A greedy or ravenous eater; a glutton.
GOR'MANDER, }

GOR'MANDIZE, *v. i.* To eat greedily; to swallow voraciously. *Shak.*

GOR'MANDIZER, *n.* A greedy voracious eater. *Cleaveland.*

GOR'MANDIZING, *ppr.* Eating greedily and voraciously.

GORSE, } *n. gors.* [Sax. *gorst.* Qu. *coarse*, L. *crassus*, or G. *kratzen*, to scratch.]
GORSS, }

Furz, or whin, a thick prickly shrub, of the genus Ulex, bearing yellow flowers in winter. *Johnson.*

GO'RY, *a.* [from *gore.*] Covered with congealed or clotted blood; as *gory* locks. *Shak.*

2. Bloody; murderous. *Shak.*

GOS'HAWK, *n.* [Sax. *goshafoc*, goose-hawk.]

A voracious fowl of the genus Falco, or hawk kind, larger than the common buzzard, but of a more slender shape. The general color of the plumage is a deep brown; the breast and belly white. *Dict. Nat. Hist.*

GOS'LING, *n.* [Sax. *gos*, goose, and *ling.*] A young goose; a goose not full grown.

2. A catkin on nut trees and pines. *Bailey. Johnson.*

GOS'PEL, *n.* [Sax. *godspell*; *god*, good, and *spell*, history, relation, narration, word, speech, that which is uttered, announced, sent or communicated; answering to the Gr. ευαγγελιον, L. *evangelium*, a good or joyful message.]

The history of the birth, life, actions, death, resurrection, ascension and doctrines of Jesus Christ; or a revelation of the grace of God to fallen man through a mediator, including the character, actions, and doctrines of Christ, with the whole scheme of salvation, as revealed by Christ and his apostles. This gospel is said to have been preached to Abraham, by the promise, "in thee shall all nations be blessed." Gal. iii. 8.

It is called the *gospel* of God. Rom. i. 1.

It is called the *gospel* of Christ. Rom. i. 16.

It is called the *gospel* of salvation. Eph. i. 13.

2. God's word. *Hammond.*

3. Divinity; theology. *Milton.*

4. Any general doctrine. *Burke.*

GOS'PEL, *v. t.* To instruct in the gospel; or to fill with sentiments of religion. *Shak.*

GOS'PEL-GOSSIP, *n.* One who is overzealous in running about among his neighbors to lecture on religious subjects. *Addison.*

GOS'PELIZE, *v. t.* To form according to the gospel. *Milton.*

2. To instruct in the gospel; to evangelize; as, to *gospelize* the savages. *E. Nott.*

GOS'PELIZED, *pp.* Instructed in the christian religion.

GOS'PELIZING, *ppr.* Evangelizing; instructing in the christian religion. *E. Stiles.*

GOS'PELLER, *n.* An evangelist; also, a follower of Wickliffe, the first Englishman who attempted a reformation from popery. [*Not much used.*] *Rowe.*

2. He who reads the gospel at the altar.

GOSS, *n.* A kind of low furz or gorse. *Shak.*

GOS'SAMER, *n.* [L. *gossipium*, cotton.] A fine filmy substance, like cobwebs, floating in the air, in calm clear weather, especially in autumn. It is seen in stubble fields and on furz or low bushes, and is probably formed by a species of spider. *Encyc.*

GOS'SAMERY, *a.* Like gossamer; flimsy; unsubstantial. *Pursuits of Literature.*

GOS'SIP, *n.* [Sax. *godsibb*; *god* and *sib* or *sibb*, peace, adoption and relation; a Saxon name of a sponsor at baptism.]

1. A sponsor; one who answers for a child in baptism; a godfather. *Obs.* *Shak. Davies.*

2. A tippling companion.

And sometimes lurk I in a *gossip's* bowl. *Shak.*

3. One who runs from house to house, tattling and telling news; an idle tattler. [*This is the sense in which the word is now used.*] *Dryden.*

4. A friend or neighbor. *Obs.*

5. Mere tattle; idle talk.

GOS'SIP, *v. i.* To prate; to chat; to talk much. *Shak.*

2. To be a pot-companion. *Shak.*

3. To run about and tattle; to tell idle tales.

GOS'SIPING, *ppr.* Prating; chatting; running from place to place and tattling.

GOS'SIPING, *n.* A prating; a running about to collect tales and tattle.

GOS'SIPRED, *n.* Compaternity; spiritual affinity, for which a juror might be challenged. [*Not used.*] *Davies.*

GOSSOON', *n.* [Fr. *garçon*, corrupted.] A boy; a servant. [*Not in use.*]

GOS'TING, *n.* An herb. *Ainsworth.*

GOT, *pret.* of *get.* The old preterit *gat*, pronounced *got*, is nearly obsolete.

GOT and GOTTEN, *pp.* of *get.*

GOTH, *n.* One of an ancient and distinguished tribe or nation, which inhabited Scandinavia, now Sweden and Norway, whose language is now retained in those countries, and a large portion of it is found in English.

2. One rude or uncivilized; a barbarian. *Addison.*

3. A rude ignorant person. *Chesterfield.*

GO'THAMIST, *n.* A person deficient in wisdom, so called from Gotham in Nottinghamshire, noted for some pleasant blunders. *Bp. Morton.*

GOTH'IC, *a.* Pertaining to the Goths; as *Gothic* customs; *Gothic* architecture; *Gothic* barbarity.

2. Rude; ancient.

3. Barbarous.

GOTH'IC, *n.* The language of the Goths.

GOTH'ICISM, *n.* Rudeness of manners; barbarousness.

2. A Gothic idiom.

3. Conformity to the Gothic style of building.

GOTH'ICIZE, *v. t.* To make Gothic; to bring back to barbarism. *Strutt.*

GOUD, *n.* Woad. [*Not used.*]

GOUGE, *n.* gouj. [Fr. *gouge*; Arm. *gouich.*] A round hollow chissel, used to cut holes, channels or grooves in wood or stone. *Moxon.*

GOUGE, *v. t.* gouj. To scoop out with a gouge.

2. To force out the eye of a person with the thumb or finger; *a barbarous practice.*

GOUL'AND, *n.* A plant or flower. *B. Jonson.*

Goulard's Extract, so called from the inventor, a saturated solution of the subacetate of lead, used as a remedy for inflammation. *Ure.*

GOURD, *n.* [Fr. *courge*; D. *kauwoerde.* Qu. the root of *gherkin.*]

A plant and its fruit, of the genus Cucurbita. There are several species, as the bottle-gourd, the shell-gourd or calabash, the warted gourd, &c. The shell is sometimes used for a piggin or for a bottle.

GOURDINESS, *n.* A swelling on a horse's leg after a journey. *Far. Dict.*

GOURDY, *a.* Swelled in the legs.

GOURD-TREE, *n.* A tree, the Crescentia, found in the W. Indies. *Fam. of Plants.*

GOURMAND. [See *Gormand.*]

GOUT, *n.* [Fr. *goutte*, a drop, the gout; the disease being considered as a defluxion; It. *gotta*; Sp. *gota*; Ir. *guta*; L. *gutta.* Qu. Pers. گوت hot, infirm in the feet.]

1. The arthritis, a painful disease of the small joints, but sometimes affecting the stomach. It is often periodical or intermitting. *Coxe.*

2. A drop. [*Not used.*] *Shak.*

GOUT, *n. goo.* [Fr. from L. *gustus*, taste.] Taste; relish.

GOUT'INESS, *n.* The state of being subject to the gout; gouty affections.

GOUT'SWELLED, *a.* Swelled with the gout.

GOUT'WÖRT, *n.* A plant, the Ægopodium.

GOUT'Y, *a.* Diseased with the gout, or subject to the gout; as a *gouty* person; a *gouty* joint; a *gouty* constitution.

2. Pertaining to the gout; as *gouty* matter. *Blackmore.*

3. Swelled; boggy; as *gouty* land. [*Not in use.*] *Spenser.*

GÖV'ERN, *v. t.* [Fr. *gouverner*; Sp. *gobernar*; It. *governare*; L. *guberno.* The L. *guberno* seems to be a compound.]

1. To direct and control, as the actions or conduct of men, either by established laws or by arbitrary will; to regulate by authority; to keep within the limits prescribed by law or sovereign will. Thus in free states, men are *governed* by the constitution and laws; in despotic states, men are *governed* by the edicts or commands of a monarch. Every man should *govern* well his own family.

2. To regulate; to influence; to direct. This is the chief point by which he is to *govern* all his counsels and actions.

3. To control; to restrain; to keep in due subjection; as, to *govern* the passions or temper.

4. To direct; to steer; to regulate the course or motion of a ship. The helm or the helmsman *governs* the ship.

5. In *grammar*, to require to be in a particular case; as, a verb transitive *governs* a word in the accusative case; or to require a particular case; as, a verb *governs* the accusative case.

GÖV'ERN, *v. i.* To exercise authority; to administer the laws. The chief magistrate should *govern* with impartiality.

2. To maintain the superiority; to have the control. *Dryden.*

GÖV'ERNABLE, *a.* That may be governed, or subjected to authority; controllable; manageable; obedient; submissive to law or rule. *Locke.*

GÖV'ERNANCE, *n.* Government; exercise of authority; direction; control; management, either of a public officer, or of a private guardian or tutor. *Maccabees. Shak.*

GÖV'ERNANT, *n.* [Fr. *gouvernante.*] A lady who has the care and management of young females; a governess. [*The latter is more generally used.*]

GÖV'ERNED, *pp.* Directed; regulated by authority; controlled; managed; influenced; restrained.

GÖV'ERNESS, *n.* A female invested with authority to control and direct; a tutoress; an instructress; a woman who has the care of instructing and directing young ladies.

GÖV'ERNING, *ppr.* Directing; controlling; regulating by laws or edicts; managing; influencing; restraining.

2. *a.* Holding the superiority; prevalent; as a *governing* wind; a *governing* party in a state. *Federalist, Jay.*

3. Directing; controlling; as a *governing* motive.

GÖV'ERNMENT, *n.* Direction; regulation. These precepts will serve for the *government* of our conduct.

2. Control; restraint. Men are apt to neglect the *government* of their temper and passions.

3. The exercise of authority; direction and restraint exercised over the actions of men in communities, societies or states; the administration of public affairs, according to established constitution, laws and usages, or by arbitrary edicts. Prussia rose to importance under the *government* of Frederick II.

4. The exercise of authority by a parent or householder. Children are often ruined by a neglect of *government* in parents.

> Let family *government* be like that of our heavenly Father, mild, gentle and affectionate. *Kollock.*

5. The system of polity in a state; that form of fundamental rules and principles by which a nation or state is governed, or by which individual members of a body politic are to regulate their social actions; a constitution, either written or unwritten, by which the rights and duties of citizens and public officers are prescribed and defined; as a monarchial *government*, or a republican *government.*

> Thirteen *governments* thus founded on the natural authority of the people alone, without the pretence of miracle or mystery, are a great point gained in favor of the rights of mankind. *J. Adams.*

6. An empire, kingdom or state; any territory over which the right of sovereignty is extended.

7. The right of governing or administering the laws. The king of England vested the *government* of Ireland in the lord lieutenant.

8. The persons or council which administer the laws of a kingdom or state; executive power.

9. Manageableness; compliance; obsequiousness. *Shak.*

10. Regularity of behavior. [*Not in use.*] *Shak.*

11. Management of the limbs or body. [*Not in use.*] *Spenser.*

12. In *grammar*, the influence of a word in regard to construction, as when established usage requires that one word should cause another to be in a particular case or mode.

GÖVERNMENT'AL, *a.* Pertaining to government; made by government. *Hamilton.*

GÖV'ERNOR, *n.* He that governs, rules or directs; one invested with supreme authority. The Creator is the rightful *governor* of all his creatures.

2. One who is invested with supreme authority to administer or enforce the laws; the supreme executive magistrate of a state, community, corporation or post. Thus, in America, each state has its *governor*; Canada has its *governor.*

3. A tutor; one who has the care of a young man; one who instructs him and forms his manners.

4. A pilot; one who steers a ship. James iii.

5. One possessing delegated authority. Joseph was *governor* over the land of Egypt. Obadiah was *governor* over Ahab's house. Damascus had a *governor* under Aretas the king.

GŎV'ERNORSHIP, *n.* The office of a governor.

GOW'AN, *n.* A plant, a species of Bellis or daisy. *Fam. of Plants.*

GOWK, *n.* [See *Gawk.*]

GOWN, *n.* [W. *gwn*; Ir. *gunna*; It. *gonna*. This is probably the *καυνακη* of Hesychius, and the *guanacum* of Varro; a garment somewhat like the *sagum* or sack, said to be of Persian origin, and among rude nations perhaps made of skins, [W. *cènysgin*,] and afterwards of wool; a kind of shag or frieze. Ch. גונכא mentioned Judges iv. 18. and 2 Kings viii. 15. See Varro de Ling. Lat. lib. 4. Bochart. De Phœn. Col. lib. 1. Cap. 42. and Cluv. Ant. Germ. Lib. 1.]

1. A woman's upper garment. *Pope.*
2. A long loose upper garment or robe, worn by professional men, as divines, lawyers, students, &c., who are called *men of the gown* or *gownmen*. It is made of any kind of cloth worn over ordinary clothes, and hangs down to the ankles or nearly so. *Encyc.*
3. A long loose upper garment, worn in sickness, &c.
4. The dress of peace, or the civil magistracy; *cedant arma togæ.*

He Mars deposed, and arms to *gowns* made yield. *Dryden.*

GOWN'ED, *a.* Dressed in a gown. *Dryden.*

GOWN'MAN, *n.* One whose professional habit is a gown.

The *gownman* learn'd. *Pope.*

2. One devoted to the arts of peace. *Rowe.*

GRAB, *n.* A vessel used on the Malabar coast, having two or three masts. *Dict.*

GRAB, *v. t.* [Dan. *greb*, a grasp; *griber*, to gripe; Sw. *grabba*, to grasp; *gripa*, to gripe; W. *grab*, a duster.]

To seize; to gripe suddenly. [*Vulgar.*]

GRAB'BLE, *v. i.* [dim. of *grab*; D. *grabbelen*; G. *grübeln*; allied to *grope*, *grovel*, and *grapple*; Arm. *scraba*; Eng. *scrabble*; allied to *rub*, or L. *rapio*, or to both.]

1. To grope; to feel with the hands. *Arbuthnot.*
2. To lie prostrate on the belly; to sprawl. *Ainsworth.*

GRAB'BLING, *ppr.* Groping; feeling along; sprawling.

GRACE, *n.* [Fr. *grace*; It. *grazia*; Sp. *gracia*; Ir. *grasa*; from the L. *gratia*, which is formed on the Celtic; W. *rhad*, grace, a blessing, a gratuity. It coincides in origin with Fr. *gré*, Eng. *agree*, *congruous*, and *ready*. The primary sense of *gratus*, is free, ready, quick, willing, prompt, from advancing. Class Rd. See *Grade.*]

1. Favor; good will; kindness; disposition to oblige another; as a grant made as an act of *grace.*

Or each, or all, may win a lady's *grace.* *Dryden.*

2. Appropriately, the free unmerited love and favor of God, the spring and source of all the benefits men receive from him.

And if by *grace*, then it is no more of works. Rom. xi.

3. Favorable influence of God; divine influence or the influence of the spirit, in renewing the heart and restraining from sin.

My *grace* is sufficient for thee. 2 Cor. xii.

4. The application of Christ's righteousness to the sinner.

Where sin abounded, *grace* did much more abound. Rom. v.

5. A state of reconciliation to God. Rom. v. 2.
6. Virtuous or religious affection or disposition, as a liberal disposition, faith, meekness, humility, patience, &c. proceeding from divine influence.
7. Spiritual instruction, improvement and edification. Eph. iv. 29.
8. Apostleship, or the qualifications of an apostle. Eph. iii. 8.
9. Eternal life; final salvation. 1 Pet. i. 13.
10. Favor; mercy; pardon.

Bow and sue for *grace*
With suppliant knee. *Milton.*

11. Favor conferred.

I should therefore esteem it a great favor and *grace.* *Prior.*

12. Privilege.

To few great Jupiter imparts this *grace.* *Dryden.*

13. That in manner, deportment or language which renders it appropriate and agreeable; suitableness; elegance with appropriate dignity. We say, a speaker delivers his address with *grace*; a man performs his part with *grace.*

Grace was in all her steps. *Milton.*

Her purple habit sits with such a *grace*
On her smooth shoulders. *Dryden.*

14. Natural or acquired excellence; any endowment that recommends the possessor to others; as the *graces* of wit and learning. *Hooker.*
15. Beauty; embellishment; in general, whatever adorns and recommends to favor; sometimes, a single beauty.

I pass their form and every charming *grace.* *Dryden.*

16. Beauty deified; among *pagans*, a goddess. The *graces* were three in number, Aglaia, Thalia, and Euphrosyne, the constant attendants of Venus. *Lempriere.*

The loves delighted, and the *graces* played. *Prior.*

17. Virtue physical; as the *grace* of plants. [*Not used.*] *Shak.*
18. The title of a duke or an archbishop, and formerly of the king of England, meaning *your goodness* or *clemency.* His *Grace* the Duke of York. Your *Grace* will please to accept my thanks.
19. A short prayer before or after meat; a blessing asked, or thanks rendered.
20. In *music*, *graces* signifies turns, trills and shakes introduced for embellishment.

Day of grace, in *theology*, time of probation, when an offer is made to sinners.

Days of grace, in *commerce*, the days immediately following the day when a bill or note becomes due, which days are allowed to the debtor or payor to make payment in. In Great Britain and the United States the days of grace are *three*, but in other countries more; the usages of merchants being different.

GRACE, *v. t.* To adorn; to decorate; to embellish and dignify.

Great Jove and Phœbus *graced* his noble line. *Pope.*

And hail, ye fair, of every charm possess'd,
Who *grace* this rising empire of the west. *D. Humphrey.*

2. To dignify or raise by an act of favor; to honor.

He might at his pleasure *grace* or disgrace whom he would in court. *Knolles.*

3. To favor; to honor. *Dryden.*
4. To supply with heavenly grace. *Bp. Hall.*

GRA'CECUP, *n.* The cup or health drank after grace. *Prior.*

GRA'CED, *pp.* Adorned; embellished; exalted; dignified; honored.

2. *a.* Beautiful; graceful. [*Not in use.*] *Sidney.*
3. Virtuous; regular; chaste. [*Not in use.*] *Shak.*

GRA'CEFUL, *a.* Beautiful with dignity; elegant; agreeable in appearance, with an expression of dignity or elevation of mind or manner; used particularly of motion, looks and speech; as a *graceful* walk; a *graceful* deportment; a *graceful* speaker; a *graceful* air.

High o'er the rest in arms the *graceful* Turnus rode. *Dryden.*

GRA'CEFULLY, *adv.* With a pleasing dignity; elegantly; with a natural ease and propriety; as, to walk or speak *gracefully.*

GRA'CEFULNESS, *n.* Elegance of manner or deportment; beauty with dignity in manner, motion or countenance. *Gracefulness* consists in the natural ease and propriety of an action, accompanied with a countenance expressive of dignity or elevation of mind. Happy is the man who can add the *gracefulness* of ease to the dignity of merit.

GRA'CELESS, *a.* Void of grace; corrupt; depraved; unregenerate; unsanctified.

GRA'CELESSLY, *adv.* Without grace.

GRA'CES, *n.* *Good graces*, favor; friendship.

GRAC'ILE, *a.* [L. *gracilis.*] Slender. [*Not in use.*]

GRACIL'ITY, *n.* Slenderness. [*Not in use.*]

GRA'CIOUS, *a.* [Fr. *gracieux*; L. *gratiosus.*]

1. Favorable; kind; friendly; as, the envoy met with a *gracious* reception.
2. Favorable; kind; benevolent; merciful; disposed to forgive offenses and impart unmerited blessings.

Thou art a God ready to pardon, *gracious* and merciful. Neh. ix.

3. Favorable; expressing kindness and favor.

All bore him witness, and wondered at the *gracious* words which proceeded from his mouth. Luke iv.

4. Proceeding from divine grace; as a person in a *gracious* state.
5. Acceptable; favored.

He made us *gracious* before the kings of Persia. [*Little used.*] 1 Esdras.

6. Renewed or implanted by grace; as *gracious* affections.
7. Virtuous; good. *Shak.*
8. Excellent; graceful; becoming. *Obs.* *Hooker.* *Camden.*

GRA'CIOUSLY, *adv.* Kindly; favorably; in a friendly manner; with kind condescension.

His testimony he *graciously* confirmed. *Dryden.*

2. In a pleasing manner.

GRA'CIOUSNESS, *n.* Kind condescension. *Clarendon.*

2. Possession of graces or good qualities. *Bp. Barlow.*

3. Pleasing manner. *Johnson.*

4. Mercifulness. *Sandys.*

GRACK'LE, *n.* [L. *graculus*, dim. of Goth. *krage*, a crow. See *Crow.* Varro's deduction of this word from *grex* is an error.]

A genus of birds, the Gracula, of which the crow-blackbird is a species.

GRADA'TION, *n.* [L. *gradatio ;* Fr. *gradation.* See *Grade.*]

1. A series of ascending steps or degrees, or a proceeding step by step ; hence, progress from one degree or state to another ; a regular advance from step to step. We observe a *gradation* in the progress of society from a rude to civilized life. Men may arrive by several *gradations* to the most horrid impiety.

2. A degree in any order or series ; we observe a *gradation* in the scale of being, from brute to man, from man to angels.

3. Order ; series ; regular process by degrees or steps ; as a *gradation* in argument or description.

GRAD'ATORY, *a.* Proceeding step by step. *Seward.*

GRAD'ATORY, *n.* Steps from the cloisters into the church. *Ainsworth.*

GRADE, *n.* [Fr. *grade ;* Sp. It. *grado ;* Port. *grao ;* from L. *gradus*, a step ; *gradior*, to step, to go ; G. *grad ;* D. *graad ;* Dan. and Sw. *grad*, a step or degree ; W. *grâz*, a step, degree, rank, from *rhâz*, a going forward or advance, Arm. *radd.* It may be from a common root with W. *rhawd*, way, course, rout ; *rhodiaw*, to walk about ; *rhod*, a wheel, L. *rota.* We observe by the Welsh that the first letter *g* is a prefix, and the root of the word then is *Rd.* We observe further that the Latin *gradior* forms *gressus*, by a common change of *d* to *s*, or as it is in Welsh *z* [*th*]. Now if *g* is a prefix, then *gressus* [*ressus*] coincides with the Sw. *resa*, Dan. *rejser*, G. *reisen*, D. *reizen*, to go, to travel, to journey ; D. *reis*, a journey or voyage. In Sw. and Dan. the verbs signify not only to travel, but to *raise.* Whether the latter word *raise* is of the same family, may be doubtful ; but the others appear to belong to one radix, coinciding with the Syr. ܪܕܐ radah, to go, to walk ; Ch. רדה to open, expand, flow, instruct ; Heb. to descend. A step then is a stretch, a reach of the foot. Class Rd. No. 1. 2. 26.]

1. A degree or rank in order or dignity, civil, military or ecclesiastical. *J. M. Mason. Walsh.*

While questions, periods, and *grades* and privileges are never once formally discussed. *S. Miller.*

2. A step or degree in any ascending series ; as crimes of every *grade.*

When we come to examine the intermediate *grades.* *S. S. Smith.*

GRA'DIENT, *a.* [L. *gradiens*, *gradior.*] Moving by steps ; walking ; as *gradient* automata. *Wilkins.*

GRAD'UAL, *a.* [Fr. *graduel*, from *grade.*] Proceeding by steps or degrees ; advancing step by step ; passing from one step to another ; regular and slow ; as a *gradual* increase of knowledge ; a *gradual* increase of light in the morning is favorable to the eyes.

2. Proceeding by degrees in a descending line or progress ; as a *gradual* decline.

GRAD'UAL, *n.* An order of steps. *Dryden.*

2. A grail ; an ancient book of hymns and prayers. *Todd.*

GRAD'UALLY, *adv.* By degrees ; step by step ; regularly ; slowly. At evening the light vanishes *gradually.*

2. In degree. [*Not used.*]

Human reason doth not only *gradually*, but specifically differ from the fantastic reason of brutes. *Grew.*

GRAD'UATE, *v. t.* [It. *graduare ;* Sp. *graduar ;* Fr. *graduer ;* from L. *gradus*, a degree.]

1. To honor with a degree or diploma, in a college or university ; to confer a degree on ; as, to *graduate* a master of arts. *Carew. Wotton.*

2. To mark with degrees, regular intervals, or divisions ; as, to *graduate* a thermometer.

3. To form shades or nice differences.

4. To raise to a higher place in the scale of metals. *Boyle.*

5. To advance by degrees ; to improve.

Dyers advance and *graduate* their colors with salts. *Brown.*

6. To temper ; to prepare.

Diseases originating in the atmosphere act exclusively on bodies *graduated* to receive their impressions. *Med. Repos.*

7. To mark degrees or differences of any kind ; as, to *graduate* punishment. *Duponceau.*

8. In *chimistry*, to bring fluids to a certain degree of consistency.

GRAD'UATE, *v. i.* To receive a degree from a college or university.

2. To pass by degrees ; to change gradually. Sandstone which *graduates* into gneiss. Carnelian sometimes *graduates* into quartz. *Kirwan.*

GRAD'UATE, *n.* One who has received a degree in a college or university, or from some professional incorporated society.

GRAD'UATED, *pp.* Honored with a degree or diploma from some learned society or college.

2. Marked with degrees or regular intervals ; tempered.

GRAD'UATESHIP, *n.* The state of a graduate. *Milton.*

GRAD'UATING, *ppr.* Honoring with a degree ; marking with degrees.

GRADUA'TION, *n.* Regular progression by succession of degrees.

2. Improvement ; exaltation of qualities. *Brown.*

3. The act of conferring or receiving academical degrees. *Charter of Dartmouth College.*

4. The act of marking with degrees.

5. The process of bringing a liquid to a certain consistence by evaporation. *Parke.*

GRAD'UATOR, *n.* An instrument for dividing any line, right or curve, into equal parts. *Journ. of Science.*

GRAFF, *n.* [See *Grave.*] A ditch or moat. *Clarendon.*

GRAFF, for *graft.* *Obs.*

GR'AFT, *n.* [Fr. *greffe ;* Arm. *id. ;* Ir. *grafchur ;* D. *griffel ;* from the root of *grave*, *engrave*, Gr. γραφω, L. *scribo*, the sense of which is to *scrape* or to dig. In Scot. *graif* signifies to bury, to inter. The sense of *graft* is that which is inserted. See *Grave.*]

A small shoot or cion of a tree, inserted in another tree as the stock which is to support and nourish it. These unite and become one tree, but the graft determines the kind of fruit.

GR'AFT, *v. t.* [Fr. *greffer.*] To insert a cion or shoot, or a small cutting of it, into another tree. *Dryden.*

2. To propagate by insertion or inoculation. *Dryden.*

3. To insert in a body to which it did not originally belong. Rom. xi. 17.

4. To impregnate with a foreign branch. *Shak.*

5. To join one thing to another so as to receive support from it.

And *graft* my love immortal on thy fame. *Pope.*

GR'AFT, *v. i.* To practice the insertion of foreign cions on a stock.

GR'AFTED, *pp.* Inserted on a foreign stock.

GR'AFTER, *n.* One who inserts cions on foreign stocks, or propagates fruit by ingrafting.

GR'AFTING, *ppr.* Inserting cions on different stocks.

Note. The true original orthography of this word is *graff ;* but *graft* has superseded the original word, as it has in the compound *ingraft.*

GRAIL, *n.* [L. *graduale.*] A book of offices in the Romish church. *Warton.*

GRAIL, *n.* [Fr. *grêle*, hail.] Small particles of any kind. *Spenser.*

GRAIN, *n.* [Fr. *grain ;* L. *granum ;* Sp. and It. *grano ;* G. *gran ;* D. *graan ;* Ir. *gran*, corn ; W. *graun*, *graen*, *gronyn*, a little pebble or gravel stone, Ir. *grean*, Arm. *gruan*, which seems to be the Eng. *ground ;* Russ. *gran*, grain, and a *corner*, a boundary. In Scot. *grain* is the branch of a tree, the stem or stalk of a plant, the branch of a river, the prong of a fork. In Sw. *gryn* is grain ; *grann*, fine ; *gren*, a branch ; and *grâns*, boundary. Dan. *gran*, a grain, a pine tree ; *grand*, a grain, an atom ; *green*, a branch, a sprig ; *grændse*, a boundary ; G. *gran*, D. *graan*, grain ; G. *gränze*, D. *grens*, a border.]

1. Any small hard mass ; as a *grain* of sand or gravel. Hence,

2. A single seed or hard seed of a plant, particularly of those kinds whose seeds are used for food of man or beast. This is usually inclosed in a proper shell or covered with a husk, and contains the embryo of a new plant. Hence,

3. Grain, without a definitive, signifies corn in general, or the fruit of certain plants which constitutes the chief food of man and beast, as wheat, rye, barley, oats and maiz.

4. A minute particle.

5. A small weight, or the smallest weight ordinarily used, being the twentieth part

of the scruple in apothecaries' weight, and the twenty fourth of a pennyweight troy.
6. A component part of stones and metals.
7. The veins or fibers of wood or other fibrous substance; whence, *cross-grained*, and *against the grain*.
8. The body or substance of wood as modified by the fibers.

Hard box, and linden of a softer *grain*. *Dryden.*

9. The body or substance of a thing considered with respect to the size, form or direction of the constituent particles; as stones of a fine *grain*. *Woodward.*

The tooth of a sea-horse, contains a curdled *grain*. *Brown.*

10. Any thing proverbially small; a very small particle or portion; as a *grain* of wit or of common sense.

Neglect not to make use of any *grain* of grace. *Hammond.*

11. Dyed or stained substance.

All in a robe of darkest *grain*. *Milton.*

12. The direction of the fibers of wood or other fibrous substance; hence the phrase, *against the grain*, applied to animals, that is, against their natural tempers.
13. The heart or temper; as brothers not united in *grain*. *Hayward.*
14. The form of the surface of any thing with respect to smoothness or roughness; state of the grit of any body composed of grains; as sandstone of a fine *grain*.
15. A tine, prong or spike. *Ray.*

A *grain of allowance*, a small allowance or indulgence; a small portion to be remitted; something above or below just weight. *Watts.*

To dye in grain, is to dye in the raw material, as wool or silk before it is manufactured.

GRAIN, *v. i.* To yield fruit. *Obs.* *Gower.*

GRAIN, or GRANE, for *groan*. [*Not in use.*]

GRA'INED, *a.* Rough; made less smooth. *Shak.*
2. Dyed in grain; ingrained. *Brown.*

GRA'INER, *n.* A lixivium obtained by infusing pigeon's dung in water; used by tanners to give flexibility to skins. *Ure.*

GRA'INING, *n.* Indentation. *Leake.*
2. A fish of the dace kind. *Dict. Nat. Hist.*

GRAINS, *n.* [in the plural.] The husks or remains of malt after brewing, or of any grain after distillation.

Grains of paradise, an Indian spice, the seeds of a species of Amomum.

GRA'INSTAFF, *n.* A quarter-staff.

GRA'INY, *a.* Full of grains or corn; full of kernels. *Johnson.*

GRAITH, *v. t.* To prepare. [See *Greith* and *Ready*.]

GRAL'LIC, *a.* [L. *grallæ*, stilts, crutches.] Stilted; an epithet given to an order of fowls having long legs, naked above the knees, which fit them for wading in water.

GRAM, *a.* [Sax. *gram*; Sw. *id.* angry; Dan. *gram*, envious, grudging.] Angry. *Obs.*

GRAM, *n.* [Fr. *gramme*, from Gr. γραμμα, whence γραμμαριον, the twenty fourth part of an ounce.]

In *the new system of French weights*, the unity of weights. It is the weight of a quantity of distilled water equal to a cubic centimeter, or 18 grains $\frac{841}{10000}$ French, or *du poids de marc*, equal to 15.444 grains troy. *Lunier.*

GRAMERCY, for Fr. *grand-merci*, is not in use. It formerly was used to express obligation. *Spenser.*

GRAMIN'EAL, GRAMIN'EOUS, } *a.* [L. *gramineus*, from *gramen*, grass.]

Grassy; like or pertaining to grass. *Gramineous* plants are those which have simple leaves, a jointed stem, a husky calyx, termed *glume*, and a single seed. This description however includes several sorts of corn, as well as grass. *Milne.*

GRAMINIV'OROUS, *a.* [L. *gramen*, grass, and *voro*, to eat.]

Feeding or subsisting on grass. The ox and all the bovine genus of quadrupeds are *graminivorous* animals; so also the horse or equine genus.

GRAM'MAR, *n.* [Fr. *grammaire*; L. *grammatica*; Gr. γραμματικη, from γραμμα, a letter, from γραφω, to write. See *Grave.*]
1. In *practice*, the art of speaking or writing a language with propriety or correctness, according to established usage.

As *a science*, grammar treats of the natural connection between ideas and words, and developes the principles which are common to all languages.

2. A system of general principles and of particular rules for speaking or writing a language; or a digested compilation of customary forms of speech in a nation; also, a book containing such principles and rules.
3. Propriety of speech. To write *grammar*, we must write according to the practice of good writers and speakers.

GRAM'MAR, *v. i.* To discourse according to the rules of grammar. *Obs.*

GRAM'MAR, *a.* Belonging to or contained in grammar; as a *grammar* rule.

GRAM'MAR-SCHOOL, *n.* A school in which the learned languages are taught. By *learned* languages, we usually mean the *Latin* and *Greek*; but others may be included.

GRAMMA'RIAN, *n.* One versed in grammar, or the construction of languages; a philologist.
2. One who teaches grammar.

GRAMMAT'ICAL, *a.* [Fr.] Belonging to grammar; as a *grammatical* rule.
2. According to the rules of grammar. We say, a sentence is not *grammatical*; the construction is not *grammatical*.

GRAMMAT'ICALLY, *adv.* According to the principles and rules of grammar; as, to write or speak *grammatically*.

GRAMMAT'ICASTER, *n.* [L.] A low grammarian; a pretender to a knowledge of grammar; a pedant. *Petty.*

GRAMMAT'ICIZE, *v. t.* To render grammatical. *Johnson.*

GRAM'MATIST, *n.* A pretender to a knowledge of grammar. *H. Tooke.*

GRAM'MATITE, *n.* [See *Tremolite.*]

GRAM'PLE, *n.* A crab-fish.

GRAM'PUS, *n.* [*grampoise*; Fr. *grand-poisson*, contracted. *Spelman.*]

A fish of the cetaceous order, and genus Delphinus. This fish grows to the length of twenty five feet, and is remarkably thick in proportion to its length. The nose is flat and turns up at the end. It has 30 teeth in each jaw. The spout-hole is on the top of the neck. The color of the back is black; the belly is of a snowy whiteness; and on each shoulder is a large white spot. This fish is remarkably voracious.

GRANADIL'LA, *n.* [Sp.] A plant; the fruit of the *Passiflora quadrangulata*. *Cyc.*

GRANADE, GRANADO. [See *Grenade.*]

GRAN'ARY, *n.* [L. *granarium*, from *granum*, grain; Fr. *grenier.*]

A store house or repository of grain after it is thrashed; a corn-house.

GRAN'ATE, *n.* Usually written *garnet*, which see.

GRAN'ATITE, *n.* [See *Grenatite.*]

GRAND, *a.* [Fr. *grand*; Sp. and It. *grande*; L. *grandis*; Norm. *grant*. If *n* is casual, this word coincides with *great*. But most probably it belongs to the Class *Rn*. The sense is to extend, to advance; hence it signifies old, advanced in age, as well as great.]
1. Great; but mostly in a figurative sense; illustrious; high in power or dignity; as a *grand* lord. *Raleigh.*
2. Great; splendid; magnificent; as a *grand* design; a *grand* parade; a *grand* view or prospect.
3. Great; principal; chief; as Satan our *grand* foe. *Milton.*
4. Noble; sublime; lofty; conceived or expressed with great dignity; as a *grand* conception.

In general, we apply the epithet *grand* to that which is great and elevated, or which elevates and expands our ideas. The ocean, the sky, a lofty tower are *grand* objects. But to constitute a thing *grand*, it seems necessary that it should be distinguished by some degree of beauty. *Elem. of Criticism.*

5. Old; more advanced; as in *grandfather*, *grandmother*, that is, old-father; and to correspond with this relation, we use *grandson*, *granddaughter*, *grandchild*.

GRAN'DAM, *n.* [*grand* and *dame.*] Grandmother. *Shak.*
2. An old woman. *Dryden.*

GRAND'CHILD, *n.* A son's or daughter's child; a child in the second degree of descent.

GRAND'DAUGHTER, *n.* The daughter of a son or daughter.

GRANDEE', *n.* [Sp. *grande.*] A nobleman; a man of elevated rank or station. In Spain, a nobleman of the first rank, who has the king's leave to be covered in his presence. *Encyc.*

GRANDEE'SHIP, *n.* The rank or estate of a grandee. *Swinburne.*

GRAND'EUR, *n.* [Fr. from *grand.*] In *a general sense*, greatness; that quality or combination of qualities in an object, which elevates or expands the mind, and excites pleasurable emotions in him who views or contemplates it. Thus the extent and uniformity of surface in the ocean constitute *grandeur*; as do the extent, the elevation, and the concave appearance or vault of the sky. So we speak of the *grandeur* of a large and well proportioned edifice, of an extensive range of lofty mountains, of a large cataract, of a pyramid, &c.

2. Splendor of appearance; state; magnificence; as the *grandeur* of a court, of a procession, &c.
3. Elevation of thought, sentiment or expression. We speak of the *grandeur* of conceptions, and of style or diction.
4. Elevation of mien or air and deportment.

GRANDEV'ITY, *n.* Great age. [*Not used.*]

GRANDE'VOUS, *a.* Of great age. [*Not used.*]

GRAND'F'ATHER, *n.* A father's or mother's father; the next degree above the father or mother in lineal ascent.

GRANDIL'OQUENCE, *n.* Lofty speaking; lofty expressions. *More.*

GRANDIL'OQUOUS, *a.* [L. *grandiloquus; grandis* and *loquor*, to speak.] Speaking in a lofty style.

GRAND'INOUS, *a.* [L. *grando.*] Consisting of hail. *Dict.*

GRAND'ITY, *n.* Greatness; magnificence. [*Not used.*] *Camden.*

GRANDJU'ROR, *n.* One of a grand jury. In Connecticut, a peace-officer.

GRAND JU'RY, *n.* [*grand* and *jury.*] A jury whose duty is to examine into the grounds of accusation against offenders, and if they see just cause, then to find bills of indictment against them to be presented to the court.

GRAND'LY, *adv.* In a lofty manner; splendidly; sublimely.

GRAND'MŎTHER, *n.* The mother of one's father or mother.

GRAND'NESS, *n.* Grandeur; greatness with beauty; magnificence. *Wollaston.*

GRAND'SIRE, *n.* A grandfather.
2. In poetry and rhetoric, any ancestor. *Dryden. Pope.*

GRAND'SŎN, *n.* The son of a son or daughter.

GRANĠE, *n.* grānj. [Fr. *grange*, a barn; *grangier*, a farmer; Sp. *grangear*, to cultivate; *grangero*, a farmer; Ir. *grainseach*, a grange; Scot. *grange*, the buildings belonging to a corn farm, originally a place where the rents and tithes, paid in grain to religious houses, were deposited; from *granum, grain.*]
A farm, with the buildings, stables, &c. *Milton. Shak.*

GRAN'ILITE, *n.* [See *Granit.*] Indeterminate granit; granit that contains more than three constituent parts. *Kirwan.*

GRAN'IT, GRAN'ITE, *n.* [Fr. *granit;* It. *granito*, grained.]
In *mineralogy*, an aggregate stone or rock, composed of crystaline grains of quartz, feldspar and mica, or at least of two of these minerals, united without a cement, or confusedly crystalized. The grains vary in size from that of a pin's head, to a mass of two or three feet; but usually the largest size is that of a nut. The color of granit is greatly diversified by the different colors and proportions of the component parts, and in general these stones are very hard. *Dict. Nat. Hist. Kirwan.*

GRAN'ITEL, *n.* [dim. of *granit.*] A binary aggregate of minerals; a granitic compound containing two constituent parts, as quartz and feldspar, or quartz and shorl or hornblend. *Kirwan.*
Italian workmen give this name to a variety of gray granit consisting of small grains. *Dict. Nat. Hist.*

GRANIT'IC, *a.* Pertaining to granit; like granit; having the nature of granit; as *granitic* texture.
2. Consisting of granit; as *granitic* mountains.
Granitic aggregates, in *mineralogy*, granular compounds of two or more simple minerals, in which only one of the essential ingredients of granit is present; as quartz and hornblend, feldspar and shorl, &c. Similar compounds occur, in which none of the ingredients of granit are present. *Cleaveland.*

GRAN'ITIN, *n.* A granitic aggregate of three species of minerals, some of which differ from the species which compose granit; as quartz, feldspar, and jade or shorl. *Kirwan.*

GRANIV'OROUS, *a.* [L. *granum*, grain, and *voro*, to eat.]
Eating grain; feeding or subsisting on seeds; as *granivorous* birds. *Brown.*

Grannam, for *grandam*, a grandmother. [*Vulgar.*] *B. Jonson.*

GR'ANT, *v. t.* [Norm. *granter*, to grant, to promise, or agree. I have not found this word in any other language. Perhaps *n* is not radical, for in some ancient charters it is written *grat.* "*Gratamus et concedimus.*" *Spelman.*]
1. To admit as true what is not proved; to allow; to yield; to concede. We take that for *granted* which is supposed to be true.

> *Grant* that the fates have firmed, by their decree— *Dryden.*

2. To give; to bestow or confer on without compensation, particularly in answer to prayer or request.

> Thou hast *granted* me life and favor. Job x.
> God *granted* him that which he requested. 1 Chron. iv.

3. To transfer the title of a thing to another, for a good or valuable consideration; to convey by deed or writing. The legislature have *granted* all the new land.

> *Grant* me the place of this threshing floor. 1 Chron. xxi.

GR'ANT, *n.* The act of granting; a bestowing or conferring.
2. The thing granted or bestowed; a gift; a boon.
3. In *law*, a conveyance in writing, of such things as cannot pass or be transferred by word only, as land, rents, reversions, tithes, &c.

> A *grant* is an executed contract. *Z. Swift.*

4. Concession; admission of something as true. *Dryden.*
5. The thing conveyed by deed or patent.

GR'ANTABLE, *a.* That may be granted or conveyed.

GR'ANTED, *pp.* Admitted as true; conceded; yielded; bestowed; conveyed.

GRANTEE', *n.* The person to whom a conveyance is made.

GR'ANTING, *ppr.* Admitting; conceding; bestowing; conveying.

GR'ANTOR, *n.* The person who grants; one who conveys lands, rents, &c.

GRAN'ULAR, *a.* [from L. *granum*, grain.]
1. Consisting of grains; as a *granular* substance.
2. Resembling grains; as a stone of *granular* appearance.

GRAN'ULATE, *v. t.* [Fr. *granuler*, from L. *granum.*]
1. To form into grains or small masses; as, to *granulate* powder or sugar.
2. To raise into small asperities; to make rough on the surface. *Ray.*

GRAN'ULATE, *v. i.* To collect or be formed into grains; as cane-juice *granulates* into sugar; melted metals *granulate* when poured into water.

GRAN'ULATED, *pp.* Formed into grains.
2. *a.* Consisting of grains; resembling grains.

GRAN'ULATING, *ppr.* Forming into grains.

GRANULA'TION, *n.* The act of forming into grains; as the *granulation* of powder and sugar. In *chimistry*, the *granulation* of metallic substances is performed by pouring the melted substances slowly into water, which is, at the same time, agitated with a broom. *Encyc.*

GRAN'ULE, *n.* [Sp. *granillo*, from L. *granum.*] A little grain; a small particle.

GRAN'ULOUS, *a.* Full of grains; abounding with granular substances.

GRAPE, *n.* [This word is from the root of *grab, gripe*, and signifies primarily a cluster or bunch; Fr. *grappe de raisin*, a bunch of grapes; W. *grab*, a cluster, a *grape; grabin*, a clasping; It. *grappa*, a grappling; *grappo*, a cluster, a bunch of grapes.]
1. Properly, a cluster of the fruit of the vine; but with us, a single berry of the vine; the fruit from which wine is made by expression and fermentation.
2. In the manege, *grapes* signifies mangy tumors on the legs of a horse.

GRAPE-HȲACINTH, *n.* A plant or flower, a species of Hyacinthus.

GRA'PELESS, *a.* Wanting the strength and flavor of the grape. *Jenyns.*

GRA'PESHOT, *n.* A cluster of small shot, confined in a canvas bag, forming a kind of cylinder, whose diameter is equal to that of the ball adapted to the cannon. *Encyc.*

GRA'PESTONE, *n.* The stone or seed of the grape.

GRAPH'IC, GRAPH'ICAL, *a.* [L. *graphicus;* Gr. γραφικος, from γραφω, to write.]
1. Pertaining to the art of writing or delineating.
2. Well delineated. *Bacon.*
3. Describing with accuracy.

GRAPH'ICALLY, *adv.* With good delineation; in a picturesque manner. *Brown.*

GRAPH'ITE, *n.* [Gr. γραφω, to write.] Carburet of iron, a substance used for pencils, and very improperly called *black-lead.* *Dict. Nat. Hist. Cleaveland.*

GRAPH'OLITE, *n.* [supra.] A species of slate proper for writing on.

GRAPHOM'ETER, *n.* [Gr. γραφω, to describe, and μετρον, measure.]
A mathematical instrument, called also a *semicircle*, whose use is to observe any angle whose vertex is at the center of the instrument in any plane, and to find how many degrees it contains. *Encyc.*

GRAPHOMET'RICAL, *a.* Pertaining to or ascertained by a graphometer.

GRAP'NEL, GRAP'LING, *n.* [Fr. *grappin.* See *Grapple.*]
1. A small anchor fitted with four or five

flukes or claws, used to hold boats or small vessels.

2. A grappling iron, used to seize and hold one ship to another in engagements. This is called a *fire grapling.*

GRAP'PLE, *v. t.* [Goth. *greipan*, to *gripe*; Ger. *greifen*; D. *grypen*; Dan. *griber*; Sw. *grabba, gripa*; It. *grappare*; W. *crapeaw.* See *Grape* and *Gripe.*]

1. To seize; to lay fast hold on, either with the hands or with hooks. We say, a man *grapples* his antagonist, or a ship *grapples* another ship.

2. To fasten; to fix, as the mind or heart. [*Not in use.*] *Shak.*

GRAP'PLE, *v. i.* To seize; to contend in close fight, as wrestlers. *Milton. Addison.*

To grapple with, to contend with, to struggle with successfully. *Shak.*

GRAP'PLE, *n.* A seizing; close hug in contest; the wrestler's hold. *Milton.*

2. Close fight. *Shak.*

3. A hook or iron instrument by which one ship fastens on another. *Dryden.*

GRAP'PLEMENT, *n.* A grappling; close fight or embrace.

GRA'PY, *a.* Like grapes; full of clusters of grapes. *Addison.*

2. Made of grapes. *Gay.*

GR'ASP, *v. t.* [It. *graspare.*] To seize and hold by clasping or embracing with the fingers or arms. We say, to *grasp* with the hand, or with the arms.

2. To catch; to seize; to lay hold of; to take possession of. Kings often *grasp* more than they can hold.

GR'ASP, *v. i.* To catch or seize; to gripe. *Dryden.*

2. To struggle; to strive. [*Not in use.*]

3. To encroach. *Dryden.*

To grasp at, to catch at; to try to seize. Alexander *grasped at* universal empire.

GR'ASP, *n.* The gripe or seizure of the hand. This seems to be its proper sense; but it denotes also a seizure by embrace, or infolding in the arms.

2. Possession; hold.

3. Reach of the arms; and figuratively, the power of seizing. Bonaparte seemed to think he had the Russian empire within his *grasp.*

GR'ASPED, *pp.* Seized with the hands or arms; embraced; held; possessed.

GR'ASPER, *n.* One who grasps or seizes; one who catches at; one who holds.

GR'ASPING, *ppr.* Seizing; embracing; catching; holding.

GR'ASS, *n.* [Sax. *græs, gærs* or *græd*; Goth. *gras*; G. D. *gras*; Sw. *gr̊as*; Dan. *græs.* In G. *rasen* is turf, sod, and *verrasen*, to overgrow with grass; hence, *g* may be a prefix. *Grass* may be allied to Gr. αγρωςις, κρασις, γρασις.]

1. In common usage, herbage; the plants which constitute the food of cattle and other beasts.

2. In *botany*, a plant having simple leaves, a stem generally jointed and tubular, a husky calyx, called *glume*, and the seed single. This definition includes wheat, rye, oats, barley, &c., and excludes clover and some other plants which are commonly called by the name of *grass.* The grasses form a numerous family of plants. *Encyc.*

Grass of Parnassus, a plant, the Parnassia.

GR'ASS, *v. t.* To cover with grass or with turf.

GR'ASS, *v. i.* To breed grass; to be covered with grass. *Tusser.*

GRASSA'TION, *n.* [L. *grassatio.*] A wandering about. [*Little used.*]

GR'ASS-GREEN, *a.* Green with grass. *Shenstone.*

2. Dark green, like the color of grass.

GR'ASS-GROWN, *a.* Overgrown with grass. *Thomson.*

GR'ASSHOPPER, *n.* [*grass* and *hop.*] An animal that lives among grass, a species of Gryllus.

GR'ASSINESS, *n.* [from *grassy.*] The state of abounding with grass; a grassy state.

GR'ASSLESS, *a.* Destitute of grass.

GR'ASSPLOT, *n.* A plat or level spot covered with grass.

GR'ASSPOLY, *n.* A plant, a species of Lythrum or willow-wort.

GR'ASSVETCH, *n.* A plant of the genus Lathyrus.

GR'ASSWRACK, *n.* A plant, the Zostera.

GR'ASSY, *a.* Covered with grass; abounding with grass. *Spenser.*

2. Resembling grass; green.

GRATE, *n.* [It. *grata*, L. *crates*, a grate, a hurdle. Qu. its alliance to the verb, to *grate.*]

1. A work or frame, composed of parallel or cross bars, with interstices; a kind of lattice-work, such as is used in the windows of prisons and cloisters.

2. An instrument or frame of iron bars for holding coals, used as fuel, in houses, stores, shops, &c.

GRATE, *v. t.* To furnish with grates; to make fast with cross bars.

GRATE, *v. t.* [Fr. *gratter*, It. *grattare*, to scratch; Dan. *grytter*, to grate, to break; Sp. *grieta*, a scratch, a crevice; W. *rhathu*, to rub off, to strip, to clear; *rhathell*, a rasp. See the Shemitic גרד, חרט, חרת and קרד. Class Rd. No. 38. 58. 62. 81. If *g* is a prefix, this word coincides with L. *rado.* See *Cry.*]

1. To rub, as a body with a rough surface against another body; to rub one thing against another, so as to produce a harsh sound; as, to *grate* the teeth.

2. To wear away in small particles, by rubbing with any thing rough or indented; as, to *grate* a nutmeg.

3. To offend; to fret; to vex; to irritate; to mortify; as, harsh words *grate* the heart; they are *grating* to the feelings; harsh sounds *grate* the ear.

4. To make a harsh sound, by rubbing or the friction of rough bodies. *Milton.*

GRATE, *v. i.* To rub hard, so as to offend; to offend by oppression or importunity.

> This *grated* harder upon the hearts of men. *South.*

2. To make a harsh sound by the friction of rough bodies. *Hooker.*

GRATE, *a.* [L. *gratus.*] Agreeable. [*Not in use.*]

GRA'TED, *pp.* Rubbed harshly; worn off by rubbing.

2. Furnished with a grate; as *grated* windows.

GRA'TEFUL, *a.* [from L. *gratus.* See *Grace.*]

1. Having a due sense of benefits; kindly disposed towards one from whom a favor has been received; willing to acknowledge and repay benefits; as a *grateful* heart.

2. Agreeable; pleasing; acceptable; gratifying; as a *grateful* present; a *grateful* offering.

3. Pleasing to the taste; delicious; affording pleasure; as food or drink *grateful* to the appetite.

> Now golden fruits on loaded branches shine,
> And *grateful* clusters swell with floods of wine. *Pope.*

GRA'TEFULLY, *adv.* With a due sense of benefits or favors; in a manner that disposes to kindness, in return for favors. The gift was *gratefully* received.

2. In a pleasing manner. Study continually furnishes something new, which may strike the imagination *gratefully.*

GRA'TEFULNESS, *n.* The quality of being grateful; gratitude.

2. The quality of being agreeable or pleasant to the mind or to the taste.

GRA'TER, *n.* [See *Grate.*] An instrument or utensil with a rough indented surface, for rubbing off small particles of a body; as a *grater* for nutmegs.

GRATIFICA'TION, *n.* [L. *gratificatio*, from *gratificor*; *gratus* and *facio*, to make.]

1. The act of pleasing, either the mind, the taste or the appetite. We speak of the *gratification* of the taste or the palate, of the appetites, of the senses, of the desires, of the mind, soul or heart.

2. That which affords pleasure; satisfaction; delight. It is not easy to renounce *gratifications* to which we are accustomed.

3. Reward; recompense. *Morton.*

GRAT'IFIED, *pp.* Pleased; indulged according to desire.

GRAT'IFIER, *n.* One who gratifies or pleases.

GRAT'IFY, *v. t.* [L. *gratificor*; *gratus*, agreeable, and *facio*, to make.]

1. To please; to give pleasure to; to indulge; as, to *gratify* the taste, the appetite, the senses, the desires, the mind, &c.

2. To delight; to please; to humor; to soothe; to satisfy; to indulge to satisfaction.

> For who would die to *gratify* a foe? *Dryden.*

3. To requite; to recompense.

GRAT'IFYING, *ppr.* Pleasing; indulging to satisfaction.

2. *a.* Giving pleasure; affording satisfaction.

GRA'TING, *ppr.* [See *Grate.*] Rubbing; wearing off in particles.

2. *a.* Fretting; irritating; harsh; as *grating* sounds, or a *grating* reflection.

GRA'TING, GRA'TINGS, *n.* [See *Grate.*] A partition of bars; an open cover for the hatches of a ship, resembling lattice-work. *Mar. Dict.*

GRA'TINGLY, *adv.* Harshly; offensively; in a manner to irritate.

GRA'TIS, *adv.* [L.] For nothing; freely; without recompense; as, to give a thing *gratis*; to perform service *gratis.*

GRAT'ITUDE, *n.* [L. *gratitudo*, from *gratus*, pleasing. See *Grace.*]

An emotion of the heart, excited by a favor or benefit received; a sentiment of kindness or good will towards a benefactor; thankfulness. Gratitude is an agreeable emotion, consisting in or accompanied with good will to a benefactor, and a disposition to make a suitable return of benefits or services, or when no return can be made, with a desire to see the benefactor prosperous and happy. Gratitude is a virtue of the highest excellence, as it implies a feeling and generous heart, and a proper sense of duty.

The love of God is the sublimest *gratitude*. *Paley.*

GRATU'ITOUS, *a.* [L. *gratuitus*, from *gratus*; Fr. *gratuit*; It. *gratuito*. See *Grace*.]

1. Free; voluntary; not required by justice; granted without claim or merit.

We mistake the *gratuitous* blessings of heaven for the fruits of our own industry. *L'Estrange.*

2. Asserted or taken without proof; as a *gratuitous* argument or affirmation.

GRATU'ITOUSLY, *adv.* Freely; voluntarily; without claim or merit; without an equivalent or compensation; as labor or services *gratuitously* bestowed.

2. Without proof; as a principle *gratuitously* assumed.

GRATU'ITY, *n.* [Fr. *gratuité*, from *gratuit*, from *gratus*.]

1. A free gift; a present; a donation; that which is given without a compensation or equivalent.

2. Something given in return for a favor; an acknowledgment.

GRAT'ULATE, *v. t.* [L. *gratulor*, from *gratus*, pleasing, grateful; Russ. with the prefix *na*, *nagrada*, recompense; *nagrajdayu*, to gratify, to reward. See *Grace*.]

1. To express joy or pleasure to a person, on account of his success, or the reception of some good; to salute with declarations of joy; to congratulate. [*The latter word is more generally used.*]

To *gratulate* the gentle princes there. *Shak.*

2. To wish or express joy to. *Shak.*

3. To declare joy for; to mention with joy. *B. Jonson.*

GRAT'ULATED, *pp.* Addressed with expressions of joy.

GRAT'ULATING, *ppr.* Addressing with expressions of joy, on account of some good received.

GRATULA'TION, *n.* [L. *gratulatio*.] An address or expression of joy to a person, on account of some good received by him; congratulation.

I shall turn my wishes into *gratulations*. *South.*

GRAT'ULATORY, *a.* Expressing gratulation; congratulatory.

GRAVE, a final syllable, is a grove, Sax. *græf*; or it is an officer, Ger. *graf*.

GRAVE, *v. t.* pret. *graved*; pp. *graven* or *graved*. [Fr. *graver*; Sp. *grabar*; Sax. *grafan*; G. *graben*; D. *graaven*; Dan. *graver*; Sw. *grafva*; Arm. *engraffi*, *engravi*; Ir. *grafadh*, *grafaim*; W. *criviaw*, from *rhiv*; Gr. γραφω, to write; originally all writing was *graving*; Eng. to *scrape*; Ch. and Syr. כרב to plow. See Class Rb. No. 30.]

1. To carve or cut letters or figures on stone or other hard substance, with a chisel or edged tool; to engrave. [*The latter word is now more generally used.*]

Thou shalt take two onyx-stones and *grave* on them the names of the children of Israel. Ex. xxviii.

2. To carve; to form or shape by cutting with a chisel; as, to *grave* an image.

Thou shalt not make unto thee any *graven* image. Ex. xx.

3. To clean a ship's bottom by burning off filth, grass or other foreign matter, and paying it over with pitch.

4. To entomb. [*Unusual.*] *Shak.*

GRAVE, *v. i.* To carve; to write or delineate on hard substances; to practice engraving.

GRAVE, *n.* [Sax. *græf*; G. *grab*; D. Sw. *graf*; Dan. *grav*; Russ. *grob*, a ditch, a trench, a grave; L. *scrobs*. See the Verb.]

1. The ditch, pit or excavated place in which a dead human body is deposited; a place for the corpse of a human being; a sepulcher.

2. A tomb.

3. Any place where the dead are reposited; a place of great slaughter or mortality. Flanders was formerly the *grave* of English armies. Russia proved to be the *grave* of the French army under Bonaparte. The tropical climates are the *grave* of American seamen and of British soldiers.

4. *Graves*, in *the plural*, sediment of tallow melted. [*Not in use or local.*]

GRA'VE-CLOTHES, *n.* The clothes or dress in which the dead are interred.

GRA'VE-DIGGER, *n.* One whose occupation is to dig graves.

GRA'VE-MAKER, *n.* A grave-digger. *Shak.*

GRA'VE-STONE, *n.* A stone laid over a grave, or erected near it, as a monument to preserve the memory of the dead.

GRAVE, *a.* [Fr. Sp. It. *grave*; Arm. *grevus*; from L. *gravis*, heavy, whence L. *gravo*, and *aggravo*, to *aggravate*. Hence *grief*, which see. Ar. كَرَبَ karaba, to overload, to press, to grieve. Class Rb. No. 30.] Properly, pressing, heavy. Hence,

1. In *music*, low; depressed; solemn; opposed to *sharp*, *acute*, or *high*; as a *grave* tone or sound. Sometimes *grave* denotes slow.

2. Solemn; sober; serious; opposed to *gay*, *light* or *jovial*; as a man of a *grave* deportment; a *grave* character.

Youth on silent wings is flown;
Graver years come rolling on. *Prior.*

3. Plain; not gay; not showy or tawdry; as a *grave* suit of clothes.

4. Being of weight; of a serious character; as a *grave* writer.

GRA'VED, *pp.* [See the Verb.] Carved; engraved; cleaned, as a ship.

GRAV'EL, *n.* [Fr. *gravelle*, *gravier*; Arm. *grevell*, or *maen-gravell*, [stone gravel;] Ger. *grober sand*, coarse sand; D. *graveel*. Probably from rubbing, grating. See *Grave*, the verb.]

1. Small stones or fragments of stone, or very small pebbles, larger than the particles of sand, but often intermixed with them.

2. In *medicine*, small calculous concretions in the kidneys and bladder. *Cyc.*

GRAV'EL, *v. t.* To cover with gravel; as, to *gravel* a walk.

2. To stick in the sand. *Camden.*

3. To puzzle; to stop; to embarrass. *Prior.*

4. To hurt the foot of a horse, by gravel lodged under the shoe.

GRAV'ELED, *pp.* Covered with gravel; stopped; embarrassed; injured by gravel.

GRA'VELESS, *a.* [from *grave*.] Without a grave or tomb; unburied. *Shak.*

GRAV'ELLY, *a.* [from *gravel*.] Abounding with gravel; consisting of gravel; as a *gravelly* soil or land.

GRAV'EL-WALK, *n.* A walk or alley covered with gravel, which makes a hard and dry bottom; *used in gardens and malls.*

GRA'VELY, *adv.* [from *grave*.] In a grave, solemn manner; soberly; seriously.

The queen of learning *gravely* smiles. *Swift.*

2. Without gaudiness or show; as, to be dressed *gravely*.

GRA'VENESS, *n.* Seriousness; solemnity; sobriety of behavior; gravity of manners or discourse. *Denham.*

GRA'VER, *n.* [See *Grave*.] One who carves or engraves; one whose profession is to cut letters or figures in stone, &c.; a sculptor.

2. An engraving tool; an instrument for graving on hard substances.

GRAV'ID, *a.* [L. *gravidus*, from *gravis*, heavy.]

Pregnant; being with child. *Herbert.*

GRAV'IDATED, *a.* Made pregnant; big. [*Not in use.*] *Barrow.*

GRAVIDA'TION, *n.* Pregnancy. [*Not in use.*] *Pearson.*

GRAVID'ITY, *n.* Pregnancy. [*Not in use.*] *Arbuthnot.*

GRA'VING, *ppr.* Engraving; carving; cutting figures on stone, copper or other hard substance.

GRA'VING, *n.* Carved work. 2 Chron. ii.

2. Impression. *King Charles.*

GRAV'ITATE, *v. i.* [Sp. *gravitar*; Fr. *graviter*; from L. *gravitas*, from *gravis*, heavy.]

To tend to the center of a body, or the central point of attraction. Thus a body elevated above the earth tends to fall, that is, it *gravitates* towards the center of the earth; and the planets are supposed to *gravitate* towards the sun, or center of the solar system.

GRAV'ITATING, *ppr.* Tending to the center of a body or system of bodies.

GRAVITA'TION, *n.* The act of tending to the center.

2. The force by which bodies are pressed or drawn, or by which they tend towards the center of the earth or other center, or the effect of that force. Thus the falling of a body to the earth is ascribed to *gravitation*. *Encyc.*

GRAV'ITY, *n.* [Fr. *gravité*; Sp. *gravidad*; L. *gravitas*, from *gravis*, heavy. See *Grave*.]

1. Weight; heaviness.

2. In *philosophy*, that force by which bodies tend or are pressed or drawn towards the center of the earth, or towards some other center, or the effect of that force; in which last sense *gravity* is synonymous with *weight*. *Encyc.*

Gravity is the tendency of great bodies to a center, or the sum or results of all the attractions of all the molecules composing a great body. *Dict. Nat. Hist.*

The force of *gravity* in a body is in direct proportion to its quantity of matter.

3. *Specific gravity*, the weight belonging to an equal bulk of every different substance. Thus the exact weight of a cubic inch of gold, compared with that of a cubic inch of water or tin, is called its *specific gravity*. The specific gravity of bodies is usually ascertained by weighing them in distilled water. *Encyc.*

4. Seriousness; sobriety of manners; solemnity of deportment or character.

Great Cato there, for *gravity* renowned. *Dryden.*

5. Weight; enormity; atrociousness; as the *gravity* of an injury. [*Not used.*] *Hooker.*

6. In *music*, lowness of sound.

GRA'VY, *n.* The fat and other liquid matter that drips from flesh in roasting, or when roasted or baked, or a mixture of that juice with flour.

GRAY, *a.* [Sax. *grig*, *græg*; G. *grau*; D. *graauw*; Dan. *graae*; Sw. *grå*; It. *grigio*; Ir. *gre*. This is probably Γραικος, *Græcus*, *Greek*, *Graii*, the name given to the Greeks, on account of their fair complexion compared with the Asiatics and Africans. [See *Europe*.]

Φορκυι δ' αυ Κητω Γραιας τεκε καλλιπαρηους,
Εκ γενετης πολιας. τας δη Γραιας καλεουσιν—
Hesiod. Theog. 270.

"Keto bore to Phorcus the Graiæ with fair cheeks, *white* from their birth, and hence they were called Graiæ." The Greek word γραια is rendered an old woman, and in this passage of Hesiod, is supposed to mean certain deities. The probability is, that it is applied to an old woman, because she is *gray*. But the fable of Hesiod is easily explained by supposing the author to have had in his mind some imperfect account of the origin of the Greeks.]

1. White, with a mixture of black.

These *gray* and dun colors may be also produced by mixing whites and blacks. *Newton.*

2. White; hoary; as *gray* hair. We apply the word to hair that is partially or wholly white.

3. Dark; of a mixed color; of the color of ashes; as *gray* eyes; the *gray*-eyed morn. *Gay. Shak.*

4. Old; mature; as *gray* experience. *Ames.*

GRAY, *n.* A gray color. *Parnel.*

2. A badger. *Ainsworth.*

GRA'Y-BEARD, *n.* An old man. *Shak.*

GRA'Y-EŸED, *a.* Having gray eyes.

GRA'YFLŸ, *n.* The trumpet-fly. *Milton.*

GRA'Y-HAIRED, *a.* Having gray hair.

GRA'Y-HEADED, *a.* Having a gray head or gray hair.

GRA'YHOUND, *n.* [Sax. *grighund*.] A tall fleet dog, used in the chase.

GRA'YISH, *a.* Somewhat gray; gray in a moderate degree.

GRA'YLING, *n.* A fish of the genus Salmo, called also umber, a voracious fish, about sixteen or eighteen inches in length, of a more elegant figure than the trout; the back and sides are of a silvery gray color. It is found in clear rapid streams in the north of Europe, and is excellent food. *Dict. Nat. Hist.*

GRA'YNESS, *n.* The quality of being gray. *Sherwood.*

GRAYWACKE, *n.* [G. *grauwacke*.] A rock somewhat remarkable in its structure and geological relations; a kind of sandstone, composed of grains or fragments of different minerals, chiefly of quartz, feldspar, siliceous slate and argillite. These fragments are sometimes angular, and sometimes their edges and angles are rounded, thus forming nodules or globular masses. The size is very variable, passing from grains to nodules of a foot in diameter. The several ingredients are united by an indurated argillaceous substance, or the interstices between the larger fragments are filled by the same materials which compose the larger parts of the rock, but in grains so comminuted as to resemble a homogeneous cement. The colors are some shade of gray or brown, as bluish gray, reddish brown, &c. *Cleaveland.*

GRAZE, *v. t.* [Sax. *grasian*; G. *grasen*; D. *graazen*; from *grass*, or from the root of L. *rado*, *rasi*, or *rodo*, *rosi*, Sp. *rozar*, Port. *roçar*, to rub against, to graze. In Russ. *grizu*, or *grezu*, signifies to bite, to gnaw.]

1. To rub or touch lightly in passing; to brush lightly the surface of a thing in passing; as, the bullet *grazed* the wall or the earth.

2. To feed or supply cattle with grass; to furnish pasture for; as, the farmer *grazes* large herds of cattle.

3. To feed on; to eat from the ground, as growing herbage.

The lambs with wolves shall *graze* the verdant mead. *Pope.*

4. To tend grazing cattle; as, Jacob *grazed* Laban's sheep. *Shak.*

GRAZE, *v. i.* To eat grass; to feed on growing herbage; as, cattle *graze* on the meadows.

2. To supply grass; as, the ground will not *graze* well. *Bacon.*

3. To move on devouring. *Bacon.*

GRA'ZED, *pp.* Touched lightly by a passing body; brushed.

2. Fed by growing grass; as, cattle are *grazed*.

3. Eaten, as growing herbage; as, the fields were *grazed*.

GRA'ZER, *n.* One that grazes or feeds on growing herbage. *Philips.*

GRA'ZIER, *n. gra'zhur.* One who feeds cattle with grass, or supplies them with pasture. *Bacon.*

GRA'ZING, *ppr.* Touching lightly, as a moving body.

2. Feeding on growing herbage; as *grazing* cattle.

3. *a.* Supplying pasture; as a *grazing* farm.

GREASE, *n.* [Fr. *graisse*; It. *grasso*; Sp. *grasa*, grease; Port. *graxa*, grease for wheels, and a distemper in a horse when his fat is melted by excessive action. *Port. Dict.*]

1. Animal fat in a soft state; oily or unctuous matter of any kind, as tallow, lard; but particularly the fatty matter of land animals, as distinguished from the oily matter of marine animals.

2. A swelling and gourdiness of a horse's legs, occasioned by traveling or by standing long in a stable. *Encyc. Johnson.*

GREASE, *v. t. greez.* To smear, anoint or daub with grease or fat.

2. To bribe; to corrupt with presents. [*Not elegant.*] *Dryden.*

GRE'ASED, *pp.* Smeared with oily matter; bribed.

GRE'ASILY, *adv.* With grease or an appearance of it; grossly.

GRE'ASINESS, *n.* The state of being greasy; oiliness; unctuousness. *Boyle.*

GRE'ASING, *ppr.* Smearing with fat or oily matter; bribing.

GRE'ASY, *a. greez'y.* Oily; fat; unctuous.

2. Smeared or defiled with grease.

3. Like grease or oil; smooth; as a fossil that has a *greasy* feel.

4. Fat of body; bulky. [*Little used.*] *Shak.*

5. Gross; indelicate; indecent. *Marston.*

GREAT, *a.* [Sax. *great*; D. *groot*; G. *gross*; Norm. *gres*; It. *grosso*; Sp. *grueso*; Port. *grosso*; Fr. *gros*; Arm. *groçz*; and probably L. *crassus*. *Great* and *gross* are the same word dialectically varied in orthography. See Class Rd. No. 59. 22. 79.]

1. Large in bulk or dimensions; a term of comparison, denoting more magnitude or extension than something else, or beyond what is usual; as a *great* body; a *great* house; a *great* farm.

2. Being of extended length or breadth; as a *great* distance; a *great* lake.

3. Large in number; as a *great* many; a *great* multitude.

4. Expressing a large, extensive or unusual degree of any thing; as *great* fear; *great* love; *great* strength; *great* wealth; *great* power; *great* influence; *great* folly.

5. Long continued; as a *great* while.

6. Important; weighty; as a *great* argument; a *great* truth; a *great* event; a thing of no *great* consequence; it is no *great* matter.

7. Chief; principal; as the *great* seal of England.

8. Chief; of vast power and excellence; supreme; illustrious; as the *great* God; the *great* Creator.

9. Vast; extensive; wonderful; admirable.

Great are thy works, Jehovah. *Milton.*

10. Possessing large or strong powers of mind; as a *great* genius.

11. Having made extensive or unusual acquisitions of science or knowledge; as a *great* philosopher or botanist; a *great* scholar.

12. Distinguished by rank, office or power; elevated; eminent; as a *great* lord; the *great* men of the nation; the *great* Mogul; Alexander the *great*.

13. Dignified in aspect, mien or manner.

Amidst the crowd she walks serenely *great*. *Dryden.*

14. Magnanimous; generous; of elevated sentiments; high-minded. He has a *great* soul.

15. Rich; sumptuous; magnificent. He disdained not to appear at *great* tables. A *great* feast or entertainment.

16. Vast; sublime; as a *great* conception or idea.

17. Dignified; noble.

Nothing can be *great* which is not right. *Rambler.*

18. Swelling; proud; as, he was not disheartened by *great* looks.

19. Chief; principal; much traveled; as a *great* road. The ocean is called the *great* highway of nations.

20. Pregnant; teeming; as *great* with young.

21. Hard; difficult. It is no *great* matter to live in peace with meek people.

22. Familiar; intimate. [*Vulgar.*]

23. Distinguished by extraordinary events, or unusual importance. Jude 6.

24. Denoting a degree of consanguinity, in the ascending or descending line, as *great* grandfather, the father of a grandfather; *great great* grandfather, the father of a *great* grandfather, and so on indefinitely; and *great* grandson, *great great* grandson. &c.

25. Superior; preeminent; as *great* chamberlain; *great* marshal.

The sense of *great* is to be understood by the things it is intended to qualify. *Great* pain or wrath is violent pain or wrath; *great* love is ardent love; *great* peace is entire peace; a *great* name is extensive renown; a *great* evil or sin, is a sin of deep malignity, &c.

GREAT, *n.* The whole; the gross; the lump or mass; as, a carpenter contracts to build a ship by the *great.*

2. People of rank or distinction. The poor envy the *great*, and the *great* despise the poor.

GREAT-BELLIED, *a.* Pregnant; teeming. *Shak.*

GREATEN, *v. t.* To enlarge. *Obs.* *Raleigh.*

GREAT-HEARTED, *a.* High-spirited; undejected. *Clarendon.*

GREATLY, *adv.* In a great degree; much.

I will *greatly* multiply thy sorrow. Gen. iii.

2. Nobly; illustriously.

By a high fate, thou *greatly* didst expire. *Dryden.*

3. Magnanimously; generously; bravely. He *greatly* scorned to turn his back on his foe. He *greatly* spurned the offered boon.

GREATNESS, *n.* Largeness of bulk, dimensions, number or quantity; as the *greatness* of a mountain, of an edifice, of a multitude, or of a sum of money. With reference to solid bodies, however, we more generally use *bulk, size, extent* or *magnitude* than *greatness;* as the *bulk* or *size* of the body; the *extent* of the ocean; the *magnitude* of the sun or of the earth.

2. Large amount; extent; as the *greatness* of a reward.

3. High degree; as the *greatness* of virtue or vice.

4. High rank or place; elevation; dignity; distinction; eminence; power; command.

Farewell, a long farewell to all my *greatness.* *Shak.*

5. Swelling pride; affected state.

It is not of pride or *greatness* that he cometh not aboard your ships. *Bacon.*

6. Magnanimity; elevation of sentiment; nobleness; as *greatness* of mind.

Virtue is the only solid basis of *greatness.* *Rambler.*

7. Strength or extent of intellectual faculties; as the *greatness* of genius.

8. Large extent or variety; as the *greatness* of a man's acquisitions.

9. Grandeur; pomp; magnificence.

Greatness with Timon dwells in such a draught,
As brings all Brobdignag before your thought. *Pope.*

10. Force; intensity; as the *greatness* of sound, of passion, heat, &c.

GREAVE, for *grove* and *groove.* [See *Grove* and *Groove.*] *Spenser.*

GREAVES, *n. plu. greevz.* [Port. Sp. *grevas.* In Fr. *greve* is the calf of the leg.]

Armor for the legs; a sort of boots. 1 Sam. xvii.

GREBE, *n.* A fowl of the genus Colymbus and order of ansers, of several species; as the tippet-grebe, the horned grebe, the eared grebe or dob-chick. *Encyc.*

GRE'CIAN, *a.* Pertaining to Greece.

GRE'CIAN, *n.* A native of Greece. Also, a Jew who understood Greek. Acts vi.

2. One well versed in the Greek language.

GRE'CISM, *n.* [L. *græcismus.*] An idiom of the Greek language. *Addison.*

GRE'CIZE, *v. t.* To render Grecian.

2. To translate into Greek.

GRE'CIZE, *v. i.* To speak the Greek language.

GREE, *n.* [Fr. *gré.* See *Agree.*] Good will. *Obs.* *Spenser.*

2. Step; rank; degree. [See *Degree.*] *Obs.* *Spenser.*

GREE. *v. i.* To agree. *Obs.* [See *Agree.*]

GREECE, *n.* [W. *grâz;* L. *gressus.* It ought to be written *grese*, but it is entirely obsolete.] A flight of steps. *Bacon.*

GREED, *n.* Greediness. *Obs.* *Graham.*

GREE'DILY, *adv.* [See *Greedy.*] With a keen appetite for food or drink; voraciously; ravenously; as, to eat or swallow *greedily.*

2. With keen or ardent desire; eagerly. Jude 11.

GREE'DINESS, *n.* Keenness of appetite for food or drink; ravenousness; voracity.

Fox in stealth, wolf in *greediness.* *Shak.*

2. Ardent desire.

GREE'DY, *a.* [Sax. *grædig;* D. *greetig;* Goth. *gredags*, from *gredon*, to hunger. It agrees in elements with L. *gradior*, and probably signifies reaching forward.]

1. Having a keen appetite for food or drink; ravenous; voracious; very hungry; followed by *of;* as a lion that is *greedy of* his prey. Ps. xvii.

2. Having a keen desire of any thing; eager to obtain; as *greedy* of gain.

GREEK, *a.* Pertaining to Greece. [See *Gray.*]

GREEK, *n.* A native of Greece.

2. The language of Greece.

Greek-fire, a combustible composition, the constituents of which are supposed to be asphalt, with niter and sulphur. *Ure.*

GREE'KISH, *a.* Peculiar to Greece. *Milton.*

GREE'KLING, *n.* An inferior Greek writer. *B. Jonson.*

GREE'KROSE, *n.* The flower campion.

GREEN, *a.* [Sax. *grene;* G. *grün;* D. *groen;* Dan. *grön;* Sw. *grön;* Heb. רען to grow, to flourish. Class Rn. No. 7.]

1. Properly, growing, flourishing, as plants; hence, of the color of herbage and plants when growing, a color composed of blue and yellow rays, one of the original prismatic colors; verdant.

2. New; fresh; recent; as a *green* wound.

The *greenest* usurpation. *Burke.*

3. Fresh; flourishing; undecayed; as *green* old age.

4. Containing its natural juices; not dry; not seasoned; as *green* wood; *green* timber.

5. Not roasted; half raw.

We say the meat is *green*, when half roasted. *Watts.*

[Rarely, if ever used in America.]

6. Unripe; immature; not arrived to perfection; as *green* fruit. Hence,

7. Immature in age; young; as *green* in age or judgment.

8. Pale; sickly; wan; of a greenish pale color. *Shak.*

GREEN, *n.* The color of growing plants; a color composed of blue and yellow rays, which, mixed in different proportions, exhibit a variety of shades; as apple *green*, meadow *green*, leek *green*, &c.

2. A grassy plain or plat; a piece of ground covered with verdant herbage.

O'er the smooth enameled *green.* *Milton.*

3. Fresh leaves or branches of trees or other plants; wreaths; *usually in the plural.*

The fragrant *greens* I seek, my brows to bind. *Dryden.*

4. The leaves and stems of young plants used in cookery or dressed for food in the spring; *in the plural.* *New England.*

GREEN, *v. t.* To make green. This is used by Thomson and by Barlow, but is not an elegant word, nor indeed hardly legitimate, in the sense in which these writers use it. "Spring *greens* the year." "God *greens* the groves." The only legitimate sense of this verb, if used, would be, to dye green, or to change to a green color. A plant growing in a dark room is yellow; let this plant be carried into the open air, and the rays of the sun will *green* it. This use would correspond with the use of *whiten, blacken, redden.*

GREE'NBROOM, **GREE'NWEED**, } *n.* A plant of the genus Genista.

GREE'NCLOTH, *n.* A board or court of justice held in the counting house of the British king's household, composed of the lord steward and the officers under him. This court has the charge and cognizance of all matters of justice in the king's household, with power to correct offenders and keep the peace of the verge, or jurisdiction of the court-royal, which extends every way two hundred yards from the gate of the palace. *Johnson. Encyc.*

GREE'N-CROP, *n.* A crop of green vegetables, such as artificial grasses, turneps, &c. *Cyc.*

GREE'N-EARTH, *n.* A species of earth or mineral, so called; the mountain green of artists. *Ure.*

GREE'N-EYED, *a.* Having green eyes; as *green-eyed* jealousy. *Shak.*

GREE'NFINCH, *n.* A bird of the genus Fringilla.

GREE'NFISH, *n.* A fish so called. *Ains.*

GREE'NGAGE, *n.* A species of plum.

GREE'N-GROCER, *n.* A retailer of greens.

GREE'NHAIRED, *a.* Having green locks or hair. *Mason.*

GREE'NHOOD, *n.* A state of greenness. *Chaucer.*

GREE'NHORN, *n.* A raw youth.

GREE'N-HOUSE, *n.* A house in which tender plants are sheltered from the weather, and preserved green during the winter or cold weather.

GREE'NISH, *a.* Somewhat green; having a tinge of green; as a *greenish* yellow. *Newton.*

GREE'NISHNESS, *n.* The quality of being greenish.

GREE'NLY, *adv.* With a green color; newly; freshly; immaturely.

GREE'NNESS, *n.* The quality of being green; viridity; as the *greenness* of grass or of a meadow.

2. Immaturity; unripeness; *in a literal or figurative sense;* as the *greenness* of fruit; the *greenness* of youth.

3. Freshness; vigor. *South.*

4. Newness.

GREE'N-SICKNESS, *n.* The chlorosis, a disease of maids, so called from the color it occasions in the face.

GREE'N-STALL, *n.* A stall on which greens are exposed to sale.

GREE'NSTONE, *n.* [so called from a tinge of green in the color.]

A rock of the trap formation, consisting of hornblend and feldspar in the state of grains or small crystals. *Ure.*

GREE'N-SWARD, *n.* Turf green with grass.

GREE'N-WEED, *n.* Dyer's weed.

GREE'NWOOD, *n.* Wood when green, as in summer.

GREE'NWOOD, *a.* Pertaining to a greenwood; as a *greenwood* shade. *Dryden.*

GREET, *v. t.* [Sax. *gretan, grettan,* to salute, to exclaim, to cry out, to bid farewell, to approach, to touch; G. *grüssen;* D. *groeten,* to greet; Sax. *grædan,* to cry; Goth. *greitan,* Sw. *gråta,* Dan. *græder,* to weep; It. *gridare;* Sp. Port. *gritar;* W. *grydian, grydiaw,* to shout, to scream or shriek, to wail, to make a vehement rough noise; perhaps L. *rudo,* to bray, to roar. See Class Rd. No. 7. 19. 43. 70. 75.]

1. To address with expressions of kind wishes; to salute in kindness and respect.

> My lord, the Mayor of London comes to *greet* you. *Shak.*

2. To address at meeting; to address in any manner. *Shak.*

3. To congratulate.

4. To pay compliments at a distance; to send kind wishes to. Col. iv. 2 Tim. iv.

5. To meet and address with kindness; or to express kind wishes accompanied with an embrace. 1 Thess. v.

6. To meet. *Shak.*

GREET, *v. i.* To meet and salute.

> There *greet* in silence, as the dead are wont,
> And sleep in peace. *Shak.*

2. To weep; written by Spenser *greit.* *Obs.*

GREE'TED, *pp.* Addressed with kind wishes; complimented.

GREE'TER, *n.* One who greets.

GREE'TING, *ppr.* Addressing with kind wishes or expressions of joy; complimenting; congratulating; saluting.

GREE'TING, *n.* Expression of kindness or joy; salutation at meeting; compliment addressed from one absent.

GREEZE, *n.* [L. *gressus.*] A step, or flight of steps. *Obs.* [See *Greece.*]

GREF'FIER, *n.* [Fr. See *Graft.*] A registrar, or recorder. *Bp. Hall.*

GRE'GAL, *a.* [L. *grex.*] Pertaining to a flock. *Dict.*

GREGA'RIAN, *a.* [See *Gregarious.*] Belonging to the herd or common sort. *Howell.*

GREGA'RIOUS, *a.* [L. *gregarius,* from *grex,* a herd.]

Having the habit of assembling or living in a flock or herd; not habitually solitary or living alone. Cattle and sheep are *gregarious* animals. Many species of birds are *gregarious.* Rapacious animals are generally not *gregarious.*

GREGA'RIOUSLY, *adv.* In a flock or herd; in a company.

GREGA'RIOUSNESS, *n.* The state or quality of living in flocks or herds.

GREGO'RIAN, *a.* Denoting what belongs to Gregory. The *Gregorian* calendar, is one which shows the new and full moon, with the time of Easter, and the movable feasts depending thereon, by means of epacts. The *Gregorian* year, is the present year, as reformed by pope Gregory XIII, in 1582; consisting of 365 days, 5 hours, 48 minutes, 47 seconds, with an additional day every fourth year. *Encyc.*

GREIT, *v. i.* [Goth. *greitan.*] To lament. *Obs.* *Spenser.*

GREITH, *v. t.* [Sax. *geredian,* to prepare; *ge* and *hræde,* ready.] To make ready. *Obs.* *Chaucer.*

GREITH, *n.* Goods; furniture. *Obs.* *Chaucer.*

GRE'MIAL, *a.* [L. *gremium.*] Belonging to the lap or bosom. *Dict.*

GRENA'DE, *n.* [Sp. *granada,* It. *granata,* Fr. *grenade,* a pomegranate, or *grained* apple.]

In *the art of war,* a hollow ball or shell of iron or other metal, about two inches and a half in diameter, to be filled with powder which is to be fired by means of a fusee, and thrown by hand among enemies. This, bursting into many pieces, does great injury, and is particularly useful in annoying an enemy in trenches and other lodgments. *Encyc.*

GRENADIE'R, *n.* [from Fr. *grenade,* Sp. *granada,* a pomegranate tree; so called, it is said, from the cap worn, which resembled the flowers of that tree; or as others alledge, so called from carrying and throwing hand grenades. The latter is the opinion of Lunier.]

1. A foot soldier, wearing a high cap. Grenadiers are usually tall, active soldiers, distinguished from others chiefly by their dress and arms; a company of them is usually attached to each battalion. *Encyc.*

2. A fowl found in Angola, in Africa.

GREN'ATITE, *n.* Staurotide or staurolite, a mineral of a dark reddish brown. It occurs imbedded in mica slate, and in talck, and is infusible by the blowpipe. It is called also prismatic garnet. *Cyc.*

GREW, *pret.* of *grow.*

GREY. [See *Gray.*]

GREYHOUND, *n.* [Sax. *grighund.*] A tall fleet dog, kept for the chase.

GRICE, *n.* A little pig.

GRID'DLE, *n.* [W. *greidell,* from *grediaw,* to heat, singe, scorch.]

A pan, broad and shallow, for baking cakes.

GRIDE, *v. t.* [It. *gridare;* Sp. *gritar;* Port. *id.;* Fr. *crier;* Eng. to *cry;* Sax. *grædan;* Dan. *græder;* Sw. *gråta.* See *Greet.*]

To grate, or to cut with a grating sound; to cut; to penetrate or pierce harshly; as the *griding* sword. *Milton.*

> That through his thigh the mortal steel did *gride.* *Spenser.*

GRID'ELIN, *n.* [Fr. *gris de lin,* flax gray.] A color mixed of white and red, or a gray violet. *Dryden.*

GRID'IRON, *n.* [W. *grediaw,* Ir. *greadam,* to heat, scorch, roast, and *iron.* See *Griddle.*]

A grated utensil for broiling flesh and fish over coals.

GRIEF, *n.* [D. *grief,* hurt; Fr. *grief,* and *grever,* to oppress; Sp. *agravio;* Norm. *grief, gref, greve;* L. *gravis.* See *Grave* and *Aggravate.* The sense is pressure or oppression.]

1. The pain of mind produced by loss, misfortune, injury or evils of any kind; sorrow; regret. We experience *grief* when we lose a friend, when we incur loss, when we consider ourselves injured, and by sympathy, we feel *grief* at the misfortunes of others.

2. The pain of mind occasioned by our own misconduct; sorrow or regret that we have done wrong; pain accompanying repentance. We feel *grief* when we have offended or injured a friend, and the consciousness of having offended the Supreme Being, fills the penitent heart with the most poignant *grief.*

3. Cause of sorrow; that which afflicts.

> Who were a *grief* of mind to Isaac and Rebekah. Gen. xxvi.
>
> A foolish son is a *grief* to his father. Prov. xvii.

GRIE'FFUL, *a.* Full of grief or sorrow. *Sackville.*

GRIE'FSHOT, *a.* Pierced with grief. *Shak.*

GRIE'VABLE, *a.* Lamentable. *Obs.* *Gower.*

GRIE'VANCE, *n.* [from *grief.*] That which causes grief or uneasiness; that which burdens, oppresses or injures, implying a sense of wrong done, or a continued injury, and therefore applied only to the effects of *human* conduct; never to providential evils. The oppressed subject has the right to petition for a redress of *grievances.*

GRIEVE, *v. t.* [D. *grieven;* Fr. *grever,* to oppress; Sp. *agraviar, agravar;* It. *gravare;* L. *gravo,* from *gravis.* See *Grave.*]

1. To give pain of mind to; to afflict; to wound the feelings. Nothing *grieves* a parent like the conduct of a profligate child.

2. To afflict; to inflict pain on.

> For he doth not afflict willingly, nor *grieve* the children of men. Lam. iii.

3. To make sorrowful; to excite regret in.

4. To offend; to displease; to provoke.

> *Grieve* not the holy Spirit of God. Eph. iv.

GRIEVE, *v. i.* To feel pain of mind or heart; to be in pain on account of an evil; to sorrow; to mourn. We *grieve at* the loss of friends or property. We *grieve at* the misfortunes of others. We *grieve for* our own misfortunes, follies and vices, as well as *for* those of our children. It is followed by *at* or *for*.

GRIE'VED, *pp.* Pained; afflicted; suffering sorrow.

GRIE'VER, *n.* He or that which grieves.

GRIE'VING, *ppr.* Giving pain; afflicting.

2. Sorrowing; exercised with grief; mourning.

GRIE'VINGLY, *adv.* In sorrow; sorrowfully. *Shak.*

GRIE'VOUS, *a.* [from *grieve*, or *grief*.] Heavy; oppressive; burdensome; as a *grievous* load of taxes.

2. Afflictive; painful; hard to be borne.

Correction is *grievous* to him that forsaketh the way. Prov. xv.

3. Causing grief or sorrow.

The thing was very *grievous* in Abraham's sight, because of his son. Gen. xxi.

4. Distressing.

The famine was very *grievous* in the land. Gen. xii.

5. Great; atrocious.

Because their sin is very *grievous*. Gen. xviii.

6. Expressing great uneasiness; as a *grievous* complaint.

7. Provoking; offensive; tending to irritate; as *grievous* words. Prov. xv.

8. Hurtful; destructive; causing mischief; as *grievous* wolves. Acts xx.

GRIE'VOUSLY, *adv.* With pain; painfully; with great pain or distress; as, to be *grievously* afflicted.

2. With discontent, ill will or grief. *Knolles.*

3. Calamitously; miserably; greatly; with great uneasiness, distress or grief.

4. Atrociously; as, to sin or offend *grievously*.

GRIE'VOUSNESS, *n.* Oppressiveness; weight that gives pain or distress; as the *grievousness* of a burden.

2. Pain; affliction; calamity; distress; as the *grievousness* of sickness, war or famine.

3. Greatness; enormity; atrociousness; as the *grievousness* of sin or offenses.

GRIF'FON, *n.* [Fr. *griffon*; Sp. *grifo*; It. *griffo*, *griffone*; G. *greif*; Dan. *grif*; D. *griffioen*; L. *gryps*, *gryphus*; Gr. γρυψ; W. *gruf*, fierce, bold, a griffon.]

In the natural history of the ancients, an imaginary animal said to be generated between the lion and eagle. It is represented with four legs, wings and a beak, the upper part resembling an eagle, and the lower part a lion. This animal was supposed to watch over mines of gold and hidden treasures, and was consecrated to the sun. The figure of the griffon is seen on ancient medals, and is still borne in coat-armor. It is also an ornament of Greek architecture. *Encyc.*

GRIF'FON-LIKE, *a.* Resembling a griffon.

GRIG, *n.* A small eel; the sand eel.

2. A merry creature. *Swift.*

3. Health. *Obs.*

GRILL, *v. t.* [Fr. *griller.*] To broil. [*Not in use.*]

GRILL, *a.* Shaking with cold. *Obs.* *Chaucer.*

GRIL'LY, *v. t.* To harass. [*Not in use.*] *Hudibras.*

GRIM, *a.* [Sax. *grim*, fierce, rough, ferocious; *gram*, raging, fury; *gremian*, to provoke; D. *gram*, angry; *grimmen*, to growl; *grimmig*, grim; *grommen*, to grumble; G. *grimm*, furious, grim; *grimmen*, to rage; *gram*, grief, sorrow; Dan. *grim*, stern, grim, peevish; *gram*, grudging, hating, peevish; W. *gremiaw*, to gnash, to snarl, from *rhem*, whence *rhemial*, to mutter. Hence Fr. *grimace*. These words belong probably to the root of L. *fremo*, which has a different prefix, Gr. βρεμω, Eng. *grumble*, *rumble*, Ir. *grim*, war. See Class Rm. No. 11. 13.]

1. Fierce; ferocious; impressing terror; frightful; horrible; as a *grim* look; a *grim* face; *grim* war. *Milton. Addison.*

2. Ugly; ill looking. *Shak.*

3. Sour; crabbed; peevish; surly.

GRIM'-FACED, *a.* Having a stern countenance.

GRIM-GRINNING, *a.* Grinning with a fierce countenance. *Shak.*

GRIM-VISAGED, *a.* Grim-faced.

GRIMA'CE, *n.* [Fr. from *grim*, or its root; Sp. *grimazo.*]

1. A distortion of the countenance, from habit, affectation or insolence. *Spectator.*

2. An air of affectation. *Granville.*

GRIMA'CED, *a.* Distorted; having a crabbed look.

GRIMAL'KIN, *n.* [Qu. Fr. *gris*, gray, and *malkin*.] The name of an old cat. *Philips.*

GRIME, *n.* [Ice. *gryma*, Sax. *hrum*, soot; Rabbinic כרום soot. Class Rm. No. 21.] Foul matter; dirt; sullying blackness, deeply insinuated. *Shak. Woodward.*

GRIME, *v. t.* To sully or soil deeply; to dirt. *Shak.*

GRIM'LY, *a.* Having a hideous or stern look. *Beaum.*

GRIM'LY, *adv.* Fiercely; ferociously; with a look of fury or ferocity. *Addison.*

2. Sourly; sullenly. *Shak.*

GRIM'NESS, *n.* Fierceness of look; sternness; crabbedness.

GRI'MY, *a.* Full of grime; foul.

GRIN, *v. i.* [Sax. *grinnian*; G. *greinen*, *grinsen*; D. *grynen*, *grinzen*; Sw. *grina*; Dan. *griner*. In W. *ysgyrnwg* is a grin or snarl, and *ysgorn*, scorn.]

1. To set the teeth together and open the lips, or to open the mouth and withdraw the lips from the teeth, so as to show them, as in laughter or scorn.

Fools *grin* on fools. *Young.*

2. To fix the teeth, as in anguish.

GRIN, *n.* The act of closing the teeth and showing them, or of withdrawing the lips and showing the teeth. *Addison. Watts.*

GRIN, *n.* A snare or trap. [*Not in use.*]

GRIN, *v. t.* To express by grinning.

He *grinned* horribly a ghastly smile. *Milton.*

GRIND, *v. t.* pret. and pp. *ground*. [Sax. *grindan*. This word, if *n* is radical, may be allied to *rend*; if not, it coincides with *grate*. See Class Rn. No. 9, to make smooth, as *mollis* in L., allied to *molo*.]

1. To break and reduce to fine particles or powder by friction; to comminute by attrition; to triturate.

Take the millstones and *grind* meal. Is. xlvii.

We say, to *grind meal*, but this is an elliptical phrase. The true phrase is, to *grind corn to meal*.

2. To break and reduce to small pieces by the teeth. *Dryden.*

3. To sharpen by rubbing or friction; to wear off the substance of a metallic instrument, and reduce it to a sharp edge by the friction of a stone; as, to *grind* an ax or sythe.

4. To make smooth; to polish by friction; as, to *grind* glass.

5. To rub one against another.

Harsh sounds—and the *grinding* of one stone against another, make a shivering or horror in the body and set the teeth on edge. *Bacon.*

6. To oppress by severe exactions; to afflict cruelly; to harass; as, to *grind* the faces of the poor. Is. iii.

7. To crush in pieces; to ruin. Matt. xxi.

8. To grate; as *grinding* pains. *Dryden.*

GRIND, *v. i.* To perform the operation of grinding; to move a mill. *Milton.*

2. To be moved or rubbed together, as in the operation of grinding; as the *grinding* jaws. *Rowe.*

3. To be ground or pulverized by friction. Corn will not *grind* well before it is dry.

4. To be polished and made smooth by friction. Glass *grinds* smooth.

5. To be sharpened by grinding. Steel *grinds* to a fine edge.

GRINDER, *n.* One that grinds, or moves a mill.

2. The instrument of grinding. *Philips.*

3. A tooth that grinds or chews food; a double tooth; a jaw-tooth.

4. The teeth in general. *Dryden.*

GRINDING, *ppr.* Reducing to powder by friction; triturating; levigating; chewing.

2. Making sharp; making smooth or polishing by friction.

GRIND'STONE, *n.* A sandstone used for grinding or sharpening tools. *Grindlestone*, used by old writers, is obsolete.

GRIN'NER, *n.* [See *Grin*.] One that grins. *Addison.*

GRIN'NING, *ppr.* Closing the teeth and showing them, as in laughter; a showing of the teeth.

GRIN'NINGLY, *adv.* With a grinning laugh.

GRIP, *n.* The griffon. [*Not in use.*] *Shak.*

GRIP, *n.* [Dan. *greb*; G. *griff*. See *Gripe*.] A grasp; a holding fast.

GRIP, *n.* [D. *groep*; Sax. *græp*.] A small ditch or furrow. [*Not used in America.*]

GRIP, *v. t.* To trench; to drain. [*Not used.*]

GRIPE, *v. t.* [Sax. *gripan*; Goth. *greipan*; D. *grypen*; G. *greifen*; Sw. *gripa*; Dan. *griber*; Fr. *gripper*; Arm. *scraba*, *scrapein*; W. *grab*, a cluster, a grape; *grabin*, a clasping; *grabiniaw*, to grapple, to scramble. Qu. Sans. *grepipan*. These words may be allied in origin to L. *rapio*.]

1. To seize; to grasp; to catch with the

hand, and to clasp closely with the fingers.

2. To hold fast; to hold with the fingers closely pressed.
3. To seize and hold fast in the arms; to embrace closely.
4. To close the fingers; to clutch. *Pope.*
5. To pinch; to press; to compress.
6. To give pain to the bowels, as if by pressure or contraction.
7. To pinch; to straiten; to distress; as *griping* poverty.

GRIPE, *v. i.* To seize or catch by pinching; to get money by hard bargains or mean exactions; as a *griping* miser.

2. To feel the colic. *Locke.*
3. To lie too close to the wind, as a ship.

GRIPE, *n.* Grasp; seizure; fast hold with the hand or paw, or with the arms. *Shak. Dryden.*

2. Squeeze; pressure. *Dryden.*
3. Oppression; cruel exactions. *Shak.*
4. Affliction; pinching distress; as the *gripe* of poverty.
5. In *seamen's language*, the fore-foot or piece of timber which terminates the keel at the fore-end. *Mar. Dict.*
6. *Gripes*, in the plural, distress of the bowels; colic.
7. *Gripes*, in *seamen's language*, an assemblage of ropes, dead-eyes and hooks, fastened to ring-bolts in the deck to secure the boats. *Mar. Dict.*

GRIPER, *n.* One who gripes; an oppressor; an extortioner.

GRIPING, *ppr.* Grasping; seizing; holding fast; pinching; oppressing; distressing the bowels.

GRIPING, *n.* A pinching or grasp; a distressing pain of the bowels; colic.

2. In *seamen's language*, the inclination of a ship to run to the windward of her course. *Mar. Dict.*

GRIPINGLY, *adv.* With a pain in the bowels.

GRIP'PLE, *a.* [from *gripe.*] Griping; greedy; covetous; unfeeling. *Obs.* *Spenser.*

2. Grasping fast; tenacious. *Obs.* *Ibid.*

GRIP'PLENESS, *n.* Covetousness. *Obs.* *Bp. Hall.*

GRIS, *n.* [Fr. *gris*, gray.] A kind of fur. *Chaucer.*

GRISAMBER, used by Milton for *ambergris.* *Obs.*

GRISE, *n.* A step, or scale of steps. [L. *gressus*, Sw. *resa.* See *Greece.*] *Obs. Shak.*

2. A swine. *Obs.*

GRISETTE, *n. griset'.* [Fr.] A tradesman's wife or daughter. [*Not used.*] *Sterne.*

GRIS'KIN, *n.* [See *Grise.*] The spine of a hog. [*Not in use.*]

GRIS'LY, *a. s* as *z.* [Sax. *grislic;* G. *grass*, *grässlich* and *graus;* W. *ecrys*, dire, shocking, that causes to start, from *rhys*, a rushing; Sax. *agrisan*, to shudder.]

Frightful; horrible; terrible; as *grisly* locks; a *grisly* countenance; a *grisly* face; a *grisly* specter; a *grisly* bear. *Shak. Milton. Dryden.*

GRIS'ONS, *n.* Inhabitants of the eastern Swiss Alps.

GRIST, *n.* [Sax. *grist;* Eth. ሐረጸ charats, to grind, coinciding with Heb. Ch. חרץ. Class Rd. No. 60. 58. &c.]

1. Properly, that which is ground; hence, corn ground; but in common usage, it signifies corn for grinding, or that which is ground at one time; as much grain as is carried to the mill at one time or the meal it produces.

   Get *grist* to the mill to have plenty in store. *Tusser.*

2. Supply; provision. *Swift.*
3. Profit; gain; [as in Latin *emolumentum*, from *molo*, to grind;] in the phrase, it brings *grist* to the mill.

GRIS'TLE, *n. gris'l.* [Sax. *gristle;* perhaps the L. *cartil*, in *cartilago; cartil* for *cratil.* Qu. Gr. χαρτερος, κρατερος, strong, or Ir. *crislion*, sinews.]

A cartilage; a smooth, solid, elastic substance in animal bodies, chiefly in those parts where a small easy motion is required, as in the nose, ears, larynx, trachea and sternum. It covers the ends of all bones which are united by movable articulations. *Quincy.*

GRIST'LY, *a.* Consisting of gristle; like gristle; cartilaginous; as the *gristly* rays of fins connected by membranes. *Ray.*

GRIST'MILL, *n.* A mill for grinding grain.

GRIT, *n.* [Sax. *greot* or *gryt*, *grytta;* G. *gries*, grit; *grütze*, groats; D. *grut*, *grutte*, and *gruis;* Dan. *grus* or *grød;* Sw. *grus;* probably allied to *grate;* Dan. *grytter*, to bruise or grate; W. *grut*, *grud*, the latter from *rhud*, a cast, or driving forward.]

1. The coarse part of meal.
2. Oats hulled, or coarsely ground; written also *groats.*
3. Sand or gravel; rough hard particles.
4. Sandstone; stone composed of particles of sand agglutinated.

GRITH, *n.* Agreement. [*Not in use.*] *Chaucer.*

GRIT'STONE, *n.* [See *Grit.*]

GRIT'TINESS, *n.* The quality of containing grit or consisting of grit, sand or small hard, rough particles of stone.

GRIT'TY, *a.* Containing sand or grit; consisting of grit; full of hard particles; sandy.

GRIZ'ELIN. [See *Gridelin.*]

GRIZ'ZLE, *n.* [Fr. Sp. Port. *gris*, gray.] Gray; a gray color; a mixture of white and black. *Shak.*

GRIZ'ZLED, *a.* Gray; of a mixed color. Gen. xxxi.

GRIZ'ZLY, *a.* Somewhat gray. *Bacon.*

GRŌAN, *v. i.* [Sax. *granian*, *grunan;* W. *grwnan;* L. *grunnio;* Fr. *gronder;* Sp. *gruñir;* It. *grugnire;* Ar. رنّ Heb. Ch. רנן to cry out, to groan; L. *rana*, a frog. Class Rn. No. 4.]

1. To breathe with a deep murmuring sound; to utter a mournful voice, as in pain or sorrow.

   For we that are in this tabernacle, do *groan*, being burdened. 2 Cor. v.

2. To sigh; to be oppressed or afflicted; or to complain of oppression. A nation *groans* under the weight of taxes.

GRŌAN, *n.* A deep mournful sound, uttered in pain, sorrow or anguish.

2. Any low, rumbling sound; as the *groans* of roaring wind. *Shak.*

GRŌANFUL, *a.* Sad; inducing groans. *Spenser.*

GRŌANING, *ppr.* Uttering a low mournful sound.

GRŌANING, *n.* The act of groaning; lamentation; complaint; a deep sound uttered in pain or sorrow.

   I have heard the *groaning* of the children of Israel. Ex. vi.

2. In *hunting*, the cry or noise of the buck. *Chamb.*

GROAT, *n. grawt.* [D. *groot*, G. *grot*, that is *great*, a *great* piece or coin; so called because before this piece was coined by Edward III. the English had no silver coin larger than a penny.]

1. An English money of account, equal to four pence.
2. A proverbial name for a small sum.

GROATS, *n.* [See *Grit.*] Oats that have the hulls taken off.

GROATS-WŌRTH, *n.* The value of a groat. *Sherwood.*

GRO'CER, *n.* [This is usually considered as formed from *gross*, but in other languages, the corresponding word is from the name of plants, herbs or spices; D. *kruidenier*, from *kruid*, an herb, wort, spices; G. *würzkrämer*, a dealer in worts, herbs or spices; Sw. *kryddkråmare.* The French, Spanish and Portuguese use words formed from the name of spice, and the Italian is from the same word as *drug.* It would seem then that a *grocer*, whatever may be the origin of the name, was originally a seller of spices and other vegetables.]

A trader who deals in tea, sugar, spices, coffee, liquors, fruits, &c.

GRO'CERY, *n.* A grocer's store.

2. The commodities sold by grocers; usually in the plural.

GROG, *n.* A mixture of spirit and water not sweetened.

GROG'-BLOSSOM, *n.* A rum bud; a redness on the nose or face of men who drink ardent spirits to excess; a deformity that marks the beastly vice of intemperance.

GROG'DRINKER, *n.* One addicted to drinking grog.

GROG'GY, *a.* A *groggy* horse is one that bears wholly on his heels in trotting. *Cyc.*

2. In *vulgar language*, tipsy; intoxicated.

GROG'RAM, } *n.* [It. *grossagrana*, gross
GROG'RAN, } grain.] A kind of stuff made of silk and mohair.

GROIN, *n.* [Ice. and Goth. *grein.* Chalmers. But I do not find this in Lye.]

1. The depressed part of the human body between the belly and the thigh.
2. Among *builders*, the angular curve made by the intersection of two semi-cylinders or arches. *Encyc.*
3. [Fr. *groin;* Gr. ῥιν.] The snout or nose of a swine. *Chaucer.*

GROIN, *v. i.* To groan. *Obs.* *Chaucer.*

GROM'WELL, } *n.* A plant of the genus
GROM'IL, } Lithospermum. The *German gromwell* is the Stellera. *Fam. of Plants.*

GROM'ET, } *n.* [Arm. *gromm*, a curb, Fr.
GROM'MET, } *gourmette.*]

Among *seamen*, a ring formed of a strand of rope laid in three times round; used to fasten the upper edge of a sail to its stay. *Mar. Dict.*

GROOM, *n.* [Pers. خرما garma, a keeper of horses. Qu. Flemish or old D. *grom*, a boy.]

1. A boy or young man; a waiter; a servant.
2. A man or boy who has the charge of horses; one who takes care of horses or the stable.
3. In *England*, an officer of the king's household; as the *groom* of the chamber; *groom* of the stole or wardrobe.
4. *Groom* for *goom*, in *bridegroom*, is a palpable mistake.

GROOVE, *n.* groov. [Ice. *groof;* Sw. *grop;* but it is merely a variation of *grave.* See *Grave* and *Grip.*]

1. A furrow, channel, or long hollow cut by a tool. Among *joiners*, a channel in the edge of a molding, style or rail.
2. Among *miners*, a shaft or pit sunk into the earth.

GROOVE, *v. t.* [Sw. *grŏpa.*] To cut a channel with an edged tool; to furrow.

GROOV'ER, *n.* A miner. [*Local.*]

GROOV'ING, *ppr.* Cutting in channels.

GROPE, *v. i.* [Sax. *gropian, grapian;* G. *grabbeln, greifen;* D. *grypen, grabbelen;* Dan. *griber*, to gripe, to grope; Sw. *grubla*, Dan. *grubler*, to search. The sense is to feel or to catch with the hand.]

1. To feel along; to search or attempt to find in the dark, or as a blind person, by feeling.

We *grope* for the wall like the blind. Is. lix.

The dying believer leaves the weeping children of mortality to *grope* a little longer among the miseries and sensualities of a worldly life. *Buckminster.*

2. To seek blindly in intellectual darkness, without a certain guide or means of knowledge.

GROPE, *v. t.* To search by feeling in the dark. We *groped* our way at midnight.

But Strephon, cautious, never meant
The bottom of the pan to *grope*. *Swift.*

GRO'PER, *n.* One who gropes; one who feels his way in the dark, or searches by feeling.

GRO'PING, *ppr.* Feeling for something in darkness; searching by feeling.

GROSS, *a.* [Fr. *gros;* It. Port. *grosso;* Sp. *grueso, grosero;* L. *crassus;* a dialectical variation of *great.*]

1. Thick; bulky; particularly applied to animals; fat; corpulent; as a *gross* man; a *gross* body.
2. Coarse; rude; rough; not delicate; as *gross* sculpture. *Wotton.*
3. Coarse, *in a figurative sense;* rough; mean; particularly, vulgar; obscene; indelicate; as *gross* language; *gross* jests.
4. Thick; large; opposed to *fine;* as wood or stone of a *gross* grain.
5. Impure; unrefined; as *gross* sensuality.
6. Great; palpable; as a *gross* mistake; *gross* injustice.
7. Coarse; large; not delicate; as *gross* features.
8. Thick; dense; not attenuated; not refined or pure; as a *gross* medium of sight; *gross* air; *gross* elements. *Bacon. Pope.*
9. Unseemly; enormous; shameful; great; as *gross* corruptions; *gross* vices.
10. Stupid; dull.

Tell her of things that no *gross* ear can hear. *Milton.*

11. Whole; entire; as the *gross* sum, or *gross* amount, as opposed to a sum consisting of separate or specified parts.

GROSS, *n.* The main body; the chief part; the bulk; the mass; as the *gross* of the people. [We now use *bulk.*] *Addison.*

2. The number of twelve dozen; twelve times twelve; as a *gross* of bottles. It never has the plural form. We say, *five gross* or *ten gross.*

In the gross, in gross, in the bulk, or the whole undivided; all parts taken together.

By the gross, in a like sense.

Gross weight, is the weight of merchandize or goods, with the dust and dross, the bag, cask, chest, &c., in which they are contained, for which an allowance is to be made of tare and tret. This being deducted, the remainder or real weight is denominated *neat* or *net* weight. *Gross weight* has lately been abolished in Connecticut by statute, May, 1827.

In English law, a *villain in gross*, was one who did not belong to the land, but immediately to the person of the lord, and was transferrable by deed, like chattels, from one owner to another. *Blackstone.*

Advowson in gross, an advowson separated from the property of a manor, and annexed to the person of its owner. *Blackstone.*

Common in gross, is common annexed to a man's person, and not appurtenant to land. *Blackstone.*

GROSSBEAK, *n.* A fowl of the genus Loxia, of several species. The bill is convex above and very thick at the base, from which circumstance it takes its name.

GROSS-HEADED, *a.* Having a thick skull; stupid. *Milton.*

GROSSLY, *adv.* In bulky or large parts; coarsely. This matter is *grossly* pulverized.

2. Greatly; palpably; enormously; as, this affair has been *grossly* misrepresented.
3. Greatly; shamefully; as *grossly* criminal.
4. Coarsely; without refinement or delicacy; as language *grossly* vulgar.
5. Without art or skill.

GROSSNESS, *n.* Thickness; bulkiness; corpulence; fatness; *applied to animal bodies.*

2. Thickness; spissitude; density; as the *grossness* of vapors.
3. Coarseness; rudeness; want of refinement or delicacy; vulgarity; as the *grossness* of language; the *grossness* of wit.

Abhor the swinish *grossness* that delights to wound the ear of delicacy. *Dwight.*

4. Greatness; enormity; as the *grossness* of vice.

GROSS'ULAR, *a.* Pertaining to or resembling a gooseberry; as *grossular* garnet.

GROSS'ULAR, *n.* A rare mineral of the garnet kind, so named from its green color. [supra.]

GROT, GROT'TO, *n.* [Fr. *grotte;* It. *grotta;* Sp. and Port. *gruta;* G. and Dan. *grotte;* D. *grot;* Sax. *grut. Grotta* is not used.]

1. A large cave or den; a subterraneous cavern, and primarily, a natural cave or rent in the earth, or such as is formed by a current of water, or an earthquake. *Pope. Prior. Dryden.*
2. A cave for coolness and refreshment.

GROTESQUE, GROTESK', *a.* [Fr. *grotesque;* Sp. Port. *grutesco;* It. *grottesca;* from *grotto.*]

Wildly formed; whimsical; extravagant; of irregular forms and proportions; ludicrous; antic; resembling the figures found in the subterraneous apartments in the ancient ruins at Rome; applied to pieces of sculpture and painting, and to natural scenery; as *grotesque* painting; *grotesque* design. *Dryden.*

GROTESQUE, GROTESK', *n.* Whimsical figures or scenery.

GROTESQUELY, GROTESK'LY, *a.* In a fantastical manner.

GROUND, *n.* [Sax. G. Dan. Sw. *grund;* D. *grond;* Russ. *grunt.* This word may be the Ir. *grian*, ground, bottom of a river or lake, from *grean*, W. *graean*, gravel. See *Grain.* It seems primarily to denote the gravelly bottom of a river or lake, or of the sea, which shows the appropriate sense of the verb to *ground*, as used by seamen.]

1. The surface of land or upper part of the earth, without reference to the materials which compose it. We apply *ground* to soil, sand or gravel indifferently, but never apply it to the whole mass of the earth or globe, nor to any portion of it when removed. We never say a shovel full or a load of *ground.* We say *under ground*, but not *under earth;* and we speak of the globe as divided into *land* and *water*, not into *ground* and *water.* Yet *ground, earth* and *land* are often used synonymously. We say, the produce or fruits of the *ground*, of the *earth*, or of *land.* The water overflows the *low ground*, or the *low land.*

There was not a man to till the *ground.* Gen. ii.

The *ground* shall give its increase. Zech. viii.

The fire ran along on the *ground.* Ex. ix.

2. Region; territory; as Egyptian *ground;* British *ground;* heavenly *ground.* *Milton.*
3. Land; estate; possession.

Thy next design is on thy neighbor's *grounds.* *Dryden.*

4. The surface of the earth, or a floor or pavement.

Dagon had fallen on his face to the *ground.* 1 Sam. v.

5. Foundation; that which supports any thing. This argument stands on defensible *ground.* Hence,
6. Fundamental cause; primary reason or original principle. He stated the *grounds* of his complaint.

Making happiness the *ground* of his unhappiness. *Sidney.*

7. First principles; as the *grounds* of religion. *Milton.*
8. In *painting*, the surface on which a figure or object is represented; that surface or substance which retains the original color,

and to which the other colors are applied to make the representation; as crimson on a white *ground*. *Encyc.*

9. In *manufactures*, the principal color, to which others are considered as ornamental. *Hakewill.*

10. *Grounds*, plural, the bottom of liquors; dregs; lees; feces; as coffee *grounds;* the *grounds* of strong beer.

11. The plain song; the tune on which descants are raised.

On that *ground*, I'll build a holy descant. *Shak.*

12. In *etching*, a gummous composition spread over the surface of the metal to be etched, to prevent the nitric acid from eating, except where the ground is opened with the point of a needle. *Encyc.*

13. Field or place of action. He fought with fury, and would not quit the *ground.*

14. In *music*, the name given to a composition in which the base, consisting of a few bars of independent notes, is continually repeated to a continually varying melody. *Busby.*

15. The foil to set a thing off. *Obs.* *Shak.*

16. Formerly, the pit of a play house. *B. Jonson.*

To gain ground, to advance; to proceed forward in conflict; as, an army in battle *gains ground.* Hence, to obtain an advantage; to have some success; as, the army *gains ground* on the enemy. Hence,

2. To gain credit; to prevail; to become more general or extensive; as, the opinion *gains ground.*

To lose ground, to retire; to retreat; to withdraw from the position taken. Hence, to lose advantage. Hence,

2. To lose credit; to decline; to become less in force or extent.

To give ground, to recede; to yield advantage.

To get ground, and *to gather ground*, are seldom used.

GROUND, *v. t.* To lay or set on the ground.

2. To found; to fix or set, as on a foundation, cause, reason or principle; as arguments *grounded* on reason; faith *grounded* on scriptural evidence.

3. To settle in first principles; to fix firmly.

Being rooted and *grounded* in love. Eph. iii.

GROUND, *v. i.* To run aground; to strike the bottom and remain fixed; as, the ship *grounded* in two fathoms of water.

GROUND, *pret.* and *pp.* of *grind.*

GROUND'AGE, *n.* A tax paid by a ship for standing in port. *Blount.*

GROUND'-ANGLING, *n.* Fishing without a float, with a bullet placed a few inches from the hook.

GROUND'-ASH, *n.* A sapling of ash; a young shoot from the stump of an ash. *Mortimer.*

GROUND'-BAIT, *n.* Bait for fish which sinks to the bottom of the water. *Walton.*

GROUND'-FLOOR, *n.* The first or lower floor of a house. But the English call the *second* floor from the ground the *first* floor.

GROUND'-IVY, *n.* A well known plant, the *Glechoma hederacea;* called also *alehoof* and *gill.*

GROUND'LESS, *a.* Wanting ground or foundation; wanting cause or reason for support; as *groundless* fear.

2. Not authorized; false; as a *groundless* report or assertion.

GROUND'LESSLY, *a.* Without reason or cause; without authority for support. *Boyle.*

GROUND'LESSNESS, *n.* Want of just cause, reason or authority for support. *Tillotson.*

GROUND'LING, *n.* A fish that keeps at the bottom of the water; hence, a low vulgar person. *Shak.*

GROUND'LY, *adv.* Upon principles; solidly. [*A bad word and not used.*] *Ascham.*

GROUND'-NUT, *n.* A plant, the Arachis, a native of South America.

GROUND'-OAK, *n.* A sapling of oak. *Mortimer.*

GROUND'-PINE, *n.* A plant, a species of Teucrium or germander; said to be so called from its resinous smell. *Encyc. Hill.*

GROUND'-PLATE, *n.* In *architecture*, the ground-plates are the outermost pieces of timber lying on or near the ground, framed into one another with mortises and tenons. *Harris.*

GROUND'-PLOT, *n.* The ground on which a building is placed.

2. The ichnography of a building. *Johnson.*

GROUND'-RENT, *n.* Rent paid for the privilege of building on another man's land. *Johnson.*

GROUND'-ROOM, *n.* A room on the ground; a lower room. *Tatler.*

GROUND'SEL, *n.* A plant of the genus Senecio, of several species.

GROUND'SEL, GROUND'-SILL, } *n.* [*ground*, and Sax. *syll*, basis, allied probably to L. *sella*, that which is set. See *Sill.*] The timber of a building which lies next to the ground; commonly called a *sill.*

GROUND'-TACKLE, *n.* In *ships*, the ropes and furniture belonging to anchors.

GROUND'WORK, *n.* The work which forms the foundation or support of any thing; the basis; the fundamentals.

2. The ground; that to which the rest are additional. *Dryden.*

3. First principle; original reason. *Dryden.*

GRÖUP, GROOP, } *n.* [It. *groppo*, a knot, a bunch; Fr. *groupe;* Sp. *grupo.* It is radically the same word as *croup, crupper*, rump; W. *grab*, a cluster, a *grape.*]

1. A cluster, crowd or throng; an assemblage, either of persons or things; a number collected without any regular form or arrangement; as a *group* of men or of trees; a *group* of isles.

2. In *painting* and *sculpture*, an assemblage of two or more figures of men, beasts or other things which have some relation to each other.

GRÖUP, GROOP, } *v. t.* [Fr. *grouper.*] To form a group; to bring or place together in a cluster or knot; to form an assemblage.

The difficulty lies in drawing and disposing, or as the painters term it, in *grouping* such a multitude of different objects. *Prior.*

GRÖUP'ED, GROOP'ED, } *pp.* Formed or placed in a crowd.

GRÖUP'ING, GROOP'ING, } *ppr.* Bringing together in a cluster or assemblage.

GRÖUP'ING, *n.* The art of composing or combining the objects of a picture or piece of sculpture. *Cyc.*

GROUSE, *n. grous.* [Pers. خُرُوس goros, gros, a cock.]

A heath-cock or cock of the wood, a fowl of the genus Tetrao. The name is given to several species, forming a particular division of the genus; such as the black game, the red game, the ptarmigan, the ruffed grouse, &c.

GROUT, *n.* [Sax. *grut.* See *Groat.*] Coarse meal; pollard.

2. A kind of wild apple. *Johnson.*

3. A thin coarse mortar.

4. That which purges off. *Warner.*

GROVE, *n.* [Sax. *græf, graf*, a *grave*, a cave, a *grove;* Goth. *groba;* from cutting an avenue, or from the resemblance of an avenue to a channel.]

1. In *gardening*, a small wood or cluster of trees with a shaded avenue, or a wood impervious to the rays of the sun. A grove is either open or close; open, when consisting of large trees whose branches shade the ground below; close, when consisting of trees and underwood, which defend the avenues from the rays of the sun and from violent winds. *Encyc.*

2. A wood of small extent. In America, the word is applied to a wood of natural growth in the field, as well as to planted trees in a garden, but only to a wood of small extent and not to a forest.

3. Something resembling a wood or trees in a wood.

Tall *groves* of masts arose in beauteous pride. *Trumbull.*

GROV'EL, *v. i. grov'l.* [Ice. *gruva;* Chaucer, *groff*, flat on the ground or face; Scot. on *groufe;* allied to *grope*, which see.]

1. To creep on the earth, or with the face to the ground; to lie prone, or move with the body prostrate on the earth; to act in a prostrate posture.

Gaze on and *grovel* on thy face. *Shak.*

To creep and *grovel* on the ground. *Milton.*

2. To be low or mean; as *groveling* sense; *groveling* thoughts. *Dryden. Addison.*

GROV'ELER, *n.* One who grovels; an abject wretch.

GROV'ELING, *ppr.* Creeping; moving on the ground.

2. *a.* Mean; without dignity or elevation.

GRO'VY, *a.* Pertaining to a grove; frequenting groves.

GROW, *v. i.* pret. *grew;* pp. *grown.* [Sax. *growan;* D. *groeyen;* Dan. *groer;* Sw. *gro;* a contracted word; W. *crotiaw, crythu*, to grow, to swell. This is probably the same word as L. *cresco*, Russ. *rastu, rostu*, a dialectical variation of *crodh* or *grodh.* The French *croître*, and Eng. *increase*, retain the final consonant.]

1. To enlarge in bulk or stature, by a natural, imperceptible addition of matter, through ducts and secreting organs, as animal and vegetable bodies; to vegetate as plants, or to be augmented by natural process, as animals. Thus, a plant *grows* from a seed to a shrub or tree, and a human being *grows* from a fetus to a man.

He causeth the grass to *grow* for cattle. Ps. civ.

2. To be produced by vegetation; as, wheat *grows* in most parts of the world; rice *grows* only in warm climates.

3. To increase; to be augmented; to wax; as, a body *grows* larger by inflation or distension; intemperance is a *growing* evil.

4. To advance; to improve; to make progress; as, to *grow* in grace, in knowledge, in piety. The young man is *growing* in reputation.

5. To advance; to extend. His reputation is *growing*.

6. To come by degrees; to become; to reach any state; as, he *grows* more skillful, or more prudent. Let not vice *grow* to a habit, or into a habit.

7. To come forward; to advance. [*Not much used.*]

Winter began to *grow* fast on. *Knolles.*

8. To be changed from one state to another; to become; as, to *grow* pale; to *grow* poor; to *grow* rich.

9. To proceed, as from a cause or reason. Lax morals may *grow* from errors in opinion.

10. To accrue; to come.

Why should damage *grow* to the hurt of the kings. Ezra iv.

11. To swell; to increase; as, the wind *grew* to a tempest.

To grow out of, to issue from; as plants from the soil, or as a branch from the main stem.

These wars have *grown out of* commercial considerations. *Federalist, Hamilton.*

To grow up, to arrive at manhood, or to advance to full stature or maturity.

To grow up, } To close and adhere;
To grow together, } to become united by growth; as flesh or the bark of a tree severed.

Grow, signifies properly to shoot out, to enlarge; but it is often used to denote a passing from one state to another, and from greater to less.

Marriages *grow* less frequent. *Paley.*

[*To grow less*, is an abuse of this word; the phrase should be to *become less.*]

GRŌW, *v. t.* To produce; to raise; as, a farmer *grows* large quantities of wheat. [This is a modern abusive use of *grow*, but prevalent in Great Britain, and the British use begins to be imitated in America. Until within a few years, we never heard *grow* used as a transitive verb in New England, and the ear revolts at the practice.]

GROWER, *n.* One who grows; that which increases.

2. In *English use*, one who raises or produces.

GRŌWING, *ppr.* Increasing; advancing in size or extent; becoming; accruing; swelling; thriving.

GROWL, *v. i.* [Gr. γρυλλη, a grunting; Flemish *grollen. Junius.* D. *krollen*, to caterwaul.]

To murmur or snarl, as a dog; to utter an angry, grumbling sound. *Gay.*

GROWL, *v. t.* To express by growling. *Thomson.*

GROWL, *n.* The murmur of a cross dog.

GROWL'ER, *n.* A snarling cur; a grumbler.

GROWL'ING, *ppr.* Grumbling; snarling.

GRŌWN, *pp.* of *grow.* Advanced; increased in growth.

2. Having arrived at full size or stature; as a *grown* woman. *Locke.*

Grown over, covered by the growth of any thing; overgrown.

GROWSE, *v. i.* [Sax. *agrisan.*] To shiver; to have chills. [*Not used.*] *Ray.*

GRŌWTH, *n.* The gradual increase of animal and vegetable bodies; the process of springing from a germ, seed or root, and proceeding to full size, by the addition of matter, through ducts and secretory vessels. In *plants*, vegetation. We speak of slow *growth* and rapid *growth;* of early *growth*; late *growth* and full *growth.*

2. Product; produce; that which has grown; as a fine *growth* of wood.

3. Production; any thing produced; as a poem of English *growth.* *Dryden.*

4. Increase in number, bulk or frequency. *Johnson.*

5. Increase in extent or prevalence; as the *growth* of trade; the *growth* of vice.

6. Advancement; progress; improvement; as *growth* in grace or piety.

GROWT'HEAD, } *n.* [probably *gross* or
GROWT'NOL, } *great-head.*]

1. A kind of fish. *Ainsworth.*

2. A lazy person; a lubber. *Obs.* *Tusser.*

GRUB, *v. i.* [Goth. *graban.* See *Grave.* The primary sense is probably to *rub*, to rake, *scrape* or scratch, as wild animals dig by scratching. Russ. *grebu*, to rake, to row; *greben*, a comb; *grob*, a grave; *groblia*, a ditch.] To dig; to be occupied in digging.

GRUB, *v. t.* To dig; mostly followed by *up.* *To grub up*, is to dig up by the roots with an instrument; to root out by digging, or throwing out the soil; as, to *grub up* trees, rushes or sedge.

GRUB, *n.* [from the Verb.] A small worm; particularly, a hexaped or six-footed worm, produced from the egg of the beetle, which is transformed into a winged insect.

2. A short thick man; a dwarf, in contempt. *Carew.*

GRUB'BER, *n.* One who grubs up shrubs, &c.

GRUB'BING-HOE, *n.* An instrument for digging up trees, shrubs, &c. by the roots; a mattoc; called also a *grub-ax.*

GRUB'BLE, *v. i.* [G. *grübeln.* See *Grovel* and *Grabble.*]

To feel in the dark; to grovel. [*Not much used.*] *Dryden.*

GRUB'STREET, *n.* Originally, the name of a street near Moorfields, in London, much inhabited by mean writers; hence applied to mean writings; as a *Grub-street* poem. *Johnson.*

GRUDĠE, *v. t.* [W. *grwg*, a broken rumbling noise; *grwgaç*, a murmur, and, as a verb, to murmur; *grwgaçu*, to grumble; from the root of *rhwciaw*, to grunt or grumble; *rhwç*, a grunt, what is *rough;* L. *rugio;* Scot. *gruch*, to grudge, to repine; Gr. γρυζω. We see the primary sense is to grumble, and this from the root of *rough.*]

1. To be discontented at another's enjoyments or advantages; to envy one the possession or happiness which we desire for ourselves.

'Tis not in thee
To *grudge* my pleasures, to cut off my train. *Shak.*

I have often heard the presbyterians say, they did not *grudge* us our employments. *Swift.*

It is followed by two objects, but probably by ellipsis; as, *grudge* us for *grudge to* us.

2. To give or take unwillingly.

Nor *grudge* my cold embraces in the grave. *Dryden.*

They have *grudged* those contributions, which have set our country at the head of all the governments of Europe. *Addison.*

GRUDĠE, *v. i.* To murmur; to repine; to complain; as, to *grudge* or complain of injustice. *Hooker.*

2. To be unwilling or reluctant. *Grudge* not to serve your country.

3. To be envious.

Grudge not one against another. James v.

4. To wish in secret. [*Not used nor proper.*]

5. To feel compunction; to grieve. *Not in use.*]

GRUDĠE, *n.* Sullen malice or malevolence; ill will; secret enmity; hatred; as an old *grudge.* *B. Jonson.*

2. Unwillingness to benefit.

3. Remorse of conscience. *Obs.*

GRUDĠ'EONS, *n. plu.* Coarse meal. [*Not in use.*] *Beaum.*

GRUDĠ'ER, *n.* One that grudges; a murmuror.

GRUDĠ'ING, *pp.* Envying; being uneasy at another's possession of something which we have a desire to possess.

GRUDĠ'ING, *n.* Uneasiness at the possession of something by another.

2. Reluctance; also, a secret wish or desire. *Dryden.*

He had a *grudging* still to be a knave. *Obs.* *Dryden.*

3. A symptom of disease. [*Not in use.*] *Jackson.*

GRUDĠ'INGLY, *adv.* Unwillingly; with reluctance or discontent; as, to give *grudgingly.*

GRU'EL, *n.* [Fr. *gruau;* W. *grual.*] A kind of light food made by boiling meal in water. It is usually made of the meal of oats or maiz.

GRUFF, *a.* [D. *grof;* G. *grob;* Dan. *grov;* Sw. *grof;* W. *gruf*, a griffon, one fierce and bold.]

Of a rough or stern countenance; sour; surly; severe; rugged; harsh. *Addison.*

GRUFF'LY, *adv.* Roughly; sternly; ruggedly; harshly.

—And *gruffly* looked the god. *Dryden.*

GRUFF'NESS, *n.* Roughness of countenance; sternness.

GRUM, *a.* [Dan. *grum*, cruel, fierce, peevish; Sw. *grym*, id.; Dan. *gremmer*, to mourn; W. *grwm*, growling, surly; *grymian*, to grumble.]

1. Morose; severe of countenance; sour; surly. *Arbuthnot.*

2. Low; deep in the throat; guttural; rumbling; as a *grum* voice.

GRUM'BLE, *v. i.* [D. *grommelen, grommen;* Sax. *grymetan;* Dan. *gremmer;* Fr. *grommeler;* W. *grymial*, to grumble; Russ. *grom*, a loud noise, thunder; *gremlyu*, to to make a loud noise, to thunder; Arm. *grommellat;* Ir. *cruim*, thunder; probably from the root of *rumble;* Heb. Ch. Syr. רעם to roar, murmur, thunder; Sax. *reo-*

mian, hremman, to scream. Class Rm. No. 11. 13.]

1. To murmur with discontent; to utter a low voice by way of complaint.

L'Avare, not using half his store,
Still *grumbles* that he has no more. *Prior.*

2. To growl; to snarl; as a lion *grumbling* over his prey.

3. To rumble; to roar; to make a harsh and heavy sound; as *grumbling* thunder; a *grumbling* storm. [In this sense, *rumble* is generally used.]

GRUM'BLER, *n.* One who grumbles or murmurs; one who complains; a discontented man. *Swift.*

GRUM'BLING, *ppr.* Murmuring through discontent; rumbling; growling.

GRUM'BLING, *n.* A murmuring through discontent; a rumbling.

GRUM'BLINGLY, *adv.* With grumbling or complaint.

GRUME, *n.* [Fr. *grumeau; L. grumus;* It. and Sp. *grumo.*]

A thick viscid consistence of a fluid; a clot, as of blood, &c.

GRUM'LY, *adv.* Morosely; with a sullen countenance.

GRU'MOUS, *a.* Thick; concreted; clotted; as *grumous* blood.

GRU'MOUSNESS, *n.* A state of being clotted or concreted. *Wiseman.*

GRUND'SEL, *n.* [See *Groundsel.*] *Milton.*

GRUNT, *v. i.* [Dan. *grynter; G. grunzen;* Sax. *grunan; Fr. grogner;* Arm. *grondal;* L. *grunnio;* Sp. *gruñir;* It. *grugnire.* See Heb. Ch. Sam. רנן, Ar. رن to cry out, to murmur. Class Rn. No. 4.]

To murmur like a hog; to utter a short groan or a deep guttural sound. *Swift. Shak.*

GRUNT, *n.* A deep guttural sound, as of a hog. *Dryden.*

GRUNT'ER, *n.* One that grunts.

2. A fish of the gurnard kind. *Dict. Nat. Hist.*

GRUNT'ING, *ppr.* Uttering the murmuring or guttural sound of swine or other animals.

GRUNT'ING, *n.* The guttural sound of swine and other animals.

GRUNT'LE, *v. i.* To grunt. [*Not much used.*]

GRUNT'LING, *n.* A young hog.

GRUTCH, for *grudge*, is now vulgar, and not to be used.

GRY, *n.* [Gr. γρυ.] A measure containing one tenth of a line. *Locke.*

2. Any thing very small or of little value. [*Not much used.*]

GRYPH'ITE, *n.* [L. *gryphites;* Gr. γρυπος, hooked.]

Crowstone, an oblong fossil shell, narrow at the head, and wider towards the extremity, where it ends in a circular limb; the head or beak is very hooked. *Encyc.*

GUAIACUM, *n. gua'cum.* Lignum vitæ, or pock wood; a tree produced in the warm climates of America. The wood is very hard, ponderous and resinous. The resin of this tree, or gum guaiacum, is of a greenish cast, and much used in medicine as a stimulant. *Encyc.*

GU'ANA, *n.* A species of lizard, found in the warmer parts of America.

GUANACO, *n.* The lama, or camel of South America, in a wild state. *Cuvier.*

GU'ANO, *n.* A substance found on many isles in the Pacific, which are frequented by fowls; used as a manure. *Ure.*

GU'ARA, *n.* A bird of Brazil, the *Tantalus ruber*, about the size of a spoonbill. When first hatched, it is black; it afterward changes to gray, and then to vivid red. *Dict. Nat. Hist.*

GUARANTEE', *n.* A warrantor. [See *Guaranty*, the noun.]

GUAR'ANTIED, *pp. gar'antied.* Warranted. [See the Verb.]

GUAR'ANTOR, *n. gar'antor.* A warrantor; one who engages to see that the stipulations of another are performed; also, one who engages to secure another in any right or possession.

GUAR'ANTY, *v. t. gar'anty.* [Fr. *garantir;* It. *guarentire;* Arm. *goaranti;* W. *gwarantu*, from *gwar*, secure, smooth, or rather from *gwara*, to fend, to fence, the root of *guard*, that is, to drive off, to hold off, to stop; D. *waaren*, to preserve, to indemnify; Sax. *werian*, to defend; Eng. to *ward;* allied to *warren*, &c. See *Warrant.*]

1. To warrant; to make sure; to undertake or engage that another person shall perform what he has stipulated; to oblige one's self to see that another's engagements are performed; to secure the performance of; as, to *guaranty* the execution of a treaty. *Madison. Hamilton.*

2. To undertake to secure to another, at all events, as claims, rights or possessions. Thus in the treaty of 1778, France *guarantied* to the United States their liberty, sovereignty and independence, and their possessions; and the United States *guarantied* to France its possessions in America.

The United States shall *guaranty* to every state in the Union a republican form of government. *Const. of U. States.*

3. To indemnify; to save harmless.

[Note. This verb, whether written *guaranty* or *guarantee*, forms an awkward participle of the present tense; and we cannot relish either *guarantying* or *guaranteeing*. With the accent on the first syllable, as now pronounced, it seems expedient to drop the *y* in the participle, and write *guaranting*.]

GUAR'ANTY, *n. gar'anty.* [Fr. *garant;* Sp. *garantia;* Arm. *goarand;* Ir. *barranta;* W. *gwarant.*]

1. An undertaking or engagement by a third person or party, that the stipulations of a treaty shall be observed by the contracting parties or by one of them; an undertaking that the engagement or promise of another shall be performed. We say, a clause of *guaranty* in a treaty. *Hamilton.*

2. One who binds himself to see the stipulations of another performed; written also *guarantee.*

GUARD, *v. t. gàrd.* [Fr. *garder;* Sp. and Port. *guardar;* It. *guardare*, to keep, preserve, defend; also, to look, to behold; Basque, *gordi;* W. *gwara*, to fend or guard, to fence, to play. The primary sense is to strike, strike back, repel, beat down, or to turn back or stop; hence, to keep or defend, as by repelling assault or danger. The sense of seeing, looking, is secondary, from the sense of *guarding*, and we retain a similar application of the root of this word in *beware;* or it is from the sense of reaching, or casting the eye, or from turning the head. This is the English to *ward.* In W. *gwar* is secure, mild, placid, that is, set, fixed, held. It seems to be allied to G. *wahr*, true, L. *verus; währen*, to keep, to last, to hold out; *bewahren*, to keep or preserve; *bewähren*, to verify, to confirm; D. *waar*, true; *waaren*, to keep, preserve, indemnify; *waarande*, a warren, and guaranty; *waarison*, a garrison; Dan. *vaer*, wary, vigilant, watching; Eng. *ware, aware;* Dan. *værger*, to *guard*, defend, maintain; *vare*, a guard or watch, *wares*, merchandize; *varer*, to keep, last, endure; Sw. *vara*, to watch, and to be, to exist; Dan. *værer*, to be; Sax. *warian, werian*, to guard, to defend, to be *wary.* The sense of *existing* implies extension or continuance. See *Regard* and *Reward.*]

1. To secure against injury, loss or attack; to protect; to defend; to keep in safety. We *guard* a city by walls and forts. A harbor is *guarded* by ships, booms or batteries. Innocence should be *guarded* by prudence and piety. Let observation and experience *guard* us against temptations to vice.

2. To secure against objections or the attacks of malevolence.

Homer has *guarded* every circumstance with caution. *Broome.*

3. To accompany and protect; to accompany for protection; as, to *guard* a general on a journey; to *guard* the baggage of an army.

4. To adorn with lists, laces or ornaments. *Obs.* *Shak.*

5. To gird; to fasten by binding. *B. Jonson.*

GUARD, *v. i.* To watch by way of caution or defense; to be cautious; to be in a state of defense or safety. *Guard* against mistakes, or against temptations.

GUARD, *n.* [Fr. *garde;* Sp. *guarda;* It. *guardia;* Eng. *ward.*]

1. Defense; preservation or security against injury, loss or attack.

2. That which secures against attack or injury; that which defends. Modesty is the *guard* of innocence.

3. A man or body of men occupied in preserving a person or place from attack or injury; he or they whose business is to defend, or to prevent attack or surprise. Kings have their *guards* to secure their persons. Joseph was sold to Potiphar, a captain of Pharaoh's *guard.*

4. A state of caution or vigilance; or the act of observing what passes in order to prevent surprise or attack; care; attention; watch; heed. Be on your *guard.* Temerity puts a man off his *guard.*

5. That which secures against objections or censure; caution of expression.

They have expressed themselves with as few *guards* and restrictions as I. *Atterbury.*

6. Part of the hilt of a sword, which protects the hand.

7. In *fencing*, a posture of defense.

8. An ornamental lace, hem or border. *Obs.*

Advanced guard, } in *military affairs*, a body
Van guard, } of troops, either horse or

foot, that march before an army or division, to prevent surprise, or give notice of danger.

Rear guard, a body of troops that march in the rear of an army or division, for its protection.

Life guard, a body of select troops, whose duty is to defend the person of a prince or other officer.

GUARD'-BOAT, *n.* A boat appointed to row the rounds among ships of war in a harbor, to observe that their officers keep a good look-out. *Mar. Dict.*

GUARD'-CHAMBER, *n.* A guard-room. 1 Kings xiv.

GUARD'-ROOM, *n.* A room for the accommodation of guards.

GUARD'-SHIP, *n.* A vessel of war appointed to superintend the marine affairs in a harbor or river, and to receive impressed seamen.

GUARD'ABLE, *a.* That may be protected. *Sir A. Williams.*

GUARD'AGE, *n.* Wardship. *Obs. Shak.*

GUARD'ANT, *a.* Acting as guardian. *Obs.*

2. In *heraldry*, having the face turned toward the spectator.

GUARD'ED, *pp.* Defended; protected; accompanied by a guard; provided with means of defense.

2. *a.* Cautious; circumspect. He was *guarded* in his expressions.

3. Framed or uttered with caution; as, his expressions were *guarded*.

GUARD'EDLY, *adv.* With circumspection.

GUARD'EDNESS, *n.* Caution; circumspection.

GUARD'ER, *n.* One that guards.

GUARD'FUL, *a.* Wary; cautious.

GUARD'IAN, *n.* [from *guard*; Fr. *gardien*; Sp. *guardian*.]

1. A warden; one who guards, preserves or secures; one to whom any thing is committed for preservation from injury.

2. In *law*, one who is chosen or appointed to take charge of the estate and education of an orphan who is a minor, or of any person who is not of sufficient discretion to manage his own concerns. The person committed to the care of a guardian is called his *ward*.

Guardian of the spiritualities, the person to whom the spiritual jurisdiction of a diocese is entrusted, during the vacancy of the see.

GUARD'IAN, *a.* Protecting; performing the office of a protector; as a *guardian* angel; *guardian* care.

GUARD'IANESS, *n.* A female guardian. [*Not in use.*] *Beaum.*

GUARD'IANSHIP, *n.* The office of a guardian; protection; care; watch.

GUARD'ING, *ppr.* Defending; protecting; securing; attending for protection.

GUARD'LESS, *a.* Without a guard or defense. *Waller.*

GUARD'SHIP, *n.* Care; protection. [*Little used.*] *Swift.*

GUA'RISH, *v. t.* [Fr. *guerir.*] To heal. *Obs. Spenser.*

GU'AVA, *n.* An American tree, and its fruit, of the genus Psidium. It is of two species, or rather varieties, the pyriferum or white guava, and pomiferum or red guava. The fruit or berry is large and oval-shaped, like a pomegranate, which it resembles in its astringent quality. The pulp is of an agreeable flavor, and of this fruit is made a delicious jelly. *Encyc.*

GU'BERNATE, *v. t.* [L. *guberno.*] To govern. [*Not used.*]

GUBERNA'TION, *n.* [L. *gubernatio.* See *Govern.*]

Government; rule; direction. [*Little used.*] *Watts.*

GU'BERNATIVE, *a.* Governing. *Chaucer.*

GUBERNATO'RIAL, *a.* [L. *gubernator.*] Pertaining to government, or to a governor.

GUD'GEON, *n. gud'jin.* [Fr. *goujon.*] A small fish of the genus Cyprinus, a fish easily caught, and hence,

2. A person easily cheated or ensnared. *Swift.*

3. A bait; allurement; something to be caught to a man's disadvantage. *Shak.*

4. An iron pin on which a wheel turns.

Sea-gudgeon, the black goby or rock fish.

GUELF, } *n.* The Guelfs, so called from
GUELPH, } the name of a family, composed a faction formerly in Italy, opposed to the Gibelines. *J. Adams.*

GUER'DON, *n. ger'don.* [Fr. from the same root as *reward*, Norm. *regarde.*]

A reward; requital; recompense; *in a good or bad sense. Obs. Spenser. Milton.*

GUER'DON, *v. t.* To reward. *Obs. B. Jonson.*

GUER'DONLESS, *a.* Unrecompensed. *Obs. Chaucer.*

GUESS, *v. t. ges.* [D. *gissen*; Sw. *gissa*; Ir. *geasam*; Dan. *gietter.* It coincides with *cast*, like the L. *conjicio*; for in Danish, *gietter* is to guess, and *giet-huus* is a casting-house or foundery, *gyder*, to pour out. Hence we see that this is the G. *giessen*, to pour, cast or found, Eng. to *gush*. In Russ. *gadayu* is to guess, and *kidayu*, to cast. Ar. حَزَي to divine or guess. Class Gs. No. 31. See also Class Gd. The sense is to *cast*, that is, to throw together circumstances, or to *cast* forward in mind.]

1. To conjecture; to form an opinion without certain principles or means of knowledge; to judge at random, either of a present unknown fact, or of a future fact.

> First, if thou canst, the harder reason *guess*. *Pope.*

2. To judge or form an opinion from some reasons that render a thing probable, but fall short of sufficient evidence. From slight circumstances or occasional expressions, we *guess* an author's meaning.

3. To hit upon by accident. *Locke.*

GUESS, *v. i.* To conjecture; to judge at random. We do not know which road to take, but we must *guess* at it.

GUESS, *n.* Conjecture; judgment without any certain evidence or grounds.

> A poet must confess
> His arts like physic, but a happy *guess*. *Dryden.*

GUESS'ED, *pp.* Conjectured; divined.

GUESS'ER, *n.* One who guesses; a conjecturer; one who judges or gives an opinion without certain means of knowing. *Pope.*

GUESS'ING, *ppr.* Conjecturing; judging without certain evidence, or grounds of opinion.

GUESS'INGLY, *adv.* By way of conjecture. *Shak.*

GUEST, *n. gest.* [Sax. *gest*; G. D. *gast*; Dan. *giest*; Sw. *gäst*; W. *gwest*, a going out, a *visit*, an inn, a lodging; also, to visit, to be a guest; *gwes*, a going; Russ. *gost*, a guest. This is the Latin *visito*, Eng. *visit*, with the Celtic prefix. See Owen's Welsh Dictionary.]

1. A stranger; one who comes from a distance, and takes lodgings at a place, either for a night or for a longer time. *Sidney.*

2. A visitor; a stranger or friend, entertained in the house or at the table of another, whether by invitation or otherwise.

> The wedding was furnished with *guests*. Matt. xxii.

GUEST'-CHAMBER, *n.* An apartment appropriated to the entertainment of guests. Mark xiv.

GUEST'-RITE, *n.* Office due to a guest. *Chapman.*

GUEST'-ROPE, } *n.* A rope to tow with,
GUESS'-ROPE, } or to make fast a boat. *Mar. Dict.*

GUEST'WISE, *adv.* In the manner of a guest.

GUGGLE. [See *Gurgle.*]

GUHR, *n.* A loose, earthy deposit from water, found in the cavities or clefts of rocks, mostly white, but sometimes red or yellow, from a mixture of clay or ocher. *Nicholson. Cleaveland.*

GUIDABLE, *a.* That may be guided or governed by counsel. *Sprat.*

GUIDAGE, *n.* [See *Guide.*] The reward given to a guide for services. [*Little used.*]

GUIDANCE, *n.* [See *Guide.*] The act of guiding; direction; government; a leading. Submit to the *guidance* of age and wisdom.

GUIDE, *v. t. gide.* [Fr. *guider*; It. *guidare*; Sp. *guiar*, to guide; *guia*, a guide, and in seamen's language, a *guy*; Port. *id.* See Class Gd. No. 17. 53.]

1. To lead or direct in a way; to conduct in a course or path; as, to *guide* an enemy or a traveler, who is not acquainted with the road or course.

> The meek will he *guide* in judgment. Ps. xxv.

2. To direct; to order.

> He will *guide* his affairs with discretion. Ps. cxii.

3. To influence; to give direction to. Men are *guided* by their interest, or supposed interest.

4. To instruct and direct. Let parents *guide* their children to virtue, dignity and happiness.

5. To direct; to regulate and manage; to superintend.

> I will that the younger women marry, bear children, and *guide* the house. 1 Tim. v.

GUIDE, *n.* [Fr. *guide*; It. *guida*; Sp. *guia.*]

1. A person who leads or directs another in his way or course; a conductor. The army followed the *guide*. The traveler may be deceived by his *guide*.

2. One who directs another in his conduct or course of life.

He will be our *guide*, even unto death. Ps. xlviii.

3. A director; a regulator; that which leads or conducts. Experience is one of our best *guides*.

GUIDED, *pp.* Led; conducted; directed in the way; instructed and directed.

GUIDELESS, *a.* Destitute of a guide; wanting a director. *Dryden.*

GUIDEPOST, *n.* A post at the forks of a road, for directing travelers the way.

GUIDER, *n.* A guide; one who guides or directs. *South.*

GUIDING, *ppr.* Leading; conducting; directing; superintending.

GUIDON, *n.* [Fr.] The flag or standard of a troop of cavalry; or the standard-bearer. *Lunier. Encyc.*

GUILD, *n. gild.* [Sax. *geld*, *gield*, *gild* or *gyld*; D. *gild*; G. *gilde*; so called, it is said, from *geldan*, *gildan*, to pay, because each member of the society was to pay something towards the charge and support of the company.]

In England, a society, fraternity or company, associated for some purpose, particularly for carrying on commerce. The merchant-guilds of our ancestors, answer to our modern corporations. They were licensed by the king, and governed by laws and orders of their own. Hence the name *Guild-hall*, the great court of judicature in London. *Cowel. Encyc.*

GUILD'ABLE, *a.* Liable to a tax. *Spelman.*

GUILDER, *n.* [See *Gilder*.]

GUILE, *n. gile.* [Qu. Old French *guille* or *gille*. It may be the Celtic form of Eng. *wile*. See Ethiopic, Cast. col. 533.]

Craft; cunning; artifice; duplicity; deceit; *usually in a bad sense.*

> We may, with more successful hope, resolve
> To wage by force or *guile* eternal war. *Milton.*

> Behold an Israelite indeed, in whom is no *guile*. John i.

GUILE, *v. t.* To disguise craftily. *Obs.* *Spenser.*

GUILEFUL, *a.* Cunning; crafty; artful; wily; deceitful; insidious; as a *guileful* person.

2. Treacherous; deceitful. *Shak.*

3. Intended to deceive; as *guileful* words.

GUILEFULLY, *adv.* Artfully; insidiously; treacherously. *Milton.*

GUILEFULNESS, *n.* Deceit; secret treachery. *Sherwood.*

GUILELESS, *a.* Free from guile or deceit; artless; frank; sincere; honest.

GUILELESSNESS, *n.* Simplicity; freedom from guile.

GUILER, *n.* One who betrays into danger by insidious arts. [*Not used.*] *Spenser.*

GUIL'LEMOT, *n.* [from the Welsh *ƈwilawg*, whirling about.]

A water fowl of the genus Colymbus, and order of ansers. It is found in the northern parts of Europe, Asia and America.

GUIL'LOTIN, *n.* [Fr. from the name of the inventor.]

An engine or machine for beheading persons at a stroke.

GUIL'LOTIN, *v. t.* To behead with the guillotin.

GUILLS, *n.* A plant, the corn marigold.

GUILT, *n. gilt.* [Sax. *gylt*, a crime, and a debt, connected with *gyldan*, to pay; or it is from the root of D. and G. *schuld*, Dan. *skyld*, a debt, fault, guilt. See *Shall*, *Should*. If the word is from *gildan*, *gyldan*, to pay, it denotes a debt contracted by an offense, a fine, and thence came the present signification.]

1. Criminality; that state of a moral agent which results from his actual commission of a crime or offense, knowing it to be a crime, or violation of law. To constitute guilt there must be a moral agent enjoying freedom of will, and capable of distinguishing between right and wrong, and a wilful or intentional violation of a known law, or rule of duty. The guilt of a person exists, as soon as the crime is committed; but to evince it to others, it must be proved by confession, or conviction in due course of law. Guilt renders a person a debtor to the law, as it binds him to pay a penalty in money or suffering. Guilt therefore implies both criminality and liableness to punishment. Guilt may proceed either from a positive act or breach of law, or from voluntary neglect of known duty.

2. Criminality in a political or civil view; exposure to forfeiture or other penalty.

> A ship incurs *guilt* by the violation of a blockade. *Kent.*

3. Crime; offense. *Shak.*

GUILT'ILY, *adv.* In a manner to incur guilt; not innocently. *Shak.*

GUILT'INESS, *n.* The state of being guilty; wickedness; criminality; guilt. *Sidney.*

GUILT'LESS, *a.* Free from guilt, crime or offense; innocent.

> The Lord will not hold him *guiltless*, that taketh his name in vain. Ex. xx.

2. Not produced by the slaughter of animals.

> But from the mountain's grassy side
> A *guiltless* feast I bring. *Goldsmith.*

GUILT'LESSLY, *adv.* Without guilt; innocently.

GUILT'LESSNESS, *n.* Innocence; freedom from guilt or crime. *Sidney.*

GUILT'-SICK, *a.* Diseased in consequence of guilt. *Beaum.*

GUILT'Y, *a. gilt'y.* [Sax. *gyltig.*] Criminal; having knowingly committed a crime or offense, or having violated a law by an overt act or by neglect, and by that act or neglect, being liable to punishment; not innocent. It may be followed by *of*; as, to be *guilty of* theft or arson.

> Nor he, nor you, were *guilty* of the strife. *Dryden.*

2. Wicked; corrupt; sinful; as a *guilty* world.

3. Conscious. *B. Jonson.*

In *Scripture*, *to be guilty of death*, is to have committed a crime which deserves death. Matt. xxvi.

To be guilty of the body and blood of Christ, is to be chargeable with the crime of crucifying Christ afresh, and offering indignity to his person and righteousness, represented by the symbols of the Lord's supper. 1 Cor. xi.

GUIN'EA, *n. gin'ny.* [from *Guinea*, in Africa, which abounds with gold.]

Formerly, a gold coin of Great Britain of the value of twenty one shillings sterling, equal to $4.66⅔, American money.

GUIN'EA-DROPPER, *n.* One who cheats by dropping guineas.

GUIN'EA-HEN, *n.* The *Numida meleagris*, a fowl of the gallinaceous order, a native of Africa. It is larger than the common domestic hen, and has a kind of colored fleshy horn on each side of the head. Its color is a dark gray, beautifully variegated with small white spots. *Encyc.*

GUIN'EA-PEP'PER, *n.* A plant, the Capsicum. The pods of some species are used for pickles.

GUIN'EA-PIG, *n.* In *zoology*, a quadruped of the genus Cavia or cavy, found in Brazil. It is about seven inches in length, and of a white color, variegated with spots of orange and black.

GUIN'IAD, } *n.* [W. *gwen*, *gwyn*, white.]
GWIN'IAD, } The whiting, a fish of the salmon or trout kind, found in many lakes in Europe and in Hudson's bay. It is gregarious, and may be taken in vast numbers at a draught. *Encyc. Pennant.*

GUISE, *n. gize.* [Fr. *guise*; It. *guisa*, way, manner; Arm. *guis*, *giz*; W. *gwez*, order, shape; Sax. *wise*; Eng. *wise*; G. *weise*; D. *guizen*, to beguile.]

1. External appearance; dress; garb. He appeared in the *guise* of a shepherd. The hypocrite wears the *guise* of religion.

> That love which is without dissimulation, wears not the *guise* of modern liberality. *J. M. Mason.*

2. Manner; mien; cast of behavior.

> By their *guise*
> Just men they seem. *Milton.*

3. Custom; mode; practice.

> The swain replied, it never was our *guise*,
> To slight the poor, or aught humane despise. *Pope.*

GUISER, *n. gi'zer.* A person in disguise; a mummer who goes about at christmas. *Eng.*

GUIT'AR, *n. git'ar.* [Fr. *guitare*; It. *chitarra*; Sp. Port. *guitarra*; L. *cithara*; Gr. *κιθαρα*.]

A stringed instrument of music; in England and the United States, used chiefly by ladies, but in Spain and Italy, much used by men. *Encyc.*

GU'LA, } *n.* An ogee or wavy member in a
GO'LA, } building; the cymatium.

GU'LAUND, *n.* An aquatic fowl of a size between a duck and a goose; the breast and belly white; the head mallard green. It inhabits Iceland. *Pennant.*

GULCH, *n.* [D. *gulzig*, greedy.] A glutton; a swallowing or devouring. [*Not used.*]

GULCH, *v. t.* To swallow greedily. [*Not used.*]

GULES, *n.* [Fr. *gueules*, red.] In *heraldry*, a term denoting red, intended perhaps to represent courage, animation or hardihood. *Encyc.*

GULF, *n.* [Fr. *golfe*; It. Sp. Port. *golfo*; Arm. *golf*; D. *golf*; Gr. *κολπος*.]

1. A recess in the ocean from the general line of the shore into the land, or a tract of water extending from the ocean or a sea into the land, between two points or promontories; a large bay; as the *gulf* of Mexico; the *gulf* of Venice; the *gulf* of Finland. A *gulf* and a *bay* differ only in extent. We apply *bay* to a large or small

recess of the sea, as the *bay* of Biscay, the *bay* of Fundy; but *gulf* is applied only to a large extent of water.

2. An abyss; a deep place in the earth; as the *gulf* of Avernus. *Spenser.*

3. A whirlpool; an absorbing eddy. *Spenser.*

4. Any thing insatiable. *Shak.*

GULF-INDENT'ED, *a.* Indented with gulfs or bays. *J. Barlow.*

GULF'Y, *a.* Full of whirlpools or gulfs; as a *gulfy* sea.

GULL, *v. t.* [D. *kullen*; Old Fr. *guiller*; allied probably to *cully.*]

To deceive; to cheat; to mislead by deception; to trick; to defraud.

The vulgar, *gull'd* into rebellion, armed. *Dryden.*

GULL, *n.* A cheating or cheat; trick; fraud. *Shak.*

2. One easily cheated. *Shak.*

GULL, *n.* [W. *gwylan*; Corn. *gullan.*] A marine fowl of the genus Larus, and order of ansers. There are several species. *Encyc.*

GULL'CATCHER, *n.* A cheat; a man who cheats or entraps silly people. *Shak.*

GULL'ED, *pp.* Cheated; deceived; defrauded.

GULL'ER, *n.* A cheat; an impostor.

GULL'ERY, *n.* Cheat. [*Not used.*] *Burton.*

GUL'LET, *n.* [Fr. *goulet*, *goulot*, from L. *gula*; Russ. *chailo*; Sans. *gola.*]

The passage in the neck of an animal by which food and liquor are taken into the stomach; the esophagus.

2. A stream or lake. [*Not used.*] *Heylin.*

GUL'LIED, *pp.* Having a hollow worn by water.

GULL'ISH, *n.* Foolish; stupid. [*Not in use.*]

GULL'ISHNESS, *n.* Foolishness; stupidity. [*Not in use.*]

GUL'LY, *n.* A channel or hollow worn in the earth by a current of water. *New England. Mitford. Hawkesworth.*

GUL'LY, *v. t.* To wear a hollow channel in the earth. *America.*

GUL'LY, *v. i.* To run with noise. [*Not in use.*]

GUL'LYHOLE, *n.* An opening where gutters empty their contents into the subterraneous sewer. *Johnson.*

GULOS'ITY, *n.* [L. *gulosus*, from *gula*, the gullet.]

Greediness; voracity; excessive appetite for food. [*Little used.*] *Brown.*

GULP, *v. t.* [D. *gulpen*; Dan. *gulper.*] To swallow eagerly, or in large draughts. *Gay.*

To gulp up, to throw up from the throat or stomach; to disgorge.

GULP, *n.* A swallow, or as much as is swallowed at once.

2. A disgorging.

GULPH. [See *Gulf.*]

GUM, *n.* [Sax. *goma.* See the next word.] The hard fleshy substance of the jaws which invests the teeth.

GUM, *n.* [Sax. *goma*; L. *gummi*; D. *gom*; Sp. *goma*; It. *gomma*; Fr. *gomme*; Gr. *χομμι*; Russ. *kamed.* See Class Gm. No. 12. 29.]

The mucilage of vegetables; a concrete juice which exudes through the bark of trees, and thickens on the surface. It is soluble in water, to which it gives a viscous and adhesive quality. It is insoluble in alcohol, and coagulates in weak acids. When dry, it is transparent and brittle, not easily pulverized, and of an insipid or slightly saccharine taste. Gum differs from resin in several particulars, but custom has inaccurately given the name of gum to several resins and gum-resins, as gum-copal, gum-sandarach, gum-ammoniac, and others. The true gums are gum-arabic, gum-senegal, gum-tragacanth, and the gums of the peach, plum and cherry trees, &c. *Nicholson. Hooper.*

Gum-elastic, or *Elastic-gum*, [*caoutchouc,*] is a singular substance, obtained from a tree in America by incision. It is a white juice, which, when dry, becomes very tough and elastic, and is used for bottles, surgical instruments, &c. *Nicholson. Encyc.*

GUM, *v. t.* To smear with gum.

2. To unite by a viscous substance.

GUM-AR'ABIC, *n.* A gum which flows from the acacia, in Arabia, Egypt, &c.

GUM'-BOIL, *n.* A boil on the gum.

GUM'LAC, *n.* The produce of an insect which deposits its eggs on the branches of a tree called *bihar*, in Assam, a country bordering on Tibet, and elsewhere in Asia. [See *Lac.*] *Nicholson.*

GUM-RESIN, *n.* [See *Resin.*] A mixed juice of plants, consisting of resin and an extractive matter, which has been taken for a gummy substance. The gum-resins do not flow naturally from plants, but are mostly extracted by incision, in the form of white, yellow or red emulsive fluids, which dry and consolidate. The most important species are olibanum, galbanum, scammony, gamboge, euphorbium, assafetida, aloes, myrrh, and gum-ammoniac. *Fourcroy.*

Gum-resins are natural combinations of gum and resin. *Webster's Manual.*

Gum-resins are composed of a gum or extractive matter, and a body intermediate between oil and resin; to which last they owe their peculiar properties. *Thomson.*

GUM-SEN'EGAL, *n.* A gum resembling gum-arabic, brought from the country of the river Senegal in Africa.

GUM-TRAG'ACANTH, *n.* The gum of a thorny shrub of that name, in Crete, Asia and Greece. *Encyc.*

GUM'MINESS, *n.* The state or quality of being gummy; viscousness.

2. Accumulation of gum. *Wiseman.*

GUMMOS'ITY, *n.* The nature of gum; gumminess; a viscous or adhesive quality. *Floyer.*

GUM'MOUS, *a.* Of the nature or quality of gum; viscous; adhesive. *Woodward.*

GUM'MY, *a.* Consisting of gum; of the nature of gum; viscous; adhesive. *Raleigh.*

2. Productive of gum. *Milton.*

3. Covered with gum or viscous matter. *Dryden.*

GUMP, *n.* [Dan. and Sw. *gump*, the rump of a fowl.] A foolish person; a dolt. [*Vulgar.*]

GUMP'TION, *n.* [Sax. *gymene*, care; *gyman*, to observe or be careful.] Care; skill; understanding. [*Vulgar.*]

GUN, *n.* [W. *gwn*; Corn. *gun.*] An instrument consisting of a barrel or tube of iron or other metal fixed in a stock, from which balls, shot or other deadly weapons are discharged by the explosion of gunpowder. The larger species of guns are called cannon; and the smaller species are called muskets, carbines, fowling pieces, &c. But one species of fire-arms, the pistol, is never called a gun.

GUN, *v. i.* To shoot. *Obs.*

GUN'-BARREL, *n.* The barrel or tube of a gun.

GUN'BOAT, *n.* A boat or small vessel fitted to carry a gun or two at the bow. *Mar. Dict.*

GUN'-CARRIAGE, *n.* A wheel carriage for bearing and moving cannon.

GUN'NEL. [See *Gunwale.*]

GUN'NER, *n.* One skilled in the use of guns; a cannonier; an officer appointed to manage artillery. The gunner of a ship of war has the charge of the ammunition and artillery, and his duty is to keep the latter in good order, and to teach the men the exercise of the guns. *Mar. Dict.*

GUN'NERY, *n.* The act of charging, directing and firing guns, as cannon, mortars and the like. Gunnery is founded on the science of projectiles.

GUN'NING, *n.* The act of hunting or shooting game with a gun.

GUN'POWDER, *n.* A composition of saltpeter, sulphur and charcoal, mixed and reduced to a fine powder, then granulated and dried. It is used in artillery, in shooting game, in blasting rocks, &c.

GUN'ROOM, *n.* In *ships*, an apartment on the after end of the lower gun-deck, occupied by the gunner, or by the lieutenants as a mess-room. *Mar. Dict.*

GUN'SHOT, *n.* The distance of the point-blank range of a cannon-shot. *Mar. Dict.*

GUN'SHOT, *a.* Made by the shot of a gun; as a *gunshot* wound.

GUN'SMITH, *n.* A maker of small arms; one whose occupation is to make or repair small fire-arms.

GUN'SMITHERY, *n.* The business of a gunsmith; the art of making small fire-arms.

GUN'STICK, *n.* A rammer, or ramrod; a stick or rod to ram down the charge of a musket, &c.

GUN'STOCK, *n.* The stock or wood in which the barrel of a gun is fixed.

GUN'STONE, *n.* A stone used for the shot of cannon. Before the invention of iron balls, stones were used for shot. *Shak.*

GUN'TACKLE, *n.* The tackle used on board of ships to run the guns out of the ports, and to secure them at sea. The tackles are pulleys affixed to the sides of a gun-carriage. *Mar. Dict.*

GUN'WALE, } *n.* The upper edge of a ship's
GUN'NEL, } side; the uppermost wale of a ship, or that piece of timber which reaches on either side from the quarter-deck to the fore-castle, being the uppermost bend which finishes the upper works of the hull. *Mar. Dict. Encyc.*

GURGE, *n.* [L. *gurges*; It. *gorgo.*] A whirlpool. [*Little used.*] *Milton.*

GURGE, *v. t.* To swallow. [*Not in use.*]

GUR'GION, *n.* The coarser part of meal separated from the bran. [*Not used.*] *Hollinshed.*

GUR'GLE, *v. i.* [It. *gorgogliare*, from *gorga*, the throat, *gorgo*, a whirlpool, L. *gurges*. See *Gargle*, which seems to be of the same family, or the same word differently applied.]

To run as liquor with a purling noise; to run or flow in a broken, irregular, noisy current, as water from a bottle, or a small stream on a stony bottom.

> Pure *gurgling* rills the lonely desert trace. *Young.*

GURG'LING, *ppr.* Running or flowing with a purling sound.

GUR'HOFITE, *n.* A subvariety of magnesian carbonate of lime, found near Gurhof, in Lower Austria. It is snow white, and has a dull, slightly conchoidal, or even fracture. *Cleaveland.*

GUR'NARD, *n.* [Ir. *guirnead*; W. *pen-gernyn*, Corn. *pengarn*, horn-head or iron-head.]

A fish of several species, of the genus Trigla. The head is loricated with rough lines, or bony plates, and there are seven rays in the membranes of the gills. *Encyc. Dict. Nat. Hist.*

GUR'RAH, *n.* A kind of plain, coarse India muslin.

GUSH, *v. i.* [Ir. *gaisim*; G. *giessen*; or D. *gudsen* or *kissen*. See *Guess.*]

1. To issue with violence and rapidity, as a fluid; to rush forth as a fluid from confinement; as, blood *gushes* from a vein in venesection.

> Behold, he smote the rock, that the waters *gushed* out. Ps. lxxviii.

2. To flow copiously. Tears *gushed* from her eyes.

GUSH, *v. t.* To emit in copious effusion.

> The gaping wound *gushed* out a crimson flood. [*Unusual.*] *Dryden.*

GUSH, *n.* A sudden and violent issue of a fluid from an inclosed place; an emission of liquor in a large quantity and with force; the fluid thus emitted. *Harvey.*

GUSH'ING, *ppr.* Rushing forth with violence, as a fluid; flowing copiously; as *gushing* waters.

2. Emitting copiously; as *gushing* eyes. *Pope.*

GUS'SET, *n.* [Fr. *gousset*, a fob, a bracket, a *gusset*, as if from *gousse*, a cod, husk or shell. But in W. *cwysed* is a gore or gusset, from *cwys*, a furrow.]

A small piece of cloth inserted in a garment, for the purpose of strengthening or enlarging some part.

GUST, *n.* [L. *gustus*, It. Sp. *gusto*, Fr. *goût*, taste; L. *gusto*, G. *kosten*, W. *çwaethu*, to taste; Gr. γευω, a contracted word, for it has γευσις, taste; W. *cwaeth*, id.]

1. Taste; tasting, or the sense of tasting. More generally, the pleasure of tasting; relish. *Tillotson.*

2. Sensual enjoyment.

> Where love is duty on the female side,
> On theirs, mere sensual *gust*, and sought with surly pride. *Dryden.*

3. Pleasure; amusement; gratification.

> Destroy all creatures for thy sport or *gust*. *Pope.*

4. Turn of fancy; intellectual taste.

> A choice of it may be made according to the *gust* and manner of the ancients. *Dryden.*

[*Taste* is now generally used.]

GUST, *v. t.* To taste; to have a relish. [*Little used.*]

GUST, *n.* [Dan. *gust*; Ir. *gaoth*, wind; W. *cwyth*, a puff, a blast of wind; allied perhaps to *gush.*]

1. A sudden squall; a violent blast of wind; a sudden rushing or driving of the wind, of short duration. *Dryden. Addison.*

2. A sudden, violent burst of passion. *Bacon.*

GUST'ABLE, *a.* That may be tasted; tastable. *Harvey.*

2. Pleasant to the taste. [*Little used.*] *Derham.*

GUSTA'TION, *n.* The act of tasting. [*Little used.*] *Brown.*

GUST'FUL, *a.* Tasteful; well-tasted; that relishes.

GUST'FULNESS, *n.* Relish; pleasantness to the taste. *Barrow.*

GUST'LESS, *a.* Tasteless. *Brown.*

GUST'O, *n.* [It. and Sp. See *Gust.*] Relish; that which excites pleasant sensations in the palate or tongue. *Derham.*

2. Intellectual taste. [*Little used.*] *Dryden.*

GUST'Y, *a.* Subject to sudden blasts of wind; stormy; tempestuous.

> Once upon a raw and *gusty* day,
> The troubled Tyber chafing with his shores— *Shak.*

GUT, *n.* [G. *kuttel*; Ch. קותלא kutla.] The intestinal canal of an animal; a pipe or tube extending, with many circumvolutions, from the pylorus to the vent. This pipe is composed of three coats, and is attached to the body by a membrane called the mesentery. This canal is of different sizes in different parts, and takes different names. The thin and small parts are called the duodenum, the ilium, and the jejunum; the large and thick parts are called the cæcum, the colon, and the rectum. By this pipe, the undigested and unabsorbed parts of food are conveyed from the stomach and discharged. This word in the plural is applied to the whole mass formed by its natural convolutions in the abdomen.

2. The stomach; the receptacle of food. [*Low.*] *Dryden.*

3. Gluttony; love of gormandizing. [*Low.*] *Hakewill.*

GUT, *v. t.* To take out the bowels; to eviscerate.

2. To plunder of contents. *Dryden.*

Gutta serena, in *medicine*, amaurosis; blindness occasioned by a diseased retina.

GUT'TED, *pp.* Deprived of the bowels; eviscerated; deprived of contents.

GUT'TER, *n.* [Fr. *gouttiere*, from *goutte*, a drop; Sp. Port. *gota*, a drop; Sp. *gotera*, a *gutter*; from L. *gutta*, a drop. A *gutter* is a dropper, that which catches drops.]

1. A channel for water; a hollow piece of timber, or a pipe, for catching and conveying off the water which drops from the eaves of a building.

2. A channel or passage for water; a hollow in the earth for conveying water; and, in popular usage, a channel worn in the earth by a current of water.

GUT'TER, *v. t.* To cut or form into small hollows. *Shak. Dryden.*

GUT'TER, *v. i.* To be hollowed or channeled. *Med. Repos.*

2. To run or sweat as a candle. [*Local.*]

GUT'TLE, *v. t.* To swallow. [*Not used.*] *L'Estrange.*

GUT'TLE, *v. i.* To swallow greedily. [*Not used.*]

GUT'TULOUS, *a.* [from L. *guttula*, a little drop.]

In the form of a small drop, or of small drops. [*Little used.*] *Brown.*

GUT'TURAL, *a.* [Fr. *guttural*, from L. *guttur*, the throat.]

Pertaining to the throat; formed in the throat; as a *guttural* letter or sound; a *guttural* voice.

GUT'TURAL, *n.* A letter pronounced in the throat; as the Gr. χ.

GUT'TURALLY, *adv.* In a guttural manner; in the throat.

GUT'TURALNESS, *n.* The quality of being guttural.

GUT'TURINE, *a.* Pertaining to the throat. [*Not in use.*] *Ray.*

GUT'TY, *a.* [from L. *gutta*, a drop.] In *heraldry*, charged or sprinkled with drops. *Encyc.*

GUT'WORT, *n.* A plant.

GUY, *n. gi.* [Sp. Port. *guia*, from *guiar*, to *guide*. See *Guide.*]

In *marine affairs*, a rope used to keep a heavy body steady while hoisting or lowering; also, a tackle to confine a boom forwards, when a vessel is going large, and to prevent the sail from gybing. *Guy* is also a large slack rope, extending from the head of the main-mast to that of the fore-mast, to sustain a tackle for loading or unloading. *Mar. Dict.*

GUZ'ZLE, *v. i.* [probably allied to Arm. *gouzoucq*, the throat. In Italian, *gozzo* is the crop of a bird.]

To swallow liquor greedily; to drink much; to drink frequently.

> Well seasoned bowls the gossip's spirits raise,
> Who, while she *guzzles*, chats the Doctor's praise. *Roscommon.*

GUZ'ZLE, *v. t.* To swallow much or often; to swallow with immoderate gust.

> —Still *guzzling* must of wine. *Dryden.*

GUZ'ZLE, *n.* An insatiable thing or person. *Marston.*

GUZ'ZLER, *n.* One who guzzles; an immoderate drinker.

GYBE, *n.* A sneer. [See *Gibe.*]

GYBE, *v. t.* In *seamen's language*, to shift a boom-sail from one side of a vessel to the other. *Mar. Dict.*

GY'BING, *ppr.* Shifting a boom-sail from one side of a vessel to the other.

GYE, *v. t.* To guide. *Obs.* *Chaucer.*

GYMNA'SIUM, *n.* [Gr. γυμνασιον, from γυμνος, naked.]

In *Greece*, a place where athletic exercises were performed. Hence, a place of exercise; a school. *Ash.*

GYMNAS'TIC, *a.* [L. *gymnasticus*; Gr. γυμναςικος, from γυμναζω, to exercise, from γυμνος, naked; the ancients being naked in their exercises.]

Pertaining to athletic exercises of the body, intended for health, defense or diversion, as running, leaping, wrestling, throwing the discus, the javelin or the hoop, playing with balls, &c. The modern gymnastic exercises are intended chiefly for the preservation and promotion of health.

ĠYMNAS′TIC, *n.* Athletic exercise.

ĠYMNAS′TICALLY, *adv.* In a gymnastic manner; athletically. *Brown.*

ĠYMNAS′TICS, *n.* The gymnastic art; the art of performing athletic exercises.

ĠYM′NIC, *a.* [Gr. γυμνικος; L. *gymnicus.*]
1. Pertaining to athletic exercises of the body.
2. Performing athletic exercises. *Milton.*

ĠYM′NIC, *n.* Athletic exercise. *Burton.*

ĠYM′NOSOPHIST, *n.* [Gr. γυμνος, naked, and σοφιςης, a philosopher.]
A philosopher of India, so called from his going with bare feet, or with little clothing. The Gymnosophists in India lived in the woods and on mountains, subsisting on wild productions of the earth. They never drank wine nor married. Some of them traveled about, and practiced physic. They believed the immortality and transmigration of the soul. They placed the chief happiness of man in a contempt of the goods of fortune, and of the pleasures of sense. *Encyc.*

ĠYM′NOSOPHY, *n.* [supra.] The doctrines of the Gymnosophists. *Good.*

ĠYM′NOSPERM, *n.* [Gr. γυμνος, naked, and σπερμα, seed.] In *botany*, a plant that bears naked seeds.

ĠYMNOSPERM′OUS, *a.* [supra.] Having naked seeds, or seeds not inclosed in a capsule or other vessel.

GYN, *v. t.* To begin. *Obs.*

ĠYNAN′DER, *n.* [Gr. γυνη, a female, and ανηρ, a male.]
In *botany*, a plant whose stamens are inserted in the pistil.

ĠYNAN′DRIAN, *a.* Having stamens inserted in the pistil.

ĠYN′ARCHY, *n.* [Gr. γυνη, woman, and αρχη, rule.] Government by a female. *Chesterfield.*

ĠYP′SEOUS, *a.* [See *Gypsum.*] Of the nature of gypsum; partaking of the qualities of gypsum.

ĠYP′SUM, *n.* [L. from Gr. γυψος; Ch. גופים and גפס to overspread with plaster; Ar. جبسين gypsum.]
Plaster stone; sulphate of lime; a mineral not unfrequently found in crystals, often in amorphous masses. There are several subspecies and varieties; as the foliated, compact, earthy, granular, snowy and branchy. *Cleaveland.*
Gypsum is of great use in agriculture and the arts. As a manure, it is invaluable.

ĠYP′SEY, ĠYP′SY, } *n.* [See *Gipsey.*]

ĠY′RAL, *a.* [See *Gyre.*] Whirling; moving in a circular form.

ĠYRA′TION, *n.* [L. *gyratio.* See *Gyre.*] A turning or whirling round; a circular motion. *Newton.*

ĠYRE, *n.* [L. *gyrus*; Gr. γυρος. Class Gr.] A circular motion, or a circle described by a moving body; a turn.

> Quick and more quick he spins in giddy *gyres.* *Dryden.*

ĠY′RED, *a.* Falling in rings. *Shak.*

ĠYR′FALCON, *n.* [Fr. *gerfault.* This is said to be in Latin *hierofalco*, from Gr. ιερος, sacred, and *falco*, and so named from the veneration of the Egyptians for hawks. *Cuvier.*] A species of Falco, or hawk.

ĠYR′OMANCY, *n.* [Gr. γυρος, a circuit, and μαντεια, divination.]
A kind of divination performed by walking round in a circle or ring. *Cyc.*

ĠYVE, *n.* [W. *gevyn*; Ir. *geibheal*, or *geibion*; from holding or making fast. See *Gavel.*] *Gyves* are fetters or shackles for the legs.

> *Gyves* and the mill had tamed thee. *Milton.*

ĠYVE, *v. t.* To fetter; to shackle; to chain. *Shak.*

H.

H, is the eighth letter of the English Alphabet. It is properly the representative of the Chaldee, Syriac and Hebrew ח, which is the eighth letter in those alphabets. Its form is the same as the Greek H *eta.* It is not strictly a vowel, nor an articulation; but the mark of a stronger breathing, than that which precedes the utterance of any other letter. It is pronounced with an expiration of breath, which, preceding a vowel, is perceptible by the ear at a considerable distance. Thus, *harm* and *arm*, *hear* and *ear*, *heat* and *eat*, are distinguished at almost any distance at which the voice can be heard. H is a letter *sui generis*, but as useful in forming and distinguishing words as any other.

In our mother tongue, the Anglo-Saxon, and other Teutonic dialects, *h* sometimes represents the L. *c*, and the Gr. κ; as in *horn*, L. *cornu*, Gr. κερας; *hide*, G. *haut*, Sw. *hud*, D. *huid*, Dan. *hud*, L. *cutis*; Sax. *hlinian*, L. *clino*, Gr. κλινω, to lean; L. *celo*, to conceal, Sax. *helan*, G. *hehlen*, Dan. *hæler.* In Latin, *h* sometimes represents the Greek χ; as in *halo*, Gr. χαλαω; *hio*, χαω. In the modern European languages, it represents other guttural letters.

In English, *h* is sometimes mute, as in *honor*, *honest*; also when united with *g*, as in *right*, *fight*, *brought.* In *which*, *what*, *who*, *whom*, and some other words in which it follows *w*, it is pronounced before it, *hwich*, *hwat*, &c. As a numeral in Latin, H denotes 200, and with a dash over it $\overline{\text{H}}$ 200,000.

As an abbreviation in Latin, H stands for *homo*, *hæres*, *hora*, &c.

HA, an exclamation, denoting surprise, joy or grief. With the first or long sound of *a*, it is used as a question, and is equivalent to "What do you say?" When repeated, *ha*, *ha*, it is an expression of laughter, or sometimes it is equivalent to "Well! it is so."

HAAK, *n.* A fish. *Ainsworth.*

Habeas Corpus, [L. have the body.] A writ for delivering a person from false imprisonment, or for removing a person from one court to another, &c. *Cowel.*

HAB′ERDASHER, *n.* [perhaps from G. *habe*, D. *have*, goods, and G. *tauschen*, to barter, to truck. If not, I can give no account of its origin.]
A seller of small wares; *a word little used or not at all in the U. States.*

HAB′ERDASHERY, *n.* The goods and wares sold by a haberdasher.

HAB′ERDINE, *n.* A dried salt cod. *Ainsworth.*

HAB′ERĠEON, *n.* [Fr. *haubergeon*; Norm. *hauberiom*; Arm. *hobregon.* It has been written also *haberge*, *hauberk*, &c. G. *halsberge*; *hals*, the neck, and *bergen*, to save or defend.]
A coat of mail or armor to defend the neck and breast. It was formed of little iron rings united, and descended from the neck to the middle of the body. *Encyc.* Ex. xxviii.

HAB′ILE, *a.* Fit; proper. [*Not in use.*] *Spenser.*

HABIL′IMENT, *n.* [Fr. *habillement*, from *habiller*, to clothe, from L. *habeo*, to have.]
A garment; clothing; usually in the plural, *habiliments*, denoting garments, clothing or dress in general.

HABIL′ITATE, *v. t.* [Fr. *habiliter.*] To qualify. [*Not used.*] *Bacon.*

HABILITA′TION, *n.* Qualification. [*Not in use.*] *Bacon.*

HABILITY. [See *Ability.*]

HAB′IT, *n.* [Fr. *habit*; Sp. *habito*; It. *abito*; L. *habitus*, from *habeo*, to have, to hold. See *Have.*]
1. Garb; dress; clothes or garments in general.

> The scenes are old, the *habits* are the same,
> We wore last year. *Dryden.*
> There are among the statues, several of Venus, in different *habits.* *Addison.*

2. A coat worn by ladies over other garments.
3. State of any thing, implying some continuance or permanence; temperament or particular state of a body, formed by nature or induced by extraneous circumstances; as a costive or lax *habit* of body; a sanguine *habit.*
4. A disposition or condition of the mind or body acquired by custom or a frequent

repetition of the same act. *Habit* is that which is held or retained, the effect of custom or frequent repetition. Hence we speak of good *habits* and bad *habits*. Frequent drinking of spirits leads to a *habit* of intemperance. We should endeavor to correct evil *habits* by a change of practice. A great point in the education of children, is to prevent the formation of bad *habits*.

Habit of plants, the general form or appearance, or the conformity of plants of the same kind in structure and growth. *Martyn.*

HAB'IT, *v. t.* To dress; to clothe; to array.

They *habited* themselves like rural deities. *Dryden.*

HAB'IT, *v. t.* To dwell; to inhabit. *Obs.* *Chaucer.*

HAB'ITABLE, *a.* [Fr. from L. *habitabilis*, from *habito*, to dwell.]

That may be inhabited or dwelt in; capable of sustaining human beings; as the *habitable* world. Some climates are scarcely *habitable.*

HAB'ITABLENESS, *n.* Capacity of being inhabited. *More. Ray.*

HAB'ITABLY, *adv.* In such a manner as to be habitable. *Forsyth.*

HAB'ITANCE, *n.* Dwelling; abode; residence. [*Not now used.*] *Spenser.*

HAB'ITANCY, *n.* Legal settlement or inhabitancy. [See *Inhabitancy.*] *Belknap.*

HAB'ITANT, *n.* [Fr. from L. *habitans.*] An inhabitant; a dweller; a resident; one who has a permanent abode in a place. *Milton. Pope.*

HAB'ITAT, *n.* Habitation. *Fleming.*

HABITA'TION, *n.* [L. *habitatio*, from *habito*, to dwell, from *habeo*, to hold, or as we say in English, to keep.]

1. Act of inhabiting; state of dwelling. *Denham.*

2. Place of abode; a settled dwelling; a mansion; a house or other place in which man or any animal dwells.

The stars may be the *habitations* of numerous races of beings.

The Lord blesseth the *habitation* of the just. Prov. iii.

HAB'ITATOR, *n.* [L.] A dweller; an inhabitant. [*Not used.*] *Brown.*

HAB'ITED, *a.* Clothed; dressed. He was *habited* like a shepherd.

2. Accustomed. [*Not usual.*]

HABIT'UAL, *a.* [Fr. *habituel*, from *habit.*] Formed or acquired by habit, frequent use or custom.

Art is properly an *habitual* knowledge of certain rules and maxims. *South.*

2. Customary; according to habit; as the *habitual* practice of sin; the *habitual* exercise of holy affections.

It is the distinguishing mark of *habitual* piety to be grateful for the most common blessings. *Buckminster.*

3. Formed by repeated impressions; rendered permanent by continued causes; as an *habitual* color of the skin. *S. S. Smith.*

HABIT'UALLY, *adv.* By habit; customarily; by frequent practice or use; as *habitually* profane; *habitually* kind and benevolent.

HABIT'UATE, *v. t.* [Fr. *habituer*, from *habit.*]

1. To accustom; to make familiar by frequent use or practice. Men may *habituate* themselves to the taste of oil or tobacco. They *habituate* themselves to vice. Let us *habituate* ourselves and our children to the exercise of charity.

2. To settle as an inhabitant in a place. *Temple.*

HABIT'UATE, *a.* Inveterate by custom. *Hammond.*

2. Formed by habit. *Temple.*

HABIT'UATED, *pp.* Accustomed; made familiar by use.

HABIT'UATING, *ppr.* Accustoming; making easy and familiar by practice.

HAB'ITUDE, *n.* [Fr. from L. *habitudo*, from *habitus.*]

1. Relation; respect; state with regard to something else. [*Little used.*] *Hale. South.*

2. Frequent intercourse; familiarity. [*Not usual.*]

To write well, one must have frequent *habitudes* with the best company. *Dryden.*

3. Customary manner or mode of life; repetition of the same acts; as the *habitudes* of fowls or insects. *Goldsmith.*

4. Custom; habit. *Dryden. Prior.*

HAB'NAB, *adv.* [*hap ne hap*, let it happen or not.]

At random; by chance; without order or rule. *Hudibras.*

HACK, *v. t.* [Sax. *haccan*; D. *hakken*; G. *hacken*; Dan. *hakker*; Sw. *hacka*; Fr. *hacher*, from which we have *hash* and *hatchet*, and from the same root, *hatchel*; Arm. *haicha*; W. *haciaw*, to hack; *hag*, a gash; and *haggle* is of the same family, as are *hew* and *hoe*. Class Cg.]

1. To cut irregularly and into small pieces; to notch; to mangle by repeated strokes of a cutting instrument.

2. To speak with stops or catches; to speak with hesitation. *Shak.*

HACK, *n.* A notch; a cut. *Shak.*

HACK, *n.* A horse kept for hire; a horse much used in draught, or in hard service; any thing exposed to hire, or used in common. [from *hackney.*]

2. A coach or other carriage kept for hire. [from *hackney.*]

3. Hesitating or faltering speech. *More.*

4. A rack for feeding cattle. [*Local.*]

HACK, *a.* Hired. *Wakefield.*

HACK, *v. i.* To be exposed or offered to common use for hire; to turn prostitute. *Hanmer.*

2. To make an effort to raise phlegm. [See *Hawk.*]

HACK'ED, *pp.* Chopped; mangled.

HACK'ING, *ppr.* Chopping into small pieces; mangling; mauling.

HACK'LE, *v. t.* [G. *hecheln*; D. *hekelen.* This is a dialectical variation of *hatchel*, *hetchel.*]

1. To comb flax or hemp; to separate the coarse part of these substances from the fine, by drawing them through the teeth of a hatchel.

2. To tear asunder. *Burke.*

HACK'LE, *n.* A hatchel. *The latter word is used in the U. States.*

2. Raw silk; any flimsy substance unspun. *Johnson. Walton.*

3. A fly for angling, dressed with feathers or silk. *Todd.*

HACK'LY, *a.* [from *hack.*] Rough; broken as if hacked.

In *mineralogy*, having fine, short, and sharp points on the surface; as a *hackly* fracture. *Cleaveland.*

HACK'MATACK, *n.* The popular name of the red larch, the *Pinus microcarpa.* *Bigelow.*

HACK'NEY, *n.* [Fr. *haquenée*, a pacing horse; Sp. *hacanea*, a nag somewhat larger than a pony; *haca*, a pony; Port. *hacanea* or *acanea*, a choice pad, or ambling nag; It. *chinea.*]

1. A pad; a nag; a pony. *Chaucer.*

2. A horse kept for hire; a horse much used.

3. A coach or other carriage kept for hire, and often exposed in the streets of cities. The word is sometimes contracted to *hack.*

4. Any thing much used or used in common; a hireling; a prostitute.

HACK'NEY, *a.* Let out for hire; devoted to common use; as a *hackney*-coach.

2. Prostitute; vicious for hire. *Roscommon.*

3. Much used; common; trite; as a *hackney* author or remark.

HACK'NEY, *v. t.* To use much; to practice in one thing; to make trite.

2. To carry in a hackney-coach. *Cowper.*

HACK'NEY-COACH. [See *Hackney.*]

HACKNEY-COACHMAN, *n.* A man who drives a hackney-coach.

HACK'NEYED, *pp.* Used much or in common.

2. Practiced; accustomed.

He is long *hackneyed* in the ways of men. *Shak.*

HACK'NEYING, *ppr.* Using much; accustoming.

HACK'NEYMAN, *n.* A man who lets horses and carriages for hire. *Barret.*

HACK'STER, *n.* A bully; a ruffian or assassin. *Obs.* *Bp. Hall.*

HAC'QUETON, *n.* [Fr. *hoqueton.*] A stuffed jacket formerly worn under armor, sometimes made of lether. [*Not used.*] *Spenser.*

HAD, *pret.* and *pp.* of *have*; contracted from Sax. *hæfd*, that is, *haved*; as, I *had*; I have *had*. In the phrase, "I *had* better go," it is supposed that *had* is used for *would*; "I'd better go." The sense of the phrase is, "it would be better for me to go."

HAD'DER, *n.* [G. *heide.*] Heath. [*Not in use.* See *Heath.*]

HAD'DOCK, *n.* [Ir. *codog.* The first syllable seems to be *cod* or *gadus*, and the last, the termination, as in *bullock.*]

A fish of the genus Gadus or cod, and order of Jugulars. It has a long body, the upper part of a dusky brown color, and the belly of a silvery hue; the lateral line is black. This fish breeds in immense numbers in the northern seas, and constitutes a considerable article of food. *Encyc.*

HADE, *n.* Among *miners*, the steep descent of a shaft; also, the descent of a hill. *Drayton.*

In *mining*, the inclination or deviation from the vertical of a mineral vein. *Cyc.*

H'AFT, *n.* [Sax. *hæft*, a haft, and *hæftan*, to seize; G. *heft*; D. *heft*; Dan. *hefte*; from the root of *have*, or of L. *capio*, W. *hafiaw*, to snatch.]

A handle; that part of an instrument or vessel which is taken into the hand, and by which it is held and used. It is used chiefly for the part of a sword or dagger by which it is held; the hilt.

H'AFT, *v. t.* To set in a haft; to furnish with a handle.

H'AFTER, *n.* [W. *hafiaw*, to catch.] A caviller; a wrangler. [*Not in use.*] *Barret.*

HAG, *n.* [In Sax. *hægesse* is a witch, fury or goblin, answering to the *Hecate* of mythology. In W. *hagyr*, ugly, is from *hag*, a gash, from the root of *hack*. In Russ. *ega* is a foolish old woman, a sorceress. See *Hagard.*]

1. An ugly old woman; as an old *hag* of threescore. *Dryden.*
2. A witch; a sorceress; an enchantress. *Shak.*
3. A fury; a she-monster. *Crashaw.*
4. A cartilaginous fish, the Gastrobranchus, which enters other fishes and devours them. It is about five or six inches long, and resembles a small eel. It is allied to the lamprey. *Cyc.*
5. Appearances of light and fire on horses' manes or men's hair, were formerly called *hags.* *Blount.*

HAG, *v. t.* To harass; to torment. *Butler.*
2. To tire; to weary with vexation.

HAG'ARD, *a.* [G. *hager*, lean; W. *hag*, a gash; *hacciaw*, to hack. See *Hack.*]

1. Literally, having a ragged look, as if hacked or gashed. Hence, lean; meager; rough; having eyes sunk in their orbits; ugly.
2. Wild; fierce; intractable; as a *hagard* hawk.

HAG'ARD, *n.* [See *Hag*. This and the other derivatives of *hag* ought to be written with a single *g.*]

1. Any thing wild and intractable. *Shak.*
2. A species of hawk. *Walton.*
3. A hag.

HAG'ARDLY, *adv.* In a hagard or ugly manner; with deformity. *Dryden.*

HAG'BORN, *n.* Born of a hag or witch. *Shak.*

HAG'GARD, *n.* [Sax. *haga*, a little field, and *geard*, a yard.] A stack-yard. *Howell.*

HAG'GESS, *n.* [from *hack.*] A mess of meat, generally pork, chopped and inclosed in a membrane. *Johnson.*
2. A sheep's head and pluck minced. *Entick.*

HAG'GLE, *v. t.* [W. *hag*, a gash or cut. It is a diminutive from the root of *hack.*]

To cut into small pieces; to notch or cut in an unskillful manner; to make rough by cutting; to mangle; as, a boy *haggles* a stick of wood.

> Suffolk first died, and York all *haggled* o'er,
> Comes to him where in gore he lay insteep'd. *Shak.*

HAG'GLE, *v. i.* To be difficult in bargaining; to hesitate and cavil. [See *Higgle.*]

HAG'GLED, *pp.* Cut irregularly into notches; made rough by cutting; mangled.

HAG'GLER, *n.* One who haggles.
2. One who cavils, hesitates and makes difficulty in bargaining.

HAG'GLING, *ppr.* Hacking; mangling; caviling and hesitating in bargaining.

HAGIOG'RAPHAL, *n.* Pertaining to hagiography, which see.

HAGIOG'RAPHER, *n.* [See the next word.] A writer of holy or sacred books.

HAGIOG'RAPHY, *n.* [Gr. αγιος, holy, and γραφη, a writing.] Sacred writings. The Jews divide the books of the Scriptures into three parts; the Law, which is contained in the five first books of the Old Testament; the Prophets, or Nevim; and the Cetuvim, or *writings*, by way of eminence. The latter class is called by the Greeks *Hagiographa*, comprehending the books of Psalms, Proverbs, Job, Daniel, Ezra, Nehemiah, Ruth, Esther, Chronicles, Canticles, Lamentations, and Ecclesiastes.

HAG'ISH, *a.* Of the nature of a hag; deformed; ugly; horrid. *Shak.*

HAG'-RIDDEN, *a.* Afflicted with the nightmar. *Cheyne.*

HAG'SHIP, *n.* The state or title of a hag or witch. *Middleton.*

HAGUEBUT. [See *Arquebuse.*]

HAH, an exclamation expressing surprise or effort.

HAIL, *n.* [Sax. *hægel* or *hagel;* G. D. Dan. and Sw. *hagel;* so called from its rough, broken form, from the root of *hack*, *haggle.*]

Masses of ice or frozen vapor, falling from the clouds in showers or storms. These masses consist of little spherules united, but not all of the same consistence; some being as hard and solid as perfect ice; others soft, like frozen snow. Hailstones assume various figures; some are round, others angular, others pyramidical, others flat, and sometimes they are stellated with six radii, like crystals of snow. *Encyc.*

HAIL, *v. i.* To pour down masses of ice or frozen vapors.

HAIL, *v. t.* To pour. *Shak.*

HAIL, *a.* [Sax. *hal*, whole, sound; *hæl*, health; G. *heil*, D. Dan. *heel*, Sw. *hel*, Gr. ουλος, whole. See *Heal.*]

Sound; whole; healthy; not impaired by disease; as a *hail* body; *hail* corn. [In this sense, it is usually written *hale.*]

HAIL, an exclamation, or rather a verb in the imperative mode, being the adjective *hail*, used as a verb. *Hail*, be well; be in health; health to you; a term of salutation, equivalent to L. *salve*, *salvete.*

> *Hail*, *hail*, brave friend. *Shak.*

HAIL, *n.* A wish of health; a salutation. This word is sometimes used as a noun; as, the angel *hail* bestowed. *Milton.*

HAIL, *v. t.* [from the same root as *call*, L. *calo*, Gr. χαλεω. See *Call* and *Heal.*]

To call; to call to a person at a distance, to arrest his attention. It is properly used in any case where the person accosted is distant, but is appropriately used by seamen. *Hoa* or *hoi*, *the ship ahoay*, is the usual manner of hailing; to which the answer is *holloa*, or *hollo*. Then follow the usual questions, whence came ye? where are you bound? &c.

HA'ILED, *pp.* Called to from a distance; accosted.

HA'ILING, *ppr.* Saluting; calling to from a distance.
2. Pouring down hail.

HA'ILSHOT, *n.* Small shot which scatter like hailstones. [*Not used.*] *Hayward.*

HA'ILSTONE, *n.* A single mass of ice falling from a cloud. *Dryden.*

HA'ILY, *a.* Consisting of hail; as *haily* showers. *Pope.*

HA'INOUS, *a.* [Fr. *haineux*, from *haine*, hatred. Qu. Gr. αινος.] Properly, hateful; odious. Hence, great, enormous, aggravated; as a *hainous* sin or crime. *Mitford.*

HA'INOUSLY, *adv.* Hatefully; abominably; enormously.

HA'INOUSNESS, *n.* Odiousness; enormity; as the *hainousness* of theft or robbery, or of any crime.

HAIR, *n.* [Sax. *hær;* G. *haar;* D. *hair;* Sw. *hår;* Dan. *haar.*]

1. A small filament issuing from the skin of an animal, and from a bulbous root. Each filament contains a tube or hollow within, occupied by a pulp or pith, which is intended for its nutrition, and extends only to that part which is in a state of growth. *Cyc.*

When *hair* means a single filament, it has a plural, *hairs.*

2. The collection or mass of filaments growing from the skin of an animal, and forming an integument or covering; as the *hair* of the head. *Hair* is the common covering of many beasts. When the filaments are very fine and short, the collection of them is called *fur*. *Wool*, also, is a kind of hair. When *hair* signifies a collection of these animal filaments, it has no plural.
3. Any thing very small or fine; or a very small distance; the breadth of a hair. He judges to a hair, that is, very exactly. *Dryden.*
4. A trifling value. It is not worth a *hair.*
5. Course; order; grain; the hair falling in a certain direction. [*Not used.*]

> You go against the *hair* of your profession. *Shak.*

6. Long, straight and distinct filaments on the surface of plants; a species of down or pubescence. *Martyn.*

HA'IRBELL, *n.* A plant, a species of hyacinth.

HA'IR-BRAINED. [See *Hare-brained.*]

HA'IR-BREADTH, *n.* [See *Breadth.*] The diameter or breadth of a hair; a very small distance.

> —Seven hundred chosen men left-handed; every one could sling stones to a *hair-breadth.* Judges xx.

It is used as an adjective; as a *hair-breadth* escape. But in New England, it is generally *hair's breadth.*

HA'IRCLOTH, *n.* Stuff or cloth made of hair, or in part with hair. In *military affairs*, pieces of this cloth are used for covering the powder in wagons, or on batteries, or for covering charged bombs, &c. *Encyc.*

HA'IRHUNG, *a.* Hanging by a hair. *Young.*

HA'IRLACE, *n.* A fillet for tying up the hair of the head. *Swift.*

HA'IRLESS, *a.* Destitute of hair; bald; as *hairless* scalps. *Shak.*

HA'IRINESS, *n.* [from *hairy.*] The state of abounding or being covered with hair. *Johnson.*

HA'IRPIN, *n.* A pin used in dressing the hair.

HA'IRPOWDER, *n.* A fine powder of flour for sprinkling the hair of the head.

HA'IR-SALT, *n.* [*haar-salz*, Werner.] A mixture of the sulphates of magnesia and iron; its taste resembles that of alum. *Cleaveland.*

HA'IRWŎRM, *n.* A genus of worms *(vermes,)* called Gordius; a filiform animal found in fresh water or in the earth. There are several species. *Encyc.*

HA'IRY, *a.* [from *hair.*] Overgrown with hair; covered with hair; abounding with hair.

Esau, my brother, is a *hairy* man. Gen. xxvii.

2. Consisting of hair; as *hairy* honors. *Dryden.*

3. Resembling hair; of the nature of hair.

HAKE, *n.* A kind of fish, the *Gadus merlucius;* called by some authors *lucius marinus.* It was formerly salted and dried. *Encyc.*

HAK'OT, *n.* A fish. *Ainsworth.*

HAL, in some names, signifies *hall.*

HAL'BERD, *n.* [Fr. *hallebarde;* G. *hellebarde;* D. *hellebaard;* It. *alabarda* or *labarda;* Sp. Port. *alabarda;* Russ. *berdish,* a halberd or battle-ax, a pole-ax. The etymology is not settled. It seems anciently to have been a battle-ax fixed to a long pole, and in Gothic *hilde* is battle.]

A military weapon, consisting of a pole or shaft of wood, with a head armed with a steel point, with a cross piece of steel, flat and pointed at both ends, or with a cutting edge at one end, and a bent point at the other. It is carried by sergeants of foot and dragoons. *Encyc.*

HALBERDIE'R, *n.* One who is armed with a halberd. *Bacon.*

HAL'CYON, *n.* *hal'shon.* [L. *halcyon,* Gr. αλκυων, a king-fisher.]

The name anciently given to the king-fisher, otherwise called *alcedo;* a bird that was said to lay her eggs in nests, on rocks near the sea, during the calm weather about the winter solstice. Hence,

HAL'CYON, *a.* Calm; quiet; peaceful; undisturbed; happy. *Halcyon days* were seven days before and as many after the winter solstice, when the weather was calm. Hence by *halcyon days* are now understood days of peace and tranquility.

HALCYO'NIAN, *a.* Halcyon; calm. *Sheldon.*

HALE, *a.* [Sax. *hal,* sound, whole. See *Hail* and *Heal.*]

Sound; entire; healthy; robust; not impaired; as a *hale* body.

HALE, *n.* Welfare. [*Not in use.*] *Spenser.*

HALE, *v. t.* [Sw. *hala;* Fr. *haler.*] To pull or draw with force; to drag. This is now more generally written and pronounced *haul,* which see. It is always to be pronounced *haul.*

H'ALF, *n.* *h'af.* plu. *halves,* pron. *h'avz.* [Sax. *half* or *healf;* Goth. *halbs;* D. *half;* Sw. *half;* Dan. *halv;* G. *halb.*]

One equal part of a thing which is divided into two parts, either in fact or in contemplation; a moiety; as *half* a pound; *half* a tract of land; *half* an orange; *half* the miseries or pleasures of life. It is applied to quantity, number, length, and every thing susceptible of division. In practice, *of* is often or usually omitted after *half.* We say, *half* a pound; *half* a mile; *half* the number.

Half the misery of life. *Addison.*

H'ALF, *v. t.* To divide into halves. [See *Halve.*]

H'ALF, *adv.* In part, or in an equal part or degree.

Half loth, and *half* consenting. *Dryden.*

In composition, *half* denotes an equal part; or indefinitely, a part, and hence, imperfect.

H'ALFBLŎOD, *n.* Relation between persons born of the same father or of the same mother, but not of both; as a brother or sister of the *half blood.* The word is sometimes used as an adjective.

H'ALF-BLŎODED, *a.* Mean; degenerate. [*Little used.*] *Shak.*

2. Proceeding from a male and female, each of full blood, but of different breeds; as a *half-blooded* sheep.

H'ALF-BRED, *a.* Mixed; mongrel; mean.

H'ALF-CAP, *n.* A cap not wholly put on. *Shak.*

H'ALF-DEAD, *a.* Almost dead; nearly exhausted.

H'ALFEN, *a.* Wanting half its due qualities. [*Not used.*] *Spenser.*

H'ALFER, *n.* One that possesses half only.

2. A male fallow deer gelded.

H'ALF-FACED, *a.* Showing only part of the face. *Shak.*

H'ALF-HATCHED, *a.* Imperfectly hatched; as *half-hatched* eggs. *Gay.*

H'ALF-HEARD, *a.* Imperfectly heard; not heard to the end.

And leave *half-heard* the melancholy tale. *Pope.*

H'ALF-LEARNED, *a.* Imperfectly learned. *South.*

H'ALF-LOST, *a.* Nearly lost. *Milton.*

H'ALF-MARK, *n.* A coin; a noble, or 6*s.* 8*d.* sterling.

H'ALF-MOON, *n.* The moon at the quarters, when half its disk appears illuminated.

2. Any thing in the shape of a half-moon. In *fortification,* an outwork composed of two faces, forming a salient angle, whose gorge is in the form of a crescent or half-moon. *Encyc.*

H'ALF-PART, *n.* An equal part. *Shak.*

H'ALF-PAY, *n.* Half the amount of wages or salary; as, an officer retires on *half-pay.*

H'ALF-PAY, *a.* Receiving or entitled to half-pay; as a *half-pay* officer.

H'ALF-PENNY, *n.* *hap'penny* or *ha'penny.* A copper coin of the value of half a penny; also, the value of half a penny. It is used in the plural.

He cheats for *half-pence.* *Dryden.*

[This coin is not current in America.]

H'ALF-PENNY, *a.* Of the price or value of half a penny; as a *half-penny* loaf. *Shak.*

H'ALF-PENNY-WŎRTH, *n.* The value of a half-penny.

H'ALF-PIKE, *n.* A small pike carried by officers. *Tatler.*

2. A small pike used in boarding ships. *Mar. Dict.*

H'ALF-PINT, *n.* The half of a pint, or fourth of a quart. *Pope.*

H'ALF-READ, *a.* Superficially informed by reading. *Dryden.*

H'ALF-SCHOLAR, *n.* One imperfectly learned. *Watts.*

Half-seas over, a low expression denoting half drunk.

H'ALF-SIGHTED, *a.* Seeing imperfectly; having weak discernment. *Bacon.*

H'ALF-SPHERE, *n.* Hemisphere. *B. Jonson.*

H'ALF-STARVED, *a.* Almost starved.

H'ALF-STRAINED, *a.* Half-bred; imperfect. *Dryden.*

H'ALF-SWŎRD, *n.* Within half the length of a sword; close fight. *Shak.*

H'ALF-WAY, *adv.* In the middle; at half the distance. *Granville.*

H'ALF-WAY, *a.* Equally distant from the extremes; as a *half-way* house.

H'ALF-WIT, *n.* A foolish person; a dolt; a blockhead. *Dryden.*

H'ALF-WITTED, *a.* Weak in intellect; silly; foolish. *Swift.*

HAL'IBUT, *n.* A fish of the genus Pleuronectes, and order of Thoracics. This fish has a compressed body, one side resembling the back, the other the belly; and both eyes on the same side of the head. It grows to a great size; some to the weight of 300 or 400 pounds. It forms an article of food, and some parts of the body are fat, tender and delicious. This fish swims on its side, and hence the name of the genus. *Encyc.*

HAL'IDOM, *n.* [Sax. *haligdome;* *holy* and *dom.*] Adjuration by what is holy. *Obs.* *Spenser.*

HALING. [See *Hauling.*]

HALIT'UOUS, *a.* [L. *halitus,* breath.] Like breath; vaporous. *Obs.* *Boyle.*

HALL, *n.* [Sax. *heal;* D. *hal* or *zaal;* G. *saal;* Sw. and Dan. *sal;* Fr. *salle;* It. and Sp. *sala;* L. *aula;* Gr. αυλη; Sans. *aala;* Copt. *auli;* Turk. *awli.* Qu. Heb. אהל, a tent, Ar. أَهَلَ to marry, and to begin housekeeping, or Heb. Ch. Syr. היכל, a palace. Qu. are these all of one family. See *Salt.*]

1. In *architecture,* a large room at the entrance of a house or palace. In the houses of ministers of state, magistrates, &c. it is the place where they give audience and dispatch business. *Encyc.*

2. An edifice in which courts of justice are held; as Westminster *Hall,* which was originally a royal palace, the kings of England formerly holding their parliaments and courts of judicature in their own dwellings, as is still the practice in Spain. *Encyc.*

3. A manor-house, in which courts were formerly held. *Addison.*

4. A college, or large edifice belonging to a collegiate institution.

5. A room for a corporation or public assembly; as a town-*hall;* Fanueil *Hall* in Boston, &c.

6. A collegiate body in the universities of Oxford and Cambridge. *Prideaux.*

HALLELU'IAH, *n.* [Heb. הללו יה praise ye Jah or Jehovah, from הלל, to praise, that is, to throw, or raise the voice, to utter a loud sound. Ar. هَلَّ halla or ealla, to appear; to begin to shine, as the new moon; to exclaim; to exult; to sing; to rejoice; to praise or worship God. Gr. ελελευ, a shout in battle. It coincides in elements with *howl,* L. *ululo.*]

Praise ye Jehovah; give praise to God; a word used in songs of praise, or a term of rejoicing in solemn ascriptions of thanksgiving to God. It is used as a noun, or as an exclamation.

[This word is improperly written with *j*, in conformity with the German and other continental languages, in which *j* has the sound of *y*. But to pronounce the word with the English sound of *j* destroys its beauty. The like mistake of the sound of *j* in *Jehovah, Jordan, Joseph*, has perverted the true pronunciation, which was *Yehovah, Yordan, Yoseph*. This perversion must now be submitted to, but in *Halleluiah* it ought not to be tolerated.]

HAL'LIARD, *n.* [from *hale, haul.*] A rope or tackle for hoisting or lowering a sail. *Mar. Dict.*

HAL'LIER, *n.* A particular kind of net for catching birds. *Encyc.*

HAL'LOO, *v. i.* [This seems to belong to the family of *call*; Fr. *haler.*]

To cry out; to exclaim with a loud voice; to call to by name, or by the word *halloo.*

Country folks *hallooed* and hooted after me. *Sidney.*

HAL'LOO, *v. t.* To encourage with shouts.

Old John *hallooes* his hounds again. *Prior.*

2. To chase with shouts. *Shak.*
3. To call or shout to. *Shak.*

[This verb is regular, and pronounced with the accent on the first syllable.]

HALLOO', an exclamation, used as a call to invite attention.

HAL'LOOING, *ppr.* Crying out; as a noun, a loud outcry.

HAL'LOW, *v. t.* [Sax. *haligan* or *halgian*, to consecrate, to sanctify, from *halig* or *halg*, holy, from *hal*, sound, safe, whole; G. *heiligen*, from *heilig*, holy, *heil*, whole; *heilen*, to heal; D. *heiligen*, from *heilig*, holy, *heil*, safety, happiness; Dan. *helliger*, from *hellig*, holy; *heel*, whole, entire; Sw. *helga*, from *helig*, holy. See *Holy.* It coincides in origin with *hold*, and L. *calleo*, to be able.]

1. To make holy; to consecrate; to set apart for holy or religious use. Ex. xxviii. xxix. 1 Kings viii.
2. To devote to holy or religious exercises; to treat as sacred.

Hallow the sabbath day, to do no work therein. Jer. xvii.

3. To reverence; to honor as sacred.

Hallowed be thy name. *Lord's Prayer.*

HAL'LOWED, *pp.* Consecrated to a sacred use, or to religious exercises; treated as sacred; reverenced.

HAL'LOWING, *ppr.* Setting apart for sacred purposes; consecrating; devoting to religious exercises; reverencing.

HAL'LOWMAS, *n.* [See *Mass.*] The feast of All Souls. *Shak.*

HALLUCINA'TION, *n.* [L. *hallucinatio*, from *hallucinor*, to blunder.]

1. Error; blunder; mistake. [*Little used.*] *Addison.*
2. In *medicine*, faulty sense [*dysæsthesia*,] or erroneous imagination. *Hallucinations of the senses*, arise from some defect in the organs of sense, or from some unusual circumstances attending the object, as when it is seen by moonlight; and they are sometimes symptoms of general disease, as in fevers. *Maniacal hallucinations* arise from some imaginary or mistaken idea. Similar hallucinations occur in *revery.* *Darwin. Parr.*

HALM, *n. haum.* [Sax. *healm*; L. *culmus.*] Straw. [See *Haum.*]

HA'LO, *n.* [Ar. هالة haulon. The verb signifies to frighten, and to adorn with necklaces.]

A circle appearing round the body of the sun, moon or stars, called also Corona, or crown. Halos are sometimes white and sometimes colored. Sometimes one only appears, and sometimes several concentric circles appear at the same time. *Encyc.*

HALSE, *n.* [Sax. *hals.*] The neck or throat. *Obs.* *Chaucer.*

HALSE, *v. i. hals.* To embrace about the neck; to adjure; to greet. *Obs.*

HAL'SENING, *a.* Sounding harshly in the throat or tongue. *Obs.* *Carew.*

HALSER, *n. hawz'er.* [Sax. G. D. Dan. Sw. *hals*, the neck; and Qu. Sax. *sæl*, a rope or strap.]

A large rope of a size between the cable and the tow-line. [See *Hawser.*]

HALT, *v. i.* [Sax. *healt*, halt, lame; *healtian*, to limp; G. *halt*, a hold, stop, halt; *halten*, to hold; Sw. *halt, halta*; Dan. *halt, halter*; from the root of *hold.*]

1. To stop in walking; to hold. In *military affairs*, the true sense is retained, to stop in a march. The army *halted* at noon.
2. To limp; that is, to stop with lameness.
3. To hesitate; to stand in doubt whether to proceed, or what to do.

How long *halt* ye between two opinions? 1 Kings xviii.

4. To fail; to falter; as a *halting* sonnet. *Shak.*

HALT, *v. t.* To stop; to cause to cease marching; *a military term.* The general *halted* his troops for refreshment. *Washington.*

HALT, *a.* [Sax. *healt.*] Lame; that is, holding or stopping in walking.

Bring hither the poor, the maimed, the *halt*, and the blind. Luke xiv.

HALT, *n.* A stopping; a stop in marching. The troops made a *halt* at the bridge.

2. The act of limping.

HALT'ER, *n.* One who halts or limps.

HALT'ER, *n.* [G. *halter*, a holder. See *Halt.*]

1. A rope or strap and head-stall for leading or confining a horse.
2. A rope for hanging malefactors.
3. A strong cord or string.

HALT'ER, *v. t.* To put a halter on; as, to *halter* a horse.

2. To catch and hold, or to bind with a rope or cord.

HALT'ING, *ppr.* Stopping; limping.

HALT'INGLY, *adv.* With limping; slowly.

H'ALVE, *v. t. h'av.* [from *half.*] To divide into two equal parts; as, to *halve* an apple.

H'ALVED, *a.* In *botany*, hemispherical; covering one side; placed on one side.

H'ALVES, *n.* plu. of *half.* Two equal parts of a thing. *To cry halves*, is to claim an equal share. *To go halves*, is to have an equal share.

HAM, Sax. *ham*, a house, is our modern word *home*, G. *heim.* It is used in *hamlet*, and in the names of places, as in *Walt-ham*, wood-house, *walt*, a wood, and *ham*, a house, [not Wal-tham, as it is often pronounced,] *Bucking-ham, Notting-ham, Wrent-ham, Dur-ham*, &c.

HAM, *n.* [Sax. *ham.*] The inner or hind part of the knee; the inner angle of the joint which unites the thigh and the leg of an animal. Hence,

2. The thigh of a beast, particularly of a hog, whether salted and cured or not. But the word is more generally understood to mean the thigh of a hog salted and dried in smoke.

HAM'ADRYAD, *n.* [Gr. αμα, together, and δρυς, a tree.] A wood nymph, feigned to live and die with the tree to which it was attached. *Spectator.*

HAM'ATE, *a.* [L. *hamatus.*] Hooked; entangled. *Berkley.*

HAM'ATED, *a.* [L. *hamatus*, from *hama*, a hook; Celtic and Pers. *cam*, crooked.] Hooked or set with hooks. *Swift.*

HAM'BLE, *v. t.* [Sax. *hamelan.*] To hamstring. [*Not used.*]

HAME, *n.* plu. *hames.* [G. *kummet*; Russ. *chomut*, a collar; but it seems to be the Scot. *haims.* In Sw. *håmma* is to stop or restrain.]

A kind of collar for a draught horse, consisting of two bending pieces of wood or bows, and these placed on curving pads or stuffed lether, made to conform to the shape of the neck.

HAM'ITE, *n.* The fossil remains of a curved shell. *Ed. Encyc.*

HAM'LET, *n.* [Sax. *ham*, a house; Fr. *hameau*; Arm. *hamell* or *hamm.* See *Home.*]

A small village; a little cluster of houses in the country.

This word seems originally to have signified the seat of a freeholder, comprehending the mansion house and adjacent buildings. It now denotes a small collection of houses in the country, in distinction from a city, a large town or township.

The country wasted and the *hamlets* burned. *Dryden.*

HAM'LETED, *a.* Accustomed to a hamlet, or to a country life. *Feltham.*

HAM'MER, *n.* [Sax. *hamer*; D. *hamer*; G. Dan. *hammer*; Sw. *hammare*; probably, the beater.]

An instrument for driving nails, beating metals, and the like. It consists of an iron head, fixed crosswise to a handle. Hammers are of various sizes; a large hammer used by smiths is called a *sledge.*

HAM'MER, *v. t.* To beat with a hammer; as, to *hamner* iron or steel.

2. To form or forge with a hammer; to shape by beating.
3. To work in the mind; to contrive by intellectual labor; usually with *out*; as, to *hammer out* a scheme.

HAM'MER, *v. i.* To work; to be busy; to labor in contrivance.

2. To be working or in agitation.

HAM'MERABLE, *a.* That may be shaped by a hammer. *Sherwood.*

HAM'MERCLOTH, *n.* The cloth which covers a coach-box, so called from the old practice of carrying a hammer, nails, &c. in a little pocket hid by this cloth. *Pegge.*

HAM'MERED, *pp.* Beaten with a hammer.

HAM'MERER, *n.* One who works with a hammer.

HAM'MERHARD, *n.* Iron or steel hardened by hammering. *Moxon.*

HAM'MERING, *ppr.* Beating with a hammer; working; contriving.

HAM'MER-MAN, *n.* One who beats or works with a hammer.

HAM'MER-WŎRT, *n.* An herb. *Todd.*

HAMMITE. [See *Ammite.*]

HAM'MOC, *n.* [Sp. *hamaca;* Port. *maca.*] A kind of hanging bed, suspended between trees or posts, or by hooks. It consists of a piece of hempen cloth about six feet long and three feet wide, gathered at the ends and suspended by cords. It forms a bed, or a receptacle for a bed, on board of ships. *Encyc. Mar. Dict.*

HAM'OUS, [L. *hamus,* a hook; Celtic, *cam,* crooked.]

Hooked; having the end hooked or curved; *a term of botany.* *Lee. Martyn.*

HAM'PER, *n.* [contracted from *hanaper,* or from *hand pannier.*]

1. A large basket for conveying things to market, &c.

2. Fetters, or some instrument that shackles. *W. Browne.*

[This signification and that of the verb following indicate that this word is from *hanaper,* and that the latter is from the sense of interweaving twigs.]

HAM'PER, *v. t.* [See the Noun.] To shackle; to entangle; hence, to impede in motion or progress, or to render progress difficult.

A lion *hampered* in a net. *L'Estrange.*

They *hamper* and entangle our souls, and hinder their flight upwards. *Tillotson.*

2. To ensnare; to inveigle; to catch with allurements. *Shak.*

3. To tangle; to render complicated. *Blackmore.*

4. To perplex; to embarrass.

Hampered by the laws. *Butler.*

HAM'PERED, *pp.* Shackled; entangled; ensnared; perplexed.

HAM'PERING, *ppr.* Shackling; entangling; perplexing.

HAM'STER, *n.* [G. *hamster;* Russ. *chomiak.*]

A species of rat, the *Mus cricetus,* or German marmot. This rat is of the size of the water rat, but is of a browner color, and its belly and legs of a dirty yellow. It is remarkable for two bags, like those of a baboon, on each side of the jaw, under the skin, in which it conveys grain, peas and acorns to its winter residence. *Encyc. Goldsmith.*

HAM'STRING, *n.* The tendons of the ham. *Wiseman.*

HAM'STRING, *v. t.* pret. and pp. *hamstrung* or *hamstringed.* To cut the tendons of the ham, and thus to lame or disable. *Dryden.*

HAN, for *have,* in the plural. *Spenser.*

HAN'APER, *n.* [Norm. *hanap,* a cup, a hamper; Sax. *hnæp,* G. *napf,* D. *nap,* Fr. *hanap,* Arm. *hanaff,* It. *nappo,* a bowl or cup. These seem to be all the same word, yet I see not how a cup and a basket should have the same name, unless the vessel was originally made of bark, and so tight as to hold liquors.] The hanaper was used in early days by the kings of England, for holding and carrying with them their money, as they journeyed from place to place. It was a kind of basket, like the *fiscus,* and hence came to be considered as the king's treasury. Hence, the clerk or warden of the *hanaper,* is an officer who receives the fees due to the king for seals of charters, patents, commissions, and writs. There is also an officer who is controller of the *hanaper.* This word therefore answered to the modern exchequer. *Spelman.*

HANCE, HAUNCE, for *enhance.* *Obs.* [See *Enhance.*]

HAN'CES, *n. plu.* [L. *ansa.*] In *architecture,* the ends of elliptical arches, which are the arches of smaller circles than the scheme or middle part of the arch. *Harris.*

2. In *a ship,* falls of the fife-rails placed on balusters on the poop and quarter-deck down to the gangway. *Harris.*

HAND, *n.* [Sax. *hand, hond;* G. and D. *hand;* Dan. *haand;* Sw. *hand.* This word may be connected in origin with Sax. *hentan,* to follow, to take or seize, Gr. χανδανω, L. *hendo,* in *prehendo;* but from its derivatives, *handy, handsome,* it would appear to proceed from a root signifying to be strong, right, straight, which would give the sense of fitness and of beauty. Chaucer has *hende, hendy,* civil, courteous.]

1. In *man,* the extremity of the arm, consisting of the palm and fingers, connected with the arm at the wrist; the part with which we hold and use any instrument.

2. In *falconry,* the foot of a hawk; and *in the manege,* the fore-foot of a horse.

3. A measure of four inches; a palm; *applied chiefly to horses;* as a horse 14 *hands* high.

4. Side; part; right or left; as on the one *hand* or the other. This is admitted on all *hands,* that is, on all sides, or by all parties.

5. Act; deed; performance; external action; that is, the effect for the cause, the *hand* being the instrument of action.

Thou sawest the contradiction between my heart and *hand.* *King Charles.*

6. Power of performance; skill.

A friend of mine has a very fine *hand* on the violin. *Addison.*

He had a mind to try his *hand* at a Spectator. *Addison.*

7. Power of making or producing.

An intelligent being coming out of the *hands* of infinite perfection. *Cheyne.*

8. Manner of acting or performance; as, he changed his *hand.* *Dryden.*

9. Agency; part in performing or executing. Punish every man who had a *hand* in the mischief. We see the *hand* of God in this event.

10. Conveyance; agency in transmitting.

11. Possession; power. The estate is in the *hands* of the owner. The papers are in my *hands.*

12. The cards held at a game; hence, a game.

13. That which performs the office of the hand or of a finger in pointing; as the *hand* of a clock; the hour *hand,* and the minute *hand.*

14. A person; an agent; a man employed in agency or service. The mason employs twenty *hands.*

15. Form of writing; style of penmanship; as a good *hand;* a bad *hand;* a fine *hand.*

16. Agency; service; ministry. Ex. iv. Lev. viii.

17. In *Scripture,* the *hand* of God, is his eternal purpose and executive power. Acts iv.

18. The providential bounty of God. Ps. civ.

19. The power of God exerted in judgments or mercies, in punishing or defending. Judges ii. Ps. xxxii.

20. The spirit of God; divine influence. 1 Kings xviii.

21. The favor of God, or his support. Neh. ii. Luke i.

At hand, near; either present and within reach, or not far distant.

Your husband is *at hand,* I hear his trumpet. *Shak.*

2. Near in time; not distant.

The day of Christ is *at hand.* 2 Thess. ii.

By hand, with the hands, in distinction from the instrumentality of tools, engines or animals; as, to weed a garden *by hand;* to lift, draw or carry *by hand.*

In hand, present payment; in respect to the receiver.

Receiving *in hand* one year's tribute. *Knolles.*

2. In a state of execution. I have a great work *in hand.*

At my hand, at his hand, &c., denote from the person or being.

Shall we receive good *at the hand* of God, and shall we not receive evil? Job ii.

On hand, in present possession; as, he has a supply of goods *on hand.*

2. Under one's care or management.

Jupiter had a farm *on his hands.* *L'Estrange.*

Off hand, without delay, hesitation or difficulty; immediately; dextrously; without previous preparation.

Out of hand, ready payment; with regard to the payer.

Let not the wages of any man tarry with thee; but give it him *out of hand.* *Tobit.*

To his hand, to my hand, &c., in readiness; already prepared; ready to be received.

The work is made *to his hands.* *Locke.*

Under his hand, under her hand, &c., with the proper writing or signature of the name. This deed is executed *under the hand* and seal of the owner.

Hand over head, negligently; rashly; without seeing what one does. [*Little used.*] *Bacon.*

Hand over hand, by passing the hands alternately one before or above another, as to climb *hand over hand;* also, rapidly, as to come up with a chase *hand over hand; used by seamen.* *Mar. Dict.*

Hand to hand, in close union; close fight. *Dryden.*

But *from hand to hand* is from one person to another.

Hand in hand, in union; conjointly; unitedly. *Swift.*

To join hand in hand, is to unite efforts and act in concert.

Hand in hand, fit; pat; suitable. *Shak.*

Hand to mouth. To live *from hand to mouth*, is to obtain food and other necessaries, as want requires, without making previous provision, or having an abundant previous supply.

To bear in hand, to keep in expectation; to elude. [*Not used.*] *Shak.*

To bear a hand, to hasten; *a seaman's phrase.*

To be hand and glove, to be intimate and familiar, as friends or associates.

To set the hand to, to engage in; to undertake.

That the Lord thy God may bless thee, in all thou *settest thine hand to.* Deut. xxiii.

To take in hand, to attempt; to undertake. Luke i.

Also, to seize and deal with.

To have a hand in, to be concerned in; to have a part or concern in doing; to have an agency in. *South.*

To put the last hand or *finishing hand to*, to complete; to perfect; to make the last corrections, or give the final polish.

To change hands, to change sides; to shift. *Butler.*

Hand, in the sense of rate, price, terms, conditions, as used by Bacon, Taylor, &c., is obsolete; as, "to buy at a dear *hand;*" "accept the mystery, but at no *hand* wrest it by pride or ignorance." So in the sense of advantage, gain, superiority, as used by Hayward; and in that of competition, content, as used by Shakspeare.

To get hand, to gain influence, is obsolete.

A heavy hand, severity or oppression.

A light hand, gentleness; moderation.

A strict hand, severe discipline; rigorous government.

Hands off, a vulgar phrase for keep off, forbear.

To pour water on the hands, in the phraseology of the Scriptures, is to serve or minister to. 2 Kings iii.

To wash the hands, to profess innocence. Matt. xxvii.

To kiss the hand, imports adoration. Job xxxi.

To lean on the hand, imports familiarity. 2 Kings v.

To strike hands, to make a contract, or to become surety for another's debt or good behavior. Prov. xvii.

Putting the hand under the thigh, was an ancient ceremony used in swearing.

To give the hand, is to make a covenant with one, or to unite with him in design. 2 Kings x.

The stretching out of the hand, denotes an exertion of power. But,

The stretching out of the hand to God, imports earnest prayer or solemn dedication of one's self to him. Ps. lxviii. and cxliii.

The lifting of the hand, was used in affirmation and swearing, and in prayer imported a solemn wishing of blessings from God. Gen. xiv. Lev. xix.

To lift the hand against a superior, to rebel. 2 Sam. xx.

To put forth the hand against one, to kill him. 1 Sam. xxiv.

To put one's hand to a neighbor's goods, to steal them. Ex. xxii.

To lay hands on in anger, to assault or seize, or to smite. Ex. xxiv. Is. xi.

To lay the hand on the mouth, imports silence. Job xl.

The laying on of hands, was also a ceremony used in consecrating one to office. Num. xxvii. 1 Tim. iv.

It was also used in blessing persons. Mark x.

Hiding the hand in the bosom, denotes idleness; inactivity; sluggishness. Prov. xix.

The clapping of hands, denotes joy and rejoicing. But in some instances, contempt or derision, or joy at the calamities of others. Ps. xlvii. Ezek. xxv.

A station at the *right hand* is honorable, and denotes favor, approbation or honor. A station on the *left hand* is less honorable. Matt. xx.

God's standing at the right hand of men, imports his regard for them, and his readiness to defend and assist them. Ps. xvi.

Satan's standing at the right hand of men, imports his readiness to accuse them, or to hinder or torment them. Zech. iii.

Clean hands, denotes innocence and a blameless and holy life. Ps. xxiv.

A slack hand, denotes idleness; carelessness; sloth. Prov. x.

The right hand, denotes power; strength. Ex. xv.

HAND, *v. t.* To give or transmit with the hand. *Hand* me a book.

2. To lead, guide and lift with the hand; to conduct. *Locke.*

3. To manage; as, I *hand* my oar. *Prior.*

4. To seize; to lay hands on. [*Not used.*] *Shak.*

5. In *seamanship*, to furl; to wrap or roll a sail close to the yard, stay or mast, and fasten it with gaskets. *Mar. Dict.*

To hand down, to transmit in succession, as from father to son, or from predecessor to successor. Fables are *handed down* from age to age.

HAND'BALL, *n.* An ancient game with a ball. *Brand.*

HAND'BARRŌW, *n.* A barrow or vehicle borne by the hands of men, and without a wheel. *Mortimer.*

HAND'BASKET, *n.* A small or portable basket. *Mortimer.*

HAND'BELL, *n.* A small bell rung by the hand; a table bell. *Bacon.*

HAND'BREADTH, *n.* A space equal to the breadth of the hand; a palm. Ex. xxv.

HAND'ЄLOTH, *n.* A handkerchief.

HAND'ЄUFF, *n.* [Sax. *handcopse.*] A manacle, consisting of iron rings for the wrists, and a connecting chain to confine the hands.

HAND'ЄUFF, *v. t.* To manacle; to confine the hands with handcuffs.

HAND'ЄR'AFT, *n.* Work performed by the hands; usually written *handicraft.*

HAND'ED, *pp.* Given or transmitted by the hands; conducted; furled.

HAND'ED, *a.* With hands joined. *Milton.*

2. In composition, as *right-handed*, most dextrous or strong with the right hand; having the right hand most able and ready.

Left-handed, having the left hand most strong and convenient for principal use.

HAND'ER, *n.* One who hands or transmits; a conveyer in succession. *Dryden.*

HAND'F'AST, *n.* Hold; custody; power of confining or keeping. *Obs.* *Shak.*

HAND'F'AST, *a.* Fast by contract; firm. *Obs.*

HAND'F'AST, *v. t.* [Sax. *handfæstan.*] To pledge; to betroth; to bind; to join solemnly by the hand. *Obs.* *B. Jonson.* *Sancroft.*

HAND'F'ASTING, *n.* A kind of betrothing, or marriage contract. *Obs.*

HAND'-FETTER, *n.* A fetter for the hand; a manacle. *Sherwood.*

HAND'FUL, *n.* As much as the hand will grasp or contain. *Addison.*

2. As much as the arms will embrace.

3. A palm; four inches. *Obs.* *Bacon.*

4. A small quantity or number. A *handful* of men. *Clarendon.*

5. As much as can be done; full employment. *Raleigh.*

In America, the phrase is, he has his *hands full.*

HAND'GALLOP, *n.* A slow and easy gallop, in which the hand presses the bridle to hinder increase of speed. *Johnson.*

HAND'GL'ASS, *n.* In *gardening*, a glass used for placing over, protecting and forwarding various plants, in winter. *Cyc.*

HAND-GRENA'DE, *n.* A grenade to be thrown by the hand.

HAND'GUN, *n.* A gun to be used by the hand. *Camden.*

HAND'IЄR'AFT, *n.* [Sax. *handcræft.*] Manual occupation; work performed by the hand. *Addison.*

2. A man who obtains his living by manual labor; one skilled in some mechanical art. *Dryden.*

HAND'IЄR'AFTSMAN, *n.* A man skilled or employed in manual occupation; a manufacturer. *Swift.*

HAND'ILY, *adv.* [See *Handy.*] With dexterity or skill; dextrously; adroitly.

2. With ease or convenience.

HAND'INESS, *n.* The ease of performance derived from practice; dexterity; adroitness. *Chesterfield.*

HAND'IWŎRK, *n.* [for *hand-work.*] Work of the hands; product of manual labor; manufacture. *Hooker.*

2. Work performed by power and wisdom. Ps. xix.

HAND'KERCHIEF, *n.* [*hand* and *kerchief.* See *Kerchief.*]

1. A piece of cloth, usually silk or linen, carried about the person for the purpose of cleaning the face or hands, as occasion requires.

2. A piece of cloth to be worn about the neck, and sometimes called a *neckerchief.*

HAND'LANGUAĠE, *n.* The art of conversing by the hands. [*Not in use.*]

HAND'LE, *v. t.* [G. *handeln*, D. *handelen*, Sw. *handla*, Dan. *handler*, to treat, to trade, to negotiate. But in English it has not the latter signification. The word is formed from *hand*, as *manage* from L. *manus.*]

1. To touch; to feel with the hand; to use or hold with the hand.

The bodies we daily *handle*—hinder the approach of the part of our hands that press them. *Locke.*

2. To manage; to use; to wield.
That fellow *handles* a bow like a crow-keeper. *Shak.*
3. To make familiar by frequent touching.
The breeders in Flanders—*handle* their colts six months every year. *Temple.*
4. To treat; to discourse on; to discuss; to use or manage in writing or speaking. The author *handled* the subject with address. The speaker *handled* the arguments to the best advantage.
5. To use; to deal with; to practice.
They that *handle* the law knew me not. Jer. ii.
6. To treat; to use well or ill.
How wert thou *handled?* *Shak.*
7. To manage; to practice on; to transact with.
You shall see how I will *handle* her. *Shak.*

HAND'LE, *n.* [Sax. Qu. L. *ansa*, Norm. *hanser.*]
1. That part of a vessel or instrument which is held in the hand when used, as the haft of a sword, the bail of a kettle, &c.
2. That of which use is made; the instrument of effecting a purpose. *South.*

HAND'LEAD, *n.* A lead for sounding.

HAND'LED, *pp.* Touched; treated; managed.

HAND'LESS, *a.* Without a hand. *Shak.*

HAND'LING, *ppr.* Touching; feeling; treating; managing.

HAND'MAID, HAND'MAIDEN, } *n.* A maid that waits at hand; a female servant or attendant. *Scripture.*

HAND'MILL, *n.* A mill moved by the hand. *Dryden.*

HAND'SAILS, *n.* Sails managed by the hand. *Temple.*

HAND'SAW, *n.* A saw to be used with the hand. *Mortimer.*

HAND'SCREW, *n.* An engine for raising heavy timbers or weights; a jack.

HAND'SEL, *n.* [Dan. *handsel;* Sax. *handselen*, from *handsyllan*, to deliver into the hand. See *Sale* and *Sell.*]
1. The first act of using any thing; the first sale. *Elyot.*
2. An earnest; money for the first sale. [*Little used.*] *Hooker.*

HAND'SEL, *v. t.* To use or do any thing the first time. *Dryden.*

HAND'SŎME, *a.* [D. *handzaam*, soft, limber, tractable; *hand* and *zaam*, together. *Zaam*, or *saam*, we see in *assemble.* The sense of docility is taken from *hand*, as in G. *behandeln*, D. *behandelen*, to handle, to manage. The Dutch sense of soft, limber, is probably from the sense of easily managed or handled.]
1. Properly, dextrous; ready; convenient.
For a thief it is so *handsome*, as it may seem it was first invented for him. *Spenser.*
This sense is either from the original meaning of hand, or from the use of the hand, or rather of the right hand. In this sense the word is still used. We say of a well fought combat and victory, it is a *handsome* affair, an affair well performed, done with dexterity or skill. [See *Handy.*]
2. Moderately beautiful, as the person or other thing; well made; having symmetry of parts; well formed. It expresses less than beautiful or elegant; as a *handsome* woman or man; she has a *handsome* person or face. So we say, a *handsome* house; a *handsome* type.
3. Graceful in manner; marked with propriety and ease; as a *handsome* address.
4. Ample; large; as a *handsome* fortune.
5. Neat; correct; moderately elegant; as a *handsome* style or composition.
6. Liberal; generous; as a *handsome* present.

The applications of this word in popular language are various and somewhat indefinite. In general, when applied to things, it imports that the form is agreeable to the eye, or to just taste; and when applied to manner, it conveys the idea of suitableness or propriety with grace.

HAND'SŎME, as a verb, to render neat or beautiful, is not an authorized word. *Donne.*

HAND'SŎMELY, *adv.* Dextrously; cleverly; with skill. *Spenser.*
2. Gracefully; with propriety and ease.
3. Neatly; with due symmetry or proportions; as, a thing is *handsomely* made or finished.
4. With a degree of beauty; as a room *handsomely* furnished or ornamented.
5. Amply; generously; liberally. She is *handsomely* endowed.

HAND'SŎMENESS, *n.* A moderate degree of beauty or elegance; as the *handsomeness* of the person or of an edifice.
2. Grace; gracefulness; ease and propriety in manner.

HAND'SPIKE, *n.* A wooden bar, used with the hand as a lever, for various purposes, as in raising weights, heaving about a windlass, &c.

HAND'STAFF, *n.* A javelin; plu. *handstaves.* Ezek. xxxix.

HAND'VISE, *n.* A vise used by hand, or for small work. *Moxon.*

HAND'WEAPON, *n.* Any weapon to be wielded by the hand. Numb. xxxv.

HAND'WRITING, *n.* The cast or form of writing peculiar to each hand or person. *Shak.*
2. Any writing.

HAND'Y, *a.* [D. *handig*, *behendig*; Dan. *hændig;* from *hand.*]
1. Performed by the hand.
They came to *handy* blows. *Obs.* *Knolles.*
2. Dextrous; ready; adroit; skilled to use the hands with ease in performance; *applied to persons.* He is *handy* with the saw or the plane. Each is *handy* in his way. *Dryden.*
3. Ingenious; performing with skill and readiness.
4. Ready to the hand; near. My books are very *handy.*
5. Convenient; suited to the use of the hand.
6. Near; that may be used without difficulty or going to a distance. We have a spring or pasture that is *handy.*

HAND'YBLŌW, *n.* A blow with the hand; an act of hostility. *Harmar.*

HAND'Y-DANDY, *n.* A play in which children change hands and places. *Shak.*

HAND'YGRIPE, *n.* Seizure by the hand. *Hudibras.*

HAND'YSTROKE, *n.* A blow inflicted by the hand. *Beaum.*

HANG, *v. t.* pret. and pp. *hanged* or *hung.* [Sax. *hangan;* Sw. *hånga;* Dan. *hænger;* G. D. *hangen;* W. *hongian*, to hang; *hong*, a hanging or dangling; *honc*, a shake, a wagging; *honcaw*, to shake, wag, stagger, to waver. The latter seems to be the primary sense.]
1. To suspend; to fasten to some fixed object above, in such a manner as to swing or move; as, to *hang* a thief. Pharaoh *hanged* the chief baker. Hence,
2. To put to death by suspending by the neck.
Many men would rebel, rather than be ruined; but they would rather not rebel than be *hanged.* *Ames.*
3. To place without any solid support or foundation.
He *hangeth* the earth upon nothing. Job xxxvi.
4. To fix in such a manner as to be movable; as, to *hang* a door or grate on hooks or by butts.
5. To cover or furnish by any thing suspended or fastened to the walls; as, to *hang* an apartment with curtains or with pictures.
Hung be the heavens with black— *Shak.*
And *hung* thy holy roofs with savage spoils. *Dryden.*

To hang out, to suspend in open view; to display; to exhibit to notice; as, to *hang out* false colors.
2. To hang abroad; to suspend in the open air.

To hang over, to project or cause to project above.

To hang down, to let fall below the proper situation; to bend down; to decline; as, to *hang down* the head, and elliptically, to *hang the head.*

To hang up, to suspend; to place on something fixed on high.
2. To suspend; to keep or suffer to remain undecided; as, to *hang up* a question in debate.

HANG, *v. i.* To be suspended; to be sustained by something above, so as to swing or be movable below.
2. To dangle; to be loose and flowing below.
3. To bend forward or downward; to lean or incline. *Addison.*
His neck obliquely o'er his shoulder *hung.* *Pope.*
4. To float; to play.
And fall those sayings from that gentle tongue,
Where civil speech and soft persuasion *hung.* *Prior.*
5. To be supported by something raised above the ground; as a *hanging* garden on the top of a house. *Addison.*
6. To depend; to rest on something for support. This question *hangs* on a single point.
7. To rest on by embracing; to cling to; as, to *hang* on the neck of a person.
Two infants *hanging* on her neck. *Peacham.*
8. To hover; to impend; with *over.* View the dangers that *hang over* the country.
9. To be delayed; to linger.
A noble stroke he lifted high,
Which *hung* not. *Milton.*
10. To incline; to have a steep declivity; as *hanging* grounds. *Mortimer.*

11. To be executed by the halter.

Sir Balaam *hangs*. *Pope.*

To hang fire, in *the military art*, is to be slow in communicating, as fire in the pan of a gun to the charge.

To hang on, to adhere to, often as something troublesome and unwelcome.

A cheerful temper dissipates the apprehensions which *hang on* the timorous. *Addison.*

2. To adhere obstinately; to be importunate.

3. To rest; to reside; to continue.

4. To be dependent on.

How wretched
Is that poor man that *hangs on* princes' favors! *Shak.*

5. In *seamen's language*, to hold fast without belaying; to pull forcibly.

To hang in doubt, to be in suspense, or in a state of uncertainty.

Thy life shall *hang in doubt* before thee. Deut. xxviii.

To hang together, to be closely united; to cling.

In the common cause we are all of a piece; we *hang together*. *Dryden.*

2. To be just united, so as barely to hold together. *Shak.*

To hang on or *upon*, to drag; to be incommodiously joined.

Life *hangs upon* me and becomes a burden. *Addison.*

To hang to, to adhere closely; to cling.

HANG, *n.* A sharp declivity. [*Colloquial.*]

HANG'BY, *n.* A dependent, in contempt. *Ray.*

HANG'ED, *pp.* Suspended; put to death by being suspended by the neck.

HANG'ER, *n.* That by which a thing is suspended.

2. A short broad sword, incurvated towards the point. *Smollett.*

3. One that hangs, or causes to be hanged. *Aubrey.*

HANG'ER-ON, *n.* One who besets another importunately in soliciting favors.

2. A dependant; one who eats and drinks without payment. *Swift.*

HANG'ING, *ppr.* Suspending to something above.

2. Being suspended; dangling; swinging.

3. *a.* Foreboding death by the halter.

What a *hanging* face! *Dryden.*

4. Requiring punishment by the halter; as a *hanging* matter. *Johnson.*

HANG'ING, *n.* Any kind of drapery hung or fastened to the walls of a room, by way of ornament.

No purple *hangings* clothe the palace walls. *Dryden.*

2. Death by the halter; as hard words or *hanging*. *Pope.*

3. Display; exhibition. *Addison.*

HANG'ING-SLEEVES, *n.* Strips of the same stuff with the gown, hanging down the back from the shoulders. *Obs.* *Halifax.*

HANG'ING-SIDE, *n.* In *mining*, the overhanging side of an inclined or hading vein. *Cyc.*

HANG'MAN, *n.* One who hangs another; a public executioner; also, a term of reproach.

HANG'NEST, *n.* The name of certain species of birds, which build nests suspended from the branches of trees, such as the Baltimore oriole or red-bird; also, the nest so suspended.

HANK, *n.* [Dan. *hank*, a handle, a hook, a tack, a clasp; Sw. *hank*, a band.]

1. A skain of thread; as much thread as is tied together; a tie.

2. In *ships*, a wooden ring fixed to a stay, to confine the stay-sails; used in the place of a grommet. *Mar. Dict.*

3. A rope or withy for fastening a gate. [*Local.*]

HANK, *v. t.* To form into hanks.

HANK'ER, *v. i.* [D. *hunkeren*. The corresponding word in Danish is *higer*, and probably *n* is casual.]

1. To long for with a keen appetite and uneasiness; *in a literal sense;* as, to *hanker for* fruit, or *after* fruit.

2. To have a vehement desire of something, accompanied with uneasiness; as, to *hanker after* the diversions of the town. *Addison.*

It is usually followed by *after*. *It is a familiar, but not a low word.*

HANK'ERING, *ppr.* Longing for with keen appetite or ardent desire.

HANK'ERING, *n.* A keen appetite that causes uneasiness till it is gratified; vehement desire to possess or enjoy.

HANK'LE, *v. t.* [See *Hank.*] To twist. [*Not in use.*]

HA'NT, a contraction of *have not*, or *has not;* as, I *ha'nt*, he *ha'nt*, we *ha'nt*.

Hanse Towns. Hanse signifies a society; Goth. *hansa*, a multitude. The *Hanse towns* in Germany were certain commercial cities which associated for the protection of commerce as early as the twelfth century. To this confederacy acceded certain commercial cities in Holland, England, France, Spain and Italy, until they amounted to seventy two, and for centuries, this confederacy commanded the respect and defied the power of kings. This confederacy at present consists of the cities of Lubeck, Hamburg and Bremen.

HANSEAT'IC, *a.* Pertaining to the Hanse towns, or to their confederacy.

HAP, *n.* [W. *hap*, or *hab*, luck, chance, fortune, that is, that which falls, or a coming suddenly. This seems to be allied to Fr. *happer*, to snap or catch; D. *happen;* Norm. *happer*, to seize; W. *hafiaw*, to snatch. In Sp. *haber* signifies to *have*, to *happen* or befall, to take. These verbs seem to unite in one radix, and all coincide with L. *capio*. The primary sense is to fall or to rush, hence, to rush on and seize.]

1. That which comes suddenly or unexpectedly; chance; fortune; accident; casual event. [See *Chance* and *Casual.*]

Whether art it was or heedless *hap*. *Spenser.*

Curs'd be good *haps*, and curs'd be they that build
Their hopes on *haps*. *Sidney.*

2. Misfortune. [But this word is obsolete or obsolescent, except in compounds and derivatives.]

HAP, *v. i.* To happen; to befall; to come by chance. *Obs.* *Spenser. Bacon.*

HAP-HAZ'ARD, *n.* [This is tautological. See *Hazard.*] Chance; accident.

We take our principles at *hap-hazard* on trust. *Locke.*

HAP'LESS, *a.* Luckless; unfortunate; unlucky; unhappy; as *hapless* youth; *hapless* maid. *Dryden.*

HAP'LY, *adv.* By chance; perhaps; it may be.

Lest *haply* ye be found to fight against God. Acts v.

2. By accident; casually. *Milton.*

HAP'PEN, *v. i.* *hap'n*. [W. *hapiaw*, to happen, to have luck. See *Hap.* Sw. *håpna*, to be surprized or amazed.]

1. To come by chance; to come without one's previous expectation; to fall out.

There shall no evil *happen* to the just. Prov. xii.

2. To come; to befall.

They talked together of all those things which had *happened*. Luke xxiv.

3. To light; to fall or come unexpectedly.

I have *happened* on some other accounts relating to mortalities. *Graunt.*

HAP'PILY, *adv.* [See *Happy.*] By good fortune; fortunately; luckily; with success.

Preferr'd by conquest, *happily* o'erthrown. *Waller.*

2. In a happy state; in a state of felicity. He lived *happily* with his consort.

3. With address or dexterity; gracefully; in a manner to ensure success.

Formed by thy converse, *happily* to steer
From grave to gay, from lively to severe. *Pope.*

4. By chance. [See *Haply.*]

HAP'PINESS, *n.* [from *happy.*] The agreeable sensations which spring from the enjoyment of good; that state of a being in which his desires are gratified, by the enjoyment of pleasure without pain; felicity; but *happiness* usually expresses less than *felicity*, and *felicity* less than *bliss*. *Happiness* is comparative. To a person distressed with pain, relief from that pain affords *happiness;* in other cases we give the name *happiness* to positive pleasure or an excitement of agreeable sensations. *Happiness* therefore admits of indefinite degrees of increase in enjoyment, or gratification of desires. Perfect *happiness*, or pleasure unalloyed with pain, is not attainable in this life.

2. Good luck; good fortune. *Johnson.*

3. Fortuitous elegance; unstudied grace.

For there's a *happiness* as well as care. *Pope.*

HAP'PY, *a.* [from *hap;* W. *hapus*, properly lucky, fortunate, receiving good from something that falls or comes to one unexpectedly, or by an event that is not within control. See *Hour.*]

1. Lucky; fortunate; successful.

Chimists have been more *happy* in finding experiments, than the causes of them. *Boyle.*

So we say, a *happy* thought; a *happy* expedient.

2. Being in the enjoyment of agreeable sensations from the possession of good; enjoying pleasure from the gratification of appetites or desires. The pleasurable sensations derived from the gratification of sensual appetites render a person temporarily *happy;* but he only can be esteemed really and permanently *happy*, who enjoys peace of mind in the favor of God. To

be in any degree *happy*, we must be free from pain both of body and of mind; to be very *happy*, we must be in the enjoyment of lively sensations of pleasure, either of body or mind.

Happy am I, for the daughters will call me blessed. Gen. xxx.

He found himself *happiest*, in communicating happiness to others. *Wirt.*

3. Prosperous; having secure possession of good.

Happy is that people whose God is Jehovah. Ps. cxliv.

4. That supplies pleasure; that furnishes enjoyment; agreeable; *applied to things*; as a *happy* condition.

5. Dextrous; ready; able.

One gentleman is *happy* at a reply, another excels in a rejoinder. *Swift.*

6. Blessed; enjoying the presence and favor of God, in a future life.

7. Harmonious; living in concord; enjoying the pleasures of friendship; as a *happy* family.

8. Propitious; favorable. *Shak.*

HARANGUE, *n.* *harang'*. *har'ang*. [Fr. *harangue*; Sp. Port. *arenga*; It. *aringa*; Arm. *harencg*; from the root of *ring*, to to sound, Sax. *hringan*.]

1. A speech addressed to an assembly or an army; a popular oration; a public address. This word seems to imply loudness or declamation, and is therefore appropriated generally to an address made to a popular assembly or to an army, and not to a sermon, or to an argument at the bar of a court, or to a speech in a deliberative council, unless in contempt.

2. Declamation; a noisy, pompous or irregular address.

HARANGUE, *v. i.* *harang'*. To make an address or speech to a large assembly; to make a noisy speech.

HARANGUE, *v. t.* *harang'*. To address by oration; as, the general *harangued* the troops.

HARANG'UER, *n.* *harang'er*. An orator; one who addresses an assembly or army; a noisy declaimer.

HARANG'UING, *ppr.* Declaiming; addressing with noisy eloquence.

HAR'ASS, *v. t.* [Fr. *harasser*. Qu. Ir. *creasam*.]

1. To weary; to fatigue to excess; to tire with bodily labor; as, to *harass* an army by a long march. *Bacon.*

2. To weary with importunity, care, or perplexity; to tease; to perplex.

Nature oppress'd and *harass'd* out with care. *Addison.*

3. To waste or desolate. *Obs.* *Hammond.*

HAR'ASS, *n.* Waste; disturbance; devastation. [*Little used.*] *Milton.*

HAR'ASSED, *pp.* Wearied; tired; teased.

HAR'ASSER, *n.* One who harasses or teases; a spoiler.

HAR'ASSING, *ppr.* Tiring; fatiguing; teasing.

H'ARBINGER, *n.* [See *Harbor*. *Harbinger* is properly a person who goes to provide *harbor* or lodgings for those that follow.]

1. In England, an officer of the king's household who rides a day's journey before the court when traveling, to provide lodgings and other accommodations. *Encyc.*

2. A forerunner; a precursor; that which precedes and gives notice of the expected arrival of something else.

H'ARBOR, *n.* [Sax. *here-berga*, the station of an army; D. *herberg*, an inn; Dan. Sw. G. *herberge*; Fr. *auberge*; Sp. Port. *albergue*; It. *albergo*. The first syllable, in the Teutonic dialects, signifies an army, or a troop, a crowd; the last syllable is *berg*, *burg*, a town, or castle, or from *bergen*, to save. But in the Celtic dialects, the first syllable, *al*, is probably different from that of the other dialects.]

1. A lodging; a place of entertainment and rest.

For *harbor* at a thousand doors they knocked. *Dryden.*

2. A port or haven for ships; a bay or inlet of the sea, in which ships can moor, and be sheltered from the fury of winds and a heavy sea; any navigable water where ships can ride in safety.

3. An asylum; a shelter; a place of safety from storms or danger.

H'ARBOR, *v. t.* To shelter; to secure; to secrete; as, to *harbor* a thief.

2. To entertain; to permit to lodge, rest or reside; as, to *harbor* malice or revenge. *Harbor* not a thought of revenge.

H'ARBOR, *v. i.* To lodge or abide for a time; to receive entertainment.

This night let's *harbor* here in York. *Shak.*

2. To take shelter.

H'ARBORAGE, *n.* Shelter; entertainment. [*Not used.*] *Shak.*

H'ARBORED, *pp.* Entertained; sheltered.

H'ARBORER, *n.* One who entertains or shelters another.

H'ARBORING, *ppr.* Entertaining; sheltering.

H'ARBORLESS, *a.* Without a harbor; destitute of shelter or a lodging.

H'ARBOR-M'ASTER, *n.* An officer who has charge of the mooring of ships, and executes the regulations respecting harbors. *New York.*

HAR'BOROUGH, *n.* A harbor or lodging. [*Not in use.*]

HAR'BOROUS, *a.* Hospitable. [*Not in use.*]

H'ARD, *a.* [Sax. *heard*; Goth. *hardu*; D. *hard*; G. *hart*; Dan. *haard*; Sw. *hård*. The primary sense is, pressed.]

1. Firm; solid; compact; not easily penetrated, or separated into parts; not yielding to pressure; applied to material bodies, and opposed to *soft*; as *hard* wood; *hard* flesh; a *hard* apple.

2. Difficult; not easy to the intellect.

In which are some things *hard* to be understood. 2 Pet. iii.

The *hard* causes they brought to Moses. Ex. xviii.

3. Difficult of accomplishment; not easy to be done or executed. A *hard* task; a disease *hard* to cure.

Is any thing too *hard* for the Lord? Gen. xviii.

4. Full of difficulties or obstacles; not easy to be traveled; as a *hard* way. *Milton.*

5. Painful; difficult; distressing.

Rachel travailed, and she had *hard* labor. Gen. xxxv.

6. Laborious; fatiguing; attended with difficulty or pain, or both; as *hard* work or labor; *hard* duty; *hard* service.

7. Oppressive; rigorous; severe; cruel; as *hard* bondage; a *hard* master. Ex. i. Is. xiv.

8. Unfeeling; insensible; not easily moved by pity; not susceptible of kindness, mercy or other tender affections; as a *hard* heart.

9. Severe; harsh; rough; abusive.

Have you given him any *hard* words of late? *Shak.*

10. Unfavorable; unkind; implying blame of another; as *hard* thoughts.

11. Severe; rigorous; oppressive. The enemy was compelled to submit to *hard* terms. So we say, a *hard* bargain; *hard* conditions.

12. Unreasonable; unjust. It is *hard* to punish a man for speculative opinions. It is a *hard* case.

13. Severe; pinching with cold; rigorous; tempestuous; as a *hard* winter; *hard* weather.

14. Powerful; forcible; urging; pressing close on.

The stag was too *hard* for the horse. *L'Estrange.*

The disputant was too *hard* for his antagonist. *Anon.*

15. Austere; rough; acid; sour; as liquors. The cider is *hard*.

16. Harsh; stiff; forced; constrained; unnatural.

Others—make the figures *harder* than the marble itself. *Dryden.*

His diction is *hard*, his figures too bold. *Dryden.*

17. Not plentiful; not prosperous; pressing; distressing; as *hard* times, when markets are bad, and money of course scarce.

18. Avaricious; difficult in making bargains; close. Matt. xxv.

19. Rough; of coarse features; as a *hard* face or countenance.

20. Austere; severe; rigorous.

21. Rude; unpolished or unintelligible.

A people of *hard* language. Ezek. iii.

22. Coarse; unpalatable or scanty; as *hard* fare.

H'ARD, *adv.* Close; near; as in the phrase, *hard by*. In this phrase, the word retains its original sense of pressed, or pressing. So in It. *presso*, Fr. *pres*, from L. *pressus*.

2. With pressure; with urgency; hence, diligently; laboriously; earnestly; vehemently; importunately; as, to work *hard* for a living.

And pray'd so *hard* for mercy from the prince. *Dryden.*

3. With difficulty; as, the vehicle moves *hard*.

4. Uneasily; vexatiously. *Shak.*

5. Closely; so as to raise difficulties.

The question is *hard* set. *Brown.*

6. Fast; nimbly; rapidly; vehemently; as, to run *hard*, that is, with pressure or urgency.

7. Violently; with great force; tempestuously; as, the wind blows *hard*, or it blows *hard*.

8. With violence; with a copious descent of water; as, it rains *hard*.

9. With force; as, to press *hard*.

Hard-a-lee, in seamen's language, an order to put the helm close to the lee side of the ship, to tack or keep her head to the wind; also, that situation of the helm. *Mar. Dict.*

Hard-a-weather, an order to put the helm close to the weather or windward side of the ship; also, that position of the helm.
Hard-a-port, an order to put the helm close to the larboard side of a ship.
Hard-a-starboard, an order to put the helm close to the starboard side of a ship. *Mar. Dict.*
HARD-BESET'TING, *a.* Closely besetting or beseiging. *Milton.*
H'ARDBOUND, *a.* Costive; fast or tight; as *hardbound* brains. *Pope.*
H'ARDEARNED, *a.* Earned with toil and difficulty. *Burke.*
H'ARDEN, *v. t.* h'ardn. To make hard or more hard; to make firm or compact; to indurate; as, to *harden* iron or steel; to *harden* clay.
2. To confirm in effrontery; to make impudent; as, to *harden* the face.
3. To make obstinate, unyielding or refractory; as, to *harden* the neck. Jer. xix.
4. To confirm in wickedness, opposition or enmity; to make obdurate.

Why then do ye *harden* your hearts, as Pharaoh and the Egyptians *hardened* their hearts? 1 Sam. vi.

So God is said to *harden* the heart, when he withdraws the influences of his spirit from men, and leaves them to pursue their own corrupt inclinations.
5. To make insensible or unfeeling; as, to *harden* one against impressions of pity or tenderness.
6. To make firm; to endure with constancy.

I would *harden* myself in sorrow. Job vi.

7. To inure; to render firm or less liable to injury, by exposure or use; as, to *harden* to a climate or to labor.
H'ARDEN, *v. i.* h'ardn. To become hard or more hard; to acquire solidity or more compactness. Mortar *hardens* by drying.
2. To become unfeeling.
3. To become inured.
4. To indurate, as flesh.
H'ARDENED, *pp.* Made hard, or more hard or compact; made unfeeling; made obstinate; confirmed in error or vice.
H'ARDENER, *n.* He or that which makes hard, or more firm and compact.
H'ARDENING, *ppr.* Making hard or more compact; making obdurate or unfeeling; confirming; becoming more hard.
H'ARDENING, *n.* The giving a greater degree of hardness to bodies than they had before. *Encyc.*
HARDFA'VORED, *a.* Having coarse features; harsh of countenance. *Dryden.*
HARDFA'VOREDNESS, *n.* Coarseness of features.
H'ARDFEATURED, *a.* Having coarse features. *Smollett.*
H'ARDFISTED, *a.* Close fisted; covetous. *Hall.*
H'ARDFOUGHT, *a.* Vigorously contested; as a *hard-fought* battle.
H'ARDGOTTEN, *a.* Obtained with difficulty.
H'ARDHANDED, *a.* Having hard hands, as a laborer. *Shak.*
H'ARDHEAD, *n.* Clash or collision of heads in contest. *Dryden.*
HARDHE'ARTED, *a.* Cruel; pitiless; merciless; unfeeling; inhuman; inexorable. *Shak. Dryden.*
HARDHE'ARTEDNESS, *n.* Want of feeling or tenderness; cruelty; inhumanity. *South.*
H'ARDIHOOD, *n.* [See *Hardy* and *Hood.*] Boldness, united with firmness and constancy of mind; dauntless bravery; intrepidity. *Milton.*

It is the society of numbers which gives *hardihood* to iniquity. *Buckminster.*

Hardihead and *hardiment*, in the sense of *hardihood*, are obsolete. *Spenser. Fairfax.*
H'ARDILY, *adv.* With great boldness; stoutly. *Scott.*
2. With hardship; not tenderly. *Goldsmith.*
H'ARDINESS, *n.* [Fr. *hardiesse.* See *Hardy.*]
1. Boldness; firm courage; intrepidity; stoutness; bravery; applied to the mind, it is synonymous with *hardihood.*
2. Firmness of body derived from laborious exercises.
3. Hardship; fatigue. *Obs.* *Spenser.*
4. Excess of confidence; assurance; effrontery.
HARD-LA'BORED, *a.* Wrought with severe labor; elaborate; studied; as a *hard-labored* poem. *Swift.*
H'ARDLY, *adv.* [See *Hard.*] With difficulty; with great labor.

Recovering *hardly* what he lost before. *Dryden.*

2. Scarcely; barely; almost not.

Hardly shall you find any one so bad, but he desires the credit of being thought good. *South.*

3. Not quite or wholly. The object is so distant we can *hardly* see it. The veal is *hardly* done. The writing is *hardly* completed.
4. Grudgingly, as an injury. *Shak.*
5. Severely; unfavorably; as, to think *hardly* of public measures.
6. Rigorously; oppressively. The prisoners were *hardly* used or treated. *Addison. Swift.*
7. Unwelcomely; harshly.

Such information comes very *hardly* and harshly to a grown man. *Locke.*

8. Coarsely; roughly; not softly.

Heaven was her canopy, bare earth her bed;
So *hardly* lodged. *Dryden.*

H'ARD-MOUTHED, *a.* Not sensible to the bit; not easily governed; as a *hard-mouthed* horse. *Dryden.*
H'ARDNESS, *n.* [See *Hard.*] Firmness; close union of the component parts; compactness; solidity; the quality of bodies which resists impression; opposed to *softness* and *fluidity.*
2. Difficulty to be understood. *Shak.*
3. Difficulty to be executed or accomplished; as the *hardness* of an enterprise. *Sidney.*
4. Scarcity; penury; difficulty of obtaining money; as the *hardness* of the times. *Swift.*
5. Obduracy; impenitence; confirmed state of wickedness; as *hardness* of heart.
6. Coarseness of features; harshness of look; as *hardness* of favor. *Ray.*
7. Severity of cold; rigor; as the *hardness* of winter.
8. Cruelty of temper; savageness; harshness.

The blame
May hang upon your *hardness.* *Shak.*

9. Stiffness; harshness; roughness; as the *hardnesses* of sculpture. *Dryden.*
10. Closeness; niggardliness; stinginess. *Johnson.*
11. Hardship; severe labor, trials or sufferings.

Endure *hardness*, as a good soldier of Jesus Christ. 2 Tim. ii.

H'ARDNIBBED, *a.* Having a hard nib or point.
H'ARDOCK, *n.* Probably *hoardock*, dock with whitish leaves. *Shak.*
H'ARDS, *n.* The refuse or coarse part of flax; tow.
H'ARDSHIP, *n.* Toil; fatigue; severe labor or want; whatever oppresses the body.
2. Injury; oppression; injustice. *Swift.*
H'ARDVISAGED, *a.* Having coarse features; of a harsh countenance. *Burke.*
H'ARDWARE, *n.* Wares made of iron or other metal, as pots, kettles, saws, knives, &c.
H'ARDWAREMAN, *n.* A maker or seller of hardwares. *Swift.*
H'ARDY, *a.* [Fr. *hardi*; Norm. *hardy*; Arm. *hardiz*, *hardih*; It. *ardire*, to dare, and boldness, assurance. The sense is shooting or advancing forward.]
1. Bold; brave; stout; daring; resolute; intrepid. Who is *hardy* enough to encounter contempt?
2. Strong; firm; compact.

An unwholesome blast may shake in pieces his *hardy* fabric. *South.*

3. Confident; full of assurance; impudent; stubborn to excess.
4. Inured to fatigue; rendered firm by exercise, as a veteran soldier.
HAR, HARE, HERE, in composition, signify an army, Sax. *here*, G. *heer*, D. *heir.* So *Harold* is a general of an army; *Herwin*, a victorious army. So in Greek, Stratocles, from *ϛρατος*, and Polemarchus, from *πολεμος.*
HARE, *n.* [Sax. *hara*; Dan. Sw. *hare.*] A quadruped of the genus Lepus, with long ears, a short tail, soft hair, and a divided upper lip. It is a timid animal, often hunted for sport or for its flesh, which is excellent food. It moves by leaps, and is remarkable for its fecundity.
2. A constellation. *Creech.*
HARE, *v. t.* [Norm. *harer*, *harier*, to stir up or provoke.]
To fright, or to excite, tease and harass, or worry. [*Not used.* See *Harry.*] *Locke.*
HA'REBELL, *n.* A plant of the genus Hyacinthus, with campaniform or bell-shaped flowers. *Fam. of Plants.*
HA'REBRAINED, *a.* [*hare* and *brain.*] Wild; giddy; volatile; heedless. *Bacon.*
HA'REFOOT, *n.* A bird; a plant. *Ainsworth.*
HA'REHE'ARTED, *a.* Timorous; easily frightened. *Ainsworth.*
HA'REHOUND, *n.* A hound for hunting hares. *Todd.*
HA'REHUNTER, *n.* One who hunts or is used to hunting hares. *Pope.*
HA'REHUNTING, *n.* The hunting of hares. *Somerville.*
HA'RELIP, *n.* A divided upper lip, like that of a hare. *Wiseman.*

HA'RELIPPED, *a.* Having a harelip.

HA'REMINT, *n.* A plant. *Ainsworth.*

HA'REPIPE, *n.* A snare for catching hares. *Stat. James I.*

HA'RE'S-EAR, *n.* A plant of the genus Bupleurum. The *Bastard Hare's Ear* is of the genus Phyllis.

HARE'S-LETTUCE, *n.* A plant of the genus Sonchus.

HA'REWORT, *n.* A plant.

HAR'EM, *n.* [Ar. حرم harama, to prohibit, drive off, or deny access.]

A seraglio; a place where Eastern princes confine their women, who are prohibited from the society of others.

HAREN'GIFORM, *a.* [See *Herring.*] Shaped like a herring. *Dict. Nat. Hist.*

HAR'ICOT, *n.* [Fr. from Gr. αραχος.] A kind of ragout of meat and roots. *Chesterfield.*

2. In *French*, beans.

HAR'IER, } *n.* [from *hare.*] A dog for HAR'RIER, } hunting hares; a kind of hound with an acute sense of smelling. *Encyc.*

HARIOLA'TION, *n.* [L. *hariolatio.*] Soothsaying. [*Not in use.*]

H'ARK, *v. i.* [contracted from *hearken*, which see.] To listen; to lend the ear. *Shak. Hudibras.*

This word is rarely or never used, except in the imperative mode, *hark*, that is, listen, hear.

H'ARL, } *n.* The skin of flax; the filaments HERL, } of flax or hemp.

2. A filamentous substance. *Mortimer.*

[In New England, I have heard this word pronounced *herl.*]

H'ARLEQUIN, *n.* [Fr. *harlequin*, a buffoon; It. *arlecchino;* Sp. *arlequin;* Arm. *harliqin, furluqin*, a juggler. I know not the origin of this word. It has been suggested that the last component part of the word is from the Gothic, Sw. *leka*, to play, and a story is told about a comedian who frequented the house of M. de Harley, but I place no reliance on these suggestions.]

A buffoon, dressed in party-colored clothes, who plays tricks, like a merry-andrew, to divert the populace. This character was first introduced into Italian comedy, but is now a standing character in English pantomime entertainments. *Encyc.*

H'ARLEQUIN, *v. i.* To play the droll; to make sport by playing ludicrous tricks.

H'ARLOCK, *n.* A plant. *Drayton.*

H'ARLOT, *n.* [W. *herlawd*, a stripling; *herlodes*, a hoiden; a word composed of *her*, a push, or challenge, and *llawd*, a *lad.* This word was formerly applied to males as well as females.

> A sturdie *harlot*—that was her hostes man. *Chaucer, Tales.*
>
> He was a gentil *harlot* and a kind. *Ibm.*

The word originally signified a bold stripling, or a hoiden. But the W. *llawd* signifies not only a *lad*, that is, a shoot, or growing youth, but as an adjective, tending forward, craving, *lewd.* See *Lewd.*]

1. A woman who prostitutes her body for hire; a prostitute; a common woman. *Dryden.*

2. In *Scripture*, one who forsakes the true God and worships idols. Is. i.

3. A servant; a rogue; a cheat. *Obs.* *Chaucer. Fox.*

H'ARLOT, *a.* Wanton; lewd; low; base. *Shak.*

H'ARLOT, *v. i.* To practice lewdness. *Milton.*

H'ARLOTRY, *n.* The trade or practice of prostitution; habitual or customary lewdness. *Dryden.*

H'ARM, *n.* [Sax. *hearm* or *harm.* In G. the word signifies grief, sorrow.]

3. Injury; hurt; damage; detriment.

> Do thyself no *harm.* Acts xvi.
>
> He shall make amends for the *harm* he hath done in the holy thing. Lev. v.

2. Moral wrong; evil; mischief; wickedness; *a popular sense of the word.*

H'ARM, *v. t.* To hurt; to injure; to damage; to impair soundness of body, either animal or vegetable. *Waller. Ray.*

HARMAT'TAN, *n.* A dry easterly wind in Africa, which destroys vegetation. *Norris.*

H'ARMED, *pp.* Injured; hurt; damaged.

H'ARMEL, *n.* The wild African rue.

H'ARMFUL, *a.* Hurtful; injurious; noxious; detrimental; mischievous.

> The earth brought forth fruit and food for man, without any mixture of *harmful* quality. *Raleigh.*

H'ARMFULLY, *adv.* Hurtfully; injuriously; with damage. *Ascham.*

H'ARMFULNESS, *n.* Hurtfulness; noxiousness.

H'ARMING, *ppr.* Hurting; injuring.

H'ARMLESS, *a.* Not hurtful or injurious; innoxious. Ceremonies are *harmless* in themselves. *Hooker.*

2. Unhurt; undamaged; uninjured; as, to give bond to save another *harmless.*

3. Innocent; not guilty.

> Who is holy, *harmless*, undefiled, separate from sinners. Heb. vii.

H'ARMLESSLY, *adv.* Innocently; without fault or crime; as, to pass the time *harmlessly* in recreations.

2. Without hurt or damage.

> Bullets fall *harmlessly* into wood or fethers. *Decay of Piety.*

H'ARMLESSNESS, *n.* The quality of being innoxious; freedom from a tendency to injure.

2. Innocence.

HARMON'IC, } *a.* [See *Harmony.*] Re- HARMON'ICAL, } lating to harmony or music; as *harmonical* use. *Bacon.*

2. Concordant; musical; consonant; as *harmonic* sounds.

> *Harmonic* twang of leather, horn and brass. *Pope.*
>
> The basis of an *harmonic* system. *Encyc.*
>
> The *harmonic* elements are the three smallest concords. *Edin. Encyc.*

3. An epithet applied to the accessary sounds which accompany the predominant and apparently simple tone of any chord or string.

Harmonical mean, in arithmetic and algebra, a term used to express certain relations of numbers and quantities, which are supposed to bear an analogy to musical consonances.

Harmonical proportion, in arithmetic and algebra, is said to obtain between three quantities, or four quantities, in certain cases.

Harmonical series, a series of many numbers in continued harmonical proportion. *Cyc.*

HARMON'ICA, *n.* A collection of musical glasses of a particular form, so arranged as to produce exquisite music. *Encyc.*

HARMON'ICS, *n.* Harmonious sounds; consonances.

2. The doctrine or science of musical sounds. *Smith.*

3. Derivative sounds, generated with predominant sounds, and produced by subordinate vibrations of a chord or string, when its whole length vibrates. These shorter vibrations produce more acute sounds, and are called *acute harmonics.*

4. *Grave harmonics* are low sounds which accompany every perfect consonance of two sounds. *Edin. Encyc.*

HARMO'NIOUS, *a.* Adapted to each other; having the parts proportioned to each other; symmetrical.

> God hath made the intellectual world *harmonious* and beautiful without us. *Locke.*

2. Concordant; consonant; symphonious; musical. *Harmonious* sounds are such as accord, and are agreeable to the ear.

3. Agreeing; living in peace and friendship; as a *harmonious* family or society.

HARMO'NIOUSLY, *adv.* With just adaptation and proportion of parts to each other.

> Distances, motions, and quantities of matter *harmoniously* adjusted in this great variety of our system. *Bentley.*

2. With accordance of sounds; musically; in concord.

3. In agreement; in peace and friendship.

HARMO'NIOUSNESS, *n.* Proportion and adaptation of parts; musicalness.

2. Agreement; concord.

H'ARMONIST, *n.* A musician; a composer of music.

2. One who brings together corresponding passages, to show their agreement.

H'ARMONIZE, *v. i.* To be in concord; to agree in sounds.

2. To agree; to be in peace and friendship; as individuals or families.

3. To agree in sense or purport; as, the arguments *harmonize;* the facts stated by different witnesses *harmonize.*

H'ARMONIZE, *v. t.* To adjust in fit proportions; to cause to agree.

2. To make musical; to combine according to the laws of counterpoint.

H'ARMONIZED, *pp.* Made to be accordant.

H'ARMONIZER, *n.* One that brings together or reconciles.

2. In *music*, a practical harmonist.

H'ARMONIZING, *ppr.* Causing to agree.

HARMONOM'ETER, *n.* [Gr. αρμονια and μετρον.]

An instrument or monochord for measuring the harmonic relations of sounds.

H'ARMONY, *n.* [L. *harmonia;* Gr. αρμονια, a setting together, a closure or seam, agreement, concert, from αρω, to fit or adapt, to square; Sp. *armonia;* It. *id.;* Fr. *harmonie.* If the Greek αρω is a contracted word, for χαρω, which is probable, it may be the French *carrer, equarrir.*]

1. The just adaptation of parts to each other, in any system or composition of things, intended to form a connected whole; as the *harmony* of the universe.

Equality and correspondence are the causes of *harmony*. *Bacon.*

All discord, *harmony* not understood. *Pope.*

2. Just proportion of sound; consonance; musical concord; the accordance of two or more intervals or sounds, or that union of different sounds which pleases the ear; or a succession of such sounds, called chords.

Ten thousand harps that tuned
Angelic *harmonies*. *Milton.*

3. Concord; agreement; accordance in facts; as the *harmony* of the gospels.

4. Concord or agreement in views, sentiments or manners, interests, &c.; good correspondence; peace and friendship. The citizens live in *harmony*.

5. *Natural harmony*, in music, consists of the harmonic triad or common chord. *Artificial harmony*, is a mixture of concords and discords. *Figured harmony*, is when one or more of the parts move, during the continuance of a chord, through certain notes which do not form any of the constituent parts of that chord. *Busby.*

6. *Perfect harmony* implies the use of untempered concords only. *Tempered harmony* is when the notes are varied by temperament. [See *Temperament.*] *Encyc.*

H'ARMOST, *n.* [Gr. αρμοςηρ, from αρμοσσω, to regulate.]

In *ancient Greece*, a Spartan governor, regulator or prefect. *Mitford.*

H'ARMOTOME, *n.* [Gr. αρμος, a joint, and τεμνω, to cut.]

In *mineralogy*, cross-stone, or staurolite, called also pyramidical zeolite. [See *Cross-stone.*]

H'ARNESS, *n.* [W. *harnaes*, from *harn*, that is, closely fitted; Fr. *harnois*; Arm. *harnes*; It. *arnese*; Sp. *arnes*; Port. *arnez*; D. *harnas*; G. *harnisch*; Sw. *harnesk*; Dan. *harnisk*. The primary sense is, to fit, prepare or put on; and in different languages, it signifies not only *harness*, but furniture and utensils.]

1. Armor; the whole accouterments or equipments of a knight or horseman; originally perhaps defensive armor, but in a more modern and enlarged sense, the furniture of a military man, defensive or offensive, as a casque, cuirass, helmet, girdle, sword, buckler, &c.

2. The furniture of a draught horse, whether for a wagon, coach, gig, chaise, &c.; called in some of the American states, *tackle* or *tackling*, with which, in its primary sense, it is synonymous. *Dryden.*

H'ARNESS, *v. t.* To dress in armor; to equip with armor for war, as a horseman.

Harnessed in rugged steel. *Rowe.*

2. To put on the furniture of a horse for draught.

Harness the horses. Jer. xlvi.

3. To defend; to equip or furnish for defense. 1 Macc. iv.

H'ARNESSED, *pp.* Equipped with armor; furnished with the dress for draught; defended.

H'ARNESSER, *n.* One who puts on the harness of a horse. *Sherwood.*

H'ARNESSING, *ppr.* Putting on armor or furniture for draught.

H'ARP, *n.* [Sax. *hearpa*; G. *harfe*; D. *harp*; Sw. *harpa*; Dan. *harpe*; Fr. *harpe*; It. Sp. Port. *arpa.*]

1. An instrument of music of the stringed kind, of a triangular figure, held upright and commonly touched with the fingers. *Encyc. Johnson.*

2. A constellation. *Creech.*

H'ARP, *v. i.* To play on the harp.

I heard the voice of harpers, *harping* with their harps. Rev. xiv.

2. To dwell on, in speaking or writing; to continue sounding.

He seems
Proud and disdainful, *harping* on what I am—
Not what he knew I was. *Shak.*

3. To touch as a passion; to affect. *Shak.*

H'ARPER, *n.* A player on the harp.

H'ARPING, *ppr.* Playing on a harp; dwelling on continually.

H'ARPING, *n.* A continual dwelling on.

Making infinite merriment by *harpings* upon old themes. *Irving.*

H'ARPING, *n.* plu. *harpings*. In *ships*, harpings are the fore-parts of the wales, which encompass the bow of the ship, and are fastened to the stem. Their use is to strengthen the ship, in the place where she sustains the greatest shock in plunging into the sea. *Encyc.*

Cat-harpings, are ropes which serve to brace in the shrouds of the lower masts, behind their respective yards. *Mar. Dict.*

H'ARPING-IRON, *n.* A harpoon, which see.

H'ARPIST, *n.* A harper. *Brown.*

HARPOON', *n.* [Fr. *harpon*; Sp. *arpon*; Port. *arpam*, *arpeo*; It. *arpione*; G. *harpune*; D. *harpoen*; from Fr. *harper*, to grapple; Sp. *arpar*, to claw; Gr. αρπαζω, from αρπαω, to seize with the claws; probably L. *rapio*, by transposition of letters. Class Rb.]

A harping-iron; a spear or javelin, used to strike whales for killing them. It consists of a long shank, with a broad flat triangular head, sharpened at both edges for penetrating the whale with facility. It is generally thrown by hand.

HARPOON', *v. t.* To strike, catch or kill with a harpoon.

The beluga is usually caught in nets, but is sometimes *harpooned*. *Pennant.*

HARPOON'ED, *pp.* Struck, caught or killed with a harpoon.

HARPOON'ER, *n.* One who uses a harpoon; the man in a whale-boat who throws the harpoon.

HARPOON'ING, *ppr.* Striking with a harpoon.

H'ARPSICHORD, *n.* [*harp* and *chord.*] An instrument of music with strings of wire, played by the fingers, by means of keys. The striking of these keys moves certain little jacks, which move a double row of chords or strings, stretched over four bridges on the table of the instrument. *Encyc.*

H'ARPY, *n.* [Fr. *harpie*; It. Sp. Port. *arpia*; L. *harpyia*; Gr. αρπυια, from the root of αρπαζω, to seize or claw.]

1. In *antiquity*, the *harpies* were fabulous winged monsters, having the face of a woman and the body of a vultur, with their feet and fingers armed with sharp claws. They were three in number, Aello, Ocypete, and Celeno. They were sent by Juno to plunder the table of Phineus. They are represented as rapacious and filthy animals. *Lempriere.*

2. Any rapacious or ravenous animal; an extortioner; a plunderer.

HARQUEBUSE. [See *Arquebuse.*]

HARRATEE'N, *n.* A kind of stuff or cloth. *Shenstone.*

HAR'RIDAN, *n.* [Fr. *haridelle*, a jade, or worn-out horse. See *Hare*, the verb.]

A decayed strumpet. *Swift.*

HAR'RIER, *n.* A hunting hound with a nice sense of smelling.

HAR'ROW, *n.* [Sw. *harf*, Dan. *harve*, a harrow. D. *hark*, G. *harke*, a rake, is probably the same word, allied to Sw. *hårja*, Dan. *herger*, Sax. *hergian*, to ravage or lay waste.]

An instrument of agriculture, formed of pieces of timber sometimes crossing each other, and set with iron teeth. It is drawn over plowed land to level it and break the clods, and to cover seed when sown.

HAR'ROW, *v. t.* [Sw. *harfva*; Dan. *harver.*] To draw a harrow over, for the purpose of breaking clods and leveling the surface, or for covering seed sown; as, to *harrow* land or ground.

2. To break or tear with a harrow.

Will he *harrow* the valleys after thee? Job xxxix.

3. To tear; to lacerate; to torment.

I could a tale unfold, whose lightest word
Would *harrow* up thy soul— *Shak.*

4. To pillage; to strip; to lay waste by violence. [*Not used.*]

5. To disturb; to agitate. *Obs.* *Shak.*

HAR'ROWED, *pp.* Broken or smoothed by a harrow.

HAR'ROWER, *n.* One who harrows.

2. A hawk.

HAR'ROWING, *ppr.* Breaking or leveling with a harrow.

HAR'RY, *v. t.* [Sax. *hergian*, to strip; *hyrwian*, to upbraid; or W. *herwa*, to rove for plunder, to scout; *her*, a push.]

1. To strip; to pillage. [See *Harrow.*]

2. To harass; to agitate; to tease. *Shak.*

HAR'RY, *v. i.* To make harassing incursions. *Obs.* *Beaum.*

H'ARSH, *a.* [G. *harsch*; Scot. *harsk*. In Dan. *harsk*, Sw. *hårsk*, is rank, rancid.]

1. Rough to the touch; rugged; grating; as *harsh* sand; *harsh* cloth; opposed to *smooth*. *Boyle.*

2. Sour; rough to the taste; as *harsh* fruit.

3. Rough to the ear; grating; discordant; jarring; as a *harsh* sound; *harsh* notes; a *harsh* voice. *Dryden.*

4. Austere; crabbed; morose; peevish. Civilization softens the *harsh* temper or nature of man.

5. Rough; rude; abusive; as *harsh* words; a *harsh* reflection.

6. Rigorous; severe.

Though *harsh* the precept, yet the preacher charm'd. *Dryden.*

H'ARSHLY, *adv.* Roughly; in a harsh manner.

2. Sourly; austerely.

3. Severely; morosely; crabbedly; as, to speak or answer *harshly*.

4. Roughly; rudely; with violence; as, to treat a person *harshly*. *Addison.*

5. Roughly; with a grating sound; unpleasantly.

It would sound *harshly* in her ears. *Shak.*

H'ARSHNESS, *n.* Roughness to the touch; opposed to *softness* and *smoothness*.

2. Sourness; austereness; as the *harshness* of fruit.

3. Roughness to the ear; as the *harshness* of sound or of a voice, or of verse.

'Tis not enough no *harshness* gives offense,
The sound must seem an echo to the sense. *Pope.*

4. Roughness of temper; moroseness; crabbedness; peevishness. *Shak.*

5. Roughness in manner or words; severity; as the *harshness* of reproof.

H'ARSLET, HAS'LET, *n.* [Ice. *hasla.* Qu.] The heart, liver, lights, &c. of a hog.

H'ART, *n.* [Sax. *heort*; Dan. and Sw. *hiort*; G. *hirsch*; D. *hert.*]
A stag or male deer, an animal of the cervine genus.

H'ARTBEEST, *n.* The quanga, or cervine antelope of Africa. *Encyc.*

H'ARTROY'AL, *n.* A plant.

H'ARTSHORN, *n.* The horn of the hart or male deer. The scrapings or raspings of this horn are medicinal, and used in decoctions, ptisans, &c. Hartshorn jelly is nutritive and strengthening. Hartshorn calcined by a strong and long continued heat, is changed into a white earth, which is employed in medicine as an absorbent. The salt of hartshorn is a powerful sudorific, and hartshorn yields also a pungent volatile spirit. *Encyc.*
The jelly of hartshorn is simply gelatine; the earth remaining after calcination, is phosphate of lime; the salt and spirit of hartshorn are muriate of ammonia, with a little animal oil. *Parr.*
Hartshorn plantain, a species of Plantago.

H'ARTSTŎNGUE, *n.* [See *Tongue.*] A plant, a species of Asplenium.

H'ARTWŎRT, *n.* The name of certain plants of the genera, Seseli, Tordylium, and Bupleurum.

HAR'USPICE, *n.* [L. *haruspex*, from *specio*, to view.]
In *Roman history*, a person who pretended to foretell future events by inspecting the entrails of beasts sacrificed, or watching the circumstances attending their slaughter, or their manner of burning and the ascent of the smoke. *Encyc. Adam.*

HAR'USPICY, *n.* Divination by the inspection of victims.

H'ARVEST, *n.* [Sax. *hærfest*, *harfest*, harvest, autumn; G. *herbst*; D. *herfst.* This word signifies autumn, and primarily had no reference to the collection of the fruits of the earth; but in German, *herbstzeit* is harvest-time. It seems to be formed from the G. *herbe*, harsh, keen, tart, *acerb*, L. *acerbus*, and primarily it refers to the cold, chilly weather in autumn in the north of Europe. This being the time when crops are collected in northern climates, the word came to signify *harvest.*]

1. The season of reaping and gathering in corn or other crops. It especially refers to the time of collecting corn or grain, which is the chief food of men, as wheat and rye. In Egypt and Syria, the wheat harvest is in April and May; in the south of Europe and of the United States, in June; in the Northern states of America, in July; and in the north of Europe, in August and September. In the United States, the harvest of maiz is mostly in October.

2. The ripe corn or grain collected and secured in barns or stacks. The *harvest* this year is abundant.

3. The product of labor; fruit or fruits.

Let us the *harvest* of our labor eat. *Dryden.*

4. Fruit or fruits; effects; consequences. He that sows iniquity will reap a *harvest* of woe.

5. In *Scripture*, *harvest* signifies figuratively the proper season for business.

He that sleepeth in *harvest*, is a son that causeth shame. Prov. x.

Also, a people whose sins have ripened them for judgment. Joel iii.
Also, the end of the world. Matt. xiii.
Also, a seasonable time for instructing men in the gospel. Matt. ix.

H'ARVEST, *v. t.* To reap or gather ripe corn and other fruits for the use of man and beast.

H'ARVESTED, *pp.* Reaped and collected, as ripe corn and fruits.

H'ARVESTER, *n.* A reaper; a laborer in gathering grain.

H'ARVEST-FLȲ, *n.* A large four-winged insect of the cicada kind, common in Italy. *Encyc.*

H'ARVEST-HOME, *n.* The time of harvest. *Dryden.*

2. The song sung by reapers at the feast made at the gathering of corn, or the feast itself. *Dryden.*

3. The opportunity of gathering treasure. *Shak.*

H'ARVESTING, *ppr.* Reaping and collecting, as ripe corn and other fruits.

H'ARVEST-LORD, *n.* The head-reaper at the harvest. *Tusser.*

H'ARVEST-MAN, *n.* A laborer in harvest.

H'ARVEST-QUEEN, *n.* An image representing Ceres, formerly carried about on the last day of harvest.

HASH, *v. t.* [Fr. *hacher*; Arm. *haicha*; Eng. to *hack.* See *Hack.*]
To chop into small pieces; to mince and mix; as, to *hash* meat. *Garth.*

HASH, *n.* Minced meat, or a dish of meat and vegetables chopped into small pieces and mixed.

HASK, *n.* A case made of rushes or flags. [*Not used.*] *Spenser.*

HAS'LET, *n.* [See *Harslet.*]

H'ASP, *n.* [Sax. *hæps*; G. *haspe*, a hinge; Dan. *hasp*; Sw. *haspe.* We probably have the word from the Danes.]

1. A clasp that passes over a staple to be fastened by a padlock. *Mortimer.*

2. A spindle to wind thread or silk on. [*Local.*]

H'ASP, *v. t.* To shut or fasten with a hasp. *Garth.*

HAS'SOC, *n.* [W. *hesor.* Qu. from *hêsg*, sedge, rushes. It signifies in Scottish, a besom, any thing bushy, and a turf of peat moss used as a seat. The sense is therefore the same as that of *mat*, a collection or mass.]
A thick mat or bass on which persons kneel in church. *Addison.*

And knees and *hassocs* are well nigh divorc'd. *Cowper.*

HAST, the second person singular of *have*, I have, thou *hast*, contracted from *havest.* It is used only in the solemn style.

HAS'TATE, HAS'TATED, *a.* [L. *hastatus*, from *hasta*, a spear.] In *botany*, spear-shaped; resembling the head of a halberd; triangular, hollowed at the base and on the sides, with the angles spreading; as a *hastate* leaf. *Martyn. Lee.*

HASTE, *n.* [G. Sw. Dan. *hast*; D. *haast*; Fr. *hâte*, for *haste*; Arm. *hast*; from hurrying, pressing, driving. See *Heat.*]

1. Celerity of motion; speed; swiftness; dispatch; expedition; applied only to voluntary beings, as men and other animals; never to other bodies. We never say, a ball flies with *haste.*

The king's business required *haste.* 1 Sam. xxi.

2. Sudden excitement of passion; quickness; precipitance; vehemence.

I said in my *haste*, all men are liars. Ps. cxvi.

3. The state of being urged or pressed by business; as, I am in great *haste.*

HĀSTE, HĀSTEN, *v. t.* *hāst*, *hāsn.* [G. *hasten*; D. *haasten*; Sw. *hasta*; Dan. *haster*; Fr. *hâter.*]
To press; to drive or urge forward; to push on; to precipitate; to accelerate movement.

I would *hasten* my escape from the windy storm. Ps. lv.

HĀSTE, HĀSTEN, *v. i.* To move with celerity; to be rapid in motion; to be speedy or quick.

They were troubled and *hasted* away. Ps. xlviii.

HĀSTED, HĀSTENED, *pp.* Moved rapidly; accelerated; urged with speed.

HĀSTENER, *n.* One that hastens or urges forward.

HĀSTING, HĀSTENING, *ppr.* Urging forward; pushing on; proceeding rapidly.

That state is *hastening* to ruin, in which no difference is made between good and bad men. *Antisthenes. Enfield.*

HĀSTILY, *adv.* [See *Hasty.*] In haste; with speed or quickness; speedily; nimbly.

Half clothed, half naked, *hastily* retire. *Dryden.*

2. Rashly; precipitately; without due reflection.

We *hastily* engaged in the war. *Swift.*

3. Passionately; under sudden excitement of passion.

HĀSTINESS, *n.* Haste; speed; quickness or celerity in motion or action, as of animals.

2. Rashness; heedless eagerness; precipitation. Our *hastiness* to engage in the war caused deep regret.

3. Irritability; susceptibility of anger, warmth or temper.

HĀSTING-PEAR, *n.* An early pear, called also *green chissel.* *Encyc.*

HĀSTINGS, *n.* [from *hasty.*] Peas that come early. *Mortimer.*

HĀSTIVE, *a.* [Fr. *hâtif*, from *haste.*] Forward; early; as fruit. [*Not much used.*] *Encyc.*

HĀSTY, *a.* Quick; speedy; opposed to *slow.*

Be not *hasty* to go out of his sight. Eccles. viii.

2. Eager; precipitate; rash; opposed to *deliberate.*

Seest thou a man that is *hasty* in his words? there is more hope of a fool than of him. Prov. xxix.

3. Irritable; easily excited to wrath; passionate.

He that is *hasty* of spirit exalteth folly. Prov. xiv.

4. Early ripe; forward; as *hasty* fruit. Is. xxviii.

HASTYPUDDING, *n.* A pudding made of the meal of maiz moistened with water and boiled, or of milk and flour boiled.

HAT, *n.* [Sax. *hæt*; G. *hut*; D. *hoed*; Dan. *hat*; Sw. *hatt*; W. *hêd* or *het*. The word signifies a cover, and in German, *fingerhut* is a thimble. The primary sense is probably to ward off, or defend.]

1. A covering for the head; a garment made of different materials, and worn by men or women for defending the head from rain or heat, or for ornament. Hats for men are usually made of fur or wool, and formed with a crown and brim. Hats for females are made of straw or grass braid, and various other materials. Of these the ever varying forms admit of no description that can long be correct.

2. The dignity of a cardinal.

HAT'-BAND, *n.* A band round the crown of a hat.

HAT'-BOX, HAT'-CASE, } *n.* A box for a hat. But a case for a lady's hat is called a *band box.*

HA'TABLE, *a.* [from *hate.*] That may be hated; odious. *Sherwood.*

HATCH, *v. t.* [G. *hecken*, *aushecken*, Dan. *hekker*, to hatch. This word seems to be connected with G. *heck*, Dan. *hekke*, Sw. *häck*, a *hedge*, Dan. *hek*, a fence of pales; and the *hatches* of a ship are doubtless of the same family. The sense probably is, to thrust out, to drive off, whence in Sw. *hägn*, a hedge, is also protection; *hägna*, to hedge, to guard. To *hatch* is to exclude.]

1. To produce young from eggs by incubation, or by artificial heat. In Egypt, chickens are *hatched* by artificial heat.

The partridge sitteth on eggs and *hatcheth* them not. Jer. xvii.

2. To contrive or plot; to form by meditation, and bring into being; to originate and produce in silence; as, to *hatch* mischief; to *hatch* heresy. *Hooker.*

HATCH, *v. t.* [Fr. *hacher*, to hack.] To shade by lines in drawing and engraving.

Those *hatching* strokes of the pencil. *Dryden.*

2. To steep. *Obs.* *Beaum.*

HATCH, *v. i.* To produce young; to bring the young to maturity. Eggs will not *hatch* without a due degree and continuance of heat.

HATCH, *n.* A brood; as many chickens as are produced at once, or by one incubation.

2. The act of exclusion from the egg.

3. Disclosure; discovery. *Shak.*

HATCH, or HATCHES, *n.* [Sax. *hæca*; D. *hek*, a railing, gate, &c. See *Hedge* and *Hatch*, supra.]

1. Properly, the grate or frame of cross-bars laid over the opening in a ship's deck, now called *hatch-bars.* The lid or cover of a hatchway is also called *hatches.*

2. The opening in a ship's deck, or the passage from one deck to another, the name of the grate itself being used for the opening; but this is more properly called the *hatchway.* *Mar. Dict.*

3. A half-door, or door with an opening over it. Qu. *Johnson.* *Shak.*

4. Floodgates. *Encyc.* *Ainsworth.*

5. In *Cornwall*, Eng. openings into mines, or in search of them. *Encyc.*

5. *To be under the hatches*, to be confined, or to be in distress, depression or slavery. *Locke.*

HATCH'EL, *n.* [G. *hechel*, D. *hekel*, Dan. *hegle*, Sw. *häckla*, whence the common pronunciation in America, *hetchel.* In Slav. *hakel* is a rake.]

An instrument formed with long iron teeth set in a board, for cleaning flax or hemp from the tow, hards or coarse part. The hatchel is a large species of comb.

HATCH'EL, *v. t.* To draw flax or hemp through the teeth of a hatchel, for separating the coarse part and broken pieces of the stalk from the fine fibrous parts.

2. To tease or vex, by sarcasms or reproaches; *a vulgar use of the word.*

HATCH'ELED, *pp.* Cleansed by a hatchel; combed.

HATCH'ELER, *n.* One who uses a hatchel.

HATCH'ELING, *ppr.* Drawing through the teeth of a hatchel.

HATCH'ET, *n.* [G. *hacke*; Dan. *hakke*; Fr. *hache*; from *hack*, which see.]

A small ax with a short handle, to be used with one hand.

To take up the hatchet, a phrase borrowed from the natives of America, is to make war.

To bury the hatchet, is to make peace.

HATCH'ET-FACE, *n.* A prominent face, like the edge of a hatchet. *Dryden.*

HATCH'ETINE, *n.* A substance of the hardness of soft tallow, of a yellowish white or greenish yellow color, found in South Wales. *Cleaveland.*

HATCH'MENT, *n.* [corrupted from *achievment.*]

An armorial escutcheon on a herse at funerals, or in a church. *Shak.*

HATCH'WAY, *n.* In *ships*, a square or oblong opening in the deck, affording a passage from one deck to another, or into the hold or lower apartments. *Mar. Dict.*

HATE, *v. t.* [Sax. *hatian*, to hate, and to heat; Goth. *hatyan*; G. *hassen*; D. *haaten*; Sw. *hata*; Dan. *hader*; L. *odi*, for *hodi.* In all the languages except the Saxon, *hate* and *heat* are distinguished in orthography; but the elements of the word are the same, and probably they are radically one word denoting to stir, to irritate, to rouse.]

1. To dislike greatly; to have a great aversion to. It expresses less than *abhor*, *detest*, and *abominate*, unless pronounced with a peculiar emphasis.

How long will fools *hate* knowledge? Prov. i.

Blessed are ye when men shall *hate* you. Luke vi.

The Roman tyrant was contented to be *hated*, if he was but feared. *Rambler.*

2. In *Scripture*, it signifies to love less.

If any man come to me, and *hate* not father and mother, &c. Luke xiv.

He that spareth the rod, *hateth* his son. Prov. xiii.

HATE, *n.* Great dislike or aversion; hatred. *Dryden.*

HA'TED, *pp.* Greatly disliked.

HA'TEFUL, *a.* Odious; exciting great dislike, aversion or disgust. All sin is *hateful* in the sight of God and of good men.

2. That feels hatred; malignant; malevolent.

And, worse than death, to view with *hateful* eyes
His rival's conquest. *Dryden.*

HA'TEFULLY, *adv.* Odiously; with great dislike.

2. Malignantly; maliciously. Ezek. xxiii.

HA'TEFULNESS, *n.* Odiousness; the quality of being hateful, or of exciting aversion or disgust.

HA'TER, *n.* One that hates.

An enemy to God, and a *hater* of all good. *Brown.*

HA'TING, *ppr.* Disliking extremely; entertaining a great aversion for.

HA'TRED, *n.* Great dislike or aversion; hate; enmity. *Hatred* is an aversion to evil, and may spring from utter disapprobation, as the *hatred* of vice or meanness; or it may spring from offenses or injuries done by fellow men, or from envy or jealousy, in which case it is usually accompanied with malevolence or malignity. Extreme hatred is abhorrence or detestation.

HAT'TED, *a.* [from *hat.*] Covered with a hat; wearing a hat.

HAT'TER, *v. t.* To harass. [*Not in use.*] *Dryden.*

HAT'TER, *n.* [from *hat.*] A maker of hats.

HAT'TOCK, *n.* [Erse, *attock.*] A shock of corn. [*Not in use.*]

HAU'BERK, *n.* A coat of mail without sleeves. *Obs.* [See *Habergeon.*]

HAUGHT, *a. haut.* [Qu. Fr. *haut*, or the root of the English *high.* If it is from the French *haut*, the orthography is corrupt, for *haut* is from the Latin *altus*, that is, *haltus*, changed to *haut.*]

High; elevated; hence, proud; insolent. *Obs.* *Spenser.* *Shak.*

HAUGHTILY, *adv. hau'tily.* [See *Haught* and *Haughty.*]

Proudly; arrogantly; with contempt or disdain; as, to speak or behave *haughtily.*

Her heavenly form too *haughtily* she prized. *Dryden.*

HAUGHTINESS, *n. hau'tiness.* The quality of being haughty; pride mingled with some degree of contempt for others; arrogance.

I will lay low the *haughtiness* of the terrible. Is. xiii.

HAUGHTY, *a. hau'ty.* [from *haught*, Fr. *haut.*]

1. Proud and disdainful; having a high opinion of one's self, with some contempt for others; lofty and arrogant; supercilious.

His wife was a woman of a *haughty* and imperious nature. *Clarendon.*

A *haughty* spirit goeth before a fall. Prov. xvi.

2. Proceeding from excessive pride, or pride mingled with contempt; manifesting pride and disdain; as a *haughty* air or walk.

3. Proud and imperious; as a *haughty* nation.
4. Lofty; bold; of high hazard; as a *haughty* enterprise. *Obs.* *Spenser.*

HAUL, *v. t.* [Fr. *haler*; Arm. *hala*; Sp. *halar*; D. *haalen.* It is sometimes written *hale*, but *haul* is preferable, as *au* represents the broad sound of *a.*]

1. To pull or draw with force; to drag; as, to *haul* a heavy body along on the ground; to *haul* a boat on shore. *Haul* is equivalent to *drag*, and differs sometimes from *pull* and *draw*, in expressing more force and labor. It is much used by seamen; as, to *haul* down the sails; *haul* in the boom; *haul* aft, &c.
2. To drag; to compel to go.

Lest he *haul* thee to the judge. Luke xii.

When applied to persons, *haul* implies compulsion or rudeness, or both.

To haul the wind, in seamanship, is to turn the head of the ship nearer to the point from which the wind blows, by arranging the sails more obliquely, bracing the yards more forward, hauling the sheets more aft, &c. *Mar. Dict.*

HAUL, *n.* A pulling with force; a violent pull. *Thomson.*

2. A draft of a net; as, to catch a hundred fish at a *haul.*

HAUL'ED, *pp.* Pulled with force; dragged; compelled to move.

HAUL'ING, *ppr.* Drawing by force or violence; dragging.

HAULM, } *n.* [Sax. *healm*; G. D. Sw. Dan.
HAUM, } *halm*; Fr. *chaume*; L. *culmus*, the stalk of corn. The sense is probably that which is set, or a shoot. It seems to be the W. *colov*, a stem or stalk, whence *columna*, a *column.*]

1. The stem or stalk of grain, of all kinds, or of pease, beans, hops, &c.
2. Straw; the dry stalks of corn, &c. in general.

H'AUNCH, *n.* [Fr. *hanche*; Arm. *hoinch*; Sp. It. Port. *anca.*]

1. The hip; that part of the body of man and of quadrupeds, which lies between the last ribs and the thigh. *Encyc.*
2. The rear; the hind part. [*Not used.*] *Shak.*

H'AUNT, *v. t.* [Fr. *hanter*; Arm. *hantein* or *henti.*]

1. To frequent; to resort to much or often, or to be much about; to visit customarily.

Celestial Venus *haunts* Idalia's groves. *Pope.*

2. To come to frequently; to intrude on; to trouble with frequent visits; to follow importunately.

You wrong me, Sir, thus still to *haunt* my house. *Shak.*

Those cares that *haunt* the court and town. *Swift.*

3. It is particularly applied to specters or apparitions, which are represented by fear and credulity as frequenting or inhabiting old, decayed and deserted houses.

Foul spirits *haunt* my resting place. *Fairfax.*

H'AUNT, *v. i.* To be much about; to visit or be present often.

I've charged thee not to *haunt* about my door. *Shak.*

H'AUNT, *n.* A place to which one frequently resorts. Taverns are often the *haunts* of tipplers. A den is the *haunt* of wild beasts.

2. The habit or custom of resorting to a place. [*Not used.*] *Arbuthnot.*
3. Custom; practice. *Obs.* *Chaucer.*

H'AUNTED, *pp.* Frequently visited or resorted to, especially by apparitions.

2. Troubled by frequent visits.

H'AUNTER, *n.* One who frequents a particular place, or is often about it.

H'AUNTING, *ppr.* Frequenting; visiting often; troubling with frequent visits.

HAUST, *n.* [Sax. *hwasta.*] A dry cough. *Obs.* *Ray.*

HAUTBOY, *n.* *ho'boy.* [Fr. *haut*, high, and *bois*, wood, or a shoot.]

A wind instrument, somewhat resembling a flute, but widening towards the bottom, and sounded through a reed. The treble is two feet long. The tenor goes a fifth lower, when blown open. It has only eight holes; but the base, which is five feet long, has eleven. *Encyc.*

HAUTEUR, *n.* [Fr.] Pride; haughtiness; insolent manner or spirit.

HAUYNE, *n.* A mineral, called by Haüy *latialite*, occurring in grains or small masses, and also in groups of minute, shining crystals. Its color is blue, of various shades. It is found imbedded in volcanic rocks, basalt, clinkstone, &c. *Cleaveland.*

HAVE, *v. t.* *hav.* pret. and pp. *had.* Indic. Present, I *have*, thou *hast*, he *has*; we, ye, they, *have.* [Sax. *habban*; Goth. *haban*; G. *haben*; D. *hebben*; Sw. *hafva*; Dan. *haver*; L. *habeo*; Sp. *haber*; Port. *haver*; It. *avere*; Fr. *avoir*; W. *hafiaw*, to snatch, or seize hastily, and *hapiaw*, to happen. The Spanish *haber* unites *have* with *happen*; *haber*, to have or possess, to take, to *happen* or befall. The primary sense then is to fall on, or to rush on and seize. See *Happen.* Class Gb. No. 74. 79.]

1. To possess; to hold in possession or power.

How many loaves *have* ye? Matt. xv.

He that gathered much *had* nothing over. Ex. xvi.

I *have* no Levite to my priest. Judges 17.

To have and *to hold*, terms in a deed of conveyance.

2. To possess, as something that is connected with, or belongs to one.

Have ye a father? *Have* ye another brother? Gen. xliii. and xliv.

—Sheep that *have* no shepherd. 1 Kings xxii.

3. To marry; to take for a wife or husband.

In the resurrection, whose wife shall she be of the seven? for they all *had* her. Matt. xxii.

4. To hold; to regard. Thus, to *have* in honor, is to hold in esteem; to esteem; to honor.

To have in derision or contempt, to hold in derision or contempt; to deride; to despise.

5. To maintain; to hold in opinion.

Sometimes they will *have* them to be the natural heat; sometimes they will *have* them to be the qualities of the tangible parts. *Bacon.*

6. To be urged by necessity or obligation; to be under necessity, or impelled by duty. I *have* to visit twenty patients every day. We *have* to strive against temptations. We *have* to encounter strong prejudices. The nation *has* to pay the interest of an immense debt.
7. To seize and hold; to catch. The hound *has* him. [*The original, but now a vulgar use of the word.*]
8. To contain. The work *has* many beauties and many faults.
9. To gain; to procure; to receive; to obtain; to purchase. I *had* this cloth very cheap. He *has* a guinea a month. He *has* high wages for his services.

Had rather, denotes wish or preference.

I *had rather* be a door-keeper in the house of my God, than dwell in the tents of wickedness. Ps. lxxxiv.

Is not this phrase a corruption of *would rather?*

To have after, to pursue. [*Not much used, nor elegant.*] *Shak.*

To have away, to remove; to take away. *Tusser.*

To have at, to encounter; to assail; as, to *have at* him; to *have at* you. [*Legitimate, but vulgar.*]

To enter into competition with; to make trial with. *Shak.*

Dryden uses in a like sense, *have with* you; but these uses are inelegant.

To have in, to contain.

To have on, to wear; to carry, as raiment or weapons.

He saw a man who *had* not *on* a wedding-garment. Matt. xxii.

To have out, to cause to depart. 2 Sam. xiii.

To have a care, to take care; to be on the guard, or to guard.

To have pleasure, to enjoy.

To have pain, to suffer.

To have sorrow, to be grieved or afflicted.

With *would* and *should.*

He would have, he desires to have, or he requires.

He should have, he ought to have.

But the various uses of *have* in such phrases, and its uses as an auxiliary verb, are fully explained in grammars. As an auxiliary, it assists in forming the perfect tense, as I *have* formed, thou *hast* formed, he *hath* or *has* formed, we *have* formed, and the prior-past tense, as I *had* seen, thou *hadst* seen, he *had* seen.

HAVELESS, *a.* *hav'les.* Having little or nothing. [*Not in use.*] *Gower.*

HA'VEN, *n.* *ha'vn.* [Sax. *hæfan*; D. *haven*; Dan. *havn*; Fr. *hâvre*; Arm. *haffn*; G. *hafen*; from *haber*, a Gaulish word, signifying the mouth of a river, says Lunier. But in Welsh, *hav* is summer, and *havyn* is a flat, extended, still place, and a *haven.*]

1. A harbor; a port; a bay, recess or inlet of the sea, or the mouth of a river which affords good anchorage and a safe station for ships; any place in which ships can be sheltered by the land from the force of tempests and a violent sea.
2. A shelter; an asylum; a place of safety. *Shak.*

HA'VENER, *n.* The overseer of a port; a harbor-master. [*Not used.*] *Carew.*

HAV'ER, *n.* One who has or possesses; a possessor; a holder. [*Little used.*] *Shak.*

HAV'ER, *n.* [G. *hafer*; D. *haver*; perhaps L. *avena.*]

Oats; a word of local use in the north of England; as *haverbread*, oaten bread. *Johnson.*

HAV'ERSACK, *n.* [Fr. *havre-sac.*] A soldier's knapsack.

HAV'ING, *ppr.* [from *have.*] Possessing; holding in power or possession; containing; gaining; receiving; taking.

HAV'ING, *n.* Possession; goods; estate. [*Not in use.*] *Shak.*

2. The act or state of possessing. *Sidney.*

HAV'OCK, *n.* [W. *havog*, a spreading about, waste, devastation; *havogi*, to commit waste, to devastate; supposed to be from *hav*, a spreading. But qu. Ir. *arvach*, havock.]

Waste; devastation; wide and general destruction.

> Ye gods! what *havock* does ambition make
> Among your works. *Addison.*

> As for Saul, he made *havock* of the church. Acts viii.

HAV'OCK, *v. t.* To waste; to destroy; to lay waste.

> To waste and *havock* yonder world. *Milton.*

HAW, *n.* [Sax. *hæg*, *hag*, G. *heck*, D. *haag*, *heg*, Dan. *hek*, *hekke*, a hedge.]

1. The berry and seed of the hawthorn, that is, *hedge-thorn*. *Bacon.*

2. [Sax. *haga.*] A small piece of ground adjoining a house; a small field; properly, an inclosed piece of land, from *hedge*, like *garden*, which also signifies an inclosure. [Dan. *hauge*, a garden.]

3. In *farriery*, an excrescence resembling a gristle, growing under the nether eyelid and eye of a horse. *Encyc.*

4. A dale. *Obs.* *Chaucer.*

HAW, *v. i.* [corrupted from *hawk*, or *hack.*] To stop in speaking with a haw, or to speak with interruption and hesitation; as, to hem and *haw*. *L'Estrange.*

HAW'FINCH, *n.* A bird, a species of Loxia.

HAW'HAW, *n.* [duplication of *haw*, a hedge.]

A fence or bank that interrupts an alley or walk, sunk between slopes and not perceived till approached. *Todd.*

HAW'ING, *ppr.* Speaking with a haw, or with hesitation.

HAWK, *n.* [Sax. *hafoc*; D. *havik*; G. *habicht*; Sw. *hök*; Dan. *hög*, *höög*; W. *hebog*, named from *heb*, utterance.]

A genus of fowls, the Falco, of many species, having a crooked beak, furnished with a cere at the base, a cloven tongue, and the head thick set with fethers. Most of the species are rapacious, feeding on birds or other small animals. Hawks were formerly trained for sport or catching small birds.

HAWK, *v. i.* To catch or attempt to catch birds by means of hawks trained for the purpose, and let loose on the prey; to practice falconry.

> He that *hawks* at larks and sparrows. *Locke.*

> A falc'ner Henry is, when Emma *hawks*. *Prior.*

2. To fly at; to attack on the wing; with *at*.

> To *hawk at* flies. *Dryden.*

HAWK, *v. i.* [W. *hoçi*; Scot. *hawgh*. Qu. Chal. כיח, and *keck* and *cough*. See Class Gk. No. 5. 29. 36.]

To make an effort to force up phlegm with noise; as, to *hawk* and spit. *Shak.* *Harvey.*

To hawk up, transitively; as, to *hawk up* phlegm.

HAWK, *n.* An effort to force up phlegm from the throat, accompanied with noise.

HAWK, *v. t.* [Qu. G. *hocken*, to take on the back; *höcken*, to higgle; *höcker*, a huckster; or the root of L. *auctio*, auction, a sale by outcry. The root of the latter probably signified to cry out.]

To cry; to offer for sale by outcry in the street, or to sell by outcry; as, to *hawk* goods or pamphlets.

HAWK'ED, *pp.* Offered for sale by outcry in the street.

2. *a.* Crooked; curving like a hawk's bill.

HAWK'ER, *n.* One who offers goods for sale by outcry in the street; a pedlar. *Swift.*

2. A falconer. [Sax. *hafcere.*]

HAWK'EYED, *a.* Having acute sight; discerning.

HAWK'ING, *ppr.* Catching wild birds by hawks.

2. Making an effort to discharge phlegm.

3. Offering for sale in the street by outcry.

HAWK'ING, *n.* The exercise of taking wild fowls by means of hawks.

HAWK'NOSED, *a.* Having an aquiline nose. *Farrand.*

HAWK'WEED, *n.* The vulgar name of several species of plants, of the genera, Hieracium, Crepis, Hyoseris, and Andryala.

HAWSE, *n. hawz.* [See *Halser.*] The situation of a ship moored with two anchors from the bows, one on the starboard, the other on the larboard bow; as, the ship has a clear *hawse*, or a foul *hawse*. A *foul hawse* is when the cables cross each other or are twisted together. *Mar. Dict.*

HAWSE-HOLE, *n.* A cylindrical hole in the bow of a ship through which a cable passes.

HAWSE-PIECE, *n.* One of the foremost timbers of a ship.

HAWS'ER, *n.* [See *Halser.*] A small cable; or a large rope, in size between a cable and a tow-line. *Mar. Dict.* *Encyc.*

HAW'THORN, *n.* [Sax. *hæg-thorn*, hedge-thorn; Sw. *hagtorn*; Dan. *hagetorn*; G. *hagedorn*; D. *haagedoorn.*]

A shrub or tree which bears the *haw*, of the genus Cratægus; the white-thorn. The hawthorn is much used for hedges, and for standards in gardens. It grows naturally in all parts of Europe. *Encyc.*

HAW'THORN-FLY, *n.* An insect so called. *Walton.*

HAY, *n.* [Sax. *heg*, *hig*; G. *heu*; D. *hooi*; Dan. *höe*; Sw. *hö.*]

Grass cut and dried for fodder; grass prepared for preservation. Make *hay* while the sun shines.

To dance the hay, to dance in a ring. *Donne.*

HAY, *v. t.* [G. *heuen.*] To dry or cure grass for preservation.

HAY, *n.* [Sax. *hæg.*] A hedge. *Obs.* *Chaucer.*

2. A net which incloses the haunt of an animal. *Harmer.*

HAY, *v. t.* To lay snares for rabbits. *Hulot.*

HA'YBOTE, *n.* Hedge-bote. In English law, an allowance of wood to a tenant for repairing hedges or fences. *Blackstone.*

HA'YCOCK, *n.* A conical pile or heap of hay, in the field.

HA'YKNIFE, *n.* A sharp instrument used in cutting hay out of a stack or mow.

HA'YLOFT, *n.* A loft or scaffold for hay, particularly in a barn.

HA'YMAKER, *n.* One who cuts and dries grass for fodder.

HA'YMAKING, *n.* The business of cutting grass and curing it for fodder.

HA'YMARKET, *n.* A place for the sale of hay.

HA'YMOW, *n.* A mow or mass of hay laid up in a barn for preservation.

HA'YRICK, *n.* A rick of hay; usually a long pile for preservation in the open air.

HA'YSTACK, *n.* A stack or large conical pile of hay in the open air, laid up for preservation.

HA'YWARD, *n.* [*hay* and *ward*, hedge-ward.]

A person who keeps the common herd or cattle of a town, and guards hedges or fences. In New England, the *hayward* is a town officer whose duty is to impound cattle, and particularly swine which are found running at large in the highways, contrary to law.

HA'YDENITE, *n.* A mineral discovered by Dr. Hayden, near Baltimore. It occurs in garnet colored crystals.

HAZ'ARD, *n.* [Fr. *hasard*; probably from the root of L. *casus*, a fall, and *ard*, the common termination.]

1. Chance; accident; casualty; a fortuitous event; that which falls or comes suddenly or unexpectedly, the cause of which is unknown, or whose operation is unforeseen or unexpected.

> I will stand the *hazard* of the die. *Shak.*

2. Danger; peril; risk. He encountered the enemy at the *hazard* of his reputation and life.

> Men are led on from one stage of life to another, in a condition of the utmost *hazard*. *Rogers.*

3. A game at dice. *Swift.*

To run the hazard, to risk; to take the chance; to do or neglect to do something, when the consequences are not foreseen, and not within the powers of calculation.

HAZ'ARD, *v. t.* [Fr. *hasarder.*] To expose to chance; to put in danger of loss or injury; to venture; to risk; as, to *hazard* life to save a friend; to *hazard* an estate on the throw of a die; to *hazard* salvation for temporal pleasure.

> Men *hazard* nothing by a course of evangelical obedience. *J. Clarke.*

2. To venture to incur, or bring on; as, to *hazard* the loss of reputation.

HAZ'ARD, *v. i.* To try the chance; to adventure; to run the risk or danger.

> Pause a day or two, before you *hazard*— *Shak.*

HAZ'ARDABLE, *a.* That is liable to hazard or chance. *Brown.*

HAZ'ARDED, *pp.* Put at risk or in danger; ventured.

HAZ'ARDER, *n.* One who ventures or puts at stake.

HAZ'ARDING, *ppr.* Exposing to danger or peril; venturing to bring on.

HAZ'ARDOUS, *a.* Dangerous; that exposes to peril or danger of loss or evil; as a *hazardous* attempt or experiment.

HAZ'ARDOUSLY, *adv.* With danger of loss or evil; with peril.

HAZ'ARDRY, *n.* Rashness; temerity. *Obs.* *Spenser.*

2. Gaming in general. *Obs.* *Chaucer.*

HAZE, *n.* [The primary sense of this word is probably to mix, or to turn, stir and make thick.]

Fog; a watery vapor in the air, or a dry vapor like smoke, which renders the air thick.

HAZE, *v. i.* To be foggy. [*A local word.*] *Ray.*

HAZE, *v. t.* To frighten. [*Not used.*] *Ainsworth.*

HAZEL, *n.* *ha'zl.* [Sax. *hæsel*, a hat or cap; *hæsl*, hazel; *hæsl-nutu*, hazel-nut; G. *hasel*; D. *hazelaar*; Dan. *hassel*, *hassel-nöd*; Sw. *hassel*. By the Saxon it appears that the word signifies a cap, and the name of the nut, a cap-nut.]

A shrub of the genus Corylus, bearing a nut containing a kernel of a mild farinaceous taste. *Encyc.*

HAZEL, *a.* *ha'zl.* Pertaining to the hazel or like it; of a light brown color, like the hazel-nut.

HA'ZEL-EARTH, *n.* A kind of red loam. *Encyc.*

HA'ZEL-NUT, *n.* The nut or fruit of the hazel.

HA'ZELLY, *a.* Of the color of the hazel-nut; of a light brown. *Mortimer.* *Encyc.*

HA'ZY, *a.* [See *Haze.*] Foggy; misty; thick with vapor; as *hazy* weather; the *hazy* north. *Thomson.*

HE, pronoun of the third person; nom. *he*; poss. *his*; obj. *him*. [Sax. mas. *he*; fem. *heo*; neut. *hit*, now contracted to *it*, L. *id*, for *hid*. It seems to be a contracted word, for the L. is *hic*, and the Saxon accusative is sometimes *hig*. In English it has no plural, but it has in Saxon, *hi*, they.]

1. A pronoun, a substitute for the third person, masculine gender, representing the man or male person named before.

> Thy desire shall be to thy husband, and *he* shall rule over thee. Gen. iii.

> Thou shalt fear Jehovah thy God; *him* shalt thou serve. Deut. x.

2. It often has reference to a person that is named in the subsequent part of the sentence. *He* is the man.

3. *He* is often used without reference to any particular person, and may be referred to any person indefinitely that answers the description. It is then synonymous with *any man*.

> *He* that walketh with wise men, shall be wise. Prov. xiii.

4. *He*, when a substitute for *man* in its general sense, expressing mankind, is of common gender, representing, like its antecedent, the whole human race.

> My Spirit shall not always strive with man, for that *he* also is flesh. Gen. vi.

5. Man; a male.

> I stand to answer thee, or any *he* the proudest of thy sort. *Shak.*

In this use of *he*, in the ludicrous style, the word has no variation of case. In the foregoing sentence, *he* is in the objective case, or position, and the word is to be considered as a noun.

6. *He* is sometimes prefixed to the names of animals to designate the male kind, as a *he-goat*, a *he-bear*. In such cases, *he* is to be considered as an adjective, or the two words as forming a compound.

HEAD, *n.* *hed.* [Sax. *heafod*, *hefed*, *heafd*; D. *hoofd*; Dan. *hoved*; Sw. *hufvud*; G. *haupt*. This word is a participle of the Sax. *heafan*, *hefan*, to *heave*, pret. *hof*, hove; G. *heben*, *hob*, &c. *Heafod*, heaved, the elevated part, the top. Class Gb.]

1. The uppermost part of the human body, or the foremost part of the body of prone and creeping animals. This part of the human body contains the organs of hearing, seeing, tasting and smelling; it contains also the brain, which is supposed to be the seat of the intellectual powers, and of sensation. Hence the *head* is the chief or most important part, and is used for the whole person, in the phrase, let the evil fall on my *head*.

2. An animal; an individual; as, the tax was raised by a certain rate per *head*. And we use the singular number to express many. The herd contains twenty *head* of oxen.

> Thirty thousand *head* of swine. *Addison.*

3. A chief; a principal person; a leader; a commander; one who has the first rank or place, and to whom others are subordinate; as the *head* of an army; the *head* of a sect or party. Eph. v.

4. The first place; the place of honor, or of command. The lord mayor sat at the *head* of the table. The general marched at the *head* of his troops.

5. Countenance; presence; in the phrases, to hide the *head*, to show the *head*.

6. Understanding; faculties of the mind; sometimes in a ludicrous sense; as, a man has a good *head*, or a strong *head*. These men laid their *heads* together to form the scheme. Never trouble your *head* about this affair. So we say, to beat the *head*; to break the *head*; that is, to study hard, to exercise the understanding or mental faculties.

7. Face; front; forepart.

> The ravishers turn *head*, the fight renews. [*Unusual.*] *Dryden.*

8. Resistance; successful opposition; in the phrase, to *make head against*, that is, to advance, or resist with success.

9. Spontaneous will or resolution; in the phrases, *of his own head*, *on their own head*. But *of* is more usual than *on*.

10. State of a deer's horns by which his age is known. The buck is called, the fifth year, a buck of the first *head*. *Shak.*

11. The top of a thing, especially when larger than the rest of the thing; as the *head* of a spear; the *head* of a cabbage; the *head* of a nail; the *head* of a mast.

12. The forepart of a thing, as the *head* of a ship, which includes the bows on both sides; also, the ornamental figure or image erected on or before the stem of a ship. *Encyc.*

13. The blade or cutting part of an ax, distinct from the helve.

14. That which rises on the top; as the *head* or yeast of beer. *Mortimer.*

15. The upper part of a bed, or bed-stead.

16. The brain.

> They turn their *heads* to imitate the sun. *Pope.*

17. The dress of the head; as a laced *head*. [*Unusual.*] *Swift.*

18. The principal source of a stream; as the *head* of the Nile.

19. Altitude of water in ponds, as applicable to the driving of mill-wheels. The mill has a good *head* of water.

20. Topic of discourse; chief point or subject; a summary; as the *heads* of a discourse or treatise.

21. Crisis; pitch; highth. The disease has grown to such a *head* as to threaten life.

22. Influence; force; strength; pitch. The sedition got to such a *head* as not to be easily quelled.

23. Body; conflux. *Obs.* *Shak.* *Spenser.*

24. Power; armed force.

> My lord, my lord, the French have gathered *head*. *Shak.*

25. Liberty; freedom from restraint; as, to give a horse the *head*. Hence,

26. License; freedom from check, control or restraint. Children should not have their *heads*.

> He has too long given his unruly passions the *head*. *South.*

27. The hair of the head; as a *head* of hair.

28. The top of corn or other plant; the part on which the seed grows.

29. The end, or the boards that form the end; as the *head* of a cask.

30. The part most remote from the mouth or opening into the sea; as the *head* of a bay, gulf or creek.

31. The maturated part of an ulcer or boil; hence, to *come to a head*, is to suppurate.

Head and ears, a phrase denoting the whole person, especially when referring to immersion. He plunged *head and ears* into the water. He was *head and ears* in debt, that is, completely overwhelmed.

Head and shoulders, by force; violently; as, to drag one *head and shoulders*.

> They bring in every figure of speech, *head and shoulders*. *Felton.*

Head or tail, or, *head nor tail*, uncertain; not reducible to certainty. *Burke.*

Head, as an adj. or in composition, chief; principal; as a *head* workman.

By the head, in seamen's language, denotes the state of a ship laden too deeply at the fore-end.

HEAD, *v. t.* *hed.* To lead; to direct; to act as leader to; as, to *head* an army; to *head* an expedition; to *head* a riot.

2. To behead; to decapitate. [*Unusual.*] *Shak.*

3. To form a head to; to fit or furnish with a head; as, to *head* a nail.

4. To lop; as, to *head* trees.

5. To go in front of; to get into the front; as, to *head* a drove of cattle.

6. To set on the head; as, to *head* a cask.

7. To oppose; to veer round and blow in opposition to the course of a ship; as, the wind *heads* us.

HEAD, *v. i.* *hed.* To originate; to spring; to have its source, as a river.

> A broad river that *heads* in the great Blue Ridge of mountains. *Adair.*

HEADACH, *n.* *hed'ake.* Pain in the head.

HEADBAND, *n. hed'band.* A fillet; a band for the head; also, the band at each end of a book. Is. iii.

HEADBOROUGH, *n. hed'burro.* In England, formerly, the chief of a frank-pledge, tithing or decennary, consisting of ten families; called in some counties, *borsholder*, that is, *borough's elder*, and sometimes *tithing man.* *Blackstone.*

HEAD-DRESS, *n. hed'dress.* The dress of the head; the covering or ornaments of a woman's head. *Pope. Addison.*

2. The crest, or tuft of fethers on a fowl's head. *Addison.*

HEADED, *pp. hed'ed.* Led; directed; furnished with a head; having a top. This is used in composition, as *clear-headed, long-headed, thick-headed*, &c.

HEADER, *n. hed'er.* One who heads nails or pins.

2. One who leads a mob or party.

3. The first brick in the angle of a wall. *Moxon.*

HEADFAST, *n. hed'fast.* A rope at the head of a ship to fasten it to a wharf or other fixed object. *Mar. Dict.*

HEADFIRST, *adv. hedfurst.* With the head foremost.

HEADGARGLE, *n. hed'gargle.* A disease of cattle. *Mortimer.*

HEADGEAR, *n. hed'gear.* The dress of a woman's head. *Burton.*

HEADINESS, *n. hed'iness.* [See *Heady.*] Rarshness; precipitation; a disposition to rush forward without due deliberation or prudence. *Spenser.*

2. Stubbornness; obstinacy.

HEADING, *n. hed'ing.* Timber for the heads of casks.

HEADLAND, *n. hed'land.* A cape; a promontory; a point of land projecting from the shore into the sea, or other expanse of water.

2. A ridge or strip of unplowed land at the ends of furrows, or near a fence.

HEADLESS, *a. hed'less.* Having no head; beheaded; as a *headless* body, neck or carcase. *Dryden. Spenser.*

2. Destitute of a chief or leader. *Raleigh.*

3. Destitute of understanding or prudence; rash; obstinate. *Spenser.*

HEADLONG, *adv. hed'long.* With the head foremost; as, to fall *headlong.* *Dryden.*

2. Rashly; precipitately; without deliberation.

—He hurries *headlong* to his fate. *Dryden.*

3. Hastily; without delay or respit.

HEADLONG, *a. hed'long.* Steep; precipitous. *Milton.*

2. Rash; precipitate; as *headlong* folly.

HEADMAN, *n. hed'man.* A chief; a leader.

HEADMŎLD-SHOT, *n.* A disease in children, in which the sutures of the skull, usually the coronal, ride, that is, when their edges shoot over one another, and are so close-locked as to compress the brain; often occasioning convulsions and death. *Encyc.*

HEAD'MŎNEY, *n. hed'munny.* A capitation-tax. *Milton.*

HEADMOST, *a. hed'most.* Most advanced; most forward; first in a line or order of progression; as the *headmost* ship in a fleet.

HEAD-PAN, *n. hed'-pan.* The brain-pan. [*Not in use.*]

HEAD-PIECE, *n. hed'-pece.* Armor for the head; a helmet; a morion. *Sidney. Dryden.*

2. Understanding; force of mind. [*Not common.*] *Prideaux.*

HEADQUA̦RT'ERS, *n. plu.* The quarters or place of residence of the commander-in-chief of an army.

2. The residence of any chief, or place from which orders are issued.

HEAD-ROPE, *n. hed'-rope.* That part of a bolt-rope which terminates any sail on the upper edge, and to which it is sewed. *Mar. Dict.*

HEAD-SAIL, *n. hed'-sail.* The *head-sails* of a ship are the sails which are extended on the fore-mast and bowsprit, as the fore-sail, foretop-sail, jib, &c. *Mar. Dict.*

HEAD-SEA, *n. hed'-sea.* Waves that meet the head of a ship or roll against her course. *Mar. Dict.*

HEADSHAKE, *n. hed'shake.* A significant shake of the head. *Shak.*

HEADSHIP, *n. hed'ship.* Authority; chief place. *Hales.*

HEADSMAN, *n. hed'sman.* One that cuts off heads; an executioner. [*Unusual.*] *Dryden.*

HEADSPRING, *n. hed'spring.* Fountain; source; origin.

HEADSTALL, *n. hed'stall.* That part of a bridle which encompasses the head.

HEADSTONE, *n. hed'stone.* The principal stone in a foundation; the chief or corner stone. *Psalms.*

2. The stone at the head of a grave.

HEADSTRONG, *a. hed'strong.* Violent; obstinate; ungovernable; resolute to run his own way; bent on pursuing his own will; not easily restrained.

Now let the *headstrong* boy my will control. *Dryden.*

2. Directed by ungovernable will or proceeding from obstinacy; as a *headstrong* course. *Dryden.*

HEAD'STRONGNESS, *n.* Obstinacy. [*Not in use.*] *Gayton.*

HEADTIRE, *n. hed'tire.* Dress or attire for the head. 1 Esdras iii.

HEADWAY, *n. hed'way.* The motion of an advancing ship. A ship makes *headway*, when she advances, as from a state of rest.

HEAD-WIND, *n. hed'-wind.* A wind that blows in a direction opposite to the ship's course.

HEAD-WŎRK'MAN, *n.* The chief workman of a party; a foreman in a manufactory. *Swift.*

HEADY, *a. hed'y.* [See *Head.*] Rash; hasty; precipitate; violent; disposed to rush forward in an enterprise without thought or deliberation; hurried on by will or passion; ungovernable.

All the talent required, is to be *heady*, to be violent on one side or the other. *Temple.*

2. Apt to affect the head; inflaming; intoxicating; strong; as spirituous liquors. Champagne is a *heady* wine.

3. Violent; impetuous; as a *heady* current. [*Not usual.*] *Shak.*

HEAL, *v. t.* [Sax. *hælan, helan, gehelan*, to heal, and to conceal, L. *celo*; Goth. *hailyan*, to heal; G. *heilen*; D. *heelen*; Sw. *hela*; Dan. *heeler*; from *hal, heil, heel, hel*, whole, sound, allied to *hold* and *holy*. Heb. כל, כלל, Ch. כלא, to be whole or entire, *all.* The primary sense of the root is to press, strain, extend; hence, to *hold*, to shut, enclose, conceal, to embrace the whole. To *heal* is to make *whole, hale*, sound, and to *conceal* is to hold, or keep close.]

1. To cure of a disease or wound and restore to soundness, or to that state of body in which the natural functions are regularly performed; as, to *heal* the sick.

Speak, and my servant shall be *healed.* Matt. viii.

2. To cure; to remove or subdue; as, to *heal* a disease.

3. To cause to cicatrize; as, to *heal* a sore or wound.

4. To restore to soundness; as, to *heal* a wounded limb.

5. To restore purity to; to remove feculence or foreign matter.

Thus saith the Lord, I have *healed* these waters. 2 Kings ii.

6. To remove, as differences or dissension; to reconcile, as parties at variance; as, to *heal* a breach or difference.

7. In *Scripture*, to forgive; to cure moral disease and restore soundness.

I will *heal* their backsliding. Hos. xiv.

8. To purify from corruptions, redress grievances and restore to prosperity. Jer. xiv.

9. To cover, as a roof with tiles, slate, lead, &c. [Sax. *helan.*] *Encyc.*

HEAL, *v. i.* To grow sound; to return to a sound state; as, the limb *heals*, or the wound *heals*; sometimes with *up* or *over*; it will *heal up* or *over.*

HE'ALABLE, *a.* That may be healed. *Sherwood.*

HE'ALED, *pp.* Restored to a sound state.

HE'ALER, *n.* He or that which cures, or restores to soundness.

HE'ALING, *ppr.* Curing; restoring to a sound state.

2. *a.* Tending to cure; mild; mollifying.

HE'ALING, *n.* The act of curing.

2. The act of covering. *Obs.*

HEALTH, *n. helth.* [from *heal.*] That state of an animal or living body, in which the parts are sound, well organized and disposed, and in which they all perform freely their natural functions. In this state the animal feels no pain. This word is applied also to plants.

Though *health* may be enjoyed without gratitude, it cannot be sported with without loss, or regained by courage. *Buckminster.*

2. Sound state of the mind; natural vigor of faculties. *Bacon.*

3. Sound state of the mind, in a moral sense; purity; goodness.

There is no *health* in us. *Common Prayer.*

4. Salvation or divine favor, or grace which cheers God's people. Ps. xliii.

5. Wish of health and happiness; used in drinking. Come, love and *health* to all; an elliptical phrase, for, I wish *health* to you.

HEALTH'FU̦L, *a. helth'ful.* Being in a sound state, as a living or organized being; having the parts or organs entire, and their functions in a free, active and undisturbed operation; free from disease. We speak of a *healthful* body, a *healthful* person, a *healthful* plant.

2. Serving to promote health; wholesome; salubrious; as a *healthful* air or climate; a *healthful* diet.

3. Indicating health or soundness; as a *healthful* condition.

4. Salutary; promoting spiritual health. *Common Prayer.*

5. Well disposed; favorable.

A *healthful* ear to hear. [*Unusual.*] *Shak.*

HEALTH'FULLY, *adv.* In health; wholesomely.

HEALTH'FULNESS, *n.* A state of being well; a state in which the parts of a living body are sound, and regularly perform their functions.

2. Wholesomeness; salubrity; state or qualities that promote health; as the *healthfulness* of the air, or of climate, or of diet, or of exercises.

HEALTH'ILY, *a.* [See *Health.*] Without disease.

HEALTH'INESS, *n.* The state of health; soundness; freedom from disease; as the *healthiness* of an animal or plant.

HEALTH'LESS, *a.* Infirm; sickly.

2. Not conducive to health. [*Little used.*] *Taylor.*

HEALTH'SÔME, *a.* Wholesome. [*Not used.*] *Shak.*

HEALTH'Y, *a.* Being in a sound state; enjoying health; hale; sound; as a *healthy* body or constitution.

2. Conducive to health; wholesome; salubrious; as a *healthy* exercise; a *healthy* climate; *healthy* recreations. *Locke.*

HEAM, *n.* In beasts, the same as afterbirth in women. *Johnson. Todd.*

HEAP, *n.* [Sax. *heap, heop;* D. *hoop;* G. *haufe;* Sw. *hop;* Dan. *hob;* Russ. *kupa;* W. *cub*, a heap, what is put together, a bundle, a *cube.* See Class Gb. No. 1. 2. 3. 4. 5.]

1. A pile or mass; a collection of things laid in a body so as to form an elevation; as a *heap* of earth or stones.

Huge *heaps* of slain around the body rise. *Dryden.*

2. A crowd; a throng; a cluster; applied to living persons. [*Inelegant and not in use.*] *Bacon. Dryden.*

3. A mass of ruins.

Thou hast made of a city a *heap.* Is. xxv.

HEAP, *v. t.* [Sax. *heapian;* Sw. *hopa;* G. *häufen;* D. *hoopen.*]

1. To throw or lay in a heap; to pile; as, to *heap* stones; often with *up;* as, to *heap up* earth; or with *on;* as, to *heap on* wood or coal.

2. To amass; to accumulate; to lay up; to collect in great quantity; with *up;* as, to *heap up* treasures.

Though the wicked *heap up* silver as the dust— Job xxvii.

3. To add something else, in large quantities. *Shak.*

4. To pile; to add till the mass takes a roundish form, or till it rises above the measure; as, to *heap* any thing in measuring.

HE'APED, *pp.* Piled; amassed; accumulated.

HE'APER, *n.* One who heaps, piles or amasses.

HE'APING, *ppr.* Piling; collecting into a mass.

HE'APY, *a.* Lying in heaps; as *heapy* rubbish. *Gay.*

HEAR, *v. t.* pret. and pp. *heard*, but more correctly *heared.* [Sax. *heoran, hyran;* G. *hören;* D. *hooren;* Dan. *hörer;* Sw. *höra.* It seems to be from *ear*, L. *auris*, or from the same root. So L. *audio* seems to be connected with Gr. *ους.* The sense is probably to lend the ear, to turn or incline the ear, and *ear* is probably a shoot or extremity.]

1. To perceive by the ear; to feel an impression of sound by the proper organs; as, to *hear* sound; to *hear* a voice; to *hear* words.

2. To give audience or allowance to speak.

He sent for Paul, and *heard* him concerning the faith in Christ. Acts xxiv.

3. To attend; to listen; to obey.

To-day, if ye will *hear* his voice, harden not your heart. Ps. xcv.

4. To attend favorably; to regard.

They think they shall be *heard* for their much speaking. Matt. vi.

5. To grant an answer to prayer.

I love the Lord, because he hath *heard* my voice. Ps. cxvi.

6. To attend to the facts, evidence, and arguments in a cause between parties; to try in a court of law or equity. The cause was *heard* and determined at the last term; or, it was *heard* at the last term, and will be determined at the next. So 2 Sam. xv.

7. To acknowledge a title; *a Latin phrase.*

Hear'st thou submissive, but a lowly birth. *Prior.*

8. To be a hearer of; to sit under the preaching of; as, what minister do you *hear?* [*A colloquial use of the word.*]

9. To learn.

I speak to the world those things which I have *heard* of him. John viii.

10. To approve and embrace.

They speak of the world, and the world *heareth* them. 1 John iv.

To hear a bird sing, to receive private communication. *Shak.*

HEAR, *v. i.* To enjoy the sense or faculty of perceiving sound. He is deaf, he cannot *hear.*

2. To listen; to hearken; to attend. He *hears* with solicitude.

3. To be told; to receive by report.

I *hear* there are divisions among you, and I partly believe it. 1 Cor. xi.

HEARD, } *pp.* Perceived by the ear. [*In* HEARED, } *pronunciation, this word should not be confounded with* herd.]

HE'ARER, *n.* One who hears; one who attends to what is orally delivered by another; an auditor; one of an audience.

HE'ARING, *ppr.* Perceiving by the ear, as sound.

2. Listening to; attending to; obeying; observing what is commanded.

3. Attending to witnesses or advocates in a judicial trial; trying.

HE'ARING, *n.* The faculty or sense by which sound is perceived.

2. Audience; attention to what is delivered; opportunity to be heard. I waited on the minister, but could not obtain a *hearing.*

3. Judicial trial; attention to the facts, testimony and arguments in a cause between parties, with a view to a just decision.

4. The act of perceiving sounds; sensation or perception of sound.

I have heard of thee by the *hearing* of the ear. Job xlii.

And to the others he said in my *hearing.* Ezek. ix.

5. Reach of the ear; extent within which sound may be heard. He was not within *hearing.*

HE'ARKEN, *v. i.* *h'arken.* [Sax. *heorcnian, hyrcnian;* G. *horchen.*]

1. To listen; to lend the ear; to attend to what is uttered, with eagerness or curiosity.

The furies *hearken*, and their snakes uncurl. *Dryden.*

2. To attend; to regard; to give heed to what is uttered; to observe or obey.

Hearken, O Israel, to the statutes and the judgments which I teach you. Deut. iv.

3. To listen; to attend; to grant or comply with.

Hearken thou to the supplication of thy servant. 1 Kings viii.

HE'ARKEN, *v. t.* *h'arken.* To hear by listening. [*Little used.*]

HE'ARKENER, *n.* *h'arkener.* A listener; one who hearkens.

HE'ARKENING, *ppr.* *h'arkening.* Listening; attending; observing.

HEARSAL, for *Rehearsal.* [*Not in use.*] *Spenser.*

HE'ARSAY, *n.* [*hear* and *say.*] Report; rumor; fame; common talk. He affirms without any authority except *hearsay.* The account we have depends on *hearsay.* It is sometimes used as an adjective; as *hearsay* evidence.

HEARSE, *n.* *hers.* [See *Herse.*] A temporary monument set over a grave. *Weever.*

2. The case or place in which a corpse is deposited. *Fairfax.*

3. A carriage for conveying the dead to the grave. [See *Herse.*]

4. A hind in the second year of her age. *Encyc.*

HEARSE, *v. t.* *hers.* To inclose in a hearse. *Shak.*

HEARSECLOTH, *n.* *hers'cloth.* A pall; a cloth to cover a hearse. *Sanderson.*

HEARSELIKE, *a.* *hers'like.* Suitable to a funeral.

HEART, *n.* *h'art.* [Sax. *heort;* G. *herz;* D. *hart;* Sw. *hierta;* Dan. *hierte;* Gr. *καρδια;* Sans. *herda.* I know not the primary sense, nor whether it is from the root of *κεαρ*, L. *cor, cordis*, and allied to Eng. *core*, or named from motion, pulsation.]

1. A muscular viscus, which is the primary organ of the blood's motion in an animal body, situated in the thorax. From this organ all the arteries arise, and in it all the veins terminate. By its alternate dilatation and contraction, the blood is received from the veins, and returned through the arteries, by which means the circulation is carried on and life preserved.

2. The inner part of any thing; the middle part or interior; as the *heart* of a country, kingdom or empire; the *heart* of a town; the *heart* of a tree.

3. The chief part; the vital part; the vigorous or efficacious part. *Bacon.*

4. The seat of the affections and passions, as of love, joy, grief, enmity, courage, pleasure, &c.

The *heart* is deceitful above all things. Every imagination of the thoughts of the *heart* is evil continually. We read of an honest and good *heart*, and an evil *heart* of unbelief, a willing *heart*, a heavy *heart*, sorrow of *heart*, a hard *heart*, a proud *heart*, a pure *heart*. The *heart* faints in adversity, or under discouragement, that is, courage fails; the *heart* is deceived, enlarged, reproved, lifted up, fixed, established, moved, &c. *Scripture.*

5. By a metonymy, *heart* is used for an affection or passion, and particularly for love.

The king's *heart* was towards Absalom. 2 Sam. xiv.

6. The seat of the understanding; as an understanding *heart*. We read of men wise in *heart*, and slow of *heart*. *Scripture.*

7. The seat of the will; hence, secret purposes, intentions or designs. There are many devices in a man's *heart*. The *heart* of kings is unsearchable. The Lord tries and searches the *heart*. David had it in his *heart* to build a house of rest for the ark. *Scripture.*

Sometimes *heart* is used for the will, or determined purpose.

The *heart* of the sons of men is fully set in them to do evil. Eccles. viii.

8. Person; character; used with respect to courage or kindness.

Cheerly, my *hearts*. *Shak.*

9. Courage; spirit; as, to take *heart*; to give *heart*; to recover *heart*. *Spenser. Temple. Milton.*

10. Secret thoughts; recesses of the mind.

Michal saw king David leaping and dancing before the Lord, and she despised him in her *heart*. 2 Sam. vi.

11. Disposition of mind.

He had a *heart* to do well. *Sidney.*

12. Secret meaning; real intention.

And then show you the *heart* of my message. *Shak.*

13. Conscience, or sense of good or ill.

Every man's *heart* and conscience—doth either like or disallow it. *Hooker.*

14. Strength; power of producing; vigor; fertility. Keep the land in *heart*.

That the spent earth may gather *heart* again. *Dryden.*

15. The utmost degree.

This gay charm—hath beguiled me
To the very *heart* of loss. *Shak.*

To get or learn by heart, to commit to memory; to learn so perfectly as to be able to repeat without a copy.

To take to heart, to be much affected; also, to be zealous, ardent or solicitous about a thing; to have concern.

To lay to heart, is used nearly in the sense of the foregoing.

To set the heart on, to fix the desires on; to be very desirous of obtaining or keeping; to be very fond of.

To set the heart at rest, to make one's self quiet; to be tranquil or easy in mind.

To find in the heart, to be willing or disposed.

I *find it in my heart* to ask your pardon. *Sidney.*

For my heart, for tenderness or affection. I could not *for my heart* refuse his request.

Or, this phrase may signify, for my life; if my life was at stake.

I could not get him *for my heart* to do it. *Shak.*

To speak to one's heart, in Scripture, to speak kindly to; to comfort; to encourage.

To have in the heart, to purpose; to have design or intention.

A hard heart, cruelty; want of sensibility.

HE'ART, *v. i.* To encourage. [*Not much used.*] *Prideaux.*

HE'ART-ACH, *n.* Sorrow; anguish of mind. *Shak.*

HE'ART-ALLU'RING, *a.* Suited to allure the affections. *Parnell.*

HEART-APPALL'ING, *a.* Dismaying the heart.

HE'ART-BREAK, *n.* Overwhelming sorrow or grief. *Shak.*

HE'ART-BREAKER, *a.* A lady's curl; a love-lock.

HE'ART-BREAKING, *a.* Breaking the heart; overpowering with grief or sorrow. *Spenser.*

HE'ART-BREAKING, *n.* Overpowering grief; deep affliction. *Hakewill.*

HE'ART-BRED, *a.* Bred in the heart. *Crashaw.*

HE'ART-BROKEN, *a.* Deeply afflicted or grieved.

HE'ART-BURIED, *a.* Deeply immersed. *Young.*

HE'ART-BURN, *n.* Cardialgy; a disease or affection of the stomach, attended with a sensation of heat and uneasiness, and occasioned by indigestion, surfeit or acidity.

HE'ART-BURNED, *a.* Having the heart inflamed. *Shak.*

HE'ART-BURNING, *a.* Causing discontent. *Middleton.*

HE'ART-BURNING, *n.* Heart-burn, which see.

2. Discontent; secret enmity. *Swift.*

HE'ART-CHILLED, *a.* Having the heart chilled. *Shenstone.*

HE'ART-CONSU'MING, *a.* Destroying peace of mind.

HE'ART-CORRO'DING, *a.* Preying on the heart.

HE'ART-DEAR, *a.* Sincerely beloved. *Shak.*

HE'ART-DEEP, *a.* Rooted in the heart. *Herbert.*

HE'ART-DISCOUR'AGING, *a.* [See *Courage.*] Depressing the spirits. *South.*

HE'ART-EASE, *n.* Quiet; tranquillity of mind. *Shak.*

HE'ART-EASING, *a.* Giving quiet to the mind. *Milton.*

HE'ART-EATING, *a.* Preying on the heart. *Burton.*

HE'ART-EXPAND'ING, *a.* Enlarging the heart; opening the feelings. *Thomson.*

HE'ART-FELT, *a.* Deeply felt; deeply affecting, either as joy or sorrow.

HE'ART-GRIEF, *n.* Affliction of the heart. *Milton.*

HE'ART-HARDENED, *a.* Obdurate; impenitent; unfeeling. *Harmer.*

HE'ART-HARDENING, *a.* Rendering cruel or obdurate. *Shak.*

HE'ART-HEAVINESS, *n.* Depression of spirits. *Shak.*

HE'ART-OFFEND'ING, *a.* Wounding the heart. *Shak.*

HE'ART-PEA, *n.* A plant, the Cardiospermum, with black seeds, having the figure of a heart of a white color on each. *Miller.*

HE'ART-QUELLING, *a.* Conquering the affection. *Spenser.*

HE'ART-RENDING, *a.* Breaking the heart; overpowering with anguish; deeply afflictive. *Waller.*

HE'ART-ROBBING, *a.* Depriving of thought; ecstatic. *Spenser.*

2. Stealing the heart; winning. *Ibm.*

HE'ART'S-BLOOD, } *n.* The blood of the heart; life; essence. *Shak.*
HE'ART-BLOOD, }

HE'ART'S-EASE, *n.* A plant, a species of Viola.

HE'ART-SEARCHING, *a.* Searching the secret thoughts and purposes.

HE'ART-SICK, *a.* Sick at heart; pained in mind; deeply afflicted or depressed.

HE'ART-SORE, *n.* That which pains the heart. *Spenser.*

HE'ART-SORE, *a.* Deeply wounded. *Shak.*

HE'ART-SOR'ROWING, *a.* Sorrowing deeply in heart. *Shak.*

HE'ART-STRING, *n.* A nerve or tendon, supposed to brace and sustain the heart. *Shak. Taylor.*

HE'ART-STRUCK, *a.* Driven to the heart; infixed in the mind.

2. Shocked with fear; dismayed. *Milton.*

HE'ART-SWELLING, *a.* Rankling in the heart. *Spenser.*

HE'ART-WHOLE, *a.* [See *Whole.*] Not affected with love; not in love, or not deeply affected.

2. Having unbroken spirits, or good courage.

HE'ART-WOUNDED, *a.* Wounded with love or grief; deeply affected with some passion. *Pope.*

HE'ART-WOUNDING, *a.* Piercing with grief. *Rowe.*

HE'ARTED, *a.* Taken to heart. [*Not used.*] *Shak.*

2. Composed of hearts. [*Not used.*] *Shak.*

3. Laid up in the heart. *Shak.*

This word is chiefly used in composition, as *hard-hearted, faint-hearted, stout-hearted*, &c.

HE'ARTEN, *v. t.* *h'artn.* To encourage; to animate; to incite or stimulate courage. *Sidney.*

2. To restore fertility or strength to; as, to *hearten* land. [*Little used.*] *May.*

HE'ARTENER, *n.* He or that which gives courage or animation. *Brown.*

HE'ARTH, *n.* *harth.* [Sax. *heorth*; G. *herd*; D. *haard*; Sw. *hård.*] A pavement or floor of brick or stone in a chimney, on which a fire is made to warm a room, and from which there is a passage for the smoke to ascend.

HE'ARTH-MONEY, } *n.* A tax on hearths. *Blackstone.*
HE'ARTH-PENNY, }

HE'ARTILY, *adv.* [from *hearty.*] From the heart; with all the heart; with sincerity; really.

I *heartily* forgive them. *Shak.*

2. With zeal; actively; vigorously. He *heartily* assisted the prince.

3. Eagerly; freely; largely; as, to eat *heartily*.

HE'ARTINESS, *n.* Sincerity; zeal; ardor; earnestness.

2. Eagerness of appetite.

HE'ARTLESS, *a.* Without courage; spiritless; faint-hearted.

Heartless they fought, and quitted soon their ground. *Dryden.*

HE'ARTLESSLY, *adv.* Without courage or spirit; faintly; timidly; feebly.

HE'ARTLESSNESS, *n.* Want of courage or spirit; dejection of mind; feebleness. *Bp. Hall.*

HE'ARTY, *a.* Having the heart engaged in any thing; sincere; warm; zealous; as, to be *hearty* in support of government.

2. Proceeding from the heart; sincere; warm; as a *hearty* welcome.

3. Being full of health; sound; strong; healthy; as a *hearty* man.

4. Strong; durable; as *hearty* timber. [*Not used in America.*] *Wotton.*

5. Having a keen appetite; eating much; as a *hearty* eater.

6. Strong; nourishing; as *hearty* food.

HE'ARTY-HALE, *a.* Good for the heart. *Obs.* *Spenser.*

HEAT, *n.* [Sax. *heat, hæt;* D. *hitte;* G. *hitze;* Sw. *hetta;* D. *hede;* L. *æstus,* for *hæstus,* or *cæstus.* See the Verb.]

1. Heat, as a cause of sensation, that is, the matter of heat, is considered to be a subtil fluid, contained in a greater or less degree in all bodies. In modern chimistry, it is called *caloric.* It expands all bodies in different proportions, and is the cause of fluidity and evaporation. A certain degree of it is also essential to animal and vegetable life. Heat is *latent,* when so combined with other matter as not to be perceptible. It is *sensible,* when it is evolved and perceptible. *Lavoisier. Encyc.*

2. Heat, as a sensation, is the effect produced on the sentient organs of animals, by the passage of caloric, disengaged from surrounding bodies, to the organs. When we touch or approach a hot body, the caloric or heat passes *from* that body *to* our organs of feeling, and gives the sensation of heat. On the contrary, when we touch a cold body, the caloric passes *from* the hand *to* that body, and causes a sensation of cold. *Lavoisier.*

Note. This theory of heat seems not to be fully settled.

3. Hot air; hot weather; as the *heat* of the tropical climates.

4. Any accumulation or concentration of the matter of heat or caloric; as the *heat* of the body; the *heat* of a furnace; a red *heat;* a white *heat;* a welding *heat.*

5. The state of being once heated or hot. Give the iron another *heat.*

6. A violent action unintermitted; a single effort.

Many causes are required for refreshment between the *heats.* *Dryden.*

7. A single effort in running; a course at a race. Hector won at the first *heat.*

8. Redness of the face; flush. *Addison.*

9. Animal excitement; violent action or agitation of the system. The body is all in a *heat.*

10. Utmost violence; rage; vehemence; as the *heat* of battle.

11. Violence; ardor; as the *heat* of party.

12. Agitation of mind; inflammation or excitement; exasperation; as the *heat* of passion.

13. Ardor; fervency; animation in thought or discourse.

With all the strength and *heat* of eloquence. *Addison.*

14. Fermentation.

HEAT, *v. t.* [Sax. *hatan,* to call, to order, command or promise; *gehatan,* to call, to promise, to grow warm; *hætan,* to heat, to command, to call; *gehætan,* to promise; *hæse,* order, command; *behæs,* a vow; *behætan,* to vow; *onhætan,* to heat, to inflame; *hatian,* to heat, to be hot, to boil, to *hate; hæt, heat,* heat; *hat,* hot; *hate,* hatred, hate; L. *odi, osus,* for *hodi, hosus;* Goth. *hatyan,* to hate; *haitan, gahaitan,* to call, to command, to vow or promise; G. *heiss,* hot; *heissen,* to call; *heitzen,* to heat; *hitze,* heat, ardor, vehemence; *geheiss,* command; *verheissen,* to promise; *hass,* hate; *hassen,* to hate; D. *heet,* hot, eager, hasty; *hitte,* heat; *heeten,* to heat, to name or call, to be called, to command; *haat,* hate; *haaten,* to hate; *verhitten,* to inflame; Sw. *het,* hot; *hetta,* heat, passion; *hetta,* to be hot, to glow; *heta,* to be called or named; *hat,* hate, hatred; *hata,* to hate; Dan. *heed,* hot; *hede,* heat, ardor; *heder,* to heat, to be called or named; *had,* hate; *hader,* to hate. With these words coincides the L. *æstus,* for *hæstus,* heat, tide, Gr. *αιθω,* to burn, and the English *haste* and *hoist* are probably of the same family. The primary and literal sense of all these words, is to stir, to rouse, to raise, to agitate, from the action of driving, urging, stimulating, whence Sw. *hetsa,* Dan. *hedser,* to excite, to set on dogs. See Class Gd. No. 39, and others. It may be further added, that in W. *câs* is hatred, a *castle,* from the sense of separating; *casau,* to hate; and if this is of the same family, it unites *castle* with the foregoing words. In these words we see the sense of repulsion.]

1. To make hot; to communicate heat to, or cause to be hot; as, to *heat* an oven or a furnace; to *heat* iron.

2. To make feverish; as, to *heat* the blood.

3. To warm with passion or desire; to excite; to rouse into action.

A noble emulation *heats* your breast. *Dryden.*

4. To agitate the blood and spirits with action; to excite animal action. *Dryden.*

HEAT, *v. i.* To grow warm or hot by fermentation, or extrication of latent heat. Green hay *heats* in a mow, and green corn in a bin.

2. To grow warm or hot. The iron or the water *heats* slowly.

HEAT, for *heated,* is in popular use and pronounced *het;* but it is not elegant.

HE'ATED, *pp.* Made hot; inflamed; exasperated.

HE'ATER, *n.* He or that which heats.

2. A triangular mass of iron, which is heated and put into a box-iron to heat it and keep it hot, for ironing or smoothing clothes. [*This utensil is going into disuse.*]

HEATH, *n.* [Sax. *hæth;* D. and G. *heide;* Dan. *hede;* Sw. *hed;* Scot. *haddyr;* W. *eiziar,* connected with *eiziaw,* to take to or possess; the clinging plant.]

1. A plant of the genus Erica, of many species. It is a shrub which is used in Great Britain for brooms, thatch, beds for the poor, and for heating ovens. Its leaves are small and continue green all the year. It is called also *ling.* *Miller. Encyc.*

2. A place overgrown with heath. *Temple.*

3. A place overgrown with shrubs of any kind. *Bacon.*

HE'ATHCOCK, *n.* A large fowl which frequents heaths, a species of grouse. *Carew.*

HE'ATHPEA, *n.* A species of bitter vetch, Orobus. *Johnson.*

HE'ATHPOUT, *n.* A bird, the same as the heath-cock. *Ed. Encyc.*

HE'ATHROSE, *n.* A plant. *Ainsworth.*

HE'ATHEN, *n.* [Sax. *hæthen;* G. *heide,* heath, and a heathen or pagan; D. *heiden;* Dan. Sw. *hedning;* Gr. *εθνος;* from *heath,* that is, one who lives in the country or woods, as *pagan* from *pagus,* a village.]

1. A pagan; a Gentile; one who worships idols, or is unacquainted with the true God. In the Scriptures, the word seems to comprehend all nations except the Jews or Israelites, as they were all strangers to the true religion, and all addicted to idolatry. The word may now be applied perhaps to all nations, except to Christians and Mohammedans.

Heathen, without the plural termination, is used plurally or collectively, for Gentiles or heathen nations.

Ask of me, and I will give thee the *heathen* for thine inheritance. Ps. ii.

Heathen, however, has a plural, expressing two or more individuals.

If men have reason to be *heathens* in Japan— *Locke.*

The precepts and examples of the ancient *heathens.* *Addison.*

2. A rude, illiterate, barbarous person.

HE'ATHEN, *a.* Gentile; pagan; as a *heathen* author. *Addison.*

HE'ATHENISH, *a.* Belonging to Gentiles or pagans; as *heathenish* rites.

2. Rude; illiterate; wild; uncivilized.

3. Barbarous; savage; cruel; rapacious. *Spenser.*

HE'ATHENISHLY, *adv.* After the manner of heathens.

HE'ATHENISM, *n.* Gentilism; paganism; ignorance of the true God; idolatry; the rites or system of religion of a pagan nation. *Hammond.*

2. Rudeness; barbarism; ignorance.

HE'ATHENIZE, *v. t.* To render heathen or heathenish. *Firmin.*

HE'ATHER, *n.* Heath.

HE'ATHY, *a.* [from *heath.*] Full of heath; abounding with heath; as *heathy* land. *Mortimer.*

HE'ATING, *ppr.* Making warm or hot; inflaming; rousing the passions; exasperating.

2. *a.* Tending to impart heat to; promoting warmth or heat; exciting action; stimulating; as *heating* medicines or applications.

HEAT'LESS, *a.* Destitute of heat; cold. *Beaum.*

HEAVE, *v. t.* *heev.* pret. *heaved,* or *hove;* pp. *heaved, hove,* formerly *hoven.* [Sax. *heafan, hefan, heofan;* Goth. *hafyan;* Sw. *häfva;* D. *heffen;* G. *heben;* Dan. *hæver,* to heave; Gr. *καφεω,* to breathe; *καπυω,* *id.* Class Gb.]

1. To lift; to raise; to move upward.

So stretch'd out huge in length the arch fiend lay,
Chain'd on the burning lake, nor ever hence
Had ris'n, or *heaved* his head. *Milton.*

2. To cause to swell.

The glittering finny swarms
That *heave* our friths and crowd upon our shores. *Thomson.*

3. To raise or force from the breast; as, to *heave* a sigh or groan, which is accompanied with a swelling or expansion of the thorax.
4. To raise; to elevate; with *high*.

One *heaved* on *high*. *Shak.*

5. To puff; to elate. *Hayward.*
6. To throw; to cast; to send; as, to *heave* a stone. This is a common use of the word in popular language, and among seamen; as, to *heave* the lead.
7. To raise by turning a windlass; with *up;* as, to *heave up* the anchor. Hence,
8. To turn a windlass or capstern with bars or levers. Hence the order, to *heave away.*

To heave ahead, to draw a ship forwards.
To heave astern, to cause to recede; to draw back.
To heave down, to throw or lay down on one side; to careen.
To heave out, to throw out. With *seamen*, to loose or unfurl a sail, particularly the stay-sails.
To heave in stays, in tacking, to bring a ship's head to the wind.
To heave short, to draw so much of a cable into the ship, as that she is almost perpendicularly above the anchor.
To heave a strain, to work at the windlass with unusual exertion.
To heave taught, to turn a capstern, &c. till the rope becomes straight. [See *Taught* and *Tight*.]
To heave to, to bring the ship's head to the wind, and stop her motion.
To heave up, to relinquish; [so to *throw up*;] as, to *heave up* a design. [*Vulgar*.]

HEAVE, *v. i. heev.* To swell, distend or dilate; as, a horse *heaves* in panting. Hence,

2. To pant; to breathe with labor or pain; as, he *heaves* for breath. *Dryden.*
3. To keck; to make an effort to vomit.
4. To rise in billows, as the sea; to swell.
5. To rise; to be lifted; as, a ship *heaves.*
6. To rise or swell, as the earth at the breaking up of frost.

To heave in sight, to appear; to make its first appearance; as a ship at sea, or as a distant object approaching or being approached.

We observe that this verb has often the sense of raising or rising in an arch or circular form, as in throwing and in distention, and from this sense is derived its application to the apparent arch over our heads, *heaven.*

HEAVE, *n. heev.* A rising or swell; an exertion or effort upward.

None could guess whether the next *heave* of the earthquake would settle or swallow them. *Dryden.*

2. A rising swell, or distention, as of the breast.

These profound *heaves.* *Shak.*

3. An effort to vomit.
4. An effort to rise. *Hudibras.*

HEAVEN, *n. hev'n.* [Sax. *heafen, hefen, heofen*, from *heafan*, to heave, and signifying elevated or arched.]

1. The region or expanse which surrounds the earth, and which appears above and around us, like an immense arch or vault, in which are seen the sun, moon and stars.
2. Among *christians*, the part of space in which the omnipresent Jehovah is supposed to afford more sensible manifestations of his glory. Hence this is called the habitation of God, and is represented as the residence of angels and blessed spirits. Deut. xxvi.

The sanctified heart loves *heaven* for its purity, and God for his goodness. *Buckminster.*

3. Among *pagans*, the residence of the celestial gods.
4. The sky or air; the region of the atmosphere; or an elevated place; *in a very indefinite sense.* Thus we speak of a mountain reaching to *heaven*; the fowls of *heaven;* the clouds of *heaven;* hail or rain from *heaven.* Jer. ix. Job xxxv.

Their cities are walled to *heaven.* Deut. i.

5. The Hebrews acknowledged three heavens; the air or aerial heavens; the firmament in which the stars are supposed to be placed; and the heaven of heavens, or third heaven, the residence of Jehovah. *Brown.*
6. Modern philosophers divide the expanse above and around the earth into two parts, the atmosphere or aerial heaven, and the etherial heaven beyond the region of the air, in which there is supposed to be a thin, unresisting medium called ether. *Encyc.*
7. The Supreme Power; the Sovereign of heaven; God; as prophets sent by *heaven.*

I have sinned against *heaven.* Luke xv.
Shun the impious profaneness which scoffs at the institutions of *heaven.* *Dwight.*

8. The pagan deities; celestials.

And show the *heavens* more just. *Shak.*

9. Elevation; sublimity.

O! for a muse of fire, that would ascend
The brightest *heaven* of invention. *Shak.*

10. Supreme felicity; great happiness.

HEAVEN-ASPI'RING, *a.* Aspiring to heaven. *Akenside.*

HEAV'EN-BANISHED, *a.* Banished from heaven. *Milton.*

HEAVEN-BEGOT', *a.* Begot by a celestial being. *Dryden.*

HEAV'EN-BORN, *a.* Born from heaven; native of heaven, or of the celestial regions; as *heaven-born* sisters. *Pope.*

HEAV'EN-BRED, *a.* Produced or cultivated in heaven; as *heaven-bred* poesy. *Shak.*

HEAV'EN-BUILT, *a.* Built by the agency or favor of the gods; as a *heaven-built* wall. *Pope.*

HEAVEN-DIRECT'ED, *a.* Pointing to the sky; as a *heaven-directed* spire. *Pope.*

2. Taught or directed by the celestial powers; as *heaven-directed* hands. *Pope.*

HEAV'EN-FALLEN, *a.* Fallen from heaven; having revolted from God. *Milton.*

HEAV'EN-GIFTED, *a.* Bestowed by heaven. *Milton.*

HEAVEN-INSPI'RED, *a.* Inspired by heaven. *Milton.*

HEAVEN-INSTRUCT'ED, *a.* Taught by heaven. *Crashaw.*

HEAVENIZE, *v. t. hev'nize.* To render like heaven. [*Unauthorized.*] *Bp. Hall.*

HEAV'EN-KISSING, *a.* Touching as it were the sky. *Shak.*

HEAV'ENLINESS, *n.* [from *heavenly.*] Supreme excellence. *Davies.*

HEAV'EN-LOVED, *a.* Beloved by heaven. *Milton.*

HEAV'ENLY, *a.* Pertaining to heaven; celestial; as *heavenly* regions; *heavenly* bliss.

2. Resembling heaven; supremely excellent; as a *heavenly* lyre; a *heavenly* temper.

The love of heaven makes one *heavenly.* *Sidney.*

3. Inhabiting heaven; as a *heavenly* race; the *heavenly* throng.

HEAV'ENLY, *adv.* In a manner resembling that of heaven.

Where *heavenly* pensive contemplation dwells. *Pope.*

2. By the influence or agency of heaven.

Our *heavenly* guided soul shall climb. *Milton.*

HEAVENLY-MINDED, *a.* Having the affections placed on heaven, and on spiritual things. *Milner.*

HEAVENLY-MINDEDNESS, *n.* The state of having the affections placed on heavenly things and spiritual objects. *Milner.*

HEAVEN-SALU'TING, *a.* Touching the sky. *Crashaw.*

HEAV'ENWARD, *adv.* Toward heaven. *Prior.*

HEAV'EN-WARRING, *a.* Warring against heaven. *Milton.*

HE'AVE-OFFERING, *n.* Among the Jews, an offering consisting of the tenth of the tithes which the Levites received, or of the first of the dough, &c. which was to be heaved or elevated. Num. xv. and xviii.

HE'AVER, *n.* One who heaves or lifts. Among *seamen*, a staff for a lever.

HEAVES, *n. heevz.* A disease of horses, characterized by difficult and laborious respiration.

HEAV'ILY, *adv. hev'ily.* [from *heavy.*] With great weight; as, to bear *heavily* on a thing; to be *heavily* loaded.

2. With great weight of grief; grievously; afflictively. When calamities fall *heavily* on the christian, he finds consolation in Christ.
3. Sorrowfully; with grief.

I came hither to transport the tidings,
Which I have *heavily* borne. *Shak.*

4. With an air of sorrow or dejection.

Why looks your Grace so *heavily* to day? *Shak.*

5. With weight; oppressively. Taxes sometimes bear *heavily* on the people.
6. Slowly and laboriously; with difficulty; as, to move *heavily.*

So they drove them *heavily.* Ex. xiv.

HEAV'INESS, *n. hev'iness.* Weight; ponderousness; gravity; the quality of being heavy; as the *heaviness* of a body.

2. Sadness; sorrow; dejection of mind; depression of spirits.

Heaviness in the heart of man maketh it stoop. Prov. xii.

Ye greatly rejoice, though now for a season ye are in *heaviness*, through manifold temptations. 1 Pet. i.

3. Sluggishness; torpidness; dullness of spirit; languidness; languor; lassitude.

What means this *heaviness* that hangs upon me? *Addison.*

5. Weight; burden; oppression; as, the *heaviness* of taxes.

6. That which it requires great strength to move or overcome; that which creates labor and difficulty; as the *heaviness* of a draught.

7. Thickness; moistness; deepness; as the *heaviness* of ground or soil.

8. Thickness; moistness; as of air.

HE'AVING, *ppr.* Lifting; swelling; throwing; panting; making an effort to vomit.

HE'AVING, *n.* A rising or swell; a panting. *Addison. Shak.*

HEAV'Y, *a.* *hev'y.* [Sax. *heafig*, *hefig*, that is, *lift-like*, lifted with labor, from *heafan*, to heave.]

1. Weighty; ponderous; having great weight; tending strongly to the center of attraction; contrary to *light; applied to material bodies;* as a *heavy* stone; a *heavy* load.

2. Sad; sorrowful; dejected; depressed in mind.

A light wife makes a *heavy* husband. *Shak.*
So is he that singeth songs to a *heavy* heart. Prov. xxv.

3. Grievous; afflictive; depressing to the spirits; as *heavy* news; a *heavy* calamity.

4. Burdensome; oppressive; as *heavy* taxes.

Make thy father's *heavy* yoke—lighter. 1 Kings xii.

5. Wanting life and animation; dull.

My *heavy* eyes you say confess
A heart to love and grief inclined. *Prior.*

6. Drowsy; dull.

Their eyes were *heavy.* Matt. xxvi. Luke ix.

7. Wanting spirit or animation; destitute of life or rapidity of sentiment; dull; as a *heavy* writer; a *heavy* style.

8. Wanting activity or vivacity; indolent.

But of a *heavy*, dull, degenerate mind. *Dryden.*

9. Slow; sluggish. He walks with a *heavy* gait.

10. Burdensome; tedious; as *heavy* hours. Time lies *heavy* on him who has no employment.

11. Loaded; encumbered; burdened.

He found his men *heavy*, and laden with booty. *Bacon.*

12. Lying with weight on the stomach; not easily digested; as, oily food is *heavy* to the stomach.

13. Moist; deep; soft; miry; as *heavy* land; a *heavy* soil. We apply *heavy* to soft loamy or clayey land, which makes the draught of a plow or wagon difficult and laborious. So we say, a *heavy* road.

14. Difficult; laborious; as a heavy *draught.*

15. Weary; supported with pain or difficulty.

And the hands of Moses were *heavy.* Ex. xvii.

16. Inflicting severe evils, punishments or judgments.

The hand of the Lord was *heavy* on them of Ashdod. I Sam. v.

17. Burdensome; occasioning great care.

This thing is too *heavy* for thee. Ex. xviii.

18. Dull; not hearing; inattentive.

Neither his ears *heavy*, that he cannot hear. Is. lix.

19. Large, as billows; swelling and rolling with great force; as a *heavy* sea.

20. Large in amount; as a *heavy* expense; a *heavy* debt.

21. Thick; dense; black; as a *heavy* cloud.

22. Violent; tempestuous; as a *heavy* wind or gale.

23. Large; abundant; as a *heavy* fall of snow or rain.

24. Great; violent; forcible; as a *heavy* fire of cannon or small arms.

25. Not raised by leaven or fermentation; not light; clammy; as *heavy* bread.

26. Requiring much labor or much expense; as a *heavy* undertaking.

27. Loud; as *heavy* thunder.

Heavy metal, in *military affairs*, signifies large guns, carrying balls of a large size, or it is applied to large balls themselves.

HEAVY, *adv.* *hev'y.* With great weight; *used in composition.*

HEAVY, *v. t.* *hev'y.* To make heavy. [*Not in use.*] *Wickliffe.*

HEAV'Y-HANDED, *a.* Clumsy; not active or dextrous.

HEAVY-LA'DEN, *a.* Laden with a heavy burden.

HEAVY SPAR, *n.* [See *Baryte.*] A genus of minerals of four species, viz. rhomboidal, prismatic, di-prismatic and axifrangible. *Jameson.*

HEB'DOMAD, *n.* [Gr. εβδομας, seven days, from επτα, seven; L. *hebdomada.*]

A week; a period of seven days. [*Not used.*] *Brown.*

HEBDOM'ADAL, } *a.* Weekly; consisting of seven days,
HEBDOM'ADARY, } or occurring every seven days. *Brown.*

HEBDOM'ADARY, *n.* A member of a chapter or convent, whose week it is to officiate in the choir, rehearse the anthems and prayers, and perform other services, which on extraordinary occasions are performed by the superiors.

HEBDOMAT'ICAL, *a.* Weekly. *Bp. Morton.*

HEB'EN, *n.* Ebony. *Spenser.*

HEB'ETATE, *v. t.* [L. *hebeto*, from *hebes*, dull, blunt, heavy.]

To dull; to blunt; to stupefy; as, to *hebetate* the intellectual faculties. *Arbuthnot.*

HEB'ETATED, *ppr.* Made blunt, dull or stupid.

HEB'ETATING, *pp.* Rendering blunt, dull or stupid.

HEBETA'TION, *n.* The act of making blunt, dull or stupid.

2. The state of being dulled.

HEBE'TE, *a.* Dull; stupid. *Obs.*

HEB'ETUDE, *n.* [L. *hebetudo.*] Dullness; stupidity. *Harvey.*

HEBRA'IC, *a.* [from *Hebrew.*] Pertaining to the Hebrews; designating the language of the Hebrews.

HEBRA'ICALLY, *adv.* After the manner of the Hebrew language; from right to left. *Swift.*

HE'BRAISM, *n.* A Hebrew idiom; a peculiar expression or manner of speaking in the Hebrew language.

HE'BRAIST, *n.* One versed in the Hebrew language.

HE'BRAIZE, *v. t.* To convert into the Hebrew idiom; to make Hebrew. *J. P. Smith.*

HE'BRAIZE, *v. i.* To speak Hebrew, or to conform to the Hebrews.

HE'BREW, *n.* [Heb. עבר Eber, either a proper name, or a name denoting passage, pilgrimage, or coming from beyond the Euphrates.]

One of the descendants of Eber, or Heber; but particularly, a descendant of Jacob, who was a descendant of Eber; an Israelite; a Jew.

2. The Hebrew language.

HE'BREW, *a.* Pertaining to the Hebrews; as the Hebrew language or rites.

HE'BREWESS, *n.* An Israelitish woman.

HEBRI''CIAN, *n.* One skilled in the Hebrew language.

HEBRID'IAN, *a.* Pertaining to the isles called Hebrides, west of Scotland. *Johnson.*

HEC'ATOMB, *n.* [L. *hecatombe;* Gr. εκατομβη; εκατον, a hundred, and βους, an ox.]

In *antiquity*, a sacrifice of a hundred oxen or beasts of the same kind, and it is said, at a hundred altars, and by a hundred priests. *Encyc.*

HECK, *n.* [See *Hatch.*] An engine or instrument for catching fish; as a salmon *heck.* *Chambers.*

2. A rack for holding fodder for cattle. [*Local.*] *Ray.*

3. A bend in a stream. [G. *ecke*, a corner.]

4. A hatch or latch of a door. [*Local.*] *Grose.*

HECK'LE, *v. t.* A different orthography of *hackle*, or *hetchel.*

HEC'TARE, *n.* [Gr. εκατον, a hundred, and L. *area.*]

A French measure containing a hundred *ares*, or ten thousand square meters. *Lunier.*

HEC'TIC, } *a.* [Gr. εκτικος, from εξις, ha-
HEC'TICAL, } bit of body, from εχω, to have.]

Habitual; denoting a slow, continual fever, marked by preternatural, though remitting heat, which precedes and accompanies the consumption or phthisis; as a *hectic* fever. *Encyc.*

2. Affected with hectic fevers; as a *hectic* patient.

3. Troubled with a morbid heat.

No *hectic* student scares the gentle maid. *Taylor.*

HEC'TIC, *n.* A hectic, or habitual fever. *Shak.*

HEC'TICALLY, *adv.* Constitutionally. *Johnson.*

HEC'TOGRAM, *n.* [Gr. εκατον, a hundred, and γραμμα, a gram.]

In the French system of weights and measures, a weight containing a hundred grams; equal to 3 ounces, 2 gros, and 12 grains, French. *Lunier.*

HEC'TOLITER, *n.* [Gr. εκατον, a hundred, and λιτρα, a pound.]

A French measure of capacity for liquids, containing a hundred liters; equal to a tenth of a cubic meter, or 107 Paris pints.

As a dry measure, it is called a *setier*, and contains 10 decaliters or bushels [*boisseaux.*] *Lunier.*

HECTOM'ETER, *n.* [Gr. εκατον, a hundred, and μετρον, measure.]

A French measure equal to a hundred meters; the meter being the unit of lineal measure. It is equivalent nearly to 308 French feet. *Lunier.*

HEC'TOR, *n.* [from *Hector*, the son of Priam, a brave Trojan warrior.]

1. A bully; a blustering, turbulent, noisy fellow.
2. One who teases or vexes.

HEC'TOR, *v. t.* To threaten; to bully; to treat with insolence. *Dryden.*

2. To tease; to vex; to torment by words.

HEC'TOR, *v. i.* To play the bully; to bluster; to be turbulent or insolent. *Swift.*

HEC'TORED, *pp.* Bullied; teased.

HEC'TORING, *ppr.* Bullying; blustering; vexing.

HEC'TORISM, *n.* The disposition or practice of a hector; a bullying. *Ch. Relig. Appeal.*

HEC'TORLY, *a.* Blustering; insolent. *Barrow.*

HEDENBERG'ITE, *n.* [from *Hedenberg*, who first analysed it.]

A mineral, or ore of iron, in masses, composed of shining plates, which break into rhombic fragments; found at Tunaborg, in Sweden. *Cleaveland.*

HEDERA'CEOUS, *a.* [L. *hederaceus*, from *hedera*, ivy; W. *eizaw*, ivy, from holding, clinging; *eiziaw*, to possess. See *Heath.*]

1. Pertaining to ivy.
2. Producing ivy.

HED'ERAL, *a.* Composed of ivy; belonging to ivy. *Bailey.*

HEDERIF'EROUS, *a.* [L. *hedera*, ivy, and *fero*, to bear.] Producing ivy.

HEDĠE, *n. hej.* [Sax. *hege*, *heag*, *hæg*, *hegge*; G. *heck*; D. *heg*, *haag*; Dan. *hekke* or *hek*; Sw. *hågn*, hedge, protection; Fr. *haie*; W. *cae*. Hence Eng. *haw*, and *Hague* in Holland. Ar. حاج a species of thorny plant.]

Properly, a thicket of thorn-bushes or other shrubs or small trees; but appropriately, such a thicket planted round a field to fence it, or in rows, to separate the parts of a garden.

Hedge, prefixed to another word, or in composition, denotes something mean, as a *hedge*-priest, a *hedge*-press, a *hedge*-vicar, that is, born in or belonging to the *hedges* or woods, low, outlandish. [*Not used in America.*]

HEDĠE, *v. t. hej.* To inclose with a hedge; to fence with a thicket of shrubs or small trees; to separate by a hedge; as, to *hedge* a field or garden.

2. To obstruct with a hedge, or to obstruct in any manner.

> I will *hedge* up thy way with thorns. Hos. ii.

3. To surround for defense; to fortify.

> England *hedged* in with the main. *Shak.*

4. To inclose for preventing escape.

> That is a law to *hedge* in the cuckow. *Locke.*

Dryden, Swift and Shakspeare have written *hedge* for *edge*, to *edge in*, but improperly.

HEDĠE, *v. i. hej.* To hide, as in a hedge; to hide; to skulk. *Shak.*

HEDĠE-BILL, } *n.* A cutting hook used
HEDĠING-BILL, } in dressing hedges.

HEDĠE-BORN, *a.* Of low birth, as if born in the woods; outlandish; obscure. *Shak.*

HEDĠE-BOTE, *n.* Wood for repairing hedges. *Blackstone.*

HEDĠE-CREEPER, *n.* One who skulks under hedges for bad purposes.

HEDĠE-FU'MITORY, *n.* A plant. *Ainsworth.*

HEDĠEHOG, *n.* A quadruped, or genus of quadrupeds, the Erinaceus. The common hedgehog has round ears, and crested nostrils; his body is about nine inches long, and the upper part is covered with prickles or spines, and the under part with hair. When attacked, this animal erects his prickles and rolls himself into a round form, which presents the points of the prickles on all sides to an assailant. *Encyc.*

2. A term of reproach. *Shak.*
3. A plant of the genus Medicago, or snail-trefoil. The seeds are shaped like a snail, downy, and armed with a few short spines. *Encyc.*
4. The globe-fish, *orbis echinatus.* *Ainsworth.*

This fish belongs to the genus Diodon. It is covered with long spines, and has the power of inflating its body, whence the name *globe-fish* [Fr. *orbe.*] *Cuvier.*

The *Sea-hedgehog*, is the Echinus, a genus of Zoophytes, generally of a spheroidal or oval form, and covered with movable spines. *Cuvier. Cyc.*

HEDĠEHOG-THISTLE, *n.* A plant, the Cactus. *Fam. of Plants.*

HEDĠE-HYSSOP, *n.* A plant, the Gratiola.

HEDĠE-MUSTARD, *n.* A plant, the Erysimum.

HEDĠE-NETTLE, *n.* A plant, the Galeopsis. The *shrubby hedge-nettle* is of the genus Prasium.

HEDĠE-NOTE, *a.* A term of contempt for low writing. *Dryden.*

HEDĠEPIG, *n.* A young hedgehog. *Shak.*

HEDĠEROW, *n.* A row or series of shrubs or trees planted for inclosure, or separation of fields. *Milton.*

HEDĠE-SPARROW, *n.* A bird of the genus Motacilla, frequenting hedges; distinguished from the sparrow that builds in thatch. *Encyc. Johnson.*

HEDĠE-WRITER, *n.* A Grub-street writer or low author. *Swift.*

HEDĠ'ER, *n.* One who makes hedges.

HEDĠ'ING, *ppr.* Inclosing with a hedge; obstructing; confining.

HEED, *v. t.* [Sax. *hedan*; G. *hüten*; D. *hoeden*; Gr. κηδεω; Sp. and Port. *cuidar.*]

To mind; to regard with care; to take notice of; to attend to; to observe.

> With pleasure Argus the musician *heeds.* *Dryden.*

HEED, *n.* Care; attention.

> With wanton *heed* and giddy cunning. *Milton.*

2. Caution; care; watch for danger; notice; circumspection; usually preceded by *take.*

Take heed of evil company. *Take heed* to your ways.

> Amasa *took* no *heed* to the sword that was in Joab's hand. 2 Sam. xx.

3. Notice; observation; regard; attention; often preceded by *give.*

> The preacher *gave* good *heed.* Eccles. xii.
> Neither *give heed* to fables. 1 Tim. i.
> Therefore we ought to *give* the more earnest *heed.* Heb. ii.

4. Seriousness; a steady look.

> A *heed*
> Was in his countenance. [*Unusual.*] *Shak.*

HEE'DED, *pp.* Noticed; observed; regarded.

HEE'DFUL, *a.* Attentive; observing; giving heed; as *heedful* of advice. *Pope.*

2. Watchful; cautious; circumspect; wary.

HEE'DFULLY, *adv.* Attentively; carefully; cautiously. Listen *heedfully* to good advice.

2. Watchfully.

HEE'DFULNESS, *n.* Attention; caution; vigilance; circumspection; care to guard against danger, or to perform duty.

HEE'DLESS, *a.* Inattentive; careless; negligent of the means of safety; thoughtless; regardless; unobserving. We say, *heedless* children; *heedless* of danger or surprise.

> The *heedless* lover does not know,
> Whose eyes they are that wound him so. *Waller.*

HEE'DLESSLY, *adv.* Carelessly; negligently; inattentively; without care or circumspection. *Brown.*

HEE'DLESSNESS, *n.* Inattention; carelessness; thoughtlessness; negligence. *Locke.*

HEEL, *n.* [Sax. *hel*, *hela*; D. *hiel*; Sw. *hål*; Dan. *hæl*; L. *calx*. Qu. its alliance to Gr. κηλη, a tumor.]

1. The hind part of the foot, particularly of man; but it is applied also to the corresponding part of the feet of quadrupeds.
2. The whole foot.

> The stag recalls his strength, his speed,
> His winged *heels*— *Denham.*

3. The hind part of a shoe, either for man or beast.
4. The part of a stocking intended for the heel.

To be out at the heels, is to have on stockings that are worn out.

5. Something shaped like the human heel; a protuberance or knob. *Mortimer.*
6. The latter part; as, a bill was introduced into the legislature at the *heel* of the session.
7. A spur.

> This horse understands the *heel* well. *Encyc.*

8. The after end of a ship's keel; the lower end of the stern-post to which it is connected; also, the lower end of a mast.

To be at the heels, to pursue closely; to follow hard; also, to attend closely.

> Hungry want is *at* my *heels.* *Otway.*

To show the heels, to flee; to run from.

To take to the heels, to flee; to betake to flight.

To lay by the heels, to fetter; to shackle; to confine. *Addison.*

To have the heels of, to outrun.

Neck and heels, the whole length of the body.

HEEL, *v. i.* To dance. *Shak.*

HEEL, *v. t.* To arm a cock. *Johnson.*

2. To add a heel to; as, to *heel* a shoe.

HEEL, *v. i.* [Sax. *hyldan*, to lean or incline; D. *hellen*; Dan. *helder*; Sw. *hålla*, to tilt.]

To incline; to lean; as a ship; as, the ship *heels* a-port, or a-starboard. *Encyc.*

HEE'LER, *n.* A cock that strikes well with his heels.

HEE'L-PIECE, *n.* Armor for the heels. *Chesterfield.*

2. A piece of lether on the heel of a shoe.

HEFT, *n.* [Sax. *hefe*, from *hefan*, to heave, to lift.]

1. Heaving; effort.

He cracks his gorge, his sides,
With violent *hefts*. [*Not used.*] *Shak.*

2. Weight; ponderousness. [This use is common in popular language in America. And we sometimes hear it used as a verb, as, to *heft*, to lift for the purpose of feeling or judging of the weight.]

3. [D. *heft.*] A handle; a haft. [*Not used.*] *Waller.*

HEFT'ED, *a.* Heaved; expressing agitation. *Shak.*

HEĠI'RA, *n.* [Ar. from هجر hajara, to remove, to desert.]

In *chronology*, an epoch among the Mohammedans, from which they compute time. The event which gave rise to it was the flight of Mohammed from Mecca; from which the magistrates, fearing his impostures might raise a sedition, expelled him, July 10, A. D. 622, under the reign of the emperor Heraclius. *Harris. Encyc.*

HEIF'ER, *n.* *hef'er.* [Sax. *heafre*, *heahfore*, *heafore.* Qu. Heb. פרה.]

A young cow. *Pope.*

HEIGH-HO. *hi-ho.* An exclamation expressing some degree of languor or uneasiness. Dryden has used it for the voice of exultation.

HEIGHT, **HIGHTH**, **HIGHT**, } *n. hite*, or *hith.* [Sax. *heahtho*, *heatho*, *hehthe*, *heotho*, *hethe*, *hihth*, *hyhthe*, contracted or changed from *heagthe*, or *higeth*, or *highthe*; G. *höhe*, *hoheit*; D. *hoogte*; Sw. *höghet*, *högd*; Dan. *höjde*, *höjhed.* This word is formed from *heah*, *hoh*, *hog*, now *high*, and as the orthography is unsettled, I should prefer to form it regularly from the present English word *high*, and write it *highth*, or *hight.* The common popular pronunciation *highth*, or *hithe*, is most regular, but in the plural *hights* is most easily pronounced.]

1. Elevation above the ground; any indefinite distance above the earth. The eagle flies at a great *hight*, or *highth.*

2. The altitude of an object; the distance which any thing rises above its foot, basis or foundation; as the *hight*, or *highth* of a tower or steeple.

3. Elevation of a star or other celestial luminary above the horizon.

4. Degree of latitude either north or south. In this application, the distance from the equator is considered as *elevation.* Latitudes are higher as they approach the pole. *Johnson.*

Guinea lieth to the north sea, in the same *height* as Peru to the south. *Abbot.*

5. Distance of one thing above another.

6. An eminence; a summit; an elevated part of any thing.

7. A hill or mountain; any elevated ground; as the *hights* of Dorchester.

8. Elevation of rank; station of dignity or office.

By him that raised me to this careful *height.* *Shak.*

9. Elevation in excellence of any kind, as in power, learning, arts.

10. Elevation in fame or reputation.

11. Utmost degree in extent or violence; as the *highth* or *hight* of a fever, of passion, of madness, of folly, of happiness, of good breeding. So we say, the *hight* of a tempest.

12. Utmost exertion.

I shall now put you to the *height* of your breeding. *Shak.*

13. Advance; degree; progress towards perfection or elevation; *speaking comparatively.*

Social duties are carried to a greater *height*— by the principles of our religion. *Addison.*

HEIGHTEN, *v. t.* *hitn.* To raise higher; *but not often used in this literal sense.*

2. To advance in progress towards a better state; to improve; to meliorate; to increase in excellence or good qualities; as, to *highten* virtue; to *highten* the beauties of description, or of poetry.

3. To aggravate; to advance towards a worse state; to augment in violence.

Foreign states have endeavored to *highten* our confusions. *Addison.*

4. To increase; as, to *highten* our relish for intellectual pleasure.

HEIGHTENED, *pp.* *hitnd.* Raised higher; elevated; exalted; advanced; improved; aggravated; increased.

HEIGHTENING, *ppr.* *hitning.* Raising; elevating; exalting; improving; increasing; aggravating.

HEIGHTENING, *n.* *hitning.* The act of elevating; increase of excellence; improvement. *Dryden.*

2. Aggravation; augmentation.

HEINOUS, *a.* an incorrect orthography. [See *Hainous.*]

HEIR, *n.* *āre.* [Norm. *hier*, *here*; Arm. *hear*, *haer*; Sp. *heredero*; Port. *herdeiro*; Fr. *heritier*; It. *erede*; L. *hæres*, *hæredis*, from the verb, Eth. ወረሰ, Heb. ירש, Ar. ورث warata, to become an heir, to inherit. The primary sense is to seize, or rush on and take, or to expel and dispossess others, and take their property, according to the practice of rude nations. We observe in the Hebrew and Ethiopic, the last consonant is a sibilant, as in the Latin nominative, but the oblique cases in the Latin correspond with the Arabic word whose final consonant is a dental. See Class Rd. No 51. 52. 68.]

1. The man who succeeds, or is to succeed another in the possession of lands, tenements and hereditaments, by descent; the man on whom the law casts an estate of inheritance by the death of the ancestor or former possessor; or the man in whom the title to an estate of inheritance is vested by the operation of law, on the death of a former owner.

We give the title to a person who is to inherit after the death of an ancestor, and during his life, as well as to the person who has actually come into possession. A man's children are his *heirs.* In most monarchies, the king's eldest son is *heir* to the throne; and a nobleman's eldest son is *heir* to his title.

Lo, one born in my house is my *heir.* Gen. xv.

2. One who inherits, or takes from an ancestor. The son is often *heir* to the disease, or to the miseries of the father.

3. One who succeeds to the estate of a former possessor. Jer. xlix. Mic. i.

4. One who is entitled to possess. In *Scripture*, saints are called *heirs* of the promise, *heirs* of righteousnes, *heirs* of salvation, &c., by virtue of the death of Christ, or of God's gracious promises.

Heir-presumptive, one who, if the ancestor should die immediately, would be heir, but whose right of inheritance may be defeated by any contingency, as by the birth of a nearer relative. *Encyc.*

HEIR, *v. t.* *āre.* To inherit; to take possession of an estate of inheritance, after the death of the ancestor. *Dryden.*

HEIR-APPA'RENT, *n.* The man who, during the life of his ancestor, is entitled to succeed to his estate or crown.

HEIRDŎM, *n.* *āredom.* Succession by inheritance. *Burke.*

HEIRESS, *n.* *āress.* A female heir; a female that inherits, or is entitled to inherit an estate; an inheritrix.

HEIRLESS, *a.* *āreless.* Destitute of an heir.

HEIR-LOOM, *n.* *āre-loom.* [*heir* and Sax. *loma*, *geloma*, *andloman*, utensils, vessels.]

Any furniture, movable, or personal chattel, which by law descends to the heir with the house or freehold; as tables, cupboards, bedsteads, &c. *Eng. Law.*

HEIRSHIP, *n.* *āreship.* The state, character or privileges of an heir; right of inheriting. *Johnson.*

2. *Heirship movables*, in *Scotland*, the best of certain kinds of movables which the heir is entitled to take, besides the heritable estate. *Encyc.*

HELD, *pret.* and *pp.* of *hold.* A court was *held* in Westminster hall. At a council *held* on the first of January.

HELE, *v. t.* [L. *celo.*] To hide. *Obs.* *Gower.*

HELI'A€AL, *a.* [L. *heliacus*; Fr. *heliaque*; from Gr. ἡλιος, the sun, W. *haul.*]

Emerging from the light of the sun, or passing into it. The *heliacal* rising of a star, is when, after being in conjunction with it and invisible, it emerges from the light so as to be visible in the morning before sunrising. On the contrary, the *heliacal* setting of a star, is when the sun approaches so near as to render it invisible by its superior splendor. *Encyc.*

HELI'A€ALLY, *adv.* A star rises *heliacally*, when it emerges from the sun's light, so as to be visible. [See the preceding word.]

HEL'I€AL, *a.* [Gr. ἑλιξ, a scroll, or spiral body.]

Spiral; winding; moving round. *Wilkins.*

HEL'ICITE, *n.* [See *Helix.*] Fossil remains of the helix, a shell.

HE'LING, *n.* [from *hele*, obs.; L. *celo.*] The covering of the roof of a building; written also *hilling.* [*Not used in the U. States.*]

HELIOCENT'RIC, *a.* [Fr. *heliocentrique*; Gr. ηλιος, the sun, and κεντρον, center.]
The *heliocentric* place of a planet, is the place of the ecliptic in which the planet would appear to a spectator at the center of the sun.
The *heliocentric* latitude of a planet, is the inclination of a line drawn between the center of the sun and the center of a planet to the plane of the ecliptic. *Encyc.*
Helioid parabola, in *mathematics*, the parabolic spiral, a curve which arises from the supposition that the axis of the common Apollonian parabola is bent round into the periphery of a circle, and is a line then passing through the extremities of the ordinates, which now converge towards the center of the said circle. *Harris.*
HELIOL'ATER, *n.* [Gr. ηλιος, the sun, and λατρευω, to worship.]
A worshiper of the sun. *Drummond.*
HELIOL'ATRY, *n.* [Gr. ηλιος, the sun, and λατρεια, service, worship.]
The worship of the sun, a branch of Sabianism.
HELIOM'ETER, *n.* [Gr. ηλιος, the sun, and μετρεω, to measure.]
An instrument for measuring with exactness the diameter of the heavenly bodies. It is called also *astrometer.* *Encyc.*
HE'LIOSCOPE, *n.* [Gr. ηλιος, the sun, and σκοπεω, to view.]
A sort of telescope fitted for viewing the sun without pain or injury to the eyes, as when made with colored glasses, or glasses blackened with smoke. *Encyc.*
HE'LIOSTATE, *n.* [Gr. ηλιος, the sun, and ϛατος.]
An instrument by which a sunbeam may be steadily directed to one spot. *Edin. Encyc.* *Ure.*
HE'LIOTROPE, *n.* [Gr. ηλιος, the sun, and τρεπω, to turn.]
1. Among the ancients, an instrument or machine for showing when the sun arrived at the tropics and the equinoctial line. *Encyc.*
2. A genus of plants, the turnsole.
3. A mineral, a subspecies of rhomboidal quartz, of a deep green color, peculiarly pleasant to the eye. It is usually variegated with blood red or yellowish dots, and is more or less translucent. Before the blowpipe, it loses its color. It is generally supposed to be chalcedony, colored by green earth or chlorite. *Cleaveland.* *Ure.*
HELISPHER'IC, **HELISPHER'ICAL**, *a.* [*helix* and *sphere.*]
Spiral. The *helispherical* line is the rhomb line in navigation, so called because on the globe it winds round the pole spirally, coming nearer and nearer to it, but never terminating in it. *Harris.*
HE'LIX, *n.* [Gr. ελιξ, a winding.] A spiral line; a winding; or something that is spiral; as a winding staircase in *architecture*, or a caulicule or little volute under the flowers of the Corinthian capital. In *anatomy*, the whole circuit or extent of the auricle, or external border of the ear. *Encyc.*
2. In *zoology*, the snail-shell.
HELL, *n.* [Sax. *hell*, *helle*; G. *hölle*; D. *hel*, *helle*; Sw. *helvete*; Dan. *helvede*. Qu. *hole*, a deep place, or from Sax. *helan*, to cover.]
1. The place or state of punishment for the wicked after death. Matt. x. Luke xii.

> Sin is *hell* begun, as religion is heaven anticipated. *J. Lathrop.*

2. The place of the dead, or of souls after death; the lower regions, or the grave; called in Hebrew, *sheol*, and by the Greeks, *hades*. Ps. xvi. Jon. ii.
3. The *pains of hell*, temporal death, or agonies that dying persons feel, or which bring to the brink of the grave. Ps. xviii.
4. The *gates of hell*, the power and policy of Satan and his instruments. Matt. xvi.
5. The infernal powers.

> While Saul and *hell* cross'd his strong fate in vain. *Cowley.*

6. The place at a running play to which are carried those who are caught. *Sidney.*
7. A place into which a tailor throws his shreds. *Hudibras.*
8. A dungeon or prison. *Obs.*
HELL'BLACK, *a.* Black as hell. *Shak.*
HELL'-BORN, *a.* Born in hell.
HELL'-BRED, *a.* Produced in hell. *Spenser.*
HELL'-BREWED, *a.* Prepared in hell.
HELL'-BROTH, *n.* A composition for infernal purposes. *Shak.*
HELL'-CAT, *n.* A witch; a hag. *Middleton.*
HELL-CONFOUND'ING, *a.* Defeating the infernal powers. *Beaum.*
HELL'-DOOMED, *a.* Doomed or consigned to hell. *Milton.*
HELL'-GOVERNED, *a.* Directed by hell. *Shak.*
HELL'-HAG, *n.* A hag of hell.
HELL'-HATED, *a.* Abhorred as hell. *Shak.*
HELL'-HAUNTED, *a.* Haunted by the devil. *Dryden.*
HELL'-HOUND, *n.* A dog of hell; an agent of hell. *Dryden.* *Milton.*
HELL'-KITE, *n.* A kite of an infernal breed. *Shak.*
HEL'LEBORE, *n.* [L. *helleborus*; Gr. ελλεβορος.]
The name of several plants of different genera, the most important of which are the black hellebore, Christmas rose, or Christmas flower, of the genus Helleborus, and the white hellebore, of the genus Veratrum. Both are acrid and poisonous, and are used in medicine as evacuants and alteratives. *Cyc.*
HEL'LEBORISM, *n.* A medicinal preparation of hellebore. *Ferrand.*
HELLE'NIAN, **HELLEN'IC**, *a.* [Gr. ελληνικος, ελληνιος.]
Pertaining to the Hellenes, or inhabitants of Greece, so called from Hellas in Greece, or from Hellen.
HEL'LENISM, *n.* [Gr. ελληνισμος.] A phrase in the idiom, genius or construction of the Greek language. *Addison.*
HEL'LENIST, *n.* [Gr. ελληνιϛης.] A Grecian Jew; a Jew who used the Greek language. *Campbell.* *Encyc.*
2. One skilled in the Greek language.
HELLENIS'TIC, *a.* Pertaining to the Hellenists. The *Hellenistic* language was the Greek spoken or used by the Jews who lived in Egypt and other countries, where the Greek language prevailed. *Campbell.*
HELLENIS'TICALLY, *adv.* According to the Hellenistic dialect. *Gregory.*
HEL'LENIZE, *v. i.* To use the Greek language. *Hammond.*
HEL'LESPONT, *n.* A narrow strait between Europe and Asia, now called the *Dardanelles*; a part of the passage between the Euxine and the Egean sea.
HELLESPONT'INE, *a.* Pertaining to the Hellespont. *Mitford.*
HEL'LIER, *n.* A tiler or slater. [See *Hele.*] [*Not in use.*]
HELL'ISH, *a.* Pertaining to hell. *Sidney.*
2. Like hell in qualities; infernal; malignant; wicked; detestable. *South.*
HELL'ISHLY, *adv.* Infernally; with extreme malignity; wickedly; detestably. *Bp. Barlow.*
HELL'ISHNESS, *n.* The qualities of hell or of its inhabitants; extreme wickedness, malignity or impiety.
HELL'WARD, *adv.* Towards hell. *Pope.*
HELL'Y, *a.* Having the qualities of hell. *Anderson.*
HELM, a termination, denotes defense; as in *Sighelm*, victorious defense. [See *Helmet.*]
HELM, *n.* [Sax. *helma*; G. *helm*, a *helm*, and a *helve*; D. Dan. *helm*; Sw. *hielm*; called in some dialects *helm-stock*, which must be the tiller only; probably from the root of *hold.*]
1. The instrument by which a ship is steered, consisting of a rudder, a tiller, and in large vessels, a wheel. [See *Rudder.*] *Mar. Dict.*
2. Station of government; the place of direction or management; as, to be at the *helm* in the administration.
HELM, *v. t.* To steer; to guide; to direct. [*Little used.*] *Shak.*
2. To cover with a helmet. *Milton.*
HELM, **HELM'ET**, *n.* [Sax. *helm.* See *Helm.*] Defensive armor for the head; a head-piece; a morion. The helmet is worn by horsemen to defend the head against the broad sword.
2. The part of a coat of arms that bears the crest. *Johnson.*
3. The upper part of a retort. *Boyle.*
4. In *botany*, the upper lip of a ringent corol. *Martyn.*
HELM'ED, **HELM'ETED**, *a.* Furnished with a helmet.
HELMIN'THIC, *a.* [Gr. ελμινς, a worm.] Expelling worms.
HELMIN'THIC, *n.* A medicine for expelling worms. *Coxe.*
HELMINTHOLOG'IC, **HELMINTHOLOG'ICAL**, *n.* [See *Helminthology.*] Pertaining to worms or vermes, or to their history.
HELMINTHOL'OGIST, *n.* One who is versed in the natural history of vermes.
HELMINTHOL'OGY, *n.* [Gr. ελμινς, a worm, and λογος, discourse.]
The science or knowledge of vermes; the description and natural history of vermes. *Ed. Encyc.*
HELM'LESS, *a.* Destitute of a helmet. *Barlow.*
2. Without a helm.
HELMS'MAN, *n.* The man at the helm.
HELM'WIND, *n.* A wind in the mountainous parts of England, so called. *Burn.*

HE'LOTISM, *n.* Slavery; the condition of the Helots, slaves in Sparta. *Stephens.*

HELP, *v. t.* a regular verb; the old past tense and participle *holp* and *holpen* being obsolete. [W. *helpu;* Sax. *helpan, hylpan;* G. *helfen;* D. *helpen;* Sw. *hielpa;* Dan. *hielper;* Goth. *hilpan.*]

1. To aid; to assist; to lend strength or means towards effecting a purpose; as, to *help* a man in his work; to *help* another in raising a building; to *help* one to pay his debts; to *help* the memory or the understanding.

2. To assist; to succor; to lend means of deliverance; as, to *help* one in distress; to *help* one out of prison.

3. To relieve; to cure, or to mitigate pain or disease.

> *Help* and ease them, but by no means bemoan them. *Locke.*
>
> The true calamus *helps* a cough. *Gerard.*

Sometimes with *of;* as, to *help* one *of* blindness. *Shak.*

4. To remedy; to change for the better.

> Cease to lament for what thou cans't not *help.* *Shak.*

5. To prevent; to hinder. The evil approaches, and who can *help* it?

6. To forbear; to avoid.

> I cannot *help* remarking the resemblance between him and our author— *Pope.*

To help forward, to advance by assistance.

To help on, to forward; to promote by aid.

To help out, to aid in delivering from difficulty, or to aid in completing a design.

> The god of learning and of light,
> Would want a god himself to *help* him *out.* *Swift.*

To help over, to enable to surmount; as, to *help* one *over* a difficulty.

To help off, to remove by help; as, to *help off* time. [*Unusual.*] *Locke.*

To help to, to supply with; to furnish with.

> Whom they would *help to* a kingdom. 1 Maccabees.

Also, to present to at table; as, to *help* one *to* a glass of wine.

HELP, *v. i.* To lend aid; to contribute strength or means.

> A generous present *helps* to persuade, as well as an agreeable person. *Garth.*

To help out, to lend aid; to bring a supply.

HELP, *n.* [W. *help.*] Aid; assistance; strength or means furnished towards promoting an object, or deliverance from difficulty or distress.

> Give us *help* from trouble; for vain is the *help* of man. Ps. lx.

2. That which gives assistance; he or that which contributes to advance a purpose.

> Virtue is a friend and a *help* to nature. *South.*
>
> God is a very present *help* in time of trouble. Ps. xlvi.

3. Remedy; relief. The evil is done; there is no *help* for it. There is no *help* for the man; his disease is incurable.

4. A hired man or woman; a servant. *U. States.*

HELP'ER, *n.* One that helps, aids or assists; an assistant; an auxiliary.

2. One that furnishes or administers a remedy.

> Compassion—is oftentimes a *helper* of evils. *More.*

3. One that supplies with any thing wanted; with *to.*

> A *helper to* a husband. *Shak.*

4. A supernumerary servant. *Swift.*

HELP'FUL, *a.* That gives aid or assistance; that furnishes means of promoting an object; useful.

2. Wholesome; salutary; as *helpful* medicines. *Raleigh.*

HELP'FULNESS, *n.* Assistance; usefulness. *Milton.*

HELP'LESS, *a.* Without help in one's self; destitute of the power or means to succor or relieve one's self. A person is rendered *helpless* by weakness, or want of means. An infant is *helpless.*

2. Destitute of support or assistance.

> How shall I then your *helpless* fame defend? *Pope.*

3. Admitting no help; irremediable. [*Not used.*] *Spenser.*

4. Unsupplied; destitute.

> *Helpless* of all that human wants require. [*Not used.*] *Dryden.*

HELP'LESSLY, *adv.* Without succor. *Kid.*

HELP'LESSNESS, *n.* Want of strength or ability; inability; want of means in one's self to obtain relief in trouble, or to accomplish one's purposes or desires.

> It is the tendency of sickness to reduce our extravagant self-estimation, by exhibiting our solitary *helplessness.* *Buckminster.*

HELTER-SKELTER, cant words denoting hurry and confusion. [*Vulgar.*] Qu. L. *hilariter* and *celeriter,* or Ch. חלט, Ar. خلط, to mix.

HELVE, *n. helv.* [Sax. *helf;* G. *helm,* a helve and a helm; probably from the root of *hold.*] The handle of an ax or hatchet.

HELVE, *v. t. helv.* To furnish with a helve, as an ax.

HELVET'IC, *a.* [Sax. *Hæfelden,* the Helvetii. Qu. hill-men or high hill-men.]

Designating what pertains to the Helvetii, the inhabitants of the Alps, now Swisserland, or what pertains to the modern states and inhabitants of the Alpine regions; as the *Helvetic* confederacy; *Helvetic* states.

HEL'VIN, *n.* [from Gr. ηλιος, the sun.] A mineral of a yellowish color, occurring in regular tetrahedrons, with truncated angles. *Cleaveland.*

HEM, *n.* [Sax. *hem;* W. *hem;* Russ. *kaima.*]

1. The border of a garment, doubled and sewed to strengthen it and prevent the raveling of the threads.

2. Edge; border. Matt. ix.

3. A particular sound of the human voice, expressed by the word *hem.*

HEM, *v. t.* To form a hem or border; to fold and sew down the edge of cloth to strengthen it.

2. To border; to edge.

> All the skirt about
> Was *hemm'd* with golden fringe. *Spenser.*

To hem in, to inclose and confine; to surround; to environ. The troops were *hemmed in* by the enemy. Sometimes perhaps to *hem about* or *round,* may be used in a like sense.

HEM, *v. i.* [D. *hemmen.*] To make the sound expressed by the word *hem.*

HEM'ACHATE, *n.* [Gr. αιμα, blood, and αχατης, agate.] A species of agate, of a blood color. *Encyc.*

HEM'ATIN, *n.* [Gr. αιμα, blood.] The coloring principle of logwood, of a red color and bitterish taste. *Chevreul.*

HEM'ATITE, *n.* [Gr. αιματιτης, from αιμα, blood.]

The name of two ores of iron, the *red hematite,* and the *brown hematite.* They are both of a fibrous structure, and the fibers, though sometimes nearly parallel, usually diverge, or even radiate from a center. They rarely occur amorphous, but almost always in concretions, reniform, globular, botryoidal, stalactitic, &c. The red hematite is a variety of the red oxyd; its streak and powder are always nearly blood red. The brown hematite is a variety of the brown oxyd or hydrate of iron; its streak and powder are always of a brownish yellow. The red hematite is also called *blood-stone.* *Cleaveland. Encyc.*

HEMATIT'IC, *a.* Pertaining to hematite, or resembling it.

HEM'ATOPE, *n.* The sea-pye, a fowl of the grallic order, that feeds on shell-fish. *Encyc.*

HEMEROBAP'TIST, *n.* [Gr. ημερα, day, and βαπτω, to wash.]

One of a sect among the Jews who bathed every day. *Fulke.*

HEM'I, in composition, from the Gr. ημισυς, signifies half, like *demi* and *semi.*

HEM'ICRANY, *n.* [Gr. ημισυς, half, and κρανιον, the skull.] A pain that affects only one side of the head.

HEM'ICYCLE, *n.* [Gr. ημικυκλος.] A half circle; more generally called a *semicircle.*

HEMID'ITONE, *n.* In *Greek music,* the lesser third. *Busby.*

HEM'INA, *n.* [L.] In *Roman antiquity,* a measure containing half a sextary, and according to Arbuthnot, about half a pint English wine measure. *Encyc.*

2. In *medicine,* a measure equal to about ten ounces. *Quincy.*

HEM'IPLEGY, *n.* [Gr. ημισυς, half, and πληγη, a stroke, from πλησσω, to strike.]

A palsy that affects one half of the body; a paralytic affection on one side of the human frame. *Encyc.*

HEMIP'TER, } *n.* [Gr. ημισυ, half, and
HEMIP'TERA, } πτερον, a wing.] The hemipters form an order of insects with the upper wings usually half crustaceous, and half membranaceous, and incumbent on each other; as the cimex.

HEMIP'TERAL, *a.* Having the upper wings half crustaceous and half membranaceous.

HEM'ISPHERE, *n.* [Gr. ημισφαιριον.] A half sphere; one half of a sphere or globe, when divided by a plane passing through its center. In *astronomy,* one half the mundane sphere. The equator divides the sphere into two equal parts. That on the north is called the *northern hemisphere;* the other, the *southern.* So the horizon divides the sphere into the *upper* and *lower hemispheres.* Hemisphere is also used for a map or projection of half the terrestrial or celestial sphere, and is then often called *planisphere.*

2. A map or projection of half the terrestrial globe.

HEMISPHER'IC, } *a.* Containing half a **HEMISPHER'ICAL,** } sphere or globe; as a *hemispheric* figure or form; a *hemispherical* body.

HEM'ISTICH, *n.* [Gr. ημιςιχιον.] Half a poetic verse, or a verse not completed. *Dryden. Encyc.*

HEMIS'TICHAL, *a.* Pertaining to a hemistich; denoting a division of the verse. *Warton.*

HEM'ITONE, *n.* [Gr. ημιτονιον.] A half tone in music; now called a *semitone.*

HEM'ITROPE, *a.* [Gr. ημισυς, half, and τρεπω, to turn.]

Half-turned; a *hemitrope crystal* is one in which one segment is turned through half the circumference of a circle. The word is used also as a noun. *Haüy.*

HEM'LOCK, *n.* [Sax. *hemleac;* the latter syllable is the same as *leek.* Qu. is it not a border-plant, a plant growing in hedges?]

1. A plant of the genus Conium, whose leaves and root are poisonous. Also, the *Cicuta maculata.* *Bigelow.*
2. A tree of the genus Pinus, an evergreen.
3. A poison, an infusion or decoction of the poisonous plant.

Popular liberty might then have escaped the indelible reproach of decreeing to the same citizens the *hemlock* on one day, and statues on the next. *Federalist, Madison.*

HEMOP'TYSIS, } *a.* [Gr. αιμα, blood, and **HEMOP'TOE,** } πτυσις, a spitting.] A spitting of blood.

HEM'ORRHAGE, } *n.* [Gr. αιμορραγια; αιμα, **HEM'ORRHAGY,** } blood, and ρηγνυω, to burst.]

A flux of blood, proceeding from the rupture of a blood-vessel, or some other cause. The ancients confined the word to a discharge of blood from the nose; but in modern use, it is applied to a flux from the nose, lungs, intestines, &c. *Encyc.*

HEM'ORRHAGIC, *a.* Pertaining to a flux of blood; consisting in hemorrhage.

HEM'ORRHOIDS, *n.* [Gr. αιμορροις; αιμα, blood, and ροος, a flowing.]

A discharge of blood from the vessels of the anus; the piles; in *Scripture,* emerods.

The term is also applied to tumors formed by a morbid dilatation of the hemorrhoidal veins. When they do not discharge blood, they are called *blind piles;* when they occasionally emit blood, *bleeding* or *open piles.* *Cyc. Parr.*

HEMORRHOID'AL, *a.* Pertaining to the hemorrhoids; as the *hemorrhoidal* vessels.

2. Consisting in a flux of blood from the vessels of the anus.

HEMP, *n.* [Sax. *henep;* G. *hanf;* D. *hennep* or *kennip;* Sw. *hampa;* Dan. *hamp;* Fr. *chanvre;* Arm. *canab;* Ir. *cannaib, cnaib;* L. *cannabis;* Gr. κανναβις; Sp. *cañamo;* It. *canapa;* Russ. *konopel.* It is found in the Arabic. See Class Nb. No. 20. 26.]

1. A fibrous plant constituting the genus Cannabis, whose skin or bark is used for cloth and cordage. Hence *canvas,* the coarse strong cloth used for sails.
2. The skin or rind of the plant, prepared for spinning. Large quantities of *hemp* are exported from Russia.

HEMP-AG'RIMONY, *n.* A plant, a species of Eupatorium.

HEMP'EN, *a. hemp'n.* Made of hemp; as a *hempen* cord.

HEMP'Y, *a.* Like hemp. [*Unusual.*] *Howell.*

HEN, *n.* [Sax. *hen, henne;* G. *henne;* D. *hen;* Sw. *höna;* Dan. *höne.* In Goth. *hana,* Sax. *han, hana,* is a cock; G. *hahn;* D. *haan.* In Sw. and Dan. *hane* is a cock, the male of a fowl, and *han* is *he,* the personal pronoun.]

The female of any kind of fowl; but it is particularly applied to the female of the domestic fowl of the gallinaceous kind, or as sometimes called, the *barn-door fowl.*

HEN'BANE, *n.* [*hen* and *bane.*] A plant, the Hyoscyamus, of several species. The roots, leaves and seeds are poisonous. *Encyc.*

HEN'BIT, *n.* A plant, the ivy-leaved speedwell. *Derham.*

HEN'-COOP, *n.* A coop or cage for fowls.

HEN'-DRIVER, *n.* A kind of hawk. *Walton.*

HEN'-HARM, } *n.* A species of kite, *py-* **HEN'-HARRIER,** } *gargus.* *Ainsworth.*

HEN'-HE'ARTED, *a.* Cowardly; timid; dastardly.

HEN'HOUSE, *n.* A house or shelter for fowls.

HEN'PECKED, *a.* Governed by the wife. *Dryden.*

HEN'ROOST, *n.* A place where poultry rest at night. *Addison.*

HENS'FEET, *n.* A plant, hedge-fumitory. *Johnson.*

HENCE, *adv. hens.* [Sax. *heona;* Scot. *hyne;* G. *hin.*]

1. From this place.

Arise, let us go *hence.* John xiv.

I will send thee far *hence* to the Gentiles. Acts xxii.

2. From this time; in the future; as a week *hence;* a year *hence.*
3. From this cause or reason, noting a consequence, inference or deduction from something just before stated.

Hence perhaps it is, that Solomon calls the fear of the Lord, the beginning of wisdom. *Tillotson.*

It sometimes denotes an inference or consequence, resulting from something that follows.

Whence come wars and fightings among you? Come they not *hence,* even from your lusts—James iv.

4. From this source or original.

All other faces borrowed *hence*— *Suckling.*

Hence signifies *from this,* and *from* before *hence* is not strictly correct. But *from hence* is so well established by custom, that it may not be practicable to correct the use of the phrase.

Hence is used elliptically and imperatively, for *go hence; depart hence; away; be gone.*

Hence, with your little ones. *Shak.*

Hence, as a verb, to send off, as used by Sidney, is improper.

HENCEFORTH, *adv. hens'forth.* From this time forward.

I never from thy side *henceforth* will stray. *Milton.*

HENCEFORWARD, *adv. hensfor'ward.* From this time forward; henceforth. *Shak. Dryden.*

HENCH'MAN, } *n.* [Sax. *hinc,* a servant.] **HENCH'BOY,** } A page; a servant. *Obs.* *Shak. Dryden.*

HEND, } *v. t.* [Sax. *hentan.*] To seize; to **HENT,** } lay hold on. *Obs.* *Fairfax.*

2. To crowd; to press on. *Obs.* *Shak.*

HEND, or **HENDY,** *a.* Gentle. *Obs.* *Chaucer.*

HENDEC'AGON, *n.* [Gr. ενδεκα, eleven, and γωνια, an angle.]

In *geometry,* a figure of eleven sides, and as many angles. *Encyc.*

HENDECASYL'LABLE, *n.* [Gr. ενδεκα and συλλαβη.] A metrical line of eleven syllables. *Warton.*

HENDI'ADIS, *n.* [Gr.] A figure, when two nouns are used instead of a noun and an adjective. *Scott.*

HE'PAR, *n.* [L. *hepar,* the liver; Gr. ηπαρ.] A combination of sulphur with an alkali was formerly called by chimists *hepar sulphuris,* liver of sulphur, from its brown red color. The term has been applied to all combinations of alkali or earth with sulphur or phosphorus. *Nicholson.*

The *hepars* are by modern chimists called *sulphurets.* *Fourcroy.*

HEPAT'IC, } *a.* [L. *hepaticus;* Gr. ηπα- **HEPAT'ICAL,** } τικος, from ηπαρ, the liver.]

Pertaining to the liver; as *hepatic* gall; *hepatic* pain; *hepatic* artery; *hepatic* flux. *Quincy. Arbuthnot.*

Hepatic air or *gas,* is a fetid vapor or elastic fluid emitted from combinations of sulphur with alkalies, earths and metals. *Nicholson. Encyc.*

This species of air is now called sulphureted hydrogen gas. *Fourcroy.*

Hepatic mercurial ore, compact sulphuret of mercury or cinnabar, a mineral of a reddish, or reddish brown, or dark red color. Its streak is dark red, and has some luster. It occurs in compact masses, with an even or fine grained fracture.

Hepatic pyrite, hepatic sulphuret of iron. During the process of decomposition of this ore, by which the sulphur is more or less disengaged, the pyrite is converted, either wholly or in part, into a compact oxyd of iron of a *liver* brown color; hence its name. *Cleaveland.*

HEP'ATITE, *n.* A gem or mineral that takes its name from the liver. Plin. L. 37. 11.

Hepatite is a name given to the fetid sulphate of baryte. It sometimes occurs in globular masses, and is either compact or of a foliated structure. By friction or the application of heat, it exhales a fetid odor, like that of sulphureted hydrogen. *Cleaveland.*

HEP'ATIZE, *v. t.* To impregnate with sulphureted hydrogen gas.

HEP'ATIZED, *pp.* Impregnated or combined with sulphureted hydrogen gas.

On the right of the river were two wells of *hepatized* water. *Barrow.*

HEPATOS'COPY, *n.* [Gr. ηπαρ, the liver, and σκοπεω, to view.]

The art or practice of divination by inspecting the liver of animals. *Encyc.*

HEPS, *n.* The berries of the hep-tree, or wild dog-rose.

HEPTACAP'SULAR, *a.* [Gr. επτα, seven, and L. *capsula,* a cell.]

Having seven cells or cavities for seeds; *a term in botany.*

HEP'TACHORD, *n.* [Gr. επτα, seven, and χορδη, chord.]

A system of seven sounds. In *ancient poetry,* verses sung or played on seven chords or different notes. In this sense the word was applied to the lyre, when it had but seven strings. One of the intervals is also called a heptachord, as containing the same number of degrees between the extremes. *Encyc.*

HEP'TAGON, *n.* [Gr. επτα, seven, and γωνια, an angle.]

In *geometry,* a figure consisting of seven sides and as many angles.

In *fortification,* a place that has seven bastions for defense. *Encyc.*

HEPTAG'ONAL, *a.* Having seven angles or sides. *Heptagonal numbers,* in *arithmetic,* a sort of polygonal numbers, wherein the difference of the terms of the corresponding arithmetical progression is 5. One of the properties of these numbers is, that if they are multiplied by 40, and 9 is added to the product, the sum will be a square number. *Encyc.*

HEP'TAGYN, *n.* [Gr. επτα, seven, and γυνη, a female.] In *botany,* a plant that has seven pistils.

HEPTAGYN'IAN, *a.* Having seven pistils.

HEPTAHEXAHE'DRAL, *a.* [Gr. επτα, seven, and *hexahedral.*]

Presenting seven ranges of faces one above another, each range containing six faces. *Cleaveland.*

HEPTAM'EREDE, *n.* [Gr. επτα, seven, and μερις, part.]

That which divides into seven parts. *A. Smith.*

HEPTAND'ER, *n.* [Gr. επτα, seven, and ανηρ, a male.] In *botany,* a plant having seven stamens.

HEPTAN'DRIAN, *a.* Having seven stamens.

HEPTAN'GULAR, *a.* [Gr. επτα, seven, and *angular.*] Having seven angles.

HEPTAPH'YLLOUS, *a.* [Gr. επτα, seven, and φυλλον, a leaf.] Having seven leaves.

HEPTAR'CHIC, *a.* Denoting a sevenfold government. *Warton.*

HEP'TARCHIST, *n.* A ruler of one division of a heptarchy. *Warton.*

HEP'TARCHY, *n.* [Gr. επτα, seven, and αρχη, rule.]

A government by seven persons, or the country governed by seven persons. But the word is usually applied to England, when under the government of seven kings, or divided into seven kingdoms; as the Saxon *heptarchy,* which comprehended the whole of England, when subject to seven independent princes. These petty kingdoms were those of Kent, the South Saxons [Sussex,] West Saxons, East Saxons [Essex,] the East Angles, Mercia, and Northumberland. *Hist. of England.*

HEP'TATEUCH, *n.* [Gr. επτα, seven, and τευχος, book.]

The first seven books of the Old Testament. [*Little used.*]

HEP'-TREE, *n.* The wild dog-rose, a species of Rosa.

HER, pronounced *hur,* an adjective, or pronominal adjective of the third person. [Sax. *hire,* sing. *heoru,* plu., the possessive case of *he, heo;* but more properly an adjective, like the L. *suus.*]

1. Belonging to a female; as *her* face; *her* head.

2. It is used before neuter nouns in personification.

> Wisdom's ways are ways of pleasantness, and all *her* paths are peace. Prov. iii.

Her is also used as a pronoun or substitute for a female in the objective case, after a verb or preposition.

> She gave also to her husband with *her,* and he did eat. Gen. iii.

Hers is primarily the objective or genitive case, denoting something that belongs to a female. But it stands as a substitute in the nominative or objective case.

> And what his fortune wanted, *hers* could mend. *Dryden.*

Here *hers* stands for *her fortune,* but it must be considered as the nominative to *could mend.* I will take back my own book and give you *hers.* Here *hers* is the object after *give.*

HER'ALD, *n.* [Fr. *heraut,* for *herault;* Arm. *herald* or *harod;* Sp. *heraldo;* Port. *arauto;* It. *araldo;* G. *herold;* W. *herodyr,* embassador and herald, from *herawd,* a defiance or challenge, *heriaw,* to brandish, to threaten, from *her,* a push, a motion of defiance, a challenge. The primary sense is to send, thrust, or drive.]

1. An officer whose business was to denounce or proclaim war, to challenge to battle, to proclaim peace, and to bear messages from the commander of an army. Hence,

2. A proclaimer; a publisher; as the *herald* of another's fame.

3. A forerunner; a precursor; a harbinger.

> It was the lark, the *herald* of the morn. *Shak.*

4. An officer in Great Britain, whose business is to marshal, order and conduct royal cavalcades, ceremonies at coronations, royal marriages, installations, creations of dukes and other nobles, embassies, funeral processions, declarations of war, proclamations of peace, &c.; also, to record and blazon the arms of the nobility and gentry, and to regulate abuses therein. *Encyc.*

5. Formerly applied by the French to a minstrel.

HER'ALD, *v. t.* To introduce, as by a herald. *Shak.*

HER'ALDIC, *a.* Pertaining to heralds or heraldry; as *heraldic* delineations. *Warton.*

HER'ALDRY, *n.* The art or office of a herald. Heraldry is the art, practice or science of recording genealogies, and blazoning arms or ensigns armorial. It also teaches whatever relates to the marshaling of cavalcades, processions and other public ceremonies. *Encyc.*

HER'ALDSHIP, *n.* The office of a herald. *Selden.*

HERB, *n. erb.* [L. *herba;* Fr. *herbe;* It. *erba;* Sp. *yerba;* Port. *erva.* Qu. Ir. *forba,* glebe, that is, food, pasture, subsistence; Gr. φερβω.]

1. A plant or vegetable with a soft or succulent stalk or stem, which dies to the root every year, and is thus distinguished from a tree and a shrub, which have ligneous or hard woody stems. *Milne. Martyn.*

2. In *the Linnean botany,* that part of a vegetable which springs from the root and is terminated by the fructification, including the stem or stalk, the leaves, the fulcra or props, and the hibernacle. *Milne. Martyn.*

The word *herb* comprehends all the grasses, and numerous plants used for culinary purposes.

HERB-CHRISTOPHER, *n.* A plant, of the genus Actæa.

HERB-ROBERT, *n.* A plant, a species of Geranium.

HERBA'CEOUS, *a.* [L. *herbaceus.*] Pertaining to herbs. *Herbaceous* plants are such as perish annually down to the root; soft, succulent vegetables. So, a *herbaceous* stem is one which is soft, not woody. *Herbaceous,* applied to animals by Derham, is not authorized. [See *Herbivorous.*]

HERB'AGE, *n.* [Fr. from *herbe.*] Herbs collectively; grass; pasture; green food for beasts.

> The influence of true religion is mild, soft and noiseless, and constant, as the descent of the evening dew on the tender *herbage.* *Buckminster.*

2. In *law,* the liberty or right of pasture in the forest or grounds of another man. *Encyc.*

HERB'AGED, *a.* Covered with grass. *Thomson.*

HERB'AL, *n.* A book that contains the names and descriptions of plants, or the classes, genera, species and qualities of vegetables. *Bacon.*

2. A hortus siccus, or dry garden; a collection of specimens of plants, dried and preserved. *Encyc.*

HERB'AL, *a.* Pertaining to herbs.

HERB'ALIST, *n.* A person skilled in plants; one who makes collections of plants.

HERB'AR, *n.* An herb. *Obs.* *Spenser.*

HERB'ARIST, *n.* A herbalist. [*Little used.*] *Derham. Boyle.*

HERBA'RIUM, *n.* A collection of dried plants. *Med. Repos.*

HERB'ARIZE. [See *Herborize.*]

HERB'ARY, *n.* A garden of plants. *Warton.*

HERB'ELET, *n.* A small herb. *Shak.*

HERBES'CENT, *a.* [L. *herbescens.*] Growing into herbs.

HERB'ID, *a.* [L. *herbidus.*] Covered with herbs. [*Little used.*]

HERBIV'OROUS, *a.* [L. *herba* and *voro,* to eat.]

Eating herbs; subsisting on herbaceous plants; feeding on vegetables. The ox and the horse are *herbivorous* animals.

HERB'LESS, *a.* Destitute of herbs. *Warton.*

HERB'ORIST. [See *Herbalist.*] *Ray.*

HERBORIZA'TION, *n.* [from *herborize.*]

1. The act of seeking plants in the field; botanical research.

2. The figure of plants in mineral substances. [See *Arborization.*] *Dict. Nat. Hist.*

HERB'ORIZE, *v. i.* To search for plants, or to seek new species of plants, with a view to ascertain their characters and to class them.

> He *herborized* as he traveled, and enriched the Flora Suecica with new discoveries. *Tooke.*

HERB'ORIZE, *v. t.* To figure; to form the figures of plants in minerals. [See *Arborize.*] *Fourcroy.*

HERB'ORIZED, *pp.* Figured; containing the figure of a plant; as a mineral body.

Daubenton has shown that *herborized* stones contain very fine mosses. *Fourcroy.*

HERB'ORIZING, *ppr.* Searching for plants.

2. Forming the figures of plants in minerals.

HERB'OUS, *a.* [L. *herbosus.*] Abounding with herbs.

HERB'WÖMAN, *n. erb'woman.* A woman that sells herbs.

HERB'Y, *a.* Having the nature of herbs. [*Little used.*] *Bacon.*

HERCU'LEAN, *a.* [from *Hercules.*] Very great, difficult or dangerous; such as it would require the strength or courage of Hercules to encounter or accomplish; as *Herculean* labor or task.

2. Having extraordinary strength and size; as *Herculean* limbs.

2. Of extraordinary strength, force or power.

HER'CULES, *n.* A constellation in the northern hemisphere, containing 113 stars. *Encyc.*

HERCYN'IAN, *a.* [from *Hercynia; G. harz*, resin.]

Denoting an extensive forest in Germany, the remains of which are now in Swabia.

HERD, *n.* [Sax. *herd, heord; G. herde;* Sw. and Dan. *hiord;* Basque, *ardi.* Words of this kind have for their primary sense, collection, assemblage. So in Saxon, *here* is an army. It may be from driving, W. *gyr.*]

1. A collection or assemblage; applied to beasts when feeding or driven together. We say, a *herd* of horses, oxen, cattle, camels, elephants, bucks, harts, and in Scripture, a *herd* of swine. But we say, a *flock* of sheep, goats or birds. A number of cattle going to market is called a *drove.*

2. A company of men or people, in contempt or detestation; a crowd; a rabble; as a vulgar *herd.*

HERD, *n.* [Sax. *hyrd; G. hirt;* Sw. *herde;* Dan. *hyrde* or *hyre;* from the same root as the preceding, that is, the holder or keeper.]

A keeper of cattle; used by Spenser, and still used in Scotland, but in English now seldom or never used, except in composition, as a *shepherd*, a *goatherd*, a *swineherd.*

HERD, *v. i.* To unite or associate, as beasts; to feed or run in collections. Most kinds of beasts manifest a disposition to *herd.*

2. To associate; to unite in companies customarily.

3. To associate; to become one of a number or party. *Walsh.*

HERD, *v. t.* To form or put into a herd. *B. Jonson.*

HERD'ESS, *n.* A shepherdess. *Obs.* *Chaucer.*

HERD'GROOM, *n.* A keeper of a herd. *Obs.* *Spenser.*

HERD'ING, *ppr.* Associating in companies.

HERD'MAN, HERDS'MAN, *n.* A keeper of herds; one employed in tending herds of cattle.

2. Formerly, the owner of a herd. *Sidney.*

HERE, *adv.* [Goth. and Sax. *her;* G. D. *hier;* Sw. *här;* Dan. *her.* It denotes this place.]

1. In this place; in the place where the speaker is present; opposed to *there.* Behold, *here* am I. Lodge *here* this night. Build *here* seven altars. *Scripture.*

2. In the present life or state.

Thus shall you be happy *here*, and more happy hereafter. *Bacon.*

3. It is used in making an offer or attempt.

Then *here's* for earnest. *Dryden.*

4. In drinking health.

Here's to thee, Dick. *Cowley.*

It is neither here nor there, it is neither in this place nor in that; neither in one place nor in another.

Here and there, in one place and another; in a dispersed manner or condition; thinly; or irregularly.

HE'REABOUT, HE'REABOUTS, *adv.* About this place. *Addison.*

HERE'AFTER, *adv.* In time to come; in some future time.

2. In a future state.

HERE'AFTER, *n.* A future state.

'Tis heaven itself that points out an *hereafter.* *Addison.*

HEREAT', *adv.* At this. He was offended *hereat*, that is, at this saying, this fact, &c.

HEREBY', *adv.* By this.

Hereby we became acquainted with the nature of things. *Watts.*

HEREIN', *adv.* In this.

Herein is my Father glorified, that ye bear much fruit. John xv.

HEREIN'TO, *adv.* Into this. *Hooker.*

HEREOF', *adv.* Of this; from this.

Hereof comes it that prince Harry is valiant. *Shak.*

HEREON', *adv.* On this. *Brown.*

HEREOUT', *adv.* Out of this place. *Spenser.*

HERETOFO'RE, *adv.* In times before the present; formerly. *Sidney.*

HEREUNTO', *adv.* To this. *Hooker.*

HEREUPON', *adv.* On this.

HEREWITH', *adv.* With this.

Most of the compounds of *here* and a preposition, are obsolete or obsolescent, or at least are deemed inelegant. But *hereafter* and *heretofore* are in elegant use. *Herein* and *hereby* are frequently used in the present version of the Scriptures, and ought not perhaps to be discarded. Indeed some of these words seem to be almost indispensable in technical law language.

HERED'ITABLE, *a.* [from the root of *heir;* L. *hæreditas.*]

That may be inherited. [*Not much used.* See *Inheritable.*] *Locke.*

HERED'ITABLY, *adv.* By inheritance; by right of descent.

The one-house-owners belong *hereditably* to no private person. *Tooke, Russ. Encyc.*

HEREDIT'AMENT, *n.* [L. *hæres, hæredium.* See *Heir.*]

Any species of property that may be inherited; lands, tenements, any thing corporeal or incorporeal, real, personal or mixed, that may descend to an heir. *Blackstone.*

A *corporeal* hereditament is visible and tangible; an *incorporeal* hereditament is an ideal right, existing in contemplation of law, issuing out of substantial corporeal property.

HERED'ITARILY, *adv.* By inheritance; by descent from an ancestor. *Pope.*

HERED'ITARY, *a.* [Fr. *hereditaire;* It. *ereditario.* See *Heir.*]

1. That has descended from an ancestor. He is in possession of a large *hereditary* estate.

2. That may descend from an ancestor to an heir; descendible to an heir at law. The crown of Great Britain is *hereditary.*

3. That is or may be transmitted from a parent to a child; as *hereditary* pride; *hereditary* bravery; *hereditary* disease.

HER'EMIT, *n.* A hermit. *Obs.* *Bp. Hall.*

HEREMIT'ICAL, *a.* [See *Hermit.* It should rather be written *hermitical.*] Solitary; secluded from society. *Pope.*

HER'ESIARCH, *n. s* as *z.* [Gr. αιρεσις, heresy, and αρχος, chief.]

A leader in heresy; the chief of a sect of heretics. *Stillingfleet.*

HER'ESIARCHY, *n.* Chief heresy.

HER'ESY, *n.* [Gr. αιρεσις, from αιρεω, to take, to hold; L. *hæresis;* Fr. *heresie.*]

1. A fundamental error in religion, or an error of opinion respecting some fundamental doctrine of religion. But in countries where there is an established church, an opinion is deemed *heresy*, when it differs from that of the church. The Scriptures being the standard of faith, any opinion that is repugnant to its doctrines, is *heresy;* but as men differ in the interpretation of Scripture, an opinion deemed *heretical* by one body of christians, may be deemed orthodox by another. In Scripture and primitive usage, *heresy* meant merely *sect, party*, or the doctrines of a sect, as we now use *denomination* or *persuasion*, implying no reproach.

2. Heresy, in *law*, is an offense against christianity, consisting in a denial of some of its essential doctrines, publicly avowed and obstinately maintained. *Blackstone.*

3. An untenable or unsound opinion or doctrine in politics. *Swift.*

HER'ETIC, *n.* [Gr. αιρετικος; It. *eretico;* Fr. *heretique.*]

1. A person under any religion, but particularly the christian, who holds and teaches opinions repugnant to the established faith, or that which is made the standard of orthodoxy. In strictness, among christians, a person who holds and avows religious opinions contrary to the doctrines of Scripture, the only rule of faith and practice.

2. Any one who maintains erroneous opinions. *Shak.*

HERET'ICAL, *a.* Containing heresy; contrary to the established faith, or to the true faith.

HERET'ICALLY, *adv.* In an heretical manner; with heresy.

HER'ETOG, HER'ETOCH, *n.* [Sax. *heretoga;* *here*, an army, and *teoche*, a leader, from *teogan, teon*, to lead, L. *duco, dux*, Eng. to *tug.*]

Among our Saxon ancestors, the leader or commander of an army, or the commander of the militia in a county or district. This officer was elected by the people in folkmote.

HER'IOT, *n.* [Sax. *heregeat;* *here*, army, and *geat*, tribute, supply, from *geotan*, to flow, to render.]

In *English law*, a tribute or fine payable to the lord of the fee on the decease of the owner, landholder or vassal. Originally this tribute consisted of military furniture, or of horses and arms, as appears by the laws of Canute, C. 69. But as defined by modern writers, a *heriot* is a customary tribute of goods and chattels, payable to the lord of the fee on the decease of the owner of the land; or a render of the best beast or other movables to the lord on the death of the tenant. Heriots were of two sorts; *heriot service*, which was due by reservation in a grant or lease of lands; and *heriot custom*, which depended solely on immemorial usage. *Wilkins. Spelman. Blackstone.*

HER'IOTABLE, *a.* Subject to the payment of a heriot. *Burn.*

HER'ISSON, *n.* [Fr. a hedgehog, from *herisser*, to bristle, to stand out as hair.]

In *fortification*, a beam or bar armed with iron spikes pointing outwards, and turning on a pivot; used to block up a passage. *Encyc.*

HER'ITABLE, *a.* [from the root of *heir*, L. *hæres.*]

1. Capable of inheriting, or taking by descent.

By the canon law this son shall be legitimate and *heritable*. *Hale.*

2. That may be inherited. [*This is the true sense.*]

3. Annexed to estates of inheritance. In Scot's law, *heritable* rights are all rights that affect lands or other immovables. *Encyc. Blackstone.*

HER'ITAGE, *n.* [Fr. from the root of *heir.*]

1. Inheritance; an estate that passes from an ancestor to an heir by descent or course of law; that which is inherited. In *Scot's law*, it sometimes signifies immovable estate, in distinction from movable.

2. In *Scripture*, the saints or people of God are called his *heritage*, as being claimed by him, and the objects of his special care. 1 Pet. v.

HERMAPHRODE'ITY, *n.* Hermaphrodism. *B. Jonson.*

HERMAPH'RODISM, *n.* [infra.] The union of the two sexes in the same individual. *Dict. Nat. Hist.*

HERMAPH'RODITE, *n.* [Fr. from Gr. ερμαφροδιτος; ερμης, Mercury, and αφροδιτη, Venus.]

1. A human being, having the parts of generation both of male and female. The term is applied also to other animals characterized by a similar formation. *Encyc.*

2. In *botany*, a flower that contains both the anther and the stigma, or the supposed male and female organs of generation, within the same calyx or on the same receptacle. *Martyn. Encyc.*

3. A plant that has only hermaphrodite flowers. *Martyn.*

HERMAPH'RODITE, *a.* Designating both sexes in the same animal, flower or plant.

HERMAPHRODIT'IC, *a.* Partaking of both sexes. *Brown.*

HERMAPHRODIT'ICALLY, *adv.* After the manner of hermaphrodites.

HERMENEU'TIC, **HERMENEU'TICAL**, *a.* [Gr. ερμηνευτικος, from ερμηνευς, an interpreter, from ερμης, Mercury.]

Interpreting; explaining; unfolding the signification; as *hermeneutic* theology, the art of expounding the Scriptures. *Bloomfield. Encyc.*

HERMENEU'TICALLY, *adv.* According to the true art of interpreting words. *M. Stuart.*

HERMENEU'TICS, *n.* The art of finding the meaning of an author's words and phrases, and of explaining it to others.

HERMET'IC, **HERMET'ICAL**, *a.* [Fr. *hermetique;* Sp. *hermetico;* from Gr. ερμης, Mercury, the fabled inventor of chimistry.]

1. Designating chimistry; chimical; as the *hermetic* art.

2. Designating that species of philosophy which pretends to solve and explain all the phenomena of nature from the three chimical principles, salt, sulphur and mercury; as the *hermetic* philosophy.

3. Designating the system which explains the causes of diseases and the operations of medicine, on the principles of the hermetical philosophy, and particularly on the system of an alkali and acid; as *hermetical* physic or medicine. *Encyc.*

4. Perfectly close, so that no air, gas, or spirit can escape; as a *hermetic* seal. The *hermetic* seal is formed by heating the neck of a vessel till it is soft, and then twisting it, till the aperture or passage is accurately closed. *Encyc.*

Hermetic books, books of the Egyptians which treat of astrology. *Bryant.*

Books which treat of universal principles, of the nature and orders of celestial beings, of medicine and other topics. *Enfield.*

HERMET'ICALLY, *adv.* According to the hermetic art; chimically; closely; accurately; as a vessel *hermetically* sealed or closed.

HER'MIT, *n.* [Fr. *hermite, ermite;* Sp. *ermitaño;* It. *eremita;* Gr. ερημιτης, from ερημος, solitary, destitute. Perhaps from the Shemitic חרם, to cut off from society, to expel, or to be separated. Class Rm. See *Harem.*]

1. A person who retires from society and lives in solitude; a recluse; an anchoret. The word is usually applied to a person who lives in solitude, disengaged from the cares and interruptions of society, for the purpose of religious contemplation and devotion.

2. A beadsman; one bound to pray for another. *Shak.*

HER'MITAGE, *n.* The habitation of a hermit; a house or hut with its appendages, in a solitary place, where a hermit dwells. *Milton.*

2. A cell in a recluse place, but annexed to an abbey. *Encyc.*

3. A kind of wine.

HER'MITARY, *n.* A cell for the religious annexed to some abbey. *Howell.*

HER'MITESS, *n.* A female hermit. *Drummond.*

HERMIT'ICAL, *a.* Pertaining to a hermit, or to retired life.

2. Suited to a hermit. *Coventry.*

HERMODAC'TYL, *n.* [Gr. ερμης, Mercury, and δακτυλος, a finger; Mercury's finger.]

In *the Materia Medica*, a root brought from Turkey. It is in the shape of a heart flatted, of a white color, compact, but easy to be cut or pulverized, of a viscous sweetish taste, with a slight degree of acrimony. Some suppose it to be the root of the Colchicum variegatum; others, the root of the Iris tuberosa. It was anciently in great repute as a cathartic; but that which is now furnished has little or no cathartic quality. *Encyc.*

HERMOGE'NIANS, *n.* A sect of ancient heretics, so called from their leader Hermogenes, who lived near the close of the second century. He held matter to be the fountain of all evil, and that souls are formed of corrupt matter. *Encyc.*

HERN, *n.* A heron, which see.

HERN'HILL, *n.* A plant.

HERN'IA, *n.* [L.] In *surgery*, a rupture; a descent of the intestines or omentum from their natural place; an unnatural protrusion of the intestines. Hernia is of various kinds. *Quincy. Coxe.*

HERN'SHAW, *n.* A heron. *Obs.* *Spenser.*

HE'RO, *n.* [L. *heros*, Gr. ηρως, a demigod. It coincides in elements with Ir. *earr*, noble, grand, a champion, and with the G. *herr*, D. *heer*, lord, master.]

1. A man of distinguished valor, intrepidity or enterprise in danger; as a *hero* in arms. *Cowley.*

2. A great, illustrious or extraordinary person; as a *hero* in learning. [*Little used.*]

3. In a *poem*, or *romance*, the principal personage, or the person who has the principal share in the transactions related; as Achilles in the Iliad, Ulysses in the Odyssey, and Æneas in the Æneid.

4. In *pagan mythology*, a hero was an illustrious person, mortal indeed, but supposed by the populace to partake of immortality, and after his death to be placed among the gods. *Encyc.*

HERO'DIANS, *n.* A sect among the Jews, which took this name from *Herod;* but authors are not agreed as to their peculiar notions.

HERO'IC, *a.* Pertaining to a hero or heroes; as *heroic* valor.

2. Becoming a hero; bold; daring; illustrious; as *heroic* action; *heroic* enterprises.

3. Brave; intrepid; magnanimous; enterprising; illustrious for valor; as Hector, the *heroic* son of Priam; a *heroic* race.

4. Productive of heroes; as a *heroic* line in pedigree.

5. Reciting the achievments of heroes; as a *heroic* poem.

6. Used in heroic poetry or hexameter; as *heroic* verse; a *heroic* foot.

Heroic age, the age when the *heroes*, or those called the children of the gods, are supposed to have lived.

HERO'ICAL, *a.* The same as *heroic.* [*Little used.*]

HERO'ICALLY, *adv.* In the manner of a hero; with valor; bravely; courageously; intrepidly. The wall was *heroically* defended.

HEROI-COM'IC, *a.* [See *Hero* and *Comic.*] Consisting of the heroic and the ludicrous; denoting the high burlesque; as a *heroi-comic* poem.

HER'OINE, *n.* *her'oin.* [Fr. *heroine*, from *hero.*]

A female hero; a woman of a brave spirit. [Heroess is not in use.] *Dryden.*

HER'OISM, *n.* [Fr. *heroisme.*] The qualities of a hero; bravery; courage; intrepidity; particularly in war. *Broome.*

HER'ON, *n.* [Fr.] A large fowl of the genus Ardea, a great devourer of fish.

HER'ONRY, HER'ONSHAW, } *n.* A place where herons breed. *Derham.*

HE'ROSHIP, *n.* The character of a hero. *Cowper.*

HER'PES, *n.* [Gr. ερπης, from ερπω, to creep.]

Tetters; an eruption on the skin; erysipelas; ringworm, &c. This disease takes various names according to its form or the part affected. *Coxe. Encyc.*

A term applied to several cutaneous eruptions, from their tendency to spread or creep from one part of the skin to another. *Cyc.*

An eruption of vesicles in small distinct clusters, accompanied with itching or tingling; including the shingles, ringworm, &c. *Good.*

HERPET'IC, *a.* Pertaining to the herpes or cutaneous eruptions; resembling the herpes, or partaking of its nature; as *herpetic* eruptions. *Darwin.*

HERPETOLOG'IC, HERPETOLOG'ICAL, } *a.* Pertaining to herpetology.

HERPETOL'OGIST, *n.* A person versed in herpetology, or the natural history of reptiles.

HERPETOL'OGY, *n.* [Gr. ερπετος, a reptile, and λογος, discourse.]

A description of reptiles; the natural history of reptiles, including oviparous quadrupeds, as the crocodile, frog and tortoise, and serpents. The history of the latter is called *ophiology.*

HER'RING, *n.* [Sax. *hæring;* Fr. *hareng;* Arm. *harincq;* G. *hering;* D. *haring;* It. *aringa;* Sp. *arenque;* Port. *id.*]

A fish of the genus Clupea. Herrings, when they migrate, move in vast shoals, and it is said that the name is formed from the Teutonic *here, heer,* an army or multitude. They come from high northern latitudes in the spring, and visit the shores of Europe and America, where they are taken and salted in great quantities.

HERRING-FISHERY, *n.* The fishing for herrings, which constitutes an important branch of business with the English, Dutch and Americans.

HERS, pron. *hurz, pron. fem. possessive;* as, this house is *hers,* that is, this is the house *of her.* But perhaps it would be more correct to consider *hers* as a substitute for the noun and adjective, in the nominative case. Of the two houses, *hers* is the best, that is, *her house* is the best.

HERSCHEL, *n. her'shel.* A planet discovered by Dr. Herschel, in 1781.

HERSE, *n. hers.* [Fr. *herse,* a harrow, a portcullis, probably from cross-work; radically the same word as *harrow,* which see.]

1. In *fortification,* a lattice or portcullis in the form of a harrow, set with iron spikes. It is hung by a rope fastened to a moulinet, and when a gate is broken, it is let down to obstruct the passage. It is called also a *sarrasin* or *cataract,* and when it consists of straight stakes without cross-pieces, it is called *orgues.*

Herse is also a harrow, used for a chevaux de frise, and laid in the way or in breaches, with the points up, to obstruct or incommode the march of an enemy. *Encyc.*

2. A carriage for bearing corpses to the grave. It is a frame only, or a box, as in England, borne on wheels.

3. A temporary monument set over a grave. [*Unusual and not legitimate.*] *Weever.*

4. A funeral eulogy. [*Not used.*] *W. Browne.*

HERSE, *v. t. hers.* To put on or in a herse. *Shak. Chapman.*

2. To carry to the grave.

HERSELF', *pron.* [*her* and *self.*] This denotes a female, the subject of discourse before mentioned, and is either in the nominative or objective case. In the nominative it usually follows *she,* and is added for the sake of emphasis, or emphatical distinction; as, *she herself* will bear the blame.

> The daughter of Pharaoh came down to wash *herself.* Ex. ii.

2. Having the command of herself; mistress of her rational powers, judgment or temper. The woman was deranged, but she is now *herself* again. She has come to *herself.*

3. In her true character; as, the woman acts like *herself.*

HERSELIKE, *a. hers'like.* Funereal; suitable to funerals. *Bacon.*

HERS'ILLON, *n.* [from *herse.*] In *the military art,* a plank or beam, whose sides are set with spikes or nails, to incommode and retard the march of an enemy. *Encyc.*

HER'Y, *v. t.* [Sax. *herian.*] To regard as holy. *Obs.* *Spenser.*

HES'ITANCY, *n.* [See *Hesitate.*] A doubting; literally, a stopping of the mind; a pausing to consider; dubiousness; suspense.

> The reason of my *hesitancy* about the air is— *Boyle.*

HES'ITANT, *a.* Hesitating; pausing; wanting volubility of speech.

HES'ITATE, *v. i. s* as *z.* [L. *hæsito;* Fr. *hesiter;* from *hæsi,* pret. of L. *hæreo,* to hang.]

1. To stop or pause respecting decision or action; to be doubtful as to fact, principle or determination; to be in suspense or uncertainty; as, he *hesitated* whether to accept the offer or not. We often *hesitate* what judgment to form.

It is never transitive, unless by poetic license.

> Just hint a fault, and *hesitate* dislike. *Pope.*

2. To stammer; to stop in speaking.

HES'ITATING, *ppr.* Doubting; pausing; stammering.

HES'ITATINGLY, *adv.* With hesitation or doubt.

HESITA'TION, *n.* A pausing or delay in forming an opinion or commencing action; doubt; suspension of opinion or decision, from uncertainty what is proper to be decided. When evidence is clear, we may decide without *hesitation.*

2. A stopping in speech; intermission between words; stammering. *Swift.*

HEST, *n.* [Sax. *hæse;* G. *geheiss,* a command; *heissen,* to call, to bid; D. *heeten.* See *Heat.*]

Command; precept; injunction; order. [Now obsolete, but it is retained in the compound, *behest.*]

HESPE'RIAN, *a.* [L. *hesperius,* western, from *hesperus, vesper,* the evening star, Venus, Gr. εσπερος.] Western; situated at the west.

HESPE'RIAN, *n.* An inhabitant of a western country. *J. Barlow.*

HET'ERARCHY, *n.* [Gr. ετερος, another, and αρχη, rule.] The government of an alien. *Bp. Hall.*

HET'EROCLITE, *n.* [Gr. ετεροχλιτον; ετερος, another, or different, and χλιτος, from χλινω, to incline, to lean.]

1. In *grammar,* a word which is irregular or anomalous either in declension or conjugation, or which deviates from the ordinary forms of inflection in words of a like kind. It is particularly applied to nouns irregular in declension.

2. Any thing or person deviating from common forms. *Johnson.*

HET'EROCLITE, HETEROCLIT'IC, HETEROCLIT'ICAL, } *a.* Irregular; anomalous; deviating from ordinary forms or rules. *Brown.*

HETEROC'LITOUS, *a.* Heteroclitic. [*Not in use.*]

HET'ERODOX, *a.* [Gr. ετερος, another, different, and δοξα, opinion.]

1. In *theology,* heretical; contrary to the faith and doctrines of the true church; or more precisely, contrary to the real doctrines of the Scriptures; as a *heterodox* opinion; opposed to *orthodox.*

2. Repugnant to the doctrines or tenets of any established church.

3. Holding opinions repugnant to the doctrines of the Scriptures, as a *heterodox* divine; or holding opinions contrary to those of an established church.

HET'ERODOXY, *n.* Heresy; an opinion or doctrine contrary to the doctrines of the Scriptures, or contrary to those of an established church.

HET'EROGENE, *a. Obs.* [See the next word.]

HETEROGE'NEAL, HETEROGE'NEOUS, } *a.* [Gr. ετερος, other, and γενος, kind.]

Of a different kind or nature; unlike or dissimilar in kind; opposed to *homogeneous.*

> The light whose rays are all alike refrangible, I call simple, homogeneal and similar; and that whose rays are some more refrangible than others, I call compound, *heterogeneal* and dissimilar. *Newton.*

Heterogeneous nouns, are such as are of different genders in the singular and plural numbers; as *hic locus,* of the masculine gender in the singular, and *hi loci* and *hæc loca,* both masculine and neuter in the plural. *Hoc cælum,* neuter in the singular; *hi cæli,* masculine in the plural.

Heterogeneous quantities, are those which are of such different kind and consideration, that one of them, taken any number of times, never equals or exceeds the other.

Heterogeneous surds, are such as have different radical signs. *Encyc.*

HETEROGENE'ITY, *n.* Opposition of nature; contrariety or dissimilitude of qualities. [*Ill formed.*]

2. Dissimilar part; something of a different kind. *Boyle.*

HETEROGE'NEOUSNESS, *n.* Difference of nature and quality; dissimilitude or contrariety in kind, nature or qualities.

HETEROPH'YLLOUS, *a.* [Gr. ετερος, diverse, and φυλλον, leaf.]

Producing a diversity of leaves; as a *heterophyllous* violet. *Journ. of Science.*

HETEROP'TICS, *n.* [See *Optics.*] False optics. *Spectator.*

HETEROS'CIAN, *n.* [Gr. ετερος, other, and σκια, shadow.]

Those inhabitants of the earth are called *Heteroscians*, whose shadows fall one way only. Such are those who live between the tropics and the polar circles. The shadows of those who live north of the tropic of Cancer, fall northward; those of the inhabitants south of the tropic of Capricorn, fall southward; whereas the shadows of those who dwell between the tropics fall sometimes to the north and sometimes to the south.

HETEROS'CIAN, *a.* Having the shadow fall one way only. *Gregory.*

HEU'LANDITE, *a.* [from *M. Heuland.*] A mineral, occurring massive, frequently globular, or crystalized in the form of a right oblique-angled prism. It has been ranked among the zeolites, but is now considered as distinct. *Phillips.*

HEW, *v. t.* pret. *hewed;* pp. *hewed* or *hewn.* [Sax. *heawian;* G. *hauen;* D. *houwen;* Sw. *hugga;* Dan. *hugger.* In Sw. *hugg* is a cut, a slash; Dan. *hug*, a beating, a striking; so that the primary sense is to strike, to drive with the hand. See *Hoe.*]

1. To cut with an ax, or other like instrument, for the purpose of making an even surface or side; as, to *hew* timber.

2. To chop; to cut; to hack; as, to *hew* in pieces.

3. To cut with a chisel; to make smooth; as, to *hew* stone.

4. To form or shape with an edged instrument; with *out;* as, to *hew out* a sepulcher. Is. xxii.

5. To form laboriously.

> I now pass my days, not studious nor idle, rather polishing old works than *hewing out* new ones. [*Unusual.*] *Pope.*

To hew down, to cut down; to fell by cutting.

To hew off, to cut off; to separate by a cutting instrument.

HEW'ED, *pp.* Cut and made smooth or even; chopped; hacked; shaped by cutting or by a chisel.

HEW'ER, *n.* One who hews wood or stone.

HEW'ING, *ppr.* Cutting and making smooth or even; chopping; hacking; forming by the chisel.

HEWN, *pp.* The same as *hewed.*

HEX'ADE, *n.* [Gr. εξ, six.] A series of six numbers. *Med. Repos.*

HEX'ACHORD, *n.* [Gr. εξ, six, and χορδη, a chord.]

In *ancient music*, an imperfect chord called a *sixth.* Also, an instrument of six chords, or system of six sounds. *Rousseau.*

HEX'AGON, *n.* [Gr. εξ, six, and γωνια, an angle.]

In *geometry*, a figure of six sides and six angles. If the sides and angles are equal, it is a *regular hexagon.* The cells of honeycomb are hexagons, and it is remarkable that bees instinctively form their cells of this figure which fills any given space without any interstice or loss of room.

HEXAG'ONAL, *a.* Having six sides and six angles.

HEXAG'ONY, for *hexagon*, is not used.

HEX'AGYN, *n.* [Gr. εξ, six, and γυνη, a female.] In *botany*, a plant that has six pistils.

HEXAGYN'IAN, *a.* Having six pistils.

HEXAHE'DRAL, *a.* Of the figure of a hexahedron; having six equal sides.

HEXAHE'DRON, *n.* [Gr. εξ, six, and εδρα, a base or seat.] A regular solid body of six sides; a cube.

HEXAHEM'ERON, *n.* [Gr. εξ, six, and ημερα, day.] The term of six days. *Good.*

HEXAM'ETER, *n.* [Gr. εξ, six, and μετρον, measure.]

In *ancient poetry*, a verse of six feet, the first four of which may be either dactyls or spondees, the fifth must regularly be a dactyl, and the sixth always a spondee. In this species of verse are composed the Iliad of Homer and the Æneid of Virgil.

> *Diva so|lo fix|os ocu|los a|versa ten|ebat.* *Virgil.*

HEXAM'ETER, *a.* Having six metrical feet.

HEXAMET'RIC, } *a.* Consisting of six metrical feet.
HEXAMET'RICAL, } *Warton.*

HEXAN'DER, *n.* [Gr. εξ, six, and ανηρ, male.] In *botany*, a plant having six stamens.

HEXAN'DRIAN, *a.* Having six stamens.

HEXAN'GULAR, *a.* [Gr. εξ, six, and *angular.*] Having six angles or corners.

HEX'APED, *a.* [Gr. εξ, six, and πους, ποδος, L. *pes, pedis*, the foot.] Having six feet.

HEX'APED, *n.* An animal having six feet. [Ray, and Johnson after him write this *hexapod;* but it is better to pursue uniformity, as in *quadruped, centiped.*]

2. A fathom. [*Not in use.*]

HEXAPET'ALOUS, *a.* [Gr. εξ, six, and πεταλον, a leaf, a petal.] Having six petals or flower-leaves.

HEXAPH'YLLOUS, *a.* [Gr. εξ, six, and φυλλον, a leaf.] Having six leaves.

HEX'APLAR, *a.* [Gr. εξ, six, and απλοω, to unfold.]

Sextuple; containing six columns; from *Hexapla*, the work of Origen, or an edition of the Bible, containing the original Hebrew, and several Greek versions.

HEXAS'TICH, *n.* [Gr. εξ, six, and ςιχος, a verse.]

A poem consisting of six verses. *Johnson. Weever.*

HEX'ASTYLE, *n.* [Gr. εξ, six, and ςυλος, a column.]

A building with six columns in front. *Encyc.*

HEY. An exclamation of joy or mutual exhortation, the contrary to the L. *hei.* *Prior.*

HEYDAY, *exclam.* [Qu. *high-day.*] An expression of frolick and exultation, and sometimes of wonder. *Shak.*

HEYDAY, *n.* A frolick; wildness. *Shak.*

HIA'TION, *n.* [L. *hio*, to gape.] The act of gaping. [*Not used.*]

HIA'TUS, *n.* [L. from *hio*, to open or gape, Gr. χαω.]

1. An opening; an aperture; a gap; a chasm.

2. The opening of the mouth in reading or speaking, when a word ends with a vowel, and the following word begins with a vowel. *Pope.*

3. A defect; a chasm in a manuscript, where some part is lost or effaced. *Encyc.*

HI'BERNACLE, *n.* [L. *hibernacula*, winter-quarters.]

1. In *botany*, the winter-quarters of a plant, that is, a bulb or a bud, in which the embryo of a future plant is inclosed by a scaly covering and protected from injuries during winter. *Barton. Martyn.*

2. The winter-lodge of a wild animal.

HIBERN'AL, *a.* [L. *hibernus.*] Belonging or relating to winter. *Brown.*

HI'BERNATE, *v. i.* [L. *hiberno;* It. *vernare.*]

To winter; to pass the season of winter in close quarters or in seclusion, as birds or beasts. *Darwin.*

HIBERNA'TION, *n.* The passing of winter in a close lodge, as beasts and fowls that retire in cold weather. *Darwin.*

HIBER'NIAN, *a.* Pertaining to Hibernia, now Ireland.

HIBER'NIAN, *n.* A native of Ireland.

HIBERN'ICISM, *n.* An idiom or mode of speech peculiar to the Irish. *Todd.*

HIBERNO-CELTIC, *n.* The native language of the Irish; the Gaelic.

Hiccius Doccius. [Qu. *hic est doctus.*] A cant word for a juggler. *Hudibras.*

HIC'COUGH, } *n.* [Dan. *hik* or *hikken;* Sw.
HICK'UP, } *hicka;* D. *hik, hikken;* Fr. *hoquet;* W. *ig, igian;* Arm. *hicq.* The English is a compound of *hic* and *cough;* and *hic* may be allied to *hitch*, to catch. The word is generally pronounced *hick-up.*]

A spasmodic affection of the stomach, esophagus, and muscles subservient to deglutition. *Encyc. Parr.*

Convulsive catch of the respiratory muscles, with sonorous inspiration; repeated at short intervals. *Good.*

HIC'COUGH, } *v. i.* To have a spasmodic affection of the stom-
HICK'UP, } ach from repletion or other cause.

HICK'ORY, *n.* A tree, a species of Juglans or walnut. Its nut is called *hickory-nut.*

HICK'WALL, } *n.* [Qu. *hitchwall.*] A small
HICK'WAY, } species of woodpecker.

HID, } *pp.* of *hide.* Concealed; placed
HID'DEN, } in secrecy.

2. *a.* Secret; unseen.

3. Mysterious.

HI'DAGE, *n.* [from *hide*, a quantity of land.] An extraordinary tax formerly paid to the kings of England for every hide of land.

HIDAL'GO, *n.* In Spain, a man of noble birth.

HID'DENLY, *adv.* In a hidden or secret manner.

HIDE, *v. t.* pret. *hid;* pp. *hid, hidden.* [Sax. *hydan;* W. *cuziaw;* Arm. *cuza*, or *cuddyo*, or *kytho;* Corn. *kitha;* Russ. *kutayu;* Gr. κευθω. In Sw. *hydda*, Dan. *hytte*, is a *hut;* and the Sw. *hyda, förhyda*, Dan. *forhuer*, to sheathe a ship, seem to be the same word. *Hood*, as well as *hut*, may belong to this root. See Class Gd. No. 26. 31. 43. 55.]

1. To conceal; to withhold or withdraw from sight; to place in any state or position in which the view is intercepted from the object. The intervention of the moon between the earth and the sun *hides* the latter from our sight. The people in Turkey *hide* their grain in the earth. No human being can *hide* his crimes or his neglect of duty from his Maker.

2. To conceal from knowledge; to keep secret.

Depart to the mountains; *hide* yourselves there three days. Josh. ii.

Tell me now what thou hast done—*hide* it not from me. Josh. vii.

3. In *Scripture*, not to confess or disclose; or to excuse and extenuate.

I acknowledged my sin to thee, and my iniquity have I not *hid*. Ps. xxxii.

4. To protect; to keep in safety.

In the time of trouble, he shall *hide* me in his pavilion. Ps. xxvii.

To hide the face from, to overlook; to pardon.

Hide thy face from my sins. Ps. li.

To hide the face, to withdraw spiritual presence, support and consolation.

Thou didst *hide thy face*, and I was troubled. Ps. xxx.

To hide one's self, to put one's self in a condition to be safe; to secure protection.

The prudent man foreseeth the evil and *hideth himself*. Prov. xxii.

HIDE, *v. i.* To lie concealed; to keep one's self out of view; to be withdrawn from sight.

Bred to disguise, in public 'tis you *hide*. *Pope.*

Hide and seek, a play of boys, in which some hide themselves and another seeks them. *Gulliver.*

HIDE, *n.* [According to Lye, Sax. Dict. under *weal-stylling*, this word signified originally a station, covered place, or place of refuge for besiegers against the attacks of the besieged. Qu.]

In the ancient laws of England, a certain portion of land, the quantity of which however is not well ascertained. Some authors consider it as the quantity that could be tilled with one plow; others, as much as would maintain a family. Some suppose it to be 60, some 80, and others 100 acres. *Spelman. Encyc.*

HIDE, *n.* [Sax. *hyd*, *hyde*; G. *haut*; D. *huid*; Sw. and Dan. *hud*; L. *cutis*; Gr. χως, χωδιον; either a peel, from stripping, separating, or a cover.]

1. The skin of an animal, either raw or dressed; more generally applied to the undressed skins of the larger domestic animals, as oxen, horses, &c.

2. The human skin; in contempt. *Dryden.*

HI'DEBOUND, *a.* A horse is *hidebound*, when his skin sticks so closely to his ribs and back, as not to be easily loosened or raised. *Far. Dict.*

Trees are said to be *hidebound*, when the bark is so close or firm that it impedes the growth. *Bacon.*

2. Harsh; untractable. [*Not used.*] *Hudibras.*

3. Niggardly; penurious. [*Not used.*] *Ainsworth.*

HID'EOUS, *a.* [Fr. *hideux*; Norm. *hidous*, from *hide*, fright, dread.]

1. Frightful to the sight; dreadful; shocking to the eye; *applied to deformity*; as a *hideous* monster; a *hideous* spectacle; *hideous* looks. *Shak. Dryden.*

2. Shocking to the ear; exciting terror; as a *hideous* noise. *Woodward.*

3. Detestable. *Spenser.*

HID'EOUSLY, *adv.* In a manner to frighten; dreadfully; shockingly. *Shak.*

HID'EOUSNESS, *n.* Frightfulness to the eye; dreadfulness; horribleness.

HI'DER, *n.* [from *hide*.] One who hides or conceals.

HI'DING, *ppr.* Concealing; covering or withdrawing from view; keeping close or secret.

HI'DING, *n.* Concealment. Hab. iii.

2. Withdrawment; a withholding; as the *hidings* of God's face. *Milner.*

HI'DING-PLACE, *n.* A place of concealment.

HIE, *v. i.* [Sax. *higan*, *higian*, to hasten, to urge forward, to press, to endeavor; also, *hiegan* and *higgan*, to be urgent, to strive.]

1. To hasten; to move or run with haste; to go in haste; *a word chiefly used in poetry.*

The youth, returning to his mistress, *hies*. *Dryden.*

2. With the reciprocal pronoun; as, *hie* thee home.

HIE, *n.* Haste; diligence. *Obs. Chaucer.*

HI'ERARCH, *n.* [Gr. ιερος, sacred, and αρχος, a ruler or prince.]

The chief of a sacred order; particularly, the chief of an order of angels. *Milton.*

HIERARCH'AL, *a.* Belonging to a hierarch. *Milton.*

HIERARCH'ICAL, *a.* Belonging to a sacred order, or to ecclesiastical government.

HI'ERARCHY, *n.* An order or rank of angels or celestial beings; or a subordination of holy beings. Some of the Rabbins reckon four, and others ten *hierarchies*, or orders of angels. *Encyc.*

2. Constitution and government of the christian church, or ecclesiastical polity, comprehending different orders of clergy; as the *hierarchy* of England. *Bacon.*

HI'EROGLYPH, HIEROGLYPH'IC, } *n.* [Gr. ιερος, sacred, and γλυφω, to carve.]

1. In *antiquity*, a sacred character; a mystical character or symbol, used in writings and inscriptions, particularly by the Egyptians, as signs of sacred, divine, or supernatural things. The hieroglyphics were figures of animals, parts of the human body, mechanical instruments, &c., which contained a meaning known only to kings and priests. It is supposed they were used to vail morality, politics, &c., from vulgar eyes. *Encyc.*

2. Pictures intended to express historical facts; supposed to be the primitive mode of writing.

3. The art of writing in picture. *Swift.*

HIEROGLYPH'IC, HIEROGLYPH'ICAL, } *a.* Emblematic; expressive of some meaning by characters, pictures or figures; as *hieroglyphic* writing; a *hieroglyphic* obelisk.

HIEROGLYPH'ICALLY, *adv.* Emblematically; by characters or pictures expressive of facts or moral qualities. The Mexicans wrote history *hieroglyphically*.

HI'EROGRAM, *n.* [Gr. ιερος, sacred, and γραμμα, letter.] A species of sacred writing.

HIEROGRAMMAT'IC, *a.* [Gr. ιερος, sacred, and γραμμα, letter.]

Denoting a kind of writing in sacred or sacerdotal characters, used only by the priests in Egypt. *Warburton.*

HIEROGRAM'MATIST, *n.* A writer of hieroglyphics.

HIEROGRAPH'IC, HIEROGRAPH'ICAL, } *a.* Pertaining to sacred writing.

HIEROG'RAPHY, *n.* [Gr. ιερος, holy, and γραφω, to write.] Sacred writing. [*Little used.*]

HIEROL'OGY, *n.* [Gr. ιερος and λογος.] A discourse on sacred things.

HIEROM'ANCY, *n.* [Gr. ιερος, sacred, and μαντεια, divination.]

Divination by observing the various things offered in sacrifice. *Encyc.*

HIEROM'NEMON, *n.* [Gr. ιερος, sacred, and μνημων, preserving memory.]

In *ancient Greece*, a magistrate who presided over the sacred rites and solemnities, &c. *Mitford.*

HI'EROPHANT, *n.* [Gr. ιεροφαντης; ιερος, sacred, and φαινω, to show.]

A priest; one who teaches the mysteries and duties of religion. *Hale.*

HIG'GLE, *v. i.* [In Dan. *hykler* signifies to flatter, fawn, disguise or play the hypocrite; Sw. *hyckla*, id. In Welsh, *hiciaw* is to snap, to catch suddenly, to trick, as if allied to *hitch*. This word may be from the same root as L. *cocio*. See *Huckster*.]

1. To carry provisions about and offer them for sale.

2. To chaffer; to be difficult in making a bargain.

It argues an ignorant mind, where we have wronged, to *higgle* and dodge in the amends. *Hale.*

HIGGLEDY-PIGGLEDY, *adv.* In confusion; *a low word.*

HIG'GLER, *n.* One who carries about provisions for sale.

2. One who chaffers in bargaining.

HIGH, *a. hi.* [Sax. *heah*, *hig*, *heh* or *hih*; G. *hoch*; D. *hoog*; Sw. *hög*; Dan. *höj*. The W. *uc*, *ucel*, may be the same word, with the loss of the first letter.]

1. Extending a great distance above the surface of the earth; elevated; lofty; of great altitude; as a *high* mountain; a *high* tower.

2. Rising, or having risen, or being far above the earth; elevated; lofty; as a *high* flight; the clouds are *high* in the atmosphere.

3. Elevated above the horizon; as, how *high* is the sun? It is an hour *high*.

4. Raised above any object.

High o'er their heads a moldering rock is placed. *Dryden.*

5. Exalted in nature or dignity.

The *highest* faculty of the soul. *Baxter.*

6. Elevated in rank, condition or office. We speak of *high* and low; of a *high* office; *high* rank; *high* station; a *high* court.

7. Possessing or governed by honorable pride; noble; exalted; magnanimous; dignified; as a man of a *high* mind.
8. Exalted in excellence or extent.

Solomon lived at ease, nor aimed beyond
Higher design than to enjoy his state. *Milton.*

9. Difficult; abstruse.

They meet to hear, and answer such *high* things. *Shak.*

10. Boastful; ostentatious.

His forces, after all the *high* discourses, amounted really but to eighteen hundred foot. *Clarendon.*

11. Arrogant; proud; lofty; loud.

The governor made himself merry with his *high* and threatening language. *Clarendon.*

12. Loud; boisterous; threatening or angry. The parties had very *high* words.
13. Violent; severe; oppressive.

When there appeareth on either side a *high* hand, violent persecution, &c. *Bacon.*

14. Public; powerful; triumphant; glorious; or under divine protection.

The children of Israel went out of Egypt with a *high* hand. Ex. xiv.

15. Noble; illustrious; honorable; as a man of *high* birth.
16. Expressive of pride and haughtiness; as *high* looks. Is. x.
17. Powerful; mighty.

Strong is thy hand, *high* is thy right hand. Ps. lxxxix.

18. Possessed of supreme power, dominion or excellence.

Thou, Lord, art *high* above all the earth. Ps. xcvii.

19. Great; important; solemn; held in veneration.

For that sabbath-day was a *high* day. John xix.

20. Violent; rushing with velocity; tempestuous; as a *high* wind.
21. Tumultuous; turbulent; inflamed; violent; as *high* passions.
22. Full; complete. It is *high* time to retire.

It is *high* time to awake from sleep. Rom. xiii.

23. Raised; accompanied by, or proceeding from great excitement of the feelings; as *high* pleasure of body or mind.
24. Rich; luxurious; well seasoned; as *high* fare; *high* living; *high* sauces. *Milton. Bacon.*
25. Strong; vivid; deep; as a *high* color.
26. Dear; of a great price, or greater price than usual; as, to purchase at a *high* rate; goods are *high*.
27. Remote from the equator north or south; as a *high* latitude.
28. Remote in past time; early in former time; as *high* antiquity.
29. Extreme; intense; as a *high* heat.
30. Loud; as a *high* sound. But more generally,
31. In *music*, acute; sharp; as a *high* note; a *high* voice; opposed to *low* or *grave*.
32. Much raised; as *high* relief [*alto relievo.*]
33. Far advanced in art or science; as *high* attainments.
34. Great; capital; committed against the king, sovereign or state; as *high* treason, distinguished from *petty* treason, which is committed against a master or other superior.
35. Great; exalted; as a *high* opinion of one's integrity.

High church and *low church*, in Great Britain, a distinction introduced after the revolution. The high church were supposed to favor the papists, or at least to support the high claims to prerogative, which were maintained by the Stuarts. The low church entertained more moderate notions, manifested great enmity to popery, and were inclined to circumscribe the royal prerogatives. This distinction is now less marked, but not wholly obliterated.

High day, high noon, the time when the sun is in the meridian.

High Dutch, is the German language, as distinguished from Low Dutch or Belgic, or the cultivated German, as opposed to the vulgar dialects.

HIGH, *adv.* Aloft; to a great altitude; as towering *high*.

2. Eminently; greatly.

Heaven and earth
Shall *high* extol thy praises. *Milton.*

3. With deep thought; profoundly.

He reasoned *high*. *Milton.*

4. Powerfully. *Milton.*

HIGH, *n.* An elevated place; superior region; as on *high*; from on *high*.

On high, aloud. *Obs.* *Spenser.*

2. Aloft.

HIGH-AIMED, *a.* Having grand or lofty designs. *Crashaw.*

HIGH-ARCHED, *a.* Having elevated arches. *May.*

HIGH-ASPI'RING, *a.* Having elevated views; aiming at elevated objects. *Bp. Hall.*

HIGH-BLEST, *a.* Supremely happy. *Milton.*

HIGH-BLOWN, *a.* Swelled much with wind; inflated, as with pride or conceit. *Shak.*

HIGH-BORN, *a.* Being of noble birth or extraction. *Rowe.*

HIGH-BUILT, *a.* Of lofty structure. *Milton.*

2. Covered with lofty buildings.

The *high-built* elephant his castle rears. *Creech.*

HIGH-CLIMBING, *a.* Climbing to a great height.

2. Difficult to be ascended. *Milton.*

HIGH-COLORED, *a.* Having a strong, deep or glaring color. *Floyer.*

2. Vivid; strong or forcible in representation; as a *high-colored* description.

HIGH-DAY, *a.* Fine; befitting a holiday. *Shak.*

HIGH-DESIGNING, *a.* Forming great schemes. *Dryden.*

HIGH-EMBOWED, *a.* Having lofty arches. *Milton.*

HIGH-ENGEN'DERED, *a.* Engendered aloft, or in the air. *Shak.*

HIGH-FED, *a.* Pampered; fed luxuriously. *Milton.*

HIGH-FLAMING, *a.* Throwing flame to a great highth. *Pope.*

HIGH-FLIER, *n.* One that carries his opinions to extravagance. *Swift.*

HIGH-FLOWN, *a.* Elevated; swelled; proud; as *high-flown* hopes. *Denham.*

2. Turgid; swelled; extravagant; as a *high-flown* hyperbole. *L'Estrange.*

HIGH-FLUSHED, *a.* Much elated. *Young.*

HIGH-FLYING, *a.* Extravagant in claims or opinions; as *high-flying*, arbitrary kings. *Dryden.*

Highgate Resin. [See *Fossil Copal.*]

HIGH-GAZING, *a.* Looking upwards. *More.*

HIGH-GOING, *a.* Moving rapidly. *Massenger.*

HIGH-GROWN, *a.* Having the crop considerably grown.

HIGH-HEAPED, *a.* Covered with high piles; as a *high-heaped* table. *Pope.*

2. Raised in high piles. *Pope.*

HIGH-HE'ARTED, *a.* Full of courage. *Beaum.*

HIGH-HEELED, *a.* Having high heels. *Swift.*

HIGH-HUNG, *a.* Hung aloft; elevated. *Dryden.*

HIGH-LIVED, *a.* Pertaining to high life. *Goldsmith.*

HIGH-METTLED, *a.* Having high spirit; ardent; full of fire; as a *high-mettled* steed.

HIGH-MINDED, *a.* Proud; arrogant.

Be not *high-minded*, but fear. Rom. xi.

2. Having honorable pride; magnanimous; opposed to *mean*.

HIGH-OPERATION, *n.* In *surgery*, a method of extracting the stone from the human bladder, by cutting the upper part of it. *Encyc.*

HIGH-PLACE, *n.* In *Scripture*, an eminence or mound on which sacrifices were offered. Before the temple was built in Jerusalem, sacrifices were offered to Jehovah by his worshipers, on *high places;* but afterwards such mounds were devoted to idolatrous sacrifices.

HIGH-PLACED, *a.* Elevated in situation or rank. *Shak.*

HIGH-PRIEST, *n.* A chief priest. *Scripture.*

HIGH-PRINCIPLED, *a.* Extravagant in notions of politics. *Swift.*

HIGH-RAISED, *a.* Elevated; raised aloft. *Dryden.*

2. Raised with great expectations or conceptions. *Milton.*

HIGH-REACHING, *a.* Reaching to a great highth.

2. Reaching upwards. *Milton.*
3. Ambitious; aspiring. *Shak.*

HIGH-REARED, *a.* Raised high; of lofty structure. *Shak.*

HIGH-RED, *a.* Having a strong red color; deeply red. *Boyle.*

HIGH-REPENT'ED, *a.* Deeply repented. [*Ill.*] *Shak.*

HIGH-RESOLV'ED, *a.* Very resolute. *Tit. Andron.*

HIGH-ROOFED, *a.* Having a lofty or sharp roof. *Milton.*

HIGH-SEASONED, *a.* Enriched with spices or other seasoning.

HIGH-SEATED, *a.* Fixed on high; seated in an elevated place. *Milton.*

HIGH-SIGHTED, *a.* Always looking upward. *Shak.*

HIGH-SOUNDING, *a.* Pompous; noisy; ostentatious; as *high-sounding* words or titles.

HIGH-SPIRITED, *a.* Full of spirit or natural fire; easily irritated; irascible.

2. Full of spirit; bold; daring.

HIGH-STOMACHED, *a.* Having a lofty spirit; proud; obstinate. *Shak.*

HIGH-SWELLING, *a.* Swelling greatly; inflated; boastful.

HIGH-SWOLN, *a.* Greatly swelled. *Shak.*

HIGH-TAPER, *n.* A plant of the genus Verbascum. *Fam. of Plants.*

HIGH-TASTED, *a.* Having a strong relish; piquant. *Denham.*

HIGH-TOWERED, *a.* Having lofty towers. *Milton.*

HIGH-VICED, *a.* Enormously wicked. *Shak.*

HIGH-WROUGHT, *a.* Wrought with exquisite art or skill; accurately finished. *Pope.*

2. Inflamed to a high degree; as *high-wrought* passion.

HIGHLAND, *n.* Elevated land; a mountainous region.

Highlands of Scotland, mountainous regions inhabited by the descendants of the ancient Celts, who retain their primitive language.

Highlands on the Hudson, sixty miles from New York. These afford most sublime and romantic scenery, and here is West Point, a fortified post during the revolution, and now the seat of one of the best military schools of the age.

HIGHLANDER, *n.* An inhabitant of the mountains; as the *Highlanders* of Scotland.

HIGHLANDISH, *a.* Denoting high or mountainous land. *Drummond.*

HIGHLY, *adv. hi'ly.* With elevation in place.

2. In a great degree. We are *highly* favored. Exercise is *highly* requisite to health.

3. Proudly; arrogantly; ambitiously. *Shak.*

4. With elevation of mind or opinion; with great estimation; as, to think *highly* of one's performances.

HIGHMOST, *a.* Highest. [*Not used.*] *Shak.*

HIGHNESS, *n. hi'ness.* Elevation above the surface; loftiness; altitude; highth.

2. Dignity; elevation in rank, character or power.

3. Excellence; value. *Howell.*

4. Violence; as the *highness* of wind.

5. Great amount; as the *highness* of price.

6. Acuteness; as the *highness* of a note or voice.

7. Intenseness, as of heat.

8. A title of honor given to princes or other men of rank.

HIGHTH, HIGHT, *n.* [See *Height.*] Elevation; altitude; loftinesss. [It is very desirable that this noun should be regularly formed from the adjective.]

Hight, to call, to promise, to command, &c. is a false orthography, from Saxon, *hatan*. It is obsolete. [See *Heat.*] *Chaucer. Spenser.*

HIGHWATER, *n.* The utmost flow or greatest elevation of the tide; also, the time of such elevation.

HIGHWATER-MARK, *n.* The line made on the shore by the tide at its utmost highth. *Mar. Dict.*

HIGHWA'Y, *n.* A public road; a way open to all passengers; so called, either because it is a great or public road, or because the earth was raised to form a dry path. *Highways* open a communication from one city or town to another.

2. Course; road; train of action. *Child.*

HIGHWA'YMAN, *n.* One who robs on the public road, or lurks in the highway for the purpose of robbing.

HILARATE, is not in use. [See *Exhilarate.*]

HILAR'ITY, *n.* [L. *hilaritas*; Gr. ιλαρος, joyful, merry. If *r* is radical, this cannot be from ιλαω, to be propitious.]

Mirth; merriment; gayety. *Hilarity* differs from *joy*; the latter, excited by good news or prosperity, is an affection of the mind; the former, by social pleasure, drinking, &c. which rouse the animal spirits.

HIL'ARY-TERM, *n.* The term of courts, &c. which begins January 23. *England.*

HILD, G. and D. *held*, Dan. *heldt*, a hero, is retained in names; as *Hildebert*, a bright hero; *Mathild, Matilda*, a heroic lady.

HILD'ING, *n.* [Qu. Sax. *hyldan*, to decline, or *hyldeleas*, destitute of affection.]

A mean, sorry, paltry man or woman. *Obs.* *Shak.*

HILL, *n.* [Sax. *hill* or *hyl*; L. *collis*; perhaps Gr. χηλη. It cannot be the G. *hügel*, D. *heuvel*, unless contracted.]

1. A natural elevation of land, or a mass of earth rising above the common level of the surrounding land; an eminence. A hill is less than a mountain, but of no definite magnitude, and is sometimes applied to a mountain. Jerusalem is seated on two *hills*. Rome stood on seven *hills*.

2. A cluster of plants, and the earth raised about them; as a *hill* of maiz or potatoes. *U. States.*

HILL, *v. t.* To raise earth about plants; to raise a little mass of earth. Farmers in New England *hill* their maiz in July. *Hilling* is generally the third hoeing.

2. To cover. *Obs.* [Sax. *helan*; L. *celo.*]

HILL'ED, *pp.* or *a.* Having hills.

HILL'ING, *n.* A covering. *Obs.*

2. The act of raising the earth around plants.

HILL'OCK, *n.* A small hill. *Milton. Dryden.*

HILL'SIDE, *n.* The side or declivity of a hill. *J. Barlow.*

HILL'Y, *a.* Abounding with hills; as a *hilly* country.

HILT, *n.* [Sax. *hilt*, the *hold*, from *healdan*, to hold.]

The handle of any thing; but chiefly applied to the handle of a sword.

HILT'ED, *a.* Having a hilt.

HI'LUM, *n.* [L.; W. *hil*, a particle, issue.] The eye of a bean or other seed; the mark or scar of the umbilical chord, by which the seed adheres to the pericarp. *Martyn.*

HIM, *pron.* The objective case of *he*, L. *eum*, anciently *em* or *im.*

> *Him* that is weak in the faith receive. Rom. xiv.

Him and *his* were formerly used for nouns of the neuter gender, but the practice is obsolete.

HIMSELF', *pron.* In the nominative or objective case. [*him* and *self.*]

1. He; but *himself* is more emphatical, or more expressive of distinct personality than *he.*

> With shame remembers, while *himself* was one
> Of the same herd, *himself* the same had done. *Denham.*

2. When *himself* is added to *he*, or to a noun, it expresses discrimination of person with particular emphasis.

> But *he himself* returned from the quarries. Judges iii.
>
> But *God himself* is with us for our captain. 2 Chron. xiii.

3. When used as the reciprocal pronoun, it is not usually emphatical.

> David hid *himself* in the field. 1 Sam. xx.

4. It was formerly used as a substitute for neuter nouns; as high as heaven *himself.* [*This use is now improper.*]

5. It is sometimes separated from *he*; as, *he* could not go *himself*, for *he himself* could not go.

6. *Himself* is used to express the proper character, or natural temper and disposition of a person, after or in opposition to wandering of mind, irregularity, or devious conduct from derangement, passion or extraneous influence. We say, a man has come to *himself*, after delirious or extravagant behavior. Let the man alone; let him act *himself.*

By himself, alone; unaccompanied; sequestered. He sits or studies *by himself.*

> Ahab went one way *by himself*, and Obadiah went another way *by himself.* 1 Kings xviii.

HIN, *n.* [Heb. הִין.] A Hebrew measure of capacity containing the sixth part of an ephah, or about five quarts English measure. *Encyc.*

HIND, *n.* [Sax. G. D. *hinde*; Sw. Dan. *hind*; allied perhaps to *han, hen.* See *Hen.*] The female of the red deer or stag.

HIND, *n.* [Sax. *hine*; Scot. *hyne.*] A domestic; a servant. *Obs.* *Shak.*

2. A peasant; a rustic; or a husbandman's servant. [*English.*] *Encyc.*

HIND, *a.* [Sax. *hyndan, hindan*; G. *hintan*; D. *hinder*. Deriv. comp. *hinder*, superl. *hindmost.*]

Backward; pertaining to the part which follows; in opposition to the fore part; as the *hind* legs of a quadruped; the *hind* toes; the *hind* shoes of a horse; the *hind* part of an animal.

HINDBERRY, *n.* A species of Rubus.

HINDER, *a. comp.* of *hind.* That is in a position contrary to that of the head or fore part; designating the part which follows; as the *hinder* part of a wagon; the *hinder* part of a ship, or the stern. Acts xxvii.

HIN'DER, *v. t.* [Sax. *henan, hynan, hindrian*; G. *hindern*; D. *hinderen*; Sw. *hindra*; Dan. *hindrer*; from *hind, hyn.* The Saxon verbs *henan, hynan*, signify to oppress, as well as to hinder, and *hean* is low, humble, poor. Qu. L. *cunctor*, or Gr. οκνεω, for οκενεω. See Class Gn. No. 4. 14. 41.]

1. To stop; to interrupt; to obstruct; to impede or prevent from moving forward by any means. It is applicable to any subject, physical, moral or intellectual.

> Them that were entering in, ye *hindered.* Luke xi.

2. To retard; to check in progression or motion; to obstruct for a time, or to render slow in motion. Cold weather *hinders* the growth of plants, or *hinders* them from

coming to maturity in due season. Let no obstacle *hinder* daily improvement.

3. To prevent.

What *hinders* younger brothers, being fathers of families, from having the same right? *Locke.*

HIN'DER, *v. i.* To interpose obstacles or impediments.

This objection *hinders* not but that the heroic action of some commander—may be written. *Dryden.*

HIN'DERANCE, *n.* The act of impeding or restraining motion.

2. Impediment; that which stops progression or advance; obstruction.

He must remove all these *hinderances* out of the way. *Atterbury.*

HIN'DERED, *pp.* Stopped; impeded; obstructed; retarded.

HIN'DERER, *n.* One who stops or retards; that which hinders.

HIN'DERING, *ppr.* Stopping; impeding; obstructing; retarding.

HINDERMOST, *a.* That which is behind all others; the last. [But we now use *hindmost.*]

HINDMOST, *a.* The last; that is in the rear of all others.

He met thee in the way, and smote the *hindmost* of thee. Deut. xxv.

HIN'DOO, *n.* An aboriginal of Hindoostan, or Hindostan.

HINGE, *n. hinj.* [This word appears to be connected with *hang*, and with *angle*, the verb; G. *angel*, a hook or hinge; D. *hengzel*, a hinge, a handle.]

1. The hook or joint on which a door or gate turns.

The gate self-opened wide
On golden *hinges* turning. *Milton.*

2. That on which any thing depends or turns; a governing principle, rule or point. This argument was the *hinge* on which the question turned.

3. A cardinal point; as east, west, north or south. [*Little used.*] *Creech.*

To be off the hinges, is to be in a state of disorder or irregularity. *Tillotson.*

HINGE, *v. t.* To furnish with hinges.

2. To bend. [*Little used.*] *Shak.*

HINGE, *v. i.* To stand, depend or turn, as on a hinge. The question *hinges* on this single point.

HING'ING, *ppr.* Depending; turning.

HINT, *v. t.* [It. *cenno*, a nod, or hint; *accennare*, to nod, or beckon.]

To bring to mind by a slight mention or remote allusion; to allude to; to suggest by a slight intimation.

Just *hint* a fault, and hesitate dislike. *Pope.*

HINT, *v. i.* To *hint at*, is to allude to; to mention slightly.

HINT, *n.* A distant allusion; slight mention; intimation; insinuation; a word or two intended to give notice, or remind one of something without a full declaration or explanation.

2. Suggestion.

HIP, *n.* [Sax. *hipe, hype, hypp*; G. *hüfte*; D. *heup*; Sw. *höft*; Dan. *hofte.* It coincides with *heap*, Sax. *hype*, and probably signifies a mass or lump.]

The projecting part of an animal formed by the os ilium or haunch bone; the haunch, or the flesh that covers the bone and the adjacent parts; the joint of the thigh.

To have on the hip, to have the advantage over one; a low phrase borrowed probably from wrestlers.

Hip and thigh, complete overthrow or defeat. Judges xv.

HIP, *v. t.* To sprain or dislocate the hip.

HIP, } *n.* The fruit of the dog-rose, or wild
HOP, } brier.

HIP'PELAPH, *n.* An animal of the deer kind, in Norway, about the size of the elk, and partaking of the nature of the horse and the stag. *Dict. Nat. Hist.*

HIP, HIPPED, HIPPISH. [See *Hyp.*]

HIP'HALT, *a.* [*hip* and *halt.*] Lame; limping. *Obs.* *Gower.*

HIP'POCAMP, *n.* [Gr. ιπποκαμπος; ιππος, a horse, and καμπτω, to bend.] A name given to the sea-horse. *Browne.*

HIPPOCEN'TAUR, *n.* [Gr. ιπποκενταυρος; ιππος, a horse, κεντεω, to spur, and ταυρος, a bull.]

In *ancient fable*, a supposed monster, half man and half horse. The hippocentaur differed from the centaur in this, that the latter rode on an ox, and the former on a horse, as the name imports. *Encyc.*

HIP'POCRAS, *n.* [Fr. quasi, *wine of Hippocrates.*]

A medicinal drink, composed of wine with an infusion of spices and other ingredients; used as a cordial. That directed by the late London Dispensary, is to be made of cloves, ginger, cinnamon and nutmegs, beat and infused in canary with sugar; to the infusion, milk, a lemon, and some slips of rosemary are to be added, and the whole strained through flannel. *Encyc.*

Hippocrates' sleeve, a kind of bag, made by uniting the opposite angles of a square piece of flannel, used for straining syrups and decoctions. *Quincy.*

Hippocratic face, [L. *facies hippocratica,*] pale, sunken, and contracted features, considered as a fatal symptom in diseases. *Parr.*

HIPPOC'RATISM, *n.* The philosophy of Hippocrates, as it regards medicine. *Chambers.*

HIP'PODAME, *n.* A sea-horse. *Spenser.*

HIP'PODROME, *n.* [Gr. ιπποδρομος; ιππος, a horse, and δρομος, a course, from δρεμω, to run.]

Anciently, a circus, or place in which horse races and chariot races were performed, and horses exercised. *Encyc.*

HIP'POGRIFF, *n.* [Fr. *hippogriffe*, from Gr. ιππος, a horse, and γρυψ, a griffon.]

A fabulous animal or monster, half horse and half griffon; a winged horse, imagined by Ariosto. *Johnson.* *Milton.*

HIP'POLITH, *n.* [Gr. ιππος, a horse, and λιθος, a stone.]

A stone found in the stomach or intestines of a horse. *Quincy.*

HIP'POMANE, *n.* [Gr. ιππος, a horse, and μανια, madness.]

1. A sort of poisonous substance, used anciently as a philter or love-charm. *Encyc.*

2. In *botany*, the manchineel-tree, which abounds with a milky juice which is acrid, caustic and poisonous. *Encyc.*

HIPPOPH'AGOUS, *a.* Feeding on horses, as the Tartars.

HIPPOPH'AGY, *n.* [Gr. ιππος, a horse, and φαγω, to eat.]

The act or practice of feeding on horses. *Quart. Rev.*

HIPPOPOT'AMY, } *n.* [Gr. ιππος, a horse,
HIPPOPOT'AMUS, } and ποταμος, a river.]

The river-horse, an animal that inhabits the Nile and other rivers in Africa. This animal resembles a hog rather than a horse, and was named perhaps from his neighing voice. He has been found of the length of 17 feet. He delights in the water, but feeds on herbage on land. *Encyc.*

HIP'ROOF, *n.* [*hip* and *roof.*] A roof that has an angle.

HIP'SHOT, *a.* [*hip* and *shot.*] Having the hip dislocated. *L'Estrange.*

HIP'WŎRT, *n.* A plant.

HIRE, *v. t.* [Sax. *hyran*; D. *huuren*; Sw. *hyra*; Dan. *hyrer*; W. *huriaw*; Ch. Syr. Sam. אגר, Ar. أَجَرَ, to hire. Class Gr. No. 10.]

1. To procure from another person and for temporary use, at a certain price, or for a stipulated or reasonable equivalent; as, to *hire* a farm for a year; to *hire* a horse for a day; to *hire* money at legal interest.

2. To engage in service for a stipulated reward; to contract with for a compensation; as, to *hire* a servant for a year; to *hire* laborers by the day or month.

3. To bribe; to engage in immoral or illegal service for a reward.

To hire out one's self, to let; to engage one's service to another for a reward.

They have *hired out themselves* for bread. 1 Sam. 2.

To hire, or *to hire out*, to let; to lease; to grant the temporary use of a thing for a compensation. He has *hired out* his house or his farm.

HIRE, *n.* [Sax. *hyre.* Qu. can the Gr. κερδος be of this family?]

1. The price, reward or compensation paid or contracted to be given for the temporary use of any thing.

2. Wages; the reward or recompense paid for personal service.

The laborer is worthy of his *hire.* Luke x.

HI'RED, *pp.* Procured or taken for use, at a stipulated or reasonable price; as a *hired* farm.

2. Employed in service for a compensation; as a *hired* man; a *hired* servant.

HI'RELING, *n.* One who is hired, or who serves for wages.

2. A mercenary; a prostitute. *Pope.*

HI'RELING, *a.* Serving for wages; venal; mercenary; employed for money or other compensation.

A tedious crew
Of *hireling* mourners. *Dryden.*

HI'RER, *n.* One that hires; one that procures the use of any thing for a compensation; one who employs persons for wages, or contracts with persons for service.

HI'RING, *ppr.* Procuring the use of for a compensation.

HIRSU'TE, *a.* [L. *hirsutus.* Qu. *hair.*]

1. Hairy; rough with hair; shaggy; set with bristles.

2. In *botany*, it is nearly synonymous with *hispid*, but it denotes having more hairs or bristles, and less stiff. *Martyn.*

HIRSU'TENESS, *n.* Hairiness. *Burton.*

HIS, *pron. possessive* of *he*, and pronounced *hiz.* [Sax. gen. *hys*, and *hyse*, male.]

1. Of him. Thus in Alfred's Orosius, "Sume for *his ege* ne dorstan." Some for fear *of him* durst not; literally, for *his awe*, for *awe of him.* Lib. 3. 8. In this instance, *his* does not express what belongs to the antecedent of *his*, [Philip,] but the fear which others entertained *of him.*
2. The present use of *his* is as a pronominal adjective, in any case indifferently, corresponding to the L. *suus.* Thus, tell John *his* papers are ready. I will deliver *his* papers to *his* messenger. He may take *his* son's books. When the noun is omitted, *his* stands as its substitute, either in the nominative or objective case. Tell John this book is *his*. He may take mine and I will take *his*.
3. *His* was formerly used for *its*, but improperly, and the use has ceased.
4. It was formerly used as the sign of the possessive. The man *his* ground, for the *man's* ground. This use has also ceased.
5. *His* is still used as a substitute for a noun, preceded by *of*; as all ye saints *of his*; ye ministers *of his*. *Scripture.*

Hisself is no longer used.

HIS'INGERITE, *n.* A mineral found in the cavities of calcarious spar, in Sudermanland. *Phillips.*

HIS'PID, *a.* [L. *hispidus.*] Rough.

2. In *botany*, having strong hairs or bristles; beset with stiff bristles. *Martyn.*

HISS, *v. i.* [Sax. *hysian, hiscan, hispan, hyspan.*]

1. To make a sound by driving the breath between the tongue and the upper teeth; to give a strong aspiration, resembling the noise made by a serpent and some other animals, or that of water thrown on hot iron. *Hissing* is an expression of contempt.

   The merchants among the people shall *hiss* at thee. Ezek. xxvii.
2. To express contempt or disapprobation by hissing.
3. To whiz, as an arrow or other thing in rapid flight.

HISS, *v. t.* To condemn by hissing; to explode. The spectators *hissed* him off the stage.

2. To procure hisses or disgrace.

   —That of an hour's age doth *hiss* the speaker. *Shak.*

HISS, *n.* The sound made by propelling the breath between the tongue and upper teeth; the noise of a serpent, a goose, &c.

   He *hiss* for *hiss* returned. *Milton.*

2. An expression of contempt or disapprobation, used in places of public exhibition.

HISS'ING, *ppr.* Making the noise of serpents.

HISS'ING, *n.* A hissing sound; an expression of scorn or contempt.

2. The occasion of contempt; the object of scorn and derision.

   I will make this city desolate, and a *hissing.* Jer. xix.

HISS'INGLY, *adv.* With a whistling sound. *Sherwood.*

HIST, *exclam.* [Dan. *hyst.* In Welsh, *hust* is a low, buzzing sound.]

A word commanding silence; equivalent to *hush*, be silent.

HISTO'RIAL, *a.* Historical. *Obs.* *Chaucer.*

HISTO'RIAN, *n.* [Fr. *historien*; L. *historicus*; It. *istorico.* See *History.*]

A writer or compiler of history; one who collects and relates facts and events in writing, particularly respecting nations. Hume is called an elegant *historian.*

HISTOR'I€, } *a.* [L. *historicus*; Fr. *historique.*] Containing
HISTOR'I€AL, } history, or the relation of facts; as a *historical* poem; the *historic* page; *historic* brass. *Pope.*

2. Pertaining to history; as *historic* care or fidelity.
3. Contained in history; deduced from history; as *historical* evidence.
4. Representing history; as a *historical* chart; *historical* painting.

HISTOR'I€ALLY, *adv.* In the manner of history; by way of narration.

   The Gospels declare *historically* something which our Lord Jesus Christ did, spoke or suffered. *Hooker.*

HIS'TORIED, *a.* Recorded in history. [*Not much in use.*]

HISTO'RIER, *n.* A historian. *Obs.*

HIS'TORIFY, *v. t.* To relate; to record in history. [*Not used.*] *Sidney.*

HISTORIOG'RAPHER, *n.* [Gr. ιςορια, history, and γραφω, to write.]

A historian; a writer of history; particularly, a professed historian; an officer employed to write the history of a prince or state; as the *historiographer* of his Britannic majesty.

HISTORIOG'RAPHY, *n.* The art or employment of a historian.

HISTORIOL'OGY, *n.* A discourse on history, or the knowledge of history. [*Not in use.*]

HIS'TORY, *n.* [Gr. ιςορια; L. Sp. Port. *historia*; It. *istoria*; Fr. *histoire*; Ir. *sdair, stair*; Sax. *stair, ster*, probably from the Latin; W. *ysdori*, history, matter of record, what is of concern or in mind, from *ysdawr*, an object of care or concern, from *dawr*, to care, to be concerned, to regard. The Greek ιςωρ signifies knowing, learned, and ιςορεω is rendered to inquire, to explore, to learn by inspection or inquiry. This would seem to be connected with W. *ystyriaw*, to consider, to regard or take notice. *History* and *story* are the same word differently written.]

1. An account of facts, particularly of facts respecting nations or states; a narration of events in the order in which they happened, with their causes and effects. *History* differs from *annals. Annals* relate simply the facts and events of each year, in strict chronological order, without any observations of the annalist. *History* regards less strictly the arrangement of events under each year, and admits the observations of the writer. This distinction however is not always regarded with strictness.

   History is of different kinds, or treats of different subjects; as a *history* of government, or political *history*; *history* of the christian church, or ecclesiastical *history*; *history* of war and conquests, or military *history*; *history* of law; *history* of commerce; *history* of the crusades, &c. In these and similar examples, *history* is written narrative or relation. What is the *history* of nations, but a narrative of the follies, crimes and miseries of man?
2. Narration; verbal relation of facts or events; story. We listen with pleasure to the soldier or the seaman, giving a *history* of his adventures.

   What *histories* of toil could I declare? *Pope.*
3. Knowledge of facts and events.

   History—is necessary to divines. *Watts.*
4. Description; an account of things that exist; as natural *history*, which comprehends a description of the works of nature, particularly of animals, plants and minerals; a *history* of animals, or zoology; a *history* of plants.
5. An account of the origin, life and actions of an individual person. We say, we have a concise *history* of the prisoner in the testimony offered to the court.

   A formal written account of an individual's life, is called *biography.*

HIS'TORY-PIECE, *n.* A representation of any remarkable event in painting, which exhibits the actors, their actions, and the attending events to the eye, by figures drawn to the life. This species of painting is called *historical* painting.

HIS'TRION, *n.* A player. [*Not in use.*] *Pope.*

HISTRION'I€, } *a.* [L. *histrionicus*, from *histrio*, a
HISTRION'I€AL, } buffoon, an actor, or stage-player.]

Pertaining to a buffoon or comedian, or to a pantomime, who represents events or characters by gestures and dancing; belonging to stage-playing; befitting a theater; theatrical. *Johnson. Encyc.*

HISTRION'I€ALLY, *adv.* In the manner of a buffoon or pantomime; theatrically.

HIS'TRIONISM, *n.* The acts or practice of buffoons or pantomimes; stage-playing. *Southey.*

HIT, *v. t.* pret. and pp. *hit.* [Sw. *hitta*, Dan. *hitter*, to find, to meet, that is, to come to, to come or fall on. This word illustrates the signification of *find.*]

1. To strike or touch, either with or without force. We *hit* a thing with the finger, or with the head; a cannon ball *hits* a mast, or a wall.
2. To strike or touch a mark with any thing directed to that object; not to miss.

   The archers *hit* him. 1 Sam. xxxi.
3. To reach; to attain to.

   Birds learning tunes, and their endeavors to *hit* the notes right— *Locke.*
4. To suit; to be conformable.

   —Melancholy,
   Whose saintly visage is too bright
   To *hit* the sense of human sight. *Milton.*
5. To strike; to touch properly; to offer the right bait.

   There you *hit* him—that argument never fails with him. *Dryden.*

To hit off, to strike out; to determine luckily. *Temple.*

2. To represent or describe exactly.

To hit out, to perform by good luck. [*Little used.*] *Spenser.*

HIT, *v. i.* To strike; to meet or come in contact; to clash; followed by *against* or *on.*

   If bodies be mere extension, how can they move and *hit* one *against* another. *Locke.*

Corpuscles meeting with or *hitting on* those bodies, become conjoined with them. *Woodward.*

2. To meet or fall on by good luck; to succeed by accident; not to miss.

And oft it *hits*
Where hope is coldest, and despair most fits. *Shak.*

3. To strike or reach the intended point; to succeed.

And millions miss for one that *hits.* *Swift.*

To hit on or *upon*, to light on; to come to or fall on by chance; to meet or find, as by accident.

None of them *hit upon* the art. *Addison.*

HIT, *n.* A striking against; the collision of one body against another; the stroke or blow that touches any thing.

So he the famed Cilician fencer prais'd,
And at each *hit* with wonder seems amaz'd. *Dryden.*

2. A chance; a casual event; as a lucky *hit.*
3. A lucky chance; a fortunate event. *Dryden.*
4. A term in back-gammon. Three *hits* are equal to a gammon.

HITCH, *v. i.* [Ar. حاك to hitch along; W. *hecian*, to halt, hop, or limp, or *hiciaw*, to snap, to catch suddenly. Both may be of one family.]

1. To move by jerks, or with stops; as, in colloquial language, to *hitch* along.

Whoe'er offends, at some unlucky time
Slides in a verse, or *hitches* in a rhyme. *Pope.*

2. To become entangled; to be caught or hooked. *South.*
3. To hit the legs together in going, as horses. [*Not used in the U. States.*]
4. To hop; to spring on one leg. [*Local.*] *Grose.*
5. To move or walk. *Grose.*

HITCH, *v. t.* To hook; to catch by a hook; as, to *hitch* a bridle.

2. To fasten by hitching; as, to *hitch* a horse by a bridle, or to *hitch* him to a post. *New England.*

HITCH, *n.* A catch; any thing that holds, as a hook; an impediment.

2. The act of catching, as on a hook, &c.
3. In *seamen's language*, a knot or noose in a rope for fastening it to a ring or other object; as a clove *hitch*; a timber *hitch*, &c. *Mar. Dict.*
4. A stop or sudden halt in walking or moving.

HITCH'ED, *pp.* Caught; hooked; fastened.

HITCH'EL, *v. t.* To hatchel. [*Not used.* See *Hatchel.*]

HITHE, *n.* [Sax. *hyth.*] A port or small haven; as in *Queenhithe*, and *Lambhithe*, now *Lambeth.* [*English.*]

HITH'ER, *adv.* [Sax. *hither* or *hider*; Goth. *hidre*; Dan. *hid*; Sw. *hit.*]

1. To this place; used with verbs signifying motion; as, to come *hither*; to proceed *hither*; to bring *hither.*
2. *Hither* and *thither*, to this place and that.
3. To this point; to this argument or topic; to this end. [*Little used and not to be encouraged.*]

Hither we refer whatever belongs to the highest perfection of man. *Hooker.*

HITH'ER, *a.* Nearest; towards the person speaking; as on the *hither* side of a hill; the *hither* end of the building.

HITH'ERMOST, *a.* Nearest on this side. *Hale.*

HITH'ERTŌ, *adv.* To this time; yet.

The Lord hath blessed me *hitherto.* Josh. xvii.

2. In any time, or every time till now; in time preceding the present.

More ample spirit than *hitherto* was wont. *Spenser.*

3. To this place; to a prescribed limit.

Hitherto shalt thou come, but no further. Job xxxviii.

HITH'ERWARD, } *adv.* This way; to-
HITH'ERWARDS, } wards this place.

A puissant and mighty power—
Is marching *hitherward* in proud array. *Shak.*

HIVE, *n.* [Sax. *hyfe*; Eth. ቀፎ kafo. Class Gb. No. 88. In W. *cyf* is the stem or stock of a tree, and *cyfgwenyn* is a beehive. So in G. *bienenstock*, Sw. *bistock*, bee-stock. The hive of wild bees is a hollow tree.]

1. A box, chest or kind of basket for the reception and habitation of a swarm of honey-bees. It is made of boards, straw or other materials.
2. A swarm of bees; or the bees inhabiting a hive. *Shak.*
3. A company or society together, or closely connected. [*Unusual.*] *Swift.*

HIVE, *v. t.* To collect into a hive; to cause to enter a hive; as, to *hive* bees. *Dryden. Mortimer.*

2. To contain; to receive, as a habitation, or place of deposit.

Where all delicious sweets are *hived.* *Cleaveland.*

HIVE, *v. i.* To take shelter or lodgings together; to reside in a collective body. *Pope.*

HI'VED, *pp.* Lodged in a hive or shelter.

HI'VER, *n.* One that collects bees into a hive. *Mortimer.*

HIVES, *n.* [Scot. Qu. *heave.*] A disease, the croup, or *cynanche trachealis*; rattles.

HO, *exclam.* A word used by teamsters, to stop their teams. It has been used as a noun, for stop, moderation, bounds.

There is no *ho* with them. *Dekker. Green.*

This word is pronounced also *whō*, or *hwō.*

HO, } *exclam.* [L. *eho.*] A call to excite
HOA, } attention, or to give notice of approach.

What noise there, *ho?* *Shak.*
Hoa, who's within? *Shak.*

HŌAR, *a.* [Sax. *har*; Heb. Ch. Syr. Ar. חור white.]

1. White; as *hoar* frost; *hoar* cliffs. *Thomson.*
2. Gray; white with age; hoary; as a matron grave and *hoar.* *Spenser.*

HŌAR, *n.* Hoariness; antiquity. *Burke.*

HŌAR, *v. i.* To become moldy or musty. [*Little used.*]

HŌAR-FROST, *n.* The white particles of ice formed by the congelation of dew or watery vapors.

HŌARD, *n.* [Sax. *hord*, from gathering, hiding, or depositing.]

A store, stock or large quantity of any thing accumulated or laid up; a hidden stock; a treasure; as a *hoard* of provisions for winter; a *hoard* of money. *Shak. Woodward.*

HŌARD, *v. t.* To collect and lay up a large quantity of any thing; to amass and deposit in secret; to store secretly; as, to *hoard* grain or provisions; to *hoard* silver and gold. *Dryden.*

It is sometimes followed by *up*, but without use; as, to *hoard up* provisions.

HŌARD, *v. i.* To collect and form a hoard; to lay up store.

Nor cared to *hoard* for those whom he did breed. *Spenser.*

HŌARDED, *pp.* Collected and laid up in store.

HŌARDER, *n.* One who lays up in store; one who accumulates and keeps in secret.

HŌARDING, *ppr.* Laying up in store.

2. *a.* Instinctively collecting and laying up provisions for winter; as, the squirrel is a *hoarding* animal.

HŌARED, *a.* Moldy; musty. [*Not in use.*]

HŌARHOUND. [See *Horehound.*]

HŌARINESS, *n.* [from *hoary.*] The state of being white, whitish or gray; as the *hoariness* of the hair or head of old men.

HŌARSE, *a.* *hōrs.* [Syr. ܚܪܫ to be rough or hoarse.]

1. Having a harsh, rough, grating voice, as when affected with a cold.
2. Rough; grating; discordant; as the voice, or as any sound. We say, the *hoarse* raven; the *hoarse* resounding shore. *Dryden.*

HŌARSELY, *adv.* With a rough, harsh, grating voice or sound. *Dryden.*

HŌARSENESS, *n.* Harshness or roughness of voice or sound; preternatural asperity of voice. *Arbuthnot.*

HŌARY, *n.* [See *Hoar.*] White or whitish; as the *hoary* willows. *Addison.*

2. White or gray with age; as *hoary* hairs; a *hoary* head.

Reverence the *hoary* head. *Dwight.*

3. Moldy; mossy, or covered with a white pubescence. *Botany.*

HŌAX, *n.* [Sax. *hucse*, or *hucx*, contempt, irony, derision; or W. *hoced*, cheat, deceit, juggle, trick.]

Something done for deception or mockery; a trick played off in sport.

HŌAX, *v. t.* To deceive; to play a trick upon for sport, or without malice. [*A colloquial word, but not elegant.*]

HOB, } *n.* [Dan. *hob*, a heap; or W. *hob*,
HUB, } that which swells.]

The nave of a wheel; a solid piece of timber in which the spokes are inserted. *Washington.*

HOB, *n.* A clown; a fairy.

HOB'BISM, *n.* The principles of the sceptical Thomas Hobbes. *Skelton.*

HOB'BIST, *n.* A follower of Hobbes.

HOB'BLE, *v. i.* [W. *hobelu*, to hop, to *hobble.* See *Hop.*]

1. To walk lamely, bearing chiefly on one leg; to limp; to walk with a hitch or hop, or with crutches.

The friar was *hobbling* the same way too. *Dryden.*

2. To walk awkwardly, as when the feet are encumbered with a clog, or with fetters.
3. To move roughly or irregularly, as verse.

While you Pindaric truths rehearse,
She *hobbles* in alternate verse. *Prior.*

HOB'BLE, *v. t.* To perplex. [*Not in use.*]

HOB'BLE, *n.* An unequal halting gait; an encumbered awkward step.

He has a *hobble* in his gait. *Swift.*

2. Difficulty; perplexity.

HOB'BLEDEHOY, *n.* A cant phrase for a boy at the age of puberty. *Swift.*

HOB'BLER, *n.* One that hobbles.

HOB'BLER, *n.* [from *hobby.*] One who by his tenure was to maintain a hobby for military service; or one who served as a soldier on a hobby with light armor. *Encyc. Davies.*

HOB'BLING, *ppr.* Walking with a halting or interrupted step.

HOB'BLINGLY, *adv.* With a limping or interrupted step.

HOB'BY, *n.* [W. *hobel,* what stops or starts suddenly; Arm. *hoberell;* Fr. *hobereau.*]

A kind of hawk; a hawk of the lure. *Encyc.*

HOB'BY, *n.* [Norm. Fr. *hobyn,* and allied to the preceding.]

1. A strong active horse, of a middle size, said to have been originally from Ireland; a nag; a pacing horse; a garran. *Johnson. Encyc.*

2. A stick, or figure of a horse, on which boys ride.

3. Any favorite object; that which a person pursues with zeal or delight.

4. A stupid fellow.

HOB'BYHORSE, *n.* [*tautological.*] A hobby; a wooden horse on which boys ride.

2. A character in the old May games. *Douce.*

3. A stupid or foolish person. *Shak.*

4. The favorite object of pursuit.

HOB'GOBLIN, *n.* [probably W. *hob,* hop, and *goblin.*] A fairy; a frightful apparition.

HO'BIT, *n.* [Sp. *hobus;* G. *haubitze.*] A small mortar, or short gun for throwing bombs. [See *Howitzer,* the common orthography.]

HOB'LIKE, *a.* Clownish; boorish. *Cotgrave.*

HOB'NAIL, *n.* [G. *hufnagel,* hoof-nail.] A nail with a thick strong head, for shoeing horses. *Shak.*

2. A clownish person; in contempt. *Milton.*

HOB'NAILED, *a.* Set with hobnails; rough. *Dryden.*

HOB'NOB, *adv.* [Qu. Sax. *habban, næbban,* have, not have.]

Take, or not take; a familiar invitation to reciprocal drinking. *Shak.*

Hobson's choice, a vulgar proverbial expression, denoting without an alternative. It is said to have had its origin in the name of a person who let horses and coaches, and obliged every customer to take in his turn that horse which stood next the stable door. *Encyc.*

HOBOY. [See *Hautboy.*]

HOCK, *n.* [Sax. *hoh.* See *Hough.*] The joint of an animal between the knee and the fetlock. *Johnson.*

2. A part of the thigh.

HOCK, HOCK'LE, } *v. t.* To hamstring; to hough; to disable by cutting the tendons of the ham.

HOCK, *n.* [from *Hochheim,* in Germany.] A sort of Rhenish wine; sometimes called *hockamore.* *Mortimer.*

HOCK'DAY, HO'KEDAY, } *n.* High day; a day of feasting and mirth, formerly held in England the second Tuesday after Easter, to commemorate the destruction of the Danes in the time of Ethelred. *Encyc.*

HOCK'EY, *n.* [G. *hoch,* Sax. *heah,* high. Qu.] Harvest-home. [*Not used.*]

HOCK'HERB, *n.* A plant, the mallows. *Ainsworth.*

HOCK'LE, *v.t.* To hamstring. *Hanmer.*

2. To mow. *Mason.*

HOCUS POCUS, *a.* [W. *hoced,* a cheat or trick, and perhaps *bwg* or *pwca,* a hobgoblin.]

A juggler; a juggler's trick; a cheat used by conjurers. *Hudibras.*

HOCUSPOCUS, *v. t.* To cheat. *L'Estrange.*

HOD, *n.* [Fr. *hotte.*] A kind of tray for carrying mortar and brick, used in bricklaying. It is fitted with a handle and borne on the shoulder.

HOD'DY-DODDY, *n.* An awkward or foolish person. *Obs.* *B. Jonson.*

HODGE-PODGE, HOTCH-POTCH, } *n.* [Qr. Fr. *hocher,* to shake, or *hachis,* minced meat.]

A mixed mass; a medley of ingredients. [*Vulgar.*] [See *Hotchpot.*]

HODIERN'AL, *a.* [L. *hodiernus,* from *hodie, hoo die,* this day.] Of this day; belonging to the present day.

HOD'MAN, *n.* A man who carries a hod; a mason's tender.

HOD'MANDOD, *n.* A shell-fish, otherwise called dodman. *Bacon.*

2. A shell-snail.

HOE, *n. ho.* [G. *haue;* Sw. *hacka,* and this is the Dan. *hakke,* G. *hacke,* a mattock; Fr. *houe.* It seems this is from the root of *hack* and *hew;* Sax. *heawian;* D. *houwen;* G. *hacken,* Sw. *hacka,* Dan. *hakker,* to chop, to hack, to hew; Fr. *houer.*]

A farmer's instrument for cutting up weeds and loosening the earth in fields and gardens. It is in shape something like an adz, being a plate of iron, with an eye for a handle, which is set at an acute angle with the plate.

HOE, *v.t.* To cut, dig, scrape or clean with a hoe; as, to *hoe* the earth in a garden; to *hoe* the beds.

2. To clear from weeds; as, to *hoe* maiz; to *hoe* cabbages.

HOE, *v. i.* To use a hoe.

HO'ED, *pp.* Cleared from weeds, or loosened by the hoe.

HO'EING, *ppr.* Cutting, scraping or digging with a hoe.

2. Clearing of weeds with a hoe.

HO'FUL, *a.* [Sax. *hohfull, hogfull;* *hoga,* care, and *full.*] Careful. *Obs.*

HOG, *n.* [W. *hwç,* a hog, a push or thrust; Arm. *houch;* probably so named from his snout, or from rooting; Sp. *hocico,* the snout of a beast; *hocicar,* to root.]

1. A swine; a general name of that species of animal.

2. In *England,* a castrated sheep of a year old. *Ash.*

3. A bullock of a year old. *Ash.*

4. A brutal fellow; one who is mean and filthy.

5. Among *seamen,* a sort of scrubbing-broom for scraping a ship's bottom under water. *Mar. Dict.*

HOG, *v. t.* To scrape a ship's bottom under water.

2. [G. *hocken.*] To carry on the back. [*Local.*] *Grose.*

3. To cut the hair short, like the bristles of a hog. [*Local.*]

HOG, *v. i.* To bend, so as to resemble in some degree a hog's back; as, a ship *hogs* in lanching.

HOG'COTE, *n.* [*hog* and *cote.*] A shed or house for swine; a sty. *Mortimer.*

HOG'GED, *pp.* Scraped under water.

2. Curving; having the ends lower than the middle. *Eton.*

HOG'GEREL, *n.* A sheep of the second year. *Ash.*

A two year old ewe. *Ainsworth.*

HOG'GET, *n.* [Norm. *hoget.*] A sheep two years old. *Skinner.*

2. A colt of a year old, called also *hog-colt.* [*Local.*] *Grose.*

3. A young boar of the second year. *Cyc.*

HOG'GISH, *a.* Having the qualities of a hog; brutish; gluttonous; filthy; meanly selfish.

HOG'GISHLY, *adv.* In a brutish, gluttonous or filthy manner.

HOG'GISHNESS, *n.* Brutishness; voracious greediness in eating; beastly filthiness; mean selfishness.

HOGH, *n.* [See *High.*] A hill; a cliff. *Obs.* *Spenser.*

HOG'HERD, *n.* [*hog* and *herd.*] A keeper of swine. *Browne.*

HOG'PEN, *n.* [*hog* and *pen.*] A hogsty.

HOG'-PLUMBTREE, *n.* A tree of the genus Spondias.

HOG'-RINGER, *n.* One whose business is to put rings in the snouts of swine.

HOG'S-BEANS, *n.* A plant. *Ainsworth.*

HOG'S-FENNEL, *n.* A plant of the genus Peucedanum.

HOG'S-MUSHROOMS, *n.* A plant. *Ainsworth.*

HOGS'HEAD, *n.* [D. *oxhoofd;* G. *oxhoft;* Dan. *oxehoved;* Sw. *oxhufvud;* that is, oxhead. The English orthography is grossly corrupt.]

1. A measure of capacity, containing 63 gallons.

2. In *America,* this name is often given to a butt, a cask containing from 110 to 120 gallons; as a *hogshead* of spirit or melasses.

3. A large cask, of indefinite contents. *Bacon.*

HOG'STY, *n.* [*hog* and *sty.*] A pen or inclosure for hogs.

HOG'WASH, *n.* [*hog* and *wash.*] Swill; the refuse matters of a kitchen or brewery, or like matter for swine. *Arbuthnot.*

HO'HLSPATH, *n.* The mineral otherwise called macle, and chiastolite.

HOI'DEN, *n.* [W. *hoeden,* a flirt, a wanton, a coquet.] A rude, bold girl; a romp.

2. A rude, bold man. [Not used in the United States.] *Milton.*

HOI'DEN, *a.* Rude; bold; inelegant; rustic. *Young.*

HOI'DEN, *v. i.* To romp rudely or indecently. *Swift.*

HOIST, *v. t.* [originally *hoise;* but corrupted, perhaps beyond remedy. G. *hissen;* D. *hyssen;* Sw. *hissa;* Dan. *hisser;* Fr. *isser;* Arm. *içza;* Sp. *izar;* Port. *içar.* This appears by the German to be radically the same word as *heat,* which see.]

1. To raise; to lift.

> We'll quickly *hoist* duke Humphrey from his seat. *Shak.*

In popular language, it is a word of general application. But the word has two appropriate uses, one by seamen, and the other by milkmaids, viz.

2. To raise, to lift or bear upwards by means of tackle; and to draw up or raise, as a sail along the masts or stays, or as a flag, though by a single block only. *Hoist* the main-sail. *Hoist* the flag. *Mar. Dict.*

3. To lift and move the leg backwards; a word of command used by milkmaids to cows, when they wish them to lift and set back the right leg.

HOIST, *n.* In *marine language,* the perpendicular highth of a flag or ensign, as opposed to the *fly,* or breadth from the staff to the outer edge. *Encyc.*

HOIST'ED, *pp.* Raised; lifted; drawn up.

HOIST'ING, *ppr.* Raising; lifting.

HOITY TOITY, an exclamation, denoting surprise or disapprobation, with some degree of contempt.

> *Hoity toity,* what have I to do with dreams? *Congreve.*

[Qu. Ice. *hauta,* to leap.]

HOLC'AD, *n.* [Gr. ὀλκαδιον.] In *ancient Greece,* a large ship of burden. *Mitford.*

HŌLD, *v. t.* pret. *held;* pp. *held.* *Holden* is obsolete in elegant writing. [Sax. *healdan;* G. *halten;* D. *houden,* *l* suppressed; Sw. *hålla;* Dan. *holder;* Gr. κωλυω, to hold or restrain; Heb. כול, to hold or contain; Ch. and Syr. to measure, that is, to limit; כלא to confine, restrain, or shut up; Ch. Syr. id; Ar. كلا to keep, guard or preserve; Ch. אכל, to take, also to eat, to roar, to thunder. See *Call.* The primary sense is, to press, to strain. Class Gl. No. 18. 32. 36. 40.]

1. To stop; to confine; to restrain from escape; to keep fast; to retain. It rarely or never signifies the first act of seizing or falling on, but the act of retaining a thing when seized or confined. To *grasp,* is to seize, or to keep fast in the hand; *hold* coincides with *grasp* in the latter sense, but not in the former. We *hold* a horse by means of a bridle. An anchor *holds* a ship in her station.

2. To embrace and confine, with bearing or lifting. We *hold* an orange in the hand, or a child in the arms.

3. To connect; to keep from separation.

> The loops *held* one curtain to another. Ex. xxxvi.

4. To maintain, as an opinion. He *holds* the doctrine of justification by free grace.

5. To consider; to regard; to think; to judge, that is, to have in the mind.

> I *hold* him but a fool. *Shak.*
>
> The Lord will not *hold* him guiltless, that taketh his name in vain. Ex. xx.

6. To contain, or to have capacity to receive and contain. Here is an empty basket that *holds* two bushels. This empty cask *holds* thirty gallons. The church *holds* two thousand people.

7. To retain within itself; to keep from running or flowing out. A vessel with holes in its bottom will not *hold* fluids.

> They have hewed them out broken cisterns that can *hold* no water. Jer. ii.

8. To defend; to keep possession; to maintain.

> With what arms
> We mean to *hold* what anciently we claim
> Of empire. *Milton.*

9. To have; as, to *hold* a place, office or title.

10. To have or possess by title; as, he *held* his lands of the king. The estate is *held* by copy of court-roll.

11. To refrain; to stop; to restrain; to withhold. *Hold* your laughter. *Hold* your tongue.

> Death! what do'st? O, *hold* thy blow. *Crashaw.*

12. To keep; as, *hold* your peace.

13. To fix; to confine; to compel to observe or fulfill; as, to *hold* one to his promise.

14. To confine; to restrain from motion.

> The Most High—*held* still the flood till they had passed. 2 Esdras.

15. To confine; to bind; in a legal or moral sense. He is *held* to perform his covenants.

16. To maintain; to retain; to continue.

> But still he *held* his purpose to depart. *Dryden.*

17. To keep in continuance or practice.

> And Night and Chaos, ancestors of nature, *hold*
> Eternal anarchy. *Milton.*

18. To continue; to keep; to prosecute or carry on.

> Seed-time and harvest, heat and hoary frost,
> Shall *hold* their course. *Milton.*

19. To have in session; as, to *hold* a court or parliament; to *hold* a council.

20. To celebrate; to solemnize; as, to *hold* a feast.

21. To maintain; to sustain; to have in use or exercise; as, to *hold* an argument or debate.

22. To sustain; to support.

> Thy right hand shall *hold* me. Ps. cxxxix.

23. To carry; to wield.

> They all *hold* swords, being expert in war. Cant. iii.

24. To maintain; to observe in practice.

> Ye *hold* the traditions of men. Mark vii.

25. To last; to endure. The provisions will *hold* us, till we arrive in port. So we say, the provisions will *last* us; but the phrase is elliptical for will hold or last *for* us, the verb being intransitive.

To hold forth, to offer; to exhibit; to propose.

> Observe the connection of ideas in the propositions which books *hold forth* and pretend to teach. *Locke.*

2. To reach forth; to put forward to view. *Cheyne.*

To hold in, to restrain; to curb; to govern by the bridle. *Swift.*

2. To restrain in general; to check; to repress. *Hooker.*

To hold off, to keep at a distance. *Pope.*

To hold on, to continue or proceed in; as, to *hold on* a course.

To hold out, to extend; to stretch forth.

> The king *held out* to Esther the golden scepter. Esther v.

2. To propose; to offer.

> Fortune *holds out* these to you as rewards. *B. Jonson.*

3. To continue to do or suffer.

> He cannot long *hold out* these pangs. [*Not used.*] *Shak.*

To hold up, to raise; as, *hold up* your head.

2. To sustain; to support.

> He *holds* himself *up* in virtue. *Sidney.*

3. To retain; to withhold.

4. To offer; to exhibit. He *held up* to view the prospect of gain.

5. To sustain; to keep from falling.

To hold one's own, to keep good one's present condition; not to fall off, or to lose ground. In *seamen's language,* a ship *holds her own,* when she sails as fast as another ship, or keeps her course.

To hold, is used by the Irish, for to lay, as a bet, to wager. I *hold* a crown, or a dollar; but this is a vulgar use of the word.

HŌLD, *v. i.* To be true; not to fail; to stand, as a fact or truth. This is a sound argument in many cases, but does not *hold* in the case under consideration.

> The rule *holds* in lands as well as in other things. *Locke.*

In this application, we often say, to *hold true,* to *hold good.* The argument *holds good* in both cases. This *holds true* in most cases.

2. To continue unbroken or unsubdued.

> Our force by land hath nobly *held.* [*Little used.*] *Shak.*

3. To last; to endure. *Bacon.*

We now say, to *hold out.*

4. To continue.

> While our obedience *holds.* *Milton.*

5. To be fast; to be firm; not to give way, or part. The rope is strong; I believe it will *hold.* The anchor *holds* well.

6. To refrain.

> His dauntless heart would fain have *held*
> From weeping. *Dryden.*

7. To stick or adhere. The plaster will not *hold.*

To hold forth, to speak in public; to harangue; to preach; to proclaim. *L'Estrange.*

To hold in, to restrain one's self. He was tempted to laugh; he could hardly *hold in.*

2. To continue in good luck. [*Unusual.*] *Swift.*

To hold off, to keep at a distance; to avoid connection.

To hold of, to be dependent on; to derive title from.

> My crown is absolute and *holds of* none. *Dryden.*

To hold on, to continue; not to be interrupted.

> The trade *held on* many years. *Swift.*

2. To keep fast hold; to cling to.

3. To proceed in a course. Job xvii.

To hold out, to last; to endure; to continue. A consumptive constitution may *hold out* a few years. He will accomplish the work, if his strength *holds out.*

2. Not to yield; not to surrender; not to be subdued. The garrison still *held out.*

To hold to, to cling or cleave to; to adhere.

> Else he will *hold to* the one, and despise the other. Matt. vi.

To hold under, or *from*, to have title from; as petty barons *holding under* the greater barons.

To hold with, to adhere to; to side with; to stand up for.

To hold plow, to direct or steer a plow by the hands, in tillage.

To hold together, to be joined; not to separate; to remain in union. *Dryden. Locke.*

To hold up, to support one's self; as, to *hold up* under misfortunes.

2. To cease raining; to cease, as falling weather; used impersonally. It *holds up*; it will *hold up*.

3. To continue the same speed; to run or move as fast. *Collier.*

But we now say, to *keep up*.

To hold a wager, to lay, to stake or to hazard a wager. *Swift.*

Hold, used imperatively, signifies stop; cease; forbear; be still.

HÖLD, *n.* A grasp with the hand; an embrace with the arms; any act or exertion of the strength or limbs which keeps a thing fast and prevents escape. Keep your *hold*; never quit your *hold*.

It is much used after the verbs to *take*, and to *lay*; to *take hold*, or to *lay hold*, is to seize. It is used in a literal sense; as to *take hold* with the hands, with the arms, or with the teeth; or in a figurative sense.

> Sorrow shall *take hold* on the inhabitants of Palestina. Ex. xv.
>
> *Take* fast *hold* of instruction. Prov. iv.
>
> My soul *took hold* on thee. *Addison.*

2. Something which may be seized for support; that which supports.

> If a man be upon a high place, without a good *hold*, he is ready to fall. *Bacon.*

3. Power of keeping.

> On your vigor now,
> My *hold* of this new kingdom all depends. *Milton.*

4. Power of seizing.

> The law hath yet another *hold* on you. *Shak.*

5. A prison; a place of confinement.

> They laid hands on them, and put them in *hold* till the next day. Acts iv.

6. Custody; safe keeping.

> King Richard, he is in the mighty *hold*
> Of Bolingbroke. *Shak.*

7. Power or influence operating on the mind; advantage that may be employed in directing or persuading another, or in governing his conduct.

> Fear—by which God and his laws take the surest *hold* of us. *Tillotson.*
>
> —Gives fortune no more *hold* of him than is necessary. *Dryden.*

8. Lurking place; a place of security; as the *hold* of a wild beast.

9. A fortified place; a fort; a castle; often called a *strong hold*. Jer. li.

10. The whole interior cavity of a ship, between the floor and the lower deck. In a vessel of one deck, the whole interior space from the keel or floor to the deck. That part of the hold which lies abaft the the main-mast is called the *after-hold*; that part immediately before the mainmast, the *main-hold*; that part about the fore-hatchway, the *fore-hold*. *Mar. Dict.*

11. In *music*, a mark directing the performer to rest on the note over which it is placed. It is called also a *pause*.

HÖLDBACK, *n.* Hinderance; restraint. *Hammond.*

HÖLDER, *n.* One who holds or grasps in his hand, or embraces with his arms.

2. A tenant; one who holds land under another. *Carew.*

3. Something by which a thing is held.

4. One who owns or possesses; as a *holder* of stock, or shares in a joint concern.

5. In *ships*, one who is employed in the hold. *Mar. Dict.*

HÖLDERFORTH, *n.* A haranguer; a preacher. *Hudibras.*

HÖLDFAST, *n.* A thing that takes hold; a catch; a hook. *Ray.*

HÖLDING, *ppr.* Stopping; confining; restraining; keeping; retaining; adhering; maintaining, &c.

HÖLDING, *n.* A tenure; a farm held of a superior. *Carew.*

2. The burden or chorus of a song. *Shak.*

3. Hold; influence; power over. *Burke.*

HOLE, *n.* [Sax. *hol*; G. *höhle*; D. *hol*; Dan. *hul, hule*; Sw. *hål*; Basque, *chiloa*; Gr. κοιλας, κοιλος. Qu. Heb. חל or Ar. خل. Class Gl. No. 20. 23.]

1. A hollow place or cavity in any solid body, of any shape or dimensions, natural or artificial. It may differ from a rent or fissure in being wider. A cell; a den; a cave or cavern in the earth; an excavation in a rock or tree; a pit, &c. Is. xi. Ezek. viii. Nah. ii. Matt. viii.

2. A perforation; an aperture; an opening in or through a solid body, left in the work or made by an instrument.

> Jehoida took a chest, and bored a *hole* in the lid of it. 2 Kings xii.

3. A mean habitation; a narrow or dark lodging. *Dryden.*

4. An opening or means of escape; a subterfuge; in the vulgar phrase, he has a *hole* to creep out at.

Arm-hole, the arm-pit; the cavity under the shoulder of a person. *Bacon.*

2. An opening in a garment for the arm.

HOLE, *v. i.* To go into a hole. *B. Jonson.*

HOLE, *v. t.* To cut, dig or make a hole or holes in; as, to *hole* a post for the insertion of rails or bars.

2. To drive into a bag, as in billiards.

HOLIBUT. [See *Halibut.*]

HO'LIDAM, *n.* [*holy* and *dame.*] Blessed lady; an ancient oath. *Hanmer.*

HOLIDAY. [See *Holyday.*]

HO'LILY, *adv.* [from *holy.*] Piously; with sanctity.

2. Sacredly; inviolably; without breach. [*Little used.*] *Shak. Sidney.*

HO'LINESS, *n.* [from *holy.*] The state of being holy; purity or integrity of moral character; freedom from sin; sanctity. *Applied to the Supreme Being*, holiness denotes perfect purity or integrity of moral character, one of his essential attributes.

> Who is like thee, glorious in *holiness?* Ex. xv.

2. *Applied to human beings*, holiness is purity of heart or dispositions; sanctified affections; piety; moral goodness, but not perfect.

> We see piety and *holiness* ridiculed as morose singularities. *Rogers.*

3. Sacredness; the state of any thing hallowed, or consecrated to God or to his worship; *applied to churches or temples.*

4. That which is separated to the service of God.

> Israel was *holiness* unto the Lord. Jer. ii.

5. A title of the pope, and formerly of the Greek emperors. *Encyc.*

HO'LING-AX, *n.* A narrow ax for cutting holes in posts.

HOL'LA, HOLLO'A, *exclam.* A word used in calling. Among *seamen*, it is the answer to one that hails, equivalent to, I hear, and am ready.

HOL'LA, HOL'LO, *v. i.* [Sax. *ahlowan.*] To call out or exclaim. [See *Halloo.*]

HOL'LAND, *n.* Fine linen manufactured in Holland.

HOL'LANDER, *n.* A native of Holland.

HOL'LEN, *n.* [See *Holly.*]

HOL'LOW, *a.* [Sax. *hol*; G. *hohl*; D. *hol*; Sw. *hålig*; Dan. *huled*; Arm. *goullo*, or *houllu*, emptied. See *Hole.*]

1. Containing an empty space, natural or artificial, within a solid substance; not solid; as a *hollow* tree; a *hollow* rock; a *hollow* sphere.

> *Hollow* with boards shalt thou make it. Ex. xxvii.

2. Sunk deep in the orbit; as a *hollow* eye.

3. Deep; low; resembling sound reverberated from a cavity, or designating such a sound; as a *hollow* roar. *Dryden.*

4. Not sincere or faithful; false; deceitful; not sound; as a *hollow* heart; a *hollow* friend. *Milton. Shak.*

Hollow spar, the mineral called also chiastolite.

HOL'LOW, *n.* A cavity, natural or artificial; any depression of surface in a body; concavity; as the *hollow* of the hand.

2. A place excavated; as the *hollow* of a tree.

3. A cave or cavern; a den; a hole; a broad open space in any thing. *Shak. Prior.*

4. A pit. *Addison.*

5. Open space of any thing; a groove; a channel; a canal. *Addison.*

HOL'LOW, *v. t.* [Sax. *holian.*] To make hollow, as by digging, cutting, or engraving; to excavate.

> Trees rudely *hollowed* did the waves sustain. *Dryden.*

HOL'LOW, *v. i.* To shout. [See *Holla* and *Hollo.*] *Dryden. Addison.*

HOL'LOWED, *pp.* Made hollow; excavated.

HOL'LOW-EYED, *a.* Having sunken eyes.

HOL'LOW-HE'ARTED, *a.* Insincere; deceitful; not sound and true; of practice or sentiment different from profession. *Butler.*

HOL'LOWING, *ppr.* Making hollow; excavating.

HOL'LOWLY, *adv.* Insincerely; deceitfully. *Shak.*

HOL'LOWNESS, *n.* The state of being hollow; cavity; depression of surface; excavation. *Bacon.*

2. Insincerity; deceitfulness; treachery. *South.*

HOL'LOW-ROOT, *n.* A plant, tuberous moschatel, or inglorious, constituting the genus Adoxa; a low plant, whose leaves and flowers smell like musk; hence it is sometimes called *musk-crowfoot*. *Encyc.*

HOL'LY, *n.* [Sax. *holegn;* D. *hulst;* perhaps L. *ilex*, for *hilex*. In Welsh, the corresponding word is *celyn*, from the root of *celu*, to conceal, L. *celo*. The *ilex* in Sw. is called iron oak.]

The holm tree, of the genus Ilex, of several species. The common holly grows from 20 to 30 feet high; the stem by age becomes large, and is covered with a grayish smooth bark, and set with branches which form a sort of cone. The leaves are oblong oval, of a lucid green on the upper surface, but pale on the under surface; the edges are indented and waved, with sharp thorns terminating each of the points. The flowers grow in clusters and are succeeded by roundish berries, which turn to a beautiful red about Michaelmas. This tree is a beautiful evergreen. *Encyc.*

Knee-Holly, a plant, the butcher's broom, of the genus Ruscus.

Sea-Holly, a plant, of the genus Eryngium.

HOL'LYHOCK, *n.* [Sax. *holihoc.*] A plant of the genus Alcea, bearing flowers of various colors. It is called also *rose-mallow.*

HOL'LYROSE, *n.* A plant. *Tate.*

HŌLM, *n.* The evergreen oak; the ilex.

2. An islet, or river isle.

3. A low flat tract of rich land on the banks of a river. *Cyc.*

HOLM'ITE, *n.* A variety of carbonate of lime; so called from Mr. Holme, who analyzed it. *Cleaveland.*

HOL'OCAUST, *n.* [Gr. ολος, whole, and καυςος, burnt, from καιω, to burn.]

A burnt-sacrifice or offering, the whole of which was consumed by fire; a species of sacrifice in use among the Jews and some pagan nations. *Ray. Encyc.*

HOL'OGRAPH, *n.* [Gr. ολος, whole, and γραφω, to write.]

A deed or testament written wholly by the grantor's or testator's own hand. *Encyc.*

HOLOGRAPH'IC, *a.* Written wholly by the grantor or testator himself.

HOLOM'ETER, *n.* [Gr. ολος, all, and μετρεω, to measure.]

An instrument for taking all kinds of measures, both on the earth and in the heavens; a pantometer. *Cyc.*

HOLP, HOLPEN, the antiquated *pret.* and *pp.* of *help.*

HŌLSTER, *n.* [Sax. *heolster*, a hiding place or recess; Port. *coldre;* from *holding*, or *concealing*, L. *celo*, Sax. *helan.*]

A lethern case for a pistol, carried by a horseman at the fore part of his saddle.

HŌLSTERED, *a.* Bearing holsters; as a *holstered* steed. *Byron.*

HŌLT, *n.* [Sax. *holt*, Ir. *coillte*, W. *cellt*, a wood, from the root of Sax. *helan*, L. *celo*, W. *celu*, to hide, to keep close; a word retained in names.]

A wood or woodland; obsolete, except in poetry. *Drayton. Browne.*

HŌ'LY, *a.* [Sax. *halig;* G. D. *heilig;* Sw. *helig;* Dan. *hellig;* from the root of *heal*, *hold*, *whole*, and *all;* Sax. *hal*, G. *heil*, D. *heel*, Sw. *hel*, Dan. *heel*, whole. See *Heal* and *Hold*, and Class Gl. No. 31, 35. 42. The sense is *whole*, entire, complete, sound, unimpaired.]

1. Properly, whole, entire or perfect, in a moral sense. Hence, pure in heart, temper or dispositions; free from sin and sinful affections. Applied to the Supreme Being, *holy* signifies perfectly pure, immaculate and complete in moral character; and man is more or less *holy*, as his heart is more or less sanctified, or purified from evil dispositions. We call a man *holy*, when his heart is conformed in some degree to the image of God, and his life is regulated by the divine precepts. Hence, *holy* is used as nearly synonymous with good, pious, godly.

> Be ye *holy;* for I am *holy.* 1 Pet. i.

2. Hallowed; consecrated or set apart to a sacred use, or to the service or worship of God; a sense frequent in Scripture; as the *holy* sabbath; *holy* oil; *holy* vessels; a *holy* nation; the *holy* temple; a *holy* priesthood.

3. Proceeding from pious principles, or directed to pious purposes; as *holy* zeal.

4. Perfectly just and good; as the *holy* law of God.

5. Sacred; as a *holy* witness. *Shak.*

Holy of holies, in Scripture, the innermost apartment of the Jewish tabernacle or temple, where the ark was kept, and where no person entered, except the high-priest, once a year.

Holy Ghost, or *Holy Spirit*, the Divine Spirit; the third person in the Trinity; the sanctifier of souls.

Holy war, a war undertaken to rescue the holy land, the ancient Judea, from the infidels; a crusade; an expedition carried on by christians against the Saracens in the eleventh, twelfth and thirteenth centuries; a war carried on in a most *unholy* manner.

HOLY-CROSS *day*, *n.* The fourteenth of September.

HOL'YDAY, *n.* A day set apart for commemorating some important event in history; a festival intended to celebrate some event deemed auspicious to the welfare of a nation; particularly an anniversary festival, devoted to religious solemnities; as christmas *holydays.*

2. A day of joy and gayety. *Shak.*

3. A day of exemption from labor; a day of amusement. *Chesterfield.*

HOL'YDAY, *a.* Pertaining to a festival; as a *holyday* suit of clothes.

HO'LY-ONE, *n.* An appellation of the Supreme Being, by way of emphasis.

2. An appellation of Christ. Is. xliii.

3. One separated to the service of God. Deut. xxxiii.

HOLY-ROOD *day*, *n.* A festival observed by Roman Catholics in memory of the exaltation of our Savior's cross. *Encyc.*

HO'LY-THISTLE, *n.* A plant of the genus Cnicus.

The blessed thistle, *Centaurea benedicta.* *Cyc.*

HO'LY-THURSDAY, *n.* The day on which the ascension of our Savior is commemorated, ten days before Whitsuntide. *Johnson.*

HO'LY-WEEK, *n.* The week before Easter, in which the passion of our Savior is commemorated. *Johnson.*

HOM'AĠE, *n.* [Fr. *hommage;* Sp. *homenage;* It. *omaggio;* from L. *homo*, man.]

1. In *feudal law*, the submission, loyalty and service which a tenant promised to his lord or superior, when first admitted to the land which he held of him in fee; or rather the act of the tenant in making this submission, on being invested with the fee. The ceremony of doing *homage* was thus performed. The tenant, being ungirt and uncovered, kneeled and held up both his hands between those of the lord, who sat before him, and there professed that "he did become his man, from that day forth, of life and limb and earthly honor," and then received a kiss from his lord. *Blackstone.*

2. Obeisance; respect paid by external action.

> Go, go, with *homage* yon proud victors meet. *Dryden.*

3. Reverence directed to the Supreme Being; reverential worship; devout affection.

HOM'AĠE, *v. t.* To pay respect to by external action; to give reverence to; to profess fealty.

HOM'AĠEABLE, *a.* Subject to homage. *Howell.*

HOM'AĠER, *n.* One who does homage, or holds land of another by homage. *Bacon.*

Homberg's Pyrophorus, ignited muriate of lime. *Ure.*

HOME, *n.* [Sax. *ham;* G. D. *heim;* Sw. *hem;* Dan. *hiem;* Gr. κωμη; properly, a house, a close place, or place of rest. Hence *hamlet*, Fr. *hameau*, Arm. *hamell.* The primary sense is probably to inclose, to cover, or to make fast. Derivatives in G. D. Sw. and Dan. signify secret, close; and we say, to bring *home* arguments, that is, press them close; to drive *home* a nail, &c. If the radical sense is close, it may be from the same root as Ar. كَمَي kamai, to cover. See *Chimistry*, and Class Gm. No. 7. 9. 20. 23.]

1. A dwelling house; the house or place in which one resides. He was not at *home.*

> Then the disciples went away again to their own *home.* John xx.
>
> *Home* is the sacred refuge of our life. *Dryden.*

2. One's own country. Let affairs at *home* be well managed by the administration.

3. The place of constant residence; the seat.

> Flandria, by plenty, made the *home* of war. *Prior.*

4. The grave; death; or a future state.

> Man goeth to his long *home.* Eccles. xii.

5. The present state of existence.

> Whilst we are at *home* in the body, we are absent from the Lord. 2 Cor. v.

HOME, *a.* Close; severe; poignant; as a *home* thrust.

HOME, *adv.* [This is merely elliptical; *to* being omitted.]

1. To one's own habitation; as in the phrases, go *home*, come *home*, bring *home*, carry *home.*

2. To one's own country. *Home* is opposed to *abroad*, or in a foreign country. My brother will return *home* in the first ship from India.

3. Close; closely; to the point; as, this consideration comes *home* to our interest, that

is, it nearly affects it. Drive the nail *home*, that is, drive it close.

To haul *home* the top-sail sheets, in seamen's language, is to draw the bottom of the top-sail *close* to the yard-arm by means of the sheets.

An anchor is said to come *home*, when it loosens from the ground by the violence of the wind or current, &c.

HO'MEBORN, *a.* Native; natural. *Donne.*

2. Domestic; not foreign. *Pope.*

HO'MEBRED, *a.* Native; natural; as *homebred* lusts. *Hammond.*

2. Domestic; originating at home; not foreign; as *homebred* evil. *Spenser.*

3. Plain; rude; artless; uncultivated; not polished by travel.

Only to me two *homebred* youths belong. *Dryden.*

HO'MEFELT, *a.* Felt in one's own breast; inward; private; as *homefelt* joys or delight. *Milton. Pope.*

HO'MEKEEPING, *a.* Staying at home. *Shak.*

HO'MELESS, *a.* Destitute of a home.

HO'MELINESS, *n.* [from *homely.*] Plainness of features; want of beauty. It expresses less than *ugliness.*

2. Rudeness; coarseness; as the *homeliness* of dress or of sentiments. *Addison.*

HO'MELOT, *n.* An inclosure on or near which the mansion house stands.

HO'MELY, *a.* [from *home.*] Of plain features; not handsome; as a *homely* face. It expresses less than *ugly.*

Let time, which makes you *homely*, make you wise.

2. Plain; like that which is made for common domestic use; rude; coarse; not fine or elegant; as a *homely* garment; a *homely* house; *homely* fare.

Now Strephon daily entertains
His Chloe in the *homeliest* strains. *Pope.*

HO'MELY, *adv.* Plainly; rudely; coarsely; as *homely* dressed. [*Little used.*]

HO'MELYN, *n.* A fish.

HO'MEMADE, *a.* Made at home; being of domestic manufacture; made either in private families, or in one's own country. *Locke.*

HO'MER, OMER, CHOMER, *n.* A Hebrew measure containing the tenth part of an epha, or about six pints. *Encyc.*

HOMER'IC, *a.* Pertaining to Homer, the great poet of Greece, or to his poetry; resembling Homer's verse.

HO'MESPEAKING, *n.* Forcible and efficacious speaking. *Milton.*

HO'MESPUN, *a.* Spun or wrought at home; of domestic manufacture. *Swift.*

2. Not made in foreign countries. *Addison.*

3. Plain; coarse; rude; homely; not elegant; as a *homespun* English proverb; a *homespun* author. *Dryden. Addison.*

HO'MESPUN, *n.* A coarse, unpolished, rustic person. *Shak.*

HO'MESTALL, HO'MESTEAD, *n.* The place of a mansion house; the inclosure or ground immediately connected with the mansion. *Dryden.*

2. Native seat; original station or place of residence.

We can trace them back to a *homestead* on the rivers Volga and Ural. *Tooke.*

[In the U. States, *homestead* is the word used.]

HO'MEWARD, HO'MEWARDS, *adv.* [Sax. *ham* and *weard.*] Toward home; toward one's habitation, or toward one's native country. *Sidney. Milton.*

HO'MEWARD-BOUND, *a.* Destined for home; returning from a foreign country to the place where the owner resides; as the *homeward-bound* fleet. We spoke a brig *homeward-bound.*

HOM'ICIDAL, *a.* [from *homicide.*] Pertaining to homicide; murderous; bloody.

HOM'ICIDE, *n.* [Fr. from L. *homicidium; homo*, man, and *cædo*, to strike, to kill.]

1. The killing of one man or human being by another. Homicide is of three kinds, *justifiable, excusable*, and *felonious; justifiable*, when it proceeds from unavoidable necessity, without an intention to kill, and without negligence; *excusable*, when it happens from misadventure, or in self-defense; *felonious*, when it proceeds from malice, or is done in the prosecution of some unlawful act, or in a sudden passion. Homicide committed with premeditated malice, is murder. Suicide also, or self-murder, is felonious homicide. Homicide comprehends murder and manslaughter. *Blackstone.*

2. A person who kills another; a manslayer. *Dryden.*

HOMILET'IC, HOMILET'ICAL, *a.* [Gr. ομιλητικος, from ομιλεω, to converse in company.]

1. Pertaining to familiar intercourse; social; conversable; companionable. *Atterbury.*

2. *Homiletic theology*, a branch of practical theology, which teaches the manner in which ministers of the gospel should adapt their discourses to the capacities of their hearers, and pursue the best methods of instructing them by their doctrines and examples. It is also called *pastoral* theology. *Encyc.*

HOM'ILIST, *n.* One that preaches to a congregation. *Beaum.*

HOM'ILY, *n.* [Fr. *homelie;* Sp. *homilia;* It. *omelia;* Gr. ομιλια, from ομιλεω, to converse in company, ομιλος, a company or assembly.]

A discourse or sermon read or pronounced to an audience; or a plain, familiar discourse on some subject of religion, such as an instructor would deliver to his pupils, or a father to his children. *Encyc.*

HOM'MOC, *n.* [I suppose this to be an Indian word.]

A hillock or small eminence of a conical form, sometimes covered with trees. *Bartram. Encyc.*

HOM'MONY, *n.* [Indian.] In *America*, maiz hulled and broken, but coarse, prepared for food by being mixed with water and boiled. *Adair.*

HOMOĠE'NEAL, HOMOĠE'NEOUS, *a.* [Fr. *homogene;* Gr. ομογενης; ομος, like, and γενος, kind.]

Of the same kind or nature; consisting of similar parts, or of elements of the like nature. Thus we say, *homogeneous* particles, elements or principles; *homogeneous* bodies.

HOMOĠE'NEALNESS, HOMOĠENE'ITY, *words not to be encouraged; equivalent to*

HOMOĠE'NEOUSNESS, *n.* Sameness of kind or nature.

HOM'OĠENY, *n.* Joint nature. *Bacon.*

HOMOL'OGATE, *v. t.* [It. *omologare;* Fr. *homologuer;* Gr. ομολογεω; ομος, like, and λεγω, to speak.] To approve; to allow. *Wheaton's Rep.* Vol. iv.

HOMOL'OGOUS, *a.* [Gr. ομος, similar, and λογος, proportion.]

Proportional to each other; a term in geometry, applied to the corresponding sides and angles of similar figures; as, *homologous* angles. *Encyc.*

HOMON'YMOUS, *a.* [Gr. ομωνυμος; ομος, like, and ονομα, name.]

Equivocal; ambiguous; that has different significations, or may be applied to different things. *Watts.*

HOMON'YMOUSLY, *adv.* In an equivocal manner. *Harris.*

HOMON'YMY, *n.* [Gr. ομωνυμια. See supra.] Ambiguity; equivocation. *Johnson.*

HOMOPH'ONY, *n.* [Gr. ομος, like, and φωνη, sound.]

Likeness of sound. Among the Greeks, a kind of music performed in unison, in opposition to *antiphony.*

HOMOT'ONOUS, *a.* [Gr. ομος, like, and τονος, tone.]

Equable; of the same tenor; applied to diseases which have a uniform tenor of rise, state, or declension. *Quincy.*

HONE, *n.* [Sw. *hen*, a hone; Sax. *hænan*, to stone. The word is found in the Greek ακονη; and in two dialects of the Burman empire, *hin, heen*, signifies a stone. Asiat. Researches, 5. 228. We find the word also in the Syriac ܐܟܢܐ akana, a hone, coticula, Lapis Lydius. Cast. Hept. 213.]

A stone of a fine grit, used for sharpening instruments that require a fine edge, and particularly for setting razors. [We never, I believe, call a *hone*, a *whet-stone.* The latter is a stone of coarse grit. See the word.]

HONE, *v. t.* To rub and sharpen on a hone; as, to *hone* a razor.

HONE, *v. i.* To pine; to long. *Obs.* [Qu. W. *hawn*, eager.]

HO'NE-WORT, *n.* A plant of the genus Sison.

HON'EST, *a. on'est.* [Fr. *honnête*, for *honeste;* Sp. Port. *honesto;* It. *onesto;* from L. *honestus*, from *honos, honor.*]

1. Upright; just; fair in dealing with others; free from trickishness and fraud; acting and having the disposition to act at all times according to justice or correct moral principles; *applied to persons.*

An *honest* man's the noblest work of God. *Pope.*

An *honest* physician leaves his patient, when he can contribute no farther to his health. *Temple.*

2. Fair; just; equitable; free from fraud; as an *honest* transaction; an *honest* transfer of property.

3. Frank; sincere; unreserved; according to truth; as an *honest* confession.

4. Sincere; proceeding from pure or just principles, or directed to a good object; as

an *honest* inquiry after truth; an *honest* endeavor; *honest* views or motives.

5. Fair; good; unimpeached.

Seek seven men of *honest* report. Acts vi.

6. Decent; honorable; or suitable.

Provide things *honest* in the sight of all men. Rom. xii.

7. Chaste; faithful.

Wives may be merry, and yet *honest* too. *Shak.*

HON'EST, *v. t. on'est.* To adorn; to grace. [*Not used.*] *Sandys.*

HONESTA'TION, *n.* Adornment; grace. [*Not used.*] *Mountague.*

HON'ESTLY, *adv. on'estly.* Uprightly; justly; with integrity and fairness; as a contract *honestly* made.

2. With frank sincerity; without fraud or disguise; according to truth; as, to confess *honestly* one's real design.

3. By upright means; with upright conduct; as, to live *honestly.*

4. Chastely; with conjugal loyalty and fidelity.

HON'ESTY, *n. on'esty.* [Fr. *honnêteté*; L. *honestas.*]

1. In *principle*, an upright disposition; moral rectitude of heart; a disposition to conform to justice and correct moral principles, in all social transactions. In *fact*, upright conduct; an actual conformity to justice and moral rectitude.

2. Fairness; candor; truth; as the *honesty* of a narrative. *Wardlaw.*

3. Frank sincerity. *Shak.*

Honesty is chiefly applicable to social transactions, or mutual dealings in the exchange of property.

HŎN'EY, *n. hun'y.* [Sax. *hunig*; G. *honig*; D. *honig, honing*; Sw. *håning*; Dan. *honning.*]

1. A sweet vegetable juice, collected by bees from the flowers of plants, and deposited in cells of the comb in hives. Honey, when pure, is of a moderate consistence, of a whitish color, tinged with yellow, sweet to the taste, of an agreeable smell, soluble in water, and becoming vinous by fermentation. In medicine, it is useful as a detergent and aperient. It is supposed to consist of sugar, mucilage, and an acid. *Encyc. Ure.*

2. Sweetness; lusciousness.

The king hath found
Matter against him, that forever mars
The *honey* of his language. *Shak.*

3. A word of tenderness; sweetness; sweet one. *Dryden.*

HŎN'EY, *v. t.* To talk fondly. [*Little used.*] *Shak.*

2. To sweeten.

HŎN'EY-BAG, *n.* The stomach of a honey-bee. *Grew.*

HŎN'EY-COMB, *n.* A substance of a firm, close texture, formed by bees into hexagonal cells for repositories of honey, and for the eggs which produce their young.

HŎNEY-COMBED, *a.* Having little flaws or cells. *Wiseman.*

HŎN'EY-DEW, *n.* A sweet saccharine substance, found on the leaves of trees and other plants in small drops like dew. It is said there are two species; one secreted from the plants, and the other deposited by a small insect called the aphis, or vine-fretter. Bees and ants are said to be fond of honey-dew. *Encyc.*

HŎN'EYED, *a.* Covered with honey. *Milton.*

2. Sweet; as *honeyed* words. *Milton. Shak.*

HŎN'EY-FLOWER, *n.* A plant of the genus Melianthus.

HŎN'EY-GNAT, *n.* An insect. *Ainsworth.*

HŎN'EY-GUIDE, *n.* A species of Cuckoo, found in Africa, which will conduct persons to hives of wild honey. *Encyc.*

HŎN'EY-H'ARVEST, *n.* Honey collected. *Dryden.*

HŎN'EYLESS, *a.* Destitute of honey. *Shak.*

HŎN'EY-LOCUST, *n.* A plant, the three-thorned Acacia, of the genus Gleditsia. *Encyc.*

HŎN'EY-MOON, } *n.* The first month after marriage.
HŎN'EY-MONTH, } *Addison.*

HŎN'EY-MOUTHED, *a.* Soft or smooth in speech. *Shak.*

HŎN'EY-STALK, *n.* Clover-flower. *Mason.*

HŎN'EY-STONE, *n.* [See *Mellite.*]

HŎN'EY-SUCKLE, *n.* A genus of plants, the Lonicera, of many species, one of which is called woodbine.

HŎN'EY-SWEET, *a.* Sweet as honey. *Chaucer.*

HŎN'EY-TŎNGUED, *a.* Using soft speech. *Shak.*

HŎN'EY-WŎRT, *n.* A plant of the genus Cerinthe.

HŎN'IED, *a.* [*Ill.* See *Honeyed.*]

HON'OR, *n. on'or.* [L. *honor, honos*; Fr. *honneur*; Sp. *honor*; Port. *honra*; It. *onore*; Arm. *enor*; Ir. *onoir.*]

1. The esteem due or paid to worth; high estimation.

A prophet is not without *honor*, except in his own country. Matt. xiii.

2. A testimony of esteem; any expression of respect or of high estimation by words or actions; as the *honors* of war; military *honors*; funeral *honors*; civil *honors.*

3. Dignity; exalted rank or place; distinction.

I have given thee riches and *honor*. 1 Kings iii.

Thou art clothed with *honor* and majesty. Ps. civ.

In doing a good thing, there is both *honor* and pleasure. *Franklin.*

4. Reverence; veneration; or any act by which reverence and submission are expressed, as worship paid to the Supreme Being.

5. Reputation; good name; as, his *honor* is unsullied.

6. True nobleness of mind; magnanimity; dignified respect for character, springing from probity, principle or moral rectitude; *a distinguishing trait in the character of good men.*

7. An assumed appearance of nobleness; scorn of meanness, springing from the fear of reproach, without regard to principle; as, shall I violate my trust? Forbid it, *honor.*

8. Any particular virtue much valued; as bravery in men, and chastity in females. *Shak.*

9. Dignity of mien; noble appearance.

Godlike erect, with native *honor* clad. *Milton.*

10. That which honors; he or that which confers dignity; as, the chancellor is an *honor* to his profession.

11. Privileges of rank or birth; *in the plural.*

Restore me to my *honors.* *Shak.*

12. Civilities paid.

Then here a slave, or if you will, a lord,
To do the *honors*, and to give the word. *Pope.*

13. That which adorns; ornament; decoration.

The sire then shook the *honors* of his head. *Dryden.*

14. A noble kind of seignory or lordship, held of the king *in capite.* *Encyc.*

On or *upon my honor*, words accompanying a declaration which pledge one's honor or reputation for the truth of it. The members of the house of lords in Great Britain are not under oath, but give their opinions *on their honor.*

Laws of honor, among persons of fashion, signify certain rules by which their social intercourse is regulated, and which are founded on a regard to reputation. These laws require a punctilious attention to decorum in external deportment, but admit of the foulest violations of moral duty. *Paley.*

Court of honor, a court of chivalry; a court of civil and criminal jurisdiction, having power to redress injuries of honor, and to hold pleas respecting matters of arms and deeds of war. *Encyc.*

HON'OR, *v. t. on'or.* [L. *honoro*; Fr. *honorer*; Sp. *honrar*; It. *onorare.*]

1. To revere; to respect; to treat with deference and submission, and perform relative duties to.

Honor thy father and thy mother. Ex. xx.

2. To reverence; to manifest the highest veneration for, in words and actions; to entertain the most exalted thoughts of; to worship; to adore.

That all men should *honor* the Son, even as they *honor* the Father. John v.

3. To dignify; to raise to distinction or notice; to elevate in rank or station; to exalt. Men are sometimes *honored* with titles and offices, which they do not merit.

Thus shall it be done to the man whom the king delighteth to *honor*. Esth. vi.

4. To glorify; to render illustrious.

I will be *honored* upon Pharaoh, and upon all his host. Ex. xiv.

5. To treat with due civility and respect in the ordinary intercourse of life. The troops *honored* the governor with a salute.

6. In *commerce*, to accept and pay when due; as, to *honor* a bill of exchange.

HON'ORABLE, *a.* [L. *honorabilis*; Fr. *honorable.*]

1. Holding a distinguished rank in society; illustrious or noble.

Shechem was more *honorable* than all the house of his father. Gen. xxxiv.

Many of them believed; also of *honorable* women who were Greeks—not a few. Acts xvii.

2. Possessing a high mind; actuated by principles of honor, or a scrupulous regard to probity, rectitude or reputation. He is an *honorable* man.

3. Conferring honor, or procured by noble deeds; as *honorable* wounds. *Dryden.*
4. Consistent with honor or reputation. It is not *honorable* to oppress the weak, or to insult the vanquished.
5. Respected; worthy of respect; regarded with esteem.

Marriage is *honorable* in all. Heb. xiii.

6. Performed or accompanied with marks of honor, or with testimonies of esteem; as an *honorable* burial.
7. Proceeding from an upright and laudable cause, or directed to a just and proper end; not base; not reproachful; as an *honorable* motive. Nothing can be *honorable* which is immoral.
8. Not to be disgraced.

Let her descend; my chambers are *honorable*. *Shak.*

9. Honest; without hypocrisy or deceit; fair. His intentions appear to be *honorable*.
10. An epithet of respect or distinction; as the *honorable* senate; the *honorable* gentleman.
11. Becoming men of rank and character, or suited to support men in a station of dignity; as an *honorable* salary. *Constitution of Massachusetts.*

HON'ORABLENESS, *n.* The state of being honorable; eminence; distinction.
2. Conformity to the principles of honor, probity or moral rectitude; fairness; *applied to disposition or to conduct.*

HON'ORABLY, *adv.* With tokens of honor or respect. The man was *honorably* received at court.
2. Magnanimously; generously; with a noble spirit or purpose. The prince *honorably* interposed to prevent a rupture between the nations.
3. Reputably; without reproach.

Why did I not more *honorably* starve? *Dryden.*

HON'ORARY, *a.* Conferring honor, or intended merely to confer honor; as an *honorary* degree; an *honorary* crown.
2. Possessing a title or place without performing services or receiving a reward; as an *honorary* member of a society.

HON'ORARY, *n.* A lawyer's fee.
2. The salary of a professor in any art or science. *Encyc.*

HON'ORED, *pp.* Respected; revered; reverenced; elevated to rank or office; dignified; exalted; glorified; accepted and paid, as a bill of exchange.

HON'ORER, *n.* One that honors; one that reveres, reverences or regards with respect.
2. One who exalts, or who confers honors.

HON'ORING, *ppr.* Respecting highly; reverencing; exalting; dignifying; conferring marks of esteem; accepting and paying, as a bill.

HON'ORLESS, *a.* Destitute of honor; not honored. *Warburton.*

HOOD, in composition, Sax. *had, hade,* G. *heit,* D. *heid,* Sw. *het,* Dan. *hed,* as in *manhood, childhood,* denotes state or fixedness, hence quality or character, from some root signifying to set, Sax. *hadian,* to ordain. It is equivalent to the termination *ness* in English, and *tas* in Latin; as *goodness,* G. *gutheit; brotherhood,* L. *fraternitas.*

HOOD, *n.* [Sax. *hod;* W. *hod.* Qu. from the root of *hut* or *hide.*]
1. A covering for the head used by females, and deeper than a bonnet.
2. A covering for the head and shoulders used by monks; a cowl.
3. A covering for a hawk's head or eyes; used in falconry.
4. Any thing to be drawn over the head to cover it.
5. An ornamental fold that hangs down the back of a graduate to mark his degree. *Johnson.*
6. A low wooden porch over the ladder which leads to the steerage of a ship; the upper part of a galley-chimney; the cover of a pump. *Mar. Dict.*

HOOD, *v. t.* To dress in a hood or cowl; to put on a hood.

The friar *hooded,* and the monarch crowned. *Pope.*

2. To cover; to blind.

I'll *hood* my eyes. *Shak.*

3. To cover.

And *hood* the flames. *Dryden.*

HOOD'MAN *blind, n.* A play in which a person blinded is to catch another and tell his name; blindman's buff. *Shak.*

HOOD'ED, *pp.* Covered with a hood; blinded.

HOOD'-WINK, *v. t.* [*hood* and *wink.*] To blind by covering the eyes.

We will blind and *hood-wink* him. *Shak.*

2. To cover; to hide.

For the prize I'll bring thee to,
Shall *hood-wink* this mischance. *Shak.*

3. To deceive by external appearances or disguise; to impose on. *Sidney.*

HOOD'-WINKED, *pp.* Blinded; deceived.

HOOD'-WINKING, *ppr.* Blinding the eyes; covering; hiding; deceiving.

HOOF, *n.* [Sax. *hof;* G. *huf;* D. *hoef;* Dan. *hov;* Sw. *hof,* a hoof, and a measure. Class Gb. No. 31.]
1. The horny substance that covers or terminates the feet of certain animals, as horses, oxen, sheep, goats, deer, &c.
2. An animal; a beast.

He had not a single *hoof* of any kind to slaughter. *Washington.*

HOOF, *v. i.* To walk, as cattle. [*Little used.*] *Scott.*

HOOF'-BOUND, *a.* A horse is said to be hoof-bound when he has a pain in the fore-feet, occasioned by the dryness and contraction of the horn of the quarters, which straitens the quarters of the heels, and often makes him lame. *Far. Dict.*

HOOF'ED, *a.* Furnished with hoofs.

Of all the *hoofed* quadrupeds, the horse is the most beautiful. *Grew.*

HOOK, *n.* [Sax. *hoc;* D. *haak;* G. *haken;* Sw. *hake;* Dan. *hage;* W. *hwg;* Heb. חכה; Ch. חכי. Class Cg. No. 22. 23. 24.]
1. A piece of iron or other metal bent into a curve for catching, holding and sustaining any thing; as a *hook* for catching fish; a tenter-hook; a chimney-hook; a pot-hook, &c.
2. A snare; a trap. *Shak.*
3. [W. *hoc,* a sythe.] A curving instrument for cutting grass or grain; a sickle; an instrument for cutting or lopping. *Mortimer. Pope.*
4. That part of a hinge which is fixed or inserted in a post. Whence the phrase, to be *off the hooks,* to be unhinged, to be disturbed or disordered. *Swift.*
5. A forked timber in a ship, placed on the keel.
6. A catch; an advantage. [*Vulgar.*]
7. In *husbandry,* a field sown two years running. [*Local.*] *Ainsworth.*

By hook and by crook, one way or other; by any means, direct or indirect. *Dryden.*

HOOK, *v. t.* To catch with a hook; as, to *hook* a fish.
2. To seize and draw, as with a hook. *Shak.*
3. To fasten with a hook.
4. To entrap; to ensnare.
5. To draw by force or artifice. *Norris.*

To hook on, to apply a hook.

HOOK, *v. i.* To bend; to be curving.

HOOK'ED, *a.* Bent into the form of a hook; curvated. The claws of a beast are *hooked.*
2. Bent; curvated; aquiline; as a *hooked* nose. *Brown.*

HOOK'ED, *pp.* Caught with a hook; fastened with a hook.

HOOK'EDNESS, *n.* A state of being bent like a hook.

HOOK'ING, *ppr.* Catching with a hook; fastening with a hook.

HOOK'NOSED, *a.* Having a curvated or aquiline nose. *Shak.*

HOOK'Y, *a.* Full of hooks; pertaining to hooks.

HOOP, *n.* [D. *hoep, hoepel.*] A band of wood or metal used to confine the staves of casks, tubs, &c. or for other similar purposes. Wooden hoops are usually made by splitting an oak or hickory sapling into two parts; but sometimes they are made of thin splints and of other species of wood.
2. A piece of whalebone in the form of a circle or ellipsis, used formerly by females to extend their petticoats; a farthingale. *Swift.*
3. Something resembling a hoop; a ring; any thing circular. *Addison.*

HOOP, *v. t.* To bind or fasten with hoops; as, to *hoop* a barrel or puncheon.
2. To clasp; to encircle; to surround. *Shak. Grew.*

HOOP, *v. i.* [Sax. *heafian, heofian,* to howl, to lament, to weep; also *hweopan,* to *whip,* to *weep,* to howl, to *whoop;* the latter is written also *weopan, wepan,* to *weep;* Goth. *wopyan,* to *whoop.* The Sax. *heafian,* seems to be connected with *heave,* and the sense is probably to raise or throw the voice. Whether *heofian* and *hweopan* are radically the same word, is not certain; most probably they are, and *whoop* and *weep* are evidently the same. *Weeping,* in rude ages, is by howling or loud outcries. See *Whoop,* the same word differently written.]
To shout; to utter a loud cry, or a particular sound by way of call or pursuit.

HOOP, *v. t.* To drive with a shout or outcry. *Shak.*
2. To call by a shout or hoop.

HOOP, *n.* A shout; also, a measure, equal to a peck. [Sw. *hof.*]
2. The hoopoe.

HOOP'ER, *n.* One who hoops casks or tubs; a cooper.

HOOP'ING, *ppr.* Fastening with hoops.

HOOP'ING, *ppr.* Crying out; shouting.

HOOP'ING-COUGH, *n.* A cough in which the patient hoops or whoops, with a deep inspiration of breath.

HOOP'OE, HOOP'OO, *n.* [Fr. *huppe*, the hoopoe, and a tuft; *huppé*, tufted; or L. *upupa, epops*; Gr. εποψ.]
A bird of the genus Upupa, whose head is adorned with a beautiful crest, which it can erect or depress at pleasure. *Encyc.*

HOOR'A, HOORAW', *exclam.* [Sw. *hurra.* The Welsh has *çwara*, play, sport; but the Swedish appears to be the English word.]
A shout of joy or exultation. [*This is the genuine English word, for which we find in books most absurdly written, huzza*, a foreign word never or rarely used.]

HOOT, *v. i.* [W. *hwd* or *hwt*, a taking off, off, away; *hwtiaw*, to take off, to push away, to *hoot*; and *udaw*, to howl or yell; Fr. *huer*, a contracted word; hence, *hue*, in *hue* and *cry*.]
1. To cry out or shout in contempt.
Matrons and girls shall *hoot* at thee no more. *Dryden.*
2. To cry, as an owl.
The clamorous owl, that nightly *hoots*. *Dryden.*

HOOT, *v. t.* To drive with cries or shouts uttered in contempt.
Partridge and his clan may *hoot* me for a cheat. *Swift.*

HOOT, *n.* A cry or shout in contempt. *Glanville.*

HOOT'ING, *n.* A shouting; clamor.

HOP, *v. i.* [Sax. *hoppan*; G. *hüpfen*; D. *huppelen*; Sw. *hoppa*; Dan. *hopper*; W. *hobelu*, to hop, to hobble. It has the elements of *caper.*]
1. To leap, or spring on one leg; *applied to persons.*
2. To leap; to spring forward by leaps; to skip, as birds.
Hopping from spray to spray. *Dryden.*
3. To walk lame; to limp; to halt. [We generally use *hobble.*]
4. To move by leaps or starts, as the blood in the veins. [*Not used.*] *Spenser.*
5. To spring; to leap; to frisk about.
6. To dance. *Chaucer.*

HOP, *n.* A leap on one leg; a leap; a jump; a spring.
2. A dance. [*Colloquial.*]

HOP, *n.* [D. *hop*; G. *hopfen*; probably *hoop*, from winding.]
A plant constituting the genus Humulus. The stalk or vine, which grows to a great length, is weak and requires to be supported. In growing, it climbs or winds round a pole or other support. This plant is of great importance in brewing, as it tends to preserve malt liquors, and renders them more aperient, diuretic and salubrious. *Encyc.*

HOP, *v. t.* To impregnate with hops. *Mortimer.*

HOP'BIND, *n.* The stalk or vine on which hops grow. *Blackstone.*

HOP'OAST, *n.* In Kent, a kiln for drying hops.

HOP'POLE, *n.* A pole used to support hops. *Tusser.*

HOP'-PICKER, *n.* One that picks hops.

HOP'VINE, *n.* The stalk of hops.

HOP'-YARD, HOP'-GARDEN, *n.* A field or inclosure where hops are raised.

HOPE, *n.* [Sax. *hopa*; D. *hoop*; Sw. *hopp*; Dan. *haab*; G. *hoffnung.* Qu. L. *cupio.* Class Gb. The primary sense is to extend, to reach forward.]
1. A desire of some good, accompanied with at least a slight expectation of obtaining it, or a belief that it is obtainable. *Hope* differs from *wish* and *desire* in this, that it implies some expectation of obtaining the good desired, or the possibility of possessing it. *Hope* therefore always gives pleasure or joy; whereas *wish* and *desire* may produce or be accompanied with pain and anxiety.
The hypocrite's *hope* shall perish. Job viii.
He wish'd, but not with *hope*— *Milton.*
Sweet *hope!* kind cheat! *Crashaw.*
He that lives upon *hope*, will die fasting. *Franklin.*
2. Confidence in a future event; the highest degree of well founded expectation of good; as a *hope* founded on God's gracious promises; *a scriptural sense.*
A well founded scriptural *hope*, is, in our religion, the source of ineffable happiness.
3. That which gives hope; he or that which furnishes ground of expectation, or promises desired good. The *hope* of Israel is the Messiah.
The Lord will be the *hope* of his people. Joel iii.
4. An opinion or belief not amounting to certainty, but grounded on substantial evidence. The christian indulges a *hope*, that his sins are pardoned.

HOPE, *v. i.* [Sax. *hopian*; G. *hoffen*; D. *hoopen*, to hope, and to heap; Dan. *haaber*; Sw. *hoppas.*]
1. To cherish a desire of good, with some expectation of obtaining it, or a belief that it is obtainable.
Hope for good success. *Taylor.*
Be sober and *hope* to the end. 1 Pet. i.
Hope humbly then, with trembling pinions soar. *Pope.*
2. To place confidence in; to trust in with confident expectation of good.
Why art thou cast down, O my soul, and why art thou disquieted within me? *Hope* thou in God. Ps. xlii.

HOPE, *v. t.* To desire with expectation of good, or a belief that it may be obtained. But as a transitive verb, it is seldom used, and the phrases in which it is so used are elliptical, *for* being understood.
So stands the Thracian herdsman with his spear,
Full in the gap, and *hopes* the hunted bear. *Dryden.*

HOPE, *n.* A sloping plain between ridges of mountains. [*Not in use.*] *Ainsworth.*

HO'PED, *pp.* Desired with expectation.

HO'PEFUL, *a.* Having qualities which excite hope; promising or giving ground to expect good or success; as a *hopeful* youth; a *hopeful* prospect.
2. Full of hope or desire, with expectation.
I was *hopeful* the success of your first attempts would encourage you to the trial of more nice and difficult experiments. *Boyle.*

HO'PEFULLY, *adv.* In a manner to raise hope; in a way promising good. He prosecutes his scheme *hopefully.*
2. In a manner to produce a favorable opinion respecting some good at the present time. The young man is *hopefully* pious.
3. With hope; with ground to expect.

HO'PEFULNESS, *n.* Promise of good; ground to expect what is desirable. *Wotton.*

HO'PELESS, *a.* Destitute of hope; having no expectation of that which is desirable; despairing.
I am a woman, friendless, *hopeless.* *Shak.*
2. Giving no ground of hope or expectation of good; promising nothing desirable; desperate; as a *hopeless* condition.

HO'PELESSLY, *adv.* Without hope. *Beaum.*

HO'PELESSNESS, *n.* A state of being desperate, or affording no hope.

HO'PER, *n.* One that hopes. *Shak.*

HO'PING, *ppr.* Having hope; indulging desire of good with the expectation of obtaining it, or a belief that it is obtainable.
2. Confiding in.

HO'PINGLY, *adv.* With hope or desire of good, and expectation of obtaining it. *Hammond.*

HOP'LITE, *n.* [Gr. οπλιτης, from οπλον, a weapon.]
In ancient Greece, a heavy-armed soldier. *Mitford.*

HOP'PER, *n.* [See *Hop.*] One who hops, or leaps on one leg.
2. Properly, a wooden trough through which grain passes into a mill; so named from its moving or shaking. But we give the name to a box or frame of boards, which receives the grain before it passes into the trough, and also to a similar box which receives apples for conducting them into a mill.
3. A vessel in which seed-corn is carried for sowing. *Encyc.*

HOP'PERS, *n.* A play in which persons hop or leap on one leg. *Johnson.*

HOP'PING, *ppr.* Leaping on one leg; dancing.

HOP'PING, *n.* A dancing; a meeting for dancing.

HOP'PLE, *v. t.* To tie the feet near together to prevent leaping; as, to *hopple* an unruly horse.

HO'RAL, *a.* [L. *hora*, an hour. See *Hour.*] Relating to an hour, or to hours. *Prior.*

HO'RALLY, *adv.* Hourly. [*Not in use.*]

HO'RARY, *a.* [L. *horarius*; Fr. *horaire*; from L. *hora*, hour.]
1. Pertaining to an hour; noting the hours; as the *horary* circle. *Encyc.*
2. Continuing an hour. *Brown.*

HORD, HORDE, *n.* [D. *horde*, a clan, and a hurdle; G. *horde*, a clan, and a pen or fold. This seems to be the Sax. *heord*, a herd.]
A company of wandering people dwelling in tents or wagons, and migrating from place to place to procure pasturage for their cattle. Such are some tribes of the Tartars in the north of Asia. A hord usually consists of fifty or sixty tents. *Encyc. Mitford.*

HORE, *n.* [Sax. *hure*, or *hor-cwen*; G. *hure*; D. *hoer*; Dan. *hore*; Sw. *hora*, and *horkåna*; W. *huren*, from *huriaw*, to hire. The common orthography *whore* is corrupt.]
A woman, married or single, who indulges unlawful sexual intercourse; also, a pros-

titute; a common woman; a harlot; a woman of ill fame. [This word comprehends *adultress* and *fornicatrix*, and all lewd women whether paid for prostitution or not.]

HORE, *v. i.* To indulge unlawful sexual commerce, as a male or female; to be habitually lewd.

HO'REDOM, *n.* The practice of unlawful sexual commerce; habitual or customary lewdness of males or females.

2. In *Scripture*, idolatry.

HO'REMASTER, } *n.* A man who is addicted to lewdness,
HO'REMÖNGER, } or frequently indulges in unlawful sexual intercourse.

HO'RESÖN, *n.* [*hore* and *son.*] A bastard; the son of a hore; a term of reproach or contempt, sometimes used in a ludicrous sense expressing dislike.

HO'RISH, *a.* Lewd; unchaste; loose; given to unlawful sexual intercourse; *applied to females only.*

HO'RISHLY, *adv.* Lewdly; unchastely.

HO'REHOUND, *n.* [Sax. *hara-hune*, white-hune.]

The name of several plants of different genera. The common horehound is the *Marrubium vulgare.* It has a bitter taste, and is used as an attenuant. *Encyc.*

HOR'IZON, *n.* [Gr. οριζων, from οριζω, to bound, ορος, a limit; Fr. *horizon*; Sp. *horizonte*; It. *orizzonte.* This word, like *contest*, *aspect*, and others in Milton, must be read in poetry with the accent on the second syllable; a harsh, unnatural pronunciation, in direct opposition to the regular analogy of English words. With the accent on the first syllable, as in common usage, it is an elegant word.]

The line that terminates the view, when extended on the surface of the earth; or a great circle of the sphere, dividing the world into two parts or hemispheres; the upper hemisphere which is visible, and the lower which is hid. The horizon is *sensible*, and *rational* or *real.* The sensible, apparent, or visible horizon, is a lesser circle of the sphere, which divides the visible part of the sphere from the invisible. It is eastern or western; the eastern is that wherein the sun and stars rise; the western, that wherein they set. The rational, true, or astronomical horizon, is a great circle whose plane passes through the center of the earth, and whose poles are the zenith and nadir. This horizon would bound the sight, if the eye could take in the whole hemisphere. *Encyc.*

HORIZON'TAL, *a.* Pertaining to the horizon, or relating to it.

2. Parallel to the horizon; on a level; as a *horizontal* line or surface.

3. Near the horizon; as *horizontal* misty air. *Milton.*

HORIZON'TALLY, *adv.* In a direction parallel to the horizon; on a level; as a ball carried *horizontally.*

HORIZONTAL'ITY, *n.* The state of being horizontal. *Kirwan.*

HORN, *n.* [Sax. G. Sw. Dan. *horn*; Goth. *haurn*; D. *hoorn*; Sw. *hörn*, a corner; W. *corn*, a horn, cornel, a corner; L. *cornu*; Sp. *cuerno*; It. Port. *corno*; Fr. *corne*; Heb. Ch. Syr. Eth. Ar. קרן. The sense is a shoot, a projection. Class Rn. No. 15.]

1. A hard substance growing on the heads of certain animals, and particularly on cloven-footed quadrupeds; usually projecting to some length and terminating in a point. Horns are generally bent or curving, and those of some animals are spiral. They serve for weapons of offense and defense. The substance of horns is gelatinous, and in Papin's digester it may be converted into jelly. *Encyc.*

Horn is an animal substance, chiefly membranous, consisting of coagulated albumen, with a little gelatin and phosphate of lime. *Ure.*

The horns of deer possess exactly the properties of bone, and are composed of the same constituents, only the proportion of cartilage is greater. *Thomson.*

2. A wind instrument of music, made of horn; a trumpet. Such were used by the Israelites.

3. In *modern times*, a wind instrument made of metal.

4. An extremity of the moon, when it is waxing or waning, and forming a crescent. *Dryden.*

5. The feeler or antenna of an insect.

6. The feeler of a snail, which may be withdrawn; hence, to *pull* or *draw in the horns*, is to repress one's ardor, or to restrain pride. *Johnson.*

7. A drinking cup; horns being used anciently for cups.

8. A winding stream. *Dryden.*

9. *Horns*, in the plural, is used to characterize a cuckold. He wears the *horns.*

10. In Scripture, *horn* is a symbol of strength or power.

> The *horn* of Moab is cut off. Jer. xlviii.

Horn is also an emblem of glory, honor, dignity.

> My *horn* is exalted in the Lord. 1 Sam. ii.

In Daniel, *horn* represents a kingdom or state.

HORN'BEAK, *n.* A fish. [See *Hornfish.*]

HORN'BEAM, *n.* [See *Beam.*] A genus of trees, the Carpinus, so named from the hardness of the wood.

HORN'BILL, *n.* A fowl of the genus Buceros, which has a flat bony forehead with two horns; a native of the E. Indies.

HORN'BLEND, *n.* [G. *horn* and *blende.*] A mineral of several varieties, called by Haüy *amphibole.* It is sometimes in regular distinct crystals; more generally the result of confused crystalization, appearing in masses, composed of lamins, acicular crystals or fibers, variously aggregated. Its prevailing colors are black and green. *Cleaveland.*

HORNBLOWER, *n.* One that blows a horn.

HORN'BOOK, *n.* The first book of children, or that in which they learn their letters and rudiments; so called from its cover of horn. [*Now little used.*] *Locke.*

HORN'-DISTEMPER, *n.* A disease of cattle, affecting the internal substance of the horn. *Encyc.*

HORN'ED, *a.* Furnished with horns; as *horned* cattle.

2. Shaped like a crescent, or the new moon. *Milton.*

HORN'EDNESS, *n.* The appearance of horns.

HORN'ER, *n.* One who works or deals in horns. *Grew.*

2. One who winds or blows the horn. *Sherwood.*

HORN'ET, *n.* [Sax. *hyrnet*, *hyrnete*; G. *horniss*; D. *horzel.*]

An insect of the genus Vespa or wasp, the *Vespa crabro.* It is much larger and stronger than the wasp, and its sting gives severe pain. This insect constructs a nest of leaves or other substance which resembles brown paper of a light color. This is attached to the branches of trees, and often of the size of a half-peck measure.

HORN'FISH, *n.* The garfish or sea-needle, of the genus Esox. *Encyc.*

HORN'FOOT, *a.* Having a hoof; hoofed. *Hakewill.*

HORN'IFY, *v. t.* To bestow horns upon. [*Not used or vulgar.*] *Beaum.*

HORN'ING, *n.* Appearance of the moon when increasing, or in the form of a crescent. *Gregory.*

HORN'ISH, *a.* Somewhat like horn; hard. *Sandys.*

HORN'LESS, *a.* Having no horns. *Journ. of Science.*

HORN'MERCURY, *n.* Muriate of mercury.

HORN'OWL, *n.* A species of owl, so called from two tufts of fethers on its head like horns. *Ainsworth.*

HORN'PIPE, *n.* An instrument of music in Wales, consisting of a wooden pipe with horns at the ends; one to collect the wind blown from the mouth; the other to carry off the sounds as modulated by the performer. [W. *pib-corn.*] *Encyc.*

2. An air or tune of triple time, with six crotchets in a bar; four to the descending beat, and two to the ascending. *Encyc.*

HORN'SHAVINGS, *n.* Scrapings or raspings of the horns of deer. *B. Jonson.*

HORN'SILVER, *n.* Muriate of silver, or chlorid of silver.

HORN'SPOON, *n.* A spoon made of horn.

HORN'SLATE, *n.* A gray siliceous stone. *Kirwan.*

HORN'STONE, *n.* A siliceous stone, a subspecies of quartz. It is divided by Jameson into splintery, conchoidal, and wood-stone. [See *Chert.*]

HORN'WORK, *n.* In *fortification*, an outwork composed of two demi-bastions joined by a curtain. *Encyc.*

HORN'Y, *a.* Consisting of horn or horns. *Milton.*

2. Resembling horn.

3. Hard; callous. *Dryden.*

HOROG'RAPHY, *n.* [Gr. ωρα, hour, and γραφω, to write.]

1. An account of hours.

2. The art of constructing dials. *Cyc.*

HO'ROLOGE, *n.* [Fr. *horloge*; L. *horologium*; Gr. ωρολογιον; ωρα, hour, and λεγω, to tell.]

An instrument that indicates the hour of the day. But *chronometer* is now generally used.

HOROLOG'ICAL, *a.* Pertaining to the horologe, or to horology.

HOROLOGIOGRAPH'IC, *a.* Pertaining to the art of dialling. *Chambers.*

HOROLOGIOG'RAPHY, *n.* [Gr. ωρα, hour λογος, discourse, and γραφω, to describe.]

An account of instruments that show the hour of the day; also, of the art of constructing dials. *Dict.*

HOROL'OGY, *n.* [Gr. ωρολογεω; ωρα, hour, and λεγω, to indicate. See *Horologe.*]
The art of constructing machines for measuring and indicating portions of time, as clocks, watches, &c. *Edin. Encyc.*

HOROMET'RICAL, *a.* [from *horometry.*] Belonging to horometry, or to the measurement of time by hours and subordinate divisions. *Asiat. Res.*

HOROM'ETRY, *n.* [Gr. ωρα, hour, and μετρον, measure.]
The art or practice of measuring time by hours and subordinate divisions.

HOR'OSCOPE, *n.* [Fr. from Gr. ωροσκοπος; ωρα, hour, and σκοπεω, to view or consider.]
1. In *astrology*, a scheme or figure of the twelve houses, or twelve signs of the zodiac, in which is marked the disposition of the heavens at a given time, and by which astrologers formerly told the fortunes of persons, according to the position of the stars at the time of their birth. *Encyc.*
2. The degree or point of the heavens arising above the eastern point of the horizon at any given time when a prediction is to be made of a future event. *Encyc.*

HOROS'COPY, *n.* The art or practice of predicting future events by the disposition of the stars and planets.

HOR'RENT, *a.* [L. *horrens.* See *Horror.*] Bristled; standing erect as bristles; pointing outward.

With bright emblazonry and *horrent* arms. *Milton.*

HOR'RIBLE, *a.* [L. *horribilis.* See *Horror.*] Exciting or tending to excite horror; dreadful; terrible; shocking; hideous; as a *horrible* figure or sight; a *horrible* story.

A dungeon *horrible* on all sides round. *Milton.*

HOR'RIBLENESS, *n.* The state or qualities that may excite horror; dreadfulness; terribleness; hideousness.

HOR'RIBLY, *adv.* In a manner to excite horror; dreadfully; terribly; as *horribly* loud; *horribly* afraid.

HOR'RID, *a.* [L. *horridus.* See *Horror.*]
1. That does or may excite horror; dreadful; hideous; shocking; as a *horrid* spectacle or sight; *horrid* sympathy. *Milton.*
2. Rough; rugged. *This is the literal and primary sense.*

Horrid with fern, and intricate with thorn. *Dryden.*

3. Shocking; very offensive; *a colloquial sense.* *Pope.*

HOR'RIDLY, *adv.* In a manner to excite horror; dreadfully; shockingly.

HOR'RIDNESS, *n.* The qualities that do or may excite horror; hideousness; enormity. *Hammond.*

HORRIF'IC, *a.* [L. *horrificus.*] Causing horror. *Thomson.*

HORRIS'ONOUS, *a.* [L. *horrisonus; horreo,* to shake, and *sonus,* sound.] Sounding dreadfully; uttering a terrible sound.

HOR'ROR, *n.* [L. from *horreo,* to shake or shiver, or to set up the bristles, to be rough.]
1. A shaking, shivering or shuddering, as in the cold fit which precedes a fever. This ague is usually accompanied with a contraction of the skin into small wrinkles, giving it a kind of roughness.
2. An excessive degree of fear, or a painful emotion which makes a person tremble; terror; a shuddering with fear; but appropriately, terror or a sensation approaching it, accompanied with hatred or detestation. *Horror* is often a passion compounded of fear and hatred or disgust. The recital of a bloody deed fills us with *horror.*

A *horror* of great darkness fell on Abram. Gen. xv.

Horror hath taken hold on me, because of the wicked that forsake thy law. Ps. cxix.

3. That which may excite horror or dread; gloom; dreariness.

And breathes a browner *horror* on the woods. *Pope.*

4. Dreadful thoughts.
5. Distressing scenes; as the *horrors* of war or famine.

HORSE, *n. hors.* [Sax. *hors;* G. *ross;* D. *ros.*]
1. A species of quadrupeds of the genus Equus, having six erect and parallel foreteeth in the upper jaw, and six somewhat prominent in the under jaw; the dog teeth are solitary, and the feet consist of an undivided hoof. The horse is a beautiful animal, and of great use for draught or conveyance on his back. *Horse,* in English, is of common gender, and may comprehend the male and female.
2. A constellation. *Creech.*
3. Cavalry; a body of troops serving on horseback. In this sense, it has no plural termination. We say, a thousand *horse;* a regiment of *horse.*
4. A machine by which something is supported; usually a wooden frame with legs. Various machines used in the arts are thus called. *Encyc.*
5. A wooden machine on which soldiers ride by way of punishment; sometimes called a *timber-mare.* *Johnson.*
6. In *seamen's language,* a rope extending from the middle of a yard to its extremity, to support the sailors while they loose, reef or furl the sails; also, a thick rope extended near the mast for hoisting a yard or extending a sail on it. *Mar. Dict.*

To take horse, to set out to ride on horseback. *Addison.*
2. To be covered, as a mare.

HORSE, *v. t.* To mount on a horse.
2. To carry on the back.

The keeper, *horsing* a deer. *Butler.*

3. To ride astride; as ridges *horsed.* *Shak.*
4. To cover a mare, as the male. *Mortimer.*

HORSEBACK, *n. hors'back.* The state of being on a horse; the posture of riding on a horse.

I saw them salute on *horseback.* *Shak.*

HORSEBEAN, *n.* A small bean usually given to horses. *Mortimer.*

HORSEBLOCK, *n.* A block or stage that assists persons in mounting and dismounting from a horse.

HORSEBOAT, *n.* A boat used in conveying horses over a river or other water.
2. A boat moved by horses; a new species of ferry-boat.

HORSEBOY, *n.* A boy employed in dressing and tending horses; a stable boy. *Knolles.*

HORSEBREAKER, *n.* One whose employment is to break horses, or to teach them to draw or carry. *Creech.*

HORSE-CHESTNUT, *n.* A large nut, the fruit of a species of Æsculus; or the tree that produces it. The tree is much cultivated for shade.

HORSECLOTH, *n.* A cloth to cover a horse.

HORSECOURSER, *n.* One that runs horses, or keeps horses for the race. *Johnson.*
2. A dealer in horses. *Wiseman.*

HORSECRAB, *n.* A crustaceous fish. *Ainsworth.*

HORSE-CU'CUMBER, *n.* A large green cucumber. *Mortimer.*

HORSEDEALER, *n.* One who buys and sells horses.

HORSEDRENCH, *n.* A dose of physic for a horse. *Shak.*

HORSEDUNG, *n.* The dung of horses.

HORSE-EMMET, *n.* A species of large ant.

HORSEFACED, *a.* Having a long coarse face; ugly.

HORSEFLESH, *n.* The flesh of a horse. *Bacon.*

HORSEFLY, *n.* A large fly that stings horses.

HORSEFOOT, *n.* A plant, called also *coltsfoot.* *Ainsworth.*

HORSEGUARDS, *n.* A body of cavalry for guards.

HORSEHAIR, *n.* The hair of horses.

HORSEHOE, *v. t.* To hoe or clean a field by means of horses.

HORSEKNAVE, *n.* A groom. *Obs.* *Chaucer.*

HORSE-KEEPER, *n.* One who keeps or takes care of horses.

HORSELAUGH, *n.* A loud, boisterous laugh. *Pope.*

HORSELEECH, *n.* A large leech. [See *Leech.*]
2. A farrier. *Ainsworth.*

HORSELITTER, *n.* A carriage hung on poles which are borne by and between two horses. *Milton.*

HORSELOAD, *n.* A load for a horse.

HORSEMAN, *n.* A rider on horseback. *Addison.*
2. A man skilled in riding. *Dryden.*
3. A soldier who serves on horseback. *Hayward.*

HORSEMANSHIP, *n.* The act of riding, and of training and managing horses. *Pope.*

HORSEMARTEN, *n.* A kind of large bee. *Ainsworth.*

HORSEMATCH, *n.* A bird. *Ainsworth.*

HORSEMEAT, *n.* Food for horses; provender. *Bacon.*

HORSE-MILL, *a.* A mill turned by a horse.

HORSE-MINT, *n.* A species of large mint.

HORSE-MUSCLE, *n.* A large muscle or shell-fish. *Bacon.*

HORSEPATH, *n.* A path for horses, as by canals.

HORSEPLAY, *n.* Rough, rugged play. *Dryden.*

HORSEPOND, *n.* A pond for watering horses.

HORSEPURSLANE, *n.* A plant of the genus Trianthema.

HORSERACE, *n.* A race by horses; a match of horses in running.

HORSERACING, *n.* The practice or act of running horses.

HORSERADISH, *n.* A plant of the genus Cochlearia, a species of scurvy grass, having a root of a pungent taste.

HORSESHOE, *n.* A shoe for horses, consisting of a plate of iron of a circular form.

HORSESHOE-HEAD, *n.* A disease of infants, in which the sutures of the skull are too open; opposed to *headmold-shot.*

HORSESTEALER, **HORSETHIEF**, } *n.* A stealer of horses.

HORSETAIL, *n.* A plant of the genus Equisetum. The *shrubby horsetail* is of the genus Ephedra. *Fam. of Plants.*

HORSETŎNGUE, *n.* A plant of the genus Ruscus.

HORSEVETCH, **HORSESHOE-VETCH**, } *n.* A plant of the genus Hippocrepis.

HORSEWAY, **HORSERŌAD**, } *n.* A way or road in which horses may travel.

HORSEWHIP, *n.* A whip for driving or striking horses.

HORSEWHIP, *v. t.* To lash; to strike with a horsewhip.

HORSEWŎRM, *n.* A worm that infests horses; a bott.

HORTA'TION, *n.* [L. *hortatio*, from *hortor*, to exhort.]
The act of exhorting, or giving advice; exhortation; advice intended to encourage. [*But* exhortation *is generally used.*]

HOR'TATIVE, *a.* Giving exhortation; advisory.

HOR'TATIVE, *n.* Exhortation; a precept given to incite or encourage. *Bacon.*

HOR'TATORY, *a.* Encouraging; inciting; giving advice; as a *hortatory* speech.

HORTEN'SIAL, *a.* [L. *hortensis.*] Fit for a garden. [*Not used.*] *Evelyn.*

HOR'TICULTOR, *n.* [L. *hortus*, a garden, and *cultor*, a tiller.] One who cultivates a garden.

HORTICUL'TURAL, *a.* Pertaining to the culture of gardens.

HOR'TICULTURE, *n.* [L. *hortus*, a garden, and *cultura*, culture, from *colo*, to till.]
The cultivation of a garden; or the art of cultivating gardens.

HORTICUL'TURIST, *n.* One who is skilled in the art of cultivating gardens.

HOR'TULAN, *a.* [L. *hortulanus.*] Belonging to a garden; as a *hortulan* calendar. *Evelyn.*

HORTUS SICCUS, *n.* [L.] Literally, a dry garden; an appellation given to a collection of specimens of plants, carefully dried and preserved. *Encyc.*

HORT'YARD, *n.* An orchard, which see.

HOSAN'NA, *n. s* as *z.* [Heb. save, I beseech you.]
An exclamation of praise to God, or an invocation of blessings. In the Hebrew ceremonies, it was a prayer rehearsed on the several days of the feast of tabernacles, in which this word was often repeated. *Encyc.*

HOSE, *n.* plu. *hosen* or *hose;* pron. *hoze, ho'zn.* [Sax. *hos*, a heel, a thorn or twig, and hose; G. *hose;* D. *kous;* W. *hos, hosan*, from *hws*, a covering, a *housing;* Fr. *chausse;* Ir. *asan.* The Welsh unites this word with *house.* The *hose* or *hosan* was a garment covering the legs and thighs, like the modern long trowsers. Hence in G. *hosen-gurt*, a *hose-girt*, is a waistband; and *hosen-träger*, hose-supporter, or shoulder-strap, indicates that the hose was sustained, as breeches and pantaloons now are, by suspenders or braces.]
1. Breeches or trowsers. *Shak.*
2. Stockings; coverings for the legs. This word, in mercantile use, is synonymous with stockings, though originally a very different garment.
3. A leathern pipe, used with fire-engines, for conveying water to extinguish fires.

HO'SIER, *n. ho'zhur.* One who deals in stockings and socks, &c.

HO'SIERY, *n. ho'zhury.* Stockings in general; socks.

HOS'PITABLE, *a.* [L. *hospitalis*, from *hospes*, a guest; It. *ospitale* and *ospitabile. Hospes*, is from the Celtic; W. *osb*, a stranger or wanderer, a guest; Arm. *osb, osp, hospyd.* See *Host.*]
1. Receiving and entertaining strangers with kindness and without reward; kind to strangers and guests; disposed to treat guests with generous kindness; as a *hospitable* man.
2. Proceeding from or indicating kindness to guests; manifesting generosity; as a *hospitable* table; *hospitable* rites. *Dryden.*
3. Inviting to strangers; offering kind reception; indicating hospitality.

> To where yon taper cheers the vale,
> With *hospitable* ray. *Goldsmith.*

HOS'PITABLY, *adv.* With kindness to strangers or guests; with generous and liberal entertainment. *Prior. Swift.*

HOS'PITAGE, *n.* Hospitality. *Obs.* *Spenser.*

HOS'PITAL, *n.* [Fr. *hôpital*, for *hospital;* L. *hospitalis*, supra.]
1. A building appropriated for the reception of sick, infirm and helpless paupers, who are supported and nursed by charity; also, a house for the reception of insane persons, whether paupers or not, or for seamen, soldiers, foundlings, &c. who are supported by the public, or by private charity, or for infected persons, &c.
2. A place for shelter or entertainment. *Obs.* *Spenser.*

HOS'PITAL, *a.* Hospitable. [*Not in use.*] *Howell.*

HOSPITAL'ITY, *n.* [Fr. *hospitalité;* L. *hospitalitas;* W. *ysbyd.* See *Hospitable.*]
The act or practice of receiving and entertaining strangers or guests without reward, or with kind and generous liberality.

> A bishop—must be given to *hospitality.* 1 Tim. iii.
>
> *Hospitality* I have found as universal as the face of man. *Ledyard.*

HOS'PITALLER, *n.* [from *hospital.*] Properly, one residing in a hospital for the purpose of receiving the poor and strangers. The *hospitallers* were an order of knights who built a hospital at Jerusalem for pilgrims. They were called *knights of St. John*, and are the same as the *knights of Malta.* *Encyc.*

HOS'PITATE, *v. i.* [L. *hospitor.*] To reside or lodge under the roof of another. [*Not used.*] *Grew.*

HOS'PITATE, *v. t.* To lodge a person. [*Not used.*]

HŌST, *n.* [Fr. *hôte*, for *hoste;* It. *oste;* Sp. *huesped;* Port. *hospede;* and L. *hostis*, a stranger, an enemy, probably of the same family. See *Hospitable.* The sense is a stranger or foreigner, that is, a wanderer or traveler, from some root signifying to wander, to go or pass, or to visit. See Class Gs. No. 5. 14. 16.]
1. One who entertains another at his own house, without reward.

> Homer never entertained guests or *hosts* with long speeches. *Sidney.*

2. One who entertains another at his house for reward; an innkeeper; a landlord.
3. A guest; one who is entertained at the house of another. The innkeeper says of the traveler, he has a good *host*, and the traveler says of his landlord, he has a kind *host.* [See *Guest.*] *Encyc.*

HŌST, *n.* [L. *hostis*, a stranger, an enemy. The sense is probably transferred from a single foe to an army of foes.]
1. An army; a number of men embodied for war.
2. Any great number or multitude.

HŌST, *n.* [L. *hostia*, a victim or sacrifice, from *hostis*, an enemy; Fr. *hostie;* applied to the Savior who was offered for the sins of men.]
In *the Romish church*, the sacrifice of the mass, or the consecrated wafer, representing the body of Christ, or as the Catholics alledge, transubstantiated into his own body. *Encyc.*

HŌST, *v. i.* To lodge at an inn; to take up entertainment. [*Little used.*] *Shak.*

HŌST, *v. t.* To give entertainment to. [*Not used.*] *Spenser.*

HOS'TAGE, *n.* [Fr. *otage*, for *ostage;* It. *ostaggio;* Arm. *ostaich;* G. *geissel;* W. *gwystyl*, a pledge, pawn, surety, hostage.]
A person delivered to an enemy or hostile power, as a pledge to secure the performance of the conditions of a treaty or stipulations of any kind, and on the performance of which the person is to be released. *Bacon. Atterbury.*

HOSTEL, HOSTELLER. [See *Hotel.*]

HŌSTESS, *n.* A female host; a woman who entertains guests at her house. *Dryden.*
2. A woman who keeps an inn. *Temple.*

HŌSTESS-SHIP, *n.* The character or business of a hostess. *Shak.*

HOS'TILE, *a.* [L. *hostilis*, from *hostis*, an enemy, that is, a foreigner.]
1. Belonging to a public enemy; designating enmity, particularly public enmity, or a state of war; inimical; as a *hostile* band or army; a *hostile* force; *hostile* intentions.
2. Possessed by a public enemy; as a *hostile* country. *Kent.*
3. Adverse; opposite; unfriendly. [*But the word is not properly applied to private enmity, or mere unfriendliness.*]

HOS'TILELY, *adv.* In a hostile manner.

HOSTIL'ITY, *n.* [Fr. *hostilité;* L. *hostilitas*, from *hostis*, an enemy.]
1. The state of war between nations or states; the actions of an open enemy; aggression; attacks of an enemy. These secret enmities broke out in *hostilities.*

> *Hostility* being thus suspended with France. *Hayward.*

We have carried on even our *hostilities* with humanity. *Atterbury.*

2. Private enmity; *a sense less proper.*

HOS'TILIZE, *v. t.* To make an enemy. [*Little used.*]

HOSTING, *n.* [from *host*, an army.] An encounter; a battle. [*Little used.*] *Milton.*

2. A muster or review. *Obs.* *Spenser.*

HOS'TLER, *n.* *hos'ler.* [from Fr. *hôtelier*, an innkeeper. See *Hotel.*]

The person who has the care of horses at an inn.

HOSTLESS, *a.* Inhospitable. [*Not in use.*]

HOSTRY, *n.* A stable for horses. *Dryden.*

2. A lodging house. *Howell.*

HOT, *a.* [Sax. *hat*; G. *heiss*; D. *heet*; Sw. *het*; Dan. *heed.* See *Heat.*]

1. Having sensible heat; opposed to *cold*; as a *hot* stove or fire; a *hot* cloth; *hot* liquors. *Hot* expresses more than *warm.*

2. Ardent in temper; easily excited or exasperated; vehement.

Achilles is impatient, *hot* and revengeful. *Dryden.*

3. Violent; furious; as a *hot* engagement or assault. *Dryden.*

4. Eager; animated; brisk; keen; as a *hot* pursuit, or a person *hot* in a pursuit.

5. Lustful; lewd. *Shak.*

6. Acrid; biting; stimulating; pungent; as *hot* as mustard or pepper.

HOT, HOTE, HOTEN, *pp.* Called; named. *Obs.* *Gower.*

HOT'BED, *n.* In *gardening*, a bed of earth and horsedung or tanner's bark, covered with glass to defend it from the cold air, intended for raising early plants, or for nourishing exotic plants of warm climates, which will not thrive in cool or temperate air. *Encyc.*

HOT'BRAINED, *a.* Ardent in temper; violent; rash; precipitate; as *hotbrained* youth. *Dryden.*

HOTCH'POT, *n.* [Fr. *hochepot*, from *hocher*, to shake, and probably *pot*, a pot or dish.]

1. Properly, a mingled mass; a mixture of ingredients. *Bacon.* *Camden.*

2. In *law*, a mixing of lands. Thus lands given in frank-marriage to one daughter, shall, after the death of the ancestor, be blended with the lands descending to her and to her sisters from the same ancestor, and then be divided in equal portions to all the daughters. *Blackstone.*

HOT'COCKLES, *n. plu.* [Qu. Fr. *hautes coquilles*, high shells.]

A play in which one covers his eyes, and guesses who strikes him, or his hand placed behind him. *Gay.*

HOTEL', *n.* [Fr. *hôtel*, for *hostel*, a palace or dwelling house of a prince or lord.]

1. A palace.

2. An inn; a house for entertaining strangers or travelers. It was formerly a house for genteel strangers or lodgers, but the name is now given to any inn.

HOT'HEADED, *a.* Of ardent passions; vehement; violent; rash. *Arbuthnot.*

HOT'HOUSE, *n.* A house kept warm to shelter tender plants and shrubs from the cold air; a place in which the plants of warmer climates may be reared, and fruits ripened.

2. A bagnio, or place to sweat and cup in. *Shak.*

3. A brothel. *B. Jonson.*

HOT'LY, *adv.* [from *hot.*] With heat.

2. Ardently; vehemently; violently; as a stag *hotly* pursued.

3. Lustfully. *Dryden.*

HOT'MOUTHED, *a.* Headstrong; ungovernable.

That *hotmouthed* beast that bears against the curb. *Dryden.*

HOT'NESS, *n.* Sensible heat beyond a moderate degree or warmth.

2. Violence; vehemence; fury.

HOT'SPUR, *n.* [*hot* and *spur.*] A man violent, passionate, heady, rash or precipitate. *Shak.*

2. A kind of pea of early growth.

HOT'SPUR, *a.* Violent; impetuous. *Spenser.*

HOT'SPURRED, *a.* Vehement; rash; heady; headstrong. *Peacham.*

HOT'TENTOT, *n.* A native of the southern extremity of Africa.

2. A savage brutal man.

HOTTENTOT-CHERRY, *n.* A plant. [See *Cherry.*] *Chambers.*

HOUGH, *n.* *hok.* [Sax. *hoh*, the heel, or the hough; G. *hacke*, D. *hak*, a heel, a hoe.]

1. The lower part of the thigh; the ham; the joint of the hind leg of a beast that connects the thigh with the leg. *Encyc.*

2. An adz; a hoe. [*Not in use.*] *Sillingfleet.*

HOUGH, *v. t.* *hok.* To hamstring; to disable by cutting the sinews of the ham.

2. To cut with a hoe. *Obs.*

HOUL'ET, *n.* An owl. [See *Howlet.*]

HOULT, *n.* [See *Holt.*]

HOUND, *n.* [Sax. G. Sw. Dan. Scot. *hund*; D. *hond*; L. *canis*; Gr. *κυων*, *κυνος*; Fr. *chien*; It. *cane.*]

A generic name of the dog; but in English it is confined to a particular breed or variety, used in the chase. It has long, smooth, pendulous ears.

HOUND, *v. t.* To set on the chase. *Bramhall.*

2. To hunt; to chase. *L'Estrange.*

HOUND'FISH, *n.* A fish, called also Galeus lævis, with a long round body, and ash-colored sides and back. *Dict. Nat. Hist.*

A species of shark, the *Squalus mustelus.* *Crabbe.* *Cyc.*

HOUNDS, *n.* In *seamen's language*, the projecting parts of the head of a mast. *Mar. Dict.*

HOUND'S TONGUE, *n.* A plant of the genus Cynoglossum.

HOUND'TREE, *n.* A kind of tree. *Ainsworth.*

HOUP. [See *Hoopoo.*]

HOUR, *n.* *our.* [L. Sp. *hora*; Gr. *ωρα*; It. *ora*; Fr. *heure*; Arm. *heur*; W. *awr*; Ir. *uair*; G. *uhr*; D. *uur.* The primary sense is time or season, occasion, from a root which signifies to come, to happen, to fall, to rush or drive. Hence the Fr. *heur* signifies luck, good fortune, and *heureux*, lucky, fortunate, happy, that is, seasonable. So in L. *tempestivus*, from *tempus.* See *Time.* But *hour*, *hora*, afterward came to signify a certain portion or division of the day. This has been different in different nations.]

1. A space of time equal to one twenty fourth part of the natural day, or duration of the diurnal revolution of the earth. An hour answers to fifteen degrees of the equator. It consists of 60 minutes, each minute of 60 seconds, &c.

2. Time; a particular time; as the *hour* of death.

Jesus saith, woman, my *hour* is not yet come. John ii.

3. The time marked or indicated by a chronometer, clock or watch; the particular time of the day. What is the *hour?* At what *hour* shall we meet? I will be with you at an early *hour.*

Good hour, signifies early or seasonably. You have arrived at a *good hour.*

To keep good hours, to be at home in good season; not to be abroad late, or at the usual hours of retiring to rest.

Hours, in the plural, certain prayers in the Romish church, to be repeated at stated times of the day, as matins and vespers. *Encyc.*

HOUR'GLASS, *n.* *our'glass.* A chronometer that measures the flux of time by the running of sand from one glass vessel to another, through a small aperture. Instead of sand, dry egg shells pulverized are sometimes used. The quantity of sand may be so proportioned as to measure an hour, a half hour, or a quarter.

2. Space of time. *Bacon.*

HOUR'HAND, *n.* The hand or pointed pin which shows the hour on a chronometer.

HOU'RI, *n.* Among Mohammedans, a nymph of paradise. *Johnson.*

HOUR'LY, *a.* *our'ly.* Happening or done every hour; occurring hour by hour; frequent; often repeated.

Observe the waning moon with *hourly* view. *Dryden.*

2. Continual.

We must live in *hourly* expectation of having the troops recalled. *Swift.*

HOUR'LY, *adv.* *our'ly.* Every hour; frequently; continually.

Great was their strife which *hourly* was renewed. *Dryden.*

HOUR'PLATE, *n.* *our'plate.* The plate of a clock or other time-piece on which the hours are marked; the dial. *Locke.*

HOUS'AGE, *n.* [from *house.*] A fee for keeping goods in a house. [*Not in use.*] *Chambers.*

HOUSE, *n.* *hous.* [Sax. Goth. Sw. Scot. *hus*; G. *haus*; D. *huis*; Dan. *huus*; L. *casa*; It. Sp. and Port. *casa*; W. *hws*, a covering or housing. If the primary sense is a covering, this word may be referred to Heb. Ch. Syr. כסה, Ar. كَسَا, to put on, to cover. Class Gs. No. 57. It corresponds to *cot*, in a different dialect.]

1. In a general sense, a building or shed intended or used as a habitation or shelter for animals of any kind; but appropriately, a building or edifice for the habitation of man; a dwelling place, mansion or abode for any of the human species. It may be of any size and composed of any materials whatever, wood, stone, brick, &c.

2. An edifice or building appropriated to the worship of God; a temple; a church; as the *house* of God.

3. A monastery; a college; as a religious *house*.
4. The manner of living; the table. He keeps a good *house*, or a miserable *house*.
5. In *astrology*, the station of a planet in the heavens, or the twelfth part of the heavens. *Johnson. Encyc.*
6. A family of ancestors; descendants and kindred; a race of persons from the same stock; a tribe. It particularly denotes a noble family or an illustrious race; as the *house* of Austria; the *house* of Hanover. So in Scripture, the *house* of Israel, or of Judah.

Two of a *house* few ages can afford. *Dryden.*

7. One of the estates of a kingdom assembled in parliament or legislature; a body of men united in their legislative capacity, and holding their place by right or by election. Thus we say, the *house* of lords or peers of Great Britain; the *house* of commons; the *house* of representatives. In most of the United States, the legislatures consist of two *houses*, the senate, and the house of representatives or delegates.
8. The quorum of a legislative body; the number of representatives assembled who are constitutionally empowered to enact laws. Hence we say, there is a sufficient number of representatives present to form a *house*.
9. In *Scripture*, those who dwell in a house and compose a family; a household.

Cornelius was a devout man, and feared God with all his *house*. Acts x.

10. Wealth; estate.

Ye devour widows' *houses*. Matt. xxiii.

11. The grave; as the *house* appointed for all living. Job xxx.
12. Household affairs; domestic concerns.

Set thy *house* in order. 2 Kings xx.

13. The body; the residence of the soul in this world; as our earthly *house*. 2 Cor. v.
14. The church among the Jews.

Moses was faithful in all his *house*. Heb. iii.

15. A place of residence. Egypt is called the *house* of bondage. Ex. xiii.
16. A square, or division on a chess board. *Encyc.*

HOUSE, *v. t. houz.* [Sw. *hysa*.] To cover from the inclemencies of the weather; to shelter; to protect by covering; as, to *house* wood; to *house* farming utensils; to *house* cattle.

2. To admit to residence; to harbor.

Palladius wished him to *house* all the Helots. *Sidney.*

3. To deposit and cover, as in the grave. *Sandys.*
4. To drive to a shelter. *Shak.*

HOUSE, *v. i. houz.* To take shelter or lodgings; to keep abode; to reside.

To *house* with darkness and with death. *Milton.*

2. To have an astrological station in the heavens.

Where Saturn *houses*. *Dryden.*

HOUSEBOAT, *n. hous'boat.* A covered boat.

HOUSEBOTE, *n. hous'bote.* [*house* and Sax. *bot*, supply.] In *law*, a sufficient allowance of wood to repair the house and supply fuel.

HOUSE-BREAK'ER, *n. hous'-breaker.* One who breaks, opens and enters a house by day with a felonious intent, or one who breaks or opens a house, and steals therefrom, by daylight. *Blackstone.*

HOUSE-BREAKING, *n. hous'-breaking.* The breaking, or opening and entering of a house by daylight, with the intent to commit a felony, or to steal or rob. The same crime committed at night is *burglary*. *Blackstone.*

HOUSEDOG, *n. hous'dog.* A dog kept to guard the house. *Addison.*

HOUSEHOLD, *n. hous'hold.* Those who dwell under the same roof and compose a family; those who belong to a family.

I baptized also the *household* of Stephanus. 1 Cor. i.

2. Family life; domestic management. *Shak.*

HOUSEHOLD, *a. hous'hold.* Belonging to the house and family; domestic; as *household* furniture; *household* affairs.

HOUSEHOLDER, *n. hous'holder.* The master or chief of a family; one who keeps house with his family. Matt. xiii.

HOUSEHOLD-STUFF, *n. hous'hold-stuff.* The furniture of a house; the vessels, utensils and goods of a family. *Bacon.*

HOUSEKEEPER, *n. hous'keeper.* One who occupies a house with his family; a man or woman who maintains a family state in a house; a householder; the master or mistress of a family. *Locke.*

2. A female servant who has the chief care of the family and superintends the other servants. *Swift.*
3. One who lives in plenty. [*Not in use.*] *Wotton.*
4. One who keeps much at home. [*Not used.*] *Shak.*
5. A housedog. [*Not used.*] *Shak.*

HOUSEKEEPING, *a. hous'keeping.* Domestic; used in a family; as *housekeeping* commodities. [*Little used.*] *Carew.*

HOUSEKEEPING, *n.* [As above.] The family state in a dwelling.

2. Hospitality; a plentiful and hospitable table. [*Not used in U. States.*]

HOUS'EL, *n. houz'l.* [Sax. *husel.* Lye supposes this to be from Goth. *hunsa*, a victim.] The eucharist; the sacred bread.

HOUS'EL, *v. t.* [Sax. *huslian.*] To give or receive the eucharist. *Obs. Chaucer.*

HOUSELAMB, *n. hous'lamb.* A lamb kept in a house for fatting.

HOUSELEEK, *n. hous'leek.* [See *Leek.*] A plant of the genus Sempervivum, which is found on the tops of houses. The *lesser houseleek* is of the genus Sedum.

HOUSELESS, *n. hous'less.* Destitute of a house or habitation; as the *houseless* child of want. *Goldsmith.*

2. Destitute of shelter.

HOUSELINE, HOUS'ING, } *n.* Among *seamen*, a small line formed of three strands, smaller than rope-yarn, used for seizings, &c. *Mar. Dict.*

HOUSEMAID, *n. hous'maid.* A female servant employed to keep a house clean, &c.

HOUSEPIGEON, *n.* A tame pigeon. *Gregory.*

HOUSEROOM, *n. hous'room.* Room or place in a house. *Dryden.*

HOUSERAISER, *n.* One who erects a house. *Wotton.*

HOUSESNAIL, *n.* A particular kind of snail. *Dict.*

HOUSEWARMING, *n. hous'warming.* A feast or merry making at the time a family enters a new house. *Johnson.*

HOUSEWIFE, *n. hous'wife.* [*house* and *wife*; contracted into *huswife, hussy.*] The mistress of a family. *Pope.*

2. A female economist; a good manager. *Dryden. Addison.*
3. One skilled in female business. *Addison.*
4. A little case or bag for articles of female work. *Shelton.*

HOUSEWIFELY, *a. hous'wifely.* Pertaining to the mistress of a family.

2. Taken from housewifery, or domestic affairs; as a *housewifely* metaphor. *Blackstone.*

HOUSEWIFERY, *n. hous'wifery.* The business of the mistress of a family; female business in the economy of a family; female management of domestic concerns. *Temple. Taylor.*

HOUSE-WRIGHT, *n. hous'-wright.* An architect who builds houses. *Fotherby.*

HOUS'ED, *pp. s* as *z.* Put under cover; sheltered.

HOUS'ING, *ppr. s* as *z.* Covering; sheltering.

2. Warped; crooked, as a brick.

HOUS'ING, *n.* Houses in general.

2. [Fr. *housse*; W. *hws*, a covering.] A cloth laid over a saddle. *Encyc.*
3. A piece of cloth fastened to the hinder part of a saddle, and covering the horse's croup; called also *boot-housing*.
4. [See *Houseline.*]

HOUS'LING, *a.* [See *Housel.*] Sacramental; as *housling* fire, used in the sacrament of marriage. *Obs. Spenser.*

HOUSS, a covering. [See *Housing.*] *Dryden.*

HOVE, *pret.* of *heave.*

HOV'EL, *n.* [Sax. *hof, hofe*, a house, a cave.] A shed; a cottage; a mean house.

HOV'EL, *v. t.* To put in a hovel; to shelter.

HOVEN, *pp.* of *heave.*

HŎV'ER, *v. i.* [W. *hoviaw*, to hang over, to fluctuate, to hover.]

1. To flap the wings, as a fowl; to hang over or about, fluttering or flapping the wings, with short irregular flights.

Great flights of birds are *hovering* about the bridge, and settling on it. *Addison.*

2. To hang over or around, with irregular motions.

A *hovering* mist came swimming o'er his sight. *Dryden.*

3. To stand in suspense or expectation. *Spenser.*
4. To wander about from place to place in the neighborhood; to move back and forth; as an army *hovering* on our borders; a ship *hovering* on our coast. *Cranch's Rep.*

HŎV'ER, *n.* A protection or shelter by hanging over. *Obs.*

HŎV'ER-GROUND, *n.* Light ground. *Ray.*

HŎV'ERING, *ppr.* Flapping the wings; hanging over or around; moving with short irregular flights.

HOW, *adv.* [Sax. *hu*; D. *hoe.*] In what manner. I know not *how* to answer.

How can a man be born when he is old? *How* can these things be? John iii.

2. To what degree or extent. *How* long shall we suffer these indignities? *How* much better is wisdom than gold!

O *how* love I thy law! *How* sweet are thy words to my taste! Ps. cxix.

3. For what reason; from what cause.

How now, my love, why is your cheek so pale? *Shak.*

4. By what means. *How* can this effect be produced?

5. In what state.

How, and with what reproach shall I return! *Dryden.*

6. It is used in a sense marking proportion; as *how* much less; *how* much more.

Behold, he putteth no trust in his servants—*how* much less in them that dwell in houses of clay— Job iv.

By *how* much they would diminish the present extent of the sea, so much they would impair the fertility and fountains and rivers of the earth. *Bentley.*

7. It is much used in exclamation.

How are the mighty fallen! 2 Sam. i.

8. In some popular phrases, *how* is superfluous or inelegant.

Thick clouds put us in some hope of land; knowing *how* that part of the South Sea was utterly unknown. *Bacon.*

HOWBE'IT, *adv.* [*how, be,* and *it.*] Be it as it may; nevertheless; notwithstanding; yet; but; however. *Obs.*

HOW'DY, *n.* A midwife. [*Local.*] *Grose.*

HOW D'YE, how do you? how is your health?

HOWEV'ER, *adv.* [*how* and *ever.*] In whatever manner or degree; as, *however* good or bad the style may be.

2. At all events; at least.

Our chief end is to be freed from all, if it may be, *however* from the greatest evils. *Tillotson.*

3. Nevertheless; notwithstanding; yet. I shall not oppose your design; I cannot *however* approve of it.

You might *howe'er* have took a fairer way. *Dryden.*

HOW'ITZ, **HOW'ITZER**, *n.* [Sp. *hobus*; G. *haubitze.*] A kind of mortar or short gun, mounted on a field carriage, and used for throwing shells. The difference between a mortar and a howitz is that the trunnions of a mortar are at the end, but those of a howitz are at the middle. *Encyc.*

HOW'KER, *n.* A Dutch vessel with two masts, a main and a mizen-mast; also, a fishing boat with one mast, used on the coast of Ireland. *Mar. Dict.*

HOWL, *v. i.* [D. *huilen*; G. *heulen*; Sw. *yla*; Dan. *hyler*; Sp. *aullar*; L. *ululo*; Gr. ὑλαω; Corn. *hoalea.* Qu. W. *wylaw*; Arm. *guela* or *iala*; Ir. *guilim*; It. *guaiolare.* The latter coincide with *wail* and *yell.*]

1. To cry as a dog or wolf; to utter a particular kind of loud, protracted and mournful sound. We say, the dog *howls*; the wolf *howls.* Hence,

2. To utter a loud, mournful sound, expressive of distress; to wail.

Howl ye, for the day of the Lord is at hand. Is. xiii.

Ye rich men, weep and *howl.* James v.

3. To roar; as a tempest.

HOWL, *v. t.* To utter or speak with outcry.

Go—*howl* it out in desarts. *Philips.*

HOWL, *n.* The cry of a dog or wolf, or other like sound.

2. The cry of a human being in horror or anguish.

HOWL'ET, *n.* [Fr. *hulotte*; from *owl.*] A fowl of the owl kind, which utters a mournful cry. It is as large as a pullet. *Dict. Nat. Hist.*

HOWL'ING, *ppr.* Uttering the cry of a dog or wolf; uttering a loud cry of distress.

HOWL'ING, *a.* Filled with howls, or howling beasts; dreary.

Innumerable artifices and stratagems are acted in the *howling* wilderness and in the great deep, that can never come to our knowledge. *Addison.*

HOWL'ING, *n.* The act of howling; a loud outcry or mournful sound.

HOWSOEV'ER, *adv.* [*how, so,* and *ever.*]

1. In what manner soever. *Raleigh.*

2. Although. *Shak.*

[For this word, *however* is generally used.]

HOX, *v. t.* To hough; to hamstring. [*Not used.* See *Hough.*] *Shak.*

HOY, *n.* A small vessel, usually rigged as a sloop, and employed in conveying passengers and goods from place to place on the sea coast, or in transporting goods to and from a ship in a road or bay. *Encyc. Mar. Dict.*

HOY, an exclamation, of no definite meaning.

HUB. [See *Hob.*]

HUB'BUB, *n.* A great noise of many confused voices; a tumult; uproar; riot. *Spenser. Clarendon.*

HUCK, *v. i.* To haggle in trading. [*Not in use.*]

HUCK, *n.* The name of a German river-trout. *Dict.*

HUCK'ABACK, *n.* A kind of linen with raised figures on it.

HUCK'LE, *n.* [infra.] The hip, that is, a bunch.

HUCK'LEBACKED, *a.* [G. *höcker*, a bunch, and *back.*] Having round shoulders.

HUCK'LEBONE, *n.* [G. *höcker*, a bunch.] The hip bone.

HUCK'STER, *n.* [G. *höcke, höcker*; Dan. *hökker.* It seems to be from *hocken*, to take on the back, and to signify primarily a pedlar, one that carries goods on his back.]

1. A retailer of small articles, of provisions, nuts, &c.

2. A mean trickish fellow. *Hub. Tale.*

HUCK'STER, *v. i.* To deal in small articles, or in petty bargains. *Swift.*

HUCK'STERESS, *n.* A female pedlar.

HUD, *n.* The shell or hull of a nut. [*Local.*] *Grose.*

HUD'DLE, *v. i.* [In Ger. *hudeln* signifies to bungle. It may be allied to *hut, hide,* or *cuddle.*]

1. To crowd; to press together promiscuously, without order or regularity. We say of a throng of people, they *huddle* together.

2. To move in a promiscuous throng without order; to press or hurry in disorder. The people *huddle* along, or *huddle* into the house.

HUD'DLE, *v. t.* To put on in haste and disorder; as, she *huddled* on her clothes.

2. To cover in haste or carelessly. *Edwards.*

3. To perform in haste and disorder. *Dryden.*

4. To throw together in confusion; to crowd together without regard to order; as, to *huddle* propositions together. *Locke.*

HUD'DLE, *n.* A crowd; a number of persons or things crowded together without order or regularity; tumult; confusion. *Glanville. Locke.*

HUD'DLED, *pp.* Crowded together without order.

HUD'DLING, *ppr.* Crowding or throwing together in disorder; putting on carelessly.

HUE, *n.* [Sax. *hiewe, hiw*, color, form, image, beauty; *hiwian*, to form, to feign, to simulate. This may be contracted, for in Sw. *hyckla*, Dan. *hykler*, is to play the hypocrite. Perhaps *how* is of this family.] Color; dye.

Flow'rs of all *hue.* *Milton.*

HUE, in the phrase *hue* and *cry*, signifies a shouting or vociferation. In *law*, a hue and cry is the pursuit of a felon or offender, with loud outcries or clamor to give an alarm. *Hue* is a contracted word, Norm. *hue*, Fr. *huer* or *hucher*, Dan. *hui*, or more propably it is from the same root as *hoot.*

HU'ER, *n.* One whose business is to cry out or give an alarm. [*Not in use.*] *Carew.*

HUFF, *n.* [Sp. *chufa*, an empty boast; *chufar*, to hector, to bully; Sw. *yfvas, yfvasig.* This word coincides in elements with *heave, hove*, Dan. *hovner*, to swell; but it may be a different word. See Class Gb. No. 4. 31.]

1. A swell of sudden anger or arrogance.

A Spaniard was wonderfully upon the *huff* about his extraction. *L'Estrange.*

2. A boaster; one swelled with a false opinion of his own value or importance.

Lewd shallow-brained *huffs* make atheism and contempt of religion the badge of wit. *South.*

HUFF, *v. t.* To swell; to enlarge; to puff up. *Grew.*

2. To hector; to bully; to treat with insolence and arrogance; to chide or rebuke with insolence.

HUFF, *v. i.* To swell; to dilate or enlarge; as, the bread *huffs.*

2. To bluster; to swell with anger, pride or arrogance; to storm.

This arrogant conceit made them *huff* at the doctrine of repentance. *South.*

A *huffing*, shining, flattering, cringing coward. *Otway.*

HUFF'ED, *pp.* Swelled; puffed up.

HUFF'ER, *n.* A bully; a swaggerer; a blusterer.

HUFF'INESS, *n.* Petulance; the state of being puffed up. *Hudibras.*

HUFF'ING, *ppr.* Swelling; puffing up; blustering.

HUFF'ISH, *a.* Arrogant; insolent; hectoring.

HUFF'ISHLY, *adv.* With arrogance or blustering.

HUFF'ISHNESS, *n.* Arrogance; petulance; noisy bluster.

HUFF'Y, *a.* Swelled or swelling; petulant.

HUG, *v. t.* [Dan. *heger*, to hug, to cherish, Sw. *hugna;* Dan. *huger*, to sit squat on the tail. The latter seems to be the G. *hocken*, to sit squat, to keep close, D. *hukken*. The sense is to press, and this word may be allied to *hedge*.]

1. To press close in an embrace.

—And *hugged* me in his arms. *Shak.*

2. To embrace closely; to hold fast; to treat with fondness.

We *hug* deformities, if they bear our names. *Glanville.*

3. To gripe in wrestling or scuffling.

To hug the land, in sailing, to sail as near the land as possible.

To hug the wind, to keep the ship close-hauled. *Mar. Dict.*

HUG, *n.* A close embrace. *Gay.*

2. A particular gripe in wrestling or scuffling.

HUGE, *a.* [This word seems to belong to the family of *high*, D. *hoog*, G. *hoch*. If so, the primary sense is to swell or rise. If not, I know not its origin.]

1. Very large or great; enormous; *applied to bulk or size;* as a *huge* mountain; a *huge* ox.

2. It is improperly applied to space and distance, in the sense of great, vast, immense; as a *huge* space; a *huge* difference. This is inelegant, or rather vulgar.

3. In *colloquial language*, very great; enormous; as a *huge* feeder. *Shak.*

HU'GELY, *adv.* Very greatly; enormously; immensely.

Doth it not flow as *hugely* as the sea? *Shak.*

HU'GENESS, *n.* Enormous bulk or largeness; as the *hugeness* of a mountain or of an elephant.

HUG'GER-MUGGER, *n.* [*Hugger* contains the elements of *hug* and *hedge*, and *mugger*, those of *smoke*, W. *mwg*, and of *smuggle*.]

In *hugger-mugger*, denotes in privacy or secrecy, and the word adverbially used, denotes secretly. [*It is a low cant word.*]

HU'GUENOT, *n.* [The origin of this word is uncertain. It is conjectured to be a corruption of G. *eidgenossen*, confederates; *eid*, oath, and *genoss*, consort.]

A name formerly given to a protestant in France.

HU'GUENOTISM, *n.* The religion of the Huguenots in France. *Sherwood.*

HU'GY, *a.* [from *huge*.] Vast in size. [*Not used.*] *Carew.*

HUISH'ER, *n.* [Fr. *huissier*.] An usher. *Obs.* [See *Usher*.] *B. Jonson.*

HUKE, *n.* [W. *hug*.] A cloke; a hyke. *Bacon.*

HULCH, *n.* A bunch. [*Not used.*]

HULCH'IS, *a.* Swelling; gibbous. [*Not used.*]

HULK, *n.* [D. *hulk;* Sax. *hulc*, a cottage or lodge, a vessel; Dan. *holk*, a hoy; Sw. *hålk*. Qu. Gr. ολκας.]

1. The body of a ship, or decked vessel of any kind; but the word is applied only to the body of an old ship or vessel which is laid by as unfit for service. A *sheer-hulk* is an old ship fitted with an apparatus to fix or take out the masts of a ship. *Encyc. Mar. Dict.*

2. Any thing bulky or unwieldy. [*Not used.*] *Shak.*

HULK, *v. t.* To take out the entrails; as, to *hulk* a hare. [*Little used.*] *Ainsworth.*

HULK'Y, *a.* Bulky; unwieldy. [*Not used.*]

HULL, *n.* [Sax. *hul*, the cover of a nut; G. *hülse;* D. *hulse;* W. *hûl*, a cover; *huliaw*, to cover, to deck, G. *hüllen*. See *Hulk*.]

1. The outer covering of any thing, particularly of a nut or of grain. Johnson says, the *hull* of a nut covers the shell.

2. The frame or body of a ship, exclusive of her masts, yards and rigging. *Mar. Dict.*

To lie a hull, in seamen's language, is to lie as a ship without any sail upon her, and her helm lashed a-lee. *Encyc.*

To strike a hull, in a storm, is to take in the sails, and lash the helm on the lee-side of a ship. *Encyc.*

HULL, *v. t.* To strip off or separate the hull or hulls; as, to *hull* grain.

2. To pierce the hull of a ship with a cannon-ball.

HULL, *v. i.* To float or drive on the water without sails. *Milton.*

HULL'Y, *a.* Having husks or pods; siliquous.

HU'LOTHEISM, *n.* [Gr. υλη, matter, and θεος, God.]

The doctrine or belief that matter is God, or that there is no God, except matter and the universe.

HUL'VER, *n.* Holly, a tree. [D. *hulst*] *Tusser.*

HUM, *v. i.* [G. *hummen;* D. *hommelen*.] To utter the sound of bees; to buzz.

2. To make an inarticulate buzzing sound.

The cloudy messenger turns me his back,
And *hums*— *Shak.*

3. To pause in speaking, and make an audible noise like the humming of bees.

He *hummed* and hawed. *Hudibras.*

4. To make a dull, heavy noise like a drone.

Still *humming*, on their drowsy course they took. *Pope.*

5. To applaud. *Obs.*

HUM, *v. t.* To sing in a low voice; as, to *hum* a tune.

2. To cause to hum; to impose on. [*Vulgar.*]

HUM, *n.* The noise of bees or insects.

2. A low confused noise, as of crowds; as the busy *hum* of men. *Milton.*

3. Any low dull noise. *Pope.*

4. A low inarticulate sound, uttered by a speaker in a pause; as *hums* and haws. *Shak. Dryden.*

5. An expression of applause. *Spectator.*

HUM, *exclam.* A sound with a pause, implying doubt and deliberation. *Pope.*

HU'MAN, *a.* [L. *humanus;* Fr. *humain;* Sp. *humano;* It. *umano*. I am not certain which are the radical letters of this word, but am inclined to believe them to be *Mn;* that the first syllable is a prefix; that *homo* in Latin is contracted, the *n* being dropped in the nominative and restored in the oblique cases; hence *homo*, and the Gothic and Sax. *guma*, a man, may be the same word, but this is doubtful. If *Mn* are the elements, this word is from the root of *man*, or rather is formed on the Teutonic word. Heb. מין form, species. The corresponding word in G. is *menschlich* [*man-like*,] D. *menschelyk*. See *Man*.]

1. Belonging to man or mankind; pertaining or relating to the race of man; as a *human* voice; *human* shape; *human* nature; *human* knowledge; *human* life.

2. Having the qualities of a man. *Swift.*

3. Profane; not sacred or divine; as a *human* author. [*Not in use.*] *Brown.*

HU'MANATE, *a.* Endued with humanity. *Obs.* *Cranmer.*

HUMA'NE, *a.* [supra.] Having the feelings and dispositions proper to man; having tenderness, compassion, and a disposition to treat others with kindness; particularly in relieving them when in distress, or in captivity, when they are helpless or defenseless; kind; benevolent.

2. Inclined to treat the lower orders of animals with tenderness.

HUMA'NELY, *adv.* With kindness, tenderness or compassion; as, the prisoners were treated *humanely*.

2. In a humane manner; with kind feelings.

HUMA'NENESS, *n.* Tenderness. *Scott.*

HU'MANIST, *n.* A professor of grammar and rhetoric; a philologist; *a term used in the universities of Scotland.*

2. One versed in the knowledge of human nature. *Shaftesbury.*

HUMAN'ITY, *n.* [L. *humanitas;* Fr. *humanité*.]

1. The peculiar nature of man, by which he is distinguished from other beings. Thus Christ, by his incarnation, was invested with *humanity*.

2. Mankind collectively; the human race.

If he is able to untie those knots, he is able to teach all *humanity*. [*Unusual.*] *Glanville.*

It is a debt we owe to *humanity*. *S. S. Smith.*

3. The kind feelings, dispositions and sympathies of man, by which he is distinguished from the lower orders of animals; kindness; benevolence; especially, a disposition to relieve persons in distress, and to treat with tenderness those who are helpless and defenseless; opposed to *cruelty*.

4. A disposition to treat the lower orders of animals with tenderness, or at least to give them no unnecessary pain.

5. The exercise of kindness; acts of tenderness.

6. Philology; grammatical studies. *Johnson.*

Humanities, in the plural, signifies grammar, rhetoric and poetry; for teaching which there are professors in the universities of Scotland. *Encyc.*

HUMANIZA'TION, *n.* The act of humanizing.

HU'MANIZE, *v. t.* To soften; to render humane; to subdue dispositions to cruelty, and render susceptible of kind feelings.

Was it the business of magic to *humanize* our natures? *Addison. Witherspoon.*

HU'MANIZED, *pp.* Softened; rendered humane.

HU'MANIZING, *ppr.* Softening; subduing cruel dispositions.

HU'MANKIND, *n.* The race of man; mankind; the human species. *Pope.*

HU'MANLY, *adv.* After the manner of men; according to the opinions or knowledge of men. The present prospects, *humanly* speaking, promise a happy issue.

2. Kindly; humanely. *Obs.* *Pope.*

HUMA'TION, *n.* Interment. [*Not used.*]

HUM'BIRD, } *n.* A very small bird
HUM'MING-BIRD, } of the genus Trochilus; so called from the sound of its wings in flight. The rostrum is subulate, filiform, and longer than the head; the tongue is filiform and tubulous. It never lights to take food, but feeds while on the wing.

HUM'BLE, *a.* [Fr. *humble*; L. *humilis*; supposed to be from *humus*, the earth, or its root.]

1. Low; opposed to *high* or *lofty.*

Thy *humble* nest built on the ground. *Cowley.*

2. Low; opposed to *lofty* or *great*; mean; not magnificent; as a *humble* cottage.

A *humble* roof, and an obscure retreat. *Anon.*

3. Lowly; modest; meek; submissive; opposed to *proud, haughty, arrogant* or *assuming*. In *an evangelical sense*, having a low opinion of one's self, and a deep sense of unworthiness in the sight of God.

God resisteth the proud, but giveth grace to the *humble*. James iv.

Without a *humble* imitation of the divine author of our blessed religion, we can never hope to be a happy nation. *Washington.*

HUM'BLE, *v. t.* To abase; to reduce to a low state. This victory *humbled* the pride of Rome. The power of Rome was *humbled*, but not subdued.

2. To crush; to break; to subdue. The battle of Waterloo *humbled* the power of Buonaparte.

3. To mortify.

4. To make humble or lowly in mind; to abase the pride of; to reduce arrogance and self-dependence; to give a low opinion of one's moral worth; to make meek and submissive to the divine will; *the evangelical sense.*

Humble yourselves under the mighty hand of God, that he may exalt you. 1 Pet. v.

Hezekiah *humbled* himself for the pride of his heart. 2 Chron. xxxii.

5. To make to condescend. He *humbles* himself to speak to them.

6. To bring down; to lower; to reduce.

The highest mountains may be *humbled* into valleys. *Hakewill.*

7. To deprive of chastity. Deut. xxi.

To humble one's self, to repent; to afflict one's self for sin; to make contrite.

HUM'BLEBEE, *n.* [G. *hummel*; D. *hommel*; Dan. *hummel*; Sw. *humla*; from *hum.* It is often called *bumblebee*, L. *bombus*, a buzzing.]

A bee of a large species, that draws its food chiefly from clover flowers.

HUM'BLED, *pp.* Made low; abased; rendered meek and submissive; penitent.

HUM'BLEMOUTHED, *a.* Mild; meek; modest. *Shak.*

HUM'BLENESS, *n.* The state of being humble or low; humility; meekness. *Bacon. Sidney.*

HUM'BLEPLANT, *n.* A species of sensitive plant. *Mortimer.*

HUM'BLER, *n.* He or that which humbles; he that reduces pride or mortifies.

HUM'BLES, } *n.* Entrails of a deer.
UM'BLES, } *Johnson.*

HUM'BLY, *adv.* In a humble manner; with modest submissiveness; with humility.

Hope *humbly* then, with trembling pinions soar,
Wait the great teacher, death, and God adore. *Pope.*

2. In a low state or condition; without elevation.

HUM'BOLDITE, *n.* [from *Humbold.*] A rare mineral recently described, occurring in small crystals, nearly colorless and transparent, or of a yellowish tinge and translucent; rarely separate, but usually aggregated; their primary form, an oblique rhombic prism. *Phillips.*

HUM'BUG, *n.* An imposition. [*A low word.*]

HUM'DRUM, *a.* [Qu. *hum*, and *drone*, or W. *trom*, heavy.] Dull; stupid. *Addison. Hudibras.*

HUM'DRUM, *n.* A stupid fellow; a drone.

HUMECT', } *v. t.* [L. *humecto*, from
HUMEC'TATE, } *humeo*, to be moist; Fr. *humecter.*]

To moisten; to wet; to water. [*Little used.*] *Brown. Howell.*

HUMECTA'TION, *n.* The act of moistening, wetting or watering. [*Little used.*] *Bacon.*

HUMEC'TIVE, *a.* Having the power to moisten.

HU'MERAL, *a.* [Fr. from L. *humerus*, the shoulder.]

Belonging to the shoulder; as the *humeral* artery.

HUM'HUM, *n.* A kind of plain, coarse India cloth, made of cotton.

HUMICUBA'TION, *n.* [L. *humus*, the ground, and *cubo*, to lie.]

A lying on the ground. [*Little used.*] *Bramhall.*

HU'MID, *a.* [L. *humidus*, from *humeo*, to be moist; Fr. *humide.*]

1. Moist; damp; containing sensible moisture; as a *humid* air or atmosphere.

2. Somewhat wet or watery; as *humid* earth.

HUMID'ITY, *n.* Moisture; dampness; a moderate degree of wetness which is perceptible to the eye or touch, occasioned by the absorption of a fluid, or its adherence to the surface of a body. When a cloth has imbibed any fluid to such a degree that it can be felt, we call it humid; but when no *humidity* is perceptible, we say it is dry. Quicksilver communicates no *humidity* to our hands or clothes, for it does not adhere to them; but it will adhere to gold, tin and lead, and render them humid and soft to the touch.

2. Moisture in the form of visible vapor, or perceptible in the air.

HU'MIDNESS, *n.* Humidity.

HUMIL'IATE, *v. t.* [L. *humilio*; Fr. *humilier.*]

To humble; to lower in condition; to depress; as *humiliated* slaves. *Eaton.*

HUMIL'IATED, *pp.* Humbled; depressed; degraded.

HUMIL'IATING, *ppr.* Humbling; depressing.

2. *a.* Abating pride; reducing self-confidence; mortifying. *Boswell.*

HUMILIA'TION, *n.* The act of humbling; the state of being humbled.

2. Descent from an elevated state or rank to one that is low or humble.

The former was a *humiliation* of deity; the latter, a *humiliation* of manhood. *Hooker.*

3. The act of abasing pride; or the state of being reduced to lowliness of mind, meekness, penitence and submission.

The doctrine he preached was *humiliation* and repentance. *Swift.*

4. Abasement of pride; mortification.

HUMIL'ITY, *n.* [L. *humilitas*; Fr. *humilité.* See *Humble.*]

1. In *ethics*, freedom from pride and arrogance; humbleness of mind; a modest estimate of one's own worth. In *theology*, humility consists in lowliness of mind; a deep sense of one's own unworthiness in the sight of God, self-abasement, penitence for sin, and submission to the divine will.

Before honor is *humility*. Prov. xv.

Serving the Lord with all *humility* of mind. Acts xx.

2. Act of submission.

With these *humilities* they satisfied the young king. *Davies.*

HU'MITE, *n.* A mineral of a reddish brown color, and a shining luster; crystalized in octahedrons, much modified by truncation and bevelment. It is named from Sir Abm. Hume. *Cleaveland.*

HUM'MER, *n.* [from *hum.*] One that hums; an applauder. *Ainsworth.*

HUM'MING, *ppr.* Making a low buzzing or murmuring sound.

HUM'MING, *n.* The sound of bees; a low murmuring sound.

HU'MOR, *n.* [L. from *humeo*, to be moist; Sans. *ama*, moist. The pronunciation, *yumor*, is odiously vulgar.]

1. Moisture; but the word is chiefly used to express the moisture or fluids of animal bodies, as the *humors* of the eye. But more generally the word is used to express a fluid in its morbid or vitiated state. Hence, in popular speech, we often hear it said, the blood is full of *humors.* But the expression is not technical nor correct.

Aqueous humor of the eye, a transparent fluid, occupying the space between the crystaline lens and the cornea, both before and behind the pupil.

Crystaline humor or *lens*, a small transparent solid body, of a softish consistence, occupying a middle position in the eye, between the aqueous and vitreous humors, and directly behind the pupil. It is of a lenticular form, or with double convex surfaces, and is the principal instrument in refracting the rays of light, so as to form an image on the retina.

Vitreous humor of the eye, a fluid contained in the minute cells of a transparent membrane, occupying the greater part of the cavity of the eye, and all the space between the crystaline and the retina. *Wistar.*

2. A disease of the skin; cutaneous eruptions. *Fielding.*

3. Turn of mind; temper; disposition, or rather a peculiarity of disposition often temporary; so called because the temper of mind has been supposed to depend on the fluids of the body. Hence we say, good *humor*; melancholy *humor*; peevish *humor.* Such humors, when temporary, we call freaks, whims, caprice. Thus a person characterized by good nature may have a fit of *ill humor*; and an ill natured person may have a fit of *good humor.* So

we say, it was the *humor* of the man at the time; it was the *humor* of the multitude.

4. That quality of the imagination which gives to ideas a wild or fantastic turn, and tends to excite laughter or mirth by ludicrous images or representations. *Humor* is less poignant and brilliant than *wit;* hence it is always agreeable. Wit, directed against folly, often offends by its severity; humor makes a man ashamed of his follies, without exciting his resentment. Humor may be employed solely to raise mirth and render conversation pleasant, or it may contain a delicate kind of satire.

5. Petulance; peevishness; better expressed by *ill humor.*

Is my friend all perfection? has he not *humors* to be endured? *South.*

6. A trick; a practice or habit.

I like not the *humor* of lying. *Shak.*

HU'MOR, *v. t.* To gratify by yielding to particular inclination, humor, wish or desire; to indulge by compliance. We sometimes *humor* children to their injury or ruin. The sick, the infirm, and the aged often require to be *humored.*

2. To suit; to indulge; to favor by imposing no restraint, and rather contributing to promote by occasional aids. We say, an actor *humors* his part, or the piece.

It is my part to invent, and that of the musicians to *humor* that invention. *Dryden.*

HU'MORAL, *a.* Pertaining to or proceeding from the humors; as a *humoral* fever. *Harvey.*

Humoral pathology, that pathology, or doctrine of the nature of diseases, which attributes all morbid phenomena to the disordered condition of the fluids or humors. *Cyc.*

HU'MORED, *pp.* Indulged; favored.

HU'MORING, *ppr.* Indulging a particular wish or propensity; favoring; contributing to aid by falling into a design or course.

HU'MORIST, *n.* One who conducts himself by his own inclination, or bent of mind; one who gratifies his own humor.

The *humorist* is one that is greatly pleased or greatly displeased with little things; his actions seldom directed by the reason and nature of things. *Watts.*

2. One that indulges humor in speaking or writing; one who has a playful fancy or genius. [See *Humor*, No. 4.]

3. One who has odd conceits; also, a wag; a droll. *Hall. Bodley.*

HU'MOROUS, *a.* Containing humor; full of wild or fanciful images; adapted to excite laughter; jocular; as a *humorous* essay; a *humorous* story.

2. Having the power to speak or write in the style of humor; fanciful; playful; exciting laughter; as a *humorous* man or author.

3. Subject to be governed by humor or caprice; irregular; capricious; whimsical.

I am known to be a *humorous* patrician. *Shak.*

Rough as a storm, and *humorous* as the wind. *Dryden.*

4. Moist; humid. [*Not in use.*] *Drayton.*

HU'MOROUSLY, *adv.* With a wild or grotesque combination of ideas; in a manner to excite laughter or mirth; pleasantly; jocosely. Addison describes *humorously* the manual exercise of ladies' fans.

2. Capriciously; whimsically; in conformity with one's humor.

We resolve by halves, rashly and *humorously.* *Calamy.*

HU'MOROUSNESS, *n.* The state or quality of being humorous; oddness of conceit; jocularity.

2. Fickleness; capriciousness.

3. Peevishness; petulance. *Goodman.*

HU'MORSŎME, *a.* Peevish; petulant; influenced by the humor of the moment.

The commons do not abet *humorsome*, factious arms. *Burke.*

2. Odd; humorous; adapted to excite laughter. *Swift.*

HU'MORSŎMELY, *adv.* Peevishly; petulantly. *Johnson.*

2. Oddly; humorously.

HUMP, *n.* [L. *umbo.*] The protuberance formed by a crooked back; as a camel with one *hump*, or two *humps.*

HUMP'BACK, *n.* A crooked back; high shoulders. *Tatler.*

HUMP'BACKED, *a.* Having a crooked back.

HUNCH, *n.* [See the Verb.] A hump; a protuberance; as the *hunch* of a camel.

2. A lump; a thick piece; as a *hunch* of bread; *a word in common vulgar use in New England.*

3. A push or jerk with the fist or elbow.

HUNCH, *v. t.* To push with the elbow; to push or thrust with a sudden jerk.

2. To push out in a protuberance; to crook the back. *Dryden.*

HUNCH'BACKED, *a.* Having a crooked back. *L'Estrange. Dryden.*

HUND'RED, *a.* [Sax. *hund* or *hundred;* Goth. *hund;* D. *honderd;* G. *hundert;* Sw. *hundra;* Dan. *hundre, hundred;* L. *centum;* W. *cant*, a circle, the hoop of a wheel, the rim of any thing, a complete circle or series, a hundred; Corn. *canz;* Arm. *cant;* Ir. *ceantr.* Lye, in his Saxon and Gothic Dictionary, suggests that this word *hund* is a mere termination of the Gothic word for ten; *taihun-taihund*, ten times ten. But this cannot be true, for the word is found in the Celtic as well as Gothic dialects, and in the Arabic خَنْدَ, Class Gn. No. 63; at least this is probably the same word. The Welsh language exhibits the true sense of the word, which is a circle, a complete series. Hence, W. *cantrev*, a division of a county, or circuit, a *canton*, a hundred. See *Canton.* The word signifies a circuit, and the sense of *hundred* is secondary. The *centuria* of the Romans, and the *hundred*, a division of a county in England, might have been merely a *division*, and not an exact hundred in number.]

Denoting the product of ten multiplied by ten, or the number of ten times ten; as a *hundred* men.

HUND'RED, *n.* A collection, body or sum, consisting of ten times ten individuals or units; the number 100.

2. A division or part of a county in England, supposed to have originally contained a hundred families, or a hundred warriors, or a hundred manors. [But as the word denotes primarily a *circuit* or *division*, it is not certain that Alfred's divisions had any reference to that number.]

HUND'RED-COURT, *n.* In *England*, a court held for all the inhabitants of a hundred. *Blackstone.*

HUND'REDER, *n.* In *England*, a man who may be of a jury in any controversy respecting land within the hundred to which he belongs.

2. One having the jurisdiction of a hundred.

HUND'REDTH, *a.* The ordinal of a hundred.

HUNG, *pret.* and *pp.* of *hang.*

HUNGARY-WATER, *n.* A distilled water prepared from the tops of flowers of rosemary; so called from a queen of Hungary, for whose use it was first made. *Encyc.*

HUN'GER, *n.* [Sax. G. Dan. Sw. *hunger*, D. *honger*, Goth. *huhrus*, hunger; Sax. *hungrian, hingrian*, Goth. *huggryan*, to hunger. It appears from the Gothic that *n* is not radical; the root then is *Hg.*]

1. An uneasy sensation occasioned by the want of food; a craving of food by the stomach; craving appetite. Hunger is not merely *want of food*, for persons when sick, may abstain long from eating without hunger, or an appetite for food. Hunger therefore is the pain or uneasiness of the stomach of a healthy person, when too long destitute of food.

2. Any strong or eager desire.

For *hunger* of my gold I die. *Dryden.*

HUN'GER, *v. i.* To feel the pain or uneasiness which is occasioned by long abstinence from food; to crave food.

2. To desire with great eagerness; to long for.

Blessed are they that *hunger* and thirst after righteousness. Matt. v.

HUN'GER, *v. t.* To famish. [*Not in use.*]

HUN'GER-BIT, } *a.* Pained, pinched
HUN'GER-BITTEN, } or weakened by hunger. *Milton.*

HUN'GERING, *ppr.* Feeling the uneasiness of want of food; desiring eagerly; longing for; craving.

HUN'GERLY, *a.* Hungry; wanting food or nourishment. *Shak.*

HUN'GERLY, *adv.* With keen appetite. [*Little used.*] *Shak.*

HUN'GER-ST'ARVED, *a.* Starved with hunger; pinched by want of food. *Shak. Dryden.*

HUN'GRED, *a.* Hungry; pinched by want of food. *Obs.* *Bacon.*

HUN'GRILY, *adv.* [from *hungry.*] With keen appetite; voraciously.

When on harsh acorns *hungrily* they fed. *Dryden.*

HUN'GRY, *a.* Having a keen appetite; feeling pain or uneasiness from want of food. Eat only when you are *hungry.*

2. Having an eager desire.

3. Lean; emaciated, as if reduced by hunger.

Cassius has a lean and *hungry* look. *Shak.*

4. Not rich or fertile; poor; barren; requiring substances to enrich itself; as a *hungry* soil; a *hungry* gravel. *Mortimer.*

HUNKS, *n.* A covetous sordid man; a miser; a niggard. *Dryden.*

HUNS, *n.* [L. *Hunni.*] The Scythians who conquered Pannonia, and gave it its present name, Hungary.

HUNT, *v. t.* [Sax. *huntian.* This word does not appear in the cognate languages. See Class Gn. No. 67.]

1. To chase wild animals, particularly quadrupeds, for the purpose of catching them for food, or for the diversion of sportsmen; to pursue with hounds for taking, as game; as, to *hunt* a stag or a hare.
2. To go in search of, for the purpose of shooting; as, to *hunt* wolves, bears, squirrels or partridges. This is the common use of the word in America. It includes fowling by shooting.
3. To pursue; to follow closely.

   Evil shall *hunt* the violent man to overthrow him. Ps. cxl.
4. To use, direct or manage hounds in the chase.

   He *hunts* a pack of dogs. *Addison.*

To hunt out or *after*, to seek; to search for. *Locke.*

To hunt from, to pursue and drive out or away.

To hunt down, to depress; to bear down by persecution or violence.

HUNT, *v. i.* To follow the chase. Gen. xxvii.

2. To seek wild animals for game, or for killing them by shooting when noxious; with *for;* as, to *hunt for* bears or wolves; to *hunt for* quails, or *for* ducks.
3. To seek by close pursuit; to search; with *for.*

   The adulteress will *hunt for* the precious life. Prov. vi.

HUNT, *n.* A chase of wild animals for catching them.

2. A huntsman. [*Not in use.*] *Chaucer.*
3. A pack of hounds. *Dryden.*
4. Pursuit; chase. *Shak.*
5. A seeking of wild animals of any kind for game; as a *hunt* for squirrels.

HUNT'ED, *pp.* Chased; pursued; sought.

HUNT'ER, *n.* One who pursues wild animals with a view to take them, either for sport or for food.

2. A dog that scents game, or is employed in the chase.
3. A horse used in the chase.

HUNT'ING, *ppr.* Chasing for seizure; pursuing; seeking; searching.

HUNT'ING, *n.* The act or practice of pursuing wild animals, for catching or killing them. Hunting was originally practiced by men for the purpose of procuring food, as it still is by uncivilized nations. But among civilized men, it is practiced mostly for exercise or diversion, or for the destruction of noxious animals, as in America.

2. A pursuit; a seeking.

HUNT'ING-HORN, *n.* A bugle; a horn used to cheer the hounds in pursuit of game.

HUNT'ING-HORSE, } *n.* A horse used in
HUNT'ING-NAG, } hunting. *Butler.*

HUNT'ING-SEAT, *n.* A temporary residence for the purpose of hunting. *Gray.*

HUNT'RESS, *n.* A female that hunts, or follows the chase. Diana is called the *huntress.*

HUNTS'MAN, *n.* One who hunts, or who practices hunting. *Waller.*

2. The servant whose office it is to manage the chase. *L'Estrange.*

HUNTS'MANSHIP, *n.* The art or practice of hunting, or the qualifications of a hunter. *Donne.*

HUR'DEN, *n.* [made of hurds, hards, or coarse flax.] A coarse kind of linen. [*Local or obs.*] *Shenstone.*

HUR'DLE, *n.* [Sax. *hyrdel;* G. *hürde*, a hurdle, a fold or pen; D. *horde*, a hurdle, a horde. The elements of this word are the same as of the L. *crates, Hrd, Crd.* It coincides also with *herd*, denoting closeness, pressure, holding.]

1. A texture of twigs, osiers or sticks; a crate of various forms, according to its destination. The English give this name to a sled or crate on which criminals are drawn to the place of execution. In this sense, it is not used in America.
2. In *fortification*, a collection of twigs or sticks interwoven closely and sustained by long stakes. It is made in the figure of a long square, five or six feet by three and a half. Hurdles serve to render works firm, or to cover traverses and lodgments for the defense of workmen against fire-works or stones. *Encyc.*
3. In *husbandry*, a frame of split timber or sticks wattled together, serving for gates, inclosures, &c. *Encyc.*

HURDS, *n.* The coarse part of flax or hemp. [See *Hards.*]

HUR'DY-GURDY, *n.* An instrument of music, said to be used in the streets of London. *Todd.*

HURL, *v. t.* [Arm. *harlua.* This may be a different spelling of *whirl.*]

1. To throw with violence; to drive with great force; as, to *hurl* a stone.

   And *hurl* them headlong to their fleet and main. *Pope.*
2. To utter with vehemence; as, to *hurl* out vows. [*Not in use.*] *Spenser.*
3. To play at a kind of game. *Carew.*

HURL, *n.* The act of throwing with violence.

2. Tumult; riot; commotion. *Knolles.*

HURL'BAT, *n.* A whirl-bat; an old kind of weapon. *Ainsworth.*

HURL'BONE, *n.* In *a horse*, a bone near the middle of the buttock. *Encyc.*

HURL'ED, *pp.* Thrown with violence.

HURL'ER, *n.* One who hurls, or who plays at hurling. *Carew.*

HURL'ING, *ppr.* Throwing with force; playing at hurling.

HURL'WIND, *n.* A whirlwind, which see. *Sandys.*

HURL'Y, } *n.* [Dan. *hurl om burl*,
HURL'Y-BURLY, } topsy turvy; Fr. *hurlu-burlu*, inconsiderately.] Tumult; bustle; confusion. *Shak.*

HURRAW, } *exclam.* Hoora; huzza. [See
HURRAH, } *Hoora.*]

HUR'RICANE, *n.* [Sp. *huracan*, for *furacan*, from the L. *furio, furo*, to rage; Port. *furaçam;* It. *oragano;* Fr. *ouragan;* D. *orkaan;* G. Dan. Sw. *orcan.* I know not the origin, nor the signification of the last syllable.]

1. A most violent storm of wind, occurring often in the West Indies, and sometimes in higher northern latitudes, and on the coast of the United States, as far north as New England. A hurricane is distinguished from every other kind of tempest by the extreme violence of the wind, and by its sudden changes; the wind often veering suddenly several points, sometimes a quarter of the circle and even more.
2. Any violent tempest. *Dryden.*

HUR'RIED, *pp.* [from *hurry.*] Hastened; urged or impelled to rapid motion or vigorous action.

HUR'RIER, *n.* One who hurries, urges or impels.

HUR'RY, *v. t.* [This word is evidently from the root of L. *curro;* Fr. *courir;* Sw. *kōra;* W. *gyru*, to drive, impel, thrust, run, ride, press forward. See Ar. جري jarai, and كار kaura, to go round, to hasten. Class Gr. No. 7. 32. 36.]

1. To hasten; to impel to greater speed; to drive or press forward with more rapidity; to urge to act or proceed with more celerity; as, to *hurry* the workmen or the work. Our business *hurries* us. The weather is hot and the load heavy; we cannot safely *hurry* the horses.
2. To drive or impel with violence.

   Impetuous lust *hurries* him on to satisfy the cravings of it. *South.*
3. To urge or drive with precipitation and confusion; for confusion is often caused by hurry.

   And wild amazement *hurries* up and down
   The little number of your doubtful friends. *Shak.*

To hurry away, to drive or carry away in haste.

HUR'RY, *v. i.* To move or act with haste; to proceed with celerity or precipitation. The business is urgent; let us *hurry.*

HUR'RY, *n.* A driving or pressing forward in motion or business.

2. Pressure; urgency to haste. We cannot wait long; we are in a *hurry.*
3. Precipitation that occasions disorder or confusion.

   It is necessary sometimes to be in haste, but never in a *hurry.* *Anon.*
4. Tumult; bustle; commotion.

   Ambition raises a tumult in the soul, and puts it into a violent *hurry* of thought. *Addison.*

HUR'RYING, *ppr.* Driving or urging to greater speed; precipitating.

HUR'RY-SKURRY, *adv.* Confusedly; in a bustle. [*Not in use.*] *Gray.*

HURST, *n.* [Sax. *hurst* or *hyrst.*] A wood or grove; a word found in many names, as in *Hazlehurst.*

HURT, *v. t.* pret. and pp. *hurt.* [Sax. *hyrt*, wounded; It. *urtare*, Fr. *heurter*, to strike or dash against; W. *hyrziaw*, to push, thrust or drive, to assault, to butt; Arm. *heurda.*]

1. To bruise; to give pain by a contusion, pressure, or any violence to the body. We *hurt* the body by a severe blow, or by tight clothes, and the feet by fetters. Ps. cv.
2. To wound; to injure or impair the sound state of the body, as by incision or fracture.
3. To harm; to damage; to injure by occasioning loss. We *hurt* a man by destroying his property.
4. To injure by diminution; to impair. A man *hurts* his estate by extravagance.

5. To injure by reducing in quality; to impair the strength, purity or beauty of.

Hurt not the wine and the oil—Rev. vi.

6. To harm; to injure; to damage, in general.

7. To wound; to injure; to give pain to; as, to *hurt* the feelings.

HURT, *n.* A wound; a bruise; any thing that gives pain to the body.

The pains of sickness and *hurts*. *Locke.*

2. Harm; mischief; injury.

I have slain a man to my wounding, and a young man to my *hurt*. Gen. iv.

3. Injury; loss.

Why should damage grow to the *hurt* of the kings? Ezra iv.

HURT'ER, *n.* One who hurts or does harm.

HURT'ERS, *n.* Pieces of wood at the lower end of a platform, to prevent the wheels of gun-carriages from injuring the parapet.

HURT'FUL, *a.* Injurious; mischievous; occasioning loss or destruction; tending to impair or destroy. Negligence is *hurtful* to property; intemperance is *hurtful* to health.

HURT'FULLY, *adv.* Injuriously; mischievously.

HURT'FULNESS, *n.* Injuriousness; tendency to occasion loss or destruction; mischievousness.

HURT'LE, *v. i.* [from *hurt.*] To clash or run against; to jostle; to skirmish; to meet in shock and encounter; to wheel suddenly. [*Not now used.*] *Spenser. Shak.*

HURT'LE, *v. t.* To move with violence or impetuosity. *Obs. Spenser.*

2. To push forcibly; to whirl.

HURT'LEBERRY, *n.* A whortleberry, which see.

HURT'LESS, *a.* Harmless; innocent; doing no injury; innoxious; as *hurtless* blows. *Dryden.*

2. Receiving no injury.

HURT'LESSLY, *adv.* Without harm. [*Little used.*] *Sidney.*

HURT'LESSNESS, *n.* Freedom from any harmful quality. [*Little used.*] *Johnson.*

HUS'BAND, *n.* *s* as *z.* [Sax. *husbonda; hus,* house, and *buend,* a farmer or cultivator, or an inhabitant, from *byan,* to inhabit or till, contracted from *bugian;* Dan. *husbonde;* Sw. *husbonde;* Sw. *byggia,* Dan. *bygger,* to build; D. *bouwen,* G. *bauen,* to build, to till, to plow or cultivate; G. *bauer,* a builder, a countryman, a clown, a rustic, a *boor;* D. *buur,* the last component part of *neighbor. Band, bond,* in this word, is the participle of *buan, byan,* that is, *buend,* occupying, tilling, and *husband* is the farmer or inhabitant of the house, in Scottish, a farmer; thence the sense of husbandry. It had no relation primarily to marriage; but among the common people, a woman calls her consort, my man, and the man calls his wife, my woman, as in Hebrew, and in this instance, the farmer or occupier of the house, or the builder, was called my farmer; or by some other means, *husband* came to denote the consort of the female head of the family.]

1. A man contracted or joined to a woman by marriage. A man to whom a woman is betrothed, as well as one actually united by marriage, is called a *husband.* Lev. xix. Deut. xxii.

2. In *seamen's language,* the owner of a ship who manages its concerns in person. *Mar. Dict.*

3. The male of animals of a lower order. *Dryden.*

4. An economist; a good manager; a man who knows and practices the methods of frugality and profit. In this sense, the word is modified by an epithet; as a good *husband;* a bad *husband.* [But in America, this application of the word is little or not at all used.] *Davies. Collier.*

5. A farmer; a cultivator; a tiller of the ground. [In this sense, it is not used in America. We always use *husbandman.*] *Bacon. Dryden.*

HUS'BAND, *v. t.* To direct and manage with frugality in expending any thing; to use or employ in the manner best suited to produce the greatest effect; to use with economy. We say, a man *husbands* his estate, his means or his time.

He is conscious how ill he has *husbanded* the great deposit of his Creator. *Rambler.*

2. To till; to cultivate with good management. *Bacon.*

3. To supply with a husband. [*Little used.*] *Shak.*

HUS'BANDABLE, *a.* Manageable with economy. [*Ill.*] *Sherwood.*

HUS'BANDED, *pp.* Used or managed with economy; well managed.

HUS'BANDING, *ppr.* Using or managing with frugality.

HUS'BANDLESS, *a.* Destitute of a husband. *Shak.*

HUS'BANDLY, *a.* Frugal; thrifty. [*Little used.*] *Tusser.*

HUS'BANDMAN, *n.* A farmer; a cultivator or tiller of the ground; one who labors in tillage. In America, where men generally own the land on which they labor, the proprietor of a farm is also a laborer or husbandman; but the word includes the lessee and the owner.

2. The master of a family. [*Not in use in America.*] *Chaucer.*

HUS'BANDRY, *n.* The business of a farmer, comprehending agriculture or tillage of the ground, the raising, managing and fattening of cattle and other domestic animals, the management of the dairy and whatever the land produces.

2. Frugality; domestic economy; good management; thrift. But in this sense we generally prefix *good;* as *good husbandry. Swift.*

3. Care of domestic affairs. *Shak.*

HUSH, *a.* [G. *husch;* Dan. *hys, hyst.* In W. *hêz* is peace; *hêzu,* to make peace; *cws* is rest, sleep; and *hust* is a low, buzzing sound; Heb. חשה to be silent. Class Gs. No. 46.]

Silent; still; quiet; as, they are *hush* as death. This adjective never precedes the noun which it qualifies, except in the compound, *hushmoney.*

HUSH, *v. t.* To still; to silence; to calm; to make quiet; to repress noise; as, to *hush* the noisy crowd; the winds were *hushed.*

My tongue shall *hush* again this storm of war. *Shak.*

2. To appease; to allay; to calm, as commotion or agitation.

Wilt thou then
Hush my cares? *Otway.*

HUSH, *v. i.* To be still; to be silent. *Spenser.*

HUSH, imperative of the verb, used as an exclamation, be still; be silent or quiet; make no noise.

To hush up, to suppress; to keep concealed.

This matter is *hushed up.* *Pope.*

HUSH'MŎNEY, *n.* A bribe to secure silence; money paid to hinder information, or disclosure of facts. *Swift.*

HUSK, *n.* [Qu. W. *gwisg,* Corn. *quesk,* a cover; or It. *guscio,* bark or shell; Sp. Port. *casca,* husks of grapes, bark. It signifies probably a cover or a peel.]

The external covering of certain fruits or seeds of plants. It is the calyx of the flower or glume of corn and grasses, formed of valves embracing the seed. The husks of the small grains, when separated, are called chaff; but in America we apply the word chiefly to the covering of the ears or seeds of maiz, which is never denominated chaff. It is sometimes used in England for the rind, skin or hull of seeds.

HUSK, *v. t.* To strip off the external integument or covering of the fruits or seeds of plants; as, to *husk* maiz.

HUSK'ED, *pp.* Stripped of its husks.

2. *a.* Covered with a husk.

HUSK'INESS, *n.* The state of being dry and rough, like a husk.

HUSK'ING, *ppr.* Stripping off husks.

HUSK'ING, *n.* The act of stripping off husks. In New England, the practice of farmers is to invite their neighbors to assist them in stripping their maiz, in autumnal evenings, and this is called a *husking.*

HUSK'Y, *a.* Abounding with husks; consisting of husks. *Dryden.*

2. Resembling husks; dry; rough.

3. Rough, as sound; harsh; whizzing.

HU'SO, *n.* A fish of the genus Accipenser, whose mouth is in the under part of the head; the body is naked, or without prickles or protuberances. It grows to the length of twenty four feet, and its skin is so tough that it is used for ropes in drawing wheel-carriages. It inhabits the Danube and the rivers of Russia, and of its sounds is made isinglass. *Encyc.*

HUS'SAR, *n.* *s* as *z.* [Tartar, *uswar,* cavalry; Sans. *uswu,* a horse. *Thomson.*]

A mounted soldier or horseman, in German cavalry. The hussars are the national cavalry of Hungary and Croatia. Their regimentals are a fur cap adorned with a fether, a doublet, a pair of breeches to which the stockings are fastened, and a pair of red or yellow boots. Their arms are a saber, a carbine and pistols. Hussars now form a part of the French and English cavalry. *Encyc.*

HUSS'ITE, *n.* A follower of John Huss, the Bohemian reformer.

HUSS'Y, *n.* [contracted from *huswife,* housewife.]

1. A bad or worthless woman. It is used also ludicrously in slight disapprobation or contempt. Go, *hussy,* go.

2. An economist; a thrifty woman. *Tusser.*

HUS'TINGS, *n.* [Sax. *hustinge;* supposed to be composed of *hus,* house, and *thing,* cause, suit; the house of trials.]

1. A court held in Guildhall, in London, before the lord mayor and aldermen of the city; the supreme court or council of the city. In this court are elected the aldermen and the four members of parliament.
2. The place where an election of a member of parliament is held. *Burke.*

HUS'TLE, *v. i.* *hus'l.* [D. *hutselen*, to shake; Sw. *hutla*, to shuffle.]
To shake together in confusion; to push or crowd.

HUS'WIFE, *n.* A worthless woman; a bad manager. [See *Hussy.*] *Shak.*
2. A female economist; a thrifty woman. *Shak.*

HUS'WIFE, *v. t.* To manage with economy and frugality. *Dryden.*

HUS'WIFERY, *n.* The business of managing the concerns of a family by a female; female management, good or bad. *Tusser.*

HUT, *n.* [G. *hütte*; D. *hut*; Dan. *hytte*; Fr. *hutte*; perhaps a dialectical orthography of Sax. *hus*, house, and *cot*; W. *cwt.*]
A small house, hovel or cabin; a mean lodge or dwelling; a cottage. It is particularly applied to log-houses erected for troops in winter.

HUT, *v. t.* To place in huts, as troops encamped in winter quarters. *Marshall. Smollett.*

HUT, *v. i.* To take lodgings in huts.

The troops *hutted* for the winter. *T. Pickering.*

HUT'TED, *pp.* Lodged in huts. *Mitford.*

HUT'TING, *ppr.* Placing in huts; taking lodgings in huts.

HUTCH, *n.* [Fr. *huche*; Sp. *hucha*; Sax. *hwæcca.*]
1. A chest or box; a corn chest or bin; a case for rabbits. *Mortimer.*
2. A rat trap.

HUX, *v. t.* To fish for pike with hooks and lines fastened to floating bladders. *Encyc.*

HUZZ, *v. i.* To buzz. [*Not in use.*] *Barret.*

HUZZ'A, *n.* A shout of joy; *a foreign word used in writing only, and most preposterously, as it is never used in practice. The word used is our native word* hoora, or hooraw. [See *Hoora.*]

HUZZ'A, *v. i.* To utter a loud shout of joy, or an acclamation in joy or praise.

HUZZ'A, *v. t.* To receive or attend with shouts of joy. *Addison.*

HY'ACINTH, *n.* [L. *hyacinthus*; Gr. υακινθος.]
1. In *botany*, a genus of plants, of several species, and a great number of varieties. The oriental hyacinth has a large, purplish, bulbous root, from which spring several narrow erect leaves; the flower stalk is upright and succulent, and adorned with many bell-shaped flowers, united in a large pyramidical spike, of different colors in the varieties. *Encyc.*
2. In *mineralogy*, a mineral, a variety of zircon, whose crystals, when distinct, have the form of a four-sided prism, terminated by four rhombic planes, which stand on the lateral edges. Its structure is foliated; its luster, strong; its fracture, conchoidal. Its prevailing color is a hyacinth red, in which the red is more or less tinged with yellow or brown. It is sometimes transparent, and sometimes only translucent. *Cleaveland.*

Hyacinth is a subspecies of pyramidical zircon. *Ure.*

HYACINTH'INE, *a.* Made of hyacinth; consisting of hyacinth; resembling hyacinth. *Milton.*

HY'ADS, *n.* [Gr. υαδες, from υω, to rain; υετος, rain.]
In *astronomy*, a cluster of seven stars in the Bull's head, supposed by the ancients to bring rain. *Encyc.*

HY'ALINE, *a.* [Gr. υαλινος, from υαλος, glass.]
Glassy; resembling glass; consisting of glass. *Milton.*

HY'ALITE, *n.* [Gr. υαλος.] Muller's glass. It consists chiefly of silex, and is white, sometimes with a shade of yellow, blue or green. *Cleaveland.*

HYBERNACLE, **HYBERNATE**, **HYBERNATION.** See *Hibernacle*, *Hibernate*, *Hibernation.*

HYB'RID, *n.* [Gr. υβρις, injury, force, rape; L. *hybrida.*]
A mongrel or mule; an animal or plant, produced from the mixture of two species. *Lee. Martyn.*

HY'BRID, **HYB'RIDOUS**, *a.* Mongrel; produced from the mixture of two species.

HY'DAGE, *n.* In *law*, a tax on lands, at a certain rate by the hyde. *Blackstone.*

HY'DATID, **HY'DATIS**, *n.* [Gr. υδατις, from υδωρ, water.] A little transparent vesicle or bladder filled with water, on any part of the body, as in dropsy. *Quincy. Darwin.*

Hydatids are certain spherical bodies, found occasionally in man, as well as in other animals, lodged in or adhering to the different viscera. Some of them, at least, are considered as possessing an independent vitality, and as constituting a distinct animal, allied to the *tænia* or tape-worm. They consist of a head, neck, and vesicular body filled with a transparent fluid. *Cyc. Parr.*

HY'DRA, *n.* [L. *hydra*; Gr. υδρα, from υδωρ, water.]
1. A water serpent. In *fabulous history*, a serpent or monster in the lake or marsh of Lerna, in Peloponnesus, represented as having many heads, one of which, being cut off, was immediately succeeded by another, unless the wound was cauterized. Hercules killed this monster by applying firebrands to the wounds, as he cut off the heads. Hence we give the name to a multitude of evils, or to a cause of multifarious evils.
2. A technical name of a genus of Zoophytes, called polypus, or polypuses.
3. A southern constellation, containing 60 stars. *Cyc.*

HYDRAC'ID, *a.* [Gr. υδωρ, water, and *acid.*] An acid formed by the union of hydrogen with a substance without oxygen. *Coxe.*

HY'DRAGOGUE, *n.* *hy'dragog.* [Gr. υδραγωγος; υδωρ, water, and αγωγη, a leading or drawing, from αγω, to lead or drive.]
A medicine that occasions a discharge of watery humors; a name that implies a supposition that every purgative has the quality of evacuating a particular humor. But in general, the stronger cathartics are hydragogues. *Quincy. Encyc.*

HYDRAN'GEA, *n.* [Gr. υδωρ, water, and αγγειον, a vessel.]
A plant which grows in the water, and bears a beautiful flower. Its capsule has been compared to a cup. *De Theis, Gloss. Botan.*

HY'DRANT, *n.* [Gr. υδραινω, to irrigate, from υδωρ, water.]
A pipe or machine with suitable valves and a spout, by which water is raised and discharged from the main conduit of an aqueduct.

HYDR'ARGILLITE, *n.* [Gr. υδωρ, water, and αργιλλος, clay.] A mineral, called also Wavellite.

HY'DRATE, *n.* [Gr. υδωρ, water.] In *chimistry*, a compound, in definite proportions, of a metallic oxyd with water. *Ure.*

A *hydrate* is a substance which has formed so intimate a union with water as to solidify it, and render it a component part. Slaked lime is a *hydrate* of lime. *Parke.*

HYDRAUL'IC, **HYDRAUL'ICAL**, *a.* [Fr. *hydraulique*; L. *hydraulicus*; Gr. υδραυλις, an instrument of music played by water; υδωρ, water, and αυλος, a pipe.]
1. Relating to the conveyance of water through pipes.
2. Transmitting water through pipes; as a *hydraulic* engine.

Hydraulic lime, a species of lime that hardens in water; used for cementing under water. *Journ. of Science.*

HYDRAUL'ICS, *n.* The science of the motion and force of fluids, and of the construction of all kinds of instruments and machines by which the force of fluids is applied to practical purposes; a branch of hydrostatics.

Hydraulics is that branch of the science of hydrodynamics which treats of fluids considered as in motion. *Ed. Encyc.*

HYDREN'TEROCELE, *n.* [Gr. υδωρ, water, εντερον, intestine, and κηλη, a tumor.]
A dropsy of the scrotum with rupture. *Coxe.*

HYDRIOD'IC, *a.* [*hydrogen* and *iodic.*] Denoting a peculiar acid or gaseous substance, produced by the combination of hydrogen and iodine.

HYD'RIODATE, *n.* A salt formed by the hydriodic acid, with a base. *De Claubry.*

HYDROC'ARBONATE, *n.* [Gr. υδωρ, water, or rather *hydrogen*, and L. *carbo*, a coal.]
Carbureted hydrogen gas, or heavy inflammable air. *Aikin.*

HYDROC'ARBURET, *n.* Carbureted hydrogen. *Henry.*

HY'DROCELE, *n.* [Gr. υδροκηλη; υδωρ, water, and κηλη, a tumor.]
Any hernia proceeding from water; a watery tumor, particularly one in the scrotum. *Encyc.*
A dropsy of the scrotum. *Coxe. Parr.*

HYDROCEPH'ALUS, *n.* [Gr. υδωρ, water, and κεφαλη, the head.]
Dropsy of the head; a preternatural distension of the head by a stagnation and extravasation of the lymph, either within or without the cranium. *Coxe. Encyc.*

HȲDROCHLO'RATE, *n.* A compound of hydrochloric acid and a base; a muriate. *Journ. of Science.*

HȲDROCHLO'RIC, *a.* [*hydrogen* and *chloric.*]

Hydrochloric acid is muriatic acid gas, a compound of chlorin and hydrogen gas. *Webster's Manual.*

HȲDROCY'ANATE, *n.* Prussiate; cyanuret.

HȲDROCYAN'IC, *a.* [Gr. υδωρ, water, or rather *hydrogen*, and κυανος, blue.]

The hydrocyanic acid is the same as the prussic acid.

HȲDRODYNAM'IC, *a.* [Gr. υδωρ, water, and δυναμις, power, force.] Pertaining to the force or pressure of water.

HȲDRODYNAM'ICS, *n.* That branch of natural philosophy which treats of the phenomena of water and other fluids, whether in motion or at rest; of their equilibrium, motion, cohesion, pressure, resistance, &c. It comprehends both hydrostatics and hydraulics. *Ed. Encyc.*

HȲDROFLU'ATE, *n.* A compound of hydrofluoric acid and a base.

HȲDROFLUOR'IC, *a.* [Gr. υδωρ, water, and *fluor.*]

Consisting of fluorin and hydrogen. The hydrofluoric acid is obtained by distilling a mixture of one part of the purest fluor spar in fine powder, with two of sulphuric acid. *Webster's Manual.*

HY'DROGEN, *n.* [Gr. υδωρ, water, and γενναω, to generate; so called as being considered the generator of water.]

In *chimistry*, a gas which constitutes one of the elements of water, of which it is said by Lavoisier to form fifteen parts in a hundred; but according to Berzelius and Dulong, hydrogen gas is 11. 1 parts in a hundred, and oxygen 88. 9. Hydrogen gas is an aeriform fluid, the lightest body known, and though extremely inflammable itself, it extinguishes burning bodies, and is fatal to animal life. Its specific gravity is 0.0694, that of air being 1.00. In consequence of its extreme lightness, it is employed for filling air balloons. *Lavoisier. Webster's Manual.*

HY'DROGENATE, *v. t.* To combine hydrogen with any thing.

HY'DROGENATED, *pp.* In combination with hydrogen.

HY'DROGENIZE, *v. t.* To combine with hydrogen.

HY'DROGENIZED, *pp.* Combined with hydrogen.

HY'DROGENIZING, *ppr.* Combining with hydrogen.

HȲDROG'RAPHER, *n.* [See *Hydrography.*] One who draws maps of the sea, lakes or other waters, with the adjacent shores; one who describes the sea or other waters. *Boyle.*

HȲDROGRAPH'IC, HȲDROGRAPH'ICAL, } *a.* Relating to or containing a description of the sea, sea coast, isles, shoals, depth of water, &c. or of a lake.

HȲDROG'RAPHY, *n.* [Gr. υδωρ, water, and γραφω, to describe.]

The art of measuring and describing the sea, lakes, rivers and other waters; or the art of forming charts, exhibiting a representation of the sea coast, gulfs, bays, isles, promontories, channels, soundings, &c.

HȲDROG'URET, *n.* A compound of hydrogen with a base.

Hydroguret is now scarcely used, except to give the derivative *hydrogureted.* *Silliman.*

HȲDROG'URETED, *a.* Denoting a compound of hydrogen with a base.

HȲDROLITE, *n.* [Gr. υδωρ, water, and λιθος, a stone.]

A mineral whose crystals are described as six sided prisms, terminated by low six sided pyramids, with truncated summits. *Cleaveland.*

HȲDROLOG'ICAL, *a.* Pertaining to hydrology.

HȲDROL'OGY, *n.* [Gr. υδωρ, water, and λογος, discourse.]

The science of water, its properties and phenomena.

HY'DROMANCY, *n.* [Gr. υδωρ, water, and μαντεια, divination.]

A method of divination or prediction of events by water; invented, according to Varro, by the Persians, and practiced by the Romans. *Encyc.*

HȲDROMAN'TIC, *a.* Pertaining to divination by water.

HY'DROMEL, *n.* [Fr. from Gr. υδωρ, water, and μελι, honey.]

A liquor consisting of honey diluted in water. Before fermentation, it is called *simple hydromel;* after fermentation, it is called *vinous hydromel* or *mead.*

HȲDROM'ETER, *n.* [See *Hydrometry.*] An instrument to measure the gravity, density, velocity, force, &c. of water and other fluids, and the strength of spirituous liquors. *Encyc.*

HȲDROMET'RIC, HȲDROMET'RICAL, } *a.* Pertaining to a hydrometer, or to the measurement of the gravity, &c. of fluids.

2. Made by a hydrometer.

HȲDROM'ETRY, *n.* [Gr. υδωρ, water, and μετρον, measure.]

The art of measuring, or the mensuration of the gravity, density, velocity, force, &c. of fluids, and the strength of rectified spirits. *Encyc.*

HȲDRO-OXYD, *n.* [Gr. υδωρ, water, and *oxyd.*]

A metallic oxyd combined with water; a metallic hydrate. *Parke. Coxe.*

HY'DROPHANE, *n.* [Gr. υδωρ, water, and φαινω, to show.]

In *mineralogy*, a variety of opal made transparent by immersion in water. *Kirwan.*

HȲDROPH'ANOUS, *a.* Made transparent by immersion in water. *Kirwan.*

HȲDROPHO'BIA, HY'DROPHOBY, } *n.* [Gr. υδωρ, water, and φοβεομαι, to fear.]

A preternatural dread of water; a symptom of canine madness, or the disease itself, which is thus denominated. This dread of water sometimes takes place in violent inflammations of the stomach, and in hysteric fits. *Encyc.*

HȲDROPHO'BIC, *a.* Pertaining to a dread of water, or canine madness. *Med. Repos.*

HȲDROP'IC, HȲDROP'ICAL, } *a.* [L. *hydrops;* Gr. υδρωψ, dropsy; υδωρ, water.]

1. Dropsical; diseased with extravasated water.

2. Containing water; caused by extravasated water; as a *hydropic* swelling.

3. Resembling dropsy.

> Every lust is a kind of *hydropic* distemper, and the more we drink the more we shall thirst. *Tillotson.*

HȲDROPNEUMAT'IC, *a.* [Gr. υδωρ, water, and πνευματικος, inflated, from πνευμα, breath, spirit.]

An epithet given to a vessel of water, with other apparatus for chimical experiments. *Med. Repos.*

HYDROPSY. [See *Dropsy.*]

HY'DROSCOPE, *n.* [Gr. υδωρ, water, and σκοπεω, to view.]

A kind of water clock, or instrument used anciently for measuring time, consisting of a cylindrical tube, conical at the bottom, perforated at the vertex, and the whole tube graduated. *Encyc.*

HȲDROSTAT'IC, HȲDROSTAT'ICAL, } *a.* [Gr. υδωρ, water, and ςατικος, static, standing or settling.]

Relating to the science of weighing fluids, or hydrostatics.

HȲDROSTAT'ICALLY, *adv.* According to hydrostatics, or to hydrostatic principles. *Bentley.*

HȲDROSTAT'ICS, *n.* The science which treats of the weight, motion, and equilibriums of fluids, or of the specific gravity and other properties of fluids, particularly of water.

Hydrostatics is that branch of the science of hydrodynamics which treats of the properties of fluids at rest. *Ed. Encyc.*

HȲDROSULPH'ATE, *n.* The same as *hydrosulphuret.*

HȲDROSULPH'URET, *n.* [*hydrogen* and *sulphuret.*]

A combination of sulphureted hydrogen with an earth, alkali or metallic oxyd.

HȲDROSULPH'URETED, *a.* Combined with sulphureted hydrogen.

Hydrosulphuric acid, is called also hydrothionic acid, or sulphureted hydrogen.

HYDROTHO'RAX, *n.* [Gr. υδωρ, water, and θωραξ.] Dropsy in the chest. *Coxe.*

HȲDROT'IC, *a.* [Gr. υδωρ, water.] Causing a discharge of water.

HȲDROT'IC, *n.* A medicine that purges off water or phlegm. *Arbuthnot.*

HȲDROXAN'THATE, *n.* [Gr. υδωρ, water, and ξανθος, yellow.]

In *chimistry*, a compound of hydroxanthic acid with a base.

HȲDROXAN'THIC, *a.* A term used to denote a new acid, formed by the action of alkalies on the bisulphuret of carbon. It is called also carbo-sulphuric acid. *Henry.*

HY'DRURET, *n.* A combination of hydrogen with sulphur, or of sulphur and sulphureted hydrogen. *Ure.*

HY'DRUS, *n.* [Gr. υδωρ, water.] A water snake; also, a constellation of the southern hemisphere.

HYE'MAL, *a.* [L. *hiems*, winter; Sans. *hima*, cold; Slav. *zima.*] Belonging to winter; done in winter.

HY'EMATE, *v. i.* To winter at a place. [*Not in use.*]

HYEMA'TION, *n.* [L. *hiemo*, to winter.] The passing or spending of a winter in a particular place.

HYE'NA, *n.* [L. *hyæna*; Gr. ὑαινα.] A quadruped of the genus Canis, having small naked ears, four toes on each foot, a straight jointed tail, and erect hair on the neck; an inhabitant of Asiatic Turkey, Syria, Persia and Barbary. It is a solitary animal, and feeds on flesh; it preys on flocks and herds, and will open graves to obtain food. It is a fierce, cruel and untamable animal, and is sometimes called the *tiger-wolf*.

HYGROM'ETER, *n.* [Gr. ὑγρος, moist, and μετρον, measure.]
An instrument for measuring the degree of moisture of the atmosphere. *Encyc.*

HYGROMET'RICAL, *a.* Pertaining to hygrometry; made by or according to the hygrometer.

HYGROM'ETRY, *n.* The act or art of measuring the moisture of the air.

HY'GROSCOPE, *n.* [Gr. ὑγρος, moist, and σκοπεω, to view.]
The same as *hygrometer*. The latter is now chiefly used.

HYGROSCOP'IC, *a.* Pertaining to the hygroscope; capable of imbibing moisture. *Adams.*

HYGROSTAT'ICS, *n.* [Gr. ὑγρος, moist, and ςατικη.]
The science of comparing degrees of moisture. *Evelyn.*

HYKE, *n.* [Ar.] A blanket or loose garment. *Parkhurst.*

HYLAR'CHICAL, *a.* [Gr. ὑλη, matter, and αρχη, rule.] Presiding over matter. *Hallywell.*

HYLOZO'IC, *n.* [Gr. ὑλη, matter, and ζωη, life.]
One who holds matter to be animated. *Clarke.*

HYM, *n.* A species of dog. Qu. *Shak.*

HY'MEN, *n.* [L. from Gr. ὑμην, membrana, pellicula, hymen.]
1. In *ancient mythology*, a fabulous deity, the son of Bacchus and Venus, supposed to preside over marriages.
2. In *anatomy*, the virginal membrane.
3. In *botany*, the fine pellicle which incloses a flower in the bud.

HYMENE'AL, HYMENE'AN, *a.* Pertaining to marriage. *Pope.*

HYMENE'AL; HYMENE'AN, *n.* A marriage song. *Milton.*

HY'MENOPTER, HYMENOP'TERA, *n.* [Gr. ὑμην, a membrane, and πτερον, a wing.]
In *entomology*, the hymenopters are an order of insects, having four membranous wings, and the tail of the female mostly armed with a sting.

HYMENOP'TERAL, *a.* Having four membranous wings.

HYMN, *n.* *hym.* [L. *hymnus*; Gr. ὑμνος; Eng. *hum.*]
A song or ode in honor of God, and among pagans, in honor of some deity. A hymn among christians is a short poem, composed for religious service, or a song of joy and praise to God. The word primarily expresses the tune, but it is used for the ode or poem.

And when they had sung a *hymn*, they went out to the mount of Olives. Matt. xxvi.

Admonishing one another in psalms and *hymns*. Col. iii.

HYMN, *v. t.* *hym.* To praise in song; to worship by singing hymns. *Milton.*
2. To sing; to celebrate in song. They *hymn* their maker's praise.

HYMN, *v. i.* *hym.* To sing in praise or adoration. *Milton.*

HYM'NED, *pp.* Sung; praised; celebrated in song.

HYM'NING, *ppr.* Praising in song; singing.

HYM'NIC, *a.* Relating to hymns. *Donne.*

HYMNOL'OGIST, *n.* A composer of hymns. *Busby.*

HYMNOL'OGY, *n.* [Gr. ὑμνος and λογος.]
A collection of hymns. *Mede.*

HYOSCIA'MA, *n.* A new vegetable alkali, extracted from the *Hyoscyamus nigra*, or henbane. *Ure.*

HYP, *n.* [a contraction of *hypochondria*.] A disease; depression of spirits.

HYP, *v. t.* To make melancholy; to depress the spirits. *Spectator.*

HYPAL'LAGE, *n.* *hypal'lagy.* [Gr. ὑπαλλαγη, change, from ὑπαλλασσω; ὑπο and αλλασσω, to change.]
In *grammar*, a figure consisting of a mutual change of cases. Thus in Virgil, *dare classibus austros*, for *dare classes austris*. Hypallage is a species of hyperbaton.

HYPAS'PIST, *n.* [Gr. ὑπασπιςης; ὑπο and ασπις, a shield.]
A soldier in the armies of Greece, armed in a particular manner. *Mitford.*

HY'PER, Gr. ὑπερ, Eng. *over*, is used in composition to denote excess, or something *over* or beyond.
2. *n.* A hypercritic. [*Not used.*] *Prior.*

HYPERAS'PIST, *n.* [Gr. ὑπερασπιςης; ὑπερ and ασπις, a shield.] A defender. *Chillingworth. Milner.*

HYPER'BATON, HY'PERBATE, *n.* [Gr. ὑπερβατον, from ὑπερβαινω, to transgress, or go beyond.]
In *grammar*, a figurative construction, inverting the natural and proper order of words and sentences. The species are the anastrophe, the hysteron proteron, the hypallage, the synchysis, the tmesis, the parenthesis, and the proper hyperbaton, which last is a long retention of the verb which completes the sentence. *Encyc.*

HYPER'BOLA, *n.* [Gr. ὑπερ, over, beyond, and βαλλω, to throw.]
In *conic sections* and *geometry*, a curve formed by cutting a cone in a direction parallel to its axis. *Encyc.*
A section of a cone, when the cutting plane makes a greater angle with the base than the side of the cone makes. *Webber.*
The latter definition is the most correct.

HYPER'BOLE, *n.* *hyper'boly.* [Fr. *hyperbole*; Gr. ὑπερβολη, excess, from ὑπερβαλλω, to throw beyond, to exceed.]
In *rhetoric*, a figure of speech which expresses much more or less than the truth, or which represents things much greater or less, better or worse than they really are. An object uncommon in size, either great or small, strikes us with surprise, and this emotion produces a momentary conviction that the object is greater or less than it is in reality. The same effect attends figurative grandeur or littleness; and hence the use of the hyperbole, which expresses this momentary conviction. The following are instances of the use of this figure.

He was owner of a piece of ground not larger than a Lacedemonian letter. *Longinus.*

If a man can number the dust of the earth, then shall thy seed also be numbered. Gen. xiii.

Ipse arduus, alta que pulsat
Sidera. *Virgil.*

He was so gaunt, the case of a flagellet was a mansion for him. *Shak.*

HYPERBOL'IC, HYPERBOL'ICAL, *n.* Belonging to the hyperbola; having the nature of the hyperbola.
2. Relating to or containing hyperbole; exaggerating or diminishing beyond the fact; exceeding the truth; as a *hyperbolical* expression.
Hyperbolic space, in *geometry*, the space or content comprehended between the curve of a hyperbole and the whole ordinate. *Bailey.*

HYPERBOL'ICALLY, *adv.* In the form of a hyperbola.
2. With exaggeration; in a manner to express more or less than the truth.

Scylla—is *hyperbolically* described by Homer as inaccessible. *Broome.*

HYPERBOL'IFORM, *a.* [*hyperbola* and *form.*]
Having the form, or nearly the form of a hyperbola. *Johnson.*

HYPER'BOLIST, *n.* One who uses hyperboles.

HYPER'BOLIZE, *v. i.* To speak or write with exaggeration. *Mountagu.*

HYPER'BOLIZE, *v. t.* To exaggerate or extenuate. *Fotherby.*

HYPER'BOLOID, *n.* [*hyperbola*, and Gr. ειδος, form.]
A hyperbolic conoid; a solid formed by the revolution of a hyperbola about its axis. *Ed. Encyc.*

HYPERBO'REAN, *a.* [L. *hyperboreus*; Gr. ὑπερβορεος; ὑπερ, beyond, and βορεας, the north.]
1. Northern; belonging to or inhabiting a region very far north; most northern.
2. Very cold; frigid.

HYPERBO'REAN, *n.* An inhabitant of the most northern region of the earth. The ancients gave this denomination to the people and places to the northward of the Scythians, people and regions of which they had little or no knowledge. The Hyperboreans then are the Laplanders, the Samoiedes, and the Russians near the White Sea.

HYPERCARBURETED, *a.* Supercarbureted; having the largest proportion of carbon. *Silliman.*

HYPERCATALEC'TIC, *a.* [Gr. ὑπερκαταληκτικος; ὑπερ and καταληξις, termination.]
A *hypercatalectic verse*, in Greek and Latin poetry, is a verse which has a syllable or two beyond the regular and just measure. *Bailey. Encyc.*

HYPERCRIT'IC, *n.* [Fr. *hypercritique*; Gr. ὑπερ, beyond, and κριτικος, critical. See *Critic.*]

One who is critical beyond measure or reason; an over rigid critic; a captious censor. *Dryden.*

HY̆PERERIT'IC, } *a.* Over critical;
HY̆PERERIT'ICAL, } critical beyond use or reason; animadverting on faults with unjust severity; as a *hypercritical* reader. *Swift.*

2. Excessively nice or exact; as a *hypercritical* punctilio. *Evelyn.*

HY̆PERERIT'ICISM, *n.* Excessive rigor of criticism. *Med. Repos. Bailey.*

HY̆PERDU'LIA, *n.* [Gr. υπερ, beyond, and δουλεια, service.]
Super-service in the Romish church, performed to the virgin Mary. *Usher.*

HY̆PER'ICON, *n.* John's wort. *Stukely.*

HY̆PER'METER, *n.* [Gr. υπερ, beyond, and μετρον, measure.]
Any thing greater than the ordinary standard of measure. *Addison.*

A verse is called a hypermeter, when it contains a syllable more than the ordinary measure. When this is the case, the following line begins with a vowel, and the redundant syllable of the former line blends with the first of the following, and they are read as one syllable.

HY̆PERMET'RICAL, *a.* Exceeding the common measure; having a redundant syllable. *Rambler.*

HY̆PEROX'YD, *a.* [Gr. υπερ and *oxyd.*] Acute to excess, as a crystal. *Cleaveland.*

HY̆PEROX'YGENATED, } *a.* [Gr. υπερ,
HY̆PEROX'YGENIZED, } beyond, and *oxygenated*, or *oxygenized.*]
Super-saturated with oxygen. *Darwin. Med. Repos.*

HY̆PEROXYMU'RIATE, *n.* The same as *chlorate.*

HY̆PEROXYMURIAT'IC, *a.* The *hyperoxymuriatic* acid is the chloric acid.

HY̆PERPHYS'ICAL, *a.* Supernatural.

HY'PERSTENE, } *n.* A mineral, Labra-
HY'PERSTHENE, } dor hornblend, or schillerspar. Its color is between grayish and greenish black, but nearly copper-red on the cleavage. So named from its difficult frangibility. [Gr. υπερ and σθενος.] *Jameson. Kirwan. Phillips.*

HY'PHEN, *n.* [Gr. υφεν, under one, or to one.]
A mark or short line made between two words to show that they form a compound word, or are to be connected; as in *preoccupied; five-leafed; ink-stand.* In writing and printing, the hyphen is used to connect the syllables of a divided word, and is placed after the syllable that closes a line, denoting the connection of that syllable or part of a word with the first syllable of the next line.

HYPNOT'IC, *a.* [Gr. υπνος, sleep.] Having the quality of producing sleep; tending to produce sleep; narcotic; soporific. *Brown.*

HYPNOT'IC, *n.* A medicine that produces, or tends to produce sleep; an opiate; a narcotic; a soporific.

HY̆PO, a Greek preposition, υπο, under, beneath; *used in composition.* Thus, *hyposulphuric* acid is an acid containing less oxygen than sulphuric acid.

HY̆POB'OLE, *n. hypob'oly.* [Gr. υπο, under, and βαλλω, to cast.]
In *rhetoric,* a figure in which several things are mentioned that seem to make against the argument or in favor of the opposite side, and each of them is refuted in order. *Encyc.*

HYP'OCAUST, *n.* [Gr. υποκαυςον; υπο and καιω, to burn.]
1. Among *the Greeks and Romans,* a subterraneous place where was a furnace to heat baths.
3. Among *the moderns,* the place where a fire is kept to warm a stove or a hot-house. *Encyc.*

HYPOCHON'DRES, } [See *Hypochon-*
HYPOCHON'DRY, } *dria.*]

HYPOCHON'DRIA, *n. plu.* [Gr. from υπο and χονδρος, a cartilage.]
1. In *anatomy,* the sides of the belly under the cartilages of the spurious ribs; the spaces on each side of the epigastric region. *Coxe. Encyc.*
2. Hypochondriac complaints. *Tatler.*

HYPOCHON'DRIAC, *a.* Pertaining to the hypochondria, or the parts of the body so called; as the *hypochondriac* region.
2. Affected by a disease, attended with debility, depression of spirits or melancholy.
3. Producing melancholy, or low spirits.

HYPOCHON'DRIAC, *n.* A person affected with debility, lowness of spirits or melancholy.

HYPOCHONDRI'ACAL, *a.* The same as *hypochondriac.*

HYPOCHONDRI'ACISM, *n.* A disease of men, characterized by languor or debility, depression of spirits or melancholy, with dyspepsy. *Darwin.*

HYPOCHONDRI'ASIS, *n.* Hypochondriacism.

HYP'OCIST, *n.* [Gr. υποκιςις, sub cisto, under the cistus.]
An inspissated juice obtained from the sessile asarum [*Cytinus hypocistis,*] resembling the true Egyptian acacia. The juice is expressed from the unripe fruit and evaporated to the consistence of an extract, formed into cakes and dried in the sun. It is an astringent, useful in diarrheas and hemorrhages. *Encyc.*

HY̆POCRATER'IFORM, *a.* [Gr. υπο, under, κρατηρ, a cup, and *form.*]
Salver-shaped; tubular, but suddenly expanding into a flat border at top; applied to a monopetalous corol. *Bigelow.*

HYPOC'RISY, *n.* [Fr. *hypocrisie; L. hypocrisis;* Gr. υποκρισις, simulation; υποκρινομαι, to feign; υπο and κρινω, to separate, discern or judge.]
1. Simulation; a feigning to be what one is not; or dissimulation, a concealment of one's real character or motives. More generally, hypocrisy is simulation, or the assuming of a false appearance of virtue or religion; a deceitful show of a good character, in morals or religion; a counterfeiting of religion.

Beware ye of the leaven of the Pharisees, which is *hypocrisy.* Luke xii.

2. Simulation; deceitful appearance; false pretence.

Hypocrisy is the necessary burden of villainy. *Rambler.*

HYP'OCRITE, *n.* [Fr. *hypocrite;* Gr. υποκριτης.]
1. One who feigns to be what he is not; one who has the form of godliness without the power, or who assumes an appearance of piety and virtue, when he is destitute of true religion.

And the *hypocrite's* hope shall perish. Job viii.

2. A dissembler; one who assumes a false appearance.

Fair *hypocrite,* you seek to cheat in vain. *Dryden.*

HY̆POCRIT'IC, } *a.* Simulating; coun-
HYPOCRIT'ICAL, } terfeiting a religious character; assuming a false and deceitful appearance; *applied to persons.*
2. Dissembling; concealing one's real character or motives.
3. Proceeding from hypocrisy, or marking hypocrisy; as a *hypocritical* face or look.

HYPOCRIT'ICALLY, *adv.* With simulation; with a false appearance of what is good; falsely; without sincerity.

HY̆POGAS'TRIC, *a.* [Gr. υπο, under, and γαςηρ, the belly.]
1. Relating to the *hypogastrium,* or middle part of the lower region of the belly.
2. An appellation given to the internal branch of the iliac artery. *Encyc.*

HY̆POGAS'TROCELE, *n.* [Gr. υπογαςριον, and κηλη, a tumor.]
A hernia or rupture of the lower belly. *Coxe.*

HY̆POGE'UM, *n.* [Gr. υπο, under, and γαια or γη, the earth.]
A name given by ancient architects to all the parts of a building which were under ground, as the cellar, &c. *Encyc.*

HY̆POG'YNOUS, *n.* [Gr. υπο, under, and γυνη, a female.]
A term applied to plants that have their corols and stamens inserted under the pistil. *Lunier.*

HY̆POPHOS'PHOROUS, *n.* [Gr. υπο and *phosphorus.*]
The hypophosphorous acid contains less oxygen than the phosphorous, and is obtained from the phosphuret of baryte. It is a liquid which may be concentrated by evaporation, till it becomes viscid. It has a very sour taste, reddens vegetable blues, and does not crystalize. *Ure.*

HY̆POPHOS'PHITE, *n.* A compound of hypophosphorous acid and a salifiable base. *Ure.*

HY̆POS'TASIS, } *n.* [L. *hypostasis;* Fr. *hy-*
HYPOS'TASY, } *postase;* Gr. υποςασις, from υπο and ιςημι, to stand.]
Properly, subsistence or substance. Hence it is used to denote distinct substance, or subsistence of the Father, Son, and Holy Spirit, in the Godhead, called by the Greek christians, three *hypostases.* The Latins more generally used *persona* to express the sense of hypostasis, and this is the modern practice. We say, the Godhead consists of three *persons.*

HY̆POSTAT'IC, } *a.* Relating to hypos-
HY̆POSTAT'ICAL, } tasis; constitutive.

Let our Carneades warn men not to subscribe to the grand doctrine of the chimists, touching their three *hypostatical* principles, till they have a little examined it. *Boyle.*

2. Personal, or distinctly personal; or constituting a distinct substance. *Pearson.*

HY̆POSUL'PHATE, *n.* A compound of hyposulphuric acid and a base.

HY̆POSUL'PHITE, *n.* A compund of hyposulphurous acid and a salifiable base.

HY̆POSUL'PHURIC, *a.* Hyposulphuric acid, is an acid combination of sulphur and oxygen, intermediate between sulphurous and sulphuric acid. *Ure.*

HY̆POSUL'PHUROUS, *a.* Hyposulphurous acid is an acid containing less oxygen than sulphurous acid. This acid is known only in combination with salifiable bases. *Ure. Henry.*

HY̆POT'ENUSE, *n.* [Gr. υποτεινουσα, part. of υποτεινω, to subtend.]
In *geometry*, the subtense or longest side of a right-angled triangle, or the line that subtends the right angle. *Encyc.*

HY̆POTH'ECATE, *v. t.* [L. *hypotheca*, a pledge; Gr. υποθηκη, from υποτιθημι, to put under, to suppose.]
1. To pledge, and properly to pledge the keel of a ship, that is, the ship itself, as security for the repayment of money borrowed to carry on a voyage. In this case the lender hazards the loss of his money by the loss of the ship; but if the ship returns safe, he receives his principal, with the premium or interest agreed on, though it may exceed the legal rate of interest. *Blackstone. Park.*
2. To pledge, as goods. *Park.*

HY̆POTH'ECATED, *pp.* Pledged, as security for money borrowed.

HY̆POTH'ECATING, *ppr.* Pledging as security.

HY̆POTHECA'TION, *n.* The act of pledging, as a ship or goods, for the repayment of money borrowed to carry on a voyage; otherwise called *bottomry.*

HY̆POTH'ECATOR, *n.* One who pledges a ship or other property, as security for the repayment of money borrowed. *Judge Johnson.*

HY̆POTH'ESIS, *n.* [L. from Gr. υποθεσις, a supposition; υποτιθημι, to suppose; υπο and τιθημι.]
1. A supposition; a proposition or principle which is supposed or taken for granted, in order to draw a conclusion or inference for proof of the point in question; something not proved, but assumed for the purpose of argument. *Encyc.*
2. A system or theory imagined or assumed to account for what is not understood. *Encyc.*

HY̆POTHET'IC, / **HY̆POTHET'ICAL,** *a.* Including a supposition; conditional; assumed without proof for the purpose of reasoning and deducing proof. *Watts.*

HY̆POTHET'ICALLY, *adv.* By way of supposition; conditionally.

HYRSE, *n. hirs.* [G. *hirse.*] Millet.

HYRST, *n.* A wood. [See *Hurst.*]

HY'SON, *n.* A species of green tea from China.

HY'SOP, / **HYSSOP,** *n. hy'sop.* [L. *hyssopus*; Gr. υσσωπος. It would be well to write this word *hysop.*]
A plant, or genus of plants, one species of which is cultivated for use. The leaves have an aromatic smell, and a warm pungent taste. Hyssop was much used by the Jews in purifications. *Encyc.*

HYSTER'IC, / **HYSTER'ICAL,** *a.* [Fr. *hysterique*; Gr. υςερικος, from υςερα, the womb.]
Disordered in the region of the womb; troubled with fits or nervous affections.

HYSTER'ICS, *n.* A disease of women, proceeding from the womb, and characterized by fits or spasmodic affections of the nervous system. *Encyc.*
A spasmodic disease of the *primæ viæ*, attended with the sensation of a ball rolling about the abdomen, stomach and throat. *Coxe.*

HYS'TEROCELE, *n.* [Gr. υςερα, the womb, and κηλη, a tumor.]
A species of hernia, caused by a displacement of the womb. *Lunier.*
A rupture containing the uterus. *Coxe.*

HYS'TERON PROT'ERON, *n.* [Gr. υςερον, last, and προτερον, first.]
A rhetorical figure, when that is said last which was done first. *Peacham.*

HYSTEROT'OMY, *n.* [Gr. υςερα, the uterus, and τομη, a cutting.]
In *surgery*, the Cesarean section; the operation of cutting into the uterus for taking out a fetus, which cannot be excluded by the usual means.

HYTHE, *n.* A port. [See *Hithe.*]

I.

I is the ninth letter, and the third vowel of the English Alphabet. We receive it through the Latin and Greek from the Shemitic *jod*, *je*, or *ye*, in Greek ιωτα, whence our English word *jot.* This vowel in French, and in most European languages, has the long fine sound which we express by *e* in *me*, or *ee* in *seen*, *meek.* This sound we retain in some foreign words which are naturalized in our language, as in *machine*, *intrigue.* But in most English words this long sound is shortened, as in *holiness*, *pity*, *gift*; in which words the sound of *i* coincides with that of *y* in *hypocrite*, *cycle*, and at the end of words, in unaccented syllables, as in *holy*, *glory.* It is this short sound of the French and Italian *i*, which we hear in the pronunciation of *been*, which we pronounce *bin.* After *l*, this letter has sometimes the liquid sound of *y*, as in *million*, pronounced *milyon.* This sound corresponds with that of the Hebrews, as in *Joseph*, which in Syria is pronounced *Yoseph*, and with the sound of the German *j*, as in *ja*, *jahr*, that is, *ya*, *yahr.*

The sound of *i* long, as in *fine*, *kind*, *arise*, is diphthongal; it begins with a sound approaching that of broad *a*, but it is not exactly the same, as the organs are not opened to the same extent, and therefore the sound begins a little above that of *aw.* The sound, if continued, closes with one that nearly approaches to that of *e* long. This sound can be learned only by the ear.

This letter enters into several digraphs, as in *fail*, *field*, *seize*, *feign*, *vein*, *friend*; and with *o* in *oil*, *join*, *coin*, it helps to form a proper diphthong.

No English word ends with *i*, but when the sound of the letter occurs at the end of a word, it is expressed by *y.*

As a numeral I signifies *one*, and stands for as many units as it is repeated in times, as II, two, III, three, &c. When it stands *before* V or X, it subtracts itself, and the numerals denote one less than the V or the X. Thus IV expresses four, one less than V, five; IX stands for nine, one less than X, ten. But when it is placed *after* V or X, it denotes the addition of an unit, or as many units as the letter is repeated in times. Thus VI is five and one, or six, and XI is ten and one, or eleven; VIII stands for five and three, or eight, &c.

Among the ancient Romans, IƆ stood for 500; CIƆ, for 1000; IƆƆ, for 5000; CCIƆƆ, for 10,000; IƆƆƆ, for 50,000; and CCCIƆƆƆ, for 100,000.

I, formerly prefixed to some English words, as in *ibuilt*, is a contraction of the Saxon prefix *ge*; and more generally this was written *y.*]

I, *pron.* [Sax. *ic*; Goth. D. *ik*; G. *ich*; Sw. *jag*; Dan. *jeg*; Gr. εγω; L. *ego*; Port. *eu*; Sp. *yo*; It. *io*; Fr. *je*; Sans. *agam.* In Armoric *me* is the nominative; so W. *mi*, Fr. *moi*, Hindoo, *me.* Either *ego* is contracted from *mego*, or *I* and *me* are from different roots. It is certain that *me* is contracted from *meg* or *mig.* See *Me.*]
The pronoun of the first person; the word which expresses one's self, or that by which a speaker or writer denotes himself. It is only the nominative case of the pronoun; in the other cases we use *me.* *I* am attached to study; study delights *me.*
We often hear in popular language the phrase *it is me*, which is now considered to be ungrammatical, for *it is I.* But the phrase may have come down to us from the use of the Welsh *mi*, or from the French use of the phrase, *c'est moi.*
In the plural, we use *we*, and *us*, which appear to be words radically distinct from *I.*
Johnson observes that Shakspeare uses *I* for *ay* or *yes.* In this he is not followed, and the use is incorrect.

IAM'BIC, *n.* [Fr. *iambique*; L. *iambicus*; Gr. ιαμβικος.]
Pertaining to the iambus, a poetic foot consisting of two syllables, a short one followed by a long one.

IAM'BUS, IAM'BUS, *n.* [L. *iambus*; Gr. ιαμβος.] In *poetry*, a foot consisting of two syllables, the first short and the last long, as in *delight*. The following line consists wholly of iambic feet.

He scorns|the force|that dares|his fu|ry stay.

IAM'BICS, *n. plu.* Verses composed of short and long syllables alternately. Anciently, certain songs or satires, supposed to have given birth to ancient comedy.

IBEX, *n.* [L.] The wild goat of the genus Capra, which is said to be the stock of the tame goat. It has large knotty horns reclining on its back, is of a yellowish color, and its beard is black. It inhabits the Alps. *Encyc.*

The *Ægagrus*, or wild goat of the mountains of Persia, appears to be the stock of the tame goat. The *Ibex* is a distinct species. *Cuvier.*

IBIS, *n.* [Gr. and L.] A fowl of the genus Tantalus, and grallic order, a native of Egypt. The bill is long, subulated, and somewhat crooked; the face naked, and the feet have four toes palmated at the base. This fowl was much valued by the Egyptians for destroying serpents. It is said by Bruce not now to inhabit Egypt, but to be found in Abyssinia. *Encyc.*

The ibis of the Egyptians is a species of the genus Scolopax. It was anciently venerated either because it devoured serpents, or because the marking of its plumage resembled one of the phases of the moon, or because it appeared in Egypt with the rising of the Nile. *Cuvier.*

The ibis is common in Egypt during the overflowing of the Nile. *Ed. Encyc.*

ICA'RIAN, *a.* [from *Icarus*, the son of Dædalus, who fled on wings to escape the resentment of Minos, but his flight being too high was fatal to him, as the sun melted the wax that cemented his wings.]
Adventurous in flight; soaring too high for safety, like Icarus.

ICE, *n.* [Sax. *is*, *isa*; G. *eis*; D. *ys*; Dan. *iis*; Sw. Ice. *is*; Ir. *cuise*. The true orthography would be *ise*. The primary sense is doubtless to set, to fix, to congeal or harden. It may be allied to the G. *eisen*, iron; perhaps also to L. *os*, a bone.]

1. Water or other fluid congealed, or in a solid state; a solid, transparent, brittle substance, formed by the congelation of a fluid, by means of the abstraction of the heat necessary to preserve its fluidity, or to use common language, congealed by cold.
2. Concreted sugar.

To break the ice, is to make the first opening to any attempt; to remove the first obstructions or difficulties; to open the way. *Shak.*

ICE, *v. t.* To cover with ice; to convert into ice. *Fletcher.*
2. To cover with concreted sugar; to frost. *Puller.*
3. To chill; to freeze.

ICEBERG, *n.* [*ice* and G. *berg*, a hill.] A hill or mountain of ice, or a vast body of ice accumulated in valleys in high northern latitudes.

This term is applied to such elevated masses as exist in the valleys of the frigid zones; to those which are found on the surface of fixed ice; and to ice of great thickness and highth in a floating state. These lofty floating masses are sometimes detached from the icebergs on shore, and sometimes formed at a distance from any land. They are found in both the frigid zones, and are sometimes carried towards the equator as low as 40°. *Ed. Encyc.*

ICEBLINK, *n.* A name given by seamen to a bright appearance near the horizon, occasioned by the ice, and observed before the ice itself is seen. *Encyc.*

ICEBOAT, *n.* A boat constructed for moving on ice.

ICEBOUND, *a.* In *seaman's language*, totally surrounded with ice, so as to be incapable of advancing. *Mar. Dict.*

ICEBUILT, *a.* Composed of ice.
2. Loaded with ice. *Gray.*

ICEHOUSE, *n.* [*ice* and *house*.] A repository for the preservation of ice during warm weather; a pit with a drain for conveying off the water of the ice when dissolved, and usually covered with a roof.

ICEISLE, *n.* *iceile*. [*ice* and *isle*.] A vast body of floating ice, such as is often seen in the Atlantic, off the banks of Newfoundland. *J. Barlow.*

When flat and extending beyond the reach of sight, it is called *field ice*; when smaller, but of very large dimensions, it is called a *floe*; when lofty, an *iceberg*. There are numerous other terms for the different appearances of floating ice. *Ed. Encyc.*

ICELANDER, *n.* A native of Iceland.

ICELAND'IC, *a.* Pertaining to Iceland; and as a noun, the language of the Icelanders.

Iceland spar, calcarious spar, in laminated masses, easily divisible into rhombs, perfectly similar to the primitive rhomb. *Cleaveland.*

ICEPLANT, *n.* A plant of the genus Mesembryanthemum, sprinkled with pellucid, glittering, icy pimples. *Encyc.*

ICESPAR, *n.* A variety of feldspar, the crystals of which resemble ice. *Jameson.*

ICHNEU'MON, *n.* [L. from the Gr. ιχνευμων, from ιχνευω, to follow the steps, ιχνος, a footstep; a follower of the crocodile.]
An animal of the genus Viverra, or weasel kind. It has a tail tapering to a point, and its toes are distant from each other. It inhabits Egypt, Barbary and India. It destroys the most venomous serpents, and seeks the eggs of the crocodile, digging them out of the sand, eating them and destroying the young. In India and Egypt, this animal is domesticated and kept for destroying rats and mice. *Encyc.*

Ichneumon-fly, a genus of flies, of the order of hymenopters, containing several hundred species. These animals have jaws, but no tongue; the antennæ have more than thirty joints, and are kept in continual motion. The abdomen is generally petiolated, or joined to the body by a pedicle. These animals are great destroyers of caterpillars, plant-lice and other insects, as the ichneumon is of the eggs and young of the crocodile. *Encyc.*

ICHNOGRAPH'IC, ICHNOGRAPH'ICAL, *a.* [See *Ichnography*.] Pertaining to ichnography; describing a ground-plot.

ICHNOG'RAPHY, *n.* [Gr. ιχνος, a footstep, and γραφω, to describe.]
In *perspective*, the view of any thing cut off by a plane parallel to the horizon, just at the base of it; a ground-plot. *Encyc.*

I'CHOR, *n.* [Gr. ιχωρ.] A thin watery humor, like serum or whey.
2. Sanious matter flowing from an ulcer. *Encyc.*

I'CHOROUS, *a.* Like ichor; thin; watery; serous.
2. Sanious.

ICH'THYOCOL, ICHTHYOCOL'LA, *n.* [Gr. ιχθυς, a fish, and κολλα, glue.] Fish-glue; isinglass; a glue prepared from the sounds of fish. *Tooke.*

ICH'THYOLITE, *n.* [Gr. ιχθυς, a fish, and λιθος, a stone.]
Fossil fish; or the figure or impression of a fish in rock. *Hitchcock.*

ICHTHYOLOG'ICAL, *a.* Pertaining to ichthyology.

ICHTHYOL'OGIST, *n.* [See *Ichthyology*.] One versed in ichthyology.

ICHTHYOL'OGY, *n.* [Gr. ιχθυς, a fish, and λογος, discourse.]
The science of fishes, or that part of zoology which treats of fishes, their structure, form and classification, their habits, uses, &c. *Encyc. Ed. Encyc.*

ICHTHYOPH'AGOUS, *a.* [Gr. ιχθυς, fish, and φαγω, to eat.] Eating or subsisting on fish. *D'Anville.*

ICHTHYOPH'AGY, *n.* [supra.] The practice of eating fish.

ICHTHYOPHTHAL'MITE, *n.* [Gr. ιχθυς, a fish, and οφθαλμος, an eye.] Fish-eye-stone. [See *Apophyllite*.]

I'CICLE, *n.* [Sax. *ises-gecel*, D. *yskegel*, ice-cone. *Kegel* is a cone or nine pin.]
A pendent conical mass of ice, formed by the freezing of water or other fluid as it flows down an inclined plane, or collects in drops and is suspended. In the north of England, it is called *ickle*.

I'CINESS, *n.* The state of being icy, or of being very cold.
2. The state of generating ice.

I'CING, *ppr.* Covering with concreted sugar.

I'CON, *n.* [Gr. εικων, an image, from εικω, to resemble.]
An image or representation. [*Not in use.*] *Brown. Hakewill.*

ICON'OCLAST, *n.* [Fr. *iconoclaste*; Gr. εικων, an image, and κλαςης, a breaker, from κλαω, to break.]
A breaker or destroyer of images; a name which Catholics give to those who reject the use of images in religious worship. *Encyc.*

ICONOCLAS'TIC, *a.* Breaking images.

ICONOG'RAPHY, *n.* [Gr. εικων, an image, and γραφω, to describe.]
The description of images or ancient statues, busts, semi-busts, paintings in fresco, mosaic works, and ancient pieces of miniature.

ICONOL'ATER, *n.* [Gr. εικων, an image, and λατρευς, a servant.]

One that worships images; a name given to the Romanists.

ICONOL'OGY, *n.* [Gr. εικων, an image, and λογος, a discourse.]

The doctrine of images or representations. *Johnson.*

ICOSAHE'DRAL, *a.* [Gr. εικοσι, twenty, and εδρα, seat, basis.] Having twenty equal sides.

ICOSAHE'DRON, *n.* [supra.] A solid of twenty equal sides.

In *geometry*, a regular solid, consisting of twenty triangular pyramids, whose vertices meet in the center of a sphere supposed to circumscribe it, and therefore have their highths and bases equal. *Encyc. Enfield.*

ICOSAN'DER, *n.* [Gr. εικοσι, twenty, and ανηρ, a male.]

In *botany*, a plant having twenty or more stamens inserted in the calyx. *Linne.*

NOTE. A writer on botany has suggested that as the proper character of plants of this class is the insertion of the stamens in the calyx, it might be expedient to denominate the class, *Calycandria.* *Journ. of Science.*

ICOSAN'DRIAN, *n.* Pertaining to the class of plants, Icosandria, having twenty or more stamens inserted in the calyx.

IC'TERIC, ICTER'ICAL, *a.* [L. *ictericus*, from *icterus*, jaundice.] Affected with the jaundice.

2. Good in the cure of the jaundice.

IC'TERIC, *n.* A remedy for the jaundice. *Swift.*

ICTERI''TIOUS, *a.* [L. *icterus*, jaundice.] Yellow; having the color of the skin when it is affected by the jaundice.

I'CY, *a.* [from *ice.*] Abounding with ice; as the *icy* regions of the north.

2. Cold; frosty; as *icy* chains. *Shak.*

3. Made of ice.

4. Resembling ice; chilling.

Religion lays not an *icy* hand on the true joys of life. *Buckminster.*

5. Cold; frigid; destitute of affection or passion. *Shak.*

6. Indifferent; unaffected; backward. *Shak.*

I'CY-PEARLED, *a.* Studded with spangles of ice. *Milton.*

I'd, contracted from *I would*, or *I had.*

IDE'A, *n.* [L. *idea*; Fr. *idée*; Gr. ιδεα, from ειδω, to see, L. *video.*]

1. Literally, that which is seen; hence, form, image, model of any thing in the mind; that which is held or comprehended by the understanding or intellectual faculties.

I have used the word *idea*, to express whatever is meant by phantasm, notion, species, or whatever it is which the mind can be employed about in thinking. *Locke.*

Whatever the mind perceives in itself, or is the immediate object of perception, thought or understanding, that I call an *idea.* *Locke.*

The attention of the understanding to the objects acting on it, by which it becomes sensible of the impressions they make, is called by logicians, *perception*; and the notices themselves as they exist in the mind, as the materials of thinking and knowledge, are distinguished by the name of *ideas.* *Encyc. art. Logic.*

An *idea* is the reflex perception of objects, after the original perception or impression has been felt by the mind. *Encyc.*

In *popular language*, idea signifies the same thing as conception, apprehension, notion. To have an idea of any thing is to conceive it. In *philosophical use*, it does not signify that act of the mind which we call thought or conception, but some *object* of thought. *Reid.*

According to modern writers on mental philosophy, an *idea* is the object of thought, or the notice which the mind takes of its perceptions.

Darwin uses *idea* for a notion of external things which our organs bring us acquainted with originally, and he defines it, a contraction, motion or configuration of the fibers which constitute the immediate organ of sense; synonymous with which he sometimes uses *sensual motion*, in contradistinction to *muscular motion.* *Zoon.*

2. In popular use, *idea* signifies notion, conception, thought, opinion, and even purpose or intention.

3. Image in the mind.

Her sweet *idea* wandered through his thoughts. *Fairfax.*

[*A bad use of the word.*]

4. An opinion; a proposition. These decisions are incompatible with the *idea*, that the principles are derived from the civil law.

IDE'AL, *a.* Existing in idea; intellectual; mental; as *ideal* knowledge.

There will always be a wide interval between practical and *ideal* excellence. *Rambler.*

2. Visionary; existing in fancy or imagination only; as *ideal* good.

3. That considers ideas as images, phantasms, or forms in the mind; as the *ideal* theory or philosophy.

IDE'ALISM, *n.* The system or theory that makes every thing to consist in ideas, and denies the existence of material bodies. *Walsh.*

IDE'ALIZE, *v. i.* To form ideas.

IDE'ALLY, *adv.* Intellectually; mentally; in idea. *Brown.*

IDE'ATE, *v. t.* To form in idea; to fancy. [*Not in use.*] *Donne.*

IDEN'TIC, IDEN'TICAL, *a.* [Fr. *identique*; Sp. *identico*; from L. *idem*, the same.]

The same; not different; as the *identical* person; the *identical* proposition. We found on the thief the *identical* goods that were lost.

IDENTIFICA'TION, *n.* The act of making or proving to be the same.

IDEN'TIFIED, *pp.* Ascertained or made to be the same.

IDEN'TIFY, *v. t.* [L. *idem*, the same, and *facio*, to make.]

1. To ascertain or prove to be the same. The owner of the goods found them in the possession of the thief, and *identified* them.

2. To make to be the same; to unite or combine in such a manner as to make one interest, purpose or intention; to treat as having the same use; to consider as the same in effect.

Paul has *identified* the two ordinances, circumcision and baptism, and thus, by demonstrating that they have one and the same use and meaning, he has exhibited to our view the very same seal of God's covenant. *J.M. Mason.*

That treaty in fact *identified* Spain with the republican government of France, by a virtual acknowledgment of unqualified vassalage, and by specific stipulations of unconditional defense. *British Declaration, Jan.* 1805.

Every precaution is taken to *identify* the interests of the people, and of the rulers. *Ramsay.*

IDEN'TIFY, *v. i.* To become the same; to coalesce in interest, purpose, use, effect, &c.

—An enlightened self-interest, which, when well understood, they tell us will *identify* with an interest more enlarged and public. *Burke.*

IDEN'TIFYING, *ppr.* Ascertaining or proving to be the same.

2. Making the same in interest, purpose, use, efficacy, &c.

IDEN'TITY, *n.* [Fr. *identité.*] Sameness, as distinguished from similitude and diversity. We speak of the *identity* of goods found, the *identity* of persons, or of personal *identity.* *Locke. South.*

IDES, *n. plu.* [L. *idus.* Qu. the Hetrurian *iduo*, to divide, the root of *wide, divide, individual.* The etymology is not ascertained.]

In the ancient Roman calendar, eight days in each month; the first day of which fell on the 13th of January, February, April, June, August, September, November and December, and on the 15th of March, May, July and October. The ides came between the calends and the nones, and were reckoned backwards. This method of reckoning is still retained in the chancery of Rome, and in the calendar of the breviary. *Encyc.*

IDIOC'RASY, *n.* [Gr. ιδιος, proper, peculiar to one's self, and κρασις, mixture, temperament, from κεραω, κεραννυμι, to mix.]

Peculiarity of constitution; that temperament, or state of constitution, which is peculiar to a person.

IDIOCRAT'IC, IDIOCRAT'ICAL, *a.* Peculiar in constitution.

ID'IOCY, *n.* [Gr. ιδιωτεια. See *Idiot.*] A defect of understanding; properly, a natural defect.

Idiocy and lunacy excuse from the guilt of crime. *Encyc.*

IDIOELEC'TRIC, *a.* [Gr. ιδιος, separate from others, peculiar to one's self, and *electric.*]

Electric *per se*, or containing electricity in its natural state. *Gregory.*

ID'IOM, *n.* [Fr. *idiome*; L. *idioma*, from Gr. ιδιωμα, from ιδιος, proper, or peculiar to one's self. The root of ιδιος is that of *divide*, Hetrurian *iduo*, Eng. *widow, wide*, Ar. بدّ badda, to separate. Class. Bd. No. 1.]

1. A mode of expression peculiar to a language; peculiarity of expression or phraseology. In this sense, it is used in the plural to denote forms of speech or phraseology, peculiar to a nation or language.

And to just *idioms* fix our doubtful speech. *Prior.*

2. The genius or peculiar cast of a language.

He followed the Latin language, but did not comply with the *idiom* of ours. *Dryden.*

3. Dialect.

IDIOMAT'IC, IDIOMAT'ICAL, *a.* Peculiar to a language; pertaining to the particular genius or modes of expression which belong to a language; as an *idiomatic* phrase.

IDIOMAT'ICALLY, *adv.* According to the idiom of a language.

IDIOPATH'IC, *a.* [See *Idiopathy.*] Pertaining to idiopathy; indicating a disease peculiar to a particular part of the body, and not arising from any preceding disease; as *idiopathic* head-ach. The epilepsy is *idiopathic*, when it proceeds from some fault in the brain; but *sympathetic*, when it is the consequence of some other disorder. *Darwin. Encyc.*

The term *idiopathic* is also applied to general as well as local diseases, as *idiopathic* fever. It then signifies, not sympathetic or symptomatic, not arising from any previous disease. *Good.*

IDIOPATH'ICALLY, *adv.* By means of its own disease or affections; not sympathetically.

IDIOP'ATHY, *n.* [Gr. ιδιος, proper, peculiar, and παθος, suffering, disease, from πασχω, to suffer.]

1. An original disease in a particular part of the body; a disease peculiar to some part of the body and not proceeding from another disease. *Coxe. Encyc.*
2. Peculiar affection. *More.*

IDIO-REPUL'SIVE, *a.* Repulsive by itself; as the *idio-repulsive* power of heat.

IDIOSYN'CRASY, *n.* [Gr. ιδιος, proper, συν, with, and κρασις, temperament.]

A peculiar temperament or organization of a body, by which it is rendered more liable to certain disorders than bodies differently constituted. *Coxe. Encyc.*

ID'IOT, *n.* [L. *idiota;* Gr. ιδιωτης, private, vulgar, unskilled, from ιδιος, peculiar, that is, separate, simple; Sp. It. *idiota;* Fr. *idiot.* See *Idiom.*]

1. A natural fool, or fool from his birth; a human being in form, but destitute of reason, or the ordinary intellectual powers of man.

   A person who has understanding enough to measure a yard of cloth, number twenty correctly, tell the days of the week, &c. is not an *idiot* in the eye of the law. *Encyc.*

2. A foolish person; one unwise.

IDIOT'IC, *a.* Like an idiot; foolish; sottish.

ID'IOTISH, *a.* Like an idiot; partaking of idiocy; foolish. *Paley.*

ID'IOTISM, *n.* [Fr. *idiotisme;* It. Sp. *idiotismo;* Gr. ιδιωτισμος, a form of speech taken from the vulgar, from ιδιος.]

1. An idiom; a peculiarity of expression; a mode of expression peculiar to a language; a peculiarity in the structure of words and phrases.

   Scholars sometimes give terminations and *idiotisms* suitable to their native language, to words newly invented. *Hale.*

2. Idiocy. *Beddoes, Hygeia.*

   But it would be well to restrain this word to its proper signification, and keep *idiocy* and *idiotism* distinct.

ID'IOTIZE, *v. i.* To become stupid. *Pers. Letters.*

I'DLE, *a.* [Sax. *idel, ydel,* vain, empty; G. *eitel,* mere, pure, idle, frivolous; D. *ydel,* vain, empty, idle; Dan. Sw. *idel,* mere, pure, unmixed. Class Dl. No. 6. 16. 25. 29.]

1. Not employed; unoccupied with business; inactive; doing nothing.

   Why stand ye here all the day *idle?* Matt. xx.

   To be *idle,* is to be vicious. *Rambler.*

2. Slothful; given to rest and ease; averse to labor or employment; lazy; as an *idle* man; an *idle* fellow.
3. Affording leisure; vacant; not occupied; as *idle* time; *idle* hours.
4. Remaining unused; unemployed; *applied to things;* as, my sword or spear is *idle.*
5. Useless; vain; ineffectual; as *idle* rage.

   Down their *idle* weapons dropped. *Milton.*

6. Unfruitful; barren; not productive of good.

   Of antres vast and *idle* desarts. *Shak.*

   Idle weeds. *Obs.* *Shak.*

7. Trifling; vain; of no importance; as an *idle* story; an *idle* reason; *idle* arguments. *Hooker. Dryden. Swift.*
8. Unprofitable; not tending to edification.

   Every *idle* word that men shall speak, they shall give an account thereof in the day of judgment. Matt. xii.

Idle differs from *lazy;* the latter implying constitutional or habitual aversion or indisposition to labor or action, sluggishness; whereas *idle,* in its proper sense, denotes merely unemployed. An industrious man may be *idle,* but he cannot be *lazy.*

I'DLE, *v. i.* To lose or spend time in inaction, or without being employed in business.

To idle away, in a transitive sense, to spend in idleness; as, to *idle away* time.

I'DLEHEADED, *a.* [*idle* and *head.*] Foolish; unreasonable. *Carew.*

2. Delirious; infatuated. [*Little used.*] *L'Estrange.*

I'DLENESS, *n.* Abstinence from labor or employment; the state of a person who is unemployed in labor, or unoccupied in business; the state of doing nothing. *Idleness* is the parent of vice.

   Through the *idleness* of the hands the house droppeth through. Eccles. x.

2. Aversion to labor; reluctance to be employed, or to exertion either of body or mind; laziness; sloth; sluggishness. This is properly *laziness;* but idleness is often the effect of laziness, and sometimes this word may be used for it.
3. Unimportance; trivialness.

   Apes of *idleness.* *Shak.*

4. Inefficacy; uselessness. [*Little used.*]
5. Barrenness; worthlessness. [*Little used.*]
6. Emptiness; foolishness; infatuation; as *idleness* of brain. [*Little used.*] *Bacon.*

I'DLEPATED, *a.* Idleheaded; stupid. *Overbury.*

I'DLER, *n.* One who does nothing; one who spends his time in inaction, or without being engaged in business.

2. A lazy person; a sluggard. *Raleigh.*

I'DLESBY, *n.* An idle or lazy person. [*Not used.*] *Whitlock.*

I'DLY, *adv.* In an idle manner; without employment.

2. Lazily; sluggishly.
3. Foolishly; uselessly; in a trifling way.

   A shilling spent *idly* by a fool, may be saved by a wiser person. *Franklin.*

4. Carelessly; without attention. *Prior.*
5. Vainly; ineffectually; as, to reason *idly* against truth.

ID'OCRASE, *n.* [Gr. ιδεα, form, and κρασις, mixture; a mixed figure.]

A mineral, the vesuvian of Werner, sometimes massive, and very often in shining prismatic crystals. Its primitive form is a four-sided prism with square bases. It is found near Vesuvius, in unaltered rocks ejected by the volcano; also in primitive rocks, in various other localities. *Cleaveland.*

I'DOL, *n.* [Fr. *idole;* It. Sp. *idolo;* L. *idolum;* Gr. ειδωλον, from ειδος, form, or ειδω, to see.]

1. An image, form or representation, usually of a man or other animal, consecrated as an object of worship; a pagan deity. *Idols* are usually statues or images, carved out of wood or stone, or formed of metals, particularly silver or gold.

   The gods of the nations are *idols.* Ps. xcvi.

2. An image.

   Nor ever *idol* seemed so much alive. *Dryden.*

3. A person loved and honored to adoration. The prince was the *idol* of the people.
4. Any thing on which we set our affections; that to which we indulge an excessive and sinful attachment.

   Little children, keep yourselves from *idols.* 1 John v.

   An *idol* is any thing which usurps the place of God in the hearts of his rational creatures. *S. Miller.*

5. A representation. [*Not in use.*] *Spenser.*

IDOL'ATER, *n.* [Fr. *idolatre;* L. *idololatra;* Gr. ειδωλολατρης. See *Idolatry.*]

1. A worshiper of idols; one who pays divine honors to images, statues, or representations of any thing made by hands; one who worships as a deity that which is not God; a pagan.
2. An adorer; a great admirer. *Hurd.*

IDOL'ATRESS, *n.* A female worshiper of idols.

IDOL'ATRIZE, *v. i.* To worship idols.

IDOL'ATRIZE, *v. t.* To adore; to worship. *Ainsworth.*

IDOL'ATROUS, *a.* Pertaining to idolatry; partaking of the nature of idolatry, or of the worship of false gods; consisting in the worship of idols; as *idolatrous* worship.

2. Consisting in or partaking of an excessive attachment or reverence; as an *idolatrous* veneration for antiquity.

IDOL'ATROUSLY, *adv.* In an idolatrous manner; with excessive reverence. *Hooker.*

IDOL'ATRY, *n.* [Fr. *idolatrie;* L. *idololatria;* Gr. ειδωλολατρεια; ειδωλον, idol, and λατρευω, to worship or serve.]

1. The worship of idols, images, or any thing made by hands, or which is not God.

   Idolatry is of two kinds; the worship of images, statues, pictures, &c. made by hands; and the worship of the heavenly bodies, the sun, moon and stars, or of demons, angels, men and animals. *Encyc.*

2. Excessive attachment or veneration for any thing, or that which borders on adoration.

I'DOLISH, *a.* Idolatrous. *Milton.*

I'DOLISM, *n.* The worship of idols. [*Little used.*] *Milton.*

I'DOLIST, *n.* A worshiper of images; *a poetical word.* *Milton.*

I'DOLIZE, *v. t.* To love to excess; to love or reverence to adoration; as, to *idolize* gold or wealth; to *idolize* children; to *idolize* a virtuous magistrate or a hero.

I'DOLIZED, *pp.* Loved or reverenced to adoration.

I'DOLIZER, *n.* One who idolizes, or loves to reverence.

I'DOLIZING, *ppr.* Loving or revering to an excess bordering on adoration.

IDO'NEOUS, *a.* [L. *idoneus*; probably from the root of Gr. δυναμαι, to be strong, able or sufficient.]

Fit; suitable; proper; convenient; adequate. [*Little used.*] *Boyle.*

IDYL, *n.* [L. *idyllium*; Gr. ειδυλλιον; supposed to be from ειδος, form.]

A short poem; properly, a short pastoral poem; as the *idyls* of Theocritus.

I. e. stands for L. *id est*, that is.

I'ELAND, *n. i'land.* [G. and D. *eiland*; Sax. *ealond*, *iegland*; composed of *ie*, *ea*, water, Fr. *eau*, contracted from L. *aqua*, and *land*. This is the genuine English word, always used in discourse, but for which is used *island*, an absurd compound of Fr. *isle* and land, which signifies *land in water-land*, or rather *ieland-land*.]

1. A portion of land surrounded by water; as Bermuda, Barbadoes, Cuba, Great Britain, Borneo.

2. A large mass of floating ice.

IF, *v. t.* imperative, contracted from Sax. *gif*, from *gifan*, Goth. *giban*, to give. It is used as the sign of a condition, or it introduces a conditional sentence. It is a verb, without a specified nominative. In like manner we use *grant*, *admit*, *suppose*. Regularly, *if* should be followed, as it was formerly, by the substitute or pronoun *that*, referring to the succeeding sentence or proposition. *If that* John shall arrive in season, I will send him with a message. But *that* is now omitted, and the subsequent sentence, proposition or affirmation may be considered as the object of the verb. *Give* John shall arrive; *grant*, *suppose*, *admit* that he shall arrive, I will send him with a message. The sense of *if*, or *give*, in this use, is grant, admit, cause to be, let the fact be, let the thing take place. *If* then is equivalent to grant, allow, admit. "*If* thou wilt, thou canst make me whole," that is, thou canst make me whole, *give* the fact, that thou wilt.

> *If* thou art the son of God, command that these stones be made bread. Matt. xiv.

2. Whether or not.

> Uncertain *if* by augury or chance. *Dryden.*

So in French, *soit que*, let it be that.

IG'NEOUS, *a.* [L. *igneus*, from *ignis*, fire, Sans. *aghni*, Bengal. *aag*, *ogin*, Slav. *ogn*.]

1. Consisting of fire; as *igneous* particles emitted from burning wood.

2. Containing fire; having the nature of fire.

3. Resembling fire; as an *igneous* appearance.

IGNES'CENT, *a.* [L. *ignescens*, *ignesco*, from *ignis*, fire.]

Emitting sparks of fire when struck with steel; scintillating; as *ignescent* stones. *Fourcroy.*

IGNES'CENT, *n.* A stone or mineral that gives out sparks when struck with steel or iron.

> Many other stones, besides this class of *ignescents*, produce a real scintillation when struck against steel. *Fourcroy.*

IG'NIFY, *v. t.* [L. *ignis* and *facio.*] To form into fire. *Stukely.*

IGNIF'LUOUS, *a.* [L. *ignifluus.*] Flowing with fire. *Cockeran.*

IGNIP'OTENT, *a.* [L. *ignis*, fire, and *potens*, powerful.]

Presiding over fire. Vulcan is called the power *ignipotent*. *Pope.*

IGNIS FATUUS, *n.* [L.] A meteor or light that appears in the night, over marshy grounds, supposed to be occasioned by phosphoric matter extricated from putrefying animal or vegetable substances, or by some inflammable gas; vulgarly called *Will with the wisp*, and *Jack with a lantern*. *Ed. Encyc.*

IGNI'TE, *v. t.* [L. *ignis*, fire.] To kindle, or set on fire.

2. More generally, to communicate fire to, or to render luminous or red by heat; as, to *ignite* charcoal or iron. Anthracite is *ignited* with more difficulty than bituminous coal.

IGNI'TE, *v. i.* To take fire; to become red with heat.

IGNI'TED, *pp.* Set on fire.

2. Rendered red or luminous by heat or fire.

IGNI'TING, *ppr.* Setting on fire; becoming red with heat.

2. Communicating fire to; heating to redness.

IGNI''TION, *n.* The act of kindling, or setting on fire.

2. The act or operation of communicating fire or heat, till the substance becomes red or luminous.

3. The state of being kindled; more generally, the state of being heated to redness or luminousness.

4. Calcination.

IGNI'TIBLE, *a.* Capable of being ignited.

IGNIV'OMOUS, *a.* [L. *ignivomus*; *ignis*, fire, and *vomo*, to vomit.]

Vomiting fire; as an *ignivomous* mountain, a volcano. *Derham.*

IGNO'BLE, *a.* [Fr. from L. *ignobilis*; *in* and *nobilis*. See *Noble*.]

1. Of low birth or family; not noble; not illustrious.

2. Mean; worthless; as an *ignoble* plant.

3. Base; not honorable; as an *ignoble* motive.

IGNOBIL'ITY, *n.* Ignobleness. [*Not in use.*] *Ball.*

IGNO'BLENESS, *n.* Want of dignity; meanness. *Ainsworth.*

IGNO'BLY, *adv.* Of low family or birth; as *ignobly* born.

2. Meanly; dishonorably; reproachfully; disgracefully; basely. The troops *ignobly* fly.

IGNOMIN'IOUS, *a.* [L. *ignominiosus*. See *Ignominy*.]

1. Incurring disgrace; cowardly; of mean character.

> Then with pale fear surprised,
> Fled *ignominious*. *Milton.*

2. Very shameful; reproachful; dishonorable; infamous. To be hanged for a crime is *ignominious*. Whipping, cropping and branding are *ignominious* punishments.

3. Despicable; worthy of contempt; as an *ignominious* projector. *Swift.*

IGNOMIN'IOUSLY, *adv.* Meanly; disgracefully; shamefully.

IG'NOMINY, *n.* [L. *ignominia*; *in* and *nomen*, against name or reputation; Fr. *ignominie*.]

Public disgrace; shame; reproach; dishonor; infamy.

> Their generals have been received with honor after their defeat; yours with *ignominy* after conquest. *Addison.*

> Vice begins in mistake, and ends in *ignominy*. *Rambler.*

IGNORA'MUS, *n.* [L. we are ignorant; from *ignoro*.]

1. The indorsement which a grand jury make on a bill presented to them for inquiry, when there is not evidence to support the charges, on which all proceedings are stopped, and the accused person is discharged.

2. An ignorant person; a vain pretender to knowledge. *South.*

IG'NORANCE, *n.* [Fr. from L. *ignorantia*; *ignoro*, not to know; *ignarus*, ignorant; *in* and *gnarus*, knowing.]

1. Want, absence or destitution of knowledge; the negative state of the mind which has not been instructed in arts, literature or science, or has not been informed of facts. Ignorance may be general, or it may be limited to particular subjects. *Ignorance* of the law does not excuse a man for violating it. *Ignorance* of facts is often venial.

> *Ignorance* is preferable to error. *Jefferson.*

2. *Ignorances*, in the plural, is used sometimes for omissions or mistakes; but the use is uncommon and not to be encouraged.

IG'NORANT, *a.* [L. *ignorans.*] Destitute of knowledge; uninstructed or uninformed; untaught; unenlightened. A man may be *ignorant* of the law, or of any art or science. He may be *ignorant* of his own rights, or of the rights of others.

2. Unknown; undiscovered; *a poetical use*: as *ignorant* concealment. *Shak.*

3. Unacquainted with.

> *Ignorant* of guilt, I fear not shame. *Dryden.*

4. Unskilfully made or done. [*Not legitimate.*]

> Poor *ignorant* baubles. *Shak.*

IG'NORANT, *n.* A person untaught or uninformed; one unlettered or unskilled.

> Did I for this take pains to teach
> Our zealous *ignorants* to preach? *Denham.*

IG'NORANTLY, *adv.* Without knowledge, instruction or information.

> Whom therefore ye *ignorantly* worship, him declare I unto you. Acts xvii.

2. Unskilfully; inexpertly. A man may mistake blunders for beauties and *ignorantly* admire them.

IGNO'RE, *v. t.* To be ignorant. [*Not in use.*] *Boyle.*

IGNOS'CIBLE, *a.* [L. *ignoscibilis.*] Pardonable. [*Not used.*]

IGNO'TE, *a.* [L. *ignotus.*] Unknown. [*Not used.*]

IGU'ANA, *n.* A species of lizard, of the genus Lacerta.

ILE, so written by Pope for *aile*, a walk or alley in a church or public building. [*Not in use.*]

2. An ear of corn. [*Not used.*] *Ainsworth.*

I'LEX, *n.* [L.] In *botany*, the generic name of the Holly-tree. Also, the *Quercus ilex*, or great scarlet oak.

IL'IAC, *a.* [L. *iliacus*, from *ilia*, the flank, or small intestines; Gr. εἰλεω, to wind.]
Pertaining to the lower bowels, or to the ileum. The *iliac* passion, is a violent and dangerous kind of colic, with an inversion of the peristaltic motion of the bowels. *Encyc. Parr.*

IL'IAD, *n.* [from *Ilium*, *Ilion*, Troy.] An epic poem, composed by Homer, in twenty four books. The subject of this poem is the wrath of Achilles; in describing which, the poet exhibits the miserable effects of disunion and public dissensions. Hence the phrase, *Ilias malorum*, an *Iliad* of woes or calamities, a world of disasters. *Cicero.*

ILK, *a.* The same; each. This is retained in Scottish, from the Saxon *elc*, each.

ILL, *n.* [supposed to be contracted from *evil*, Sax. *yfel*; but this is doubtful. It is in Swedish, *illa*, and Dan. *ilde*.]
1. Bad or evil, in a general sense; contrary to good, physical or moral; *applied to things;* evil; wicked; wrong; iniquitous; as, his ways are *ill;* he sets an *ill* example.
2. Producing evil or misfortune; as an *ill* star or planet.
3. Bad; evil; unfortunate; as an *ill* end; an *ill* fate.
4. Unhealthy; insalubrious; as an *ill* air or climate.
5. Cross; crabbed; surly; peevish; as *ill* nature; *ill* temper.
6. Diseased; disordered; sick or indisposed; *applied to persons;* as, the man is *ill;* he has been *ill* a long time; he is *ill* of a fever.
7. Diseased; impaired; as an *ill* state of health.
8. Discordant; harsh; disagreeable; as an *ill* sound.
9. Homely; ugly; as *ill* looks, or an *ill* countenance.
10. Unfavorable; suspicious; as when we say, this affair bears an *ill* look or aspect.
11. Rude; unpolished; as *ill* breeding; *ill* manners.
12. Not proper; not regular or legitimate; as an *ill* expression in grammar.

ILL, *n.* Wickedness; depravity; evil.

> Strong virtue, like strong nature, struggles still,
> Exerts itself and then throws off the *ill.* *Dryden.*

2. Misfortune; calamity; evil; disease; pain; whatever annoys or impairs happiness, or prevents success.

> Who can all sense of other's *ills* escape,
> Is but a brute at best in human shape. *Tate.*

ILL, *adv.* Not well; not rightly or perfectly. He is *ill* at ease.
2. Not easily; with pain or difficulty. He is *ill* able to sustain the burden.

> *Ill* bears the sex the youthful lovers' fate,
> When just approaching to the nuptial state. *Dryden.*

ILL, prefixed to participles of the present tense, and denoting evil or wrong, may be considered as a noun governed by the participle, or as making a part of a compound word; as an *ill meaning* man, an *ill designing* man, an *ill boding* hour; that is, a man meaning ill, an hour boding ill. It is more consonant, however, to the genius of our language, to treat these and similar words as compounds. In some cases, as before the participles of intransitive verbs, *ill must* be considered as a part of the compound, as in *ill-looking.* When used before the perfect participle, *ill* is to be considered as an adverb, or modifying word, or to be treated as a part of the compound; as in *ill-bred, ill-governed, ill-fated, ill-favored, ill-formed, ill-minded.* In these and all similar connections, it might be well to unite the two words in a compound by a hyphen. As *ill* may be prefixed to almost any participle, it is needless to attempt to collect a list of such words for insertion.

Il, prefixed to words beginning with *l*, stands for *in*, as used in the Latin language, and usually denotes a negation of the sense of the simple word, as *illegal*, not legal; or it denotes *to* or *on*, and merely augments or enforces the sense, as in *illuminate.*

ILLAB'ILE, *a.* [See *Labile.*] Not liable to fall or err; infallible. [*Not used.*] *Cheyne.*

ILLABIL'ITY, *n.* The quality of not being liable to err, fall or apostatize. [*Not used.*] *Cheyne.*

ILLAC'ERABLE, *a.* [See *Lacerate.*] That cannot be torn or rent.

ILLAPSE, *n.* *illaps'.* [See *Lapse.*] A sliding in; an immission or entrance of one thing into another. *Norris.*
2. A falling on; a sudden attack. *Thomson.*

ILLAQ'UEATE, *v. t.* [L. *illaqueo; in* and *laqueo*, to ensnare; *laqueus*, a snare.]
To ensnare; to entrap; to entangle; to catch. [*Little used.*] *More.*

ILLAQ'UEATED, *pp.* Ensnared.

ILLAQUEA'TION, *n.* The act of ensnaring; a catching or entrapping. [*Little used.*] *Brown.*
2. A snare.

ILLA'TION, *n.* [L. *illatio; in* and *latio*, a bearing; *latus*, from *fero.*]
An inference from premises; a conclusion; deduction. [*Little used.*] *Locke.*

IL'LATIVE, *a.* [See *Illation.*] Relating to illation; that may be inferred; as an *illative* consequence.
2. That denotes an inference; as an *illative* word or particle, as *then* and *therefore.* *Watts.*

IL'LATIVE, *n.* That which denotes illation or inference. *Bp. Hall.*

ILLAUD'ABLE, *a.* [See *Laudable.*] Not laudable; not worthy of approbation or commendation; as an *illaudable* motive or act.
2. Worthy of censure or dispraise.

ILLAUD'ABLY, *adv.* In a manner unworthy of praise; without deserving praise. *Broome.*

ILL-BRED, *a.* Not well bred; unpolite.

ILL-BREE'DING, *n.* Want of good breeding; unpoliteness.

ILL-CONDI''TIONED, *a.* [See *Condition.*] Being in bad order or state.

ILLE'CEBROUS, *a.* [L. *illecebrosus.*] Alluring; full of allurement. *Elyot.*

ILLE'GAL, *a.* [See *Legal.*] Not legal; unlawful; contrary to law; illicit; as an *illegal* act; *illegal* trade.

ILLEGAL'ITY, *n.* Contrariety to law; unlawfulness; as the *illegality* of trespass, or of false imprisonment.

ILLE'GALIZE, *v. t.* To render unlawful.

ILLE'GALLY, *adv.* In a manner contrary to law; unlawfully; as a man *illegally* imprisoned. *Blackstone.*

ILLEĠIBIL'ITY, *n.* The quality of being illegible.

ILLEĠ'IBLE, *a.* [See *Legible.*] That cannot be read; obscure or defaced so that the words cannot be known. It is a disgrace to a gentleman to write an *illegible* hand. The manuscripts found in the ruins of Herculaneum are mostly *illegible.*

ILLEĠ'IBLY, *adv.* In a manner not to be read; as a letter written *illegibly.*

ILLEĠIT'IMACY, *n.* [See *Legitimate.*]
1. The state of being born out of wedlock; the state of bastardy. *Blackstone.*
2. The state of being not genuine, or of legitimate origin.

ILLEĠIT'IMATE, *a.* [See *Legitimate.*]
1. Unlawfully begotten; born out of wedlock; spurious; as an *illegitimate* son or daughter.
2. Unlawful; contrary to law.
3. Not genuine; not of genuine origin; as an *illegitimate* inference.
4. Not authorized by good usage; as an *illegitimate* word.

ILLEĠIT'IMATE, *v. t.* To render illegitimate; to prove to be born out of wedlock; to bastardize. *Wotton.*

ILLEĠIT'IMATELY, *adv.* Not in wedlock; without authority.

ILLEĠITIMA'TION, *n.* The state of one not born in wedlock. *Bacon.*
2. Want of genuineness. *Martin.*

ILLEV'IABLE, *a.* [*in*, not, and Fr. *lever*, to raise or levy.] That cannot be levied or collected. *Hale.*

ILL'-FACED, *a.* Having an ugly face. *Hall.*

ILL-FA'VORED, *a.* [*ill* and *favored.*] Ugly; ill-looking; wanting beauty; deformed.

> *Ill-favored* and lean fleshed. Gen. xli.

ILL-FA'VOREDLY, *adv.* With deformity.
2. Roughly; rudely. *Howell.*

ILL-FA'VOREDNESS, *n.* Ugliness; deformity.

ILLIB'ERAL, *a.* [See *Liberal.*] Not liberal; not free or generous.
2. Not noble; not ingenuous; not catholic; of a contracted mind. Cold in charity; in religion, *illiberal.* *K. Charles.*
3. Not candid; uncharitable in judging.
4. Not generous; not munificent; sparing of gifts. *Woodward.*
5. Not becoming a well bred man. *Harris.*
6. Not pure; not well authorized or elegant; as *illiberal* words in Latin. [*Unusual.*] *Chesterfield.*

ILLIBERAL'ITY, *n.* Narrowness of mind; contractedness; meanness; want of catholic opinions.
2. Parsimony; want of munificence. *Bacon.*

ILLIB'ERALLY, *adv.* Ungenerously; uncandidly; uncharitably; disingenuously.
2. Parsimoniously.

ILLIC'IT, *a.* [L. *illicitus; in* and *licitus*, from *liceo*, to permit.]
Not permitted or allowed; prohibited; unlawful; as an *illicit* trade; *illicit* intercourse or connection.

ILLIC'ITLY, *adv.* Unlawfully.

ILLIC'ITNESS, *n.* Unlawfulness.

ILLIC'ITOUS, *a.* Unlawful.

ILLI'GHTEN, *v. t.* [See *Light*, *Lighten*.] To enlighten. [*Not in use.*] *Raleigh.*

ILLIM'ITABLE, *a.* [*in*, not, and *limit*, or L. *limes*.]

That cannot be limited or bounded; as the *illimitable* void. *Thomson.*

ILLIM'ITABLY, *adv.* Without possibility of being bounded.

2. Without limits.

ILLIM'ITED, *a.* [Fr. *illimité*; *in* and L. *limes*, a limit.]

Unbounded; not limited; interminable. *Bp. Hall.*

ILLIM'ITEDNESS, *n.* Boundlessness; the state of being without limits or restriction.

The absoluteness and *illimitedness* of his commission was much spoken of. *Clarendon.*

ILLINI''TION, *n.* [L. *illinitus*, *illinio*, to anoint; *in* and *lino*, to besmear.]

A thin crust of some extraneous substance formed on minerals.

It is sometimes disguised by a thin crust or *illinition* of black manganese. *Kirwan.*

ILLIT'ERACY, *n.* [from *illiterate*.] The state of being untaught or unlearned; want of a knowledge of letters; ignorance. *Encyc.*

ILLIT'ERATE, *a.* [L. *illiteratus*; *in* and *literatus*; from *litera*, a letter.]

Unlettered; ignorant of letters or books; untaught; unlearned; uninstructed in science; as an *illiterate* man, nation or tribe. *Wotton.*

ILLIT'ERATENESS, *n.* Want of learning; ignorance of letters, books or science. *Boyle.*

ILLIT'ERATURE, *n.* Want of learning. [*Little used.*] *Ayliffe.*

ILL-LI'VED, *a.* Leading a wicked life. [*Little used.*] *Bp. Hall.*

ILL-NA'TURE, *n.* [*ill* and *nature*.] Crossness; crabbedness; habitual bad temper, or want of kindness; fractiousness. *South.*

ILL-NA'TURED, *a.* Cross; crabbed; surly; intractable; of habitual bad temper; peevish; fractious. An *ill-natured* person may disturb the harmony of a whole parish.

2. That indicates ill-nature.

The *ill-natured* task refuse. *Addison.*

3. Intractable; not yielding to culture; as *ill-natured* land. [*Not legitimate.*] *Philips.*

ILL-NA'TUREDLY, *adv.* In a peevish or froward manner; crossly; unkindly.

ILL-NA'TUREDNESS, *n.* Crossness; want of a kind disposition.

ILL'NESS, *n.* [from *ill*.] Badness; unfavorableness; as the *illness* of the weather. [*Not used.*] *Locke.*

2. Disease; indisposition; malady; disorder of health; sickness. He has recovered from his *illness*.

3. Wickedness; iniquity; wrong moral conduct. *Shak.*

ILLOĠ'ICAL, *a.* [See *Logical*.] Ignorant or negligent of the rules of logic or correct reasoning; as an *illogical* disputant.

2. Contrary to the rules of logic or sound reasoning; as an *illogical* inference.

ILLOĠ'ICALLY, *adv.* In a manner contrary to the rules of correct reasoning.

ILLOĠ'ICALNESS, *n.* Contrariety to sound reasoning. *Hammond.*

ILL'STARRED, *a.* [*ill* and *star*.] Fated to be unfortunate. *Beddoes.*

ILL'-TRAINED, *a.* Not well trained or disciplined. *Milford.*

ILLU'DE, *v. t.* [L. *illudo*; *in* and *ludo*, to play. See *Ludicrous*.]

To play upon by artifice; to deceive; to mock; to excite hope and disappoint it.

ILLU'DED, *pp.* Deceived; mocked.

ILLU'DING, *ppr.* Playing on by artifice; deceiving.

ILLU'ME, ILLU'MINE, *v. t.* [Fr. *illuminer*; L. *illumino*; *in* and *lumino*, to enlighten, from *lumen*, light. See *Luminous*.]

1. To illuminate; to enlighten; to throw or spread light on; to make light or bright. *Milton.*

[*These words are used chiefly in poetry.*]

2. To enlighten, as the mind; to cause to understand.

3. To brighten; to adorn.

The mountain's brow,
Illum'd with fluid gold— *Thomson.*

ILLU'MINANT, *n.* That which illuminates or affords light. *Boyle.*

ILLU'MINATE, *v. t.* [See *Illume*.] To enlighten; to throw light on; to supply with light. [*This word is used in poetry or prose.*]

2. To adorn with festal lamps or bonfires.

3. To enlighten intellectually with knowledge or grace. Heb. x.

4. To adorn with pictures, portraits and other paintings; as, to *illuminate* manuscripts or books, according to ancient practice. *Encyc.*

5. To illustrate; to throw light on, as on obscure subjects. *Watts.*

ILLU'MINATE, *a.* Enlightened. *Bp. Hall.*

ILLU'MINATE, *n.* One of a sect of heretics pretending to possess extraordinary light and knowledge.

ILLU'MINATED, *pp.* Enlightened; rendered light or luminous; illustrated; adorned with pictures, as books.

ILLU'MINATING, *ppr.* Enlightening; rendering luminous or bright; illustrating; adorning with pictures.

ILLU'MINATING, *n.* The act, practice or art of adorning manuscripts and books by paintings.

ILLUMINA'TION, *n.* The act of illuminating or rendering luminous; the act of supplying with light.

2. The act of rendering a house or a town light, by placing lights at the windows, or in elevated situations, as a manifestation of joy; or the state of being thus rendered light.

3. That which gives light.

The sun—is an *illumination* created. *Raleigh.*

4. Brightness; splendor.

5. Infusion of intellectual light; an enlightening of the understanding by knowledge, or the mind by spiritual light.

6. The act, art or practice of adorning manuscripts and books with pictures. *Encyc.*

7. Inspiration; the special communication of knowledge to the mind by the Supreme Being.

Hymns and psalms—are framed by meditation beforehand, or by prophetical *illumination* are inspired. *Hooker.*

ILLU'MINATIVE, *a.* [Fr. *illuminatif*.] Having the power of giving light. *Digby.*

ILLU'MINATOR, *n.* He or that which illuminates or gives light.

2. One whose occupation is to decorate manuscripts and books with pictures, portraits and drawings of any kind. This practice began among the Romans, and was continued during the middle ages. The manuscripts containing portraits, pictures and emblematic figures, form a valuable part of the riches preserved in the principal libraries in Europe. *Encyc.*

From this word, by contraction, is formed *limner*.

ILLUMINEE', ILLUMINA'TI, *n.* A church term anciently applied to persons who had received baptism; in which ceremony they received a lighted taper, as a symbol of the faith and grace they had received by that sacrament. *Encyc.*

2. The name of a sect of heretics, who sprung up in Spain about the year 1575, and who afterward appeared in France. Their principal doctrine was, that by means of a sublime manner of prayer, they had attained to so perfect a state as to have no need of ordinances, sacraments and good works. *Encyc.*

3. The name given to certain associations of men in modern Europe, who combined to overthrow the existing religious institutions, and substitute reason, by which they expected to raise men and society to perfection. *Robison.*

ILLU'MINISM, *n.* The principles of the Illuminati.

ILLU'MINIZE, *v. t.* To initiate into the doctrines or principles of the Illuminati. *Am. Review.*

ILLU'SION, *n.* *s* as *z*. [Fr. *illusion*; L. *illusio*, from *illudo*, to *illude*.]

Deceptive appearance; false show, by which a person is or may be deceived, or his expectations disappointed; mockery.

Ye soft *illusions*, dear deceits, arise! *Pope.*

ILLU'SIVE, *a.* Deceiving by false show; deceitful; false.

While the fond soul,
Wrapt in gay visions of unreal bliss,
Still paints th' *illusive* form. *Thomson.*

ILLU'SIVELY, *adv.* By means of a false show.

ILLU'SIVENESS, *n.* Deception; false show. *Ash.*

ILLU'SORY, *a.* [Fr. *illusoire*, from L. *illusus*, *illudo*.]

Deceiving or tending to deceive by false appearances; fallacious. His offers were *illusory*.

ILLUS'TRATE, *v. t.* [Fr. *illustrer*; L. *illustro*; *in* and *lustro*, to illuminate. See *Luster*.]

1. To make clear, bright or luminous.

2. To brighten with honor; to make distinguished.

Matter to me of glory! whom their hate
Illustrates— *Milton.*

3. To brighten; to make glorious, or to display the glory of; as, to *illustrate* the perfections of God.

4. To explain or elucidate; to make clear, intelligible or obvious, what is dark or obscure; as, to *illustrate* a passage of Scripture by comments, or of a profane author by a gloss.

ILLUS'TRATED, *pp.* Made bright or glorious.

2. Explained; elucidated; made clear to the understanding.

ILLUS'TRATING, *ppr.* Making bright or glorious; rendering distinguished; elucidating.

ILLUSTRA'TION, *n.* The act of rendering bright or glorious.

2. Explanation; elucidation; a rendering clear what is obscure or abstruse. *Locke.*

ILLUS'TRATIVE, *a.* Having the quality of elucidating and making clear what is obscure; as an argument or simile *illustrative* of the subject. *Brown.*

2. Having the quality of rendering glorious, or of displaying glory.

ILLUS'TRATIVELY, *adv.* By way of illustration or elucidation. *Brown.*

ILLUS'TRATOR, *n.* One who illustrates or makes clear.

ILLUS'TRIOUS, *a.* [Fr. *illustre;* L. *illustris.*]

1. Conspicuous; distinguished by the reputation of greatness; renowned; eminent; as an *illustrious* general or magistrate; an *illustrious* prince.

2. Conspicuous; renowned; conferring honor; as *illustrious* actions.

3. Glorious; as an *illustrious* display of the divine perfections.

4. A title of honor.

ILLUS'TRIOUSLY, *adv.* Conspicuously; nobly; eminently; with dignity or distinction.

2. Gloriously; in a way to manifest glory. The redemption of man displays *illustriously* the justice as well as the benevolence of God.

ILLUS'TRIOUSNESS, *n.* Eminence of character; greatness; grandeur; glory.

ILLUXU'RIOUS, *a.* Not luxurious. *Drury.*

ILL-WILL', *n.* Enmity; malevolence.

ILL-WILL'ER, *n.* One who wishes ill to another.

I'M, contracted from *I am.*

IM, in composition, is usually the representative of the Latin *in;* *n* being changed to *m,* for the sake of easy utterance, before a labial, as in *imbibe, immense, impartial.* We use the same prefix in compounds not of Latin origin, as in *imbody, imbitter.* For *im,* the French write *em,* which we also use in words borrowed from their language.

IM'AGE, *n.* [Fr. *image;* L. *imago;* Sp. *imagen;* It. *image, immagine;* Ir. *iomaigh.*]

1. A representation or similitude of any person or thing, formed of a material substance; as an *image* wrought out of stone, wood or wax.

Whose is this *image* and superscription? Matt. xxii.

2. A statue.

3. An idol; the representation of any person or thing, that is an object of worship. The second commandment forbids the worship of *images.*

4. The likeness of any thing on canvas; a picture; a resemblance painted.

5. Any copy, representation or likeness. The child is the *image* of its mother.

6. Semblance; show; appearance.

The face of things a frightful *image* bears. *Dryden.*

7. An idea; a representation of any thing to the mind; a conception; a picture drawn by fancy.

Can we conceive
Image of aught delightful, soft or great? *Prior.*

8. In *rhetoric,* a lively description of any thing in discourse, which presents a kind of picture to the mind. *Encyc.*

9. In *optics,* the figure of any object, made by rays of light proceeding from the several points of it. Thus a mirror reflects the *image* of a person standing before it, as does water in a vessel or stream, when undisturbed.

IM'AGE, *v. t.* To imagine; to copy by the imagination; to form a likeness in the mind by the fancy or recollection.

And *image* charms he must behold no more. *Pope.*

IM'AGERY, *n. im'ajry.* Sensible representations, pictures, statues.

Rich carvings, portraitures and *imagery.* *Dryden.*

2. Show; appearance.

What can thy *imagery* and sorrow mean? *Prior.*

3. Forms of the fancy; false ideas; imaginary phantasms.

The *imagery* of a melancholic fancy— *Atterbury.*

4. Representations in writing or speaking; lively descriptions which impress the images of things on the mind; figures in discourse.

I wish there may be in this poem any instance of good *imagery.* *Dryden.*

5. Form; make.

IM'AGE-WORSHIP, *n.* The worship of images; idolatry.

IMAG'INABLE, *a.* [Fr. See *Imagine.*] That may be imagined or conceived. This point is proved with all *imaginable* clearness.

IMAG'INANT, *a.* Imagining; conceiving. [*Not used.*] *Bacon.*

IMAG'INARY, *a.* Existing only in imagination or fancy; visionary; fancied; not real.

Imaginary ills and fancied tortures. *Addison.*

IMAGINA'TION, *n.* [L. *imaginatio;* Fr. *imagination.*]

The power or faculty of the mind by which it conceives and forms ideas of things communicated to it by the organs of sense. *Encyc.*

Imagination I understand to be the representation of an individual thought. *Bacon.*

Our simple apprehension of corporeal objects, if present, is sense; if absent, is *imagination* [conception.] *Glanville.*

Imagination, in its proper sense, signifies a lively conception of objects of sight. It is distinguished from conception, as a part from a whole. *Reid.*

The business of conception is to present us with an exact transcript of what we have felt or perceived. But we have also a power of modifying our conceptions, by combining the parts of different ones so as to form new wholes of our own creation. I shall employ the word *imagination* to express this power. I apprehend this to be the proper sense of the word, if imagination be the power which gives birth to the productions of the poet and the painter. *Stewart.*

We would define *imagination* to be the will working on the materials of memory; not satisfied with following the order prescribed by nature, or suggested by accident, it selects the parts of different conceptions, or objects of memory, to form a whole more pleasing, more terrible, or more awful, than has ever been presented in the ordinary course of nature. *Ed. Encyc.*

The two latter definitions give the true sense of the word, as now understood.

2. Conception; image in the mind; idea.

Sometimes despair darkens all her *imaginations.* *Sidney.*

His *imaginations* were often as just as they were bold and strong. *Dennis.*

3. Contrivance; scheme formed in the mind; device.

Thou hast seen all their vengeance, and all their *imaginations* against me. Lam. iii.

4. Conceit; an unsolid or fanciful opinion.

We are apt to think that space, in itself, is actually boundless; to which *imagination,* the idea of space of itself leads us. *Locke.*

5. First motion or purpose of the mind. Gen. vi.

IMAG'INATIVE, *a.* [Fr. *imaginatif.*] That forms imaginations. *Taylor.*

2. Full of imaginations; fantastic. *Bacon.*

IMAG'INE, *v. t.* [Fr. *imaginer;* Sp. *imaginar;* L. *imaginor,* from *imago,* image.]

1. To form a notion or idea in the mind; to fancy. We can *imagine* the figure of a horse's head united to a human body.

In this sense, *fancy* is the more proper word.

2. To form ideas or representations in the mind, by modifying and combining our conceptions. *Stewart.*

3. To contrive in purpose; to scheme; to devise.

How long will ye *imagine* mischief against a man? Ps. lxii.

IMAG'INE, *v. i.* To conceive; to have a notion or idea. I cannot *imagine* how this should have happened.

IMAG'INED, *pp.* Formed in the mind; fancied; contrived.

IMAG'INER, *n.* One who forms ideas; one who contrives. *Bacon.*

IMAG'INING, *ppr.* Forming ideas in the mind; devising.

IM'AM, } *n.* A minister or priest among the
IM'AN, } Mohammedans.

Imbalm, Imbargo, Imbark, Imbase. See *Embalm, Embargo, Embark, Embase.*

IMBAN', *v. t.* [*in* and *ban.*] To excommunicate, in a civil sense; to cut off from the rights of man, or exclude from the common privileges of humanity. [*Not well authorized.*] *J. Barlow.*

IMBAND', *v. t.* [*in* and *band.*] To form into a band or bands.

Beneath full sails *imbanded* nations rise. *J. Barlow.*

IMBAND'ED, *pp.* Formed into a band or bands.

IMBANK', *v. t.* [*in* and *bank.*] To inclose with a bank; to defend by banks, mounds or dikes.

IMBANK'ED, *pp.* Inclosed or defended with a bank.

IMBANK'ING, *ppr.* Inclosing or surrounding with a bank.

IMBANK'MENT, *n.* The act of surrounding or defending with a bank.

2. Inclosure by a bank; the banks or mounds of earth that are raised to defend a place, especially against floods.

IMB'ARN, *v. t.* To deposit in a barn. [*Not used.*] *Herbert.*

IMB'ASTARDIZE, *v. t.* To bastardize, which see. *Milton.*

IMBE'AD, *v. t.* [*in* and *bead.*] To fasten with a bead.

> The strong bright bayonet *imbeaded* fast. *J. Barlow.*

IMBE'ADED, *pp.* Fastened with a bead.

IM'BECILE, *a. im'becil.* [L. *imbecillis;* Fr. *imbecile.* This seems to be a compound word, of which the primitive *bec*, is not now to be found or recognized.]

Weak; feeble; destitute of strength, either of body or of mind; impotent. *Barrow.*

IMBECIL'ITY, *n.* [L. *imbecillitas;* Fr. *imbecillité.*]

1. Want of strength; weakness; feebleness of body or of mind. We speak of the *imbecility* of the body or of the intellect, when either does not possess the usual strength and vigor that belongs to men, and which is necessary to a due performance of its functions. This may be natural, or induced by violence or disease.

2. Impotence of males; inability to procreate children.

IMBED', *v. t.* [*in* and *bed.*] To sink or lay in a bed; to place in a mass of earth, sand or other substance, so as to be partly inclosed.

IMBED'DED, *pp.* Laid or inclosed, as in a bed or mass of surrounding matter.

IMBED'DING, *ppr.* Laying, as in a bed.

IMBEL'LIC, *a.* [L. *in* and *bellicus.*] Not warlike or martial. [*Little used.*] *Junius.*

IMBENCH'ING, *n.* [*in* and *bench.*] A raised work like a bench. *Parkhurst.*

IMBI'BE, *v. t.* [L. *imbibo; in* and *bibo*, to drink; Fr. *imbiber.*]

1. To drink in; to absorb; as, a dry or porous body *imbibes* a fluid; a spunge *imbibes* moisture.

2. To receive or admit into the mind and retain; as, to *imbibe* principles; to *imbibe* errors. Imbibing in the mind always implies retention, at least for a time.

3. To imbue, as used by Newton; but he has not been followed.

IMBI'BED, *pp.* Drank in, as a fluid; absorbed; received into the mind and retained.

IMBI'BER, *n.* He or that which imbibes.

IMBI'BING, *ppr.* Drinking in; absorbing; receiving and retaining.

IMBIBI''TION, *n.* The act of imbibing. *Bacon.*

IMBIT'TER, *v. t.* [*in* and *bitter.*] To make bitter.

2. To make unhappy or grievous; to render distressing. The sins of youth often *imbitter* old age. Grief *imbitters* our enjoyments.

3. To exasperate; to make more severe, poignant or painful. The sorrows of true penitence are *imbittered* by a sense of our ingratitude to our Almighty Benefactor.

4. To exasperate; to render more violent or malignant; as, to *imbitter* enmity, anger, rage, passion, &c.

IMBIT'TERED, *pp.* Made unhappy or painful; exasperated.

IMBIT'TERING, *ppr.* Rendering unhappy or distressing; exasperating.

IMBOD'IED, *pp.* [See *Imbody.*] Formed into a body.

IMBOD'Y, *v. t.* [*in* and *body.*] To form into a body; to invest with matter; to make corporeal; as, to *imbody* the soul or spirit.

> An opening cloud reveals
> A heavenly form, *imbodied* and array'd
> With robes of light. *Dryden.*

2. To form into a body, collection or system; as, to *imbody* the laws of a state in a code.

3. To bring into a band, company, regiment, brigade, army, or other regular assemblage; to collect; as, to *embody* the forces of a nation.

> Then Clausus came, who led a numerous band
> Of troops *imbodied.* *Dryden.*

IMBOD'Y, *v. i.* To unite in a body, mass or collection; to coalesce. *Milton. Locke.*

IMBOD'YING, *ppr.* Forming into a body; investing with a corporeal body.

2. Collecting and uniting in a body.

IMBOIL', *v. i.* To effervesce. *Spenser.*

IMBŌLDEN, *v. t. imbōldn.* [*in* and *bold;* It. *imbaldanzire.*]

To encourage; to give confidence to.

> Nothing *imboldens* sin so much as mercy. *Shak.*

IMBŌLDEN, *pp.* Encouraged; having received confidence.

IMBŌLDENING, *ppr.* Encouraging; giving confidence.

IMBORD'ER, *v. t.* [*in* and *border.*] To furnish or inclose with a border; to adorn with a border.

2. To terminate; to bound. *Milton.*

IMBORD'ERED, *pp.* Furnished, inclosed or adorned with a border; bounded.

IMBORD'ERING, *ppr.* Furnishing, inclosing or adorning with a border; bounding.

IMBOSK', *v. t.* [It. *imboscare.* See *Bush.*] To conceal, as in bushes; to hide. *Milton.*

IMBŎ'SOM, *v. t. s* as *z.* [*in* and *bosom.*] To hold in the bosom; to cover fondly with the folds of one's garment.

2. To hold in nearness or intimacy.

> —The Father infinite,
> By whom in bliss *imbosomed* sat the Son. *Milton.*

3. To admit to the heart or affection; to caress.

> But glad desire, his late *imbosom'd* guest— *Sidney.*

4. To inclose in the midst; to surround.

> Villages *imbosomed* soft in trees— *Thomson.*

5. To inclose in the midst; to cover; as pearls *imbosomed* in the deep.

IMBŎ'SOMED, *pp.* Held in the bosom or to the breast; caressed; surrounded in the midst; inclosed; covered.

IMBŎ'SOMING, *ppr.* Holding in the bosom; caressing; holding to the breast; inclosing or covering in the midst.

IMBOUND', *v. t.* [*in* and *bound.*] To inclose in limits; to shut in. [*Little used.*] *Shak.*

IMBŌW, *v. t.* [*in* and *bow.*] To arch; to vault; as an *imbowed* roof. *Milton.*

2. To make of a circular form; as *imbowed* windows. *Bacon.*

IMBŌWED, *pp.* Arched; vaulted; made of a circular form.

IMBOW'ER, *v. t.* [*in* and *bower.*] To cover with a bower; to shelter with trees. *Thomson.*

IMBOW'ERED, *pp.* Covered with a bower; sheltered with trees.

IMBOW'ERING, *ppr.* Covering with a bower or with trees.

IMBŌWING, *ppr.* Arching; vaulting; making of a circular form.

IMBŌWMENT, *n.* An arch; a vault. *Bacon.*

IMBOX', *v. t.* To inclose in a box.

IMBRAN'GLE, *v. t.* To entangle. *Hudibras.*

IMBREE'D, *v. t.* To generate within.

IM'BRICATE, } *a.* [L. *imbricatus, imbrico*,
IM'BRICATED, } from *imbrex*, a tile.]

1. Bent and hollowed like a roof or gutter tile. *Johnson.*

2. In *botany*, lying over each other, like tiles on a roof; parallel, with a strait surface, and lying one over the other; as leaves in the bud. *Lee. Martyn.*

IMBRICA'TION, *n.* A concave indenture, like that of tiles; tiling. *Derham.*

IMBROWN', *v. t.* [*in* and *brown.*] To make brown; to darken; to obscure.

> The unpierc'd shade
> *Imbrown'd* the noon-tide bowers. *Milton.*

2. To darken the color of; to make dirty.

> The foot grows black that was with dirt *imbrown'd.* *Gay.*

3. To tan; to darken the complexion.

IMBROWN'ED, *pp.* Made brown; darkened; tanned.

IMBROWN'ING, *ppr.* Rendering brown; darkening; tanning.

IMBRUE, *v. t. imbru'.* [Gr. εμβρεχω, to moisten; εν and βρεχω. Hence it is allied to *embrocate*, and Sp. *embriagar*, to intoxicate. See *Ebriety, Brook* and *Rain.*]

1. To wet or moisten; to soak; to drench in a fluid, chiefly in blood.

> Whose arrows in my blood their wings *imbrue.* *Sandys.*

> Lucius pities the offenders,
> That would *imbrue* their hands in Cato's blood. *Addison.*

2. To pour out liquor. *Obs.* *Spenser.*

IMBRU'ED, *pp.* Wet; moistened; drenched.

IMBRU'ING, *ppr.* Wetting; moistening; drenching.

IMBRU'TE, *v. t.* [*in* and *brute.*] To degrade to the state of a brute; to reduce to brutality.

> —And mix with bestial slime
> This essence to incarnate and *imbrute.* *Milton.*

IMBRU'TE, *v. i.* To sink to the state of a brute. *Milton.*

IMBRU'TED, *pp.* Degraded to brutism.

IMBRU'TING, *ppr.* Reducing to brutishness.

IMBUE, *v. t. imbu'.* [L. *imbuo; in* and the root of Eng. *buck*, to buck cloth, that is, to dip, drench or steep in water.]

1. To tinge deeply; to dye; as, to *imbue* cloth. *Boyle.*

2. To tincture deeply; to cause to imbibe; as, to *imbue* the minds of youth with good principles.

IMBU'ED, *pp.* Tinged; dyed; tinctured.

IMBU'ING, *ppr.* Tinging; dyeing; tincturing deeply.

IMITABIL'ITY, *n.* [See *Imitable, Imitate.*] The quality of being imitable. *Norris.*

IM'ITABLE, *a.* [Fr. from L. *imitabilis.* See *Imitate.*]

1. That may be imitated or copied. Let us follow our Savior in all his *imitable* conduct and traits of character. There are some works of the ancients that are hardly *imitable.* The dignified style of Johnson is scarcely *imitable.*
2. Worthy of imitation.

IMI'TATE, *v. t.* [Fr. *imiter;* Sp. Port. *imitar;* It. *imitare;* L. *imitor;* allied perhaps to Gr. ὁμος, similar, equal.]

1. To follow in manners; to copy in form, color or quality. We *imitate* another in dress or manners; we *imitate* a statue, a painting, a sound, an action, when we make or do that which resembles it. We should seek the best models to *imitate,* and in morals and piety, it is our duty to *imitate* the example of our Savior. But as we cannot always make an exact similitude of the original, hence,
2. To attempt or endeavor to copy or resemble; as, to *imitate* the colors of the rainbow, or any of the beauties of nature. Cicero appears to have *imitated* the Greek orators.
3. To counterfeit.

> This hand appear'd a shining sword to wield,
> And that sustain'd an *imitated* shield. *Dryden.*

4. To pursue the course of a composition, so as to use like images and examples. *Johnson. Gay.*

IM'ITATED, *pp.* Followed; copied.

IM'ITATING, *ppr.* Following in manner; copying.

IMITA'TION, *n.* [Fr. from L. *imitatio; imitor,* to imitate.]

1. The act of following in manner, or of copying in form; the act of making the similitude of any thing, or of attempting a resemblance. By the *imitation* of bad men or of evil examples, we are apt to contract vicious habits. In the *imitation* of natural forms and colors, we are often unsuccessful. *Imitation* in music, says Rousseau, is a reiteration of the same air, or of one which is similar, in several parts where it is repeated by one after the other, either in unison, or at the distance of a fourth, a fifth, a third, or any interval whatever. *Imitation* in oratory, is an endeavor to resemble a speaker or writer in the qualities which we propose to ourselves as patterns. *Encyc.*
2. That which is made or produced as a copy; likeness; resemblance. We say, a thing is a true *imitation* of nature.
3. A method of translating, in which modern examples and illustrations are used for ancient, or domestic for foreign, or in which the translator not only varies the words and sense, but forsakes them as he sees occasion. *Johnson. Dryden.*

IM'ITATIVE, *a.* Inclined to follow in manner; as, man is an *imitative* being.

2. Aiming at resemblance; that is used in the business of forming resemblances. Painting is an *imitative* art.
3. Formed after a model, pattern or original.

> This temple, less in form, with equal grace,
> Was *imitative* of the first in Thrace. *Dryden.*

Imitative music, is that which is intended to resemble some natural operation, the passions, and the like. *Busby.*

IM'ITATOR, *n.* One that follows in manners or deportment.

2. One that copies, or attempts to make the resemblance of any thing.

IMITA'TORSHIP, *n.* The office or state of an imitator. *Marston.*

IMMAC'ULATE, *n.* [L. *immaculatus; in* and *macula,* a spot.]

1. Spotless; pure; unstained; undefiled; without blemish; as *immaculate* reputation; *immaculate* thoughts. Our Savior has set us an example of an *immaculate* life and conversation.
2. Pure; limpid; not tinged with impure matter; as an *immaculate* fountain. *Shak.*

Immaculate conception, the conception of our Savior by the virgin Mary.

IMMAC'ULATELY, *adv.* With spotless purity.

IMMAC'ULATENESS, *n.* Spotless purity.

IMMA'ILED, *a.* Wearing mail or armor. *Browne.*

IMMAL'LEABLE, *a.* [*in* and *malleable.*] Not malleable; that cannot be extended by hammering. *Med. Repos.*

IMMAN'ACLE, *v. t.* [*in* and *manacle.*] To put manacles on; to fetter or confine; to restrain from free action. *Milton.*

IMMAN'ACLED, *pp.* Fettered; confined.

IMMAN'ACLING, *ppr.* Fettering; confining.

IMMA'NE, *a.* [L. *immanis.*] Vast; huge; very great. [*Little used.*]

IMMA'NELY, *adv.* Monstrously; cruelly. *Milton.*

IM'MANENCY, *n.* Internal dwelling. *Pearson.*

IM'MANENT, *a.* [L. *in* and *manens, maneo,* to abide.] Inherent; intrinsic; internal. *South.*

IMMAN'ITY, *n.* [L. *immanitas.*] Barbarity; savageness. *Shak.*

IMMARCES'SIBLE, *a.* [L. *in* and *marcesco,* to fade.] Unfading. *Dict.*

IMM'ARTIAL, *a.* [*in* and *martial.*] Not martial; not warlike. *Chapman.*

IMM'ASK, *v. t.* [*in* and *mask.*] To cover, as with a mask; to disguise. *Shak.*

IMM'ASKED, *pp.* Covered; masked.

IMM'ASKING, *ppr.* Covering; disguising.

IMMATCH'ABLE, *a.* That cannot be matched; peerless.

IMMATE'RIAL, *a.* [Fr. *immateriel; in* and *material.*]

1. Incorporeal; not material; not consisting of matter; as *immaterial* spirits. The mind or soul is *immaterial.*
2. Unimportant; without weight; not material; of no essential consequence. *Melmoth. Aikin. Hayley. Ruffhead.*

IMMATE'RIALISM, *n.* The doctrine of the existence or state of immaterial substances or spiritual beings.

IMMATE'RIALIST, *n.* One who professes immateriality. *Swift.*

IMMATERIAL'ITY, *n.* The quality of being immaterial, or not consisting of matter; destitution of matter; as the *immateriality* of the soul.

IMMATE'RIALIZED, *a.* Rendered or made immaterial. *Glanville.*

IMMATE'RIALLY, *adv.* In a manner not depending on matter.

2. In a manner unimportant.

IMMATE'RIALNESS, *n.* The state of being immaterial; immateriality.

IMMATE'RIATE, *a.* Not consisting of matter; incorporeal; immaterial. [*Little used.*] *Bacon.*

IMMATU'RE, *a.* [L. *immaturus; in* and *maturus.*]

1. Not mature or ripe; unripe; that has not arrived to a perfect state; *applied to fruit.*
2. Not perfect; not brought to a complete state; as *immature* plans or counsels.
3. Hasty; too early; that comes before the natural time. *Taylor.*

[In this sense, *premature* is generally used.]

IMMATU'RELY, *adv.* Too soon; before ripeness or completion; before the natural time.

IMMATU'RENESS, } *n.* Unripeness; in-
IMMATU'RITY, } completeness; the state of a thing which has not arrived to perfection.

IMMEABIL'ITY, *n.* [L. *in* and *meo,* to pass.] Want of power to pass. *Arbuthnot.*

The proper sense is, the quality of not being *permeable,* or not affording a passage through the pores. [*Little used.*]

IMMEAS'URABLE, *a. immezh'urable.* [*in* and *measure.*] That cannot be measured; immense; indefinitely extensive; as an *immeasurable* distance or space; an *immeasurable* abyss. *Milton. Addison.*

IMMEAS'URABLY, *adv.* To an extent not to be measured; immensely; beyond all measure. *Milton.*

IMMEAS'URED, *a.* Exceeding common measure.

IMMECHAN'ICAL, *a.* [*in* and *mechanical.*] Not consonant to the laws of mechanics. *Cheyne.*

IMME'DIACY, *n.* [from *immediate.*] Power of acting without dependence. *Shak.*

IMME'DIATE, *a.* [Fr. *immediat;* It. *immediato;* L. *in* and *medius,* middle.]

1. Proximate; acting without a medium, or without the intervention of another cause or means; producing its effect by its own direct agency. An *immediate* cause is that which is exerted directly in producing its effect, in opposition to a *mediate* cause, or one more remote.
2. Not acting by second causes; as the *immediate* will of God. *Abbot.*
3. Instant; present; without the intervention of time. We must have an *immediate* supply of bread.

> *Immediate* are my needs— *Shak.*
> Death—inflicted—by an *immediate* stroke. *Milton.*

IMME'DIATELY, *adv.* Without the intervention of any other cause or event; opposed to *mediately.*

> The transfer, whether accepted *immediately* by himself, or *mediately* by his agent, vests in him the property. *Anon.*

2. Instantly; at the present time; without delay, or the intervention of time.

> And Jesus put forth his hand, and touched him, saying, I will, be thou clean. And *immediately* his leprosy was cleansed. Matt. viii.

IMME'DIATENESS, *n.* Presence with regard to time.

2. Exemption from second or intervening causes.

IMMED'ICABLE, *a.* [L. *immedicabilis; in* and *medicabilis*, from *medico*, to heal.] Not to be healed; incurable. *Milton.*

IMMELO'DIOUS, *a.* Not melodious. *Drummond.*

IMMEM'ORABLE, *a.* [L. *immemorabilis; in* and *memorabilis.* See *Memory.*]
Not to be remembered; not worth remembering. *Johnson.*

IMMEMO'RIAL, *a.* [Fr. from L. *in* and *memor, memoria.*]
Beyond memory; an epithet given to time or duration, &c., whose beginning is not remembered, or cannot be traced and ascertained; as when it is said a man has possessed an estate in fee from time *immemorial*, or time out of mind. Such possession constitutes *prescription*, or *prescriptive right.* So we speak of *immemorial* use, custom or practice. In England, a thing is said to be *immemorial*, when it commenced before the reign of Edward II.

IMMEMO'RIALLY, *adv.* Beyond memory. *Bentley.*

IMMENSE, *a. immens'.* [Fr. from L. *immensus; in* and *mensus, metior*, to measure.]
1. Unlimited; unbounded; infinite.

> O goodness infinite! goodness *immense!* *Milton.*

2. Vast in extent; very great; as an *immense* distance.
3. Huge in bulk; very large; as the *immense* body of Jupiter.

IMMENSELY, *adv. immens'ly.* Infinitely; without limits or measure.
2. Vastly; very greatly.

IMMENS'ITY, *n.* Unlimited extension; an extent not to be measured; infinity.

> By the power we find in ourselves of repeating, as often as we will, any idea of space, we get the idea of *immensity.* *Locke.*

2. Vastness in extent or bulk; greatness.

IMMENSURABIL'ITY, *n.* [from *immensurable.*]
The quality of not being capable of measure; impossibility to be measured.

IMMEN'SURABLE, *a.* [L. *in* and *mensurabilis*, from *mensura*, measure; *mensus, metior.*] Not to be measured; immeasurable.

> The law of nature—a term of *immensurable* extent. *Ward.*

IMMEN'SURATE, *a.* Unmeasured. *W. Mountagu.*

IMMERGE, *v. t. immerj'.* [L. *immergo; in* and *mergo*, to plunge.]
1. To plunge into or under a fluid. [See *Immerse*, which is generally used.]
2. *v. i.* To enter the light of the sun, as a star, or the shadow of the earth, as the moon.

IMMER'IT, *n.* Want of worth. [*Not used.*]

IMMER'ITED, *a.* Unmerited. [*Not used.*]

IMMER'ITOUS, *a.* Undeserving. [*Not used.*]

IMMERSE, *v. t. immers'.* [L. *immersus*, from *immergo; in* and *mergo*, to plunge.]
1. To put under water or other fluid; to plunge; to dip.
2. To sink or cover deep; to cover wholly; as, to be *immersed* in a wood. *Dryden.*
3. To plunge; to overwhelm; to involve; to engage deeply; as, to *immerse* in business or cares.

> It is impossible for a man to have a lively hope in another life, and yet be deeply *immersed* in the enjoyment of this. *Atterbury.*

IMMERS'ED, *pp.* Put into a fluid; plunged; deeply engaged; enveloped in the light of the sun, as a star, or in the shadow of the earth, as the moon.

IMMERS'ING, *ppr.* Plunging into a fluid; dipping; overwhelming; deeply engaging.

IMMER'SION, *n.* The act of putting into a fluid below the surface; the act of plunging into a fluid till covered.
2. The state of sinking into a fluid.
3. The state of being overwhelmed or deeply engaged; as an *immersion* in the affairs of life. *Atterbury.*
4. In *astronomy*, the act of entering into the light of the sun, as a star, so as to be enveloped and invisible to the eye; or the state of being so enveloped. Also, the entrance of the moon into the shadow of the earth, at the commencement of an eclipse; or the state of being enveloped in the shadow. It is opposed to *emersion.*
The time when a star or planet is so near the sun as to be invisible; also, the moment when the moon begins to be darkened, and to enter the shadow of the earth. *Encyc.*

IMMESH', *v. t.* [*in* and *mesh.*] To entangle in the meshes of a net, or in a web. Observe whether the fly is completely *immeshed.* The spider used his efforts to *immesh* the scorpion. *Goldsmith.*

IMMESH'ED, *pp.* Entangled in meshes or webs.

IMMESH'ING, *ppr.* Entangling in meshes or webs.

IMMETHOD'ICAL, *a.* [*in* and *methodical.* See *Method.*]
Having no method; without systematic arrangement; without order or regularity; confused. *Addison.*

IMMETHOD'ICALLY, *adv.* Without order or regularity; irregularly.

IMMETHOD'ICALNESS, *n.* Want of method; confusion.

IM'MIGRANT, *n.* A person that removes into a country for the purpose of permanent residence.

IM'MIGRATE, *v. i.* [L. *immigro; in* and *migro*, to migrate.]
To remove into a country for the purpose of permanent residence. [See *Emigrate.*] *Belknap.*

IMMIGRA'TION, *n.* The passing or removing into a country for the purpose of permanent residence.

IM'MINENCE, *n.* [L. *imminentia, immineo*, to hang over.]
Properly, a hanging over, but used by Shakspeare for impending evil or danger. [*Little used.*]

IM'MINENT, *a.* [L. *imminens*, from *immineo*, to hang over; *in* and *minor*, to threaten. See *Menace.*]
Literally, shooting over; hence, hanging over; impending; threatening; near; appearing as if about to fall on; *used of evils;* as *imminent* danger; *imminent* judgments, evils or death. *Hooker. Milton.*

IMMIN'GLE, *v. t.* [*in* and *mingle.*] To mingle; to mix; to unite with numbers. *Thomson.*

IMMIN'GLED, *pp.* Mixed; mingled.

IMMIN'GLING, *ppr.* Mixing; mingling.

IMMINU'TION, *n.* [L. *imminutio, imminuo; in* and *minuo*, to lessen.] A lessening; diminution; decrease. *Ray.*

IMMISCIBIL'ITY, *n.* [L. *immisceo; in* and *misceo*, to mix.] Incapacity of being mixed.

IMMIS'CIBLE, *a.* [*in* and *miscible.*] Not capable of being mixed. *Med. Repos.*

IMMIS'SION, *n.* [L. *immissio, immitto; in* and *mitto*, to send.]
The act of sending or thrusting in; injection; contrary to *emission.*

IMMIT', *v. t.* [L. *immitto; in* and *mitto*, to send.] To send in; to inject. *Greenhill.*

IMMIT'IGABLE, *a.* [*in* and *mitigate.*] That cannot be mitigated or appeased. *Harris.*

IMMIX', *v. t.* [*in* and *mix.*] To mix; to mingle.

IMMIX'ABLE, *a.* Not capable of being mixed. *Wilkins.*

IMMIX'ED, } IMMIXT', } *a.* Unmixed. *Herbert.*

IMMOBIL'ITY, *n.* [Fr. *immobilité;* L. *immobilitas*, from *immobilis; in* and *mobilis*, from *moveo*, to move.]
Unmovableness; fixedness in place or state; resistance to motion. *Arbuthnot.*

IMMOD'ERACY, *n.* Excess. *Brown.*

IMMOD'ERATE, *a.* [L. *immoderatus; in* and *moderatus.* See *Moderate.*]
Exceeding just or usual bounds; not confined to suitable limits; excessive; extravagant; unreasonable; as *immoderate* demands; *immoderate* passions, cares or grief.

IMMOD'ERATELY, *adv.* Excessively; to an undue degree; unreasonably; as, to weep *immoderately.*

IMMOD'ERATENESS, *n.* Excess; extravagance. *Shelford.*

IMMOD'ERATION, *n.* Excess; want of moderation. *Hammond.*

IMMOD'EST, *a.* [Fr. *immodeste;* L. *immodestus; in* and *modestus*, modest. See the latter.]
1. Literally, not limited to due bounds. Hence, in a general sense, immoderate; exorbitant; unreasonable; arrogant.
2. Appropriately, wanting in the reserve or restraint which decency requires; wanting in decency and delicacy. It is *immodest* to treat superiors with the familiarity that is customary among equals.
3. Wanting in chastity; unchaste; lewd; as an *immodest* female.
4. Impure; indelicate; as an *immodest* thought. *Dryden.*
5. Obscene; as an *immodest* word.

IMMOD'ESTLY, *adv.* Without due reserve; indecently; unchastely; obscenely.

IMMOD'ESTY, *n.* [L. *immodestia.*] Want of modesty; indecency; unchastity.
2. Want of delicacy or decent reserve.

IM'MOLATE, *v. t.* [Fr. *immoler;* L. *immolo*, to sacrifice; *in* and *mola*, meal sprinkled with salt, which was thrown on the head of the victim.]
1. To sacrifice; to kill, as a victim offered in sacrifice. *Boyle.*
2. To offer in sacrifice.

Now *immolate* the tongues and mix the wine. *Pope.*

IM'MOLATED, *pp.* Sacrificed; offered in sacrifice.

From the same altar on which the small states shall be *immolated,* will rise the smoke of sacrificed liberty, and despotism must be the dreadful successor. *U. Tracy.*

IM'MOLATING, *ppr.* Sacrificing; offering, as a victim.

IMMOLA'TION, *n.* The act of sacrificing. *Brown.*

2. A sacrifice offered.

IM'MOLATOR, *n.* One who offers in sacrifice.

IMMO'MENT, *a.* Trifling. [*Not English.*] *Shak.*

IMMOMENT'OUS, *a.* Unimportant. *Seward.*

IMMOR'AL, *a.* [*in* and *moral.*] Inconsistent with moral rectitude; contrary to the moral or divine law; wicked; unjust; dishonest; vicious. Every action is *immoral* which contravenes any divine precept, or which is contrary to the duties which men owe to each other.

2. Wicked or unjust in practice; vicious; dishonest; as an *immoral* man. Every man who violates a divine law or a social duty, is *immoral,* but we particularly apply the term to a person who habitually violates the laws.

IMMORAL'ITY, *n.* Any act or practice which contravenes the divine commands or the social duties. Injustice, dishonesty, fraud, slander, profaneness, gaming, intemperance, lewdness, are *immoralities.* All crimes are immoralities; but *crime* expresses more than *immorality.*

IMMOR'ALLY, *adv.* Wickedly; viciously; in violation of law or duty.

IMMORIG'EROUS, *a.* [Low L. *immoriger.*] Rude; uncivil. *Stackhouse.*

IMMORIG'EROUSNESS, *n.* Rudeness; disobedience. *Bp. Taylor.*

IMMOR'TAL, *a.* [L. *immortalis.* See *Mortal.*]

1. Having no principle of alteration or corruption; exempt from death; having life or being that shall never end; as an *immortal* soul.

To the King eternal, *immortal,* invisible, the only wise God, be honor and glory forever. 1 Tim. i.

2. Never ending; everlasting; continual.

I have
Immortal longings in me. *Shak.*

3. Perpetual; having unlimited existence. A corporation is called an *immortal* being.

4. Destined to live in all the ages of this world; imperishable; as *immortal* fame. So Homer is called the *immortal* bard.

IMMORTAL'ITY, *n.* The quality of never ceasing to live or exist; exemption from death and annihilation; life destined to endure without end; as the *immortality* of the human soul.

—Jesus Christ, who hath abolished death, and hath brought life and *immortality* to light through the gospel. 2 Tim. i.

2. Exemption from oblivion.

3. Perpetuity; existence not limited; as the *immortality* of a corporation. *J. Marshall.*

IMMORTALIZA'TION, *n.* The act of immortalizing.

IMMOR'TALIZE, *v. t.* [Fr. *immortaliser;* Sp. *immortalizar.*]

1. To render immortal; to make perpetual; to cause to live or exist while the world shall endure. The Iliad has *immortalized* the name of Homer.

Alexander had no Homer to *immortalize* his guilty name. *T. Dawes.*

2. To exempt from oblivion; to make perpetual.

IMMOR'TALIZE, *v. i.* To become immortal. [*Not in use.*] *Pope.*

IMMOR'TALIZED, *pp.* Rendered immortal or perpetual.

IMMOR'TALIZING, *ppr.* Making immortal or perpetual.

IMMOR'TALLY, *adv.* With endless existence; with exemption from death.

IMMORTIFICA'TION, *n.* [*in* and *mortification.*] Want of subjection of the passions. *Bp. Taylor.*

IMMÖVABIL'ITY, *n.* Stedfastness that cannot be moved or shaken.

IMMÖV'ABLE, *a.* [*in* and *movable.*] That cannot be moved from its place; as an *immovable* foundation.

2. Not to be moved from a purpose; stedfast; fixed; that cannot be induced to change or alter; as a man who remains *immovable.*

3. That cannot be altered or shaken; unalterable; unchangeable; as an *immovable* purpose or resolution.

4. That cannot be affected or moved; not impressible; not susceptible of compassion or tender feelings; unfeeling. *Dryden.*

5. Fixed; not liable to be removed; permanent in place; as *immovable* estate. *Blackstone. Ayliffe.*

6. Not to be shaken or agitated.

IMMÖV'ABLENESS, *n.* The quality of being immovable.

IMMÖV'ABLY, *adv.* In a manner not to be moved from its place or purpose; or in a manner not to be shaken; unalterably; unchangeably. *Immovably* firm to their duty; *immovably* fixed or established.

IMMUND', *a.* [L. *immundus.*] Unclean.

IMMUNDIC'ITY, *n.* Uncleanness. *Mountagu.*

IMMU'NITY, *n.* [Fr. *immunité;* L. *immunitas,* from *immunis,* free, exempt; *in* and *munus,* charge, office, duty.]

1. Freedom or exemption from obligation. To be exempted from observing the rites or duties of the church, is an *immunity.*

2. Exemption from any charge, duty, office, tax or imposition; a particular privilege; as the *immunities* of the free cities of Germany; the *immunities* of the clergy.

3. Freedom; as an *immunity* from error. *Dryden.*

IMMU'RE, *v. t.* [Norm. *emmurrer,* to wall in; Sw. *inmura;* L. *in* and *murus,* a wall.]

1. To inclose within walls; to shut up; to confine; as, to *immure* nuns in cloisters. The student *immures* himself voluntarily.

2. To wall; to surround with walls.

Lysimachus *immured* it with a wall. [*Not usual.*] *Sandys.*

3. To imprison. *Denham.*

IMMU'RE, *n.* A wall. [*Not used.*] *Shak.*

IMMU'RED, *pp.* Confined within walls.

IMMU'SICAL, *a.* [*in* and *musical.*] Not musical; inharmonious; not accordant; harsh. *Bacon. Brown.*

IMMUTABIL'ITY, *n.* [Fr. *immutabilité;* L. *immutabilitas; in* and *mutabilis,* mutable, from *muto,* to change.]

Unchangeableness; the quality that renders change or alteration impossible; invariableness. *Immutability* is an attribute of God.

IMMU'TABLE, *a.* [L. *immutabilis; in* and *mutabilis.*]

Unchangeable; invariable; unalterable; not capable or susceptible of change.

That by two *immutable* things, in which it was impossible for God to lie, we might have strong consolation. Heb. vi.

IMMU'TABLENESS, *n.* Unchangeableness; immutability.

IMMU'TABLY, *adv.* Unchangeably; unalterably; invariably; in a manner that admits of no change. *Boyle.*

IMMU'TATE, *a.* [L. *immutatus.*] Unchanged. *Lee.*

IMMUTA'TION, *n.* [L. *immutatio.*] Change; alteration. *More.*

IMP, *n.* [W. *imp,* a shoot or cion; Sw. *ymp,* Dan. *ympe,* id.]

1. A son; offspring; progeny.

The tender *imp* was weaned. *Fairfax.*
A lad of life, an *imp* of fame. *Shak.*

2. A subaltern or puny devil. *Hooker. Milton.*

IMP, *v. t.* [W. *impiaw,* G. *impfen,* Sw. *ympa,* Dan. *ymper,* to engraft; D. *ent,* a graft; *enten,* to engraft.]

1. To graft. *Chaucer.*

2. To lengthen; to extend or enlarge by something inserted or added; a term originally used by falconers, who repair a hawk's wing by adding fethers.

Imp out our drooping country's broken wings. *Shak.*

—The false north displays
Her broken league to *imp* her serpent wings. *Milton.*

This verb is, I believe, used only in poetry.

IMPA'CABLE, *a.* [L. *in* and *paco,* to appease.]

Not to be appeased or quieted. *Spenser.*

IMPACT', *v. t.* [L. *impactus,* from *impingo; in* and *pango,* to drive.]

To drive close; to press or drive firmly together. *Woodward.*

IM'PACT, *n.* Touch; impression. *Darwin.*

IMPACT'ED, *pp.* Driven hard; made close by driving. *Woodward.*

IMPA'INT, *v. t.* To paint; to adorn with colors. *Shak.*

IMPA'IR, *v. t.* [Fr. *empirer;* Sp. *empeorar;* Port. *empeiorar,* from *peior,* worse, Sp. *peor,* Fr. *pire,* from L. *pejor.*]

1. To make worse; to diminish in quantity, value or excellence. An estate is *impaired* by extravagance or neglect. The profligate *impairs* his estate and his reputation. Imprudence *impairs* a man's usefulness.

2. To weaken; to enfeeble. The constitution is *impaired* by intemperance, by infirmity and by age. The force of evidence may be *impaired* by the suspicion of interest in the witness.

IMPA'IR, *v. i.* To be lessened or worn out. [*Little used.*] *Spenser.*

IM'PAIR, *a.* [L. *impar,* unequal.] In *crystalography,* when a different number of faces is presented by the prism, and by each summit; but the three numbers follow no law of progression. *Cleaveland.*

IMPA'IR, } *n.* Diminution; decrease;
IMPA'IRMENT, } injury. [*Not used.*] *Brown.*

IMPA'IRED, *pp.* Diminished; injured; weakened.

IMPA'IRER, *n.* He or that which impairs. *Warburton.*

IMPA'IRING, *ppr.* Making worse; lessening; injuring; enfeebling.

IMPAL'ATABLE, *a.* Unpalatable. [*Little used.*]

IMPA'LE, *v. t.* [L. *in* and *palus*, a pole, a stake.]
1. To fix on a stake; to put to death by fixing on an upright sharp stake. [See *Empale.*]
2. To inclose with stakes, posts or palisades.
3. In *heraldry*, to join two coats of arms pale-wise. *Encyc.*

IMPAL'LID, *v. t.* To make pallid or pale. [*Not in use.*] *Feltham.*

IMP'ALM, *v. t.* *imp'am.* [L. *in* and *palma*, the hand.]
To grasp; to take in the hand. *J. Barlow.*

IMPALPABIL'ITY, *n.* The quality of not being palpable, or perceptible by the touch. *Jortin.*

IMPAL'PABLE, *a.* [Fr. from L. *in* and *palpo*, to feel. [See *Palpable.*]
Not to be felt; that cannot be perceived by the touch; as an *impalpable* powder, whose parts are so minute that they cannot be distinguished by the senses, particlarly by feeling. *Encyc.*
2. Not coarse or gross. *Warton.*

IMPAL'SY, *v. t.* *s* as *z.* [*in* and *palsy.*] To strike with palsy; to paralize; to deaden.

IM'PANATE, *a.* [L. *in* and *panis*, bread.] Embodied in bread. *Cranmer.*

IM'PANATE, *v. t.* To embody with bread. *Waterland.*

IMPANA'TION, *n.* The supposed substantial presence of the body and blood of Christ, with the substance of the bread and wine, after consecration, in the eucharist; a tenet of the Lutheran church; otherwise called *consubstantiation.* *Encyc.*

IMPAN'NEL, *v. t.* [*in* and *pannel.*] To write or enter the names of a jury in a list or on a piece of parchment, called a *pannel;* to form, complete or enroll a list of jurors in a court of justice.

IMPAN'NELED, *pp.* Having the names entered in a pannel; formed, as a jury.

IMPAN'NELING, *ppr.* Writing the names on a pannel; forming, as a jury.

IMPAR'ADISE, *v. t.* [It. *imparadisare; in* and *paradise.*]
To put in a place of felicity; to make happy.

IMPAR'ADISED, *pp.* Placed in a condition resembling that of paradise; made happy.

IMPAR'ADISING, *ppr.* Making very happy.

IMPAR'ALLELED, *a.* Unparalleled. [*Not used.*] *Burnet.*

IMPARASYLLAB'IC, *a.* [L. *in*, *par*, and *syllaba.*]
Not consisting of an equal number of syllables. An *imparasyllabic* noun is one which has not the same number of syllables in all the cases; as *lapis, lapidis; mens, mentis.* *Bryant.*

IMP'ARDONABLE, *a.* Unpardonable. *South.*

IMPAR'ITY, *n.* [*in* and *parity;* L. *par*, equal.]
1. Inequality; disproportion. *Bacon.*
2. Oddness; indivisibility into equal parts. *Brown.*
3. Difference of degree, rank or excellence *Sancroft.*

IMP'ARK, *v. t.* [*in* and *park.*] To inclose for a park; to make a park by inclosure; to sever from a common. *Johnson.*

IMP'ARL, *v. i.* [Norm. *emperler; in* and Fr. *parler*, to speak.]
To hold mutual discourse; appropriately, in law, to have licence to settle a lawsuit amicably; to have delay for mutual adjustment. *Blackstone.*

IMP'ARLANCE, *n.* Properly, leave for mutual discourse; appropriately, in law, the licence or privilege of a defendant, granted on motion, to have delay of trial, to see if he can settle the matter amicably by talking with the plaintiff, and thus to determine what answer he shall make to the plaintiff's action. Hence,
2. The continuance of a cause till another day, or from day to day. *Blackstone.*

IMPARSONEE', *a.* A *parson imparsonee*, is a parson presented, instituted and inducted into a rectory, and in full possession. *Blackstone.*

IMP'ART, *v. t.* [L. *impertior; in* and *partio*, to divide; from *pars*, a part.]
1. To give, grant or communicate; to bestow on another a share or portion of something; as, to *impart* a portion of provisions to the poor.
2. To grant; to give; to confer; as, to *impart* honor or favor.
3. To communicate the knowledge of something; to make known; to show by words or tokens.

> Gentle lady,
> When first I did *impart* my love to you—
> *Shak.* *Milton.*

IMP'ARTANCE, *n.* Communication of a share; grant.

IMPARTA'TION, *n.* The act of imparting or conferring. [*Not much used.*] *Chauncey.*

IMP'ARTED, *pp.* Communicated; granted; conferred.

IMP'ARTIAL, *a.* [*in* and *partial*, from *part*, L. *pars.*]
1. Not partial; not biased in favor of one party more than another; indifferent; unprejudiced; disinterested; as an *impartial* judge or arbitrator.
2. Not favoring one party more than another; equitable; just; as an *impartial* judgment or decision; an *impartial* opinion.

IMP'ARTIALIST, *n.* One who is impartial. [*Little used.*] *Boyle.*

IMPARTIAL'ITY, *n.* *imparshal'ity.* Indifference of opinion or judgment; freedom from bias in favor of one side or party more than another; disinterestedness. *Impartiality* is indispensable to an upright judge.
2. Equitableness; justice; as the *impartiality* of a decision.

IMP'ARTIALLY, *adv.* Without bias of judgment; without prejudice; without inclination to favor one party or side more than another; equitably; justly.

IMPARTIBIL'ITY, *n.* The quality of not being subject to partition.
2. The quality of being capable of being communicated.

IMP'ARTIBLE, *a.* [Sp. *impartible; in* and *partible.*]
1. Not partible or subject to partition; as an *impartible* estate. *Blackstone.*
2. [from *impart.*] That may be imparted, conferred, bestowed or communicated. *Digby.*

IMP'ARTING, *ppr.* Communicating; granting; bestowing.

IMP'ARTMENT, *n.* The act of imparting; the communication of knowledge; disclosure. *Shak.*

IMP'ASSABLE, *a.* [*in* and *passable.* See *Pass.*]
That cannot be passed; not admitting a passage; as an *impassable* road, mountain or gulf. *Milton.* *Temple.*

IMP'ASSABLENESS, *n.* The state of being impassable.

IMP'ASSABLY, *adv.* In a manner or degree that prevents passing, or the power of passing.

IMPASSIBIL'ITY, } *n.* [from *impassible.*]
IMPAS'SIBLENESS, }
Exemption from pain or suffering; insusceptibility of injury from external things. *Dryden.*

IMPAS'SIBLE, *a.* [Fr. *impassible;* Sp. *impasible;* L. *impassibilis*, from *passus, patior*, to suffer.]
Incapable of pain, passion or suffering; that cannot be affected with pain or uneasiness. Whatever is destitute of sensation is *impassible.*

> Though naked and *impassible*, depart. *Dryden.*

IMPAS'SION, *v. t.* [*in* and *passion.*] To move or affect strongly with passion.

IMPAS'SIONATE, *v. t.* To affect powerfully. *More.*

IMPAS'SIONATE, *a.* Strongly affected.
2. Without passion or feeling. *Burton.*

IMPAS'SIONED, *a.* Actuated or agitated by passion.

> The tempter all *impassioned*, thus began. *Milton.*

2. Animated; excited; having the feelings warmed; as an *impassioned* orator.
3. Animated; expressive of passion or ardor; as an *impassioned* discourse.

IMPAS'SIVE, *a.* [L. *in* and *passus, patior*, to suffer.]
Not susceptible of pain or suffering; as the *impassive* air; *impassive* ice. *Dryden.* *Pope.*

IMPAS'SIVELY, *adv.* Without sensibility to pain or suffering.

IMPAS'SIVENESS, *n.* The state of being insusceptible of pain. *Mountagu.*

IMPASSIV'ITY, *n.* The quality of being insusceptible of feeling, pain or suffering. *Pausanias, Trans*

IMPASTA'TION, *n.* [*in* and *paste.*] The mixtion of various materials of different colors and consistences, baked or united by a cement, and hardened by the air or by fire. *Chambers.*

IMPA'STE, *v. t.* [Fr. *empâter; in* and *pâte*, paste.]
1. To knead; to make into paste.
2. In *painting*, to lay on colors thick and bold.

IMPA'STED, *a.* Concreted, as into paste. *Shak.*

2. Pasted over; covered with paste, or with thick paint.

IMPAT'IBLE, *a.* [L. *impatibilis.*] Intolerable; that cannot be borne.

IMPA'TIENCE, *n.* [Fr.; L. *impatientia*, from *impatiens; in* and *patior*, to suffer.]
Uneasiness under pain or suffering; the not enduring pain with composure; restlessness occasioned by suffering positive evil, or the absence of expected good. Impatience is not *rage*, nor absolute *inability* to bear pain; but it implies want of fortitude, or of its exercise. It usually springs from irritability of temper.

IMPA'TIENT, *a.* [L. *impatiens.*] Uneasy or fretful under suffering; not bearing pain with composure; not enduring evil without fretfulness, uneasiness, and a desire or effort to get rid of the evil. Young men are *impatient* of restraint. We are all apt to be *impatient* under wrongs; but it is a christian duty not to be *impatient* in sickness, or under any afflictive dispensation of Providence.

2. Not suffering quietly; not enduring.

> Fame, *impatient* of extremes, decays
> Not more by envy than excess of praise. *Pope.*

3. Hasty; eager; not enduring delay. The *impatient* man will not wait for information; he often acts with precipitance. Be not *impatient for* the return of spring.

4. Not to be borne; as *impatient* smart. *Spenser.*

This word is followed by *of, at, for*, or *under*. We are *impatient of* restraint, or *of* wrongs; *impatient at* the delay of expected good; *impatient for* the return of a friend, or *for* the arrival of the mail; *impatient under* evils of any kind. The proper use of these particles can be learnt only by practice or observation.

IMPA'TIENT, *n.* One who is restless under suffering. [*Unusual.*]

IMPA'TIENTLY, *adv.* With uneasiness or restlessness; as, to bear disappointment *impatiently.*

2. With eager desire causing uneasiness; as, to wait *impatiently* for the arrival of one's friend.

3. Passionately; ardently. *Clarendon.*

IMPATRONIZA'TION, *n.* Absolute seignory or possession. *Cotgrave.*

IMPAT'RONIZE, *v. t.* [Fr. *impatroniser.*] To gain to one's self the power of any seignory. *Bacon.*

IMPAWN', *v. t.* [*in* and *pawn.*] To pawn; to pledge; to deposit as security. *Shak.*

IMPE'ACH, *v. t.* [Fr. *empêcher*; Arm. *ampeich, ampechein*; Port. Sp. *empachar*; It. *impacciare*; to hinder, to stop. It signifies also in Portuguese, to surfeit, to overload, to glut. It belongs to the family of *pack*; L. *pango, pactus*; Ar. بَكَّ bakka, to press or compress. Class Bg. No. 18. 20. 61. The literal sense of *impeach* is to thrust or send against; hence, to hinder, to stop.]

1. To hinder; to impede. This sense is found in our early writers.

> These ungracious practices of his sons did *impeach* his journey to the Holy Land. *Davies.*

> A defluxion on my throat *impeached* my utterance. *Howell.*

[*This application of the word is obsolete.*]

2. To accuse; to charge with a crime or misdemeanor; but *appropriately*, to exhibit charges of maladministration against a public officer before a competent tribunal, that is, to send or put on, to load. The word is now restricted to accusations made by authority; as, to *impeach* a judge. [See *Impeachment.*]

3. To accuse; to censure; to call in question; as, to *impeach* one's motives or conduct.

4. To call to account; to charge as answerable.

IMPE'ACH, *n.* Hinderance. *Obs.*

IMPE'ACHABLE, *a.* Liable to accusation; chargeable with a crime; accusable; censurable.

2. Liable to be called in question; accountable.

> Owners of lands in fee simple are not *impeachable* for waste. *Z. Swift.*

IMPE'ACHED, *pp.* Hindered. *Obs.*

2. Accused; charged with a crime, misdemeanor or wrong; censured.

> The first donee in tail may commit waste, without being *impeached.* *Z. Swift.*

IMPE'ACHER, *n.* An accuser by authority; one who calls in question.

IMPE'ACHING, *ppr.* Hindering. *Obs.*

2. Accusing by authority; calling in question the purity or rectitude of conduct or motives.

IMPE'ACHMENT, *n.* Hinderance; impediment; stop; obstruction. *Obs.* *Spenser. Shak.*

2. An accusation or charge brought against a public officer for maladministration in his office. In *Great Britain*, it is the privilege or right of the house of commons to impeach, and the right of the house of lords to try and determine impeachments. In the U. States, it is the right of the house of representatives to impeach, and of the senate to try and determine impeachments. In Great Britain, the house of peers, and in the U. States, the senate of the United States, and the senates in the several states, are the high courts of impeachment.

3. The act of impeaching.

4. Censure; accusation; a calling in question the purity of motives or the rectitude of conduct, &c. This declaration is no *impeachment* of his motives or of his judgment.

5. The act of calling to account, as for waste.

6. The state of being liable to account, as for waste.

IMPEARL, *v. t.* *imperl'.* [*in* and *pearl.*] To form in the resemblance of pearls.

> —Dew-drops which the sun
> *Impearls* on every leaf, and every flower. *Milton.*

2. To decorate with pearls, or with things resembling pearls.

> The dews of the morning *impearl* every thorn. *Digby.*

IMPECCABIL'ITY, IMPEC'CANCY, *n.* [See *Impeccable.*] The quality of not being liable to sin; exemption from sin, error or offense. *Pope.*

IMPEC'CABLE, *a.* [Sp. *impecable*; Fr. *impeccable*; *in* and Sp. *pecable*, Fr. *peccable*, from L. *pecco*, to err, to sin.]
Not liable to sin; not subject to sin; exempt from the possibility of sinning. No mere man is *impeccable.*

IMPE'DE, *v. t.* [Sp. *impedir*; It. *impedire*; L. *impedio*; supposed to be compounded of *in* and *pedes*, feet, to catch or entangle the feet.]
To hinder; to stop in progress; to obstruct; as, to *impede* the progress of troops.

IMPE'DED, *pp.* Hindered; stopped; obstructed.

IMPED'IMENT, *n.* [L. *impedimentum.*] That which hinders progress or motion; hinderance; obstruction; obstacle; *applicable to every subject, physical or moral.* Bad roads are *impediments* in marching and travelling. Idleness and dissipation are *impediments* to improvement. The cares of life are *impediments* to the progress of vital religion.

2. That which prevents distinct articulation; as an *impediment* in speech.

IMPED'IMENT, *v. t.* To impede. [*Not in use.*] *Bp. Reynolds.*

IMPEDIMENT'AL, *a.* Hindering; obstructing. *Mountagu.*

IMPE'DING, *ppr.* Hindering; stopping; obstructing.

IM'PEDITE, *v. t.* To impede. [*Not in use.*]

IMPED'ITIVE, *a.* Causing hinderance. *Sanderson.*

IMPEL', *v. t.* [Sp. *impeler*; It. *impellere*; L. *impello*; *in* and *pello*, to drive.]
To drive or urge forward; to press on; to excite to action or to move forward, by the application of physical force, or moral suasion or necessity. A ball is *impelled* by the force of powder; a ship is *impelled* by wind; a man may be *impelled* by hunger or a regard to his safety; motives of policy or of safety *impel* nations to confederate.

> The surge *impelled* me on a craggy coast. *Pope.*

> And several men *impel* to several ends. *Pope.*

IMPEL'LED, *pp.* Driven forward; urged on; moved by any force or power, physical or moral.

IMPEL'LENT, *n.* A power or force that drives forward; impulsive power. *Glanville.*

IMPEL'LER, *n.* He or that which impels.

IMPEL'LING, *ppr.* Driving forward; urging; pressing.

IMPEN', *v. t.* [*in* and *pen.*] To pen; to shut or inclose in a narrow place. *Feltham.*

IMPEND', *v. i.* [L. *impendeo*; *in* and *pendeo*, to hang.]

1. To hang over; to be suspended above; to threaten. A dark cloud *impends* over the land.

> Destruction sure o'er all your heads *impends.* *Pope.*

2. To be near; to be approaching and ready to fall on.

> It expresses our deep sense of God's *impending* wrath. *Smalridge.*

> Nor bear advices of *impending* foes. *Pope.*

IMPEND'ENCE, IMPEND'ENCY, *n.* The state of hanging over; near approach; a menacing attitude. *Hammond.*

IMPEND'ENT, *a.* Hanging over; imminent; threatening; pressing closely; as an *impendent* evil. *Hale.*

IMPEND'ING, *ppr.* Hanging over; approaching near; threatening.

IMPENETRABIL'ITY, *n.* [from *impenetrable.*]
1. The quality of being impenetrable.
2. In *philosophy*, that quality of matter which prevents two bodies from occupying the same space at the same time. *Good.*
3. Insusceptibility of intellectual impression. *Johnson.*

IMPEN'ETRABLE, *a.* [L. *impenetrabilis; in* and *penetrabilis*, from *penetro*, to penetrate.]
1. That cannot be penetrated or pierced; not admitting the passage of other bodies; as an *impenetrable* shield.
2. Not to be affected or moved; not admitting impressions on the mind. The hardened sinner remains *impenetrable* to the admonitions of the gospel.
3. Not to be entered by the sight; as *impenetrable* darkness. Hence,
4. Not to be entered and viewed by the eye of the intellect; as *impenetrable* obscurity or abstruseness.

IMPEN'ETRABLENESS, *n.* Impenetrability, which see.

IMPEN'ETRABLY, *adv.* With solidity that admits not of being penetrated.
2. With hardness that admits not of impression; as *impenetrably* dull. *Pope.*

IMPEN'ITENCE, IMPEN'ITENCY, *n.* [Fr. *impenitence;* Sp. *impenitencia;* It. *impenitenza;* L. *in* and *pœnitens*, from *pœniteo*, to repent, *pœna*, pain.]
Want of penitence or repentance; absence of contrition or sorrow for sin; obduracy; hardness of heart. Final *impenitence* dooms the sinner to inevitable punishment.

> He will advance from one degree of *impenitence* to another. *Rogers.*

IMPEN'ITENT, *a.* [Fr.; *in* and *penitent*, supra.]
Not penitent; not repenting of sin; not contrite; obdurate; of a hard heart.

> They died
> *Impenitent.* *Milton.*

IMPEN'ITENT, *n.* One who does not repent; a hardened sinner.

IMPEN'ITENTLY, *adv.* Without repentance or contrition for sin; obdurately.

IMPEN'NOUS, *a.* [*in* and *pennous.*] Wanting wings.

IMPE'OPLE, *v. t.* To form into a community. [See *People.*] *Beaum.*

IM'PERATE, *a.* [L. *imperatus*, *impero*, to command.]
Done by impulse or direction of the mind. [*Not used.*] *South. Hale.*

IMPER'ATIVE, *a.* [Fr. *imperatif;* L. *imperativus*, from *impero*, to command. See *Empire.*]
1. Commanding; expressive of command; containing positive command, as distinguished from *advisory*, or *discretionary.* The orders are *imperative.*
2. In *grammar*, the *imperative* mode of a verb is that which expresses command, entreaty, advice or exhortation; as, *go, write, attend.*

IMPER'ATIVELY, *adv.* With command; authoritatively.

IMPERATO'RIAL, *a.* Commanding. [*Not in use.*] *Norris.*

IMPERCEP'TIBLE, *a.* [Fr.; *in* and *perceptible.*]
1. Not to be perceived; not to be known or discovered by the senses. We say a thing is *imperceptible* to the touch, to the eye or sight, to the ear, to the taste or smell. Hence,
2. Very small; fine; minute in dimensions; or very slow in motion or progress; as, the growth of a plant or animal is *imperceptible;* it is too slow to be perceived by the eye.

IMPERCEP'TIBLE, *n.* That which cannot be perceived by the senses on account of its smallness. [*Little used.*] *Tatler.*

IMPERCEP'TIBLENESS, *n.* The quality of being imperceptible. *Hale.*

IMPERCEP'TIBLY, *adv.* In a manner not to be perceived. *Addison.*

IMPERCIP'IENT, *a.* Not perceiving or having power to perceive. *Baxter.*

IMPER'DIBLE, *a.* Not destructible. [*Not a legitimate word.*]

IMPER'FECT, *a.* [L. *imperfectus; in* and *perfectus*, finished, perfect; *perficio*, to perfect; *per* and *facio*, to make.]
1. Not finished; not complete. The work or design is *imperfect.*
2. Defective; not entire, sound or whole; wanting a part; impaired. The writings of Livy are *imperfect.*
3. Not perfect in intellect; liable to err; as, men are *imperfect;* our minds and understandings are *imperfect.*
4. Not perfect in a moral view; not according to the laws of God, or the rules of right. Our services and obedience are *imperfect.*
5. In *grammar*, the *imperfect* tense denotes an action in time past, then present, but not finished.
6. In *music*, incomplete; not having all the accessary sounds; as an *imperfect* chord. An *imperfect* interval is one which does not contain its complement of simple sounds. *Busby.*

IMPERFEC'TION, *n.* [Fr. from L. *imperfectio*, supra.]
Defect; fault; the want of a part or of something necessary to complete a thing; *equally applicable to physical or moral subjects.* When fruit fails to come to maturity, and after it begins to decay, we denominate the defect, an *imperfection.* Laws sometimes fail of the intended effect, either from their *imperfection*, or from the *imperfection* of the administration. Men are all chargeable with *imperfections*, both in character and in conduct.

IMPER'FECTLY, *adv.* In an imperfect manner or degree; not fully; not entirely; not completely; not in the best manner; not without fault or failure.

IMPER'FECTNESS, *n.* The state of being imperfect.

IMPER'FORABLE, *a.* [infra.] That cannot be perforated or bored through.

IMPER'FORATE, *a.* [L. *in* and *perforatus*, *perforo.*]
Not perforated or pierced; having no opening. *Sharpe.*

IMPER'FORATED, *a.* Not perforated. *Brown.*
2. Having no pores. *Sir J. Banks.*

IMPERFORA'TION, *n.* The state of being not perforated, or without any aperture.

IMPE'RIAL, *a.* [Fr. from L. *imperialis*, from *impero*, to command. See *Emperor.*]
1. Pertaining to an empire, or to an emperor; as an *imperial* government; an *imperial* diadem; *imperial* authority or edict; *imperial* power or sway.
2. Royal; belonging to a monarch; as an *imperial* palace; *imperial* arts. *Dryden.*
3. Pertaining to royalty; denoting sovereignty.
4. Commanding; maintaining supremacy; as the *imperial* democracy of Athens. *Mitford.*

Imperial chamber, the sovereign court of the German empire. *Encyc.*

Imperial city, a city in Germany which has no head but the emperor.

Imperial diet, an assembly of all the states of the German empire. *Encyc.*

IMPE'RIALIST, *n.* One who belongs to an emperor; a subject or soldier of an emperor. The denomination, *imperialists*, is often given to the troops or armies of the emperor of Austria.

IMPERIAL'ITY, *n.* Imperial power.
2. The right of an emperor to a share of the produce of mines, &c.

> The late empress having by ukases of grace, relinquished her *imperialities* on the private mines, viz. the tenths of the copper, iron, silver and gold— *Tooke.*

IMPE'RIALLY, *adv.* In a royal manner.

IMPER'IL, *v. t.* [*in* and *peril.*] To bring into danger. *Spenser.*

IMPE'RIOUS, *a.* [L. *imperiosus;* It. Sp. *imperioso;* Fr. *imperieux.* See *Imperial.*]
1. Commanding; dictatorial; haughty; arrogant; overbearing; domineering; as an *imperious* tyrant; an *imperious* dictator; an *imperious* man; an *imperious* temper. *More. Shak.*
2. Commanding; indicating an imperious temper; authoritative; as *imperious* words. *Locke.*
3. Powerful; overbearing; not to be opposed by obstacles; as a man of a vast and *imperious* mind. *Tillotson.*
4. Commanding; urgent; pressing; as *imperious* love; *imperious* circumstances; *imperious* appetite. *Dryden. S. S. Smith.*
5. Authoritative; commanding with rightful authority.

> The commandment high and *imperious* in its claims. *D. A. Clark.*

IMPE'RIOUSLY, *adv.* With arrogance of command; with a haughty air of authority; in a domineering manner. *South.*
2. With urgency or force not to be opposed.

IMPE'RIOUSNESS, *n.* Authority; air of command. *South.*
2. Arrogance of command; haughtiness.

> *Imperiousness* and severity is an ill way of treating men who have reason to guide them. *Locke.*

IMPER'ISHABLE, *a.* [Fr. *imperissable; in* and *perish.*]
Not subject to decay; not liable to perish; indestructible; enduring permanently; as an *imperishable* monument; *imperishable* renown.

> Elegant discourses on virtue—will not supply the consolations of *imperishable* hope.

IMPER'ISHABLENESS, *n.* The quality of being imperishable.

IMPER'MANENCE, *n.* Want of permanence or continued duration. *W. Mountague.*

IMPER'MANENT, *a.* [*in* and *permanent.*] Not permanent; not enduring. *Gregory.*

IMPERMEABIL'ITY, *n.* The quality of being impermeable by a fluid. *Cavallo. Asiat. Res.*

IMPER'MEABLE, *a.* [L. *in* and *permeo*; *per* and *meo*, to pass.]
Not to be passed through the pores by a fluid; as *impermeable* lether.

IMPER'SONAL, *a.* [Fr. *impersonnel*: L. *impersonalis*; *in* and *personalis*, from *persona.* See *Person.*]
In *grammar*, an impersonal verb is one which is not employed with the first and second persons, *I* and *thou* or *you*, *we* and *ye*, for nominatives, and which has no variation of ending to express them, but is used only with the termination of the third person singular, with *it* for a nominative in English, and without a nominative in Latin; as, *it rains*; *it becomes* us to be modest; L. *tœdet*; *libet*; *pugnatur.*

IMPERSONAL'ITY, *n.* Indistinction of personality. *Draper.*

IMPER'SONALLY, *adv.* In the manner of an impersonal verb.

IMPER'SONATE, *v. t.* To personify. *Warton.*

IMPER'SONATED, *a.* Made persons of. [See *Personated.*] *Warton.*

IMPERSPICU'ITY, *n.* Want of perspicuity, or clearness to the mind.

IMPERSPIC'UOUS, *a.* [*in* and *perspicuous.*] Not perspicuous; not clear; obscure. *Bailey.*

IMPERSUA'SIBLE, *a.* [L. *in* and *persuasibilis.* See *Persuade.*]
Not to be moved by persuasion; not yielding to arguments. *Decay of Piety.*

IMPER'TINENCE, IMPER'TINENCY, *n.* [Fr. *impertinence*, from L. *impertinens*; *in* and *pertinens*, *pertineo*, to pertain; *per* and *teneo*, to hold.]
1. That which is not pertinent; that which does not belong to the subject in hand; that which is of no weight. *Bacon.*
2. The state of not being pertinent.
3. Folly; rambling thought. [*Little used.*] *Shak.*
4. Rudeness; improper intrusion; interference by word or conduct which is not consistent with the age or station of the person. [*This is the most usual sense.*]

> We should avoid the vexation and *impertinence* of pedants. *Swift.*

5. A trifle; a thing of little or no value.

> There are many subtile *impertinencies* learnt in schools— *Watts.*

IMPER'TINENT, *a.* [L. *impertinens*, supra.]
1. Not pertaining to the matter in hand; of no weight; having no bearing on the subject; as an *impertinent* remark. *Hooker. Tillotson.*
2. Rude; intrusive; meddling with that which does not belong to the person; as an *impertinent* coxcomb.
3. Trifling; foolish; negligent of the present purpose. *Pope.*

IMPER'TINENT, *n.* An intruder; a meddler; one who interferes in what does not belong to him. *L'Estrange.*

IMPER'TINENTLY, *adv.* Without relation to the matter in hand.
2. Officiously; intrusively; rudely. *Addison.*

IMPERTRANSIBIL'ITY, *n.* The quality of not being capable of being passed through. *Hale.*

IMPERTRAN'SIBLE, *a.* [L. *in* and *pertranseo*; *per* and *transeo*, to pass over or through; *trans* and *eo*, to go.] Not to be passed through. [*Little used.*]

IMPERTURB'ABLE, *a.* [L. *in* and *perturbo*, to disturb; *per* and *turbo.*]
That cannot be disturbed or agitated; permanently quiet. *Encyc.*

IMPERTURBA'TION, *n.* Freedom from agitation of mind; calmness. *W. Mountague.*

IMPERTURB'ED, *a.* Undisturbed. [*Not in use.*] *Bailey.*

IMPER'VIOUS, *a.* [L. *impervius*; *in* and *pervius*, passable; *per* and *via*, way.]
1. Not to be penetrated or passed through; impenetrable; as an *impervious* gulf; an *impervious* forest.
2. Not penetrable; not to be pierced by a pointed instrument; as an *impervious* shield.
3. Not penetrable by light; not permeable to fluids. Glass is pervious to light, but *impervious* to water. Paper is *impervious* to light. In the latter sense only, *impervious* is synonymous with *impermeable.*

IMPER'VIOUSLY, *adv.* In a manner to prevent passage or penetration.

IMPER'VIOUSNESS, *n.* The state of not admitting a passage.

IMPETIG'INOUS, *a.* [L. *impetigo*, a ring-worm.]
Resembling the ring-worm or tetters; covered with scales or scabs; scurfy.

IM'PETRABLE, *a.* [See *Impetrate.*] That may be obtained by petition.

IM'PETRATE, *v. t.* [L. *impetro.*] To obtain by request or entreaty. *Usher.*

IMPETRA'TION, *n.* The act of obtaining by prayer or petition. *Herbert.*
2. In *law*, the preobtaining of benefices from the church of Rome, which belonged to the disposal of the king and other lay patrons of the realm. *Encyc.*

IM'PETRATIVE, *a.* Obtaining; tending to obtain by entreaty. *Bp. Hall.*

IM'PETRATORY, *a.* Beseeching; containing entreaty. *Taylor.*

IMPETUOS'ITY, *n.* [See *Impetuous.*] A rushing with violence and great force; fury; violence.
2. Vehemence; furiousness of temper.

IMPET'UOUS, *a.* [Fr. *impetueux*; L. *impetuosus*, from *impetus*, *impeto*; *in* and *peto*, to urge, to rush. See *Bid.*]
1. Rushing with great force and violence; moving rapidly; furious; forcible; fierce; raging; as an *impetuous* wind; an *impetuous* torrent.
2. Vehement of mind; fierce; hasty; passionate; violent; as a man of *impetuous* temper.

IMPET'UOUSLY, *adv.* Violently; fiercely; forcibly; with haste and force. *Addison.*

IMPET'UOUSNESS, *n.* A driving or rushing with haste and violence; furiousness; fury; violence.
2. Vehemence of temper; violence.

IM'PETUS, *n.* [L. supra.] Force of motion; the force with which any body is driven or impelled.
2. The force with which one body in motion strikes another.

IMPIC'TURED, *a.* Painted; impressed. *Spenser.*

IMPIER. [See *Umpire.*]

IMPIERCEABLE, *a.* *impers'able.* [*in* and *pierce.*] Not to be pierced or penetrated. *Spenser.*

IMPI'ETY, *n.* [Fr. *impieté*; L. *impietas*; *in* and *pietas*, *pius.*]
1. Ungodliness; irreverence towards the Supreme Being; contempt of the divine character and authority; neglect of the divine precepts. These constitute different degrees of *impiety.*
2. Any act of wickedness, as blasphemy and scoffing at the Supreme Being, or at his authority; profaneness. Any expression of contempt for God or his laws, constitutes an *impiety* of the highest degree of criminality. Disobedience to the divine commands or neglect of duty implies contempt for his authority, and is therefore *impiety. Impiety*, when it expresses the temper or disposition, has no plural; but it is otherwise when it expresses an act of wickedness, for all such acts are *impieties.*

IMPIG'NORATE, *v. t.* To pledge or pawn. [*Not in use.*]

IMPIGNORA'TION, *n.* The act of pawning. [*Not in use.*]

IMPINGE, *v. i.* *impinj'.* [L. *impingo*; *in* and *pango*, to strike. See *Pack.*]
To fall against; to strike; to dash against; to clash upon.

> The cause of reflection is not the *impinging* of light on the solid or impervious parts of bodies. *Newton.*

IMPING'ING, *ppr.* Striking against.

IMPIN'GUATE, *v. t.* [L. *in* and *pinguis*, fat.] To fatten; to make fat. [*Not in use.*] *Bacon.*

IM'PIOUS, *a.* [L. *impius*; *in* and *pius*, pious.]
1. Irreverent towards the Supreme Being; wanting in veneration for God and his authority; irreligious; profane. The scoffer at God and his authority is *impious.* The profane swearer is *impious.*

> When vice prevails and *impious* men bear sway,
> The post of honor is a private station. *Addison.*

2. Irreverent towards God; proceeding from or manifesting a contempt for the Supreme Being; tending to dishonor God or his laws, and bring them into contempt; as an *impious* deed; *impious* language; *impious* writings.

IM'PIOUSLY, *adv.* With irreverence for God, or contempt for his authority; profanely; wickedly.

IM'PIOUSNESS, *n.* Impiety; contempt of God and his laws.

IMPLACABIL'ITY, IMPLA'CABLENESS, *n.* [from *implacable.*] The quality of not being appeasable; inexorableness; irreconcilable enmity or anger.

IMPLA'CABLE, *a.* [Fr. from L. *implacabilis; in* and *placabilis*, from *placo*, to appease.]
1. Not to be appeased; that can not be pacified and rendered peaceable; inexorable; stubborn or constant in enmity; as an *implacable* prince.
2. Not to be appeased or subdued; as *implacable* anger; *implacable* enmity, malice or revenge.

IMPLA'CABLY, *adv.* With enmity not to be pacified or subdued; inexorably; as, to hate a person *implacably*.

IMPLANT', *v. t.* [*in* and *plant*, L. *planto.*] To set, plant or infix for the purpose of growth; as, to *implant* the seeds of virtue, or the principles of knowledge in the minds of youth; to *implant* grace in the heart. [*It is now seldom or never used in its literal sense for setting plants or seeds in the earth.*]

IMPLANTA'TION, *n.* The act of setting or infixing in the mind or heart, as principles or first rudiments. *Brown.*

IMPLANT'ED, *pp.* Set; infixed in the mind, as principles or rudiments.

IMPLANT'ING, *ppr.* Setting or infixing in the mind, as principles.

IMPLAUSIBIL'ITY, *n.* [from *implausible.*] The quality of not being plausible or specious.

IMPLAUS'IBLE, *a. s* as *z.* [*in* and *plausible.*] Not specious; not wearing the appearance of truth or credibility, and not likely to be believed; as an *implausible* harangue. *Swift.*

IMPLAUS'IBLY, *adv.* Without an appearance of probability.

IMPLE'ACH, *v. t.* [*in* and *pleach.*] To interweave. [*Not in use.*] *Shak.*

IMPLE'AD, *v. t.* [*in* and *plead.*] To institute and prosecute a suit against one in court; to sue at law. The corporation shall have power to plead and be *impleaded.*

Let them *implead* one another. Acts xix.

IMPLE'ADED, *pp.* Prosecuted; sued; subject to answer to a suit in court.

IMPLE'ADER, *n.* One who prosecutes another.

IMPLE'ADING, *ppr.* Prosecuting a suit.

IMPLE'ASING, *a.* Unpleasing. [*Not in use.*]

IMPLEDGE, *v. t.* To pawn. [*Not used.*]

IM'PLEMENT, *n.* [Low L. *implementum*, from *impleo*, to fill; *in* and *pleo.*]
Whatever may supply wants; particularly, as now used, tools, utensils, vessels, instruments; the tools or instruments of labor; the vessels used in a kitchen, &c.; as the *implements* of trade or of husbandry. [*It is a word of very extensive signification.*]

IMPLE'TION, *n.* [L. *impleo*, to fill; *in* and *pleo.*] The act of filling; the state of being full.

The *impletion* is either in simple or compound flowers. The *impletion* of simple flowers, is by the increase either of the petals, or of the nectary. *Lee.*

IM'PLEX, *a.* [L. *implexus.* See *Implicate.*] Infolded; intricate; entangled; complicated.

Every poem is simple or *implex*; it is called simple, when there is no change of fortune in it; *implex*, when the fortune of the chief actor changes from bad to good, or from good to bad. *Spectator.*

IMPLEX'ION, *n.* [See *Implicate.*] The act of infolding or involving; the state of being involved; involution. [*Little used.*] *Dict.*

IM'PLICATE, *v. t.* [Fr. *impliquer*; It. *implicare*; L. *implico, implicatus*; *in* and *plico*, to fold, Gr. πλεκω, W. *plygu.*]
1. To infold; to involve; to entangle. [*Seldom used in its literal sense.*] *Boyle.*
2. To involve; to bring into connection with; also, to show or prove to be connected or concerned; as, the evidence does not *implicate* the accused person in this conspiracy.

IM'PLICATED, *pp.* Infolded; involved.
2. Involved; connected; concerned; proved to be concerned or to have had a part. Twenty persons are *implicated* in the plot.

IM'PLICATING, *ppr.* Involving; proving to be concerned.

IMPLICA'TION, *n.* [L. *implicatio*, supra.]
1 The act of infolding or involving.
2. Involution; entanglement.

Three principal causes of firmness are, the grossness, the quiet contact, and the *implication* of the component parts. *Boyle.*

3. An implying, or that which is implied, but not expressed; a tacit inference, or something fairly to be understood, though not expressed in words.

The doctors are, by *implication*, of a different opinion. *Ayliffe.*

IM'PLICATIVE, *a.* Having implication.

IM'PLICATIVELY, *adv.* By implication. *Buck.*

IMPLIC'IT, *a.* [L. *implicitus*, from *implico*, supra.]
1. Infolded; entangled; complicated.

In his woolly fleece
I cling *implicit*. [*Little used.*] *Pope.*

2. Implied; tacitly comprised; fairly to be understood, though not expressed in words; as an *implicit* contract or agreement.
3. Resting on another; trusting to the word or authority of another, without doubting or reserve, or without examining into the truth of the thing itself. Thus we give *implicit* credit or confidence to the declarations of a person of known veracity. We receive with *implicit* faith whatever God has clearly revealed.

IMPLIC'ITLY, *adv.* By inference deducible, but not expressed in words; virtually; in reality, but not in name.

He that denies the providence of God, *implicitly* denies his existence. *Bentley.*

2. By connection with something else; dependently; with unreserved confidence; without doubting, or without examining evidence. We are disposed to believe *implicitly* what a man of veracity testifies.

Learn not to dispute the methods of his providence, but humbly and *implicitly* to acquiesce in and adore them. *Atterbury.*

IMPLIC'ITNESS, *n.* The state of being implicit; the state of trusting without reserve.

IMPLI'ED, *pp.* [See *Imply.*] Involved; contained virtually, though not expressed; as an *implied* promise.

IMPLI'EDLY, *adv.* By implication.

IMPLORA'TION, *n.* Earnest supplication. *Bp. Hall.*

IMPLO'RE, *v. t.* [Fr. *implorer*; Sp. *implorar*; It. *implorare*; L. *imploro*; *in* and *ploro*, to cry out.]
1. To call upon or for, in supplication; to beseech; to pray earnestly; to petition with urgency; to entreat; as, to *implore* the forgiveness of sins; to *implore* mercy.

Imploring all the gods that reign above. *Pope.*

2. To ask earnestly; to beg.

IMPLO'RE, *v. i.* To entreat; to beg.

IMPLO'RE, *n.* Earnest supplication. [*Not used.*] *Spenser.*

IMPLO'RED, *pp.* Earnestly supplicated; besought.

IMPLO'RER, *n.* One who prays earnestly.

IMPLO'RING, *ppr.* Beseeching; entreating; praying earnestly.

IMPLU'MED, } *a.* Having no plumes or
IMPLU'MOUS, } fethers. *Johnson.*

IMPLUNGE, *v. t. implunj'.* To plunge; to immerse. *Fuller.*

IMPLY', *v. t.* [Fr. *impliquer*; Sp. *implicar*; It. *implicare*; L. *implico*; *in* and *plico*, to fold. See *Implicate.*]
1. Literally, to infold or involve; to wrap up. *Obs.* *Spenser.*
2. To involve or contain in substance or essence, or by fair inference, or by construction of law, when not expressed in words.

Where a malicious act is proved, a malicious intention is *implied.* *Sherlock.*

When a man employs a laborer to work for him, or an agent to transact business for him, the act of hiring *implies* an obligation, and a promise that he shall pay him a reasonable reward for his services. Contracts are express or *implied*; express contracts are those in which an agreement or promise is expressed by words or in writing; *implied* contracts are such as arise from the presumption of law, or the justice and reason of the transaction. *Blackstone.*

IMPLY'ING, *ppr.* Involving; containing in substance, or by fair inference, or by construction of law.

IMPOCK'ET, *v. t.* To pocket. [*Not used.*]

IMPOIS'ON, *v. t. s* as *z.* [Fr. *empoisonner.* See *Poison.*]
1. To poison; to impregnate with poison; to corrupt with poison.
2. To embitter; to impair; as, grief *impoisons* the pleasures of life.
3. To kill with poison. [*Rare.*] *Shak.*

IMPOIS'ONED, *pp.* Poisoned; corrupted; embittered.

IMPOIS'ONING, *ppr.* Poisoning; corrupting; embittering.

IMPOIS'ONMENT, *n.* The act of poisoning. *Pope.*

IM'POLARLY, *adv.* Not according to the direction of the poles. [*Not used.*] *Brown.*

IMPOL'ICY, *n.* [*in* and *policy.*] Inexpedience; unsuitableness to the end proposed; bad policy; defect of wisdom; *a word applied to private as well as public affairs.* *Washington.*

IMPOLI'TE, *a.* [*in* and *polite.*] Not of polished manners; unpolite; uncivil; rude in manners.

IMPOLI'TELY, *adv.* Uncivilly.

IMPOLI'TENESS, *n.* Incivility; want of good manners. *Chesterfield.*

IMPOL'ITIC, *a.* Not wise; devising and pursuing measures adapted to injure the

public interest; as an *impolitic* prince or minister.
2. Unwise; adapted to injure the public interest; as an *impolitic* law, measure or scheme.
3. Not wise in private concerns; pursuing measures ill suited to promote private welfare; not prudent.
4. Not suited to promote private interest.

IMPOLIT'ICAL, for *impolitic*, is obsolete.

IMPOL'ITICLY, *adv.* Not wisely; not with due forecast and prudence; in a manner to injure public or private interest.

IMPONDERABIL'ITY, *n.* Absolute levity; destitution of sensible weight.

IMPON'DERABLE, IMPON'DEROUS, } *a.* [*in* and *ponderable, ponderous.*] Not having sensible weight. *Brown.*

IMPOOR', *v. t.* [*in* and *poor.*] To impoverish. [*Not in use.*] *Browne.*

IMPOROS'ITY, *n.* [*in* and *porosity.*] Want of porosity; closeness of texture; compactness that excludes pores. *Bacon.*

IMPO'ROUS, *a.* Destitute of pores; very close or compact in texture; solid. *Brown. Ray.*

IMPO'RT, *v. t.* [Fr. *importer;* L. *importo; in* and *porto*, to bear. See *Bear.*]
1. To bring from a foreign country or jurisdiction, or from another state, into one's own country, jurisdiction or state; opposed to *export.* We *import* teas and silks from China, wines from Spain and France, and dry goods from Great Britain. Great Britain *imports* cotton from America and India. We may say also that Connecticut, Massachusetts and Maine *import* flour from the middle states.
2. To bear or convey, as signification or meaning; to mean; to signify; to imply. We are to understand by a term, what it clearly *imports.*
3. To be of weight to; to be of moment or consequence to; to bear on the interest of, or to have a bearing on.

> Her length of sickness, with what else more serious
> *Importeth* thee to know, this bears. *Shak.*
> If I endure it, what *imports* it you? *Dryden.*

IM'PORT, *n.* That which is borne or conveyed in words; meaning; signification; the sense which words are intended to convey to the understanding, or which they bear in sound interpretation. *Import* differs from *implication* in this, that the meaning of a term or number of words in connection is less obscurely expressed. *Import* depends less on inference or deduction than *implication*, and is also applied more frequently to a single word. In all philosophical discussions, it is useful to ascertain the *import* of the terms employed. In the construction of laws and treaties, we are to examine carefully the *import* of words and phrases.
2. That which is imported or brought into a country from another country or state; generally in the plural. Our *imports* exceed our exports; the balance must be paid in specie; hence the scarcity of coin.
3. Importance; weight; consequence. [*Formerly accented on the second syllable.*] *Shak. Dryden.*

IMPO'RTABLE, *a.* That may be imported.
2. Insupportable; not to be endured. *Obs.* *Spenser.*

IMPORT'ANCE, *n.* [Fr.; Sp. *importancia;* It. *importanza; from import.*]
1. Weight; consequence; a bearing on some interest; that quality of any thing by which it may affect a measure, interest or result. The education of youth is of great *importance* to a free government. A religious education is of infinite *importance* to every human being.
2. Weight or consequence in the scale of being.

> Thy own *importance* know,
> Nor bound thy narrow views to things below. *Pope.*

3. Weight or consequence in self-estimation. He believes himself a man of *importance.*
4. Thing implied; matter; subject; importunity. [*In these senses, obsolete.*] *Shak.*

IMPORT'ANT, *a.* [Fr.] Literally, bearing on or to. Hence, weighty; momentous; of great consequence; having a bearing on some interest, measure or result by which good or ill may be produced. Truth is *important* to happiness as well as to knowledge, but none so *important* as religious truth. The commerce of Great Britain is *important* to her navy, and her navy is *important* to her independence. Men often forget the *important* end for which they were created.
2. Bearing on; forcible; driving.

> He fiercely at him flew,
> And with *important* outrage him assailed. *Spenser.*

3. Importunate. [*Not used.*] *Shak.*

IMPORT'ANTLY, *adv.* Weightily; forcibly. *Hammond.*

IMPORTA'TION, *n.* [Fr.; from *import.*]
1. The act or practice of importing, or of bringing from another country or state; opposed to *exportation.* Nations forbid the *importation* of commodities which are produced or manufactured in sufficient abundance at home.
2. The wares or commodities imported. The *importations*, this season, exceed those of the last.
3. Conveyance.

IMPO'RTED, *pp.* Brought from another country or state.

IMPO'RTER, *n.* He that imports; the merchant who, by himself or his agent, brings goods from another country or state.

IMPO'RTING, *ppr.* Bringing into one's own country or state from a foreign or distant state.
2. Bearing, as a signification; meaning.
3. Having weight or consequence.

IMPO'RTLESS, *a.* Of no weight or consequence. [*Not used.*] *Shak.*

IMPORT'UNACY, *n.* The act of importuning; importunateness.

IMPORT'UNATE, *a.* [L. *importunus.* See *Importune.*]
1. Bearing on; pressing or urging in request or demand; urgent and pertinacious in solicitation; as an *importunate* suitor or petitioner.
2. Pressing; urgent; as an *importunate* demand.
3. Inciting urgently for gratification; as *importunate* passions and appetites.

IMPORT'UNATELY, *adv.* With urgent request; with pressing solicitation.

IMPORT'UNATENESS, *n.* Urgent and pressing solicitation. *Digby.*

IMPORT'UNATOR, *n.* One that importunes. [*Not in use.*] *Sandys.*

IMPORTU'NE, *v. t.* [Fr. *importuner;* Sp. *importunar;* It. *importunare;* from L. *importunus; in* and *porto*, to bear on.]
To request with urgency; to press with solicitation; to urge with frequent or unceasing application.

> Their ministers and residents here have perpetually *importuned* the court with unreasonable demands. *Swift.*

IMPORTU'NE, *a.* [L. *importunus.* Formerly accented on the second syllable.]
1. Pressing in request; urgent; troublesome by frequent demands; vexatious; unreasonable. *Spenser. Bacon.*
2. Unseasonable. *Milton.*
[This word is obsolete; being superseded by *importunate*, unless perhaps in poetry.]

IMPORTU'NELY, *adv.* With urgent solicitation; incessantly; continually; troublesomely. *Obs.* *Spenser.*
2. Unseasonably; improperly. *Obs.* *Sanderson.*

IMPORTU'NITY, *n.* [Fr. *importunité;* L. *importunitas.*]
Pressing solicitation; urgent request; application for a claim or favor, which is urged with troublesome frequency or pertinacity. Men are sometimes overcome by the *importunity* of their wives or children.

IMPO'RTUOUS, *a.* [L. *importuosus; in* and *portus.*] Without a port, haven or harbor.

IMPO'SABLE, *a.* That may be imposed or laid on. *Hammond.*

IMPO'SE, *v. t. s* as *z.* [Fr. *imposer;* L. *impositum*, from *impono; in* and *pono*, to put. *Pono*, as written, belongs to Class *Bn;* and *posui, positum*, to Class *Bs.* or *Bd.* The latter coincide with Eng. *put.*]
1. To lay on; to set on; to lay on, as a burden, tax, toll, duty or penalty. The legislature *imposes* taxes for the support of government; toll is *imposed* on passengers to maintain roads, and penalties are *imposed* on those who violate the laws. God *imposes* no burdens on men which they are unable to bear.

> On impious realms and barb'rous kings *impose*
> Thy plagues— *Pope.*

2. To place over by authority or by force. The Romans often *imposed* rapacious governors on their colonies and conquered countries.
3. To lay on, as a command; to enjoin, as a duty.

> Thou on the deep *imposest* nobler laws. *Waller.*
> *Impose* but your commands— *Dryden.*

4. To fix on; to impute. [*Little used.*] *Brown.*
5. To lay on, as hands in the ceremony of ordination, or of confirmation.
6. To obtrude fallaciously.

> Our poet thinks not fit
> T' *impose* upon you what he writes for wit. *Dryden.*

7. Among *printers*, to put the pages on the stone and fit on the chase, and thus prepare the form for the press.
To impose on, to deceive; to mislead by a trick or false pretense; vulgarly, to *put*

upon. We are liable to be *imposed on* by others, and sometimes we *impose on* ourselves.

IMPO'SE, *n.* *s* as *z.* Command; injunction. [*Not used.*] *Shak.*

IMPO'SED, *pp.* Laid on, as a tax, burden, duty or penalty; enjoined.

Imposed on, deceived.

IMPO'SER, *n.* One who lays on; one who enjoins.

—The *imposers* of these oaths might repent. *Walton.*

IMPO'SING, *ppr.* Laying on; enjoining; deceiving.

2. *a.* Commanding; adapted to impress forcibly; as an *imposing* air or manner.

—Large and *imposing* edifices, embosomed in the groves of some rich valley. *Bishop Hobart.*

IMPO'SING-STONE, *n.* Among *printers,* the stone on which the pages or columns of types are imposed or made into forms.

IMPOSI''TION, *n.* *s* as *z.* [Fr. from L. *impositio.* See *Impose.*]

1. In a general sense, the act of laying on.
2. The act of laying on hands in the ceremony of ordination, when the bishop in the episcopal church, and the ministers in congregational churches, place their hands on the head of the person whom they are ordaining, while one prays for a blessing on his labors. The same ceremony is used in other cases.
2. The act of setting on or affixing to; as the *imposition* of names. *Boyle.*
3. That which is imposed; a tax, toll, duty or excise laid by authority. Tyrants oppress their subjects with grievous *impositions.*
4. Injunction, as of a law or duty. *Milton.*
5. Constraint; oppression; burden.

Let it not be made, contrary to its own nature, the occasion of strife, a narrow spirit, and unreasonable *impositions* on the mind and practice. *Watts.*

6. Deception; imposture.

Being acquainted with his hand, I had no reason to suspect an *imposition.* *Smollet.*

7. A supernumerary exercise enjoined on students as a punishment. *Warton.*

IMPOSSIBIL'ITY, *n.* [from *impossible.*]

1. That which cannot be; the state of being not possible to exist. That a thing should be and not be at the same time, is an *impossibility.*
2. Impracticability; the state or quality of being not feasible or possible to be done. That a man by his own strength should lift a ship of the line, is to him an *impossibility,* as the means are inadequate to the end. [See *Impossible.*]

IMPOSS'IBLE, *a.* [Fr. from L. *impossibilis; in* and *possibilis,* from *possum,* to be able.]

1. That cannot be. It is *impossible* that two and two should make five, or that a circle and a square should be the same thing, or that a thing should be, and not be at the same time.
2. Impracticable; not feasible; that cannot be done.

With men this is *impossible;* but with God all things are possible. Matt. xix.

Without faith it is *impossible* to please God. Heb. xi.

There are two kinds of impossibilities; *physical* and *moral.* That is a *physical impossibility,* which is contrary to the law of nature. A thing is said to be *morally impossible,* when in itself it is possible, but attended with difficulties or circumstances which give it the appearance of being impossible. [See *Possible, Practicable* and *Impracticable.*] *Encyc.*

IM'POST, *n.* [Sp. It. *imposta;* Fr. *impôt,* for *impost;* L. *impositum, impono.*]

1. Any tax or tribute imposed by authority; particularly, a duty or tax laid by government on goods imported, and paid or secured by the importer at the time of importation. *Imposts* are also called *customs.*
2. In *architecture,* that part of a pillar in vaults and arches, on which the weight of the building rests; or the capital of a pillar, or cornice which crowns the pier and supports the first stone or part of an arch. *Ainsworth. Ash.*

IMPOS'THUMATE, *v. i.* *impos'tumate.* [See *Imposthume.*]

To form an abscess; to gather; to collect pus or purulent matter in any part of an animal body. *Arbuthnot.*

IMPOS'THUMATE, *v. t.* To affect with an imposthume or abscess.

IMPOS'THUMATED, *pp.* Affected with an imposthume.

IMPOSTHUMA'TION, *n.* The act of forming an abscess; also, an abscess; an imposthume. *Coxe. Bacon.*

IMPOS'THUME, *n.* *impos'tume.* [This word is a corruption of *apostem,* L. *apostema,* Gr. αποςημα, from αφιςημι, to separate, to withdraw, or to stand off; απο and ιςημι, to stand.]

An abscess; a collection of pus or purulent matter in any part of an animal body. *Encyc.*

[This word and its derivatives, being mere corruptions, might well be suffered to pass into oblivion.]

IMPOS'THUME, *v. i.* The same as *imposthumate.*

IMPOS'TOR, *n.* [Fr. *imposteur;* Sp. Port. *impostor;* It. *impostore;* from Low L. *impostor,* from *impono.* See *Impose.*]

One who imposes on others; a person who assumes a character for the purpose of deception; a deceiver under a false character. It seems to be yet unsettled, whether Perkin Warbeck was an *impostor.* A religious impostor may be one who assumes the character of a preacher, without authority; or one who falsely pretends to an extraordinary commission from heaven, and terrifies people with denunciations of judgments. *Encyc.*

IMPOS'TURAGE, *n.* Imposition. [*Not in use.*] *Bp. Taylor.*

IMPOS'TURE, *n.* [Fr. from L. *impostura.* See *Impose.*]

Deception practised under a false or assumed character; fraud or imposition practiced by a false pretender.

—Form new legends,
And fill the world with follies and *impostures.* *Irene.*

IMPOS'TURED, *a.* Having the nature of imposture. *Beaum.*

IMPOS'TUROUS, *a.* Deceitful. [*Not used.*] *Beaum.*

IM'POTENCE, } *n.* [L. *impotentia; in* and
IM'POTENCY, } *potens,* from *possum,* the root of It. *potere,* Sp. *poder.* See *Power.*]

1. Want of strength or power, animal or intellectual; weakness; feebleness; inability; imbecility; defect of power, natural or adventitious, to perform any thing.

Some were poor by the *impotency* of nature; as young fatherless children, old decrepit persons, idiots and cripples. *Hayward.*

The *impotence* of exercising animal motion attends fevers. *Arbuthnot.*

2. Moral inability; the want of power or inclination to resist or overcome habits and natural propensities.
3. Inability to beget.
4. Ungovernable passion; *a Latin signification.* [*Little used.*] *Milton.*

IM'POTENT, *a.* [Fr. from L. *impotens.*]

1. Weak; feeble; wanting strength or power; unable by nature, or disabled by disease or accident to perform any act.

I know thou wast not slow to hear,
Nor *impotent* to save. *Addison.*

2. Wanting the power of propagation, as males.
3. Wanting the power of restraint; not having the command over; as *impotent* of tongue. *Dryden.*

IM'POTENT, *n.* One who is feeble, infirm, or languishing under disease. *Shak.*

IM'POTENTLY, *adv.* Weakly; without power over the passions.

IMPOUND', *v. t.* [*in* and *pound.* See *Pound.*]

1. To put, shut or confine in a pound or close pen; as, to *impound* unruly or stray horses, cattle, &c.
2. To confine; to restrain within limits. *Bacon.*

IMPOUND'ED, *pp.* Confined in a pound.

IMPOUND'ER, *n.* One who impounds the beasts of another.

IMPOUND'ING, *ppr.* Confining in a pound; restraining.

IMPOV'ERISH, *v. t.* [Fr. *appauvrir, appauvrissant,* from *pauvre,* poor; It. *impoverire.* See *Poor.*]

1. To make poor; to reduce to poverty or indigence. Idleness and vice are sure to *impoverish* individuals and families.
2. To exhaust strength, richness or fertility; as, to *impoverish* land by frequent cropping.

IMPOV'ERISHED, *pp.* Reduced to poverty; exhausted.

IMPOV'ERISHER, *n.* One who makes others poor.

2. That which impairs fertility.

IMPOV'ERISHING, *ppr.* Making poor; exhausting.

IMPOV'ERISHMENT, *n.* Depauperation; a reducing to indigence; exhaustion; drain of wealth, richness or fertility.

IMPOWER. [See *Empower.*]

IMPRACTICABIL'ITY, } *n.* [See *Im-*
IMPRAC'TICABLENESS, } *practicable.*]

1. The state or quality of being beyond human power, or the means proposed; infeasibility.
2. Untractableness; stubbornness. *Burnet.*

IMPRAC'TICABLE, *a.* [*in* and *practicable;* Fr. *impraticable.* See *Practice.*]

1. That cannot be done or performed; infeasible; not to be effected by human means, or by the means proposed. It is

impracticable for a man to lift a tun by his unassisted strength; but not *impracticable* for a man aided by a mechanical power.

2. Untractable; unmanageable; stubborn; as a fierce, *impracticable* nature. *Rowe.*

3. That cannot be passed or traveled; as an *impracticable* road; *a colloquial sense.*

IMPRAC'TICABLY, *adv.* In a manner or degree that hinders practice.

—Morality not *impracticably* rigid. *Johnson.*

IM'PRECATE, *v. t.* [L. *imprecor; in* and *precor*, to pray. See *Pray.*]

To invoke, as an evil on any one; to pray that a curse or calamity may fall on one's self or on another person.

IM'PRECATED, *pp.* Invoked on one, as some evil.

IM'PRECATING, *ppr.* Calling for evil on one's self or another.

IMPRECA'TION, *n.* [L. *imprecatio.*] The act of imprecating, or invoking evil on any one; a prayer that a curse or calamity may fall on any one.

IM'PRECATORY, *a.* Containing a prayer for evil to befall a person.

IMPRECIS'ION, *n. s* as *z.* [*in* and *precision.*] Want of precision or exactness; defect of accuracy. *Taylor.*

IMPRE'GN, *v. t. impre'ne.* [It. *impregnare;* Fr. *impregner;* L. *in* and *prægnans.* See *Pregnant.*]

To impregnate; to infuse the seed of young, or other prolific principle. [Used in poetry. See *Impregnate.*] *Milton. Thomson.*

IMPREG'NABLE, *a.* [Fr. *imprenable.*]

1. Not to be stormed, or taken by assault; that cannot be reduced by force; able to resist attack; as an *impregnable* fortress.

2. Not to be moved, impressed or shaken; invincible.

The man's affection remains wholly unconcerned and *impregnable.* *South.*

IMPREG'NABLY, *adv.* In a manner to resist penetration or assault; in a manner to defy force; as a place *impregnably* fortified. *Sandys.*

IMPREG'NATE, *v. t.* [It. *impregnare;* Fr. *impregner;* Sp. *impregnar.* See *Pregnant.*]

1. To infuse the principle of conception; to make pregnant, as a female animal.

2. To deposit the fecundating dust of a flower on the pistils of a plant; to render prolific.

3. To infuse particles of one thing into another; to communicate the virtues of one thing to another, as in pharmacy, by mixture, digestion, &c.

IMPREG'NATE, *a.* Impregnated; rendered prolific or fruitful.

IMPREG'NATED, *a.* Made pregnant or prolific; fecundated; filled with something by mixture, &c.

IMPREG'NATING, *ppr.* Infusing seed or pollen; rendering pregnant; fructifying; fecundating; filling by infusion or mixture.

IMPREGNA'TION, *n.* [Fr.] The act of fecundating and rendering fruitful; *applied to animals or plants.*

2. The communication of the particles or virtues of one thing to another.

3. That with which any thing is impregnated. *Derham.*

4. Saturation. *Ainsworth.*

IMPREJU'DICATE, *a.* [L. *in, præ,* and *judico.*]

Not prejudged; unprejudiced; not prepossessed; impartial. [*Not used.*] *Brown.*

IMPREPARA'TION, *n.* [*in* and *preparation.*]

Want of preparation; unpreparedness; unreadiness. [*Little used.*] *Hooker.*

IMPRESCRIPTIBIL'ITY, *n.* [Fr. *imprescriptibilité*, from *imprescriptible.*]

The state of being independent of prescription; the state which renders a thing not liable to be lost or impaired by the prescription of another, or by one's own non-user. *Vattel, Trans.*

IMPRESCRIP'TIBLE, *a.* [Fr. from *prescriptible*, from L. *præscribo; præ* and *scribo*, to write.]

That cannot be lost or impaired by non-user, or by the claims of another founded on prescription.

Rights of mere ability which a man may use or not at pleasure, without any person's having a right to prescribe to me on that subject, are *imprescriptible.* *Vattel, Trans.*

The rights of navigation, fishing, and others that may be exercised on the sea, belonging to the right of mere ability, are *imprescriptible.* *Vattel.*

IMPRESS', *v. t.* [L. *impressum*, from *imprimo; in* and *premo*, to press.]

1. To imprint; to stamp; to make a mark or figure on any thing by pressure; as, to *impress* coin with the figure of a man's head, or with that of an ox or sheep; to *impress* a figure on wax or clay.

2. To print, as books.

3. To mark; to indent.

4. To fix deep; as, to *impress* truth on the mind, or facts on the memory. Hence, to convict of sin.

5. To compel to enter into public service, as seamen; to seize and take into service by compulsion, as nurses in sickness. In this sense, we use *press* or *impress* indifferently.

6. To seize; to take for public service; as, to *impress* provisions. *Marshall.*

IM'PRESS, *n.* A mark or indentation, made by pressure.

2. The figure or image of any thing made by pressure; stamp; likeness.

3. Mark of distinction; stamp; character.

God leaves us this general *impress* or character on the works of creation, that they were very good. *South.*

4. Device; motto.

To describe emblazoned shields,
Impresses quaint— *Milton.*

5. The act of compelling to enter into public service. [See *Press.*] *Shak.*

IMPRESS'ED, *pp.* Imprinted; stamped; marked by pressure; compelled to enter public service; seized for public use; fixed in the mind; made sensible; convinced.

IMPRESSIBIL'ITY, *n.* The quality of being impressible.

IMPRESS'IBLE, *a.* That may be impressed; that yields to pressure; that may receive impressions. Solid bodies are not easily *impressible.*

2. That may be impressed; that may have its figure stamped on another body.

IMPRESS'ING, *ppr.* Imprinting; stamping; fixing in the mind; compelling into service.

IMPRES'SION, *n.* [Fr.; L. *impressio.*] The act of impressing, as one body on another; as a figure made by *impression.*

2. Mark; indentation; stamp made by pressure; as, a seal makes an *impression* on wax.

3. The effect which objects produce on the mind. Thus we say, the truths of the gospel make an *impression* on the mind; they make no *impression*, or a deep and lasting *impression.* The heart is *impressed* with love or gratitude. We lie open to the *impressions* of flattery.

4. Image in the mind; idea.

5. Sensible effect. The artillery made no *impression* on the fort. The attack made no *impression* on the enemy.

6. A single edition of a book; the books printed at once; as a copy of the last *impression.* The whole *impression* of the work was sold in a month.

7. Slight, indistinct remembrance. I have an *impression* that the fact was stated to me, but I cannot clearly recollect it.

IMPRESS'IVE, *a.* Making or tending to make an impression; having the power of affecting, or of exciting attention and feeling; adapted to touch sensibility or the conscience; as an *impressive* discourse; an *impressive* scene.

2. Capable of being impressed; susceptible. *Spenser.*

IMPRESS'IVELY, *adv.* In a manner to touch sensibility, or to awaken conscience; in a manner to produce a powerful effect on the mind.

IMPRESS'IVENESS, *n.* The quality of being impressive.

IMPRESS'MENT, *n.* The act of impressing men into public service; as the *impressment* of seamen.

2. The act of compelling into any service; as the *impressment* of nurses to attend the sick.

3. The act of seizing for public use; as the *impressment* of provisions for the army. *Marshall.*

IMPRESS'URE, *n.* The mark made by pressure; indentation; dent; impression. *Shak.*

IM'PREST, *n.* [It. *imprestare.*] A kind of earnest-money; loan; money advanced. *Burke.*

IMPREST', *v. t.* To advance on loan.

IMPREV'ALENCE, *n.* Incapability of prevailing. *Hall.*

IMPRIMA'TUR, *n.* [L. let it be printed.] A license to print a book, &c.

IMPRIM'ERY, *n.* [Fr. *imprimerie.*] A print; impression; a printing-house; art of printing. [*Not in use.*]

IM'PRIMIS, *adv.* [L. *imprimis*, for *in primis.*] In the first place; first in order.

IMPRINT', *v. t.* [It. *imprimere;* Sp. *imprimir;* Fr. *imprimer;* L. *imprimo; in* and *premo*, to press. See *Print.*]

1. To impress; to mark by pressure; as a character or device *imprinted* on wax or cloth.

2. To stamp letters and words on paper by means of types; to print.

3. To fix on the mind or memory; to impress. Let your father's admonitions and instructions be *imprinted* on your mind.

IMPRINT'ED, *pp.* Marked by pressure; printed; fixed in the mind or memory.

IMPRINT'ING, *ppr.* Marking by pressure; printing; fixing on the mind or memory.

IMPRIS'ON, *v. t.* impriz'n. [Fr. *emprisonner; in* and *prison.*]

1. To put into a prison; to confine in a prison or jail, or to arrest and detain in custody in any place.

2. To confine; to shut up; to restrain from escape; to deprive of the liberty to move from place to place; as, to be *imprisoned* in a cell.

He *imprisoned* was in chains remediless. *Spenser.*

Try to *imprison* the resistless winds. *Dryden.*

IMPRIS'ONED, *pp.* Confined in a prison or jail; restrained from escape or from going at large.

IMPRIS'ONING, *ppr.* Shutting up in prison; confining in a place.

IMPRIS'ONMENT, *n.* The act of putting and confining in prison; the act of arresting and detaining in custody.

2. Confinement in a place; restraint of liberty to go from place to place at pleasure. Appropriately, the confinement of a criminal or debtor within the walls of a prison, or in the custody of a sheriff, &c.

False imprisonment is any confinement of the person, or restraint of liberty, without legal or sufficient authority. The arrest or detention of the person by an officer without warrant, or by an illegal warrant, or by a legal warrant executed at an unlawful time, is *false imprisonment.* *Blackstone.*

IMPROBABIL'ITY, *n.* [See *Improbable.*] The quality of being improbable, or not likely to be true; unlikelihood.

IMPROB'ABLE, *a.* [Sp. Fr. from L. *improbabilis; in* and *probabilis*, from *probo*, to prove.]

Not likely to be true; not to be expected under the circumstances of the case. It is always *improbable* that men will knowingly oppose their own interest; yet the fact is possible. It is *improbable* that snow will fall in July, but not incredible.

IMPROB'ABLY, *adv.* In a manner not likely to be true.

2. In a manner not to be approved. *Obs.* *Boyle.*

IM'PROBATE, *v. t.* [L. *improbo.*] To disallow; not to approve. [*Not used.*] *Ainsworth.*

IMPROBA'TION, *n.* The act of disapproving. [*Not in use.*] *Ainsworth.*

IMPROB'ITY, *n.* [L. *improbitas; in* and *probitas*, from *probo*, to approve.]

That which is disapproved or disallowed; want of integrity or rectitude of principle; dishonesty. A man of known *improbity* is always suspected, and usually despised.

IMPRODU'CED, *a.* Not produced. [*Not in use.*] *Ray.*

IMPROFI''CIENCY, *n.* Want of proficiency. *Bacon.*

IMPROF'ITABLE, *a.* Unprofitable. [*Not in use.*] *Elyot.*

IMPROMP'TU, *adv.* [L. *in promptu*, in readiness, from *promptus*, ready, quick.]

Off hand; without previous study; as a verse uttered or written *impromptu.*

IMPROMP'TU, *n.* A piece made off hand, at the moment, or without previous study; an extemporaneous composition.

IMPROP'ER, *a.* [L. *improprius; in* and *proprius*, proper.]

1. Not proper; not suitable; not adapted to its end; unfit; as an *improper* medicine for a particular disease; an *improper* regulation.

2. Not becoming; not decent; not suited to the character, time or place; as *improper* conduct in church; *improper* behavior before superiors; an *improper* speech.

3. Not according to the settled usages or principles of a language; as an *improper* word or phrase.

4. Not suited to a particular place or office; unqualified; as, he is an *improper* man for the office.

IMPROP'ERLY, *adv.* Not fitly; in a manner not suited to the end; in a manner not suited to the company, time, place and circumstances; unsuitably; incongruously.

2. In a manner not according with established usages; inaccurately; ungrammatically; as, to speak or write *improperly.*

IMPROPI''TIOUS, *a.* Not propitious; unpropitious. *Wotton.*

[*The latter is the word in use.*]

IMPROPO'RTIONABLE, *a.* Not proportionable. [*Little used.*] *B. Jonson.*

IMPROPO'RTIONATE, *a.* Not proportionate; not adjusted. [*Little used.*] *Smith.*

IMPRO'PRIATE, *v. t.* [L. *in* and *proprius*, proper.]

1. To appropriate to private use; to take to one's self; as, to *impropriate* thanks to one's self. [*Not used.*] *Bacon.*

2. To annex the possessions of the church or a benefice to a layman. *Spelman.*

IMPRO'PRIATE, *a.* Devolved into the hands of a layman.

IMPRO'PRIATED, *pp.* Appropriated to one's self. [See *Appropriated.*]

2. Put in possession of a layman.

IMPRO'PRIATING, *ppr.* Appropriating to one's self.

2. Annexing to a lay proprietor.

IMPROPRIA'TION, *n.* The act of putting an ecclesiastical benefice into the hands of a layman. *Ayliffe.*

2. The benefice impropriated.

IMPRO'PRIATOR, *n.* A layman who has possession of the lands of the church or an ecclesiastical living. *Ayliffe.*

IMPROPRI'ETY, *n.* [Fr. *impropriété*, from L. *improprius.* See *Improper.*]

1. Unfitness; unsuitableness to character, time, place or circumstances; as *impropriety* of behavior or manners. Levity of conduct is an *impropriety* in a religious assembly and at a funeral. Rudeness or forwardness in young persons before their superiors, is *impropriety.* Indecency and indecorum are *improprieties.*

2. Inaccuracy in language; a word or phrase not according with the established usages or principles of speaking or writing.

Many gross *improprieties*, however authorized by practice, ought to be discarded. *Swift.*

IMPROSPER'ITY, *n.* Unprosperity; want of success. *Naunton.*

IMPROS'PEROUS, *a.* [*in* and *prosperous.*] Not prosperous; not successful; unfortunate; not yielding profit; not advancing interest; as an *improsperous* undertaking or voyage. *Dryden.*

[*Unprosperous* is the word most generally used in this sense.]

IMPROS'PEROUSLY, *adv.* Unsuccessfully; unprosperously; unfortunately. *Boyle.*

IMPROS'PEROUSNESS, *n.* Ill success; want of prosperity. *Hammond.*

IMPRÖVABIL'ITY, *n.* [See *Improvable.*] The state or quality of being capable of improvement; susceptibility of being made better.

IMPRÖV'ABLE, *a.* [See *Improve.*] Susceptible of improvement; capable of growing or being made better; that may be advanced in good qualities.

We have stock enough, and that too of an *improvable* nature, that is capable of infinite advancement. *Decay of Piety.*

Man is accommodated with moral principles, *improvable* by the exercise of his faculties. *Hale.*

I have a fine spread of *improvable* lands. *Addison.*

2. That may be used to advantage, or for the increase of any thing valuable.

The essays of weaker heads afford *improvable* hints to better. *Brown.*

3. Capable of tillage or cultivation.

A scarcity of *improvable* lands began to be felt in these colonies. *Ramsay, Hist. Carolina.* *B. Trumbull.*

IMPRÖV'ABLENESS, *n.* Susceptibility of improvement; capableness of being made better, or of being used to advantage.

IMPRÖVE, *v. t.* improov'. [Norm. *prover*, to improve; *improwment*, improving. The French and Italians use the same compound in a different sense. It is from the Latin *in* and *probo*, to prove, or the adjective *probus.*]

1. To make better; to advance in value or good qualities. We *amend* a bad, but *improve* a good thing. *Johnson.*

A good education *improves* the mind and the manners. A judicious rotation of crops tends to *improve* land.

2. To use or employ to good purpose; to make productive; to turn to profitable account; to use for advantage; to employ for advancing interest, reputation or happiness.

Many opportunities occur of *improving* money, which, if a man misses, he may not afterwards recover. *Rambler.*

Melissus was a man of parts, capable of enjoying and *improving* life. *Ibm.*

True policy as well as good faith, in my opinion, binds us to *improve* the occasion. *Washington.*

This success was not *improved.* *Marshall.*

Those who enjoy the advantage of better instruction, should *improve* their privileges. *Milner.*

They were aware of the advantages of their position, and *improved* them with equal skill and diligence. *Walsh, Rev. of Hamilton's Works.*

Those moments were diligently *improved.* *Gibbon.*

The candidate *improved* his advantages. *Gibbon.*

A hint that I do not remember to have seen opened and *improved.* *Addison. Spect.* iii.

Whatever interest we have at the throne of grace, should be *improved* in behalf of others. *Scott. Com.* Ex. xxxiii.

The court seldom fails to *improve* the opportunity. *Blackstone.*

My lords, no time should be lost, which may promise to *improve* this disposition in America. *Lord Chatham.*

If we neglect to *improve* our knowledge to the ends for which it was given— *Locke.*

It is the fault of persons not *improving* that light. *S. Clarke.*

The shorter the time—the more eager were they to *improve* it. *Lardner.*

A young minister wishing to *improve* the occasion— *C. Simeon.*

3. To apply to practical purposes; as, to *improve* a discourse, or the doctrines stated and proved in a sermon. *Owen.*

4. To advance or increase by use; *in a bad sense.*

I fear we have not a little *improved* the wretched inheritance of our ancestors. [*Ill.*] *Porteus.*

5. To use; to employ; as, to *improve* a witness or a deposition.

Let even the coach, the inns, or the ships be *improved* as openings for useful instruction. *T. Scott.*

6. To use; to occupy; to cultivate. The house or the farm is now *improved* by an industrious tenant.

This application is perhaps peculiar to some parts of the U. States. It however deviates little from that in some of the foregoing definitions.

IMPRÖVE, *v. i. improov'.* To grow better or wiser; to advance in goodness, knowledge, wisdom or other excellence. We are pleased to see our children *improve* in knowledge and virtue. A farm *improves* under judicious management. The artisan *improves* by experience. It is the duty, as it is the desire of a good man, to *improve* in grace and piety.

We take care to *improve* in our frugality and diligence. *Atterbury.*

2. To advance in bad qualities; to grow worse.

Domitian *improved* in cruelty toward the end of his reign. *Milner.*

[*I regret to see this word thus used, or rather perverted.*]

3. To increase; to be enhanced; to rise. The price of cotton *improves,* or is *improved.* [*A mercantile and modern use of the word.*]

To improve on, to make useful additions or amendments to; to bring nearer to perfection; as, to *improve on* the mode of tillage usually practiced.

IMPRÖV'ED, *pp.* Made better, wiser or more excellent; advanced in moral worth, knowledge or manners.

2. Made better; advanced in fertility or other good qualities.

3. Used to profit or good purpose; as opportunities of learning *improved.*

4. Used; occupied; as *improved* land.

IMPRÖVEMENT, *n. improov'ment.* Advancement in moral worth, learning, wisdom, skill or other excellence; as the *improvement* of the mind or of the heart by cultivation; *improvement* in classical learning, science or mechanical skill; *improvement* in music; *improvement* in holiness.

2. Melioration; a making or growing better, or more valuable; as the *improvement* of barren or exhausted land; the *improvement* of the roads; the *improvement* of the breed of horses or cattle.

3. A valuable addition; excellence added, or a change for the better; sometimes with *on.*

The parts of Sinon, Camilla, and some few others, are *improvements on* the Greek poet. *Addison.*

4. Advance or progress from any state to a better.

There is a design of publishing the history of architecture, with its several *improvements* and decays. *Addison.*

5. Instruction; growth in knowledge or refinement; edification.

I look upon your city as the best place of *improvement.* *South.*

6. Use or employment to beneficial purposes; a turning to good account; as the *improvement* of natural advantages or spiritual privileges.

A good *improvement* of his reason. *S. Clarke.*

7. Practical application; as the *improvement* of the doctrines and principles of a sermon.

I shall make some *improvement* of this doctrine. *Tillotson.*

Hence,

8. The part of a discourse intended to enforce and apply the doctrines, is called the *improvement.*

9. Use; occupancy.

10. *Improvements,* plu., valuable additions or melioration, as buildings, clearings, drains, fences, &c., on a farm. *Kent.*

IMPRÖV'ER, *n.* One who improves; one who makes himself or any thing else better; as an *improver* of horses or cattle.

2. That which improves, enriches or meliorates; as, chalk is an *improver* of lands. *Mortimer.*

IMPROVI'DED, *a.* [L. *improvisus; in* and *provideo,* to foresee or provide.]

Unforeseen; unexpected; not provided against. *Obs.* *Spenser.*

IMPROV'IDENCE, *n.* [L. *in* and *providens, providentia,* from *pro,* before, and *video,* to see.]

Want of providence or forecast; neglect of foresight, or of the measures which foresight might dictate for safety or advantage. Half the inconveniences and losses which men suffer are the effects of *improvidence.*

IMPROV'IDENT, *a.* [L. *in* and *providens; pro* and *video,* supra.]

Wanting forecast; not foreseeing what will be necessary or convenient, or neglecting the measures which foresight would dictate; wanting care to make provision for future exigences. Seamen are proverbially *improvident.* It is sometimes followed by *of;* as *improvident of* harm.

IMPROV'IDENTLY, *adv.* Without foresight or forecast; without care to provide against future wants.

IMPRÖV'ING, *ppr.* Making better; growing better; using to advantage.

IMPROVIS'ION, *n. s* as *z.* [*in* and *provision.*]

Want of forecast; improvidence. [*Little used.*] *Brown.*

IMPRU'DENCE, *n.* [Fr. from L. *imprudentia; in* and *prudentia,* prudence.]

Want of prudence; indiscretion; want of caution, circumspection, or a due regard to the consequences of words to be uttered or actions to be performed, or their probable effects on the interest, safety, reputation or happiness of one's self or others; heedlessness; inconsiderateness; rashness. Let a man of sixty attempt to enumerate the evils which his *imprudence* has brought on himself, his family, or his neighbors.

IMPRU'DENT, *a.* [Fr. from L. *imprudens; in* and *prudens,* prudent.]

Wanting prudence or discretion; indiscrete; injudicious; not attentive to the consequences of words or actions; rash; heedless. The *imprudent* man often laments his mistakes, and then repeats them.

IMPRU'DENTLY, *adv.* Without the exercise of prudence; indiscretely.

IM'PUDENCE, *n.* [Fr. from L. *impudens; in* and *pudens,* from *pudeo,* to be ashamed.]

Shamelessness; want of modesty; effrontery; assurance accompanied with a disregard of the opinions of others.

Those clear truths, that either their own evidence forces us to admit, or common experience makes it *impudence* to deny. *Locke.*

IM'PUDENT, *a.* [Fr. from L. *impudens.*] Shameless; wanting modesty; bold with contempt of others; saucy.

When we behold an angel, not to fear
Is to be *impudent.* *Dryden.*

IM'PUDENTLY, *adv.* Shamelessly; with indecent assurance.

At once assail
With open mouths, and *impudently* rail. *Sandys.*

IMPUDIC'ITY, *n.* [L. *impudicitia.*] Immodesty. *Sheldon.*

IMPU'GN, *v. t. impu'ne.* [Fr. *impugner;* Sp. *impugnar;* L. *impugno; in* and *pugno,* to fight or resist.]

To oppose; to attack by words or arguments; to contradict. The lawfulness of lots is *impugned* by some, and defended by others.

The truth hereof I will not rashly *impugn,* or over-boldly affirm. *Peacham.*

IMPUGNA'TION, *n.* Opposition. [*Little used.*] *Bp. Hall.*

IMPU'GNED, *pp.* Opposed; contradicted; disputed.

IMPU'GNER, *n.* One who opposes or contradicts.

IMPU'GNING, *ppr.* Opposing; attacking; contradicting.

IMPUIS'SANCE, *n.* [Fr.; *in* and *puissance.*] Impotence; weakness. *Obs.* *Bacon.*

IM'PULSE, *n. im'puls.* [L. *impulsus,* from *impello.* See *Impel.*]

1. Force communicated; the effect of one body acting on another. *Impulse* is the effect of motion, and is in proportion to the quantity of matter and velocity of the impelling body.

2. Influence acting on the mind; motive.

These were my natural *impulses* for the undertaking. *Dryden.*

3. Impression; supposed supernatural influence on the mind.

Meantime, by Jove's *impulse,* Mezentius armed,
Succeeded Turnus— *Dryden.*

IMPUL'SION, *n.* [Fr. from L. *impulsio.* See *Impel.*]

1. The act of driving against or impelling; the agency of a body in motion on another body. *Bacon.*

2. Influence on the mind; impulse. *Milton.*

IMPULS'IVE, *a.* [Fr. *impulsif.* See *Impel.*] Having the power of driving or impelling; moving; impellent.

Poor men! poor papers! We and they
Do some *impulsive* force obey. *Prior.*

IMPULS'IVELY, *adv.* With force; by impulse.

IMPU'NITY, *n.* [Fr. *impunité*; L. *impunitas*; *in* and *punio*, to punish.]

1. Exemption from punishment or penalty. No person should be permitted to violate the laws with *impunity. Impunity* encourages men in crimes.

2. Freedom or exemption from injury. Some ferocious animals are not to be encountered with *impunity.*

IMPU'RE, *a.* [Fr. *impur*; L. *impurus*; *in* and *purus*, pure.]

1. Not pure; foul; feculent; tinctured; mixed or impregnated with extraneous substance; as *impure* water or air; *impure* salt or magnesia.

2. Obscene; as *impure* language or ideas.

3. Unchaste; lewd; unclean; as *impure* actions.

4. Defiled by sin or guilt; unholy; as *persons.*

5. Unhallowed; unholy; as *things.*

6. Unclean; *in a legal sense*; not purified according to the ceremonial law of Moses.

IMPU'RE, *v. t.* To render foul; to defile. [*Not used.*] *Bp. Hall.*

IMPU'RELY, *adv.* In an impure manner; with impurity.

IMPU'RENESS, IMPU'RITY, *n.* [Fr. *impureté*; L. *impuritas*, supra.]

1. Want of purity; foulness; feculence; the admixture of a foreign substance in any thing; as the *impurity* of water, of air, of spirits, or of any species of earth or metal.

2. Any foul matter.

3. Unchastity; lewdness.

The foul *impurities* that reigned among the monkish clergy. *Atterbury.*

4. Want of sanctity or holiness; defilement by guilt.

5. Want of ceremonial purity; legal pollution or uncleanness. By the Mosaic law, a person contracted *impurity* by touching a dead body or a leper.

6. Foul language; obscenity.

Profaneness, *impurity*, or scandal, is not wit. *Buckminster.*

IMPUR'PLE, *v. t.* [*in* and *purple*; Fr. *empourprer.*]

To color or tinge with purple; to make red or reddish; as a field *impurpled* with blood.

The bright
Pavement, that like a sea of jasper shone,
Impurpled with celestial roses, smil'd. *Milton.*

IMPUR'PLING, *ppr.* Tinging or coloring with purple.

IMPU'TABLE, *a.* [See *Impute.*] That may be imputed or charged to a person; chargeable. Thus we say, crimes, sins, errors, trespasses are *imputable* to those who commit them.

2. That may be ascribed to; *in a good sense.* This favor is *imputable* to your goodness, or to a good motive.

3. Accusable; chargeable with a fault. [*Not proper.*] *Ayliffe.*

4. That may be set to the account of another. It has been a question much agitated, whether Adam's sin is *imputable* to his posterity.

IMPU'TABLENESS, *n.* The quality of being imputable. *Norris.*

IMPUTA'TION, *n.* [Fr. from *imputer.*] The act of imputing or charging; attribution; generally in *an ill sense*; as the *imputation* of crimes or faults to the true authors of them. We are liable to the *imputation* of numerous sins and errors, to the *imputation* of pride, vanity and self-confidence; to the *imputation* of weakness and irresolution, or of rashness.

2. Sometimes in *a good sense.*

If I had a suit to Master Shallow, I would humor his men with the *imputation* of being near their master. *Shak.*

3. Charge or attribution of evil; censure; reproach.

Let us be careful to guard ourselves against these groundless *imputations* of our enemies, and to rise above them. *Addison.*

4. Hint; slight notice. Qu. *intimation.* *Shak.*

IMPU'TATIVE, *a.* That may be imputed.

IMPU'TATIVELY, *adv.* By imputation. *Encyc.*

IMPU'TE, *v. t.* [Fr. *imputer*; It. *imputare*; Sp. *imputar*; L. *imputo*; *in* and *puto*, to think, to reckon; properly, to set, to put, to throw to or on.]

1. To charge; to attribute; to set to the account of; generally *ill*, sometimes *good.* We *impute* crimes, sins, trespasses, faults, blame, &c., to the guilty persons. We *impute* wrong actions to bad motives, or to ignorance, or to folly and rashness. We *impute* misfortunes and miscarriages to imprudence.

And therefore it was *imputed* to him for righteousness. Rom. iv.

2. To attribute; to ascribe.

I have read a book *imputed* to lord Bathurst. *Swift.*

3. To reckon to one what does not belong to him.

It has been held that Adam's sin is *imputed* to all his posterity. *Encyc.*

Thy merit
Imputed shall absolve them who renounce
Their own both righteous and unrighteous deeds. *Milton.*

IMPU'TED, *pp.* Charged to the account of; attributed; ascribed.

IMPU'TER, *n.* One that imputes or attributes.

IMPU'TING, *ppr.* Charging to the account of; attributing; ascribing.

IMPUTRES'CIBLE, *a.* [*in* and L. *putresco*, to putrefy.]

Not subject to putrefaction or corruption.

IN, a prefix, L. *in*, is used in composition as a particle of negation, like the English *un*, of which it seems to be a dialectical orthography; or it denotes *within*, *into*, or *among*, as in *inbred*, *incase*; or it serves only to augment or render emphatical the sense of the word to which it is prefixed, as in *inclose*, *increase.*

In, before *l*, is changed into *il*, as in *illusion*; and before *r*, into *ir*, as in *irregular*; and into *im*, before a labial, as in *imbitter*, *immaterial*, *impatient.*

IN, *prep.* [L. *in*; Gr. εν; Goth. and Sax. *in*; Fr. *en*; Sp. *en*; It. *in*; G. *in* or *ein*; D. *in*; Dan. *ind*; Sw. *in*; W. *yn*; Sans. *antu.*]

In denotes present or inclosed, surrounded by limits; as *in* a house; *in* a fort; *in* a city. It denotes a state of being mixed, as sugar *in* tea; or combined, as carbonic acid *in* coal, or latent heat *in* air. It denotes present in any state; as *in* sickness or health. It denotes present in time; as *in* that hour or day. The uses of *in*, however, cannot, in all cases, be defined by equivalent words, except by explaining the phrase in which it is used; as *in* deed; *in* fact; *in* essence; *in* quality; *in* reason; *in* courage; *in* spirits, &c. A man *in* spirits or good courage, denotes one who possesses at the time spirits or courage; *in* reason is equivalent to *with* reason; one *in* ten denotes one of that number, and we say also one *of* ten, and one *out of* ten.

In the name, is used in phrases of invoking, swearing, declaring, praying, &c. In prayer, it denotes by virtue of, or for the sake of. *In the name of the people*, denotes on their behalf or part; in their stead, or for their sake.

In, in many cases, is equivalent to *on.* This use of the word is frequent in the Scriptures; as, let fowls multiply *in* the earth. This use is more frequent in England than in America. We generally use *on*, in all similar phrases.

In signifies by or through. *In* thee shall all nations be blessed. I am glorified *in* them.

In that, is sometimes equivalent to *because.*

Some things they do *in that* they are men; some things *in that* they are men misled and blinded with error. *Hooker.*

In these and similar phrases, *that* is an antecedent, substitute, or pronoun relating to the subsequent part of the sentence, or the subsequent clause. God commendeth his love towards us, *in that* while we were yet sinners, Christ died for us. That is, in the fact stated in the latter clause, for which *that* is the substitute. Rom. v.

In as much, seeing; seeing that; this being the fact. I will ride for health, *inasmuch* as I am infirm.

In is often used without the noun to which it properly belongs. I care not who is *in*, or who is *out*, that is, *in office*, or *out of office.* Come *in*, that is, into the house or other place. Who has or will come *in*, that is, into office. A vessel has come *in*, that is, into port, or has arrived.

To be or *keep in with*, to be close or near. *Keep* the ship *in with* the land.

INABIL'ITY, *n.* [Fr. *inhabilité*; L. *inhabilis*; *in* and *habilis*, Norm. *hable*, able.]

1. Want of sufficient physical power or strength; as the *inability* of a man to raise an arm or a leg.

3. Want of adequate means; as an *inability* to purchase a farm, or to fit out a ship.

3. Want of moral power. *Moral inability* is considered to be want of inclination, disposition or will, or a deep-rooted aversion to act, and therefore improperly so called.

Moral *inability* aggravates our guilt. *Scott.*

4. Want of intellectual strength or force; as an *inability* to comprehend a mathematical demonstration.
5. Want of knowledge or skill; as an *inability* to read or write.

INA′BLEMENT, *n.* [See *Enable.*] Ability. [*Not in use.*] *Bacon.*

INAB′STINENCE, *n.* [*in* and *abstinence.*] A not abstaining; a partaking; indulgence of appetite; as the *inabstinence* of Eve. *Milton.*

INABU′SIVELY, *adv.* Without abuse. *L. North.*

INAƐCESSIBIL′ITY, } *n.* [from *inac-*
INAƐCESS′IBLENESS, } *cessible.*]
The quality or state of being inaccessible, or not to be reached.

INAƐCESS′IBLE, *a.* [*in* and *accessible.*]
1. Not to be reached; as an *inaccessible* highth or rock. The depths of the sea are *inaccessible.*
2. Not to be obtained. The necessary vouchers are *inaccessible.*
3. Not to be approached; forbidding access; as an *inaccessible* prince.

INAƐCESS′IBLY, *adv.* So as not to be approached. *Warton.*

INAƐ′ƐURACY, *n.* [from *inaccurate.*] Want of accuracy or exactness; mistake; fault; defect; error; as an *inaccuracy* in writing, in a transcript, or in a calculation.

INAƐ′ƐURATE, *a.* [*in* and *accurate.*] Not accurate; not exact or correct; not according to truth; erroneous; as an *inaccurate* man; he is *inaccurate* in narration; the transcript or copy is *inaccurate;* the instrument is *inaccurate.*

INAƐ′ƐURATELY, *adv.* Not according to truth; incorrectly; erroneously. The accounts are *inaccurately* stated.

INAƐ′TION, *n.* [Fr.; *in* and *action.*] Want of action; forbearance of labor; idleness; rest. *Pope.*

INAƐ′TIVE, *a.* [*in* and *active.*] Not active; inert; having no power to move. Matter is, per se, *inactive.*
2. Not active; not diligent or industrious; not busy; idle. Also, habitually idle; indolent; sluggish; as an *inactive* officer.

INAƐ′TIVELY, *adv.* Idly; sluggishly; without motion, labor or employment.

INAƐTIV′ITY, *n.* [*in* and *activity.*] Inertness; as the *inactivity* of matter.
2. Idleness, or habitual idleness; want of action or exertion; sluggishness. *Swift.*

INAƐ′TUATE, *v. t.* To put in action. [*Not used.*] *Glanville.*

INAƐTUA′TION, *n.* Operation. [*Not used.*] *Glanville.*

INAD′EQUACY, *n.* [from *inadequate.*] The quality of being unequal or insufficient for a purpose.

The *inadequacy* and consequent inefficacy of the alledged causes— *Dwight.*

2. Inequality.

Dr. Price considers this *inadequacy* of representation as our fundamental grievance. *Burke.*

3. Incompleteness; defectiveness; as the *inadequacy* of ideas.

INAD′EQUATE, *a.* [*in* and *adequate*, L. *adæquatus*, from *adæquo*, to equal.]
1. Not equal to the purpose; insufficient to effect the object; unequal; as *inadequate* power, strength, resources.
2. Not equal to the real state or condition of a thing; not just or in due proportion; partial; incomplete; as *inadequate* ideas of God, of his perfections, or moral government; an *inadequate* compensation for services.
3. Incomplete; defective; not just; as *inadequate* representation or description.

INAD′EQUATELY, *adv.* Not fully or sufficiently; not completely.

INAD′EQUATENESS, *n.* The quality of being inadequate; inadequacy; inequality; incompleteness.

INADEQUA′TION, *n.* Want of exact correspondence. *Puller.*

INADHE′SION, *n.* *s* as *z.* [*in* and *adhesion.*] Want of adhesion; a not adhering.

Porcelain clay is distinguished from colorific earths by *inadhesion* to the fingers. *Kirwan.*

INADMISSIBIL′ITY, *n.* [from *inadmissible.*] The quality of being inadmissible, or not proper to be received; as the *inadmissibility* of an argument, or of evidence in court, or of a proposal in a negotiation.

INADMIS′SIBLE, *a.* [Fr.; *in* and *admissible*, from *admitto*, to admit.]
Not admissible; not proper to be admitted, allowed or received; as *inadmissible* testimony; an *inadmissible* proposition.

INADVERT′ENCE, } *n.* [Fr. *inadvertance*,
INADVERT′ENCY, } from L. *in* and *advertens, adverto.* See *Advert.*]
1. A not turning the mind to; inattention; negligence; heedlessness. Many mistakes and some misfortunes proceed from *inadvertence.*
2. The effect of inattention; any oversight, mistake or fault which proceeds from negligence of thought.

The productions of a great genius, with many lapses and *inadvertencies*, are infinitely preferable to works of an inferior kind of author. *Addison.*

INADVERT′ENT, *a.* [L. *in* and *advertens.*] Not turning the mind to; heedless; careless; negligent.

INADVERT′ENTLY, *adv.* Heedlessly; carelessly; from want of attention; inconsiderately.

INAFFABIL′ITY, *n.* Reservedness in conversation.

INAF′FABLE, *a.* Not affable; reserved.

INAFFEƐTA′TION, *n.* Destitution of affected manner.

INAFFEƐT′ED, *a.* Unaffected. [*Not used.*]

INA′IDABLE, *a.* That cannot be assisted. *Shak.*

INA′LIENABLE, *a.* [Fr.; *in* and *alienable*, from L. *alieno, alienus.*]
Unalienable; that cannot be legally or justly alienated or transferred to another. The dominions of a king are *inalienable.* All men have certain natural rights which are *inalienable.* The estate of a minor is *inalienable*, without a reservation of the right of redemption, or the authority of the legislature.

INA′LIENABLENESS, *n.* The state of being inalienable. *Scott.*

INA′LIENABLY, *adv.* In a manner that forbids alienation; as rights *inalienably* vested.

INALIMENT′AL, *a.* [*in* and *aliment.*] Affording no nourishment. *Bacon.*

INALTERABIL′ITY, *n.* [from *inalterable.*] The quality of not being alterable or changeable. *Fourcroy.*

INAL′TERABLE, *a.* [*in* and *alterable.*] That cannot or may not be altered or changed; unalterable. *Hakewill.*

INA′MIABLE, *a.* Unamiable. [*Not in use.*]

INA′MIABLENESS, *n.* Unamiableness. [*Not in use.*]

INAMIS′SIBLE, *a.* [L. *in* and *amitto*, to lose.] Not to be lost. [*Little used.*] *Hammond.*

INAMIS′SIBLENESS, *n.* The state of not being liable to be lost.

INAMORA′TO, *n.* [L. *in* and *amor*, love.] A lover. *Marston.*

INA′NE, *a.* [L. *inanis*, empty.] Empty; void; sometimes used as a noun, to express a void space. *Locke.*

INAN′GULAR, *a.* Not angular. [*Little used.*] *Brown.*

INAN′IMATE, *v. t.* [infra.] To animate. [*Little used.*]

INAN′IMATE, *a.* [L. *inanimatus; in* and *animo, animatus.*]
1. Destitute of animal life. Plants, stones and earth are *inanimate* substances; a corpse is an *inanimate* body.
2. Destitute of animation or life.

INAN′IMATED, *a.* Destitute of animal life. *Cheyne.*
2. Not animated; not sprightly. [See *Unanimated.*]

INANI′′TION, *n.* [Fr. from L. *inanis*, empty.]
Emptiness; want of fullness; as *inanition* of body or of the vessels. *Burton.*

INAN′ITY, *n.* [L. *inanitas*, from *inanis*, void.] Emptiness; void space; vacuity. *Digby.*

INAP′PETENCE, } *n.* [*in* and *appetence*, L.
INAP′PETENCY, } *appetentia.*] Want of appetence, or of a disposition to seek, select or imbibe nutriment. [See *Appetence.*]
2. Want of desire or inclination. *Cheyne.*

INAPPLIƐABIL′ITY, *n.* [from *inapplicable.*] The quality of not being applicable; unfitness.

INAP′PLIƐABLE, *a.* [*in* and *applicable.*] Not applicable; that cannot be applied; not suited or suitable to the purpose. The argument or the testimony is *inapplicable* to the case.

INAPPLIƐA′TION, *n.* [Fr.; *in* and *application.*]
Want of application; want of attention or assiduity; negligence; indolence; neglect of study or industry.

INAP′POSITE, *a.* *s* as *z.* [*in* and *apposite.*] Not apposite; not fit or suitable; not pertinent; as an *inapposite* argument.

INAPPRE′CIABLE, *a.* [*in* and *appreciable*, from *appreciate.*]
1. Not to be appreciated; that cannot be duly valued.
2. That cannot be estimated. *Ure.*

INAPPREHENS′IBLE, *a.* Not intelligible. *Milton.*

INAPPREHENS′IVE, *a.* Not apprehensive; regardless. *Taylor.*

INAPPROACHABLE, *a.* [*in* and *approachable.*] Not to be approached; inaccessible.

INAPPRO′PRIATE, *a.* [*in* and *appropriate.*] Not appropriate; unsuited; not proper. *J. P. Smith.*

2. Not appropriate; not belonging to. *Med. Repos.*

INAPT'ITUDE, *n.* [*in* and *aptitude.*] Want of aptitude; unfitness; unsuitableness. *Burke.*

INA'QUATE, *a.* [L. *in* and *aquatus.*] Embodied in water. *Cranmer.*

INAQUA'TION, *n.* The state of being inaquate. *Gardner.*

INAR'ABLE, *a.* [*in* and *arable.*] Not arable; not capable of being plowed or tilled. *Dict.*

IN'ARCH, *v. t.* [*in* and *arch.*] To graft by approach; to graft by uniting a cion to a stock without separating it from its parent tree. *Miller. Encyc.*

IN'ARCHED, *pp.* Grafted by approach.

IN'ARCHING, *ppr.* Grafting by approach.

IN'ARCHING, *n.* A method of ingrafting, by which a cion, without being separated from its parent tree, is joined to a stock standing near. *Encyc.*

INARTIC'ULATE, *a.* [*in* and *articulate.*] Not uttered with articulation or junction of the organs of speech; not articulate; not distinct, or with distinction of syllables. The sounds of brutes and fowls are, for the most part, *inarticulate.*

INARTIC'ULATELY, *adv.* Not with distinct syllables; indistinctly.

INARTIC'ULATENESS, *n.* Indistinctness of utterance by animal voices; want of distinct articulation.

INARTICULA'TION, *n.* Indistinctness of sounds in speaking.

INARTIFI''CIAL, *a.* [*in* and *artificial.*]
1. Not done by art; not made or performed by the rules of art; formed without art; as an *inartificial* style of composition.
2. Simple; artless.

INARTIFI''CIALLY, *adv.* Without art; in an artless manner; contrary to the rules of art. *Collier.*

INATTEN'TION, *n.* [*in* and *attention.*] The want of attention, or of fixing the mind steadily on an object; heedlessness; neglect.

Novel lays attract our ravished ears,
But old, the mind with *inattention* hears. *Pope.*

INATTENT'IVE, *a.* [*in* and *attentive.*] Not fixing the mind on an object; heedless; careless; negligent; regardless; as an *inattentive* spectator or hearer; an *inattentive* habit. *Watts.*

INATTENT'IVELY, *adv.* Without attention; carelessly; heedlessly. *Johnson.*

INAUD'IBLE, *a.* [*in* and *audible.*] That cannot be heard; as an *inaudible* voice or sound.
2. Making no sound; as the *inaudible* foot of time. *Shak.*

INAUD'IBLY, *adv.* In a manner not to be heard. *Colebrooke.*

INAUG'URAL, *a.* [L. *inauguro; in* and *augur.*]
1. Pertaining to inauguration; as *inaugural* ceremonies.
2. Made or pronounced at an inauguration; as an *inaugural* address.

INAUG'URATE, *v. t.* [supra.] To introduce or induct into an office with solemnity or suitable ceremonies; to invest with an office in a formal manner; a word borrowed from the ceremonies used by the Romans when they were received into the college of augurs. Kings and emperors are *inaugurated* by coronation; a prelate, by consecration; and the president of a college by such ceremonies and forms as give weight and authority to the transaction.
2. To begin with good omens. [*Not used.*] *Wotton.*

INAUG'URATE, *a.* Invested with office. *Drayton.*

INAUG'URATED, *pp.* Inducted into office with appropriate ceremonies.

INAUG'URATING, *ppr.* Inducting into office with solemnities.

INAUGURA'TION, *n.* The act of inducting into office with solemnity; investiture with office by appropriate ceremonies.

INAUG'URATORY, *a.* Suited to induction into office; pertaining to inauguration; as *inauguratory* gratulations. *Johnson's Lives of the Poets.*

INAURA'TION, *n.* [L. *inauro, inauratus; in* and *aurum,* gold.]
The act or process of gilding, or covering with gold. *Arbuthnot.*

INAUS'PICATE, *a.* Ill omened. *Buck.*

IMAUSPI''CIOUS, *a.* [*in* and *auspicious.*] Ill omened; unfortunate; unlucky; evil; unfavorable. The war commenced at an *inauspicious* time, and its issue was *inauspicious.* The counsels of a bad man have an *inauspicious* influence on society.

INAUSPI''CIOUSLY, *adv.* With ill omens; unfortunately; unfavorably.

INAUSPI''CIOUSNESS, *n.* Unluckiness; unfavorableness.

IN'BEING, *n.* [*in* and *being.*] Inherence; inherent existence; inseparableness. *Watts.*

IN'BORN, *a.* [*in* and *born.*] Innate; implanted by nature; as *inborn* passions; *inborn* worth. *Dryden. Addison.*

IN'BREATHED, *a.* [*in* and *breathe.*] Infused by inspiration. *Milton.*

IN'BRED, *a.* [*in* and *bred, breed.*] Bred within; innate; natural; as *inbred* worth; *inbred* affection. *Dryden.*

INBREE'D, *v. t.* To produce or generate within. *Bp. Reynolds.*

IN'CA, *n.* The name or title given by the natives of Peru to their kings and to the princes of the blood, before the conquest of that country by the Spaniards.

INCA'GE, *v. t.* [*in* and *cage.*] To confine in a cage; to coop up; to confine to any narrow limits. *Shak.*

INCA'GED, *pp.* Cooped up; confined to a cage or to narrow limits.

INCA'GING, *ppr.* Confining to a cage or to narrow limits.

INCA'GEMENT, *n.* Confinement in a cage. *Shelton.*

INCAL'CULABLE, *a.* That cannot be calculated; beyond calculation.

INCAL'CULABLY, *adv.* In a degree beyond calculation.

INCALES'CENCE, } *n.* [L. *incalescens, incalesco; in* and *calesco, caleo,* to be hot.]
INCALES'CENCY, }
A growing warm; incipient or increasing heat. *Ray.*

INCALES'CENT, *a.* Growing warm; increasing in heat.

INCAMERA'TION, *n.* [*in* and *camera,* a chamber, or arched roof.]
The act or process of uniting lands, revenues or other rights to the pope's domain. *Encyc.*

INCANDES'CENCE, *n.* [L. *incandescens, incandesco; in* and *candesco; candeo, caneo,* to be white, to shine; *canus,* white.]
A white heat; or the glowing whiteness of a body caused by intense heat. We say, a metal is heated to *incandescence.*

INCANDES'CENT, *a.* White or glowing with heat.

INCANTA'TION, *n.* [L. *incantatio, incanto; in* and *canto,* to sing.]
The act of enchanting; enchantment; the act of using certain formulas of words and ceremonies, for the purpose of raising spirits. *Encyc. Bacon.*

INCANT'ATORY, *a.* Dealing by enchantment; magical. *Brown.*

INCANT'ING, *a.* Enchanting. [*Not used.*]

INCAN'TON, *v. t.* [*in* and *canton.*] To unite to a canton or separate community. *Addison.*

INCAPABIL'ITY, } *n.* [from *incapable.*] The quality of being incapable; natural incapacity or want of power; as the *incapableness* of a child to comprehend logical syllogisms.
INCA'PABLENESS, }
2. Want of legal qualifications or of legal power; as the *incapability* of holding an office.

INCA'PABLE, *a.* [Fr.; *in* and *capable.*]
1. Wanting capacity sufficient; not having room sufficient to contain or hold; followed by *of.* We say, a vessel is *incapable of* containing or holding a certain quantity of liquor; but I believe we rarely or never say, a vessel is *incapable of* that quantity.
2. Wanting natural power or capacity to learn, know, understand or comprehend. Man is *incapable* of comprehending the essence of the Divine Being. An idiot is *incapable* of learning to read.
3. Not admitting; not in a state to receive; not susceptible of; as, a bridge is *incapable* of reparation.
4. Wanting power equal to any purpose.

Is not your father grown *incapable*
Of reasonable affairs? *Shak.* [See No. 2.]

5. Wanting moral power or disposition. He is *incapable* of a dishonorable act.
6. Unqualified or disqualified, in a legal sense; not having the legal or constitutional qualifications. A man not thirty years of age is *unqualified,* and therefore *incapable* of holding the office of president of the United States; a man convicted on impeachment is *disqualified,* and therefore *incapable* of holding any office of honor or profit under the government.

Incapable properly denotes a want of passive power, the power of receiving, and is applicable particularly to the mind; *unable* denotes the want of active power or power of performing, and is applicable to the body or the mind. [See *Incapacity.*]

INCAPA'CIOUS, *a.* [*in* and *capacious.*] Not capacious; not large or spacious; narrow; of small content; as an *incapacious* soul. *Burnet.*

INCAPA'CIOUSNESS, *n.* Narrowness; want of containing space.

INCAPAC'ITATE, *v. t.* [*in* and *capacitate.*]
1. To deprive of capacity or natural power

of learning, knowing, understanding or performing. Old age and infirmity often *incapacitate* men to exercise the office of a judge.

2. To render or make incapable; as, infancy *incapacitates* a child for learning algebra.

3. To disable; to weaken; to deprive of competent power or ability. This is an improper use of the word. The loss of an arm *disables* a soldier, but does not *incapacitate* him.

4. To render unfit; as, infancy *incapacitates* one for marriage.

5. To disqualify; to deprive of legal or constitutional requisites; as, conviction of a crime *incapacitates* one to be a witness.

INCAPACITA'TION, *n.* Want of capacity; disqualification. *Burke.*

INCAPAC'ITY, *n.* [*in* and *capacity.*] Want of capacity, intellectual power, or the power of receiving, containing or understanding; *applied to the mind, and it may be natural or casual.* There is a *natural incapacity* in children to comprehend difficult propositions in logic or metaphysics, and a *natural incapacity* in men to comprehend the nature of spiritual beings. The defect of understanding proceeding from intoxication, or from an injury done to the brain, is a *casual incapacity.*

2. Want of qualification or legal requisites; inability; as the *incapacity* of minors to make binding contracts.

3. Disqualification; disability by deprivation of power; as the *incapacity* of a convict to give testimony in a court of law.

INC'ARCERATE, *v. t.* [L *incarcero*; *in* and *carcer*, a prison, Sp. *carcel*, Sax. *carcœrn*, Goth. *karkara*, G. D. *kerker*, W. *carcar*. *Carcer* seems to be allied to W. *carc*, Eng. *cark*, care; showing that the primary sense is to press or strain.]

1. To imprison; to confine in a jail.

2. To confine; to shut up or inclose. *Harvey.*

INC'ARCERATE, *a.* Imprisoned; confined. *More.*

INCARCERA'TION, *n.* The act of imprisoning or confining; imprisonment.

INC'ARN, *v. t.* [L. *incarno; in* and *caro, carnis*, flesh.]

To cover with flesh; to invest with flesh. *Wiseman.*

INC'ARN, *v. i.* To breed flesh. *Wiseman.*

INC'ARNADINE, *a.* [Fr. *incarnadin;* It. *incarnatino*; L. *in* and *caro*, flesh.]

Flesh-colored; of a carnation color; pale red. *Shak.*

INC'ARNADINE, *v. t.* To dye red or flesh-color. [*Little used.*]

INC'ARNATE, *v. t.* [Fr. *incarner*; Sp. *encarnar*; It. *incarnare*; L. *incarno*; *in* and *caro*, flesh.]

To clothe with flesh; to embody in flesh. *Milton. Asiat. Res.*

INC'ARNATE, *a.* Invested with flesh; embodied in flesh; as the *incarnate* Son of God.

2. In *Scotland*, of a red color; flesh-colored.

INCARNA'TION, *n.* The act of clothing with flesh.

2. The act of assuming flesh, or of taking a human body and the nature of man; as the *incarnation* of the Son of God.

3. In *surgery*, the process of healing wounds and filling the part with new flesh. *Encyc.*

INC'ARNATIVE, *a.* [Fr. *incarnatif.*] Causing new flesh to grow; healing. *Encyc.*

INC'ARNATIVE, *n.* A medicine that tends to promote the growth of new flesh, and assist nature in the healing of wounds. *Encyc.*

INCA'SE, *v. t.* [*in* and *case.*] To inclose in a case.

2. To inclose; to cover or surround with something solid.

> Rich plates of gold the folding doors *incase.* *Pope.*

INCA'SED, *pp.* Inclosed as in a case, sheath or box.

INCA'SING, *ppr.* Inclosing as in a case.

INC'ASK, *v. t.* To put into a cask. *Sherwood.*

INCAS'TELLATED, *a.* Confined or inclosed in a castle.

INCATENA'TION, *n.* [L. *catena*, a chain.] The act of linking together. *Goldsmith.*

INCAU'TIOUS, *a.* [*in* and *cautious.*] Not cautious; unwary; not circumspect; heedless; not attending to the circumstances on which safety and interest depend; as *incautious* youth.

INCAU'TIOUSLY, *adv.* Unwarily; heedlessly; without due circumspection.

INCAU'TIOUSNESS, *n.* Want of caution; unwariness; want of foresight.

IN'CAVATED, *a.* [L. *in* and *cavo*, to make hollow.] Made hollow; bent round or in.

INCAVA'TION, *n.* The act of making hollow.

2. A hollow made.

INCEND', *v. t.* [L. *incendo.*] To inflame; to excite. [*Little used.*] *Marston.*

INCEND'IARY, *n.* [L. *incendiarius*, from *incendo*, to burn; *in* and *candeo*, to shine, or be on fire.]

1. A person who maliciously sets fire to another man's dwelling house, or to any outhouse, being parcel of the same, as a barn or stable; one who is guilty of arson.

2. Any person who sets fire to a building.

3. A person who excites or inflames factions, and promotes quarrels.

> Several cities of Greece drove them out as *incendiaries.* *Bentley.*
>
> *Incendiaries* of figure and distinction, who are the inventors and publishers of gross falsehoods, cannot be regarded but with the utmost detestation. *Addison.*

4. He or that which excites.

INCEND'IARY, *a.* Pertaining to the malicious burning of a dwelling; as an *incendiary* purpose.

2. Tending to excite or inflame factions, sedition or quarrels.

IN'CENSE, *n. in'cens.* [L. *incensum*, burnt, from *incendo*, to burn; It. *incenso*; Fr. *encens.*]

1. Perfume exhaled by fire; the odors of spices and gums, burnt in religious rites, or as an offering to some deity.

> A thick cloud of *incense* went up. Ezek. viii.

2. The materials burnt for making perfumes. The incense used in the Jewish offerings was a mixture of sweet spices, stacte, onycha, galbanum, and the gum of the frankincense tree.

> Nadab and Abihu, the sons of Aaron, took either of them his censer, and put fire therein and put *incense* thereon. Lev. x.

3. Acceptable prayers and praises. Mal. i.

4. In *the Materia Medica*, a dry resinous substance known by the name of thus and olibanum. *Encyc.*

IN'CENSE, *v. t. in'cens.* To perfume with incense. In the Romish church, it is the deacon's office to *incense* the officiating priest or prelate, and the choir. *Encyc.*

INCENSE, *v. t. incens.'* To enkindle or inflame to violent anger; to excite angry passions; to provoke; to irritate; to exasperate; to heat; to fire. It expresses less than *enrage.*

> How could my pious son thy power *incense?* *Dryden.*

INCENS'ED, *pp.* Inflamed to violent anger; exasperated.

INCENSEMENT, *n. incens'ment.* Violent irritation of the passions; heat; exasperation. It expresses less than *rage* and *fury.* *Shak.*

INCENS'ING, *ppr.* Inflaming to anger; irritating; exasperating.

INCEN'SION, *n.* [L. *incensio*, from *incendo*, to burn.]

The act of kindling; the state of being on fire. *Bacon.*

INCENS'IVE, *a.* Tending to excite or provoke. *Barrow.*

INCENS'OR, *n.* [L.] A kindler of anger; an inflamer of the angry passions.

INCENS'ORY, *n.* The vessel in which incense is burnt and offered. [We generally use *censer.*] *Ainsworth.*

INCEN'TIVE, *a.* [Low L. *incentivus*, from *incendo*, to burn.] Inciting; encouraging or moving.

> Competency is the most *incentive* to industry. *Decay of Piety.*

INCEN'TIVE, *n.* [Low L. *incentivum.*]

1. That which kindles or inflames; *used now in a figurative sense only.*

2. That which moves the mind or operates on the passions; that which incites or has a tendency to incite to determination or action; that which prompts to good or ill; motive; spur. The love of money, and the desire of promotion, are two most powerful *incentives* to action.

INCEP'TION, *n.* [L. *inceptio*, from *incipio*, to begin; *in* and *capio*, to take.] Beginning. *Bacon.*

> I hope this society will not be marked with vivacity of *inception*, apathy of progress, and prematureness of decay. *Rawle.*

INCEP'TIVE, *a.* [L. *inceptivus*, from *incipio*, to begin.]

Beginning; noting beginning; as an *inceptive* proposition; an *inceptive* verb, which expresses the beginning of action.

> A point is *inceptive* of a line, and a line is *inceptive* of a surface.

INCEP'TOR, *n.* A beginner; one in the rudiments. *Walton.*

INCERA'TION, *n.* [L. *incero*, from *cera.*] The act of covering with wax.

INCER'TAIN, *a.* [*in* and *certain.*] Uncertain; doubtful; unsteady. *Fairfax.*

INCER'TAINLY, *adv.* Doubtfully.

INCER'TAINTY, *n.* Uncertainty; doubt. *Davies.*

INCER'TITUDE, *n.* [L. *incertitudo*, from *incertus*; *in* and *certus*, certain.] Uncertainty; doubtfulness; doubt.

INCES'SABLE, *a.* Unceasing; continual. [*Little used.*] *Shelton.*

INCES'SANCY, *n.* [from *incessant.*] Unintermitted continuance; unceasingness. *Dwight.*

INCES'SANT, *a.* [L. *in* and *cessans*, from *cesso*, to cease.]
Unceasing; unintermitted; uninterrupted; continual; as *incessant* rains; *incessant* clamors. *Milton. Pope.*

INCES'SANTLY, *adv.* Without ceasing; continually. *Spenser.*

IN'CEST, *n.* [Fr. *inceste*; L. *incestum*; *in* and *castus*, chaste.]
The crime of cohabitation or sexual commerce between persons related within the degrees wherein marriage is prohibited by the law of a country.
Spiritual incest, is a like crime committed between persons who have a spiritual alliance by means of baptism or confirmation. It is also understood of a vicar or other beneficiary, who holds two benefices, the one depending on the collation of the other. *Encyc.*

INCEST'UOUS, *a.* Guilty of incest; as an *incestuous* person.
2. Involving the crime of incest; as an *incestuous* connection.

INCEST'UOUSLY, *adv.* In an incestuous manner; in a manner to involve the crime of incest.

INCEST'UOUSNESS, *n.* The state or quality of being incestuous. *Bp. Hall.*

INCH, *n.* [Sax. *ince*; L. *uncia*, the twelfth part; Gr. ουγγια, but said to be from the Latin.]
1. A lineal measure in Great Britain and the United States, being the twelfth part of a foot, and equal to the length of three barley corns.
2. Proverbially, a small quantity or degree; as, to die by *inches*; to gain ground by *inches.*
3. A precise point of time.

Beldame, I think, we watch'd you at an *inch.* [*Unusual.*] *Shak.*

INCH, *v. t.* To drive by inches or small degrees. [*Little used.*] *Dryden.*
2. To deal out by inches; to give sparingly. [*Little used.*] *Ainsworth.*

INCH, *v. i.* To advance or retire by small degrees. [*Little used.*] *Johnson.*
Inched, is added to words of number; as *four-inched.* *Shak.*
But in America the common practice is to add only *inch*; as a *seven-inch* cable.

INCHAR'ITABLE, *a.* Uncharitable. [*The latter is the word used.*]

INCHAS'TITY, *n.* [*in* and *chastity.*] Lewdness; impurity; unchastity. *J. Edwards.*

INCHEST', *v. t.* To put into a chest. *Sherwood.*

INCH'-MEAL, *n.* [*inch* and *meal.*] A piece an inch long. *Shak.*

IN'CHOATE, *v. t.* [L. *inchoo.*] To begin. [*Little used.*] *More.*

IN'CHOATE, *a.* Begun; commenced.

It is neither a substance perfect, nor a substance *inchoate.* *Raleigh.*

IN'CHOATELY, *adv.* In an incipient degree.

INCHOA'TION, *n.* The act of beginning; commencement; inception.

The setting on foot some of those arts in those parts, would be looked on as the first *inchoation* of them. [*Little used.*] *Hale.*

INCHO'ATIVE, *a.* Noting beginning; inceptive; as an *inchoative* verb, otherwise called *inceptive.*

INCI'DE, *v. t.* [L. *incido*; *in* and *cædo*, to strike.]
To cut; to separate; as medicines. *Obs.* *Quincy. Arbuthnot.*

IN'CIDENCE, *n.* [L. *incidens*; *incido*, to fall on; *in* and *cado*, to fall.]
1. Literally, a falling on; whence, an accident or casualty. *Shak.*
2. The manner of falling on, or the direction in which one body falls on or strikes another. The angle which the line of falling, or the direction of a moving body striking another, makes with the plane struck, is called the *angle of incidence.* When rays of light striking a body are reflected, the angle of *incidence* and the angle of reflection are equal.

In equal *incidences* there is a considerable inequality of refractions. *Newton.*

IN'CIDENT, *a.* Falling; casual; fortuitous; coming or happening occasionally, or not in the usual course of things, or not according to expectation or in connection with the main design.

As the ordinary course of common affairs is disposed of by general laws, so man's rarer *incident* necessities and utilities should be with special equity considered. *Hooker.*

A proposition introduced by *who, which, whose, whom*, &c. is called an *incident* proposition; as, Julius, *whose* surname was Cesar, overcame Pompey. *Watts.*

2. Happening; apt to happen; as intemperate passions *incident* to human nature; diseases *incident* to a climate; misfortunes *incident* to the poor.
3. Appertaining to or following the chief or principal. A court baron is *incident* to a manor. *Encyc.*

IN'CIDENT, *n.* That which falls out; an event; casualty.
2. That which happens aside of the main design; an episode or subordinate action.

No person, no *incident* in a play but must be of use to carry on the main design. *Dryden.*

INCIDENT'AL, *a.* Happening; coming without design; casual; accidental; as an *incidental* conversation; an *incidental* occurrence.
2. Not necessary to the chief purpose; occasional.

By some persons, religious duties appear to be regarded as an *incidental* business. *Rogers.*

INCIDENT'AL, *n.* An incident. [*Little used.*] *Pope.*

INCIDENT'ALLY, *adv.* Casually; without intention; accidentally. I was *incidentally* present when the conversation took place.
2. Beside the main design; occasionally.

I treat either purposely or *incidentally* of colors. *Boyle.*

IN'CIDENTLY, *adv.* Occasionally; by the way. [*Not used.*] *Bacon.*

INCIN'ERATE, *v. t.* [L. *in* and *cinis, cineris*, ashes.] To burn to ashes. *Bacon.*

INCIN'ERATED, *pp.* Burnt to ashes.

INCIN'ERATING, *ppr.* Reducing to ashes by combustion.

INCINERA'TION, *n.* The act of reducing to ashes by combustion. *Boyle. Encyc.*

INCIP'IENCY, *n.* Beginning; commencement.

INCIP'IENT, *a.* [L. *incipiens, incipio*; *in* and *capio*, to take.]
Beginning; commencing; as the *incipient* stage of a fever; *incipient* light or day.

INCIR'CLET, *n.* A small circle. *Sidney.*

INCIRCUMSCRIP'TIBLE, *a.* That cannot be circumscribed or limited. *Cranmer.*

INCIRCUMSPEC'TION, *n.* [*in* and *circumspection.*] Want of circumspection; heedlessness. *Brown.*

INCI'SE, *v. t.* *s* as *z.* [Fr. *inciser.*] To cut in; to carve. *Carew.*

INCI'SED, *a.* [L. *incisus*, from *incido*, to cut.]
Cut; made by cutting; as an *incised* wound; *incised* lips. *Wiseman.*

INCI'SELY, *adv.* In the manner of incisions or notches. *Eaton.*

INCIS'ION, *n.* *s* as *z.* [Fr.; L. *incisio*, from *incido*, to cut.]
1. A cutting; the act of cutting into a substance.
2. A cut; a gash; the separation of the surface of any substance made by a sharp instrument. The surgeon with his knife makes an *incision* in the flesh, and the gardener, in a tree; but we do not say, an *incision* is made with a plow or a spade; at least such phraseology is unusual.
3. Separation of viscid matter by medicines. *Obs.* *Bacon.*

INCI'SIVE, *a.* [Fr. *incisif.*] Having the quality of cutting or separating the superficial part of any thing.
Incisive teeth, in animals, are the fore teeth, the cutters.

INCI'SOR, *n.* [L.] A cutter; a fore tooth, which cuts, bites or separates.

INCI'SORY, *a.* Having the quality of cutting.

INCIS'URE, *n.* [L. *incisura.*] A cut; a place opened by cutting; an incision. *Derham.*

INCI'TANT, *n.* [from *incite.*] That which excites action in an animal body. *Darwin.*

INCITA'TION, *n.* [L. *incitatio.* See *Incite.*]
1. The act of inciting or moving to action; incitement. *Brown.*
2. Incitement; incentive; motive; that which excites to action; that which rouses or prompts. *Government of the Tongue.*

INCI'TE, *v. t.* [L. *incito*; *in* and *cito*, to call, to stir up.]
1. To move the mind to action by persuasion or motives presented; to stir up; to rouse; to spur on.

Antiochus, when he *incited* Prusias to join in war, set before him the greatness of the Romans. *Bacon.*

2. To move to action by impulse or influence.

No blown ambition does our arms *incite.* *Shak.*

3. To animate; to encourage.

INCI'TED, *pp.* Moved to action; stirred up; spurred on.

INCI'TEMENT, *n.* That which incites the mind or moves to action; motive; incentive; impulse.

From the long records of a distant age,
Derive *incitements* to renew thy rage. *Pope.*

INCI'TER, *n.* He or that which incites or moves to action.

INCI'TING, *ppr.* Exciting to action; stirring up.

In general, *incite* denotes to operate on the mind or will; *excite* has the same sense, but it extends also to the passions and to material substances; as, to *excite* action in the heart and arteries.

INCIV'IL, *a.* [*in* and *civil.*] Uncivil; rude; unpolite. [But *uncivil* is generally used.]

INCIVIL'ITY, *n.* [Fr. *incivilité.*] Want of courtesy; rudeness of manners towards others; impoliteness. *Tillotson.*

2. Any act of rudeness or ill breeding; *with a plural.* Loud laughter and uncomely jests in respectable company, are *incivilities* and indecencies.

INCIV'ILLY, *adv.* Uncivilly; rudely.

INCIV'ISM, *n.* [*in* and *civism.*] Want of civism; want of love to one's country or of patriotism; unfriendliness to the state or government of which one is a citizen. *Ames.*

INCL'ASP, *v. t.* To clasp; to hold fast. *Cudworth.*

IN'CLAVATED, *a.* Set; fast fixed. *Dict.*

IN'CLE, *n.* A kind of tape made of linen yarn. *Encyc.*

INCLEM'ENCY, *n.* [Fr. *inclemence;* L. *inclementia.* See *Clemency.*]

1. Want of clemency; want of mildness of temper; unmercifulness; harshness; severity; *applied to persons.*

2. Roughness; boisterousness; storminess; or simply raininess; severe cold, &c.; *applied to the weather.* We were detained by the *inclemency* of the weather.

INCLEM'ENT, *a.* Destitute of a mild and kind temper; void of tenderness; unmerciful; severe; harsh.

2. Rough; stormy; boisterous; rainy; rigorously cold, &c.; as *inclement* weather; *inclement* sky. *Pope.*

INCLI'NABLE, *a.* [L. *inclinabilis.* See *Incline.*]

1. Leaning; tending; as a tower *inclinable* to fall. *Bentley.*

2. Having a propension of will; leaning in disposition; somewhat disposed; as a mind *inclinable* to truth. *Milton.*

INCLINA'TION, *n.* [Fr. from L. *inclinatio.* See *Incline.*]

1. A leaning; any deviation of a body or line from an upright position, or from a parallel line, towards another body; as the *inclination* of the head in bowing.

2. In *geometry*, the angle made by two lines or planes that meet; as, the *inclination* of axis of the earth to the plane of the ecliptic is 23° 28′.

3. A leaning of the mind or will; propension or propensity; a disposition more favorable to one thing than to another. The prince has no *inclination* to peace. The bachelor has manifested no *inclination* to marry. Men have a natural *inclination* to pleasure.

A mere *inclination* to a thing is not properly a willing of that thing. *South.*

4. Love; affection; regard; desire; with *for.* Some men have an *inclination for* music, others *for* painting.

5. Disposition of mind. *Shak.*

6. The dip of the magnetic needle, or its tendency to incline towards the earth; also, the angle made by the needle with the horizon. *Enfield.*

7. The act of decanting liquors by stooping or inclining the vessel. *Quincy.*

INCLI'NATORILY, *adv.* Obliquely; with inclination. *Brown.*

INCLI'NATORY, *a.* Having the quality of leaning or inclining. *Brown.*

INCLI'NE, *v. i.* [L. *inclino; in* and *clino,* Gr. κλινω, Sax. *hlinian, hleonian, hlynian,* Eng. to *lean,* G. *lehnen,* D. *leunen,* Russ. *klonyu* and *nakloniayu,* Ir. *cleonaim;* Fr. *incliner;* Port. Sp. *inclinar;* It. *inclinare, inchinare, chinare.* Class Ln.]

1. To lean; to deviate from an erect or parallel line toward any object; to tend. Converging lines *incline* toward each other. A road *inclines* to the north or south. Connecticut river runs south, *inclining* in some part of its course to the west, and below Middletown, it *inclines* to the east.

2. To lean; *in a moral sense;* to have a propension; to be disposed; to have some wish or desire.

Their hearts *inclined* to follow Abimelech. Judges ix.

3. To have an appetite; to be disposed; as, to be *inclined* to eat.

INCLI'NE, *v. t.* To cause to deviate from an erect, perpendicular or parallel line; to give a leaning to; as, *incline* the column or post to the east; *incline* your head to the right.

2. To give a tendency or propension to the will or affections; to turn; to dispose.

Incline our hearts to keep this law. *Common Prayer.*

Incline my heart to thy testimonies. Ps. cxix.

3. To bend; to cause to stoop or bow; as, to *incline* the head or the body in acts of reverence or civility.

INCLI'NED, *pp.* Having a leaning or tendency; disposed.

Inclined plane, in *mechanics,* is a plane that makes an oblique angle with the plane of the horizon; a sloping plane.

INCLI'NER, *n.* An inclined dial.

INCLI'NING, *ppr.* Leaning; causing to lean.

INCLI'NING, *a.* Leaning.

INCLIP', *v. t.* [*in* and *clip.*] To grasp; to inclose; to surround. *Shak.*

INCLOIS'TER, *v. t.* [*in* and *cloister.*] To shut up or confine in a cloister. [But *cloister* is generally used.]

INCLO'SE, *v. t. s* as *z.* [Fr. *enclos;* Sp. It. *incluso;* L. *inclusus, includo; in* and *claudo,* or *cludo.*]

1. To surround; to shut in; to confine on all sides; as, to *inclose* a field with a fence; to *inclose* a fort or an army with troops; to *inclose* a town with walls.

2. To separate from common grounds by a fence; as, to *inclose* lands.

3. To include; to shut or confine; as, to *inclose* trinkets in a box.

4. To environ; to encompass.

5. To cover with a wrapper or envelop; to cover under seal; as, to *inclose* a letter or a bank note.

INCLO'SED, *pp.* Surrounded; encompassed; confined on all sides; covered and sealed; fenced.

INCLO'SER, *n.* He or that which incloses; one who separates land from common grounds by a fence.

INCLO'SING, *ppr.* Surrounding; encompassing; shutting in; covering and confining.

INCLO'SURE, *n.* The act of inclosing.

2. The separation of land from common ground into distinct possessions by a fence.

3. The appropriation of things common. *Taylor.*

4. State of being inclosed, shut up or encompassed. *Ray.*

5. A space inclosed or fenced; a space comprehended within certain limits.

6. Ground inclosed or separated from common land.

7. That which is inclosed or contained in an envelop, as a paper. *Washington.*

INCLOUD', *v. t.* [*in* and *cloud.*] To darken; to obscure. *Shak.*

INCLOUD'ED, *pp.* Involved in obscurity.

INCLOUD'ING, *ppr.* Darkening; obscuring.

INCLU'DE, *v. t.* [L. *includo; in* and *cludo,* to shut up; Fr. *enclorre.*]

1. To confine within; to hold; to contain; as, the shell of a nut *includes* the kernel; a pearl is *included* in a shell. [But in these senses we more commonly use *inclose.*]

2. To comprise; to comprehend; to contain. The history of England necessarily *includes* a portion of that of France. The word duty, *includes* what we owe to God, to our fellow men, and to ourselves; it *includes* also a tax payable to the government.

INCLU'DED, *pp.* Contained; comprehended.

INCLU'DING, *ppr.* Containing; comprising.

INCLU'SION, *n. s* as *z.* [L. *inclusio.*] The act of including.

INCLU'SIVE, *a.* [Fr. *inclusif.*] Inclosing; encircling. *Shak.*

2. Comprehended in the number or sum; as from Monday to Saturday *inclusive,* that is, taking in both Monday and Saturday.

INCLU'SIVELY, *adv.* Comprehending the thing mentioned; as from Monday to Saturday *inclusively.*

INCOAG'ULABLE, *a.* [*in* and *coagulable.*] That cannot be coagulated or concreted.

INCOER'CIBLE, *a.* [*in* and *coercible,* from *coerce.*]
Not to be coerced or compelled; that cannot be forced. *Black.*

INCOEXIST'ENCE, *n.* [*in* and *coexistence.*] A not existing together. [*Not common.*] *Locke.*

INCOG', *adv.* [contracted from *incognito.*] In concealment; in disguise; in a manner not to be known.

INCOG'ITANCY, *n.* [L. *incogitantia; in* and *cogito,* to think.]
Want of thought, or want of the power of thinking. *Decay of Piety.*

INCOG'ITANT, *a.* Not thinking; thoughtless. *Milton.*

INCOG'ITANTLY, *adv.* Without consideration. *Boyle.*

INCOG'ITATIVE, *a.* [*in* and *cogitative.*] Not thinking; wanting the power of thought; as, a vegetable is an *incogitative* being. *Locke.*

INCOG'NITO, *adv.* [L. *incognitus; in* and *cognitus*, known.] In concealment; in a disguise of the real person.

INCOGN'IZABLE, *a. incon'izable.* [*in* and *cognizable.*]
That cannot be recognized, known or distinguished.

The Lettish race, not a primitive stock of the Slavi, but a distinct branch, now become *incognizable*— *Tooke.*

INCOHE'RENCE, INCOHE'RENCY, *n.* [*in* and *coherence.*]
1. Want of coherence; want of cohesion or adherence; looseness or unconnected state of parts, as of a powder. *Boyle.*
2. Want of connection; incongruity; inconsistency; want of agreement, or dependence of one part on another; as the *incoherence* of arguments, facts or principles.
3. Inconsistency; that which does not agree with other parts of the same thing.

INCOHE'RENT, *a.* [*in* and *coherent.*]
1. Wanting cohesion; loose; unconnected; not fixed to each other; *applied to material substances.* *Woodward.*
2. Wanting coherence or agreement; incongruous; inconsistent; having no dependence of one part on another; as, the thoughts of a dreaming man, and the language of a madman, are *incoherent.*

INCOHE'RENTLY, *adv.* Inconsistently; without coherence of parts; as, to talk *incoherently.*

INCOIN'CIDENCE, *n.* [*in* and *coincidence.*] Want of coincidence or agreement.

INCOIN'CIDENT, *a.* [*in* and *coincident.*] Not coincident; not agreeing in time, place or principle.

INCOLU'MITY, *n.* [L. *incolumitas.*] Safety; security. *Howell.*

INCOMBI'NE, *v. i.* To differ. [*Ill formed.*] *Milton.*

INCOMBUSTIBIL'ITY, *n.* [from *incombustible.*]
The quality of being incapable of being burnt or consumed. *Ray.*

INCOMBUST'IBLE, *a.* [*in* and *combustible.*] Not to be burnt, decomposed or consumed by fire. Amianth is an *incombustible* substance.

INCOMBUST'IBLENESS, *n.* Incombustibility.

IN'COME, *n. in'cum.* [*in* and *come.*] That gain which proceeds from labor, business or property of any kind; the produce of a farm; the rent of houses; the proceeds of professional business; the profits of commerce or of occupation; the interest of money or stock in funds. *Income* is often used synonymously with *revenue*, but *income* is more generally applied to the gain of private persons, and *revenue* to that of a sovereign or of a state. We speak of the annual *income* of a gentleman, and the annual *revenue* of the state.
2. A coming in; admission; introduction. [*Not in use.*]

IN'COMING, *a.* Coming in. *Burke.*

IN'COMING, *n.* [*in* and *come.*] Income; gain.

Many *incomings* are subject to great fluctuations. *Tooke.*

INCOMMENSURABIL'ITY, *n.* [from *incommensurable.*]
The quality or state of a thing, when it has no common measure with another thing, or when the same thing will not exactly measure both.

INCOMMEN'SURABLE, *a.* [*in* and *commensurable.*]
Having no common measure. Two lines are *incommensurable*, when, compared to each other, they have no common measure, that is, no measure that will exactly measure both. Quantities are *incommensurable*, when no third quantity can be found that is an aliquot part of both. *Encyc.*

INCOMMEN'SURATE, *a.* [*in* and *commensurate.*]
1. Not admitting of a common measure. *More.*
2. Not of equal measure or extent; not adequate. Our means are *incommensurate* to our wants.

INCOMMEN'SURATELY, *adv.* Not in equal or due measure or proportion. *Cheyne.*

INCOMMIS'CIBLE, *a.* [*in* and *commix.*] That cannot be commixed or mutually mixed.

INCOMMIX'TURE, *n.* A state of being unmixed. *Brown.*

INCOMMO'DE, *v. t.* [L. *incommodo; in* and *commodo, con* and *modus.*]
To give inconvenience to; to give trouble to; to disturb or molest in the quiet enjoyment of something, or in the facility of acquisition. It denotes less than *annoy, vex* or *harass.* We are *incommoded* by want of room to sit at ease. Visits of strangers at unseasonable hours, *incommode* a family. Often we are *incommoded* by a fashionable dress.

INCOMMO'DED, *pp.* Put to inconvenience; molested.

INCOMMO'DING, *ppr.* Subjecting to trouble or inconvenience.

INCOMMO'DIOUS, *a.* [L. *incommodus.*] Inconvenient; not affording ease or advantage; unsuitable; giving trouble, without much injury. A seat in church, or the site of a house may be *incommodious.*

INCOMMO'DIOUSLY, *adv.* In a manner to create inconvenience; inconveniently; unsuitably.

INCOMMO'DIOUSNESS, *n.* Inconvenience; unsuitableness.

INCOMMOD'ITY, *n.* [Fr. *incommodité;* L. *incommoditas.*] Inconvenience; trouble. [*Now little used.*] *Bacon.*

INCOMMUNICABIL'ITY, INCOMMU'NICABLENESS, *n.* [from *incommunicable.*] The quality of not being communicable, or capable of being imparted to another.

INCOMMU'NICABLE, *a.* [*in* and *communicable.*]
1. That cannot be communicated or imparted to others.
2. That cannot or may not be communicated, told or revealed to others. *South.*

INCOMMU'NICABLY, *adv.* In a manner not to be imparted or communicated. *Hakewill.*

INCOMMU'NICATED, *a.* Not imparted.

INCOMMU'NICATING, *a.* Having no communion or intercourse with each other; as an administration in *incommunicating* hands. *Hale.*

INCOMMU'NICATIVE, *a.* Not communicative; not free or apt to impart to others in conversation.
2. Not disposed to hold communion, fellowship or intercourse with.

The Chinese—an *incommunicative* nation. *Buchanan.*

INCOMMUTABIL'ITY, INCOMMU'TABLENESS, *n.* The quality of being incommutable.

INCOMMU'TABLE, *a.* [*in* and *commutable.*]
Not to be exchanged or commuted with another.

INCOMMU'TABLY, *adv.* Without reciprocal change. *Ch. Relig. Appeal.*

INCOMPACT', INCOMPACT'ED, *a.* [*in* and *compact.*] Not compact; not having the parts firmly united; not solid. *Boyle.*

INCOM'PARABLE, *a.* [*in* and *comparable.*] That admits of no comparison with others; usually in *a good sense*, but it may be properly used in *a bad sense.* When we say, an *incomparable* man, we mean a man of good qualities, or of some excellence that raises him above comparison or equality with others. So we say, *incomparable* excellence, virtue, wit, &c. But *incomparable* baseness or malignity may be used with propriety.

INCOM'PARABLENESS, *n.* Excellence beyond comparison.

INCOM'PARABLY, *adv.* Beyond comparison; without competition. Newton was *incomparably* the greatest philosopher the English nation had produced.

INCOMPA'RED, *a.* Not matched; peerless. *Spenser.*

INCOMPAS'SIONATE, *a.* [*in* and *compassionate.*]
Void of compassion or pity; destitute of tenderness. *Johnson.*

INCOMPAS'SIONATELY, *adv.* Without pity or tenderness.

INCOMPAS'SIONATENESS, *n.* Want of pity. *Granger.*

INCOMPATIBIL'ITY, *n.* [from *incompatible.*]
1. Inconsistency; that quality or state of a thing which renders it impossible that it should subsist or be consistent with something else. There is a permanent *incompatibility* between truth and falsehood.
2. Irreconcilable disagreement. During the revolution in France, *incompatibility* of temper was deemed a sufficient cause for divorcing man and wife.

INCOMPAT'IBLE, *a.* [Fr. from the L. *in* and *competo*, to suit, to be proper or convenient; *con* and *peto*, to press toward, to seek, or press on. It was formerly *incompetible.*]
1. Inconsistent; that cannot subsist with something else. Thus, truth and falsehood are essentially *incompatible*, as are virtue and vice. A degree of cold that congeals water is *incompatible* with vege-

tation. Dissipation is *incompatible* with health, reputation and virtue.

2. Irreconcilably different or disagreeing; incongruous; as *incompatible* tempers.

3. Legally or constitutionally inconsistent; that cannot be united in the same person, without violating the law or constitution. By our constitution, the offices of a legislator and of a judge are *incompatible*, as they cannot be held at the same time by the same person.

INCOMPAT'IBLY, *adv.* Inconsistently; incongruously.

INCOM'PETENCE, INCOM'PETENCY, *n.* [Fr. *incompetence*, from *incompetent*.]

1. Inability; want of sufficient intellectual powers or talents; as the *incompetency* of infants or idiots.

2. Want of natural adequate strength of body or of suitable faculties; as the *incompetency* of the eyes to discern the motions of the heavenly bodies.

3. Want of legal or constitutional qualifications; as the *incompetency* of a witness.

4. Want of adequate means.

5. Insufficiency; inadequacy; as the *incompetency* of testimony.

INCOM'PETENT, *a.* [Fr. from L. *in* and *competens, competo.* See *Incompatible.*]

1. Wanting adequate powers of mind or suitable faculties; as an *incompetent* judge. Infancy, derangement, want of learning or dotage may render a person *incompetent* to fill an office or to transact business.

2. Wanting due strength or suitable faculties; unable.

3. Wanting the legal or constitutional qualifications. A person convicted of a crime, is an *incompetent* witness in a court of law or equity.

4. Destitute of means; unable.

5. Inadequate; insufficient; as *incompetent* testimony.

6. Unfit; improper; legally unavailable.

It is *incompetent* for the defendant to make this defense. *Mass. Rep.*

INCOM'PETENTLY, *adv.* Insufficiently; inadequately; not suitably.

INCOMPLE'TE, *a.* [*in* and *complete.*] Not finished. The building is *incomplete.*

2. Imperfect; defective.

INCOMPLE'TELY, *adv.* Imperfectly.

INCOMPLE'TENESS, *n.* An unfinished state; imperfectness; defectiveness.

INCOMPLEX', *a.* [*in* and *complex.*] Not complex; uncompounded; simple.

INCOMPLI'ANCE, *n.* [*in* and *compliance.*]

1. Defect of compliance; refusal to comply with solicitations.

2. Untractableness; unyielding temper or constitution.

Self-conceit produces peevishness and *incompliance* of humor in things lawful and indifferent. *Tillotson.*

INCOMPLI'ANT, *a.* [*in* and *compliant.*] Unyielding to request or solicitation; not disposed to comply.

INCOMPO'SED, *a.* [*in* and *composed.*] Disordered; disturbed. [But this word is little used. Instead of it we use *discomposed.*]

INCOM'POSITE, *a.* *incom'pozit.* [*in* and *composite.*] Uncompounded; simple.

INCOMPOSSIBIL'ITY, *n.* [*in* and *compossible.*]

The quality of not being possible but by the negation or destruction of something; inconsistency with something. [*Little used.*] *More. Hale.*

INCOMPOS'SIBLE, *a.* [*in, con,* and *possible.*]

Not possible to be or subsist with something else. [*This and the preceding word are little used, and can hardly be considered as legitimate English words.*]

INCOMPREHENSIBIL'ITY, *n.* [See the next word.]

The quality of being incomprehensible, or beyond the reach of human intellect; inconceivableness. *Campbell.*

INCOMPREHENS'IBLE, *a.* [Fr. See *Comprehend.*]

1. That cannot be comprehended or understood; that is beyond the reach of human intellect; inconceivable. The nature of spiritual being is *incomprehensible to* us, or *by* us.

2. Not to be contained. [*Little used.*] *Hooker.*

INCOMPREHENS'IBLENESS, *n.* Incomprehensibility, which see.

INCOMPREHENS'IBLY, *adv.* In a manner which the human mind cannot comprehend or understand; inconceivably. *Locke.*

INCOMPREHEN'SION, *n.* Want of comprehension or understanding. *Bacon.*

INCOMPREHENS'IVE, *a.* Not comprehensive; not extensive. *Warton.*

INCOMPRESSIBIL'ITY, *n.* [See *Incompressible.*]

The quality of resisting compression, or of being incapable of reduction by force into a smaller compass.

INCOMPRESS'IBLE, *a.* [*in* and *compressible.*]

Not to be compressed; not capable of being reduced by force into a smaller compass; resisting compression. Water is not wholly *incompressible.*

INCONCE'ALABLE, *a.* [*in* and *concealable.*]

Not concealable; not to be hid or kept secret. *Brown.*

INCONCE'IVABLE, *a.* [*in* and *conceivable*; Fr. *inconcevable.*]

1. That cannot be conceived by the mind; incomprehensible. It is *inconceivable* to us, how the will acts in producing muscular motion.

2. That cannot be understood.

INCONCE'IVABLENESS, *n.* The quality of being inconceivable; incomprehensibility.

INCONCE'IVABLY, *adv.* In a manner beyond comprehension, or beyond the reach of human intellect. *South.*

INCONCEP'TIBLE, *a.* Inconceivable. [*Little used.*] *Hale.*

INCONCIN'NITY, *n.* [L. *inconcinnitas.*] Unsuitableness; want of proportion. *More.*

INCONCLU'DENT, *a.* [L. *in* and *concludens, concludo,* to conclude.]

Not inferring a conclusion or consequence. [*Little used.*] *Ayliffe.*

INCONCLU'DING, *a.* Inferring no consequence. *Pearson.*

INCONCLU'SIVE, *a.* [*in* and *conclusive.*] Not producing a conclusion; not closing, concluding or settling a point in debate or a doubtful question. An argument or evidence is *inconclusive*, when it does not exhibit the truth of a disputed case in such a manner as to satisfy the mind, and put an end to debate or doubt.

INCONCLU'SIVELY, *adv.* Without such evidence as to determine the understanding in regard to truth or falsehood.

INCONCLU'SIVENESS, *n.* Want of such evidence as to satisfy the mind of truth or falsehood, and put an end to debate.

INCONCOCT', *a.* Inconcocted.

INCONCOCT'ED, *a.* [*in* and *concoct.*] Not fully digested; not matured; unripened. *Bacon.*

INCONCOC'TION, *n.* [*in* and *concoction.*] The state of being indigested; unripeness; immaturity. *Bacon.*

INCONCUR'RING, *a.* [*in* and *concurring*, from *concur.*] Not concurring; not agreeing. *Brown.*

INCONCUS'SIBLE, *a.* That cannot be shaken. *Reynolds.*

INCONDENSABIL'ITY, *n.* [See *Incondensable.*] The quality of being not condensable.

INCONDENS'ABLE, *a.* [*in* and *condensable.*]

1. Not capable of condensation; that cannot be made more dense or compact. *Black.*

2. Not to be converted from a state of vapor to a fluid.

INCON'DITE, *a.* [L. *inconditus*; *in* and *condo*, to build.]

Rude; unpolished; irregular. [*Little used.*] *Philips.*

INCONDI''TIONAL, *a.* [*in* and *conditional.*] Without any condition, exception or limitation; absolute. [*Not now used.* See *Unconditional.*] *Brown.*

INCONDI''TIONATE, *a.* [*in* and *condition.*]

Not limited or restrained by conditions; absolute. [*Not now used.*] *Boyle.*

INCONFIRMED, for *unconfirmed*, is not in use.

INCONFORM'ITY, *n.* [*in* and *conformity.*] Want of conformity; incompliance with the practice of others, or with the requisitions of law, rule or custom; non-conformity. [The latter word is more commonly used, especially to express dissent in religion.]

INCONFU'SED, *a.* *s* as *z.* Not confused; distinct. *Bacon.*

INCONFU'SION, *n.* Distinctness. *Bacon.*

INCONGE'NIAL, *a.* [*in* and *congenial.*] Not congenial; not of a like nature; unsuitable.

INCONGENIAL'ITY, *n.* Unlikeness of nature; unsuitableness.

INCON'GRUENCE, *n.* [*in* and *congruence.*] Want of congruence, adaptation or agreement; unsuitableness. [*Little used.* We now use *incongruity.*] *Boyle.*

INCON'GRUENT, *a.* Unsuitable; inconsistent. *Elyot.*

INCONGRU'ITY, *n.* [*in* and *congruity.*]

1. Want of congruity; impropriety; inconsistency; absurdity; unsuitableness of one thing to another. The levity of youth in a grave divine, is deemed an *incongruity* between manners and profession.

2. Disagreement of parts; want of symmetry. *Donne.*

INCON'GRUOUS, *a.* [L. *incongruus.*] Not congruous; unsuitable; not fitting; inconsistent; improper. The dress of a seaman on a judge, would be deemed *incongruous* with his character and station.

INCON'GRUOUSLY, *adv.* Unsuitably; unfitly; improperly.

INCONNEC'TION, *n.* [*in* and *connection.*] Want of connection; loose, disjointed state. *Bp. Hall.*

INCON'SCIONABLE, *a.* Having no sense of good and evil. *Spenser.*

INCON'SEQUENCE, *n.* [L. *inconsequentia.*] Want of just inference; inconclusiveness. *Stillingfleet.*

INCON'SEQUENT, *a.* Not following from the premises; without regular inference; as an *inconsequent* deduction or argument. *Brown.*

INCONSEQUEN'TIAL, *a.* Not regularly following from the premises.

2. Not of consequence; not of importance; of little moment. *Chesterfield.*

INCONSID'ERABLE, *a.* [*in* and *considerable.*]
Not worthy of consideration or notice; unimportant; small; trivial. We speak of an *inconsiderable* distance; an *inconsiderable* quantity or amount; *inconsiderable* value. No sin is *inconsiderable* in the sight of a holy God.

INCONSID'ERABLENESS, *n.* Small importance. *Tillotson.*

INCONSID'ERABLY, *adv.* In a small degree; to a small amount; very little.

INCONSID'ERACY, *n.* Thoughtlessness; want of consideration. [*Unusual.*] *Chesterfield.*

INCONSID'ERATE, *a.* [L. *inconsideratus.* See *Consider.*]

1. Not considerate; not attending to the circumstances which regard safety or propriety; hasty; rash; imprudent; careless; thoughtless; heedless; inattentive. The young are generally *inconsiderate.*

2. Proceeding from heedlessness; rash; as *inconsiderate* conduct.

3. Not duly regarding; with *of*, before the subject; as *inconsiderate of* consequences.

INCONSID'ERATELY, *adv.* Without due consideration or regard to consequences; heedlessly; carelessly; rashly; imprudently. *Addison.*

INCONSID'ERATENESS, *n.* Want of due regard to consequences; carelessness; thoughtlessness; inadvertence; inattention; imprudence. *Tillotson.*

INCONSIDERA'TION, *n.* [Fr.; *in* and *consideration.*]
Want of due consideration; want of thought; inattention to consequences. *Taylor.*

INCONSIST'ENCE, INCONSIST'ENCY, *n.* [*in* and *consistence.*]

1. Such opposition or disagreement as that one proposition infers the negation of the other; such contrariety between things that both cannot subsist together.

> There is a perfect *inconsistency* between that which is of debt and that which is of free gift. *South.*

2. Absurdity in argument or narration; argument or narrative where one part destroys the other; self-contradiction. *Johnson.*

3. Incongruity; want of agreement or uniformity; as the *inconsistency* of a man with himself.

4. Unsteadiness; changeableness.

INCONSIST'ENT, *a.* Incompatible; incongruous; not suitable. Loud laughter in grave company is *inconsistent* with good breeding. Habitual gloom is *inconsistent* with health and happiness.

2. Not consistent; contrary, so that one infers the negation or destruction of the other; or so that the truth of one proves the other to be false. Two covenants, one that a man shall have an estate in fee, and the other that he shall hold it for years, are *inconsistent.*

3. Not uniform; being contrary at different times. Men are sometimes *inconsistent* with themselves.

INCONSIST'ENTLY, *adv.* With absurdity; incongruously; with self-contradiction; without steadiness or uniformity.

INCONSIST'ENTNESS, *n.* Inconsistency. [*Not in use.*] *More.*

INCONSIST'ING, *a.* Inconsistent. [*Not used.*] *Dryden.*

INCONSO'LABLE, *a.* [*in* and *consolable.*] Not to be consoled; grieved beyond susceptibility of comfort. *Addison.*

INCONSO'LABLY, *adv.* In a manner or degree that does not admit of consolation.

INCON'SONANCE, *n.* Disagreement of sounds; discordance. *Busby.*

INCON'SONANCY, *n.* [*in* and *consonancy.*] Disagreement; inconsistency. In *music*, disagreement of sounds; discordance.

INCON'SONANT, *a.* Not agreeing; inconsistent; discordant.

INCONSPIC'UOUS, *a.* [*in* and *conspicuous.*]

1. Not discernible; not to be perceived by the sight. *Boyle.*

2. Not conspicuous.

INCON'STANCY, *n.* [L. *inconstantia.* See *Constancy.*]

1. Mutability or instability of temper or affection; unsteadiness; fickleness. *Addison.*

2. Want of uniformity; dissimilitude. *Woodward.*

INCON'STANT, *a.* [L. *inconstans*; Fr. *inconstant.*]

1. Mutable; subject to change of opinion, inclination or purpose; not firm in resolution; unsteady; fickle; *used of persons*; as *inconstant* in love or friendship.

2. Mutable; changeable; variable; *used of things.*

INCON'STANTLY, *adv.* In an inconstant manner; not steadily.

INCONSU'MABLE, *a.* [*in* and *consumable.*]
Not to be consumed; that cannot be wasted. *Brown.*

INCONSUM'MATE, *a.* [*in* and *consummate.*]
Not consummate; not finished; not complete.

INCONSUM'MATENESS, *n.* State of being incomplete.

INCONSUMP'TIBLE, *a.* [L. *in* and *consumptus.*]

1. Not to be spent, wasted or destroyed by fire. [*Not used.*] *Digby.*

2. Not to be destroyed. [*Not used.*]

INCONTEST'ABLE, *a.* [Fr.] Not contestable; not to be disputed; not admitting debate; too clear to be controverted; incontrovertible; as *incontestable* evidence, truth or facts.

INCONTEST'ABLY, *adv.* In a manner to preclude debate; indisputably; incontrovertibly; indubitably. *Reid.*

INCONTIG'UOUS, *a.* [*in* and *contiguous.*] Not contiguous; not adjoining; not touching; separate. *Boyle.*

INCON'TINENCE, INCON'TINENCY, *n.* [L. *incontinentia*; Fr. *incontinence.* See *Continence.*]

1. Want of restraint of the passions or appetites; free or uncontrolled indulgence of the passions or appetites, as of anger. *Gillies' Aristotle.*

2. Want of restraint of the sexual appetite; free or illegal indulgence of lust; lewdness; used of either sex, but appropriately of the male sex. *Incontinence* in men is the same as *unchastity* in women.

3. Among *physicians*, the inability of any of the animal organs to restrain discharges of their contents, so that the discharges are involuntary; also, the involuntary discharge itself; as an *incontinence* of urine in diabetes.

INCON'TINENT, *a.* [L. *incontinens.*] Not restraining the passions or appetites, particularly the sexual appetite; indulging lust without restraint or in violation of law; unchaste; lewd.

2. Unable to restrain discharges.
In the sense of *immediate* or *immediately*, *obs.*

INCON'TINENT, *n.* One who is unchaste. *B. Jonson.*

INCON'TINENTLY, *adv.* Without due restraint of the passions or appetites; unchastely.

2. Immediately. *Obs.* *Pope.*

INCONTRACT'ED, *a.* Not contracted; not shortened. *Blackwall.*

INCONTROLLABLE, *a.* [*in* and *controllable.*]
Not to be controlled; that cannot be restrained or governed; uncontrollable. *Walsh.*

INCONTROLLABLY, *adv.* In a manner that admits of no control.

INCONTROVERT'IBLE, *a.* [*in* and *controvertible.*]
Indisputable; too clear or certain to admit of dispute.

INCONTROVERT'IBLY, *adv.* In a manner or to a degree that precludes debate or controversy.

INCONVE'NIENCE, INCONVE'NIENCY, *n.* [L. *inconveniens*; *in* and *convenio*, *conveniens.*]

1. Unfitness; unsuitableness; inexpedience.

> They plead against the *inconvenience*, not the unlawfulness of popish apparel. *Hooker.*

2. That which gives trouble or uneasiness; disadvantage; any thing that disturbs quiet, impedes prosperity, or increases the difficulty of action or success. Rain and bad roads are *inconveniences* to the traveler; want of utensils is a great *inconvenience* to a family; but the great *inconvenience* of human life is the want of money and the means of obtaining it.

INCONVE'NIENT, *a.* [Fr. from the L. supra.]

1. Incommodious; unsuitable; disadvantageous; giving trouble or uneasiness; in-

creasing the difficulty of progress or success; as an *inconvenient* dress or garment; an *inconvenient* house; *inconvenient* customs; an *inconvenient* arrangement of business.

2. Unfit; unsuitable. *Hooker.*

INCONVE'NIENTLY, *adv.* Unsuitably; incommodiously; in a manner to give trouble; unseasonably.

INCONVERS'ABLE, *a.* [*in* and *conversable.*]
Not inclined to free conversation; incommunicative; unsocial; reserved. *More.*

INCON'VERSANT, *a.* Not conversant; not familiar; not versed. *Shaw's Zool.*

INCONVERTIBIL'ITY, *n.* [from *inconvertible.*]
The quality of not being changeable or convertible into something else; as the *inconvertibility* of bank notes or other currency into gold or silver. *Walsh.*

INCONVERT'IBLE, *a.* [*in* and *convertible.*]
Not convertible; that cannot be transmuted or changed into something else. One metal is *inconvertible* into another. Bank notes are sometimes *inconvertible* into specie. *Walsh.*

INCONVIN'CIBLE, *a.* [*in* and *convincible.*] Not convincible; that cannot be convinced; not capable of conviction.

INCONVIN'CIBLY, *adv.* In a manner not admitting of conviction.

INCO'NY, *a.* or *n.* [Qu. *in* and *con*, to know.] Unlearned; artless; an accomplished person, in contempt. [*Ill.*] *Shak.*

INCOR'PORAL, *a.* [*in* and *corporal.*] Not consisting of matter or body; immaterial. [*Incorporeal is generally used.*] *Raleigh.*

INCORPORAL'ITY, *n.* The quality of not consisting of matter; immateriality.

INCOR'PORALLY, *adv.* Without matter or a body; immaterially.

INCOR'PORATE, *a.* [*in* and *corporate.*]
1. Not consisting of matter; not having a material body. [*Little used.*]
2. Mixed; united in one body; associated. *Bacon. Shak.*

INCOR'PORATE, *v. t.* [Fr. *incorporer*; Sp. *incorporar*; It. *incorporare*; L. *incorporo*; *in* and *corpus*, a body.]
1. In *pharmacy*, to mix different ingredients in one mass or body; to reduce dry substances to the consistence of paste by the admixture of a fluid, as in making pills, &c. *Encyc.*
2. To mix and embody one substance in another; as, to *incorporate* copper with silver.
3. To unite; to blend; to work into another mass or body; as, to *incorporate* plagiarisms into one's own composition.
4. To unite; to associate in another government or empire. The Romans *incorporated* conquered countries into their government. *Addison.*
5. To embody; to give a material form to.

The idolaters, who worshiped their images as gods, supposed some spirit to be *incorporated* therein. *Stillingfleet.*

6. To form into a legal body, or body politic; to constitute a body, composed of one or more individuals, with the quality of perpetual existence or succession, unless limited by the act of incorporation; as, to *incorporate* the inhabitants of a city, town or parish; to *incorporate* the proprietors of a bridge, the stockholders of a bank, of an insurance company, &c. New Haven was *incorporated* in January 1784; Hartford in May 1784. *Stat. of Connecticut.*

INCOR'PORATE, *v. i.* To unite so as to make a part of another body; to be mixed or blended; to grow into, &c.; usually followed by *with.*

Painters' colors and ashes do better *incorporate with* oil. *Bacon.*

INCOR'PORATED, *pp.* Mixed or united in one body; associated in the same political body; united in a legal body.

INCOR'PORATING, *ppr.* Mixing or uniting in one body or mass; associating in the same political body; forming a legal body.

INCORPORA'TION, *n.* The act of incorporating.
2. Union of different ingredients in one mass.
3. Association in the same political body; as the *incorporation* of conquered countries into the Roman republic.
4. Formation of a legal or political body by the union of individuals, constituting an artificial person. *Blackstone.*

INCORPO'REAL, *a.* [Fr. *incorporel*; L. *incorporalis, incorporeus.*]
Not consisting of matter; not having a material body; immaterial. Spirits are deemed *incorporeal* substances.

INCORPO'REALLY, *adv.* Without body; immaterially. *Bacon.*

INCORPORE'ITY, *n.* The quality of being not material; immateriality.

INCORPSE, *v. t.* *incorps'.* To incorporate. [*Barbarous.*] *Shak.*

INCORRECT', *a.* [*in* and *correct.*] Not correct; not exact; not according to a copy or model, or to established rules; inaccurate; faulty.

The piece, you think, is *incorrect.* *Pope.*

2. Not according to truth; inaccurate; as an *incorrect* statement, narration or calculation.
3. Not according to law or morality.

INCORREC'TION, *n.* Want of correction. *Arnway.*

INCORRECT'LY, *adv.* Not in accordance with truth or other standard; inaccurately; not exactly; as a writing *incorrectly* copied; testimony *incorrectly* stated.

INCORRECT'NESS, *n.* Want of conformity to truth or to a standard; inaccuracy. *Incorrectness* may consist in defect or in redundance.

INCOR'RIGIBLE, *a.* [Fr.; *in* and *corrigible*; L. *corrigo*; *con* and *rego.*]
1. That cannot be corrected or amended; bad beyond correction; as *incorrigible* error.
2. Too depraved to be corrected or reformed; as an *incorrigible* sinner; an *incorrigible* drunkard.

INCOR'RIGIBLENESS, } *n.* The quality of
INCORRIGIBIL'ITY, } being bad, erroneous or depraved beyond correction; hopeless depravity in persons and error in things. *Locke.*

INCOR'RIGIBLY, *adv.* To a degree of depravity beyond all means of amendment. *Roscommon.*

INCORRUPT', } *a.* [L. *incorruptus*; *in*
INCORRUPT'ED, } and *corrumpo*, *corruptus*; *con* and *rumpo*, to break.]
Not corrupt; not marred, impaired or spoiled; not defiled or depraved; pure; sound; untainted; *applicable to persons, principles or substances.* *Milton.*

INCORRUPTIBIL'ITY, *n.* [from *incorruptible.*]
The quality of being incapable of decay or corruption.

INCORRUPT'IBLE, *a.* [Fr.; *in* and *corruptible.*]
1. That cannot corrupt or decay; not admitting of corruption. Thus gold, glass, mercury, &c., are *incorruptible.* Spirits are supposed to be *incorruptible.*

Our bodies shall be changed into *incorruptible* and immortal substances. *Wake.*

2. That cannot be bribed; inflexibly just and upright.

INCORRUPT'IBLENESS, *n.* The quality of being incorruptible, or not liable to decay. *Boyle.*

INCORRUP'TION, *n.* [*in* and *corruption.*] Incapacity of being corrupted.

It is sown in corruption; it is raised in *incorruption.* 1 Cor. xv.

INCORRUPT'IVE, *a.* Not liable to corruption or decay. *Akenside.*

INCORRUPT'NESS, *n.* Exemption from decay or corruption.
2. Purity of mind or manners; probity; integrity; honesty. *Woodward.*

INCRAS'SATE, *v. t.* [L. *incrasso, incrassatus*; *in* and *crassus*, thick.]
1. To make thick or thicker; to thicken; the contrary to *attenuate.*
2. In *pharmacy*, to make fluids thicker by the mixture of other substances less fluid, or by evaporating the thinner parts.

Acids dissolve or attenuate; alkalies precipitate or *incrassate.* *Newton.*

INCRAS'SATE, *v. i.* To become thick or thicker.

INCRAS'SATE, } *a.* In *botany*, thickened
INCRAS'SATED, } or becoming thicker towards the flower, as a peduncle. *Martyn.*
2. Fattened.

INCRAS'SATED, *pp.* Made thick or thicker.

INCRAS'SATING, *ppr.* Rendering thick or thicker; growing thicker.

INCRASSA'TION, *n.* The act of thickening, or state of becoming thick or thicker. *Brown.*

INCRAS'SATIVE, *a.* Having the quality of thickening.

INCRAS'SATIVE, *n.* That which has the power to thicken. *Harvey.*

INCRE'ASABLE, *a.* That may be increased. *Sherwood.*

INCRE'ASE, *v. i.* [L. *incresco*; *in* and *cresco*, to grow, Fr. *croître*, Sp. *crecer*, It. *crescere*, Arm. *cresqi.* As the Latin pret. is *crevi*, this word and the Eng. *grow*, are probably of the same family. Class Rd. No. 59. 75.]
1. To become greater in bulk or quantity; to grow; to augment; as plants. Hence, to become more in number; to advance in value, or in any quality good or bad. Animal and vegetable bodies *increase* by natural growth; wealth *increases* by industry; heat *increases*, as the sun advances towards the meridian; a multitude *increases* by accession of numbers; knowledge *increases* with age and study; passion and

enmity *increase* by irritation, and misery *increases* with vice.

The Lord make you to *increase* and abound in love one toward another. 1 Thess. iii.

2. To become more violent; as, the fever *increases;* the pain *increases;* cold, wind or a storm *increases.*
3. To become more bright or vivid; as, the light *increases.*
4. To swell; to rise.

The waters *increased* and bore up the ark. Gen. vii.

5. To swell; to become louder, as sound.
6. To become of more esteem and authority.

He must *increase,* but I must decrease. John iii.

7. To enlarge, as the enlightened part of the moon's disk.

INCRE'ASE, *v. t.* To augment or make greater in bulk, quantity or amount; as, to *increase* wealth or treasure; to *increase* a sum or value.

2. To advance in quality; to add to any quality or affection; as, to *increase* the strength of moral habits; to *increase* love, zeal or passion.
3. To extend; to lengthen; as, to *increase* distance.
4. To extend; to spread; as, to *increase* fame or renown.
5. To aggravate; as, to *increase* guilt or trespass.

INCRE'ASE, *n.* Augmentation; a growing larger; extension.

Of the *increase* of his government and peace, there shall be no end. Is. ix.

2. Increment; profit; interest; that which is added to the original stock.

Take thou no interest of him or *increase;* but fear thy God. Lev. xxv.

3. Produce, as of land.

Then shall the earth yield her *increase.* Ps. lxvii.

4. Progeny; issue; offspring.

All the *increase* of thy house shall die in the flower of their age. 1 Sam. ii.

5. Generation. *Shak.*
6. The waxing of the moon; the augmentation of the luminous part of the moon, presented to the inhabitants of the earth.

Seeds, hair, nails, hedges and herbs will grow soonest, if set or cut in the *increase* of the moon. *Bacon.*

7. Augmentation of strength or violence; as *increase* of heat, love or other passion; *increase* of force.
8. Augmentation of degree; as *increase* of happiness or misery.

INCRE'ASED, *pp.* Augmented; made or grown larger.

INCRE'ASEFUL, *a.* Abundant of produce. *Shak.*

INCRE'ASER, *n.* He or that which increases.

INCRE'ASING, *ppr.* Growing; becoming larger; advancing in any quality, good or bad.

INCREA'TE, INCREA'TED, *a.* Uncreated, which see. [*The latter is the word mostly used.*]

INCREDIBIL'ITY, *n.* [Fr. *incredibilité.* See *Incredible.*]

The quality of surpassing belief, or of being too extraordinary to admit of belief. *Dryden.*

INCRED'IBLE, *a.* [L. *incredibilis; in* and *credibilis,* credible.]

That cannot be believed; not to be credited; too extraordinary and improbable to admit of belief.

Why should it be thought a thing *incredible* with you, that God should raise the dead? Acts xxvi.

INCRED'IBLENESS, *n.* Incredibility, which see.

INCRED'IBLY, *adv.* In a manner to preclude belief.

INCREDU'LITY, *n.* [Fr. *incredulité.*] The quality of not believing; indisposition to believe; a withholding or refusal of belief. *Raleigh.*

Of every species of *incredulity,* religious unbelief is infinitely the most irrational. *Buckminster.*

INCRED'ULOUS, *a.* [L. *incredulus; in* and *credulus; credo,* to believe.]

Not believing; indisposed to admit the truth of what is related; refusing or withholding belief. *Bacon.*

INCRED'ULOUSNESS, *n.* Incredulity, which see.

INCREM'ABLE, *a.* [L. *in* and *cremo.*] That cannot be burnt. [*Not used.*] *Brown.*

IN'CREMENT, *n.* [L. *incrementum,* from *incresco.* See *Increase.*]

1. Increase; a growing in bulk, quantity, number, value or amount; augmentation.
2. Produce; production.
3. Matter added; increase.
4. In *mathematics,* the quantity by which a variable quantity increases; a differential quantity.

IN'CREPATE, *v. t.* [L. *increpo.*] To chide; to rebuke. [*Not in use.*]

INCREPA'TION, *n.* [It. *increpazione.*] A chiding or rebuking; rebuke; reprehension. *Hammond.*

INCRES'CENT, *a.* [L. *increscens.* See *Increase.*]

Increasing; growing; augmenting; swelling.

INCRIM'INATE, *v. t.* [L. *in* and *criminor,* to accuse. See *Crime.*]

To accuse; to charge with a crime or fault.

INCRUENT'AL, *a.* [L. *incruentus.*] Unbloody; not attended with blood. [*Not in use.*]

INCRUST', *v. t.* [L. *incrusto; in* and *crusto,* to crust.]

To cover with a crust or with a hard coat; to form a crust on the surface of any substance; as iron *incrusted* with oxyd or rust; a vessel *incrusted* with salt.

INCRUST'ATE, *v. t.* To incrust. [*Less frequently used.*]

INCRUSTA'TION, *n.* [Fr. from L. *incrustatio.*]

1. A crust or rough coat of any thing on the surface of a body.
2. A covering or lining of marble or other stone. *Addison.*

INCRYS'TALIZABLE, *a.* [*in* and *crystalizable.*]

That will not crystalize; that cannot be formed into crystals.

IN'CUBATE, *v. i.* [L. *incubo; in* and *cubo,* to lie down.] To sit, as on eggs for hatching.

INCUBA'TION, *n.* [Fr. from L. *incubatio.*] The act of sitting on eggs for the purpose of hatching young. *Ray.*

INCU'BATURE, *n.* Incubation. [*Not used.*]

IN'CUBUS, *n.* [L. from *incubo,* to lie on.]

1. The nightmar; an oppression of the breast in sleep, or sense of weight, with an almost total loss of the power of moving the body, while the imagination is frightened or astonished.
2. A demon; an imaginary being or fairy. *Bp. Hall.*

INCUL'CATE, *v. t.* [L. *inculco,* to drive or force on; *in* and *calco,* to tread, *calx,* the heel.]

To impress by frequent admonitions; to teach and enforce by frequent repetitions; to urge on the mind. Our Savior *inculcates* on his followers humility and forgiveness of injuries.

INCUL'CATED, *pp.* Impressed or enforced by frequent admonitions.

INCUL'CATING, *ppr.* Impressing or enforcing by repeated instruction.

INCULCA'TION, *n.* The action of impressing by repeated admonitions.

INCULP'ABLE, *a.* [L. *in* and *culpabilis,* from *culpa,* a fault.]

Without fault; unblamable; that cannot be accused. *South.*

INCULP'ABLENESS, *n.* Unblamableness. *Mountagu.*

INCULP'ABLY, *a.* Unblamably; without blame. *South.*

INCULT', *a.* [L. *incultus; in* and *cultus,* from *colo.*]

Untilled; uncultivated. *Thomson.*

INCUL'TIVATED, *a.* Not cultivated; uncultivated.

INCULTIVA'TION, *n.* Neglect or want of cultivation. *Berington.*

INCUL'TURE, *n.* Want or neglect of cultivation. *Feltham.*

INCUM'BENCY, *n.* [from *incumbent.*] A lying or resting on something.

2. The state of holding or being in possession of a benefice, or of an office.

These fines are to be paid to the bishop, only during his *incumbency.* *Swift.*

There is no test of the tenure, but *incumbency* on the part of the king. *E. Everett.*

INCUM'BENT, *a.* [L. *incumbens, incumbo; in* and *cumbo,* to lie down; Sp. *incumbir.*]

1. Lying or resting on.

And when to move th' *incumbent* load they try. *Addison.*

2. Supported; buoyed up.

And fly *incumbent* on the dusky air. *Dryden.*

3. Leaning on, or resting against; as *incumbent* stamens or anthers, in botany. *Martyn.*
4. Lying on, as duty or obligation; imposed and emphatically urging or pressing to performance; indispensable.

All men, truly zealous, will perform those good works which are *incumbent* on all christians. *Sprat.*

INCUM'BENT, *n.* The person who is in present possession of a benefice, or of any office. [*It is applied to civil officers as well as to ecclesiastical.*]

INCUM'BER, *v. t.* [Fr. *encombrer;* It. *ingombrare.*]

To burden with a load; to embarrass. [See *Encumber,* and its derivatives.]

INCUM'BRANCE, *n.* A burdensome and troublesome load; any thing that impedes motion or action, or renders it difficult or laborious; clog; impediment; embarrassment.

2. A legal claim on the estate of another.

INCUM'BRANCER, *n.* One who has an incumbrance, or some legal claim on an estate. *Kent.*

INCUM'BROUS, *a.* Cumbersome; troublesome. *Obs.* *Chaucer.*

INCUR', *v. t.* [L. *incurro*, to run against; *in* and *curro*, to run; It. *incorrere;* Sp. *incurrir.*]

1. Literally, to run against; hence, to become liable to; to become subject to. Thus, a thief *incurs* the punishment of the law by the act of stealing, before he is convicted, and we have all *incurred* the penalties of God's law.

2. To bring on; as, to *incur* a debt; to *incur* guilt; to *incur* the displeasure of God; to *incur* blame or censure.

3. To occur; to meet; to press on. *Obs.* *Bacon.*

INCURABIL'ITY, *n.* [Fr. *incurabilité.*] The state of being incurable; impossibility of cure; insusceptibility of cure or remedy. *Harvey.*

INCU'RABLE, *a.* [Fr.; *in* and *curable.*]

1. That cannot be cured; not admitting of cure; beyond the power of skill or medicine; as an *incurable* disease.

2. Not admitting remedy or correction; irremediable; remediless; as *incurable* evils.

INCU'RABLE, *n.* A person diseased beyond the reach of cure.

INCU'RABLENESS, *n.* The state of not admitting cure or remedy.

INCU'RABLY, *adv.* In a manner or degree that renders cure impracticable.

INCURIOS'ITY, *n.* Want of curiosity; inattentiveness; indifference. *Wotton.*

INCU'RIOUS, *a.* [*in* and *curious.*] Destitute of curiosity; not curious or inquisitive; inattentive. *Swift.*

INCU'RIOUSNESS, *n.* Want of curiosity or inquisitiveness. *Chesterfield.*

INCUR'RED, *pp.* Brought on.

INCUR'RING, *ppr.* Becoming subject or liable to; bringing on.

INCUR'SION, *n.* [Fr. *incursion;* L. *incursio*, from *incurro.* See *Incur.*]

1. Literally, a running into; hence, an entering into a territory with hostile intention; an inroad; applied to the expeditions of small parties or detachments of an enemy's army, entering a territory for attack, plunder or destruction of a post or magazine. Hence it differs from *invasion*, which is the hostile entrance of an army for conquest. During the revolution, the British troops made an *incursion* to Danbury, and destroyed the magazines. In opposing this *incursion*, Gen. Wooster was killed.

2. Attack; occurrence; as sins of daily *incursion.* [*Unusual.*] *South.*

INCURV'ATE, *v. t.* [L. *incurvo; in* and *curvus*, bent.]

To bend; to crook; to turn from a right line or straight course.

INCURV'ATE, *a.* Curved inwards or upwards.

INCURV'ATED, *pp.* Bent; turned from a rectilinear direction.

INCURV'ATING, *ppr.* Bending; turning from a right line.

INCURVA'TION, *n.* The act of bending.

2. The state of being bent, or turned from a rectilinear course; curvity; crookedness.

3. The act of bowing, or bending the body in respect or reverence. *Stillingfleet.*

INCURVE, *v. t. incurv'.* To bend; to make crooked.

INCURV'ITY, *n.* [from L. *incurvus.*] A state of being bent or crooked; crookedness; a bending inward. *Brown.*

IN'DAGATE, *v. t.* [L. *indago.*] To seek or search out. [*Not used.*]

INDAGA'TION, *n.* The act of searching; search; inquiry; examination. [*Little used.*] *Boyle. Brown.*

IN'DAGATOR, *n.* A searcher; one who seeks or inquires with diligence. [*Little used.*] *Boyle.*

IND'ART, *v. t.* [*in* and *dart.*] To dart in; to thrust or strike in. *Shak.*

Indebitatus assumpsit. [See *Assumpsit.*]

INDEBT, a verb, is never used.

INDEBT'ED, *a. indet'ted.* [It. *indebitato.*]

1. Being in debt; having incurred a debt; held or obliged to pay. A is indebted to B; he is indebted *in* a large sum, or *to* a large amount.

2. Obliged by something received, for which restitution or gratitude is due. We are *indebted to* our parents *for* their care of us in infancy and youth. We are *indebted to* God *for* life. We are *indebted to* the christian religion *for* many of the advantages, and much of the refinement of modern times.

INDEBT'EDNESS, *n. indet'tedness.* The state of being indebted.

INDEBT'MENT, *n. indet'ment.* The state of being indebted. [*Little used.*] *Hall.*

INDE'CENCY, *n.* [Fr. *indecence;* It. *indecenza;* L. *indecens, indeceo; in* and *deceo*, to become.]

That which is unbecoming in language or manners; any action or behavior which is deemed a violation of modesty, or an offense to delicacy, as rude or wanton actions, obscene language, and whatever tends to excite a blush in a spectator. Extreme assurance or impudence may also be deemed *indecency* of behavior towards superiors. [See *Indecorum.*]

INDE'CENT, *a.* [Fr. from L. *indecens.*] Unbecoming; unfit to be seen or heard; offensive to modesty and delicacy; as *indecent* language; *indecent* manners; an *indecent* posture or gesture. *Dryden.*

INDE'CENTLY, *adv.* In a manner to offend modesty or delicacy.

INDECID'UOUS, *a.* [*in* and *deciduous.*] Not falling, as the leaves of trees in autumn; lasting; evergreen.

INDEC'IMABLE, *a.* Not liable to the payment of tithes. *Cowel.*

INDECIS'ION, *n. s* as *z.* [*in* and *decision.*] Want of decision; want of settled purpose or of firmness in the determinations of the will; a wavering of mind; irresolution. *Burke.*

INDECI'SIVE, *a.* [*in* and *decisive.*] Not decisive; not bringing to a final close or ultimate issue; as an *indecisive* battle or engagement; an argument *indecisive* of the question.

2. Unsettled; wavering; vacillating; hesitating; as an *indecisive* state of mind; an *indecisive* character.

INDECI'SIVELY, *adv.* Without decision.

INDECI'SIVENESS, *n.* The state of being undecided; unsettled state; state of not being brought to a final issue.

INDECLI'NABLE, *a.* [Fr. from L. *indeclinabilis; in* and *declino.*]

Not declinable; not varied by terminations; as, *pondo*, in Latin, is an *indeclinable* noun.

INDECLI'NABLY, *adv.* Without variation. *Mountagu.*

INDECOMPO'SABLE, *a. s* as *z.* [*in* and *decomposable, decompose.*]

Not capable of decomposition, or of being resolved into the primary constituent elements. *Encyc.*

INDECOMPO'SABLENESS, *n.* Incapableness of decomposition.

INDEC'OROUS, *a.* [L. *indecorus; in* and *decor, decus, deceo*, to become.]

Unbecoming; violating good manners; contrary to the established rules of good breeding, or to the forms of respect which age and station require. It is *indecorous* in a young person to take the highest place in company, when his superiors are present. *Indecorous* is sometimes equivalent to *indecent*; but it is less frequently applied to actions which offend modesty and chastity.

INDEC'OROUSLY, *adv.* In an unbecoming manner.

INDEC'OROUSNESS, *n.* Violation of good manners in words or behavior.

INDECO'RUM, *n.* [L. *in* and *decorum.*] Impropriety of behavior; that in behavior or manners which violates the established rules of civility, or the duties of respect which age or station requires; an unbecoming action. It is sometimes synonymous with *indecency;* but *indecency*, more frequently than *indecorum*, is applied to words or actions which refer to what nature and propriety require to be concealed or suppressed.

INDEE'D, *adv.* [*in* and *deed.*] In reality; in truth; in fact.

> The carnal mind is enmity against God; for it is not subject to the law of God, neither *indeed* can be. Rom. viii.

Indeed is usually emphatical, but in some cases more so than in others; as, this is true; it is *indeed.*

> I were a beast *indeed* to do you wrong. *Dryden.*

> Some sons *indeed*, some very few we see,
> Who keep themselves from this infection free. *Dryden.*

> There is *indeed* no greater pleasure in visiting these magazines of war— *Addison.*

It is used to note concession or admission; as, ships not so large *indeed*, but better manned.

Indeed is used as an expression of surprise, or for the purpose of obtaining confirmation of a fact stated. *Indeed!* is it possible? is it so *in fact ?*

INDEFAT'IGABLE, *a.* [L. *indefatigabilis; in* and *defatigo, fatigo*, to fatigue.]

Unwearied; not tired; not exhausted by labor; not yielding to fatigue; as *indefatigable* exertions; *indefatigable* attendance or perseverance.

> Upborne with *indefatigable* wings. *Milton.*

INDEFAT'IGABLENESS, *n.* Unweariedness; persistency. *Parnell.*

INDEFAT'IGABLY, *adv.* Without weariness; without yielding to fatigue. *Dryden.*

INDEFATIGA'TION, *n.* Unweariedness. [*Not used.*]

INDEFEASIBIL'ITY, *n.* [from *indefeasible.*]
The quality or state of being not subject to be made void; as the *indefeasibility* of a title.

INDEFE'ASIBLE, *a.* *s* as *z.* [*in* and *defeasible; Fr. defaire, defait,* to undo, to defeat; *de* and *faire,* to make, L. *facio.*]
Not to be defeated; that cannot be made void; as an *indefeasible* estate or title.

INDEFE'ASIBLY, *adv.* In a manner not to be defeated or made void.

INDEFECTIBIL'ITY, *n.* [from *indefectible.*]
The quality of being subject to no defect or decay. *Ch. Observer.*

INDEFECT'IBLE, *a.* [*in* and *defect.*] Unfailing; not liable to defect, failure or decay.

INDEFECT'IVE, *a.* Not defective; perfect; complete. *South.*

INDEFE'ISIBLE, *a.* Indefeasible. [*Not used.*]

INDEFENSIBIL'ITY, *n.* [from *indefensible.*]
The quality or state of not being capable of defense or vindication. *Walsh.*

INDEFENS'IBLE, *a.* [*in* and *defensible,* from *defend.*]
1. That cannot be defended or maintained. A military post may be *indefensible.* A bad cause is *indefensible.*
2. Not to be vindicated or justified. An improper action or indecent expression is *indefensible.*

INDEFENS'IVE, *a.* Having no defense. *Herbert.*

INDEFI''CIENCY, *n.* The quality of not being deficient, or of suffering no delay.

INDEFI''CIENT, *a.* Not deficient; not failing; perfect.

INDEFI'NABLE, *a.* That cannot be defined. *Reynolds.*

INDEF'INITE, *a.* [L. *indefinitus; in* and *definitus, definio,* to define; *de* and *finio,* to end, *finis,* end.]
1. Not limited or defined; not determinate; not precise or certain; as an *indefinite* time. An *indefinite* proposition, term or phrase, is one which has not a precise meaning or limited signification.
2. That has no certain limits, or to which the human mind can affix none; as *indefinite* space. A space may be *indefinite,* though not *infinite.*

INDEF'INITELY, *adv.* Without any settled limitation; as space *indefinitely* extended.
2. Not precisely; not with certainty or precision; as, to use a word *indefinitely.*

INDEF'INITENESS, *n.* The quality of being undefined, unlimited, or not precise and certain.

INDEFIN'ITUDE, *n.* Quantity not limited by our understanding, though yet finite. [*Not used.*] *Hale.*

INDELIB'ERATE, *a.* [*in* and *deliberate;* Fr. *indeliberé.*]
Done or performed without deliberation or consideration; sudden; unpremeditated; as the *indeliberate* commission of sin.

INDELIB'ERATELY, *adv.* Without deliberation or premeditation.

INDELIBIL'ITY, *n.* The quality of being indelible. *Horsley.*

INDEL'IBLE, *a.* [Fr. *indelebile;* L. *indelebilis; in* and *delebilis,* from *deleo,* to blot out.]
1. Not to be blotted out; that cannot be effaced or canceled; as *indelible* letters or characters. *Indelible* ink is such as cannot be taken out of paper or cloth, or not by ordinary means.
2. Not to be annulled.

They are endued with *indelible* power from above, to feed and govern this household. [*Unusual.*] *Sprat.*

3. That cannot be effaced or lost; as, impressions on the mind may be *indelible;* reproach or stain on reputation may be *indelible.*

INDEL'IBLY, *adv.* In a manner not to be blotted out or effaced; too deeply imprinted to be effaced, or to vanish.

INDEL'ICACY, *n.* [*in* and *delicacy.*] Want of delicacy; want of decency in language or behavior, regarding what nature and manners require to be concealed. *Addison.*
2. Want of a nice sense of propriety, or nice regard to refinement in manners or in the treatment of others; rudeness; coarseness of manners or language; that which is offensive to refined taste or purity of mind.

INDEL'ICATE, *a.* Wanting delicacy; indecent; but it expresses less than *indecent;* as an *indelicate* word or expression; *indelicate* behavior; *indelicate* customs.
2. Offensive to good manners, or to purity of mind.

INDEL'ICATELY, *adv.* Indecently; in a manner to offend against good manners or purity of mind.

INDEMNIFICA'TION, *n.* [from *indemnify.*]
1. The act of indemnifying, saving harmless, or securing against loss, damage or penalty.
2. Security against loss.
3. Reimbursement of loss, damage or penalty.

INDEM'NIFIED, *pp.* Saved harmless; secured against damage.

INDEM'NIFY, *v. t.* [*in* and *damnify;* L. *damnificus; damnum,* loss.]
1. To save harmless; to secure against loss, damage or penalty.
2. To make good; to reimburse to one what he has lost. We *indemnify* a man, by giving sufficient security to make good a future loss, or by actual reimbursement of loss, after it has occurred.

INDEM'NIFYING, *ppr.* Saving harmless; securing against loss; reimbursing loss.

INDEM'NITY, *n.* [Fr. *indemnité;* Sp. *indemnidad;* It. *indennità;* L. *in* and *damnum,* loss.]
1. Security given to save harmless; a writing or pledge by which a person is secured against future loss.
2. Security against punishment.

INDEMON'STRABLE, *a.* [*in* and *demonstrable.*] That cannot be demonstrated.

INDENIZA'TION, *n.* The act of naturalizing, or the patent by which a person is made free.

IN'DENIZE, *v. t.* To endenize, which see.

INDEN'IZEN, *v. t.* To invest with the privileges of a free citizen. *Overbury.*

INDENT', *v. t.* [*in* and Fr. *dent,* L. *dens,* a tooth; Fr. *denteler;* Arm. *danta.*]
1. To notch; to jag; to cut any margin into points or inequalities, like a row of teeth; as, to *indent* the edge of paper.

The margins—are *indented.* *Woodward.*

2. To bind out by indentures or contract; as, to *indent* a young man to a shoemaker; to *indent* a servant.

INDENT', *v. i.* To contract; to bargain or covenant. [From the practice of using indented writings or counterparts.] *Shak.*

INDENT', *n.* Incisure; a cut or notch in the margin of any thing, or a recess like a notch. *Shak.*
2. A stamp.

IN'DENT, *n.* A certificate or indented certificate issued by the government of the United States at the close of the revolution, for the principal or interest of the public debt. *Ramsay. Hamilton.*

INDENTA'TION, INDENT'MENT, *n.* A notch; a cut in the margin of paper or other things. *Woodward.*
2. A recess or depression in any border.

INDENT'ED, *pp.* Cut in the edge into points, like teeth.
2. Bound out by indented writings; as an *indented* apprentice or servant.
3. Bound out by writings, or covenants in writing. [The practice of indenting writings is in some places discontinued, but the term remains in use.]

INDENT'ING, *ppr.* Cutting into notches.
2. Binding out by covenants in writing.

INDENT'MENT, *n.* Indenture.

INDENT'URE, *n.* A writing containing a contract. Indentures are generally duplicates, laid together and indented, so that the two papers or parchments correspond to each other. But indenting is often neglected, while the writings or counterparts retain the name of *indentures.*

INDENT'URE, *v. t.* To indent; to bind by indentures; as, to *indenture* an apprentice.

INDEPEND'ENCE, *n.* [*in* and *dependence.*]
1. A state of being not dependent; complete exemption from control, or the power of others; as the *independence* of the Supreme Being.
2. A state in which a person does not rely on others for subsistence; ability to support one's self.
3. A state of mind in which a person acts without bias or influence from others; exemption from undue influence; self-direction. *Independence* of mind is an important qualification in a judge.

Declaration of Independence, the solemn declaration of the Congress of the United States of America, on the 4th of July 1776, by which they formally renounced their subjection to the government of Great Britain.

INDEPEND'ENT, *a.* [*in* and *dependent.*]
1. Not dependent; not subject to the control of others; not subordinate. God is the only being who is perfectly *independent.*
2. Not holding or enjoying possessions at the will of another; not relying on others;

not dependent. We all wish to be *independent* in property; yet few men are wholly *independent*, even in property, and none *independent* for the supply of their wants.

3. Affording the means of independence; as an *independent* estate.
4. Not subject to bias or influence; not obsequious; self-directing; as a man of an *independent* mind.
5. Not connected with. It is believed the soul may exist *independent* of matter.
6. Free; easy; self-commanding; bold; unconstrained; as an *independent* air or manner.
7. Separate from; exclusive.

I mean the account of that obligation in general, under which we conceive ourselves bound to obey a law, *independent* of those resources which the law provides for its own enforcement. *Ward.*

8. Pertaining to an independent or congregational church. It is followed by *of* or *on*, both of which are well authorized. *On* is most conformable to analogy, for it always follows *depend*, but *of* is most common.

INDEPEND'ENT, *n.* One who, in religious affairs, maintains that every congregation of christians is a complete church, subject to no superior authority, and competent to perform every act of government in ecclesiastical affairs.

INDEPEND'ENTLY, *adv.* Without depending or relying on others; without control.

2. Without undue bias or influence; not obsequiously.
3. Without connection with other things.

INDEP'RECABLE, *a.* That cannot be deprecated.

INDEPREHENS'IBLE, *a.* That cannot be found out. *Bp. Morton.*

INDEPRI'VABLE, *a.* That cannot be deprived.

INDESCRI'BABLE, *a.* That cannot be described.

INDESCRIP'TIVE, *a.* Not descriptive or containing just description.

INDESERT', *n.* *s* as z. [*in* and *desert.*] Want of merit or worth. *Addison.*

INDES'INENT, *a.* [L. *in* and *desino*, to cease; *de* and *sino.*] Not ceasing; perpetual.

INDES'INENTLY, *adv.* Without cessation. *Ray.*

INDESTRUCTIBIL'ITY, *n.* [from *indestructible.*] The quality of resisting decomposition, or of being incapable of destruction.

INDESTRUC'TIBLE, *a.* [*in* and *destructible.*] That cannot be destroyed; incapable of decomposition; as a material substance. *Boyle.*

INDETERM'INABLE, *a.* [*in* and *determinable.*]

1. That cannot be determined, ascertained or fixed. *Brown.*
2. Not to be determined or ended.

INDETERM'INATE, *a.* [*in* and *determinate.*]

1. Not determinate; not settled or fixed; not definite; uncertain; as an *indeterminate* number of years.
2. Not certain; not precise.

INDETERM'INATELY, *adv.* Not in any settled manner; indefinitely; not with precise limits; as a space *indeterminately* large.

2. Not with certainty or precision of signification; as an idea *indeterminately* expressed.

INDETERM'INATENESS, *n.* Indefiniteness; want of certain limits; want of precision. *Paley.*

INDETERMINA'TION, *n.* [*in* and *determination.*]

1. Want of determination; an unsettled or wavering state, as of the mind.
2. Want of fixed or stated direction. *Bramhall.*

INDETERM'INED, *a.* [*in* and *determined.*] Undetermined; unsettled; unfixed.

INDEVO'TE, *a.* Not devoted. *Bentley.*

INDEVO'TED, *a.* Not devoted. *Clarendon.*

INDEVO'TION, *n.* [Fr.; *in* and *devotion.*] Want of devotion; absence of devout affections. *Decay of Piety.*

INDEVOUT', *a.* [Fr. *indevot.*] Not devout; not having devout affections. *Ibm.*

INDEVOUT'LY, *adv.* Without devotion.

IN'DEX, *n.* plu. *indexes*, sometimes *indices.* [L. connected with *indico*, to show; *in* and *dico*, Gr. δειχνυω.]

1. That which points out; that which shows or manifests.

Tastes are the *indexes* of the different qualities of plants. *Arbuthnot.*

2. The hand that points to any thing, as the hour of the day, the road to a place, &c. *Bentley.*
3. A table of the contents of a book. *Watts.*

A table of references in an alphabetical order.

4. In *anatomy*, the fore finger, or pointing finger.
5. In *arithmetic* and *algebra*, that which shows to what power any quantity is involved; the exponent. *Encyc.*
6. The *index of a globe*, or *the gnomon*, is a little style fitted on the north pole, which by turning with the globe, serves to point to certain divisions of the hour circle. *Encyc.*
7. In *music*, a direct, which see.

Index expurgatory, in catholic countries, a catalogue of prohibited books.

INDEX'ICAL, *a.* Having the form of an index; pertaining to an index.

INDEX'ICALLY, *adv.* In the manner of an index. *Swift.*

INDEXTER'ITY, *n.* [*in* and *dexterity.*]

1. Want of dexterity or readiness in the use of the hands; clumsiness; awkwardness.
2. Want of skill or readiness in any art or occupation. *Harvey.*

IN'DIA, *n.* A country in Asia, so named from the river Indus.

IN'DIAN, *a.* [from India, and this from *Indus*, the name of a river in Asia.] Pertaining to either of the Indies, East or West.

IN'DIAN, *n.* A general name of any native of the Indies; as an East *Indian*, or West *Indian*. It is particularly applied to any native of the American continent.

INDIAN *Arrow Root*, *n.* A plant of the genus Maranta.

INDIAN *Berry*, *n.* A plant of the genus Menispermum.

INDIAN *Bread*, *n.* A plant of the genus Jatropha.

INDIAN *Corn*, *n.* A plant, the maiz, of the genus Zea; a native of America.

INDIAN *Cress*, *n.* A plant of the genus Tropæolum.

INDIAN *Fig*, *n.* A plant of the genus Cactus.

INDIAN *Ink*, *n.* A substance brought from China, used for water colors. It is in rolls or in square cakes, and is said to consist of lampblack and animal glue. *Encyc.*

IN'DIANITE, *n.* [from *India.*] A mineral occurring in masses having a foliated structure and shining luster. Its color is white or gray. *Cleaveland.*

INDIAN *Reed*, *n.* A plant of the genus Canna.

INDIAN *Red*, *n.* A species of ocher, a very fine purple earth, of a firm, compact texture and great weight. *Hill.*

INDIA *Rubber*, *n.* The caoutchouc, a substance of extraordinary elasticity, called also *elastic gum* or *resin*. It is produced by incision from the syringe tree of Cayenne.

IN'DICANT, *a.* [L. *indicans*; *in* and *dico*, to show.] Showing; pointing out what is to be done for the cure of disease. *Coxe.*

IN'DICATE, *v. t.* [L. *indico*; *in* and *dico*, to show, Gr. δειχνυμι.]

1. To show; to point out; to discover; to direct the mind to a knowledge of something not seen, or something that will probably occur in future. Thus, fermentation *indicates* a certain degree of heat in a liquor. A heavy swell of the sea in calm weather often *indicates* a storm at a distance. A particular kind of cloud in the west at evening, *indicates* the approach of rain.
2. To tell; to disclose.
3. In *medicine*, to show or manifest by symptoms; to point to as the proper remedies; as, great prostration of strength *indicates* the use of stimulants.

IN'DICATED, *pp.* Shown; pointed out; directed.

IN'DICATING, *ppr.* Showing; pointing out; directing.

INDICA'TION, *n.* The act of pointing out.

2. Mark; token; sign; symptom; whatever serves to discover what is not before known, or otherwise obvious.

The frequent stops they make in the most convenient places, are plain *indications* of their weariness. *Addison.*

3. In *medicine*, any symptom or occurrence in a disease, which serves to direct to suitable remedies.
4. Discovery made; intelligence given. *Bentley.*
5. Explanation; display. [*Little used.*] *Bacon.*

INDIC'ATIVE, *a.* [L. *indicativus.*] Showing; giving intimation or knowledge of something not visible or obvious. Reserve is not always *indicative* of modesty; it may be *indicative* of prudence.

2. In *grammar*, the *indicative* mode is the form of the verb that *indicates*, that is, which affirms or denies; as, he *writes*, he

is writing; they *run*; we *misimprove* advantages. It also asks questions; as, *has* the mail *arrived*?

INDIC'ATIVELY, *adv.* In a manner to show or signify. *Grew.*

IN'DICATOR, *n.* He or that which shows or points out. *Smith.*

IN'DICATORY, *a.* Showing; serving to show or make known.

INDICE. [See *Index.*]

IN'DICOLITE, *n.* [*indigo*, or *indico*, and λιθος, a stone.]

In *mineralogy*, a variety of shorl or tourmalin, of an indigo blue color, sometimes with a tinge of azure or green. *Cleaveland.*

INDICT, *v. t.* *indi'te.* [L. *indictus*, from *indico*; *in* and *dico*, to speak.]

In *law*, to accuse or charge with a crime or misdemeanor, in writing, by a grand jury under oath. It is the peculiar province of a grand jury to *indict*, as it is of a house of representatives to *impeach*. It is followed by *of*; as *indicted of* treason or arson.

INDICTABLE, *a.* *indi'table.* That may be indicted; as an *indictable* offender.

2. Subject to be presented by a grand jury; subject to indictment; as an *indictable* offense.

INDICTED, *pp.* *indi'ted.* Accused by a grand jury.

INDICTER, *n.* *indi'ter.* One who indicts.

INDICTING, *ppr.* *indi'ting.* Accusing, or making a formal or written charge of a crime by a grand jury.

INDIC'TION, *n.* [Fr. from Low L. *indictio*, *indico.*]

1. Declaration; proclamation. *Bacon.*

2. In *chronology*, a cycle of fifteen years, instituted by Constantine the Great; originally, a period of taxation. Constantine having reduced the time which the Romans were obliged to serve in the army to fifteen years, imposed a tax or tribute at the end of that term, to pay the troops discharged. This practice introduced the keeping of accounts by this period. But, as it is said, in honor of the great victory of Constantine over Mezentius, Sep. 24, A. D. 312, by which christianity was more effectually established, the council of Nice ordained that accounts of years should no longer be kept by Olympiads, but that the *indiction* should be used as the point from which to reckon and date years. This was begun Jan. 1, A. D. 313. *Johnson. Encyc.*

INDIC'TIVE, *a.* Proclaimed; declared. *Kennet.*

INDICTMENT, *n.* *indi'tement.* A written accusation or formal charge of a crime or misdemeanor, preferred by a grand jury under oath to a court. *Blackstone.*

2. The paper or parchment containing the accusation of a grand jury.

IN'DIES, *n. plu.* of *India.*

INDIF'FERENCE, *n.* [Fr. from L. *indifferentia*; *in* and *differo*, to differ. *Indifferency* is little used.]

1. Equipoise or neutrality of mind between different persons or things; a state in which the mind is not inclined to one side more than the other; as when we see a contest of parties with *indifference.*

2. Impartiality; freedom from prejudice, prepossession or bias; as when we read a book on controverted points with *indifference.* [*This is a different application of the first definition.*]

3. Unconcernedness; a state of the mind when it feels no anxiety or interest in what is presented to it. No person of humanity can behold the wretchedness of the poor with *indifference.*

4. State in which there is no difference, or in which no moral or physical reason preponderates; as when we speak of the *indifference* of things in themselves. *Hooker.*

INDIF'FERENT, *a.* [Fr. from L. *indifferens.*]

1. Neutral; not inclined to one side, party or thing more than to another.

> Cato knows neither of them,
> *Indifferent* in his choice to sleep or die. *Addison.*

2. Unconcerned; feeling no interest, anxiety or care respecting any thing. It seems to be impossible that a rational being should be *indifferent* to the means of obtaining endless happiness.

> It was a remarkable law of Solon, that any person who, in the commotions of the republic, remained neuter, or an *indifferent* spectator of the contending parties, should be condemned to perpetual banishment. *Addison.*

3. Having no influence or preponderating weight; having no difference that gives a preference. It is *indifferent* which road we take.

4. Neutral, as to good or evil. Things in themselves *indifferent*, may be rendered evil by the prohibition of law.

5. Impartial; disinterested; as an *indifferent* judge, juror or arbitrator.

6. Passable; of a middling state or quality; neither good, nor the worst; as *indifferent* writing or paper.

Indifferent, used adverbially, as *indifferent* honest, is ungrammatical and vulgar.

INDIF'FERENTLY, *adv.* Without distinction or preference; as, to offer pardon *indifferently* to all. *Addison.*

2. Equally; impartially; without favor, prejudice or bias.

> —They may truly and *indifferently* minister justice. *Com. Prayer.*

3. In a neutral state; without concern; without wish or aversion.

> Set honor in one eye and death i' th' other,
> And I will look on death *indifferently*. *Shak.*

4. Not well; tolerably; passably; as *indifferently* well; to be *indifferently* entertained.

IN'DIGENCE, IN'DIGENCY, } *n.* [Fr. *indigence*, from L. *indigentia*, from *indigeo*; *in* or *ind*, and *egeo*, to want, to lack.]

Want of estate, or means of comfortable subsistence; penury; poverty. A large portion of the human race live in *indigence*, while others possess more than they can enjoy.

IN'DIGENE, *n.* [L. *indigena*; *in* or *ind*, and *geno*, *gigno*, to beget, or to be born.]

One born in a country; a native animal or plant. *Evelyn. Vattel.*

INDIG'ENOUS, *a.* [L. *indigena*, supra.]

1. Native; born in a country; *applied to persons.*

2. Native; produced naturally in a country or climate; not exotic; *applied to vegetables.*

IN'DIGENT, *a.* [L. *indigens*; Fr. *indigent.*]

Destitute of property or means of comfortable subsistence; needy; poor.

> Charity consists in relieving the *indigent*. *Addison.*

INDIGEST', *n.* A crude mass. [*Not used.*] *Shak.*

INDIGEST'ED, *a.* [*in* and *digested*; L. *indigestus.*]

1. Not digested; not concocted in the stomach; not changed or prepared for nourishing the body; undigested; crude.

2. Not separated into distinct classes or orders, or into proper form; not regularly disposed and arranged. Chaos is represented as a rude or *indigested* mass.

3. Not methodized; not reduced to due form; crude; as an *indigested* scheme.

4. Not prepared by heat.

5. Not brought to suppuration, as the contents of an abscess or boil; as an *indigested* wound. *Wiseman.*

INDIGEST'IBLE, *a.* [*in* and *digestible.*]

1. Not digestible; not easily converted into chyme, or prepared in the stomach for nourishing the body. *Arbuthnot.*

2. Not to be received or patiently endured.

INDIGES'TION, *n.* [*in* and *digestion.*]

Want of due coction in the stomach; a failure of that change in food which prepares it for nutriment; crudity. *Encyc.*

As *a disease*, dyspepsy; that state of the stomach, in which it is incapable of performing its natural healthy functions.

INDIG'ITATE, *v. t.* To point out with the finger. *Brown.*

INDIGITA'TION, *n.* The act of pointing out with the finger. *More.*

INDIGN, *a.* *indi'ne.* [L. *indignus.*] Unworthy; disgraceful. *Obs.* *Chaucer.*

INDIG'NANCE, *n.* Indignation. [*Not in use.*] *Spenser.*

INDIG'NANT, *a.* [L. *indignans*, from *indignor*, to disdain; *in* and *dignor*, *dignus.*]

Affected at once with anger and disdain; feeling the mingled emotions of wrath and scorn or contempt, as when a person is exasperated at one despised, or by a mean action, or by the charge of a dishonorable act. Goliath was *indignant* at the challenge of David.

> He strides *indignant*, and with haughty cries
> To single fight the fairy prince defies. *Tickell.*

INDIGNA'TION, *n.* [Fr. from L. *indignatio.*]

1. Anger or extreme anger, mingled with contempt, disgust or abhorrence.

> When Haman saw Mordecai in the king's gate, that he stood not up, nor moved for him, he was full of *indignation* against Mordecai. Esth. v.

2. The anger of a superior; extreme anger; particularly, the wrath of God against sinful men for their ingratitude and rebellion. 2. Kings iii.

3. The effects of anger; the dreadful effects of God's wrath; terrible judgments. Is. xxvi.

4. Holy displeasure at one's self for sin. 2 Cor. vii.

INDIG'NIFY, *v. t.* To treat disdainfully. [*Not used.*] *Spenser.*

INDIG'NITY, *n.* [L. *indignitas.*] Unmerited, contemptuous conduct towards another; any action towards another which manifests contempt for him; contumely; incivility or injury, accompanied with insult. Contemptuous words respecting one, or foul language in the presence of persons of character and delicacy, and indecent behavior, are *indignities.* Christ on the cross was treated with the foulest *indignity.*

INDIGNLY, *adv.* *indi'nely.* Unworthily. *Obs.* *Hall.*

IN'DIGO, *n.* [L. *indicum*, from *India*; Fr. It. Sp. *indigo.*]
A substance or dye, prepared from the leaves and stalks of the indigo-plant, which are steeped in water till the pulp is extracted, when the tincture is drawn off and churned or agitated, till the dye begins to granulate. The flakes are then left to settle; the liquor is drawn off, and the indigo is drained in bags and dried in boxes. It is used for dyeing blue. *Edwards, W. Ind.*

INDIGOM'ETER, *n.* An instrument for ascertaining the strength of indigo. *Ure.*

IN'DIGO-PLANT, *n.* A plant of the genus Indigofera, from which is prepared indigo. It is a native of Asia, Africa and America, and called by the native Americans, *anil.* The calyx is patent; the carina of the corol is furnished with a subulate, patulous spur on each side; the legume or pod is linear. Several species are cultivated for making indigo, of which the most important are the *tinctoria*, or common indigo-plant, the *anil*, a larger species, and the *disperma*, which furnishes the Guatimala indigo. *Encyc. Miller. Edin. Encyc.*

INDIL'ATORY, *n.* [*in* and *dilatory.*] Not dilatory or slow. *Cornwallis.*

INDIL'IGENCE, *n.* [*in* and *diligence.*] Want of diligence; slothfulness. *B. Jonson.*

INDIL'IGENT, *a.* Not diligent; idle; slothful. *Feltham.*

INDIL'IGENTLY, *adv.* Without diligence. *Bp. Hall.*

INDIMIN'ISHABLE, *a.* That cannot be diminished. *Milton.*

INDIRECT', *a.* [L. *indirectus*; *in* and *directus*, from *dirigo.*]
1. Not straight or rectilinear; deviating from a direct line or course; circuitous. From New York to England by Bordeaux, is an *indirect* course.
2. Not direct, in *a moral sense;* not tending to a purpose by the shortest or plainest course, or by the obvious, ordinary means, but obliquely or consequentially; by remote means; as an *indirect* accusation; an *indirect* attack on reputation; an *indirect* answer or proposal. Hence,
3. Wrong; improper. *Shak.*
4. Not fair; not honest; tending to mislead or deceive.

> *Indirect* dealing will be discovered one time or other. *Tillotson.*

5. *Indirect tax*, is a tax or duty on articles of consumption, as an excise, customs, &c.

INDIREC'TION, *n.* [*in* and *direction.*] Oblique course or means. *Shak.*
2. Dishonest practice. *Obs.* *Shak.*

INDIRECT'LY, *adv.* Not in a straight line or course; obliquely.
2. Not by direct means.
3. Not in express terms. He *indirectly* mentioned the subject.
4. Unfairly.

> Your crown and kingdom *indirectly* held. *Shak.*

INDIRECT'NESS, *n.* Obliquity; devious course.
2. Unfairness; dishonesty. *Mountagu.*

INDISCERN'IBLE, *a.* [*in* and *discernible.*] That cannot be discerned; not visible or perceptible; not discoverable. *Denham.*

INDISCERN'IBLENESS, *n.* Incapability of being discerned. *Hammond.*

INDISCERN'IBLY, *adv.* In a manner not to be seen or perceived.

INDISCERP'IBLE, *a.* Indiscerptible. *Obs.* *More.*

INDISCERPTIBIL'ITY, *n.* The quality of being incapable of dissolution, or separation of parts.

INDISCERP'TIBLE, *a.* [*in* and *discerptible.*] Incapable of being destroyed by dissolution, or separation of parts. *Bp. Butler.*

INDIS'CIPLINABLE, *a.* [*in* and *disciplinable.*]
That cannot be disciplined or subjected to discipline; not capable of being improved by discipline. *Hale.*

INDISCOV'ERABLE, *a.* [*in* and *discoverable.*] That cannot be discovered; undiscoverable.

INDISCOV'ERY, *n.* [*in* and *discovery.*] Want of discovery. [*Unusual.*] *Brown.*

INDISCREE'T, *a.* [*in* and *discreet.*] Not discreet; wanting in discretion; imprudent; inconsiderate; injudicious; as *persons.*
2. Not according to discretion or sound judgment; as *indiscreet* behavior.

INDISCREE'TLY, *adv.* Not discreetly; without prudence; inconsiderately; without judgment.

INDISCRE'TE, *a.* Not discrete or separated. *Pownal.*

INDISCRE''TION, *n.* [*in* and *discretion.*] Want of discretion; imprudence. The grossest vices pass under the fashionable name, *indiscretions.*

INDISCRIM'INATE, *a.* [L. *indiscriminatus.* See *Discriminate.*]
1. Undistinguishing; not making any distinction; as the *indiscriminate* voraciousness of a glutton. *Chesterfield.*
2. Not having discrimination; confused.
3. Undistinguished or undistinguishable.

INDISCRIM'INATELY, *adv.* Without distinction; in confusion.

INDISCRIMIN'ATING, *ppr.* or *a.* Not making any distinction; as the victims of an *indiscriminating* spirit of rapine. *Marshall.*

INDISCRIMINA'TION, *n.* Want of discrimination or distinction. *Jefferson.*

INDISCUS'SED, *a.* Not discussed. *Donne.*

INDISPENSABIL'ITY, *a.* Indispensableness. [*Little used.*] *Skelton.*

INDISPENS'ABLE, *a.* [Fr.; *in* and *dispensable.*]
Not to be dispensed with; that cannot be omitted, remitted or spared; absolutely necessary or requisite. Air and water are *indispensable* to the life of man. Our duties to God and to our fellow men are of *indispensable* obligation.

INDISPENS'ABLENESS, *n.* The state or quality of being absolutely necessary.

INDISPENS'ABLY, *adv.* Necessarily; in a manner or degree that forbids dispensation, omission or want.

INDISPERS'ED, *a.* Not dispersed. *More.*

INDISPO'SE, *v. t.* *s* as *z.* [Fr. *indisposer*; *in* and *disposer*, to dispose or fit. See *Dispose.*]
1. To disincline; to alienate the mind and render it averse or unfavorable to any thing. A love of pleasure *indisposes* the mind *to* severe study and steady attention to business. The pride and selfishness of men *indispose* them *to* religious duties.
2. To render unfit; to disqualify for its proper functions; to disorder; as the distemperature of *indisposed* organs. *Glanville.*
3. To disorder slightly, as the healthy functions of the body.

> It made him rather *indisposed* than sick. *Walton.*

4. To make unfavorable or disinclined; with *towards.*

> The king was sufficiently *indisposed towards* the persons, or the principles of Calvin's disciples. *Clarendon.*

INDISPO'SED, *pp.* or *a.* Disinclined; averse; unwilling; unfavorable.
2. Disordered; disqualified for its functions; unfit.
3. Slightly disordered; not in perfect health.

INDISPO'SEDNESS, *n.* Disinclination; slight aversion; unwillingness; unfavorableness.
2. Unfitness; disordered state.

INDISPO'SING, *ppr.* Disinclining; rendering somewhat averse, unwilling or unfavorable.
2. Disordering; rendering unfit.

INDISPOSI''TION, *n.* [Fr.; *in* and *disposition.*]
1. Disinclination; aversion; unwillingness; dislike; as the *indisposition* of men to submit to severe discipline; an *indisposition* to abandon vicious practices.

> A general *indisposition* towards believing. *Atterbury.*

2. Slight disorder of the healthy functions of the body; tendency to disease. *Indisposition* is a slight defect of healthy action in bodily functions, rather than settled or marked disease.
3. Want of tendency or natural appetency or affinity; as the *indisposition* of two substances to combine.

INDIS'PUTABLE, *a.* [Fr.; *in* and *disputable.*]
Not to be disputed; incontrovertible; incontestable; too evident to admit of dispute. *Addison.*

INDIS'PUTABLENESS, *n.* The state or quality of being indisputable, or too clear to admit of controversy.

INDIS'PUTABLY, *adv.* Without dispute; in a manner or degree not admitting of controversy; unquestionably; without opposition.

INDISPU'TED, *a.* Not disputed or controverted; undisputed. *Encyc.*

INDISSOLUBIL'ITY, *n.* [Fr. *indissolubilité.* See *Indissoluble.*]
1. The quality of being indissoluble, or not capable of being dissolved, melted or liquefied. *Locke.*

2. The quality of being incapable of a breach; perpetuity of union, obligation or binding force. *Warburton.*

INDIS'SOLUBLE, *a.* [Fr. from L. *indissolubilis; in* and *dissolubilis*, from *dissolvo; dis* and *solvo*, to loosen.]

1. Not capable of being dissolved, melted or liquefied, as by heat or water. Few substances are absolutely *indissoluble* by heat; many are *indissoluble* in water.
2. That cannot be broken or rightfully violated; perpetually binding or obligatory; as an *indissoluble* league or covenant. The marriage covenant is *indissoluble*, except in certain specified cases.
3. Not to be broken; firm; stable; as *indissoluble* friendship; *indissoluble* bands of love.

INDIS'SOLUBLENESS, *n.* The quality of being incapable of dissolution, separation or breach; indissolubility. *Hale.*

INDIS'SOLUBLY, *adv.* In a manner resisting separation; firmly united beyond the power of separation; in a manner not to be dissolved or broken.

On they move
Indissolubly firm. *Milton.*

INDISSOLV'ABLE, *a.* [*in* and *dissolvable.*]

1. That cannot be dissolved; not capable of being melted or liquefied.
2. Indissoluble; that cannot be broken; perpetually firm and binding; as an *indissolvable* bond of union.
3. Not capable of separation into parts by natural process.

INDIS'TANCY, *n.* Want of distance or separation. [*A bad word and not used.*] *Pearson.*

INDISTINCT', *a.* [Fr.; L. *indistinctus; in* and *distinctus.* See *Distinct.*]

1. Not distinct or distinguishable; not separate in such a manner as to be perceptible by itself. The parts of a substance are *indistinct*, when they are so blended that the eye cannot separate them, or perceive them as separate. Sounds are *indistinct*, when the ear cannot separate them. Hence,
2. Obscure; not clear; confused; as *indistinct* ideas or notions.
3. Imperfect; faint; not presenting clear and well defined images; as *indistinct* vision; an *indistinct* view.
4. Not exactly discerning. [*Unusual.*] *Shak.*

INDISTINCT'IBLE, *a.* Undistinguishable. [*Little used.*] *Warton.*

INDISTINC'TION, *n.* Want of distinction; confusion; uncertainty.

The *indistinction* of many of the same name—hath made some doubt. *Brown.*

2. Indiscrimination; want of distinction. *Sprat.*
3. Equality of condition or rank. *Coxe, Switz.*

INDISTINCT'LY, *adv.* Without distinction or separation; as when parts of a thing are *indistinctly* seen.

2. Confusedly; not clearly; obscurely; as when ideas are *indistinctly* comprehended.
3. Not definitely; not with precise limits; as when the border of a thing is *indistinctly* marked.

INDISTINCT'NESS, *n.* Want of distinction or discrimination; confusion; uncertainty.

2. Obscurity; faintness; as the *indistinctness* of vision.

INDISTIN'GUISHABLE, *a.* [*in* and *distinguishable.*]
That cannot be distinguished or separated; undistinguishable. *Tytler.*

INDISTIN'GUISHING, *a.* Making no difference; as *indistinguishing* liberalities. *Johnson.*

INDISTURB'ANCE, *n.* [*in* and *disturbance.*]
Freedom from disturbance; calmness; repose; tranquillity. *Temple.*

INDITCH', *v. t.* To bury in a ditch. [*Little used.*] *Bp. Hall.*

INDI'TE, *v. t.* [L. *indico, indictum; in* and *dico*, to speak.]

1. To compose; to write; to commit to words in writing.

Hear how learn'd Greece her useful rules *indites.* *Pope.*

2. To direct or dictate what is to be uttered or written. The late President Dwight *indited* his sermons.

My heart is *inditing* a good matter. Ps. xlv.

INDI'TE, *v. i.* To compose an account of. *Waller.*

[This is from the same original as *indict.* The different applications of the word have induced authors to express each in a different orthography, but without good reason.]

INDI'TED, *pp.* Composed; written; dictated.

INDI'TEMENT, *n.* The act of inditing.

INDI'TING, *ppr.* Committing to words in writing; dictating what shall be written.

INDIVI'DABLE, *a.* Not capable of division. *Shak.*

INDIVI'DED, *a.* Undivided. *Patrick.*

INDIVID'UAL, *a.* [Fr. *individuel;* L. *individuus; in* and *dividuus*, from *divido*, to divide.]

1. Not divided, or not to be divided; single; one; as an *individual* man or city.

—Under his great vicegerent reign abide
United, as one *individual* soul. *Milton.*

2. Pertaining to one only; as *individual* labor or exertions.

INDIVID'UAL, *n.* A single person or human being. This is the common application of the word; as, there was not an *individual* present.

2. A single animal or thing of any kind. But this word, as a noun, is rarely applied except to human beings.

INDIVIDUAL'ITY, *n.* Separate or distinct existence; a state of oneness. *Arbuthnot.*

INDIVID'UALIZE, *v. t.* To distinguish; to select or mark as an individual, or to distinguish the peculiar properties of a person from others. *Drake.*

INDIVID'UALIZED, *pp.* Distinguished as a particular person or thing. *Drake.*

INDIVID'UALIZING, *ppr.* Distinguishing as an individual.

INDIVID'UALLY, *adv.* Separately; by itself; to the exclusion of others. Thirty men will unitedly accomplish what each of them *individually* cannot perform.

2. With separate or distinct existence.

How should that subsist solitarily by itself, which hath no substance, but *individually* the very same whereby others subsist with it? *Hooker.*

3. Inseparably; incommunicably.

Omniscience—an attribute *individually* proper to the Godhead. *Hakewill.*

INDIVID'UATE, *a.* Undivided.

INDIVID'UATE, *v. t.* To make single; to distinguish from others of the species.

Life is *individuated* into infinite numbers, that have their distinct sense and pleasure. *More.*

INDIVIDUA'TION, *a.* The act of making single or the same, to the exclusion of others. *Watts.*

2. The act of separating into individuals by analysis. *Etymol. Vocabulary.*

INDIVIDU'ITY, *n.* Separate existence. [*Not used.*]

INDIVIN'ITY, *n.* Want of divine power. *Brown.*

INDIVISIBIL'ITY, *n.* [See *Indivisible.*] The state or property of being indivisible. *Locke.*

INDIVIS'IBLE, *a.* *s* as *z.* [*in* and *divisible.* See *Divide.*]
That cannot be divided, separated or broken; not separable into parts. Perhaps the particles of matter, however small, cannot be considered as *indivisible.* The mind or soul must be *indivisible.* A mathematical point is *indivisible.*

INDIVIS'IBLE, *n.* In *geometry*, indivisibles are the elements or principles into which a body or figure may be resolved; elements infinitely small. *Encyc.*

INDIVIS'IBLENESS, *n.* Indivisibility, which see.

INDIVIS'IBLY, *adv.* So as not to be capable of division.

INDO'CIBLE, *a.* [*in* and *docible;* L. *doceo*, to teach.]

1. Unteachable; not capable of being taught, or not easily instructed; dull in intellect. *Bp. Hall.*
2. Intractable, as a beast.

INDO'CILE, *a.* [Fr.; L. *indocilis; in* and *docilis; doceo*, to teach.]

1. Not teachable; not easily instructed; dull. *Bentley.*
2. Intractable, as a beast.

INDOCIL'ITY, *n.* [Fr. *indocilité.*] Unteachableness; dullness of intellect. *Bp. Hall.*

2. Intractableness, as of a beast.

INDOC'TRINATE, *v. t.* [Fr. *endoctriner;* L. *in* and *doctrina*, learning.]
To teach; to instruct in rudiments or principles.

He took much delight in *indoctrinating* his young unexperienced favorite. *Clarendon.*

INDOC'TRINATED, *pp.* Taught; instructed in the principles of any science.

INDOC'TRINATING, *ppr.* Teaching; instructing in principles or rudiments.

INDOCTRINA'TION, *n.* Instruction in the rudiments and principles of any science; information. *Brown.*

IN'DOLENCE, *n.* [Fr. from L. *indolentia; in* and *doleo*, to be pained.]

1. Literally, freedom from pain. *Burnet.*
2. Habitual idleness; indisposition to labor; laziness; inaction or want of exertion of body or mind, proceeding from love of ease or aversion to toil. *Indolence*, like *laziness*, implies a constitutional or habitual love of ease; *idleness* does not.

IN'DOLENT, *a.* [Fr.] Habitually idle or indisposed to labor; lazy; listless; sluggish; indulging in ease; *applied to persons.*
2. Inactive; idle; as an *indolent* life.
3. Free from pain; as an *indolent* tumor.

IN'DOLENTLY, *adv.* In habitual idleness and ease; without action, activity or exertion; lazily.

Calm and serene you *indolently* sit. *Addison.*

INDOM'ITABLE, *a.* Untamable. [*Not used.*] *Herbert.*

INDOMPT'ABLE, *a.* [Fr.; *in* and *dompter*, L. *domo*, to tame.] Not to be subdued. [*Unusual.*] *Tooke.*

INDORS'ABLE, *a.* That may be indorsed, assigned and made payable to order.

INDORSE, *v. t. indors'.* [L. *in* and *dorsum*, the back.]
1. To write on the back of a paper or written instrument; as, to *indorse* a note or bill of exchange; to *indorse* a receipt or assignment on a bill or note. Hence,
2. To assign by writing an order on the back of a note or bill; to assign or transfer by indorsement. The bill was *indorsed* to the bank.

To indorse in blank, to write a name only on a note or bill, leaving a blank to be filled by the indorsee.

INDORSEE', *n.* The person to whom a note or bill is indorsed, or assigned by indorsement.

INDORSEMENT, *n. indors'ment.* The act of writing on the back of a note, bill, or other written instrument.
2. That which is written on the back of a note, bill, or other paper, as a name, an order for payment, the return of an officer, or the verdict of a grand jury.

INDORS'ER, *n.* The person who indorses, or writes his name on the back of a note or bill of exchange, and who, by this act, as the case may be, makes himself liable to pay the note or bill.

IN'DRAUGHT, *n. in'dràft.* [*in* and *draught.*] An opening from the sea into the land; an inlet. *Obs.* *Raleigh.*

INDRENCH', *v. t.* [*in* and *drench.*] To overwhelm with water; to drown; to drench. *Shak.*

INDU'BIOUS, *a.* [L. *indubius*; *in* and *dubius*, doubtful.]
1. Not dubious or doubtful; certain.
2. Not doubting; unsuspecting; as *indubious* confidence. *Harvey.*

INDU'BITABLE, *a.* [Fr. from L. *indubitabilis*; *in* and *dubitabilis*, from *dubito*, to doubt.]

Not to be doubted; unquestionable; evident; apparently certain; too plain to admit of doubt. *Watts.*

INDU'BITABLENESS, *n.* State of being indubitable. *Ash.*

INDU'BITABLY, *adv.* Undoubtedly; unquestionably; in a manner to remove all doubt. *Sprat.*

INDU'BITATE, *a.* [L. *indubitatus.*] Not questioned; evident; certain. [*Not used.*] *Bacon.*

INDU'CE, *v. t.* [L. *induco*; *in* and *duco*, to lead; Fr. *induire*; It. *indurre.*]
1. To lead, as by persuasion or argument; to prevail on; to incite; to influence by motives. The emperor could not be *induced* to take part in the contest.
2. To produce by influence.

As this belief is absolutely necessary for all mankind, the evidence for *inducing* it must be of that nature as to accommodate itself to all species of men. *Forbes.*

3. To produce; to bring on; to cause; as a fever *induced* by extreme fatigue. The revolution in France has *induced* a change of opinions and of property.
4. To introduce; to bring into view.

The poet may be seen *inducing* his personages in the first Iliad. *Pope.*

5. To offer by way of induction or inference. [*Not used.*] *Brown.*

INDU'CED, *pp.* Persuaded by motives; influenced; produced; caused.

INDU'CEMENT, *n.* Motive; any thing that leads the mind to will or to act; any argument, reason or fact that tends to persuade or influence the mind. The love of ease is an *inducement* to idleness. The love of money is an *inducement* to industry in good men, and to the perpetration of crimes in the bad.

INDU'CER, *n.* He or that which induces, persuades or influences.

INDU'CIBLE, *a.* That may be induced; that may be offered by induction. *Brown.*
2. That may be caused. *Barrow.*

INDU'CING, *ppr.* Leading or moving by reason or arguments; persuading; producing; causing.

INDUCT', *v. t.* [L. *inductus*, from *induco*; *in* and *duco*, to lead.] *Literally*, to bring in or introduce. Hence, *appropriately*,
2. To introduce, as to a benefice or office; to put in actual possession of an ecclesiastical living or of any other office, with the customary forms and ceremonies. Clerks or parsons are *inducted* by a mandate from the bishop to the archdeacon, who usually issues a precept to other clergymen to perform the duty. In the United States, certain civil officers and presidents of colleges, are *inducted* into office with appropriate ceremonies.

INDUCT'ED, *pp.* Introduced into office with the usual formalities.

INDUCT'ILE, *a.* [*in* and *ductile.*] Not capable of being drawn into threads, as a metal. [See *Ductile.*]

INDUCTIL'ITY, *n.* The quality of being inductile.

INDUCT'ING, *ppr.* Introducing into office with the usual formalities.

INDUC'TION, *n.* [Fr. from L. *inductio.* See *Induct.*]
1. Literally, a bringing in; introduction; entrance. Hence,
2. In *logic* and *rhetoric*, the act of drawing a consequence from two or more propositions, which are called premises. *Watts.*
3. The method of reasoning from particulars to generals, or the inferring of one general proposition from several particular ones.
4. The conclusion or inference drawn from premises or from propositions which are admitted to be true, either in fact, or for the sake of argument. *Encyc.*
5. The introduction of a clergyman into a benefice, or giving possession of an ecclesiastical living; or the introduction of a person into an office by the usual forms and ceremonies. *Induction* is applied to the introduction of officers, only when certain oaths are to be administered or other formalities are to be observed, which are intended to confer authority or give dignity to the transaction. In Great Britain, *induction* is used for giving possession of ecclesiastical offices. In the United States, it is applied to the formal introduction of civil officers, and the higher officers of colleges.

INDUCT'IVE, *a.* Leading or drawing; with *to.*

A brutish vice,
Inductive mainly *to* the sin of Eve. *Milton.*

2. Tending to induce or cause.

They may be *inductive* of credibility. [*Unusual.*] *Hale.*

3. Leading to inferences; proceeding by induction; employed in drawing conclusions from premises; as *inductive* reasoning.

INDUCT'IVELY, *adv.* By induction or inference.

INDUCT'OR, *n.* The person who inducts another into an office or benefice.

INDUE, *v. t. indu'.* [L. *induo*; Gr. ενδυω; Fr. *enduire.* This word coincides nearly in signification with *endow*, that is, to put on, to furnish. *Duo* is evidently a contracted word.]
1. To put on something; to invest; to clothe; as, to *indue* matter with forms, or man with intelligence.
2. To furnish; to supply with; to endow.

INDU'ED, *pp.* Clothed; invested.

INDUEMENT, *n. indu'ment.* A putting on; endowment. *Mountagu.*

INDU'ING, *ppr.* Investing; putting on.

INDULGE, *v. t. indulj'.* [L. *indulgeo.* This word is compound, but the primitive simple verb is not known, nor the radical sense. If allied to G. and D. *dulden*, to bear, to tolerate, it is from the root of L. *tolero.*]
1. To permit to be or to continue; to suffer; not to restrain or oppose; as, to *indulge* sloth; to *indulge* the passions; to *indulge* pride, selfishness or inclinations.
2. To gratify, *negatively*; not to check or restrain the will, appetite or desire; as, to *indulge* children in amusements.
2. To gratify, *positively*; to grant something not of right, but as a favor; to grant in compliance with wishes or desire.

Yet, yet a moment, one dim ray of light
Indulge, dread Chaos and eternal Night! *Pope.*

4. In *general*, to gratify; to favor; to humor; to yield to the wishes of; to withhold restraint from.

It is remarked by Johnson, that if the matter of indulgence is a single thing, it has *with* before it; if it is a habit, it has *in*. He indulged himself *with* a glass of wine; he indulges himself *in* sloth or intemperance.

INDULGE, *v. i. indulj'.* To permit to enjoy or practice; or to yield to the enjoyment or practice of, without restraint or control; as, to *indulge* in sin, or in sensual pleasure. This form of expression is elliptical, a pronoun being omitted; as, to indulge *myself* or *himself.*

Most men are more willing to *indulge* in easy vices, than to practice laborious virtues. *Johnson.*

2. To yield; to comply; to be favorable. [*Little used.*]

INDUL'ĠED, *pp.* Permitted to be and to operate without check or control; as love of pleasure *indulged* to excess.

2. Gratified; yielded to; humored in wishes or desires; as a child *indulged* by his parents.

3. Granted.

INDUL'ĠENCE, } *n.* Free permission to **INDUL'ĠENCY**, } the appetites, humor, desires, passions or will to act or operate; forbearance of restraint or control. How many children are ruined by *indulgence!* *Indulgence* is not kindness or tenderness, but it may be the effect of one or the other, or of negligence.

2. Gratification; as the *indulgence* of lust or of appetite.

3. Favor granted; liberality; gratification.

If all these gracious *indulgencies* are without effect on us, we must perish in our folly. *Rogers.*

4. In *the Romish church*, remission of the punishment due to sins, granted by the pope or church, and supposed to save the sinner from purgatory; absolution from the censures of the church and from all transgressions. *Encyc.*

INDUL'ĠENT, *a.* Yielding to the wishes, desires, humor or appetites of those under one's care; compliant; not opposing or restraining; as an *indulgent* parent.

2. Mild; favorable; not severe; as the *indulgent* censure of posterity. *Waller.*

3. Gratifying; favoring; with *of.*

The feeble old, *indulgent of* their ease. *Dryden.*

INDULĠEN'TIAL, *a.* Relating to the indulgencies of the Romish church. [*Not well authorized.*] *Brevint.*

INDUL'ĠENTLY, *adv.* With unrestrained enjoyment. *Hammond.*

2. Mildly; favorably; not severely.

INDUL'ĠER, *n.* One who indulges. *Mountagu.*

INDUL'ĠING, *ppr.* Permitting to enjoy or to practice; gratifying.

INDULT', } *n.* [It. *indulto*, a pardon; L. **INDULT'O**, } *indultus*, indulged.]

1. In *the church of Rome*, the power of presenting to benefices, granted to certain persons, as to kings and cardinals. *Encyc.*

2. In *Spain*, a duty, tax or custom, paid to the king for all goods imported from the West Indies in the galleons. *Encyc.*

IN'DURATE, *v. i.* [L. *induro; in* and *duro*, to harden.]

To grow hard; to harden or become hard. Clay *indurates* by drying, and by extreme heat.

IN'DURATE, *v. t.* To make hard. Extreme heat *indurates* clay. Some fossils are *indurated* by exposure to the air.

2. To make unfeeling; to deprive of sensibility; to render obdurate; as, to *indurate* the heart. *Goldsmith.*

IN'DURATED, *pp.* Hardened; made obdurate.

IN'DURATING, *ppr.* Hardening; rendering insensible.

INDURA'TION, *n.* The act of hardening, or process of growing hard. *Bacon.*

2. Hardness of heart; obduracy. *Decay of Piety.*

INDUS'TRIOUS, *a.* [L. *industrius*, from *industria.*]

1. Diligent in business or study; constantly, regularly or habitually occupied in business; assiduous; opposed to *slothful* and *idle.*

Frugal and *industrious* men are commonly friendly to the established government. *Temple.*

2. Diligent in a particular pursuit, or to a particular end; opposed to *remiss* or *slack;* as *industrious* to accomplish a journey, or to reconcile contending parties.

3. Given to industry; characterized by diligence; as an *industrious* life.

4. Careful; assiduous; as the *industrious* application of knowing men. *Watts.*

INDUS'TRIOUSLY, *adv.* With habitual diligence; with steady application of the powers of body or of mind.

2. Diligently; assiduously; with care; *applied to a particular purpose.* He attempted *industriously* to make peace. He *industriously* concealed his name.

IN'DUSTRY, *n.* [L. *industria;* Fr. *industrie.* This is a compound word, and the root probably of the Class Ds.]

Habitual diligence in any employment, either bodily or mental; steady attention to business; assiduity; opposed to *sloth* and *idleness.* We are directed to take lessons of *industry* from the bee. *Industry* pays debts, while idleness or despair will increase them.

INDWELL'ER, *n.* An inhabitant. *Spenser.*

INDWELL'ING, *a.* [*in* and *dwelling.*] Dwelling within; remaining in the heart, even after it is renewed; as *indwelling* sin. *Panoplist. Macknight. Milner.*

INDWELL'ING, *n.* Residence within, or in the heart or soul.

INE'BRIANT, *a.* [See *Inebriate.*] Intoxicating.

INE'BRIANT, *n.* Any thing that intoxicates, as opium. *Encyc.*

INE'BRIATE, *v. t.* [L. *inebrio, inebriatus; in* and *ebrio*, to intoxicate; *ebrius*, soaked, drenched, drunken. The Latin *ebrius* is contracted from *ebrigus* or *ebregus*, as appears from the Spanish *embriagar*, to intoxicate; *embriago*, inebriated; It. *briaco*, drunk; *imbriacare, imbriacarsi.* The sense is to wash or drench, and it is evidently from the common root of the Gr. βρεχω, to water or irrigate. See *Rain.*]

1. To make drunk; to intoxicate. *Sandys.*

2. To disorder the senses; to stupefy, or to make furious or frantic; to produce effects like those of liquor, which are various in different constitutions.

INE'BRIATE, *v. i.* To be or become intoxicated. *Bacon.*

INE'BRIATE, *n.* A habitual drunkard.

Some *inebriates* have their paroxysms of inebriety terminated by much pale urine, profuse sweats, &c. *Darwin.*

INE'BRIATED, *pp.* Intoxicated.

INE'BRIATING, *ppr.* Making drunk; intoxicating.

INEBRIA'TION, *n.* Drunkenness; intoxication. *Brown.*

INEBRI'ETY, *n.* Drunkenness; intoxication. *Darwin.*

INED'ITED, *a.* [*in* and *edited.*] Unpublished. *Warton.*

INEF'FABLE, *a.* [Fr. from L. *ineffabilis; in* and *effabilis*, from *effor*, to speak.]

Unspeakable; unutterable; that cannot be expressed in words; *usually in a good sense;* as the *ineffable* joys of heaven; the *ineffable* glories of the Deity.

INEF'FABLENESS, *n.* Unspeakableness; quality of being unutterable. *Scott.*

INEF'FABLY, *adv.* Unspeakably; in a manner not to be expressed in words. *Milton.*

INEFFE€T'IVE, *a.* [*in* and *effective.*] Not effective; not producing any effect, or the effect intended; inefficient; useless.

The word of God, without the spirit, is a dead and *ineffective* letter. *Taylor.*

2. Not able; not competent to the service intended; as *ineffective* troops; *ineffective* force.

3. Producing no effect.

INEFFE€T'UAL, *a.* [*in* and *effectual.*] Not producing its proper effect, or not able to produce its effect; inefficient; weak; as an *ineffectual* remedy; the Spaniards made an *ineffectual* attempt to reduce Gibraltar. [See *Inefficacious.*]

INEFFE€T'UALLY, *adv.* Without effect; in vain.

INEFFE€T'UALNESS, *n.* Want of effect, or of power to produce it; inefficacy.

James speaks of the *ineffectualness* of some men's devotion. *Wake.*

INEFFERVES'CENCE, *n.* [*in* and *effervescence.*]

Want of effervescence; a state of not effervescing. *Kirwan.*

INEFFERVES'CENT, *a.* Not effervescing, or not susceptible of effervescence.

INEFFERVESCIBIL'ITY, *n.* The quality of not effervescing, or not being susceptible of effervescence. *Kirwan.*

INEFFERVES'CIBLE, *a.* Not capable of effervescence.

INEFFI€A'CIOUS, *a.* [It. and Fr. *inefficace;* L. *inefficax; in* and *efficax, efficio*, to effect; *ex* and *facio*, to make.]

Not efficacious; not having power to produce the effect desired, or the proper effect; of inadequate power or force.

Ineffectual, says Johnson, rather denotes an actual failure, and *inefficacious*, an habitual impotence to any effect. But the distinction is not always observed, nor can it be; for we cannot always know whether means are *inefficacious*, till experiment has proved them *ineffectual;* nor even then, for we cannot be certain that the failure of means to produce an effect is to be attributed to habitual want of power, or to accidental and temporary causes. *Inefficacious* is therefore sometimes synonymous with *ineffectual.*

INEFFI€A'CIOUSLY, *adv.* Without efficacy or effect.

INEFFI€A'CIOUSNESS, *n.* Want of power to produce the effect, or want of effect.

INEF'FICACY, *n.* [*in* and *efficacy*, L. *efficacia.*]

1. Want of power to produce the desired or proper effect; inefficiency; as the *inefficacy* of medicines or of means.

2. Ineffectualness; failure of effect.

INEFFI′′CIENCY, *n.* [*in* and *efficiency.*] Want of power or exertion of power to produce the effect; inefficacy.

INEFFI′′CIENT, *a.* [*in* and *efficient.*] Not efficient; not producing the effect; inefficacious.

2. Not active; effecting nothing; as an *inefficient* force. *Chesterfield.*

INEFFI′′CIENTLY, *adv.* Ineffectually; without effect.

INELAB′ORATE, *a.* Not elaborate; not wrought with care. *Cockeram.*

INELAS′TIC, *a.* [*in* and *elastic.*] Not elastic; wanting elasticity; unelastic.

INELASTIC′ITY, *n.* The absence of elasticity; the want of elastic power.

INEL′EGANCE, INEL′EGANCY, *n.* [See *Inelegant.*] Want of elegance; want of beauty or polish in language, composition or manners; want of symmetry or ornament in building; want of delicacy in coloring, &c.

INEL′EGANT, *a.* [L. *inelegans; in* and *elegans*, from the root of *eligo*, to choose.]

Not elegant; wanting beauty or polish, as language, or refinement, as manners; wanting symmetry or ornament, as an edifice; in short, wanting in any thing which correct taste requires.

INEL′EGANTLY, *adv.* In an inelegant or unbecoming manner; coarsely; roughly. *Chesterfield.*

INELIGIBIL′ITY, *n.* [from *ineligible.*] Incapacity of being elected to an office.

2. State or quality of not being worthy of choice.

INEL′IGIBLE, *a.* [*in* and *eligible.*] Not capable of being elected to an office.

2. Not worthy to be chosen or preferred; not expedient.

INEL′OQUENT, *a.* [*in* and *eloquent.*] Not eloquent; not speaking with fluency, propriety, grace and pathos; not persuasive; *used of persons.*

2. Not fluent, graceful or pathetic; not persuasive; as language or composition. *Milton.*

INEL′OQUENTLY, *adv.* Without eloquence.

INELUCT′ABLE, *a.* [L. *ineluctabilis.*] Not to be resisted by struggling; not to be overcome. [*Not used.*] *Pearson.*

INELU′DIBLE, *a.* [*in* and *eludible.*] That cannot be eluded or defeated. *Glanville.*

INENAR′RABLE, *a.* [L. *inenarrabilis.*] That cannot be narrated or told.

INEPT′, *a.* [L. *ineptus; in* and *aptus*, fit, *apt.*]

1. Not apt or fit; unfit; unsuitable. *Woodward.*

2. Improper; unbecoming; foolish. *More.*

INEPT′ITUDE, *n.* Unfitness; inaptitude; unsuitableness; as an *ineptitude* to motion. *Arbuthnot.*

INEPT′LY, *adv.* Unfitly; unsuitably; foolishly. *Glanville.*

INEPT′NESS, *n.* Unfitness. *More.*

INE′QUAL, *a.* [*in* and *equal.*] Unequal; uneven; various. *Shenstone.*

INEQUAL′ITY, *n.* [L. *inæqualitas; in* and *æqualis*, equal; Fr. *inegalité.*]

1. Difference or want of equality in degree, quantity, length, or quality of any kind; the state of not having equal measure, degree, dimensions or amount; as an *inequality* in size or stature; an *inequality* of numbers or of power; *inequality* of distances or of motions.

2. Unevenness; want of levelness; the alternate rising and falling of a surface; as the *inequalities* of the surface of the earth, or of a marble slab.

3. Disproportion to any office or purpose; inadequacy; incompetency; as the *inequality* of terrestrial things to the wants of a rational soul.

4. Diversity; want of uniformity in different times or places; as the *inequality* of air or temperature.

5. Difference of rank, station or condition; as the *inequalities* of men in society; *inequalities* of rank or property.

INEQUIDIS′TANT, *a.* Not being equally distant. *Say.*

INEQUILAT′ERAL, *a.* Having unequal sides. *Say.*

INEQ′UITABLE, *a.* [*in* and *equitable.*] Not equitable; not just.

INE′QUIVALVE, INEQUIVAL′VULAR, *a.* Having unequal valves.

INERM′, INERM′OUS, *a.* [L. *inermis; in* and *arma*, arms.]

Unarmed; destitute of prickles or thorns, as a leaf; *a botanical word.* *Martyn.*

INERRABIL′ITY, *n.* [from *inerrable.*] Exemption from error or from the possibility of erring; infallibility. *King Charles.*

INER′RABLE, *a.* [*in* and *err.*] That cannot err; exempt from error or mistake; infallible. *Hammond.*

INER′RABLENESS, *n.* Exemption from error; inerrability. *Hammond.*

INER′RABLY, *adv.* With security from error; infallibly.

INERRAT′IC, *a.* [*in* and *erratic.*] Not erratic or wandering; fixed. *Paus. Trans.*

INER′RINGLY, *adv.* Without error, mistake or deviation. *Glanville.*

INERT′, *a.* [L. *iners; in* and *ars*, art. The English sense is drawn not from *art*, but from the primary sense, strength or vigorous action.]

1. Destitute of the power of moving itself, or of active resistance to motion impressed; as, matter is *inert.*

2. Dull; sluggish; indisposed to move or act. *Thomson.*

INER′TION, *n.* Want of activity; want of action or exertion.

> These vicissitudes of exertion and *inertion* of the arterial system, constitute the paroxysms of remittent fever. *Darwin.*

INERT′ITUDE, *n.* The state of being inert, or a tendency to remain quiescent till impelled by external force to move. *Good.*

INERT′LY, *adv.* Without activity; sluggishly. *Dunciad.*

INERT′NESS, *n.* The state or quality of being inert, or destitute of the power to move *per se;* that quality of passiveness by which bodies persist in a state of rest, or of motion given to them by external force. In the language of philosophy, this quality is called *vis inertiæ*, or *inertia.* *Newton.*

2. Want of activity or exertion; habitual indisposition to action or motion; sluggishness.

In esse, [L.] in being; actually existing; distinguished from *in posse*, or *in potentia*, which denote that a thing is not, but may be.

INES′CATE, *v. t.* [L. *inesco.*] To bait; to lay a bait for.

INESCA′TION, *n.* The act of baiting. *Hallowell.*

INES′TIMABLE, *a.* [L. *inæstimabilis.* See *Estimate.*]

1. That cannot be estimated or computed; as an *inestimable* sum of money.

2. Too valuable or excellent to be rated; being above all price; as *inestimable* rights. The privileges of American citizens, civil and religious, are *inestimable.*

INES′TIMABLY, *adv.* In a manner not to be estimated or rated.

INEV′IDENCE, *n.* Want of evidence; obscurity. *Barrow.*

INEV′IDENT, *a.* [*in* and *evident.*] Not evident; not clear or obvious; obscure. *Brown.*

INEVITABIL′ITY, *n.* [from *inevitable.*] Impossibility to be avoided; certainty to happen. *Bramhall.*

INEV′ITABLE, *a.* [Fr. from L. *inevitabilis; in* and *evitabilis*, from *evito*, to shun.]

Not to be avoided; that cannot be shunned; unavoidable; that admits of no escape or evasion. To die is the *inevitable* lot of man; we are all subjected to many *inevitable* calamities.

INEV′ITABLENESS, *n.* The state of being unavoidable.

INEV′ITABLY, *adv.* Without possibility of escape or evasion; unavoidably; certainly.

> How *inevitably* does immoderate laughter end in a sigh! *South.*

INEXACT′, *a.* [*in* and *exact.*] Not exact; not precisely correct or true.

INEXACT′NESS, *n.* Incorrectness; want of precision.

INEXCI′TABLE, *a.* [*in* and *excitable.*] Not susceptible of excitement; dull; lifeless; torpid.

INEXCU′SABLE, *a. s* as *z.* [L. *inexcusabilis; in* and *excusabilis, excuso.* See *Excuse.*]

Not to be excused or justified; as *inexcusable* folly.

INEXCU′SABLENESS, *n.* The quality of not admitting of excuse or justification; enormity beyond forgiveness or palliation.

> This *inexcusableness* is stated on the supposition that they knew God, but did not glorify him. *South.*

INEXCU′SABLY, *adv.* With a degree of guilt or folly beyond excuse or justification.

INEXECU′TION, *n.* Neglect of execution; non-performance; as the *inexecution* of a treaty.

INEXER′TION, *n.* [*in* and *exertion.*] Want of exertion; want of effort; defect of action. *Darwin.*

INEXHA′LABLE, *a.* [*in* and *exhalable*, L. *exhalo.*]

Not to be exhaled or evaporated; not evaporable. *Brown.*

INEXHAUST′ED, *a.* [*in* and *exhausted.*]

1. Not exhausted; not emptied; unexhausted.

2. Not spent; not having lost all strength or resources; unexhausted.

INEXHAUST'IBLE, *a.* [*in* and *exhaustible.*]

1. That cannot be exhausted or emptied; unfailing; as an *inexhaustible* quantity or supply of water.
2. That cannot be wasted or spent; as *inexhaustible* stores of provisions.

INEXHAUST'IBLENESS, *n.* The state of being inexhaustible.

INEXHAUST'IVE, *a.* Not to be exhausted or spent.

INEXIST'ENCE, *n.* [*in* and *existence.*]

1. Want of being or existence. *Broome.*
2. Inherence.

INEXIST'ENT, *a.* [*in* and *existent.*] Not having being; not existing. *South. Brown.*

2. Existing in something else. *Boyle.*

INEXORABIL'ITY, *n.* The quality of being inexorable or unyielding to entreaty. *Paley.*

INEX'ORABLE, *a.* [Fr. from L. *inexorabilis; in* and *exorabilis*, from *exoro*, to entreat; *ex* and *oro*, to pray.]

1. Not to be persuaded or moved by entreaty or prayer; too firm and determined in purpose to yield to supplication; as an *inexorable* prince or tyrant; an *inexorable* judge.
2. Unyielding; that cannot be made to bend.

Inexorable equality of laws. *Gibbon.*

INEX'ORABLY, *adv.* So as to be immovable by intreaty.

INEXPECTA'TION, *n.* State of having no expectation. *Feltham.*

INEXPECT'ED, *a.* Not expected. [*Not in use.*]

INEXPE'DIENCE, } *n.* [*in* and *expedience.*]
INEXPE'DIENCY, } Want of fitness; impropriety; unsuitableness to the purpose. The *inexpedience* of a measure is to be determined by the prospect of its advancing the purpose intended or not.

INEXPE'DIENT, *a.* [*in* and *expedient.*] Not expedient; not tending to promote a purpose; not tending to a good end; unfit; improper; unsuitable to time and place. Whatever tends to retard or defeat success in a good cause is *inexpedient.* What is expedient at one time, may be *inexpedient* at another.

INEXPE'RIENCE, *n.* [*in* and *experience.*] Want of experience or experimental knowledge; as the *inexperience* of youth, or their *inexperience* of the world.

INEXPE'RIENCED, *a.* Not having experience; unskillled.

INEXPERT', *a.* [*in* and *expert.*] Not expert; not skilled; destitute of knowledge or dexterity derived from practice.

In letters and in laws
Not *inexpert.* *Prior.*

INEX'PIABLE, *a.* [Fr. from L. *inexpiabilis.* See *Expiate.*]

1. That admits of no atonement or satisfaction; as an *inexpiable* crime or offense.
2. That cannot be mollified or appeased by atonement; as *inexpiable* hate. *Milton.*

INEX'PIABLY, *adv.* To a degree that admits of no atonement. *Roscommon.*

INEXPLA'INABLE, *a.* That cannot be explained; inexplicable. [*The latter word is generally used.*]

INEXPLE'ABLY, *adv.* Insatiably. [*Not used.*] *Sandys.*

INEX'PLICABLE, *a.* [Fr. from L. *inexplicabilis; in* and *explico*, to unfold.]

That cannot be explained or interpreted; not capable of being rendered plain and intelligible; as an *inexplicable* mystery.

INEX'PLICABLY, *adv.* In a manner not to be explained.

INEXPLO'RABLE, *a.* [*in* and *explorable*, from *explore.*]

That cannot be explored, searched or discovered. *Tooke.*

INEXPRESS'IBLE, *a.* [*in* and *expressible*, from *express.*]

Not to be expressed in words; not to be uttered; unspeakable; unutterable; as *inexpressible* grief, joy or pleasure.

INEXPRESS'IBLY, *adv.* In a manner or degree not to be told or expressed in words; unspeakably; unutterably. *Hammond.*

INEXPRESS'IVE, *a.* Not tending to express; not expressing; inexpressible.

INEXPO'SURE, *n.* [*in* and *exposure.*] A state of not being exposed. *Med. Repos.*

INEXPUG'NABLE, *a.* [Fr. from L. *inexpugnabilis; in* and *expugno; ex* and *pugno*, to fight.]

Not to be subdued by force; not to be taken by assault; impregnable. *Ray.*

INEXSU'PERABLE, *a.* [L. *inexsuperabilis.*] Not to be passed over or surmounted.

INEXTEND'ED, *a.* Having no extension. *Good.*

INEXTEN'SION, *n.* [*in* and *extension.*] Want of extension; unextended state. *Encyc.*

INEXTERM'INABLE, *a.* [*in* and *exterminable.*] That cannot be exterminated. *Rush.*

INEXTINCT', *a.* Not quenched; not extinct.

INEXTIN'GUISHABLE, *a.* [*in* and *extinguishable.*]

That cannot be extinguished; unquenchable; as *inextinguishable* flame, thirst or desire.

INEXTIR'PABLE, *a.* That cannot be extirpated.

INEX'TRICABLE, *a.* [Fr. from L. *inextricabilis.* See *Extricate.*]

1. Not to be disentangled; not to be freed from intricacy or perplexity; as an *inextricable* maze or difficulty. *Sherlock.*
2. Not to be untied; as an *inextricable* knot.

INEX'TRICABLENESS, *n.* The state of being inextricable. *Donne.*

INEX'TRICABLY, *adv.* To a degree of perplexity not to be disentangled. *Pope.*

INEYE, *v. t.* To inoculate, as a tree or a bud. *Philips.*

INFAB'RICATED, *a.* Unfabricated; unwrought. [*Not used.*]

INFALLIBIL'ITY, } *n.* [from *infallible.*]
INFAL'LIBLENESS, } The quality of being incapable of error or mistake; entire exemption from liability to error; inerrability. No human being can justly lay claim to *infallibility.* This is an attribute of God only.

INFAL'LIBLE, *a.* [F. *infaillible; in* and *faillir*, L. *fallo.*]

1. Not fallible; not capable of erring; entirely exempt from liability to mistake; *applied to persons.* No man is *infallible;* to be *infallible* is the prerogative of God only.
2. Not liable to fail, or to deceive confidence; certain; as *infallible* evidence; *infallible* success.

To whom he showed himself alive after his passion, by many *infallible* proofs— Acts i.

INFAL'LIBLY, *adv.* Without a possibility of erring or mistaking. *Smalridge.*

2. Certainly; without a possibility of failure. Our Savior has directed us to conduct that will *infallibly* render us happy.

INFA'ME, *v. t.* To defame. [*Not used.*] *Bacon.*

IN'FAMOUS, *a.* [Fr. *infame;* L. *infamis; infamo*, to defame; *in* and *fama*, fame.]

1. Of ill report, *emphatically;* having a reputation of the worst kind; publicly branded with odium for vice or guilt; base; scandalous; notoriously vile; *used of persons;* as an *infamous* liar; an *infamous* rake or gambler.
2. Odious; detestable; held in abhorrence; that renders a person infamous; as an *infamous* vice.
3. Branded with infamy by conviction of a crime. An *infamous* person cannot be a witness.

IN'FAMOUSLY, *adv.* In a manner or degree to render infamous; scandalously; disgracefully; shamefully.

2. With open reproach.

IN'FAMOUSNESS, } *n.* [Fr. *infamie;* L.
IN'FAMY, } *infamia; in* and *fama*, report.]

1. Total loss of reputation; public disgrace. Avoid the crimes and vices which expose men to *infamy.*
2. Qualities which are detested and despised; qualities notoriously bad and scandalous; as the *infamy* of an action.
3. In *law*, that loss of character or public disgrace which a convict incurs, and by which a person is rendered incapable of being a witness or juror. *Encyc.*

IN'FANCY, *n.* [L. *infantia.* See *Infant.*]

1. The first part of life, beginning at the birth. In common usage, *infancy* extends not beyond the first year or two of life, but there is not a defined limit where *infancy* ends, and childhood begins.
2. In *law*, infancy extends to the age of twenty one years.
3. The first age of any thing; the beginning or early period of existence; as the *infancy* of the Roman republic; the *infancy* of a college or of a charitable society; the *infancy* of agriculture, of manufactures, or of commerce.

INFAND'OUS, *a.* [L. *infandus.*] Too odious to be expressed. [*Not in use.*] *Howell.*

INFANG'THEF, *n.* [Sax. *in, fangan*, to take, and *theof*, thief.]

In *English law*, the privilege granted to lords to judge thieves taken on their manors, or within their franchises. *Cowel.*

IN'FANT, *n.* [Fr. *enfant;* L. *infans; in* and *fans*, speaking, *fari*, to speak.]

1. A child in the first period of life, beginning at his birth; a young babe. In common usage, a child ceases to be called an

infant within the first or second year, but at no definite period. In some cases, authors indulge a greater latitude, and extend the term to include children of several years of age.

2. In *law*, a person under the age of twenty one years, who is incapable of making valid contracts.

IN'FANT, *a.* Pertaining to infancy or the first period of life.

2. Young; tender; not mature; as *infant* strength.

INFANT'A, *n.* In *Spain* and *Portugal*, any princess of the royal blood, except the eldest daughter when heiress apparent.

INFANT'E, *n.* In *Spain* and *Portugal*, any son of the king, except the eldest or heir apparent.

INFANT'ICIDE, *n.* [Low L. *infanticidium; infans*, an infant, and *cædo*, to kill.]

1. The intentional killing of an infant.

2. The slaughter of infants by Herod. Matt. ii.

3. A slayer of infants.

IN'FANTILE, *a.* [L. *infantilis.*] Pertaining to infancy, or to an infant; pertaining to the first period of life.

IN'FANTINE, *a.* Pertaining to infants or to young children.

IN'FANTLIKE, *a.* Like an infant. *Shak.*

IN'FANTLY, *a.* Like a child's. *Beaum.*

IN'FANTRY, *n.* [Fr. *infanterie;* Sp. *infanteria;* It. *fanteria.* See *Infant.*]

In *military affairs*, the soldiers or troops that serve on foot, as distinguished from *cavalry;* as a company, regiment or brigade of *infantry.* In some armies, there have been *heavy-armed infantry*, and *light-armed* or *light infantry*, according to their manner of arming and equipping.

INF'ARCE, *v. t. infars.* To stuff. [*Not in use.*]

INFARC'TION, *n.* [L. *infarcio, infercio*, to stuff; *in* and *farcio.*]

The act of stuffing or filling; constipation. *Harvey.*

INFASH'IONABLE, *a.* Unfashionable. [*Not used.*] *Beaum.*

INFAT'IGABLE, *a.* Indefatigable. *Obs.*

INFAT'UATE, *v. t.* [L. *infatuo; in* and *fatuus*, foolish.]

1. To make foolish; to affect with folly; to weaken the intellectual powers, or to deprive of sound judgment. In general, this word does not signify to deprive absolutely of rational powers and reduce to idiocy, but to deprive of sound judgment, so that a person *infatuated* acts in certain cases as a fool, or without common discretion and prudence. Whom God intends to destroy, he first *infatuates.*

The judgment of God will be very visible in *infatuating* a people, ripe and prepared for destruction. *Clarendon.*

2. To prepossess or incline to a person or thing in a manner not justified by prudence or reason; to inspire with an extravagant or foolish passion, too obstinate to be controlled by reason. Men are often *infatuated* with a love of gaming, or of sensual pleasure.

INFAT'UATED, *pp.* Affected with folly.

INFAT'UATING, *ppr.* Affecting with folly.

INFATUA'TION, *n.* The act of affecting with folly.

2. A state of mind in which the intellectual powers are weakened, either generally, or in regard to particular objects, so that the person affected acts without his usual judgment, and contrary to the dictates of reason. All men who waste their substance in gaming, intemperance or any other vice, are chargeable with *infatuation.*

INFAUST'ING, *n.* [L. *infaustus.*] The act of making unlucky. *Obs.* *Bacon.*

INFEASIBIL'ITY, **INFE'ASIBLENESS**, } *n. s* as z. [from *infeasible.*]

Impracticability; the quality of not being capable of being done or performed.

INFE'ASIBLE, *a. s* as z. [*in* and *feasible*, Fr. *faisable*, from *faire*, to make or do, L. *facio.*]

Not to be done; that cannot be accomplished; impracticable. *Glanville.*

INFECT', *v. t.* [Fr. *infecter;* Sp. *infectar;* It. *infettare;* L. *inficio, infectus; in* and *facio.* In this application of *inficio*, as in *inficior*, to deny, we find the radical sense of *facio*, to make, which is to thrust, to drive. To *infect* is to *thrust in;* to *deny* is to *thrust against*, that is, to thrust away, to repel. And here we observe the different effects of the prefix *in*, upon the verb.]

1. To taint with disease; to infuse into a healthy body the virus, miasma, or morbid matter of a diseased body, or any pestilential or noxious air or substance by which a disease is produced. Persons in health are *infected* by the contagion of the plague, of syphilis, of small pox, of measles, of malignant fevers. In some cases, persons can be *infected* only by contact, as in syphilis; in most cases, they may be *infected* without contact with the diseased body.

2. To taint or affect with morbid or noxious matter; as, to *infect* a lancet; to *infect* clothing; to *infect* an apartment.

3. To communicate bad qualities to; to corrupt; to taint by the communication of any thing noxious or pernicious. It is melancholy to see the young *infected* and corrupted by vicious examples, or the minds of our citizens *infected* with errors.

4. To contaminate with illegality.

INFECT', *a.* Infected. [*Not used.*]

INFECT'ED, *pp.* Tainted with noxious matter; corrupted by poisonous exhalations; corrupted by bad qualities communicated.

INFECT'ER, *n.* He or that which infects.

INFECT'ING, *ppr.* Tainting; corrupting.

INFEC'TION, *n.* [Fr. from L. *inficio.*] The act of infecting, or the act by which poisonous matter, morbid miasmata or exhalations produce disease in a health body. The words *contagion* and *infection* are frequently confounded. The proper distinction between them is this. *Contagion* is the virus or effluvium generated in a diseased body, and capable of producing the specific disease in a healthy body by contact or otherwise. Marsh miasm is not properly contagion. *Infection* is any thing that taints or corrupts; hence it includes contagion, and any other morbid, noxious matter which may excite disease in a healthy body. Hence,

2. The morbid cause which excites disease in a healthy or uninfected body. This cause may be contagion from a diseased body, or other poisonous or noxious matter received into the body or under the skin. The *infection* of the plague and of yellow fever, is said to be imported in ships and conveyed in clothing; persons are said to take the *infection* from a diseased person, or from the air of apartments where the sick are confined. The *infection* spreads in a city, or it is free from *infection.* Pestilential exhalations are called *infections.*

Tooke, Russ. Encyc. art. Plague. Rush.

Infection is used in two acceptations; first, as denoting the effluvium or infectious matter exhaled from the person of one diseased, in which sense it is synonymous with *contagion;* and secondly, as signifying the act of communication of such morbid effluvium, by which disease is transferred. *Cyc.*

3. That which taints, poisons or corrupts by communication from one to another; as the *infection* of error or of evil example.

4. Contamination by illegality, as in cases of contraband goods.

5. Communication of like qualities.

Mankind are gay or serious by *infection.* *Rambler.*

INFEC'TIOUS, *a.* Having qualities that may taint, or communicate disease to; as an *infectious* fever; *infectious* clothing; *infectious* air; *infectious* miasma.

2. Corrupting; tending to taint by communication; as *infectious* vices or manners.

3. Contaminating with illegality; exposing to seizure and forfeiture.

Contraband articles are said to be of an *infectious* nature. *Kent.*

4. Capable of being communicated by near approach.

Grief as well as joy is *infectious.* *Kames.*

INFEC'TIOUSLY, *adv.* By infection.

INFEC'TIOUSNESS, *n.* The quality of being infectious, or capable of communicating disease or taint from one to another.

INFECT'IVE, *a.* Having the quality of communicating disease or taint from one to another. *Sidney.*

INFE'CUND, *a.* [L. *infæcundus; in* and *fæcundus*, prolific.] Unfruitful; not producing young; barren.

INFECUND'ITY, *n.* [L. *infæcunditas.*] Unfruitfulness; barrenness. *Med. Repos.*

INFELIC'ITY, *n.* [Fr. *infelicité;* L. *infelicitas.* See *Felicity.*] Unhappiness; misery; misfortune.

2. Unfortunate state; unfavorableness; as the *infelicity* of the times, or of the occasion.

INFER', *v. t.* [Fr. *inferer;* L. *infero; in* and *fero*, to bear or produce.]

1. Literally, to bring on; to induce. [*Little used.*] *Harvey.*

2. To deduce; to draw or derive, as a fact or consequence. From the character of God, as creator and governor of the world, we *infer* the indispensable obligation of all his creatures to obey his commands. We *infer* one proposition or truth from another, when we perceive that if one is true, the other must be true also.

3. To offer; to produce. [*Not used.*] *Shak.*

INFER'ABLE, *a.* That may be inferred or deduced from premises. *Burke.*

IN'FERENCE, *n.* [Fr. from *inferer.*] A truth or proposition drawn from another which is admitted or supposed to be true; a conclusion. *Inferences* result from reasoning, as when the mind perceives such a connection between ideas, as that, if certain propositions called premises are true, the conclusions or propositions deduced from them must also be true.

INFEOFF. [See *Enfeoff.*]

INFE'RIOR, *a.* [L. comp. from *inferus*, low; Sp. *id;* Fr. *inferieur.*]

1. Lower in place.
2. Lower in station, age, or rank in life. Pay due respect to those who are superior in station, and due civility to those who are *inferior.*
3. Lower in excellence or value; as a poem of *inferior* merit; cloth of *inferior* quality or price.
4. Subordinate; of less importance. Attend to health and safety; ease and convenience are *inferior* considerations.

INFE'RIOR, *n.* A person who is younger, or of a lower station or rank in society.

A person gets more by obliging his *inferior*, than by disdaining him. *South.*

INFERIOR'ITY, *n.* [Fr. *inferiorité.*] A lower state of dignity, age, value or quality. We speak of the *inferiority* of rank, of office, of talents, of age, of worth.

INFERN'AL, *a.* [Fr. from L. *infernus.*]

1. Properly, pertaining to the lower regions, or regions of the dead, the Tartarus of the ancients. Hence,
2. Pertaining to hell; inhabiting hell; as *infernal* spirits.
3. Hellish; resembling the temper of *infernal* spirits; malicious; diabolical; very wicked and detestable.

INFERN'AL, *n.* An inhabitant of hell, or of the lower regions.

Infernal stone [*lapis infernalis,*] a name formerly given to lunar caustic, a substance prepared from an evaporated solution of silver, or from crystals of silver. *Hill.*

Lunar caustic is nitrate of silver fused and cast in small cylinders. *Webster's Manual.*

INFER'TILE, *a.* [Fr. from L. *infertilis; in* and *fertilis.*]

Not fertile; not fruitful or productive; barren; as an *infertile* soil.

INFERTIL'ITY, *n.* Unfruitfulness; unproductiveness; barrenness; as the *infertility* of land. *Hale.*

INFEST', *v. t.* [Fr. *infester*; L. *infesto.*] To trouble greatly; to disturb; to annoy; to harass. In warm weather, men are *infested* with musketoes and gnats; flies *infest* horses and cattle. The sea is often *infested* with pirates. Small parties of the enemy *infest* the coast.

These, said the genius, are envy, avarice, superstition, love, with the like cares and passions that *infest* human life. *Addison.*

INFESTA'TION, *n.* The act of infesting; molestation. *Bacon.*

INFEST'ED, *pp.* Troubled; annoyed; harassed; plagued.

INFES'TERED, *a.* [*in* and *fester.*] Rankling; inveterate.

INFEST'ING, *ppr.* Annoying; harassing; disturbing.

INFEST'IVE, *a.* [*in* and *festive.*] Having no mirth.

INFESTIV'ITY, *n.* [*in* and *festivity.*] Want of festivity, or of cheerfulness and mirth at entertainments.

INFEST'UOUS, *a.* [L. *infestus.*] Mischievous. [*Not used.*] *Bacon.*

INFEUDA'TION, *n.* [*in* and *feudum*, feud.]

1. The act of putting one in possession of an estate in fee. *Hale.*
2. The granting of tithes to laymen. *Blackstone.*

IN'FIDEL, *a.* [Fr. *infidele; L. infidelis; in* and *fidelis*, faithful.]

Unbelieving; disbelieving the inspiration of the Scriptures, or the divine institution of christianity.

The *infidel* writer is a great enemy to society. *Knox.*

IN'FIDEL, *n.* One who disbelieves the inspiration of the Scriptures, and the divine origin of christianity.

INFIDEL'ITY, *n.* [Fr. *infidelité; L. infidelitas.*]

1. In general, want of faith or belief; a withholding of credit.
2. Disbelief of the inspiration of the Scriptures, or the divine original of christianity; unbelief.

There is no doubt that vanity is one principal cause of *infidelity.* *Knox.*

3. Unfaithfulness, particularly in married persons; a violation of the marriage covenant by adultery or lewdness.
4. Breach of trust; treachery; deceit; as the *infidelity* of a friend or a servant. In this sense, *unfaithfulness* is most used.

INFIL'TRATE, *v. i.* [Fr. *filtrer*, to filter.] To enter by penetrating the pores or interstices of a substance.

INFIL'TRATING, *ppr.* Penetrating by the pores or interstices.

INFILTRA'TION, *n.* The act or process of entering the pores or cavities of a body.

2. The substance which has entered the pores or cavities of a body.

Calcarious *infiltrations*, filling the cavities of other stones. *Kirwan.*

IN'FINITE, *a.* [L. *infinitus; in* and *finitus*, terminated; Fr. *infini*; Sp. *infinito.*]

1. Without limits; unbounded; boundless; not circumscribed; applied to *time, space* and *qualities.* God is *infinite* in duration, having neither beginning nor end of existence. He is also *infinite* in presence, or omnipresent, and his perfections are *infinite.* We also speak of *infinite* space.
2. That will have no end. Thus angels and men, though they have had a beginning, will exist in *infinite* duration.
3. That has a beginning in space, but is infinitely extended; as, a line beginning at a point, but extended indefinitely, is an *infinite* line.
4. Infinite is used loosely and hyperbolically for indefinitely large, immense, of great size or extent.

Infinite canon, in *music*, a perpetual fugue.

IN'FINITELY, *adv.* Without bounds or limits.

2. Immensely; greatly; to a great extent or degree; as, I am *infinitely* obliged by your condescension.

IN'FINITENESS, *n.* Boundless extent of time, space or qualities; infinity. *Taylor.*

2. Immensity; greatness.

INFINITES'IMAL, *a.* Indefinitely small. *Johnson. Encyc.*

INFINITES'IMAL, *n.* An indefinitely small quantity. *Encyc.*

INFIN'ITIVE, *a.* [L. *infinitivus;* Fr. *infinitif.*]

In *grammar*, the *infinitive* mode expresses the action of the verb, without limitation of person or number; as, *to love.*

INFIN'ITUDE, *n.* Infinity; infiniteness; the quality or state of being without limits; infinite extent; as the *infinitude* of space, of time, or of perfections.

2. Immensity; greatness.
3. Boundless number. *Addison.*

INFIN'ITY, *n.* [Fr. *infinité;* L. *infinitas.*]

1. Unlimited extent of time, space or quantity; boundlessness. We apply *infinity* to God and his perfections; we speak of the *infinity* of his existence, his knowledge, his power, his goodness and holiness.
2. Immensity; indefinite extent.
3. Endless or indefinite number; *a hyperbolical use of the word;* as an *infinity* of beauties.

INFIRM, *a.* *inferm'.* [Fr. *infirme;* L. *infirmus; in* and *firmus.*]

1. Not firm or sound; weak; feeble; as an *infirm* body; an *infirm* constitution.
2. Weak of mind; irresolute; as *infirm* of purpose. *Shak.*
3. Not solid or stable.

He who fixes on false principles, treads on *infirm* ground. *South.*

INFIRM, *v. t.* *inferm'.* To weaken. [*Not used.*] *Raleigh.*

INFIRMARY, *n.* *inferm'ary.* A hospital or place where the sick are lodged and nursed.

INFIRMITY, *n.* *inferm'ity.* [Fr. *infirmité;* L. *infirmitas.*]

1. An unsound or unhealthy state of the body; weakness; feebleness. Old age is subject to *infirmities.*
2. Weakness of mind; failing; fault; foible.

A friend should bear a friend's *infirmities.* *Shak.*

3. Weakness of resolution.
4. Any particular disease; malady; *applied rather to chronic, than to violent diseases.* *Hooker.*
5. Defect; imperfection; weakness; as the *infirmities* of a constitution of government. *Hamilton.*

INFIRMNESS, *n.* *inferm'ness.* Weakness; feebleness; unsoundness. *Boyle.*

INFIX', *v. t.* [L. *infixus, infigo; in* and *figo*, to fix.]

1. To fix by piercing or thrusting in; as, to *infix* a sting, spear or dart.
2. To set in; to fasten in something.
3. To implant or fix, as principles, thoughts, instructions; as, to *infix* good principles in the mind, or ideas in the memory.

INFIX'ED, *pp.* Thrust in; set in; inserted; deeply implanted.

INFIX'ING, *ppr.* Thrusting in; setting in; implanting.

INFLA'ME, *v. t.* [L. *inflammo; in* and *flamma*, flame.]
1. To set on fire; to kindle; to cause to burn; *in a literal sense.* But more generally,
2. To excite or increase, as passion or appetite; to enkindle into violent action; as, to *inflame* love, lust or thirst; to *inflame* desire or anger.
3. To exaggerate; to aggravate in description.

A friend exaggerates a man's virtues, an enemy *inflames* his crimes. [*Unusual.*] *Addison.*

4. To heat; to excite excessive action in the blood; as, to *inflame* the blood or body; to *inflame* with wine.
5. To provoke; to irritate; to anger.
6. To increase; to exasperate; as, to *inflame* the enmity of parties, or the spirit of sedition.
7. To increase; to augment; as, to *inflame* a presumption. *Kent.*

INFLA'ME, *v. i.* To grow hot, angry and painful. *Wiseman.*

INFLA'MED, *pp.* Set on fire; enkindled; heated; provoked; exasperated.

INFLA'MER, *n.* The person or thing that inflames. *Addison.*

INFLA'MING, *ppr.* Kindling; heating; provoking; exasperating.

INFLAMMABIL'ITY, *n.* Susceptibility of taking fire.

INFLAM'MABLE, *a.* That may be set on fire; easily enkindled; susceptible of combustion; as *inflammable* oils or spirits.

INFLAM'MABLENESS, *n.* The quality of being susceptible of flame, or capable of taking fire; inflammability. *Boyle.*

INFLAMMA'TION, *n.* [L. *inflammatio.*]
1. The act of setting on fire or inflaming.
2. The state of being in flame. *Temple. Wilkins.*
3. In *medicine* and *surgery*, a redness and swelling of any part of an animal body, attended with heat, pain and febrile symptoms. *Encyc.*
4. Violent excitement; heat; animosity; turbulence; as an *inflammation* of the body politic, or of parties.

INFLAM'MATORY, *a.* Inflaming; tending to excite heat or inflammation; as medicines of an *inflammatory* nature.
2. Accompanied with preternatural heat and excitement of arterial action; as an *inflammatory* fever or disease.
3. Tending to excite anger, animosity, tumult or sedition; as *inflammatory* libels, writings, speeches or publications.

INFLA'TE, *v. t.* [L. *inflatus*, from *inflo; in* and *flo*, to blow.]
1. To swell or distend by injecting air; as, to *inflate* a bladder; to *inflate* the lungs.
2. To fill with the breath; to blow in. *Dryden.*
3. To swell; to puff up; to elate; as, to *inflate* one with pride or vanity.

INFLA'TE, **INFLA'TED**, } *a.* In *botany*, puffed; hollow and distended; as a perianth, corol, nectary, or pericarp. *Martyn.*

INFLA'TED, *pp.* Swelled or distended with air; puffed up.

INFLA'TING, *ppr.* Distending with air; puffing up.

INFLA'TION, *n.* [L. *inflatio.*] The act of inflating.
2. The state of being distended with air injected or inhaled.
3. The state of being puffed up, as with vanity.
4. Conceit. *B. Jonson.*

INFLECT', *v. t.* [L. *inflecto; in* and *flecto*, to bend.]
1. To bend; to turn from a direct line or course.

Are not the rays of the sun reflected, refracted and *inflected* by one and the same principle? *Newton.*

2. In *grammar*, to vary a noun or a verb in its terminations; to decline, as a noun or adjective, or to conjugate, as a verb.
3. To modulate, as the voice.

INFLECT'ED, *pp.* Bent or turned from a direct line or course; as an *inflected* ray of light; varied in termination.

INFLECT'ING, *ppr.* Bending or turning from its course; varying in termination; modulating, as the voice.

INFLEC'TION, *n.* [L. *inflectio.*] The act of bending or turning from a direct line or course.
2. In *optics*, a property of light by which its rays, when they approach a body, are bent towards it or from it. *Encyc. Cyc.*
3. In *grammar*, the variation of nouns, &c. by declension, and verbs by conjugation. *Encyc.*
4. Modulation of the voice in speaking. *Hooker.*

More commonly *inflection* gives significance to tones. *E. Porter.*

Point of inflection, in *geometry*, the point where a curve begins to bend the contrary way. *Encyc.*

INFLECT'IVE, *a.* Having the power of bending; as the *inflective* quality of the air. *Derham.*

INFLEX'ED, *a.* [L. *inflexus.*] Turned; bent. *Feltham.*

INFLEXIBIL'ITY, **INFLEX'IBLENESS**, } *n.* [Fr. *inflexibilité*, from *inflexible*; L. *in* and *flexibilis*, from *flecto*, to bend.]
1. The quality of being inflexible, or not capable of being bent; unyielding stiffness.
2. Obstinacy of will or temper; firmness of purpose that will not yield to importunity or persuasion; unbending pertinacity.

INFLEX'IBLE, *a.* [Fr.; L. *inflexibilis.*]
1. That cannot be bent; as an *inflexible* oak.
2. That will not yield to prayers or arguments; firm in purpose; not to be prevailed on; that cannot be turned; as a man of upright and *inflexible* temper. *Addison.*
3. Not to be changed or altered.

The nature of things is *inflexible.* *Watts.*

INFLEX'IBLY, *adv.* With a firmness that resists all importunity or persuasion; with unyielding pertinaciousness; inexorable. A judge should be *inflexibly* just and impartial.

INFLEXION. [See *Inflection.*]

INFLICT', *v. t.* [L. *inflictus, infligo; in* and *fligo*, to strike, Eng. to *flog.*]
To lay on; to throw or send on; to apply; as, to *inflict* pain or disgrace; to *inflict* punishment on an offender.
To *inflict* an office, condition, knowledge, tenderness, &c. on one, as used by Chesterfield, is not an authorized use of the word.

INFLICT'ED, *pp.* Laid on; applied; as punishment or judgments.

INFLICT'ER, *n.* He who lays on or applies.

INFLICT'ING, *ppr.* Laying on; applying.

INFLIC'TION, *n.* [L. *inflictio.*] The act of laying on or applying; as the *infliction* of torment or of punishment.
2. The punishment applied.

His severest *inflictions* are in themselves acts of justice and righteousness. *Rogers.*

INFLICT'IVE, *a.* Tending or able to inflict.

INFLORES'CENCE, *n.* [L. *inflorescens, infloresco, infloreo; in* and *floreo*, to blossom.]
1. In *botany*, a mode of flowering, or the manner in which flowers are supported on their foot-stalks or peduncles.

Inflorescence affords an excellent characteristic mark in distinguishing the species of plants. *Milne.*

2. A flowering; the unfolding of blossoms. *Journ. of Science.*

IN'FLUENCE, *n.* [Fr. from L. *influens, influo*, to flow in; *in* and *fluo*, to flow; Sp. *influencia*; It. *influenza.*] Literally, a flowing in, into or on, and referring to substances spiritual or too subtil to be visible, like inspiration. Hence the word was formerly followed by *into.*

God hath his *influence into* the very essence of all things. *Hooker.*

It is now followed by *on* or *with.*
2. In *a general sense*, influence denotes power whose operation is invisible and known only by its effects, or a power whose cause and operation are unseen.
3. The power which celestial bodies are supposed to exert on terrestrial; as the *influence* of the planets on the birth and fortunes of men; *an exploded doctrine of astrology.*
4. Moral power; power of truth operating on the mind, rational faculties or will, in persuading or dissuading, as the *influence* of motives, of arguments, or of prayer. We say, arguments had no *influence on* the jury. The magistrate is not popular; he has no *influence with* the people; or he has great *influence with* the prince.
5. Physical power; power that affects natural bodies by unseen operation; as, the rays of the sun have an *influence* in whitening cloth, and in giving a green color to vegetables.
6. Power acting on sensibility; as the *influence* of love or pity in sympathy.
7. Spiritual power, or the immediate power of God on the mind; as divine *influence*; the *influences* of the Holy Spirit.

IN'FLUENCE, *v. t.* To move by physical power operating by unseen laws or force; to affect.

These experiments succeed after the same manner *in vacuo*, as in the open air, and therefore are not *influenced* by the weight or pressure of the atmosphere. *Newton.*

2. To move by moral power; to act on and affect, as the mind or will, in persuading or dissuading; to induce. Men are *influenced* by motives of interest or pleasure. An orator may *influence* the people to take arms, or to abandon an enterprise.

3. To move, as the passions; as, to *influence* one by pity.
4. To lead or direct. This revelation is sufficient to *influence* our faith and practice.

IN'FLUENCED, *pp.* Moved; excited; affected; persuaded; induced.

IN'FLUENCING, *ppr.* Moving; affecting; inducing.

IN'FLUENT, *a.* Flowing in. [*Little used.*] *Arbuthnot.*

INFLUEN'TIAL, *a.* Exerting influence or power by invisible operation, as physical causes on bodies, or as moral causes on the mind. It is particularly used to express the operation of moral causes. *Milner.*

Influential characters, persons who possess the power of inclining or controlling the minds of others. *Hamilton.*

INFLUEN'TIALLY, *adv.* By means of influence, so as to incline, move or direct.

INFLUEN'ZA, *n.* [It. *influenza*, influence.] An epidemic catarrh. The *influenza* of October and November, 1789, and that of April and May, 1790, were very general or universal in the United States, and unusually severe. A like *influenza* prevailed in the winters of 1825 and 1826.

IN'FLUX, *n.* [L. *influxus, influo; in* and *fluo*, to flow.]

1. The act of flowing in; as an *influx* of light or other fluid.
2. Infusion; intromission.

The *influx* of the knowlege of God, in relation to everlasting life, is infinitely of moment. *Hale.*

3. Influence; power. [*Not used.*] *Hale.*
4. A coming in; introduction; importation in abundance; as a great *influx* of goods into a country, or an *influx* of gold and silver.

INFLUX'ION, *n.* Infusion; intromission. *Bacon.*

INFLUX'IOUS, *a.* Influential. [*Not used.*]

INFLUX'IVE, *a.* Having influence, or having a tendency to flow in. *Halesworth.*

INFŌLD, *v. i.* [*in* and *fold.*] To involve; to wrap up or enwrap; to inclose.

Infold his limbs in bands. *Blackmore.*

2. To clasp with the arms; to embrace.

Noble Banco, let me *infold* thee,
And hold thee to my heart. *Shak.*

INFŌLDED, *pp.* Involved; enwrapped; inclosed; embraced.

INFŌLDING, *ppr.* Involving; wrapping up; clasping.

INFŌ'LIATE, *v. t.* [L. *in* and *folium*, a leaf.]

To cover or overspread with leaves. [*Not much used.*] *Howell.*

INFORM', *v. t.* [Fr. *informer;* Sp. *informar;* It. *informare;* L. *informo*, to shape; *in* and *formo, forma*, form.] Properly, to give form or shape to, but in this sense not used.

1. To animate; to give life to; to actuate by vital powers.

Let others better mold the running mass
Of metals, and *inform* the breathing brass. *Dryden.*

Breath *informs* this fleeting frame. *Prior.*

—Breathes in our soul, *informs* our vital part. *Pope.*

[*This use is chiefly or wholly poetical.*]

2. To instruct; to tell to; to acquaint; to communicate knowledge to; to make known to by word or writing; usually followed by *of.* Before we judge, we should be well *informed of* the facts relating to the case. A messenger arrived and *informed* the commander *of* the state of the troops. Letters from Europe *inform* us *of* the commencement of hostilities between the Persians and Turks.
3. To communicate a knowledge of facts to one by way of accusation.

Tertullus *informed* the governor against Paul. Acts xxiv.

In this application the verb is usually intransitive; as, A *informed* against B.

INFORM', *v. i.* To give intelligence. *Shak.*

He might either teach in the same manner, or *inform* how he had been taught— *Monthly Rev.*

To inform against, to communicate facts by way of accusation; to give intelligence of a breach of law. Two persons came to the magistrate, and *informed against* A.

INFORM', *a.* [L. *informis.*] Without regular form; shapeless; ugly.

INFORM'AL, *a.* [*in* and *formal.*] Not in the regular or usual form; as an *informal* writing; *informal* proceedings.

2. Not in the usual manner; not according to custom; as an *informal* visit.
3. Not with the official forms; as, the secretary made to the envoy an *informal* communication.

INFORMAL'ITY, *n.* [from *informal.*] Want of regular or customary form. The *informality* of legal proceedings may render them void.

INFORM'ALLY, *adv.* In an irregular or informal manner; without the usual forms.

INFORM'ANT, *n.* One who informs, or gives intelligence.

2. One who offers an accusation. [See *Informer*, which is generally used.]

INFORMA'TION, *n.* [Fr. from L. *informatio.*]

1. Intelligence; notice, news or advice communicated by word or writing. We received *information* of the capture of the ship by an arrival at Boston. The *information* by the messenger is confirmed by letters.
2. Knowledge derived from reading or instruction.

He should get some *information* in the subject he intends to handle. *Swift.*

3. Knowledge derived from the senses or from the operation of the intellectual faculties.

The active *informations* of the intellect— *South.*

4. Communication of facts for the purpose of accusation; a charge or accusation exhibited to a magistrate or court. An *information* is the accusation of a common informer or of a private person; the accusation of a grand jury is called an *indictment* or a *presentment.* *Blackstone.*

INFORM'ATIVE, *a.* Having power to animate. *More.*

INFORM'ED, *pp.* Told; instructed; made acquainted.

INFORM'ER, *n.* One who animates, informs or gives intelligence.

2. One who communicates, or whose duty it is to communicate to a magistrate a knowledge of the violations of law, and bring the offenders to trial.

INFORM'IDABLE, *a.* [*in* and *formidable.*] Not formidable; not to be feared or dreaded.

Foe not *informidable.* *Milton.*

INFORM'ING, *ppr.* Giving notice or intelligence; telling.

2. Communicating facts by way of accusation.

Informing officer, is an officer whose duty it is to inform against persons for breaches of law, as an attorney-general, a sheriff, constable, or grand juror.

A common informer, is any person who informs against another.

INFORM'ITY, *n.* [L. *informis.*] Want of regular form; shapelessness. *Brown.*

INFORM'OUS, *a.* [Fr. *informe;* L. *informis.*] Of no regular form or figure; shapeless. *Brown. Wilford.*

INFOR'TUNATE, *a.* [L. *infortunatus.*] Unlucky; unfortunate. [The latter is commonly used.]

INFOR'TUNATELY, *adv.* Unfortunately. [*Not used.*]

INFOR'TUNE, *n.* Misfortune. [*Not used.*] *Elyot.*

INFRA€T', *v. t.* [L. *infractus*, from *infringo; in* and *frango*, to break.]

To break; to violate. [This is synonymous with *infringe;* it is an unnecessary word and little used.]

INFRA€'TION, *n.* [Fr. from L. *infractio.* See *Infract.*]

The act of breaking; breach; violation; non-observance; as an *infraction* of a treaty, compact, agreement or law. *Watts.*

INFRA€T'OR, *n.* One that violates an agreement, &c.

INFRAMUND'ANE, *a.* [L. *infra*, below, and *mundanus, mundus*, the world.] Lying or being beneath the world.

INFRAN'GIBLE, *a.* [*in* and *frangible.*]

1. Not to be broken or separated into parts; as *infrangible* atoms. *Cheyne.*
2. Not to be violated.

INFRE'QUENCE, } *n.* [L. *infrequentia.*] Uncommonness;
INFRE'QUENCY, } rareness; the state of rarely occurring. *Broome.*

INFRE'QUENT, *a.* [L. *infrequens; in* and *frequens*, frequent.]

Rare; uncommon; seldom happening or occurring to notice; unfrequent.

INFRIG'IDATE, *v. t.* [L. *in* and *frigidus*, cold.] To chill; to make cold. [*Little used.*] *Boyle.*

INFRIGIDA'TION, *n.* The act of making cold. *Tatler.*

INFRINGE, *v. t.* *infrinj'.* [L. *infringo; in* and *frango*, to break. See *Break.*]

1. To break, as contracts; to violate, either positively by contravention, or negatively by non-fulfillment or neglect of performance. A prince or a private person *infringes* an agreement or covenant by neglecting to perform its conditions, as well as by doing what is stipulated not to be done.
2. To break; to violate; to transgress; to neglect to fulfill or obey; as, to *infringe* a law.
3. To destroy or hinder; as, to *infringe* efficacy. [*Little used.*] *Hooker.*

INFRING'ED, *pp.* Broken; violated; transgressed.

INFRINGEMENT, *n.* *infrinj'ment.* Act of violating; breach; violation; non-fulfillment; as the *infringement* of a treaty, compact or other agreement; the *infringement* of a law or constitution.

INFRING'ER, *n.* One who violates; a violator.

INFRING'ING, *ppr.* Breaking; violating; transgressing; failing to observe or fulfill.

IN'FUCATE, *v. t.* [L. *infuco; in* and *fuco*, to paint.] To stain; to paint; to daub.

INFU'MED, *a.* [L. *infumatus.*] Dried in smoke.

INFUNDIB'ULIFORM, *a.* [L. *infundibulum*, a funnel, and *form.*]
In *botany*, having the shape of a funnel, as the corol of a flower; monopetalous, having a conical border rising from a tube. *Martyn.*

INFU'RIATE, *a.* [L. *in* and *furiatus*, from *furia*, fury.] Enraged; mad; raging. *Milton. Thomson.*

INFU'RIATE, *v. t.* To render furious or mad; to enrage. *Decay of Piety.*

INFUS'CATE, *v. t.* [L. *infuscatus, infusco*, to make black; *in* and *fusco, fuscus*, dark.] To darken; to make black.

INFUSCA'TION, *n.* The act of darkening or blackening.

INFU'SE, *v. t. s* as *z.* [Fr. *infuser*, from L. *infusus, infundo*, to pour in; *in* and *fundo*, to pour.]
1. To pour in, as a liquid.

That strong Circean liquor cease t' *infuse.* *Denham.*

2. To instill, as principles or qualities.

Why should he desire to have qualities *infused* into his son, which himself never possessed? *Swift.*

3. To pour in or instill, as into the mind. *Infuse* into young minds a noble ardor.
4. To introduce; as, to *infuse* Gallicisms into a composition.
5. To inspire with; as, to *infuse* the breast with magnanimity. [*Not used.*] *Shak.*
6. To steep in liquor without boiling, for the purpose of extracting medicinal qualities.

One scruple of dried leaves is *infused* in ten ounces of warm water. *Coxe.*

7. To make an infusion with an ingredient. [*Not used.*] *Bacon.*

INFU'SE, *n.* Infusion. *Obs.* *Spenser.*

INFU'SED, *pp.* Poured in; instilled; steeped.

INFU'SER, *n.* One who infuses.

INFUSIBIL'ITY, *n.* [from *infusible.*] The capacity of being infused or poured in.
2. The incapacity of being fused or dissolved.

INFU'SIBLE, *a.* [from the verb.] That may be infused. Good principles are *infusible* into the minds of youth.

INFU'SIBLE, *a.* [*in*, not, and *fusible*, from *fuse.*]
Not fusible; incapable of fusion; that cannot be dissolved or melted.

The best crucibles are made of Limoges earth, which seems absolutely *infusible.* *Lavoisier.*

INFU'SING, *ppr.* Pouring in; instilling; steeping.

INFU'SION, *n. s* as *z.* The act of pouring in or instilling; instillation; as the *infusion* of good principles into the mind; the *infusion* of ardor or zeal.
2. Suggestion; whisper.

His folly and his wisdom are of his own growth, not the echo or *infusion* of other men. *Swift.*

3. In *pharmacy*, the process of steeping in liquor, an operation by which the medicinal qualities of plants may be extracted by a liquor without boiling. *Encyc.*
4. The liquor in which plants are steeped, and which is impregnated with their virtues or qualities. *Coxe.*

INFU'SIVE, *a.* Having the power of infusion. *Thomson.*

INFU'SORY, *a.* The infusory order of worms [*vermes*] comprehends those minute and simple animalcules which are seldom capable of being traced except by the microscope. *Good.*

Ing, in Saxon, signifies a pasture or meadow, Goth. *winga.* [See *English.*]

INGANNA'TION, *n.* [It. *ingannare*, to cheat.] Cheat; fraud. [*Not used.*]

IN'GATE, *n.* [*in* and *gate.*] Entrance; passage in. *Obs.* *Spenser.*

INGATH'ERING, *n.* [*in* and *gathering.*] The act or business of collecting and securing the fruits of the earth; harvest; as the feast of *ingathering.* Ex. xxiii.

INGEL'ABLE, *a.* [*in* and *gelable.*] That cannot be congealed.

INGEM'INATE, *a.* [L. *ingeminatus.*] Redoubled. *Taylor.*

INGEM'INATE, *v. t.* [L. *ingemino; in* and *gemino.*] To double or repeat. *Sandys.*

INGEMINA'TION, *n.* Repetition; reduplication. *Walsall.*

INGENDER. [See *Engender.*]

INGENERABIL'ITY, *n.* [infra.] Incapacity of being engendered.

INGEN'ERABLE, *a.* [*in* and *generate.*] That cannot be engendered or produced. *Boyle.*

INGEN'ERATE, *v. t.* [L. *ingenero; in* and *genero*, to generate.] To generate or produce within. *Fellows.*

INGEN'ERATE, *a.* Generated within; inborn; innate; inbred; as *ingenerate* powers of body. *Wotton.*

INGEN'ERATED, *pp.* Produced within.

Noble habits *ingenerated* in the soul. *Hale.*

INGEN'ERATING, *ppr.* Generating or producing within.

INGE'NIOUS, *a.* [L. *ingeniosus*, from *ingenium: in* and *genius, geno, gigno*, to beget, Gr. γεινομαι.]
1. Possessed of genius, or the faculty of invention; hence, skillful or prompt to invent; having an aptitude to contrive, or to form new combinations of ideas; as an *ingenious* author; an *ingenious* mechanic.

The more *ingenious* men are, the more apt are they to trouble themselves. *Temple.*

2. Proceeding from genius or ingenuity; of curious design, structure or mechanism; as an *ingenious* performance of any kind; an *ingenious* scheme or plan; an *ingenious* model or machine; *ingenious* fabric; *ingenious* contrivance.
3. Witty; well formed; well adapted; as an *ingenious* reply.
4. Mental; intellectual. [*Not used.*] *Shak.*

INGE'NIOUSLY, *adv.* With ingenuity; with readiness in contrivance; with skill.

INGE'NIOUSNESS, *n.* The quality of being ingenious or prompt in invention; ingenuity; *used of persons.*
2. Curiousness of design or mechanism; *used of things.*

INGEN'ITE, *a.* [L. *ingenitus; in* and *genitus*, born.]
Innate; inborn; inbred; native; ingenerate. *South.*

INGENU'ITY, *n.* [Fr. *ingenuité.*] The quality or power of ready invention; quickness or acuteness in combining ideas, or in forming new combinations; ingeniousness; skill; *used of persons.* How many machines for saving labor has the *ingenuity* of men devised and constructed.
2. Curiousness in design, the effect of ingenuity; as the *ingenuity* of a plan or of mechanism.
3. Openness of heart; fairness; candor.

[This sense of the word was formerly common, and is found in good authors down to the age of Locke, and even later; but it is now wholly obsolete. In lieu of it, *ingenuousness* is used.]

INGEN'UOUS, *a.* [L. *ingenuus.*] Open; frank; fair; candid; free from reserve, disguise, equivocation or dissimulation; *used of persons or things.* We speak of an *ingenuous* mind; an *ingenuous* man; an *ingenuous* declaration or confession.
2. Noble; generous; as an *ingenuous* ardor or zeal; *ingenuous* detestation of falsehood. *Locke.*
3. Of honorable extraction; freeborn; as *ingenuous* blood or birth.

INGEN'UOUSLY, *adv.* Openly; fairly; candidly; without reserve or dissimulation. *Dryden.*

INGEN'UOUSNESS, *n.* Openness of heart; frankness; fairness; freedom from reserve or dissimulation; as, to confess our faults with *ingenuousness.*
2. Fairness; candidness; as the *ingenuousness* of a confession.

IN'GENY, *n.* Wit; ingenuity. *Obs.* *Bacon.*

INGEST', *v. t.* [L. *ingestus*, from *ingero; in* and *gero*, to bear.] To throw into the stomach. [*Little used.*] *Brown.*

INGES'TION, *n.* The act of throwing into the stomach; as the *ingestion* of milk or other food. *Harvey.*

IN'GLE, *n.* [Qu. L. *igniculus, ignis.*] Flame; blaze. [*Not in use.*] *Ray.*
2. In *Scottish*, a fire, or fireplace. *Burns.*

INGLO'RIOUS, *a.* [L. *inglorius; in* and *gloria.*]
1. Not glorious; not bringing honor or glory; not accompanied with fame or celebrity; as an *inglorious* life of ease.
2. Shameful; disgraceful. He charged his troops with *inglorious* flight.

INGLO'RIOUSLY, *adv.* With want of glory; dishonorably; with shame.

IN'GOT, *n.* [Fr. *lingot.* Qu. L. *lingua.*] A mass or wedge of gold or silver cast in a mold; a mass of unwrought metal. *Encyc.*

INGR'AFT, *v. t.* [*in* and *graff.* The original word is *ingraff* or *graff*, but it is corrupted beyond recovery.]
1. To insert a cion of one tree or plant into another for propagation; as, to *ingraft* the cion of an apple-tree on a pear-tree, as its stock; to *ingraft* a peach on a plum.
2. To propagate by insition. *May.*
3. To plant or introduce something foreign

into that which is native, for the purpose of propagation.

This fellow would *ingraft* a foreign name
Upon our stock. *Dryden.*

4. To set or fix deep and firm.

Ingrafted love he bears to Cesar. *Shak.*

INGR'AFTED, *pp.* Inserted into a stock for growth and propagation; introduced into a native stock; set or fixed deep.

INGR'AFTING, *ppr.* Inserting, as cions in stocks; introducing and inserting on a native stock what is foreign; fixing deep.

INGR'AFTMENT, *n.* The act of ingrafting.

2. The thing ingrafted.

IN'GRAIN, *v. t.* [*in* and *grain.*] To dye in the grain, or before manufacture.

IN'GRAINED, *pp.* Dyed in the grain or in the raw material; as *ingrained* carpets.

IN'GRAINING, *ppr.* Dyeing in the raw material.

INGRAP'PLED, *a.* Grappled; seized on; entwined. *Drayton.*

IN'GRATE, } *a.* [L. *ingratus; in* and
INGRA'TEFUL, } *gratus;* Fr. *ingrat.*]

1. Ungrateful; unthankful; not having feelings of kindness for a favor received. *Milton. Pope.*

2. Unpleasing to the sense.

He gives no *ingrateful* food. *Milton.*

IN'GRATE, *n.* [Fr. *ingrat.*] An ungrateful person.

INGRA'TEFULLY, *adv.* Ungratefully.

INGRA'TEFULNESS, *n.* Ungratefulness.

INGRA'TIATE, *v. t. ingra'shate.* [It. *ingrazianarsi;* L. *in* and *gratia*, favor.]

1. To commend one's self to another's good will, confidence or kindness. It is always used as a reciprocal verb, and followed by *with*, before the person whose favor is sought. Ministers and courtiers *ingratiate* themselves *with* their sovereign. Demagogues *ingratiate* themselves *with* the populace.

2. To recommend; to render easy; *used of things.* *Hammond.*

INGRA'TIATING, *ppr.* Commending one's self to the favor of another.

INGRA'TIATING, *n.* The act of commending one's self to another's favor.

INGRAT'ITUDE, *n.* [Fr.; *in* and *gratitude.*]

1. Want of gratitude or sentiments of kindness for favors received; insensibility to favors, and want of a disposition to repay them; unthankfulness.

Ingratitude is abhorred by God and man. *L'Estrange.*

No man will own himself guilty of *ingratitude.*

2. Retribution of evil for good.

Nor was it with *ingratitude* returned. *Dryden.*

INGRA'VE, *v. t.* To bury. [*Not used.*]

INGRAV'IDATE, *v. t.* [L. *gravidus.*] To impregnate. *Fuller.*

INGREAT, *v. t.* To make great. [*Not in use.*] *Fotherby.*

INGRE'DIENT, *n.* [Fr. from L. *ingrediens*, entering into; *ingredior; in* and *gradior.* See *Grade.*]

That which enters into a compound, or is a component part of any compound or mixture. It is particularly applied to the simples in medicinal compositions, but admits of a very general application. We say, an ointment or a decoction is composed of certain *ingredients;* and Addison wondered that learning was not thought a proper *ingredient* in the education of a woman of quality or fortune.

IN'GRESS, *n.* [L. *ingressus, ingredior,* supra.]

1. Entrance; as the *ingress* of air into the lungs. It is particularly applied to the entrance of the moon into the shadow of the earth in eclipses, the sun's entrance into a sign, &c.

2. Power of entrance; means of entering. All *ingress* was prohibited.

INGRES'SION, *n.* [Fr. from L. *ingressio, ingredior.*] The act of entering; entrance. *Digby.*

IN'GUINAL, *a.* [from L. *inguen*, the groin.] Pertaining to the groin; as an *inguinal* tumor.

INGULF', *v. t.* [*in* and *gulf.*] To swallow up in a vast deep, gulf or whirlpool. *Milton.*

2. To cast into a gulf. *Hayward.*

INGULF'ED, *pp.* Swallowed up in a gulf or vast deep; cast into a gulf.

INGULF'ING, *ppr.* Swallowing up in a gulf, whirlpool or vast deep.

INGUR'GITATE, *v. t.* [L. *ingurgito; in* and *gurges*, a gulf.] To swallow greedily or in great quantity. *Dict.*

INGUR'GITATE, *v. i.* To drink largely; to swill.

INGURGITA'TION, *n.* The act of swallowing greedily, or in great quantity. *Darwin.*

INGUST'ABLE, *a.* [L. *in* and *gusto*, to taste.] That cannot be tasted. [*Little used.*] *Brown.*

INHAB'ILE, *a.* [Fr. from L. *inhabilis; in* and *habilis*, apt, fit.]

1. Not apt or fit; unfit; not convenient; as *inhabile* matter. *Encyc.*

2. Unskilled; unready; unqualified; *used of persons.* [*Little used.* See *Unable.*]

INHABIL'ITY, *n.* [from *inhabile.*] Unaptness; unfitness; want of skill. [*Little used.* See *Inability.*]

INHAB'IT, *v. t.* [L. *inhabito; in* and *habito*, to dwell.]

To live or dwell in; to occupy as a place of settled residence. Wild beasts *inhabit* the forest; fishes *inhabit* the ocean, lakes and rivers; men *inhabit* cities and houses.

Thus saith the high and lofty One, that *inhabiteth* eternity—Is. lvii.

INHAB'IT, *v. i.* To dwell; to live; to abide.

They say wild beasts *inhabit* here. *Waller.*

INHAB'ITABLE, *a.* [from *inhabit.*] Habitable; that may be inhabited; capable of affording habitation to animals. The stars may be *inhabitable* worlds. Some regions of the earth are not *inhabitable* by reason of cold or sterility. A building may be too old and decayed to be *inhabitable.*

2. Not habitable. [Fr. *inhabitable;* L. *inhabitabilis.*] [*Not in use.*] *Shak.*

INHAB'ITANCE, *n.* Residence of dwellers. [*Little used.*] *Carew.*

INHAB'ITANCY, *n.* Residence; habitancy; permanent or legal residence in a town, city or parish; or the domiciliation which the law requires to entitle a pauper to demand support from the town, city or parish in which he lives, otherwise called a legal settlement, which subjects a town to support a person, if a pauper. *Laws of Mass. Blackstone.*

INHAB'ITANT, *n.* A dweller; one who dwells or resides permanently in a place, or who has a fixed residence, as distinguished from an occasional lodger or visitor; as the *inhabitant* of a house or cottage; the *inhabitants* of a town, city, county or state. So brute animals are *inhabitants* of the regions to which their natures are adapted; and we speak of spiritual beings, as *inhabitants* of heaven.

2. One who has a legal settlement in a town, city or parish. The conditions or qualifications which constitute a person an inhabitant of a town or parish, so as to subject the town or parish to support him, if a pauper, are defined by the statutes of different governments or states.

INHABITA'TION, *n.* The act of inhabiting, or state of being inhabited. *Raleigh.*

2. Abode; place of dwelling. *Milton.*

3. Population; whole mass of inhabitants. *Brown.*

[*This word is little used.*]

INHAB'ITED, *pp.* Occupied by inhabitants, human or irrational.

INHAB'ITER, *n.* One who inhabits; a dweller; an inhabitant. *Derham.*

INHAB'ITING, *ppr.* Dwelling in; occupying as a settled or permanent inhabitant; residing in.

INHAB'ITRESS, *n.* A female inhabitant. *Bp. Richardson.*

INHA'LE, *v. t.* [L. *inhalo; in* and *halo*, to breathe.]

To draw into the lungs; to inspire; as, to *inhale* air; opposed to *exhale* and *expire.*

Martin was walking forth to *inhale* the fresh breeze of the evening. *Arbuthnot and Pope.*

INHA'LED, *pp.* Drawn into the lungs.

INHA'LER, *n.* One who inhales.

2. In *medicine*, a machine for breathing or drawing warm steam into the lungs, as a remedy for coughs and catarrhal complaints. *Encyc.*

INHA'LING, *ppr.* Drawing into the lungs; breathing.

INHARMON'IC, } *a.* Unharmonious;
INHARMON'ICAL, } discordant.

INHARMO'NIOUS, *a.* [*in* and *harmonious.*] Not harmonious; unmusical; discordant. *Broome.*

INHARMO'NIOUSLY, *adv.* Without harmony; discordantly.

INHE'RE, *v. i.* [L. *inhæreo; in* and *hæreo*, to hang.]

To exist or be fixed in something else; as, colors *inhere* in cloth; a dart *inheres* in the flesh.

INHE'RENCE, *n.* Existence in something; a fixed state of being in another body or substance.

INHE'RENT, *a.* Existing in something else, so as to be inseparable from it.

Inherent baseness. *Shak.*

2. Innate; naturally pertaining to; as the *inherent* qualities of the magnet; the *inherent* right of men to life, liberty and protection.

INHE'RENTLY, *adv.* By inherence. *Bentley.*

INHE'RING, *ppr.* Existing or fixed in something else.

INHER'IT, *v. t.* [Sp. *heredar;* Port. *herdar;* It. *eredare;* Fr. *heriter;* from L. *hæres,* an heir. See *Heir.*]

1. To take by descent from an ancestor; to take by succession, as the representative of the former possessor; to receive, as a right or title descendible by law from an ancestor at his decease. The heir *inherits* the lands or real estate of his father; the eldest son of the nobleman *inherits* his father's title, and the eldest son of a king *inherits* the crown.
2. To receive by nature from a progenitor. The son *inherits* the virtues of his father; the daughter *inherits* the temper of her mother, and children often *inherit* the constitutional infirmities of their parents.
3. To possess; to enjoy; to take as a possession, by gift or divine appropriation; as, to *inherit* everlasting life; to *inherit* the promises.

—That thou mayest live, and *inherit* the land which Jehovah thy God giveth thee. Deut. xvi.

The meek shall *inherit* the earth. Matt. v.

INHER'IT, *v. i.* To take or have possession or property.

—Thou shall not *inherit* in our father's house. Judges xi.

INHER'ITABLE, *a.* That may be inherited; transmissible or descendible from the ancestor to the heir by course of law; as an *inheritable* estate or title.

2. That may be transmitted from the parent to the child; as *inheritable* qualities or infirmities.
3. Capable of taking by inheritance, or of receiving by descent.

By attainder—the blood of the person attainted is so corrupted as to be rendered no longer *inheritable.* *Blackstone.*

INHER'ITABLY, *adv.* By inheritance. *Sherwood.*

INHER'ITANCE, *n.* An estate derived from an ancestor to an heir by succession or in course of law; or an estate which the law casts on a child or other person, as the representative of the deceased ancestor.

2. The reception of an estate by hereditary right, or the descent by which an estate or title is cast on the heir; as, the heir received the estate by *inheritance.*
3. The estate or possession which may descend to an heir, though it has not descended.

And Rachel and Leah answered and said, is there yet any portion or *inheritance* for us in our father's house? Gen. xxxi.

4. An estate given or possessed by donation or divine appropriation. Num. xxvi.
5. That which is possessed or enjoyed.

Ask of me, and I will give thee the heathen for thine *inheritance.* Ps. ii.

INHER'ITED, *pp.* Received by descent from an ancestor; possessed.

INHER'ITING, *ppr.* Taking by succession or right of representation; receiving from ancestors; possessing.

INHER'ITOR, *n.* An heir; one who inherits or may inherit.

INHER'ITRESS, INHER'ITRIX, } *n.* An heiress; a female who inherits or is entitled to inherit, after the death of her ancestor.

INHERSE, *v. t.* *inhers'.* [*in* and *herse.*] To inclose in a funeral monument. *Shak.*

INHE'SION, *n.* *s* as *z.* [L. *inhæsio, inhæreo.*] Inherence; the state of existing or being fixed in something.

INHIA'TION, *n.* [L. *inhiatio.*] A gaping after; eager desire. [*Not used.*]

INHIB'IT, *v. t.* [Fr. *inhiber;* L. *inhibeo;* *in* and *habeo,* to hold, properly to rush or drive.]

1. To restrain; to hinder; to check or repress.

Their motions also are excited or *inhibited*—by the objects without them. *Bentley.*

2. To forbid; to prohibit; to interdict.

All men were *inhibited* by proclamation at the dissolution so much as to mention a parliament. *Clarendon.*

INHIB'ITED, *pp.* Restrained; forbid.

INHIB'ITING, *ppr.* Restraining; repressing; prohibiting.

INHIBI''TION, *n.* [Fr. from L. *inhibitio.*]

1. Prohibition; restraint; embargo.
2. In *law,* a writ to forbid or inhibit a judge from farther proceedings in a cause depending before him; commonly, a writ issuing from a higher ecclesiastical court to an inferior one, on appeal. *Cowel.*

INHŌLD, *v. t.* pret. and pp. *inheld.* [*in* and *hold.*]

To have inherent; to contain in itself. [*Little used.*] *Raleigh.*

INHŌLDER, *n.* An inhabitant. *Obs.* *Spenser.*

INHOOP', *v. t.* [*in* and *hoop.*] To confine or inclose in any place. *Shak.*

INHOS'PITABLE, *a.* [*in* and *hospitable.*]

1. Not hospitable; not disposed to entertain strangers gratuitously; declining to entertain guests, or entertaining them with reluctance; as an *inhospitable* person or people.
2. Affording no conveniences, subsistence or shelter to strangers; as *inhospitable* deserts or rocks. *Milton. Dryden.*

INHOS'PITABLY, *adv.* Unkindly to strangers. *Milton.*

INHOS'PITABLENESS, INHOSPITAL'ITY, } *n.* Want of hospitality or kindness to strangers; refusal or unwillingness to entertain guests or strangers without reward. *Chesterfield.*

INHU'MAN, *a.* [Fr. *inhumain;* L. *inhumanus;* *in* and *humanus,* humane.]

1. Destitute of the kindness and tenderness that belong to a human being; cruel; barbarous; savage; unfeeling; as an *inhuman* person or people.
2. Marked with cruelty; as an *inhuman* act.

INHUMAN'ITY, *n.* [Fr. *inhumanité.*] Cruelty in disposition; savageness of heart; *used of persons.*

2. Cruelty in act; barbarity; *used of actions.*

INHU'MANLY, *adv.* With cruelty; barbarously. *Swift.*

INHU'MATE, INHU'ME, } *v. t.* [Fr. *inhumer;* L. *inhumo, humo,* to bury.]

1. To bury; to inter; to deposit in the earth, as a dead body.
2. To digest in a vessel surrounded with warm earth. *Encyc.*

INHUMA'TION, *n.* The act of burying; interment.

2. In *chimistry,* a method of digesting substances by burying the vessel containing them in warm earth, or a like substance. *Encyc.*

INHU'MED, *pp.* Buried; interred.

INHU'MING, *ppr.* Burying; interring.

INIMAG'INABLE, *a.* Unimaginable; inconceivable. *Pearson.*

INIM'ICAL, *a.* [L. *inimicus;* *in* and *amicus,* a friend.]

1. Unfriendly; having the disposition or temper of an enemy; applied to *private* enmity, as *hostile* is to *public.*
2. Adverse; hurtful; repugnant.

—Savage violences *inimical* to commerce. *Ward.*

INIMITABIL'ITY, *n.* [from *inimitable.*] The quality of being incapable of imitation. *Norris.*

INIM'ITABLE, *a.* [Fr. from L. *inimitabilis;* *in* and *imitabilis,* from *imitor,* to imitate.]

That cannot be imitated or copied; surpassing imitation; as *inimitable* beauty or excellence; an *inimitable* description; *inimitable* eloquence.

INIM'ITABLY, *adv.* In a manner not to be imitated; to a degree beyond imitation.

Charms such as thine, *inimitably* great. *Broome.*

INIQ'UITOUS, *a.* [See *Iniquity.*] Unjust; wicked; as an *iniquitous* bargain; an *iniquitous* proceeding. [It is applied to things rather than to persons, but may be applied to persons.]

INIQ'UITY, *n.* [Fr. *iniquité;* L. *iniquitas;* *in* and *æquitas,* equity.]

1. Injustice; unrighteousness; a deviation from rectitude; as the *iniquity* of war; the *iniquity* of the slave trade.
2. Want of rectitude in principle; as a malicious prosecution originating in the *iniquity* of the author.
3. A particular deviation from rectitude; a sin or crime; wickedness; any act of injustice.

Your *iniquities* have separated between you and your God. Is. lix.

4. Original want of holiness or depravity.

I was shapen in *iniquity.* Ps. li.

INIQ'UOUS, *a.* Unjust. [*Not used.*]

INIRRITABIL'ITY, *n.* [*in* and *irritability.*] The quality of being inirritable, or not susceptible of contraction by excitement. *Darwin.*

INIR'RITABLE, *a.* [*in* and *irritable.*] Not irritable; not susceptible of irritation, or contraction by excitement. *Darwin.*

INIR'RITATIVE, *a.* Not accompanied with excitement; as an *inirritative* fever. *Darwin.*

INISLE, *v. t.* *ini'le.* [*in* and *isle.*] To surround; to encircle. [*Not in use.*] *Drayton.*

INI''TIAL, *a.* [Fr. from L. *initialis, initium,* beginning.]

1. Beginning; placed at the beginning; as the *initial* letters of a name.
2. Beginning; incipient; as the *initial* symptoms of a disease.

INI''TIAL, *n.* The first letter of a name.

INI''TIALLY, *adv.* In an incipient degree. *Barrow.*

INI''TIATE, *v. t.* [Low L. *initio,* to enter or begin, from *initum, ineo,* to enter; *in* and *eo,* to go.]

1. To instruct in rudiments or principles; or to introduce into any society or sect by in-

structing the candidate in its principles or ceremonies; as, to *initiate* a person into the mysteries of Ceres.

2. To introduce into a new state or society; as, to *initiate* one into a club. *Addison.*

3. To instruct; to acquaint with; as, to *initiate* one in the higher branches of mathematics.

4. To begin upon. *Clarendon.*

INI''TIATE, *v. i.* To do the first act; to perform the first rite. *Pope.*

INI''TIATE, *a.* Unpracticed. *Shak.*

2. Begun; commenced. A tenant by the curtesy *initiate*, becomes so by the birth of a child, but his estate is not consummate till the death of the wife. *Blackstone.*

INI''TIATE, *n.* One who is initiated. *J. Barlow.*

INI''TIATED, *pp.* Instructed in the first principles; entered.

INI''TIATING, *ppr.* Introducing by instruction, or by appropriate ceremonies. *J. M. Mason.*

INITIA'TION, *n.* [L. *initiatio.*] The act or process of introducing one into a new society, by instructing him in its principles, rules or ceremonies; as, to *initiate* a person into a christian community.

2. The act or process of making one acquainted with principles before unknown.

3. Admission by application of ceremonies or use of symbols; as, to *initiate* one into the visible church by baptism. *Hammond.*

INI''TIATORY, *a.* Initiating or serving to initiate; introducing by instruction, or by the use and application of symbols or ceremonies.

Two *initiatory* rites of the same general import cannot exist together. *J. M. Mason.*

INI''TIATORY, *n.* [supra.] Introductory rite. *L. Addison.*

INJECT', *v. t.* [L. *injectus, injicio; in* and *jacio*, to throw.]

1. To throw in; to dart in; as, to *inject* any thing into the mouth or stomach.

2. To cast or throw on.

—And mound *inject* on mound. *Pope.*

INJECT'ED, *pp.* Thrown in or on.

INJECT'ING, *ppr.* Throwing in or on.

INJECT'ION, *n.* [Fr. from L. *injectio.*] The act of throwing in, particularly that of throwing a liquid medicine into the body by a syringe or pipe.

2. A liquid medicine thrown into the body by a syringe or pipe; a clyster.

3. In *anatomy*, the act of filling the vessels of an animal body with some colored substance, in order to render visible their figures and ramifications. *Encyc.*

INJOIN. [See *Enjoin.*]

INJUCUND'ITY, *n.* [L. *injucunditas.*] Unpleasantness; disagreeableness. [*Little used.*]

INJU'DICABLE, *a.* Not cognizable by a judge. [*Little used.*]

INJUDI''CIAL, *a.* Not according to the forms of law. *Dict.*

INJUDI''CIOUS, *a.* [*in* and *judicious.*] Not judicious; void of judgment; acting without judgment; unwise; as an *injudicious* person.

2. Not according to sound judgment or discretion; unwise; as an *injudicious* measure.

INJUDI''CIOUSLY, *adv.* Without judgment; unwisely.

INJUDI''CIOUSNESS, *n.* The quality of being injudicious or unwise. *Whitlock.*

INJUNC'TION, *n.* [L. *injunctio*, from *injungo*, to enjoin; *in* and *jungo*, to join.]

1. A command; order; precept; the direction of a superior vested with authority.

For still they knew, and ought t' have still remembered
The high *injunction*, not to taste that fruit. *Milton.*

2. Urgent advice or exhortation of persons not vested with absolute authority to command.

3. In *law*, a writ or order of the court of chancery, directed to an inferior court, or to parties and their counsel, directing them to stay proceedings, or to do some act, as to put the plaintiff in possession for want of the defendant's appearance, to stay waste or other injury, &c. When the reason for granting an injunction ceases, the injunction is dissolved. *Blackstone.*

IN'JURE, *v. t.* [Fr. *injure, injurier;* L. *injuria*, injury; Sp. *injuriar;* It. *ingiuriare.* See *Injury.*]

1. To hurt or wound, as the person; to impair soundness, as of health.

2. To damage or lessen the value of, as goods or estate.

3. To slander, tarnish or impair, as reputation or character.

4. To impair or diminish; to annoy; as happiness.

5. To give pain to; to grieve; as sensibility or feelings.

6. To impair, as the intellect or mind.

7. To hurt or weaken; as, to *injure* a good cause.

8. To impair; to violate; as, to *injure* rights.

9. To make worse; as, great rains *injure* the roads.

10. In *general*, to wrong the person, to damage the property, or to lessen the happiness of ourselves or others. A man *injures* his person by wounds, his estate by negligence or extravagance, and his happiness by vices. He *injures* his neighbor by violence to his person, by fraud, by calumny, and by non-fulfillment of his contracts.

IN'JURED, *pp.* Hurt; wounded; damaged; impaired; weakened; made worse.

IN'JURER, *n.* One who injures or wrongs.

IN'JURING, *ppr.* Hurting; damaging; impairing; weakening; rendering worse.

INJU'RIOUS, *a.* [L. *injurius;* Fr. *injurieux.*]

1. Wrongful; unjust; hurtful to the rights of another. That which impairs rights or prevents the enjoyment of them, is *injurious.*

2. Hurtful to the person or health. Violence is *injurious* to the person, as intemperance is to the health.

3. Affecting with damage or loss. Indolence is *injurious* to property.

4. Mischievous; hurtful; as the *injurious* consequences of sin or folly.

5. Lessening or tarnishing reputation. The very suspicion of cowardice is *injurious* to a soldier's character.

6. Detractory; contumelious; hurting reputation; as, obscure hints as well as open detraction, are sometimes *injurious* to reputation.

7. In *general*, whatever gives pain to the body or mind, whatever impairs or destroys property or rights, whatever tarnishes reputation, whatever disturbs happiness, whatever retards prosperity or defeats the success of a good cause, is deemed *injurious.*

INJU'RIOUSLY, *adv.* Wrongfully; hurtfully; with injustice; mischievously.

INJU'RIOUSNESS, *n.* The quality of being injurious or hurtful; injury.

IN'JURY, *n.* [L. *injuria; in* and *jus, juris*, right; Fr. *injure;* It. *ingiuria;* Sp. *injuria.*]

1. In *general*, any wrong or damage done to a man's person, rights, reputation or goods. That which impairs the soundness of the body or health, or gives pain, is an *injury*. That which impairs the mental faculties, is an *injury*. These *injuries* may be received by a fall or by other violence. Trespass, fraud, and non-fulfillment of covenants and contracts are *injuries* to rights. Slander is an *injury* to reputation, and so is cowardice and vice. Whatever impairs the quality or diminishes the value of goods or property, is an *injury*. We may receive *injury* by misfortune as well as by injustice.

2. Mischief; detriment.

Many times we do *injury* to a cause by dwelling on trifling arguments. *Watts.*

3. Any diminution of that which is good, valuable or advantageous.

INJUS'TICE, *n.* [Fr. from L. *injustitia; in* and *justitia*, justice.]

1. Iniquity; wrong; any violation of another's rights, as fraud in contracts, or the withholding of what is due. It has a particular reference to an *unequal* distribution of rights, property or privileges among persons who have *equal* claims.

2. The withholding from another merited praise, or ascribing to him unmerited blame.

INK, *n.* [D. *inkt;* Fr. *encre.*] A black liquor or substance used for writing, generally made of an infusion of galls, copperas and gum-arabic.

2. Any liquor used for writing or forming letters, as red ink, &c.

3. A pigment.

Printing ink is made by boiling lintseed oil, and burning it about a minute, and mixing it with lampblack, with an addition of soap and rosin.

Ink for the rolling press, is made with lintseed oil burnt as above, and mixed with Frankfort black.

Indian ink, from China, is composed of lampblack, and size or animal glue. *Nicholson.*

Sympathetic ink, a liquor used in writing, which exhibits no color or appearance till some other means are used, such as holding it to the fire, or rubbing something over it. *Encyc.*

INK, *v. t.* To black or daub with ink.

INK'HORN, *n.* [*ink* and *horn;* horns being formerly used for holding ink.]

1. A small vessel used to hold ink on a writing table or desk, or for carrying it about the person. Inkhorns are made of horn, glass or stone.

2. A portable case for the instruments of writing. *Johnson.*

INK'INESS, *n.* [from *inky.*] The state or quality of being inky.

INK'LE, *n.* A kind of narrow fillet; tape. *Shak.*

INK'LING, *n.* A hint or whisper; an intimation. [*Little used.*] *Bacon.*

INK'MAKER, *n.* One whose occupation is to make ink.

INKNOT, *v. t.* *innot'.* [*in* and *knot.*] To bind as with a knot.

INK'STAND, *n.* A vessel for holding ink and other writing utensils.

INK'-STONE, *n.* A kind of small round stone of a white, red, gray, yellow or black color, containing a quantity of native vitriol or sulphate of iron; used in making ink. *Encyc.*

INK'Y, *a.* Consisting of ink; resembling ink; black.

2. Tarnished or blackened with ink.

INLA'CE, *v. t.* [*in* and *lace.*] To embellish with variegations. *Fletcher.*

INLA'ID, *pp.* of *inlay,* which see.

IN'LAND, *a.* [*in* and *land.*] Interior; remote from the sea. Worcester in Massachusetts, and Lancaster in Pennsylvania, are large *inland* towns.

2. Within land; remote from the ocean; as an *inland* lake or sea. *Spenser.*

3. Carried on within a country; domestic, not foreign; as *inland* trade or transportation; *inland* navigation.

4. Confined to a country; drawn and payable in the same country; as an *inland* bill of exchange, distinguished from a *foreign* bill, which is drawn in one country on a person living in another.

IN'LAND, *n.* The interior part of a country. *Shak. Milton.*

IN'LANDER, *n.* One who lives in the interior of a country, or at a distance from the sea. *Brown.*

INLAND'ISH, *a,* Denoting something inland; native.

INLAP'IDATE, *v. t.* [*in* and *lapido, lapis,* a stone.]
To convert into a stony substance; to petrify. [*Little used.*] *Bacon.*

INLA'Y, *v. t.* pret. and pp. *inlaid.* [*in* and *lay.*] To veneer; to diversify cabinet or other work by laying in and fastening with glue, thin slices or leaves of fine wood, on a ground of common wood. This is used in making compartments. *Encyc.*

IN'LAY, *n.* Matter or pieces of wood inlaid, or prepared for inlaying. *Milton.*

INLA'YER, *n.* The person who inlays or whose occupation it is to inlay.

INLA'YING, *ppr.* The operation of diversifying or ornamenting work with thin pieces of wood, set in a ground of other wood.

INLAW', *v. t.* To clear of outlawry or attainder. *Bacon.*

IN'LET, *n.* [*in* and *let.*] A passage or opening by which an inclosed place may be entered; place of ingress; entrance. Thus, a window is an *inlet* for light into a house; the senses are the *inlets* of ideas or perceptions into the mind.

2. A bay or recess in the shore of the sea or of a lake or large river, or between isles.

In limine, [L.] at the threshold; at the beginning or outset.

INLIST', *v. i.* [*in* and *list.*] To enter into military service by signing articles and receiving a sum of money. [See *List.*]

INLIST', *v. t.* To engage or procure to enter into military service. [See *Enlist,* a common spelling, but *inlist* is preferable.]

INLIST'ED, *pp.* Engaged in military service, as a soldier.

INLIST'ING, *ppr.* Entering or engaging in military service.

INLIST'MENT, *n.* The act of inlisting.

These *inlistments* were for one year only. *Marshall.*

2. The writing containing the terms of military service, and a list of names of those who enter into the service.

INLOCK', *v. t.* To lock or inclose one thing within another.

IN'LY, *a.* [*in* and *like.*] Internal; interior; secret. *Shak.*

IN'LY, *adv.* Internally; within; in the heart; secretly; as, to be *inly* pleased or grieved. *Milton. Spenser.*

IN'MATE, *n.* [*in* or *inn,* and *mate.*] A person who lodges or dwells in the same house with another, occupying different rooms, but using the same door for passing in and out of the house. *Cowel.*

2. A lodger; one who lives with a family, but is not otherwise connected with it than as a lodger.

IN'MATE, *a.* Admitted as a dweller. *Milton.*

IN'MOST, *a.* [*in* and *most.*] Deepest within; remotest from the surface or external part.

The silent, slow, consuming fires
Which on my *inmost* vitals prey. *Addison.*

I got into the *inmost* court. *Gulliver.*

INN, *n.* [Sax. *inn,* probably from the Heb. and Ch. חנה to dwell or to pitch a tent, whence Ch. חנות an inn. Class Gn. No. 19.]

1. A house for the lodging and entertainment of travelers. In *America,* it is often a tavern, where liquors are furnished for travelers and others.

There was no room for them in the *inn.* Luke ii.

2. In *England,* a college of municipal or common law professors and students; formerly, the town-house of a nobleman, bishop or other distinguished personage, in which he resided when he attended the court.

Inns of court, colleges in which students of law reside and are instructed. The principal are the Inner Temple, the Middle Temple, Lincoln's Inn, and Gray's Inn.

Inns of chancery, colleges in which young students formerly began their law studies. These are now occupied chiefly by attorneys, solicitors, &c. *Encyc.*

INN'HOLDER, *n.* [*inn* and *hold.*] A person who keeps an inn or house for the entertainment of travelers; also, a taverner.

2. An inhabitant. *Obs.* *Spenser.*

INN'KEEPER, *n.* [*inn* and *keep.*] An innholder. In *America,* the innkeeper is often a tavern keeper or taverner, as well as an innkeeper, the inn for furnishing lodgings and provisions being usually united with the tavern for the sale of liquors.

INN, *v. i.* To take up lodging; to lodge. *Donne.*

INN, *v. t.* To house; to put under cover. *Bacon.*

IN'NATE, *a.* [L. *innatus,* from *innascor; in* and *nascor,* to be born.]
Inborn; native; natural. *Innate* ideas are such as are supposed to be stamped on the mind, at the moment when existence begins. Mr. Locke has taken great pains to prove that no such ideas exist. *Encyc.*

INNATED, for *innate,* is not used.

IN'NATELY, *adv.* Naturally.

IN'NATENESS, *n.* The quality of being innate.

INNAV'IGABLE, *a.* [L. *innavigabilis; in* and *navigabilis.* See *Navigate.*]
That cannot be navigated; impassable by ships or vessels. *Dryden.*

IN'NER, *a.* [from *in.*] Interior; farther inward than something else; as an *inner* chamber; the *inner* court of a temple or palace.

2. Interior; internal; not outward; as the *inner* man. Eph. iii.

IN'NERLY, *adv.* More within. *Barret.*

IN'NERMOST, *a.* Farthest inward; most remote from the outward part. Prov. xviii.

INNERVE, *v. t.* *innerv'.* [*in* and *nerve.*] To give nerve to; to invigorate; to strengthen. *Dwight.*

IN'NING, *n.* The ingathering of grain.

2. A term in cricket, a turn for using the bat.

INN'INGS, *n.* Lands recovered from the sea. *Ainsworth.*

IN'NOCENCE, } *n.* [Fr. from L. *innocentia;*
IN'NOCENCY, } *in* and *noceo,* to hurt.]

1. Properly, freedom from any quality that can injure; innoxiousness; harmlessness; as the *innocence* of a medicine which can do no harm. In this sense, the noun is not obsolete, though less used than the adjective.

2. In *a moral sense,* freedom from crime, sin or guilt; untainted purity of heart and life; unimpaired integrity.

Enjoyment left nothing to ask—*innocence* left nothing to fear. *Johnson.*

3. Freedom from guilt or evil intentions; simplicity of heart; as the *innocence* of a child.

4. Freedom from the guilt of a particular sin or crime. This is the sense in which the word is most generally used, for perfect *innocence* cannot be predicated of man. A man charged with theft or murder may prove his *innocence.*

5. The state of being lawfully conveyed to a belligerent, or of not being contraband; as the *innocence* of a cargo, or of any merchandize. *Kent.*

IN'NOCENT, *a.* [Fr. from L. *innocens.*]

1. Properly, not noxious; not producing injury; free from qualities that can injure; harmless; innoxious; as an *innocent* medicine or remedy.

2. Free from guilt; not having done wrong or violated any law; not tainted with sin; pure; upright. In this general sense, no human being that is a moral agent, can be *innocent.* It is followed by *of.*

3. Free from the guilt of a particular crime or evil action; as, a man is *innocent* of the crime charged in the indictment.

4. Lawful; permitted; as an *innocent* trade.

5. Not contraband; not subject to forfeiture; as *innocent* goods carried to a belligerent nation. *Kent.*

IN'NOCENT, *n.* One free from guilt or harm. *Shak.*

2. A natural; an idiot. [*Unusual.*] *Hooker.*

IN'NOCENTLY, *adv.* Without harm; without incurring guilt.

2. With simplicity; without evil design.

3. Without incurring a forfeiture or penalty; as goods *innocently* imported.

INNOC'UOUS, *a.* [L. *innocuus; in* and *noceo*, to hurt.]

Harmless; safe; producing no ill effect; innocent. Certain poisons used as medicines in small quantities, prove not only *innocuous*, but beneficial. It applied only to *things;* not to *persons.*

INNOC'UOUSLY, *adv.* Without harm; without injurious effects.

INNOC'UOUSNESS, *n.* Harmlessness; the quality of being destitute of mischievous qualities or effects. *Digby.*

INNOM'INABLE, *a.* Not to be named. *Chaucer.*

INNOM'INATE, *a.* Having no name; anonymous. *Ray.*

IN'NOVATE, *v. t.* [Fr. *innover;* L. *innovo; in* and *novo*, to make new, *novus*, new.]

1. To change or alter by introducing something new.

From his attempts upon the civil power, he proceeds to *innovate* God's worship. *South.*

2. To bring in something new. *Bacon.*

IN'NOVATE, *v. i.* To introduce novelties; to make changes in any thing established; with *on.* It is often dangerous to *innovate on* the customs of a nation.

IN'NOVATED, *pp.* Changed by the introduction of something new.

IN'NOVATING, *ppr.* Introducing novelties.

INNOVA'TION, *n.* [from *innovate.*] Change made by the introduction of something new; change in established laws, customs, rites or practices. *Innovation* is expedient, when it remedies an evil, and safe, when men are prepared to receive it. *Innovation* is often used in an ill sense, for a change that disturbs settled opinions and practices without an equivalent advantage.

IN'NOVATOR, *n.* An introducer of changes.

Time is the greatest *innovator.* *Bacon.*

2. One who introduces novelties, or who makes changes by introducing something new. *South.*

INNOX'IOUS, *a.* [L. *innoxius; in* and *noxius, noceo*, to hurt.]

1. Free from mischievous qualities; innocent; harmless; as an *innoxious* drug.

2. Not producing evil; harmless in effects.

Innoxious flames are often seen on the hair of men's heads, and on horses' manes. *Digby.*

3. Free from crime; pure; innocent. *Pope.*

INNOX'IOUSLY, *adv.* Harmlessly; without mischief.

2. Without harm suffered. *Brown.*

INNOX'IOUSNESS, *n.* Harmlessness.

The *innoxiousness* of the small pox. *Tooke.*

INNUEND'O, *n.* [L. from *innuo*, to nod; *in* and *nuo.*]

1. An oblique hint; a remote intimation or reference to a person or thing not named.

Mercury—owns it a marriage by *innuendo.* *Dryden.*

2. In *law*, a word used to point out the precise person.

IN'NUENT, *a.* [L. *innuens.*] Significant. *Burton.*

INNUMERABIL'ITY, INNU'MERABLENESS, *n.* State of being innumerable. *Fotherby. Sherwood.*

INNU'MERABLE, *a.* [L. *innumerabilis.* See *Number.*]

1. Not to be counted; that cannot be enumerated or numbered for multitude.

2. In *a loose sense*, very numerous.

INNU'MERABLY, *adv.* Without number.

INNU'MEROUS, *a.* [L. *innumerus; in* and *numerus*, number.]

Too many to be counted or numbered; innumerable. *Milton. Pope.*

INNUTRI''TION, *n.* [*in* and *nutrition.*] Want of nutrition; failure of nourishment. *Darwin.*

INNUTRI''TIOUS, *a.* [*in* and *nutritious.*] Not nutritious; not supplying nourishment; not nourishing. *Darwin.*

INOBE'DIENCE, *n.* Disobedience; neglect of obedience. *Bp. Bedell.*

INOBE'DIENT, *a.* Not yielding obedience; neglecting to obey.

INOBSERV'ABLE, *a.* [*in* and *observable.*] That cannot be seen, perceived or observed.

INOBSERV'ANCE, *n.* Want of observance; neglect of observing; disobedience. *Bacon.*

INOBSERV'ANT, *a.* [*in* and *observant.*] Not taking notice. *Beddoes.*

INOBSERVA'TION, *n.* Neglect or want of observation. *Shuckford.*

INOC'ULATE, *v. t.* [L. *inoculo; in* and *oculus*, the eye.]

1. To bud; to insert the bud of a tree or plant in another tree or plant, for the purpose of growth on the new stock. All sorts of stone fruit, apples, pears, &c. may be *inoculated.* We *inoculate* the stock with a foreign bud.

2. To communicate a disease to a person by inserting infectious matter in his skin or flesh; as, to *inoculate* a person with the matter of small pox or cow pox. When the latter disease is communicated, it is called *vaccination.*

INOC'ULATE, *v. i.* To propagate by budding; to practice inoculation. The time to *inoculate* is when the buds are formed at the extremities of the same year's shoot, indicating that the spring growth for that season is complete.

INOC'ULATED, *pp.* Budded; as an *inoculated* stock.

2. Inserted in another stock, as a bud.

3. Infected by inoculation with a particular disease.

INOC'ULATING, *ppr.* Budding; propagating by inserting a bud on another stock.

2. Infecting by inoculation.

INOCULA'TION, *n.* [L. *inoculatio.*] The act or practice of inserting buds of one plant under the bark of another for propagation.

2. The act or practice of communicating a disease to a person in health, by inserting contagious matter in his skin or flesh. This practice is limited chiefly to the communication of the small pox, and of the cow pox, which is intended as a substitute for it. [See *Vaccination.*]

INOC'ULATOR, *n.* A person who inoculates; one who propagates plants or diseases by inoculation.

INO'DIATE, *v. t.* [L. *in* and *odium.*] To make hateful. [*Not in use.*] *South.*

INO'DORATE, *a.* [L. *in* and *odoratus.*] Having no scent or odor. *Bacon.*

INO'DOROUS, *a.* [L. *inodorus; in* and *odor.*] Wanting scent; having no smell.

The white of an egg is an *inodorous* liquor. *Arbuthnot.*

INOFFENS'IVE, *a.* [*in* and *offensive.*]

1. Giving no offense or provocation; as an *inoffensive* man; an *inoffensive* answer.

2. Giving no uneasiness or disturbance; as an *inoffensive* appearance or sight.

3. Harmless; doing no injury or mischief.

Thy *inoffensive* satires never bite. *Dryden.*

4. Not obstructing; presenting no hinderance.

—From hence a passage broad,
Smooth, easy, *inoffensive*, down to hell.
[*Unusual.*] *Milton.*

INOFFENS'IVELY, *adv.* Without giving offense; without harm; in a manner not to offend.

INOFFENS'IVENESS, *n.* Harmlessness; the quality of being not offensive either to the senses or to the mind.

INOFFI''CIAL, *a.* [*in* and *official.*] Not official; not proceeding from the proper officer; not clothed with the usual forms of authority, or not done in an official character; as an *inofficial* communication; *inofficial* intelligence.

Pinckney and Marshall would not make *inofficial* visits to discuss official business. *Pickering.*

INOFFI''CIALLY, *adv.* Without the usual forms, or not in the official character.

INOFFI''CIOUS, *a.* [*in* and *officious.*]

1. Unkind; regardless of natural obligation; contrary to natural duty.

—Suggesting that the parent had lost the use of his reason, when he made the *inofficious* testament. *Blackstone.*

Let not a father hope to excuse an *inofficious* disposition of his fortune, by alledging that every man may do what he will with his own. *Paley.*

2. Unfit for an office.

Thou drown'st thyself in *inofficious* sleep. *B. Jonson.*

3. Not civil or attentive. *B. Jonson.*

INOPERA'TION, *n.* Agency; influence; production of effects. [*Not used.*] *Bp. Hall.*

INOP'ERATIVE, *a.* [*in* and *operative.*] Not operative; not active; having no operation; producing no effect; as laws rendered *inoperative* by neglect; *inoperative* remedies.

INOPPORTU'NE, *a.* [L. *inopportunus.* See *Opportune.*]

Not opportune; inconvenient; unseasonable in time.

INOPPORTU'NELY, *adv.* Unseasonably; at an inconvenient time.

INOPPRESS'IVE, *a.* [*in* and *oppressive.*] Not oppressive; not burdensome. *O. Wolcott.*

INOP'ULENT, *a.* [*in* and *opulent.*] Not opulent; not wealthy; not affluent or rich.

INOR'DINACY, *n.* [from *inordinate.*] Deviation from order or rule prescribed; irregularity; disorder; excess, or want of moderation; as the *inordinacy* of desire or other passion. *Bp. Taylor.*

INOR'DINATE, *a.* [L. *inordinatus; in* and *ordo*, order.]
Irregular; disorderly; excessive; immoderate; not limited to rules prescribed, or to usual bounds; as an *inordinate* love of the world; *inordinate* desire of fame.

INOR'DINATELY, *adv.* Irregularly; excessively; immoderately. *Skelton.*

INOR'DINATENESS, *n.* Deviation from order; excess; want of moderation; inordinacy; intemperance in desire or other passion. *Bp. Hall.*

INORDINA'TION, *n.* Irregularity; deviation from rule or right. *South.*

INORGAN'IC, INORGAN'ICAL, *a.* [*in* and *organic.*] Devoid of organs; not formed with the organs or instruments of life; as the *inorganic* matter that forms the earth's surface. *Kirwan.*
Inorganic bodies, are such as have no organs, as minerals.

INORGAN'ICALLY, *adv.* Without organs.

INOR'GANIZED, *a.* Not having organic structure; void of organs; as earths, metals and other minerals.

INOS'CULATE, *v. i.* [L *in* and *osculatus*, from *osculor*, to kiss.]
In *anatomy*, to unite by apposition or contact; to unite, as two vessels at their extremities; as, one vein or artery *inosculates* with another; a vein *inosculates* with an artery.

INOS'CULATE, *v. t.* To unite, as two vessels in an animal body.

INOS'CULATING, *ppr.* Uniting, as the extremities of two vessels.

INOSCULA'TION, *n.* The union of two vessels of an animal body at their extremities, by means of which a communication is maintained, and the circulation of fluids is carried on; anastomosy. *Ray.*

IN'QUEST, *n.* [Fr. *enquête*; L. *inquisitio*, *inquiro; in* and *quæro*, to seek.]
1. Inquisition; judicial inquiry; official examination. An *inquest* of office, is an inquiry made by the king's officer, his sheriff, coroner, or escheator, concerning any matter that entitles the king to the possession of lands or tenements, goods or chattels. It is made by a jury of no dedeterminate number. *Blackstone.*
In *the United States*, a similar inquiry, made by the proper officer, under the authority of a state.
2. A jury.
3. Inquiry; search. *South.*

INQUI'ET, *v. t.* To disturb; to trouble. [*Not used.*]

INQUIETA'TION, *n.* Disturbance. [*Not used.*]

INQUI'ETUDE, *n.* [Fr. from L. *inquietudo; in* and *quies*, rest.]
Disturbed state; want of quiet; restlessness; uneasiness, either of body or mind; disquietude. *Pope.*

IN'QUINATE, *v. t.* [L. *inquino*, to defile; *in* and Gr. κοινοω, from κοινος, common.] To defile; to pollute; to contaminate. [*Little used.*] *Brown.*

INQUINA'TION, *n.* The act of defiling, or state of being defiled; pollution; corruption. [*Little used.*] *Bacon.*

INQUI'RABLE, *a.* [from *inquire.*] That may be inquired into; subject to inquisition or inquest. *Bacon.*

INQUI'RE, *v. i.* [Fr. *enquerir;* Sp. *inquirir;* L. *inquiro; in* and *quæro*, to seek; Malayan, *charee*, to seek. See *Acquire.*]
1. To ask a question; to seek for truth or information by asking questions.
We will call the damsel and *inquire* at her mouth. Gen. xxiv.
It has *of* before the person asked. *Enquire of* them, or *of* him. It has *of, concerning*, or *after*, before the subject of inquiry.
He sent Hadoram, his son, to king David to *inquire of* his welfare. 1 Chron. xviii.
For thou dost not *inquire* wisely *concerning* this. Eccl. vii.
When search is to be made for particular knowledge or information, it is followed by *into*. The coroner by jury *inquires into* the cause of a sudden death. When a place or person is sought, or something hid or missing, *for* is commonly used. *Inquire for* one Saul of Tarsus. He was *inquiring for* the house to which he was directed. *Inquire for* the cloke that is lost. *Inquire for* the right road. Sometimes it is followed by *after*. *Inquire after* the right way.
When some general information is sought, this verb is followed by *about;* sometimes by *concerning*. His friends *inquired about* him; they *inquired concerning* his welfare.
2. To seek for truth by argument or the discussion of questions, or by investigation.
To inquire into, to make examination; to seek for particular information. *Inquire into* the time, manner and place. *Inquire into* all the circumstances of the case.

INQUI'RE, *v. t.* To ask about; to seek by asking; as, he *inquired* the way; but the phrase is elliptical, for *inquire for* the way.

INQUI'RENT, *a.* Making inquiry.

INQUI'RER, *n.* One who asks a question; one who interrogates; one who searches or examines; one who seeks for knowledge or information.

INQUI'RING, *ppr.* Seeking for information by asking questions; asking; questioning; interrogating; examining.

INQUI'RY, *n.* [Norm. *enquerre*, from *querer*, to inquire.]
1. The act of inquiring; a seeking for information by asking questions; interrogation.
The men who were sent from Cornelius, had made *inquiry* for Simon's house, and stood before the gate. Acts x.
2. Search for truth, information or knowledge; research; examination into facts or principles by proposing and discussing questions, by solving problems, by experiments or other modes; as physical *inquiries; inquiries* about philosophical knowledge. *Locke.*
The first *inquiry* of a rational being should be, who made me? the second, why was I made? who is my Creator, and what is his will?

INQUISI''TION, *n.* *s* as *z.* [Fr. from L. *inquisitio, inquiro.* See *Inquire.*]
1. Inquiry; examination; a searching or search. Ps. ix.
2. Judicial inquiry; official examination; inquest.
The justices in eyre had it formerly in charge to make *inquisition* concerning them by a jury of the county. *Blackstone.*
3. Examination; discussion. *Bacon.*
4. In some catholic couutries, a court or tribunal established for the examination and punishment of heretics. This court was established in the twelfth century by father Dominic, who was charged by pope Innocent III. with orders to excite catholic princes and people to extirpate heretics. *Encyc.*

INQUISI''TIONAL, *a.* Making inquiry; busy in inquiry. *Sterne.*

INQUIS'ITIVE, *a.* *s* as *z.* Apt to ask questions; addicted to inquiry; inclined to seek information by questions; followed by *about* or *after*. He was very *inquisitive about* or *after* news. Children are usually *inquisitive.*
2. Inclined to seek knowledge by discussion, investigation or observation; given to research. He possesses an *inquisitive* mind or disposition. We live in an *inquisitive* age.

INQUIS'ITIVE, *n.* A person who is inquisitive; one curious in research. *Temple.*

INQUIS'ITIVELY, *adv.* With curiosity to obtain information; with scrutiny.

INQUIS'ITIVENESS, *n.* The disposition to obtain information by questioning others, or by researches into facts, causes or principles; curiosity to learn what is not known. The works of nature furnish ample matter for the *inquisitiveness* of the human mind.

INQUIS'ITOR, *n.* [L. See *Inquire.*] One who inquires; particularly, one whose official duty it is to inquire and examine. *Dryden.*
2. A member of the court of inquisition in Catholic countries. *Encyc.*

INQUISITO'RIAL, *a.* Pertaining to inquisition; as *inquisitorial* power.
2. Pertaining to the catholic court of inquisition; as *inquisitorial* tragedy. *Encyc.*
Inquisitorial robes. *Buchanan.*

INQUISITO'RIOUS, *a.* Making strict inquiry. *Milton.*

INRA'IL, *v. t.* [*in* and *rail.*] To rail in; to inclose with rails. *Hooker. Gay.*

INRA'ILED, *pp.* Inclosed with rails.

INRA'ILING, *ppr.* Inclosing with rails.

INREG'ISTER, *v. t.* [Fr. *enregistrer.* See *Register.*]
To register; to record; to enter in a register. *Walsh.*

IN'ROAD, *n.* [*in* and *road.*] The entrance of an enemy into a country with purposes of hostility; a sudden or desultory incursion or invasion. The confines of England and Scotland were formerly harassed with frequent *inroads*. The English made *inroads* into Scotland, and the Scots into England, and the country was sometimes desolated.
2. Attack; encroachment.

INSA'FETY, *n.* Want of safety. [*Ill.*] *Naunton.*

INSALU'BRIOUS, *a.* [*in* and *salubrious.*] Not salubrious; not healthful; unfavorable to health; unwholesome; as an *insalubrious* air or climate.

INSALU'BRITY, *n.* [*in* and *salubrity.*] Want of salubrity; unhealthfulness; unwholesomeness; as the *insalubrity* of air, water or climate.

INSAL'UTARY, *a.* [*in* and *salutary.*] Not salutary; not favorable to health or soundness.

2. Not tending to safety; productive of evil.

INSAN'ABLE, *a.* [L. *insanabilis; in* and *sano*, to heal.] Incurable; that cannot be healed. *Johnson.*

INSA'NE, *a.* [L. *insanus; in* and *sanus*, sound.]

1. Unsound in mind or intellect; mad; deranged in mind; delirious; distracted. *Shak.*

[In the sense of making mad, it is little used.]

2. Used by or appropriated to insane persons; as an *insane* hospital.

INSA'NE, *n.* An insane person; as a hospital for the *insane.*

INSA'NELY, *adv.* Madly; foolishly; without reason. *Montgomery.*

INSA'NENESS, INSAN'ITY, *n.* The state of being unsound in mind; derangement of intellect; madness. *Insanity* is chiefly used, and the word is applicable to any degree of mental derangement, from slight delirium or wandering, to distraction. It is however rarely used to express slight, temporary delirium, occasioned by fever or accident.

INSAP'ORY, *a.* [L. *in* and *sapor*, taste.] Tasteless; wanting flavor. [*Not used.*] *Herbert.*

INSA'TIABLE, *a. insa'shable.* [Fr. from L. *insatiabilis; in* and *satio*, to satisfy.]

Incapable of being satisfied or appeased; very greedy; as an *insatiable* appetite or desire; *insatiable* thirst.

INSA'TIABLENESS, *n. insa'shableness.* Greediness of appetite that cannot be satisfied or appeased. *King Charles.*

INSA'TIABLY, *adv. insa'shably.* With greediness not to be satisfied. *South.*

INSA'TIATE, *a. insa'shate.* [L. *insatiatus.*] Not to be satisfied; insatiable; as *insatiate* thirst. *Philips.*

INSA'TIATELY, *adv.* So greedily as not to be satisfied.

INSATI'ETY, *n.* Insatiableness. *Granger.*

INSATISFAC'TION, *n.* Want of satisfaction. *Bacon.*

INSAT'URABLE, *a.* [L. *insaturabilis; in* and *satur*, full.]

Not to be saturated, filled or glutted. *Johnson.*

INSCI'ENCE, *n.* [*in* and *science.*] Ignorance; want of knowledge. *Ch. Relig. Appeal.*

INSCRI'BE, *v. t.* [L. *inscribo; in* and *scribo*, to write, Eng. to *scrape.* See *Scribe.*]

1. To write on; to engrave on for perpetuity or duration; as, to *inscribe* a line or verse on a monument, on a column or pillar.

2. To imprint on; as, to *inscribe* any thing on the mind or memory.

3. To assign or address to; to commend to by a short address, less formal than a dedication; as, to *inscribe* an ode or a book to a prince.

4. To mark with letters, characters or words; as, to *inscribe* a stone with a name.

5. To draw a figure within another, so that all the angles of the figure inscribed touch the angles, sides or planes of the other figure. *Johnson. Encyc.*

INSCRI'BED, *pp.* Written on; engraved; marked; addressed.

INSCRI'BER, *n.* One who inscribes. *Pownall.*

INSCRI'BING, *ppr.* Writing on; engraving; marking; addressing.

INSCRIP'TION, *n.* [Fr. from L. *inscriptio.* See *Inscribe.*]

1. Something written or engraved to communicate knowledge to after ages; any character, word, line or sentence written or engraved on a solid substance for duration; as *inscriptions* on monuments, called epitaphs, on pillars, &c. We do not call by this name, writings on paper or parchment.

2. A title.

3. An address or consignment of a book to a person, as a mark of respect, or an invitation of patronage. It is less formal than a dedication.

INSCRIP'TIVE, *a.* Bearing inscription.

INSCRÖLL, *v. t.* To write on a scroll. *Shak.*

INSCRUTABIL'ITY, INSCRU'TABLENESS, *n.* The quality of being inscrutable.

INSCRU'TABLE, *a.* [Fr. from L. *inscrutabilis; in* and *scrutor*, to search.]

1. Unsearchable; that cannot be searched into and understood by inquiry or study. The designs of the emperor appear to be *inscrutable.*

2. That cannot be penetrated, discovered or understood by human reason. The ways of Providence are often *inscrutable.* Mysteries are *inscrutable.*

INSCRU'TABLY, *adv.* In a manner or degree not to be found out or understood. The moral government of an infinite being must often be *inscrutably* dark and mysterious.

INSCULP', *v. t.* [L. *insculpo; in* and *sculpo*, to engrave.] To engrave; to carve. [*Little used.*] *Shak.*

INSCULP'TION, *n.* Inscription. [*Little used.*] *Tourneur.*

INSCULP'TURE, *n.* An engraving; sculpture. [See *Sculpture*, which is generally used.] *Shak.*

INSE'AM, *v. t.* [*in* and *seam.*] To impress or mark with a seam or cicatrix. [*Poetical.*] *Pope.*

INSEARCH, *v. t. inserch'.* To make search. [*Not used.*] *Elyot.*

INSEC'ABLE, *a.* [L. *insecabilis; in* and *seco*, to cut.]

That cannot be divided by a cutting instrument; indivisible. *Encyc.*

IN'SECT, *n.* [L. *insecta*, plu., from *inseco*, to cut in; *in* and *seco*, to cut. This name seems to have been originally given to certain small animals whose bodies appear *cut in*, or almost divided. So in Greek, *εντομα.*]

1. In *zoology*, a small invertebral animal, breathing by lateral spiracles, and furnished with articulated extremities and movable antennæ. Most insects pass through three states or metamorphoses, the larva, the chrysalis, and the perfect insect. The class of insects, in the Linnean system, is divided into seven orders, the last of which *(Aptera)* includes the *Crustacea*, which breathe by gills, and the *Arachnides*, which have no antennæ, now forming two distinct classes. *Linne. Cuvier.*

The term *insect* has been applied, but improperly, to other small invertebral animals of the Linnean class *Vermes.* *Encyc.*

2. Any thing small or contemptible. *Thomson.*

IN'SECT, *a.* Small; mean; contemptible.

INSECTA'TOR, *n.* [L.] A persecutor. [*Little used.*]

INSECT'ED, *a.* Having the nature of an insect. *Howell.*

INSECT'ILE, *a.* Having the nature of insects. *Bacon.*

INSECT'ILE, *n.* An insect. [*Not used.*] *Wotton.*

INSEC'TION, *n.* A cutting in; incisure; incision.

INSECTIV'OROUS, *a.* [*insect* and L. *voro*, to eat.]

Feeding or subsisting on insects. Many winged animals are *insectivorous.* *Dict. Nat. Hist.*

INSECTOL'OGER, *n.* [*insect* and Gr. *λογος.*] One who studies insects. [*Not in use.* See *Entomologist.*]

INSECU'RE, *a.* [*in* and *secure.*] Not secure; not safe; not confident of safety; *used of persons.* No man can be quiet, when he feels *insecure.*

2. Not safe; not effectually guarded or protected; unsafe; exposed to danger or loss. Goods on the ocean are *insecure.* Hay and grain unhoused are *insecure.* Debts are often *insecure.*

INSECU'RELY, *adv.* Without security or safety; without certainty. *Chesterfield.*

INSECU'RITY, *n.* [*in* and *security.*] Want of safety, or want of confidence in safety. Seamen in a tempest must be conscious of their *insecurity.*

2. Uncertainty. With what *insecurity* of truth we ascribe effects to unseen causes.

3. Want of safety; danger; hazard; exposure to destruction or loss; *applied to things;* as the *insecurity* of a building exposed to fire; the *insecurity* of a debt.

INSECU'TION, *n.* [L. *insecutio.*] Pursuit. *Chapman.*

INSEM'INATE, *v. t.* [L. *insemino.*] To sow. [*Little used.*]

INSEMINA'TION, *n.* The act of sowing. [*Little used.*]

INSENS'ATE, *a.* [Fr. *insensé;* L. *in* and *sensus*, sense.]

Destitute of sense; stupid; foolish; wanting sensibility. *Milton. Hammond.*

INSENSIBIL'ITY, *n.* [from *insensible.*]

1. Want of sensibility, or the power of feeling or perceiving. A frozen limb is in a state of *insensibility*, as is an animal body after death.

2. Want of the power to be moved or affected; want of tenderness or susceptibility of emotion and passion. Not to be moved at the distresses of others denotes an *insensibility* extremely unnatural.
3. Dullness; stupidity; torpor.

INSENS'IBLE, *a.* [Fr. Sp. from L. *in* and *sensus*, sense, *sentio*, to feel.]
1. Imperceptible; that cannot be felt or perceived. The motion of the earth is *insensible* to the eye. A plant grows, and the body decays by *insensible* degrees. The humors of the body are evacuated by *insensible* perspiration.

The dense and bright light of the circle will obscure the rare and weak light of these dark colors round about it, and render them almost *insensible*. *Newton.*

2. Destitute of the power of feeling or perceiving; wanting corporeal sensibility. An injury to the spine often renders the inferior parts of the body *insensible*.
3. Not susceptible of emotion or passion; void of feeling; wanting tenderness. To be *insensible* to the sufferings of our fellow men is inhuman. To be *insensible* of danger is not always evidence of courage.
4. Dull; stupid; torpid.
5. Void of sense or meaning; as *insensible* words. *Hale. Du Ponceau.*

INSENS'IBLENESS, *n.* Inability to perceive; want of sensibility. [See *Insensibility*, which is generally used.]

INSENS'IBLY, *adv.* Imperceptibly; in a manner not to be felt or perceived by the senses.

The hills rise *insensibly*. *Addison.*

2. By slow degrees; gradually. Men often slide *insensibly* into vicious habits.

INSENT'IENT, *a.* [*in* and *sentient.*] Not having perception or the power of perception. *Reid.*

INSEP'ARABLE, *a.* [Fr. from L. *inseparabilis; in* and *separabilis, separo*, to separate.]
That cannot be separated or disjoined; not to be parted. There is an *inseparable* connection between vice and suffering or punishment.

INSEP'ARABLENESS, } *n.* The quality of being inseparable, or incapable of disjunction.
INSEPARABIL'ITY, }
[*The latter word is rarely used.*] *Locke.*

INSEP'ARABLY, *adv.* In a manner that prevents separation; with indissoluble union. *Bacon. Temple.*

INSEP'ARATE, *a.* Not separate. [*Not used.*]

INSEP'ARATELY, *adv.* So as not to be separated. [*Not used.*] *Cranmer.*

INSERT', *v. t.* [Fr. *inserer;* L. *insero, insertum; in* and *sero*, to thrust.]
Literally, to thrust in; hence, to set in or among; as, to *insert* a cion in a stock; to *insert* a letter, word or passage in a composition; to *insert* an advertisement or other writing in a paper.

INSERT'ED, *pp.* Set in or among.

INSERT'ING, *ppr.* Setting in or among.

INSER'TION, *n.* [Fr. from L. *insertio.*]
1. The act of setting or placing in or among other things; as the *insertion* of cions in stocks; the *insertion* of words or passages in writings; the *insertion* of notices or essays in a public paper; the *insertion* of vessels, tendons, &c. in other parts of the body.
2. The thing inserted. *Broome.*

INSERV'IENT, *a.* Conducive.

INSET', *v. t.* To infix or implant. *Chaucer.*

INSHA'DED, *a.* Marked with different shades. *Browne.*

INSHELL', *v. t.* To hide in a shell. *Shak.*

INSHEL'TER, *v. i.* To shelter. *Shak.*

INSHIP', *v. t.* To ship; to embark. *Shak.*

INSHRINE. [See *Enshrine.*]

IN'SIDE, *n.* [*in* and *side.*] The interior part of a thing; internal part; opposed to *outside;* as the *inside* of a church; the *inside* of a letter.

INSID'IATE, *v. t.* [L. *insidior.*] To lie in ambush for.

INSID'IATOR, *n.* One who lies in ambush. *Barrow.*

INSID'IOUS, *a.* [L. *insidiosus*, from *insideo*, to lie in wait; *in* and *sedeo*, to sit.]
1. Properly, lying in wait; hence, watching an opportunity to insnare or entrap; deceitful; sly; treacherous; *used of persons.*
2. Intended to entrap; as *insidious* arts.

INSID'IOUSLY, *adv.* With intention to insnare; deceitfully; treacherously; with malicious artifice or stratagem. *Bacon.*

INSID'IOUSNESS, *n.* A watching for an opportunity to insnare; deceitfulness; treachery. *Barrow.*

IN'SIGHT, *n.* *in'site.* [*in* and *sight.*] Sight or view of the interior of any thing; deep inspection or view; introspection; thorough knowledge or skill.

A garden gives us a great *insight* into the contrivance and wisdom of Providence. *Spectator.*

INSIG'NIA, *n.* [L. plu.] Badges or distinguishing marks of office or honor. *Burke.*
2. Marks, signs or visible impressions, by which any thing is known or distinguished. *Beattie.*

INSIGNIF'ICANCE, } *n.* [*in* and *significance.*]
INSIGNIF'ICANCY, }
1. Want of significance or meaning; as the *insignificance* of words or phrases.
2. Unimportance; want of force or effect; as the *insignificance* of human art or of ceremonies. *Addison.*
3. Want of weight; meanness.

INSIGNIF'ICANT, *a.* [*in* and *significant.*]
1. Void of signification; destitute of meaning; as *insignificant* words.
2. Unimportant; answering no purpose; having no weight or effect; as *insignificant* rites.
3. Without weight of character; mean; contemptible; as an *insignificant* being or fellow.

INSIGNIF'ICANT, *n.* An insignificant, trifling or worthless thing. *Tatler.*

INSIGNIF'ICANTLY, *adv.* Without meaning, as words.
2. Without importance or effect; to no purpose.

INSIGNIF'ICATIVE, *a.* Not expressing by external signs.

INSINCE'RE, *a.* [L. *insincerus; in* and *sincerus*, sincere.]
1. Not sincere; not being in truth what one appears to be; dissembling; hypocritical; false; *used of persons;* as an *insincere* heart.
2. Deceitful; hypocritical; false; *used of things;* as *insincere* declarations or professions.
3. Not sound.

INSINCE'RELY, *adv.* Without sincerity; hypocritically.

INSINCER'ITY, *n.* Dissimulation; want of sincerity or of being in reality what one appears to be; hypocrisy; *used of persons.*
2. Deceitfulness; hollowness; *used of things;* as the *insincerity* of professions.

INSIN'EW, *v. t.* [*in* and *sinew.*] To strengthen; to give vigor to. *Shak.*

INSIN'UANT, *a.* [Fr. from L. *insinuans.*] Insinuating; having the power to gain favor. [*Little used.*] *Wotton.*

INSIN'UATE, *v. t.* [Fr. *insinuer;* L. *insinuo; in* and *sinus*, the bosom, a bay, inlet or recess.]
1. To introduce gently, or into a narrow passage; to wind in. Water *insinuates* itself into the crevices of rocks.
2. To push or work one's self into favor; to introduce by slow, gentle or artful means.

He *insinuated* himself into the very good grace of the duke of Buckingham. *Clarendon.*

3. To hint; to suggest by remote allusion.

And all the fictions bards pursue,
Do but *insinuate* what's true. *Swift.*

4. To instill; to infuse gently; to introduce artfully.

All the art of rhetoric, besides order and clearness, are for nothing else but to *insinuate* wrong ideas, move the passions and thereby mislead the judgment. *Locke.*

INSIN'UATE, *v. i.* To creep in; to wind in; to flow in; to enter gently, slowly or imperceptibly, as into crevices.
2. To gain on the affections by gentle or artful means, or by imperceptible degrees; as *insinuating* flattery.
3. To wind along. *Milton.*

INSIN'UATED, *pp.* Introduced or conveyed gently, imperceptibly or by winding into crevices; hinted.

INSIN'UATING, *ppr.* Creeping or winding in; flowing in; gaining on gently; hinting.
2. *a.* Tending to enter gently; insensibly winning favor and confidence.

INSINUA'TION, *n.* [Fr. from L. *insinuatio.*]
1. The act of insinuating; a creeping or winding in; a flowing into crevices.
2. The act of gaining on favor or affections, by gentle or artful means.
3. The art or power of pleasing and stealing on the affections.

He had a natural *insinuation* and address, which made him acceptable in the best company. *Clarendon.*

4. A hint; a suggestion or intimation by distant allusion. Slander may be conveyed by *insinuations.*

INSIN'UATIVE, *a.* Stealing on the affections. *Bacon.*

INSIN'UATOR, *n.* One who insinuates; one that hints.

INSIP'ID, *a.* [Fr. *insipide;* L. *insipidus; in* and *sapidus, sapio*, to taste.]
1. Tasteless; destitute of taste; wanting the qualities which affect the organs of taste; vapid; as *insipid* liquor.
2. Wanting spirit, life or animation; wanting pathos, or the power of exciting emotions; flat; dull; heavy; as an *insipid* address; an *insipid* composition.

3. Wanting power to gratify desire; as *insipid* pleasures.

INSIPID'ITY, } n. [Fr. *insipidité.*]
INSIP'IDNESS, }

1. Want of taste, or the power of exciting sensation in the tongue.

2. Want of life or spirit.

Dryden's lines shine strongly through the *insipidity* of Tate's. *Pope.*

INSIP'IDLY, *adv.* Without taste; without spirit or life; without enjoyment. *Locke.*

INSIP'IENCE, *n.* [L. *insipientia; in* and *sapio*, to be wise.]

Want of wisdom; folly; foolishness; want of understanding.

INSIST', *v. i.* [Fr. *insister*; L. *insisto*; *in* and *sisto*, to stand.]

1. Literally, to stand or rest on. [*Rarely used.*] *Ray.*

2. In *geometry*, an angle is said to *insist upon* the arc of the circle intercepted between the two lines which contain the angle.

3. To dwell on in discourse; as, to *insist on* a particular topic.

To insist on, to press or urge for any thing with immovable firmness; to persist in demands; as, to *insist on* oppressive terms in a treaty; to *insist on* immediate payment of a debt.

INSIST'ENT, *a.* Standing or resting on; as an *insistent* wall. [*Little used.*] *Wotton.*

INSIST'URE, *n.* A dwelling or standing on; fixedness. *Obs.* *Shak.*

INSIT'IENCY, *n.* [L. *in* and *sitio*, to thirst.] Freedom from thirst. *Grew.*

INSI''TION, *n.* [L. *insitio*, from *insitus*, *insero*, to plant.]

The insertion of a cion in a stock; ingraftment. *Ray.*

INSNA'RE, *v. t.* [*in* and *snare.*] To catch in a snare; to entrap; to take by artificial means.

2. To inveigle; to seduce by artifice; to take by wiles, stratagem or deceit. The flattering tongue is apt to *insnare* the artless youth.

3. To entangle; to involve in difficulties or perplexities.

[This word is often written *ensnare*, but *insnare* is the true orthography.]

INSNA'RED, *pp.* Caught in a snare; entrapped; inveigled; involved in perplexities.

INSNA'RER, *n.* One that insnares.

INSNA'RING, *ppr.* Catching in a snare; entrapping; seducing; involving in difficulties.

INSOBRI'ETY, *n.* [*in* and *sobriety.*] Want of sobriety; intemperance; drunkenness. *Decay of Piety.*

INSO'CIABLE, *a.* [Fr. from L. *insociabilis*; *in* and *sociabilis*, *socio*, to unite.]

1. Not inclined to unite in social converse; not given to conversation; unsociable; taciturn.

2. That cannot be joined or connected.

Lime and wood are *insociable.* [*Not in use.*] *Wotton.*

IN'SOLATE, *v. t.* [L. *insolo*; *in* and *sol*, the sun.]

To dry in the sun's rays; to expose to the heat of the sun; to ripen or prepare by exposure to the sun.

IN'SOLATED, *pp.* Exposed to the sun; dried or matured in the sun's rays.

IN'SOLATING, *ppr.* Exposing to the action of sun-beams.

INSOLA'TION, *n.* The act of exposing to the rays of the sun for drying or maturing, as fruits, drugs, &c. or for rendering acid, as vinegar, or for promoting some chimical action of one substance on another.

2. A stroke of the sun; the action of extreme heat on the brain. *Battie.*

IN'SOLENCE, *n.* [Fr. from L. *insolentia*; *in* and *soleo*, to be accustomed.]

Pride or haughtiness manifested in contemptuous and overbearing treatment of others; petulant contempt; impudence. *Johnson.*

Blown with *insolence* and wine. *Milton.*

IN'SOLENCE, *v. t.* To treat with haughty contempt. [*Not used.*] *K. Charles.*

IN'SOLENT, *a.* Proud and haughty, with contempt of others; overbearing; domineering in power; as an *insolent* master. *Atterbury.*

2. Proceeding from insolence; haughty and contemptuous; as *insolent* words or behavior.

3. Unaccustomed; *the primary sense.* [*Not used.*]

IN'SOLENTLY, *adv.* With contemptuous pride; haughtily; rudely; saucily. *Dryden.*

INSOLID'ITY, *n.* [*in* and *solidity.*] Want of solidity; weakness. *More.*

INSOLUBIL'ITY, *n.* [from *insoluble.*] The quality of not being soluble or dissolvable, particularly in a fluid.

INSOL'UBLE, *a.* [Fr. from L. *insolubilis*; *in* and *solvo*, to dissolve.]

1. That cannot be dissolved, particularly by a liquid. We say a substance is *insoluble* in water, when its parts will not separate and mix with that fluid.

2. Not to be solved or explained; not to be resolved; as a doubt or difficulty. [*Not much used.*]

INSOLV'ABLE, *a.* [Fr. from L. *in* and *solvo*, to loosen or dissolve.]

1. Not to be cleared of difficulty or uncertainty; not to be solved or explained; not admitting solution or explication; as an *insolvable* problem or difficulty. *Watts.*

2. That cannot be paid or discharged. *Pope.*

INSOLV'ENCY, *n.* [infra.] Inability of a person to pay all his debts; or the state of wanting property sufficient for such payment; as a merchant's *insolvency.*

2. Insufficiency to discharge all debts of the owner; as the *insolvency* of an estate.

Act of insolvency. [See infra, *Insolvent law.*]

INSOLV'ENT, *a.* [L. *in* and *solvens*, *solvo*, to solve, to free, to pay.]

1. Not having money, goods or estate sufficient to pay all debts; as an *insolvent* debtor.

2. Not sufficient to pay all the debts of the owner; as an *insolvent* estate.

3. Respecting insolvent debtors; relieving an insolvent debtor from imprisonment for debt, or from liability to arrest and imprisonment for debts previously contracted; as an *insolvent* law. *Daggett. Sergeant.*

Insolvent law, or *act of insolvency*, a law which liberates a debtor from imprisonment, or exempts him from liability to arrest and imprisonment on account of any debt previously contracted. These terms may be considered as *generic*, comprehending also bankrupt laws, which protect a man's future acquisitions from his creditors. But in a limited sense, as the words are now generally used, an insolvent law extends only to protect the person of the debtor from imprisonment on account of debts previously contracted. *Stat. of Conn.* *Wheaton's Rep.*

INSOLV'ENT, *n.* A debtor unable to pay his debts. *Sergeant.*

INSOM'NIOUS, *a.* [L. *insomniosus*; or *in* and *somnus*, sleep.] Troubled with dreams; restless in sleep.

INSOMUCH', *adv.* [*in*, *so*, and *much.*] So that; to that degree.

Simonides was an excellent poet, *insomuch* that he made his fortune by it. *L'Estrange.*

[This word or combination of words is not deemed elegant, and is obsolescent, at least in classical composition.]

INSPECT', *v. t.* [L. *inspicio*, *inspectum*; *in* and *specio*, to view.]

1. To look on; to view or oversee for the purpose of examination. It is the duty of parents to *inspect* the conduct or manners of their children.

2. To look into; to view and examine, for the purpose of ascertaining the quality or condition of a thing; as, to *inspect* potash; to *inspect* flour; to *inspect* arms.

3. To view and examine for the purpose of discovering and correcting errors; as, to *inspect* the press, or the proof-sheets of a book.

4. To superintend.

INSPECT', *n.* Close examination. [*Not used.*] *Thomson.*

INSPECT'ED, *pp.* Viewed with care; examined by the eye or officially.

INSPECT'ING, *ppr.* Looking on or into; viewing with care; examining for ascertaining the quality or condition.

INSPEC'TION, *n.* [Fr. from L. *inspectio.*]

1. A looking on or into; prying examination; close or careful survey; as the divine *inspection* into the affairs of the world. *Bentley.*

2. Watch; guardianship; as a youth placed at school under the *inspection* of a friend.

3. Superintendence; oversight. The fortifications are to be executed under the *inspection* of an officer of the army.

4. Official view; a careful viewing and examining of commodities or manufactures, to ascertain their quality; as the *inspection* of flour.

5. Official examination, as of arms, to see that they are in good order for service.

INSPECT'OR, *n.* One who inspects, views or oversees; as an *inspector* of morals; an *inspector* of the press.

2. A superintendent; one to whose care the execution of any work is committed, for the purpose of seeing it faithfully performed.

3. An officer whose duty is to examine the quality of goods or commodities offered for sale.

4. An officer of the customs.

5. A military officer whose duty is to inspect the troops and examine their arms.

INSPECT'ORATE, } *n.* The office of an
INSPECT'ORSHIP, } inspector. *Washington.*

INSPERS'ED, *a.* Sprinkled on. [*Not used.*]

INSPER'SION, *n.* [L. *inspersio, inspergo; in* and *spargo*, to scatter.] The act of sprinkling on. *Ainsworth.*

INSPEX'IMUS, *n.* [we have inspected; *the first word of ancient charters, &c.*] An exemplification.

INSPHE'RE, *v. t.* [*in* and *sphere.*] To place in an orb or sphere. *Milton.*

INSPI'RABLE, *a.* [from *inspire.*] That may be inspired.

2. That may be drawn into the lungs; inhalable; as air or vapors.

INSPIRA'TION, *n.* [Fr. from L. *inspiro.*]

1. The act of drawing air into the lungs; the inhaling of air; a branch of respiration, and opposed to *expiration.*

2. The act of breathing into any thing.

3. The infusion of ideas into the mind by the Holy Spirit; the conveying into the minds of men, ideas, notices or monitions by extraordinary or supernatural influence; or the communication of the divine will to the understanding by suggestions or impressions on the mind, which leave no room to doubt the reality of their supernatural origin.

> All Scripture is given by *inspiration* of God. 2 Tim. iii.

4. The infusion of ideas or directions by the supposed deities of pagans.

5. The infusion or communication of ideas or poetic spirit, by a superior being or supposed presiding power; as the *inspiration* of Homer or other poet.

IN'SPIRATORY, *a.* Pertaining to inspiration, or inhaling air into the lungs. *Med. Repos.*

INSPI'RE, *v. i.* [L. *inspiro; in* and *spiro*, to breathe; Fr. *inspirer.*]

To draw in breath; to inhale air into the lungs; opposed to *expire.*

INSPI'RE, *v. t.* To breathe into.

> Ye nine, descend and sing,
> The breathing instruments *inspire.* *Pope.*

2. To infuse by breathing.

> He knew not his Maker, and him that *inspired* into him an active soul. *Wisdom.*

3. To infuse into the mind; as, to *inspire* with new life.

4. To infuse or suggest ideas or monitions supernaturally; to communicate divine instructions to the mind. In this manner, we suppose the prophets to have been *inspired*, and the Scriptures to have been composed under divine influence or direction.

5. To infuse ideas or poetic spirit.

6. To draw into the lungs; as, to *inspire* and *expire* the air with difficulty. *Harvey.*

INSPI'RED, *pp.* Breathed in; inhaled; infused.

2. Informed or directed by the Holy Spirit.

INSPI'RER, *n.* He that inspires.

INSPI'RING, *ppr.* Breathing in; inhaling into the lungs; infusing into the mind supernaturally.

2. *a.* Infusing spirit or courage; animating.

INSPIR'IT, *v. t.* [*in* and *spirit.*] To infuse or excite spirit in; to enliven; to animate; to give new life to; to encourage; to invigorate.

> The courage of Agamemnon is *inspirited* by the love of empire and ambition. *Pope.*

INSPIR'ITED, *pp.* Enlivened; animated; invigorated.

INSPIR'ITING, *ppr.* Infusing spirit; giving new life to.

INSPIS'SATE, *v. t.* [L. *in* and *spissus*, thick.] To thicken, as fluids; to bring to greater consistence by evaporating the thinner parts, &c.

INSPIS'SATED, *pp.* Thickened, as a liquor.

INSPIS'SATING, *ppr.* Thickening, as a liquor.

INSPISSA'TION, *n.* The act or operation of rendering a fluid substance thicker by evaporation, &c.

INSTABIL'ITY, *n.* [Fr. *instabilité;* L. *instabilitas, instabilis; in* and *stabilis*, from *sto*, to stand.]

1. Want of stability; want of firmness in purpose; inconstancy; fickleness; mutability of opinion or conduct. *Instability* is the characteristic of weak minds.

2. Changeableness; mutability; as the *instability* of laws, plans or measures.

INSTA'BLE, *a.* [L. *instabilis.*] Inconstant; prone to change or recede from a purpose; mutable; *of persons.*

2. Not steady or fixed; changeable; *of things.*

[*Instable* and *unstable* are synonymous, and the latter is more commonly used.]

INSTA'BLENESS, *n.* Unstableness; mutability; instability.

INSTALL', *v. t.* [Fr. *installer;* Sp. *instalar;* It. *installare;* from G. *stall*, from *stellen*, D. *stellen*, to set, Gr. στελλω, to send.]

To set, place or instate, in an office, rank or order; to invest with any charge, office or rank, with the customary ceremonies. To *install* a clergyman or minister of the gospel, is to place one who has been previously ordained, over a particular church and congregation, or to invest an ordained minister with a particular pastoral charge; in England, to induct a dean, prebendary or other ecclesiastical dignitary into possession of the church to which he belongs.

INSTALLA'TION, *n.* The act of giving possession of an office, rank or order, with the customary ceremonies.

> On the election, the bishop gives a mandate for his *installation.* *Ayliffe.*

INSTALL'ED, *pp.* Placed in a seat, office or order.

INSTALL'ING, *ppr.* Placing in a seat, office or order.

INSTALL'MENT, *n.* The act of installing, or giving possession of an office with the usual ceremonies or solemnities. *Shak.*

2. The seat in which one is placed. [*Unusual.*] *Shak.*

3. In *commerce*, a part of a large sum of money paid or to be paid at a particular period. In constituting a capital stock by subscriptions of individuals, it is customary to afford facilities to subscribers by dividing the sum subscribed into *installments*, or portions payable at distinct periods. In large contracts also, it is not unusual to agree that the money shall be paid by *installments.*

IN'STANCE, *n.* [Fr. from L. *insto*, to press; *in* and *sto*, to stand.] Literally, a standing on. Hence,

1. Urgency; a pressing; solicitation; importunity; application. The request was granted at the *instance* of the defendant's advocate.

2. Example; a case occurring; a case offered. Howard furnished a remarkable *instance* of disinterested benevolence. The world may never witness a second *instance* of the success of daring enterprise and usurpation, equal to that of Buonaparte.

> Suppose the earth should be removed nearer to the sun, and revolve, for *instance*, in the orbit of Mercury, the whole ocean would boil with heat. *Bentley.*

> The use of *instances*, is to illustrate and explain a difficulty. *Baker.*

3. Time; occasion; occurrence.

> These seem as if, in the time of Edward I, they were drawn up into the form of a law, in the first *instance.* *Hale.*

4. Motive; influence. *Obs.* *Shak.*

5. Process of a suit. *Obs.* *Ayliffe.*

Instance-court, a branch of the court of admiralty, in England, distinct from the prize-court.

IN'STANCE, *v. i.* To give or offer an example or case.

> As to false citations—I shall *instance* in two or three. *Tillotson.*

IN'STANCE, *v. t.* To mention as an example or case. He *instanced* the event of Cesar's death.

IN'STANCED, *pp.* or *a.* Given in proof or as an example. *Bp. Hall.*

IN'STANT, *a.* [Fr. from L. *instans, insto.*]

1. Pressing; urgent; importunate; earnest.

> Rejoicing in hope; patient in tribulation; continuing *instant* in prayer. Rom. xii.

2. Immediate; without intervening time; present.

> Impending death is thine and *instant* doom. *Prior.*

3. Quick; making no delay.

> *Instant* he flew with hospitable haste. *Pope.*

4. Present; current. On the tenth of July *instant.*

IN'STANT, *n.* A point in duration; a moment; a part of duration in which we perceive no succession, or a part that occupies the time of a single thought.

2. A particular time. *Shak.*

INSTANTANE'ITY, *n.* Unpremeditated production. *Shenstone.*

INSTANTA'NEOUS, *a.* [Fr. *instantané;* Sp. It. *instantaneo.*]

Done in an instant; occurring or acting without any perceptible succession; very speedily. The passage of electricity through any given space appears to be *instantaneous.*

INSTANTA'NEOUSLY, *adv.* In an instant; in a moment; in an indivisible point of duration. The operations of the human mind are wonderful; our thoughts fly from world to world *instantaneously.* In the western parts of the Atlantic states of America, showers of rain sometimes begin *instantaneously.*

INSTANTA'NEOUSNESS, *n.* The quality of being done in an instant.

INSTANT'ER, *adv.* [L.] In *law*, immediately; at the present time; without delay.

The party was compelled to plead *instanter.*

IN'STANTLY, *adv.* Immediately; without any intervening time; at the moment. Lightning often kills *instantly.*

2. With urgent importunity.

And when they came to Jesus, they besought him *instantly,* saying, that he was worthy for whom he should do this. Luke vii.

3. With diligence and earnestness. Acts xxvi.

INST'AR, *v. t.* [*in* and *star.*] To set or adorn with stars, or with brilliants.

A golden throne
Instarr'd with gems. *J. Barlow.*

INSTA'TE, *v. t.* [*in* and *state.*] To set or place; to establish, as in a rank or condition; as, to *instate* a person in greatness or in favor. *South. Atterbury.*

2. To invest. *Obs.* *Shak.*

INSTA'TED, *pp.* Set or placed.

INSTA'TING, *ppr.* Setting or placing.

INSTAURA'TION, *n.* [Fr. from L. *instauratio, instauro,* to renew.]

Renewal; repair; re-establishment; the restoration of a thing to its former state, after decay, lapse or dilapidation.

INSTAURA'TOR, *n.* One who renews or restores to a former condition. *More.*

INSTEAD, *insted'.* [a compound of *in* and *stead,* place; but *stead* retains its character of a noun, and is followed by *of; instead of,* in the same manner as *in the stead of.*]

In the place or room of.

Let thistles grow *instead of* wheat. Job xxxi.

Absalom made Amasa captain of the host *instead of* Joab. 2 Sam. xvii.

This consideration is *instead of* a thousand arguments. In this use, *instead* may be equivalent to *equal to.*

When *instead* is used without *of* following, there is an ellipsis, or some words are understood.

INSTEE'P, *v. t.* [*in* and *steep.*] To steep or soak; to drench; to macerate in moisture. *Shak.*

2. To keep under or in water.

INSTEE'PED, *ppr.* Steeped; soaked; drenched; lying under water.

INSTEE'PING, *ppr.* Steeping; soaking.

IN'STEP, *n.* [*in* and *step.*] The *instep* of the human foot, is the fore part of the upper side of the foot, near its junction with the leg.

2. The *instep* of a horse, is that part of the hind leg, which reaches from the ham to the pastern-joint. *Encyc.*

IN'STIGATE, *v. t.* [L. *instigo; in* and *stigo,* inusit., Gr. ςιζω, to prick.]

To incite; to set on; to provoke; to urge; *used chiefly or wholly in an ill sense;* as, to *instigate* one to evil; to *instigate* to a crime.

IN'STIGATED, *pp.* Incited or persuaded, as to evil.

IN'STIGATING, *ppr.* Inciting; tempting to evil.

INSTIGA'TION, *n.* Incitement, as to evil or wickedness; the act of encouraging to commit a crime or some evil act.

2. Temptation; impulse to evil; as the *instigation* of the devil.

IN'STIGATOR, *n.* One who incites another to an evil act; a tempter.

2. That which incites; that which moves persons to commit wickedness.

INSTILL', *v. t.* [L. *instillo; in* and *stillo,* to drop.]

1. To infuse by drops. *Milton.*

2. To infuse slowly, or by small quantities; as, to *instill* good principles into the mind.

INSTILLA'TION, *n.* [L. *instillatio.*] The act of infusing by drops or by small quantities.

2. The act of infusing slowly into the mind.

3. That which is instilled or infused.

INSTILL'ED, *pp.* Infused by drops or by slow degrees.

INSTILL'ER, *n.* He that instills.

INSTILL'ING, *ppr.* Infusing by drops or by slow degrees. *Shak.*

INSTILL'MENT, *n.* Any thing instilled. *Shak.*

INSTIM'ULATE, *v. t.* To stimulate; to excite. [*Not used.*]

INSTIM'ULATING, *ppr.* Not stimulating; not exciting vital powers. *Cheyne.*

INSTIMULA'TION, *n.* [*in* and *stimulation.*]

The act of stimulating, inciting or urging forward.

INSTINCT', *a.* [L. *instinctus.* See the Noun.]

Moved; animated; excited; as *instinct* with spirit. *Obs.* *Milton.*

Betulia—*instinct* with life. *Faber.*

IN'STINCT, *n.* [Fr.; It. *instinto, istinto;* Sp. Port. *instinto;* from L. *instinctus,* inwardly moved; *in* and *stinguo,* Gr. ςιζω, ςιγω. See *Distinguish, Extinguish.* The sense of the root is to thrust; hence the compound, *instinctus,* signifies properly, thrust in, infixed. See *Instigate.*]

A certain power or disposition of mind by which, independent of all instruction or experience, without deliberation and without having any end in view, animals are unerringly directed to do spontaneously whatever is necessary for the preservation of the individual, or the continuation of the kind. Such, in the human species, is the instinct of sucking exerted immediately after birth, and that of insects in depositing their eggs in situations most favorable for hatching. *Encyc.*

Instinct may be defined, the operation of the principle of organized life by the exercise of certain natural powers directed to the present or future good of the individual. *Instinct* is the general property of the living principle, or the law of organized life in a state of action. *Good.*

And *reason* raise o'er *instinct* as you can,
In *this* 'tis God directs, in *that* 'tis man.
Pope.

INSTINCT'ED, *a.* Impressed; as an animating power. [*Little used.*] *Bentley.*

INSTINC'TION, *n.* Instinct. [*Not in use.*] *Elyot.*

INSTINCT'IVE, *a.* Prompted by instinct; spontaneous; acting without reasoning, deliberation, instruction or experience; determined by natural impulse or propensity. The propensity of bees to form hexagonal cells for holding their honey and their young, must be *instinctive.*

INSTINCT'IVELY, *adv.* By force of instinct; without reasoning, instruction or experience; by natural impulse.

IN'STITUTE, *v. t.* [L. *instituo; in* and *statuo,* to set.]

1. To establish; to appoint; to enact; to form and prescribe; as, to *institute* laws; to *institute* rules and regulations.

2. To found; to originate and establish; as, to *institute* a new order of nobility; to *institute* a court.

3. To ground or establish in principles; to educate; to instruct; as, to *institute* children in the principles of a science.

4. To begin; to commence; to set in operation; as, to *institute* an inquiry; to *institute* a suit.

5. To invest with the spiritual part of a benefice or the care of souls. *Blackstone.*

IN'STITUTE, *n.* [L. *institutum;* Fr. *institut.*]

1. Established law; settled order.

2. Precept; maxim; principle.

To make the Stoic *institutes* thy own. *Dryden.*

3. A book of elements or principles; particularly, a work containing the principles of the Roman law. *Encyc.*

4. In *Scots law,* when a number of persons in succession hold an estate in tail, the first is called the *institute,* the others *substitutes.* *Encyc.*

IN'STITUTED, *pp.* Established; appointed; founded; enacted; invested with the care of souls.

IN'STITUTING, *ppr.* Establishing; founding; enacting; investing with the care of souls.

INSTITU'TION, *n.* [Fr. from L. *institutio.*]

1. The act of establishing.

2. Establishment; that which is appointed, prescribed or founded by authority, and intended to be permanent. Thus we speak of the *institutions* of Moses or Lycurgus. We apply the word *institution* to laws, rites, and ceremonies, which are enjoined by authority as permanent rules of conduct or of government.

3. A system, plan or society established, either by law or by the authority of individuals for promoting any object, public or social. We call a college or an academy, a literary *institution;* a bible society, a benevolent or charitable *institution;* a banking company and an insurance company are commercial *institutions.*

4. A system of the elements or rules of any art or science. *Encyc.*

5. Education; instruction.

His learning was not the effect of precept or *institution.* *Bentley.*

6. The act or ceremony of investing a clerk with the spiritual part of a benefice, by which the care of souls is committed to his charge. *Blackstone.*

INSTITU'TIONAL, *a.* Enjoined; instituted by authority. *Etym. Vocabulary.*

INSTITU'TIONARY, *a.* Elemental; containing the first principles or doctrines. *Brown.*

IN'STITUTIST, *n.* A writer of institutes or elementary rules and instructions. *Harvey.*

IN'STITUTIVE, *a.* That establishes; having power to establish. *Barrow.*

2. Established; depending on institution. *Milton.*

IN'STITUTOR, *n.* [L.] The person who establishes; one who enacts laws, rites and ceremonies, and enjoins the observance of them.

2. The person who founds an order, sect, society or scheme for the promotion of a public or social object.

3. An instructor; one who educates; as an *institutor* of youth. *Walker.*

INSTOP′, *v. t.* [*in* and *stop.*] To stop; to close; to make fast. [*Little used.*] *Dryden.*

INSTRA′TIFIED, *a.* Stratified within something else. *Journ. of Science.*

INSTRUCT′, *v. t.* [L. *instruo, instructum; in* and *struo*, to set or to put on, to furnish; Fr. It. *instruire;* Sp. *instruir.* The L. *struo* is contracted from *struco* or *strugo.* See *Destroy.*]

1. To teach; to inform the mind; to educate; to impart knowledge to one who was destitute of it. The first duty of parents is to *instruct* their children in the principles of religion and morality.

2. To direct; to enjoin; to persuade or admonish.

She being before *instructed* by her mother, said, give me here the head of John the Baptist in a charger. Matt. xiv.

3. To direct or command; to furnish with orders. The president *instructed* his envoy to insist on the restitution of the property.

4. To inform; to advise or give notice to. On this question the court is not *instructed.*

5. To model; to form; to prepare. [*Not used.*] *Ayliffe.*

INSTRUCT′ED, *pp.* Taught; informed; trained up; educated.

INSTRUCT′IBLE, *a.* Able to instruct. [*Ill.*] *Bacon.*

INSTRUCT′ING, *ppr.* Teaching; informing the mind; directing.

INSTRUC′TION, *n.* [Fr. from L. *instructio.*]

1. The act of teaching or informing the understanding in that of which it was before ignorant; information.

2. Precepts conveying knowledge.

Receive my *instruction* and not silver. Prov. viii.

3. Direction; order; command; mandate. The minister received *instructions* from his sovereign to demand a categorical answer.

INSTRUCT′IVE, *a.* [Sp. *instructivo;* It. *instruttivo;* Fr. *instructif.*]

Conveying knowledge; serving to instruct or inform. Affliction furnishes very *instructive* lessons.

INSTRUCT′IVELY, *adv.* So as to afford instruction. *Pope.*

INSTRUCT′OR, *n.* A teacher; a person who imparts knowledge to another by precept or information. 1 Cor. iv.

2. The preceptor of a school or seminary of learning; any president, professor or tutor, whose business is to teach languages, literature or the sciences; any professional man who teaches the principles of his profession.

INSTRUCT′RESS, *n.* A female who instructs; a preceptress; a tutoress.

IN′STRUMENT, *n.* [Fr. from L. *instrumentum*, from *instruo*, to prepare; that which is prepared.]

1. A tool; that by which work is performed or any thing is effected; as a knife, a hammer, a saw, a plow, &c. Swords, muskets and cannon are *instruments* of destruction. A telescope is an astronomical *instrument.*

2. That which is subservient to the execution of a plan or purpose, or to the production of any effect; means used or contributing to an effect; *applicable to persons or things.* Bad men are often *instruments* of ruin to others. The distribution of the Scriptures may be the *instrument* of a vastly extensive reformation in morals and religion.

3. An artificial machine or body constructed for yielding harmonious sounds; as an organ, a harpsichord, a violin, or flute, &c., which are called musical *instruments*, or *instruments* of music.

4. In *law*, a writing containing the terms of a contract, as a deed of conveyance, a grant, a patent, an indenture, &c.; in general, a writing by which some fact is recorded for evidence, or some right conveyed.

5. A person who acts for another, or is employed by another for a special purpose, and if the purpose is dishonorable, the term implies degradation or meanness.

INSTRUMENT′AL, *a.* Conducive as an instrument or means to some end; contributing aid; serving to promote or effect an object; helpful. The press has been *instrumental* in enlarging the bounds of knowledge.

2. Pertaining to instruments; made by instruments; as *instrumental* music, distinguished from *vocal* music, which is made by the human voice.

INSTRUMENTAL′ITY, *n.* Subordinate or auxiliary agency; agency of any thing as means to an end; as the *instrumentality* of second causes.

INSTRUMENT′ALLY, *adv.* By way of an instrument; in the nature of an instrument; as means to an end. *South.*

2. With instruments of music.

INSTRUMENT′ALNESS, *n.* Usefulness, as of means to an end; instrumentality. *Hammond.*

INSTY̆LE, *v. t.* [*in* and *style.*] To call; to denominate. [*Not used.*] *Crashaw.*

INSUAV′ITY, *n.* [L. *insuavitas.*] Unpleasantness. *Burton.*

INSUBJEC′TION, *n.* State of disobedience to government.

INSUBMIS′SION, *n.* Defect of submission; disobedience.

INSUBORD′INATE, *a.* Not submitting to authority.

INSUBORDINA′TION, *n.* Want of subordination; disorder; disobedience to lawful authority. *Marshall. J. M. Mason.*

INSUBSTAN′TIAL, *a.* Unsubstantial; not real. *Shak.*

INSUCCA′TION, *n.* [L. *insucco*, to moisten; *in* and *succus*, juice.]

The act of soaking or moistening; maceration; solution in the juice of herbs. *Coxe.*

INSUF′FERABLE, *a.* [*in* and *sufferable.*]

1. Intolerable; that cannot be borne or endured; as *insufferable* heat, cold or pain.

2. That cannot be permitted or tolerated. Our wrongs are *insufferable.*

3. Detestable; contemptible; disgusting beyond endurance.

A multitude of scribblers who daily pester the world with their *insufferable* stuff— *Dryden.*

INSUF′FERABLY, *adv.* To a degree beyond endurance; as a blaze *insufferably* bright; a person *insufferably* proud.

INSUFFI′′CIENCY, *n.* [*in* and *sufficiency.*]

1. Inadequateness; want of sufficiency; deficiency; as an *insufficiency* of provisions to supply the garrison.

2. Inadequacy of power or skill; inability; incapacity; incompetency; as the *insufficiency* of a man for an office.

3. Want of the requisite strength, value or force; defect.

The *insufficiency* of the light of nature is supplied by the light of Scripture. *Hooker.*

INSUFFI′′CIENT, *a.* [*in* and *sufficient.*]

1. Not sufficient; inadequate to any need, use or purpose. The provisions are *insufficient* in quantity and defective in quality.

2. Wanting in strength, power, ability, or skill; incapable; unfit; as a person *insufficient* to discharge the duties of an office.

INSUFFI′′CIENTLY, *adv.* With want of sufficiency; with want of proper ability or skill; inadequately.

INSUFFLA′TION, *n.* [L. *in* and *sufflo*, to blow.]

1. The act of breathing on.

2. The act of blowing a substance into a cavity of the body. *Coxe.*

INSU′ITABLE, *a.* Unsuitable. [*Little used.*] *Burnet.*

IN′SULAR, *a.* [L. *insularis*, from *insula*, an isle.]

Belonging to an isle; surrounded by water; as an *insular* situation.

IN′SULAR, *n.* One who dwells in an isle. *Berkeley.*

IN′SULATE, *v. t.* [L. *insula*, an isle.] To place in a detached situation, or in a state to have no communication with surrounding objects.

2. In *architecture*, to set a column alone or not contiguous to a wall.

3. In *electrical experiments*, to place on a non-conducting substance, or in a situation to prevent communication with the earth.

4. To make an isle. [*Little used.*]

IN′SULATED, *pp.* or *a.* Standing by itself; not being contiguous to other bodies; as an *insulated* house or column.

2. In *electrical experiments*, placed on an electric or non-conducting substance; not communicating with the earth.

IN′SULATING, *ppr.* Setting in a detached position. In *electrical experiments*, preventing communication by the interposition of an electric body.

INSULA′TION, *n.* The act of insulating; the state of being detached from other objects.

2. In *electrical experiments*, that state in which the communication of electrical fluid is prevented by the interposition of an electric body.

IN′SULATOR, *n.* In *electrical experiments*, the substance or body that insulates, or interrupts the communication of electricity to surrounding objects; a non-conductor or electric. *Ed. Encyc.*

INSULSE, *a. insuls′.* [L. *insulsus.*] Dull; insipid. [*Not used.*] *Milton.*

IN'SULT, *n.* [Fr. *insulte*; L. *insultus*, from *insilio*, to leap on; *in* and *salio*, to leap.]
1. The act of leaping on. [*Little used.*] *Dryden.*
2. Any gross abuse offered to another, either by words or actions; act or speech of insolence or contempt.

The ruthless sneer that *insult* adds to grief. *Savage.*

INSULT', *v. t.* [Fr. *insulter*; It. *insultare*; Sp. *insultar*; L. *insulto*. See the Noun.]
To treat with gross abuse, insolence or contempt, by words or actions; as, to call a man a coward or a liar, or to sneer at him, is to *insult* him.
To insult over, to triumph over with insolence and contempt.

INSULT', *v. i.* To behave with insolent triumph. *B. Jonson.*

INSULTA'TION, *n.* The act of insulting; abusive treatment. *Feltham.*

INSULT'ED, *pp.* Abused or treated with insolence and contempt.

INSULT'ER, *n.* One who insults. *Rowe.*

INSULT'ING, *ppr.* Treating with insolence or contempt.

INSULT'INGLY, *adv.* With insolent contempt; with contemptuous triumph. *Dryden.*

INSU'ME, *v. t.* [L. *insumo.*] To take in. [*Not used.*] *Evelyn.*

INSUPERABIL'ITY, *n.* [from *insuperable.*] The quality of being insuperable. [*Little used.*]

INSU'PERABLE, *a.* [L. *insuperabilis*; *in* and *superabilis*, from *supero*, to overcome or surpass.]
1. That cannot be overcome or surmounted; insurmountable; as *insuperable* difficulties, objections or obstacles.
2. That cannot be passed over.

And middle natures, how they long to join,
Yet never pass th' *insuperable* line. *Pope.*

The latter application is unusual. This word is rarely or never used in reference to an enemy, in the sense of invincible or unconquerable. We do not say that troops or enemies are *insuperable*; but the word is applied chiefly to difficulties, objections, obstacles or impediments.

INSU'PERABLENESS, *n.* The quality of being insuperable or insurmountable.

INSU'PERABLY, *adv.* In a manner or degree not to be overcome; insurmountably. *Grew.*

INSUPPÖRTABLE, *a.* [Fr. *in* and *supportable.*]
1. That cannot be supported or borne; as the weight or burden is *insupportable.*
2. That cannot be borne or endured; insufferable; intolerable. We say of heat or cold, insult, indignity or disgrace, it is *insupportable.*

INSUPPÖRTABLENESS, *n.* The quality of being insupportable; insufferableness; the state of being beyond endurance. *Sidney.*

INSUPPÖRTABLY, *adv.* In a manner or degree that cannot be supported or endured. *Dryden.*

INSUPPRESS'IBLE, *a.* Not to be suppressed or concealed. *Young.*

INSUPPRESS'IVE, *a.* Not to be suppressed. *Shak.*

INSU'RABLE, *a.* [from *insure.*] That may be insured against loss or damage; proper to be insured.

The French law annuls the latter policies so far as they exceed the *insurable* interest which remained in the insured at the time of the subscription thereof. *Walsh.*

INSU'RANCE, *n.* [from *insure.*] The act of insuring or assuring against loss or damage; or a contract by which one engages for a stipulated consideration or premium per cent. to make up a loss which another may sustain. *Insurance* is usually made on goods or property exposed to uncommon hazard, or on lives.
2. The premium paid for insuring property or life.
Insurance company, a company or corporation whose business is to insure against loss or damage.

INSU'RANCER, *n.* An underwriter. [*Not in use.*]

INSU'RE, *v. t.* *inshu're.* [*in* and *sure.* The French use *assurer*; we use indifferently *assure* or *insure.*]
To make sure or secure; to contract or covenant for a consideration to secure a person against loss; or to engage to indemnify another for the loss of any specified property, at a certain stipulated rate per cent., called a premium. The property usually *insured* is such as is exposed to extraordinary hazard. Thus the merchant *insures* his ship or its cargo, or both, against the dangers of the sea; houses are *insured* against fire; sometimes hazardous debts are *insured*, and sometimes lives.

INSU'RE, *v. i.* To underwrite; to practice making insurance. This company *insures* at 3 per cent., or at a low premium.

INSU'RED, *pp.* Made sure; assured; secured against loss.

INSU'RER, *n.* One who insures; the person who contracts to pay the losses of another for a premium; an underwriter.

INSURǴ'ENT, *a.* [L. *insurgens*; *in* and *surgo*, to rise.]
Rising in opposition to lawful civil or political authority; as *insurgent* chiefs. *Stephens.*

INSURǴ'ENT, *n.* A person who rises in opposition to civil or political authority; one who openly and actively resists the execution of laws. [See *Insurrection.*] An *insurgent* differs from a *rebel*. The *insurgent* opposes the execution of a particular law or laws; the *rebel* attempts to overthrow or change the government, or he revolts and attempts to place his country under another jurisdiction. All *rebels* are *insurgents*, but all *insurgents* are not *rebels.*

INSU'RING, *ppr.* Making secure; assuring against loss; engaging to indemnify for losses.

INSURMOUNT'ABLE, *a.* [Fr. *insurmontable.* See *Surmount.*]
1. Insuperable; that cannot be surmounted or overcome; as an *insurmountable* difficulty, obstacle or impediment.
2. Not to be surmounted; not to be passed by ascending; as an *insurmountable* wall or rampart.

INSURMOUNT'ABLY, *adv.* In a manner or degree not to be overcome.

INSURREC'TION, *n.* [L. *insurgo*; *in* and *surgo*, to rise.]
1. A rising against civil or political authority; the open and active opposition of a number of persons to the execution of law in a city or state. It is equivalent to *sedition*, except that *sedition* expresses a less extensive rising of citizens. It differs from *rebellion*, for the latter expresses a revolt, or an attempt to overthrow the government, to establish a different one or to place the country under another jurisdiction. It differs from *mutiny*, as it respects the civil or political government; whereas a *mutiny* is an open opposition to law in the army or navy. *Insurrection* is however used with such latitude as to comprehend either sedition or rebellion.

It is found that this city of old time hath made *insurrection* against kings, and that rebellion and sedition have been made therein. Ezra iv.

2. A rising in mass to oppose an enemy. [*Little used.*]

INSURREC'TIONAL, *a.* Pertaining to insurrection; consisting in insurrection. *Amer. Review.*

INSURREC'TIONARY, *a.* Pertaining or suitable to insurrection. *Burke.*

INSUSCEPTIBIL'ITY, *n.* [from *insusceptible.*]
Want of susceptibility, or capacity to feel or perceive. *Med. Repos.*

INSUSCEPT'IBLE, *a.* [*in* and *susceptible.*]
1. Not susceptible; not capable of being moved, affected or impressed; as a limb *insusceptible* of pain; a heart *insusceptible* of pity.
2. Not capable of receiving or admitting.

INSUSURRA'TION, *n.* [L. *insusurro.*] The act of whispering into something.

INTAC'TABLE, *a.* [L. *intactum*; *in* and *tactum*, *tango*, to touch.] Not perceptible to the touch. *Dict.*

INTAGLIATED, *a.* *intal'yated.* [See *Intaglio.*] Engraved or stamped on. *Warton.*

INTAGLIO, *n.* *intal'yo.* [It. from *intagliare*, to carve; *in* and *tagliare*, to cut, Fr. *tailler.*]
Literally, a cutting or engraving; hence, any thing engraved, or a precious stone with a head or an inscription engraved on it. *Addison.*

INTANǴ'IBLE, *a.* [*in* and *tangible.*] That cannot or may not be touched. *Wilkins.*
2. Not perceptible to the touch.

A corporation is an artificial, invisible, *intangible* being. *Marshall.*

INTAN'ǴIBLENESS, } *n.* The quality of being intangible.
INTANǴIBIL'ITY, }

INTĀSTABLE, *a.* [*in* and *tastable*, *taste.*] That cannot be tasted; that cannot affect the organs of taste. *Grew.*

IN'TEǴER, *n.* [L. See *Entire.*] The whole of any thing; particularly, in arithmetic, a whole number, in contradistinction to a fraction. Thus in the number 54. 7, in decimal arithmetic, 54 is an integer, and 7 a fraction, or seven tenths of a unit.

IN'TEGRAL, *a.* [Fr. from *integer.*] Whole; entire. *Bacon.*

A local motion keepeth bodies *integral.* *Bacon.*

2. Making part of a whole, or necessary to make a whole.
3. Not fractional.
4. Uninjured; complete; not defective. *Holder.*

IN'TEGRAL, *n.* A whole; an entire thing.

INTEGRAL'ITY, *n.* Entireness. [*Not used.*] *Whitaker.*

IN'TEGRALLY, *adv.* Wholly; completely. *Whitaker.*

IN'TEGRANT, *a.* Making part of a whole; necessary to constitute an entire thing. *Burke.*

Integrant particles of bodies, are those into which bodies are reduced by solution or mechanical division, as distinct from *elementary particles*.

IN'TEGRATE, *v. t.* [L. *integro.*] To renew; to restore; to perfect; to make a thing entire. *South.*

IN'TEGRATED, *pp.* Made entire.

INTEGRA'TION, *n.* The act of making entire.

INTEG'RITY, *n.* [Fr. *integrité*; L. *integritas*, from *integer.*]

1. Wholeness; entireness; unbroken state. The constitution of the U. States guaranties to each state the *integrity* of its territories. The contracting parties guarantied the *integrity* of the empire.
2. The entire, unimpaired state of any thing, particularly of the mind; moral soundness or purity; incorruptness; uprightness; honesty. *Integrity* comprehends the whole moral character, but has a special reference to uprighness in mutual dealings, transfers of property, and agencies for others.

> The moral grandeur of independent *integrity* is the sublimest thing in nature, before which the pomp of eastern magnificence and the splendor of conquest are odious as well as perishable. *Buckminster.*

3. Purity; genuine, unadulterated, unimpaired state; as the *integrity* of language.

INTEGUMA'TION, *n.* [L. *intego*, to cover.]

That part of physiology, which treats of the integuments of animals and plants. *Encyc.*

INTEG'UMENT, *n.* [L. *integumentum*, *intego*, to cover; *in* and *tego*. See *Deck.*]

That which naturally invests or covers another thing; but appropriately and chiefly, in *anatomy*, a covering which invests the body, as the skin, or a membrane that invests a particular part. The skin of seeds and the shells of crustaceous animals are denominated *integuments*. *Encyc.*

IN'TELLECT, *n.* [Fr. from L. *intellectus*, from *intelligo*, to understand. See *Intelligence.*]

That faculty of the human soul or mind, which receives or comprehends the ideas communicated to it by the senses or by perception, or by other means; the faculty of thinking; otherwise called the *understanding*. A clear *intellect* receives and entertains the same ideas which another communicates with perspicuity.

INTELLEC'TION, *n.* [Fr. from L. *intellectio*, from *intelligo.*]

The act of understanding; simple apprehension of ideas. *Bentley.*

INTELLEC'TIVE, *a.* [Fr. *intellectif.*] Having power to understand. *Glanville.*

2. Produced by the understanding. *Harris.*
3. To be perceived by the understanding, not by the senses. *Milton.*

INTELLEC'TUAL, *a.* [Fr. *intellectuel.*]

1. Relating to the intellect or understanding; belonging to the mind; performed by the understanding; mental; as *intellectual* powers or operations.
2. Ideal; perceived by the intellect; existing in the understanding; as an *intellectual* scene. *Pope.*
3. Having the power of understanding; as an *intellectual* being.
4. Relating to the understanding; treating of the mind; as *intellectual* philosophy, now sometimes called *mental* philosophy.

INTELLEC'TUAL, *n.* The intellect or understanding. [*Little used.*] *Milton.*

INTELLEC'TUALIST, *n.* One who overrates the understanding. *Bacon.*

INTELLECTUAL'ITY, *n.* The state of intellectual power. [*Not used.*] *Hallywell.*

INTELLEC'TUALLY, *adv.* By means of the understanding.

INTEL'LIGENCE, *n.* [Fr. from L. *intelligentia*, from *intelligo*, to understand. This verb is probably composed of *in*, *inter*, or *intus*, within, and *lego*, to collect. The primary sense of *understand* is generally to take or hold, as we say, to *take* one's ideas or meaning.]

1. Understanding; skill. *Spenser.*
2. Notice; information communicated; an account of things distant or before unknown. *Intelligence* may be transmitted by messengers, by letters, by signals or by telegraphs.
3. Commerce of acquaintance; terms of intercourse. Good *intelligence* between men is harmony. So we say, there is a good *understanding* between persons, when they have the same views, or are free from discord.
4. A spiritual being; as a *created intelligence*. It is believed that the universe is peopled with innumerable superior *intelligences*.

INTEL'LIGENCE, *v. t.* To inform; to instruct. [*Little used.*]

INTEL'LIGENCED, *pp.* Informed; instructed. [*Little used.*] *Bacon.*

INTEL'LIGENCE-OFFICE, *n.* An office or place where information may be obtained, particularly respecting servants to be hired.

INTEL'LIGENCER, *n.* One who sends or conveys intelligence; one who gives notice of private or distant transactions; a messenger. *Bacon. Addison.*

2. A public paper; a newspaper.

INTEL'LIGENCING, *ppr.* or *a.* Giving or conveying notice to from a distance.

INTEL'LIGENT, *a.* [Fr. from L. *intelligens.*]

1. Endowed with the faculty of understanding or reason. Man is an *intelligent* being.
2. Knowing; understanding; well informed; skilled; as an *intelligent* officer; an *intelligent* young man; an *intelligent* architect; sometimes followed by *of*; as *intelligent of* seasons. *Milton.*
2. Giving information. [*Not used nor proper.*] *Shak.*

INTELLIGEN'TIAL, *a.* Consisting of unbodied mind.

> Food alike those pure
> *Intelligential* substances require. *Milton.*

2. Intellectual; exercising understanding. *Milton.*

INTELLIGIBIL'ITY, **INTEL'LIGIBLENESS**, *n.* [from *intelligible.*] The quality or state of being intelligible; the possibility of being understood. *Locke. Tooke.*

INTEL'LIGIBLE, *a.* [Fr. from L. *intelligibilis.*]

That may be understood or comprehended; as an *intelligible* account. The rules of human duty are *intelligible* to minds of the smallest capacity.

INTEL'LIGIBLY, *adv.* In a manner to be understood; clearly; plainly; as, to write or speak *intelligibly.*

INTEM'ERATE, *a.* [L. *intemeratus.*] Pure; undefiled. [*Not in use.*]

INTEM'ERATENESS, *n.* State of being unpolluted. [*Not used.*] *Donne.*

INTEM'PERAMENT, *n.* [*in* and *temperament.*]

A bad state or constitution; as the *intemperament* of an ulcerated part. *Harvey.*

INTEM'PERANCE, *n.* [Fr. from L. *intemperantia.*]

1. In *a general sense*, want of moderation or due restraint; excess in any kind of action or indulgence; any exertion of body or mind, or any indulgence of appetites or passions which is injurious to the person or contrary to morality; as *intemperance* in study or in labor, in eating or drinking, or in any other gratification. Hence, appropriately and emphatically,
2. Habitual indulgence in drinking spirituous liquors, with or without intoxication.

> Should a foreign army land on our shores, to levy such a tax upon us as *intemperance* levies—no mortal power could resist the swelling tide of indignation that would overwhelm it. *L. Beecher.*

INTEM'PERATE, *a.* [L. *intemperatus*; *in* and *temperatus*, from *tempero*, to moderate or restrain.]

1. Not moderate or restrained within due limits; indulging to excess any appetite or passion, either habitually or in a particular instance; immoderate in enjoyment or exertion. A man may be *intemperate* in passion, *intemperate* in labor, *intemperate* in study or zeal. Hence by customary application, *intemperate* denotes indulging to excess in the use of food or drink, but particularly in the use of spirituous liquors. Hence,
2. Addicted to an excessive or habitual use of spirituous liquors.
3. Passionate; ungovernable. *Shak.*
4. Excessive; exceeding the convenient mean or degree; as an *intemperate* climate. The weather may be rendered *intemperate* by violent winds, rain or snow, or by excessive cold or heat.

INTEM'PERATE, *v. t.* To disorder. [*Not in use.*] *Whitaker.*

INTEM'PERATELY, *adv.* With excessive indulgence of appetite or passion; with undue exertion; immoderately; excessively.

INTEM'PERATENESS, *n.* Want of moderation; excessive degree of indulgence; as the *intemperateness* of appetite or passion.
2. Immoderate degree of any quality in the weather, as in cold, heat or storms.

INTEM'PERATURE, *n.* Excess of some quality.

INTEMPEST'IVE, *a.* [L. *intempestivus.*] Untimely. [*Not used.*] *Burton.*

INTEMPEST'IVELY, *adv.* Unseasonably. [*Not used.*]

INTEMPESTIV'ITY, *n.* Untimeliness. [*Not used.*]

INTEN'ABLE, *a.* [*in* and *tenable.*] That cannot be held or maintained; that is not defensible; as an *intenable* opinion; an *intenable* fortress. *Warburton.*
[*Untenable*, though not more proper, is more generally used.]

INTEND', *v. t.* [L. *intendo*; *in* and *tendo*, to stretch or strain, from *teneo*, Gr. τεινω, to stretch.]
1. To stretch; to strain; to extend; to distend.

By this the lungs are *intended* or remitted. *Hale.*

[*This literal sense is now uncommon.*]
2. To mean; to design; to purpose, that is, to stretch or set forward in mind. [*This is now the usual sense.*]

For they *intended* evil against thee. Ps. xxi.

3. To regard; to fix the mind on; to attend; to take care of.

Having no children, she did with singular care and tenderness *intend* the education of Philip. *Bacon.*

[This use of the word is now obsolete. We now use *tend* and *superintend* or *regard.*]
4. To enforce; to make intense. *Brown.*

INTEND'ANT, *n.* [Fr. from L. *intendo.*]
1. One who has the charge, oversight, direction or management of some public business; as an *intendant* of marine; an *intendant* of finance: a word much used in France, and sometimes in England and America, but we generally use in lieu of it *superintendent.*
2. In *Charleston*, S. Carolina, the mayor or chief municipal officer of the city.

INTEND'ED, *pp.* Designed; purposed; as, the insult was *intended.*
2. Stretched; made intense. [*Little used.*]

INTEND'ER, *pp.* One who intends.

INTEND'IMENT, *n.* Attention; understanding; consideration. *Obs.*

INTEND'ING, *ppr.* Meaning; designing; purposing.
2. Stretching; distending. [*Little used.*]

INTEND'MENT, *n.* [Fr. *entendement*, with a sense somewhat different.]
Intention; design; in *law*, the true meaning of a person or of a law, or of any legal instrument. In the construction of statutes or of contracts, the *intendment* of the same is, if possible, to be ascertained, that is, the true meaning or intention of the legislator or contracting party.

INTEN'ERATE, *v. t.* [L. *in* and *tener*, tender.] To make tender; to soften.

Autumn vigor gives,
Equal, *intenerating*, milky grain. *Philips.*

INTEN'ERATED, *pp.* Made tender or soft.

INTEN'ERATING, *ppr.* Making tender.

INTENERA'TION, *n.* The act of making soft or tender. *Bacon.*
[*Intenerate* and its derivatives are little used.]

INTENSE, *a.* *intens'.* [L. *intensus*, from *intendo*, to stretch.]
1. Literally, strained, stretched; hence, very close, strict, as when the mind is fixed or bent on a particular subject; as, *intense* study or application; *intense* thought.
2. Raised to a high degree; violent; vehement; as *intense* heat.
3. Very severe or keen; as *intense* cold.
4. Vehement; ardent; as *intense* phrases in language.
5. Extreme in degree.

The doctrine of the atonement supposes that the sins of men were so laid on Christ, that his sufferings were inconceivably *intense* and overwhelming. *S. E. Dwight.*

6. Kept on the stretch; anxiously attentive; opposed to *remiss.* *Milton.*

INTENSELY, *adv.* *intens'ly.* To an extreme degree; vehemently; as a furnace *intensely* heated; weather *intensely* cold.
2. Attentively; earnestly. *Spenser.*

INTENSENESS, *n.* *intens'ness.* The state of being strained or stretched; intensity; as the *intenseness* of a cord.
2. The state of being raised or concentrated to a great degree; extreme violence; as the *intenseness* of heat or cold.
3. Extreme closeness; as the *intenseness* of study or thought.

INTEN'SION, *n.* [L. *intensio.*] A straining, stretching or bending; the state of being strained; as the *intension* of a musical string.
2. Increase of power or energy of any quality; opposed to *remission.*

INTENS'ITY, *n.* [Fr. *intensité.*] The state of being strained or stretched; intenseness, as of a musical chord.
2. The state of being raised to a great degree; extreme violence; as the *intensity* of heat.
3. Extreme closeness; as *intensity* of application.
4. Excess; extreme degree; as the *intensity* of guilt. *Burke.*

INTENS'IVE, *a.* Stretched, or admitting of extension.
2. Intent; unremitted; assiduous; as *intensive* circumspection. *Wotton.*
3. Serving to give force or emphasis; as an *intensive* particle or preposition.

INTENS'IVELY, *adv.* By increase of degree; in a manner to give force. *Bramhall.*

INTENT', *a.* [L. *intentus*, from *intendo.* See *Intend.*]
Literally, having the mind strained or bent on an object; hence, fixed closely; sedulously applied; eager in pursuit of an object; anxiously diligent; formerly with *to*, but now with *on*; as *intent on* business or pleasure; *intent on* the acquisition of science.

Be *intent* and solicitous to take up the meaning of the speaker— *Watts.*

INTENT', *n.* Literally, the stretching of the mind towards an object; hence, a design; a purpose; intention; meaning; drift; aim; applied to *persons* or *things.*

The principal *intent* of Scripture is to deliver the laws of duties supernatural. *Hooker.*

I ask therefore, for what *intent* ye have sent for me? Acts x.

To all intents, in all senses; whatever may be designed.

He was miserable *to all intents* and purposes. *L'Estrange.*

INTEN'TION, *n.* [Fr. from L. *intentio.* See *Intend.*]
1. Primarily, a stretching or bending of the mind towards an object; hence, uncommon exertion of the intellectual faculties; closeness of application; fixedness of attention; earnestness.

Intention is when the mind, with great earnestness and of choice, fixes its view on any idea, considers it on every side, and will not be called off by the ordinary solicitation of other ideas. *Locke.*

2. Design; purpose; the fixed direction of the mind to a particular object, or a determination to act in a particular manner. It is my *intention* to proceed to Paris.
3. End or aim; the object to be accomplished.

In chronical distempers, the principal *intention* is to restore the tone of the solid parts. *Arbuthnot.*

4. The state of being strained. [See *Intension.*]

INTEN'TIONAL, *a.* Intended; designed; done with design or purpose. The act was *intentional*, not accidental.

INTEN'TIONALLY, *adv.* By design; of purpose; not casually.

INTEN'TIONED, in composition; as *well-intentioned*, having good designs, honest in purpose; *ill-intentioned*, having ill designs. *Milner. Ch. Obs.*

INTENT'IVE, *a.* Attentive; having the mind closely applied. *Bacon.*
[This word is nearly superseded by *attentive.*]

INTENT'IVELY, *adv.* Closely; with close application. *Bp. Hall.*

INTENT'IVENESS, *n.* Closeness of attention or application of mind. *W. Mountague.*

INTENT'LY, *adv.* With close attention or application; with eagerness or earnestness; as the mind *intently* directed to an object; the eyes *intently* fixed; the man is *intently* employed in the study of geology.

INTENT'NESS, *n.* The state of being intent; close application; constant employment of the mind. *Swift.*

IN'TER, a Latin preposition, signifying *among* or *between*; used as a prefix.

INTER', *v. t.* [Fr. *enterrer*; *en* and *terre*, L. *terra*, the earth; Sp. *enterrar*; It. *interrare.*]
1. To bury; to deposit and cover in the earth; as, to *inter* a dead animal body.
2. To cover with earth.
But it is used almost exclusively to denote the depositing and covering of dead animal bodies.

IN'TERACT, *n.* [*inter* and *act.*] Intermediate employment or time; a short piece between others. *Chesterfield.*

INTERAM'NIAN, *a.* [L. *inter* and *amnis*, river.] Situated between rivers. *Bryant.*

INTERAN'IMATE, *v. t.* To animate mutually. [*Little used.*] *Donne.*

INTERBASTA'TION, *n.* [Sp. *bastear*, to baste.] Patch-work. [*Not in use.*] *Smith.*

INTER'CALAR, } *a.* [Fr. *intercalaire*; L.
INTER'CALARY, } *intercalarius*; *inter* and *calo*, to call or proclaim.]
Inserted; an epithet given to the odd day inserted in leap year. The twenty ninth of February in leap year is called the *intercalary* day. We read in Livy of an *intercalary* month.

IN'TERCALATE, *v. t.* [L. *intercalo*; *inter* and *calo*, to call.]
To insert an extraordinary day or other portion of time.

IN'TERCALATED, *pp.* Inserted.

IN'TERCALATING, *ppr.* Inserting.

INTERCALA'TION, *n.* [L. *intercalatio*.] The insertion of an odd or extraordinary day in the calendar, as the 29th of February in leap year.

INTERCE'DE, *v. i.* [L. *intercedo*; *inter* and *cedo*; literally, to move or pass between.]
1. To pass between.

He supposes that a vast period *interceded* between that origination and the age in which he lived. *Hale.*

2. To mediate; to interpose; to make intercession; to act between parties with a view to reconcile those who differ or contend; usually followed by *with*. *Calamy.*
3. To plead in favor of one.

INTERCE'DENT, *a.* Passing between; mediating; pleading for.

INTERCE'DER, *n.* One who intercedes or interposes between parties, to effect a reconciliation; a mediator; an intercessor.

INTERCE'DING, *ppr.* Mediating; pleading.

INTERCEPT', *v. t.* [Fr. *intercepter*; L. *interceptus*, *intercipio*, to stop; *inter* and *capio*, to take.]
1. To take or seize on by the way; to stop on its passage; as, to *intercept* a letter. The prince was *intercepted* at Rome. The convoy was *intercepted* by a detachment of the enemy.
2. To obstruct; to stop in progress; as, to *intercept* rays of light; to *intercept* the current of a river, or a course of proceedings.
3. To stop, as a course or passing; as, to *intercept* a course. *Dryden.*
4. To interrupt communication with, or progress towards.

While storms vindictive *intercept* the shore. *Pope.*

5. To take, include or comprehend between.

Right ascension is an arch of the equator, reckoning towards the east, *intercepted* between the beginning of Aries, and the point of the equator which rises at the same time with the sun or star in a right sphere. *Bailey.*

INTERCEPT'ED, *pp.* Taken on the way; seized in progress; stopped.

INTERCEPT'ER, *n.* One who intercepts.

INTERCEPT'ING, *ppr.* Seizing on its passage; hindering from proceeding; comprehending between.

INTERCEP'TION, *n.* The act of seizing something on its passage; a stopping; obstruction of a course or proceeding; hinderance. *Wotton.*

INTERCES'SION, *n.* [Fr. from L. *intercessio*, from *intercedo*. See *Intercede*.] The act of interceding; mediation; interposition between parties at variance, with a view to reconciliation; prayer or solicitation to one party in favor of another, sometimes against another.

Your *intercession* now is needless grown;
Retire and let me speak with her alone. *Dryden.*

He bore the sin of many, and made *intercession* for the transgressors. Is. liii.

INTERCES'SOR, *n.* [L. See *Intercede*.]
1. A mediator; one who interposes between parties at variance, with a view to reconcile them; one who pleads in behalf of another. *Milton.*
2. A bishop who, during a vacancy of the see, administers the bishopric till a successor is elected. *Encyc.*

INTERCES'SORY, *a.* Containing intercession; interceding.

INTERCHA'IN, *v. t.* [*inter* and *chain*.] To chain; to link together. *Shak.*

INTERCHA'INED, *pp.* Chained together.

INTERCHA'INING, *ppr.* Chaining or fastening together.

INTERCHANGE, *v. t.* [*inter* and *change*.]
1. To put each in the place of the other; to give and take mutually; to exchange; to reciprocate; as, to *interchange* places; to *interchange* cares or duties.

I shall *interchange*
My waned state for Henry's regal crown. *Shak.*

2. To succeed alternately. *Sidney.*

IN'TERCHANGE, *n.* Mutual change, each giving and receiving; exchange; permutation of commodities; barter; as the *interchange* of commodities between New York and Liverpool.
2. Alternate succession; as the *interchange* of light and darkness.

Sweet *interchange*
Of hill and valley, rivers, woods and plains. *Milton.*

3. A mutual giving and receiving; reciprocation; as an *interchange* of civilities or kind offices.

INTERCHANGEABLE, *a.* That may be interchanged; that may be given and taken mutually. *Bacon.*
2. Following each other in alternate succession; as the four *interchangeable* seasons. *Holder.*

INTERCHANGEABLENESS, *n.* The state of being interchangeable.

INTERCHANGEABLY, *adv.* Alternately; by reciprocation; in a manner by which each gives and receives. *Hooker.*

INTERCHANGED, *pp.* Mutually exchanged; reciprocated.

INTERCHANGEMENT, *n.* Exchange; mutual transfer. [*Little used.*] *Shak.*

INTERCHANGING, *ppr.* Mutually giving and receiving; taking each other's place successively; reciprocating.

INTERCI'DENT, *a.* [L. *intercido*.] Falling or coming between. *Boyle.*

INTERCIP'IENT, *a.* [L. *intercipiens*. See *Intercept*.] Intercepting; seizing by the way; stopping.

INTERCIP'IENT, *n.* He or that which intercepts or stops on the passage. *Wiseman.*

INTERCIS'ION, *n. s* as *z.* [L. *intercido*; *inter* and *cædo*, to cut.] Interruption. [*Little used.*] *Brown.*

INTERCLU'DE, *v. t.* [L. *intercludo*; *inter* and *claudo*, to shut.]
1. To shut from a place or course by something intervening; to intercept. *Holder.*
2. To cut off; to interrupt. *Mitford.*

INTERCLU'DED, *pp.* Intercepted; interrupted.

INTERCLU'DING, *ppr.* Interrupting.

INTERCLU'SION, *n. s* as *z.* Interception; a stopping.

INTERCOLUMNIA'TION, *n.* [L. *inter* and *columna*, a column.]
In *architecture*, the space between two columns. By the rules of the art, this should be in proportion to the highth and bulk of the columns. *Encyc.*

INTERCOM'MON, *v. i.* [*inter* and *common*.]
1. To feed at the same table. *Bacon.*
2. To graze cattle in a common pasture; to use a common with others, or to possess or enjoy the right of feeding in common.

Common because of vicinage, is where the inhabitants of two townships contiguous to each other, have usually *intercommoned* with one another. *Blackstone.*

INTERCOM'MONING, *ppr.* Feeding at the same table, or using a common pasture; enjoying a common field with others.

INTERCOMMU'NICATE, *v. i.* [*inter* and *communicate*.]
To communicate mutually; to hold mutual communication.

INTERCOMMU'NICATION, *n.* Reciprocal communication.

INTERCOMMU'NION, *n.* [*inter* and *communion*.]
Mutual communion; as an *intercommunion* of deities. *Faber.*

INTERCOMMU'NITY, *n.* [*inter* and *community*.]
A mutual communication or community; mutual freedom or exercise of religion; as the *intercommunity* of pagan theology. *Paley.*

INTERCOST'AL, *a.* [Fr. from L. *inter*, between, and *costa*, a rib.]
Placed or lying between the ribs; as an *intercostal* muscle, artery or vein. *Encyc.*

INTERCOST'AL, *n.* A part lying between the ribs. *Derham.*

IN'TERCOURSE, *n.* [L. *intercursus*, *intercurro*; *inter* and *curro*, to run.] Literally, a running or passing between. Hence,
1. Communication; commerce; connection by reciprocal dealings between persons or nations, either in common affairs and civilities, in trade, or correspondence by letters. We have an *intercourse* with neighbors and friends in mutual visits and in social concerns; nations and individuals have *intercourse* with foreign nations or individuals by an interchange of commodities, by purchase and sale, by treaties, contracts, &c.
2. Silent communication or exchange.

This sweet *intercourse*
Of looks and smiles. *Milton.*

INTERCUR', *v. i.* [L. *intercurro*.] To intervene; to come in the mean time. *Shelton.*

INTERCUR'RENCE, *n.* [L. *intercurrens*, *intercurro*.] A passing or running between. *Boyle.*

INTERCUR'RENT, *a.* [L. *intercurrens*.]
1. Running between or among. *Boyle.*

2. Occurring; intervening. *Barrow.*

INTERCUTA'NEOUS, *a.* [L. *inter* and *cutis*, the skin.] Being within or under the skin.

IN'TERDEAL, *n.* [*inter* and *deal.*] Mutual dealing; traffick. *Spenser.*

INTERDICT', *v. t.* [L. *interdico, interdictum; inter* and *dico*, to speak.]

1. To forbid; to prohibit. An act of congress *interdicted* the sailing of vessels from our ports. Our intercourse with foreign nations was *interdicted.*

2. To forbid communion; to cut off from the enjoyment of communion with a church.

An archbishop may not only excommunicate and *interdict* his suffragans, but his vicar-general may do the same. *Ayliffe.*

IN'TERDICT, *n.* [L. *interdictum.*] Prohibition; a prohibiting order or decree.

2. A papal prohibition by which the clergy are restrained from performing divine service; a species of ecclesiastical censure. The pope has sometimes laid a whole kingdom under an *interdict.*

3. A papal prohibition by which persons are restrained from attending divine service, or prevented from enjoying some privilege.

INTERDICT'ED, *pp.* Forbid; prohibited.

INTERDICT'ING, *ppr.* Forbidding; prohibiting; cutting off from the enjoyment of some privilege.

INTERDIC'TION, *n.* [Fr. from L. *interdictio.*]

The act of interdicting; prohibition; prohibiting decree; curse. *Milton. Shak.*

INTERDICT'IVE, *a.* Having power to prohibit.

INTERDICT'ORY, *a.* Serving to prohibit.

INTEREQUINOC'TIAL, *a.* [*inter* and *equinox.*]

Coming between the vernal and autumnal equinoxes.

Spring and autumn I have denominated equinoctial periods. Summer and winter I have called *interequinoctial* intervals. *Balfour. Asiat. Res.*

INTERESS, for *interest*, is obsolete.

IN'TEREST, *v. t.* [Fr. *interesser;* It. *interessare;* Sp. *interesar;* L. *inter* and *esse.*]

1. To concern; to affect; to excite emotion or passion, usually in favor, but sometimes against a person or thing. A narration of suffering *interests* us in favor of the sufferer. We are *interested* in the story or in the fate of the sufferer. We are *interested* to know the result, issue or event of an enterprise. It is followed by *in* or *for.* We are *interested in* the narration, but *for* the sufferer.

2. To give a share in. Christ, by his atonement, has *interested* believers in the blessings of the covenant of grace.

3. To have a share.

We are not all *interested* in the public funds, but we are all *interested* in the happiness of a free government.

4. To engage; as, to *interest* one in our favor.

To interest one's self, is to take a share or concern in.

IN'TEREST, *n.* Concern; advantage; good; as private *interest; public interest.*

Divisions hinder the common *interest* and public good. *Temple.*

2. Influence over others. They had now lost their *interest* at court.

He knew his *interest* sufficient to procure the office. *Rambler.*

3. Share; portion; part; participation in value. He has parted with his *interest* in the stocks. He has an *interest* in a manufactory of cotton goods.

4. Regard to private profit.

'Tis *interest* calls off all her sneaking train. *Pope.*

5. Premium paid for the use of money; the profit per cent. derived from money lent, or property used by another person, or from debts remaining unpaid. Commercial states have a legal rate of *interest.* Debts on book bear an *interest* after the expiration of the credit. Courts allow *interest* in many cases where it is not stipulated. A higher rate of *interest* than that which the law allows, is called *usury.*

Simple interest is that which arises from the principal sum only.

Compound interest is that which arises from the principal with the interest added; interest on interest.

6. Any surplus advantage.

With all speed,
You shall have your desires with *interest.* *Shak.*

IN'TERESTED, *pp.* Made a sharer; as one *interested* in the funds.

2. Affected; moved; having the passions excited; as one *interested* by a story.

3. *a.* Having an interest; concerned in a cause or in consequences; liable to be affected; as an *interested* witness.

IN'TERESTING, *ppr.* Giving a share or concern; as by *interesting* one in a voyage, or in a banking company.

2. Engaging the affections; as by *interesting* a person in one's favor.

3. *a.* Engaging the attention or curiosity; exciting emotions or passions; as an *interesting* story.

INTERFE'RE, *v. i.* [L. *inter* and *fero*, to bear, or *ferio*, to strike.]

1. To interpose; to intermeddle; to enter into or take a part in the concerns of others. It is prudence not to *interfere* in party disputes, but from necessity.

2. To clash; to come in collision; to be in opposition. The claims of two nations may *interfere.*

3. A horse is said to *interfere*, when one hoof or shoe strikes against the fetlock of the opposite leg, and breaks the skin or injures the flesh. *Far. Dict.*

INTERFE'RENCE, *n.* Interposition; an intermeddling; mediation. *Burke.*

2. A clashing or collision.

3. A striking of one foot against the other.

INTERFE'RING, *ppr.* Interposing; meddling.

2. Clashing; coming in collision.

3. Striking one foot against the fetlock of the opposite leg.

INTERFE'RING, *n.* Interference. *Bp. Butler.*

INTER'FLUENT, } *a.* [L. *interfluo; inter*
INTER'FLUOUS, } and *fluo*, to flow.]
Flowing between. *Boyle.*

INTERFOLIA'CEOUS, *a.* [L. *inter* and *folium*, a leaf.]

Being between opposite leaves, but placed alternately with them; as *interfoliaceous* flowers or peduncles. *Martyn.*

INTERFULG'ENT, *a.* [L. *inter* and *fulgens*, shining.] Shining between. *Johnson.*

INTERFU'SED, *a.* *s* as *z.* [L. *interfusus; inter* and *fundo*, to pour.] Poured or spread between.

The ambient air, wide *interfused*,
Embracing round this florid earth. *Milton.*

IN'TERIM, *n.* [L.] The mean time; time intervening. *Tatler.*

INTE'RIOR, *a.* [L. comp. formed from *inter* or *intra*, in or within.]

1. Internal; being within any limits, inclosure or substance; inner; opposed to *exterior* or superficial; as the *interior* apartments of a house; the *interior* ornaments; the *interior* surface of a hollow ball; the *interior* parts of the earth.

2. Inland; remote from the limits, frontier or shore; as the *interior* parts of a country, state or kingdom.

INTE'RIOR, *n.* The internal part of a thing; the inside.

2. The inland part of a country, state or kingdom.

INTERJA'CENCY, *n.* [L. *interjacens; inter* and *jacens*, lying.]

1. A lying between; a being between; intervention; as the *interjacency* of the Tweed between England and Scotland. *Hale.*

2. That which lies between. [*Little used.*] *Brown.*

INTERJA'CENT, *a.* [L. *interjacens*, supra.] Lying or being between; intervening; as *interjacent* isles. *Raleigh.*

INTERJECT', *v. t.* [L. *interjicio; inter* and *jacio*, to throw.]

To throw between; to throw in between other things; to insert.

A circumstance—may be *interjected* even between a relative word and that to which it relates. *Encyc.*

INTERJECT'ED, *pp.* Thrown in or inserted between.

INTERJECT'ING, *ppr.* Throwing or inserting between.

INTERJEC'TION, *n.* The act of throwing between.

2. A word in speaking or writing, thrown in between words connected in construction, to express some emotion or passion. "These were delightful days, but, *alas*, they are no more." [See *Exclamation.*]

INTERJECT'IONAL, *a.* Thrown in between other words or phrases; as an *interjectional* remark. *Observer.*

INTERJOIN', *v. t.* [*inter* and *join.*] To join mutually; to intermarry. [*Little used.*] *Shak.*

INTERKNOWL'EDGE, *n.* [*inter* and *knowledge.*] Mutual knowledge. [*Little used.*] *Bacon.*

INTERLA'CE, *v. t.* [Fr. *entrelacer;* It. *intralciare;* Sp. *entrelazar.* See *Lace.*]

To intermix; to put or insert one thing with another.

They *interlaced* some errors. *Hayward.*

The epic way is every where *interlaced* with dialogue. *Dryden.*

INTERLA'CED, *pp.* Intermixed; inserted between other things.

INTERLA'CING, *ppr.* Intermixing; inserting between.

INTERLAPSE, *n.* *interlaps'.* [*inter* and *lapse.*]

The lapse or flow of time between two events. *Harvey.*

INTERL'ARD, *v. t.* [Fr. *entrelarder; entre,* among, and *larder,* to lard.]

1. Primarily, to mix fat with lean; hence, to interpose; to insert between. *Carew.*

2. To mix; to diversify by mixture. *Hale.*

INTERL'ARDED, *pp.* Interposed; inserted between; mixed.

INTERL'ARDING, *ppr.* Inserting between; intermixing.

IN'TERLEAF, *n.* [See *Leaf.*] A leaf inserted between other leaves; a blank leaf inserted. *Chesterfield.*

INTERLE'AVE, *v. t.* [*inter* and *leaf.*] To insert a leaf; to insert a blank leaf or blank leaves in a book, between other leaves.

INTERLE'AVED, *pp.* Inserted between leaves, or having blank leaves inserted between other leaves.

INTERLE'AVING, *ppr.* Inserting blank leaves between other leaves.

INTERLI'NE, *v. t.* [*inter* and *line.*] To write in alternate lines; as, to *interline* Latin and English. *Locke.*

2. To write between lines already written or printed, for the purpose of adding to or correcting what is written. *Swift.*

INTERLIN'EAR, INTERLIN'EARY, *a.* [*inter* and *linear.*] Written between lines before written or printed.

INTERLIN'EARY, *n.* A book having insertions between the leaves.

INTERLINEA'TION, *n.* [*inter* and *lineation.*]

1. The act of inserting words or lines between lines before written or printed.

2. The words, passage or line inserted between lines before written or printed.

INTERLI'NED, *pp.* Written between lines; as an *interlined* word.

2. Containing a line or lines written between lines; as an *interlined* manuscript.

INTERLI'NING, *ppr.* Writing between lines already written or printed.

INTERLI'NING, *n.* Correction or alteration by writing between the lines. *Burnet.*

INTERLINK', *v. t.* [*inter* and *link.*] To connect by uniting links; to join one chain to another. *Dryden.*

INTERLINK'ED, *pp.* Connected by union of links; joined.

INTERLINK'ING, *ppr.* Connecting by uniting links; joining.

INTERLOCA'TION, *n.* A placing between; interposition.

INTERLOCU'TION, *n.* [L. *interlocutio; inter* and *locutio, loquor,* to speak.]

1. Dialogue; conference; interchange of speech. *Hooker.*

2. In *law,* an intermediate act or decree before final decision. *Ayliffe.*

INTERLOC'UTOR, *n.* [L. *interloquor,* supra.]

1. One who speaks in dialogue; a dialogist. *Boyle.*

2. In *Scots law,* an interlocutory judgment or sentence. *Encyc.*

INTERLOC'UTORY, *a.* [Fr. *interlocutoire,* supra.]

1. Consisting of dialogue.

There are several *interlocutory* discourses in the holy Scriptures. *Fiddes.*

2. In *law,* intermediate; not final or definitive. An order, sentence, decree or judgment, given in an intermediate stage of a cause, or on some intermediate question before the final decision, is called *interlocutory;* as a decree in chancery referring a question of fact to a court of law, or a judgment on default in a court of law. *Blackstone.*

INTERLO'PE, *v. i.* [*inter* and D. *loopen,* G. *laufen,* to run, Eng. to *leap.* See *Leap.*] To run between parties and intercept the advantage that one should gain from the other; to traffick without a proper license; to forestall; to prevent right. *Johnson.*

INTERLO'PER, *n.* One who runs into business to which he has no right; one who interferes wrongfully; one who enters a country or place to trade without license.

INTERLO'PING, *ppr.* Interfering wrongfully. *Encyc.*

INTERLU'CATE, *v. t.* To let in light by cutting away branches of trees.

INTERLUCA'TION, *n.* The act of thinning a wood to let in light. *Evelyn.*

INTERLU'CENT, *a.* [L. *interlucens; inter* and *luceo,* to shine.] Shining between. *Dict.*

IN'TERLUDE, *n.* [L. *inter* and *ludus,* play.]

An entertainment exhibited on the stage between the acts of a play, or between the play and the afterpiece, to amuse the spectators, while the actors take breath and shift their dress, or the scenes and decorations are changed. In *ancient tragedy,* the chorus sung the interludes. In *modern times,* interludes consist of songs, feats of activity, dances, concerts of music, &c. *Encyc.*

IN'TERLUDER, *n.* One that performs in an interlude. *B. Jonson.*

INTERLU'ENCY, *n.* [L. *interluens, interluo,* to flow between.]

A flowing between; water interposed. [*Little used.*] *Hale.*

INTERLU'NAR, INTERLU'NARY, *a.* [L. *inter* and *luna,* the moon.] Belonging to the time when the moon, at or near its conjunction with the sun, is invisible. *Brown. Milton.*

INTERMAR'RIAGE, *n.* [*inter* and *marriage.*]

Marriage between two families, where each takes one and gives another. *Johnson. Addison.*

INTERMAR'RIED, *pp.* Mutually connected by marriage.

INTERMAR'RY, *v. i.* [*inter* and *marry.*]

1. To marry one and give another in marriage, as two families.

2. To marry some of each order, family, tribe or nation with the other.

About the middle of the fourth century from the building of Rome, it was declared lawful for nobles and plebeians to *intermarry.* *Swift.*

INTERMAR'RYING, *ppr.* Mutually giving and receiving in marriage; mutually connecting by marriage.

IN'TERMEAN, *n.* [*inter* and *mean.*] Interact; something done in the mean time. [*Not used.*] *Todd.*

INTERMEA'TION, *n.* [L. *inter* and *meo,* to flow.] A flowing between. [*Not in use.*]

INTERMED'DLE, *v. i.* [*inter* and *meddle.*] To meddle in the affairs of others, in which one has no concern; to meddle officiously; to interpose or interfere improperly.

The practice of Spain has been, by war and by conditions of treaty, to *intermeddle* with foreign states. *Bacon.*

INTERMED'DLER, *n.* One that interposes officiously; one who meddles, or intrudes into business to which he has no right. *Swift.*

INTERMED'DLING, *ppr.* Interposing officiously; intruding.

INTERMED'DLING, *n.* Officious interposition. *Hamilton.*

INTERME'DIAL, *a.* [L. *inter* and *medius,* middle.]

Lying between; intervening; intervenient. *Evelyn.*

INTERME'DIARY, *n.* [from *intermediate.*]

1. Interposition; intervention. [*Not much used.*] *Derham.*

2. Something interposed.

INTERME'DIATE, *a.* [Fr. *intermediat;* L. *inter* and *medius,* middle.]

Lying or being in the middle place or degree between two extremes; intervening; interposed; as an *intermediate* space between hills or rivers; *intermediate* colors. Man has an *intermediate* nature and rank between angels and brutes.

INTERME'DIATE, *n.* In *chimistry,* a substance which is the intermedium or means of chemical affinity, as an alkali, which renders oil combinable with water.

INTERME'DIATELY, *adv.* By way of intervention.

INTERMEDIA'TION, *n.* Intervention; common means. *Cheyne.*

INTERME'DIUM, *n.* Intermediate space. *Ash.*

2. An intervening agent. *Cowper.*

INTERMELL', *v. t.* or *i.* [Fr. *entremêler.*] To intermix or intermeddle. [*Not in use.*] *Marston. Fisher.*

INTER'MENT, *n.* [from *inter.*] The act of depositing a dead body in the earth; burial; sepulture.

INTERMEN'TION, *v. t.* To mention among other things; to include. [*Not used.*]

INTERMICA'TION, *n.* [L. *intermico; inter* and *mico,* to shine.] A shining between or among.

INTERMIGRA'TION, *n.* [L. *inter* and *migro,* to migrate.]

Reciprocal migration; removal from one country to another by men or tribes which take the place each of the other. *Hale.*

INTERM'INABLE, *a.* [L. *in* and *terminus,* end; *termino,* to end.]

Boundless; endless; admitting no limit; as *interminable* space or duration; *interminable* sufferings. Milton uses this word as an appellation of the Godhead.

INTERM'INATE, *a.* [L. *interminatus, intermino.*]

Unbounded; unlimited; endless; as *interminate* sleep. *Chapman.*

INTERM'INATE, *v. t.* [L. *interminor.*] To menace. [*Not used.*] *Bp. Hall.*

INTERMINA'TION, *n.* [L. *interminor,* to menace or forbid.] A menace or threat. [*Not used.*] *Hall.*

INTERMIN'GLE, *v. t.* [*inter* and *mingle.*] To mingle or mix together; to put some things with others. *Hooker.*

INTERMIN'GLE, *v. i.* To be mixed or incorporated.

INTERMIN'GLED, *pp.* Intermixed.

> There trees and *intermingled* temples rise. *Pope.*

INTERMIN'GLING, *ppr.* Mingling or mixing together.

INTERMIS'SION, *n.* [Fr. from L. *intermissio.* See *Intermit.*]

1. Cessation for a time; pause; intermediate stop; as, to labor without *intermission;* service or business will begin after an *intermission* of one hour.
2. Intervenient time. *Shak.*
3. The temporary cessation or subsidence of a fever; the space of time between the paroxysms of a disease. *Intermission* is an entire cessation, as distinguished from *remission* or abatement of fever.
4. The state of being neglected; disuse; as of words. [*Little used.*] *B. Jonson.*

INTERMIS'SIVE, *a.* Coming by fits or after temporary cessations; not continual. *Howell.*

INTERMIT', *v. t.* [L. *intermitto; inter* and *mitto,* to send.]

To cause to cease for a time; to interrupt; to suspend.

> Pray to the gods, to *intermit* the plague
> That needs must light on this ingratitude. *Shak.*

INTERMIT', *v. i.* To cease for a time; to go off at intervals; as a fever. A tertian fever *intermits* every other day. The pulse sometimes *intermits* for a second of time.

INTERMIT'TED, *pp.* Caused to cease for a time; suspended.

INTERMIT'TENT, *a.* Ceasing at intervals; as an *intermittent* fever.

INTERMIT'TENT, *n.* A fever which entirely subsides or ceases at certain intervals. The ague and fever is called an *intermittent.*

INTERMIT'TING, *ppr.* Ceasing for a time; pausing.

2. Causing to cease.

INTERMIT'TINGLY, *adv.* With intermissions; at intervals.

INTERMIX', *v. t.* [*inter* and *mix.*] To mix together; to put some things with others; to intermingle.

> In yonder spring of roses, *intermix'd*
> With myrtle, find what to redress 'till noon. *Milton.*

INTERMIX', *v. i.* To be mixed together; to be intermingled.

INTERMIX'ED, *pp.* Mingled together.

INTERMIX'ING, *ppr.* Intermingling.

INTERMIX'TURE, *n.* A mass formed by mixture; a mass of ingredients mixed.

2. Admixture; something additional mingled in a mass.

> In this height of impiety there wanted not an *intermixture* of levity and folly. *Bacon.*

INTERMONT'ANE, *a.* [L. *inter* and *montanus, mons,* a mountain.]

Between mountains; as *intermontane* soil. *Mease.*

INTERMUND'ANE, *a.* [L. *inter* and *mundanus, mundus,* the world.]

Being between worlds or between orb and orb; as *intermundane* spaces. *Locke.*

INTERMU'RAL, *a.* [L. *inter* and *muralis, murus,* a wall.] Lying between walls. *Ainsworth.*

INTERMUSC'ULAR, *a.* [*inter* and *muscle.*] Between the muscles. *Beverly.*

INTERMUTA'TION, *n.* [*inter* and *mutation.*]

Interchange; mutual or reciprocal change. *Thomson.*

INTERMU'TUAL, for *mutual,* is an illegitimate word.

INTERN', *a.* Internal. [*Not much used.*] *Howell.*

INTERN'AL, *a.* [L. *internus.*] Inward; interior; being within any limit or surface; not external. We speak of the *internal* parts of a body, of a bone, of the earth, &c. *Internal* excellence is opposed to *external.* The *internal* peace of man, is peace of mind or conscience. The *internal* evidence of the divine origin of the Scriptures, is the evidence which arises from the excellence of its precepts and their adaptation to the condition of man, or from other peculiarities.

2. Pertaining to the heart.

> With our Savior, *internal* purity is every thing. *Paley.*

3. Intrinsic; real; as the *internal* rectitude of actions.
4. Confined to a country; domestic; not foreign; as the *internal* trade of a state or kingdom; *internal* troubles or dissensions; *internal* war. *Internal* taxes are taxes on the lands and other property within a state or kingdom; opposed to *external* taxes. *Hamilton.*

INTERN'ALLY, *adv.* Inwardly; within the body; beneath the surface.

2. Mentally; intellectually.
3. Spiritually.

INTERNA'TIONAL, *a.* [*inter* and *national.*] Existing and regulating the mutual intercourse between different nations; as *international* law. *J. Q. Adams. Baring.*

INTERNE'CINE, *a.* [L. *internecinus, interneco,* to kill; *inter* and *neco.*] Deadly; destructive. [*Little used.*] *Hudibras.*

INTERNE'CION, *n.* [L. *internecio.*] Mutual slaughter or destruction. [*Little used.*] *Hale.*

INTERNEC'TION, *n.* Connection. [*Useless.*] *W. Mountague.*

IN'TERNODE, *n.* [L. *internodium; inter* and *nodus,* knot.]

In *botany,* the space between two joints of a plant. *Martyn.*

INTERNUN'CIO, *n.* [L. *internuncius; inter* and *nuncius,* a messenger.] A messenger between two parties. *Johnson.*

INTEROS'SEAL, } *a.* [L. *inter* and *os,* a
INTEROS'SEOUS, } bone.] Situated between bones; as an *interosseous* ligament.

INTERPE'AL, *v. t.* [L. *interpello.*] To interrupt. [*Not used.*] *More.*

INTERPEL', *v. t.* To set forth. [*Not used.*] *B. Jonson. Mason.*

INTERPELLA'TION, *n.* [L. *interpellatio, interpello; inter* and *pello,* to drive or thrust.] A summons; a citation. *Ayliffe.*

2. Interruption. *More.*
3. An earnest address; intercession. *Bp. Taylor.*

INTERPLE'AD, *v. i.* [*inter* and *plead.*] In *law,* to discuss a point incidentally happening, before the principal cause can be tried. *Jameson.*

INTERPLE'ADER, *n.* A bill of *interpleader,* in chancery, is where a person owes a debt or rent to one of the parties in suit, but, till the determination of it, he knows not to which, and he desires that they may *interplead* or settle their claims between themselves, that he may be safe in the payment. *Blackstone.*

INTERPLEDGE, *v. t.* *interplej'.* To give and take as a mutual pledge. *Davenant.*

INTERPOINT', *v. t.* To point; to distinguish by stops or marks.

IN'TERPOLATE, *v. t.* [Fr. *interpoler;* L. *interpolo; inter* and *polio,* to polish.]

1. To renew; to begin again; to carry on with intermission; as a succession of *interpolated* motions. *Obs. Hale.*
2. To foist in; to insert, as a spurious word or passage in a manuscript or book; to add a spurious word or passage to the original.

> The Athenians were put in possession of Salamis by another law which was cited by Solon, or as some think, *interpolated* by him for that purpose. *Pope.*

IN'TERPOLATED, *pp.* Inserted or added to the original.

IN'TERPOLATING, *ppr.* Foisting in a spurious word or passage.

INTERPOLA'TION, *n.* The act of foisting a word or passage into a manuscript or book.

2. A spurious word or passage inserted in the genuine writings of an author.

> I have changed the situation of some of the Latin verses, and made some *interpolations.* *Cromwell to Pope.*

3. In *mathematics,* that branch of analysis, which treats of the methods by which, when a series of quantities succeeding each other, and formed all according to some determinate law, are given, others subject to the same law may be interposed between them. *Ed. Encyc.*

IN'TERPOLATOR, *n.* [L.] One who foists into a book or manuscript, spurious words or passages; one who adds something to genuine writings. *Swift.*

INTERPOL'ISH, *v. t.* To polish between.

INTERPO'NE, *v. t.* [L. *inter* and *pono.*] To set or insert between. [*Not in use.*] *Ch. Relig. Appeal.*

INTERPO'SAL, *n.* *s* as *z.* [from *interpose.*]

1. The act of interposing; interposition; interference; agency between two persons. *South.*
2. Intervention; a coming or being between. *Glanville.*

INTERPO'SE, *v. t.* *s* as *z.* [Fr. *interposer;* L. *interpono, interpositum; inter* and *pono,* to place.]

1. To place between; as, to *interpose* a body between the sun and the earth.
2. To place between or among; to thrust in; to intrude, as an obstruction, interruption or inconvenience.

> What watchful cares do *interpose* themselves
> Betwixt your eyes and night. *Shak.*
> Human frailty will too often *interpose* itself among persons of the holiest function. *Swift.*

3. To offer, as aid or services, for relief or the adjustment of differences. The emperor *interposed* his aid or services to reconcile the contending parties.

The common Father of mankind seasonably *interposed* his hand and rescued miserable man— *Woodward.*

INTERPO'SE, *v. i.* To step in between parties at variance; to mediate. The prince *interposed* and made peace.

2. To put in by way of interruption.

But, *interposes* Eleutherius, this objection may be made against almost any hypothesis. *Boyle.*

INTERPO'SE, *n.* Interposal. [*Not used.*] *Spenser.*

INTERPO'SED, *pp.* Placed between or among; thrust in.

INTERPO'SER, *n.* One that interposes or comes between others; a mediator or agent between parties.

INTERPO'SING, *ppr.* Placing between; coming between; offering aid or services.

INTERPOS'IT, *n.* A place of deposit between one commercial city or country and another. *Mitford.*

INTERPOSI''TION, *n.* [Fr. from L. *interpositio.*]

1. A being, placing or coming between; intervention; as the *interposition* of the Baltic sea between Germany and Sweden. The *interposition* of the moon between the earth and the sun occasions a solar eclipse.

2. Intervenient agency; as the *interposition* of the magistrate in quieting sedition. How many evidences have we of divine *interposition* in favor of good men!

3. Mediation; agency between parties. By the *interposition* of a common friend, the parties have been reconciled.

4. Any thing interposed. *Milton.*

INTERPO'SURE, *n.* Interposal. [*Not in use.*] *Glanville.*

INTER'PRET, *v. t.* [Fr. *interpreter*; L. *interpretor*, from *interpres.* The word is compounded of *inter* and *pres, pretis*; but the latter is not found in its simple form, and its origin is uncertain. It coincides in elements with פרד or פרש to part, to spread.]

1. To explain the meaning of words to a person who does not understand them; to expound; to translate unintelligible words into intelligible ones; as, to *interpret* the Hebrew language to an Englishman.

—Immanuel, which being *interpreted*, signifies, God with us. Matt. i.

2. To explain or unfold the meaning of predictions, visions, dreams or enigmas; to expound and lay open what is concealed from the understanding; as, Joseph *interpreted* the dream of Pharaoh.

3. To decipher.

4. To explain something not understood; as, to *interpret* looks or signs.

5. To define; to explain words by other words in the same language.

INTER'PRETABLE, *a.* That may be interpreted or explained. *Collier.*

INTERPRETA'TION, *n.* [Fr. from L. *interpretatio.*]

1. The act of interpreting; explanation of unintelligible words in language that is intelligible. *Interpretation* is the design of translation.

2. The act of expounding or unfolding what is not understood or not obvious; as the *interpretation* of dreams and prophecy.

Look how we can, or sad or merrily,
Interpretation will misquote our looks. *Shak.*

3. The sense given by an interpreter; exposition. We sometimes find various *interpretations* of the same passage of Scripture and other ancient writings.

4. The power of explaining. *Bacon.*

INTER'PRETATIVE, *a.* Collected or known by interpretation.

An *interpretative* siding with heretics. *Hammond.*

2. Containing explanation. *Barrow.*

INTER'PRETATIVELY, *adv.* As may be collected by interpretation. *Ray.*

INTER'PRETED, *pp.* Explained; expounded.

INTER'PRETER, *n.* One that explains or expounds; an expositor; as an *interpreter* of the Scriptures.

2. A translator; one who renders the words of one language in words of corresponding signification in another.

INTER'PRETING, *ppr.* Explaining; expounding; translating.

INTERPUNC'TION, *n.* [L. *interpunctio, interpungo*; *inter* and *pungo*, to point.]

The making of points between sentences or parts of a sentence. But *punctuation* is generally used.

INTERREG'NUM, *n.* [L. *inter* and *regnum*, rule or reign.]

The time in which a throne is vacant, between the death or abdication of a king and the accession of his successor. An *interregnum*, in strictness, can happen only in governments where the king is elective; for in hereditary kingdoms, the reign of the successor commences at the moment of his predecessor's death or demise. The word however is used with more latitude.

INTERREIGN, *n.* *interra'ne.* [A translation of *interregnum*, Fr. *interregne.*] An interregnum, or vacancy of the throne. [*supra.*] *Bacon.*

INTER'RER, *n.* [from *inter.*] One that inters or buries.

IN'TERREX, *n.* [L. *inter* and *rex*, king.] A regent; a magistrate that governs during an interregnum.

INTER'ROGATE, *v. t.* [Fr. *interroger*; L. *interrogo*; *inter* and *rogo*, to ask.]

To question; to examine by asking questions; as, to *interrogate* a witness.

INTER'ROGATE, *v. i.* To ask questions. *Bacon.*

INTER'ROGATED, *pp.* Examined by questions.

INTER'ROGATING, *ppr.* Asking questions of one; examining by questions.

INTERROGA'TION, *n.* The act of questioning; examination by questions.

2. A question put; inquiry. *Pope.*

3. A note that marks a question; as, does Job serve God for naught?

INTERROG'ATIVE, *a.* [Fr. *interrogatif.*] Denoting a question; expressed in the form of a question; as an *interrogative* phrase or sentence.

INTERROG'ATIVE, *n.* A word used in asking questions; as *who? what? which? why?*

INTERROG'ATIVELY, *adv.* In the form of a question.

INTER'ROGATOR, *n.* One who asks questions.

INTERROG'ATORY, *n.* [Fr. *interrogatoire.*] A question or inquiry. In *law*, a particular question to a witness, who is to answer it under the solemnities of an oath. This may be in open court or before commissioners.

INTERROG'ATORY, *a.* Containing a question; expressing a question; as an *interrogatory* sentence. *Johnson.*

INTERRUPT', *v. t.* [L. *interrumpo, interruptus*; *inter* and *rumpo*, to break.]

1. To stop or hinder by breaking in upon the course or progress of any thing; to break the current or motion of; as, a fall of rain *interrupted* our journey. There was not a tree nor a bush to *interrupt* the charge of the enemy. The speaker was *interrupted* by shouts of acclamation. We apply the word both to the agent and to his progress. We say, an alarm *interrupted* the speaker, or his argument or discourse.

2. To divide; to separate; to break continuity or a continued series. The road was on a plain, not *interrupted* by a single hill, or *interrupted* here and there by a hill.

INTERRUPT', *a.* Broken; containing a chasm. *Milton.*

INTERRUPT'ED, *pp.* Stopped; hindered from proceeding.

INTERRUPT'EDLY, *adv.* With breaks or interruptions. *Boyle.*

INTERRUPT'ER, *n.* One that interrupts.

INTERRUPT'ING, *ppr.* Hindering by breaking in upon.

INTERRUP'TION, *n.* [Fr. from L. *interruptio.*]

1. The act of interrupting, or breaking in upon progression.

2. Breach of any thing extended; interposition; as an isle separated from the continent by the *interruption* of the sea. *Hale.*

3. Intervention; interposition.

Lest the *interruption* of time cause you to lose the idea of one part. *Dryden.*

4. Stop; hinderance; obstruction caused by breaking in upon any course, current, progress or motion. An *interruption* may be temporary or durable. The work of the Erie canal has suffered few *interruptions* from storms and floods. The lava met with no *interruption* till it descended to the foot of the mountain. The author has met with many *interruptions* in the execution of his work. The speaker or the argument proceeds without *interruption.*

5. Stop; cessation; intermission. *Locke.*

INTERSCAP'ULAR, *a.* [L. *inter* and *scapula*, the shoulder-blade.] Situated between the shoulders.

INTERSCIND', *v. t.* [L. *inter* and *scindo.*] To cut off. *Dict.*

INTERSCRI'BE, *v. t.* [L. *inter* and *scribo.*] To write between. *Dict.*

INTERSE'CANT, *a.* [L. *intersecans, interseco*; *inter* and *seco*, to cut.] Dividing into parts; crossing. *Dict.*

INTERSECT', *v. t.* [L. *interseco*; *inter*, between, and *seco*, to cut.]

To cut or cross mutually; to divide into parts. Thus two lines or two planes may *intersect* each other. The ecliptic *intersects* the equator.

INTERSECT', *v. i.* To meet and cross each other; as, the point where two lines *intersect*. [*This is elliptical.*]

INTERSECT'ED, *pp.* Cut or divided into parts; crossed.

INTERSECT'ING, *ppr.* Cutting; crossing; as lines.

INTERSEC'TION, *n.* [L. *intersectio.*] The act or state of intersecting.

2. The point or line in which two lines or two planes cut each other.

INTERSEM'INATE, *v. t.* [L. *interseminatus; inter*, between, and *semino*, to sow.] To sow between or among. [*Little used.*]

INTERSERT', *v. t.* [L. *intersero; inter*, between, and *sero*, to throw.]

To set or put in between other things. *Brerewood.*

INTERSER'TION, *n.* An insertion, or thing inserted between other things. *Hammond.*

IN'TERSPACE, *n.* [*inter* and *space.*] A space between other things.

INTERSPERSE, *v. t.* *interspers'.* [L. *interspersus; inter*, between, and *spargo*, to scatter.]

To scatter or set here and there among other things; as an able argument *interspersed* with flowers of rhetoric. *Intersperse* shrubs among trees.

INTERSPERS'ED, *pp.* Scattered or situated here and there among other things.

INTERSPERS'ING, *ppr.* Scattering here and there among other things.

INTERSPER'SION, *n.* The act of scattering or setting here and there among other things.

INTERSTEL'LAR, *a.* [L. *inter* and *stella*, a star.]

Situated beyond the solar system. *Bacon.*

IN'TERSTICE, *n.* [Fr. from L. *interstitium; inter* and *sto*, to stand.]

1. A space between things; but chiefly, a narrow or small space between things closely set, or the parts which compose a body. We speak of the *interstices* between the teeth, or between the parts of wood or stone.

2. Time between one act and another; interval. *Ayliffe.*

INTERSTINCT'IVE, *a.* Distinguishing. [*Not used.*] *Wallis.*

INTERSTI''TIAL, *a.* Pertaining to or containing interstices. *Encyc.*

INTERSTRA'TIFIED, *a.* Stratified among or between other bodies. *Encyc.*

INTERTALK, *v. t.* *intertauk'.* To exchange conversation. [*Not used.*] *Carew.*

INTERTAN'GLE, *v. t.* To intertwist; to entangle. *Beaum.*

INTERTEX'TURE, *n.* [L. *intertextus; inter* and *texo*, to weave.]

The act of interweaving, or the state of things interwoven. *More.*

IN'TERTIE, **IN'TERDUCE**, } *n.* In *carpentry*, a small timber between summers.

INTERTROP'ICAL, *a.* [*inter* and *tropical.*] Situated between the tropics. *J. Morse.*

INTERTWI'NE, *v. t.* [*inter* and *twine.*] To unite by twining or twisting one with another. *Milton.*

INTERTWI'NED, *pp.* Twined or twisted one with another.

INTERTWI'NING, *ppr.* Twining one with another.

INTERTWIST', *v. t.* [*inter* and *twist.*] To twist one with another.]

INTERTWIST'ED, *pp.* Twisted one with another.

INTERTWIST'ING, *ppr.* Twisting one with another.

IN'TERVAL, *n.* [Fr. *intervalle;* L. *intervallum; inter* and *vallum*, a wall, or *vallus*, a stake.]

1. A space between things; a void space intervening between any two objects; as an *interval* between two columns, between two pickets or palisades, between two houses or walls, or between two mountains or hills.

2. Space of time between any two points or events; as the *interval* between the death of Charles I. of England and the accession of Charles II.; the *interval* between two wars. Hence we say, an *interval* of peace.

3. The space of time between two paroxysms of disease, pain or delirium; remission; as an *interval* of ease, of peace, of reason.

4. The distance between two given sounds in music, or the difference in point of gravity or acuteness. *Encyc.*

5. A tract of low or plain ground between hills, or along the banks of rivers, usually alluvial land enriched by the overflowings of rivers, or by fertilizing deposits of earth from the adjacent hills. *Hutchinson.*

[Dr. Belknap writes this *intervale;* I think improperly.]

INTERVEINED, *a.* [*inter* and *vein.*] Intersected as with veins.

> Fair champaign with less rivers interveined. *Milton.*

INTERVE'NE, *v. i.* [L. *intervenio; inter* and *venio*, to come.]

1. To come or be between persons or things; to be situated between. Thus the Atlantic *intervenes* between Europe and America; the Mediterranean *intervenes* between Europe and Africa.

2. To come between points of time or events; as the period that *intervened* between the treaty of Ryswick and the treaty of Utrecht.

3. To happen in a way to disturb, cross or interrupt. Events may *intervene* to frustrate our purposes or wishes.

4. To interpose or undertake voluntarily for another. A third party may *intervene* and accept a bill of exchange for another.

INTERVE'NE, *n.* A coming between. [*Not used.*] *Wotton.*

INTERVE'NIENT, *a.* Coming or being between; intercedent; interposed. [*Little used.*] *Bacon.*

INTERVE'NING, *ppr.* or *a.* Coming or being between persons or things, or between points of time; as *intervening* space or time; *intervening* events or misfortunes; *intervening* peace.

INTERVEN'TION, *n.* [Fr. from L. *interventio.*]

1. A state of coming or being between; interposition. Light is not interrupted by the *intervention* of a transparent body.

2. Agency of persons between persons; interposition; mediation; any interference that may affect the interests of others.

> Let us decide our quarrels at home without the *intervention* of a foreign power. *Temple.*

3. Agency of means or instruments; as, effects are produced by the *intervention* of natural causes.

4. Interposition in favor of another; a voluntary undertaking of one party for another. A bill of exchange may be accepted by the *intervention* of a third person in behalf of the drawer or of one of the indorsers. *French Commercial Code. Walsh.*

INTERVEN'UE, *n.* [Fr. *intervenu.*] Interposition. [*Not used.*] *Blount.*

INTERVERT', *v. t.* [L. *interverto; inter* and *verto*, to turn.]

To turn to another course or to another use. [*Little used.*] *Wotton.*

IN'TERVIEW, *n.* [*inter* and *view;* Fr. *entrevue.*]

A mutual sight or view; a meeting; usually a formal meeting for some conference on an important subject; hence the word implies a conference or mutual communication of thoughts. The envoy had an *interview* with the king or with the secretary of foreign affairs. The parties had an *interview* and adjusted their differences.

INTERVOLVE, *v. t.* *intervolv'.* [L. *intervolvo; inter* and *volvo*, to roll.]

To involve one within another. *Milton.*

INTERVOLV'ED, *pp.* Involved one within another; wrapped together.

INTERVOLV'ING, *ppr.* Involving one within another.

INTERWE'AVE, *v. t.* pret. *interwove;* pp. *interwoven.* [*inter* and *weave.*]

1. To weave together; to intermix or unite in texture or construction; as threads of silk and cotton *interwoven.*

2. To intermix; to set among or together; as a covert of *interwoven* trees.

3. To intermingle; to insert together; as, to *interweave* truth with falsehood.

INTERWE'AVING, *ppr.* Weaving together.

INTERWE'AVING, *n.* Intertexture. *Milton.*

INTERWISH', *v. t.* [*inter* and *wish.*] To wish mutually to each other. [*Little used.*] *Donne.*

INTERWORK'ING, *n.* The act of working together.

INTERWRE'ATHED, *a.* Woven into a wreath.

INTEST'ABLE, *a.* [L. *intestabilis; in* and *testabilis; testis*, a witness; *testor*, to testify.]

Not capable of making a will; legally unqualified or disqualified to make a testament; as, a person unqualified for want of discretion, or disqualified by loss of reason, is *intestable.* *Ayliffe.*

INTEST'ACY, *n.* [from *intestate.*] The state of dying without making a will or disposing of one's effects. *Blackstone.*

INTEST'ATE, *a.* [Fr. *intestat;* L. *intestatus; in* and *testatus, testor*, to make a will.]

1. Dying without having made a will. When a man dies *intestate*, his estate is committed for settlement to administrators.

2. Not devised; not disposed of by will; as an *intestate* estate. *Laws of Mass. and Conn.*

INTEST'ATE, *n.* A person who dies without making a will. *Blackstone.*

INTEST'INAL, *a.* [from *intestine.*] Pertaining to the intestines of an animal body; as the *intestinal* tube or canal. *Arbuthnot.*

INTEST'INE, *a.* [Fr. *intestin;* L. *intestinus*, from *intus*, within.]
1. Internal; inward; opposed to *external;* applied to the human or other animal body; as an *intestine* disease.
2. Internal with regard to a state or country; domestic, not foreign; as *intestine* feuds; *intestine* war; *intestine* enemies. It is to be remarked that this word is usually or always applied to evils. We never say, *intestine* happiness or prosperity; *intestine* trade, manufactures or bills; but *intestine* broils, trouble, disorders, calamities, war, &c. We say, *internal* peace, welfare, prosperity, or *internal* broils, war, trade, &c. This restricted use of *intestine* seems to be entirely arbitrary.

INTEST'INE, *n.* usually in the plural, *intestines.* The bowels; the canal or tube that extends, with convolutions, from the right orifice of the stomach to the anus.

INTHIRST, *v. t. inthurst'.* [*in* and *thirst.*] To make thirsty. [*Not used.*] *Bp. Hall.*

INTHRALL', *v. t.* [*in* and *thrall;* Sax. *threal*, a servant; Ir. *traill.*]
To enslave; to reduce to bondage or servitude; to shackle. The Greeks have been *inthralled* by the Turks.

She soothes, but never can *inthrall* my mind. *Prior.*

INTHRALL'ED, *pp.* Enslaved; reduced to servitude.

INTHRALL'ING, *ppr.* Enslaving.

INTHRALL'MENT, *n.* Servitude; slavery; bondage. *Milton.*

INTHRO'NE, *v. t.* [*in* and *throne.*] To seat on a throne; to raise to royalty or supreme dominion. [See *Enthrone*, which is the more common orthography.]

INTHRONIZA'TION, *n.* The act of enthroning. [*Not in use.*]

INTHRO'NIZE, *v. t.* To enthrone. [*Not in use.*]

IN'TIMACY, *n.* [from *intimate.*] Close familiarity or fellowship; nearness in friendship. *Rogers.*

IN'TIMATE, *a.* [L. *intimus*, superl. of *intus*, or *interus*, within.]
1. Inmost; inward; internal; as *intimate* impulse. *Milton.*
2. Near; close.

He was honored with an *intimate* and immediate admission. *South.*

3. Close in friendship or acquaintance; familiar; as an *intimate* friend; *intimate* acquaintance.

IN'TIMATE, *n.* A familiar friend or associate; one to whom the thoughts of another are entrusted without reserve.

IN'TIMATE, *v. i.* To share together. [*Not in use.*] *Spenser.*

IN'TIMATE, *v. t.* [Fr. *intimer;* Sp. *intimar;* It. *intimare;* Low L. *intimo*, to intimate, to register, to love entirely, to make one intimate, to enter, from *intimus.*]
To hint; to suggest obscurely, indirectly or not very plainly; to give slight notice of. He *intimated* his intention of resigning his office.

'Tis heaven itself that points out an hereafter,
And *intimates* eternity to man. *Addison.*

IN'TIMATED, *pp.* Hinted; slightly mentioned or signified.

IN'TIMATELY, *adv.* Closely; with close intermixture and union of parts; as two fluids *intimately* mixed.
2. Closely; with nearness of friendship or alliance; as two friends *intimately* united; two families *intimately* connected.
3. Familiarly; particularly; as, to be *intimately* acquainted with facts or with a subject.

IN'TIMATING, *ppr.* Hinting; suggesting.

INTIMA'TION, *n.* [Fr. from *intimate.*] Hint; an obscure or indirect suggestion or notice; a declaration or remark communicating imperfect information. Our friend left us without giving any previous *intimation* of his design.

IN'TIME, *a.* [L. *intimus.*] Inward; internal. [*Not used.*] *Digby.*

INTIM'IDATE, *v. t.* [Fr. *intimider;* *in* and L. *timidus*, fearful; *timeo*, to fear.]
To make fearful; to inspire with fear; to dishearten; to abash.

Now guilt once harbor'd in the conscious breast,
Intimidates the brave, degrades the great. *Irene.*

INTIM'IDATED, *pp.* Made fearful; abashed.

INTIM'IDATING, *ppr.* Making fearful; abashing.

INTIMIDA'TION, *n.* The act of making fearful; the state of being abashed.

INTINCTIV'ITY, *n.* [L. *in* and *tinctus*, dipped, stained.]
The want of the quality of coloring or tinging other bodies. Fuller's earth is distinguished from colorific earths by its *intinctivity.* *Kirwan.*

INTIRE, INTIRELY. [See *Entire* and its derivatives.]

INTITLE. [See *Entitle.*]

IN'TO, *prep.* [*in* and *to.*] Noting entrance or a passing from the outside of a thing to its interior parts. It follows verbs expressing motion. Come *into* the house; go *into* the church; one stream falls or runs *into* another. Water enters *into* the fine vessels of plants.
2. Noting penetration beyond the outside or surface, or access to it. Look *into* a letter or book; look *into* an apartment.
3. Noting insertion. Infuse more spirit or animation *into* the composition.
4. Noting mixture. Put other ingredients *into* the compound.
5. Noting inclusion. Put these ideas *into* other words.
6. Noting the passing of a thing from one form or state to another. Compound substances may be resolved *into* others which are more simple; ice is convertible *into* water, and water *into* vapor. Men are more easily drawn than forced *into* compliance. We reduce many distinct substances *into* one mass. We are led by evidence *into* belief of truth. Men are often enticed *into* the commission of crimes. Children are sometimes frightened *into* fits, and we are all liable to be seduced *into* error and folly.

INTOL'ERABLE, *a.* [Fr. from L. *intolerabilis;* *in* and *tolerabilis*, *tolero*, to bear.]
1. Not to be borne; that cannot be endured; as *intolerable* pain; *intolerable* heat or cold; an *intolerable* burden.
2. Insufferable; as *intolerable* laziness.

INTOL'ERABLENESS, *n.* The quality of being not tolerable or sufferable.

INTOL'ERABLY, *adv.* To a degree beyond endurance; as *intolerably* cold; *intolerably* abusive.

INTOL'ERANCE, *n.* [from *intolerant.*] Want of toleration; the not enduring at all or not suffering to exist without persecution; as the *intolerance* of a prince or a church towards a religious sect. *Burke.*

INTOL'ERANT, *a.* [Fr. from L. *in* and *tolero*, to endure.]
1. Not enduring; not able to endure.

The powers of the human body being limited and *intolerant* of excesses. *Arbuthnot.*

2. Not enduring difference of opinion or worship; refusing to tolerate others in the enjoyment of their opinions, rights and worship.

INTOL'ERANT, *n.* One who does not favor toleration. *Lowth.*

INTOL'ERATED, *a.* Not endured; not tolerated. *Chesterfield.*

INTOLERA'TION, *n.* Intolerance; refusal to tolerate others in their opinions or worship. *Chesterfield.*

INTÖMB, *v. t. intoom'.* [*in* and *tomb.*] To deposit in a tomb; to bury. *Dryden.*

INTÖMBED, *pp. intoom'ed.* Deposited in a tomb; buried.

INTÖMBING, *ppr. intoom'ing.* Depositing in a tomb; interring.

IN'TONATE, *v. i.* [L. *intono*, *intonatus;* *in* and *tono*, to sound or thunder.]
1. To sound; to sound the notes of the musical scale.
2. To thunder.

INTONA'TION, *n.* In *music*, the action of sounding the notes of the scale with the voice, or any other given order of musical tones. *Encyc.*
2. The manner of sounding or tuning the notes of a musical scale.
3. In *speaking*, the modulation of the voice in expression.

INTO'NE, *v. i.* [L. *intono*, supra.] To utter a sound, or a deep protracted sound.

Ass *intones* to ass. *Pope.*

INTOR'SION, *n.* [L. *intorqueo*, *intorsum*, to twist.]
A winding, bending or twisting. In *botany*, the bending or twining of any part of a plant towards one side or the other, or in any direction from the vertical. *Martyn.*

INTORT', *v. t.* [L. *intortus*, from *intorqueo*, to twist.]
To twist; to wreath; to wind; to wring. *Pope.*

INTORT'ED, *pp.* Twisted; made winding. *Arbuthnot. Pope.*

INTORT'ING, *ppr.* Winding; twisting.

INTOX'ICATE, *v. t.* [*in* and L. *toxicum*, which, Pliny informs us, is from *taxa*, a species of tree, in Greek, σμιλαξ. Lib. xvi. 10.]
1. To inebriate; to make drunk; as with spirituous liquor.

As with new wine *intoxicated* both,
They swim in mirth— *Milton.*

2. To excite the spirits to a kind of delirium; to elate to enthusiasm, frenzy or madness. Success may sometimes *intoxicate* a man

of sobriety. An enthusiast may be *intoxicated* with zeal.

INTOX'ICATE, *a.* Inebriated. *More.*

INTOX'ICATED, *pp.* Inebriated; made drunk; excited to frenzy.

INTOX'ICATING, *ppr.* Inebriating; elating to excess or frenzy.

2. *a.* Having qualities that produce inebriation; as *intoxicating* liquors.

INTOXICA'TION, *n.* Inebriation; ebriety; drunkenness; the act of making drunk. *South.*

INTRACT'ABLE, *a.* [L. *intractabilis; in* and *tractabilis, tracto,* to handle, manage, govern; Fr. *intraitable;* It. *intrattabile.*]

1. Not to be governed or managed; violent; stubborn; obstinate; refractory; as an *intractable* temper.

2. Not to be taught; indocile.

INTRACT'ABLENESS, INTRACTABIL'ITY, } *n.* The quality of being ungovernable; obstinacy; perverseness. *Porteus.*

2. Indocility.

INTRACT'ABLY, *adv.* In a perverse, stubborn manner.

INTRAFOLIA'CEOUS, *a.* [L. *intra* and *folium,* a leaf.]

In *botany,* growing on the inside of a leaf; as *intrafoliaceous* stipules. *Lee. Martyn.*

INTRANCE. [See *Entrance.*]

INTRANQUIL'LITY, *n.* [*in* and *tranquillity.*]

Unquietness; inquietude; want of rest. *Temple.*

INTRAN'SIENT, *a.* Not transient; not passing suddenly away. *Killingbeck.*

INTRANS'ITIVE, *a.* [L. *intransitivus; in* and *transeo,* to pass over.]

In *grammar,* an *intransitive* verb is one which expresses an action or state that is limited to the agent, or in other words, an action that does not *pass over* to, or operate upon an object; as, I *walk;* I *run;* I *sleep.*

INTRANS'ITIVELY, *adv.* Without an object following; in the manner of an intransitive verb. *Lowth.*

INTRANSMIS'SIBLE, *a.* That cannot be transmitted. *J. P. Smith.*

INTRANSMUTABIL'ITY, *n.* The quality of not being transmutable. *Ray.*

INTRANSMU'TABLE, *a.* [*in* and *transmutable.*]

That cannot be transmuted or changed into another substance. *Ray.*

IN'TRANT, *a.* [L. *intrans.*] Entering; penetrating.

INTREASURE, *v. t.* *intrezh'ur.* [*in* and *treasure.*]

To lay up as in a treasury. [*Little used.*] *Shak.*

INTRE'ATFUL, *a.* Full of entreaty.

INTRENCH', *v. t.* [*in* and Fr. *trancher,* to cut. See *Trench.*]

1. To dig or cut a trench around a place, as in fortification; to fortify with a ditch and parapet. The army *intrenched* their camp, or they were *intrenched.*

2. To furrow; to make hollows in.

> His face
> Deep scars of thunder had *intrenched.* *Milton.*

To intrench on, literally, to cut into; hence, to invade; to encroach; to enter on and take possession of that which belongs to another. In the contest for power, the king was charged with *intrenching on* the rights of the nobles, and the nobles were accused of *intrenching on* the prerogatives of the crown.

INTRENCH'ANT, *a.* Not to be divided or wounded; indivisible. [*Not used.*] *Shak.*

INTRENCH'ED, *pp.* Fortified with a ditch and parapet.

INTRENCH'ING, *ppr.* Fortifying with a trench and parapet.

INTRENCH'MENT, *n.* Properly, a trench or ditch only; but as the earth thrown out of a trench forms a part, and often the most necessary and useful part of a fortification, hence *intrenchment* is generally understood to signify a ditch and parapet, and sometimes it signifies fascines covered with earth, gabions, bags filled with earth, or other materials collected to cover men from an enemy's fire.

> On our side we have thrown up *intrenchments* on Winter and Prospect hills. *Washington.*

INTREP'ID, *a.* [L. *intrepidus; in* and *trepidus, trepido,* to tremble.]

Literally, not trembling or shaking with fear; hence, fearless; bold; brave; undaunted; as an *intrepid* soldier.

INTREPID'ITY, *n.* [Fr. *intrepidité.*] Fearlessness; fearless bravery in danger; undaunted courage or boldness. The troops engaged with *intrepidity.*

INTREP'IDLY, *adv.* Without trembling or shrinking from danger; fearlessly; daringly; resolutely. *Pope.*

IN'TRICABLE, *a.* Entangling. [*Not in use.*] *Shelton.*

IN'TRICACY, *n.* [from *intricate.*] The state of being entangled; perplexity; involution; complication; as the *intricacy* of a knot, and figuratively, the *intricacy* of accounts, the *intricacy* of a cause in controversy, the *intricacy* of a plot. *Addison.*

IN'TRICATE, *a.* [L. *intricatus,* from *intrico,* to fold; *in* and *tricor;* It. *intrecciare.* See *Trick.*]

Entangled; involved; perplexed; complicated; obscure. We passed through *intricate* windings. We found the accounts *intricate.* The case on trial is *intricate.* The plot of a tragedy may be too *intricate* to please.

IN'TRICATE, *v. t.* To perplex; to make obscure. [*Little used.*] *Camden.*

IN'TRICATELY, *adv.* With involution or infoldings; with perplexity or intricacy. *Wotton.*

IN'TRICATENESS, *n.* The state of being involved; involution; complication; perplexity. *Sidney.*

INTRICA'TION, *n.* Entanglement. [*Not used.*]

INTRIGUE, *n.* *intree'g.* [Fr. *id.;* It. *intrigo;* verbs, Fr. *intriguer,* to perplex, embroil, intrigue; It. *intricare, intrigare,* to perplex, to make intricate; Low L. *intrico, intricor,* to enwrap; *tricor,* to trifle, to show tricks; allied to Gr. θριξ, τριχος, hair or a lock of hair, as we should say, a plexus. In D. *bedriegen,* G. *betriegen,* signify to cheat; D. *driegen,* to tack, to baste; G. *triegen,* to deceive; *trug,* deceit, fraud. The primary sense seems to be to fold, lay over, or to draw together.]

1. A plot or scheme of a complicated nature, intended to effect some purpose by secret artifices. An *intrigue* may be formed and prosecuted by an individual, and we often hear of the *intrigues* of a minister or a courtier, but often several projectors are concerned in an *intrigue.* The word is usually applied to affairs of love or of government.

2. The plot of a play or romance; a complicated scheme of designs, actions and events, intended to awaken interest in an audience or reader, and make them wait with eager curiosity for the solution or development.

3. Intricacy; complication. [*Not in use.*] *Hale.*

INTRIGUE, *v. i.* *intree'g.* To form a plot or scheme, usually complicated, and intended to effect some purpose by secret artifices. The courtier *intrigues* with the minister, and the lover with his mistress.

INTRIGUE, *v. t.* *intree'g.* To perplex or render intricate. [*Not used.*] *L. Addison.*

INTRIGUER, *n.* *intree'ger.* One who intrigues; one who forms plots, or pursues an object by secret artifices.

INTRIGUING, *ppr.* *intree'ging.* Forming secret plots or schemes.

2. *a.* Addicted to intrigue; given to secret machinations.

INTRIGUINGLY, *a.* *intree'gingly.* With intrigue; with artifice or secret machinations.

INTRIN'SECATE, *a.* Entangled; perplexed. [*Not in use.*]

INTRIN'SIC, INTRIN'SICAL, } *a.* [Fr. *intrinseque;* Sp. *intrinseco;* It. *intrinsico;* L. *intrinsecus; intra* and *secus.* It was formerly written *intrinsecal.*]

1. Inward; internal; hence, true; genuine; real; essential; inherent; not apparent or accidental; as the *intrinsic* value of gold or silver; the *intrinsic* merit of an action; the *intrinsic* worth or goodness of a person. *Prior.*

2. Intimate; closely familiar. *Obs.* *Wotton.*

INTRIN'SICALLY, *adv.* Internally; in its nature; really; truly.

> A lie is a thing absolutely and *intrinsically* evil. *South.*

INTRODU'CE, *v. t.* [L. *introduco; intro,* within, and *duco,* to lead; Fr. *introduire;* It. *introdurre.*]

1. To lead or bring in; to conduct or usher into a place; as, to *introduce* a person into a drawing room.

2. To conduct and make known; to bring to be acquainted; as, to *introduce* a stranger to a person; to *introduce* a foreign minister to a prince.

3. To bring something new into notice or practice; as, to *introduce* a new fashion, or a new remedy for a disease; to *introduce* an improved mode of tillage.

4. To bring in; to import; as, to *introduce* foreign goods.

5. To produce; to cause to exist; as, to *introduce* habits into children. *Locke.*

6. To begin; to open to notice. He *introduced* the subject with a long preface.

7. To bring before the public by writing or discourse; as, to *introduce* one's self to notice or to the public.

INTRODU'CED, *pp.* Led or conducted in; brought in; made acquainted; imported.

INTRODU'CER, *n.* One who introduces; one who conducts another to a place or person; one who makes strangers known to each other; one who brings any thing into notice or practice.

INTRODU'CING, *ppr.* Conducting or bringing in; making known, as one stranger to another; bringing any thing into notice or practice.

INTRODUC'TION, *n.* [Fr. from L. *introductio.*]

1. The action of conducting or ushering into a place; *used of persons.* We speak of the *introduction* of one stranger to another; the *introduction* of a foreign minister to a prince or court, and the *introduction* of company to a levee.
2. The act of bringing into a country; as the *introduction* of gold or bullion, or of merchandise.
3. The act of bringing something into notice, practice or use; as the *introduction* of new modes of dress or of tillage.
4. The part of a book which precedes the main work; a preface or preliminary discourse.
5. The first part of an oration or discourse, in which the speaker gives some general account of his design and subject, and prepares the minds of his audience for a favorable reception of his remarks or arguments.

INTRODUC'TIVE, *a.* Serving to introduce; serving as the means to bring forward something. *Lowth.*

INTRODUC'TOR, *n.* An introducer. [*Not used.*]

INTRODUC'TORY, *a.* Serving to introduce something else; previous; prefatory; preliminary; as *introductory* remarks; an *introductory* discourse.

INTROGRES'SION, *n.* [L. *introgressio.*] Entrance. [*Not used.*]

INTROMIS'SION, *n.* [L. *intromissus, intromitto; intro* and *mitto,* to send.]

1. The action of sending in. *Peacham.*
2. In *Scot's law,* an intermeddling with the effects of another. *Johnson.*

INTROMIT', *v. t.* [L. *intromitto,* supra.] To send in; to let in; to admit. *Greenhill.*

2. To allow to enter; to be the medium by which a thing enters. Glass in the window *intromits* light without cold into a room.

INTROMIT', *v. i.* To intermeddle with the effects of another. *Stuart.*

INTRORECEP'TION, *n.* The act of admitting into or within. *Hammond.*

INTROSPECT', *v. t.* [L. *introspicio; intro* and *specio,* to look.]

To look into or within; to view the inside.

INTROSPEC'TION, *n.* A view of the inside or interior.

> I was forced to make an *introspection* into my own mind. *Dryden.*

INTROSUSCEP'TION, **INTUSSUSCEP'TION**, *n.* The falling of one part of an intestine into another, or the passing of one part within another, causing a duplicature of the intestine. *Coxe. Hooper.*

INTROVE'NIENT, *a.* [L. *intro* and *veniens, venio,* to come.]

Coming in or between; entering. [*Little used.*] *Brown.*

INTROVER'SION, *n.* The act of turning inwards. *Berkeley.*

INTROVERT', *v. t.* [L. *intro* and *verto.*] To turn inwards. *Cowper.*

INTRU'DE, *v. i.* [L. *intrudo; in* and *trudo,* to thrust. See *Thrust.*]

1. To thrust one's self in; to come or go in without invitation or welcome; to enter, as into company, against the will of the company or the host; as, to *intrude* on families at unseasonable hours. Never *intrude* where your company is not desired.
2. To encroach; to enter or force one's self in without permission; as, to *intrude* on the lands of another.
3. To enter uncalled or uninvited, or without just right. Col. ii.

INTRU'DE, *v. t.* To thrust one's self in, or to enter into some place without right or welcome.

2. To force or cast in. *Greenhill.*

INTRU'DED, *pp.* Thrust in.

INTRU'DER, *n.* One who intrudes; one who thrusts himself in, or enters where he has no right or is not welcome.

> They were but *intruders* on the possession, during the minority of the heir. *Davies.*
>
> They were all strangers and *intruders.* *Locke.*

INTRU'DING, *ppr.* Entering without invitation, right or welcome.

INTRU'SION, *n.* *s* as *z.* [Fr. from L. *intrusio,* from *intrudo.*]

1. The action of thrusting in, or of entering into a place or state without invitation, right or welcome. The company may be disturbed by the *intrusion* of an unwelcome guest.

> —Many excellent strains which have been jostled off by the *intrusions* of poetical fictions. *Brown.*
>
> Why this *intrusion?*
> Were not my orders that I should be private? *Addison.*

2. Encroachment; entrance without right on the property or possessions of another.
3. Voluntary entrance on an undertaking unsuitable for the person. *Wotton.*

INTRU'SIVE, *a.* Thrusting in or entering without right or welcome; apt to intrude. *Thomson.*

INTRUST', *v. t.* [*in* and *trust.*] To deliver in trust; to confide to the care of; to commit to another with confidence in his fidelity; as, to *intrust* a servant *with* one's money or goods, or to *intrust* money or goods *to* a servant. We *intrust* an agent or factor *with* commercial business, or we *intrust* commercial concerns *to* an agent. We *intrust* our friends *with* secrets, or *intrust* secrets *to* them.

INTRUST'ED, *pp.* Delivered in trust; committed to the hands or care of another, in confidence that he will be faithful in discharging his duty.

INTRUST'ING, *ppr.* Delivering in trust; confiding to the care of.

INTUI''TION, *n.* [Sp. *intuicion;* L. *intuitus, intueor; in* and *tueor.*]

A looking on; a sight or view; *but restricted to mental view or perception.* Particularly and appropriately, the act by which the mind perceives the agreement or disagreement of two ideas, or the truth of things, immediately, or the moment they are presented, without the intervention of other ideas, or without reasoning and deduction.

> We know by *intuition,* that a part is less than the whole. *Encyc.*

INTU'ITIVE, *a.* [Sp. and It. *intuitivo;* Fr. *intuitif.*]

1. Perceived by the mind immediately, without the intervention of argument or testimony; exhibiting truth to the mind on bare inspection; as *intuitive* evidence.
2. Received or obtained by intuition or simple inspection; as *intuitive* judgment or knowledge.
3. Seeing clearly; as an *intuitive* view; *intuitive* vision. *Hooker.*
4. Having the power of discovering truth without reasoning; as the *intuitive* powers of celestial beings.

INTU'ITIVELY, *adv.* By immediate perception; without reasoning; as, to perceive truth *intuitively.*

INTUMESCE, *v. i.* *intumes'.* [L. *intumesco; in* and *tumeo,* to swell.]

To swell; to enlarge or expand with heat.

> In a higher heat it *intumesces* and melts into a yellowish black mass. *Kirwan.*

INTUMES'CENCE, *n.* [supra.] The action of swelling.

2. A swell; a swelling with bubbles; a rising and enlarging; a tumid state. *Woodward.*

INTURGES'CENCE, *n.* [L. *in* and *turgesco,* to swell.]

A swelling; the action of swelling or state of being swelled. *Brown.*

INTU'SE, *n.* [L. *intusus.*] A bruise. [*Not in use.*] *Spenser.*

INTWI'NE, *v. t.* [*in* and *twine.*] To twine or twist together; to wreath; as a wreath of flowers *intwined.*

INTWI'NED, *pp.* Twisted together.

INTWI'NING, *ppr.* Wreathing together.

INTWIST', *v. t.* [*in* and *twist.*] To twist together; to interweave. *Parkhurst.*

INTWIST'ED, *pp.* Twisted together.

INTWIST'ING, *ppr.* Twisting together.

IN'ULIN, *n.* A peculiar vegetable principle extracted from the Inula helenium, or elecampane. *Ure.*

INUM'BRATE, *v. t.* [L. *inumbro.*] To shade.

INUNC'TION, *n.* [L. *inunctus, inungo; in* and *ungo,* to anoint.]

The action of anointing; unction. *Ray.*

INUNCTUOS'ITY, *n.* [L *in* and *unctus,* or Eng. *unctuous.*]

The want of unctuosity; destitution of greasiness or oiliness which is perceptible to the touch; as the *inunctuosity* of porcelain clay. *Kirwan.*

INUN'DANT, *a.* [L. *inundans,* infra.] Overflowing. *Shenstone.*

INUN'DATE, *v. t.* [L. *inundo, inundatus; in* and *unda,* a wave, or its root.]

1. To overflow; to deluge; to spread over with a fluid. The low lands along the Mississippi are *inundated* almost every spring.
2. To fill with an overflowing abundance or superfluity; as, the country was once *inundated* with bills of credit. The presses *inundate* the country with papers.

INUN'DATED, *pp.* Overflowed; spread over with a fluid; copiously supplied.

INUN'DATING, *ppr.* Overflowing; deluging; spreading over.

INUNDA'TION, *n.* [L. *inundatio.*] An overflow of water or other fluid; a flood; a rising and spreading of water over low grounds. Holland has frequently suffered immensely by *inundations* of the sea. The Delta in Egypt is annually enriched by the *inundation* of the Nile.

2. An overspreading of any kind; an overflowing or superfluous abundance.

INUNDERSTAND'ING, *a.* Void of understanding. [*A bad word and not used.*] *Pearson.*

INURBAN'ITY, *n.* [*in* and *urbanity.*] Incivility; rude, unpolished manners or deportment; want of courteousness. *Bp. Hall.*

INU'RE, *v. t.* [*in* and *ure. Ure* signifies use, practice, in old English, and in Norman French. In Chaucer, it seems to bear rather the signification of luck or fortune. In Scottish, it is used in both senses. See *Ure.*]

1. To habituate; to accustom; to apply or expose in use or practice till use gives little or no pain or inconvenience, or makes little impression. Thus a man *inures* his body to labor and toil, till he sustains that which would destroy a body unaccustomed to it. So we *inure* ourselves to cold or heat. Warriors are *inured* to blood, and seamen are *inured* to hardships and deprivations.

INU'RE, *v. i.* To pass in use; to take or have effect; to be applied; to serve to the use or benefit of; as, a gift of lands *inures* to the heirs of the grantee, or it *inures* to their benefit.

INU'RED, *pp.* Accustomed; hardened by use.

INU'REMENT, *n.* Use; practice; habit; custom; frequency. *Johnson. Wotton.*

INU'RING, *ppr.* Habituating; accustoming.

2. Passing in use to the benefit of.

INURN', *v. t.* [*in* and *urn.*] To bury; to inter; to intomb.

—The sepulcher
Wherein we saw thee quietly *inurned.* *Shak.*

2. To put in an urn.

INURN'ED, *pp.* Deposited in a tomb.

INURN'ING, *ppr.* Interring; burying.

INUSITA'TION, *n.* Want of use; disuse. [*Little used.*] *Paley.*

INUS'TION, *n.* [L. *inustio, inuro*; *in* and *uro*, to burn.] The action of burning.

2. A branding; the action of marking by burning.

INU'TILE, *a.* [Fr. from L. *inutilis.*] Unprofitable; useless. [*Not in use.*] *Bacon.*

INUTIL'ITY, *n.* [Fr. *inutilité*; L. *inutilitas*; *in* and *utilitas.* See *Utility.*]

Uselessness; the quality of being unprofitable; unprofitableness; as the *inutility* of vain speculations and visionary projects.

INUT'TERABLE, *a.* That cannot be uttered. *Milton.*

INVA'DE, *v. t.* [L. *invado*; *in* and *vado*, to go.]

1. To enter a country, as an army with hostile intentions; to enter as an enemy, with a view to conquest or plunder; to attack. The French armies *invaded* Holland in 1795. They *invaded* Russia and perished.

2. To attack; to assail; to assault.

There shall be seditions among men and *invading* one another. 2 Esdras.

3. To attack; to infringe; to encroach on; to violate. The king *invaded* the rights and privileges of the people, and the people *invaded* the prerogatives of the king.

4. To go into; *a Latinism.* [*Not used.*] *Spenser.*

5. To fall on; to attack; to seize; as a disease.

INVA'DED, *pp.* Entered by an army with a hostile design; attacked; assaulted; infringed; violated.

INVA'DER, *n.* One who enters the territory of another with a view to war, conquest or plunder. *Bacon. Swift.*

2. An assailant.

3. An encroacher; an intruder; one who infringes the rights of another. *Hammond.*

INVA'DING, *ppr.* Entering on the possessions of another with a view to war, conquest or plunder; assaulting; infringing; attacking.

INVALES'CENCE, *n.* [L. *invalesco.*] Strength; health. *Dict.*

INVALETU'DINARY, *a.* Wanting health.

INVAL'ID, *a.* [L. *invalidus*; *in* and *validus*, strong, from *valeo*, to be strong, to avail.]

1. Weak; of no force, weight or cogency. *Milton.*

2. In *law*, having no force, effect or efficacy; void; null; as an *invalid* contract or agreement.

IN'VALID, *n.* [Fr. *invalide*; L. *invalidus*, supra.]

1. A person who is weak and infirm; a person sickly or indisposed.

2. A person who is infirm, wounded, maimed, or otherwise disabled for active service; a soldier or seaman worn out in service. The hospitals for *invalids* at Chelsea and Greenwich, in England, are institutions honorable to the English nation.

INVAL'IDATE, *v. t.* [from *invalid*; Fr. *invalider.*]

1. To weaken or lessen the force of; *more generally*, to destroy the strength or validity of; to render of no force or effect; as, to *invalidate* an agreement or a contract.

2. To overthrow; to prove to be of no force; as, to *invalidate* an argument.

INVAL'IDATED, *pp.* Rendered invalid or of no force.

INVAL'IDATING, *ppr.* Destroying the force and effect of.

INVALID'ITY, *n.* [Fr. *invalidité.*] Weakness; want of cogency; want of legal force or efficacy; as the *invalidity* of an agreement or of a will.

INVAL'IDNESS, *n.* Invalidity; as the *invalidness* of reasoning.

INVAL'UABLE, *a.* [*in* and *valuable.*] Precious above estimation; so valuable that its worth cannot be estimated; inestimable. The privileges of christians are *invaluable.*

INVAL'UABLY, *adv.* Inestimably. *Bp. Hall.*

INVA'RIABLE, *a.* [Fr.; *in* and *variable*, from *vary.*]

Constant in the same state; immutable; unalterable; unchangeable; that does not vary; always uniform. The character and the laws of the Supreme Being must necessarily be *invariable.*

INVA'RIABLENESS, *n.* Constancy of state, condition or quality; immutability; unchangeableness.

INVA'RIABLY, *adv.* Constantly; uniformly; without alteration or change. We are bound to pursue *invariably* the path of duty.

INVA'RIED, *a.* Unvaried; not changing or altering. *Blackwall.*

INVA'SION, *n.* *s* as *z.* [L. *invasio*, from *invado.* See *Invade.*]

1. A hostile entrance into the possessions of another; particularly, the entrance of a hostile army into a country for the purpose of conquest or plunder, or the attack of a military force. The north of England and south of Scotland were for centuries subject to *invasion*, each from the other. The *invasion* of England by William the Norman, was in 1066.

2. An attack on the rights of another; infringement or violation.

3. Attack of a disease; as the *invasion* of the plague, in Egypt. *Arbuthnot.*

INVA'SIVE, *a.* [from *invade.*] Entering on another's possessions with hostile designs; aggressive.

2. Infringing another's rights.

INVEC'TION, *n.* Invective, which see. [*Invection* is little used.]

INVEC'TIVE, *n.* [Fr. *invective*; Sp. *invectiva*; It. *invettiva*; from L. *inveho.* See *Inveigh.*]

A railing speech or expression; something uttered or written, intended to cast opprobrium, censure or reproach on another; a harsh or reproachful accusation. It differs from *reproof*, as the latter may come from a friend and be intended for the good of the person reproved; but *invective* proceeds from an enemy, and is intended to give pain or to injure. *Encyc.*

It is followed by *against.* He uttered severe *invectives against* the unfortunate general.

INVEC'TIVE, *a.* Satirical; abusive; railing. *Dryden.*

INVEC'TIVELY, *adv.* Satirically; abusively. *Shak.*

INVEIGH, *v. i.* *inva'y.* [L. *inveho*, to bear, throw or bring on or against; *in* and *veho*, to carry.]

To exclaim or rail against; to utter censorious and bitter language against any one; to reproach; with *against.* The author *inveighed* sharply *against* the vices of the clergy in his age. Men *inveigh against* the follies of fashion.

INVEIGHER, *n.* *inva'yer.* One who rails; a railer.

INVEIGHING, *ppr.* *inva'ying.* Exclaiming against; railing at; uttering bitter words.

INVE'IGLE, *v. t.* [Norm. *enveogler*, to inveigle, to blind; Fr. *aveugler.* The affinities of this word are obscure.]

To entice; to seduce; to wheedle; to persuade to something evil by deceptive arts or flattery.

Yet have they many baits and guileful spells
To *inveigle* and invite th' unwary sense— *Milton.*

INVE'IGLED, *pp.* Enticed; wheedled; seduced from duty.

INVE'IGLEMENT, *n.* Seduction to evil; enticement. *South.*

INVE'IGLER, *n.* One who entices or draws into any design by arts and flattery.

INVE'IGLING, *ppr.* Enticing; wheedling; persuading to any thing bad.

INVEILED, *a.* Covered as with a veil. *Browne.*

INVENT', *v. t.* [Fr. *inventer;* Sp. *inventar;* It. *inventare;* L. *invenio, inventum; in* and *venio,* to come; literally, to come to, to fall on, to meet, Eng. to *find.*]

1. To find out something new; to devise something not before known; to contrive and produce something that did not before exist; as, to *invent* a new instrument of music; to *invent* a machine for spinning; to *invent* gunpowder. [See *Invention.*]

2. To forge; to fabricate; to contrive falsely; as, to *invent* falsehoods.

3. To feign; to frame by the imagination; as, to *invent* the machinery of a poem.

4. To light on; to meet with. [*This is the literal sense, but not now used.*] *Spenser.*

INVENT'ED, *pp.* Found out; devised; contrived; forged; fabricated.

INVENT'ER, *n.* [See *Inventor.*]

INVENT'ING, *ppr.* Finding out what was before unknown; devising or contriving something new; fabricating.

INVEN'TION, *n.* [Fr. from L. *inventio.*]

1. The action or operation of finding out something new; the contrivance of that which did not before exist; as the *invention* of logarithms; the *invention* of the art of printing; the *invention* of the orrery. *Invention* differs from *discovery. Invention* is applied to the contrivance and production of something that did not before exist. *Discovery* brings to light that which existed before, but which was not known. We are indebted to *invention* for the thermometer and barometer. We are indebted to *discovery* for the knowledge of the isles in the Pacific ocean, and for the knowledge of galvanism, and many species of earth not formerly known. This distinction is important, though not always observed.

2. That which is invented. The cotton gin is the *invention* of Whitney; the steam boat is the *invention* of Fulton. The Doric, Ionic and Corinthian orders are said to be *inventions* of the Greeks; the Tuscan and Composite are *inventions* of the Latins.

3. Forgery; fiction. Fables are the *inventions* of ingenious men.

4. In *painting,* the finding or choice of the objects which are to enter into the composition of the piece. *Encyc.*

5. In *poetry,* it is applied to whatever the poet adds to the history of the subject.

6. In *rhetoric,* the finding and selecting of arguments to prove and illustrate the point in view.

7. The power of inventing; that skill or ingenuity which is or may be employed in contriving any thing new. Thus we say, a man of *invention.* *Encyc.*

8. Discovery; the finding of things hidden or before unknown. [*Less proper.*] *Ray.*

INVENT'IVE, *a.* [Fr. *inventif.*] Able to invent; quick at contrivance; ready at expedients; as an *inventive* head or genius. *Dryden.*

INVENT'OR, *n.* One who finds out something new; one who contrives and produces any thing not before existing; a contriver. The *inventors* of many of the most useful arts are not known.

INVENTO'RIALLY, *adv.* In the manner of an inventory. *Shak.*

IN'VENTORIED, *pp.* Inserted or registered in an inventory.

IN'VENTORY, *n.* [Sp. It. *inventario;* Fr. *inventaire;* from *invent.*]

1. An account, catalogue or schedule of all the goods and chattels of a deceased person. In some of the United States, the *inventory* must include an account of the real as well as the personal estate of the deceased.

2. A catalogue of movables.

3. A catalogue or account of particular things. [*An indefinite use of the word.*]

IN'VENTORY, *v. t.* [Fr. *inventorier.*] To make an inventory of; to make a list, catalogue or schedule of; as, to *inventory* the goods and estate of the deceased. *Blackstone.*

2. To insert or register in an account of goods.

INVENT'RESS, *n.* [from *invent.*] A female that invents. *Dryden.*

INVERSE, *a.* *invers'.* [L. *inversus.* See *Invert.*]

Inverted; reciprocal. *Inverse* proportion or ratio, is when the effect or result of any operation is *less* in proportion as the cause is *greater,* or is *greater* in proportion as the cause is *less.* Thus the time in which a quantity of work may be performed, will be *less* in proportion as the number of workmen is *greater,* and *greater* in proportion as the number of workmen is *less.* If *ten* men can perform a certain quantity of work in *six* days, then *twenty* men will perform the same work in *three* days. *Inverse* proportion is opposed to *direct.*

INVERSELY, *adv.* *invers'ly.* In an inverted order or manner; when more produces less, and less produces more; or when one thing is greater or less, in proportion as another is less or greater.

INVER'SION, *n.* [Fr. from L. *inversio.* See *Invert.*]

1. Change of order, so that the last becomes first and the first last; a turning or change of the natural order of things.

> It is just the *inversion* of an act of parliament; your Lordship first signed it, and then it was passed among the lords and commons. *Dryden.*

2. Change of places, so that each takes the place of the other.

3. A turning backwards; a contrary rule of operation. Problems in geometry and arithmetic are often proved by *inversion,* as division by multiplication, and multiplication by division.

4. In *grammar,* a change of the natural order of words; as, "of all vices, impurity is one of the most detestable," instead of "impurity is one of the most detestable of all vices."

5. In *music,* the change of position either of a subject or of a chord. *Busby.*

INVERT', *v. t.* [L. *inverto; in* and *verto,* to turn.]

1. To turn into a contrary direction; to turn upside down; as, to *invert* a cone; to *invert* a hollow vessel.

2. To place in a contrary order or method; as, to *invert* the rules of justice; to *invert* the order of words.

> And winter storms *invert* the year. *Dryden.*

3. In *music,* to change the order of the notes which form a chord, or the parts which compose harmony. *Encyc.*

4. To divert; to turn into another channel; to embezzle. [*Not in use.*] *Knolles.*

INVERT'EBRAL, *a.* Destitute of a vertebral column, as animals. *Ed. Encyc.*

INVERT'EBRATED, *a.* Destitute of a back bone or vertebral chain. [See *Vertebrated.*] *Good.*

INVERT'ED, *pp.* Turned to a contrary direction; turned upside down; changed in order.

INVERT'EDLY, *adv.* In a contrary or reversed order. *Derham.*

INVERT'ENT, *n.* A medicine intended to invert the natural order of the successive irritative motions in the system. *Darwin.*

INVERT'ING, *ppr.* Turning in a contrary direction; changing the order.

INVEST', *v. t.* [Fr. *investir;* L. *investio; in* and *vestio,* to clothe. See *Vest.*]

1. To clothe; to dress; to put garments on; to array; usually and most correctly followed by *with,* before the thing put on; as, to *invest* one *with* a mantle or robe. In this sense, it is used chiefly in poetry and elevated prose, not in colloquial discourse.

2. To clothe with office or authority; to place in possession of an office, rank or dignity; as, to *invest* a person with a civil office, or with an ecclesiastical dignity.

3. To adorn; to grace; as, to *invest* with honor. *Shak.*

4. To clothe; to surround; as, to be *invested* with light, splendor or glory.

5. To confer; to give. [*Little used.*] *Bacon.*

6. To inclose; to surround; to block up, so as to intercept succors of men and provisions and prevent escape; to lay siege to; as, to *invest* a town.

7. To clothe money in something permanent or less fleeting; as, to *invest* money *in* funded or bank stock; to *invest* it *in* lands or goods. In this application, it is always followed by *in.*

INVEST'ED, *pp.* Clothed; dressed; adorned; inclosed.

INVEST'IENT, *a.* Covering; clothing. *Woodward.*

INVEST'IGABLE, *a.* [from *investigate.*] That may be investigated or searched out; discoverable by rational search or disquisition. The causes or reasons of things are sometimes *investigable.*

INVEST'IGATE, *v. t.* [L. *investigo; in* and *vestigo,* to follow a track, to search; *vestigium,* a track or *footstep.*]

To search into; to inquire and examine into with care and accuracy; to find out by careful disquisition; as, to *investigate* the powers and forces of nature; to *investigate* the causes of natural phenomena; to *investigate* the principles of moral duty; to *investigate* the conduct of an agent or the motives of a prince.

INVEST'IGATED, *pp.* Searched into; examined with care.

INVEST'IGATING, *ppr.* Searching into; inquiring into with care.

INVESTIGA'TION, *n.* [Fr. from L. *investigatio.*] The action or process of searching minutely for truth, facts or principles; a careful inquiry to find out what is unknown, either in the physical or moral world, and either by observation and experiment, or by argument and discussion. Thus we speak of the *investigations* of the philosopher and the mathematician; the *investigations* of the judge, the moralist and the divine.

INVEST'IGATIVE, *a.* Curious and deliberate in researches. *Pegge.*

INVEST'IGATOR, *n.* One who searches diligently into a subject.

INVEST'ITURE, *n.* [Fr. See *Invest.*] The action of giving possession, or livery of seizin.

The grant of land or a feud was perfected by the ceremony of corporal *investiture*, or open delivery of possession. *Blackstone.*

It was customary for princes to make *investiture* of ecclesiastical benefices. *Encyc.*

2. The right of giving possession of any manor, office or benefice.

He had refused to yield to the pope the *investiture* of bishops. *Raleigh.*

INVEST'IVE, *a.* Clothing; encircling.

INVEST'MENT, *n.* The action of investing.

2. Clothes; dress; garment; habit. *Shak.* [We now use *vestment.*]

3. The act of surrounding, blocking up or besieging by an armed force.

The capitulation was signed by the commander of the fort, within six days after its *investment.* *Marshall.*

4. The laying out of money in the purchase of some species of property; literally, the clothing of money with something.

Before the *investment* could be made, a change of the market might render it ineligible. *Hamilton.*

INVET'ERACY, *n.* [L. *inveteratio.* See *Inveterate.*] Long continuance, or the firmness or deep rooted obstinacy of any quality or state acquired by time; as the *inveteracy* of custom and habit: usually or always applied in a bad sense; as the *inveteracy* of prejudice, of error, or of any evil habit.

INVET'ERATE, *a.* [L. *inveteratus, invetero; in* and *vetero*, from *vetus*, old.]

1. Old; long established.

It is an *inveterate* and received opinion—*Obs.* *Bacon.*

2. Deep rooted; firmly established by long continuance; obstinate; *used of evils;* as an *inveterate* disease; an *inveterate* abuse; an *inveterate* course of sin.

3. Having fixed habits by long continuance; *used of persons;* as an *inveterate* sinner.

4. Violent; deep rooted; obstinate; as *inveterate* enmity or malice.

INVET'ERATE, *v. t.* [L. *invetero*, to grow old.] To fix and settle by long continuance. [*Obsolete or little used.*] *Bacon.*

INVET'ERATELY, *adv.* With obstinacy; violently.

INVET'ERATENESS, *n.* Obstinacy confirmed by time; inveteracy; as the *inveterateness* of a mischief. *Locke.*

INVETERA'TION, *n.* The act of hardening or confirming by long continuance.

INVID'IOUS, *a.* [L. *invidiosus*, from *invideo*, to envy; *in* and *video*, to see. *Invideo* signifies properly, to look against.]

1. Envious; malignant. *Evelyn.*

2. Likely to incur ill will or hatred, or to provoke envy; hateful. [*This is the usual sense.*]

Agamemnon found it an *invidious* affair to give the preference to any one of the Grecian heroes. *Broome.*

INVID'IOUSLY, *adv.* Enviously; malignantly.

2. In a manner likely to provoke hatred.

INVID'IOUSNESS, *n.* The quality of provoking envy or hatred.

INVIG'ILANCE, *n.* Want of vigilance; neglect of watching.

INVIG'ORATE, *v. t.* [It. *invigorire; in* and *vigor.*] To give vigor to; to strengthen; to animate; to give life and energy to. Exercise *invigorates* the body; cheerfulness *invigorates* the mind.

Christian graces and virtues they cannot be, unless fed, *invigorated* and animated by universal charity. *Atterbury.*

INVIG'ORATED, *pp.* Strengthened; animated.

INVIG'ORATING, *ppr.* Giving fresh vigor to; strengthening.

INVIGORA'TION, *n.* The action of invigorating, or state of being invigorated.

INVIL'LAGED, *a.* Turned into a village. *Browne.*

INVIN'CIBLE, *a.* [Fr. *invincible; L. in* and *vinco*, to conquer.]

1. Not to be conquered or subdued; that cannot be overcome; unconquerable; as an *invincible* army.

2. Not to be overcome; insuperable; as, an *invincible* obstacle, error, habit or objection.

INVIN'CIBLENESS, **INVINCIBIL'ITY**, *n.* The quality of being unconquerable; insuperableness.

INVIN'CIBLY, *adv.* Unconquerably; insuperably.

INVI'OLABLE, *a.* [Fr. from L. *inviolabilis; in* and *violabilis, violo*, to violate.]

1. Not to be profaned; that ought not to be injured, polluted or treated with irreverence; as, a sacred place and sacred things should be considered *inviolable.* *Milton.*

2. Not to be broken; as an *inviolable* league, covenant, agreement, contract, vow or promise.

3. Not to be injured or tarnished; as *inviolable* chastity or honor.

4. Not susceptible of hurt or wound; as *inviolable* saints. *Milton.*

INVI'OLABLENESS, **INVIOLABIL'ITY**, *n.* [from *inviolable.*] The quality or state of being inviolable; as the *inviolability* of crowned heads. *Ward.*

2. The quality of not being subject to be broken.

INVI'OLABLY, *adv.* Without profanation; without breach or failure; as a sanctuary *inviolably* sacred; to keep a promise *inviolably.*

INVI'OLATE, *a.* [L. *inviolatus.*] Unhurt; uninjured; unprofaned; unpolluted; unbroken.

But let *inviolate* truth be always dear
To thee. *Denham.*

INVI'OLATED, *a.* Unprofaned; unbroken; unviolated. *Drayton.*

IN'VIOUS, *a.* [L. *invius; in* and *via*, way.] Impassable; untrodden. *Hudibras.*

IN'VIOUSNESS, *n.* State of being impassable. *Ward.*

INVISC'ATE, *v. t.* [L. *in* and *viscus*, glue, birdlime.]

1. To lime; to daub with glue.

2. To catch with glue or birdlime; to entangle with glutinous matter. [*Little used.*] *Brown.*

INVIS'CERATE, *v. t.* To breed; to nourish. [*A bad word.*] *Mountague.*

INVISIBIL'ITY, **INVIS'IBLENESS**, *n.* [Fr. *invisibilité*, from *invisible.*] The state of being invisible; imperceptibleness to the sight. *Ray.*

INVIS'IBLE, *a. s* as *z.* [Fr. from L. *invisibilis; in* and *visibilis, viso*, to see.] That cannot be seen; imperceptible by the sight. Millions of stars, *invisible* to the naked eye, may be seen by the telescope.

He endured, as seeing him who is *invisible.* Heb. xi.

INVIS'IBLY, *adv.* In a manner to escape the sight; imperceptibly to the eye. *Denham.*

INVIS'ION, *n. s* as *z.* [*in* and *vision.*] Want of vision, or the power of seeing. [*Little used.*] *Brown.*

INVITA'TION, *n.* [Fr. from L. *invitatio.* See *Invite.*] The act of inviting; solicitation; the calling or requesting of a person's company to visit, to dine, or to accompany him to any place.

INVI'TATORY, *a.* Using or containing invitations. *Wheatley.*

INVI'TATORY, *n.* A part of the service in the catholic church; a psalm or anthem sung in the morning.

—Antiphonary, a service-book, which contained all the *invitatories*, responsories and collects. *Encyc.*

INVI'TE, *v. t.* [L. *invito;* It. *invitare;* Fr. *inviter.* This word is formed by *in* and the Teutonic *bid*, or its root; *inbid.* See *Bid.*]

1. To ask to do some act or to go to some place; to request the company of a person; as, to *invite* one to dine or sup; to *invite* friends to a wedding; to *invite* company to an entertainment; to *invite* one to an excursion into the country.

2. To allure; to draw to; to tempt to come; to induce by pleasure or hope.

—Shady groves, that easy sleep *invite.* *Dryden.*

3. To present temptations or allurements to.

The people should be in a situation not to *invite* hostilities. *Federalist, Jay.*

INVI'TED, *pp.* Solicited; requested to come or go in person; allured.

INVI'TER, *n.* One who invites. *Pope.*

INVI'TING, *ppr.* Soliciting the company of; asking to attend.

2. *a.* Alluring; tempting; drawing to; as an *inviting* amusement or prospect.

Nothing is so easy and *inviting* as the retort of abuse and sarcasm. *Irving.*

INVI'TING, *n.* Invitation. *Shak.*

INVI'TINGLY, *adv.* In such a manner as to invite or allure.

INVI'TINGNESS, *n.* The quality of being inviting. *Taylor.*

INVIT'RIFIABLE, *a.* [*in* and *vitrifiable*, from *vitrify*.]
That cannot be vitrified or converted into glass. *Kirwan.*

IN'VOCATE, *v. t.* [L. *invoco; in* and *voco*, to call.]
To invoke; to call on in supplication; to implore; to address in prayer.

If Dagon be thy god,
Go to his temple, *invocate* his aid— *Milton.*

[Instead of this word, *invoke* is generally used.]

IN'VOCATED, *pp.* Invoked; called on in prayer.

IN'VOCATING, *ppr.* Invoking.

INVOCA'TION, *n.* [Fr. from L. *invocatio*.]
1. The act of addressing in prayer. *Hooker.*
2. The form or act of calling for the assistance or presence of any being, particularly of some divinity; as the *invocation* of the muses.

The whole poem is a prayer to Fortune, and the *invocation* is divided between the two deities. *Addison.*

3. A judicial call, demand or order; as the *invocation* of papers or evidence into a court. *Wheaton's Rep.*

IN'VOICE, *n.* [Fr. *envoi*, a sending or thing sent, from *envoyer*, to send, It. *inviare; envois*, plu. things sent.]
1. In *commerce*, a written account of the particulars of merchandise, shipped or sent to a purchaser, consignee, factor, &c. with the value or prices and charges annexed.
2. A written account of ratable estate. *Laws of New Hampshire.*

IN'VOICE, *v. t.* To make a written account of goods or property with their prices.

Goods, wares and merchandise imported from Norway, and *invoiced* in the current dollar of Norway— *Madison's Proclamation.*
It is usual to *invoice* goods in the currency of the country in which the seller resides.

IN'VOICED, *pp.* Inserted in a list with the price or value annexed. *Robinson, Adm. Reports.*

IN'VOICING, *ppr.* Making an account in writing of goods, with their prices or values annexed; inserting in an invoice.

INVO'KE, *v. t.* [L. *invoco; in* and *voco*, to call; *vox*, a word.]
1. To address in prayer; to call on for assistance and protection; as, to *invoke* the Supreme Being. Poets *invoke* the muses for assistance.
2. To order; to call judicially; as, to *invoke* depositions or evidence into a court. *Wirt.*

INVO'KED, *pp.* Addressed in prayer for aid; called.

INVO'KING, *ppr.* Addressing in prayer for aid; calling.

INVOL'UCEL, *n.* [dim. of *involucre*.] A partial involucre; an involucret. *Eaton.*

INVOLU'CELLATE, *a.* [supra.] Surrounded with involucels. *Barton.*

INVOLU'CRUM, **INVOLU'CRE**, *n.* [L. from *involvo*.] In *botany*, a calyx remote from the flower, particularly in the umbel, but applied also to the whorl and other kinds of inflorescence. *Martyn.*

INVOLU'CRED, *a.* Having an involucre, as umbels, whorls, &c. *Martyn.*

INVOLU'CRET, *n.* A small or partial involucrum. *Martyn.*

INVOL'UNTARILY, *adv.* [from *involuntary*.]
1. Not by choice; not spontaneously; against one's will. *Baxter.*
2. In a manner independent of the will.

INVOL'UNTARINESS, *n.* Want of choice or will. *Bp. Hall.*
2. Independence on the will.

INVOL'UNTARY, *a.* [Fr. *involontaire*; L. *in* and *voluntarius*. See *Voluntary*.]
1. Not having will or choice; unwilling.
2. Independent of will or choice. The motion of the heart and arteries is *involuntary*, but not against the will.
3. Not proceeding from choice; not done willingly; opposed to the will. A slave and a conquered nation yield an *involuntary* submission to a master.

IN'VOLUTE, *n.* [L. *involutus*.] A curve traced by the end of a string folded upon a figure, or unwound from it.

IN'VOLUTE, **IN'VOLUTED**, *a.* [L. *involutus*, *involvo*. See *Involve*.] In *botany*, rolled spirally inwards. *Involuted* foliation or vernation, is when the leaves within the bud have their edges rolled spirally inwards on both sides towards the upper surface. *Martyn.*

INVOLU'TION, *n.* [Fr.; L. *involutio*. See *Involve*.]
1. The action of involving or infolding.
2. The state of being entangled or involved; complication.

All things are mixed and causes blended by mutual *involutions*. *Glanville.*

3. In *grammar*, the insertion of one or more clauses or members of a sentence between the agent or subject and the verb; a third intervening member within a second, &c; as, habitual falsehood, *if we may judge from experience*, infers absolute depravity.
4. In *algebra*, the raising of a quantity from its root to any power assigned. Thus $2\times2\times2=8$. Here 8, the third power of 2, is found by *involution*, or multiplying the number into itself, and the product by the same number.

INVOLVE, *v. t.* *involv'.* [L. *involvo; in* and *volvo*, to roll, Eng. to *wallow*.]
1. To envelop; to cover with surrounding matter; as, to *involve* one in smoke or dust.
2. To envelop in any thing which exists on all sides; as, to *involve* in darkness or obscurity.
3. To imply; to comprise. To be and not to be at the same time, *involves* a contradiction.
4. To entwist; to join; to connect.

He knows his end with mine *involved*. *Milton.*

5. To take in; to catch; to conjoin.

The gathering number, as it moves along,
Involves a vast involuntary throng. *Pope.*

6. To entangle. Let not our enemy *involve* the nation in war, nor our imprudence *involve* us in difficulty.
7. To plunge; to overwhelm. Extravagance often *involves* men in debt and distress.
8. To inwrap; to infold; to complicate or make intricate.

Some *involved* their snaky folds. *Milton.*
Florid, witty, *involved* discourses. *Locke.*

9. To blend; to mingle confusedly. *Milton.*
10. In *algebra*, to raise a quantity from the root to any assigned power; as a quantity *involved* to the third or fourth power.

INVOLV'ED, *pp.* Enveloped; implied; inwrapped; entangled.

INVOLV'ING, *ppr.* Enveloping; implying; comprising; entangling; complicating.

INVULNERABIL'ITY, **INVUL'NERABLENESS**, *n.* [from *invulnerable*.]
The quality or state of being invulnerable, or secure from wounds or injury. *Walsh.*

INVUL'NERABLE, *a.* [Fr. from L. *invulnerabilis*. See *Vulnerable*.]
That cannot be wounded; incapable of receiving injury.

Nor vainly hope
To be *invulnerable* in those bright arms. *Milton.*

INWALL', *v. t.* [*in* and *wall*.] To inclose or fortify with a wall. *Spenser.*

IN'WARD, *a.* [Sax. *inweard*; G. *einwärts*; *in* and *ward*. See *Ward*.]
1. Internal; interior; placed or being within; as the *inward* structure of the body.
2. Intimate; domestic; familiar. *Spenser.*
3. Seated in the mind or soul. *Shak.*

IN'WARD, **IN'WARDS**, *adv.* Toward the inside. Turn the attention *inward*.
2. Toward the center or interior; as, to bend a thing *inward*.
3. Into the mind or thoughts.

Celestial light shine *inward*. *Milton.*

IN'WARDLY, *adv.* In the inner parts; internally.

Let Benedict, like covered fire,
Consume away in sighs, waste *inwardly*. *Shak.*

2. In the heart; privately; secretly. He *inwardly* repines. It is not easy to treat with respect a person whom we *inwardly* despise.
3. Towards the center.

IN'WARDNESS, *n.* Intimacy; familiarity. [*Not used.*] *Shak.*
2. Internal state. [*Unusual.*]

IN'WARDS, *n. plu.* The inner parts of an animal; the bowels; the viscera. *Milton.* Ex. xxix.

INWE'AVE, *v. t.* pret. *inwove*; pp. *inwoven*, *inwove*. [*in* and *weave*.] To weave together; to intermix or intertwine by weaving.

Down they cast
Their crowns *inwove* with amaranth and gold. *Milton.*

INWHEE'L, *v. t.* [*in* and *wheel*.] To encircle. *Beaum.*

IN'WIT, *n.* [*in* and *wit*.] Mind; understanding. *Obs.*

INWOOD', *v. t.* To hide in woods. *Sidney.*

INWORK'ING, *ppr.* or *a.* [*in* and *work*.] Working or operating within.

INWORK'ING, *n.* Internal operation; energy within. *Macknight.*

INWO'VE, **INWO'VEN**, *pp.* of *inweave*. Woven in; intertwined by weaving.

INWRAP, *v. t.* *inrap'.* [*in* and *wrap*.] To involve; to infold; to cover by wrapping; as, to be *inwrapped* in smoke or in a cloud; to *inwrap* in a cloke.
2. To involve in difficulty or perplexity; to perplex. *Bacon.*
3. To ravish or transport. [*Ill.* See *Rap.*]

INWREATHE, *v. t.* *inre'the.* [*in* and *wreathe*.]

To surround or encompass as with a wreath, or with something in the form of a wreath.

Resplendent locks *inwreathed* with beams. *Milton.*

INWROUGHT, *pp.* or *a.* *inraut'.* [*in* and *wrought*, from *work.*]
Wrought or worked in or among other things; adorned with figures. *Milton.*

I'ODATE, *n.* [See *Iodine.*] A compound consisting of oxygen, iodin and a base. *Gay Lussac. Henry.*

I'ODIC, *a.* *Iodic* acid is a compound of iodin and oxygen.

I'ODIDE, *n.* A compound of iodin with a metal or other substance.

I'ODIN, I'ODINE, *n.* [Gr. ιωδης, resembling a violet.] In *chimistry*, a peculiar substance recently discovered by Courtois, a manufacturer of salt-peter in Paris. It is obtained from certain sea-weeds or marine plants. At the ordinary temperature of the atmosphere it is a solid, apparently a simple substance, at least hitherto undecomposed. It is incombustible, but in combining with several bodies, it exhibits the phenomena of combustion; hence it has been considered a supporter of combustion. Like chlorin, it destroys vegetable colors, but with less energy. Its color is bluish black or grayish black, of a metallic luster. It is often in scales, resembling those of micaceous iron ore; sometimes in brilliant rhomboidal plates, or in elongated octahedrons. Its taste is acrid, and it is somewhat poisonous. It is fusible at 225° of Fahrenheit. The color of its vapor is a beautiful violet, whence its name. *Henry. Ure.*

I'ODOUS, *a.* *Iodous* acid is a compound of iodin and oxygen, containing less of the latter than *iodic* acid.

IOD'URET, *n.* A compound of iodin and a metallic or other base.

I'OLITE, *n.* [Gr. ιον, a violet, and λιθος, stone.]
A mineral of a violet blue color, with a shade of purple or black, called also *dichroit* and *cordierite.* It occurs in regular six-sided prisms. Its varieties are peliom and steinheilite. *Cleaveland.*

[NOTE. By the regular principles of pronouncing the Greek *iota* and the Shemitic *jod*, this word ought to be pronounced *yolite.*]

ION'IC, *a.* [from *Ionia.*] The *Ionic order*, in architecture, is that species of column named from Ionia, in Greece. It is more slender than the Doric and Tuscan, but less slender and less ornamented than the Corinthian and Composite. It is simple, but majestic; its highth is 18 modules, and that of the entablature four and a half. *Encyc.*

2. The *Ionic dialect* of the Greek language, is the dialect used in Ionia.

3. The *Ionic sect* of philosophers, was that founded by Thales of Miletus, in Ionia. Their distinguishing tenet was, that water is the principle of all natural things. *Encyc.*

4. Denoting an airy kind of music. The *Ionic* or *Ionian mode* was, reckoning from grave to acute, the second of the five middle modes. *Busby.*

IPECACUAN'HA, *n.* A root produced in South America. Four sorts are mentioned, gray, brown, white, and yellow. The gray, or genuine kind, is referred by Mutis to the *Psychotria emetica*, but more recently by Brotero to the *Callicocca Ipecacuanha*, a plant growing in Brazil. These plants have been considered by some as the same, or as species of the same genus. This root is used as an emetic. *Parr.*

Ipecacuanha is a little wrinkled root about the thickness of a moderate quill, much used as an emetic, and against diarrheas and dysenteries. *Cyc.*

IRASCIBIL'ITY, IRAS'CIBLENESS, *n.* [from *irascible.*] The quality of being irascible, or easily inflamed by anger; irritability of temper.

IRAS'CIBLE, *a.* [Fr. from L. *irascor*, from *ira.* See *Ire.*]
Very susceptible of anger; easily provoked or inflamed with resentment; irritable; as an *irascible* man; an *irascible* temper.

IRE, *n.* [Fr. from L. *ira*, wrath; W. *irad*, pungency, passion, rage. See Eng. *Wrath.*]
Anger; wrath; keen resentment; *a word chiefly used in poetry.*

Thus will persist, relentless in his *ire.* *Dryden.*

I'REFUL, *a.* [*ire* and *full.*] Angry; wroth; furious with anger.

The *ireful* bastard Orleans. *Shak.*

I'REFULLY, *adv.* In an angry manner.

I'RENARCH, *n.* [Gr. ειρηναρχης.] An officer formerly employed in the Greek empire, to preserve the public tranquillity.

IRIDES'CENCE, *n.* Exhibition of colors like those of the rainbow.

IRIDES'CENT, *a.* [from *iris.*] Having colors like the rainbow. *Fourcroy. Barrow.*

IRID'IUM, *n.* [from *iris.*] A metal of a whitish color, not malleable, found in the ore of platinum, and in a native alloy with osmium. Its specific gravity is above 18. It takes its name from the variety of colors which it exhibits while dissolving in muriatic acid. The native alloy with osmium, or native iridium, is of a steel gray color and shining metallic luster. It usually occurs in small irregular flat grains, in alluvial soil, in S. America. *Cleaveland. Webster's Manual.*

I'RIS, *n.* plu. *irises.* [L. *iris, iridis*, the rainbow, Gr. ιρις.]
1. The rainbow. *Brown.*
2. An appearance resembling the rainbow. *Newton.*
3. The colored circle which surrounds the pupil of the eye, by means of which that opening is enlarged and diminished.
4. The changeable colors which sometimes appear in the glasses of telescopes, microscopes, &c.
5. A colored spectrum which a triangular glass prism casts on a wall, when placed at a due angle in the sun-beams.
6. The flower-de-lis, or flag-flower, a genus of many species.

I'RISATED, *a.* Exhibiting the prismatic colors; resembling the rainbow. *Phillips.*

I'RISED, *a.* Containing colors like those of the rainbow. *Chaptal.*

I'RISH, *a.* Pertaining to Ireland.

I'RISH, *n.* A native of Ireland.
2. The language of the Irish; the Hiberno-Celtic.

I'RISHISM, *n.* A mode of speaking peculiar to the Irish.

IRK, *v. t.* *urk.* [Scot. *irk*, to weary; *irk*, indolent. Lye suggests that this may be from Sax. *weorce*, work, which signifies also pain, or anxiety; but it seems more probably to be connected with Sax. *earg*, slothful, lazy, Gr. αργος.]
To weary; to give pain to; used only impersonally; as, it *irketh* me, it gives me uneasiness. It is nearly obsolete. *Shak.*

IRK'SŎME, *a.* Wearisome; tedious; tiresome; giving uneasiness; used of something troublesome by long continuance or repetition; as *irksome* hours; *irksome* toil or task. *Addison. Milton.*

IRK'SŎMELY, *adv.* In a wearisome or tedious manner.

IRK'SŎMENESS, *n.* Tediousness; wearisomeness.

IRON, *n.* *i'urn*, or *i'rn.* [Sax. *iren*; Scot. *irne, yrn*, or *airn*; Isl. *iarn*; Sw. *järn* or *iärn*; Dan. *iern*; W. *haiarn*; Ir. *iarann*; Arm. *hoarn.* Qu. L. *ferrum*, for *herrum.* The radical elements of this word are not easily ascertained.]
1. A metal, the hardest, most common and most useful of all the metals; of a livid whitish color inclined to gray, internally composed, to appearance, of small facets, and susceptible of a fine polish. It is so hard and elastic as to be capable of destroying the aggregation of any other metal. Next to tin, it is the lightest of all metallic substances, and next to gold, the most tenacious. It may be hammered into plates, but not into leaves. Its ductility is more considerable. It has the property of magnetism; it is attracted by the lodestone, and will acquire its properties. It is found rarely in native masses; but in ores, mineralized by different substances, it abounds in every part of the earth. Its medicinal qualities are valuable. *Fourcroy. Encyc.*
2. An instrument or utensil made of iron; as a flat-*iron*, a smoothing-*iron*.

Canst thou fill his skin with barbed *irons?* Job xli.

3. *Figuratively*, strength; power; as a rod of *iron.* Dan. ii.
4. *Irons*, plu., fetters; chains; manacles; handcuffs. Ps. cv.

I'RON, *a.* Made of iron; consisting of iron; as an *iron* gate; an *iron* bar; *iron* dust.
2. Resembling iron in color; as an *iron* gray color.
3. Harsh; rude; severe; miserable; as the *iron* age of the world.

Iron years of wars and dangers. *Rowe.*
Jove crush'd the nations with an *iron* rod. *Pope.*

4. Binding fast; not to be broken; as the *iron* sleep of death. *Philips.*
5. Hard of understanding; dull; as an *iron* witted fool. *Shak.*
6. Firm; robust; as an *iron* constitution.

I'RON, *v. t.* To smooth with an instrument of iron.
2. To shackle with irons; to fetter or handcuff.
3. To furnish or arm with iron.

I'RON-CLAY, *n.* A substance intermediate between basalt and wacky, of a reddish brown color, and occurring massive or vesicular. *Cyc.*

I'RONED, *pp.* Smoothed with an iron; shackled; armed with iron.

I'RONFLINT, *n.* Ferruginous quartz; a subspecies of quartz, opake or translucent at the edges, with a fracture more or less conchoidal, shining and nearly vitreous. It is sometimes in very minute and perfect six-sided prisms, terminated at both extremities by six-sided pyramids. It occurs also in masses, and in small grains. Its varieties are red, yellow, and greenish. *Cleaveland.*

I'RONHE'ARTED, *a.* Hardhearted; unfeeling; cruel.

I'RONMÖLD, *n.* A spot on cloth made by applying rusty iron to the cloth when wet.

I'RONMÖNGER, *n.* A dealer in iron wares or hardware.

I'RONSICK, *a.* In *seamen's language*, a ship is said to be *ironsick*, when her bolts and nails are so much corroded or eaten with rust that she has become leaky. *Encyc.*

I'RONSTONE, *n.* An ore of iron.

I'RONWOOD, *n.* The popular name of a genus of trees called Sideroxylon, of several species; so called from their hardness.

I'RONWÖRK, *n.* A general name of the parts or pieces of a building which consist of iron; any thing made of iron.

I'RONWÖRKS, *n. plu.* The works or establishment where pig-iron is wrought into bars, &c.

I'RONWÖRT, *n.* A genus of plants called Sideritis, of several species.

IRON'ICAL, *a.* [Fr. *ironique.* See *Irony.*] Expressing one thing and meaning another. An *ironical* expression is often accompanied with a manner of utterance which indicates that the speaker intends to be understood in a sense directly contrary to that which the words convey.

IRON'ICALLY, *adv.* By way of irony; by the use of irony. A commendation may be *ironically* severe.

I'RONIST, *n.* One who deals in irony. *Pope.*

I'RONY, *a.* [from *iron.*] Made or consisting of iron; partaking of iron; as *irony* chains; *irony* particles. *Hammond.*

2. Resembling iron; hard.

I'RONY, *n.* [Fr. *ironie;* L. *ironia;* Gr. *ειρωνια*, from *ειρων*, a dissembler in speech.] A mode of speech expressing a sense contrary to that which the speaker intends to convey; as, Nero was a very virtuous prince; Pope Hildebrand was remarkable for his meekness and humility. When irony is uttered, the dissimulation is generally apparent from the manner of speaking, as by a smile or an arch look, or perhaps by an affected gravity of countenance. Irony in writing may also be detected by the manner of expression.

I'ROUS, *a.* [from *ire.*] Apt to be angry. *Obs.* *Chaucer.*

IRRA'DIANCE, IRRA'DIANCY, *n.* [L. *irradians*, from *irradio.* See *Irradiate.*]

1. Emission of rays of light on an object.
2. Beams of light emitted; luster; splendor. *Milton.*

IRRA'DIATE, *v. t.* [L. *irradio; in* and *radio*, to shine. See *Ray.*]

1. To illuminate; to brighten; to make splendid; to adorn with luster. *South.*
2. To enlighten intellectually; to illuminate; as, to *irradiate* the mind. *Milton.*
3. To animate by heat or light. *Hale.*
4. To decorate with shining ornaments. *Pope.*

IRRA'DIATE, *v. i.* To emit rays; to shine.

IRRA'DIATE, *a.* Adorned with shining ornaments. *Mason.*

IRRA'DIATED, *pp.* Illuminated; enlightened; made luminous or bright; decorated with rays of light or with something shining.

IRRA'DIATING, *ppr.* Illuminating; decorating with beams of light.

IRRADIA'TION, *n.* The act of emitting beams of light.

2. Illumination; brightness.
3. Intellectual light. *Hale.*
4. The act of emitting minute particles or effluvia from some substance. *Encyc.*

IRRA'TIONAL, *a.* [L. *irrationalis; in* and *rationalis*, from *ratio.*]

1. Not rational; void of reason or understanding. Brutes are *irrational* animals.
2. Not according to the dictates of reason; contrary to reason; absurd. To pursue a course of life which destroys happiness, is *irrational.*

IRRATIONAL'ITY, *n.* Want of reason or the powers of understanding.

IRRA'TIONALLY, *adv.* Without reason; in a manner contrary to reason; absurdly.

IRRECLA'IMABLE, *a.* [*in* and *reclaimable.*]

1. Not to be reclaimed; that cannot be recalled from error or vice; that cannot be brought to reform. *Addison.*
2. That cannot be tamed.

IRRECLA'IMABLY, *adv.* So as not to admit of reformation.

IRRECONCI'LABLE, *a.* [*in* and *reconcilable.*]

1. Not to be recalled to amity, or a state of friendship and kindness; retaining enmity that cannot be appeased or subdued; as an *irreconcilable* enemy or faction.
2. That cannot be appeased or subdued; as *irreconcilable* enmity or hatred.
3. That cannot be made to agree or be consistent; incongruous; incompatible; as *irreconcilable* absurdities. It is followed by *with* or *to.* A man's conduct may be *irreconcilable to* or *with* his avowed principles.

IRRECONCI'LABLENESS, *n.* The quality of being irreconcilable; incongruity; incompatibility.

IRRECONCI'LABLY, *adv.* In a manner that precludes reconciliation. Men may be *irreconcilably* opposed to each other.

IRREC'ONCILE, *v. t.* To prevent from being reconciled. [*Ill.*] *Bp. Taylor.*

IRRECONCI'LED, *a.* [*in* and *reconciled.*]

1. Not reconciled.
2. Not atoned for. *Shak.*

IRRECONCI'LEMENT, *n.* Want of reconciliation; disagreement.

IRRECONCILIA'TION, *n.* Want of reconciliation. *Prideaux.*

IRRECÖV'ERABLE, *a.* [*in* and *recoverable.*]

1. Not to be recovered or repaired; as an *irrecoverable* loss.
2. That cannot be regained. Time past is *irrecoverable.* *Rogers.*
3. That cannot be obtained by demand or suit; as a debt. *Franklin.*
4. Not be remedied; as *irrecoverable* misery. *Tillotson.*

IRRECÖV'ERABLENESS, *n.* The state of being irrecoverable. *Donne.*

IRRECÖV'ERABLY, *adv.* Beyond recovery; beyond the possibility of being regained, repaired or remedied. Happiness may be *irrecoverably* lost.

2. Beyond the possibility of being reclaimed. A profligate may be *irrecoverably* abandoned to vice.

IRRECU'PERABLE, *a.* [L. *in* and *recupero*, to recover.] Irrecoverable. [*Not used.*]

IRRECU'PERABLY, *adv.* Irrecoverably. [*Not used.*]

IRREDEE'MABLE, *a.* [*in* and *redeemable.*]

1. That cannot be redeemed.
2. Not subject to be paid at the pleasure of government; as *irredeemable* debts; *irredeemable* certificates or stock. *Hamilton. Smollett.*

IRREDEE'MABLENESS, IRREDEEMABIL'ITY, *n.* The quality of being not redeemable.

IRREDU'CIBLE, *a.* [*in* and *reducible.*] Not to be reduced; that cannot be brought back to a former state.

2. That cannot be reduced or changed to a different state; as corpuscles of air *irreducible* into water. *Boyle.*

IRREDU'CIBLENESS, *n.* The quality of being irreducible.

IRREFRA'GABLE, *a.* [*in* and *refragable*, L. *refragor; re* and the root of *frango*, to break.] That cannot be refuted or overthrown; incontestable; undeniable; as an *irrefragable* argument; *irrefragable* reason or evidence. *Atterbury. Swift.*

IRREFRA'GABLENESS, IRREFRAGABIL'ITY, *n.* The quality of being irrefragable or incapable of refutation.

IRREFRA'GABLY, *adv.* With force or strength that cannot be overthrown; with certainty beyond refutation. We say, the point in debate was *irrefragably* proved.

IRREFU'TABLE, *a.* [Low L. *irrefutabilis.* See *Refute.*] That cannot be refuted or disproved. *Bp. Hall.*

IRREFU'TABLY, *adv.* Beyond the possibility of refutation. *Romeyn.*

IRREGEN'ERACY, *n.* Unregeneracy. *J. M. Mason.*

IRREG'ULAR, *a.* [Fr. *irregulier;* L. *irregularis; in* and *regularis, regula.* See *Regular.*]

1. Not regular; not according to common form or rules; as an *irregular* building or fortification.
2. Not according to established principles or customs; deviating from usage; as the *irregular* proceedings of a legislative body.
3. Not conformable to nature or the usual operation of natural laws; as an *irregular* action of the heart and arteries.
4. Not according to the rules of art; immethodical; as *irregular* verse; an *irregular* discourse.
5. Not in conformity to laws, human or divine; deviating from the rules of moral rectitude; vicious; as *irregular* conduct or propensities.

6. Not straight; as an *irregular* line or course.
7. Not uniform; as *irregular* motion.
8. In *grammar*, an *irregular* noun or verb is one which deviates from the common rules in its inflections.

IRREG'ULAR, *n.* A soldier not in regular service. *Kent.*

IRREGULAR'ITY, *n.* [Fr. *irregularité.*]
1. Deviation from a straight line or from any common or established rule; deviation from method or order; as the *irregularity* of proceedings.
2. Deviation from law, human or divine, or from moral rectitude; inordinate practice; vice. It is a favorable symptom when a profligate man becomes ashamed of his *irregularities.*

IRREG'ULARLY, *adv.* Without rule, method or order.

IRREG'ULATE, *v. t.* To make irregular; to disorder. [*Not in use.*] *Brown.*

IRREL'ATIVE, *a.* [*in* and *relative.*] Not relative; unconnected.

Irrelative chords, in music, have no common sound.

IRREL'ATIVELY, *adv.* Unconnectedly. *Boyle.*

IRREL'EVANCY, *n.* [from *irrelevant.*] Inapplicability; the quality of not being applicable, or of not serving to aid and support; as the *irrelevancy* of an argument or of testimony to a case in question.

IRREL'EVANT, *a.* [*in* and Fr. *relever*, to raise, from *elever*, *lever*, L. *elevo*, *levo*, to raise.]

Not relevant; not applicable or pertinent; not serving to support. We call evidence, testimony and arguments *irrelevant* to a cause, when they are inapplicable to it, or do not serve to support it.

IRREL'EVANTLY, *adv.* Without being to the purpose.

IRRELIE'VABLE, *a.* Not admitting relief. *Hargrave.*

IRRELIG'ION, *n.* [Fr.; *in* and *religion.*] Want of religion, or contempt of it; impiety. *Dryden.*

IRRELIG'IONIST, *n.* One who is destitute of religious principles; a despiser of religion. *Nott.*

IRRELIG'IOUS, *a.* [Fr. *irreligieux.*] Destitute of religious principles; contemning religion; impious; ungodly.

Shame and reproach are generally the portion of the impious and *irreligious.* *South.*

2. Contrary to religion; profane; impious; wicked; as an *irreligious* speech; *irreligious* conduct.

IRRELIG'IOUSLY, *adv.* With impiety; wickedly.

IRRELIG'IOUSNESS, *n.* Want of religious principles or practices; ungodliness.

IRRE'MEABLE, *a.* [L. *irremeabilis; in* and *remeo*, to return; *re* and *meo*, to pass.]

Admitting no return; as an *irremeable* way. *Dryden.*

IRREME'DIABLE, *a.* [Fr.; *in* and *remediable*, from *remedy.*]
1. Not to be remedied; that cannot be cured; as an *irremediable* disease or evil.
2. Not to be corrected or redressed; as *irremediable* error or mischief.

IRREME'DIABLENESS, *n.* State of being irremediable.

IRREME'DIABLY, *adv.* In a manner or degree that precludes remedy, cure or correction. *Bp. Taylor.*

IRREMIS'SIBLE, *a.* [Fr.; *in* and *remissible*; L. *remitto.* See *Remit.*]

Not to be pardoned; that cannot be forgiven or remitted. *Whiston.*

IRREMIS'SIBLENESS, *n.* The quality of being unpardonable. *Hammond.*

IRREMIS'SIBLY, *adv.* So as not to be pardoned. *Sherwood.*

IRREMÖVABIL'ITY, *n.* [See *Irremovable.*] The quality or state of being irremovable, or not removable from office.

IRREMÖV'ABLE, *a.* [*in* and *removable.*]
1. That cannot be moved or changed. *Shak.*
2. That cannot be legally or constitutionally removed from office.

IRREMU'NERABLE, *a.* [*in* and *remunerable.*] That cannot be rewarded.

IRRENOWN'ED, *a.* Not renowned; not celebrated. *Spenser.*

IRREPARABIL'ITY, *n.* [See *Irreparable.*] The quality or state of being irreparable, or beyond repair or recovery. *Sterne.*

IRREP'ARABLE, *a.* [Fr. from L. *irreparabilis.* See *Repair.*]
1. That cannot be repaired or mended; as an *irreparable* breach.
2. That cannot be recovered or regained; as an *irreparable* loss. *Milton. Addison.*

IRREP'ARABLY, *adv.* In a manner or degree that precludes recovery or repair.

IRREPEALABIL'ITY, *n.* [from *irrepealable.*] The quality of being irrepealable.

IRREPE'ALABLE, *a.* [*in* and *repealable.*] See *Repeal.*]

That cannot be legally repealed or annulled. *Sullivan.*

IRREPE'ALABLENESS, *n.* Irrepealability.

IRREPE'ALABLY, *adv.* Beyond the power of repeal.

IRREPENT'ANCE, *n.* Want of repentance; impenitence. *Mountagu.*

IRREPLEV'IABLE, *a.* [*in* and *repleviable.*] That cannot be replevied.

IRREPLEV'ISABLE, *a.* [*in* and *replevisable.*] That cannot be replevied.

IRREPREHENS'IBLE, *a.* [*in* and *reprehensible.*]

Not reprehensible; not to be blamed or censured; free from fault. *Vattel, Trans.*

IRREPREHENS'IBLENESS, *n.* The quality of being irreprehensible.

IRREPREHENS'IBLY, *adv.* In a manner not to incur blame; without blame. *Sherwood.*

IRREPRESENT'ABLE, *a.* [*in* and *represent.*]

Not to be represented; that cannot be figured or represented by any image. *Stillingfleet.*

IRREPRESS'IBLE, *a.* [*in* and *repressible.*] That cannot be repressed.

IRREPRŌACHABLE, *a.* [*in* and *reproachable.*]

That cannot be justly reproached; free from blame; upright; innocent. An *irreproachable* life is the highest honor of a rational being.

IRREPRŌACHABLENESS, *n.* The quality or state of being not reproachable.

IRREPRŌACHABLY, *adv.* In a manner not to deserve reproach; blamelessly; as deportment *irreproachably* upright.

IRREPRÖV'ABLE, *a.* [*in* and *reprovable.*] That cannot be justly reproved; blameless; upright.

IRREPRÖV'ABLY, *adv.* So as not to be liable to reproof or blame. *Weever.*

IRRESIST'ANCE, *n.* *s* as *z.* [*in* and *resistance.*]

Forbearance to resist; non-resistance; passive submission. *Paley.*

IRRESISTIBIL'ITY, } *n.* [from *irresistible.*]
IRRESIST'IBLENESS,

The quality of being irresistible; power or force beyond resistance or opposition. *Hammond.*

IRRESIST'IBLE, *a.* [Fr.; *in* and *resistible.* See *Resist.*]

That cannot be successfully resisted or opposed; superior to opposition.

An *irresistible* law of our nature impels us to seek happiness. *J. M. Mason.*

IRRESIST'IBLY, *adv.* With a power that cannot be successfully resisted or opposed. *Dryden.*

IRRES'OLUBLE, *a.* *s* as *z.* [L. *in* and *resolvo.*]

Not to be dissolved; incapable of dissolution. *Boyle.*

IRRES'OLUBLENESS, *n.* The quality of being indissoluble; resistance to separation of parts by heat. *Boyle.*

IRRES'OLUTE, *a.* *s* as *z.* [*in* and *resolute.*] Not firm or constant in purpose; not decided; not determined; wavering; given to doubt. *Irresolute* men either resolve not at all, or resolve and re-resolve.

IRRES'OLUTELY, *adv.* Without firmness of mind; without decision.

IRRES'OLUTENESS, *n.* Want of firm determination or purpose; vacillation of mind.

IRRESOLU'TION, *n.* [Fr.; *in* and *resolution.*]

Want of resolution; want of decision in purpose; a fluctuation of mind, as in doubt, or between hope and fear. *Addison.*

IRRESOLV'EDLY, *adv.* *s* as *z.* [*in* and *resolved.*]

Without settled determination. [*Little used.*] *Boyle.*

IRRESPEȻT'IVE, *a.* [*in* and *respective.*] Not regarding circumstances.

According to this doctrine, it must be resolved wholly into the absolute, *irrespective* will of God. *Rogers.*

IRRESPEȻT'IVELY, *adv.* Without regard to circumstances, or not taking them into consideration. *Hammond.*

IRRES'PIRABLE, *a.* [*in* and *respirable.*] Unfit for respiration; not having the qualities which support animal life; as *irrespirable* air.

IRRESPONSIBIL'ITY, *n.* Want of responsibility.

IRRESPŌNS'IBLE, *a.* [*in* and *responsible.*] Not responsible; not liable or able to answer for consequences; not answerable.

IRRETEN'TIVE, *a.* Not retentive or apt to retain. *Skelton.*

IRRETRIE'VABLE, *a.* [*in* and *retrievable*, from *retrieve.*]

Not to be recovered or repaired; irrecoverable; irreparable; as an *irretrievable* loss.

IRRETRIE'VABLENESS, *n.* The state of being irretrievable.

IRRETRIE'VABLY, *adv.* Irreparably; irrecoverably; in a manner not to be regained. *Woodward.*

IRRETURN'ABLE, *a.* Not to be returned.

IRREV'ERENCE, *n.* [L. *irreverentia; in* and *reverentia.* See *Reverence.*]

1. Want of reverence, or want of veneration; want of a due regard to the authority and character of the Supreme Being. *Irreverence* toward God is analagous to *disrespect* toward man.

2. The state of being disregarded; *applied to men.* But this word is appropriately applicable to the Supreme Being and to his laws and institutions.

IRREV'ERENT, *a.* [Fr.; *in* and *reverent.*]

1. Wanting in reverence and veneration; not entertaining or manifesting due regard to the Supreme Being.

2. Proceeding from irreverence; expressive of a want of veneration; as an *irreverent* thought, word or phrase.

3. Wanting in respect to superiors. *Milton.*

IRREV'ERENTLY, *adv.* Without due regard to the authority and character of the Supreme Being; in an irreverent manner.

2. Without due respect to superiors.

IRREVERS'IBLE, *a.* [*in* and *reversible.*] That cannot be reversed; that cannot be recalled, repealed or annulled; as an *irreversible* decree or sentence.

IRREVERS'IBLENESS, *n.* State of being irreversible.

IRREVERS'IBLY, *adv.* In a manner which precludes a reversal or repeal.

IRREVOCABIL'ITY, } *n.* State of being
IRREV'OCABLENESS, } irrevocable.

IRREV'OCABLE, *a.* [Fr. from L. *irrevocabilis; in* and *revocabilis, revoco; re* and *voco,* to call.]

Not to be recalled or revoked; that cannot be reversed, repealed or annulled; as an *irrevocable* decree, sentence, edict or doom; *irrevocable* fate; an *irrevocable* promise. *Milton. Dryden.*

IRREV'OCABLY, *adv.* Beyond recall; in a manner precluding repeal.

IRREVO'KABLE, *a.* [*in* and *revokable.*] Not to be recalled; irrevocable. *Asiat. Res.*

IRREV'OLUBLE, *a.* That has no revolution. [*Not used.*] *Milton.*

IR'RIGATE, *v. t.* [L. *irrigo; in* and *rigo,* to water.]

1. To water; to wet; to moisten; to bedew. *Ray.*

2. To water, as land, by causing a stream to flow upon it and spread over it.

IR'RIGATED, *pp.* Watered; moistened.

IR'RIGATING, *ppr.* Watering; wetting; moistening.

IRRIGA'TION, *n.* The act of watering or moistening.

2. In *agriculture,* the operation of causing water to flow over lands for nourishing plants.

IRRIG'UOUS, *a.* [L. *irriguus.* See *Irrigate.*]

1. Watered; watery; moist.

> The flowery lap
> Of some *irriguous* valley spreads her store. *Milton.*

2. Dewy; moist. *Philips.*

IRRIS'ION, *n.* *s* as *z.* [L. *irrisio, irrideo; in* and *rideo,* to laugh.] The act of laughing at another. *Woodward.*

IRRITABIL'ITY, *n.* [from *irritable.*] Susceptibility of excitement; the quality of being easily irritated or exasperated; as *irritability* of temper.

2. In *physiology,* one of the four faculties of the sensorium, by which fibrous contractions are caused in consequence of the irritations excited by external bodies. *Darwin.*

Irritability differs from *sensibility;* the most *irritable* parts of the body not being at all *sensible,* and vice versa. The heart is endued with the greatest *irritability.* *Haller. Encyc.*

IR'RITABLE, *a.* [from *irritate.*] Susceptible of excitement, or of heat and action, as animal bodies.

2. Very susceptible of anger or passion; easily inflamed or exasperated; as an *irritable* temper.

3. In *physiology,* susceptible of contraction, in consequence of the appulse of an external body.

> In general, there is nothing *irritable* in the animal body, but the muscular fibers. *Haller. Encyc.*

IR'RITANT, *a.* Irritating.

IR'RITANT, *n.* That which excites or irritates. *Rush.*

IR'RITATE, *v. t.* [L. *irrito; in* and *ira,* wrath; W. *irad,* pungency, passion, rage; or perhaps more properly from Sw. *reta,* to provoke; G. *reitzen,* to tickle, vellicate, irritate.]

1. To excite heat and redness in the skin or flesh of living animal bodies, as by friction; to inflame; to fret; as, to *irritate* a wounded part by a coarse bandage.

2. To excite anger; to provoke; to tease; to exasperate. Never *irritate* a child for trifling faults. The insolence of a tyrant *irritates* his subjects.

3. To increase action or violence; to highten excitement in.

> Air, if very cold, *irritateth* the flame. *Bacon.*

4. To cause fibrous contractions in an extreme part of the sensorium, as by the appulse of an external body. *Darwin.*

IR'RITATED, *pp.* Excited; provoked; caused to contract.

IR'RITATING, *ppr.* Exciting; angering; provoking; causing to contract.

IRRITA'TION, *n.* The operation of exciting heat, action and redness in the skin or flesh of living animals, by friction or other means.

2. The excitement of action in the animal system by the application of food, medicines and the like.

3. Excitement of anger or passion; provocation; exasperation; anger.

4. In *physiology,* an exertion or change of some extreme part of the sensorium residing in the muscles or organs of sense, in consequence of the appulses of external bodies. *Darwin.*

> *Irritation* is the effect of a stimulus applied to an irritable part. *Coxe.*

IR'RITATIVE, *a.* Serving to excite or irritate.

2. Accompanied with or produced by increased action or irritation; as an *irritative* fever. *Darwin.*

IR'RITATORY, *a.* Exciting; stimulating. *Hales.*

IRRORA'TION, *n.* [L. *irroratio; in* and *ros.*]

The act of bedewing; the state of being moistened with dew. *Spallanzani, Trans.*

IRRUP'TION, *n.* [Fr. from L. *irruptio; in* and *rumpo,* to break or burst.]

1. A bursting in; a breaking or sudden, violent rushing into a place. Holland has been often inundated by *irruptions* of the sea.

2. A sudden invasion or incursion; a sudden, violent inroad, or entrance of invaders into a place or country; as the *irruption* of the northern nations into France and Italy.

IRRUP'TIVE, *a.* Rushing in or upon.

IS, *v. i.* *iz.* [Sax. *is;* G. *ist;* D. *is;* L. *est;* Gr. εςι; Sans. *asti;* Pers. *est* or *hist.*]

The third person singular of the substantive verb, which is composed of three or four distinct roots, which appear in the words *am, be, are,* and *is.* *Is* and *was* coincide with the Latin *esse,* and Goth. *wesan.* In the indicative, present tense, it is thus varied; I am, thou art, he, she, or it, *is;* we, ye or you, they, are. In writing and speaking, the vowel is often dropped; as, he's gone; there's none left.

IS'ABEL, *n.* [Fr. *isabelle.*] Isabel yellow is a brownish yellow, with a shade of brownish red. *Kirwan.*

ISAGOG'IC, } *a.* [Gr. εισαγωγικος.] In-
ISAGOG'ICAL, } troductory. *Gregory.*

IS'AGON, *n.* [Gr. ισος, equal, and γωνια, an angle.] A figure whose angles are equal.

IS'ATIS, *n.* In *zoology,* the arctic fox or Canis lagopus. *Encyc.*

ISCHIAD'IC, *a.* [L. *ischiadicus,* from *ischias,* the *sciatica,* from *ischium,* the hip; Gr. ισχιον, ισχιαδικος.]

Pertaining to the hip. The ischiadic passion or disease is ranked by Cullen with rheumatism. It is a rheumatic affection of the hip joint. It is called also *sciatica.* It is sometimes seated in the tendinous expansion which covers the muscles of the thigh, but its most common seat is in the muscles, or in the capsular ligament, and it is then either rheumatic or gouty. *Parr. Johnson.*

ISCHURET'IC, *a.* [See *Ischury.*] Having the quality of relieving ischury.

ISCHURET'IC, *n.* A medicine adapted to relieve ischury. *Coxe.*

IS'CHURY, *n.* [Gr. ισχουρια, from ισχω, to stop, and ουρον, urine.]

A stoppage or suppression of urine. *Coxe. Encyc.*

IS'ERIN, } *n.* [G. *eisen,* iron.] A mineral
IS'ERINE, } of an iron black color, and of a splendent metallic luster, occurring in small obtuse angular grains. It is harder than feldspar, and consists of the oxyds of iron and titanium, with a small portion of uranium. *Ure.*

Ish, a termination of English words, is, in Sax. *isc,* Dan. *isk,* G. *isch;* and not improbably, it is the termination *esque,* in French, as in *grotesque,* It. *esco,* in *grotesco,* and the Latin termination of the inceptive verb, as in *fervesco*. Annexed to English adjectives, *ish* denotes diminution, or a small degree of the quality; as *whitish*, from *white*; *yellowish*, from *yellow*.

Ish annexed to names forms a possessive adjective; as in *Swedish*, *Danish*, *English*.

Ish annexed to common nouns forms an adjective denoting a participation of the qualities expressed by the noun; as *foolish*, from *fool*; *roguish*, from *rogue*; *brutish*, from *brute*. This is the more common use of this termination.

I'SICLE, a pendant shoot of ice, is more generally written *icicle*. [See *Ice* and *Icicle*.]

I'SINGLASS, *n. i'zinglass.* [that is, *ise* or *ice-glass*.]

A substance consisting chiefly of gelatin, of a firm texture and whitish color, prepared from the sounds or air-bladders of certain fresh water fishes, particularly of the huso, a fish of the sturgeon kind, found in the rivers of Russia. It is used as an agglutinant, and in fining wines. *Encyc.*

ISINGLASS-STONE. [See *Mica*.]

IS'LAMISM, *n.* [from the Ar. سلم salama, to be free, safe or devoted to God.]

The true faith, according to the Mohammedans; Mohammedanism. *Encyc.*

ISLAND, *n. i'land.* [This is an absurd compound of *isle* and *land*, that is, *land-in-water land*, or *ieland-land*. There is no such legitimate word in English, and it is found only in books. The genuine word always used in discourse is our native word, Sax. *ealond*, D. G. *eiland*.]

1. A tract of land surrounded by water.
2. A large mass of floating ice, is called an *island of ice*.

I'SLANDER, *n. i'lander.* An inhabitant of an ieland.

ISLE, } *n. ile.* [Fr. *isle* or *île*, from It. *isola*,
ILE, } L. *insula*.]

1. A tract of land surrounded by water, or a detached portion of land embosomed in the ocean, in a lake or river.

The *isles* shall wait for his law. Is. xlii.

2. A passage in a church. [See *Aisle*.]

ISLET, *n. i'let.* A little ieland.

ISOCH'RONAL, } *a.* [Gr. ισος, equal, and
ISOCH'RONOUS, } χρονος, time.]

Uniform in time; of equal time; performed in equal times.

An *isochronal* line, is that in which a heavy body is supposed to descend without acceleration. *Bailey.*

Isochronal vibrations of a pendulum are such as are performed in the same space of time. *Encyc.*

IS'OLATE, *v. t.* [It. *isola*, an isle or ieland.] To place in a detached situation; to place by itself; to insulate. *Med. Repos.*

IS'OLATED, *pp.* or *a.* [Fr. *isolé*; It. *isolato*, from *isola*, an isle.]

Standing detached from others of a like kind; placed by itself or alone.

IS'OLATING, *ppr.* Placing by itself or detached like an isle.

ISOMORPH'ISM, *n.* [Gr. ισος, like, and μορφη, form.]

The quality of a substance by which it is capable of replacing another in a compound, without an alteration of its primitive form.

ISOMORPH'OUS, *a.* Capable of retaining its primitive form in a compound. *Ed. Rev.*

IS'ONOMY, *n.* [Gr. ισος, equal, and νομος, law.]

Equal law; equal distribution of rights and privileges. *Mitford.*

ISOPERIMET'RICAL, *a.* [See *Isoperimetry*.]

Having equal boundaries; as *isoperimetrical* figures or bodies.

ISOPERIM'ETRY, *n.* [Gr. ισος, equal, περι, around, and μετρον, measure.]

In *geometry*, the science of figures having equal perimeters or boundaries.

ISOS'CELES, *a.* [Gr. ισοσκελης; ισος, equal, and σκελος, leg.]

Having two legs only that are equal; as an *isosceles* triangle.

IS'RAELITE, *n.* A descendant of Israel or Jacob; a Jew.

ISRAELIT'IC, } *a.* Pertaining to Israel.
ISRAELI'TISH, } *J. P. Smith.*

ISOTHERM'AL, *a.* [Gr. ισος, equal, proper, and θερμα, heat.] Warmed by its own heat. *Ure.*

ISOTON'IC, *a.* [Gr. ισος, equal, and τονος, tone.]

Having equal tones. The *isotonic* system, in music, consists of intervals, in which each concord is alike tempered, and in which there are twelve equal semitones.

IS'SUABLE, *a.* [from *issue*.] That may be issued. In *law*, an *issuable* term, is one in which issues are made up. *Blackstone.*

ISSUE, *n. ish'u.* [Fr. *issue*; It. *uscio*, a door, and *uscire*, to go out. It may coincide in origin with Heb. Ch. יצא, Eth. ወፀአ watsa.]

1. The act of passing or flowing out; a moving out of any inclosed place; egress; applied to water or other fluid, to smoke, to a body of men, &c. We say, an *issue* of water from a pipe, from a spring, or from a river; an *issue* of blood from a wound, of air from a bellows; an *issue* of people from a door or house.
2. A sending out; as the *issue* of an order from a commanding officer or from a court; the *issue* of money from a treasury.
3. Event; consequence; end or ultimate result. Our present condition will be best for us in the *issue*.
4. Passage out; outlet.

To God the Lord belong the *issues* from death. Ps. lxviii.

5. Progeny; a child or children; offspring; as, he had *issue*, a son; and we speak of *issue* of the whole blood or half blood. A man dies without *issue*.
6. Produce of the earth, or profits of land, tenements or other property. A conveyed to B all his right to a term for years, with all the *issues*, rents and profits.
7. In *surgery*, a fontanel; a little ulcer made in some part of an animal body, to promote discharges. *Encyc.*
8. Evacuation; discharge; a flux or running. Lev. xii. Matt. ix.
9. In *law*, the close or result of pleadings; the point of matter depending in suit, on which the parties join, and put the case to trial by a jury. *Cowel.*
10. A giving out from a repository; delivery; as an *issue* of rations or provisions from a store, or of powder from a magazine.

IS'SUE, *v. i.* [It. *uscire*. See the Noun.]

1. To pass or flow out; to run out of any inclosed place; to proceed, as from a source; as, water *issues* from springs; blood *issues* from wounds; sap or gum *issues* from trees; light *issues* from the sun.
2. To go out; to rush out. Troops *issued* from the town and attacked the besiegers.
3. To proceed, as progeny; to spring.

Of thy sons that shall *issue* from thee—2 Kings xx.

4. To proceed; to be produced; to arise; to grow or accrue; as rents and profits *issuing* from land, tenements, or a capital stock.
5. In *legal pleadings*, to come to a point in fact or law, on which the parties join and rest the decision of the cause. Our lawyers say, a cause *issues* to the court or to the jury; it *issues* in demurrer.
6. To close; to end. We know not how the cause will *issue*.

IS'SUE, *v. t.* To send out; to put into circulation; as, to *issue* money from a treasury, or notes from a bank.

2. To send out; to deliver from authority; as, to *issue* an order from the department of war; to *issue* a writ or precept.
3. To deliver for use; as, to *issue* provisions from a store.

IS'SUED, *pp.* Descended; sent out. *Shak.*

IS'SUELESS, *a.* Having no issue or progeny; wanting children. *Shak.*

IS'SUING, *ppr.* Flowing or passing out; proceeding from; sending out.

IS'SUING, *n.* A flowing or passing out.

2. Emission; a sending out, as of bills or notes.

ISTHMUS, *n. ist'mus.* [L. from Gr. ισθμος.] A neck or narrow slip of land by which two continents are connected, or by which a peninsula is united to the main land. Such is the Neck, so called, which connects Boston with the main land at Roxbury. But the word is applied to land of considerable extent, between seas; as the *isthmus* of Darien, which connects North and South America, and the *isthmus* between the Euxine and Caspian seas.

IT, *pron.* [Sax. *hit*; D. *het*; G. *es*; L. *id*.]

1. A substitute or pronoun of the neuter gender, sometimes called demonstrative, and standing for any thing except males and females. "Keep thy heart with all diligence, for out of *it* are the issues of life." Prov. iv. Here *it* is the substitute for *heart*.
2. *It* is much used as the nominative case or word to verbs called impersonal; as *it* rains; *it* snows. In this case, there is no determinate thing to which it can be referred.

In other cases, *it* may be referred to *matter*, *affair*, or some other word. Is *it* come to this?

3. Very often, *it* is used to introduce a sentence, preceding a verb as a nominative, but referring to a clause or distinct member of the sentence. "*It* is well ascertained, that the figure of the earth is an oblate spheroid." What is well ascertained?

The answer will show: the figure of the earth is an oblate spheroid; *it* [that] is well ascertained. Here *it* represents the clause of the sentence, "the figure of the earth," &c. If the order of the sentence is inverted, the use of *it* is superseded. The figure of the earth is an oblate spheroid; *that* is well ascertained.

It, like *that*, is often a substitute for a sentence or clause of a sentence.

4. *It* often begins a sentence, when a personal pronoun, or the name of a person, or a masculine noun follows. *It* is I: be not afraid. *It* was Judas who betrayed Christ. When a question is asked, *it* follows the verb; as, who was *it* that betrayed Christ?

5. *It* is used also for the state of a person or affair.

> How is *it* with our general? *Shak.*

6. *It* is used after intransitive verbs very indefinitely and sometimes ludicrously, but rarely in an elevated style.

> If Abraham brought all with him, it is not probable he meant to walk *it* back for his pleasure. *Raleigh.*

> The Lacedemonians, at the straits of Thermopylae, when their arms failed them, fought *it* out with nails and teeth. *Dryden.*

> Whether the charmer sinner *it*, or saint *it*. *Pope.*

ITAL'IAN, *a.* Pertaining to Italy.

ITAL'IAN, *n.* A native of Italy.

2. The language used in Italy, or by the Italians.

ITAL'IANATE, *v. t.* To render Italian, or conformable to Italian customs.

ITAL'IANIZE, *v. i.* To play the Italian; to speak Italian. *Cotgrave.*

ITAL'IC, *a.* Relating to Italy or its characters.

ITAL'ICIZE, *v. t.* To write or print in Italic characters.

ITAL'ICS, *n. plu.* Italic letters or characters; characters first used in Italy, and which stand inclining; *the letters in which this clause is printed.* They are used to distinguish words for emphasis, importance, antithesis, &c.

ITCH, *n.* [Sax. *gictha*; D. *jeukte*; Ch. חכוך; Ar. حَكَّة; Eth. ሐከከ hakke. See the Verb.]

1. A cutaneous disease of the human race, appearing in small watery pustules on the skin, accompanied with an uneasiness or irritation that inclines the patient to use friction. This disease is supposed by some authors to be occasioned by a small insect, a species of Acarus, as the microscope detects these insects in the vesicles. Others suppose the pustules only form a nidus for the insects. This disease is taken only by contact or contagion.

2. The sensation in the skin occasioned by the disease.

3. A constant teasing desire; as an *itch* for praise; an *itch* for scribbling. *Dryden.*

ITCH, *v. i.* [G. *jucken*, D. *jeuken*, to itch; Ch. חכך; Ar. حَكَّ; Eth. ሐከከ hakak, to scratch. Hence Ar. to be affected with the itch. Class Cg. No. 22.]

1. To feel a particular uneasiness in the skin, which inclines the person to scratch the part.

2. To have a constant desire or teasing inclination; as *itching* ears. 2 Tim. iv.

ITCH'ING, *ppr.* Having a sensation that calls for scratching.

2. Having a constant desire.

ITCH'Y, *a.* Infected with the itch.

I'TEM, *adv.* [L. *item*, also.] Also; a word used when something is to be added.

I'TEM, *n.* An article; a separate particular in an account. The account consists of many *items.*

2. A hint; an innuendo.

I'TEM, *v. t.* To make a note or memorandum of. *Addison.*

IT'ERABLE, *a.* That may be repeated. [*Not used.*] *Brown.*

IT'ERANT, *a.* [See *Iterate.*] Repeating; as an *iterant* echo. *Bacon.*

IT'ERATE, *v. t.* [L. *itero*, to repeat, from *iter*, a going.]

To repeat; to utter or do a second time; as, to *iterate* advice or admonition; to *iterate* a trespass.

IT'ERATED, *pp.* Repeated.

IT'ERATING, *ppr.* Repeating; uttering or doing over again.

ITERA'TION, *n.* [L. *iteratio.*] Repetition; recital or performance a second time. *Bacon.*

IT'ERATIVE, *a.* Repeating.

ITIN'ERANT, *a.* [L. *iter*, a way or journey.]

Passing or traveling about a country; wandering; not settled; as an *itinerant* preacher.

ITIN'ERANT, *n.* One who travels from place to place, particularly a preacher; one who is unsettled.

ITIN'ERARY, *n.* [Fr. *itineraire*; Low L. *itinerarium*, from *iter*, a going.]

An account of travels or of the distances of places; as the *itinerary* of Antoninus.

ITIN'ERARY, *a.* Traveling; passing from place to place, or done on a journey. *Bacon.*

ITIN'ERATE, *v. i.* [L. *iter*, a going; Low L. *itinero.*]

To travel from place to place, particularly for the purpose of preaching; to wander without a settled habitation.

ITSELF', *pron.* [*it* and *self.*] The neutral reciprocal pronoun, or substitute applied to things. The thing is good in *itself*; it stands by *itself.*

> Borrowing of foreigners, in *itself*, makes not the kingdom rich or poor. *Locke.*

IT'TRIUM, *n.* The undecomposable base of yttria; but better written *yttrium*, unless *yttria* should be written *ittria.*

I'VORY, *n.* [Fr. *ivoire*; It. *avorio*; L. *ebur.*] The tusk of an elephant, a hard, solid substance, of a fine white color. This tooth is sometimes six or seven feet in length, hollow from the base to a certain highth, and filled with a compact medullary substance, seeming to contain a great number of glands. The ivory of Ceylon and Achem does not become yellow in wearing, and hence is preferred to that of Guinea. *Encyc.*

I'VORY, *a.* Consisting of ivory; as an *ivory* comb.

I'VORY-BLACK, *n.* A fine kind of soft blacking.

I'VY, *n.* [Sax. *ifig*; G. *epheu.*] A parasitic plant of the genus Hedera, which creeps along the ground, or if it finds support, rises on trees or buildings, climbing to a great highth.

> Direct the clasping *ivy* where to climb. *Milton.*

I'VYED, *a.* Overgrown with ivy. *Warton.*

END OF VOL I.

VOL. II.

AN AMERICAN DICTIONARY OF THE ENGLISH LANGUAGE.

J. This letter has been added to the English Alphabet in modern days; the letter I being written formerly in words where J is now used. It seems to have had the sound of *y*, in many words, as it still has in the German. The English sound of this letter may be expressed by *dzh*, or *edzh*, a compound sound coinciding exactly with that of *g*, in *genius;* the French *j*, with the articulation *d* preceding it. It is the tenth letter of the English Alphabet.

JAB'BER, *v. i.* [D. *gabberen*, or Fr. *jaboter*. Class Gb.]

To talk rapidly or indistinctly; to chatter; to prate. *Swift.*

JAB'BER, *n.* Rapid talk with indistinct utterance of words. *Swift.*

JAB'BERER, *n.* One that talks rapidly, indistinctly or unintelligibly.

JAB'BERING, *ppr.* Prating; talking rapidly and confusedly.

JAB'BERMENT, *n.* Idle prate. *Obs.* *Milton.*

JAB'IRU, *n.* An aquatic fowl of the crane kind.

The Jabiru is the *Mycteria Americana.* It resembles the stork. *Cuvier.*

JAC'AMAR, *n.* A kind of fowls arranged by Linne under the genus Alcedo; but their toes are differently placed, and their food consists of insects. They are about the size of a lark. Numerous species are described. *Encyc.*

The Jacamars are arranged in a separate genus, Galbula, and along with the woodpeckers in the order of climbers. *Cuvier.*

JA'CENT, *a.* [L. *jacens, jaceo*, to lie.] Lying at length. *Wotton.*

JA'CINTH, *n.* [a different orthography of *Hyacinth.*]

1. A genus of plants. [See *Hyacinth.*]

2. A species of pellucid gems. [See *Hyacinth.*] Rev. xxi.

JACK, *n.* [*zeku*, in Ethiopic, is the pronoun *he*, or *she.*]

1. A nickname or diminutive of John, used as a general term of contempt for any saucy or paltry fellow. *Johnson.*

2. The name of an instrument that supplies the place of a boy; an instrument to pull off boots. *Watts.*

3. An engine to turn a spit; as a kitchen *jack;* a smoke *jack.*

4. A young pike. *Mortimer.*

5. A coat of mail. [Sp. *xaco, xaqueta.*] *Hayward.*

6. A pitcher of waxed lether. *Dryden.*

7. A small bowl thrown out for a mark to the bowlers.

8. Part of a musical instrument called a virginal. *Bacon.*

9. The male of certain animals, as of the ass. [Arm. *ozach*, a husband.] *Arbuthnot.*

10. A horse or wooden frame on which wood or timber is sawed. *Ainsworth.*

11. In *sea-language*, a flag, ensign or colors, displayed from a staff on the end of a bowsprit. *Mar. Dict.*

12. In *Yorkshire*, half a pint. *Grose.* A quarter of a pint. *Pegge.*

Jack at all trades, a person who can turn his hand to any kind of business.

Jack by the hedge, a plant of the genus Erysimum, that grows under hedges. *Fam. of Plants.*

Jack in a box, a plant of the genus Hernandia.

2. A large wooden male screw, turning in a female one. *Mar. Dict.*

Jack with a lantern, an ignis fatuus, a meteor that appears in low moist lands.

Jack of the clock-house, a little man that strikes the quarters in a clock.

JACK'ALENT, *n.* [*Jack in lent*, a poor starved fellow.]

A simple sheepish fellow. *Shak.*

JACK'ANAPES, *n.* [*jack* and *ape.*] A monkey; an ape.

2. A coxcomb; an impertinent fellow.

A young upstart *jackanapes.* *Arbuthnot.*

JACK'ASS, *n.* The male of the ass.

JACK'-BLOCK, *n.* A block attached to the top-gallant-tie of a ship, to sway up or to strike the yard. *Mar. Dict.*

JACK'BOOTS, *n.* [See No. 5. supra.] Boots that serve as armor for the legs. *Spectator.*

JACK'DAW, *n.* [*jack* and *daw.*] A fowl of the genus Corvus, thievish and mischievous to the farmer. *Encyc.*

JACK'FLAG, *n.* A flag hoisted at the spritsail top-mast-head. *Encyc.*

JACK'PUDDING, *n.* [*jack* and *pudding.*] A merry Andrew; a buffoon; a zany. *Gay.*

JACK'SMITH, *n.* A smith who makes jacks for the chimney.

JACK'AL, *n.* [Sp. *chacal;* Turk. *chical.*] An animal of the genus Canis, resembling a dog and a fox; a native of Asia and Africa. It preys on poultry and other small animals. It is the *Canis aureus* of Linne. *Encyc. Cyc.*

JACK'ET, *n.* [Sp. *xaqueta*, a short loose coat; *xaco*, a short jacket; *xaquetilla*, a jacket; Fr. *jaquette;* Basque, *jacaya.*] A short close garment worn by males, extending downwards to the hips; a short coat.

JACK'ETED, *a.* Wearing a jacket.

JAC'OBIN, *n.* [So named from the place of meeting, which was the monastery of the monks called Jacobines.]

The *Jacobins*, in France, during the late revolution, were a society of violent revolutionists, who held secret meetings in which measures were concerted to direct the proceedings of the National Assembly. Hence, a Jacobin is the member of a club, or other person, who opposes government in a secret and unlawful manner or by violent means; a turbulent demagogue.

JAC'OBINE, *n.* A monk of the order of Dominicans.

2. A pigeon with a high tuft. *Ainsworth.*

JACOBIN'IC, } *a.* Resembling the Jaco-
JACOBIN'ICAL, } bins of France; turbulent; discontented with government; holding democratic principles.

JAC'OBINISM, *n.* Jacobinic principles; unreasonable or violent opposition to legitimate government; an attempt to overthrow or change government by secret cabals or irregular means; popular turbulence.

JAC'OBINIZE, *v. t.* To taint with Jacobinism. *Burke.*

JAC'OBITE, *n.* [from *Jacobus*, James.] A partizan or adherent of James II. king of England, after he abdicated the throne, and of his descendants; of course, an opposer of the revolution in 1688, in favor of William and Mary. *Bolingbroke.*

2. One of a sect of christians in Syria and Mesopotamia, who hold that Jesus Christ had but one nature. *Encyc. Cyc.*

JAC'OBITE, *a.* Pertaining to the partizans of James II.

JAC'OBITISM, *n.* The principles of the partizans of James II. *Mason.*

JACOB'S-LADDER, *n.* A plant of the genus Polemonium. *Fam. of Plants.*

JACOB'S-STAFF, *n.* A pilgrim's staff.

2. A staff concealing a dagger.

3. A cross staff; a kind of astrolabe. *Johnson.*

JAC'OBUS, *n.* [*Jacobus*, James.] A gold coin, value twenty-five shillings sterling, struck in the reign of James I. *L'Estrange.*

JACONET', *n.* A kind of coarse muslin.

JAC'TANCY, *n.* [L. *jactantia.*] A boasting. [*Not used.*]

JAC'TITATION, *n.* [L. *jactito*, *jacto.* It ought rather to be *jactation*, L. *jactatio.*]

1. A tossing of the body; restlessness. *Harvey.*

2. A term in the canon law for a false pretension to marriage; vain boasting. *Johnson.*

JAC'ULATE, *v. t.* [L. *jaculor.*] To dart.

JACULA'TION, *n.* The action of darting, throwing or lanching, as missive weapons. *Milton.*

JAC'ULATOR, *n.* The shooting fish, a species of Chætodon.

JAC'ULATORY, *a.* Darting or throwing out suddenly, or suddenly thrown out; uttered in short sentences. [See *Ejaculatory.*]

JADE, *n.* [of unknown origin. Qu. Sp. *jadear*, to pant.]

1. A mean or poor horse; a tired horse; a worthless nag.

Tired as a *jade* in overloaden cart. *Sidney.*

2. A mean woman; a word of contempt, noting sometimes age, but generally vice. *Johnson.*

She shines the first of battered *jades.* *Swift.*

3. A young woman; in irony or slight contempt. *Addison.*

JADE, *n.* A mineral called also nephrite or nephritic stone, remarkable for its hardness and tenacity, of a color more or less green, and of a resinous or oily aspect when polished. It is fusible into a glass or enamel. Cleaveland divides jade into three subspecies, *nephrite*, *saussurite*, and *axestone.* It is found in detached masses or inhering in rocks. *Werner. Jameson. Cleaveland.*

JADE, *v. t.* To tire; to fatigue; to weary with hard service; as, to *jade* a horse.

2. To weary with attention or study; to tire.

The mind once *jaded* by an attempt above its power, is very hardly brought to exert its force again. *Locke.*

3. To harass; to crush. *Shak.*

4. To tire or wear out in mean offices; as a *jaded* groom. *Shak.*

5. To ride; to rule with tyranny.

I do not now fool myself, to let imagination *jade* me. *Shak.*

JADE, *v. i.* To become weary; to lose spirit; to sink.

They are promising in the beginning, but they fail and *jade* and tire in the prosecution. *South.*

JA'DED, *pp.* Tired; wearied; fatigued; harassed.

JA'DERY, *n.* The tricks of a jade. *Beaum.*

JA'DING, *ppr.* Tiring; wearying; harassing.

JA'DISH, *a.* Vitious; bad, like a jade.

2. Unchaste. *L'Estrange.*

JAG, *n.* [Sp. *zaga*, a load, packed on the back part of a carriage. Qu.] A small load. *New-England.*

JAGG, *v. t.* [perhaps G. *zacken*, a tooth, a prong, to indent; Sw. *tagg*, a sharp point.]

To notch; to cut into notches or teeth like those of a saw.

JAGG, } *n.* A tooth of a saw; a denticula-
JAG, } tion. In *botany*, a cleft or division. *Martyn.*

JAG'GED, *pp.* Notched; uneven.

2. *a.* Having notches or teeth; cleft; divided; laciniate; as *jagged* leaves.

JAG'GEDNESS, *n.* The state of being denticulated; unevenness. *Peacham.*

JAG'GING, *ppr.* Notching; cutting into teeth; dividing.

JAG'GY, *a.* Set with teeth; denticulated; uneven. *Addison.*

JAGUAR', *n.* The American tiger, or ounce of Brasil, belonging to the genus Felis. *Cyc.*

JAH, *n.* Jehovah.

JAIL, *n.* [Fr. *geole;* Arm. *geol* or *jol;* Sp. *jaula*, a cage, a cell. Sometimes written very improperly *gaol*, and as improperly pronounced *gole.*]

A prison; a building or place for the confinement of persons arrested for debt or for crime, and held in the custody of the sheriff.

JA'ILBIRD, *n.* A prisoner; one who has been confined in prison.

JA'ILER, *n.* The keeper of a prison.

JA'ILFEVER, *n.* A contagious and fatal fever generated in jails and other places crowded with people.

JAKES, *n.* [Qu. L. *jacio*, to throw.] A house of office or back-house; a privy. *Swift.*

JAL'AP, *n.* [Port. *jalapa;* Fr. *jalap;* Sp. *xalapa;* so called from *Xalapa*, a province in Mexico, whence it is imported.]

The root of a plant, a species of Convolvulus. It is brought in thin transverse slices, and also whole, of an oval shape, hard, solid and heavy. It has little or no taste or smell, but is much used in powder as a cathartic. *Cyc.*

JAM, *n.* A conserve of fruits boiled with sugar and water.

2. A kind of frock for children.

JAM, *v. t.* [Russ. *jem*, a press; *jmu*, to press.]

1. To press; to crowd; to wedge in.

2. In *England*, to tread hard or make firm by treading, as land by cattle. *Grose.*

JAM, } *n.* Among the lead miners of Men-
JAMB, } dip, a thick bed of stone which hinders them when pursuing the veins of ore. *Cyc.*

JAMB, *n. jam.* [Fr. *jambe*, a leg; *jambes de force*, a corbel or pier; It. *gamba*, a leg; *gambo*, a stem or stalk.]

In *architecture*, a supporter; the side-piece or post of a door; the side-piece of a fire-place.

JAMBEE', *n.* A name formerly given to a fashionable cane. *Tatler.*

JAM'BEUX, *n.* [supra.] Armor for the legs. *Obs.* *Dryden.*

JANE, *n.* A coin of Genoa. *Spenser.*

2. A kind of fustian.

JAN'GLE, *v. i.* [G. *zanken.*] To quarrel in words; to altercate; to bicker; to wrangle. *Shak.*

JAN'GLE, *v. t.* To cause to sound untunably or discordantly.

—E'er monkish rhymes
Had *jangl'd* their fantastic chimes. *Prior.*

JAN'GLER, *n.* A wrangling, noisy fellow.

JAN'GLING, *ppr.* Wrangling; quarreling; sounding discordantly.

JAN'GLING, *n.* A noisy dispute; a wrangling.

JAN'ITOR, *n.* [L.] A door-keeper; a porter. *Warton.*

JANIZA'RIAN, *n.* Pertaining to the Janizaries, or their government. *Burke.*

JAN'IZARY, *n.* [Turkish, *yeniskeri; yeni* and *askari*, new troops. *Eton.*]

A soldier of the Turkish foot guards. The Janizaries were a body of infantry, and reputed the Grand Seignor's guards. They became turbulent, and rising in arms against the Sultan, were attacked, defeated and destroyed in Constantinople, in June 1826.

JAN'NOCK, *n.* Oat-bread. [*Local.*]

JAN'SENISM, *n.* The doctrine of Jansen in regard to free will and grace.

JAN'SENIST, *n.* A follower of Jansen, bishop of Ypres, in Flanders.

J'ANT, *v. i.* [In Fr. *jante* is the felly of a wheel, and the original root signified probably to extend or to run, to ramble.]

To ramble here and there; to make an excursion. *Shak.*

J'ANT, *n.* An excursion; a ramble; a short journey. *Milton.*

J'ANTILY, *adv.* [from *janty.*] Briskly; airily; gayly.

J'ANTINESS, *n.* Airiness; flutter; briskness.

J'ANTY, *a.* Airy; showy; fluttering; finical. *Hobbes.*

JAN'UARY, *n.* [Ir. *gionbhar* or *gionvar*; Russ. *genvar*; Fr. *janvier*; It. *gennaio*; Sp. *enero*; Port. *janeiro*; L. *januarius*. It is evident from the Irish and Russian words, that the first syllable of *January*, is from the root of L. *geno*, to beget, Eng. to *begin*, Sax. *aginnan*. *Var* is said to signify a revolution. *January* then signifies the *beginning*, or first month. *Janus* is probably from the same root.]

The first month of the year, according to the present computation. At the foundation of Rome, March was considered the first month. January and February were introduced by Numa Pompilius. *Encyc.*

JAPAN', *n.* [from the country in Asia, so called.]

This name is given to work varnished and figured in the manner practiced by the natives of Japan. *Encyc. Cyc.*

JAPAN-EARTH, *n.* Catechu, a combination of gummy and resinous matter, obtained from the juice of a species of palm tree. *Nicholson.*

Japan-earth or catechu, is obtained by decoction and evaporation from a species of Mimosa. It consists chiefly of tannin combined with a peculiar species of extractive. *Thomson.*

JAPAN', *v. t.* To varnish in the manner of the Japanese.

2. To black and gloss, as in blacking shoes or boots. *Gay.*

JAPANE'SE, *a.* Pertaining to Japan or its inhabitants.

JAPANE'SE, *n.* A native of Japan; or the language of the inhabitants.

JAPAN'NED, *pp.* Varnished in a particular manner.

JAPAN'NER, *n.* One who varnishes in the manner of the Japanese, or one skilled in the art.

2. A shoe-blacker. *Pope.*

JAPAN'NING, *ppr.* Varnishing in the manner of the Japanese; giving a glossy black surface.

JAPAN'NING, *n.* The art of varnishing and drawing figures on wood or other material, in the manner practiced by the Japanese. *Encyc.*

JAPE, *v. i.* [Ice. *geipa.*] To jest. *Obs.* *Chaucer.*

JAPE, *v. t.* [Sax. *geap*, deceitful.] To cheat. *Obs.* *Chaucer.*

JAPE, *n.* A jest; a trick. *Obs.* *Chaucer.*

JA'PER, *n.* A jester. *Obs.*

JAPHET'IC, *a.* Pertaining to Japheth, the eldest son of Noah; as the *Japhetic* nations, which people the North of Asia and all Europe; *Japhetic* languages.

JAP'U, *n.* A bird of Brasil that suspends its nest.

J'AR, *v. i.* To strike together with a short rattle or tremulous sound; to strike untunably or harshly; to strike discordantly; as a *jarring* sound.

> A string may *jar* in the best master's hand. *Roscommon.*

2. To clash; to interfere; to act in opposition; to be inconsistent.

> For orders and degrees
> *Jar* not with liberty, but well consist. *Milton.*

3. To quarrel; to dispute; to clash in words. *Dryden.*

4. To vibrate regularly; to repeat the same sound. *Shak.*

J'AR, *v. t.* To shake; to cause to tremble; to cause a short tremulous motion in a thing.

J'AR, *n.* A rattling vibration of sound; a shake; as a trembling *jar*. *Holder.*

2. A harsh sound; discord.

3. Clash of interest or opinions; collision; discord; debate.

> And yet his peace is but continual *jar*. *Spenser.*

4. The state of a door half open, or ready to move and strike the post. *Swift.*

5. Repetition of the noise made by the pendulum of a clock. *Shak.*

J'AR, *n.* [Sp. *jarra*, *jarro*; Port. *id.*; It. *giarro.*]

A vessel with a large belly and broad mouth, made of earth or glass; as a *jar* of honey. *Dryden.*

> We say, an electrical battery of nine *jars*.

2. A certain measure; as a *jar* of oil.

JARARACA, *n.* A species of serpent in America, seldom exceeding 18 inches in length, having prominent veins on its head, and of a dusky brownish color, variegated with red and black spots. It is very poisonous. *Cyc.*

J'ARBLE, } *v. t.* To bemire. [*Not in use.*]
JAV'EL, } *Spenser.*

JARDES, *n.* [Fr.] Callous tumors on the legs of a horse, below the bend of the ham on the outside. *Far. Dict.*

J'ARGLE, *v. i.* To emit a harsh or shrill sound. [*Not in use.*] *Bp. Hall.*

J'ARGON, *n.* [Fr. *jargon*; It. *gergo*, *gergone*; Sp. *xerga*, jargon, and coarse frieze, *serge.*]

1. Confused, unintelligible talk or language; gabble; gibberish; cant.

> All *jargon* of the schools. *Prior.*

2. A mineral, usually of a gray or greenish white color, in small irregular grains, or crystalized in quadrangular prisms surmounted with pyramids, or in octahedrons consisting of double quadrangular prisms. [See *Zircon.*] *Kirwan.*

JARGONELLE, *n.* *jargonel'.* A species of pear.

JARGON'IC, *a.* Pertaining to the mineral jargon.

J'ARRED, *pp.* [from *jar.*] Shaken.

J'ARRING, *ppr.* Shaking; making a harsh sound; discordant.

J'ARRING, *n.* A shaking; discord; dispute; collision. *Burnet.*

JAS'HAWK, *n.* A young hawk. *Ainsworth.*

JAS'MIN, } *n.* [Fr. *jasmin*; Sp. *jazmin*;
JAS'MINE, } It. *gelsomino.* The Ar. is ياسمين. It is sometimes written in English *jessamine.*]

A plant of the genus Jasminum, bearing beautiful flowers. There are several species. The common white jasmin is a climbing shrub, rising on supports 15 or 20 feet high. The name is also given to several plants of different genera; as the *Arabian Jasmin*, of the genus Nyctanthes; the *bastard Jasmin*, of the genus Cestrum, and also of the genus Lycium; the *Persian Jasmin*, of the genus Syringa; the *red Jasmin*, of the genus Plumeria; the *scarlet* and *yellow Jasmin*, of the genus Bignonia, &c. *Encyc.*

JAS'PACHATE, *n.* A name anciently given to some varieties of agate jasper. *Cyc.*

J'ASPER, *n.* [Fr. *jaspe*; L. *iaspis*; Gr. ιασπις; It. *diaspro*; Ar. يشب; Heb. ישפה.]

A mineral of the siliceous kind, and of several varieties. It is less hard than flint or even than common quartz, but gives fire with steel. It is entirely opake, or sometimes feebly translucent at the edges, and it presents almost every variety of color. Its varieties are common jasper, striped jasper, Egyptian jasper, &c. It admits of an elegant polish, and is used for vases, seals, snuff-boxes, &c. *Cleaveland. Kirwan.*

Jasper is a subspecies of rhomboidal quartz, of five kinds, Egyptian, striped, porcelain, common, and agate jasper. *Jameson.*

J'ASPERATED, *a.* Mixed with jasper; containing particles of jasper; as *jasperated* agate. *Fourcroy.*

JASPIDE'AN, *a.* Like jasper; consisting of jasper, or partaking of jasper. *Kirwan.*

J'ASPONYX, *n.* The purest horn-colored onyx, with beautiful green zones, composed of genuine matter of the finest jaspers. *Encyc.*

JAUNCE, *v. i.* [Fr. *jancer.*] To bustle; to jaunt. *Obs.* *Shak.*

JAUNDICE, *n.* *j'andis.* [Fr. *jaunisse*, from *jaune*, yellow.]

A disease which is characterized by a suffusion of bile over the coats of the eye and the whole surface of the body, by which they are tinged with a yellow color. Hence its name.

JAUNDICED, *a.* *j'andised.* Affected with the jaundice; suffused with a yellow color; as a *jaundiced* eye.

2. Prejudiced; seeing with discolored organs.

JAUNT. [See *Jant.*]

JAV'EL, *v. t.* To bemire; and as a noun, a wandering or dirty fellow. *Obs.* *Spenser.*

JAV'ELIN, *n.* [Fr. *javeline*; It. *giavellotto*; Sp. *jabalina*, the female of the wild boar, and a javelin, from *jabali*, a wild boar.]

A sort of spear about five feet and a half long, the shaft of which was of wood, but pointed with steel; used by horse or foot. Every Roman soldier carried seven *javelins*.

JAW, *n.* [Fr. *joue*, the cheek. It coincides in origin with *chaw*, *chew*, Arm. *joaga*, to chew; *javed* or *gaved*, a jaw. In old authors, *jaw* is written *chaw*. It belongs to Class Cg. See *Chaw* and *Chew.*]

1. The bones of the mouth in which the teeth are fixed. They resemble a horse shoe. In most animals, the under jaw only is movable.

2. The mouth.

3. In *vulgar language*, scolding, wrangling, abusive clamor.

JAW, *v. i.* To scold; to clamor. [*Vulgar.*]

JAW, *v. t.* To abuse by scolding. [*Vulgar.*]

JAW'ED, *a.* Denoting the appearance of the jaws. *Skelton.*

JAW'FALL, *n.* [*jaw* and *fall.*] Depression of the jaw; figuratively, depression of spirits. *M. Griffith.*

JAW'FALLEN, *a.* Depressed in spirits; dejected.

JAWN, *v. i.* To yawn. [*Not in use.* See *Yawn.*]

JAW'Y, *a.* Relating to the jaws. *Gayton.*

JAY, *n.* [Fr. *geai*; Sp. *gayo.*] A bird, the Corvus glandarius. *Encyc.*

JAYET. [See *Jet.*]

JA'ZEL, *n.* A gem of an azure blue color. [Qu. Sp. *azul*, corrupted.]

JEALOUS, *a. jel'us.* [Fr. *jaloux*; It. *geloso.* The Spanish use *zeloso* from *zelo*, zeal; but the Italian word seems to be of distinct origin from *zeal*, and to belong to Class Gl.]

1. Suspicious; apprehensive of rivalship; uneasy through fear that another has withdrawn or may withdraw from one the affections of a person he loves, or enjoy some good which he desires to obtain; followed by *of*, and applied both to the object of love and to the rival. We say, a young man is *jealous of* the woman he loves, or *jealous of* his rival. A man is *jealous of* his wife, and the wife *of* her husband.
2. Suspicious that we do not enjoy the affection or respect of others, or that another is more loved and respected than ourselves.
3. Emulous; full of competition. *Dryden.*
4. Solicitous to defend the honor of; concerned for the character of.

> I have been very *jealous* for the Lord God of hosts. 1 Kings xix.

5. Suspiciously vigilant; anxiously careful and concerned for.

> I am *jealous* over you with a godly jealousy. 2 Cor. xi.

6. Suspiciously fearful.

> 'Tis doing wrong creates such doubts as these,
> Renders us *jealous* and destroys our peace. *Waller.*

JEALOUSLY, *adv. jel'usly.* With jealousy or suspicion; emulously; with suspicious fear, vigilance or caution.

JEALOUSNESS, *n. jel'usness.* The state of being jealous; suspicion; suspicious vigilance. *King Charles.*

JEALOUSY, *n. jel'usy.* [Fr. *jalousie*; It. *gelosia.*]

1. That passion or peculiar uneasiness which arises from the fear that a rival may rob us of the affection of one whom we love, or the suspicion that he has already done it; or it is the uneasiness which arises from the fear that another does or will enjoy some advantage which we desire for ourselves. A man's *jealousy* is excited by the attentions of a rival to his favorite lady. A woman's *jealousy* is roused by her husband's attentions to another woman. The candidate for office manifests a *jealousy* of others who seek the same office. The *jealousy* of a student is awakened by the apprehension that his fellow will bear away the palm of praise. In short, *jealousy* is awakened by whatever may exalt others, or give them pleasures and advantages which we desire for ourselves. *Jealousy* is nearly allied to *envy*, for *jealousy*, before a good is lost by ourselves, is converted into *envy*, after it is obtained by others.

> *Jealousy* is the apprehension of superiority. *Shenstone.*
>
> Whoever had qualities to alarm our *jealousy*, had excellence to deserve our fondness. *Rambler.*

2. Suspicious fear or apprehension. *Clarendon.*
3. Suspicious caution or vigilance; an earnest concern or solicitude for the welfare or honor of others. Such was Paul's godly *jealousy* for the Corinthians.
4. Indignation. God's *jealousy* signifies his concern for his own character and government, with a holy indignation against those who violate his laws, and offend against his majesty. Ps. lxxix.

JEARS, *n.* In *sea-language*, an assemblage of tackles by which the lower yards of a ship are hoisted or lowered. Hoisting is called *swaying*, and lowering is called *striking*. This word is sometimes written *geers* or *gears.* [See *Gear.*] *Mar. Dict.*

JEAT, *n.* A fossil of a fine black color. [See *Jet.*]

JEER, *v. i.* [G. *scheren*, to rail at, to jeer, to *shear*, to shave, D. *scheeren*, Dan. *skierer*, Sw. *skåra*, Gr. κειρω, without a prefix. These all seem to be of one family, Class Gr. The primary sense is probably to *rub*, or to cut by rubbing; and we use *rub* in a like sense; a *dry rub*, is a keen, cutting, sarcastic remark.]

To utter severe, sarcastic reflections; to scoff; to deride; to flout; to make a mock of; as, to *jeer* at one in sport. *Herbert.*

JEER, *v. t.* To treat with scoffs or derision. *Howell.*

JEER, *n.* Railing language; scoff; taunt; biting jest; flout; jibe; mockery; derision; ridicule with scorn.

> Midas exposed to all their *jeers*,
> Had lost his art, and kept his ears. *Swift.*

JEE'RED, *pp.* Railed at; derided.

JEE'RER, *n.* A scoffer; a railer; a scorner; a mocker.

JEE'RING, *ppr.* Scoffing; mocking; deriding.

JEE'RING, *n.* Derision.

JEE'RINGLY, *adv.* With raillery; scornfully; contemptuously; in mockery. *Derham.*

JEF'FERSONITE, *n.* A mineral occurring in crystaline masses, of a dark olive green color passing into brown, found imbedded in Franklinite and garnet, in New Jersey. *Phillips.*

JEG'GET, *n.* A kind of sausage. [*Not in use.*] *Ainsworth.*

JEHO'VAH, *n.* The Scripture name of the Supreme Being, Heb. יהוה. If, as is supposed, this name is from the Hebrew substantive verb, the word denotes the PERMANENT BEING, as the primary sense of the substantive verb in all languages, is to be fixed, to stand, to remain or abide. This is a name peculiarly appropriate to the eternal Spirit, the unchangeable God, who describes himself thus, I AM THAT I AM. Ex. iii.

JEHO'VIST, *n.* Among critics, one who maintains that the vowel-points annexed to the word Jehovah in Hebrew, are the proper vowels of the word and express the true pronunciation. The *Jehovists* are opposed to the *Adonists*, who hold that the points annexed to the word *Jehovah*, are the vowels of the word *Adonai*. *Encyc.*

JEJU'NE, *a.* [L. *jejunus*, empty, dry.]

1. Wanting; empty; vacant. *Bacon.*
2. Hungry; not saturated.
3. Dry; barren; wanting interesting matter; as a *jejune* narrative.

JEJU'NENESS, *n.* Poverty; barrenness; particularly, want of interesting matter; a deficiency of matter that can engage the attention and gratify the mind; as the *jejuneness* of style or narrative. [*Jejunity* is not used.]

JEL'LIED, *a.* [See *Jelly* and *Gelly.*] Brought to the consistence of jelly.

JEL'LY, *n.* [Sp. *jalea*, from L. *gelo*, to congeal. See *Gelly.*]

1. The inspissated juice of fruit, boiled with sugar.
2. Something viscous or glutinous; something of the consistency of jelly; a transparent sizy substance, obtained from animal substances by decoction; portable soup.

JEL'LYBAG, *n.* A bag through which jelly is distilled.

JEN'ITE, *n.* A different orthography of *yenite*, which see.

JEN'NET, *n.* A small Spanish horse, properly *genet.*

JEN'NETING, *n.* [said to be corrupted from *juneting*, an apple ripe in June, or at St. Jean.] A species of early apple. *Mortimer.*

JEN'NY, *n.* A machine for spinning, moved by water or steam and used in manufactories.

JENT'LING, *n.* A fish, the blue chub, found in the Danube.

JEOFAIL, *n. jef'fail.* [Fr. *j'ai failli*, I have failed.]

An oversight in pleading or other proceeding at law; or the acknowledgment of a mistake. *Blackstone.*

JEOPARD, *v. t. jep'ard.* [See *Jeopardy.*] To hazard; to put in danger; to expose to loss or injury.

> Zebulon and Naphtali were a people that *jeoparded* their lives to the death in the high places of the field. Judges v.

JEOPARDER, *n. jep'arder.* One who puts to hazard.

JEOPARDIZE, *v. t. jep'ardize.* To expose to loss or injury; to jeopard. [This is a modern word, used by respectable writers in America, but synonymous with *jeopard* and therefore useless.]

JEOPARDOUS, *a. jep'ardous.* Exposed to danger; perilous; hazardous.

JEOPARDOUSLY, *adv. jep'ardously.* With risk or danger.

JEOPARDY, *n. jep'ardy.* [The origin of this word is not settled. Some authors suppose it to be Fr. *j'ai perdu*, I have lost, or *jeu perdu*, a lost game. Tyrwhitt supposes it to be *jeu parti*, an even game, or game in which the chances are even. "Si nous les voyons a jeu parti." If we see them at an even game. *Froissart*, vol. i. c. 234. But *jeopardy* may be corrupted from the G. *gefahr*, danger, hazard; *gefährden*, to hazard, to jeopard. See *Fare.*]

Exposure to death, loss or injury; hazard; danger; peril.

> They were filled with water and were in *jeopardy.* Luke viii.

JER'BOA, *n.* A quadruped having very short fore legs.

JERK, *v. t.* [This is probably the Ch. Heb. ירק, to *reach*, to spit, that is, to throw out with a sudden effort, Sax. *hræcan*, *herca*. If not, I know not its origin or affinities. It seems to be a different orthography of *yerk.*]

1. To thrust out; to thrust with a sudden effort; to give a sudden pull, twitch, thrust or push; as, to *jerk* one under the ribs; to *jerk* one with the elbow.

2. To throw with a quick, smart motion; as, to *jerk* a stone. We apply this word to express the mode of throwing to a little distance by drawing the arm back of the body, and thrusting it forward against the side or hip, which stops the arm suddenly.

JERK, *v. t.* To accost eagerly. [*Not in use.*] *Dryden.*

JERK, *n.* A short sudden thrust, push or twitch; a striking against something with a short quick motion; as a *jerk* of the elbow.

His jade gave him a *jerk*. *B. Jonson.*

2. A sudden spring.

Lobsters swim by *jerks*. *Grew.*

JERK'IN, *n.* A jacket; a short coat; a close waistcoat. *Shak. South.*

2. A kind of hawk. *Ainsworth.*

JER'SEY, *n.* [from the ieland so called.]

1. Fine yarn of wool. *Johnson.*

2. The finest of wool separated from the rest; combed wool. *Bailey. Encyc.*

JERUSALEM ARTICHOKE, *n.* A plant, a species of Helianthus or Sunflower.

JESS, *n.* Short straps of lether tied round the legs of a hawk, by which she is held on the fist. *Hanmer.*

2. A ribin that hangs down from a garland or crown in falconry. *Encyc.*

JES'SAMIN, *n.* A genus of plants and their flowers. [See *Jasmin.*]

JES'SE, *n.* A large brass candlestick branched into many sconces, hanging down in the middle of a church or choir. *Cowel.*

JESS'ED, *a.* Having jesses on; *a term in heraldry.*

JEST, *n.* [Sp. and Port. *chiste*, a witty saying, a jest or joke; *chistoso*, gay, facetious; allied perhaps to L. *gestio.*]

1. A joke; something ludicrous uttered and meant only to excite laughter. Religion should never be the subject of *jest.*

2. The object of laughter or sport; a laughing stock.

Then let me be your *jest*, I deserve it. *Shak.*

In jest, for mere sport or diversion; not in truth and reality; not in earnest.

—And given in earnest what I begged *in jest*. *Shak.*

3. A mask.

4. A deed; an action. *Obs.*

JEST, *v. i.* To divert or make merry by words or actions; to joke.

Jest not with a rude man, lest thy ancestors be disgraced. *Ecclus.*

2. To utter in sport; to say what is not true, merely for diversion.

3. To play a part in a mask. *Shak.*

JEST'ER, *n.* A person given to jesting, sportive talk and merry pranks.

—He rambled up and down
With shallow *jesters*. *Shak.*

2. One given to sarcasm.

Now, as a *jester*, I accost you. *Swift.*

3. A buffoon; a merry-andrew, a person formerly retained by princes to make sport for them.

JEST'ING, *ppr.* Joking; talking for diversion or merriment.

JEST'ING, *n.* A joking; concise wit; wit that consists in a trope or verbal figure, in a metaphorical sense of words, or in a double sense of the same word, or in similitude of sound in different words. *Encyc.*

JEST'INGLY, *adv.* In a jocose manner; not in earnest. *Herbert.*

JEST'ING-STOCK, *n.* A laughing stock; a butt of ridicule. *Googe.*

JES'UIT, *n.* *s* as *z.* One of the society of Jesus, so called, founded by Ignatius Loyola; a society remarkable for their cunning in propagating their principles.

JES'UITED, *a.* Conforming to the principles of the Jesuits. *White.*

JES'UITESS, *n.* A female Jesuit in principle. *Bp. Hall.*

JESUIT'IC, } *a.* Pertaining to the Jesuits
JESUIT'ICAL, } or their principles and arts.

2. Designing; cunning; deceitful; prevaricating.

JESUIT'ICALLY, *adv.* Craftily.

JES'UITISM, *n.* The arts, principles and practices of the Jesuits.

2. Cunning; deceit; hypocrisy; prevarication; deceptive practices to effect a purpose.

JES'UITS'-BARK, *n.* Peruvian bark; the bark of the Cinchona, a tree of Peru.

JET, *n.* [D. *git*; Fr. *jayet*; L. *gagates.*] A solid, dry, black, inflammable fossil substance, harder than asphalt, susceptible of a good polish, and glossy in its fracture, which is conchoidal or undulating. It is found not in strata or continued masses, but in unconnected heaps. It is wrought into toys, buttons, mourning jewels, &c. *Nicholson. Encyc.*

Jet is regarded as a variety of lignite, or coal originating in wood. *Haüy. Cleaveland.*

JET, *n.* [Fr. *jet*, It. *getto*, a cast; probably from L. *jactus*, whence Fr. *jetter*, It. *gettare*, to throw.]

1. A spout, spouting or shooting of water; a *jet d' eau.*

2. A yard. *Tusser.* Drift; scope. [*Not in use or local.*]

JET, *v. i.* [See the Noun.] To shoot forward; to shoot out; to project; to jut; to intrude. *Shak.*

2. To strut; to throw or toss the body in haughtiness. *Shak.*

3. To jerk; to jolt; to be shaken. *Wiseman.*

[*This orthography is rarely used.* See *Jut.*]

JETTEAU, *n.* *jet'to.* [Fr. *jet d'eau.*] A throw or spout of water. *Addison.*

JET'SAM, }
JET'SON, } *n.* [Fr. *jetter*, to throw.] In *law* and *commerce*, properly,
JET'TISON, } the throwing of goods overboard in order to lighten a ship in a tempest for her preservation. The word may however be used for the goods thus thrown away, or adverbially.

Jetsam is where goods are cast into the sea, and there sink and remain under water; *flotsam*, is where they continue swimming; *ligan* is where they are sunk in the sea, but tied to a cork or buoy. *Park. Blackstone.*

JET'TEE, *n.* A projection in a building.

JET'TY, *v. i.* To jut.

JET'TY, *n.* A small pier or projection into a river for narrowing it and raising the water above that place. *Cyc.*

JET'TY, *a.* Made of jet, or black as jet. *Prior. Pope.*

JET'TYHEAD, *n.* The projecting part of a wharf; the front of a wharf whose side forms one of the cheeks of a dock. *Mar. Dict.*

JEW, *n.* [a contraction of Judas or Judah.] A Hebrew or Israelite.

JEW'EL, *n.* [It. *gioia*, joy, mirth, a jewel; *gioiello*, a jewel; Fr. *joyau*; Sp. *joya*, *joyel*; G. *juwel*; D. *juweel*. It is from the root of *joy*. Low L. *jocale*. Class Cg.]

1. An ornament worn by ladies, usually consisting of a precious stone, or set with one or more; a pendant worn in the ear.

2. A precious stone. *Shak.*

3. A name expressive of fondness. A mother calls her child, her *jewel.*

JEW'EL, *v. t.* To dress or adorn with jewels. *B. Jonson.*

JEW'EL-HOUSE, } *n.* The place where
JEW'EL-OFFICE, } the royal ornaments are reposited. *Shak.*

JEW'EL-LIKE, *a.* Brilliant as a jewel. *Shak.*

JEW'ELED, *pp.* Adorned with jewels.

JEW'ELER, *n.* One who makes or deals in jewels and other ornaments.

JEW'ELING, *ppr.* Adorning with jewels.

JEW'ELRY, *n.* Jewels in general.

JEW'ESS, *n.* A Hebrew woman. Acts xxiv.

JEW'ISH, *a.* Pertaining to the Jews or Hebrews. Tit. i.

JEW'ISHLY, *adv.* In the manner of the Jews. *Donne.*

JEW'ISHNESS, *n.* The rites of the Jews. *Martin.*

JEW'RY, *n.* Judea; also, a district inhabited by Jews, whence the name of a street in London. *Chaucer.*

JEWS-EAR, *n.* The name of a species of Fungus, the *Peziza auricula*, bearing some resemblance to the human ear. *Johnson. Lee.*

JEWS-FRANKINCENSE, *n.* A plant, a species of Styrax.

JEWS-HARP, *n.* [*Jew* and *harp.*] An instrument of music shaped like a harp, which, placed between the teeth and by means of a spring struck by the finger, gives a sound which is modulated by the breath into soft melody. It is called also *Jews-trump.*

JEWS-MALLOW, *n.* A plant, a species of Corchorus.

JEWS-PITCH, *n.* Asphaltum, which see.

JEWS-STONE, *n.* The clavated spine of a very large egg-shaped sea urchin petrified. It is a regular figure, oblong and rounded, about three quarters of an inch in length, and half an inch in diameter. Its color is a pale dusky gray, with a tinge of dusky red. *Hill.*

JEZ'EBEL, *n.* An impudent, daring, vitious woman. *Spectator.*

JIB, *n.* The foremost sail of a ship, being a large stay-sail extended from the outer end of the jib-boom towards the fore-top-mast-head. In sloops, it is on the bowsprit, and extends towards the lower mast-head. *Mar. Dict.*

JIB-BOOM, *n.* A spar which is run out from the extremity of the bowsprit, and which serves as a continuation of it. Beyond this is sometimes extended the *flying-jib-boom.*

JIBOY'A, *n.* An American serpent of the largest kind.

JIG, *n.* [It. *giga*; Fr. *gigue*. See *Gig*.] A kind of light dance, or a tune or air.

2. A ballad. *B. Jonson.*

JIG, *v. i.* To dance a jig.

JIG'GER, *n.* In *sea-language*, a machine consisting of a rope about five feet long, with a block at one end and a sheave at the other, used to hold on the cable when it is heaved into the ship, by the revolution of the windlass. *Mar. Dict.*

JIG'GISH, *a.* Suitable to a jig.

JIG'MAKER, *n.* One who makes or plays jigs. *Shak.*

2. A ballad maker. *Dekker.*

JIG'PIN, *n.* A pin used by miners to hold the turn-beams, and prevent them from turning. *Cyc.*

JILL, *n.* A young woman; in contempt. [See *Gill*.]

JILL'-FLIRT, *n.* A light wanton woman. *Guardian.*

JILT, *n.* [of uncertain etymology.] A woman who gives her lover hopes and capriciously disappoints him; a woman who trifles with her lover. *Otway.*

2. A name of contempt for a woman. *Pope.*

JILT, *v. t.* To encourage a lover and then frustrate his hopes; to trick in love; to give hopes to a lover and then reject him. *Dryden.*

JILT, *v. i.* To play the jilt; to practice deception in love and discard lovers. *Congreve.*

JIM'MERS, *n.* Jointed hinges. *Bailey.*

JIN'GLE, *v. i.* [Qu. Ch. and Syr. זג, זגא a little bell; or Persian زنك zank, a little brass ball or bell. It may be allied to *jangle.*]
To sound with a fine sharp rattle; to clink; as *jingling* chains or bells.

JIN'GLE, *v. t.* To cause to give a sharp sound, as a little bell or as pieces of metal.

> The bells she *jingled*, and the whistle blew. *Pope.*

JIN'GLE, *n.* A rattling or clinking sound, as of little bells or pieces of metal.

2. A little bell or rattle.

3. Correspondence of sound in rhymes. *Dryden.*

JIN'GLING, *ppr.* Giving a sharp fine rattling sound, as a little bell or as pieces of metal.

JIP'PO, *n.* [Fr. *jupe*.] A waistcoat or kind of stays for females.

JOB, *n.* [of unknown origin, but perhaps allied to *chop*, primarily to strike or drive.]

1. A piece of work; any thing to be done, whether of more or less importance. The carpenter or mason undertakes to build a house by the *job*. The erection of Westminster bridge was a heavy *job*; and it was a great *job* to erect Central wharf, in Boston. The mechanic has many small *jobs* on hand.

2. A lucrative business; an undertaking with a view to profit.

> No cheek is known to blush nor heart to throb,
> Save when they lose a question or a *job*. *Pope.*

3. A sudden stab with a pointed instrument. [This seems to be nearly the original sense.]

To do the job for one, to kill him.

JOB, *v. t.* To strike or stab with a sharp instrument. *L'Estrange.*

2. To drive in a sharp pointed instrument. *Moxon.*

JOB, *v. i.* To deal in the public stocks; to buy and sell as a broker.

> The judge shall *job*, the bishop bite the town,
> And mighty dukes pack cards for half a crown. *Pope.*

JOB'BER, *n.* One who does small jobs.

2. A dealer in the public stocks or funds; usually called a *stock-jobber.* *Swift.*

3. One who engages in a low, lucrative affair.

JOB'BERNOWL, *n.* [said to be from Flemish *jobbe*, dull, and Sax. *knol*, head or top.]
A loggerhead; a blockhead. [*A low word.*] *Hudibras.*

JOB'S-TEARS, *n.* A plant of the genus Coix.

JOCK'EY, *n.* [said to be from *Jackey*, a diminutive of *Jack*, John; primarily, a boy that rides horses.]

1. A man that rides horses in a race. *Addison.*

2. A dealer in horses; one who makes it his business to buy and sell horses for gain. Hence,

3. A cheat; one who deceives or takes undue advantage in trade.

JOCK'EY, *v. t.* To cheat; to trick; to deceive in trade.

2. To jostle by riding against one. *Johnson.*

JOCK'EYSHIP, *n.* The art or practice of riding horses. *Cowper.*

JOCO'SE, *a.* [L. *jocosus*, from *jocus*, a *joke*.]

1. Given to jokes and jesting; merry; waggish; *used of persons.*

2. Containing a joke; sportive; merry; as *jocose* or comical airs. *Watts.*

JOCO'SELY, *adv.* In jest; for sport or game; waggishly. *Broome.*

JOCO'SENESS, *n.* The quality of being jocose; waggery; merriment. [*Jocosity* is not used.]

JOCO-SE'RIOUS, *a.* Partaking of mirth and seriousness. *Green.*

JOC'ULAR, *a.* [L. *jocularis*, from *jocus*, a *joke*.]

1. Jocose; waggish; merry; given to jesting; *used of persons.*

2. Containing jokes; sportive; not serious; as a *jocular* expression or style.

JOCULAR'ITY, *n.* Merriment; jesting. *Brown.*

JOC'ULARLY, *adv.* In jest; for sport or mirth. *Bp. Lavington.*

JOC'ULARY, *a.* Jocular. [*Not in use.*] *Ash. Bacon.*

JOC'ULATOR, *n.* [L.] A jester; a droll; a minstrel. *Strutt.*

JOC'ULATORY, *a.* Droll; merrily said.

JOC'UND, *a.* [L. *jocundus*, from *jocus*, a *joke*.] Merry; gay; airy; lively; sportive.

> Rural sports and *jocund* strains. *Prior*

JOCUND'ITY, **JOC'UNDNESS**, *n.* State of being merry; gayety.

JOC'UNDLY, *adv.* Merrily; gayly.

JOG, *v. t.* [Qu. W. *gogi*, to shake, or D. *schokken*, to jolt or shake, which seems to be the Fr. *choquer*, Eng. *shock*, *shake*.]
To push or shake with the elbow or hand; to give notice or excite attention by a slight push.

> Sudden I *jogged* Ulysses. *Pope.*

JOG, *v. i.* To move by jogs or small shocks, like those of a slow trot.

> So hung his destiny, never to rot,
> While he might still *jog* on, and keep his trot. *Milton.*

2. To walk or travel idly, heavily or slowly.

> Thus they *jog* on, still tricking, never thriving. *Dryden.*

JOG, *n.* A push; a slight shake; a shake or push intended to give notice or awaken attention. When your friend falls asleep at church, give him a *jog*.

2. A rub; a small stop; obstruction. *Glanville.*

JOG'GER, *n.* One who walks or moves heavily and slowly.

2. One who gives a sudden push.

JOG'GING, *ppr.* Pushing slightly.

JOG'GING, *n.* A slight push or shake.

JOG'GLE, *v. t.* [from *jog*.] To shake slightly; to give a sudden but slight push.

JOG'GLED, *pp.* Slightly shaken.

JOG'GLING, *ppr.* Shaking slightly.

JOHAN'NES, *n.* [*John*, latinized.] A Portuguese gold coin of the value of eight dollars; contracted often into *joe*; as a *joe*, or half-*joe*. It is named from the figure of king John, which it bears.

JOHN'APPLE, *n.* A sort of apple, good for spring use, when other fruit is spent. *Mortimer.*

JOIN, *v. t.* [Fr. *joindre*; It. *giugnere*; from L. *jungo*, *jungere*; *jungo* for *jugo*; Sp. and Port. *juntar*, to join; L. *jugum*; Eng. *yoke*; Gr. ζυγος and ζευγος, a yoke, and a pair; ζυγοω, to yoke; ζευγνυμι, to join; Ch. זוג; Syr. ܙܘܓ zug; Ar. زاج to join, to couple, to marry, to pair; Eth. ዘወገ zog, a pair, as in Arabic. It signifies also in Syriac, to rage, to cry out; showing that the primary sense is to strain, to stretch, to extend, precisely as in *span*.]

1. To set or bring one thing in contiguity with another.

> Woe to them that *join* house to house, that lay field to field. Is. v.

2. To couple; to connect; to combine; as, to *join* ideas. *Locke.*

3. To unite in league or marriage.

> Now Jehoshaphat had riches and honor in abundance, and *joined* affinity with Ahab. 2 Ch. xviii.

> What God hath *joined* together, let not man put asunder. Matt. xix.

4. To associate.

> Go near and *join* thyself to this chariot. Acts viii.

5. To unite in any act.

> Thy tuneful voice with numbers *join*. *Dryden.*

6. To unite in concord.

But that ye be perfectly *joined* together in the same mind, and in the same judgment. 1 Cor. i.

The phrase, to *join battle*, is probably elliptical, for *join in battle;* or it is borrowed from the Latin, *committere prœlium*, to send together the battle.

In general, *join* signifies to unite two entire things without breach or intermixture, by contact or contiguity, either temporary or permanent. It differs from *connect*, which signifies properly, to unite by an intermediate substance. But *join*, *unite*, and *connect* are often used synonymously.

JOIN, *v. i.* To grow to; to adhere. The place where two bones of the body *join*, is called a joint or articulation.

2. To be contiguous, close or in contact; as when two houses *join*.

3. To unite with in marriage, league, confederacy, partnership or society. Russia and Austria *joined* in opposition to Buonaparte's ambitious views. Men *join* in great undertakings, and in companies for trade or manufacture. They *join* in entertainments and amusements. They *join* in benevolent associations. It is often followed by *with*.

Any other may *join with* him that is injured, and assist him in recovering satisfaction. *Locke.*

Should we again break thy commandments, and *join* in affinity with the people of these abominations? Ezra ix.

JOIN'DER, *n.* A joining; as a *joinder* in demurrer. *Blackstone.*

JOIN'ED, *pp.* Added; united; set or fastened together; associated; confederated.

JOIN'ER, *n.* One whose occupation is to construct things by joining pieces of wood; but appropriately and usually, a mechanic who does the wood-work in the covering and finishing of buildings. This is the true and original sense of the word in Great Britain and in New England. This person is called in New York, a *carpenter.* [See *Carpenter.*]

JOIN'ERY, *n.* The art of fitting and joining pieces of timber in the construction of utensils or parts of a building, so as to form one entire piece.

JOIN'HAND, *n.* Writing in which letters are joined in words; as distinguished from writing in single letters. *Addison.*

JOIN'ING, *ppr.* Adding; making contiguous; uniting; confederating.

JOINT, *n.* [Fr. *joint;* Sp. *junta, juntura;* It. *giuntura;* L. *junctura.* See *Join.*]

1. The joining of two or more things.

2. In *anatomy*, the joining of two or more bones; an articulation; as the elbow, the knee, or the knuckle.

3. A knot; the union of two parts of a plant; or the space between two joints; an internode; as the *joint* of a cane, or of a stalk of maiz.

4. A hinge; a juncture of parts which admits of motion.

5. The place where two pieces of timber are united.

6. In *joinery*, straight lines are called a joint, when two pieces of wood are planed. *Moxon.*

7. One of the limbs of an animal cut up by the butcher.

Out of joint, luxated; dislocated; as when the head of a bone is displaced from its socket. Hence figuratively, confused; disordered; misplaced.

JOINT, *a.* Shared by two or more; as *joint* property.

2. United in the same profession; having an interest in the same thing; as a *joint*-heir or heiress.

3. United; combined; acting in concert; as a *joint* force; *joint* efforts; *joint* vigor.

JOINT, *v. t.* To form with joints or articulations; *used mostly in the participle;* as the fingers are *jointed;* a cane has a *jointed* stalk.

2. To form many parts into one; as *jointed* wood. *Dryden.*

3. To cut or divide into joints or quarters. *Dryden.*

JOINT'ED, *pp.* Formed with articulations, as the stem of a plant.

2. Separated into joints or quarters.

JOINT'ER, *n.* A long plane, a joiner's utensil.

JOINT'-HEIR, *n.* [*joint* and *heir.*] An heir having a joint interest with another. Rom. viii.

JOINT'LY, *adv.* Together; unitedly; in concert; with cooperation.

2. With union of interest; as, to be *jointly* concerned in a voyage.

JOINT'RESS, *n.* A woman who has a jointure. *Blackstone.*

JOINT'STOOL, *n.* A stool consisting of parts inserted in each other. *South.*

JOINT-TEN'ANCY, *n.* [*joint* and *tenant.*] A tenure of estate by unity of interest, title, time and possession. *Blackstone.*

JOINT-TEN'ANT, *n.* [*joint* and *tenant.*] One who holds an estate by joint-tenancy.

JOINT'URE, *n.* [Fr.] An estate in lands or tenements, settled on a woman in consideration of marriage, and which she is to enjoy after her husband's decease. *Blackstone.*

JOINT'URE, *v. t.* To settle a jointure upon. *Cowley.*

JOINT'URED, *pp.* Endowed with a jointure.

JOIST, *n.* [Scot. *geist* or *gest.* Qu. Fr. *gesir*, to lie.]

A small piece of timber, such as is framed into the girders and summers of a building to support a floor. *Encyc.*

JOIST, *v. t.* To fit in joists; to lay joists.

JOKE, *n.* [L. *jocus;* Dan. *giek*, a joke; *giekker*, to joke; Sw. *gäcka*, to ridicule; G. *schäkern.*]

1. A jest; something said for the sake of exciting a laugh; something witty or sportive; raillery. A jealous person will rarely bear a *joke.*

2. An illusion; something not real, or to no purpose.

Inclose whole downs in walls, 'tis all a *joke!* *Pope.*

In joke, in jest; for the sake of raising a laugh; not in earnest.

JOKE, *v. i.* [L. *jocor.*] To jest; to be merry in words or actions.

JOKE, *v. t.* To rally; to cast jokes at; to make merry with.

JO'KER, *n.* A jester; a merry fellow. *Dennis.*

JO'KING, *ppr.* Jesting; making merry with.

JOLE, *n.* [sometimes written *jowl;* Sax. *ceole*, the jaw or cheek; Ir. *gial.* Qu. Arm. *chagell*, contracted.]

1. The cheek; used in the phrase, *cheek by jole*, that is, with the cheeks together, close, tête à tête. *Dryden.*

2. The head of a fish. *Pope.*

JOLE, *v. t.* To strike the head against any thing; to clash with violence. [*Not used.*] *Shak.*

JOL'LILY, *adv.* [See *Jolly.*] With noisy mirth; with a disposition to noisy mirth. *Dryden.*

JOL'LIMENT, *n.* Mirth; merriment. *Obs.* *Spenser.*

JOL'LINESS, } *n.* [from *jolly.*] Noisy mirth;
JOL'LITY, } gayety; merriment; festivity.

All was now turned to *jollity* and game. *Milton.*

2. Elevation of spirit; gayety.

He with a proud *jollity* commanded him to leave that quarrel for him who was only worthy to enter into it. *Sidney.*

[This word in America is not now applied to respectable company.]

JOL'LY, *a.* [Fr. *joli*, pretty; It. *giulivo*, joyful, merry. Qu. Sax. *geola, gehol*, a feast, the *yule*, or feast of the nativity.]

1. Merry; gay; lively; full of life and mirth; jovial. It expresses more life and noise than *cheerful;* as a *jolly* troop of huntsmen. *Shak.*

[It is seldom applied in colloquial usage to respectable company. We rarely say of respectable persons, they are *jolly.* It is applied to the young and the vulgar.]

2. Expressing mirth or inspiring it.

And with his *jolly* pipe delights the groves. *Prior.*

The coachman is swelled into *jolly* dimensions by frequent potations of malt liquors. *Irving.*

3. Exciting mirth and gayety; as *jolly* May. *Dryden.*

4. Like one in high health; pretty. *South.*

JOL'LY-BOAT, *n.* A small boat belonging to a ship. [Sw. *julle*, a yawl.]

JOLT, *v. i.* To shake with short abrupt risings and fallings; as a carriage moving on rough ground. The carriage *jolts.*

JOLT, *v. t.* To shake with sudden jerks, as in a carriage on rough ground, or on a high trotting horse; as the horse or carriage *jolts* the rider.

JOLT, *n.* A shock or shake by a sudden jerk, as in a carriage. *Swift.*

JOLTER, *n.* He or that which jolts.

JOLTHEAD, *n.* A greathead; a dunce; a blockhead. *Shak.*

JOLTING, *ppr.* Giving sudden jerks or shakes.

JON'QUIL, *n.* [Fr. *jonquille;* It. *giunchiglia; giunco*, L. *juncus*, a rush, and It. *giglio*, a lily. It is sometimes called the rush leafed daffodil.]

A plant of the genus Narcissus or daffodil, bearing beautiful flowers, of various colors, yellow and white. *Encyc.*

JOR'DEN, *n.* A vessel for chamber uses. *Swift.*

JO'SO, *n.* A small fish of the gudgeon kind.

JOS'TLE, *v. t. jos'l.* [Fr. *jouter*, for *jouster;* It. *giostrare;* Sp. *justar.* Written also *justle.*] To run against; to push.

JOS'TLED, *pp.* Run against; pushed. We say, a thing is *jostled* out of its place.

JOS'TLING, *ppr.* Running against; pushing.

JOS'TLING, *n.* A running against; a crowding.

JOT, *n.* [Gr. ιωτα, Ch. Heb. *yod*, Syr. *yudh*, the name of the letter י or *i*.]
An iota; a point; a tittle; the least quantity assignable.

Till heaven and earth pass, one *jot* or one tittle shall in no wise pass from the law till all shall be fulfilled. Matt. v.

A man may read much, and acquire not a *jot* of knowledge, or be a *jot* the wiser. *Anon.*

JOT, *v. t.* To set down; to make a memorandum of.

JOT'TING, *n.* A memorandum. *Todd.*

JÖUIS'SANCE, *n.* [Fr.] Jollity; merriment. [*Not in use.*] *Spenser.*

JOURNAL, *n. jur'nal.* [Fr. *journal*; It. *giornale*, from *giorno*, a day; Corn. *jurna*; W. *diurnod*; L. *diurnum.* This was originally an adjective, signifying daily, as in Spenser and Shakspeare; but the adjective is obsolete.]
1. A diary; an account of daily transactions and events; or the book containing such account.
2. Among *merchants*, a book in which every particular article or charge is fairly entered from the waste book or blotter.
3. In *navigation*, a daily register of the ship's course and distance, the winds, weather, and other occurrences.
4. A paper published daily, or other newspaper; also, the title of a book or pamphlet published at stated times, containing an account of inventions, discoveries and improvements in arts and sciences; as the *Journal* de Savans; the *Journal* of Science.

JOURNALIST, *n. jur'nalist.* The writer of a journal or diary.

JOURNALIZE, *v. t. jur'nalize.* To enter in a journal.

JOURNEY, *n. jur'ny.* [Fr. *journée*, a day or day's work; It. *giornata*, a day; Sp. *jornada*, a journey, or travel of a day; It. *giorno*, a day, from L. *diurnus, dies.*]
1. The travel of a day. *Obs.* *Milton.*
2. Travel by land to any distance and for any time, indefinitely; as a *journey* from London to Paris, or to Rome; a *journey* to visit a brother; a week's *journey*; we made two *journeys* to Philadelphia.
3. Passage from one place to another; as a long *journey* from the upper regions. *Burnet.*
4. It may sometimes include a passing by water.

JOURNEY, *v. i. jur'ny.* To travel from place to place; to pass from home to a distance.

Abram *journeyed*, going on still towards the south. Gen. xii.

JOUR'NEYING, *ppr.* Traveling; passing from place to place.

JOUR'NEYING, *n.* A traveling or passing from one place to another; as the *journeyings* of the children of Israel.

JOUR'NEYMAN, *n.* [*journey* and *man.*] Strictly, a man hired to work by the day, but in fact, any mechanic who is hired to work for another in his employment, whether by the month, year or other term. It is applied only to mechanics in their own occupations.

JOUR'NEY-WŎRK, *n.* Work done for hire by a mechanic in his proper occupation. [*This word is never applied to farming.*]

JOUST. [See *Just.*]

JOVE, *n.* [L. *Jovis*, gen. of *Jupiter*, Gr. ζευς.]
1. The name of the Supreme Deity among the Romans.
2. The planet Jupiter.

Or ask of yonder argent fields above
Why *Jove's* satellites are less than *Jove.* *Pope.*

3. The air or atmosphere, or the god of the air.

And *Jove* descends in showers of kindly rain. *Dryden.*

JO'VIAL, *a.* [from *Jove*, supra.] Under the influence of Jupiter, the planet.

—The fixed stars astrologically differenced by the planets, and esteemed Martial or *Jovial* according to the colors whereby they answer these planets. *Brown.*

JO'VIAL, *a.* [Fr. and Sp. *id.*; It. *gioviale*; probably from the root of *giovane*, young, or from that of *joy.* If it is from *Jove*, it must be from the sense of airy or fresh.]
1. Gay; merry; airy; joyous; jolly; as a *jovial* youth; a *jovial* throng.
2. Expressive of mirth and hilarity.

His odes are some of them panegyrical, others moral, the rest are *jovial* or bacchanalian. *Dryden.*

JO'VIALIST, *n.* One who lives a jovial life. *Hall.*

JO'VIALLY, *adv.* Merrily; gayly; with noisy mirth.

JO'VIALNESS, *n.* Noisy mirth; gayety.

JOWL, *n.* The cheek. [See *Jole.*]

JOWL'ER, *n.* The name of a hunting dog, beagle or other dog. *Dryden.*

JOW'TER, *n.* A fish driver. *Carew.*

JOY, *n.* [Fr. *joie*; It. *gioia*; Arm. *joa*, contracted; G. *jauchzen*, to shout; D. *juichen*, to rejoice; Sp. *gozo*; Port. *id.* This word belongs to the Class Cg, and its radical sense is probably, to shout, or to leap, or to play or sport, and allied perhaps to *joke* and *juggle.*]
1. The passion or emotion excited by the acquisition or expectation of good; that excitement of pleasurable feelings which is caused by success, good fortune, the gratification of desire or some good possessed, or by a rational prospect of possessing what we love or desire; gladness; exultation; exhilaration of spirits.

Joy is a delight of the mind, from the consideration of the present or assured approaching possession of a good. *Locke.*

—Peace,
Bring heavenly balm to heal my country's wounds,
Joy to my soul and transport to my lay. *D. Humphrey.*

2. Gayety; mirth; festivity.

The roofs with *joy* resound. *Dryden.*

3. Happiness; felicity.

Her heavenly form beheld, all wished her *joy.* *Dryden.*

4. A glorious and triumphant state.

—Who for the *joy* that was set before him, endured the cross. Heb. xii.

5. The cause of joy or happiness.

For ye are our glory and *joy.* 1 Thess. ii.

6. A term of fondness; the cause of joy.

JOY, *v. i.* To rejoice; to be glad; to exult.

I will *joy* in the God of my salvation. Hab. iii.

JOY, *v. t.* To give joy to; to congratulate; to entertain kindly.
2. To gladden; to exhilarate.

My soul was *joyed* in vain. *Pope.*

3. [Fr. *jouir.*] To enjoy; to have or possess with pleasure, or to have pleasure in the possession of. [*Little used.* See *Enjoy.*] *Milton. Dryden.*

JOY'ANCE, *n.* [Old Fr. *joiant.*] Gayety; festivity. *Obs.* *Spenser.*

JOY'ED, *pp.* Gladdened; enjoyed.

JOY'FUL, *a.* Full of joy; very glad; exulting.

My soul shall be *joyful* in my God. Is. lxi.

Rarely, it has *of* before the cause of joy.

Sad for their loss, but *joyful of* our life. *Pope.*

JOY'FULLY, *adv.* With joy; gladly.

Never did men more *joyfully* obey. *Dryden*

JOY'FULNESS, *n.* Great gladness; joy. Deut. xxviii.

JOY'LESS, *a.* Destitute of joy; wanting joy.

With downcast eyes the *joyless* victor sat. *Dryden.*

Rarely followed by *of*; as *joyless of* the grove. *Dryden.*

2. Giving no joy or pleasure.

A *joyless*, dismal, black and sorrowful issue. *Shak.*

JOY'LESSLY, *adv.* Without joy. *Milton.*

JOY'LESSNESS, *n.* State of being joyless. *Donne.*

JOY'OUS, *a.* [Fr. *joyeux.*] Glad; gay; merry; joyful.

Joyous the birds; fresh gales and gentle airs
Whispered it. *Milton.*

2. Giving joy.

They, all as glad as birds of *joyous* prime— *Spenser.*

It has *of*, before the cause of joy.

And *joyous of* our conquest early won. *Dryden.*

JOY'OUSLY, *adv.* With joy or gladness.

JOY'OUSNESS, *n.* The state of being joyous.

JUB, *n.* A bottle or vessel. *Obs.* *Chaucer.*

JU'BILANT, *a.* [L. *jubilans.* See *Jubilee.*] Uttering songs of triumph; rejoicing; shouting with joy.

While the bright pomp ascended *jubilant.* *Milton.*

JUBILA'TION, *n.* [Fr. from L. *jubilatio.* See *Jubilee.*] The act of declaring triumph.

JU'BILEE, *n.* [Fr. *jubilé*; L. *jubilum*, from *jubilo*, to shout for joy; Sp. *jubileo*; It. *giubbileo*; Heb. יבל or יובל, the blast of a trumpet, coinciding with Eng. *bawl, peal*, L. *pello.*]
1. Among the Jews, every fiftieth year, being the year following the revolution of seven weeks of years, at which time all the slaves were liberated, and all lands which had been alienated during the whole period, reverted to their former owners. This was a time of great rejoicing. Hence,
2. A season of great public joy and festivity. *Milton.*
3. A church solemnity or ceremony celebrated at Rome, in which the pope grants plenary indulgence to sinners, or to as many as visit the churches of St. Peter and St. Paul at Rome. *Encyc.*

JU€UND'ITY, *n.* [L. *jucunditas*, from *jucundus*, sweet, pleasant.]
Pleasantness; agreeableness. [*Little used.*] *Brown.*

JUDA'I€, } *a.* Pertaining to the Jews.
JUDA'I€AL, } *Milner.*

JUDA'I€ALLY, *adv.* After the Jewish manner. *Milton.*

JU'DAISM, *n.* [Fr. *judaisme*, from *Judah*, whence *Jew.*]
1. The religious doctrines and rites of the Jews, as enjoined in the laws of Moses. *Judaism* was a temporary dispensation.
2. Conformity to the Jewish rites and ceremonies. *Encyc.*

JU'DAIZE, *v. i.* [Fr. *judaiser*, from *Judah.*] To conform to the religious doctrines and rites of the Jews.

They—prevailed on the Galatians to *judaize* so far as to observe the rites of Moses in various instances. *Milner.*

JU'DAIZER, *n.* One who conforms to the religion of the Jews. *Macknight.*

JU'DAIZING, *ppr.* Conforming to the doctrines and rites of the Jews.

JU'DAS-TREE, *n.* A plant of the genus Cercis.

JUD'DOCK, *n.* A small snipe, called also Jack-snipe.

JUDĠE, *n.* [Fr. *juge*; Sp. *juez*; Port. *juiz*; It. *giudice*; L. *judex*, supposed to be compounded of *jus*, law or right, and *dico*, to pronounce. "Hinc *judex*, quod jus dicat accepta potestate." *Varro.*]
1. A civil officer who is invested with authority to hear and determine causes, civil or criminal, between parties, according to his commission; as the *judges* of the king's bench, or of the common pleas; *judges* of the supreme court, of district courts, or of a county court. The *judge* of a court of equity is called a *chancellor.*
2. The Supreme Being.

Shall not the *judge* of all the earth do right? Gen. xviii.

3. One who presides in a court of judicature.
4. One who has skill to decide on the merits of a question, or on the value of any thing; one who can discern truth and propriety.

A man who is no *judge* of law, may be a good *judge* of poetry or eloquence, or of the merits of a painting. *Dryden.*

5. In *the history of Israel*, a chief magistrate, with civil and military powers. The Israelites were governed by *judges* more than three hundred years, and the history of their transactions is called the *book of Judges.*
6. A juryman or juror. In criminal suits, the jurors are *judges* of the law as well as of the fact.

JUDĠE, *v. i.* [Fr. *juger*; L. *judico*; It. *giudicare*; Sp. *juzgar.*]
1. To compare facts or ideas, and perceive their agreement or disagreement, and thus to distinguish truth from falsehood.

Judge not according to the appearance. John vii.

2. To form an opinion; to bring to issue the reasoning or deliberations of the mind.

If I did not know the originals, I should not be able to *judge*, by the copies, which was Virgil and which Ovid. *Dryden.*

3. To hear and determine, as in causes on trial; to pass sentence. He was present on the bench, but could not *judge* in the case.

The Lord *judge* between thee and me. Gen. xvi.

4. To discern; to distinguish; to consider accurately for the purpose of forming an opinion or conclusion.

Judge in yourselves; is it comely that a woman pray unto God uncovered? 1 Cor. xi.

JUDĠE, *v. t.* To hear and determine a case; to examine and decide.

Chaos shall *judge* the strife. *Milton.*

2. To try; to examine and pass sentence on.

Take ye him and *judge* him according to your law. John xviii.

God shall *judge* the righteous and the wicked. Eccles. iii.

3. Rightly to understand and discern.

He that is spiritual, *judgeth* all things. 1 Cor. ii.

4. To censure rashly; to pass severe sentence.

Judge not, that ye be not *judged.* Matt. vii.

5. To esteem; to think; to reckon.

If ye have *judged* me to be faithful to the Lord— Acts xvi.

6. To rule or govern.

The Lord shall *judge* his people. Heb. x.

7. To doom to punishment; to punish.

I will *judge* thee according to thy ways. Ezek. vii.

JUDĠ'ED, *pp.* Heard and determined; tried judicially; sentenced; censured; doomed.

JUDĠ'ER, *n.* One who judges or passes sentence.

JUDĠESHIP, *n. judj'ship.* The office of a judge.

JUDĠ'ING, *ppr.* Hearing and determining; forming an opinion; dooming.

JUDĠ'MENT, *n.* [Fr. *jugement.*] The act of judging; the act or process of the mind in comparing its ideas, to find their agreement or disagreement, and to ascertain truth; or the process of examining facts and arguments, to ascertain propriety and justice; or the process of examining the relations between one proposition and another. *Locke. Encyc. Johnson.*
2. The faculty of the mind by which man is enabled to compare ideas and ascertain the relations of terms and propositions; as a man of clear *judgment* or sound *judgment.* The *judgment* may be biased by prejudice. *Judgment* supplies the want of certain knowledge.
3. The determination of the mind, formed from comparing the relations of ideas, or the comparison of facts and arguments. In the formation of our *judgments*, we should be careful to weigh and compare all the facts connected with the subject.
4. In *law*, the sentence or doom pronounced in any cause, civil or criminal, by the judge or court by which it is tried. *Judgment* may be rendered on demurrer, on a verdict, on a confession or default, or on a non-suit. *Judgment*, though pronounced by the judge or court, is properly the determination or sentence of the *law.* A pardon may be pleaded in arrest of *judgment.*
5. The right or power of passing sentence. *Shak.*
6. Determination; decision.

Let reason govern us in the formation of our *judgment* of things proposed to our inquiry.

7. Opinion; notion.

She, in my *judgment*, was as fair as you. *Shak.*

8. In *Scripture*, the spirit of wisdom and prudence, enabling a person to discern right and wrong, good and evil.

Give the king thy *judgments*, O God. Ps. lxxii.

9. A remarkable punishment; an extraordinary calamity inflicted by God on sinners.

Judgments are prepared for scorners. Prov. xix. Is. xxvi.

10. The spiritual government of the world.

The Father hath committed all *judgment* to the Son. John v.

11. The righteous statutes and commandments of God are called his *judgments.* Ps. cxix.
12. The doctrines of the gospel, or God's word. Matt. xii.
13. Justice and equity. Luke xi. Is. i.
14. The decrees and purposes of God concerning nations. Rom. xi.
15. A court or tribunal. Matt. v.
16. Controversies, or decisions of controversies. 1 Cor. vi.
17. The gospel, or kingdom of grace. Matt. xii.
18. The final trial of the human race, when God will decide the fate of every individual, and award sentence according to justice.

For God shall bring every work into *judgment*, with every secret thing, whether it be good, or whether it be evil. Eccles. xii.

Judgment of God. Formerly this term was applied to extraordinary trials of secret crimes, as by arms and single combat, by ordeal, or hot plowshares, &c.; it being imagined that God would work miracles to vindicate innocence.

JUDĠ'MENT-DAY, *n.* The last day, or day when final judgment will be pronounced on the subjects of God's moral government.

JUDĠ'MENT-HALL, *n.* The hall where courts are held.

JUDĠ'MENT-SEAT, *n.* The seat or bench on which judges sit in court.
2. A court; a tribunal.

We shall all stand before the *judgment-seat* of Christ. Rom. xiv.

JU'DI€ATIVE, *a.* Having power to judge. *Hammond.*

JU'DI€ATORY, *a.* Dispensing justice.

JU'DI€ATORY, *n.* [L. *judicatorium.*] A court of justice; a tribunal. *Atterbury.*
2. Distribution of justice. *Clarendon.*

JU'DI€ATURE, *n.* [Fr.] The power of distributing justice by legal trial and determination. A court of *judicature* is a court invested with powers to administer justice between man and man.
2. A court of justice; a judicatory. *South.*

JUDI''CIAL, *a.* Pertaining to courts of justice; as *judicial* power.
2. Practiced in the distribution of justice; as *judicial* proceedings.
3. Proceeding from a court of justice; as a *judicial* determination.
4. Issued by a court under its seal; as a *judicial* writ.
5. Inflicted, as a penalty or in judgment; as *judicial* hardness of heart; a *judicial* punishment.

JUDI''CIALLY, *adv.* In the forms of legal justice; as a sentence *judicially* declared.

2. By way of penalty or judgment; as, to be *judicially* punished.

JUDI″CIARY, *n.* [Fr. *judiciaire;* L. *judicia-rius.*]

1. Passing judgment or sentence. *Boyle.*
2. Pertaining to the courts of judicature or legal tribunals.

JUDI″CIARY, *n.* That branch of government which is concerned in the trial and determination of controversies between parties, and of criminal prosecutions; the system of courts of justice in a government. An independent *judiciary* is the firmest bulwark of freedom. *United States.*

JUDI″CIOUS, *a.* [Fr. *judicieux;* It. *giudi-cioso.*]

1. According to sound judgment; wise; prudent; rational; adapted to obtain a good end by the best means; *used of things.* Nothing is more important to success in the world than a *judicious* application of time, unless it may be a *judicious* expenditure of money.
2. Acting according to sound judgment; possessing sound judgment; wise; directed by reason and wisdom; *used of persons;* as a *judicious* magistrate; a *judicious* historian.

JUDI″CIOUSLY, *adv.* With good judgment; with discretion or wisdom; skillfully.

Longinus has *judiciously* preferred the sublime genius that sometimes errs, to the middling or indifferent one, which makes few faults, but seldom rises to excellence. *Dryden.*

JUDI″CIOUSNESS, *n.* The quality of acting or being according to sound judgment.

JUG, *n.* [Junius mentions the Danish *jugge,* an urn or water-pot, and the Sax. has *ceac,* Low L. *caucus.* Qu.]

A vessel, usually earthen, with a swelling belly and narrow mouth, used for holding and conveying liquors. *Swift.*

JUG′GLE, *v. i.* [D. *guichelen* or *goochelen;* G. *gaukeln;* It. *giocolare;* Dan. *gögler,* to juggle; *giekker,* to joke; Sw. *gäck,* a jester; *gäcka,* to mock, to make sport; L. *joculor,* to jest, from *jocus,* a joke; *jocor,* to joke, which coincides with the Sp. and Port. *jugar,* to play, to sport; Fr. *jouer,* contracted. It is certain that *joke* and *jocular,* and probable that *joy,* are from the same root as *juggle;* perhaps Ch. חוך *hukk,* or *chuk,* to laugh, to play, to sport. Class Gk. No. 18.]

1. To play tricks by slight of hand; to amuse and make sport by tricks, which make a false show of extraordinary powers.
2. To practice artifice or imposture.

Be these *juggling* fiends no more believed. *Shak.*

JUG′GLE, *v. t.* To deceive by trick or artifice.

Is't possible the spells of France should *juggle*
Men into such strange mockeries? *Shak.*

JUG′GLE, *n.* A trick by legerdemain.

2. An imposture; a deception. *Tillotson.*

JUG′GLER, *n.* [Sp. *juglar;* Fr. *jongleur;* It. *giocolatore;* D. *güichelær.*]

1. One who practices or exhibits tricks by slight of hand; one who makes sport by tricks of extraordinary dexterity, by which the spectator is deceived. *Jugglers* are punishable by law.
2. A cheat; a deceiver; a trickish fellow. *Shak.*

JUG′GLING, *ppr.* Playing tricks by slight of hand; deceiving.

JUG′GLING, *n.* The act or practice of exhibiting tricks of legerdemain.

JUG′GLINGLY, *adv.* In a deceptive manner.

JU′GULAR, *a.* [L. *jugulum,* the neck, either from *jugum,* a yoke, or from its radical sense, to extend, to join. See *Join.*]

Pertaining to the neck or throat; as the *jugular* vein.

JU′GULAR, *n.* A large vein of the neck.

JUICE, } *n. juse.* [D. *juys;* Fr. *jus.* The reg-
JUSE, } ular orthography is *juse.*]

The sap of vegetables; the fluid part of animal substances. *Encyc.*

JUICE, *v. t.* To moisten.

JUICELESS, *a. ju′seless.* Destitute of juice; dry; without moisture. *More.*

JUICINESS, *n. ju′siness.* The state of abounding with juice; succulence in plants.

JUICY, *a. ju′sy.* Abounding with juice; moist; succulent. *Bacon.*

JUISE, *n.* [L. *jus.*] Judgment; justice. *Obs.* *Gower.*

JU′JUB, } *n.* [L. *zizyphum;* Pers. زيزفون.]
JU′JUBE, }

The name of a plant and of its fruit, which is pulpy and resembles a small plum. The plant is arranged under the genus Rhamnus. The fruit was formerly used in pectoral decoctions, but it is now in little reputation. *Encyc. Miller.*

JUKE, *v. i.* [Fr. *jucher.*] To perch. [*Not used.*]

JU′LEP, *n.* [Ar. جلاب julabon; Pers. id.; Fr. *julep;* It. *giulebbo.*]

In *pharmacy,* a medicine composed of some proper liquor and a sirup of sugar, of extemporaneous preparation, serving as a vehicle to other forms of medicine. *Encyc. Quincy.*

JU′LIAN, *a.* Noting the old account of the year, as regulated by Julius Cesar, which continued to be used till 1752, when the Gregorian year, or new style, was adopted.

Julian Alps, called also Carnian, between Venetia and Noricum. *D'Anville.*

JU′LIS, *n.* A small fish with a green back.

JU′LUS, *n.* [Gr. ιουλος, a handful or bundle.]

1. In *botany,* a catkin or ament, a species of calyx or inflorescence, consisting of chaffy scales arranged along a stalk, as in hazle, birch, willow, &c. *Martyn.*
2. A genus of multiped insects, of the order of Apters, of a semi-cylindrical form, with moniliform antennæ, and two articulated palpi. *Encyc.*

JULY′, *n.* The seventh month of the year, during which the sun enters the sign Leo. It is so called from *Julius,* the surname of Caius Cesar, who was born in this month. Before that time, this month was called *Quintilis,* or the fifth month, according to the old Roman calendar, in which March was the first month of the year.

JULȲ-FLOWER, *n.* The name of certain species of plants. The *clove July-flower* is of the genus Dianthus; the *queen's July-flower* of the genus Hesperis; and the *stock July-flower* of the genus Cheiranthus. [See *Gilly-flower.*] *Lee.*

JU′MART, *n.* [Fr.] The offspring of a bull and a mare. *Locke.*

JUM′BLE, *v. t.* [Chaucer, *jombre.*] To mix in a confused mass; to put or throw together without order. It is often followed by *together.*

One may observe how apt that is to *jumble together* passages of Scripture. *Locke.*

JUM′BLE, *v. i.* To meet, mix or unite in a confused manner. *Swift.*

JUM′BLE, *n.* Confused mixture, mass or collection without order. *Swift.*

JUM′BLED, *pp.* Mixed or collected in a confused mass.

JUM′BLEMENT, *n.* Confused mixture. [*Not in use.*]

JUM′BLER, *a.* One who mixes things in confusion.

JUM′BLING, *ppr.* Putting or mixing in a confused mass.

JU′MENT, *n.* [Fr. from L. *jumentum,* a beast.]

A beast of burden. [*Not used.*] *Brown.*

JUMP, *v. i.* [Qu. the root of It. *zampillare,* to spring.]

1. To leap; to skip; to spring. *Applied to men,* it signifies to spring upwards or forwards with both feet, in distinction from *hop,* which signifies to spring with one foot. A man *jumps* over a ditch; a beast *jumps* over a fence. A man *jumps* upon a horse; a goat *jumps* from rock to rock.
2. To spring over any thing; to pass to at a leap.

Here, upon this bank and shelve of time,
We'd *jump* the life to come. *Shak.*

We see a little, presume a great deal, and so *jump* to the conclusion. *Spectator.*

3. To bound; to pass from object to object; to jolt.

The noise of the rattling of the wheels, and of the prancing horses, and of the *jumping* chariots. Nahum iii.

4. To agree; to tally; to coincide.

In some sort it *jumps* with my humor. *Shak.*

[This use of the word is now vulgar, and in America, I think, is confined to the single phrase, to *jump in judgment.*]

JUMP, *v. t.* To pass by a leap; to pass over eagerly or hastily; as, to *jump* a stream. [But *over* is understood.]

JUMP, *n.* The act of jumping; a leap; a spring; a bound.

2. A lucky chance. *Shak.*

JUMP, *n.* [Fr. *jupe;* It. *giubba.*] A kind of loose or limber stays or waistcoat, worn by females.

JUMP, *adv.* Exactly; nicely. *Obs.* *Hooker.*

JUMP′ER, *n.* One who jumps.

JUMP′ING, *ppr.* Leaping; springing; bounding.

JUN′CATE, *n.* [It. *giuncata,* cream cheese; Fr. *jonchée de crême,* a kind of cream cheese served in a frail of green rushes, and for that reason so called, or because made in a frail or basket of rushes; L. *juncus,* a rush.]

1. A cheese-cake; a kind of sweetmeat of curds and sugar. *Johnson.*
2. Any kind of delicate food. *Milton.*
3. A furtive or private entertainment. [It is now written *junket.*]

JUNC'OUS, *a.* [L. *junceus* or *juncosus*, from *juncus*, a rush.]
Full of bulrushes. [*Little used.*]

JUNC'TION, *n.* [Fr. from L. *junctio*, from *jungo*, to join.]
1. The act or operation of joining; as the *junction* of two armies or detachments.
2. Union; coalition; combination.
3. The place or point of union.

JUNC'TURE, *n.* [L. *junctura*; Sp. *juntura*; It. *giuntura*; from L. *jungo*, to join.]
1. A joining; union; amity; as the *juncture* of hearts. [*Little used.*] *King Charles.*
2. A union of two bodies; a seam; particularly, a joint or articulation. *Encyc.*
3. The line or point at which two bodies are joined. *Boyle.*
4. A point of time; particularly, a point rendered critical or important by a concurrence of circumstances. *Addison.*

JUNE, *n.* [L *junius*; Fr. *juin*; It. *giugno*; Sp. *junio.*]
The sixth month of the year, when the sun enters the sign Cancer.

JUN'GLE, *n.* [Hindoo.] In Hindoostan, a thick wood of small trees or shrubs. *Asiat. Res.*

JUN'GLY, *a.* Consisting of jungles; abounding with jungles. *Ibm.*

JU'NIOR, *a.* [L. from *juvenis*, young; quasi, *juvonior.*]
Younger; not as old as another; as a *junior* partner in a company. It is applied to distinguish the younger of two persons bearing the same name in one family or town, and opposed to *elder*; as John Doe *junior.*

JU'NIOR, *n.* A person younger than another.

> The fools, my *juniors* by a year— *Swift.*

JUNIOR'ITY, *n.* The state of being junior. *Bullokar.*

JU'NIPER, *n.* [L. *juniperus*; It. *ginepro*; Fr. *genevre*; Sp. *enebro.*]
A tree or shrub bearing berries of a bluish color, of a warm, pungent, sweet taste, yielding when fresh, by expression, a rich, sweet, aromatic juice. They are useful carminatives and stomachics. The wood of the tree is of a reddish color, hard and durable, and is used in cabinet work and veneering. The oil of juniper mixed with that of nuts makes an excellent varnish; and the resin powdered is used under the name of *pounce.* *Encyc.*

JUNK, *n.* [L. *juncus*, It. *giunco*, Sp. *junco*, Fr. *jonc*, a bulrush, of which ropes were made in early ages.]
1. Pieces of old cable or old cordage, used for making points, gaskets, mats, &c., and when untwisted and picked to pieces, it forms oakum for filling the seams of ships. *Mar. Dict.*
2. A small ship used in China; a Chinese vessel. [*An eastern word.*]

JUNK'ET, *n.* [See *Juncate.*] A sweetmeat. *Shak.*
2. A stolen entertainment.

JUNK'ET, *v. i.* To feast in secret; to make an entertainment by stealth. *Swift.*
2. To feast.

> Job's children *junketed* and feasted together often. *South.*

JUN'TO, *n.* [Sp. *junta*, a meeting or council, from L. *junctus*, joined; It. *giunto.*]
1. Primarily, a select council or assembly, which deliberates in secret on any affair of government. In a good sense, it is not used in English; but hence,
2. A cabal; a meeting or collection of men combined for secret deliberation and intrigue for party purposes; a faction; as a *junto* of ministers. *Gulliver.*

JU'PITER, *n.* [L. the air or heavens; *Jovis pater.*]
1. The supreme deity among the Greeks and Romans.
2. One of the superior planets, remarkable for its brightness. Its diameter is about eighty-nine thousand miles; its distance from the sun, four hundred and ninety millions of miles, and its revolution round the sun a little less than twelve years.

JUPPON', *n.* [Fr. *jupon*; It. *giubbone.*] A short close coat. *Dryden.*

JU'RAT, *n.* [Fr. from L. *juratus*, sworn, from *juro*, to swear.]
In *England*, a magistrate in some corporations; an alderman, or an assistant to a bailiff. *Encyc.*

JU'RATORY, *a.* [Fr. *juratoire*, from L. *juro*, to swear.]
Comprising an oath; as *juratory* caution. [*Little used.*] *Ayliffe.*

JURID'ICAL, *a.* [L. *juridicus*; *jus*, *juris*, law, and *dico*, to pronounce.]
1. Acting in the distribution of justice; pertaining to a judge.
2. Used in courts of law or tribunals of justice. *Hale.*

JURID'ICALLY, *adv.* According to forms of law, or proceedings in tribunals of justice; with legal authority.

JURISCON'SULT, *n.* [L. *juris consultus*; *jus* and *consultus*, *consulo*, to consult.]
Among the Romans, a man learned in the law; a counselor at law; a master of Roman jurisprudence, who was consulted on the interpretation of the laws. *Encyc.*

JURISDIC'TION, *n.* [Fr. from L. *jurisdictio*; *jus*, *juris*, law, and *dictio*, from *dico*, to pronounce; It. *giuridizione*; Sp. *jurisdiccione*; Port. *jurisdiçam.*]
1. The legal power or authority of doing justice in cases of complaint; the power of executing the laws and distributing justice. Thus we speak of certain suits or actions, or the cognizance of certain crimes being within the *jurisdiction* of a court, that is, within the limits of their authority or commission. Inferior courts have *jurisdiction* of debt and trespass, or of smaller offenses; the supreme courts have *jurisdiction* of treason, murder, and other high crimes. *Jurisdiction* is secular or ecclesiastical.
2. Power of governing or legislating. The legislature of one state can exercise no *jurisdiction* in another.
3. The power or right of exercising authority. Nations claim exclusive *jurisdiction* on the sea, to the extent of a marine league from the main land or shore.
4. The limit within which power may be exercised.
Jurisdiction, in its most general sense, is the power to make, declare or apply the law; when confined to the judiciary department, it is what we denominate the *judicial power*, the right of administering justice through the laws, by the means which the laws have provided for that purpose. Jurisdiction, is limited to place or territory, to persons, or to particular subjects. *Du Ponceau.*

JURISDIC'TIONAL, *a.* Pertaining to jurisdiction; as *jurisdictional* rights.

JURISDIC'TIVE, *a.* Having jurisdiction. *Milton.*

JURISPRU'DENCE, *n.* [Fr. from L. *jurisprudentia*; *jus*, law, and *prudentia*, science.]
The science of law; the knowledge of the laws, customs and rights of men in a state or community, necessary for the due administration of justice. The study of *jurisprudence*, next to that of theology, is the most important and useful to men.

JURISPRU'DENT, *a.* Understanding law. *West.*

JURISPRUDEN'TIAL, *a.* Pertaining to jurisprudence. *Ward.*

JU'RIST, *n.* [Fr. *juriste*; It. *giurista*; Sp. *jurista*; from L. *jus*, *juris*, law.]
1. A man who professes the science of law; one versed in the law, or more particularly, in the civil law; a civilian. *Bacon.*
2. One versed in the law of nations, or who writes on the subject.

JU'ROR, *n.* [L. *jurator*; or rather *juro*, to swear.]
One that serves on a jury; one sworn to deliver the truth on the evidence given him concerning any matter in question or on trial.

JU'RY, *n.* [Fr. *juré*, sworn, L. *juro*, to swear.]
A number of freeholders, selected in the manner prescribed by law, empanneled and sworn to inquire into and try any matter of fact, and to declare the truth on the evidence given them in the case. *Grand juries* consist usually of twenty four freeholders at least, and are summoned to try matters alledged in indictments. *Petty juries*, consisting usually of twelve men, attend courts to try matters of fact in civil causes, and to decide both the law and the fact in criminal prosecutions. The decision of a petty jury is called a *verdict.*

JU'RYMAN, *n.* One who is empanneled on a jury, or who serves as a juror.

JU'RYM'AST, *n.* A mast erected in a ship to supply the place of one carried away in a tempest or an engagement, &c. The most probable origin of the word *jury*, in this compound, is that proposed by Thomson, viz. from the Fr. *jour*, day, quasi, *jouré*, temporary, or from L. *juvare*, to assist.

JUST, *a.* [Fr. *juste*; Sp. *justo*; It. *giusto*; L. *justus*. The primary sense is probably straight or close, from the sense of setting, erecting, or extending.]
1. Regular; orderly; due; suitable.

> When all
> The war shall stand ranged in its *just* array. *Addison.*

2. Exactly proportioned; proper.

> Pleaseth your lordship
> To meet his grace, *just* distance 'tween our armies? *Shak.*

3. Full; complete to the common standard.

> He was a comely personage, a little above *just* stature. *Bacon.*

4. Full; true; a sense allied to the preceding, or the same.

—So that once the skirmish was like to have come to a *just* battle. *Knolles.*

5. In *a moral sense*, upright; honest; having principles of rectitude; or conforming exactly to the laws, and to principles of rectitude in social conduct; equitable in the distribution of justice; as a *just* judge.

6. In *an evangelical sense*, righteous; religious; influenced by a regard to the laws of God; or living in exact conformity to the divine will.

There is not a *just* man on earth, that doeth good, and sinneth not. Eccles. vii.

7. Conformed to rules of justice; doing equal justice.

Just balances, *just* weights, a *just* ephah and a *just* hin shall ye have. Lev. xix.

8. Conformed to truth; exact; proper; accurate; as *just* thoughts; *just* expressions; *just* images or representations; a *just* description; a *just* inference.

9. True; founded in truth and fact; as a *just* charge or accusation.

10. Innocent; blameless; without guilt.

How should man be *just* with God? Job ix.

11. Equitable; due; merited; as a *just* recompense or reward.

—Whose damnation is *just*. Rom. iii.

12. True to promises; faithful; as *just* to one's word or engagements.

13. Impartial; allowing what is due; giving fair representation of character, merit or demerit.

JUST, *adv.* Close or closely; near or nearly, in place. He stood *just* by the speaker, and heard what he said. He stood *just* at the entrance of the city.

2. Near or nearly in time; almost. *Just* at that moment he arose and fled.

3. Exactly; nicely; accurately. They remain *just* of the same opinion.

'Tis with our judgments as our watches; none
Go *just* alike, yet each believes his own. *Pope.*

4. Merely; barely; exactly.

—And having *just* enough, not covet more. *Dryden.*

5. Narrowly. He *just* escaped without injury.

JUST, *n.* [Fr. *jouste*, now *joute*; Sp. *justa*; Port. *id.*; It. *giostra*; probably from the root of *jostle* or *justle*. The primary sense is to thrust, to drive, to push.]

A mock encounter on horseback; a combat for sport or for exercise, in which the combatants pushed with lances and swords, man to man, in mock fight; a tilt; one of the exercises at tournaments. *Encyc.*

JUST, *v. i.* [Fr. *jouter*; Sp. and Port. *justar*; It. *giostrare.*]

1. To engage in mock fight on horseback.
2. To push; to drive; to justle.

JUST'ICE, *n.* [Fr.; Sp. *justicia*; It. *giustizia*; from L. *justitia*, from *justus*, just.]

2. The virtue which consists in giving to every one what is his due; practical conformity to the laws and to principles of rectitude in the dealings of men with each other; honesty; integrity in commerce or mutual intercourse. *Justice* is *distributive* or *commutative*. *Distributive justice* belongs to magistrates or rulers, and consists in distributing to every man that right or equity which the laws and the principles of equity require; or in deciding controversies according to the laws and to principles of equity. *Commutative justice* consists in fair dealing in trade and mutual intercourse between man and man.

2. Impartiality; equal distribution of right in expressing opinions; fair representation of facts respecting merit or demerit. In criticisms, narrations, history or discourse, it is a duty to do *justice* to every man, whether friend or foe.

3. Equity; agreeableness to right; as, he proved the *justice* of his claim. This should, in strictness, be *justness.*

4. Vindictive retribution; merited punishment. Sooner or later, *justice* overtakes the criminal.

5. Right; application of equity. His arm will do him *justice.*

6. [Low L. *justiciarius.*] A person commissioned to hold courts, or to try and decide controversies and administer justice to individuals; as the Chief *Justice* of the king's bench, or of the common pleas, in England; the Chief *Justice* of the supreme court in the United States, &c. and *justices* of the peace.

JUST'ICE, *v. t.* To administer justice. [*Little used.*] *Bacon.*

JUST'ICEABLE, *a.* Liable to account in a court of justice. [*Little used.*] *Hayward.*

JUST'ICER, *n.* An administrator of justice. [*Little used.*] *Bp. Hall.*

JUST'ICESHIP, *n.* The office or dignity of a justice. *Swift.*

JUSTI''CIARY, } *n.* [L. *justiciarius.*] An
JUSTI''CIAR, } administrator of justice. *Burke.*

2. A chief justice. *Blackstone.*

3. One that boasts of the justice of his own act. [*Not used.*] *Dering.*

JUST'IFIABLE, *a.* [from *justify.*] That may be proved to be just; that may be vindicated on principles of law, reason, rectitude or propriety; defensible; vindicable. No breach of law or moral obligation is *justifiable*. The execution of a malefactor in pursuance of a sentence of court, is *justifiable* homicide.

JUST'IFIABLENESS, *n.* The quality of being justifiable; rectitude; possibility of being defended or vindicated. *King Charles.*

JUST'IFIABLY, *adv.* In a manner that admits of vindication or justification; rightly.

JUSTIFICA'TION, *n.* [Fr. from *justifier*, to *justify.*]

1. The act of justifying; a showing to be just or conformable to law, rectitude or propriety; vindication; defense. The court listened to the evidence and arguments in *justification* of the prisoner's conduct. Our disobedience to God's commands admits no *justification.*

2. Absolution.

I hope, for my brother's *justification*, he wrote this but as an essay of my virtue. *Shak.*

3. In *law*, the showing of a sufficient reason in court why a defendant did what he is called to answer. Pleas in *justification* must set forth some special matter.

4. In *theology*, remission of sin and absolution from guilt and punishment; or an act of free grace by which God pardons the sinner and accepts him as righteous, on account of the atonement of Christ.

JUSTIF'ICATIVE, *a.* Justifying; that has power to justify.

JUSTIFICA'TOR, *n.* One who justifies. [*Little used.*]

JUST'IFIER, *n.* One who justifies; one who vindicates, supports or defends.

2. He who pardons and absolves from guilt and punishment.

That he might be just, and the *justifier* of him who believeth in Jesus. Rom. iii.

JUST'IFY̆, *v. t.* [Fr. *justifier*; Sp. *justificar*; It. *giustificare*; L. *justus*, just, and *facio*, to make.]

1 To prove or show to be just, or conformable to law, right, justice, propriety or duty; to defend or maintain; to vindicate as right. We cannot *justify* disobedience or ingratitude to our Maker. We cannot *justify* insult or incivility to our fellow men. Intemperance, lewdness, profaneness and dueling are in no case to be *justified.*

2. In *theology*, to pardon and clear from guilt; to absolve or acquit from guilt and merited punishment, and to accept as righteous on account of the merits of the Savior, or by the application of Christ's atonement to the offender. *St. Paul.*

3. To cause another to appear comparatively righteous, or less guilty than one's self. Ezek. xvi.

4. To judge rightly of.

Wisdom is *justified* by her children. Matt. xi.

5. To accept as just and treat with favor. James ii.

JUST'IFY̆, *v. i.* In *printing*, to agree; to suit; to conform exactly; to form an even surface or true line with something else. Types of different sizes will not *justify* with each other.

JUS'TLE, *v. i. jus'l.* [See *Jostle* and *Just.*] To run against; to encounter; to strike against; to clash.

The chariots shall rage in the streets; they shall *justle* one against another in the broad ways. Nah. ii.

JUS'TLE, *v. t. jus'l.* To push; to drive; to force by rushing against; commonly followed by *off* or *out*; as, to *justle* a thing *off* the table, or *out* of its place.

JUST'LY, *adv.* [from *just.*] In conformity to law, justice or propriety; by right. The offender is *justly* condemned. The hero is *justly* rewarded, applauded or honored.

2. According to truth and facts. His character is *justly* described.

3. Honestly; fairly; with integrity; as, to do *justly*. Mic. vi.

4. Properly; accurately; exactly.

Their feet assist their hands, and *justly* beat the ground. *Dryden.*

JUST'NESS, *n.* Accuracy; exactness; as the *justness* of proportions.

2. Conformity to truth; as the *justness* of a description or representation.

3. Justice; reasonableness; equity; as the *justness* of a cause or of a demand. [*Justness* is properly applied to things, and *justice* to persons; but the distinction is not always observed.]

JUT, *v. i.* [a different spelling of *jet.*] To

shoot forward; to project beyond the main body; as the *jutting* part of a building. A point of land *juts* into the sea.

JUT, *n.* A shooting forward; a projection.

JUT'TING, *ppr.* Shooting out; projecting.

JUT'TY, *v. i.* To jut. [*Not used.*] *Shak.*

JUT'TY, *n.* A projection in a building; also, a pier or mole.

JUT-WINDOW, *n.* A window that projects from the line of a building.

JU'VENILE, *a.* [L. *juvenilis*, from *juvenis*, young.]

1. Young; youthful; as *juvenile* years or age.

2. Pertaining or suited to youth; as *juvenile* sports.

JUVENIL'ITY, *n.* Youthfulness; youthful age. *Glanville.*

2. Light and careless manner; the manners or customs of youth. *Glanville.*

JUXTAPOS'ITED, *a.* [L. *juxta*, near, and *posited.*] Placed near; adjacent or contiguous. *Macquer.*

JUXTAPOSI''TION, *n.* [L. *juxta*, near, and *position.*]

A placing or being placed in nearness or contiguity; as the parts of a substance or of a composition. The connection of words is sometimes to be ascertained by *juxtaposition.*

K.

K, the eleventh letter of the English Alphabet, is borrowed from the Greeks, being the same character as the Greek *kappa*, answering to the oriental *kaph.* It represents a close articulation, formed by pressing the root of the tongue against the upper part of the mouth, with a depression of the lower jaw and opening of the teeth. It is usually denominated a guttural, but is more properly a palatal. Before all the vowels, it has one invariable sound, corresponding with that of *c*, before *a*, *o* and *u*, as in *keel*, *ken.* In monosyllables, it is used after *c*, as in *crack*, *check*, *deck*, being necessary to exhibit a correct pronunciation in the derivatives, *cracked*, *checked*, *decked*, *cracking*, for without it, *c*, before the vowels *e* and *i*, would be sounded like *s.*

Formerly, *k* was added to *c*, in certain words of Latin origin, as in *musick*, *publick*, *republick.* But in modern practice, *k* is very properly omitted, being entirely superfluous, and the more properly, as it is never written in the derivatives, *musical*, *publication*, *republican.* It is retained in *traffick*, as in monosyllables, on account of the pronunciation of the derivatives, *trafficked*, *trafficking.*

K is silent before *n*, as in *know*, *knife*, *knee.*

As a numeral, K stands for 250; and with a stroke over it, thus, $\bar{K}$, for 250,000.

This character was not used by the ancient Romans, and rarely in the later ages of their empire. In the place of *k*, they used c, as in *clino*, for the Greek *κλινω.* In the Teutonic dialects, this Greek letter is sometimes represented by *h.* [See *H.*]

KAALING, *n.* A bird, a species of starling, found in China.

KAB'BOS, *n.* A fish of a brown color, without scales.

KALE, *n.* [L. *caulis*; W. *cawl.*] Sea-cale, an esculent plant of the genus Crambe.

KAL'ENDAR, *n.* [See *Calendar.*]

KA'LI, *n.* [Ar. قَلِي the ashes of the Salicornia, from قَلَي kalai, to fry.]

A plant, a species of Salsola, or glass-wort, the ashes of which are used in making glass. Hence *alkali*, which see.

KA'LIF, *n.* [See *Calif.*]

KAL'MIA, *n.* The name of a genus of evergreen shrubs, natives of N. America, called laurel, ivy-bush, calico-bush, &c.

KAM, *a.* [W. *cam.*] Crooked. [*Not used.*] *Shak.*

KAN, KAUN, KHAN, } *n.* In Persia, an officer answering to a governor in Europe or America. Among the Tartars, a chief or prince. [See *Khan.*]

KANGAROO', *n.* A singular animal found in New Holland, resembling in some respects the opossum. It belongs to the genus Didelphis. It has a small head, neck and shoulders, the body increasing in thickness to the rump. The fore legs are very short, useless in walking, but used for digging or bringing food to the mouth. The hind legs, which are long, are used in moving, particularly in leaping. *Encyc.*

KA'OLIN, *n.* A species of earth or variety of clay, used as one of the two ingredients in the oriental porcelain. The other ingredient is called in China *petunse.* Its color is white, with a shade of gray, yellow or red. *Encyc. Cleaveland.*

KAR'AGANE, *n.* A species of gray fox found in the Russian empire. *Tooke.*

KARPH'OLITE, *n.* [Gr. *καρφος*, straw, and *λιθος*, a stone.]

A mineral recently discovered. It has a fibrous structure and a yellow color. *Werner. Cleaveland.*

KA'TA, *n.* In Syria, a fowl of the grous kind.

KAW, *v. i.* [from the sound.] To cry as a raven, crow or rook. *Locke.*

KAW, *n.* The cry of the raven, crow or rook. *Dryden.*

KAWN, *n.* In Turkey, a public inn.

KAYLE, *n.* [Fr. *quille*, a nine-pin, a *keel.*]

1. A nine-pin, a kettle-pin; sometimes written *keel.* *Sidney. Carew.*

2. A kind of play in Scotland, in which nine holes ranged in threes, are made in the ground, and an iron ball rolled in among them. *Johnson.*

KECK, *v. i.* [G. *köken.*] To heave the stomach; to reach, as in an effort to vomit. [*Little used.*] *Bacon. Swift.*

KECK, *n.* A reaching or heaving of the stomach. *Cheyne.*

KECK'LE, *v. t.* [Qu. G. *kugeln*, to roll.] To wind old rope round a cable to preserve its surface from being fretted, or to wind iron chains round a cable to defend it from the friction of a rocky bottom, or from the ice. *Mar. Dict.*

KECK'SY, *n.* [Qu. Fr. *cigue*, L. *cicuta.* It is said to be commonly pronounced *kex.*] Hemlock; a hollow jointed plant. [*Not used in America.*] *Shak.*

KECK'Y, *a.* Resembling a kex.

2. An Indian scepter. *Grew.*

KEDĠE, *n.* [allied probably to *cag* and *keg.*] A small anchor, used to keep a ship steady when riding in a harbor or river, and particularly at the turn of the tide, to keep her clear of her bower anchor, also to remove her from one part of a harbor to another, being carried out in a boat and let go, as in warping or kedging. [Sometimes written *kedger.*] *Mar. Dict.*

KEDĠE, *v. t.* To warp, as a ship; to move by means of a kedge, as in a river.

KED'LACK, *n.* A weed that grows among wheat and rye; charlock. [*I believe not used in America.*] *Tusser. Johnson.*

KEE, *plu.* of *cow.* [*Local in England and not used in America.*] *Gay.*

KEECH, *n.* A mass or lump. [*Not in use.*] *Percy.*

KEEL, *n.* [Sax. *cœle*; G. and D. *kiel*; Dan. *kiil*, *kiol*; Russ. *kil*; Sw. *kȯl*; Fr. *quille*; Sp. *quilla*; Port. *quilha.* The word, in different languages, signifies a *keel*, a pin, *kayle*, and a *quill*; probably from extending.]

1. The principal timber in a ship, extending from stem to stern at the bottom, and supporting the whole frame. *Mar. Dict.*

2. A low flat-bottomed vessel, used in the river Tyne, to convey coals from Newcastle for loading the colliers.

3. In *botany*, the lower petal of a papilionaceous corol, inclosing the stamens and pistil. *Martyn.*

False keel, a strong thick piece of timber, bolted to the bottom of the keel, to preserve it from injury.

On an even keel, in a level or horizontal position.

KEEL, *v. t.* [Sax. *cœlan.*] To cool. *Obs.* *Gower.*

KEEL, *v. t.* To plow with a keel; to navigate. *J. Barlow.*

2. To turn up the keel; to show the bottom. *Shak.*

To keel the pot, in Ireland, to scum it. *Shak.*

KEE'LAĠE, *n.* Duty paid for a ship entering Hartlepool, Eng.

KEE'LED, *a.* In *botany*, carinated; having a longitudinal prominence on the back; as a *keeled* leaf, calyx or nectary. *Martyn.*

KEE'LFAT, *n.* [Sax. *cœlan*, to cool, and *fat*, vat.]

A cooler; a vessel in which liquor is set for cooling. [*Not used.*]

KEE'LHAUL, *v. t.* [D. *kielhaalen; keel* and *haul.*]

To haul under the keel of a ship. Keel-hauling is a punishment inflicted in the Dutch navy for certain offenses. The offender is suspended by a rope from one yard arm, with weights on his legs, and a rope fastened to him, leading under the ship's bottom to the opposite yard arm, and being let fall into the water, he is drawn under the ship's bottom and raised on the other side. *Mar. Dict.*

KEE'LING, *n.* A kind of small cod, of which stock fish is made.

KEELSON, *n. kel'son.* A piece of timber in a ship, laid on the middle of the floor timbers over the keel, fastened with long bolts and clinched, and thus binding the floor timbers to the keel. *Mar. Dict.*

KEEN, *a.* [Sax. *cene; G. kühn; D. koen;* properly, bold, stout, eager, daring, from shooting forward. Class Gn.]

1. Eager; vehement; as hungry curs too *keen* at the sport. *Tatler.*

   The sheep were so *keen* on the acorns— *L'Estrange.*

2. Eager; sharp; as a *keen* appetite.
3. Sharp; having a very fine edge; as a *keen* razor, or a razor with a *keen* edge. We say a *keen* edge, but a *sharp* point.
4. Piercing; penetrating; severe; applied to cold or to wind; as a *keen* wind; the cold is very *keen*.
5. Bitter; piercing; acrimonious; as *keen* satire or sarcasm.

   Good father cardinal, cry thou amen,
   To my *keen* curses. *Shak.*

KEEN, *v. t.* To sharpen. [*Unusual.*] *Thomson.*

KEE'NLY, *adv.* Eagerly; vehemently.

2. Sharply; severely; bitterly.

KEE'NNESS, *n.* Eagerness; vehemence; as the *keenness* of hunger.

2. Sharpness; fineness of edge; as the *keenness* of a razor.
3. The quality of piercing; rigor; sharpness; as the *keenness* of the air or of cold.
4. Asperity; acrimony; bitterness; as the *keenness* of satire, invective or sarcasm.
5. Acuteness; sharpness; as the *keenness* of wit.

KEEP, *v. t.* pret. and pp. *kept.* [Sax. *cepan*, Syr. ܟܒܐ kaba, Eth. ዐቀበ akab, to keep. Class Gb. No. 68. 85. The word coincides in elements with *have*, L. *habeo*, and *capio*, but I think the radical sense to be different.]

1. To hold; to retain in one's power or possession; not to lose or part with; as, to *keep* a house or a farm; to *keep* any thing in the memory, mind or heart.
2. To have in custody for security or preservation.

   The crown of Stephanus, first king of Hungary, was always *kept* in the castle of Vicegrade. *Knolles.*

3. To preserve; to retain.

   The Lord God, merciful and gracious, *keeping* mercy for thousands— Ex. xxxiv.

4. To preserve from falling or from danger; to protect; to guard or sustain.

   And behold, I am with thee, and will *keep* thee. Gen. xxviii. Luke iv.

5. To hold or restrain from departure; to detain.

   —That I may know what *keeps* me here with you. *Dryden.*

6. To tend; to have the care of.

   And the Lord God took the man and put him in the garden of Eden, to dress it and to *keep* it. Gen. ii.

7. To tend; to feed; to pasture; as, to *keep* a flock of sheep or a herd of cattle in a yard or in a field. He *keeps* his horses on oats or on hay.
8. To preserve in any tenor or state. *Keep* a stiff rein.

   Keep the constitution sound. *Addison.*

9. To regard; to attend to.

   While the stars and course of heaven I *keep*— *Dryden.*

10. To hold in any state; as, to *keep* in order.
11. To continue any state, course or action; as, to *keep* silence; to *keep* the same road or the same pace; to *keep* reading or talking; to *keep* a given distance.
12. To practice; to do or perform; to obey; to observe in practice; not to neglect or violate; as, to *keep* the laws, statutes or commandments of God. *Scripture.*
13. To fulfill; to perform; as, to *keep* one's word, promise or covenant.
14. To practice; to use habitually; as, to *keep* bad hours. *Pope.*
15. To copy carefully.

   Her servant's eyes were fix'd upon her face,
   And as she moved or turned, her motions viewed,
   Her measures *kept*, and step by step pursued. *Dryden.*

16. To observe or solemnize.

   Ye shall *keep* it a feast to the Lord. Ex. xii.

17. To board; to maintain; to supply with necessaries of life. The men are *kept* at a moderate price per week.
18. To have in the house; to entertain; as, to *keep* lodgers.
19. To maintain; not to intermit; as, to *keep* watch or guard.
20. To hold in one's own bosom; to confine to one's own knowledge; not to disclose or communicate to others; not to betray; as, to *keep* a secret; to *keep* one's own counsel.
21. To have in pay; as, to *keep* a servant.

To keep back, to reserve; to withhold; not to disclose or communicate.

   I will *keep* nothing *back* from you. Jer. xlii.

2. To restrain; to prevent from advancing.

   Keep back thy servant also from presumptuous sins. Ps. xix.

3. To reserve; to withhold; not to deliver. Acts v.

To keep company with, to frequent the society of; to associate with. Let youth *keep company with* the wise and good.

2. To accompany; to go with; as, to *keep company with* one on a journey or voyage.

To keep down, to prevent from rising; not to lift or suffer to be raised.

To keep in, to prevent from escape; to hold in confinement.

2. To conceal; not to tell or disclose.
3. To restrain; to curb. *Locke.*

To keep off, to hinder from approach or attack; as, to *keep off* an enemy or an evil.

To keep under, to restrain; to hold in subjection; as, to *keep under* an antagonist or a conquered country; to *keep under* the appetites and passions.

To keep up, to maintain; to prevent from falling or diminution; as, to *keep up* the price of goods; to *keep up* one's credit.

2. To maintain; to continue; to hinder from ceasing.

   In joy, that which *keeps up* the action is the desire to continue it. *Locke.*

To keep out, to hinder from entering or taking possession.

To keep bed, to remain in bed without rising; to be confined to one's bed.

To keep house, to maintain a family state. His income enables him to *keep house*.

2. To remain in the house; to be confined. His feeble health obliges him to *keep house*.

To keep from, to restrain; to prevent approach.

To keep a school, to maintain or support it; as, the town or its inhabitants *keep* ten *schools;* more properly, to govern and instruct or teach a school, as a preceptor.

KEEP, *v. i.* To remain in any state; as, to *keep* at a distance; to *keep* aloft; to *keep* near; to *keep* in the house; to *keep* before or behind; to *keep* in favor; to *keep* out of company, or out of reach.

2. To last; to endure; not to perish or be impaired. Seek for winter's use apples that will *keep*.

   If the malt is not thoroughly dried, the ale it makes will not *keep*. *Mortimer.*

3. To lodge; to dwell; to reside for a time.

   Knock at the study, where, they say, he *keeps*. *Shak.*

To keep to, to adhere strictly; not to neglect or deviate from; as, to *keep to* old customs; to *keep to* a rule; to *keep to* one's word or promise.

To keep on, to go forward; to proceed; to continue to advance. *Dryden.*

To keep up, to remain unsubdued; or not to be confined to one's bed.

In *popular language*, this word signifies to continue; to repeat continually; not to cease.

KEEP, *n.* Custody; guard. [*Little used.*] *Dryden.*

2. *Colloquially*, case; condition; as in good *keep*. *English.*
3. Guardianship; restraint. [*Little used.*] *Ascham.*
4. A place of confinement; in old castles, the dungeon.

KEE'PER, *n.* One who keeps; one that holds or has possession of any thing.

2. One who retains in custody; one who has the care of a prison and the custody of prisoners.
3. One who has the care of a park or other inclosure, or the custody of beasts; as the *keeper* of a park, a pound, or of sheep.
4. One who has the care, custody or superintendence of any thing.

In Great Britain, the *keeper of the great seal*, is a lord by his office, and one of the privy council. All royal grants, commissions and charters pass through his hands. He is constituted lord-keeper by the delivery of the great seal. The *keeper of the privy seal* is also a lord by his office, and a member of the privy council.

KEE'PERSHIP, *n.* The office of a keeper. [*Little used.*] *Carew.*

KEE'PING, *ppr.* Holding; restraining; preserving; guarding; protecting; performing.

KEE'PING, *n.* A holding; restraint; custody; guard; preservation.

2. Feed; fodder. The cattle have good *keeping.*

3. In *painting*, a representation of objects in the manner they appear to the eye at different distances from it.

KEE'PSAKE, *n.* Any thing kept, or given to be kept for the sake of the giver; a token of friendship.

KEF'FEKIL, *n.* A stone, white or yellow, which hardens in the fire, and of which Turkey pipes are made. *Nicholson.*

KEG, *n.* [Fr. *caque.*] A small cask or barrel; written more correctly *cag.*

KELL, *n.* A sort of pottage. [*Not used in America.*] *Ainsworth.*

KELL, *n.* The caul or omentum. [See *Caul*, the usual orthography of the word.] *Wiseman.*

2. The chrysalis of the caterpillar. *B. Jonson.*

KELP, *n.* [Ar. and Pers.] The calcined ashes of sea weed, used in the manufacture of glass. This is a dark colored alkaline substance, which, in a furnace, vitrifies and becomes transparent. *Encyc.*

KELP'Y, *n.* An imaginary spirit of the waters, in the form of a horse. [*Local and vulgar.*]

KEL'SON. [See *Keelson.*]

KELT'ER, *n.* [Dan. *kilter*, to gird, to truss up; *kilte*, a folding.]

The phrase, *he is not in kelter*, signifies, he is not in a proper dress or equipage, or not in readiness.

KEMB, *v. t.* [Sax. *cemban*, to comb.] To comb, which see. *Kemb* is an obsolete orthography. *B. Jonson. Dryden.*

KEM'ELIN, *n.* [Qu. Gr. *χειμηλιον*, furniture.] A tub; a brewer's vessel. [*Not in use.*] *Chaucer.*

KEN, *v. t.* [W. *ceniaw*, to see; *ceiniaw*, to take a view, to perceive; which Owen deduces from *càn*, *cain*, clear, bright, fair, white, and sight, brightness, and this coincides with L. *canus*, white, *caneo*, to be white, and this with L. *cano*, to sing, *canto*, Eng. to *cant*, to chant. These coincide in elements with G. *kennen*, to know, *erkennen*, to see, know, discern; D. *kennen*. Sw. *kunna*, Dan. *kiender*, to know, to be able; Sax. *connan*, *cunnan*, Goth. *kunnan*, to know. In Sax. *cennan* is to bear, L. *gigno*, Gr. *γενναω*. The radical sense is to strain, extend, reach. In Sans. *kanna* is an eye. See *Can.*]

1. To see at a distance; to descry.

We *ken* them from afar. *Addison.*

2. To know; to understand. *Obs. Shak. Gay.* [*This verb is used chiefly in poetry.*]

KEN, *v. i.* To look round. *Burton.*

KEN, *n.* View; reach of sight.

Coasting they kept the land within their *ken.* *Dryden.*

KEN'DAL-GREEN, *n.* A species of green cloth made of kendal. *Shak.*

KEN'NEL, *n.* [Fr. *chenil*; It. *canile*; from L. *canis*, a dog.]

1. A house or cot for dogs, or for a pack of hounds.

2. A pack of hounds or their cry. *Encyc.*

3. The hole of a fox or other beast; a haunt.

KEN'NEL, *n.* [It. *canale*; Fr. *canal*; Eng. *channel.*]

1. The water-course of a street; a little canal or channel.

2. A puddle.

KEN'NEL, *v. i.* To lodge; to lie; to dwell; as a dog or a fox.

The dog *kenneled* in a hollow tree. *L'Estrange.*

KEN'NEL, *v. t.* To keep or confine in a kennel. *Tatler.*

KEN'NING, *n.* View; sight. *Bacon.*

KEN'TLE, *n.* [W. *cant*, a hundred; L. *centum.*]

In *commerce*, a hundred pounds in weight; as a *kentle* of fish. [It is written and pronounced also *quintal.*]

KENT'LEDGE, *n.* In *seamen's language*, pigs of iron for ballast laid on the floor of a ship. *Mar. Dict.*

KEPT, *pret.* and *pp.* of *keep.*

KERB-STONE, KIRB-STONE. [See *Curb-stone.*]

KER'CHIEF, *n.* [contracted from *coverchief*; Fr. *couvrir*, to cover, and *chef*, the head. *Chaucer.*]

1. A head dress; a cloth to cover the head. *Shak.*

2. A cloth used in dress. *Hayward.*

The word is now seldom used, except in its compound, *handkerchief*, and sometimes *neckerchief.*

KER'CHIEFED, } *a.* Dressed; hooded;
KER'CHIEFT, } covered. *Milton.*

KERF, *n.* [Sax. *cyrf*; *ceorfan*, *cearfan*, to cut, Eng. to *carve*; D. *kerf*, a notch; *kerven*, to cut; G. *kerb*, *kerben*, Ir. *cearb.*]

The cut of an ax, a saw, or other instrument; the notch or slit made in wood by cutting.

KERM'ES, *n.* [Ar. قرمز kirmiran, coccus baphica. *Castell.*]

In *zoology*, an insect produced in the excrescences of a species of small oak, or the body of an insect transformed into a grain, berry, or husk. This body is full of reddish juice, which is used in dyeing red. Hence the word *crimson.* *Encyc.*

KERM'ES-MINERAL, *n.* A mineral substance, so called from its color. It is a precipitate of antimony, obtained by fusion with a fixed alkali and subsequent solution in boiling water, or by simple ebullition. *Nicholson. Encyc.*

KERN, *n.* An Irish footman or foot-soldier. *Spenser.*

2. In *English laws*, an idle person or vagabond. *Encyc.*

KERN, *n.* A hand-mill consisting of two stones, one of which is turned by the hand; usually written *quern*, which see.

2. A churn. *Obs.*

KERN, *v. i.* [G. and D. *kern*, a kernel; G. *kernen*, to curdle.]

1. To harden, as corn in ripening. *Carew.*

2. To take the form of corns; to granulate. *Grew.*

KERN'-BABY, *n.* [*corn-baby.*] An image dressed with corn, and carried before reapers to their harvest-home.

KERN'EL, *n.* [Sax. *cyrnel*, a little *corn*, grain or nut; G. and D. *kern*; Fr. *cerneau*; W. *cwaren*, a gland, a kernel.]

1. The edible substance contained in the shell of a nut. *More.*

2. Any thing included in a shell, husk or integument; a grain or corn; as a *kernel* of wheat or oats.

3. The seed of pulpy fruit; as the *kernel* of an apple. *Bacon.*

4. The central part of any thing; a small mass around which other matter is concreted; a nucleus. *Arbuthnot.*

5. A hard concretion in the flesh.

KERN'EL, *v. i.* To harden or ripen into kernels; as the seeds of plants.

KERN'ELLY, *a.* Full of kernels; resembling kernels.

KER'SEY, *n.* [D. *kerzaai*; Fr. *cariset*; Sp. *carisea.*]

A species of coarse woolen cloth; a coarse stuff made chiefly in Kent and Devonshire in England. *Encyc.*

KERVE, *v. t.* To carve. [*Not used.*]

KERV'ER, *n.* A carver. [*Not used.*]

KE'SAR, *n.* [from *Cesar.*] An emperor. *Obs.* *Spenser.*

KES'TREL, *n.* A fowl of the genus Falco, or hawk kind; called also *stannel* and *windhover.* It builds in hollow oaks, and feeds on quails and other small birds. *Encyc.*

KETCH, *n.* [Fr. *quaiche*; G. and D. *kits.*] A vessel with two masts, a main and mizen-mast, usually from 100 to 250 tons burden. Ketches are generally used as yachts or as bomb-vessels. The latter are called *bomb-ketches.* *Mar. Dict.*

KETCH'UP, *n.* A sauce. [See *Catchup.*]

KET'TLE, *n.* [Sax. *cetl*, *cetel* or *cytel*; G. *kessel*; D. *ketel*; Dan. *kedel*; Sw. *kittel*; Russ. *kotel.*]

A vessel of iron or other metal, with a wide mouth, usually without a cover, used for heating and boiling water or other liquor.

Among *the Tartars*, a *kettle* represents a family, or as many as feed from one kettle.

Among *the Dutch*, a battery of mortars sunk in the earth, is called a *kettle.* *Encyc.*

KET'TLE-DRUM, *n.* An instrument of martial music, composed of two basins of copper or brass, rounded at the bottom and covered with vellum or goat-skin. *Encyc.*

KET'TLE-DRUMMER, *n.* The man who beats the kettle-drum.

KET'TLE-PINS, *n.* Nine pins; skittles.

KEV'EL, *n.* In *ships*, a piece of timber serving to belay the sheets or great ropes by which the bottoms of the fore-sail and main-sail are extended. *Mar. Dict.*

KEX, *n.* Hemlock; the stem of the teasel; a dry stalk. [See *Kecksy.*]

KEY, *n. kē.* [Sax. *cæg.*] In a general sense, a fastener; that which fastens; as a piece of wood in the frame of a building, or in a chain, &c.

2. An instrument for shutting or opening a lock, by pushing the bolt one way or the other. Keys are of various forms, and fitted to the wards of the locks to which they belong.

3. An instrument by which something is screwed or turned; as the *key* of a watch or other chronometer.

4. The stone which binds an arch. [See *Key-stone.*]

5. In *an organ* or *harpsichord*, the key, or finger key is a little lever or piece in the fore part by which the instrument is played on by the fingers.

6. In *music*, the key, or key note, is the fundamental note or tone, to which the whole piece is accommodated, and with which it usually begins and always ends. There are two *keys*, one of the major, and one of the minor mode. *Key* sometimes signifies a scale or system of intervals. *Rousseau.*

7. An index, or that which serves to explain a cypher. Hence,

8. That which serves to explain any thing difficult to be understood.

9. In *the Romish church*, ecclesiastical jurisdiction, or the power of the pope; or the power of excommunicating or absolving. *Encyc.*

10. A ledge or lay of rocks near the surface of the water.

11. The husk containing the seed of an ash. *Evelyn.*

KEY, *n.* [Ir. *ceigh*; D. *kaai*; G. *kai*; Fr. *quai*; Arm. *qae*. The word is probably contracted from the root of the preceding word, signifying, to hold, make fast, restrain. Class Cg.]

A bank or wharf built on the side of a river or harbor, for the convenience of loading and unloading ships, and securing them in their stations. Hence keys are furnished with posts, rings, cranes, capstans, &c. It is sometimes written *quay*. *Encyc.*

KE'YAGE, *n.* Money paid for the use of a key or quay.

KE'Y-COLD, *a.* Lifeless. [*Not in use.*]

KE'YED, *a.* Furnished with keys; as a *keyed* instrument.

2. Set to a key, as a tune.

KE'YHOLE, *n.* A hole or aperture in a door or lock, for receiving a key.

KE'YSTONE, *n.* The stone on the top or middle of an arch or vault, which being wider at the top than at the bottom, enters like a wedge and binds the work; properly, the *fastening-stone*.

KHAN, *n.* *kaun.* In *Asia*, a governor; a king; a prince; a chief. In Persia, the word denotes the governor of a province; among the Tartars, it is equivalent to king or prince. *Eton.*

2. An inn.

KHANATE, *n.* *kaun'ate.* The dominion or jurisdiction of a khan. *Tooke.*

KIBE, *n.* [This word has the elements of *chap, gap, gape.* Class Gb. No. 7. Perhaps it is of Persian origin, كفيدن kafidan, to crack, to split. Qu. Dan. *kiebe*, the chops.]

A chap or crack in the flesh occasioned by cold; an ulcerated chilblain; as in the heels.

KI'BED, *a.* Chapped; cracked with cold; affected with chilblains; as *kibed* heels. *Darwin.*

KI'BY, *a.* Affected with kibes.

KICK, *v. t.* [W. *ciciaw*, from *cic*, the foot. *Owen.* Pers. كج a kicking.]

To strike with the foot; as, a horse *kicks* a servant; a man *kicks* a dog.

KICK, *v. i.* To practice striking with the foot or feet; as a horse accustomed to *kick.*

2. To thrust out the foot or feet with violence, either in wantonness, resistance, anger or contempt; to manifest opposition.

> Wherefore *kick* ye at my sacrifice? 1 Sam. ii.
>
> Jeshurun waxed fat and *kicked.* Deut. xxxii.
>
> It is hard for thee to *kick* against the goads. Acts ix.

KICK, *n.* A blow with the foot or feet; a striking or thrust of the foot.

KICK'ED, *pp.* Struck with the foot or feet.

KICK'ER, *n.* One that kicks.

KICK'ING, *ppr.* Striking with the foot; thrusting out the foot with violence.

KICK'ING, *n.* The act of striking with the foot, or of yerking the foot with violence. What cannot be effected by *kicking*, may sometimes be done by coaxing.

KICK'SHAW, *n.* [corrupted from Fr. *quelque chose*, something.]

1. Something fantastical or uncommon, or something that has no particular name.

2. A dish so changed by cooking, that it can scarcely be known. *Johnson.*

KICK'SHOE, *n.* A dancer, in contempt; a caperer; a buffoon. [A word used only by Milton.]

KID, *n.* [Dan. *kid*; Sw. *kid, kidling*; W. *cidws*, a goat, *cidysen*, a young goat; L. *hædus*; vulgar Gr. γιδα; Sans. *ada*; Turk. *getsi*; Heb. Ch. גדי; Syr. [Syriac] a kid; Russ. *kidayu*, to throw, to bring forth young.]

1. A young goat.

2. A faggot; a bundle of heath and furze. *Eng.*

KID, *v. t.* or *i.* To bring forth a young goat.

2. To make into a bundle, as faggots. *Eng.*

KID, *v. t.* [Sax. *cythan.*] To show, discover or make known. *Obs.* *Gower.*

KID'DER, *n.* [Sw. *kyta*, to truck.] An engrosser of corn, or one who carries corn, provisions and merchandize about the country for sale. *Eng.*

KID'DLE, *n.* A kind of wear in a river for catching fish; corruptly pronounced *kittle.* *Mag. Charta.*

KID'DŌW, *n.* A web-footed fowl, called also guillemot, sea-hen, or skout. *Chambers.*

KID'LING, *n.* [Sw.] A young kid. *Browne.*

KID'NAP, *v. t.* [G. *kinderdieb*; D. *kinderdief*, child-thief. *Kid* is usually supposed to be contracted from *kind*, a child, in which case, *nap* may be the oriental גנב, to steal. See *Knab.*]

To steal a human being, man, woman or child; or to seize and forcibly carry away any person whatever from his own country or state into another. *Encyc.*

KID'NAPPED, *pp.* Stolen or forcibly carried away; as a human being.

KID'NAPPER, *n.* One who steals or forcibly carries away a human being; a man-stealer.

KID'NAPPING, *ppr.* Stealing or forcibly carrying away human beings.

KID'NAPPING, *n.* The act of stealing, or forcible abduction of a human being from his own country or state. This crime was capital by the Jewish law, and in modern times is highly penal.

KID'NEY, *n.* [I have not found this word in any other language.]

1. The kidneys are two oblong flattened bodies, extending from the eleventh and twelfth ribs to the fourth lumbar vertebra, behind the intestines. Their use is to separate the urine from the blood. *Parr. Quincy.*

2. Sort; kind. [*A ludicrous use of the word.*] *Shak.*

3. A cant term for a waiting servant. *Tatler.*

KID'NEY-BEAN, *n.* A sort of bean so named from its resemblance to the kidney. It is of the genus Phaseolus.

KID'NEY-FORM, } *a.* Having the form
KID'NEY-SHAPED, } or shape of a kidney. *Kirwan.*

KID'NEY-VETCH, *n.* A plant of the genus Anthyllis.

KID'NEY-WŎRT, *n.* A plant of the genus Saxifraga.

KIF'FEKILL, } *n.* A mineral, the meer-
KEF'FEKILL, } schaum, which see.

KIL, *n.* A Dutch word, signifying a channel or bed of a river, and hence a stream.

KIL'DERKIN, *n.* [Qu. D. *kinderkin.*] A small barrel; a liquid measure containing two firkins, or 16 or 18 gallons. *Encyc.*

KILL, *v. t.* [The Dutch has *keel*, the throat, and *keelen*, to cut the throat, to kill. In Russ. *kolyu* is to stab. But this word seems to be allied to Sax. *cwellan*, to kill, to quell, that is, to beat down, to lay; and if so, it may be connected with D. *kwellen*, G. *quälen*, Sw. *quälia*, Dan. *quæler*, to torment, but in Danish to stifle, choke or quell. This affinity is rendered probable by the seamen's phrase, to *kill* the wind, that is, to allay or destroy it.]

1. To deprive of life, animal or vegetable, in any manner or by any means. To *kill* an animal or a plant, is to put an end to the vital functions, either by destroying or essentially injuring the organs necessary to life, or by causing them to cease from action. An animal may be *killed* by the sword or by poison, by disease or by suffocation. A strong solution of salt will *kill* plants.

2. To butcher; to slaughter for food; as, to *kill* an ox.

3. To quell; to appease; to calm; to still; as, in seamen's language, a shower of rain *kills* the wind.

KIL'LAS, *n.* An argillaceous stone of a pale gray or greenish gray, of a lamellar or coarsely granular texture, found in Cornwall, England. *Nicholson.*

KILL'DEE, *n.* A small bird in America, so called from its voice or note; a species of plover.

KILL'ED, *pp.* Deprived of life; quelled; calmed.

KILL'ER, *n.* One who deprives of life; he or that which kills.

KILL'ING, *ppr.* Depriving of life; quelling.

KIL'LINITE, *n.* A mineral, a variety of spodumene, found at Killeney, in Ireland. *Taylor.*

KIL'LOW, *n.* An earth of a blackish or deep blue color. *Woodward.*

KILN, *n.* *kil.* [Sax. *cyln*, from *cylene*, a furnace or kitchen; L. *culina*; W. *cyl* and *cylyn.*]

1. A large stove or oven; a fabric of brick or stone which may be heated for the purpose of hardening, burning or drying any thing; as a *kiln* for baking or hardening earthen vessels; a *kiln* for drying grain or meal.
2. A pile of brick constructed for burning or hardening; called also a *brick-kiln.*

KIL'N-DRIED, *pp.* Dried in a kiln.

KIL'N-DRY̆, *v. t. kil-dry.* To dry in a kiln; as, to *kiln-dry* meal or grain.

KIL'N-DRY̆ING, *ppr.* Drying in a kiln.

KIL'OGRAM, *n.* [Fr. *kilogramme*; Gr. χιλιοι, a thousand, and γραμμα. See *Gram.*]
In the new system of French weights and measures, a thousand grams. According to Lunier, the kilogram is equal in weight to a cubic decimeter of water, or two pounds, five drams and a half.

KIL'OLITER, *n.* [Fr. *kilolitre*; Gr. χιλιοι, a thousand, and λιτρα, a Greek measure. See *Liter.*]
In the new French measures, a thousand liters; or 264 gallons and 44,231 cubic inches. According to Lunier, it is nearly equal to a tun of wine of Bourdeaux.

KILOM'ETER, *n.* [Fr. *kilometre*; Gr. χιλιοι, a thousand, and μετρον, a meter.]
In the French system of measures, a thousand meters; the meter being the unit of linear measure. The kilometer is nearly equal to a quarter of a French league. *Lunier.*

KILT, *n.* A kind of short petticoat worn by the highlanders of Scotland.

KILT, *pp.* Killed. *Obs.*

KIM'BO, KIM'BOW, } *a.* [probably from the Celtic *cam*, crooked. The Italian *sghembo*, crooked, awry, is from the same source.]
Crooked; arched; bent; as a *kimbo* handle. *Dryden.*
To set the arms a kimbo, is to set the hands on the hips, with the elbows projecting outward.

KIN, *n.* [Sax. *cyn*, *cynn*, or *cind*, *gecynd*, kind, genus, race, relation; Ir. *cine*; G. *kind*, a child; D. *kind*; W. *cenal, cenaw*; L. *genus*; Gr. γενος; connected with L. *gigno*, *geno*, Gr. γινομαι. Class Gn. No. 29. See *Begin.*]
1. Relation, properly by consanguinity or blood, but perhaps sometimes used for relation by affinity or marriage.

> This man is of *kin* to me. *Bacon. Dryden.*

2. Relatives; kindred; persons of the same race.

> —The father, mother and the *kin* beside. *Dryden.*

3. A relation; a relative. *Davies.*
4. The same generical class; a thing related.

> And the ear-deafening voice of th' oracle,
> *Kin* to Jove's thunder. *Shak.*

5. As a termination, *kin* is used as a diminutive, denoting small, from the sense of *child*; as in *manikin*, a little man; *Tomkin, Wilkin, Pipkin.*

KIN, *a.* Of the same nature; kindred; congenial. *Chaucer.*

KIN'ATE, *n.* A salt formed by the union of kinic acid with a base. *Ure.*

KIND, *n.* [Sax. *cyn*, or *cynn*. See *Kin.*]
1. Race; genus; generic class; as in *mankind* or human *kind.* In technical language, *kind* answers to *genus.*
2. Sort, in a sense more loose than genus; as, there are several *kinds* of eloquence and of style, many *kinds* of music, many *kinds* of government, various *kinds* of architecture or of painting, various *kinds* of soil, &c.
3. Particular nature; as laws most perfect in their *kind.* *Baker.*
4. Natural state; produce or commodity, as distinguished from money; as taxes paid in *kind.*
5. Nature; natural propensity or determination.

> Some of you, on pure instinct of nature,
> Are led by *kind* t' admire your fellow creature. *Dryden.*

6. Manner; way. [*Little used.*] *Bacon.*
7. Sort. He spoke with a *kind* of scorn or contempt.

KIND, *a.* [W. and Arm. *cun*, kind, favorable, attractive. In Ir. *ceann*, is affection. This word would seem to be connected with the preceding, but in sense it coincides best with the Teutonic *gunstig*, favorable, kind, from G. *gönnen*, to be glad or pleased, to love to see, to favor, D. *gunnen*, to grant or vouchsafe.]
1. Disposed to do good to others, and to make them happy by granting their requests, supplying their wants or assisting them in distress; having tenderness or goodness of nature; benevolent; benignant.

> God is *kind* to the unthankful, and to the evil. Luke vi.

> Be ye *kind* one to another, tender-hearted. Eph. iv.

2. Proceeding from tenderness or goodness of heart; benevolent; as a *kind* act; a *kind* return of favors.

KIND'ED, *a.* Begotten. *Obs.* [See *Kin.*] *Spenser.*

KIN'DLE, *v. t.* [W. *cynneu*; L. *accendo*; from the root of *candeo, caneo*, to be light or white, to shine.]
1. To set on fire; to cause to burn with flame; to light; as, to *kindle* a fire.
2. To inflame, as the passions; to exasperate; to rouse; to provoke; to excite to action; to heat; to fire; to animate; as, to *kindle* anger or wrath; to *kindle* resentment; to *kindle* the flame of love, or love into a flame.

> So is a contentious woman to *kindle* strife. Prov. xxvi.

3. To bring forth. [Sax. *cennan.*] [*Not used.*] *Shak.*

KIN'DLE, *v. i.* To take fire; to begin to burn with flame. Fuel and fire well laid, will *kindle* without a bellows.
2. To begin to rage, or be violently excited; to be roused or exasperated.

> It shall *kindle* in the thickets of the forest. Is. ix.

KIN'DLED, *pp.* Set on fire; inflamed; excited into action.

KIN'DLER, *n.* He or that which kindles or sets on fire.

KINDLESS, *a.* Destitute of kindness; unnatural. *Shak.*

KINDLINESS, *n.* Affection; affectionate disposition; benignity.
2. Natural disposition. *Milton.*

KIN'DLING, *ppr.* Setting on fire; causing to burn with flame; exciting into action.

KINDLY, *a.* [See *Kind*, the noun.] Homogeneal; congenial; kindred; of the same nature. This Johnson supposes to be the original sense; but it is also used as a derivative of the adjective, in the sense of
2. Mild; bland; softening; as *kindly* showers. *Prior.*

KINDLY, *adv.* With good will; with a disposition to make others happy or to oblige; benevolently; favorably. Let the poor be treated *kindly.*

> Be *kindly* affectioned one to another, with brotherly love— Rom. xii.

> And he comforted them, and spake *kindly* unto them. Gen. l.

KINDNESS, *n.* [from *kind*, the adjective.]
1. Good will; benevolence; that temper or disposition which delights in contributing to the happiness of others, which is exercised cheerfully in gratifying their wishes, supplying their wants or alleviating their distresses; benignity of nature. *Kindness* ever accompanies love.

> There is no man whose *kindness* we may not sometime want, or by whose malice we may not sometime suffer. *Rambler.*

2. Act of good will; beneficence; any act of benevolence which promotes the happiness or welfare of others. Charity, hospitality, attentions to the wants of others, &c., are deemed acts of *kindness*, or *kindnesses.* Acts xxviii.

KIN'DRED, *n.* [from *kin, kind*; Sax. *cynren*; W. *cenal, cenedyl.*]
1. Relation by birth; consanguinity.

> Like her, of equal *kindred* to the throne. *Dryden.*

2. Relation by marriage; affinity.
3. Relatives by blood or marriage, more properly the former.

> Thou shalt go unto my country and to my *kindred.* Gen. xxiv.

4. Relation; suit; connection in kind. *Shak.*

KIN'DRED, *a.* Related; congenial; of the like nature or properties; as *kindred* souls; *kindred* skies. *Dryden.*

KINE, *plu.* of *cow*; D. *koeyen.* But *cows*, the regular plural, is now in general use.

KING, *n.* [Sax. *cyng, cynig*, or *cyning*; G. *könig*; D. *koning*; Sw. *konung, kung*; Dan. *konge*; W. *cūn*, a chief, a leader, one that attracts or draws. If the Welsh word is the same or of the same family, it proves that the primary sense is a leader, a guide, or one who goes before, for the radical sense of the verb must be to *draw.* It coincides in elements with the Ir. *cean*, head, and with the oriental *khan*, or *kaun.* The primary sense is probably a head, a leader.]
1. The chief or sovereign of a nation; a man invested with supreme authority over a nation, tribe or country; a monarch. Kings are *absolute* monarchs, when they possess the powers of government without control, or the entire sovereignty over a nation; they are *limited* monarchs, when their power is restrained by fixed laws; and they are *absolute*, when they possess the whole legislative, judicial, and executive power, or when the legislative or judicial powers, or both, are vested in other bodies of men. Kings are *hereditary* sovereigns, when they hold the powers of gov-

ernment by right of birth or inheritance, and *elective*, when raised to the throne by choice.

Kings will be tyrants from policy, when subjects are rebels from principle. *Burke.*

2. A sovereign; a prince; a ruler. Christ is called the *king* of his church. Ps. ii.
3. A card having the picture of a king; as the *king* of diamonds.
4. The chief piece in the game of chess.

King at arms, an officer in England of great antiquity, and formerly of great authority, whose business is to direct the heralds, preside at their chapters, and have the jurisdiction of armory. There are three kings at arms, viz. garter, clarencieux, and norroy. The latter [*northroy*] officiates north of the Trent. *Encyc.*

KING, *v. t.* In *ludicrous language*, to supply with a king, or to make royal; to raise to royalty. *Shak.*

KING′APPLE, *n.* A kind of apple, so called.

KING'S BENCH, *n.* A high court or tribunal in England; so called because the king used to sit there in person. It is the supreme court of common law, consisting of a chief justice and three other justices. *Blackstone.*

KING′BIRD, *n.* A fowl of the genus Paradisea; also, a species of the genus Muscicapa, so called from its courage in attacking larger fowls.

KING′CR′AFT, *n.* The craft of kings; the act of governing; *usually in a bad sense.*

KING′CUP, *n.* A flower, crowfoot. *Gay.*

KING'S-EVIL, *n.* A disease of the scrofulous kind.

KING′FISHER, *n.* A fowl of the genus Alcedo.

KING'S-SPEAR, *n.* A plant of the genus Asphodelus.

KING′STONE, *n.* A fish. *Ainsworth.*

KING′DŎM, *n.* [*king* and *dom*, jurisdiction.]

1. The territory or country subject to a king; an undivided territory under the dominion of a king or monarch. The foreign possessions of a king are not usually included in the term *kingdom.* Thus we speak of the *kingdom* of England, of France or of Spain, without including the East or West Indies.
2. The inhabitants or population subject to a king. The whole *kingdom* was alarmed.
3. In *natural history*, a division; as the animal, vegetable and mineral *kingdoms.*
4. A region; a tract; the place where any thing prevails and holds sway; as the watery *kingdom.* *Shak.*
5. In *Scripture*, the government or universal dominion of God. 1 Chron. xxix. Ps. cxlv.
6. The power of supreme administration. 1 Sam. xviii.
7. A princely nation or state.

Ye shall be unto me a *kingdom* of priests. Ex. xix.

8. Heaven. Matt. xxvi.
9. State of glory in heaven. Matt. v.
10. The reign of the Messiah. Matt. iii.
11. Government; rule; supreme administration.

KING′DŎMED, *a.* Proud of royalty. *Shak.*

KING′HOOD, *n.* State of being a king. *Obs.* *Gower.*

KING′LESS, *a.* Having no king. *Byron.*

KING′LIKE, *a.* Like a king.

KING′LING, *n.* A little king.

KING′LY, *a.* Belonging to a king; suitable to a king; as a *kingly* couch. *Shak.*

2. Royal; sovereign; monarchical; as a *kingly* government.
3. Noble; august; splendid; becoming a king; as *kingly* magnificence.

KING′LY, *adv.* With an air of royalty; with a superior dignity.

Low bow'd the rest; he, *kingly*, did but nod. *Pope.*

KING′SHIP, *n.* Royalty; the state, office or dignity of a king. *King Charles.*

KIN′IC, *a.* Pertaining to cinchona; as the *kinic* acid. *Ure.*

KINK, *n.* [Sw. *kink*, D. *kink*, a bend or turn. Qu. L. *cingo.*]

The twist of a rope or thread, occasioned by a spontaneous winding of the rope or thread when doubled, that is, by an effort of hard twisted ropes or threads to untwist, they wind about each other.

KINK, *v. i.* To wind into a kink; to twist spontaneously.

KINK′HAUST, *n.* The chincough. [*Not used.*]

KI′NO, *n.* An astringent resin obtained from an African tree. *Hooper.*

Kino consists of tannin and extractive. *Ure.*

KINS′FŌLK, *n.* [*kin* and *folk.*] Relations; kindred; persons of the same family. *Obs.*

KINS′MAN, *n.* [*kin* and *man.*] A man of the same race or family; one related by blood. *Dryden.*

KINS′WŎMAN, *n.* A female relation. *Dennis.*

KIP′PER, *n.* A term applied to a salmon, when unfit to be taken, and to the time when they are so considered. *Eng.*

KIRK, *n. kurk.* [Sax. *cyrc* or *ciric*; Gr. *κυριακη*, from *κυριος*, lord.]

In *Scotland*, a church. This is the same word as *church*, differently written and pronounced. [See *Church.*]

KIRK′MAN, *n.* One of the church of Scotland.

KIR′TLE, *n. ker'tl.* [Sax. *cyrtel*; Sw. *kiortel.*]

1. An upper garment; a gown; a petticoat; a short jacket; a mantle. *Johnson. Encyc.*
2. A quantity of flax, about a hundred pounds. *Encyc.*

[*I know not that this word is used in America.*]

KIR′TLED, *a.* Wearing a kirtle.

KISS, *v. t.* [Sax. *cyssan*; G. *küssen*; D. *kuschen*; Sw. *kyssa*; Dan. *kysser.*]

1. To salute with the lips.
2. To treat with fondness; to caress.

The hearts of princes *kiss* obedience. *Shak.*

3. To touch gently.

When the sweet wind did gently *kiss* the trees. *Shak.*

KISS, *n.* A salute given with the lips; a common token of affection.

KISS′ED, *pp.* Saluted with a kiss.

KISS′ER, *n.* One that kisses.

KISS′ING, *ppr.* Saluting with the lips.

KISS′ING-COMFIT, *n.* Perfumed sugar plums to sweeten the breath. *Shak.*

KISS′ING-CRUST, *n.* In *cookery*, the crust of a loaf that touches another.

KIST, *n.* A chest. [*Not used.*]

KIT, *n.* [D. *kit.*] A large bottle. *Skinner.*

2. A small fiddle. *Grew.*
3. A kind of fish-tub, and a milk-pail. *Entick.*

[*I know not that this word is used in America.*]

KIT′-CAT, *n.* A term applied to a club in London, to which Addison and Steele belonged; so called from Christopher Cat, a pastry cook, who served the club with mutton pies; applied also to a portrait three fourths less than a half length, placed in the club-room. *Todd.*

KITCH′EN, *n.* [Sax. *cycene*; G. *küche*; D. *keuken*; Sw. *kok*; Dan. *kokke*; W. *cegin*; It. *cucina*; L. *coquina*; Sp. *cocina*; from the root of L. *coquo*, to cook.]

1. A cook-room; the room of a house appropriated to cookery.

A fat *kitchen* makes a lean will. *Franklin.*

2. In ships, the galley or caboose.
3. A utensil for roasting meat; as a tin *kitchen.*

KITCH′EN-G′ARDEN, *n.* A garden or piece of ground appropriated to the raising of vegetables for the table.

KITCH′EN-MAID, *n.* A female servant whose business is to clean the kitchen and utensils of cookery, or in general, to do the work of a kitchen.

KITCH′EN-STUFF, *n.* Fat collected from pots and dripping pans. *Donne.*

KITCH′EN-WENCH, *n.* The woman who cleans the kitchen and utensils of cookery.

KITCH′EN-WŎRK, *n.* Work done in the kitchen; as cookery, washing, &c.

KITE, *n.* [Sax. *cyta.*] A rapacious fowl of the genus Falco or hawk, remarkable for *gliding* through the air without frequently moving its wings; hence called *glide.*

2. A name of reproach, denoting rapacity. *Shak.*
3. A light frame of wood and paper constructed for flying in the air for the amusement of boys.

KITE, *n.* In the north of England, the belly.

KI′TEFOOT, *n.* A sort of tobacco, so called.

KI′TESFOOT, *n.* A plant. *Ainsworth.*

KITH, *n.* [Sax. *cyththe.*] Acquaintance. *Obs.* *Gower.*

KIT′LING, *n.* [L. *catulus.*] A whelp; the young of a beast. *B. Jonson.*

KIT′TEN, *n. kit'n.* [D. *katje.*] A young cat, or the young of the cat.

KIT′TEN, *v. i. kit'n.* To bring forth young, as a cat.

KIT′TIWAKE, *n.* A fowl of the genus Larus, or gull kind.

KIT′TLE, *v. t.* [Sax. *citelan.*] To tickle. [*Not used.*] *Sherwood.*

KLICK, *v. i.* [a different orthography or diminutive of *clack.*]

1. To make a small, sharp sound by striking two things together.
2. In *Scotland*, to pilfer, by taking with a snatch.

KLICK, *n.* A stroke or blow. [*A word in vulgar use.*]

KNAB, *v. t. nab.* [D. *knappen*; G. *id.*] To bite; to gnaw; to nibble. [This word may belong to the root of *nibble*, and it properly signifies to catch or seize suddenly with the teeth.] *L'Estrange.*

KNAB'BLE, *v. i.* To bite or nibble. [*Not used.*] *Brown.*

KNACK, *n. nak.* A little machine; a petty contrivance; a toy.

A *knack*, a toy, a trick, a baby's cap. *Shak.*

2. A readiness; habitual facility of performance; dexterity; adroitness.

My author has a great *knack* at remarks. *Atterbury.*

The Dean was famous in his time,
And had a kind of *knack* at rhyme. *Swift.*

3. A nice trick.

For how should equal colors do the *knack*?
Cameleons who can paint in white and black? *Pope.*

KNACK, *v. i. nak.* [G. *knacken*; Dan. *knager.*]

To crack; to make a sharp abrupt noise. [*Little used.*] *Johnson.*

KNACK'ER, *n. nak'er.* A maker of knacks, toys or small work. *Mortimer.*

2. A rope-maker, or collar-maker. [*Not in use.*] *Ainsworth. Entick.*

KNAG, *n. nag.* [Dan. *knag*, Sw. *knagg*, a knot in wood, Ir. *cnag*, W. *cnwc.*]

1. A knot in wood, or a protuberant knot; a wart.

2. A peg for hanging things on.

3. The shoot of a deer's horns.

KNAG'GY, *n. nag'gy.* Knotty; full of knots; rough with knots; hence, rough in temper.

KNAP, *n. nap.* [Sax. *cnæp*, W. *cnap*, a button, a knob, D. *knop.*]

A protuberance; a swelling. [*Little used.* See *Knob.*] *Bacon.*

KNAP, *v.t. nap.* [D. *knappen.* See *Knab.*]

1. To bite; to bite off; to break short. [*Little used.*] *More.*

2. To strike with a sharp noise. [*Little used.*] *Bacon.*

KNAP, *v. i. nap.* To make a short, sharp sound. *Wiseman.*

KNAP'BOTTLE, *n. nap'bottle.* A plant.

KNAP'PISH, *a. nap'pish.* Snappish. [See *Snap.*]

KNAP'PLE, *v. i. nap'ple.* To break off with an abrupt sharp noise.

KNAP'SACK, *n. nap'sack.* [G. *knappsack*; D. *knapzak*, from *knappen*, to eat.]

A soldier's bag, carried on his back, and containing necessaries of food and clothing. It may be of lether or coarse cloth.

KNAP'WEED, *n. nap'weed.* A plant of the genus Centaurea, so called probably from *knap*, a button. *Fam. of Plants.*

KN'AR, *n. n'ar.* [G. *knor* or *knorren*; D. *knor.*] A knot in wood. *Dryden.*

KN'ARLED, *a.* Knotted. [See *Gnarled.*]

KN'ARRY, *a.* Knotty. *Chaucer.*

KNAVE, *n. nave.* [Sax. *cnapa* or *cnafa*, a boy; G. *knabe*; D. *knaap*; Dan. *knab*; originally, a boy or young man, then a servant, and lastly a rogue.]

1. A boy; a man-child. *Obs.*

2. A servant. *Obs.* *Dryden.*

3. A false deceitful fellow; a dishonest man or boy.

In defiance of demonstration, *knaves* will continue to proselyte fools. *Ames.*

4. A card with a soldier painted on it. *Hudibras.*

KNA'VERY, *n. na'very.* Dishonesty; deception in traffick; trick; petty villainy; fraud. *Shak. Dryden.*

2. Mischievous tricks or practices.

KNA'VISH, *a. na'vish.* Dishonest; fraudulent; as a *knavish* fellow, or a *knavish* trick or transaction.

2. Waggish; mischievous.

Cupid is a *knavish* lad,
Thus to make poor females mad. *Shak.*

KNA'VISHLY, *na'vishly.* Dishonestly; fraudulently.

2. Waggishly; mischievously.

KNA'VISHNESS, *n. na'vishness.* The quality or habit of knavery; dishonesty.

KNAW'EL, *n. naw'el.* A species of plant.

KNEAD, *v. t. nead.* [Sax. *cnædan*; G. *kneten*; D. *kneeden*; Dan. *kneder*; Sw. *knåda.*]

To work and press ingredients into a mass, usually with the hands; particularly, to work into a well mixed mass the materials of bread, cake or paste; as, to *knead* dough.

The cake she *kneaded* was the savory meat. *Prior.*

KNE'ADED, *pp. ne'aded.* Worked and pressed together.

KNE'ADING, *ppr. ne'ading.* Working and mixing into a well mixed mass.

KNE'ADING-TROUGH, *n. ne'ading-trauf.* A trough or tray in which dough is worked and mixed.

KNEB'ELITE, *n. neb'elite.* [from *Von Knebel.*]

A mineral of a gray color, spotted with dirty white, brownish green, or green. *Phillips.*

KNEE, *n. nee.* [Sax. *cneow*; G. *knie*; D. *knie*; Sw. *knä*; Dan. *knæ*; Fr. *genou*; It. *ginocchio*; L. *genu*; Gr. γονυ; Sans. *janu.* As the same word in Saxon signifies generation, it appears to belong to the family of γινομαι, *geno*, and to signify a shoot or protuberance.]

1. In *anatomy*, the articulation of the thigh and leg bones.

2. In *ship-building*, a piece of timber somewhat in the shape of the human knee when bent, having two branches or arms, and used to connect the beams of a ship with her sides or timbers. *Mar. Dict.*

KNEE, *v. t. nee.* To supplicate by kneeling. [*Not used.*] *Shak.*

KNEE-CROOKING, *a. nee'crooking.* Obsequious. *Shak.*

KNEED, *a. need.* Having knees; as *in-kneed, out-kneed.*

2. In *botany*, geniculated; forming an obtuse angle at the joints, like the knee when a little bent; as *kneed*-grass. *Martyn.*

KNEE-DEEP, *a. nee'-deep.* Rising to the knees; as water or snow *knee-deep.*

2. Sunk to the knees; as wading in water or mire *knee-deep.*

KNEE-HIGH, *a. nee-hi.* Rising to the knees; as water *knee-high.*

KNEE'HOLLY, *n. nee'holly.* A plant of the genus Ruscus.

KNEE'HOLM, *n. nee'home.* Kneeholly.

KNEE'PAN, *n. nee'pan.* The round bone on the fore part of the knee.

KNEEL, *v. i. neel.* [D. *knielen*; Dan. *knæler*; Fr. *agenouiller*, from *genouil*, the knee.]

To bend the knee; to fall on the knees; sometimes with *down.*

As soon as you are dressed, *kneel down* and say the Lord's prayer. *Taylor.*

KNEE'LER, *n. nee'ler.* One who kneels or worships by kneeling.

KNEE'LING, *ppr. nee'ling.* Falling on the knees.

KNEE'TRIBUTE, *n. nee'tribute.* Tribute paid by kneeling; worship or obeisance by genuflection. *Milton.*

KNELL, *n. nell.* [Sax. *cnyll*; *cnyllan*, to beat or knock; W. *cnul*, a passing bell; G. *knallen*, to clap or crack; Sw. *knalla*; Dan. *gneller*, to bawl.]

Properly, the stroke of a bell; hence, the sound caused by striking a bell; appropriately and perhaps exclusively, the sound of a bell rung at a funeral; a tolling.

KNEW, *pret.* of *know.*

KNIFE, *n. nife*; plu. *knives*; *nives.* [Sax. *cnif*; Dan. *kniv*; Sw. *knif*; Fr. *ganif* or *canif.* This word seems to have a connection with the D. *knippen*, Sw. *knipa*, to clip or pinch, to nip; Dan. *kniber*, G. *kneifen*, W. *cneiviaw*, to clip, to shear. Its primary sense then is an instrument that *nips* off, or cuts off with a stroke.]

1. A cutting instrument with a sharp edge. Knives are of various shapes and sizes, adapted to their respective uses; as table *knives*; carving *knives* or carvers; pen-*knives*, &c.

2. A sword or dagger. *Spenser.*

KNIGHT, *n. nite.* [Sax. *cniht*, *cneoht*, a boy, a servant, Ir. *cniocht*, G. *knecht*, D. *knegt*, Sw. *knecht*, Dan. *knegt.*]

1. Originally, a knight was a youth, and young men being employed as servants, hence it came to signify a servant. But among our warlike ancestors, the word was particularly applied to a young man after he was admitted to the privilege of bearing arms. The admission to this privilege was a ceremony of great importance, and was the origin of the institution of knighthood. Hence, in feudal times, a *knight* was a man admitted to military rank by a certain ceremony. This privilege was conferred on youths of family and fortune, and hence sprung the honorable title of knight, in modern usage. A knight has the title of *Sir.* *Encyc. Johnson.*

2. A pupil or follower. *Shak.*

3. A champion. *Drayton.*

Knight of the post, a knight dubbed at the whipping post or pillory; a hireling witness. *Johnson.*

Knight of the shire, in England, one of the representatives of a county in parliament, originally a knight, but now any gentleman having an estate in land of six hundred pounds a year is qualified. *Johnson.*

KNIGHT, *v. t. nite.* To dub or create a knight, which is done by the king who gives the person kneeling a blow with a sword, and says, *rise, Sir.* *Johnson.*

KNIGHT-ER'RANT, *n.* [*knight* and L. *errans*, *erro*, to wander.]

A wandering knight; a knight who traveled in search of adventures, for the purpose of exhibiting military skill, prowess and generosity.

KNIGHT-ER'RANTRY, *n.* The practice of wandering in quest of adventures; the manners of wandering knights.

KNIGHT-HEADS, *n.* In *ships*, bollard timbers, two pieces of timber rising just within the stem, one on each side of the bowsprit to secure its inner end; also, two strong frames of timber which inclose and support the ends of the windlass. *Mar. Dict.*

KNIGHTHOOD, *n.* The character or dignity of a knight.

2. A military order, honor, or degree of ancient nobility, conferred as a reward of valor or merit. It is of four kinds, military, regular, honorary, and social. *Encyc.*

KNIGHTLINESS, *n.* Duties of a knight. *Spenser.*

KNIGHTLY, *a.* Pertaining to a knight; becoming a knight; as a *knightly* combat. *Sidney.*

KNIGHT-M'ARSHAL, *n.* An officer in the household of the British king, who has cognizance of transgressions within the king's household and verge, and of contracts made there. *Encyc.*

KNIGHT-SERVICE, *n.* In *English feudal law*, a tenure of lands held by knights on condition of performing military service, every possessor of a *knight's fee*, or estate originally of twenty pounds annual value, being obliged to attend the king in his wars.

KNIT, *v. t. nit.* pret. and pp. *knit* or *knitted.* [Sax. *cnyttan;* Sw. *knyta;* Dan. *knytter*; probably L. *nodo*, whence *nodus*, Eng. *knot.*]

1. To unite, as threads by needles; to connect in a kind of net-work; as, to *knit* a stocking.

2. To unite closely; as, let our hearts be *knit* together in love.

3. To join or cause to grow together.

Nature cannot *knit* the bones, while the parts are under a discharge. *Wiseman.*

4. To tie; to fasten.

And he saw heaven opened, and a certain vessel descending to him, as it were a great sheet *knit* at the four corners. Acts x.

5. To draw together; to contract; as, to *knit* the brows.

KNIT, *v. i. nit.* To unite or interweave by needles.

2. To unite closely; to grow together. Broken bones will in time *knit* and become sound.

KNIT, *n. nit.* Union by knitting; texture. [*Little used.*]

KNIT'TABLE, *a. nit'table.* That may be knit.

KNIT'TER, *n. nit'ter.* One that knits.

KNIT'TING, *ppr. nit'ting.* Uniting by needles; forming texture; uniting in growth.

KNIT'TING, *n.* Junction. *Wotton.*

KNIT'TING-NEEDLE, *n. nit'ting-needle.* A long needle usually made of wire, used for knitting threads into stockings, garters, &c.

KNIT'TLE, *n. nit'l.* [from *knit.*] A string that gathers or draws together a purse.

2. A small line used in ships to sling hammocs. *Mar. Dict.*

KNOB, *n. nob.* [Sax. *cnæp;* G. *knopf;* D. *knoop;* Sw. *knopp;* Dan. *knop, knub, knap;* W. *cnwb, cnwpa.* The word signifies a button, a top, a bunch.]

A hard protuberance; a hard swelling or rising; a bunch; as a *knob* in the flesh or on a bone. *Ray.*

KNOB'BED, *a. nob'bed.* Containing knobs; full of knobs.

KNOB'BINESS, *n. nob'biness.* [from *knobby.*]

The quality of having knobs, or of being full of protuberances.

KNOB'BY, *a. nob'by.* Full of knobs or hard protuberances; hard.

KNOCK, *v. i. nok.* [Sax. *cnucian;* W. *cnociaw;* Sw. *knacka.*]

1. To strike or beat with something thick or heavy; as, to *knock* with a club or with the fist; to *knock* at the door. We never use this word to express beating with a small stick or whip.

2. To drive or be driven against; to strike against; to clash; as when one heavy body *knocks* against another.

To knock under, to yield; to submit; to acknowledge to be conquered; an expression borrowed from the practice of *knocking under the table*, when conquered. *Johnson.*

KNOCK, *v. t. nok.* To strike; to drive against; as, to *knock* the head against a post.

2. To strike a door for admittance; to rap.

To knock down, to strike down; to fell; to prostrate by a blow or by blows; as, to *knock down* an ox.

To knock out, to force out by a blow or by blows; as, to *knock out* the brains.

To knock up, to arouse by knocking. In *popular use*, to beat out; to fatigue till unable to do more.

To knock off, to force off by beating. At *auctions*, to assign to a bidder by a blow on the counter.

To knock on the head, to kill by a blow or by blows.

KNOCK, *n. nok.* A blow; a stroke with something thick or heavy.

2. A stroke on a door, intended as a request for admittance; a rap.

KNOCK'ER, *n. nok'er.* One that knocks.

2. An instrument or kind of hammer, fastened to a door to be used in seeking for admittance.

KNOCK'ING, *ppr. nok'ing.* Beating; striking.

KNOCK'ING, *n. nok'ing.* A beating; a rap.

KNOLL, *v. t. nōll.* [Sax. *cnyllan*, to beat or strike. See *Knell.*]

To ring a bell, usually for a funeral. *Shak.*

KNOLL, *v. i. nōll.* To sound, as a bell. *Shak.*

[This word, I believe, is not used in America.]

KNOLL, *n. nōll.* [Sax. *cnoll;* Sw. *knyl, knōl;* W. *cnol.*]

The top or crown of a hill; but more generally, a little round hill or mount; a small elevation of earth.

KNOP, *n. nop.* [a different spelling of *knap* or *nob.*]

A knob; a tufted top; a bud; a bunch; a button.

KNOP'PED, *a. nop'ped.* Having knops or knobs; fastened as with buttons.

KNOT, *n. not.* [Sax. *cnotta;* G. *knoten;* D. *knot;* Sw. *knota;* Dan. *knude;* L. *nodus;* probably connected with *knit*, but perhaps from *swelling* or *gathering.*]

1. The complication of threads made by knitting; a tie; union of cords by interweaving; as a *knot* difficult to be untied.

2. Any figure, the lines of which frequently intersect each other; as a *knot* in gardening.

In beds and curious *knots.* *Milton.*

3. A bond of association or union; as the nuptial *knot.*

4. The part of a tree where a branch shoots.

5. The protuberant joint of a plant. *Martyn.*

6. A cluster; a collection; a group; as a *knot* of ladies; a *knot* of figures in painting.

7. Difficulty; intricacy; something not easily solved. *South.*

8. Any intrigue or difficult perplexity of affairs. *Dryden.*

9. A bird of the genus Tringa.

10. An epaulet.

11. In *seamen's language*, a division of the logline, which answers to half a minute, as a mile does to an hour, or it is the hundred and twentieth part of a mile. Hence, when a ship goes eight miles an hour, she is said to go eight *knots.* *Mar. Dict.*

KNOT, *v. t. not.* To complicate or tie in a knot or knots; to form a knot.

2. To entangle; to perplex.

3. To unite closely. *Bacon.*

KNOT, *v. i. not.* To form knots or joints, as in plants.

2. To knit knots for fringe.

KNOT'BERRY, *n. not'berry.* A plant of the genus Rubus.

KNOT'GRASS, *n. not'grass.* The name of several species of plants, so denominated from the joints of the stem. The *common knotgrass* is the Polygonum aviculare.

KNOT'LESS, *a. not'less.* Free from knots; without knots. *Martyn.*

KNOT'TED, *a. not'ted.* Full of knots; having knots; as the *knotted* oak. *Dryden.*

2. Having intersecting figures. *Shak.*

KNOT'TINESS, *n. not'tiness.* [from *knotty.*]

1. Fullness of knots; the quality of having many knots or swellings.

2. Difficulty of solution; intricacy.

KNOT'TY, *a. not'ty.* Full of knots; having many knots; as *knotty* timber.

2. Hard; rugged; as a *knotty* head. *Rowe.*

3. Difficult; intricate; perplexed; as a *knotty* question or point.

KNOUT, *n. nout.* A punishment in Russia, inflicted with a whip.

KNOW, *v. t. no.* pret. *knew;* pp. *known.* [Sax. *cnawan;* Russ. *znayu*, with a prefix. This is probably from the same original as the L. *nosco, cognosco*, Gr. γινωσκω, although much varied in orthography. *Nosco* makes *novi*, which, with *g* or *c* prefixed, *gnovi* or *cnovi*, would coincide with *know, knew.* So L. *cresco, crevi*, coincides with *grow, grew.* The radical sense of *knowing* is generally to take, receive, or hold.]

1. To perceive with certainty; to understand clearly; to have a clear and certain perception of truth, fact, or any thing that actually exists. To *know* a thing pre-

cludes all doubt or uncertainty of its existence. We *know* what we see with our eyes, or perceive by other senses. We *know* that fire and water are different substances. We *know* that truth and falsehood express ideas incompatible with each other. We *know* that a circle is not a square. We do not *know* the truth of reports, nor can we always *know* what to believe.

2. To be informed of; to be taught. It is not unusual for us to say we *know* things from information, when we rely on the veracity of the informer.

3. To distinguish; as, to *know* one man from another. We *know* a fixed star from a planet by its twinkling.

4. To recognize by recollection, remembrance, representation or description. We do not always *know* a person after a long absence. We sometimes *know* a man by having seen his portrait, or having heard him described.

5. To be no stranger to; to be familiar. This man is well *known* to us.

6. In *Scripture*, to have sexual commerce with. Gen. iv.

7. To approve.

The Lord *knoweth* the way of the righteous. Ps. i.

8. To learn. Prov. i.

9. To acknowledge with due respect. 1. Thess. v.

10. To choose; to favor or take an interest in. Amos iii.

11. To commit; to have.

He hath made him to be sin for us, who *knew* no sin. 2 Cor.

12. To have full assurance of; to have satisfactory evidence of any thing, though short of certainty.

KNOW, *v. i.* *no.* To have clear and certain perception; not to be doubtful; sometimes with *of*.

If any man will do his will, he shall *know of* the doctrine, whether it be of God, or whether I speak of myself. John vii.

2. To be informed.

Sir John must not *know of* it. *Shak.*

3. To take cognizance of; to examine.

Know of your youth—examine well your blood. *Shak.*

KNOWABLE, *a.* *no'able.* That may be known; that may be discovered, understood or ascertained. *Locke. Bentley.*

KNOWER, *n.* *no'er.* One who knows.

KNOWING, *ppr.* *no'ing.* Having clear and certain perception of.

2. *a.* Skillful; well informed; well instructed; as a *knowing* man.

The *knowing* and intelligent part of the world. *South.*

3. Conscious; intelligent.

A *knowing* prudent cause. *Blackmore.*

KNOWING, *n.* *no'ing.* Knowledge. *Shak.*

KNOWINGLY, *adv.* *no'ingly.* With knowledge. He would not *knowingly* offend.

KNOWL'EDGE, *n.* *nol'lej.* [Chaucer, *knowleching*, from *knowleche*, to acknowledge. Qu. the sense of *lech.*]

1. A clear and certain perception of that which exists, or of truth and fact; the perception of the connection and agreement, or disagreement and repugnancy of our ideas. *Encyc. Locke.*

We can have no *knowledge* of that which does not exist. God has a perfect *knowledge* of all his works. Human *knowledge* is very limited, and is mostly gained by observation and experience.

2. Learning; illumination of mind.

Ignorance is the curse of God,
Knowledge the wing wherewith we fly to heaven. *Shak.*

3. Skill; as a *knowledge* of seamanship.

4. Acquaintance with any fact or person. I have no *knowledge* of the man or thing.

5. Cognizance; notice. Ruth ii.

6. Information; power of knowing. *Sidney.*

7. Sexual intercourse. But it is usual to prefix *carnal*; as *carnal* knowledge.

KNOWLEDGE, for *acknowledge* or *avow*, is not used. *Bacon.*

KNUB, **KNUB'BLE**, } *v. t.* *nub*, *nub'ble.* } To beat; to strike with the knuckle. [*Not used.*]

KNUCK'LE, *n.* *nuk'l.* [Sax. *cnucl*; G. *knöchel*; D. *kneukel*; W. *cnuc*, a joint or junction; *cnuciaw*, to join, to couple.]

1. The joint of a finger, particularly when protuberant by the closing of the fingers.

2. The knee joint of a calf; as a *knuckle* of veal.

3. The joint of a plant. [*Not used.*] *Bacon.*

KNUCK'LE, *v. i.* *nuk'l.* To yield; to submit in contest to an antagonist.

KNUCK'LED, *a.* Jointed. *Bacon.*

KNUFF, *n.* *nuff.* A lout; a clown. [*Not used.*]

KNUR, **KNURLE**, } *n.* *nur*, *nurle.* } [G. *knorren*, a knot, a knag, a gnar.]

A knot; a hard substance. *Woodward.*

KNURL'ED, *a.* *nurl'ed.* Full of knots.

KNUR'LY, *a.* *nur'ly.* [from *knur.*] Full of knots; hard. This seems to be the same as *gnarly.*

KNUR'RY, *a.* *nur'ry.* Full of knots.

KOBA, *n.* An antelope, with horns close at the base.

KO'KOB, *n.* A venomous serpent of America.

KOL'LYRITE, *n.* [Gr. κολλυριον.] A variety of clay whose color is pure white, or with a shade of gray, red or yellow. *Cleaveland.*

KOM'MANIC, *n.* The crested lark of Germany.

KON'ILITE, *n.* [Gr. κονος, dust, and λιθος, a stone.]

A mineral in the form of a loose powder, consisting chiefly of silex, and remarkably fusible. *Phillips.*

KONITE. [See *Conite.*]

KO'PECK, *n.* A Russian coin, about the value of a cent.

KO'RAN, *n.* pronounced by oriental scholars *korawn.* [Ar. قُرْآن from قَرَأَ to read, to call, to teach.]

The Mohammedan book of faith; the alkoran.

KO'RET, *n.* A delicious fish of the East Indies.

KO'RIN, *n.* An antelope with slender smooth horns.

KOUPH'OLITE, *n.* [Gr. κουφος, light, and λιθος, stone.]

A mineral, regarded as a variety of prehnite. It occurs in minute rhomboidal plates, of a greenish or yellowish white, translucid, glistening and pearly. It is found in the Pyrenees. *Cleaveland.*

KRAAL, *n.* In the southern part of Africa, among the Hottentots, a village; a collection of huts.

KRAG, *n.* A species of argillaceous earth.

KRA'KEN, *n.* A supposed enormous sea animal. *Guthrie.*

KRU'KA, *n.* A bird of Russia and Sweden, resembling a hedge sparrow. *Pennant.*

KU'FIC, *a.* The Kufic letters were the ancient letters of the Arabic, so called from Kufa, on the Euphrates.

KU'MISS, *n.* A liquor or drink made from mare's milk fermented and distilled; milk-spirit, used by the Tartars. *Tooke.*

KU'RIL, *n.* A bird, the black petrel. *Pennant.*

KURIL'IAN, *a.* The Kurilian isles are a chain in the Pacific, extending from the southern extremity of Kamschatka to Jesso.

KȲ, *n.* Kine. [*Not in use.*]

KY'ANITE, *n.* [G. *kyanit*, Werner; from the Gr. κυανος, sky-colored. It is written also *cyanite*, but most improperly, if pronounced *kyanite*. *Kyanite* is doubtless the preferable orthography.]

A mineral found both massive and in regular crystals. It is frequently in broad or compressed six-sided prisms, with bases a little inclined; or this crystal may be viewed as a four-sided prism, truncated on two of its lateral edges, diagonally opposite. Its prevailing color is *blue*, whence its name, but varying from a fine Prussian blue to sky-blue, or bluish white. It occurs also of various shades of green, and even gray, or white and reddish. It is infusible by the common blowpipe. This mineral is called by Haüy and Brongniart, *disthene*, and by Saussure, *sappare.* *Cleaveland.*

KȲAN'OGEN, *n.* [Gr. κυανος, blue, and γενναω, to beget.]

Carbureted azote; the compound base of prussic acid, called also prussine.

L.

L, the twelfth letter of the English Alphabet, is usually denominated a *semi-vowel*, or a *liquid*. It represents an imperfect articulation, formed by placing the tip of the tongue against the gum that incloses the roots of the upper teeth; but the sides of the tongue not being in close contact with the roof of the mouth, the breath of course not being entirely intercepted, this articulation is attended with an imperfect sound. The shape of the letter is evidently borrowed from that of the oriental *lamed*, or *lomad*, nearly coinciding with the Samaritan ࠋ.

L has only one sound in English, as in *like*, *canal*. At the end of monosyllables, it is often doubled, as in *fall*, *full*, *tell*, *bell*; but not after diphthongs and digraphs; *foul*, *fool*, *prowl*, *growl*, *foal*, &c. being written with a single *l*.

With some nations, *l* and *r* are commutable; as in Greek, λιριον, L. *lilium*; It. *scorta*, an escort, Sp. Port. *escolta*. Indeed, *l* and *r* are letters of the same organ.

By some nations of Celtic origin, *l*, at the beginning of words, is aspirated and doubled in writing, as in the W. *lled*, L. *latus*; *llan*, a *lawn*; *llawr*, a *floor*; Sp. *llamar*, L. *clamo*.

In some words, *l* is mute, as in *half*, *calf*, *walk*, *talk*, *chalk*.

In our mother tongue, the Anglo-Saxon, *l* is sometimes preceded by *h*, and aspirated, as in *hlaf*, loaf; *hladan*, to lade or load; *hlot*, lot; *hlinian*, *hleonian*, to lean, Gr. κλινω, L. *clino*. In the latter word, the Saxon *h* represents the Greek κ and Latin *c*, as it does in many other words.

In English words, the terminating syllable *le* is unaccented, the *e* is silent, and *l* has a feeble sound; as in *able*, *eagle*, pronounced *abl*, *eagl*.

As a numeral, L denotes 50, and with a dash, L̄, 50,000. As an abbreviation, in Latin, it stands for Lucius; and L.L.S. for a sesterce, or two *libræ* and a half. *Encyc.*

LA, *exclam.* [perhaps corrupted from *look*, but this is doubtful.]
Look; see; behold. *Shak.*

LA, in *music*, the syllable by which Guido denotes the last sound of each hexachord. *Encyc.*

LAB, *n.* A great talker; a blabber. *Obs.* *Chaucer.*

LAB'ADIST, *n.* The Labadists were followers of Jean de Labadie, who lived in the 17th century. They held that God can and does deceive men, that the observance of the sabbath is a matter of indifference, and other peculiar or heretical opinions. *Encyc.*

LABDANUM. [See *Ladanum*.]

LABEFAC'TION, *n.* [L. *labefactio*, from *labefacio*; *labo*, to totter, and *facio*, to make.]
A weakening or loosening; a failing; decay; downfall; ruin.

LAB'EFY, *v. t.* To weaken or impair. [*Not used.*] *Dict.*

LA'BEL, *n.* [W. *llab*, a strip; *labed*, a label.]
1. A narrow slip of silk, paper or parchment, containing a name or title, and affixed to any thing, denoting its contents. Such are the *labels* affixed to the vessels of an apothecary. *Labels* also are affixed to deeds or writings to hold the appended seal. *Harris.*
2. Any paper annexed to a will by way of addition; as a codicil. *Encyc.*
3. In *heraldry*, a fillet usually placed in the middle, along the chief of the coat, without touching its extremities. It is adorned with pendants, and used on the arms of the eldest son, to distinguish him from the younger sons, while the father is living. *Encyc.*
4. A long thin brass rule, with a small sight at one end, and a center-hole at the other, commonly used with a tangent line on the edge of a circumferentor, to take altitudes, &c. *Encyc.*

LA'BEL, *v. t.* To affix a label to.

LA'BELED, *pp.* Furnished with a label.

LA'BELING, *ppr.* Distinguishing by a label.

LA'BENT, *a.* [L. *labens*.] Sliding; gliding. *Dict.*

LA'BIAL, *a.* [Fr. from L. *labium*, a lip. See *Lip*.]
Pertaining to the lips; formed by the lips; as a *labial* articulation. Thus *b*, *p*, and *m* are *labial* articulations, and *oo*, Fr. *ou*, It. *u*, is a *labial* vowel.

LA'BIAL, *n.* A letter or character representing an articulation of the lips; as *b*, *f*, *m*, *p*, *v*.

LA'BIATE, } *a.* [from L. *labium*, lip.]
LA'BIATED, } In *botany*, a *labiate* corol is irregular, monopetalous, with two lips, or monopetalous, consisting of a narrow tube with a wide mouth, divided into two or more segments arranged in two opposite divisions or lips. A *labiate* flower has a *labiate* corol. *Martyn.* *Encyc.*

LA'BILE, *a.* [Low L. *labilis*.] Liable to err, fall or apostatize. [*Not used.*] *Cheyne.*

LABIODENT'AL, *a.* [*labium*, a lip, and *dens*, a tooth.]
Formed or pronounced by the cooperation of the lips and teeth; as *f* and *v*. *Holder.*

LA'BOR, *n.* [L. *labor*. from *labo*, to fail.]
Exertion of muscular strength, or bodily exertion which occasions weariness; particularly, the exertion of the limbs in occupations by which subsistence is obtained, as in agriculture and manufactures, in distinction from exertions of strength in play or amusements, which are denominated *exercise*, rather than *labor*. Toilsome work; pains; travail; any bodily exertion which is attended with fatigue. After the *labors* of the day, the farmer retires, and rest is sweet. Moderate *labor* contributes to health.

> What is obtained by *labor*, will of right be the property of him by whose *labor* it is gained. *Rambler.*

2. Intellectual exertion; application of the mind which occasions weariness; as the *labor* of compiling and writing a history.
3. Exertion of mental powers, united with bodily employment; as the *labors* of the apostles in propagating christianity.
4. Work done, or to be done; that which requires wearisome exertion.

> Being a *labor* of so great difficulty, the exact performance thereof we may rather wish than look for. *Hooker.*

5. Heroic achievment; as the *labors* of Hercules.
6. Travail; the pangs and efforts of childbirth.
7. The evils of life; trials; persecution, &c.

> They rest from their *labors*— Rev. xiv.

LA'BOR, *v. i.* [L. *laboro*.] To exert muscular strength; to act or move with painful effort, particularly in servile occupations; to work; to toil.

> Six days shalt thou *labor*, and do all thy work— Ex. xx.

2. To exert one's powers of body or mind, or both, in the prosecution of any design; to strive; to take pains.

> *Labor* not for the meat which perisheth. John vi.

3. To toil; to be burdened.

> Come unto me all ye that *labor*, and are heavy laden, and I will give you rest. Matt. xi.

4. To move with difficulty.

> The stone that *labors* up the hill. *Glanville.*

5. To move irregularly with little progress; to pitch and roll heavily; as a ship in a turbulent sea. *Mar. Dict.*
6. To be in distress; to be pressed.

> —As sounding cymbals aid the *laboring* moon. *Dryden.*

7. To be in travail; to suffer the pangs of childbirth.
8. To journey or march.

> Make not all the people to *labor* thither. Josh. vii.

9. To perform the duties of the pastoral office. 1 Tim. v.
10. To perform christian offices.

To labor under, to be afflicted with; to be burdened or distressed with; as, to *labor under* a disease or an affliction.

LA'BOR, *v. t.* To work at; to till; to cultivate.

> The most excellent lands are lying fallow, or only *labored* by children. *Tooke.*

2. To prosecute with effort; to urge; as, to *labor* a point or argument.

3. To form or fabricate with exertion; as, to *labor* arms for Troy. *Dryden.*
4. To beat; to belabor. [*The latter word is generally used.*] *Dryden.*
5. To form with toil and care; as a *labored* composition.

LA'BORANT, *n.* A chimist. [*Not used.*] *Boyle.*

LAB'ORATORY, *n.* [Fr. *laboratoire*, from *labor.*]
1. A house or place where operations and experiments in chimistry, pharmacy, pyrotechny, &c., are performed.
2. A place where arms are manufactured or repaired, or fire-works prepared; as the *laboratory* in Springfield, in Massachusetts.
3. A place where work is performed, or any thing is prepared for use. Hence the stomach is called the grand *laboratory* of the human body; the liver, the *laboratory* of the bile.

LA'BORED, *pp.* Tilled; cultivated; formed with labor.

LA'BORER, *n.* One who labors in a toilsome occupation; a man who does work that requires little skill, as distinguished from an artisan.

LA'BORING, *ppr.* Exerting muscular strength or intellectual power; toiling; moving with pain or with difficulty; cultivating.
2. A *laboring man*, or *laborer*, is often used for a man who performs work that requires no apprenticeship or professional skill, in distinction from an artisan; but this restricted sense is not always observed. A *hard laboring man*, is one accustomed to hard labor.

LABO'RIOUS, *a.* [L. *laboriosus*; Fr. *laborieux.*]
1. Using exertion; employing labor; diligent in work or service; assiduous; *used of persons*; as a *laborious* husbandman or mechanic; a *laborious* minister or pastor.
2. Requiring labor; toilsome; tiresome; not easy; as *laborious* duties or services.
3. Requiring labor, exertion, perseverance or sacrifices.

Dost thou love watchings, abstinence or toil,
Laborious virtues all? Learn these from Cato. *Addison.*

LABO'RIOUSLY, *adv.* With labor, toil or difficulty. *Pope.*

LABO'RIOUSNESS, *n.* The quality of being laborious, or attended with toil; toilsomeness; difficulty.
2. Diligence; assiduity.

LA'BORLESS, *a.* Not laborious. *Brerewood.*

LA'BORSŌME, *a.* Made with great labor and diligence. [*Not in use.*] *Sandys.*

LABURN'UM, *n.* A tree of the genus Cytisus.

LAB'YRINTH, *n.* [L. *labyrinthus*; Gr. λαβυρινθος.]
1. Among the ancients, an edifice or place full of intricacies, or formed with winding passages, which rendered it difficult to find the way from the interior to the entrance. The most remarkable of these edifices mentioned, are the Egyptian and the Cretan labyrinths. *Encyc. Lempriere.*
2. A maze; an inexplicable difficulty.
3. Formerly, an ornamental maze or wilderness in gardens. *Spenser.*
4. A cavity in the ear. *Quincy.*

LABYRINTH'IAN, *a.* Winding; intricate; perplexed. *Bp. Hall.*

LA€, *n.* [Sp. *laca*; G. *lack*; Dan. D. *lak*; said to be from the Arabic.]
Gum-lac, so called, but improperly, not being a gum, but a *resin*. It is deposited on different species of trees in the East Indies, by an insect called *Chermes lacca*. *Stick lac* is the substance in its natural state, encrusting small twigs. When broken off and boiled in water, it loses its red color, and is called *seed lac*. When melted and reduced to a thin crust, it is called *shell lac*. United with ivory black or vermilion, it forms black and red *sealing wax*. A solution with borax, colored by lampblack, constitutes *Indian ink*. Lac dissolved in alcohol or other menstrua, by different methods of preparation, constitutes various kinds of *varnishes* and *lackers*. *Thomson.*

LA€'CI€, *a.* Pertaining to lac, or produced from it; as laccic acid.

LACE, *n.* [Sp. *lazo*, a tie or knot, Fr. *lacet*, It. *laccio*, L. *laqueus.*]
1. A work composed of threads interwoven into a net, and worked on a pillow with spindles or pins. Fine *laces* are manufactured in France, Italy and England.
2. A string; a cord. *Spenser.*
3. A snare; a gin. *Fairfax.*
4. A plaited string with which females fasten their clothes.

Doll ne'er was called to cut her *lace*. *Swift.*

LACE, *v. t.* To fasten with a string through eyelet holes.

When Jenny's stays are newly *laced*— *Prior.*

2. To adorn with lace; as cloth *laced* with silver. *Shak.*
3. To embellish with variegations or stripes.

Look, love, what envious streaks
Do *lace* the severing clouds in yonder east. *Shak.*

4. To beat; to lash; [probably to make stripes on.]

I'll *lace* your coat for ye. *L'Estrange.*

LA'CE-BARK, *n.* A shrub in the W. Indies, the Daphne lagetto, so called from the texture of its inner bark.

LA'CED, *pp.* Fastened with lace or a string; also, tricked off with lace.

Laced coffee, coffee with spirits in it. *Addison.*

LA'CEMAN, *n.* A man who deals in lace. *Addison.*

LA'CEWŌMAN, *n.* A woman who makes or sells lace.

LAC'ERABLE, *a.* [See *Lacerate.*] That may be torn. *Harvey.*

LAC'ERATE, *v. t.* [L. *lacero*, to tear.] To tear; to rend; to separate a substance by violence or tearing; as, to *lacerate* the flesh. It is applied chiefly to the flesh, or figuratively to the heart. But sometimes it is applied to the political or civil divisions in a state.

LAC'ERATE, } *pp.* or *a.* Rent; torn.
LAC'ERATED, }

2. In *botany*, having the edge variously cut into irregular segments; as a *lacerated* leaf. *Martyn.*

LACERA'TION, *n.* The act of tearing or rending; the breach made by rending. *Arbuthnot.*

LAC'ERATIVE, *a.* Tearing; having the power to tear; as *lacerative* humors. *Harvey.*

LAC'ERTINE, *a.* [L. *lacertus.*] Like a lizard. *Journ. of Science.*

LACER'TUS, *n.* The girroc, a fish of the gar-fish kind; also, the lizard-fish. *Dict. Nat. Hist. Cyc.*

LACHE, } *n.* [Norm. Fr. *lachesse*, from
LACH'ES, } *lache*; L. *laxus*, lax, slow.]
In *law*, neglect; negligence.

LA€H'RYMABLE, *a.* Lamentable. *Morley.*

LA€H'RYMAL, *a.* [Fr. from L. *lachryma*, a tear.]
1. Generating or secreting tears; as the *lachrymal* gland.
2. Pertaining to tears; conveying tears.

LA€H'RYMARY, *a.* Containing tears. *Addison.*

LA€HRYMA'TION, *n.* The act of shedding tears.

LA€H'RYMATORY, *n.* [Fr. *lachrymatoire.*] A vessel found in sepulchers of the ancients, in which it has been supposed the tears of a deceased person's friends were collected and preserved with the ashes and urn. It was a small glass or bottle like a phial. *Encyc.*

LA'CING, *ppr.* Fastening with a string; adorned or trimmed with lace.

LACIN'IATE, } *a.* [L. *lacinia*, a hem.]
LACIN'IATED, } Adorned with fringes.
2. In *botany*, jagged. *Martyn.*

LACK, *v. t.* [D. *leeg*, empty; *leegen*, to empty; Dan. *lak*, a fault; *lakker*, to decline or wear away; Goth. *ufligan*, to lack or fail; L. *deliquium*, which seems to be connected with *linquo*, to leave, to faint, and with *liquo*, to melt, *liquid*, &c.]
1. To want; to be destitute of; not to have or possess.

If any of you *lack* wisdom, let him ask it of God— James i.

2. To blame. [*Not in use.*] *Chaucer.*

LACK, *v. i.* To be in want.

The young lions do *lack* and suffer hunger. Ps. xxxiv.

2. To be wanting.

Perhaps there shall *lack* five of the fifty righteous. Gen. xviii.

LACK, *n.* Want; destitution; need; failure.

He that gathered little, had no *lack*. Ex. xvi.

Lack of rupees is one hundred thousand rupees, which at 55 cents each, amount to fifty five thousand dollars, or at 2s. 6d. sterling, to £12,500.

LACK-A-DAY, *exclam.* of sorrow or regret; alas.

LACK'BRAIN, *n.* One that wants brains, or is deficient in understanding. *Shak.*

LACK'ER, } *n.* [Fr. *laque.*] A kind of
LAC'QUER, } varnish. The basis of lackers is a solution of the substance called *seed-lac* or *shell-lac*, in spirit of wine or alcohol. Varnishes applied to metals improve their color and preserve them from tarnishing. *Encyc. Cyc.*

Lackers consist of different resins in a state of solution, of which the most common are mastick, sandarach, lac, benzoin, copal, amber, and asphalt. The menstrua are either expressed or essential oils, or spirit of wine. *Nicholson.*

LACK'ER, *v. t.* To varnish; to smear over with lacker, for the purpose of improving color or preserving from tarnishing and decay.

LACK'ERED, *pp.* Covered with lacker; varnished.

LACK'EY, *n.* [Fr. *laquais*; Sp. *lacayo*; Port. *lacaio*; It. *lacchè*; Eth. ለአከ lak, to send, whence ለአክ lake, a servant; L. *lego*, to send. From this root is the Shemitic מלאך, a messenger.]
An attending servant; a footboy or footman. *Addison.*

LACK'EY, *v. t.* To attend servilely. *Milton.*

LACK'EY, *v. i.* To act as footboy; to pay servile attendance.

> Oft have I servants seen on horses ride,
> The free and noble *lackey* by their side. *Sandys.*

LACK'LINEN, *a.* Wanting shirts. [*Little used.*] *Shak.*

LACK'LUSTER, *a.* Wanting luster or brightness. *Shak.*

LACON'IC, **LACON'ICAL**, } *a.* [Fr. *laconique*; L. *laconicus*; from *Laconia* or *Lacones*, the Spartans.]
1. Short; brief; pithy; sententious; expressing much in few words, after the manner of the Spartans; as a *laconic* phrase. *Pope.*
2. Pertaining to Sparta or Lacedemonia. *Trans. of Pausanias. D'Anville.*

LACON'ICALLY, *adv.* Briefly; concisely; as a sentiment *laconically* expressed.

LACON'ICS, *n.* A book of Pausanias, which treats of Lacedemonia.

LA'CONISM, **LACON'ICISM**, } *n.* [L. *laconismus*.] A concise style.
2. A brief sententious phrase or expression.

LAC'TAGE, *n.* The produce of animals yielding milk. *Shuckford.*

LAC'TANT, *a.* [L. *lactans*, from *lacto*, to give suck; *lac*, milk.] Suckling; giving suck. [*Little used.*]

LAC'TARY, *a.* [L. *lactarius*, from *lacto*; *lac*, milk.]
Milky; full of white juice like milk. [*Little used.*] *Brown.*

LAC'TARY, *n.* [L. *lactarius*.] A dairy-house.

LAC'TATE, *n.* In *chimistry*, a salt formed by the lactic acid, or acid of milk, with a base. *Fourcroy.*

LACTA'TION, *n.* [L. *lacto*, to give suck.] The act of giving suck; or the time of suckling. *Johnson. Encyc.*

LAC'TEAL, *a.* Pertaining to milk.
2. Conveying chyle; as a *lacteal* vessel.

LAC'TEAL, *n.* A vessel or slender tube of animal bodies, for conveying chyle from the intestines to the common reservatory. *Encyc.*

LAC'TEOUS, *a.* [L. *lacteus*, from *lac*, milk.]
1. Milky; resembling milk. *Brown.*
2. Lacteal; conveying chyle; as a *lacteous* vessel. *Bentley.*

LACTES'CENCE, *n.* [L. *lactescens*, *lactescp*, from *lacto*; *lac*, milk.]
1. Tendency to milk; milkiness or milky color. *Boyle.*
2. In *botany*, milkiness; the liquor which flows abundantly from a plant, when wounded; commonly white, but sometimes yellow or red. *Martyn.*

LACTES'CENT, *a.* Producing milk or white juice. *Arbuthnot.*
2. Abounding with a thick colored juice. *Encyc.*

LAC'TIC, *a.* Pertaining to milk, or procured from sour milk or whey; as the *lactic* acid. *Fourcroy.*

LACTIF'EROUS, *a.* [L. *lac*, milk, and *fero*, to bear.]
1. Bearing or conveying milk or white juice; as a *lactiferous* duct. *Boyle.*
2. Producing a thick colored juice; as a plant. *Encyc.*

LAC'UNAR, *n.* [L.] An arched roof or ceiling.

LACU'NOUS, **LACUNO'SE**, } *a.* [L. *lacunosus*, from *lacuna*, a ditch or hollow.]
Furrowed or pitted. A *lacunose* leaf has the disk depressed between the veins. *Martyn.*

LAD, *n.* [W. *llawd*, a lad; and Sax. *leod*, G. *leute*, Russ. *lead*, people, are probably from the same root; Ir. *lath*, a youth, D. *loot*, a shoot; Heb. Ch. Syr. Sam. ילד, to procreate or bear young; Eth. ወለደ Ar. ولد, walada, id. Class Ld. No 29.] A young man or boy; a stripling. *Locke.*

LAD'ANUM, *n.* [said to be Arabic.] The resinous juice which exudes from the leaves of the *Cistus ladanifera*, a shrub which grows in Arabia, Candia, and other parts of the Archipelago. It is collected with a kind of rake, with lether thongs attached to it, with which the shrubs are brushed. The best sort is in dark-colored black masses, of the consistence of a soft plaster. The other sort is in long rolls coiled up, harder than the former, and of a paler color. It is chiefly used in external applications. *Encyc. Parr.*

LAD'DER, *n.* [Sax. *hlædder*; D. *ladder* or *leder*; G. *leiter*, a ladder, a leader, a guide; *leiten*, to lead.]
1. A frame of wood, consisting of two side-pieces, connected by rounds inserted in them at suitable distances, aud thus forming steps, by which persons may ascend a building, &c.
2. That by which a person ascends or rises; means of ascending; as a *ladder* made of cords. *Shak.*

> Lowliness is young ambition's *ladder*. *Shak.*

3. Gradual rise; elevation.

> Mounting fast towards the top of the *ladder* ecclesiastical. *Swift.*

LADE, *v. t.* pret. *laded*; pp. *laded*, *laden*. [Sax. *ladan* and *hladan*; G. *laden*; D. *laaden*; Sw. *ladda*; Dan. *ladder*; Russ. *klad*, a load or cargo; *kladu*, to put, to lay, to make, build or found, to lay eggs, to give, to suppose, &c. Here we observe that to *load* or *lade* is to throw, that is, to put on or in, for to send, thrust, throw, is the sense of laying eggs. Now this is precisely the radical signification of the words *loud*, *lad*, W. *llawd*, *clod*, L. *plaudo*, &c.]
1. To load; to put on or in, as a burden or freight. We *lade* a ship with cotton. We *lade* a horse or other beast with corn.

> And they *laded* their asses with the corn and departed thence. Gen. xlii.

2. To dip; to throw in or out, as a fluid, with a ladle or dipper; as, to *lade* water out of a tub or into a cistern.
3. To draw water. [*Not in use.*]

LADE, *n.* The mouth of a river. *Obs.* *Gibson.*

LA'DED, **LA'DEN**, } *pp.* Loaded; charged with a burden or freight.
2. *a.* Oppressed; burdened.

LA'DING, *ppr.* Loading; charging with a burden or freight; throwing or dipping out.

LA'DING, *n.* That which constitutes a load or cargo; freight; burden; as the *lading* of a ship. Acts xxvii.

LAD'KIN, *n.* A little lad; a youth. [*Little used.*]

LA'DLE, *n.* [Sax. *hlædle*, from *hladan*, supra.]
1. An utensil somewhat like a dish, with a long handle, used for throwing or dipping out liquor from a vessel.
2. The receptacle of a mill wheel, which receives the water which moves it.
3. In *gunnery*, an instrument for drawing the charge of a cannon. *Mar. Dict.*

LA'DLE-FUL, *n.* The quantity contained in a ladle. *Swift.*

LA'DY, *n.* [Sax. *hlafdig*, *hlæfdiga*, *hlæfdia*. The first syllable of this word occurs in *hlaford*, lord, and this is supposed to be *hlaf*, a loaf, and the words to signify *bread-givers*. But this is doubtful; the meaning of the last syllable not being ascertained in either word.]
1. A woman of distinction. Originally, the title of lady was given to the daughters of earls and others in high rank, but by custom, the title belongs to any woman of genteel education.
2. A word of complaisance; used of women. *Guardian.*
3. Mistress; the female who presides or has authority over a manor or a family.

LA'DY-BIRD, **LA'DY-BUG**, **LA'DY-COW**, **LA'DY-FLY**, } *n.* A small red vaginopennous or sheath-winged insect. *Gay.*
A coleopterous insect of the genus Coccinella. *Linne.*

LADY'S BED-STRAW, *n.* A plant of the genus Galium.

LADY'S BOWER, *n.* A plant of the genus Clematis.

LADY'S COMB, *n.* A plant of the genus Scandix.

LADY'S CUSHION, *n.* A plant of the genus Saxifraga.

LADY'S FINGER, *n.* A plant of the genus Anthyllis.

LADY'S MANTLE, *n.* A plant of the genus Alchemilla.

LADY'S SEAL, *n.* A plant of the genus Tamus.

LADY'S SLIPPER, *n.* A plant of the genus Cypripedium.

LADY'S SMOCK, *n.* A plant of the genus Cardamine.

LADY'S TRACES, *n.* A plant of the genus Ophrys.

LA'DY-DAY, *n.* The day of the annunciation of the holy virgin, March 25th.

LA'DY-LIKE, *a.* Like a lady in manners; genteel; well bred.
2. Soft; tender; delicate. *Dryden.*

LA'DYSHIP, *n.* The title of a lady. *Shak. Dryden.*

LAG, *a.* [This word belongs to the root of *slack, slow, sluggish, languish, long*; Goth. *laggs*; W. *llag, llac*; Gr. λαγγευω, λαγγαζω. Class Lg. See the Verb.]

1. Coming after or behind; slow; sluggish; tardy. *Shak.*
2. Last; long delayed; as the *lag* end. *Shak.*

[This adjective is not now in use.]

LAG, *n.* The lowest class; the rump; the fag end.

2. He that comes behind. [*Not in use.*] *Shak.*

LAG, *v. i.* [W. *llag, llac*, slack, loose; Goth. *laggs*, long; Eng. to *flag*, and *flacceo, langueo*, to *languish*, &c. The sense is to extend or draw out, or to become lax or loose. Class Lg.]

To walk or move slowly; to loiter; to stay behind.

I shall not *lag* behind. *Milton.*

LAG'GARD, *n.* Slow; sluggish; backward. [*Not used.*] *Collins.*

LAG'GER, *a.* A loiterer; an idler; one who moves slowly and falls behind.

LAG'GING, *ppr.* Loitering; moving slowly and falling behind.

The nurse went *lagging* after with the child. *Dryden.*

LAGOON,' } **LAGU'NE,** } *n.* [It. Sp. *laguna*, from the root of *lake.*] A fen, moor, marsh, shallow pond or lake; as the *lagunes* of Venice. *Ray. Smollet.*

LA'IC, } **LA'ICAL,** } *a.* [It. *laico, laicale*, Fr. *laique*, Sp. *laycal*, D. *leek*, L. *laicus*, from Gr. λαικος, from λαος, people. The Greek λαος is probably a contracted word.]

Belonging to the laity or people, in distinction from the clergy.

LA'IC, *n.* A layman. *Bp. Morton.*

LAID, *pret.* and *pp.* of *lay*; so written for *layed.*

LAIN, *pp.* of *lie. Lien* would be a more regular orthography, but *lain* is generally used.

LAIR, *n.* [G. *lager*, from the root of *lay*, L. *locus.*]

1. A place of rest; the bed or couch of a boar or wild beast. *Milton. Dryden.*
2. Pasture; the ground. *Spenser.*

LAIRD, *n.* [contracted from Sax. *hlaford*, lord.]

In the Scots dialect, a lord; the proprietor of a manor. *Cleaveland.*

LA'ITY, *n.* [Gr. λαος, people. See *Laic.*]

1. The people, as distinguished from the clergy; the body of the people not in orders. *Swift.*
2. The state of a layman, or of not being in orders. [*Not used.*] *Ayliffe.*

LAKE, *v. i.* [Sw. *leka*; Dan. *leger*; Goth. *laikon.*]

To play; to sport. *North of England.* This is *play*, Sax. *plegan*, without a prefix.

LAKE, *n.* [G. *lache*, a puddle; Fr. *lac*; L. *lacus*; Sp. It. *lago*; Sax. *luh*; Scot. *loch*; Ir. *lough*; Ice. *laugh.* A lake is a stand of water, from the root of *lay.* Hence L. *lagena*, Eng. *flagon*, and Sp. *laguna*, lagoon.]

1. A large and extensive collection of water contained in a cavity or hollow of the earth. It differs from a *pond* in size, the latter being a collection of small extent; but sometimes a collection of water is called a pond or a lake indifferently. North America contains some of the largest *lakes* on the globe, particularly the *lakes* Ontario, Erie, Huron, Michigan and Superior.
2. A middle color between ultramarine and vermilion, made of cochineal. *Dryden.*

LA'KY, *a.* Pertaining to a lake or lakes. *Sherwood.*

LAMA, *n.* The sovereign pontiff, or rather the god of the Asiatic Tartars. *Encyc.*

2. A small species of camel, the Camelus lama of South America.

LAM'ANTIN, } **LAM'ENTIN,** } *n.* A species of the walrus or sea-cow, the Trichechus manatus. *Encyc.*

LAMB, *n. lam.* [Goth. and Sax. *lamb*; D. Dan. *lam*; G. *lamm*; Sw. *lamb.* The letter *b* is casual and useless. I suspect the word to signify a shoot, as in other cases of the young of animals, from a root which is retained in the Welsh *llamu*, to bound, to skip.]

1. The young of the sheep kind.
2. The *Lamb of God*, in Scripture, the Savior Jesus Christ, who was typified by the paschal lamb.

Behold the *lamb of God*, who taketh away the sin of the world. John i.

LAMB, *v. t.* To bring forth young, as sheep.

LAM'BATIVE, *a.* [L. *lambo*, to lick; W. *llaib, lleibiaw*, to lap.]

Taken by licking. [*Little used.*] *Brown.*

LAM'BATIVE, *n.* A medicine taken by licking with the tongue. *Wiseman.*

LAM'BENT, *a.* [L. *lambens, lambo*, to lick.] Playing about; touching lightly; gliding over; as a *lambent* flame. *Dryden.*

LAMBKIN, *n. lam'kin.* A small lamb. *Gay.*

LAMBLIKE, *a. lam'like.* Like a lamb; gentle; humble; meek; as a *lamblike* temper.

LAMDOID'AL, *a.* [Gr. λαμδα, the name of the letter Λ, and ειδος, form.]

In the form of the Greek Λ, the English L; as the *lamdoidal* suture. *Sharp.*

LAME, *a.* [Sax. *lame* or *lama*; G. *lahm*; D. Dan. *lam*; Sw. *lahm.* It is probably allied to *limp.*]

1. Crippled or disabled in a limb, or otherwise injured so as to be unsound and impaired in strength; as a *lame* arm or leg, or a person *lame* in one leg.
2. Imperfect; not satisfactory; as a *lame* excuse. *Swift.*
3. Hobbling; not smooth; as numbers in verse. *Dryden.*

LAME, *v. t.* To make lame; to cripple or disable; to render imperfect and unsound; as, to *lame* an arm or a leg. *Dryden.*

LAM'EL, *n.* [L. *lamella*; W. *llavyn.* See *Lamin.*] A thin plate or scale of any thing.

LAM'ELLAR, *a.* [from *lamel.*] Disposed in thin plates or scales.

LAM'ELLARLY, *adv.* In thin plates or scales.

LAM'ELLATE, } **LAM'ELLATED,** } *a.* Formed in thin plates or scales, or covered with them.

LAMELLIF'EROUS, *a.* [L. *lamella* and *fero*, to produce.]

Producing plates; an epithet of polypiers presenting lamellar stars, or waved furrows garnished with plates. *Dict. Nat. Hist.*

LAM'ELLIFORM, *a.* [L. *lamella*, a plate, and *form.*] Having the form of a plate. *Journ. of Science.*

LA'MELY, *adv.* [See *Lame.*] Like a cripple; with impaired strength; in a halting manner; as, to walk *lamely.*

2. Imperfectly; without a complete exhibition of parts; as a figure *lamely* drawn; a scene *lamely* described.
3. Weakly; poorly; unsteadily; feebly.

LA'MENESS, *n.* An impaired state of the body or limbs; loss of natural soundness and strength by a wound or by disease; particularly applied to the limbs, and implying a total or partial inability; as the *lameness* of the leg or arm.

2. Imperfection; weakness; as the *lameness* of an argument or of a description.

LAMENT', *v. i.* [L. *lamentor.*] To mourn; to grieve; to weep or wail; to express sorrow.

Jeremiah *lamented* for Josiah. 2 Chron. xxxv.

2. To regret deeply; to feel sorrow.

LAMENT', *v. t.* To bewail; to mourn for; to bemoan; to deplore.

One laughed at follies, one *lamented* crimes. *Dryden.*

LAMENT', *n.* [L. *lamentum.*] Grief or sorrow expressed in complaints or cries; lamentation; a weeping.

Torment, and loud *lament*, and furious rage. *Milton.*

[*This noun is used chiefly or solely in poetry.*]

LAM'ENTABLE, *a.* [Fr. from L. *lamentabilis.*]

1. To be lamented; deserving sorrow; as a *lamentable* declension of morals.
2. Mournful; adapted to awaken grief; as a *lamentable* tune.
3. Expressing sorrow; as *lamentable* cries.
4. Miserable; pitiful; low; poor; *in a sense rather ludicrous.* [*Little used.*] *Stillingfleet.*

LAM'ENTABLY, *adv.* Mournfully; with expressions or tokens of sorrow. *Sidney.*

2. So as to cause sorrow. *Shak.*
3. Pitifully; despicably.

LAMENTA'TION, *n.* [L. *lamentatio.*] Expression of sorrow; cries of grief; the act of bewailing.

In Rama was there a voice heard, *lamentation* and weeping. Matt. ii.

2. In *the plural*, a book of Scripture, containing the lamentations of Jeremiah.

LAMENT'ED, *pp.* Bewailed; mourned for.

LAMENT'ER, *n.* One who mourns, or cries out with sorrow.

LAMENTIN. [See *Lamantin.*]

LAMENT'ING, *ppr.* Bewailing; mourning; weeping.

LAMENT'ING, *n.* A mourning; lamentation.

LA'MIA, *n.* [L.] A hag; a witch; a demon.

LAM'IN, } **LAM'INA,** } *n.* [L. *lamina*; W. *llavyn*, from extending, W. *llav.*]

1. A thin plate or scale; a layer or coat lying over another; applied to the plates of minerals, bones, &c. *Encyc.*
2. A bone, or part of a bone, resembling a thin plate, such as the cribriform plate of the ethmoid bone. *Parr.*
3. The lap of the ear. *Parr.*
4. The border, or the upper, broad or spreading part of the petal, in a polypetalous corol. *Martyn.*

LAM'INABLE, *a.* Capable of being formed into thin plates. *Kirwan.*

LAM'INAR, *a.* In plates; consisting of thin plates or layers.

LAM'INATE, LAM'INATED, *a.* Plated; consisting of plates, scales or layers, one over another.

LAMM, *v. t.* To beat. [*Not in use.*] *Beaum.*

LAM'MAS, *n.* [Sax. *hlammæsse*, from *hlafmæsse*, *loaf-mass*, bread-feast, or feast of first fruits. *Lye.*]
The first day of August. *Bacon.*

LAMP, *n.* [Fr. *lampe*; L. *lampas*; Gr. λαμπας, from λαμπω, to shine; Heb. and Ch. לפיד. Qu.]
1. A vessel for containing oil to be burned by means of a wick; or a light, a burning wick inserted in a vessel of oil. Hence,
2. *Figuratively*, a light of any kind. The moon is called the *lamp* of heaven.

> Thy gentle eyes send forth a quickening spirit,
> To feed the dying *lamp* of life within me. *Rowe.*

Lamp of safety, or *safety lamp*, a lamp for lighting coal mines, without exposing workmen to the explosion of inflammable air. *Davy.*

LAM'PAS, *n.* [Fr.] A lump of flesh of the size of a nut, in the roof of a horse's mouth, and rising above the teeth. *Far. Dict.*

LAMP'BLACK, *n.* [*lamp* and *black*; being originally made by means of a lamp or torch.]
A fine soot formed by the condensation of the smoke of burning pitch or resinous substances, in a chimney terminating in a cone of cloth. *Fourcroy.*

LAMP'IATE, *n.* A compound salt, composed of lampic acid and a base. *Ure.*

LAMP'IC, *a.* The lampic acid is obtained by the combustion of ether by means of a lamp. *Ure.*

LAMP'ING, *a.* [It. *lampante.*] Shining; sparkling. [*Not used.*] *Spenser.*

LAMPOON', *n.* [Qu. Old Fr. *lamper.*]
A personal satire in writing; abuse; censure written to reproach and vex rather than to reform. *Johnson. Dryden. Pope.*

LAMPOON', *v. t.* To abuse with personal censure; to reproach in written satire.

LAMPOON'ER, *n.* One who abuses with personal satire; the writer of a lampoon.

> The squibs are those who are called libelers, *lampooners*, and pamphleteers. *Tatler.*

LAMPOON'ING, *ppr.* Abusing with personal satire.

LAMPOON'RY, *n.* Abuse.

LAM'PREY, *n.* [Fr. *lamproie*; Sax. *lampræda*; G. *lamprete*; D. *lamprei*; Dan. *lampret*; Sp. and Port. *lamprea*; It. *lampreda*; W. *lleiprog*; Arm. *lamprezenn*. In Arm. *lampra* signifies to *slip* or glide. In Welsh *lleipiaw*, is to *lick* or *lap*, and *lleipraw*, to make flabby. If *m* is casual, which is probable, the Armoric *lampra* for *lapra*, coincides with L. *labor*, to *slip*, and most probably the animal is named from *slipping*. If, however, the sense is taken from *licking* the rocks, as Camden supposes, it accords with the sense of the technical name of the genus *petromyzon*, the *rock-sucker.*]
A genus of anguilliform fishes, resembling the eel, and moving in water by winding, like the serpent on land. This fish has seven spiracles on each side of the neck, and a fistula or aperture on the top of the head, but no pectoral or ventral fins. The marine or sea lamprey is sometimes found so large as to weigh four or five pounds. *Encyc.*

Lamprel and *lampron.* [See *Lamprey.*]

LA'NATE, LAN'ATED, *a.* [L. *lanatus*, from *lana*, wool.] Wooly. In *botany*, covered with a substance like curled hairs; as a *lanated* leaf or stem.

LANCE, *n.* *l'ans.* [L. *lancea*; Fr. *lance*; Sp. *lanza*; It. *lancia*; G. *lanze*; D. Sw. *lans*; Dan. *lantse*; Slav. *lanzha*; Gr. λογχη. This word probably belongs to Class *Lg*, and is named from shooting, sending.]
A spear, an offensive weapon in form of a half pike, used by the ancients and thrown by the hand. It consisted of the shaft or handle, the wings and the dart. *Encyc.*

LANCE, *v. t.* [Arm. *lançza*, to shoot, to vomit.]
1. To pierce with a lance or with a sharp pointed instrument.

> —Seized the due victim, and with fury *lanc'd*
> Her back. *Dryden.*

2. To pierce or cut; to open with a lancet; as, to *lance* a vein or an abscess.

LANCELY, *a.* *l'ansly.* Suitable to a lance. *Sidney.*

LAN'CEOLAR, *a.* In *botany*, tapering towards each end. *As. Res.*

LAN'CEOLATE, LAN'CEOLATED, *a.* Shaped like a lance; oblong and gradually tapering toward each extremity; spear-shaped; as a *lanceolate* leaf. *Martyn.*

LANCEPESA'DE, *n.* [It. *lancia-spezzata*, a demi-lance-man, a light horseman.] An officer under the corporal. *J. Hall.*

L'ANCER, *n.* One who lances; one who carries a lance.

L'ANCET, *n.* [Fr. *lancette*, from *lance.*] A surgical instrument, sharp-pointed and two-edged; used in venesection, and in opening tumors, abscesses, &c. *Encyc.*
2. A pointed window. *Warton.*

L'ANCH, *v. t.* [from *lance*, Fr. *lancer.*] To throw, as a lance; to dart; to let fly.

> See whose arm can *lanch* the surer bolt. *Dryden. Lee.*

2. To move, or cause to slide from the land into the water; as, to *lanch* a ship.

L'ANCH, *v. i.* To dart or fly off; to push off; as, to *lanch* into the wide world; to *lanch* into a wide field of discussion.

L'ANCH, *n.* The sliding or movement of a ship from the land into the water, on ways prepared for the purpose.
2. A kind of boat, longer, lower, and more flat-bottomed than a long boat. *Mar. Dict.*

LAND, *n.* [Goth. Sax. G. D. Dan. Sw. *land.* I suppose this to be the W. *llan*, a clear place or area, and the same as *lawn*; Cantabrian, *landa*, a plain or field, It. Sp. *landa*. The final *d* is probably adventitious. The primary sense is a lay or spread. Class Ln.]
1. Earth, or the solid matter which constitutes the fixed part of the surface of the globe, in distinction from the sea or other waters, which constitute the fluid or movable part. Hence we say, the globe is terraqueous, consisting of land and water. The seaman in a long voyage longs to see *land.*
2. Any portion of the solid, superficial part of the globe, whether a kingdom or country, or a particular region. The United States is denominated the *land* of freedom.

> Go, view the *land*, even Jericho. Josh. ii.

3. Any small portion of the superficial part of the earth or ground. We speak of the quantity of *land* in a manor. Five hundred acres of *land* is a large farm.
4. Ground; soil, or the superficial part of the earth in respect to its nature or quality; as good *land*; poor *land*; moist or dry *land.*
5. Real estate. A traitor forfeits all his *lands* and tenements.
6. The inhabitants of a country or region; a nation or people.

> These answers in the silent night received,
> The king himself divulged, the *land* believed. *Dryden.*

7. The ground left unplowed between furrows, is by some of our farmers called a *land.*

To make the land, To make land, In *seaman's language*, is to discover land from sea, as the ship approaches it.

To shut in the land, to lose sight of the land left, by the intervention of a point or promontory.

To set the land, to see by the compass how it bears from the ship.

LAND, *n.* [Sax. *hland* or *hlond.*] Urine; whence the old expression, *land dam*, to kill. *Obs.* *Shak.*

LAND, *v. t.* To set on shore; to disembark; to debark; as, to *land* troops from a ship or boat; to *land* goods.

LAND, *v. i.* To go on shore from a ship or boat; to disembark.

LAN'DAU, *n.* A kind of coach or carriage whose top may be opened and thrown back; so called from a town in Germany.

LAND'-BREEZE, *n.* [*land* and *breeze.*] A current of air setting from the land towards the sea.

LAND'ED, *pp.* Disembarked; set on shore from a ship or boat.
2. *a.* Having an estate in land; as a *landed* gentleman.

> The house of commons must consist, for the most part, of *landed* men. *Addison.*

3. Consisting in real estate or land; as *landed* security; *landed* property. The *landed* interest of a nation is the interest consisting in land; but the word is used also for the owners of that interest, the proprietors of land.

LAND'FALL, *n.* [*land* and *fall.*] A sudden translation of property in land by the death of a rich man. *Johnson.*
2. In *seamen's language*, the first land discovered after a voyage. *Mar. Dict.*

LAND'FLOOD, *n.* [*land* and *flood.*] An overflowing of land by water; an inundation. Properly, a flood from the land from the swelling of rivers; but I am not sure that it is always used in this sense.

LAND'-FORCE, *n.* [*land* and *force.*] A military force, army or troops serving on land, as distinguished from a naval force.

LAND'GRAVE, *n.* [G. *landgraf*; D. *landgraaf*. *Graf* or *graaf* is an earl or count,

Sax. *gerefa*, a companion or count. It is contracted into *reeve*, as in *sheriff*, or *shire-reeve*.]

In *Germany*, a count or earl; or an officer nearly corresponding to the earl of England, and the count of France. It is now a title of certain princes who possess estates or territories called landgraviates. *Encyc.*

LANDGRA'VIATE, *n.* The territory held by a landgrave, or his office, jurisdiction or authority. *Encyc.*

LAND'HOLDER, *n.* A holder, owner or proprietor of land.

LAND'ING, *ppr.* Setting on shore; coming on shore.

LAND'ING, LAND'ING-PLACE, } *n.* A place on the shore of the sea or of a lake, or on the bank of a river, where persons land or come on shore, or where goods are set on shore.

LAND'JOBBER, *n.* A man who makes a business of buying land on speculation, or of buying and selling for the profit of bargains, or who buys and sells for others.

LAND'LADY, *n.* [See *Landlord.*] A woman who has tenants holding from her. *Johnson.*

2. The mistress of an inn. *Swift.*

LAND'LESS, *a.* Destitute of land; having no property in land. *Shak.*

LAND'LOCK, *v.t.* [*land* and *lock.*] To inclose or encompass by land.

LAND'LOCKED, *pp.* Encompassed by land, so that no point of the compass is open to the sea. *Encyc.*

LAND'LOPER, *n.* [See *Leap* and *Interloper.*]

A landman; literally, a *land runner;* a term of reproach among seamen to designate a man who passes his life on land.

LAND'LORD, *n.* [Sax. *land-hlaford*, lord of the land. But in German *lehen-herr*, D. *leen-herr*, is lord of the *loan* or fief. Perhaps the Saxon is so written by mistake, or the word may have been corrupted.]

1. The lord of a manor or of land; the owner of land who has tenants under him. *Johnson.*

2. The master of an inn or tavern. *Addison.*

LAND'MAN, *n.* A man who serves on land; opposed to *seaman.*

LAND'MARK, *n.* [*land* and *mark.*] A mark to designate the boundary of land; any mark or fixed object; as a marked tree, a stone, a ditch, or a heap of stones, by which the limits of a farm, a town or other portion of territory may be known and preserved.

Thou shalt not remove thy neighbor's *landmark.* Deut. xix.

2. In *navigation*, any elevated object on land that serves as a guide to seamen.

LAND'-OFFICE, *n.* In *the United States*, an office in which the sales of new land are registered, and warrants issued for the location of land, and other business respecting unsettled land is transacted.

LAND'SCAPE, *n.* [D. *landschap;* G. *landschaft;* Dan. *landskab;* Sw. *landskap;* *land* and *skape.*]

1. A portion of land or territory which the eye can comprehend in a single view, including mountains, rivers, lakes, and whatever the land contains.

—Whilst the *landscape* round it measures,
Russet lawns and fallows gray,
Where the nibbling flocks do stray. *Milton.*

2. A picture, exhibiting the form of a district of country, as far as the eye can reach, or a particular extent of land and the objects it contains, or its various scenery. *Addison. Pope.*

3. The view or prospect of a district of country.

LAND'SLIP, *n.* A portion of a hill or mountain, which *slips* or slides down; or the sliding down of a considerable tract of land from a mountain. *Landslips* are not unfrequent in Swisserland. *Goldsmith.*

LAND'SMAN, *n.* In *seaman's language*, a sailor on board a ship, who has not before been at sea.

LAND'STREIGHT, *n.* A narrow slip of land. [*Not used.*] *Mountague.*

LAND'-TAX, *n.* A tax assessed on land and buildings.

LAND'-TURN, *n.* A land breeze. *Encyc.*

LAND'-WAITER, *n.* An officer of the customs, whose duty is to *wait* or attend on the landing of goods, and to examine, weigh or measure, and take an account of them. *Encyc.*

LAND'WARD, *adv.* Toward the land. *Sandys.*

LAND'-WIND, *n.* A wind blowing from the land.

LAND'-WORKER, *n.* One who tills the ground. *Pownall.*

LANE, *n.* [D. *laan*, a lane, a walk. Class Ln.]

1. A narrow way or passage, or a private passage, as distinguished from a public road or highway. A lane may be open to all passengers, or it may be inclosed and appropriated to a man's private use. In *the U. States*, the word is used chiefly in the country, and answers in a degree, to an *alley* in a city. It has sometimes been used for *alley*. In London, the word *lane* is added to the names of streets; as *chancery lane.*

2. A passage between lines of men, or people standing on each side. *Bacon.*

LAN'GRAGE, LAN'GREL, } *n.* *Langrel shot* or *langrage*, is a particular kind of shot used at sea for tearing sails and rigging, and thus disabling an enemy's ship. It consists of bolts, nails and other pieces of iron fastened together. *Mar. Dict.*

LANGTERALOO', *n.* A game at cards. *Tatler.*

LAN'GUAGE, *n.* [Fr. *langage;* Sp. *lengua*, *lenguage;* Port. *linguagem;* It. *linguaggio;* Arm. *langaich;* from L. *lingua*, the tongue, and speech. It seems to be connected with *lingo*, to *lick;* the *n* is evidently casual, for *ligula*, in Latin, is a little tongue, and this signifies also a strap or lace, as if the primary sense were to extend.]

1. Human speech; the expression of ideas by words or significant articulate sounds, for the communication of thoughts. *Language* consists in the oral utterance of sounds, which usage has made the representatives of ideas. When two or more persons customarily annex the same sounds to the same ideas, the expression of these sounds by one person communicates his ideas to another. This is the primary sense of *language*, the use of which is to communicate the thoughts of one person to another through the organs of hearing. Articulate sounds are represented by letters, marks or characters which form words. Hence language consists also in

2. Words duly arranged in sentences, written, printed or engraved, and exhibited to the eye.

3. The speech or expression of ideas peculiar to a particular nation. Men had originally one and the same *language*, but the tribes or families of men, since their dispersion, have distinct *languages.*

4. Style; manner of expression.

Others for *language* all their care express. *Pope.*

5. The inarticulate sounds by which irrational animals express their feelings and wants. Each species of animals has peculiar sounds, which are uttered instinctively, and are understood by its own species, and its own species only.

6. Any manner of expressing thoughts. Thus we speak of the *language* of the eye, a *language* very expressive and intelligible.

7. A nation, as distinguished by their speech. Dan. iii.

LAN'GUAGED, *a.* Having a language; as many-*languaged* nations. *Pope.*

LAN'GUAGE-MASTER, *n.* One whose profession is to teach languages. *Spectator.*

LAN'GUET, *n.* [Fr. *languette.*] Any thing in the shape of the tongue. [*Not English.*] *Johnson.*

LAN'GUID, *a.* [L. *languidus*, from *langueo*, to droop or *flag*. See *Languish.*]

1. Flagging; drooping; hence, feeble; weak; heavy; dull; indisposed to exertion. The body is *languid* after excessive action, which exhausts its powers.

2. Slow; as *languid* motion.

3. Dull; heartless; without animation.

And fire their *languid* soul with Cato's virtue. *Addison.*

LAN'GUIDLY, *adv.* Weakly; feebly; slowly. *Boyle.*

LAN'GUIDNESS, *n.* Weakness from exhaustion of strength; feebleness; dullness; languor.

2. Slowness.

LAN'GUISH, *v. i.* [Fr. *languir*, *languissant;* Arm. *languiçza;* It. *languire;* L. *langueo*, *lachinisso;* Gr. λαγγευω, to *flag*, to *lag*. This word is of the family of W. *llac*, slack, loose; *llaciaw*, to *slacken*, to relax. L. *laxo*, *laxus*, *flacceo*, and Goth. *laggs*, long, may be of the same family.]

1. To lose strength or animation; to be or become dull, feeble or spiritless; to pine; to be or to grow heavy. We *languish* under disease or after excessive exertion.

She that hath borne seven *languisheth.* Jer. xv.

2. To wither; to fade; to lose the vegetating power.

For the fields of Heshbon *languish.* Is. xvi.

3. To grow dull; to be no longer active and vigorous. The war *languished* for want of supplies. Commerce, agriculture, manufactures *languish*, not for want of money, but for want of good markets.

4. To pine or sink under sorrow or any continued passion; as, a woman *languishes* for the loss of her lover.

Therefore shall the land mourn, and every oné that dwelleth therein shall *languish*. Hosea iv.

5. To look with softness or tenderness, as with the head reclined and a peculiar cast of the eye. *Dryden.*

LAN'GUISH, *v. t.* To cause to droop or pine. [*Little used.*] *Shak.*

LAN'GUISH, *n.* Act of pining; also, a soft and tender look or appearance.

And the blue *languish* of soft Allia's eye. *Pope.*

LAN'GUISHER, *n.* One who languishes or pines.

LAN'GUISHING, *ppr.* Becoming or being feeble; losing strength; pining; withering; fading.

2. *a.* Having a languid appearance; as a *languishing* eye.

LAN'GUISHINGLY, *adv.* Weakly; feebly; dully; slowly.

2. With tender softness.

LAN'GUISHMENT, *n.* The state of pining. *Spenser.*

2. Softness of look or mien, with the head reclined. *Dryden.*

LAN'GUOR, *n.* [L. *languor*; Fr. *langueur.*]

1. Feebleness; dullness; heaviness; lassitude of body; that state of the body which is induced by exhaustion of strength, as by disease, by extraordinary exertion, by the relaxing effect of heat, or by weakness from any cause.

2. Dullness of the intellectual faculty; listlessness. *Watts.*

3. Softness; laxity.

To isles of fragrance, lily-silvered vales,
Diffusing *languor* in the parting gales. *Dunciad.*

LAN'GUOROUS, *a.* Tedious; melancholy. *Obs.* *Spenser.*

LAN'GURE, *v. t.* To languish. [*Not in use.*] *Chaucer.*

LANIARD, *n.* *lan'yard.* [Fr. *laniere*, a strap.]

A short piece of rope or line, used for fastening something in ships, as the *laniards* of the gun-ports, of the buoy, of the cathook, &c., but especially used to extend the shrouds and stays of the masts, by their communication with the dead eyes, &c. *Mar. Dict.*

LA'NIATE, *v. t.* [L. *lanio.*] To tear in pieces. [*Little used.*]

LANIA'TION, *n.* A tearing in pieces. [*Little used.*]

LANIF'EROUS, *a.* [L. *lanifer*; *lana*, wool, and *fero*, to produce.] Bearing or producing wool.

LAN'IFICE, *n.* [L. *lanificium*; *lana*, wool, and *facio*, to make.]

Manufacture of wool. [*Little used.*] *Bacon.*

LANIG'EROUS, *a.* [L. *laniger*; *lana*, wool, and *gero*, to bear.] Bearing or producing wool.

LANK, *a.* [Sax. *hlanca*; Gr. λαγαρος; probably allied to *flank*, and W. *llac*, slack, lax; *llaciaw*, to slacken; G. *schlank.*]

1. Loose or lax and easily yielding to pressure; not distended; not stiff or firm by distension; not plump; as a *lank* bladder or purse.

The clergy's bags
Are *lank* and lean with thy extortions. *Shak.*

2. Thin; slender; meager; not full and firm; as a *lank* body.

3. Languid; drooping. [See *Languish.*] *Milton.*

LANK'LY, *adv.* Thinly; loosely; laxly.

LANK'NESS, *n.* Laxity; flabbiness; leanness; slenderness.

LANK'Y, *n.* Lank. [*Vulgar.*]

LAN'NER, LAN'NERET, } *n.* [Fr. *lanier*; L. *laniarius*, *lanius*, a butcher.] A species of hawk.

LANS'QUENET, *n.* [*lance* and *knecht*, a boy, a knight.]

1. A common foot soldier.

2. A game at cards. *Johnson. Encyc.*

LAN'TERN, *n.* [Fr. *lanterne*; L. *laterna*; G. *laterne*; D. *lantaarn*; Sp. *linterna.*]

1. A case or vessel made of tin perforated with many holes, or of some transparent substance, as glass, horn, or oiled paper; used for carrying a candle or other light in the open air, or into stables, &c. *Locke.*

A *dark lantern* is one with a single opening, which may be closed so as to conceal the light.

2. A light-house or light to direct the course of ships. *Addison.*

3. In *architecture*, a little dome raised over the roof of a building to give light, and to serve as a crowning to the fabric. *Encyc.*

4. A square cage of carpentry placed over the ridge of a corridor or gallery, between two rows of shops, to illuminate them. *Encyc.*

Magic lantern, an optical machine by which painted images are represented so much magnified as to appear like the effect of magic.

LAN'TERN-FLY, *n.* An insect of the genus Fulgora. *Encyc.*

LAN'TERN-JAWS, *n.* A thin visage. *Spectator.*

LANU'GINOUS, *a.* [L. *lanuginosus*, from *lanugo*, down, from *lana*, wool.]

Downy; covered with down, or fine soft hair.

LAODICE'AN, *a.* Like the christians of Laodicea; lukewarm in religion.

LAODICE'ANISM, *n.* Lukewarmness in religion. *E. Stiles.*

LAP, *n.* [Sax. *læppe*; G. *lappen*; D. Dan. *lap*; Sw. *lapp*. This word seems to be a different orthography of *flap.*]

1. The loose part of a coat; the lower part of a garment that plays loosely. *Swift.*

2. The part of clothes that lies on the knees when a person sits down; hence, the knees in this position.

Men expect that happiness should drop into their *laps*. *Tillotson.*

LAP, *v. t.* To fold; to bend and lay over or on; as, to *lap* a piece of cloth.

To lap boards, is to lay one partly over another.

2. To wrap or twist round.

I *lapped* a slender thread about the paper. *Newton.*

3. To infold; to involve.

Her garment spreads, and *laps* him in the folds. *Dryden.*

LAP, *v. i.* To be spread or laid; to be turned over.

The upper wings are opacous; at their hinder ends where they *lap* over, transparent like the wing of a fly. *Grew.*

LAP, *v. i.* [Sax. *lappian*; D. *labben*; Arm. *lappa*; Fr. *laper*; Dan. *laber*; W. *llepiaw*, *lleibiaw*; Gr. λαπτω. If *m* is casual in L. *lambo*, as it probably is, this is the same word. Class Lb. No. 22.]

To take up liquor or food with the tongue; to feed or drink by licking.

The dogs by the river Nilus' side being thirsty, *lap* hastily as they run along the shore. *Digby.*

And the number of them that *lapped* were three hundred men. Judg. vii.

LAP, *v. t.* To take into the mouth with the tongue; to lick up; as, a cat *laps* milk. *Shak.*

LAP'DOG, *n.* A small dog fondled in the lap. *Dryden.*

LAP'FULL, *n.* As much as the lap can contain. 2 Kings iv.

LAP'ICIDE, *n.* A stone-cutter. [*Not used.*] *Dict.*

LAPIDA'RIOUS, *a.* [L. *lapidarius*, from *lapis*, a stone.] Stony; consisting of stones.

LAP'IDARY, *n.* [Fr. *lapidaire*; L. *lapidarius*, *lapis*, a stone.]

1. An artificer who cuts precious stones.

2. A dealer in precious stones.

3. A virtuoso skilled in the nature and kinds of gems or precious stones. *Encyc.*

LAP'IDARY, *a.* Pertaining to the art of cutting stones. The *lapidary* style denotes that which is proper for monumental and other inscriptions. *Encyc.*

LAP'IDATE, *v. t.* [L. *lapido.*] To stone. [*Not used.*]

LAPIDA'TION, *n.* The act of stoning a person to death. *Hall.*

LAPID'EOUS, *a.* [L. *lapideus.*] Stony; of the nature of stone; as *lapideous* matter. [*Little used.*] *Ray.*

LAPIDES'CENCE, *n.* [L. *lapidesco*, from *lapis*, a stone.]

1. The process of becoming stone; a hardening into a stony substance.

2. A stony concretion. *Brown.*

LAPIDES'CENT, *a.* Growing or turning to stone; that has the quality of petrifying bodies. *Encyc.*

LAPIDES'CENT, *n.* Any substance which has the quality of petrifying a body, or converting it to stone.

LAPIDIF'IC, *a.* [L. *lapis*, a stone, and *facio*, to make.] Forming or converting into stone.

LAPIDIFICA'TION, *n.* The operation of forming or converting into a stony substance, by means of a liquid charged with earthy particles in solution, which crystalize in the interstices, and end in forming free stone, pudding stone, &c. *Dict. Nat. Hist.*

LAPID'IFY, *v. t.* [L. *lapis*, a stone, and *facio*, to form.] To form into stone.

LAPID'IFY, *v. i.* To turn into stone; to become stone.

LAP'IDIST, *n.* A dealer in precious stones. [See *Lapidary.*]

LAPIS, in Latin, a stone. Hence,

Lapis Bononiensis, the Bolognian stone.

Lapis Hepaticus, liver stone.

Lapis Lazuli, azure stone, an aluminous mineral, of a rich blue color, resembling the blue carbonate of copper. [See *Lazuli*.]

Lapis Lydius, touch-stone; basanite; a variety of siliceous slate.

LAP′PED, *pp.* [See *Lap*.] Turned or folded over.

LAP′PER, *n.* One that laps; one that wraps or folds.

2. One that takes up with his tongue.

LAP′PET, *n.* [*dim.* of *lap*.] A part of a garment or dress that hangs loose. *Swift.*

LAP′PING, *ppr.* Wrapping; folding; laying on.

2. Licking; taking into the mouth with the tongue.

LAPSE, *n. laps.* [L. *lapsus*, from *labor*, to slide, to fall. Class Lb.]

1. A sliding, gliding or flowing; a smooth course; as the *lapse* of a stream; the *lapse* of time.

2. A falling or passing.

> The *lapse* to indolence is soft and imperceptible, but the return to diligence is difficult. *Rambler.*

3. A slip; an error; a fault; a failing in duty; a slight deviation from truth or rectitude.

> This Scripture may be usefully applied as a caution to guard against those *lapses* and failings to which our infirmities daily expose us. *Rogers.*

So we say, a *lapse* in style or propriety.

4. In *ecclesiastical law*, the slip or omission of a patron to present a clerk to a benefice, within six months after it becomes void. In this case, the benefice is said to be *lapsed*, or *in lapse*. *Encyc.*

5. In *theology*, the fall or apostasy of Adam.

LAPSE, *v. i. laps.* To glide; to pass slowly, silently or by degrees.

> This disposition to shorten our words by retrenching the vowels, is nothing else but a tendency to *lapse* into the barbarity of those northern nations from which we descended. *Swift.*

2. To slide or slip in moral conduct; to fail in duty; to deviate from rectitude; to commit a fault.

> To *lapse* in fullness
> Is sorer than to lie for need. *Shak.*

3. To slip or commit a fault by inadvertency or mistake.

> Homer, in his characters of Vulcan and Thersites, has *lapsed* into the burlesque character. *Addison.*

4. To fall or pass from one proprietor to another, by the omission or negligence of the patron.

> If the archbishop shall not fill it up within six months ensuing, it *lapses* to the king. *Ayliffe.*

5. To fall from a state of innocence, or from truth, faith or perfection.

> Once more I will renew
> His *lapsed* powers. *Milton.*

LAPS′ED, *pp.* Fallen; passed from one proprietor to another by the negligence of the patron; as a *lapsed* benefice. A *lapsed* legacy is one which falls to the heirs through the failure of the legatee, as when the legatee dies before the testator.

LAP′SIDED, *a.* [*lap* and *side*.] Having one side heavier than the other, as a ship. *Mar. Dict.*

LAPS′ING, *ppr.* Gliding; flowing; failing; falling to one person through the omission of another.

LAP′WING, *n.* A bird of the genus Tringa; the tewit.

LAP′WŌRK, *n.* Work in which one part laps over another. *Grew.*

L′AR, *n.* plu. *lares.* [L.] A household deity. *Lovelace.*

L′ARBŌARD, *n.* [*Board*, *bord*, is a side; but I know not the meaning of *lar*. The Dutch use *bakboord*, and the Germans *backbord*.]

The left hand side of a ship, when a person stands with his face to the head; opposed to *starboard*.

L′ARBŌARD, *a.* Pertaining to the left hand side of a ship; as the *larboard* quarter.

L′ARCENY, *n.* [Fr. *larcin*; Norm. *larcim*; Arm. *laeroncy*, or *lazroncy*, contracted from L. *latrocinium*, from the Celtic; W. *lladyr*, theft; *lladron*, thieves; Sp. *ladron*; It. *ladro*, *ladrone*.]

Theft; the act of taking and carrying away the goods or property of another feloniously. Larceny is of two kinds; *simple larceny*, or theft, not accompanied with any atrocious circumstance; and *mixed* or *compound larceny*, which includes in it the aggravation of taking from one's house or person, as in burglary or robbery. The stealing of any thing below the value of twelve pence, is called *petty larceny*; above that value, it is called *grand larceny*. *Blackstone.*

L′ARCH, *n.* [L. *larix*; Sp. *alerce*; It. *larice*; G. *lerchenbaum*; D. *lorkenboom*.]

The common name of a division of the genus Pinus, species of which are natives of America, as well as of Europe.

L′ARD, *n.* [Fr. *lard*; L. *lardum*, *laridum*; It. and Sp. *lardo*; Arm. *lardt*. Qu. W. *llâr*, that spreads or drops, soft.]

1. The fat of swine, after being melted and separated from the flesh.

2. Bacon; the flesh of swine. *Dryden.*

L′ARD, *v. t.* [Fr. *larder*; Arm. *larda*.] To stuff with bacon or pork.

> The *larded* thighs on loaded altars laid. *Dryden.*

2. To fatten; to enrich.

> Now Falstaff sweats to death,
> And *lards* the lean earth. *Shak.*

3. To mix with something by way of improvement.

> —Let no alien interpose,
> To *lard* with wit thy hungry Epsom prose. *Dryden.*

L′ARD, *v. i.* To grow fat. *Drayton.*

LARDA′CEOUS, *a.* Of the nature of lard; consisting of lard. *Coxe.*

L′ARDED, *pp.* Stuffed with bacon; fattened; mixed.

L′ARDER, *n.* A room where meat is kept or salted. *Bacon.*

L′ARDRY, *n.* A larder. [*Not used.*]

L′ARĠE, *a. larj.* [Fr. *large*; Sp. Port. It. *largo*; Arm. *larg*; L. *largus*. The primary sense is to spread, stretch or distend, to diffuse, hence to loosen, to relax; Sp. *largar*, to loosen, to slacken, as a rope. Class Lr. It seems to be connected with Gr. λαυρος, wide, copious, and perhaps with *floor*, W. *llawr*, and with *llawer*, much, many. In Basque, *larria*, is gross, and *larritu*, to grow.]

1. Big; of great size; bulky; as a *large* body; a *large* horse or ox; a *large* mountain; a *large* tree; a *large* ship.

2. Wide; extensive; as a *large* field or plain; a *large* extent of territory.

3. Extensive or populous; containing many inhabitants; as a *large* city or town.

4. Abundant; plentiful; ample; as a *large* supply of provisions.

5. Copious; diffusive.

> I might be very *large* on the importance and advantages of education. *Felton.*

6. In *seamen's language*, the wind is *large* when it crosses the line of a ship's course in a favorable direction, particularly on the beam or quarter. *Encyc.*

7. Wide; consisting of much water; as a *large* river.

8. Liberal; of a great amount; as a *large* donation.

At large, without restraint or confinement; as, to go *at large*; to be left *at large*.

2. Diffusely; fully; in the full extent; as, to discourse on a subject *at large*.

L′ARĠE, *n.* Formerly, a musical note equal to four breves. *Busby.*

LARĠEHE′ARTEDNESS, *n.* Largeness of heart; liberality. [*Not used.*] *Bp. Reynolds.*

L′ARĠELY, *adv.* Widely; extensively.

2. Copiously; diffusely; amply. The subject was *largely* discussed.

3. Liberally; bountifully.

> —How he lives and eats;
> How *largely* gives. *Dryden.*

4. Abundantly.

> They their fill of love and love's disport
> Took *largely*. *Milton.*

L′ARĠENESS, *n.* Bigness; bulk; magnitude; as the *largeness* of an animal.

2. Greatness; comprehension; as the *largeness* of mind or of capacity.

3. Extent; extensiveness; as *largeness* of views.

4. Extension; amplitude; liberality; as the *largeness* of an offer; *largeness* of heart. *Hooker. Waller.*

5. Wideness; extent; as the *largeness* of a river.

L′ARĠESS, *n.* [Fr. *largesse*; L. *largitio*; from *largus*, large.]

A present; a gift or donation; a bounty bestowed. *Bacon. Dryden.*

L′ARĠISH, *a.* Somewhat large. [*Unusual.*] *Cavallo.*

L′ARGO, **LARGHET′TO**, } [It.] Musical terms, directing to slow movement. *Largo* is one degree quicker than *grave*, and two degrees quicker than *adagio*. *Dict.*

L′ARK, *n.* [Sax. *laferc*, *lauerce*; Scot. *laverok*, *lauerok*; G. *lerche*; D. *leeuwrik*; Dan. *lerke*; Sw. *lärka*; Icl. *lava*, *loova*. As the Latin *alauda* coincides with *laudo*, Eng. *loud*, so the first syllable of *lark*, *laf*, *lau*, *lave*, may coincide with the Dan. *lover*, to praise, to sing or cry out. But I know not the sense of the word.]

A bird of the genus Alauda, distinguished for its singing.

L′ARKER, *n.* A catcher of larks. *Dict.*

L′ARKLIKE, *a.* Resembling a lark in manners.

L′ARK'S-HEEL, *n.* A flower called Indian cress.

L'ARKSPUR, *n.* A plant of the genus Delphinium.

L'ARMIER, *n.* [Fr. from *larme*, a tear or drop.]
The flat jutting part of a cornice; literally, the dropper; the eave or drip of a house.

LAR'UM, *n.* [G. *lärm*, bustle, noise; Dan. *id.*]
Alarm; a noise giving notice of danger. [See *Alarm*, which is generally used.]

L'ARVA, } *n.* [L. *larva*, a mask; Sw. *larf*;
L'ARVE, } Dan. G. *larve*.]
An insect in the caterpillar state; eruca; the state of an insect when the animal is masked, and before it has attained its winged or perfect state; the first stage in the metamorphoses of insects, preceding the chrysalis and perfect insect. *Linne.*

L'ARVATED, *a.* Masked; clothed as with a mask.

LARYN'GEAN, *a.* [See *Larynx.*] Pertaining to the larynx.

LARYNGOT'OMY, *n.* [*larynx* and Gr. τεμνω, to cut.]
The operation of cutting the larynx or windpipe; the making of an incision into the larynx for assisting respiration when obstructed, or removing foreign bodies; bronchotomy; tracheotomy. *Coxe. Quincy.*

LAR'YNX, *n.* [Gr. λαρυγξ.] In *anatomy*, the upper part of the windpipe or trachea, a cartilaginous cavity, which modulates the voice in speaking and singing. *Quincy.*

LAS'CAR, *n.* In *the East Indies*, a native seaman, or a gunner.

LASCIVIENCY, LASCIVIENT. [*Not used.* See the next words.]

LASCIV'IOUS, *a.* [Fr. *lascif*; It. Sp. *lascivo*; from L. *lascivus*, from *laxus*, *laxo*, to relax, to loosen. Class Lg.]
1. Loose; wanton; lewd; lustful; as *lascivious* men; *lascivious* desires; *lascivious* eyes. *Milton.*
2. Soft; wanton; luxurious.

He capers nimbly in a lady's chamber,
To the *lascivious* pleasing of a lute. *Shak.*

LASCIV'IOUSLY, *adv.* Loosely; wantonly; lewdly.

LASCIV'IOUSNESS, *n.* Looseness; irregular indulgence of animal desires; wantonness; lustfulness.

Who, being past feeling, have given themselves over to *lasciviousness*. Eph. iv.

2. Tendency to excite lust, and promote irregular indulgences.

The reason pretended by Augustus was, the *lasciviousness* of his Elegies and his Art of Love. *Dryden.*

LASH, *n.* [This may be the same word as *leash*, Fr. *laisse*, or it may be allied to the G. *lasche*, a slap, *laschen*, to lash or slap, and both may be from one root.]
1. The thong or braided cord of a whip.

I observed that your whip wanted a *lash* to it. *Addison.*

2. A leash or string.
3. A stroke with a whip, or any thing pliant and tough. The culprit was whipped thirty nine *lashes*.
4. A stroke of satire; a sarcasm; an expression or retort that cuts or gives pain.

The moral is a *lash* at the vanity of arrogating that to ourselves which succeeds well. *L'Estrange.*

LASH, *v. t.* To strike with a lash or any thing pliant; to whip or scourge.

We *lash* the pupil and defraud the ward. *Dryden.*

2. To throw up with a sudden jerk.

He falls; and *lashing* up his heels, his rider throws. *Dryden.*

3. To beat, as with something loose; to dash against.

And big waves *lash* the frighted shores— *Prior.*

4. To tie or bind with a rope or cord; to secure or fasten by a string; as, to *lash* any thing to a mast or to a yard; to *lash* a trunk on a coach.
5. To satirize; to censure with severity; as, to *lash* vice.

LASH, *v. i.* To ply the whip; to strike at.

To laugh at follies, or to *lash* at vice. *Dryden.*

To lash out, is to be extravagant or unruly. *Feltham.*

LASH'ED, *pp.* Struck with a lash; whipped; tied; made fast by a rope.
2. In *botany*, ciliate; fringed. *Lee.*

LASH'ER, *n.* One that whips or lashes.

LASH'ER, } *n.* A piece of rope for binding
LASH'ING, } or making fast one thing to another. *Mar. Dict.*

LASH'ING, *n.* Extravagance; unruliness. *South.*

L'ASS, *n.* [Qu. from *laddess*, as Hickes suggests.]
A young woman; a girl. *Philips.*

LAS'SITUDE, *n.* [Fr. from L. *lassitudo*, from *lassus*, and this from *laxus*, *laxo*, to relax.]
1. Weakness; dullness; heaviness; weariness; languor of body or mind, proceeding from exhaustion of strength by excessive labor or action, or other means.
2. Among *physicians*, lassitude is a morbid sensation or languor which often precedes disease, in which case it proceeds from an impaired or diseased action of the organs.

L'ASSLORN, *a.* Forsaken by his lass or mistress. *Shak.*

L'AST, *a.* [contracted from *latest*; Sax. *last*, from *latost*; G. *letzt*; D. *laatst*, from *laat*, late. Qu. is the Gr. λοισθος from the same root? See *Late* and *Let.*]
1. That comes after all the others; the latest; *applied to time*; as the *last* hour of the day; the *last* day of the year.
2. That follows all the others; that is behind all the others in place; hindmost; as, this was the *last* man that entered the church.
3. Beyond which there is no more.

Here, *last* of Britons, let your names be read. *Pope.*

4. Next before the present; as the *last* week; the *last* year.
5. Utmost.

Their *last* endeavors bend,
T' outshine each other. *Dryden.*
It is an object of the *last* importance. *Ellicott.*

6. Lowest; meanest.

Antilochus
Takes the *last* prize. *Pope.*

At last, at the last, at the end; in the conclusion.

Gad, a troop shall overcome him; but he shall overcome *at the last*. Gen. xlix.

To the last, to the end; till the conclusion.

And blunder on in business *to the last*. *Pope.*

In the phrases, "you are the *last* man I should consult," "this is the *last* place in which I should expect to find you," the word *last* implies improbability; this is the most improbable place, and therefore I should resort to it *last*.

L'AST, *adv.* The last time; the time before the present. I saw him *last* at New York.
2. In conclusion; finally.

Pleased with his idol, he commends, admires,
Adores; and *last*, the thing adored desires. *Dryden.*

L'AST, *v. i.* [Sax. *lastan*, *læstan*. This verb seems to be from the adjective *last*, the primary sense of which is continued, drawn out. See *Let.*]
1. To continue in time; to endure; to remain in existence. Our government cannot *last* long unless administered by honest men.
2. To continue unimpaired; not to decay or perish. Select for winter the best apples to *last*. This color will *last*.
3. To hold out; to continue unconsumed. The captain knew he had not water on board to *last* a week.

L'AST, *n.* [Sax. *hlæste*; G. Sw. D. Dan. *last*; Russ. *laste*; Fr. *lest*; Arm. *lastr*; W. *llwyth*. See *Load.*]
A load; hence, a certain weight or measure. A *last* of codfish, white herrings, meal, and ashes, is twelve barrels; a *last* of corn is ten quarters or eighty bushels; of gunpowder, twenty four barrels; of red herrings, twenty cades; of hides, twelve dozen; of lether, twenty dickers; of pitch and tar, fourteen barrels; of wool, twelve sacks; of flax or fethers, 1700 lbs. *Encyc.*

L'AST, *n.* [Sax. *laste*, *læste*; G. *leisten*; D. *leest*; Dan. *læst*; Sw. *läst.*]
A mold or form of the human foot, made of wood, on which shoes are formed.

The cobler is not to go beyond his *last*. *L'Estrange.*

L'ASTAGE, *n.* [Fr. *lestage*. See *Last*, a load.]
1. A duty paid for freight or transportation. [*Not used in the U. States.*]
2. Ballast. [*Not used.*]
3. The lading of a ship. [*Not used.*]

L'ASTERY, *n.* A red color. [*Not in use.*] *Spenser.*

L'ASTING, *ppr.* Continuing in time; enduring; remaining.
2. *a.* Durable; of long continuance; that may continue or endure; as a *lasting* good or evil; a *lasting* color.

L'ASTINGLY, *adv.* Durably; with continuance.

L'ASTINGNESS, *n.* Durability; the quality or state of long continuance. *Sidney.*

L'ASTLY, *adv.* In the last place.
2. In the conclusion; at last; finally.

LATCH, *n.* [Fr. *loquet*; Arm. *licqed* or *clicqed*, coinciding with L. *ligula*, from *ligo*, to tie, and with English *lock*, Sax. *læcan*, to catch. The G. *klinke*, D. *klink*, coincide with Fr. *clenche*, which, if *n* is casual, are the Arm. *clicqed*, Eng. to *clinch*. The same word in W. is *clicied*, a latch, and the It. *laccio*, a snare, L. *laqueus*, from which we have *lace*, may belong to the same root. The primary sense of the root is to catch, to close, stop or make fast.]

1. A small piece of iron or wood used to fasten a door. *Gay.*

2. A small line like a loop, used to lace the bonnets to the courses, or the drabblers to the bonnets. *Dict.*

LATCH, *v. t.* To fasten with a latch; to fasten. *Locke.*

2. [Fr. *lecher.*] To smear. [*Not used.*] *Shak.*

LATCH'ET, *n.* [from *latch*, Fr. *lacet.*] The string that fastens a shoe. Mark i.

LATE, *a.* [Sax. *læt, lat*; Goth. *lata*; D. *laat*; Sw. *lat*; Dan. *lad*, idle, lazy; Goth. *latyan*, Sax. *latian*, to delay or retard. This word is from the root of *let*, the sense of which is to draw out, extend or prolong, hence to be slow or late. See *Let.* This adjective has regular terminations of the comparative and superlative degrees, *later, latest*, but it has also *latter*, and *latest* is often contracted into *last.*]

1. Coming after the usual time; slow; tardy; long delayed; as a *late* spring; a *late* summer. The crops or harvest will be *late.*

2. Far advanced towards the end or close; as a *late* hour of the day. He began at a *late* period of his life.

3. Last, or recently in any place, office or character; as the *late* ministry; the *late* administration.

4. Existing not long ago, but now decayed or departed; as the *late* bishop of London.

5. Not long past; happening not long ago; recent; as the *late* rains. We have received *late* intelligence.

LATE, *adv.* After the usual time, or the time appointed; after delay; as, he arrived *late.*

2. After the proper or usual season. This year the fruits ripen *late.*

3. Not long ago; lately.

> And round them throng
> With leaps and bounds the *late* imprison'd young. *Pope.*

4. Far in the night, day, week, or other particular period; as, to lie a-bed *late*; to sit up *late* at night.

Of late, lately, in time not long past, or near the present. The practice is *of late* uncommon.

Too late, after the proper time; not in due time. We arrived *too late* to see the procession.

LA'TED, *a.* Belated; being too late. [*Not used.*] *Shak.*

LAT'EEN, *a.* A *lateen* sail is a triangular sail, extended by a *lateen* yard, which is slung about one quarter the distance from the lower end, which is brought down at the tack, while the other end is elevated at an angle of about 45 degrees; used in xebecs, polacres and setees, in the Mediterranean. *Mar. Dict.*

LA'TELY, *adv.* Not long ago; recently. We called on a gentleman who has *lately* arrived from Italy.

LA'TENCY, *n.* [See *Latent.*] The state of being concealed; abstruseness. *Paley.*

LA'TENESS, *n.* The state of being tardy, or of coming after the usual time; as the *lateness* of spring or of harvest.

2. Time far advanced in any particular period; as *lateness* of the day or night; *lateness* in the season; *lateness* in life.

3. The state of being out of time, or after the appointed time; as the *lateness* of one's arrival.

LA'TENT, *a.* [L. *latens, lateo*; Gr. ληθω, λανθανω; Heb. לאט, to cover, or rather Ch. לטא, to hide or be hid. Class Ld. No. 1. 11.]

Hid; concealed; secret; not seen; not visible or apparent. We speak of *latent* motives; *latent* reasons; *latent* springs of action.

Latent heat, is heat in combination, in distinction from sensible heat; the portion of heat which disappears, when a body changes its form from the solid to the fluid, or from the fluid to the aeriform state. *Black.*

LA'TER, *a.* [comp. deg. of *late.*] Posterior; subsequent.

LAT'ERAL, *a.* [Fr. from L. *lateralis*, from *latus*, a side, and broad, Gr. πλατυς; coinciding with W. *llêd, llyd*, breadth, and probably with Eng. *flat*, W. *plad* or *llez*, or both. The primary sense of these words is to extend, as in *late, let.*]

1. Pertaining to the side; as the *lateral* view of an object.

2. Proceeding from the side; as the *lateral* branches of a tree; *lateral* shoots.

LATERAL'ITY, *n.* The quality of having distinct sides. [*Not used.*] *Brown.*

LAT'ERALLY, *adv.* By the side; sideways. *Holder.*

2. In the direction of the side.

LAT'ERAN, *n.* One of the churches at Rome. The name is said to have been derived from that of a man. *Encyc.*

A latere, [L.] A legate *a latere*, is a pope's legate or envoy, so called because sent from his *side*, from among his favorites and counselors.

LA'TERED, *a.* Delayed. *Obs.* *Chaucer.*

LATERIFO'LIOUS, *a.* [L. *latus*, side, and *folium*, leaf.]

In *botany*, growing on the side of a leaf at the base; as a *laterifolious* flower. *Lee. Martyn.*

LATERI''TIOUS, *a.* [L. *lateritius*, from *later*, a brick.] Like bricks; of the color of bricks. *Med. Repos.*

Lateritious sediment, a sediment in urine resembling brick dust, observed after the crises of fevers, and at the termination of gouty paroxysms. *Parr.*

L'ATH, *n.* [W. *clawd*, a thin board, or *llâth*, a rod; Fr. *latte*; Sp. *latas*, plu.; G. *latte*; D. *lat.*]

1. A thin, narrow board or slip of wood nailed to the rafters of a building to support the tiles or covering.

2. A thin narrow slip of wood nailed to the studs, to support the plastering.

L'ATH, *v. t.* To cover or line with laths. *Mortimer.*

L'ATH, *n.* [Sax. *leth.* The signification of this word is not clearly ascertained. It may be from Sax. *lathian*, to call together, and signify primarily, a meeting or assembly. See *Wapenktae.*]

In some parts of England, a part or division of a county. Spenser, Spelman and Blackstone do not agree in their accounts of the *lath*; but according to the laws of Edward the Confessor, the *lath*, in some counties, answered to the *trithing* or third part of a county in others. *Wilkins.*

LATHE, *n.* [Qu. *lath*, supra, or W. *lathru*, to make smooth.]

An engine by which instruments of wood, ivory, metals and other materials, are turned and cut into a smooth round form.

LATH'ER, *v. i.* [Sax. *lethrian*, to lather, to anoint. Qu. W. *llathru*, to make smooth, or *llithraw*, to glide; *llithrig*, slippery, or *llyth*, soft; *llyzu*, to spread.]

To form a foam with water and soap; to become froth, or frothy matter.

LATH'ER, *v. t.* To spread over with the foam of soap.

LATH'ER, *n.* Foam or froth made by soap moistened with water.

2. Foam or froth from profuse sweat, as of a horse.

L'ATHY, *a.* Thin as a lath; long and slender. *Todd.*

L'ATHY, *a.* [W. *lleth, llyth.*] Flabby; weak. *New England.*

LATIB'ULIZE, *v. i.* [L. *latibulum*, a hiding place.]

To retire into a den, burrow or cavity, and lie dormant in winter; to retreat and lie hid.

> The tortoise *latibulizes* in October. *Shaw's Zool.*

LAT'ICLAVE, *n.* [L. *laticlavium*; *latus*, broad, and *clavus*, a stud.]

An ornament of dress worn by Roman senators. It is supposed to have been a broad stripe of purple on the fore part of the tunic, set with knobs or studs. *Encyc.*

LAT'IN, *a.* Pertaining to the Latins, a people of Latium, in Italy; Roman; as the *Latin* language.

Latin church, the western church; the christian church in Italy, France, Spain and other countries where the Latin language was introduced, as distinct from the Greek or eastern church. *Encyc.*

LAT'IN, *n.* The language of the ancient Romans.

2. An exercise in schools, consisting in turning English into Latin. *Ascham.*

LAT'INISM, *n.* A Latin idiom; a mode of speech peculiar to the Latins. *Addison.*

LAT'INIST, *n.* One skilled in Latin.

LATIN'ITY, *n.* Purity of the Latin style or idiom; the Latin tongue.

LAT'INIZE, *v. t.* To give to foreign words Latin terminations and make them Latin. *Watts.*

LAT'INIZE, *v. i.* To use words or phrases borrowed from the Latin. *Dryden.*

LATIROS'TROUS, *a.* [L. *latus*, broad, and *rostrum*, beak.] Having a broad beak, as a fowl. *Brown.*

LA'TISH, *a.* [from *late.*] Somewhat late.

LAT'ITANCY, *n.* [L. *latitans, latito*, to lie hid, from *lateo.* See *Latent.*]

The state of lying concealed; the state of lurking. *Brown.*

LAT'ITANT, *a.* Lurking; lying hid; concealed. *Boyle.*

[These words are rarely used. See *Latent.*]

LAT'ITAT, *n.* [L. he lurks.] A writ by which a person is summoned into the king's bench to answer, as supposing he lies concealed. *Blackstone.*

LAT'ITUDE, *n.* [Fr. from L. *latitudo*, breadth; *latus*, broad; W. *llyd*, breadth.]

1. Breadth; width; extent from side to side. *Wotton.*
2. Room; space. *Locke.*
[*In the foregoing senses, little used.*]
3. In *astronomy*, the distance of a star north or south of the ecliptic.
4. In *geography*, the distance of any place on the globe, north or south of the equator. Boston is situated in the forty third degree of north *latitude.*
5. Extent of meaning or construction; indefinite acceptation. The words will not bear this *latitude* of construction.
6. Extent of deviation from a settled point; freedom from rules or limits; laxity.

In human actions, there are no degrees and precise natural limits described, but a *latitude* is indulged. *Taylor.*

7. Extent.

I pretend not to treat of them in their full *latitude.* *Locke.*

LATITU'DINAL, *a.* Pertaining to latitude; in the direction of latitude. *Gregory.*

LATITUDINA'RIAN, *a.* [Fr. *latitudinaire.*] Not restrained; not confined by precise limits; free; thinking or acting at large; as *lattudinarian* opinions or doctrines.

LATITUDINA'RIAN, *n.* One who is moderate in his notions, or not restrained by precise settled limits in opinion; one who indulges freedom in thinking.

2. In *theology*, one who departs in opinion from the strict principles of orthodoxy; or one who indulges a latitude of thinking and interpretation; a moderate man.

LATITUDINA'RIANISM, *n.* Freedom or liberality of opinion, particularly in theology. *Ch. Obs.*

2. Indifference to religion. *W. Jones.*

LA'TRANT, *a.* [L. *latro*, to bark.] Barking. *Tickell.*

LA'TRATE, *v. i.* To bark as a dog. [*Not used.*]

LATRA'TION, *n.* A barking. [*Not used.*]

LA'TRIA, *n.* [L. from Gr. λατρεια.] The highest kind of worship, or that paid to God; distinguished by the catholics from *dulia*, or the inferior worship paid to saints. *Encyc.*

LATRO'BITE, *n.* [from *Latrobe.*] A newly described mineral of a pale pink red color, massive or crystalized, from an isle near the Labrador coast. *Phillips.*

LAT'ROCINY, *n.* [L. *latrocinium.*] Theft; larceny. [*Not in use.*]

LAT'TEN, *n.* [Fr. *leton* or *laiton*; D. *latoen*; Arm. *laton.*] Iron plate covered with tin. *Encyc.*

LAT'TEN-BRASS, *n.* Plates of milled brass reduced to different thicknesses, according to the uses they are intended for. *Encyc.*

LAT'TER, *a.* [an irregular comparative of *late.*]

1. Coming or happening after something else; opposed to *former*; as the former and *latter* rain; former or *latter* harvest.
2. Mentioned the last of two.

The difference between reason and revelation—and in what sense the *latter* is superior. *Watts.*

3. Modern; lately done or past; as in these *latter* ages.

LAT'TERLY, *adv.* Of late; in time not long past; lately. *Richardson.*

LAT'TERMATH, *n.* The latter mowing; that which is mowed after a former mowing.

LAT'TICE, *n.* [Fr. *lattis*, a covering of *laths*, from *latte*, a *lath*; W. *cledrwy*, from *cledyr*, a board, shingle or rail.]

Any work of wood or iron, made by crossing laths, rods or bars, and forming open squares like net-work; as the *lattice* of a window.

The mother of Sisera looked out at a window, and cried through the *lattice.* Judg. v.

LAT'TICE, *a.* Consisting of cross pieces; as *lattice* work.

2. Furnished with lattice work; as a *lattice* window.

LAT'TICE, *v. t.* To form with cross bars, and open work.

2. To furnish with a lattice.

LAT'TICED, *pp.* Furnished with a lattice.

LAUD, *n.* [L. *laus, laudis*; W. *clod*; Ir. *cloth*; allied to Gr. κλειω, κλεος. This is from the same root as Eng. *loud*, G. *laut*, and the primary sense is to strain, to utter sound, to cry out. See *Loud.*]

1. Praise; commendation; an extolling in words; honorable mention. [*Little used.*] *Pope.*
2. That part of divine worship which consists in praise. *Bacon.*
3. Music or singing in honor of any one.

LAUD, *v. t.* [L. *laudo.*] To praise in words alone, or with words and singing; to celebrate. *Bentley.*

LAUD'ABLE, *a.* [L. *laudabilis.*] Praiseworthy; commendable; as *laudable* motives; *laudable* actions.

2. Healthy; salubrious; as *laudable* juices of the body. *Arbuthnot.*
3. Healthy; well digested; as *laudable* pus.

LAUD'ABLENESS, *n.* The quality of deserving praise; praiseworthiness; as the *laudableness* of designs, purposes, motives or actions. [*Laudability*, in a like sense, has been used, but rarely.]

LAUD'ABLY, *adv.* In a manner deserving praise.

LAUD'ANUM, *n.* [from L. *laudo*, to praise.] Opium dissolved in spirit or wine; tincture of opium. *Coxe.*

LAUD'ATIVE, *n.* [L. *laudativus.*] A panegyric; an eulogy. [*Little used.*] *Bacon.*

LAUD'ATORY, *a.* Containing praise; tending to praise.

LAUD'ATORY, *n.* That which contains praise. *Milton.*

LAUD'ER, *n.* One who praises.

LAUGH, *v. i.* *l'aff.* [Sax. *hlihan*; Goth. *hlahyan*; G. *lachen*; D. *lachgen*; Sw. *le*; Dan. *leer*; Heb. and Ch. לעג, laag. Class Lg. No. 17.]

1. To make the noise and exhibit the features which are characteristic of mirth in the human species. Violent *laughter* is accompanied with a shaking of the sides, and all *laughter* expels breath from the lungs. *Bacon.*
2. In *poetry*, to be gay; to appear gay, cheerful, pleasant, lively or brilliant.

Then *laughs* the childish year with flow'rets crown'd. *Dryden.*

And o'er the foaming bowl, the *laughing* wine. *Pope.*

To laugh at, to ridicule; to treat with some degree of contempt.

No fool to *laugh at*, which he valued more. *Pope.*

To laugh to scorn, to deride; to treat with mockery, contempt and scorn. Neh. ii.

LAUGH, *n.* *l'aff.* An expression of mirth peculiar to the human species.

But feigns a *laugh*, to see me search around,
And by that *laugh* the willing fair is found. *Pope.*

LAUGHABLE, *a.* *l'affable.* That may justly excite laughter; as a *laughable* story; a *laughable* scene.

LAUGHER, *n.* *l'affer.* One who laughs, or is fond of merriment.

The *laughers* are a majority. *Pope.*

LAUGHING, *ppr.* *l'affing.* Expressing mirth in a particular manner.

LAUGHINGLY, *adv.* *l'affingly.* In a merry way; with laughter.

LAUGHING-STOCK, *n.* An object of ridicule; a butt of sport. *Spenser. Shak.*

LAUGHTER, *n.* *l'affter.* Convulsive merriment; an expression of mirth peculiar to man, consisting in a peculiar noise and configuration of features, with a shaking of the sides and expulsion of breath.

I said of *laughter*, it is mad. Eccles. ii.

LAUGH-WORTHY, *a.* Deserving to be laughed at. *B. Jonson.*

LAU'MONITE, *n.* Efflorescent zeolite; so called from Laumont, its discoverer. It is found in laminated masses, in groups of prismatic crystals or prismatic distinct concretions. Exposed to the air, it disintegrates. *Cleaveland.*

LAUNCH. [See *Lanch*, the more correct orthography.]

LAUND, *n.* A lawn. [*Not used.*] *Chaucer.*

LAUNDER, *n.* *l'ander.* [from L. *lavo*, to wash.]

A washer-woman; also, a long and hollow trough, used by miners to receive the powdered ore from the box where it is beaten. *Encyc.*

LAUNDER, *v. t.* *l'ander.* To wash; to wet. *Shak.*

LAUNDERER, *n.* *l'anderer.* A man who follows the business of washing clothes. *Butler.*

LAUNDRESS, *n.* *l'andress.* [Fr. *lavandiere*; Sp. *lavandera*; It. *lavandaia*; from L. *lavo*, Sp. *lavar*, to wash.]

A washer-woman; a female whose employment is to wash clothes.

LAUNDRESS, *v. i.* *l'andress.* [supra.] To practice washing. *Blount.*

LAUNDRY, *n.* *l'andry.* [Sp. *lavadero.*]

1. A washing. *Bacon.*
2. The place or room where clothes are washed.

LAU'REATE, *a.* [L. *laureatus*, from *laurea*, a laurel.]

Decked or invested with laurel; as *laureate* hearse. *Milton.*

Soft on her lap her *laureate* son reclines. *Pope.*

Poet laureate, in *Great Britain*, an officer of the king's household, whose business is to compose an ode annually for the king's birth day, and for the new year. It is said this title was first given him in the time of Edward IV. *Encyc.*

LAU'REATE, *v. t.* To honor with a degree in the university, and a present of a wreath of laurel. *Warton.*

LAU'REATED, *pp.* Honored with a degree and a laurel wreath.

LAUREA'TION, *n.* The act of conferring a degree in the university, together with a wreath of laurel; an honor bestowed on those who excelled in writing verse. This was an ancient practice at Oxford, from which probably originated the denomination of *poet laureate.* *Warton.*

LAU'REL, *n.* [L. *laurus*; It. *lauro*; Fr. *laurier*; Sp. *laurel*; Port. *laureiro*; W. *llorwyz, llorwyzen,* laurel wood, from the root of *llawr*, a floor, *llor*, that spreads; Dan. *laur-bær-tree*; G. *lorbeer*, the laurel or bay-berry. *Laur* coincides in elements with *flower, floreo.*]

The bay-tree or Laurus, a genus of plants of several species. *Encyc.*

LAU'RELED, *a.* Crowned or decorated with laurel, or with a laurel wreath; laureate.

LAURIF'EROUS, *a.* [L. *laurus* and *fero*, to bear.] Producing or bringing laurel.

LAU'RUSTIN, *n.* [L. *laurustinus.*] A plant of the genus Viburnum, an evergreen shrub or tree, whose flowers are said to continue through the winter.

LAUS'KRAUT, *n.* [G. *läusekraut*, louse-plant.] A plant of the genus Delphinium.

LAU'TU, *n.* A band of cotton, twisted and worn on the head of the Inca of Peru, as a badge of royalty. *J. Barlow.*

L'AVA, *n.* [probably from flowing, and from the root of L. *fluo*, or *lavo*; It. *laua*, a stream, now *lava.*]

1. A mass or stream of melted minerals or stony matter which bursts or is thrown from the mouth or sides of a volcano, and is sometimes ejected in such quantities as to overwhelm cities. Catana, at the foot of Etna, has often been destroyed by it, and in 1783, a vast tract of land in Iceland was overspread by an eruption of lava from mount Hecla.

2. The same matter when cool and hardened.

LAVA'TION, *n.* [L. *lavatio*, from *lavo.*] A washing or cleansing. *Hakewill.*

LAV'ATORY, *n.* [See *Lave.*] A place for washing.

2. A wash or lotion for a diseased part.

3. A place where gold is obtained by washing. *Encyc.*

LAVE, *v. t.* [Fr. *laver*; Sp. *lavar*; It. *lavare*; L. *lavo*; Gr. λουω; Sans. *allava*; probably contracted from *lago* or *laugo.*]

To wash; to bathe; *a word used chiefly in poetry or rhetoric.* *Milton. Dryden.*

LAVE, *v. i.* To bathe; to wash one's self. *Pope.*

LAVE, *v. t.* [Fr. *lever.*] To throw up or out; to lade out. [*Not in use.*] *B. Jonson.*

LA'VE-EARED, *a.* Having large pendant ears. [*Not in use.*] *Bp. Hall.*

LAVEE'R, *v. t.* [Fr. *louvoyer* or *louvier*; D. *laveeren.*] In seamen's language, to tack; to sail back and forth. [I believe this word is not in common use.]

LAV'ENDER, *n.* [L. *lavendula.*] A plant, or a genus of aromatic plants, Lavandula.

LA'VER, *n.* [Fr. *lavoir*, from *laver*, to lave.] A vessel for washing; a large bason; in scripture history, a bason placed in the court of the Jewish tabernacle, where the officiating priests washed their hands and feet and the entrails of victims. *Encyc.*

LAVEROCK. [See *Lark.*]

LA'VING, *ppr.* Washing; bathing.

LAV'ISH, *a.* [I know not from what source we have received this word. It coincides in elements with L. *liber*, free, *liberal*, and L. *lavo*, to wash.]

1. Prodigal; expending or bestowing with profusion; profuse. He was *lavish* of expense; *lavish* of praise; *lavish* of encomiums; *lavish* of censure; *lavish* of blood and treasure.

2. Wasteful; expending without necessity; liberal to a fault. *Dryden.*

3. Wild; unrestrained.

> Curbing his *lavish* spirit. *Shak.*

LAV'ISH, *v. t.* To expend or bestow with profusion; as, to *lavish* praise or encomiums.

2. To waste; to expend without necessity or use; to squander; as, to *lavish* money on vices and amusements.

LAV'ISHED, *pp.* Expended profusely; wasted.

LAV'ISHER, *n.* A prodigal; a profuse person.

LAV'ISHING, *ppr.* Expending or laying out with profusion; wasting.

LAV'ISHLY, *adv.* With profuse expense; prodigally; wastefully. *Dryden. Pope.*

LAV'ISHNESS, *n.* Profusion; prodigality. *Spenser.*

LAVOL'TA, *n.* [It. *la volta*, the turn.] An old dance in which was much turning and capering. *Shak.*

LAW, *n.* [Sax. *laga, lage, lag,* or *lah*; Sw. *lag*; Dan. *lov*; It. *legge*; Sp. *ley*; Fr. *loi*; L. *lex*; from the root of *lay*, Sax. *lecgan*, Goth. *lagyan.* See *Lay.* A law is that which is *laid*, set or fixed, like *statute, constitution*, from L. *statuo.*]

1. A rule, particularly an established or permanent rule, prescribed by the supreme power of a state to its subjects, for regulating their actions, particularly their social actions. Laws are *imperative* or *mandatory*, commanding what shall be done; *prohibitory*, restraining from what is to be forborn; or *permissive*, declaring what may be done without incurring a penalty. The *laws* which enjoin the duties of piety and morality, are prescribed by God and found in the Scriptures.

> *Law* is beneficence acting by rule. *Burke.*

2. *Municipal law*, is a rule of civil conduct prescribed by the supreme power of a state, commanding what its subjects are to do, and prohibiting what they are to forbear; a statute.

Municipal or civil laws are established by the decrees, edicts or ordinances of absolute princes, as emperors and kings, or by the formal acts of the legislatures of free states. *Law* therefore is sometimes equivalent to *decree, edict*, or *ordinance.*

3. *Law of nature*, is a rule of conduct arising out of the natural relations of human beings established by the Creator, and existing prior to any positive precept. Thus it is a *law of nature*, that one man should not injure another, and murder and fraud would be crimes, independent of any prohibition from a supreme power.

4. *Laws of animal nature*, the inherent principles by which the economy and functions of animal bodies are performed, such as respiration, the circulation of the blood, digestion, nutrition, various secretions, &c.

5. *Laws of vegetation*, the principles by which plants are produced, and their growth carried on till they arrive to perfection.

6. *Physical laws*, or *laws of nature.* The invariable tendency or determination of any species of matter to a particular form with definite properties, and the determination of a body to certain motions, changes, and relations, which uniformly take place in the same circumstances, is called a *physical law.* These tendencies or determinations, whether called laws or affections of matter, have been established by the Creator, and are, with a peculiar felicity of expression, denominated in Scripture, *ordinances of heaven.*

7. *Laws of nations*, the rules that regulate the mutual intercourse of nations or states. These rules depend on natural law, or the principles of justice which spring from the social state; or they are founded on customs, compacts, treaties, leagues and agreements between independent communities.

> By the *law of nations*, we are to understand that code of public instruction, which defines the rights and prescribes the duties of nations, in their intercourse with each other. *Kent.*

8. *Moral law*, a law which prescribes to men their religious and social duties, in other words, their duties to God and to each other. The moral law is summarily contained in the decalogue or ten commandments, written by the finger of God on two tables of stone, and delivered to Moses on mount Sinai. Ex. xx.

9. *Ecclesiastical law*, a rule of action prescribed for the government of a church; otherwise called *canon law.*

10. *Written law*, a law or rule of action prescribed or enacted by a sovereign, and promulgated and recorded in writing; a written statute, ordinance, edict or decree.

11. *Unwritten* or *common law*, a rule of action which derives its authority from long usage, or established custom, which has been immemorially received and recognized by judicial tribunals. As this law can be traced to no positive statutes, its rules or principles are to be found only in the records of courts, and in the reports of judicial decisions.

12. *By-law*, a law of a city, town or private corporation. [See *By.*]

13. *Mosaic law*, the institutions of Moses, or the code of laws prescribed to the Jews, as distinguished from the *gospel.*

14. *Ceremonial law*, the Mosaic institutions which prescribe the external rites and ceremonies to be observed by the Jews, as distinct from the *moral precepts*, which are of perpetual obligation.

15. A rule of direction; a directory; as reason and natural conscience.

> These, having not the *law*, are a *law* to themselves. Rom. ii.

16. That which governs or has a tendency to rule; that which has the power of controlling.

But I see another *law* in my members warring against the *law* of my mind, and bringing me into captivity to the *law* of sin which is in my members. Rom. 7.

17. The word of God; the doctrines and precepts of God, or his revealed will.

But his delight is in the *law* of the Lord, and in his *law* doth he meditate day and night. Ps. i.

18. The Old Testament.

Is it not written in your *law*, I said, ye are gods? John x.

19. The institutions of Moses, as distinct from the other parts of the Old Testament; as the *law* and the prophets.

20. A rule or axiom of science or art; settled principle; as the *laws* of versification or poetry.

21. *Law martial*, or *martial law*, the rules ordained for the government of an army or military force.

22. *Marine laws*, rules for the regulation of navigation, and the commercial intercourse of nations.

23. *Commercial law*, *law-merchant*, the system of rules by which trade and commercial intercourse are regulated between merchants.

24. Judicial process; prosecution of right in courts of law.

Tom Touchy is a fellow famous for taking the *law* of every body. *Spectator.*

Hence the phrase, *to go to law*, to prosecute; to seek redress in a legal tribunal.

25. Jurisprudence; as in the title, *Doctor of Laws.*

26. In general, *law* is a rule of action prescribed for the government of rational beings or moral agents, to which rule they are bound to yield obedience, in default of which they are exposed to punishment; or *law* is a settled mode or course of action or operation in irrational beings and in inanimate bodies.

Civil law, criminal law. [See *Civil* and *Criminal.*]

Laws of honor. [See *Honor.*]

Law language, the language used in legal writings and forms, particularly the Norman dialect or Old French, which was used in judicial proceedings from the days of William the conqueror to the 36th year of Edward III.

Wager of law, a species of trial formerly used in England, in which the defendant gave security that he would, on a certain day, make his law, that is, he would make oath that he owed nothing to the plaintiff, and would produce eleven of his neighbors as compurgators, who should swear that they believed in their consciences that he had sworn the truth. *Blackstone.*

LAW'-BREAKER, *n.* One who violates the law. *Milton.*

LAW-DAY, *n.* A day of open court. *Shak.*

2. A leet or sheriff's tourn.

LAW'FUL, *a.* Agreeable to law; conformable to law; allowed by law; legal; legitimate. That is deemed *lawful* which no law forbids, but many things are *lawful* which are not expedient.

2. Constituted by law; rightful; as the *lawful* owner of lands.

LAW'FULLY, *adv.* Legally; in accordance with law; without violating law. We may *lawfully* do what the laws do not forbid.

LAW'FULNESS, *n.* The quality of being conformable to law; legality. The *lawfulness* of an action does not always prove its propriety or expedience.

LAW'GIVER, *n.* [*law* and *give.*] One who makes or enacts a law; a legislator. *Swift.*

LAW'GIVING, *a.* Making or enacting laws; legislative. *Waller.*

LAW'ING, *n.* Expeditation; the act of cutting off the claws and balls of the fore feet of mastiffs to prevent them from running after deer. *Blackstone.*

LAW'LESS, *a.* Not subject to law; unrestrained by law; as a *lawless* tyrant; *lawless* men.

2. Contrary to law; illegal; unauthorized; as a *lawless* claim.

He needs no indirect nor *lawless* course. *Shak.*

3. Not subject to the ordinary laws of nature; uncontrolled.

He, meteor-like, flames *lawless* through the void. *Pope.*

LAW'LESSLY, *adv.* In a manner contrary to law. *Shak.*

LAW'LESSNESS, *n.* The quality or state of being unrestrained by law; disorder. *Spenser.*

LAW'-MAKER, *n.* One who enacts or ordains laws; a legislator; a lawgiver. *Law-makers* should not be law-breakers. *Adage.*

LAW'-MONGER, *n.* A low dealer in law; a pettifogger. *Milton.*

LAWN, *n.* [W. *llan*, an open, clear place. It is the same word as *land*, with an appropriate signification, and coincides with *plain, planus*, Ir. *cluain.*]

An open space between woods, or a plain in a park or adjoining a noble seat.

Betwixt them *lawns* or level downs, and flocks
Grazing the tender herbs, were interspers'd. *Milton.*

LAWN, *n.* [Fr. *linon*, from *lin*, flax, L. *linum.*]

A sort of fine linen. Its use in the sleeves of bishops, explains the following line.

A saint in crape is twice a saint in *lawn.* *Pope.*

LAWN, *a.* Made of lawn.

LAWN'Y, *a.* Level, as a plain; like a lawn.

2. Made of lawn. *Bp. Hall.*

LAW'SUIT, *n.* [See *Suit.*] A suit in law for the recovery of a supposed right; a process in law instituted by a party to compel another to do him justice.

LAW'YER, *n.* [that is, *lawer*, contracted from *law-wer, law-man.*]

One versed in the laws, or a practitioner of law; one whose profession is to institute suits in courts of law, and to prosecute or defend the cause of clients. This is a general term, comprehending attorneys, counselors, solicitors, barristers, serjeants and advocates.

LAW'YER-LIKE, *a.* Like a real lawyer.

LAW'YERLY, *a.* Judicial. *Milton.*

LAX, *a.* [L. *laxus*; Sp. *laso*; It. *lasso*; Fr. *lache*, for *lasche.*]

1. Loose; flabby; soft; not tense, firm or rigid; as *lax* flesh; a *lax* fiber.

2. Slack; not tight or tense; as a *lax* cord.

3. Not firmly united; of loose texture; as gravel and the like *laxer* matter. *Woodward.*

4. Not rigidly exact; as a *lax* moral discourse. *Baker.*

5. Not strict; as *lax* morals.

6. Loose in the bowels; having too frequent discharges.

LAX, *n.* A looseness; diarrhæa.

2. A species of fish or salmon. [Sax. *lœx.*] [*Not in use.*]

LAXA'TION, *n.* [L. *laxatio.*] The act of loosening or slackening; or the state of being loose or slackened.

LAX'ATIVE, *a.* [Fr. *laxatif*, from L. *laxo.*] Having the power or quality of loosening or opening the bowels, and relieving from constipation.

LAX'ATIVE, *n.* A medicine that relaxes the bowels and relieves from costiveness; a gentle purgative. *Coxe.*

LAX'ATIVENESS, *n.* The quality of relaxing.

LAX'ITY, *n.* [L. *laxitas.*] Looseness; slackness; the opposite of *tenseness* or *tension.*

2. Looseness of texture. *Bentley.*

3. Want of exactness or precision; as *laxity* of expression.

4. Looseness; defect of exactness; as *laxity* of morals.

5. Looseness, as of the bowels; the opposite of *costiveness.*

6. Openness; not closeness.

LAX'LY, *adv.* Loosely; without exactness. *Rees.*

LAX'NESS, *n.* Looseness; softness; flabbiness; as the *laxness* of flesh or of muscles.

2. Laxity; the opposite of *tension.*

3. Looseness, as of morals or discipline.

4. Looseness, as of the bowels.

5. Slackness, as of a cord.

LAY, *pret.* of *lie.* The estate *lay* in the county of Hartford.

When Ahab heard these words, he rent his clothes, and put sackcloth upon his head, and fasted and *lay* in sackcloth. 1 Kings xxi.

LAY, *v. t.* pret. and pp. *laid.* [Sax. *lecgan, legan*; D. *leggen*; G. *legen*; Sw. *lägga*; Dan. *legger*; Russ. *loju*; L. *loco*, whence *locus*, W. *lle*, place, Eng. *ley* or *lea*; W. *lleau*, to lay. Hence Fr. *lieu*, Arm. *lech*, a place; Ir. *legadh*, Arm. *lacqaat*, to lay. The primary sense is to send or throw; hence this word is the L. *lego, legare*, differently applied; Gr. λεγομαι, to lie down; Eth. ለአከ lak, to send, whence *lackey.* Class Lg. No 1. and 21. It coincides with *lodge* and with *lie.*]

1. Literally, to throw down; hence, to put or place; applied to things *broad* or *long*, and in this respect differing from *set.* We *lay* a book on the table, when we place it on its side, but we *set* it on the end. We *lay* the foundation of a house, but we *set* a building on its foundation.

He *laid* his robe from him. Jonah iii.
Soft on the flowery herb I found me *laid.* *Milton.*

A stone was brought and *laid* on the mouth of the den. Dan. vi.

2. To beat down; to prostrate. Violent winds with rain *lay* corn and grass.

3. To settle; to fix and keep from rising. A shower *lays* the dust.

4. To place in order; to dispose with regularity in building; as, to *lay* bricks or stones in constructing walls.

5. To spread on a surface; as, to *lay* plaster or paint.

6. To spread or set; as, to *lay* snares.

7. To calm; to appease; to still; to allay.

After a tempest, when the winds are *laid*. *Waller.*

8. To quiet; to still; to restrain from walking; as, to *lay* the devil. *L'Estrange.*

9. To spread and set in order; to prepare; as, to *lay* a table for dinner.

10. To place in the earth for growth.

The chief time of *laying* gilliflowers, is in July. *Mortimer.*

11. To place at hazard; to wage; to stake; as, to *lay* a crown or an eagle; to *lay* a wager.

12. To bring forth; to exclude; as, to *lay* eggs.

13. To add; to join.

Wo to them that join house to house, that *lay* field to field. Is. v.

14. To put; to apply.

She *layeth* her hand to the spindle. Prov. xxxi.

15. To assess; to charge; to impose; as, to *lay* a tax on land; to *lay* a duty on salt.

16. To charge; to impute; as, to *lay* blame on one; to *lay* want of prudence to one's charge.

17. To impose, as evil, burden, or punishment.

The Lord hath *laid* on him the iniquity of us all. Is. liii.

18. To enjoin as a duty; as, to *lay* commands on one.

19. To exhibit; to present or offer; as, to *lay* an indictment in a particular county.

20. To prostrate; to slay.

The leaders first
He *laid* along. *Dryden.*

21. To depress and lose sight of, by sailing or departing from; as, to *lay* the land; *a seaman's phrase.*

22. To station; to set; as, to *lay* an ambush.

23. To contrive; to scheme; to plan.

To lay a cable, to twist or unite the strands.

To lay apart, to put away; to reject.

Lay apart all filthiness. James i.

To lay aside, to put off or away; not to retain.

Let us *lay aside* every weight, and the sin that doth so easily beset us. Heb. xii.

2. To discontinue; as, to *lay aside* the use of any thing.

To lay away, to reposit in store; to put aside for preservation.

To lay before, to exhibit; to show; to present to view. The papers are *laid before* Congress.

To lay by, to reserve for future use.

Let every one of you *lay by* him in store, as God hath prospered him. 1 Cor. xvi.

2. To put away; to dismiss.

Let brave spirits not be *laid by*, as persons unnecessary for the time. *Bacon.*

3. To put off.

And she arose and went away, and *laid by* her veil. Gen. xxxviii.

To lay down, to deposit, as a pledge, equivalent or satisfaction; to resign.

I *lay down* my life for the sheep. John x.

2. To give up; to resign; to quit or relinquish; as, to *lay down* an office or commission.

3. To quit; to surrender the use of; as, to *lay down* one's arms.

4. To offer or advance; as, to *lay down* a proposition or principle. *Addison.*

To lay one's self down, to commit to repose.

I will both *lay me down* in peace and sleep—Ps. iv.

To lay hold of, to seize; to catch. *To lay hold on*, is used in a like sense. *Locke.*

To lay in, to store; to treasure; to provide previously. *Addison.*

To lay on, to apply with force; to inflict; as, to *lay on* blows.

To lay open, to open; to make bare; to uncover; also, to show; to expose; to reveal; as, to *lay open* the designs of an enemy.

To lay over, to spread over; to incrust; to cover the surface; as, to *lay over* with gold or silver.

To lay out, to expend; as, to *lay out* money, or sums of money.

2. To display; to discover.

He takes occasion to *lay out* bigotry and false confidence in all its colors. *Atterbury. Obs.*

3. To plan; to dispose in order the several parts; as, to *lay out* a garden.

4. To dress in grave clothes and place in a decent posture; as, to *lay out* a corpse. Shakspeare uses to *lay forth.*

5. To exert; as, to *lay out* all one's strength. So with the reciprocal pronoun, to *lay one's self out*, is to exert strength.

To lay to, to charge upon; to impute. *Sidney.*

2. To apply with vigor. *Tusser.*

3. To attack or harass. *Obs.* *Knolles.*

4. To check the motion of a ship, and cause her to be stationary.

To lay together, to collect; to bring to one place; also, to bring into one view.

To lay to heart, to permit to affect greatly.

To lay under, to subject to; as, to *lay* one *under* restraint or obligation.

To lay up, to store; to treasure; to reposit for future use.

Lay up for yourselves treasures in heaven. Matt. vi.

2. To confine to the bed or chamber. He is *laid up* with the gout.

To lay siege, to besiege; to encompass with an army.

To lay wait, to station for private attack; to lay in ambush for.

To lay the course, in sailing, is to sail towards the port intended, without gibing.

To lay waste, to destroy; to desolate; to deprive of inhabitants, improvements and productions.

To lay the land, in *seamen's language*, is to cause the land apparently to sink or appear lower, by sailing from it; the distance diminishing the elevation.

LAY, *v. i.* To bring or produce eggs.

Hens will greedily eat the herb that will make them *lay* the better. *Mortimer.*

2. To contrive; to form a scheme. [*Unusual.*]

To lay about, to strike or throw the arms on all sides; to act with vigor. *Spenser. South.*

To lay at, to strike or to endeavor to strike.

The sword of him that *layeth at* him cannot hold. Job xli.

To lay in for, to make overtures for; to engage or secure the possession of.

I have laid in for these. *Dryden.*

To lay on, to strike; to beat; to deal blows incessantly and with vehemence.

2. To act with vehemence; *used of expenses. Shak.*

To lay out, to purpose; to intend. He *lays out* to make a journey.

2. To take measures.

I made strict inquiry wherever I came, and *laid out* for intelligence of all places. *Woodward.*

To lay upon, to importune. *Obs.*

LAY, *n.* That which lies or is laid; a row; a stratum; a layer; one rank in a series reckoned upward; as a *lay* of wood.

A viol should have a *lay* of wire-strings below. *Bacon.*

2. A bet; a wager. [*Little used.*] *Graunt.*

3. Station; rank. [*Not used.*]

LAY, *n.* [Sax. *leag, leah, lege*; W. *lle*; Russ. *lug*; L. *locus*; Fr. *lieu*. See *Lay*, the verb. The words which signify *place*, are from verbs which express *setting* or *laying*. It is written also *ley*, and *lea*, but less properly.]

A meadow; a plain or plat of grass land.

A tuft of daisies on a flowery *lay*. *Dryden.*
The lowing herd wind slowly o'er the *lea*. *Gray.*

LAY, *n.* [Sax. *legh* or *ley*; Gr. ληχεω, to sound. It might also be deduced from G. *lied*, a song; D. *id.*; Sax. *leoth*; Scot. *leid, lede*, or *luid*; Ir. *lyidh*; Gael. *laoidh*; from the root of *loud*, L. *laudo, plaudo*, Sax. *hlydan*.]

A song; as a loud or soft *lay*; immortal *lays*. *Spenser. Milton.*

[It is used chiefly in poetry.]

LAY, *a.* [Fr. *lai*, L. *laicus*, It. *laico*, Sp. *lego*, a layman; Gr. λαικος, from λαος, people.]

Pertaining to the laity or people, as distinct from the clergy; not clerical; as a *lay* person; a *lay* preacher; a *lay* brother.

LAY-CLERK, *n.* A vocal officiate in a cathedral. *Busby.*

LA'YER, *n. la'er.* [from *lay*, the verb.] A stratum; a bed; a body spread over another; as a *layer* of clay or of sand.

2. A shoot or twig of a plant, not detached from the stock, laid under ground for growth or propagation. *Encyc.*

3. A hen that lays eggs. *Mortimer.*

LA'YING, *ppr.* Putting; placing; applying; imputing; wagering.

LA'YLAND, *n.* Land lying untilled; fallow ground. [*Local.*]

LA'YMAN, *n. la'man.* [*lay* and *man.*] A man who is not a clergyman; one of the laity or people, distinct from the clergy. *Dryden. Swift.*

2. An image used by painters in contriving attitudes. *Dryden.*

3. A lay-clerk.

LA'YSTALL, *n.* [*lay* and *stall.*] A heap of dung, or a place where dung is laid. *Ash.*

LA'ZAR, *n.* [from *Lazarus;* Sp. *lazaro.*] A person infected with nauseous and pestilential disease. *Shak. Dryden.*

LAZARET', LAZARET'TO, *n.* [Sp. *lazareto;* It. *lazzeretto;* Fr. *lazaret;* from *Lazarus.*]
A public building, hospital or pest-house for the reception of diseased persons, particularly for those affected with contagious distempers.

LA'ZAR-HOUSE, *n.* A lazaretto; also, a hospital for quarantine.

LA'ZAR-LIKE, LA'ZARLY, *a.* Full of sores; leprous. *Bp. Hall.*

LA'ZARWŎRT, LA'SERWŎRT, *n.* Laserpitium, a genus of plants of several species, natives of Germany, Italy, France, &c.

LAZE, *v. i.* To live in idleness. [*Vulgar.*]

LAZE, *v. t.* To waste in sloth. [*Vulgar.*]

LA'ZILY, *adv.* [from *lazy.*] In a heavy, sluggish manner; sluggishly.

Whether he *lazily* and listlessly dreams away his time. *Locke.*

LA'ZINESS, *n.* [from *lazy.*] The state or quality of being lazy; indisposition to action or exertion; indolence; sluggishness; heaviness in motion; habitual sloth. *Laziness* differs from *idleness;* the latter being a mere defect or cessation of action, but *laziness* is sloth, with natural or habitual disinclination to action.

Laziness travels so slowly, that poverty soon overtakes him. *Franklin.*

2. Slowness; tardiness.

LA'ZING, *a.* Spending time in sluggish inaction. *L'Estrange.*

[*This is an ill-formed, inelegant word.*]

LAZ'ULI. *Lapis Lazuli* is a mineral of a fine, azure blue color, usually amorphous, or in rounded masses of a moderate size. It is often marked by yellow spots or veins of sulphuret of iron, and is much valued for ornamental work. It is distinguished from *lazulite,* by the intenseness of its color. [Qu. Ar. *azul.*] *Cleaveland.*

LAZ'ULITE, *n.* A mineral of a light, indigo blue color, occurring in small masses, or crystalized in oblique four-sided prisms. *Cleaveland.*

LA'ZY, *a.* [G. *lass, lässig;* W. *llesg.* The Fr. *lâche* is from L. *laxus,* and it is doubtful whether this is of the same family.]

1. Disinclined to action or exertion; naturally or habitually slothful; sluggish; indolent; averse to labor; heavy in motion.

Wicked men will ever live like rogues, and not fall to work, but be *lazy* and spend victuals. *Bacon.*

2. Slow; moving slowly or apparently with labor; as a *lazy* stream.

The night-owl's *lazy* flight. *Shak.*

LD, stands for *lord.*

LEA, LEY, *n.* [See *Lay.*] A meadow or plain. The Welsh write *lle,* but as this word is from the root of *lay,* the latter is the more correct orthography.

LEACH, *v. t.* [Sw. *laka,* to fall in drops, to distill; *lăka,* to leak; Dan. *lekker,* to drop, to *leak.* See *Leak.* Perhaps L. *lix* may be from the same root.]

To wash, as ashes, by percolation, or causing water to pass through them, and thus to separate from them the alkali. The water thus charged with alkali, is called *lye.*

LEACH, *n.* A quantity of wood ashes, through which water passes, and thus imbibes the alkali.

LE'ACH-TUB, *n.* A wooden vessel or tub in which ashes are leached. It is sometimes written *letch-tub.*

LEAD, *n. led.* [Sax. *læd;* G. *loth;* D. *lood;* Dan. Sw. *lod;* Russ. *lot,* probably a mass, like *clod.*]

A metal of a dull white color, with a cast of blue. It is the least elastic and sonorous of all the metals, and at the same time it is soft and easily fusible. It is found native in small masses, but generally mineralized by sulphur, and sometimes by other substances. Lead fused in a strong heat, throws off vapors which are unwholesome.

2. A plummet or mass of lead, used in sounding at sea.

3. *Leads,* a flat roof covered with lead. *Shak. Bacon.*

White lead, the oxyd of lead, ground with one third part of chalk. *Fourcroy.*

LEAD, *v. t. led.* To cover with lead; to fit with lead.

LEAD, *v. t.* pret. and pp. *led.* [Sax. *lædan;* G. *leiten;* D. *leiden;* Sw. *leda;* Dan. *leder;* probably to draw, to strain, or extend.]

1. To guide by the hand; as, to *lead* a child. It often includes the sense of drawing as well as of directing.

2. To guide or conduct by showing the way; to direct; as, the Israelites were *led* by a pillar of a cloud by day, and by a pillar of fire by night.

3. To conduct to any place.

He *leadeth* me beside the still waters. Ps. xxiii.

4. To conduct, as a chief or commander, implying authority; to direct and govern; as, a general *leads* his troops to battle and to victory.

Christ took not on him flesh and blood, that he might conquer and rule nations, *lead* armies— *South.*

5. To precede; to introduce by going first.

As Hesperus that *leads* the sun his way. *Fairfax.*

6. To guide; to show the method of attaining an object. Self-examination may *lead* us to a knowledge of ourselves.

7. To draw; to entice; to allure. The love of pleasure *leads* men into vices which degrade and impoverish them.

8. To induce; to prevail on; to influence.

He was driven by the necessities of the times more than *led* by his own disposition to any rigor of actions. *K. Charles.*

9. To pass; to spend, that is, to draw out; as, to *lead* a life of gayety, or a solitary life.

That we may *lead* a quiet and peaceable life in all godliness and honesty. 1 Tim. ii.

To lead astray, to guide in a wrong way or into error; to seduce from truth or rectitude.

To lead captive, to carry into captivity.

LEAD, *v. i.* To go before and show the way.

I will *lead* on softly. Gen. xxxiii.

2. To conduct, as a chief or commander. Let the troops follow, where their general *leads.*

3. To draw; to have a tendency to. Gaming *leads* to other vices.

4. To exercise dominion. *Spenser.*

To lead off or *out,* to go first; to begin. *Cumberland.*

LEAD, *n.* Precedence; a going before; guidance. Let the general take the *lead.* [A colloquial word in reputable use.]

LEADEN, *a. led'n.* [from *lead.*] Made of lead; as a *leaden* ball.

2. Heavy; indisposed to action. *Shak.*

3. Heavy; dull. *Shak.*

LEADEN-HE'ARTED, *a.* Stupid; destitute of feeling. *Thomson.*

LEADEN-HEE'LED, *a.* Moving slowly. *Ford.*

LEADEN-STEP'PING, *a.* Moving slowly. *Milton.*

LE'ADER, *n.* One that leads or conducts; a guide; a conductor.

2. A chief; a commander; a captain.

3. One who goes first.

4. The chief of a party or faction; as the *leader* of the whigs or of the tories; a *leader* of the Jacobins.

5. A performer who leads a band or choir in music.

LE'ADING, *ppr.* Guiding; conducting; preceding; drawing; alluring; passing life.

2. *a.* Chief; principal; capital; most influential; as a *leading* motive; a *leading* man in a party.

3. Showing the way by going first.

He left his mother a countess by patent, which was a new *leading* example— *Wotton.*

LE'ADING, *n.* Guidance; the act of conducting; direction. *Shak. Spenser.*

LE'ADING-STRINGS, *n.* Strings by which children are supported when beginning to walk. *Dryden.*

To be in leading strings, to be in a state of infancy or dependence, or in pupilage under the guidance of others.

LE'ADMAN, *n.* One who begins or leads a dance. *Obs.* *B. Jonson.*

LEADWŎRT, *n. led'wort.* Plumbago, a genus of plants.

LEADY, *a. led'dy.* Of the color of lead.

LEAF, *n.* plu. *leaves.* [Sax. *leafe;* D. *loof;* G. *laub;* Sw. *lof;* Dan. *löv;* Goth. *lauf.*]

1. In *botany,* leaves are organs of perspiration and inhalation in plants. They usually shoot from the sides of the stems and branches, but sometimes from the root; sometimes they are sessile; more generally supported by petioles. They are of various forms, flat, extended, linear, cylindric, &c.

2. The thin, extended part of a flower; a petal.

3. A part of a book containing two pages.

4. The side of a double door. 1 Kings vi.

5. Something resembling a leaf in thinness and extension; a very thin plate; as gold *leaf.*

6. The movable side of a table.

LEAF, *v. i.* To shoot out leaves; to produce leaves. The trees *leaf* in May.

LE'AFAGE, *n.* Abundance of leaves.

LE'AFED, *pp.* Having leaves.

LE'AFLESS, *a.* Destitute of leaves; as a *leafless* tree. *Pope.*

LE'AFLET, *n.* A little leaf.

2. In *botany,* one of the divisions of a compound leaf; a foliole.

LE'AF-STALK, *n.* The petiole or stalk which supports a leaf. *Martyn.*

LE'AFY, *a.* Full of leaves; as the *leafy* forest. *Dryden.*

LEAGUE, *n.* leeg. [Fr. *ligue*; It. *lega*; Sp. *liga*; from L. *ligo*, to bind.]

An alliance or confederacy between princes or states for their mutual aid or defense; a national contract or compact. A league may be *offensive* or *defensive*, or both. It is *offensive*, when the contracting parties agree to unite in attacking a common enemy; *defensive*, when the parties agree to act in concert in defending each other against an enemy.

2. A combination or union of two or more parties for the purpose of maintaining friendship and promoting their mutual interest, or for executing any design in concert.

> And let there be
> 'Twixt us and them no *league*, nor amity. *Denham.*

LEAGUE, *v. i.* leeg. To unite, as princes or states in a contract of amity for mutual aid or defense; to confederate. Russia and Austria *leagued* to oppose the ambition of Buonaparte.

2. To unite or confederate, as private persons for mutual aid.

LEAGUE, *n.* leeg. [of Celtic origin. W. *llec*, a flat stone, whence Low L. *leuca*, Sp. *legua*, It. *lega*, Fr. *lieue*, Ir. *leac*. It appears from the Welsh, that this word is from the root of *lay*.]

1. Originally, a stone erected on the public roads, at certain distances, in the manner of the modern mile-stones. Hence,

2. The distance between two stones. With the English and Americans, a *league* is the length of three miles; but this measure is used chiefly at sea. The *league* on the continent of Europe, is very different among different nations. The Dutch and German *league* contains four geographical miles. *Encyc.*

LE'AGUED, *pp.* lee'ged. United in mutual compact; confederated.

LE'AGUER, *n.* lee'ger. One who unites in a league; a confederate. *Encyc.*

LE'AGUER, *n.* [D. *beleggeren*. See *Beleaguer*.]

Siege; investment of a town or fort by an army. [*Little used.*] *Shak.*

LEAK, *n.* [D. *lek*, a leak, and leaky; *lekken*, to leak, to drop, to *sleek* or make smooth; *lekker*, dainty, delicate, nice, delicious; G. *leck*, a leak, and leaky; *lecken*, to leak, to drop out, to jump, to *lick*; *lecker*, dainty, delicious, *lickerish*; Sw. *laka*, to distill or drop, and *lǎka*, to leak; Dan. *lek*, leaky; *lekke*, a leak; *lekkefad*, a dripping pan; *lekker*, to leak, to drop; *lekker*, dainty, delicate, nice, *lickerish*; Sax. *hlece*, leaky. If the noun is the primary word, it may be the Gr. λακις, a fissure or crevice, from ληκεω, Dor. λακεω, to crack, to sound, or to burst with sound, coinciding with L. *lacero* and *loquor*, and perhaps Eng. *clack*. It seems that *lickerish* is from the root of *leak*, and signifies properly watery.]

1. A crack, crevice, fissure or hole in a vessel, that admits water, or permits a fluid to escape.

2. The oozing or passing of water or other fluid or liquor through a crack, fissure or aperture in a vessel, either *into* it, as into a ship, or *out of* it, as out of a cask.

To spring a leak, is to open or crack so as to let in water; to begin to let in water.

LEAK, *a.* Leaky. [*Not in use.*] *Spenser.*

LEAK, *v. i.* To let water or other liquor into or out of a vessel, through a hole or crevice in the vessel. A ship *leaks*, when she admits water through her seams or an aperture in her bottom or sides, into the hull. A pail or a cask *leaks*, when it admits liquor to pass out through a hole or crevice.

To leak out, to find vent; to escape privately from confinement or secresy; as a fact or report.

LE'AKAGE, *n.* A leaking; or the quantity of a liquor that enters or issues by leaking.

2. An allowance, in commerce, of a certain rate per cent. for the leaking of casks, or the waste of liquors by leaking.

LE'AKY, *a.* That admits water or other liquor to pass in or out; as a *leaky* vessel; a *leaky* ship or barrel.

2. Apt to disclose secrets; tattling; not close. *L'Estrange.*

LE'AMER, *n.* A dog; a kind of hound.

LEAN, *v. i.* [Sax. *hlinian*, *hleonian*, to lean; *linian*, to recline; G. *lehnen*; D. *leunen*; Dan. *læner*; Sw. *lǎna sig*; Ir. *claonaim*; Russ. *klonyu*; Gr. κλινω; L. *clino*. Class Ln. No. 3.]

1. To deviate or move from a straight or perpendicular line; or to be in a position thus deviating. We say, a column *leans* to the north or to the east; it *leans* to the right or left.

2. To incline or propend; to tend toward.

> They delight rather to *lean* to their old customs— *Spenser.*

> Trust in the Lord with all thine heart, and *lean* not to thine own understanding. Prov. iii.

3. To bend or incline so as to rest on something; as, to *lean* against a wall or a pillar; to *lean* on the arm of another.

4. To bend; to be in a bending posture.

LEAN, *v. t.* To incline; to cause to lean. *Shak.*

2. To conceal. [Ice. *luna.*] [*Not in use.*] *Ray.*

LEAN, *a.* [Sax. *læne* or *hlæne*; D. Dan. G. *klein*, small, lean; Sw. *klen*; allied perhaps to L. *lenis*, and Eng. *slender*.]

1. Wanting flesh; meager; not fat; as a *lean* body; a *lean* man or animal.

2. Not rich; destitute of good qualities; bare; barren; as *lean* earth.

3. Low; poor; in opposition to *rich* or *great*; as a *lean* action. [*Unusual.*]

4. Barren of thought; destitute of that which improves or entertains; jejune; as a *lean* discourse or dissertation.

LEAN, *n.* That part of flesh which consists of muscle without the fat. *Farquhar.*

LE'ANLY, *adv.* Meagerly; without fat or plumpness.

LE'ANNESS, *n.* Destitution of fat; want of flesh; thinness of body; meagernsss; *applied to animals.*

2. Want of matter; poverty; emptiness; as the *leanness* of a purse. *Shak.*

3. In *Scripture*, want of grace and spiritual comfort.

> He sent *leanness* into their soul. Ps. cvi.

LE'ANY, *a.* Alert; brisk; active. [*Not in use.*] *Spenser.*

LEAP, *v. i.* [Sax. *hleapan*, Goth. *hlaupan*, to leap; G. *laufen*; D. *loopen*, Sw. *lŏpa*, Dan. *löber*, to run, to pass rapidly, to flow, *slip* or glide; W. *llwf*, a *leap*. From these significations, it may be inferred that this word belongs to the family of L. *labor*, perhaps Heb. Ch. Syr. Sam. Eth. חלף. Class Lb. No. 30. Qu. L. *lupus*, a wolf, the *leaper*.]

1. To spring or rise from the ground with both feet, as man, or with all the feet, as other animals; to jump; to vault; as, a man *leaps* over a fence, or *leaps* upon a horse.

> A man *leapeth* better with weights in his hands than without. *Bacon.*

2. To spring or move suddenly; as, to *leap* from a horse.

3. To rush with violence.

> And the man in whom the evil spirit was, *leaped* on them and overcame them— Acts xix.

4. To spring; to bound; to skip; as, to *leap* for joy.

5. To fly; to start. Job xli.

> He parted frowning from me, as if ruin
> *Leaped* from his eyes. *Shak.*

[Our common people retain the Saxon aspirate of this word in the phrase, *to clip it*, to run fast.]

LEAP, *v. t.* To pass over by leaping; to spring or bound from one side to the other; as, to *leap* a wall, a gate or a gulf; to *leap* a stream. [But the phrase is elliptical, and *over* is understood.]

2. To compress; as the male of certain beasts. *Dryden.*

LEAP, *n.* A jump; a spring; a bound; act of leaping.

2. Space passed by leaping.

3. A sudden transition or passing. *Swift.*

4. The space that may be passed at a bound.

> 'Tis the convenient *leap* I mean to try. *Dryden.*

5. Embrace of animals. *Dryden.*

6. Hazard, or effect of leaping. *Shak.*

7. A basket; a weel for fish. [*Not in use.*] *Wickliffe. Sherwood.*

LE'APER, *n.* One that leaps. A horse is called a good *leaper*.

LE'AP-FROG, *n.* A play of children, in which they imitate the leap of frogs. *Shak.*

LE'APING, *ppr.* Jumping; springing; bounding; skipping.

LE'APINGLY, *adv.* By leaps.

LE'AP-YEAR, *n.* Bissextile, a year containing 366 days; every fourth year, which *leaps* over a day more than a common year. Thus in common years, if the first day of March is on Monday, the present year, it will, the next year, fall on Tuesday, but in leap-year it will leap to Wednesday; for leap-year contains a day more than a common year, a day being added to the month of February. *Brown.*

LEARN, *v. t.* lern. [Sax. *leornian*; G. *lernen*; D. *leeren*; Dan. *lærer*; Sw. *lǎra*. The latter coincides with the Sax. *læran*, to teach, the same word having both significations, to teach and to learn. In popular use, *learn* still has both senses.]

1. To gain knowledge of; to acquire knowledge or ideas of something before unknown. We *learn* the use of letters, the meaning of words and the principles of science. We *learn* things by instruction, by study, and by experience and observation. It is much easier to *learn* what is right, than to unlearn what is wrong.

Now *learn* a parable of the fig-tree. Matt. xxiv.

2. To acquire skill in any thing; to gain by practice a faculty of performing; as, to *learn* to play on a flute or an organ.

The chief art of *learning* is to attempt but little at a time. *Locke.*

3. To teach; to communicate the knowledge of something before unknown.

Hast thou not *learned* me how
To make perfumes? *Shak.*

[This use of *learn* is found in respectable writers, but is now deemed inelegant as well as improper.]

LEARN, *v. i. lern.* To gain or receive knowledge; to receive instruction; to take pattern; with *of.*

Take my yoke upon you, and *learn of* me; for I am meek and lowly—. Matt. xi.

2. To receive information or intelligence.

LEARNED, } *pp.* lern'ed, } Obtained as
LEARNT, } lernt. } knowledge or information.

LEARNED, *a. lern'ed.* Versed in literature and science; as a *learned* man.

2. Skillful; well acquainted with arts; knowing; with *in;* as *learned in* martial arts.

3. Containing learning; as a *learned* treatise or publication. *Coxe.*

4. Versed in scholastic, as distinct from other knowledge.

Men of much reading are greatly *learned*, but may be little knowing. *Locke.*

The *learned*, learned men; men of erudition; literati.

LEARNEDLY, *adv. lern'edly.* With learning or erudition; with skill; as, to discuss a question *learnedly.*

Every coxcomb swears as *learnedly* as they. *Swift.*

LEARNER, *n. lern'er.* A person who is gaining knowledge from instruction, from reading or study, or by other means; one who is in the rudiments of any science or art.

LEARNING, *ppr. lern'ing.* Gaining knowledge by instruction or reading, by study, by experience or observation; acquiring skill by practice.

LEARNING, *n. lern'ing.* The knowledge of principles or facts received by instruction or study; acquired knowledge or ideas in any branch of science or literature; erudition; literature; science. The Scaligers were men of great *learning.* [*This is the proper sense of the word.*]

2. Knowledge acquired by experience, experiment or observation.

3. Skill in any thing good or bad. *Hooker.*

LE'ASABLE, *a.* That may be leased. *Sherwood.*

LEASE, *n.* [Fr. *laisser.* See the Verb.]

1. A demise or letting of lands, tenements or hereditaments to another for life, for a term of years, or at will, for a rent or compensation reserved; also, the contract for such letting. *Encyc.*

2. Any tenure by grant or permission.

Our high placed Macbeth
Shall live the *lease* of nature. *Shak.*

LEASE, *v. t.* [Fr. *laisser;* a different orthography of Eng. *let.* See *Let.*]

To let; to demise; to grant the temporary possession of lands, tenements or hereditaments to another for a rent reserved. A *leased* to B his land in Dale for the annual rent of a pepper corn.

LEASE, *v. i. leez.* [Sax. *lesan*, to collect, also to free, to liberate, to redeem; D. *leezen;* G. *lesen*, to gather, to cull, to sift, also to read, like L. *lego;* Dan. *leser*, Sw. *låsa*, to read.]

To glean; to gather what harvest men have left. *Obs.* *Dryden.*

LE'ASED, *pp.* Demised or let, as lands or tenements.

LE'ASEHOLD, *a.* Held by lease; as a *leasehold* tenement. *Swift.*

LE'ASER, *n.* A gleaner; a gatherer after reapers.

LEASH, *n.* [Fr. *laisse, lesse;* D. *letse.* Qu. It. *laccio*, L. *laqueus.*]

1. A thong of lether, or long line by which a falconer holds his hawk, or a courser his dog. *Shak.*

2. Among sportsmen, a brace and a half; tierce; three; three creatures of any kind, especially greyhounds, foxes, bucks and hares. *Shak.* *Dennis.*

3. A band wherewith to tie any thing. *Boyle.*

LEASH, *v. t.* To bind; to hold by a string. *Shak.*

LE'ASING, *n. s* as *z.* [Sax. *leasunge*, from *lease, leasa*, false.]

Falsehood; lies. [*Obsolete or nearly so.*]

LE'ASOW, *n.* [Sax. *læswe.*] A pasture. *Obs.* *Wickliffe.*

LEAST, *a.* [superl. of Sax. *læs*, less, contracted from *læsest.* It cannot be regularly formed from *little.*]

Smallest; little beyond others, either in size or degree; as the *least* insect; the *least* mercy.

Least is often used without the noun to which it refers. "I am the *least* of the apostles," that is, the *least* apostle of all the apostles. 1 Cor. xv.

LEAST, *adv.* In the smallest or lowest degree; in a degree below all others; as, to reward those who *least* deserve it.

At least, } to say no more; not to de-
At the least, } mand or affirm more than is barely sufficient; at the lowest degree. If he has not incurred a penalty, he *at least* deserves censure.

He who tempts, though vain, *at least* asperses
The tempted with dishonor. *Milton.*

2. To say no more. Let useful observations be *at least* a part of your conversation.

The least, in the smallest degree. His faculties are not in *the least* impaired.

At leastwise, in the sense of *at least*, is obsolete.

LE'ASY, *a. s* as *z.* Thin; flimsy. It is usually pronounced *sleazy.* *Ascham.*

LEAT, *n.* [Sax. *læt, duxit.*] A trench to conduct water to or from a mill.

LEATH'ER, } *n.* [Sax. *lether;* G. D. *leder;*
LETH'ER, } Sw. *läder;* Dan. *læther;* Arm. *lezr;* Ir. *leather.* The most correct orthography is *lether.*]

1. The skin of an animal dressed and prepared for use.

2. Dressed hides in general.

3. Skin; in an ironical sense.

LEATH'ER, } *a.* Lethern; consisting of
LETH'ER, } lether; as a *lether* glove.

LEATH'ER-COAT, *n.* An apple with a tough coat or rind. *Shak.*

LEATH'ER-DRESSER, *n.* One who dresses lether; one who prepares hides for use. *Pope.*

LEATH'ER-JACKET, *n.* A fish of the Pacific ocean. *Cook.*

LEATH'ER-MOUTHED, *a.*

By *leather-mouthed* fish, I mean such as have their teeth in their throat, as the chub. *Walton.*

LEATH'ERN, } *a.* Made of lether; consist-
LETH'ERN, } ing of lether; as a *lethern* purse; a *lethern* girdle.

LEATH'ER-SELLER, } *n.* A seller or deal-
LETH'ER-SELLER, } er in lether.

LEATH'ER-WINGED, } *a.* Having wings
LETH'ER-WINGED, } like lether. *Spenser.*

LEATH'ERY, } *a.* Resembling lether;
LETH'ERY, } tough. *Grew.*

LEAVE, *n.* [Sax. *leaf, lefe*, from *leafan, lefan, lyfan*, to permit, to grant, to trust, to believe; G. *erlaub*, D. *oorlof, verlof*, leave, *furlow;* Sax. *leofan*, to *live*, and to *leave.*]

1. Permission; allowance; license; liberty granted by which restraint or illegality is removed.

No friend has *leave* to bear away the dead. *Dryden.*

David earnestly asked *leave* of me. 1 Sam. xx.

2. Farewell; adieu; ceremony of departure; a formal parting of friends; used chiefly in the phrase to *take leave.* Acts xviii.

LEAVE, *v. t.* pret. and pp. *left.* [Sax. *læfan*, to leave; *lefan*, to permit, to believe; *lefe*, leave; *lcfian*, to live; *leofan*, to leave, to live; *leofa*, leave, permission, licence; *lyfan*, to permit, also to live. But *live* is also written *liban, libban*, with *b*, which *leave* is not. *Belifan*, to remain or be left; *alyfan*, to permit; *ge-læfan*, to leave, to permit, to believe; *ge-leaf*, leave, license, assent, consent, faith or belief; *ge-lefan*, to believe, to think or suppose, to permit, to *live;* *ge-leofan*, id.; *ge-lyfan*, to believe, to trust; *ge-lyfed*, permitted or allowed, believed, lawful, also alive, having life; *leof*, loved; *lufa*, love, also belief; *leoflic*, faithful; *luflic*, willingly, *lubenter;* *luflic*, lovely. The German has *leave* in *urlaub*, a furlow, and *belief* in *glaube;* *live* in *leben;* and *love* in *liebe, lieben*, the Latin *libet, lubet.* Gr. λειπω. Dan. *lever*, Sw. *lefva*, to live. These are a small part of the affinities of this word. The Germans and Dutch express the sense of *leave*, by *lassen, laaten*, which is our *let*, Fr. *laisser;* and *let* in English has the sense both of permit and of hinder. The most prominent significations of *leave*, are to stop or forbear, and to withdraw.]

1. To withdraw or depart from; to quit for a longer or shorter time indefinitely, or for perpetuity. We *left* Cowes on our return to the United States, May 10, 1825. We *leave* home for a day or a year. The

fever *leaves* the patient daily at a certain hour. The secretary has *left* the business of his office with his first clerk.

A man shall *leave* his father and his mother, and cleave to his wife. Gen. ii.

2. To forsake; to desert; to abandon; to relinquish.

We have *left* all and followed thee. Mark x.

3. To suffer to remain; not to take or remove.

Let no man *leave* of it till the morning. Ex. xvi.

4. To have remaining at death; as, to *leave* a good name.

5. To commit or trust to, as a deposit; or to suffer to remain. I *left* the papers in the care of the consul.

6. To bequeath; to give by will. The deceased has *left* his lands to his sons, but he has *left* a legacy to his only daughter.

7. To permit without interposition. Of this, he *leaves* the reader to judge.

8. To cease to do; to desist from; to forbear.

Let us return, lest my father *leave* caring for the asses and take thought for us. 1 Sam. ix.

9. To refer; to commit for decision.

To be left to one's self, to be deserted or forsaken; to be permitted to follow one's own opinions or desires.

To leave off, to desist from; to forbear; as, to *leave off* work at six o'clock.

To leave off, to cease wearing; as, to *leave off* a garment.

2. To forsake; as, to *leave off* an old acquaintance. *Arbuthnot.*

To leave out, to omit; as, to *leave out* a word or name in writing.

LEAVE, *v. i.* To cease; to desist.

He began at the eldest and *left* at the youngest. Gen. xliv.

To leave off, to cease; to desist; to stop.

But when you find that vigorous heat abate,
Leave off, and for another summons wait. *Roscommon.*

LEAVE, *v. t.* [Fr. *lever.*] To raise. [*Not used.*] *Spenser.*

LE'AVED, *a.* [from *leaf*; but *leafed* would be preferable.]

1. Furnished with foliage or leaves.

2. Having a leaf, or made with leaves or folds; as a two-*leaved* gate.

LEAVEN, *n. lev'n.* [Fr. *levain*, from *lever*, to raise, L. *levo*, Eng. to *lift.*]

1. A mass of sour dough, which, mixed with a larger quantity of dough or paste, produces fermentation in it and renders it light. During the seven days of the passover, no *leaven* was permitted to be in the houses of the Jews. Ex. xii.

2. Any thing which makes a general change in the mass. It generally means something which corrupts or depraves that with which it is mixed.

Beware of the *leaven* of the Pharisees and of the Sadducees. Matt. xvi.

LEAVEN, *v. t. lev'n.* To excite fermentation in; to raise and make light, as dough or paste.

A little leaven *leaveneth* the whole lump. 1 Cor. v.

2. To taint; to imbue. *Prior.*

LEAVENED, *pp. lev'ened.* Raised and made light by fermentation.

LEAVENING, *ppr. lev'ening.* Making light by fermentation.

LEAVENING, *n. lev'ening.* That which leavens or makes light. *Bacon.*

LEAVENOUS, *a. lev'enous.* Containing leaven; tainted. *Milton.*

LE'AVER, *n.* [from *leave.*] One who leaves or relinquishes; one who forsakes. *Shak.*

LEAVES, *n. plu.* of *leaf.*

LE'AVING, *ppr.* Quitting; withdrawing from; relinquishing; suffering to remain; ceasing; desisting from.

LE'AVINGS, *n. plu.* Things left; remnant; relics.

The *leavings* of Pharsalia. *Addison.*

2. Refuse; offal. *Swift.*

LE'AVY, *a.* [from *leaf.*] Full of leaves; covered with leaves. [An improper word; it ought to be *leafy.*] *Sidney. Shak.*

LECH, for *lick. Obs.* [See *Lick.*]

LECH'ER, *n.* [It. *lecco*, gluttony, lechery; *leccare*, to lick; *leccardo*, greedy; G. *lecken*; D. *likker.* See *lick*, *leak* and *lickerish.* But in Saxon *leger-scipe* is lewdness, from *leger*, a layer, or a lying down; *lecgan*, to lay; *ligan*, to lie. See *Lubricity.*]

A man given to lewdness; one addicted, in an exorbitant degree, to the indulgence of the animal appetite, and an illicit commerce with females.

LECH'ER, *v. i.* To practice lewdness; to indulge lust. *B. Jonson.*

LECH'EROUS, *a.* Addicted to lewdness; prone to indulge lust; lustful; lewd. *Derham.*

2. Provoking lust. *Chaucer.*

LECH'EROUSLY, *adv.* Lustfully; lewdly.

LECH'EROUSNESS, *n.* Lust, or strong propensity to indulge the sexual appetite.

LECH'ERY, *n.* Lewdness; free indulgence of lust; practice of indulging the animal appetite. *Shak.*

LEC'TION, *n.* [L. *lectio*, from *lego*, to read, Ir. *leighim*, *leagham*, Gr. λεγω, Fr. *lire.*]

1. A reading.

2. A difference or variety in copies of a manuscript or book. *Watts.*

3. A lesson or portion of Scripture read in divine service.

LEC'TIONARY, *n.* The Romish service-book, containing portions of Scripture.

LEC'TURE, *n.* [Fr. *lecture*, from L. *lectura*, from *lego*, to read.]

1. A discourse read or pronounced on any subject; usually, a formal or methodical discourse, intended for instruction; as a *lecture* on morals, philosophy, rhetoric, or theology.

2. A reading; the act or practice of reading; as in the *lecture* of Holy Scripture. [*Little used.*] *Brown.*

3. A magisterial reprimand; a formal reproof. *Addison.*

4. A recitation; rehearsal of a lesson. *Eng. Univ.*

LEC'TURE, *v. i.* To read or deliver a formal discourse.

2. To practice reading lectures for instruction. We say, the professor *lectures* on geometry, or on chimistry.

LEC'TURE, *v. t.* To instruct by discourses.

2. To instruct dogmatically or authoritatively; to reprove; as, to *lecture* one for his faults.

LEC'TURER, *n.* One who reads or pronounces lectures; a professor or an instructor who delivers formal discourses for the instruction of others.

2. A preacher in a church, hired by the parish to assist the rector, vicar or curate. *Johnson.*

LEC'TURESHIP, *n.* The office of a lecturer. *Swift.*

LEC'TURING, *ppr.* Reading or delivering a discourse; reproving.

LEC'TURN, *n.* A reading desk. [*Not in use.*] *Chaucer.*

LED, *pret.* and *pp.* of *lead.*

LED'EN, *n.* [Sax. *lyden.*] Language; true meaning. *Obs.* *Chaucer. Spenser.*

LEDGE, *n.* [Sax. *leger*, a layer; D. *leggen*, to lay, Sax. *lecgan.*]

1. A stratum, layer or row.

The lowest *ledge* or row should be merely of stone. *Wotton.*

2. A ridge; a prominent row; as a *ledge* of rocks.

3. A prominent part; a regular part rising or projecting beyond the rest. *Swift.*

4. A small molding.

5. A small piece of timber placed athwart ships, under the deck between the beams.

6. A long ridge of rocks near the surface of the sea. *Mar. Dict.*

LEDG'ER, *n.* The principal book of accounts among merchants; the book into which the accounts of the journal are carried in a summary form. [See *Leger.*]

LEE, *n.* plu. *lees.* [Fr. *lie.*] Dregs; sediment. [See *Lees.*]

LEE, *n.* [Sw. *lă*; Dan. *læ.* In Sax. *hleo*, *hleow*, is a bower or shelter; Scot. *le*, calm, sheltered; Ice. *hle*, D. *ly*, *lee*, and *luw*, sheltered from the wind; W. *clyd*, sheltering, warm; Sp. *lua*, lee.]

Literally, a calm or sheltered place, a place defended from the wind; hence, that part of the hemisphere towards which the wind blows, as opposed to that from which it proceeds.

Under the lee, denotes properly, in the part defended from the wind.

Under the lee of the land, is properly, near the shore which breaks the force of the wind.

Under the lee of a ship, on the side opposite to that on which the wind blows.

LEE, *v. i.* To lie. [*Not used.* See *Lie.*] *Chaucer.*

LEE'-BOARD, *n.* A frame of plank affixed to the side of a flat-bottomed vessel, to prevent it from falling to leeward when close-hauled.

LEE'-GAGE, *n.* A greater distance from the point whence the wind blows, than another vessel has.

LEE'-LURCH, *n.* A sudden and violent roll of a ship to leeward in a high sea.

LEE'-SHORE, *n.* The shore under the lee of a ship, or that towards which the wind blows.

LEE'-SIDE, *n.* The side of a ship or boat farthest from the point whence the wind blows; opposed to the *weather*-side.

LEE'-TIDE, *n.* A tide running in the same direction that the wind blows. *A tide under the lee*, is a stream in an opposite direction to the wind.

LEE'WARD, *a.* Pertaining to the part towards which the wind blows; as a *leeward* ship.

LEE'WARD, *adv.* Towards the lee, or that part towards which the wind blows; opposed to *windward;* as fall to *leeward.*

LEE'WAY, *n.* The lateral movement of a ship to the leeward of her course, or the angle which the line of her way makes with her keel, when she is close-hauled. *Mar. Dict.*

LEECH, *n.* [Goth. *leikeis*, Sax. *læc*, a host or innkeeper, a physician; Dan. *læge; læger*, to heal; Sw. *läkia*, to heal; *läkiare*, a physician; Ir. *liagh;* Russ. *liakar.*]

A physician; a professor of the art of healing. *Spenser. Dryden. Gay.*

[This word, in the United States, is nearly or wholly obsolete. Even *cow leech* is not used.]

2. [Sax. *læccan*, to seize.] A blood-sucker; an animal of the genus Hirudo, a species of aquatic worm, which is used in the medical art for topical bleeding. One large species of this animal is called *horse-leech.*

3. In *seamen's language*, the border or edge of a sail, which is sloping or perpendicular; as the *fore-leech*, the *after-leech*, &c.

LEE'CH-CRAFT, *n.* The art of healing. *Obs.* *Davies.*

LEE'CH-LINE, *n.* Leech-lines are ropes fastened to the middle of the leeches of the main-sail and fore-sail, serving to truss them up to the yards.

LEE'CH-ROPE, *n.* That part of the bolt-rope to which the skirt or border of a sail is sewed. *Mar. Dict.*

LEEF, *a.* Kind; fond; pleasing; willing. *Obs.* [See *Lief.*] *Spenser.*

LEEK, *n.* [Sax. *leac;* G. *lauch;* D. *look;* Sw. *lök;* Dan. *lög.*]

A plant of the genus Allium, with a bulbous root. Numb. xi.

LEE'LITE, *n.* A mineral, so called from Dr. Lee, of St. John's College, Cambridge. It is described as a siliceous stone, and by some mineralogists considered to be a hydrate of silica. *Phillips.*

LEER, *v. i.* [D. *gluuren, begluuren.*] To look obliquely; to turn the eye and cast a look from a corner, either in contempt, defiance or frowning, or for a sly look. *Swift.*

2. To look with a forced countenance. *Dryden.*

LEER, *v. t.* To allure with smiles. *Dryden.*

LEER, *n.* [Sax. *hleare, hleor*, the cheek.]

1. The cheek. *Obs.*
2. Complexion; hue; face. *Obs.* *Shak.*
3. An oblique view.

—With jealous *leer* malign
Eyed them askance. *Milton.*

4. An affected cast of countenance.

Damn with faint praise, concede with civil *leer.* *Pope.*

LEER, *a.* [Sax. *gelær.*] Empty; also, trifling; frivolous. *Obs.* *B. Jonson.*

LEE'RING, *ppr.* Looking obliquely; casting a look askance.

LEE'RINGLY, *adv.* With an arch oblique look or smile.

LEES, *n.* [Fr. *lie;* Arm. *ly;* probably a contracted word. It is used in the plural only.]

The grosser parts of any liquor which have settled on the bottom of a vessel; dregs; sediment; as the *lees* of wine.

LEESE, *v. t.* To lose. *Obs.* [See *Lose.*] *B. Jonson.*

LEESE, *v. t.* [L. *læsus.*] To hurt. *Obs.* *Wickliffe.*

LEET, *n.* In Great Britain, a court. The *court-leet* or view of frankpledge, is a court of record held once a year and not oftener, within a particular hundred, lordship or manor, before the steward of the leet. Its original intent was to view the frankpledges or freemen within the liberty, to preserve the peace, and punish certain minute offenses. All freeholders within the precinct are obliged to attend this court. *Blackstone.*

The court-leet is for the most part superseded by the county court.

LEET-ALE, *n.* A feast or merry making in the time of leet. *Eng.*

LEFT, *pret.* and *pp.* of *leave.*

LEFT, *a.* [L. *lævus;* Gr. λαιος, Hesych. λαφος; probably from the root of *leave*, Gr. λειπω, and properly weak, deficient. Applied to the hand or arm, it denotes the weak arm, as opposed to the *right*, the strong or dextrous. Hence the ancient idea of sinister, unfortunate, attached to the left arm or side.]

1. Denoting the part opposed to the *right* of the body; as the *left* hand, arm or side. Hence, the noun being omitted, we say, on the *left*, that is, on the *left* side or wing, as of an army.

2. The *left* bank of a river, is that which is on the *left* hand of a person whose face is towards the mouth of the river.

LEFT-HAND'ED, *a.* Having the left hand or arm more strong and dextrous than the right; using the left hand and arm with more dexterity than the right.

2. Unlucky; inauspicious; unseasonable. *Obs.* *B. Jonson.*

LEFT-HAND'EDNESS, *n.* Habitual use of the left hand, or rather the ability to use the left hand with more ease and strength than the right.

LEFT-HAND'INESS, *n.* Awkwardness. *Chesterfield.*

LEG, *n.* [Dan. *læg;* It. *lacca.*] The limb of an animal, used in supporting the body and in walking and running; properly, that part of the limb from the knee to the foot, but in a more general sense, the whole limb, including the thigh, the leg and the foot.

2. The long or slender support of any thing; as the *leg* of a table.

To make a leg, to bow; a phrase introduced probably by the practice of drawing the right leg backward. [*Little used.*] *Locke. Swift.*

To stand on one's own legs, to support one's self; to trust to one's own strength or efforts without aid.

LEG'ACY, *n* [Sp. *legado;* Fr. *legs;* L. *legatum*, from *lego*, to send, to bequeath; Eth. ለአከ lak, Ar. ألك alaka, to send. Class Lg. No. 1.]

A bequest; a particular thing, or certain sum of money given by last will or testament.

Good counsel is the best *legacy* a father can leave to his child. *L. Estrange.*

LEG'ACY-HUNTER, *n.* One who flatters and courts for legacies.

LE'GAL, *a.* [Fr. from L. *legalis*, from *lex*, *legis*, law.]

1. According to law; in conformity with law; as a *legal* standard or test; a *legal* procedure.

2. Lawful; permitted by law; as a *legal* trade. Any thing is *legal* which the laws do not forbid.

3. According to the law of works, as distinguished from free grace; or resting on works for salvation. *Scott. Milton.*

4. Pertaining to law; created by law.

The exception must be confined to *legal* crimes. *Paley.*

So we use the phrase, *criminal* law.

LEGAL'ITY, *n.* Lawfulness; conformity to law.

2. In *theology*, a reliance on works for salvation. *Scott.*

LE'GALIZE, *v. t.* To make lawful; to render conformable to law; to authorize. What can *legalize* revenge?

2. To sanction; to give the authority of law to that which is done without law or authority. Irregular proceedings may be *legalized* by a subsequent act of the legislature.

LE'GALLY, *adv.* Lawfully; according to law; in a manner permitted by law.

LEG'ATARY, *n.* [Fr. *legataire;* L. *legatarius*, from *lego*, to bequeath.]

A legatee; one to whom a legacy is bequeathed.

[But *legatee* is generally used.]

LEG'ATE, *n.* [Fr. *legat;* L. *legatus*, from *lego*, to send. See *Lackey.*] An embassador; but especially,

2. The pope's embassador to a foreign prince or state; a cardinal or bishop sent as the pope's representative or commissioner to a sovereign prince. Legates are of three kinds; legates *a latere*, or counselors and assistants of his holiness, legates *de latere*, who are not cardinals, and legates *by office.* *Encyc.*

LEGATEE', *n.* [L. *lego*, to send.] One to whom a legacy is bequeathed. *Swift.*

LEG'ATESHIP, *n.* The office of a legate.

LEG'ATINE, *a.* Pertaining to a legate; as *legatine* power. *Shak.*

2. Made by or proceeding from a legate; as a *legatine* constitution. *Ayliffe.*

LEGA'TION, *n.* [L. *legatio*, from *lego*, to send.] An embassy; a deputation; properly a sending, but generally, the person or persons sent as envoys or embassadors to a foreign court. *Bacon.*

LEGA'TOR, *n.* [L.] A testator; one who bequeaths a legacy. [*Little used.*] *Dryden.*

LEGE, *v. t.* To allege; to lighten. [*Not in use.*] *Chaucer.*

LEG'END, *n.* [It. *leggenda;* L. *legenda*, from *lego*, to read; originally, in the Romish church, a book of service or lessons to be read in worship.]

1. A chronicle or register of the lives of saints, formerly read at matins and at the refectories of religious houses. Hence,

2. An idle or ridiculous story told respecting saints. *Encyc.*

3. Any memorial or relation. *Johnson.*

4. An incredible, unauthentic narrative. *Blackmore.*

5. An inscription, particularly on medals and on coins. *Addison.*

LEǴEND, *v. t.* To tell or narrate, as a legend. *Hall.*

LEǴENDARY, *a.* Consisting of legends; fabulous; strange.

LEǴENDARY, *n.* A book of legends; a relater of legends. *Sheldon.*

LEǴER, *n.* [D. *leggen*, to lie, Sax. *lecgan.*] Any thing that lies in a place; that which rests or remains; sometimes used as a noun, but more frequently as an adjective, as a *leger* ambassador, that is, resident; but the word is now obsolete, except in particular phrases.

A *leger-line*, in music, a line added to the staff of five lines, when more lines than five are wanted, for designating notes ascending or descending.

A *leger-book*, or *leger*, a book that lies in the counting house, the book into which merchants carry a summary of the accounts of the journal; usually written *ledger*.

LEǴERDEMAIN, *n.* [Fr. *leger*, It. *leggiero*, light, slight, and Fr. *de main*, of hand. See *Light.*]

Slight of hand; a deceptive performance which depends on dexterity of hand; a trick performed with such art and adroitness, that the manner or art eludes observation. The word is sometimes used adjectively; as a *legerdemain* trick.

LEǴER'ITY, *n.* [Fr. *legereté.*] Lightness; nimbleness. [*Not in use.*] *Shak.*

LEG'GED, *a.* [from *leg.*] Having legs; used in composition; as a two-*legged* animal.

LEG'GIN, *n.* [from *leg.*] A cover for the leg; a garment that incloses the leg. *Mackenzie.*

LEGIBIL'ITY, *n.* Legibleness; the quality or state of being legible.

LEǴIBLE, *a.* [L. *legibilis*, from *lego*, to read.]

1. That may be read; consisting of letters or figures that may be distinguished by the eye; as a fair, *legible* manuscript.

2. That may be discovered or understood by apparent marks or indications. The thoughts of men are often *legible* in their countenances.

LEǴIBLENESS, *n.* The quality or state of being legible.

LEǴIBLY, *adv.* In such a manner as may be read; as a manuscript *legibly* written.

LE'ǴION, *n.* [L. *legio*, from *lego*, to collect.]

1. In Roman antiquity, a body of infantry consisting of different numbers of men at different periods, from three to five thousand. Each legion was divided into ten cohorts, each cohort into ten companies, and each company into two centuries. *Encyc.*

2. A military force; military bands. *Shak.*

3. A great number.

Where one sin has entered, *legions* will force their way through the same breach. *Rogers.*

My name is *legion*, for we are many. Mark v.

LE'ǴIONARY, *a.* Relating to a legion or to legions.

2. Consisting of a legion or of legions; as a *legionary* force.

3. Containing a great number; as a *legionary* body of errors. *Brown.*

LE'ǴIONARY, *n.* One of a legion. *Milton.*

LEǴ'ISLATE, *v. i.* [L. *lex*, *legis*, law, and *fero*, *latum*, to give, pass or enact.]

To make or enact a law or laws. It is a question whether it is expedient to *legislate* at present on the subject. Let us not *legislate*, when we have no power to enforce our laws.

LEǴISLA'TION, *n.* [Fr.] The act of passing a law or laws; the enacting of laws.

Pythagoras joined *legislation* to his philosophy. *Littleton.*

LEǴ'ISLATIVE, *a.* [Fr. *legislatif.*] Giving or enacting laws; as a *legislative* body.

2. Capable of enacting laws; as *legislative* power.

3. Pertaining to the enacting of laws; suitable to laws; as the *legislative* style.

4. Done by enacting; as a *legislative* act.

[*Note.* In this word, and in *legislator*, *legislatrix*, *legislature*, the accent is nearly equal on the first and third syllables, and *a*, in the third, has its first or long sound.]

LEǴISLA'TOR, *n.* [L.] A lawgiver; one who makes laws for a state or community. This word is limited in its use to a supreme lawgiver, the lawgiver of a sovereign state or kingdom, and is not applied to men that make the by-laws of a subordinate corporation.

LEǴISLA'TORSHIP, *n.* The office of a legislator. [*Not in use.*] *Halifax.*

LEǴISLA'TRESS, } *n.* A female who
LEǴISLA'TRIX, } makes laws. *Tooke.*

LEǴ'ISLATURE, *n.* [Sp. *legislatura.*] The body of men in a state or kingdom, invested with power to make and repeal laws; the supreme power of a state. The *legislature* of Great Britain consists of the house of lords and the house of commons with the king, whose sanction is necessary to every bill before it becomes a law. The *legislatures* of most of the states in America, consist of two houses or branches, but the sanction of the governor is required to give their acts the force of law, or a concurrence of two thirds of the two houses, after he has declined and assigned his objections.

LE'ǴIST, *n.* One skilled in the laws. *Marston.*

LEǴIT'IMACY, *n.* [from *legitimate.*] Lawfulness of birth; opposed to *bastardy.* *Ayliffe.*

2. Genuineness; opposed to *spuriousness.* The *legitimacy* of his conclusions is not to be questioned.

LEǴIT'IMATE, *a.* [Fr. *legitime*; L. *legitimus*; from *lex*, law.]

1. Lawfully begotten or born; born in wedlock; as *legitimate* heirs or children.

2. Genuine; real; proceeding from a pure source; not false or spurious; as *legitimate* arguments or inferences.

LEǴIT'IMATE, *v. t.* [Fr. *legitimer*; Sp. *legitimar*; It. *legittimare.*]

1. To make lawful.

2. To render legitimate; to communicate the rights of a legitimate child to one that is illegitimate; to invest with the rights of a lawful heir. *Ayliffe.*

LEǴIT'IMATELY, *adv.* Lawfully; according to law.

2. Genuinely; not falsely. *Dryden.*

LEǴIT'IMATENESS, *n.* Legality; lawfulness; genuineness.

LEǴITIMA'TION, *n.* [Fr.] The act of rendering legitimate, or of investing an illegitimate child with the rights of one born in wedlock.

2. Lawful birth. [*Unusual.*] *Shak.*

LEG'UME, } *n.* [L. *legumen*; Fr. *legume*;
LEGU'MEN, } probably from L. *lego*, to collect, and signifying that which collects, or holds, or a collection.]

In *botany*, a pericarp or seed-vessel, of two valves, in which the seeds are fixed to one suture only. In the latter circumstance it differs from a siliqua, in which the seeds are attached to both sutures. In popular use, a *legume* is called a pod, or a cod; as a *pea-pod*, or *peas-cod.* *Martyn.*

2. In *the plural*, pulse, peas, beans, &c.

LEGU'MINOUS, *a.* Pertaining to pulse; consisting of pulse. *Leguminous* plants are such as have a legume for a pericarp, as peas and beans.

LEIS'URABLE, *a.* *s* as *z.* [See *Leisure.*] Vacant of employment; not occupied; as *leisurable* hours. [*Little used.*] *Brown.*

LEIS'URABLY, *adv.* At leisure; without hurry. [*Little used.*] *Hooker.*

LEISURE, *n.* *lezh'ur* or *lee'zhur.* [Fr. *loisir.* This is doubtless from the same root as Sw. and Dan. *ledig*, void, empty, vacant, free, eased; Sw. *ledighet*, Dan. *ledighed*, leisure.]

1. Freedom from occupation or business; vacant time; time free from employment.

The desire of *leisure* is much more natural than of business and care. *Temple.*

I shall leave with him that rebuke to be considered at his *leisure.* *Locke.*

2. Convenience of time.

He sigh'd, and had no *leisure* more to say.
[*Not used.*] *Dryden.*

LEIS'URELY, *a.* Done at leisure; not hasty; deliberate; slow; as a *leisurely* walk or march; a *leisurely* survey of life.

LEIS'URELY, *adv.* Not in haste or hurry; slowly; at leisure; deliberately.

We descended very *leisurely*, my friend being careful to count the steps. *Addison.*

LE'MAN, *n.* [probably contracted from *lifman*, *leveman*; Sax. *leof*, loved, and *man.* See *Love* and *Lief.*]

A sweetheart; a gallant, or a mistress. *Obs.* *Chaucer. Spenser. Shak.*

LEME, *n.* [Sax. *leoma.*] A ray of light. [*Not in use.*] *Chaucer.*

LEME, *v. i.* To shine. *Obs.*

LEM'MA, *n.* [Gr. λημμα, from λαμβανω, to receive.]

In *mathematics*, a previous proposition proved, or a proposition demonstrated for the purpose of being used in the demonstration of some other proposition. It is therefore a *received* truth. *Day.*

LEM'MING, } *n.* A species of animal be-
LE'MING, } longing to the genus Mus; a kind of rat, in the north of Europe, which sometimes migrates from north to south in immense numbers. *Encyc.*

Lemnian earth, or *sphragide*, from the isle of Lemnos, in the Egean sea, a kind of astringent medicinal earth, of a fatty consistence and reddish color, used in the same cases as *bole.* It has the external appearance of clay, with a smooth surface resembling agate, especially in recent fractures. It removes impurities like soap. *Encyc. Nicholson.*

LEM'NISCATE, *n.* [L. *lemniscus*, a ribin; *lemniscatus*, adorned with ribins.] A curve in the form of the figure 8.

LEM'ON, *n.* [Fr. Sp. *limon*; It. *limone*. This word is found in the Arabic of Avicenna, and in the Amharic dialect of Ethiopia, we find *lime* or *lome*, the same word.]

1. The fruit of a tree belonging to the genus Citrus, which grows in warm climates. This fruit furnishes a cooling acid juice, which forms an ingredient in some of our most delicious liquors.

2. *Lemon* or *lemon tree*, the tree that produces lemons.

LEMONA'DE, *n.* [Fr. *limonade*; Sp. *limonada*; from *limon*.]

A liquor consisting of lemon juice mixed with water and sweetened.

LE'MUR, *n.* [L.] A genus of quadrupeds, the Makis, natives of Africa and the East Indies.

LE'MURES, *n.* [L.] Hobgoblins; evil spirits. [*Not English.*]

LEND, *v. t.* pret. and pp. *lent*. [Sax. *lænan*; Sw. *låna*; Dan. *laaner*; G. *leihen*; D. *leenen*. *Lend* is a corrupt orthography of *len*, or *loan*, or derived from it. See *Loan*.]

1. To grant to another for temporary use, on the express or implied condition that the thing shall be returned; as, to *lend* a book; or

2. To grant a thing to be used, on the condition that its equivalent in kind shall be returned; as, to *lend* a sum of money, or a loaf of bread.

3. To afford; to grant; to furnish, in general; as, to *lend* assistance; to *lend* an ear to a discourse.

> Cato, *lend* me for a while thy patience. *Addison.*

4. To grant for temporary use, on condition of receiving a compensation at certain periods for the use of the thing, and an ultimate return of the thing, or its full value. Thus money is *lent* on condition of receiving interest for the use, and of having the principal sum returned at the stipulated time. *Lend* is correlative to *borrow.*

5. To permit to use for another's benefit. A *lent* his name to obtain money from the bank.

6. To let for hire or compensation; as, to *lend* a horse or gig. [This sense is used by Paley, and probably may be common in England. But in the United States, I believe, the word is never thus used, except in reference to money. We *lend* money upon interest, but never *lend* a coach or horse for a compensation. We use *let*.]

LEND'ABLE, *a.* That may be lent. *Sherwood.*

LEND'ER, *n.* One who lends.

> The borrower is servant to the *lender*. Prov. xxii.

2. One who makes a trade of putting money to interest. *Bacon. Dryden.*

LEND'ING, *ppr.* Granting for temporary use. [See *Lend*.]

LEND'ING, *n.* The act of loaning.

2. That which is lent or furnished. *Shak.*

LENDS, *n.* [Sax.] Loins. [*Not in use.*] *Wickliffe.*

LENGTH, *n.* [Sax. *lengthe*, from *leng*, long; D. *lengte*.]

1. The extent of any thing material from end to end; the longest line which can be drawn through a body, parallel to its sides; as the *length* of a church or of a ship; the *length* of a rope or line.

2. Extent; extension.

> Stretch'd at his *length* he spurns the swarthy ground. *Dryden.*

3. A certain extent; a portion of space; with a plural.

> Large *lengths* of seas and shores— *Shak.*

4. Space of time; duration, indefinitely; as a great *length* of time. What *length* of time will this enterprise require for its accomplishment?

5. Long duration.

> May heaven, great monarch, still augment your bliss,
> With *length* of days, and every day like this. *Dryden.*

6. Reach or extent; as, to pursue a subject to a great *length*.

7. Extent; as the *length* of a discourse, essay, or argument.

8. Distance.

> He had marched to the *length* of Exeter. [*Unusual and inelegant.*] *Clarendon.*

At length, at or in the full extent. Let the name be inserted *at length*.

2. At last; at the end or conclusion. *Dryden.*

LENGTH, *v. t.* To extend. [*Not used.*]

LENGTH'EN, *v. t.* *length'n*. To extend in length; to make longer; to elongate; as, to *lengthen* a line.

2. To draw out or extend in time; to protract; to continue in duration; as, to *lengthen* life. The days *lengthen* from December to June.

3. To extend; as, to *lengthen* a discourse or a dissertation.

4. To draw out in pronunciation; as, to *lengthen* a sound or a syllable. This verb is often followed by *out*, which may be sometimes emphatical, but in general is useless.

> What if I please to *lengthen out* his date? *Dryden.*

LENGTH'EN, *v. i.* To grow longer; to extend in length. A hempen rope contracts when wet, and *lengthens* when dry.

LENGTH'ENED, *pp.* Made longer; drawn out in length; continued in duration.

LENGTH'ENING, *ppr.* Making longer; extending in length or in duration.

LENGTH'ENING, *n.* Continuation; protraction. Dan. iv.

LENGTH'FUL, *a.* Of great length in measure. *Pope.*

LENGTH'WISE, *adv.* In the direction of the length; in a longitudinal direction.

LENGTH'Y, *a.* Being long or moderately long; not short; not brief; *applied mostly to moral subjects*, as to discourses, writings, arguments, proceedings, &c.; as a *lengthy* sermon; a *lengthy* dissertation; a *lengthy* detail.

> *Lengthy* periods. *Washington's Letter to Plater.*

> No ministerial act in France, in matters of judicial cognizance, is done without a *proces verbal*, in which the facts are stated amidst a great deal of *lengthy* formality, with a degree of minuteness, highly profitable to the verbalizing officers and to the revenue. *Am. Review, Ap. Oct. 1811.*

> P. S. Murray has sent or will send a double copy of the Bride and Giaour; in the last one, some *lengthy* additions; pray accept them, according to old customs— *Lord Byron's Letter to Dr. Clarke, Dec. 13, 1813.*

> Chalmers' Political Annals, in treating of South Carolina—is by no means as *lengthy* as Mr. Hewitt's History. *Drayton's View of South Carolina.*

LE'NIENT, *a.* [L. *leniens*, from *lenio*, *lenis*, soft, mild; Ar. لين laina, to be soft, or smooth. Class Ln. No 4. The primary sense probably is smooth, or to make smooth, and *blandus* may be of the same family.]

1. Softening; mitigating; assuasive.

> Time, that on all things lays his *lenient* hand,
> Yet tames not this. *Pope.*

Sometimes with *of*; as *lenient of* grief. *Milton.*

2. Laxative; emollient.

> Oils relax the fibers, are *lenient*, balsamic— *Arbuthnot.*

LE'NIENT, *n.* That which softens or assuages; an emollient. *Wiseman.*

LEN'IFY, *v. t.* To assuage; to soften; to mitigate. [*Little used.*] *Bacon. Dryden.*

LEN'IMENT, *n.* An assuasive. [*Not used.*]

LEN'ITIVE, *a.* [It. *lenitivo*; Fr. *lenitif*; from L. *lenio*, to soften.]

Having the quality of softening or mitigating, as pain or acrimony; assuasive; emollient. *Bacon. Arbuthnot.*

LEN'ITIVE, *n.* A medicine or application that has the quality of easing pain; that which softens or mitigates.

2. A palliative; that which abates passion. *South.*

LEN'ITY, *n.* [L. *lenitas*, from *lenis*, mild, soft.]

Mildness of temper; softness; tenderness; mercy. Young offenders may be treated with *lenity*. It is opposed to *severity* and *rigor*.

LENS, *n.* plu. *lenses*. [L *lens*, a lentil.] A transparent substance, usually glass, so formed that rays of light passing through it are made to change their direction, and to magnify or diminish objects at a certain distance. Lenses are double-convex, or convex on both sides; double-concave, or concave on both sides; plano-convex, or plano-concave, that is, with one side plane, and the other convex or concave; or convex on one side and concave on the other: the latter is called a *meniscus*. *Encyc.*

LENT, *pp.* of *lend*.

LENT, *n.* [Sax. *lencten*, spring, lent, from *leng*, long; *lenegan*, to lengthen; so called from the lengthening of the days.]

The quadragesimal fast, or fast of forty days, observed by the christian church before Easter, the festival of our Savior's resurrection. It begins at Ash-Wednesday, and continues till Easter.

LENT'EN, *a.* Pertaining to lent; used in lent; sparing; as a *lenten* entertainment; a *lenten* sallad. *Shak.*

LENTIC'ULAR, *a.* [L. *lenticularis*, from *lens*, supra.]

1. Resembling a lentil.

2. Having the form of a lens; lentiform.

LENTIC'ULARLY, *adv.* In the manner of a lens; with a curve.

LENTIC'ULITE, *n.* A petrified shell.

LENT'IFORM, *a.* [L. *lens* and *forma*, form.] Of the form of a lens.

LENTIG'INOUS, *a.* [L. *lentigo*, a freckle, from L. *lens*.] Freckly; scurfy; furfuraceous.

LENTI'GO, *n.* A freckly eruption on the skin.

LEN'TIL, *n.* [Fr. *lentille*, from L. lens.] A plant of the genus Ervum. It is an annual plant, rising with weak stalks about 18 inches. The seeds, which are contained in a pod, are round, flat, and a little convex in the middle. It is cultivated for fodder, and for its seeds. *Encyc.*

LEN'TISK, } *n.* [Fr. *lentisque; It. lentischio; Sp. lentisco;* L. *lentiscus*.]
LENTIS'CUS, }

A tree of the genus Pistacia, the mastich-tree, a native of Arabia, Persia, Syria, and the south of Europe. The wood is of a pale brown, resinous and fragrant. [See *Mastich*.]

LENT'ITUDE, *n.* [L. *lentus*, slow.] Slowness. [*Not used.*] *Dict.*

LENT'NER, *n.* A kind of hawk. *Walton.*

LENT'OR, *n.* [L. from *lentus*, slow, tough, clammy; Fr. *lenteur*.]

1. Tenacity; viscousness. *Bacon.*

2. Slowness; delay; sluggishness. *Arbuthnot.*

3. Siziness; thickness of fluids; viscidity; *a term used in the humoral pathology.* *Coxe. Quincy.*

LENT'OUS, *a.* [L. *lentus*, slow, thick.] Viscid; viscous; tenacious. *Brown.*

LEN'ZINITE, *n.* [from *Lenzius*, a German mineralogist.]

A mineral of two kinds, the opaline and argillaceous; a variety of clay, occurring usually in small masses of the size of a nut. *Cleaveland. Phillips.*

LE'O, *n.* [L.] The Lion, the fifth sign of the zodiac.

LE'ONINE, *a.* [L. *leoninus*, from *leo*, lion.] Belonging to a lion; resembling a lion, or partaking of his qualities; as *leonine* fierceness or rapacity.

Leonine verses, so named from Leo, the inventor, are those, the end of which rhymes with the middle; as,

Gloria *factorum* temere conceditur *horum*. *Johnson.*

LE'ONINELY, *adv.* In the manner of a lion. *Harris.*

LEOPARD, *n. lep'ard.* [L. *leo*, lion, and *pardus*, pard, Gr. παρδος, from Heb. פרד to separate, that is, spotted, broken into spots.]

A rapacious quadruped of the genus Felis. It differs from the panther and the once in the beauty of its color, which is of a lively yellow, with smaller spots than those of the two latter, and disposed in groups. It is larger than the once and less than the panther. This animal is found in Africa and Asia, and so rapacious as to spare neither man nor beast. *Encyc.*

LEOP'ARD'S-BANE, *n.* A plant of the genus Doronicum. The *German Leopard's-bane* is of the genus Arnica. *Lee.*

LEP'ER, *n.* [L. *lepra*, leprosy, Fr. *lepre*, Ir. *lobhar*, Gr. λεπρα.] A person affected with leprosy.

LEP'ID, *a.* [L. *lepidus*.] Pleasant; jocose. [*Little used.*]

LEP'IDOLITE, *n.* [Gr. λεπις, a scale.] A mineral found in scaly masses, ordinarily of a violet or lilac color; allied to mica. *Dict.*

Lepidolite is of a peach-blossom red color, sometimes gray; massive and in small concretions. On account of its beautiful color, it has been cut into snuff-boxes. It is sometimes called *lilalite*. *Jameson. Ure.*

LEP'IDOPTER, } *n.* [Gr. λεπις, a scale, and πτερον, a wing.]
LEPIDOP'TERA, }

The *Lepidopters* are an order of insects having four wings covered with fine scales, like powder, as the butterfly.

LEPIDOP'TERAL, *a.* Belonging to the order of Lepidopters.

LEP'ORINE, *a.* [L. *leporinus*, from *lepus*, a hare. Qu. the Teutonic *leap*, to run.]

Pertaining to a hare; having the nature or qualities of the hare. *Johnson.*

LEPROS'ITY, *n.* Squamousness. [*Little used.*] *Bacon.*

LEP'ROSY, *n.* [See *Leper*.] A foul cutaneous disease, appearing in dry, white, thin, scurfy scabs, attended with violent itching. It sometimes covers the whole body, rarely the face. One species of it is called elephantiasis. *Encyc.*

The term *leprosy* is applied to two very distinct diseases, the scaly and the tuberculated, or the proper leprosy and the elephantiasis. The former is characterized by smooth laminated scales, sometimes livid, but usually whitish; in the latter, the skin is thickened, livid and tuberculated. It is called the black leprosy, but this term is also applied to the livid variety of the scaly leprosy. *Good.*

LEP'ROUS, *a.* [Fr. *lepreux*. See *Leper*.]

Infected with leprosy; covered with white scales.

His hand was *leprous* as snow. Ex. iv.

LEP'ROUSLY, *adv.* In an infectious degree.

LERE, *n.* Learning; lesson; lore. *Obs.* *Spenser.*

LERE, *v. t.* To learn; to teach. *Obs.* *Chaucer.*

LE'SION, *n. le'zhun.* [L. *læsio*, from *lædo*, to hurt.]

A hurting; hurt; wound; injury. *Rush.*

LESS, for *unless*. [*Not in use.*]

LESS, a terminating syllable of many nouns and some adjectives, is the Sax. *leas*, Goth. *laus*, belonging to the verb *lysan*, *lausyan*, to loose, free, separate. Hence it is a privative word, denoting destitution; as a *witless* man, a man destitute of wit; *childless*, without children; *fatherless; faithless; pennyless; lawless*, &c.

LESS, *a.* [Sax. *læs;* perhaps allied to Dan. *liser*, to abate, to *lessen*, to relieve, to ease. *Less* has the sense of the comparative degree of *little*.]

Smaller; not so large or great; as a *less* quantity or number; a horse of *less* size or value. We are all destined to suffer affliction in a greater or *less* degree.

LESS, *adv.* Not so much; in a smaller or lower degree; as *less* bright or loud; *less* beautiful; *less* obliging; *less* careful. The *less* a man praises himself, the more disposed are others to praise him.

LESS, *n.* Not so much.

They gathered some more, some *less*. Ex. xvi.

2. An inferior.

The *less* is blessed by the better. Heb. vii.

LESS, *v. t.* To make less. [*Not in use.*] *Gower*

LESSEE', *n.* [from *lease*.] The person to whom a lease is given, or who takes an estate by lease. *Blackstone.*

LESS'EN, *v. t. les'n.* [from *less*.] To make less; to diminish; to reduce in bulk, size, quantity, number or amount; to make smaller; as, to *lessen* a kingdom or its population.

2. To diminish in degree, state or quality; as, awkward manners tend to *lessen* our respect for men of merit.

3. To degrade; to reduce in dignity.

St. Paul chose to magnify his office, when ill men conspired to *lessen* it. *Atterbury.*

LESS'EN, *v. i. les'n.* To become less; to shrink; to contract in bulk, quantity, number or amount; to be diminished. The apparent magnitude of objects *lessens* as we recede from them.

2. To become less in degree, quality or intensity; to decrease. The strength of the body, and the vivacity of the temper usually *lessen* as we advance in age.

LESS'ENED, *pp.* Made smaller; diminished.

LESS'ENING, *ppr.* Reducing in bulk, amount or degree; degrading.

LESS'ER, *a.* [Sax. *læssa*, *læsse*, from *læs*. This word is a corruption; but too well established to be discarded.]

Less; smaller. Authors always write the *Lesser* Asia.

By the same reason, may a man in a state of nature, punish the *lesser* breaches of that law. *Locke.*

God made the *lesser* light to rule the night. Gen. i.

LES'SON, *n. les'n.* [This word we probably have received from the Fr. *leçon*, L. *lectio*, from *lego*, to read, Fr. *lire*, *lisant;* Sp. *leccion;* It. *lezione;* Sw. *lexa;* and not from the D. *leezen*, G. *lesen*, to read.]

1. Any thing read or recited to a teacher by a pupil or learner for improvement; or such a portion of a book as a pupil learns and repeats at one time. The instructor is pleased when his pupils recite their *lessons* with accuracy and promptness.

2. A portion of Scripture read in divine service. Thus endeth the first *lesson*.

3. A portion of a book or manuscript assigned by a preceptor to a pupil to be learnt, or for an exercise; something to be learnt. Give him his *lesson*.

4. Precept; doctrine or notion inculcated.

Be not jealous over the wife of thy bosom, and teach her not an evil *lesson* against thyself. *Ecclus.*

5. Severe lecture; reproof; rebuke.

She would give her a *lesson* for walking so late. *Sidney.*

6. Tune written for an instrument. *Davies.*

7. Instruction or truth, taught by experience. The *lessons* which sickness imparts, she leaves to be practiced when health is established.

LES'SON, *v. t. les'n.* To teach; to instruct.

Children should be *lessoned* into a contempt and detestation of this vice. *L'Estrange.*

LES'SONED, *pp.* Taught; instructed.

LES'SONING, *ppr.* Teaching.

LES'SOR, *n.* [from *lease.*] One who leases; the person who lets to farm, or gives a lease. *Blackstone.*

LEST, *con.* [from the Sax. *leas*, Goth. *laus*, loose, separate. In Saxon it was preceded by *the, the leas*, that less, that not, *ne forte.* Hence it denotes a *loosing* or separation, and hence it comes to express prevention.] That not; for fear that.

Ye shall not eat of it, neither shall ye touch it, *lest* ye die. Gen. iii.

The phrase may be thus explained. Ye shall not touch it; that separated or dismissed, ye die. *That* here refers to the preceding command or sentence; that being removed or not observed, the fact being not so, ye will die.

Sin no more, *lest* a worse thing come to thee. John v.

Sin no more; that fact not taking place, a worse thing will happen to thee.

LET, *v. t.* pret. and pp. *let. Letted* is obsolete. [Sax. *lætan, letan*, Goth. *letan*, to permit, to hinder, to dismiss or send away, to let go, to leave, to admit, to think or suppose, to dissemble, to retard, to be *late* or slow, to dally or trifle, to lease or let out; *letan aweg*, to *let away*, to throw; W. *lluz*, hinderance; *lluziaw*, to hinder; D. *laaten*, to permit, to suffer, to give, to leave, to loose, to put, to stow; G. *lassen*, to let, to permit, grant, allow, suffer; *verlassen*, to forsake; *unterlassen*, to cease, to forbear; Sw. *låta*, to permit; Dan. *lader*, to let, permit, allow, grant, suffer, give leave. But in the four latter dialects, there is another verb, which corresponds with *let* in some of its significations; D. *lyden*, G. *leiden*, Sw. *lida*, Dan. *lider*, to suffer, endure, undergo, to permit. With this verb corresponds the English *late*, D. *laat*, Sw. *lat*, Dan. *lad*, slothful, lazy; and the G. *lass*, feeble, lazy, coincides with *lassen*, supra, and this may be the Eng. *lazy.* To *let out*, like L. *elocare*, is to *lease*, Fr. *laisser. Let* is the Fr. *laisser*, in a different dialect. By the German and Welsh it appears that the last radical may have originally been *th*, *ts* or *tz*, or other compound. See Class Ld. No. 2. 15. 19. 23. 32. and Class Ls. No. 30.]

1. To permit; to allow; to suffer; to give leave or power by a positive act, or negatively, to withhold restraint; not to prevent. A leaky ship *lets* water enter into the hold. *Let* is followed by the infinitive without the sign *to.*

Pharaoh said, I will *let* you go. Ex. viii.

When the ship was caught and could not bear up into the wind, we *let* her drive. Acts xxvii.

2. To lease; to grant possession and use for a compensation; as, to *let* to farm; to *let* an estate for a year; to *let* a room to lodgers; often followed by *out*, as, to *let out* a farm; but the use of *out* is unnecessary.

3. To suffer; to permit; with the usual sign of the infinitive.

There's a letter for you, Sir, if your name be Horatio, as I am *let* to know it is. [*Not used.*] *Shak.*

4. In *the imperative mode, let* has the following uses. Followed by the first and third persons, it expresses desire or wish; hence it is used in prayer and entreaty to superiors, and to those who have us in their power; as, *let me* not wander from thy commandments. Ps. cxix.

Followed by the first person plural, *let* expresses exhortation or entreaty; as, rise, *let us* go.

Followed by the third person, it implies permission or command addressed to an inferior. *Let him* go, *let them* remain, are commands addressed to the second person. *Let thou*, or *let ye*, that is, do thou or you permit him to go.

Sometimes *let* is used to express a command or injunction to a third person. When the signal is given to engage, *let* every man do his duty.

When applied to things not rational, it implies allowance or concession.

O'er golden sands *let* rich Pactolus flow. *Pope.*

5. To retard; to hinder; to impede; to interpose obstructions. 2 Thess. 2.

[This sense is now obsolete, or nearly so.]

To let alone, to leave; to suffer to remain without intermeddling; as, *let alone* this idle project; *let* me *alone.*

To let down, to permit to sink or fall; to lower.

She *let* them *down* by a cord through the window. Josh. ii.

To let loose, to free from restraint; to permit to wander at large.

To let in or *into*, to permit or suffer to enter; to admit. Open the door, *let in* my friend. We are not *let into* the secrets of the cabinet.

To let blood, to open a vein and suffer the blood to flow out.

To let out, to suffer to escape; also, to lease or let to hire.

To let off, to discharge, to let fly, as an arrow; or cause to explode, as a gun.

LET, *v. i.* To forbear. *Obs.* *Bacon.*

LET, *n.* A retarding; hinderance; obstacle; impediment; delay. [*Obsolete, unless in some technical phrases.*]

LET, a termination of diminutives; as *hamlet*, a little house; *rivulet*, a small stream. [Sax. *lyt*, small, less, few. See *Little.*]

LE'THAL, *a.* [L. *lethalis*, mortal, from Gr. ληθη, oblivion.] Deadly; mortal; fatal. *Richardson.*

LETHAL'ITY, *n.* Mortality. *Akins.*

LETHAR'ĠIC, LETHAR'ĠICAL, *a.* [L. *lethargicus*; Fr. *lethargique.*] Preternaturally inclined to sleep; drowsy; dull; heavy. *Arbuthnot.*

LETHAR'ĠICALLY, *adv.* In a morbid sleepiness.

LETHAR'ĠICALNESS, LETHAR'ĠICNESS, *n.* Preternatural or morbid sleepiness or drowsiness. *More. Herbert.*

LETH'ARĠIED, *pp.* or *a.* Laid asleep; entranced. *Shak.*

LETH'ARĠY, *n.* [L. *lethargia*; Gr. ληθαργια; ληθη, oblivion, and αργος, idle.]

1. Preternatural sleepiness; morbid drowsiness; continued or profound sleep, from which a person can scarcely be awaked, and if awaked, remains stupid.

2. Dullness; inaction; inattention.

Europe lay then under a deep *lethargy.* *Atterbury.*

LETH'ARĠY, *v. t.* To make lethargic or dull. *Churchill.*

LE'THE, *n. le'thee.* [Gr. ληθη, forgetfulness; ληθω, L. *lateo*, to be hid.] Oblivion; a draught of oblivion. *Milton.*

LETHE'AN, *a.* Inducing forgetfulness or oblivion. *Lempriere. As. Res.*

LETHIF'EROUS, *a.*[L. *lethum*, death, and *fero*, to bring.]

Deadly; mortal; bringing death or destruction. *Robinson.*

LET'TER, *n.* [from *let.*] One who permits.

2. One who retards or hinders.

3. One who gives vent; as a blood-*letter.*

LET'TER, *n.* [Fr. *lettre*; It. *lettera*; L. *litera*; W. *llythyr.*]

1. A mark or character, written, printed, engraved or painted; used as the representative of a sound, or of an articulation of the human organs of speech. By sounds, and articulations or closures of the organs, are formed syllables and words. Hence a letter is the first element of *written* language, as a simple sound is the first element of *spoken* language or speech. As *sounds* are audible and communicate ideas to others by the ear, so *letters* are visible representatives of sounds, and communicate the thoughts of others by means of the eye.

2. A written or printed message; an epistle; a communication made by visible characters from one person to another at a distance.

The style of *letters* ought to be free, easy and natural. *Walsh.*

3. The verbal expression; the literal meaning.

We must observe the *letter* of the law, without doing violence to the reason of the law, and the intentions of the lawgiver. *Taylor.*

4. Type; a character formed of metal or wood, usually of metal, and used in printing books.

5. *Letters*, in the plural, learning; erudition; as a man of *letters.*

Dead letter, a writing or precept, which is without authority or force. The best law may become a *dead letter.*

Letter of attorney, a writing by which one person authorizes another to act in his stead.

Letter of marque, a private ship commissioned or authorized by a government to make reprisals on the ships of another state. [See *Marque.*]

Letters patent, or *overt, open*, a writing executed and sealed, by which power and authority are granted to a person to do some act, or enjoy some right; as *letters patent* under the seal of England.

LET'TER, *v. t.* To impress or form letters on; as, to *letter* a book; a book gilt and *lettered.*

LET'TER-CASE, *n.* A case or book to put letters in.

LET'TERED, *pp.* Stamped with letters.

LET'TERED, *a.* Literate; educated; versed in literature or science. *Collier.*

2. Belonging to learning; suiting letters.

LET'TER-FOUNDER, *n.* One who casts letters; a type-founder.

LET'TERING, *ppr.* Impressing or forming letters on; as *lettering* a book on the cover.

LET'TERLESS, *a.* Illiterate; unlettered; not learned. *Waterland.*

LET'TER-PRESS, *n.* [*letter* and *press.*] Print; letters and words impressed on paper or other material by types.

LETTUCE, *n. let'tis.* [Fr. *laitue;* It. *lattuga;* Sp. *lechuga;* Arm. *lactuzen;* G. *lattich;* D. *latuw;* from L. *lactuca*, according to Varro, from *lac*, milk.]
A genus of plants, the Lactuca, of many species, some of which are used as salads.

LEU'CIN, LEU'CINE, *n.* [Gr. λευκος, white.] A peculiar white pulverulent substance obtained from beef-fibers, treated with sulphuric acid, and afterwards with alcohol. *Braconnet. Webster's Manual.*

LEU'CITE, *n.* [Gr. λευκος, white.] A stony substance, so called from its whiteness, found among volcanic productions in Italy, in crystals, or in irregular masses; formerly called crystals of white shorl, or white granite or granilite. *Dict. Nat. Hist.*
Haüy calls this mineral, *amphigene.* It is called by some writers *leucolite*, and by others, *dodecahedral zeolite.*

LEUCO-ETHIOP'IC, *a.* [Gr. λευκος, white, and αιθιοψ, black.]
White and black; designating a white animal of a black species, or the albino. *Lawrence.*

LEUCOPHLEG'MACY, *n.* [Gr. λευκος, white, and φλεγμα, phlegm.]
A dropsical habit of body, or the commencement of anasarca; paleness, with viscid juices and cold sweats. *Coxe. Parr. Arbuthnot.*

LEUCOPHLEGMAT'IC, *a.* Having a dropsical habit of body with a white bloated skin.

LEUCO'THIOP, *n.* [See *Leuco-ethiopic.*] An albino; a white man of a black race.

LEU'THRITE, *n.* [from *Leuthra*, in Saxony.]
A substance that appears to be a recomposed rock, of a loose texture, gritty and harsh to the touch. Its color is a grayish white, tinged here and there with an ocherous brown. It includes small fragments of mica. *Phillips.*

LE'VANT, *a.* [Fr. *levant*, rising, from *lever*, L. *levo.*]
Eastern; denoting the part of the hemisphere where the sun rises.
Forth rush the *levant* and the ponent winds. *Milton.*

LEVANT', *n.* [It. *levante*, the East, supra.] Properly, a country to the eastward; but appropriately, the countries of Turkey, Syria, Asia Minor, Greece, Egypt, &c. which are washed by the Mediterranean and its contiguous waters.

LEV'ANTINE, *a.* Pertaining to the Levant. *D'Anville.*
2. Designating a particular kind of silk cloth.

LEV'ANTINE, *n.* A particular kind of silk cloth.

LEVA'TOR, *n.* [L. from *levo*, to raise.] In *anatomy*, a muscle that serves to raise some part, as the lip or the eyelid.
2. A surgical instrument used to raise a depressed part of the skull. *Wiseman.*

LEVE, for *believe. Obs.* *Gower.*

LEV'EE, *n.* [Fr. from *lever*, to raise, L. *levo.*]
1. The time of rising.
2. The concourse of persons who visit a prince or great personage in the morning. *Johnson.*
3. A bank or causey, particularly along a river to prevent inundation; as the *levees* along the Mississippi.

LEV'EL, *a.* [Sax. *læfe*, id.; W. *llyvn*, smooth, even, *level*, sleek, slippery; *llyvelu*, to level, to render uniform, to devise, invent, guess; *llyvnu*, to make smooth. This seems to be connected with *llyvu*, to lick. So *like*, D. *gelyk*, G. *gleich*, is smooth, even, level, equal, coinciding with Eng. *sleek.* The L. *libella*, *libra*, belong to this root; It. *livella.*]
1. Horizontal; coinciding with the plane of the horizon. To be perfectly *level* is to be exactly horizontal.
2. Even; flat; not having one part higher than another; not ascending or descending; as a *level* plain or field; *level* ground; a *level* floor or pavement. In common usage, *level* is often applied to surfaces that are not perfectly horizontal, but which have no inequalities of magnitude.
3. Even with any thing else; of the same highth; on the same line or plane.
4. Equal in rank or degree; having no degree of superiority.
Be *level* in preferments, and you will soon be as *level* in your learning. *Bentley.*

LEV'EL, *v. t.* To make horizontal.
2. To make even; to reduce or remove inequalities of surface in any thing; as, to *level* a road or walk.
3. To reduce or bring to the same highth with something else.
And their proud structures *level* with the ground. *Sandys.*
4. To lay flat; to reduce to an even surface or plain.
He *levels* mountains, and he raises plains. *Dryden.*
5. To reduce to equality of condition, state or degree; as, to *level* all ranks and degrees of men.
6. To point, in taking aim; to elevate or depress so as to direct a missile weapon to an object; to aim; as, to *level* a cannon or musket.
7. To aim; to direct; as severe remarks *leveled* at the vices and follies of the age.
8. To suit; to proportion; as, to *level* observations to the capacity of children.

LEV'EL, *v. i.* To accord; to agree; to suit. [*Little used.*] *Shak.*
2. To aim at; to point a gun or an arrow to the mark.
3. To aim at; to direct the view or purpose.
The glory of God and the good of his church, ought to be the mark at which we *level.* *Hooker.*
4. To be aimed; to be in the same direction with the mark.
He raised it till he *level'd* right. *Butler.*
5. To aim; to make attempts.
Ambitious York did *level* at thy crown. *Shak.*
6. To conjecture; to attempt to guess. [*Not used.*] *Shak.*

LEV'EL, *n.* A horizontal line, or a plane; a surface without inequalities. *Hale.*
2. Rate; standard; usual elevation; customary highth; as the ordinary *level* of the world.
3. Equal elevation with something else; a state of equality.
Providence, for the most part, sets us on a *level.* *Spectator.*
4. The line of direction in which a missile weapon is aimed.
5. An instrument in mechanics by which to find or draw a horizontal line, as in setting buildings, or in making canals and drains. The instruments for these purposes are various; as the air *level*, the carpenter's *level*, the mason's *level*, and the gunner's *level.*
6. Rule; plan; scheme: borrowed from the mechanic's level.
Be the fair *level* of thy actions laid— *Prior.*

LEV'ELED, *pp.* Reduced to a plane; made even.
2. Reduced to an equal state, condition or rank.
3. Reduced to an equality with something else.
4. Elevated or depressed to a right line towards something; pointed to an object; directed to a mark.
5. Suited; proportioned.

LEV'ELER, *n.* One that levels or makes even.
2. One that destroys or attempts to destroy distinctions, and reduce to equality.

LEV'ELING, *ppr.* Making level or even.
2. Reducing to an equality of condition.

LEV'ELING, *n.* The art or practice of finding a horizontal line, or of ascertaining the different elevations of objects on the surface of the earth; in other words, the difference in the distance of objects from the center of the earth. *Encyc.*

LEV'ELNESS, *n.* Evenness; equality of surface.
2. Equality with something else.

LEVEN. [See *Leaven.*]

LEV'EN, *n.* [Sax. *hlifian.*] Lightning. *Obs.* *Chaucer.*

LEV'ER, *n.* [Fr. *levier;* It. *leva;* from *lever*, *levare*, L. *levo*, to raise.]
In *mechanics*, a bar of metal, wood, or other substance, turning on a support called the fulcrum or prop. Its arms are equal, as in the *balance;* or unequal, as in *steelyards.* It is one of the mechanical powers, and is of three kinds, viz. 1. When the fulcrum is between the weight and the power, as in the *handspike*, *crowbar*, &c. 2. When the weight is between the power and the fulcrum, as in *rowing a boat.* 3. When the power is between the weight and the fulcrum, as in *raising a ladder* from the ground, by applying the hands to one of the lower rounds. The bones of animals are levers of the third kind.

LEV'ERET, *n.* [Fr. *lievret*, from *lievre*, a hare.] A hare in the first year of her age.

LEV'EROCK, *n.* A bird, a lark. [See *Lark.*] *Johnson.*

LEV'ET, *n.* [Qu. Fr. *lever*, to raise.] A blast of a trumpet; probably that by which soldiers are called in the morning. [*Not used.*] *Hudibras.*

LEV'IABLE, *a.* [from *levy.*] That may be levied; that may be assessed and collected; as sums *leviable* by course of law. *Bacon.*

LEVI'ATHAN, *n.* [Heb. לויתן.] An aquatic animal, described in the book of Job, ch. xli, and mentioned in other passages of Scripture. In Isaiah, it is called the crooked serpent. It is not agreed what animal is intended by the writers, whether the crocodile, the whale, or a species of serpent.
2. The whale, or a great whale. *Milton.*

LEV'IGATE, *v. t.* [L. *lævigo*, from *lævis*, smooth, Gr. λειος.]
1. In *pharmacy* and *chimistry*, to rub or grind to a fine impalpable powder; to make fine, soft and smooth.
2. To plane; to polish. *Barrow.*

LEV'IGATE, *a.* Made smooth.

LEV'IGATED, *pp.* Reduced to a fine impalpable powder.

LEV'IGATING, *ppr.* Rendering very fine, soft and smooth, by grinding or rubbing.

LEVIGA'TION, *n.* The act or operation of grinding or rubbing a solid substance to a fine impalpable powder. *Encyc.*

LEVITA'TION, *n.* [L. *levis*, *levitas*.] Lightness; buoyancy; act of making light.

LE'VITE, *n.* [from *Levi*, one of the sons of Jacob.]
One of the tribe or family of Levi; a descendant of Levi; more particularly, an officer in the Jewish church, who was employed in manual service, as in bringing wood and other necessaries for the sacrifices. The Levites also sung and played on instruments of music. They were subordinate to the priests, the descendants of Aaron, who was also of the family of Levi. *Encyc.*

LEVIT'ICAL, *a.* Belonging to the Levites, or descendants of Levi; as the *levitical* law, the law given by Moses, which prescribed the duties and rights of the priests and Levites, and regulated the civil and religious concerns of the Jews.
2. Priestly. *Milton.*

LEVIT'ICALLY, *adv.* After the manner of the Levites.

LEVIT'ICUS, *n.* [from *Levi*, *Levite*.] A canonical book of the Old Testament, containing the laws and regulations which relate to the priests and Levites among the Jews, or the body of the ceremonial law.

LEV'ITY, *n.* [L. *levitas*, from *levis*, light; connected perhaps with Eng. *lift*.]
1. Lightness; the want of weight in a body, compared with another that is heavier. The ascent of a balloon in the air is owing to its *levity*, as the gas that fills it is lighter than common air.
2. Lightness of temper or conduct; inconstancy; changeableness; unsteadiness; as the *levity* of youth. *Hooker.*
3. Want of due consideration; vanity; freak. He never employed his omnipotence out of *levity* or ostentation.
4. Gayety of mind; want of seriousness; disposition to trifle. The spirit of religion and seriousness was succeeded by *levity*.

LEV'Y, *v. t.* [Fr. *lever*; It. *levare*; Sp. *levar*; L. *levo*; Eng. to *lift*.]
1. To raise; to collect. To *levy* troops, is to enlist or to order men into public service. To *levy* an army, is to collect troops and form an army by enrollment, conscription or other means.
2. To raise; to collect by assessment; as, to *levy* taxes, toll, tribute, or contributions.
To levy war, is to raise or begin war; to take arms for attack; to attack. *Blackstone.*
To levy a fine, to commence and carry on a suit for assuring the title to lands or tenements. *Blackstone.*

LEV'Y, *n.* The act of collecting men for military, or other public service, as by enlistment, enrollment or other means. 1 Kings ix.
2. Troops collected; an army raised. 1 Kings v.
3. The act of collecting money for public use by tax or other imposition.
4. War raised. [*Not in use.*] *Shak.*

LEW, *a.* [D. *laauw*.] Tepid; lukewarm; pale; wan. *Obs.*

LEWD, *a.* [W. *llodig*, having a craving; *llodi*, to reach out, to crave; *llodineb*, lewdness; *llawd*, that shoots out or is growing, a *lad*; G. *luder*, lewdness; Heb. Ch. Syr. Sam. ילד to beget, to bring forth; Ar. ولد, Eth. ወለደ id.]
1. Given to the unlawful indulgence of lust; addicted to fornication or adultery; dissolute; lustful; libidinous. Ezek. xxiii.
2. Proceeding from unlawful lust; as *lewd* actions.
3. Wicked; vile; profligate; licentious. Acts xvii.

LEWD, *a.* [Sax. *læwed*, *lewd*. This seems to be a contracted word, and either from the root of *laical*, *lay*, or from the Sax. *leod*, G. *leute*, people, which seems to be from the same root as the foregoing word, like L. *gens*, from *geno*.] Lay; laical; not clerical. *Obs.* *Davies.*

LEWD'LY, *adv.* With the unlawful indulgence of lust; lustfully.
2. Wickedly; wantonly.

LEWD'NESS, *n.* The unlawful indulgence of lust; fornication, or adultery.
2. In *Scripture*, it generally denotes idolatry.
3. Licentiousness; shamelessness. *Spenser.*

LEWD'STER, *n.* One given to the criminal indulgence of lust; a lecher. [*Not used.*] *Shak.*

LEXICOG'RAPHER, *n.* [See *Lexicography*.] The author of a lexicon or dictionary.

LEXICOGRAPH'IC, *a.* Pertaining to the writing or compilation of a dictionary. *Boswell.*

LEXICOG'RAPHY, *n.* [Gr. λεξικον, a dictionary, and γραφω, to write.]
1. The act of writing a lexicon or dictionary, or the art of composing dictionaries.
2. The composition or compilation of a dictionary.

LEXICOL'OGY, *n.* [Gr. λεξικον, a dictionary, and λογος, discourse.]
The science of words; that branch of learning which treats of the proper signification and just application of words. *Med. Repos.*

LEX'ICON, *n.* [Gr. λεξικον, a dictionary, from λεξις, λεγω, to speak.]
A dictionary; a vocabulary or book containing an alphabetical arrangement of the words in a language, with the definition of each, or an explanation of its meaning.

LEX'ICONIST, *n.* A writer of a lexicon. [*Little used.*] *Orient. Col.*

LEX'IGRAPHY, *n.* [Gr. λεξις, a word, and γραφω, to write.] The art or practice of defining words. *Med. Repos.*

LEY, a different orthography of *lay* and *lea*, a meadow or *field*.

LHER'ZOLITE, *n.* [from *Lherz*, in the Pyrenees.]
A mineral, a variety of pyroxene. When crystalized, its crystals are brilliant, translucid, very small, and of an emerald green. *Dict.*

LI'ABLE, *a.* [Fr. *lier*, to bind, L. *ligo*; Norm. *lige*, a bond. See *Liege*.]
1. Bound; obliged in law or equity; responsible; answerable. The surety is *liable* for the debt of his principal. The parent is not *liable* for debts contracted by a son who is a minor, except for necessaries.
This use of *liable* is now common among lawyers. The phrase is abridged. The surety is *liable*, that is, bound to pay the debt of his principal.
2. Subject; obnoxious; exposed.
Proudly secure, yet *liable* to fall. *Milton.*
Liable, in this sense, is always applied to evils. We never say, a man is *liable* to happiness or prosperity, but he is *liable* to disease, calamities, censure; he is *liable* to err, to sin, to fall.

LI'ABLENESS, } *n.* The state of being
LIABIL'ITY, } bound or obliged in law or justice; responsibility. The officer wishes to discharge himself from his *liability*.
2. Exposedness; tendency; a state of being subject; as the *liableness* of a man to contract disease in an infected room; a *liability* to accidents.

LIA'R, *n.* [from *lie*.] A person who knowingly utters falsehood; one who declares to another as a fact what he knows to be not true, and with an intention to deceive him. The uttering of falsehood by mistake, and without an intention to deceive, does not constitute one a liar.
2. One who denies Christ. 1 John ii.

LI'ARD, *a.* Gray. *Obs.* *Chaucer.*

LI'AS, *n.* A species of limestone, occurring in flat, horizontal strata, and supposed to be of recent formation. *Encyc.*

LIB, *v. t.* [D. *lubben*.] To castrate. [*Not in use.*] *Chapman.*

LIBA'TION, *n.* [L. *libatio*, from *libo*, to pour out, to taste.]
1. The act of pouring a liquor, usually wine, either on the ground, or on a victim in sacrifice, in honor of some deity. The Hebrews, Greeks and Romans practiced *libation*. This was a solemn act and accompanied with prayer. *Encyc.*
2. The wine or other liquor poured out in honor of a deity. *Stillingfleet.* *Dryden.*

LIBBARD, an obsolete spelling of *leopard*. *Spenser.* *Milton.*

LIB'BARD'S-BANE, *n.* A poisonous plant. *B. Jonson.*

LI'BEL, *n.* [L. *libellus*, a little book, from *liber*, a book, from the sense of bark, and this from stripping, separating. Hence *liber*, a book, and *liber*, free, are the same word. Class Lb. No. 24. 27. 30. 31.]

1. A defamatory writing, L. *libellus famosus.* Hence, the epithet being omitted, *libel* expresses the same thing. Any book, pamphlet, writing or picture, containing representations, maliciously made or published, tending to bring a person into contempt, or expose him to public hatred and derision. The communication of such defamatory writing to a single person, is considered in law a publication. It is immaterial with respect to the essence of a libel, whether the matter of it is true or false, since the provocation and not the falsity is the thing to be punished *criminally.* But in a *civil* action, a libel must appear to be false, as well as scandalous. *Blackstone.*

In a more extensive sense, any blasphemous, treasonable or immoral writing or picture made public, is a libel, and punishable by law.

2. In *the civil law,* and *in courts of admiralty,* a declaration or charge in writing exhibited in court, particularly against a ship or goods, for violating the laws of trade or of revenue.

LI'BEL, *v. t.* To defame or expose to public hatred and contempt by a writing or picture; to lampoon.

> Some wicked wits have *libeled* all the fair. *Pope.*

2. To exhibit a charge against any thing in court, particularly against a ship or goods, for a violation of the laws of trade or revenue.

LI'BEL, *v. i.* To spread defamation, written or printed; with *against.* He *libels against* the peers of the realm. [*Not now in use.*]

LI'BELANT, *n.* One who libels; one who brings a libel or institutes a suit in an admiralty court.

> The counsel for the *libelant,* contended they had a right to read the instructions— *Cranch, Rep.*

LI'BELED, *pp.* Defamed by a writing or picture made public.

2. Charged or declared against in an admiralty court.

LI'BELER, *n.* One who libels or defames by writing or pictures; a lampooner.

> It is ignorance of ourselves which makes us the *libelers* of others. *Buckminster.*

LI'BELING, *ppr.* Defaming by a published writing or picture.

2. Exhibiting charges against in court.

LI'BELOUS, *a.* Defamatory; containing that which exposes a person to public hatred, contempt and ridicule; as a *libelous* pamphlet or picture.

LIB'ERAL, *a.* [Fr. from L. *liberalis,* from *liber,* free. See *Libel.*]

1. Of a free heart; free to give or bestow; not close or contracted; munificent; bountiful; generous; giving largely; as a *liberal* donor; the *liberal* founders of a college or hospital. It expresses less than *profuse* or *extravagant.*

2. Generous; ample; large; as a *liberal* donation; a *liberal* allowance.

3. Not selfish, narrow or contracted; catholic; enlarged; embracing other interests than one's own; as *liberal* sentiments or views; a *liberal* mind; *liberal* policy.

4. General; extensive; embracing literature and the sciences generally; as a *liberal* education. This phrase is often but not necessarily synonymous with *collegiate;* as a *collegiate* education.

5. Free; open; candid; as a *liberal* communication of thoughts.

6. Large; profuse; as a *liberal* discharge of matter by secretions or excretions.

7. Free; not literal or strict; as a *liberal* construction of law.

8. Not mean; not low in birth or mind.

9. Licentious; free to excess. *Shak.*

Liberal arts, as distinguished from *mechanical arts,* are such as depend more on the exertion of the mind than on the labor of the hands, and regard amusement, curiosity or intellectual improvement, rather than the necessity of subsistence, or manual skill. Such are grammar, rhetoric, painting, sculpture, architecture, music, &c.

Liberal has *of* before the thing bestowed, and *to* before the person or object on which any thing is bestowed; as, to be *liberal of* praise or censure; *liberal to* the poor.

LIBERAL'ITY, *n.* [L. *liberalitas;* Fr. *libéralité.* See *Liberal.*]

1. Munificence; bounty.

> That *liberality* is but cast away,
> Which makes us borrow what we cannot pay. *Denham.*

2. A particular act of generosity; a donation; a gratuity. In this sense, it has the plural number. A prudent man is not impoverished by his *liberalities.*

3. Largeness of mind; catholicism; that comprehensiveness of mind which includes other interests beside its own, and duly estimates in its decisions the value or importance of each. It is evidence of a noble mind to judge of men and things with *liberality.*

> Many treat the gospel with indifference under the name of *liberality.* *J. M. Mason.*

4. Candor; impartiality.

LIB'ERALIZE, *v. t.* To render liberal or catholic; to enlarge; to free from narrow views or prejudices; as, to *liberalize* the mind. *Burke. Walsh.*

LIB'ERALIZED, *pp.* Freed from narrow views and prejudices; made liberal.

LIB'ERALIZING, *ppr.* Rendering liberal; divesting of narrow views and prejudices.

LIB'ERALLY, *adv.* Bountifully; freely; largely; with munificence.

> If any of you lack wisdom, let him ask of God, who giveth to all men *liberally,* and upbraideth not. James i.

2. With generous and impartial regard to other interests than our own; with enlarged views; without selfishness or meanness; as, to think or judge *liberally* of men and their actions.

3. Freely; not strictly; not literally.

LIB'ERATE, *v. t.* [L. *libero,* from *liber,* free; Fr. *liberer;* It. *liberare.*]

1. To free; to release from restraint or bondage; to set at liberty; as, to *liberate* one from duress or imprisonment; to *liberate* the mind from the shackles of prejudice.

2. To manumit; as, to *liberate* a slave.

LIB'ERATED, *pp.* Freed; released from confinement, restraint or slavery; manumitted.

LIB'ERATING, *ppr.* Delivering from restraint or slavery.

LIBERA'TION, *n.* [L. *liberatio.*] The act of delivering from restraint, confinement or slavery.

LIB'ERATOR, *n.* One who liberates or delivers.

LIBERTA'RIAN, *a.* [L. *liber,* free; *libertas,* liberty.]

Pertaining to liberty, or to the doctrine of free will, as opposed to the doctrine of necessity.

> Remove from their mind *libertarian* prejudice. *Encyc.*

LIB'ERTINAĠE, *n.* Libertinism, which is most used.

LIB'ERTINE, *n.* [L. *libertinus,* from *liber,* free.]

1. Among the Romans, a freedman; a person manumitted or set free from legal servitude.

2. One unconfined; one free from restraint. *Shak.*

3. A man who lives without restraint of the animal passion; one who indulges his lust without restraint; one who leads a dissolute, licentious life; a rake; a debauchee.

LIB'ERTINE, *a.* Licentious; dissolute; not under the restraint of law or religion; as *libertine* principles; a *libertine* life.

LIB'ERTINISM, *n.* State of a freedman. [*Little used.*] *Hammond.*

2. Licentiousness of opinion and practice; an unrestrained indulgence of lust; debauchery; lewdness. *Atterbury.*

LIB'ERTY, *n.* [L. *libertas,* from *liber,* free; Fr. *liberté;* It. *libertà;* Sp. *libertad.* Class Lb. No. 24. 27. 30. 31.]

1. Freedom from restraint, in a general sense, and applicable to the body, or to the will or mind. The body is at *liberty,* when not confined; the will or mind is at *liberty,* when not checked or controlled. A man enjoys *liberty,* when no physical force operates to restrain his actions or volitions.

2. *Natural liberty,* consists in the power of acting as one thinks fit, without any restraint or control, except from the laws of nature. It is a state of exemption from the control of others, and from positive laws and the institutions of social life. This liberty is abridged by the establishment of government.

3. *Civil liberty,* is the liberty of men in a state of society, or natural liberty, so far only abridged and restrained, as is necessary and expedient for the safety and interest of the society, state or nation. A restraint of natural liberty, not necessary or expedient for the public, is tyranny or oppression. Civil liberty is an exemption from the arbitrary will of others, which exemption is secured by established laws, which restrain every man from injuring or controlling another. Hence the restraints of law are essential to *civil liberty.*

> The *liberty* of one depends not so much on the removal of all restraint from him, as on the due restraint upon the *liberty* of others. *Ames.*

In this sentence, the latter word *liberty* denotes *natural liberty.*

4. *Political liberty,* is sometimes used as synonymous with *civil liberty.* But it more properly designates the *liberty of a nation,* the freedom of a nation or state from all unjust abridgment of its rights and independence by another nation. Hence we

often speak of the *political liberties* of Europe, or the nations of Europe.

5. *Religious liberty*, is the free right of adopting and enjoying opinions on religious subjects, and of worshiping the Supreme Being according to the dictates of conscience, without external control.

6. *Liberty*, in metaphysics, as opposed to *necessity*, is the power of an agent to do or forbear any particular action, according to the determination or thought of the mind, by which either is preferred to the other. *Locke.*

Freedom of the will; exemption from compulsion or restraint in willing or volition.

7. Privilege; exemption; immunity enjoyed by prescription or by grant; with a plural. Thus we speak of the *liberties* of the commercial cities of Europe.

8. Leave; permission granted. The witness obtained *liberty* to leave the court.

9. A space in which one is permitted to pass without restraint, and beyond which he may not lawfully pass; with a plural; as the *liberties* of a prison.

10. Freedom of action or speech beyond the ordinary bounds of civility or decorum. Females should repel all improper *liberties.*

To take the liberty to do or say any thing, to use freedom not specially granted.

To set at liberty, to deliver from confinement; to release from restraint.

To be at liberty, to be free from restraint.

Liberty of the press, is freedom from any restriction on the power to publish books; the free power of publishing what one pleases, subject only to punishment for abusing the privilege, or publishing what is mischievous to the public or injurious to individuals. *Blackstone.*

LIB'IDINIST, *n.* One given to lewdness. *Junius.*

LIBID'INOUS, *a.* [L. *libidinosus*, from *libido*, *lubido*, lust, from *libeo*, *libet*, *lubet*, to please, it pleaseth; G. *liebe*, love; *lieben*, to love; Eng. *love*, which see. The root is *lib* or *lub.*]

Lustful; lewd; having an eager appetite for venereal pleasure. *Bentley.*

LIBID'INOUSLY, *a.* Lustfully; with lewd desire.

LIBID'INOUSNESS, *n.* The state or quality of being lustful; inordinate appetite for venereal pleasure.

LI'BRA, *n.* [L.] The balance; the seventh sign in the zodiac, which the sun enters at the autumnal equinox, in September.

LIBRA'RIAN, *n.* [L. *librarius*, with a different signification, from *liber*, bark, a book.]

1. The keeper or one who has the care of a library or collection of books.

2. One who transcribes or copies books. [*Not now used.*] *Broome.*

LI'BRARY, *n.* [L. *librarium*, *libraria*, from *liber*, a book.]

1. A collection of books belonging to a private person, or to a public institution or a company.

2. An edifice or an apartment for holding a collection of books.

LI'BRATE, *v. t.* [L. *libro*, from *libra*, a balance, a level; allied perhaps to Eng. *level.*]

To poise; to balance; to hold in equipoise.

LI'BRATE, *v. i.* To move, as a balance; to be poised.

> Their parts all *librate* on too nice a beam. *Clifton.*

LIBRA'TION, *n.* The act of balancing or state of being balanced; a state of equipoise, with equal weights on both sides of a center.

2. In *astronomy*, an apparent irregularity of the moon's motions, by which it seems to librate about its axis. *Encyc.*

> *Libration* is the balancing motion or trepidation in the firmament, whereby the declination of the sun and the latitude of the stars change from time to time. *Dict. Trev.*

3. A balancing or equipoise between extremes. *Darwin.*

LI'BRATORY, *a.* Balancing; moving like a balance, as it tends to an equipoise or level.

LICE, *plu.* of *louse.*

LICE-BANE, *n.* A plant.

LI'CENSE, *n.* [Fr. from L. *licentia*, from *liceo*, to be permitted, Ir. *leighim*, *ligim*, to allow or permit.]

1. Leave; permission; authority or liberty given to do or forbear any act. A *license* may be verbal or written; when *written*, the paper containing the authority is called a *license.* A man is not permitted to retail spirituous liquors till he has obtained a *license.*

2. Excess of liberty; exorbitant freedom; freedom abused, or used in contempt of law or decorum.

> *License* they mean, when they cry liberty. *Milton.*

LI'CENSE, *v. t.* To permit by grant of authority; to remove legal restraint by a grant of permission; as, to *license* a man to keep an inn.

2. To authorize to act in a particular character; as, to *license* a physician or a lawyer.

3. To dismiss. [*Not in use.*] *Wotton.*

LI'CENSER, *n.* One who grants permission; a person authorized to grant permission to others; as a *licenser* of the press.

LICEN'TIATE, *n.* [from L. *licentia.*] One who has a license; as a *licentiate* in physic or medicine.

2. In *Spain*, one who has a degree; as a *licentiate* in law or divinity. The officers of justice are mostly distinguished by this title. *Encyc.*

LICEN'TIATE, *v. t.* To give license or permission. *L'Estrange.*

LICEN'TIOUS, *a.* [L. *licentiosus.*] Using license; indulging freedom to excess; unrestrained by law or morality; loose; dissolute; as a *licentious* man.

2. Exceeding the limits of law or propriety; wanton; unrestrained; as *licentious* desires. *Licentious* thoughts precede *licentious* conduct.

LICEN'TIOUSLY, *adv.* With excess of liberty; in contempt of law and morality.

LICEN'TIOUSNESS, *n.* Excessive indulgence of liberty; contempt of the just restraints of law, morality and decorum. The *licentiousness* of authors is justly condemned; the *licentiousness* of the press is punishable by law.

> Law is the god of wise men; *licentiousness* is the god of fools. *Plato.*

LICH, *a.* [Sax. *lic.* See *Like.*] Like; even; equal. *Obs.* *Gower.*

LICH, *n.* [Sax. *lic* or *lice*, a body, the flesh, a dead body or corpse; *lichama*, a living body; hence *lichwake*, watching with the dead; *Lichfield*, the field of dead bodies; Goth. *leik*, the flesh, a body; *leikan*, to please, Sax. *licean*; Goth. *leiks*, like; G. *gleich*, D. *lyk* and *gelyk*, like; G. *leiche*, a dead body, D. *lyk*; Heb. חלק chalak, smooth; Ar. حلق chalaka, to shave, to make smooth; خلق galaka, to measure, to form, to create, to make smooth and equable, to be beautiful; derivatives, creature, man, people. We see the radical sense is smooth, or rather to make even, equal, smooth; hence like, likeness, and a body. We have here an instance of the radical sense of *man* and *body*, almost exactly analogous to that of *Adam*, from דמה to make equal, to be like.]

LICH'EN, *n.* [L. from Gr. λειχην.] In *botany*, the name for an extensive division of cryptogamian plants, constituting a genus in the order of Algæ, in the Linnean system, but now forming a distinct natural order. They appear in the form of thin flat crusts, covering rocks and the bark of trees, or in foliaceous expansions, or branched like a shrub in miniature, or sometimes only as a gelatinous mass, or a powdery substance. They are called rock moss and tree moss, and some of the liverworts are of this order. They also include the Iceland moss and the reindeer moss; but they are entirely distinct from the true mosses *(Musci.)* *Ed. Encyc.*

2. In *surgery*, a species of impetigo, appearing in the form of a red, dry, rough, and somewhat prurient spot, that gives off small furfuraceous scales. *Hooper.*

LICHENOGRAPH'IC, **LICHENOGRAPH'ICAL**, *a.* Pertaining to lichenography.

LICHENOG'RAPHIST, *n.* One who describes the lichens.

LICHENOG'RAPHY, *n.* [*lichen* and γραφω, to write.]

A description of the vegetables called lichens; the science which illustrates the natural history of the lichens. *Acharius.*

LIC'IT, *a.* [L. *licitus.*] Lawful.

LIC'ITLY, *adv.* Lawfully.

LIC'ITNESS, *n.* Lawfulness.

LICK, *v. t.* [Sax. *liccian*; Goth. *laigwan*; G. *lecken*, *schlecken*; D. *likken*; Dan. *likker*, *slikker*; Sw. *slekia*, *slikia*; Fr. *lecher*; It. *leccare*; Ir. *leagaim*, *lighim*; Russ. *lokayu*, *liju*; L. *lingo*; Gr. λειχω. Class Lg. No. 12. 18. See *Like* and *Sleek.*]

1. To pass or draw the tongue over the surface; as, a dog *licks* a wound. *Temple.*

2. To lap; to take in by the tongue; as, a dog or cat *licks* milk. 1 Kings xxi.

To lick up, to devour; to consume entirely.

> Now shall this company *lick up* all that are round about us, as an ox *licketh up* the grass of the field. Numb. xxii.

To lick the dust, to be slain; to perish in battle.

> His enemies shall *lick the dust.* Ps. lxxii.

LICK, *n.* In *America*, a place where beasts of the forest lick for salt, at salt springs.

LICK, *n.* [W. *llaç*, a lick, a slap, a ray, a blade; *llaçiaw*, to lick, to shoot out, to throw or lay about, to cudgel. Qu. the root of *flog* and *slay*, to strike. See Ar. لَكَّ lakka, to strike. Class Lg. No. 14.]

1. A blow; a stroke. [*Not an elegant word.*]
2. A wash; something rubbed on. [*Not in use.*]

LICK, *v. t.* To strike repeatedly for punishment; to flog; to chastise with blows. [Not an elegant word; but probably *flog*, L. *fligo*, is from the root of this word.]

LICK'ER, *n.* One that licks.

LICK'ERISH, *a.* [D. Dan. *lekker*, G. *lecker*, Sw. *läcker*, nice, dainty, delicate. This seems to be connected with D. *lekken*, G. *lecken*, Dan. *lekker*, Sw. *läcka*, to leak, for in D. the verb signifies also to make *sleek* or smooth, and in G. to *lick*, which unites the word with *lick*, and perhaps with *like*. In Sax. *liccera* is a glutton, and this is the It. *lecco*, a glutton, a *lecher*; *leccardo*, greedy; *leccare*, to lick. The Arm. has *lickez*, lickerish. The phrase, the *mouth waters for a thing*, may throw light on this word, and if the first syllable of *delight*, *delicious* and *delicate*, is a prefix, these are of the same family, as may be the Gr. γλυκυς, sweet. The senses of *watery*, *smooth*, *sweet*, are allied; *likeness* is often connected with *smoothness*, in radical sense, and *sleek* is probably from the root of *lick*, *like*.]

1. Nice in the choice of food; dainty; as a *lickerish* palate. *L'Estrange.*
2. Eager; greedy to swallow; eager to taste or enjoy; having a keen relish. *Sidney. Dryden. Locke.*
3. Dainty; tempting the appetite; as *lickerish* baits. *Milton.*

LICK'ERISHLY, *adv.* Daintily.

LICK'ERISHNESS, *n.* Niceness of palate; daintiness.

LIC'ORICE, *n.* [It. *liquirizia*; L. *glycyrrhiza*; Gr. γλυκυρριζα; γλυκυς, sweet, and ριζα, root.]

A plant of the genus Glycyrrhiza. The root of this plant abounds with a sweet balsamic juice, much used in pectoral compositions. *Encyc.*

LICOROUS, LICOROUSNESS, for *lickerish*, &c. not used.

LIC'TOR, *n.* [L. Qu. *lick*, to strike.] An officer among the Romans, who bore an ax and fasces or rods, as ensigns of his office. The duty of a lictor was to attend the chief magistrates when they appeared in public, to clear the way and cause due respect to be paid to them. A dictator was attended by twenty four lictors, a consul by twelve, and a master of the horse by six. It was also the duty of lictors to apprehend and punish criminals. *Encyc. Johnson.*

LID, *n.* [Sax. *hlid*, a cover; *hlidan*, to cover; *ge-hlid*, a roof; D. Dan. *lid*; L. *claudo*, *cludo*; Gr. κλειω, contracted from κλειδοω; Heb. לאט or לוט to cover, Ar. لَطَّ latta. Class Ld. No. 1. 8. 9.]

A cover; that which shuts the opening of a vessel or box; as the *lid* of a chest or trunk; also, the cover of the eye, the membrane which is drawn over the eyeball of an animal at pleasure, and which is intended for its protection; the *eyelid*.

LIE, water impregnated with alkaline salt, is written *lye*, to distinguish it from *lie*, a falsehood.

LIE, *n.* [Sax. *lig* or *lyge*; Sw. *lögn*; Dan. *lögn*; D. *leugen*; G. *lug*, *lüge*; Russ. *loj*. The verb is probably the primary word.]

1. A criminal falsehood; a falsehood uttered for the purpose of deception; an intentional violation of truth. Fiction, or a false statement or representation, not intended to deceive, mislead or injure, as in fables, parables and the like, is not a lie.

> It is willful deceit that makes a *lie*. A man may act a *lie*, as by pointing his finger in a wrong direction, when a traveler inquires of him his road. *Paley.*

2. A fiction; *in a ludicrous sense.* *Dryden.*
3. False doctrine. 1 John ii.
4. An idolatrous picture of God, or a false god. Rom. i.
5. That which deceives and disappoints confidence. Micah i.

To give the lie, to charge with falsehood. A man's actions may *give the lie* to his words.

LIE, *v. i.* [Sax. *ligan*, *leogan*; Dan. *lyver*; Sw. *liuga*; G. *lügen*; D. *leugenen*; Russ. *lgu*.]

1. To utter falsehood with an intention to deceive, or with an immoral design.

> Thou hast not *lied* to men, but to God. Acts v.

2. To exhibit a false representation; to say or do that which deceives another, when he has a right to know the truth, or when morality requires a just representation.

LIE, *v. i.* pret. *lay*; pp. *lain*, [*lien*, *obs.*] [Sax. *ligan* or *licgan*; Goth. *ligan*; Sw. *liggia*; Dan. *ligger*; D. *liggen*; G. *liegen*; Russ. *leju*; Gr. λεγομαι. The Gr. word usually signifies to speak, which is to utter or throw out sounds. Hence to *lie down* is to throw one's self down, and probably *lie* and *lay* are of one family, as are *jacio* and *jaceo*, in Latin.]

1. To be in a horizontal position, or nearly so, and to rest on any thing lengthwise, and not on the end. Thus a person *lies* on a bed, and a fallen tree on the ground. A cask stands on its end, but *lies* on its side.
2. To rest in an inclining posture; to lean; as, to *lie* on or against a column.
3. To rest; to press on.
4. To be reposited in the grave.

> All the kings of the earth, even all of them, *lie* in glory. Is. xiv.

5. To rest on a bed or couch; to be prostrate; as, to *lie* sick.

> My little daughter *lieth* at the point of death. Mark v.

6. To be situated. New Haven *lies* in the forty second degree of north latitude. Ireland *lies* west of England.

> Envy *lies* between beings equal in nature, though unequal in circumstances. *Collier.*

7. To be; to rest; to abide; to remain; often followed by some word denoting a particular condition; as, to *lie* waste; to *lie* fallow; to *lie* open; to *lie* hid; to *lie* pining or grieving; to *lie* under one's displeasure; to *lie* at the mercy of a creditor, or at the mercy of the waves.
8. To consist.

> He that thinks that diversion may not *lie* in hard labor, forgets the early rising of the huntsman. *Locke.*

9. To be sustainable in law; to be capable of being maintained. An action *lies* against the tenant for waste.

> An appeal *lies* in this case. *Ch. J. Parsons.*

To lie at, to teaze or importune. [*Little used.*]

To lie at the heart, to be fixed as an object of affection or anxious desire.

> The Spaniards have but one temptation to quarrel with us, the recovering of Jamaica, for that has ever *lain at their hearts*. *Temple.*

To lie by, to be reposited, or remaining with. He has the manuscript *lying by* him.

2. To rest; to intermit labor. We *lay by* during the heat of the day.

To lie in the way, to be an obstacle or impediment. Remove the objections that *lie in the way* of an amicable adjustment.

To lie hard or *heavy*, to press; to oppress; to burden.

To lie on hand, to be or remain in possession; to remain unsold or undisposed of. Great quantities of wine *lie on hand*, or have *lain* long *on hand*.

To lie on the hands, to remain unoccupied or unemployed; to be tedious. Men are sometimes at a loss to know how to employ the time that *lies on their hands*.

To lie on the head, to be imputed.

> What he gets more of her than sharp words, let it *lie on my head*. *Shak.*

To lie in wait, to wait for in concealment; to lie in ambush; to watch for an opportunity to attack or seize.

To lie in one, to be in the power of; to belong to.

> As much as *lieth in you*, live peaceably with all men. Rom. xii.

To lie down, to lay the body on the ground or other level place; also, to go to rest.

To lie in, to be in childbed; to bring forth young.

To lie under, to be subject to; to suffer; to be oppressed by.

To lie on or *upon*, to be a matter of obligation or duty. It *lies on* the plaintiff to maintain his action.

To lie with, to lodge or sleep with; also, to have carnal knowledge of.

2. To belong to. It *lies with* you to make amends.

To lie over, to remain unpaid, after the time when payment is due; as a note in bank.

To lie to, to be stationary, as a ship.

LIEF, *a.* [Sax. *leof*, loved, D. *lief*, G. *lieb*. See *Love*.] Dear; beloved. *Obs.* *Spenser. Shak.*

LIEF, *adv.* [supra. This word coincides with *love*, L. *lubet*, *libet*, and the primary sense is to be free, prompt, ready.]

Gladly; willingly; freely; used in familiar speech, in the phrase, I had as *lief* go as not. It has been supposed that *had* in this phrase is a corruption of *would*. At any rate it is anomalous.

LIEGE, *a.* [It. *ligio*; Fr. *lige*; from L. *ligo*, to bind; Gr. λυγοω, to bind, to bend; λυγος, a withe.]

Bound by a feudal tenure; obliged to be faithful and loyal to a superior, as a vassal to his lord; subject; faithful; as a *liege* man. By *liege* homage, a vassal was bound to serve his lord against all, without excepting his sovereign; or against all, excepting a former lord to whom he owed like service. *Encyc.*

2. Sovereign; as a *liege* lord. [See the Noun.]

LIEGE, *n.* [supra.] A vassal holding a fee by which he is bound to perform certain services and duties to his lord.

2. A lord or superior; a sovereign.

[Note. This is a false application of the word, arising probably from transferring the word from the vassal to the lord; the lord of *liege men*, being called *liege lord.* *Johnson.*]

LIE'GE-MAN, *n.* A vassal; a subject. *Obs.* *Spenser. Shak.*

LIEN, the obsolete participle of *lie.* [See *Lain.*]

LIEN, *n.* [supra.] A legal claim; as a *lien* upon land.

LIENTER'IC, *a.* [from *lientery.*] Pertaining to a lientery. *Grew.*

LI'ENTERY, *n.* [Fr. *lienterie;* L. It. *lienteria;* Gr. λειον, smooth, and εντερον, an intestine.]

A flux of the bowels, in which the aliments are discharged undigested, and with little alteration either in color or substance. *Encyc.*

LIER, *n.* [from *lie.*] One who lies down; one who rests or remains; as a *lier* in wait or in ambush. Josh. viii.

LIEU, *n.* [Fr. from the root of L. *locus*, Eng. *ley* or *lea.* See *Ley.*]

Place; room; stead. It is used only with *in.* Let me have gold *in lieu* of silver. *In lieu* of fashionable honor, let justice be substituted.

LIEUTENANCY, *n.* *luten'ancy.* [See *Lieutenant.*]

1. The office or commission of a lieutenant. *Shak.*

2. The body of lieutenants. *Felton.*

LIEUTENANT, *n.* *luten'ant.* [Fr.; composed of *lieu*, place, and *tenant*, L. *tenens*, holding.]

1. An officer who supplies the place of a superior in his absence. Officers of this kind are civil, as the lord-*lieutenant* of a kingdom or county; or military, as a *lieutenant* general, a *lieutenant* colonel.

2. In *military affairs*, the second commissioned officer in a company of infantry cavalry or artillery.

3. In *ships of war*, the officer next in rank to the captain.

LIEUTENANTSHIP. [See *Lieutenancy.*]

LIEVE, for *lief*, is vulgar. [See *Lief.*]

LIE'VRITE, *n.* A mineral, called also *yenite*, which see.

LIFE, *n.* plu. *lives.* [Sax. *lif, lyf;* Sw. *lif;* Dan. *liv;* G. *leben;* D. *leeven.* See *Live.*]

1. In *a general sense*, that state of animals and plants, or of an organized being, in which its natural functions and motions are performed, or in which its organs are capable of performing their functions. A tree is not destitute of life in winter, when the functions of its organs are suspended; nor man during a swoon or syncope; nor strictly birds, quadrupeds or serpents during their torpitude in winter. They are not strictly dead, till the functions of their organs are incapable of being renewed.

2. In *animals*, animation; vitality; and in *man*, that state of being in which the soul and body are united.

He entreated me not to take his *life.* *Broome.*

3. In *plants*, the state in which they grow or are capable of growth, by means of the circulation of the sap. The *life* of an oak may be two, three, or four hundred years.

4. The present state of existence; the time from birth to death. The *life* of man seldom exceeds seventy years.

If in this *life* only we have hope in Christ, we are of all men most miserable. 1 Cor. xv.

5. Manner of living; conduct; deportment, in regard to morals.

I will teach my family to lead good *lives.* *Mrs. Barker.*

6. Condition; course of living, in regard to happiness and misery. We say, a man's *life* has been a series of prosperity, or misfortune.

7. Blood, the supposed vehicle of animation.

And the warm *life* came issuing through the wound. *Pope.*

8. Animals in general; animal being.

Full nature swarms with *life.* *Thomson.*

9. System of animal nature.

Lives through all *life.* *Pope.*

10. Spirit; animation; briskness; vivacity; resolution.

They have no notion of *life* and fire in fancy and words. *Felton.*

11. The living form; real person or state; in opposition to a *copy;* as, a picture is taken from the *life*; a description from the *life.*

12. Exact resemblance; with *to*, before *life.* His portrait is drawn *to* the *life.*

13. General state of man, or of social manners; as the studies and arts that polish *life.*

14. Condition; rank in society; as high *life* and low *life.*

15. Common occurrences; course of things; human affairs.

But to know
That which before us lies in daily *life*,
Is the prime wisdom. *Milton.*

16. A person; a living being; usually or always, a human being. How many *lives* were sacrificed during the revolution!

17. Narrative of a past life; history of the events of life; biographical narration. Johnson wrote the *life* of Milton, and the *lives* of other poets.

18. In *Scripture*, nourishment; support of life.

For the tree of the field is man's *life.* Deut. xx.

19. The stomach or appetite.

His *life* abhorreth bread. Job xxxiii.

20. The enjoyments or blessings of the present life.

Having the promise of the *life* that now is, and of that which is to come. 1 Tim. iv.

21. Supreme felicity.

To be spiritually minded is *life* and peace. Rom. viii.

22. Eternal happiness in heaven. Rom. v.

23. Restoration to life. Rom. v.

24. The author and giver of supreme felicity.

I am the way, the truth, and the *life.* John xiv.

25. A quickening, animating and strengthening principle, in a moral sense. John vi.

LI'FE-BLOOD, *n.* The blood necessary to life; vital blood. *Dryden.*

2. That which constitutes or gives strength and energy.

Money, the *life-blood* of the nation. *Swift.*

LI'FE-BLOOD, *a.* Necessary as blood to life; essential. *Milton.*

LIFE-ESTA'TE, *n.* An estate that continues during the life of the possessor.

LIFE-EVERL'ASTING, *n.* A plant of the genus Gnaphalium.

LI'FE-GIVING, *a.* Having power to give life; inspiriting; invigorating. *Spenser. Milton.*

LI'FEGUARD, *n.* A guard of the life or person; a guard that attends the person of a prince, or other person.

LI'FELESS, *a.* Dead; deprived of life; as a *lifeless* body.

2. Destitute of life; unanimated; as *lifeless* matter.

3. Destitute of power, force, vigor or spirit; dull; heavy; inactive.

4. Void of spirit; vapid; as liquor.

5. Torpid.

6. Wanting physical energy.

LI'FELESSLY, *adv.* Without vigor; dully; frigidly; heavily.

LI'FELESSNESS, *n.* Destitution of life, vigor and spirit; inactivity.

LI'FELIKE, *a.* Like a living person. *Pope.*

LI'FERENT, *n.* The rent of an estate that continues for life.

LI'FESTRING, *n.* A nerve or string that is imagined to be essential to life.

LI'FETIME, *n.* The time that life continues; duration of life. *Addison.*

LI'FEWEARY, *a.* Tired of life; weary of living. *Shak.*

LIFT, *v. t.* [Sw. *lyfta*, Dan. *löfter*, to lift; Goth. *hlifan*, to steal; Sax. *hlifian*, to be high or conspicuous; Goth. *hliftus*, a thief. We retain this sense in *shoplifter.* L. *levo*, *elevo*, It. *levare*, to lift; Sp. *levar*, to carry or transport; Fr. *lever;* perhaps L. *levis*, light.]

1. To raise; to elevate; as, to *lift* the foot or the hand; to *lift* the head.

2. To raise; to elevate mentally.

To thee, O Lord, do I *lift* up my soul. Ps. xxv.

3. To raise in fortune.

The eye of the Lord *lifted* up his head from misery. *Ecclus.*

4. To raise in estimation, dignity or rank. His fortune has *lifted* him into notice, or into office.

The Roman virtues *lift* up mortal man. *Addison.*

5. To elate; to cause to swell, as with pride. *Up* is often used after *lift*, as a qualifying word; sometimes with effect or emphasis; very often, however, it is useless.

6. To bear; to support. *Spenser.*

7. To steal, that is, to take and carry away. Hence we retain the use of *shoplifter*, although the verb in this sense is obsolete.

8. In *Scripture*, to crucify.

When ye have *lifted* up the Son of man. John viii.

To lift up the eyes, to look; to fix the eyes on.

Lot *lifted up his eyes* and beheld Jordan. Gen. xiii.

2. To direct the desires to God in prayer. Ps. cxxi.

To lift up the head, to raise from a low condition; to exalt. Gen. xl.

2. To rejoice. Luke xxi.

To lift up the hand, to swear, or to confirm by oath. Gen. xiv.

2. To raise the hands in prayer. Ps. xxviii.
3. To rise in opposition to; to rebel; to assault. 2 Sam. xviii.
4. To injure or oppress. Job xxxi.
5. To shake off sloth and engage in duty. Heb. xii.

To lift up the face, to look to with confidence, cheerfulness and comfort. Job xxii.

To lift up the heel against, to treat with insolence and contempt.

To lift up the horn, to behave arrogantly or scornfully. Ps. lxxv.

To lift up the feet, to come speedily to one's relief. Ps. lxxiv.

To lift up the voice, to cry aloud; to call out, either in grief or joy. Gen. xxi. Is. xxiv.

LIFT, *v. i.* To try to raise; to exert the strength for the purpose of raising or bearing.

The body strained by *lifting* at a weight too heavy— *Locke.*

2. To practice theft. *Obs.* *Spenser.*

LIFT, *n.* The act of raising; a lifting; as the *lift* of the feet in walking or running. *Bacon.*

The goat gives the fox a *lift*. *L'Estrange.*

2. An effort to raise; as, give us a *lift*. [*Popular use.*]
3. That which is to be raised.
4. A *dead lift*, an ineffectual effort to raise; or the thing which the strength is not sufficient to raise.
5. Any thing to be done which exceeds the strength; or a state of inability; as, to help one at a *dead lift*. *Butler. Swift.*
6. A rise; a degree of elevation; as the *lift* of a lock in canals. *Gallatin.*
7. In *Scottish*, the sky; the atmosphere; the firmament. [Sax. *lyft*, air, Sw. *luft*.]
8. In *seamen's language*, a rope descending from the cap and mast-head to the extremity of a yard. Its use is to support the yard, keep it in equilibrio, and raise the end, when occasion requires. *Mar. Dict.*

LIFT'ED, *pp.* Raised; elevated; swelled with pride.

LIFT'ER, *n.* One that lifts or raises.

LIFT'ING, *ppr.* Raising; swelling with pride.

LIFT'ING, *n.* The act of lifting; assistance.

LIG, *v. i.* To lie. [See *Lie.*] *Obs.* *Chaucer.*

LIG'AMENT, *n.* [L. *ligamentum*, from *ligo*, to bind, that is, to strain.]

1. Any thing that ties or unites one thing or part to another.

Interwoven is the love of liberty with every *ligament* of your hearts. *Washington.*

2. In *anatomy*, a strong, compact substance, serving to bind one bone to another. It is a white, solid, inelastic, tendinous substance, softer than cartilage, but harder than membrane. *Encyc. Quincy. Coxe.*
3. Bond; chain; that which binds or restrains. *Addison.*

LIGAMENT'AL, LIGAMENT'OUS, *a.* Composing a ligament; of the nature of a ligament; binding; as a strong *ligamentous* membrane. *Wiseman.*

LIGA'TION, *n.* [L. *ligatio.*] The act of binding, or state of being bound. *Addison.*

LIG'ATURE, *n.* [Fr. from L. *ligatura.*]

1. Any thing that binds; a band or bandage. *Ray.*
2. The act of binding; as, by a strict *ligature* of the parts. *Arbuthnot.*
3. Impotence induced by magic. *Coxe. Encyc.*
4. In *music*, a band or line connecting notes.
5. Among *printers*, a double character, or a type consisting of two letters or characters united; as *ﬂ*, *ﬁ*, in English. The old editions of Greek authors abound with *ligatures*.
6. The state of being bound. *Mortimer.*
7. In *medicine*, stiffness of a joint. *Coxe.*
8. In *surgery*, a cord or string for tying the blood vessels, particularly the arteries, to prevent hemorrhage.

LIGHT, *n. lite.* [Sax. *leoht, liht;* D. G. *licht;* L. *lux*, light, and *luceo*, to shine; Port. Sp. *luz*, light; W. *llug*, tending to break out or open, or to shoot, to gleam, and as a noun, a breaking out in blotches, a gleam, indistinct light; *llwg*, that is apt to break out, that is bright, a tumor, an eruption; *llygu*, to make bright, to clear, to break out, to appear in spots; *lluç*, a darting, sudden throw, glance, flash; *lluçiaw*, to throw, to fling, to pelt; *lluçed*, a gleam, lightning. This word furnishes a full and distinct explanation of the original sense of light, to throw, dart, shoot, or break forth; and it accords with Eng. *luck*, both in elements and radical sense. Class Lg. No. 6. 7. 23. 24.]

1. That ethereal agent or matter which makes objects perceptible to the sense of seeing, but the particles of which are separately invisible. It is now generally believed that light is a fluid, or real matter, existing independent of other substances, with properties peculiar to itself. Its velocity is astonishing, as it passes through a space of nearly twelve millions of miles in a minute. Light, when decomposed, is found to consist of rays differently colored; as red, orange, yellow, green, blue, indigo, and violet. The sun is the principal source of light in the solar system; but light is also emitted from bodies ignited, or in combustion, and is reflected from enlightened bodies, as the moon. Light is also emitted from certain putrefying substances. It is usually united with heat, but it exists also independent of it. *Hooper. Nicholson. Encyc.*
2. That flood of luminous rays which flows from the sun, and constitutes day.

God called the *light* day, and the darkness he called night. Gen. i.

3. Day; the dawn of day.

The murderer rising with the *light*, killeth the poor and needy. Job. xxiv.

4. Life.

O, spring to *light*, auspicious babe, be born! *Pope.*

5. Any thing that gives light; as a lamp, candle, taper, lighted tower, star, &c.

Then he called for a *light*, and sprang in— Acts xvi.

I have set thee to be a *light* to the Gentiles. Acts xiii.

And God made two great *lights*. Gen. i.

6. The illuminated part of a picture; the part which lies open to the luminary by which the piece is supposed to be enlightened, and is painted in vivid colors; opposed to *shade*.
7. Illumination of mind; instruction; knowledge.

I opened Ariosto in Italian, and the very first two lines gave me *light* to all I could desire. *Dryden.*

Light, understanding and wisdom—was found in him. Dan. v.

8. Means of knowing. By using such *lights* as we have, we may arrive at probability, if not at certainty.
9. Open view; a visible state; a state of being seen by the eye, or perceived, understood or known. Further researches will doubtless bring to *light* many isles yet undiscovered; further experiments will bring to *light* properties of matter yet unknown.
10. Public view or notice.

Why am I ask'd what next shall see the *light?* *Pope.*

11. Explanation; illustration; means of understanding. One part of Scripture throws *light* on another.
12. Point of view; situation to be seen or viewed; *a use of the word taken from painting.* It is useful to exhibit a subject in a variety of *lights*. Let every thought be presented in a strong *light*. In whatever *light* we view this event, it must be considered an evil.
13. A window; a place that admits light to enter. 1 Kings vii.
14. A pane of glass; as a window with twelve *lights*.
15. In *Scripture*, God, the source of knowledge.

God is *light*. 1 John i.

16. Christ.

That was the true *light*, that lighteth every man that cometh into the world. John i.

17. Joy; comfort; felicity.

Light is sown for the righteous. Ps. xcvii.

18. Saving knowledge.

It is because there is no *light* in them. Is. viii.

19. Prosperity; happiness.

Then shall thy *light* break forth as the morning. Is. lviii.

20. Support; comfort; deliverance. Mic. vii.
21. The gospel. Matt. iv.
22. The understanding or judgment. Matt. vi.
23. The gifts and graces of christians. Matt. v.
24. A moral instructor, as John the Baptist. John v.
25. A true christian, a person enlightened. Eph. v.
26. A good king, the guide of his people. Sam. xxi.

The light of the countenance, favor; smiles. Ps. iv.

To stand in one's own light, to be the means of preventing good, or frustrating one's own purposes.

To come to light, to be detected; to be discovered or found.

LIGHT, *a. lite.* Bright; clear; not dark or obscure; as, the morning is *light;* the apartment is *light.*

2. In *colors*, white or whitish; as a *light* color; a *light* brown; a *light* complexion.

LIGHT, *a. lite.* [Sax. *liht, leoht;* D. *ligt;* G. *leicht;* Fr. *leger;* It. *leggiero;* Port. *ligeiro;* Sp. *ligero;* Russ. *legkei;* Sans. *leka.* The Sw. *lätt*, Dan. *let*, may be contractions of the same word. The Slavonic also has *lehek* and *legok.* Qu. L. *alacer.* This word accords with *light*, the fluid, in orthography, and may be from the same radix.]

1. Having little weight; not tending to the center of gravity with force; not heavy. A fether is *light*, compared with lead or silver; but a thing is *light* only comparatively. That which is *light* to a man, may be heavy to a child. A *light* burden for a camel, may be insupportable to a horse.

2. Not burdensome; easy to be lifted, borne or carried by physical strength; as a *light* burden, weight or load.

3. Not oppressive; easy to be suffered or endured; as a *light* affliction. 2 Cor. iv.

4. Easy to be performed; not difficult; not requiring great strength or exertion. The task is *light;* the work is *light.*

5. Easy to be digested; not oppressive to the stomach; as *light* food. It may signify also, containing little nutriment.

6. Not heavily armed, or armed with light weapons; as *light* troops; a troop of *light* horse.

7. Active; swift; nimble.

Asahel was as *light* of foot as a wild roe. 2 Sam. ii.

8. Not encumbered; unembarrassed; clear of impediments.

Unmarried men are best masters, but not best subjects; for they are *light* to run away. *Bacon.*

9. Not laden; not deeply laden; not sufficiently ballasted. The ship returned *light.*

10. Slight; trifling; not important; as a *light* error. *Boyle.*

11. Not dense; not gross; as *light* vapors; *light* fumes. *Dryden.*

12. Small; inconsiderable; not copious or vehement; as a *light* rain; a *light* snow.

13. Not strong; not violent; moderate; as a *light* wind.

14. Easy to admit influence; inconsiderate; easily influenced by trifling considerations; unsteady; unsettled; volatile; as a *light*, vain person; a *light* mind.

There is no greater argument of a *light* and inconsiderate person, than profanely to scoff at religion. *Tillotson.*

15. Gay; airy; indulging levity; wanting dignity or solidity; trifling.

Seneca cannot be too heavy, nor Plautus too *light.* *Shak.*

We may neither be *light* in prayer, nor wrathful in debate. *J. M. Mason.*

16. Wanton; unchaste; as a woman of *light* carriage.

A *light* wife doth make a heavy husband. *Shak.*

17. Not of legal weight; clipped; diminished; as *light* coin.

To set light by, to undervalue; to slight; to treat as of no importance; to despise.

To make light of, to treat as of little consequence; to slight; to disregard.

LIGHT, *v. t. lite.* To kindle; to inflame; to set fire to; as, to *light* a candle or lamp; sometimes with *up;* as, to *light up* an inextinguishable flame. We often hear *lit* used for *lighted*, as, he *lit* a candle; but this is inelegant.

2. To give light to.

Ah hopeless, lasting flames! like those that burn
To *light* the dead— *Pope.*

3. To illuminate; to fill or spread over with light; as, to *light* a room; to *light* the streets of a city.

4. To lighten; to ease of a burden. [*Not in use.* See *Lighten.*] *Spenser.*

LIGHT, *v. i. lite.* [Sax. *lihtan, alihtan, gelihtan*, to *light* or kindle, to *lighten* or alleviate, and to *alight; hlihtan*, to *alight;* D. *lichten*, to shine; *ligten*, to heave or lift; G. *lichten*, to weigh, to lighten.]

1. To fall on; to come to by chance; to happen to find; with *on.*

A weaker man may sometimes *light on* notions which had escaped a wiser. *Watts.*

2. To fall on; to strike.

They shall hunger no more, neither thirst any more; neither shall the sun *light on* them, nor any heat. Rev. vii.

3. To descend, as from a horse or carriage; with *down, off*, or *from.*

He *lighted down* from his chariot. 2 Kings v. She *lighted off* the camel. Gen. xxiv.

4. To settle; to rest; to stoop from flight. The bee *lights* on this flower and that.

LI'GHT-ARMED, *a.* Armed with light weapons.

LI'GHT-BEARER, *n.* A torch-bearer. *B. Jonson.*

LI'GHT-BRAIN, *n.* An empty headed person. *Martin.*

LIGHTED, *pp. li'ted.* Kindled; set on fire; caused to burn. [*Lit*, for *lighted*, is inelegant.]

LIGHTEN, *v. i. li'tn.* [from *light*, the fluid; Sax. *lihtan.*]

1. To flash; to burst forth or dart, as lightning; to shine with an instantaneous illumination.

This dreadful night
That thunders, *lightens*, opens graves, and roars
As doth the lion. *Shak.*

2. To shine like lightning. *Shak.*

3. To fall; to light. *Obs.*

LIGHTEN, *v. t. li'tn.* To dissipate darkness; to fill with light; to spread over with light; to illuminate; to enlighten; as, to *lighten* an apartment with lamps or gas; to *lighten* the streets.

A key of fire ran all along the shore,
And *lightened* all the river with a blaze. *Dryden.*

2. To illuminate with knowledge; *in a moral sense.*

A light to *lighten* the Gentiles. Luke ii.

3. To free from trouble and fill with joy.

They looked to him and were *lightened.* Ps. xxxiv.

LIGHTEN, *v. t. li'tn.* [from *light*, not heavy; Sax. *lihtan.*]

1. To make lighter; to reduce in weight; to make less heavy; as, to *lighten* a ship by unloading; to *lighten* a load or burden.

2. To alleviate; to make less burdensome or afflictive; as, to *lighten* the cares of life; to *lighten* the burden of grief.

3. To cheer; to exhilarate.

He *lightens* my humor with his merry jest. *Shak.*

LIGHTER, *n. li'ter.* One that lights; as a *lighter* of lamps.

2. A large open flat-bottomed boat, used in loading and unloading ships.

LIGHTERMAN, *n. li'terman.* A man who manages a lighter; a boatman.

LIGHTFINGERED, *a. li'tefingered.* Dextrous in taking and conveying away; thievish; addicted to petty thefts.

LIGHTFOOT, } *a.* *li'tefoot,* } Nimble
LIGHTFOOTED, } *li'tefooted.* } in running or dancing; active. [*Little used.*] *Spenser.*

LI'GHTHEADED, *a.* [See *Head.*] Thoughtless; heedless; weak; volatile; unsteady. *Clarendon.*

2. Disordered in the head; dizzy; delirious.

LI'GHTHEADEDNESS, *n.* Disorder of the head; dizziness; deliriousness.

LI'GHTHE'ARTED, *a.* Free from grief or anxiety; gay; cheerful; merry.

LI'GHT-HORSE, *n.* Light armed cavalry.

LI'GHT-HOUSE, *n.* A pharos; a tower or building erected on a rock or point of land, or on an isle in the sea, with a light or number of lamps on the top, intended to direct seamen in navigating ships at night.

LI'GHTLEGGED, *a.* Nimble; swift of foot. *Sidney.*

LIGHTLESS, *a. li'teless.* Destitute of light; dark.

LIGHTLY, *adv. li'tely.* With little weight; as, to tread *lightly;* to press *lightly.*

2. Without deep impression.

The soft ideas of the cheerful note,
Lightly received, were easily forgot. *Prior.*

3. Easily; readily; without difficulty; of course.

4. Without reason, or for reasons of little weight.

Flatter not the rich, neither do thou willingly or *lightly* appear before great personages. *Taylor.*

5. Without dejection; cheerfully.

Bid that welcome
Which comes to punish us, and we punish it,
Seeming to bear it *lightly.* *Shak.*

6. Not chastely; wantonly. *Swift.*

7. Nimbly; with agility; not heavily or tardily.

He led me *lightly* o'er the stream.

8. Gayly; airily; with levity; without heed or care.

LIGHTMINDED, *a.* Unsettled; unsteady; volatile; not considerate.

He that is hasty to give credit, is *lightminded.* *Ecclus.*

LIGHTNESS, *n. li'teness.* Want of weight; levity; the contrary to *heaviness;* as the *lightness* of air, compared with water.

2. Inconstancy; unsteadiness; the quality of mind which disposes it to be influenced by trifling considerations.

—Such is the *lightness* of you common men. *Shak.*

3. Levity; wantonness; lewdness; unchastity. *Shak. Sidney.*

4. Agility; nimbleness.

LIGHTNING, *n. li'tening.* [that is, *lighte'ing*, the participle present of *lighten.*]

1. A sudden discharge of electricity from a cloud to the earth, or from the earth to a cloud, or from one cloud to another, that

is, from a body positively charged to one negatively charged, producing a vivid flash of light, and usually a loud report, called thunder. Sometimes lightning is a mere instantaneous flash of light without thunder, as *heat-lightning*, lightning seen by reflection, the flash being beyond the limits of our horizon.

2. [from *lighten*, to diminish weight.] Abatement; alleviation; mitigation. *Spectator.*

LI'GHTROOM, *n.* In a ship of war, a small apartment, having double glass windows towards the magazine, and containing lights by which the gunner fills cartridges. *Mar. Dict.*

LIGHTS, *n. lites.* plu. [so called from their *lightness.*]

The lungs; the organs of breathing in animals. These organs in man we call *lungs*; in other animals, *lights*.

LIGHTSŎME, *a. li'tesome.* Luminous; not dark; not obscure.

White walls make rooms more *lightsome* than black. [*Little used.*] *Bacon.*

The *lightsome* realms of love. *Dryden.*

[*In the latter passage, the word is elegant.*]

2. Gay; airy; cheering; exhilarating.

That *lightsome* affection of joy. *Hooker.*

LI'GHTSŎMENESS, *n.* Luminousness; the quality of being light; opposed to *darkness* or *darksomeness*. *Cheyne.*

2. Cheerfulness; merriment; levity.

[*This word is little used.*]

LIGN-AL'OES, *n.* [L. *lignum*, wood, and *aloes.*] Aloes-wood. Num. xxiv.

LIG'NEOUS, *a.* [L. *ligneus.*] Wooden; made of wood; consisting of wood; resembling wood. The harder part of a plant is *ligneous*.

LIGNIFICA'TION, *n.* The process of becoming or of converting into wood, or the hard substance of a vegetable. *Good.*

LIG'NIFORM, *a.* [L. *lignum*, wood, and *form.*] Like wood; resembling wood. *Kirwan.*

LIG'NIFȲ, *v. t.* [L. *lignum*, wood, and *facio*, to make.] To convert into wood.

LIG'NIFȲ, *v. i.* To become wood.

LIG'NITE, *n.* [L. *lignum.*] Fossil or bituminous wood, a mineral combustible substance. *Dict. Nat. Hist.*

LIG'NOUS, *a.* Ligneous. [*Little used.*] *Evelyn.*

LIGNUM-VITÆ, *n.* [L.] Guaiacum or pockwood, a genus of plants, natives of warm climates. The common Lignum-vitæ is a native of the warm latitudes of America. It becomes a large tree, having a hard, brownish, brittle bark, and its wood firm, solid, ponderous, very resinous, of a blackish yellow color in the middle, and of a hot aromatic taste. It is of considerable use in medicine and the mechanical arts, being wrought into utensils, wheels, cogs, and various articles of turnery. *Encyc.*

LIG'ULATE, LIG'ULATED, } *a.* [L. *ligula*, a strap.] Like a bandage or strap; as a *ligulate* flower, a species of compound flower, the florets of which have their corollets flat, spreading out towards the end, with the base only tubular. This is the semi-floscular flower of Tournefort. *Botany.*

LIG'URE, *n.* A kind of precious stone. Ex. xxviii.

LIG'URITE, *n.* [from *Liguria.*] A mineral occurring in oblique rhombic prisms, of an apple green color, occasionally speckled. *Phillips.*

LIKE, *a.* [Sax. *lic*, *gelic*, Goth. *leiks*, D. *lyk*, *gelyk*, G. *gleich*, Sw. *lik*, Dan. *lig*, *lige*, like, plain, even, equal, smooth. The sense of *like*, similar, is even, smooth, equal, but this sense may be from *laying*, pressing, and hence this word may be allied to the Eth. ለከዐ lakeo, to stamp, seal, impress, whence its derivative, an image; or the sense be taken from rubbing or shaving. We observe that *like* has also the sense of *please; to like* is to be pleased. Now, if *p* in L. *placeo*, is a prefix, the latter may be formed on the root of *like*. And if *de* is a prefix, in *delight*, *delecto*, *delicious*, *delicate*, these may be of the same family. *Like* is evidently from the same root as the Ch. and Heb. חלק, Ar. حلق chalaka, to be or make smooth. Qu. Gr. ηλικος, ηλικια. See *Lick* and *Lickerish.*]

1. Equal in quantity, quality or degree; as a territory of *like* extent with another; men of *like* excellence.

More clergymen were impoverished by the late war, than ever in the *like* space before. *Sprat.*

2. Similar; resembling; having resemblance.

Elias was a man subject to *like* passions as we are. James v.

Why might not other planets have been created for *like* uses with the earth, each for its own inhabitants? *Bentley.*

Like is usually followed by *to* or *unto*, but it is often omitted.

What city is *like unto* this great city? Rev. xviii.

I saw three unclean spirits *like* frogs. Rev. xvi.

Among them all was found none *like* Daniel, Hananiah, Mishael, and Azariah. Dan. i.

3. Probable; likely, that is, having the resemblance or appearance of an event; giving reason to expect or believe.

He is *like* to die of hunger in the place where he is, for there is no more bread. Jer. xxxviii.

Many were not easy to be governed, nor *like* to conform themselves to strict rules. *Clarendon.*

LIKE, *n.* [elliptically, for *like thing*, *like event*, *like person.*]

1. Some person or thing resembling another; an equal. The *like* may never happen again.

He was a man, take him for all and all,
I shall not look upon his *like* again. *Shak.*

2. *Had like*, in the phrase, "he *had like* to be defeated," seems to be a corruption; but perhaps *like* here is used for resemblance or probability, and has the character of a noun. At any rate, as a phrase, it is authorized by good usage.

LIKE, *adv.* In the same manner.

—Solomon in all his glory was not arrayed *like* one of these. Matt. vi. Luke xii.

Like as a father pitieth his children, so the Lord pitieth them that fear him. Ps. ciii.

2. In a manner becoming.

Be strong, and quit yourselves *like* men. 1 Sam. iv.

3. Likely; probably; as *like* enough it will. *Shak.*

LIKE, *v. t.* [Sax. *licean*, *lician*; Goth. *leikan*; probably L. *placeo* and *delecto*, with prefixes.]

1. To be pleased with in a moderate degree; to approve. It expresses less than *love* and *delight*. We *like* a plan or design, when we approve of it as correct or beneficial. We *like* the character or conduct of a man when it comports with our view of rectitude. We *like* food that the taste relishes. We *like* whatever gives us pleasure.

He proceeded from looking to *liking*, and from *liking* to loving. *Sidney.*

2. To please; to be agreeable to.

This desire being recommended to her majesty, it *liked* her to include the same within one entire lease. *Obs.* *Bacon.*

3. To liken. *Obs.* *Shak.*

LIKE, *v. i.* To be pleased; to choose.

He may go or stay, as he *likes*. *Locke.*

2. *To like of*, to be pleased. *Obs.* *Knolles.*

LI'KELIHOOD, *n.* [*likely* and *hood.*] Probability; verisimilitude; appearance of truth or reality. There is little *likelihood* that an habitual drunkard will become temperate. There is little *likelihood* that an old offender will be reformed. Prudence directs us not to undertake a design, when there is little or no *likelihood* of success.

2. Appearance; show; resemblance. *Obs.* *Shak.*

LI'KELINESS, *n.* [from *likely.*] Probability.

2. The qualities that please. [See *Likely.*]

LI'KELY, *a.* [that is, *like-like.*] Probable; that may be rationally thought or believed to have taken place in time past, or to be true now or hereafter; such as is more reasonable than the contrary. A *likely* story, is one which evidence, or the circumstances of the case render probable, and therefore credible.

2. Such as may be liked; pleasing; as a *likely* man or woman.

[This use of *likely* is not obsolete, as Johnson affirms, nor is it vulgar. But the English and their descendants in America differ in the application. The English apply the word to external appearance, and with them, *likely* is equivalent to *handsome*, *well formed*; as a *likely* man, a *likely* horse. In America, the word is usually applied to the endowments of the mind, or to pleasing accomplishments. With us, a *likely* man, is a man of good character and talents, or of good dispositions or accomplishments, that render him pleasing or respectable.]

LI'KELY, *adv.* Probably.

While man was innocent, he was *likely* ignorant of nothing important for him to know. *Glanville.*

LIKE-MINDED, *a.* Having a like disposition or purpose. Rom. xv.

LIKEN, *v. t. li'kn.* [Sw. *likna*; Dan. *ligner.*] To compare; to represent as resembling or similar.

Whosoever heareth these sayings of mine, and doeth them, I will *liken* him unto a wise man, that built his house on a rock. Matt. vi.

LI'KENED, *pp.* Compared.

LI'KENESS, *n.* Resemblance in form; similitude. The picture is a good *likeness* of the original.

2. Resemblance; form; external appearance. Guard against an enemy in the *likeness* of a friend.

3. One that resembles another; a copy; a counterpart.

I took you for your *likeness*, Chloe. *Prior.*

4. An image, picture or statue, resembling a person or thing. Ex. xx.

LI'KENING, *ppr.* Comparing; representing as similar.

LI'KEWISE, *adv.* [*like* and *wise.*] In like manner; also; moreover; too.

For he seeth that wise men die, *likewise* the fool and the brutish person perish, and leave their wealth to others. Ps. xlix.

LI'KING, *ppr.* of *like.* Approving; being pleased with.

2. *a.* Plump; full; of a good appearance. Dan. i. *Obs.*

LI'KING, *n.* A good state of body; healthful appearance; plumpness.

Their young ones are in good *liking*— Job xxxix.

2. State of trial. [*Not used.*] *Dryden.*

3. Inclination; pleasure; as, this is an amusement to your *liking.* *Spenser.*

4. Delight in; pleasure in; with *to.*

He who has no *liking to* the whole, ought not to censure the parts. *Dryden.*

LI'LAC, *n.* [Fr. *lilas;* Sp. *lilac.*] A plant or shrub of the genus Syringa, a native of Persia. The common lilac is cultivated for its flowers, which are purple or white.

LIL'ALITE, *n.* A species of earth of the argillaceous kind; called also *lepidolite*, which see. *Kirwan.*

LILIA'CEOUS, *a.* [L. *liliaceus*, from *lilium*, a lily.]

Pertaining to lilies; lily-like. A *liliaceous* corol is one that has six regular petals. *Martyn.*

LIL'IED, *a.* Embellished with lilies.

By sandy Ladon's *lilied* banks. *Milton.*

LILL, *v. t.* [See *Loll.* But *lill* is used in New England.] *Spenser.*

LILT, *v. i.* To do any thing with dexterity or quickness. [*Local.*] *Pegge.*

2. To sing or play on the bagpipe.

LIL'Y, *n.* [L. *lilium;* Gr. λειριον; Sp. *lirio.*] A genus of plants of many species, which are all bulbous-rooted, herbaceous perennials, producing bell-shaped, hexapetalous flowers of great beauty and variety of colors. *Encyc.*

Lily of the valley, a plant of the genus Convallaria, with a monopetalous, bell-shaped corol, divided at the top into six segments. *Miller.*

LILY-DAF'FODIL, *n.* A plant and flower.

LIL'Y-HANDED, *a.* Having white delicate hands. *Spenser.*

LIL'Y-HYACINTH, *n.* A plant. *Miller.*

LILY-LIV'ERED, *a.* White-livered; cowardly. [*Not used.*] *Shak.*

LIMA'TION, *n.* [L. *limo*, to file.] The act of filing or polishing.

LI'MATURE, *n.* [L. *limo*, to file.] A filing.

2. Filings; particles rubbed off by filing. *Johnson.*

LIMB, *n. lim.* [Sax. *lim;* Dan. Sw. *lem;* L. *limbus*, edge or border, extremity; *limes*, limit, coinciding perhaps with W. *llem*, *llym*, sharp, or *llamu*, to leap. The sense of *limb* is from shooting or extending.]

1. Edge or border. This is the proper signification of the word; but in this sense it is limited chiefly to technical use, and applied to the sun, moon, or a star, to a leaf, to a quadrant, &c. We say, the sun or moon is eclipsed on its northern *limb.* But we never say, the *limb* of a board, of a tract of land or water, &c.

2. In *anatomy*, and in *common use*, an extremity of the human body; a member; a projecting part; as the arm or leg; that is, a shoot.

3. The branch of a tree; applied only to a branch of some size, and not to a small twig.

4. In *botany*, the border or upper spreading part of a monopetalous corol. *Martyn.*

LIMB, *v. t. lim.* To supply with limbs. *Milton.*

2. To dismember; to tear off the limbs.

LIM'BAT, *n.* A cooling periodical wind in the isle of Cyprus, blowing from the north west from eight o'clock, A. M. to the middle of the day or later. *Encyc.*

LIM'BEC, *n.* [contracted from *alembic.*] A still; *a word not now used.*

LIM'BEC, *v. t.* To strain or pass through a still. *Obs.* *Sandys.*

LIMB'ED, *a.* In composition, formed with regard to limbs; as well-*limbed;* large-*limbed;* short-*limbed.* *Pope.*

LIM'BER, *a.* [perhaps from the W. *llib*, *llibin;* for *m* and *b* are convertible, and *m* before *b*, is often casual.]

Easily bent; flexible; pliant; yielding. In America, it is applied to material things; as a *limber* rod; a *limber* joint.

LIM'BER, *n.* In a *ship*, a square hole cut through the floor timbers, as a passage for water to the pump-well. *Mar. Dict.*

LIM'BERNESS, *n.* The quality of being easily bent; flexibleness; pliancy.

LIM'BERS, *n.* A two-wheeled carriage, having boxes for ammunition.

2. Thills; shafts of a carriage. [*Local.*]

LIM'BILITE, *n.* A mineral from Limbourg, in Swabia, of a honey yellow color, and compact texture. *Saussure.*

LIMB'LESS, *a.* Destitute of limbs. *Massinger.*

LIMB'-MEAL, *a.* Piece-meal. *Shak.*

LIM'BO, } *n.* [L. *limbus.*] A region border-
LIM'BUS, } ing on hell, or hell itself. *Shak.*

Among catholics, a place where the souls of persons are lodged after death.

2. A place of restraint. *Dryden.*

LIME, *n.* [Sax. *lim*, lime, whence *geliman*, to glue; Sw. Dan. *lim*, D. *lym*, G. *leim* and *lehem*, loam; L. *limus;* It. Sp. *limo;* probably Gr. λημη, γλημη, and allied to *clammy.* On this word is formed *slime.*]

1. A viscous substance, sometimes laid on twigs for catching birds. *Dryden.*

2. Calcarious earth, oxyd of calcium, procured from chalk and certain stones and shells, by expelling from them the carbonic acid, by means of a strong heat in a furnace. The best lime for mortar or cement is obtained from limestone, or carbonate of lime, of which marble is a fine species. *Hooper. Nicholson.*

3. The linden tree.

4. [Fr. *lime.* See *Lemon.*] A species of acid fruit, smaller than the lemon.

LIME, *v. t.* [Sax. *geliman.*] To smear with a viscous substance. *L'Estrange.*

2. To entangle; to ensnare. *Shak.*

3. To manure with lime.

Land may be improved by draining, marling and *liming.* *Child.*

4. To cement. *Shak.*

LI'ME-BURNER, *n.* One who burns stones to lime.

LI'MED, *pp.* Smeared with lime; entangled; manured with lime.

LI'MEHOUND, *n.* A dog used in hunting the wild boar; a limer. *Spenser.*

LIMEKILN, *n. li'mekil.* A kiln or furnace in which stones or shells are exposed to a strong heat and reduced to lime.

LI'MESTONE, *n.* Stone of which lime is made by the expulsion of its carbonic acid, or fixed air. It is called carbonate of lime. Of this there are several species.

LI'METWIG, *n.* A twig smeared with lime. *Milton.*

LI'METWIGGED, *a.* Smeared with lime. *Addison.*

LI'MEWATER, *n.* Water impregnated with lime.

LI'MING, *ppr.* Daubing with viscous matter; entangling; manuring with lime.

LIM'IT, *n.* [L. *limes;* Fr. *limites.* See *Limb.*]

1. Bound; border; utmost extent; the part that terminates a thing; as the *limit* of a town, city or empire; the *limits* of human knowledge.

2. The thing which bounds; restraint.

3. *Limits*, plu., the extent of the liberties of a prison.

LIM'IT, *v. t.* To bound; to set bounds to.

2. To confine within certain bounds; to circumscribe; to restrain. The government of England is a *limited* monarchy.

They tempted God and *limited* the Holy One of Israel. Ps. lxxviii.

3. To restrain from a lax or general signification. *World* sometimes signifies the universe, and sometimes its signification is *limited* to this earth.

LIM'ITABLE, *a.* That may be limited, circumscribed, bounded or restrained. *Hume.*

LIM'ITANEOUS, *a.* Pertaining to bounds. *Dict.*

LIMITA'RIAN, *a.* That limits or circumscribes.

LIMITA'RIAN, *n.* One that limits; one who holds the doctrine that a part of the human race only are to be saved; opposed to *universalist.* *Huntington.*

LIM'ITARY, *a.* Placed at the limit, as a guard.

—Proud *limitary* cherub. *Milton.*

LIMITA'TION, *n.* [L. *limitatio.*] The act of bounding or circumscribing.

2. Restriction; restraint; circumscription. The king consented to a *limitation* of his prerogatives. Government by the *limitation* of natural rights secures civil liberty.

3. Restriction; confinement from a lax indeterminate import. Words of general import are often to be understood with *limitations.*

4. A certain precinct within which friars were allowed to beg or exercise their functions. *Gilping.*

LIM'ITED, *pp.* Bounded; circumscribed; restrained.

2. *a.* Narrow; circumscribed. Our views of nature are very *limited.*

LIM'ITEDLY, *adv.* With limitation.

LIM'ITEDNESS, *n.* State of being limited. *Parker.*

LIM'ITER, *n.* He or that which limits or confines.

2. A friar licenced to beg within certain bounds, or whose duty was limited to a certain district.

LIM'ITLESS, *a.* Having no limits; unbounded. *Davies.*

LIM'MER, *n.* A limehound; a mongrel. *Johnson.*

2. A dog engendered between a hound and a mastiff. *Bailey.*

3. A thill or shaft. [*Local.* See *Limber.*]

4. A thill-horse. [*Local.*]

LIMN, *v. t. lim.* [Fr. *enluminer*; L. *lumino.*] To draw or paint; or to paint in water colors. *Encyc.*

LIM'NED, *pp. lim'med.* Painted.

LIM'NER, *n.* [Fr. *enlumineur*; L. *illuminator*, in the middle ages, *alluminor.*]

1. One that colors or paints on paper or parchment; one who decorates books with initial pictures. *Encyc.*

2. A portrait painter.

LIMN'ING, *ppr.* Drawing; painting; painting in water colors.

LIM'NING, *n.* The act or art of drawing or painting in water colors. *Addison.*

LI'MOUS, *a.* [L. *limosus*, from *limus*, slime.] Muddy; slimy; thick. *Brown.*

LIMP, *v. i.* [Sax. *lemp-healt*, lamo; *gelimpan*, to happen, that is, to fall; allied perhaps to *lame.*] To halt; to walk lamely. *Bacon.*

LIMP, *n.* A halt; act of limping.

LIMP, *a.* Vapid; weak. [*Not used.*] *Walton.*

LIMP'ER, *n.* One that limps.

LIM'PET, *n.* [L. *lepas*; Gr. λεπας, from λεπω, to peel or strip off bark.]

A univalve shell of the genus Patella, adhering to rocks.

LIM'PID, *a.* [L. *limpidus.*] Pure; clear; transparent; as a *limpid* stream.

LIM'PIDNESS, *n.* Clearness; purity.

LIM'PING, *ppr.* Halting; walking lamely.

LIM'PINGLY, *adv.* Lamely; in a halting manner.

LIM'SY, *a.* [W. *llymsi.*] Weak; flexible. *N. England.*

LI'MY, *a.* [See *Lime.*] Viscous; glutinous; as *limy* snares.

2. Containing lime; as a *limy* soil.

3. Resembling lime; having the qualities of lime.

LIN, *v. i.* [Ice. *linna.*] To yield. *Obs.*

LIN, *n.* [Celtic.] A pool or mere. [*Not used.*]

LINCH'PIN, *n.* [Sax. *lynis*, an axis, D. *lens.*]

A pin used to prevent the wheel of a carriage from sliding off the axle-tree.

LINC'TURE, *n.* [L. *lingo*, *linctus.*] Medicine taken by licking. *Burton.*

LIN'DEN, *n.* [Sax. Sw. Dan. *lind*; D. *linde* or *linde-boom*; G. *linde*, *lindenbaum.*]

The lime-tree, or teil-tree, of the genus Tilia. *Dryden.*

LINE, *n.* [L. *linea*; Fr. *ligne*, from L. *linum*; Gr. λινον, flax; G. *leine*; D. *lyn*; Sw. *lina*; Dan. *line.*]

1. In *geometry*, a quantity extended in length, without breadth or thickness; or a limit terminating a surface. *Encyc.*

2. A slender string; a small cord or rope. The angler uses a *line* and hook. The seaman uses a hand *line*, a hauling *line*, spilling *lines*, &c.

3. A thread, string or cord extended to direct any operation.

> We as by *line* upon the ocean go. *Dryden.*

4. Lineament; a mark in the hand or face.

> He tipples palmistry, and dines
> On all her fortune-telling *lines.* *Cleaveland.*

5. Delineation; sketch; as the *lines* of a building. *Temple.*

6. Contour; outline; exterior limit of a figure.

> Free as thy stroke, yet faultless as thy *line.* *Pope.*

7. In *writing*, *printing* and *engraving*, the words and letters which stand on a level in one row, between one margin and another; as a page of thirty *lines.*

8. In *poetry*, a verse, or the words which form a certain number of feet, according to the measure.

9. A short letter; a note. I received a *line* from my friend by the last mail.

10. A rank or row of soldiers, or the disposition of an army drawn up with an extended front; or the like disposition of a fleet prepared for engagement.

11. A trench or rampart; an extended work in fortification.

> Unite thy forces and attack their *lines.* *Dryden.*

12. Method; disposition; as *line* of order. *Shak.*

13. Extension; limit; border.

> Eden stretched her *line*
> From Auran eastward to the royal towers
> Of great Seleucia. *Milton.*

14. Equator; equinoctial circle.

> When the sun below the *line* descends— *Creech.*

15. A series or succession of progeny or relations, descending from a common progenitor. We speak of the ascending or descending *line*; the *line* of descent; the male *line*; a *line* of kings.

16. The twelfth part of an inch.

17. A straight extended mark.

18. A straight or parallel direction. The houses must all stand in a *line.* Every new building must be set in a *line* with others on the same street.

19. Occupation; employment; department or course of business. We speak of men in the same *line* of business. *Washington.*

20. Course; direction.

> What general *line* of conduct ought to be pursued? *Washington.*

21. Lint or flax. [*Seldom used.*] *Spenser.*

22. In *heraldry*, lines are the figures used in armories to divide the shield into different parts, and to compose different figures. *Encyc.*

23. In *Scripture*, *line* signifies a cord for measuring; also, instruction, doctrine. Ps. xix. Is. xxviii.

A right line, a straight or direct line; the shortest line that can be drawn between two points.

Horizontal line, a line drawn parallel to the horizon.

Equinoctial line, in *geography*, a great circle on the earth's surface, at 90 degrees distance from each pole, and bisecting the earth at that part. In *astronomy*, the circle which the sun seems to describe, in March and September, when the days and nights are of equal length.

Meridian line, an imaginary circle drawn through the two poles of the earth, and any part of its surface.

A ship of the line, a ship of war large enough to have a place in the line of battle. All ships carrying seventy four or more large guns, are ships of the line. Smaller ships may sometimes be so called.

LINE, *v. t.* [supposed to be from L. *linum*, flax, whence *linen*, which is often used for linings.]

1. To cover on the inside; as a garment *lined* with linen, fur or silk; a box *lined* with paper or tin.

2. To put in the inside.

> —What if I do *line* one of their hands? *Shak.*

3. To place along by the side of any thing for guarding; as, to *line* a hedge with riflemen; to *line* works with soldiers.

4. To strengthen by additional works or men.

> *Line* and new repair your towns of war
> With men of courage. *Shak.*

5. To cover; to add a covering; as, to *line* a crutch. *Shak.*

6. To strengthen with any thing added.

> Who *lined* himself with hope. *Shak.*

7. To impregnate; applied to irrational animals. *Creech.*

LIN'EAGE, *n.* [Fr. *lignage*, from *ligne*, *line.*]

Race; progeny; descendants in a line from a common progenitor.

LIN'EAL, *a.* [L. *linealis*, from *linea*, line.]

1. Composed of lines; delineated; as *lineal* designs. *Wotton.*

2. In a direct line from an ancestor; as *lineal* descent; *lineal* succession. *Locke.*

3. Hereditary; derived from ancestors. *Shak.*

4. Allied by direct descent.

> For only you are *lineal* to the throne. *Dryden.*

5. In the direction of a line; as *lineal* measure.

Lineal measure, the measure of length.

LINEAL'ITY, *n.* The state of being in the form of a line. *Am. Review.*

LIN'EALLY, *adv.* In a direct line; as, the prince is *lineally* descended from the conqueror.

LIN'EAMENT, *n.* [Fr. from L. *lineamentum.*]

Feature; form; make; the outline or exterior of a body or figure, particularly of the face.

> Man he seems
> In all his *lineaments.* *Milton.*
> —The *lineaments* of the body. *Locke.*
> —*Lineaments* of a character. *Swift.*

LIN'EAR, *a.* [L. *linearis.*] Pertaining to a line; consisting of lines; in a straight direction.

2. In *botany*, like a line; slender; of the same breadth throughout, except at the extremities; as a *linear* leaf.

Linear numbers, in mathematics, such as have relation to length only; such is a number which represents one side of a plane figure. If the plane figure is a square, the linear figure is called a root. *Encyc.*

Linear problem, that which may be solved geometrically by the intersection of two right lines. *Encyc.*

LIN'EATE, *a.* In *botany*, marked longitudinally with depressed parallel lines; as a *lineate* leaf.

LINEA'TION, *n.* Draught; delineation, which see. *Woodward.*

LI'NED, *pp.* Covered on the inside.

LIN'EN, *n.* [L. *linum*, flax, Gr. λινον, W. *llin*, Ir. *lin*, Russ. *len*, G. *lein*. The sense is probably long, extended or smooth. In the latter sense, it would accord with L. *linio, lenio.*]

1. Cloth made of flax or hemp.
2. An under garment.

LIN'EN, *a.* [L. *lineus.*] Made of flax or hemp; as *linen* cloth; a *linen* stocking.

2. Resembling linen cloth; white; pale. *Shak.*

Fossil-linen, a kind of amianth, with soft, parallel, flexible fibers. *Encyc.*

LIN'EN-DRAPER, *n.* A person who deals in linens.

Linener and *linen-man*, in a like sense, are obsolete.

LING, *n.* [D. *leng*; Ir. *long*; probably Sax. *leng*, long.]

A fish of the genus Gadus, or cod kind, which grows to the length of four feet or more, is very slender, with a flat head. This fish abounds on the coasts of Scotland and Ireland, and forms a considerable article of commerce. *Encyc.*

LING, *n.* [Ice. *ling*, from *leng*, long.] A species of long grass; heath. *Jamieson. Cyc.*

Ling, a Saxon termination, as in *darling*, *firstling*, denotes primarily state, condition, or subject. In some words, it denotes the young of an animal, or a small one.

LIN'GER, *v. i.* [from the root of *long*, Sax. *leng.*]

1. To delay; to loiter; to remain or wait long; to be slow.

> Nor cast one longing, *lingering* look behind. *Gray.*

> Whose judgment now of a long time *lingereth* not. 2 Pet. ii.

2. To hesitate; to be slow in deciding; to be in suspense.

> Perhaps thou *lingerest*, in deep thought detained. *Milton.*

3. To remain long in any state. The patient *lingers* on a bed of sickness.

LIN'GER, *v. t.* To protract. *Shak.*

LIN'GERER, *n.* One who lingers.

LIN'GERING, *ppr.* Delaying; loitering.

2. *a.* Drawing out in time; remaining long; protracted; as a *lingering* disease.

> To die is the fate of man; but to die with *lingering* anguish is generally his folly. *Rambler.*

LIN'GERING, *n.* A delaying; a remaining long; tardiness; protraction.

> The *lingerings* of holyday customs. *Irving.*

LIN'GERINGLY, *adv.* With delay; slowly; tediously. *Hale.*

LIN'GET, *n.* [Fr. *lingot*, from *languette*, a tongue.]

A small mass of metal. *Camden.*

LIN'GLE, *n.* [Fr. *ligneul*, from *ligne.*] Shoemaker's thread. [*Not in use or local.*] *Drayton.*

LIN'GO, *n.* [L. *lingua.*] Language; speech. [*Vulgar.*]

LINGUADENT'AL, *a.* [L. *lingua*, tongue, and *dens*, a tooth.]

Formed or uttered by the joint use of the tongue and teeth; as the letters *d* and *t*. *Holder.*

LINGUADENT'AL, *n.* An articulation formed by the tongue and teeth.

LIN'GUAFORM, *a.* [*lingua* and *form.*] Having the form or shape of the tongue. *Martyn.*

LIN'GUAL, *a.* [L. *lingua*, the tongue.] Pertaining to the tongue; as the *lingual* nerves, the ninth pair, which go to the tongue; the *lingual* muscle, or muscle of the tongue.

LIN'GUIST, *n.* [L. *lingua*, tongue.] A person skilled in languages; usually applied to a person well versed in the languages taught in colleges, Greek, Latin, and Hebrew. *Milton.*

LIN'GULATE, *a.* [L. *lingulatus*, from *lingua*, tongue.]

Shaped like the tongue or a strap. [But *ligulate* is more generally used.] *Martyn.*

LINGWORT, *n.* An herb.

LIN'IMENT, *n.* [Fr. from L. *linimentum*, from *linio, lino*, to anoint.]

A species of soft ointment; a composition of a consistence somewhat thinner than an unguent, but thicker than oil. *Encyc.*

LI'NING, *ppr.* [See *Line.*] Covering on the inside, as a garment.

LI'NING, *n.* The inner covering of any thing, as of a garment or a box. The pleura is called the *lining* of the thorax.

2. That which is within. *Shak.*

LINK, *n.* [G. *gelenk*, a joint, a ring, a swivel, a link, and as an adjective, flexible, limber, from *lenken*, to bend; Dan. *lenke*, a chain.]

1. A single ring or division of a chain.
2. Any thing doubled and closed like a link; as a *link* of horse hair. *Mortimer.*
3. A chain; any thing connecting.

> —And love, the common *link*, the new creation crowned. *Dryden.*

4. Any single constituent part of a connected series. This argument is a *link* in the chain of reasoning.
5. A series; a chain.

LINK, *n.* [Gr. λυχνος, L. *lychnus*, a lamp or candle, coinciding in elements with *light.*]

A torch made of tow or hards, &c., and pitch. *Shak. Dryden.*

LINK, *v. t.* To complicate. *Johnson.*

2. To unite or connect by something intervening or in other manner.

> —*Link* towns to towns by avenues of oak. *Pope.*

> —And creature *link'd* to creature, man to man. *Pope.*

LINK, *v. i.* To be connected. *Burke.*

LINK'BOY, } *n.* A boy or man that carries
LINK'MAN, } a link or torch to light passengers. *More. Gay.*

LINK'ED, *pp.* United; connected.

LINK'ING, *ppr.* Uniting; connecting.

LIN'NET, *n.* [Fr. *linot*; W. *llinos*, from *llîn*, flax, and called also in W. *adern y llin*, flax-bird; Sax. *linetwege.* So in L. *carduelis*, from *carduus*, a thistle.]

A small singing bird of the genus Fringilla.

LINSEED. [See *Lintseed.*]

LIN'SEY-WOOLSEY, *a.* Made of linen and wool; hence, vile; mean; of different and unsuitable parts. *Johnson.*

LIN'STOCK, *n.* [*lint* and *stock.*] A pointed staff with a crotch or fork at one end, to hold a lighted match; used in firing cannon. It may be stuck in the ground or in the deck of a ship. *Encyc.*

LINT, *n.* [Sax. *linet*, L. *linteum, linteus*, from *linum*, flax.]

Flax; but more generally, linen scraped into a soft substance, and used for dressing wounds and sores.

LINT'EL, *n.* [Fr. *linteau*; Sp. *lintel* or *dintel.*]

The head-piece of a door-frame or window-frame; the part of the frame that lies on the side-pieces. Ex. xii.

LINT'SEED, *n.* [*lint*, flax, and *seed*; Sax. *linsæd.*] Flaxseed.

LI'ON, *n.* [Fr. from L. *leo, leonis*, Gr. λεων, Arm. *leon*, W. *llew*, a lion; *llewa*, to swallow, to devour.]

1. A quadruped of the genus Felis, very strong, fierce and rapacious. The largest lions are eight or nine feet in length. The male has a thick head, beset with long bushy hair of a yellowish color. The lion is a native of Africa and the warm climates of Asia. His aspect is noble, his gait stately, and his roar tremendous.
2. A sign in the zodiac.

LI'ONESS, *n.* The female of the lion kind.

LI'ONLIKE, *a.* Like a lion; fierce. *Camden.*

LI'ON-METTLED, *a.* Having the courage and spirit of a lion. *Hillhouse.*

LION'S FOOT, *n.* A plant of the genus Catananche.

LION'S LEAF, *n.* A plant of the genus Leontice.

LION'S TAIL, *n.* A plant of the genus Leonurus.

LIP, *n.* [Sax. *lippa, lippe*; D. *lip*; G. Dan. *lippe*; Sw. *läpp*; L. *labium, labrum*; It. *labbro*; Sp. *labio*; Fr. *levre*; Ir. *clab* or *liobhar*; Pers. لب. It may be connected with W. *llavaru*, Ir. *labhraim*, to speak, that is, to thrust out. The sense is probably a border.]

1. The edge or border of the mouth. The lips are two fleshy or muscular parts, composing the exterior of the mouth in man and many other animals. In man, the lips, which may be opened or closed at pleasure, form the covering of the teeth, and are organs of speech essential to certain articulations. Hence the lips, by a figure, denote the mouth, or all the organs of speech, and sometimes speech itself. Job ii.
2. The edge of any thing; as the *lip* of a vessel. *Burnet.*
3. In *botany*, one of the two opposite divisions of a labiate corol. The upper is called the *helmet*, and the lower the *beard*. Also, an appendage to the flowers of the orchises, considered by Linne as a nectary. *Martyn. Smith.*

To *make a lip*, to drop the under lip in sullenness or contempt. *Shak.*

LIP, *v. t.* To kiss. *Shak.*

LIP-DEVO'TION, *n.* Prayers uttered by the lips without the desires of the heart.

LIP'-GOOD, *a.* Good in profession only. *B. Jonson.*

LIP'-LABOR, *n.* Labor or action of the lips without concurrence of the mind; words without sentiments.

LIP'OGRAM, *n.* [Gr. λειπω, to leave, and γραμμα, a letter.]

A writing in which a single letter is wholly omitted.

LIPOGRAM'MATIST, *n.* One who writes any thing, dropping a single letter. *Addison.*

LIPOTH'YMOUS, *a.* [See *Lipothymy.*] Swooning; fainting.

LIPOTH'YMY, *n.* [Gr. λειποθυμια; λειπω, to fail, and θυμος, soul.]

A fainting; a swoon. *Coxe. Taylor.*

LIP'PED, *a.* Having lips.

2. In *botany*, labiate.

LIP'PITUDE, *n.* [L. *lippitudo*, from *lippus*, blear-eyed.]

Soreness of eyes; blearedness. *Bacon.*

LIP'-WISDOM, *n.* Wisdom in talk without practice; wisdom in words not supported by experience. *Sidney.*

LIQ'UABLE, *a.* [See *Liquate.*] That may be melted.

LIQUA'TION, *n.* [L. *liquatio*. See *Liquate.*]

1. The act or operation of melting.

2. The capacity of being melted; as a substance congealed beyond *liquation*. *Brown.*

LI'QUATE, *v. i.* [L. *liquo.*] To melt; to liquefy; to be dissolved. [*Little used.*] *Woodward.*

LIQUEFAC'TION, *n.* [L. *liquefactio*, from *liquefacio.*]

The act or operation of melting or dissolving; the conversion of a solid into a liquid by the sole agency of heat or caloric. *Liquefaction*, in common usage, signifies the melting of any substance, but by some authors it is applied to the melting of substances, which pass through intermediate states of softness before they become fluid, as tallow, wax, resin, &c. *Coxe's Dispensatory.*

2. The state of being melted.

LIQ'UEFIABLE, *a.* That may be melted, or changed from a solid to a liquid state. *Bacon.*

LIQ'UEFIER, *n.* That which melts any solid substance.

LIQ'UEFY, *v. t.* [Fr. *liquefier*, from L. *liquefacio*. See *Liquid.*]

To melt; to dissolve; to convert from a fixed or solid form to that of a liquid, and technically, to melt by the sole agency of heat or caloric.

LIQ'UEFY, *v. i.* To be melted; to become liquid. *Addison.*

LIQ'UEFYING, *ppr.* Melting; becoming liquid.

LIQUES'CENCY, *n.* [L. *liquescentia.*] Aptness to melt. *Johnson.*

LIQUES'CENT, *a.* Melting; becoming fluid.

LIQUEUR, *n.* [Fr.] A spirituous cordial.

LIQ'UID, *a.* [L. *liquidus*, from *liquo*, to melt, Ir. *leagham*; probably from flowing, and coinciding with Sax. *loge*, water, L. *lix*, and *lug*, in *Lugdunum*, *Leyden*, *Lyons.*]

Fluid; flowing or capable of flowing; not fixed or solid. But *liquid* is not precisely synonymous with *fluid*. Mercury and air are *fluid*, but not *liquid*.

2. Soft; clear; flowing; smooth; as *liquid* melody. *Crashaw.*

3. Pronounced without any jar; smooth; as a *liquid* letter.

4. Dissolved; not obtainable by law; as a *liquid* debt. *Obs.* *Ayliffe.*

LIQ'UID, *n.* A fluid or flowing substance; a substance whose parts change their relative position on the slightest pressure, and which flows on an inclined plane; as water, wine, milk, &c.

2. In *grammar*, a letter which has a smooth flowing sound, or which flows smoothly after a mute; as *l* and *r*, in *bla*, *bra*. *M* and *n* are also called liquids.

LIQ'UIDATE, *v. t.* [Fr. *liquider*; L. *liquido.*] To clear from all obscurity.

> Time only can *liquidate* the meaning of all parts of a compound system. *Hamilton.*

2. To settle; to adjust; to ascertain or reduce to precision in amount.

> Which method of *liquidating* the amercement to a precise sum, was usually performed in the superior courts. *Blackstone.*
>
> The clerk of the commons' house of assembly in 1774, gave certificates to the public creditors that their demands were *liquidated*, and should be provided for in the next tax-bill. *Ramsay.*
>
> The domestic debt may be subdivided into *liquidated* and *unliquidated*. *Hamilton.*

3. To pay; to settle, adjust and satisfy; as a debt. *Wheaton.*

> Kyburgh was ceded to Zuric by Sigismond, to *liquidate* a debt of a thousand florins. *Coxe's Switz.*

LIQ'UIDATED, *pp.* Settled; adjusted; reduced to certainty; paid.

LIQ'UIDATING, *ppr.* Adjusting; ascertaining; paying.

LIQUIDA'TION, *n.* The act of settling and adjusting debts, or ascertaining their amount or balance due.

LIQ'UIDATOR, *n.* He or that which liquidates or settles. *E. Everett.*

LIQUID'ITY, *n.* [Fr. *liquidité.*] The quality of being fluid or liquid.

2. Thinness. *Glanville.*

LIQ'UIDNESS, *n.* The quality of being liquid; fluency. *Boyle.*

LIQ'UOR, *n.* *lik'or.* [Sax. *loge*; Fr. *liqueur*; L. *liquor.*]

A liquid or fluid substance. [See *Liquid.*] *Liquor* is a word of general signification, extending to water, milk, blood, sap, juice, &c.; but its most common application is to spirituous fluids, whether distilled or fermented, to decoctions, solutions, tinctures. *Milton.*

LIQ'UOR, *v. t.* To moisten; to drench. [*Little used.*] *Bacon.*

LIQUORICE. [See *Licorice.*]

LIS'BON, *n.* A species of wine exported from Lisbon, in Portugal.

LISNE, *n.* A cavity or hollow. [*Not in use.*] *Hale.*

LISP, *v. i.* [G. *lispeln*, D. *lispen*, to lisp; Sax. *vlisp* or *vlips*, a lisping; Sw. *läspa*, Russ. *lepetzu*, to lisp.]

To speak with a particular articulation of the tongue and teeth, nearly as in pronouncing *th*. *Lisping* is particularly noticed in uttering *th* for *s*, as *yeth* for *yes*. It is most common in children.

> I *lisped* in numbers, for the numbers came. *Pope.*

LISP, *v. t.* To pronounce with a lisp; as, she *lisped* a few words.

LISP, *n.* The act of lisping, as in uttering an aspirated *th* for *s*.

LISP'ER, *n.* One that lisps.

LISP'ING, *ppr.* Uttering with a lisp.

LISP'INGLY, *adv.* With a lisp. *Holder.*

LIST, *n.* [Sax. Sw. *list*; It. Sp. *lista*; Fr. Dan. *liste*; D. *lyst*; G. *litze*. If *list*, a roll or catalogue, and *list*, a border or strip of cloth, are from the same root, we find the original orthography in the Arm. *lez*, and Sp. *liza*, and perhaps the L. *licium*, Fr. *lice*. But in some languages the words are distinguished; Fr. *liste*, a roll, and *lisiere*, a list or selvage of cloth.]

1. In *commerce*, the border, edge or selvage of cloth; a strip of cloth forming the border, particularly of broadcloth, and serving to strengthen it.

2. A line inclosing or forming the extremity of a piece of ground, or field of combat; hence, the ground or field inclosed for a race or combat. Hence, to *enter the lists*, is to accept a challenge or engage in contest. Hence,

3. A limit or boundary; a border.

4. In *architecture*, a little square molding; a fillet; called also a *listel*.

5. A roll or catalogue, that is, a row or line; as a *list* of names; a *list* of books; a *list* of articles; a *list* of ratable estate.

6. A strip of cloth; a fillet. *Swift.*

Civil list, in Great Britain and the United States, the civil officers of government, as judges, embassadors, secretaries, &c. Hence it is used for the revenues or appropriations of public money for the support of the civil officers.

LIST, *v. t.* [from *list*, a roll.] To enroll; to register in a list or catalogue; to enlist. The latter is the more elegant word. Hence,

2. To engage in the public service, as soldiers.

> They in my name are *listed*. *Dryden.*

3. To inclose for combat; as, to *list* a field. *Dryden.*

4. To sew together, as strips of cloth; or to form a border. *Wotton.*

5. To cover with a list, or with strips of cloth; as, to *list* a door.

6. To hearken; to attend; a contraction of *listen*, which see.

LIST, *v. i.* To engage in public service by enrolling one's name; to enlist. [The latter is the more elegant word. See *Enlist.*]

LIST, *v. i.* [Sax. *lystan*; G. *lüsten*; D. *lusten*; Sw. *lysta*; Dan. *lyster*. See *Lust*. The primary sense seems to be to lean, incline, advance or stretch toward. [See the Noun.]

Properly, to lean or incline; to be propense; hence, to desire or choose.

> Let other men think of your devices as they *list*. *Whitgifte.*
>
> The wind bloweth where it *listeth*. John iii.

LIST, *n.* In the language of seamen, an inclination to one side. The ship has a *list* to port. *Mar. Dict.*

LIST'ED, *pp.* Striped; particolored in stripes.

2. Covered with list.

3. Inclosed for combat.

4. Engaged in public service; enrolled.

LIST'EL, *n.* A list in architecture; a fillet. *Encyc.*

LIST'EN, *v. i.* lis'n. [Sax. *lystan* or *hlystan*; D. *luisteren.* Qu. G. *lauschen*; Scot. *lith.*]

1. To hearken; to give ear; to attend closely with a view to hear.

On the green bank I sat, and *listened* long. *Dryden.*

2. To obey; to yield to advice; to follow admonition.

LIS'TEN, *v. t.* lis'n. To hear; to attend. *Shak.*

LIST'ENER, *n.* One who listens; a hearkener.

LIST'ER, *n.* One who makes a list or roll.

LIST'FUL, *a.* Attentive. *Obs.* *Spenser.*

LIST'ING, *ppr.* Inclosing for combat; covering with list; enlisting.

LIST'LESS, *a.* Not listening; not attending; indifferent to what is passing; heedless; inattentive; thoughtless; careless; as a *listless* hearer or spectator.

LIST'LESSLY, *adv.* Without attention; heedlessly.

LIST'LESSNESS, *n.* Inattention; heedlessness; indifference to what is passing and may be interesting.

LIT, *pret.* of *light.* The bird *lit* on a tree before me.

I *lit* my pipe with the paper. *Addison.*

[This word, though used by some good writers, is very inelegant.]

LIT'ANY, *n.* [Fr. *litanie*, Gr. λιτανεια, supplication, from λιτανευω, λιτομαι, λισσομαι, to pray.]

A solemn form of supplication, used in public worship.

Supplications for the appeasing of God's wrath, were by the Greek church termed *litanies*, by the Latin, rogations. *Hooker.*

LITE, *a.* Little. [*Not in use.*]

LĪTER, *n.* [Fr. *litre*, from Gr. λιτρα.] A French measure of capacity, being a cubic decimeter, containing, according to Lunier, about a pint and a half old French measure. The liter is equal to 60,02800 cubic inches, or nearly 2⅛ wine pints. *Cyc.*

LIT'ERAL, *a.* [Fr. from L. *litera*, a letter.]

1. According to the letter; primitive; real; not figurative or metaphorical; as the *literal* meaning of a phrase.

2. Following the letter or exact words; not free; as a *literal* translation.

3. Consisting of letters.

The *literal* notation of numbers was known to Europeans before the ciphers. *Johnson.*

LIT'ERAL, *n.* Literal meaning. [*Not used.*] *Brown.*

LIT'ERALISM, *n.* That which accords with the letter. *Milton.*

LITERAL'ITY, *n.* Original or literal meaning. *Brown.*

LIT'ERALLY, *adv.* According to the primary and natural import of words; not figuratively. A man and his wife cannot be *literally* one flesh.

2. With close adherence to words; word by word.

So wild and ungovernable a poet cannot be translated *literally.* *Dryden.*

LIT'ERARY, *a.* [L. *literarius.*] Pertaining to letters or literature; respecting learning or learned men; as a *literary* history; *literary* conversation.

2. Derived from erudition; as *literary* fame.

3. Furnished with erudition; versed in letters; as a *literary* man.

4. Consisting in letters, or written or printed compositions; as *literary* property.

LIT'ERATE, *a.* [L. *literatus.*] Learned; lettered; instructed in learning and science. *Johnson.*

LITERA'TI, *n. plu.* [L. *literatus.*] The learned; men of erudition. *Spectator.*

LIT'ERATOR, *n.* [L.] A petty schoolmaster. *Burke.*

LIT'ERATURE, *n.* [L. *literatura.*] Learning; acquaintance with letters or books. *Literature* comprehends a knowledge of the ancient languages, denominated classical, history, grammar, rhetoric, logic, geography, &c. as well as of the sciences. A knowledge of the world and good breeding give luster to *literature.*

LITH, *n.* [Sax.] A joint or limb. *Obs.* *Chaucer.*

LITHAN'THRAX, *n.* [Gr. λιθος, a stone, and ανθραξ, a coal.]

Stone-coal, a black, compact, brittle, inflammable substance, of laminated texture, more or less shining. *Nicholson.*

LITH'ARĠE, *n.* [Fr. from L. *lithargyros*, Gr. λιθαργυρος, the spume or scum of silver.]

A semi-vitreous oxyd of lead, produced in refining silver by cupellation with lead. It appears in the form of soft flakes, or semi-transparent shining plates.

Dict. Nat. Hist. *Encyc.* *Nicholson.*

LITHE, *a.* [Sax. *lith, lithe*; W. *llyth.*] That may be easily bent; pliant; flexible; limber; as the elephant's *lithe* proboscis. *Milton.*

LITHE, *v. t.* To smooth; to soften; to palliate. *Obs.* *Chaucer.*

2. To listen. *Obs.* [See *Listen.*]

LI'THENESS, *n.* Flexibility; limberness.

LI'THER, *a.* Soft; pliant. *Obs.* *Shak.*

2. [Sax. *lythr.*] Bad; corrupt. *Obs.* *Woolton.*

LI'THERLY, *adv.* Slowly; lazily. *Obs.* *Barret.*

LI'THERNESS, *n.* Idleness; laziness. *Obs.* *Barret.*

LITH'IA, *n.* A new alkali, found in a mineral called petalite, of which the basis is a metal called *lithium.* *Davy.* *Ure.*

LITH'IATE, *n.* [Gr. λιθος, a stone.] A salt or compound formed by the lithic acid combined with a base. *Hooper.*

LITH'IC, *a.* [supra.] Pertaining to the stone in the bladder. The *lithic* acid is obtained from a calculus in the bladder.

LITHOBIBLION. [See *Lithophyl.*]

LITH'OCARP, *n.* [Gr. λιθος, a stone, and καρπος, fruit.] Fossil fruit; fruit petrified. *Dict. Nat. Hist.*

LITH'OCOLLA, *n.* [Gr. λιθος, a stone, and κολλα, glue.] A cement that unites stones. *Ash.*

LITHODEN'DRON, *n.* [Gr. λιθος, stone, and δενδρον, tree.] Coral; so called from its resembling a petrified branch. *Parr.*

LITHOĠEN'ESY, *n.* [Gr. λιθος, stone, and γενεσις, generation.]

The doctrine or science of the origin of minerals composing the globe, and of the causes which have produced their form and disposition. *Dict. Nat. Hist.*

LITHOGLYPH'ITE, *n.* [Gr. λιθος, stone, and γλυφω, to engrave.]

A fossil that presents the appearance of being engraved or shaped by art. *Lunier.*

LITHOG'RAPHER, *n.* [See *Lithography.*] One who practices lithography.

LITHOGRAPH'IC, **LITHOGRAPH'ICAL**, } *a.* Pertaining to lithography.

LITHOGRAPH'ICALLY, *adv.* By the lithographic art.

LITHOG'RAPHY, *n.* [Gr. λιθος, stone, and γραφω, to engrave or write.]

The art of engraving, or of tracing letters, figures or other designs on stone, and of transferring them to paper by impression; an art recently invented by Mr. Sennefelder of Munich, in Bavaria. *Journ. of Science.*

LITHOLOĠ'IC, **LITHOLOĠ'ICAL**, } *a.* [See *Lithology.*]

Pertaining to the science of stones.

LITHOL'OĠIST, *n.* A person skilled in the science of stones.

LITHOL'OĠY, *n.* [Gr. λιθος, stone, and λογος, discourse.]

1. The science or natural history of stones. *Fourcroy.*

2. A treatise on stones found in the body. *Coxe.*

LITH'OMANCY, *n.* [Gr. λιθος, stone, and μαντεια, divination.]

Divination or prediction of events by means of stones. *Brown.*

LITHOMAR'GA, **LITH'OMARĠE**, } *n.* [Gr. λιθος, stone, and L. *marga*, marl.]

An earth of two species, friable and indurated, more siliceous than aluminous, distinguished by its great fineness and its fusibility into a soft slag.

Dict. Nat. Hist. *Kirwan.* *Ure.*

LITHONTRIP'TIC, *a.* [Gr. λιθος, stone, and τριβω, to wear or break.]

Having the quality of dissolving the stone in the bladder or kidneys.

LITHONTRIP'TIC, *n.* A medicine which has the power of dissolving the stone in the bladder or kidneys; a solvent of stone in the human urinary passages. *Coxe.*

LITH'ONTRIPTOR, **LITH'OTRITOR**, } *n.* An instrument for triturating the stone in the bladder, so that it may be extracted without cutting; recently invented by Dr. Civiale.

LITH'ONTRIPTY, **LITH'OTRITY**, } *n.* The operation of triturating the stone in the bladder, by means of an instrument called *lithotritor.*

LITHOPH'AGOUS, *a.* [Gr. λιθος, stone, and φαγω, to eat.]

Eating or swallowing stones or gravel, as the ostrich.

LITH'OPHOSPHOR, *n.* [Gr. λιθος, stone, and φωσφορος.]

A stone that becomes phosphoric by heat. *Dict. Nat. Hist.*

LITHOPHOSPHOR'IC, *a.* Pertaining to lithophosphor; becoming phosphoric by heat.

LITH'OPHYL, *n.* [Gr. λιθος, stone, and φυλλον, a leaf.]

Bibliolite or lithobiblion, fossil leaves, or the figures of leaves on fossils.

LITH'OPHYTE, *n.* [Gr. λιθος, stone, and φυτον, a plant; literally, stone-plant.]

Stone-coral; a name given to those species

of polypiers, whose substance is stony. The older naturalists classed them with vegetables. *Cuvier. Ray.*

LITHOPHYT'IC, *a.* Pertaining to lithophytes.

LITH'OPHYTOUS, *a.* Pertaining to or consisting of lithophytes.

LITH'OTOME, *n.* [Gr. λιθος, stone, and τεμνω, to cut.]
A stone so formed naturally as to appear as if cut artificially. *Dict. Nat. Hist.*

LITHOTOM'IC, *a.* Pertaining to or performed by lithotomy.

LITHOT'OMIST, *n.* [See *Lithotomy.*] One who performs the operation of cutting for the stone in the bladder; or one who is skilled in the operation.

LITHOT'OMY, *n.* [Gr. λιθος, stone, and τεμνω, to cut.]
The operation, art or practice of cutting for the stone in the bladder.

LITHOX'YLE, *n.* [Gr. λιθος, stone, and ξυλον, wood.]
Petrified wood. It differs from *lignite*, being really changed into stone; such as silicified woods, which are changed into varieties of silex, &c. *Dict. Nat. Hist.*

LITH'Y, *a.* [See *Lithe.*] Easily bent; pliable. [This is probably the word which, in our popular use, is pronounced *lathy.*]

LIT'IGANT, *a.* [See *Litigate.*] Contending in law; engaged in a lawsuit; as the parties *litigant.* *Ayliffe.*

LIT'IGANT, *n.* A person engaged in a lawsuit. *L'Estrange.*

LIT'IGATE, *v. t.* [L. *litigo*, from *lis*, *litis*, a contest or debate; Ar. لدّ ladda, to dispute. Class Ld. No. 2. *Lis, litis*, coincides with the Sax. *flit*, contention; *flitan*, to contend.]
To contest in law; to prosecute or defend by pleadings, exhibition of evidence, and judicial debate; as, to *litigate* a cause or a question.

LIT'IGATE, *v. i.* To dispute in law; to carry on a suit by judicial process.

LIT'IGATED, *pp.* Contested judicially.

LIT'IGATING, *ppr.* Contesting in law.

LITIGA'TION, *n.* The act or process of carrying on a suit in a court of law or equity for the recovery of a right or claim; a judicial contest.

LITIG'IOUS, *a.* [Fr. *litigieux*; L. *litigiosus.*]
1. Inclined to judicial contest; given to the practice of contending in law; quarrelsome; contentious; *applied to persons.* A *litigious* man is a bad neighbor and a bad citizen.
2. Disputable; controvertible; subject to contention; as *litigious* right. *Blackstone.*

> No fences, parted fields, nor marks nor bounds,
> Distinguish'd acres of *litigious* grounds. *Dryden.*

LITIG'IOUSLY, *adv.* In a contentious manner.

LITIG'IOUSNESS, *n.* A disposition to engage in or to carry on lawsuits; inclination to judicial contests.

LIT'MUS, } *n.* A blue pigment, formed
LAC'MUS, } from archil, a species of lichen. [See *Archil.*] It is prepared by bruising the archil, and adding quick lime and putrefied urine, or spirit of urine distilled from lime. The mixture, after cooling and the evaporation of the fluid, becomes a mass of the consistence of paste, which is laid on a board to dry in square lumps. *Encyc.*

LIT'ORN, *n.* A bird, a species of thrush, in size and shape resembling the hen-blackbird. *Dict. Nat. Hist.*

LIT'OTE, *n.* [Gr. λιτος, slender.] Diminution; extenuation. *Pope.*

LIT'TER, *n.* [Fr. *litiere*, from *lit*; contracted from L. *lectus*, from the root of *lego*, Eng. *lay*; It. *lettica* or *lettiga*; Sp. *litera*; Port. *liteira*; Arm. *leter.*]
1. A vehicle formed with shafts supporting a bed between them, in which a person may be borne by men or by a horse. If by the latter, it is called a horse-litter. A similar vehicle in India is called a *palanquin.*
2. Straw, hay or other soft substance, used as a bed for horses and for other purposes.
3. [Ice. *lider*, generation, from the root of *lad, leod.*] A brood of young pigs, kittens, puppies, or other quadrupeds. The word is applied only to certain quadrupeds of the smaller kinds. [Qu. the root of *lad.*]
4. A birth of pigs or other small animals.
5. Waste matters, shreds, fragments and the like, scattered on a floor or other clean place.

LIT'TER, *v. t.* To bring forth young, as swine and other small quadrupeds. It is sometimes applied to human beings in contempt. *Shak.*
2. To scatter over carelessly with shreds, fragments and the like; as, to *litter* a room or a carpet. *Swift.*
3. To cover with straw or hay; as, to *litter* a stable. *Dryden.*
4. To supply with litter; as, to *litter* cattle.

LIT'TERED, *pp.* Furnished with straw.
2. *a.* Covered or overspread with litter, pieces, shreds, &c.

LIT'TLE, *a.* comp. *less, lesser*; sup. *least.* [Sax. *lytel, lytle*; Scot. *lite, lyte*, adv. *lyt*; Goth. *leitil*; Sw. *liten*; Dan. *liden*; D. *luttel*; probably from the sense of diminishing. Class Ld. No. 15. 22. 31.]
1. Small in size or extent; not great or large; as a *little* body; a *little* animal; a *little* piece of ground; a *little* table; a *little* book; a *little* hill; a *little* distance; a *little* child.
2. Short in duration; as a *little* time or season; a *little* sleep.
3. Small in quantity or amount; as a *little* hay or grass; a *little* food; a *little* sum; a *little* light; a *little* air or water.
4. Of small dignity, power or importance.

> When thou wast *little* in thy own sight, wast thou not made the head of the tribes? 1 Sam. xv.

5. Of small force or effect; slight; inconsiderable; as *little* attention or exertions; *little* effort; *little* care or diligence; *little* weight.

LIT'TLE, *n.* A small quantity or amount. He demanded much and obtained *little.* He had *little* of his father's liberality.
2. A small space.

> Much was in *little* writ— *Dryden.*

3. Any thing small, slight, or of inconsiderable importance.

> I view with anger and disdain,
> How *little* gives thee joy and pain. *Prior.*

4. Not much.

> These they are fitted for, and *little* else. *Cheyne.*

LIT'TLE, *adv.* In a small degree; slightly; as, he is *little* changed. It is a *little* discolored.
2. Not much; in a small quantity or space of time. He sleeps *little.*
3. In some degree; slightly; sometimes preceded by *a.* The liquor is *a little* sour or astringent.

LIT'TLENESS, *n.* Smallness of size or bulk; as the *littleness* of the body or of an animal.
2. Meanness; want of grandeur; as *littleness* of conception.
3. Want of dignity. Contemplations on the majesty of God displayed in his works, may awaken in us a sense of our own *littleness.*
4. Meanness; penuriousness.

LIT'TORAL, *a.* [L. *littoralis*, from *littus*, shore.] Belonging to a shore. [*Little used.*]

LIT'UITE, *n.* A fossil shell.

LITUR'GICAL, *a.* [See *Liturgy.*] Pertaining to a liturgy.

LIT'URGY, *n.* [Fr. *liturgie*; Sp. It. *liturgia*; Gr. λειτουργια; λειτος, public, and εργον, work.]
In a general sense, all public ceremonies that belong to divine service; hence, in a restricted sense, among the Romanists, the mass; and among protestants, the common prayer, or the formulary of public prayers. *Johnson. Encyc.*

LIVE, *v. i.* liv. [Sax. *liban, leofan, lifian*; Goth. *liban*; Sw. *lefwa*; Dan. *lever*; G. *leben*; D. *lieven.* It coincides with *leave.* The primary sense probably is to rest, remain, abide. If so, the root may be Ar. لبّ labba, to be, to abide. Class Lb. No. 1.]
1. To abide; to dwell; to have settled residence in any place. Where do you *live*? I *live* in London. He *lives* in Philadelphia. He *lives* in a large house in Second street. The Swiss *live* on mountains. The Bedouin Arabs *live* in the desert.
2. To continue; to be permanent; not to perish.

> Men's evil manners *live* in brass; their virtues
> We write in water. *Shak.*

3. To be animated; to have the vital principle; to have the bodily functions in operation, or in a capacity to operate, as respiration, circulation of blood, secretions, &c.; *applied to animals.*

> I am Joseph; doth my father yet *live*? Gen. xlv.

4. To have the principles of vegetable life; to be in a state in which the organs do or may perform their functions in the circulation of sap and in growth; *applied to plants.* This tree will not *live*, unless watered; it will not *live* through the winter.
5. To pass life or time in a particular manner, with regard to habits or condition. In what manner does your son *live*? Does

he *live* in ease and affluence? Does he *live* according to the dictates of reason and the precepts of religion?

If we act by several broken views, we shall *live* and die in misery. *Spectator.*

6. To continue in life. The way to *live* long is to be temperate.

7. To live, emphatically; to enjoy life; to be in a state of happiness.

What greater curse could envious fortune give,
Than just to die, when I began to *live?* *Dryden.*

8. To feed; to subsist; to be nourished and supported in life; as, horses *live* on grass or grain; fowls *live* on seeds or insects; some kinds of fish *live* on others; carnivorous animals *live* on flesh.

9. To subsist; to be maintained in life; to be supported. Many of the clergy are obliged to *live* on small salaries. All men in health may *live* by industry with economy, yet some men *live* by robbery.

10. To remain undestroyed; to float; not to sink or founder. It must be a good ship that *lives* at sea in a hurricane.

Nor can our shaken vessels *live* at sea. *Dryden.*

11. To exist; to have being.

As I *live*, saith the Lord— Ezek. xviii.

12. In *Scripture*, to be exempt from death, temporal or spiritual.

Ye shall therefore keep my statutes and judgments, which if a man do, he shall *live* in them. Lev. xviii.

13. To recover from sickness; to have life prolonged.

Thy son *liveth*. John iv.

14. To be inwardly quickened, nourished and actuated by divine influence or faith. Gal. ii.

15. To be greatly refreshed, comforted and animated.

For now we *live*, if ye stand fast in the Lord. 1 Thess. iii.

16. To appear as in life or reality; to be manifest in real character.

And all the writer *lives* in every line. *Pope.*

To live with, to dwell or to be a lodger with.

2. To cohabit; to have intercourse, as male and female. *Shak.*

LIVE, *v. t. liv.* To continue in constantly or habitually; as, to *live* a life of ease.

2. To act habitually in conformity to.

It is not enough to say prayers, unless they *live* them too. *Parker.*

LIVE, *a.* Having life; having respiration and other organic functions in operation, or in a capacity to operate; not dead; as a *live* ox.

2. Having vegetable life; as a *live* plant.

3. Containing fire; ignited; not extinct; as a *live* coal.

4. Vivid, as color. *Thomson.*

LIVELESS, not used. [See *Lifeless.*]

LI'VELIHOOD, *n.* [*lively* and *hood*, or *lifelode*, from *lead*. I find in Saxon *lif-lade*, lead or course of life, *vitæ iter.*]

Means of living; support of life; maintenance. Trade furnishes many people with an honest *livelihood*. Men of enterprise seek a *livelihood* where they can find it.

LI'VELINESS, *n.* [from *lively.*] The quality or state of being lively or animated; sprightliness; vivacity; animation; spirit; as the *liveliness* of youth, contrasted with the gravity of age.

2. An appearance of life, animation or spirit; as the *liveliness* of the eye or countenance in a portrait.

3. Briskness; activity; effervescence, as of liquors.

LIVELODE, for *livelihood*, not used. *Hubberd's Tale.*

LIVELONG, *a. liv'long.* [*live* and *long.*]

1. Long in passing.

How could she sit the *livelong* day,
Yet never ask us once to play? *Swift.*

2. Lasting; durable; as a *livelong* monument. [*Not used.*] *Milton.*

3. A plant of the genus Sedum.

LI'VELY, *a.* Brisk; vigorous; vivacious; active; as a *lively* youth.

2. Gay; airy.

From grave to gay, from *lively* to severe. *Pope.*

3. Representing life; as a *lively* imitation of nature.

4. Animated; spirited; as a *lively* strain of eloquence; a *lively* description.

5. Strong; energetic; as a *lively* faith or hope; a *lively* persuasion.

Lively stones, in Scripture. Saints are called *lively stones*, as being quickened by the Spirit and active in holiness. *Brown.*

LI'VELY, *adv.* Briskly; vigorously. [*Little used.*] *Hayward.*

2. With strong resemblance of life.

That part of poetry must needs be best, which describes most *lively* our actions and passions. [*Little used.*] *Dryden.*

LIV'ER, *n.* One who lives.

And try if life be worth the *liver's* care. *Prior.*

It is often used with a word of qualification; as a *high liver;* a *loose liver*, &c.

LIV'ER, *n.* [Sax. *lifer, lifre;* D. *leever;* G. *leber;* Sw. *lefver;* Dan. *lever;* Russ. *liber.* The Saxon word is rendered also *libramentum*, and this viscus may be named from its *weight.*]

A viscus or intestine of considerable size and of a reddish color, convex on the anterior and superior side, and of an unequal surface on the inferior and posterior side. It is situated under the false ribs, in the right hypochondrium. It consists of two lobes, of a glandular substance, and destined for the secretion of the bile. *Encyc.*

LIV'ERCŎLOR, *a.* Dark red; of the color of the liver. *Woodward.*

LIV'ERED, *a.* Having a liver; as white-*livered*. *Sherwood.*

LIV'ERGROŴN, *a.* Having a large liver. *Graunt.*

LIV'ERSTONE, *n.* [G. *leber-stein.*] A stone or species of earth of the barytic genus, of a gray or brown color, which, when rubbed or heated to redness, emits the smell of liver of sulphur, or alkaline sulphuret. *Kirwan.*

LIV'ERWŎRT, *n.* The name of many species of plants. Several of the lichens are so called. The liverworts *(Hepaticæ)* are a natural order of cryptogamian plants, whose herbage is generally frondose, and resembling the leafy lichens, but whose seeds are contained in a distinct capsule. The *noble liverwort* is the Anemone hepatica. *Smith. Lee.*

LIV'ERY, *n.* [Norm. from Fr. *livrer*, to deliver.]

1. The act of delivering possession of lands or tenements; a term of English law. It is usual to say, *livery of seisin*, which is a feudal investiture, made by the delivery of a turf, of a rod or twig, from the feoffor to the feoffee. In America, no such ceremony is necessary to a conveyance of real estate, the delivery of a deed being sufficient.

2. Release from wardship; deliverance. *King Charles.*

3. The writ by which possession is obtained. *Johnson.*

4. The state of being kept at a certain rate; as, to keep horses at *livery*. *Spenser.*

5. A form of dress by which noblemen and gentlemen distinguish their servants. The Romish church has also *liveries* for confessors, virgins, apostles, martyrs, penitents, &c. Hence,

6. A particular dress or garb, appropriate or peculiar to particular times or things; as the *livery* of May; the *livery* of autumn.

Now came still evening on, and twilight gray
Had in her sober *livery* all things clad. *Milton.*

7. The whole body of liverymen in London.

LIV'ERY, *v. t.* To clothe in livery. *Shak.*

LIV'ERYMAN, *n.* One who wears a livery; as a servant.

2. In London, a freeman of the city, of some distinction. The liverymen are chosen from among the freemen of each company, and from their number are elected the common council, sheriff and other superior officers of the city. They alone have the right of voting for members of parliament. *Encyc.*

LIV'ERY-STABLE, *n.* A stable where horses are kept for hire.

LIVES, *n. plu.* of *life.*

LI'VESTOCK, *n.* [*live* and *stock.*] Horses, cattle and smaller domestic animals; a term applied in America to such animals as may be exported alive for foreign market.

LIV'ID, *a.* [Fr. *livide;* It. *livido;* L. *lividus;* from *liveo*, to be black and blue.]

Black and blue; of a lead color; discolored, as flesh by contusion.

Upon my *livid* lips bestow a kiss. *Dryden.*

LIVID'ITY, LIV'IDNESS, } *n.* A dark color, like that of bruised flesh. [*Lividness* is the preferable word.]

LIV'ING, *ppr.* [from *live.*] Dwelling; residing; existing; subsisting; having life or the vital functions in operation; not dead.

2. *a.* Issuing continually from the earth; running; flowing; as a *living* spring or fountain; opposed to *stagnant.*

3. *a.* Producing action, animation and vigor; quickening; as a *living* principle; a *living* faith.

LIV'ING, *n.* He or those who are alive; usually with a plural signification; as in the land of the *living.*

The *living* will lay it to his heart. Eccles. vii.

LIV'ING, *n.* Means of subsistence; estate.

He divided to them his *living*. Luke xv.

She of her want, did cast in all that she had, even all her *living*. Mark xii.

2. Power of continuing life. There is no *living* with a scold.

There is no *living* without trusting some body or other in some cases. *L'Estrange.*

3. Livelihood. He made a *living* by his occupation. The woman spins for a *living*.
4. The benefice of a clergyman. He lost his *living* by non-conformity.

LIV'INGLY, *adv.* In a living state. *Brown.*

Livonica terra, a species of fine bole found in Livonia, brought to market in little cakes.

LI'VRE, *n.* [Fr.; L. *libra.*] A French money of account, equal to 20 sous, or ten pence sterling.

LIXIV'IAL, LIXIV'IOUS, } *a.* [L. *lixivius*, from *lix*, lye.]
1. Obtained by lixiviation; impregnated with alkaline salt extracted from wood ashes. *Lixivial* salts are those which are obtained by passing water through ashes, or by pouring it on them.
2. Containing salt extracted from the ashes of wood.
3. Of the color of lye; resembling lye.
4. Having the qualities of alkaline salts from wood ashes.

LIXIV'IATE, LIXIV'IATED, } *a.* Pertaining to lye or lixivium; of the quality of alkaline salts.
2. Impregnated with salts from wood ashes.

LIXIV'IATE, *v. t.* [L. *lixivia*, *lixivium*, lye.] To form lye; to impregnate with salts from wood ashes. Water is *lixiviated* by passing through ashes.

LIXIVIA'TION, *n.* The operation or process of extracting alkaline salts from ashes by pouring water on them, the water passing through them imbibing the salts.

LIXIV'IUM, *n.* [L. from *lix*, lye, Sp. *lexia*, Fr. *lessive.*]
Lye; water impregnated with alkaline salts imbibed from wood ashes. It is sometimes applied to other extracts. *Boyle.*

LIZ'ARD, *n.* [Fr. *lezarde*; L. *lacertus*; Sp. *lagarto*; It. *lucerta*, *lucertola*; Arm. *glasard.* If *lizard* is the L. *lacerta*, there has been a change of *c* into *z* or *s*, which may be the fact. In Ethiopic, *latsekat* is lizard. Gebelin deduces the word from an oriental word *leza*, to hide. But this is doubtful.]
In *zoology*, a genus of amphibious animals, called Lacerta, and comprehending the crocodile, alligator, chamelion, salamander, &c. But the name, in common life, is applied to the smaller species of this genus, and of these there is a great variety. These animals are ranked in the order of reptiles. The body is naked, with four feet and a tail. The body is thicker and more tapering than that of the serpent. *Encyc.*

LIZ'ARD-TAIL, *n.* A plant of the genus Saururus, and another of the genus Piper. *Fam. of Plants.*

LL. D. letters standing for *Doctor of Laws*, the title of an honorary degree.

LO, *exclam.* [Sax. *la.* Whether this is a contracted word or not, does not appear.]
Look; see; behold; observe. This word is used to excite particular attention in a hearer to some object of sight, or subject of discourse.

> *Lo*, here is Christ. Matt. xxiv.
> *Lo*, we turn to the Gentiles. Acts xiii.

LOACH, LOCHE, } *n.* [Fr. *loche.*] A small fish of the genus Cobitis, inhabiting small clear streams, and esteemed dainty food. *Walton.*

LOAD, *n.* [Sax. *hlad* or *lade*; W. *llwyth.* See *Lade.*]
1. A burden; that which is laid on or put in any thing for conveyance. Thus we lay a *load* on a beast or on a man's shoulders, or on a cart or wagon; and we say, a light *load*, a heavy *load.* A *load* then is indefinite in quantity or weight. But by usage, in some cases, the word has a more definite signification, and expresses a certain quantity or weight, or as much as is usually carried, or as can be well sustained. *Load* is never used for the cargo of a ship; this is called *loading*, *lading*, freight, or cargo.
2. Any heavy burden; a large quantity borne or sustained. A tree may be said to have a *load* of fruit upon it.
3. That which is borne with pain or difficulty; a grievous weight; encumbrance; in a literal sense.

> Jove lightened of its *load*
> Th' enormous mass— *Pope.*

In a figurative sense, we say, a *load* of care or grief; a *load* of guilt or crimes.
4. Weight or violence of blows. *Milton.*
5. A quantity of food or drink that oppresses, or as much as can be borne. *Dryden.*
6. Among *miners*, the quantity of nine dishes of ore, each dish being about half a hundred weight. *Encyc. Cyc.*

LOAD, *v. t.* pret. and pp. *loaded.* [*loadon*, formerly used, is obsolete, and *laden* belongs to *lade.* *Load*, from the noun, is a regular verb.]
1. To lay on a burden; to put on or in something to be carried, or as much as can be carried; as, to *load* a camel or a horse; to *load* a cart or wagon. To *load* a gun, is to charge, or to put in a sufficient quantity of powder, or powder and ball or shot.
2. To encumber; to lay on or put in that which is borne with pain or difficulty; in a literal sense, as to *load* the stomach with meat; or in a figurative sense, as to *load* the mind or memory.
3. To make heavy by something added or appended.

> Thy dreadful vow, *loaden* with death— *Addison.*

So in a literal sense, to *load* a whip.
4. To bestow or confer on in great abundance; as, to *load* one with honors; to *load* with reproaches.

LOADED, *pp.* Charged with a load or cargo; having a burden; freighted, as a ship; having a charge of powder, or powder and shot, as a gun.
2. Burdened with any thing oppressive; as *loaded* with cares, with guilt or shame.

LOADER, *n.* One who puts on a load.

LOADING, *ppr.* Charging with a load; burdening; encumbering; charging, as a gun.

LOADING, *n.* A cargo; a burden; also, any thing that makes part of a load.

LOADMANAGE, *n.* Pilotage; skill of a pilot. [*Not used.*]

LOADSMAN, *n.* [*load* and *man.*] A pilot. *Obs.*

LOADSTAR, LODESTAR, } *n.* [*lead* and *star.*] The star that leads; the polestar; the cynosure. *Obs.* *Shak.*

LOADSTONE, *n.* [from the verb *lead* and *stone.* The old orthography, *lodestone*, is most correct, as this word has no connection with the verb to *load.*]
The native magnet, an ore of iron in the lowest state of oxydation, which has the power of attracting metallic iron, as iron filings, and of communicating to masses of iron the same property of attraction, forming *artificial magnets.* [See *Lodestone.*]

LOAF, *n.* plu. *loaves.* [Sax. *hlaf* or *laf*; Goth. *hlaibs*; G. *leib*; Polish, *chlieb*; Bohemian, *chleb*; Russ. *chlib* or *chleb*; Croatian, *hlib*; Finnish, *leipa* or *leipam*; Laponic, *laibe.* The German *leib* is rendered a *loaf*, and body, waist, belly; *leiblich*, which in English, would be *loaf-like*, signifies corporeal, bodily. *Loaf* then signifies a lump or mass, from some root that signifies to set, or to collect, or to form.]
1. A mass of bread when baked. It is larger than a *cake.* The size and price of a *loaf*, in large cities, are regulated by law.
2. A mass or lump, as of sugar.
3. Any thick mass.

LOAF-SUGAR, *n.* Sugar refined and formed into a conical mass.

LOAM, *n.* [Sax. *lam*; D. *leem*; G. *lehm*; L. *limus*; Sw. *lim*; Dan. *lim*, *liim*; so named probably from smoothness or softness; W. *llim.*]
A natural mixture of sand and clay with oxyd of iron; a species of earth or soil of different colors, whitish, brown or yellow, readily diffusible in water. *Cleaveland. Encyc.*

LOAM, *v. t.* To cover with loam. *Moxon.*

LOAMY, *a.* Consisting of loam; partaking of the nature of loam, or resembling it.

LOAN, *n.* [Sax. *læn*, *hlæn*; Sw. *lån*; Dan. *laan*; D. *leen*; G. *lehen.* See *Lend.*]
1. The act of lending; a lending.
2. That which is lent; any thing furnished for temporary use to a person at his request, on the express or implied condition that the specific thing shall be returned, or its equivalent in kind, but without compensation for the use; as a *loan* of a book or of bread.
3. Something furnished for temporary use, on the condition that it shall be returned or its equivalent, but with a compensation for the use. In this sense, *loan* is generally applied to money. [See *Lend.*]
4. A furnishing; permission to use; grant of the use; as a *loan* of credit. *Kent.*

LOAN, *v. t.* [Sax. *lænan*; G. *lehnen*; D. *leenen*; Sw. *låna*; Dan. *laaner.*]
To lend; to deliver to another for temporary use, on condition that the thing shall be returned, as a book; or to deliver for use, on condition that an equivalent in kind shall be returned, as bread; or to deliver for temporary use, on condition that an equivalent in kind shall be returned, with a compensation for the use, as in the case of money at interest. Bills of credit were issued, to be *loaned* on interest.
Ramsay. Kent. Laws of the U. States. Stat. of Conn. and of New York.

LO'AN-OFFICE, *n.* In *America*, a public office in which loans of money are negotiated for the public, or in which the accounts of loans are kept and the interest paid to the lenders.

LO'AN-OFFICER, *n.* A public officer empowered to superintend and transact the business of a loan-office.

LOATH, } *a.* [Sax. *lath*, hateful; *lathian*, to
LOTH, } lothe; Sw. *ledas*, to lothe or nauseate; Dan. *leede*, lothesome; *lee*, aversion. In America, the primitive pronunciation of *lath*, that is, *lawth*, is retained in the adjective, which is written *loth.* The verb would be better written *lothe*, in analogy with *cloth, clothe.* See *Loth.*]
Disliking; unwilling; reluctant. He was *loth* to leave the company. [See *Loth.*]

LOATHE, } *v. t.* To hate; to look on with
LOTHE, } hatred or abhorrence; particularly, to feel disgust at food or drink, either from natural antipathy, or a sickly appetite, or from satiety, or from its ill taste. [See *Lothe.*]

LOATHER, *n.* One that lothes.

LOATHFUL, *a.* Hating; abhorring through disgust. *Hubberd's Tale.*
2. Abhorred; hated. *Spenser.*

LOATHING, *ppr.* Hating from disgust; abhorring.

LOATHINGLY, *adv.* In a fastidious manner.

LOATHLY, *a.* Hateful; exciting hatred. *Obs.* *Spenser.*

LOATHLY, *adv.* Unwillingly; reluctantly. [See *Lothly.*]

LOATHNESS, *n.* Unwillingness; reluctance. [See *Lothness.*]

LOATHSOME, *a.* Disgusting; exciting disgust.
2. Hateful; abhorred; detestable.
3. Causing fastidiousness. [See *Lothesome.*]

LOATHSOMENESS, *n.* The quality which excites disgust, hatred or abhorrence. *Addison.*

LOAVES, *plu.* of *loaf.*

LOB, *n.* [W. *llob*, allied to *lubber, looby, club*, &c. Qu. G. *laff.*]
1. A dull, heavy, sluggish person.
2. Something thick and heavy; as in *lob-worm.* *Walton.*

LOB, *v. t.* To let fall heavily or lazily.

> And their poor jades
> *Lob* down their heads. *Shak.*

LO'BATE, } *a.* [from *lobe.*] Consisting of
LO'BED, } lobes. In *botany*, divided to the middle into parts distant from each other, with convex margins. *Martyn.*

LOB'BY, *n.* [Qu. G. *laube*, an arbor or bower.]
1. An opening before a room, or an entrance into a principal apartment, where there is a considerable space between that and the portico or vestibule. *Encyc.*
2. A small hall or waiting room. *Encyc.*
3. A small apartment taken from a hall or entry.
4. In *a ship*, an apartment close before the captain's cabin. *Cyc.*
5. In *agriculture*, a confined place for cattle, formed by hedges, trees or other fencing, near the farm-yard. *Cyc.*

LOBE, *n.* [Fr. *lobe*; Sp. Port. *lobo*; L. *lobus*; Gr. λοβος.]
1. A part or division of the lungs, liver, &c.
2. The lower soft part of the ear.
3. A division of a simple leaf.
4. The cotyledon or placenta of a seed.

LO'BED, *a.* Lobate, which see.

LOBSPOUND, *n.* A prison. *Hudibras.*

LOB'STER, *n.* [Sax. *loppestre* or *lopystre.* The first syllable coincides with Sax. *lobbe*, a spider, and with *loppe*, a flea; probably all named from their shape or legs. The last syllable coincides with *ster*, in *spinster, minister.*]
A crustaceous fish of the genus Cancer. Lobsters have large claws and fangs, and four pair of legs. They are said to change their crust annually, and to be frightened at thunder or other loud report. They constitute an article of food.

LOB'ULE, *n.* [Sp. *lobulo.*] A small lobe.

LO'CAL, *a.* [Fr. Sp. *local*; It. *locale*; L. *localis*; from *locus*, place, Sans. *log*; from the root of *lay*, L. *loco.* See *Lay.*]
1. Pertaining to a place, or to a fixed or limited portion of space. We say, the *local* situation of the house is pleasant. We are often influenced in our opinions by *local* circumstances.
2. Limited or confined to a spot, place, or definite district; as a *local* custom. The yellow fever is *local* in its origin, and often continues for a time, to be a *local* disease.
3. In law, *local* actions are such as must be brought in a particular county, where the cause arises; distinguished from *transitory* actions. *Blackstone.*

LOCAL'ITY, *n.* Existence in a place, or in a certain portion of space.

> It is thought that the soul and angels are devoid of quantity and dimension, and that they have nothing to do with grosser *locality.* *Glanville.*

2. Limitation to a county, district or place; as *locality* of trial. *Blackstone.*
3. Position; situation; place; particularly, geographical place or situation, as of a mineral or plant.

LO'CALLY, *adv.* With respect to place; in place; as, to be *locally* separated or distant.

LO'CATE, *v. t.* [L. *loco, locatus*; It. *locare.*]
1. To place; to set in a particular spot or position.
2. To select, survey and settle the bounds of a particular tract of land; or to designate a portion of land by limits; as, to *locate* a tract of a hundred acres in a particular township. *U. States.*
3. To designate and determine the place of; as, a committee was appointed to *locate* a church or a court house. *N. England.*

LO'CATED, *pp.* Placed; situated; fixed in place.

LO'CATING, *ppr.* Placing; designating the place of.

LOCA'TION, *n.* The act of placing, or of designating the place of.
2. Situation with respect to place. The *location* of the city on a large river is favorable for commerce.
3. That which is located; a tract of land designated in place. *U. States.*
4. In *the civil law*, a leasing on rent.

LOCH, *n.* [Gaelic.] A lake; a bay or arm of the sea; used in Scotland.

LOCH, *n.* *Loch* or *lohoch*, is an Arabian name for the forms of medicines called eclegmas, lambatives, linctures, and the like. *Quincy.*

LOCH'AGE, *n.* [Gr. λοχαγος; λοχος, a body of soldiers, and αγω, to lead.]
In *Greece*, an officer who commanded a lochus or cohort, the number of men in which is not certainly known. *Mitford.*

LOCHE. [See *Loach.*]

LO'CHIA, *n.* [Gr. λοχεια.] Evacuations which follow childbirth.

LO'CHIAL, *a.* Pertaining to evacuations from the womb after childbirth.

LOCK, *n.* [Sax. *loc* or *loce*, an inclosed place, the fastening of a door, a tuft or curl of hair. In the latter sense, it is the G. *locke*, D. *lok*, L. *floccus*, Eng. *lock*; Ir. *loc*, a stop, hinderance; W. *lloc*, a mound, an inclosed place; Russ. *lokon*, a lock of hair; Sax. *lucan*, Goth. *lukan*, to lock; Dan. *lukke*, a hedge, fence or bar; *lukker*, to shut, to inclose, to fasten, to lock; Fr. *loquet*, a latch; Arm. *licqued*, or *clicqed*, W. *clicied.* *Lock* and *flock* may be of one family. The primary sense is to shut, to close, to press, strain or drive, which may be the radical sense of *flock*, Gr. πλεκω, πλοκος, L. *plico*, as well as of *lock.* But see Class Lg. No. 48. and 13. 14. 16.]
1. Lock, in its primary sense, is any thing that fastens; but we now appropriate the word to an instrument composed of a spring, wards, and a bolt of iron or steel, used to fasten doors, chests and the like. The bolt is moved by a key.
2. The part of a musket or fowling-piece or other fire-arm, which contains the pan, trigger, &c.
3. The barrier or works of a canal, which confine the water, consisting of a dam, banks or walls, with two gates or pairs of gates, which may be opened or shut at pleasure.
4. A grapple in wrestling. *Milton.*
5. Any inclosure. *Dryden.*
6. A tuft of hair; a plexus of wool, hay or other like substance; a flock; a ringlet of hair.

> A *lock* of hair will draw more than a cable rope. *Grew.*

Lock of water, is the measure equal to the contents of the chamber of the locks by which the consumption of water on a canal is estimated.

LOCK'-KEEPER, *n.* One who attends the locks of a canal.

LOCK'-PADDLE, *n.* A small sluse that serves to fill and empty a lock.

LOCK'-SIL, *n.* An angular piece of timber at the bottom of a lock, against which the gates shut.

LOCK'-WEIR, *n.* A paddle-weir, in canals, an over-fall behind the upper gates, by which the waste water of the upper pound is let down through the paddle-holes into the chamber of the lock. *Cyc.*

LOCK, *v. t.* To fasten with a particular instrument; as, to *lock* a door; to *lock* a trunk.
2. To shut up or confine, as with a lock; as, to be *locked* in a prison. *Lock* the secret in your breast.
3. To close fast. The frost *locks* up our rivers.
4. To embrace closely; as, to *lock* one in the arms.
5. To furnish with locks, as a canal.
6. To confine; to restrain. Our shipping was *locked* up by the embargo.
7. In *fencing*, to seize the sword-arm of an antagonist, by turning the left arm around it, after closing the parade, shell to shell, in order to disarm him. *Cyc.*

LOCK, *v. i.* To become fast. The door *locks* close.

2. To unite closely by mutual insertion; as, they *lock* into each other. *Boyle.*

LOCK'AGE, *n.* Materials for locks in a canal. *Gallatin.*

2. Works which form a lock on a canal. *Journ. of Science.*

3. Toll paid for passing the locks of a canal.

LOCK'ED, *pp.* Made fast by a lock; furnished with a lock or locks; closely embraced.

LOCK'ER, *n.* A close place, as a drawer or an apartment in a ship, that may be closed with a lock.

A *shot-locker* is a strong frame of plank near the pump-well in the hold, where shot are deposited. *Mar. Dict.*

LOCK'ET, *n.* [Fr. *loquet.*] A small lock; a catch or spring to fasten a necklace or other ornament. *Johnson.*

LOCK'RAM, *n.* A sort of coarse linen. *Hanmer.*

LOCK'SMITH, *n.* An artificer whose occupation is to make locks.

LOCK'Y, *a.* Having locks or tufts. *Sherwood.*

LOCOMO'TION, *n.* [L. *locus*, place, and *motio*, motion.]

1. The act of moving from place to place. *Brown.*

2. The power of moving from place to place. Most animals possess *locomotion;* plants have life, but not *locomotion.*

LOCOMO'TIVE, *a.* Moving from place to place; changing place, or able to change place; as a *locomotive* animal. Most animals are distinguished from plants by their *locomotive* faculty.

Locomotive engine, a steam engine employed in land carriage; chiefly on railways.

LOCOMOTIV'ITY, *n.* The power of changing place. *Bryant.*

LOC'ULAMENT, *n.* [L. *loculamentum*, from *locus, loculus.*]

In *botany*, the cell of a pericarp in which the seed is lodged. A pericarp is unilocular, bilocular, &c. *Martyn.*

LO'CUST, *n.* [L. *locusta.*] An insect of the genus Gryllus. These insects are at times so numerous in Africa and the S. of Asia, as to devour every green thing, and when they migrate, they fly in an immense cloud.

LO'CUST, *n.* A name of several plants and trees; as a species of Melianthus, and of Ceratonia.

LO'CUST-TREE, *n.* A tree of the genus Hymenæa, and another of the genus Robinia. The *Honey-Locust-tree*, is of the genus Gleditsia.

LODE, *n.* [from Sax. *lædan*, to lead.]

1. Among *miners*, a metallic vein, or any regular vein or course, whether metallic or not, but commonly a metallic vein. *Encyc. Cyc.*

2. A cut or reach of water. *Cyc.*

LO'DE-STONE, *n.* [from the verb to *lead*, and *stone.*]

1. A magnet, an ore of iron; a stone found in iron mines, of a dark or black lead color, and of considerable hardness and weight. It attracts iron filings, and communicates to iron the same property of attraction. But its peculiar value consists in its communicating to a needle the property of taking a direction to the north and south, a property of inestimable utility in navigation and surveying.

2. A name given by Cornish miners to a species of stones, called also tin-stones; a compound of stones and sand, of different kinds and colors. *Nicholson.*

LODG'ABLE, *a.* Capable of affording a temporary abode. [*Not used.*]

LODGE, *v. t.* [Fr. *loger*, to lodge; It. *loggia*, a lodge; *alloggiare*, to lodge; Sp. *alojar;* Arm. *logea;* Dan. *logerer.* The sense is to set or throw down. In Sax. *logian* is to compose, to deposit or lay up, also to repair; Russ. *loju*, to lay, to put. It is probably allied to *lay.*]

1. To set, lay or deposit for keeping or preservation, for a longer or shorter time. The men *lodged* their arms in the arsenal.

2. To place; to plant; to infix.

> He *lodged* an arrow in a tender breast. *Addison.*

3. To fix; to settle in the heart, mind or memory.

> I can give no reason
> More than a *lodged* hate— *Shak.*

4. To furnish with a temporary habitation, or with an accommodation for a night. He *lodged* the prince a month, a week, or a night. [*The word usually denotes a short residence, but for no definite time.*]

5. To harbor; to cover.

> The deer is *lodged.* *Addison.*

6. To afford place to; to contain for keeping.

> The memory can *lodge* a greater store of images, than the senses can present at one time. *Cheyne.*

7. To throw in or on; as, to *lodge* a ball or a bomb in a fort.

8. To throw down; to lay flat.

> Our sighs, and they shall *lodge* the summer corn. *Shak.*

LODGE, *v. i.* To reside; to dwell; to rest in a place.

> And *lodge* such daring souls in little men. *Pope.*

2. To rest or dwell for a time, as for a night, a week, a month. We *lodged* a night at the Golden Ball. We *lodged* a week at the City Hotel. Soldiers *lodge* in tents in summer, and in huts in winter. Fowls *lodge* on trees or rocks.

3. To fall flat, as grain. Wheat and oats on strong land are apt to *lodge.*

LODGE, *n.* A small house in a park or forest, for a temporary place of rest at night; a temporary habitation; a hut. *Sidney. Shak.*

2. A small house or tenement appended to a larger; as a porter's *lodge.*

3. A den; a cave; any place where a wild beast dwells.

LODG'ED, *pp.* Placed at rest; deposited; infixed; furnished with accommodations for a night or other short time; laid flat.

LODG'ER, *n.* One who lives at board, or in a hired room, or who has a bed in another's house for a night.

2. One that resides in any place for a time. *Pope.*

LODG'ING, *ppr.* Placing at rest; depositing; furnishing lodgings.

2. Resting for a night; residing for a time.

LODG'ING, *n.* A place of rest for a night, or of residence for a time; temporary habitation; apartment.

> Wits take *lodgings* in the sound of Bow. *Pope.*

2. Place of residence.

> Fair bosom—the *lodging* of delight. *Spenser.*

3. Harbor; cover; place of rest. *Sidney.*

4. Convenience for repose at night. *Sidney.*

LODG'MENT, *n.* [Fr. *logement.*] The act of lodging, or the state of being lodged; a being placed or deposited at rest for keeping for a time or for permanence.

2. Accumulation or collection of something deposited or remaining at rest.

3. In *military affairs*, an encampment made by an army.

4. A work cast up by besiegers, during their approaches, in some dangerous post which they have gained, and where it is necessary to secure themselves against the enemy's fire. *Cyc.*

LOFFE, *v. i.* To laugh. [*Not used.*] *Shak.*

LOFT, *n.* [Dan. *loft*, Sax. *lyfte*, the air, an arch, vault or ceiling; probably allied to *lift*, Dan. *löfter.* Qu. Gr. λοφος.]

1. Properly, an elevation; hence, in a building, the elevation of one story or floor above another; hence, a floor above another; as the second *loft;* third *loft;* fourth *loft.* Spenser seems to have used the word for the highest floor or top, and this may have been its original signification.

2. A high room or place. *Pope.*

LOFT'ILY, *adv.* [from *lofty.*] On high; in an elevated place.

2. Proudly; haughtily.

> They are corrupt and speak wickedly concerning oppression; they speak *loftily.* Ps. lxxiii.

3. With elevation of language, diction or sentiment; sublimely.

> My lowly verse may *loftily* arise. *Spenser.*

4. In an elevated attitude. A horse carries his head *loftily.*

LOFT'INESS, *n.* Highth; elevation in place or position; altitude; as the *loftiness* of a mountain.

2. Pride; haughtiness.

> Augustus and Tiberius had *loftiness* enough in their tempers— *Collier.*

3. Elevation of attitude or mien; as *loftiness* of carriage.

4. Sublimity; elevation of diction or sentiment.

> Three poets in three distant ages born:
> The first in *loftiness* of thought surpass'd;
> The next in majesty; in both the last. *Dryden.*

LOFT'Y, *a.* Elevated in place; high; as a *lofty* tower; a *lofty* mountain. [*But it expresses more than high, or at least is more emphatical, poetical and elegant.*]

> See *lofty* Lebanon his head advance. *Pope*

2. Elevated in condition or character.

> Thus saith the high and *lofty* One, that inhabiteth eternity, whose name is Holy— Is. lvii.

3. Proud; haughty; as *lofty* looks. Is. ii.

4. Elevated in sentiment or diction; sublime; as *lofty* strains; *lofty* rhyme. *Milton.*

5. Stately; dignified; as *lofty* steps.

LOG, *n.* [This word is probably allied to D. *log, logge*, heavy, dull, sluggish; a sense retained in *water-logged*; and to *lug*, *luggage*, perhaps to *clog*.]

1. A bulky piece or stick of timber unhewed. Pine *logs* are floated down rivers in America, and stopped at saw-mills. A piece of timber when hewed or squared, is not called a *log*, unless perhaps in constructing log-huts.

2. In *navigation*, a machine for measuring the rate of a ship's velocity through the water. The common log is a piece of board, forming the quadrant of a circle of about six inches radius, balanced by a small plate of lead nailed on the circular part, so as to swim perpendicular. *Mar. Dict.*

3. [Heb. לג.] A Hebrew measure of liquids, containing, according to some authors, three quarters of a pint; according to others, five sixths of a pint. According to Arbuthnot, it was the seventy second part of the bath or ephah, and the twelfth part of a hin. *Johnson. Encyc.*

LOG, *v. i.* To move to and fro. [*Not used.*] *Polwhele.*

LOG'-BOARD, *n.* In *navigation*, two boards, shutting like a book, and divided into columns, containing the hours of the day and night, direction of the wind, course of the ship, &c., from which is formed the log-book. *Mar. Dict.*

LOG'-BOOK, *n.* A book into which are transcribed the contents of the log-board. *Mar. Dict.*

LOG'-HOUSE, } *n.* A house or hut whose
LOG'-HUT, } walls are composed of logs laid on each other.

LOG'-LINE, *n.* A line or cord about a hundred and fifty fathoms in length, fastened to the log by means of two legs. This is wound on a reel, called the *log-reel*. *Encyc. Mar. Dict.*

LOG'-REEL, *n.* A reel in the gallery of a ship, on which the log-line is wound. *Encyc. Mar. Dict.*

LOG'ARITHM, *n.* [Fr. *logarithme*; Gr. λογος, ratio, and αριθμος, number.]

Logarithms are the exponents of a series of powers and roots. *Day.*

The logarithm of a number is that exponent of some other number, which renders the power of the latter, denoted by the exponent, equal to the former. *Cyc.*

When the logarithms form a series in arithmetical progression, the corresponding natural numbers form a series in geometrical progression. Thus,

Logarithms	0	1	2	3	4	5
Natural numbers,	1	10	100	1000	10000	100000

The addition and subtraction of logarithms answer to the multiplication and division of their natural numbers. In like manner, involution is performed by multiplying the logarithm of any number by the number denoting the required power; and evolution, by dividing the logarithm by the number denoting the required root.

Logarithms are the invention of Baron Napier, lord of Marchiston in Scotland; but the kind now in use, were invented by Henry Briggs, professor of geometry in Gresham college, at Oxford. They are extremely useful in abridging the labor of trigonometrical calculations.

LOGARITHMET'IC, } Pertaining to
LOGARITHMET'ICAL, } *a.* logarithms;
LOGARITH'MIC, } consisting of logarithms. *Encyc. Lavoisier.*

LOG'GATS, *n.* The name of a play or game, the same as is now called *kittle-pins*. It was prohibited by Stat. 33, Henry VIII. [*Not in use.*] *Hanmer.*

LOG'GERHEAD, *n.* [*log* and *head.*] A blockhead; a dunce; a dolt; a thick-skull. *Shak.*

2. A spherical mass of iron, with a long handle; used to heat tar. *Mar. Dict.*

To fall to loggerheads, } to come to blows;
To go to loggerheads, } to fall to fighting without weapons. *L'Estrange.*

LOG'GERHEADED, *a.* Dull; stupid; doltish. *Shak.*

LOG'IC, *n.* [Fr. *logique*; It. *logica*; L. *id.*; from the Gr. λογικη, from λογος, reason, λεγω, to speak.]

The art of thinking and reasoning justly.

> *Logic* is the art of using reason well in our inquiries after truth, and the communication of it to others. *Watts.*

Logic may be defined, the science or history of the human mind, as it traces the progress of our knowledge from our first conceptions through their different combinations, and the numerous deductions that result from comparing them with one another. *Encyc.*

Correct reasoning implies correct thinking and legitimate inferences from premises, which are principles assumed or admitted to be just. *Logic* then includes the art of thinking, as well as the art of reasoning. *W.*

> The purpose of *logic* is to direct the intellectual powers in the investigation of truth, and in the communication of it to others. *Hedge.*

LOG'ICAL, *a.* Pertaining to logic; used in logic; as *logical* subtilties. *Hooker.*

2. According to the rules of logic; as a *logical* argument or inference. This reasoning is strictly *logical*.

3. Skilled in logic; versed in the art of thinking and reasoning; discriminating; as a *logical* head. *Spectator.*

LOG'ICALLY, *adv.* According to the rules of logic; as, to argue *logically*.

LOGI''CIAN, *n.* A person skilled in logic, or the art of reasoning.

> Each fierce *logician* still expelling Locke. *Pope.*

LOGIS'TIC, *a.* Relating to sexagesimal fractions. *Cyc.*

LOG'MAN, *n.* A man who carries logs. *Shak.*

2. One whose occupation is to cut and convey logs to a mill. [*Local.*] *U. States.*

LOGOGRAPH'IC, } *a.* Pertaining to lo-
LOGOGRAPH'ICAL, } gography.

LOGOG'RAPHY, *n.* [Gr. λογος, a word, and γραφω, to write.]

A method of printing, in which a type represents a word, instead of forming a letter. *Encyc.*

LOG'OGRIPHE, *n.* [Gr. λογος and γριφος.] A sort of riddle. *Obs.* *B. Jonson.*

LOGOM'ACHIST, *n.* One who contends about words. *E. T. Fitch.*

LOGOM'ACHY, *n.* [Gr. λογος, word, and μαχη, contest, altercation.]

Contention in words merely, or rather a contention about words; a war of words. *Howell.*

LOGOMET'RIC, *a.* [Gr. λογος, ratio, and μετρεω, to measure.]

A *logometric* scale is intended to measure or ascertain chimical equivalents. *Wollaston.*

LOG'WOOD, *n.* A species of tree and wood, called also Campeachy-wood, from the bay of Campeachy in Spanish America, of the genus Hæmatoxylon, of which there is one species only. This tree has a crooked, deformed stem, growing to the highth of 20 or 24 feet, with crooked irregular branches, armed with strong thorns. The wood is of a firm texture and a red color. It is much used in dyeing. *Encyc.*

LO'HOCH, } *n.* [Ar.] A medicine of a mid-
LO'HOCK, } dle consistence between a soft electuary and a syrup. [See *Loch.*] *Encyc.*

LOIN, *n.* [Sax. *lend*; G. D. *lende*; Sw. *länd*; Dan. *lænd*; W. *clun*; Arm. *lænienn* or *loinch*; Ir. *luan* or *bleun*; L. *clunis.*]

The *loins* are the space on each side of the vertebræ, between the lowest of the false ribs and the upper portion of the os ilium or haunch bone, or the lateral portions of the lumbar region; called also the *reins*.

LOIT'ER, *v. i.* [D. *leuteren*; Russ. *leitayu* or *letäyu*. Qu. its alliance to *late* and *let.*]

To linger; to be slow in moving; to delay; to be dilatory; to spend time idly.

> If we have *loitered*, let us quicken our pace. *Rogers.*

LOIT'ERER, *n.* A lingerer; one that delays or is slow in motion; an idler; one that is sluggish or dilatory.

> Ever listless *loiterers*, that attend
> No cause, no trust, no duty and no friend. *Pope.*

LOIT'ERING, *ppr.* Lingering; delaying; moving slowly.

LOKE, *n.* [Qu. Ir. *loch*, dark; Gr. λυγη, darkness.]

1. In the Scandinavian mythology, the evil deity, the author of all calamities; answering to the Arimanes of the Persians. *Mallet. Edda.*

2. A close narrow lane. [*Local.*]

LOLL, *v. i.* [Eth. አለወለወ alolo, to thrust out the tongue. The sense of this word is to throw, to send. Hence it coincides with the Gr. λαλεω, W. *lloliaw*, to speak, to prate, Dan. *laller*, G. *lallen*. It coincides also with *lull*, to appease, that is, to throw down.]

1. To recline; to lean; properly, to throw one's self down; hence, to lie at ease.

> Void of care he *lolls* supine in state. *Dryden.*

2. To suffer the tongue to hang extended from the mouth, as an ox or a dog when heated with labor or exertion.

> The triple porter of the Stygian seat,
> With *lolling* tongue lay fawning at his feet. *Dryden.*

LOLL, *v. t.* To thrust out, as the tongue.

> Fierce tigers couched around, and *lolled* their tongues. *Dryden.*

LOLL'ARD, *n.* [Qu. G. *lallen*, *lollen*, to prate or to sing.]

The *Lollards* were a sect of early reformers

in Germany and England, the followers of Wickliffe.

LOLL'ARDY, *n.* The doctrines of the Lollards.

LOLL'ING, *ppr.* Throwing down or out; reclining at ease; thrusting out the tongue.

LOMBARD'IC, *a.* Pertaining to the Lombards; an epithet applied to one of the ancient alphabets derived from the Roman, and relating to the manuscripts of Italy. *Astle.*

LO'MENT, *n.* [L. *lomentum.*] An elongated pericarp, which never bursts. It consists, like the legume, of two valves, with the seeds attached to the under suture, but is divided into small cells, each containing a single seed. *Ed. Encyc.*

LOMENTA'CEOUS, *a.* [L. *lomentum*, bean meal, a color.]
Furnished with a loment. The *lomentaceæ* are a natural order of plants, many of which furnish beautiful tinctures or dyes, and whose seeds are contained in a loment or legume. *Linne.*

LOM'ONITE, *n.* Laumonite, or di-prismatic zeolite. *Ure.*

LOMP, *n.* A kind of roundish fish. *Johnson.*

LŎN'DONISM, *n.* A mode of speaking peculiar to London. *Pegge.*

LONE, *a.* [Dan. *lön*, a corner, nook, a lurking place, secrecy; *lönlig*, Sw. *lönnlig*, private, close, clandestine. The radical sense is probably to separate, or rather to withdraw or retire, and the word may be allied to Fr. *loin.* If *alone* is composed of *all* and *one*, which the Teutonic dialects indicate, it has no connection with *lone.*]

1. Solitary; retired; unfrequented; having no company.

And leave you in *lone* woods or empty walls. *Pope.*

2. Single; standing by itself; not having others in the neighborhood; as a *lone* house. *Pope.*

3. Single; unmarried, or in widowhood. *Shak.*

LONE, *n.* A lane. [*Local.*]

LO'NELINESS, *n.* Solitude; retirement; seclusion from company. He was weary of the *loneliness* of his habitation.

2. Love of retirement; disposition to solitude.

I see
The mystery of your *loneliness.* *Shak.*

LO'NELY, *a.* Solitary; retired; sequestered from company or neighbors; as a *lonely* situation; a *lonely* cell. *Dryden.*

2. Solitary; as the *lonely* traveler.

3. Addicted to solitude or seclusion from company. *Rowe.*

LO'NENESS, *n.* Solitude; seclusion. *Donne.*

LO'NESŎME, *a.* Solitary; secluded from society.

How horrid will these *lonesome* seats appear! *Blackmore.*

LO'NESŎMENESS, *n.* The state of being solitary; solitude.

LONG, *a.* [Sax. *long*, *lang* and *leng*; G. *lange*; D. Dan. *lang*; Sw. *lång*; Goth. *laggs*; L. *longus*; It. *lungo*; Fr. *long.* The Gothic word seems to connect this word with *lag*, in the sense of drawing out, whence delaying.]

1. Extended; drawn out in a line, or in the direction of length; opposed to *short*, and contradistinguished from *broad* or *wide.* *Long* is a relative term; for a thing may be *long* in respect to one thing, and *short* with respect to another. We apply *long* to things greatly extended, and to things which exceed the common measure. We say, a *long* way, a *long* distance, a *long* line, and *long* hair, *long* arms. By the latter terms, we mean *hair* and *arms* exceeding the usual length.

2. Drawn out or extended in time; as a *long* time; a *long* period of time; a *long* while; a *long* series of events; a *long* sickness or confinement; a *long* session; a *long* debate.

3. Extended to any certain measure expressed; as a span *long*; a yard *long*; a mile *long*, that is, extended to the measure of a mile, &c.

4. Dilatory; continuing for an extended time.

Death will not be *long* in coming. *Ecclus.*

5. Tedious; continued to a great length.

A tale should never be too *long.* *Prior.*

6. Continued in a series to a great extent; as a *long* succession of princes; a *long* line of ancestors.

7. Continued in sound; protracted; as a *long* note; a *long* syllable.

8. Continued; lingering or longing.

Praying for him, and casting a *long* look that way, he saw the galley leave the pursuit. *Sidney.*

9. Extensive; extending far in prospect or into futurity.

The perennial existence of bodies corporate and their fortunes, are things particularly suited to a man who has *long* views. *Burke.*

Long home, the grave or death. Eccles. xii.

LONG, *n.* Formerly, a musical note equal to two breves. *Obs.*

LONG, *adv.* To a great extent in space; as a *long* extended line.

2. To a great extent in time; as, they that tarry *long* at the wine. Prov. xxiii.

When the trumpet soundeth *long.* Ex. xix.

So in composition we say, *long*-expected, *long*-forgot.

3. At a point of duration far distant, either prior or posterior; as not *long* before; not *long* after; *long* before the foundation of Rome; *long* after the conquest of Gaul by Julius Cesar.

4. Through the whole extent or duration of.

The God who fed me all my life *long* to this day. Gen. xlviii.

The bird of dawning singeth all night *long.* *Spenser.*

LONG, *adv.* [Sax. *gelang*, cause or fault. Qu. *belonging to*, as the cause.]
By means of; by the fault of; owing to. *Obs.*

Mistress, all this evil is *long* of you. *Shak.*

LONG, *v. t.* To belong. [*Not used.*] *Chaucer.*

LONG, *v. i.* [Sax. *langian*, with *æfter.* We now say, to *long after*, or to *long for.* The sense is to reach or stretch toward.]

1. To desire earnestly or eagerly.

I *long* to see you. Rom. i.

I have *longed* after thy precepts. Ps. cxix.

I have *longed* for thy salvation. Ps. cxix.

2. To have a preternatural craving appetite; as a *longing* woman.

3. To have an eager appetite; as, to *long* for fruit.

LONGANIM'ITY, *n.* [L. *longanimitas*; *longus*, long, and *animus*, mind.]
Forbearance; patience; disposition to endure long under offenses. *Brown. Howell.*

LONG'BOAT, *n.* The largest and strongest boat belonging to a ship. *Mar. Dict.*

LON'GER, *a.* [comp. of *long.*] More long; of greater length; as a *longer* course.

LON'GER, *adv.* For a greater duration. This evil can be endured no *longer.*

LON'GEST, *a.* Of the greatest extent; as the *longest* line.

LON'GEST, *adv.* For the greatest continuance of time. They who live *longest*, are most convinced of the vanity of life.

LONGE'VAL, *a.* [L. *longus* and *ævum.*] Long lived. *Pope.*

LONGEV'ITY, *n.* [L. *longævitas*; *longus*, long, and *ævum*, age.]
Length or duration of life; more generally, great length of life.

The instances of *longevity* are chiefly among the abstemious. *Arbuthnot.*

LONGE'VOUS, *a.* [L. *longævus*, supra.] Living a long time; of great age.

LONG'-HEADED, *a.* Having a great extent of thought.

LONGIM'ANOUS, *a.* [L. *longus*, long, and *manus*, hand.] Having long hands. *Brown.*

LONGIM'ETRY, *n.* [L. *longus*, long, and Gr. *μετρον*, measure.]
The art or practice of measuring distances or lengths, whether accessible or inaccessible. *Encyc.*

LONG'ING, *ppr.* Earnestly desiring; having a craving or preternatural appetite.

LONG'ING, *n.* An eager desire; a craving or preternatural appetite.

LONG'INGLY, *adv.* With eager wishes or appetite.

LONGIN'QUITY, *n.* [L. *longinquitas.*] Great distance. *Barrow.*

LONG'ISH, *a.* Somewhat long; moderately long.

LON'GITUDE, *n.* [L. *longitudo*, from *longus*, long.]

1. Properly, length; as the *longitude* of a room; but in this sense not now used. Appropriately, in geography,

2. The distance of any place on the globe from another place, eastward or westward; or the distance of any place from a given meridian. Boston, in Massachusetts, is situated in the 71st degree of *longitude* west from Greenwich. To be able to ascertain precisely the *longitude* of a ship at sea, is a great desideratum in navigation.

3. The longitude of a star, is its distance from the equinoctial points, or the beginning of Aries or Libra. *Bailey.*

LONGITU'DINAL, *a.* Pertaining to longitude or length; as *longitudinal* distance.

2. Extending in length; running lengthwise, as distinguished from transverse or across; as the *longitudinal* diameter of a body. The *longitudinal* suture of the head runs between the coronal and lamdoidal sutures. *Bailey.*

LONGITU'DINALLY, *adv.* In the direction of length.

Some of the fibers of the human body are placed *longitudinally*, others transversely. *Encyc.*

LONG'LEGGED, *a.* Having long legs.

LONG'LIVED, *a.* Having a long life or existence; living long; lasting long.

LONG'LY, *adv.* With longing desire. [*Not used.*] *Shak.*

LONG-MEASURE, *n.* Lineal measure; the measure of length.

LONG'NESS, *n.* Length. [*Little used.*]

LONG-PRIM'ER, *n.* A printing type of a particular size, between small pica and bourgeois.

LONG'SHANKED, *a.* Having long legs. *Burton.*

LONG-SIGHT, *n.* Long-sightedness. *Good.*

LONG-SIGHTED, *a.* Able to see at a great distance; used literally of the eyes, and figuratively of the mind or intellect.

LONG-SIGHTEDNESS, *n.* The faculty of seeing objects at a great distance.

2. In *medicine*, presbyopy; that defect of sight by which objects near at hand are seen confusedly, but at remoter distances distinctly. *Hooper.*

LONG'SOME, *a.* Extended in length; tiresome; tedious; as a *longsome* plain. *Obs.* *Prior.*

LONG'SPUN, *a.* Spun or extended to a great length. *Addison.*

LONG-SUF'FERANCE, *n.* Forbearance to punish; clemency; patience. *Com. Prayer.*

LONG-SUF'FERING, *a.* Bearing injuries or provocation for a long time; patient; not easily provoked.

The Lord God, merciful and gracious, *long-suffering* and abundant in goodness. Ex. xxxiv.

LONG-SUF'FERING, *n.* Long endurance; patience of offense.

Despisest thou the riches of his goodness, and forbearance, and *long-suffering?* Rom. ii.

LONG'-TONGUED, *a.* Rating; babbling. *Shak.*

LONGWAYS, a mistake for *longwise.*

LONG-WIND'ED, *a.* Long breathed; tedious in speaking, argument or narration; as a *long-winded* advocate.

LONG'-WISE, *adv.* In the direction of length; lengthwise. [*Little used.*] *Hakewill.*

LO'NISH, *a.* Somewhat solitary. [*Not used and inelegant.*]

LOO, *n.* A game at cards. *Pope.*

LOOB'ILY, *adv.* [See *Looby.*] Like a looby; in an awkward, clumsy manner. *L'Estrange.*

LOOB'Y, *n.* [W. *llabi*, a tall lank person, a looby, a lubber, a clumsy fellow; *llob*, a blockhead, an unwieldy lump.] An awkward, clumsy fellow; a lubber.

Who could give the *looby* such airs? *Swift.*

LOOF, *n.* The after part of a ship's bow, or the part where the planks begin to be incurvated, as they approach the stem. *Mar. Dict.*

LOOF. [See *Luff*, which is the word used.]

LOOF'ED, *a.* [See *Aloof.*] Gone to a distance. [*Not used.*] *Shak.*

LOOK, *v. i.* [Sax. *locian*; G. *lugen*; Sans. *lokhan*. It is perhaps allied to W. *lygu*, to appear, to shine. See *Light.* The primary sense is to stretch, to extend, to shoot, hence to direct the eye. We observe its primary sense is nearly the same as that of *seek.* Hence, to *look for* is to *seek.*]

1. To direct the eye towards an object, with the intention of seeing it.

When the object is within sight, *look* is usually followed by *on* or *at.* We *look on* or *at* a picture; we *look on* or *at* the moon; we cannot *look on* or *at* the unclouded sun, without pain.

At, after *look*, is not used in our version of the Scriptures. In common usage, *at* or *on* is now used indifferently in many cases, and yet in other cases, usage has established a preference. In general, *on* is used in the more solemn forms of expression. Moses was afraid to *look on* God. The Lord *look on* you and judge. In these and similar phrases, the use of *at* would be condemned, as expressing too little solemnity.

In some cases, *at* seems to be more properly used before very distant objects; but the cases can hardly be defined.

The particular direction of the eye is expressed by various modifying words; as, to *look down*, to *look up*, to *look back*, to *look forward*, to *look from*, to *look round*, to *look out*, to *look under.* When the object is not in sight, *look* is followed by *after*, or *for.* Hence, to *look after*, or *look for*, is equivalent to *seek* or *search*, or to *expect.*

2. To see; to have the sight or view of.

Fate sees thy life lodged in a brittle glass,
And *looks* it through, but to it cannot pass. *Dryden.*

3. To direct the intellectual eye; to apply the mind or understanding; to consider; to examine. *Look* at the conduct of this man; view it in all its aspects. Let every man *look* into the state of his own heart. Let us *look* beyond the received notions of men on this subject.

4. To expect.

He must *look* to fight another battle, before he could reach Oxford. [*Little used.*] *Clarendon.*

5. To take care; to watch.

Look that ye bind them fast. *Shak.*

6. To be directed.

Let thine eyes *look* right on. Prov. iv.

7. To seem; to appear; to have a particular appearance. The patient *looks* better than he did. The clouds *look* rainy.

I am afraid it would *look* more like vanity than gratitude. *Addison.*

Observe how such a practice *looks* in another person. *Watts.*

So we say, to *look* stout or big; to *look* peevish; to *look* pleasant or graceful.

8. To have a particular direction or situation; to face; to front.

The gate that *looketh* toward the north. Ezek. viii.

The east gate of the Lord's house, that *looketh* eastward. Ezek. xi.

To look about, to look on all sides, or in different directions.

To look about one, to be on the watch; to be vigilant; to be circumspect or guarded. *Arbuthnot.*

To look after, to attend; to take care of; as, to *look after* children.

2. To expect; to be in a state of expectation.

Men's hearts failing them for fear, and for *looking after* those things which are coming on the earth. Luke xxi.

3. To seek; to search.

My subject does not oblige me to *look after* the water, or point forth the place whereunto it has now retreated. *Woodward.*

To look for, to expect; as, to *look for* news by the arrival of a ship.

Look now *for* no enchanting voice. *Milton.*

2. To seek; to search; as, to *look for* lost money, or lost cattle.

To look into, to inspect closely; to observe narrowly; to examine; as, to *look into* the works of nature; to *look into* the conduct of another; to *look into* one's affairs.

Which things the angels desire to *look into.* I Pet. i.

To look on, to regard; to esteem.

Her friends would *look on* her the worse. *Prior.*

2. To consider; to view; to conceive of; to think.

I *looked on* Virgil as a succinct, majestic writer. *Dryden.*

3. To be a mere spectator.

I'll be a candle-holder and *look on.* *Shak.*

To look over, to examine one by one; as, to *look over* a catalogue of books; to *look over* accounts.

To overlook, has a different sense, to pass over without seeing.

To look out, to be on the watch. The seaman *looks out* for breakers.

To look to, or *unto*, to watch; to take care of.

Look well *to* thy herds. Prov. xxvii.

2. To resort to with confidence or expectation of receiving something; to expect to receive from. The creditor may *look to* the surety for payment.

Look to me and be ye saved, all the ends of the earth. Is. xlv.

To look through, to penetrate with the eye, or with the understanding; to see or understand perfectly.

LOOK, *v. t.* To seek; to search for.

Looking my love, I go from place to place. *Obs.* *Spenser.*

2. To influence by looks or presence; as, to *look* down opposition.

A spirit fit to start into an empire,
And *look* the world to law. *Dryden.*

To look out, to search for and discover. *Look out* associates of good reputation.

To look one another in the face, to meet for combat. 2 Kings xiv.

LOOK, in the imperative, is used to excite attention or notice. *Look* ye, *look* you; that is, see, behold, observe, take notice.

LOOK, *n.* Cast of countenance; air of the face; aspect; as, a high *look* is an index of pride; a downcast *look* indicates modesty, bashfulness, or depression of mind.

Pain, disgrace and poverty have frightful *looks.* *Locke.*

2. The act of looking or seeing. Every *look* filled him with anguish.

3. View; watch. *Swinburne.*

LOOK'ER, *n.* One who looks.

A *looker on*, a mere spectator; one that *looks on*, but has no agency or interest in the affair.

LOOK'ING-GLASS, *n.* A glass which reflects the form of the person who looks on it; a mirror.

There is none so homely but loves a *looking-glass.* *South.*

LOOK'-OUT, *n.* A careful looking or watching for any object or event. *Mar. Dict.*

LOOL, *n.* In *metallurgy*, a vessel used to receive the washings of ores of metals. *Encyc.*

LOOM, *n.* [Sax. *loma*, *geloma*, utensils.] In composition, *heir-loom*, in law, is a personal chattel that by special custom descends to an heir with the inheritance, being such a thing as cannot be separated from the estate, without injury to it; such as jewels of the crown, charters, deeds, and the like. *Blackstone.*

2. A frame or machine of wood or other material, in which a weaver works threads into cloth.

Hector, when he sees Andromache overwhelmed with terror, sends her for consolation to the *loom* and the distaff. *Rambler.*

3. [Dan. *lom* or *loom*, G. *lohme*.] A fowl of the size of a goose.

4. That part of an oar which is within board. *Mar. Dict.*

LOOM, *v. i.* [Qu. Sax. *leoman*, to shine, from *leoma*, a beam of light. This does not give the exact sense of the word as now used.]

To appear above the surface either of sea or land, or to appear larger than the real dimensions and indistinctly; as a distant object, a ship at sea, or a mountain. The ship *looms* large, or the land *looms* high. *Mar. Dict.*

LOOM'-GALE, *n.* A gentle gale of wind. *Encyc.*

LOOM'ING, *ppr.* Appearing above the surface, or indistinctly, at a distance.

LOON, *n.* [Scot. *loun* or *loon*. Qu. Sax. *lun*, needy, or Ir. *liun*, sluggish.]

1. A sorry fellow; a rogue; a rascal. *Dryden. Shak.*

2. A sea-fowl of the genus Colymbus. [Ice. *lunde*.]

LOOP, *n.* [Ir. *lubam*, to bend or fold; *lub*, *luba*, a thong, a loop.]

1. A folding or doubling of a string or a noose, through which a lace or cord may be run for fastening.

That the probation bear no hinge, nor *loop*
To hang a doubt on. *Shak.*

2. In *iron-works*, the part of a row or block of cast iron, melted off for the forge or hammer.

LOOP'ED, *a.* Full of holes. *Shak.*

LOOP'HOLE, *n.* A small aperture in the bulk-head and other parts of a merchant ship, through which small arms are fired at an enemy. *Mar. Dict.*

2. A hole or aperture that gives a passage.

3. A passage for escape; means of escape. *Dryden.*

LOOP'HOLED, *a.* Full of holes or openings for escape. *Hudibras.*

LOOP'ING, *n.* In *metallurgy*, the running together of the matter of an ore into a mass, when the ore is only heated for calcination. [D. *loopen*, to run.] *Encyc.*

LOORD, *n.* [D. *lær*, a clown; Fr. *lourd*, Sp. *lerdo*, heavy, dull, gross.]

A dull stupid fellow; a drone. [*Not in use.*] *Spenser.*

LOOSE, *v. t. loos.* [Sax. *lysan*, *alysan*, *leosan*; Sw. *lősa*; D. *lossen*, *loozen*; G. *lösen*; Dan. *löser*; Goth. *lausyan*; Gr. λυω, contracted from the same root. The W. *llaesu*, signifies to relax, but may be from the root of *lax*. These words coincide with the Ch. Syr. Ar. Heb. חלץ. Class Ls. No. 30.]

1. To untie or unbind; to free from any fastening.

Canst thou *loose* the bands of Orion? Job xxxviii.

Ye shall find an ass tied, and a colt with her; *loose* them, and bring them to me. Matt. xxi.

2. To relax.

The joints of his loins were *loosed*. Dan. v.

3. To release from imprisonment; to liberate; to set at liberty.

The captive exile hasteneth that he may be *loosed*. Is. li.

4. To free from obligation.

Art thou *loosed* from a wife? seek not a wife. 1 Cor. vii.

5. To free from any thing that binds or shackles; as a man *loosed* from lust and pelf. *Dryden.*

6. To relieve; to free from any thing burdensome or afflictive.

Woman, thou art *loosed* from thine infirmity. Luke xiii.

7. To disengage; to detach; as, to *loose* one's hold.

8. To put off.

Loose thy shoe from off thy foot. Josh. v.

9. To open.

Who is worthy to open the book, and to *loose* the seals thereof? Rev. v.

10. To remit; to absolve.

Whatsoever thou shalt *loose* on earth, shall be *loosed* in heaven. Matt. xvi.

LOOSE, *v. i.* To set sail; to leave a port or harbor.

Now when Paul and his company *loosed* from Paphos, they came to Perga, in Pamphylia. Acts xiii.

LOOSE, *a.* [Goth. *laus*; D. *los*, *losse*; G. *los*; Dan. *lös*; Sw. *lős*. Qu. W. *llæs*, loose, lax.]

1. Unbound; untied; unsewed; not fastened or confined; as the *loose* sheets of a book.

2. Not tight or close; as a *loose* garment.

3. Not crowded; not close or compact.

With horse and chariots rank'd in *loose* array. *Milton.*

4. Not dense, close or compact; as a cloth or fossil of *loose* texture.

5. Not close; not concise; lax; as a *loose* and diffuse style.

6. Not precise or exact; vague; indeterminate; as a *loose* way of reasoning.

7. Not strict or rigid; as a *loose* observance of rites.

8. Unconnected; rambling; as a *loose* indigested play.

Vario spends whole mornings in running over *loose* and unconnected pages. *Watts.*

9. Of lax bowels. *Locke.*

10. Unengaged; not attached or enslaved.

Their prevailing principle is, to sit as *loose* from pleasures, and be as moderate in the use of them as they can. *Atterbury.*

11. Disengaged; free from obligation; with *from* or *of*.

Now I stand
Loose of my vow; but who knows Cato's thought? [*Little used.*] *Addison.*

12. Wanton; unrestrained in behavior; dissolute; unchaste; as a *loose* man or woman.

13. Containing unchaste language; as a *loose* epistle. *Dryden.*

To break loose, to escape from confinement; to gain liberty by violence. *Dryden.*

To let loose, to free from restraint or confinement; to set at liberty. *Locke.*

LOOSE, *n.* Freedom from restraint; liberty.

Come, give thy soul a *loose*. *Dryden.*
Vent all its griefs, and give a *loose* to sorrow. *Addison.*

We use this word only in the phrase, *give a loose*. The following use of it, "he runs with an unbounded *loose*," is obsolete. *Prior.*

LOOS'ED, *pp.* Untied; unbound; freed from restraint.

LOOSELY, *adv. loos'ly.* Not fast; not firmly; that may be easily disengaged; as things *loosely* tied or connected.

2. Without confinement.

Her golden locks for haste were *loosely* shed
About her ears. *Spenser.*

3. Without union or connection.

Part *loosely* wing the region. *Milton.*

4. Irregularly; not with the usual restraints.

A bishop living *loosely*, was charged that his conversation was not according to the apostle's lives. *Camden.*

5. Negligently; carelessly; heedlessly; as a mind *loosely* employed. *Locke.*

6. Meanly; slightly.

A prince should not be so *loosely* studied, as to remember so weak a composition. *Shak.*

7. Wantonly; dissolutely; unchastely. *Pope.*

LOOS'EN, *v. t. loos'n.* [from *loose*, or it is the Saxon infinitive retained.]

1. To free from tightness, tension, firmness or fixedness; as, to *loosen* a string when tied, or a knot; to *loosen* a joint; to *loosen* a rock in the earth.

2. To render less dense or compact; as, to *loosen* the earth about the roots of a tree.

3. To free from restraint.

It *loosens* his hands and assists his understanding. *Dryden.*

4. To remove costiveness from; to facilitate or increase alvine discharges.

Fear *looseneth* the belly. *Bacon.*

LOOS'EN, *v. i.* To become loose; to become less tight, firm or compact.

LOOS'ENED, *pp.* Freed from tightness or fixedness; rendered loose.

LOOSENESS, *n. loos'ness.* The state of being loose or relaxed; a state opposite to that of being tight, fast, fixed or compact; as the *looseness* of a cord; the *looseness* of a robe; the *looseness* of the skin; the *looseness* of earth, or of the texture of cloth.

2. The state opposite to rigor or rigidness; laxity; levity; as *looseness* of morals or of principles.

3. Irregularity; habitual deviation from strict rules; as *looseness* of life. *Hayward.*

4. Habitual lewdness; unchastity. *Spenser.*

5. Flux from the bowels; diarrhæa. *Bacon.*

LOOS'ENING, *ppr.* Freeing from tightness, tension or fixedness; rendering less compact.

LOOSESTRIFE, *n. loos'strife.* In *botany*, the name of several species of plants, of the genera Lysimachia, Epilobium, Lythrum, and Gaura. *Lee.*

LOOS'ING, *ppr.* Setting free from confinement.

LOP, *v. t.* [I know not the affinities of this word, unless it is *lob*, or the W. *llab*, a stroke; *llabiaw*, to *slap* or strike, or the Eng. *flap*, or Ir. *lubam*, to bend The primary sense is evidently to fall or fell, or to strike down, and I think it connected with *flap*.]

1. To cut off, as the top or extreme part of any thing; to shorten by cutting off the extremities; as, to *lop* a tree or its branches.

With branches *lopp'd* in wood, or mountain fell'd. *Milton.*

2. To cut off, as exuberances; to separate, as superfluous parts.

Expunge the whole, or *lop* the excrescent parts. *Pope.*

3. To cut partly off and bend down; as, to *lop* the trees or saplings of a hedge.

4. To let fall; to *flap*; as, a horse *lops* his ears.

LOP, *n.* That which is cut from trees.

Else both body and *lop* will be of little value. *Mortimer.*

LOP, *n.* [Sax. *loppe*.] A flea. [*Local.*]

LOPE, pret. of *leap*. [Sw. *lŏpa*; D. *loopen*.] *Obs.* *Spenser.*

LOPE, *n.* [Sw. *lŏpa*, D. *loopen*, to run. See *Leap*.]

A leap; a long step. [*A word in popular use in America.*]

LOPE, *v. i.* To leap; to move or run with a long step, as a dog.

LO'PING, *ppr.* Leaping; moving or running with a long step.

LOP'PED, *pp.* Cut off; shortened by cutting off the top or end; bent down.

LOP'PER, *n.* One that lops.

LOP'PING, *ppr.* Cutting off; shortening by cutting off the extremity; letting fall.

LOP'PING, *n.* That which is cut off.

LOQUA'CIOUS, *a.* [L. *loquax*, from *loquor*, to speak. Qu. Eng. to *clack*.] Talkative; given to continual talking.

Loquacious, brawling, ever in the wrong. *Dryden.*

2. Speaking; noisy.

Blind British bards, with volant touch,
Traverse *loquacious* strings. *Philips.*

3. Apt to blab and disclose secrets.

LOQUA'CIOUSNESS, } *n.* [L. *loquacitas*.] Talkativeness;
LOQUAC'ITY, }
the habit or practice of talking continually or excessively.

Too great *loquacity* and too great taciturnity by fits. *Arbuthnot.*

LORD, *n.* [Sax. *hlaford*. This has been supposed to be compounded of *hlaf*, loaf, and *ford*, *afford*, to give; and hence a *lord* is interpreted, a *bread-giver*. But *lady*, in Saxon, is in like manner written *hlæfdæg*; and *dæg* can hardly signify a giver. The word occurs in none of the Teutonic dialects, except the Saxon; and it is not easy to ascertain the original signification of the word. I question the correctness of the common interpretation.]

1. A master; a person possessing supreme power and authority; a ruler; a governor.

Man over man
He made not *lord*. *Milton.*
But now I was the *lord*
Of this fair mansion. *Shak.*

2. A tyrant; an oppressive ruler. *Dryden.*

3. A husband.

I oft in bitterness of soul deplored
My absent daughter, and my dearer *lord*. *Pope.*

My *lord* also being old. Gen. xviii.

4. A baron; the proprietor of a manor; as the *lord* of the manor.

5. A nobleman; a title of honor in Great Britain given to those who are noble by birth or creation; a peer of the realm, including dukes, marquises, earls, viscounts and barons. Archbishops and bishops also, as members of the house of lords, are lords of parliament. Thus we say, *lords* temporal and spiritual. By courtesy also the title is given to the sons of dukes and marquises, and to the eldest sons of earls. *Encyc.*

6. An honorary title bestowed on certain official characters; as *lord* advocate, *lord* chamberlain, *lord* chancellor, *lord* chief justice, &c.

7. In *Scripture*, the Supreme Being; Jehovah. When *Lord*, in the Old Testament, is printed in capitals, it is the translation of JEHOVAH, and so might, with more propriety, be rendered. The word is applied to Christ, Ps. cx. Col. iii. and to the Holy Spirit, 2 Thess. iii. As a title of respect, it is applied to kings, Gen. xl. 2 Sam. xix. to princes and nobles, Gen. xlii. Dan. iv. to a husband, Gen. xviii. to a prophet, 1 Kings xviii. 2 Kings ii. and to a respectable person, Gen. xxiv. Christ is called the *Lord of glory*, 1 Cor. ii. and *Lord of lords*, Rev. xix.

LORD, *v. t.* To invest with the dignity and privileges of a lord. *Shak.*

LORD, *v. i.* To domineer; to rule with arbitrary or despotic sway; sometimes followed by *over*, and sometimes by *it*, in the manner of a transitive verb.

The whiles she *lordeth* in licentious bliss. *Spenser.*

I see them *lording it* in London streets. *Shak.*

They *lorded over* them whom now they serve. *Milton.*

LORD'ING, *n.* A little lord; a lord, in contempt or ridicule. [*Little used.*] *Swift.*

LORD'LIKE, *a.* Becoming a lord.

2. Haughty; proud; insolent. *Dryden.*

LORD'LINESS, *n.* [from *lordly*.] Dignity; high station. *Shak.*

2. Pride; haughtiness. *More.*

LORD'LING, *n.* A little or diminutive lord. *Swift.*

LORD'LY, *a.* [*lord* and *like*.] Becoming a lord; pertaining to a lord.

Lordly sins require *lordly* estates to support them. *South.*

2. Proud; haughty; imperious; insolent.

Every rich and *lordly* swain,
With pride would drag about her chain. *Swift.*

LORD'LY, *adv.* Proudly; imperiously; despotically.

A famished lion, issuing from the wood,
Roars *lordly* fierce. *Dryden.*

LORD'SHIP, *n.* The state or quality of being a lord; hence, a title of honor given to noblemen, except to dukes, who have the title of *grace*.

2. A titulary compellation of judges and certain other persons in authority and office. *Johnson.*

3. Dominion; power; authority.

They who are accounted to rule over the Gentiles, exercise *lordship* over them. Mark x.

4. Seigniory; domain; the territory of a lord over which he holds jurisdiction; a manor.

What lands and *lordships* for their owner know
My quondam barber. *Dryden.*

LORE, *n.* [Sax. *lar*, from the root of *læran*, to learn; D. *leer*; G. *lehre*; Dan. *lære*; Sw. *lăra*.] Learning; doctrine; lesson; instruction.

The law of nations, or the *lore* of war. *Fairfax.*

Lo! Rome herself, proud mistress now no more
Of arts, but thundering against heathen *lore*. *Pope.*

LOR'EL, *n.* [Sax. *leoran*, to wander.] An abandoned scoundrel; a vagrant. *Obs.* *Chaucer.*

LO'RESMAN, *n.* [*lore* and *man*.] An instructor. *Obs.* *Gower.*

LOR'ICATE, *v. t.* [L. *lorico*, *loricatus*, from *lorica*, a coat of mail.]

1. To plate over; to spread over, as a plate for defense.

Nature hath *loricated* the sides of the tympanum in animals with ear-wax. *Ray.*

2. To cover with a crust, as a chimical vessel, for resisting fire.

LOR'ICATED, *pp.* Covered or plated over; encrusted.

LOR'ICATING, *ppr.* Covering over with a plate or crust.

LORICA'TION, *n.* The act or operation of covering any thing with a plate or crust for defense; as the *lorication* of a chimical vessel, to enable it to resist the action of fire, and sustain a high degree of heat.

LOR'IMER, *n.* [L. *lorum*, a thong; Fr. *lormier*.]

A bridle-maker; one that makes bits for bridles, &c. [*Not used.*]

LO'RING, *n.* Instructive discourse. *Obs.* *Spenser.*

LO'RIOT, *n.* [Fr.] A bird called witwal; the oriole.

LO'RIS, *n.* A small quadruped of Ceylon.

LORN, *a.* [Sax. Dan. *forloren*, lost. See *Forlorn*.] Lost; forsaken; lonely. *Spenser.*

LO'RY, *n.* A subordinate genus of fowls of the parrot kind, forming the link between the parrot and parroquet. *Dict. Nat. Hist.*

LÖSABLE, *a.* That may be lost. [*Little used.*] *Boyle.*

LÖSE, *v. t.* looz. pret. and pp. *lost*. [Sax. *losian*, *forlosian*, *forlysan*; D. *verliezen*; Goth. *liusan*. The sense is probably to part, to separate, and from the root of *loose*.]

1. To mislay; to part or be separated from a thing, so as to have no knowledge of the place where it is; as, to *lose* a book or a paper; to *lose* a record; to *lose* a dollar or a ducat.

2. To forfeit by unsuccessful contest; as, to *lose* money in gaming.

3. Not to gain or win; as, to *lose* a battle, that is, to be defeated.

4. To be deprived of; as, to *lose* men in battle; to *lose* an arm or a leg by a shot or by amputation; to *lose* one's life or honor.

5. To forfeit, as a penalty. Our first parents *lost* the favor of God by their apostasy.

6. To suffer diminution or waste of.

If the salt hath *lost* its savor, wherewith shall it be salted? Matt. v.

7. To ruin; to destroy.

The woman that deliberates is *lost*. *Addison.*

8. To wander from; to miss, so as not to be able to find; as, to *lose* the way.

9. To bewilder.

Lost in the maze of words. *Pope.*

10. To possess no longer; to be deprived of; contrary to *keep;* as, to *lose* a valuable trade.

11. Not to employ or enjoy; to waste. Titus sighed to *lose* a day.

Th' unhappy have but hours, and these they *lose*. *Dryden.*

12. To waste; to squander; to throw away; as, to *lose* a fortune by gaming, or by dissipation.

13. To suffer to vanish from view or perception. We *lost* sight of the land at noon. I *lost* my companion in the crowd.

Like following life in creatures we dissect,
We *lose* it in the moment we detect. *Pope.*

14. To ruin; to destroy by shipwreck, &c. The Albion was *lost* on the coast of Ireland, April 22, 1822. The admiral *lost* three ships in a tempest.

15. To cause to perish; as, to be *lost* at sea.

16. To employ ineffectually; to throw away; to waste. Instruction is often *lost* on the dull; admonition is *lost* on the profligate. It is often the fate of projectors to *lose* their labor.

17. To be freed from.

His scaly back the bunch has got
Which Edwin *lost* before. *Parnell.*

18. To fail to obtain.

He shall in no wise *lose* his reward. Matt. x.

To lose one's self, to be bewildered; also, to slumber; to have the memory and reason suspended.

LÖSE, *v. i. looz.* To forfeit any thing in contest; not to win.

We'll talk with them too,
Who *loses* and who wins; who's in, who's out. *Shak.*

2. To decline; to fail.

Wisdom in discourse with her
Loses discountenanced, and like folly shows. *Milton.*

LOS'EL, *n. s* as *z.* [from the root of *loose.*] A wasteful fellow, one who loses by sloth or neglect; a worthless person. *Obs.* *Spenser.*

LOS'ENGER, *n.* [Sax. *leas*, false; *leasunge*, falsity.] A deceiver. *Obs.* *Chaucer.*

LÖSER, *n. looz'er.* One that loses, or that is deprived of any thing by defeat, forfeiture or the like; the contrary to *winner* or *gainer*. A *loser* by trade may be honest and moral; this cannot be said of a *loser* by gaming.

LÖSING, *ppr. looz'ing.* Parting from; missing; forfeiting; wasting; employing to no good purpose.

LOSS, *n.* Privation; as the *loss* of property; *loss* of money by gaming; *loss* of health or reputation. Every *loss* is not a detriment. We cannot regret the *loss* of bad company or of evil habits.

2. Destruction; ruin; as the *loss* of a ship at sea; the *loss* of an army.

3. Defeat; as the *loss* of a battle.

4. Waste; useless application; as a *loss* of time or labor.

5. Waste by leakage or escape; as a *loss* of liquors in transportation.

To bear a loss, to make good; also, to sustain a loss without sinking under it.

To be at a loss, to be puzzled; to be unable to determine; to be in a state of uncertainty.

LOSS'FUL, *a.* Detrimental. [*Not used.*] *Bp. Hall.*

LOSS'LESS, *a.* Free from loss. [*Not used.*] *Milton.*

LOST, *pp.* [from *lose.*] Mislaid or left in a place unknown or forgotten; that cannot be found; as a *lost* book.

2. Ruined; destroyed; wasted or squandered; employed to no good purpose; as *lost* money; *lost* time.

3. Forfeited; as a *lost* estate.

4. Not able to find the right way, or the place intended. A stranger is *lost* in London or Paris.

5. Bewildered; perplexed; being in a maze; as, a speaker may be *lost* in his argument.

6. Alienated; insensible; hardened beyond sensibility or recovery; as a profligate *lost* to shame; *lost* to all sense of honor.

7. Not perceptible to the senses; not visible; as an isle *lost* in fog; a person *lost* in a crowd.

8. Shipwrecked or foundered; sunk or destroyed; as a ship *lost* at sea, or on the rocks.

LOT, *n.* [Sax. *hlot, hlodd, hlet, hlyt;* Goth. *hlauts;* D. Fr. *lot;* Sw. *lott;* Dan. Arm. *lod;* G. *los;* It. *lotto;* Sp. *loteria*, a lottery. The primary sense is that which comes, falls or happens, or a part, a division or share. The French, from *lot*, have *lotir*, to divide; Arm. *loda*, id. whence *lodecq*, a co-heir.]

1. That which, in human speech, is called chance, hazard, fortune; but in strictness of language, is the determination of Providence; as, the land shall be divided by *lot*. Num. xxvi.

2. That by which the fate or portion of one is determined; that by which an event is committed to chance, that is, to the determination of Providence; as, to cast *lots*; to draw *lots*.

The *lot* is cast into the lap, but the whole disposing thereof is of the Lord. Prov. xvi.

3. The part, division or fate which falls to one by chance, that is, by divine determination.

The second *lot* came forth to Simeon. Josh. xix.

He was but born to try
The *lot* of man, to suffer and to die. *Pope.*

4. A distinct portion or parcel; as a *lot* of goods; a *lot* of boards.

5. Proportion or share of taxes; as, to pay scot and *lot*.

6. In *the U. States*, a piece or division of land; perhaps originally assigned by drawing lots, but now any portion, piece or division. So we say, a man has a *lot* of land in Broadway, or in the meadow; he has a *lot* in the plain, or on the mountain; he has a home-*lot*, a house-*lot*, a wood-*lot*.

The defendants leased a house and *lot* in the city of New York. *Kent. Franklin, Law of Penn.*

To cast lots, is to use or throw a die, or some other instrument, by the unforeseen turn or position of which, an event is by previous agreement determined.

To draw lots, to determine an event by drawing one thing from a number whose marks are concealed from the drawer, and thus determining an event.

LOT, *v. t.* To allot; to assign; to distribute; to sort; to catalogue; to portion. *Prior.*

LOTE, *n.* [L. *lotus, lotos.*] A plant of the genus Celtis, the lote-tree, of several species. The wood of one species is very durable, and is used for timber. In Italy, flutes and other wind-instruments are made of it, and in England it is used for the frames of coaches, &c. *Encyc.*

2. A little fish.

LOTH, *a.* [Sax. *lath*, Sw. *led*, Dan. *leede*, odious, hated. The common orthography is *loath*, pronounced with *o* long, but both the orthography and pronunciation are corrupt. This word follows the analogy of *cloth*, Sax. *clath.* I have followed Milton, Dryden, Waller, Spenser and Shakspeare in the orthography of the adjective, and Cruden in that of the verb. The primary sense is to thrust, to turn or drive away. See the verb, and Class Ld. No. 9.15.]

1. Literally, hating, detesting; hence,

2. Unwilling; disliking; not inclined; reluctant.

Long doth he stay, as *loth* to leave the land. *Davies.*

To pardon willing, and to punish *loth*. *Waller.*

LOTHE, *v. t.* [Sax. *lathian*, to hate, to detest, to call, to invite; *gelathian*, to call; Goth. *lathon*, to call; Sw. *ledas*, to lothe; G. *einladen*, to invite, to lade or load, from *laden*, to lade, to invite, to cite or summon. See *Lade.*]

1. To feel disgust at any thing; properly, to have an extreme aversion of the appetite to food or drink.

Our soul *lotheth* this light bread. Num. xxi.

Lothing the honey'd cakes, I long'd for bread. *Cowley.*

2. To hate; to dislike greatly; to abhor.

Ye shall *lothe* yourselves in your own sight for all your evils— Ezek. xx.

Not to reveal the secret which I *lothe*. *Waller.*

LOTHE, *v. i.* To create disgust. *Obs.* *Spenser.*

LO'THED, *pp.* Hated; abhorred; turned from with disgust.

LO'THER, *n.* One that lothes or abhors.

LO'THFUL, *a.* Hating; abhorring.

Which he did with *lothful* eyes behold. *Hubberd.*

2. Disgusting; hated; exciting abhorrence.

Above the reach of *lothful* sinful lust. *Spenser.*

LO'THING, *ppr.* Feeling disgust at; having extreme aversion to; as *lothing* food.

2. Hating; abhorring; as *lothing* sin.

LO'THING, *n.* Extreme disgust; abhorrence. Ezek. xvi.

LO'THINGLY, *adv.* With extreme disgust or abhorrence; in a fastidious manner.

LOTH'LY, *adv.* Unwillingly; reluctantly.

This shows that you from nature *lothly* stray. *Donne.*

LOTH'NESS, *n.* Unwillingness; reluctance.

There grew among them a general silence and *lothness* to speak. *Bacon.*

LO'THSÔME, *a.* [Sw. *ledesam.*] Causing an extreme aversion of appetite; exciting fastidiousness. Num. xi.

2. Exciting extreme disgust; offensive; as a *lothsome* disease. Ps. xxxviii.

3. Odious; exciting hatred or abhorrence; detestable; as *lothsome* sloth. *Spenser.*

LO'THSÔMENESS, *n.* The quality of exciting extreme disgust or abhorrence. *Addison.*

LO'TION, *n.* [L. *lotio*, from *lavo*, to wash.]

1. A washing; particularly, a washing of the skin for the purpose of rendering it fair. *Encyc.*

2. A liquid preparation for washing some part of the body, to cleanse it of foulness or deformity. *Encyc.*

3. In *pharmacy*, a preparation of medicines, by washing them in some liquid, to remove foreign substances, impurities, &c. *Encyc.*

LOT'TERY, *n.* [Fr. *loterie*: Sp. *loteria.* See *Lot.*]

1. A scheme for the distribution of prizes by chance, or the distribution itself. *Lotteries* are often authorized by law, but many good men deem them immoral in principle, and almost all men concur in the opinion that their effects are pernicious.

2. Allotment. [*Not used.*]

LOUD, *a.* [Sax. *hlud* or *lud*; G. *laut*; D. *luid*; Dan. *lyd*; L. *laudo*, to praise, and with a prefix, *plaudo*; W. *clod*, praise, formed from *llod*, which signifies what is forcibly uttered; *llodi*, to reach out; *llawd*, that shoots out, that is productive, also a *lad.* This is the Ch. Syr. Heb. Sam. ילד, Eth. ወለደ walad, Ar. وَلَدَ walada, to bring forth. The primary sense is obvious. Qu. its connection with the Ir. *blaodh* and *glaodh*, a calling, and Sax. *lathian*, to call. See Class Ld. No. 8. 29.]

1. Having a great sound; high sounding; noisy; striking the ear with great force; as a *loud* voice; a *loud* cry; *loud* thunder.

2. Uttering or making a great noise; as *loud* instruments. 2 Chron. xxx.

3. Clamorous; noisy.

She is *loud* and stubborn. Prov. vii.

4. Emphatical; impressive; as a *loud* call to avoid danger.

LOUD'LY, *adv.* With great sound or noise; noisily.

Who long and *loudly* in the schools declaimed. *Denham.*

2. Clamorously; with vehement complaints or importunity. He *loudly* complained of intolerance.

LOUD'NESS, *n.* Great sound or noise; as the *loudness* of a voice or of thunder.

2. Clamor; clamorousness; turbulence; uproar.

LOUGH, *n.* *lok.* [Ir. and Scot. *loch.*] A lake; a different orthography of *loch* and *lake.* *Fairfax.*

LOUIS D'OR, *n.* [a Lewis of gold.] A gold coin of France, first struck in 1640, in the reign of Louis XIII., value, twenty shillings sterling, equal to $4.4444.

LOUNGE, *v. i.* [Fr. *longis*, a lingerer, from *long.*] To live in idleness; to spend time lazily.

LOUNG'ER, *n.* An idler; one who loiters away his time in indolence.

LOUR. [See *Lower.*]

LOUSE, *n.* *lous.* plu. *lice.* [Sax. *lus*, plu. *lys*; D. *luis*; G. *laus*; Sw. Dan. *lus.*]

A small insect of the genus Pediculus. It has six feet, two eyes, with long feelers and a sting in the mouth. It infests the bodies of men and other animals; but different animals are infested with different species. *Encyc.*

LOUSE, *v. t.* *louz.* To clean from lice. *Swift.*

LOUSE-WÔRT, *n.* *lous'-wort.* A plant of the genus Pedicularis. The yellow lousewort is of the genus Rhinanthus. *Fam. of Plants.*

LOUS'ILY, *adv.* *s* as *z.* [from *lousy.*] In a mean, paltry manner; scurvily.

LOUS'INESS, *n.* *s* as *z.* The state of abounding with lice.

LOUS'Y, *a.* *s* as *z.* [from *louse.*] Swarming with lice; infested with lice. *Dryden.*

2. Mean; low; contemptible; as a *lousy* knave. *Shak.*

LOUT, *n.* [Qu. Sax. *leod*, G. *leute*, people.] A mean awkward fellow; a bumpkin; a clown. *Shak. Gay.*

LOUT, *v. i.* [Sax. *hlutan.*] To bend; to bow; to stoop. [*Obsolete or local.*] *Spenser. B. Jonson.*

LOUT'ISH, *a.* Clownish; rude; awkward. *Sidney.*

LOUT'ISHLY, *adv.* Like a clown; in a rude, clumsy, awkward manner.

LOUVER, *n.* *loo'ver.* [Fr. *l'ouvert.*] An opening in the roof of a cottage for the smoke to escape. *Spenser.*

LÔV'ABLE, *a.* Worthy of love; amiable. *Sherwood.*

LÔV'AGE, *n.* A plant of the genus Ligusticum. *Fam. of Plants.*

LÔVE, *v. t.* *luv.* [Sax. *lufian*, *luvian*; D. *lieven*; G. *lieben*; Russ. *lioblyu*; L. *libeo*, *lubeo*; Sans. *loab*, love, desire. See *Lief.* The sense is probably to be prompt, free, willing, from leaning, advancing, or drawing forward.]

1. In a general sense to be pleased with; to regard with affection, on account of some qualities which excite pleasing sensations or desire of gratification. We *love* a friend, on account of some qualities which give us pleasure in his society. We *love* a man who has done us a favor; in which case, gratitude enters into the composition of our affection. We *love* our parents and our children, on account of their connection with us, and on account of many qualities which please us. We *love* to retire to a cool shade in summer. We *love* a warm room in winter. We *love* to hear an eloquent advocate. The christian *loves* his Bible. In short, we *love* whatever gives us pleasure and delight, whether animal or intellectual; and if our hearts are right, we *love* God above all things, as the sum of all excellence and all the attributes which can communicate happiness to intelligent beings. In other words, the christian *loves* God with the love of complacency in his attributes, the love of benevolence towards the interests of his kingdom, and the love of gratitude for favors received.

Thou shalt *love* the Lord thy God with all thy heart, and with all thy soul, and with all thy mind—

Thou shalt *love* thy neighbor as thyself. Matt. xxii.

2. To have benevolence or good will for. John iii.

LÔVE, *n.* An affection of the mind excited by beauty and worth of any kind, or by the qualities of an object which communicate pleasure, sensual or intellectual. It is opposed to *hatred.* *Love* between the sexes, is a compound affection, consisting of esteem, benevolence, and animal desire. *Love* is excited by pleasing qualities of any kind, as by kindness, benevolence, charity, and by the qualities which render social intercourse agreeable. In the latter case, *love* is ardent friendship, or a strong attachment springing from good will and esteem, and the pleasure derived from the company, civilities and kindnesses of others.

Between certain natural relatives, *love* seems to be in some cases instinctive. Such is the *love* of a mother for her child, which manifests itself toward an infant, before any particular qualities in the child are unfolded. This affection is apparently as strong in irrational animals as in human beings.

We speak of the *love* of amusements, the *love* of books, the *love* of money, and the *love* of whatever contributes to our pleasure or supposed profit.

The *love* of God is the first duty of man, and this springs from just views of his attributes or excellencies of character, which afford the highest delight to the sanctified heart. Esteem and reverence constitute ingredients in this affection, and a fear of offending him is its inseparable effect.

2. Courtship; chiefly in the phrase, to *make love*, that is, to court; to woo; to solicit union in marriage.

3. Patriotism; the attachment one has to his native land; as the *love* of country.

4. Benevolence; good will.

God is *love.* 1 John iv.

5. The object beloved.

The lover and the *love* of human kind. *Pope.*

6. A word of endearment.

Trust me, *love.* *Dryden.*

7. Picturesque representation of love.

Such was his form as painters, when they show
Their utmost art, on naked *loves* bestow. *Dryden.*

8. Lewdness.

He is not lolling on a lewd *love*-bed. *Shak.*

9. A thin silk stuff. *Obs.* *Boyle.*

Love in idleness, a kind of violet. *Shak.*

Free of love, a plant of the genus Cercis. *Fam. of Plants.*

LÔVE-APPLE, *n.* A plant of the genus Solanum.

LÔVE-BROKER, *n.* A third person who acts as agent between lovers. *Shak.*

LÔVED, *pp.* Having the affection of any one.

LÔVE-DARTING, *a.* Darting love. *Milton.*

LÔVE-DAY, *n.* A day formerly appointed for an amicable adjustment of differences. *Chaucer.*

LŎVE-FAVOR, *n.* Something given to be worn in token of love. *Bp. Hall.*

LŎVE-KNOT, *n.* *luv'-not.* A knot so called, used as a token of love or representing mutual affection.

LŎVE-LABORED, *a.* Labored by love. *Milton.*

LŎVE-LASS, *n.* A sweetheart.

LŎVELESS, *a.* Void of love; void of tenderness or kindness. *Milton. Shelton.*

LŎVE-LETTER, *n.* A letter professing love; a letter of courtship.

LŎVELILY, *adv.* *luv'lily.* [from *lovely.*] Amiably; in a manner to excite love. *Otway.*

LŎVELINESS, *n.* *luv'liness.* [from *lovely.*] Amiableness; qualities of body or mind that may excite love.

If there is such a native *loveliness* in the sex, as to make them victorious when in the wrong, how resistless their power when they are on the side of truth. *Spectator.*

LŎVE-LOCK, *n.* A curl or lock of hair so called; worn by men of fashion in the reigns of Elizabeth and James I. *Lily.*

LŎVE-LORN, *a.* [*love* and *lorn.*] Forsaken by one's love; as the *love-lorn* nightingale. *Milton.*

LŎVELY, *a.* *luv'ly.* Amiable; that may excite love; possessing qualities which may invite affection.

Saul and Jonathan were *lovely* and pleasant in their lives— 2 Sam. i.

LŎVE-MŎNGER, *n.* [*love* and *monger.*] One who deals in affairs of love. [*Not used.*] *Shak.*

LŎVE-PINED, *a.* Wasted by love. *Spenser.*

LŎV'ER, *n.* One who loves; one who has a tender affection, particularly for a female.

Love is blind, and *lovers* cannot see— *Shak.*

2. A friend; one who regards with kindness.

Your brother and his *lover* have embraced. *Shak.*

3. One who likes or is pleased with any thing; as a *lover* of books or of science; a *lover* of wine; a *lover* of religion.

Lover and *loover.* [See *Louver.*]

LŎVE-SECRET, *n.* A secret between lovers. *Dryden.*

LŎVE-SHAFT, *n.* Cupid's arrow. *Shak.*

LŎVE-SICK, *a.* Sick or languishing with love or amorous desire; as a *love-sick* maid.

To the dear mistress of my *love-sick* mind. *Dryden.*

2. Dictated by a languishing lover, or expressive of languishing love.

Where nightingales their *love-sick* ditty sing. *Dryden.*

LŎVESŎME, *a.* Lovely. [*Not used.*] *Dryden.*

LŎVE-SONG, *n.* A song expressing love. *Shak.*

LŎVE-SUIT, *n.* Courtship; solicitation of union in marriage. *Shak.*

LŎVE-TALE, *n.* A narrative of love.

Cato's a proper person to entrust
A *love-tale* with. *Addison.*

LŎVE-THOUGHT, *n.* Amorous fancy. [*Not used.*] *Shak.*

LŎVE-TOKEN, *n.* A present in token of love. *Shak.*

LŎVE-TOY, *n.* A small present from a lover. *Arbuthnot.*

LŎVE-TRICK, *n.* Art or artifice expressive of love.

Other *love-tricks* than glancing with the eyes. *Donne.*

LŎVING, *ppr.* Entertaining a strong affection for; having tender regard for.

2. *a.* Fond; affectionate; as a *loving* friend.

3. Expressing love or kindness; as *loving* words.

LŎVING-KINDNESS, *n.* Tender regard; mercy; favor; *a scriptural word.*

My *loving-kindness* will I not utterly take from him. Ps. lxxxix.

LŎVINGLY, *adv.* With love; with affection; affectionately.

It is no great matter to live *lovingly* with meek persons. *Taylor.*

LŎVINGNESS, *n.* Affection; kind regard.

The only two bands of good will, loveliness and *lovingness.* *Sidney.*

LŌW, *a.* [D. *laag*, G. *leg*, Sw. *låg*, low; Sax. *loh*, a pit or gulf; Russ. *log*, a low place, a hollow; Dan. *lag*, a bed or layer, a row; from the root of *lay.*]

1. Not high or elevated; depressed below any given surface or place. *Low* ground or land, is land below the common level. *Low* is opposed to *high*, and both are relative terms. That which is *low* with respect to one thing, may be *high* with respect to another. A *low* house would be a *high* fence. A *low* flight for an eagle, would be a *high* flight for a partridge.

2. Not rising to the usual highth; as a man of *low* stature.

3. Declining near the horizon. The sun is *low* at four o'clock in winter, and at six in summer.

4. Deep; descending far below the adjacent ground; as a *low* valley.

The *lowest* bottom shook of Erebus. *Milton.*

5. Sunk to the natural level of the ocean by the retiring of the tide; as *low* water.

6. Below the usual rate or amount, or below the ordinary value; as a *low* price of corn; *low* wages.

7. Not high or loud; as a *low* voice.

8. Grave; depressed in the scale of sounds; as a *low* note.

9. Near or not very distant from the equator; as a *low* latitude. We say, the *low* southern latitudes; the *high* northern latitudes.

10. Late in time; modern; as the *lower* empire.

11. Dejected; depressed in vigor; wanting strength or animation; as *low* spirits; *low* in spirits. His courage is *low.*

12. Depressed in condition; in a humble state.

Why but to keep you *low* and ignorant? *Milton.*

13. Humble in rank; in a mean condition; as men of high and *low* condition; the *lower* walks of life; a *low* class of people.

14. Mean; abject; groveling; base; as a person of *low* mind.

15. Dishonorable; mean; as a *low* trick or stratagem.

16. Not elevated or sublime; not exalted in thought or diction; as a *low* comparison; a *low* metaphor; *low* language.

In comparison of these divine writers, the noblest wits of the heathen world are *low* and dull. *Felton.*

17. Vulgar; common; as a *low* education.

18. Submissive; humble; reverent.

And pay their fealty
With *low* subjection. *Milton.*
But first *low* reverence done. *Ibm.*

19. Weak; exhausted of vital energy. His disease has brought him very *low.*

20. Feeble; weak; without force; as a *low* pulse.

21. Moderate; not inflammatory; as a *low* fever.

22. Moderate; not intense; as a *low* heat; a *low* temperature.

23. Impoverished; in reduced circumstances. The rich are often reduced to a *low* condition.

24. Moderate; as a *low* calculation or estimate.

25. Plain; simple; not rich, high seasoned or nourishing; as a *low* diet.

LŌW, *adv.* Not aloft; not on high; *often in composition;* as *low*-brow'd rocks. *Milton. Pope.*

2. Under the usual price; at a moderate price. He sold his wheat *low.*

3. Near the ground; as, the bird flies very *low.*

4. In a mean condition; *in composition;* as a *low*-born fellow; a *low*-born lass. *Shak.*

5. In time approaching our own.

In the part of the world which was first inhabited, even as *low* down as Abraham's time, they wandered with their flocks and herds. *Locke.*

6. With a depressed voice; not loudly; as, speak *low.*

7. In a state of subjection, poverty or disgrace; as, to be brought *low* by oppression, by want or by vice.

LŌW, *v. t.* To sink; to depress. [*Not used.*] *Wickliffe.*

LŌW, *v. i.* [Sax. *hleowan;* D. *lœijen.* It is probably a contracted word, coinciding with L. *lugeo*, to weep, the sense of which is, to *cry out.*]

To bellow, as an ox or cow.

The *lowing* herd wind slowly o'er the lea. *Gray.*

LŌWBELL, *n.* [Sw. *låge*, flame; *låga*, to flame; Sax. *lœg*, *leg*, *lig*, id.; Scot. *lowe;* G. *loke.*]

A kind of fowling in the night, in which the birds are wakened by a bell, and blinded by light, so as to be easily taken. *Cowel.*

LŌWBELL, *v. t.* To scare, as with a lowbell. *Hammond.*

LŌW, LŌWE, a termination of names, as in Bed-*low.* [Sax. *hlaw*, a hill, heap or barrow, Goth. *hlaiw.*]

LŌW-BORN, *a.* Born in low life.

LŌW-BRED, *a.* Bred in a low condition or manner; vulgar.

LŌWER, *v. t.* [from *low.*] To cause to descend; to let down; to take or bring down; as, to *lower* the main-sail of a sloop.

2. To suffer to sink downwards. *Woodward.*

3. To bring down; to reduce or humble; as, to *lower* the pride of man.

4. To lessen; to diminish; to reduce, as value or amount; as, to *lower* the price or value of goods, or the rate of interest.

LŌWER, *v. i.* To fall; to sink; to grow less. *Shak.*

LOW'ER, *v. i.* To appear dark or gloomy; to be clouded; to threaten a storm.

And all the clouds that *lowered* upon your house. *Shak.*

The *lowering* spring. *Dryden.*

2. To frown; to look sullen.

But sullen discontent sat *lowering* on her face. *Dryden.*

LOW'ER, *n.* Cloudiness; gloominess.

2. A frowning; sullenness. *Sidney.*

LŌWER, *a.* [comp. of *low.*] Less high or elevated.

LOW'ERINGLY, *adv.* With cloudiness or threatening gloom.

LŌWERMOST, *a.* [from *low.*] Lowest.

LOW'ERY, *a.* Cloudy; gloomy.

LŌWEST, *a.* [superl. of *low.*] Most low; deepest; most depressed or degraded, &c.

LŌWING, *ppr.* Bellowing, as an ox.

LŌWING, *n.* The bellowing or cry of cattle.

LŌWLAND, *n.* Land which is low with respect to the neighboring country; a low or level country. Thus the Belgic states are called *Lowlands.* The word is sometimes opposed to a mountainous country; as the *Lowlands* of Scotland. Sometimes it denotes a marsh. *Dryden.*

LŌWLIHOOD, *n.* A humble state. *Obs.* *Chaucer.*

LŌWLINESS, *n.* [from *lowly.*] Freedom from pride; humility; humbleness of mind. *Milton.*

Walk—with all *lowliness* and meekness. Eph. iv. Phil. ii.

2. Meanness; want of dignity; abject state. [*In this sense little used.*] *Spenser. Dryden.*

LŌWLY, *a.* [*low* and *like.*] Having a low esteem of one's own worth; humble; meek; free from pride.

Take my yoke upon you and learn of me, for I am meek and *lowly* in heart. Matt. xi.

He scorneth the scorners; but he giveth grace to the *lowly.* Prov. iii.

2. Mean; low; wanting dignity or rank.

One common right the great and *lowly* claim. *Pope.*

3. Not lofty or sublime; humble.

These rural poems, and their *lowly* strain. *Dryden.*

4. Not high; not elevated in place. *Dryden.*

LŌWLY, *adv.* Humbly; meekly; modestly.

Be *lowly* wise. *Milton.*

2. Meanly; in a low condition; without grandeur or dignity.

I will show myself highly fed and *lowly* taught. *Shak.*

LOWN, *n.* [See *Loon.*] A low fellow; a scoundrel. *Shak.*

LŌWNESS, *n.* The state of being low or depressed; the state of being less elevated than something else; as the *lowness* of the ground, or of the water after the ebb-tide.

2. Meanness of condition. Men are not to be despised or oppressed on account of the *lowness* of their birth or condition.

3. Meanness of mind or character; want of dignity. Haughtiness usually springs from *lowness* of mind; real dignity is distinguished by modesty.

4. Want of sublimity in style or sentiment; the contrary to *loftiness.* *Dryden.*

5. Submissiveness; as the *lowness* of obedience. *Bacon.*

6. Depression of mind; want of courage or fortitude; dejection; as *lowness* of spirits.

7. Depression in fortune; a state of poverty; as the *lowness* of circumstances.

8. Depression in strength or intensity; as the *lowness* of heat or temperature; *lowness* of zeal.

9. Depression in price or worth; as the *lowness* of price or value; the *lowness* of the funds or of the markets.

10. Graveness of sound; as the *lowness* of notes.

11. Softness of sound; as the *lowness* of the voice.

LŌW-SPIR'ITED, *a.* Not having animation and courage; dejected; depressed; not lively or sprightly. Losses of property often render men *low-spirited.* Excessive severity breaks the mind, and renders the child or pupil *low-spirited.*

LŌW-SPIR'ITEDNESS, *n.* Dejection of mind or courage; a state of low spirits. *Cheyne.*

LŌW-THOUGHT'ED, *a.* Having the thoughts employed on low subjects; not having sublime and elevated thoughts or contemplations; mean of sentiment; as *low-thoughted* care. *Milton. Pope.*

LŌW-WINES, *n.* [*low* and *wine.*] The liquor produced by the first distillation of melasses, or fermented liquors; the first run of the still. *Edwards, W. Ind.*

LOXODROM'I€, *a.* [Gr. λοξος, oblique, and δρομος, a course.]

Pertaining to oblique sailing by the rhomb; as *loxodromic* tables.

LOXODROM'I€S, *n.* The art of oblique sailing by the rhomb, which always makes an equal angle with every meridian; that is, when a ship sails neither directly under the equator, nor under the same meridian, but obliquely. *Harris. Bailey.*

LOY'AL, *a.* [Fr. *loyal*; It. *leale*; Sp. *leal*; from L. *lex*, law.]

Faithful to a prince or superior; true to plighted faith, duty or love; not treacherous; used of subjects to their prince, and of husband, wife and lovers; as a *loyal* subject; a *loyal* wife.

There Laodamia with Evadne moves,
Unhappy both! but *loyal* in their loves. *Dryden.*

LOY'ALIST, *n.* A person who adheres to his sovereign; particularly, one who maintains his allegiance to his prince, and defends his cause in times of revolt or revolution.

LOY'ALLY, *adv.* With fidelity to a prince or sovereign, or to a husband or lover.

LOY'ALTY, *n.* Fidelity to a prince or sovereign, or to a husband or lover.

He had such *loyalty* to the king as the law requires. *Clarendon.*

LOZ'ENGE, *n.* [Fr. *losange*; Gr. λοξος, oblique, and γωνια, a corner.]

1. Originally, a figure with four equal sides, having two acute and two obtuse angles; a rhomb.

2. In *heraldry*, a four-cornered figure, resembling a pane of glass in old casements. *Encyc.*

3. Among jewelers, lozenges are common to brilliants and rose diamonds. In brilliants, they are formed by the meeting of the skill and the star facets on the bezil; in the latter, by the meeting of the facets in the horizontal ribs of the crown. *Encyc.*

4. A form of medicine in small pieces, to be chewed or held in the mouth till melted. *Johnson.*

5. In confectionary, a small cake of preserved fruit, or of sugar, &c.

LOZ'ENGED, *a.* Made into the shape of lozenges.

LOZ'ENGY, *a.* In *heraldry*, having the field or charge covered with lozenges.

LP, a contraction of lordship.

LU. [See *Loo.*]

LUBBARD. [*Not used.* See *Lubber.*]

LUB'BER, *n.* [W. *llabi*, a tall lank fellow, a clumsy man, a stripling, a *lubber*, a *looby*; *llab*, a flag or thin strip, a stripe or stroke; *llabiaw*, to *slap*; *llob*, an unwieldy lump, a dull fellow. From the significations of *llabi*, it appears that the primary sense is tall and lank, like a stripling who gains his highth before he does his full strength, and hence is clumsy. But *looby* seems rather to be from *llob.*]

A heavy, clumsy fellow; a sturdy drone; a clown.

And lingering *lubbers* lose many a penny. *Tusser.*

LUB'BERLY, *a.* Properly, tall and lank without activity; hence, bulky and heavy; clumsy; lazy; as a *lubberly* fellow or boy.

LUB'BERLY, *adv.* Clumsily; awkwardly. *Dryden.*

LU'BRI€, *a.* [L. *lubricus*, slippery.] Having a smooth surface; slippery; as a *lubric* throat. *Crashaw.*

2. Wavering; unsteady; as the *lubric* waves of state. *Wotton.*

3. Lascivious; wanton; lewd.

This *lubric* and adulterate age. *Dryden.*

[*This word is now little used.*]

LU'BRI€ANT, *n.* [See *Lubricate.*] That which lubricates.

LU'BRI€ATE, *v. t.* [L. *lubrico*, from *lubricus*, slippery; allied to *labor*, to slip or slide.]

To make smooth or slippery. Mucilaginous and saponaceous medicines *lubricate* the parts to which they are applied.

LU'BRI€ATED, *pp.* Made smooth and slippery.

LU'BRI€ATING, *ppr.* Rendering smooth and slippery.

LU'BRI€ATOR, *n.* That which lubricates.

LUBRIC'ITY, *n.* [Fr. *lubricité.*] Smoothness of surface; slipperiness.

2. Smoothness; aptness to glide over any thing, or to facilitate the motion of bodies in contact by diminishing friction. *Ray.*

3. Slipperiness; instability; as the *lubricity* of fortune. *L'Estrange.*

4. Lasciviousness; propensity to lewdness; lewdness; lechery; incontinency. *Dryden.*

LU'BRI€OUS, *a.* [L. *lubricus.*] Smooth; slippery. *Woodward.*

2. Wavering; unstable; as *lubricous* opinions. *Glanville.*

LUBRIFA€'TION, *n.* [infra.] The act of lubricating or making smooth. *Bacon.*

LUBRIFI€A'TION, *n.* [L. *lubricus* and *facio*, to make.]

The act or operation of making smooth and slippery. *Ray.*

LUCE, *n.* A pike full grown. *Johnson. Shak.*

LU'CENT, *a.* [L. *lucens*, from *luceo*, to shine. See *Light.*]
Shining; bright; resplendent; as the sun's *lucent* orb. *Milton.*

LU'CERN, *n.* [Qu. W. *llysau*, plants; *llysieuyn*, a plant; Corn. *lyzuan;* or from Lucerne, in Switzerland.]
A plant of the genus Medicago, cultivated for fodder.

LU'CID, *a.* [L. *lucidus*, from *luceo*, to shine. See *Light.*]
1. Shining; bright; resplendent; as the *lucid* orbs of heaven.
2. Clear; transparent; pellucid; as a *lucid* stream. *Milton.*
3. Bright with the radiance of intellect; not darkened or confused by delirium or madness; marked by the regular operations of reason; as the *lucid* intervals of a deranged man.
4. Clear; distinct; presenting a clear view; easily understood; as a *lucid* order or arrangement.

LUCID'ITY, *n.* Brightness. [*Not used.*]

LU'CIDNESS, *n.* Brightness; clearness.

LU'CIFER, *n.* [L. *lux*, *lucis*, light, and *fero*, to bring.]
1. The planet Venus, so called from its brightness.
2. Satan.

> And when he falls, he falls like *Lucifer*,
> Never to hope again. *Shak.*

LUCIFE'RIAN, *a.* Pertaining to Lucifer, or to the Luciferians.

LUCIFE'RIANS, *n.* A sect that followed Lucifer, bishop of Cagliari, in the fourth century. They held to the carnal nature of the soul, and that there is no place for repentance for such as fall.

LUCIF'EROUS, *a.* [L. *lucifer*, supra.] Giving light; affording light or means of discovery. *Boyle.*

LUCIF'IC, *a.* [L. *lux*, light, and *facio*, to make.]
Producing light. *Grew.*

LU'CIFORM, *a.* [L. *lux*, light, and *forma*, form.]
Having the form of light; resembling light.

> The water prepares us, and purifies our *luciform* spirit to receive the divinity. *Paus. Trans.*

LUCK, *n.* [D. *luk*, *geluk*; G. *glück*; Sw. *lycka*; Dan. *lykke*; Sans. *lakki*. The sense is that which comes, falls, happens. W. *lluç*, a dart or throw; *lluçiaw*, to throw. Qu. Gr. λαγχανω; Ar. لقي. Class Lg. No. 21.]
That which happens to a person; an event, good or ill, affecting a man's interest or happiness, and which is deemed casual; fortune. *Luck* respects persons and their proceedings. We never say, in a literal sense, that a plant has the *luck* to grow in a particular place; or a fossil has the *luck* to be of a particular form. We say, a person has the good *luck* to escape from danger; or the ill *luck* to be ensnared or to suffer loss. He has had good *luck*, or bad *luck* in gaming, fishing or hunting. *Luck*, or what we call chance, accident, fortune, is an event which takes place without being intended or foreseen, or from some cause not under human control; that which cannot be previously known or determined with certainty by human skill or power.

> Consider the gift of *luck* as below the care of a wise man. *Rambler.*

LUCK'ILY, *adv.* [from *lucky.*] Fortunately; by good fortune; with a favorable issue; *in a good sense.* *Luckily*, we escaped injury.

LUCK'INESS, *n.* The state of being fortunate; as the *luckiness* of a man or of an event.
2. Good fortune; a favorable issue or event. [In this sense, *luck* is generally used.]

LUCK'LESS, *a.* Unfortunate; meeting with ill success; as a *luckless* gamester; a *luckless* maid.
2. Unfortunate; producing ill or no good.

> Prayers made and granted in a *luckless* hour. *Dryden.*

LUCK'Y, *a.* Fortunate; meeting with good success; as a *lucky* adventurer.
2. Fortunate; producing good by chance; favorable; as a *lucky* adventure; a *lucky* time; a *lucky* cast.

LU'CRATIVE, *a.* [Fr. *lucratif;* L. *lucrativus*, from *lucror*, to gain profit.]
Gainful; profitable; making increase of money or goods; as a *lucrative* trade; *lucrative* business or office.

LU'CRE, *n.* *lu'ker.* [L. *lucrum;* Fr. *lucre.*]
Gain in money or goods; profit; usually in an ill sense, or with the sense of something base or unworthy.

> The lust of *lucre*, and the dread of death. *Pope.*

> A bishop must be blameless—not given to filthy *lucre.* Tit. i.

LUCRIF'EROUS, *a.* [L. *lucrum*, gain, and *fero*, to produce.] Gainful; profitable. [*Little used.*] *Boyle.*

LUCRIF'IC, *a.* [L. *lucrum*, gain, and *facio*, to make.] Producing profit; gainful. [*Not used.*]

LUCTA'TION, *n.* [L. *luctatio*, from *luctor*, to wrestle or strive.]
Struggle; contest; effort to overcome in contest. [*Little used.*]

LUC'TUAL, *a.* [L. *luctus*, grief.] Producing grief. [*Not used.*] *Buck.*

LU'CUBRATE, *v. i.* [L. *lucubro*, to study by candle-light, from *lucubrum*, from *lux*, light.]
To study by candle-light or a lamp; to study by night.

LUCUBRA'TION, *n.* Study by a lamp or by candle-light; nocturnal study.
2. That which is composed by night; that which is produced by meditation in retirement. *Tatler.*

LU'CUBRATORY, *a.* Composed by candle-light or by night. *Pope.*

LU'CULENT, *a.* [L. *luculentus*, from *luceo*, to shine.]
1. Lucid; clear; transparent; as *luculent* rivers. *Thomson.*
2. Clear; evident; luminous.

> The most *luculent* testimonies that the christian religion hath. *Hooker.*

LU'CULLITE, *n.* A subspecies of carbonate of lime, of three kinds. *Ure. Jameson.*

LUDIB'RIOUS, *a.* [L. *ludibriosus*, from *ludo*, to sport.] Sportive; wanton. *J. Barlow.*

LU'DICROUS, *a.* [L. *ludicer*, from *ludo*, to sport.]
Sportive; burlesque; adapted to raise laughter, without scorn or contempt. *Ludicrous* differs from *ridiculous;* the latter implying contempt or derision.

> Plutarch quotes this instance of Homer's judgment, in closing a *ludicrous* scene with decency and instruction. *Broome.*

LU'DICROUSLY, *adv.* Sportively; in burlesque; in a manner to raise laughter without contempt.

LU'DICROUSNESS, *n.* Sportiveness; the quality of exciting laughter without contempt; merry cast.

LUDIFICA'TION, *n.* [L. *ludificor.*] The act of deriding.

LUDIF'ICATORY, *a.* Making sport; tending to excite derision. *Barrow.*

LUFF, *n.* [Goth. *lofa;* Scot. *loof;* Ir. *lav*, *lamh;* W. *law.*] The palm of the hand.

LUFF, *n.* [Fr. *lof;* G. *loof;* D. *loef;* Arm. *loff.*]
Weather-gage, or part towards the wind; or the sailing of a ship close to the wind.

LUFF, *v. i.* [D. *loeven;* Arm. *loffi.*] To turn the head of a ship towards the wind; to sail nearer the wind. Hence, in the imperative, *luff*, is an order to put the tiller on the lee-side, in order to make the ship sail nearer the wind. *Luff round*, or *luff a-lee*, is the extreme of this movement, intended to throw the ship's head into the wind. A ship is said to *spring her luff*, when she yields to the helm by sailing nearer the wind. *Encyc.*

LUFF'-TACKLE, *n.* A large tackle not destined for any particular place in the ship, but movable at pleasure. *Mar. Dict.*

LUG, *v. t.* [Sax. *lyccan*, *aluccan*, *geluggian*, to pull, to *pluck*, Ir. *luighim.* See *Pluck.*]
1. To haul; to drag; to pull with force, as something heavy and moved with difficulty.

> Jowler *lugs* him still
> Through hedges. *Dryden.*

2. To carry or convey with labor.

> They must divide the image among them, and so *lug* off every one his share. *Collier.*

To lug out, to draw a sword, in burlesque. *Dryden.*

LUG, *v. i.* To drag; to move heavily. [Qu.] *Dryden.*

LUG, *n.* A small fish. *Carew.*
2. In Scotland, an ear. *Obs.* *Johnson.*
3. A pole or perch, a land-measure. *Obs.* *Spenser.*
4. Something heavy to be drawn or carried. [*Vulgar.*]

LUG'GAGE, *n.* [from *lug.*] Any thing cumbersome and heavy to be carried; traveling baggage.

> I am gathering up my *luggage* and preparing for my journey. *Swift.*

2. Something of more weight than value.

> What do you mean
> To dote on such *luggage?* *Shak.*

LUG'GER, *n.* [D. *loger.*] A vessel carrying three masts with a running bowsprit and lug-sails. *Mar. Dict.*

LUGGS, *n.* An insect like an earth-worm, but having legs.

LUG'-SAIL, *n.* A square sail bent upon a yard that hangs obliquely to the mast at one third of its length. *Mar. Dict.*

LUGU'BRIOUS, *a.* [L. *lugubris*, from *lugeo*, to weep.]
Mournful; indicating sorrow; as a *lugubrious* look. *Decay of Piety.*

LU'KEWARM, *a.* [Sax. *vlaco*, tepid, moderately warm; *vlacian*, to warm; D. *laauw*, *laauwen*; G. *lau*; Dan. *lunken*, lukewarm; *lunker*, to make tepid; allied to *flag*, *lag*, or to *lay*, *allay*, or to *slack*.]
1. Moderately warm; tepid; as *lukewarm* water; *lukewarm* heat. *Wiseman. Newton.*
2. Not ardent; not zealous; cool; indifferent; as *lukewarm* obedience; *lukewarm* patriots. Rev. iii. *Dryden. Addison.*

LU'KEWARMLY, *adv.* With moderate warmth.
2. With indifference; coolly.

LU'KEWARMNESS, *n.* A mild or moderate heat.
2. Indifference; want of zeal or ardor; coldness.

The defect of zeal is *lukewarmness*, or coldness in religion. *Sprat.*

LULL, *v. t.* [Dan. *luller*; G. D. *lullen*; L. *lallo*. Qu. Russ. *leleyu*, to dandle or fondle. The sense is to throw down, to still, to appease. Seamen say, the wind *lulls*, when it subsides.]
To quiet; to compose; to cause to rest. The nation may be *lulled* into security.

—To *lull* him soft asleep. *Spenser.*
Such sweet compulsion doth in music lie,
To *lull* the daughters of necessity. *Milton.*

LULL, *v. i.* To subside; to cease; to become calm; as, the wind *lulls*.

LULL, *n.* Power or quality of soothing. *Young.*

LULL'ABY, *n.* [*lull* and *by*, Russ. *bayu*. See *By*.]
A song to quiet babes; that which quiets. *Shak. Locke.*

LULL'ED, *pp.* Quieted; appeased; composed to rest.

LULL'ER, *n.* One that lulls; one that fondles.

LULL'ING, *ppr.* Stilling; composing to rest.

LUM, *n.* [Qu. Sax. *leoma*.] The chimney of a cottage. *Todd.*

LUM'ACHEL, } *n.* A calcarious stone
LUMACHEL'LA, } composed of shells and coral conglutinated, but so far retaining their organization as to exhibit different colors, and so hard as to admit of polish. *Nicholson. Fourcroy.*

LUMBAG'INOUS, *a.* Pertaining to lumbago. *Cheyne.*

LUMBA'GO, *n.* [L. *lumbus*, loins.] A pain in the loins and small of the back, such as precedes certain fevers. *Quincy.*
A rheumatic affection of the muscles about the loins. *Hooper.*

LUM'BAR, *a.* [L. *lumbus*, loins.] Pertaining to the loins. The *lumbar region* is the posterior portion of the body between the false ribs and the upper edge of the haunch bone. *Parr.*

LUM'BER, *n.* [allied to Sax. *leoma*, utensils, or to *lump*, *clump*, a mass, or Dan. *lumpe*, a rag; *lumperie*, trifles; Sw. *lumpor*, rags, old cloths; D. *lomp*; G. *lumpen*; Fr. *lambeau*. In French, *lambourde* is a joist.]
1. Any thing useless and cumbersome, or things bulky and thrown aside as of no use.

The very bed was violated—
And thrown among the common *lumber*. *Otway.*

2. In America, timber sawed or split for use; as beams, joists, boards, planks, staves, hoops and the like.
3. Harm; mischief. [*Local.*] *Pegge.*

LUM'BER, *v. t.* To heap together in disorder. *Rymer.*
2. To fill with lumber; as, to *lumber* a room.

LUM'BER-ROOM, *n.* A place for the reception of lumber or useless things.

LUM'BRIC, *n.* [L. *lumbricus*, a worm.] A worm. *Med. Repos.*

LUM'BRICAL, *a.* [L. *lumbricus*, a worm.] Resembling a worm; as the *lumbrical* muscles.

LUM'BRICAL, *a.* Pertaining to the loins.

LUM'BRICAL, *n.* A muscle of the fingers and toes, so named from its resembling a worm. Of these muscles, there are four of the fingers and as many of the toes.

LUMBRIC'IFORM, *a.* [L. *lumbricus*, a worm, and *form*.] Resembling a worm in shape.

LU'MINARY, *n.* [L. *luminare*, from *lumen*, light. *Lumen* is the Saxon *leoma*, a ray, or from *luceo*, by contraction, for *lucmen*, *lugmen*.]
1. Any body that gives light, but chiefly one of the celestial orbs. The sun is the principal *luminary* in our system. The stars are inferior *luminaries*.
2. One that illustrates any subject, or enlightens mankind; as, Bacon and Newton were distinguished *luminaries*.

LUMINATION. [See *Illumination*.]

LU'MINE, *v. t.* To enlighten. [*Not used*. See *Illumine*.]

LUMINIF'EROUS, *a.* [L. *lumen*, light, and *fero*, to produce.] Producing light. *Ure.*

LU'MINOUS, *a.* [L. *luminosus*; Fr. *lumineux*.]
1. Shining; emitting light. The sun is a most *luminous* body.
2. Light; illuminated. The moon is rendered *luminous* by the rays of the sun.
3. Bright; shining; as a *luminous* color.
4. Clear; as a *luminous* essay or argument.

LU'MINOUSLY, *adv.* With brightness or clearness.

LU'MINOUSNESS, *n.* The quality of being bright or shining; brightness; as the *luminousness* of the sea. *Encyc.*
2. Clearness; perspicuity; as the *luminousness* of ideas, arguments or method. *Cheyne.*

LUMP, *n.* [G. Dan. and Sw. *klump*; D. *klomp*; W. *clamp* and *clap*. If *m* is not radical, this belongs to Class Lb. *Lump* is *clump*, without the prefix.]
1. A small mass of matter of no definite shape; as a *lump* of earth; a *lump* of butter; a *lump* of sugar.
2. A mass of things blended or thrown together without order or distinction; as copper, iron, gold, silver, lead, tin, promiscuously in one *lump*.
3. A cluster; as a *lump* of figs. 2 Kings xx.
In the lump, the whole together; in gross.

They may buy my papers *in the lump*. *Addison.*

LUMP, *v. t.* To throw into a mass; to unite in a body or sum without distinction of particulars.

The expenses ought to be *lumped*. *Ayliffe.*

2. To take in the gross.

LUMP'EN, *n.* A long fish of a greenish color, and marked with lines.

LUMP'FISH, *n.* A thick fish of the genus Cyclopterus. The back is sharp and elevated; the belly flat, and of a crimson color. Along the body run five rows of sharp bony tubercles. It swims edgewise; called also a sea-owl. *Encyc.*

LUMP'ING, *ppr.* Throwing into a mass or sum.
2. *a.* Bulky; heavy. [*A low word.*] *Arbuthnot.*

LUMP'ISH, *a.* Like a lump; heavy; gross; bulky. *Raleigh. Dryden.*
2. Dull; inactive. *Shak.*

LUMP'ISHLY, *adv.* Heavily; with dullness or stupidity.

LUMP'ISHNESS, *n.* Heaviness; dullness; stupidity.

LUMP'Y, *a.* Full of lumps or small compact masses. *Mortimer.*

Luna cornea, muriate of silver. *Ure.*

LU'NACY, *n.* [from L. *luna*, the moon; W. *llun*, form, figure, image, the moon.]
1. A species of insanity or madness, supposed to be influenced by the moon, or periodical in the month.
2. Madness in general.

LU'NAR, } *a.* [L. *lunaris*.] Pertaining to
LU'NARY, } the moon; as *lunar* observations.
2. Measured by the revolutions of the moon; as *lunar* days or years.
3. Resembling the moon; orbed. *Dryden.*
4. Under the influence of the moon. *Obs.* *Bacon.*

Lunar caustic, nitrate of silver, fused in a low heat. *Nicholson.*

LUNA'RIAN, *n.* An inhabitant of the moon.

LU'NARY, *n.* Moonwort, a plant of the genus Lunaria.

LU'NATED, *a.* Formed like a half-moon.

LU'NATIC, *a.* Affected by a species of madness, supposed to be influenced by the moon.

LU'NATIC, *n.* A person affected by insanity, supposed to be influenced or produced by the moon, or by its position in its orbit; a madman. *Swift.*

LUNA'TION, *n.* [L. *lunatio*.] A revolution of the moon.

LUNCH, } *n.* [W. *llwnc*, a gulp, a
LUNCH'EON, } swallow, the gullet; Arm. *louncqa*, *longein*, to swallow greedily.]
Literally, a swallow; but in usage, a portion of food taken at any time, except at a regular meal. It is not unusual to take a *luncheon* before dinner. The passengers in the line-ships regularly have their *lunch*.

I sliced the *luncheon* from the barley loaf. *Gay.*

LUNE, *n.* [L. *luna*, the moon.] Any thing in the shape of a half-moon. [*Little used.*] *Watts.*
2. A fit of lunacy or madness, or a freak. [*Not used.*] *Shak.*
3. A leash; as the *lune* of a hawk.

LU'NET, } *n.* [Fr. *lunette*, from *lune*, the
LUNETTE, } moon.]
1. In *fortification*, an enveloped counterguard, or elevation of earth made beyond

the second ditch, opposite to the places of arms; or a covered place before the courtine, consisting of two faces that form an angle inward. It is commonly raised in ditches full of water, to serve instead of fausse brays, to dispute the enemy's passage of the ditch. *Encyc. Trevoux.*

2. In *the manege*, a half horse-shoe, which wants the spunge, or that part of the branch which runs towards the quarters of the foot. *Encyc.*

3. A piece of felt to cover the eye of a vicious horse. *Encyc.*

LU'NET, *n.* A little moon. *Bp. Hall.*

LUNG, *n.* [Sax. *lungen*; D. *long*; G. Dan. *lunge*; Sw. *lunga.*]

1. The lungs are the organs of respiration in man and many other animals. There are two of these organs, each of which occupies its cavity in the thorax. They alternately inhale and expel the air, by means of which the necessary function of respiration is carried on.

Each *lung* fills completely the cavity in which it is placed. *Wistar.*

2. Formerly, a person having a strong voice, and a sort of servant. *B. Jonson.*

LUNGE, *n.* [See *Allonge.*] A sudden push or thrust.

LUNG'ED, *a.* Having lungs, or the nature or resemblance of lungs; drawing in and expelling air. *Dryden.*

LUNG'-GROWN, *a.* Having lungs that adhere to the pleura. *Harvey.*

LUN'GIS, *n.* [Fr. *longis*, from *long.*] A lingerer; a dull, drowsy fellow.

LUNG'WORT, *n.* A plant of the genus Pulmonaria.

LU'NIFORM, *a.* [L. *luna*, the moon, and *form.*] Resembling the moon.

LUNISO'LAR, *a.* [L. *luna*, moon, and *solaris*, *sol*, sun.]

Compounded of the revolutions of the sun and moon. *Johnson.*

The *lunisolar* year consists of 532 common years; found by multiplying the cycle of the sun by that of the moon. *Encyc.*

LU'NISTICE, *n.* [L. *luna*, the moon, and *sto*, *steti*, or *sisto*, to stand.]

The farthest point of the moon's northing and southing, in its monthly revolution. *Encyc.*

LUNT, *n.* [D. *lont*, Dan. *lunte*, a match.] The match-cord used for firing cannon. *Johnson.*

LU'NULAR, *a.* [from L. *luna*, the moon.] In *botany*, like the new moon; shaped like a small crescent.

LU'NULATE, *a.* [from L. *luna*, the moon.] In *botany*, resembling a small crescent.

LU'PERCAL, *a.* Pertaining to the Lupercalia, or feasts of the Romans in honor of Pan; as a noun, the feast itself.

LU'PINE, *n.* [Fr. *lupin*; L. *lupinus.*] A kind of pulse. The genus Lupinus contains several species, mostly annual plants, bearing digitate leaves, and papilionaceous flowers. The seeds of the white lupine have a leguminous taste, accompanied with a disagreeable bitterness, and are said to be anthelmintic. *Encyc.*

LU'PULIN, *n.* [L. *lupulus*, hops.] The fine yellow powder of hops. *A. W. Ives.*

LURCH, *n.* [W. *llerc*, a frisk, or frisking about, a loitering or lurking; *llercian*, to loiter about, to lurk. This is the same word radically as *lurk*. The primary sense is to run, start, leap or frisk about, as a man or beast that flies from one tree or other object to another to conceal himself. Hence we see the peculiar applicability of this word in seamen's language.]

In *seamen's language*, a sudden roll of a ship. A *lee-lurch* is a sudden roll to the leeward, as when a heavy sea strikes the ship on the weather side. *Cyc.*

To leave in the lurch, to leave in a difficult situation, or in embarrassment; to leave in a forlorn state or without help. *Denham.*

LURCH, *v. i.* To roll or pass suddenly to one side, as a ship in a heavy sea.

2. To withdraw to one side, or to a private place; to lie in ambush or in secret; to lie close. [For this, *lurk* is now used.] *L'Estrange.*

3. To shift; to play tricks.

I am fain to shuffle, to hedge and to *lurch*. *Shak.*

LURCH, *v. t.* To defeat; to disappoint, that is, to evade; as, to *lurch* the expectation. [*Little used.*] *South.*

2. To steal; to filch; to pilfer. [*Little used.*] *Johnson.*

LURCH, *v. t.* [L. *lurco*, a glutton.] To swallow or eat greedily; to devour. [*Not used.*] *Bacon.*

LURCH'ER, *n.* One that lies in wait or lurks; one that watches to pilfer, or to betray or entrap; a poacher.

Swift from the play the scudding *lurcher* flies. *Gay.*

2. A dog that watches for his game. *Tatler.*

3. [L. *lurco*, a glutton.] A glutton; a gormandizer.

LUR'DAN, *a.* Blockish. [*Not used.*] *Johnson.*

LUR'DAN, *n.* A clown; a blockhead. [*Not used.*]

LURE, *n.*]Fr. *leurre.*] Something held out to call a hawk; hence,

2. Any enticement; that which invites by the prospect of advantage or pleasure; as the *lures* of beauty or of gain.

LURE, *v. i.* To call hawks.

Standing by one that *lured* loud and shrill. *Bacon.*

LURE, *v. t.* To entice; to attract; to invite by any thing that promises pleasure or advantage.

Lured on by the pleasure of the bait. *Temple.*

And various science *lures* the learned eye. *Gay.*

LU'RED, *pp.* Enticed; attracted; invited by the hope of pleasure or advantage.

LU'RID, *a.* [L. *luridus*; W. *llur*, livid, a gloom. Qu. the root of *lower.*] Gloomy; dismal. *Thomson.*

LU'RING, *ppr.* Enticing; calling.

LURK, *v. i.* [W. *llercian*, to frisk or loiter about, to lurk; G. *lauern*; D. *loeren*; Sw. *lura*; Dan. *lurer*. See *Lurch.*]

1. To lie hid; to lie in wait.

Let us lay wait for blood; let us *lurk* privily for the innocent. Prov. i.

2. To lie concealed or unperceived. See that no selfish motive *lurks* in the heart.

See
The *lurking* gold upon the fatal tree. *Dryden.*

3. To retire from public observation; to keep out of sight.

The defendant *lurks* and wanders about in Berks. *Blackstone.*

LURK'ER, *n.* One that lurks or keeps out of sight.

LURK'ING, *ppr.* Lying concealed; keeping out of sight.

LURK'ING-PLACE, *n.* A place in which one lies concealed; a secret place; a hiding place; a den. 1 Sam. xxiii.

LUS'CIOUS, *a.* [I know not the origin and affinities of this word. The Dutch express it by *zoetlustig*, sweet-lusty. Qu. the root of *luxury.*]

1. Sweet or rich so as to cloy or nauseate; sweet to excess; as *luscious* food.

2. Very sweet; delicious; grateful to the taste.

And raisins keep their *luscious* native taste. *Dryden.*

3. Pleasing; delightful.

He will bait him in with the *luscious* proposal of some gainful purchase. *South.*

4. Fullsome; as *luscious* flattery.

5. Smutty; obscene. [*Unusual.*] *Steele.*

LUS'CIOUSLY, *adv.* With sweetness or richness that cloys or nauseates.

2. Obscenely. *Steele.*

LUS'CIOUSNESS, *n.* Immoderate richness or sweetness that cloys or offends. *Mortimer.*

LU'SERN, *n.* A lynx. *Johnson.*

LUSH, *a.* Of a dark, deep, full color.

How *lush* and lusty the grass looks; how green! *Obs.* *Shak.*

LUSK, *a.* [Fr. *lasche.*] Lazy; slothful. [*Not in use.*]

LUSK, *n.* A lazy fellow; a lubber. [*Not in use.*]

LUSK'ISH, *a.* Inclined to be lazy. *Marston.*

LUSK'ISHLY, *adv.* Lazily.

LUSK'ISHNESS, *n.* Disposition to indolence; laziness. *Obs.* *Spenser.*

LUSO'RIOUS, *a.* [L. *lusorius*, from *ludo*, *lusi*, to sport.]

Used in play; sportive. [*Little used.*] *Sanderson.*

LU'SORY, *a.* [L. *lusorius*, as above.] Used in play; playful; as *lusory* methods of instructing children. *Watts.*

LUST, *n.* [Sax. G. D. Sw. *lust*; Dan. *lyst*; Ir. *lasadh*, lust, and a burning. The primary sense is to extend, reach, expand, to stretch forward. It is the same as *list.*]

1. Longing desire; eagerness to possess or enjoy; as the *lust* of gain.

My *lust* shall be satisfied upon them. Ex. xv.

2. Concupiscence; carnal appetite; unlawful desire of carnal pleasure. Rom. i. 2 Pet. ii.

3. Evil propensity; depraved affections and desires. James i. Ps. lxxxi.

4. Vigor; active power. [*Not used.*] *Bacon.*

LUST, *v. i.* [Sax. *lustan*; G. *lüsten*; D. *lusten*; Sw. *lysta*; Dan. *lyster.*]

1. To desire eagerly; to long; with *after*.

Thou mayest kill and eat flesh in all thy gates, whatsoever thy soul *lusteth after*. Deut. xii.

2. To have carnal desire; to desire eagerly the gratification of carnal appetite.

Lust not after her beauty in thy heart. Prov. vi.

Whosoever looketh on a woman to *lust* after her, hath committed adultery with her already in his heart. Matt. v.

3. To have irregular or inordinate desires.

The spirit that dwelleth in us *lusteth* to envy. James iv.

Lust not after evil things as they also *lusted*. 1 Cor. x.

4. To list; to like.

LUST'FUL, *a.* Having lust, or eager desire of carnal gratification; libidinous; as an intemperate and *lustful* man.

2. Provoking to sensuality; inciting to lust or exciting carnal desire. *Tillotson.*

Thence his *lustful* orgies he enlarged. *Milton.*

3. Vigorous; robust; stout. *Sackville.*

LUST'FULLY, *adv.* With concupiscence or carnal desire.

LUST'FULNESS, *n.* The state of having carnal desires; libidinousness.

LUST'IHOOD, *n.* [*lusty* and *hood.*] Vigor of body. *Obs.* *Spenser.*

LUST'ILY, *adv.* With vigor of body; stoutly; with vigorous exertion.

I determine to fight *lustily* for him. *Shak.*

LUST'INESS, *n.* Vigor of body; stoutness; strength; robustness; sturdiness.

Cappadocian slaves were famous for their *lustiness*. *Dryden.*

LUST'ING, *ppr.* Having eager desire; having carnal appetite.

LUST'ING, *n.* Eager desire; inordinate desire; desire of carnal gratification.

LUST'LESS, *a.* Listless; not willing. *Obs.* *Spenser.*

2. Not vigorous. *Gower.*

LUS'TRAL, *a.* [L. *lustralis*, from *lustro*, to purify.]

1. Used in purification; as *lustral* water; *lustral* waves.

2. Pertaining to purification; as *lustral* days.

LUS'TRATE, *v. t.* [L. *lustro*, to cleanse. See *Luster.*]

1. To make clear or pure; to purify. [See *Illustrate.*]

2. To view; to survey.

LUSTRA'TION, *n.* The act or operation of making clear or pure; a cleansing or purifying by water.

And holy water for *lustration* bring. *Dryden.*

2. In *antiquity*, the sacrifices or ceremonies by which cities, fields, armies or people defiled by crimes, were purified. *Encyc.*

LUS'TER, *n.* [Fr. *lustre*; L. *lustrum*; It. *lustro*; from L. *lustro*, to purify; Dan. *lys*, light; *lyser*, to shine; Sw. *lysa*; D. *luister*, splendor; Ir. *lasadh*, *lasaim*, *leosam*, to give light, to burn; *leos*, light.]

1. Brightness; splendor; gloss; as the *luster* of the sun or stars; the *luster* of silk.

The sun's mild *luster* warms the vital air. *Pope.*

2. The splendor of birth, of deeds or of fame; renown; distinction.

His ancestors continued about four hundred years, rather without obscurity than with any great share of *luster*. *Wotton.*

3. A sconce with lights; a branched candlestick of glass. *Pope.* *Encyc.*

4. The space of five years. [L. *lustrum.*] *Bolingbroke.*

LUS'TRICAL, *a.* Pertaining to purification. *Middleton.*

LUS'TRING, *n.* A species of glossy silk cloth. [Corruptly written and pronounced *lutestring.*]

LUS'TROUS, *a.* Bright; shining; luminous.

Good sparks and *lustrous*. *Shak.*

LUS'TRUM, *n.* In ancient Rome, the space of five years.

LUST'-STAINED, *a.* Defiled by lust. *Shak.*

LUST'WÖRT, *n.* [*lust* and *wort.*] A plant of the genus Drosera.

LUST'Y, *a.* [from *lust*; D. *lustig.*] Stout; vigorous; robust; healthful; able of body. This is the correct sense of the word, comprehending full health and strength; as a *lusty* youth. But it is now used in the sense of,

2. Bulky; large; of great size. This sense does not always include that of vigor.

3. Handsome; pleasant; saucy. *Obs.* *Gower.* *Spenser.* *Shak.*

4. Copious; plentiful; as a *lusty* draught. *Tatler.*

5. Pregnant; *a colloquial use.*

LU'TANIST, *n.* [from *lute.*] A person that plays on the lute.

A celebrated *lutanist* was playing to a large company. *Asiat. Res.*

LUTA'RIOUS, *a.* [L. *lutarius*, from *lutum*, mud.]

1. Pertaining to mud; living in mud.

2. Of the color of mud. *Grew.*

LUTA'TION, *n.* [See *Lute.*] The act or method of luting vessels.

LUTE, *n.* [Fr. *luth*; It. *liuto*; Sp. *laud*; D. *luit*; G. *laute*; Sw. *luta*; Dan. *lut*; Russ. *liotnia*. Qu. *loud*, L. *laudo.*]

An instrument of music with strings. It consists of four parts, viz; the table, the body or belly which has nine or ten sides, the neck, which has nine or ten stops or divisions marked with strings, and the head or cross. In the middle of the table there is a passage for the sound. There is also a bridge to which the strings are fastened. The strings are struck with the right hand, and with the left the stops are pressed. *Encyc.*

LUTE, **LU'TING**, } *n.* [L. *lutum*, mud, clay.] Among chimists, a composition of clay or other tenacious substance used for stopping the juncture of vessels so closely as to prevent the escape or entrance of air.

LUTE, *v. t.* To close or coat with lute. *Bacon.*

LU'TE-CASE, *n.* A case for a lute. *Shak.*

LU'TED, *pp.* Closed with lute.

LU'TENIST, *n.* A performer on the lute. *Busby.*

LU'TER, **LU'TIST**, } *n.* One who plays on a lute.

LU'TE-STRING, *n.* The string of a lute. *Shak.*

LU'THERAN, *a.* Pertaining to Luther, the reformer; as the *Lutheran* church.

LU'THERAN, *n.* A disciple or follower of Luther; one who adheres to the doctrines of Luther.

LU'THERANISM, *n.* The doctrines of religion as taught by Luther.

LU'THERN, *n.* In *architecture*, a kind of window over the cornice, in the roof of a building, to admit light into the upper story. *Encyc.*

LU'TING, *ppr.* Closing with lute.

LU'TULENT, *a.* [L. *lutulentus*, from *lutum*, mud.] Muddy; turbid; thick.

LUX'ATE, *v. t.* [L. *luxo*, Fr. *luxer*, to loosen; probably from the same root as *lax*, L. *laxo*, *laxus.*]

To displace, or remove from its proper place, as a joint; to put out of joint; to dislocate. *Lux*, in a like sense, is, I believe, not now used. *Encyc.*

LUX'ATED, *pp.* Put out of joint; dislocated.

LUX'ATING, *ppr.* Removing or forcing out of its place, as a joint; dislocating.

LUXA'TION, *n.* The act of moving or forcing a joint from its proper place or articulation; or the state of being thus put out of joint.

2. A dislocation; that which is dislocated.

LUXE, *n.* Luxury. [*Not used.*]

LUXU'RIANCE, **LUXU'RIANCY**, } *n.* [L. *luxurians*, *luxurio*, to grow rank, or to wanton.]

1. Rank growth; strong, vigorous growth; exuberance.

Flowers grow up in the garden with the greatest *luxuriancy* and profusion. *Spectator.*

2. Excessive or superfluous growth.

A fungus prevents healing only by its *luxuriancy*. *Wiseman.*

LUXU'RIANT, *a.* Exuberant in growth; abundant; as a *luxuriant* growth of grass.

2. Exuberant in plenty; superfluous in abundance.

Prune the *luxuriant*, the uncouth refine. *Pope.*

3. A *luxuriant* flower multiplies the covers of the fructification so as to destroy the essential parts. *Martyn.*

LUXU'RIANTLY, *adv.* With exuberant growth.

LUXU'RIATE, *v. i.* To grow exuberantly, or to grow to superfluous abundance.

LUXURIA'TION, *n.* The process of growing exuberantly, or beyond the natural growth. *Lee.*

LUXU'RIOUS, *a.* [Fr. *luxurieux*; L. *luxuriosus*, from *luxo*, to loosen; *luxor*, to riot.]

1. Voluptuous; indulging freely or excessively in the pleasures of the table, the gratification of appetite, or in rich and expensive dress and equipage; as a *luxurious* life; *luxurious* cities.

2. Administering to luxury; contributing to free or extravagant indulgence in diet, dress and equipage; as *luxurious* wealth. *Milton.*

3. Furnished with luxuries; as a *luxurious* table.

4. Softening by pleasure, or free indulgence in luxury; as *luxurious* ease.

5. Lustful; libidinous; given to the gratification of lust; as a *luxurious* bed. *Shak.*

6. Luxuriant; exuberant.

The work under our labor grows
Luxurious by restraint. [*Not used.*] *Milton.*

LUXU'RIOUSLY, *adv.* In abundance of rich diet, dress or equipage; deliciously; voluptuously. *Dryden.*

LUX'URIST, *n.* One given to luxury. *Temple.*

LUX'URY, *n.* [L. *luxuria*, from *luxo*, to loosen.]

1. A free or extravagant indulgence in the pleasures of the table, as in rich and expensive diet, or delicious food and liquors; voluptuousness in the gratification of appetite; or the free indulgence in costly dress and equipage.

Riches expose a man to pride and *luxury*. *Spectator.*

2. That which gratifies a nice and fastidious appetite; a dainty; any delicious food or drink. The canvas-back duck is a *luxury* for an epicure.

3. Any thing delightful to the senses.

He cut the side of a rock for a garden, and by laying on it earth, furnished a kind of *luxury* for a hermit. *Addison.*

4. Lust; lewd desire. [*Not now used.*] *Shak.*

5. Luxuriance; exuberance of growth. [*Not now used.*] *Bacon.*

LY, a termination of adjectives, is a contraction of Sax. *lic*, G. *lich*, D. *lyk*, Dan. *lige*, Sw. *lik*, Eng. *like*; as in *lovely*, *manly*, that is, *love-like*, *man-like*. As the termination of names, *ly* signifies field or plain, Sax. *leag*, Eng. *lay*, *lea* or *ley*, L. *locus*.

LY'AM, *n.* A leash for holding a hound. *Drayton.*

LYCAN'THROPY, *n.* [Gr. λυκανθρωπια; λυκος, a wolf, and ανθρωπος, man.] A kind of erratic melancholy. *Coxe.*

LYCOS'TOM, *n.* A Baltic fish resembling a herring.

LYD'IAN, *a.* [from *Lydia.*] Noting a kind of soft slow music anciently in vogue. *Milton.*

Lydian stone, flinty slate. *Ure.*

LYE, *n.* [Sax. *leah*; G. *lauge*; D. *loog*; Arm. *ligeou* or *lichou*; Sp. *lexia*; Fr. *lessive*; L. *lix*, whence *lixivium*. It coincides with Sax. *loge*, water; Ant. L. *lixa*, whence *Lugdunum*, *Leyden*, *Lyons*, that is, *Water*-town.]

Water impregnated with alkaline salt imbibed from the ashes of wood.

LYE, *n.* A falsehood. [See *Lie.*]

LY'ING, *ppr.* of *lie*. Being prostrate. [See *Lie.*]

LY'ING, *ppr.* of *lie*. Telling falsehood.

Lying in, being in childbirth.

2. *n.* The act of bearing a child.

LYM'NITE, *n.* A kind of freshwater snail, found fossil.

LYMPH, *n.* [L. *lympha.*] Water, or a colorless fluid in animal bodies, separated from the blood and contained in certain vessels called *lymphatics*. *Encyc.*

LYMPH'ATE, **LYMPH'ATED**, *a.* Frightened into madness; raving.

LYMPHAT'IC, *a.* Pertaining to lymph.

2. Enthusiastic. [*Not used.*] *Shaftsbury.*

LYMPHAT'IC, *n.* A vessel of animal bodies which contains or conveys lymph.

The *lymphatics* seem to perform the whole business of absorption. *Encyc.*

2. A mad enthusiast; a lunatic. [*Not used.*] *Shaftsbury.*

LYMPH'EDUCT, *n.* [L. *lympha*, lymph, and *ductus*, a duct.]

A vessel of animal bodies which conveys the lymph.

LYMPHOG'RAPHY, *n.* [L. *lympha*, lymph, and Gr. γραφω, to describe.]

A description of the lymphatic vessels, their origin and uses. *Encyc.*

LYNX, *n.* [L. *lynx*; Gr. λογξ; D. *lochs*; G. *luchs*; It. *lince.*]

A quadruped of the genus Felis, resembling the common cat, but his ears are longer and his tail shorter. His hair is streaked with yellow, white and black colors. His air is sprightly; he howls like the wolf, and walks and leaps like a cat. This animal is celebrated for the sharpness of his sight. *Encyc.*

LY'RATE, **LY'RATED**, *a.* [from *lyre.*] In *botany*, divided transversely into several jags, the lower ones smaller and more remote from each other than the upper ones; as a *lyrate* leaf. *Martyn.*

LYRE, *n.* [Fr. *lyre*; L. *lyra*; Gr. λυρα; It. and Sp. *lira*; D. *lier*; G. *leier.*]

A stringed instrument of music, a kind of harp much used by the ancients.

LYR'IC, **LYR'ICAL**, *a.* [L. *lyricus*; Fr. *lyrique.*] Pertaining to a lyre or harp. *Lyric* poetry is such as is sung to the harp or lyre. This was much cultivated by the ancients, among whom Anacreon, Alcæus, Stesichorus, Sappho and Horace are distinguished as lyric poets.

LYR'IC, *n.* A composer of lyric poems. *Addison.*

LYR'ICISM, *n.* A lyric composition. *Gray.*

LY'RIST, *n.* A musician who plays on the harp or lyre. *Pope.*

LYS, *n.* A Chinese measure of length, equal to 533 yards. *Grosier.*

LYTE'RIAN, *a.* [Gr. λυτηριος, from λυω, to loosen.]

In *medical science*, terminating a disease; indicating the solution of a disease. *Jones.*

LYTH'RODE, *n.* A mineral found in Norway; its color, an aurora-red, passing into brownish red or brown. It appears to be allied to elaolite, or fettstein. *Dict. Nat. Hist.*

Lythrode is probably a variety of fettstein. *Cleaveland.*

M.

M is the thirteenth letter of the English Alphabet, and a labial articulation, formed by a compression of the lips. It is called a semi-vowel, as the articulation or compression of the lips is accompanied with a humming sound through the nose, which constitutes a difference between this letter and *b*. Its sound is uniform; as in *man*, *time*, *rim*.

M is a numeral letter, and among the ancients stood for a thousand; a use which is retained by the moderns. With a dash or stroke over it, $\overline{\text{M}}$, it stands for a thousand times a thousand, or a million.

As an abbreviation, M stands for Marcus, Martius, Manlius or Mutius.

A. M. or M. A. stands for *artium magister*, master of arts; M. D. for *medicinæ doctor*, doctor of medicine; A. M. for *anno mundi*, the year of the world; MS. for *manuscript*; MSS. for *manuscripts*.

In astronomical tables, M stands for *meridian*, *meridional*, or *mid-day*.

In medical prescriptions, M stands for *maniple*, or handful, or *misce*, mix, or *mixtura*, a mixture. *Encyc.*

In the late British Pharmacopæias it signifies *mensurâ*, by measure. *Parr.*

In law, M is a brand or stigma impressed on one convicted of *manslaughter*, and admitted to the benefit of clergy.

MAB, *n.* [W. *mab*, a child.] In *northern mythology*, the queen of the imaginary beings called fairies.

2. A slattern. *Ray.*

MAB, *v. i.* To dress negligently. *Ray.*

MAC, in names of Scotch and Irish origin, signifies *son*. [See *Maid.*]

MACARO'NI, *n.* [It. *maccheroni*, a sort of paste; Fr. *macaroni*; Gr. μακαρ, happy.]

1. A kind of biscuit made of flour, eggs, sugar and almonds, and dressed with butter and spices. *B. Jonson.*

2. A sort of droll or fool, and hence, a fop; a fribble; a finical fellow.

MACARON'IC, *a.* Pertaining to or like a macaroni; empty; trifling; vain; affected.

2. Consisting of a mixture or jumble of ill formed or ill connected words.

MACARON'IC, *n.* A kind of burlesque poetry, in which native words are made to end in Latin terminations, or Latin words are modernized. *Jones. Encyc.*

MACAROON, the same as *macaroni*.

MACAU'CO, *n.* A name of several species of quadrupeds of the genus Lemur. *Encyc.*

MACAW′, MACA′O, n. The name of a race of beautiful fowls of the parrot kind, under the genus Psittacus. *Dict. Nat. Hist.*

MACAW′-TREE, n. A species of palm tree. *Miller.*

MAC′CABEES, n. The name of two apocryphal books in the Bible.

MAC′COBOY, n. A kind of snuff.

MACE, n. [It. *mazza*, Sp. *maza*, Port. *maça*, Fr. *masse*, a club.]
An ensign of authority borne before magistrates. Originally, the mace was a club or instrument of war, made of iron and much used by cavalry. It was in the shape of a coffee mill. Being no longer a weapon of war, its form is changed; it is made of silver or copper gilt, and ornamented with a crown, globe and cross. *Encyc.*

A leaden *mace*. *Shak.*
A heavy iron *mace*. *Knolles.*

MACE, n. [L. *macis.*] A spice; the second coat which covers the nutmeg, a thin and membranaceous substance of an oleaginous nature and yellowish color, being in flakes divided into many ramifications; it is extremely fragrant and aromatic. *Encyc.*

MA′CE-ALE, n. Ale spiced with mace. *Wiseman.*

MA′CE-BEARER, n. A person who carries a mace before men in authority. *Spectator.*

MAC′ERATE, v. t. [L. *macero*, from *macer*, thin, lean; *maceo*, to be thin or lean; Fr. *maigre;* Eng. *meager;* It. *macro;* Sp. *magro;* probably allied to Eng. *meek*, Ch. מאך mak. Class Mg. No. 2. and 9.]
1. To make lean; to wear away. *Harvey.*
2. To mortify; to harass with corporeal hardships; to cause to pine or waste away.

Out of excessive zeal they *macerate* their bodies and impair their health. *Fiddes.*

3. To steep almost to solution; to soften and separate the parts of a substance by steeping it in a fluid, or by the digestive process. So we say, food is *macerated* in the stomach.

MAC′ERATED, pp. Made thin or lean; steeped almost to solution.

MAC′ERATING, ppr. Making lean; steeping almost to solution; softening.

MACERA′TION, n. The act or the process of making thin or lean by wearing away, or by mortification.
2. The act, process or operation of softening and almost dissolving by steeping in a fluid.

The saliva serves for the *maceration* and dissolution of the meat into chyle. *Ray.*

MACE-REED, or REED-MACE, n. A plant of the genus Typha.

MACHIAVE′LIAN, a. [from *Machiavel*, an Italian writer, secretary and historiographer to the republic of Florence.]
Pertaining to Machiavel, or denoting his principles; politically cunning; crafty; cunning in political management.

MACHIAVE′LIAN, n. One who adopts the principles of Machiavel.

MACH′IAVELISM, n. The principles of Machiavel, or practice in conformity to them; political cunning and artifice, intended to favor arbitrary power. *Cyc.*

MACHICOLA′TION, n. [Fr. *meche*, a match, and *couler*, to flow.]
In *old castles*, the pouring of hot substances through apertures in the upper part of the gate upon assailants; or the apertures themselves. *Cyc.*

MACH′INAL, a. [See *Machine.*] Pertaining to machines. *Dict.*

MACH′INATE, v. t. [L. *machinor*, from Gr. μαχανα or μηχανη.] To plan; to contrive; to form a scheme. *Sandys.*

MACH′INATED, pp. Planned; contrived.

MACH′INATING, ppr. Contriving; scheming.

MACHINA′TION, n. [Fr. See *Machine.*] The act of planning or contriving a scheme for executing some purpose, particularly an evil purpose; an artful design formed with deliberation. *Shak.*

MACH′INATOR, n. One that forms a scheme, or who plots with evil designs. *Glanville.*

MACHİNE, n. [Fr. from L. *machina.*] An artificial work, simple or complicated, that serves to apply or regulate moving power, or to produce motion, so as to save time or force. The simple machines are the six mechanical powers, viz.; the lever, the pulley, the axis and wheel, the wedge, the screw, and the inclined plane. Complicated machines are such as combine two or more of these powers for the production of motion or force. *Encyc.*
2. An engine; an instrument of force.

With inward arms the dire *machine* they load. *Dryden.*

3. Supernatural agency in a poem, or a superhuman being introduced into a poem to perform some exploit. *Pope.*

MACHİNERY, n. A complicated work, or combination of mechanical powers in a work, designed to increase, regulate or apply motion and force; as the *machinery* of a watch or other chronometer.
2. Machines in general. The *machinery* of a cotton-mill is often moved by a single wheel.
3. In *epic* and *dramatic poetry*, superhuman beings introduced by the poet to solve difficulty, or perform some exploit which exceeds human power; or the word may signify the agency of such beings, as supposed deities, angels, demons and the like.

Nec Deus intersit, nisi dignus vindice nodus
Incidit. *Horace.*

A deity is not to be introduced, unless a difficulty occurs that requires the intervention of a god.

The *machinery* of Milton's Paradise Lost, consists of numerous superhuman personages. Pope's Rape of the Lock is rendered very interesting by the *machinery* of sylphs.

MACHİNING, a. Denoting the machinery of a poem. [*Not used.*] *Dryden.*

MACH′INIST, n. [Fr. *machaniste.*] A constructor of machines and engines, or one well versed in the principles of machines.

MACIG′NO, n. [It.] A species of stone of two varieties, one of a grayish yellow color, the other of a bluish gray color. *Cyc.*

MAC′ILENCY, n. [See *Macilent.*] Leanness.

MAC′ILENT, a. [L. *macilentus*, from *macer*, lean, thin. See *Macerate.*] Lean; thin; having little flesh.

MACK′EREL, n. [D. *mackreel;* G. *mackrele;* Fr. *maquereau;* Ir. *mackreil;* W. *macrell;* from the root of L. *macula*, a spot; the spotted fish. So in British, it is called *brithilh*, Arm. *bresell*, for the like reason.]
A species of fish of the genus Scomber, an excellent table fish.

MACK′EREL, n. [Old Fr. *maquerel.*] A pander or pimp.

Mackerel-gale, in Dryden, may mean a a gate that ripples the surface of the sea, or one which is suitable for catching mackerel, as this fish is caught with the bait in motion.

MACK′EREL-SKY̆, n. A sky streaked or marked like a mackerel. *Hooke.*

MAC′LE, n. A name given to chiastolite or hollow spar. *Cyc.*

MACLU′RITE, n. A mineral of a brilliant pale green color, so called in honor of Maclure, the mineralogist. *Nuttall.*

MAC′ROCOSM, n. [Gr. μακρος, great, and κοσμος, world.]
The great world; the universe, or the visible system of worlds; opposed to *microcosm*, or the world of man. *Encyc.*

MACROL′OG̈Y, n. [Gr. μακρος, great, and λογος, discourse.]
Long and tedious talk; prolonged discourse without matter; superfluity of words. *Bullokar.*

MACTA′TION, n. [L. *macto*, to kill.] The act of killing a victim for sacrifice. *Encyc.*

MAC′ULA, n. [L.] A spot, as on the skin, or on the surface of the sun or other luminous orb.

MAC′ULATE, v. t. [L. *maculo.*] To spot; to stain. *Elyot.*

MAC′ULATE, MAC′ULATED, a. Spotted.

MACULA′TION, n. The act of spotting; a spot; a stain. *Shak.*

MAC′ULE, n. A spot. [supra.] [*Little used.*]

MAD, a. [Sax. *gemaad;* Ir. *amad;* It. *matto*, mad, foolish; *mattone*, a brick, and an arrant fool; *matteria* and *mattezza*, foolishness; *ammattire*, to become distracted.]
1. Disordered in intellect; distracted; furious.

We must bind our passions in chains, lest like *mad* folks, they break their locks and bolts. *Taylor.*

2. Proceeding from disordered intellect or expressing it; as a *mad* demeanor. *Milton.*
3. Enraged; furious; as a *mad* bull.

And being exceedingly *mad* against them, I persecuted them, even to strange cities. Acts xxvi.

4. Inflamed to excess with desire; excited with violent and unreasonable passion or appetite; infatuated; followed properly by *after*.

The world is running *mad after* farce, the extremity of bad poetry. *Dryden.*

"*Mad upon* their idols," would be better rendered, "*Mad after* their idols." Jer. l.

5. Distracted with anxiety or trouble; extremely perplexed.

Thou shalt be *mad* for the sight of thine eyes—Deut. xxviii.

6. Infatuated with folly.

The spiritual man is *mad*. Hos. ix.

7. Inflamed with anger; very angry. [*This is a common and perhaps the most general sense of the word in America. It is thus used by Arbuthnot, and is perfectly proper.*]

8. Proceeding from folly or infatuation.

Mad wars destroy in one year the works of many years of peace. *Franklin.*

MAD, *v. t.* To make mad, furious or angry. *Sidney.*

MAD, *v. i.* To be mad, furious or wild. *Wickliffe. Spenser.*

MAD, MADE, *n.* [Sax. Goth. *matha.*] An earth-worm. [But this is the Eng. *moth.*] *Ray.*

MAD'AM, *n.* [Fr. *ma*, my, and *dame.*] An appellation or complimentary title given to married and elderly ladies, or chiefly to them.

MAD'APPLE, *n.* A plant of the genus Solanum.

MAD'BRAIN, MAD'BRAINED, *a.* Disordered in mind; hot-headed; rash. *Shak.*

MAD'CAP, *a.* [*mad-caput* or *cap.*] A violent, rash, hot-headed person; a madman.

MAD'DEN, *v. t. mad'n.* To make mad. *Thomson.*

MAD'DEN, *v. i.* To become mad; to act as if mad.

They rave, recite and *madden* round the land. *Pope.*

MAD'DENED, *pp.* Rendered mad.

MAD'DENING, *ppr.* Making mad or angry.

MAD'DER, *n.* [Sax. *mæddere.*] A plant of the genus Rubia, one species of which is much used in dyeing red. The root is used in medicine as an aperient and detergent, and is in great reputation as an emmenagogue. It is cultivated in France and Holland. *Encyc. Hill.*

MAD'DING, *ppr.* of *mad.* Raging; furious. *Milton. Dryden.*

MADE, *pret.* and *pp.* of *make.*

MADEFAC'TION, *n.* [L. *madefacio.*] The act of making wet.

MAD'EFIED, *pp.* Made wet. *Bacon.*

MAD'EFY, *v. t.* [L. *madefio.*] To make wet or moist; to moisten. [*Not much used.*]

MAD'EFYING, *ppr.* Making moist or wet.

MADEIRA, *n.* A rich wine made on the isle of Madeira.

MADEMOISELLE, *n.* [Fr. *ma*, my, and *demoiselle*, damsel. See *Damsel.*]

A young woman, or the title given to one; miss; also, the puppet sent from the French metropolis to exhibit the prevailing fashions. *Spectator.*

MAD'HEADED, *n.* Hot brained; rash. *Shak.*

MAD'HOUSE, *n.* A house where insane persons are confined for cure or for restraint.

MAD'ID, *a.* [L. *madidus.*] Wet; moist. [*Not in use.*]

MAD'LY, *adv.* [from *mad.*] Without reason or understanding; rashly; wildly.

2. With extreme folly or infatuated zeal or passion.

MAD'MAN, *n.* A man raving or furious with disordered intellect; a distracted man.

2. A man without understanding.

3. One inflamed with extravagant passion, and acting contrary to reason.

MAD'NESS, *n.* [from *mad.*] Distraction; a state of disordered reason or intellect, in which the patient raves or is furious.

There are degrees of *madness* as of folly. *Locke.*

2. Extreme folly; headstrong passion and rashness that act in opposition to reason; as the *madness* of a mob.

3. Wildness of passion; fury; rage; as the *madness* of despair.

MADO'NA, MADON'NA, *n.* [Sp. *madona*, It. *madonna*, my lady.] A term of compellation equivalent to *madam.* It is given to the virgin Mary.

MAD'REPORE, *n.* [Fr. *madre*, spotted, and *pore.*]

A submarine substance of a stony hardness, resembling coral. It consists of carbonate of lime with some animal matter. It is of a white color, wrinkled on the surface, and full of cavities or cells, inhabited by a small animal. From a liquor discharged by this animal, the substance is said to be formed. Madrepores constitute a genus of polypiers, of variable forms, always garnished with radiated plates. *Encyc. Dict. Nat. Hist.*

MAD'REPORITE, *n.* A name given to certain petrified bones found in Normandy, in France, belonging to a cetaceous fish or to a species of crocodile. These bones contain many little brown lines in zigzag, resembling entangled threads. They have none of the properties of madrepore. *Dict. Nat. Hist.*

MAD'REPORITE, *n.* A variety of limestone, so called on account of its occurring in radiated prismatic concretions resembling the stars of madrepores. When rubbed, it emits the smell of sulphureted hydrogen gas.

2. Fossil madrepore.

MADRIE'R, *n.* [Fr.] A thick plank armed with iron plates, with a cavity to receive the mouth of a petard, with which it is applied to any thing intended to be broken down; also, a plank used for supporting the earth in mines. *Chambers. Bailey.*

MAD'RIGAL, *n.* [Sp. Port. Fr. id.; It. *madrigale.* Its origin is not ascertained.]

1. A little amorous poem, sometimes called a pastoral poem, containing a certain number of free unequal verses, not confined to the scrupulous regularity of a sonnet or the subtilty of the epigram, but containing some tender and delicate, though simple thought, suitably expressed. *Cyc.*

2. An elaborate vocal composition in five or six parts. *Busby.*

MAD'WORT, *n.* A plant of the genus Alyssum.

MÆSTO'SO, an Italian word signifying *majestic*, a direction in music to play the part with grandeur and strength.

MAF'FLE, *v. i.* To stammer. [*Not in use.*] *Barret.*

MAGAZI'NE, *n.* [Fr. *magazin*; It. *magazzino*; Sp. *magacen* and *almacen*; Port. *almazem* or *armazem*; from Ar. خزن *gazana*, to deposit or lay up for preservation. This word is formed with the Shemitic prefix *m.*]

1. A store of arms, ammunition or provisions; or the building in which such store is deposited. It is usually a public store or storehouse.

2. In *ships of war*, a close room in the hold, where the gunpowder is kept. Large ships have usually two *magazines*. *Mar. Dict.*

3. A pamphlet periodically published, containing miscellaneous papers or compositions. The first publication of this kind in England, was the *Gentleman's Magazine*, which first appeared in 1731, under the name of *Sylvanus Urban*, by Edward Cave, and which is still continued.

MAGAZI'NER, *n.* One who writes for a magazine. [*Little used.*] *Goldsmith.*

MAGE, *n.* A magician. [*Not used.*] *Spenser.*

Magellanic clouds, whitish clouds, or appearances like clouds near the south pole, which revolve like the stars; so called from Magellan, the navigator. They are three in number. *Cyc.*

MAG'GOT, *n.* [W. *macai*, plu. *maceiod*, *magiod*, a maggot or grub, from *magu*, to breed.

1. A worm or grub; particularly, the fly-worm, from the egg of the large blue or green fly. This maggot changes into a fly.

2. A whim; an odd fancy.

MAG'GOTY, *a.* Full of maggots.

MAG'GOTY-HEADED, *a.* Having a head full of whims. *L. of Wood.*

MA'GI, *n. plu.* [L.] Wise men or philosophers of the East. *Fotherby.*

MA'GIAN, *a.* [L. *magus*; Gr. *μαγος.*] Pertaining to the Magi, a sect of philosophers in Persia.

MA'GIAN, *n.* One of the sect of the Persian Magi, who hold that there are two principles, one the cause of good, the other of evil. The knowledge of these philosophers was deemed by the vulgar to be supernatural. *Encyc.*

MA'GIANISM, *n.* The philosophy or doctrines of the Magi.

MAG'IC, *n.* [L. *magia*; Gr. *μαγεια*, from *μαγος*, a philosopher among the Persians.]

1. The art or science of putting into action the power of spirits; or the science of producing wonderful effects by the aid of superhuman beings, or of departed spirits; sorcery; enchantment. [*This art or science is now discarded.*]

2. The secret operations of natural causes. *Bacon.*

Natural magic, the application of natural causes to passive subjects, by which surprising effects are produced. *Encyc.*

Celestial magic, attributes to spirits a kind of dominion over the planets, and to the planets an influence over men.

Superstitious or *geotic magic*, consists in the invocation of devils or demons, and supposes some tacit or express agreement between them and human beings. *Encyc.*

Magic square, a square figure, formed by a series of numbers in mathematical proportion, so disposed in parallel and equal ranks, as that the sums of each row or line taken perpendicularly, horizontally, or diagonally, are equal. *Encyc.*

Magic lantern, a dioptric machine invented by Kircher, which, by means of a lamp in a dark room, exhibits images of objects in their distinct colors and proportions, with the appearance of life itself. *Encyc.*

MAG'IC, MAG'ICAL, } *a.* Pertaining to magic; used in magic; as a *magic* wand; *magic* art.

2. Performed by magic, the agency of spirits, or by the invisible powers of nature; as *magical* effects.

MAG'ICALLY, *adv.* By the arts of magic; according to the rules or rites of magic; by enchantment. *Camden.*

MAGI''CIAN, *n.* One skilled in magic; one that practices the black art; an enchanter; a necromancer; a sorcerer or sorceress. *Locke. Waller.*

MAGISTE'RIAL, *a.* [See *Magistrate.*] Pertaining to a master; such as suits a master; authoritative. *Dryden.*

2. Proud; lofty; arrogant; imperious; domineering.

Pretenses go a great way with men that take fair words and *magisterial* looks for current payment. *L'Estrange.*

3. In *chimistry*, pertaining to magistery, which see.

MAGISTE'RIALLY, *adv.* With the air of a master; arrogantly; authoritatively. *Bacon. South.*

MAGISTE'RIALNESS, *n.* The air and manner of a master; haughtiness; imperiousness; peremptoriness. *Nelson.*

MAG'ISTERY, *n.* [L. *magisterium.*] Among chimists, a precipitate; a fine substance deposited by precipitation; usually applied to particular kinds of precipitate, as that of bismuth, coal, crab's eyes, sulphur, &c. *Obs. Encyc.*

MAG'ISTRACY, *n.* [See *Magistrate.*] The office or dignity of a magistrate.

Duelling is not only an usurpation of the divine prerogative, but it is an insult upon *magistracy*. *Clarissa.*

2. The body of magistrates.

MAG'ISTRAL, *a.* Suiting a magistrate; authoritative. *Obs.*

MAG'ISTRAL, *n.* A sovereign medicine or remedy. *Obs.*

MAGISTRAL'ITY, *n.* Despotic authority in opinion. *Obs. Bacon.*

MAG'ISTRALLY, *adv.* Authoritatively; with imperiousness. *Obs. Bramhall.*

MAG'ISTRATE, *n.* [L. *magistratus*, from *magister*, master; *magis*, *major*, and *ster*, Teutonic *steora*, a director; *steoran*, to steer; the principal director.]

A public civil officer, invested with the executive government or some branch of it. In this sense, a king is the highest or first magistrate, as is the President of the United States. But the word is more particularly applied to subordinate officers, as governors, intendants, prefects, mayors, justices of the peace, and the like.

The *magistrate* must have his reverence; the laws their authority. *Burke.*

MAGISTRAT'IC, *a.* Having the authority of a magistrate. *Taylor.*

MAG'ISTRATURE, *n.* [Fr.] Magistracy. [*Little used.*]

MAGNA CHARTA, *n.* [L .great charter.]

1. The great charter, so called, obtained by the English barons from king John, A. D. 1215. This name is also given to the charter granted to the people of England in the ninth year of Henry III. and confirmed by Edward I.

2. A fundamental constitution which guarantees rights and privileges.

MAGNANIM'ITY, *n.* [L. *magnanimitas*; *magnus*, great, and *animus*, mind.]

Greatness of mind; that elevation or dignity of soul, which encounters danger and trouble with tranquillity and firmness, which raises the possessor above revenge, and makes him delight in acts of benevolence, which makes him disdain injustice and meanness, and prompts him to sacrifice personal ease, interest and safety for the accomplishment of useful and noble objects.

MAGNAN'IMOUS, *a.* [L. *magnanimus.*]

1. Great of mind; elevated in soul or in sentiment; brave; disinterested; as a *magnanimous* prince or general.

2. Dictated by magnanimity; exhibiting nobleness of soul; liberal and honorable; not selfish.

There is an indissoluble union between a *magnanimous* policy and the solid rewards of public prosperity and felicity. *Washington.*

MAGNAN'IMOUSLY, *adv.* With greatness of mind; bravely; with dignity and elevation of sentiment. *Milton.*

MAGNE'SIA, *n. s* as *z.* [Fr. *magnesie.* Qu. from *Magnesia*, the place where first found. Lunier says, from Gr. μαγνης, the lodestone; but the reason he does not assign.]

A primitive earth, having for its base a metallic substance, called magnesium. It is generally found in combination with other substances. It is absorbent and antacid, and moderately cathartic. *Ure.*

MAGNE'SIAN, *a.* Pertaining to magnesia, or partaking of its qualities.

MAG'NESITE, *n.* Carbonated magnesia, or magnesia combined with silex. It occurs in amorphous masses, or in masses tuberous and spungiform; its color is yellowish gray, or white with spots, and dendritic delineations of blackish brown. *Haüy. Cyc.*

MAGNE'SIUM, *n.* The undecomposable base of magnesia.

MAG'NET, *n.* [L. from Gr. μαγνης, from *Magnesia*, in Asia Minor.]

The lodestone; an ore of iron which has the peculiar properties of attracting metallic iron, of pointing to the poles, and of dipping or inclining downwards. These properties it communicates to iron by contact. A bar of iron to which these properties are imparted, is called an *artificial magnet*. *Encyc.*

MAGNET'IC, MAGNET'ICAL, } *a.* Pertaining to the magnet; possessing the properties of the magnet, or corresponding properties; as a *magnetic* bar of iron, or a *magnetic* needle.

2. Attractive.

She that had all *magnetic* force alone— *Donne.*

MAGNET'ICALLY, *adv.* By means of magnetism; by the power of attraction. *Burton.*

MAGNET'ICALNESS, *n.* The quality of being magnetic.

MAGNET'ICS, *n.* The science or principles of magnetism.

MAGNETIF'EROUS, *a.* Producing or conducting magnetism. *Journ. of Science.*

MAG'NETISM, *n.* That branch of science which treats of the properties of the magnet, the power of the lodestone, &c.

2. Power of attraction; as the *magnetism* of interest. *Glanville.*

Animal magnetism, a sympathy supposed to exist between the magnet and the human body, by means of which the magnet is said to be able to cure diseases; or a fluid supposed to exist throughout nature, and to be the medium of influence between celestial bodies, and the earth and human bodies.

MAG'NETIZE, *v. t.* To communicate magnetic properties to any thing; as, to *magnetize* a needle.

Seven of Deslon's patients were *magnetized* at Dr. Franklin's house. *Encyc.*

MAG'NETIZE, *v. i.* To acquire magnetic properties; to become magnetic. A bar of iron standing some time in an inclined position, will *magnetize*.

MAG'NETIZED, *pp.* Made magnetic.

MAG'NETIZING, *ppr.* Imparting magnetism to.

MAG'NIFIABLE, *a.* [See *Magnify.*] That may be magnified; worthy of being magnified or extolled. *Brown.*

MAGNIF'IC, MAGNIF'ICAL, } *a.* [L. *magnificus.*]

Grand; splendid; illustrious. *Milton.*

MAGNIF'ICATE, *v. t.* To magnify or extol. [*Not used.*] *Marston.*

MAGNIF'ICENCE, *n.* [L. *magnificentia.*] Grandeur of appearance; greatness and splendor of show or state; as the *magnificence* of a palace or of a procession; the *magnificence* of a Roman triumph.

MAGNIF'ICENT, *a.* Grand in appearance; splendid; pompous.

Man he made, and for him built
Magnificent this world. *Milton.*

2. Exhibiting grandeur. *Sidney.*

MAGNIF'ICENTLY, *adv.* With splendor of appearance, or pomp of show. The minister was *magnificently* entertained at court.

2. With exalted sentiments. We can never conceive too *magnificently* of the Creator and his works.

MAGNIF'ICO, *n.* A grandee of Venice. *Shak.*

MAG'NIFIER, *n.* [from *magnify.*] One who magnifies; one who extols or exalts in praises.

2. A glass that magnifies; a convex lens which increases the apparent magnitude of bodies.

MAGNIFY, *v. t.* [L. *magnifico*; *magnus*, great, and *facio*, to make.]

1. To make great or greater; to increase the apparent dimensions of a body. A convex lens *magnifies* the bulk of a body to the eye.

2. To make great in representation; to extol; to exalt in description or praise. The embassador *magnified* the king and queen.

3. To extol; to exalt; to elevate; to raise in estimation.

Thee that day
Thy thunders *magnified*. *Milton.*
The Lord *magnified* Solomon exceedingly. 1 Chron. xxix.

To magnify one's self, to raise in pride and pretensions.

He shall *magnify* himself in his heart Dan. viii.

MAG'NIFYING, *ppr.* Enlarging apparent bulk or dimensions; extolling; exalting.

MAGNIL'OQUENCE, *n.* [L. *magnus*, great, and *loquens*, speaking.]
A lofty manner of speaking; tumid, pompous words or style. *Bentley.*

MAG'NITUDE, *n.* [L. *magnitudo.*] Extent of dimensions or parts; bulk; size; *applied to things that have length, breadth or thickness.*
2. Greatness; grandeur.

With plain heroic *magnitude* of mind. *Milton.*

3. Greatness, in reference to influence or effect; importance. In affairs of *magnitude*, disdain not to take counsel.

MAGNO'LIA, *n.* The laurel-leafed tuliptree, of several species.

MAG'PIE, *n.* [W. *piog*, L. *pica*, with *mag.*]
A chattering bird of the genus Corvus.

MAG'UEY, *n.* A species of aloe in Mexico, which furnished the natives with timber for their buildings. Its leaves were used for covering the roofs of their houses, and for paper, clothing and cordage. *Encyc.*
The maguey is a species of the genus Agave, and is now cultivated in Mexico, for the purpose of preparing from its leaves a spirituous liquor called *pulque*. *Humboldt.*

MAHOG'ANY, *n.* A tree of the genus Swietenia, growing in the tropical climates of America. The wood is of a reddish or brown color, very hard, and susceptible of a fine polish. Of this are made our most beautiful and durable pieces of cabinet furniture.

MAHOM'ETAN, } This word and the
MOHAM'MEDAN. } name of the Arabian prophet, so called, are written in many different ways. The best authorized and most correct orthography seems to be *Mohammed, Mohammedan.* [See *Mohammedan.*]

MA'HOUND, *n.* Formerly a contemptuous name for Mohammed and the devil, &c. *Skelton.*

MAID, *n.* A species of skate fish.

MAID, } *n.* [Sax. *mægth*, from *mæg*, a
MA'IDEN, } general name of relation, man, boy, or woman; Goth. *magath*; D. *maagd*; G. *magd*; Ir. *mogh*, a man; Sp. *mozo*, a man-servant, a bachelor; *moza*, a maid; Port. *macho*, a male; Russ. *muj*. It coincides in elements with Sax. *magan*, to be able, Eng. *may.*]
1. An unmarried woman, or a young unmarried woman; a virgin.
2. A female servant. *Dryden.*
3. It is used in composition, to express the feminine gender, as in *maid-servant.*

MA'IDEN, *n.* A maid; also, an instrument for beheading criminals, and another for washing linen.

MA'IDEN, *a.* Pertaining to a young woman or virgin; as *maiden* charms.
2. Consisting of young women or virgins.

Amid the *maiden* throng. *Addison.*

3. Fresh; new; unused.

He fleshed his *maiden* sword. *Shak.*

MA'IDEN, *v. i.* To speak and act demurely or modestly. *Bp. Hall.*

MA'IDENHAIR, *n.* A plant of the genus Adiantum.

MA'IDENHOOD, *n.* [Sax. *mægdenhad*, *mædenhad.*]
1. The state of being a maid or virgin; virginity.

The modest lore of *maidenhood.* *Milton.*

2. Newness; freshness; uncontaminated state. *Shak.*

MA'IDENLIKE, *a.* Like a maid; modest. *Shak.*

MA'IDENLINESS, *n.* The behavior that becomes a maid; modesty; gentleness. *Sherwood.*

MA'IDENLIP, *n.* A plant. *Ainsworth.*

MA'IDENLY, *a.* Like a maid; gentle; modest; reserved. *Shak.*

MA'IDENLY, *adv.* In a maidenlike manner. *Skelton.*

MA'IDHOOD, *n.* Virginity. *Shak.*

MAIDMAR'IAN, *n.* A dance; so called from a buffoon dressed like a man. *Obs.* *Temple.*

MA'IDPALE, *a.* Pale, like a sick girl. *Shak.*

MA'ID-SERVANT, *n.* A female servant. *Swift.*

MAIL, *n.* [Fr. *maille*, a stitch in knitting, a mail; Sp. *malla*, a mesh, net-work, a coat of mail; Port. id. and a spot; It. *maglia* and *camaglio*; Arm. *mailh*; D. *maal*; W. *magyl*, a knot, a mesh; *maglu*, to knit, to entangle, to entrap, to form meshes. The sense of *spot*, which occurs in the French and Portuguese, indicates this word to be from the root of L. *macula*, and the Welsh words prove it to be contracted from *magel.*]
1. A coat of steel net-work, formerly worn for defending the body against swords, poniards, &c. The mail was of two sorts, chain and plate mail; the former consisting of iron rings, each having four others inserted into it; the latter consisting of a number of small lamins of metal, laid over one another like the scales of a fish, and sewed down to a strong linen or lethern jacket. *Cyc.*
2. Armor; that which defends the body.

We strip the lobster of his scarlet *mail.* *Gay.*

We read also of shirts of *mail*, and gloves of *mail.*

3. In *ships*, a square machine composed of rings interwoven, like net-work, used for rubbing off the loose hemp on lines and white cordage.
4. A rent. [Sax. *mal.*] Also, a spot. *Obs.*

MAIL, *n.* [Fr. *malette*; Ir. *mala*; Fr. *malle*; Arm. *mal.*]
A bag for the conveyance of letters and papers, particularly letters conveyed from one post office to another, under public authority.

MAIL, *v. t.* To put on a coat of mail or armor; to arm defensively. *Shak.*
2. To inclose in a wrapper and direct to a post office. We say, letters were *mailed* for Philadelphia.

MA'IL-COACH, *n.* A coach that conveys the public mails.

MA'ILED, *pp.* Covered with a mail or with armor; inclosed and directed, as letters in a bundle.
2. *a.* Spotted; speckled. *Sherwood.*

MA'ILING, *ppr.* Investing with a coat of mail; inclosing in a wrapper and directing to a post office.

MAIM, *v. t.* [Old Fr. *mahemer* or *mahaigner*; Arm. *mahaigna, mahagnein.*]
1. To deprive of the use of a limb, so as to render a person less able to defend himself in fighting, or to annoy his adversary. *Blackstone.*
2. To deprive of a necessary part; to cripple; to disable.

You *maim'd* the jurisdiction of all bishops. *Shak.*

MAIM, *n.* [written in law-language, *mayhem.*]
1. The privation of the use of a limb or member of the body, so as to render the sufferer less able to defend himself or to annoy his adversary.
2. The privation of any necessary part; a crippling.

Surely there is more cause to fear lest the want thereof be a *maim*, than the use of it a blemish. *Hooker.*

3. Injury; mischief. *Shak.*
4. Essential defect.

A noble author esteems it to be a *maim* in history. [*Not used.*] *Hayward.*

MA'IMED, *pp.* Crippled; disabled in limbs; lame.

MA'IMING, *ppr.* Disabling by depriving of the use of a limb; crippling; rendering lame or defective.

MA'IMEDNESS, *n.* A state of being maimed. *Bolton.*

MAIN, *a.* [Sax. *mægn*, strength, force, power, from *magan*, to be able or strong, that is, to strain or stretch, Eng. *may, might.* If *g* is radical in the L. *magnus*, this may be of the same family; Goth. *mickels*; Eng. *much.*]
1. Principal; chief; that which has most power in producing an effect, or which is mostly regarded in prospect; as the *main* branch or tributary stream of a river; the *main* timbers of an edifice; a *main* design; a *main* object.

Our *main* interest is to be as happy as we can, and as long as possible. *Tillotson.*

2. Mighty; vast; as the *main* abyss. *Milton.*
3. Important; powerful.

This young prince, with a train of young noblemen and gentlemen, not with any *main* army, came over to take possession of his patrimony. *Davies.*

MAIN, *n.* Strength; force; violent effort; as in the phrase, "with might and *main.*" *Dryden.*
2. The gross; the bulk; the greater part.

The *main* of them may be reduced to language and an improvement in wisdom— *Locke.*

3. The ocean; the great sea, as distinguished from rivers, bays, sounds and the like.

He fell, and struggling in the *main*— *Dryden.*

4. The continent, as distinguished from an isle. We arrived at Nantucket on Saturday, but did not reach the *main* till Monday. In this use of the word, *land* is omitted; *main* for *main land.*
5. A hamper. *Ainsworth.*

6. A course; a duct. *Act of Parliament.*
For the main, in the main, for the most part; in the greatest part.

MAIN, *n.* [L. *manus*, hand; Fr. *main.*] A hand at dice. We throw a merry *main.*

And lucky *mains* make people wise. [*Not used.*] *Prior.*

2. A match at cock fighting.

MA'IN-LAND, *n.* The continent; the principal land, as opposed to an *isle.* *Dryden.*

MA'INLY, *adv.* Chiefly; principally. He is *mainly* occupied with domestic concerns.

2. Greatly; to a great degree; mightily. *Bacon.*

MA'IN-MAST, *n.* The principal mast in a ship or other vessel.

MA'IN-KEEL, *n.* The principal keel, as distinguished from the false keel.

MA'INOR, *n.* [Old Fr. *manoevre, meinour*, L. *a manu*, from the hand, or in the work.] The old law phrase, *to be taken as a thief with the mainor*, signifies, to be taken in the very act of killing venison or stealing wood, or in preparing so to do; or it denotes the being taken with the thing stolen upon him. *Blackstone.*

MAINPERN'ABLE, *a.* That may be admitted to give surety by mainpernors; that may be mainprized.

MAINPERN'OR, *n.* [Old Fr. *main*, the hand, and *prendre*, to take; *pernon, pernez*, for *prenon, prenez.*] In *law*, a surety for a prisoner's appearance in court at a day. *Mainpernors* differ from *bail*, in that a man's *bail* may imprison or surrender him before the stipulated day of appearance; *mainpernors* can do neither; they are bound to produce him to answer all charges whatsoever. *Blackstone.*

MA'INPRIZE, *n.* [Fr. *main*, hand, and *prendre, pris*, to take.]

1. In *law*, a writ directed to the sheriff, commanding him to take sureties for the prisoner's appearance, and to let him go at large. These sureties are called *mainpernors.* *Blackstone.*

2. Deliverance of a prisoner on security for his appearance at a day.

MA'INPRIZE, *v. t.* To suffer a prisoner to go at large, on his finding sureties, mainpernors, for his appearance at a day.

MA'IN-SAIL, *n.* The principal sail in a ship. The main-sail of a ship or brig is extended by a yard attached to the main-mast, and that of a sloop, by the boom.

MA'IN-SHEET, *n.* The sheet that extends and fastens the main-sail.

MA'INSWEAR, *v. i.* [Sax. *manswerian; man*, evil, and *swerian*, to swear.] To swear falsely; to perjure one's self. *Blount.*

MAINTA'IN, *v. t.* [Fr. *maintenir; main*, hand, and *tenir*, to hold; L. *manus* and *teneo.*]

1. To hold, preserve or keep in any particular state or condition; to support; to sustain; not to suffer to fail or decline; as, to *maintain* a certain degree of heat in a furnace; to *maintain* the digestive process or powers of the stomach; to *maintain* the fertility of soil; to *maintain* present character or reputation.

2. To hold; to keep; not to lose or surrender; as, to *maintain* a place or post.

3. To continue; not to suffer to cease; as, to *maintain* a conversation.

4. To keep up; to uphold; to support the expense of; as, to *maintain* state or equipage.

What *maintains* one vice would bring up two children. *Franklin.*

5. To support with food, clothing and other conveniences; as, to *maintain* a family by trade or labor.

6. To support by intellectual powers, or by force of reason; as, to *maintain* an argument.

7. To support; to defend; to vindicate; to justify; to prove to be just; as, to *maintain* one's right or cause.

8. To support by assertion or argument; to affirm.

In tragedy and satire, I *maintain* that this age and the last have excelled the ancients. *Dryden.*

MAINTA'INABLE, *a.* That may be maintained, supported, preserved or sustained.

2. That may be defended or kept by force or resistance; as, a military post is not *maintainable.*

3. That may be defended by argument or just claim; vindicable; defensible.

MAINTA'INED, *pp.* Kept in any state; preserved; upheld; supported; defended; vindicated.

MAINTA'INER, *n.* One who supports, preserves, sustains or vindicates.

MAINTA'INING, *ppr.* Supporting; preserving; upholding; defending; vindicating.

MA'INTENANCE, *n.* Sustenance; sustentation; support by means of supplies of food, clothing and other conveniences; as, his labor contributed little to the *maintenance* of his family.

2. Means of support; that which supplies conveniences.

Those of better fortune not making learning their *maintenance.* *Swift.*

3. Support; protection; defense; vindication; as the *maintenance* of right or just claims.

4. Continuance; security from failure or decline.

Whatever is granted to the church for God's honor and the *maintenance* of his service, is granted to God. *South.*

5. In *law*, an officious intermeddling in a suit in which the person has no interest, by assisting either party with money or means to prosecute or defend it. This is a punishable offense. But to assist a poor kinsman from compassion, is not maintenance. *Encyc.*

MA'IN-TOP, *n.* The top of the main-mast of a ship or brig.

MA'IN-YARD, *n.* The yard on which the main-sail is extended, supported by the main-mast.

MAISTER, for *master*, is obsolete. *Spenser.*

MAISTRESS, for *mistress*, is obsolete. *Chaucer.*

MAIZ, *n.* A plant of the genus Zea, the native corn of America, called Indian corn. [In the Lettish and Livonic languages, in the north of Europe, *mayse* is bread. *Tooke.* In Ir. *maise* is food; perhaps a different orthography of *meat.*]

MA'JA, *n.* A bird of Cuba, of a beautiful yellow color, whose flesh is accounted a delicacy. *Dict. Nat. Hist.*

MAJES'TIC, *a.* [from *majesty.*] August; having dignity of person or appearance; grand; princely. The prince was *majestic* in person and appearance.

In his face
Sat meekness, hightened with *majestic* grace. *Milton.*

2. Splendid; grand.

Get the start of this *majestic* world. *Shak.*

3. Elevated; lofty.

The least portions must be of the epic kind; all must be grave, *majestic* and sublime. *Dryden.*

4. Stately; becoming majesty; as a *majestic* air or walk.

MAJES'TICAL, *a.* Majestic. [*Little used.*]

MAJES'TICALLY, *adv.* With dignity; with grandeur; with a lofty air or appearance.

MAJ'ESTY, *n.* [L. *majestas*, from the root of *magis, major*, more, greater.]

1. Greatness of appearance; dignity; grandeur; dignity of aspect or manner; the quality or state of a person or thing which inspires awe or reverence in the beholder; applied with peculiar propriety to God and his works.

Jehovah reigneth; he is clothed with *majesty.* Ps. xciii.

The voice of Jehovah is full of *majesty.* Ps. xxix.

It is applied to the dignity, pomp and splendor of earthly princes.

When he showed the riches of his glorious kingdom—the honor of his excellent *majesty* many days— Esth. i.

2. Dignity; elevation of manner.

The first in loftiness of thought surpass'd,
The next in *majesty*— *Dryden.*

3. A title of emperors, kings and queens; as most royal *majesty;* may it please your *majesty.* In this sense, it admits of the plural; as, their *majesties* attended the concert.

MA'JOR, *a.* [L.] Greater in number, quantity or extent; as the *major* part of the assembly; the *major* part of the revenue; the *major* part of the territory.

2. Greater in dignity.

My *major* vow lies here. *Shak.*

3. In *music*, an epithet applied to the modes in which the third is four semitones above the tonic or key-note, and to intervals consisting of four semitones. *Busby.*

Major and *minor*, in music, are applied to concords which differ from each other by a semitone.

Major tone, the difference between the fifth and fourth, and major semitone is the difference between the major fourth and the third. The major tone surpasses the minor by a comma. *Encyc.*

MA'JOR, *n.* In *military affairs*, an officer next in rank above a captain, and below a lieutenant colonel; the lowest field officer.

2. The mayor of a town. [See *Mayor.*]

Aid-major, an officer appointed to act as major on certain occasions.

Brigade-major. [See *Brigade.*]

Drum-major, the first drummer in a regiment, who has authority over the other drummers.

Fife-major, the first or chief fifer.

Sergeant-major, a non-commissioned officer, subordinate to the adjutant.

MA'JOR, *n.* In *law*, a person of full age to manage his own concerns.

MAJOR, *n.* In *logic*, the first proposition of a regular syllogism, containing the principal term; as, no unholy person is qualified for happiness in heaven, [the major.] Every man in his natural state is unholy, [minor.] Therefore, no man in his natural state, is qualified for happiness in heaven, [conclusion or inference.]

MAJORA'TION, *n.* Increase; enlargement. [*Not used.*] *Bacon.*

MAJOR-DO'MO, *n.* [*major* and *domus*, house.]

A man who holds the place of master of the house; a steward; also, a chief minister. *Encyc.*

MA'JOR-ĠENERAL, *n.* A military officer who commands a division or a number of regiments; the next in rank below a lieutenant general.

MAJOR'ITY, *n.* [Fr. *majorité*; from *major.*]

1. The greater number; more than half; as a *majority* of mankind; a *majority* of votes in Congress. A measure may be carried by a large or small *majority.*

2. Full age; the age at which the laws of a country permit a young person to manage his own affairs. Henry III. had no sooner come to his *majority*, than the barons raised war against him.

3. The office, rank or commission of a major.

4. The state of being greater.

It is not a plurality of parts, without *majority* of parts. [*Little used.*] *Grew.*

5. [L. *majores.*] Ancestors; ancestry. [*Not used.*] *Brown.*

6. Chief rank. [*Not used.*] *Shak.*

MAKE, *v. t.* pret. and pp. *made.* [Sax. *macian*; G. *machen*; D. *maaken*; Dan. *mager*, to contrive; *mager paa*, to make, to form, to mold, to contrive, to practice. The primary sense is to cause to act or do, to press, drive, strain or compel, as in the phrases, *make* your servant work, *make* him go.]

1. To compel; to constrain.

They should be *made* to rise at an early hour. *Locke.*

2. To form of materials; to fashion; to mold into shape; to cause to exist in a different form, or as a distinct thing.

He fashioned it with a graving tool, after he had *made* it a molten calf. Ex. xxxii.

God not only *made*, but created; not only *made* the work, but the materials. *Dwight, Theol.*

3. To create; to cause to exist; to form from nothing. God *made* the materials of the earth and of all worlds.

4. To compose; to constitute as parts, materials or ingredients united in a whole. These several sums *make* the whole amount.

The heaven, the air, the earth, and boundless sea,
Make but one temple for the deity. *Waller.*

5. To form by art.

And art with her contending, doth aspire
T' excel the natural with *made* delights. *Spenser.*

6. To produce or effect, as the agent.

Call for Sampson, that he may *make* us sport. Judges xvi.

7. To produce, as the cause; to procure; to obtain. Good tillage is necessary to *make* good crops.

Wealth *maketh* many friends. Prov. xix.

8. To do; to perform; to execute; as, to *make* a journey; to *make* a long voyage.

9. To cause to have any quality, as by change or alteration. Wealth may *make* a man proud; beauty may *make* a woman vain; a due sense of human weakness should *make* us humble.

10. To bring into any state or condition; to constitute.

See I have *made* thee a god to Pharaoh. Ex. vii.

Who *made* thee a prince and a judge over us? Ex. ii.

11. To contract; to establish; as, to *make* friendship. *Rowe.*

12. To keep; as, to *make* abode. *Dryden.*

13. To raise to good fortune; to secure in riches or happiness; as when it is said, he is *made* for this world.

Who *makes* or ruins with a smile or frown. *Dryden.*

14. To suffer.

He accuses Neptune unjustly, who *makes* shipwreck a second time. *Bacon.*

15. To incur; as, to *make* a loss. [*Improper.*] *Dryden.*

16. To commit; to do.

I will neither plead my age nor sickness in excuse of the faults which I *made.* [*Little used.*] *Dryden.*

17. To intend or to do; to purpose to do.

Gomez, what *mak'st* thou here, with a whole brotherhood of city bailiffs? [*Not used.*] *Dryden.*

We now say, what *doest* thou here?

18. To raise, as profit; to gain; to collect; as, to *make* money in trade or by husbandry; to *make* an estate by steady industry.

19. To discover; to arrive in sight of; *a seaman's phrase.* They *made* the land at nine o'clock on the larboard bow, distant five leagues.

20. To reach; to arrive at; as, to *make* a port or harbor; *a seaman's phrase.*

21. To gain by advance; as, to *make* little way with a head wind; we *made* our way to the next village. *This phrase often implies difficulty.*

22. To provide; as, to *make* a dinner or entertainment.

23. To put or place; as, to *make* a difference between strict right and expedience.

24. To turn; to convert, as to use.

Whate'er they catch,
Their fury *makes* an instrument of war. *Dryden.*

25. To represent. He is not the fool you *make* him, that is, as your representation exhibits him.

26. To constitute; to form. It is melancholy to think that sensual pleasure *makes* the happiness of a great part of mankind.

27. To induce; to cause. Self-confidence *makes* a man rely too much on his own strength and resources.

28. To put into a suitable or regular form for use; as, to *make* a bed.

29. To fabricate; to forge. He *made* the story himself.

30. To compose; to form and write; as, to *make* verses or an oration.

31. To cure; to dry and prepare for preservation; as, to *make* hay.

To make amends, to make good; to give adequate compensation; to replace the value or amount of loss.

To make account of, to esteem; to regard. *Bacon.*

To make away, to kill; to destroy. *Sidney. Addison.*

2. To alienate; to transfer. *Waller.*

We now usually say, to *make over* property.

To make free with, to treat with freedom; to treat without ceremony. *Pope.*

To make good, to maintain; to defend.

I'll either die, or I'll *make good* the place. *Dryden.*

2. To fulfill; to accomplish; as, to *make good* one's word, promise or engagement.

3. To make compensation for; to supply an equivalent; as, to *make good* a loss or damage.

To make light of, to consider as of no consequence; to treat with indifference or contempt.

They *made light of* it, and went their way. Matt. xxii.

To make love, } to court; to attempt to gain
To make suit, } the favor or affection.

To make merry, to feast; to be joyful or jovial. *Bacon.*

To make much of, to treat with fondness or esteem; to consider as of great value, or as giving great pleasure.

To make of, to understand. He knows not what to *make of* the news, that is, he does not well understand it; he knows not how to consider or view it.

2. To produce from; to effect.

I am astonished that those who have appeared against this paper, have *made* so very little *of* it. *Addison.*

3. To consider; to account; to esteem.

Makes she no more *of* me than of a slave? *Dryden.*

To make over, to transfer the title of; to convey; to alienate. He *made over* his estate in trust or in fee.

To make out, to learn; to discover; to obtain a clear understanding of. I cannot *make out* the meaning or sense of this difficult passage. Antiquaries are not able to *make out* the inscription on this medal.

2. To prove; to evince; to establish by evidence or argument. The plaintiff, not being able to *make out* his case, withdrew the suit.

In the passages from divines, most of the reasonings which *make out* both my propositions are already suggested. *Atterbury.*

3. To furnish; to find or supply. He promised to pay, but was not able to *make out* the money or the whole sum.

To make sure of, to consider as certain. *Dryden.*

2. To secure to one's possession; as, to *make sure of* the game.

To make up, to collect into a sum or mass; as, to *make up* the amount of rent; to *make up* a bundle or package.

2. To reconcile; to compose; as, to *make up* a difference or quarrel.

3. To repair; as, to *make up* a hedge. Ezek. xiii.

4. To supply what is wanting. A dollar is wanted to *make up* the stipulated sum.
5. To compose, as ingredients or parts.

Oh, he was all *made up* of love and charms! *Addison.*

The parties among us are *made up* of moderate whigs and presbyterians. *Swift.*

6. To shape; as, to *make up* a mass into pills.
7. To assume a particular form of features; as, to *make up* a face; whence, to *make up* a lip, is to pout.
8. To compensate; to make good; as, to *make up* a loss.
9. To settle; to adjust, or to arrange for settlement; as, to *make up* accounts.
10. To determine; to bring to a definite conclusion; as, to *make up* one's mind.

In *seamen's language*, to *make sail*, to increase the quantity of sail already extended.

To make sternway, to move with the stern foremost.

To make water, to leak.

To make words, to multiply words.

MAKE, *v. i.* To tend; to proceed; to move. He *made* towards home. The tiger *made* at the sportsman. Formerly authors used to *make way*, to *make on*, to *make forth*, to *make about*; but these phrases are obsolete. We now say, to *make at*, to *make towards*.

2. To contribute; to have effect. This argument *makes* nothing in his favor. He believes wrong to be right, and right to be wrong, when it *makes* for his advantage.
3. To rise; to flow toward land; as, the tide *makes* fast.

To make as if, to show; to appear; to carry appearance.

Joshua and all Israel *made as if* they were beaten before them, and fled. Josh. viii.

To make away with, to kill; to destroy.

To make for, to move towards; to direct a course towards; as, we apprehended a tempest approaching, and *made for* a harbor.

2. To tend to advantage; to favor. A war between commercial nations *makes for* the interest of neutrals.

To make against, to tend to injury. This argument *makes against* his cause.

To make out, to succeed; to have success at last. He *made out* to reconcile the contending parties.

To make up, to approach. He *made up* to us with boldness.

To make up for, to compensate; to supply by an equivalent.

Have you a supply of friends to *make up for* those who are gone? *Swift.*

To make up with, to settle differences; to become friends.

To make with, to concur. *Hooker.*

MAKE, *n.* Structure; texture; constitution of parts in a body. It may sometimes be synonymous with *shape* or *form*, but more properly, the word signifies the manner in which the parts of a body are united; as a man of slender *make*, or feeble *make*.

Is our perfection of so frail a *make*
As every plot can undermine and shake? *Dryden.*

MAKE, *n.* [Sax. *maca, gemaca*; Dan. *mage*; Eng. *match*. It seems allied to *make*, as *peer*, L. *par*, to Heb. ברא.]
A companion; a mate. *Obs.* *Spenser. B. Jonson.*

MA'KEBATE, *n.* [*make* and Sax. *bate*, contention.]
One who excites contention and quarrels. *Sidney.*

MA'KELESS, *a.* Matchless; without a mate. *Obs.*

MA'KER, *n.* The Creator.

The universal *Maker* we may praise. *Milton.*

2. One that makes, forms, shapes or molds; a manufacturer; as a *maker* of watches, or of jewelry; a *maker* of cloth.
3. A poet.

MA'KEPEACE, *n.* A peace-maker; one that reconciles persons when at variance. *Shak.*

MA'KEWEIGHT, *n.* That which is thrown into a scale to make weight. *Philips.*

MA'KI, *n.* An animal of the genus Lemur. The *ring-tailed maki* is of the size of a cat. *Encyc.*
The common name of a subdivision of the Linnean genus Lemur, including the macauco, the mongooz, and the vari. *Cuvier.*

MA'KING, *ppr.* Forming; causing; compelling; creating; constituting.

MA'KING, *n.* The act of forming, causing or constituting.

2. Workmanship. This is cloth of your own *making*.
3. Composition; structure.
4. A poem.

MAL, or MALE, as a prefix, in composition, denotes ill or evil, Fr. *mal*, L. *malus*. [See *Malady*.]

MAL'ACHITE, *n.* [Gr. μαλαχη, mallows, L. *malva*, from μαλακος, soft, so named from its resembling the color of the leaf of mallows.]
An oxyd of copper, combined with carbonic acid, found in solid masses of a beautiful green color. It consists of layers, in the form of nipples or needles converging towards a common center. It takes a good polish and is often manufactured into toys. *Fourcroy. Dict. Nat. Hist.*

MAL'ACOLITE, *n.* [Gr. μαλαχη, mallows, from its color.]
Another name for diopside, a variety of pyroxene. *Cleaveland. Lunier.*

MALACOPTERYG'EOUS, *a.* [Gr. μαλακος, soft, and πτερυγιον, a point or fether.]
Having bony rays of fins, not sharp or pointed at the extremity; as a fish.

MALACOS'TOMOUS, *a.* [Gr. μαλακος, soft, and στομα, mouth.]
Having soft jaws without teeth; as a fish. *Encyc.*

MALADMINISTRA'TION, *n.* [See *Mal* and *Administer*.]
Bad management of public affairs; vicious or defective conduct in administration, or the performance of official duties, particularly of executive and ministerial duties, prescribed by law; as the *maladministration* of a king, or of any chief magistrate.

MAL'ADY, *n.* [Fr. *maladie*; It. *malattia*, from the W. *mall*, softness, debility, an evil, a malady; L. *malum*; W. *mallu*, to make soft or flaccid, to deprive of energy, to make insipid, to make evil, to become evil. This coincides in origin with Eng. *mellow*, L. *mollis*, Gr. μαλακος. In opposition to this, *virtue*, *value* and *health*, are from the sense of strength, vigor.]

1. Any sickness or disease of the human body; any distemper, disorder or indisposition, proceeding from impaired, defective or morbid organic functions; more particularly, a lingering or deep seated disorder or indisposition. It may be applied to any animal body, but is, I believe, rarely or never applied to plants.

The *maladies* of the body may prove medicines to the mind. *Buckminster.*

2. Defect or corruption of the heart; depravity; moral disorder or corruption of moral principles. Depravity of heart is a moral *malady*.
3. Disorder of the understanding or mind.

MAL'AGA, *n.* A species of wine imported from Malaga, in Spain.

MALAN'DERS, *n.* [from *mal*, ill, and It. *andare*, to go.]
A dry scab on the pastern of a horse. *Johnson.*

MAL'APERT, *a.* [*mal* and *pert*.] Saucy; quick, with impudence; sprightly, without respect or decency; bold; forward.

Are you growing *malapert*? *Dryden.*

MAL'APERTLY, *adv.* Saucily; with impudence. *Skelton.*

MAL'APERTNESS, *n.* Sauciness; impudent pertness or forwardness; sprightliness of reply without decency.

MALAPROPOS, *adv. malap'ropo.* [Fr. *mal*, evil, and *apropos*, to the purpose.] Unsuitably. *Dryden.*

MA'LAR, *a.* [L. *mala*, the cheek.] Pertaining to the cheek.

MAL'ATE, *n.* [L. *malum*, an apple.] A salt formed by the malic acid, the acid of apples, combined with a base. *Chimistry.*

MAL'AXATE, *v. t.* [Gr. μαλασσω.] To soften; to knead to softness. [*Not used.*]

MALAXA'TION, *n.* The act of moistening and softening; or the forming of ingredients into a mass for pills or plasters. [*Little used.*] *Bailey.*

MALCONFORMA'TION, *n.* Ill form; disproportion of parts. *Tully.*

MAL'CONTENT, *n.* [*mal* and *content*.] A discontented subject of government; one who murmurs at the laws and administration, or who manifests his uneasiness by overt acts, as in sedition or insurrection.

MAL'CONTENT, } *a.* Discontented
MALCONTENT'ED, } with the laws or the administration of government; uneasy; dissatisfied with the government.

The famous *malcontent* earl of Leicester. *Milner.*

MALCONTENT'EDLY, *adv.* With discontent.

MALCONTENT'EDNESS, *n.* Discontentedness with the government; dissatisfaction; want of attachment to the government, manifested by overt acts. *Spectator.*

MALE, *a.* [Fr. *male*, for *masle*, from L. *masculus*, from *mas*, *maris*.]

1. Pertaining to the sex that procreates young, and applied to animals of all kinds; as a *male* child; a *male* beast, fish or fowl.
2. Denoting the sex of a plant which produces the fecundating dust, or a flower or plant that bears the stamens only, without pistils.

3. Denoting the screw whose threads enter the grooves or channels of the corresponding or female screw.

MALE, *n.* Among *animals*, one of the sex whose office is to beget young; a he-animal.

2. In *botany*, a plant or flower which produces stamens only, without pistils.

3. In *mechanics*, the screw whose threads enter the grooves or channels of the corresponding part or female screw.

MALEDIC'ENCY, *n.* [L. *maledicentia*; *male* and *dico*.]

Evil speaking; reproachful language; proneness to reproach. [*Little used.*] *Atterbury.*

MAL'EDICENT, *a.* Speaking reproachfully; slanderous. [*Little used.*] *Sandys.*

MALEDIC'TION, *n.* [L. *maledictio*; *male*, evil, and *dico*, to speak.]

Evil speaking; denunciation of evil; a cursing; curse or execration. *Hooker.*

MALEFAC'TION, *n.* [L. *male*, evil, and *facio*, to do.]

A criminal deed; a crime; an offense against the laws. [*Little used.*] *Shak.*

MALEFAC'TOR, *n.* [supra.] One who commits a crime; one guilty of violating the laws, in such a manner as to subject him to public prosecution and punishment, particularly to capital punishment; a criminal. *Dryden.*

MAL'EFICE, *n.* [Fr. See *Malefaction.*] An evil deed; artifice; enchantment. [*Not in use.*] *Chaucer.*

MALEFI''CIATE, *v. t.* To bewitch. [*Not in use.*] *Burton.*

MALEFICIA'TION, *n.* A bewitching. [*Not in use.*]

MALEFI''CIENCE, *n.* [L. *maleficientia.*] The doing of evil, harm or mischief.

MALEFI''CIENT, *a.* Doing evil, harm or mischief. *Burke.*

MALEN'GINE, *n.* [Fr. *malengin.*] Guile; deceit. [*Not in use.*] *Spenser.*

MAL'ET, *n.* [Fr. *malette.* See *Mail.*] A little bag or budget; a portmanteau. [*Not used.*] *Shelton.*

MALEV'OLENCE, *n.* [L. *malevolentia*; *malum*, evil, and *volens*, *volo*, to will.]

Ill will; personal hatred; evil disposition towards another; enmity of heart; inclination to injure others. It expresses less than *malignity.* *Shak.*

MALEV'OLENT, *a.* Having an evil disposition towards another or others; wishing evil to others; ill disposed, or disposed to injure others. A *malevolent* heart rejoices in the misfortunes of others.

2. Unfavorable; unpropitious; bringing calamity.

MALEV'OLENTLY, *adv.* With ill will or enmity; with the wish or design to injure.

MALEV'OLOUS, *a.* Malevolent. [*Not in use.*] *Warburton.*

MALFE'ASANCE, *n.* [Fr.] Evil doing; wrong; illegal deed.

MALFORMA'TION, *n.* [*mal* and *formation.*]

Ill or wrong formation; irregular or anomalous formation or structure of parts. *Darwin.*

MA'LIC, *a.* [L. *malum*, an apple.] Pertaining to apples; drawn from the juice of apples; as *malic* acid. *Chimistry.*

MAL'ICE, *n.* [Fr. It. *malizia*; Sp. *malicia*; L. *malitia*, from *malus*, evil; W. *mall.* See *Malady.*]

Extreme enmity of heart, or malevolence; a disposition to injure others without cause, from mere personal gratification or from a spirit of revenge; unprovoked malignity or spite.

—Nor set down aught in *malice.* *Shak.*

MAL'ICE, *v. t.* To regard with extreme ill will. [*Not used.*] *Spenser.*

MALI''CIOUS, *a.* Harboring ill will or enmity without provocation; malevolent in the extreme; malignant in heart.

I grant him bloody,
Sudden, *malicious*, smacking of every sin
That has a name. *Shak.*

2. Proceeding from extreme hatred or ill will; dictated by malice; as a *malicious* report.

MALI''CIOUSLY, *adv.* With malice; with extreme enmity or ill will; with deliberate intention to injure. *Swift.*

MALI''CIOUSNESS, *n.* The quality of being malicious; extreme enmity or disposition to injure; malignity. *Herbert.*

MALIGN, *a.* *mali'ne.* [Fr. *maligne*; L. *malignus*, from *malus*, evil. See *Malady.*]

1. Having a very evil disposition towards others; harboring violent hatred or enmity; malicious; as *malign* spirits. *Milton.*

2. Unfavorable; pernicious; tending to injure; as a *malign* aspect of planets. *Milton.*

3. Malignant; pernicious; as a *malign* ulcer. *Bacon.*

MALIGN, *v. t.* To regard with envy or malice; to treat with extreme enmity; to injure maliciously.

The people practice mischief against private men, whom they *malign* by stealing their goods and murdering them. *Spenser.*

2. To traduce; to defame.

MALIGN, *v. i.* To entertain malice. *Milton.*

MALIG'NANCY, *n.* [See *Malignant.*] Extreme malevolence; bitter enmity; malice; as *malignancy* of heart.

2. Unfavorableness; unpropitiousness; as the *malignancy* of the aspect of planets.

The *malignancy* of my fate might distemper yours. *Shak.*

3. Virulence; tendency to mortification or to a fatal issue; as the *malignancy* of an ulcer or of a fever.

MALIG'NANT, *a.* [L. *malignus*, *maligno*, from *malus*, evil.]

1. Malicious; having extreme malevolence or enmity; as a *malignant* heart.

2. Unpropitious; exerting pernicious influence; as *malignant* stars. *Shak.*

3. Virulent; as a *malignant* ulcer.

4. Dangerous to life; as a *malignant* fever.

5. Extremely hainous; as the *malignant* nature of sin.

MALIG'NANT, *n.* A man of extreme enmity or evil intentions. [*Not used.*] *Hooker.*

MALIG'NANTLY, *adv.* Maliciously; with extreme malevolence.

2. With pernicious influence.

MALIGNER, *n.* One who regards or treats another with enmity; a traducer; a defamer. *Swift.*

MALIG'NITY, *n.* [L. *malignitas.*] Extreme enmity, or evil dispositions of heart towards another; malice without provocation, or malevolence with baseness of heart; deep rooted spite.

2. Virulence; destructive tendency; as the *malignity* of an ulcer or disease.

3. Extreme evilness of nature; as the *malignity* of fraud.

4. Extreme sinfulness; enormity or hainousness; as the *malignity* of sin.

MALIGNLY, *adv.* With extreme ill will.

2. Unpropitiously; perniciously.

MAL'ISON, *n.* Malediction. [*Not in use.*] *Chaucer.*

MALKIN, *n.* *maw'kin.* A mop; also, a low maid-servant. *Shak.*

MALL, *n.* *maul.* [Fr. *mail*; Sp. *mallo*; Port. *malho*; from L. *malleus.*]

1. A large heavy wooden beetle; an instrument for driving any thing with force.

2. A blow. *Obs.* *Spenser.*

MALL, *n.* *mal.* [Arm. *mailh.* Qu. from a play with mall and ball, or a beaten walk.]

A public walk; a level shaded walk. *Allée d'arbres battue et bordée.* *Gregoire's Arm. Dict.*

MALL, *v. t.* *maul.* To beat with a mall; to beat with something heavy; to bruise.

MAL'LARD, *n.* A species of duck of the genus Anas. *Pennant.*

MALLEABIL'ITY, *n.* [from *malleable.*] That quality of bodies which renders them susceptible of extension by beating. It is opposed to *friability* or *brittleness.* *Locke.*

MAL'LEABLE, *a.* [Fr. from L. *malleus.* See *Mall.*]

That may be drawn out and extended by beating; capable of extension by the hammer; a quality of metals, particularly of gold. *Newton.*

MAL'LEABLENESS, *n.* Malleability, which see.

MAL'LEATE, *v. t.* To hammer; to draw into a plate or leaf by beating.

MALLEA'TION, *n.* The act of beating into a plate or leaf, as a metal; extension by beating.

MAL'LET, *n.* [Fr. *maillet*; Russ. *molot*; Slav. *mlat*; L. *malleus.*]

A wooden hammer or instrument for beating, or for driving pins; particularly used in carpentry, for driving the chisel.

MALLOW, } *n.* [Sax. *malu*, *mealwe*, *malwe*; Fr. *mauve*; L. Sp. It.
MALLOWS, } *malva*; Gr. μαλαχη, from μαλαχος, soft, Eng. *mellow*, W. *mall.* See *Malady.*]

A plant of the genus Malva; so called from its emollient qualities.

Marsh-mallows, a plant of the genus Althæa.

MALM'SEY, *n.* [Fr. *malvoisie*; It. *malvosio*; Sp. *marvisia*, from *Malvasia*, in Greece; L. *vinum arvisium.*]

The name of a species of grape, and also of a kind of wine.

MALPRAC'TICE, *n.* [*mal* and *practice.*] Evil practice; illegal or immoral conduct; practice contrary to established rules.

MALT, *n.* [Sax. *mealt*; D. *mout*; G. *malz*; Sw. Dan. *malt.* Qu. W. *mall*, soft.]

Barley steeped in water, fermented and dried in a kiln, and thus prepared for brewing into ale or beer.

MALT, *v. t.* To make into malt; as, to *malt* barley.

MALT, *v. i.* To become malt.

To house it green will make it *malt* worse. *Mortimer.*

MALT'-DRINK, MALT'-LIQUOR, } *n.* A liquor prepared for drink by an infusion of malt; as beer, ale, porter, &c.

MALT'-DUST, *n.* The grains or remains of malt.

Malt-dust is an enricher of barren land. *Mortimer.*

MALT'-FLOOR, *n.* A floor for drying malt. *Mortimer.*

MALT'-HORSE, *n.* A horse employed in grinding malt; hence, a dull fellow. *Shak.*

MALTMAN, MALTSTER, } *n.* A man whose occupation is to make malt. *Swift.*

MALTWORM, *n.* [*malt* and *worm.*] A tippler. *Shak.*

MAL'TALENT, *n.* [Old Fr.] Ill humor. [*Not in use.*] *Chaucer.*

MAL'THA, *n.* A variety of bitumen, viscid and tenacious, like pitch; unctuous to the touch and exhaling a bituminous odor. *Cleaveland.*

MALTRE'AT, *v. t.* [*mal* and *treat.*] To treat ill; to abuse; to treat roughly, rudely, or with unkindness.

MALTRE'ATED, *pp.* Ill treated; abused.

MALTRE'ATING, *ppr.* Abusing; treating unkindly.

MALTRE'ATMENT, *n.* Ill treatment; ill usage; abuse.

MALVA'CEOUS, *a.* [L. *malvaceus,* from *malva,* mallows.] Pertaining to mallows.

MALVERSA'TION, *n.* [L. *male,* ill, and *versor,* to behave.]

Evil conduct; improper or wicked behavior; mean artifices, or fraudulent tricks. *Burke.*

MAM, MAMM'A, } *n.* [L. *mamma,* the breast or pap, and mother; W. *mam;* Arm. *mamm;* Ir. *muime,* a nurse; Antiq. Gr. *μαμμη.*]

A familiar word for mother, used by young children.

MAM'ALUKE, MAM'ELUKE, } *n.* The military force of Egypt consisted of soldiers called Mamelukes, who were originally mercenaries, but afterwards masters of the country. Their power has been recently annihilated by the present Pashaw of Egypt.

MAM'MAL, *n.* [L. *mamma,* the breast.] In *zoology,* an animal that suckles its young. [See *Mammifer.*] *Good.*

MAMMA'LIAN, *a.* Pertaining to the mammals.

MAMMAL'OGIST, *n.* One who treats of mammiferous animals.

MAMMAL'OGY, *n.* [L. *mamma,* breast, and *λογος,* discourse.]

The science or doctrine of mammiferous animals. [See *Mammifer.*]

MAM'MARY, *a.* [See *Mamma.*] Pertaining to the breasts or paps; as the *mammary* arteries and veins.

MAMMEE', *n.* A tree of the genus Mammea, of two species, both large evergreens produced in hot climates. *Encyc.*

MAM'MET, *n.* A puppet; a figure dressed.

MAM'MIFER, *n.* [L. *mamma,* the breast, and *fero,* to bear.]

An animal which has breasts for nourishing its young. The mammifers have a double system of circulation, red and warm blood; the fetus is nourished in the matrix by means of one or more placentas, and the young by milk secreted by the breasts. *Dict. Nat. Hist.*

MAMMIF'EROUS, *a.* [supra.] Having breasts and nourishing the young by the milk secreted by them.

MAM'MIFORM, *a.* [L. *mamma* and *form.*] Having the shape or form of paps.

MAM'MILLARY, *a.* [L. *mamilla.*] Pertaining to the paps; resembling a pap; an epithet applied to two small protuberances, like nipples, found under the fore ventricles of the brain, and to a process of the temporal bone.

2. In *mineralogy,* applied to minerals composed of convex concretions.

MAM'MILLATED, *a.* Having small nipples, or little globes like nipples. *Say.*

MAM'MOC, *n.* A shapeless piece. [*Not used.*] *Herbert.*

MAM'MOC, *v. t.* To tear in pieces. [*Not used.*] *Milton.*

MAM'MODIS, *n.* Coarse, plain India muslins.

MAM'MON, *n.* [Syr.] Riches; wealth; or the god of riches.

Ye cannot serve God and *mammon.* Matt. vi.

MAM'MONIST, *n.* A person devoted to the acquisition of wealth; one whose affections are placed supremely on riches; a worldling. *Hammond.*

MAM'MOTH, *n.* [Russ. *mamant,* the skeleton of a huge animal, now extinct.]

This name has been given to a huge quadruped, now extinct, whose bones are found on both continents.

MAN, *n.* plu. *men.* [Sax. *man, mann* and *mon,* mankind, man, a woman, a vassal, also one, any one, like the Fr. *on;* Goth. *manna;* Sans. *man;* D. *man,* a man, a husband; *mensch,* a human being, man, woman, person; G. *id.;* Dan. *man, menneske;* Sw. *man, meniskia;* Sax. *mennesc,* human; Ice. *mann,* a man, a husband; W. *mynw,* a person, a body, from *mwn,* that which rises up or stretches out. The primary sense is, form, image, whence species, coinciding probably with the Fr. *mine,* Eng. *mien,* Arm. *man* or *min,* look, aspect, countenance; Ch. and Heb. מין species, kind; Heb. תמונה image, similitude; Syr. [illegible], progeny. It is remarkable that in the Icelandic, this word, a little varied, is used in Gen. i. 26, 27. "Og Gud sagde, ver vilium gera mannenn, epter *mind* og liking vorre." And God said, let us make man after our *image* and likeness. "Og Gud skapade mannenn epter sinne *mind,* epter Guds *mind* skapade hann hann, og han skapade thau karlman og kvinnu." Literally, and God shaped man after his *image,* after God's *image* shaped he them, and he shaped them male and female; *karlman,* male, [See *Carle* and *Churl,*] and *kvinnu,* female, that is *queen,* woman. *Icelandic Bible. Man* in its radical sense, agrees almost precisely with *Adam,* in the Shemitic languages.]

1. Mankind; the human race; the whole species of human beings; beings distinguished from all other animals by the powers of reason and speech, as well as by their shape and dignified aspect. "Os homini sublime dedit."

And God said, Let us make *man* in our image, after our likeness, and let *them* have dominion— Gen. i.

Man that is born of a woman, is of few days and full of trouble. Job xiv.

My spirit shall not always strive with *man.* Gen. vi.

I will destroy *man* whom I have created. Gen. vi.

There hath no temptation taken you, but such as is common to *man.* 1 Cor. x.

It is written, *man* shall not live by bread alone. Matt. iv.

There must be somewhere such a rank as *man.* *Pope.*

Respecting *man,* whatever wrong we call— *Pope.*

But vindicate the ways of God to *man.* *Pope.*

The proper study of mankind is *man.* *Pope.*

In the System of Nature, *man* is ranked as a distinct genus. *Encyc.*

When opposed to *woman,* man sometimes denotes the male sex in general.

Woman has, in general, much stronger propensity than *man* to the discharge of parental duties. *Cowper.*

2. A male individual of the human race, of adult growth or years.

The king is but a *man* as I am. *Shak.*

And the *man* dreams but what the boy believed. *Dryden.*

3. A male of the human race; used often in compound words, or in the nature of an adjective; as a *man*-child; *men*-cooks; *men*-servants.

4. A servant, or an attendant of the male sex.

I and my *man* will presently go ride. *Cowley.*

5. A word of familiar address.

We speak no treason, *man.* *Shak.*

6. It sometimes bears the sense of a male adult of some uncommon qualifications; particularly, the sense of strength, vigor, bravery, virile powers, or magnanimity, as distinguished from the weakness, timidity or impotence of a boy, or from the narrow mindedness of low bred men.

I dare do all that may become a *man.* *Shak.*

Will reckons he should not have been the *man* he is, had he not broke windows— *Addison.*

So in popular language, it is said, he is no *man.* Play your part like a *man.* He has not the spirit of a *man.*

Thou art but a youth, and he a *man* of war from his youth. 1 Sam. xvii.

7. An individual of the human species.

In matters of equity between *man* and *man*— *Watts.*

Under this phraseology, females may be comprehended. So a law restraining *man,* or *every man* from a particular act, comprehends women and children, if of competent age to be the subjects of law.

8. *Man* is sometimes opposed to *boy* or *child,* and sometimes to *beast.*

9. One who is master of his mental powers, or who conducts himself with his usual judgment. When a person has lost his senses, or acts without his usual judgment, we say, he is not his own *man.* *Ainsworth.*

10. It is sometimes used indefinitely, without reference to a particular individual;

any person; one. This is as much as a *man* can desire.

A *man*, in an instant, may discover the assertion to be impossible. *More.*

This word however is always used in the singular number, referring to an individual. In this respect it does not answer to the French *on*, nor to the use of *man* by our Saxon ancestors. In Saxon, *man ofsloh*, signifies, *they slew; man sette ut, they set* or *fitted out*. So in German, *man sagt*, may be rendered, *one says, it is said, they say*, or *people say*. So in Danish, *man siger, one says, it is said, they say.*

11. In *popular usage*, a husband.

Every wife ought to answer for her *man*. *Addison.*

12. A movable piece at chess or draughts.

13. In *feudal law*, a vassal, a liege subject or tenant.

The vassal or tenant, kneeling, ungirt, uncovered and holding up his hands between those of his lord, professed that he did become his *man*, from that day forth, of life, limb, and earthly honor. *Blackstone.*

Man of war, a ship of war; an armed ship.

MAN-MIDWIFE, *n.* A man who practices obstetrics.

MAN, *v. t.* To furnish with men; as, to *man* the lines of a fort or fortress; to *man* a ship or a boat; to *man* the yards; to *man* the capstan; to *man* a prize. It is, however, generally understood to signify, to supply with the full complement or with a sufficient number of men.

2. To guard with men. *Shak.*

3. To strengthen; to fortify.

Theodosius having *manned* his soul with proper reflections— *Addison.*

4. To tame a hawk. [*Little used.*] *Shak.*

5. To furnish with attendants or servants. [*Little used.*] *Shak. B. Jonson.*

6. To point; to aim.

Man but a rush against Othello's breast,
And he retires. [*Not used.*] *Shak.*

MAN'ACLE, *n.* [Fr. *manicles*; It. *manette*; Sp. *maniota*; L. *manica*; from *manus*, the hand; W. *man.*]

An instrument of iron for fastening the hands; hand-cuffs; shackles. It is generally used in the plural, *manacles*. *Shak.*

MAN'ACLE, *v. t.* To put on hand-cuffs or other fastening for confining the hands.

2. To shackle; to confine; to restrain the use of the limbs or natural powers.

Is it thus you use this monarch, to *manacle* him hand and foot? *Arbuthnot.*

MAN'ACLED, *pp.* Hand-cuffed; shackled.

MAN'ACLING, *ppr.* Confining the hands; shackling.

MAN'AGE, *v. t.* [Fr. *menager*; *menage*, house, household, house-keeping; It. *maneggiare*; Sp. Port. *manejar*. The primary sense seems to be to *lead.*]

1. To conduct; to carry on; to direct the concerns of; as, to *manage* a farm; to *manage* the affairs of a family.

What wars I *manage*, and what wreaths I gain. *Prior.*

2. To train or govern, as a horse.

They vault from hunters to the *managed* steed. *Young.*

3. To govern; to control; to make tame or tractable; as, the buffalo is too refractory to be *managed*.

4. To wield; to move or use in the manner desired; to have under command.

Long tubes are cumbersome, and scarce to be easily *managed*. *Newton.*

5. To make subservient.

Antony *managed* him to his own views. *Middleton.*

6. To husband; to treat with caution or sparingly.

The less he had to lose, the less he car'd
To *manage* lothesome life, when love was the reward. *Dryden.*

7. To treat with caution or judgment; to govern with address.

It was much his interest to *manage* his protestant subjects. *Addison.*

MAN'AGE, *v. i.* To direct or conduct affairs; to carry on concerns or business.

Leave them to *manage* for thee. *Dryden.*

MAN'AGE, *n.* Conduct; administration; as the *manage* of the state or kingdom. *Obs.* *Shak.*

2. Government; control, as of a horse, or the exercise of riding him.

3. Discipline; governance; direction. *L'Estrange.*

4. Use; application or treatment.

Quicksilver will not endure the *manage* of the fire. *Bacon.*

[This word is nearly obsolete in all its applications, unless in reference to horses. We now use *management.*]

MAN'AGEABLE, *a.* Easy to be used or directed to its proper purpose; not difficult to be moved or wielded. Heavy cannon are not very *manageable*.

2. Governable; tractable; that may be controlled; as a *manageable* horse.

3. That may be made subservient to one's views or designs.

MAN'AGEABLENESS, *n.* The quality of being easily used, or directed to its proper purpose; as the *manageableness* of an instrument. *Boyle.*

2. Tractableness; the quality of being susceptible of government and control; easiness to be governed.

MAN'AGED, *pp.* Conducted; carried on; trained by discipline; governed; controlled; wielded.

MAN'AGEMENT, *n.* Conduct; administration; manner of treating, directing or carrying on; as the *management* of a family or of a farm; the *management* of state affairs.

2. Cunning practice; conduct directed by art, design or prudence; contrivance.

Mark with what *management* their tribes divide. *Dryden.*

3. Practice; transaction; dealing.

He had great *management* with ecclesiastics, in the view to be advanced to the pontificate. *Addison.*

4. Modulation; variation.

All directions as to the *management* of the voice, must be regarded as subsidiary to the expression of feeling. *Porter's Analysis.*

MAN'AGER, *n.* One who has the conduct or direction of any thing; as the *manager* of a theater; the *manager* of a lottery, of a ball, &c.

A skilful *manager* of the rabble. *South.*

An artful *manager*, that crept between— *Pope.*

2. A person who conducts business with economy and frugality; a good husband.

A prince of great aspiring thoughts; in the main, a *manager* of his treasure. *Temple.*

MAN'AGERY, *n.* [from *manage.*] Conduct; direction; administration. *Clarendon.*

2. Husbandry; economy; frugality. *Decay of Piety.*

3. Manner of using. *Ibm.*

[*Little used or obsolete in all its applications.*]

MAN'AGING, *ppr.* Conducting; regulating; directing; governing; wielding.

MAN'AKIN, *n.* The name of a beautiful race of birds found in warm climates. *Dict. Nat. Hist.*

MANA'TI, } *n.* The sea-cow, or fish-tailed
MANA'TUS, } walrus, an animal of the genus Trichechus, which grows to an enormous size; sometimes it is said, to the length of twenty three feet. Of this animal there are two varieties, the australis, or lamentin, and borealis, or whale-tailed manati. It has fore feet palmated, and furnished with claws, but the hind part ends in a tail like that of a fish. The skin is of a dark color, the eyes small, and instead of teeth, the mouth is furnished with hard bones, extending the whole length of the jaws. [There are eight grinders on each side in each jaw. *Cuvier.*] It never leaves the water, but frequents the mouths of rivers, feeding on grass that grows in the water. *Encyc. Dict. Nat. Hist.*

MANA'TION, *n.* [L. *manatio*, from *mano*, to flow.]

The act of issuing or flowing out. [*Little used.*]

MAN'CHET, *n.* A small loaf of fine bread. [*Not used.*] *Bacon.*

MANCHINEE'L, *n.* [L. *mancanilla.*] A tree of the genus Hippomane, growing in the West Indies to the size of a large oak. It abounds in an acrid, milky juice of a poisonous quality. It bears a fruit of the size of a pippin, which, when eaten, causes inflammation in the mouth and throat, pains in the stomach, &c. The wood is valuable for cabinet work. *Encyc.*

MAN'CIPATE, *v. t.* [L. *mancipo*, from *manceps, mancipium*; *manu capio*, to take with the hand.]

To enslave; to bind; to restrict. [*Little used.*] *Hale.*

MANCIPA'TION, *n.* Slavery; involuntary servitude. [*Little used.*] *Johnson.*

MAN'CIPLE, *n.* [L. *manceps*; *manu capio*, supra.]

A steward; an undertaker; a purveyor, particularly of a college. *Johnson.*

MANDA'MUS, *n.* [L. *mando*, to command; *mandamus*, we command. The primary sense is to send.]

In *law*, a command or writ, issuing from the king's bench in England, and in America, from some of the higher courts, directed to any person, corporation, or inferior court, requiring them to do some act therein specified, which appertains to their office and duty; as to admit or restore a person to an office or franchise, or to an academical degree, or to deliver papers, annex a seal to a paper, &c. *Blackstone.*

MANDARI'N, *n.* In *China*, a magistrate or governor of a province; also, the court language of China.

MAN'DATARY, } *n.* [Fr. *mandataire*, from
MAN'DATORY, } L. *mando*, to command.]

1. A person to whom the pope has by his prerogative given a mandate or order for his benefice. *Ayliffe.*

2. One to whom a command or charge is given.

MAN'DATE, *n.* [L. *mando*, to command.]

1. A command; an order, precept or injunction; a commission.

This dream all powerful Juno sends; I bear
Her mighty *mandates*, and her words you hear. *Dryden.*

2. In *canon law*, a rescript of the pope, commanding an ordinary collator to put the person therein named in possession of the first vacant benefice in his collation. *Encyc.*

MANDA'TOR, *n.* [L.] A director. *Ayliffe.*

MAN'DATORY, *a.* Containing a command; preceptive; directory.

MAN'DIBLE, *n.* [L. *mando*, to chew; W. *mant*, a jaw, that which shuts.]

The jaw, the instrument of chewing; *applied particularly to fowls.*

MANDIB'ULAR, *a.* Belonging to the jaw. *Gayton.*

MAN'DIL, *n.* [Fr. *mandille*, from the root of *mantle*; W. *mant.*] A sort of mantle. [*Not in use.*] *Herbert.*

MANDIL'ION, *n.* [supra.] A soldier's coat; a loose garment. *Ainsworth.*

MAN'DLESTONE, *n.* [G. *mandelstein*, almond-stone.]

Kernel-stone; almond-stone, called also amygdaloid; a name given to stones or rocks which have kernels enveloped in paste. *Dict. Nat. Hist.*

MANDMENT, for *commandment*, is not in use.

MAN'DOLIN, *n.* [It. *mandola.*] A cithern or harp. [*Not in use.*]

MAN'DRAKE, *n.* [L. *mandragoras*; It. *mandragola*; Fr. *mandragore.*]

A plant of the genus Atropa, growing naturally in Spain, Italy and the Levant. It is a narcotic, and its fresh roots are a violent cathartic. Its effect in rendering barren women prolific is supposed to be imaginary. *Encyc.*

MAN'DREL, *n.* An instrument for confining in the lathe the substance to be turned. *Moxon.*

MAN'DRILL, *n.* A species of monkey. *Dict. Nat. Hist.*

MAN'DUCABLE, *a.* That can be chewed; fit to be eaten. *Herbert.*

MAN'DUCATE, *v. t.* [L. *mando*, whence Fr. *manger.*] To chew.

MAN'DUCATED, *pp.* Chewed.

MAN'DUCATING, *ppr.* Chewing; grinding with the teeth.

MANDUCA'TION, *n.* The act of chewing or eating.

MANE, *n.* [D. *maan*, mane, and moon; G. *mähne*; Sw. *man* or *mahn*; Dan. *man*; probably from extending, like *man.*]

The hair growing on the upper side of the neck of a horse or other animal, usually hanging down on one side.

MAN'EATER, *n.* A human being that feeds on human flesh; a cannibal; an anthropophagite.

MA'NED, *a.* Having a mane.

MAN'EGE, *n.* [Fr.] A school for teaching horsemanship, and for training horses.

MANERIAL. [See *Manorial.*]

MA'NES, *n. plu.* [L.] The ghost, shade or soul of a deceased person; and among the ancient pagans, the infernal deities.

2. The remains of the dead.

Hail, O ye holy *manes!* *Dryden.*

MANEU'VER, *n.* [Fr. *manœuvre*; *main*, L. *manus*, the hand, and *œuvre*, work, L. *opera.*]

1. Management; dextrous movement, particularly in an army or navy; any evolution, movement or change of position among companies, battalions, regiments, ships, &c. for the purpose of distributing the forces in the best manner to meet the enemy.

2. Management with address or artful design.

MANEU'VER, *v. i.* To move or change positions among troops or ships, for the purpose of advantageous attack or defense; or in military exercise, for the purpose of discipline.

2. To manage with address or art.

MANEU'VER, *v. t.* To change the positions of troops or ships.

MANEU'VERED, *pp.* Moved in position.

MANEU'VERING, *ppr.* Changing the position or order for advantageous attack or defense.

MAN'FUL, *a.* [*man* and *full.*] Having the spirit of a man; bold; brave; courageous.

2. Noble; honorable.

MAN'FULLY, *adv.* Boldly; courageously; honorably.

MAN'FULNESS, *n.* Boldness; courageousness.

MAN'GABY, *n.* A monkey with naked eyelids; the white-eyed monkey. *Dict. Nat. Hist.*

MAN'GANESE, *n.* A metal of a dusky white, or whitish gray color, very hard and difficult to fuse. It never occurs as a natural product in a metallic state. The substance usually so called is an oxyd of manganese, but not pure. *Cyc. Henry.*

MANGANE'SIAN, *a.* Pertaining to manganese; consisting of it or partaking of its qualities. *Seybert.*

MANGANE'SIATE, *n.* A compound of manganesic acid, with a base.

MANGANE'SIC, *a.* Obtained from manganese; as the *manganesic* acid. *Henry.*

[*Manganic* is ill formed.]

MANGANE'SIOUS, *a.* *Manganesious* acid is an acid with a minimum of oxygen. *Henry.*

MANG'CORN, *n.* [Sax. *mengan*, to mix, and *corn.*]

A mixture of wheat and rye, or other species of grain. [*Not used in America.*]

MANGE, *n.* [Fr. *mangeaison.*] The scab or itch in cattle, dogs and other beasts.

MANGEL-WURZEL, *n.* [G. *mangel*, want, and *wurzel*, root.]

The root of scarcity, a plant of the beet kind.

MANGER, *n.* [Fr. *mangeoire*, from *manger*, to eat, L. *mando.*]

1. A trough or box in which fodder is laid for cattle, or the place in which horses and cattle are fed.

2. In *ships of war*, a space across the deck, within the hawse-holes, separated from the after part of the deck, to prevent the water which enters the hawse-holes from running over the deck.

MANGER-BOARD, *n.* The bulk-head on a ship's deck that separates the manger from the other part of the deck. *Mar. Dict.*

MANGINESS, *n.* [from *mangy.*] Scabbiness; infection of the mange.

MAN'GLE, *v. t.* [D. *mangelen*, G. *mangeln*, to want. Qu.]

1. To cut with a dull instrument and tear, or to tear in cutting; to cut in a bungling manner; *applied chiefly to the cutting of flesh.*

And seized with fear, forgot his *mangled* meat. *Dryden.*

2. To curtail; to take by piece-meal.

MAN'GLE, *n.* [Dan. *mangle*; G. *mange*; D. *mangel*; from L. *mango.*]

1. A rolling press or calender for smoothing cloth.

2. A name of the mangrove, which see.

MAN'GLE, *v. t.* To smooth cloth with a mangle; to calender.

MAN'GLED, *pp.* Torn in cutting; smoothed with a mangle.

MAN'GLER, *n.* One who tears in cutting; one who uses a mangle.

MAN'GLING, *ppr.* Lacerating in the act of cutting; tearing.

2. Smoothing with a mangle.

MAN'GO, *n.* The fruit of the mango tree, a native of the East Indies, of the genus Mangifera. It is brought to us only when pickled. Hence *mango* is the green fruit of the tree pickled. *Encyc.*

2. A green muskmelon pickled.

MAN'GONEL, *n.* [Fr. *mangoneau.*] An engine formerly used for throwing stones and battering walls.

MAN'GONISM, *n.* The art of setting off to advantage. *Obs.*

MAN'GONIZE, *v. t.* To polish for setting off to advantage. *Obs.* *B. Jonson.*

MAN'GOSTAN, } *n.* A tree of the East
MANGOSTEE'N, } Indies, of the genus Garcinia, so called from Dr. Garcin, who described it. The tree grows to the highth of 18 feet, and bears fruit of the size of a crab apple, the pulp of which is very delicious food. *Encyc.*

MAN'GROVE, *n.* A tree of the East and West Indies, otherwise called mangle, and of the genus Rhizophora. One species, the black mangle, grows in waters on the sides of rivers. The red mangrove does not grow in water. Its wood is of a deep red color, compact and heavy. The soft part of the bark of the white mangrove is formed into ropes. *Encyc.*

2. The name of a fish. *Pennant.*

MANGY, *a.* [from *mange.*] Scabby; infected with the mange. *Shak.*

MAN'HATER, *n.* [*man* and *hate.*] One who hates mankind; a misanthrope.

MAN'HOOD, *n.* [*man* and *hood.*] The state of one who is a man, of an adult male, or one who is advanced beyond puberty, boyhood or childhood; virility.

2. Virility; as opposed to *womanhood.* *Dryden*

3. Human nature; as the *manhood* of Christ.
4. The qualities of a man; courage; bravery; resolution. [*Little used.*] *Sidney.*

MA'NIA, *n.* [L. and Gr.] Madness.

MAN'IABLE, *a.* Manageable; tractable. [*Not in use.*] *Bacon.*

MA'NIAC, *a.* [L. *maniacus.*] Mad; raving with madness; raging with disordered intellect. *Grew.*

MA'NIAC, *n.* A madman; one raving with madness. *Shenstone.*

MANI'ACAL, *a.* Affected with madness.

MANICHE'AN, *a.* Pertaining to the Manichees.

MANICHE'AN, MANICHEE', *n.* One of a sect in Persia, who maintained that there are two supreme principles, the one good, the other evil, which produce all the happiness and calamities of the world. The first principle, or *light*, they held to be the author of all good; the second, or *darkness*, the author of all evil. The founder of the sect was Manes. *Encyc.*

MAN'ICHEISM, *n.* [supra.] The doctrines taught, or system of principles maintained by the Manichees. *Encyc. Milner.*

MAN'ICHORD, MANICORD'ON, *n.* [Fr. *manichordion.*] A musical instrument in the form of a spinnet, whose strings, like those of the clarichord, are covered with little pieces of cloth to deaden and soften their sounds; whence it is called the *dumb spinnet.* *Encyc.*

MAN'ICON, *n.* A species of nightshade.

MAN'IFEST, *a.* [L. *manifestus*, Ir. *meanan*, plain, clear; *minighim*, to make smooth, to polish, to explain. Clearness may be from polishing, or from opening, expanding, extending.]

1. Plain; open; clearly visible to the eye or obvious to the understanding; apparent; not obscure or difficult to be seen or understood. From the testimony, the truth we conceive to be *manifest.*

> Thus *manifest* to sight the god appeared. *Dryden.*

> That which may be known of God is *manifest* in them. Rom. i.

2. Detected; with *of.*

> Calistho there stood *manifest of* shame. [*Unusual.*] *Dryden.*

MAN'IFEST, *n.* An invoice of a cargo of goods, imported or laden for export, to be exhibited at the custom-house by the master of the vessel, or the owner or shipper.

MAN'IFEST, MANIFEST'O, *n.* [It. *manifesto;* L. *manifestus*, manifest.] A public declaration, usually of a prince or sovereign, showing his intentions, or proclaiming his opinions and motives; as a *manifesto* declaring the purpose of a prince to begin war, and explaining his motives. [*Manifesto* only is now used.] *Addison.*

MAN'IFEST, *v. t.* [L. *manifesto.*] To reveal; to make to appear; to show plainly; to make public; to disclose to the eye or to the understanding.

> Nothing is hid, which shall not be *manifested.* Mark iv.

> He that loveth me, shall be loved of my Father, and I will love him, and will *manifest* myself to him. John iv.

> Thy life did *manifest* thou lov'dst me not. *Shak.*

2. To display; to exhibit more clearly to the view. The wisdom of God is *manifested* in the order and harmony of creation.

MANIFESTA'TION, *n.* The act of disclosing what is secret, unseen or obscure; discovery to the eye or to the understanding; the exhibition of any thing by clear evidence; display; as the *manifestation* of God's power in creation, or of his benevolence in redemption.

> The secret manner in which acts of mercy ought to be performed, requires this public *manifestation* of them at the great day. *Atterbury.*

MAN'IFESTED, *pp.* Made clear; disclosed; made apparent, obvious or evident.

MANIFEST'IBLE, *a.* That may be made evident. *Brown.*

MAN'IFESTING, *ppr.* Showing clearly; making evident; disclosing; displaying. *Bacon.*

MAN'IFESTLY, *adv.* Clearly; evidently; plainly; in a manner to be clearly seen or understood.

MAN'IFESTNESS, *n.* Clearness to the sight or mind; obviousness.

MANIFESTO. [See *Manifest.*]

MAN'IFOLD, *a.* [*many* and *fold.*] Of divers kinds; many in number; numerous; multiplied.

> O Lord, how *manifold* are thy works! Ps. civ.

> I know your *manifold* transgressions. Amos v.

2. Exhibited or appearing at divers times or in various ways; *applied to words in the singular number;* as the *manifold* wisdom of God, or his *manifold* grace. Eph. iii. 1 Pet. iv.

MAN'IFOLDED, *a.* Having many doublings or complications; as a *manifolded* shield. [*Not used.*] *Spenser.*

MAN'IFOLDLY, *adv.* In a manifold manner; in many ways. *Sidney.*

MAN'IFOLDNESS, *n.* Multiplicity. *Sherwood.*

MANIG'LIONS, *n.* In *gunnery*, two handles on the back of a piece of ordnance, after the German way of casting. *Bailey.*

MAN'IKIN, *n.* A little man. *Shak.*

MAN'IL, MANIL'LA, *n.* [Sp. *manilla*, a bracelet, from L. *manus*, Sp. *mano*, the hand.] A ring or bracelet worn by persons in Africa. *Herbert.*

MA'NIOC, MA'NIHOC, MA'NIHOT, *n.* A plant of the genus Jatropha, or Cassada plant. It has palmated leaves, with entire lobes. *Encyc.*

Manioc is an acrid plant, but from its root is extracted a pleasant nourishing substance, called *cassava.* This is obtained by grating the root, and pressing out the juice, which is an acrid and noxious poison. The substance is then dried and baked, or roasted on a plate of hot iron. *Fourcroy.*

MAN'IPLE, *n.* [L. *manipulus*, a handful. Qu. L. *manus* and the Teutonic *full.*]

1. A handful.
2. A small band of soldiers; *a word applied only to Roman troops.*
3. A fanon, or kind of ornament worn about the arm of a mass priest; or a garment worn by the Romish priests when they officiate. *Sp. Dict.*

MANIP'ULAR, *a.* Pertaining to the maniple.

MANIPULA'TION, *n.* [Fr. id.; It. *manipolazione*, from *manipolare*, to work with the hand, from L. *manipulus*, supra.] In *general*, work by hand; manual operation; as in *mining*, the manner of digging ore; in *chimistry*, the operation of preparing substances for experiments; in *pharmacy*, the preparation of drugs.

MAN'KILLER, *n.* [*man* and *kill.*] One who slays a man.

MAN'KILLING, *a.* Used to kill men. *Dryden.*

MANKIND, *n.* [*man* and *kind.* This word admits the accent either on the first or second syllable; the distinction of accent being inconsiderable.]

1. The race or species of human beings.

> The proper study of *mankind* is man. *Pope.*

2. A male, or the males of the human race.

> Thou shalt not lie with *mankind* as with womankind. Lev. xviii.

MANKIND, *a.* Resembling man in form, not woman. *Frobisher.*

MAN'LESS, *a.* [*man* and *less.*] Destitute of men; not manned; as a boat. [*Little used.*] *Bacon.*

MAN'LIKE, *a.* Having the proper qualities of a man. *Sidney.*

2. Of man's nature. *Milton.*

MAN'LINESS, *n.* [from *manly.*] The qualities of a man; dignity; bravery; boldness. *Locke.*

MAN'LING, *n.* A little man. *B. Jonson.*

MAN'LY, *a.* [*man* and *like.*] Manlike; becoming a man; firm; brave; undaunted.

> Serene and *manly*, hardened to sustain
> The load of life— *Dryden.*

2. Dignified; noble; stately.

> He moves with *manly* grace. *Dryden.*

3. Pertaining to the adult age of man; as a *manly* voice.
4. Not boyish or womanish; as a *manly* stride. *Shak.*

MAN'LY, *adv.* With courage like a man.

MAN'NA, *n.* [Ar. مَانَ mauna, to provide necessaries for one's household, to sustain, to feed them; مُونَةٌ munahon, provisions for a journey. This seems to be the true original of the word. In Irish, *mann* is wheat, bread or food. Class Mn. No. 3.]

1. A substance miraculously furnished as food for the Israelites in their journey through the wilderness of Arabia. Ex. xvi.

Josephus, Ant. B. iii. 1. considers the Hebrew word מן man, to signify *what.* In conformity with this idea, the seventy translate the passage, Ex. xvi. 15. τι εστι τουτο? what is this? which rendering seems to accord with the following words, for they knew not what it was. And in the Encyclopedia, the translators are charged with making Moses fall into a plain contradiction. Art. *Manna.* But Christ and his apostles confirm the common version: "Not as your fathers ate *manna*, and are dead." John vi. 58. Heb. ix. 4. And we have other evidence, that the present version is correct; for in the same chapter, Moses directed Aaron to "take a pot and put a homer full of *manna* therein." Now it would be strange language to say, put an homer full of *what*, or *what is it*. So also verse 35. "The children of Israel ate *manna* forty years, &c." In both verses, the Hebrew word is the same as in verse 15.

2. In *the materia medica*, the juice of a certain tree of the ash-kind, the Fraxinus ornus, or flowering ash, a native of Sicily, Calabria, and other parts of the south of Europe. It is either naturally concreted, or exsiccated and purified by art. The best manna is in oblong pieces or flakes of a whitish or pale yellow color, light, friable, and somewhat transparent. It is a mild laxative. *Encyc. Hooper.*

MAN'NER, *n.* [Fr. *maniere*; It. *maniera*; Sp. *manera*; Arm. *manyell*; D. G. *manier*; Dan. *maneer*; Sw. *maner*. This word seems to be allied to Fr. *manier*, Arm. *manea*, to handle, from Fr. *main*, Sp. It. *mano*, Port. *mam*, L. *manus*, the hand.]

1. Form; method; way of performing or executing.

Find thou the *manner*, and the means prepare. *Dryden.*

2. Custom; habitual practice.

Show them the *manner* of the king that shall reign over them. This will be the *manner* of the king. 1 Sam. viii.

Paul, as his *manner* was— Acts xvii.

3. Sort; kind.

Ye tithe mint and rue, and all *manner* of herbs. Luke xi.

They shall say all *manner* of evil against you falsely— Matt. v.

In this application, *manner* has the sense of a plural word; *all sorts* or *kinds*.

4. Certain degree or measure. It is in a *manner* done already.

The bread is in a *manner* common. 1 Sam. xxi.

This use may also be sometimes defined by *sort* or *fashion*; as we say, a thing is done after a sort or fashion, that is, not well, fully or perfectly.

Augustinus does in a *manner* confess the charge. *Baker.*

5. Mien; cast of look; mode.

Air and *manner* are more expressive than words. *Clarissa.*

6. Peculiar way or carriage; distinct mode.

It can hardly be imagined how great a difference was in the humor, disposition and *manner* of the army under Essex and that under Waller. *Clarendon.*

A man's company may be known by his *manner* of expressing himself. *Swift.*

7. Way; mode; *of things*.

The temptations of prosperity insinuate themselves after a gentle, but very powerful *manner*. *Atterbury.*

8. Way of service or worship.

The nations which thou hast removed and placed in the cities of Samaria, know not the *manner* of the god of the land— 2 Kings vii.

9. In *painting*, the particular habit of a painter in managing colors, lights and shades. *Encyc.*

MAN'NER, *v. t.* To instruct in manners. *Shak.*

MAN'NERISM, *n.* Adherence to the same manner; uniformity of manner. *Edin. Rev.*

MAN'NERIST, *n.* An artist who performs his work in one unvaried manner. *Churchill.*

MAN'NERLINESS, *n.* The quality of being civil and respectful in behavior; civility; complaisance. *Hale.*

MAN'NERLY, *a.* Decent in external deportment; civil; respectful; complaisant; not rude or vulgar.

What thou think'st meet and is most *mannerly*. *Shak.*

MAN'NERLY, *adv.* With civility; respectfully; without rudeness. *Shak.*

MAN'NERS, *n. plu.* Deportment; carriage; behavior; conduct; course of life; *in a moral sense.*

Evil communications corrupt good *manners*. 1 Cor. xv.

2. Ceremonious behavior; civility; decent and respectful deportment.

Shall we, in our applications to the great God, take that to be religion, which the common reason of mankind will not allow to be *manners*? *South.*

3. A bow or courtesy; as, make your *manners*; *a popular use of the word.*

MAN'NISH, *a.* [from *man.*] Having the appearance of a man; bold; masculine; as a *mannish* countenance.

A woman impudent and mannish grown. *Shak.*

MANOM'ETER, *n.* [Gr. μανος, rare, and μετρον, measure.]

An instrument to measure or show the alterations in the rarity or density of the air. *Encyc.*

MANOMET'RICAL, *a.* Pertaining to the manometer; made by the manometer.

MAN'OR, *n.* [Fr. *manoir*, Arm. *maner*, a country house, or gentleman's seat; W. *maenan* or *maenawr*, a manor, a district bounded by stones, from *maen*, a stone. The word in French and Armoric signifies a house, a habitation, as well as a manor; and in this sense, the word would be naturally deducible from L. *maneo*, to abide. But the etymology in Welsh is not improbably the true one.]

The land belonging to a lord or nobleman, or so much land as a lord or great personage formerly kept in his own hands for the use and subsistence of his family. In these days, a *manor* rather signifies the jurisdiction and royalty incorporeal, than the land or site; for a man may have a manor in gross, as the law terms it, that is, the right and interest of a court-baron, with the perquisites thereto belonging. *Cowel.*

MAN'OR-HOUSE, } *n.* The house belonging to a manor.
MAN'OR-SEAT, }

MANO'RIAL, } *a.* Pertaining to a manor.
MANE'RIAL, }

They have no civil liberty; their children belong not to them, but to their *manorial* lord. *Tooke.*

MAN'PLEASER, *n.* [*man* and *pleaser.*] One who pleases men, or one who takes uncommon pains to gain the favor of men. *Swift.*

MAN'QUELLER, *n.* [*man* and *quell.*] A mankiller; a manslayer; a murderer. [*Not used.*] *Carew.*

MANSE, *n. mans.* [L. *mansio*, from *maneo*, to abide.]

1. A house or habitation; particularly, a parsonage house. A *capital manse* is the manor-house or lord's court.

2. A farm.

MAN'SERVANT, *n.* A male servant.

MAN'SION, *n.* [L. *mansio*, from *maneo*, to dwell.]

1. Any place of residence; a house; a habitation.

Thy *mansion* wants thee, Adam, rise. *Milton.*

In my Father's house are many *mansions*. John xiv.

2. The house of the lord of a manor.

3. Residence; abode.

These poets near our princes sleep,
And in one grave their *mansions* keep. *Denham.*

MAN'SION, *v. i.* To dwell; to reside. *Mede.*

MAN'SIONARY, *a.* Resident; residentiary; as *mansionary* canons. *Encyc.*

MAN'SION-HOUSE, *n.* The house in which one resides; an inhabited house. *Blackstone.*

MAN'SIONRY, *n.* A place of residence. [*Not used.*] *Shak.*

MAN'SLAUGHTER, *n.* [*man* and *slaughter.* See *Slay.*]

1. In *a general sense*, the killing of a man or of men; destruction of the human species; murder. *Ascham.*

2. In *law*, the unlawful killing of a man without malice, express or implied. This may be voluntary, upon a sudden heat or excitement of anger; or involuntary, but in the commission of some unlawful act. *Manslaughter* differs from murder in not proceeding from malice prepense or deliberate, which is essential to constitute murder. It differs from homicide excusable, being done in consequence of some unlawful act, whereas excusable homicide happens in consequence of misadventure. *Blackstone.*

MAN'SLAYER, *n.* One that has slain a human being. The Israelites had cities of refuge for *manslayers*.

MAN'STEALER, *n.* One who steals and sells men.

MAN'STEALING, *n.* The act of stealing a human being.

MAN'SUETE, *a.* [L. *mansuetus.*] Tame; gentle; not wild or ferocious. [*Little used.*] *Ray.*

MAN'SUETUDE, *n.* [L. *mansuetudo.*] Tameness; mildness; gentleness. *Herbert.*

MAN'TA, *n.* [Sp. *manta*, a blanket.] A flat fish that is very troublesome to pearl-fishers. *Encyc.*

MANTEL. [See *Mantle.*]

MAN'TELET, } *n.* [dim. of *mantle.*] A small cloke worn by women. *Johnson.*
MANT'LET, }

2. In *fortification*, a kind of movable parapet or penthouse, made of planks, nailed one over another to the highth of almost six feet, cased with tin and set on wheels. In a siege, this is driven before pioneers, to protect them from the enemy's small shot. *Harris.*

MANT'IGER, rather *mantichor*, or *manticor*, *n.* [L. *manticora*, *mantichora*, Gr. μαντιχωρας.]

A large monkey or baboon. *Arbuthnot.*

MAN'TLE, *n.* [Sax. *mæntel*, *mentel*; It. Sp. *manto*; G. D. *mantel*; W. *mantell*. Qu. Gr. μανδυς, μανδυας, a cloke, from the Persic. In W. *mant* is that which shuts.]

1. A kind of cloke or loose garment to be worn over other garments.

The herald and children are clothed with *mantles* of satin. *Bacon.*

2. A cover.

Well covered with the night's black *mantle.* *Shak.*

3. A cover; that which conceals; as the *mantle* of charity.

MAN'TLE, *v. t.* To cloke; to cover; to disguise.

So the rising senses
Begin to chase th' ignorant fumes, that *mantle*
Their clearer reason. *Shak.*

MAN'TLE, *v. i.* To expand; to spread.

The swan with arched neck
Between her white wings *mantling*, rows
Her state with oary feet. *Milton.*

2. To joy; to revel. *Johnson.*

My frail fancy, fed with full delights,
Doth bathe in bliss, and *mantleth* most at ease. *Spenser.*

[Qu. is not the sense to be covered or wrapped, to rest collected and secure?]

3. To be expanded; to be spread or extended.

He gave the *mantling* vine to grow,
A trophy to his love. *Fenton.*

4. To gather over and form a cover; to collect on the surface, as a covering.

There is a sort of men, whose visages
Do cream and *mantle* like a standing pond. *Shak.*

And the brain dances to the *mantling* bowl. *Pope.*

5. To rush to the face and cover it with a crimson color.

When *mantling* blood
Flow'd in his lovely cheeks. *Smith.*

[Fermentation cannot be deduced from *mantling*, otherwise than as a secondary sense.]

MAN'TLE, MAN'TLE-TREE, } *n.* The piece of timber or stone in front of a chimney, over the fire-place, resting on the jambs. *Encyc.*

[This word, according to Johnson, signifies the work over the fire-place, which we call a mantle-piece.]

MAN'TLE-PIECE, MAN'TLE-SHELF, } *n.* The work over a fire-place, in front of the chimney.

MANT'LING, *n.* In *heraldry*, the representation of a mantle, or the drapery of a coat of arms.

MAN'TO, *n.* [It.] A robe; a cloke. *Ricaut.*

MANTOL'OGY, *n.* [Gr. μαντεια, divination, and λογος, discourse.]

The act or art of divination or prophesying. [*Little used.*]

MAN'TUA, *n.* [Fr. *manteau.* See *Mantle.*] A lady's gown. *Pope.*

MAN'TUA-MAKER, *n.* One who makes gowns for ladies. *Addison.*

MAN'UAL, *a.* [L. *manualis*, from *manus*, the hand, W. *man.*]

1. Performed by the hand; as *manual* labor or operation.

2. Used or made by the hand; as a deed under the king's sign *manual.*

MAN'UAL, *n.* A small book, such as may be carried in the hand, or conveniently handled; as a *manual* of laws. *Hale.*

2. The service book of the Romish church. *Stillingfleet.*

Manual exercise, in the military art, the exercise by which soldiers are taught the use of their muskets and other arms.

MAN'UARY, *a.* Done by the hand. [*Not used.*] *Fotherby.*

MANU'BIAL, *a.* [L. *manubialis*, from *manubiæ*, spoils.]

Belonging to spoils; taken in war. [*Little used.*]

MANUDUC'TION, *n.* [L. *manus*, hand, and *ductio*, a leading.] Guidance by the hand. *Glanville. South.*

MANUDUC'TOR, *n.* [L. *manus*, hand, and *ductor*, a leader.]

An officer in the ancient church, who gave the signal for the choir to sing, who beat time and regulated the music. *Encyc.*

MANUFAC'TORY, *n.* [See *Manufacture.*] A house or place where goods are manufactured.

MANUFAC'TURAL, *a.* Pertaining or relating to manufactures.

MANUFAC'TURE, *n.* [Fr. from L. *manus*, hand, and *facio*, to make.]

1. The operation of making cloth, wares, utensils, paper, books, and whatever is used by man; the operation of reducing raw materials of any kind into a form suitable for use, by the hands, by art or machinery.

2. Any thing made from raw materials by the hand, by machinery, or by art; as cloths, iron utensils, shoes, cabinet work, sadlery, and the like.

MANUFAC'TURE, *v. t.* To make or fabricate from raw materials, by the hand, by art or machinery, and work into forms convenient for use; as, to *manufacture* cloth, nails, or glass.

2. To work raw materials into suitable forms for use; as, to *manufacture* wool, cotton, silk or iron.

MANUFAC'TURE, *v. i.* To be occupied in manufactures. *Boswell.*

MANUFAC'TURED, *pp.* Made from raw materials into forms for use.

MANUFAC'TURER, *n.* One who works raw materials into wares suitable for use.

2. One who employs workmen for manufacturing; the owner of a manufactory.

MANUFAC'TURING, *ppr.* Making goods and wares from raw materials.

MANUMISE, for *manumit*, not used.

MANUMIS'SION, *n.* [L. *manumissio.* See *Manumit.*]

The act of liberating a slave from bondage, and giving him freedom. *Arbuthnot.*

MAN'UMIT, *v. t.* [L. *manumitto*; *manus*, hand, and *mitto*, to send.]

To release from slavery; to liberate from personal bondage or servitude; to free, as a slave. *Dryden.*

MAN'UMITTED, *pp.* Released from slavery.

MAN'UMITTING, *ppr.* Liberating from personal bondage.

MANU'RABLE, *a.* [from *manure.*] That may be cultivated. This, though the original sense, is rarely or never used. The present sense of *manure*, would give the following signification.

2. That may be manured, or enriched by manure.

MANU'RAGE, *n.* Cultivation. [*Not used.*] *Warner.*

MANU'RANCE, *n.* Cultivation. [*Not used.*] *Spenser.*

MANU'RE, *v. t.* [Fr. *manœuvrer*, but in a different sense; Norm. *mainoverer*, to manure; *main*, L. *manus*, hand, and *ouvrer*, to work, L. *operor.*]

1. To cultivate by manual labor; to till. [*In this sense not now used.*] *Milton.*

2. To apply to land any fertilizing matter, as dung, compost, ashes, lime, fish, or any vegetable or animal substance.

3. To fertilize; to enrich with nutritive substances.

The corps of half her senate
Manure the fields of Thessaly. *Addison.*

MANU'RE, *n.* Any matter which fertilizes land, as the contents of stables and barnyards, marl, ashes, fish, salt, and every kind of animal and vegetable substance applied to land, or capable of furnishing nutriment to plants.

MANU'RED, *pp.* Dressed or overspread with a fertilizing substance.

MANU'REMENT, *n.* Cultivation; improvement. [*Little used.*] *Warton.*

MANU'RER, *n.* One that manures lands.

MANU'RING, *ppr.* Dressing or overspreading land with manure; fertilizing.

MANU'RING, *n.* A dressing or spread of manure on land. *Mitford.*

MAN'USCRIPT, *n.* [L. *manu scriptum*, written with the hand; It. *manuscritto*; Fr. *manuscrit.*]

A book or paper written with the hand or pen.

MAN'USCRIPT, *a.* Written with the hand; not printed.

MANUTEN'ENCY, *n.* Maintenance. [*Not in use.*] *Sancroft.*

MANY, *a.* *men'ny.* [Sax. *mæneg*, *maneg*, or *menig*; D. *menig*; G. *mancher*; Dan. *mange*; Sw. *månge*; Sax. *menigeo*, a multitude; Goth. *managa*, many; *managei*, a multitude; Russ. *mnogei*, many; *mnoju*, to multiply. It has no variation to express degrees of comparison; *more* and *most*, which are used for the comparative and superlative degrees, are from a different root.]

1. Numerous; comprising a great number of individuals.

Thou shalt be a father of *many* nations. Gen. xvii.

Not *many* wise men after the flesh, not *many* mighty, not *many* noble, are called. 1 Cor. i.

Many are the afflictions of the righteous. Ps. xxxiv.

It is often preceded by *as* or *so*, and followed by *so*, indicating an equal number. *As many* books as you take, *so many* shall be charged to your account.

So many laws argue *so many* sins. *Milton.*

It is also followed by *as.*

As *many as* were willing-hearted brought bracelets. Ex. xxxiv.

It precedes *an* or *a*, before a noun in the singular number.

Full *many a* gem of purest ray serene. *Gray.*

2. In *low language*, preceded by *too*, it denotes powerful or much; as, they are *too many* for us. *L'Estrange.*

MANY, *n.* *men'ny.* A multitude; a great number of individuals; the people.

O thou fond *many.* *Shak.*

The vulgar and the *many* are fit only to be led or driven. *South.*

MANY, *n.* *men'ny.* [Norm. Fr. *meignee.*] A retinue of servants; household. *Obs.* *Chaucer.*

MANY-CLEFT', *a.* Multifid; having many fissures. *Martyn.*

MANY-COL'ORED, *a.* Having many colors or hues. *Pope.*

MANY-COR'NERED, *a.* Having many corners, or more than twelve; polygonal. *Dryden.*

MANY-FLOW'ERED, *a.* Having many flowers. *Martyn.*

MANY-HEAD'ED, *a.* Having many heads; as a *many-headed* monster; *many-headed* tyranny. *Dryden.*

MANY-LAN'GUAGED, *a.* Having many languages. *Pope.*

MANY-LE'AVED, *a.* Polyphyllous; having many leaves. *Martyn.*

MANY-M'ASTERED, *a.* Having many masters. *J. Barlow.*

MANY-P'ARTED, *a.* Multipartite; divided into several parts; as a corol. *Martyn.*

MANY-PE'OPLED, *a.* Having a numerous population. *Sandys.*

MANY-PET'ALED, *a.* Having many petals. *Martyn.*

MANY-TWINK'LING, *a.* Variously twinkling or gleaming. *Gray.*

MANY-VALV'ED, *a.* Multivalvular; having many valves. *Martyn.*

MAP, *n.* [Sp. *mapa*; Port. *mappa*; It. *mappamonda.* Qu. L. *mappa*, a cloth or towel, a Punic word; Rabbinic מפא. Maps may have been originally drawn on cloth.]

A representation of the surface of the earth or of any part of it, drawn on paper or other material, exhibiting the lines of latitude and longitude, and the positions of countries, kingdoms, states, mountains, rivers, &c. A *map* of the earth, or of a large portion of it, comprehends a representation of land and water; but a representation of a continent or any portion of land only, is properly a *map*, and a representation of the ocean only or any portion of it, is called a *chart.* We say, a *map* of England, of France, of Europe; but a *chart* of the Atlantic, of the Pacific, &c.

MAP, *v. t.* To draw or delineate, as the figure of any portion of land. *Shak.*

MA'PLE, } *n.* A tree of the genus
MA'PLE-TREE, } Acer, of several species. Of the sap of the rock maple, sugar is made in America, in great quantities, by evaporation.

MAPLE-SU'GAR, *n.* Sugar obtained by evaporation from the juice of the rock maple.

MAP'PERY, *n.* [from *map.*] The art of planning and designing maps. *Shak.*

M'AR, *v. t.* [Sax. *merran, mirran, myrran, amyrran*, to err, to deviate, to hinder, to lose, scatter or waste, to draw from or mislead, to corrupt or deprave; Sp. *marrar*, to deviate from truth and justice; *marro*, want, defect; Ir. *mearaighim*; Gr. *αμαρτανω*, [qu. Gr. *μαραινω*, L. *marceo*;] It. *smarrire*, to miss, to lose; *smarrimento*, a wandering.]

1. To injure by cutting off a part, or by wounding and making defective; as, to *mar* a tree by incision.

> I pray you, *mar* no more trees by writing songs in their barks. *Shak.*
>
> Neither shalt thou *mar* the corners of thy beard. Lev. xix.

2. To injure; to hurt; to impair the strength or purity of.

> When brewers *mar* their malt with water. *Shak.*

3. To injure; to diminish; to interrupt.

> But mirth is *marred*, and the good cheer is lost. *Dryden.*

4. To injure; to deform; to disfigure.

> Ire, envy and despair
> *Marr'd* all his borrow'd visage. *Milton.*
>
> His visage was so *marred* more than any man. Is. lii.
>
> Moral evil alone *mars* the intellectual works of God. *Buckminster.*

[This word is not obsolete in America.]

MAR, in *nightmar.* [See *Nightmar.*]

M'AR, *n.* An injury. *Obs.*

2. A lake. [See *Mere.*]

MAR'ACAN, *n.* A species of parrot in Brazil.

MAR'ACOCK, *n.* A plant of the genus Passiflora.

MARANA'THA, *n.* [Syriac.] The Lord comes or has come; a word used by the apostle Paul in expressing a curse. This word was used in anathematizing persons for great crimes; as much as to say, "may the Lord come quickly to take vengeance on thee for thy crimes." *Calmet.*

MAR'ANON, *n.* The proper name of a river in South America, the largest in the world; most absurdly called Amazon. *Garcilasso.*

MARAS'MUS, *n.* [Gr. *μαρασμος*, from *μαραινω*, to cause to pine or waste away.]

Atrophy; a wasting of flesh without fever or apparent disease; a kind of consumption. *Coxe. Encyc.*

MARAUD', *v. i.* [Fr. *maraud*, a rascal; Eth. ወረደ marad, to hurry, to run. The Heb. מרד to rebel, may be the same word differently applied. Class Mr. No. 22. The Danish has the word in *maroder*, a robber in war, a corsair. So *corsair* is from L. *cursus, curro.*]

To rove in quest of plunder; to make an excursion for booty; to plunder.

MARAUD'ER, *n.* A rover in quest of booty or plunder; a plunderer; *usually applied to small parties of soldiers.*

MARAUD'ING, *ppr.* Roving in search of plunder.

MARAUD'ING, *n.* A roving for plunder; a plundering by invaders.

MARAVE'DI, *n.* A small copper coin of Spain, equal to three mills American money, less than a farthing sterling.

M'ARBLE, *n.* [Fr. *marbre*; Sp. *marmol*; It. *marmo*; L. *marmor*; Gr. *μαρμαρος*, white.]

1. The popular name of any species of calcarious stone or mineral, of a compact texture, and of a beautiful appearance, susceptible of a good polish. The varieties are numerous, and greatly diversified in color. Marble is limestone, or a stone which may be calcined to lime, a carbonate of lime; but limestone is a more general name, comprehending the calcarious stones of an inferior texture, as well as those which admit a fine polish. Marble is much used for statues, busts, pillars, chimney pieces, monuments, &c.

2. A little ball of marble or other stone, used by children in play.

3. A stone remarkable for some inscription or sculpture.

Arundel marbles, } marble pieces with a
Arundelian marbles, } chronicle of the city of Athens inscribed on them; presented to the university of Oxford, by Thomas, earl of Arundel. *Encyc.*

M'ARBLE, *a.* Made of marble; as a *marble* pillar.

2. Variegated in color; stained or veined like marble; as the *marble* cover of a book.

3. Hard; insensible; as a *marble* heart.

M'ARBLE, *v. t.* To variegate in color; to cloud; to stain or vein like marble; as, to *marble* the cover of a book.

M'ARBLED, *pp.* Diversified in color; veined like marble.

M'ARBLE-HE'ARTED, *a.* Having a heart like marble; hard hearted; cruel; insensible; incapable of being moved by pity, love or sympathy. *Shak.*

M'ARBLING, *ppr.* Variegating in colors; clouding or veining like marble.

M'ARBLING, *n.* The art or practice of variegating in color, in imitation of marble.

M'ARCASITE, *n.* [It. *marcassita*; Fr. *marcassite.*]

A name which has been given to all sorts of minerals, to ores, pyrites, and semi-metals. It is now obsolete. *Nicholson. Hill. Encyc.*

MARCASIT'IC, *a.* Pertaining to marcasite; of the nature of marcasite. *Encyc.*

MARCES'CENT, *a.* [L. *marcescens, marcesco.*] Withering; fading; decaying.

MARCES'SIBLE, *a.* That may wither; liable to decay.

M'ARCH, *n.* [L. *Mars*, the god of war.] The third month of the year.

M'ARCH, *v. i.* To border on; to be contiguous to. *Obs.* *Gower.*

M'ARCH, *v. i.* [Fr. *marcher*; Sp. Port. *marchar*; G. *marschiren*; It. *marciare*, to march, to putrefy, L. *marceo*, Gr. *μαραινω*; Basque, *mariatu*, to rot. The senses of the Italian word unite in that of passing, departing. See *Mar.*]

1. To move by steps and in order, as soldiers; to move in a military manner. We say, the army *marched*, or the troops *marched.*

2. To walk in a grave, deliberate or stately manner.

> Like thee, great son of Jove, like thee,
> When clad in rising majesty,
> Thou *marchest* down o'er Delos' hills. *Prior.*

M'ARCH, *v. t.* To cause to move, as an army. Buonaparte *marched* an immense army to Moscow, but he did not *march* them back to France.

2. To cause to move in order or regular procession. *Prior.*

M'ARCH, *n.* [Fr. *marche*; It. *marzo*; D. *mark*; G. *marsch.*]

1. The walk or movement of soldiers in order, whether infantry or cavalry. The troops were fatigued with a long *march.*

2. A grave, deliberate or solemn walk.

> The long majestic *march.* *Pope.*

3. A slow or laborious walk. *Addison.*

4. A signal to move; a particular beat of the drum. *Knolles.*

5. Movement; progression; advance; as the *march* of reason; the *march* of mind.

M'ARCHER, *n.* The lord or officer who defended the *marches* or borders of a territory. *Davies.*

M'ARCHES, *n. plu.* [Sax. *mearc*; Goth. *marka*; Fr. *marches*; D. *mark*; Basque, *marra.* It is radically the same word as *mark* and *march.*]

Borders; limits; confines; as lord of the *marches.* *England.*

M'ARCHING, *ppr.* Moving or walking in order or in a stately manner.

M'ARCHING, *n.* Military movement; passage of troops.

M'ARCHIONESS, *n.* The wife or widow of a marquis; or a female having the rank and dignity of a marquis. *Spelman.*

M'ARCHPANE, *n.* [Fr. *massepain*; L. *panis*, bread.]

A kind of sweet bread or biscuit. [*Not used.*] *Sidney.*

M'ARCID, *a.* [L. *marcidus*, from *marceo*, to pine.]

Pining; wasted away; lean; withered. *Dryden.*

M'ARCOR, *n.* [L.] The state of withering or wasting; leanness; waste of flesh. [*Little used.*] *Harvey.*

MARE, *n.* [Sax. *myra*; G. *mahre.*] The female of the horse, or equine genus of quadrupeds.

2. [Sax. *mara*, D. *merrie*, the name of a spirit imagined by the nations of the north of Europe to torment persons in sleep.] A kind of torpor or stagnation which seems to press the stomach in sleep; the incubus. [It is now used only in the compound, *nightmare*, which ought to be written *nightmar.*]

MAR'ECA, *n.* A species of duck in South America.

MARE'NA, *n.* A kind of fish somewhat like a pilchard.

M'ARESCHAL, *n. m'arshal.* [Fr. *marechal*; D. G. *marschalk*; Dan. *marskalk*, composed of W. *marc*, a horse, and the Teutonic *scalk* or *skalk*, *schalk*, a servant. This word is now written *marshal*, which see.] The chief commander of an army. *Prior.*

M'ARGARATE, *n.* [L. *margarita*, a pearl, from the Greek.]

In chimistry, a compound of margaric acid with a base.

MARGAR'IC, *a.* [supra.] Pertaining to pearl. The *margaric* acid is obtained by digesting soap made of hog's lard and potash, in water. It appears in the form of pearly scales. *Cyc.*

M'ARGARIN, } *n.* A peculiar pearl-like substance, extracted
M'ARGARINE, } from hog's lard; called also margarite and margaric acid. *Silliman.*

M'ARGARITE, *n.* A pearl. *Peacham.*

2. Margaric acid.

3. A mineral of a grayish white color found in Tyrol. *Phillips.*

M'ARGAY, *n.* An American animal of the cat kind.

M'ARGIN, *n.* [formerly *marge* or *margent.* Fr. *marge*; Arm. *marz*; It. *margine*; Sp. *margen*; L. *margo*; Dan. *marg.* It coincides in elements with *marches.*]

1. A border; edge; brink; verge; as the *margin* of a river or lake.

2. The edge of the leaf or page of a book, left blank or filled with notes.

3. The edge of a wound.

4. In *botany*, the edge of a leaf. *Lee.*

M'ARGIN, *v. t.* To furnish with a margin; to border.

2. To enter in the margin.

M'ARGINAL, *a.* Pertaining to a margin.

2. Written or printed in the margin; as a *marginal* note or gloss.

M'ARGINALLY, *adv.* In the margin of a book.

M'ARGINATED, *a.* Having a margin.

M'ARGODE, *n.* A bluish gray stone, resembling clay in external appearance, but so hard as to cut spars and zeolites. *Nicholson.*

M'ARGOT, *n.* A fish of the perch kind, found in the waters of Carolina. *Pennant.*

M'ARGRAVE, *n.* [D. *markgraff*; G. *markgraf*; Dan. *margraeve*; compounded of *mark*, *march*, a border, and *graff*, *graf* or *grave*, an earl or count. See *Reeve* and *Sheriff.*] Originally, a lord or keeper of the marches or borders; now a title of nobility in Germany, &c.

MARGRA'VIATE, *n.* The territory or jurisdiction of a margrave.

MAR'IETS, *n.* A kind of violet, [*violæ marianæ.*]

MARIG'ENOUS, *a.* [L. *mare*, the sea, and *gigno*, to produce.] Produced in or by the sea. *Kirwan.*

MAR'IGOLD, *n.* [It is called in Welsh *gold*, which is said to be from *gol*, going round or covering. In D. it is called *goudsbloem*, gold-flower; in G. *ringelblume*, ring-flower; in Dan. *guldblomst*, gold-flower.]

A plant of the genus Calendula, bearing a yellow flower. There are several plants of different genera bearing this name; as the African *marigold*, of the genus Tagetes; corn-*marigold*, of the genus Chrysanthemum; fig-*marigold*, of the genus Mesembryanthemum; marsh-*marigold*, of the genus Caltha.

MAR'IKIN, *n.* A species of monkey having a mane. *Dict. Nat. Hist.*

MAR'INATE, *v. t.* [Fr. *mariner*, from *marine.*]

To salt or pickle fish, and then preserve them in oil or vinegar. [*Little used.*] *Johnson.*

MARI'NE, *a.* [Fr. from L. *marinus*, from *mare*, the sea, W. *mor.* The seven lakes within the Delta Venetum were formerly called *septem maria*, and *mare* may signify a stand of water.]

1. Pertaining to the sea; as *marine* productions or bodies; *marine* shells.

2. Transacted at sea; done on the ocean; as a *marine* engagement.

3. Doing duty on the sea; as a *marine* officer; *marine* forces.

MARI'NE, *n.* A soldier that serves on board of a ship in naval engagements. In the plural, *marines*, a body of troops trained to do military service on board of ships.

2. The whole navy of a kingdom or state. *Hamilton.*

3. The whole economy of naval affairs, comprehending the building, rigging, equipping, navigating and management of ships of war in engagements.

MAR'INER, *n.* [Fr. *marinier*, from L. *mare*, the sea.]

A seaman or sailor; one whose occupation is to assist in navigating ships.

MAR'IPUT, *n.* The zoril, an animal of the skunk tribe.

MAR'ISH, *n.* [Fr. *marais*; Sax. *mersc*; D. *moeras*; G. *morast*; from L. *mare*, W. *mor*, the sea.]

Low ground, wet or covered with water and coarse grass; a fen; a bog; a moor. It is now written *marsh*, which see. *Sandys. Milton.*

MAR'ISH, *a.* Moory; fenny; boggy. *Bacon.*

MAR'ITAL, *a.* [Fr. from L. *maritus*, Fr. *mari*, a husband.] Pertaining to a husband. *Ayliffe.*

MAR'ITIME, *a.* [L. *maritimus*, from *mare*, the sea.]

1. Relating or pertaining to the sea or ocean; as *maritime* affairs.

2. Performed on the sea; naval; as *maritime* service.

3. Bordering on the sea; as a *maritime* coast.

4. Situated near the sea; as *maritime* towns.

5. Having a navy and commerce by sea; as *maritime* powers.

Maritimal is not now used.

[Note. We never say, a *maritime* body, a *maritime* shell or production, a *maritime* officer or engagement, a *maritime* league. See *Marine.*]

M'ARJORAM, *n.* [Fr. *marjolaine*; It. *maggiorana*; G. *majoran*; D. *mariolien*; Sp. *mejorana*; Arm. *marjol*; Port. *mangerona.*]

A plant of the genus Origanum, of several species. The sweet marjoram is peculiarly aromatic and fragrant, and much used in cookery. The Spanish marjoram is of the genus Urtica. *Fam. of Plants.*

M'ARK, *n.* [Sax. *marc*, *mearc*; D. *merk*; G. *marke*; Dan. *mærke*; Sw. *märke*; W. *marc*; Fr. *marque*; Arm. *mercq*; Sp. Port. It. *marca*; Sans. *marcca.* The word coincides in elements with *march*, and with *marches*, borders, the utmost extent, and with *market*, and L. *mercor*, the primary sense of which is to go, to pass; as we see by the Greek εμπορευομαι, from πορευομαι, to pass, Eng. *fair*, and *fare.* Thus in Dutch, *mark* signifies a *mark*, a boundary, and a *march.* Class Mr. No. 7. Ar.]

1. A visible line made by drawing one substance on another; as a *mark* made by chalk or charcoal, or a pen.

2. A line, groove or depression made by stamping or cutting; an incision; a channel or impression; as the *mark* of a chisel, of a stamp, of a rod or whip; the *mark* of the finger or foot.

3. Any note or sign of distinction.

The Lord set a *mark* upon Cain. Gen. 4.

4. Any visible effect of force or agency.

There are scarce any *marks* left of a subterraneous fire. *Addison.*

5. Any apparent or intelligible effect; proof, evidence.

The confusion of tongues was a *mark* of separation. *Bacon.*

6. Notice taken.

The laws
Stand like the forfeits in a barber's shop,
As much for mock as *mark.* *Shak.*

7. Any thing to which a missile weapon may be directed.

France was a fairer *mark* to shoot at than Ireland. *Davies.*

8. Any object used as a guide, or to which the mind may be directed. The dome of the State house in Boston is a good *mark* for seamen.

9. Any thing visible by which knowledge of something may be obtained; indication; as the *marks* of age in a horse. Civility is a *mark* of politeness or respect. Levity is a *mark* of weakness.

10. A character made by a person who cannot write his name, and intended as a substitute for it.
11. [Fr. *marc*, Sp. *marco*.] A weight of certain commodities, but particularly of gold and silver, used in several states of Europe; in Great Britain, a money of account, equal to thirteen shillings and four pence. In some countries, it is a coin.
12. A license of reprisals. [See *Marque*.]

M'ARK, *v. t.* [Sax. *mearcian*; D. *merken*; G. *marken*; Dan. *mærker*; Sw. *mårka*; Fr. *marquer*; Arm. *mercqa*; Port. and Sp. *marcar*; It. *marcare*; W. *marciaw*.]
1. To draw or make a visible line or character with any substance; as, to *mark* with chalk or with compasses.
2. To stamp; to impress; to make a visible impression, figure or indenture; as, to *mark* a sheep with a brand.
3. To make an incision; to lop off a part; to make any sign of distinction; as, to *mark* sheep or cattle by cuts in their ears.
4. To form a name or the initials of a name for distinction; as, to *mark* cloth; to *mark* a handkerchief.
5. To notice; to take particular observation of.

> *Mark* them who cause divisions and offenses. Rom. xvi.
>
> *Mark* the perfect man, and behold the upright, for the end of that man is peace. Ps. xxxvii.

6. To heed; to regard. *Smith.*

To mark out, to notify, as by a mark; to point out; to designate. The ringleaders were *marked out* for seizure and punishment.

M'ARK, *v. i.* To note; to observe critically; to take particular notice; to remark.

> *Mark*, I pray you, and see how this man seeketh mischief. 1 Kings xx.

M'ARKABLE, *a.* Remarkable. [*Not in use.*] *Sandys.*

M'ARKED, *pp.* Impressed with any note or figure of distinction; noted; distinguished by some character.

M'ARKER, *n.* One who puts a mark on any thing.
2. One that notes or takes notice.

M'ARKET, *n.* [D. G. *markt*; Dan. *marked*; Fr. *marché*; Arm. *marchad*; It. *mercato*; Sp. Port. *mercado*; L. *mercatus*, from *mercor*, to buy; W. *marcnat*; Ir. *margadh*. See *Mark*.]
1. A public place in a city or town, where provisions or cattle are exposed to sale; an appointed place for selling and buying at private sale, as distinguished from an auction.
2. A public building in which provisions are exposed to sale; a market-house.
3. Sale; the exchange of provisions or goods for money; purchase or rate of purchase and sale. The seller says he comes to a bad *market*, when the buyer says he comes to a good *market*. We say, the *markets* are low or high; by which we understand the price or rate of purchase. We say that commodities find a quick or ready *market*; *markets* are dull. We are not able to find a *market* for our goods or provisions.
4. Place of sale; as the British *market*; the American *market*.
5. The privilege of keeping a public market.

M'ARKET, *v. i.* To deal in market; to buy or sell; to make bargains for provisions or goods.

M'ARKET-BELL, *n.* The bell that gives notice of the time or day of market.

M'ARKET-CROSS, *n.* A cross set up where a market is held.

M'ARKET-DAY, *n.* The day of a public market.

M'ARKET-FOLKS, *n.* People that come to the market. *Shak.*

M'ARKET-HOUSE, *n.* A building for a public market.

M'ARKET-MAID, *n.* A woman that brings things to market.

M'ARKET-MAN, *n.* A man that brings things to market.

M'ARKET-PLACE, *n.* The place where provisions or goods are exposed to sale.

M'ARKET-PRICE, } *n.* The current price
M'ARKET-RATE, } of commodities at any given time.

M'ARKET-TOWN, *n.* A town that has the privilege of a stated public market.

M'ARKET-WÖMAN, *n.* A woman that brings things to market or that attends a market for selling any thing.

M'ARKETABLE, *a.* That may be sold; salable. *Shak.*
2. Current in market; as *marketable* value. *Locke. Edwards.*

M'ARKSMAN, *n.* [*Mark* and *man*.] One that is skillful to hit a mark; he that shoots well. *Shak. Dryden.*
2. One who, not able to write, makes his mark instead of his name.

M'ARL, *n.* [W. *marl*; D. Sw. Dan. G. *mergel*; L. Sp. It. *marga*; Ir. *marla*; Arm. *marg*. It seems to be allied to Sax. *merg*, *mearh*; D. *merg*, marrow, and to be named from its softness; Eth. መረገ clay, gypsum, or mortar. See *Marrow*.]
A species of calcarious earth, of different composition, being united with clay or fuller's earth. In a crude state, it effervesces with acids. It is found loose and friable, or more or less indurated. It possesses fertilizing properties and is much used for manure.
Marl is composed of carbonate of lime and clay in various proportions. *Cleaveland.*

M'ARL, *v. t.* To overspread or manure with marl.
2. To fasten with marline. *Ainsworth.*

MARLA'CEOUS, *a.* Resembling marl; partaking of the qualities of marl.

M'ARLINE, *n.* [Sp. *merlin*; Port. *merlim*.] A small line composed of two strands little twisted, and either tarred or white; used for winding round ropes and cables, to prevent their being fretted by the blocks, &c. *Mar. Dict.*

M'ARLINE, *v. t.* To wind marline round a rope.

M'ARLINE-SPIKE, *n.* A small iron like a large spike, used to open the bolt rope when the sail is to be sewed to it, &c. *Bailey.*

M'ARLING, *n.* The act of winding a small line about a rope, to prevent its being galled.

M'ARLITE, *n.* A variety of marl. *Kirwan.*

MARLIT'IC, *a.* Partaking of the qualities of marlite.

M'ARLPIT, *n.* A pit where marl is dug. *Woodward.*

M'ARLY, *a.* Consisting in or partaking of marl.
2. Resembling marl. *Mortimer.*
3. Abounding with marl.

M'ARMALADE, *n.* [Fr. *marmelade*; Sp. *mermelada*; Port. *marmelada*, from *marmelo*, a quince, L. *melo*, or Sp. *melado*, like honey, L. *mel*.]
The pulp of quinces boiled into a consistence with sugar, or a confection of plums, apricots, quinces, &c. boiled with sugar. In Scotland, it is made of Seville oranges and sugar only. *Quincy. Encyc.*

M'ARMALITE, *n.* [Gr. μαρμαιρω, to shine.] A mineral of a pearly or metallic luster; a hydrate of magnesia. *Nuttall.*

MARMORA'CEOUS, *a.* Pertaining to or like marble. [See *Marmorean*, the more legitimate word.]

M'ARMORATED, *a.* [L. *marmor*, marble.] Covered with marble. [*Little used.*]

MARMORA'TION, *n.* A covering or incrusting with marble. [*Little used.*]

MARMO'REAN, *a.* [L. *marmoreus*.] Pertaining to marble.
2. Made of marble.

M'ARMOSE, *n.* An animal resembling the opossum, but less. Instead of a bag, this animal has two longitudinal folds near the thighs, which serve to inclose the young. *Dict. Nat. Hist.*

M'ARMOSET, *n.* A small monkey. *Shak.*

M'ARMOT, *n.* [It. *marmotta*.] A quadruped of the genus Arctomys, allied to the murine tribe. It is about the size of the rabbit, and inhabits the higher region of the Alps and Pyrenees. The name is also given to other species of the genus. The woodchuck of North America is called the Maryland marmot. *Ed. Encyc.*

MAROON', *n.* A name given to free blacks living on the mountains in the West India isles.

MAROON', *v. t.* To put a sailor ashore on a desolate isle, under pretence of his having committed some great crime. *Encyc.*

M'ARQUE, } *n.* [Fr.] Letters of *marque*
M'ARK, } are letters of reprisal; a license or extraordinary commission granted by a sovereign of one state to his subjects, to make reprisals at sea on the subjects of another, under pretense of indemnification for injuries received. *Marque* is said to be from the same root as *marches*, limits, frontiers, and literally to denote a license to pass the limits of a jurisdiction on land, for the purpose of obtaining satisfaction for theft by seizing the property of the subjects of a foreign nation. I can give no better account of the origin of this word. *Lunier.*
2. The ship commissioned for making reprisals.

M'ARQUETRY, *n.* [Fr. *marqueterie*, from *marque*, *marqueter*, to spot.]
Inlaid work; work inlaid with variegations of fine wood, shells, ivory and the like.

M'ARQUIS, *n.* [Fr. id.; Sp. *marques*; It. *marchese*; from *march*, marches, limits. See *Marches*.]
A title of honor in Great Britain, next to that of duke. Originally, the marquis was an officer whose duty was to guard the

marches or frontiers of the kingdom. The office has ceased, and marquis is now a mere title conferred by patent. *Encyc.*

M'ARQUIS, *n.* A marchioness. *Obs.* *Shak.*

M'ARQUISATE, *n.* The seigniory, dignity, or lordship of a marquis.

M'ARRER, *n.* [from *mar.*] One that mars, hurts or impairs. *Ascham.*

MARRIABLE, for *marriageable.* [*Not used.*]

MAR'RIAGE, *n.* [Fr. *mariage*, from *marier*, to marry, from *mari*, a husband; L. *mas, maris;* Sp. *maridage.*]

The act of uniting a man and woman for life; wedlock; the legal union of a man and woman for life. Marriage is a contract both civil and religious, by which the parties engage to live together in mutual affection and fidelity, till death shall separate them. Marriage was instituted by God himself for the purpose of preventing the promiscuous intercourse of the sexes, for promoting domestic felicity, and for securing the maintenance and education of children.

> *Marriage* is honorable in all and the bed undefiled. Heb. xiii.

2. A feast made on the occasion of a marriage.

> The kingdom of heaven is like a certain king, who made a *marriage* for his son. Matt. xxii.

3. In *a scriptural sense*, the union between Christ and his church by the covenant of grace. Rev. xix.

MAR'RIAGEABLE, *a.* Of an age suitable for marriage; fit to be married. Young persons are *marriageable* at an earlier age in warm climates than in cold.

2. Capable of union. *Milton.*

MAR'RIAGE-ARTICLES, *n.* Contract or agreement on which a marriage is founded.

MAR'RIED, *pp.* [from *marry.*] United in wedlock.

2. *a.* Conjugal; connubial; as the *married* state.

MAR'ROW, *n.* [Sax. *merg, mearh;* D. *merg;* G. *mark;* Dan. *marv;* Sw. *mårg;* Corn. *maru;* Ir. *smir* and *smear;* W. *mêr*, marrow; Ch. מרא mera, to make fat; Ar. to be manly. See *Marl.*]

1. A soft oleaginous substance contained in the cavities of animal bones.
2. The essence; the best part.
3. In the Scottish dialect, a companion; fellow; associate; match. *Tusser.*

MAR'ROW, *v. t.* To fill with marrow or with fat; to glut.

MAR'ROW-BONE, *n.* A bone containing marrow, or boiled for its marrow. *L'Estrange.*

2. The bone of the knee; *in ludicrous language.* *Dryden.*

MAR'ROWFAT, *n.* A kind of rich pea.

MAR'ROWISH, *a.* Of the nature of marrow. *Burton.*

MAR'ROWLESS, *a.* Destitute of marrow. *Shak.*

MAR'ROWY, *a.* Full of marrow; pithy.

MAR'RY, *v. t.* [Fr. *marier*, from *mari*, a husband; L. *mas, maris*, a male; Finnish, *mari* or *mord*, id.; Ar. مرا mara, to be manly, masculine, brave; whence its derivatives, a man, L. *vir*, a husband, a lord or master. See also Ludolf, Eth. Lex. Col. 68.]

1. To unite in wedlock or matrimony; to join a man and woman for life, and constitute them man and wife according to the laws or customs of a nation. By the laws, ordained clergymen have a right to *marry* persons within certain limits prescribed.

> Tell him he shall *marry* the couple himself. *Gay.*

2. To dispose of in wedlock.

> Mecænas told Augustus he must either *marry* his daughter Julia to Agrippa, or take away his life. *Bacon.*

[*In this sense, it is properly applicable to females only.*]

3. To take for husband or wife. We say, a man *marries* a woman; or a woman *marries* a man. The first was the original sense, but both are now well authorized.
4. In *Scripture*, to unite in covenant, or in the closest connection.

> Turn, O backsliding children, saith Jehovah, for I am *married* to you. Jer. iii.

MAR'RY, *v. i.* To enter into the conjugal state; to unite as husband and wife; to take a husband or a wife.

> If the case of the man be so with his wife, it is not good to *marry*. Matt. xix.
>
> I will therefore that the younger women *marry.* I Tim. v.

MAR'RY, a term of asseveration, is said to have been derived from the practice of swearing by the virgin Mary. It is obsolete.

M'ARS, *n.* In *mythology*, the god of war; in *modern usage*, a planet; and in the *old chimistry*, a term for iron.

M'ARSH, *n.* [Sax. *mersc;* Fr. *marais;* D. *moeras;* G. *morast.* It was formerly written *marish*, directly from the French. We have *morass* from the Teutonic. See *Moor.*]

A tract of low land, usually or occasionally covered with water, or very wet and miry, and overgrown with coarse grass or with detached clumps of sedge; a fen. It differs from swamp, which is merely moist or spungy land, but often producing valuable crops of grass. Low land occasionally overflowed by the tides, is called *salt marsh.*

M'ARSH-EL'DER, *n.* The gelder rose, a species of Viburnum. *Lee.*

M'ARSH-MAL'LOW, *n.* A plant of the genus Althæa.

M'ARSH-MAR'IGOLD, *n.* A plant of the genus Caltha.

M'ARSH-ROCK'ET, *n.* A species of water cresses. *Johnson.*

M'ARSHAL, *n.* [Fr. *marechal;* D. G. *marschalk;* Dan. *marshalk;* compounded of W. *marc*, a horse, and Teut. *scealc*, or *schalk*, or *skalk*, a servant. The latter word now signifies a rogue. In Celtic, *scal* or *scalc* signified a man, boy, or servant. In Fr. *marechal*, Sp. *mariscal*, signify a marshal, and a farrier.] Originally, an officer who had the care of horses; a groom. In more modern usage,

1. The chief officer of arms, whose duty it is to regulate combats in the lists. *Johnson.*
2. One who regulates rank and order at a feast or any other assembly, directs the order of procession and the like.
3. A harbinger; a pursuivant; one who goes before a prince to declare his coming and provide entertainment. *Johnson.*
4. In France, the highest military officer. In other countries of Europe, a marshal is a military officer of high rank, and called *field-marshal.*
5. In *America*, a civil officer, appointed by the President and Senate of the United States, in each judicial district, answering to the sheriff of a county. His duty is to execute all precepts directed to him, issued under the authority of the United States.
6. An officer of any private society, appointed to regulate their ceremonies and execute their orders.

Earl marshal of England, the eighth officer of state; an honorary title, and personal, until made hereditary by Charles II, in the family of Howard. During a vacancy in the office of high constable, the earl marshal has jurisdiction in the court of chivalry. *Encyc.*

Earl marshal of Scotland. This officer formerly had command of the cavalry, under the constable. This office was held by the family of Keith, but forfeited by rebellion in 1715. *Encyc.*

Knight marshal, or *marshal of the king's house*, formerly an officer who was to execute the commands of the lord steward, and have the custody of prisoners committed by the court of verge; hence, the name of a prison in Southwark. *Encyc.*

Marshal of the king's bench, an officer who has the custody of the prison called the *king's bench*, in Southwark. He attends on the court and has the charge of the prisoners committed by them. *Encyc.*

MA'RSHAL, *v. t.* To dispose in order; to arrange in a suitable manner; as, to *marshal* an army; to *marshal* troops. *Dryden.*

2. To lead, as a harbinger. [*Not used.*] *Shak.*
3. To dispose in due order the several parts of an escutcheon, or the coats of arms of distinct families. *Encyc.*

M'ARSHALED, *pp.* Arranged in due order.

M'ARSHALER, *n.* One who disposes in due order.

M'ARSHALING, *ppr.* Arranging in due order.

M'ARSHALSEA, *n.* In *England*, the prison in Southwark, belonging to the marshal of the king's household. *Johnson.*

Court of marshalsea, a court formerly held before the steward and marshal of the king's house, to administer justice between the king's domestic servants. *Blackstone.*

M'ARSHALSHIP, *n.* The office of a marshal.

M'ARSHY, *a.* [from *marsh.*] Wet; boggy; fenny. *Dryden.*

2. Produced in marshes; as a *marshy* weed. *Dryden.*

M'ART, *n.* [from *market.*] A place of sale or traffick. It was formerly applied chiefly to markets and fairs in cities and towns, but it has now a more extensive application. We say, the United States are a principal *mart* for English goods; England and France are the *marts* of American cotton.

2. Bargain; purchase and sale. [*Not used.*] *Shak.*

M'ART, *v. t.* To buy and sell; to traffick. [*Not used.*] *Shak.*

M'ARTAGON, *n.* A kind of lily. *Herbert.*

M'ARTEL, *v. t.* [Fr. *marteler.*] To strike. *Obs.* *Obs.*

MARTEN. [See *Martin.*]

M'ARTEN, *n.* [D. *marter*; G. *marder*; Fr. *marte*; Arm. *mart*, *martr*; Sp. *marta*; It. *martora.*]

An animal of the genus Mustela, or weasel kind, whose fur is used in making hats and muffs.

M'ARTIAL, *a.* [Fr. from L. *martialis*; Sp. *marcial*; It. *marziale*; from L. *Mars*, the god of war.]

1. Pertaining to war; suited to war; as *martial* equipage; *martial* music; a *martial* appearance.

2. Warlike; brave; given to war; as a *martial* nation or people.

3. Suited to battle; as a *martial* array.

4. Belonging to war, or to an army and navy; opposed to *civil*; as *martial* law; a court *martial*.

5. Pertaining to Mars, or borrowing the properties of that planet.

> The natures of the fixed stars are esteemed *martial*, or jovial, according to the colors by which they answer to those planets. *Obs.* *Brown.*

6. Having the properties of iron, called by the old chimists, *Mars*.

M'ARTIALISM, *n.* Bravery; martial exercises. [*Not in use.*] *Prince.*

M'ARTIALIST, *n.* A warrior; a fighter. [*Not used.*] *Howel.*

M'ARTIN, *n.* [Fr. *martinet*; Sp. *martinete.* The Germans call it *mauer-schwalbe*, wall-swallow, and perhaps the word is formed from the root of L. *murus*, W. *mur*, a wall.]

A bird of the genus Hirundo, which forms its nest in buildings. It was formerly written by some authors *martlet*. *Dryden.*

M'ARTINET, } *n.* In *military language*, a
M'ARTLET, } strict disciplinarian; so called from an officer of that name.

M'ARTINETS, *n.* In *ships*, martinets are small lines fastened to the leech of a sail, to bring it close to the yard when the sail is furled. *Bailey.*

M'ARTINGAL, *n.* [Fr. *martingale*; It. Sp. *martingala.* The Portuguese call it *gamarra.*]

1. A strap or thong fastened to the girth under a horse's belly, and at the other end to the muss-roll, passing between the fore legs. *Encyc.*

2. In *ships*, a rope extending from the jib-boom, to the end of a bumpkin under the cap of the bowsprit. *Mar. Dict.*

M'ARTINMAS, *n.* [*Martin* and *mass.*] The feast of St. Martin, the eleventh of November. *Johnson.*

M'ARTLET, *n.* [See *Martin.*] Martlets, in heraldry, are little birds represented without feet, used as a mark of distinction for younger brothers of a family, who are thus admonished that they are to trust for promotion to the wings of merit. *Encyc.*

M'ARTYR, *n.* [Gr. μαρτυρ, a witness.] One who, by his death, bears witness to the truth of the gospel. Stephen was the first christian *martyr*.

> To be a *martyr* signifies only to witness the truth of Christ. *South.*

2. One who suffers death in defense of any cause. We say, a man dies a *martyr* to his political principles or to the cause of liberty.

M'ARTYR, *v. t.* To put to death for adhering to what one believes to be the truth; to sacrifice one on account of his faith or profession. *Pearson.*

2. To murder; to destroy. *Chaucer.*

M'ARTYRDOM, *n.* The death of a martyr; the suffering of death on account of one's adherence to the faith of the gospel.

> He intends to crown their innocence with the glory of *martyrdom*. *Bacon.*

M'ARTYRIZE, *v. t.* To offer as a martyr. [*Little used.*] *Spenser.*

MARTYROLOĠ'ICAL, *a.* Registering or registered in a catalogue of martyrs.

MARTYROL'OĠIST, *n.* A writer of martyrology, or an account of martyrs.

MARTYROL'OĠY, *n.* [Gr. μαρτυρ, a witness, and λογος, discourse.]

A history or account of martyrs with their sufferings; or a register of martyrs. *Stillingfleet.*

M'ARVEL, *n.* [Fr. *merveille*; Ir. *miorbhaille*; It. *maraviglia*; Sp. *maravilla*; Port. *maravilha*; Arm. *marz*; L. *mirabilis*, wonderful, from *miror*, Ch. Syr. דמר demar, to wonder, L. *demiror*. We have the primary sense in the Armoric *miret*, to stop, hold, keep, guard, hinder; for to wonder, admire or be astonished, is to stop, to hold, to be fixed, which exactly expresses the fact. The Russian *zamirayu*, to be astonished, is the same word with a prefix, and from *miryu*, to pacify or appease, that is, to stop, to allay. From the same root or family, probably, we have *moor*, to moor a ship, Sp. Port. *amarrar*, Fr. *amarrer*, to *moor*, and *demeurer*, to dwell or abide. So also L. *mora*, delay, and perhaps *morior*, W. *maru*, to die, *murus*, a wall, Eng. *demur*, &c. Class Mr. No. 32.]

1. A wonder; that which arrests the attention and causes a person to stand or gaze, or to pause. [This word is nearly obsolete, or at least little used in elegant writings.]

2. Wonder; admiration.

Marvel of Peru, a plant of the genus Mirabilis.

M'ARVEL, *v. i.* To wonder. It expresses less than *astonish* or *amaze*. [*Nearly obsolete.*]

M'ARVELING, *ppr.* Wondering.

M'ARVELOUS, *a.* [Fr. *merveilleux*; It. *marviglioso.*]

1. Wonderful; strange; exciting wonder or some degree of surprise.

> This is the Lord's doing; it is *marvelous* in our eyes. Ps. cxviii.

2. Surpassing credit; incredible. *Pope.*

3. The *marvelous*, in writings, is that which exceeds natural power, or is preternatural; opposed to *probable*. *Johnson.*

4. Formerly used adverbially for *wonderfully, exceedingly*.

M'ARVELOUSLY, *adv.* Wonderfully; strangely; in a manner to excite wonder or surprise. *Clarendon.*

M'ARVELOUSNESS, *n.* Wonderfulness; strangeness.

MA'RY-BUD, *n.* The marigold. *Shak.*

M'ASCLE, *n.* m'asl. In *heraldry*, a lozenge, as it were perforated. *Todd.*

M'ASCULINE, *a.* [Fr. *masculin*; L. *masculinus*, from *masculus*, *mas*, or the Ir. *modh*, Polish *maz*, Bohemian *muz*, Slavonic, *mosch.*]

1. Having the qualities of a man; strong; robust; as a *masculine* body.

2. Resembling man; coarse; opposed to *delicate* or *soft*; as *masculine* features.

3. Bold; brave; as a *masculine* spirit or courage.

4. In *grammar*, the *masculine* gender of words is that which expresses a male, or something analagous to it; or it is the gender appropriated to males, though not always expressing the male sex. *Encyc.* *Johnson.*

M'ASCULINELY, *adv.* Like a man. *B. Jonson.*

M'ASCULINENESS, *n.* The quality or state of being manly; resemblance of man in qualities; as in coarseness of features, strength of body, boldness, &c.

MASH, *n.* [G. *meischen*, to mix, to mash; Sp. *mascar*, to chew, Fr. *macher*, for *mascher*, L. *mastico.*]

1. A mixture or mass of ingredients, beaten or blended together in a promiscuous manner.

2. A mixture for a horse. *Far. Dict.*

3. A mesh. [See *Mesh*, the more common orthography.]

MASH, *v. t.* To beat into a confused mass.

2. To bruise; to crush by beating or pressure; as, to *mash* apples in a mill.

3. To mix malt and water together in brewing.

MASH'ED, *pp.* Beat into a mass; bruised; crushed; mixed into a mash.

MASH'ING, *ppr.* Beating into a mass; bruising; crushing.

MASH'ING-TUB, *n.* A tub for containing the mash in breweries.

MASH'Y, *a.* Produced by crushing or bruising. *Thomson.*

M'ASK, *n.* [Fr. *masque*; It. *maschera*; Sp. Port. *mascara*; Arm. *masel*; D. *masker*; G. *maske.*]

1. A cover for the face; that which conceals the face, especially a cover with apertures for the eyes and mouth; a visor. A *mask* is designed to conceal the face from beholders, or to preserve the complexion from injury by exposure to the weather and the rays of the sun. *Encyc.*

2. That which disguises; any pretense or subterfuge. *Prior.*

3. A festive entertainment of dancing or other diversions, in which the company all wear masks; a masquerade. *Shak.*

4. A revel; a bustle; a piece of mummery.

> This thought might lead through this world's vain *mask*. *Milton.*

5. A dramatic performance written in a tragic style, without attention to rules or probability. *Peacham.*

6. In *architecture*, a piece of sculpture representing some grotesque form, to fill and

adorn vacant places, as in friezes, pannels of doors, keys of arches, &c. *Encyc.*

M'ASK, *v. t.* To cover the face for concealment or defense against injury; to conceal with a mask or visor. *Addison.*

2. To disguise; to cover; to hide.

Masking the business from the common eye. *Shak.*

M'ASK, *v. i.* To revel; to play the fool in masquerade.

2. To be disguised in any way. *Shak.*

M'ASKED, *pp.* Having the face covered; concealed; disguised.

2. *a.* In *botany*, personate.

M'ASKER, *n.* One that wears a mask; one that plays the fool at a masquerade.

M'ASKERY, *n.* The dress or disguise of a masker. *Marston.*

M'ASK-HOUSE, *n.* A place for masquerades. *Bp. Hall.*

M'ASKING, *ppr.* Covering with a mask; concealing.

MASLIN. [See *Meslin.*]

MA'SON, *n. ma'sn.* [Fr. *maçon*; Arm. *maçzonn*; D. *metselaar.* In Sp. *mazoneria* is masonry, as if from *mazo*, a mallet, *maza*, a club, a *mace.* It is probably from the root of *mix* or *mash*, or more probably of *mass*, and denotes one that works in mortar. See *Mass.*]

1. A man whose occupation is to lay bricks and stones, or to construct the walls of buildings, chimneys and the like, which consist of bricks or stones.

2. A member of the fraternity of free masons.

MASON'IC, *a.* Pertaining to the craft or mysteries of free masons.

MA'SONRY, *n.* [Fr. *maçonnerie*; Sp. *mazoneria.*]

1. The art or occupation of a mason.

2. The work or performance of a mason; as when we say, the wall is good *masonry.*

3. The craft of free masons.

MAS'ORA, *n.* [Heb.] A Hebrew work on the bible, by several Rabbins.

MASORET'IC, *a.* [Heb. מסר, to deliver, whence *masora*, tradition, whence the *Masorites*, the adherents to the traditionary readings of the Scriptures.]

Relating to the Masorites, who interpreted the Scriptures by tradition, and invented the Hebrew points to fix the true reading and pronunciation. Whence the vowel-points are denominated *masoretic.*

MAS'ORITE, *n.* One of the writers of the Masora.

MASQUERA'DE, *n.* [It. *mascherata.* See *Mask.*]

1. A nocturnal assembly of persons wearing masks, and amusing themselves with dancing, conversation and other diversions.

In courtly balls and midnight *masquerades.* *Pope.*

2. Disguise.

I came to visit thee in *masquerade.* *Dryden.*

3. A Spanish diversion on horseback. *Clarendon.*

MASQUERA'DE, *v. i.* To go in disguise.

2. To assemble in masks. *Swift.*

MASQUERA'DE, *v. t.* To put in disguise. *Killingbeck.*

MASQUERA'DER, *n.* A person wearing a mask; one disguised. *L'Estrange.*

MASQUERA'DING, *ppr.* Assembling in masks for diversion.

M'ASS, *n.* [Fr. *masse*, a mass, a heap, a *mace*, or club; Port. *maça*, dough, and a *mace*; Sp. *masa*, dough, mortar, a mass, and *maza*, a club, a *mace*; *mazo*, a mallet; It. *massa*, a heap, and *mazza*, a *mace*; G. *masse*; L. *massa*, a mass. These words seem to belong to the root of the Greek μασσω, to beat or pound, the root of which is μαγ; hence the connection between *mass*, and *mace*, a club. If any of these words are of a different origin, they may belong to the root of *mix.*]

1. A lump; a body of matter concreted, collected or formed into a lump; applied to any solid body; as a *mass* of iron or lead; a *mass* of flesh; a *mass* of ice; a *mass* of dough.

2. A collective body of fluid matter. The ocean is a *mass* of water.

3. A heap; as a *mass* of earth.

4. A great quantity collected; as a *mass* of treasure.

5. Bulk; magnitude.

This army of such *mass* and charge. *Shak.*

6. An assemblage; a collection of particulars blended, confused or indistinct; as a *mass* of colors. *Addison.*

They lose their forms, and make a *mass*
Confused and black, if brought too near. *Prior.*

7. Gross body of things considered collectively; the body; the bulk; as the *mass* of people in a nation. A small portion of morbid matter may infect the whole *mass* of fluids in the body.

Comets have power over the *mass* of things. *Bacon.*

M'ASS, *n.* [Sax. *mæsa*, *mæsse*; Fr. *messe*; It. *messa*; Sp. *misa*; D. *misse*; G. Dan. *messe*; Sw. *messa*; Low L. *missa.* The word signifies primarily leisure, cessation from labor, from the L. *missus*, *remissus*, like the L. *feriæ*; hence a feast or holiday. Laws of Alfred, 39. "Be mæsse dæge freolse." *De festivitate diei festi.* See also Laws of Cnute, Lib. 1. 14. and 2. 42. Hence Sax. *hlafmæsse*, lemmas, bread-feast, and *Martin-mas*, *Michael-mas*, *candlemas*, *christmas.*]

The service of the Romish church; the office or prayers used at the celebration of the eucharist; the consecration of the bread and wine. *Lye. Encyc. Wilkins.*

M'ASS, *v. i.* To celebrate mass. [*Not used.*] *Hooker.*

M'ASS, *v. t.* To fill; to stuff; to strengthen. [*Not used.*] *Hayward.*

MAS'SACER, } *n.* [Fr. *massacre*; Arm.
MAS'SACRE, } *maçzaer*; It. *mazzicare*, to beat, from *mazza*, a club, a *mace.* So *smite* in English signifies to kill, as well as to beat.]

1. The murder of an individual, or the slaughter of numbers of human beings, with circumstances of cruelty; the indiscriminate killing of human beings, without authority or necessity, and without forms civil or military. It differs from *assassination*, which is a *private* killing. It differs from *carnage*, which is rather the effect of slaughter than slaughter itself, and is applied to the authorized destruction of men in battle. *Massacre* is sometimes called *butchery*, from its resemblance to the killing of cattle. If a soldier kills a man in battle in his own defense, it is a lawful act; it is killing, and it is slaughter, but it is not a *massacre.* Whereas, if a soldier kills an enemy after he has surrendered, it it is *massacre*, a killing without necessity, often without authority, contrary to the usages of nations, and of course with cruelty. The practice of killing prisoners, even when authorized by the commander, is properly *massacre*; as the authority given proceeds from cruelty. We have all heard of the *massacre* of the protestants in France, in the reign of Charles IX. and frequent instances of barbarous *massacre* occur in the war between the Turks and Greeks.

2. Murder. *Shak.*

MAS'SACER, } *v. t.* To murder human be-
MAS'SACRE, } ings with circumstances of cruelty; to kill men with indiscriminate violence, without authority or necessity, and contrary to the usages of nations; to butcher human beings.

MAS'SACRER, *n.* One who massacres. [*A very bad word.*] *Burke.*

M'ASSER, *n.* A priest who celebrates mass.

MAS'SETER, *n.* [Gr. from μασσαομαι, to chew.] A muscle which raises the under jaw.

MAS'SICOT, } *n.* [Fr. *massicot.*] Calcined
MAS'TICOT, } white lead; yellow oxyd of lead. Lead exposed to the air while melting, is covered with a gray, dusky pellicle. This pellicle carefully taken off, is reduced by agitation to a greenish gray powder, inclining to yellow. This oxyd, separated from the grains of lead by sifting, and exposed to a more intense heat, sufficient to make it red hot, assumes a deep yellow color. In this state it is called *massicot.* Massicot, slowly heated by a moderate fire, takes a beautiful red color, and obtains the name of minium. *Fourcroy.*

Massicot is sometimes used by painters, and it is used as a drier in the composition of ointments and plasters. *Encyc.*

M'ASSINESS, } *n.* [See *Massy*, *Mass-*
M'ASSIVENESS, } *ive.*] The state of being massy; great weight or weight with bulk; ponderousness.

M'ASSIVE, } *a.* [Fr. *massif*, from *mass.*]
M'ASSY, } Heavy; weighty; ponderous; bulky and heavy; as a *massy* shield; a *massy* rock.

The yawning rocks in *massy* fragments fly. *Pope.*

M'ASSIVE, *a.* In *mineralogy*, in mass; having a crystaline structure, but not a regular form. We say, a mineral occurs *massive.*

M'AST, *n.* [Sax. *mæst*; D. G. Sw. Dan. *mast*; Fr. *mât*, for *mast*; Port. *masto* or *mastro*; Sp. *mastiles*, masts; *masteleros*, top-masts; *masto*, a trunk, a stock in which any cion is ingrafted.]

A long, round piece of timber, elevated or designed to be raised perpendicularly or nearly so, on the keel of a ship or other vessel, to which the yards, sails and rigging are attached, and by which they are supported. A mast is a single stick, formed from the trunk of a tree, or it consists of many pieces of timber united by iron bands. Masts are of several kinds, as the main-mast, fore-mast, mizzen-mast, top-mast, top-gallant-mast, &c.

M'AST, *n.* [Sax. *mæste*, acorns, food; Goth. *mats*, food, *meat;* Ir. *mais*, *meas*, an acorn; *maise*, food; W. *mes*, acorns, a portion, a meal; *mesen*, an acorn. This may be the American *maiz*, and signify food in general, from eating, chewing, masticating, or primarily a nut kernel, or acorn, the food of the primitive tribes of men. It seems to be radically the same word as *meat.*]
The fruit of the oak and beech, or other forest trees; nuts; acorns. [*It has no plural.*]

M'ASTED, *a.* Furnished with a mast or masts.

M'ASTER, *n.* [Fr. *maitre*, for *maister;* Russ. *master;* D. *meester;* G. *meister*; Sw. *mästare;* Dan. *mester;* Arm. *meastr;* It. Sp. *maestro;* L. *magister*, compounded of the root of *magis*, *major*, greater, and the Teutonic *ster*, Sax. *steoran*, to *steer*. See *Steer*. The word then signifies a chief director. See *Minister*.]

1. A man who rules, governs or directs either men or business. A man who owns slaves is their *master;* he who has servants is their *master;* he who has apprentices is their *master*, as he has the government and direction of them. The man who superintends and directs any business, is *master*, or *master* workman.
   O thou my friend, my genius, come along,
   Thou *master* of the poet and the song. *Pope.*
   Nations that want protectors, will have *masters.* *Ames.*
2. A director, head, or chief manager; as the *master* of a feast.
3. The owner; proprietor; with the idea of governing. The *master* of a house may be the owner, or the occupant, who has a temporary right of governing it.
   It would be believed that he rather took the horse for his subject, than his *master.* *Dryden.*
4. A lord; a ruler; one who has supreme dominion.
   Cesar, the world's great *master* and his own. *Pope.*
5. A chief; a principal; as the *master* root of a plant. *Mortimer.*
   One *master* passion swallows up the rest. *Pope.*
6. One who has possession, and the power of controlling or using at pleasure.
   When I have made myself *master* of a hundred thousand drachmas— *Addison.*
7. The commander of a merchant ship.
8. In *ships of war*, an officer who takes rank immediately after the lieutenants, and navigates the ship under the direction of the captain.
9. The director of a school; a teacher; an instructor. In this sense the word is giving place to the more appropriate words teacher, instructor and preceptor; at least it is so in the United States.
10. One uncontrolled.
   Let every man be *master* of his time. *Shak.*
11. An appellation of respect.
   Master doctor, you have brought those drugs. *Shak.*
12. An appellation given to young men.
   Where there are little *masters* and misses in a house— *Swift.*
13. A man eminently or perfectly skilled in any occupation, art or science. We say, a man is *master* of his business; a great *master* of music, of the flute or violin; a *master* of his subject, &c.
14. A title of dignity in colleges and universities; as *Master* of Arts.
15. The chief of a society; as the Grand *Master* of Malta, of free-masons, &c.
16. The director of ceremonies at public places, or on public occasions.
17. The president of a college. *England.*

Master in chancery, an assistant of the lord chancellor, chosen from among the barristers to sit in chancery, or at the rolls. *Encyc.*

Master of the rolls, an officer who has charge of the rolls and patents that pass the great seal, and of the records of the chancery. *Encyc.*

To be master of one's self, to have the command or control of one's own passions.

The word *master* has numerous applications, in all of which it has the sense of director, chief or superintendent.

As a title of respect given to adult persons, it is pronounced *mister;* a pronunciation which seems to have been derived from some of the northern dialects. [supra.]

M'ASTER, *v. t.* To conquer; to overpower; to subdue; to bring under control.
   Obstinacy and willful neglect must be *mastered*, even though it costs blows. *Locke.*
   Evil customs must be *mastered* by degrees. *Calamy.*
2. To execute with skill.
   I will not offer that which I cannot *master.* *Bacon.*
3. To rule; to govern.
   —And rather father thee than *master* thee. [*Not used.*] *Shak.*

M'ASTER, *v. i.* To be skillful; to excel. *Obs.* *Spenser.*

M'ASTERDOM, *n.* Dominion; rule. [*Not used.*] *Shak.*

M'ASTERFUL, *a.* Having the skill of a master; also, imperious; arbitrary. *Obs.*

M'ASTER-HAND, *n.* The hand of a man eminently skillful. *Pope.*

M'ASTER-JEST, *n.* Principal jest. *Hudibras.*

M'ASTER-KEY, *n.* The key that opens many locks, the subordinate keys of which open only one each. *Dryden.*

M'ASTERLESS, *a.* Destitute of a master or owner. *Spenser.*
2. Ungoverned; unsubdued.

M'ASTER-LODE, *n.* In mining, the principal vein of ore. *Encyc.*

M'ASTERLY, *a.* Formed or executed with superior skill; suitable to a master; most excellent; skillful; as a *masterly* design; a *masterly* performance; a *masterly* stroke of policy.
2. Imperious.

M'ASTERLY, *adv.* With the skill of a master.
   Thou dost speak *masterly.* *Shak.*
   "I think it very *masterly* written," in Swift, is improper or unusual.

M'ASTER-PIECE, *n.* A capital performance; any thing done or made with superior or extraordinary skill.
   This wondrous *master-piece* I fain would see. *Dryden.*
2. Chief excellence or talent.
   Dissimulation was his *master-piece.* *Clarendon.*

M'ASTERSHIP, *n.* Dominion; rule; supreme power.
2. Superiority; preeminence.
   Where noble youths for *mastership* should strive. *Dryden.*
3. Chief work; master-piece. [*Not used.*] *Dryden.*
4. Superior skill. *Shak.*
5. Title of respect; in irony.
   How now, signior Launce, what new with your *mastership.* *Shak.*
6. The office of president of a college, or other institution.

M'ASTER-SINEW, *n.* A large sinew that surrounds the hough of a horse, and divides it from the bone by a hollow place, where the wind-galls are usually seated. *Far. Dict.*

M'ASTER-STRING, *n.* Principal string. *Rowe.*

M'ASTER-STROKE, *n.* Capital performance. *Blackmore.*

M'ASTER-TOOTH, *n.* A principal tooth. *Bacon.*

M'ASTER-TOUCH, *n.* Principal performance. *Tatler.*

M'ASTER-WORK, *n.* Principal performance. *Thomson.*

M'ASTER-WORT, *n.* A plant of the genus Imperatoria.

M'ASTERY, *n.* Dominion; power of governing or commanding.
   If divided by mountains, they will fight for the *mastery* of the passages of the tops— *Raleigh.*
2. Superiority in competition; preeminence.
   Every man that striveth for the *mastery*, is temperate in all things. 1 Cor. ix.
3. Victory in war.
   It is not the voice of them that shout for *mastery.* Ex. xxxii.
4. Eminent skill; superior dexterity.
   He could attain to a *mastery* in all languages. *Tillotson.*
5. Attainment of eminent skill or power.
   The learning and *mastery* of a tongue being unpleasant in itself, should not be cumbered with other difficulties. *Locke.*

M'ASTFUL, *a.* [from *mast.*] Abounding with mast, or fruit of oak, beech and other forest trees; as the *mastful* chesnut. *Dryden.*

MAS'TIC, } *n.* [Fr. *mastic;* It. *mastice;* D.
MAS'TICH, } *mastik;* Sp. *almaciga;* Port. *almecega;* Ir. *maisteog;* L. *mastiche;* Gr. *μαςιχη.*]
1. A resin exuding from the mastic-tree, a species of Pistacia, and obtained by incision. It is in white farinaceous tears, of a faint smell, and is used as an astringent and an aromatic. It is used also as an ingredient in drying varnishes. *Fourcroy. Encyc.*
2. A kind of mortar or cement. *Addison.*

MAS'TICATE, *v. t.* [L. *mastico.* Qu. W. *mesigaw*, from *mes*, mast, acorns, food.]
To chew; to grind with the teeth and prepare for swallowing and digestion; as, to *masticate* food.

MAS'TICATED, *pp.* Chewed.

MAS'TICATING, *ppr.* Chewing; breaking into small pieces with the teeth.

MASTICA'TION, *n.* The act or operation of chewing solid food, breaking it into small pieces, and mixing it with saliva; thus preparing it for deglutition, and more easy digestion in the stomach.
   Mastication is a necessary preparation of solid aliment, without which there can be no good digestion. *Arbuthnot.*

MAS'TICATORY, *a.* Chewing; adapted to perform the office of chewing food. *Lawrence's Lect.*

MAS'TICATORY, *n.* A substance to be chewed to increase the saliva. *Coxe.*

M'ASTIFF, *n.* plu. *mastiffs.* *Mastives* is irregular. [Sp. *mastin;* It. *mastino;* Fr. *matin;* Arm. *mastin;* Low L. *mastivus.*]

A large species of dog, remarkable for strength and courage. Strabo informs us that the *mastiffs* of Britain were trained for war, and used by the Gauls in battle. *Encyc.*

M'ASTLESS, *a.* Having no mast; as a vessel.

2. Bearing no mast; as a *mastless* oak or beech. *Dryden.*

MASTLIN. [See *Meslin.*]

MAS'TODON, *n.* [Gr. μαςος, mamilla, and οδους, a tooth.]

A genus of mammiferous animals resembling the elephant, now extinct, and known only by their fossil remains. It includes the N. American mammoth.

MAS'TOID, *a.* [Gr. μαστος, the nipple or breast, and ειδος, form.]

Resembling the nipple or breast; as the *mastoid* muscle; the *mastoid* process.

MASTRESS, for *mistress*, is not used. *Chaucer.*

M'ASTY, *a.* Full of mast; abounding with acorns, &c.

MAT, *n.* [W. *mat;* Sax. *meatta;* D. *mat;* G. *matte;* L. *matta;* Sp. *mata;* Ir. *matta;* Russ. *mat;* W. *math*, that is spread. The sense is probably a lay or spread, from falling, throwing, or stretching. Class Md. No. 6. 8. 9.]

1. A texture of sedge, rushes, flags, husks, straw, or other material, to be laid on a floor for cleaning the boots and shoes of those who enter a house, and for other purposes. *Carew.*

2. A web of rope-yarn, used in ships to secure the standing rigging from the friction of the yards, &c.

MAT, *v. t.* To cover or lay with mats. *Evelyn.*

2. To twist together; to interweave like a mat; to entangle.

> And o'er his eyebrows hung his *matted* hair. *Dryden.*

3. To press together; to lay flat; as *matted* grass.

MAT'ACHIN, *n.* [Sp. a buffoon, a grotesque dance.]

An old dance. *Sidney.*

MAT'ADORE, *n.* [Sp. *matador*, a murderer, and a card, from *matar*, to kill.]

One of the three principal cards in the game of omber and quadrille, which are always two black aces and the deuce in spades and clubs, and the seven in hearts and diamonds. *Johnson. Pope.*

MATCH, *n.* [Fr. *meche;* It. *miccia;* Sp. Port. *mecha;* Arm. *mechenn, mech.*]

1. Some very combustible substance used for catching fire from a spark, as hemp, flax, cotton, tow dipped in sulphur, or a species of dry wood, called vulgarly touchwood.

2. A rope or cord made of hempen tow, composed of three strands slightly twisted, and again covered with tow and boiled in the lees of old wine. This when lighted at one end, retains fire and burns slowly till consumed. It is used in firing artillery, &c. *Encyc.*

MATCH, *n.* [Sax. *maca* and *gemaca*, an equal, fellow, companion, D. *makker*, Dan. *maga*, Sw. *make.*]

1. A person who is equal to another in strength or other quality; one able to cope with another.

> Government—makes an innocent man of the lowest ranks a *match* for the mightiest of his fellow subjects. *Addison.*

2. One that suits or tallies with another; or any thing that equals another.

3. Union by marriage.

> Love doth seldom suffer itself to be confined by other *matches* than those of its own making. *Boyle.*

In popular language, it is applied to the engagement of lovers before marriage.

4. One to be married.

> She inherited a fair fortune of her own—and was looked upon as the richest *match* in the west. *Clarendon.*

MATCH, *n.* [Gr. μαχη, a battle, a fight; but probably of the same family as the preceding.]

A contest; competition for victory; or a union of parties for contest; as in games or sports.

> A solemn *match* was made; he lost the prize. *Dryden.*

MATCH, *v. t.* To equal.

> No settled senses of the world can *match*
> The pleasure of that madness. *Shak.*

2. To show an equal.

> No history or antiquity can *match* his policies and his conduct. *South.*

3. To oppose as equal; to set against as equal in contest.

> Eternal might
> To *match* with their inventions they presumed
> So easy, and of his thunder made a scorn. *Milton.*

4. To suit; to make equal; to proportion.

> Let poets *match* their subject to their strength— *Roscommon.*
> —To *match* patterns and colors. *Swift.*

5. To marry; to give in marriage.

> A senator of Rome, while Rome survived,
> Would not have *match'd* his daughter with a king. *Addison.*

6. To purify vessels by burning a match in them.

MATCH, *v. i.* To be united in marriage.

> I hold it a sin to *match* in my kindred. *Shak.*

> Let tigers *match* with hinds, and wolves with sheep. *Dryden.*

2. To suit; to correspond; to be of equal size, figure or quality; to tally. We say of a piece of cloth, it does not *match* with another.

MATCH'ABLE, *a.* Equal; suitable; fit to be joined. *Spenser.*

2. Correspondent. [*Little used.*] *Woodward.*

MATCH'ED, *pp.* Equaled; suited; placed in opposition; married.

MATCH'ING, *ppr.* Equaling; suiting; setting in opposition; uniting in marriage.

MATCH'LESS, *a.* Having no equal; as *matchless* impudence; a *matchless* queen; *matchless* love or charms.

MATCH'LESSLY, *adv.* In a manner or degree not to be equaled.

MATCH'LESSNESS, *n.* The state or quality of being without an equal.

MATCH'LOCK, *n.* Formerly, the lock of a musket which was fired by a match.

MATCH'MAKER, *n.* One who makes matches for burning.

2. One who contrives or effects a union by marriage.

MATE, *n.* [D. *maat;* Ar. مطا matau, to associate. Class Md. No. 11.]

1. A companion; an associate; one who customarily associates with another. Young persons nearly of an age, and frequently associating, are called *mates* or *playmates.*

2. A husband or wife.

3. The male or female of animals which associate for propagation and the care of their young. *Milton.*

4. One that eats at the same table.

5. One that attends the same school; a school-mate.

6. An officer in a merchant ship or ship of war, whose duty is to assist the master or commander. In a merchant ship, the mate, in the absence of the master, takes command of the ship. Large ships have a first, second, and third *mate.*

In general, *mate*, in compound words, denotes an assistant, and ranks next in subordination to the principal; as master's *mate;* surgeon's *mate*, &c.

MATE, *n.* [Sp. Port. *mate;* Fr. *mat;* from Sp. *matar*, to kill.]

In chess, the state of the king so situated that he cannot escape.

MATE, *v. t.* To match; to marry. *Spenser. Shak.*

2. To equal; to be equal to.

> For thus the mastful chesnut *mates* the skies. *Dryden.*

3. To oppose; to equal.

> —I i' th' way of loyalty and truth,
> Dare *mate* a sounder man than Surrey can be. *Shak.*

MATE, *v. t.* [Fr. *mater*, to mate in chess; Sw. *matta*, to weaken, to enervate; Sp. *matar*, to kill.]

To enervate; to subdue; to crush.

> Audacity doth almost bind and *mate* the weaker sort of minds. [*Not used.*] *Bacon.*

MA'TELESS, *a.* Having no mate or companion. *Peacham.*

Materia Medica, a general name for every substance used in medicine. *Encyc.*

2. An auxiliary branch of the science of medicine, which treats of the nature and properties of all the substances that are employed for the cure of diseases. *Ed. Encyc.*

MATE'RIAL, *a.* [It. *materiale;* Fr. *materiel;* Sp. *material;* from L. *materia*, matter.]

1. Consisting of matter; not spiritual; as *material* substance; *material* bodies.

2. Important; momentous; more or less necessary; having influence or effect.

> Hold them for catholics or heretics, it is not a thing very *material* in this question. *Hooker.*

> In the account of simple ideas, I shall set down only such as are most *material* to our present purpose. *Locke.*

So we say, a *material* point; a *material*

fault or error; a *material* fact or consideration.

3. Not formal; substantial.

4. Furnishing materials; as *material* men. *Wheaton, Rep.*

MATE'RIAL, *n.* The substance or matter of which any thing is made; as, wool is the *material* of cloth; rags are the *material* of paper.

MATE'RIALISM, *n.* The doctrine of materialists; the opinion of those who maintain that the soul of man is not a spiritual substance distinct from matter, but that it is the result or effect of the organization of matter in the body.

> The irregular fears of a future state had been supplanted by the *materialism* of Epicurus. *Buckminster.*

MATE'RIALIST, *n.* One who denies the existence of spiritual substances, and maintains that the soul of man is the result of a particular organization of matter in the body.

MATERIAL'ITY, *n.* Material existence; corporeity; not spirituality. *Digby.*

2. Importance; as the *materiality* of facts. *Judge Chase.*

MATE'RIALIZE, *v. t.* To reduce to a state of matter; also, to regard as matter. *Reid.*

MATE'RIALLY, *adv.* In the state of matter. *Boyle.*

2. Not formally; substantially.

> An ill intention may spoil an act *materially* good. *South.*

3. In an important manner or degree; essentially. It *materially* concerns us to know the real motives of our actions.

MATE'RIALNESS, *n.* The state of being material; importance.

MATE'RIATE, MATE'RIATED, *a.* [L. *materiatus.*] Consisting of matter. [*Little used.*] *Bacon.*

MATERIA'TION, *n.* The act of forming matter. [*Not used.*] *Brown.*

MATERN'AL, *a.* [L. *maternus*, from *mater*, mother.]

Motherly; pertaining to a mother; becoming a mother; as *maternal* love; *maternal* tenderness.

MATERN'ITY, *n.* [Fr. *maternité.*] The character or relation of a mother.

MAT'FELON, *n.* [Sp. Port. *matar*, D. *matsen*, to kill, and *felon.*]

A plant of the genus Centaurea, knap-weed.

MATH, *n.* [Sax. *mæth.*] A mowing; as in *aftermath.*

MATHEMAT'IC, MATHEMAT'ICAL, *a.* [L. *mathematicus.*] Pertaining to mathematics; as *mathematical* knowledge; *mathematical* instruments.

2. According to the principles of mathematics; as *mathematical* exactness.

MATHEMAT'ICALLY, *adv.* According to the laws or principles of mathematical science.

2. With mathematical certainty; demonstrably. *Bentley.*

MATHEMATI''CIAN, *n.* [Fr. *mathematicien.*] One versed in mathematics.

MATHEMAT'ICS, *n.* [L. *mathematica*, from Gr. μαθηματικη, from μανθανω, to learn; the ν is probably casual, and the root belongs to Class Md. No. 10.]

The science of quantity; the science which treats of magnitude and number, or of whatever can be measured or numbered. This science is divided into *pure* or *speculative*, which considers quantity abstractly, without relation to matter; and *mixed*, which treats of magnitude as subsisting in material bodies, and is consequently interwoven with physical considerations. It is the peculiar excellence of *mathematics*, that its principles are demonstrable. Arithmetic, geometry, algebra, trigonometry, and conic sections, are branches of *mathematics.*

MATH'EMEG, *n.* A fish of the cod kind, inhabiting Hudson's bay. *Pennant.*

MATH'ES, *n.* An herb. *Ainsworth.*

MATH'ESIS, *n.* [Gr. μαθησις.] The doctrine of mathematics. *Pope.*

MAT'IN, *a.* [Fr. *matin*, morning; G. *mette*, matins; L. *matutinus.*]

Pertaining to the morning; used in the morning; as a *matin* trumpet.

MAT'IN, *n.* Morning. [*Not used.*] *Shak.*

MAT'INS, *n.* Morning worship or service; morning prayers or songs.

> The vigils are celebrated before them, and the noctum and *matins*, for the saints whose the relics are. *Stillingfleet.*

> The winged choristers began
> To chirp their *matins.* *Cleaveland.*

2. Time of morning service; the first canonical hour in the Romish church.

MAT'RASS, *n.* [Fr. *matras*; D. *id.* In French, the word signifies an arrow; Arm. *matara*, to throw a dart. This verb coincides with L. *mitto.* It seems then to be so called from its long neck.]

A cucurbit; a chimical vessel in the shape of an egg, or with a tapering neck, open at the top, serving the purposes of digestion, evaporation, &c. *Nicholson. Quincy.*

MAT'RESS, *n.* [W. *matras*; D. *id.*; It. *materasso*; G. *matratze*; Fr. *matelas*; Arm. *matelacz*, from *mat.*]

A quilted bed; a bed stuffed with hair, moss or other soft material, and quilted.

MA'TRICE, MA'TRIX, *n.* [L. *matrix*, from *mater*, mother.]

1. The womb; the cavity in which the fetus of an animal is formed and nourished till its birth. *Encyc.*

2. A mold; the cavity in which any thing is formed, and which gives it shape; as the *matrix* of a type.

3. The place where any thing is formed or produced; as the *matrix* of metals; gang.

4. In *dyeing*, the five simple colors, black, white, blue, red and yellow, of which all the rest are composed. *Encyc.*

MAT'RICIDAL, *a.* Pertaining to matricide.

MAT'RICIDE, *n.* [L. *matricidium*; *mater*, mother, and *cædo*, to slay.]

1. The killing or murder of a mother. *Brown.*

2. The killer or murderer of his mother.

MATRIC'ULATE, *v. t.* [L. *matricula*, a roll or register, from *matrix.*]

To enter or admit to membership in a body or society, particularly in a college or university, by enrolling the name in a register. *Wotton.*

MATRIC'ULATE, *n.* One enrolled in a register, and thus admitted to membership in a society. *Arbuthnot.*

MATRICULA'TION, *n.* The act of registering a name and admitting to membership. *Ayliffe.*

MATRIMO'NIAL, *a.* [It. *matrimoniale.* See *Matrimony.*]

1. Pertaining to marriage; connubial; nuptial; hymeneal; as *matrimonial* rights or duties.

2. Derived from marriage.

> If he relied on that title, he could be but a king at curtesy, and have rather a *matrimonial*, than a regal power. *Bacon.*

MATRIMO'NIALLY, *adv.* According to the manner or laws of marriage. *Ayliffe.*

MATRIMO'NIOUS, *a.* Matrimonial. [*Little used.*] *Milton.*

MAT'RIMONY, *n.* [L. *matrimonium*, from *mater*, mother.]

Marriage; wedlock; the union of man and woman for life; the nuptial state.

> If any man know cause why this couple should not be joined in holy *matrimony*, they are to declare it. *Com. Prayer.*

MATRIX. [See *Matrice.*]

MAT'RON, *n.* [Fr. *matrone*; L. *matrona*; from *mater*, mother.]

An elderly married woman, or an elderly lady. *Johnson. Encyc.*

MAT'RONAL, *a.* [L. *matronalis.*] Pertaining to a matron; suitable to an elderly lady or to a married woman; grave; motherly. *Bacon.*

MAT'RONIZE, *v. t.* To render matronlike. *Richardson.*

MAT'RONLIKE, *a.* Having the manners of an elderly woman; grave; sedate; becoming a matron.

MAT'RONLY, *a.* Elderly; advanced in years. *L'Estrange.*

MATROSS', *n.* [D. *matroos*; Sw. Dan. Russ. *matros*, a sailor; D. *maat*, a mate; *maats*, fellows, sailors; Fr. *matelot.* In Arm. *martelot* is a colleague. The word seems to be from *mate.*]

Matrosses are soldiers in a train of artillery, who are next to the gunners and assist them in loading, firing and spunging the guns. They carry fire-locks, and march with the store waggons as guards and assistants. *Bailey. Encyc.*

MAT'TAMORE, *n.* In the east, a subterranean repository for wheat. *Parkhurst. Shaw.*

MAT'TER, *n.* [L. Sp. It. *materia*; Fr. *matiere*; Arm. *matery*; W. *mater*, what is produced, occasion, affair, *matter*; *madrez*, pus, matter; *madru*, to putrefy or dissolve. Owen deduces *mater* from *mâd*, what proceeds or advances, a good; *madu*, to cause to proceed, to render productive; *mâd*, good, beneficial, that is, advancing, progressive. Here we have a clear idea of the radical sense of *good*, which is proceeding, advancing. A *good* is that which advances or promotes; and hence we see the connection between this word *mâd*, and matter, pus, both from *progressiveness.*

The original verb is in the Ar. مدّ madda, to extend, to reach or stretch, to be tall, to thrust out, to excrete, to produce pus, to yawn; derivatives, pus, sanies, *matter.* This verb in Heb. and Ch. signifies to measure, and is the same as the L. *metior*, Gr. μετρεω. In Syriac, it signifies to escape.]

1. Substance excreted from living animal bodies; that which is thrown out or discharged in a tumor, boil or abscess; pus; purulent substance collected in an abscess, the effect of suppuration more or less perfect; as digested *matter;* sanious *matter.*

2. Body; substance extended; that which is visible or tangible; as earth, wood, stone, air, vapor, water.

3. In *a more general and philosophic sense,* the substance of which all bodies are composed; the substratum of sensible qualities, though the parts composing the substratum may not be visible or tangible. *Encyc.*

Matter is usually divided by philosophical writers into four kinds or classes; *solid, liquid, aeriform,* and *imponderable. Solid* substances are those whose parts firmly cohere and resist impression, as wood or stone; *liquids* have free motion among their parts, and easily yield to impression, as water and wine. *Aeriform* substances are elastic fluids, called vapors and gases, as air and oxygen gas. The *imponderable* substances are destitute of weight, as light, caloric, electricity, and magnetism.

4. Subject; thing treated; that about which we write or speak; that which employs thought or excites emotion; as, this is *matter* of praise, of gratitude, or of astonishment.

> Son of God, Savior of men, thy name
> Shall be the copious *matter* of my song. *Milton.*

5. The very thing supposed or intended.

> He grants the deluge to have come so very near the *matter,* that few escaped. *Tillotson.*

6. Affair; business; event; thing; course of things. *Matters* have succeeded well thus far; observe how *matters* stand; thus the *matter* rests at present; thus the *matter* ended.

> To help the *matter,* the alchimists call in many vanities from astrology. *Bacon.*

> Some young female seems to have carried *matters* so far, that she is ripe for asking advice. *Spectator.*

7. Cause of any event, as of any disturbance, of a disease, or of a difficulty. When a moving machine stops suddenly, we ask, what is the *matter?* When a person is ill, we ask, what is the *matter?* When a tumult or quarrel takes place, we ask, what is the *matter?*

8. Subject of complaint; suit; demand.

> If the *matter* should be tried by duel between two champions— *Bacon.*

> Every great *matter* they shall bring to thee, but every small *matter* they shall judge— Ex. xviii.

9. Import; consequence; importance; moment.

> A prophet some, and some a poet cry,
> No *matter* which, so neither of them lie. *Dryden.*

10. Space of time; a portion of distance.

> I have thoughts to tarry a small *matter.* *Congreve.*

> Away he goes, a *matter* of seven miles— *L'Estrange.*

[In these last senses, the use of *matter* is now vulgar.]

Upon the matter, considering the whole; taking all things into view. This phrase is now obsolete; but in lieu of it, we sometimes use, *upon the whole matter.*

> Waller, with Sir William Balfour, exceeded in horse, but were, *upon the whole matter,* equal in foot. *Clarendon.*

Matter of record, that which is recorded, or which may be proved by record.

MAT'TER, *v. i.* To be of importance; to import; used with *it, this, that,* or *what. This matters* not; *that matters* not; chiefly used in negative phrases; as, *what matters* it?

> *It matters* not how they are called, so we know who they are. *Locke.*

2. To maturate; to form pus; to collect, as matter in an abscess.

> Each slight sore *mattereth.* [*Little used.*] *Sidney.*

[We now use *maturate.*]

MAT'TER, *v. t.* To regard. [*Not used.*]

MAT'TERLESS, *a.* Void of matter. *B. Jonson.*

MAT'TERY, *a.* Purulent; generating pus; as a *mattery* cough. *Harvey.*

MAT'TOCK, *n.* [Sax. *mattuc;* W. *matog.*] A tool to grub up weeds or roots; a grubbing hoe. *Bailey.*

MATTRESS. [See *Matress,* a more correct orthography.]

MAT'URANT, *n.* [L. *maturo,* from *maturus,* mature, ripe.] In *pharmacy,* a medicine or application to a tumor, which promotes suppuration. *Encyc.*

MAT'URATE, *v. t.* [L. *maturo,* to hasten, from *maturus,* ripe.] To ripen; to hasten or promote suppuration.

MAT'URATE, *v. i.* To become ripe; to suppurate, as a tumor, and form pus.

MATURA'TION, *n.* The process of ripening or coming to maturity; ripeness. *Bacon.*

2. The process of suppurating; suppuration; the forming of pus in tumors. *Quincy.*

MAT'URATIVE, *a.* Ripening; conducing to ripeness.

2. Conducing to suppuration, or the formation of matter in a tumor or abscess.

MATU'RE, *a.* [L. *maturus;* Dan. *moed, moeden.* In W. *mêd,* is complete, perfect, mature; and *medi* signifies to reap, L. *meto.* So *ripe,* in English, seems to be connected with *reap.* In Ch. מטא signifies to come to, to reach, to be mature. See *Meet.*]

1. Ripe; perfected by time or natural growth; as a man of *mature* age. We apply it to a young man who has arrived to the age when he is supposed to be competent to manage his own concerns; to a young woman who is fit to be married; and to elderly men who have much experience.

> Their prince is a man of learning and virtue, *mature* in years— *Addison.*

> *Mature* the virgin was, of Egypt's race. *Prior.*

> How shall I meet or how accost the sage,
> Unskilled in speech, nor yet *mature* of age. *Pope.*

2. Brought to perfection; *used of plants.* The wheat is *mature.*

3. Completed; prepared; ready. The plan or scheme was *mature.*

> This lies glowing, and is *mature* for the violent breaking out. *Shak.*

4. Ripe; come to suppuration; as, the tumor is *mature.*

MATU'RE, *v. t.* [L. *maturo.*] To ripen; to hasten to a perfect state; to promote ripeness.

> Prick an apple with a pin full of holes, not deep, and smear it with sack, to see if the virtual heat of the wine will not *mature* it. *Bacon.*

2. To advance towards perfection.

> Love indulged my labors past,
> *Matures* my present, and shall bound my last. *Pope.*

MATU'RE, *v. i.* To advance toward ripeness; to become ripe or perfect. Wine *matures* by age, or by agitation in a long voyage. The judgment *matures* by age and experience.

MATU'RED, *pp.* Ripened; advanced to perfection; prepared.

MATU'RELY, *adv.* With ripeness; completely.

2. With full deliberation. A prince entering on war, ought *maturely* to consider the state of his finances.

3. Early; soon. [*A Latinism, little used.*] *Bentley.*

MATU'RING, *ppr.* Ripening; being in or coming to a complete state.

MATU'RITY, }
MATU'RENESS, } *n.* Ripeness; a state of perfection or completeness; as the *maturity* of age or of judgment; the *maturity* of corn or of grass; the *maturity* of a plan or scheme.

MAT'UTINAL, }
MAT'UTINE, } *a.* [L. *matutinus.*] Pertaining to the morning. *Herbert.*

MAT'WEED, *n.* A plant of the genus Lygeum.

MAUD'LIN, *a.* [corrupted from Magdelen, who is drawn by painters with eyes swelled and red with weeping.] Drunk; fuddled; approaching to intoxication; stupid.

> And the kind *maudlin* crowd melts in her praise. *Southern.*

MAUD'LIN, *n.* A plant of the genus Achillea.

MAU'GER, *adv.* [Fr. *malgré,* ill will; *mal* and *gré.*] In spite of; in opposition to; notwithstanding; *used only in burlesque.*

> This, *mauger* all the world, will I keep safe. *Shak.*

MAUKIN. [See *Malkin.*]

MAUL, *n.* [L. *malleus.* See *Mall.*] A heavy wooden hammer; written also *mall.*

MAUL, *v. t.* To beat and bruise with a heavy stick or cudgel; to wound in a coarse manner.

> Meek modern faith to murder, hack and *maul.* *Pope.*

MAUNCH, *n.* [Fr. *manche.*] A loose sleeve. [*Not used.*] *Herbert.*

MAUND, *n.* [Sax. and D. *mand.*] A hand-basket; *a word used in Scotland.*

MAUND, }
MAUND'ER, } *v. t.* and *i.* To mutter; to murmur; to grumble; to beg. *Obs.*

MAUND'ER, *n.* A beggar. *Obs.*

MAUND'ERER, *n.* A grumbler. *Obs.*

MAUND'ERING, *n.* Complaint. *Obs.*

MAUNDY-THURSDAY, *n.* [supposed to be from Sax. *mand,* a basket; because on that day, princes used to give alms to the poor from their baskets; or from *dies mandati,* the day of command, on which day our Savior gave his great *mandate,* that we should love one another. *Lye. Johnson.*]

The Thursday in passion week, or next before Good Friday.

MAUSOLE'AN, *a.* Pertaining to a mausoleum; monumental. *Burton.*

MAUSOLE'UM, *n.* [L.; Fr. *mausolée;* from Mausolus, king of Caria, to whom Artemisia, his widow, erected a stately monument.]

A magnificent tomb, or stately sepulchral monument.

MAU'THER, *n.* A foolish young girl. [*Not used.*] *B. Jonson.*

MA'VIS, *n.* [Fr. *mauvis.*] A bird, a species of Turdus.

MAW, *n.* [Sax. *maga;* Sw. *mage;* D. *maag;* G. *magen.*]

1. The stomach of brutes; applied to the stomach of human beings in contempt only.

2. The craw of fowls. *Arbuthnot.*

MAWK, *n.* A maggot; a slattern. [*Not in use.*]

MAWK'INGLY, *adv.* Slatternly; sluttishly. *Bp. Taylor.*

MAWK'ISH, *a.* Apt to cause satiety or lothing.

So sweetly *mawkish,* and so smoothly dull. *Pope.*

MAWK'ISHNESS, *n.* Aptness to cause lothing.

MAWK'Y, *a.* Maggoty. [*Local.*] *Grose.*

MAW'MET, *n.* [from *Mahomet.*] A puppet; anciently, an idol. *Obs.* *Wickliffe.*

MAW'METRY, *n.* The religion of Mohammed; also, idolatry. *Obs.* *Chaucer.*

MAW'MISH, *a.* [from *maw,* or *mawmet.*] Foolish; silly; idle; nauseous. *L'Estrange.*

MAW'WÖRM, *n.* A worm that infests the stomach. *Harvey.*

MAX'ILLAR, MAX'ILLARY, } *a.* [L. *maxillaris,* from *maxilla,* the jaw-bone; probably from the root of *mash.*]

Pertaining to the jaw; as the *maxillary* bones or glands.

MAX'IM, *n.* [Fr. *maxime,* It. *massima,* L. *maximum,* literally the greatest.]

1. An established principle or proposition; a principle generally received or admitted as true. It is nearly the same in popular usage, as *axiom* in philosophy and mathematics.

It is a *maxim* of state, that countries newly acquired and not settled, are matters of burden, rather than of strength. *Bacon.*

It is their *maxim,* love is love's reward. *Dryden.*

2. In *music,* the longest note formerly used, equal to two longs, or four breves. *Busby.*

MAX'IM-MÖNGER, *n.* One who deals much in maxims. *Chesterfield.*

MAX'IMUM, *n.* [L.] In *mathematics,* the greatest number or quantity attainable in any given case; opposed to *minimum.*

MAY, *n.* [L. *Maius;* Fr. *Mai;* It. *Maggio;* Sp. *Mayo.*]

1. The fifth month of the year, beginning with January, but the third, beginning with March, as was the ancient practice of the Romans.

2. [Goth. *mawi.* See *Maid.*] A young woman. *Obs.*

3. The early part of life.

His *May* of youth and bloom of lustihood. *Shak.*

MAY, *v. i.* To gather flowers in May-morning. *Sidney.*

MAY, *verb aux.*; pret. *might.* [Sax. *magan,* to be strong or able, to avail; D. *meijen* or *moogen;* G. *mögen;* Russ. *mogu.* The old pret. *mought* is obsolete, but not wholly extinct among our common people. The sense is to strain or press.]

1. To be possible. We say, a thing *may* be, or *may* not be; an event *may* happen; a thing *may* be done, if means are not wanting.

2. To have physical power; to be able.

Make the most of life you *may.* *Bourne.*

3. To have moral power; to have liberty, leave, license or permission; to be permitted; to be allowed. A man *may* do what the laws permit. He *may* do what is not against decency, propriety or good manners. We *may* not violate the laws, or the rules of good breeding. I told the servant he *might* be absent.

Thou *mayest* be no longer steward. Luke xvi.

4. It is used in prayer and petitions to express desire. O *may* we never experience the evils we dread. So also in expressions of good will. *May* you live happily, and be a blessing to your country. It was formerly used for *can,* and its radical sense is the same.

May be, it may be, are expressions equivalent to *perhaps, by chance, peradventure,* that is, it is possible to be.

MA'Y-APPLE, *n.* A plant of the genus Podophyllum.

MA'Y-BLOOM, *n.* The hawthorn.

MA'Y-BUG, *n.* A chaffer. *Ainsworth.*

MA'Y-BUSH, *n.* A plant of the genus Cratægus.

MA'Y-DAY, *n.* The first day of May.

MA'Y-DEW, *n.* The dew of May, which is said to whiten linen, and to afford by repeated distillations, a red and odoriferous spirit. It has been supposed that from the preparation of this dew, the Rosicrucians took their name. *Encyc.*

MA'Y-DUKE, *n.* A variety of the common cherry.

MA'Y-FLOWER, *n.* A plant; a flower that appears in May. *Bacon.*

MA'Y-FLY, *n.* An insect or fly that appears in May. *Walton.*

MA'Y-GAME, *n.* Sport or diversion; play, such as is used on the first of May. *Dryden.*

MA'YING, *n.* The gathering of flowers on May-day.

MA'Y-LADY, *n.* The queen or lady of May, in old May-games. *Dryden.*

MA'Y-LILY, *n.* The lily of the valley, of the genus Convallaria.

MA'Y-MORN, *n.* Freshness; vigor. *Shak.*

MA'Y-POLE, *n.* A pole to dance round in May; a long pole erected.

MA'Y-WEED, *n.* A plant of the genus Anthemis.

MAYHEM. [See *Maim.*]

MA'YOR, *n.* [Fr. *maire;* Norm. *maeur, mair, meyre;* Arm. *mear;* W. *maer,* one stationed, one that looks after or tends, one that keeps or guards, a provost, a *mayor,* a bailiff; *maer y biswal,* a land steward, the keeper of a cow-lare; *maerdrev,* a dairy hamlet; *maerdy,* a dairy-farm; *maeron,* a male-keeper or dairy-farmer; *maeres,* a female who looks after, a dairy-woman; *maeroni,* the office of a keeper, superintendency, *mayoralty;* Arm. *miret,* to keep, stop, hold, coinciding with Fr. *mirer,* L. *miror,* the primary sense of which is precisely the same as in the Armoric. See *Admirable* and *Miracle.* A *mayor,* then, was originally an overseer, and among country gentlemen, a steward, a kind of domestic bailiff; rendered in the writings of the middle ages, *villicus.* See *Spelman ad voc.* The derivation of the word from L. *major,* is undoubtedly an error.]

The chief magistrate of a city, who, in London and York, is called lord mayor. The mayor of a city, in America, is the chief judge of the city court, and is assisted, in some cases at least, by two or more aldermen. To the lord mayor of London belong several courts of judicature, as the hustings, court of requests, and court of common council.

MA'YORALTY, *n.* The office of a mayor. *Bacon.*

MA'YORESS, *n.* The wife of a mayor.

MAZ'AGAN, *n.* A variety of the common bean, [*vicia faba.*]

MAZ'ARD, *n.* [probably from the root of *marsh;* Fr. *machoire.*]

1. The jaw. [*Not used.*] *Shak. Hudibras.*

2. A kind of cherry.

MAZ'ARD, *v. t.* To knock on the head. [*Not in use.*] *B. Jonson.*

MAZARI'NE, *n.* A deep blue color.

2. A particular way of dressing fowls.

3. A little dish set in a larger one. *Ash.*

MAZE, *n.* [Sax. *mase,* a whirlpool; Arm. *mez,* confusion or shame. The origin and affinities of this word are not ascertained.]

1. A winding and turning; perplexed state of things; intricacy; a state that embarrasses.

The ways of heaven are dark and intricate,
Puzzled with *mazes,* and perplexed with error. *Addison.*

2. Confusion of thought; perplexity; uncertainty.

3. A labyrinth.

MAZE, *v. t.* To bewilder; to confound with intricacy; to amaze. *Spenser.*

MAZE, *v. i.* To be bewildered. *Obs.* *Chaucer.*

MA'ZEDNESS, *n.* Confusion; astonishment. *Obs.* *Chaucer.*

MA'ZER, *n.* A maple cup. *Obs.* *Spenser.*

MAZOLOG'ICAL, *a.* Pertaining to mazology.

MAZOL'OGIST, *n.* One versed in mazology.

MAZOL'OGY, *n.* [Gr. *μαζα,* a breast, and *λογος,* discourse.]

The doctrine or history of mammiferous animals.

MA'ZY, *a.* Winding; perplexed with turns and windings; intricate; as *mazy* error. *Milton.*

To run the ring and trace the *mazy* round. *Dryden.*

M. D. *Medicinæ Doctor,* doctor of medicine.

ME, *pron. pers.*; the objective case of *I,* answering to the oblique cases of *ego,* in Latin. [Sax. *me;* Goth. *mik;* G. *mich;* Fr. *moi;* L. *mihi;* Sp. *mi;* It. *mi* or *me;* Arm. *me;*

Port. *mim;* D. *my;* Galic, *mo;* Hindoo, *mejko;* Sans. *me.* The Hindoos use *me* in the nominative, as in Celtic and French, *mi, moi.*]

Follow *me;* give to *me;* go with *me.* The phrase "I followed *me* close," is not in use. Before *think*, as in *methinks*, *me* is properly in the dative case, and the verb is impersonal; the construction is, *it appears to me.*

ME'ACOCK, *n.* [Qu. *meek* and *cock.*] An uxorious, effeminate man. [*Not used.*] *Johnson.*

ME'ACOCK, *a.* Lame; timorous; cowardly. [*Not used.*] *Shak.*

MEAD, *n.* [Sax. *medo, medu*, mead or wine; D. *meede;* G. *meth;* Dan. *miöd;* W. *mez;* Ir. *miodh* or *meadh;* Arm. *mez.* In Gr. *μεθυ* is wine, as is *madja* in Sanscrit, and *medo* in Zend. In Russ. *med* or *meda* is honey. If the word signifies primarily liquor in general, it may be allied to Gr. *μυδαω*, L. *madeo*, to be wet. But it may have had its name from honey.]

A fermented liquor consisting of honey and water, sometimes enriched with spices. *Encyc.*

MEAD, } *n.* *meed*, **MEADOW**, } *med'o.* } [Sax. *mæde, mædewe;* G. *matte*, a mat, and a meadow; Ir. *madh.* The sense is extended or flat depressed land. It is supposed that this word enters into the name *Mediolanum*, now *Milan*, in Italy; that is, *mead-land.*]

A tract of low land. In America, the word is applied particularly to the low ground on the banks of rivers, consisting of a rich mold or an alluvial soil, whether grass land, pasture, tillage or wood land; as the *meadows* on the banks of the Connecticut. The word with us does not necessarily imply wet land. This species of land is called, in the western states, *bottoms*, or *bottom land.* The word is also used for other low or flat lands, particularly lands appropriated to the culture of grass.

The word is said to be applied in Great Britain to land somewhat watery, but covered with grass. *Johnson.*

Meadow means pasture or grass land, annually mown for hay; but more particularly, land too moist for cattle to graze on in winter, without spoiling the sward. *Encyc. Cyc.*

[*Mead* is used chiefly in poetry.]

MEAD'OW-ORE, *n.* In mineralogy, conchoidal bog iron ore. *Ure.*

MEAD'OW-RUE, *n.* A plant of the genus Thalictrum.

MEAD'OW-SAFFRON, *n.* A plant of the genus Colchicum.

MEAD'OW-SAXIFRAGE, *n.* A plant of the genus Peucedanum.

MEAD'OW-SWEET, *n.* A plant of the genus Spiræa.

MEAD'OW-WORT, *n.* A plant. *Drayton.*

MEAD'OWY, *a.* Containing meadow. *J. Barlow.*

ME'AGER, *a.* [Fr. *maigre;* Sp. It. *magro;* L. *macer;* D. G. Dan. Sw. *mager;* Gr. *μικκος, μικρος*, small; allied to Eng. *meek;* Ch. מאך, to be thin, to be depressed, to subdue; Heb. מוך id. Class Mg. No. 2. 9. and 10. 13.]

1. Thin; lean; destitute of flesh or having little flesh; *applied to animals.*

> *Meager* were his looks,
> Sharp misery had worn him to the bones. *Shak.*

2. Poor; barren; destitute of richness, fertility, or any thing valuable; as a *meager* soil; *meager* limestone. *Journ. of Science.*

3. Barren; poor; wanting strength of diction, or richness of ideas or imagery; as a *meager* style or composition; *meager* annals.

ME'AGER, *v.t.* To make lean. [*Not used.*] *Knolles.*

ME'AGERLY, *adv.* Poorly; thinly.

ME'AGERNESS, *n.* Leanness; want of flesh.

2. Poorness; barrenness; want of fertility or richness.

3. Scantiness; barrenness; as the *meagerness* of service. *Bacon.*

MEAK, *n.* A hook with a long handle. *Tusser.*

MEAL, *n.* [Sax. *mæl*, a part or portion; D. *maal;* G. *mahl;* probably from breaking. See the next word.]

1. A portion of food taken at one time; a repast. It is customary in the U. States to eat three *meals* in a day. The principal *meal* of our ancestors was dinner, at noon.

2. A part; a fragment; in the word *piecemeal.*

MEAL, *n.* [Sax. *mealewe, melewe;* G. *mehl;* Sw. *miöl;* Dan. D. *meel;* G. *mehlicht*, mealy, mellow; W. *mâl*, bruised, ground, smooth. This word seems to be allied to *mill*, L. *mola*, and to L. *mollis*, Eng. *mellow.* The radical sense is probably to break, comminute, or grind to fine particles, and hence the sense of softness; or the sense of softness may be from yielding or smoothness, and the verb may be from the noun.]

1. The substance of edible grain ground to fine particles, and not bolted or sifted. Meal primarily includes the bran as well as the flour. Since bolting has been generally practiced, the word *meal* is not generally applied to the finer part, or flour, at least in the United States, though I believe it is sometimes so used. In New England, *meal* is now usually applied to ground maiz, whether bolted or unbolted, called *Indian meal*, or *corn-meal.* The words *wheat-meal* and *rye-meal* are rarely used, though not wholly extinct; and *meal* occurs also in *oatmeal.*

2. Flour; the finer part of pulverized grain. [*This sense is now uncommon.*]

MEAL, *v. t.* To sprinkle with meal, or to mix meal with. [*Little used.*]

ME'ALINESS, *n.* The quality of being mealy; softness or smoothness to the touch.

MEA'L-MAN, *n.* A man that deals in meal.

ME'AL-TIME, *n.* The usual time of eating meals.

ME'ALY, *a.* Having the qualities of meal; soft; smooth to the feel.

2. Like meal; farinaceous; soft, dry and friable; as a *mealy* potatoe; a *mealy* apple.

3. Overspread with something that resembles meal; as the *mealy* wings of an insect. *Thomson.*

ME'ALY-MOUTHED, *a.* Literally, having a soft mouth; hence, unwilling to tell the truth in plain language; inclined to speak of any thing in softer terms than the truth will warrant. *L'Estrange.*

MEALY-MOUTH'EDNESS, *n.* Inclination to express the truth in soft words, or to disguise the plain fact; reluctance to tell the plain truth.

MEAN, *a.* [Sax. *mæne, gemæne;* the latter word signifies *common*, L. *communis.* *Mean* coincides in elements with Sax. *mæneg*, many, and the primary sense may be a crowd, like *vulgar*, from L. *vulgus.* If the primary sense is small, it coincides with Ir. *mion*, W. *mân* or *main*, Fr. *menu*, It. *meno*, L. *minor* and *minuo*, to diminish; but I think the word belongs to the root of *common.* See Class Mn. No. 2 and 5.]

1. Wanting dignity; low in rank or birth; as a man of *mean* parentage, *mean* birth or origin.

2. Wanting dignity of mind; low minded; base; destitute of honor; spiritless.

> Can you imagine I so *mean* could prove,
> To save my life by changing of my love? *Dryden.*

3. Contemptible; despicable.

> The Roman legions and great Cesar found
> Our fathers no *mean* foes. *Philips.*

4. Of little value; low in worth or estimation; worthy of little or no regard.

> We fast, not to please men, nor to promote any *mean* worldly interest. *Smalridge.*

5. Of little value; humble; poor; as a *mean* abode; a *mean* dress.

MEAN, *a.* [Fr. *moyen;* Sp. Port. *mediano;* L. *medium, medius;* Ir. *meadhan.* See *Middle.*]

1. Middle; at an equal distance from the extremes; as the *mean* distance; the *mean* proportion between quantities; the *mean* ratio.

> According to the fittest style of lofty, *mean*, or lowly. *Milton.*

2. Intervening; intermediate; coming between; as in the *mean* time or while.

MEAN, *n.* The middle point or place; the middle rate or degree; mediocrity; medium. Observe the golden *mean.*

> There is a *mean* in all things. *Dryden.*
> But no authority of gods or men
> Allow of any *mean* in poesy. *Roscommon.*

2. Intervening time; interval of time; interim; meantime.

> And in the *mean*, vouchsafe her honorable tomb. *Spenser.*

Here is an omission of *time* or *while.*

3. Measure; regulation. [*Not in use.*] *Spenser.*

4. Instrument; that which is used to effect an object; the medium through which something is done.

> The virtuous conversation of christians was a *mean* to work the conversion of the heathen to Christ. *Hooker.*

In this sense, *means*, in the plural, is generally used, and often with a definitive and verb in the singular.

> By *this means* he had them more at vantage. *Bacon.*

> A good character, when established, should not be rested on as an end, but employed as *a means* of doing good. *Atterbury.*

5. *Means*, in the plural, income, revenue, resources, substance or estate, considered as the instrument of effecting any purpose. He would have built a house, but he wanted *means.*

Your *means* are slender. *Shak.*

6. Instrument of action or performance.

By all means, without fail. Go, *by all means*.

By no means, not at all; certainly not; not in any degree.

The wine on this side of the lake is *by no means* so good as that on the other. *Addison.*

By no manner of means, by no means; not the least. *Burke.*

By any means, possibly; at all.

If *by any means* I might attain to the resurrection of the dead. Phil. iii.

Meantime, *Meanwhile*, } in the intervening time. [In this use of these words there is an omission of *in* or *in the*; *in the meantime.*]

MEAN, *v. t.* pret. and pp. *meant*; pronounced *ment.* [Sax. *mænan*, *menan*, to mean, to intend, also to relate, to recite or tell, also to *moan*, to lament; G. *meinen*; D. *meenen*; Sw. *mena*; Dan. *meener*, *mener*; Russ. *mnyu*, to think or believe; Ir. *smuainim.* It coincides in origin with L. *mens*, Eng. *mind.* The primary sense is to set or to thrust forward, to reach, stretch or extend. So in L. *intendo*, to stretch onward or towards, and *propono*, to propose, to set or put forward.]

1. To have in the mind, view or contemplation; to intend.

What *mean* you by this service? Ex. xii.

2. To intend; to purpose; to design, with reference to a future act.

Ye thought evil against me, but God *meant* it for good. Gen. l.

3. To signify; to indicate.

What *mean* these seven ewe lambs? Gen. xxi.

What *meaneth* the noise of this great shout in the camp of the Hebrews? 1 Sam. iv.

Go ye, and learn what that *meaneth*— Matt. ix.

MEAN, *v. i.* To have thought or ideas; or to have meaning. *Pope.*

MEAN'DER, *n.* [the name of a winding river in Phrygia.]

1. A winding course; a winding or turning in a passage; as the *meanders* of the veins and arteries. *Hale.*

While lingering rivers in *meanders* glide. *Blackmore.*

2. A maze; a labyrinth; perplexity; as the *meanders* of the law. *Arbuthnot.*

MEAN'DER, *v. t.* To wind, turn or flow round; to make flexuous. *Drayton.*

MEAN'DER, *v. i.* To wind or turn in a course or passage; to be intricate. *Shenstone.*

MEAN'DERING, *ppr.* or *a.* Winding in a course, passage or current.

MEAN'DRIAN, *a.* Winding; having many turns.

ME'ANING, *ppr.* Having in mind; intending; signifying.

ME'ANING, *n.* That which exists in the mind, view or contemplation as a settled aim or purpose, though not directly expressed. We say, this or that is not his *meaning.*

2. Intention; purpose; aim; with reference to a future act.

I am no honest man, if there be any good *meaning* towards you. *Shak.*

3. Signification. What is the *meaning* of all this parade? The *meaning* of a hieroglyphic is not always obvious.

4. The sense of words or expressions; that which is to be understood; signification; that which the writer or speaker intends to express or communicate. Words have a literal *meaning*, or a metaphorical *meaning*, and it is not always easy to ascertain the real *meaning.*

5. Sense; power of thinking. [*Little used.*]

ME'ANLY, *adv.* [See *Mean.*] Moderately; not in a great degree.

In the reign of Domitian, poetry was *meanly* cultivated. [*Not used.*] *Dryden.*

2. Without dignity or rank; in a low condition; as *meanly* born.

3. Poorly; as *meanly* dressed.

4. Without greatness or elevation of mind; without honor; with a low mind or narrow views. He *meanly* declines to fulfill his promise.

Would you *meanly* thus rely
On power, you know, I must obey? *Prior.*

5. Without respect; disrespectfully. We cannot bear to hear others speak *meanly* of our kindred.

ME'ANNESS, *n.* Want of dignity or rank; low state; as *meanness* of birth or condition. Poverty is not always *meanness*; it may be connected with it, but men of dignified minds and manners are often poor.

2. Want of excellence of any kind; poorness; rudeness.

This figure is of a later date, by the *meanness* of the workmanship. *Addison.*

3. Lowness of mind; want of dignity and elevation; want of honor. *Meanness* in men incurs contempt. All dishonesty is *meanness.*

4. Sordidness; niggardliness; opposed to *liberality* or *charitableness. Meanness* is very different from frugality.

5. Want of richness; poorness; as the *meanness* of dress or equipage.

MEANT, *pret.* and *pp.* of *mean.*

MEAR. [See *Mere.*]

ME'ASE, *n.* [from the root of *measure.*] The quantity of 500; as a *mease* of herrings. [*Not used in America.*]

MEASLE, *n.* mee'zl. A leper. [*Not in use.*] *Wickliffe.*

MEASLED, *a.* mee'zled. [See *Measles.*] Infected or spotted with measles.

MEASLES, *n.* mee'zles; with a plural termination. [G. *maser*, a spot; *masig*, measled; D. *mazelen*; from sprinkling or from mixing. Class Ms. No. 14. 15.]

1. A contagious disease of the human body, usually characterized by an eruption of small red points or spots, from which it has its name.

2. A disease of swine. *B. Jonson.*

3. A disease of trees. *Mortimer.*

MEASLY, *a.* mee'zly. Infected with measles or eruptions. *Swift.*

MEASURABLE, *a.* mezh'urable. [See *Measure.*]

1. That may be measured; susceptible of mensuration or computation. *Bentley.*

2. Moderate; in small quantity or extent.

MEASURABLENESS, *n.* mezh'urableness. The quality of admitting mensuration.

MEASURABLY, *adv.* mezh'urably. Moderately; in a limited degree.

MEASURE, *n.* mezh'ur. [Fr. *mesure*; It. *misura*; Sp. *medida*; Arm. *musur* or *musul*; Ir. *meas*; W. *meidyr* and *mesur*; G. *mass*, measure, and *messen*, to measure; D. *maat*; Sw. *matt*; Dan. *maade*, measure, and mode; L. *mensura*, from *mensus*, with a casual *n*, the participle of *metior*, to measure, Eng. to *mete*; Gr. μετρον, μετρεω. With these correspond the Eng. *meet*, fit, proper, and *meet*, the verb; Sax. *gemet*, meet, fit; *metan* and *gemettan*, to meet or meet with, to find, to mete or measure, and to paint. The sense is to come to, to fall, to happen, and this sense is connected with that of stretching, extending, that is, reaching to; the latter gives the sense of *measure.* We find in Heb. מר measure; מדד, to mete, to measure. This word in Ar. مد madda, signifies to stretch or extend, to draw out in length or time; as do other verbs with the same elements, under one of which we find the *meta* of the Latins. The Ch. מטא signifies to come to, to arrive, to reach, to be *mature*, and מצא, in Heb. Ch. and Eth. signifies to find, to come to. Now the Saxon verb unites in itself the significations of all three of the oriental verbs.]

1. The whole extent or dimensions of a thing, including length, breadth and thickness.

The *measure* thereof is longer than the earth and broader than the sea. Job xi.

It is applied also to length or to breadth separately.

2. That by which extent or dimension is ascertained, either length, breadth, thickness, capacity, or amount; as, a rod or pole is a *measure* of five yards and a half; an inch, a foot, a yard, are *measures* of length; a gallon is a *measure* of capacity. Weights and *measures* should be uniform. Silver and gold are the common *measure* of value.

3. A limited or definite quantity; as a *measure* of wine or beer.

4. Determined extent or length; limit.

Lord, make me to know my end, and the *measure* of my days. Ps. xxxix.

5. A rule by which any thing is adjusted or proportioned.

God's goodness is the *measure* of his providence. *More.*

6. Proportion; quantity settled.

I enter not into the particulars of the law of nature, or its *measures* of punishment; yet there is such a law. *Locke.*

7. Full or sufficient quantity.

I'll never pause again,
Till either death hath clos'd these eyes of mine,
Or fortune given me *measure* of revenge. *Shak.*

8. Extent of power or office.

We will not boast of things without our *measure.* 2 Cor. x.

9. Portion allotted; extent of ability.

If else thou seekest
Aught not surpassing human *measure*, say. *Milton.*

10. Degree; quantity indefinite.

I have laid down, in some *measure*, the description of the old world. *Abbot.*

A great *measure* of discretion is to be used in the performance of confession. *Taylor.*

11. In *music*, that division by which the motion of music is regulated; or the interval or space of time between the rising and falling of the hand or foot of him who beats time. This measure regulates the time of

dwelling on each note. The ordinary or common *measure* is one second. *Encyc.*

12. In *poetry*, the measure or meter is the manner of ordering and combining the quantities, or the long and short syllables. Thus hexameter, pentameter, Iambic, Sapphic verses, &c. consist of different *measures*. *Encyc.*

13. In *dancing*, the interval between steps, corresponding to the interval between notes in the music.

My legs can keep no *measure* in delight. *Shak.*

14. In *geometry*, any quantity assumed as one or unity, to which the ratio of other homogeneous or similar quantities is expressed. *Encyc.*

15. Means to an end; an act, step or proceeding towards the accomplishment of an object; *an extensive signification of the word, applicable to almost every act preparatory to a final end, and by which it is to be attained.* Thus we speak of legislative *measures*, political *measures*, public *measures*, prudent *measures*, a rash *measure*, effectual *measures*, inefficient *measures*.

In measure, with moderation; without excess.

Without measure, without limits; very largely or copiously.

To have hard measure, to be harshly or oppressively treated.

Lineal or *long measure*, measure of length; the measure of lines or distances.

Liquid measure, the measure of liquors.

MEASURE, *v. t. mezh'ur.* To compute or ascertain extent, quantity, dimensions or capacity by a certain rule; as, to *measure* land; to *measure* distance; to *measure* the altitude of a mountain; to *measure* the capacity of a ship or of a cask.

2. To ascertain the degree of any thing; as, to *measure* the degrees of heat, or of moisture.

3. To pass through or over.

We must *measure* twenty miles to day. *Shak.*

The vessel plows the sea,
And *measures* back with speed her former way. *Dryden.*

4. To judge of distance, extent or quantity; as, to *measure* any thing by the eye.

Great are thy works, Jehovah, infinite
Thy power; what thought can *measure* thee? *Milton.*

5. To adjust; to proportion.

To secure a contented spirit, *measure* your desires by your fortunes, not your fortunes by your desires. *Taylor.*

6. To allot or distribute by measure.

With what measure ye mete, it shall be *measured* to you again. Matt. vii.

MEASURED, *pp. mezh'ured.* Computed or ascertained by a rule; adjusted; proportioned; passed over.

2. *a.* Equal; uniform; steady. He walked with *measured* steps.

MEASURELESS, *a. mezh'urless.* Without measure; unlimited; immeasurable. *Shak.*

MEASUREMENT, *n. mezh'urment.* The act of measuring; mensuration. *Burke.*

MEASURER, *n. mezh'urer.* One who measures; one whose occupation or duty is to measure commodities in market.

MEASURING, *ppr. mezh'uring.* Computing or ascertaining length, dimensions, capacity or amount.

2. *a.* A *measuring* cast, a throw or cast that requires to be measured, or not to be distinguished from another but by measuring. *Waller.*

MEAT, *n.* [Sax. *mæte, mete*; Goth. *mats*; Sw. *mat*; Dan. *mad*; Hindoo, *mas*. In W. *maethu* signifies to feed, to nourish, Corn. *methia*. In the language of the Mohegans, in America, *meetseh* signifies, eat thou; *meetsoo*, he eats. Qu. *maiz* and *mast*.]

1. Food in general; any thing eaten for nourishment, either by man or beast.

And God said, Behold, I have given you every herb—to you it shall be for *meat*. Gen. i.

Every moving thing that liveth, shall be *meat* for you. Gen. ix.

Thy carcase shall be *meat* to all fowls of the air. Deut. xxviii.

2. The flesh of animals used as food. *This is now the more usual sense of the word.* The *meat* of carnivorous animals is tough, coarse and ill flavored. The *meat* of herbivorous animals is generally palatable.

3. In *Scripture*, spiritual food; that which sustains and nourishes spiritual life or holiness.

My flesh is *meat* indeed. John vi.

4. Spiritual comfort; that which delights the soul.

My *meat* is to do the will of him that sent me. John iv.

5. Products of the earth proper for food. Hab. iii.

6. The more abstruse doctrines of the gospel, or mysteries of religion. Heb. v.

7. Ceremonial ordinances. Heb. xiii.

To sit at meat, to sit or recline at the table. *Scripture.*

ME'ATED, *a.* Fed; fattened. [*Not used.*] *Tusser.*

MEATHE, *n.* [W. *mez*. See *Mead*.] Liquor or drink. [*Not used.*] *Milton.*

ME'AT-OFFERING, *n.* An offering consisting of meat or food.

ME'ATY, *a.* Fleshy, but not fat. [*Local.*] *Grose.*

MEAWL. [See *Mewl*.]

ME'AZLING, *ppr.* Falling in small drops; properly *mizzling*, or rather *mistling*, from *mist*. *Arbuthnot.*

MECHAN'IC, MECHAN'ICAL, *a.* [L. *mechanicus*; Fr. *mechanique*; Gr. μηχανικος, from μηχανη, a machine.]

1. Pertaining to machines, or to the art of constructing machines; pertaining to the art of making wares, goods, instruments, furniture, &c. We say, a man is employed in *mechanical* labor; he lives by *mechanical* occupation.

2. Constructed or performed by the rules or laws of mechanics. The work is not *mechanical*.

3. Skilled in the art of making machines; bred to manual labor. *Johnson.*

4. Pertaining to artisans or mechanics; vulgar.

To make a god, a hero or a king,
Descend to a *mechanic* dialect. *Roscommon.*

5. Pertaining to the principles of mechanics, in philosophy; as *mechanical* powers or forces; a *mechanical* principle.

6. Acting by physical power; as *mechanical* pressure.

The terms *mechanical* and *chimical*, are thus distinguished: those changes which bodies undergo without altering their constitution, that is, losing their identity, such as changes of place, of figure, &c. are *mechanical*; those which alter the constitution of bodies, making them different substances, as when flour, yeast and water unite to form bread, are *chimical*. In the one case, the changes relate to *masses* of matter, as the motions of the heavenly bodies, or the action of the wind on a ship under sail; in the other case, the changes occur between the *particles* of matter, as the action of heat in melting lead, or the union of sand and lime forming mortar. Most of what are usually called the *mechanic arts*, are partly mechanical, and partly chimical.

MECHAN'IC, *n.* A person whose occupation is to construct machines, or goods, wares, instruments, furniture, and the like.

2. One skilled in a mechanical occupation or art.

MECHAN'ICALLY, *adv.* According to the laws of mechanism, or good workmanship.

2. By physical force or power.

3. By the laws of motion, without intelligence or design, or by the force of habit. We say, a man arrives to such perfection in playing on an instrument, that his fingers move *mechanically*.

Mechanically turned or *inclined*, naturally or habitually disposed to use mechanical arts. *Swift.*

MECHAN'ICALNESS, *n.* The state of being mechanical, or governed by mechanism.

MECHANI''CIAN, *n.* One skilled in mechanics.

MECHAN'ICS, *n.* That science which treats of the doctrines of motion. It investigates the forces by which bodies are kept either in equilibrium or in motion, and is accordingly divided into statics and dynamics.

A mathematical science which shows the effects of powers or moving forces, so far as they are applied to engines, and demonstrates the laws of motion. *Harris.*

It is a well known truth in *mechanics*, that the actual and theoretical powers of a machine will never coincide. *J. Appleton.*

MECH'ANISM, *n.* The construction of a machine, engine or instrument, intended to apply power to a useful purpose; the structure of parts, or manner in which the parts of a machine are united to answer its design.

2. Action of a machine, according to the laws of mechanics.

MECH'ANIST, *n.* The maker of machines, or one skilled in mechanics.

MECH'LIN, *n.* A species of lace, made at Mechlin.

MECHO'ACAN, *n.* White jalap, the root of an American species of Convolvulus, from Mechoacan, in Mexico; a purgative of slow operation, but safe. *Encyc.*

MECO'NIATE, *n.* A salt consisting of meconic acid and a base.

MECON'IC, *a.* Meconic acid is an acid contained in opium.

MEC'ONITE, *n.* A small sandstone; ammite. *Coxe. De Costa.*

MEC͡O'NIUM, *n.* [Gr. μηκωνιον, from μηκων, poppy.]

1. The juice of the white poppy, which has the virtues of opium. *Coxe. Encyc.*
2. The first fæces of infants. *Coxe.*

MED'AL, *n.* [Fr. *medaille*; It. *medaglia*; Sp. *medalla*; Arm. *metallinn*; from L. *metallum*, metal. Qu. Ar. مَطَلَ matala, to beat or extend by beating. Class Md. No. 45.]

An ancient coin, or a piece of metal in the form of a coin, stamped with some figure or device to preserve the portrait of some distinguished person, or the memory of an illustrious action or event.

MEDAL'LIC͡, *a.* Pertaining to a medal or to medals. *Addison.*

MEDAL'LION, *n.* [Fr.; from *medal.*] A large antique stamp or medal.

2. The representation of a medallion.

MED'ALLIST, *n.* A person that is skilled or curious in medals. *Johnson.*

MED'DLE, *v. i.* [D. *middelen*, to mediate; G. *mittler*, middle, and mediator; Sw. *medlare*; Dan. *midler*, a mediator. Qu. Sw. *meddela*, Dan. *meddeler*, to communicate or participate; *med*, with, and *dela*, *deeler*, to deal. *Meddle* seems to be connected with *medley*, a mixture. Chaucer and Spenser use *medle*, to mix, and the G. *mittler* is evidently from *mitte*, *mittel*, middle, which seems to be connected with *mit*, with. In W. *mid* signifies an inclosure. Perhaps all these words may belong to one family.]

1. To have to do; to take part; to interpose and act in the concerns of others, or in affairs in which one's interposition is not necessary; often with the sense of intrusion or officiousness.

> I have thus far been an upright judge, not *meddling* with the design nor disposition. *Dryden.*

> What hast thou to do to *meddle* with the affairs of my family? *Arbuthnot.*

> Why should'st thou *meddle* to thy hurt? 2 Kings xiv.

2. To have to do; to touch; to handle. *Meddle* not with edge-tools, is an admonition to children. When the object is specified, *meddle* is properly followed by *with* or *in;* usually by the former.

> The civil lawyers—have *meddled in* a matter that belongs not to them. *Locke.*

MED'DLE, *v. t.* To mix; to mingle.

> He *meddled* his talk with many a tear. *Obs. Spenser.*

MED'DLER, *n.* One that meddles; one that interferes or busies himself with things in which he has no concern; an officious person; a busy body. *Bacon.*

MED'DLESŌME, *a.* Given to meddling; apt to interpose in the affairs of others; officiously intrusive.

MED'DLESŌMENESS, *n.* Officious interposition in the affairs of others. *Barrow.*

MED'DLING, *ppr.* Having to do; touching; handling; officiously interposing in other men's concerns.

2. *a.* Officious; busy in other men's affairs; as a *meddling* neighbor.

ME'DIAL, *a.* [L. *medius*, middle.] Mean; noting a mean or average.

Medial alligation, is a method of finding the mean rate or value of a mixture consisting of two or more ingredients of different quantities and values. In this case, the quantity and value of each ingredient are given.

ME'DIANT, *n.* In *music*, an appellation given to the third above the key-note, because it divides the interval between the tonic and dominant into two thirds. *Rousseau. Busby.*

ME'DIATE, *a.* [Fr *mediat;* It. *mediato;* from L. *medius*, middle.] Middle; being between the two extremes.

> Anxious we hover in a *mediate* state. *Prior.*

2. Interposed; intervening; being between two objects.

> Soon the *mediate* clouds shall be dispelled. *Prior.*

3. Acting by means, or by an intervening cause or instrument. Thus we speak of *mediate* and *immediate* causes. The wind that propels a ship is the *immediate* cause of its motion; the oar with which a man rows a boat is the *immediate* cause of its motion; but the rower is the *mediate* cause, acting by means of the oar.

ME'DIATE, *v. i.* To interpose between parties, as the equal friend of each; to act indifferently between contending parties, with a view to reconciliation; to intercede. The prince that *mediates* between nations and prevents a war, is the benefactor of both parties.

2. To be between two. [*Little used.*] *Digby.*

ME'DIATE, *v. t.* To effect by mediation or interposition between parties; as, to *mediate* a peace. *Clarendon.*

2. To limit by something in the middle. [*Not used.*] *Holder.*

ME'DIATELY, *adv.* By means or by a secondary cause, acting between the first cause and the effect.

> God worketh all things amongst us *mediately*, by secondary means. *Raleigh.*

> The king grants a manor to A, and A grants a portion of it to B. In this case, B holds his lands immediately of A, but *mediately* of the king. *Blackstone.*

MEDIA'TION, *n.* [Fr. from L. *medius*, middle.]

1. Interposition; intervention; agency between parties at variance, with a view to reconcile them. The contentions of individuals and families are often terminated by the *mediation* of friends. The controversies of nations are sometimes adjusted by *mediation*. The reconciliation of sinners to God by the *mediation* of Christ, is a glorious display of divine benevolence.
2. Agency interposed; intervenient power.

> The soul, during its residence in the body, does all things by the *mediation* of the passions. *South.*

3. Intercession; entreaty for another.

MEDIA'TOR, *n.* [Fr. *mediateur.*] One that interposes between parties at variance for the purpose of reconciling them.

2. By way of eminence, Christ is THE MEDIATOR, the divine intercessor through whom sinners may be reconciled to an offended God. Tim. 2.

> Christ is a *mediator* by nature, as partaking of both natures divine and human; and *mediator* by office, as transacting matters between God and man. *Waterland.*

MEDIATO'RIAL, *a.* Belonging to a mediator; as *mediatorial* office or character. [*Mediatory* is not used.]

MEDIA'TORSHIP, *n.* The office of a mediator.

MEDIA'TRESS, } *n.* A female mediator.
MEDIA'TRIX, } *Ainsworth.*

MED'IC͡, *n.* A plant of the genus Medicago. The *sea-medic* is of the same genus; the *medic vetch* is of the genus Hedysarum. *Fam. of Plants.*

MED'IC͡ABLE, *a.* [See *Medical.*] That may be cured or healed.

MED'IC͡AL, *a.* [L. *medicus*, from *medeor*, to heal; Gr. μηδικος, μηδομαι; μηδος, cure.]

1. Pertaining to the art of healing diseases; as the *medical* profession; *medical* services.
2. Medicinal; containing that which heals; tending to cure; as the *medical* properties of a plant.

MED'IC͡ALLY, *adv.* In the manner of medicine; according to the rules of the healing art, or for the purpose of healing; as a simple or mineral *medically* used or applied.

2. In relation to the healing art; as a plant *medically* considered.

MED'IC͡AMENT, *n.* [Fr. from L. *medicamentum.*]

Any thing used for healing diseases or wounds; a medicine; a healing application. *Coxe.*

MEDIC͡AMENT'AL, *a.* Relating to healing applications; having the qualities of medicaments.

MEDIC͡AMENT'ALLY, *adv.* After the manner of healing applications.

MED'IC͡ASTER, *n.* A quack. *Whitlock.*

MED'IC͡ATE, *v. t.* [L. *medico.*] To tincture or impregnate with healing substances, or with any thing medicinal. *Arbuthnot.*

MED'IC͡ATED, *pp.* Prepared or furnished with any thing medicinal.

MED'IC͡ATING, *ppr.* Impregnating with medical substances; preparing with any thing medicinal.

MEDIC͡A'TION, *n.* The act or process of impregnating with medicinal substances; the infusion of medicinal virtues. *Bacon.*

2. The use of medicine. *Brown.*

MEDIC'INABLE, *a.* Having the properties of medicine; medicinal. [*The latter is the word now used.*] *Bacon. Wotton.*

MEDIC'INAL, *a.* [L. *medicinalis.*] Having the property of healing or of mitigating disease; adapted to the cure or alleviation of bodily disorders; as *medicinal* plants; *medicinal* virtues of minerals; *medicinal* springs. The waters of Saratoga and Ballston are remarkably *medicinal.*

2. Pertaining to medicine; as *medicinal* days or hours. *Quincy.*

MEDIC'INALLY, *adv.* In the manner of medicine; with medicinal qualities.

2. With a view to healing; as, to use a mineral *medicinally.*

MED'ICINE, *n.* [L. *medicina*, from *medeor*, to cure; vulgarly and improperly pronounced *med'sn.*]

1. Any substance, liquid or solid, that has the property of curing or mitigating disease in animals, or that is used for that purpose. Simples, plants and minerals furnish most of our *medicines.* Even poisons used with judgment and in moderation, are safe and efficacious *medicines.* Medicines are *internal* or *external*, *simple* or *compound.*

2. The art of preventing, curing or alleviating the diseases of the human body. Hence we say, the study of *medicine*, or a student of *medicine*.

3. In the French sense, a physician. [*Not in use.*] *Shak.*

MED'ICINE, *v. t.* To affect or operate on as medicine. [*Not used.*] *Shak.*

MEDI'ETY, *n.* [Fr. *medieté*; L. *medietas*; from L. *medius*, middle.]

The middle state or part; half; moiety. [*Little used.*] *Brown.*

ME'DIN, *n.* A small coin.

MEDIO'CRAL, *a.* [L. *mediocris.*] Being of a middle quality; indifferent; ordinary; as *mediocral* intellect. [*Rare.*] *Addison.*

ME'DIOCRIST, *n.* A person of middling abilities. [*Not used.*] *Swift.*

MEDIOC'RITY, *n.* [L. *mediocritas*, from *mediocris*, middling; *medius*, middle.]

1. A middle state or degree; a moderate degree or rate. A *mediocrity* of condition is most favorable to morals and happiness. A *mediocrity* of talents well employed will generally ensure respectability.

Men of age seldom drive business home to the full period, but content themselves with a *mediocrity* of success. *Bacon.*

2. Moderation; temperance.

We owe obedience to the law of reason, which teacheth *mediocrity* in meats and drinks. *Hooker.*

MED'ITATE, *v. i.* [L. *meditor*; Sp. *meditar*; Fr. *mediter.*]

1. To dwell on any thing in thought; to contemplate; to study; to turn or revolve any subject in the mind; appropriately but not exclusively used of pious contemplation, or a consideration of the great truths of religion.

His delight is in the law of the Lord, and in his law doth he *meditate* day and night. Ps. i.

2. To intend; to have in contemplation.

I *meditate* to pass the remainder of life in a state of undisturbed repose. *Washington.*

MED'ITATE, *v. t.* To plan by revolving in the mind; to contrive; to intend.

Some affirmed that I *meditated* a war. *King Charles.*

2. To think on; to revolve in the mind.

Blessed is the man that doth *meditate* good things. *Ecclus.*

MED'ITATED, *pp.* Planned; contrived.

MED'ITATING, *ppr.* Revolving in the mind; contemplating; contriving.

MEDITA'TION, *n.* [L. *meditatio.*] Close or continued thought; the turning or revolving of a subject in the mind; serious contemplation.

Let the words of my mouth and the *meditations* of my heart be acceptable in thy sight, O Lord, my strength and my Redeemer. Ps. xix.

MED'ITATIVE, *a.* Addicted to meditation. *Ainsworth.*

2. Expressing meditation or design. *Johnson.*

MEDITERRA'NE, **MEDITERRA'NEAN**, **MEDITERRA'NEOUS**, } *a.* [L. *medius*, middle, and *terra*, land.]

1. Inclosed or nearly inclosed with land; as the *Mediterranean* sea, between Europe and Africa. [*Mediterrane* is not used.]

2. Inland; remote from the ocean or sea; as *mediterraneous* mountains. *Burnet.*

ME'DIUM, *n.* plu. *mediums*; *media* not being generally, though sometimes used. [L.] In *philosophy*, the space or substance through which a body moves or passes to any point. Thus ether is supposed to be the *medium* through which the planets move; air is the *medium* through which bodies move near the earth; water the *medium* in which fishes live and move; glass a *medium* through which light passes; and we speak of a resisting *medium*, a refracting *medium*, &c.

2. In *logic*, the mean or middle term of a syllogism, or the middle term in an argument, being the reason why a thing is affirmed or denied.

Nothing can be honorable that violates moral principle.

Dueling violates moral principle.

Therefore dueling is not honorable.

Here the second term is the *medium*, mean, or middle term.

3. *Arithmetical medium*, that which is equally distant from each extreme, or which exceeds the lesser extreme as much as it is exceeded by the greater, in respect of quantity, not of proportion. Thus, 9 is a *medium* between 6 and 12.

4. *Geometrical medium*, is that wherein the same ratio is preserved between the first and second terms, as between the second and third. Thus, 6 is a *geometrical medium* between 4 and 9. *Encyc.*

In the three last senses or applications, *mean* is more generally used for *medium*.

5. The means or instrument by which any thing is accomplished, conveyed or carried on. Thus money is the *medium* of commerce; coin is the common *medium* of trade among all civilized nations, but wampum is the *medium* of trade among the Indian tribes, and bills of credit or bank notes are often used as *mediums* of trade in the place of gold and silver. Intelligence is communicated through the *medium* of the press.

6. The middle place or degree; the mean.

The just *medium* of this case lies between pride and abjection. *L'Estrange.*

7. A kind of printing paper of middle size.

MED'LAR, *n.* [L. *mespilus.*] A tree and a genus of trees, called Mespilus; also, the fruit of the tree. The German or common medlar is cultivated in gardens for its fruit. *Encyc.*

MED'LE, *v. t.* To mix; not used, but hence,

MED'LEY, *n.* A mixture; a mingled and confused mass of ingredients; used often or commonly with some degree of contempt.

This *medley* of philosophy and war. *Addison.*

Love is a *medley* of endearments, jars, suspicions, reconcilements, wars—then peace again. *Walsh.*

MED'LEY, *a.* Mingled; confused. [*Little used.*] *Dryden.*

MEDUL'LAR, **MED'ULLARY**, } *a.* [L. *medullaris*, from *medulla*, marrow; W. *madruz*; allied to *matter*, that is, soft.]

Pertaining to marrow; consisting of marrow; resembling marrow; as *medullary* substance.

MEDUL'LIN, *n.* [L. *medulla.*] The pith of the sunflower, which has neither taste nor smell. It is insoluble in water, ether, alcohol and oils, but soluble in nitric acid, and instead of yielding suberic acid, it yields the oxalic. *Cyc.*

MEED, *n.* [Sax. *med*, Gr. *μισθος*, G. *miethe*, hire; Sans. *medha*, a gift.]

1. Reward; recompense; that which is bestowed or rendered in consideration of merit.

Thanks to men
Of noble minds is honorable *meed*. *Shak.*

2. A gift or present. [*Not used.*] *Shak.*

MEEK, *a.* [Sw. *miuk*, soft, tender; Dan. *myg*; Sp. *mego*; Port. *meigo*; G. *gemach.* The primary sense is flowing, liquid, or thin, attenuated, and allied to *muck*, L. *mucus*, Eng. *mucilage*, Heb. Ch. מוג, to melt. Class Mg. No. 8. See also No. 10. and No. 2. 9. 13.]

1. Mild of temper; soft; gentle; not easily provoked or irritated; yielding; given to forbearance under injuries.

Now the man Moses was very *meek*, above all men. Num. xii.

2. *Appropriately*, humble, in an evangelical sense; submissive to the divine will; not proud, self-sufficient or refractory; not peevish and apt to complain of divine dispensations. Christ says, "Learn of me, for I am *meek* and lowly in heart, and ye shall find rest to your souls." Matt. xi.

Blessed are the *meek*, for they shall inherit the earth. Matt. v.

MEE'KEN, *v. t.* *mee'kn.* To make meek; to soften; to render mild. *Thomson.*

MEE'KLY, *adv.* Mildly; gently; submissively; humbly; not proudly or roughly.

And this mis-seeming discord *meekly* lay aside. *Spenser.*

MEE'KNESS, *n.* Softness of temper; mildness; gentleness; forbearance under injuries and provocations.

2. In *an evangelical sense*, humility; resignation; submission to the divine will, without murmuring or peevishness; opposed to *pride*, *arrogance* and *refractoriness.* Gal. v.

I beseech you by the *meekness* of Christ. 1 Cor. x.

Meekness is a grace which Jesus alone inculcated, and which no ancient philosopher seems to have understood or recommended. *Buckminster.*

MEER, *a.* Simple; unmixed; usually written *mere.*

MEER, *n.* A lake; a boundary. [See *Mere.*]

MEE'RED, *a.* Relating to a boundary. [See *Mere.*] *Shak.*

MEER'SCHAUM, *n.* [G. sea-foam.] A hydrate of magnesia combined with silex. It occurs in beds in Natolia, and when first taken out, is soft, and makes lather like soap. It is manufactured into tobacco pipes, which are boiled in oil or wax, and baked. *Cyc.*

MEET, *a.* [Sax. *gemet*, with a prefix, from the root of *metan*, *gemetan*, to *meet*, to find, that is, to come to, to come together. So the equivalent word *convenient*, is from L. *convenio.*]

Fit; suitable; proper; qualified; convenient; adapted, as to a use or purpose.

Ye shall pass over armed before your brethren, the children of Israel, all that are *meet* for the war. Deut. iii.

It was *meet* that we should make merry— Luke xv.

Bring forth fruits *meet* for repentance. Matt. iii.

MEET, *v. t.* pret. and pp. *met.* [Sax. *metan*, *mætan*, *gemetan*, to meet, to find, to measure, to *mete*; Goth. *motyan*; D. *ontmoeten*, *gemoetan*, to meet, and *gemoet*, a meeting; Sw. *möta*, to meet, to fall, come or happen; *möte*, a meeting; *mot*, toward, against; Dan. *möder*, to meet; *möde*, a meeting; *mod*, contrary, against, towards. The sense is to come to, to fall to or happen, to reach to; Gr. μετα, with; G. *mit*, D. *met*, *mede*, Sw. and Dan. *med*, with or by; W. *med*, to; Ch. Syr. מטה מטא, to come to, to arrive, to happen; Heb. Ch. Eth. מצא. Qu. W. *ammod*, a covenant; *commod*, agreement.]

1. To come together, approaching in opposite or different directions; to come face to face; as, to *meet* a man in the road.

   His daughter came out to *meet* him with timbrels and with dances. Judges xi.

2. To come together in any place; as, we *met* many strangers at the levee.
3. To come together in hostility; to encounter. The armies *met* on the plains of Pharsalia.
4. To encounter unexpectedly. *Milton.*
5. To come together in extension; to come in contact; to join. The line A *meets* the line B and forms an angle.
6. To come to; to find; to light on; to receive. The good man *meets* his reward; the criminal in due time *meets* the punishment he deserves.

   Of vice or virtue, whether blest or curst,
   Which *meets* contempt, or which compassion first. *Pope.*

MEET, *v. i.* To come together or to approach near, or into company with. How pleasant it is for friends to *meet* on the road; still more pleasant to *meet* in a foreign country.

2. To come together in hostility; to encounter. The armies *met* at Waterloo, and decided the fate of Buonaparte.
3. To assemble; to congregate. The council *met* at 10 o'clock. The legislature will *meet* on the first Wednesday in the month.
4. To come together by being extended; to come in contact; to join. Two converging lines will *meet* in a point.

To meet with, to light on; to find; to come to; often with the sense of an unexpected event.

   We *met with* many things worthy of observation. *Bacon.*

2. To join; to unite in company.

   Falstaff at that oak shall *meet with* us. *Shak.*

3. To suffer unexpectedly; as, to *meet with* a fall; to *meet with* a loss.
4. To encounter; to engage in opposition.

   Royal mistress,
   Prepare to *meet with* more than brutal fury
   From the fierce prince. *Rowe.*

5. To obviate; a Latinism. [*Not used.*] *Bacon.*

To meet half way, to approach from an equal distance and meet; metaphorically, to make mutual and equal concessions, each party renouncing some pretensions.

MEE'TER, *n.* One that meets another; one that accosts another. *Shak.*

MEE'TING, *ppr.* Coming together; encountering; joining; assembling.

MEE'TING, *n.* A coming together; an interview; as a happy *meeting* of friends.

2. An assembly; a congregation; a collection of people; a convention. The *meeting* was numerous; the *meeting* was clamorous; the *meeting* was dissolved at sunset.
3. A conflux, as of rivers; a joining, as of lines.

MEE'TING-HOUSE, *n.* A place of worship; a church.

MEE'TLY, *adv.* [from *meet.*] Fitly; suitably; properly.

MEE'TNESS, *n.* [from *meet.*] Fitness; suitableness; propriety. *Bp. Hall.*

MEG'ACOSM, *n.* [Gr. μεγας, great, and κοσμος, world.] The great world. *Bp. Croft.*

MEGALON'YX, *n.* [Gr. μεγαλη, great, and ονυξ, a nail.]

An animal now extinct, whose bones have been found in Virginia. *Cuvier.*

MEGALOP'OLIS, *n.* [Gr. μεγαλη, great, and πολις, city.]

A chief city; a metropolis. [*Not in use.*] *Herbert.*

MEGATHE'RIUM, } *n.* [Gr. μεγας, great,
MEGATH'ERY, } and θηρα, a wild beast.]

A quadruped now extinct, but whose remains have been found in South America. It was larger than the megalonyx. *Cyc.*

ME'GRIM, *n.* [Fr. *migraine*, corrupted from L. and G. *hemicrania*, half the head.]

Properly, a pain in the side of the head; hence, a disorder of the head; vertigo. *Bacon.*

MEINE, *v. t.* [Sax. *mengan.*] To mingle. *Obs.* *Chaucer.*

MEINE, } *n.* [See *Menial.*] A retinue or
ME'NY, } family of servants; domestics. *Obs.* *Shak.*

MEIONITE, *n.* [Gr. μειων, less; from its low pyramids.]

Prismato-pyramidical feldspar, of a grayish white color. It occurs massive and crystalized. *Ure.*

MEIO'SIS, *n.* [Gr. μειωσις.] Diminution; a rhetorical figure, a species of hyperbole, representing a thing less than it is. *Beattie.*

MEL'AMPODE, *n.* [Gr. μελαμποδιον, blackfoot.] The black hellebore. *Spenser.*

MELANAGOGUE, *n.* *melan'agog.* [Gr. μελας, μελανος, black, and αγω, to drive.]

A medicine supposed to expel black bile or choler. [*Old.*]

MEL'ANCHOLIC, *a.* [See *Melancholy.*]

1. Depressed in spirits; affected with gloom; dejected; hypochondriac. Grief indulged to excess, has a tendency to render a person *melancholic.*
2. Produced by melancholy; expressive of melancholy; mournful; as *melancholic* strains.

   Just as the *melancholic* eye,
   Sees fleets and armies in the sky. *Prior.*

3. Unhappy; unfortunate; causing sorrow; as accidents and *melancholic* perplexities. *Clarendon.*

MEL'ANCHOLIC, *n.* One affected with a gloomy state of mind. [*Melancholian*, in a like sense, is not used.] *Spenser.*

2. A gloomy state of mind. *Clarendon.*

MEL'ANCHOLILY, *adv.* With melancholy. *Keepe.*

MEL'ANCHOLINESS, *n.* State of being melancholy; disposition to indulge gloominess of mind. *Aubrey.*

MELANCHO'LIOUS, *a.* Gloomy. [*Not in use.*] *Gower.*

MEL'ANCHOLIST, *n.* One affected with melancholy. *Glanville.*

MEL'ANCHOLIZE, *v. i.* To become gloomy in mind. *Burton.*

MEL'ANCHOLIZE, *v. t.* To make melancholy. *More.*

[*This verb is rarely or never used.*]

MEL'ANCHOLY, *n.* [Gr. μελαν, black, and χολη, bile; L. *melancholia.*]

1. A gloomy state of mind, often a gloomy state that is of some continuance, or habitual; depression of spirits induced by grief; dejection of spirits. This was formerly supposed to proceed from a redundance of black bile. *Melancholy*, when extreme and of long continuance, is a disease, sometimes accompanied with partial insanity. Cullen defines it, partial insanity without dyspepsy.

In *nosology*, mental alienation restrained to a single object or train of ideas, in distinction from *mania*, in which the alienation is general. *Good.*

   Moon-struck madness, moping *melancholy.* *Milton.*

MEL'ANCHOLY, *a.* Gloomy; depressed in spirits; dejected; *applied to persons.* Overwhelming grief has made me *melancholy.*

2. Dismal; gloomy; habitually dejected; as a *melancholy* temper.
3. Calamitous; afflictive; that may or does produce great evil and grief; as a *melancholy* event. The *melancholy* fate of the Albion! The *melancholy* destruction of Scio and of Missolonghi!

MELANGE, *n.* *melanj'.* [Fr.] A mixture. [*Not English.*] *Drummond.*

MEL'ANITE, *n.* [Gr. μελας, black.] A mineral, a variety of garnet, of a velvet black or grayish black, occurring always in crystals of a dodecahedral form. *Cleaveland.* *Ure.*

Melanite is perfectly opake. It is found among volcanic substances. *Dict. Nat. Hist.*

MELANIT'IC, *a.* Pertaining to melanite.

MEL'ANTERI, *n.* [Gr. μελαν, black.] Salt of iron, or iron in a saline state, mixed with inflammable matter. *Fourcroy.*

MEL'ANURE, } *n.* A small fish of the
MELANU'RUS, } Mediterranean. *Dict. Nat. Hist.*

MEL'ASSES, *n. sing.* [It. *melassa*; Sp. *melaza*; Fr. *melasse*; from Gr. μελας black, or from μελι, honey; Sans. *mali*, black.]

The sirup which drains from Muscovado sugar when cooling; treacle. *Nicholson.* *Edwards.*

MEL'ILOT, *n.* [Fr.] A plant of the genus Trifolium.

ME'LIORATE, *v. t.* [Fr. *ameliorer*; Sp. *mejorar*; It. *migliorare*; from L. *melior*, better; W. *mall*, gain, profit; Ir. *meall*, good.]

To make better; to improve; as, to *meliorate* fruit by grafting, or soil by cultivation. Civilization has done much, but christianity more, to *meliorate* the condition of men in society.

   Nature by art we nobly *meliorate.* *Denham.*

ME'LIORATE, *v. i.* To grow better.

ME'LIORATED, *pp.* Made better; improved.

ME'LIORATING, *ppr.* Improving; advancing in good qualities.

The pure and benign light of revelation has had a *meliorating* influence on mankind. *Washington.*

MELIORA'TION, *n.* The act or operation of making better; improvement.

MELIOR'ITY, *n.* The state of being better. [*Not in use.*] *Bacon.*

MELL, *v. i.* [Fr. *mêler.*] To mix; to meddle. [*Not in use.*] *Spenser.*

MELL, *n.* [L. *mel.*] Honey. [*Not English.*]

MEL'LATE, *n.* [L. *mel*, honey, Gr. μελι, W. *mel.*]

A combination of the mellitic acid with a base.

MELLIF'EROUS, *a.* [L. *mel*, honey, and *fero*, to produce.] Producing honey.

MELLIFICA'TION, *n.* [L. *mellifico.*] The making or production of honey.

MELLIF'LUENCE, *n.* [L. *mel*, honey, and *fluo*, to flow.]

A flow of sweetness, or a sweet smooth flow. *Watts.*

MELLIF'LUENT, } *a.* Flowing with hon-
MELLIF'LUOUS, } ey; smooth; sweetly flowing; as a *mellifluous* voice.

MEL'LIT, *n.* In *farriery*, a dry scab on the heel of a horse's fore foot, cured by a mixture of honey and vinegar.

MEL'LITE, *n.* [L. *mel.*] Honey stone; a mineral of a honey color, found only in very minute regular crystals. *Cleaveland.*

MELLIT'IC, *a.* Pertaining to honey stone.

MEL'LOW, *a.* [Sax. *melewe;* G. *mehl*, D. Dan. *meel*, meal; G. *mehlig*, *mehlicht*, mellow, mealy; Dan. *meelagtig*, mellow; L. *mollis*, Fr. *mol*, *molle*, soft, Gr. μαλακος; W. *mall*, soft, melting, insipid, evil, and as a noun, a *malady.* The Welsh unites the word with L. *malus.* These words are evidently allied to *mild* and *melt*, and *meal* would seem to be connected with *mill.* I am not certain which is the primary word. See Class Ml. No. 2. 4. 9. 12.]

1. Soft with ripeness; easily yielding to pressure; as a *mellow* peach or apple; *mellow* fruit.
2. Soft to the ear; as a *mellow* sound; a *mellow* pipe.
3. Soft; well pulverized; not indurated or compact; as *mellow* ground or earth.
4. Soft and smooth to the taste; as *mellow* wine.
5. Soft with liquor; intoxicated; merry. *Addison.*
6. Soft or easy to the eye.

The tender flush whose *mellow* stain imbues
Heaven with all freaks of light. *Percival.*

MEL'LOW, *v. t.* To ripen; to bring to maturity; to soften by ripeness or age.

On foreign mountains may the sun refine
The grape's soft juice and *mellow* it to wine. *Addison.*

2. To soften; to pulverize. Earth is *mellowed* by frost.
3. To mature; to bring to perfection.

This episode—*mellowed* into that reputation which time has given it. *Dryden.*

MEL'LOW, *v. i.* To become soft; to be ripened, matured or brought to perfection. Fruit, when taken from the tree, soon *mellows.* Wine *mellows* with age.

MEL'LOWNESS, *n.* Softness; the quality of yielding easily to pressure; ripeness, as of fruit.

2. Maturity; softness or smoothness from age, as of wine.

MEL'LOWY, *a.* Soft; unctuous. *Drayton.*

MELOCOTO'NE, *n.* [Sp. *melocoton*, a peach-tree grafted into a quince-tree, or the fruit of the tree; It. *melocotogno*, quince-tree; L. *malum cotoneum*, quince-apple. *Cotoneum* is probably our *cotton*, and the fruit so named from its pubescence.]

A quince. But the name is sometimes given to a large kind of peach.

MELO'DIOUS, *a.* [See *Melody.*] Containing melody; musical; agreeable to the ear by a sweet succession of sounds; as a *melodious* voice; *melodious* strains.

And music more *melodious* than the spheres. *Dryden.*

MELO'DIOUSLY, *adv.* In a melodious manner; musically.

MELO'DIOUSNESS, *n.* The quality of being agreeable to the ear by a sweet succession of sounds; musicalness.

MEL'ODIZE, *v. t.* To make melodious.

MEL'ODRAME, *n.* [Gr. μελος, a song, and *drama.*]

A dramatic performance in which songs are intermixed. *Todd.*

MEL'ODY, *n.* [Gr. μελωδια; μελος, a limb, or a song, and ωδη, an ode; L. *melos.*]

An agreeable succession of sounds; a succession of sounds so regulated and modulated as to please the ear. To constitute melody, the sounds must be arranged according to the laws of rythmus, measure, or the due proportion of the movements to each other. *Melody* differs from *harmony*, as it consists in the agreeable succession and modulation of sounds by a single voice; whereas *harmony* consists in the accordance of different voices or sounds. *Melody* is *vocal* or *instrumental.* *Hooker.*

To make melody in the heart, to praise God with a joyful and thankful disposition, ascribing to him the honor due to his name. Eph. v.

MEL'ON, *n.* [Fr. from L. *melo;* Sp. *melon;* It. *mellone*, a melon; Gr. μηλον, an apple; D. *meloen;* G. *melone;* Dan. Sw. *melon;* Slav. *mlun.* This word has the elements of *mellow*, L. *mollis*, W. *mall.*]

The name of certain plants and their fruit, as the water-*melon*, the musk-*melon.*

MEL'ON-THISTLE, *n.* A plant of the genus Cactus.

MEL'ROSE, *n.* [*mel* and *rose.*] Honey of roses. *Fordyce.*

MELT, *v. t.* [Sax. *meltan;* Gr. μελδω; D. *smelten;* G. *schmelzen;* Sw. *smälta;* Dan. *smelter;* whence Eng. *smelt*, *smalt.* We have in these words decisive evidence that *s*, in *smelten*, &c. is a prefix. *Melt*, in English, is regular, forming *melted* for its past tense and passive participle. The old participle *molten*, is used only as an adjective. This verb belongs to a numerous class of words in Ml, denoting soft or softness. See Class Ml. No. 10. 18. 19.]

1. To dissolve; to make liquid; to liquefy; to reduce from a solid to a liquid or flowing state by heat; as, to *melt* wax, tallow or lead; to *melt* ice or snow.
2. To dissolve; to reduce to first principles. *Burnet.*
3. To soften to love or tenderness.

For pity *melts* the mind to love. *Dryden.*

4. To waste away; to dissipate.

In general riot *melted* down thy youth. *Shak.*

5. To dishearten. Josh. xiv.

MELT, *v. i.* To become liquid; to dissolve; to be changed from a fixed or solid to a flowing state.

And whiter snow in minutes *melts* away. *Dryden.*

2. To be softened to love, pity, tenderness or sympathy; to become tender, mild or gentle.

Melting with tenderness and mild compassion. *Shak.*

3. To be dissolved; to lose substance.

—And what seem'd corporal,
Melted as breath into the wind. *Shak.*

4. To be subdued by affliction; to sink into weakness.

My soul *melteth* for heaviness—strengthen thou me. Ps. cxix.

5. To faint; to be discouraged or disheartened.

As soon as we heard these things, our heart *melted.* Josh. ii.

MELT'ED, *pp.* Dissolved; made liquid; softened; discouraged.

MELT'ER, *n.* One that melts any thing. *Derham.*

MELT'ING, *ppr.* Dissolving; liquefying; softening; discouraging.

2. *a.* Tending to soften; softening into tenderness; as *melting* eloquence.

MELT'ING, *n.* The act of softening; the act of rendering tender. *South.*

MELT'INGLY, *adv.* In a manner to melt or soften.

2. Like something melting. *Sidney.*

MELT'INGNESS, *n.* The power of melting or softening.

MEL'WEL, *n.* A fish.

MEM'BER, *n.* [Fr. *membre;* L. *membrum.*]

1. A limb of animal bodies, as a leg, an arm, an ear, a finger, that is, a subordinate part of the main body.
2. A part of a discourse, or of a period or sentence; a clause; a part of a verse. Harmony in poetry is produced by a proportion between the *members* of the same verse, or between the *members* of different verses.
3. In *architecture*, a subordinate part of a building, as a frieze or cornice; sometimes a molding.
4. An individual of a community or society. Every citizen is a *member* of the state or body politic. So the individuals of a club, a corporation or confederacy, are called its *members.* Students of an academy or college are its *members.* Professed christians are called *members* of the church.
5. The appetites and passions, considered as tempting to sin. Rom. vii. Col. iii.

MEM'BERED, *a.* Having limbs.

MEM'BERSHIP, *n.* The state of being a member.

2. Community; society. *Beaum.*

MEM'BRANE, *n.* [Fr. from L. *membrana;* Ir. *meambrum.* The last component part of this word is found in the Ethiopic and Amharic; Eth. ብሬሃ ና bereana, parchment, vellum, from በረሀ barah, to shine or be clear. Ludolf, Col. 231. 2. The substance then is named from its clearness or transparency.]

In *anatomy*, a thin, white, flexible skin, formed by fibers interwoven like net-work, and serving to cover some part of the body. *Encyc.*

The term is applied to the thin expanded parts, of various texture, both in animals and vegetables.

MEMBRA'NEOUS, MEM'BRANOUS, MEMBRANA'CEOUS, } *a.* Belonging to a membrane; consisting of membranes; as a *membraneous* covering.

Birds of prey have *membranaceous* stomachs, not muscular. *Arbuthnot.*

2. In *botany*, a *membranaceous* leaf has no distinguishable pulp between the two surfaces. In general, it denotes flatted or resembling parchment. *Martyn.*

MEMBRA'NIFORM, *a.* Having the form of a membrane or of parchment.

MEMENT'O, *n.* [L. from *memini.* See *Memory.*]

A hint, suggestion, notice or memorial to awaken memory; that which reminds.

He is but a man, and seasonable *mementos* may be useful. *Bacon.*

MEM'OIR, *n.* [Fr. *memoire*, memory.] A species of history written by a person who had some share in the transactions related. Persons often write their own *memoirs.*

2. A history of transactions in which some person had a principal share, is called his *memoirs*, though compiled or written by a different hand.

3. The history of a society, or the journals and proceedings of a society; as *memoirs* of the Royal Society.

4. A written account; register of facts. *Arbuthnot.*

MEM'ORABLE, *a.* [Fr. from L. *memorabilis.* See *Memory.*]

Worthy to be remembered; illustrious; celebrated; distinguished.

By tombs, by books, by *memorable* deeds. *Davies.*

MEM'ORABLY, *adv.* In a manner worthy to be remembered.

MEMORAND'UM, *n.* plu. *memorandums* or *memoranda.* [L.] A note to help the memory.

I entered a *memorandum* in my pocket-book. *Guardian.*

MEM'ORATIVE, *a.* Adapted or tending to preserve the memory of any thing. *Hammond.*

MEMO'RIAL, *a.* [Fr. from L. *memorialis.* See *Memory.*]

1. Preservative of memory.

There high in air *memorial* of my name,
Fix the smooth oar, and bid me live to fame. *Pope.*

2. Contained in memory; as *memorial* possession. *Watts.*

MEMO'RIAL, *n.* That which preserves the memory of something; any thing that serves to keep in memory. A monument is a *memorial* of a deceased person, or of an event. The Lord's supper is a *memorial* of the death and sufferings of Christ.

Churches have names; some as *memorials* of peace, some of wisdom, some of the Trinity. *Hooker.*

2. Any note or hint to assist the memory.

Memorials written with king Edward's hand shall be the ground of this history. *Hayward.*

3. A written representation of facts, made to a legislative or other body as the ground of a petition, or a representation of facts accompanied with a petition.

MEMO'RIALIST, *n.* One who writes a memorial. *Spectator.*

2. One who presents a memorial to a legislative or any other body, or to a person. *U. States.*

MEMO'RIALIZE, *v. t.* To present a memorial to; to petition by memorial. *U. States.*

MEM'ORIST, *n.* One who causes to be remembered. [*Not used.*] *Brown.*

MEM'ORIZE, *v. t.* To record; to commit to memory by writing.

They neglect to *memorize* their conquest of the Indians. *Spenser.*

2. To cause to be remembered.

They meant to *memorize* another Golgotha. *Shak.*

MEM'ORY, *n.* [L. *memoria*; Fr. *memoire*; Sw. *minne*; Ir. *meamhair* or *meabhair*, *meanma.* This word is from *memini*, which is probably corrupted from the Greek *μναομαι*, to remember, from *μενος*, mind, or the same root. See *Mind.*]

1. The faculty of the mind by which it retains the knowledge of past events, or ideas which are past. A distinction is made between *memory* and *recollection.* *Memory* retains past ideas without any, or with little effort; *recollection* implies an effort to recall ideas that are past. *Beattie. Reid. Stewart.*

Memory is the purveyor of reason. *Rambler.*

2. A retaining of past ideas in the mind; remembrance. Events that excite little attention are apt to escape from *memory.*

3. Exemption from oblivion.

That ever-living man of *memory*,
Henry the fifth. *Shak.*

4. The time within which past events can be remembered or recollected, or the time within which a person may have knowledge of what is past. The revolution in England was before my *memory*; the revolution in America was within the author's *memory.*

5. Memorial; monumental record; that which calls to remembrance. A monument in London was erected in *memory* of the conflagration in 1666.

6. Reflection; attention. *Shak.*

MEM'ORY, *v. t.* To lay up in the mind or memory. [*Not used.*] *Chaucer.*

MEMPH'IAN, *a.* [from *Memphis*, the ancient metropolis of Egypt, said to be altered from *Menuf, Memf. Ludolf.*]

Pertaining to Memphis; very dark; a sense borrowed from the darkness of Egypt in the time of Moses.

MEN, *plu.* of *man.* Two or more males, individuals of the human race.

2. Males of bravery. We will live in honor, or die like *men.*

3. Persons; people; mankind; in an indefinite sense. *Men* are apt to forget the benefactor, while they riot on the benefit.

MEN'ACE, *v. t.* [Fr. *menacer*; It. *minacciare*; Sp. *amenazar*; L. *minor.* The primary sense is to rush, throw or push forward. The sense is more clearly expressed by *emineo* and *promineo*, to jut forward, from the same root. See *Mind*, which is of the same family.]

1. To threaten; to express or show a disposition or determination to inflict punishment or other evil. The combined powers *menaced* France with war on every side.

2. To show or manifest the probability of future evil or danger to. The spirit of insubordination *menaced* Spain with the horrors of civil war.

3. To exhibit the appearance of any catastrophe to come; as, a hanging rock *menaces* a fall, or *menaces* the plain or the inhabitants below.

MEN'ACE, *n.* A threat or threatening; the declaration or show of a disposition or determination to inflict an evil; *used of persons.*

2. The show of a probable evil or catastrophe to come.

MEN'ACED, *pp.* Threatened.

MEN'ACER, *n.* One that threatens.

MEN'AȻHANITE, *n.* An oxyd of titanium, or mineral of a grayish or iron black color, occurring in very small rounded grains, imperfectly lamellar, and of a glistening luster; found near Menachan, in Cornwall, Eng. *Ure. Phillips. Cleaveland.*

MENAȻHANIT'IȻ, *a.* Pertaining to menachanite.

MEN'ACING, *ppr.* Threatening; declaring a disposition or determination to inflict evil.

2. *a.* Exhibiting the danger or probability of an evil or catastrophe to come; as a *menacing* attitude.

MEN'AĠE, *n.* [Fr. a family. See *Manage.*] A collection of brute animals. *Addison.*

MEN'AĠERY, *n.* [Fr. *menagerie*; It. *menageria.*]

A yard or place in which wild animals are kept, or a collection of wild animals.

MENAGOGUE, *n.* *men'agog.* [Gr. *μηνες*, menstrua, and *αγω*, to drive.]

A medicine that promotes the menstrual flux. *Quincy.*

MEND, *v. t.* [L. *emendo*; Fr. *amender*; It. *mendare*; from L. *menda*, a fault, spot or blemish. *Mend* is contracted from *emendo*, *amend*, for the L. negative *e* for *ex*, is necessary to express the removal of a fault.]

1. To repair, as a breach; to supply a part broken or defective; as, to *mend* a garment, a road, a mill-dam, a fence, &c.

2. To correct; to set right; to alter for the better; as, to *mend* the life or manners.

3. To repair; to restore to a sound state; as, to *mend* a feeble or broken constitution. *Locke.*

4. To help; to advance; to make better. This plausible apology does not *mend* the matter.

Though in some lands the grass is but short, yet it *mends* garden herbs and fruit. *Mortimer.*

5. To improve; to hasten.

He saw the monster *mend* his pace. *Dryden.*

MEND, *v. i.* To grow better; to advance to a better state; to improve. We say, a feeble constitution *mends* daily; a sick man *mends*, or is convalescent.

MEND'ABLE, *a.* Capable of being mended.

MENDA'CIOUS, *a.* [L. *mendax.*] Lying; false. [*Little used.*]

MENDAC'ITY, *n.* [L. *mendax*, false, lying. See Class Mn. No. 4.] Falsehood. *Brown.*

[The proper signification of this word would be a disposition to lie, or habitual lying.]

MEND'ED, *pp.* Repaired; made better; improved.

MEND'ER, *n.* One who mends or repairs.

MEND'ICANCY, *a.* [L. *mendicans.*] Beggary; a state of begging.

MEND'ICANT, *a.* [L. *mendicans*, from *mendico*, to beg, Fr. *mendier*; allied to L. *mando*, to command, demand.]

1. Begging; poor to a state of beggary; as reduced to a *mendicant* state.

2. Practicing beggary; as a *mendicant* friar.

MEND'ICANT, *n.* A beggar; one that makes it his business to beg alms; one of the begging fraternity of the Romish church.

MEND'ICATE, *v. t.* To beg, or practice begging. [*Not used.*]

MENDIC'ITY, *n.* [L. *mendicitas.*] The state of begging; the life of a beggar.

MENDMENT, for *amendment.* [*Not in use.*]

MENDS, for *amends*, not used. *Shak*

MENHA'DEN, *n.* A species of fish.

ME'NIAL, *a.* [Norm. *meignal*, *meynal*, from *meignee* or *meiny*, a family. The Norm. has also *mesnie* and *mesnee*, a family, household or company, and *meinez*, many. Qu. the root of *maison*, *messuage*, or of *many.*]

1. Pertaining to servants, or domestic servants; low; mean.

The women attendants perform only the most *menial* offices. *Swift.*

[Johnson observes on this passage, that Swift seems not to have known the meaning of this word. But this is the only sense in which it is now used.]

2. Belonging to the retinue or train of servants. *Johnson.*

Two *menial* dogs before their master pressed. *Dryden.*

[If this definition of Johnson is correct, it indicates that *menial* is from *meinez*, many, rather than from *mesnie*, family. But the sense may be *house-dogs.*]

ME'NIAL, *n.* A domestic servant.

MEN'ILITE, *n.* A mineral substance found at Menil Montant near Paris, of the nature of silex, of a brown liver color on the interior, and ordinarily of a clear blue on the surface. It is found in the shape of the kidneys, of the size of the hand or larger; sometimes in globules of the size of a nut. *Dict. Nat. Hist.*

MENIS'CUS, *n.* plu. *meniscuses.* [Gr. μηνισκος, a little moon.]

A lens convex on one side, and concave on the other. *Encyc.*

MENISPERM'ATE, *n.* A compound of menispermic acid and a salifiable base.

MENISPERM'IC, *a.* The menispermic acid is obtained from the seeds of the menispermum cocculus. *Ure.*

MEN'IVER, *n.* A small white animal in Russia, or its fur which is very fine. *Chaucer.*

MENOL'OGY, *n.* [Gr. μην, μηνος, month, and λογος, discourse.]

1. A register of months. *Stillingfleet.*

2. In *the Greek church*, martyrology, or a brief calendar of the lives of the saints, for each day in the year, or a simple remembrance of those whose lives are not written. *Lunier.*

MEN'OW, *n.* [Fr. *menu*, small. Qu.] A small fresh water fish, the minnow. *Bailey.*

MEN'PLEASER, *n.* One who is solicitous to please men, rather than to please God, by obedience to his commands.

MEN'SAL, *a.* [L. *mensalis*, from *mensa*, a table.]

Belonging to the table; transacted at table. [*Little used.*] *Clarissa.*

MEN'STRUAL, *a.* [Fr. from L. *menstrualis*, from *mensis*, month.]

1. Monthly; happening once a month; as the *menstrual* flux.

2. Lasting a month; as the *menstrual* orbit of the moon. *Bentley.*

3. Pertaining to a menstruum. *Bacon.*

MEN'STRUANT, *a.* Subject to monthly flowings. *Brown.*

MEN'STRUOUS, *a.* [L. *menstruus*, from *mensis*, a month.]

1. Having the monthly flow or discharge; as a female. *Sandys.*

2. Pertaining to the monthly flow of females. *Brown.*

MEN'STRUUM, *n.* plu. *menstruums.* [from L. *mensis*, month. The use of this word is supposed to have originated in some notion of the old chimists, about the influence of the moon in the preparation of dissolvents. *Johnson.*]

A dissolvent or solvent; any fluid or subtilized substance which dissolves a solid body.

All liquors are called *menstruums* which are used as dissolvents, or to extract the virtues of ingredients by infusion or decoction. *Quincy.*

Inquire what is the proper *menstruum* to dissolve a metal. *Bacon.*

MENSURABIL'ITY, *n.* [from *mensurable.*] Capacity of being measured.

MEN'SURABLE, *a.* [L. *mensura*, measure. The *n* is probably casual, and the word is the same as *measurable.*]

Measurable; capable of being measured. *Holder.*

MEN'SURAL, *a.* Pertaining to measure.

MEN'SURATE, *v. t.* [L. *mensura*, measure.] To measure. [*Little used.*]

MENSURA'TION, *n.* The act, process or art of measuring, or taking the dimensions of any thing.

2. Measure; the result of measuring. *Arbuthnot.*

MEN'TAL, *a.* [It. *mentale*; Fr. *mental*; from L. *mens*, mind.]

Pertaining to the mind; intellectual; as *mental* faculties; *mental* operations; *mental* sight; *mental* taste. *Milton. Addison.*

MEN'TALLY, *adv.* Intellectually; in the mind; in thought or meditation; in idea. *Bentley.*

MEN'TION, *n.* [Fr. from L. *mentio*, from Gr. μνεια, from μναω, to put in mind; It. *menzione*; Sp. *mencion*; Port. *mençaõ*; allied probably to L. *moneo* and *mind.* Mention is a throwing out.]

A hint; a suggestion; a brief notice or remark expressed in words or writing; used chiefly after *make.*

Make no *mention* of other gods. Josh. xxiii.

I will *make mention* of thy righteousness. Ps. lxxi.

Without ceasing I *make mention* of you always in my prayers. Rom. i.

MEN'TION, *v. t.* [Fr. *mentionner*; It. *menzionare.*]

To speak; to name; to utter a brief remark; to state a particular fact, or to express it in writing. It is applied to something thrown in or added incidentally in a discourse or writing, and thus differs from the sense of *relate*, *recite*, and *narrate.* I *mentioned* to him a fact that fell under my own observation. In the course of conversation, that circumstance was *mentioned.*

I will *mention* the loving-kindness of the Lord. Is. lxiii.

MEN'TIONED, *pp.* Named; stated.

MEN'TIONING, *ppr.* Naming; uttering.

MENTO'RIAL, *a.* [from *Mentor*, the friend and adviser of Ulysses.]

Containing advice or admonition.

MEPHIT'IC, *a.* [L. *mephitis*, an ill smell.] Offensive to the smell; foul; poisonous; noxious; pestilential; destructive to life. *Mephitic* acid is carbonic acid.

MEPH'ITIS, MEPH'ITISM, } *n.* Foul, offensive or noxious exhalations from dissolving substances, filth or other source; also, carbonic acid gas. *Med. Repos.*

MERCANTAN'TE, *n.* [It. *mercatante.*] A foreign trader. [*Not in use.*] *Shak.*

MER'CANTILE, *a.* [It. and Fr. from L. *mercans*, *mercor*, to buy; Port. Sp. *mercantil.*]

1. Trading; commercial; carrying on commerce; as *mercantile* nations; the *mercantile* class of men.

2. Pertaining or relating to commerce or trade; as *mercantile* business.

MER'CAT, *n.* [L. *mercatus.*] Market; trade. [*Not in use.*] *Sprat.*

MER'CENARILY, *adv.* In a mercenary manner. *Spectator.*

MER'CENARINESS, *n.* [from *mercenary.*] Venality; regard to hire or reward. *Boyle.*

MER'CENARY, *a.* [Fr. *mercenaire*; L. *mercenarius*, from *merces*, reward, wages; *mercor*, to buy.]

1. Venal; that may be hired; actuated by the hope of reward; moved by the love of money; as a *mercenary* prince or judge.

2. Hired; purchased by money; as *mercenary* services; *mercenary* soldiers.

3. Sold for money; as *mercenary* blood. *Shak.*

4. Greedy of gain; mean; selfish; as a *mercenary* disposition.

5. Contracted from motives of gain; as a *mercenary* marriage.

MER'CENARY, *n.* One who is hired; a soldier that is hired into foreign service; a hireling.

MER'CER, *n.* [Fr. *mercier*; It. *merciaio*; from L. *merx*, wares, commodities.]

One who deals in silks. *Howel.*

MER'CERSHIP, *n.* The business of a mercer.

MER'CERY, *n.* [Fr. *mercerie*; It. *merceria.*]

The commodities or goods in which a mercer deals; trade of mercers. *Graunt.*

MER'CHAND, *v. i.* [Fr. *marchander.*] To trade. [*Not used.*] *Bacon.*

MER'CHANDISE, *n.* [Fr. from *marchand*, a merchant, or *marchander*, to cheapen.]

1. The objects of commerce; wares, goods, commodities, whatever is usually bought or sold in trade. But provisions daily sold in market, horses, cattle, and fuel are not usually included in the term, and real estate never.
2. Trade; traffick; commerce. *Shak.*

MER'CHANDISE, *v. i.* To trade; to carry on commerce.

MER'CHANDRY, *n.* Trade; commerce. [*Not in use.*] *Saunderson.*

MER'CHANT, *n.* [Fr. *marchand*; It. *mercante*; Sp. *merchante*; Arm. *marchadour*; from L. *mercor*, to buy.]

1. A man who trafficks or carries on trade with foreign countries, or who exports and imports goods and sells them by wholesale.
2. In *popular usage*, any trader, or one who deals in the purchase and sale of goods.
3. A ship in trade. [*Not used.*]

MER'CHANT, *v. i.* To trade. [*Not in use.*]

MER'CHANTABLE, *a.* Fit for market; such as is usually sold in market, or such as will bring the ordinary price; as *merchantable* wheat or timber.

MER'CHANTLIKE, *a.* Like a merchant.

MER'CHANTMAN, *n.* A ship or vessel employed in the transportation of goods, as distinguished from a ship of war.

MER'CIABLE, *a.* Merciful. [*Not in use.*] *Gower.*

MER'CIFUL, *a.* [from *mercy.*] Having or exercising mercy; compassionate; tender; disposed to pity offenders and to forgive their offenses; unwilling to punish for injuries; *applied appropriately to the Supreme Being.*

The Lord passed before him and proclaimed, the Lord, the Lord God, *merciful* and gracious, long-suffering and abundant in goodness and truth. Ex. xxxiv.

2. Compassionate; tender; unwilling to give pain; not cruel. A *merciful* man will be *merciful* to his beast.

MER'CIFULLY, *adv.* With compassion or pity; tenderly; mildly.

MER'CIFULNESS, *n.* Tenderness towards offenders; willingness to forbear punishment; readiness to forgive. *Hammond.*

MER'CIFY, *v. t.* To pity. [*Not in use.*] *Spenser.*

MER'CILESS, *a.* Destitute of mercy; unfeeling; pitiless; hard-hearted; cruel; as a *merciless* tyrant. *Dryden.*

2. Not sparing; as the *merciless* waves or tempest.

MER'CILESSLY, *adv.* In a manner void of mercy or pity; cruelly.

MER'CILESSNESS, *n.* Want of mercy or pity.

MERCU'RIAL, *a.* [from *Mercury*; L. *mercurialis.*]

1. Formed under the influence of Mercury; active; sprightly; full of fire or vigor; as a *mercurial* youth; a *mercurial* nation. *Bacon. Swift.*
2. Pertaining to quicksilver; containing quicksilver, or consisting of mercury; as *mercurial* preparations or medicines.

MERCU'RIALIST, *n.* One under the influence of Mercury, or one resembling Mercury in variety of character.

MERCU'RIATE, *n.* A combination of the oxyd of mercury with another substance.

Mercuric acid, a saturated combination of mercury and oxygen.

MERCURIFICA'TION, *n.* In *metallurgic chimistry*, the process or operation of obtaining the mercury from metallic minerals in its fluid form. *Encyc.*

2. The act of mixing with quicksilver. *Boyle.*

MERCU'RIFY, *v. t.* To obtain mercury from metallic minerals, which it is said may be done by a large lens, the intense heat of which expels the mercury in fumes, which are afterwards condensed. *Encyc.*

MER'CURY, *n.* [L. *Mercurius.* In mythology, *Mercury* is the god of eloquence and of commerce, called by the Greeks *Hermes*, and his name is said to be formed from *merces*, or *mercor.* But in antiquity, there were several persons or deities of this name.]

1. Quicksilver, a metal remarkable for its fusibility, which is so great that to fix or congeal it, requires a degree of cold which is marked on Fahrenheit's scale at thirty nine degrees below zero. Its specific gravity is greater than that of any other metal, except platina, gold and tungsten. Under a heat of 660 degrees, it rises in fumes and is gradually converted into a red oxyd. Mercury is used in barometers to ascertain the weight of the atmosphere, and in thermometers to determine the temperature of the air, for which purposes it is well adapted by its expansibility, and the extensive range between its freezing and boiling points. Preparations of this metal are among the most powerful poisons, and are extensively used as medicines. The preparation called calomel, is a most efficacious deobstruent.
2. Heat of constitutional temperament; spirit; sprightly qualities. *Pope.*
3. A genus of plants, the Mercurialis, of several species.
4. One of the planets nearest the sun. It is 3224 miles in diameter, and revolves round the sun in about 88 days. Its mean distance from the sun is thirty seven millions of miles.
5. The name of a newspaper or periodical publication, and in some places, the carrier of a newspaper or pamphlet.

MER'CURY, *v. t.* To wash with a preparation of mercury. *B. Jonson.*

MER'CY, *n.* [Fr. *merci*; Norm. *merce*, *meer* or *mers*; supposed to be a contraction of L. *misericordia.* But qu. Eth. መሐረ meher, to pity.]

1. That benevolence, mildness or tenderness of heart which disposes a person to overlook injuries, or to treat an offender better than he deserves; the disposition that tempers justice, and induces an injured person to forgive trespasses and injuries, and to forbear punishment, or inflict less than law or justice will warrant. In this sense, there is perhaps no word in our language precisely synonymous with *mercy.* That which comes nearest to it is *grace.* It implies benevolence, tenderness, mildness, pity or compassion, and clemency, but exercised only towards offenders. *Mercy* is a distinguishing attribute of the Supreme Being.

The Lord is long-suffering and of great *mercy*, forgiving iniquity and transgression, and by no means clearing the guilty. Num. xiv.

2. An act or exercise of mercy or favor. It is a *mercy* that they escaped.

I am not worthy of the least of all thy *mercies.* Gen. xxxii.

3. Pity; compassion manifested towards a person in distress.

And he said, he that showed *mercy* on him. Luke x.

4. Clemency and bounty.

Mercy and truth preserve the king; and his throne is upheld by *mercy.* Prov. xxviii.

5. Charity, or the duties of charity and benevolence.

I will have *mercy* and not sacrifice. Matt. ix.

6. Grace; favor. 1 Cor. vii. Jude 2.
7. Eternal life, the fruit of mercy. 2 Tim. i.
8. Pardon.

I cry thee *mercy* with all my heart. *Dryden.*

9. The act of sparing, or the forbearance of a violent act expected. The prisoner cried for *mercy.*

To be or *to lie at the mercy of*, to have no means of self-defense, but to be dependent for safety on the mercy or compassion of another, or in the power of that which is irresistible; as, to be at the *mercy* of a foe, or of the waves.

MER'CY-SEAT, *n.* The propitiatory; the covering of the ark of the covenant among the Jews. This was of gold, and its ends were fixed to two cherubs, whose wings extended forward, and formed a kind of throne for the majesty of God, who is represented in Scripture as sitting between the cherubs. It was from this seat that God gave his oracles to Moses, or to the high priest who consulted him. *Calmet.*

MERD, *n.* [Fr. *merde*; L. *merda.*] Ordure; dung. *Burton.*

MERE, *a.* [L. *merus*; It. *mero.*] This or that only; distinct from any thing else.

From *mere* success nothing can be concluded in favor of a nation. *Atterbury.*

What if the head, the eye or ear repin'd
To serve *mere* engines to the ruling mind? *Pope.*

2. Absolute; entire. *Spenser.*

MERE, *n.* [Sax. *mære* or *mere*, a pool, lake or the sea; D. *meir*; L. *mare.* See *Moor.*]

A pool or lake.

MERE, *n.* [Sax. *mæra*, *gemæra*; Gr. μειρω, to divide, or Russ. *miryu*, to measure.]

A boundary; used chiefly in the compound, *mere-stone.* *Bacon.*

MERE, *v. t.* To divide, limit or bound. *Obs.* *Spenser.*

ME'RELY, *adv.* Purely; only; solely; thus and no other way; for this and no other purpose.

Prize not your life for other ends
Than *merely* to oblige your friends. *Swift.*

MERETRI''CIOUS, *a.* [L. *meretricius*, from *meretrix*, a prostitute.]

1. Pertaining to prostitutes; such as is practiced by harlots; as *meretricious* arts.

2. Alluring by false show; worn for disguise; having a gaudy but deceitful appearance; false; as *meretricious* dress or ornaments.

MERETRI''CIOUSLY, *adv.* In the manner of prostitutes; with deceitful enticements.

MERETRI''CIOUSNESS, *n.* The arts of a prostitute; deceitful enticements.

MERGAN'SER, *n.* [Sp. *merganser*, from L. *mergo*, to dive.]
A water fowl of the genus Mergus; called also *goosander.*

MERǴE, *v. t.* [L. *mergo.*] To immerse; to cause to be swallowed up.

The plaintiff became the purchaser and *merged* his term in the fee. *Kent.*

MERǴE, *v. i.* To be sunk, swallowed or lost. *Law Term.*

MERǴ'ER, *n.* [L. *mergo*, to merge.] In *law*, a merging or drowning of a less estate in a greater; as when a reversion in fee simple descends to or is purchased by a tenant of the same estate for years, the term for years is *merged*, lost, annihilated in the inheritance or fee simple estate. *Blackstone.*

MERID'IAN, *n.* [Fr. *meridien*; It. *meridiano*; L. *meridies.* Qu. Ir. *mir*, a part; Gr. *μειρω*, to divide. Varro testifies that this word was originally *medidies* [mid-day,] and that he had seen it so written on a sun-dial.]

1. In astronomy and geography, a great circle supposed to be drawn or to pass through the poles of the earth, and the zenith and nadir of any given place, intersecting the equator at right angles, and dividing the hemisphere into eastern and western. Every place on the globe has its *meridian*, and when the sun arrives at this circle, it is mid-day or noon, whence the name. This circle may be considered to be drawn on the surface of the earth, or it may be considered as a circle in the heavens coinciding with that on the earth.
2. Mid-day; noon.
3. The highest point; as the *meridian* of life; the *meridian* of power or of glory.
4. The particular place or state, with regard to local circumstances or things that distinguish it from others. We say, a book is adapted to the *meridian* of France or Italy; a measure is adapted to the *meridian* of London or Washington.

Magnetic meridian, a great circle, parallel with the direction of the magnetic needle, and passing through its poles.

MERID'IAN, *a.* Being on the meridian or at mid-day.

The sun sat high in his *meridian* tower. *Milton.*

2. Pertaining to the meridian or to mid-day; as the sun's *meridian* heat or splendor.
3. Pertaining to the highest point; as, the hero enjoyed his *meridian* glory.
4. Pertaining to the magnetic meridian.

MERID'IONAL, *a.* [Fr.] Pertaining to the meridian.
2. Southern. *Brown.*
3. Southerly; having a southern aspect. *Wotton.*

Meridional distance is the departure from the meridian, or easting or westing.

MERIDIONAL'ITY, *n.* The state of being in the meridian.
2. Position in the south; aspect towards the south. *Johnson.*

MERID'IONALLY, *adv.* In the direction of the meridian. *Brown.*

MER'IT, *n.* [L. *meritum*, from *mereo*, to earn or deserve; It. Sp. *merito*; Fr. *merite.*]
1. Desert; goodness or excellence which entitles one to honor or reward; worth; any performance or worth which claims regard or compensation; *applied to morals, to excellence in writing, or to valuable services of any kind.* Thus we speak of the inability of men to obtain salvation by their own *merits.* We speak of the *merits* of an author; the *merits* of a soldier, &c.
2. Value; excellence; *applied to things;* as the *merits* of an essay or poem; the *merits* of a painting; the *merits* of a heroic achievment.
3. Reward deserved; that which is earned or merited.

Those laurel groves, the *merits* of thy youth. *Prior.*

MER'IT, *v. t.* [Fr. *meriter*; L. *merito.*] To deserve; to earn by active service, or by any valuable performance; to have a right to claim reward in money, regard, honor or happiness. Watts, by his writings, *merited* the gratitude of the whole christian world. The faithful laborer *merits* his wages.

A man at best is incapable of *meriting* any thing from God. *South.*

2. To deserve; to have a just title to. Fidelity *merits* and usually obtains confidence.
3. To deserve, in an ill sense; to have a just title to. Every violation of law *merits* punishment. Every sin *merits* God's displeasure.

MER'ITABLE, *a.* Deserving of reward. [*Not in use.*] *B. Jonson.*

MER'ITED, *pp.* Earned; deserved.

MER'ITING, *ppr.* Earning; deserving.

MER'IT-MONGER, *n.* One who advocates the doctrine of human merit, as entitled to reward, or depends on merit for salvation. *Milner.*

MERITO'RIOUS, *a.* [It. *meritorio*; Fr. *meritoire.*]
Deserving of reward or of notice, regard, fame or happiness, or of that which shall be a suitable return for services or excellence of any kind. We applaud the *meritorious* services of the laborer, the soldier and the seaman. We admire the *meritorious* labors of a Watts, a Doddridge, a Carey and a Martyn. We rely for salvation on the *meritorious* obedience and sufferings of Christ.

MERITO'RIOUSLY, *adv.* In such a manner as to deserve reward. *Wotton.*

MERITO'RIOUSNESS, *n.* The state or quality of deserving a reward or suitable return.

MER'ITORY, *a.* Deserving of reward. [*Not used.*] *Gower.*

MERLE, *n.* [L. *merula.*] A blackbird. *Drayton.*

MER'LIN, *n.* [Fr.] A species of hawk of the genus Falco.

MER'LON, *n.* [It. *merlo*; Fr. *merlon.*] In *fortification*, that part of a parapet which lies between two embrasures. *Encyc.*

MER'MAID, *n.* [Fr. *mer*, L. *mare*, the sea, and *maid.*]
A marine animal, said to resemble a woman in the upper parts of the body, and a fish in the lower part. The male is called the *merman.*

ME'ROPS, *n.* A genus of birds called bee-eaters.

MER'RILY, *adv.* [from *merry.*] With mirth; with gayety and laughter; jovially. [See *Mirth* and *Merry.*]

Merrily sing and sport and play. *Glanville.*

MER'RIMAKE, *n.* [*merry* and *make.*] A meeting for mirth; a festival; mirth. *Spenser.*

MER'RIMAKE, *v. i.* To be merry or jovial; to feast. *Gay.*

MER'RIMENT, *n.* Mirth; gayety with laughter or noise; noisy sports; hilarity; frolick. *Milton.*

MER'RINESS, *n.* Mirth; gayety with laughter. *Shak.*

MER'RY, *a.* [Sax. *mirige, myrig*; Ar. مرح to be joyful. Class Mr. No. 10.]
1. Gay and noisy; jovial; exhilarated to laughter.

Man is the *merriest* species of the creation. *Addison.*

They drank and were *merry* with him. Gen. xliii.

2. Causing laughter or mirth; as a *merry* jest. *Shak.*
3. Brisk; as a *merry* gale. [*This is the primary sense of the word.*] *Dryden.*
4. Pleasant; agreeable; delightful. *Chaucer.*

To make merry, to be jovial; to indulge in hilarity; to feast with mirth. Judges ix.

MERRY-AN'DREW, *n.* A buffoon; a zany; one whose business is to make sport for others. *Spectator.*

MER'RY-MAKING, *a.* Producing mirth.

Mirth, music, *merry-making* melody
Speed the light hours no more at Holyrood. *Hillhouse.*

MER'RY-MEETING, *n.* A festival; a meeting for mirth. *Bp. Taylor.*

MER'RY-THOUGHT, *n.* The forked bone of a fowl's breast, which boys and girls break by pulling each one side; the longest part broken betokening priority of marriage. *Echard.*

MER'SION, *n.* [L. *mersio*, from *mergo*, to dive or sink.]
The act of sinking or plunging under water. But *immersion* is generally used.

MESARA'IC, *a.* [Gr. *μεσαραιον*; *μεσος*, middle, and *αραια*, intestines.]
The same as *mesenteric;* pertaining to the mesentery.

MESEE'MS, *verb impersonal.* [*me* and *seems.*] It seems to me. It is used also in the past tense, *meseemed.* *Spenser.*

MESENTER'IC, *a.* [See *Mesentery.*] Pertaining to the mesentery; as *mesenteric* glands or arteries.

MES'ENTERY, *n.* [Gr. *μεσεντεριον*; *μεσος*, middle, and *εντερον*, intestine.]
A fatty membrane placed in the middle of the intestines, and to which they are attached. This prevents them from becoming entangled with each other by convolutions. It is formed by a duplicature of the peritoneum. *Encyc. Quincy.*

MESH, *n.* [W. *masg*, net-work, a mesh; D. *maas*; G. *masche*, a mesh or a stitch.]

1. The opening or space between the threads of a net.
2. The grains or wash of a brewery.

MESH, *v. t.* To catch in a net; to ensnare. *Drayton.*

MESH'Y, *a.* Formed like net-work; reticulated. *Thomson.*

MES'LIN, *n.* [from Fr. *mesler*, *mêler*, to mix, or L. *miscellaneus*, from *misceo*, to mix.]
A mixture of different sorts of grain; in America, a mixture of wheat and rye.

MESNE, *a. meen.* [Old Fr.] In *law*, middle; intervening; as a *mesne* lord, that is, a lord who holds land of a superior, but grants a part of it to another person. In this case, he is a *tenant* to the superior, but *lord* or superior to the second grantee, and called the *mesne* lord.
Mesne process, that part of the proceedings in a suit which intervenes between the original process or writ and the final issue, and which issues, pending the suit, on some collateral matter; and sometimes it is understood to be the whole process preceding the execution. *Blackstone.*
Mesne profits, the profits of an estate which accrue to a tenant in possession, after the demise of the lessor.

MES'OCOLON, *n.* [Gr. μεσος, middle, and *colon.*]
In *anatomy*, that part of the mesentery, which, having reached the extremity of the ileum, contracts and changes its name, or that part of the mesentery to which the colon is attached. *Encyc. Hooper.*

MESOLEU'CYS, *n.* [Gr. μεσος, middle, and λευκος, white.]
A precious stone with a streak of white in the middle. *Dict.*

MES'OLITE, *n.* A mineral of the zeolite family.

MESOLOG'ARITHM, *n.* [Gr. μεσος, middle, and *logarithm.*]
A logarithm of the co-sines and co-tangents. *Kepler. Harris.*
The former is called by Napier an antilogarithm, the latter a differential. *Encyc.*

MESOM'ELAS, *n.* [Gr. μεσος, middle, and μελας, black.]
A precious stone with a black vein parting every color in the midst.

MES'OTYPE, *n.* [Gr. μεσος, middle, and τυπος, form, type.]
Prismatic zeolite; a mineral divided into three subspecies, fibrous zeolite, natrolite, and mealy zeolite. This is said by some writers to be so named from its property, when transparent, of doubling images. Others say it is a *mean form* between stilbite and analcime. *Dict. Jameson. Phillips.*

MESPRISE, *n.* Contempt; *a French word.* [*Not in use.*]

MESS, *n.* [In Fr. *mets* is a mess of meat, perhaps *meat.* In Goth. *mes* is a dish, Ir. *meis.* In Sax. *mese* is a table, Sp. *mesa*, L. *mensa.* But *mets*, mess, is probably a different word.]
1. A dish or a quantity of food prepared or set on a table at one time; as a *mess* of pottage; a *mess* of herbs; a *mess* of broth. *Milton. Pope.*
2. A medley; a mixed mass; a quantity.
3. As much provender or grain as is given to a beast at once.
4. A number of persons who eat together; *among seamen and soldiers.*

MESS, *v. i.* To eat; to feed.
2. To associate at the same table; to eat in company, as seamen.

MESS, *v. t.* To supply with a mess.

MES'SAGE, *n.* [Fr. from L. *missus*, *mitto*, to send; Sp. *mensage.*]
1. Any notice, word or communication, written or verbal, sent from one person to another. We send a servant with a verbal or written *message.*

> The welcome *message* made, was soon received. *Dryden.*

2. An official written communication of facts or opinions sent by a chief magistrate to the two houses of a legislature or other deliberative body. Congress receives a *message* from the President of the United States at the opening of the session. The Governors of some of the states communicate to the legislature by *message*, others by address.
3. An official verbal communication from one branch of a legislature to the other.

MES'SAGER, } *n.* [Fr. *messager*; It. *messaggiere*; Sp. *mensagero.* The correct orthography is *messager.*]
MES'SENGER, }
1. One who bears a message or an errand; the bearer of a verbal or written communication, notice or invitation from one person to another, or to a public body; one who conveys dispatches from one prince or court to another.
2. A harbinger; a forerunner; he or that which foreshows.

> Yon gray lines
> That fret the clouds, are *messengers* of day. *Shak.*

MESSI'AH, *n.* [Heb. משיח, anointed.] Christ, the anointed; the Savior of the world.

> I know that when *Messiah* cometh, who is called Christ, he will tell us all things. Jesus answered her, I that speak to thee am he. John iv.

MESSI'AHSHIP, *n.* The character, state or office of the Savior.

> Josephus—whose prejudices were against the *Messiahship* and religion of Jesus. *Buckminster.*

MES'SIEURS, *n.* [*plu.* of *monsieur*, my lord.] Sirs; gentlemen.

MESS'-MATE, *n.* An associate in eating; one who eats ordinarily at the same table.

MESS'UAGE, *n.* [from Old Fr. *meson*, *mesonage*, a house or house-room; *mesuenges*, household. The French now write *maison.*]
In *law*, a dwelling house and adjoining land, appropriated to the use of the household, including the adjacent buildings. *Encyc.*

MET, *pret.* and *pp.* of *meet.*

METAB'ASIS, *n.* [Gr. from μετα, beyond, and βαινω, to go.]
In *rhetoric*, transition; a passing from one thing to another.

METAB'OLA, *n.* [Gr. μετα, beyond, and βολη, a casting.]
In *medicine*, a change of air, time or disease. [*Little used.*] *Dict.*

METACARP'AL, *a.* [from *metacarpus.*] Belonging to the metacarpus.

METACARP'US, *n.* [Gr. μεταχαρπιον; μετα, beyond, and χαρπος, the wrist.]
In *anatomy*, the part of the hand between the wrist and the fingers.

METACH'RONISM, *n.* [Gr μετα, beyond, and χρονος, time.]
An error in chronology, by placing an event after its real time.

ME'TAGE, *n.* [from *mete.*] Measurement of coal; price of measuring.

METAGRAM'MATISM, *n.* [Gr. μετα, beyond, and γραμμα, a letter.]
Anagrammatism, or *metagrammatism*, is a transposition of the letters of a name into such a connection as to express some perfect sense applicable to the person named. *Camden.*

METAL, *n. met'l.* [Fr. from L. *metallum*; Gr. μεταλλον; Sw. G. *metall*; D. *metaal*; *id.*; Dan. *metal*; Sp. *id.*; It. *metallo*; Ir. *miotal*; W. *mettel.*]
A simple, fixed, shining, opake body or substance, insoluble in water, fusible by heat, a good conductor of heat and electricity, capable when in the state of an oxyd, of uniting with acids and forming with them metallic salts. Many of the metals are also malleable or extensible by the hammer, and some of them extremely ductile. Metals are mostly fossil, sometimes found native or pure, but more generally combined with other matter. Some metals are more malleable than others, and this circumstance gave rise to the distinction of metals and semi-metals; a distinction little regarded at the present day. Recent discoveries have enlarged the list of the metals, and the whole number now recognized is thirty, exclusive of those which have been recently discovered, as the bases of the earths and alkalies. Twelve of these are malleable, viz. platina, gold, silver, mercury, lead, copper, tin, iron, zink, palladium, nickel, and cadmium. The following sixteen are not sufficiently tenacious to bear extension by beating, viz. arsenic, antimony, bismuth, cobalt, manganese, tellurium, titanium, columbium, molybden, tungsten, chrome, osmium, iridium, rhodium, uranium, and cerium. *Encyc. Nicholson. Thomson. Phillips. Ure.*
To these may be added potassium, sodium, barium, strontium, calcium, and lithium. *Henry.*
The following have not been exhibited in a separate form; magnesium, glucinum, yttrium, aluminum, thorinum, zirconium, and silicium.
2. Courage; spirit; so written by mistake for *mettle.*

METALEP'SIS, *n.* [Gr. μεταληπσις, participation; μετα, beyond, and λαμβανω, to take.]
In *rhetoric*, the continuation of a trope in one word through a succession of significations, or the union of two or more tropes of a different kind in one word, so that several gradations or intervening senses come between the word expressed and the thing intended by it; as "in one Cesar there are many Mariuses." Here Marius, by a synecdoche or antonomasy, is put for any ambitious, turbulent man, and this, by a metonymy of the cause, for the ill effects of such a temper to the public. *Bailey. Encyc.*

METALEP'TIC, *a.* Pertaining to a metalepsis or participation; translative.

2. Transverse; as the *metaleptic* motion of a muscle. *Bailey.*

METALEP'TICALLY, *adv.* By transposition.

METAL'LIC, *a.* [L. *metallicus.*] Pertaining to a metal or metals; consisting of metal; partaking of the nature of metals; like a metal; as a *metallic* substance; *metallic* ore; *metallic* brightness.

METALLIF'EROUS, *a.* [L. *metallum,* metal, and *fero,* to produce.] Producing metals. *Kirwan.*

METAL'LIFORM, *a.* Having the form of metals; like metal. *Kirwan.*

MET'ALLINE, *a.* Pertaining to a metal; consisting of metal.

2. Impregnated with metal; as *metalline* water. *Bacon.*

MET'ALLIST, *n.* A worker in metals, or one skilled in metals. *Moxon.*

METALLIZA'TION, *n.* The act or process of forming into a metal; the operation which gives to a substance its proper metallic properties. *Encyc. Dict.*

MET'ALLIZE, *v. t.* To form into metal; to give to a substance its proper metallic properties. *Dict.*

METALLOG'RAPHY, *n.* [Gr. μεταλλον, metal, and γραφη, description.] An account of metals, or a treatise on metallic substances. *Dict.*

MET'ALLOID, *n.* [*metal,* and Gr. ειδος.] A name sometimes applied to the metallic bases of the alkalies and earths.

METALLOID'AL, *a.* Having the form or appearance of a metal.

MET'ALLURGIC, *a.* [See *Metallurgy.*] Pertaining to metallurgy, or the art of working metals.

MET'ALLURGIST, *n.* One whose occupation is to work metals, or to purify, refine and prepare metals for use.

MET'ALLURGY, *n.* [Gr. μεταλλον, metal, and εργον, work.]
The art of working metals, comprehending the whole process of separating them from other matters in the ore, smelting, refining and parting them. Gilding is also a branch of metallurgy. But in a more limited and usual sense, metallurgy is the operation of separating metals from their ores. *Encyc.*
The French include in metallurgy the art of drawing metals from the earth. *Dict.*

MET'ALMAN, *n.* A worker in metals; a coppersmith or tinman.

METAMORPH'IC, METAMORPH'OSIC, } *a.* [See *Metamorphose.*] Changing the form; transforming.

METAMORPH'OSE, *v. t.* [Gr. μεταμορφοω; μετα, over, beyond, and μορφη, form.] To change into a different form; to transform; particularly, to change the form of insects, as from the larva to a winged animal. The ancients pretended that Jupiter was *metamorphosed* into a bull, and Lycaon into a wolf.

And earth was *metamorphosed* into man. *Dryden.*

METAMORPH'OSER, *n.* One that transforms or changes the shape.

METAMORPH'OSING, *ppr.* Changing the shape.

METAMORPH'OSIS, *n.* Change of form or shape; transformation; particularly, a change in the form of being; as the *metamorphosis* of an insect from the aurelia or chrysalis state into a winged animal.

2. Any change of form or shape.

METAMORPHOS'TICAL, *a.* Pertaining to or effected by metamorphosis. *Pope.*

MET'APHOR, *n.* [Gr. μεταφορα, from μεταφερω, to transfer; μετα, over, and φερω, to carry.]
A short similitude; a similitude reduced to a single word; or a word expressing similitude without the signs of comparison. Thus "that man is a fox," is a metaphor; but "that man is like a fox," is a similitude or comparison. So when I say, "the soldiers were lions in combat," I use a metaphor; but when I say, "the soldiers fought like lions," I use a similitude. In *metaphor,* the similitude is contained in the name; a man is a *fox,* means, a man is as crafty as a fox. So we say, a man *bridles* his anger, that is, restrains it as a bridle restrains a horse. Beauty *awakens* love or tender passions; opposition *fires* courage.

METAPHOR'IC, METAPHOR'ICAL, } *a.* Pertaining to metaphor; comprising a metaphor; not literal; as a *metaphorical* use of words; a *metaphorical* expression; a *metaphorical* sense.

METAPHOR'ICALLY, *adv.* In a metaphorical manner; not literally.

MET'APHORIST, *n.* One that makes metaphors. *Pope.*

MET'APHRASE, *n.* [Gr. μεταφρασις; μετα, over, according to or with, and φρασις, phrase.]
A verbal translation; a version or translation of one language into another, word for word. *Dryden.*

MET'APHRAST, *n.* A person who translates from one language into another, word for word. *Encyc.*

METAPHRAS'TIC, *a.* Close or literal in translation.

METAPHYS'IC, METAPHYS'ICAL, } *a. s* as *z.* [See *Metaphysics.*]

1. Pertaining or relating to metaphysics.

2. According to rules or principles of metaphysics; as *metaphysical* reasoning.

3. Preternatural or supernatural. [*Not used.*] *Shak.*

METAPHYS'ICALLY, *adv.* In the manner of metaphysical science.

METAPHYSI"CIAN, *n. s* as *z.* One who is versed in the science of metaphysics.

METAPHYS'ICS, *n. s* as *z.* [Gr. μετα, after, and φυσικη, physics. It is said that this name was given to the science by Aristotle or his followers, who considered the science of natural bodies, *physics,* as the first in the order of studies, and the science of mind or intelligence to be the second.]
The science of the principles and causes of all things existing; hence, the science of mind or intelligence. This science comprehends *ontology,* or the science which treats of the nature, essence, and qualities or attributes of being; *cosmology,* the science of the world, which treats of the nature and laws of matter and of motion; *anthroposophy,* which treats of the powers of man, and the motions by which life is produced; *psychology,* which treats of the intellectual soul; *pneumatology,* or the science of spirits or angels, &c. *Metaphysical theology,* called by Leibnitz and others *theodicy,* treats of the existence of God, his essence and attributes. These divisions of the science of metaphysics, which prevailed in the ancient schools, are now not much regarded. The natural division of things that exist is into body and mind, things material and immaterial. The former belong to physics, and the latter to the science of metaphysics. *Encyc.*

MET'APLASM, *n.* [Gr. μεταπλασμος, transformation; μετα, over, and πλασσω, to form.]
In *grammar,* a transmutation or change made in a word by transposing or retrenching a syllable or letter.

METAS'TASIS, *n.* [Gr. μεταστασις, mutation; μετα, over, and ιστημι, to place.]
A translation or removal of a disease from one part to another, or such an alteration as is succeeded by a solution. *Coxe. Encyc.*

METATAR'SAL, *a.* [from *metatarsus.*] Belonging to the metatarsus.

METATAR'SUS, *n.* [Gr. μετα, beyond, and ταρσος, tarsus.] The middle of the foot, or part between the ankle and the toes. *Coxe.*

METATH'ESIS, *n.* [Gr. μεταθεσις; μετα, over, and τιθημι, to set.]

1. Transposition; a figure by which the letters or syllables of a word are transposed; as *pistris* for *pristis.* *Encyc.*

2. In *medicine,* a change or removal of a morbid cause, without expulsion. *Coxe. Encyc.*

METE, *v. t.* [Sax. *metan, ametan, gemetan;* D. *meeten;* G. *messen;* Sw. *måta;* Sp. *medir;* L. *metior;* Gr. μετρεω; W. *meidraw;* Ch. and Heb. מדד, to measure; Ar. مدّ madda, to extend. See *Measure,* and Class Md. No. 2.]
To measure; to ascertain quantity, dimensions or capacity by any rule or standard. [*Obsolescent.*]

METE, *n.* [Sax. *mitta.*] Measure; limit; boundary; used chiefly in the plural, in the phrase, *metes and bounds.*

METEMP'SYCHOSE, *v. t.* To translate from one body to another, as the soul.

METEMPSYCHO'SIS, *n.* [Gr. μετεμψυχωσις; μετα, beyond, and ψυχωσις, animation, life; ψυχοω, to animate.]
Transmigration; the passing of the soul of a man after death into some other animal body. Pythagoras and his followers held that after death the souls of men pass into other bodies, and this doctrine still prevails in some parts of Asia, particularly in India and China. *Encyc.*

METEMP'TOSIS, *n.* [Gr. μετα, after, and πιπτω, to fall.]
In *chronology,* the solar equation necessary to prevent the new moon from happening a day too late, or the suppression of the bissextile once in 134 years. The opposite to this is the *proemptosis,* or the addition of a day every 300 years, and another every 2400 years. *Encyc.*

ME'TEOR, *n.* [Gr. μετεωρος, sublime, lofty.]

1. In *a general sense,* a body that flies or floats in the air, and in this sense it includes rain, hail, snow, &c. But in a restricted sense, in which it is commonly understood,

2. A fiery or luminous body or appearance flying or floating in the atmosphere, or in a more elevated region. We give this name to the brilliant globes or masses of matter which are occasionally seen moving rapidly through our atmosphere, and which throw off, with loud explosions, fragments that reach the earth, and are called falling stones. We call by the same name those fire balls which are usually denominated falling stars, supposed to be owing to gelatinous matter inflated by phosphureted hydrogen gas; also, the lights which appear over moist grounds and grave yards, called *ignes fatui*, which are ascribed to the same cause.

And *meteor*-like flame lawless through the sky. *Pope.*

METEOR'IC, *a.* Pertaining to meteors; consisting of meteors.

2. Proceeding from a meteor; as *meteoric* stones.

ME'TEORIZE, *v. i.* To ascend in vapors. [*Not used.*] *Evelyn.*

MET'EOROLITE, } *n.* A meteoric stone;
MET'EROLITE, } a stone or solid compound of earthy and metallic matter which falls to the earth after the displosion of a luminous meteor or fire ball; called also aerolite. *Cleaveland.*

METEOROLOG'IC, } *a.* Pertaining to
METEOROLOG'ICAL, } the atmosphere and its phenomena. A *meteorological* table or register is an account of the state of the air and its temperature, weight, dryness or moisture, winds, &c. ascertained by the barometer, thermometer, hygrometer, anemometer and other *meteorological* instruments.

METEOROL'OGIST, } *n.* A person skilled
METEROL'OGIST, } in meteors; one who studies the phenomena of meteors, or keeps a register of them. *Howell.*

METEOROL'OGY, *n.* [Gr. μετεωρος, lofty, and λογος, discourse.] The science which treats of the atmosphere and its phenomena, particularly in its relation to heat and moisture. *D. Olmsted.*

METEOROM'ANCY, } *n.* [Gr. μετεωρον, a
METEROM'ANCY, } meteor, and μαντεια, divination.]
A species of divination by meteors, chiefly by thunder and lightning; held in high estimation by the Romans. *Encyc.*

METEOROS'COPY, *n.* [Gr. μετεωρος, lofty, and σκοπεω, to view.]
That part of astronomy which treats of sublime heavenly bodies, distance of stars, &c. *Bailey.*

METE'OROUS, *a.* Having the nature of a meteor. *Milton.*

ME'TER, *n.* [from *mete.*] One who measures; used in compounds, as in coal-*meter*, land-*meter*.

ME'TER, *n.* [Sax. *meter*; Fr. *metre*; L. *metrum*; Gr. μετρον, from μετρεω.]

1. Measure; verse; arrangement of poetical feet, or of long and short syllables in verse. Hexameter is a *meter* of six feet. This word is most improperly written *metre.* How very absurd to write the simple word in this manner, but in all its numerous compounds, *meter*, as in *diameter*, *hexameter*, *thermometer*, &c.

2. A French measure of length, equal to $39\frac{37}{100}$ English inches, the standard of linear measure, being the ten millionth part of the distance from the equator to the North Pole, as ascertained by actual measurement of an arc of the meridian. *Lunier. D. Olmsted.*

ME'TEWAND, *n.* [*mete* and *wand.*] A staff or rod of a certain length, used as a measure. [*Obs.*] *Ascham.*

ME'TEYARD, *n.* [Sax. *metgeard.*] A yard, staff or rod, used as a measure. *Obs.* [We now use *yard.*]

METHEG'LIN, *n.* [W. *mezyglin*, according to Owen, from W. *mezyg*, a physician, and *llyn*, water; a medicinal liquor. But *mez* is mead, and *mezu* is to be strong or able.]
A liquor made of honey and water boiled and fermented, often enriched with spices. *Encyc.*

METHINKS, *v. impers.* pp. *methought.* [*me* and *think.*] It seems to me; it appears to me; I think. *Me* is here in the dative. The word is not antiquated, but is not elegant.

METH'OD, *n.* [L. *methodus*; Gr. μεθοδος; μετα, with, and οδος, way.]

1. A suitable and convenient arrangement of things, proceedings or ideas; the natural or regular disposition of separate things or parts; convenient order for transacting business, or for comprehending any complicated subject. Without *method*, business of any kind will fall into confusion. To carry on farming to advantage, to keep accounts correctly, *method* is indispensable.

2. Way; manner. Let us know the nature of the disease, and the *method* of cure.

3. Classification; arrangement of natural bodies according to their common characteristics; as the *method* of Theophrast; the *method* of Ray; the Linnean *method.*
In natural arrangements a distinction is sometimes made between *method* and *system. System* is an arrangement founded, throughout all its parts, on some one principle. *Method* is an arrangement less fixed and determinate, and founded on more general relations. Thus we say, the *natural method*, and the *artificial* or *sexual system* of Linne, though the latter is not a perfect system. *Ed. Encyc.*

METHOD'IC, } *a.* Arranged in conven-
METHOD'ICAL, } ient order; disposed in a just and natural manner, or in a manner to illustrate a subject, or to facilitate practical operations; as a *methodical* arrangement of the parts of a discourse or of arguments; a *methodical* treatise; *methodical* accounts.

METHOD'ICALLY, *adv.* In a methodical manner; according to natural or convenient order.

METH'ODISM, *n.* The doctrines and worship of the sect of Christians called *Methodists.*

METH'ODIST, *n.* One that observes method.

2. One of a sect of christians, founded by Morgan, or rather by John Wesley, and so called from the exact regularity of their lives, and the strictness of their principles and rules.

3. A physician who practices by method or theory. *Boyle.*

4. In *the cant of irreligious men*, a person of strict piety; one who lives in the exact observance of religious duties.

METHODIS'TIC, *a.* Resembling the Methodists; partaking of the strictness of Methodists. *Ch. Obs.*

METH'ODIZE, *v. t.* To reduce to method; to dispose in due order; to arrange in a convenient manner.

One who brings with him any observations he has made in reading the poets, will find his own reflections *methodized* and explained in the works of a good critic. *Spectator.*

METHOUGHT, *pret.* of *methinks.* It seemed to me; I thought. *Milton. Dryden.*

ME'TIC, *n.* [Gr. μετοικος; μετα and οικος, house.]
In ancient Greece, a sojourner; a resident stranger in a Grecian city or place. *Mitford.*

METIC'ULOUS, *a.* [L. *Feticulosus.*] Timid. [*Not used.*] *Coles.*

METON'IC CYCLE, } the cycle of the
METON'IC YEAR, } moon, or period of nineteen years, in which the lunations of the moon return to the same days of the month; so called from its discoverer Meton the Athenian. *Encyc. Baily.*

METONYM'IC, } *a.* [See *Metonymy.*]
METONYM'ICAL, } Used by way of metonymy, by putting one word for another.

METONYM'ICALLY, *adv.* By putting one word for another.

MET'ONYMY, *n.* [Gr. μετωνυμια; μετα, over, beyond, and ονομα, name.]
In *rhetoric*, a trope in which one word is put for another; a change of names which have some relation to each other; as when we say, "a man keeps a good *table*," instead of good *provisions*. "We read *Virgil*," that is, his *poeFs* or *writings*. "They have *Moses* and the *prophets*," that is, their *books* or *writings*. A man has a clear *head*, that is, *understanding*, *intellect*; a warm *heart*, that is, *affections*.

METOPE, *n.* met'opy. [Gr. μετοπη; μετα, with, near or by, and οπη, an aperture or hollow.]
In *architecture*, the space between the triglyphs of the Doric frieze, which among the ancients used to be painted or adorned with carved work. *Encyc.*

METOPOS'COPIST, *n.* [infra.] One versed in physiognomy.

METOPOS'COPY, *n.* [Gr. μετωπον, the forehead, and σκοπεω, to view.]
The study of physiognomy; the art of discovering the character or the dispositions of men by their features, or the lines of the face. *Encyc.*

METRE. [See *Meter.*]

MET'RICAL, *a.* [L. *metricus*; Fr. *metrique.*]

1. Pertaining to measure, or due arrangement or combination of long and short syllables.

2. Consisting of verses; as *metrical* compositions.

METROL'OGY, *n.* [Gr. μετρον, measure, and λογος, discourse.]

1. A discourse on measures or mensuration; the description of measures.

2. An account of measures, or the science of weights and measures. *J. Q. Adams.*

METROP'OLIS, *n.* [L. from Gr. *μητροπολις*; *μητηρ*, mother, and *πολις*, city. It has no plural.]

Literally, the mother-city, that is, the chief city or capital of a kingdom, state or country, as Paris in France, Madrid in Spain, London in Great Britain. In the United States, Washington, in the District of Columbia, is the *metropolis*, as being the seat of government; but in several of the states, the largest cities are not the seats of the respective governments. Yet New York city, in the state of that name, and Philadelphia in Pennsylvania, are the chief cities, and may be called each the *metropolis* of the state in which it is situated, though neither of them is the seat of government in the state.

METROPOL'ITAN, *a.* Belonging to a metropolis, or to the mother church; residing in the chief city.

METROPOL'ITAN, *n.* The bishop of the mother church; an archbishop. *Clarendon.*

METROP'OLITE, *n.* A metropolitan. [*Not used.*]

METROPOL'ITIC, METROPOLIT'ICAL, *a.* Pertaining to a metropolis; chief or principal of cities; archiepiscopal. *Knolles. Milner. Selden.*

METTLE, *n.* *met'l.* [usually supposed to be corrupted from *metal*. But it may be from W. *mezwl* or *methwl*, mind, connected with *mezu*, to be able, and coinciding with the root of the Eng. *moody*; D. *moed*, courage, heart, spirit; G. *muth*, mind, courage, mettle; Sax. Sw. *mod*; Dan. *mod* or *mood*; Goth. *mod*, angry. The Sax. *modig*, L. *animus*, *animosus*, furnish an analogy in point. The radical sense of *mind*, is to advance, to push forward, whence the sense of briskness, ardor.]

Spirit; constitutional ardor; that temperament which is susceptible of high excitement. It is not synonymous with *courage*, though it may be accompanied with it, and is sometimes used for it.

> The winged courser, like a generous horse,
> Shows most true *mettle* when you check his course. *Pope.*

MET'TLED, *a.* High spirited; ardent; full of fire. *Pope.*

MET'TLESOME, *a.* Full of spirit; possessing constitutional ardor; brisk; fiery; as a *mettlesome* horse. *Tatler.*

MET'TLESOMENESS, *n.* The state of being high spirited.

MEW, *n.* [Sax. *mæw*; Dan. *maage*; D. *meeuw*; G. *mewe*; Fr. *mouette*.] A sea-fowl of the genus Larus; a gull.

MEW, *n.* [Fr. *mue*; Arm. *muz*; W. *mud*, a *mew* and *mute*; D. *muite*. See the verb to *mew*, to shed fethers.]

A cage for birds; an inclosure; a place of confinement.

MEW, *v. t.* [from the noun.] To shut up; to inclose; to confine, as in a cage or other inclosure.

> More pity that the eagle should be *mew'd*. *Shak.*

> Close *mew'd* in their sedans, for fear of air. *Dryden.*

MEW, *v. t.* [W. *miw*, a shedding of fethers; It. *mudare*, to mew; Fr. *muer*; Arm. *muza*; G. *mausen*; D. *muiten*, to mew or molt, to *mutiny*; Sp. *muda*, change, alteration, a *mute* letter, time of molting or shedding fethers, roost of a hawk; Port. *mudar*, to change, to mew or cast fethers or a slough; *muda*, a dumb woman, the mewing or molting of birds. The W. *mud*, a mew, is also removal, a pass or move, a change of residence, and *mute*; and the verb *mudaw* is to change, to remove, comprehending the L. *muto* and *moto*. We have then clear evidence that *mew*, a cage, *mew*, to molt, and the L. *muto*, *moto*, and *mutus*, and Eng. *mutiny*, are all from one root. The primary sense is to press or drive, whence to move, to change, and to shut up, that is, to press or drive close; and this is the sense of *mute*. *Mutiny* is from motion or change.]

To shed or cast; to change; to molt. The hawk *mewed* his fethers.

> Nine times the moon had *mew'd* her horns— *Dryden.*

MEW, *v. i.* [W. *mewian*; G. *miauen*; coinciding probably with L. *mugio*.] To cry as a cat.

MEW, *v. i.* To change; to put on a new appearance.

MEW'ING, *ppr.* Casting the fethers or skin; crying.

MEWL, *v. i.* [Fr. *miauler*; It. *miagolare*; Sp. *maullar* or *mayar*; coinciding in elements with L. *mugio*, to low; G. *mucken*; Dan. *mukker*, to mutter; Gr. *μηκαομαι*, to bleat; Ir. *meigiollam*; W. *migiaw*.] To cry or squall, as a child. *Shak.*

MEWL'ER, *n.* One that squalls or mewls.

MEZE'REON, *n.* A plant of the genus Daphne; the spurge olive. *Encyc.*

MEZZO, in music, denotes middle, mean.

MEZZORELIE'VO, *n.* [It. *mezzorilievo*.] Middle relief.

MEZZOTINT'O, *n.* [It. *mezzo*, middle, half, and *tinto*, L. *tinctus*, painted.]

A particular manner of engraving or representation of figures on copper, in imitation of painting in Indian ink. To perform this the plate is scratched and furrowed in different directions; the design is then drawn on the face, then the dents and furrows are erased from the parts where the lights of the piece are to be; the parts which are to represent shades being left. *Encyc.*

MI'ASM, MIAS'MA, *n.* [Gr. from *μιαινω*, to pollute.] Infecting substances floating in the air; the effluvia or fine particles of any putrefying bodies, rising and floating in the atmosphere, and considered to be noxious to health.

MIASMAT'IC, *a.* Pertaining to miasma; partaking of the qualities of noxious effluvia.

MI'CA, *n.* [L. *mica*, a grain or particle; *mico*, to shine.]

A mineral of a foliated structure, consisting of thin flexible lamels or scales, having a shining surface. The scales are sometimes parallel, sometimes interwoven, sometimes wavy or undulated, sometimes representing filaments. It is called also *talck*, *glimmer*, *muscovy-glass*, and *glist*. *Nicholson. Encyc.*

Jameson subdivides mica into ten subspecies, viz. mica, pinite, lepidolite, chlorite, green earth, talck, nacrite, potstone, steatite and figure stone. *Ure.*

MICA'CEOUS, *a.* Pertaining to mica; resembling mica or partaking of its properties.

MIC'AREL, *n.* A species of argillaceous earth; a mineral of a brownish or blackish red color, commonly crystalized in rhomboidal prisms, or in prisms of six sides. *Dict.*

MICE, *plu.* of *mouse.*

MI'CHAELITE, *n.* A subvariety of siliceous sinter, found in the isle of St. Michael. *J. W. Webster.*

MICH'AELMAS, *n.* The feast of St. Michael, a festival of the Romish church, celebrated Sept. 29; hence,

2. In colloquial language, autumn.

MICHE, *v. i.* [allied perhaps to Sw. *maka*, to withdraw; Sax. *smugan*, to creep. *Meeching* or *meaching*, is still used by some of our common people in the sense of mean, cowardly, retiring.]

1. To lie hid; to skulk; to retire or shrink from view.

2. To pilfer. *Obs.* *Shak.*

MICH'ER, *n.* One who skulks, or creeps out of sight; a thief. *Obs.* *Chaucer. Sidney. Shak.*

MICH'ERY, *n.* Theft; cheating. *Obs.* *Gower.*

MICH'ING, *ppr.* Retiring; skulking; creeping from sight; mean; cowardly. [*Vulgar.*]

MICK'LE, *a.* [Sax. *micel*, *mucel*; Scot. *myche*, *mekyl*, *muckle*; Sw. *mycken*; Sp. *mucho*; Gr. *μεγας*, *μεγαλη*. See *Much*.]

Much; great. [Obsolete, but retained in the Scottish language.]

MI'CO, *n.* A beautiful species of monkey.

MIC'ROCOSM, *n.* [Gr. *μικρος*, small, and *κοσμος*, world.]

Literally, the little world; but used for man, supposed to be an epitome of the universe or great world. *Swift. Encyc.*

Microcosmic salt, a triple salt of soda, ammonia and phosphoric acid, obtained from urine. *Ure.*

MICROCOS'MICAL, *a.* Pertaining to the microcosm.

MICROCOUS'TIC, *n.* [Gr. *μικρος*, small, and *ακουω*, to hear.]

An instrument to augment small sounds, and assist in hearing.

MICROG'RAPHY, *n.* [Gr. *μικρος*, small, and *γραφω*, to describe.]

The description of objects too small to be discerned without the aid of a microscope. *Encyc. Grew.*

MICROM'ETER, *n.* [Gr. *μικρος*, small, and *μετρον*, measure.]

An instrument for measuring small objects or spaces, by the help of which, the apparent magnitude of objects viewed through the microscope or telescope, is measured with great exactness. *Encyc.*

MIC'ROPHONE, *n.* [Gr. *μικρος*, small, and *φωνη*, sound.]

An instrument to augment small sounds; a microcoustic. *Bailey.*

MIC'ROSCOPE, *n.* [Gr. *μικρος*, small, and *σκοπεω*, to view.]

An optical instrument consisting of lenses or mirrors, which magnify objects, and thus render visible minute objects which cannot be seen by the naked eye, or enlarge the apparent magnitude of small visible bodies, so as to enable us to examine their texture or construction.

MI€ROS€OP'I€, MI€ROS€OP'I€AL, *a.* Made by the aid of a microscope; as *microscopic* observation. *Arbuthnot.*

2. Assisted by a microscope.

> Evading even the *microscopic* eye. *Thomson.*

3. Resembling a microscope; capable of seeing small objects.

> Why has not man a *microscopic* eye? *Pope.*

4. Very small; visible only by the aid of a microscope; as a *microscopic* insect.

MI€ROS€OP'I€ALLY, *adv.* By the microscope; with minute inspection. *Good.*

MI€TURI''TION, *n.* [L. *micturio.*] The act of making water, or passing the urine. *Darwin.*

MID, *a.* [Sax. *midd, midde*; L. *medius*; W. *mid*, an inclosure.]

1. Middle; at equal distance from extremes; as the *mid* hour of night. *Rowe.*

2. Intervening.

> No more the mounting larks, while Daphne sings,
> Shall, lifting in *mid* air, suspend their wings. *Pope.*

MI'DA, *n.* [Gr. μιδας.] A worm, or the bean-fly. *Chambers.*

MID'-AĠE, *n.* The middle of life, or persons of that age. *Shak.*

MID-€OURSE, *n.* The middle of the course or way. *Milton.*

MID'-DAY, *a.* Being at noon; meridional; as the *mid-day* sun. *Addison.*

MID'-DAY, *n.* The middle of the day; noon. *Donne.*

MID'DEST, *a. superl.* of *mid.*

> Among the *middest* crowd. [*Not used.*] *Spenser.*

MIDDLE, *a. mid'l.* [Sax. D. *middel*; G. *mittel*; Dan. *middel*; perhaps *mid* and *deel*; Sans. *medhi* and *madhyam*; L. *medius*; Gr. μεσος; It. *mezzo*; Sp. *medio*; Port. *mayo, mediano*; Ir. *modham, muadh*; Fr. *midi, moyen,* [*mitan, obs.*;] Ch. מצע. This word has the elements of the Sax. *mid*, D. *mede*, Sw. and Dan. *mede*, G. *mit*, with, Gr. μετα, which is from the root of the English *meet*, which see. Qu. has not the L. *medius*, in the phrase *medius fidius*, the sense of *with* or *by*; *by* or *with my faith.* In W. *mid* signifies an inclosure, a hem or list round a place. In Russ. *mejdu* signifies *among*. See Class Ms. No. 21. 27.]

1. Equally distant from the extremes; as the *middle* point of a line or circle; the *middle* station of life. The *middle* path or course is most safe.

2. Intermediate; intervening.

> Will, seeking good, finds many *middle* ends. *Davies.*

Middle ages, the ages or period of time about equally distant from the decline of the Roman empire and the revival of letters in Europe, or from the eighth to the fifteenth century of the christian era.

MID'DLE, *n.* The point or part equally distant from the extremities.

> See, there come people down by the *middle* of the land. Judges ix.

2. The time that passes, or events that happen between the beginning and the end. *Dryden.*

MID'DLE-AĠED, *a.* Being about the middle of the ordinary age of man. A *middle-aged* man is so called from the age of thirty five or forty to forty five or fifty.

MID'DLE-EARTH, *n.* [Sax. *middan-eard.*] The world. *Obs.* *Shak.*

MID'DLEMOST, *a.* Being in the middle, or nearest the middle of a number of things that are near the middle. If a thing is in the middle, it cannot be more so, and in this sense the word is improper. But when two or more things are near the middle, one may be nearer than another.

MID'DLING, *a.* [Sax. *midlen.*] Of middle rank, state, size or quality; about equally distant from the extremes; moderate. Thus we speak of people of the *middling* class or sort, neither high nor low; of a man of *middling* capacity or understanding; a man of *middling* size; fruit of a *middling* quality.

MIDĠE, *n.* [Sax. *myge, mygge.*] A gnat or flea. [*Not used.*]

MID'-HEAVEN, *n.* The middle of the sky or heaven. *Milton.*

MID'LAND, *a.* Being in the interior country; distant from the coast or sea shore; as *midland* towns or inhabitants. *Howell. Hale.*

2. Surrounded by the sea; mediterranean.

> And on the *midland* sea the French had aw'd. *Dryden.*

MID'LEG, *n.* Middle of the leg. *Bacon.*

MID'MOST, *a.* Middle; as the *midmost* battles. *Dryden.*

MID'NIGHT, *n.* The middle of the night; twelve o'clock at night.

MID'NIGHT, *a.* Being in the middle of the night; as *midnight* studies. *Bacon.*

2. Dark as midnight; very dark; as *midnight* gloom.

MID'RIFF, *n.* [Sax. *midhrife*; *mid* and *hrife*, the belly.]

In *anatomy*, the diaphragm; the muscle which divides the trunk into two cavities, the thorax and abdomen. *Quincy.*

MID'SEA, *n.* The Mediterranean sea. *Dryden.*

MID'SHIP, *a.* Being or belonging to the middle of a ship; as a *midship* beam.

MID'SHIPMAN, *n.* In *ships of war*, a kind of naval cadet, whose business is to second the orders of the superior officers and assist in the necessary business of the ship, particularly in managing the sails, that he may be trained to a knowledge of the machinery, discipline and operations of ships of war, and qualified for naval service. *Mar. Dict.*

MID'SHIPS, *adv.* In the middle of a ship; properly *amidships.*

MIDST, *n.* [contracted from *middest*, the superlative of *mid.*] The middle.

> There is nothing said or done in the *midst* of the play, which might not have been placed in the beginning. *Dryden.*

The phrase, *in the midst*, often signifies involved in, surrounded or overwhelmed by, or in the thickest part, or in the depths of; as *in the midst* of afflictions, troubles or cares; *in the midst* of our contemplations; *in the midst* of the battle; *in the midst* of pagan darkness and error; *in the midst* of gospel light; *in the midst* of the ocean; *in the midst* of civil dissensions.

From the midst, from the middle, or from among. Deut. xviii.

MIDST, *adv.* In the middle.

> On earth, join all ye creatures to extol
> Him first, Him last, Him *midst*, and without end. *Milton.*

MID'STREAM, *n.* The middle of the stream. *Dryden.*

MID'SUMMER, *n.* The middle of summer; the summer solstice, about the 21st of June. *Swift. Gay.*

MID'WARD, *adv.* Midst. [*Not in use.*]

MID'WAY, *n.* The middle of the way or distance.

> Paths indirect, or in the *midway* faint. *Milton.*

MID'WAY, *a.* Being in the middle of the way or distance; as the *midway* air. *Shak.*

MID'WAY, *adv.* In the middle of the way or distance; half way.

> She met his glance *midway.* *Dryden.*

MID'WIFE, *n.* [supposed by Junius and Skinner to be *meedwife*, a woman that has a reward. This is probably a mistake. The word is a compound of *mid*, with, and *wif*, a woman; in analogy with the L. *obstetrix*, from *obsto, obstiti*, to stand before. The Dutch use *vroedvrouw*, a wise or skillful woman. The Danish equivalent word is *iordemoder*, earth-mother; the Swedish, *iord-gumma.* The Spanish and Portuguese word is *comadre*; *co* for L. *cum*, with, and *madre*, mother, which is precisely analogous to *midwife.*]

A woman that assists other women in childbirth.

MID'WIFE, *v. i.* To perform the office of midwife.

MID'WIFE, *v. t.* To assist in childbirth.

MID'WIFERY, *n.* The art or practice of assisting women in childbirth; obstetrics.

2. Assistance at childbirth.

3. Help or cooperation in production. *Stepney.*

MID'-WINTER, *n.* The middle of winter, or the winter solstice, December 21. As the severity of winter in North America falls in January and February, the word ordinarily denotes this period, or some weeks after the winter solstice.

MI'EMITE, *n.* Granular miemite is a subvariety of magnesian limestone, first found at Miemo, in Tuscany. It occurs massive, or crystalized in flat, double, three-sided pyramids. Its color is light green or greenish white. *Jameson. Cyc.*

MIEN, *n.* [Fr. *mine*; Dan. Sw. *id.*; Arm. *man*; Corn. *mein*, the face; Ice. *mind*, image. See *Man.*]

Look; air; manner; external appearance; carriage; as a lofty *mien*; a majestic *mien.* *Waller. Pope.*

MIFF, *n.* A slight degree of resentment. [*Colloquial.*]

MIF'FED, *a.* Slightly offended. [In Norman French, *mefet* is offense or misdeed, and *meffet*, misdone; *mes* and *faire*; whence *meffere*, to do mischief. But qu. whether this is the English *miff.*]

MIGHT, *n. pret.* of *may.* Had power or liberty. He *might* go, or *might* have gone.

2. It sometimes denotes *was possible*, implying ignorance of the fact in the speaker. Orders *might* have been given for the purpose.

MIGHT, *n.* [Sax. *might*, *meht* ; G. *macht* ; D. Sw. Dan. *magt* ; from the root of *may*, Sax. *magan*, to be able ; Sans. *mahat*, strong. See *May*.]

1. Strength ; force ; power ; primarily and chiefly, bodily strength or physical power ; as, to work or strive with all one's *might*.
   There shall be no *might* in thy hand. Deut. xxviii.
2. Political power or great achievments.
   The acts of David—with all his reign and his *might*. 1 Chron. xxix. 1 Kings xv.
3. National strength ; physical power or military force.
   We have no *might* against this great company that cometh against us. 2 Chron. xx.
4. Valor with bodily strength ; military prowess ; as men of *might*. 1 Chron. xii.
5. Ability ; strength or application of means.
   I have prepared with all my *might* for the house of my God— 1 Chron. xxix.
6. Strength or force of purpose.
   Like him was no king that turned to the Lord with all his *might*. 2 Kings xxiii.
7. Strength of affection.
   Thou shalt love the Lord thy God with all thine heart, and with all thy soul, and with all thy *might*. Deut. vi.
8. Strength of light ; splendor ; effulgence.
   Let them that love him be as the sun when he goeth forth in his *might*. Judges v.

Shakspeare applies the word to an oath. "An oath of mickle *might*." This application is obsolete. We now use *strength* or *force* ; as the *strength* or *force* of an oath or covenant.

With might and main, with the utmost strength or bodily exertion ; a tautological phrase, as both words are from the same root, and mean the same thing.

MI'GHTILY, *adv.* [from *mighty*.] With great power, force or strength ; vigorously ; as, to strive *mightily*.

2. Vehemently ; with great earnestness.
   Cry *mightily* to God. Jonah iii.
3. Powerfully ; with great energy.
   Whereto I also labor, striving according to his working, which worketh in me *mightily*. Col. i.
4. With great strength of argument.
   He *mightily* convinced the Jews. Acts xviii.
5. With great or irresistible force ; greatly ; extensively.
   So *mightily* grew the word of God and prevailed. Acts xix.
6. With strong means of defense.
   Fortify thy power *mightily*. Nah. ii.
7. Greatly ; to a great degree ; very much.
   I was *mightily* pleased with a story applicable to this piece of philosophy. *Spectator.*
   [*Admissible in colloquial and familiar language.*]

MI'GHTINESS, *n.* Power ; greatness ; highth of dignity.

How soon this *mightiness* meets misery ! *Shak.*

2. A title of dignity ; as their High *Mightinesses*.

MI'GHTY, *a.* [Sax. *mihtig*.] Having great bodily strength or physical power ; very strong or vigorous ; as a *mighty* arm.

2. Very strong ; valiant ; bold ; as a *mighty* man of valor. Judges vi.
3. Very powerful ; having great command.
   Cush begat Nimrod ; he began to be a *mighty* one on the earth. Gen. x.
4. Very strong in numbers ; as a *mighty* nation. Gen. xviii.
5. Very strong or great in corporeal power ; very able.
   Wo to them that are *mighty* to drink wine. Is. v.
6. Violent ; very loud ; as *mighty* thunderings. Ex. ix. Ps. lxviii.
7. Vehement ; rushing with violence ; as a *mighty* wind or tempest. Ex. x. Rev. vi.
8. Very great ; vast ; as *mighty* waters. Neh. ix.
9. Very great or strong ; as *mighty* power. 2 Chron. xxvi.
10. Very forcible ; efficacious ; as, great is truth and *mighty*. *Esdras.*
11. Very great or eminent in intellect or acquirements ; as the *mighty* Scaliger and Selden. *Echard.*
12. Great ; wonderful ; performed with great power ; as *mighty* works. Matt. xi.
13. Very severe and distressing ; as a *mighty* famine. Luke xv.
14. Very great, large or populous ; as a *mighty* city. Rev. xviii.
15. Important ; momentous.
    I'll sing of heroes and of kings,
    In mighty numbers *mighty* things. *Cowley.*

MI'GHTY, *adv.* In a great degree ; very ; as *mighty* wise ; *mighty* thoughtful. [*Colloquial.*] *Prior.*

MIGNIARD, *a.* [Fr. *mignard*.] Soft ; dainty ; delicate ; pretty. *B. Jonson.*

MIGNONETTE, **MIG'ONET**, } *n.* [Fr.] An annual flower or plant of the genus Reseda, having the scent of raspberries. *Mason.*

MI'GRATE, *v. i.* [L. *migro*.] To pass or remove from one country or from one state to another, with a view to permanent residence, or residence of some continuance. The first settlers of New England *migrated* first to Holland, and afterwards to America. Some species of fowls *migrate* in autumn to a warmer climate for a temporary residence. To change residence in the same city or state is not to *migrate*.

2. To pass or remove from one region or district to another for a temporary residence ; as, the Tartars *migrate* for the sake of finding pasturage.

MI'GRATING, *ppr.* Removing from one state to another for a permanent residence. The people of the eastern states are continually *migrating* to the western states.

MIGRA'TION, *n.* [L. *migratio*.] The act of removing from one kingdom or state to another, for the purpose of permanent residence, or a residence of some continuance.

2. Change of place ; removal ; as the *migration* of the center of gravity. *Woodward.*

MI'GRATORY, *a.* Removing or accustomed to remove from one state or country to another for permanent residence.

2. Roving ; wandering ; occasionally removing for pasturage ; as the *migratory* Tartars.
3. Passing from one climate to another ; as fowls.

MILCH, *a.* [Sax. *melce*. See *Milk*.] Giving milk ; as a *milch* cow. It is now applied only to beasts.

MILD, *a.* [Sax. *mild* ; G. D. Sw. Dan. *id.* ; Russ. *melayu*, to pity. The primary sense is soft or smooth, L. *mollis*, Eng. *mellow*, W. *mall* ; allied perhaps to *melt*. Class Ml. No. 9. 16. 18.]

1. Soft ; gently and pleasantly affecting the senses ; not violent ; as a *mild* air ; a *mild* sun ; a *mild* temperature ; a *mild* light.
   The rosy morn resigns her light
   And *milder* glory to the noon. *Waller.*
   And with a *milder* gleam refreshed the sight. *Addison.*
2. Not acrid, pungent, corrosive or drastic ; operating gently ; not acrimonious ; demulcent ; mollifying ; lenitive ; assuasive ; as a *mild* liquor ; a *mild* cataplasm ; a *mild* cathartic or emetic.
3. Tender and gentle in temper or disposition ; kind ; compassionate ; merciful ; clement ; indulgent ; not severe or cruel.
   It teaches us to adore him as a *mild* and merciful Being. *Rogers.*
4. Not fierce, rough or angry ; as *mild* words.
5. Placid ; not fierce ; not stern ; not frowning ; as a *mild* look or aspect.
6. Not sharp, tart, sour or bitter ; moderately sweet or pleasant to the taste ; as *mild* fruit.
7. Calm ; tranquil. When passion subsides the temper becomes *mild*.
8. Moderate ; not violent or intense ; as a *mild* heat.

MIL'DEW, *n.* [Sax. *mildeaw* ; L. *melligo*, from *mel*, honey ; G. *mehlthau*, as if from *mehl*, meal.]

1. Honey dew ; a thick, clammy, sweet juice, found on the leaves of plants, which is said to injure the plants by corroding them, or otherwise preventing them from coming to perfection. *Hill. Encyc.*
2. Spots on cloth or paper caused by moisture.

MIL'DEW, *v. t.* To taint with mildew. *Shak.*

MIL'DEWED, *pp.* Tainted or injured by mildew.

MIL'DEWING, *ppr.* Tainting with mildew.

MILDLY, *adv.* Softly ; gently ; tenderly ; not roughly or violently ; moderately ; as, to speak *mildly* ; to burn *mildly* ; to operate *mildly*.

MILDNESS, *n.* Softness ; gentleness ; as the *mildness* of words or speech ; *mildness* of voice.

2. Tenderness ; mercy ; clemency ; as *mildness* of temper.
3. Gentleness of operation ; as the *mildness* of a medicine.
4. Softness ; the quality that affects the senses pleasantly ; as the *mildness* of fruit or of liquors.
5. Temperateness ; moderate state ; as the *mildness* of weather.

MILD-SPIR'ITED, *a.* Having a mild temper. *Arbuthnot.*

MILE, *n.* [L. *mille passus*, a thousand paces ; *passus* being dropped in common usage, the word became a noun ; Sax. Sw. *mil* ; Dan. *miil* ; G. *meile* ; D. *myl* ; Fr. *mille* ; Sp. *milla* ; Port. *milha* ; It. *miglio*.]

A measure of length or distance, containing eight furlongs, 320 rods, poles or perches, 1760 yards, 5280 feet, or 80 chains. The Roman mile was a thousand paces, equal to 1600 yards English measure.

MI'LEAGE, *n.* Fees paid for travel by the mile.

MI'LESTONE, *n.* A stone set to mark the distance or space of a mile.

MIL'FOIL, *n.* [L. *millefolium*, a thousand leaves.]
A plant of the genus Achillea ; yarrow.

MIL'IARY, *a.* [Fr. *miliaire*, L. *milium*, millet.]
1. Resembling millet seeds ; as a *miliary* eruption ; *miliary* glands. The *miliary* glands are the sebaceous glands of the skin. *Coxe.*
2. Accompanied with an eruption like millet seeds ; as a *miliary* fever.

MILICE, for *militia*, is not in use.

MIL'IOLITE, *n.* Fossil remains of the Miliola, a genus of univalve shells. *Ed. Encyc.*

MIL'ITANCY, *n.* Warfare. [*Little used.*] *Mountague.*

MIL'ITANT, *a.* [L. *militans, milito*, to fight.]
1. Fighting ; combating ; serving as a soldier. *Spenser.*
2. The *church militant*, is the christian church on earth, which is supposed to be engaged in a constant warfare against its enemies ; thus distinguished from the *church triumphant*, or in heaven. *Hooker.*

MIL'ITARILY, *adv.* In a soldierly manner.

MIL'ITARY, *a.* [Fr. *militaire ;* L. *militaris*, from *miles*, a soldier ; *milito*, to fight; Gr. *αμιλλα*, contest.]
1. Pertaining to soldiers or to arms; as a *military* parade or appearance ; *military* discipline.
2. Engaged in the service of soldiers or arms ; as a *military* man.
3. Warlike ; becoming a soldier ; as *military* virtue ; *military* bravery.
4. Derived from the services or exploits of a soldier ; as *military* renown.
5. Conformable to the customs or rules of armies or militia. The conduct of the officer was not *military.*
6. Performed or made by soldiers ; as a *military* election. *Bacon.*
Military tenure, a tenure of land, on condition of performing military service.

MIL'ITARY, *n.* The whole body of soldiers; soldiery ; militia ; an army. *U. States. Mitford.*

MIL'ITATE, *v. i.* [L. *milito.*] To *militate against*, is to oppose ; to be or to act in opposition. *Smollet.*
Paley writes, to *militate with ;* but in America, *against* is generally used.

MILI''TIA, *n.* [L. from *miles*, a soldier ; Ir. *mal* or *mil ;* W. *milwr ;* Gr. *μωλος*, war ; *μωλεω*, to fight ; *αμιλλα*, combat, contention. The primary sense of fighting is to strive, struggle, drive, or to strike, to beat, Eng. *moil*, L. *molior*, Heb. Ch. Syr. Sam. Ar. עמל, to labor or toil. So *exercitus*, from *exerceo*, to exert, to strive. Class Ml. No. 15.]
The body of soldiers in a state enrolled for discipline, but not engaged in actual service except in emergencies; as distinguished from regular troops, whose sole occupation is war or military service. The militia of a country are the able bodied men organized into companies, regiments and brigades, with officers of all grades, and required by law to attend military exercises on certain days only, but at other times left to pursue their usual occupations.

MILK, *n.* [Sax. *melce ;* G. *milch ;* D. *melk ;* Sw. *miölk ;* Dan. *mælk ;* Russ. *mleko* or *moloko ;* Bohemian, *mliko ;* Ir. *meilg.* See the Verb.]
1. A white fluid or liquor, secreted by certain glands in female animals, and drawn from the breasts for the nourishment of their young.
2. The white juice of certain plants.
3. Emulsion made by bruising seeds. *Bacon.*

MILK, *v. t.* [Sax. *melcan, meolcian ;* G. D. *melken ;* Sw. *miölka ;* Dan. *mælker ;* Russ. *melzyu ;* L. *mulgeo ;* Gr. *αμελγω.*]
1. To draw or press milk from the breasts by the hand ; as, to *milk* a cow.
2. To suck. [*Not used.*] *Shak.*

MILK'EN, *a.* Consisting of milk. [*Not used.*] *Temple.*

MILK'ER, *n.* One that milks.

MILK'-FEVER, *n.* A fever which accompanies the first flowing of milk in females after childbirth.

MILK'-HEDGE, *n.* A shrub growing on the Coromandel coast, containing a milky juice.

MILK'INESS, *n.* Qualities like those of milk ; softness. *Dryden.*

MILK'-LIVERED, *a.* Cowardly ; timorous. *Shak.*

MILK'MAID, *n.* A woman that milks or is employed in the dairy.

MILK'MAN, *n.* A man that sells milk or carries milk to market.

MILK'PAIL, *n.* A pail which receives the milk drawn from cows.

MILK'PAN, *n.* A pan in which milk is set.

MILK'PORRIDGE, } *n.* A species of food
MILK'POTTAGE, } composed of milk or milk and water, boiled with meal or flour. *Locke.*

MILK'SCORE, *n.* An account of milk sold or purchased in small quantities, scored or marked. *Addison.*

MILK'SOP, *n.* A soft, effeminate, feeble-minded man. *Addison. Prior.*

MILK'-THISTLE, *n.* A plant of the genus Carduus.

MILK'TOOTH, *n.* The fore tooth of a foal, which is cast within two or three years. *Far. Dict.*

MILK-TRE'FOIL, *n.* A plant, the cytisus. *Johnson.*

MILK'-VETCH, *n.* A plant of the genus Astragalus.

MILK'-WORT, *n.* A plant of the genus Euphorbia ; spurge.

MILK'-WEED, *n.* A plant, the *Asclepias Syriaca.*

MILK'WHITE, *a.* White as milk. *Dryden.*

MILK'WÖMAN, *n.* A woman that sells milk. *Arbuthnot.*

MILK'Y, *a.* Made of milk.
2. Resembling milk ; as *milky* sap or juice. *Pope.*
3. Yielding milk ; as *milky* mothers. *Roscommon.*
4. Soft ; mild ; gentle ; timorous ; as a *milky* heart. *Shak.*

MILK'Y-WAY, *n.* The galaxy ; a broad luminous path or circle in the heavens, supposed to be the blended light of innumerable fixed stars, which are not distinguishable with ordinary telescopes. *Harris.*

MILL, *n.* [L. *mille*, a thousand.] A money of account of the United States, value the tenth of a cent, or the thousandth of a dollar.

MILL, *n.* [Sax. *miln ;* W. *melin ;* Ir. *meile* or *muilean ;* Corn. *melyn ;* Arm. *mell* or *melin ;* Fr. *moulin ;* L. *mola ;* Gr. *μυλη, μυλος ;* G. *mühle ;* D. *molen ;* Sw. *möl ;* Dan. *mölle ;* Sp. *molino ;* It. *mulino ;* Russ. *melnitsa ;* Goth. *malan*, to grind, Ir. *meilim*, Fr. *moudre*, for *mouldre*, W. *malu*, Arm. *mala* or *malein*, Sp. *moler*, L. *molo*, G. *mahlen*, D. *maalen*, Sw. *måla*, Dan. *maler*, Port. *moer*, by contraction, Russ. *melyu.* It is not certain which is the original word, the noun or the verb ; or whether both are from a prior radical sense. We observe that the elements of this word coincide with those of L. *mel*, honey, *mollis*, Eng. *mellow, mild, mold, meal*, W. *mall*, &c. all expressive of softness. Grinding is now breaking by friction or pressure, but not improbably grain was pulverized by breaking before the use of the quern. If so, *mill* may coincide in origin with *mallet.* We observe that this word is in the languages of all the great European families, Celtic, Teutonic and Slavonic.]
1. A complicated engine or machine for grinding and reducing to fine particles, grain, fruit or other substance, or for performing other operations by means of wheels and a circular motion ; as a grist-*mill* for grain ; a coffee-*mill* ; a cider-*mill ;* a bark-*mill.* The original purpose of mills was to comminute grain for food, but the word *mill* is now extended to engines or machines moved by water, wind or steam, for carrying on many other operations. We have *oil-mills, saw-mills, slitting-mills, bark-mills, fulling-mills*, &c.
2. The house or building that contains the machinery for grinding, &c.

MILL, *v. t.* To grind ; to comminute ; to reduce to fine particles or to small pieces.
2. To beat up chocolate. *Johnson.*
3. To stamp coin.
4. To full, as cloth.

MILL'COG, *n.* The cog of a mill wheel. *Mortimer.*

MILL'DAM, *n.* A dam or mound to obstruct a water course, and raise the water to an altitude sufficient to turn a mill wheel. *Mortimer.*

MILL'HORSE, *n.* A horse that turns a mill.

MILL'POND, *n.* A pond or reservoir of water raised for driving a mill wheel.

MILL'RACE, *n.* The current of water that drives a mill wheel, or the canal in which it is conveyed. *Franklin.*

MILL'-SIXPENCE, *n.* An old English coin first milled in 1561. *Douce.*

MILL'STONE, *n.* A stone used for grinding grain.

MILL'-TOOTH, *n.* plu. *mill-teeth.* A grinder, *dens molaris.* *Arbuthnot.*

MILLENA'RIAN, *a.* [Fr. *millenaire.* See *Millenium.*]
Consisting of a thousand years ; pertaining to the millenium. *Encyc.*

MILLENA'RIAN, *n.* A chiliast ; one who believes in the millenium, and that Christ will reign on earth with his saints a thousand years before the end of the world. *Encyc.*

MIL'LENARY, *a.* [Fr. *millenaire.*] Consisting of a thousand. *Arbuthnot.*

MILLEN'IAL, *a.* Pertaining to the millenium, or to a thousand years; as *millenial* period; *millenial* happiness. *Burnet.*

MIL'LENIST, *n.* One who holds to the millenium. [*Not used.*] *Johnson.*

MILLEN'IUM, *n.* [L. *mille*, a thousand, and *annus*, year.]

A thousand years; a word used to denote the thousand years mentioned in Revelations xx. during which period Satan shall be bound and restrained from seducing men to sin, and Christ shall reign on earth with his saints.

MIL'LEPED, *n.* [L. *mille*, a thousand, and *pes*, foot.]

The wood-louse, an insect having many feet, a species of Oniscus.

MIL'LEPORE, *n.* [L. *mille*, a thousand, and *porus*, a pore.]

A genus of lithophytes or polypiers of various forms, which have the surface perforated with little holes or pores, or even without any apparent perforation. *Cuvier.*

MIL'LEPORITE, *n.* Fossil millepores.

MIL'LER, *n.* [from *mill.*] One whose occupation is to attend a grist-mill.

2. An insect whose wings appear as if covered with white dust or powder, like a miller's clothes.

MIL'LER'S-THUMB, *n.* A small fish found in small streams.

MILLES'IMAL, *a.* [L. *millesimus*, from *mille*, a thousand.]

Thousandth; consisting of thousandth parts; as *millesimal* fractions. *Watts.*

MIL'LET, *n.* [Fr. *millet* or *mil*; It. *miglio*; Sp. *mijo*; L. *milium*; Sax. *mil.*]

A plant of the genus Milium, of several species, one of which is cultivated as an esculent grain. *Encyc.*

The *Indian millet* is of the genus Holcus. *Lee.*

MIL'LIARY, *a.* [L. *milliarium*, a milestone.]

Pertaining to a mile; denoting a mile; as a *milliary* column. *D'Anville.*

MIL'LIGRAM, *n.* [L. *mille*, a thousand, and Gr. γραμμα, a gram.]

In the system of French weights and measures, the thousandth part of a gram, equal to a cubic millimeter of water. *Lunier.*

The milligram is equal to .0154 English grains. *Cyc.*

MIL'LILITER, *n.* [L. *mille*, a thousand, and *liter.*]

A French measure of capacity containing the thousandth part of a liter or cubic decimeter, equal to .06103 decimals of a cubic inch. *Cyc.*

MILLIM'ETER, *n.* [L. *mille*, a thousand, and *metrum*, a measure.]

A French lineal measure containing the thousandth part of a meter; equal to .03937 decimals of an inch. It is the least measure of length. *Lunier. Cyc.*

MIL'LINER, *n.* [Johnson supposes this word to be *Milaner*, from *Milan*, in Italy.]

A woman who makes and sells head-dresses, hats or bonnets, &c. for females.

MIL'LINERY, *n.* The articles made or sold by milliners, as head-dresses, hats or bonnets, laces, ribins and the like.

MILLION, *n.* *mil'yun.* [Fr. *million*; It. *milione*; Sp. *millon*; Port. *milham*; probably from L. *mille*, a thousand.]

1. The number of ten hundred thousand, or a thousand thousand. It is used as a noun or an adjective; as a *million* of men, or a *million* men. As a noun, it has a regular plural, *millions.*

2. In common usage, a very great number, indefinitely.

> There are *millions* of truths that men are not concerned to know. *Locke.*

MILL'IONARY, *a.* Pertaining to millions; consisting of millions; as the *millionary* chronology of the Pundits. *Pinkerton.*

MILL'IONED, *a.* Multiplied by millions. [*Not used.*] *Shak.*

MILL'IONTH, *a.* The ten hundred thousandth.

MILLRE'A, } *n.* A coin of Portugal of the
MILLREE', } value of $1.24 cents.

MILT, *n.* [Sax. Dan. D. *milt*; G. *milz*; Sw. *mjälte*; It. *milza*; probably so named from its softness, and allied to *mild*, *mellow*, *melt.*]

1. In *anatomy*, the spleen, a viscus situated in the left hypochondrium under the diaphragm.

2. The soft roe of fishes, or the spermatic part of the males. *Encyc.*

MILT, *v. t.* To impregnate the roe or spawn of the female fish. *Johnson.*

MILT'ER, *n.* A male fish. *Walton.*

MILT'WÖRT, *n.* A plant of the genus Asplenium.

MIME, *n.* A buffoon. *Obs.* [See *Mimic.*]

2. A kind of dramatic farce. *Obs.*

MIME, *v. i.* To mimic, or play the buffoon. *Obs.* [See *Mimic.*]

MI'MER, *n.* A mimic. *Obs.* [See *Mimic.*]

MIME'SIS, *n.* [Gr.] In *rhetoric*, imitation of the voice or gestures of another. *Encyc.*

MIMET'IC, *a.* [Gr. μιμητικος.] Apt to imitate; given to aping or mimicry.

MIM'IC, } *a.* [L. *mimus*, *mimicus*; Gr.
MIM'ICAL, } μιμος, μιμικος; μιμεομαι, to imitate; allied probably to μωμος.]

1. Imitative; inclined to imitate or to ape; having the practice or habit of imitating.

> Man is of all creatures the most *mimical* in gestures, speech, &c. *Wotton.*

2. Consisting of imitation; as *mimic* gestures.

Mimic implies often something droll or ludicrous, or less dignified than *imitative.*

MIM'IC, *n.* One who imitates or mimics; a buffoon who attempts to excite laughter or derision by acting or speaking in the manner of another. *Prior.*

2. A mean or servile imitator.

> Of France the *mimic*, and of Spain the prey. *Anon.*

MIM'ICK, *v. t.* To imitate or ape for sport; to attempt to excite laughter or derision by acting or speaking like another; to ridicule by imitation.

> —The walk, the words, the gesture, could supply,
> The habit *mimick*, and the mien belie. *Dryden.*

MIM'ICRY, *n.* Ludicrous imitation for sport or ridicule. *Spectator.*

MIMOG'RAPHER, *n.* [Gr. μιμος and γραφω.]

A writer of farces. *Herbert.*

MI'NA, *n.* [Gr. μνα; L. *mina.* Ar. Class Mn. No. 5. 9. 7.] A weight or denomination of money. The mina of the Old Testament was valued at sixty shekels. The Greek or Attic mina, was valued at a hundred drachmas, about £2. 17*s.* sterling, $10. 44 cents. *Encyc.*

MINA'CIOUS, *a.* [L. *minax*, from *minor*, to threaten.]

Threatening; menacing. *More.*

MINAC'ITY, *n.* [L. *minax.*] Disposition to threaten. [*Little used.*]

MIN'ARET, *n.* [W. *mwn*, a spire. See *Mound.*]

A small spire or steeple, or spire-like ornament in Saracen architecture. *Mason.*

MIN'ATORY, *a.* Threatening; menacing. *Bacon.*

MINCE, *v. t.* *mins.* [Sax. *minsian*, from the root of L. *minuo*, to diminish; W. *main*, Arm. *maon*, Fr. *menu*, *mince*, Ir. *min*, *mion*, small, fine; L. *minor*, smaller; *minuo*, to diminish; Gr. μινυος, small, slender; μινυθω, to diminish; L. *minutus*, minute; Sw. *minska*, to diminish; Ar. مَنَّ manna, to weaken, to diminish. Class Mn. No. 5.]

1. To cut or chop into very small pieces; as, to *mince* meat. *Dryden.*

2. To diminish in speaking; to retrench, cut off or omit a part for the purpose of suppressing the truth; to extenuate in representation.

> I know no way to *mince* it in love, but to say directly, I love you. *Shak.*

> Siren, now *mince* the sin,
> And mollify damnation with a phrase— *Dryden.*

> If, to *mince* his meaning, I had either omitted some part of what he said, or taken from the strength of his expression, I certainly had wronged him. *Dryden.*

> These—were forced to *mince* the matter. *Woodward.*

3. To speak with affected softness; to clip words; not to utter the full sound. *Shak.*

4. To walk with short or diminished steps.

MINCE, *v. i.* To walk with short steps; to walk with affected nicety; to affect delicacy in manner.

> I'll turn two *mincing* steps
> Into a manly stride. *Shak.*

> Because the daughters of Zion are haughty—walking and *mincing* as they go. Is. iii.

2. To speak softly, or with affected nicety. *Dryden.*

MIN'CED, *pp.* Cut or chopped into very small pieces.

MINCE-PIE, } *n.* A pie made with minc-
MINCED-PIE, } ed meat and other ingredients, baked in paste. *Spectator.*

MIN'CING, *ppr.* Cutting into small pieces; speaking or walking affectedly.

MIN'CINGLY, *adv.* In small parts; not fully. *Hooker.*

MIND, *n.* [Sax. *gemind*, *gemynde*; Ir. *mein*, *mian*; W. *myn* or *menw*, mind or will; *govyn*, a demand; Dan. *minde*, mind, vote, consent; *minder*, to remind; Sw. *minne*, memory; *minnas*, to remember, to call to mind, as L. *reminiscor*; L. *mens*; Gr. μνεια, memory, mention; μναομαι, to remember; μενος, mind, ardor of mind, vehemence; μηνις, anger; Sans. *man*, *mana*, mind, will, heart, thought; Zend, *meno.*

Mind signifies properly intention, a reaching or inclining forward to an object, from the primary sense of extending, stretching or inclining, or advancing eagerly, pushing or setting forward, whence the Greek sense of the word, in analogy with the Teutonic *mod, moed, muth,* mind, courage, spirit, mettle. So L. *animus, animosus.* The Russ. has *pominayu,* to mention, to remember; *pomin,* remembrance, and *umenie* or *umeinie,* understanding. Qu. *Minos, Menu, Menes, Mentor.* Class Mn. No. 1. 9.]

1. Intention; purpose; design.

The sacrifice of the wicked is abomination; how much more, when he bringeth it with a wicked *mind.* Prov. xxi.

2. Inclination; will; desire; *a sense much used, but expressing less than settled purpose;* as in the common phrases, "I wish to know your *mind;*" "let me know your *mind;*" "he had a *mind* to go;" "he has a partner to his *mind.*"
3. Opinion; as, to express one's *mind.* We are of one *mind.*
4. Memory; remembrance; as, to put one in *mind;* to call to *mind;* the fact is out of my *mind;* time out of *mind.* From the operations of the intellect in man, this word came to signify,
5. The intellectual or intelligent power in man; the understanding; the power that conceives, judges or reasons.

I fear I am not in my perfect *mind.* *Shak.*

So we speak of a sound *mind,* a disordered *mind,* a weak *mind,* a strong *mind,* with reference to the *active* powers of the understanding; and in a *passive* sense, it denotes capacity, as when we say, the *mind* cannot comprehend a subject.

6. The heart or seat of affection.

Which were a grief of *mind* to Isaac and Rebekah. Gen. xxvi.

7. The will and affection; as readiness of *mind.* Acts xvii.
8. The implanted principle of grace. Rom. vii.

MIND, *v. t.* To attend to; to fix the thoughts on; to regard with attention.

Cease to request me; let us *mind* our way. *Dryden.*

Mind not high things. Rom. xii.

2. To attend to or regard with submission; to obey. His father told him to desist, but he would not *mind* him.
3. To put in mind; to remind. *Obs.* *Locke.*
4. To intend; to mean. *Chapman.*

MIND, *v. i.* To be inclined or disposed to incline.

When one of them *mindeth* to go into rebellion. *Obs.* *Spenser.*

MINDED, *a.* Disposed; inclined.

If men were *minded* to live virtuously. *Tillotson.*

Joseph was *minded* to put her away privily. Matt. i.

Minded is much used in composition; as high-*minded;* low-*minded;* feeble-*minded;* sober-*minded;* double-*minded.*

MINDEDNESS, *n.* Disposition; inclination towards any thing; as heavenly *mindedness.* *Milner.*

MINDFILLING, *a.* Filling the mind. *Mitford.*

MINDFUL, *a.* Attentive; regarding with care; bearing in mind; heedful; observant.

I promise to be *mindful* of your admonitions. *Hammond.*

What is man, that thou art *mindful* of him? Ps. vii.

MINDFULLY, *adv.* Attentively; heedfully.

MINDFULNESS, *n.* Attention; regard; heedfulness.

MINDING, *ppr.* Regarding; heeding.

MINDING, *n.* Regard.

MINDLESS, *a.* Inattentive; heedless; forgetful; negligent; careless.

Cursed Athens, *mindless* of thy worth. *Shak.*

2. Not endued with mind or intellectual powers; as *mindless* bodies. *Davies.*
3. Stupid; unthinking; as a *mindless* slave. *Shak.*

MIND-STRICKEN, *a.* Moved; affected in mind. [*Not used.*] *Sidney.*

MINE, *a.* called sometimes a *pronominal adj.* [Sax. Sw. Dan. *min;* Goth. *meins;* Fr. *mon;* D. *myn;* G. *mein,* contracted from *migen;* for *me,* in Gothic is *mik,* Dan. *mig,* G. *mich.* The L. *meus,* and Russ. *moi,* are also contracted.]

My; belonging to me. It was formerly used before nouns beginning with vowels. "I kept myself from *mine* iniquity." Ps. xviii. But this use is no longer retained. We now use *my* before a vowel as well as before an articulation; as *my* iniquity. In present usage, *my* always precedes the noun, and *mine* follows the noun, and usually the verb; as, this is *my* book; this book is *mine;* it is called *my* book; the book is called *mine:* it is acknowledged to be *mine.*

Mine sometimes supplies the place of a noun. Your sword and *mine* are different in construction.

MINE, *n.* [Fr. *mine,* a mine or ore, whence *mineral;* It. *mina, miniera;* Sp. *mina,* a mine, a conduit, a subterraneous canal, a spring or source of water; Port. *id.;* Ir. *men, mianach;* Dan. G. *mine;* Sw. *mina;* D. *myn;* W. *mwn,* whence *mwnai,* money; Arm. *min.* The radical signification is not obvious.]

1. A pit or excavation in the earth, from which metallic ores, mineral substances and other fossil bodies are taken by digging. The pits from which stones only are taken, are called *quarries.*
2. In *the military art,* a subterraneous canal or passage dug under the wall or rampart of a fortification, where a quantity of powder may be lodged for blowing up the works.
3. A rich source of wealth or other good.

MINE, *v. i.* To dig a mine or pit in the earth. *Woodward.*

2. To form a subterraneous canal or hole by scratching; to form a burrow or lodge in the earth, as animals; as the *mining* coney. *Wotton.*
2. To practice secret means of injury.

MINE, *v. t.* To sap; to undermine; to dig away or otherwise remove the substratum or foundation; hence, to ruin or destroy by slow degrees or secret means.

They *mined* the walls. *Hayward.*

In a metaphorical sense, *undermine* is generally used.

MI'NE-DIGGER, *n.* One that digs mines.

MI'NER, *n.* One that digs for metals and other fossils.

2. One who digs canals or passages under the walls of a fort, &c. Armies have sappers and *miners.*

MIN'ERAL, *n.* [Fr. Sp. *mineral;* Low L. *minera,* a matrix or vein of metals, whence *mineralia;* all from *mine.*]

A body destitute of organization, and which naturally exists within the earth or at its surface. *Cleaveland.*

Minerals were formerly divided into *salts, earths, inflammables* and *ores;* a division which serves for a general distribution, but a more scientific arrangement into *classes, orders, genera, species, subspecies* and *varieties,* has been adopted to meet the more precise views of modern mineralogists.

MIN'ERAL, *a.* Pertaining to minerals; consisting of fossil substances; as the *mineral* kingdom.

2. Impregnated with minerals or fossil matter; as *mineral* waters; a *mineral* spring.

MIN'ERALIST, *n.* One versed or employed in minerals.

MINERALIZA'TION, *n.* [See *Mineralize.*]

1. The process of forming an ore by combination with another substance; the natural operation of uniting a metallic substance with another.
2. The process of converting into a mineral, as a bone or a plant.
3. The act of impregnating with a mineral, as water.

MIN'ERALIZE, *v. t.* [from *mineral.*] In *mineralogy,* to combine with a metal in forming an ore or mineral. Sulphur *mineralizes* many of the metals.

2. To convert into a mineral.

In these caverns, the bones are not *mineralized.* *Buckland.*

3. To impregnate with a mineral substance; as, to *mineralize* water.

MIN'ERALIZED, *pp.* Deprived of its usual properties by being combined with another substance or formed into an ore; as, metallic substances are *mineralized.*

2. Converted into a mineral.
3. Impregnated with a mineral.

MIN'ERALIZER, *n.* A substance which mineralizes another or combines with it in an ore, and thus deprives it of its usual and peculiar properties. Sulphur is one of the most common *mineralizers.* *Nicholson.*

MINERALOG'ICAL, *a.* [See *Mineralogy.*] Pertaining to the science of minerals; as a *mineralogical* table.

MINERALOG'ICALLY, *adv.* In mineralogy. *Phillips.*

MINERAL'OGIST, *n.* One who is versed in the science of minerals, or one who treats or discourses of the properties of mineral bodies.

MINERAL'OGY, *n.* [*mineral* and Gr. λογος, discourse.]

The science which treats of the properties of mineral substances, and teaches us to characterize, distinguish and class them according to their properties. It comprehends the study or science of all inorganic substances in the earth or on its surface. *Encyc.* *Cyc.*

MIN'GLE, *v. t.* [Sax. *mengan* or *mencgan*; G. D. *mengen*. This word seems to be a derivative from G. *menge*, Sax. *menigo*, a multitude, or from the same root. Hence *among* signifies *mingled*, or in the crowd.]
1. To mix; to blend; to unite in one body; as, to *mingle* liquors of different kinds.
2. To mix or blend without order or promiscuously.

There was fire *mingled* with hail. Ex. ix.

3. To compound; to unite in a mass, as solid substances; as, to *mingle* flour, sugar and eggs in cookery.
4. To join in mutual intercourse or in society.

The holy seed have *mingled* themselves with the people of those lands. Ezra ix. Ps. cvi.

5. To contaminate; to render impure; to debase by mixture.

The best of us appear contented with a *mingled* imperfect virtue. *Rogers.*

6. To confuse.

There *mingle* broils. *Milton.*

MIN'GLE, *v. i.* To be mixed; to be united with.

She, when she saw her sister nymphs, suppressed
Her rising fears, and *mingled* with the rest. *Addison.*

MIN'GLE, *n.* Mixture; medley; promiscuous mass. [*Not used.*] *Dryden.*

MIN'GLED, *pp.* Mixed; united promiscuously.

MIN'GLEDLY, *adv.* Confusedly. *Barret.*

MIN'GLER, *n.* One that mingles.

MIN'GLING, *ppr.* Mixing; uniting without order.

MIN'IARD, *a.* [Fr. *mignard.*] Soft; dainty. [*Little used.*]

MIN'IARDIZE, *v. t.* To render soft, delicate or dainty. *Howell.*

MIN'IATE, *v. t.* [It. *miniare*, from *minio*, L. *minium*, vermillion.] To paint or tinge with vermillion. *Warton.*

MIN'IATURE, *n.* [It. Sp. *miniatura*, from It. *miniare*, supra; Fr. *miniature.*]
1. A painting in water colors on vellum, ivory or paper, with points or dots; sometimes in oil colors. The term is usually applied to portraits painted on a very small scale.
2. A picture or representation in a small compass, or less than the reality. *Encyc.*
3. Red letter; rubric distinction. *Hickes.*

MIN'IKIN, *a.* [Qu. W. *main*, small, and *kin.*] Small; diminutive; *used in slight contempt.*

MIN'IKIN, *n.* A small sort of pins.
2. A darling; a favorite. [See *Minion.*]

MIN'IM, *n.* [W. *main*, small. See *Mince.*]
1. A little man or being; a dwarf. *Milton.*
2. One of a certain reformed order of Franciscans or Minimi. *Weever.*
3. A note in music, equal to half a semibreve or two crotchets.
4. A short poetical encomium. *Obs.* *Spenser.*
5. A small fish.

MIN'IMUM, *n.* [L.] The least quantity assignable in a given case. *Encyc.*

MIN'IMUS, *n.* [L.] A being of the smallest size. *Shak.*

MI'NING, *ppr.* Digging into the earth, as for fossils and minerals; sapping.
2. *a.* Designating the business of digging mines; as the *mining* districts of Siberia. *Sparks.*

MIN'ION, *a.* [infra.] Fine; trim; dainty. [*Not used.*]

MINION, *n.* *min'yon.* [Fr. *mignon*; It. *mignone*, a darling; from W. *main*, Fr. *menu*, small; W. *mwyn*, tender, gentle.] A favorite; a darling; particularly, the favorite of a prince, on whom he lavishes his favors; one who gains favors by flattery or mean adulation.

Edward sent an army into Ireland, not for conquest, but to guard the person of his *minion*, Piers Gaviston. *Davies.*

The drowsy tyrant by his *minions* led. *Swift.*

MIN'ION, *n.* [W. *main*, Fr. *menu*, small; L. *minor.* See *Mince.*] A small kind of printing types.

MIN'IONING, *n.* Kind treatment. *Marston.*

MIN'IONLIKE, } *adv.* Finely; daintily.
MIN'IONLY, }

MIN'IONSHIP, *n.* State of being a minion.

MIN'IOUS, *n.* [from L. *minium.*] Of the color of red lead or vermillion. *Brown.*

MIN'ISH, *v. t.* [L. *minuo*, to lessen.] To lessen; to diminish. *Obs.* [See *Diminish.*]

MIN'ISTER, *n.* [L.; probably from Ar. مهن to serve, wait, attend, Class Mn. No. 2. and Sax. *steore*, helm, direction; *steoran*, to *steer.*]
1. Properly, a chief servant; hence, an agent appointed to transact or manage business under the authority of another; *in which sense, it is a word of very extensive application.*

Moses rose up and his *minister* Joshua. Ex. xxiv.

2. One to whom a king or prince entrusts the direction of affairs of state; as *minister* of state; the prime *minister.* In modern governments, the secretaries or heads of the several departments or branches of government are the *ministers* of the chief magistrate.
3. A magistrate; an executive officer.

For he is the *minister* of God to thee for good. Rom. xiii.

4. A delegate; an embassador; the representative of a sovereign at a foreign court; usually such as is resident at a foreign court, but not restricted to such.
5. One who serves at the altar; one who performs sacerdotal duties; the pastor of a church, duly authorized or licensed to preach the gospel and administer the sacraments. Eph. iii.
6. Christ is called a *minister* of the sanctuary. Heb. viii.
7. An angel; a messenger of God.

Who maketh his angels spirits, his *ministers* a flaming fire. Ps. civ.

MIN'ISTER, *v. t.* [L. *ministro.*] To give; to afford; to supply.

He that *ministereth* seed to the sower— 2 Cor. ix.

That it may *minister* grace to the hearers. Eph. iv.

MIN'ISTER, *v. i.* To attend and serve; to perform service in any office, sacred or secular.

I will sanctify also both Aaron and his sons, to *minister* to me in the priest's office. Ex. xxix.

2. To afford supplies; to give things needful; to supply the means of relief; to relieve.

When saw we thee hungry, or thirsty, or a stranger, or naked, or sick, or in prison, and did not *minister* unto thee? Matt. xxv.

3. To give medicines.

Canst thou not *minister* to a mind diseased? *Shak.*

In this sense, we commonly use *administer.*

MIN'ISTERED, *pp.* Served; afforded; supplied.

MINISTE'RIAL, *a.* Attending for service; attendant; acting at command.

Enlight'ning spirits and *ministerial* flames. *Prior.*

2. Acting under superior authority; pertaining to a minister.

For the *ministerial* offices in court, there must be an eye to them. *Bacon.*

3. Pertaining to executive offices, as distinct from judicial. The office and acts of a sheriff are *ministerial.*
4. Sacerdotal; pertaining to ministers of the gospel; as *ministerial* garments; *ministerial* duties.

Genuine *ministerial* prudence keeps back no important truth, listens to no compromise with sin, connives at no fashionable vice, cringes before no lordly worldling. *H. Humphrey.*

5. Pertaining to ministers of state; as *ministerial* circles; *ministerial* benches. *Burke.*

MINISTE'RIALLY, *adv.* In a ministerial manner or character. *Waterland.*

MIN'ISTERING, *ppr.* Attending and serving as a subordinate agent; serving under superior authority. Heb. i.
2. Affording aid or supplies; administering things needful.

MINISTERY. [See *Ministry.*]

MIN'ISTRAL, *a.* Pertaining to a minister. [*Little used.*] *Johnson.*

MIN'ISTRANT, *a.* Performing service as a minister; attendant on service; acting under command.

Princedoms and dominations *ministrant.* *Milton.*

MINISTRA'TION, *n.* [L. *ministratio.*] The act of performing service as a subordinate agent; agency; intervention for aid or service.

—Because their widows were neglected in the daily *ministrations.* Acts vi.

2. Office of a minister; service; ecclesiastical function.

As soon as the days of his *ministration* were ended. Luke i.

MIN'ISTRESS, *n.* A female that ministers. *Akenside.*

MIN'ISTRY, *n.* [L. *ministerium.*] The office, duties or functions of a subordinate agent of any kind.
2. Agency; service; aid; interposition; instrumentality.

He directs the affairs of this world by the ordinary *ministry* of second causes. *Atterbury.*

3. Ecclesiastical function; agency or service of a minister of the gospel or clergyman in the modern church, or of priests, apostles and evangelists in the ancient. Acts i. Rom. xii. 2 Tim. iv. Num. iv.
4. Time of ministration; duration of the office of a minister, civil or ecclesiastical.

The war with France was during the *ministry* of Pitt.

5. Persons who compose the executive government or the council of a supreme magistrate; the body of ministers of state. *Swift.*

6. Business; employment.

He abhorred the wicked *ministry* of arms. *Dryden.*

MINISTRYSHIP, for *ministry*, is little used and hardly proper. *Swift.*

MIN'IUM, *n.* [L.] The red oxyd of lead, produced by calcination. Lead exposed to air while melting is covered with a gray dusky pellicle. This taken off and agitated becomes a greenish gray powder, inclining to yellow. This oxyd, separated by sifting from the grains of lead which it contains, and exposed to a more intense heat, takes a deep yellow color, and in this state it is called *massicot.* The latter, slowly heated, takes a beautiful red color, and is called *minium.* *Fourcroy.*

MINK, *n.* An American quadruped of the genus Mustela, an amphibious animal that burrows in the earth on the side of a river or pond, whose fur is more valuable than that of the muskrat. *Belknap.*

MINNOC, used by Shakspeare, is supposed by Johnson to be the same as *minx.* Qu. *mimic.*

MIN'NOW, MIN'OW, *n.* [Fr. *menu*, small.] A very small fish, a species of Cyprinus. *Encyc. Walton.*

MI'NOR, *a.* [L.; the comparative degree of a word not found in that language, but existing in the Celtic dialects, W. *main*, Arm. *moan*, Ir. *min*, *mion*, the root of L. *minuo*, to diminish. See *Mince.*]

1. Less; smaller; sometimes applied to the bulk or magnitude of a single object; more generally to amount, degree or importance. We say, the *minor* divisions of a body, the *minor* part of a body; opposed to the *major* part. We say, *minor* sums, *minor* faults, *minor* considerations, details or arguments. In the latter phrases, *minor* is equivalent to small, petty, inconsiderable, not principal, important or weighty.

2. In *music*, less or lower by a lesser semitone; as a third *minor.* *Encyc.*

Asia Minor, the Lesser Asia, that part of Asia which lies between the Euxine on the north, and the Mediterranean on the south.

MI'NOR, *n.* A person of either sex under age; one who is under the authority of his parents or guardians, or who is not permitted by law to make contracts and manage his own property. By the laws of Great Britain and of the United States, persons are *minors* till they are twenty one years of age.

2. In *logic*, the second proposition of a regular syllogism, as in the following:

Every act of injustice partakes of meanness.

To take money from another by gaming, or reputation by seduction, are acts of injustice.

Therefore the taking of money from another by gaming, or reputation by seduction, partake of meanness.

3. A Minorite, a Franciscan friar.

4. A beautiful bird of the East Indies. *Dict. Nat. Hist.*

MI'NORATE, *v. t.* To diminish. [*Not used.*]

MINORA'TION, *n.* A lessening; diminution.

MI'NORITE, *n.* A Franciscan friar.

MINOR'ITY, *n.* [Fr. *minorité*, from L. *minor.*]

1. The state of being under age. [See *Minor.*]

2. The smaller number; as the *minority* of the senate or house of representatives; opposed to *majority.* We say, the *minority* was large or small; AB was in the *minority*; the *minority* must be ruled by the majority.

MIN'OTAUR, *n.* [Fr. *minotaure*; It. *minotauro*; L. *minotaurus*; from *man*, which must have been in early ages a Latin word, and *taurus*, a bull.]

A fabled monster, half man and half bull. *Ovid. Virgil. Shak.*

MIN'STER, *n.* [Sax. *minstre* or *mynster.* See *Monastery.*]

A monastery; an ecclesiastical convent or fraternity; but it is said originally to have been the church of a monastery; a cathedral church. *Encyc.*

MIN'STREL, *n.* [Fr. *menetrier*, for *menestrier*; Sp. *ministril*, a minstrel, and a tipstaff, or petty officer of justice; Port. *menestral*; perhaps a derivative from *menear*, to move, stir, wag, wield. If so, the word originally signified a performer on a musical instrument, who accompanied his performances with gestures, like the *histrio* and *joculator.*]

A singer and musical performer on instruments. Minstrels were formerly poets as well as musicians, and held in high repute by our rude ancestors. Their attendance was sought and their performances lavishly rewarded by princes. It was in the character of a minstrel that king Alfred entered the camp of the Danes his enemies, and explored their situation.

MIN'STRELSY, *n.* The arts and occupations of minstrels; instrumental music.

2. A number of musicians.

The *minstrelsy* of heaven. *Milton.*

MINT, *n.* [Sax. *mynet*, money or stamped coin; D. *munt*, *mint*, coin; G. *münze*; Sw. *mynt*; Dan. *myndt*, coin. This word is doubtless a derivative from *mine*, or L. *moneta*, from the same root.]

1. The place where money is coined by public authority. In Great Britain, formerly, there was a *mint* in almost every county; but the privilege of coining is now considered as a royal prerogative in that country, and as the prerogative of the sovereign power in other countries. The only *mint* now in Great Britain is in the Tower of London. The *mint* in the United States is in Philadelphia.

2. A place of invention or fabrication; as a *mint* of phrases; a *mint* of calumny. *Shak. Addison.*

3. A source of abundant supply.

MINT, *v. t.* [Sax. *mynetian.*] To coin; to make and stamp money. *Bacon.*

2. To invent; to forge; to fabricate. *Bacon.*

MINT, *n.* [Sax. *mint*; Sw. *mynta*; Dan. *mynte*; G. *münze*; L. *mentha*; It. Sp. *menta*; Fr. *mente*; D. *kruismunt*, cross-mint; Ir. *miontas*; Arm. *mendt* or *mintys.*]

A plant of the genus Mentha.

MINT'AGE, *n.* That which is coined or stamped. *Milton.*

2. The duty paid for coining.

MINT'ER, *n.* A coiner; also, an inventor.

MINT'MAN, *n.* A coiner; one skilled in coining or in coins.

MINT'MASTER, *n.* The master or superintendent of a mint. *Boyle.*

2. One who invents or fabricates. *Locke.*

MIN'UEND, *n.* [L. *minuendus*, *minuo*, to lessen.]

In *arithmetic*, the number from which another number is to be subtracted.

MIN'UET, *n.* [Sp. *minueto*; Fr. *menuet*, from *menu*, small, W. *main.* See *Mince.*]

1. A slow graceful dance, consisting of a coupee, a high step and a balance. *Encyc.*

2. A tune or air to regulate the movements in the dance so called; a movement of three crotchets or three quavers in a bar.

MIN'UM, *n.* [from W. *main*, Fr. *menu*, small. See *Mince.*]

1. A small kind of printing types; now written *minion.*

2. A note of slow time containing two crotchets; now written *minim*, which see.

MINU'TE, *a.* [L. *minutus*; Fr. *menu*, W. *main*, small. See *Mince.*]

1. Very small, little or slender; of very small bulk or size; small in consequence; as a *minute* grain of sand; a *minute* filament. The blood circulates through very *minute* vessels. *Minute* divisions of a subject often perplex the understanding. *Minute* details are tedious.

2. Attending to small things; critical; as *minute* observation.

MINUTE, *n.* *min'it.* [L. *minutum*, that is, a small portion.]

1. A small portion of time or duration, being the sixtieth part of an hour.

Since you are not sure of a *minute*, throw not away an hour. *Franklin.*

2. In *geometry*, the sixtieth part of a degree of a circle.

3. In *architecture*, the sixtieth, but sometimes the thirtieth part of a module. *Encyc.*

4. A space of time indefinitely small. I will be with you in a *minute*, or in a few *minutes*, that is, in a short time.

5. A short sketch of any agreement or other subject, taken in writing; a note to preserve the memory of any thing; as, to take *minutes* of a contract; to take *minutes* of a conversation or debate.

MINUTE, *v. t.* *min'it.* To set down a short sketch or note of any agreement or other subject in writing. *Spectator.*

MIN'UTE-BOOK, *n.* A book of short hints.

MIN'UTE-GLASS, *n.* A glass, the sand of which measures a minute.

MIN'UTE-GUNS, *n.* Guns discharged every minute.

MIN'UTE-HAND, *n.* The hand that points to the minutes on a clock or watch.

MINU'TELY, *adv.* [from *minute.*] To a small point of time, space or matter; exactly; nicely; as, to measure the length of any thing *minutely*; to ascertain time *minutely*; to relate a story *minutely.*

MINUTELY, *a.* *min'illy.* Happening every minute. *Hammond.*

MIN'UTELY, *adv.* [from *minute.*] Every minute; with very little time intervening.

As if it were *minutely* proclaimed in thunder from heaven. *Hammond.*

MINU'TENESS, *n.* Extreme smallness, fineness or slenderness; as the *minuteness* of the particles of air or of a fluid; the *minuteness* of the filaments of cotton; the *minuteness* of details in narration.

2. Attention to small things; critical exactness; as the *minuteness* of observation or distinction.

MIN'UTE-WATCH, *n.* A watch that distinguishes minutes of time, or on which minutes are marked. *Boyle.*

MINU'TIÆ, *n.* [L.] The smaller particulars.

MINX, *n.* [Qu. *minnoc.*] A pert, wanton girl. *Shak.*

2. A she-puppy.

MI'NY, *a.* [from *mine.*] Abounding with mines.

2. Subterraneous. *Thomson.*

MI'RABLE, *a.* Wonderful. [*Not in use.*] *Shak.*

MIR'ACLE, *n.* [Fr. from L. *miraculum*, from *miror*, to wonder; Arm. *miret*, to hold. See *Marvel.*]

1. Literally, a wonder or wonderful thing; but appropriately,

2. In *theology*, an event or effect contrary to the established constitution and course of things, or a deviation from the known laws of nature; a supernatural event. *Miracles* can be wrought only by Almighty power, as when Christ healed lepers, saying, "I will, be thou clean," or calmed the tempest, "Peace, be still."

They considered not the *miracle* of the loaves. Mark vi.

A man approved of God by *miracles* and signs. Acts ii.

3. Anciently, a spectacle or dramatic representation exhibiting the lives of the saints. *Chaucer.*

MIR'ACLE, *v. t.* To make wonderful. [*Not used.*] *Shak.*

MIR'ACLE-MÖNGER, *n.* An impostor who pretends to work miracles. *Hallywell.*

MIRAC'ULOUS, *a.* Performed supernaturally, or by a power beyond the ordinary agency of natural laws; effected by the direct agency of Almighty power, and not by natural causes; as the *miraculous* healing of the sick or raising the dead by Christ.

2. Supernatural; furnished supernaturally, or competent to perform miracles; as the *miraculous* powers of the Apostles. *Miraculous*, applied to the extraordinary powers of the Apostles, may mean conferred by supernatural agency, or competent to work miracles. I believe it is generally used in the latter sense.

3. In *a less definite sense*, wonderful; extraordinary.

MIRAC'ULOUSLY, *adv.* By miracle; supernaturally.

Æneas, wounded as he was, could not have engaged him in single combat, unless his hurt had been *miraculously* healed. *Dryden.*

2. Wonderfully; by extraordinary means.

MIRAC'ULOUSNESS, *n.* The state of being effected by miracle or by supernatural agency.

MIRADŌR, *n.* [Sp. from L. *miror.*] A balcony or gallery commanding an extensive view. *Dryden.*

MIRE, *n.* [See Class Mr. No. 16.] Deep mud; earth so wet and soft as to yield to the feet and to wheels.

MIRE, *v. t.* To plunge and fix in mire; to set or stall in mud. We say, a horse, an ox or a carriage is *mired*, when it has sunk deep into mud and its progress is stopped.

2. To soil or daub with mud or foul matter. *Shak.*

MIRE, *v. i.* To sink in mud, or to sink so deep as to be unable to move forward.

MIRE, *n.* An ant. [See *Pismire.*]

MIRE-CRŌW, *n.* The sea-crow or pewit gull, of the genus Larus.

MI'RINESS, *n.* [from *miry.*] The state of consisting of deep mud.

MIRK, *a.* [Sax. *mirce.*] Dark. *Obs.* [See *Murky.*]

MIRK'SŌME, *a.* Dark; obscure. [See *Murky.*]

MIRK'SŌMENESS, *n.* Obscurity. [See *Murky.*]

MIR'RŌR, *n.* [Fr. *miroir*; Sp. *mirar*, Corn. *miras*, to look; L. *miror*, to admire.]

1. A looking glass; any glass or polished substance that forms images by the reflection of rays of light.

In the clear *mirror* of thy ruling star
I saw, alas! some dread event depend. *Pope.*

2. A pattern; an exemplar; that on which men ought to fix their eyes; that which gives a true representation, or in which a true image may be seen.

O goddess, heavenly bright,
Mirror of grace and majesty divine. *Spenser.*

MIR'ROR-STONE, *n.* A bright stone. *Obs.*

MIRTH, *n. merth.* [Sax. *mirht*, *myrhth*; *mirig*, merry; Ar. مرح to be very brisk or joyful. Class Mr. No. 10.] Social merriment; hilarity; high excitement of pleasurable feelings in company; noisy gayety; jollity. *Mirth* differs from *joy* and *cheerfulness*, as always implying noise.

With genial joy to warm the soul,
Bright Helen mixed a *mirth*-inspiring bowl. *Pope.*

I will cause to cease the voice of *mirth* from Judah and Jerusalem. Jer. vii.

MIRTH'FUL, *a.* Merry; jovial; festive.

The feast was served, the bowl was crown'd,
To the king's pleasure went the *mirthful* round. *Prior.*

MIRTH'FULLY, *adv.* In a jovial manner.

MIRTH'LESS, *a.* Without mirth or hilarity.

MI'RY, *a.* [from *mire.*] Abounding with deep mud; full of mire; as a *miry* road; a *miry* lane. *Gay.*

2. Consisting of mire. *Shak.*

MIS, a prefix, denotes error, or erroneous, wrong, from the verb *miss*, to err, to go wrong, Goth. *missa;* Sax. *mis*, from *missian*, to err, to deviate or wander; D. *mis*, *missen;* G. *miss*, *missen;* Dan. *mis*, *mister;* Sw. *mis*, *mista;* W. *méth*, a failing, a miss; Fr. *mes*, or *me*, in composition; It. *mis.*

MISACCEPTA'TION, *n.* The act of taking or understanding in a wrong sense.

MISADVEN'TURE, *n.* Mischance; misfortune; ill luck; an unlucky accident.

2. In *law*, homicide by misadventure, is when a man, doing a lawful act, without any intention of injury, unfortunately kills another. This is called *excusable homicide.* *Blackstone.*

MISADVEN'TURED, *a.* Unfortunate. *Shak.*

MISADVI'SED, *a.* [See *Advise.*] Ill advised; ill directed. *Johnson.*

MISAFFECT', *v. t.* To dislike.

MISAFFECT'ED, *a.* Ill disposed.

MISAFFIRM', *v. t.* To affirm incorrectly.

MISA'IMED, *a.* Not rightly aimed or directed. *Spenser.*

MISALLEDGE, *v. t. misallej'.* To state erroneously.

MISALLEGA'TION, *n.* Erroneous statement.

MISALLI'ANCE, *n.* Improper association.

MISALLI'ED, *a.* Ill allied or associated. *Burke.*

MIS'ANTHROPE, } *n.* [Gr. μισανθρωπος; μισεω, to hate,
MISAN'THROPIST, } and ανθρωπος, man.] A hater of mankind. *Swift.*

MISANTHROP'IC, } *a.* Hating or having a dislike to
MISANTHROP'ICAL, } mankind. *Walsh.*

MISAN'THROPY, *n.* Hatred or dislike to mankind; opposed to *philanthropy.*

MISAPPLICA'TION, *n.* A wrong application; an application to a wrong person or purpose.

MISAPPLI'ED, *pp.* Applied to a wrong person or purpose.

MISAPPLY', *v. t.* To apply to a wrong person or purpose; as to *misapply* a name or title; to *misapply* our talents or exertions; to *misapply* public money.

MISAPPLY'ING, *ppr.* Applying to a wrong person or purpose.

MISAPPREHEND', *v. t.* To misunderstand; to take in a wrong sense. *Locke.*

MISAPPREHEND'ED, *pp.* Not rightly understood.

MISAPPREHEND'ING, *ppr.* Misunderstanding.

MISAPPREHEN'SION, *n.* A mistaking or mistake; wrong apprehension of one's meaning or of a fact.

MISASCRI'BE, *v. t.* To ascribe falsely or erroneously. *Boyle.*

MISASSIGN, *v. t.* [See *Assign.*] To assign erroneously. *Boyle.*

MISATTEND', *v. t.* To disregard. *Milton.*

MISBECŌME, *v. t. misbecum'.* [See *Become.*] Not to become; to suit ill; not to befit.

Thy father will not act what *misbecomes* him. *Addison.*

MISBECŌM'ING, *ppr.* or *a.* Unseemly; unsuitable; improper; indecorous.

MISBECŌM'INGNESS, *n.* Unbecomingness; unsuitableness. *Boyle.*

MISBEGOT', } *ppr.* or *a.* Unlawfully or irregu-
MISBEGOT'TEN, } larly begotten. *Shak. Dryden.*

MISBEHA'VE, *v. i.* To behave ill; to conduct one's self improperly.

MISBEHA'VED, *a.* Guilty of ill behavior; ill bred; rude. *Shak.*

MISBEHA'VIOR, *n. misbeha'vyor.* Ill conduct; improper, rude or uncivil behavior. *Addison.*

MISBELIE'F, *n.* Erroneous belief; false religion. *Massinger.*

MISBELIE'VE, *v. t.* To believe erroneously. *Shak.*

MISBELIE'VER, *n.* One who believes wrongly; one who holds a false religion. *Dryden.*

MISBELIE'VING, *a.* Believing erroneously; irreligious. *Shak.*

MISBESEE'M, *v. t.* To suit ill.

MISBESTOW, *v. t.* To bestow improperly. *Milton.*

MIS'BORN, *a.* Born to evil. *Spenser.*

MISCAL'CULATE, *v. t.* To calculate erroneously. *Arbuthnot.*

MISCAL'CULATED, *pp.* Erroneously calculated.

MISCAL'CULATING, *ppr.* Committing errors in calculation.

MISCALCULA'TION, *n.* Erroneous calculation.

MISCALL', *v. t.* To call by a wrong name; to name improperly.

MISCALL'ED, *pp.* Misnamed.

MISCALL'ING, *ppr.* Misnaming.

MISCAR'RIAGE, *n.* Unfortunate event of an undertaking; failure.

When a counselor, to save himself,
Would lay *miscarriages* upon his prince. *Dryden.*

2. Ill conduct; evil or improper behavior; as the failings and *miscarriages* of the righteous. *Rogers.*

3. Abortion; the act of bringing forth before the time. *Encyc.*

MISCAR'RY, *v. i.* To fail of the intended effect; not to succeed; to be unsuccessful; to suffer defeat; *applied to persons or undertakings, and to things.* We say, a project, scheme, design, enterprise, attempt, has *miscarried.*

Have you not heard of Frederick, the great soldier, who *miscarried* at sea? *Shak.*

My ships have all *miscarried.* *Shak.*

2. To bring forth young before the proper time; to suffer abortion.

MISCAR'RYING, *ppr.* Failing of the intended effect; suffering abortion. Hos. ix.

MISC'AST, *v. t.* To cast or reckon erroneously. *Brown.*

MISC'AST, *pp.* Erroneously cast or reckoned.

MISC'AST, *n.* An erroneous cast or reckoning.

MISC'ASTING, *ppr.* Casting or reckoning erroneously.

MISCELLANA'RIAN, *a.* [See *Miscellany.*] Belonging to miscellanies; of miscellanies.

Miscellanarian authors. *Shaftsbury.*

MISCELLANA'RIAN, *n.* A writer of miscellanies. *Shaftsbury.*

MIS'CELLANE, *n.* [L. *miscellaneus.*] A mixture of two or more sorts of grain; now called *meslin.* *Bacon.*

MISCELLA'NEOUS, *a.* [L. *miscellaneus,* from *misceo,* to mix.]

Mixed; mingled; consisting of several kinds; as a *miscellaneous* publication; a *miscellaneous* rabble. *Milton.*

MISCELLA'NEOUSNESS, *n.* The state of being mixed; composition of various kinds.

MIS'CELLANY, *n.* [Fr. *miscellanées;* Sp. *miscelanea;* L. *miscellanea,* from *misceo,* to mix; Ch. Ar. מזג, to mix. Class Ms. No. 7.]

1. A mass or mixture of various kinds; particularly,

2. A book or pamphlet containing a collection of compositions on various subjects, or a collection of various kinds of compositions. *Pope. Swift.*

MIS'CELLANY, *a.* Miscellaneous. *Obs.* *Bacon.*

MISCEN'TER, *v. t.* To place amiss. [*Not in use.*] *Donne.*

MISCH'ANCE, *n.* Ill luck; ill fortune; misfortune; mishap; misadventure.

It is a man's unhappiness, his *mischance* or calamity, but not his fault. *South.*

MISCHAR'ACTERIZE, *v. t.* [See *Character.*] To characterize falsely or erroneously; to give a wrong character to.

They totally *mischaracterize* the action. *Eton.*

MISCH'ARGE, *v. t.* To mistake in charging, as an account.

MISCH'ARGE, *n.* A mistake in charging, as an account; an erroneous entry in an account.

MIS'CHIEF, *n.* [Old Fr. *meschef; mes,* wrong, and *chef,* head or end, the root of *achieve,* Fr. *achever.*]

1. Harm; hurt; injury; damage; evil, whether intended or not. A new law is made to remedy the *mischief.*

2. Intentional injury; harm or damage done by design.

Thy tongue deviseth *mischief.* Ps. lii.

3. Ill consequence; evil; vexatious affair.

The *mischief* was, these allies would never allow that the common enemy was subdued. *Swift.*

MIS'CHIEF, *v. t.* To hurt; to harm; to injure. *Sprat.*

MIS'CHIEF-MAKER, *n.* One who makes mischief; one who excites or instigates quarrels or enmity.

MIS'CHIEF-MAKING, *a.* Causing harm; exciting enmity or quarrels. *Rowe.*

MIS'CHIEVOUS, *a.* Harmful; hurtful; injurious; making mischief; *of persons;* as a *mischievous* man or disposition.

2. Hurtful; noxious; as a *mischievous* thing. *Arbuthnot.*

3. Inclined to do harm; as a *mischievous* boy.

MIS'CHIEVOUSLY, *adv.* With injury, hurt, loss or damage. We say, the law operates *mischievously.*

2. With evil intention or disposition. The injury was done *mischievously.*

MIS'CHIEVOUSNESS, *n.* Hurtfulness; noxiousness.

2. Disposition to do harm, or to vex or annoy; as the *mischievousness* of youth.

Mischief denotes injury, harm or damage of less malignity and magnitude than what are usually called crimes. We never give the name of mischief to theft, robbery or murder. And it so commonly implies *intention* in committing petty offenses, that it shocks us to hear the word applied to the calamities inflicted by Providence. We say, a tempest has done great *damage,* but not *mischief.* In like manner, the adjective *mischievous* is not applied to thieves, pirates and other felons, but to persons committing petty trespasses and offenses.

MISCH'NA, *n.* A part of the Jewish Talmud. [See *Mishna.*]

MISCHOOSE, *v. t. mischooz'.* To choose wrong; to make a wrong choice. *Milton.*

MISCHO'SEN, *pp.* Chosen by mistake.

MIS'CIBLE, *a.* [Fr. from L. *misceo,* to mix.] That may be mixed. Oil and water are not *miscible.*

MISCITA'TION, *n.* A wrong citation; erroneous quotation. *Collier.*

MISCI'TE, *v. t.* To cite erroneously or falsely.

MISCLA'IM, *n.* A mistaken claim or demand. *Bacon.*

MISCOMPUTA'TION, *n.* Erroneous computation; false reckoning. *Clarendon.*

MISCOMPU'TE, *v. t.* To compute or reckon erroneously.

MISCONCE'IT, } *n.* Erroneous conception; false opinion; wrong notion or understanding of a thing.
MISCONCEP'TION, }

Great errors and dangers result from a *misconception* of the names of things. *Harvey.*

MISCONCE'IVE, *v. t.* or *i.* To receive a false notion or opinion of any thing; to misjudge; to have an erroneous understanding of any thing.

To yield to others just and reasonable causes of those things, which, for want of due consideration heretofore, they have *misconceived.* *Hooker.*

MISCONCE'IVED, *pp.* Wrongly understood; mistaken.

MISCONCE'IVING, *ppr.* Mistaking; misunderstanding.

MISCON'DUCT, *n.* Wrong conduct; ill behavior; ill management. *Addison.*

MISCONDUCT', *v. t.* To conduct amiss; to mismanage.

MISCONDUCT', *v. i.* To behave amiss.

MISCONDUCT'ED, *pp.* Ill managed; badly conducted.

MISCONDUCT'ING, *ppr.* Mismanaging; misbehaving.

MISCONJEC'TURE, *n.* A wrong conjecture or guess.

MISCONJEC'TURE, *v. t.* or *i.* To guess wrong.

MISCONSTRUC'TION, *n.* Wrong interpretation of words or things; a mistaking of the true meaning; as a *misconstruction* of words or actions.

MISCON'STRUE, *v. t.* To interpret erroneously either words or things. It is important not to *misconstrue* the Scriptures.

Do not, great sir, *misconstrue* his intent. *Dryden.*

A virtuous emperor was much affected to find his actions *misconstrued.* *Addison.*

MISCON'STRUED, *pp.* Erroneously interpreted.

MISCON'STRUER, *n.* One who makes a wrong interpretation.

MISCON'STRUING, *ppr.* Interpreting wrongly.

MISCORRECT', *v. t.* To correct erroneously; to mistake in attempting to correct another.

He passed the first seven years of his life at Mantua, not seventeen, as Scaliger *miscorrects* his author. *Dryden.*

MISCORRECT'ED, *pp.* Mistaken in the attempt to correct.

MISCOUN'SEL, *v. t.* To advise wrong. *Spenser.*

MISCOUNT', *v. t.* To count erroneously; to mistake in counting.

MISCOUNT', *v. i.* To make a wrong reckoning. *Bp. Patrick.*

MISCOUNT′, *n.* An erroneous counting or numbering.

MIS′CREANCE, } *n.* [See *Miscreant.*] Un-
MIS′CREANCY, } belief; false faith; adherence to a false religion. *Obs.* *Spenser.*

MIS′CREANT, *n.* [Fr. *mécréant*; Norm. *mescreaunt*; *mes*, wrong, and *creance*, belief, from L. *credens*, *credo*.]

1. An infidel, or one who embraces a false faith.

2. A vile wretch; an unprincipled fellow. *Addison.*

MISCREA′TE, } *a.* Formed unnaturally
MISCREA′TED, } or illegitimately; deformed. *Obs.* *Spenser.*

MISDA′TE, *n.* A wrong date.

MISDA′TE, *v. i.* To date erroneously.

MISDEE′D, *n.* An evil deed; a wicked action.

> Evils which our own *misdeeds* have wrought. *Milton.*

MISDEE′M, *v. t.* To judge erroneously; to misjudge; to mistake in judging. *Spenser.*

MISDEME′AN, *v. t.* To behave ill. *Shak.*

MISDEME′ANOR, *n.* Ill behavior; evil conduct; fault; mismanagement. *South.*

2. In *law*, an offense of a less atrocious nature than a crime. Crimes and misdemeanors are mere synonymous terms; but in common usage, the word *crime* is made to denote offenses of a deeper and more atrocious dye, while small faults and omissions of less consequence are comprised under the gentler name of *misdemeanors*. *Blackstone.*

MISDESERT′, *n.* Ill desert. *Spenser.*

MISDEVO′TION, *n.* False devotion; mistaken piety. [*Little used.*] *Donne.*

MISDI′ET, *n.* Improper diet or food. [*Not used.*] *Spenser.*

MISDIRECT′, *v. t.* To give a wrong direction to; as, to *misdirect* a passenger.

2. To direct to a wrong person or place; as, to *misdirect* a letter.

MISDIRECT′ED, *pp.* Directed wrong, or to a wrong person or place.

MISDIRECT′ING, *ppr.* Directing wrong, or to a wrong person or place.

MISDISPOSI′′TION, *n.* Disposition to evil. [*Not in use.*] *Bp. Hall.*

MISDISTIN′GUISH, *v. t.* To make wrong distinctions. *Hooker.*

MISDÖ, *v. t.* [See *Do.*] To do wrong; to do amiss; to commit a crime or fault. *Milton.*

MISDÖER, *n.* One who does wrong; one who commits a fault or crime. *Spenser.*

MISDÖING, *ppr.* Doing wrong; committing a fault or crime.

MISDÖING, *n.* A wrong done; a fault or crime; an offense. *L'Estrange.*

MISDOUBT, *v. t.* *misdout′*. [See *Doubt.*] To suspect of deceit or danger. [*An ill formed word and not in use.*] *Sidney. Shak. Dryden.*

MISDOUBT′, *n.* Suspicion of crime or danger. [*Not used.*] *Shak.*

2. Irresolution; hesitation. [*Not used.*] *Shak.*

MISDOUBT′FUL, *a.* Misgiving. [*Not used.*] *Spenser.*

MISE, *n.* *meze.* [Fr. *mis*, put, laid, *pp.* of *mettre*, L. *mitto*; Norm. *mise.*]

1. In *law*, an issue to be tried at the grand assize.

2. Expense; cost.

3. A tax or tallage; in Wales, an honorary gift of the people to a new king or prince of Wales; also, a tribute paid in the county Palatine of Chester at the change of the owner of the earldoms. *Encyc.*

MISEMPLOY′, *v. t.* To employ to no purpose, or to a bad purpose; as, to *misemploy* time, power, advantages, talents, &c. *Locke. Addison.*

MISEMPLOY′ED, *pp.* Used to no purpose, or to a bad one.

MISEMPLOY′ING, *ppr.* Using to no purpose, or to a bad one.

MISEMPLOY′MENT, *n.* Ill employment; application to no purpose, or to a bad purpose. *Hale.*

MISEN′TRY, *n.* An erroneous entry or charge, as of an account.

MI′SER, *n.* *s* as *z*. [L. *miser*, miserable.] A miserable person; one wretched or afflicted. *Obs.* *Spenser.*

2. A wretch; a mean fellow. *Obs.* *Shak.*

3. An extremely covetous person; a sordid wretch; a niggard; one who in wealth makes himself miserable by the fear of poverty. [*This is the only sense in which it is now used.*]

> No silver saints by dying *misers* given. *Pope.*

MIS′ERABLE, *a.* *s* or *z*. [Fr. *miserable*, from L. *miser*, *miserabilis.*]

1. Very unhappy from grief, pain, calamity, poverty, apprehension of evil, or other cause. It however expresses somewhat less than *wretched*.

> What hopes delude thee, *miserable* man? *Dryden.*

2. Very poor; worthless.

> *Miserable* comforters are ye all. Job xvi.

3. Causing unhappiness or misery.

> What's more *miserable* than discontent? *Shak.*

4. Very poor or mean; as a *miserable* hut; *miserable* clothing.

5. Very poor or barren; as a *miserable* soil.

6. Very low or despicable; as a *miserable* person.

MIS′ERABLENESS, *n.* State of misery; poorness.

MIS′ERABLY, *adv.* Unhappily; calamitously.

> The fifth was *miserably* stabbed to death. *South.*

2. Very poorly or meanly; wretchedly. They were *miserably* entertained. *Sidney.*

3. In misery or unhappiness.

MI′SERLY, *a.* [See *Miser.*] Very covetous; sordid; niggardly; parsimonious.

MIS′ERY, *n.* *s* as *z*. [L. *miseria*; Fr. *misère.*]

1. Great unhappiness; extreme pain of body or mind. A man suffers *misery* from the gout, or from great afflictions, distress, calamity, and other evils. *Misery* expresses somewhat less than *wretchedness*.

> *Misery* is as really the fruit of vice reigning in the heart, as tares are the produce of tares sown in the field. *J. Lathrop.*

2. Calamity; misfortune; natural evils which are the cause of misery.

> And mourn the *miseries* of human life. *Dryden.*

3. Covetousness. [*Not used.*] *Shak.*

MISES′TIMATE, *v. t.* To estimate erroneously. *Mitford.*

MISFALL′, *v. t.* To befall, as ill luck; to happen to unluckily. *Spenser.*

MISFA′RE, *n.* Ill fare; misfortune. *Spenser.*

MISFASH′ION, *v. t.* To form wrong. *Hakewill.*

MISFE′ASANCE, *n.* *misfe′zance.* [Fr. *mes* and *faisance*, from *faire*, to do.] In *law*, a trespass; a wrong done. *Encyc.*

MISFORM′, *v. t.* To make of an ill form; to put in an ill shape. *Spenser.*

MISFOR′TUNE, *n.* Ill fortune; ill luck; calamity; an evil or cross accident; as loss of property at sea or by fire.

> Consider why the change was wrought,
> You'll find it his *misfortune*, not his fault. *Addison.*

MISFOR′TUNED, *a.* Unfortunate. *Milton.*

MISGIVE, *v. t.* *misgiv′*. [See *Give.*] To fill with doubt; to deprive of confidence; to fail; usually applied to the heart.

> So doth my heart *misgive* me. *Shak.*
> His heart *misgave* him. *Addison.*

2. To give or grant amiss. [*Not in use.*] *Laud.*

MISGIV′ING, *ppr.* Filling with doubt or distrust; failing.

MISGIV′ING, *n.* A failing of confidence; doubt; distrust.

> Doubts, suspicions and *misgivings*. *South.*

MISGOT′TEN, *a.* Unjustly obtained.

MISGŎV′ERN, *v. t.* To govern ill; to administer unfaithfully.

> Solyman charged him bitterly that he had *misgoverned* the state. *Knolles.*

MISGŎV′ERNANCE, *n.* Ill government; disorder; irregularity. *Spenser.*

MISGŎV′ERNED, *pp.* Ill governed; badly administered.

2. Rude; unrestrained; as rude, *misgoverned* hands. *Shak.*

MISGŎV′ERNMENT, *n.* Ill administration of public affairs. *Raleigh.*

2. Ill management in private affairs. *Taylor.*

3. Irregularity; disorder. *Shak.*

MISGR′AFF, *v. t.* To graft amiss.

MISGROUND′, *v. t.* To found erroneously. *Hall.*

MISGUI′DANCE, *n.* Wrong direction; guidance into error. *South.*

MISGUI′DE, *v. t.* To lead or guide into error; to direct ill; as, to *misguide* the understanding or mind. *Locke. Pope.*

MISGUI′DED, *pp.* Led astray by evil counsel or wrong direction; as a *misguided* prince. *Prior.*

MISGUI′DING, *ppr.* Giving wrong direction to; leading into error.

MIS′GUM, } *n.* An anguilliform fish about
MIS′GURN, } the size of a common eel. *Dict. Nat. Hist.*

MISHAP′, *n.* Ill chance; evil accident; ill luck; misfortune.

> Secure from worldly chances and *mishaps*. *Shak.*

MISHAP′PEN, *v. i.* To happen ill. *Spenser.*

MISHE′AR, *v. t.* To mistake in hearing.

MISH′NA, *n.* A collection or digest of Jewish traditions and explanations of Scripture.

MISH'NIC, *a.* Pertaining or relating to the Mishna. *Enfield. Encyc.*

MISIMPRÖVE, *v. t.* *misimproov'.* To improve to a bad purpose; to abuse; as, to *misimprove* time, talents, advantages.

MISIMPRÖVED, *pp.* Used to a bad purpose.

MISIMPRÖVEMENT, *n.* *misimproov'ment.* Ill use or employment; improvement to a bad purpose.

MISINFER', *v. t.* To draw a wrong inference. *Hooker.*

MISINFORM', *v. t.* To give erroneous information to; to communicate an incorrect statement of facts. *Bacon.*

MISINFORMA'TION, *n.* Wrong informations; false account or intelligence received. *Bacon. South.*

MISINFORM'ED, *pp.* Wrongly informed.

MISINFORM'ER, *n.* One that gives wrong information.

MISINFORM'ING, *ppr.* Communicating erroneous information to.

MISINSTRUCT', *v. t.* To instruct amiss. *Hooker.*

MISINSTRUC'TION, *n.* Wrong instruction. *More.*

MISINTEL'LIĠENCE, *n.* Wrong information; disagreement.

MISINTER'PRET, *v. t.* To interpret erroneously; to understand or to explain in a wrong sense. *Arbuthnot.*

MISINTERPRETA'TION, *n.* The act of interpreting erroneously.

MISINTER'PRETED, *a.* Erroneously understood or explained.

MISINTER'PRETER, *n.* One who interprets erroneously.

MISINTER'PRETING, *ppr.* Erroneously interpreting.

MISJOIN', *v. t.* To join unfitly or improperly. *Milton. Dryden.*

MISJOIN'ED, *pp.* Improperly united.

MISJOIN'ING, *ppr.* Joining unfitly or improperly.

MISJUDĠE, *v. t.* *misjudj'.* To mistake in judging of; to judge erroneously. *L'Estrange.*

MISJUDĠE, *v. i.* *misjudj'.* To err in judgment; to form false opinions or notions.

MISJUDĠ'ED, *pp.* Judged erroneously.

MISJUDĠ'ING, *ppr.* Judging erroneously of; forming a wrong opinion or inference.

MISJUDĠ'MENT, *n.* A wrong or unjust determination. *Hale.*

MIS'KIN, *n.* A little bagpipe.

MISKIN'DLE, *v. t.* To kindle amiss; to inflame to a bad purpose.

MISLA'ID, *pp.* Laid in a wrong place, or place not recollected; lost.

MISLA'Y, *v. t.* To lay in a wrong place.

> The fault is generally *mislaid* upon nature. *Locke.*

2. To lay in a place not recollected; to lose.

> If the butler be the tell-tale, *mislay* a spoon so as he may never find it. *Swift.*

MISLA'YER, *n.* One that lays in a wrong place; one that loses. *Bacon.*

MISLA'YING, *ppr.* Laying in a wrong place, or place not remembered; losing.

MISLE, *v. i.* *mis'l.* [from *mist*, and properly *mistle.*]

To rain in very fine drops, like a thick mist. *Gay. Derham.*

MISLE'AD, *v. t.* pret. and pp. *misled.* [See *Lead.*]

To lead into a wrong way or path; to lead astray; to guide into error; to cause to mistake; to deceive.

> Trust not servants who *mislead* or misinform you. *Bacon.*

> But of the two, less dangerous is th' offense,
> To tire our patience, than *mislead* our sense. *Pope.*

MISLE'ADER, *n.* One who leads into error.

MISLE'ADING, *ppr.* Leading into error; causing to err; deceiving.

MISLED', *pp.* of *mislead.* Led into error; led a wrong way.

> —To give due light
> To the *misled* and lonely traveller. *Milton.*

MISLI'KE, *v. t.* To dislike; to disapprove; to have aversion to; as, to *mislike* a man or an opinion. *Raleigh. Sidney.*
[For this word, *dislike* is generally used.]

MISLI'KE, *n.* Dislike; disapprobation; aversion.

MISLI'KED, *pp.* Disliked; disapproved.

MISLI'KER, *n.* One that dislikes.

MISLI'KING, *ppr.* Disliking; disapproving.

MISLIN, [See *Meslin.*]

MISLIVE, *v. i.* *misliv'.* To live amiss. [*Not used.*] *Spenser.*

MISLUCK', *n.* Ill luck; misfortune.

MIS'LY, *a.* [See *Misle* and *Mist.*] Raining in very small drops.

MISMAN'AĠE, *v. t.* To manage ill; to administer improperly; as, to *mismanage* public affairs.

MISMAN'AĠE, *v. i.* To behave ill; to conduct amiss.

MISMAN'AĠED, *pp.* Ill managed or conducted.

MISMAN'AĠEMENT, *n.* Ill or improper management; ill conduct; as the *mismanagement* of public or private affairs.

MISMAN'AĠER, *n.* One that manages ill. *Burke.*

MISMAN'AĠING, *ppr.* Managing ill.

MISM'ARK, *v. t.* To mark with the wrong token; to mark erroneously. *Collier.*

MISM'ARKED, *pp.* Wrongly marked.

MISM'ARKING, *ppr.* Marking erroneously.

MISMATCH', *v. t.* To match unsuitably. *Southern.*

MISMATCH'ED, *pp.* Unsuitably matched; ill joined.

MISMATCH'ING, *ppr.* Matching in an unsuitable manner.

MISNA'ME, *v. t.* To call by the wrong name. *Boyle.*

MISNA'MED, *pp.* Called by a wrong name.

MISNA'MING, *ppr.* Calling by a wrong name.

MISNO'MER, *n.* [Old Fr. *mes*, wrong, and *nommer*, to name.]

In *law*, the mistaking of the true name of a person; a misnaming. [*Misnosmer*, as written by Blackstone, must be a corrupt orthography. In no dialect has *name*, L. *nomen*, been written with *s*, unless by mistake.]

MISOBE'DIENCE, *n.* Erroneous obedience or disobedience. [*Not used.*] *Milton.*

MISOBSERVE, *v. t.* *misobzerv'.* To observe inaccurately; to mistake in observing. *Locke.*

MISOG'AMIST, *n.* [Gr. μισεω, to hate, and γαμος, marriage.]

A hater of marriage.

MISOĠ'YNIST, *n.* [Gr. μισεω, to hate, and γυνη, woman.]

A woman hater. [*Unusual.*] *Fuller.*

MISOĠ'YNY, *n.* [supra.] Hatred of the female sex.

MISOPIN'ION, *n.* Erroneous opinion. *Bp. Hall.*

MISOR'DER, *v. t.* To order ill; to manage erroneously. *Obs.* *Ascham.*

2. To manage ill; to conduct badly. *Obs.* *Shak.*

MISOR'DER, *n.* Irregularity; disorderly proceedings. [We now use *disorder.*] *Camden.*

MISOR'DERLY, *a.* Irregular; disorderly. *Ascham.*

MISPELL, MISPEND, &c. [See *Miss-spell, Miss-spend.*]

MISPERSUA'DE, *v. t.* To persuade amiss, or to lead to a wrong notion. *Hooker.*

MISPERSUA'SION, *n.* A false persuasion; wrong notion or opinion. *Decay of Piety.*

MISPIK'EL, *n.* Arsenical pyrite; an ore of arsenic, containing this metal in combination with iron, sometimes found in cubic crystals, but more often without any regular form. *Fourcroy.*

MISPLA'CE, *v. t.* To put in a wrong place; as, the book is *misplaced.*

2. To place on an improper object; as, he *misplaced* his confidence. *South.*

MISPLA'CED, *pp.* Put in a wrong place, or on an improper object.

MISPLA'CING, *ppr.* Putting in a wrong place, or on a wrong object.

MISPLE'AD, *v. i.* To err in pleading. *Blackstone.*

MISPLE'ADING, *ppr.* Making a mistake in pleading.

MISPLE'ADING, *n.* A mistake in pleading.

MISPOINT', *v. t.* To point improperly; to err in punctuation.

MISPRINT', *v. t.* To mistake in printing; to print wrong.

MISPRINT', *n.* A mistake in printing; a deviation from the copy. *Ch. Obs.*

MISPRINT'ED, *pp.* Erroneously printed.

MISPRINT'ING, *ppr.* Printing wrong.

MISPRI'SE, MISPRI'ZE, *v. t.* [Fr. *meprendre*, *mepris*; *mes*, wrong, and *prendre*, to take.]

1. To mistake. *Shak.*

2. To slight or undervalue.

> O for those vanish'd hours, so much *mispris'd.* *Hillhouse.*

MISPRISION, *n.* *misprizh'un.* [supra.] Neglect; contempt.

2. In *law*, any high offense under the degree of capital, but nearly bordering thereon. *Misprision* is contained in every treason and felony. *Misprisions* are divided into *negative* and *positive*; *negative*, which consist in the concealment of something which ought to be revealed; and *positive*, which consist in the commission of something which ought not to be done. *Misprision of treason*, consists in a bare knowledge and concealment of treason, without assenting to it. *Blackstone.*

> Maladministration in offices of high public trust, is a *positive misprision.* *Ibm.*

3. Mistake; oversight; contempt. [*Not in use.*] *Shak.*

MISPROCEE'DING, *n.* Wrong or irregular proceeding. *Bacon.*

MISPROFESS′, *v. t.* To make a false profession; to make pretensions to skill which is not possessed. *Donne.*

MISPRONOUNCE, *v. t. mispronouns′.* To pronounce erroneously; as, to *mispronounce* a word, a name, &c.

MISPRONOUNCE, *v. i. mispronouns′.* To speak incorrectly. *Milton.*

MISPRONUNCIA′TION, *n.* A wrong or improper pronunciation. *Swift.*

MISPROPO′RTION, *v. t.* To err in proportioning one thing to another; to join without due proportion.

MISPROUD′, *a.* Vitiously proud. [*Not used.*] *Shak.*

MISQUOTA′TION, *n.* An erroneous quotation; the act of quoting wrong.

MISQUO′TE, *v. t.* To quote erroneously; to cite incorrectly.

MISQUO′TED, *pp.* Incorrectly quoted or cited.

MISQUO′TING, *ppr.* Quoting or citing erroneously.

MISRA′TE, *v. t.* To rate erroneously; to estimate falsely. *Barrow.*

MISRECI′TAL, *n.* An inaccurate recital.

MISRECI′TE, *v. t.* To recite erroneously. *Bramhall.*

MISRECI′TED, *pp.* Recited incorrectly.

MISRECI′TING, *ppr.* Reciting erroneously.

MISRECK′ON, *v. t.* To reckon or compute wrong. *Swift.*

MISRECK′ONED, *pp.* Reckoned or computed erroneously.

MISRECK′ONING, *ppr.* Reckoning wrong; and as a noun, an erroneous computation.

MISRELA′TE, *v. t.* To relate falsely or inaccurately. *Boyle.*

MISRELA′TED, *pp.* Erroneously related or told.

MISRELA′TING, *ppr.* Relating or telling erroneously.

MISRELA′TION, *n.* Erroneous relation or narration. *Bramhall.*

MISREMEM′BER, *v. t.* To mistake in remembering; not to remember correctly. *Boyle.*

MISREMEM′BERED, *pp.* Inaccurately recollected.

MISREMEM′BERING, *ppr.* Remembering inaccurately.

MISREPORT, *v. t.* To report erroneously; to give an incorrect account of. *Locke.*

MISREPORT, *n.* An erroneous report; a false or incorrect account given. *Denham. South.*

MISREPORTED, *pp.* Incorrectly reported.

MISREPORTING, *ppr.* Reporting incorrectly.

MISREPRESENT′, *v. t.* To represent falsely or incorrectly; to give a false or erroneous representation, either maliciously, ignorantly or carelessly. *Swift.*

MISREPRESENTA′TION, *n.* The act of giving a false or erroneous representation. *Swift.*

2. A false or incorrect account given, either from mistake, carelessness or malice. *Atterbury.*

MISREPRESENT′ED, *pp.* Falsely or erroneously represented.

MISREPRESENT′ER, *n.* One who gives a false or erroneous account.

MISREPRESENT′ING, *ppr.* Giving a false or erroneous representation.

[*Note.* This word is so customarily used for an euphemism, or as a softer expression for *lie* or *falsehood*, as to convey the idea generally of intentional falsehood. This signification however is not necessarily implied.]

MISREPU′TE, *v. t.* To have in wrong estimation.

MISREPU′TED, *pp.* or *a.* Erroneously reputed. *Milton.*

MISRU′LE, *n.* Disorder; confusion; tumult from insubordination.

> Enormous riot and *misrule*— *Pope.*

2. Unjust domination.

MISRU′LY, *a.* Unruly; ungovernable; turbulent. *Hall.*

MISS, *n.* [supposed by Bailey to be contracted from *mistress.* But probably it is from the Armoric *mesell*, a young lady, or contracted from Fr. *demoiselle*, Sp. *damisola.* See *Damsel.*]

1. The title of a young woman or girl; as little masters and *misses.* *Swift.*

2. A kept mistress; a prostitute retained; a concubine. *Dryden.*

MISS, *v. t.* [Sax. *missian*; D. G. *missen*; Sw. *mista*; Dan. *mister*; allied perhaps to L. *mitto, misi*; *omitto, omisi.* But this is not certain. The Welsh has the word in *methu*, to fail, to miss, to become abortive, to miscarry, to decay. See Class Md. No. 8. 12. 13. 14. 16. Hence the prefix *mis.*]

1. To fail in aim; to fail of reaching the object; not to hit; as, to *miss* the mark; to *miss* the object intended.

2. To fail of finding the right way; to err in attempting to find; as, to *miss* the way or the road.

3. To fail of obtaining.

> Orgalus feared nothing but to *miss* Parthenia. *Sidney.*

4. To learn or discover that something is wanting, or not where it was supposed to be; as, to *miss* one's snuff-box; I *missed* the first volume of Livy.

> Neither *missed* we any thing—. Nothing was *missed* of all that pertained to him. 1 Sam. xxv.

5. To be without; as, we cannot *miss* him. *Obs.* *Shak.*

6. To omit; to pass by; to go without; to fail to have; as, to *miss* a meal of victuals.

> She would never *miss* one day
> A walk so fine, a sight so gay. *Prior.*

7. To perceive the want of.

> What by me thou hast lost, thou least shalt *miss.* *Milton.*

> He who has a firm sincere friend, may want all the rest without *missing* them. *South.*

8. To fail of seeing or finding.

MISS, *v. i.* To fail to hit; to fly wide; to deviate from the true direction.

> Flying bullets now,
> To execute his rage, appear too slow;
> They *miss*, or sweep but common souls away. *Waller.*

2. Not to succeed; to fail.

> Men observe when things hit, and not when they *miss*— *Bacon.*

3. To fail; to miscarry, as by accident.

> The invention all admired, and each, how he
> To be the inventor *missed.* *Milton.*

4. To fail to obtain, learn or find; with *of.*

> On the least reflection, we cannot *miss of* them. *Atterbury.*

5. To fail; to mistake. *Spenser.*

MISS, *n.* Loss; want.

> There will be no great *miss* of those which are lost. *Locke.*

2. Mistake; error.

> He did without any great *miss* in the hardest points of grammar. [*Little used.*] *Ascham.*

3. Harm from mistake. *Obs.* *Spenser.*

MIS′SAL, *n.* [It. *messale*; Fr. *missel.* See *Mass.*] The Romish mass-book. *Stillingfleet.*

MISSA′Y, *v. t.* To say wrong; to slander. [*Little used.*] *Spenser.*

MISSA′Y, *v. i.* To speak ill. *Spenser.*

MISSA′YING, *n.* Wrong expression. *Milton.*

MISSEE′M, *v. i.* To make a false appearance. *Spenser.*

2. To misbecome. *Obs.* *Spenser.*

MIS′SEL, } **MIS′SEL-BIRD**, } *n.* A species of thrush.

MIS′SELDINE, *n.* The mistletoe. [*Not used.*] *Barret.*

MISSEM′BLANCE, *n.* False resemblance. *Spelman.*

MISSERVE, *v. t. misserv′.* To serve unfaithfully. *Arbuthnot.*

MISSHA′PE, *v. t.* [See *Shape.*] To shape ill; to give an ill form to; to deform.

> And horribly *misshapes* with ugly sights. *Spenser.*

> A *misshaped* figure. *Pope.*
> *Misshapen* mountains. *Bentley.*

MISSHA′PED, } **MISSHA′PEN**, } *pp.* Ill formed; deformed; ugly.

MISSHA′PING, *ppr.* Giving an ill shape to.

MIS′SILE, *a.* [L. *missilis*, from *missus*, sent; *mitto*, to send.] Thrown or sent, or that may be thrown.

A *missile* weapon is one that is thrown by the hand, or from an engine in war, in distinction from such as are held or retained in the hand, or fixed. An arrow, a dart, a javelin, a stone, a bullet, a bomb, are *missile* weapons.

MISS′ING, *ppr.* [from *miss.*] Failing to hit, to reach or to find; discovering to be wanting.

2. *a.* Lost; absent from the place where it was expected to be found; wanting. My horse is *missing*; my pen or my book is *missing.*

> For a time caught up to God, as once
> Moses was in the mount, and *missing* long. *Milton.*

MIS′SION, *n.* [L. *missio*, from *mitto*, to send.]

1. A sending or being sent, usually the latter; a being sent or delegated by authority, with certain powers for transacting business; commission; as sent on a foreign *mission.*

> How to begin, how to accomplish best
> His end of being on earth, and *mission* high. *Milton.*

2. Persons sent; any number of persons appointed by authority to perform any service; particularly, the persons sent to propagate religion, or evangelize the heathen. The societies for propagating the gospel have *missions* in almost every country. Last week a *mission* sailed for the Sandwich isles. We have domestic *missions* and foreign *missions.*

3. Dismission; discharge from service; *a Roman use of the word; in English, obsolete.* *Bacon.*

4. Faction; party. [*Not in use.*] *Shak.*

MIS′SIONARY, *n.* [Fr. *missionaire.*] One sent to propagate religion. Christian *missionaries* are called *missionaries of the cross.*

MIS'SIONARY, *a.* Pertaining to missions; as a *missionary* meeting; a *missionary* fund.

MISSIONER, for *missionary*, is not used.

MIS'SIVE, *a.* [Fr.] Such as is sent; as a letter *missive.*

2. Thrown or sent, or such as may be sent; as a *missive* weapon. *Dryden.*

MIS'SIVE, *n.* A letter sent, or a messenger. *Bacon. Shak.*

MISSPE'AK, *v. i.* [See *Speak.*] To err or mistake in speaking. *Shak.*

MISSPE'AK, *v. t.* To utter wrong. *Donne.*

MISSPELL', *v. t.* To spell wrong; to write or utter with wrong letters.

MISSPELL'ED, } *pp.* Spelled wrong, or
MISSPELT', } with wrong letters.

MISSPELL'ING, *ppr.* Spelling wrong.

MISSPELL'ING, *n.* A wrong spelling; false orthography.

MISSPEND', *v. t.* To spend amiss; to waste or consume to no purpose, or to a bad one; as, to *misspend* time or money; to *misspend* life. *Dryden. Rogers.*

2. To waste.

The genial moisture due
To apples, otherwise *misspends* itself. *Philips.*

MISSPEND'ER, *n.* One that consumes prodigally or improperly. *Norris.*

MISSPEND'ING, *pp.* Spending to no purpose, or to a bad one.

MISSPENSE, *n. misspens'.* A spending improperly; a wasting.

MISSPENT', *ppr.* Ill spent; expended or consumed to no purpose, or to a bad one; as *misspent* time or life.

MISSPO'KE, } *pp.* Uttered or spoken
MISSPO'KEN, } amiss.

MISSTA'TE, *v. t.* To state wrong; to make an erroneous representation of facts; as, to *misstate* a question in debate. *Sanderson.*

MISSTA'TED, *pp.* Stated erroneously.

MISSTA'TEMENT, *n.* A wrong statement; an erroneous representation, verbal or written; as a *misstatement* of facts in testimony, or of accounts in a report. *Hamilton.*

MISSTA'TING, *ppr.* Stating falsely or erroneously.

MIS'SY, *n.* The sulphate of iron, having lost the water of its crystalization, is called *sori;* more thoroughly calcined, it is yellow, and called *missy.* *Fourcroy.*

MIST, *n.* [Sax. D. *mist;* L. *mixtus, mistus,* from *misceo,* to *mix.*]

1. Water falling in very numerous, but fine and almost imperceptible drops.

A *mist* is a multitude of small but solid globules, which therefore descend. *Grew.*

2. That which dims or darkens, and obscures or intercepts vision.

His passion cast a *mist* before his sense. *Dryden.*

MIST, *v. t.* To cloud; to cover with vapor. *Shak.*

MIST-ENCUM'BERED, *a.* Loaded with mist. *J. Barlow.*

MISTA'KABLE, *a.* That may be misconceived or mistaken. *Brown.*

MISTA'KE, *v. t.* To take wrong; to conceive or understand erroneously; to misunderstand or misapprehend.

'Tis to *mistake* them costs the time and pain. *Pope.*

2. To take one thing or person for another.

We *mistake* the eloquence of self-apology for the animation of conscious integrity. *Buckminster.*

A man may *mistake* the love of virtue for the practice of it. *Johnson.*

MISTA'KE, *v. i.* To err in opinion or judgment.

Servants *mistake,* and sometimes occasion misunderstanding among friends. *Swift.*

MISTA'KE, *n.* An error in opinion or judgment; misconception.

Infallibility is an absolute security of the understanding from all possibility of *mistake.* *Tillotson.*

2. A slip; a fault; an error. There is a *mistake* in the account or in the date.

MISTA'KEN. In the use of this participle, there is a peculiarity which ought to be carefully noticed. When used of *persons,* it signifies to *be in an error, to be wrong;* as, I am *mistaken,* you are *mistaken,* he is *mistaken.* But when used of *things,* it signifies *misunderstood, misconceived;* as, the sense of the passage is *mistaken,* that is, not rightly understood.

MISTA'KER, *n.* One that mistakes or misunderstands.

MISTA'KING, *ppr.* Making a mistake; erring from the truth; misconceiving.

MISTA'KING, *n.* An error; a mistake. *Hall.*

MISTA'KINGLY, *adv.* Erroneously; falsely. *Boyle.*

MISTAUGHT', *pp.* Wrongly taught; as a *mistaught* youth. *L'Estrange.*

MISTE'ACH, *v. t.* [See *Teach.*] To teach wrong; to instruct erroneously. *Sanderson.*

MISTE'ACHING, *ppr.* Instructing erroneously.

MISTELL', *v. t.* [See *Tell.*] To tell erroneously.

MISTEM'PER, *v. t.* To temper ill; to disorder. *Shak.*

MISTEM'PERED, *pp.* Tempered ill.

MIS'TER, *n.* [The pronunciation of this word is probably from the Welsh, German or Dutch dialect. See *Master.*]

The common title of address to gentlemen, and to men of all classes. In writing, it is expressed by the abbreviation *Mr.*

MIS'TER, *v. t.* To occasion loss. [Sw. *mista.*] [*Not in use.*]

MISTERM', *v. t.* To term or denominate erroneously. *Shak.*

MISTERM'ED, *pp.* Wrongly denominated.

MISTERM'ING, *ppr.* Denominating erroneously.

MIST'FUL, *a.* Clouded with mist.

MISTHINK', *v. i.* [See *Think.*] To think wrong. [*Little used.*] *Shak.*

MISTHOUGHT', *pp.* of *misthink.* Thought wrong of.

Adam, *misthought* of her to thee so dear. *Milton.*

MISTI'ME, *v. t.* To time wrong; not to adapt to the time.

MISTI'ME, *v. i.* To neglect the proper time.

MISTI'MED, *pp.* Ill timed; done at a wrong time.

MISTI'MING, *ppr.* Ill timing; doing unseasonably.

MIST'INESS, *n.* [See *Mist.*] A state of being misty; a state of thick rain in very small drops. *Bacon.*

MIS'TION, *n.* [L. *mistus, mixtus.* See *Mix.*]

1. A state of being mixed.

2. Mixture; a mingling. *Boyle.*

MISTI'TLE, *v. t.* To call by a wrong title or name. *Warburton.*

MISTI'TLED, *pp.* Wrongly named.

MISTLE, *v. i. mis'l.* [from *mist.*] To fall in very fine drops, as rain. [See *Missle.*]

MISTLETOE, } *n. mis'lto.* [Sax. *mistelta;*
MISLETOE, } Dan. *mistel,* the same shrub, and birdlime; G. *id.*]

A plant or shrub that grows on trees. It is of the genus Viscum. The berry contains a glutinous substance, and the shrub is said to be propagated by birds. This plant was held in great veneration by the Druids. *Bacon. Miller. Encyc.*

MIST'LIKE, *a.* Resembling mist. *Shak.*

MISTOLD, *pp.* Erroneously told. [See *Tell.*]

MISTOOK', *pret.* of *mistake.*

MISTRA'IN, *v. t.* To train or educate amiss. *Spenser.*

MISTRANSLA'TE, *v. t.* To translate erroneously. *Macknight.*

MISTRANSLA'TED, *pp.* Erroneously rendered into another language.

MISTRANSLA'TING, *ppr.* Translating incorrectly.

MISTRANSLA'TION, *n.* An erroneous translation or version.

MIS'TRESS, *n.* [Fr. *maîtresse;* It. *maestra, maestressa;* Sp. *maestra;* L. *magistra;* Ir. *maigh is treas.* See *Master.*]

1. A woman who governs; correlative to *servant, slave,* or *subject.*

My *mistress* here lies murdered in her bed. *Shak.*

2. The female head of a family.

3. That which governs; a sovereign. Rome was *mistress* of the world.

4. One that commands, or has possession and sovereignty. The queen is *mistress* of the Indies.

5. A female who is well skilled in any thing; as, she is *mistress* of arithmetic.

6. A woman teacher; an instructress of a school. *Swift.*

7. A woman beloved and courted. *Clarendon.*

8. A woman in keeping for lewd purposes.

9. A term of contemptuous address. *Shak.*

MIS'TRESS, *v. t.* To wait upon a mistress; to be courting. *Donne.*

MIS'TRESS-SHIP, *n.* Female rule or dominion. *Hall.*

MISTRUST', *n.* [Dan. *mistrøst.* See *Trust.*] Want of confidence or trust; suspicion. *Milton.*

MISTRUST', *v. t.* [Dan. *mistroer;* Sw. *misstro.* See *Trust.*]

To suspect; to doubt; to regard with jealousy or suspicion.

Fate her own book *mistrusted* at the sight. *Cowley.*

MISTRUST'ED, *pp.* Suspected.

MISTRUST'FUL, *a.* Suspicious; doubting; wanting confidence in. *Waller.*

MISTRUST'FULNESS, *n.* Suspicion; doubt. *Sidney.*

MISTRUST′FULLY, *adv.* With suspicion or doubt.

MISTRUST′ING, *ppr.* Suspecting; having no confidence in.

MISTRUST′INGLY, *adv.* With distrust or suspicion.

MISTRUST′LESS, *a.* Unsuspecting; unsuspicious. *Carew.*

MISTU′NE, *v. t.* To tune wrong or erroneously; to put out of tune. *Skelton.*

MISTURN′, *v. t.* To pervert. [*Not used.*]

MISTU′TOR, *v. t.* To instruct amiss.

MIST′Y, *a.* [from *mist.*] Overspread with mist; filled with very minute drops of rain; as *misty* weather; a *misty* atmosphere; a *misty* night or day. *Spenser. Pope.*

2. Dim; obscure; clouded; as *misty* sight.

MISUNDERSTAND′, *v. t.* To misconceive; to mistake; to take in a wrong sense. *Locke. Addison.*

MISUNDERSTAND′ING, *ppr.* Mistaking the meaning.

MISUNDERSTAND′ING, *n.* Misconception; mistake of the meaning; error. *Bacon.*

2. Disagreement; difference; dissension; sometimes a softer name for *quarrel.* *Swift.*

MISUNDERSTOOD′, *pp.* Misconceived; mistaken; understood erroneously. *South.*

MISUSAGE, *n.* *misyu′zage.* Ill usage; abuse.

MISUSE, *v. t.* *misyu′ze.* [Fr. *mesuser.* See *Use.*]

1. To treat or use improperly; to use to a bad purpose. *Milton.*

2. To abuse; to treat ill.

MISUSE, *n.* *misyu′se.* Ill treatment; improper use; employment to a bad purpose; as the *misuse* of mercies. *Addison.*

2. Abuse; ill treatment. *Shak.*

3. Wrong application; misapplication; erroneous use; as the *misuse* of words. *Locke.*

MISUSED, *pp.* *misyu′zed.* Improperly used or applied; misapplied; misemployed; abused.

MISUSING, *ppr.* *misyu′zing.* Using improperly; abusing; misapplying.

MISVOUCH′, *v. t.* To vouch falsely.

MISWEAR, *v. t.* To swear ill. *Obs.* *Bacon.*

MISWED′, *v. t.* To wed improperly.

MISWED′DED, *pp.* Ill matched.

MISWEE′N, *v. i.* To misjudge; to distrust. *Spenser.*

MISWEND′, *v. i.* To go wrong. *Obs.* *Spenser.*

MISWRI′TE, *v. t.* [See *Write.*] To write incorrectly. *Bp. Cosin.*

MISWROUGHT, *a.* *misraut′.* Badly wrought. *Bacon.*

MISY. [See *Missy.*]

MISZEALOUS, *a.* *miszel′ous.* Actuated by false zeal. *Bp. Hall.*

MITE, *n.* [Sax. *mite*; D. *myt*; Dan. *mid*; Fr. *mite*; Heb. Ch. מעט, small. Class Md. No. 17.]

1. A very small insect of the genus Acarus.

2. In *Scripture*, a small piece of money, the quarter of a denarius, or about seven English farthings. *Encyc.*

3. Any thing proverbially very small; a very little particle or quantity. *Dryden.*

4. The twentieth part of a grain. *Arbuthnot.*

MITEL′LA, *n.* A plant.

MI′TER, *n.* [It. Sp. *mitra*; Fr. *mitre*; Arm. *mintr.*]

1. A sacerdotal ornament worn on the head by bishops and certain abbots, on solemn occasions. *Encyc.*

2. In *architecture*, an angle of 45°. *Encyc.*

3. In *Irish history*, a sort of base money or coin. *Encyc.*

4. Figuratively, the dignity of bishops or abbots.

MI′TER, *v. t.* To adorn with a miter.

2. To unite at an angle of 45°.

MI′TERED, *pp.* or *a.* Wearing a miter.

2. Honored with the privilege of wearing a miter.

3. Cut or joined at an angle of 45°.

MITHIC. [See *Mythic.*]

MITH′RIDATE, *n.* In *pharmacy*, an antidote against poison, or a composition in form of an electuary, supposed to serve either as a remedy or a preservative against poison. It takes its name from Mithridates, king of Pontus, the inventor. *Encyc.*

MITHRIDAT′IC, *a.* Pertaining to mithridate, or its inventor, Mithridates.

MIT′IGABLE, *a.* That may be mitigated. *Barrow.*

MIT′IGANT, *a.* [L. *mit′gans*, *mitigo*, from *mitis*, mild; W. *mezal*, soft.]

1. Softening; lenient; lenitive.

2. Diminishing; easing; as pain.

MIT′IGATE, *v. t.* [L. *mitigo*, from *mitis*, soft, mild, W. *mezal*, Ir. *maoth*, *muadh*; Ar. ماد to be tender or smooth. Class Md. No. 1. 6. 25. 28.]

1. To alleviate, as suffering; to assuage; to lessen; as, to *mitigate* pain or grief.

> And counsel *mitigates* the greatest smart. *Spenser.*

2. To make less severe; as, to *mitigate* doom. *Milton.*

3. To abate; to make less rigorous; to moderate; as, to *mitigate* cold; to *mitigate* the severity of the season.

4. To temper; to moderate; to soften in harshness or severity.

> We could wish that the rigor of their opinions were allayed and *mitigated.* *Hooker.*

5. To calm; to appease; to moderate; as, to *mitigate* the fierceness of party. *Spectator.*

6. To diminish; to render more tolerable; as, to *mitigate* the evils or calamities of life; to *mitigate* punishment.

7. To reduce in amount or severity; as, to *mitigate* a penalty.

8. To soften, or make mild and accessible; *in a literal sense.*

> It was this opinion which *mitigated* kings into companions. [*Unusual.*] *Burke.*

MIT′IGATED, *pp.* Softened; alleviated; moderated; diminished.

MIT′IGATING, *ppr.* Softening; alleviating; tempering; moderating; abating.

MITIGA′TION, *n.* [L. *mitigatio.*] Alleviation; abatement or diminution of any thing painful, harsh, severe, afflictive or calamitous; as the *mitigation* of pain, grief, rigor, severity, punishment or penalty.

MIT′IGATIVE, *a.* Lenitive; tending to alleviate.

MIT′IGATOR, *n.* He or that which mitigates.

MIT′TEN, *n.* [Fr. *mitaine*; Ir. *mitog*, perhaps from *math*, the hand.]

1. A cover for the hand, worn to defend it from cold or other injury. It differs from a glove, in not having a separate cover for each finger.

2. A cover for the arm only.

To handle without mittens, to treat roughly; *a popular colloquial phrase.*

MIT′TENT, *a.* [L. *mittens*, from *mitto*, to send.]

Sending forth; emitting. [*Not used.*] *Wiseman.*

MIT′TIMUS, *n.* [L. we send.] In *law*, a precept or command in writing, under the hand or hand and seal of a justice of the peace or other proper officer, directed to the keeper of a prison, requiring him to imprison an offender; a warrant of commitment to prison.

2. A writ for removing records from one court to another. *Encyc.*

MITU, *n.* A fowl of the turkey kind, found in Brazil.

MI′TY, *a.* [from *mite.*] Having or abounding with mites.

MIX, *v. t.* pret. and pp. *mixed* or *mixt.* [Sax. *miscan*; G. *mischen*; Sp. *mecer*; Port. *mexer*, to stir, shake, mix; L. *misceo*, *mixtum*; It. *mischiare*; Ir. *measgadh*; W. *mysgu*; Arm. *gemesga*; Russ. *meshayu.* The Gr. *μιγνυω* forms *μιξω.* These words seem to coincide with the Heb. and Ch. מסך, and Ar. مشج to mix. The Sanscrit *misra*, to mix, may be the same word. The radical sense is probably to stir, shake or agitate.]

1. To unite or blend promiscuously two or more ingredients into a mass or compound; applied both to solids and liquids; as, to *mix* flour and salt; to *mix* wines.

2. To join; to associate; to unite with in company.

> Ephraim, he hath *mixed* himself among the people. Hos. vii.

3. To join; to mingle.

> You *mix* your sadness with some fear. *Shak.*

4. To unite with a crowd or multitude.

MIX, *v. i.* To become united or blended promiscuously in a mass or compound. Oil and water will not *mix* without the intervention of a third substance.

2. To be joined or associated; as, to *mix* with the multitude, or to *mix* in society.

MIX′ED, *pp.* United in a promiscuous mass or compound; blended; joined; mingled; associated.

2. *a.* Promiscuous; consisting of various kinds or different things; as a *mixed* multitude.

MIX′EN, *n.* A dunghill; a laystall. *Johnson.*

MIX′ER, *n.* One who mixes or mingles.

MIX′ING, *ppr.* Uniting or blending in a mass or compound; joining in company; associating.

MIXTILIN′EAL, } *a.* [L. *mixtus*, mixed, and
MIXTILIN′EAR, } *linea*, line.]

Containing a mixture of lines, right, curved, &c. *Duncan.*

MIX'TION, *n.* [Fr.; from L. *mixtus.*] Mixture; promiscuous assemblage. *Brown.*

MIXT'LY, *adv.* With mixture. *Bacon.*

MIX'TURE, *n.* [L. *mixtura.*] The act of mixing, or state of being mixed. Compounds are made by the *mixture* of different substances.

2. A mass or compound, consisting of different ingredients blended without order. In this life there is a *mixture* of good and evil. Most wines in market are base *mixtures.*

3. The ingredient added and mixed. Cicero doubted whether it is possible for a community to exist without a prevailing *mixture* of piety in its constitution.

4. In *pharmacy*, a liquid medicine which receives into its composition not only extracts, salts and other substances dissolvable in water, but earths, powders and other substances not dissolvable. *Encyc.*

5. In *chimistry*, mixture differs from combination. In *mixture*, the several ingredients are blended without an alteration of the substances, each of which still retains its own nature and properties. In *combination*, the substances unite by chimical attraction, and losing their distinct properties, they form a compound differing in its properties from either of the ingredients.

MIZ'MAZE, *n.* A cant word for a maze or labyrinth. *Locke.*

MIZZEN, *n.* *miz'n.* [It. *mezzana*, mizzen, that is, middle, from *mezzo*, middle, half.]

In *sea-language*, the aftermost of the fixed sails of a ship, extended sometimes by a gaff, and sometimes by a yard which crosses the mast obliquely. *Mar. Dict.*

MIZ'ZEN-MAST, *n.* The mast which supports the after-sails, and stands nearest to the stern.

MIZ'ZLE, *v. i.* To mistle. [See *Mistle.*]

MIZ'ZY, *n.* A bog or quagmire. *Ainsworth.*

MNEMONIC, *a.* *nemon'ic.* [infra.] Assisting the memory.

MNEMON'ICS, *n.* [from Gr. μνημονικος, from μναομαι, to remember.]

The art of memory; the precepts and rules intended to teach the method of assisting the memory. *Bailey.*

MO, *a.* [Sax. *ma*; Scot. *mæ.*] More. *Obs.* *Spenser.*

MOAN, *v. t.* [Sax. *mænan*, to moan, also to *mean*, intend, signify. The primary sense is to reach or stretch forward, or to throw out.]

To lament; to deplore; to bewail with an audible voice.

> Ye floods, ye woods, ye echoes, *moan*
> My dear Columbo dead and gone. *Prior.*

MOAN, *v. i.* To grieve; to make lamentations.

> Unpitied and unheard, where misery *moans.* *Thomson.*

MOAN, *n.* Lamentation; audible expression of sorrow; grief expressed in words or cries.

> Sullen *moans*,
> Hollow groans. *Pope.*

MOANED, *pp.* Lamented; deplored.

MOANFUL, *a.* Sorrowful; expressing sorrow.

MOANFULLY, *adv.* With lamentation.

MOANING, *ppr.* Lamenting; bewailing.

MOAT, *n.* [Ir. *mota*; Sp. *id.*; Fr. *motte.* The word signifies a bank or mound, that is, a mass or collection. This sense is transferred to the ditch adjoining, as *dike* is transferred to the bank.]

In *fortification*, a ditch or deep trench round the rampart of a castle or other fortified place. It is sometimes filled with water. *Encyc.*

MOAT, *v. t.* To surround with a ditch for defense; as a *moated* castle. *Dryden.*

MOB, *n.* [from L. *mobilis*, movable, variable.]

1. A crowd or promiscuous multitude of people, rude, tumultuous and disorderly.

2. A disorderly assembly.

> Had every Athenian citizen been a Socrates, every Athenian assembly would still have been a *mob.* *Federalist, Madison.*

3. A huddled dress. *Steele.*

MOB, *v. t.* To attack in a disorderly crowd; to harass tumultuously.

2. To wrap up in a cowl or vail.

MOB'BISH, *a.* Like a mob; tumultuous; mean; vulgar.

MOB'CAP, *n.* [D. *mop.*] A plain cap or head-dress for females.

MO'BILE, *a.* [Fr.] Movable. [*Not used.*] *Skelton.*

MO'BILE, *n.* [Fr. from L. *mobilis.*] The mob; the populace. *South.*

Primum mobile, [L.] in *the ancient astronomy*, a ninth heaven or sphere, supposed to be beyond the fixed stars, and to be the first mover of all the lower spheres.

MOBIL'ITY, *n.* [Fr. *mobilité*; L. *mobilitas*, from *moveo*, to move.]

1. Susceptibility of motion; capacity of being moved. *Wotton.*

2. Aptitude to motion; activity; readiness to move. *Arbuthnot.*

3. In *cant language*, the populace. *Dryden.*

4. Fickleness; inconstancy. *Ainsworth.*

MOB'LE, *v. t.* To wrap the head in a hood. *Shak.*

MOC'CASON, *n.* A shoe or cover for the feet, made of deer-skin or other soft lether, without a sole, and ornamented on the upper side; the customary shoe worn by the native Indians.

MO'CHA-STONE, *n.* [from *Mocha*, in Arabia.]

Dendritic agate; a mineral in the interior of which appear brown, reddish brown, blackish or green delineations of shrubs destitute of leaves. These in some cases may have been produced by the filtration of the oxyds of iron and manganese; but in other cases they appear to be vegetable fibers, sometimes retaining their natural form and color, and sometimes coated by oxyd of iron. *Cleaveland.*

MOCK, *v. t.* [Fr. *moquer*; Gr. μωκαω; W. *mociaw*, to mock, and *moc*, a mimic; Ir. *magadh* or *mogadh*, a mocking; Ch. Syr. מוק. Class Mg. No. 10.]

1. Properly, to imitate; to mimick; hence, to imitate in contempt or derision; to mimick for the sake of derision; to deride by mimicry.

2. To deride; to laugh at; to ridicule; to treat with scorn or contempt.

> As he was going up by the way, there came forth little children out of the city, and *mocked* him, saying, go up, thou bald head. 2 Kings ii. Mark x.

3. To defeat; to illude; to disappoint; to deceive; as, to *mock* expectation.

> Thou hast *mocked* me and told me lies. Judg. xvi.

4. To fool; to tantalize; to play on in contempt.

> He will not
> *Mock* us with his blest sight, then snatch him hence. *Milton.*

MOCK, *v. i.* To make sport in contempt or in jest, or to speak jestingly.

> When thou *mockest*, shall no man make thee ashamed? Job xi.

MOCK, *n.* Ridicule; derision; sneer; an act manifesting contempt.

> Fools make a *mock* at sin. Prov. xiv.
> What shall be the portion of those who make a *mock* at every thing sacred? *Tillotson.*

2. Imitation; mimicry. [*Little used.*] *Crashaw.*

MOCK, *a.* False; counterfeit; assumed; imitating reality, but not real.

> That superior greatness and *mock* majesty— *Spectator.*

MOCK'ABLE, *a.* Exposed to derision. [*Little used.*] *Shak.*

MOCK'AGE, *n.* Mockery. [*Not used.*] *Elyot.*

MOCK'ED, *pp.* Imitated or mimicked in derision; laughed at; ridiculed; defeated; illuded.

MOCK'ER, *n.* One that mocks; a scorner; a scoffer; a derider. *South.*

2. A deceiver; an impostor.

MOCK'ERY, *n.* The act of deriding and exposing to contempt, by mimicking the words or actions of another.

2. Derision; ridicule; sportive insult or contempt; contemptuous merriment at persons or things.

> Grace at meals is now generally so performed as to look more like *mockery* upon devotion, than any solemn application of the mind to God. *Law.*

3. Sport; subject of laughter.

> Of the holy place they made a *mockery.* *Maccabees.*

4. Vain imitation or effort; that which deceives, disappoints or frustrates.

> It is as the air, invulnerable,
> And our vain blows malicious *mockery.* *Shak.*

5. Imitation; counterfeit appearance; false show.

> And bear about the *mockery* of woe
> To midnight dances. *Pope.*

MOCK'ESON, *n.* The name of a serpent.

MOCK'ING, *ppr.* Imitating in contempt; mimicking; ridiculing by mimicry; treating with sneers and scorn; defeating; deluding.

MOCK'ING, *n.* Derision; insult.

MOCK'ING-BIRD, *n.* The mocking thrush of America; a bird of the genus Turdus.

MOCK'INGLY, *adv.* By way of derision; in contempt.

MOCK'ING-STOCK, *n.* A butt of sport.

MOCKLE. [See *Mickle.*]

MOCK'-LEAD, } *n.* A sulphuret of zink, the
MOCK'-ORE, } same as *blend*, which see.

MOCK'-ORANGE, *n.* A plant of the genus Philadelphus.

MOCK'-PRIVET, *n.* A plant of the genus Phillyrea.

MO'DAL, *a.* [See *Mode.*] Consisting in mode only; relating to form; having the form without the essence or reality; as the *modal* diversity of the faculties of the soul. *Glanville.*

MODAL'ITY, *n.* The quality of being modal, or being in form only.

MODE, *n.* [Fr. *mode*; L. *modus*; Sp. It. *modo*; W. *moz*; Ir. *modh*; Sax. *mete*, *gemet* or *gemett*, from *metan*, *gemetan*, to *meet*, to find, to measure or *mete*, L. *metior*. The primary sense of *mode* is measure, hence form. Measure is from extending, the extent, hence a limit, and hence the derivative sense of restraining. See *Meet* and *Measure.*]

1. Manner of existing or being; manner; method; form; fashion; custom; way; as the *mode* of speaking; the *mode* of dressing; *modes* of receiving or entertaining company.

The duty of itself being resolved on, the *mode* of doing it may be easily found. *Taylor.*

It is applicable to particular acts, or to a series of acts, or to the common usage of a city or nation. One man has a particular *mode* of walking; another has a singular *mode* of dressing his hair. We find it necessary to conform in some measure to the usual *modes* of dress.

2. Gradation; degree.

What *modes* of sight between each wide extreme! *Pope.*

3. State; quality. *Shak.*

4. In *metaphysics*, the dependence or affection of a substance. Such complex ideas as contain not in them the supposition of subsisting by themselves, but are considered as dependencies or affections of substances, Locke calls *modes*. Of these he makes two kinds; *simple modes*, which are only variations or different combinations of the same idea, as a *dozen*, which consists of so many units added together; and *mixed modes*, which are compounded of simple ideas of several kinds, as *beauty*, which is compounded of color and figure.

A *mode* is that which cannot subsist in and of itself, but is esteemed as belonging to and subsisting by the help of some substance, which for that reason is called its subject. *Watts.*

5. In *music*, a regular disposition of the air and accompaniments relative to certain principal sounds, on which a piece of music is formed, and which are called the essential sounds of the mode. *Encyc.*

6. In *grammar*, a particular manner of conjugating verbs to express manner of action or being, as affirmation, command, condition and the like; usually and not very properly written *mood*. *Mood* is a word of different signification. [See *Mood.*]

7. A kind of silk.

MODEL, *n.* *mod'l*. [Fr. *modelle*; L. *modulus*, from *modus.*]

1. A pattern of something to be made; any thing of a particular form, shape or construction, intended for imitation; primarily, a small pattern; a form in miniature of something to be made on a larger scale; as the *model* of a building; the *model* of a fort.

2. A mold; something intended to give shape to castings. *Shak.*

3. Pattern; example; as, to form a government on the *model* of the British or American constitution.

4. Standard; that by which a thing is to be measured.

He that despairs, measures Providence by his own contracted *model*. *South.*

5. In *painting* and *sculpture*, that which is to be copied or imitated; as the naked human form.

6. A pattern; any thing to be imitated. Take Cicero, lord Chatham or Burke, as a *model* of eloquence; take Washington as a *model* of prudence, integrity and patriotism; above all, let Christ be the *model* of our benevolence, humility, obedience and patience.

7. A copy; representation; something made in imitation of real life; as anatomical *models*, representing the parts of the body. General Pfiffer constructed a *model* of the mountainous parts of Switzerland.

MOD'EL, *v. t.* [Fr. *modeler.*] To plan or form in a particular manner; to shape; to imitate in planning or forming; as, to *model* a house or a government; to *model* an edifice according to the plan delineated.

MOD'ELED, *pp.* Formed according to a model; planned; shaped; formed.

MOD'ELER, *n.* A planner; a contriver. *Spectator.*

MOD'ELING, *ppr.* Forming according to a model; planning; forming; shaping.

MOD'ERATE, *a.* [L. *moderatus*, from *moderor*, to limit, from *modus*, a limit.]

1. Literally, limited; restrained; hence, temperate; observing reasonable bounds in indulgence; as *moderate* in eating or drinking, or in other gratifications.

2. Limited in quantity; not excessive or expensive. He keeps a *moderate* table.

3. Restrained in passion, ardor or temper; not violent; as *moderate* men of both parties.

4. Not extreme in opinion; as a *moderate* Calvinist or Lutheran.

5. Placed between extremes; holding the mean or middle place; as reformation of a *moderate* kind.

6. Temperate; not extreme, violent or rigorous; as *moderate* weather; a *moderate* winter; *moderate* heat; a *moderate* breeze of wind.

7. Of a middle rate; as men of *moderate* abilities.

8. Not swift; as a *moderate* walk.

MOD'ERATE, *v. t.* To restrain from excess of any kind; to reduce from a state of violence; to lessen; to allay; to repress; as, to *moderate* rage, action, desires, &c.; to *moderate* heat or wind.

2. To temper; to make temperate; to qualify.

By its astringent quality, it *moderates* the relaxing quality of warm water. *Arbuthnot.*

MOD'ERATE, *v. i.* To become less violent, severe, rigorous or intense. The cold of winter usually *moderates* in March; the heat of summer *moderates* in September.

MOD'ERATED, *pp.* Reduced in violence, rigor or intensity; allayed; lessened; tempered; qualified.

MOD'ERATELY, *adv.* Temperately; mildly; without violence.

2. In a middle degree; not excessively; as water *moderately* warm.

Each nymph but *moderately* fair. *Waller.*

MOD'ERATENESS, *n.* State of being moderate; temperateness; a middle state between extremes; as the *moderateness* of the weather; used commonly of *things*, as *moderation* is of *persons*. *Johnson.*

MOD'ERATING, *ppr.* Reducing in violence or excess; allaying; tempering; becoming more mild.

MODERA'TION, *n.* [L. *moderatio.*] The state of being moderate, or of keeping a due mean between extremes or excess of violence. The General's *moderation* after victory was more honorable than the victory itself.

In *moderation* placing all my glory,
While tories call me whig, and whigs a tory. *Pope.*

2. Restraint of violent passions or indulgence of appetite. Eat and drink with *moderation*; indulge with *moderation* in pleasures and exercise.

3. Calmness of mind; equanimity; as, to bear prosperity or adversity with *moderation*.

4. Frugality in expenses. *Ainsworth.*

MODERA'TOR, *n.* He or that which moderates or restrains. Contemplation is an excellent *moderator* of the passions.

2. The person who presides over a meeting or assembly of people to preserve order, propose questions, regulate the proceedings and declare the vote; as the *moderator* of a town meeting or of a society. *Watts.*

MODERA'TORSHIP, *n.* The office of a moderator. *Elyot.*

MOD'ERN, *a.* [Fr. *moderne*; It. Sp. *moderno*. This word seems to be formed from L. *modo*, and *ern*, which we find in other Latin words that have reference to time, as in *hodiernus*, *hesternus*.]

1. Pertaining to the present time, or time not long past; late; recent; not ancient or remote in past time; as *modern* days, ages or time; *modern* authors; *modern* fashions; *modern* taste; *modern* practice. *Bacon. Prior.*

2. Common; mean; vulgar. [*Not used.*] *Shak.*

MOD'ERNISM, *n.* Modern practice; something recently formed, particularly in writing. *Swift.*

MOD'ERNIST, *n.* One who admires the moderns. *Swift.*

MOD'ERNIZE, *v. t.* To render modern; to adapt ancient compositions to modern persons or things, or rather to adapt the ancient style or idiom to modern style and taste.

MOD'ERNIZED, *pp.* Rendered conformable to modern usage.

MOD'ERNIZER, *n.* He that renders modern.

MOD'ERNIZING, *ppr.* Rendering modern.

MOD'ERNLY, *adv.* In modern times. [*Not in use.*] *Milton.*

MOD'ERNNESS, *n.* The quality of being modern; recentness; novelty.

MOD'ERNS, *n.* Those who have lived in times recently past, or are now living; opposed to the *ancients*. *Boyle. Pope.*

MOD'EST, *a.* [Fr. *modeste*; L. *modestus*, from *modus*, a limit.]

1. Properly, restrained by a sense of propriety; hence, not forward or bold; not pre-

sumptuous or arrogant; not boastful; as a *modest* youth; a *modest* man.

2. Not bold or forward; as a *modest* maid. The word may be thus used without reference to chastity.

The blushing beauties of a *modest* maid. *Dryden.*

3. Not loose; not lewd.

Mrs. Ford, the honest woman, the *modest* wife. *Shak.*

4. Moderate; not excessive or extreme; not extravagant; as a *modest* request; *modest* joy; a *modest* computation. *Addison.*

MOD'ESTLY, *adv.* Not boldly; not arrogantly or presumptuously; with due respect. He *modestly* expressed his opinions.

2. Not loosely or wantonly; decently; as, to be *modestly* attired; to behave *modestly.*

3. Not excessively; not extravagantly.

MOD'ESTY, *n.* [L. *modestia.*] That lowly temper which accompanies a moderate estimate of one's own worth and importance. This temper when natural, springs in some measure from timidity, and in young and inexperienced persons, is allied to bashfulness and diffidence. In persons who have seen the world, and lost their natural timidity, *modesty* springs no less from principle than from feeling, and is manifested by retiring, unobtrusive manners, assuming less to itself than others are willing to yield, and conceding to others all due honor and respect, or even more than they expect or require.

2. Modesty, as an act or series of acts, consists in humble, unobtrusive deportment, as opposed to extreme boldness, forwardness, arrogance, presumption, audacity or impudence. Thus we say, the petitioner urged his claims with *modesty;* the speaker addressed the audience with *modesty.*

3. Moderation; decency. *Shak.*

4. In *females,* modesty has the like character as in males; but the word is used also as synonymous with chastity, or purity of manners. In this sense, modesty results from purity of mind, or from the fear of disgrace and ignominy fortified by education and principle. Unaffected *modesty* is the sweetest charm of female excellence, the richest gem in the diadem of their honor.

MOD'ESTY-PIECE, *n.* A narrow lace worn by females over the bosom. *Addison.*

MOD'ICUM, *n.* [L.] A little; a small quantity. *Dryden.*

MOD'IFIABLE, *a.* [from *modify.*] That may be modified or diversified by various forms and differences; as *modifiable* matter. *Locke.*

MODIFICA'TION, *n.* [from *modify.*] The act of modifying, or giving to any thing new forms, or differences of external qualities or modes.

If these powers of cogitation, volition and sensation are not inherent in matter as such, nor acquirable to matter by any motion or *modification* of it— *Bentley.*

2. Particular form or manner; as the various *modifications* of light or sound. The treaty, in several of its *modifications,* was held to be objectionable. *Newton. Holder.*

MOD'IFIED, *pp.* Changed in form or external qualities; varied; diversified.

2. Moderated; tempered; qualified in exceptionable parts.

MOD'IFIER, *n.* He or that which modifies.

MOD'IFȲ, *v. t.* [Fr. *modifier;* It. *modificare;* Sp. *modificar;* L. *modificor; modus,* limit, manner, and *facio,* to make.]

1. To change the form or external qualities of a thing; to shape; to give a new form of being to; as, to *modify* matter, light or sound. *Newton. Holder.*

2. To vary; to give a new form to any thing; as, to *modify* the terms of a contract. A prefix *modifies* the sense of a verb.

3. To moderate; to qualify; to reduce in extent or degree.

Of his grace
He *modifies* his first severe decree. *Dryden.*

MOD'IFȲ, *v. i.* To extenuate. *L'Estrange.*

MOD'IFȲING, *ppr.* Changing the external qualities; giving a new form to; moderating.

MODILLION, *n.* *modil'yun.* [It. *modiglione;* Fr. *modillon;* from L. *modiolus,* from *modus.*]

In *architecture,* an ornament in the cornice of the Ionic, Corinthian and Composite columns; a sort of bracket serving to support the projecture of the larmier or drip; a dental. *Encyc. Harris.*

MO'DISH, *a.* [from *mode.*] According to the mode or customary manner; fashionable; as a *modish* dress; a *modish* feast. *Dryden.*

MO'DISHLY, *adv.* Fashionably; in the customary mode. *Locke.*

MO'DISHNESS, *n.* The state of being fashionable.

2. Affectation of the fashion. *Johnson.*

MOD'ULATE, *v. t.* [L. *modulor,* from *modus,* limit, measure.]

1. To form sound to a certain key, or to a certain proportion. *Johnson. Encyc.*

2. To vary or inflect sound in a natural, customary or musical manner. Thus the organs of speech *modulate* the voice in reading or speaking.

Could any person so *modulate* her voice as to deceive so many. *Broome.*

MOD'ULATED, *pp.* Formed to a certain key; varied; inflected.

MOD'ULATING, *ppr.* Forming to a certain proportion; varying; inflecting.

MODULA'TION, *n.* [L. *modulatio;* Fr. *modulation.*]

1. The act of forming any thing to a certain proportion; as the different proportion and *modulation* of matter. *Woodward.*

2. The act of inflecting the voice in reading or speaking; a rising or falling of the voice. *Encyc.*

3. In *music,* the art of composing melody or harmony agreeable to the laws prescribed by any particular key, or of changing the key, or of passing from one key to another. *Encyc.*

Modulation is the manner of ascertaining and managing the modes; or more generally, the art of conducting the harmony and air through several modes in a manner agreeable to the ear and conformed to rules. *Rousseau.*

4. Sound modulated; melody. *Thomson.*

MOD'ULATOR, *n.* He or that which modulates. The tongue is a principal *modulator* of the human voice.

MOD'ULE, *n.* [Fr.; from L. *modulus.*] A model or representation.

2. In *architecture,* a certain measure or size taken at pleasure for regulating the proportion of columns, and the symmetry or disposition of the whole building. The usual *module* of a column is its semidiameter at the base. This is divided into parts or minutes. *Encyc.*

MOD'ULE, *v. t.* To model; to shape; to modulate. [*Little used.*]

MO'DUS, *n.* [L.] A compensation for tithes; an equivalent in money or other certain thing, given to a parson or vicar by the owners of land in lieu of tithes. The whole phrase is *modus decimandi;* but *modus* alone is commonly used. *Blackstone.*

MOD'WALL, *n.* A bird.

MOE, *a.* More. [*Not used.*] *Hooker.*

MOGUL', *n.* The name of a prince or emperor of the nation in Asia called Moguls, or Monguls.

MO'HAIR, *n.* [G. *mohr,* mohair, and a moor; Fr. *moire;* Russ. *mor.*]

The hair of a kind of goat in Turkey, of which are made camlets, which are sometimes called by the same name. *Encyc.*

MO'HAIR-SHELL, *n.* In *conchology,* a peculiar species of Voluta, of a closely and finely reticulated texture, resembling on the surface mohair, or a close web of the silkworm. *Encyc.*

MOHAM'MEDAN, *a.* Pertaining to Mohammed or Mahomet.

MOHAM'MEDAN, *n.* A follower of Mohammed, the founder of the religion of Arabia and Persia.

MOHAM'MEDANISM, *n.* The religion or doctrines and precepts of Mohammed, contained in a book called the Koran or Alkoran.

MOHAM'MEDANIZE, *v. t.* To render conformable to the modes or principles of the Mohammedans.

MO'HAWK, } *n.* The appellation given to
MO'HOCK, } certain ruffians who infested the streets of London; so called from the nation of Indians of that name in America. *Prior.*

MOI'DORE, *n.* A gold coin of Portugal, valued at $6, or £1. 7*s.* sterling.

MOI'ETY, *n.* [Fr. *moitié;* L. *medietas;* It. *meta;* Sp. *mitad.*]

The half; one of two equal parts; as a *moiety* of an estate, of goods or of profits; the *moiety* of a jury or of a nation. *Clarendon. Addison.*

MOIL, *v. t.* [Fr. *mouiller.*] To daub; to make dirty. [*Little used.*] *Knolles.*

2. To weary. [See the next word.] *Chapman.*

MOIL, *v. i.* [Gr. μολος, μωλος, labor, combat; μωλεω, to strive, to fight; L. *molior,* and *miles;* Ar. عمل to work, labor, perform, to strive, to war; Heb. Ch. Syr. Sam. עמל id. Class Ml. No. 15. 12.]

To labor; to toil; to work with painful efforts.

Now he must *moil* and drudge for one he lothes. *Dryden.*

MOIL, *n.* A spot. [Sax. *mal.*] [*Not in use.*]

MOIST, *a.* [Fr. *moite*, for *moiste* ; Arm. *mouest* ; Russ. *motzu*, to wet. If the last radical letter is a dental, this word may belong to the family of L. *madeo*, Gr. μυδαω. See Class Ms. No. 1. and Class Md. No. 1.]

1. Moderately wet ; damp ; as a *moist* atmosphere or air.

Exhalation dusk and *moist*. *Milton.*

2. Containing water or other liquid in a perceptible degree.

MOISTEN, *v. t. mois'n.* To make damp ; to wet in a small degree.

A pipe a little *moistened* on the inside. *Bacon.*

His bones are *moistened* with marrow. Job xxi.

MOIST, as a verb, is obsolete.

MOISTENED, *pp. mois'nd.* Made wet in a small degree.

MOISTENER, *n. mois'ner.* He or that which moistens.

MOISTENING, *ppr. mois'ning.* Wetting moderately.

MOIST'FUL, *a.* Full of moisture. *Drayton.*

MOIST'NESS, *n.* Dampness ; a small degree of wetness. *Addison.*

MOIST'URE, *n.* [Fr *moiteur.*] A moderate degree of wetness.

Set such plants as require much *moisture*, on sandy, dry grounds. *Bacon.*

2. A small quantity of any liquid ; as the *moisture* of the body. *Shak.*

MOIST'Y, *a.* Drizzling. [*Not in use.*]

MŌKES, of a net, the meshes. [*Not in use.*] *Ainsworth.*

MO'KY, *a.* [W. *mwg* ; from the root of *smoke.*] Muggy ; dark ; murky. *Obs.*

MO'LAR, *a.* [L. *molaris.*] Having power to grind ; grinding ; as the *molar* teeth. *Bacon.*

MOLASSES, an incorrect orthography of *melasses.*

MŌLD, *n.* [Sax. *mold, molda, myl* ; W. *mol* ; D. Dan. *mul* ; Sw. G. *mull* ; probably allied to *mellow*, L. *mollis.* See *Mellow, Meal* and *Mill.* It is incorrectly written *mould.*]

1. Fine soft earth, or earth easily pulverized, such as constitutes soil ; as black *mold.* *Ed. W. Indies.*

A mortal substance of terrestrial *mold.* *Hoole.*

2. A substance like down which forms on bodies which lie long in warm and damp air. The microscope exhibits this substance as consisting of small plants. *Encyc.*

3. Matter of which any thing is formed.

Nature formed me of her softest *mold.* *Addison.*

MŌLD, *n.* [Sp. *molde*, a mold or matrix ; *moldar, amoldar*, to cast ; Port. *molde, moldar*, id. ; Fr. *moule* ; Arm. *moul* ; Dan. *mul, muld* ; W. *mold*, whence *moldiaw*, to mold, work or knead. This may be radically the same word as *mold*, fine earth ; a name taken from the material of *molds.* The connection of *matrix* with *mater* and *materia*, fortifies this conjecture.]

1. The matrix in which any thing is cast and receives its form. Molds are of various kinds. Molds for casting cannon and various vessels, are composed of some species of earth, particularly clay. Molds for other purposes consist of a cavity in some species of metal, cut or formed to the shape designed, or are otherwise formed, each for its particular use.

2. Cast ; form ; as a writer of vulgar *mold.* *Waller.*

3. The suture or contexture of the skull. *Ainsworth.*

4. In *ship-building*, a thin flexible piece of timber, used as a pattern by which to form the curves of the timbers and compassing pieces. *Encyc.*

5. Among *gold beaters*, a number of pieces of vellum or a like substance, laid over one another, between which the leaves of gold and silver are laid for beating. *Encyc.*

MŌLD, *v. t.* To cause to contract mold. *Knolles.*

2. To cover with mold or soil. *Edwards.*

MŌLD, *v. i.* To contract mold ; to become moldy. *Bacon.*

MŌLD, *v. t.* To form into a particular shape ; to shape ; to model.

He forgeth and *moldeth* metals. *Hall.*

Did I request thee, Maker, from my clay
To *mold* me man ? *Milton.*

2. To knead ; as, to *mold* dough or bread. *Ainsworth.*

MŌLDABLE, *a.* That may be molded or formed. *Bacon.*

MŌLDED, *pp.* Formed into a particular shape ; kneaded.

2. Covered with mold.

MŌLDER, *n.* He who molds or forms into shape.

MŌLDER, *v. i.* [Dan. *mulner*, Sw. *multna*, to grow moldy.]

1. To turn to dust by natural decay ; to crumble ; to perish ; to waste away by a gradual separation of the component particles, without the presence of water. In this manner, animal and vegetable substances *molder*, and so also do stones and shells.

When statues *molder*, and when arches fall. *Prior.*

2. To be diminished ; to waste away gradually.

If he had sat still, the enemy's army would have *moldered* to nothing. *Clarendon.*

MŌLDER, *v. t.* To turn to dust ; to crumble ; to waste.

Some felt the silent stroke of *moldering* age. *Pope.*

MŌLDERING, *ppr.* Turning to dust ; crumbling ; wasting away.

MŌLDINESS, *n.* [from *moldy.*] The state of being moldy. *Bacon.*

MŌLDING, *ppr.* [from *mold.*] Forming into shape ; kneading.

MŌLDING, *n.* Any thing cast in a mold, or which appears to be so ; hence, in *architecture*, a projecture beyond the wall, column, wainscot, &c. an assemblage of which forms a cornice, a door-case, or other decoration. *Encyc.*

MŌLD-WARP, *n.* [Sax. *mold* and *weorpan*, to turn. See *Mole.*]

A mole ; a small animal of the genus Talpa, that moves under ground and turns up the mold or surface of the earth. *Spenser. Carew.*

MŌLDY, *a.* [from *mold.*] Overgrown with mold. *Addison.*

MOLE, *n.* [Sax. *mæl, mal* ; D. *maal* ; G. *mahl.*]

1. A spot, mark or small permanent protuberance on the human body, from which usually issue one or more hairs.

2. [L. *mola.*] A mass of fleshy matter of a spherical figure, generated in the uterus. *Encyc.*

MOLE, *n.* [L. *moles* ; Fr. *mole* ; W. *moel*, a heap, or *mwl*, a mass.]

1. A mound or massive work formed of large stones laid in the sea by means of coffer dams, extended either in a right line or an arch of a circle before a port, which it serves to defend from the violent impulse of the waves ; thus protecting ships in a harbor. The word is sometimes used for the harbor itself. *Encyc.*

2. Among *the Romans*, a kind of mausoleum, built like a round tower on a square base, insulated, encompassed with columns and covered with a dome. *Encyc.*

MOLE, *n.* [D. *mol* ; G. *maulwurf*, moldwarp ; Sw. *mullsork, mullvad* or *mullwarpel* ; Dan. *muldvarp.*]

A small animal of the genus Talpa, which in search of worms or other insects, forms a road just under the surface of the ground, raising the soil into a little ridge ; from which circumstance it is called a *moldwarp*, or *mold-turner.* The mole has very small eyes. *Ray.*

Learn of the *mole* to plow, the worm to weave. *Pope.*

MOLE, *v. t.* To clear of mole-hills. [*Local.*] *Pegge.*

MO'LE-BAT, *n.* A fish. *Ainsworth.*

MO'LE-CAST, *n.* A little elevation of earth made by a mole. *Mortimer.*

MO'LE-CATCHER, *n.* One whose employment is to catch moles. *Tusser.*

MO'LE-CRICKET, *n.* An insect of the genus Gryllus.

MO'LECULE, *n.* [Fr. from *mole.*] A very minute particle of matter. Molecules are elementary, constituent, or integrant. The latter result from the union of the elementary. *Dict. Nat. Hist. Fourcroy. Kirwan.*

MO'LE-EYED, *a.* Having very small eyes ; blind.

MO'LE-HILL, *n.* [W. *malur.*] A little hillock or elevation of earth thrown up by moles working under ground ; hence proverbially, a very small hill, or other small thing, compared with a larger.

—Having leaped over such mountains, lie down before a *mole-hill.* *South.*

MOLEST', *v. t.* [Fr. *molester* ; It. *molestare* ; Sp. *molestar* ; from L. *molestus*, troublesome ; Sp. *moler*, to grind, to molest, to vex, L. *molo.* See *Mill.*]

To trouble ; to disturb ; to render uneasy.

They have *molested* the church with needless opposition. *Hooker.*

MOLESTA'TION, *n.* Disturbance ; annoyance ; uneasiness given. [It usually expresses less than *vexation.*] *Brown.*

MOLEST'ED, *pp.* Disturbed ; troubled ; annoyed.

MOLEST'ER, *n.* One that disturbs.

MOLEST'FUL, *a.* Troublesome.

MOLEST'ING, *ppr.* Disturbing ; troubling.

MO'LE-TRACK, *n.* The course of a mole under ground. *Mortimer.*

MO'LE-WARP, *n.* A mole. [See *Mole* and *Mold-warp.*]

MO'LIEN, *n.* A flowering tree of China. *Grosier.*

MOLIM'INOUS, *a.* [from L. *molimen.*] Very important. [*Not used.*] *More.*

MO'LINIST, *n.* A follower of the opinions of Molina, a Spanish Jesuit, in respect to grace; an opposer of the Jansenists.

MOL'LIENT, *a.* [L. *molliens, mollio.* See *Mellow.*]
Softening; assuaging; lessening. [See *Emollient,* which is generally used.]

MOL'LIFIABLE, *a.* [from *mollify.*] That may be softened.

MOLLIFICA'TION, *n.* The act of mollifying or softening.
2. Mitigation; an appeasing. *Shak.*

MOL'LIFIED, *pp.* Softened; appeased.

MOL'LIFIER, *n.* That which softens, appeases or mitigates.
2. He that softens, mitigates or pacifies.

MOL'LIFY, *v. t.* [L. *mollio;* Fr. *mollir.* See *Mellow.*] To soften; to make soft or tender. Is. i.
2. To assuage, as pain or irritation.
3. To appease; to pacify; to calm or quiet. *Dryden.*
4. To qualify; to reduce in harshness or asperity. *Clarendon.*

MOLLUS'CA, *n.* [from L. *mollis,* soft.] In *zoology,* a division or class of animals whose bodies are soft, without an internal skeleton, or articulated covering. Some of them breathe by lungs, others by gills; some live on land, others in water. Some of them are naked; others testaceous or provided with shells. Many of them are furnished with feelers or tentacula. *Cuvier. Ed. Encyc.*

MOLLUS'CAN, MOLLUS'COUS, *a.* Pertaining to the mollusca, or partaking of their properties. [*Molluscous* is used, but is less analogical than *molluscan.*]

MOLOS'SUS, *n.* [Gr.] In *Greek and Latin verse,* a foot of three long syllables.

MOLT, *v. i.* [W. *moel,* bald, bare, also as a noun, a heap, pile or conical hill with a smooth top; *moeli,* to heap or pile, to make bald. So *bald,* in English, seems to be connected with *bold,* that is, prominent.]
To shed or cast the hair, fethers, skin, horns, &c.; as an animal. Fowls *molt* by losing their fethers, beasts by losing their hair, serpents by casting their skins, and deer their horns. The molting of the hawk is called *mewing.*

MOLTEN, *pp.* of *melt.* Melted. *Obs.*
2. *a.* Made of melted metal; as a *molten* image.

MOLTING, *ppr.* Casting or shedding a natural covering, as hair, fethers, skin or horns.

MOLTING, *n.* The act or operation by which certain animals, annually or at certain times, cast off or lose their hair, fethers, skins, horns, &c.

MO'LY, *n.* [L. from Gr. μωλυ.] Wild garlic, a plant having a bulbous root.

MOLYB'DEN, MOLYB'DENA, *n.* [Gr. μολυβδαινα, a mass of lead.]
An ore of molybdenum, a scarce mineral of a peculiar form, and sometimes confounded with plumbago, from which however it is distinguished by its more shining, scaly appearance, and a more greasy feel. *Encyc.*

MOLYB'DENOUS, *a.* Pertaining to molybden, or obtained from it. The *molybdenous* acid is the deutoxyd of molybdenum.

MOLYB'DENUM, *n.* A metal which has not been reduced into masses of any magnitude, but has been obtained only in small separate globules, in a blackish, brilliant mass. These are brittle and extremely infusible. *Nicholson. Ure.*
The most common natural compound of this metal is a sulphuret. *Webster's Manual.*

MOME, *n.* [Fr. *momon.* See *Mum.*] A dull, silent person; a stupid fellow; a stock; a post. *Johnson. Spenser.*

MO'MENT, *n.* [L. *momentum.* This word is contracted from *motamentum,* or some other word, the radical verb of which signifies to move, rush, drive or fall suddenly, which sense gives that of *force.* The sense of an instant of time is from falling or rushing, which accords well with that of *meet.*]
1. The most minute and indivisible part of time; an instant.

In a *moment,* in the twinkling of an eye. 1 Cor. xv.

2. Force; impulsive power.

—Touch with lightest *moment* of impulse,
His free will. *Milton.*

Little used; but hence,
3. Importance in influence or effect; consequence; weight or value.

It is an abstruse speculation, but also of far less *moment* to us than the others. *Bentley.*

MOMENT'AL, *a.* Important. [*Not in use.*]

MOMENT'ALLY, *adv.* For a moment. *Brown.*

MOMENTANEOUS, MOMENTANY, *not used.* [See *Momentary.*]

MO'MENTARILY, *adv.* Every moment. *Shenstone.*

MO'MENTARY, *a.* Done in a moment; continuing only a moment; lasting a very short time; as a *momentary* pang.

Momentary as a sound,
Swift as a shadow, short as any dream. *Shak.*

MO'MENTLY, *adv.* For a moment.
2. In a moment; every moment. We *momently* expect the arrival of the mail.

MOMENT'OUS, *a.* Important; weighty; of consequence. Let no false step be made in the *momentous* concerns of the soul.

MOMENT'UM, *n.* [L.] In *mechanics,* impetus; the quantity of motion in a moving body. This is always equal to the quantity of matter multiplied into the velocity. *Encyc.*

MOM'MERY, MUM'MERY, *n.* [Fr. *momerie,* from *Momus,* the god of raillery and jesting.]
An entertainment or frolick in masks; a farcical entertainment in which masked persons play antic tricks. *Rowe.*

MO'MOT, *n.* The name of a genus of birds in S. America, whose beak and tongue resemble the toucan's. *Ed. Encyc.*

MON'ACHAL, *a.* [Fr. from L. *monachus,* Gr. μοναχος, a monk.]
Pertaining to monks or a monastic life; monastic.

MON'ACHISM, *n.* [Fr. *monachisme;* It. *monachismo.* See *Monk.*] The state of monks; a monastic life.

MON'AD, *n.* [Gr. μονας, unity, from μονος, sole.]
1. An ultimate atom, or simple unextended point. *Leibnitz.*
2. An indivisible thing. *Good.*

MON'ADELPH, *n.* [Gr. μονος, sole, and αδελφος, brother.]
In *botany,* a plant whose stamens are united in one body by the filaments.

MONADELPH'IAN, *a.* Having the stamens united in one body by the filaments.

MONAD'IC, MONAD'ICAL, *a.* Having the nature or character of a monad. *More.*

MONAN'DER, *n.* [Gr. μονος, one, and ανηρ, a male.]
In *botany,* a plant having one stamen only.

MONAN'DRIAN, *a.* Having one stamen only.

MON'ARCH, *n.* [It. Sp. *monarca;* Fr. *monarque;* Gr. μοναρχης; μονος, sole, and αρχος, a chief.]
1. The prince or ruler of a nation, who exercises all the powers of government without control, or who is vested with absolute sovereign power; an emperor, king or prince invested with an unlimited power. This is the strict sense of the word.
2. A king or prince, the supreme magistrate of a nation, whose powers are in some respects limited by the constitution of the government. Thus we call the king of Great Britain a *monarch,* although he can make no law without the consent of parliament.
3. He or that which is superior to others of the same kind; as, an oak is called the *monarch* of the forest; a lion the *monarch* of wild beasts.
4. One that presides; president; as Bacchus, *monarch* of the vine. *Shak.*

MON'ARCH, *a.* Supreme; ruling; as a *monarch* savage. *Pope.*

MONARCH'AL, *a.* Pertaining to a monarch; suiting a monarch; sovereign; regal; imperial.

Satan, whom now transcendant glory raised
Above his fellows, with *monarchal* pride—
Milton.

MON'ARCHESS, *n.* A female monarch; an empress.

MONARCH'IC, MONARCH'ICAL, *a.* Vested in a single ruler; as *monarchical* government or power.
2. Pertaining to monarchy.

MON'ARCHIST, *n.* An advocate of monarchy. *Barrow.*

MON'ARCHIZE, *v. i.* To play the king; to act the monarch. *Shak.*

MON'ARCHIZE, *v. t.* To rule; to govern.

MON'ARCHY, *n.* [Gr. μοναρχια. See *Monarch.*]
1. A state or goverment in which the supreme power is lodged in the hands of a single person. Such a state is usually called an empire or a kingdom; and we usually give this denomination to a large state only. But the same name is sometimes given to a kingdom or state in which the power of the king or supreme magistrate is limited by a constitution, or by fundamental laws. Such is the British *monarchy.* Hence we speak of absolute or despotic *monarchies,* and of limited *monarchies.*

A free government has a great advantage over a simple *monarchy.* *J. Adams.*

2. A kingdom; an empire. *Shak.*

MON'ASTERY, *n.* [Fr. *monastère*; It. *monastero*; Sp. *monasterio*; Low L. *monasterium*; Gr. μοναςηριον, from μονος, sole, separate; W. *môn.*]
A house of religious retirement, or of seclusion from ordinary temporal concerns, whether an abbey, a priory or a nunnery. The word is usually applied to the houses of monks, mendicant friars and nuns. *Encyc.*

MONAS'TIC, } *a.* [Fr. *monastique*; It. *monastico*; Low L. *monasticus*; Gr. μοναςικος, from μονος, sole, separate.]
MONAS'TICAL,
Pertaining to monasteries, monks and nuns; recluse; secluded from the temporal concerns of life and devoted to religion; as a *monastic* life; *monastic* orders. *Denham.*

MONAS'TIC, *n.* A monk.

MONAS'TICALLY, *adv.* Reclusely; in a retired manner; in the manner of monks. *Swift.*

MONAS'TICISM, *n.* Monastic life. *Milner.*

MŎNDAY, *n.* [Sax. *monandæg*; D. *maandag*; G. *montag*; *moon* and *day*; being formerly sacred to that planet.] The second day of the week.

MONDE, *n.* [Fr.] The world; also, a globe, an ensign of authority. *Drummond.*

MONE'CIAN, *n.* [Gr. μονος, sole, and οικος, house.]
In *botany*, one of that class of plants, whose male and female flowers are on the same plant.

MONE'CIAN, *a.* Pertaining to the class of plants above described.

MŎNEY, *n.* plu. *moneys.* [Sax. *mynet*; D. *munt*, mint; G. *münze*; Sw. *mynt*; Dan. *myndt*, money or mint; Fr. *monnoie*; Ir. *monadh*; W. *mwnai*; Sp. *moneda*; Port. *moeda*, contracted; L. It. *moneta.* *Money* and *mint* are the same word varied.]
1. Coin; stamped metal; any piece of metal, usually gold, silver or copper, stamped by public authority, and used as the medium of commerce. We sometimes give the name of money to other coined metals, and to any other material which rude nations use as a medium of trade. But among modern commercial nations, gold, silver and copper are the only metals used for this purpose. Gold and silver, containing great value in a small compass, and being therefore of easy conveyance, and being also durable and little liable to diminution by use, are the most convenient metals for coin or money, which is the representative of commodities of all kinds, of lands, and of every thing that is capable of being transferred in commerce.
2. Bank notes or bills of credit issued by authority, and exchangeable for coin or redeemable, are also called *money*; as such notes in modern times represent coin, and are used as a substitute for it. If a man pays in hand for goods in bank notes which are current, he is said to pay in ready *money.*
3. Wealth; affluence.

> *Money* can neither open new avenues to pleasure, nor block up the passages of anguish. *Rambler.*

MŎNEYAĠE, *n.* Anciently, in England, a general land tax levied by the two first Norman kings, a shilling on each hearth. *Hume.*

MŎNEY-BAG, *n.* A bag or purse for holding money. *Addison.*

MŎNEY-BOX, *n.* A box or till to hold money.

MŎNEY-BRŎKER, *n.* A broker who deals in money. *Johnson.*

MŎNEY-CHANĠER, *n.* A broker who deals in money or exchanges. *Arbuthnot.*

MŎNEYED, *a.* Rich in money; having money; able to command money; used often in opposition to such as have their wealth in real estate.

> Invite *moneyed* men to lend to the merchants. *Bacon.*

2. Consisting in money; as *moneyed* capital. *Hamilton's Report.*

MŎNEYER, *n.* A banker; one who deals in money.
2. A coiner of money. [*Little used in either sense.*]

MŎNEY-LENDER, *n.* One who lends money.

MŎNEYLESS, *a.* Destitute of money; pennyless. *Swift.*

MŎNEY-MATTER, *n.* An account consisting of charges of money; an account between debtor and creditor. *Arbuthnot.*

MŎNEY-SCRIVENER, *n.* A person who raises money for others. *Arbuthnot.*

MŎNEY-SPINNER, *n.* A small spider.

MŎNEY'S-WŎRTH, *n.* Something that will bring money.
2. Full value; the worth of a thing in money.

MŎNEY-WŎRT, *n.* A plant of the genus Lysimachia.

MŎNGER, *n.* [Sax. *mangere*, from *mangian*, to trade, D. *manger.*]
A trader; a dealer; now used only or chiefly in composition; as fish-*monger*, iron-*monger*, news-*monger*, cheese-*monger.*

MŎNGREL, *a.* [from Sax. *mengan*, to mix. See *Mingle.*]
Of a mixed breed; of different kinds. *Swift.*

MŎNGREL, *n.* An animal of a mixed breed.

MONIL'IFORM, *a.* [L. *monile*, a necklace, and *form.*]
Like a necklace. *Encyc.*

MON'IMENT, *n.* [L. *monimentum*, from *moneo*, to admonish.]
1. An inscription; something to preserve memory. *Obs.*
2. A mark; an image; a superscription. *Spenser.*

MON'ISH, *v. t.* To admonish; to warn. [*Not used.*] [See *Admonish.*]

MON'ISHER, *n.* An admonisher, which see.

MON'ISHMENT, *n.* Admonition. *Obs.*

MONI''TION, *n.* [Fr. from L. *monitio.*]
1. Warning; instruction given by way of caution; as the *monitions* of a friend. *Swift.*
2. Information; indication.

> We have no visible *monitions* of other periods, such as we have of the day by successive light and darkness. *Holder.*

MON'ITIVE, *a.* Admonitory; conveying admonition. *Barrow.*

MON'ITOR, *n.* [L.] One who warns of faults or informs of duty; one who gives advice and instruction by way of reproof or caution.

> You need not be a *monitor* to the king. *Bacon.*

2. In *schools*, a person authorized to look to the scholars in the absence of the instructor, or to notice the absence or faults of the scholars, or to instruct a division or class.

MON'ITORY, *a.* Giving admonition; warning; instructing by way of caution.

> Losses, miscarriages and disappointments are *monitory* and instructive. *L'Estrange.*

MON'ITORY, *n.* Admonition; warning. *Bacon.*

MON'ITRESS, *n.* A female monitor.

MŎNK, *n.* [Gr. μοναχος, from μονος, W. *môn*, sole, separate; whence L. *monachus*; Sax. *monec, munuc*; Fr. *moine*; Arm. *mannach*; W. *mynaç*; Sans. *muni.*]
A man who retires from the ordinary temporal concerns of the world, and devotes himself to religion. Monks usually live in monasteries, on entering which they take a vow to observe certain rules. Some however live as hermits in solitude, and others have lived a strolling life without any fixed residence. *Encyc.*

MŎNKERY, *n.* The life of monks; the monastic life.

MŎNKEY, *n.* [It. *monicchio.*] The popular name of the ape and baboon. But in zoology, monkey is more properly the name of those animals of the genus Simia, which have long tails. Ray distributes animals of this kind into three classes; apes which have no tails; monkeys with long tails; and baboons with short tails. *Encyc.*
2. A name of contempt or of slight kindness. *Johnson.*

MŎNKHOOD, *n.* The character of a monk. *Atterbury.*

MŎNKISH, *a.* Like a monk, or pertaining to monks; monastic; as *monkish* manners; *monkish* dress; *monkish* solitude.

MŎNK'S HEAD, *n.* A plant of the genus Leontodon.

MŎNK'S HOOD, *n.* A plant of the genus Aconitum.

MŎNK'S RHUBARB, *n.* A plant of the genus Rumex, a species of dock.

MONOC'EROS, *n.* [Gr. μονος, sole, and κερας, horn.] The unicorn.

MON'OCHORD, *n.* [Gr. μονος, sole, only, and χορδη, chord.]
A musical instrument of one string. As its name imports, it had originally but one string; but it is generally constructed with two, by means of which the musician is better enabled to try the proportions of sounds and intervals, and judge of the harmony of two tempered notes. *Encyc.*

In the proper sense of the word, a trumpet marine is considered a *monochord.*

MONOCHROMAT'IC, *a.* [Gr. μονος, sole, and χρωμα, color.]
Consisting of one color, or presenting rays of light of one color only.
Quart. Journ. Journ. of Science.

MON'OCOTYLE, } *a.* Having only one seed-lobe or seminal leaf.
MONOCOTYLED'ONOUS,
Martyn. Milne.

MONOCOTYL'EDON, *n.* [Gr. μονος, sole, and κοτυληδων, a hollow.]
In *botany*, a plant with only one cotyledon or seed-lobe.

MONOC'ULAR, **MONOC'ULOUS**, *a.* [Gr. μονος, sole, and L. *oculus*, eye.]
Having one eye only. *Howell.*

MON'OCULE, *n.* [supra.] An insect with one eye. *Pennant.*

MON'ODON, *n.* [Gr. μονοδους, having one tooth or shoot.]
The unicorn fish, or sea-unicorn, which has a remarkable horn projecting from its head. [This horn is really a tusk, of which there are two, but only one of them is usually developed. *Cuvier.*] It is called also the monoceros, or horned narwhal. Its usual size is from sixteen to twenty feet. *Encyc.*

MON'ODY, *n.* [Gr. μονωδια; μονος, sole, and ωδη, song.] A song or poem sung by one person only. *Johnson.*

MON'OGAM, *n.* [Gr. μονος, sole, and γαμη, marriage.]
In *botany*, a plant that has a simple flower, though the anthers are united. *Lee.*

MONOGAM'IAN, *a.* Pertaining to the order of plants that have a simple flower. *Lee.*

MONOG'AMIST, *n.* [supra.] One who disallows second marriages. *Johnson.*

MONOG'AMOUS, *a.* Having one wife only and not permitted to marry a second.

MONOG'AMY, *n.* [supra.] The marriage of one wife only, or the state of such as are restrained to a single wife. *Bp. Hall.*

MON'OGRAM, *n.* [Gr. μονος, sole, and γραμμα, letter.]
A character or cypher composed of one, two or more letters interwoven, being an abbreviation of a name; used on seals, &c. *Encyc.*

MON'OGRAMMAL, *a.* Sketching in the manner of a monogram. *Fotherby.*

MON'OGRAPH, *n.* [Gr. μονος, sole, and γραφω, to describe.]
An account or description of a single thing or class of things; as a *monograph* of violets in botany; a *monograph* of an Egyptian mummy. *Journ. of Science.*

MONOGRAPH'IC, **MONOGRAPH'ICAL**, *a.* Drawn in lines without colors. *Bailey. Ash.*
2. Pertaining to a monograph.

MONOG'RAPHY, *n.* [Gr. μονος, sole, and γραφω, to describe.]
A description drawn in lines without colors. Qu. should not this be *monogram?*

MON'OGYN, *n.* [Gr. μονος, sole, and γυνη, a female.]
In *botany*, a plant having only one style or stigma. *Smith.*

MONOGYN'IAN, *a.* Pertaining to the order monogynia; having only one style or stigma.

MONOLOGUE, *n.* mon'olog. [Gr. μονολογια; μονος, sole, and λογος, speech.]
1. A soliloquy; a speech uttered by a person alone. *Dryden.*
2. A poem, song or scene composed for a single performer. *Busby.*

MONOM'ACHY, *n.* [Gr. μονομαχια; μονος, sole, and μαχη, combat.] A duel; a single combat.

MON'OME, *n.* [Gr. μονος, sole, and ονομα, name.]
In *algebra*, a quantity that has one name only. *Harris.*

MONO'MIAL, *n.* In *algebra*, a quantity expressed by one name or letter.

MONOP'ATHY, *n.* [Gr. μονος, sole, and παθεια, suffering.] Solitary suffering or sensibility. *Whitlock.*

MONOPET'ALOUS, *a.* [Gr. μονος, only, and πεταλον, flower-leaf.]
In *botany*, having only one petal, or a one-petaled corol; as a *monopetalous* corol or flower. *Martyn.*

MON'OPHTHONG, *n.* [Gr. μονος, sole, and φθογγος, sound.] A simple vowel-sound. *Beattie.*

MONOPHTHON'GAL, *a.* Consisting of a simple vowel-sound. *Beattie.*

MONOPH'YLLOUS, *a.* [Gr. μονος, sole, and φυλλον, leaf.] Having one leaf only.

MONOPH'YSITE, *n.* [Gr. μονος, only, and φυσις, nature.]
One who maintains that Jesus Christ had but one nature, or that the human and divine nature were so united as to form one nature only. *Encyc.*

MONOP'OLIST, **MONOP'OLIZER**, *n.* [Sp. It. *monopolista*. See *Monopolize.*]
One that monopolizes; a person who engrosses a commodity by purchasing the whole of that article in market for the purpose of selling it at an advanced price; or one who has a license or privilege granted by authority, for the sole buying or selling of any commodity. The man who retains in his hands his own produce or manufacture, is not a monopolist within the meaning of the laws for preventing monopolies.

MONOP'OLIZE, *v. t.* [Gr. μονος, sole, and πωλεω, to sell; Fr. *monopoler.*]
1. To purchase or obtain possession of the whole of any commodity or goods in market with the view of selling them at advanced prices, and of having the power of commanding the prices; as, to *monopolize* sugar or tea.
2. To engross or obtain by any means the exclusive right of trading to any place, and the sole power of vending any commodity or goods in a particular place or country; as, to *monopolize* the India or Levant trade.
3. To obtain the whole; as, to *monopolize* advantages. *Federalist, Jay.*

MONOP'OLY, *n.* [Fr. *monopole;* L. *monopolium*; Gr. μονοπωλια; μονος and πωλεω.]
The sole power of vending any species of goods, obtained either by engrossing the articles in market by purchase, or by a license from the government confirming this privilege. Thus the East India Company in Great Britain has a *monopoly* of the trade to the East Indies, granted to them by charter. *Monopolies* by individuals obtained by engrossing, are an offense prohibited by law. But a man has by natural right the exclusive power of vending his own produce or manufactures, and to retain that exclusive right is not a *monopoly* within the meaning of law.

MONOP'TOTE, *n.* [Gr. μονος, only, and πτωσις, case.] A noun having only one oblique case. *Clarke.*

MONOSPERM'OUS, *a.* [Gr. μονος, only, and σπερμα, seed.] Having one seed only.

MON'OSTICH, *n.* [Gr. μονοςιχον; μονος, only, and ςιχος, verse.] A composition consisting of one verse only.

MONOSTROPH'IC, *a.* [Gr. μονοςροφος, having one strophe.]
Having one strophe only; not varied in measure; written in unvaried measure. *Mason.*

MONOSYLLAB'IC, *a.* [See *Monosyllable.*]
1. Consisting of one syllable; as a *monosyllabic* word.
2. Consisting of words of one syllable; as a *monosyllabic* verse.

MONOSYL'LABLE, *n.* [Gr. μονος, only, and συλλαβη, a syllable.] A word of one syllable.

MONOSYL'LABLED, *a.* Formed into one syllable. *Cleaveland.*

MON'OTHEISM, *n.* [Gr. μονος, only, and θεος, God.]
The doctrine or belief of the existence of one God only. *Asiat. Res.*

MONOTH'ELITE, *n.* [Gr. μονος, one, and θελησις, will.]
One who holds that Christ had but one will. *Milner.*

MON'OTONE, *n.* [See *Monotony.*] In *rhetoric*, a sameness of sound, or the utterance of successive syllables on one unvaried key, without inflection or cadence. *Mason. E. Porter.*

MONOTON'IC, *a.* Monotonous. [*Little used.*]

MONOT'ONOUS, *a.* Continued in the same tone without inflection or cadence; unvaried in tone.

MONOT'ONOUSLY, *adv.* With one uniform tone; without inflection of voice. *Nares.*

MONOT'ONY, *n.* [Gr. μονοτονια; μονος, sole, and τονος, sound.]
1. Uniformity of tone or sound; want of inflections of voice in speaking; want of cadence or modulation.
2. Uniformity; sameness.

At sea, every thing that breaks the *monotony* of the surrounding expanse attracts attention. *Irving.*

MONSIEUR, *n.* [Fr.] Sir; Mr. *Pope.*

MONSOON', *n.* A periodical wind, blowing six months from the same quarter or point of the compass, then changing and blowing the same time from the opposite quarter. The monsoons prevail in the East Indies, and are called also *trade winds.* But we usually give the denomination of trade winds to those which blow the whole year from the same point, as the winds within the tropics on the Atlantic.

MON'STER, *n.* [L. *monstrum*, from *monstro*, to show. So we say in English, a *sight.* See *Muster.*]
1. An animal produced with a shape or with parts that are not natural, as when the body is ill formed or distorted, or the limbs too few or too many, or when any part is extravagantly out of proportion, either through defect or excess.
2. Any unnatural production; something greatly deformed. *Monsters* are common in the vegetable kingdom. *Encyc.*
3. A person so wicked as to appear horrible; one unnaturally wicked or mischievous. So a parricide is called a *monster.*

MON'STER, *v. t.* To make monstrous. [*Not used.*] *Shak.*

MON'STER-TAMING, *a.* Taming monsters. *Hamilton.*

MONSTROS'ITY, *n.* The state of being monstrous, or out of the common order of nature.

We often read of monstrous births; but we see a greater *monstrosity* in education, when a father begets a son and trains him up into a beast. *South.*

2. An unnatural production; that which is monstrous.

Fabri arranges distortions, gibbosities, tumors, &c. in the class of morbific *monstrosities*. *Encyc.*

A *monstrosity* never changes the name or affects the immutability of a species. *Adanson.*

MON'STROUS, *a.* [L. *monstrosus.*] Unnatural in form; deviating greatly from the natural form; out of the common course of nature; as a *monstrous* birth or production.

2. Strange; very wonderful; generally expressive of *dislike.* *Shak.*

3. Enormous; huge; extraordinary; as a *monstrous* highth; a *monstrous* tree or mountain. *Pope.*

4. Shocking to the sight or other senses; hateful.

MON'STROUS, *adv.* Exceedingly; very much; as *monstrous* hard; *monstrous* thick.

And will be *monstrous* witty on the poor. *Dryden.*

[This use is colloquial and vulgar.]

MON'STROUSLY, *adv.* In a manner out of the common order of nature; hence, shockingly; terribly; hideously; horribly; as a man *monstrously* wicked.

2. To a great degree; enormously; extravagantly.

Who with his wife is *monstrously* in love. *Dryden.*

MON'STROUSNESS, *n.* The state of being monstrous.

2. Enormity; irregular nature or behavior. *Shak.*

MONTAN'IC, *a.* [L. *montanus*, from *mons*, mountain.]

Pertaining to mountains; consisting in mountains. *Kirwan.*

MON'TANISM, *n.* The tenets of Montanus.

MON'TANIST, *n.* A follower of the heresiarch Montanus, a Phrygian by birth, who pretended he was inspired by the Holy Spirit and instructed in several points not revealed to the apostles. His sect sprung up in the second century. *Encyc.*

MONTANIST'IC, *a.* Pertaining to the heresy of Montanus.

MON'TANIZE, *v. i.* To follow the opinions of Montanus. *Hooker.*

MONT'ANT, *n.* [Fr. from *monter*, to mount.] A term in fencing. *Shak.*

MONTE'RO, *n.* [Sp. *montera.*] A horseman's cap. *Bacon.*

MONTETH', *n.* A vessel in which glasses are washed; so called from the name of the inventor. *King.*

MŎNTH, *n.* [Sax. *monath*, from *mona*, the moon; D. *maand;* G. *monath;* Sw. *månad;* Dan. *maaned;* L. *mensis;* Gr. *μην*, a month, from *μηνη*, the moon.]

A space or period of time constituting a division of the year. *Month* originally signified the time of one revolution of the moon, a lunation, or the period from one change or conjunction of the moon with the sun to another, a period of 27 days, 7 hours, 43 minutes and 5 seconds. This is the *periodical month*, or as we generally call it, the *lunar month*. In this sense we still use the word *month*. But we also apply the term to the space of time in which the sun passes through one sign, or a twelfth part of the zodiac. This period contains 30 days, 10 hours, 29 minutes, 5 seconds, and is called a *solar month*. In the year, there are twelve solar months, and thirteen lunar months.

In popular language, four weeks are called a month, being nearly the length of the lunar month. A calendar month differs in some degree from a solar month; consisting of twenty eight, twenty nine, thirty or thirty one days, as the months stand in calendars or almanacks.

MŎNTHLY, *a.* Continued a month or performed in a month; as the *monthly* revolution of the moon.

2. Done or happening once a month, or every month; as the *monthly* concert of prayer; a *monthly* visit.

MŎNTHLY, *adv.* Once a month; in every month. The moon changes *monthly*.

2. As if under the influence of the moon; in the manner of a lunatic. [*Not used.*] *Middleton.*

MŎNTH'S-MIND, *n.* Earnest desire; strong inclination. *Hudibras.*

MONTM'ARTRITE, *n.* A mineral of a yellowish color, occurring massive, and found at Montmartre, near Paris. It is soft, but resists the weather. It is a compound of the sulphate and carbonate of lime. *Ure.*

MONTOIR, *n.* [Fr.] In horsemanship, a stone used for aiding to mount a horse.

MON'UMENT, *n.* [L. *monumentum*, from *moneo*, to admonish or remind.]

1. Any thing by which the memory of a person or an event is preserved or perpetuated; a building, stone or other thing placed or erected to remind men of the person who raised it, or of a person deceased, or of any remarkable event; as a mausoleum, a pillar, a pyramid, a triumphal arch, a tombstone and the like. A pillar of 200 feet in highth, composed of Portland stone, was erected in London as a *monument* to preserve the memory of the great conflagration in 1666. A *monument* is erected on Bunker Hill to commemorate the battle of June 17, 1775.

2. A stone or a heap of stones or other durable thing, intended to mark the bounds of states, towns or distinct possessions, and preserve the memory of divisional lines. *New England.*

3. A thing that reminds or gives notice.

MONUMENT'AL, *a.* Pertaining to a monument; as a *monumental* inscription.

2. Serving as a monument; memorial; preserving memory.

Of pine or *monumental* oak. *Milton.*

A work outlasting *monumental* brass. *Pope.*

3. Belonging to a tomb; as *monumental* rest. *Crashaw.*

MONUMENT'ALLY, *adv.* By way of memorial. *Gayton.*

MOOD, *n.* [Fr. *mode;* L. *modus.* See *Mode.*]

1. The form of an argument; the regular determination of propositions according to their quantity, as universal or particular, and their quality, as affirmative or negative. *Watts. Encyc.*

2. Style of music. *Milton. Encyc.*

3. The variation of a verb to express manner of action or being. [See *Mode.*]

In the foregoing senses, and in all cases, this word when derived from the Latin *modus*, ought to be written *mode*, it being a distinct word from the following.

MOOD, *n.* [Goth. *mod*, anger; Sax. Sw. *mod*, the mind, a lofty mind, pride, violence; *modig*, proud, spirited; G. *muth*, mind, mood, courage, mettle, spirit; D. *moed;* Dan. *mood, mod*, heart, courage, mettle. We observe these words unite the sense of *mind* with that of *spirit, courage, anger*, for the primary sense is derived from moving, driving or rushing forward, or from exciting. We observe analogous cases in the L. *animus* and Gr. *θυμος*. Class Md. No. 19. 24. 25.]

1. Temper of mind; temporary state of the mind in regard to passion or feeling; humor; as a melancholy *mood;* an angry *mood;* a suppliant *mood.* *Dryden. Addison.*

2. Anger; heat of temper. *Hooker.*

[In this sense little used, unless qualified by an adjective.]

MOOD'ILY, *adv.* [from *moody.*] Sadly. *Obs.*

MOOD'INESS, *n.* Anger; peevishness.

MOOD'Y, *a.* [Sax. *modig*, angry.] Angry; peevish; fretful; out of humor.

Every peevish *moody* malcontent. *Rowe.*

2. Mental; intellectual; as *moody* food. *Obs.* *Shak.*

3. Sad; pensive.

4. Violent; furious.

MOON, *n.* [Sax. *mona;* Goth. *mena;* Dan. *maane;* Sw. *måna;* D. *maan;* G. *mond;* Gr. *μηνη*, Doric, *μανα;* Lapponic, *mana.*]

1. The heavenly orb which revolves round the earth; a secondary planet or satellite of the earth, whose borrowed light is reflected to the earth and serves to dispel the darkness of night. Its mean distance from the earth is 60½ semidiameters of the earth, or 240,000 miles. Its revolution round the earth in 27 days, 7 hours, 43 minutes, constitutes the lunar month.

2. A month. This is the sense in which rude nations use the name of the moon; as seven *moons.*

Half-moon, in fortification, a figure resembling a crescent.

MOON'-BEAM, *n.* A ray of light from the moon. *Dryden.*

MOON'-CALF, *n.* A monster; a false conception. *Shak.*

2. A mole or mass of fleshy matter generated in the uterus.

3. A dolt; a stupid fellow. *Dryden.*

MOON'ED, *a.* Taken for the moon. *Milton.*

MOON'ET, *n.* A little moon. *Hall.*

MOON'-EYE, *n.* An eye affected by the moon.

MOON'-EYED, *a.* Having eyes affected by the revolutions of the moon.

2. Dim-eyed; purblind. *Ainsworth.*

MOON'-FISH, *n.* A fish whose tail is shaped like a half-moon. *Grew.*

MOON'ISH, *a.* Like the moon; variable. *Shak.*

MOON'LESS, *a.* Not favored with moonlight. *Dryden.*

MOON'LIGHT, *n.* The light afforded by the moon.

MOON'LIGHT, *a.* Illuminated by the moon; as *moonlight* revels. *Shak.*

MOON'LING, *n.* A simpleton. *B. Jonson.*

MOON'LÖVED, *a.* Loved when the moon shines. *Milton.*

MOON'-SAD, *n.* A plant of the genus Menispermum, having a rosaceous flower. *Miller.*

MOON'SHINE, *n.* The light of the moon. *Dryden.*

2. In burlesque, a month. *Shak.*

A matter of moonshine, a matter of no consequence or of indifference.

MOON'SHINE, }
MOON'SHINY, } *a.* Illuminated by the moon; as a fair *moonshine* night. *Clarendon.*

I went to see them in a *moonshiny* night. *Addison.*

MOON'STONE, *n.* A variety of adularia, of a white color, or a yellowish or greenish white, somewhat iridescent, found in blunt amorphous masses, or crystalized in truncated rhomboidal prisms, or in rectangular tables, or in hexahedral prisms beveled at both ends. The surface is often sulcated. *Kirwan.*

MOON'STRUCK, *a.* Affected by the influence of the moon; lunatic; as *moonstruck* madness. *Milton.*

MOON-TRE'FOIL, *n.* A plant of the genus Medicago.

MOON'-WÖRT, *n.* A plant of the genus Lunaria; satin-flower; honesty.

MOON'Y, *a.* Lunated; having a crescent for a standard; in resemblance of the moon; as the *moony* troops or *moony* host of the sultans of Turkey. *Philips. Fenton.*

MOOR, *n.* [Sax. *mor*, a mountain, a pool or lake, a plain; D. *moer;* G. *mohr;* Fr. *mare;* Dan. *myre.*]

1. A tract of land overrun with heath. *Encyc.*

2. A marsh; a fen; a tract of wet low ground, or ground covered with stagnant water.

MOOR, *n.* [D. *moor;* G. *mohr;* Fr. *maure;* Gr. αμαυρος, μαυρος, dark, obscure.]

A native of the northern coast of Africa, called by the Romans from the color of the people, *Mauritania*, the country of dark-complexioned people. The same country is now called Morocco, Tunis, Algiers, &c.

MOOR, *v. t.* [Sp. Port. *amarra*, a cable, and a command to belay or fasten; *amarrar*, to moor, as a ship; Fr. *amarrer;* Arm. *amarra;* D. *maaren;* allied probably to L. *moror*, Fr. *demeurer*, to delay. It is composed of the same elements as the Saxon *merran, amerran, amyrran*, to hinder, to *mar.*]

To confine or secure a ship in a particular station, as by cables and anchors or by chains. A ship is never said to be *moored*, when she rides by a single anchor. *Mar. Dict.*

MOOR, *v. i.* To be confined by cables or chains.

On oozy ground his galleys *moor.* *Dryden.*

MOOR'COCK, }
MOOR'FOWL, } *n.* A fowl of the genus Tetrao, found in moors;
MOOR'HEN, } red-game; gor-cock.

MOOR'ED, *pp.* Made fast in a station by cables or chains.

MOOR'ING, *ppr.* Confining to a station by cables or chains.

MOOR'ING, *n.* In *seamen's language*, moorings are the anchors, chains and bridles laid athwart the bottom of a river or harbor to confine a ship.

MOOR'ISH, *a.* Marshy; fenny; watery.

Along the *moorish* fens. *Thomson.*

2. Pertaining to the Moors in Africa.

MOOR'LAND, *n.* A marsh or tract of low watery ground. *Mortimer. Swift.*

2. Land rising into moderate hills, foul, cold and full of bogs, as in Staffordshire, England.

MOOR'STONE, *n.* A species of granite. *Woodward.*

MOOR'Y, *a.* Marshy; fenny; boggy; watery.

As when thick mists arise from *moory* vales. *Fairfax.*

MOOSE, *n. moos.* [a native Indian name.] An animal of the genus Cervus, and the largest of the deer kind, growing sometimes to the highth of 17 hands, and weighing 1200 pounds. This animal has palmated horns, with a short thick neck, and an upright mane of a light brown color. The eyes are small, the ears a foot long, very broad and slouching; the upper lip is square, hangs over the lower one, and has a deep sulcus in the middle so as to appear bifid. This animal inhabits cold northern climates, being found in the American forests of Canada and New England, and in the corresponding latitudes of Europe and Asia. It is the elk of Europe. *Encyc.*

MOOT, *v. t.* [Sax. *motian*, to *meet*, to debate; Sw. *möta*, to meet, to fall, to come to or on; Goth. *motyan.* See *Meet*, of which this word is a different orthography. The sense of debate is from *meeting*, like *encounter*, from the French; for *meeting* gives rise to the sense of opposing, and the Dan. *mod* and Sw. *emot*, against, a preposition answering to L. *contra*, Fr. *contre*, is from this root.]

To debate; to discuss; to argue for and against. The word is applied chiefly to the disputes of students in law, who state a question and discuss it by way of exercise to qualify themselves for arguing causes in court.

MOOT, *v. i.* To argue or plead on a supposed cause.

MOOT, }
MOOT'-CASE, } *n.* A point, case or question to be mooted or
MOOT'-POINT, } debated; a disputable case; an unsettled question.

In this *moot-case* your judgment to refuse. *Dryden.*

MOOT'ED, *pp.* Debated; disputed; controverted.

MOOT'ER, *n.* A disputer of a mooted case.

MOOT'-HALL, }
MOOT'-HOUSE, } *n.* A town hall; hall of judgment. *Obs.* *Wickliffe.*

MOOT'ING, *ppr.* Disputing; debating for exercise.

MOOT'ING, *n.* The exercise of disputing.

MOP, *n.* [W. *mop* or *mopa;* L. *mappa.*] A piece of cloth, or a collection of thrums or coarse yarn fastened to a handle and used for cleaning floors. *Swift.*

2. A wry mouth. [*Not used.*] *Shak.*

MOP, *v. t.* To rub or wipe with a mop.

MOP, *v. i.* To make a wry mouth. [*Not used.*] *Shak.*

MOPE, *v. i.* [I have not found this word, unless in the D. *moppen*, to pout.]

To be very stupid; to be very dull; to drowse; to be spiritless or gloomy.

Demoniac phrensy, *moping* melancholy. *Milton.*

—Or but a sickly part of one true sense
Could not so *mope.* *Shak.*

MOPE, *v. t.* To make stupid or spiritless.

MOPE, *n.* A stupid or low spirited person; a drone.

MO'PED, *pp.* Made stupid.

A young, low spirited, *moped* creature. *Locke.*

MO'PE-EYED, *a.* [Qu. Gr. μυωψ.] Short-sighted; purblind. *Bramhall.*

MO'PING, *ppr.* Affected with dullness; spiritless; gloomy.

MO'PISH, *a.* Dull; spiritless; stupid; dejected.

MO'PISHNESS, *n.* Dejection; dullness; stupidity.

MOP'PET, }
MOP'SEY, } *n.* [from *mop;* L. *mappa.*] A rag-baby; a puppet made of cloth; a fondling name of a little girl. *Dryden.*

MO'PUS, *n.* A mope; a drone. *Swift.*

MOR'AL, *a.* [Fr. Sp. *moral;* It. *morale;* L. *moralis*, from *mos, moris*, manner. The elements of this word are probably *Mr.;* but I know not the primary sense. The word coincides in elements with Ar. مر to pass, to walk.]

1. Relating to the practice, manners or conduct of men as social beings in relation to each other, and with reference to right and wrong. The word *moral* is applicable to actions that are good or evil, virtuous or vicious, and has reference to the law of God as the standard by which their character is to be determined. The word however may be applied to actions which affect only, or primarily and principally, a person's own happiness.

Keep at the least within the compass of *moral* actions, which have in them vice or virtue. *Hooker.*

Mankind is broken loose from *moral* bands. *Dryden.*

2. Subject to the moral law and capable of moral actions; bound to perform social duties; as a *moral* agent or being.

3. Supported by the evidence of reason or probability; founded on experience of the ordinary course of things; as *moral* certainty, distinguished from *physical* or *mathematical* certainty or demonstration.

Physical and mathematical certainty may be stiled infallible, and *moral* certainty may be properly stiled indubitable. *Wilkins.*

Things of a moral nature may be proved by *moral* arguments. *Tillotson.*

4. Conformed to rules of right, or to the divine law respecting social duties; vir-

tuous; just; as when we say, a particular action is not *moral.*

5\. Conformed to law and right in exterior deportment; as, he leads a good *moral* life.

6\. Reasoning or instructing with regard to vice and virtue.

Whilst thou, a *moral* fool, sitt'st still and cri'st. *Shak.*

7\. In general, *moral* denotes something which respects the conduct of men and their relations as social beings whose actions have a bearing on each other's rights and happiness, and are therefore right or wrong, virtuous or vicious; as *moral* character; *moral* views; *moral* knowledge; *moral* sentiments; *moral* maxims; *moral* approbation; *moral* doubts; *moral* justice; *moral* virtue; *moral* obligations, &c. Or *moral* denotes something which respects the intellectual powers of man, as distinct from his physical powers. Thus we speak of *moral* evidence, *moral* arguments, *moral* persuasion, *moral* certainty, *moral* force; which operate on the mind.

Moral law, the law of God which prescribes the moral or social duties, and prohibits the transgression of them.

Moral sense, an innate or natural sense of right and wrong; an instinctive perception of what is right or wrong in moral conduct, which approves some actions and disapproves others, independent of education or the knowledge of any positive rule or law. But the existence of any such moral sense is very much doubted. *Paley. Encyc.*

Moral philosophy, the science of manners and duty; the science which treats of the nature and condition of man as a social being, of the duties which result from his social relations, and the reasons on which they are founded.

MOR'AL, *n.* Morality; the doctrine or practice of the duties of life. [*Not much used.*] *Prior.*

2\. The doctrine inculcated by a fiction; the accommodation of a fable to form the morals.

The *moral* is the first business of the poet. *Dryden.*

MOR'AL, *v. i.* To moralize. [*Not in use.*]

MOR'ALER, *n.* A moralizer. [*Not in use.*] *Shak.*

MOR'ALIST, *n.* [It. *moralista*; Fr. *moraliste.*]

1\. One who teaches the duties of life, or a writer of essays intended to correct vice and inculcate moral duties. *Addison.*

2\. One who practices moral duties; a mere moral person. *Hammond.*

MORAL'ITY, *n.* [Fr. *moralité.*] The doctrine or system of moral duties, or the duties of men in their social character; ethics.

The system of *morality* to be gathered from the writings of ancient sages, falls very short of that delivered in the gospel. *Swift.*

2\. The practice of the moral duties; virtue. We often admire the politeness of men whose *morality* we question.

3\. The quality of an action which renders it good; the conformity of an act to the divine law, or to the principles of rectitude. This conformity implies that the act must be performed by a free agent, and from a motive of obedience to the divine will. This is the strict theological and scriptural sense of morality. But we often apply the word to actions which accord with justice and human laws, without reference to the motives from which they proceed.

MORALIZA'TION, *n.* Moral reflections, or the act of making moral reflections. *Warton.*

2\. Explanation in a moral sense. *Elyot.*

MOR'ALIZE, *v. t.* [Fr. *moraliser*; Sp. *moralizar*; It. *moralizzare.*]

1\. To apply to a moral purpose, or to explain in a moral sense.

This fable is *moralized* in a common proverb. *L'Estrange.*

Did he not *moralize* this spectacle? *Shak.*

2\. To furnish with manners or examples. *Spenser.*

3\. To render moral or virtuous; to correct the morals of.

It had a large share in *moralizing* the poor white people of the country. *Ramsay.*

[This sense, though the most strictly etymological, is rare, but not to be condemned.]

MOR'ALIZE, *v. i.* To speak or write on moral subjects, or to make moral reflections.

MOR'ALIZED, *pp.* Applied to a moral purpose, or explained in a moral sense.

2\. Rendered moral or less corrupt. *Ch. Relig. Appeal.*

MOR'ALIZER, *n.* One who moralizes.

MOR'ALIZING, *ppr.* Applying to a moral purpose, or explaining in a moral sense.

2\. Making moral reflections in words or writing.

MOR'ALIZING, *n.* The application of facts to a moral purpose, or the making of moral reflections.

His *moralizings* are always pleasant, and he does not spare, where he thinks it useful to moralize. *Ch. Obs.*

MOR'ALLY, *adv.* In a moral or ethical sense; according to the rules of morality.

By good, *morally* so called, *bonum honestum* ought chiefly to be understood. *South.*

2\. Virtuously; honestly; according to moral rules in external deportment. He resolves to live *morally.*

3\. According to the rules of the divine law. An action is not in strictness *morally* good, which does not proceed from good motives, or a principle of love and obedience to the divine law and to the lawgiver. Charity bestowed to gratify pride, or justice done by compulsion, cannot be *morally* good in the sight of God.

4\. According to the evidence of human reason or of probabilities, founded on facts or experience; according to the usual course of things and human judgment.

It is *morally* impossible for a hypocrite to keep himself long on his guard. *L'Estrange.*

From the nature of things, I am *morally* certain that a mind free from passion and prejudice is more fit to pass a true judgment than one biased by affection and interest. *Wilkins.*

MOR'ALS, *n. plu.* The practice of the duties of life; as a man of correct *morals.*

2\. Conduct; behavior; course of life, in regard to good and evil.

Some, as corrupt in their *morals* as vice could make them, have been solicitous to have their children virtuously and piously educated. *South.*

What can laws do without *morals?* *Franklin.*

MORASS', *n.* [D. *moeras*, from *moer*, a marsh; Sw. *moras*; G. *morast*; Sax. *mersc*; Fr. *marais*; from *mare* or *moor*, a tract of level ground.]

A marsh; a fen; a tract of low moist ground. *Watts. Thomson.*

MORASS'Y, *a.* Marshy; fenny. *Pennant.*

MORA'VIAN, *a.* Pertaining to Moravia.

MORA'VIAN, *n.* One of a religious sect, called the United Brethren.

MOR'BID, *a.* [L. *morbidus*, from *morbus*, a disease, from the root of *morior*, to die; W. *marw*, to die, from *mar*, laid flat. The sense of the verb then is to fall, fail or sink; Ir. *marbh*, W. *marw*, dead. In Ch. מרע is to be sick. Class Mr. No. 12.]

Diseased; sickly; not sound and healthful; as *morbid* humors; a *morbid* constitution; a *morbid* state of the juices of a plant; a *morbid* sensibility.

MOR'BIDNESS, *n.* A state of being diseased, sickly or unsound.

MORBIF'IC, MORBIF'ICAL, } *a.* [Fr. *morbifique*; L. *morbus*, disease, and *facio*, to make.]

Causing disease; generating a sickly state; as *morbific* matter.

MORBIL'LOUS, *a.* [L. *morbilli*, measles, a medical term from *morbus.*]

Pertaining to the measles; measly; partaking of the nature of measles, or resembling the eruptions of that disease.

MORBO'SE, *a.* [L. *morbosus.*] Proceeding from disease; unsound; unhealthy; as a *morbose* tumor or excrescence in plants. *Ray.*

MORBOS'ITY, *n.* A diseased state. *Brown.*

MORDA'CIOUS, *a.* [L. *mordax*, infra.] Biting; given to biting. *Evelyn.*

MORDA'CIOUSLY, *adv.* In a biting manner; sarcastically. *Waterhouse.*

MORDAC'ITY, *n.* [L. *mordacitas*, from *mordeo*, to bite.]

The quality of biting.

MOR'DANT, *n.* [Fr. biting.] A substance which has a chimical affinity for coloring matter and serves to fix colors; such as alum. *Fourcroy.*

MOR'DICANCY, *n.* A biting quality; corrosiveness. *Evelyn.*

MOR'DICANT, *a.* [Fr.; from L. *mordeo*, to bite.]

Biting; acrid; as the *mordicant* quality of a body. *Boyle.*

MORDICA'TION, *n.* [from L. *mordeo*, to bite.]

The act of biting or corroding; corrosion.

Another cause is the *mordication* of the orifices, especially of the mesentery veins. *Bacon.*

MORE, *a.* [Sax. *more*, *mara* or *mare*, more or greater; D. *meer*; G. *mehr*; Dan. *meere*; Sw. *mer.* The Saxon *ma* and *mo*, in Chaucer, have the same sense. In W. *mawr*, Ir. *mor*, signifies *great*, in the positive degree. The word may be contracted from *mag*, the root of L. *magis*; *mare*, for *mager*; but this is conjecture.]

1\. Greater in quality, degree or amount; *in a general sense*; as *more* land; *more* water; *more* courage; *more* virtue; *more* power or wisdom; *more* love; *more* praise; *more* light. It is applicable to every thing, material or immaterial.

2. Greater in number; exceeding in numbers; as *more* men; *more* virtues; *more* years.

The children of Israel are *more* than we. Ex. i.

3. Greater.

The *more* part knew not why they had come together. Acts xix.

4. Added to some former number; additional.

But Montague demands one labor *more*. *Addison.*

MORE, *adv.* To a greater degree.

Israel loved Joseph *more* than all his children. Gen. xxxvii.

2. It is used with *the*.

They hated him yet *the more*. Gen. xxxvii.

3. It is used to modify an adjective and form the comparative degree, having the same force and effect as the termination *er*, in monosyllables; as *more* wise; *more* illustrious; *more* contemptible; *more* durable. It *may* be used before all adjectives which admit of comparison, and *must* be used before polysyllables.

4. A second or another time; again. I expected to hear of him no *more*.

The dove returned not to him again any *more*. Gen. viii.

No more, not continuing; existing no longer; gone; deceased or destroyed. Cassius is *no more*. Troy is *no more*.

No more is used in commands, in an elliptical form of address. *No more!* that is, say *no more*; let me hear *no more*. In this use however, *more*, when the sentence is complete, is a noun or substitute for a noun.

Much more, in a greater degree or with more readiness; more abundantly.

More and more, with continual increase.

Amon trespassed *more and more*. 2 Chron. xxxiii.

MORE, *a noun or substitute for a noun*. A greater quantity, amount or number.

They gathered some *more*, some less. Ex. xvi.

They were *more* who died by hail-stones, than they whom the children of Israel slew with the sword. Josh. x.

God do so to thee and *more* also. 1 Sam. iii.

There were *more* than forty who had made this conspiracy. Acts xxiii.

2. Greater thing; other thing; something further. Here we rest; we can do no *more*. He conquered his enemies; he did *more*, he conquered himself.

MORE, *v. t.* To make more. *Obs.* *Gower.*

MOREE'N, *n.* A stuff used for curtains, &c.

MOREL', *n.* [It. *morella*; Fr. *morelle*.] Garden nightshade, a plant of the genus Solanum.

2. A kind of cherry.

MORELAND. [See *Moorland*.]

MO'RENESS, *n.* Greatness. *Obs.* *Wickliffe.*

MOREO'VER, *adv.* [*more* and *over*.] Beyond what has been said; further; besides; also; likewise.

Moreover, by them is thy servant warned. Ps. xix.

MORESK', } *a.* [Fr. from It. *moresco*,
MORESQUE, } from *Moro*, a Moor.]
Done after the manner of the Moors.

MORESK', *n.* A species of painting or carving done after the Moorish manner, consisting of grotesque pieces and compartments promiscuously interspersed. *Encyc.*

MOR'GLAY, *n.* [L. *mors*, death, and Celtic *glaive*, sword.]
A deadly weapon.

MOR'GRAY, *n.* A Mediterranean fish of a pale reddish gray color, spotted with brown and white. It is called also the rough hound-fish. It weighs about twenty ounces and is well tasted. *Dict. Nat. Hist.*

MORICE. [See *Morisco*.]

MORIGERA'TION, *n.* [See *Morigerous*.] Obsequiousness; obedience. *Obs.* *Bacon.*

MORIG'EROUS, *a.* [L. *morigerus*; *mos*, *moris*, manner, and *gero*, to carry.]
Obedient; obsequious. [*Little used.*] *Dict.*

MOR'IL, *n.* [Fr. *morille*.] A mushroom of the size of a walnut, abounding with little holes. *Encyc.*

MORIL'LIFORM, *a.* Having the form of the moril, a mushroom.

MOR'ILLON, *n.* A fowl of the genus Anas. *Pennant.*

MOR'INEL, *n.* A bird, called also dotteril.

MORIN'GA, *n.* A plant.

MOR'ION, *n.* [Fr. from It. *morione*.] Armor for the head; a helmet or casque to defend the head. *Raleigh. Dryden.*

MORIS'CO, } *n.* [from *Moor*.] A dance, or
MO'RISK, } a dancer of the morris or moorish dance. [See *Morris*.] *Shak.*

MOR'KIN, *n.* [Sw. *murken*, putrefied; or Fr. *mort*, L. *mortuus*, dead, and *kin*, kind.]
Among *hunters*, a beast that has died by sickness or mischance. *Bailey.*

MOR'LAND, } *n.* Moorland, which see.
MO'RELAND, }

MOR'LING, } *n.* [Fr. *mort*, dead.] Wool
MORT'LING, } plucked from a dead sheep. *Ainsworth.*

MOR'MO, *n.* [Gr. μορμω.] A bugbear; false terror. *Johnson.*

MORN, *n.* [Sax. *marne*, *margene*, *mergen*, *morgen*, Dan. D. G. *morgen*, Sw. *morgon*, morn, morning or morrow. In W. *mory*, Ir. *marach* is morrow; Scot. *morn* or *morne*, morrow. In Goth. *meryan* signifies to publish, that is, to open or throw forth; Orient. אמר. In Russ. *morgayu* signifies to wink or twinkle; Ice. *morgnar*, to grow light.]
The first part of the day; the morning; a word used chiefly in poetry.

And blooming peace shall ever bless thy *morn*. *Prior.*

MORN'ING, *n.* [Sax. *margene*, *morgen*. See *Morn*.]

1. The first part of the day, beginning at twelve o'clock at night and extending to twelve at noon. Thus we say, a star rises at one o'clock in the *morning*. In a more limited sense, *morning* is the time beginning an hour or two before sunrise, or at break of day, and extending to the hour of breakfast and of beginning the labors of the day. Among men of business in large cities, the *morning* extends to the hour of dining.

2. The first or early part.

In the *morning* of life, devote yourself to the service of the Most High. *J. Clarke.*

MORN'ING, *a.* Pertaining to the first part or early part of the day; being in the early part of the day; as *morning* dew; *morning* light; *morning* service.

She looks as clear
As *morning* roses newly washed with dew. *Shak.*

MORNING-GOWN, *n.* A gown worn in the morning before one is formally dressed. *Addison.*

MORNING-STAR, *n.* The planet Venus, when it precedes the sun in rising, and shines in the morning.

MOROC'CO, *n.* A fine kind of lether; lether dressed in a particular manner; said to be borrowed from the Moors.

MORO'SE, *a.* [L. *morosus*; It. Sp. *moroso*, slow, tardy. In Portuguese, *moroso* signifies dwelling on lewd thoughts; *morosidade*, the act of dwelling on such thoughts. *Morose* then is from the root of L. *moror*, to delay, stop, hinder, whence *commoror*, to dwell, Fr. *demeurer*, Eng. *demur*. The customary sense then is derived from the gloomy, sullen temper formed by habitually fixing the thoughts on some object.]
Of a sour temper; severe; sullen and austere.

Some have deserved censure for a *morose* and affected taciturnity; others have made speeches though they had nothing to say. *Watts.*

MORO'SELY, *adv.* Sourly; with sullen austerity.

MORO'SENESS, *n.* Sourness of temper; sullenness. *Moroseness* is not precisely *peevishness* or *fretfulness*, though often accompanied with it. It denotes more of silence and severity or ill humor, than the irritability or irritation which characterizes peevishness.

Learn good humor, never to oppose without just reason; abate some degrees of pride and *moroseness*. *Watts.*

MOROS'ITY, *n.* Moroseness. [*Not used.*] *Shak.*

MOROX'YLIC, *a.* Moroxylic acid is obtained from a saline exudation from the morus alba or white mulberry.

MOR'PHEW, *n.* [It. *morfea*.] A scurf on the face.

MOR'PHEW, *v. t.* To cover with scurf. *Bp. Hall.*

MOR'PHIA, *n.* A vegetable alkali extracted from opium, of which it constitutes the narcotic principle. *Bigelow. Ure.*

MOR'RICE, } [Fr. *moresque*; from
MOR'RIS, } *n.* *Moor*.] A moorish
MOR'RIS-DANCE, } dance; a dance in imitation of the Moors, as sarabands, chacons, &c. usually performed with castanets, tambours, &c. by young men in their shirts, with bells at their feet and ribins of various colors tied round their arms and flung across their shoulders. *Encyc.*

Nine men's morrice, a kind of play with nine holes in the ground. *Shak.*

MOR'RIS-DANCER, *n.* One who dances a morris-dance. *Temple.*

MOR'RIS-PIKE, *n.* A moorish pike.

MOR'ROW, *n.* [Sax. *morgen*. But it seems rather to be the Welsh *mory*, morrow.]

1. The day next after the present.

Till this stormy night is gone,
And th' eternal *morrow* dawn. *Crashaw.*

This word is often preceded by *on* or *to*.

The Lord did that thing *on the morrow*. Ex. ix.

To morrow shall this sign be. Ex. viii.

So we say, *to* night, *to'* day. *To morrow* is equivalent to *on the morrow.*

2. The next day subsequent to any day specified.

But if the sacrifice of his offering shall be a vow or a voluntary offering, it shall be eaten the same day that he offereth his sacrifice; and on the *morrow* also the remainder of it shall be eaten. Lev. vii.

Good morrow, a term of salutation; good morning.

MORSE, *n. mors.* [Russ. *morj.*] In *zoology*, the sea-horse or walrus, an animal of the genus Trichechus, which sometimes grows to the length of 18 feet. This animal has a round head, small mouth and eyes, thick lips, a short neck, and a body thick in the middle and tapering towards the tail. His skin is wrinkled, with short hairs thinly dispersed. His legs are short and loosely articulated, and he has five toes on each foot connected by webs. Teeth of this animal have been found which weighed thirty pounds. These animals are gregarious, but shy and very fierce when attacked. They inhabit the shores of Spitzbergen, Hudson's bay and other places in high northern latitudes. *Encyc.*

MOR'SEL, *n.* [from L. *morsus*, a bite, from *mordeo.*]

1. A bite; a mouthful; a small piece of food.

Every *morsel* to a satisfied hunger is only a new labor to a tired digestion. *South.*

2. A piece; a meal; something to be eaten.

On these herbs and fruits and flowers
Feed first, on each beast next and fish and fowl,
No homely *morsels.* *Milton.*

3. A small quantity of something not eatable. [*Improper.*] *Boyle.*

MOR'SURE, *n.* The act of biting.

MORT, *n.* [Fr. See *Mortal.*] A tune sounded at the death of game. *Shak.*

2. A salmon in his third year. *Todd.*

MOR'TAL, *a.* [L. *mortalis*, from *mors*, death, or *morior*, to die, that is, to fall; W. *marw*; Fr. *mourir;* Arm. *mervel;* It. *morire* : Sp. *morir.* See Class Mr. No. 12. 14.]

1. Subject to death; destined to die. Man is *mortal.*

2. Deadly; destructive to life; causing death, or that must cause death; as a *mortal* wound; *mortal* poison.

The fruit
Of that forbidden tree whose *mortal* taste
Brought death into the world, and all our woe— *Milton.*

3. Bringing death; terminating life.

Safe in the hand of one disposing power,
Or in the natal or the *mortal* hour. *Pope.*

4. Deadly in malice or purpose; as a *mortal* foe. In colloquial language, a *mortal* foe is an inveterate foe.

5. Exposing to certain death; incurring the penalty of death; condemned to be punished with death; not venial; as a *mortal* sin.

6. Human; belonging to man who is mortal; as *mortal* wit or knowledge; *mortal* power.

The voice of God
To *mortal* ear is dreadful. *Milton.*

7. Extreme; violent. [*Not elegant.*]

The nymph grew pale, and in a *mortal* fright— *Dryden.*

MOR'TAL, *n.* Man; a being subject to death; a human being.

Warn poor *mortals* left behind. *Tickel.*

It is often used in ludicrous and colloquial language.

I can behold no *mortal* now. *Prior.*

MORTAL'ITY, *n.* [L. *mortalitas.*] Subjection to death or the necessity of dying.

When I saw her die,
I then did think on your *mortality.* *Carew.*

2. Death.

Gladly would I meet
Mortality, my sentence. *Milton.*

3. Frequency of death; actual death of great numbers of men or beasts; as a time of great *mortality.* *Graunt.*

4. Human nature.

Take these tears, *mortality's* relief. *Pope.*

5. Power of destruction.

Mortality and mercy in Vienna,
Live in thy tongue and heart. *Shak.*

MOR'TALIZE, *v. t.* To make mortal. *Broome.*

MOR'TALLY, *adv.* Irrecoverably; in a manner that must cause death; as *mortally* wounded. *Dryden.*

2. Extremely.

Adrian *mortally* envied poets, painters and artificers, in works wherein he had a vein to excel. *Bacon.*

MOR'TAR, *n.* [L. *mortarium*; Fr. *mortier*; Sp. *mortero*; It. *mortaio*; Dan. *morter*; D. *mortier*; G. *mörser*; Russ. *morter*; Arm. *mortez*; Ir. *moirteal*; allied perhaps to Fr. *marteau*, Sp. *martillo*, a hammer, and named from beating. See Class Mr. No. 10. 16. 25.]

1. A vessel of wood or metal in form of an inverted bell, in which substances are pounded or bruised with a pestle.

2. A short piece of ordnance, thick and wide, used for throwing bombs, carcases, shells, &c.; so named from its resemblance in shape to the utensil above described.

MOR'TAR, *n.* [D. *mortel*; Fr. *mortier*; G. *mörtel*; Sp. *mortero*; Ir. *moirteal.* In other languages, as in English, the orthography of this word and of the last is the same, and perhaps this name is taken from beating and mixing.]

A mixture of lime and sand with water, used as a cement for uniting stones and bricks in walls. If the lime is slaked and the materials mixed with lime water, the cement will be much stronger. *Encyc.*

Mort d'ancestor. [Fr. death of the ancestor.] In *law*, a writ of assize, by which a demandant recovers possession of an estate from which he has been ousted, on the death of his ancestor. *Blackstone.*

MOR'TER, *n.* [Fr. *mortier.*] A lamp or light. *Obs.* *Chaucer.*

MORTGAGE, *n. mor'gage.* [Fr. *mort*, dead, and *gage*, pledge.]

1. Literally, a dead pledge; the grant of an estate in fee as security for the payment of money, and on the condition that if the money shall be paid according to the contract, the grant shall be void, and the mortgagee shall re-convey the estate to the mortgager. Formerly the condition was, that if the mortgager should repay the money at the day specified, he might then re-enter on the estate granted in pledge; but the modern practice is for the mortgagee, on receiving payment, to re-convey the land to the mortgager. Before the time specified for payment, that is, between the time of contract and the time limited for payment, the estate is conditional, and the mortgagee is called *tenant in mortgage*; but on failure of payment at the time limited, the estate becomes absolute in the mortgagee. But in this case, courts of equity interpose, and if the estate is of more value than the debt, they will on application grant a reasonable time for the mortgager to redeem the estate. This is called the *equity of redemption.* *Blackstone.*

2. The state of being pledged; as lands given in *mortgage.*

[The term *mortgage* is applicable only to real estate.]

MORTGAGE, *v. t. mor'gage.* To grant an estate in fee as security for money lent or contracted to be paid at a certain time, on condition that if the debt shall be discharged according to the contract, the grant shall be void, otherwise to remain in full force. It is customary to give a mortgage for securing the repayment of money lent, or the payment of the purchase money of an estate, or for any other debt.

2. To pledge; to make liable to the payment of any debt or expenditure.

Already a portion of the entire capital of the nation is *mortgaged* for the support of drunkards. *L. Beecher.*

MORTGAGED, *pp. mor'gaged.* Conveyed in fee as security for the payment of mo-money.

MORTGAGEE, *n. morgagee'.* The person to whom an estate is mortgaged.

MORTGAGER, *n. mor'gager.* [from *mortgage. Mortgagor* is an orthography that should have no countenance.]

The person who grants an estate as security for a debt, as above specified.

MORTIF'EROUS, *a.* [L. *mortifer*; *mors*, death, and *fero*, to bring.]

Bringing or producing death; deadly; fatal; destructive. *Hammond.*

MORTIFICA'TION, *n.* [Fr. See *Mortify.*]

1. In *medicine* and *surgery*, the death and consequent putrefaction of one part of an animal body, while the rest is alive; or the loss of heat and action in some part of a living animal, followed by a dissolution of organic texture; gangrene; sphacelus. *Mortification* is the local or partial death of a living animal body, and if not arrested, soon extinguishes life in the whole body. We usually apply *mortification* to the *local* extinction of life and loss of organic texture in a living body. The dissolution of the *whole* body after death, is called *putrefaction.*

2. In *Scripture*, the act of subduing the passions and appetites by penance, abstinence or painful severities inflicted on the body. The *mortification* of the body by fasting has been the practice of almost all nations, and the *mortification* of the appetites and passions by self-denial is always a christian duty.

3. Humiliation or slight vexation; the state of being humbled or depressed by disappointment, vexation, crosses, or any thing that wounds or abases pride.

It is one of the vexatious *mortifications* of a

studious man to have his thoughts disordered by a tedious visit. *L'Estrange.*

We had the *mortification* to lose sight of Munich, Augsburg and Ratisbon. *Addison.*

4. Destruction of active qualities; applied to metals. [See *Mortify;* but I believe not used.] *Bacon.*

MOR'TIFIED, *pp.* Affected by sphacelus or gangrene.

2. Humbled; subdued; abased.

MOR'TIFIEDNESS, *n.* Humiliation; subjection of the passions. *Taylor.*

MOR'TIFIER, *n.* He or that which mortifies.

MOR'TIFY, *v. t.* [Fr. *mortifier;* It. *mortificare;* Sp. *mortificar;* L. *mors,* death, and *facio,* to make.]

1. To destroy the organic texture and vital functions of some part of a living animal; to change to sphacelus or gangrene. Extreme inflammation speedily *mortifies* flesh.

2. To subdue or bring into subjection, as the bodily appetites by abstinence or rigorous severities.

We *mortify* ourselves with fish. *Brown.*

With fasting *mortified,* worn out with tears. *Harte.*

3. To subdue; to abase; to humble; to reduce; to restrain; as inordinate passions.

Mortify thy learned lust. *Prior.*

Mortify therefore your members which are upon the earth. Col. iii.

4. To humble; to depress; to affect with slight vexation.

How often is the ambitious man *mortified* with the very praises he receives, if they do not rise so high as he thinks they ought. *Addison.*

He is controlled by a nod, *mortified* by a frown, and transported with a smile. *Addison.*

5. To destroy active powers or essential qualities.

He *mortified* pearls in vinegar— *Hakewill.*

Quicksilver—*mortified* with turpentine. *Bacon.*

[*I believe this application is not now in use.*]

MOR'TIFY, *v. i.* To lose vital heat and action and suffer the dissolution of organic texture, as flesh; to corrupt or gangrene.

2. To be subdued. *Johnson.*

3. To practice severities and penance from religious motives.

This makes him give alms of all that he hath, watch, fast and *mortify.* *Law.*

MOR'TIFYING, *ppr.* Changing from soundness to gangrene or sphacelus.

2. Subduing; humbling; restraining.

3. *a.* Humiliating; tending to humble or abase. He met with a *mortifying* repulse.

MORTISE, *n. mor'tis.* [Fr. *mortaise;* Arm. *mortez;* Sp. *mortaja;* Ir. *mortis.* The Armoric *mortez* signifies both a *mortar* and a *mortise,* and the Spanish *mortaja* signifies a mortise and a winding sheet or shroud. In the latter sense, the Portuguese use *mortalha,* from *mortal.* These alliances indicate that these words are all from the root of *mors,* death, which may be from beating or throwing down.]

A cut or hollow place made in timber by the augur and chisel, to receive the tenon of another piece of timber.

MOR'TISE, *v. t.* To cut or make a mortise in.

2. To join timbers by a tenon and mortise; as, to *mortise* a beam into a post, or a joist into a girder.

MOR'TISED, *pp.* Having a mortise; joined by a mortise and tenon.

MOR'TISING, *ppr.* Making a mortise; uniting by a mortise and tenon.

MORT'MAIN, *n.* [Fr. *mort,* dead, and *main,* hand.]

In *law,* possession of lands or tenements in dead hands, or hands that cannot alienate. Alienation in *mortmain* is an alienation of lands or tenements to any corporation, sole or aggregate, ecclesiastical or temporal, particularly to religious houses, by which the estate becomes perpetually inherent in the corporation and unalienable. *Blackstone.*

MORT'PAY, *n.* [Fr. *mort,* dead, and *pay.*] Dead pay; payment not made. [*Not used.*] *Bacon.*

MOR'TRESS, *n.* [from *mortar.*] A dish of meat of various kinds beaten together. [*Not used.*] *Bacon.*

MOR'TUARY, *n.* [Fr. *mortuaire,* pertaining to the dead.]

1. A sort of ecclesiastical heriot, a customary gift claimed by and due to the minister of a parish on the death of a parishioner. It seems to have been originally a voluntary bequest or donation, intended to make amends for any failure in the payment of tithes of which the deceased had been guilty. *Blackstone.*

2. A burial place. *Whitlock.*

MOR'TUARY, *a.* Belonging to the burial of the dead.

MOSA'IC, *a. s* as z. [Fr. *mosaique;* It. *mosaico;* Sp. *mosayco;* L. *musivum.*]

1. Mosaic work is an assemblage of little pieces of glass, marble, precious stones, &c. of various colors, cut square and cemented on a ground of stucco, in such a manner as to imitate the colors and gradations of painting. *Encyc.*

2. [from *Moses.*] Pertaining to Moses, the leader of the Israelites; as the *Mosaic* law, rites or institutions.

MOS'CHATEL, *n.* [from Gr. μοσχος, L. *muscus,* musk.]

A plant of the genus Adoxa, hollow root or inglorious. There is one species only, whose leaves and flowers smell like musk; and hence it is sometimes called *musk-crowfoot.* *Encyc.*

MOSK, *n.* [Fr. *mosquée;* It. *moschea;* Sp. *mezquita;* Ar. مَسْجِدٌ *masjidon,* from سَجَدَ sajada, to bend, bow, adore.]

A Mohammedan temple or place of religious worship. Mosks are square buildings, generally constructed of stone. Before the chief gate is a square court paved with white marble, and surrounded with a low gallery whose roof is supported by pillars of marble. In this gallery the worshipers wash themselves before they enter the mosk. *Encyc.*

MOSS, *n.* [Sax. *meos;* G. *moos;* D. *mos;* Sw. *mossa;* W. *mwswg,* from *mws,* that shoots up, and of a strong scent; L. *muscus;* Gr. μοσχος. The two latter signify *moss* and *musk,* both from shooting out; hence It. *musco, muschio;* Sp. *musco;* Port. *musgo;* Fr. *mousse.* The Greek word signifies also a young animal, and a shoot or twig. From the French *mousse,* comes *mousseline,* muslin, from its softness or resemblance to moss. Lunier says it is from *Mossoul,* a city of Mesopotamia.]

The mosses are one of the seven families or classes into which all vegetables are divided by Linne in the Philosophia Botanica. In Ray's method, the mosses form the third class, and in Tournefort's, they constitute a single genus. In the sexual system, they are the second order of the class cryptogamia, which contains all the plants in which the parts of the flower and fruit are wanting or not conspicuous. *Milne.*

The mosses, *musci,* form a natural order of small plants, with leafy stems and narrow simple leaves. Their flowers are generally monecian or diecian, and their seeds are contained in a capsule covered with a calyptra or hood. *Ed. Encyc.*

The term *moss* is also applied to many other small plants, particularly *lichens,* species of which are called *tree-moss, rock-moss, coral-moss,* &c. The *fir-moss* and *club-moss* are of the genus Lycopodium.

2. [Sw. *måse.*] A bog; a place where peat is found.

MOSS, *v. t.* To cover with moss by natural growth.

An oak whose boughs were *mossed* with age. *Shak.*

MOSS'-CLAD, *a.* Clad or covered with moss. *Littleton.*

MOSS'ED, *pp.* Overgrown with moss.

MOSS-GROWN, *a.* Overgrown with moss; as *moss-grown* towers.

MOSS'INESS, *n.* [from *mossy.*] The state of being overgrown with moss. *Bacon.*

MOSS'-TROOPER, *n.* [*moss* and *trooper.*] A robber; a bandit. *Bp. of Dromore.*

MOSS'Y, *a.* Overgrown with moss; abounding with moss.

Old trees are more *mossy* than young. *Bacon.*

2. Shaded or covered with moss, or bordered with moss; as *mossy* brooks; *mossy* fountains. *Pope. Cowley.*

MŌST, *a. superl.* of *more.* [Sax. *mæst,* that is, *ma* and *est;* Goth. *maists;* D. Dan. *meest;* G. *meist;* Sw. *mest, måst.*]

1. Consisting of the greatest number. That scheme of life is to be preferred, which presents a prospect of the *most* advantages with the fewest inconveniences.

Most men will proclaim every one his own goodness. Prov. xx.

2. Consisting of the greatest quantity; greatest; as the *most* part of the land or the mountain.

MŌST, *adv.* In the greatest or highest degree. Pursue that course of life which will *most* tend to produce private happiness and public usefulness. Contemplations on the works of God expand the mind and tend to produce *most* sublime views of his power and wisdom.

As *most* is used to express the superlative degree, it is used before any adjective; as *most* vile, *most* wicked, *most* illustrious.

MŌST, *n.* [used as a substitute for a noun, when the noun is omitted or understood.]

1. The greatest number or part.

Then he began to upbraid the cities wherein *most* of his mighty works were done. Matt. xi.

[This use seems to have resulted from the omission of *part*, or some similar word, and *most* in this case signifies *greatest*, that is, the *greatest part*.]

2. *The most*, the greatest value, amount or advantage, or the utmost in extent, degree or effect.

A covetous man makes *the most* of what he has, and can get. *L'Estrange.*

At the most, the greatest degree or quantity; the utmost extent. Stock brings six per cent. interest *at the most*, often less.

MOS'TIC, *n.* [G. *mahlerstock*, contracted.] A painter's staff or stick on which he rests his hand in painting. *Ainsworth.*

MŎSTLY, *adv.* For the greatest part. The exports of the U. States consist *mostly* of cotton, rice, tobacco, flour and lumber.

MŎSTWHAT, *adv.* For the most part. *Obs.* *Hammond.*

MOT. [See *Motto.*]

MO'TACIL, *n.* [L. *motacilla.*] A bird of the genus Motacilla or wagtail.

MOTE, in *folkmote*, &c. signifies a meeting, Sax. *mot*, *gemot.*

MOTE, *n.* [Sax. *mot;* Sp. *mota;* W. *ysmot*, a patch or spot.]

A small particle; any thing proverbially small; a spot.

Why beholdest thou the *mote* in thy brother's eye? Matt. vii.

The little *motes* in the sun do ever stir, though there is no wind. *Bacon.*

MOTE, for *mought*, *might* or *must*, obsolete. *Spenser.*

MO'TET, *n.* [Fr.] A musical composition; an air or hymn. *Herbert.*

MOTH, *n.* [Sax. *mogthe*, *mohth*, *moth* or *matha;* Goth. *matha;* D. *mot;* G. *motte.*]

1. An animal of the genus Phalæna, which breeds in yarn and garments, and often does injury by eating the substance and destroying the texture. Matt. vi.

The name is also applied to the whole genus.

2. *Figuratively*, that which gradually and silently eats, consumes or wastes any thing. Idle persons are a *moth* to the community.

MOTH'EAT, *v. t.* [*moth* and *eat.*] To eat or prey upon, as a moth eats a garment. *Herbert.*

MOTH'EATEN, *a.* Eaten by moths. Job xiii.

MOTH'EN, *a.* Full of moths. [*Not in use.*] *Falke.*

MŎTHER, *n.* [Sax. *moder;* D. *moeder*, mother, and *modder*, mud; *baar-moeder*, the womb; *moer*, mother, dam, womb, lees; *moerspul*, hysterics; [*moer* seems to be a contraction of *moeder;*] *moeder-naakt*, stark naked; G. *mutter*, mother, and the thick slimy concretion in vinegar; *bärmutter*, the womb or matrix; *mutter-fieber*, a hysteric fit; *mutter-lamm* and *mutterschaf*, a ewe or female sheep; *mutterflecken* and *mutter-mahl*, a mole; *mutterpferd*, a mare, the female of the horse kind; *mutter-scheide*, the vagina; *mutternackt*, stark naked; *moder*, mud, mold.

Sw. *moder*, mother; *vin-moder*, mother of wine; *moderfall*, prolapsus uteri; *moderlif*, the womb or matrix.

Dan. *moder*, mother; *moderskeede*, the vagina; *moderen i quinder*, the matrix; *modder* or *mudder*, mud.

Ir. *mathair*, a mother, and matter, pus.

Gr. *ματηρ*, mother, and *μητρα*, matrix.

L. *mater*, mother; *matrix*, the womb; *materia*, matter, stuff, materials of which any thing is made.

It. *madre*, mother, cause, origin, root, spring, a mold or form for castings; *matera* or *materia*, matter, subject, cause; *matrice*, the matrix.

Sp. *madre*, mother, matrix, womb, the bed of a river, a sink or sewer; *madriz*, matrix; *materia*, matter, purulent running.

Port. *madre*, a mother, the matrix, the channel of a river; *materia*, matter, pus.

Pers. مادر madar, a mother.

Sans. *mada*, *madra*, *meddra* or *mata*, mother.

Russ. *mat*, mother; *matka*, a female, a matrix.

Fr. *mere*, mother, contracted from the Latin.

W. *madrez*, matter, purulent discharge.

We observe that in some other languages, as well as in English, the same word signifies a female parent, and the thick slime formed in vinegar; and in all the languages of Europe here cited, the orthography is nearly the same as that of *mud* and *matter.* The question then occurs whether the name of a female parent originated in a word expressing *matter*, mold; either the soil of the earth, as the producer, or the like substance, when shaped and fitted as a mold for castings; or whether the name is connected with the opinion that the earth is the *mother* of all productions; whence the word *mother-earth.* We are informed by a fragment of Sanchoniathon, that the ancient Phenicians considered *mud*, *μωτ*, to be the substance from which all things were formed. See *Mud.* The word *matter* is evidently from the Ar. مدّ *madda*, to secrete, eject or discharge a purulent substance; and I think cannot have any direct connection with *mud.* But in the Italian, Spanish and Portuguese, the same word *madre* signifies mother, and a mold for castings; and the northern languages, particularly the German and Danish, seem to establish the fact that the proper sense of *mother* is matrix. Hence *mother* of pearl, the matrix of pearl. If this word had its origin in the name of the earth used for the forms of castings, it would not be a singular fact; for our word *mold*, in this sense, I suppose to be so named from *mold*, fine earth. The question remains *sub judice.*]

1. A female parent; especially, one of the human race; a woman who has borne a child; correlative to *son* or *daughter.*

2. That which has produced any thing.

Alas, poor country! it cannot
Be called our *mother*, but our grave. *Shak.*

So our native land is called *mother* country, and a plant from which a slip or cion is taken, is called the *mother* plant. In this use, *mother* may be considered as an adjective.

3. That which has preceded in time; the oldest or chief of any thing; as a *mother*-church.

4. Hysterical passion. [*Not used.*] *Graunt.*

5. A familiar term of address or appellation of an old woman or matron.

6. An appellation given to a woman who exercises care and tenderness towards another, or gives parental advice; as when one says, "a woman has been a *mother* to me."

7. A thick slimy substance concreted in liquors, particularly in vinegar, very different from scum or common lees.

MŎTHER *of pearl*, *n.* The matrix of pearl; the shell in which pearls are generated; a species of Mytilus or Mussel. *Encyc.*

MŎTHER *of thyme*, *n.* A plant of the genus Thymus.

MŎTHER, *a.* Native; natural; received by birth; as *mother*-wit.

2. Native; vernacular; received from parents or ancestors; as *mother*-tongue.

MŎTHER, *v. i.* To concrete, as the thick matter of liquors. *Dryden.*

MŎTHER, *v. t.* To adopt as a son or daughter. *Howell.*

MŎTHERHOOD, *n.* The state of being a mother. *Donne.*

MŎTHER-IN-LAW, *n.* The mother of a husband or wife.

MŎTHERLESS, *a.* Destitute of a mother; having lost a mother; as *motherless* children.

MŎTHERLY, *a.* Pertaining to a mother; as *motherly* power or authority. *Hooker.*

2. Becoming a mother; tender; parental; as *motherly* love or care. *Arbuthnot.*

MŎTHERLY, *adv.* In the manner of a mother. *Donne.*

MŎTHER-WATER, *n.* A fluid remaining after the evaporation of salt water, and containing deliquescent salts and impurities. *Ure.*

MŎTHER-WIT, *n.* Native wit; common sense.

MŎTHER-WŎRT, *n.* A plant of the genus Leonurus.

MŎTHERY, *a.* Concreted; resembling or partaking of the nature of mother; as the *mothery* substance in liquors.

MOTH'MULLEN, *n.* A plant. *Miller.*

MOTH'WŎRT, *n.* A plant.

MOTH'Y, *a.* [from *moth.*] Full of moths; as an old *mothy* saddle. *Shak.*

MO'TION, *n.* [L. *motio;* Fr. *motion.* See *Move.*] The act or process of changing place; change of local position; the passing of a body from one place to another; change of distance between bodies; opposed to *rest.*

Animal motion is that which is performed by animals in consequence of volition or an act of the will; but how the will operates on the body in producing motion, we cannot explain. *Mechanical motion* is effected by the force or power of one body acting on another. *Perpetual motion* is that which is effected or supplied by itself, without the impulse or intervention of any external cause. Hitherto it has been found impossible to invent a machine that has this principle.

2. Animal life and action.

Devoid of sense and *motion.* *Milton.*

3. Manner of moving the body; port; gait; air.

Each member move and every *motion* guide. *Blackmore.*

4. Change of posture; action.

Watching the *motion* of her patron's eye. *Dryden.*

5. Military march or movement. *Milton.*
6. Agitation; as the *motions* of the sea.
7. Internal action; excitement; as the *motions* of the breast. *Gay.*
8. Direction; tendency.

In our proper *motion* we ascend. *Milton.*

9. The effect of impulse; action proceeding from any cause, external or internal. In the growth of plants and animals, there must be a *motion* of the component parts, though invisible. Attraction or chimical affinity produces sensible *motion* of the parts of bodies. *Motions* of the mind ascribed to the invisible agency of the Supreme Being, are called good *motions.*

Let a good man obey every good *motion* rising in his heart, knowing that every such *motion* proceeds from God. *South.*

10. Proposal made; proposition offered; particularly, a proposition made in a deliberative assembly. A *motion* is made for a committee; a *motion* for introducing a bill; a *motion* to adjourn.
11. A puppet-show or puppet. [*Not used.*] *Shak.*

MO'TION, *v. t.* To propose. [*Little used.* See *Move.*]

MO'TIONER, *n.* A mover. [*Not used.*]

MO'TIONLESS, *a.* Wanting motion; being at rest.

I grow a statue, fixed and *motionless.* *Dryden.*

MO'TIVE, *a.* [See the Noun.] Causing motion; having power to move or tending to move; as a *motive* argument; *motive* power. *Hooker. Bentley.*

MO'TIVE, *n.* [It. Sp. Port. *motivo*; Fr. *motif.* See *Move.*]

1. That which incites to action; that which determines the choice, or moves the will. Thus we speak of good *motives,* and bad *motives;* strong and weak *motives.* The *motive* to continue at rest is ease or satisfaction; the *motive* to change is uneasiness, or the prospect of good.
2. That which may or ought to incite to action; reason; cause.
3. A mover. [*Not in use.*] *Shak.*

MOTIV'ITY, *n.* The power of producing motion.

MOT'LEY, *a.* [W. *ysmot,* a spot; *ysmotiaw,* to spot, to dapple; Sp. *motear,* id.; Eng. *mote.*]

1. Variegated in color; consisting of different colors; dappled; as a *motley* coat. *Shak.*
2. Composed of different or various parts, characters or kinds; diversified; as a *motley* style.

And doubts of *motley* hue. *Dryden.*

[This word primarily means *spotted;* but it may signify also *striped.*]

MO'TOR, *n.* [L. from *moveo,* to move.] A mover. The metals are called *motors* of electricity. *Volta.*

MO'TORY, *a.* Giving motion; as *motory* muscles. *Ray.*

MOT'TO, *n.* [It. *id.*; Sp. Port. *mote;* Fr. *mot;* Sax. *mæthelan,* to speak; Ir. *meadhair,* talk, discourse; Goth. *mathlei,* id.; Gr. *μυθος, μυθενω, μυθεομαι.*]

Primarily, a word; but more commonly, a sentence or phrase prefixed to an essay or discourse, containing the subject of it, or added to a device.

In *heraldry,* the motto is carried in a scroll, alluding to the bearing or to the name of the bearer, or expressing some important idea.

MOULD, an incorrect orthography. [See *Mold,* and its derivatives.]

MOULT. [See *Molt.*]

MOUNCH, MAUNCH, } *v. t.* To chew. *Obs. Chaucer.*

MOUND, *n.* [Sax. *mund;* W. *mwnt,* from *mwn;* L. *mons.* See *Mount.*]

Something raised as a defense or fortification, usually a bank of earth or stone; a bulwark; a rampart or fence.

God has thrown
That mountain as his garden *mound,* high raised. *Milton.*

To thrid the thickets or to leap the *mounds.* *Dryden.*

MOUND, *v. t.* To fortify with a mound. *Johnson.*

MOUND'ED, *pp.* Surrounded or defended by mounds.

The lakes high *mounded.* *J. Barlow.*

MOUND'ING, *ppr.* Defending by a mound.

MOUNT, *n.* [Fr. *mont;* Sax. *munt;* It. Port. Sp. *monte;* Arm. *menez, mene;* W. *mwnt,* a mount, mountain or mound, a heap; L. *mons,* literally a heap or an elevation; Ir. *moin* or *muine;* Basque, *mendia.* Qu. Gr. *βουνος.*]

1. A mass of earth, or earth and rock, rising considerably above the common surface of the surrounding land. *Mount* is used for an eminence or elevation of earth, indefinite in highth or size, and may be a hillock, hill or mountain. We apply it to *Mount* Blanc, in Switzerland, to *Mount* Tom and *Mount* Holyoke, in Massachusetts, and it is applied in Scripture to the small hillocks on which sacrifice was offered, as well as to *Mount* Sinai. Jacob offered sacrifice on the *mount* or heap of stones raised for a witness between him and Laban. Gen. xxxi.
2. A mound; a bulwark for offense or defense.

Hew ye down trees and cast a *mount* against Jerusalem. Jer. vi.

3. Formerly, a bank or fund of money. *Obs. Bacon.*

MOUNT, *v. i.* [Fr. *monter;* It. *montare;* Sp. *montar.*]

1. To rise on high; to ascend; with or without *up.*

Doth the eagle *mount up* at thy command? Job xxxix.

The fire of trees and houses *mounts* on high. *Cowley.*

2. To rise; to ascend; to tower; to be built to a great altitude.

Though Babylon should *mount* up to heaven. Jer. li.

3. To get on horseback. *Shak.*
4. To leap upon any animal.
5. To amount; to rise in value.

Bring then these blessings to a strict account,
Make fair deductions, see to what they *mount.* *Pope.*

MOUNT, *v. t.* To raise aloft; to lift on high.

What power is it which *mounts* my love so high? *Shak.*

2. To ascend; to climb; to get upon an elevated place; as, to *mount* a throne.
3. To place one's self on horseback; as, to *mount* a horse.
4. To furnish with horses; as, to *mount* a troop. The dragoons were well *mounted.*
5. To put on or cover with something; to embellish with ornaments; as, to *mount* a sword.
6. To carry; to be furnished with; as, a ship of the line *mounts* seventy four guns; a fort *mounts* a hundred cannon.
7. To raise and place on a carriage; as, to *mount* a cannon.

To mount guard, to take the station and do the duty of a sentinel.

MOUNT'AIN, *n.* [Fr. *montagne;* Sp. *montaña;* It. *montagna;* L. adjective, *montanus.*]

A large mass of earth and rock, rising above the common level of the earth or adjacent land, but of no definite altitude. We apply *mountain* to the largest eminences on the globe; but sometimes the word is used for a large hill. In general, *mountain* denotes an elevation higher and larger than a hill; as the Altaic *mountains* in Asia, the Alps in Switzerland, the Andes in South America, the Alleghany *mountains* in Virginia, the Kaatskill in New-York, the White *mountains* in New-Hampshire, and the Green *mountains* in Vermont. The word is applied to a single elevation, or to an extended range.

MOUNT'AIN, *a.* Pertaining to a mountain; found on mountains; growing or dwelling on a mountain; as *mountain* air; *mountain* pines; *mountain* goats.

MOUNT'AIN-BLUE, *n.* Malachite; carbonate of copper.

MOUNTAINE'ER, MOUNT'AINER, } *a.* An inhabitant of a mountain.

2. A rustic; a freebooter; a savage. *Milton.*

MOUNT'AINET, *n.* A small mountain; a hillock. [*Not used.*] *Sidney.*

MOUNT'AIN-GREEN, *n.* A carbonate of copper.

MOUNT'AINOUS, *a.* Full of mountains; as the *mountainous* country of the Swiss.

2. Large as a mountain; huge; as a *mountainous* heap. *Prior.*
3. Inhabiting mountains. [*Not used.*] *Bacon.*

MOUNT'AINOUSNESS, *n.* The state of being full of mountains. *Brerewood.*

MOUNT'AIN-PARSLEY, *n.* A plant of the genus Athamanta. *Lee.*

MOUNT'AIN-ROSE, *n.* A plant.

MOUNT'AIN-SOAP, *n.* A mineral of a pale brownish black color. *Ure.*

MOUNT'ANT, *a.* [Fr. *montant.*] Rising on high. *Shak.*

MOUNT'EBANK, *n.* [It. *montare,* to mount, and *banco,* bench.]

1. One who mounts a bench or stage in the market or other public place, boasts of his skill in curing diseases, vends medicines which he pretends are infallible remedies, and thus deludes the ignorant multitude. Persons of this character may be indicted and punished.
2. Any boastful and false pretender.

Nothing so impossible in nature, but *mountebanks* will undertake. *Arbuthnot.*

MOUNT'EBANK, *v. t.* To cheat by boasting and false pretenses; to gull. *Shak.*

MOUNT'EBANKERY, *n.* Quackery; boastful and vain pretenses. *Hammond.*

MOUNT'ED, *pp.* Raised; seated on horseback; placed on a carriage; covered or embellished; furnished with guns.

MOUNT'ENAUNCE, *n.* Amount in space. [*Not used.*] *Spenser.*

MOUNT'ER, *n.* One that mounts or ascends. *Swift.*

MOUNT'ING, *ppr.* Rising; soaring; placing on horseback; ascending an eminence; embellishing.

MOUNT'INGLY, *adv.* By rising or ascending.

MOUNT'Y, *n.* The rise of a hawk. *Sidney.*

MOURN, *v. i.* [Sax. *murnan, myrnan;* L. *mæreo;* allied perhaps to G. D. *murren,* to *murmur;* Fr. *morne,* sad, sullen. See *Murmur,* and the root of *amarus,* bitter. Class Mr. No. 7.]

1. To express grief or sorrow; to grieve; to be sorrowful. Mourning may be expressed by weeping or audible sounds, or by sobs, sighs or inward silent grief.

> Abraham came to *mourn* for Sarah and to weep. Gen. 23.

> Blessed are they that *mourn,* for they shall be comforted. Matt. v.

2. To wear the customary habit of sorrow.

> We *mourn* in black. *Shak.*

> Grieve for an hour perhaps, then *mourn* a year. *Pope.*

MOURN, *v. t.* To grieve for; to lament. But there is an ellipsis of *for,* the verb not being transitive. When we say, we *mourn* a friend or a child, the real sense and complete phrase is, we *mourn for* a friend, or *mourn for the loss of* a friend. "He *mourn'd* his rival's ill success," that is, he *mourned for* his rival's ill success. *Addison.*

2. To utter in a sorrowful manner.

> The love lorn nightingale
> Nightly to thee her sad song *mourneth* well. *Milton.*

MOURNE, *n. mōrn.* [Fr. *morne.*] The round end of a staff; the part of a lance to which the steel is fixed, or the ferrel. [*Not used.*] *Sidney. Johnson.*

MOURNER, *n.* One that mourns or is grieved at any loss or misfortune.

2. One that follows a funeral in the habit of mourning. *L'Estrange.*

3. Something used at funerals.

> The *mourner* eugh and builder oak were there. *Dryden.*

MOURNFUL, *a.* Intended to express sorrow, or exhibiting the appearance of grief; as a *mournful* bell; *mournful* music. *Shak. Dryden.*

> No funeral rites nor man in *mournful* weeds. *Shak.*

2. Causing sorrow; sad; calamitous; as a *mournful* death. *Shak.*

3. Sorrowful; feeling grief.

> The *mournful* fair—
> Shall visit her distinguished urn. *Prior.*

MOURNFULLY, *adv.* In a manner expressive of sorrow; with sorrow. Mal. iii.

MOURNFULNESS, *n.* Sorrow; grief; state of mourning.

2. Appearance or expression of grief.

MOURNING, *ppr.* Grieving; lamenting; sorrowing; wearing the appearance of sorrow.

MOURNING, *n.* The act of sorrowing or expressing grief; lamentation; sorrow.

2. The dress or customary habit worn by mourners.

> And ev'n the pavements were with *mourning* hid. *Dryden.*

MOURNING-DOVE, *n.* A species of dove found in the U. States, the *Columba Caroliniensis.*

MOURNINGLY, *adv.* With the appearance of sorrow. *Shak.*

MOUSE, *n.* plu. *mice.* [Sax. Sw. *mus;* D. *muis;* G. *maus;* Dan. *mus, muus;* L. *mus;* Gr. *μυς;* Russ. *mishe.* The L. *mus* forms *muris* in the genitive, and the root is not obvious.]

1. A small animal of the genus Mus, inhabiting houses. The name is also applied to many other species of the genus, as the *field mouse, meadow mouse, rock mouse, &c.*

2. Among *seamen,* a knob formed on a rope by spun yarn or parceling. *Mar. Dict.*

MOUSE, *v. i. mouz.* To catch mice. *Shak.*

MOUSE, *v. t. mouz.* To tear, as a cat devours a mouse.

To mouse a hook, with seamen, is to fasten a small line across the upper part to prevent unhooking. *Mar. Dict.*

MOUSE-EAR, *n. mous'-ear.* A plant of the genus Hieracium; also, a plant of the genus Myosotis, called likewise *mouse-ear scorpion grass.* The *mouse-ear chickweed* is of the genus Cerastium. *Lee. Encyc.*

MOUSE-HOLE, *n. mous'hole.* A hole where mice enter or pass; a very small hole or entrance.

> He can creep in at a *mouse-hole.* *Stillingfleet.*

MOUSE-HUNT, *n. mous'-hunt.* A hunting for mice.

2. A mouser; one that hunts mice. *Shak.*

MOUSER, *n. mouz'er.* One that catches mice. The cat is a good *mouser.*

MOUSE-TAIL, *n. mous'-tail.* A plant of the genus Myosurus.

MOUSE-TRAP, *n. mous'-trap.* A trap for catching mice. *Prior.*

MOUTH, *n.* [Sax. *muth.* As this word does not occur in the other Teutonic dialects, and as *n* is sometimes casually introduced into words before dentals, it is not improbable that the Goth. *munths,* G. Dan. *mund,* Sw. *mun,* and D. *mond,* may be the same word. The Saxon *muth* coincides in elements with *motto,* Gr. *μυθος.*]

1. The aperture in the head of an animal, between the lips, by which he utters his voice and receives food. In a more general sense, the mouth consists of the lips, the gums, the insides of the cheeks, the palate, the salival glands, the uvula and tonsils. *Encyc.*

2. The opening of a vessel by which it is filled or emptied; as the *mouth* of a jar or pitcher.

3. The part or channel of a river by which its waters are discharged into the ocean or into a lake. The Mississippi and the Nile discharge their waters by several *mouths.*

4. The opening of a piece of ordnance at the end, by which the charge issues.

5. The aperture of a vessel in animal bodies, by which fluids or other matter is received or discharged; as the *mouth* of the lacteals.

6. The opening or entrance of a cave, pit, well or den. Dan. viii.

7. The instrument of speaking; as, the story is in every body's *mouth.* *South. Locke.*

8. A principal speaker; one that utters the common opinion.

> Every coffee house has some statesman belonging to it, who is the *mouth* of the street where he lives. *Addison.*

9. Cry; voice.

> The fearful dogs divide,
> All spend their *mouth* aloft, but none abide. *Dryden.*

10. In Scripture, words uttered. Job xix. Is. xlix. Ps. lxxiii.

11. Desires; necessities. Ps. ciii.

12. Freedom and boldness of speech; force of argument. Luke xxi.

13. Boasting; vaunting. Judges ix.

14. Testimony. Deut. xvii.

15. Reproaches; calumnies. Job v.

To make a mouth, } *To make mouths,* } to distort the mouth; to make a wry face; hence, to deride or treat with scorn. *Shak. Addison.*

2. To pout; to treat disdainfully.

Down in the mouth, dejected; mortified. *L'Estrange.*

To have God's law in the mouth, to converse much on it and delight in it. Ex. xiii.

To draw near to God with the mouth, to make an external appearance of devotion and worship, while there is no regard to him in the heart. Is. xxix.

A froward mouth, contradictions and disobedience. Prov. iv.

A smooth mouth, soft and flattering language. Prov. v.

To stop the mouth, to silence or to be silent; to put to shame; to confound. Rom. iii.

To lay the hand on the mouth, to be struck silent with shame. Mic. vii.

To set the mouth against the heavens, to speak arrogantly and blasphemously. Ps. lxxiii.

MOUTH, *v. t.* To utter with a voice affectedly big or swelling; as, to *mouth* words or language.

> Twitch'd by the sleeve, he *mouths* it more and more. *Dryden.*

2. To take into the mouth; to seize with the mouth. *Dryden.*

3. To chew; to grind, as food; to eat; to devour. *Shak.*

4. To form by the mouth, as a bear her cub. [*Not used.*] *Brown.*

5. To reproach; to insult. *Blair.*

MOUTH, *v. i.* To speak with a full, round, or loud, affected voice; to vociferate; to rant; as a *mouthing* actor. *Dryden.*

> I'll bellow out for Rome and for my country,
> And *mouth* at Cesar, till I shake the senate. *Addison.*

MOUTH'ED, *pp.* Uttered with a full, swelling, affected voice.

2. Taken into the mouth; chewed.

3. *a.* Furnished with a mouth; used chiefly in composition; as well-*mouthed;* foul-*mouthed,* contumelious, reproachful or obscene; mealy-*mouthed,* bashful, reserved in speaking the plain truth; hard-*mouthed,* as a horse, not obedient to the bit, difficult to be restrained or governed by the bridle.

4. Borne down or overpowered by clamor.

MOUTH'FRIEND, *n.* One who professes friendship without entertaining it; a pretended friend. *Shak.*

MOUTH'FUL, *n.* As much as the mouth contains at once.

2. A quantity proverbially small; a small quantity. *L'Estrange. Dryden.*

MOUTH'HONOR, *n.* Civility expressed without sincerity. *Shak.*

MOUTH'ING, *ppr.* Uttering with an affected swelling voice.

MOUTH'LESS, *a.* Destitute of a mouth.

MOUTH'MADE, *a.* Expressed without sincerity; hypocritical.

MOUTH'PIECE, *n.* The piece of a musical wind instrument to which the mouth is applied.

2. One who delivers the opinions of others.

MÖVABLE, *a.* [from *move.*] That may be moved; that can or may be lifted, carried, drawn, turned or conveyed, or in any way made to change place or posture; susceptible of motion.

2. That may or does change from one time to another; as a *movable* feast.

A movable letter, in Hebrew grammar, is one that is pronounced, as opposed to one that is quiescent.

MÖVABLENESS, *n.* The state or quality of being movable; mobility; susceptibility of motion.

MÖVABLES, *n. plu.* Goods, wares, commodities, furniture; any species of property not fixed, and thus distinguished from houses and lands.

MÖVABLY, *adv.* So that it may be moved. *Grew.*

MÖVE, *v. t. moov.* [L. *moveo;* It. *movere;* Sp. *mover;* Fr. *mouvoir;* W. *mudaw.* It is probably a contracted word. Class Md.]

1. To impel; to carry, convey or draw from one place to another; to cause to change place or posture in any manner or by any means. The wind *moves* a ship; the cartman *moves* goods; the horse *moves* a cart or carriage. Mere matter cannot *move* itself. Machines are *moved* by springs, weights, or force applied.

2. To excite into action; to affect; to agitate; to rouse; as, to *move* the passions.

3. To cause to act or determine; as, to *move* the will.

4. To persuade; to prevail on; to excite from a state of rest or indifference.

> Minds desirous of revenge were not *moved* with gold. *Knolles.*

> But when no female arts his mind could *move*,
> She turn'd to furious hate her impious love. *Dryden.*

5. To excite tenderness, pity or grief in the heart; to affect; to touch pathetically; to excite feeling in.

> The use of images in orations and poetry is to *move* pity or terror. *Felton.*

> When he saw the multitudes, he was *moved* with compassion on them— Matt. ix.

6. To make angry; to provoke; to irritate. *Shak.*

7. To excite tumult or commotion.

> When they had come to Bethlehem, all the city was *moved* about them. Ruth i. Matt. xxi.

8. To influence or incite by secret agency.

> God *moved* them to depart from him. 2 Chron. xviii. 2 Pet. i.

9. To shake; to agitate.

> The kingdoms were *moved.* Ps. xlvi. Jer. xlix.

10. To propose; to offer for consideration and determination; as, to *move* a resolution in a deliberative assembly.

11. To propose; to recommend.

> They are to be blamed alike who *move* and who decline war upon particular respects. *Hayward.*

12. To prompt; to incite; to instigate. Acts xvii.

MÖVE, *v. i.* To change place or posture; to stir; to pass or go in any manner or direction from one place or part of space to another. The planets *move* in their orbits; the earth *moves* on its axis; a ship *moves* at a certain rate an hour. We *move* by walking, running or turning; animals *move* by creeping, swimming or flying.

> On the green bank I sat and listened long,
> Nor till her lay was ended could I *move.* *Dryden.*

2. To have action.

> In him we live, and *move*, and have our being. Acts xvii.

3. To have the power of action.

> Every *moving* thing that liveth, shall be meat for you. Gen. ix.

4. To walk.

> He *moves* with manly grace. *Dryden.*

5. To march. The army *moved* and took a position behind a wood.

6. To tremble; to shake.

> The foundations also of the hills *moved* and were shaken, because he was wroth. Ps. xviii.

7. To change residence. Men *move* with their families from one house, town or state to another.

MÖVE, *n.* The act of moving; the act of transferring from place to place, as in chess. *Cowley.*

MÖVED, *pp.* Stirred; excited.

MÖVELESS, *a.* That cannot be moved; fixed.

> The Grecian phalanx, *moveless* as a tower. *Pope.*

MÖVEMENT, *n.* [Fr. *mouvement.*] Motion; a passing, progression, shaking, turning or flowing; any change of position in a material body; as the *movement* of an army in marching or maneuvering; the *movement* of a wheel or a machine.

2. The manner of moving.

3. Excitement; agitation; as the *movement* of the mind. *Pope.*

4. In *music*, any single strain or part having the same measure or time.

> Any change of time is a change of *movement.* *Busby.*

MO'VENT, *a.* [L. *movens.*] Moving; not quiescent. [*Little used.*] *Grew.*

MO'VENT, *n.* That which moves any thing. [*Little used.*] *Glanville.*

MÖVER, *n.* The person or thing that gives motion or impels to action. *Shak. Wilkins.*

2. He or that which moves.

3. A proposer; one that offers a proposition, or recommends any thing for consideration or adoption; as the *mover* of a resolution in a legislative body.

MÖVING, *ppr.* Causing to move or act; impelling; instigating; persuading; influencing.

2. *a.* Exciting the passions or affections; touching; pathetic; affecting; adapted to excite or affect the passions; as a *moving* address or discourse.

MÖVING, *n.* Motive; impulse. *South.*

MÖVINGLY, *adv.* In a manner to excite the passions or affect sensibility; pathetically.

> His air, his voice, his looks and honest soul,
> Speak all so *movingly* in his behalf. *Addison.*

MÖVINGNESS, *n.* The power of affecting, as the passions.

MOW, *n.* [Sax. *mowe* or *muga;* It. *mucchio*, a heap or mass; Sp. *mucho*, much; Sw. *mycken*, many, much.]

A heap, mass or pile of hay deposited in a barn.

[We never give this name to hay piled in the field or open air. The latter is called a *stack* or *rick.*]

MOW, *v. t.* To lay hay in a heap or mass in a barn, or to lay it in a suitable manner.

MŌW, *v. t.* pret. *mowed;* pp. *mowed* or *mown.* [Sax. *mawan;* D. *maaijen* or *maayen;* Sw. *meya;* Dan. *mejer;* G. *mähen.* In Sp. and Port. *mochar* is to cut off. The L. has *meto*, and the Gr. *αμαω*, to mow or reap. The last radical letter is not ascertained.]

1. To cut down with a sythe, as grass or other plants. We say, to *mow* grass.

2. To cut the grass from; as, to *mow* a meadow.

3. To cut down with speed; to cut down indiscriminately, or in great numbers or quantity. We say, a discharge of grape shot *mows* down whole ranks of men. Hence Saturn or Time is represented with a sythe, an emblem of the general and indiscriminate destruction of the human race by death.

MOW, *v. i.* To cut grass; to practice mowing; to use the sythe. Does the man *mow* well?

2. To perform the business of mowing; to cut and make grass into hay; to gather the crop of grass, or other crop.

[In America, *mow* is not applied to the cutting of wheat or rye. When these are cut with a sythe, they are said to be *cradled.* Oats and barley are sometimes mowed.]

MOW, *n.* [from *mouth.*] A wry face. *Obs.* *Shak.*

MOW, *v. i.* To make mouths. *Obs.* *Ascham.*

MOW'BURN, *v. i.* To heat and ferment in the mow, as hay when housed too green. *Mortimer.*

MOWE, *v. i.* To be able; must; may. *Obs.* *Chaucer.*

MŌWED, } **MŌWN**, } *pp.* Cut with a sythe.

2. Cleared of grass with a sythe, as land.

MŌWER, *n.* One who mows; a man dextrous in the use of the sythe.

MOW'ING, *ppr.* Putting into a mow.

MŌWING, *ppr.* Cutting down with a sythe.

MŌWING, *n.* The act of cutting with a sythe.

2. Land from which grass is cut.

MOX'A, *n.* The down of the mugwort of China; a soft lanuginous substance prepared in Japan from the young leaves of a species of Artemisia. In the eastern countries, it is used for the gout, &c. by burning it on the skin. This produces a dark colored spot, the exulceration of which is promoted by applying a little garlic. *Encyc. Coxe.*

MOYLE, *n.* A mule. [See *Mule.*]

MUCH, *a.* [Sw. *mycken*; Sp. *mucho*; It. *mucchio.* See *Mow.* The sense is probably a heap or mass, and it may be allied to *mickle*, great, Gr. μεγα.]

1. Great in quantity or amount.

Thou shalt carry *much* seed into the field, and gather but little in. Deut. xxviii.

Manasseh wrought *much* wickedness in the sight of the Lord to provoke him to anger. 2 Kings xxi.

Return with *much* riches to your tents. Josh. xxii.

2. Long in duration. How *much* time is spent in trifling amusements!

3. Many in number.

Edom came out against him with *much* people. Num. xx.

[This application of *much* is no longer used.]

MUCH, *adv.* In a great degree; by far; *qualifying adjectives of the comparative degree*; as *much* more, *much* stronger, *much* heavier, *much* more splendid, *much* higher. So we say, *much* less, *much* smaller, *much* less distinguished, *much* weaker, *much* finer.

2. To a great degree or extent; *qualifying verbs and participles.*

Jonathan, Saul's son, delighted *much* in David. 1 Sam. xix.

It is a night to be *much* observed. Ex. xii.

The soul of the people was *much* discouraged because of the way. Num. xxi.

A *much* afflicted, *much* enduring man. *Pope.*

3. Often or long.

Think *much*, speak little. *Dryden.*

4. Nearly.

All left the world *much* as they found it. *Temple.*

MUCH, *n.* A great quantity; a great deal.

He that gathered *much* had nothing over. Ex. xvi.

To whom *much* is given, of him *much* shall be required. Luke xii.

They have *much* of the poetry of Mæcenas, but little of his liberality. *Dryden.*

2. More than enough; a heavy service or burden.

He thought not *much* to clothe his enemies. *Milton.*

Who thought it *much* a man should die of love. *Dryden.*

3. An uncommon thing; something strange.

It was *much* that one who was so great a lover of peace should be happy in war. *Bacon.*

As much, an equal quantity; *used as an adjective or noun.* Return *as much* bread as you borrowed. If you borrow money, return *as much* as you receive. So we say, *twice as much, five times as much*, that is, twice or five times the quantity.

2. A certain or suitable quantity.

Then take *as much* as thy soul desireth. 1 Sam. ii.

3. To an equal degree; *adverbially.* One man loves power *as much* as another loves gold.

So much, an equal quantity or a certain quantity, *as a noun*; to an equal degree, or to a certain degree, *as an adverb.*

Of sweet cinnamon half *so much.* Ex. xxx.

In all Israel, there was none to be *so much* praised as Absalom. 2 Sam. xiv.

Too much, an excessive quantity, *as a noun*; to an excessive degree, *as an adverb.*

To make much of, to value highly; to prize or to treat with great kindness and attention. *Milner.*

2. To fondle.

Much at one, nearly of equal value, effect or influence. *Dryden.*

MUCHWHAT, *adv.* Nearly; almost. [*Not elegant.*] *Locke.*

MU'CIC, *a.* [from *mucus.*] The mucic acid is the same as the saccholactic. It is obtained from gums, &c. *Ure.*

MU'CID, *a.* [L. *mucidus*, from *muceo.*] Musty; moldy; slimy.

MU'CIDNESS, *n.* Mustiness; sliminess. *Ainsworth.*

MU'CILAGE, *n.* [Fr. from L. *mucus*, the slimy discharges from the nose; *muceo*, to grow moldy or musty; It. *mucillaggine*; Sp. *mucilago.* The L. *mucus*, in Ir. is *smug*; *smugaim*, to blow the nose. It is probably allied to Eng. *muck*; Heb. Ch. מוג or מוק, to dissolve, to putrefy. Class Mg. No. 8. 10.]

1. In *chimistry*, one of the proximate elements of vegetables. The same substance is a gum when solid, and a mucilage when in solution. *Thomson.*

Both the ingredients improve one another; for the *mucilage* adds to the lubricity of the oil, and the oil preserves the *mucilage* from inspissation. *Ray.*

Mucilage is obtained from vegetable or animal substances. *Nicholson.*

2. The liquor which moistens and lubricates the ligaments and cartilages of the articulations or joints in animal bodies. *Encyc.*

MUCILAG'INOUS, *a.* Pertaining to or secreting mucilage; as the *mucilaginous* glands. *Encyc.*

2. Slimy; ropy; moist, soft and lubricous; partaking of the nature of mucilage; as a *mucilaginous* gum. *Grew.*

MUCILAG'INOUSNESS, *n.* Sliminess; the state of being mucilaginous.

MU'CITE, *n.* A combination of a substance with mucous acid. *Parke.*

MUCK, *n.* [Sax. *meox, miox*; Dan. *mög*, dung; *mug*, mold, soil; L. *mucus*; qu. from moisture or putrefaction. In W. *mwg* is *smoke*, which may be allied to Eng. *muggy*, from dissolving, wasting. So in French *fumer*, to smoke, to dung or muck. See the Heb. and Ch. verbs under *mucilage.* In Russ. *mochu* is to moisten, and *makayu*, to dip, to soak.]

1. Dung in a moist state, or a mass of dung and putrefied vegetable matter.

With fattening *muck* besmear the roots. *Philips.*

2. Something mean, vile or filthy.

To run a muck, to run madly and attack all we meet. *Pope. Dryden.*

Running a muck, is a phrase derived from the Malays, (in whose language *amock* signifies to kill,) applied to desperate persons who intoxicate themselves with opium and then arm themselves with a dagger and attempt to kill all they meet. *Ed. Encyc.*

MUCK, *v. t.* To manure with muck. *Tusser.*

MUCK'ENDER, *n.* [Sp. *mocadero*, from *moco*, mucus; Fr. *mouchoir.*] A pocket handkerchief. [*Not used.*] *Dorset.*

MUCK'ER, *v. t.* [from *muck.*] To scrape together money by mean labor or shifts. [Not used in America.]

MUCK'ERER, *n.* A miser; a niggard. [*Not used.*] *Chaucer.*

MUCK'HEAP, } **MUCK'HILL**, } *n.* A dunghill. *Burton.*

MUCK'INESS, *n.* Filthiness; nastiness. *Johnson.*

MUCK'LE, *a.* [Sax. *mycel.*] Much. *Obs.*

MUCK'SWEAT, *n.* Profuse sweat. *Johnson.*

MUCK'WORM, *n.* A worm that lives in muck.

2. A miser; one who scrapes together money by mean labor and devices. *Bunyan.*

MUCK'Y, *a.* Filthy; nasty. *Spenser.*

MUCOSO-SACCHARINE, *a.* Partaking of the qualities of mucilage and sugar. *Fourcroy.*

MU'COUS, *a.* [See *Mucus.*] Pertaining to mucus or resembling it; slimy, ropy and lubricous; as a *mucous* substance.

2. Secreting a slimy substance; as the *mucous* membrane.

The mucous membrane lines all the cavities of the body which open externally, and secretes the fluid called *mucus.* *Bichat.*

MU'COUSNESS, *n.* The state of being mucous; sliminess.

MU'CRONATE, } **MU'CRONATED**, } *a.* [L. *mucronatus*, from *mucro*, a point.] Narrowed to a point; terminating in a point. *Woodward.*

MU'CULENT, *a.* [L. *muculentus.*] Slimy; moist and moderately viscous.

MU'CUS, *n.* [L. See *Mucilage* and *Muck.*]

1. A viscid fluid secreted by the mucous membrane, which it serves to moisten and defend. It covers the lining membranes of all the cavities which open externally, such as those of the mouth, nose, lungs, intestinal canal, urinary passages, &c. It differs from gelatine. *Parr. Ure.*

In the action of chewing, the *mucus* mixeth with the aliment. *Arbuthnot.*

2. This term has also been applied to other animal fluids of a viscid quality, as the synovial fluid, which lubricates the cavities of the joints.

MUD, *n.* [D. *modder*; G. *moder.* See *Mother.* Εχ του αυτου συμπλοχης του πνευματος εγενετο μωτ. Τουτο τινες φασιν ιλυν, οιδε υδατωδους μιξεως σηψιν. *Mot*, id est, *mod*; Phœnices ita scribebant. Bochart, Phœn. Lib. 2. Chap. 2.

This is said to be a fragment of Sanchoniathon's Phenician history, translated by Philo and preserved by Eusebius. This Phenician word *mod*, μωτ, rendered in Gr. ιλυς, is precisely the English *mud*, the matter, material or substance of which, according to the ancients, all things were formed. See Castel. Col. 2010, and the word *mother.* Plutarch, de Iside, says the Egyptians called Isis *muth*, that is, mother. This is a remarkable fact, and proves beyond controversy the common origin of the Phenician, Celtic and Teutonic nations. *Mud* may perhaps be named from wetness, and be connected with L. *madeo*, Gr. μυδαω, W. *mwydaw*, to wet.]

Moist and soft earth of any kind, such as is found in marshes and swamps, at the bottom of rivers and ponds, or in highways after rain.

MUD, *v. t.* To bury in mud or slime. *Shak.*

2. To make turbid or foul with dirt; to stir the sediment in liquors. *Glanville.*

MUD'DILY, *adv.* [from *muddy*.] Turbidly; with foul mixture.

Lucilius—writ loosely and *muddily*. *Dryden.*

MUD'DINESS, *n.* Turbidness; foulness caused by mud, dirt or sediment; as the *muddiness* of a stream. *Addison.*

MUD'DLE, *v. t.* [from *mud*.] To make foul, turbid or muddy, as water.

He did ill to *muddle* the water. *L'Estrange.*

2. To intoxicate partially; to cloud or stupefy, particularly with liquor.

He was often drunk, always *muddled*. *Arbuthnot.*

Epicurus seems to have had his brains *muddled*. *Bentley.*

MUD'DLED, *pp.* Made turbid; half drunk; stupefied.

MUD'DLING, *ppr.* Making foul with dirt or dregs; making half drunk; stupefying.

MUD'DY, *a.* [from *mud*.] Foul with dirt or fine earthy particles; turbid, as water or other fluids; as a *muddy* stream. Water running on fine clay always appears *muddy*.

2. Containing mud; as a *muddy* ditch; a *muddy* road. *Shak.*

3. Dirty; dashed, soiled or besmeared with mud; as *muddy* boots.

4. Consisting of mud or earth; gross; impure; as this *muddy* vesture of decay. *Shak.*

5. Dark; of the color of mud; as *muddy* cheeks. *Swift.*

6. Cloudy in mind; dull; heavy; stupid.

Dost think I am so *muddy?* *Shak.*

MUD'DY, *v. t.* To soil with mud; to dirty.

2. To cloud; to make dull or heavy. *Grew.*

MUDDY-HEADED, *a.* Having a dull understanding.

MUD'-FISH, *n.* A fish, a species of the cyprinus kind. *Dict. Nat. Hist.*

MUD'-SILL, *n.* In bridges, the sill that is laid at the bottom of a river, lake, &c. [See *Sill*.]

MUD'-SUCKER, *n.* An aquatic fowl. *Derham.*

MUD'-WALL, *n.* A wall composed of mud, or of materials laid in mud without mortar. *South.*

2. A bird, the apiaster. *Ainsworth.*

MUD'-WALLED, *a.* Having a mud wall. *Prior.*

MUD'WŎRT, *n.* A species of Limosella, the least water plantain. *Lee.*

MUE. [See *Mew*.]

MUFF, *n.* [Dan. *muff* or *muffe*; D. *mof*; G. *muff*; Fr. *moufle*, mittens; Sp. *muflas*, thick gloves.]

A warm cover for the hands, usually made of fur or dressed skins. *Locke. Dryden.*

MUF'FIN, *n.* A delicate or light cake.

MUF'FLE, *v. t.* [D. *moffelen*; G. *muffeln*; It. *camuffare*, to disguise or mask.]

1. To cover from the weather by cloth, fur or any garment; to cover close, particularly the neck and face.

You must be *muffled* up like ladies. *Dryden.*

The face lies *muffled* up within the garment. *Addison.*

2. To blindfold.

Alas! that love whose view is *muffled* still— *Shak.*

He *muffled* with a cloud his mournful eyes. *Dryden.*

3. To cover; to conceal; to involve.

They were in former ages *muffled* in darkness and superstition. *Arbuthnot.*

4. In *seamanship*, to put matting or other soft substance round an oar, to prevent its making a noise.

5. To wind something round the strings of a drum to prevent a sharp sound, or to render the sound grave and solemn.

MUF'FLE, *v. i.* To mutter; to speak indistinctly or without clear articulation. *Holder.*

MUF'FLE, *n.* [Sp. *mufla*.] In *chimistry*, a vessel in the shape of an oblong arch or vault, closed behind by a semi-circular plane, the floor of which is a rectangular plane; or in other words, a little oven to be placed in a furnace, and under which small cupels and crucibles are placed, in which substances are subjected to heat without coming in contact with fuel, smoke or ashes; used in metallurgic operations. *Fourcroy. Encyc.*

MUF'FLED, *pp.* Covered closely, especially about the face; involved; blindfolded.

MUF'FLER, *n.* A cover for the face; a part of female dress. *Shak. Arbuthnot.*

MUF'FLING, *ppr.* Covering closely, especially about the face; wrapping close; involving; blindfolding.

MUF'FLON, *n.* The wild sheep or musmon.

MUF'TI, *n.* The high priest or chief of the ecclesiastical order among the Mohammedans.

MUG, *n.* [I know not whence derived.] A kind of cup from which liquors are drank. In America, the word is applied chiefly or solely to an earthen cup.

MUG'GARD, *a.* [See *Muggy*.] Sullen; displeased. [*Not in use.*]

MUG'GENT, *n.* A species of wild fresh water duck. *Dict. Nat. Hist.*

MUG'GISH, } *a.* [W. *mwcan*, a cloud of fog;
MUG'GY, } *mwg*, smoke; or from the root of *muck*.]

1. Moist; damp; moldy; as *muggy* straw. *Mortimer.*

2. Moist; damp; close; warm and unelastic; as *muggy* air. [*This is the principal use of the word in America.*]

MUG'HOUSE, *n.* [from *mug*.] An alehouse. *Tickel.*

MU'ĠIENT, *a.* [L. *mugio*, to bellow.] Lowing; bellowing. [*Not used.*] *Brown.*

MU'ĠIL, *n.* [L.] The mullet, a genus of fishes of the order of abdominals.

MUG'WEED, *n.* A plant of the genus Valantia.

MUG'WŎRT, *n.* [Sax. *mugwyrt*.] A plant of the genus Artemisia.

MULAT'TO, *n.* [Sp. *mulato*, that is, muled, of a mixed breed, from *mulo*, L. *mulus*, a mule; Fr. *mulatre*.]

A person that is the offspring of a negress by a white man, or of a white woman by a negro.

MUL'BERRY, *n.* [Sw. *mulbär*; G. *maulbeere*.]

The berry or fruit of a tree of the genus Morus.

MUL'BERRY-TREE, *n.* The tree which produces the mulberry.

MULCH, *n.* [Heb. מלח, to dissolve.] Half rotten straw. *Bailey.*

MULCT, *n.* [L. *mulcta* or *multa*.] A fine imposed on a person guilty of some offense or misdemeanor, usually a pecuniary fine.

MULCT, *v. t.* [L. *mulcto*; Fr. *mulcter*.] To fine; to punish for an offense or misdemeanor by imposing a pecuniary fine. *Bacon.*

MULCT'UARY, *a.* Imposing a pecuniary penalty. *Overbury.*

MULE, *n.* [Sp. It. *mulo*; L. *mulus*; Sax. *mul*; D. *muil* or *muilezel*; G. *maulesel*; Sw. *mulåsne*; Dan. *mule*; Fr. *id.*; Arm. *mules*; Ir. *muile*; W. *mul*. The latter signifies a mule, and bashful, simple.]

1. A quadruped of a mongrel breed, usually generated between an ass and a mare, sometimes between a horse and a she-ass. But the name is applied to any animal produced by a mixture of different species. *Encyc.*

2. A plant or vegetable produced by impregnating the pistil of one species of plant with the farin or fecundating dust of another. This is called also a *hybrid*. *Encyc. Martyn.*

MULETEE'R, *n.* [It. *mulattiere*; Fr. *muletier*.]

A mule-driver.

MU'LE-WŎRT, *n.* A plant of the genus Hemionitis.

MULIEB'RITY, *n.* [from L. *muliebris*, from *mulier*, a woman.]

Womanhood; the state of being a woman; a state in females corresponding to virility in man; also, effeminacy; softness.

MU'LIER, *n.* [L.] In *law*, lawful issue born in wedlock though begotten before. *Encyc.*

MU'LISH, *a.* Like a mule; sullen; stubborn.

MULL, *v. t.* [qu. L. *mollio*, to soften, or W. *mwll*, warm, or Sp. *mullir*, to beat.]

1. To soften; or to heat, sweeten and enrich with spices; as, to *mull* wine.

Drink new cider, *mull'd* with ginger warm. *Gay.*

2. To dispirit or deaden. *Shak.*

MULL, *n.* In *Scottish*, a snuff-box, made of the small end of a horn. *Obs.* *Cumberland.*

MULL, *n.* Dust. [*Not in use.*] *Gower.*

MUL'LEN, *n.* [Old Fr. *molene*; probably so named from the root of L. *mollis*, soft. So in German, *wollkraut*, wool-plant.]

A plant of the genus Verbascum.

MUL'LER, *n.* [Fr. *moliere*, *molette*; L. *molaris*, from *mola*, a mill-stone.]

1. A stone held in the hand with which colors and other matters are ground on another stone; used by painters and apothecaries. *Bailey. Encyc.*

2. An instrument used by glass grinders, being a piece of wood with the piece of glass to be ground cemented to one end, either convex in a bason, or concave in a sphere or bowl. *Encyc.*

MUL'LET, *n.* [Fr. *mulet*, a mullet, and a great mule; Gr. μυλλος; L. *mullus.*]
A fish of the genus Mugil. The lips are membranaceous; the inferior one carinated inwards; it has no teeth, and the body is of a whitish color. This fish frequents the shore and roots in the sand like a hog. It is an excellent fish for the table. *Encyc.*

MUL'LIGRUBS, *n.* A twisting of the intestines; sullenness. [A low word.]

MUL'LION, *n.* [Fr. *moulure.*] A division in a window frame; a bar.

MUL'LION, *v. t.* To shape into divisions. *Shak.*

MUL'LOCK, *n.* Rubbish.

MULSE, *n.* [L. *mulsus.*] Wine boiled and mingled with honey.

MULTAN'GULAR, *a.* [L. *multus*, many, and *angulus*, angle; Basque, *mola*, a multitude; *multsa*, much.]
Having many angles; polygonal. *Martyn.*

MULTAN'GULARLY, *adv.* With many angles or corners. *Grew.*

MULTIEAP'SULAR, *a.* [L. *multus*, many, and *capsula*, a chest.]
In *botany*, having many capsules. *Martyn.*

MULTIEA'VOUS, *a.* [L. *multus*, many, and *cavus*, hollow.]
Having many holes or cavities. *Dict.*

MULTIFA'RIOUS, *a.* [L. *multifarius.* Qu. *varius.*]
Having great multiplicity; having great diversity or variety; as *multifarious* artifice. *More.*

MULTIFA'RIOUSLY, *adv.* With great multiplicity and diversity; with great variety of modes and relations. *Bentley.*

MULTIFA'RIOUSNESS, *n.* Multiplied diversity. *Norris.*

MUL'TIFID, *a.* [L. *multifidus*; *multus*, many, and *findo*, to divide.]
Having many divisions; many-cleft; divided into several parts by linear sinuses and straight margins; as a *multifid* leaf or corol. *Martyn.*

MULTIF'LOROUS, *a.* [L. *multus*, many, and *flos*, flower.]
Many-flowered; having many flowers. *Martyn.*

MUL'TIFORM, *a.* [L. *multiformis*; *multus*, many, and *forma*, form.]
Having many forms, shapes or appearances; as the *multiform* operations of the air-pump. *Watts.*

MULTIFORM'ITY, *n.* Diversity of forms; variety of shapes or appearances in the same thing. *Johnson.*

MULTIGEN'EROUS, *a.* [L. *multigenus*; *multus*, many, and *genus*, kind.]
Having many kinds. *Dict.*

MULTIJU'GOUS, *a.* [L. *multus*, many, and *jugum*, a yoke, a pair.]
Consisting of many pairs.

MULTILAT'ERAL, *a.* [L *multus*, many, and *latus*, side.]
Having many sides. A *multilateral* figure must also be multangular.

MULTILIN'EAL, *a.* Having many lines.

MULTILOE'ULAR, *a.* [L. *multus*, many, and *loculus*, a cell.]
Having many cells; as a *multilocular* pericarp. *Martyn.*

MULTIL'OQUOUS, *a.* [L. *multus*, many, and *loquor*, to speak.]
Speaking much; very talkative; loquacious. *Dict.*

MULTINO'MIAL, **MULTINOM'INAL**, *a.* [L. *multus*, many, and *nomen*, name.]
Having many names or terms. *Dict.*

MULTIP'AROUS, *a.* [L. *multus*, many, and *pario*, to bear.]
Producing many at a birth. A serpent is a *multiparous* animal.

MULTIP'ARTITE, *a.* [L. *multus*, many, and *partitus*, divided.]
Divided into many parts; having several parts.

MUL'TIPED, *n.* [L. *multus*, many, and *pes*, foot.]
An insect that has many feet.

MUL'TIPED, *a.* Having many feet.

MUL'TIPLE, *a.* [L. *multiplex*; *multus*, many, and *plico*, to fold.]
Containing many times.

MUL'TIPLE, *n.* In *arithmetic*, a *common multiple* of two or more numbers contains each of them a certain number of times exactly; thus 24 is a common multiple of 3 and 4. But the *least common multiple*, is the least number which will do this; thus 12 is the least common multiple of 3 and 4.

MUL'TIPLEX, *a.* [L.] Many-fold; having petals lying over each other in folds. *Martyn.*

MUL'TIPLIABLE, *a.* [Fr. See *Multiply.*] That may be multiplied.

MUL'TIPLIABLENESS, *n.* Capacity of being multiplied.

MUL'TIPLIEABLE, *a.* That may be multiplied.

MULTIPLIEAND', *n.* [L. *multiplicandus.* See *Multiply.*]
In *arithmetic*, the number to be multiplied by another, which is called the multiplier.

MUL'TIPLIEATE, *a.* [L. *multiplicatus.*]
1. Consisting of many, or more than one. *Derham.*
2. A *multiplicate* flower is a sort of luxuriant flower, having the corol multiplied so far as to exclude only some of the stamens. *Martyn.*

MULTIPLIEA'TION, *n.* [L. *multiplicatio.*]
1. The act of multiplying or of increasing number; as the *multiplication* of the human species by natural generation.
2. In *arithmetic*, a rule or operation by which any given number may be increased according to any number of times proposed. Thus 10 multiplied by 5 is increased to 50.

MUL'TIPLIEATIVE, *a.* Tending to multiply; having the power to multiply or increase numbers. *Med. Repos.*

MULTIPLIEA'TOR, *n.* The number by which another number is multiplied; a multiplier.

MULTIPLIC'ITY, *n.* [Fr. *multiplicité*, from L. *multiplex.*]
1. A state of being many; as a *multiplicity* of thoughts or objects.
2. Many of the same kind. The pagans of antiquity had a *multiplicity* of deities.

MUL'TIPLIED, *pp.* Increased in numbers.
2. Numerous; often repeated; as *multiplied* aggressions.

MUL'TIPLIER, *n.* One who multiplies, or increases number.
2. The number in arithmetic by which another is multiplied; the multiplicator.

MUL'TIPLȲ, *v. t.* [L. *multiplico*; *multus*, many, and *plico*, to fold or double, Gr. πλεκω, W. *plygu*, Fr. *plier*, *multiplier.*]
1. To increase in number; to make more by natural generation or production, or by addition; as, to *multiply* men, horses or other animals; to *multiply* evils.

> I will *multiply* my signs and wonders in Egypt. Ex. vii.

> Impunity will *multiply* motives to disobedience. *Ames.*

2. In *arithmetic*, to increase any given number as many times as there are units in any other given number. Thus 7×8=56, that is, 7 *multiplied* by 8 produces the number 56.

MUL'TIPLȲ, *v. i.* To grow or increase in number.

> Be fruitful and *multiply*. Gen. i.

> When men began to *multiply* on the face of the earth. Gen. vi.

2. To increase in extent; to extend; to spread.

> The word of God grew and *multiplied*. Acts xii.

MUL'TIPLȲING, *ppr.* Increasing in number.
2. Growing or becoming numerous.

MULTIP'OTENT, *a.* [L. *multipotens*; *multus*, many, much, and *potens*, powerful.]
Having manifold power, or power to do many things; as Jove *multipotent*. *Shak.*

MULTIPRES'ENCE, *n.* [L. *multus*, many, and *præsentia*, presence.]
The power or act of being present in many places at once, or in more places than one. *Hall.*

MULTISIL'IQUOUS, *a.* [L. *multus*, many, and *siliqua*, a pod.]
Having many pods or seed-vessels. *Bailey.*

MULTIS'ONOUS, *a.* [L. *multus*, many, and *sonus*, sound.]
Having many sounds, or sounding much. *Bailey.*

MULTISYL'LABLE, *n.* A word of many syllables; a polysyllable. [*The latter is mostly used.*]

MUL'TITUDE, *n.* [Fr. from L. *multitudo*, from *multus*, many.]
1. The state of being many; a great number.
2. A number collectively; the sum of many. *Hale.*
3. A great number, indefinitely.

> It is a fault in a *multitude* of preachers, that they utterly neglect method in their harangues. *Watts.*

4. A crowd or throng; the populace; applied to the populace when assembled in great numbers, and to the mass of men without reference to an assemblage.

> He the vast hissing *multitude* admires. *Addison.*

> The *multitude* have always been credulous, and the few artful. *J. Adams.*

MULTITU'DINOUS, *a.* Consisting of a multitude or great number.
2. Having the appearance of a multitude; as the *multitudinous* sea. *Shak.*
3. Manifold; as the *multitudinous* tongue. *Shak.*

MULTIV'AGANT, **MULTIV'AGOUS**, *a.* [L. *multivagus.*] Wandering much. [*Not used.*] *Dict.*

MUL'TIVALVE, *n.* [L. *multus*, many, and *valvæ*, valves, folding doors.]

An animal which has a shell of many valves. *Zoology.*

MUL'TIVALVE, } *a.* Having many
MULTIVALV'ULAR, } valves.

MULTIV'ERSANT, *a.* [L. *multus*, many, and *verto*, to form.]
Protean; turning into many shapes; assuming many forms. *Journ. of Science.*

MULTIV'IOUS, *a.* [L. *multus*, many, and *via*, way.]
Having many ways or roads. [*Little used.*] *Dict.*

MULTOC'ULAR, *a.* [L. *multus*, many, and *oculus*, eye.]
Having many eyes, or more eyes than two. *Derham.*

MUL'TURE, *n.* [L. *molitura*, a grinding. See *Mill.*]
1. In *Scots law*, the toll or emolument given to the proprietor of a mill for grinding corn. *Encyc.*
2. A grist or grinding.

MUM, *a.* [See *Mumble*, *Mumm*, and *Mummery.*]
1. Silent; not speaking.

The citizens are *mum*; say not a word. *Shak.*

2. As an exclamation or command, be silent; hush.

Mum then, and no more proceed. *Shak.*

3. As a noun, silence. *Hudibras.*

MUM, *n.* [G. Dan. *mumme*; D. *mom.*] A species of malt liquor much used in Germany. It is made of the malt of wheat, seven bushels, with one bushel of oat meal and a bushel of ground beans, or in the same proportion. This is brewed with 63 gallons of water, and boiled till one third is evaporated. *Encyc.*

MUM'-CHANCE, *n.* A game of hazard with dice. [*Local.*]
2. A fool. [*Local.*]

MUM'BLE, *v. i.* [G. *mummeln*; D. *mommelen, mompelen*; Sw. *mumla*; Dan. *mumler.* This word seems to be connected with *mum*, in the sense of closeness of the lips.]
1. To mutter; to speak with the lips or other organs partly closed, so as to render the sounds inarticulate and imperfect; to utter words with a grumbling tone.

Peace, you *mumbling* fool. *Shak.*

—A wrinkled hag, with age grown double,
Picking dry sticks and *mumbling* to herself. *Otway.*

2. To chew or bite softly; to eat with the lips close. *Dryden.*

MUM'BLE, *v. t.* To utter with a low inarticulate voice.

He with *mumbled* prayers atones the deity. *Dryden.*

2. To mouth gently, or to eat with a muttering sound. *Pope.*
3. To suppress or utter imperfectly. *Dryden.*

MUM'BLED, *pp.* Uttered with a low inarticulate voice; chewed softly or with a low muttering sound.

MUM'BLER, *n.* One that speaks with a low inarticulate voice.

MUM'BLING, *ppr.* Uttering with a low inarticulate voice; chewing softly or with a grumbling sound.

MUM'BLINGLY, *adv.* With a low inarticulate utterance. [*Mumble* and *mutter* are not always synonymous; *mutter* often expresses peevishness, which *mumble* does not.]

MUMM, *v. t.* [Dan. *mumme*, a mask; D. *mommen*, to mask; G. *mumme*, a mask or muffle; *mummeln*, to mask, to mumble; Fr. *mummer*; Sw. *förmumma*, to personate; probably allied to the Gr. μωμος, Momus, the deity of sport and ridicule, a buffoon; for in Rabbinic, this word is used for a mask. Buxt. 1219. The primary sense of this word and *mum* is evidently to close, shut or cover.]
To mask; to sport or make diversion in a mask or disguise. *Hubberd's Tale.*

MUM'MER, *n.* One who masks himself and makes diversion in disguise; originally, one who made sport by gestures without speaking.

Jugglers and dancers, anticks, *mummers.* *Milton.*

MUM'MERY, *n.* [Fr. *momerie*; Sp. *momeria.* See *Mumm.*]
1. Masking; sport; diversion; frolicking in masks; low contemptible amusement; buffoonery.

Your fathers
Disdained the *mummery* of foreign strollers. *Fenton.*

2. Farcical show; hypocritical disguise and parade to delude vulgar minds.

MUM'MIFY, *v. t.* [infra.] To make into a mummy. *Journ. of Science.*

MUM'MY, *n.* [It. *mummia*; Sp. Port. *momia.* In Arabic, موميا momia, is wax, bees-wax, and a mummy; Pers. موم moum, wax. A substance thus called is found in Corasan and in the deserts of Kerman, in Persia, and according to Chardin, it is a gum distilling from rocks. It seems to have some resemblance to asphalt. Qu. the *pissasphaltus* of Pliny.]
1. A dead human body embalmed and dried after the Egyptian manner; a name perhaps given to it from the substance used in preserving it. There are two kinds of mummies. The first are bodies dried by the heat of the sun. Such are found in the sands of Libya. The other kind is taken from the catacombs in Egypt. *Encyc.*
2. The name of two substances prepared for medicinal use, which according to Hill are, the one, the dried flesh of human bodies embalmed with myrrh and spice; the other, a liquor running from such mummies when newly prepared, or when affected by great heat and damps. This is preserved in vials, and if suffered to dry, becomes solid. But it is alledged that the first sort consists of pieces of the flesh of executed criminals, or other flesh filled with bitumen and other ingredients. But see the opinion of Chardin, supra.
3. There are found in Poland natural mummies lying in caverns, supposed to be the remains of persons who in time of war took refuge in caves, but being discovered were suffocated by their enemies. These bodies are dried, with the flesh and skin shrunk almost close to the bones, and are of a blackish color. *Encyc.*
4. Among gardeners, a sort of wax used in grafting and planting trees. *Chambers.*

To beat to a mummy, to beat soundly, or to a senseless mass.

MUM'MY-CHOG, *n.* A small fish of the carp kind. *Pennant.*

MUMP, *v. t.* [D. *mompen.* See *Mum* and *Mumble.*]
1. To nibble; to bite quick; to chew with continued motion; as a *mumping* squirrel. *Otway.*
2. To talk loud and quick.
3. To go begging. *Ainsworth.*
4. To deceive; to cheat.

MUMP'ER, *n.* A beggar. *Johnson.*

MUMP'ING, *n.* Begging tricks; foolish tricks; mockery.

MUMP'ISH, *a.* Dull; heavy; sullen; sour.

MUMPS, *n.* [See *Mum*, *Mumble*, *Mumm.*]
1. Sullenness; silent displeasure. [*Little used.*] *Skinner.*
2. A disease, the *cynanche parotidæa*, a swelling of the parotid glands. *Coxe.*

MUNCH, *v. t.* [perhaps Fr. *manger*, or from the same root.]
To chew by great mouthfuls. [*Vulgar.*] *Shak.*

MUNCH, *v. i.* To chew eagerly by great mouthfuls. [*Vulgar.*] *Dryden.*

MUNCH'ER, *n.* One that munches. *Johnson.*

MUND, Sax. *mund*, protection, patronage, peace, is found in old laws; as *mundbrece*, that is, a *breaking* or violation of the peace. It is retained in names, as in *Edmund*, Sax. *eadmund*, happy peace, as in Greek *Irenæus, Hesychius.* *Gibson.*

MUN'DANE, *a.* [L. *mundanus*, from *mundus*, the world.]
Belonging to the world; as *mundane* sphere; *mundane* space. *Bentley.*

MUNDAN'ITY, *n.* Worldliness. [*Not used.*] *Mountague.*

MUNDA'TION, *n.* [L. *mundus*, clean.] The act of cleansing. [*Not used.*]

MUN'DATORY, *a.* [L. *mundo*, to cleanse.] Cleansing; having power to cleanse. [*Little used.*]

MUN'DIC, *n.* A kind of marcasite; a mineral substance, so called from its shining appearance. *Obs.* *Woodward.*

MUNDIFICA'TION, *n.* [L. *mundus*, clean, and *facio*, to make.]
The act or operation of cleansing any body from dross or extraneous matter. *Quincy.*

MUNDIF'ICATIVE, *a.* Cleansing; having the power to cleanse. *Wiseman.*

MUNDIF'ICATIVE, *n.* A medicine that has the quality of cleansing.

MUN'DIFY, *v. t.* [L. *mundus*, clean, and *facio*, to make.]
To cleanse. [*Little used.*] *Harvey.*

MU'NERARY, *a.* [L. *munus*, a gift.] Having the nature of a gift. [*Little used.*] *Johnson.*

MUNERATE, MUNERATION. [*Not used.* See *Remunerate.*]

MUN'GREL, *n.* [See *Mongrel.*] An animal generated between different kinds, as a dog.

MUN'GREL, *a.* Generated between different kinds; degenerate. *Shak. Dryden.*

MUNIC'IPAL, *a.* [Fr. from L. *municipalis*, from *municeps*, a person who enjoys the rights of a free citizen; *munus*, office, duty, and *capio*, to take.]

1. Pertaining to a corporation or city; as *municipal* rights; *municipal* officers.
2. Pertaining to a state, kingdom or nation.

Municipal law is properly defined to be a rule of civil conduct prescribed by the supreme power in a state— *Blackstone.*

Municipal, as used by the Romans, originally designated that which pertained to a *municipium*, a free city or town. It still retains this limited sense; but we have extended it to what belongs to a state or nation, as a distinct, independent body. *Municipal* law or regulation respects solely the citizens of a state, and is thus distinguished from *commercial* law, *political* law, and the *law of nations.*

MUNICIPAL'ITY, *n.* In France, a certain district or division of the country; also, its inhabitants. *Burke.*

MUNIF'ICENCE, *n.* [Fr. from L. *munificentia; munus*, a gift or favor, and *facio*, to make.]

1. A giving or bestowing liberally; bounty; liberality. To constitute *munificence*, the act of conferring must be free, and proceed from generous motives.

A state of poverty obscures all the virtues of liberality and *munificence.* *Addison.*

2. In Spenser, fortification or strength. [L. *munio*, to fortify.] [*Not used.*]

MUNIF'ICENT, *a.* Liberal in giving or bestowing; generous; as a *munificent* benefactor or patron. *Atterbury.*

MUNIF'ICENTLY, *adv.* Liberally; generously.

MU'NIMENT, *n.* [L. *munimentum*, from *munio*, to fortify.]

1. A fortification of any kind; a strong hold; a place of defense.
2. Support; defense. *Shak.*
3. Record; a writing by which claims and rights are defended or maintained. *Termes de la ley. Johnson's Rep.*

MU'NITE, *v. t.* To fortify. [*Not in use.*] *Bacon.*

MUNI''TION, *n.* [Fr. from L. *munitio*, from *munio*, to fortify. The primary sense is that which is set or fixed, or that which defends, drives back or hinders. Indeed, both senses may be from the same root, Heb. Ch. מנע, Ar. مَنَعَ, or Heb. אמן amen. Class Mn. No. 10. 12.]

1. Fortification. *Obs.* *Hale.*
2. Ammunition; whatever materials are used in war for defense, or for annoying an enemy. The word includes guns of all kinds, mortars, &c. and their loading.
3. Provisions of a garrison or fortress, or for ships of war, and in general for an army; stores of all kinds for a fort, an army or navy.

Munition-ships, ships which convey military and naval stores of any kind, and attend or follow a fleet to supply ships of war.

MU'NITY, *n.* Freedom; security. [*Not used.*] [See *Immunity.*]

MUNNION, *n. mun'yon.* [See *Munition.*] An upright piece of timber which separates the several lights in a window-frame. [See *Mullion.*] *Moxon.*

MUNS, MUNDS, } *n.* The mouth. [*Vulgar.*]

MU'RAGE, *n.* [L. *murus*, a wall.] Money paid for keeping walls in repair. *Termes de la ley. Johnson.*

MU'RAL, *a.* [L. *muralis*, from *murus*, a wall; W. *mur*, that which is fixed or firm; *muriaw*, to fix or establish. It seems to belong to the root of *moor*, to make fast, as a ship.]

1. Pertaining to a wall.

—Soon repaired her *mural* breach. *Milton.*

2. Resembling a wall; perpendicular or steep; as a *mural* precipice.

Mural crown, among the ancient Romans, a golden crown or circle of gold, indented and embattled, bestowed on him who first mounted the wall of a besieged place and there lodged a standard. *Encyc.*

MUR'DER, *n.* [Sax. *morther*, from *morth*, death; *myrthian*, to murder; D. *moord;* G. Dan. Sw. *mord;* Ir. *marbh;* L. *mors;* Sp. *muerte;* It. *morte;* Pehlavi, *murdan*, to die; Sans. *marana;* W. *marw*, to die, which seems to be from *marth*, lying flat or plain; *marthu*, to flatten, to deaden. If this is the sense, the primary idea is to fail or fall, or to beat down. The old orthography, *murther*, is obsolete.]

1. The act of unlawfully killing a human being with premeditated malice, by a person of sound mind. To constitute murder in law, the person killing another must be of sound mind or in possession of his reason, and the act must be done with malice prepense, aforethought or premeditated; but malice may be implied, as well as express. *Coke. Blackstone*
2. An outcry, when life is in danger.

MUR'DER, *v. t.* [Sax. *myrthian;* D. *moorden;* G. *morden;* Sw. *mörda.*]

1. To kill a human being with premeditated malice. [See the Noun.]
2. To destroy; to put an end to.

Canst thou *murder* thy breath in middle of a word? *Shak.*

MUR'DERED, *pp.* Slain with malice prepense.

MUR'DERER, *n.* A person who in possession of his reason, unlawfully kills a human being with premeditated malice.

2. A small piece of ordnance.

MUR'DERESS, *n.* A female who commits murder. *Dryden.*

MUR'DERING, *ppr.* Killing a human being with malice premeditated.

MUR'DEROUS, *a.* Guilty of murder; as the *murderous* king. *Milton.*

2. Consisting in murder; done with murder; bloody; cruel; as *murderous* rapine.
3. Bloody; sanguinary; committing murder; as *murderous* tyranny.
4. Premeditating murder; as *murderous* intent or design.

MUR'DEROUSLY, *adv.* In a murderous or cruel manner.

MURE, *n.* [L. *murus.*] A wall. [*Not used.*] *Shak.*

MURE, *v. t.* [Fr. *murer.*] To inclose in walls; to wall. *Knolles.*

[But *immure* is chiefly used.]

MU'RIACITE, *n.* [See *Muriate.*] A stone composed of salt, sand and gypsum.

MU'RIATE, *n.* [L. *muria, muries*, salt water, brine; *amarus*, bitter; Heb. Ch. Syr. Sam. Eth. Ar. מרר, to be bitter. Class Mr. No. 7.]

A salt formed by muriatic acid combined with a base.

MU'RIATED, *a.* Combined with muriatic acid. *Kirwan.*

2. Put in brine. *Evelyn.*

MURIAT'IC, *a.* Having the nature of brine or salt water; pertaining to sea salt. The *muriatic* acid is the acid of marine salt.

MURIATIF'EROUS, *a.* Producing muriatic substances or salt.

MURICAL'CITE, *n.* Rhomb-spar. *Ure.*

MU'RICATED, *a.* [L. *muricatus*, from *murex*, the point of a rock.]

1. Formed with sharp points; full of sharp points or prickles.
2. In *botany*, having the surface covered with sharp points, or armed with prickles. *Lee. Martyn.*

MU'RICITE, *n.* Fossil remains of the murex, a genus of shells.

MU'RINE, *a.* [L. *murinus*, from *mus, muris*, a mouse.] Pertaining to a mouse or to mice.

MURK, *n.* [Sw. *mörker;* Dan. *mörkhed;* Russ. *mrak.*] Darkness. [*Little used.*] *Shak.*

MURK'Y, *a.* [Dan. *mörk;* Sw. *mörk*, dark, obscure; *mörka*, to darken; Russ. *merknu*, to obscure; allied perhaps to *Moor*, an African; Gr. αμαυρος.]

Dark; obscure; gloomy.

A *murky* storm deep lowering o'er our heads. *Addison.*

MUR'MUR, *n.* [L. See the Verb.] A low sound continued or continually repeated, as that of a stream running in a stony channel, or that of flame.

Black melancholy sits,
Deepens the *murmur* of the falling floods,
And breathes a browner horror on the woods. *Pope.*

2. A complaint half suppressed, or uttered in a low, muttering voice.

Some discontents there are, some idle *murmurs.* *Dryden.*

MUR'MUR, *v. i.* [L. *murmuro;* Gr. μορμυρω; Fr. *murmurer;* Arm. *murmuli;* Sp. Port. *murmurar;* It. *mormorare.* This seems to be a duplication of the root, which is retained in the D. *morren*, G. *murren*, Sw. *murra*, Dan. *murrer*, to mutter, growl or murmur; Sp. *morro*, purring, as a cat; Sw. *morr*, a grumbling; Ar. مرمر. Class Mr. No. 7. It seems also to be connected with *mourn*, Sax. *murnan, murcnian*, to murmur.]

1. To make a low continued noise, like the hum of bees, a stream of water, rolling waves, or like the wind in a forest; as the *murmuring* surge. *Shak.*

The forests *murmur* and the surges roar. *Pope.*

2. To grumble; to complain; to utter complaints in a low, half articulated voice; to utter sullen discontent; with *at*, before the thing which is the cause of discontent; as, *murmur* not *at* sickness; or with *at* or *against*, before the active agent which produces the evil.

The Jews *murmured at* him. John vi.

The people *murmured against* Moses. Ex. xiii.

MUR'MURER, *n.* One who murmurs; one who complains sullenly; a grumbler.

MUR'MURING, *ppr.* Uttering complaints in a low voice or sullen manner; grumbling; complaining.

MUR'MURINGLY, *adv.* With a low sound; with complaints.

MUR'MUROUS, *a.* Exciting murmur or complaint.

MURR, *n.* A catarrh. [*Not in use.*] *Gascoigne.*

MURRAIN, *n. mur'rin.* [Sp. *morrina*, a disease among cattle, sadness; Port. *morrinha*; It. *moria*; *morire*, Port. *morrêr*, Sp. *morir*, L. *morior*, to die.]

An infectious and fatal disease among cattle. Ex. ix. *Bacon. Garth.*

MUR'RE, *n.* A kind of bird. *Carew.*

MUR'REY, *a.* [from the root of *Moor*, an African.] Of a dark red color. *Bacon. Boyle.*

MUR'RHINE, *a.* [L. *murrhinus.*] An epithet given to a delicate kind of ware or porcelain brought from the east; Pliny says from Carmania, now Kerman, in Persia. *Encyc. Pinkerton.*

MUR'RION, *n.* [Port. *morriam*; It. *morione*; from the root of L. *murus*, a wall. See *Mural.*]

A helmet; a casque; armor for the head; written also *morion.* *King.*

MUS'ARD, *n.* [Fr. See *Muse.*] A dreamer; one who is apt to be absent in mind. *Obs.* *Chaucer.*

MUS'ƐADEL, MUS'ƐADINE, MUSƐAT', MUS'ƐATEL, *a.* [It. *moscatello*; Port. Sp. *moscatel*; Fr. *muscat*, *muscadin*, *muscadet*; from It. *moscado*, musk, or *muscata* [*noce moscada*,] a nutmeg, Fr. *muscade*, from *musc.* Hence, in Italian, *vin muscato*, muscat, or muscadine wine.]

1. An appellation given to a kind of rich wine, and to the grapes which produce it. The word is also used as a noun.
2. A sweet pear.

MUS'CLE, *n.* [Fr. from L. *musculus*, a muscle, and a little *mouse*; D. Sw. Dan. *muskel*; G. *muschel*; Gr. *μυς*, a mouse, and a muscle.]

1. In *anatomy*, the muscles are the organs of motion, consisting of fibers or bundles of fibers inclosed in a thin cellular membrane. The muscles are susceptible of contraction and relaxation, and in a healthy state the proper muscles are subject to the will, and are called *voluntary* muscles. But other parts of the body, as the heart, the urinary bladder, the stomach, &c. are of a muscular texture, and susceptible of contraction and dilatation, but are not subject to the will, and are therefore called *involuntary* muscles. The red color of the muscles is owing to the blood vessels which they contain. The ends of the muscles are fastened to the bones which they move, and when they act in opposition to each other, they are called *antagonists.* *Encyc.*

Muscles are divided into the head, belly and tail. The head is the part fixed on the immovable joint called its origin, and is usually tendinous; the belly is the middle fleshy part, which consists of the true muscular fibers; the tail is the tendinous portion inserted into the part to be moved, called the insertion; but in the tendon, the fibers are more compact than in the belly of the muscle, and do not admit the red globules. *Parr.*

2. A bivalvular shell fish of the genus Mytilus; sometimes written *mussel.*

MUSƐOS'ITY, *n.* Mossiness.

MUSƐOVA'DO, *n.* Unrefined sugar; the raw material from which loaf and lump sugar are procured by refining. Muscovado is obtained from the juice of the sugar cane by evaporation and draining off the liquid part called *melasses.* *Edwards.*

[This word is used either as a noun or an adjective.]

MUS'ƐOVY-DUCK, *n.* The musk-duck, *Anas moschata.*

MUS'ƐOVY-GLASS, *n.* Mica, which see.

MUS'ƐULAR, *a.* [from *muscle.*] Pertaining to a muscle; as a *muscular* fiber.

2. Performed by a muscle; as *muscular* motion.
3. Strong; brawny; vigorous; as a *muscular* body or frame.

MUSƐULAR'ITY, *n.* The state of being muscular. *Grew.*

MUS'ƐULITE, *n.* A petrified muscle or shell. *Kirwan.*

MUS'ƐULOUS, *a.* [L. *musculosus.*] Full of muscles.

2. Strong; brawny.
3. Pertaining to a muscle or to muscles.

MUSE, *n.* *s* as *z.* [L. *musa*; Gr. *μουσα.* See the Verb.]

1. Properly, song; but in usage, the deity or power of poetry. Hence poets in modern times, as in ancient, invoke the aid of the Muse or Muses, or in other words, the genius of poetry.

> Granville commands; your aid, O *Muses*, bring,
> What *Muse* for Granville can refuse to sing? *Pope.*

2. Deep thought; close attention or contemplation which abstracts the mind from passing scenes; hence sometimes, absence of mind.

> As in great *muse*, no word to creature spake. *Spenser.*

> He was fill'd
> With admiration and deep *muse* to hear
> Of things so high and strange. *Milton.*

MUSE, *v. i.* *s* as *z.* [Fr. *muser*, to loiter or trifle; It. *musare*, to gaze, to stand idle; allied to this word probably are L. *musso* and *mussito*, to mutter or murmur, to demur, to be silent. The Greek *μυζω* signifies to press, or utter sound with the lips compressed. The latter verb belongs to Class *Mg*; for *μυγμα*, a sound uttered through the nose or with close lips, is of the same family, L. *mussitatio.* The word then primarily denotes what we call humming, to hum, as persons do when idle, or alone and steadily occupied. If the elements of the word are *Ms*, it may be referred to the Ar. Syr. همس. Class Ms. No. 35.]

1. To ponder; to think closely; to study in silence.

> He *mused* upon some dangerous plot. *Sidney.*

> I *muse* on the works of thy hands. Ps. cxliii.

2. To be absent in mind; to be so occupied in study or contemplation, as not to observe passing scenes or things present. *Shak.*
3. To wonder.

> Do not *muse* of me. *Obs.* *Shak.*

MUSE, *v. t.* To think on; to meditate on. *Thomson.*

MU'SEFUL, *a.* Thinking deeply or closely; silently thoughtful.

> Full of *museful* mopings. *Dryden.*

MU'SELESS, *a.* Disregarding the power of poetry. *Milton.*

MU'SER, *n.* One who thinks closely in silence, or one apt to be absent in mind. *Johnson.*

MU'SET, *n.* The place through which the hare goes to relief; *a hunting term.* *Bailey.*

MUSE'UM, *n.* [Gr. *μουσειον*, a place for the muses or for study.]

A house or apartment appropriated as a repository of things that have an immediate relation to the arts; a cabinet of curiosities.

MUSH, *n.* [G. *mus*, pap.] The meal of maiz boiled in water.

MUSH'ROOM, *n.* [Fr. *mousseron*, the white mushroom, from *mousse*, moss, or the same root, bearing the sense of softness or nap.]

1. The common name of numerous cryptogamian plants of the natural order of Fungi. Some of them are esculent, others poisonous. Mushrooms grow on dunghills and in moist rich ground, and often spring up in a short time.

> The origin of man, in the view of the atheist, is the same with that of the *mushroom.* *Dwight.*

2. An upstart; one that rises suddenly from a low condition in life. *Bacon.*

MUSH'ROOM-STONE, *n.* A fossil or stone that produces mushrooms; the Lyncurius. *Woodward.*

MU'SIƐ, *n.* *s* as *z.* [L. *musica*; Gr. *μουσικη*; Fr. *musique.* See *Muse.*]

1. Melody or harmony; any succession of sounds so modulated as to please the ear, or any combination of simultaneous sounds in accordance or harmony. Music is *vocal* or *instrumental.* *Vocal* music is the melody of a single voice, or the harmony of two or more voices in concert. *Instrumental* music is that produced by one or more instruments.

> By *music* minds an equal temper know. *Pope.*

2. Any entertainment consisting in melody or harmony.

> What *music* and dancing and diversions and songs are to many in the world, that prayers and devotions and psalms are to you. *Law.*

3. The science of harmonical sounds, which treats of the principles of harmony, or the properties, dependencies and relations of sounds to each other. This may be called *speculative* or *theoretical* music. *Encyc.*
4. The art of combining sounds in a manner to please the ear. This is *practical* music or composition. *Encyc.*
5. Order; harmony in revolutions; as the *music* of the spheres.

MU'SIƐAL, *a.* Belonging to music; as *musical* proportion; a *musical* instrument.

2. Producing music or agreeable sounds; as a *musical* voice.
3. Melodious; harmonious; pleasing to the ear; as *musical* sounds or numbers.

MU'SIƐALLY, *adv.* In a melodious or harmonious manner; with sweet sounds.

MU'SIƐALNESS, *n.* The quality of being melodious or harmonious.

MU'SIƐ-BOOK, *n.* A book containing tunes or songs for the voice or for instruments.

MUSI''CIAN, *n.* A person skilled in the science of music, or one that sings or performs on instruments of music according to the rules of the art. *Bacon. Dryden.*

MU'SIC-M'ASTER, *n.* One who teaches music.

MU'SING, *ppr.* Meditating in silence.

MU'SING, *n.* Meditation; contemplation.

MUSK, *n.* [L. *muscus*; Gr. *μοσχος*, musk, and moss; It. *musco* and *muschio*; Sp. *musco*; Fr. Arm. *musc*; W. *mwsg*. The latter Owen derives from *mws*, which as a noun signifies something that shoots out, effluvia, and as an adjective, of a strong scent. The Arabic word coinciding with these is found under مسك masaka, to hold or contain, and the name is interpreted to signify both the follicle containing the matter, and the substance contained.]

A strong scented substance obtained from a cyst or bag near the navel of the Thibet musk [*Moschus moschiferus*,] an animal that inhabits the Asiatic Alps, especially the Altaic chain. This animal is a little more than three feet in length; the head resembles that of the roe, the fur is coarse, like that of the cervine race, but thick, erect, smooth and soft. It has no horns, but the male has two long tusks, one on each side, projecting from the mouth. The female is smaller than the male, and has neither tusks nor follicle. The cyst of the male is about the size of a hen's egg, oval, flat on one side and rounded on the other, having a small orifice. This contains a clotted, oily, friable matter of a dark brown color, which is the true musk, one of the strongest odors or perfumes in nature. We give the name to the substance and to the animal. *Encyc.*

MUSK, *n.* Grape-hyacinth or grape-flower. *Johnson.*

MUSK, *v. t.* To perfume with musk.

MUSK'-APPLE, *n.* A particular kind of apple.

MUSK'-CAT, *n.* The musk, which see.

MUSK'-CHERRY, *n.* A kind of cherry.

MUSK'ET, *n.* [It. *moschetto*; Sp. *mosquete*; Fr. *mousquet*. It seems to be formed from Sp. *mosca*, L. *musca*, a fly.]

1. A species of fire-arms used in war, and fired by means of a lighted match. This manner of firing was in use as late as the civil war in England. But the proper musket is no longer in use. The name, however, in common speech, is yet applied to fusees or fire-locks fired by a spring lock. *Encyc.*

2. A male hawk of a small kind, the female of which is the sparrow hawk. *Dryden. Hanmer.*

MUSKETEE'R, *n.* A soldier armed with a musket. *Clarendon.*

MUSKE'TOE, *n.* [Sp. Port. *mosquito*, from Sp. *mosca*, L. *musca*, a fly.]

A small insect of the genus Culex, that is bred in water; a species of gnat that abounds in marshes and low lands, and whose sting is peculiarly painful and vexatious.

MUSKETOON', *n.* [Fr. *mousqueton*. See *Musket*.]

A short thick musket, carrying five ounces of iron, or seven and a half of lead; the shortest kind of blunderbuss. *Encyc.*

2. One who is armed with a musketoon. *Herbert.*

MUSK'INESS, *n.* [from *musk*.] The scent of musk. *Johnson.*

MUSK'MELON, *n.* [*musk* and *melon*.] A delicious species of melon; named probably from its fragrance.

MUSK'-OX, *n.* A species of the genus Bos, which inhabits the country about Hudson's Bay. It has large horns united at the skull, but turned downward on each side of the head. The hair of this animal is very long and fine. *Encyc.*

MUSK'-PEAR, *n.* A fragrant kind of pear. *Johnson.*

MUSK'RAT, } *n.* An American animal of
MUS'QUASH, } the murine genus, the *Mus zibethicus*. It has a compressed, lanceolated tail, with toes separate. It has the smell of musk in summer, but loses it in winter. The fur is used by hatters. Its popular name in America is *musquash*. *Belknap.*

MUSK'-ROSE, *n.* A species of rose; so called from its fragrance. *Bacon. Milton.*

MUSK'-SEED, *n.* A plant of the genus Hibiscus.

MUSK'-WOOD, *n.* A species of plant of the genus Trichilia.

MUSK'Y, *a.* Having the odor of musk; fragrant. *Milton.*

MUS'LIN, *n. s* as *z*. [Fr. *mousseline*; It. *mussolina*, *mussolo*; Sp. *moselina* or *musulina*. This, if a compound word, is formed of Fr. *mousse*, moss, or its root, on account of its soft nap, and *lin*, flax. The opinion of Lunier that it is named from Moussoul, in Mesopotamia, is probably unfounded.]

A sort of fine cotton cloth, which bears a downy knot on its surface. *Encyc.*

MUS'LIN, *a.* Made of muslin; as a *muslin* gown.

MUSLINET', *n.* A sort of coarse cotton cloth.

MUS'MON, } *n.* An animal esteemed a spe-
MUS'IMON, } cies of sheep, described by the ancients as common in Corsica, Sardinia and Barbary. Buffon considers it to be the sheep in a wild state. *Encyc.*

MUS'ROLE, *n.* [Fr. *muserolle*, from *museau*, muzzle.] The nose band of a horse's bridle. *Bailey.*

MUSS, *n.* A scramble. [*Not used.*] *Shak.*

MUSSEL. [See *Muscle*.]

MUS'SITE, *n.* [from the valley of Mussa, in Piedmont.]

A variety of pyroxene of a greenish white color; otherwise called diopside. *Dict. Nat. Hist.*

MUS'SULMAN, *n.* A Mohammedan or follower of Mohammed. The word, it is said, signifies in the Turkish language a true believer, or orthodox. It may be from Ar. *eslam*, salvation. *Cyc. Thomson.*

MUS'SULMANISH, *a.* Mohammedan. *Herbert.*

MUST, *v. i.* [Sax. *most*; D. *moeten*, *moest*; Sw. *måste*; G. *müssen*. It is used as an auxiliary verb, and has no variation to express person, time or number. Its primary sense is probably to be strong or able, as it is rendered in Saxon; from pressing, straining. Class Ms. No. 25. Ch. and No. 31.]

1. To be obliged; to be necessitated. It expresses both physical and moral necessity. A man *must* eat for nourishment, and he *must* sleep for refreshment. We *must* submit to the laws or be exposed to punishment. A bill in a legislative body *must* have three readings before it can pass to be enacted.

2. It expresses moral fitness or propriety, as necessary or essential to the character or end proposed. "Deacons *must* be grave;" "a bishop *must* have a good report of them that are without." 1 Tim. iii.

MUST, *n.* [L. *mustum*; Sax. *must*; It. Sp. Port. *mosto*; Russ. *mst*; Fr. *moût*; D. G. *most*; Heb. Ch. חמץ to ferment. Class Ms. No. 38.]

New wine; wine pressed from the grape but not fermented. *Encyc.*

MUST, *v. t.* [Fr. *moisi*, moldy; Ir. *musgam*, to be musty. Qu. W. *mws*, of a strong scent.] To make moldy and sour. *Mortimer.*

MUST, *v. i.* To grow moldy and sour; to contract a fetid smell.

MUS'TAC, *n.* A small tufted monkey.

MUSTA'CHES, *n.* [Fr. *moustaches*; Sp. *mostacho*, a whisker; It. *mostacchio*; Gr. *μυςαξ*, the upper lip, and the hair growing on it.]

Whiskers; long hair on the upper lip.

MUS'TARD, *n.* [It. *mostarda*; Fr. *moutarde*; Arm. *mustard*; Port. *mostarda*; Sp. *mostaza*; W. *mwstarz*; *mws*, that has a strong scent, and *tarz*, a breaking out.]

A plant of the genus Sinapis, and its seed, which has a pungent taste and is a powerful stimulant. It is used externally in cataplasms, and internally as a diuretic and stimulant. *Encyc.*

MUSTEE', } *n.* A person of a mixed breed.
MESTEE', } *W. Indies.*

MUS'TELINE, *a.* [L. *mustelinus*, from *mustela*, a weasel.]

Pertaining to the weasel or animals of the genus Mustela; as a *musteline* color; the *musteline* genus.

MUS'TER, *v. t.* [G. *mustern*, D. *monsteren*, Sw. *mönstra*, Dan. *mynstrer*, to muster; It. *mostrare*, Sp. Port. *mostrar*, Fr. *montrer*, L. *monstro*, to show. Either *n* has been lost in some of these languages, or it is not radical in the Latin.]

Properly, to collect troops for review, parade and exercise; but in general, to collect or assemble troops, persons or things. The officers *muster* their soldiers regularly; they *muster* all their forces. The philosopher *musters* all the wise sayings of the ancients. *Spenser. Locke. Tillotson.*

MUS'TER, *v. i.* To assemble; to meet in one place.

MUS'TER, *n.* [It. Port. *mostra*, a show or muster; Sp. *muestra*, a pattern, a model, a *muster*-roll; G. *muster*, a pattern, a sample; D. *monster*; Dan. *mynster*; L. *monstrum*, a show or prodigy.]

1. An assembling of troops for review, or a review of troops under arms. *Encyc.*

2. A register or roll of troops mustered.

> Ye publish the *musters* of your own bands. *Hooker.*

3. A collection, or the act of collecting. *Ainsworth.*

To pass muster, to be approved or allowed. *South.*

MUS'TER-BOOK, *n.* A book in which forces are registered. *Shak.*

MUS'TER-M'ASTER, *n.* One who takes an account of troops, and of their arms and other military apparatus. The chief officer of this kind is called *muster-master-general.* *Encyc.*

MUS'TER-ROLL, *n.* A roll or register of the troops in each company, troop or regiment. *Encyc.*

MUS'TILY, *adv.* [from *musty.*] Moldily; sourly.

MUS'TINESS, *n.* The quality of being musty or sour; moldiness; damp foulness. *Evelyn.*

MUS'TY, *a.* [from *must.*] Moldy; sour; foul and fetid; as a *musty* cask; *musty* corn or straw; *musty* books.

2. Stale; spoiled by age.

> The proverb is somewhat *musty.* *Shak.*

3. Having an ill flavor; as *musty* wine. *Pope.*

4. Dull; heavy; spiritless.

> That he may not grow *musty* and unfit for conversation. *Addison.*

MUTABIL'ITY, *n.* [Fr. *mutabilité*; It. *mutabilità*; L. *mutabilitas*, from *mutabilis*, *muto*, to change.]

1. Changeableness; susceptibility of change; the quality of being subject to change or alteration, either in form, state or essential qualities.

> Plato confesses that the heavens and the frame of the world are corporeal, and therefore subject to *mutability.* *Stillingfleet.*

2. The state of habitually or frequently changing.

3. Changeableness, as of mind, disposition or will; inconstancy; instability; as the *mutability* of opinion or purpose.

MU'TABLE, *a.* [It. *mutabile*; L. *mutabilis*, from *muto*, to change, W. *mudaw.* See *Mew.*]

1. Subject to change; changeable; that may be altered in form, qualities or nature. Almost every thing we see on earth is *mutable*; substances are *mutable* in their form, and we all know by sad experience how *mutable* are the conditions of life.

2. Inconstant; unsettled; unstable; susceptible of change. Our opinions and our purposes are *mutable.*

MU'TABLENESS, *n.* Changeableness; mutability; instability.

MUTA'TION, *n.* [L. *mutatio.*] The act or process of changing.

2. Change; alteration, either in form or qualities.

> The vicissitude or *mutations* in the superior globe are no fit matter for this present argument. *Bacon.*

MUTE, *a.* [L. *mutus*; W. *mûd*; Fr. *muet*; It. *muto*; Sp. *mudo*; Ir. *muite*; Arm. *mud* or *simudet.*]

1. Silent; not speaking; not uttering words, or not having the power of utterance; dumb. *Mute* may express temporary silence, or permanent inability to speak.

> To the *mute* my speech is lost. *Dryden.*

In this phrase, it denotes unable to utter words. More generally, it denotes temporarily silent; as, all sat *mute.*

> All the heavenly choir stood *mute.* *Milton.*

2. Uttering no sound; as *mute* sorrow.

3. Silent; not pronounced; as a *mute* letter.

MUTE, *n.* In *law*, a person that stands speechless when he ought to answer or plead.

2. In *grammar*, a letter that represents no sound; a close articulation which intercepts the voice. Mutes are of two kinds, *pure* and *impure.* The *pure mutes* instantly and entirely intercept the voice, as *k*, *p* and *t*, in the syllables *ek*, *ep*, *et.* The *impure mutes* intercept the voice less suddenly, as the articulations are less close. Such are *b*, *d* and *g*, as in the syllables *eb*, *ed*, *eg.*

3. In *music*, a little utensil of wood or brass, used on a violin to deaden or soften the sounds. *Busby.*

MUTE, *v. i.* [Fr. *mutir.*] To eject the contents of the bowels, as birds. *B. Jonson.*

MUTE, *n.* The dung of fowls.

MU'TELY, *adv.* Silently; without uttering words or sounds. *Milton.*

MU'TENESS, *n.* Silence; forbearance of speaking.

MU'TILATE, *v. t.* [L. *mutilo*, probably from the root of *meto*, to cut off; Fr. *mutiler*; It. *mutilare.*]

1. To cut off a limb or essential part of an animal body. To cut off the hand or foot is to *mutilate* the body or the person.

2. To cut or break off, or otherwise separate any important part, as of a statue or building. *Encyc.*

3. To retrench, destroy or remove any material part, so as to render the thing imperfect; as, to *mutilate* the poems of Homer or the orations of Cicero.

> Among the *mutilated* poets of antiquity, there is none whose fragments are so beautiful as those of Sappho. *Addison.*

MU'TILATED, *pp.* Deprived of a limb or of an essential part.

MU'TILATED, MU'TILATE, } *a.* In *botany*, the reverse of *luxuriant*; not producing a corol, when not regularly apetalous; *applied to flowers.* *Lee. Martyn.*

MU'TILATING, *ppr.* Retrenching a limb or an essential part.

MUTILA'TION, *n.* [L. *mutilatio.*] The act of mutilating; deprivation of a limb or of an essential part.

2. *Mutilation* is a term of very general import, applied to bodies, to statues, to buildings and to writings; but appropriately, it denotes the retrenchment of a human limb or member, and particularly of the male organs of generation.

MU'TILATOR, *n.* One who mutilates.

MU'TILOUS, *a.* Mutilated; defective; imperfect. *Ray.*

Mutine, a mutineer, and *mutine*, to mutiny, are not in use.

MUTINE'ER, *n.* [See *Mutiny.*] One guilty of mutiny; a person in military or naval service, who rises in opposition to the authority of the officers, who openly resists the government of the army or navy, or attempts to destroy due subordination.

MU'TING, *n.* The dung of fowls. *More.*

MU'TINOUS, *a.* Turbulent; disposed to resist the authority of laws and regulations in an army or navy, or openly resisting such authority.

2. Seditious. [See *Mutiny.*]

MU'TINOUSLY, *adv.* In a manner or with intent to oppose lawful authority or due subordination in military or naval service.

MU'TINOUSNESS, *n.* The state of being mutinous; opposition to lawful authority among military men.

MU'TINY, *n.* [Fr. *mutin*, refractory, stubborn; *mutiner*, to mutiny or rise in arms; *mutinerie*, mutiny; Sp. *motin*, a mutiny; *amotinar*, to excite rebellion; It. *mutinare*, to mutiny; Port. *motim*; D. *muiten*, mutiny, and as a verb, to mutiny, and to *mew*, to molt or cast the fethers, coinciding with the Fr. *muer*, Eng. to *mew*; G. *meuterey*, mutiny, and *mausen*, to mew or molt; Dan. *myterie*; Sw. *mytteri*, mutiny; Arm. *muza*, to mew or molt. We see that these words, *mutiny* and *mew*, are from the same root as L. *muto*, to change, W. *mudaw*, which is radically the same word as L. *moto*, to move. *Mutiny* is formed from the French *mutin*, a derivative word, and *mew* from the root or verb. So *motin*, in Spanish, is a derivative, while *muda*, change, and Port. *mudar*, to change fethers, are directly from the verb; Eth. መረበ to turn; Ar. مَطَا to move or drive, or مَاطَ to drive. Class Md. No. 14. 10.]

An insurrection of soldiers or seamen against the authority of their commanders; open resistance of officers or opposition to their authority. A mutiny is properly the act of numbers, but by statutes and orders for governing the army and navy in different countries, the acts which constitute mutiny are multiplied and defined; and acts of individuals, amounting to a resistance of the authority or lawful commands of officers, are declared to be mutiny. Any attempt to excite opposition to lawful authority, or any act of contempt towards officers, or disobedience of commands, is by the British mutiny act declared to be mutiny. Any concealment of mutinous acts, or neglect to attempt a suppression of them, is declared also to be mutiny.

[*Note.* In good authors who lived a century ago, *mutiny* and *mutinous* were applied to insurrection and sedition in civil society. But I believe these words are now applied exclusively to soldiers and seamen.]

MU'TINY, *v. i.* To rise against lawful authority in military and naval service; to excite or attempt to excite opposition to the lawful commands of military and naval officers; to commit some act which tends to bring the authority of officers into contempt, or in any way to promote insubordination.

MUT'TER, *v. i.* [L. *mutio*, *muttio*, and *musso*, *mussito*; allied perhaps to *muse*, which see.]

1. To utter words with a low voice and compressed lips, with sullenness or in complaint; to grumble; to murmur.

> Meantime your filthy foreigner will stare,
> And *mutter* to himself. *Dryden.*

2. To sound with a low rumbling noise.

> Thick lightnings flash, the *muttering* thunder rolls. *Pope.*

MUT'TER, *v. t.* To utter with imperfect articulations, or with a low murmuring voice.

> Your lips have spoken lies, your tongue hath *muttered* perverseness. Is. lix.
>
> They in sleep will *mutter* their affairs. *Shak.*

MUT'TER, *n.* Murmur; obscure utterance. *Milton.*

MUT'TERED, *pp.* Uttered in a low murmuring voice.

MUT'TERER, *n.* A grumbler; one that mutters.

MUT'TERING, *ppr.* Uttering with a low murmuring voice; grumbling; murmuring.

MUT'TERINGLY, *adv.* With a low voice; without distinct articulation.

MUTTON, *n.* mut'n. [Fr. *mouton*, for *moulton;* W. *mollt*, a wether; Arm. *maud;* Ir. *molt.* Qu. Gr. μηλον.]
1. The flesh of sheep, raw or dressed for food.
2. A sheep. [*But this sense is now obsolete or ludicrous.*] *Bacon.*

MUT'TONFIST, *n.* A large red brawny hand. *Dryden.*

MU'TUAL, *a.* [Fr. *mutuel;* L. *mutuus*, from *muto*, to change.]
Reciprocal; interchanged, each acting in return or correspondence to the other; given and received. *Mutual* love is that which is entertained by two persons each for the other; *mutual* advantage is that which is conferred by one person on another, and received by him in return. So we say, *mutual* assistance, *mutual* aversion.

And, what should most excite a *mutual* flame,
Your rural cares and pleasures are the same. *Pope.*

MUTUAL'ITY, *n.* Reciprocation; interchange. *Shak.*

MU'TUALLY, *adv.* Reciprocally; in the manner of giving and receiving.

The tongue and the pen *mutually* assist one another. *Holder.*

[Note. *Mutual* and *mutually* properly refer to two persons or their intercourse; but they may be and often are applied to numbers acting together or in concert.]

MUTUA'TION, *n.* [L. *mutuatio.*] The act of borrowing. [*Little used.*] *Hall.*

MU'TULE, *n.* [Fr. *mutule.*] In *architecture*, a square modillion under the cornice. In French, it is rendered a corbel or bracket.

MUZ'ZLE, *n.* [Fr. *museau*, muzzle or snout; Arm. *musell;* probably from the root of *mouth.*]
1. The mouth of a thing; the extreme or end for entrance or discharge; applied chiefly to the end of a tube, as the open end of a common fusee or pistol, or of a bellows.
2. A fastening for the mouth which hinders from biting.

With golden *muzzles* all their mouths were bound. *Dryden.*

MUZ'ZLE, *v. t.* To bind the mouth; to fasten the mouth to prevent biting or eating.

Thou shalt not *muzzle* the ox when he treadeth out the corn. Deut. xxv.

2. To fondle with the mouth close. [*Low.*]
3. To restrain from hurt.

My dagger *muzzled*— *Shak.*

MUZ'ZLE, *v. i.* To bring the mouth near.

The bear *muzzles* and smells to him. *L'Estrange.*

MUZ'ZLE-RING, *n.* The metalline ring or circle that surrounds the mouth of a cannon or other piece. *Encyc.*

MŸ, *pronom. adj.* [contracted from *migen*, *mine. Me* was originally *mig*, and the adjective *migen.* So in L. *meus.* See *Mine.*]
Belonging to me; as, this is *my* book. Formerly, *mine* was used before a vowel, and *my* before a consonant; *my* is now used before both. We say, *my* book; *my* own book; *my* old friend. *Mine* is still used after a verb; as, this book is *mine.*

MYNHEE'R, *n.* [D. my lord or master.] A Dutchman.

MŸOGRAPH'IĊAL, *a.* [See *Myography.*] Pertaining to a description of the muscles.

MŸOG'RAPHIST, *n.* One who describes the muscles of animals.

MŸOG'RAPHY, *n.* [Gr. μυς, μυος, a muscle, and γραφω, to describe.] A description of the muscles of the body.

MŸOLOĠ'IĊAL, *a.* [See *Myology.*] Pertaining to the description and doctrine of the muscles.

MŸOL'OĠY, *n.* [μυς, μυος, muscle, and λογος, discourse.]
A description of the muscles, or the doctrine of the muscles of the human body. *Cheyne. Encyc.*

MY'OPE, *n.* [Gr. μυωψ; μυω, to shut, and ωψ, the eye.] A short-sighted person. *Adams.*

MY'OPY, *n.* Short-sightedness. *Encyc.*

MYR'IAD, *n.* [Gr. μυριας, from μυριος, extreme, innumerable; W. *myr*, that is infinite, fluctuating, ants, emmets; *myrz*, infinity, a myriad, ten thousand. Here we see the origin of the Gr. μυρμος, μυρμηξ, an ant, so named from numbers or motion. See *Fervent.*]
1. The number of ten thousand.
2. An immense number, indefinitely. *Milton.*

MYRIAM'ETER, *n.* [Gr. μυρια, ten thousand, and μετρον, measure.]
In the new system of French measures, the length of ten thousand meters, equal to two mean leagues of the ancient measure. *Lunier.*

MYR'IARĊH, *n.* [Gr. μυρια, ten thousand, and αρχος, chief.]
A captain or commander of ten thousand men.

MYR'IARE, *n.* [Gr. μυρια and *are*, L. *area.*]
A French linear measure of ten thousand ares, or 100,000 square meters. *Lunier.*

MYR'ICIN, *n.* The substance which remains after bees-wax, or the wax of the Myrica cordifolia, has been digested in alcohol. *Dr. John.*

MYRIOL'ITER, *n.* [Gr. μυριος and λιτρα, a pound.] A French measure of capacity containing ten thousand liters, or 610,280 cubic inches.

MYR'MIDON, *n.* [Gr. μυρμηδων, a multitude of ants; W. *myr;* qu. so called from their numbers or from their industry.]
Primarily, the Myrmidons are said to have been a people on the borders of Thessaly, who accompanied Achilles to the war against Troy. Hence the name came to signify a soldier of a rough character, a desperate soldier or ruffian.

MYROB'ALAN, *n.* [L. *myrobolanum;* Gr. μυροβαλανος; μυρον, unguent, and βαλανος, a nut.]
A dried fruit of the plum kind brought from the East Indies, of which there are several kinds, all slightly purgative and astringent, but not now used in medicine. *Parr. Encyc.*

MYROP'OLIST, *n.* [Gr. μυρον, unguent, and πωλεω, to sell.] One that sells unguents. [*Little used.*]

MYRRH, *n.* mer. [L. *myrrha;* Gr. μυρρα or σμυρνα; Sp. It. *mirra;* Fr. *myrrhe;* Arabic, from مُرّ marra, to be bitter. Class Mr.]
A gum-resin that comes in the form of drops or globules of various colors and sizes, of a pretty strong but agreeable smell, and of a bitter taste. It is imported from Egypt, but chiefly from the southern or eastern parts of Arabia; from what species of tree or plant it is procured, is unknown. As a medicine, it is a good stomachic, antispasmodic and cordial. *Parr. Fourcroy. Encyc.*

MYR'RHINE, *a.* [L. *myrrhinus.*] Made of the myrrhine stone. [See *Murrine.*] *Milton.*

MYR'TIFORM, *a.* [L. *myrtus*, myrtle, and *form.*] Resembling myrtle or myrtle berries.

MYR'TLE, *n.* [L. *myrtus;* Gr. μυρτος.] A plant of the genus Myrtus, of several species. The common myrtle rises with a shrubby upright stem, eight or ten feet high. Its branches form a close full head, closely garnished with oval lanceolate leaves. It has numerous small, pale flowers from the axillas, singly on each footstalk. *Encyc.*

MY'RUS, *n.* A species of sea-serpent, of the anguilliform kind. *Dict. Nat. Hist.*

MŸSELF', *pron.* A compound of *my* and *self*, used after I, to express emphasis, marking emphatically the distinction between the speaker and another person; as, I *myself* will do it; I have done it *myself.*
2. In the objective case, the reciprocal of I. I will defend *myself.*
3. It is sometimes used without I, particularly in poetry.

Myself shall mount the rostrum in his favor. *Addison.*

MYSTAGOGUE, *n.* mys'tagog. [Gr. μυςης, one initiated in mysteries, and αγωγος, a leader.]
1. One who interprets mysteries. *Bailey.*
2. One that keeps church relics and shows them to strangers. *Bailey.*

MYSTE'RIAL, *a.* Containing a mystery or enigma. *B. Jonson.*

MYSTE'RIARĊH, *n.* [Gr. μυςηριον, mystery, and αρχος, chief.]
One presiding over mysteries. *Johnson.*

MYSTE'RIOUS, *a.* [See *Mystery.*] Obscure; hid from the understanding; not clearly understood. The birth and connections of the man with the iron mask in France are *mysterious*, and have never been explained.
2. In *religion*, obscure; secret; not revealed or explained; hidden from human understanding, or unintelligible; beyond human comprehension. Applied to the divine counsels and government, the word often implies something awfully obscure; as, the ways of God are often *mysterious.*

MYSTE'RIOUSLY, *adv.* Obscurely; enigmatically.
2. In a manner wonderfully obscure and unintelligible.

MYSTE'RIOUSNESS, *n.* Obscurity; the quality of being hid from the understanding, and calculated to excite curiosity or wonder.

2. Artful perplexity.

MYS'TERY, *n.* [L. *mysterium*, Gr. μυςηριον, a secret. This word in Greek is rendered also *murium latibulum;* but probably both senses are from that of hiding or shutting; Gr. μυω, to shut, to conceal.]

1. A profound secret; something wholly unknown or something kept cautiously concealed, and therefore exciting curiosity or wonder; such as the *mystery* of the man with the iron mask in France.

2. In *religion*, any thing in the character or attributes of God, or in the economy of divine providence, which is not revealed to man. *President Moore.*

3. That which is beyond human comprehension until explained. In this sense, *mystery* often conveys the idea of something awfully sublime or important; something that excites wonder.

Great is the *mystery* of godliness. 1 Tim. iii.

Having made known to us the *mystery* of his will. Eph. i.

We speak the wisdom of God in a *mystery*. 1 Cor. ii.

4. An enigma; any thing artfully made difficult.

5. A kind of ancient dramatic representation. *Bp. Percy.*

6. A trade; a calling; any mechanical occupation which supposes skill or knowledge peculiar to those who carry it on, and therefore a secret to others.

[The word in the latter sense has been supposed to have a different origin from the foregoing, viz. Fr. *metier*, Norm. *mestier*, business, trade, occupation, as if from Norm. *mestie*, master. But this is probably incorrect.]

MYS'TIC, **MYS'TICAL**, *a.* [L. *mysticus*; Gr. μυςικος.] Obscure; hid; secret. *Dryden.*

2. Sacredly obscure or secret; remote from human comprehension.

God hath revealed a way *mystical* and supernatural. *Hooker.*

3. Involving some secret meaning; allegorical; emblematical; as *mystic* dance; *mystic* Babylon. *Milton. Burnet.*

MYS'TICALLY, *adv.* In a manner or by an act implying a secret meaning. *Donne.*

MYS'TICALNESS, *n.* The quality of being mystical, or of involving some secret meaning.

MYS'TICISM, *n.* Obscurity of doctrine.

2. The doctrine of the Mystics, who profess a pure, sublime and perfect devotion, wholly disinterested, and maintain that they hold immediate intercourse with the divine Spirit.

MYS'TICS, *n.* A religious sect who profess to have direct intercourse with the Spirit of God.

MYTH'IC, *a.* [from Gr. μυθος, a fable.] Fabulous. *Shuckford.*

MYTHOLOG'ICAL, *a.* [See *Mythology.*] Relating to mythology; fabulous.

MYTHOLOG'ICALLY, *adv.* In a way suited to the system of fables.

MYTHOL'OGIST, *n.* One versed in mythology; one who writes on mythology, or explains the fables of the ancient pagans. *Norris.*

MYTHOL'OGIZE, *v. i.* To relate or explain the fabulous history of the heathen.

MYTHOL'OGY, *n.* [Gr. μυθος, a fable, and λογος, discourse.]

A system of fables or fabulous opinions and doctrines respecting the deities which heathen nations have supposed to preside over the world or to influence the affairs of it.

MYT'ILITE, *n.* [Gr. μυτιλος, a kind of shell.]

In *geology*, a petrified muscle or shell of the genus Mytilus. *Kirwan.*

N.

N is the fourteenth letter of the English Alphabet, and an articulation formed by placing the end of the tongue against the root of the upper teeth. It is an imperfect mute or semi-vowel, and a nasal letter; the articulation being accompanied with a sound through the nose. It has one sound only, and after *m* is silent or nearly so, as in *hymn* and *condemn.*

N, among the ancients, was a numeral letter signifying 900, and with a stroke over it, N̄, 9000. Among the lawyers, N. L. stood for *non liquet*, the case is not clear.

In commerce, No. is an abbreviation of the French *nombre*, and stands for *number.*

N. S. stands for New Style.

NAB, *n.* The summit of a mountain or rock. [*Local.*] *Grose.*

NAB, *v. t.* [Sw. *nappa;* Dan. *napper;* G. D. *knappen.* See *Knap.*]

To catch suddenly; to seize by a sudden grasp or thrust; *a word little used and only in low language.*

NA'BOB, *n.* A deputy or prince in India, subordinate to the Subahs; hence,

2. A man of great wealth.

NACKER. [See *Naker.*]

NA'CREOUS, *a.* [See *Naker.*] Having a pearly luster. *Phillips.*

NA'CRITE, *n.* [See *Naker.*] A rare mineral, called also talckite, consisting of scaly parts; glimmering, pearly, friable, with a greasy feel; the color, a greenish white. *Jameson. Ure.*

NA'DIR, *n.* [Ar. نظير, from نظر natara, to be like, proportional, corresponding to, opposite.]

That point of the heavens or lower hemisphere directly opposite to the zenith; the point directly under the place where we stand.

NA'DLE-STEIN, *n.* [G. *nadel* and *stein.*] Needle-stone; rutile. *Ure.*

NÆVE, *n.* [L. *nævus.*] A spot. *Dryden.*

NAFE, **NAFF**, *n.* A kind of tufted sea-fowl. *Todd.*

NAG, *n.* A small horse; a horse in general, or rather a sprightly horse. *L'Estrange.*

2. A paramour; *in contempt.* *Shak.*

NAID, **NA'IAD**, *n.* [Gr. ναιαδες, naiads, from ναω, to flow.]

In *mythology*, a water nymph; a deity that presides over rivers and springs.

NAIL, *n.* [Sax. *nægel;* Sw. G. D. *nagel;* Dan. *nagle;* Russ. *nagot;* Sans. *naga* or *nakha.* If the word was originally applied to a claw or talon, the primary sense may be to catch, or it may be a shoot.]

1. The claw or talon of a fowl or other animal.

2. The horny substance growing at the end of the human fingers and toes.

3. A small pointed piece of metal, usually with a head, to be driven into a board or other piece of timber, and serving to fasten it to other timber. The larger kinds of instruments of this sort are called *spikes;* and a long thin kind with a flattish head, is called a *brad.*

4. A stud or boss; a short nail with a large broad head. *Swift.*

5. A measure of length, being two inches and a quarter, or the 16th of a yard.

On the nail, in hand; immediately; without delay or time of credit; as, to pay money *on the nail.* *Swift.*

To hit the nail on the head, to hit or touch the exact point.

NAIL, *v. t.* To fasten with nails; to unite, close or make compact with nails.

2. To stud with nails.

The rivets of your arms were *nail'd* with gold. *Dryden.*

3. To stop the vent of a cannon; to spike.

NA'ILED, *pp.* Fastened with nails; studded.

NA'ILER, *n.* One whose occupation is to make nails.

NA'ILERY, *n.* A manufactory where nails are made.

NA'ILING, *ppr.* Fastening with nails; studding.

NA'IVELY, *adv.* [Fr. *naïf*, from L. *nativus.*] With native or unaffected simplicity.

NA'IVETE, **NA'IVTY**, *n.* Native simplicity; unaffected plainness or ingenuousness. *Gray.*

NA'KED, *a.* [Sax. *nacod;* G. *nacket, nackt;* D. *naakt;* Sw. *naken;* Dan. *nögen;* Russ. *nagei*, *nagost* and *nagota*, nakedness; Ir. *nochta*, open, discovered; *nochduighe*, naked; *nochduighim*, to strip. Class Ng. No. 5. 10. 47. and 15. 16.]

1. Not covered; bare; having no clothes on; as a *naked* body or a *naked* limb.

2. Unarmed; defenseless; open; exposed; having no means of defense or protection against an enemy's attack, or against other injury.

Behold my bosom *naked* to your swords. *Addison.*

3. Open to view; not concealed; manifest. Heb. iv.

4. Destitute of worldly goods. Job i.

5. Exposed to shame and disgrace. Ex. xxxii.

6. Guilty and exposed to divine wrath. Rev. iii.

7. Plain; evident; undisguised; as the *naked* truth.

8. Mere; bare; simple; wanting the necessary additions. God requires of man something besides the *naked* belief of his being and his word.

9. Not inclosed in a pod or case; as *naked* seeds of a plant.

10. Without leaves, fulcres or arms; as a *naked* stem or trunk. *Martyn.*

11. Not assisted by glasses; as the *naked* eye.

NA'KEDLY, *adv.* Without covering.

2. Simply; barely; merely; in the abstract. *Holder.*

3. Evidently.

NA'KEDNESS, *n.* Want of covering or clothing; nudity; bareness.

Ham, the father of Canaan, saw the *nakedness* of his father. Gen. ix.

2. Want of means of defense.

Ye are spies; to see the *nakedness* of the land are ye come. Gen. xlii.

3. Plainness; openness to view. *Shak.*

To uncover nakedness, in Scripture, is to have incestuous or unlawful commerce with a female.

NA'KER, *n.* A violent flatulence passing from one limb to another with pain. *Parr.*

NA'KER, *n.* [Sp. *nacar*; It. *nacchera*; Fr. *nacre.*]

Mother of pearl; the white substance which constitutes the interior surface of a shell producing a pearl.

NALL, *n.* [Dan. *naal*, a needle.] An awl, such as collar-makers or shoe-makers use. [*Not used or local.*] *Johnson.*

NAME, *n.* [Sax. *nama*; D. *naam*; G. *name*; Sw. *namn*; Dan. *navn*; Ice. *nafn*; L. *nomen*; Gr. *ονομα*; It. Port. *nome*; Sp. *nombre*; Fr. *nom*; Pers. *nam, namah*; Sans. and Hindoo, *nama, nom*; Malay and Bengalee, *namma*; Ostiak, *nemen*. Qu. Heb. נאם.]

1. That by which a thing is called; the sound or combination of sounds used to express an idea, or any material substance, quality or act; an appellation attached to a thing by customary use, by which it may be vocally distinguished from other things. A name may be attached to an individual only, and is then *proper* or *appropriate*, as *John, Thomas, London, Paris*; or it may be attached to a species, genus or class of things, as *sheep, goat, horse, tree, animal*, which are called *common names, specific* or *generic*.

2. The letters or characters written or engraved, expressing the sounds by which a person or thing is known and distinguished.

3. A person.

They list with women each degenerate *name*. *Dryden.*

4. Reputation; character; that which is commonly said of a person; as a good *name*; a bad name. *Clarendon.*

5. Renown; fame; honor; celebrity; eminence; praise; distinction.

What men of *name* resort to him? *Shak.*

But in this sense, the word is often qualified by an epithet; as a *great name*; a *mighty name.*

6. Remembrance; memory.

The Lord shall blot out his *name* from under heaven. Deut. xxix.

7. Appearance only; sound only; not reality; as a friend in *name*. Rev. iii.

8. Authority; behalf; part; as in the *name* of the people. When a man speaks or acts in the *name* of another, he does it by their authority or in their behalf, as their representative.

9. Assumed character of another.

—Had forged a treason in my patron's *name*. *Dryden.*

10. In *Scripture*, the *name* of God signifies his titles, his attributes, his will or purpose, his honor and glory, his word, his grace, his wisdom, power and goodness, his worship or service, or God himself.

11. Issue; posterity that preserves the name. Deut. xxv.

12. In *grammar*, a noun.

To call names, to apply opprobrious names; to call by reproachful appellations. *Swift.*

To take the name of God in vain, to swear falsely or profanely, or to use the name of God with levity or contempt. Ex. xx.

To know by name, to honor by a particular friendship or familiarity. Ex. xxxiii.

Christian name, the name a person receives by baptism, as distinguished from *surname.*

NAME, *v. t.* [Sax. *naman, nemnan*, Goth. *namnyan*, to call, to name, to invoke; D. *noemen*; G. *nennen*; Sw. *nåmna*; Dan. *nævner.*]

1. To set or give to any person or thing a sound or combination of sounds by which it may be known and distinguished; to call; to give an appellation to.

She *named* the child Ichabod. 1 Sam. iv.

Thus was the building left
Ridiculous, and the work confusion *named*. *Milton.*

2. To mention by name; to utter or pronounce the sound or sounds by which a person or thing is known and distinguished.

Neither use thyself to the *naming* of the Holy One. *Ecclus.*

3. To nominate; to designate for any purpose by name.

Thou shalt anoint to me him whom I *name* to thee. 1 Sam. xvi.

4. To entitle. *Milton.*

To name the name of Christ, to make profession of faith in him. 2 Tim. iv.

NA'MED, *pp.* Called; denominated; designated by name.

NA'MELESS, *a.* Without a name; not distinguished by an appellation; as a *nameless* star. *Waller.*

2. He or that whose name is not known or mentioned. *Atterbury.*

NA'MELY, *adv.* To mention by name; particularly.

For the excellency of the soul, *namely*, its power of divining in dreams; that several such divinations have been made, none can question. *Addison.*

NA'MER, *n.* One that names or calls by name.

NA'MESAKE, *n.* One that has the same name as another. *Addison.*

NA'MING, *ppr.* Calling; nominating; mentioning.

NAN, a Welsh word signifying *what*, used as an interrogative. [This word has been extensively used within my memory by the common people of New England.]

NANKEE'N, *n.* [*Nankin*, a Chinese word.] A species of cotton cloth of a firm texture, from China, now imitated by the manufacturers in Great Britain.

NAP, *n.* [Sax. *hnappian*. Qu. its connection with *hnepan*, to lean, that is, to nod.]

A short sleep or slumber. *Sidney.*

NAP, *v. i.* To have a short sleep; to be drowsy.

2. To be in a careless, secure state. *Wickliffe.*

NAP, *n.* [Sax. *hnoppa*, nap; It. *nappa*, a tassel; Ar. كناب kinabon. Class Nb. No. 20.]

1. The woolly or villous substance on the surface of cloth.

2. The downy or soft hairy substance on plants. *Martyn.*

3. A knop. [See *Knop.*]

NAPE, *n.* [Sax. *cnæp*, a knob; Ar. كنب kanaba, to be hard or callous, whence a callus. Class Nb. No. 20.]

The prominent joint of the neck behind. *Bacon.*

NA'PERY, *n.* [Fr. *nappe*; It. *nappa, napparie.*]

Linen for the table; table cloths or linen cloth in general. *Obs.* *Shelton.*

NAPH'EW, *n.* [L. *napus*, a turnep; Sax. *cnæp*, a knob.] A plant.

NAPH'THA, *n.* [L. Gr. Ch. Syr. Ar. from نفط nafata, to push out, as pustules, to throw out, to boil, to be angry. In Amharic, *neft* or *nepht*, from this sense, signifies a gun or musket.]

An inflammable mineral substance of the bituminous kind, of a light brown or yellowish color, sharp taste, and incapable of decomposition. By long keeping it hardens into a substance resembling vegetable resin, and becomes black. It is as inflammable as ether. It is said to issue from the earth at Baku, in Persia, and to be received into cisterns. *Encyc. Kirwan.*

Naphtha consists of carbon and hydrogen. *Thomson.*

NAPH'THALINE, *n.* A peculiar crystalizable substance, deposited from naphtha distilled from coal tar, consisting of hydrogen and carbon. *Webster's Manual.*

NAP'KIN, *n.* [Fr. *nape*, cloth; of which *napkin* is a diminutive.]

1. A cloth used for wiping the hands; a towel.

2. A handkerchief. *Obs.* *Shak.*

NAP'LESS, *a.* Without nap; threadbare. *Shak.*

NAP'PAL, *n.* Soap rock. *Pinkerton.*

NAP'PINESS, *n.* The quality of being sleepy or inclined to take naps.

2. The quality of having a nap; abundance of nap; as on cloth.

NAP'PY, *a.* [from *nap.*] Frothy; spumy; as *nappy* beer. *Gay.*

NAP'TAKING, *a.* Taking naps.

NAP'TAKING, *n.* A taking by surprise, as when one is not on his guard; unexpected onset when one is unprepared. *Carew.*

NARCIS'SUS, *n.* [L.; Gr. ναρκισσος.] In *botany*, the daffodil, a genus of plants of several species. They are of the bulbous-rooted tribe, perennial in root, but with annual leaves and flower stalks. *Encyc.*

NARCOT'IC, NARCOT'ICAL, } *a.* [Gr. ναρκωτικος, from ναρκοω, to render torpid.]

Causing stupor, stupefaction, or insensibility to pain; soporific; inducing sleep. *Quincy. Encyc.*

NARCOT'IC, *n.* A medicine which stupefies the senses and renders insensible to pain; hence, a medicine which induces sleep; a soporific; an opiate. *Quincy. Encyc.*

NARCOT'ICALLY, *adv.* By producing torpor or drowsiness. *Whitlock.*

NARCOT'ICNESS, *n.* The quality of inducing sleep or removing pain.

N'ARCOTINE, *n.* The pure narcotic principle of opium. *Journ. of Science.*

N'ARD, *n.* [L. *nardus, nardum*; Gr. ναρδος; from the Arabic, Phenician, Syriac or Persian, probably the latter. It is a native of India, where it is called *jatamansi* and *sumbul.* *Sir Wm. Jones.*]

1. A plant usually called spikenard, *spica nardi;* highly valued by the ancients, both as an article of luxury and of medicine. It is an odorous or aromatic plant.

2. An unguent prepared from the plant.

N'ARDINE, *a.* Pertaining to nard; having the qualities of spikenard. *Asiat. Res.*

NARE, *n.* [L. *naris.*] The nostril. [*Not used.*] *Hudibras.*

NAR'RABLE, *a.* [L. *narrabilis.* See *Narrate.*]

That may be related, told or narrated. [*Not used.*]

NAR'RATE, *v. t.* [L. *narro*; It. *narrare*; Sp. *narrar*; Fr. *narrer.* Class Nr. No. 2. 5. 6.]

1. To tell, rehearse or recite, as a story; to relate the particulars of any event or transaction, or any series of incidents.

2. To write, as the particulars of a story or history. We never say, to *narrate* a sentence, a sermon or an oration, but we *narrate* a story, or the particular events which have fallen under our observation, or which we have heard related.

NAR'RATED, *pp.* Related; told.

NAR'RATING, *ppr.* Relating; telling; reciting.

NARRA'TION, *n.* [L. *narratio.*] The act of telling or relating the particulars of an event; rehearsal; recital.

2. Relation; story; history; the relation in words or writing, of the particulars of any transaction or event, or of any series of transactions or events.

3. In *oratory*, that part of a discourse which recites the time, manner or consequences of an action, or simply states the facts connected with the subject.

NAR'RATIVE, *a.* [Fr. *narratif.*] Relating the particulars of an event or transaction; giving a particular or continued account.

2. Apt or inclined to relate stories, or to tell particulars of events; story-telling.

> But wise through time and *narrative* with age. *Pope.*

NAR'RATIVE, *n.* The recital of a story, or a continued account of the particulars of an event or transaction; story.

> Cynthio was much taken with my *narrative.* *Tatler.*

NAR'RATIVELY, *adv.* By way of narration, story or recital. *Ayliffe.*

NARRA'TOR, *n.* One that narrates; one that relates a series of events or transactions. *Watts.*

NAR'RATORY, *a.* Giving an account of events. *Howell.*

NAR'ROW, *a.* [Sax. *neara, nearo, nearu, nearew.* I suspect this word and *near* to be contracted by the loss of *g*, W. *nig*, narrow, strait; *nigiaw*, to narrow; for the D. has *naauw*, narrow, close, G. *genau*, with a prefix. In this case, the word belongs to the root of *nigh;* D. *naaken*, to approach.]

1. Of little breadth; not wide or broad; having little distance from side to side; as a *narrow* board; a *narrow* street; a *narrow* sea; a *narrow* hem or border. It is only or chiefly applied to the surface of flat or level bodies.

2. Of little extent; very limited; as a *narrow* space or compass.

3. Covetous; not liberal or bountiful; as a *narrow* heart.

4. Contracted; of confined views or sentiments; very limited.

> The greatest understanding is *narrow.* *Grew.*

In this sense and the former, it is often prefixed to mind or soul, &c.; as *narrow*-minded; *narrow*-souled; *narrow*-hearted.

5. Near; within a small distance. *Dryden.*

6. Close; near; accurate; scrutinizing; as a *narrow* search; *narrow* inspection.

7. Near; barely sufficient to avoid evil; as a *narrow* escape.

NAR'ROW, NAR'ROWS, } *n.* A strait; a narrow passage through a mountain, or a narrow channel of water between one sea or lake and another; a sound. It is usually in the plural, but sometimes in the singular. *Washington. Mitford.*

NAR'ROW, *v. t.* To lessen the breadth of; to contract.

> A government, by alienating the affections of the people, may be said to *narrow* its bottom. *Temple.*

2. To contract in extent; as, to *narrow* one's influence; to *narrow* the faculties or capacity.

3. To draw into a smaller compass; to contract; to limit; to confine; as, to *narrow* our views or knowledge; to *narrow* a question in discussion.

4. In knitting, to contract the size of a stocking by taking two stitches into one.

NAR'ROW, *v. i.* To become less broad; to contract in breadth. At that place, the sea *narrows* into a strait.

2. In *horsemanship*, a horse is said to *narrow*, when he does not take ground enough, or bear out enough to the one hand or the other. *Far. Dict.*

3. To contract the size of a stocking by taking two stitches into one.

NAR'ROWED, *pp.* Contracted; made less wide.

NAR'ROWING, *ppr.* Contracting; making less broad.

NAR'ROWINGS, *n.* The part of a stocking which is narrowed.

NAR'ROWLY, *adv.* With little breadth.

2. Contractedly; without much extent.

3. Closely; accurately; with minute scrutiny; as, to look or watch *narrowly;* to search *narrowly.*

4. Nearly; within a little; by a small distance; as, he *narrowly* escaped.

5. Sparingly.

NAR'ROWNESS, *n.* Smallness of breadth or distance from side to side; as the *narrowness* of cloth, of a street or highway, of a stream or sea.

2. Smallness of extent; contractedness; as the *narrowness* of capacity or comprehension; *narrowness* of knowledge or attainments.

3. Smallness of estate or means of living; poverty; as the *narrowness* of fortune or of circumstances. *South.*

4. Contractedness; penuriousness; covetousness; as *narrowness* of heart.

5. Illiberality; want of generous, enlarged or charitable views or sentiments; as *narrowness* of mind or views.

N'ARWAL, N'ARWHAL, } *n.* [G. *narwall.*] The *Monodon monoceros*, a cetaceous animal found in the northern seas, which grows to twenty feet in length. The spiracle of this animal is on the anterior part of the skull. When young it has two teeth or horns, but when old it has but one, which projects from the upper jaw and is spiral. From this circumstance of its having one horn only, it has obtained the name of the *sea unicorn*, or *unicorn fish.* *Pennant. Encyc.*

NAS, for *ne has*, has not. *Obs.* *Spenser.*

NA'SAL, *a.* *s* as *z.* [L. *nasus*, nose; It. *nasale.*]

Pertaining to the nose; formed or affected by the nose; as a *nasal* sound; a *nasal* letter.

NA'SAL, *n.* *s* as *z.* A letter whose sound is affected by the nose.

2. A medicine that operates through the nose; an errhine. *Barton.*

NAS'CAL, *n.* A kind of medicated pessary. *Ferrand.*

A pessary made of wool or cotton, to raise the nose when compressed. *Parr.*

NAS'CENT, *a.* [L. *nascens, nasco*, to be born.]

Beginning to exist or to grow; coming into being. *Black.*

NA'SEBERRY, *n.* The naseberry tree is a species of the genus Sloanea. *Fam. of Plants.*

NAS'ICORNOUS, *a.* [L. *nasus*, nose, and *cornu*, horn.]

Having a horn growing on the nose. *Brown.*

N'ASTILY, *adv.* [from *nasty.*] In a nasty manner; filthily; dirtily.

2. Obscenely.

N'ASTINESS, *n.* Extreme filthiness; dirtiness; filth.
2. Obscenity; ribaldry. *South.*

NASTUR'TION, *n.* [L. *nasturtium; quod* nasum torqueat. *Varro.*]
A plant of the genus Tropœolum; Indian cresses.

N'ASTY, *a.* [origin unknown. Qu. G. *nass*, wet.]
1. Disgustingly filthy; very dirty, foul or defiled; nauseous. *Atterbury.*
2. Obscene.

NA'SUS, *n.* A fresh water fish, about nine inches in length, resembling the chub. It is found in the Danube, Rhine and other large rivers of Germany. *Dict. Nat. Hist.*

NA'TAL, *a.* [L. *natalis*, from *nascor*, to be born.]
Pertaining to birth. The *natal* day is the day of birth or nativity. So we say, *natal* hour; *natal* place. *Camden. Prior.*

NATALI''TIAL, } *a.* [L. *natalitius*, from NATALI''TIOUS, } *nascor*, to be born.]
Pertaining to one's birth or birth day, or consecrated to one's nativity. *Evelyn.*

NA'TANT, *a.* [L. *natans*, from *nato*, to swim.]
In *botany*, swimming; floating on the surface of water; as the leaf of an aquatic plant. *Lee. Martyn.*

NATA'TION, *n.* [L. *natatio*, from *nato*, to swim.]
A swimming; the act of floating on the water. [*Little used.*] *Brown.*

NA'TATORY, *a.* Enabling to swim. *Brit. Crit.*

NATCH, *n.* [for *notch.*] The part of an ox between the loins, near the rump. *Marshal.*

NATH'LESS, *adv.* [Sax. *natheles; na, the* and *less*, not the less.]
Nevertheless; not the less; notwithstanding. *Obs.* *Milton.*

NATH'MORE, *adv.* [*na, the* and *more.*] Not the more; never the more. *Obs.* *Spenser.*

NA'TION, *n.* [L. *natio*, from *natus*, born; *nascor*, to be born; perhaps Heb. נין.]
1. A body of people inhabiting the same country, or united under the same sovereign or government; as the English *nation;* the French *nation.* It often happens that many nations are subject to one government; in which case, the word *nation* usually denotes a body of people speaking the same language, or a body that has formerly been under a distinct government, but has been conquered, or incorporated with a larger nation. Thus the empire of Russia comprehends many *nations*, as did formerly the Roman and Persian empires. *Nation*, as its etymology imports, originally denoted a family or race of men descended from a common progenitor, like *tribe*, but by emigration, conquest and intermixture of men of different families, this distinction is in most countries lost.
2. A great number, by way of emphasis. *Young.*

NA'TIONAL, *a.* Pertaining to a nation; as *national* customs, dress or language.
2. Public; general; common to a nation; as a *national* calamity.
3. Attached or unduly attached to one's own country. The writer manifested much *national* prejudice. He was too *national* to be impartial.

NATIONAL'ITY, *n.* National character; also, the quality of being national, or strongly attached to one's own nation. *Boswell.*

NA'TIONALIZE, *v. t.* To make national; to give to one the character and habits of a nation, or the peculiar attachments which belong to citizens of the same nation.

NA'TIONALLY, *adv.* In regard to the nation; as a whole nation.
> The Jews—being *nationally* espoused to God by covenant. *South.*

NA'TIVE, *a.* [L. *nativus*, from *nascor, natus*, to be born.]
1. Produced by nature; original; born with the being; natural; not acquired; as *native* genius; *native* affections; a *native* talent or disposition; *native* cheerfulness; *native* simplicity.
2. Produced by nature; not factitious or artificial; as *native* ore; *native* color.
3. Conferred by birth; as *native* rights and privileges.
4. Pertaining to the place of birth; as *native* soil; *native* country; *native* graves. *Shak.*
5. Original; that of which any thing is made; as man's *native* dust. *Milton.*
6. Born with; congenial. *Shak.*

NA'TIVE, *n.* One born in any place is said to be a *native* of that place, whether country, city or town.
2. Offspring. [*Not in use.*] *Shak.*

NA'TIVELY, *adv.* By birth; naturally; originally. *Taylor. Lightfoot.*

NA'TIVENESS, *n.* State of being produced by nature. *Johnson.*

NATIV'ITY, *n.* Birth; the coming into life or the world. The feast of Christmas is observed in memory of Christ's *nativity.*
2. Time, place and manner of birth; as, to calculate one's *nativity.*
3. State or place of being produced.
> These, in their dark *nativity*, the deep
> Shall yield us pregnant with infernal flame. *Milton.*

NAT'KA, *n.* A bird, a species of shrike. *Pennant.*

NA'TROLITE, *n.* A variety of mesotype or zeolite, so called by Klaproth on account of the great quantity of soda it contains. *Dict. Nat. Hist.*

NA'TRON, *n.* Native carbonate of soda, or mineral alkali. [See *Niter.*]

NAT'URAL, *a.* [Fr. *naturel;* L. *naturalis*, from *natura*, nature, from *nascor*, to be born or produced.]
1. Pertaining to nature; produced or effected by nature, or by the laws of growth, formation or motion impressed on bodies or beings by divine power. Thus we speak of the *natural* growth of animals or plants; the *natural* motion of a gravitating body; *natural* strength or disposition; the *natural* heat of the body; *natural* color; *natural* beauty. In this sense, *natural* is opposed to *artificial* or *acquired.*
2. According to the stated course of things. Poverty and shame are the *natural* consequences of certain vices.
3. Not forced; not far fetched; such as is dictated by nature. The gestures of the orator are *natural.*
4. According to the life; as a *natural* representation of the face.
5. Consonant to nature.
> Fire and warmth go together, and so seem to carry with them as *natural* an evidence as self-evident truths themselves. *Locke.*

6. Derived from nature, as opposed to *habitual.* The love of pleasure is *natural;* the love of study is usually habitual or acquired.
7. Discoverable by reason; not revealed; as *natural* religion.
8. Produced or coming in the ordinary course of things, or the progress of animals and vegetables; as a *natural* death; opposed to *violent* or *premature.*
9. Tender; affectionate by nature. *Shak.*
10. Unaffected; unassumed; according to truth and reality.
> What can be more *natural* than the circumstances of the behavior of those women who had lost their husbands on this fatal day? *Addison.*

11. Illegitimate; born out of wedlock; as a *natural* son.
12. Native; vernacular; as one's *natural* language. *Swift.*
13. Derived from the study of the works of nature; as *natural* knowledge. *Addison.*
14. A *natural* note, in music, is that which is according to the usual order of the scale; opposed to *flat* and *sharp* notes, which are called *artificial.*

Natural history, in its most extensive sense, is the description of whatever is created, or of the whole universe, including the heavens and the earth, and all the productions of the earth. But more generally, natural history is limited to a description of the earth and its productions, including zoology, botany, geology, mineralogy, meteorology, &c.

Natural philosophy, the science of material natural bodies, of their properties, powers and motions. It is distinguished from intellectual and moral philosophy, which respect the mind or understanding of man and the qualities of actions. Natural philosophy comprehends mechanics, hydrostatics, optics, astronomy, chimistry, magnetism, electricity, galvanism, &c.

NAT'URAL, *n.* An idiot; one born without the usual powers of reason or understanding. This is probably elliptical for *natural fool.*
2. A native; an original inhabitant. [*Not in use.*] *Raleigh.*
3. Gift of nature; natural quality. [*Not in use.*] *B. Jonson. Wotton.*

NAT'URALISM, *n.* Mere state of nature. *Lavington.*

NAT'URALIST, *n.* One that studies natural history and philosophy or physics; one that is versed in natural history or philosophy. It is more generally applied to one that is versed in *natural history.*

NATURALIZA'TION, *n.* [See *Naturalize.*] The act of investing an alien with the rights and privileges of a native subject or citizen. *Naturalization* in Great Britain is only by act of parliament. In the United States, it is by act of Congress, vesting certain tribunals with the power.

NAT'URALIZE, *v. t.* [from *natural, nature.*]
1. To confer on an alien the rights and privileges of a native subject or citizen; to adopt foreigners into a nation or state, and place them in the condition of natural born subjects.
2. To make natural; to render easy and familiar by custom and habit; as, custom *naturalizes* labor or study. *South.*
3. To adapt; to make suitable; to acclimate; as, to *naturalize* one to a climate.
4. To receive or adopt as native, natural or vernacular; to make our own; as, to *naturalize* foreign words.
5. To accustom; to habituate; as, to *naturalize* the vine to a cold climate. *Gibbon.*

NAT'URALIZED, *pp.* Invested with the privileges of natives; rendered easy and familiar; adapted to a climate; acclimated; received as native.

NAT'URALIZING, *ppr.* Vesting with the rights of native subjects; making easy; acclimating; adopting.

NAT'URALLY, *adv.* According to nature; by the force or impulse of nature; not by art or habit. We are *naturally* prone to evil.
2. According to nature; without affectation; with just representation; according to life.
3. According to the usual course of things; as, the effect or consequence *naturally* follows.
4. Spontaneously; without art or cultivation. Every plant must have grown *naturally* in some place or other.

NAT'URALNESS, *n.* The state of being given or produced by nature; as the *naturalness* of desire. *South.*
2. Conformity to nature, or to truth and reality; not affectation; as the *naturalness* of the eyebrows. *Dryden.*

NAT'URALS, *n. plu.* Among physicians, whatever belongs naturally to an animal; opposed to *non-naturals.* [*It may perhaps be sometimes used in the singular.*]

NA'TURE, *n.* [Fr. *id.*; L. Sp. It. *natura;* from *natus*, born, produced, from *nascor.*]
1. In *a general sense*, whatever is made or produced; a word that comprehends all the works of God; the universe. Of a phenix we say, there is no such thing in *nature.*

And look through *nature* up to *nature's* God. *Pope.*

2. By a metonymy of the effect for the cause, *nature* is used for the agent, creator, author, producer of things, or for the powers that produce them. By the expression, "trees and fossils are produced by *nature*," we mean, they are formed or produced by certain inherent powers in matter, or we mean that they are produced by God, the Creator, the Author of whatever is made or produced. The opinion that things are produced by inherent powers of matter, independent of a supreme intelligent author, is atheism. But generally men mean by *nature*, thus used, the Author of created things, or the operation of his power.
3. The essence, essential qualities or attributes of a thing, which constitute it what it is; as the *nature* of the soul; the *nature* of blood; the *nature* of a fluid; the *nature* of plants, or of a metal; the *nature* of a circle or an angle. When we speak of the *nature* of man, we understand the peculiar constitution of his body or mind, or the qualities of the species which distinguish him from other animals. When we speak of the *nature* of *a* man, or an individual of the race, we mean his particular qualities or constitution; either the peculiar temperament of his body, or the affections of his mind, his natural appetites, passions, disposition or temper. So of irrational animals.
4. The established or regular course of things; as when we say, an event is not according to *nature*, or it is out of the order of *nature.* *Boyle.*
5. A law or principle of action or motion in a natural body. A stone by *nature* falls, or inclines to fall. *Boyle.*
6. Constitution; aggregate powers of a body, especially a living one. We say, *nature* is strong or weak; *nature* is almost exhausted. *Boyle.*
7. The constitution and appearances of things.

The works, whether of poets, painters, moralists or historians, which are built upon general *nature*, live forever. *Reynolds.*

8. Natural affection or reverence.

Have we not seen
The murdering son ascend his parent's bed,
Through violated *nature* force his way? *Pope.*

9. System of created things.

He binding *nature* fast in fate,
Left conscience free and will. *Pope.*

10. Sort; species; kind; particular character.

A dispute of this *nature* caused mischief to a king and an archbishop. *Dryden.*

11. Sentiments or images conformed to nature, or to truth and reality.

Only *nature* can please those tastes which are unprejudiced and refined. *Addison.*

12. Birth. No man is noble by *nature.*

NA'TURE, *v. t.* To endow with natural qualities. [*Not in use.*] *Gower.*

NA'TURIST, *n.* One who ascribes every thing to nature. *Boyle.*

NATU'RITY, *n.* The quality or state of being produced by nature. [*A very bad word and not used.*] *Brown.*

NAU'FRAGE, *n.* [L. *naufragium; navis*, a ship, and *frango*, to break. See *Wreck*, which is from the same root, *break*, L. *fractus.*] Shipwreck. [*Not in use.*] *Brown.*

NAU'FRAGOUS, *a.* Causing shipwreck. [*Little used.*] *Taylor.*

NAUGHT, *n. naut.* [Sax. *naht, nauht;* compounded of *ne* and *aught* or *wiht*, a creature, wight; Goth. *niwaiht. Waiht* coincides with *wight*, L. *quid, quod.* See *Aught.*] Nothing.

Doth Job serve God for *naught?* Job i.
Thou sellest thy people for *naught.* Ps. xliv.

To set at naught, to slight, disregard or despise.

Ye have *set at naught* all my counsel. Prov. i.

NAUGHT, *adv. naut.* In no degree.

To wealth or sovereign power he *naught* applied. *Fairfax.*

NAUGHT, *a. naut.* Bad; worthless; of no value or account.

Things *naught* and things indifferent. *Hooker.*

It is *naught*, it is *naught*, says the buyer. Prov. xx.

NAUGHTILY, *adv. naut'ily.* Wickedly; corruptly.

NAUGHTINESS, *n. naut'iness.* Badness; wickedness; evil principle or purpose.

I know thy pride and the *naughtiness* of thy heart. 1 Sam. xvii.

2. Slight wickedness of children; perverseness; mischievousness. *Dryden. Shak. Sidney.*

NAUGHTY, *a. naut'y.* Wicked; corrupt.

A *naughty* person, a wicked man, walketh with a froward mouth. Prov. 6.

2. Bad; worthless.

The other basket had very *naughty* figs. Jer. xxiv.

3. Mischievous; perverse; froward; as a *naughty* child. It is now seldom used except in the latter sense, as applied to children.

NAUL'AGE, *n.* [L. *naulum.*] The freight of passengers in a ship. [*Little used.*]

NAU'MACHY, *n.* [L. *naumachia;* Gr. ναυμαχια; ναυς, a ship, and μαχη, fight.]
1. Among the ancient Romans, a show or spectacle representing a sea-fight.
2. The place where these shows were exhibited. *Encyc.*

NAU'SEA, *n.* [L. from Gr. ναυσια, from ναυς, a ship.]
Originally and properly, sea-sickness; hence, any similar sickness of the stomach, accompanied with a propensity to vomit; qualm; lothing; squeamishness of the stomach.

NAU'SEATE, *v. i.* [L. *nauseo.*] To become squeamish; to feel disgust; to be inclined to reject from the stomach.

NAU'SEATE, *v. t.* To lothe; to reject with disgust.

The patient *nauseates* and lothes wholesome foods. *Blackmore.*

Old age, with silent pace, comes creeping on,
Nauseates the praise which in her youth she won. *Dryden.*

2. To affect with disgust. *Swift.*

NAU'SEOUS, *a.* Lothesome; disgustful; disgusting; regarded with abhorrence; as a *nauseous* drug or medicine.

NAU'SEOUSLY, *adv.* Lothesomely; disgustfully.

NAU'SEOUSNESS, *n.* Lothesomeness; quality of exciting disgust; as the *nauseousness* of a drug or medicine.

The *nauseousness* of such company disgusts a reasonable man. *Dryden.*

NAU'TIC, NAU'TICAL, *a.* [L. *nauticus*, from *nauta*, a seaman, from *navis*, a ship. See *Navy.*]
Pertaining to seamen or navigation; as *nautical* skill; a *nautical* almanack.

NAU'TILITE, *n.* [from L. *nautilus*, a shell-fish.] A fossil nautilus. *Kirwan. Dict.*

NAU'TILUS, *n.* [L.; Gr. ναυτιλος, from ναυς, a ship.]
A genus of marine animals, whose shell consists of one spiral valve divided into several apartments by partitions. There are many species. This animal, when it sails, extends two of its arms, and between these supports a membrane that serves as a sail. With two other arms it rows or steers. *Encyc.*

Learn of the little *nautilus* to sail. *Pope.*

NA'VAL, *a.* [L. *navalis*, from *navis*, Gr. ναυς, a ship.]

1. Consisting of ships; as a *naval* force or armament.
2. Pertaining to ships; as *naval* stores.

NA'VALS, *n.* Naval affairs. [*Not used.*] *Clarendon.*

NA'VARCH, *n.* [Gr. ναυαρχος.] In ancient Greece, the commander of a fleet. *Mitford.*

NAV'ARCHY, *n.* [from L. *navarchus*, an admiral.] Knowledge of managing ships. *Petty.*

NAVE, *n.* [Sax. *nafa, nafu*; Dan. *nav*; G. *nabe*; Sw. *naf.*]
1. The thick piece of timber in the center of a wheel, in which the spokes are inserted; called also the *hob.*
2. The middle or body of a church extending from the balluster or rail of the door, to the chief choir. *Encyc.*

NAVEL, *n.* *na'vl.* [Sax. *nafela*, from *nafa*, nave; D. *navel*; G. *nabel*; Sw. *nafle*; Dan. *navle*; Zend, *nafo*; Pehlavi, *naf*; Sans. *nabha*; Pers. ناف naf.]
The center of the lower part of the abdomen, or the point where the umbilical cord passes out of the fetus. The umbilical cord is a collection of vessels by which the fetus of an animal communicates with the parent by means of the placenta, to which it is attached. *Encyc.*

NA'VEL-GALL, *n.* A bruise on the top of the chine of the back of a horse, behind the saddle. *Johnson.*

NA'VEL-STRING, *n.* The umbilical cord. [See *Navel.*]

NA'VEL-WORT, *n.* A plant of the genus Cotyledon. It has the appearance of houseleek. *Miller.*

NAV'EW, *n.* [L. *napus*; Sax. *næpe.*] A plant of the genus Brassica. It has a spindle-shaped root, less than the turnep. *Encyc. Miller.*

NAVIC'ULAR, *a.* [L. *navicula*, a little ship.]
1. Relating to small ships or boats. *Bryant.*
2. Shaped like a boat; cymbiform. The *navicular* bone is the scaphoid bone of the wrist. *Coxe. Quincy.*

NAV'IGABLE, *a.* [L. *navigabilis*, from *navigo*, to sail, from *navis*, a ship.]
That may be navigated or passed in ships or vessels; as a *navigable* river.

NAV'IGABLENESS, *n.* The quality or state of being navigable.

NAV'IGATE, *v. i.* [L. *navigo*, from *navis*, a ship; Ir. *snamhaim.*]
To pass on water in ships; to sail.

The Phœnicians *navigated* to the extremities of the Western ocean. *Arbuthnot.*

NAV'IGATE, *v. t.* To pass over in ships; to sail on; as, to *navigate* the Atlantic.
2. To steer, direct or manage in sailing; as, to *navigate* a ship.

NAV'IGATED, *pp.* Steered or managed in passing on the water; passed over in sailing.

NAV'IGATING, *ppr.* Passing on or over in sailing; steering and managing in sailing.

NAVIGA'TION, *n.* [L. *navigatio.*] The act of navigating; the act of passing on water in ships or other vessels.
2. The art of conducting ships or vessels from one place to another. This art comprehends not only the management of the sails, but the directing and measuring of the course of ships by the laws of geometry, or by astronomical principles and observations. *Encyc.*
3. Ships in general.
Aerial navigation, the sailing or floating in the air by means of balloons.
Inland navigation, the passing of boats or small vessels on rivers, lakes or canals, in the interior of a country; conveyance by boats or vessels in the interior of a country.

NAV'IGATOR, *n.* One that navigates or sails; chiefly, one who directs the course of a ship, or one who is skillful in the art of navigation. We say, a bold *navigator*, an experienced *navigator*, an able *navigator.*

NA'VY, *n.* [L. *navis*; Gr. ναυς, from νεω, to swim, L. *no, nato*; Sans. *nau*; Armenian, *naw*; Pers. *naodan.* The elements of the verb are probably *Nd*, coinciding with Eng. *nod*, L. *nuto.* To swim then is to move up and down. Class Nd. No. 3. 9.]
1. A fleet of ships; an assemblage of merchantmen, or so many as sail in company.

The *navy* of Hiram brought gold from Ophir. 1 Kings x.

2. The whole of the ships of war belonging to a nation or king. The *navy* of Great Britain is the defense of the kingdom and its commerce. This is the usual acceptation of the word.

NAWL, *n.* An awl. [*Not in use.*]

NAY, *adv.* [a contracted word; L. *nego*; Sw. *ney* or *nej*, from *neka*, to deny; W. *nac*, from *naca*, to deny.]
1. No; a word that expresses negation.

I tell you *nay*, but except ye repent, ye shall all likewise perish. Luke xiii.

2. It expresses also refusal.

He that will not when he may,
When he would he shall have *nay.* *Proverb.*

[In these senses it is now rarely used; *no* being substituted.]
3. Not only so; not this alone; intimating that something is to be added by way of amplification. He requested an answer; *nay*, he urged it.

NAY, *n.* Denial; refusal.

NAY, *v. t.* To refuse. [*Not in use.*]

NA'YWARD, *n.* Tendency to denial. [*Not used.*] *Shak.*

NA'YWORD, *n.* A by-word; a proverbial reproach; a watch-word. *Obs. Ibm.*

NAZARE'NE, *n.* An inhabitant of Nazareth; one of the early converts to Christianity; in contempt. Acts xxiv.

NAZ'ARITE, *n.* A Jew who professed extraordinary purity of life and devotion. *Encyc.*

NAZ'ARITISM, *n.* The doctrines or practice of the Nazarites. *Burder.*

NE, [Sax.] not, is obsolete. We find it in early English writers, prefixed to other words; as *nill*, for *ne will*, will not; *nas*, for *ne has*, has not; *nis*, for *ne is*, is not. *Spenser.*

NEAF, *n.* [Ice. *nefi*; Scot. *nieve.*] The fist. *Obs.* *Shak.*

NEAL, *v. t.* [Sax. *anælan*, to kindle.] To temper and reduce to a due consistence by heat. But *neal* is now rarely used. [See *Anneal.*]

NEAL, *v. i.* To be tempered by heat. [*Little used.*] [See *Anneal.*] *Bacon.*

NEAP, *n.* [This word may belong to the root of *neb, nib*; Ice. *nif*, nose; Eth. *anaf.*]
The tongue or pole of a cart, sled or wagon. *N. England.*

NEAP, *a.* [Sax. *hnipan*, to incline, to fall.] Low. The *neap tides* are those which happen in the middle of the second and fourth quarters of the moon. They are low tides, and opposed to *spring tides.*

NEAP, *n.* Low water. [*Little used.*]

NE'APED, BENE'APED, } *a.* Left aground. A ship is said to be *neaped*, when left aground, particularly on the highth of a spring tide, so that she will not float till the return of the next spring tide. *Mar. Dict.*

NEAPOL'ITAN, *a.* Belonging to Naples, in Italy.

NEAPOL'ITAN, *n.* An inhabitant or native of the kingdom of Naples.

NE'AP-TIDE, *n.* Low tide. [See *Neap.*]

NEAR, *a.* [Sax. *ner* or *neara*, nigher. This seems to be a contracted word, from *nigher*, the comparative of *neh, nih* or *nieh*, D. *naauw*, G. *nahe*, Sw. *når*, Dan. *nær*; W. *nig*, strait, narrow; *nigiaw*, to narrow.]
1. Nigh; not far distant in place, time or degree. Regularly, *near* should be followed by *to*, but this is often omitted. We say, a house stands *near* a river; a friend sits *near* me; the man fell and was *near* destruction.

And Jacob went *near to* Isaac his father. Gen. xxvii.

Now is our salvation *nearer* than when we believed. Rom. xiii.

2. Closely related by blood.

She is thy father's *near* kinswoman. Lev. xviii.

3. Not distant in affection, support or assistance; present; ready; willing to aid.

Call upon the Lord, while he is *near.* Is. lv.

4. Intimate; united in close ties of affection or confidence; as a *near* friend.
5. Dear; affecting one's interest or feelings; as a *near* concern.

My *nearest* life. *Shak.*

6. Close; parsimonious.
7. Close; not loose, free or rambling; as a version *near* the original.
8. Next to one; opposed to *off*; as the *near* horse or ox in a team.

NEAR, *adv.* Almost; within a little. It is *near* twelve o'clock. The payment of such a sum would go *near* to ruin him. *Addison.*

NEAR, *v. t.* To approach; to come nearer; as, the ship *neared* the land; *a seaman's phrase.*

NE'AREST, *a.* [*superl.* of *near.*] Shortest; most direct; as the *nearest* way to London. So we use *nearer* for *shorter.* [This use of these words is not correct, but very common.]

NE'ARLY, *adv.* At no great distance; not remotely.
2. Closely; as two persons *nearly* related or allied.
3. Intimately; pressingly; with a close relation to one's interest or happiness. It *nearly* concerns us to preserve peace with our neighbor.
4. Almost; within a little. The fact is *nearly* demonstrated.
5. In a parsimonious or niggardly manner.

NE'ARNESS, *n.* Closeness; small distance. The *nearness* of a place to a market enhances the value of lands.

2. Close alliance by blood; propinquity; as the *nearness* of brothers and sisters, parents and children.

3. Close union by affection; intimacy of friendship.

4. Parsimony; closeness in expenses. *Bacon.*

NEAT, *n.* [Sax. *neat, neten, niten, nyten*; Sw. *nöt*; Dan. *nöd.* In Sax. *geneat* is a herdsman. In Spanish, *ganado* is cattle, and vermin; doubtless the same word with a prefix. In W. *cnud* is a group. *Neat* coincides with the root of *need* in elements, and if connected with it, the sense is a herd or collection, from crowding, pressing; but this is doubtful.]

1. Cattle of the bovine genus, as bulls, oxen and cows. In America, this word is used in composition, as in *neat's* tongue, *neat's* foot oil, and tautologically in *neat cattle.*

2. A single cow. *Tusser.*

NEAT, *a.* [It. *netto*; Sp. *neto*; Fr. *net*; Arm. *neat* or *neet*; L. *nitidus, niteo*, to shine, to be clean, fair or fine; W. *nith*, pure; *nithiaw*, to purify, to winnow.]

1. Very clean; free from foul or extraneous matter; as *neat* clothes. The vessels are kept *neat*; the woman keeps her house very *neat.*

2. Pure; free from impure words and phrases; as a *neat* style.

3. Cleanly; preserving neatness; as a *neat* woman.

4. Pure; unadulterated; as *neat* wine. *Obs.* *Chapman.*

5. Free from tawdry appendages and well adjusted; as a *neat* dress.

6. Clear of the cask, case, bag, box, &c.; as *neat* weight. It is usually written *net* or *nett.*

NE'ATHERD, *n.* [Sax. *neathyrd.*] A person who has the care of cattle; a cow-keeper. *Dryden.*

NE'ATLY, *adv.* With neatness; in a neat manner; in a cleanly manner; as a garment *neatly* washed.

2. With good taste; without tawdry ornaments; as a lady *neatly* dressed.

3. Nicely; handsomely; as a vessel *neatly* gilt.

NE'ATNESS, *n.* Exact cleanliness; entire freedom from foul matter; as the *neatness* of a floor or of a garment.

2. Purity; freedom from ill chosen words; as the *neatness* of style.

3. Freedom from useless or tawdry ornaments; with good adjustment of the several parts; as the *neatness* of a dress.

NE'ATRESS, *n.* [from *neat*, cattle.] A female who takes care of cattle. [*Not used in the United States.*] *Warner.*

NEB, *n.* [Sax. *neb* or *nebbe*; Ice. *nebbe* or *nef*; Dan. *neb, næb*, and with a prefix, *snabel*; Sw. *näf*; D. *neb, sneb*; G. *schnabel.* In the different dialects, it signifies a bill, beak, the nose, or the face, from extending or shooting. See Class Nb. No. 2. 3. 6. 8. 10. 13. 15. 21. 24. It is also written *nib.*]

The nose; the beak of a fowl; the bill; the mouth.

NEB'ULA, **NEB'ULE**, *n.* [L. *nebula*; Gr. νεφος, νεφελη; G. *nebel*; D. *nevel*; Ir. *neall, neul*, by contraction; It. *nebbia*; Sp. *niebla*, fog, mist. Probably the primary sense is thick or mixed.]

1. A dark spot, a film in the eye, or a slight opacity of the cornea. *Cyc.*

2. In *astronomy*, a cluster of fixed stars, not distinguishable from each other or scarcely visible to the naked eye, and exhibiting a dim hazy light, appearing like dusky specks or clouds through the telescope. *Cyc.*

NEBULOS'ITY, *n.* [from *nebulous.*] The state of being cloudy or hazy. *Med. Repos.*

NEB'ULOUS, *a.* [L. *nebulosus.*] Cloudy; hazy. [See *Nebule.*]

2. Resembling a small cloud or collection of vapors.

NECESSA'RIAN, *n.* [See *Necessary.*] An advocate for the doctrine of philosophical necessity; more properly *necessitarian.* *Priestley.*

NEC'ESSARIES, *n. plu.* [from *necessary.*] Things necessary for some purpose; as the *necessaries* of life. *Locke.*

NEC'ESSARILY, *adv.* By necessity; in such a manner that it cannot be otherwise. Truth is *necessarily* opposite to falsehood. A square is *necessarily* different from a circle.

2. Indispensably. Most men are *necessarily* occupied in procuring their subsistence.

3. By unavoidable consequence. Certain inferences *necessarily* result from particular premises.

NEC'ESSARINESS, *n.* The state of being necessary.

NEC'ESSARY, *a.* [L. *necessarius.*] That must be; that cannot be otherwise; indispensably requisite. It is *necessary* that every effect should have a cause.

2. Indispensable; requisite; essential; that cannot be otherwise without preventing the purpose intended. Air is *necessary* to support animal life; food is *necessary* to nourish the body; holiness is a *necessary* qualification for happiness; health is *necessary* to the enjoyment of pleasure; subjection to law is *necessary* to the safety of persons and property.

3. Unavoidable; as a *necessary* inference or consequence from facts or arguments.

4. Acting from necessity or compulsion; opposed to *free.* Whether man is a *necessary* or a free agent is a question much discussed.

NEC'ESSARY, *n.* A privy.

NECESSITA'RIAN, **NECESSA'RIAN**, *n.* One who maintains the doctrine of philosophical necessity in regard to the origin and existence of things. *Beattie.*

NECES'SITATE, *v. t.* [from L. *necessitas.*] To make necessary or indispensable; to render unavoidable; to compel.

> The marquis of Newcastle, being pressed on both sides, was *necessitated* to draw all his army into York. *Clarendon.*
>
> Sickness might *necessitate* his removal from court. *South.*

NECES'SITATED, *pp.* Made necessary, indispensable or unavoidable.

NECES'SITATING, *ppr.* Making necessary or indispensable.

NECESSITA'TION, *n.* The act of making necessary; compulsion. [*Little used.*] *Bramhall.*

NECES'SITIED, *a.* In a state of want. [*Not in use.*] *Shak.*

NECES'SITOUS, *a.* Very needy or indigent; pressed with poverty.

> There are multitudes of *necessitous* heirs and penurious parents. *Arbuthnot.*

2. Narrow; destitute; pinching; as *necessitous* circumstances.

NECES'SITOUSNESS, *n.* Extreme poverty or destitution of the means of living; pressing want. *Burnet.*

NECES'SITUDE, *n.* Necessitousness; want. [*Not used.*] *Hale.*

NECES'SITY, *n.* [L. *necessitas.*] That which must be and cannot be otherwise, or the cause of that which cannot be otherwise. It is of *necessity* that a thing cannot be and not be at the same time. It is of *necessity* that two contradictory propositions cannot both be true.

2. Irresistible power; compulsive force, physical or moral. If man's actions are determined by causes beyond his control, he acts from *necessity*, and is not a free agent. *Necessity* compelled the general to act on the defensive.

3. Indispensableness; the state of being requisite. The *necessity* of funds to support public credit, no man questions. The *necessity* of economy in domestic concerns is admitted. No man can plead *necessity* in excuse for crimes.

4. Extreme indigence; pinching poverty; pressing need.

> The cause of all the distractions in his court or army proceeded from the extreme poverty and *necessity* his majesty was in. *Clarendon.*

5. Unavoidableness; inevitableness; as the *necessity* of a consequence from certain premises.

6. In *the plural*, things requisite for a purpose.

> These should be hours for *necessities*,
> Not for delights. *Shak.*

NECK, *n.* [Sax. *hnece, hnecca, necca*; G. *nick, genick*, the nape of the neck; D. *nek*; Sw. *nacke*; Dan. *nakke*; It. Port. Sp. *nuca.* This word is properly the nape or vertebræ of the neck behind, and is so rendered in other languages, L. *nux*, that is, a knob or mass; W. *cnwc.*]

1. The part of an animal's body which is between the head and the trunk, and connects them. In man and many other animals, this part is more slender than the trunk; hence,

2. A long narrow tract of land projecting from the main body, or a narrow tract connecting two larger tracts; as the *neck* of land between Boston and Roxbury.

3. The long slender part of a vessel, as a retort; or of a plant, as a gourd; or of any instrument, as a guitar.

A stiff neck, in Scripture, denotes obstinacy in sin.

On the neck, immediately after; following closely.

> First by committing one sin *on the neck* of another. *Perkins.*

[This phrase is not much used. We more frequently say, *on the heels.*]

To break the neck of an affair, to hinder, or to do the principal thing to prevent.

To harden the neck, to grow obstinate; to be more and more perverse and rebellious. Neh. ix.

NECK'BEEF, *n.* The coarse flesh of the neck of cattle, sold at a low price.

As cheap as *neckbeef*. *Swift.*

NECK'CLOTH, *n.* A piece of cloth worn on the neck.

NECK'ED, *a.* Having a neck; as in *stiff-necked*.

NECK'ERCHIEF, **NECK'ATEE**, *n.* A gorget; a kerchief for a woman's neck. [*Not in much use.*] *Bailey.*

NECK'LACE, *n.* A string of beads or precious stones, worn by women on the neck. *Arbuthnot.*

NECK'LACED, *a.* Marked as with a necklace. *Sir W. Jones.*

NECK'LAND, *n.* A neck or long tract of land. *Hakewill.*

NECK'VERSE, *n.* The verse formerly read to entitle a party to the benefit of clergy, said to be the first verse of the fifty first Psalm, "*Miserere mei, &c.*" *Tindall.*

NECK'WEED, *n.* Hemp; in ridicule.

NECROLOG'ICAL, *a.* Pertaining to or giving an account of the dead or of deaths.

NECROL'OGIST, *n.* One who gives an account of deaths.

NECROL'OGY, *n.* [Gr. *νεκρος*, dead, and *λογος*, discourse.]
An account of the dead or of deaths; a register of deaths.

NEC'ROMANCER, *n.* [See *Necromancy.*] One who pretends to foretell future events by holding converse with departed spirits; a conjurer. *Swift.*

NEC'ROMANCY, *n.* [Gr. *νεκρος*, dead, and *μαντεια*, divination.]
1. The art of revealing future events by means of a pretended communication with the dead. This imposture is prohibited. Deut. xviii.
2. Enchantment; conjuration. *Abbot.*

NECROMAN'TIC, *a.* Pertaining to necromancy; performed by necromancy.

NECROMAN'TIC, *n.* Trick; conjuration. *Young.*

NECROMAN'TICALLY, *adv.* By necromancy or the black art; by conjuration. *Gregory.*

NEC'RONITE, *n.* [Gr. *νεκρος*, dead.] Fetid feldspar, a mineral which when struck or pounded, exhales a fetid odor like that of putrid flesh. *Hayden.*

NEC'TAR, *n.* [L. from the Greek.]
1. In *fabulous history* and *poetry*, the drink of the gods; hence,
2. Any very sweet and pleasant drink.

NECTA'REAN, **NECTA'REOUS**, *a.* Resembling nectar; very sweet and pleasant.

The juice *nectareous* and the balmy dew. *Pope.*

NEC'TARED, *a.* Imbued with nectar; mingled with nectar; abounding with nectar. *Milton.*

NECTA'RIAL, *a.* Pertaining to the nectary of a plant.

Stamens inserted into the margin of a glandulous *nectarial* ring. *As. Res.*

NECTARIF'EROUS, *a.* [*nectar* and L. *fero*, to bear.]
Producing nectar or nomus; as a *nectariferous* glandule. *Lee.*

NEC'TARINE, *a.* Sweet as nectar. *Milton.*

NEC'TARINE, *n.* A fruit, a variety of the peach with a smooth rind.

NEC'TARIZE, *v. t.* To sweeten. *Cockeram.*

NEC'TAROUS, *a.* Sweet as nectar. *Milton.*

NEC'TARY, *n.* [from *nectar.*] In *botany*, the melliferous part of a vegetable, peculiar to the flower. It usually makes a part of the corol, but is sometimes distinct from it. Sometimes it is in the form of a horn or spur; sometimes in that of a cup; whence it is called the honey cup. *Martyn.*

NED'DER, *n.* [W. *nadyr*; Sax. *nedder.*] An adder. *Obs.*

NEED, *n.* [Sax. *nead, neod, nyd*; D. *nood*; G. *noth*; Sw. *nöd*; Dan. *nöd*; Eth. ነደየ nadei, to be in want. The primary sense is to press. Class Nd. No. 7. 24.]
1. Want; occasion for something; necessity; a state that requires supply or relief. It sometimes expresses urgent want; pressing exigency.

What further *need* have we of witnesses? Matt. xxvi.

For ye have *need* of patience— Heb. x.

2. Want of the means of subsistence; poverty; indigence.

I know how to abound and to suffer *need*. Phil. iv.

NEED, *v. t.* [Sax. *geneadan, genedan*, to compel; Dan. *nöder.*]
To want; to lack; to require, as supply or relief.

They that be whole *need* not a physician, but they that are sick. Matt. ix.

NEED, *v. i.* To be wanted; to be necessary.

When we have done it, we have done all that is in our power, and all that *needs*. [*Not used.*] *Locke.*

Need is often used as an auxiliary, or at least without the personal termination.

And the lender *need* not fear he shall be injured. *Anacharsis, Trans.*

NEE'DED, *pp.* Wanted.

NEE'DER, *n.* One that wants.

NEE'DFUL, *a.* Necessary, as supply or relief; requisite.

All things *needful* for defense abound. *Dryden.*

NEE'DFULLY, *adv.* Necessarily. *B. Jonson.*

NEE'DILY, *adv.* [from *needy.*] In want or poverty.

NEE'DINESS, *n.* [from *needy.*] Want; poverty; indigence. *Bacon.*

NEE'DING, *ppr.* Wanting; requiring, as supply or relief.

NEE'DLE, *n.* [Sax. *nedl, nædl*; G. *nadel*; Goth. *nethal*; Arm. *nadoz*; Ir. *snathad*; W. *nydwyz*, from *nwd*, something sharp or pointed. It may be allied to *nettle.*]
1. A small instrument of steel pointed at one end, with an eye at the other to receive a thread; used in sewing and embroidery. Needles are also used by surgeons in sewing up wounds.
2. A small pointed piece of steel used in the mariner's compass, which by its magnetic quality is attracted and directed to the pole, and thus enables navigators to steer their ships the course intended.
3. Any crystalized substance in the form of a needle.

Dipping needle, a magnetic needle that dips or inclines downwards.

NEE'DLE, *v. t.* To form crystals in the shape of a needle.

NEE'DLE, *v. i.* To shoot in crystalization into the form of needles; as *needled* prisms. *Fourcroy.*

NEE'DLE-FISH, *n.* A fish of the genus Syngnathus. The middle of the body is hexangular. Also, the sea-urchin.

NEE'DLEFUL, *n.* As much thread as is put at once in a needle.

NEE'DLE-MAKER, **NEE'DLER**, *n.* One who manufactures needles.

NEE'DLE-ORE, *n.* Acicular bismuth glance. *Ure.*

NEE'DLE-SHELL, *n.* The sea-urchin. *Dict. Nat. Hist.*

NEE'DLE-STONE, *n.* A mineral of the zeolite family. *Cleaveland.*

NEE'DLEWORK, *n.* Work executed with a needle; or the business of a seamstress. It is used particularly for embroidery.

NEEDLE-ZE'OLITE, *n.* A species of zeolite of a grayish white color. *Ure.*

NEE'DLESS, *a.* Not wanted; unnecessary; not requisite; as *needless* labor; *needless* expenses.
2. Not wanting. *Obs.* *Shak.*

NEE'DLESSLY, *adv.* Without necessity.

NEE'DLESSNESS, *n.* Unnecessariness. *Locke.*

NEE'DMENT, *n.* Something needed or wanted. [*Not used.*] *Shak.*

NEEDS, *adv.* [from *need*; Sax. *nedes.*] Necessarily; indispensably; generally used with *must.*

A trial at law *must needs* be innocent in itself. *Kettlewell.*

NEE'DY, *a.* Necessitous; indigent; very poor; distressed by want of the means of living.

To relieve the *needy* and comfort the afflicted, are duties that fall in our way every day. *Addison.*

Spare the blushes of *needy* merit. *Dwight.*

NE'ER, a contraction of *never.*

NEESE, *v. i.* *neez.* [G. *neesen*; D. *niezen*; Sw. *niusa*; Dan. *nyser*; Ar. نشع nashaa; hence *sneeze.* Class Ns. No. 30.]
To sneeze. *Obs.* [See *Sneeze*, which is formed on this word.]

NEE'SEWORT, *n.* A plant. *Sherwood.*

NEE'SING, *n.* A sneezing. *Obs.*

NEF, *n.* The nave of a church. [*Not used.* See *Nave.*]

NEFAND'OUS, *a.* [L. *nefandus*, not to be spoken.]
Not to be named; abominable. *Sheldon.*

NEFA'RIOUS, *a.* [L. *nefarius*, from *nefas*, unlawful, or *ne* and *for, fari*, to utter.]
Wicked in the extreme; abominable; atrociously sinful or villainous; detestably vile.

NEFA'RIOUSLY, *adv.* With extreme wickedness; abominably. *Milton.*

NEGA'TION, *n.* [L. *negatio*, from *nego*, to deny, Sw. *neka*, Dan. *nægter*, W. *naca, nacâu, nagu*, Fr. *nier*, from L. *nego*. The sense is to thrust, to stop or repel; for in Italian, *negare* is to deny, and *annegare* is to deny, and to drown, to stifle in water;

Sp. *negar*, to deny; *anegar*, to drown or inundate, Fr. *noyer*.]

1. Denial; a declaration that something is not; opposed to *affirmation*; as, the soul is *not* matter.
2. In *logic*, description by denial, exclusion or exception.

Negation is the absence of that which does not belong to the thing we are speaking of. *Watts.*

3. Argument drawn from denial.

It may be proved by way of *negation*, that they came not from Europe, as having no remainder of the arts, learning and civilities of it. *Heylin.*

NEG'ATIVE, *a.* [Fr. *negatif*; L. *negativus*.]

1. Implying denial or negation; opposed to *affirmative*, as a *negative* proposition is that which *denies*. Matter is not spirit.
2. Implying absence; opposed to *positive*.

There is a *negative* way of denying Christ, when we do not acknowledge and confess him. *South.*

3. Having the power of stopping or restraining. A *negative* voice in legislation is a voice or vote to prevent the passing of a law or decree.

Negative sign, in algebra, the sign of subtraction, a sign which indicates that the quantity to which it is prefixed is to be subtracted. It is opposed to *positive* or *affirmative*; as *ab—n*.

Negative electricity, according to Dr. Franklin, is a deficiency of the fluid in a substance, or less than the substance naturally contains.

NEG'ATIVE, *n.* A proposition by which something is denied; as, matter has not the power of moving itself.

2. A word that denies; as *not*, *no*.
3. In *legislation*, the right or power of preventing the enaction of a law or decree. The governor has not a *negative* on the proceedings of the legislature, but each branch has a *negative* on the other.

Negative pregnant, a negation of one thing, implying the affirmation of another.

NEG'ATIVE, *v. t.* To disprove; to prove the contrary.

The omission or infrequency of such recitals does not *negative* the existence of miracles. *Paley.*

2. To reject by vote; to refuse to enact or sanction. The senate *negatived* the bill.
3. To resist a choice or what is proposed.

NEG'ATIVELY, *adv.* With or by denial; as, he answered *negatively*. *Boyle.*

2. In the form of speech implying the absence of something; opposed to *positively*.

I shall show what this image of God in man is, *negatively*, by showing wherein it does not consist, and positively, by showing wherein it it does consist. *South.*

3. Negatively charged or electrified. [See *Positively*.]

NEG'ATORY, *a.* That denies; belonging to negation. [*Little used.*]

NE'GER, *n.* [L. *niger*.] A black person; one of the African race. [See *Negro*.]

NEGLECT', *v. t.* [L. *neglectus*, from *negligo*. In G. the corresponding word is *nachlassen*, D. *nalaaten*, compounds of *nach*, *na*, after, and *lassen*, *laaten*, to let, to leave, to suffer to pass, Eng. *let*, Fr. *laisser*. The sense of the latter words then is to leave behind, or permit to remain; Dan. *nachlæssig*, negligent. I suspect the L. *negligo* to be composed of the same prefix, *neg* for *nach*, and *linquo*, *lictum*, as *n* is not radical in the latter. But of this I am not confident.]

1. To omit by carelessness or design; to forbear to do, use, employ, promote or attend to; as, to *neglect* duty or business; to *neglect* to pay honest debts; to *neglect* our interest or policy; to *neglect* the means in our power.
2. To omit to receive or embrace; to slight.

How shall we escape, if we *neglect* so great salvation? Heb. ii.

3. To slight; not to notice; to forbear to treat with attention or respect. Among people of good breeding, strangers seldom complain of being *neglected*.
4. To postpone. [*Not in use.*] *Shak.*

NEGLECT', *n.* Omission; forbearance to do any thing that can be done or that requires to be done. *Neglect* may be from carelessness or intention. The *neglect* of business is the cause of many failures, but *neglect* of economy is more frequent and more injurious.

2. Slight; omission of attention or civilities. *Neglect* of due notice and attention to strangers is characteristic of ill breeding.
3. Negligence; habitual want of regard.

Age breeds *neglect* in all. *Denham.*

4. State of being disregarded.

Rescue my poor remains from vile *neglect*. *Prior.*

NEGLECT'ED, *pp.* Omitted to be done; slighted; disregarded.

NEGLECT'ER, *n.* One that neglects.

NEGLECT'FUL, *a.* Heedless; careless; inattentive. *Locke.*

2. Accustomed or apt to omit what may or ought to be done.
3. Treating with neglect or slight.
4. Indicating neglect, slight or indifference; as a *neglectful* countenance. *Locke.*

NEGLECT'FULLY, *adv.* With neglect; with heedless inattention; with careless indifference.

NEGLECT'ING, *ppr.* Omitting; passing by; forbearing to do; slighting; treating with indifference.

NEGLECT'INGLY, *adv.* Carelessly; heedlessly. *Shak.*

NEGLEC'TION, *n.* The state of being negligent. [*Not used.*] *Shak.*

NEGLECT'IVE, *a.* Inattentive; regardless of. [*Little used.*] *K. Charles.*

NEGLIGEE', *n.* A kind of gown formerly worn. *Goldsmith.*

NEG'LIGENCE, *n.* [L. *negligentia*.] Neglect; omission to do; more generally,

2. Habitual omission of that which ought to be done, or a habit of omitting to do things, either from carelessness or design. *Negligence* is usually the child of sloth or laziness, and the parent of disorders in business, often of poverty.

NEG'LIGENT, *a.* Careless; heedless; apt or accustomed to omit what ought to be done; inattentive to business or necessary concerns. It is applied to a particular instance of neglect, or it denotes habitually careless or inattentive. 2 Chron. xxix. 2 Pet. i.

He that thinks he can afford to be *negligent*, is not far from being poor. *Rambler.*

2. Regardless.

Be thou *negligent* of fame. *Swift.*

NEG'LIGENTLY, *adv.* Carelessly; heedlessly; without exactness; as a person *negligently* dressed; a piece *negligently* written; a farm *negligently* cultivated.

2. With slight, disregard or inattention.

NEGOTIABIL'ITY, *n.* The quality of being negotiable or transferable by indorsment. *Sewall. Walsh.*

NEGO'TIABLE, *a.* [from *negotiate*.] That may be transferred by assignment or indorsment; that may be passed from the owner to another person so as to vest the property in the assignee; as a *negotiable* note or bill of exchange. *Walsh.*

NEGO'TIANT, *n.* One who negotiates; a negotiator. [*Not used.*] *Raleigh.*

NEGO'TIATE, *v. i.* [L. *negotior*; It. *negoziare*; Sp. *negociar*; Fr. *negocier*; from L. *negotium*, business, employment; W. *neges*, an errand, business; *negeseua*, to go on errands, to negotiate.]

1. To transact business; to treat with another respecting purchase and sale; to hold intercourse in bargaining or trade, either in person or by a broker or substitute; as, to *negotiate with* a man *for* the purchase of goods or a farm.
2. To hold intercourse with another respecting a treaty, league or convention; to treat with respecting peace or commerce.

It is a crime for an embassador to betray his prince for whom he should *negotiate*. *Decay of Piety.*

NEGOTIATE, *v. t. nego'shate.* To procure by mutual intercourse and agreement with another; as, to *negotiate* a loan of money.

Ship brokers and interpreters *negotiate* affreightments. *Walsh.*

2. To procure, make or establish by mutual intercourse and agreement with others. Mr. Jay *negotiated* a treaty with the British ministry in 1794.
3. To sell; to pass; to transfer for a valuable consideration; as, to *negotiate* a bill of exchange.

The notes were not *negotiated* to them in the usual course of business or trade. *Kent.*

NEGO'TIATED, *pp.* Procured or obtained by agreement with another; sold or transferred for a valuable consideration.

NEGO'TIATING, *ppr.* Treating with; transacting business.

NEGOTIA'TION, *n.* The act of negotiating; the transacting of business in traffick; the treating with another respecting sale or purchase.

2. The transaction of business between nations; the mutual intercourse of governments by their agents, in making treaties and the like; as the *negotiations* at Ghent.

NEGO'TIATOR, *n.* One that negotiates; one that treats with others either as principal or agent, in respect to purchase and sale, or public compacts. *Swift.*

NE'GRESS, *n.* [See *Negro*.] A female of the black race of Africa.

NE'GRO, *n.* [It. Sp. *negro*, black, from L. *niger*. It is remarkable that our common people retain the exact Latin pronunciation of this word, *neger*.]

A native or descendant of the black race of men in Africa. The word is never applied to the tawny or olive colored inhabitants of the northern coast of Africa, but to the more southern race of men who are quite black.

NE'GUS, *n.* A liquor made of wine, water, sugar, nutmeg and lemon juice; so called, it is said, from its first maker, Col. *Negus.*

NEIF, *n.* [Ice. *nefi.*] The neaf or fist. [*Not used.*] *Shak.*

2. A slave. [*Not used.*]

NEIGH, *v. i. na.* [Sax. *hnægan;* Sw. *gnägga;* Dan. *knægger;* It. *annicchiare.* In W. *cnecu* signifies to jar or quarrel; *cnec,* a sharp noise.]

To utter the voice of a horse, expressive of want or desire; to whinny.

NEIGH, *n. na.* The voice of a horse; a whinnying.

NEIGHBOR, } *n.* *na'bur.* [Sax. *nehbur,*
NEHBOOR, } *nehgebur,* a nigh boor, a *boor* or countryman living *nigh,* [see *Nigh;*] G. *nachbar;* D. *nabuur;* Sw. *nabo;* Dan. *naboe.* See *Boor.* The true orthography, as this word is now pronounced, is *nehboor;* Sax. *neh,* nigh, and *boor.*]

1. One who lives near another. In large towns, a *neighbor* is one who lives within a few doors. In the country, a *neighbor* may live at a greater distance; and in new settlements, where the people are thinly scattered over the country, a *neighbor* may be distant several miles. Such is the use of the word in the United States.

2. One who lives in familiarity with another; a word of civility. *Shak.*

3. An intimate; a confidant. [*Not used.*] *Shak.*

4. A fellow being. Acts. vii.

5. One of the human race; any one that needs our help, or to whom we have an opportunity of doing good. Luke x.

6. A country that is near.

NEIGHBOR, *v. t.* To adjoin; to confine on or be near to.

> These grow on the hills that *neighbor* the shore. *Sandys.*

2. To acquaint with; to make near to or make familiar. [*Not used.*] *Shak.*

To neighbor it, in colloquial language, to cultivate friendly intercourse by mutual visits.

NEIGHBORHOOD, *n.* A place near; vicinity; the adjoining district or any place not distant. He lives in my *neighborhood.*

2. State of being near each other; as several states in a *neighborhood.* *Swift.*

3. The inhabitants who live in the vicinity of each other. The fire alarmed all the *neighborhood.*

NEIGHBORING, *a.* Living or being near; as the *neighboring* inhabitants; *neighboring* countries or nations. *Paley.*

NEIGHBORLINESS, *n.* State or quality of being neighborly. *Scott.*

NEIGHBORLY, *a.* Becoming a neighbor; kind; civil.

> Judge if this be *neighborly* dealing. *Arbuthnot.*

2. Cultivating familiar intercourse; interchanging frequent visits; social. Friend, you are not *neighborly.*

NEIGHBORLY, *adv.* With social civility; as, to live *neighborly.*

NEIGHBORSHIP, *n.* State of being neighbors. [*Not in use.*] *Miss Baillie.*

NE'ITHER, *n. compound pronoun, pronominal adjective, or a substitute.* [Sax. *nather, nathor, nauther* or *nouther;* *na,* not, and *either* or *other,* not either, or not other. So in L. *neuter, ne* and *uter.*] Not either; not the one nor the other.

1. It refers to individual things or persons; as, which road shall I take? *Neither,* take *neither* road. The upright judge inclines to *neither* party.

It is used as a substitute; as, the upright judge inclines to *neither* of the parties.

> He *neither* loves
> Nor either cares for him. *Shak.*

2. It refers to a sentence; as, "ye shall not eat of it, *neither* shall ye touch it." That is, ye shall not eat, *not either* or *other* shall ye touch it; ye shall not eat, nor shall ye do the other thing here mentioned, that is, touch it. Gen. iii.

"Fight *neither* with small nor great, save only with the king;" that is, fight not, either with small or great. 1 Kings xxii.

Neither, in the first part of a negative sentence, is followed by *nor,* in the subsequent part. It is *neither* the one *nor* the other. But *or* would be most proper, for the negative in *neither,* applies to both parts of the sentence.

It is often used in the last member of a negative sentence instead of *nor,* as in the passage above cited. "Ye shall not eat it, *neither* shall ye touch it." Here *neither* is improperly used for *nor,* for *not* in the first clause refers only to that clause, and the second negative refers only to the second clause. "Ye shall *not* eat it, *nor* shall ye touch it.

In the sentences above, *neither* is considered to be a conjunction or connecting word, though in fact it is a pronoun or representative of a clause of a sentence.

3. *Neither* primarily refers to *two;* not *either* of two. But by usage it is applicable to any number, referring to individuals separately considered. Five or ten persons being charged with a misdemeanor or riot, each may say, *neither* of us was present.

4. *Neither* sometimes closes a sentence in a peculiar manner, thus, "men come not to the knowledge of ideas thought to be innate, till they come to the use of reason; nor then *neither.*" *Locke.*

That is, *not either* when they come to the use of reason, or before.

Formerly, in English, as in Greek and French, two negatives were used for one negation. But in such phrases as that above, good speakers now use *either;* "nor then *either.*"

NEM. CON. for *nemine contradicente.* [L.] No one contradicting or opposing, that is, unanimously; without opposition.

NEM'OLITE, *n.* [Gr. νεμος, a wood, and λιθος, a stone.] An arborized stone. *Dict. Nat. Hist.*

NEM'ORAL, *a.* [L. *nemoralis,* from *nemus,* a wood.]

Pertaining to a wood or grove. *Dict.*

NEM'OROUS, *a.* [L. *nemorosus.*] Woody. *Evelyn.*

NEMP'NE, *v. t.* [Sax. *nemnan,* to name or call.] To call. *Obs.* *Chaucer.*

NE'NIA, *n.* [Gr.] A funeral song; an elegy. [*Not used.*]

NEN'UPHAR, *n.* The water lily or water rose, a species of Nymphæa.

NEOD'AMODE, *n.* [Gr. νεοδαμωδης; νεος, new, and δημωδης, popular; δημος, people.]

In ancient Greece, a person newly admitted to citizenship. *Mitford.*

NEOLOG'IC, } *a.* [from *neology.*] Pertaining to neology;
NEOLOG'ICAL, } employing new words. *Chesterfield.*

NEOL'OGISM, *n.* A new word or expression.

NEOL'OGIST, *n.* One who introduces new words into a language. Lavoisier has been a successful *neologist.* *Med. Repos.*

NEOL'OGY, *n.* [Gr. νεος, new, and λογος, a word.]

The introduction of a new word or of new words into a language. The present nomenclature of chimistry is a remarkable instance of *neology.*

NEONO'MIAN, *n.* [Gr. νεος, new, and νομος, law.]

One who advocates new laws, or desires God's law to be altered. *Scott.*

NE'OPHYTE, *n.* [Gr. νεος, new, and φυτον, a plant.]

1. A new convert or proselyte; a name given by the early christians to such heathens as had recently embraced the christian faith, and were considered as regenerated by baptism. *Encyc.*

2. A novice; one newly admitted to the order of priest.

3. A tyro; a beginner in learning.

NEOTER'IC, } *a.* [Gr. νεωτερικος, young, from νεος, new; Low
NEOTER'ICAL, } L. *neotericus.*]

New; recent in origin; modern. *Bacon.*

NEOTER'IC, *n.* One of modern times. *Burton.*

NEP, *n.* A plant of the genus Nepeta; catmint.

NEPEN'THE, *n.* [Gr. νηπενθης; νη, not, and πενθος, grief.]

A drug or medicine that drives away pain and grief. [*Little used.*] *Milton.*

NEPH'ELIN, } *n.* [Gr. νεφελη, a cloud.]
NEPH'ELINE, } A mineral found mixed with other substances, primitive or volcanic, in small masses or veins, granolamellar and in hexahedral crystals. It is white or yellow. *Dict. Nat. Hist.* *Ure.*

NEPH'EW, *n.* [Fr. *neveu;* L. *nepos;* It. *nepote;* D. *neef;* G. *neffe;* Sans. *naptri;* W. *nai,* contracted.]

1. The son of a brother or sister. *Dryden.*

2. A grandson; also, a descendant. [*Not much used.*] *Hooker.*

NEPH'RITE, *n.* [Gr. νεφριτης, from νεφρος, the kidneys.]

A mineral, a subspecies of jade, of a leek green color, massive and in rolled pieces. It occurs in granite and gneiss, and is remarkable for its hardness and tenacity. It was formerly worn as a remedy for diseases of the kidneys, but is now cut into handles of sabers and daggers. *Cleaveland. Ure. Cyc.*

NEPHRIT'IC, } *a.* [Gr. νεφριτικος, from
NEPHRIT'ICAL, } νεφρος, the kidneys.]

1. Pertaining to the kidneys or organs of urine; as a *nephritic* disease.

2. Affected with the stone or gravel; as a *nephritic* patient.

3. Relieving or curing the stone or gravel, or disorders of the kidneys in general; as a *nephritic* medicine.

Nephritic stone, a stone of the silicious kind, called jade.

Nephritic wood, a species of compact wood of a fine grain, brought from New Spain, which gives a blue color to spirit of wine and to water; which color is changed to yellow by acids, and again to blue by alkalies. *Nicholson. Encyc.*

NEPHRIT'IC, *n.* A medicine adapted to relieve or cure the diseases of the kidneys, particularly the gravel or stone in the bladder. *Cyc.*

NEPH'RITIS, *n.* In *medicine*, an inflammation of the kidneys.

NEPHROT'OMY, *n.* [Gr. νεφρος, a kidney, and τεμνω, to cut.]

In *surgery*, the operation of extracting a stone from the kidney. *Cyc.*

NEP'OTISM, *n.* [Fr. *nepotisme*, from L. *nepos*, nephew.]

1. Fondness for nephews. *Addison.*
2. Undue attachment to relations; favoritism shown to nephews and other relations.

NEPTU'NIAN, *a.* [from *Neptunus*, the fabled deity of the ocean.]

1. Pertaining to the ocean or sea.
2. Formed by water or aqueous solution; as *neptunian* rocks.

NEPTU'NIAN, NEP'TUNIST, *n.* One who adopts the theory that the whole earth was once covered with water, or rather that the substances of the globe were formed from aqueous solution; opposed to the *Plutonic* theory. *Pinkerton. Good.*

NE'REID, *n.* [Gr. νηρηιδες, *plu.* of νηρηις, from Νηρευς, a marine deity; Sans. *nara*, water; Ar. Heb. נהר, to flow. See *Narrate.*]

In *mythology*, a sea nymph. In ancient monuments, the Nereids are represented as riding on sea horses, sometimes with the human form entire, and sometimes with the tail of a fish. They were the daughters of Nereus, and constantly attended Neptune. *Encyc.*

NERF'LING, *n.* A fresh water fish of Germany, of the lether-mouthed kind, and apparently a variety of the rudd. *Dict. Nat. Hist.*

NER'ITE, *n.* A genus of univalvular shells.

NER'ITITE, *n.* A petrified shell of the genus Nerita.

NERVE, *n. nerv.* [L. *nervus*; Fr. *nerf*; W. *nerth*, strength; Gr. νευρον, nerve; probably allied to ανηρ, a man, L. *vir*; Pers. نر nar, the male of any animal; Sans. *nar*, a man. In Welsh, *nêr* denotes one that possesses self-energy, and hence an epithet of God.]

1. An organ of sensation and motion in animals. The nerves are prolongations of the medullary substance of the brain, which ramify and extend to every part of the body. *Encyc. Parr.*
2. A sinew or tendon. *Pope.*
3. Strength; firmness of body; as a man of *nerve.*
4. Fortitude; firmness of mind; courage.
5. Strength; force; authority; as the *nerves* of discipline. *Gibbon.*

NERVE, *v. t.* To give strength or vigor; to arm with force; as, fear *nerved* his arm. *Ames.*

NERV'ED, *pp.* Armed with strength.

2. *a.* In *botany*, having vessels simple and unbranched, extending from the base towards the tip; as a *nerved* leaf.

NERVELESS, *a. nerv'less.* Destitute of strength; weak. *Pope.*

NERV'INE, *a.* [Low L. *nervinus.*] That has the quality of relieving in disorders of the nerves.

NERV'INE, *n.* A medicine that affords relief from disorders of the nerves.

NERV'OUS, *a.* [L. *nervosus.*] Strong; vigorous; as a *nervous* arm.

2. Pertaining to the nerves; seated in or affecting the nerves; as a *nervous* disease or fever.
3. Having the nerves affected; hypochondriac; *a colloquial use of the word.*
4. Possessing or manifesting vigor of mind; characterized by strength in sentiment or style; as a *nervous* historian. *Adams.*

NERV'OUS, NERV'OSE, *a.* In *botany.* [See *Nerved*, No. 2.]

NERV'OUSLY, *adv.* With strength or vigor. *Warton.*

NERV'OUSNESS, *n.* Strength; force; vigor. *Warton.*

2. The state of being composed of nerves. *Goldsmith.*

NERV'Y, *a.* Strong; vigorous. *Shak.*

NESCIENCE, *n. nesh'ens.* [L. *nesciens*, *nescio*; *ne* and *scio.*]

Want of knowledge; ignorance. *Bp. Hall.*

NESH, *a.* [Sax. *nesc.*] Soft; tender; nice. [*Not used.*] *Chaucer.*

NESS, a termination of names, signifies a promontory, from the root of *nose*, which see.

NESS, a termination of appellatives, [Sax. *nesse, nysse,*] denotes state or quality, as in *goodness*, *greatness.*

NEST, *n.* [Sax. G. D. *id.*; Sw. *nåste*; W. *nyth*; L. *nidus*; Fr. *nid*; It. Sp. *nido*; Arm. *neiz*; Ir. *nead*; Russ. *gnizdo*; Gr. νεοσσος, νεοσσια, νεοττια, unless the latter are from νεος. In Persic, *nisim* is a nest, *nashiman*, a mansion, and *nishashtan*, to sit down, to dwell or remain.]

1. The place or bed formed or used by a bird for incubation or the mansion of her young, until they are able to fly. The word is used also for the bed in which certain insects deposit their eggs.
2. Any place where irrational animals are produced. *Bentley.*
3. An abode; a place of residence; a receptacle of numbers, or the collection itself; *usually in an ill sense*; as a *nest* of rogues.
4. A warm close place of abode; generally in contempt. *Spenser.*
5. A number of boxes, cases or the like, inserted in each other.

NEST, *v. i.* To build and occupy a nest.

> The king of birds *nested* with its leaves. *Howell.*

NEST'EGG, *n.* An egg left in the nest to prevent the hen from forsaking it. *Hudibras.*

NESTLE, *v. i. nes'l.* To settle; to harbor; to lie close and snug, as a bird in her nest.

> The king-fisher *nestles* in hollow banks. *L'Estrange.*

> Their purpose was to fortify in some strong place of the wild country, and there *nestle* till succors came. *Bacon.*

2. To move about in one's seat, like a bird when forming her nest; as, a child *nestles.*

NESTLE, *v. t. nes'l.* To house, as in a nest. *Donne.*

2. To cherish, as a bird her young. *Chapman.*

NEST'LING, *n.* A young bird in the nest, or just taken from the nest.

2. A nest. [*Not used.*]

NEST'LING, *a.* Newly hatched; being yet in the nest. *Barrington.*

NESTO'RIAN, *n.* A follower of Nestorius, a heretic of the fifth century, who taught that Christ was divided into two persons.

NET, *n.* [Sax. *net*, *nyt*; D. Dan. *net*; G. *netz*; Sw. *nât*, *not*; Goth. *nati*, from the root of *knit*, Sax. *cnyttan*, whence *knot*, L. *nodus.*]

1. An instrument for catching fish and fowls, or wild beasts, formed with twine or thread interwoven with meshes.
2. A cunning device; a snare. Micah vii.
3. Inextricable difficulty. Job xviii.
4. Severe afflictions. Job xix.

NET, *v. t.* To make a net or net-work; to knot. *Seward.*

NET, *a.* [Fr. *net*; It. *netto.* See *Neat.*]

1. Neat; pure; unadulterated. [*Little used.*]
2. Being without flaw or spot. [*Little used.*]
3. Being beyond all charges or outlay; as *net* profits.
4. Being clear of all tare and tret, or all deductions; as *net* weight. It is sometimes written *nett*, but improperly. *Net* is properly a mercantile appropriation of *neat.*

NET, *v. t.* To produce clear profit.

NETH'ER, *a.* [Sax. *neother*; G. *nieder*; D. Dan. *neder.* This word is of the comparative degree; the positive occurs only in composition, as in *beneath*, Sax. *neothan.* It is used only in implied comparison, as in the *nether* part, the *nether* millstone; but we never say, one part is *nether* than another. It is not much used.]

1. Lower; lying or being beneath or in the lower part; opposed to *upper*; as the *nether* millstone.

> Distorted all my *nether* shape thus grew
> Transform'd. *Milton.*

2. In a lower place.

> 'Twixt upper, *nether* and surrounding fires. *Milton.*

3. Belonging to the regions below. *Dryden.*

NETH'ERMOST, *a.* Lowest; as the *nethermost* hell; the *nethermost* abyss. *South. Milton.*

NET'TING, *n.* [from *net.*] A piece of net-work.

2. A complication of ropes fastened across each other, to be stretched along the upper part of a ship's quarter to contain hammocks. Netting is also employed to hold the fore and main-top-mast sails when stowed. Netting is also extended along a ship's gunwale in engagements, to prevent the enemy from boarding. *Mar. Dict.*

NETTLE, *n. net'l.* [Sax. *nell*, *netele*; D. *netel*; G. *nessel*; Sw. *nâssla*; Gr. κνιδη, from the root of κνιζω, κναω, to scratch.]

A plant of the genus Urtica, whose prickles

fret the skin and occasion very painful sensations.

And near the noisome *nettle* blooms the rose. *Rambler, motto.*

NET'TLE, *v. t.* To fret or sting; to irritate or vex; to excite sensations of displeasure or uneasiness, not amounting to wrath or violent anger.

The princes were *nettled* at the scandal of this affront. *L'Estrange.*

NET'TLED, *pp.* Fretted; irritated.

NET'TLER, *n.* One that provokes, stings or irritates. *Milton.*

NET'TLE-TREE, *n.* A tree of the genus Celtis, whose leaves are deeply serrated, and end in a sharp point. *Encyc.*

NET'TLING, *ppr.* Irritating; vexing.

NET'-WÖRK, *n.* A complication of threads, twine or cords united at certain distances, forming meshes, interstices or open spaces between the knots or intersections; reticulated or decussated work. *Addison.*

NEUROLOG'IEAL, *a.* [See *Neurology.*] Pertaining to neurology, or to a description of the nerves of animals.

NEUROL'OGIST, *n.* One who describes the nerves of animals.

NEUROL'OGY, *n.* [Gr. νευρον, a nerve, and λογος, discourse.]

A description of the nerves of animal bodies, or the doctrine of the nerves.

NEU'ROPTER, } *n.* [Gr. νευρον, a nerve,
NEUROP'TERA, } and πτερον, a wing.]

The *neuropters* are an order of insects having four membranous, transparent, naked wings, reticulated with veins.

NEUROP'TERAL, *a.* Belonging to the order of neuropters.

NEU'ROSPAST, *n.* [Gr. νευροσπαςεω, to draw with strings.]

A puppet; a little figure put in motion. *More.*

NEUROT'IE, *a.* [Gr. νευρον, a nerve.] Useful in disorders of the nerves.

NEUROT'IE, *n.* A medicine useful in disorders of the nerves. *Encyc.*

NEUROTOM'IEAL, *a.* [See *Neurotomy.*] Pertaining to the anatomy or dissection of nerves.

NEUROT'OMIST, *n.* One who dissects the nerves.

NEUROT'OMY, *n.* [Gr. νευρον, a nerve, and τεμνω, to cut.]

1. The dissection of a nerve. *Coxe.*
2. The art or practice of dissecting the nerves.

NEUTER, *a.* nu'ter. [L.; compounded of *ne* and *uter*, not either.]

1. Not adhering to either party; taking no part with either side, either when persons are contending, or questions are discussed. It may be synonymous with *indifferent*, or it may not. The United States remained *neuter* during the French revolution, but very few of the people were *indifferent* as to the success of the parties engaged. A man may be *neuter* from feeling, and he is then *indifferent;* but he may be *neuter* in fact, when he is not in feeling or principle. A judge should be perfectly *neuter* in feeling, that he may decide with impartiality.
2. In *grammar*, of neither gender; an epithet given to nouns that are neither masculine nor feminine; primarily to nouns which express neither sex.

NEU'TER, *n.* A person that takes no part in a contest between two or more individuals or nations; a person who is either indifferent to the cause, or forbears to interfere.

2. An animal of neither sex, or incapable of propagation. The working bees are *neuters.* *Ed. Encyc.*

Neuter verb, in grammar, a verb which expresses an action or state limited to the subject, and which is not followed by an object; as, I *go;* I *sit;* I *am;* I *run;* I *walk.* It is better denominated *intransitive.*

NEU'TRAL, *a.* [Fr. *neutre;* L. *neutralis*, from *neuter.*]

1. Not engaged on either side; not taking an active part with either of contending parties. It is policy for a nation to be *neutral* when other nations are at war. Belligerents often obtain supplies from *neutral* states.
2. Indifferent; having no bias in favor of either side or party.
3. Indifferent; neither very good nor bad.

Some things good, and some things ill do seem,
And *neutral* some in her fantastic eye. *Davies.*

Neutral salt, in chimistry, a salt or body composed of two primitive saline substances in combination, and possessing the character neither of an acid or alkaline salt; or a combination of an acid with any substance which destroys its acidity; any salt saturated with an alkali, an earth or a metal. But it is more usual to denominate *neutral*, a salt which is united with an alkaline substance, and to call the others earthy or metallic. *Hooper. Nicholson. Encyc.*

NEU'TRAL, *n.* A person or nation that takes no part in a contest between others.

The *neutral*, as far as his commerce extends, becomes a party in the war. *R. G. Harper.*

NEU'TRALIST, *n.* A neutral. [*Little used.*]

NEUTRAL'ITY, *n.* The state of being unengaged in disputes or contests between others; the state of taking no part on either side. States often arm to maintain their *neutrality.*

2. A state of indifference in feeling or principle.
3. Indifference in quality; a state neither very good nor evil. [*Little used.*] *Donne.*
4. A combination of neutral powers or states; as the armed *neutrality.*

NEUTRALIZA'TION, *n.* [from *neutralize.*]

1. The act of neutralizing or destroying the peculiar properties of a body by combination with another body or substance.
2. The act of reducing to a state of indifference or neutrality.

NEU'TRALIZE, *v. t.* To render neutral; to reduce to a state of indifference between different parties or opinions.

2. In *chimistry*, to destroy or render inert or imperceptible the peculiar properties of a body by combining it with a different substance. Thus to *neutralize* acids and alkalies, is to combine them in such proportions that the compound will not exhibit the qualities of either. This is called a *neutral* salt.
3. To destroy the peculiar properties or opposite dispositions of parties or other things, or reduce them to a state of indifference or inactivity; as, to *neutralize* parties in government; to *neutralize* opposition.

The benefits of universities—*neutralized* by moral evils. *Ch. Obs.*

A cloud of counter citations that *neutralize* each other. *E. Everett.*

NEU'TRALIZED, *pp.* Reduced to neutrality or indifference.

NEU'TRALIZER, *n.* That which neutralizes; that which destroys, disguises or renders inert the peculiar properties of a body. The base of a salt is its *neutralizer.*

NEU'TRALIZING, *ppr.* Destroying or rendering inert the peculiar properties of a substance; reducing to indifference or inactivity.

NEU'TRALLY, *adv.* Without taking part with either side; indifferently.

NEV'ER, *adv.* [Sax. *næfre;* ne, not, and *æfre*, ever.]

1. Not ever; not at any time; at no time. It refers to the past or the future. This man was *never* at Calcutta; he will *never* be there.
2. It has a particular use in the following sentences.

"Ask me *never* so much dower and gift." Gen. xxxiv.

"Which will not hearken to the voice of charmers, charming *never* so wisely." Ps. lviii.

"A fear of battery—though *never* so well grounded, is no duress." *Blackstone.*

This is a genuine English use of *never*, found in our Saxon authors, and it ought to be retained. "Ask me so much dower as *never* was done;" that is, dower to any extent. The practice of using *ever* in such phrases, is corrupt. It not only destroys the force but the propriety of the phrase. *Burke. Camden. Washington. Goldsmith. Hooke.*

3. In no degree; not.

Whoever has a friend to guide him, may carry his eyes in another man's head and yet see *never* the worse. *South.*

4. It is used for *not.* He answered him *never* a word; that is, *not ever.* This use is not common.
5. It is much used in composition; as in *never-ending*, *never-failing*, *never-dying*, *never-ceasing*, *never-fading*; but in all such compounds, *never* retains its true meaning.

NEVERTHELESS', *adv.* [*never, the* and *less.*] Not the less; notwithstanding; that is, in opposition to any thing, or without regarding it. "It rained, *nevertheless*, we proceeded on our journey;" we did *not the less* proceed on our journey; we proceeded in opposition to the rain, without regarding it, or without being prevented.

NEW, *a.* [Sax. *neow;* D. *nieuw;* G. *neu;* Sw. Dan. *ny;* L. *novus;* It. *nuovo;* Sp. *nuevo;* Gr. νεος; Fr. *neuf;* Arm. *nevez;* Ir. *nua, nuadh;* W. *newyz;* Russ. *novie;* Hindoo, *nava, nou;* Sans. *nawa;* Pers. نو.]

1. Lately made, invented, produced or come into being; that has existed a short time only; recent in origin; novel; opposed to *old*, and used of things; as a *new* coat; a *new* house; a *new* book; a *new* fashion;

a *new* theory; the *new* chimistry; a *new* discovery.

2. Lately introduced to our knowledge; not before known; recently discovered; as a *new* metal; a *new* species of animals or plants found in foreign countries; the *new* continent.

3. Modern; not ancient.

4. Recently produced by change; as a *new* life.

Put on the *new* man. Eph. iv.

5. Not habituated; not familiar; unaccustomed.

Heretics and such as instill their poison into *new* minds. *Hooker.*

New to the plough, unpracticed in the trace. *Pope.*

6. Renovated; repaired so as to recover the first state.

Men, after long emaciating diets, wax plump, fat and almost *new*. *Bacon.*

7. Fresh after any event.

New from her sickness to that northern air. *Dryden.*

8. Not of ancient extraction or a family of ancient distinction.

By superior capacity and extensive knowledge, a *new* man often mounts to favor. *Addison.*

9. Not before used; strange; unknown.

They shall speak with *new* tongues. Mark xvi.

10. Recently commenced; as the *new* year.

11. Having passed the change or conjunction with the sun; as the *new* moon.

12. Not cleared and cultivated, or lately cleared; as *new* land. *America.*

13. That has lately appeared for the first time; as a *new* star.

New is much used in composition to qualify other words, and always bears its true sense of late, recent, novel, fresh; as in *new*-born, *new*-made, *new*-grown, *new*-formed, *new*-found. In this use, *new* may be considered as adverbial, or as a part of the compound.

NEW, *v. t.* To make new. [*Not used.*] *Gower.*

NEW'EL, *n.* In *architecture*, the upright post about which are formed winding stairs, or a cylinder of stone formed by the end of the steps of the winding stairs.

2. Novelty. [*Not used.*] *Spenser.*

NEW-FANG'LED, *a.* [*new* and *fangle.*] New made; formed with the affectation of novelty; in contempt.

New-fangled devices. *Atterbury.*

NEW-FANG'LEDNESS, *n.* Vain or affected fashion or form. *Sidney. Carew.*

NEW-FASH'IONED, *a.* Made in a new form, or lately come into fashion.

NEW'ING, *n.* Yeast or barm. *Ainsworth.*

NEW'ISH, *a.* Somewhat new; nearly new. *Bacon.*

NEW'LY, *adv.* Lately; freshly; recently.

He rubb'd it o'er with *newly* gathered mint. *Dryden.*

2. With a new form, different from the former.

And the refined mind doth *newly* fashion
Into a fairer form. *Spenser.*

3. In a manner not existing before.

NEW-MOD'EL, *v. t.* To give a new form to.

NEW-MOD'ELED, *a.* Formed after a new model.

NEW-MOD'ELING, *ppr.* Giving a new form to.

NEW'NESS, *n.* Lateness of origin; recentness; state of being lately invented or produced; as the *newness* of a dress; the *newness* of a system.

2. Novelty; the state of being first known or introduced. The *newness* of the scene was very gratifying.

3. Innovation; recent change.

And happy *newness* that intends old right. *Shak.*

4. Want of practice or familiarity.

His *newness* shamed most of the others' long exercise. *Sidney.*

5. Different state or qualities introduced by change or regeneration.

Even so we also should walk in *newness* of life. Rom. vi.

NEWS, *n.* [from *new*; Fr. *nouvelles.* This word has a plural form, but is almost always united with a verb in the singular.]

1. Recent account; fresh information of something that has lately taken place at a distance, or of something before unknown; tidings. We have *news* from Constantinople. *News* has just arrived. This *news* is favorable.

Evil *news* rides fast, while good *news* baits. *Milton.*

It is no *news* for the weak and poor to be a prey to the strong and rich. *L'Estrange.*

2. A newspaper.

NEWS'-MONGER, *n.* One that deals in news; one who employs much time in hearing and telling news. *Arbuthnot.*

NEWS'PAPER, *n.* A sheet of paper printed and distributed for conveying news; a public print that circulates news, advertisements, proceedings of legislative bodies, public documents and the like.

NEWT, *n.* A small lizard; an eft. *Encyc.*

NEWTO'NIAN, *a.* Pertaining to Sir Isaac Newton, or formed or discovered by him; as the *Newtonian* philosophy or system.

NEWTO'NIAN, *n.* A follower of Newton in philosophy.

NEW-YEAR'S GIFT, *n.* A present made on the first day of the year.

NEXT, *a. superl.* of *nigh.* [Sax. *next* or *nexsta*, from *neh*, *neah*, nigh; G. *nächst*; D. *naast*; Sw. *năst*; Dan. *næs*.]

1. Nearest in place; that has no object intervening between it and some other; immediately preceding, or preceding in order. We say, the *next* person before or after another.

Her princely guest
Was *next* her side, in order sat the rest. *Dryden.*

2. Nearest in time; as the *next* day or hour; the *next* day before or after Easter.

3. Nearest in degree, quality, rank, right or relation; as, one man is *next* to another in excellence; one is *next* in kindred; one is *next* in rank or dignity. Assign the property to him who has the *next* claim.

NEXT, *adv.* At the time or turn nearest or immediately succeeding. It is not material who follows *next.*

NIAS, for *an eyas*, a young hawk. *B. Jonson.*

NIB, *n.* [Sax. *neb*, *nebb.* See *Neb*, the same word differently written.]

1. The bill or beak of a fowl.

2. The point of any thing, particularly of a pen.

NIB'BED, *a.* Having a nib or point.

NIB'BLE, *v. t.* [from *nib.*] To bite by little at a time; to eat slowly or in small bits. So sheep are said to *nibble* the grass. *Shak.*

2. To bite, as a fish does the bait; to carp at; just to catch by biting. *Gay.*

NIB'BLE, *v. i.* To bite at; as, fishes *nibble* at the bait. *Grew.*

2. To carp at; to find fault; to censure little faults.

Instead of returning a full answer to my book, he manifestly *nibbles* at a single passage. *Tillotson.*

NIB'BLE, *n.* A little bite, or seizing to bite.

NIB'BLER, *n.* One that bites a little at a time; a carper.

NIB'BLING, *ppr.* Biting in small bits; carping.

NICE, *a.* [Sax. *nesc* or *hnesc*; D. *nesch*, soft, tender; G. *naschen*, to eat dainties or sweetmeats; Dan. *knæs*, dainties.]

1. Properly, soft; whence, delicate; tender; dainty; sweet or very pleasant to the taste; as a *nice* bit; *nice* food.

2. Delicate; fine; *applied to texture, composition or color*; as cloth of a *nice* texture; *nice* tints of color.

3. Accurate; exact; precise; as *nice* proportions; *nice* symmetry; *nice* workmanship; *nice* rules.

4. Requiring scrupulous exactness; as a *nice* point.

5. Perceiving the smallest difference; distinguishing accurately and minutely by perception; as a person of *nice* taste; hence,

6. Perceiving accurately the smallest faults, errors or irregularities; distinguishing and judging with exactness; as a *nice* judge of a subject; *nice* discernment.

Our author happy in a judge so *nice*. *Pope.*

7. Over scrupulous or exact.

Curious, not knowing; not exact, but *nice*. *Pope.*

8. Delicate; scrupulously and minutely cautious.

The letter was not *nice*, but full of charge
Of dear import. *Shak.*
Dear love, continue *nice* and chaste. *Donne.*

9. Fastidious; squeamish.

And to taste,
Think not I shall be *nice*. *Milton.*

10. Delicate; easily injured.

How *nice* the reputation of the maid! *Roscommon.*

11. Refined; as *nice* and subtle happiness. *Milton.*

12. Having lucky hits. [*Not used.*] *Shak.*

13. Weak; foolish; effeminate. *Obs.* *Gower.*

14. Trivial; unimportant. *Shak.*

To make nice, to be scrupulous. *Shak.*

NI'CELY, *adv.* With delicate perception; as, to be *nicely* sensible.

2. Accurately; exactly; with exact order or proportion; as the parts of a machine or building *nicely* adjusted; a shape *nicely* proportioned; a dress *nicely* fitted to the body; the ingredients of a medicine *nicely* proportioned and mixed.

3. In *colloquial language*, well; cleverly; dextrously; handsomely; in the best manner; as, a feat is *nicely* done.

NI'CENE, *a.* Pertaining to Nice, a town of Asia Minor. The *Nicene creed*, was a summary of christian faith composed by the council of Nice against Arianism, A. D. 325, altered and confirmed by the council of Constantinople, A. D. 381. *Encyc.*

NI'CENESS, *n.* Delicacy of perception; the quality of perceiving small differences; as *niceness* of taste.

2. Extreme delicacy; excess of scrupulousness or exactness.

Unlike the *niceness* of our modern dames. *Dryden.*

3. Accuracy; minute exactness; as *niceness* of work; *niceness* of texture or proportion.

Where's now the labored *niceness* in thy dress? *Dryden.*

NI'CETY, *n.* Niceness; delicacy of perception.

2. Excess of delicacy; fastidiousness; squeamishness.

So love doth lothe disdainful *nicety.* *Spenser.*

3. Minute difference; as the *niceties* of words.

4. Minuteness of observation or discrimination; precision. The connoisseur judges of the beauties of a painting with great *nicety.*

5. Delicate management; exactness in treatment.

Love such *nicety* requires,
One blast will put out all his fires. *Swift.*

6. *Niceties*, in the plural, delicacies for food; dainties.

NICH, NICHE, } *n.* [Fr. *niche;* Sp. Port. *nicho;* It. *nicchia*, properly a *nook*, corner, and *nicchio*, a shell. It seems to be a different orthography of *nook.*]

A cavity, hollow or recess within the thickness of a wall, for a statue or bust. *Pope.*

NICK, *n.* In *the northern mythology*, an evil spirit of the waters; hence the modern vulgar phrase, *Old Nick*, the evil one.

NICK, *n.* [Sw. *nick;* Dan. *nik;* D. *knik*, a nod; G. *nicken*, to nod; *genick*, the nape; *genicke*, a continual nodding. The word seems to signify a point, from shooting forward.]

1. The exact point of time required by necessity or convenience; the critical time. *L'Estrange.*

2. [G. *knick*, a flaw.] A notch or score for keeping an account; a reckoning. *Obs.* *Shak.*

3. A winning throw. *Prior.*

NICK, *v. t.* To hit; to touch luckily; to perform by a slight artifice used at the lucky time.

The just reason of doing things must be *nicked*, and all accidents improved. *L'Estrange.*

2. To cut in nicks or notches. [See *Notch.*] *Shak.*

3. To suit, as lattices cut in nicks. *Obs.* *Camden.*

4. To defeat or cozen, as at dice; to disappoint by some trick or unexpected turn. *Obs.* *Shak.*

NICK, *v. t.* [G. *knicken*, to flaw.] To notch or make an incision in a horse's tail, to make him carry it higher.

NICKAR-TREE, *n.* A tree of the genus Guilandina, which grows in the western parts of the U. States, and bears a nut of the size of a pignut. *Mease.*

NICK'EL, *n.* A metal of a white or reddish white color, of great hardness, very difficult to be purified, always magnetic, and when perfectly pure, malleable. It is generally obtained from its sulphuret.

NICK'ELIC, *a.* The nickelic acid is a saturated combination of nickel and oxygen.

NICK'ER, *n.* One who watches for opportunities to pilfer or practice knavery. *Arbuthnot.*

NICK'NAME, *n.* [In Fr. *nique* is a term of contempt. In G. *necken* is to banter. In Ch. חנך signifies to surname, to call by a name of reproach.]

A name given in contempt, derision or reproach; an opprobrious appellation. *Bacon.*

NICK'NAME, *v. t.* To give a name of reproach; to call by an opprobrious appellation.

You *nickname* virtue vice. *Shak.*

NICK'NAMED, *pp.* Named in derision.

NICK'NAMING, *ppr.* Calling by a name in contempt or derision.

NICOLA'ITAN, *n.* One of a sect in the ancient christian church, so named from Nicolas, a deacon of the church of Jerusalem. They held that all married women should be common to prevent jealousy. They are not charged with erroneous opinions respecting God, but with licentious practices. Rev. ii.

NICO'TIAN, *a.* Pertaining to or denoting tobacco; and as a noun, tobacco; so called from Nicot, who first introduced it into France, A. D. 1560.

NIC'OTIN, *n.* The peculiar principle in the leaves of tobacco; a colorless substance of an acrid taste. It is precipitated from its solution by the tincture of nutgalls. *Vauquelin.*

NIC'TATE, *v. i.* [L. *nicto*, to wink.] To wink. *Ray.*

NIC'TATING, NIC'TITATING, } *ppr.* or *a.* Winking. The nictitating membrane is a thin membrane that covers and protects the eyes of some animals, without entirely obstructing the sight. *Paley.*

NICTA'TION, *n.* The act of winking.

NIDE, *n.* [L. *nidus*, a nest.] A brood; as a *nide* of pheasants. [*Not in use.*]

NIDG'ET, *n.* A dastard. [*Not in use.*] *Camden.*

NID'IFICATE, *v. i.* [L. *nidifico*, from *nidus*, a nest.] To make a nest.

NIDIFICA'TION, *n.* The act or operation of building a nest, and the hatching and feeding of young in the nest. *Derham.*

NID'ING, *n.* [Sax. *nithing;* Dan. Sw. *niding.*] A despicable coward; a dastard. *Obs.*

NI'DOR, *n.* [L.] Scent; savor. *Bp. Taylor.*

NIDOROS'ITY, *n.* Eructation with the taste of undigested roast meat. *Floyer.*

NI'DOROUS, *a.* Resembling the smell or taste of roasted meat. *Bacon.*

NID'ULANT, *a.* [L. *nidulor*, from *nidus*, nest.]

In *botany*, nestling; lying loose in pulp or cotton, within a berry or pericarp. *Martyn. Lee.*

NIDULA'TION, *n.* The time of remaining in the nest; as of a bird. *Brown.*

NI'DUS, *n.* [L.] A nest; a repository for the eggs of birds, insects, &c.

NIECE, *n.* *nese.* [Fr. *nièce;* Arm. *nizes*, *nyes;* W. *nith;* qu. The D. has *nigt*, and the G. *nichte.*] The daughter of a brother or sister.

NIF'LE, *n.* [Norm.] A trifle. *Obs.* *Chaucer.*

NIG'GARD, *n.* [W. *nig*, straight, narrow, or G. *knicker*, a niggard, and a nod or nodding; *knickern*, to haggle, to be sordidly parsimonious; Dan. *gnier*, for *gniker* or *gniger*, a niggard. This word seems to belong to the family of D. *knikken*, G. *nicken*, Dan. *nikker*, to nod, and this to Dan. *knikker*, to crack; exhibiting analogies similar to those of *wretch*, *wreck* and *haggle.* *Ard* is a termination, as in *dotard.*]

A miser; a person meanly close and covetous; a sordid wretch who saves every cent, or spends grudgingly.

Serve him as a grudging master,
As a penurious *niggard* of his wealth. *Milton.*

Be *niggards* of advice on no pretense. *Pope.*

NIG'GARD, *a.* Miserly; meanly covetous; sordidly parsimonious. *Dryden.*

2. Sparing; wary.

Most free of question, but to our demands
Niggard in his reply. *Shak.*

NIG'GARD, *v. t.* To stint; to supply sparingly. [*Little used.*] *Shak.*

NIG'GARDISE, *n.* Niggardliness. [*Not in use.*] *Spenser.*

NIG'GARDISH, *a.* Somewhat covetous or niggardly. *Johnson.*

NIG'GARDLINESS, *n.* Mean covetousness; sordid parsimony; extreme avarice manifested in sparing expense.

Niggardliness is not good husbandry. *Addison.*

NIG'GARDLY, *a.* Meanly covetous or avaricious; sordidly parsimonious; extremely sparing of expense.

Where the owner of the house will be bountiful, it is not for the steward to be *niggardly.* *Hall.*

2. Sparing; wary; cautiously avoiding profusion. *Sidney.*

NIG'GARDLY, *adv.* Sparingly; with cautious parsimony. *Shak.*

NIG'GARDNESS, *n.* Niggardliness. [*Not used.*] *Sidney.*

NIG'GARDY, *n.* Niggardliness. [*Not used.*]

NIG'GLE, *v. t.* and *i.* To mock; to trifle with. [*Not in use.*] *Beaum.*

NIGH, *a.* *ni.* [Sax. *neah*, *neahg*, *neh*, for *nig;* G. *nahe*, nigh. This is the G. *nach*, D. *na*, a preposition signifying to, on or after, that is, approaching, pressing on, making towards; D. *naaken*, to approach; W. *nig*, strait, narrow.]

1. Near; not distant or remote in place or time.

The loud tumult shows the battle *nigh.* *Prior.*

When the fig-tree putteth forth leaves, ye know that summer is *nigh.* Matt. xxiv.

2. Closely allied by blood; as a *nigh* kinsman. *Knolles.*

3. Easy to be obtained or learnt; of easy access.

The word is very *nigh* unto thee. Deut. xxx.

4. Ready to support, to forgive, or to aid and defend.

The Lord is *nigh* unto them who are of a broken heart. Ps. xxxiv.

5. Close in fellowship; intimate in relation,

Ye are made *nigh* by the blood of Christ. Eph. ii.

6. Near in progress or condition. Heb. vi.

NIGH, *adv. ni.* Near; at a small distance in place or time, or in the course of events.

He was sick, *nigh* to death. Phil. ii.

2. Near to a place.

He drew *nigh*. *Milton.*

3. Almost; near. He was *nigh* dead.

Nigh is never a preposition. In the phrase, "*nigh* this recess, with terror they survey," there is an ellipsis of *to*. They, *nigh to* this recess, survey, &c.

NIGH, *v. i. ni.* To approach; to advance or draw near. [*Not used.*] *Hubberd.*

NIGHLY, *adv. ni'ly.* Nearly; within a little.

A cube and a sphere *nighly* of the same bigness. [*Not used.*] *Locke.*

NIGHNESS, *n. ni'ness.* Nearness; proximity in place, time or degree.

NIGHT, *n. nite.* [Sax. *niht*; Goth. *nahts*; D. *nagt*; G. *nacht*; Sw. *natt*; Dan. *nat*, contracted; L. *nox*; Gr. *νυξ*; Sp. *noche*; Port. *nôite*; It. *notte*; Fr. *nuit*; Ir. *nocht*; Russ. *noch*; Slav. *nosch*; Sans. *nischa*. The sense may be dark, black, or it may be the decline of the day, from declining, departing, like the Shemitic ערב.]

1. That part of the natural day when the sun is beneath the horizon, or the time from sunset to sunrise.

2. The time after the close of life; death. John ix.

She closed her eyes in everlasting *night*. *Dryden.*

3. A state of ignorance; intellectual and moral darkness; heathenish ignorance. Rom. xiii.

4. Adversity; a state of affliction and distress. Is. xxi.

5. Obscurity; a state of concealment from the eye or the mind; unintelligibleness.

Nature and nature's works lay hid in *night*. *Pope.*

In the night, suddenly; unexpectedly. Luke xii.

To-night, in this night. *To-night* the moon will be eclipsed.

NIGHT-ANGLING, *n.* The angling for or catching fish in the night. *Encyc.*

NIGHT-BIRD, *n.* A bird that flies only in the night. *Hall.*

NIGHT-BORN, *a.* Produced in darkness.

NIGHT-BRAWLER, *n.* One who excites brawls or makes a tumult at night. *Shak.*

NIGHT-CAP, *n.* A cap worn in bed or in undress. *Swift.*

NIGHT-CROW, *n.* A fowl that cries in the night. *Shak.*

NIGHT-DEW, *n.* The dew formed in the night. *Dryden.*

NIGHT-DOG, *n.* A dog that hunts in the night; used by deer-stealers. *Shak.*

NIGHT-DRESS, *n.* A dress worn at night. *Pope.*

NIGHTED, *a.* Darkened; clouded; black. [*Little used.*] *Shak.*

NIGHTFALL, *n.* The close of the day; evening. *Swift.*

NIGHT-FARING, *a.* Traveling in the night. *Gay.*

NIGHT-FIRE, *n.* Ignis fatuus; Will with a wisp; Jack with a lantern. *Herbert.*

2. Fire burning in the night.

NIGHT-FLY, *n.* An insect that flies in the night. *Shak.*

NIGHT-FOUNDERED, *a.* Lost or distressed in the night. *Milton.*

NIGHT-GOWN, *n.* A loose gown used for undress. *Addison.*

NIGHT-HAG, *n.* A witch supposed to wander in the night. *Milton.*

NIGHTINGALE, *n.* [Sax. *nihtegale*; Sw. *näktergal*; D. *nagtegaal*; G. *nachtigall*; Dan. *nattergal*; composed of *night* and Sax. *galan*, to sing.]

1. A small bird that sings at night, of the genus Motacilla; Philomela or Philomel. *Shak. Waller.*

2. A word of endearment. *Shak.*

NIGHTISH, *a.* Pertaining to night, or attached to the night.

NIGHTLY, *a.* Done by night; happening in the night, or appearing in the night; as *nightly* sports; *nightly* dews.

2. Done every night. The watch goes his *nightly* round.

NIGHTLY, *adv.* By night.

Thee, Sion, and the flowery brooks beneath,
Nightly I visit. *Milton.*

2. Every night. *Addison.*

NIGHT-MAN, *n.* One who removes filth from cities in the night.

NIGHTMAR, *n.* [*night* and Sax. *mara*, incubus, nightmar. *Mara* may be from the root of *merran*, to stop, to hinder, [see *Moor*;] or it may be the Rabbinic מריא, an evil spirit or demon.]

Incubus; a sensation in sleep resembling the pressure of a weight on the breast or about the præcordia. It is usually the effect of indigestion or of a loaded stomach.

NIGHT-PIECE, *n.* A piece of painting so colored as to be supposed seen by candle-light. *Addison.*

NIGHT-RAIL, *n.* [*night* and Sax. *regl*, or rather *hrægle*, a garment or robe.]

A loose robe or garment worn over the dress at night. [*Not used.*] *Addison.*

NIGHT-RAVEN, *n.* A fowl of ill omen that cries in the night. *Spenser. Shak.*

NIGHT-REST, *n.* Rest or repose at night. *Shak.*

NIGHT-ROBBER, *n.* One that robs or steals in the night. *Spenser.*

NIGHT-RULE, *n.* A tumult or frolick in the night. *Shak.*

NIGHTSHADE, *n.* [Sax. *nihtscada.*]

A plant of the genus Solanum. The *deadly nightshade* is of the genus Atropa; the *American nightshade* of the genus Phytolacea; the *bastard nightshade* of the genus Rivina; the *enchanter's nightshade* of the genus Circæa; the *Malabar nightshade* of the genus Basella; and the *three-leaved nightshade* of the genus Trillium. *Fam. of Plants.*

NIGHT-SHINING, *a.* Shining in the night; luminous in darkness. *Wilkins.*

NIGHT-SHRIEK, *n.* A shriek or outcry in the night. *Shak.*

NIGHT-SPELL, *n.* A charm against accidents at night. *Chaucer.*

NIGHT-TRIPPING, *a.* Tripping about in the night; as a *night-tripping* fairy. *Shak.*

NIGHT-VISION, *n.* A vision at night. Dan. ii.

NIGHT-WAKING, *a.* Watching in the night.

NIGHT-WALK, *n.* A walk in the evening or night. *Walton.*

NIGHT-WALKER, *n.* One that walks in his sleep; a somnambulist.

2. One that roves about in the night for evil purposes. *Night-walkers* are punishable by law.

NIGHT-WALKING, *a.* Roving in the night.

NIGHT-WALKING, *n.* A roving in the streets at night with evil designs.

NIGHT-WANDERER, *n.* One roving at night. *Shak.*

NIGHT-WANDERING, *a.* Wandering in the night. *Shak.*

NIGHT-WARBLING, *a.* Warbling or singing in the night. *Milton.*

NIGHTWARD, *a.* Approaching towards night. *Milton.*

NIGHT-WATCH, *n.* A period in the night, as distinguished by the change of the watch. *Night-watches*, however, in the Psalms, seems to mean the night or time of sleep in general.

2. A watch or guard in the night.

NIGHT-WATCHER, *n.* One that watches in the night with evil designs.

NIGHT-WITCH, *n.* A night hag; a witch that appears in the night.

NIGRES'CENT, *a.* [L. *nigresco*, to grow black.

Growing black; changing to a black color; approaching to blackness.

NIG'RIN, NIG'RINE, } *n.* An ore of titanium, found in black grains or rolled pieces. *Ure.*

NIHIL'ITY, *n.* [L. *nihilum*, *nihil*, nothing; *ne* and *hilum.*]

Nothingness; a state of being nothing. *Watts.*

NILL, *v. t.* [Sax. *nillan*, that is, *ne*, not, and *willan*, to will; L. *nolo*; *ne* and *volo.*]

Not to will; to refuse; to reject. *Obs.* *Spenser.*

NILL, *v. i.* To be unwilling. *Shak.*

NILL, *n.* The shining sparks of brass in trying and melting the ore. *Johnson.*

NILOM'ETER, *n.* [*Nile* and Gr. *μετρον*, measure.

An instrument for measuring the rise of water in the Nile during the flood.

NIM, *v. t.* [Sax. *neman*, *niman*, Goth. *niman*, D. *neemen*, Gr. *nehmen*, to take.]

To take; to steal; to filch. *Obs.* *Hudibras. L'Estrange.*

NIM'BLE, *a.* [qu. W. *nwyv*, liveliness. In Dan. *nem* is sharp, acute.]

Light and quick in motion; moving with ease and celerity; lively; swift. It is applied chiefly to motions of the feet and hands, sometimes to other things; as a *nimble* boy; the *nimble*-footed deer.

Through the mid seas the *nimble* pinnace sails. *Pope.*

NIM'BLE-FOOTED, *a.* Running with speed; light of foot.

NIM'BLENESS, *n.* Lightness and agility in motion; quickness; celerity; speed; swiftness. It implies lightness and springiness.

The stag thought it better to trust to the *nimbleness* of his feet. *Sidney.*

Ovid ranged over Parnassus with great *nimbleness* and agility. *Addison.*

NIM'BLESS, *n.* Nimbleness. *Obs.* *Spenser.*

NIM'BLE-WITTED, *a.* Quick; ready to speak. *Bacon.*

NIM'BLY, *adv.* With agility; with light, quick motion.

He capers *nimbly* in a lady's chamber. *Shak.*

NIM'IETY, *n.* [L. *nimietas.*] The state of being too much. [*Not in use.*]

NIM'MER, *n.* [Sax. *niman*, to take.] A thief. [*Not in use.*] *Hudibras.*

NIN'COMPOOP, *n.* [said to be a corruption of L. *non compos*, not of sound mind.] A fool; a blockhead; a trifling dotard. [*A low word.*] *Addison.*

NINE, *a.* [Goth. *niun*; G. *neun*; Sw. *nijo*; Dan. *ni*; L. *nonus*; probably contracted, as the Saxon is *nigan*, and the Dutch *negen*, Hindoo *now*, Burman *no* or *nonaw.*] Denoting the number composed of eight and one; as *nine* men; *nine* days.

NINE, *n.* The number composed of eight and one; or the number less by a unit than ten; three times three.

NI'NE-FOLD, *a.* Nine times repeated. *Milton.*

NI'NE-HOLES, *n.* A game in which holes are made in the ground, into which a pellet is to be bowled. *Drayton.*

NI'NE-PENCE, *n.* A silver coin of the value of nine pence.

NI'NE-PINS, *n.* A play with nine pins or sharpened pieces of wood set on end, at which a bowl is rolled for throwing them down. We say, to play at *nine-pins*, or a game at *nine-pins.*

NI'NE-SCORE, *a.* Noting nine times twenty, or one hundred and eighty. [See *Score.*]

NI'NE-SCORE, *n.* The number of nine times twenty.

NI'NETEEN, *a.* [Sax. *nigantyne.*] Noting the number of *nine* and *ten* united; as *nineteen* years.

NI'NETEENTH, *a.* [Sax. *nigantothe.*] The ordinal of nineteen; designating nineteen.

NI'NETIETH, *a.* The ordinal of ninety.

NI'NETY, *a.* Nine times ten; as *ninety* years.

NIN'NY, *n.* [Sp. *niño*; L. *nanus*, a dwarf; Ar. نانا weak in mind.] A fool; a simpleton. *Swift.*

NIN'NYHAMMER, *n.* A simpleton. [*Little used.*] *Arbuthnot.*

NINTH, *a.* [Sax. *nigetha*, *nigotha*; but *ninth*, in English, is formed directly from *nine*; Sw. *nijnde.*] The ordinal of nine; designating the number nine, the next preceding ten; as the *ninth* day or month.

NINTH, *n.* In *music*, an interval containing an octave and a tone.

NIP, *v. t.* [D. *knippen*, to nip, to clip, to pinch; Sw. *knipa*; G. *kneif*, a knife, a *nipping* tool; *kneifen*, to *nip*, to cut off, to pinch; *kniff*, a pinch, a *nipping*; *knipp*, a fillip, a snap; W. *cneiviaw*, to clip. These words coincide with *knife*, Sax. *cnif*, Fr. *ganif* or *canif.*]

1. To cut, bite or pinch off the end or nib, or to pinch off with the ends of the fingers. The word is used in both senses; the former is probably the true sense. Hence,

2. To cut off the end of any thing; to clip, as with a knife or scissors; as, to *nip* off a shoot or twig.

3. To blast; to kill or destroy the end of any thing; hence, to kill; as, the frost has *nipped* the corn; the leaves are *nipped*; the plant was *nipped* in the bud. Hence, to *nip in the bud*, is to kill or destroy in infancy or youth, or in the first stage of growth.

4. To pinch, bite or affect the extremities of any thing; as a *nipping* frost; hence, to pinch or bite in general; to check growth.

5. To check circulation.

When blood is *nipt.* [*Unusual.*] *Shak.*

6. To bite; to vex.

And sharp remorse his heart did prick and *nip.* *Spenser.*

7. To satirize keenly; to taunt sarcastically. *Hubberd.*

NIP, *n.* A pinch with the nails or teeth. *Ascham.*

2. A small cut, or a cutting off the end.

3. A blast; a killing of the ends of plants; destruction by frost.

4. A biting sarcasm; a taunt. *Stepney.*

5. A sip or small draught; as a *nip* of toddy. [G. *nippen*, Dan. *nipper*, to sip.]

NIP'PED, NIPT, *pp.* Pinched; bit; cropped; blasted.

NIP'PER, *n.* A satirist. [*Not used.*] *Ascham.*

2. A fore tooth of a horse. The nippers are four.

NIP'PERS, *n.* Small pinchers.

NIP'PING, *ppr.* Pinching; pinching off; biting off the end; cropping; clipping; blasting; killing.

NIP'PINGLY, *adv.* With bitter sarcasm. *Johnson.*

NIP'PLE, *n.* [Sax. *nypele*; *dim.* of *nib*, *neb.*]

1. A teat; a dug; the spungy protuberance by which milk is drawn from the breasts of females. *Ray.* *Encyc.*

2. The orifice at which any animal liquor is separated. *Derham.*

NIP'PLEWÖRT, *n.* A plant of the genus Lapsana.

NIS'AN, *n.* A month of the Jewish calendar, the first month of the sacred year and seventh of the civil year, answering nearly to our March. It was originally called Abib, but began to be called Nisan after the captivity. *Encyc.*

NISI PRIUS, *n.* [L.] In *law*, a writ which lies in cases where the jury being impanneled and returned before the justices of the bench, one of the parties requests to have this writ for the ease of the country, that the cause may be tried before the justices of the same county. The purport of the writ is, that the sheriff is commanded to bring to Westminster the men impanneled at a certain day, before the justices, *nisi prius*, that is, unless the justices shall first come into the county to take assizes. Hence the courts directed to try matters of fact in the several counties are called courts of *Nisi Prius*, or *Nisi Prius* courts. In some of the United States, similar courts are established, with powers defined by statute.

NIT, *n.* [Sax. *hnitu*; G. *niss*; D. *neet*; Sw. *gnet*; Dan. *gnid*; W. *nezen*, *nêz.*] The egg of a louse or other small insect. *Derham.*

NI'TENCY, *n.* [from L. *niteo*, to shine.]

1. Brightness; luster. [*Little used.*]

2. [L. *nitor*, to strive.] Endeavor; effort; spring to expand itself. [*Little used.*] *Boyle.*

NIT'ID, *a.* [L. *nitidus.*] Bright; lustrous; shining. *Boyle.*

2. Gay; spruce; fine; *applied to persons.* [*Little used.*] *Reeve.*

NI'TER, *n.* [Fr. *nitre*; Sp. It. *nitro*; L. *nitrum*; Gr. νιτρον; Heb. Syr. נתר; Ar. نطرون nitrona. In Hebrew, the verb under which this word appears signifies to spring, leap, shake, and to strip or break; in Ch. to strip or to fall off; in Syriac, the same; in Sam. to keep, to watch or guard; in Ar. the same; in Eth. to shine.] A salt, called also salt-peter [stone-salt,] and in the modern nomenclature of chimistry, nitrate of potash. It exists in large quantities in the earth, and is continually formed in inhabited places, on walls sheltered from rain, and in all situations where animal matters are decomposed, under stables and barns, &c. It is of great use in the arts; is the principal ingredient in gunpowder, and is useful in medicines, in preserving meat, butter, &c. It is a white substance, and has an acrid, bitterish taste. *Hooper.* *Fourcroy.*

NITH'ING, *n.* [Sax.] A coward; a dastard; a poltroon. [See *Niding.*]

NI'TRATE, *n.* A salt formed by the union of the nitric acid with a base; as *nitrate* of soda. *Lavoisier.* *Fourcroy.*

NI'TRATED, *a.* Combined with niter. *Kirwan.*

NI'TRIC, *a.* Impregnated with niter. *Nitric acid* is the acid saturated with oxygen, or an acid composed of oxygen and nitrogen or azote.

NI'TRITE, *n.* A salt formed by the combination of the nitrous acid with a base.

NI'TROGEN, *n.* [Gr. νιτρον, niter, and γενναω, to produce.] The element of niter; that which produces niter; that element or component part of air which is called azote. [See *Azote.*]

NITROG'ENOUS, *a.* Pertaining to nitrogen; producing niter.

NITROLEU'CIC, *a.* Designating an acid obtained from leucine acted on by niter. *Braconnet.*

NITROM'ETER, *n.* [Gr. νιτρον and μετρεω, to measure.] An instrument for ascertaining the quality or value of niter. *Ure.*

NITRO-MŪRIAT'IC, *a.* Partaking of niter and muria or sea-salt. The nitro-muriatic acid is a combination or mixture of nitric and muriatic acid.

NI'TROUS, *a.* Pertaining to niter; partaking of the qualities of niter, or resembling it. *Nitrous* acid is one of the compounds formed of nitrogen and oxygen, in which the oxygen is in a lower proportion than that in which the same elements form *nitric* acid.

NI'TRY, *a.* Nitrous; pertaining to niter; producing niter. *Gay.*

NIT'TER, *n.* [from *nit.*] The horse bee that deposits nits on horses. *Med. Repos.*

NIT'TILY, *adv.* [from *nitty.*] Lousily. [*Not used.*] *Hayward.*

NIT'TY, *a.* [from *nit.*] Full of nits; abounding with nits. *Johnson.*

NI'VAL, *a.* [L. *nivalis*, from *nix, nivis*, snow.]

Abounding with snow; snowy. [*Not used.*] *Dict.*

NI'VEOUS, *a.* [L. *niveus.*] Snowy; resembling snow; partaking of the qualities of snow. *Brown.*

NO. an abbreviation of *number*, Fr. *nombre*; as *No.* 8. *No.* 10.

NO, *adv.* [Sax. *na* or *ne*; W. *na*; Russ. *ne*; Sans. *na*; Pers. Zend, *id.*]

1. A word of denial or refusal, expressing a negative, and equivalent to *nay* and *not.* When it expresses a negative answer, it is opposed to *yes* or *yea.* Will you go? *No.*

It is frequently used in denying propositions, and opposed to affirmation or concession. "That I may prove them, whether they will walk in my law, or *no.*" Ex. xvi. *No*, in this use, is deemed less elegant than *not*, but the use is very general.

2. After another negative, it repeats the negation with great emphasis.

There is none righteous, *no*, not one. Rom. iii. 1 Cor. v.

Sometimes it follows an affirmative proposition in like manner, but still it denies with emphasis and gives force to the following negative.

To whom we gave place by subjection, *no*, not for an hour. Gal. ii.

Sometimes it begins a sentence with a like emphatical signification, strengthening the following negative.

No, not the bow which so adorns the skies,
So glorious is, or boasts so many dyes. *Waller.*

3. Not in any degree; as *no* longer; *no* shorter; *no* more; *no* less.

4. When *no* is repeated, it expresses negation or refusal with emphasis; as *no, no.*

NO, *a.* Not any; none.

Let there be *no* strife between thee and me. Gen. xiii.

2. Not any; not one.

Thou shalt worship *no* other God. Ex. xxxiv.

3. When it precedes *where*, as in *no where*, it may be considered as adverbial, though originally an adjective.

NOBIL'IARY, *n.* [See *Noble.*] A history of noble families. *Encyc.*

NOBIL'ITATE, *v. t.* [L. *nobilito.* See *Noble.*] To make noble; to ennoble.

NOBILITA'TION, *n.* The act of making noble. *More.*

NOBIL'ITY, *n.* [L. *nobilitas.*] Dignity of mind; greatness; grandeur; that elevation of soul which comprehends bravery, generosity, magnanimity, intrepidity, and contempt of every thing that dishonors character.

Though she hated Amphialus, yet the *nobility* of her courage prevailed over it. *Sidney.*

They thought it great their sovereign to control,
And named their pride, *nobility* of soul. *Dryden.*

2. Antiquity of family; descent from noble ancestors; distinction by blood, usually joined with riches.

When I took up Boccace unawares, I fell on the same argument of preferring virtue to *nobility* of blood and titles, in the story of Sigismunda. *Dryden.*

3. The qualities which constitute distinction of rank in civil society, according to the customs or laws of the country; that eminence or dignity which a man derives from birth or title conferred, and which places him in an order above common men. In Great Britain, nobility is extended to five ranks, those of duke, marquis, earl, viscount and baron.

4. The persons collectively who enjoy rank above commoners; the peerage; as the English *nobility*; French, German, Russian *nobility.*

NO'BLE, *a.* [Fr. Sp. *noble*; Port. *nobre*; It. *nobile*; L. *nobilis*, from *nosco, novi*, to know.]

1. Great; elevated; dignified; being above every thing that can dishonor reputation; as a *noble* mind; a *noble* courage; *noble* deeds of valor. *Milton.*

2. Exalted; elevated; sublime.

Statues, with winding ivy crown'd, belong
To *nobler* poets for a *nobler* song. *Dryden.*

3. Magnificent; stately; splendid; as a *noble* parade; a *noble* edifice.

4. Of an ancient and splendid family; as *noble* by descent.

5. Distinguished from commoners by rank and title; as a *noble* personage.

6. Free; generous; liberal; as a *noble* heart.

7. Principal; capital; as the *noble* parts of the body. *Johnson.*

8. Ingenuous; candid; of an excellent disposition; ready to receive truth. Acts. xvii.

9. Of the best kind; choice; excellent; as a *noble* vine. Jer. ii.

NO'BLE, *n.* A person of rank above a commoner; a nobleman; a peer; as a duke, marquis, earl, viscount or baron.

2. In *Scripture*, a person of honorable family or distinguished by station. Ex. xxiv. Neh. vi.

3. Originally, a gold coin, but now a money of account, value 6s. 8d. sterling, or $1 48 cts. *Camden.*

NO'BLEMAN, *n.* A noble; a peer; one who enjoys rank above a commoner, either by virtue of birth, by office or patent. *Dryden.*

NO'BLEWÖMAN, *n.* A female of noble rank. *Cavendish.*

NO'BLENESS, *n.* Greatness; dignity; ingenuousness; magnanimity; elevation of mind or of condition, particularly of the mind.

His purposes are full of honesty, *nobleness* and integrity. *Taylor.*

Greatness of mind and *nobleness* their seat
Build in her loveliest. *Milton.*

The *nobleness* of life is to do this— *Shak.*

2. Distinction by birth; honor derived from a noble ancestry.

NOBLESS', *n.* [Fr. *noblesse*, from Sp. *nobleza.*]

1. The nobility; persons of noble rank collectively, including males and females. *Dryden.*

2. Dignity; greatness; noble birth or condition. [*In these senses, not now used.*] *Spenser. B. Jonson.*

NO'BLY, *adv.* Of noble extraction; descended from a family of rank; as *nobly* born or descended. *Dryden.*

2. With greatness of soul; heroically; with magnanimity; as a deed *nobly* done. He *nobly* preferred death to disgrace.

3. Splendidly; magnificently. He was *nobly* entertained.

Where could an emperor's ashes have been so *nobly* lodged as in the midst of his metropolis and on the top of so exalted a monument? *Addison.*

NO'BODY, *n.* [*no* and *body.*] No person; no one. *Swift.*

NO'CENT, *a.* [L. *nocens*, from *noceo*, to hurt, from striking. See *Annoy.*]

Hurtful; mischievous; injurious; doing hurt; as *nocent* qualities. *Watts.*

NO'CIVE, *a.* [L. *nocivus.*] Hurtful; injurious. *Hooker.*

NOCK, *n.* A notch. *Obs.* [See *Notch.*]

NOCK, *v. t.* To place in the notch. *Obs.* *Chapman.*

NOCTAMBULA'TION, *n.* [L. *nox*, night, and *ambulo*, to walk.]

A rising from bed and walking in sleep. *Beddoes.*

NOCTAM'BULIST, *n.* One who rises from bed and walks in his sleep. Arbuthnot uses *noctambulo* in the same sense; but it is a less analogical word.

NOCTID'IAL, *a.* [L. *nox*, night, and *dies*, day.]

Comprising a night and a day. [*Little used.*] *Holder.*

NOCTIF'EROUS, *a.* [L. *nox*, night, and *fero*, to bring.] Bringing night. [*Not used.*] *Dict.*

NOCTIL'UCA, *n.* [L. *nox*, night, and *luceo*, to shine.]

A species of phosphorus which shines in darkness without the previous aid of solar rays. *Encyc.*

NOCTIL'UCOUS, *a.* Shining in the night. *Pennant.*

NOCTIV'AGANT, *a.* [L. *nox*, night, and *vagor*, to wander.] Wandering in the night.

NOCTIVAGA'TION, *n.* A roving in the night. *Gayton.*

NOC'TUARY, *n.* [from L. *nox*, night.] An account of what passes in the night. *Addison.*

NOC'TULE, *n.* [from L. *nox*, night.] A large species of bat.

NOC'TURN, *n.* [L. *nocturnus*, by night.] An office of devotion, or religious service by night. *Stillingfleet.*

NOCTURN'AL, *a.* [L. *nocturnus*, from *nox*, night.]

1. Pertaining to night; as *nocturnal* darkness.

2. Done or happening at night; as a *nocturnal* expedition or assault; a *nocturnal* visit.

3. Nightly; done or being every night.

From gilded roofs depending lamps display
Nocturnal beams, that emulate the day. *Dryden.*

NOCTURN'AL, *n.* An instrument, chiefly used at sea to take the altitude of stars about the pole, in order to ascertain the latitude. This may be a hemisphere, or a planisphere on the plane of the equinoctial. *Encyc.*

NOC'UMENT, *n.* [L. *nocumentum*, from *noceo*, to hurt.] Harm. [*Not used.*]

NOD, *v. i.* [L. *nuto*; Gr. νευω, contracted; W. *amnaid*, a nod; *amneidiaw*, to nod, to beckon, from *naid*, a leap, a spring; *neidiaw*, to leap, to throb or beat, as the pulse; Ar. نَادَ to nod, to shake; Heb. Ch. Syr. נוד to move, to shake, to wander. It coincides in elements with L. *nato*, to swim. Class Nd. No. 3. 9. 10.]

1. To incline the head with a quick motion, either forward or sidewise, as persons *nod* in sleep.
2. To bend or incline with a quick motion; as *nodding* plumes.

The *nodding* verdure of its brow. *Thomson.*

3. To be drowsy.

Your predecessors, contrary to other authors, never pleased their readers more than when they were *nodding*. *Addison.*

4. To make a slight bow; also, to beckon with a nod.

NOD, *v. t.* To incline or bend; to shake. *Shak.*

NOD, *n.* A quick declination of the head.

A look or a *nod* only ought to correct them when they do amiss. *Locke.*

2. A quick declination or inclination.

Like a drunken sailor on a mast,
Ready with every *nod* to tumble down. *Shak.*

3. A quick inclination of the head in drowsiness or sleep. *Locke.*
4. A slight obeisance. *Shak.*
5. A command; as in L. *numen*, for *nutamen.*

NO'DATED, *a.* [L. *nodatus.*] Knotted. A *nodated* hyperbola is one that by turning round crosses itself.

NODA'TION, *n.* [L. *nodatio*, from *nodo*, to tie.]

The act of making a knot, or state of being knotted. [*Little used.*]

NOD'DEN, *a.* Bent; inclined. [*Not in use.*] *Thomson.*

NOD'DER, *n.* One who nods; a drowsy person. *Pope.*

NOD'DING, *ppr.* Inclining the head with a short quick motion.

NOD'DLE, *n.* [qu. L. *nodulus*, a lump; or from *nod.*] The head; in contempt.

Come, master, I have a project in my *noddle*. *L'Estrange.*

NOD'DY, *n.* [qu. Gr. νωθης.] A simpleton; a fool.

2. A fowl of the genus Sterna, very simple and easily taken.
3. A game at cards. *B. Jonson.*

NODE, *n.* [L. *nodus*; Eng. *knot*; allied probably to *knit*, Sax. *cnyttan.*]

1. Properly, a knot; a knob; hence,
2. In *surgery*, a swelling of the periosteum, tendons or bones.
3. In *astronomy*, the point where the orbit of a planet intersects the ecliptic. These points are two, and that where a planet ascends northward above the plane of the ecliptic, is called the *ascending node*, or *dragon's head*; that where a planet descends to the south, is called the *descending node*, or *dragon's tail*. *Encyc.*
4. In *poetry*, the knot, intrigue or plot of a piece, or the principal difficulty.
5. In *dialing*, a point or hole in the gnomon of a dial, by the shadow or light of which, either the hour of the day in dials without furniture, or the parallels of the sun's declination and his place in the ecliptic, &c. in dials with furniture, are shown.

NODO'SE, *a.* [L. *nodosus*, from *nodus*, knot.]

Knotted; having knots or swelling joints. *Martyn.*

NODOS'ITY, *n.* Knottiness. *Brown.*

NO'DOUS, *a.* [L. *nodosus.*] Knotty; full of knots. *Brown.*

NOD'ULAR, *a.* Pertaining to or in the form of a nodule or knot.

NOD'ULE, *n.* [L. *nodulus.*] A little knot or lump.

NOD'ULED, *a.* Having little knots or lumps. *Darwin.*

NOG, *n.* [*abbrev.* of *noggen.*] A little pot; also, ale. *Skinner. Swift.*

NOG'GEN, *a.* Hard; rough; harsh. [*Not used.*] *King Charles.*

NOG'GIN, *n.* A small mug or wooden cup.

NOG'GING, *n.* A partition of scantlings filled with bricks. *Mason.*

NOI'ANCE, *n.* [See *Annoy.*] Annoyance; trouble; mischief; inconvenience. [*Not used.*] *Shak.*

NOIE, for *annoy*,
NOIER, for *annoyer*, } are not in use.
NOIOUS, troublesome, } *Tusser.*

NOISE, *n. noiz.* [Fr. *noise*, strife, squabble, dispute; Arm. *noes.* Class Ns. Ar. 11. Syr. 24. and L. *noxa*, *noxia.* Class Ng. No. 23.]

1. Sound of any kind, or proceeding from any cause, as the sound made by the organs of speech, by the wings of an insect, the rushing of the wind, or the roaring of the sea, of cannon or thunder, a low sound, a high sound, &c.; *a word of general signification.*
2. Outcry; clamor; loud, importunate or continued talk expressive of boasting, complaint or quarreling. In quarreling, it expresses less than *uproar.*

What *noise* have we about transplantation of diseases and transfusion of blood? *Baker.*

3. Frequent talk; much public conversation.

Socrates lived in Athens during the great plague which has made so much *noise* in all ages, and never caught the least infection. *Spectator.*

NOISE, *v. i. noiz.* To sound loud.

Harm those terrors did me none, though *noising* loud. *Milton.*

NOISE, *v. t. noiz.* To spread by rumor or report.

All these sayings were *noised* abroad—Luke i.

2. To disturb with noise. [*Not authorized.*] *Dryden.*

NOIS'ED, *pp. s* as *z.* Spread by report; much talked of.

NOISEFUL, *a. noiz'ful.* Loud; clamorous; making much noise or talk. *Dryden.*

NOISELESS, *a. noiz'less.* Making no noise or bustle; silent; as the *noiseless* foot of time. *Shak.*

So *noiseless* would I live. *Dryden.*

NOISE-MAKER, *n. noiz'-maker.* One who makes a clamor. *L'Estrange.*

NOISILY, *adv. noiz'ily.* With noise; with making a noise.

NOISINESS, *n. noiz'iness.* The state of being noisy; loudness of sound; clamorousness.

NOISING, *ppr. noiz'ing.* Spreading by report.

NOISÔME, *a. noi'sum.* [Norm. *noisife*; It. *nocivo*, *noioso.* This word is formed with the Teutonic *some*, united with the It. *noiare*, Fr. *nuire*, *nuisant*, from the L. *noxa*, *noceo*, to hurt. Class Ng.]

1. Noxious to health; hurtful; mischievous; unwholesome; insalubrious; destructive; as *noisome* winds; *noisome* effluvia or miasmata; *noisome* pestilence. *Milton. Dryden.*
2. Noxious; injurious.
3. Offensive to the smell or other senses; disgusting; fetid.

Foul breath is *noisome*. *Shak.*

NOI'SÔMELY, *adv.* With a fetid stench; with an infectious steam.

NOI'SÔMENESS, *n.* Offensiveness to the smell; quality that disgusts. *South.*

NOISY, *a. noiz'y.* [from *noise.*] Making a loud sound.

2. Clamorous; turbulent; as the *noisy* crowd.
3. Full of noise.

O leave the *noisy* town. *Dryden.*

Nolens volens, [L.] unwilling or willing; whether he will or not.

NOLI-ME-TANĠERE, *n.* [L. touch me not.]

1. A plant of the genus Impatiens, called also balsamine; also, a plant of the genus Momordica, or male balsam apple, one species of which is called the wild or spurting cucumber. *Encyc.*
2. Among *physicians*, an ulcer or cancer, a species of herpes. *Coxe.*

NOLI''TION, *n.* [L. *nolo*, that is, *ne volo*, I will not.]

Unwillingness; opposed to *volition.* [*Little used.*] *Hale.*

NOLL, *n.* [Sax. *hnol*, *cnoll*, knoll.] The head; the noddle. [*Not used.*]

NO'MAD, *n.* [Gr. νομας, νομαδος, living on pasturage, from νεμω, to distribute or divide, to feed. This verb is connected with νεμος, L. *nemus*, a wood, a place overgrown with trees, and also a pasture, the primary sense of which is probably to spring or shoot, for the verb νεμω signifies among other things, to leap, to dance, and may be allied to Eng. *nimble.* Cattle originally subsisted by browsing, as they still do in new settlements.]

One who leads a wandering life, and subsists by tending herds of cattle which graze on herbage of spontaneous growth. Such is the practice at this day in the central and northern parts of Asia, and the Numidians in Africa are supposed to have been so called from this practice. *Tooke. Encyc.*

NOMAD'IC, *a.* [Gr. νομαδικος.] Pastoral; subsisting by the tending of cattle, and wandering for the sake of pasturage; as the *nomadic* tribes of Asia.

NO'MADIZE, *v. i.* To wander with flocks and herds for the sake of finding pasturage; to subsist by the grazing of herds on herbage of natural growth.

The Vogules *nomadize* chiefly about the rivers Irtish, Oby, Kama and Volga. *Tooke.*

NO'MADIZING, *ppr.* Leading a pastoral life and wandering or removing from place to place for the sake of finding pasture.

NO'MANCY, *n.* [Gr. ονομα, L. *nomen*, name, and μαντεια, divination.]
The art or practice of divining the destiny of persons by the letters which form their names. *Dict.*

NÔM'BLES, *n.* [Fr.] The entrails of a deer. *Johnson.*

NOM'BRIL, *n.* [Fr. the navel.] The center of an escutcheon. *Cyc.*

NOME, *n.* [Gr. νομος.] A province or tract of country; an Egyptian government or division. *Maurice.*
2. In *the ancient Greek music*, any melody determined by inviolable rules. *Cyc.*
3. [L. *nomen.*] In *algebra*, a quantity with a sign prefixed or added to it, by which it is connected with another quantity, upon which the whole becomes a binomial, trinomial, and the like. *Cyc.*
4. [Gr. νεμω, to eat.] In *surgery*, a phagedenic ulcer, or species of herpes. *Cyc.*

NÔMENCLA'TOR, *n.* [L.; Fr. *nomenclateur*; L. *nomen*, name, and *calo*, Gr. χαλεω, to call.]
1. A person who calls things or persons by their names. In Rome, candidates for office were attended each by a *nomenclator*, who informed the candidate of the names of the persons they met, and whose votes they wished to solicit. *Cyc.*
2. In *modern usage*, a person who gives names to things, or who settles and adjusts the names of things in any art or science.

NÔMENCLA'TRESS, *n.* A female nomenclator. *Addison.*

NÔMENCLA'TURAL, *a.* Pertaining or according to a nomenclature. *Barton.*

NO'MENCLATURE, *n.* [L. *nomenclatura.* See *Nomenclator.*]
1. A list or catalogue of the more usual and important words in a language, with their significations; a vocabulary or dictionary.
2. The names of things in any art or science, or the whole vocabulary of names or technical terms which are appropriated to any particular branch of science; as the *nomenclature* of botany or of chimistry; the new *nomenclature* of Lavoisier and his associates.

NO'MIAL, *n.* [from L. *nomen*, name.] A single name or term in mathematics.

NOM'INAL, *a.* [L. *nominalis*, from *nomen.* See *Name.*]
1. Titular; existing in name only; as, a *nominal* distinction or difference is a difference in name and not in reality.
2. Pertaining to a name or names; consisting in names.

NOM'INAL, NOM'INALIST, } *n.* The Nominalists were a sect of school philosophers, the disciples of Ocham or Occam, in the 14th century, who maintained that words and not things are the object of dialectics. They were the founders of the university of Leipsic. *Encyc.*

NOM'INALIZE, *v. t.* To convert into a noun. [*Not in use and ill formed.*]

NOM'INALLY, *adv.* By name or in name only.

NOM'INATE, *v. t.* [L. *nomino*, from *nomen*, name. See *Name.*]
1. To name; to mention by name. *Wotton.*
2. To call; to entitle; to denominate. *Spenser.*
3. To name or designate by name for an office or place; to appoint; as, to *nominate* an heir or an executor. *Locke.*
4. Usually, to name for an election, choice or appointment; to propose by name, or offer the name of a person as a candidate for an office or place. This is the principal use of the word in the United States; as in a public assembly, where men are to be selected and chosen to office, any member of the assembly or meeting *nominates*, that is, proposes to the chairman the name of a person whom he desires to have elected.

NOM'INATED, *pp.* Named; mentioned by name; designated or proposed for an office or for election.

NOM'INATELY, *adv.* By name; particularly. *Spelman.*

NOM'INATING, *ppr.* Naming; proposing for an office or for choice by name.

NOMINA'TION, *n.* The act of naming or of nominating; the act of proposing by name for an office.
2. The power of nominating or appointing to office.

The *nomination* of persons to places being a prerogative of the king— *Clarendon.*

3. The state of being nominated. AB is in *nomination* for governor.

NOM'INATIVE, *a.* Pertaining to the name which precedes a verb, or to the first case of nouns; as the *nominative* case or *nominative* word.

NOM'INATIVE, *n.* In *grammar*, the first case of names or nouns and of adjectives which are declinable.

NOM'INATOR, *n.* One that nominates.

NOMINEE', *n.* In *law*, the person who is named to receive a copy-hold estate on surrender of it to the lord; the cestuy que use, sometimes called the surrenderee. *Blackstone.*
2. A person named or designated by another. *Paley.*
3. A person on whose life depends an annuity.

NOMOTHET'IC, NOMOTHET'ICAL, } *a.* [Gr. νομοθετης.] Legislative; enacting laws. *Bp. Barlow.*

NON, *adv.* [L.] Not. This word is used in the English language as a prefix only, for giving a negative sense to words; as in *non*-residence, *non*-performance, *non*-existence, *non*-payment, *non*-concurrence, *non*-admission, *non*-appearance, *non*-attendance, *non*-conformity, *non*-compliance, *non*-communion, and the like.

NON-ABIL'ITY, *n.* A want of ability; in *law*, an exception taken against a plaintiff in a cause, when he is unable legally to commence a suit.

NON'AGE, *n.* [*non*, not, and *age.*] Minority; the time of life before a person, according to the laws of his country, becomes of age to manage his own concerns. Legal maturity of age is different in different countries. In this country, as in Great Britain, a man's *nonage* continues till he has completed twenty one years. Nonage is sometimes the period under 14 years of age, as in case of marriage. *Bailey. Encyc.*

NONAGES'IMAL, *a.* [L. *nonagesimus*, ninetieth.]
Noting the 90th degree of the ecliptic; being in the highest point of the ecliptic.

NON'AGON, *n.* [L. *nonus*, nine, and Gr. γωνια, an angle.]
A figure having nine sides and nine angles. *Bailey.*

NON-APPE'ARANCE, *n.* Default of appearance, as in court, to prosecute or defend.

NON-APPOINT'MENT, *n.* Neglect of appointment. *Franklin.*

NON-ATTEND'ANCE, *n.* A failure to attend; omission of attendance.

NON-ATTEN'TION, *n.* Inattention. *Swift.*

NON-BITU'MINOUS, *a.* Containing no bitumen. *Journ. of Science.*

NONCE, *n.* Purpose; intent; design. [*Not in use.*] *Spenser. B. Jonson.*

NON'-CLAIM, *n.* A failure to make claim within the time limited by law; omission of claim. *Bailey.*

NON-COMMU'NION, *n.* Neglect or failure of communion. *B. Trumbull.*

NON-COMPLI'ANCE, *n.* Neglect or failure of compliance.

NON-COMPLY'ING, *a.* Neglecting or refusing to comply. *Hamilton.*

Non compos mentis, or *non compos*, [L.] not of sound mind; not having the regular use of reason; as a noun, an idiot; a lunatic; one devoid of reason, either by nature or by accident.

NON-CONDUCT'ING, *a.* Not conducting; not transmitting another fluid. Thus in electricity, wax is a *non-conducting* substance.

NON-CONDUC'TION, *n.* A non-conducting. *Ure.*

NON-CONDUCT'OR, *n.* A substance which does not conduct, that is, transmit another substance or fluid, or which transmits it with difficulty. Thus wool is a *non-conductor* of heat; glass and dry wood are *non-conductors* of the electrical fluid.

NON-CONFORM'IST, *n.* One who neglects or refuses to conform to the rites and mode of worship of an established church. *Blackstone. Swift.*

NON-CONFORM'ITY, *n.* Neglect or failure of conformity.
2. The neglect or refusal to unite with an established church in its rites and mode of worship. *Blackstone.*

NON-CONTA'GIOUS, *a.* Not contagious.

NON-CONTA'GIOUSNESS, *n.* The quality or state of being not communicable from a diseased to a healthy body.

NON-COTEMPORA'NEOUS, *a.* Not being cotemporary, or not of cotemporary origin. *Journ. of Science.*

NON-DESCRIPT', *a.* [L. *non*, not, and *descriptus*, described.] That has not been described.

NON-DESCRIPT', *n.* Any thing that has not been described. Thus a plant or animal newly discovered is called a *non-descript.*

NONE, *a.* [Sax. *nan*; *ne*, not, and *ane*, one. The Latins use *nemo*, *neminis*, that is, *ne* and *man.*]

1. Not one; *used of persons or things.*
There is *none* that doeth good; no, not one. Ps. xiv.
2. Not any; not a part; not the least portion.
Six days shall ye gather it, but on the seventh day, which is the sabbath, in it there shall be *none*. Ex. xvi.
3. It was formerly used before nouns; as, "thou shalt have *none* assurance of thy life." This use is obsolete; we now use *no*; thou shalt have *no* assurance. "This is *none* other but the house of God;" we now say, *no* other.
4. It is used as a substitute, the noun being omitted. "He walketh through dry places, seeking rest and finding *none*;" that is, no rest. Matt. xii.
5. In the following phrase, it is used for *nothing*, or *no concern*. "Israel would *none* of me," that is, Israel would not listen to me at all; they would have no concern with me; they utterly rejected my counsels.
6. As a substitute, *none* has a plural signification.
Terms of peace were *none* vouchsafed. *Milton.*

NON-ELECT', *n.* [L. *non*, not, and *electus*, elected.]
One who is not elected or chosen to salvation. *Huntington.*

NON-ELEC'TRIC, *a.* Conducting the electric fluid.

NON-ELEC'TRIC, *n.* A substance that is not an electric, or which transmits the fluid; as metals.

NON-EMPHAT'IC, } *a.* Having no emphasis; unemphatic. *Beattie.*
NON-EMPHAT'ICAL, }

NON-EN'TITY, *n.* Non-existence; the negation of being. *Bentley.*
2. A thing not existing.
There was no such thing as rendering evil for evil, when evil was a *non-entity*. *South.*

NON-EPIS'COPAL, *a.* Not episcopal; not of the episcopal church or denomination. *J. M. Mason.*

NON-EPISCOPA'LIAN, *n.* One who does not belong to the episcopal church or denomination. *J. M. Mason.*

NONES, *n. plu.* [L. *nonæ*; perhaps Goth. *niun*, Eng. *nine.*]
1. In *the Roman calendar*, the fifth day of the months January, February, April, June, August, September, November and December, and the seventh day of March, May, July and October. The *nones* were *nine* days from the ides.
2. Prayers, formerly so called. *Todd.*

NON-ESSEN'TIAL, *n.* Non-essentials are things not essential to a particular purpose. *J. M. Mason.*

NO'NESUCH, *n.* [*none* and *such.*] An extraordinary thing; a thing that has not its equal.
2. A plant of the genus Lychnis. *Lee.*

NON-EXECU'TION, *n.* Neglect of execution; non-performance.

NON-EXIST'ENCE, *n.* Absence of existence; the negation of being.
2. A thing that has no existence or being. *Brown.*

NON-EXPŌRTA'TION, *n.* A failure of exportation; a not exporting goods or commodities.

NONIL'LION, *n.* [L. *nonus*, nine, and *million.*] The number of nine million millions.

NON-IMPORTA'TION, *n.* Want or failure of importation; a not importing goods.

NON-JU'RING, *a.* [L. *non*, not, and *juro*, to swear.]
Not swearing allegiance; an epithet applied to the party in Great Britain that would not swear allegiance to the Hanoverian family and government.

NON-JU'ROR, *n.* In *Great Britain*, one who refused to take the oath of allegiance to the government and crown of England at the revolution, when James II. abdicated the throne, and the Hanoverian family was introduced. The non-jurors were the adherents of James.

NON-MANUFAC'TURING, *a.* Not carrying on manufactures; as *non-manufacturing* states. *Hamilton.*

NON-METAL'LIC, *a.* Not consisting of metal. *Coxe's Orfila.*

NON-NAT'URALS, *n.* In *medicine*, things which, by the abuse of them, become the causes of disease, as meat, drink, sleep, rest, motion, the passions, retentions, excretions, &c.
Functions or accidents not strictly belonging to man. *Parr.*

NON-OBSERV'ANCE, *n.* Neglect or failure to observe or fulfill.

Non obstante, [L. *notwithstanding*,] a clause in statutes and letters patent, importing a license from the king to do a thing which at common law might be lawfully done, but being restrained by act of parliament, cannot be done without such license. *Encyc.*

NONPAREIL, *n. nonparel'.* [Fr. *non*, not or no, and *pareil*, equal.]
1. Excellence unequaled. *Shak.*
2. A sort of apple.
3. A sort of printing type very small, and the smallest now used except three.

NONPAREIL, *a. nonparel'.* Having no equal; peerless. *Whitlock.*

NON-PA'YMENT, *n.* Neglect of payment. *S. E. Dwight.*

NON'PLUS, *n.* [L. *non*, not, and *plus*, more, further.]
Puzzle; insuperable difficulty; a state in which one is unable to proceed or decide. *Locke. South.*

NON'PLUS, *v. t.* To puzzle; to confound; to put to a stand; to stop by embarrassment. *Dryden.*
Your situation has *nonplussed* me. *Th. Scott.*

NON-PONDEROS'ITY, *n.* Destitution of weight; levity. *Black.*

NON-PON'DEROUS, *a.* Having no weight.

NON-PRODUC'TION, *n.* A failure to produce or exhibit.

NON-PROFI''CIENCY, *n.* Failure to make progress.

NON-PROFI''CIENT, *n.* One who has failed to improve or make progress in any study or pursuit. *Bp. Hall.*

Non Pros. contraction of *nolle prosequi*, the plaintiff will not prosecute. It is used also as a verb.

NON-REG'ARDANCE, *n.* Want of due regard. *Dict.*

NON-RENDI''TION, *n.* Neglect of rendition; the not rendering what is due.
The non-payment of a debt, or the *non-rendition* of a service which is due, is an injury for which the subsequent reparation of the loss sustained—is an atonement. *S. E. Dwight.*

NON-RESEM'BLANCE, *n.* *s* as *z*. Unlikeness; dissimilarity.

NON-RES'IDENCE, *n.* *s* as *z*. Failure or neglect of residing at the place where one is stationed, or where official duties require one to reside, or on one's own lands. *Swift.*

NON-RES'IDENT, *a.* Not residing in a particular place, on one's own estate, or in one's proper place; as a *non-resident* clergyman or proprietor of lands.

NON-RES'IDENT, *n.* One who does not reside on one's own lands, or in the place where official duties require. In the United States, lands in one state or township belonging to a person residing in another state or township, are called the lands of *non-residents.*

NON-RESIST'ANCE, *n.* *s* as *z*. The omission of resistance; passive obedience; submission to authority, power or usurpation without opposition.

NON-RESIST'ANT, *a.* Making no resistance to power or oppression. *Arbuthnot.*

NON-SA'NE, *a.* [L. *non*, not, and *sanus*, sound.]
Unsound; not perfect; as a person of *non-sane* memory. *Blackstone.*

NON'SENSE, *n.* No sense; words or language which have no meaning, or which convey no just ideas; absurdity. *Dryden.*
2. Trifles; things of no importance. *Thomson.*

NONSENS'ICAL, *a.* Unmeaning; absurd; foolish. *Ray.*

NONSENS'ICALLY, *adv.* Absurdly; without meaning.

NONSENS'ICALNESS, *n.* Jargon; absurdity; that which conveys no proper ideas.

NONSENS'ITIVE, *a.* Wanting sense or perception. *Feltham.*

NON-SOLU'TION, *n.* Failure of solution or explanation. *Broome.*

NON-SOLV'ENCY, *n.* Inability to pay debts. *Swift.*

NON-SOLV'ENT, *a.* Not able to pay debts; insolvent. *Johnson.*

NON-SPA'RING, *a.* Sparing none; all-destroying; merciless. *Shak.*

NONSUCH. [See *Nonesuch.*]

NON'SUIT, *n.* In *law*, the default, neglect or non-appearance of the plaintiff in a suit, when called in court, by which the plaintiff signifies his intention to drop the suit. Hence a *nonsuit* amounts to a stoppage of the suit. A *nonsuit* differs from a *retraxit*; a *nonsuit* is the default or neglect of the plaintiff, and after this he may bring another suit for the same cause; but a *retraxit* is an open positive renunciation of the suit, by which he forever loses his action. [See the Verb.] *Blackstone.*

NON'SUIT, *v. t.* To determine or record that the plaintiff drops his suit, on default of appearance when called in court. When a plaintiff being called in court, declines to answer, or when he neglects to deliver his declaration, he is supposed to drop his suit; he is therefore *nonsuited*, that is, his non-appearance is entered on the record, and this entry amounts to a judgment of the court that the plaintiff has dropped the suit.

When two are joined in a writ, and one is *nonsuited*— *Z. Swift.*

NON'SUIT, *a.* Nonsuited.

The plaintiff must become *nonsuit.* *Tyng's Rep.*

NON'SUITED, *pp.* Adjudged to have deserted the suit by default of appearance; as a plaintiff.

NON'SUITING, *ppr.* Adjudging to have abandoned the suit by non-appearance or other neglect; as a plaintiff.

NON-USANCE, *n. non-yu'zance.* Neglect of use. *Brown.*

NON-USER, *n. non-yu'zer.* A not using; failure to use; neglect of official duty; default of performing the duties and services required of an officer.

An office may be forfeited by misuser or *non-user.* *Blackstone.*

2. Neglect or omission of use.

A franchise may be lost by *misuser* or *non-user.* *Supreme Court, U. S.*

NOO'DLE, *n.* A simpleton. [*A vulgar word.*]

NOOK, *n.* [See *Nich.*] A corner; a narrow place formed by an angle in bodies or between bodies; as a hollow *nook.* *Milton.*

NOON, *n.* [Sax. *non;* D. *noen;* W. *nawn*, that is at the summit; said to be from *naw*, that is up or ultimate, that limits, also *nine.* It has been supposed that the *ninth* hour, among the Romans, was the time of eating the chief meal; this hour was three o'clock, P. M. In Danish, *none* is an afternooning, a collation.]

1. The middle of the day; the time when the sun is in the meridian; twelve o'clock.

2. Dryden used the word for midnight. "At the *noon* of night."

NOON, *a.* Meridional.

How of the *noon* bell. *Young.*

NOON'DAY, *n.* Mid-day; twelve o'clock in the day. *Boyle.*

NOON'DAY, *a.* Pertaining to mid-day; meridional; as the *noonday* heat.

NOON'ING, *n.* Repose at noon; sometimes, repast at noon. *Addison.*

NOON'STEAD, *n.* The station of the sun at noon. *Drayton.*

NOON'TIDE, *n.* [See *Tide*, which signifies *time.*]

The time of noon; mid-day. *Shak.*

NOON'TIDE, *a.* Pertaining to noon; meridional. *Milton.*

NOOSE, *n. nooz.* [Ir. *nas*, a band or tie; *nasgaim*, to bind or tie.]

A running knot, which binds the closer the more it is drawn.

Where the hangman does dispose
To special friend the knot of *noose.* *Hudibras.*

NOOSE, *v. t. nooz.* To tie in a noose; to catch in a noose; to entrap; to ensnare.

NO'PAL, *n.* A plant of the genus Cactus, from which the cochineal is collected in Mexico; Indian fig or raquette. The fruit resembles a fig. *Encyc.*

NOPE, *n.* A provincial name for the bullfinch or red tail. *Eng. Dict.*

NOR, *connective.* [*ne* and *or.*] A word that denies or renders negative the second or subsequent part of a proposition, or a proposition following another negative proposition; correlative to *neither* or *not.*

I neither love *nor* fear thee. *Shak.*
Fight neither with small *nor* great. 1 Kings xxii.
Eye hath not seen, *nor* ear heard— 1 Cor. ii.

2. *Nor* sometimes begins a sentence, but in this case a negative proposition has preceded it in the foregoing sentence.

3. In some cases, usually in poetry, *neither* is omitted, and the negation which it would express is included in *nor.*

Simois *nor* Xanthus shall be wanting there. *Dryden.*

That is, *neither* Simois *nor* Xanthus.

4. Sometimes in poetry, *nor* is used for *neither*, in the first part of the proposition.

I whom *nor* avarice *nor* pleasures move. *Walsh.*

NOR'MAL, *a.* [L. *normalis*, from *norma*, a square, a rule.]

1. According to a square or rule; perpendicular; forming a right angle.

2. According to a rule or principle.

3. Relating to rudiments or elements; teaching rudiments or first principles; as *normal* schools in France.

NOR'MAN, *n.* In *seamen's language*, a short wooden bar to be thrust into a hole of the windlass, on which to fasten the cable. *Mar. Dict.*

NOR'MAN, *n.* [*north-man* or *nord-man.*] A Norwegian, or a native of Normandy.

NOR'MAN, *a.* Pertaining to Normandy; as the *Norman* language.

NOR'ROY, *n.* [*north* and *roy*, north king.] The title of the third of the three kings at arms or provincial heralds. *Burke.*

NORTH, *n.* [Sax. *north;* G. Sw. Dan. *nord;* D. *noord;* It. *norte;* Fr. *nord;* Arm. *id.;* Sp. *nord*, the north wind, and *norte*, north, the arctic pole, and a rule or guide. I know not the origin of this word, nor its primary sense. It may have been applied first to the pole star, or to the wind, like *Boreas.*]

One of the cardinal points, being that point of the horizon which is directly opposite to the sun in the meridian, on the left hand when we stand with the face to the east; or it is that point of intersection of the horizon and meridian which is nearest our pole. *Cyc.*

NORTH, *a.* Being in the north; as the *north* polar star.

NORTHE'AST, *n.* The point between the north and east, at an equal distance from each.

NORTHE'AST, *a.* Pertaining to the northeast, or proceeding from that point; as a *northeast* wind.

NORTH'ERLY, *a.* Being towards the north, or nearer towards the north than to any other cardinal point. [We use this word and *northern* with considerable latitude.]

NORTH'ERLY, *adv.* Towards the north; as, to sail *northerly.*

2. In a northern direction; as a *northerly* course.

3. Proceeding from a northern point.

NORTH'ERN, *a.* Being in the north, or nearer to that point than to the east or west.

2. In a direction towards the north, or a point near it; as, to steer a *northern* course.

NORTH'ERNLY, *adv.* Toward the north. [*Not used.*] *Hakewill.*

NORTH'ING, *n.* The motion or distance of a planet from the equator northward.

As the tides of the sea obey the southing and *northing* of the sea— *Darwin.*

2. Course or distance northward of the equator.

NORTH'-STAR, *n.* The north polar star.

NORTH'WARD, *a.* [Sax. *north* and *weard.*] Being towards the north, or nearer to the north than to the east and west points.

NORTH'WARD, *adv.* Towards the north, or towards a point nearer to the north than the east and west points. *Bacon. Dryden.*

NORTHWEST', *n.* The point in the horizon between the north and west, and equally distant from each.

NORTHWEST', *a.* Pertaining to the point between the north and west; being in the northwest; as the *northwest* coast.

2. Proceeding from the northwest; as a *northwest* wind.

NORTHWEST'ERN, *a.* Pertaining to or being in the northwest, or in a direction to the northwest; as a *northwestern* course.

NORTH'-WIND, *n.* The wind that blows from the north. *Watts.*

NORWE'GIAN, *a.* Belonging to Norway.

NORWE'GIAN, *n.* A native of Norway.

NOSE, *n.* *s* as *z.* [Sax. *nose, næse, nase;* G. *nase;* D. *neus;* Sw. *näsa;* Dan. *næse;* L. *nasus;* It. *naso;* Fr. *nez;* Russ. *nos;* Dalmatian, *nooss;* Sans. *nasa.* Qu. Gr. *νησος*, an isle. It occurs in *Peloponnesus*, the promontory of Pelops. It seems to be the same word, or from the same root as *ness*, in *Sheerness.*]

1. The prominent part of the face which is the organ of smell, consisting of two similar cavities called nostrils. The nose serves also to modulate the voice in speaking, and to discharge the tears which flow through the lachrymal ducts. Through this organ also the air usually passes in respiration, and it constitutes no small part of the beauty of the face. In man, the nose is situated near the middle of the face; but in quadrupeds, the nose is at or near the lower extremity of the head.

2. The end of any thing; as the *nose* of a bellows. *Holder.*

3. Scent; sagacity.

We are not offended with a dog for a better *nose* than his master. *Collier.*

To lead by the nose, to lead blindly.

To be led by the nose, to follow another obsequiously, or to be led without resistance or enquiring the reason.

To thrust one's nose into the affairs of others, to meddle officiously in other people's matters; to be a busy-body.

To put one's nose out of joint, to alienate the affections from another.

NOSE, *v. t.* To smell; to scent. *Shak.*

2. To face; to oppose to the face. *Wood.*

NOSE, *v. i.* To look big; to bluster. [*Not used.*] *Shak.*

NO'SEBLEED, *n.* A hemorrhage or bleeding at the nose.

2. A plant of the genus Achillea.

NO'SED, *a.* Having a nose; as in long-*nosed.*
2. Having sagacity. *Middleton.*
NO'SE-FISH, *n.* A fish of the lether-mouthed kind, with a flat blunt snout; called also *broad-snout.* *Dict. Nat. Hist.*
NO'SEGAY, *n.* [*nose* and Celtic *geac*, a bough.]
A bunch of flowers used to regale the sense of smelling.
As on the *nosegay* in her breast reclined. *Pope.*
NO'SELESS, *a.* Destitute of a nose. *Shak.*
NO'SE-SMART, *n.* A plant, nasturtium; cresses.
NOSETHRIL. [See *Nostril.*]
NOS'LE, *n.* [from *nose.*] A little nose; the extremity of a thing; as the *nosle* of a bellows. [See *Nozzle.*]
NOSOLOĠ'ICAL, *a.* [See *Nosology.*] Pertaining to nosology, or a systematic classification of diseases.
NOSOL'OĠIST, *n.* One who classifies diseases, arranges them in order and gives them suitable names.
NOSOL'OĠY, *n.* [Gr. νοσος, disease, and λογος, discourse.]
1. A treatise on diseases, or a systematic arrangement or classification of diseases with names and definitions, according to the distinctive character of each class, order, genus and species. *Encyc.*
2. That branch of medical science which treats of the classification of diseases.
NOSOPOET'IC, *a.* [Gr. νοσος, disease, and ποιεω, to produce.] Producing diseases. [*Little used.*] *Arbuthnot.*
NOS'TRIL, *n.* [Sax. *nosethyrl, næsethyrl. Thyrl* or *thirel* is an opening or perforation; *thirlian, thyrlian,* to bore, to perforate, to *thrill,* to *drill.* See *Drill.*]
An aperture or passage through the nose. The nostrils are the passages through which air is inhaled and exhaled in respiration.
NOS'TRUM, *n.* [L. from *noster,* ours.] A medicine, the ingredients of which are kept secret for the purpose of restricting the profits of sale to the inventor or proprietor. *Pope.*
NOT, *adv.* [Sax. *naht* or *noht,* naught, that is, *ne* and *awiht,* not any thing; D. *niet;* G. *nicht;* Russ. *niete;* Scot. *nocht.* See *Naught.*]
1. A word that expresses negation, denial or refusal; as, he will *not* go; will you remain? I will *not.* In the first member of a sentence, it may be followed by *nor* or *neither;* as *not* for a price *nor* reward; I was *not* in safety, *neither* had I rest.
2. With the substantive verb in the following phrase, it denies being, or denotes extinction of existence.
Thine eyes are open upon me, and I am *not.* Job vii.
NOT'ABLE, *a.* [Fr. *notable;* L. *notabilis,* from *notus,* known; *nosco,* to know.]
1. Remarkable; worthy of notice; memorable; observable; distinguished or noted.
They bore two or three charges from the horse with *notable* courage. *Clarendon.*
Two young men of *notable* strength. 2 Macc.
2. Active; industrious; careful; as a *notable* woman.
[*In both senses, this word is obsolete in elegant style, or used only in irony. The second sense is in colloquial use in New England.*]
3. In Scripture, conspicuous; sightly; as a *notable* horn. Dan. viii.
4. Notorious. Matt. xxvii.
5. Terrible. Acts ii.
6. Known or apparent. Acts iv.
NOT'ABLE, *n.* In France, the nobles or persons of rank and distinction were formerly called *notables.*
2. A thing worthy of observation. *Addison.*
NOT'ABLENESS, *n.* Activity; industriousness; care. [*Little used.*]
2. Remarkableness.
NOT'ABLY, *adv.* Memorably; remarkably; eminently. *Bacon.*
2. With show of consequence or importance. *Addison.*
NOTA'RIAL, *a.* [from *notary.*] Pertaining to a notary; as a *notarial* seal; *notarial* evidence or attestation.
2. Done or taken by a notary.
NO'TARY, *n.* [L. *notarius,* from *notus,* known, from *nosco.*]
1. Primarily, a person employed to take notes of contracts, trials and proceedings in courts among the Romans.
2. In *modern usage,* an officer authorized to attest contracts or writings of any kind, to give them the evidence of authenticity. This officer is often styled *notary public.*
NOTA'TION, *n.* [L. *notatio,* from *noto,* to mark.]
1. The act or practice of recording any thing by marks, figures or characters; particularly in arithmetic and algebra, the expressing of numbers and quantities by figures, signs or characters appropriate for the purpose.
2. Meaning; signification.
Conscience, according to the very *notation* of the word, imports a double knowledge. [*Unusual.*] *South.*
NOTCH, *n.* [qu. G. *knicken,* to crack or flaw, Dan. *knikker.* It seems to be the same word in origin as *niche, nick.* Class Ng. No. 49.]
1. A hollow cut in any thing; a nick; an indentation.
And on the stick ten equal *notches* makes. *Swift.*
2. An opening or narrow passage through a mountain or hill. We say, the *notch* of a mountain. *U. States.*
NOTCH, *v. t.* To cut in small hollows; as, to *notch* a stick. *Pope.*
NOTCH'-WEED, *n.* A plant called orach. *Johnson.*
NOTE, for *ne wote,* knew not or could not. *Chaucer. Spenser.*
NOTE, *n.* [L. *nota;* Fr. *note;* W. *nod;* from L. *notus, nosco,* to know.]
1. A mark or token; something by which a thing may be known; a visible sign.
They who appertain to the visible church have all the *notes* of external profession. *Hooker.*
2. A mark made in a book, indicating something worthy of particular notice.
3. A short remark; a passage or explanation in the margin of a book.
4. A minute, memorandum or short writing intended to assist the memory.
5. Notice; heed.
Give order to my servants that they take
No *note* at all of our being absent hence. *Shak.*
6. Reputation; consequence; distinction; as men of *note.* Acts xvi.
7. State of being observed.
Small matters, continually in use and *note.* [*Little used.*] *Bacon.*
8. In *music,* a character which marks a sound, or the sound itself; as a semibreve, a minim, &c. Notes are marks of sounds in relation to elevation or depression, or to the time of continuing sounds.
9. Tune; voice; harmonious or melodious sounds.
The wakeful bird tunes her nocturnal *note.* *Milton.*
One common *note* on either lyre did strike. *Dryden.*
10. Abbreviation; symbol. *Baker.*
11. A short letter; a billet. *Dryden.*
12. Annotation; commentary; as the *notes* in Scott's Bible; to write *notes* on Homer.
13. A written or printed paper acknowledging a debt and promising payment; as a promissory *note;* a bank-*note;* a *note* of hand; a negotiable *note.*
14. *Notes,* plu. a writing; a written discourse; applied equally to minutes or heads of a discourse or argument, or to a discourse fully written. The advocate often has *notes* to assist his memory, and clergymen preach with *notes* or without them.
15. A diplomatic communication in writing; an official paper sent from one minister or envoy to another.
My *note* of January 10th still remains unanswered. *Gallatin.*
NOTE, *v. t.* [L. *noto.*] To observe; to notice with particular care; to heed; to attend to.
No more of that; I have *noted* it well. *Shak.*
Their manners *noted* and their states survey'd. *Pope.*
2. To set down in writing.
Note it in a book. Is. xxx.
3. To charge, as with a crime; with *of* or *for.*
They were both *noted of* incontinency. *Obs.* *Dryden.*
NOTE, *v. t.* [Sax. *hnitan.*] To butt; to push with the horns. [*Not used.*] *Ray.*
NO'TE-BOOK, *n.* A book in which memorandums are written. *Shak.*
2. A book in which notes of hand are registered.
NO'TED, *pp.* Set down in writing.
2. Observed; noticed.
3. *a.* Remarkable; much known by reputation or report; eminent; celebrated; as a *noted* author; a *noted* commander; a *noted* traveler.
NO'TEDLY, *adv.* With observation or notice. *Shak.*
NO'TEDNESS, *n.* Conspicuousness; eminence; celebrity. *Boyle.*
NO'TELESS, *a.* Not attracting notice; not conspicuous. *Decker.*
NO'TER, *n.* One who takes notice; an annotator. *Gregory.*
NO'TEWORTHY, *a.* Worthy of observation or notice. *Shak.*
NOTH'ING, *n.* [*no* and *thing.*] Not any thing; not any being or existence; a word that denies the existence of any thing; non-entity; opposed to *something.* The world was created from *nothing.*

2. Non-existence; a state of annihilation. *Shak.*

3. Not any thing; not any particular thing, deed or event. *Nothing* was done to redeem our character. He thought *nothing* done, while any thing remained to be done.

A determination to choose *nothing* is a determination not to choose the truth. *J. M. Mason.*

4. No other thing.

Nothing but this will entitle you to God's acceptance. *Wake.*

5. No part, portion, quantity or degree. The troops manifested *nothing* of irresolution in the attack.

Yet had his aspect *nothing* of severe. *Dryden.*

6. No importance; no value; no use.

Behold, ye are of *nothing*, and your work of naught. Is. xli.

7. No possession of estate; a low condition.

A man that from very *nothing* is grown to an unspeakable estate. *Shak.*

8. A thing of no proportion to something, or of trifling value or advantage.

The charge of making the ground, and otherwise, is great, but *nothing* to the profit. *Bacon.*

9. A trifle; a thing of no consideration or importance.

'Tis *nothing*, says the fool; but says the friend,
This *nothing*, sir, will bring you to your end. *Dryden.*

To make nothing of, to make no difficulty or to consider as trifling, light or unimportant.

We are industrious to preserve our bodies from slavery, but we *make nothing of* suffering our souls to be slaves to our lusts. *Ray.*

NOTH'ING, *adv.* In no degree; not at all.

Adam, with such counsel *nothing* sway'd— *Milton.*

In the phrase, *nothing worth*, the words are transposed; the natural order being, *worth nothing*.

NOTH'INGNESS, *n.* Nihility; non-existence. *Donne.*

2. Nothing; a thing of no value. *Hudibras.*

NO'TICE, *n.* [Fr. from L. *notitia*, from *noto* or *notus.*]

1. Observation by the eye or by the other senses. We take *notice* of objects passing or standing before us; we take *notice* of the words of a speaker; we take *notice* of a peculiar taste of food, or of the smell of an orange, and of our peculiar sensations. Notice then is the act by which we gain knowledge of something within the reach of the senses, or the effect of an impression on some of the senses.

2. Observation by the mind or intellectual power; as, to take *notice* of a distinction between truth and veracity.

3. Information; intelligence by whatever means communicated; knowledge given or received; as, I received *notice* by a messenger or by letter. He gave *notice* of his arrival. The bell gives *notice* of the hour of the day. The merchant gives *notice* that a bill of exchange is not accepted.

4. A paper that communicates information.

5. Attention; respectful treatment; civility.

6. Remark; observation.

NO'TICE, *v. t.* To observe; to see. We *noticed* the conduct of the speaker; we *noticed* no improper conduct.

2. To heed; to regard. His conduct was rude, but I did not *notice* it.

3. To remark; to mention or make observations on.

This plant deserves to be *noticed* in this place. *Tooke.*

Another circumstance was *noticed* in connection with the suggestion last discussed. *Hamilton.*

4. To treat with attention and civilities; as, to *notice* strangers.

5. To observe intellectually.

NO'TICEABLE, *a.* That may be observed; worthy of observation.

NO'TICED, *pp.* Observed; seen; remarked; treated with attention.

NO'TICING, *ppr.* Observing; seeing; regarding; remarking on; treating with attention.

NOTIFICA'TION, *n.* [See *Notify.*] The act of notifying or giving notice; the act of making known, particularly the act of giving official notice or information to the public, or to individuals, corporations, companies or societies, by words, by writing or by other means.

2. Notice given in words or writing, or by signs.

3. The writing which communicates information; an advertisement, citation, &c.

NO'TIFIED, *pp.* Made known; *applied to things.* This design of the king was *notified* to the court of Berlin.

2. Informed by words, writing or other means; *applied to persons.* The inhabitants of the city have been *notified* that a meeting is to be held at the State House.

NO'TIFY, *v. t.* [Fr. *notifier;* It. *notificare;* L. *notus*, known, and *facio*, to make.]

1. To make known; to declare; to publish. The laws of God *notify* to man his will and our duty.

2. To make known by private communication; to give information of. The allied sovereigns have *notified* the Spanish court of their purpose of maintaining legitimate government.

3. To give notice to; to inform by words or writing, in person or by message, or by any signs which are understood. The constable has *notified* the citizens to meet at the City Hall. The bell *notifies* us of the time of meeting.

The President of the United States has *notified* the House of Representatives, that he has approved and signed the act. *Journals of the Senate.*

[*Note.* This application of *notify* has been condemned, but it is in constant good use in the U. States, and in perfect accordance with the use of *certify.*]

NO'TIFYING, *ppr.* Making known; giving notice to.

NO'TION, *n.* [Fr. from L. *notio*, from *notus*, known; *nosco*, to know.]

1. Conception; mental apprehension of whatever may be known or imagined. We may have a just *notion* of power, or false *notions* respecting spirit.

Notion and *idea* are primarily different; *idea* being the conception of something visible, as the *idea* of a square or a triangle; and *notion* the conception of things invisible or intellectual, as the *notion* we have of spirits. But from negligence in the use of *idea*, the two words are constantly confounded.

What hath been generally agreed on, I content myself to assume under the *notion* of principles. *Newton.*

Few agree in their *notions* about these words. *Cheyne.*

That *notion* of hunger, cold, sound, color, thought, wish or fear, which is in the mind, is called the *idea* of hunger, cold, &c. *Watts.*

2. Sentiment; opinion; as the extravagant *notions* they entertain of themselves. *Addison.*

3. Sense; understanding; intellectual power. [*Not used.*] *Shak.*

4. Inclination; *in vulgar use;* as, I have a *notion* to do this or that.

NO'TIONAL, *a.* Imaginary; ideal; existing in idea only; visionary; fantastical.

Notional good, by fancy only made. *Prior.*

A *notional* and imaginary thing. *Bentley.*

2. Dealing in imaginary things; whimsical; fanciful; as a *notional* man.

NOTIONAL'ITY, *n.* Empty ungrounded opinion. [*Not used.*] *Glanville.*

NO'TIONALLY, *adv.* In mental apprehension; in conception; not in reality.

Two faculties *notionally* or really distinct. *Norris.*

NO'TIONIST, *n.* One who holds to an ungrounded opinion. *Bp. Hopkins.*

NOTORI'ETY, *n.* [Fr. *notorieté*, from *notoire.* See *Notorious.*]

1. Exposure to the public knowledge; the state of being publicly or generally known; as the *notoriety* of a crime.

2. Public knowledge.

They were not subjects in their own nature so exposed to public *notoriety.* *Addison.*

NOTO'RIOUS, *a.* [It. Sp. *notorio;* Fr. *notoire;* from Low L. *notorius*, from *notus*, known.]

1. Publicly known; manifest to the world; evident; usually, known to disadvantage; hence almost always used in an ill sense; as a *notorious* thief; a *notorious* crime or vice; a man *notorious* for lewdness or gaming.

2. In a good sense.

Your goodness,
Since you provoke me, shall be most *notorious.* *Shak.*

NOTO'RIOUSLY, *adv.* Publicly; openly; in a manner to be known or manifest. *Swift. Dryden.*

NOTO'RIOUSNESS, *n.* The state of being open or known; notoriety. *Overbury.*

NOTT, *a.* [Sax. *hnot.*] Shorn. *Obs.* *Chaucer.*

NOTT, *v. t.* To shear. *Obs.* *Stowe.*

NO'TUS, *n.* [L.] The south wind. *Milton.*

NOT'WHEAT, *n.* [Sax. *hnot*, smooth, shorn.] Wheat not bearded. *Carew.*

NOTWITHSTAND'ING, the participle of *withstand*, with *not* prefixed, and signifying not opposing; nevertheless. It retains in all cases its participial signification. For example, "I will surely rend the kingdom from thee, and will give it to thy servant; *notwithstanding*, in thy days I will not do it, for David thy father's sake." 1 Kings xi. In this passage there is an ellipsis of *that*, after *notwithstanding*. *That* refers to the former part of the sentence, *I will rend the kingdom from thee;* notwithstanding *that* (declaration or determination,) in thy days I will not do it. In this and in all cases, *notwithstanding*, either with or without *that* or *this*, constitutes the case absolute or independent.

"It is a rainy day, but *notwithstanding that*, the troops must be reviewed;" that is, the rainy day not opposing or preventing. *That*, in this case, is a substitute for the whole first clause of the sentence. It is to that clause what a relative is to an antecedent noun, and *which* may be used in the place of it; *notwithstanding which*, that is, the rainy day.

"Christ enjoined on his followers not to publish the cures he wrought; but *notwithstanding his injunctions*, they proclaimed them." Here, *notwithstanding his injunctions*, is the case independent or absolute; the injunctions of Christ not opposing or preventing.

This word answers precisely to the Latin *non obstante*, and both are used with nouns or with substitutes for nouns, for sentences or for clauses of sentences. So in the Latin phrase, *hoc non obstante*, *hoc* may refer to a single word, to a sentence or to a series of sentences.

NOUGHT. See *Naught.*

NOUL, *n.* [Sax. *hnol.*] The top of the head. [*Not in use.*] *Spenser.*

NOULD, *ne would*, would not. *Spenser.*

NOUN, *n.* [altered from L. *nomen*, name.] In *grammar*, a name; that sound or combination of sounds by which a thing is called, whether material or immaterial. [See *Name.*]

NOURISH, *v. t. nur'ish.* [Fr. *nourrir;* It. *nutrire;* Sp. Port. *nutrir;* from L. *nutrio.* The G. *nähren*, Sw. *nåra*, Dan. *nærer*, to nourish, cannot be the same word unless they have lost a dental, which may perhaps be the fact.]

1. To feed and cause to grow; to supply a living or organized body, animal or vegetable, with matter which increases its bulk or supplies the waste occasioned by any of its functions; to supply with nutriment.

2. To support; to maintain by feeding. Gen. xlvii.

> Whilst I in Ireland *nourish* a mighty band,
> I will stir up in England some black storm. *Shak.*

3. To supply the means of support and increase; to encourage; as, to *nourish* rebellion; to *nourish* the virtues.

> What madness was it, with such proofs, to *nourish* their contentions! *Hooker.*

4. To cherish; to comfort. James v.

5. To educate; to instruct; to promote growth in attainments. 1 Tim. iv.

NOURISH, *v. i. nur'ish.* To promote growth.

> Grains and roots *nourish* more than leaves. [*Elliptical.*] *Bacon.*

2. To gain nourishment. [*Unusual.*] *Bacon.*

NOURISHABLE, *a. nur'ishable.* Susceptible of nourishment; as the *nourishable* parts of the body. *Grew.*

NOURISHED, *pp. nur'ished.* Fed; supplied with nutriment; caused to grow.

NOURISHER, *n. nur'isher.* The person or thing that nourishes. *Bacon. Milton.*

NOURISHING, *ppr. nur'ishing.* Feeding; supplying with aliment; supporting with food.

2. *a.* Promoting growth; nutritious; as a *nourishing* diet.

NOURISHMENT, *n. nur'ishment.* That which serves to promote the growth of animals or plants, or to repair the waste of animal bodies; food; sustenance; nutriment. *Newton.*

2. Nutrition; support of animal or vegetable bodies. *Blackmore.*

3. Instruction, or that which promotes growth in attainments; as *nourishment* and growth in grace.

> So they may learn to seek the *nourishment* of their souls. *Hooker.*

NOURITURE. [See *Nurture.*]

NOURSLING. [See *Nursling.*]

NOVAC'ULITE, *n.* [L. *novacula*, a razor.] Razor-stone; Turkey-hone; coticular shist; whet-slate, a variety of argillaceous slate. *Brogniart. Ure.*

NOVA'TIAN, *n.* In *church history*, one of the sect of Novatus or Novatianus, who held that the lapsed might not be received again into communion with the church, and that second marriages are unlawful.

NOVA'TIANISM, *n.* The opinions of the Novatians.

> One Hypolitus, a Roman presbyter, had been seduced into *Novatianism.* *Milner.*

NOVATION. [See *Innovation.*]

NOVATOR. [See *Innovator.*]

NOV'EL, *a.* [L. *novellus*, from *novus*, new; It. *novello;* Sp. *novel.*]

1. New; of recent origin or introduction; not ancient; hence, unusual; as a *novel* heresy; *novel* opinions. The proceedings of the court were *novel.*

2. In *the civil law*, the *novel* constitutions are those which are supplemental to the code, and posterior in time to the other books. These contained new decrees of successive emperors.

3. In *the common law*, the assize of *novel* disseizin is an action in which the demandant recites a complaint of the disseizin in terms of direct averment, whereupon the sheriff is commanded to reseize the land and chattels thereon, and keep the same in custody till the arrival of the justices of assize. *Blackstone.*

NOV'EL, *n.* A new or supplemental constitution or decree. [See the Adjective.]

2. A fictitious tale or narrative in prose, intended to exhibit the operation of the passions, and particularly of love.

> The coxcomb's *novel* and the drunkard's toast. *Prior.*

NOV'ELISM, *n.* Innovation. [*Little used.*] *Dering.*

NOV'ELIST, *n.* An innovator; an asserter of novelty. *Bacon. White.*

2. A writer of a novel or of novels. *Warton.*

3. A writer of news. [*Not used.*] *Tatler.*

NOV'ELIZE, *v. i.* To innovate. [*Not in use.*]

NOV'ELTY, *n.* Newness; recentness of origin or introduction. *Hooker.*

> *Novelty* is the great parent of pleasure. *South.*

NOVEM'BER, *n.* [L. from *novem*, nine; the ninth month, according to the ancient Roman year, beginning in March.] The eleventh month of the year.

NO'VENARY, *n.* [L. *novenarius*, from *novem*, nine.] The number nine; nine collectively.

NOVENARY, *a.* Pertaining to the number nine.

NO'VEN'NIAL, *a.* [L. *novem*, nine, and *annus*, year.] Done every ninth year. *Potter.*

NOVER'CAL, *a.* [L. *noverca*, a step-mother.]

Pertaining to a step-mother; suitable to a step-mother; in the manner of a step-mother. *Derham.*

NOV'ICE, *n.* [Fr. from L. *novitius*, from *novus*, new.]

1. One who is new in any business; one unacquainted or unskilled; one in the rudiments; a beginner.

> I am young, a *novice* in the trade. *Dryden.*

2. One that has entered a religious house, but has not taken the vow; a probationer. *Shak.*

3. One newly planted in the church, or one newly converted to the christian faith. 1 Tim. iii.

NOVI''TIATE, *n.* [Fr. *noviciat;* It. *noviziato.* See *Novice.*]

1. The state or time of learning rudiments.

2. In *religious houses*, a year or other time of probation for the trial of a novice, to determine whether he has the necessary qualities for living up to the rule to which his vow is to bind him.

NOVI''TIOUS, *a.* [L. *novitius.*] Newly invented. [*Not used.*] *Pearson.*

NOV'ITY, *n.* [L. *novitas.*] Newness. [*Not used.*] *Brown.*

NOW, *adv.* [Sax. D. Sw. Dan. Goth. *nu.* The G. has *nun*, Gr. *νυν*, L. *nunc.*]

1. At the present time.

> I have a patient *now* living at an advanced age, who discharged blood from his lungs thirty years ago. *Arbuthnot.*

2. A little while ago; very lately.

> They that but *now* for honor and for plate,
> Made the sea blush with blood, resign their hate. *Waller.*

3. At one time; at another time.

> *Now* high, *now* low, *now* master up, *now* miss. *Pope.*

4. *Now* sometimes expresses or implies a connection between the subsequent and preceding proposition; often it introduces an inference or an explanation of what precedes.

> Not this man, but Barabbas; *now* Barabbas was a robber. John xviii.

> Then said Micah, *now* I know that the Lord will do me good, seeing I have a Levite for my priest. Judges xvii.

> The other great mischief which befalls men, is by their being misrepresented. *Now* by calling evil good, a man is misrepresented to others in the way of slander— *South.*

5. After this; things being so.

> How shall any man distinguish *now* betwixt a parasite and a man of honor? *L'Estrange.*

6. In supplication, it appears to be somewhat emphatical.

> I beseech thee, O Lord, remember *now* how I have walked before thee in truth and with a perfect heart. 2 Kings xx.

7. *Now* sometimes refers to a particular time past specified or understood, and may be defined, *at that time.* He was *now* sensible of his mistake.

Now and then, at one time and another, indefinitely; occasionally; not often; at intervals.

They *now and then* appear in offices of religion. *Rogers.*

If there were any such thing as spontaneous generation, a new species would *now and then* appear.

2. Applied to places which appear at intervals or in succession.

A mead here, there a heath, and *now and then* a wood. *Drayton.*

Now, now, repeated, is used to excite attention to something immediately to happen.

NOW, *n.* The present time or moment.

Nothing is there to come, and nothing past,
But an eternal *now* does ever last. *Cowley.*

Now a days, adv. In this age.

What men of spirit *now a days*,
Come to give sober judgment of new plays? *Garrick.*

[*This is a common colloquial phrase, but not elegant in writing, unless of the more familiar kinds.*]

NO'WAY, NO'WAYS, *adv.* [*no* and *way.*] In no manner or degree. [These can hardly be considered as compound words.]

NOW'ED, *a.* [Fr. *noué.*] Knotted; tied in a knot; used in heraldry. *Encyc.*

NOW'EL, *n.* [Fr. *noel.*] A shout of joy or christmas song. *Obs.* *Chaucer.*

NOWES, *n.* [Fr. *nou.*] The marriage knot. *Obs.* *Crashaw.*

NO'WHERE, *adv.* [*no* and *where*; Sax. *na-whære.*]

Not in any place or state. Happiness is *nowhere* to be found but in the practice of virtue.

But it is better to write *no* and *where* as separate words.

NO'WISE, *adv.* [*no* and *wise*; often by mistake written *noways.*]

Not in any manner or degree. *Bentley.*

NOXIOUS, *a. nok'shus.* [L. *noxius*, from *noceo*, to hurt.]

1. Hurtful; harmful; baneful; pernicious; destructive; unwholesome; insalubrious; as *noxious* air, food, climate; pernicious; corrupting to morals; as *noxious* practices or examples; *noxious* haunts of vice.

2. Guilty; criminal.

Those who are *noxious* in the eye of the law.
[*Little used.*] *Bramhall.*

3. Unfavorable; injurious.

Too frequent appearance in places of public resort is *noxious* to spiritual promotion. *Swift.*

NOX'IOUSLY, *adv.* Hurtfully; perniciously.

NOX'IOUSNESS, *n.* Hurtfulness; the quality that injures, impairs or destroys; insalubrity; as the *noxiousness* of foul air.

2. The quality that corrupts or perverts; as the *noxiousness* of doctrines.

Noy, noyance, noyer, noyful, noyous, noysance. [See *Annoy* and *Nuisance.*]

NOYAU, *n. noy'o.* A rich cordial.

NOZ'LE, NOZ'ZLE, *n.* [from *nose.*] The nose; the extremity of any thing; the snout. *Arbuthnot.*

NUB'BLE, *v. t.* [for *knubble*, from *knob*, the fist.]

To beat or bruise with the fist. [*Not used.*] *Ainsworth.*

NUBIF'EROUS, *a.* [L. *nubifer*; *nubes*, a cloud or fog, and *fero*, to produce.] Bringing or producing clouds. *Dict.*

NU'BILE, *a.* [Fr. from L. *nubilis*, from *nubo*, to marry.]

Marriageable; of an age suitable for marriage. *Prior.*

NU'BILOUS, *a.* [L. *nubilus*, from *nubes.*] Cloudy. *Bailey.*

NUCIF'EROUS, *a.* [L. *nux*, nut, and *fero*, to bear.] Bearing or producing nuts. *Dict.*

NU'CLEUS, *n.* [L. from *nux*, a nut.]

1. Properly, the kernel of a nut; but in usage, any body about which matter is collected. *Woodward.*

2. The body of a comet, called also its head, which appears to be surrounded with light.

NUDA'TION, *n.* [L. *nudatio*, from *nudo*, to make bare.]

The act of stripping or making bare or naked.

NUDE, *a.* [L. *nudus.*] Bare.

2. In *law*, void; of no force. *Blackstone.*

NU'DITY, *n.* [L. *nuditas.*] Nakedness.

2. *Nudities*, in the plural, naked parts which decency requires to be concealed. *Dryden.*

3. In *painting* and *sculpture*, the naked parts of the human figure, or parts not covered with drapery.

Nudum Pactum, [L.] in *law*, an agreement that is void or not valid according to the laws of the land. *Blackstone.*

NUGAC'ITY, *n.* [L. *nugax*, from *nugæ*, trifles.]

Futility; trifling talk or behavior. *More. Johnson.*

NUGA'TION, *n.* [L. *nugor*, to trifle.] The act or practice of trifling. [*Little used.*] *Bacon.*

NU'GATORY, *a.* [L. *nugatorius.*] Trifling; vain; futile; insignificant. *Bentley.*

2. Of no force; inoperative; ineffectual. The laws are sometimes rendered *nugatory* by inexecution. Any agreement may be rendered *nugatory* by something which contravenes its execution.

NU'ISANCE, NU'SANCE, *n.* [Fr. *nuisance*, from *nuire*, L. *noceo*, to annoy. Blackstone writes *nusance*, and it is desirable that his example may be followed.]

1. That which annoys or gives trouble and vexation; that which is offensive or noxious. A liar is a *nusance* to society.

2. In *law*, that which incommodes or annoys; something that produces inconvenience or damage. Nusances are public or private; *public*, when they annoy citizens in general, as obstructions of the highway; *private*, when they affect individuals only, as when one man erects a house so near his neighbor's as to throw the water off the roof upon his neighbor's land or house, or to intercept the light that his neighbor before enjoyed. *Blackstone.*

Nul, in law, signifies *no*, not any; as *nul* disseizin; *nul* tiel record; *nul* tort.

NULL, *v. t.* [L. *nullus*; *ne* and *ullus*, not any.]

To annul; to deprive of validity; to destroy. [*Not much used.*] [See *Annul.*] *Milton.*

NULL, *a.* [L. *nullus.*] Void; of no legal or binding force or validity; of no efficacy; invalid. The contract of a minor is *null* in law, except for necessaries.

NULL, *n.* Something that has no force or meaning. A cipher is called a *null.* [*Not used.*] *Bacon.*

NULLIFID'IAN, *a.* [L. *nullus*, none, and *fides*, faith.]

Of no faith; of no religion or honesty. [*Not used.*] *Feltham.*

NUL'LIFIED, *pp.* Made void.

NUL'LIFY, *v. t.* [L. *nullus*, none, and *facio*, to make.]

To annul; to make void; to render invalid; to deprive of legal force or efficacy. *Ames.*

NUL'LITY, *n.* [It. *nullità*; Fr. *nullité*; from L. *nullus.*]

1. Nothingness; want of existence. *Bacon.*

2. Want of legal force, validity or efficacy. *South.*

NUMB, *a. num.* [Sax. *numen*, the participle of Sax. Goth. *niman*, to take, to seize, whence *beniman* or *benyman*, to deprive; *benum*, *benuman*, stupefied, that is, seized, arrested, held, stopped; D. *neemen*; G. *nehmen*. Class Nm. No. 7. 9.]

1. Torpid; destitute of the power of sensation and motion; as, the fingers or limbs are *numb* with cold.

2. Producing numbness; benumbing; as the *numb* cold night. [*Not used nor proper.*] *Shak.*

NUMB, *v. t. num.* To make torpid; to deprive of the power of sensation or motion; to deaden; to benumb; to stupefy.

For lazy winter *numbs* the laboring hand. *Dryden.*

And *numbing* coldness has embraced the ear. *Prior.*

NUMBED, *pp. num'med.* Rendered torpid.

NUM'BER, *n.* [Fr. *nombre*; L. *numerus*; It. Sp. Port. *numero*; Arm. W. *niver*; Ir. *nuimhir*. I know not whether the elements are *Nm*, or *Nb*. Probably the radical sense is to speak, name or tell, as our word *tell*, in the other dialects, is to number. *Number* may be allied to *name*, as the Spaniards use *nombre* for name, and the French word written with the same letters, is *number*. Class Nm. No. 1.]

1. The designation of a unit in reference to other units, or in reckoning, counting, enumerating; as, one is the first *number*; a simple *number*.

2. An assemblage of two or more units. Two is a *number* composed of one and one added. Five and three added make the *number* eight. *Number* may be applied to any collection or multitude of units or individuals, and therefore is indefinite, unless defined by other words or by figures or signs of definite signification. Hence,

3. More than one; many.

Ladies are always of great use to the party they espouse, and never fail to win over *numbers*. *Addison.*

4. Multitude.

Number itself importeth not much in armies, where the men are of weak courage. *Bacon.*

5. In *poetry*, measure; the order and quantity of syllables constituting feet, which render verse musical to the ear. The har-

mony of verse consists in the proper distribution of the long and short syllables, with suitable pauses.

In *oratory*, a judicious disposition of words, syllables and cadences constitutes a kind of measure resembling poetic *numbers*.

6. Poetry; verse.

I lisped in *numbers*, for the *numbers* came. *Pope.*

Here the first word *numbers* may be taken for *poetry* or *verse*, and the second for *measure*.

Yet should the Muses bid my *numbers* roll. *Pope.*

7. In *grammar*, the difference of termination or form of a word, to express unity or plurality. The termination which denotes one or an individual, is the singular *number*; the termination that denotes two or more individuals or units, constitutes the plural *number*. Hence we say, a noun, an adjective, a pronoun or a verb is in the *singular* or the *plural* number.

8. In *mathematics*, number is variously distinguished. *Cardinal numbers* are those which express the amount of units; as 1. 2. 3. 4. 5. 6. 7. 8. 9. 10. *Ordinal numbers* are those which express order; as first, second, third, fourth, &c.

Determinate number, is that referred to a given unit, as a ternary or three; an *indeterminate number*, is referred to unity in general, and called quantity.

Homogeneal numbers, are those referred to the same units; those referred to different units are termed *heterogeneal*.

Whole numbers, are called *integers*.

A *rational number*, is one commensurable with unity. A number incommensurable with unity, is termed *irrational* or *surd*.

A *prime* or *primitive number*, is divisible only by unity; as three, five, seven, &c.

A *perfect number*, is that whose aliquot parts added together, make the whole number, as 28, whose aliquot parts, 14. 7. 4. 2. 1. make the number 28.

An *imperfect number*, is that whose aliquot parts added together, make more or less than the number. This is abundant or defective; abundant, as 12, whose aliquot parts, 6. 4. 3. 2. 1. make 16; or defective, as 16, whose aliquot parts, 8. 4. 2. 1. make 15 only.

A *square number*, is the product of a number multiplied by itself; as, 16 is the square number of 4.

A *cubic number*, is the product of a square number by its root; as, 27 is the product of the square number 9 by its root 3. *Encyc.*

Golden number, the cycle of the moon, or revolution of 19 years, in which time the conjunctions, oppositions and other aspects of the moon are nearly the same as they were on the same days of the month 19 years before.

NUM'BER, *v. t.* [L. *numero.*] To count; to reckon; to ascertain the units of any sum, collection or multitude.

If a man can *number* the dust of the earth, then shall thy seed also be *numbered*. Gen. xiii.

2. To reckon as one of a collection or multitude.

He was *numbered* with the transgressors. Is. liii.

NUM'BERED, *pp.* Counted; enumerated.

NUM'BERER, *n.* One that numbers.

NUM'BERING, *ppr.* Counting; ascertaining the units of a multitude or collection.

NUM'BERLESS, *a.* That cannot be counted; innumerable. *Milton.*

NUM'BERS, *n.* The title of the fourth book of the Pentateuch.

NUMBING, *ppr. num'ming.* Making torpid.

NUM'BLES, *n.* [Fr. *nombles.*] The entrails of a deer. *Bailey.*

NUMBNESS, *n. num'ness.* Torpor; that state of a living body in which it has not the power of feeling or motion, as when paralytic or chilled by cold.

NU'MERABLE, *a.* [L. *numerabilis.*] That may be numbered or counted.

NU'MERAL, *a.* [Fr.; L. *numeralis.*] Pertaining to number; consisting of number.

The dependence of a long train of *numeral* progressions. *Locke.*

2. Expressing number; representing number; standing as a substitute for figures; as *numeral* letters; as X for 10; L for fifty; C for 100; D for 500; M for 1000.

3. Expressing numbers; as *numeral* characters. The figures we now use to express numbers are 1. 2. 3. 4. 5. 6. 7. 8. 9. 0. They are said to be of Arabian origin; but the Arabians might have received them from India. This is a controverted question.

NU'MERALLY, *adv.* According to number; in number.

NU'MERARY, *a.* Belonging to a certain number.

A supernumerary canon, when he obtains a prebend, becomes a *numerary* canon. *Ayliffe.*

NU'MERATE, *v. t.* To count or reckon in numbers; to calculate. [But *enumerate* is generally used.] *Lancaster.*

NUMERA'TION, *n.* [L. *numeratio.*] The act or art of numbering.

Numeration is but still the adding of one unit more, and giving to the whole a new name or sign. *Locke.*

2. In *arithmetic*, notation; the art of expressing in characters any number proposed in words, or of expressing in words any number proposed in characters; the act or art of writing or reading numbers. Thus we write 1000, for thousand, and 50, we read fifty.

NU'MERATOR, *n.* [L.] One that numbers.

2. In *arithmetic*, the number in vulgar fractions which shows how many parts of a unit are taken. Thus when a unit is divided into 9 parts, and we take 5, we express it thus, $\frac{5}{9}$, that is, five ninths; 5 being the *numerator*, and 9 the denominator.

NUMER'IC, NUMER'ICAL, *a.* [It. *numerico*; Fr. *numerique*; from L. *numerus*, number.]

1. Belonging to number; denoting number; consisting in numbers; as *numerical* algebra; *numerical* characters.

2. *Numerical* difference, is that by which one individual is distinguished from another. The same *numerical* body is identically the same.

NUMER'ICALLY, *adv.* In numbers; as parts of a thing *numerically* expressed.

2. With respect to number or sameness in number; as, a thing is *numerically* the same, or *numerically* different.

NU'MERIST, *n.* One that deals in numbers. [*Not used.*] *Brown.*

NUMEROS'ITY, *n.* The state of being numerous. [*Not used.*] *Brown.*

NU'MEROUS, *a.* [L. *numerosus.*] Being many, or consisting of a great number of individuals; as a *numerous* army; a *numerous* body; a *numerous* people.

2. Consisting of poetic numbers; melodious; musical. In prose, a style becomes *numerous* by the alternate disposition or intermixture of long and short syllables, or of long and short words; or by a judicious selection and disposition of smooth flowing words, and by closing the periods with important or well sounding words. *Encyc.*

NU'MEROUSNESS, *n.* The quality of being numerous or many; the quality of consisting of a great number of individuals; as the *numerousness* of an army or of an assembly.

2. The quality of consisting of poetic numbers; melodiousness; musicalness. *Encyc.*

NUMISMAT'IC, *a.* [L. *numisma*, money, coin; Gr. νομισμα, from νομιζω, to suppose, to sanction, from νομος, law or custom.] Pertaining to money, coin or medals.

NUMISMAT'ICS, *n.* The science of coins and medals.

NUMISMATOL'OGIST, *n.* One versed in the knowledge of coins and medals.

NUMISMATOL'OGY, *n.* [Gr. νομισμα, coin, and λογος, discourse.]

The branch of historical science which treats of coins and medals.

NUM'MARY, NUM'MULAR, *a.* [L. *nummus*, a coin.] Pertaining to coin or money. *Arbuthnot. Dict.*

NUM'MULITE, *n.* [L. *nummus*, money.] Fossil remains of a chambered shell of a flattened form, formerly mistaken for money. *Ed. Encyc.*

NUMPS, *n.* A dolt; a blockhead. [*Not used.*] *Parker.*

NUM'SKULL, *n.* [*numb* and *skull.*] A dunce; a dolt; a stupid fellow. *Prior.*

NUM'SKULLED, *a.* Dull in intellect; stupid; doltish. *Arbuthnot.*

NUN, *n.* [Sax. Dan. *nunne*; D. *non*; G. *nonne*; Sw. *nunna*; Fr. *nonne.*]

A woman devoted to a religious life, and who lives in a cloister or nunnery, secluded from the world, under a vow of perpetual chastity.

NUN, *n.* A web-footed fowl of the size of a duck, with a white head and neck. *Dict.*

2. The blue titmouse. *Sherwood.*

NUN'CHION, *n.* A portion of food taken between meals. [qu. from *noon*, or a corruption of *luncheon.*] *Ainsworth.*

NUN'CIATURE, *n.* [See *Nuncio.*] The office of a nuncio. *Clarendon.*

NUN'CIO, *n.* [It. *nunzio*, from L. *nuncius*, a messenger.]

1. An embassador from the pope to some catholic prince or state, or who attends some congress or assembly as the pope's representative. *Encyc.*

2. A messenger; one who brings intelligence. *Shak.*

NUN'CUPATE, *v. t.* [L. *nuncupo.*] To declare publicly or solemnly. [*Not used.*] *Barrow.*

NUNCUPA'TION, *n.* A naming. *Chaucer.*

NUNCU'PATIVE, NUNCU'PATORY, *a.* [It. *nuncupativo;* Fr. *nuncupatif;* from L. *nuncupo,* to declare.]

1. Nominal; existing only in name. *Encyc.*
2. Publicly or solemnly declaratory. *Fotherby.*
3. Verbal, not written. A *nuncupative* will or testament is one which is made by the verbal declaration of the testator, and depends merely on oral testimony for proof, though afterwards reduced to writing. *Blackstone.*

NUN'DINAL, *a.* [L. *nundinalis,* from *nundinæ,* a fair or market, quasi *novem-dinæ,* every nine days.]

1. Pertaining to a fair or to a market day.
2. A *nundinal* letter, among the Romans, was one of the eight first letters of the alphabet, which were repeated successively from the first to the last day of the year. One of these always expressed the market days, which returned every nine days.

NUN'DINAL, *n.* A nundinal letter.

NUN'DINATE, *v. i.* To buy and sell at fairs. [*Not used.*]

NUNDINA'TION, *n.* Traffick in fairs. [*Not used.*]

NUNNA'TION, *n.* In *Arabic grammar,* from the name of *N,* the pronunciation of *n* at the end of words.

NUN'NERY, *n.* A house in which nuns reside; a cloister in which females under a vow of chastity and devoted to religion, reside during life.

NUP'TIAL, *a.* [L. *nuptialis,* from *nuptus, nubo,* to marry.]

1. Pertaining to marriage; done at a wedding; as *nuptial* rites and ceremonies; *nuptial* torch.
2. Constituting marriage; as the *nuptial* knot or band.

The Bible has mitigated the horrors of war; it has given effectual obligation to the *nuptial* vow. *G. Spring.*

NUP'TIALS, *n. plu.* Marriage, which see. *Dryden.*

NURSE, *n. nurs.* [Fr. *nourrice,* from *nourrir,* to nourish.]

1. A woman that has the care of infants, or a woman employed to tend the children of others.
2. A woman who suckles infants.
3. A woman that has the care of a sick person.
4. A man who has the care of the sick.
5. A person that breeds, educates or protects; hence, that which breeds, brings up or causes to grow; as Greece, the *nurse* of the liberal arts.
6. An old woman; in contempt. *Blackmore.*
7. The state of being nursed; as, to put a child to *nurse.* *Cleaveland.*
8. In *composition,* that which supplies food; as a *nurse*-pond. *Walton.*

NURSE, *v. t. nurs.* To tend, as infants; as, to *nurse* a child.

2. To suckle; to nourish at the breast.
3. To attend and take care of in child-bed; as, to *nurse* a woman in her illness.
4. To tend the sick; *applied to males and females.*
5. To feed; to maintain; to bring up. Is. lx.
6. To cherish; to foster; to encourage; to promote growth in. We say, to *nurse* a feeble animal or plant.

By what hands has vice been *nursed* into so uncontrolled a dominion? *Locke.*

7. To manage with care and economy, with a view to increase; as, to *nurse* our national resources.

NURS'ED, *pp.* Tended in infancy or sickness; nourished from the breast; maintained; cherished.

NURS'ER, *n.* One that cherishes or encourages growth.

NURS'ERY, *n.* The place or apartment in a house appropriated to the care of children. *Bacon.*

2. A place where young trees are propagated for the purpose of being transplanted; a plantation of young trees. *Bacon.*
3. The place where any thing is fostered and the growth promoted.

To see fair Padua, *nursery* of arts. *Shak.*

So we say, a *nursery* of thieves or of rogues. Alehouses and dram-shops are the *nurseries* of intemperance.

Christian families are the *nurseries* of the church on earth, as she is the *nursery* of the church in heaven. *J. M. Mason.*

4. That which forms and educates. Commerce is the *nursery* of seamen.
5. The act of nursing. [*Little used.*] *Shak.*
6. That which is the object of a nurse's care. *Milton.*

NURS'ING, *ppr.* Tending; nourishing at the breast; educating; maintaining.

NURS'LING, *n.* An infant; a child. *Dryden.*

2. One that is nursed. *Spenser.*

NUR'TURE, *n.* [Fr. *nourriture,* from *nourrir,* to nourish.]

1. That which nourishes; food; diet. *Milton.*
2. That which promotes growth; education; instruction. Eph. vi.

NUR'TURE, *v. t.* To feed; to nourish.

2. To educate; to bring or train up.

He was *nurtured* where he was born. *Wotton.*

NUSANCE. [See *Nuisance.*]

NUT, *n.* [Sax. *hnut;* D. *noot;* G. *nuss;* Sw. *nöt;* Dan. *nödd;* Ir. *cnudh;* W. *cna, cnau.* It seems to be allied to *knot,* a bunch or hard lump.]

1. The fruit of certain trees and shrubs, consisting of a hard shell inclosing a kernel. A nut is properly the pericarp of the fruit. Various kinds of *nuts* are distinguished; as *walnut, chestnut, hazlenut, butternut.*
2. In *mechanics,* a small cylinder or other body, with teeth or projections corresponding with the teeth or grooves of a wheel. *Wilkins. Ray.*
3. The projection near the eye of an anchor. *Mar. Dict.*

NUT, *v. t.* To gather nuts. *Wood.*

NUTA'TION, *n.* [L. *nutatio,* a nodding, from *nuto,* to nod.]

In *astronomy,* a kind of tremulous motion of the axis of the earth, by which in its annual revolution it is twice inclined to the ecliptic, and as often returns to its former position. *Encyc.*

NUT-BREAKER. [See *Nutcracker.*]

NUT'-BROWN, *a.* Brown as a nut long kept and dried. *Milton.*

NUT'-CRACKER, *n.* An instrument for cracking nuts. *Addison.*

2. A bird of the genus Corvus; the nut-breaker. *Pennant.*

NUT'GALL, *n.* An excrescence of the oak. *Brown.*

NUT'-HATCH, *n.* The common name of birds of the genus Sitta. The common European nut-hatch is called also *nut-jobber* and *nut-pecker.* *Encyc. Johnson.*

NUT'-HOOK, *n.* A pole with a hook at the end to pull down boughs for gathering the nuts; also, the name given to a thief that stole goods from a window by means of a hook. *Shak.*

NUT'MEG, *n.* [L. *nux moschata;* It. *noce moscada;* Port. *noz moscada;* Fr. *muscade* or *noix muscade.* But it may be questioned whether the last syllable in English, *meg,* is not from L. *macis,* mace, the bark that envelops the nut.]

The fruit of a tree of the genus Myristica, growing in the isles of the East Indies and South Sea. The tree grows to the highth of thirty feet, producing numerous branches. The color of the bark of the trunk is a reddish brown; that of the young branches a bright green. The fruit is of the kind called *drupe,* that is, a pulpy pericarp without valves, containing a nut or kernel. The covering of this nut is the mace. The nutmeg is an aromatic, very grateful to the taste and smell, and much used in cookery.

NUTRICA'TION, *n.* Manner of feeding or being fed. [*Not in use.*]

NU'TRIENT, *a.* [L. *nutrio.*] Nourishing; promoting growth.

NU'TRIENT, *n.* Any substance which nourishes by promoting the growth or repairing the waste of animal bodies.

NU'TRIMENT, *n.* [L. *nutrimentum,* from *nutrio,* to nourish.]

1. That which nourishes; that which promotes the growth or repairs the natural waste of animal bodies, or that which promotes the growth of vegetables; food; aliment. *South.*
2. That which promotes enlargement or improvement; as the *nutriment* of the mind.

NUTRIMENT'AL, *a.* Having the qualities of food; alimental. *Arbuthnot.*

NUTRI''TION, *n.* [L. *nutritio,* from *nutrio,* to nourish.]

1. The act or process of promoting the growth or repairing the waste of animal bodies; the act or process of promoting growth in vegetables. *Darwin.*
2. That which nourishes; nutriment.

Fixed like a plant on his peculiar spot,
To draw *nutrition,* propagate, and rot. *Pope.*

There is no *nutrition* in ardent spirits. *L. Beecher.*

NUTRI''TIOUS, *a.* Nourishing; promoting the growth or repairing the waste of animal bodies. Milk is very *nutritious.*

NU'TRITIVE, *a.* Having the quality of nourishing; nutrimental; alimental; as a *nutritive* food.

NU'TRITURE, *n.* The quality of nourishing. [*Not used.*] *Harvey.*

NUT'-SHELL, *n.* The hard shell of a nut; the covering of the kernel.

2. Proverbially, a thing of little compass or of little value. *L'Estrange.*

NUT'-TREE, *n.* A tree that bears nuts.

NUZ'ZLE, *v. t.* [qu. from *noursle.*] To nurse; to foster. [*Vulgar.*]

NUZ'ZLE, *v. t.* [qu. from *nose* or *noursle.*] To hide the head, as a child in the mother's bosom. *Bailey.*

NUZ'ZLE, *v. t.* [qu. *noursle* or *nestle.*] To nestle; to house as in a nest.

NUZ'ZLE, *v. i.* [qu. from *nose.*] To go with the nose near the ground, or thrusting the nose into the ground like a swine. *Arbuthnot. Pope.*

NYC'TALOPS, *n.* [Gr. νυκταλωψ; νυξ, night, and ωψ, the eye.]

1. One that sees best in the night. *Coles.*

2. One who loses his sight as night comes on, and remains blind till morning.

NYC'TALOPY, *n.* The faculty of seeing best in darkness, or the disorder from which this faculty proceeds. *Todd.*

2. In *present usage*, the disorder in which the patient loses his sight as night approaches, and remains blind till morning.

NYE, *n.* A brood or flock of pheasants.

NYL'GAU, *n.* A quadruped of the genus Bos, a native of the interior of India, of a middle size between the cow and the deer. Its body, horns and tail are not unlike those of a bull; the head, neck and legs resemble those of the deer. The color is an ash gray. *Encyc.*

NYMPH, *n.* [L. *nympha*; Gr. νυμφη.] In *mythology*, a goddess of the mountains, forests, meadows and waters. According to the ancients, all the world was full of nymphs, some terrestrial, others celestial; and these had names assigned to them according to their place of residence, or the parts of the world over which they were supposed to preside. *Encyc.*

2. In *poetry*, a lady. *Waller.*

NYMPH, NYMPH'A, } *n.* Another name of the pupa, chrysalis, or aurelia; the second state of an insect, passing to its perfect form.

NYMPHE'AN, *a.* Pertaining to nymphs; inhabited by nymphs; as a *nymphean* cave. *Faber.*

NYMPH'ICAL, *a.* Pertaining to nymphs. *Pausanias, Trans.*

NYMPH'ISH, *a.* Relating to nymphs; ladylike. *Drayton.*

NYMPH'LIKE, NYMPH'LY, } *a.* Resembling nymphs. *Drayton.*

NYS, [*ne* and *is.*] None is; is not. *Obs.* *Spenser.*

O.

O is the fifteenth letter, and the fourth vowel in the English Alphabet. The shape of this letter seems to have been taken from the circular configuration of the lips in uttering the sound. It corresponds in figure with the Coptic O, and nearly with the Syriac initial and final *vau*, and the Ethiopic *ain.* In words derived from the oriental languages, it often represents the *vau* of those languages, and sometimes the *ain*; the original sound of the latter being formed deep in the throat, and with a greater aperture of the mouth.

In English, O has a long sound, as in *tone, hone, groan, cloke, roll, droll*; a short sound, as in *lot, plod, rod, song, lodge*, and the sound of *oo*, or the Italian *u*, and French *ou*, as in *move, prove.* This sound is shortened in words ending in a close articulation, as in *book, foot.*

The long sound of O, is usually denoted by *e*, at the end of a word or syllable, as in *bone, lonely*; or by a servile *a*, as in *moan, foal.* It is generally long before *ll*, as in *roll*; but it is short in *doll, loll*, and in words of more syllables than one, as in *folly, volley.*

As a numeral, O was sometimes used by the ancients for 11, and with a dash over it, Ō, for 11,000.

Among the Irish, O prefixed to the name of a family, denotes progeny, or is a a character of dignity; as O'Neil; O'Carrol.

Among the ancients, O was a mark of triple time, from the notion that the ternary or number 3, is the most perfect of numbers, and properly expressed by a circle, the most perfect figure.

O is often used as an exclamation, expressing a wish.

O, were he present. *Dryden.*

It sometimes expresses surprise.

Shakspeare uses O for a circle or oval.

Within this wooden *O.*

O. S. stands for Old Style.

ŌAF, *n.* [said to be a corruption of *ouph* or *elf*, a fairy or demon, and to denote a foolish child left by fairies in the place of one of better intellects which they steal. *Johnson.*]

1. A changeling; a foolish child left by fairies in the place of another. *Drayton.*

2. A dolt; an idiot; a blockhead.

ŌAFISH, *a.* Stupid; dull; doltish. [*Little used.*]

ŌAFISHNESS, *n.* Stupidity; dullness; folly. [*Little used.*]

ŌAK, *n.* [Sax. *ac, æc*; D. *eik* or *eikboom*; G. *eiche* or *eichbaum*; Sw. *ek*; Dan. *eegetræe*, oak-tree. It is probable that the first syllable, *oak*, was originally an adjective expressing some quality, as hard or strong, and by the disuse of *tree, oak* became the name of the tree.]

A tree of the genus Quercus, or rather the popular name of the genus itself, of which there are several species. The white oak grows to a great size, and furnishes a most valuable timber; but the live oak of the United States is the most durable timber for ships. In Hartford still stands the venerable *oak*, in the hollow stem of which was concealed and preserved the colonial charter of Connecticut, when Sir E. Andros, by authority of a writ of quo warranto from the British crown, attempted to obtain possession of it, in 1687. As it was then a large tree, it must now be nearly three hundred years old.

ŌAK-APPLE, *n.* A kind of spungy excrescence on oak leaves or tender branches, &c. produced in consequence of the puncture of an insect. It is called also oak leaf gall, or gall-nut. *Bacon. Encyc.*

ŌAKEN, *a.* *o'kn.* Made of oak or consisting of oak; as an *oaken* plank or bench; an *oaken* bower. *Milton.*

2. Composed of branches of oak; as an *oaken* garland. *Addison.*

ŌAKENPIN, *n.* An apple; so called from its hardnesss. *Mortimer.*

ŌAKLING, *n.* A young oak. *Evelyn.*

ŌAKUM, *n.* [Sax. *æcemba, æcumbe*, tow. The latter part of the word may be Sax. *cemb*, a comb.]

The substance of old ropes untwisted and pulled into loose hemp; used for calking the seams of ships, stopping leaks, &c. That formed from untarred ropes is called white oakum.

ŌAKY, *a.* [from *oak.*] Hard; firm; strong. *Hall.*

ŌAR, *n.* [Sax. *ar*; Sw. *åra*; Norm. *ower.*] An instrument for rowing boats, being a piece of timber round or square at one end, and flat at the other. The round end is the handle, and the flat end the blade.

To boat the oars, in seamanship, to cease rowing and lay the oars in the boat.

To ship the oars, to place them in the rowlocks.

To unship the oars, to take them out of the row-locks. *Mar. Dict.*

ŌAR, *v. i.* To row. *Pope.*

ŌAR, *v. t.* To impel by rowing. *Shak.*

ŌARY, *a.* Having the form or use of an oar; as the swan's *oary* feet. *Milton. Addison.*

ŌAST, OST, OUST, } *n.* [qu. εςια, or L. *ustus.*] A kiln to dry hops or malt. *Mortimer.*

ŌAT, *n.* [Sax. *ate*, oat or cockle, darnel; Russ. *oves* or *ovetzi.*]

A plant of the genus Avena, and more usually, the seed of the plant. The word is commonly used in the plural, *oats.* This plant flourishes best in cold latitudes, and degenerates in the warm. The meal of this grain, *oatmeal*, forms a considerable and very valuable article of food for man in Scotland, and every where oats are excellent food for horses and cattle.

ŌATCAKE, *n.* A cake made of the meal of oats. *Peacham.*

OATEN, *a.* o'tn. Made of oatmeal; as *oaten* cakes.

2. Consisting of an oat straw or stem; as an *oaten* pipe. *Milton.*

OATH, *n.* [Sax. *ath*; Goth. *aiths*; D. *eed*; G. *eid*; Sw. *ed*; Dan. *æed.*]

A solemn affirmation or declaration, made with an appeal to God for the truth of what is affirmed. The appeal to God in an oath, implies that the person imprecates his vengeance and renounces his favor if the declaration is false, or if the declaration is a promise, the person invokes the vengeance of God if he should fail to fulfill it. A false oath is called perjury.

OATHABLE, *a.* Capable of having an oath administered to. [*Not used.*] *Shak.*

OATHBREAKING, *n.* The violation of an oath; perjury. *Shak.*

OATMALT, *n.* Malt made of oats. *Mortimer.*

OATMEAL, *n.* Meal of oats produced by grinding or pounding. *Gay.*

2. A plant. [*Not used.*]

OAT-THISTLE, *n.* A plant. [*Not used.*] *Ainsworth.*

OB, a Latin preposition, signifies primarily, in front, before, and hence against, towards; as in *objicio*, to object, that is, to throw against. It has also the force of *in* or *on*; as in *obtrude.* In composition, the letter *b* is often changed into the first letter of the word to which it is prefixed; as in *occasion*, *offer*, *oppose.*

OBAM'BULATE, *v. i.* [L. *obambulo.*] To walk about. [*Not used.*] *Cockeram.*

OBAMBULA'TION, *n.* A walking about. [*Not used.*] *Dict.*

OBBLIGA'TO, *a.* [It. bound.] A term in music, signifying on purpose for the instrument named. *Cyc.*

OBCORD'ATE, *a.* [L. from *ob* and *cor*, the heart.]

In *botany*, shaped like a heart, with the apex downward; as an *obcordate* petal or legume. *Martyn.*

OBDORMI''TION, *n.* [L. *obdormio*, to sleep.] Sleep; sound sleep. [*Little used.*] *Hall.*

OBDU'CE, *v. t.* [L. *obduco*; *ob* and *duco*, to lead.] To draw over, as a covering. [*Little used.*] *Hale.*

OBDUCT', *v. t.* [L. *obduco.*] To draw over; to cover. [*Not in use.*] *Brown.*

OBDUC'TION, *n.* [L. *obductio.*] The act of drawing over, as a covering; the act of laying over. [*Little used.*] *Cockeram.*

OB'DURACY, *n.* [See *Obdurate.*] Invincible hardness of heart; impenitence that cannot be subdued; inflexible persistency in sin; obstinacy in wickedness.

> God may by almighty grace hinder the absolute completion of sin in final *obduracy.* *South.*

OB'DURATE, *a.* [L. *obduro*, to harden; *ob* and *duro.*]

1. Hardened in heart; inflexibly hard; persisting obstinately in sin or impenitence.

2. Hardened against good or favor; stubborn; unyielding; inflexible.

> The custom of evil makes the heart *obdurate* against whatsoever instructions to the contrary. *Hooker.*

3. Harsh; rugged; as an *obdurate* consonant. [*Little used.*] *Swift.*

OB'DURATE, *v. t.* To harden. [*Not used.*] *More.*

OB'DURATELY, *adv.* Stubbornly; inflexibly; with obstinate impenitence.

OB'DURATENESS, *n.* Stubbornness; inflexible persistence in sin.

OBDURA'TION, *n.* The hardening of the heart; hardness of heart; stubbornness. *Hooker. Hammond.*

OBDU'RE, *v. t.* [L. *obduro.*] To harden; to render obstinate in sin. [*Little used.*] *Herbert.*

2. To render inflexible. [*Little used.*] *Hall.*

OBDU'RED, *pp.* or *a.* Hardened; inflexible; impenitent. *Milton.*

OBDU'REDNESS, *n.* Hardness of heart; stubbornness. [*Little used.*] *Hall.*

OBE'DIENCE, *n.* [Fr. from L. *obedientia.* See *Obey.*]

Compliance with a command, prohibition or known law and rule of duty prescribed; the performance of what is required or enjoined by authority, or the abstaining from what is prohibited, in compliance with the command or prohibition. To constitute obedience, the act or forbearance to act must be in submission to authority; the command must be known to the person, and his compliance must be in consequence of it, or it is not obedience. *Obedience* is not synonymous with *obsequiousness*; the latter often implying meanness or servility, and obedience being merely a proper submission to authority. That which duty requires implies dignity of conduct rather than servility. Obedience may be *voluntary* or *involuntary*. *Voluntary obedience* alone can be acceptable to God.

> Government must compel the *obedience* of individuals; otherwise who will seek its protection or fear its vengeance? *Ames.*

OBE'DIENT, *a.* [L. *obediens.*] Submissive to authority; yielding compliance with commands, orders or injunctions; performing what is required, or abstaining from what is forbid.

> The chief his orders gives; the *obedient* band,
> With due observance, wait the chief's command. *Pope.*

OBEDIEN'TIAL, *a.* [Fr. *obedienciel.*] According to the rule of obedience; in compliance with commands; as *obediential* submission. *Hammond.*

OBE'DIENTLY, *adv.* With obedience; with due submission to commands; with submission or compliance with orders. *Tillotson.*

OBE'ISANCE, *n.* [Fr. *obeissance*, from *obeir*, to obey, L. *obedio.*]

A bow or courtesy; an act of reverence made by an inclination of the body or the knee. Gen. xxxvii.

OBELIS'CAL, *a.* In the form of an obelisk. *Stukeley.*

OB'ELISK, *n.* [L. *obeliscus*; Gr. ὀβελισκος, *dim.* of ὀβελος, a spit.]

1. A truncated, quadrangular and slender pyramid intended as an ornament, and often charged with inscriptions or hieroglyphics. Some ancient obelisks appear to have been erected in honor of distinguished persons or their achievments. Ptolemy Philadelphus raised one of 88 cubits high in honor of Arsinoe. Augustus erected one in the Campus Martius at Rome, which served to mark the hours on a horizontal dial drawn on the pavement. *Encyc.*

2. In *writing* and *printing*, a reference or mark referring the reader to a note in the margin, thus, †. It is used also for a mark of censure, or for designating obsolete words, or for other purposes at the pleasure of the writer.

OBEQ'UITATE, *v. i.* [L. *obequito*; *ob* and *equito*, to ride; *equus*, a horse.] To ride about. [*Not used.*] *Cockeram.*

OBEQUITA'TION, *n.* The act of riding about. [*Not used.*] *Cockeram.*

OBERRA'TION, *n.* [L. *oberro*; *ob* and *erro*, to wander.] The act of wandering about. [*Little used.*] *Johnson.*

OBE'SE, *a.* [L. *obesus.*] Fat; fleshy. [*Little used.*] *Gayton.*

OBE'SENESS, } *n.* [L. *obesitas.*] Fatness;
OBES'ITY, } fleshiness; incumbrance of flesh. *Grew.*

OBEY, *v. t.* [Fr. *obeir*, contracted from L. *obedio*, It. *ubbidire*; supposed to be contracted from *ob* and *audio*, to hear. See Gr. ἐξακουω.]

1. To comply with the commands, orders or instructions of a superior, or with the requirements of law, moral, political or municipal; to do that which is commanded or required, or to forbear doing that which is prohibited.

> Children, *obey* your parents in the Lord. Eph. vi.

> Servants, *obey* in all things your masters. Col. iii.

> He who has learned to *obey*, will know how to command.

2. To submit to the government of; to be ruled by.

> All Israel *obeyed* Solomon. 1 Chron. xxix. Dan. vii.

3. To submit to the direction or control of. Seamen say, the ship will not *obey* the helm.

> Let not sin therefore reign in your mortal body, that ye should *obey* it in the lusts thereof. Rom. vi. James iii.

4. To yield to the impulse, power or operation of; as, to *obey* stimulus. *Darwin.*

> Relentless time, destroying power,
> Whom stone and brass *obey.*

OBEYED, *pp.* Complied with; performed; as a command; yielded to.

OBEYER, *n.* One who yields obedience.

OBEYING, *ppr.* Complying with commands; submitting to.

OBFIRM, } *v. t.* obferm', } To make
OBFIRMATE, } obferm'ate. } firm; to harden in resolution. [*Not used.*] *Hall. Sheldon.*

OBFUS'CATE, *v. t.* [L. *ob* and *fusco*, to obscure.] To darken; to obscure. *Waterhouse.*

OBFUS'CATED, *pp.* Darkened in color. *Shenstone.*

OBFUS'CATION, *n.* The act of darkening or rendering obscure; a clouding.

> *Obfuscations* of the cornea. *Darwin.*

OB'IT, *n.* [L. *obiit*, *obivit*; *ob* and *eo*, to go.] Properly, death; decease; hence, funeral solemnities or anniversary service for the soul of the deceased on the day of his death. *Encyc. Mountagu.*

OBIT'UAL, *a.* [L. *obeo*, to die; *obitus*, death.]

Pertaining to obits, or the days when funeral solemnities are celebrated; as *obitual* days. *Encyc.*

OBIT'UARY, *n.* [Fr. *obituaire.*] A list of the dead, or a register of obitual anniversary days, when service is performed for the dead. *Encyc.*

2. An account of persons deceased; notice of the death of a person, often accompanied with a brief biographical sketch of his character.

OBIT'UARY, *a.* Relating to the decease of a person or persons; as an *obituary* notice.

OB'JECT, *n.* [Fr. *objet; L. objectum, objectus.* See the Verb.]

1. That about which any power or faculty is employed, or something apprehended or presented to the mind by sensation or imagination. Thus that quality of a rose which is perceived by the sense of smell, is an *object* of perception. When the *object* is not in contact with the organ of sense, there must be some medium through which we obtain the perception of it. The impression which *objects* make on the senses, must be by the immediate application of them to the organs of sense, or by means of the medium that intervenes between the organs and the *objects*.

2. That to which the mind is directed for accomplishment or attainment; end; ultimate purpose. Happiness is the *object* of every man's desires; we all strive to attain that *object*. Wealth and honor are pursued with eagerness as desirable *objects*.

3. Something presented to the senses or the mind, to excite emotion, affection or passion.

This passenger felt some degree of concern at the sight of so moving an *object*. *Atterbury.*

In this sense, the word uttered with a particular emphasis, signifies something that may strongly move our pity, abhorrence or disgust. What an *object!*

4. In *grammar*, that which is produced, influenced or acted on by something else; that which follows a transitive verb. When we say, "God created the world," *world* denotes the thing produced, and is the *object* after the verb *created*. When we say, "the light affects the eye," *eye* denotes that which is affected or acted on. When we say, "instruction directs the mind or opinions," *mind* and *opinions* are the *objects* influenced.

OB'JECT-GLASS, *n.* In *a telescope* or *microscope*, the glass placed at the end of a tube next the object.

OBJECT', *v. t.* [L. *objicio; ob* and *jacio*, to throw against.]

1. To oppose; to present in opposition.

Pallas to their eyes
The mist *objected*, and condens'd the skies. *Pope.*

2. To present or offer in opposition, as a charge criminal, or as a reason adverse to something supposed to be erroneous or wrong; with *to* or *against*.

The book—giveth liberty to *object* any crime *against* such as are to be ordered. *Whitgifte.*

The adversaries of religion *object against* professors the irregularity of their lives, and too often with justice.

There was this single fault that Erasmus, though an enemy, could *object to* him. *Atterbury.*

OBJECT', *v. i.* To oppose in words or arguments; to offer reasons against. The council *objected* to the admission of the plaintiff's witnesses.

OBJECT', *a.* Opposed; presented in opposition. [*Not used.*] *Sandys.*

OBJECT'ABLE, *a.* That may be opposed. *Taylor.*

OBJEC'TION, *n.* [L. *objectio.*] The act of objecting.

2. That which is presented in opposition; adverse reason or argument. The defendant urged several *objections* to the plaintiff's claims. The plaintiff has removed or overthrown those *objections*.

3. That which may be offered in opposition; reason existing, though not offered, against a measure or an opinion. We often have *objections* in our minds which we never offer or present in opposition.

4. Criminal charge; fault found.

OBJEC'TIONABLE, *a.* Justly liable to objections; such as may be objected against.

OBJECT'IVE, *a.* [Fr. *objectif.*] Belonging to the object; contained in the object.

Objective certainty, is when the proposition is certainly true in itself; and subjective, when we are certain of the truth of it. The one is in things, the other in our minds. *Watts.*

2. In *grammar*, the *objective* case is that which follows a transitive verb or a preposition; that case in which the *object* of the verb is placed, when produced or affected by the act expressed by the verb. This case in English answers to the oblique cases of the Latin. *Lowth.*

OBJECT'IVELY, *adv.* In the manner of an object; as a determinate idea *objectively* in the mind. *Locke.*

2. In the state of an object. *Brown.*

OBJECT'IVENESS, *n.* The state of being an object.

Is there such a motion or *objectiveness* of external bodies, which produceth light? *Hale.*

OBJECT'OR, *n.* One that objects; one that offers arguments or reasons in opposition to a proposition or measure. *Bentley.*

OBJUR'GATE, *v. t.* [L. *objurgo; ob* and *jurgo*, to chide.] To chide; to reprove. [*Not used.*]

OBJURGA'TION, *n.* [L. *objurgatio.*] The act of chiding by way of censure; reproof; reprehension. [*Little used.*] *Bramhall.*

OBJUR'GATORY, *a.* Containing censure or reproof; culpatory. [*Little used.*] *Howell.*

OBLA'DA, *n.* A fish of the sparus kind, variegated with longitudinal lines, and having a large black spot on each side, near the tail. *Dict. Nat. Hist.*

OBLA'TE, *a.* [L. *oblatus, offero; ob* and *fero*, to bear.]

Flattened or depressed at the poles; as an *oblate* spheroid, which is the figure of the earth. *Cheyne.*

OBLA'TENESS, *n.* The quality or state of being oblate. *Fleming.*

OBLA'TION, *n.* [L. *oblatio*, from *offero; ob* and *fero*, to bear or bring.]

Any thing offered or presented in worship or sacred service; an offering; a sacrifice.

Bring no more vain *oblations*. Is. i.

OBLEC'TATE, *v. t.* [L. *oblecto.*] To delight; to please highly. [*Not used.*]

OBLECTA'TION, *n.* The act of pleasing highly; delight. *Feltham.*

OB'LIGATE, *v. t.* [L. *obligo; ob* and *ligo*, to bind.]

To bind, as one's self, in a moral and legal sense; to impose on, as a duty which the law or good faith may enforce. A man may *obligate* himself to pay money, or erect a house, either by bond, by covenant or by a verbal promise. A man *obligates* himself only by a positive act of his own. We never say, a man *obligates* his heirs or executors. Until recently, the sense of this word has been restricted to positive and personal acts; and when moral duty or law binds a person to do something, the word *oblige* has been used. But this distinction is not now observed.

The millions of mankind, as one vast fraternity, should feel *obligated* by a sense of duty and the impulse of affection, to realize the equal rights and to subserve the best interests of each other. *Proudfit.*

That's your true plan, to *obligate*
The present minister of state. *Churchill.*

OB'LIGATED, *pp.* Bound by contract or promise.

OB'LIGATING, *ppr.* Bound by covenant, contract, promise or bond.

OBLIGA'TION, *n.* [L. *obligatio.*] The binding power of a vow, promise, oath or contract, or of law, civil, political or moral, independent of a promise; that which constitutes legal or moral duty, and which renders a person liable to coercion and punishment for neglecting it. The laws and commands of God impose on us an *obligation* to love him supremely, and our neighbor as ourselves. Every citizen is under an *obligation* to obey the laws of the state. Moral *obligation* binds men without promise or contract.

2. The binding force of civility, kindness or gratitude, when the performance of a duty cannot be enforced by law. Favors conferred impose on men an *obligation* to make suitable returns.

3. Any act by which a person becomes bound to do something to or for another, or to forbear something. *Taylor.*

4. In *law*, a bond with a condition annexed and a penalty for non-fulfillment.

OBLIGATO. [See *Obbligato.*]

OB'LIGATORY, *a.* Binding in law or conscience; imposing duty; requiring performance or forbearance of some act; followed by *on; to* is obsolete.

As long as law is *obligatory*, so long our obedience is due. *Taylor.*

OBLI'GE, *v. t.* pronounced as written, not *obleege.* [Fr. *obliger;* It. *obbligare;* Sp. *obligar;* from L. *obligo; ob* and *ligo*, to bind; Russ. *oblagayu* or *oblegayu*, to encompass or surround.]

1. To constrain by necessity; to compel by physical force. An admiral may be *obliged* to surrender his ships, or he may be *obliged* by adverse winds to delay sailing.

2. To constrain by legal force; to bind in law. We are *obliged* to pay toll for supporting roads and bridges.

3. To bind or constrain by moral force. We are *obliged* to believe positive and unsuspected testimony.

4. To bind in conscience or honor; to constrain by a sense of propriety. We are

often *obliged* to conform to established customs, rites or ceremonies. To be *obliged* to yield to fashion is often the worst species of tyranny.
5. To do a favor to; to lay under obligation of gratitude; as, to *oblige* one with a loan of money.
6. To do a favor to; to please; to gratify. *Oblige* us with your company at dinner.
7. To indebt.
To those hills we are *obliged* for all our metals. *Bentley.*

OBLI'ĠED, *pp.* Bound in duty or in law; compelled; constrained; favored; indebted.

OBLIĠEE', *n.* The person to whom another is bound, or the person to whom a bond is given. *Blackstone.*

OBLI'ĠEMENT, *n.* Obligation. [*Little used.*] *Milton. Dryden.*

OBLI'ĠER, *n.* One that obliges.

OBLI'ĠING, *ppr.* Binding in law or conscience; compelling; constraining.
2. Doing a favor to.
No man can long be the enemy of one whom he is in the habit of *obliging*. *H. Humphrey.*

OBLI'ĠING, *a.* [Fr. *obligeant.*] Having the disposition to do favors, or actually conferring them; as an *obliging* man; a man of an *obliging* disposition; hence, civil; complaisant; kind.
Mons. Strozzi has many curiosities, and is very *obliging* to a stranger that desires the sight of them. *Addison.*

OBLI'ĠINGLY, *adv.* With civility; kindly; complaisantly. *Addison. Swift.*

OBLI'ĠINGNESS, *n.* Obligation. [*Little used.*] *Hammond.*
2. Civility; complaisance; disposition to exercise kindness. *Walton.*

OBLIGOR', *n.* The person who binds himself or gives his bond to another. *Blackstone.*

OBLIQUA'TION, *n.* [L. *obliquo*, from *obliquus*, oblique.]
1. Declination from a strait line or course; a turning to one side; as the *obliquation* of the eyes. *Newton.*
2. Deviation from moral rectitude.

OBLI'QUE, OBLI'KE, } *a. obli'ke.* [L. *obliquus*; Fr. *oblique.*]
1. Deviating from a right line; not direct; not perpendicular; not parallel; aslant.
It has a direction *oblique* to that of the former motion. *Cheyne.*
An *oblique* angle is either acute or obtuse; any angle except a right one.
An *oblique* line is one that, falling on another, makes *oblique* angles with it.
Oblique planes, in dialing, are those which decline from the zenith, or incline towards the horizon.
Oblique sailing, is when a ship sails upon some rhomb between the four cardinal points, making an oblique angle with the meridian. *Encyc.*
2. Indirect; by a side glance; as an *oblique* hint. *Shak.*
3. In *grammar*, an *oblique* case is any case except the nominative.

OBLI'QUELY, *adv.* In a line deviating from a right line; not directly; not perpendicularly.
Declining from the noon of day,
The sun *obliquely* shoots his burning ray. *Pope.*
2. Indirectly; by a side glance; by an allusion; not in the direct or plain meaning.
His discourse tends *obliquely* to the detracting from others. *Addison.*

OBLI'QUENESS, *n.* Obliquity.

OBLIQ'UITY, *n.* [L. *obliquitas*; Fr. *obliquité.*]
1. Deviation from a right line; deviation from parallelism or perpendicularity; as the *obliquity* of the ecliptic to the equator.
2. Deviation from moral rectitude.
To disobey God or oppose his will in any thing imports a moral *obliquity*. *South.*
3. Irregularity; deviation from ordinary rules.

OBLIT'ERATE, *v. t.* [L. *oblitero*; *ob* and *litera*, letter.]
1. To efface; to erase or blot out any thing written; or to efface any thing engraved. A writing may be *obliterated* by erasure, by blotting, or by the slow operation of time or natural causes.
2. To efface; to wear out; to destroy by time or other means; as, to *obliterate* ideas or impressions; to *obliterate* the monuments of antiquity; to *obliterate* reproach. *Hale. Locke.*
3. To reduce to a very low or imperceptible state.
The torpor of the vascular system and *obliterated* pulse. *Med. Repos.*

OBLIT'ERATED, *pp.* Effaced; erased; worn out; destroyed.

OBLIT'ERATING, *ppr.* Effacing; wearing out; destroying.

OBLITERA'TION, *n.* The act of effacing; effacement; a blotting out or wearing out; extinction. *Hale.*

OBLIV'ION, *n.* [L. *oblivio.*] Forgetfulness; cessation of remembrance.
Among our crimes *oblivion* may be set. *Dryden.*
2. A forgetting of offenses, or remission of punishment. An act of *oblivion* is an amnesty, or general pardon of crimes and offenses, granted by a sovereign, by which punishment is remitted.

OBLIV'IOUS, *a.* [L. *obliviosus.*] Causing forgetfulness. *Shak.*
The *oblivious* calm of indifference. *J. M. Mason.*
Behold the wonders of th' *oblivious* lake. *Pope.*
2. Forgetful. *Cavendish.*

OB'LOCUTOR, *n.* A gainsayer. [*Not in use.*] *Bull.*

OB'LONG, *a.* [Fr. from L. *oblongus.*] Longer than broad. *Harris.*

OB'LONG, *n.* A figure or solid which is longer than it is broad.

OB'LONGISH, *a.* Somewhat oblong.

OB'LONGLY, *a.* In an oblong form. *Cheyne.*

OB'LONGNESS, *n.* The state of being longer than broad.

OBLONG-OVATE, *a.* In *botany*, between oblong and ovate, but inclined to the latter. *Martyn.*

OBLO'QUIOUS, *a.* [See *Obloquy.*] Containing obloquy; reproachful. [*Little used.*] *Naunton.*

OB'LOQUY, *n.* [L. *obloquor*; *ob* and *loquor*, to speak.]
1. Censorious speech; reproachful language; language that casts contempt on men or their actions.
Shall names that made your city the glory of the earth, be mentioned with *obloquy* and detraction? *Addison.*
2. Cause of reproach; disgrace. [*Not used.*] *Shak.*

OBLUCTA'TION, *n.* [L. *obluctor*; *ob* and *luctor*, to struggle.]
A struggling or striving against; resistance. [*Little used.*] *Fotherby.*

OBMUTES'CENCE, *n.* [L. *obmutesco*, to be silent.]
1. Loss of speech; silence. *Brown.*
2. A keeping silence. *Paley.*

OBNOX'IOUS, *a.* [L. *obnoxius*; *ob* and *noxius*, hurtful, from *noceo.*]
1. Subject; answerable.
The writings of lawyers, which are tied and *obnoxious* to their particular laws. *Bacon.*
2. Liable; subject to cognizance or punishment.
We know ourselves *obnoxious* to God's severe justice. *Calamy.*
3. Liable; exposed; as friendship *obnoxious* to jealousies. *Hayward.*
4. Reprehensible; censurable; not approved; as *obnoxious* authors. *Fell.*
5. Odious; hateful; offensive; with *to*; as, the minister was *obnoxious to* the whigs.

OBNOX'IOUSLY, *adv.* In a state of subjection or liability.
2. Reprehensibly; odiously; offensively.

OBNOX'IOUSNESS, *n.* Subjection or liableness to punishment. *Hall.*
2. Odiousness; offensiveness. The *obnoxiousness* of the law rendered the legislature unpopular.

OBNU'BILATE, *v. t.* [L. *obnubilor*; *ob* and *nubilo*; *nubes*, mist, cloud.]
To cloud; to obscure. *Burton.*

OBNUBILA'TION, *n.* The act or operation of making dark or obscure. *Beddoes. Waterhouse.*

OB'OLE, *n.* [L. *obolus.*] In *pharmacy*, the weight of ten grains or half a scruple. *Encyc.*

OB'OLUS, *n.* [L. from Gr. οβολος.] A small silver coin of Athens, the sixth part of a drachma, about two cents in value, or a penny farthing sterling.

OBO'VATE, *a.* In *botany*, inversely ovate; having the narrow end downward; as an *obovate* leaf. *Martyn.*

OBREP'TION, *n.* [L. *obrepo*; *ob* and *repo*, to creep.]
The act of creeping on with secrecy or by surprise. *Cudworth.*

OBREPTI''TIOUS, *a.* [supra.] Done or obtained by surprise; with secrecy or by concealment of the truth. *Encyc.*

OBSCE'NE, *a.* [Fr. from L. *obscœnus.*] Offensive to chastity and delicacy; impure; expressing or presenting to the mind or view something which delicacy, purity and decency forbid to be exposed; as *obscene* language; *obscene* pictures.
2. Foul; filthy; offensive; disgusting.
A girdle foul with grease binds his *obscene* attire. *Dryden.*
3. Inauspicious; ill omened.
At the cheerful light,
The groaning ghosts and birds *obscene* take flight. *Dryden.*

OBSCE'NELY, *adv.* In a manner offensive to chastity or purity; impurely; unchastely. *Milton.*

OBSCE'NENESS, } *n.* [Fr. *obscenité*; L.
OBSCEN'ITY, } *obscœnitas.*]
1. Impurity in expression or representation; that quality in words or things which presents what is offensive to chastity or purity of mind; ribaldry.

Cowley asserts plainly that *obscenity* has no place in wit. *Dryden.*

Those fables were tempered with the Italian severity, and free from any note of infamy or *obsceneness.* *Dryden.*

No pardon vile *obscenity* should find. *Pope.*

2. Unchaste actions; lewdness.

To wash th' *obscenities* of night away. *Dryden.*

OBSCURA'TION, *n.* [L. *obscuratio.*] The act of darkening.
2. The state of being darkened or obscured; as the *obscuration* of the moon in an eclipse.

OBSCU'RE, *a.* [L. *obscurus*; It. *oscuro.*]
1. Dark; destitute of light.

Whoso curseth his father or mother, his lamp shall be put out in *obscure* darkness. Prov. xx.

2. Living in darkness; as the *obscure* bird. *Shak.*
3. Not easily understood; not obviously intelligible; abstruse; as an *obscure* passage in a writing. *Dryden.*
4. Not much known or observed; retired; remote from observation; as an *obscure* retreat.
5. Not noted; unknown; unnoticed; humble; mean; as an *obscure* person; a person of *obscure* birth. *Atterbury.*
6. Not easily legible; as an *obscure* inscription.
7. Not clear, full or distinct; imperfect; as an *obscure* view of remote objects.

OBSCU'RE, *v. t.* [L. *obscuro.*] To darken; to make dark. The shadow of the earth *obscures* the moon, and the body of the moon *obscures* the sun, in an eclipse.
2. To cloud; to make partially dark. Thick clouds *obscure* the day.
3. To hide from the view; as, clouds *obscure* the sun.
4. To make less visible.

Why, 'tis an office of discovery, love,
And I should be *obscured.* *Shak.*

5. To make less legible; as, time has *obscured* the writing.
6. To make less intelligible.

There is scarce any duty which has been so *obscured* by the writings of the learned as this. *Wake.*

7. To make less glorious, beautiful or illustrious.

—And see'st not sin *obscures* thy godlike frame? *Dryden.*

8. To conceal; to make unknown. *Milton.*
9. To tarnish; as, to *obscure* brightness.

OBSCU'RELY, *adv.* Darkly; not clearly; imperfectly; as an object *obscurely* seen; *obscurely* visible.
2. Out of sight; in a state not to be noticed; privately; in retirement; not conspicuously.

There live retired,
Content thyself to be *obscurely* good. *Addison.*

3. Not clearly; not plainly to the mind; darkly; as future events *obscurely* revealed.
4. Not plainly; indirectly; by hints or allusion.

OBSCU'RENESS, } *n.* [L. *obscuritas.*] Dark-
OBSCU'RITY, } ness; want of light.

We wait for light, but behold *obscurity.* Is. lix.

2. A state of retirement from the world; a state of being unnoticed; privacy.

You are not for *obscurity* designed. *Dryden.*

3. Darkness of meaning; unintelligibleness; as the *obscurity* of writings or of a particular passage.
4. Illegibleness; as the *obscurity* of letters or of an inscription.
5. A state of being unknown to fame; humble condition; as the *obscurity* of birth or parentage.

OB'SECRATE, *v. t.* [L. *obsecro.*] To beseech; to intreat; to supplicate; to pray earnestly. *Cockeram.*

OBSECRA'TION, *n.* Intreaty; supplication. *Stillingfleet.*
2. A figure of rhetoric, in which the orator implores the assistance of God or man. *Encyc.*

OB'SEQUENT, *a.* [L. *obsequens.*] Obedient; submissive to. [*Little used.*] *Fotherby.*

OB'SEQUIES, *n. plu.* [Fr. *obsèques*, from L. *obsequium*, complaisance, from *obsequor*, to follow.]
Funeral rites and solemnities; the last duties performed to a deceased person. *Dryden.*
[Milton uses the word in the singular, but the common usage is different.]

OBSE'QUIOUS, *a.* [from L. *obsequium*, complaisance, from *obsequor*, to follow; *ob* and *sequor.*]
1. Promptly obedient or submissive to the will of another; compliant; yielding to the desires of others, properly to the will or command of a superior, but in actual use, it often signifies yielding to the will or desires of such as have no right to control.

His servants weeping,
Obsequious to his orders, bear him hither. *Addison.*

2. Servilely or meanly condescending; compliant to excess; as an *obsequious* flatterer, minion or parasite.
3. Funereal; pertaining to funeral rites. [*Not used.*] *Shak.*

OBSE'QUIOUSLY, *adv.* With ready obedience; with prompt compliance.

They rise and with respectful awe,
At the word given, *obsequiously* withdraw. *Dryden.*

2. With reverence for the dead. [*Not used.*] *Shak.*

OBSE'QUIOUSNESS, *n.* Ready obedience; prompt compliance with the orders of a superior.
2. Servile submission; mean or excessive complaisance.

They apply themselves both to his interest and humor, with all the arts of flattery and *obsequiousness.* *South.*

OBSERV'ABLE, *a. s* as *z.* [See *Observe.*]
1. That may be observed or noticed.
2. Worthy of observation or of particular notice; remarkable.

I took a just account of every *observable* circumstance of the earth, stone, metal or other matter. *Woodward.*

OBSERV'ABLY, *adv. s* as *z.* In a manner worthy of note. *Brown.*

OBSERV'ANCE, *n. s* as *z.* [Fr. See *Observe.*]
1. The act of observing; the act of keeping or adhering to in practice; performance; as the *observance* of rules, rites, ceremonies or laws.

Love rigid honesty,
And strict *observance* of impartial laws. *Roscommon.*

2. Respect; ceremonial reverence in practice.

To do *observance* on the morn of May. *Shak.*

3. Performance of rites, religious ceremonies or external service.

Some represent to themselves the whole of religion as consisting in a few easy *observances.* *Rogers.*

4. Rule of practice; thing to be observed. *Shak.*
5. Observation; attention to. [*Little used.*] *Hale.*
6. Obedient regard or attention.

Having had experience of his fidelity and *observance* abroad. [*Not used.*] *Wotton.*

OBSERVAND'A, *n. plu. s* as *z.* [L.] Things to be observed. *Swift.*

OBSERV'ANT, *a. s* as *z.* Taking notice; attentively viewing or noticing; as an *observant* spectator or traveler.
2. Obedient; adhering to in practice; with *of.* He is very *observant of* the rules of his order.

We are told how *observant* Alexander was *of* his master Aristotle. *Digby.*

3. Carefully attentive; submissive. *Raleigh.*

OBSERV'ANT, *n. s* as *z.* A slavish attendant. [*Not in use.*] *Shak.*
2. A diligent observer. *Hooker.*

OBSERVA'TION, *n. s* as *z.* [L. *observatio.* See *Observe.*]
1. The act of observing or taking notice; the act of seeing or of fixing the mind on any thing. We apply the word to simple vision, as when one says, a spot on the sun's disk did not fall under his *observation*; or to the notice or cognizance of the mind, as when one says, the distinction made by the orator escaped his *observation.* When however it expresses vision, it often represents a more fixed or particular view than a mere transient sight; as an astronomical *observation.*
2. Notion gained by observing; the effect or result of seeing or taking cognizance in the mind, and either retained in the mind or expressed in words; inference or something arising out of the act of seeing or noticing, or that which is produced by thinking and reflecting on a subject; note; remark; animadversion. We often say, I made the *observation* in my own mind; but properly an *observation* is that which is expressed as the result of viewing or of thinking.

In matters of human prudence, we shall find the greatest advantage by making wise *observations* on our conduct. *Watts.*

3. Observance; adherence to in practice; performance of what is prescribed.

He freed the christian church from the external *observation* and obedience of legal precepts not formally moral. *White.*

4. In *navigation*, the taking of the altitude

of the sun or a star in order to find the latitude. *Encyc.*

OBSERVA'TOR, *n. s* as z. [Fr. *observateur.*]
1. One that observes or takes notice. *Hale.*
2. A remarker. *Dryden.*

OBSERV'ATORY, *n. s* as z. [Fr. *observatoire.*]
A place or building for making observations on the heavenly bodies; as the royal *observatory* at Greenwich.

OBSERVE, *v. t. obzerv'.* [L. *observo; ob* and *servo*, to keep or hold. The sense is to hold in view, or to keep the eyes on. See Class Sr. No. 34. 38. 45. and Class Dr. No. 32.]
1. To see or behold with some attention; to notice; as, to *observe* a halo round the moon; I *observed* a singular phenomenon; we *observe* strangers or their dress. I saw the figure, but *observed* nothing peculiar in it.
2. To take notice or cognizance of by the intellect. We *observe* nice distinctions in arguments, or a peculiar delicacy of thought.
3. To utter or express, as a remark, opinion or sentiment; to remark. He *observed* that no man appears great to his domestics.
4. To keep religiously; to celebrate.

A night to be much *observed* to the Lord. Ex. xii.

Ye shall *observe* the feast of unleavened bread. Ex. xii.

Ye *observe* days, and months, and times, and years. Gal. iv.

5. To keep or adhere to in practice; to comply with; to obey; as, to *observe* the laws of the state; to *observe* the rules and regulations of a society.

Teaching them to *observe* all things whatsoever I have commanded you. Matt. xxviii.

6. To practice.

In the days of Enoch, the people *observed* not circumcision or the sabbath. *White.*

OBSERVE, *v. i. obzerv'.* To remark. I have heard the gentleman's arguments, and shall hereafter *observe* upon them.
2. To be attentive.

OBSERV'ED, *pp. s* as z. Noticed by the eye or the mind.
2. Kept religiously; celebrated; practiced.

OBSERV'ER, *n. s* as z. One who observes; one that takes notice; particularly, one who looks to with care, attention or vigilance.

Careful *observers* may foretell the hour,
By sure prognostic, when to dread a shower. *Swift.*

Creditors are great *observers* of set days and times. *Franklin.*

2. A beholder; a looker on; a spectator. *South.*
3. One who keeps any law, custom, regulation or rite; one who adheres to any thing in practice; one who performs; as a great *observer* of forms; an *observer* of old customs. *Bacon.*
4. One who fulfills or performs; as, he is a strict *observer* of his word or promise. *Prior.*
5. One who keeps religiously; as an *observer* of the sabbath. *Atterbury.*

OBSERV'ING, *ppr. s* as z. Taking notice by the eye or the intellect.
2. Remarking.
3. Keeping; adhering to in practice; fulfilling.
4. *a.* Giving particular attention; habitually taking notice; attentive to what passes. He is an *observing* man.

OBSERV'INGLY, *adv. s* as z. Attentively; carefully; with close observation. *Shak.*

OBSESS', *v. t.* [L. *obsideo, obsessus; ob* and *sedeo*, to sit.] To besiege. [*Not used.*] *Elyot.*

OBSESS'ION, *n.* [L. *obsessio.*] The act of besieging; the first attack of Satan antecedent to possession. [*Little used.*] *Burton.*

OBSID'IAN, *n.* A mineral of two kinds, translucent and transparent. The translucent has a velvet black color; the transparent is of a dark blue. These occur massive in porphyry, gneiss or granite, generally invested with a gray opake crust. *Dict. Nat. Hist. Ure. Kirwan.*

The fracture of obsidian is vitreous or pearly; hence the two varieties, *vitreous obsidian* and *pearlstone.* *Jameson.*

OBSID'IONAL, *a.* [L. *obsidionalis; ob* and *sedeo*, to sit.] Pertaining to a siege. *Brown.*

OB'SIGNATE, *v. t.* [L. *obsigno; ob* and *signo*, to seal.] To seal up; to ratify. [*Little used.*] *Barrow.*

OBSIGNA'TION, *n.* The act of sealing; ratification by sealing; confirmation. *Taylor.*

OBSIG'NATORY, *a.* Ratifying; confirming by sealing. *Ward.*

OBSOLES'CENT, *a.* [L. *obsolesco*, to go out of use.]
Going out of use; passing into desuetude.

All the words compounded of *here* and a preposition, except *hereafter*, are obsolete or *obsolescent.* *Campbell.*

OBSOLE'TE, *a.* [L. *obsoletus.*] Gone into disuse; disused; neglected; as an *obsolete* word; an *obsolete* statute; applied chiefly to words or writings. *Dryden. Swift.*
2. In *botany*, obscure; not very distinct. *Eaton.*

OBSOLE'TENESS, *n.* The state of being neglected in use; a state of desuetude. *Johnson.*
2. In *botany*, indistinctness.

OB'STACLE, *n.* [Fr. from L. *obsto*, to withstand; *ob* and *sto.*]
That which opposes; any thing that stands in the way and hinders progress; hinderance; obstruction, either in a physical or moral sense. An army may meet with *obstacles* on its march; bad roads are *obstacles* to traveling; prejudice is an *obstacle* to improvement; want of union is often an insuperable *obstacle* to beneficial measures.

OB'STANCY, *n.* [L. *obstantia; ob* and *sto.*] Opposition; impediment; obstruction. [*Not used.*] *B. Jonson.*

OBSTET'RIC, *a.* [L. *obstetrix*, a midwife; *ob* and *sto*, to stand before.]
Pertaining to midwifery, or the delivery of women in childbed; as the *obstetric* art.

OBSTET'RICATE, *v. i.* [See *Obstetric.*] To perform the office of a midwife. [*Little used.*] *Evelyn.*

OBSTET'RICATE, *v. t.* To assist as a midwife. [*Little used.*] *Waterhouse.*

OBSTETRICA'TION, *n.* The act of assisting as a midwife.
2. The office of a midwife. *Hall.*

OBSTETRI''CIAN, *n.* One skilled in the art of assisting women in parturition. *Med. Repos.*

OBSTET'RICS, *n.* The art of assisting women in parturition; midwifery. *Encyc.*

OB'STINACY, *n.* [L. *obstinatio*, from *obsto*, to stand against, to oppose; *ob* and *sto.*]
1. A fixedness in opinion or resolution that cannot be shaken at all, or not without great difficulty; firm and usually unreasonable adherence to an opinion, purpose or system; a fixedness that will not yield to persuasion, arguments or other means. *Obstinacy* may not always convey the idea of unreasonable or unjustifiable firmness; as when we say, soldiers fight with *obstinacy.* But often, and perhaps usually, the word denotes a fixedness of resolution which is not to be vindicated under the circumstances; stubbornness; pertinacity; persistency.
2. Fixedness that will not yield to application, or that yields with difficulty; as the *obstinacy* of a disease or evil.

OB'STINATE, *a.* [L. *obstinatus.*] Stubborn; pertinaciously adhering to an opinion or purpose; fixed firmly in resolution; not yielding to reason, arguments or other means.

I have known great cures done by *obstinate* resolutions of drinking no wine. *Temple.*

No ass so meek, no ass so *obstinate.* *Pope.*

2. Not yielding or not easily subdued or removed; as an *obstinate* fever; *obstinate* obstructions; an *obstinate* cough.

OB'STINATELY, *adv.* Stubbornly; pertinaciously; with fixedness of purpose not to be shaken, or not without difficulty; as a sinner *obstinately* bent on his own destruction.

Inflexible to ill and *obstinately* just. *Addison.*

OB'STINATENESS, *n.* Stubbornness; pertinacity in opinion or purpose; fixed determination. *Hall.*

OBSTIPA'TION, *n.* [L. *obstipo; ob* and *stipo*, to crowd.
1. The act of stopping up; as a passage.
2. In *medicine*, costiveness.

OBSTREP'EROUS, *a.* [L. *obstreperus*, from *obstrepo*, to roar; *ob* and *strepo.*]
Loud; noisy; clamorous; vociferous; making a tumultuous noise.

The players do not only connive at his *obstreperous* approbation, but repair at their own cost whatever damages he makes. *Addison.*

OBSTREP'EROUSLY, *adv.* Loudly; clamorously; with tumultuous noise.

OBSTREP'EROUSNESS, *n.* Loudness; clamor; noisy turbulence.

OBSTRIC'TION, *n.* [L. *obstrictus, obstringo; ob* and *stringo*, to strain.]
Obligation; bond. *Milton.*

OBSTRUCT', *v. t.* [L. *obstruo; ob* and *struo*, to set.]
1. To block up; to stop up or close; as a way or passage; to fill with obstacles or impediments that prevent passing; as, to *obstruct* a road, highway or channel; to *obstruct* the canals or fine vessels of the body.
2. To stop; to impede; to hinder in passing; as, the bar at the mouth of the river *obstructs* the entrance of ships; clouds *obstruct* the light of the sun.

3. To retard; to interrupt; to render slow. Progress is often *obstructed* by difficulties, though not entirely stopped.

OBSTRUCT'ED, *pp.* Blocked up; stopped; as a passage.
2. Hindered; impeded; as progress.
3. Retarded; interrupted.

OBSTRUCT'ER, *n.* One that obstructs or hinders.

OBSTRUCT'ING, *ppr.* Blocking up; stopping; impeding; interrupting.

OBSTRUC'TION, *n.* [L. *obstructio.*] The act of obstructing.
2. Obstacle; impediment; any thing that stops or closes a way or channel. Bars of sand at the mouths of rivers are often *obstructions* to navigation.
3. That which impedes progress; hinderance. Disunion and party spirit are often *obstructions* to legislative measures and to public prosperity.
4. A heap. [*Not proper.*] *Shak.*

OBSTRUCT'IVE, *a.* [Fr. *obstructif*; It. *osstruttivo.*]
Presenting obstacles; hindering; causing impediment. *Hammond.*

OBSTRUCT'IVE, *n.* Obstacle; impediment. [*Little used.*] *Hammond.*

OB'STRUENT, *a.* [L *obstruens.*] Blocking up; hindering.

OB'STRUENT, *n.* Any thing that obstructs the natural passages in the body. *Quincy.*

OBSTUPEFAC'TION, *n.* [L. *obstupefacio.*] The act of making stupid or insensible. [See *Stupefaction*, which is generally used.]

OBSTUPEFAC'TIVE, *a.* [L. *obstupefacio.*] Stupefying; rendering insensible, torpid or inert. [*Little used.*] [See *Stupefactive.*] *Abbot.*

OBTA'IN, *v. t.* [L. *obtineo*; *ob* and *teneo*, to hold; Fr. *obtenir*; It. *ottenere.*]
1. To get; to gain; to procure; in *a general sense*, to gain possession of a thing, whether temporary or permanent; to acquire. This word usually implies exertion to get possession, and in this it differs from *receive*, which may or may not imply exertion. It differs from *acquire*, as genus from species; *acquire* being properly applied only to things permanently possessed; but *obtain* is applied both to things of temporary and of permanent possession. We *obtain* loans of money on application; we *obtain* answers to letters; we *obtain* spirit from liquors by distillation and salts by evaporation. We *obtain* by seeking; we often *receive* without seeking. We *acquire* or *obtain* a good title to lands by deed, or by a judgment of court; but we do not *acquire* spirit by distillation; nor do we *acquire* an answer to a letter or an application.

> He shall *obtain* the kingdom by flatteries. Dan. xi.

> In whom we have *obtained* an inheritance. Eph. i.

2. To keep; to hold. *Milton.*

OBTA'IN, *v. i.* To be received in customary or common use; to continue in use; to be established in practice.

> The Theodosian code, several hundred years after Justinian's time, *obtained* in the western parts of the empire. *Baker.*

2. To be established; to subsist in nature.

> The general laws of fluidity, elasticity and gravity, *obtain* in animal and inanimate tubes. *Cheyne.*

3. To prevail; to succeed. [*Little used.*] *Bacon.*

OBTA'INABLE, *a.* That may be obtained; that may be procured or gained. *Arbuthnot. Kettlewell.*

OBTA'INED, *pp.* Gained; procured; acquired.

OBTA'INER, *n.* One who obtains.

OBTA'INING, *ppr.* Gaining; procuring; acquiring.

OBTA'INMENT, *n.* The act of obtaining. *Milton.*

OBTEND', *v. t.* [L. *obtendo*; *ob* and *tendo*; literally, to stretch against or before.]
1. To oppose; to hold out in opposition. *Dryden.*
2. To pretend; to offer as the reason of any thing. [*Not used.*] *Dryden.*
[*This word is rarely used.*]

OBTENEBRA'TION, *n.* [from L. *ob* and *tenebræ*, darkness.]
A darkening; act of darkening; darkness.

> In every megrim or vertigo there is an *obtenebration* joined with a semblance of turning round. [*Little used.*] *Bacon.*

OBTEN'SION, *n.* The act of obtending. [*Not used.*]

OBTEST', *v. t.* [L. *obtestor*; *ob* and *testor*, to witness.] To beseech; to supplicate.

> *Obtest* his clemency. *Dryden.*

OBTEST', *v. i.* To protest. *Waterhouse.*

OBTESTA'TION, *n.* Supplication; entreaty. *Elyot.*
2. Solemn injunction. *Hall.*

OBTEST'ING, *ppr.* Beseeching; supplicating.

OBTRECTA'TION, *n.* [L. *obtrectatio*, from *obtrecto*; *ob* and *tracto.*]
Slander; detraction; calumny. [*Little used.*] *Barrow.*

OBTRU'DE, *v. t.* [L. *obtrudo*; *ob* and *trudo*, Eng. to *thrust.*]
1. To thrust in or on; to throw, crowd or thrust into any place or state by force or imposition, or without solicitation. Men *obtrude* their vain speculations upon the world.

> A cause of common error is the credulity of men, that is, an easy assent to what is *obtruded.* *Brown.*

> The objects of our senses *obtrude* their particular ideas upon our minds, whether we will or not. *Locke.*

2. To offer with unreasonable importunity; to urge upon against the will.

> Why shouldst thou then *obtrude* this diligence
> In vain, where no acceptance it can find? *Milton.*

To obtrude one's self, to enter a place where one is not desired; to thrust one's self in uninvited, or against the will of the company.

OBTRU'DE, *v. i.* To enter when not invited.
2. To thrust or be thrust upon.

OBTRU'DED, *pp.* Thrust in by force or unsolicited.

OBTRU'DER, *n.* One who obtrudes. *Boyle.*

OBTRU'DING, *ppr.* Thrusting in or on; entering uninvited.

OBTRUN'CATE, *v. t.* [L. *obtrunco*; *ob* and *trunco*, to cut off.] To deprive of a limb; to lop. [*Little used.*] *Cockeram.*

OBTRUNCA'TION, *n.* The act of lopping or cutting off. [*Little used.*] *Cockeram.*

OBTRU'SION, *n.* *s* as *z.* [L. *obtrudo*, *obtrusus.*]
The act of obtruding; a thrusting upon others by force or unsolicited; as the *obtrusion* of crude opinions on the world.

OBTRU'SIVE, *a.* Disposed to obtrude any thing upon others; inclined to intrude or thrust one's self among others, or to enter uninvited.

> Not obvious, not *obtrusive*, but retired,
> The more desirable. *Milton.*

OBTRU'SIVELY, *adv.* By way of obtrusion or thrusting upon others, or entering unsolicited.

OBTUND', *v. t.* [L. *obtundo*; *ob* and *tundo*, to beat.]
To dull; to blunt; to quell; to deaden; to reduce the edge, pungency or violent action of any thing; as, to *obtund* the acrimony of the gall. *Harvey.*

OBTURA'TION, *n.* [L. *obturatus*, from *obturo*, to stop up.]
The act of stopping by spreading over or covering.

OB'TURA'TOR, *n.* In *anatomy*, the obturators are muscles which rise from the outer and inner side of the pelvis around the foramen thyroideum, and are rotators of the thigh. *Wistar. Coxe.*

OBTUSANG'ULAR, *a.* [*obtuse* and *angular.*]
Having angles that are obtuse, or larger than right angles.

OBTU'SE, *a.* [L. *obtusus*, from *obtundo*, to beat against.]
1. Blunt; not pointed or acute. Applied to angles, it denotes one that is larger than a right angle, or more than ninety degrees.
2. Dull; not having acute sensibility; as *obtuse* senses. *Milton.*
3. Not sharp or shrill; dull; obscure; as *obtuse* sound.

OBTU'SELY, *adv.* Without a sharp point.
2. Dully; stupidly.

OBTU'SENESS, *n.* Bluntness; as the *obtuseness* of an edge or a point.
2. Dullness; want of quick sensibility; as the *obtuseness* of the senses.
3. Dullness of sound.

OBTU'SION, *n.* *s* as *z.* The act of making blunt.
2. The state of being dulled or blunted; as the *obtusion* of the senses.

OBUM'BRATE, *v. t.* [L. *obumbro*; *ob* and *umbra*, a shade.]
To shade; to darken; to cloud. [*Little used.*] *Howell.*

OBUMBRA'TION, *n.* The act of darkening or obscuring.

OBVEN'TION, *n.* [L. *obvenio*; *ob* and *venio*, to come.]
Something occasional; that which happens not regularly, but incidentally. [*Not used.*] *Spenser.*

OBVERS'ANT, *a.* [L. *obversans*, *obversor*; *ob* and *versor*, to turn.] Conversant; familiar. [*Not used.*] *Bacon.*

OBVERSE, *a.* *obvers'.* In *botany*, having the base narrower than the top; as a leaf.

OB'VERSE, *n.* The face of a coin; opposed to *reverse.*

OBVERT′, *v. t.* [L. *obverto; ob* and *verto*, to turn.] To turn towards. *Watts.*

OBVERT′ED, *pp.* Turned towards.

OBVERT′ING, *ppr.* Turning towards.

OB′VIATE, *v. t.* [Fr. *obvier;* It. *ovviare;* Sp. *obviar;* from L. *obvius; ob* and *via*, way.]

Properly, to meet in the way; to oppose; hence, to prevent by interception, or to remove at the beginning or in the outset; hence in present usage, to remove in general, as difficulties or objections; to clear the way of obstacles in reasoning, deliberating or planning.

To lay down every thing in its full light, so as to *obviate* all exceptions. *Woodward.*

OB′VIATED, *pp.* Removed, as objections or difficulties.

OB′VIATING, *ppr.* Removing, as objections in reasoning or planning.

OB′VIOUS, *a.* [L. *obvius.* See the Verb.]

1. Meeting; opposed in front.

I to the evil turn
My *obvious* breast. [*Not now used.*] *Milton.*

2. Open; exposed. [*Little used.*] *Milton.*

3. Plain; evident; easily discovered, seen or understood; readily perceived by the eye or the intellect. We say, a phenomenon *obvious* to the sight, or a truth *obvious* to the mind. *Milton. Dryden.*

OB′VIOUSLY, *adv.* Evidently; plainly; apparently; manifestly. Men do not always pursue what is *obviously* their interest.

2. Naturally. *Holyday.*

3. Easily to be found. *Selden.*

OB′VIOUSNESS, *n.* State of being plain or evident to the eye or the mind. *Boyle.*

OB′VOLUTE, **OB′VOLUTED**, } *a.* [L. *obvolutus, obvolvo; ob* and *volvo*, to roll.]

In *botany*, obvolute foliation is when the margins of the leaves alternately embrace the straight margin of the opposite leaf. *Martyn.*

OCCA′SION, *n. s* as *z.* [L. *occasio*, from *occido*, to fall; *ob* and *cado.*]

1. Properly, a falling, happening or coming to; an occurrence, casualty, incident; something distinct from the ordinary course or regular order of things. *Hooker.*

2. Opportunity; convenience; favorable time, season or circumstances.

I'll take th' *occasion* which he gives to bring
Him to his death. *Waller.*

Use not liberty for an *occasion* to the flesh. Gal. v.

Sin taking *occasion* by the commandment, deceived me. Rom. vii.

3. Accidental cause; incident, event or fact giving rise to something else. What was the *occasion* of this custom?

Her beauty was the *occasion* of the war. *Dryden.*

4. Incidental need; casual exigency; opportunity accompanied with need or demand. So we say, we have *occasion* for all our resources. We have frequent *occasions* for assisting each other.

The ancient canons were well fitted for the *occasion* of the church in its purer ages. *Baker.*

My *occasions* have found time to use them toward a supply of money. *Shak.*

OCCA′SION, *v. t.* [Fr. *occasionner.*] To cause incidentally; to cause; to produce. The expectation of war *occasions* a depression in the price of stocks. Consumptions are often *occasioned* by colds. Indigestion *occasions* pain in the head. Heat *occasions* lassitude.

2. To influence; to cause.

If we inquire what it is that *occasions* men to make several combinations of simple ideas into distinct modes— *Locke.*

OCCA′SIONABLE, *a. s* as *z.* That may be caused or occasioned. [*Little used.*] *Barrow.*

OCCA′SIONAL, *a. s* as *z.* [Fr. *occasionnel.*]

1. Incidental; casual; occurring at times, but not regular or systematic; made or happening as opportunity requires or admits. We make *occasional* remarks on the events of the age.

2. Produced by accident; as the *occasional* origin of a thing. *Brown.*

3. Produced or made on some special event; as an *occasional* discourse.

OCCA′SIONALLY, *adv. s* as *z.* According to incidental exigence; at times, as convenience requires or opportunity offers; not regularly. He was *occasionally* present at our meetings. We have *occasionally* lent our aid.

OCCA′SIONED, *pp. s* as *z.* Caused incidentally; caused; produced.

OCCA′SIONER, *n. s* as *z.* One that causes or produces, either incidentally or otherwise.

He was the *occasioner* of loss to his neighbor. *Sanderson.*

OCCA′SIONING, *ppr. s* as *z.* Causing incidentally or otherwise.

OCCA′SIVE, *a.* Falling; descending; western; pertaining to the setting sun.

Amplitude is ortive or *occasive.* *Encyc.*

OCCECA′TION, *n.* [L. *occæcatio; ob* and *cæco*, to blind.]

The act of making blind. [*Little used.*] *Sanderson.*

OC′CIDENT, *n.* [L. *occidens, occido*, to fall; *ob* and *cado.*]

The west; the western quarter of the hemisphere; so called from the decline or fall of the sun. *Encyc.*

OCCIDENT′AL, *a.* [L. *occidentalis.*] Western; opposed to *oriental;* pertaining to the western quarter of the hemisphere, or to some part of the earth westward of the speaker or spectator; as *occidental* climates; *occidental* pearl; *occidental* gold. *Encyc. Howell.*

OCCID′UOUS, *a.* [L. *occido, occiduus.*] Western. [*Little used.*]

OCCIP′ITAL, *a.* [from L. *occiput*, the back part of the head; *ob* and *caput.*]

Pertaining to the back part of the head, or to the occiput.

OC′CIPUT, *n.* [L *ob* and *caput*, head.] The hinder part of the head, or that part of the skull which forms the hind part of the head.

OCCIS′ION, *n. s* as *z.* [L. *occisio*, from *occido*, to kill; *ob* and *cædo.*]

A killing; the act of killing. [*Not used.*] *Hall.*

OCCLU′DE, *v. t.* [L. *occludo; ob* and *cludo, claudo*, to shut.]

To shut up; to close. [*Little used.*] *Brown.*

OCCLU′SE, *a.* [L. *occlusus.*] Shut; closed. [*Little used.*] *Holder.*

OCCLU′SION, *n. s* as *z.* [L. *occlusio.*] A shutting up; a closing. *Howell.*

[This is an elegant word, though little used.]

OCCULT′, *a.* [L. *occultus, occulo; ob* and *celo*, to conceal.]

Hidden from the eye or understanding; invisible; secret; unknown; undiscovered; undetected; as the *occult* qualities of matter. *Newton.*

The *occult* sciences are magic, necromancy, &c.

Occult lines, in geometry, are such as are drawn with the compasses or a pencil, and are scarcely visible. *Encyc.*

OCCULTA′TION, *n.* [L. *occultatio.*] A hiding; also, the time a star or planet is hid from our sight, when eclipsed by the interposition of the body of a planet. *Encyc.*

2. In *astronomy*, the hiding of a star or planet from our sight, by passing behind some other of the heavenly bodies.

OCCULT′ED, *a.* Hid; secret. [*Not used.*] *Shak.*

OCCULT′NESS, *n.* The state of being concealed from view; secretness.

OC′CUPANCY, *n.* [L. *occupo*, to take or seize; *ob* and *capio*, to seize.]

1. The act of taking possession.

2. In *law*, the taking possession of a thing not belonging to any person. The person who first takes possession of land is said to have or hold it by right of *occupancy.*

Occupancy gave the original right to the property in the substance of the earth itself. *Blackstone.*

OC′CUPANT, *n.* He that occupies or takes possession; he that has possession.

3. In *law*, one that first takes possession of that which has no legal owner. The right of property, either in wild beasts and fowls, or in land belonging to no person, vests in the first *occupant.* The property in these cases follows the possession.

OC′CUPATE, *v. t.* [L. *occupo.*] To hold; to possess; to take up. [*Not used.*] *Bacon.*

OCCUPA′TION, *n.* [L. *occupatio.*] The act of taking possession. *Bacon.*

2. Possession; a holding or keeping; tenure; use; as lands in the *occupation* of AB.

3. That which engages the time and attention; employment; business. He devotes to study all the time that his other *occupations* will permit.

4. The principal business of one's life; vocation; calling; trade; the business which a man follows to procure a living or obtain wealth. Agriculture, manufactures and commerce furnish the most general *occupations* of life. Painting, statuary, music, are agreeable *occupations.* Men not engaged in some useful *occupation* commonly fall into vicious courses.

OC′CUPIER, *n.* One that occupies or takes possession. *Raleigh.*

2. One who holds possession.

3. One who follows an employment. Ezek. xxvii.

OC′CUPY, *v. t.* [L. *occupo; ob* and *capio*, to seize or take.]

1. To take possession. The person who first *occupies* land which has no owner, has the right of property.

2. To keep in possession; to possess; to hold or keep for use. The tenant *occupies* a farm under a lease of twenty one years. A lodger *occupies* an apartment; a man *occupies* the chair in which he sits.
3. To take up; to possess; to cover or fill. The camp *occupies* five acres of ground. Air may be so rarefied as to *occupy* a vast space. The writing *occupies* a sheet of paper, or it *occupies* five lines only.
4. To employ; to use.

The archbishop may have occasion to *occupy* more chaplains than six. *Eng. Statute.*

5. To employ; to busy one's self. Every man should be *occupied*, or should *occupy* himself, in some useful labor.
6. To follow, as business.

All the ships of the sea with their mariners were in thee to *occupy* thy merchandise. Ezek. xxvii.

7. To use; to expend.

All the gold that was *occupied* for the work—Ex. xxxviii. [*Not now in use.*]

OC'CUPY, *v. i.* To follow business; to negotiate.

Occupy till I come. Luke xix.

OC'CUPYING, *ppr.* Taking or keeping possession; employing.

OCCUR', *v. i.* [L. *occurro; ob* and *curro*, to run.]

1. Primarily, to meet; to strike against; to clash; and so used by Bentley, but this application is obsolete.
2. To meet or come to the mind; to be presented to the mind, imagination or memory. We say, no better plan *occurs* to me or to my mind; it does not *occur* to my recollection; the thought did not *occur* to me.

There doth not *occur* to me any use of this experiment for profit. *Bacon.*

3. To appear; to meet the eye; to be found here and there. This word *occurs* in twenty places in the Scriptures; the other word does not *occur* in a single place; it does not *occur* in the sense suggested.
4. To oppose; to obviate. [*Not used.*] *Bentley.*

OCCUR'RENCE, *n.* [Fr.] Literally, a coming or happening; hence, any incident or accidental event; that which happens without being designed or expected; any single event. We speak of an unusual *occurrence*, or of the ordinary *occurrences* of life.

2. Occasional presentation.

Voyages detain the mind by the perpetual *occurrence* and expectation of something new. *Watts.*

OCCUR'RENT, *n.* Incident; any thing that happens. *Obs.* *Bacon.*

OCCUR'SION, *n.* [L. *occursio*, from *occurro*, to meet.] A meeting of bodies; a clash. *Boyle.*

OCEAN, *n. o'shun.* [L. *oceanus;* Gr. ωκεανος; Fr. *ocean;* Ir. *ocein, aigein;* W. *eigiawn, aig* or *eigion.* In Welsh, the word is rendered the great source, the middle, the abyss or great deep, and is allied in orthography to *eigian*, force, or a forcing out, a producing; *eigiaw*, to bring forth, from *aig*, what brings forth, the female, the womb, the sea, a shoal of fishes, a flock or herd. Bochart cites many authorities to prove that the ancients understood the ocean to encompass the earth, and he supposes it to be derived from the Heb. Ch. Syr. חוג hog, to encompass, whence a circle. This is probably an error. The word seems to have for its origin greatness or extent.]

1. The vast body of water which covers more than three fifths of the surface of the globe, called also the sea, or great sea. It is customary to speak of the ocean as if divided into three parts, the Atlantic ocean, the Pacific ocean, and the Indian ocean; but the ocean is *one* mass or body, partially separated by the continents of Europe, Asia and Africa on one side, and by America on the other.
2. An immense expanse; as the boundless *ocean* of eternity; *oceans* of duration and space. *Locke.*

OCEAN, *a. o'shun.* Pertaining to the main or great sea; as the *ocean* wave; *ocean* stream. *Milton.*

OCEANIC, *a. oshean'ic.* Pertaining to the ocean. *Cook.*

O'CELLATED, *a.* [L. *ocellatus*, from *ocellus*, a little eye.]

1. Resembling an eye. *Derham.*
2. Formed with the figures of little eyes.

O'CELOT, *n.* The Mexican panther.

O'CHER, *n.* [Fr. *ocre;* L. *ochra;* Gr. ωχρα, from ωχρος, pale.]

A variety of clay deeply colored by the oxyd of iron. Its most common colors are red, yellow and brown. It is used as a pigment.

O'CHEROUS, *a.* Consisting of ocher; as *ocherous* matter.

2. Resembling ocher; as an *ocherous* color.

OCH'IMY, *n.* [corrupted from *alchimy.*] A mixed base metal. *Johnson. Todd.*

OCHLOC'RACY, *n.* [Gr. οχλοκρατια; οχλος, the people or a multitude, and κρατεω, to govern.]

A form of government in which the multitude or common people rule. *Encyc. Jones.*

O'CHREY, *a.* Partaking of ocher. [*Not used.*] *Woodward.*

OCH'ROITS, *n.* Cerite.

O'CRA, *n.* A viscous vegetable substance in the W. Indies, used in soups, &c. *Encyc.*

It is obtained by boiling the green pods of the *Hibiscus esculentus.* Also, the name of the plant itself.

OC'TACHORD, *n.* An instrument or system of eight sounds. *Busby.*

OC'TAGON, *n.* [Gr. οκτω, eight, and γωνια, angle.]

1. In *geometry*, a figure of eight sides and eight angles. When the sides and angles are equal, it is a regular octagon which may be inscribed in a circle. *Harris. Encyc.*
2. In *fortification*, a place with eight bastions. *Encyc.*

OCTAG'ONAL, *a.* Having eight sides and eight angles.

OCTAHE'DRAL, *a.* [See *Octahedron.*] Having eight equal sides.

OCTAHE'DRITE, *n.* Pyramidical ore of titanium. *Ure.*

OCTAHE'DRON, *n.* [Gr. οκτω, eight, and εδρα, a base.]

In *geometry*, a solid contained by eight equal and equilateral triangles. It is one of the five regular bodies. *Encyc.*

OCTAN'DER, *n.* [Gr. οκτω, eight, and ανηρ, a male.] In *botany*, a plant having eight stamens.

OCTAN'DRIAN, *a.* Having eight stamens.

OCTAN'GULAR, *a.* [L. *octo*, eight, and *angular.*] Having eight angles.

OC'TANT, *n.* [L. *octans*, an eighth part, from *octo*, eight.]

In *astronomy*, that aspect of two planets in which they are distant from each other the eighth part of a circle or 45°. *Encyc.*

OC'TAVE, *a.* [infra.] Denoting eight. *Dryden.*

OC'TAVE, *n.* [Fr. from L. *octavus*, eighth.]

1. The eighth day after a festival. *Johnson.*
2. Eight days together after a festival. *Ainsworth.*
3. In *music*, an eighth, or an interval of seven degrees or twelve semitones. The octave is the most perfect of the chords, consisting of six full tones and two semitones major. It contains the whole diatonic scale. *Encyc.*

OCTA'VO, *n.* [L. *octavus*, eighth.] A book in which a sheet is folded into eight leaves. The word is used as a noun or an adjective. We say, an *octavo*, or an *octavo* volume. The true phrase is, a *book in octavo.*

OCTEN'NIAL, *a.* [L. *octo*, eight, and *annus*, year.]

1. Happening every eighth year.
2. Lasting eight years.

OC'TILE, *n.* The same as *octant*, supra.

OCTO'BER, *n.* [L. from *octo*, eighth; the eighth month of the primitive Roman year which began in March.]

The tenth month of the year in our calendar, which follows that of Numa and Julius Cesar.

OCTODEC'IMAL, *a.* [L. *octo*, eight, and *decem*, ten.]

In *crystalography*, designating a crystal whose prisms, or the middle part, has eight faces, and the two summits together ten faces.

OCTODEN'TATE, *a.* [L. *octo*, eight, and *dentatus*, toothed.] Having eight teeth.

OC'TOFID, *a.* [L. *octo*, eight, and *findo*, to cleave.]

In *botany*, cleft or separated into eight segments; as a calyx. *Martyn.*

OC'TOGENARY, *a.* [L. *octogenarius*, from *octogeni*, eighty.] Of eighty years of age.

OC'TOGENARY, *n.* A person eighty years of age. *J. Adams.*

OCTOLOC'ULAR, *a.* [L. *octo*, eight, and *locus*, place.] In *botany*, having eight cells for seeds.

OC'TONARY, *a.* [L. *octonarius.*] Belonging to the number eight.

OCTONOC'ULAR, *a.* [L. *octo*, eight, and *oculus*, eye.] Having eight eyes. *Derham.*

OCTOPET'ALOUS, *a.* [Gr. οκτω, eight, and πεταλον, a petal.] Having eight petals or flower-leaves. *Dict.*

OCTORA'DIATED, *a.* [L. *octo*, eight, and *radius*, ray.] Having eight rays.

OCTOSPERM'OUS, *a.* [Gr. οκτω, eight, and σπερμα, seed.] Containing eight seeds.

OC'TOSTYLE, *n.* [Gr. οκτω, eight, and ϛυλος, style.]

In *ancient architecture*, the face of an edifice adorned with eight columns, or a range of eight columns. *Encyc.*

OCTOSYL'LABLE, *a.* [L. *octo*, eight, and *syllaba*, syllable.] Consisting of eight syllables.

OC'TUPLE, *a.* [L. *octuplus; octo*, eight, and *plico*, to fold.] Eight-fold. *Dict.*

OC'ULAR, *a.* [Fr. *oculaire;* L. *ocularius*, from *oculus*, eye.]
Depending on the eye; known by the eye; received by actual sight; as *ocular* proof; *ocular* demonstration or evidence.

OC'ULARLY, *adv.* By the eye, sight or actual view. *Brown.*

OC'ULATE, *a.* [L. *oculatus.*] Furnished with eyes; knowing by the eye. *Johnson.*

OC'ULIFORM, *a.* [L. *oculus*, eye, and *forma*, form.]
In the form of an eye; resembling the eye in form; as an *oculiform* pebble. *Fourcroy.*

OC'ULIST, *n.* [from L. *oculus*, the eye.] One skilled in diseases of the eyes, or one who professes to cure them.

Oculus beli, a semi-pellucid gem, a variety of agate of a grayish white color, variegated with yellow, and with a black central nucleus. Its variegations resemble the pupil and iris of the eye. *Encyc.*

Oculus cati, cat's eye or asteria, a beautiful gem approaching the nature of the opal, having a bright color which seems to be lodged deep in the stone, and which shifts as it is moved in various directions. It is larger than a pea, and generally of a semicircular form, naturally smooth. It is found in the East and West Indies, and in Europe. *Encyc.*

Oculus mundi, otherwise called hydrophane and lapis mutabilis, a precious stone of an opake whitish brown color, but becoming transparent by infusion in an aqueous fluid, and resuming its opacity when dry. It is found in beds over the opals in Hungary, Silesia and Saxony, and over the chalcedonies and agates in Iceland. *Encyc.*

ODD, *a.* [Sw. *udda*, odd, and *udd, udde*, a point; Dan. *odd*, a point or tip. In W. *od* is notable, singular, and *odid*, a rarity. In Russ. *odin* or *odno* is one.]

1. Not even; not divisible into equal numbers; as one, three, five, seven, &c.

   Good luck lies in *odd* numbers. *Shak.*

2. Left or remaining after the union, estimate or use of even numbers; or remaining after round numbers or any number specified; as the *odd* number; the *odd* man.

   Sixteen hundred and *odd* years after the earth was made, it was destroyed by a deluge. *Burnet.*

3. Singular; extraordinary; differing from what is usual; strange; as an *odd* phenomenon. *Newton.*

   It sometimes implies dislike or contempt; as an *odd* fellow.

4. Not noted; unheeded; not taken into the common account.

   There are yet missing some few *odd* lads that you remember not. *Shak.*

5. Uncommon; particular.

   The *odd* man to perform all three perfectly is Joannes Sturmius. *Ascham.*

6. Uncommon; in appearance improper or not likely to answer the purpose. This is an *odd* way of doing things.

   Locke's Essay would be an *odd* book for a man to make himself master of, who would get a reputation by his critical writings. *Spectator.*

7. Separate from that which is regularly occupied; remaining unemployed. I will take some *odd* time to do this business. He may do it at *odd* times.

ODD'ITY, *n.* Singularity; strangeness; as the *oddity* of dress, manners or shape; *oddity* of appearance.

2. A singular person; *in colloquial language.* This man is an *oddity.*

ODD'LY, *adv.* Not evenly. [*Little used.*]

2. Strangely; unusually; irregularly; singularly; uncouthly; as *oddly* dressed; *oddly* formed.

   A figure *oddly* turned. *Locke.*

   A black substance lying on the ground very *oddly* shaped. *Swift.*

ODD'NESS, *n.* The state of being not even.

2. Singularity; strangeness; particularity; irregularity; uncouthness; as the *oddness* of dress or shape; the *oddness* of an event or accident. *Dryden. Swift.*

ODDS, *n.* *s* as *z.* [It is used both in the singular and plural.]

1. Inequality; excess of either compared with the other; difference in favor of one and against another.

   Preeminent by so much *odds.* *Milton.*

   In this example, *much* marks the singular number, and *many* cannot be used.

   Cromwell, with *odds* of number and of fate— *Waller.*

   All the *odds* between them has been the different scope given to their understandings to range in. *Locke.*

   Judging is balancing an account and determining on which side the *odds* lie. *Locke.*

   There appeared at least four to one *odds* against them. *Swift.*

2. Advantage; superiority. *Hudibras.*

3. Quarrel; dispute; debate. *Shak.*

It is odds, more likely than the contrary.

   It is odds that he will find a shrewd temptation. *South.*

At odds, in dispute; at variance; in controversy or quarrel.

   That sets us all *at odds.* *Shak.*

   Or they must always be *at odds.* *Swift.*

ODE, *n.* [L. *ode;* Gr. ωδη.] A short poem or song; a poetical composition proper to be set to music or sung; a lyric poem. The ode is of the greater or less kind; the less is characterized by sweetness and ease; the greater by sublimity, rapture and quickness of transition. *Johnson.*

   Pindar has left Olympic *odes*, Pythian *odes*, Nemean *odes*, and Isthmian *odes.*

   The *ode* consists of unequal verses in stanzas or strophes. *Busby.*

O'DIOUS, *a.* [L. *odiosus*, from *odi*, I hated, Eng. *hate.*]

1. Hateful; deserving hatred. It expresses something less than *detestable* and *abominable;* as an *odious* name; *odious* vice.

   All wickedness is *odious.* *Sprat.*

2. Offensive to the senses; disgusting; as an *odious* sight; an *odious* smell.

3. Causing hate; invidious; as, to utter *odious* truth.

4. Exposed to hatred.

   He rendered himself *odious* to the parliament. *Clarendon.*

O'DIOUSLY, *adv.* Hatefully; in a manner to deserve or excite hatred. *Milton.*

2. Invidiously; so as to cause hate. *Dryden.*

O'DIOUSNESS, *n.* Hatefulness; the quality that deserves or may excite hatred; as the *odiousness* of sin. *Wake.*

2. The state of being hated. [*Not usual.*] *Sidney.*

O'DIUM, *n.* [L.] Hatred; dislike. This measure brought a general *odium* on his government.

2. The quality that provokes hatred; offensiveness.

   She threw the *odium* of the fact on me. *Dryden.*

ODONTAL'ĠIC, *a.* [Gr. οδους, a tooth, and αλγος, pain.]
Pertaining to the tooth-ache.

ODONTAL'ĠIC, *n.* A remedy for the tooth-ache.

ODONTAL'ĠY, *n.* Tooth-ache.

O'DOR, *n.* [L.] Smell; scent; fragrance; a sweet or an offensive smell; perfume. *Bacon. Addison.*

O'DORAMENT, *n.* [L. *odoramentum.*] A perfume; a strong scent. *Burton.*

O'DORATE, *a.* [L. *odoratus.*] Scented; having a strong scent, fetid or fragrant. *Bacon.*

O'DORATING, *a.* Diffusing odor or scent; fragrant.

ODORIF'EROUS, *a.* [L. *odoriferus; odor* and *fero*, to bear.]

1. Giving scent; diffusing fragrance; fragrant; perfumed; usually, sweet of scent; as *odoriferous* spices; *odoriferous* flowers.

2. Bearing scent; as *odoriferous* gales.

ODORIF'EROUSNESS, *n.* The quality of diffusing scent; fragrance; sweetness of scent.

O'DOROUS, *a.* Sweet of scent; fragrant. *Spenser. Waller.*

O'DOROUSNESS, *n.* Fragrance; the quality of diffusing scent, or of exciting the sensation of smell.

ŒCONOMICAL, ŒCONOMY, ŒDEMATOUS, ŒSOPHAGUS. [See *Economical, Economy, Edematous, Esophagus.*]

OEILIAD, *n.* [Fr. *œillade*, from *œil*, the eye.] A glance; a wink. [*Not English nor used.*] *Shak.*

O'ER, contracted from *over*, which see.

OF, *prep.* *ov.* [Sax. *of;* G. *ab;* Sw. Ice. Dan. D. *af;* L. *ab*, but originally *af;* Gr. απο. The primary sense is departing, issuing or proceeding from; but this sense has been modified by usage.]

1. From or out of; proceeding from, as the cause, source, means, author or agent bestowing.

   I have received *of* the Lord that which also I delivered to you. 1 Cor. xi.

   For it was *of* the Lord to harden their hearts. Josh. xi.

   It is *of* the Lord's mercies that we are not consumed. Lam. iii.

   The whole disposing thereof is *of* the Lord. Prov. xvi.

   Go, inquire *of* the Lord for me. 2 Chron. xxxiv.

   That holy thing that shall be born *of* thee. Luke i.

   Hence *of* is the sign of the genitive case, the case that denotes production; as the son *of* man, the son proceeding from man, produced from man. This is the primary sense, although we now say, produced *by* man. "Part *of* these were slain;" that is, a number separate, for *part* denotes a division; the sense then is, a number *from* or *out of* the whole were slain. So also, "some *of* these were slain;" that is, some *from* or *out of* the others. "I have known him *of* old, or *of* a child;" that is, *from* old times, *from* a child. "He is *of* the race of kings;" that is, descended *from* kings. "He is *of* noble blood or birth, or *of* ignoble origin." "No particle of matter, or no body can move *of* itself;" that is, by force or strength *proceeding from* itself, derived *from* itself.

"The quarrel is not now *of* fame and tribute, or *of* wrongs done;" that is, *from* fame or wrongs, as the cause, and we may render it *concerning, about, relating to.*

"*Of* this little he had some to spare;" that is, some *from* the whole. It may be rendered *out of.*

"*Of* all our heroes thou canst boast alone;" that is, thou alone *from* the number of heroes. This may be rendered *among.*

"The best *of* men, the most renowned *of* all;" that is, the best *from* the number of men, the most renowned *from* the whole; denoting primarily separation, like *part.*

"I was well entertained *of* the English Consul;" that is, entertained *from* the Consul; my entertainment was *from* the Consul. This use is obsolete, and we use *by* in lieu of it.

"This does *of* right belong to us;" that is, *from* right, *de jure;* our title proceeds *from* right.

"The chariot was all *of* cedar;" that is, made *from* cedar. So we say, made *of* gold, made *of* clay; an application corresponding with our modern use of *from;* manufactured *from* wool, or *from* raw materials. Hence we say, cloth consisting *of* wool. "This is a scheme *of* his own devising;" that is, *from* his own devising or device. "If any man minister, let him do it as *of* the ability which God giveth;" that is, as *from* the ability, as the source of action.

"*Of* happy, he is become miserable;" that is, *from* happy; *from* being happy, he has passed to being miserable. "*Of* necessity this must prove ruinous;" that is, *from* necessity, as the cause or source. "*Of* a hundred take fifty;" that is, *from* a hundred, or *out of* a hundred, *from* among a hundred.

Of sometimes implies a part or share.

It is a duty to communicate *of* those blessings we have received. *Franklin.*

From is then the primary sense of this preposition; a sense retained in *off,* the same word differently written for distinction. But this sense is appropriately lost in many of its applications; as a man *of* genius, a man *of* courage, a man *of* rare endowments, a fossil *of* a red color, or *of* a hexagonal figure. He lost all hope *of* relief. This is an affair *of* the cabinet. He is a man *of* decayed fortune. What is the price *of* corn? We say that *of,* in these and similar phrases, denotes property or possession, making *of* the sign of the genitive or possessive case. These applications, however, all proceeded from the same primary sense. That which proceeds from or is produced by a person, is naturally the property or possession of that person, as the son *of* John; and this idea of property in the course of time would pass to things not thus produced, but still bearing a relation to another thing. Thus we say, the father *of* a son, as well as the son *of* a father. In both senses, other languages also use the same word, as in the French *de, de la,* and Italian *di, dell. Of* then has one primary sense, *from,* departing, issuing, proceeding *from* or *out of,* and a derivative sense denoting possession or property.

OFF, *a. auf.* Most distant; as the *off* horse in a team.

OFF, *adv. auf.* From, noting distance. The house is a mile *off.*

2. From, with the action of removing or separating; as, to take *off* the hat or cloke. So we say, to cut *off,* to pare *off,* to clip *off,* to peel *off,* to tear *off,* to march *off,* to fly *off.*

3. From, noting separation; as, the match is *off.*

4. From, noting departure, abatement, remission or a leaving. The fever goes *off;* the pain goes *off.*

5. In *painting,* it denotes projection or relief.

This comes *off* well and excellent. *Shak.*

6. From; away; not towards; as, to look *off;* opposed to *on* or *toward.*

7. On the opposite side of a question.

The questions no way touch upon puritanism, either *off* or on. *Sanderson.*

Off hand, without study or preparation. She plays a tune *off hand.* He speaks fluently *off hand.*

Off and on, at one time applying and engaged, then absent or remiss.

To be off, in colloquial language, to depart or to recede from an agreement or design.

To come off, to escape, or to fare in the event.

To get off, to alight; to come down.

2. To make escape.

To go off, to depart; to desert.

2. To take fire; to be discharged; as a gun.

Well off, ill off, badly off, having good or ill success.

OFF, *prep.* Not on; as, to be *off* one's legs. He was not *off* the bed the whole day.

2. Distant from; as about two miles *off* this town. [*Not now used.*] *Addison.*

OFF, as an exclamation, is a command to depart, either with or without contempt or abhorrence.

OF'FAL, *n.* [D. *afval; af* and *vallen,* to fall; G. *abfall;* Dan. *affald;* Sw. *affall; off* and *fall.*]

1. Waste meat; the parts of an animal butchered which are unfit for use or rejected. *Arbuthnot.*

2. Carrion; coarse meat. *Milton. Shak.*

3. Refuse; that which is thrown away as of no value, or fit only for beasts. *Dryden. Mortimer.*

4. Any thing of no value; rubbish. *Shak.*

OFFEND', *v. t.* [L. *offendo; ob* and *fendo, obs.* to strike, hit, meet, or thrust against. We use the simple verb in *fend,* to *fend off,* to *fence.*]

1. To attack; to assail. [*Not used.*] *Sidney.*

2. To displease; to make angry; to affront. It expresses rather less than *make angry,* and without any modifying word, it is nearly synonymous with *displease.* We are *offended* by rudeness, incivility and harsh language. Children *offend* their parents by disobedience, and parents *offend* their children by unreasonable austerity or restraint.

The emperor was grievously *offended* with them who had kept such negligent watch. *Knolles.*

A brother *offended* is harder to be won than a strong city. Prov. xviii.

3. To shock; to wound; as, to *offend* the conscience. *Law.*

4. To pain; to annoy; to injure; as, a strong light *offends* weak eyes.

5. To transgress; to violate; as, to *offend* the laws. But we generally use the intransitive verb in this sense, with *against;* to *offend against* the law.

6. To disturb, annoy, or cause to fall or stumble.

Great peace have they that love thy law, and nothing shall *offend* them. Ps. cxix.

7. To draw to evil, or hinder in obedience; to cause to sin or neglect duty.

If thy right eye *offend* thee, pluck it out—if thy right hand *offend* thee, cut it off. Matt. v.

OFFEND', *v. i.* To transgress the moral or divine law; to sin; to commit a crime.

Whoever shall keep the whole law, and yet *offend* in one point, is guilty of all. James ii.

In many things we *offend* all. James iii.

2. To cause dislike or anger.

I shall *offend,* either to detain or to give it. *Shak.*

But this phrase is really elliptical, some person being understood.

3. To be scandalized; to be stumbled.

If meat make my brother to *offend*— 1 Cor. viii.

To offend against, to act injuriously or unjustly.

Nor yet *against* Cesar have I *offended* any thing at all. Acts xxv.

2. To transgress; to violate; as, to *offend against* the laws of society, the laws of God, or the rules of civility or propriety.

We have *offended against* the Lord already. 2 Chron. xxviii.

OFFEND'ED, *pp.* Displeased.

OFFEND'ER, *n.* One that offends; one that violates any law, divine or human; a criminal; a trespasser; a transgressor; one that does an injury. The man who robs, steals, or commits an assault, is an *offender.*

OFFEND'ING, *ppr.* Displeasing; making angry; causing to stumble; committing sin.

OFFEND'RESS, *n.* A female that offends. *Shak.*

OFFENSE, *n. offens'.* [L. *offensus, offensa;* It. *offesa;* Sp. *ofensa;* Fr. *offence.*]

1. Displeasure; anger, or moderate anger. He gave them just cause of *offense.* He took *offense.*

2. Scandal; cause of stumbling. Christ is called a stone of stumbling and rock of *offense* to both the houses of Israel. Ps. viii.

3. Any transgression of law, divine or human; a crime; sin; act of wickedness or omission of duty.

Christ was delivered for our *offenses,* and raised again for our justification. Rom. iv.

4. An injury.

I have given my opinion against the authority of two great men, but I hope without *offense* to their memories. *Dryden.*

5. Attack; assault; as a weapon of *offense.* *Richardson.*
6. Impediment. Matt. xvi.

OFFENSEFUL, *a. offens'ful.* Giving displeasure; injurious. [*Not used.*] *Shak.*

OFFENSELESS, *a. offens'less.* Unoffending; innocent; inoffensive. *Milton.*

OFFENS'IVE, *a.* [Fr. *offensif;* It. *offensivo;* Sp. *ofensivo.*]

1. Causing displeasure or some degree of anger; displeasing. All sin is *offensive* to God. Rude behavior is *offensive* to men. Good breeding forbids us to use *offensive* words.
2. Disgusting; giving pain or unpleasant sensations; disagreeable; as an *offensive* taste or smell; an *offensive* sight. Discordant sounds are *offensive* to the ears.
3. Injurious.

   It is an excellent opener for the liver, but *offensive* to the stomach. *Bacon.*
4. Assailant; used in attack; opposed to *defensive;* as an *offensive* weapon or engine. *Wilkins.*
5. Assailant; invading; making the first attack; opposed to *defensive;* as an *offensive* war.

A *league offensive and defensive,* is one that requires both or all parties to make war together against a nation, and each party to defend the other in case of being attacked.

OFFENS'IVE, *n.* The part of attacking; as, to act on the *offensive.*

OFFENS'IVELY, *adv.* In a manner to give displeasure; as language *offensively* harsh or sarcastic.

2. Injuriously; mischievously. *Hooker.*
3. By way of invasion or first attack. The enemy was not in a condition to act *offensively.*
4. Unpleasantly to the senses.

OFFENS'IVENESS, *n.* The quality that offends or displeases; as the *offensiveness* of rude language or behavior.

2. Injuriousness; mischief.
3. Cause of disgust; the quality that gives pain to the senses, or unpleasant sensations; as the *offensiveness* of smell or taste.

OF'FER, *v. t.* [L. *offero; ob* and *fero,* to bring.]

1. Literally, to bring to or before; hence, to present for acceptance or rejection; to exhibit something that may be taken or received or not. He *offered* me a sum of money. He *offered* me his umbrella to defend me from the rain.

   The heathen women under the Mogul, *offer* themselves to the flames at the death of their husbands. *Collier.*
2. To present in words; to proffer; to make a proposal to.

   I *offer* thee three things. 2 Sam. xxiv.
3. To present, as an act of worship; to immolate; to sacrifice; often with *up.*

   Thou shalt *offer* every day a bullock as a sin-offering for atonement. Ex. xxix.

   The one lamb shalt thou *offer* in the morning. Ibm.

   A holy priesthood to *offer up* spiritual sacrifices. 1 Pet. 2.
4. To present in prayer or devotion.

   Offer to God thanksgiving. Ps. l.
5. To bid, as a price, reward or wages; as, to *offer* ten eagles for a ring; to *offer* a hundred dollars a year for a laborer; to *offer* a salary.
6. To present to the view or to the mind; as ideas which sense or reflection *offers* to the mind. *Locke.*

To offer violence, to assault; to attack or commence attack.

OF'FER, *v. i.* To present itself; to be at hand.

Th' occasion *offers* and the youth complies. *Dryden.*

2. To present verbally; to declare a willingness. He *offered* to accompany his brother.
3. To make an attempt.

   We came close to the shore and *offered* to land. *Bacon.*

   Formerly with *at.*

   I will not *offer at* that I cannot master. *Obs.* *Bacon.*

OF'FER, *n.* [Fr. *offre.*] A proposal to be accepted or rejected; presentation to choice. The prince made liberal *offers,* but they were rejected.

When *offers* are disdained, and love deny'd. *Pope.*

2. First advance.

   Force compels this *offer.* *Shak.*
3. The act of bidding a price, or the sum bid. By an *offer* we manifest a desire to buy. When the seller declines accepting, he manifests that he thinks the *offer* not sufficient.
4. Attempt; endeavor; essay.

   It is in the power of every one to make some essay, some *offer* and attempt. [*Nearly obsolete.*] *South.*

OF'FERABLE, *a.* That may be offered. *Mountague.*

OF'FERED, *pp.* Presented for acceptance or rejection; presented in worship or devotion; immolated; bid; presented to the eye or the mind.

OF'FERER, *n.* One that offers; one that sacrifices or dedicates in worship. *Chapman. Hooker.*

OF'FERING, *ppr.* Presenting; proposing; sacrificing; bidding; presenting to the eye or mind.

OF'FERING, *n.* That which is presented in divine service; an animal or a portion of bread or corn, or of gold and silver, or other valuable articles, presented to God as an atonement for sin, or as a return of thanks for his favors, or for other religious purpose; a sacrifice; an oblation. In the Mosaic economy, there were burnt-*offerings,* sin-*offerings,* peace-*offerings,* trespass-*offerings,* thank-*offerings,* wave-*offerings,* and wood-*offerings.* Pagan nations also present *offerings* to their deities. Christ by the *offering* of himself has superseded the use of all other *offerings,* having made atonement for all men.

When thou shalt make his soul an *offering* for sin, he shall see his seed— Is. liii.

OF'FERTORY, *n.* [Fr. *offertoire.*] The act of offering, or the thing offered. [*Little used.*] *Bacon. Fell.*

1. Offertory was properly an anthem chanted or a voluntary played on the organ during the offering and a part of the mass, in the Catholic church; but since the reformation it denotes certain sentences in the communion-office, read while the alms are collecting. *Todd. Cyc.*
2. Anciently, the linen on which the offering was laid. *Cyc.*

OF'FERTURE, *n.* Offer; proposal. [*Not used.*] *K. Charles.*

OF'FICE, *n.* [Fr. from L. *officium; ob* and *facio,* to make or do.]

1. A particular duty, charge or trust conferred by public authority and for a public purpose; an employment undertaken by commission or authority from government or those who administer it. Thus we speak of the *office* of secretary of state, of treasurer, of a judge, of a sheriff, of a justice of the peace, &c. *Offices* are civil, judicial, ministerial, executive, legislative, political, municipal, diplomatic, military, ecclesiastical, &c.
2. A duty, charge or trust of a sacred nature, conferred by God himself; as the *office* of priest, in the Old Testament; and that of the apostles, in the New Testament.

   Inasmuch as I am the apostle of the Gentiles, I magnify my *office.* Rom. xi.
3. Duty or employment of a private nature; as the *office* of a midwife. Ex. i.
4. That which is performed, intended or assigned to be done by a particular thing, or that which any thing is fitted to perform; answering to *duty* in intelligent beings. We enjoy health when the several organs of the body perform their respective *offices.*

   In this experiment, the several intervals of the teeth of the comb do the *office* of so many prisms. *Newton.*
5. Business; particular employment.

   Hesperus, whose *office* is to bring
   Twilight upon the earth. *Milton.*
6. Act of good or ill voluntarily tendered; usually in a good sense; as kind *offices;* *offices* of pity; pious *offices.*
7. Act of worship. *Shak.*
8. Formulary of devotion.

   The Lord's prayer, the ten commandments and the creed, is a very good *office* for children if they are not fitted for more regular *offices.* *Taylor.*
9. A house or apartment in which public officers and others transact business; as the register's *office;* a lawyer's *office.*
10. In *architecture,* an apartment appropriated for the necessary business or occasions of a palace or nobleman's house. The word is used also for a building pertaining to a farm. *Encyc. Cyc.*
11. In *the canon law,* a benefice which has no jurisdiction annexed to it. *Encyc.*
12. The person or persons entrusted with particular duties of a public nature.

    —This *office* [of quarter-master-general] not to have the disposal of public money, except small occasional sums. *Marshall.*

OF'FICE, *v. t.* To perform; to do; to discharge. [*Not used.*] *Shak.*

OF'FICER, *n.* A person commissioned or authorized to perform any public duty. *Officers* are civil, military or ecclesiastical. There are great *officers* of state, and subordinate *officers.* Military and naval *officers* of the same grade usually take rank according to the dates of their commissions. Non-commissioned *officers* are nominated by their captains, and appointed by the commanding *officers* of regiments.

OF'FICER, *v. t.* To furnish with officers; to appoint officers over.

Count Pulaski raised a legionary corps, which he *officered* principally with foreigners. *Marshall.*

OF'FICERED, *pp.* Furnished with officers. *Addison.*

OFFI''CIAL, *a.* [Fr. *officiel; from office.*] Pertaining to an office or public trust. The secretary is engaged in *official* duties.

2. Derived from the proper office or officer, or from the proper authority; made or communicated by virtue of authority; as an *official* statement or report. We have *official* intelligence of the battle.

3. Conducive by virtue of appropriate powers.

The stomach and other parts *official* to nutrition. [*Unusual.*] *Brown.*

OFFI''CIAL, *n.* An eclesiastical judge appointed by a bishop, chapter, archdeacon, &c., with charge of the spiritual jurisdiction. *Blackstone.*

OFFI''CIALLY, *adv.* By the proper officer; by virtue of the proper authority; in pursuance of the special powers vested; as accounts or reports *officially* verified or rendered; letters *officially* communicated; persons *officially* notified.

OFFI''CIALTY, *n.* The charge or office of an official. *Ayliffe.*

OFFI''CIATE, *v. i.* To act as an officer in his office, to transact the appropriate business of an office or public trust. At this court the chief justice *officiated.*

The bishops and priests *officiate* at the altar. *Stillingfleet.*

2. To perform the appropriate official duties of another.

OFFI''CIATE, *v. t.* To give in consequence of office.

The stars *officiate* light. [*Improper.*] *Milton.*

OFFI''CIATING, *ppr.* Performing the appropriate duties of an office; performing the office of another.

OFFIC'INAL, *a.* [Fr.; from L. *officina*, a shop.]

Used in a shop or belonging to it. *Officinal* drugs, medicines and simples are such as are required to be constantly kept in the shops of apothecaries. *Encyc.*

OFFI''CIOUS, *a.* [L. *officiosus.*] Kind; obliging; doing kind offices.

Yet not to earth are those bright luminaries
Officious. *Milton.*

2. Excessively forward in kindness; importunately interposing services.

You are too *officious*
In her behalf that scorns your services. *Shak.*

3. Busy; intermeddling in affairs in which one has no concern.

OFFI''CIOUSLY, *adv.* Kindly; with solicitous care.

Let thy goats *officiously* be nurs'd. *Dryden.*

2. With importunate or excessive forwardness.

Flattering crowds *officiously* appear,
To give themselves, not you, a happy year. *Dryden.*

3. In a busy meddling manner.

OFFI''CIOUSNESS, *n.* Eagerness to serve; usually, an excess of zeal to serve others, or improper forwardness, interposing in affairs without being desired, or with a disposition to meddle with the concerns of others.

2. Service. [*Little used.*] *Brown.*

OFF'ING, *n.* [from *off.*] That part of the sea which is at a good distance from the shore, or at a competent distance, where there is deep water and no need of a pilot. We saw a ship in the *offing.* *Mar. Dict. Encyc.*

OFF'SCOURING, *n.* [*off* and *scour.*] That which is scoured off; hence, refuse; rejected matter; that which is vile or despised. Lam. iii. 1 Cor. iv.

OFF'SET, *n.* [*off* and *set.*] A shoot; a sprout from the roots of a plant. *Locke. Ray.*

2. In *surveying*, a perpendicular let fall from the stationary lines to the hedge, fence or extremity of an inclosure.

3. In *accounts*, a sum, account or value *set off* against another sum or account, as an equivalent. *O. Wolcott.*

[This is also written *set-off.*]

OFF'SET, *v. t.* To set one account against another; to make the account of one party pay the demand of another. *Judge Sewall.*

OFF'SPRING, *n.* [*off* and *spring.*] A child or children; a descendant or descendants, however remote from the stock. Acts xvii. Rev. xxii.

2. Propagation; generation. *Hooker.*

3. Production of any kind. *Denham.*

OFFUSCATE, OFFUSCATION. [See *Obfuscate, Obfuscation.*]

OFF'WARD, *adv.* [*off* and *ward.*] Leaning off, as a ship on shore.

OFT, *adv.* [Sax. *oft;* Sw. *ofta;* Dan. *ofte.*] Often; frequently; not rarely. It was formerly used in prose and may be so used still; but is more generally used in poetry.

Oft she rejects, but never once offends. *Pope.*

OFTEN, *adv. of'n.* comp. *oftener;* superl. *oftenest.* [Sax. *oft;* Goth. *ufta.*] Frequently; many times; not seldom. *Addison.*

OFTEN, *a. of'n.* Frequent. [*Improper.*]

OFTENNESS, *n. of'nness.* Frequency. [*Not used.*] *Hooker.*

OFTENTIMES, *adv. of'ntimes.* [*often* and *times.*] Frequently; often; many times. *Hooker. Atterbury.*

OFT'TIMES, *adv.* [*oft* and *times.*] Frequently; often. *Milton.*

OG. [See *Ogee.*]

OGDOAS'TICH, *n.* [Gr. ογδοος, eighth, and ςιχος, a verse.] A poem of eight lines. [*Little used.*] *Selden.*

OGEE', *n.* [Fr. *ogive, augive.*] In *architecture*, a molding consisting of two members, the one concave, the other convex, or of a round and a hollow somewhat like an S. *Encyc.*

2. In *gunnery*, an ornamental molding in the shape of an S, used on guns, mortars and howitzers. *Cyc.*

OGGANI''TION, *n.* [L. *obgannio, ogganio*, to growl.]

The murmuring of a dog; a grumbling or snarling. [*Not used.*] *Mountagu.*

O'GHAM, *n.* A particular kind of stenography or writing in cipher practiced by the Irish. *Astle. Encyc.*

OGIVE, *n. o'jiv.* In *architecture*, an arch or branch of the Gothic vault, which passing diagonally from one angle to another forms a cross with the other arches. The middle where the ogives cross each other, is called the key. The members or moldings of the ogives are called nerves, branches or reins, and the arches which separate the ogives, double arches. *Encyc.*

O'GLE, *v. t.* [from D. *oog*, the eye, Sax. *eag*, L. *oculus.* See *Eye.*]

To view with side glances, as in fondness or with design to attract notice.

And *ogling* all their audience, then they speak. *Dryden.*

O'GLE, *n.* A side glance or look. *Addison.*

O'GLER, *n.* One that ogles. *Addison.*

O'GLING, *ppr.* Viewing with side glances.

O'GLING, *n.* The act of viewing with side glances.

OGLIO, now written *olio*, which see.

O'GRE, } *n.* [Fr. *ogre.*] An imaginary
O'GRESS, } monster of the East. *Ar. Nights.*

O'GRESS, *n.* In *heraldry*, a cannon ball of a black color. *Ashmole.*

OH, *exclam.* denoting surprise, pain, sorrow or anxiety.

OIL, *n.* [Sax. *œl.* It seems to be named from its inflammability, for *œlan*, is to kindle, and to oil; hence *anœlan*, to *anneal; œled*, fire; Dan. *ild*, whence the name of *Hildebrand*, Dan. *Ildebrand*, fire-brand; D. *oly;* G. *oel;* Sw. *olja;* Dan. *olie;* Fr. *huile;* It. *olio;* L. *oleum;* Gr. ελαιον; W. *olew;* Ir. *ola;* Arm. Sp. Port. *oleo.*]

An unctuous substance expressed or drawn from several animal and vegetable substances. The distinctive characters of oil are inflammability, fluidity, and insolubility in water. Oils are fixed or fat, and volatile or essential. They have a smooth feel, and most of them have little taste or smell. Animal oil is found in all animal substances. Vegetable oils are produced by expression, infusion or distillation. *Encyc. Nicholson.*

OIL, *v. t.* To smear or rub over with oil; to lubricate with oil; to anoint with oil. *Wotton. Swift.*

OIL'-BAG, *n.* A bag, cyst or gland in animals containing oil.

OIL'-COLOR, *n.* A color made by grinding a coloring substance in oil. *Boyle.*

OIL'ED, *pp.* Smeared or anointed with oil. *Huloet.*

OIL'ER, *n.* One who deals in oils and pickles.

OIL'-GAS, *n.* Inflammable gas procured from oil, and used for lighting streets and apartments in buildings.

OIL'INESS, *n.* The quality of being oily; unctuousness; greasiness; a quality approaching that of oil. *Bacon. Arbuthnot.*

OIL'ING, *ppr.* Smearing or anointing with oil.

OIL'MAN, *n.* One who deals in oils and pickles. *Johnson.*

OIL'-NUT, *n.* The butternut of N. America. *Carver.*

OIL'-NUT, } *n.* A plant, a species of Ri-
OIL'-TREE, } cinus, the palma Christi, or castor, from which is procured castor oil. *Fam. of Plants. Encyc.*

OIL'-SHOP, *n.* A shop where oils and pickles are sold.

OIL'Y, *a.* Consisting of oil; containing oil; having the qualities of oil; as *oily* matter or substance. *Bacon.*

2. Resembling oil; as an *oily* appearance.

3. Fatty; greasy. *Shak.*

OILY-GRAIN, *n.* A plant. *Miller.*

OILY-PALM, *n.* A tree. *Miller.*

OINT, *v. t.* [Fr. *oindre, oint;* Sp. Port. *untar.* The French *oindre* is formed from the L. *ungo,* like *joindre* from *jungo.*]

To anoint; to smear with an unctuous substance.

They *oint* their naked limbs with mother'd oil. *Dryden.*

OINT'ED, *pp.* Anointed; smeared with an oily or greasy matter.

OINT'ING, *ppr.* Anointing.

OINT'MENT, *n.* Unguent; any soft, unctuous substance or compound, used for smearing, particularly the body or a diseased part.

OIS'ANITE, *n.* Pyramidical ore of titanium. *Ure.*

OKE, *n.* An Egyptian and Turkish weight, equal to about two pounds and three quarters, English avoirdupois weight. *Eton.*

OKER. [See *Ocher.*]

ŌLD, *a.* [Sax. *eald;* G. *alt;* D. *oud;* Dan. *ælde,* old age.]

1. Advanced far in years or life; having lived beyond the middle period, or rather towards the end of life, or towards the end of the ordinary term of living; applied to animals or plants; as an *old* man; an *old* age; an *old* camel or horse; an *old* tree. This adjective is placed after the noun that designates the time lived.

Abraham was seventy five years *old* when he departed from Haran. Gen. xii.

2. Having been long made or used; decayed by time; as an *old* garment; an *old* house.

3. Being of long continuance; begun long ago; as an *old* acquaintance.

4. Having been long made; not new or fresh; as *old* wine.

5. Being of a former year's growth; not of the last crop; as *old* wheat; *old* hay.

6. Ancient; that existed in former ages; as the *old* inhabitants of Britain; the *old* Romans.

7. Of any duration whatever; as a year *old;* seven years *old.* How *old* art thou?

8. Subsisting before something else. He built a new house on the site of the *old* one. The *old* law is repealed by the new.

9. Long practiced. He is grown *old* in vice. He is an *old* offender.

10. That has been long cultivated; as *old* land; an *old* farm; opposed to *new* land, land lately cleared and cultivated. *America.*

11. More than enough; great.

If a man were porter of hellgate, he should have *old* turning of the key. *Shak.*

12. In vulgar language, crafty; cunning.

Of old, long ago; from ancient times; as in days *of old.* *Dryden.*

We apply *old* chiefly to things subject to decay. We never say, the *old* sun, or an *old* mountain.

ŌLDEN, *a.* Old; ancient. [*Used in poetry.*] *Shak.*

ŌLD-FASH'IONED, *a.* Formed according to obsolete fashion or custom; as an *old-fashioned* dress.

Old-fashioned men of wit. *Addison.*

ŌLDNESS, *n.* Old age; an advanced state of life or existence; as the *oldness* of a man, of an elephant or a tree.

2. The state of being old, or of a long continuance; as the *oldness* of a building or a garment.

3. Antiquity; as the *oldness* of monuments.

ŌLD-WIFE, *n.* A contemptuous name for an old prating woman. 1 Tim. iv.

2. A fish of the genus Labrus, and another of the genus Balistes. *Encyc.*

OLEAǴINOUS, *a.* [L. *oleaginus,* from *oleum,* oil.] Having the qualities of oil; oily; unctuous. *Arbuthnot.*

OLEAǴINOUSNESS, *n.* Oiliness. *Boyle.*

OLEAN'DER, *n.* A plant of the genus Nerium, the rose-bay or South sea rose; a beautiful shrub with flowers in clusters, of a fine purple color, but of an indifferent smell. The plant, especially the bark of the roots, is said to be poisonous. *Encyc.*

OLEAS'TER, *n.* [L. from *olea,* the olive tree.]

A plant of the genus Elæagnus; the wild olive. *Miller.*

O'LEATE, *n.* A compound of oleic acid with a salifiable base. *Chevreul.*

OLEF'IANT, *a.* [L. *oleo, olfacio.*] Olefiant gas is a compound of one prime of carbon and one of hydrogen, called by Ure carbureted hydrogen, to distinguish it from the gas resulting from one prime of carbon and two of hydrogen, which he calls subcarbureted hydrogen.

Olefiant gas, is so called from its property of forming with chlorin a compound resembling oil.

O'LEIC, *a.* [from *oil.*] The oleic acid is obtained from a soap made by digesting hog's lard in potash lye. *Chevreul.*

OLEOSAC'CHARUM, *n.* A mixture of oil and sugar. *Ure.*

O'LEOSE, } *a.* [L. *oleosus.*] Oily. [*Little*
O'LEOUS, } *used.*] *Ray.*

OLERA'CEOUS, *a.* [L. *oleraceus,* from *olus, oleris,* pot-herbs.]

Pertaining to pot-herbs; of the nature or qualities of herbs for cookery. *Lee. Brown.*

OLFACT', *v. t.* [L. *olfacto, olfacio; oleo,* to smell, and *facio,* to make.]

To smell; used in burlesque, but not otherwise authorized. *Hudibras.*

OLFACT'ORY, *a.* [L. *olfacio,* supra.] Pertaining to smelling; having the sense of smelling; as *olfactory* nerves. *Locke.*

OL'IBAN, } *n.* [Ar. لبان lubanon;
OLIBA'NUM, } with the adjective *al, the,* corrupted into *ol.* The word signifies then frankincense, and it is so named from its whiteness.]

A gum-resin consisting of tears or drops, of a yellow transparent color and disagreeable smell. It is brought from Turkey and the East Indies. It is not, as Linne supposed, produced by the Juniperus Lycia, but from a different tree growing in Arabia and Hindoostan. See Asiatic Researches, 9. 377. In Arabia, *luban* is applied to benzoin, which is generally used for incense, and oliban is called condur, whence Gr. χονδρος. In medicine, it is used in fumigations as a resolvent. *Fourcroy. Encyc.*

Thompson says olibanum is produced by different trees and in different countries.

OL'ID, } *a.* [L. *olidus,* from *oleo,* to
OL'IDOUS, } smell.] Fetid; having a strong disagreeable smell. [*Little used.*] *Boyle. Brown.*

OLIGARCH'AL, } *a.* [See *Oligarchy.*]
OLIGARCH'ICAL, } Pertaining to oligarchy, or government by a few. *Burke.*

OL'IGARCHY, *n.* [Gr. ολιγαρχια; ολιγος, few, and αρχη, rule.]

A form of government in which the supreme power is placed in a few hands; a species of aristocracy. *Swift.*

OL'IǴIST, } *a.* [Gr. ολιγιςος, least.] Oli-
OLIǴIST'IC, } gist iron, so called, is a crystalized tritoxyd of iron.

O'LIO, *n.* [It. from Sp. *olla;* Port. *olha,* a dish of meat boiled or stewed; L. *olla,* a pot.]

1. A mixture; a medley. *Dryden.*

2. A miscellany; a collection of various pieces; *applied to musical collections.*

OL'ITORY, *a.* [L. *olitor,* a gardener, from *olus,* pot-herbs.]

Belonging to a kitchen garden; as *olitory* seeds. *Evelyn.*

It may perhaps be used as a noun.

OLIVA'CEOUS, *a.* [from L. *oliva,* olive.] Of the color of the olive. *Pennant.*

OLIVAS'TER, *n.* [Fr. *olivâtre,* from L. *oliva,* olive.] Of the color of the olive; tawny. *Bacon.*

OL'IVE, *n.* [L. *oliva,* from *olea,* an olive tree; Fr. *olive;* Gr. ελαια. See *Oil.*]

A plant or tree of the genus Olea. The common olive tree grows in warm climates and rises to the highth of twenty or thirty feet, having an upright stem with numerous branches. This tree is much cultivated in the south of Europe for its fruit, from which is expressed the olive oil, and which is used also for pickles. *Encyc.*

OL'IVED, *a.* Decorated with olive trees. *Warton.*

OL'IVENITE, *n.* An ore of copper. *Ure.*

OL'IVE-YARD, *n.* An inclosure or piece of ground in which olives are cultivated. Ex. xxiii.

OL'IVIN, } *n.* [from *olive.*] A subspecies
OL'IVINE, } of prismatic chrysolite of a brownish green, often inclining to a yellowish or grayish green, usually found in roundish grains in other stones; sometimes in large masses, but not crystalized. It is a constituent of many lavas and frequently occurs in basaltic rocks. *Kirwan. Ure.*

OLYM'PIAD, *n.* [L. *Olympias;* Gr. Ολυμπιας, from Ολυμπος, Olympus, a mountain of Macedonia.]

A period of four years reckoned from one celebration of the Olympic games to another, and constituting an important epoch in history and chronology. The first Olympiad commenced 775 years before the birth of Christ, and 22 years before the foundation of Rome. The computation by Olympiads ceased at the three hundred and sixty fourth Olympiad, in the year 440 of the christian era. *Encyc.*

OLYM'PEAN, *a.* Pertaining to Olympus; or to Olympia, a town in Greece.

Olympic games, or *Olympics*, solemn games among the ancient Greeks, dedicated to Olympian Jupiter, and celebrated once in four years at Olympia. [See *Olympiad*.]

OM'BER, } *n.* [Fr. from Sp. *hombre*, man,
OM'BRE, } L. *homo*.]
A game at cards, borrowed from the Spaniards, usually played by three persons, though sometimes by two or five. *Encyc.*

OMBROM'ETER, *n.* [Gr. ομβρος, rain, and μετρον, measure.]
A machine or instrument to measure the quantity of rain that falls. *Encyc.*

OME'GA, *n.* [Gr. great O.] The name of the last letter of the Greek alphabet, as Alpha, A, is the first. Hence in Scripture, *Alpha and Omega* denotes the first and the last, the beginning and the ending. Rev.

OM'ELET, *n.* [Fr. *omelette*.] A kind of pancake or fritter made with eggs and other ingredients. *Encyc.*

O'MEN, *n.* [L. *omen*; but according to Varro, it was originally *osmen*, that which is uttered by the mouth, denoting wish or vow, and with him agree Festus and Nonius, says Vossius. Another author derives the word from the Heb. ענן, an augur. Cicero assigns to the word the same origin as Varro. "Voces hominum, quæ vocent omina." But the word came afterwards to denote things rather than words.]
A sign or indication of some future event; a prognostic. Superstition and ignorance multiply *omens*; philosophy and truth reject all *omens*, except such as may be called *causes* of the events. Without a miracle, how can one event be the *omen* of another with which it has no connection?

O'MENED, *a.* Containing an omen or prognostic. *Pope.*

OMENT'UM, *n.* [L.] In *anatomy*, the caul or epiploon; a membranaceous covering of the bowels, being placed under the peritoneum and immediately above the intestines. *Encyc.*

O'MER, *n.* [Heb.] A Hebrew measure containing ten baths, or seventy five gallons and five pints of liquids, and eight bushels of things dry. It was the largest measure used by the Jews. It is written also *homer* and *chomer*. This word is used by the prophets, but the corresponding measure is called by the historical writers *corus*. *Encyc.*

OM'INATE, *v. t.* [L. *ominor*, from *omen*.] To presage; to foreshow; to foretoken. [*Little used.*] *Decay of Piety.*

OM'INATE, *v. i.* To foretoken.

OMINA'TION, *n.* A foreboding; a presaging; prognostic. [*Little used.*] *Brown.*

OM'INOUS, *a.* [L. *ominosus*.] Foreboding or presaging evil; indicating a future evil event; inauspicious.

In the heathen worship of God, a sacrifice without a heart was accounted *ominous*. *South.*

2. Foreshowing or exhibiting signs of good.

Though he had a good *ominous* name to have made peace, nothing followed. *Bacon.*

OM'INOUSLY, *adv.* With good or bad omens. *Fotherby.*

OM'INOUSNESS, *n.* The quality of being ominous. *Burnet.*

OMIS'SIBLE, *a.* [L. *omissus*. See *Omit*.] That may be omitted. *Parkhurst.*

OMIS'SION, *n.* [Fr. from L. *omissio*, from *omitto*, *omissus*.]
1. Neglect or failure to do something which a person had power to do, or which duty required to be done. *Omission* may be innocent or criminal; *innocent*, when no duty demands performance, but *criminal* when duty is neglected.

The most natural division of all offenses, is into those of *omission* and those of *commission*. *Addison.*

2. A leaving out; neglect or failure to insert or mention; as the *omission* of a word or clause.

OMIS'SIVE, *a.* Leaving out. *Stackhouse.*

OMIT', *v. t.* [L. *omitto*; *ob* and *mitto*, to send.]
1. To leave, pass by or neglect; to fail or forbear to do or to use; as, to *omit* an opportunity of writing a letter. To *omit* known duty is criminal.
2. To leave out; not to insert or mention; as, to *omit* an important word in a deed; to *omit* invidious comparisons; to *omit* a passage in reading or transcribing.

OMIT'TANCE, *n.* Forbearance; neglect. [*Not used.*] *Shak.*

OMIT'TED, *pp.* Neglected; passed by; left out.

OMIT'TING, *ppr.* Neglecting or failing to do or use; passing by; leaving out.

OMNIFA'RIOUS, *a.* [Low L. *omnifarius*.] Of all varieties, forms or kinds. *Bentley.*

OMNIF'EROUS, *a.* [L. *omnifer*; *omnis*, all, and *fero*, to bear.] All-bearing; producing all kinds. *Dict.*

OMNIF'IC, *a.* [L. *omnis*, all, and *facio*, to make.] All-creating.

Thou deep, peace!
Said then th' *omnific* word, your discord end. *Milton.*

OM'NIFORM, *a.* [L. *omnis*, all, and *forma*, form.] Having every form or shape. *Dict.*

OMNIFORM'ITY, *n.* The quality of having every form. *More.*

OMNIG'ENOUS, *a.* [L. *omnigenus*; *omnis*, all, every, and *genus*, kind.]
Consisting of all kinds. *Dict.*

OMNIPAR'ITY, *n.* [L. *omnis*, all, and *par*, equal.] General equality. *White.*

OMNIPERCIP'IENCE, *n.* [L. *omnis*, and *percipiens*, perceiving.] Perception of every thing. *More.*

OMNIPERCIP'IENT, *a.* Perceiving every thing. *More.*

OMNIP'OTENCE, } *n.* [L. *omnipotens*;
OMNIP'OTENCY, } *omnis*, all, and *potens*, powerful.]
Almighty power; unlimited or infinite power; a word in strictness applicable only to God. Hence it is sometimes used for God. The works of creation demonstrate the *omnipotence* of God.

Will *Omnipotence* neglect to save
The suffering virtue of the wise and brave? *Pope.*

2. Unlimited power over particular things; as the *omnipotence* of love.

OMNIP'OTENT, *a.* [supra.] Almighty; possessing unlimited power; all powerful. The being that can create worlds must be *omnipotent*.
2. Having unlimited power of a particular kind; as *omnipotent* love. *Shak.*

OMNIP'OTENTLY, *adv.* With almighty power. *Young.*

OMNIPRES'ENCE, *n.* *s* as *z*. [L. *omnis*, and *presens*, present.]
Presence in every place at the same time; unbounded or universal presence; ubiquity. *Omnipresence* is an attribute peculiar to God.

OMNIPRES'ENT, *a.* Present in all places at the same time; ubiquitary; as the *omnipresent* Jehovah.

OMNIPRESEN'TIAL, *a.* Implying universal presence. *South.*

OMNIS'CIENCE, } *n.* [L. *omnis*, all, and
OMNIS'CIENCY, } *scientia*, knowledge.]
The quality of knowing all things at once; universal knowledge; knowledge unbounded or infinite. *Omniscience* is an attribute peculiar to God.

OMNIS'CIENT, *a.* Having universal knowledge or knowledge of all things; infinitely knowing; all-seeing; as the *omniscient* God.

OMNIS'CIOUS, *a.* [L. *omnis*, all, and *scio*, to know.] All-knowing. [*Not used.*] *Hakewill.*

OM'NIUM, *n.* [L. *omnis*, all.] The aggregate of certain portions of different stocks in the public funds; *a word in use among dealers in the English stocks.*

Omnium denotes *all* the particulars included in the contract between government and the public for a loan. *Cyc.*

OMNIV'OROUS, *a.* [L. *omnivorus*; *omnis*, all, and *voro*, to eat.]
All-devouring; eating every thing indiscriminately. *Burke.*

OM'OPLATE, *n.* [Gr. ωμος, shoulder, and πλατυς, broad.] The shoulder blade or scapula.

OM'PHACINE, *a.* [Gr. ομφακινος, from ομφαξ, unripe fruit.]
Pertaining to or expressed from unripe fruit. *Omphacine* oil is a viscous brown juice extracted from green olives. With this the wrestlers in the ancient gymnastic exercises used to anoint their bodies. *Encyc.*

OM'PHACITE, *n.* A mineral of a pale leek green color, massive or disseminated, and in narrow radiated concretions. *Ure.*

OM'PHALIC, *n.* [Gr. ομφαλος, the navel.] Pertaining to the navel. *Asiat. Res.*

OMPHAL'OCELE, *n.* [Gr. ομφαλος, navel, and κηλη, tumor.] A rupture at the navel. *Coxe.*

OM'PHALOPTER, } *n.* [Gr. ομφαλος, navel,
OMPHALOP'TIC, } and οπτικος, optic.]
An optical glass that is convex on both sides; commonly called a convex lens. *Dict.*

OMPHALOT'OMY, *n.* [Gr. ομφαλος, the navel, and τεμνω, to cut.]
The operation of dividing the navel string.

O'MY, *a.* Mellow; as land. [*Not in use.*] *Ray.*

ON, *prep.* [G. *an*; D. *aan*; Goth. *ana*; Gr. ανω; L. *in*; Gr. εν. The Sax. *in* is our *in*, and *un* is a negative; but probably all these words are radically the same. The primary sense of the verb from which these words must be derived, is to pass, to approach, to come to or to meet. Hence they denote nearness, closeness or contiguity, and from meeting the Latin *in* and the English *un* have their power of negation or opposing.]
1. Being in contact with the surface or upper part of a thing and supported by it; placed or lying in contact with the surface; as, my book is *on* the table; the table

stands *on* the floor; the house rests *on* its foundation; we lie *on* a bed, or stand *on* the earth.

2. Coming or falling to the surface of any thing; as, rain falls *on* the earth.

Whosoever shall fall *on* this stone, shall be broken. Matt. xxi.

3. Performing or acting by contact with the surface, upper part or outside of any thing; as, to play *on* a harp, a violin, or a drum.

4. Noting addition; as heaps *on* heaps; mischief *on* mischief; loss *on* loss.

5. At or near. When we say, a vessel is *on* shore, we mean that she is aground; but when we say, a fleet or a ship is *on* the American coast, or an isle is situated *on* the coast of England, we mean only that it is near the coast. So we say, *on* each side stands an armed man, that is, at or near each side.

So we say, Philadelphia is situated *on* the Delaware; Middlebury is *on* the Otter Creek; Guilford stands *on* the Sound; that is, near the river or Sound, instead of *on* the bank, side or shore.

6. It denotes resting for support; as, to depend *on*, to rely *on*; hence, the ground of any thing; as, he will covenant *on* certain considerations or conditions; the considerations being the support of the covenant.

7. At or in the time of; as, *on* the sabbath we abstain from labor. We usually say, *at* the hour, *on* or *in* the day, *in* or *on* the week, month or year.

8. At the time of, with some reference to cause or motive. *On* public occasions, the officers appear in full dress or uniform.

9. It is put before the object of some passion, with the sense of *towards* or *for*. Have pity or compassion *on* him.

10. At the peril of, or for the safety of.

Hence, *on* thy life. *Dryden.*

11. Denoting a pledge or engagement, or put before the thing pledged. He affirmed or promised *on* his word, or *on* his honor.

12. Noting imprecation or invocation, or coming to, falling or resting on. *On* us be all the blame.

His blood be *on* us, and *on* our children. Matt. xxvii.

13. In consequence of, or immediately after. *On* the ratification of the treaty, the armies were disbanded.

14. Noting part, distinction or opposition; as *on* one side and *on* the other. *On* our part, expect punctuality.

On the way, on the road, denote proceeding, traveling, journeying, or making progress.

On the alert, in a state of vigilance or activity.

On high, in an elevated place; sublimely.

On fire, in a state of burning or inflammation, and metaphorically, in a rage or passion.

On a sudden, suddenly.

On the wing, in flight; flying; metaphorically, departing.

On it, on't, is used for *of it*. I heard nothing *on't*. The gamester has a poor trade *on't*. [*This use is now vulgar.*]

Upon is used in the same sense with *on*, often with elegance, and frequently without necessity or advantage.

ON, *adv.* Forward, in progression; as, move *on*; go *on*.

2. Forward, in succession. From father to son, from the son to the grandson, and so *on*.

3. In continuance; without interruption or ceasing; as, sleep *on*, take your ease; say *on*; sing *on*; write *on*.

4. Adhering; not off; as in the phrase, "he is neither *on* nor *off*," that is, he is not steady; he is irresolute.

5. Attached to the body; as, his clothes are not *on*.

To put on, to attach to the body, as clothes or arms.

On, when it expresses contact with the surface of a thing, is opposed to *under, off*, or *within*, and when it expresses contact with the side of a thing, is opposed to *off*.

On is sometimes used as an exclamation, or rather as a command to move or proceed, some verb being understood; as, cheerly *on*, courageous friends; that is, *go on, move on*.

ON'AGER, *n.* [L.] The wild ass.

O'NANISM, *n.* [from *Onan*, in Scripture.] The crime of self-pollution.

ONCE, *adv. wuns.* [from *one*. So D. *eens*, from *een*, and G. *einst*, from *ein*, one.]

1. One time.

Trees that bear mast are fruitful but *once* in two years. *Bacon.*

2. One time, though no more. The mind *once* tainted with vice, is prone to grow worse and worse.

3. At one former time; formerly.

My soul had *once* some foolish fondness for thee,
But hence 'tis gone. *Addison.*

4. At the same point of time; not gradually.

At *once* the winds arise,
The thunders roll. *Dryden.*

At once, at the same time; as, they all moved *at once*; hence, when it refers to two or more, the sense is *together, as one*.

This hath all its force *at once*, on the first impression. *Atterbury.*

Once is used as a noun, when preceded by *this* or *that*; as *this once, that once*.

ONCE, *n. ons.* [Fr.] A quadruped of the genus Felis, less than the panther, of a whitish gray color. It is found in Africa and Asia, is easily tamed and is employed like a dog in hunting. *Encyc.*

ONE, *a. wun.* [Sax. *an, æn*; D. *een*; G. *ein*; Sw. *en*; Dan. *en* or *een*; Ice. *einn*; W. *un* or *yn*; L. *unus*; Gr. εν; It. Sp. *uno*; Port. *hum*; Fr. *un*; Arm. *unan*; Ir. *an, aon*.]

1. Single in number; individual; as *one* man; *one* book. There is *one* sun only in our system of planets.

2. Indefinitely, some or any. You will *one* day repent of your folly. But in this phrase, *one day* is equivalent to *some future time*.

3. It follows *any*.

When *any one* heareth the word of the kingdom. Matt. xiii.

4. Different; diverse; opposed to *another*. It is *one* thing to promise, and *another* to fulfill.

5. It is used with *another*, to denote mutuality or reciprocation. Be kind and assist *one another*.

6. It is used with *another*, to denote average or mean proportion. The coins *one* with *another*, weigh seven penny weight each.

7. One of two; opposed to *other*.

Ask from *one* side of heaven to the *other*. Deut. iv.

8. Single by union; undivided; the same.

The church is therefore *one*, though the members may be many. *Pearson.*

9. Single in kind; the same.

One plague was on you all and on your lords. 1 Sam. iv.

One day, on a certain or particular day, referring to time past.

One day when Phœbe fair
With all her band was following the chase. *Spenser.*

2. Referring to future time; at a future time, indefinitely. [See *One*, No. 2.]

At one, in union; in agreement or concord.

The king resolved to keep Ferdinand and Philip *at one* with themselves. *Bacon.*

In one, in union; in one united body.

One, like many other adjectives, is used without a noun, and is to be considered as a substitute for some noun understood. Let the men depart *one* by *one*; count them *one* by *one*; every *one* has his peculiar habits; we learn of *one* another, that is, we learn, *one* of us learns of another.

In this use, as a substitute, *one* may be plural; as the great *ones* of the earth; they came with their little *ones*.

It also denotes union, a united body.

Ye are all *one* in Christ Jesus. Gal. iii.

One o'clock, one hour of the clock, that is, as signified or represented by the clock.

One is used indefinitely for any person; as, *one* sees; *one* knows; after the French manner, *on voit*. Our ancestors used *man* in this manner; *man* sees; *man* knows; "*man* brohte," *man* brought, that is, they brought. *Saxon.*

This word we have received from the Latin through the Italian and French. The same word from our Saxon ancestors we write *an*.

ONE-BERRY, *n. wun'-berry.* A plant of the genus Paris; true love. *Fam. of Plants.*

ONE-EYED, *a. wun'-eyed.* Having one eye only. *Dryden.*

ONEIROCRIT'IC, *n.* [Gr. ονειροκριτικος; ονειρον, a dream, and κριτικος, discerning.] An interpreter of dreams; one who judges what is signified by dreams. *Warburton. Addison.*

ONEIROCRIT'IC, *n.* The art of interpreting dreams. *Warburton.*

ONEIROCRIT'IC, ONEIROCRIT'ICAL, ONIROCRIT'IC, } *a.* Having the power of interpreting dreams, or pretending to judge of future events signified by dreams.

My *oneirocritical* correspondent. *Addison.*

ONEIROM'ANCY, *n.* [Gr. ονειρον, a dream, and μαντεια, divination.] Divination by dreams. *Spenser.*

ONEMENT, *n. wun'ment.* State of being one. [*Not in use.*] *Bp. Hall.*

ONENESS, *n. wun'ness.* [from *one*.] Singleness in number; individuality; unity; the quality of being one.

Our God is one, or rather very *oneness*. *Hooker.*

ON'ERARY, *a.* [L. *onerarius*, from *onus*, a load; *onero*, to load.]

Fitted or intended for the carriage of burdens; comprising a burden.

ON'ERATE, *v. t.* [L. *onero*, from *onus*, a burden.] To load; to burden.

ONERA'TION, *n.* The act of loading.

ON'EROUS, *a.* [L. *onerosus*, from *onus*, a load.] Burdensome; oppressive. *Ayliffe. Burton.*

2. In *Scots law*, being for the advantage of both parties; as an *onerous* contract; opposed to *gratuitous.*

ONION, *n. un'yun.* [Fr. *ognon;* Arm. *ouignoun;* Ir. *uinnium.* In W. *ceninen* is a leek.]

A plant of the genus Allium; and particularly, its bulbous root, much used as an article of food.

ONKOT'OMY, *n.* [Gr. ογκος, tumor, and τεμνω, to cut.]

In *surgery*, the opening of a tumor or abscess. *Encyc.*

ONLY, *a.* [Sax. *ænlic*, one-like.] Single; one alone; as, John was the *only* man present.

2. This and no other. This is an *only* child.

3. This above all others. He is the *only* man for music. *Johnson.*

ONLY, *adv.* Singly; merely; barely; in one manner or for one purpose alone.

> I purpose my thoughts *only* as conjectures. *Burnet.*

> And to be loved himself, needs *only* to be known. *Dryden.*

2. This and no other wise.

> Every imagination of the thoughts of his heart was *only* evil continually. Gen. vi.

3. Singly; without more; as *only*-begotten.

ON'OMANCY, *n.* [Gr. ονομα, name, and μαντεια, divination.] Divination by the letters of a name.

> Destinies were superstitiously, by *onomancy*, deciphered out of names. *Camden.*

ONOMAN'TIC, ONOMAN'TICAL, } *a.* Predicting by names, or the letters composing names. *Camden.*

ON'OMATOPE, ON'OMATOPY, } *n.* [Gr. ονοματοποιια; ονομα, name, and ποιεω, to make.]

1. In *grammar* and *rhetoric*, a figure in which words are formed to resemble the sound made by the thing signified; as, to *buzz*, as bees; to *crackle*, as burning thorns or brush. *Encyc.*

2. A word whose sound corresponds to the sound of the thing signified.

ON'SET, *n.* [*on* and *set.*] A rushing or setting upon; a violent attack; assault; a storming; appropriately, the assault of an army or body of troops upon an enemy or a fort.

> The shout
> Of battle now began and rushing sound
> Of *onset.* *Milton.*

2. An attack of any kind; as the impetuous *onset* of grief. *Philips.*

ON'SET, *v. t.* To assault; to begin. [*Not used.*] *Carew.*

ONSLAUGHT, *n. on'slaut.* [*on* and *slay.*] Attack; storm; onset. [*Not used.*] *Hudibras.*

ONTOLOG'IC, ONTOLOG'ICAL, } *a.* [See *Ontology.*] Pertaining to the science of being in general and its affections.

ONTOL'OGIST, *n.* One who treats of or considers the nature and qualities of being in general.

ONTOL'OGY, *n.* [Gr. οντα, from ειμι, and λογος, discourse.]

That part of the science of metaphysics which investigates and explains the nature and essence of all beings, their qualities and attributes. *Encyc.*

ON'WARD, *adv.* [Sax. *ondward, andweard; on* and *weard*, L. *versus.*]

1. Toward the point before or in front; forward; progressively; in advance; as, to move *onward.*

> Not one looks backward, *onward* still he goes. *Pope.*

2. In a state of advanced progression.

3. A little further or forward.

ON'WARD, *a.* Advanced or advancing; as an *onward* course.

2. Increased; improved. *Sidney.*

3. Conducting; leading forward to perfection. *Home.*

ON'YCHA, *n.* [from Gr. ονυξ.] Supposed to be the odoriferous shell of the onyx-fish, or the onyx. Ex. xxx.

ON'YX, *n.* [Gr. ονυξ, a nail, L. *onyx.*] A semi-pellucid gem with variously colored zones or veins, a variety of chalcedony. *Encyc. Nicholson.*

O'OLITE, *n.* [Gr. ωον, an egg, and λιθος, stone, from its resemblance to the roes of fish.]

Egg-stone, a variety of concreted carbonate of lime; oviform limestone. *Jameson.*

OOZE, *v. i. ooz.* [The origin of this word is not easily ascertained. In Eth. ወሐዘ signifies to flow. In Amharic, ወዘዐ signifies to sweat. In Ethiopic, ወፀአ signifies to *issue*, to come or go out, and this is the Heb. יצא. In Sax. *wæs* is water, G. *wasser.* These words seem to be nearly allied. See *Issue.*]

To flow gently; to percolate, as a liquid through the pores of a substance, or through small openings. Water *oozes* from the earth and through a filter.

> The latent rill, scarce *oozing* through the grass. *Thomson.*

OOZE, *n.* Soft mud or slime; earth so wet as to flow gently or easily yield to pressure. *Carew.*

2. Soft flow; spring. *Prior.*

3. The liquor of a tan-vat.

OOZ'ING, *ppr.* Flowing gently; percolating.

OOZ'Y, *a.* Miry; containing soft mud; resembling ooze; as the *oozy* bed of a river. *Pope.*

O'PACATE, *v. t.* [L. *opaco.*] To shade; to darken; to obscure; to cloud. [*Not used.*] *Boyle.*

OPAC'ITY, *n.* [L. *opacitas.*] Opakeness; the quality of a body which renders it impervious to the rays of light; want of transparency. *Opacity* may exist in bodies of any color.

2. Darkness; obscurity. *Glanville.*

OPA'COUS, *a.* [L. *opacus.*] Not pervious to the rays of light; not transparent.

2. Dark; obscure. [See *Opake.*]

OPA'COUSNESS, *n.* Imperviousness to light. *Evelyn.*

O'PAH, *n.* A fish of a large kind with a smooth skin, found on the coast of Guinea. *Dict. Nat. Hist.*

OPA'KE, *a.* [L. *opacus;* Fr. *opaque.*] Impervious to the rays of light; not transparent. [*This is the word now generally used.*] Chalk is an *opake* substance.

2. Dark; obscure.

OPA'KENESS, *n.* The quality of being impervious to light; want of transparency; opacity.

O'PAL, *n.* [L. *opalus* or *opalum.*] A stone of the silicious genus, and of several varieties. It is one of the most beautiful of this genus, by reason of its changeableness of color by reflection and refraction. Kirwan distributes opals into four families, opal, semi-opal, pitch stone [pechstein,] and ligniform. Jameson divides opal into seven kinds. *Encyc. Kirwan. Nicholson.*

Opal is a subspecies of indivisible quartz. *Ure.*

OPALES'CENCE, *n.* A colored shining luster reflected from a single spot in a mineral. It is sometimes simple and sometimes stellar.

OPALES'CENT, *a.* Resembling opal; reflecting a colored luster from a single spot. *Kirwan.*

O'PALINE, *a.* Pertaining to or like opal.

O'PALIZE, *v. t.* To make to resemble opal; as *opalized* wood. *Cleaveland.*

OPAQUE. [See *Opake.*]

OPAQUENESS. [See *Opakeness.*]

OPE, *a.* Open. *Obs.*

OPE, *v. t.* To open; used only in poetry, and probably a contracted word.

OPEN, *a. o'pn.* [Sax. D. *open;* G. *offen;* Sw. *öpen;* Dan. *aaben.*]

1. Unclosed; not shut; as, the gate is *open;* an *open* door or window; an *open* book; *open* eyes.

2. Spread; expanded. He received his son with *open* arms.

3. Unsealed; as an *open* letter.

4. Not shut or fast; as an *open* hand.

5. Not covered; as the *open* air; an *open* vessel.

6. Not covered with trees; clear; as an *open* country or field.

7. Not stopped; as an *open* bottle.

8. Not fenced or obstructed; as an *open* road.

9. Not frosty; warmer than usual; not freezing severely; as an *open* winter.

> An *open* and warm winter portendeth a hot and dry summer. *Bacon.*

Johnson interprets *open*, in this passage, by not cloudy, not gloomy. I think the definition wrong. In America, an *open* winter is one in which the earth is not bound with frost and covered with snow.

10. Public; before a court and its suitors. His testimony was given in *open* court.

11. Admitting all persons without restraint; free to all comers. He keeps *open* house at the election.

12. Clear of ice; as, the river or the harbor is *open.*

13. Plain; apparent; evident; public; not secret or concealed; as an *open* declaration; *open* avowal; *open* shame; *open* defiance. The nations contend in *open* war or in *open* arms.

14. Not wearing disguise; frank; sincere; unreserved; candid; artless.

> He was held a man *open* and of good faith. *Bacon.*

> His generous, *open*, undesigning heart. *Addison.*

15. Not clouded; not contracted or frowning; having an air of frankness and sincerity; as an *open* look.

With aspect *open* shall erect his head. *Pope.*

16. Not hidden; exposed to view.

We are to exercise our thoughts and lay *open* the treasures of divine truth. *Burnet.*

17. Ready to hear or receive what is offered.

His ears are *open* to their cry. Ps. xxxiv.

18. Free to be employed for redress; not restrained or denied; nct precluding any person.

The law is *open*. Acts xix.

19. Exposed; not protected; without defense. The country is *open* to invaders.

—Hath left me *open* to all injuries. *Shak.*

20. Attentive; employed in inspection.

Thine eyes are *open* upon all the ways of the sons of men— Jer. xxxii.

21. Clear; unobstructed; as an *open* view.

22. Unsettled; not balanced or closed; as an *open* account.

Open accounts between merchants. *Johnson's Rep.*

23. Not closed; free to be debated; as a question *open* for discussion.

24. In *music*, an *open* note is that which a string is tuned to produce. *Busby.*

OPEN, *v. t. o'pn.* [Sax. *openian*; D. *openen*; G. *öffnen*; Sw. *öpna*; Dan. *aabner*; Ar. بان. Class Bn. No. 3.]

1. To unclose; to unbar; to unlock; to remove any fastening or cover and set open; as, to *open* a door or gate; to *open* a desk.

2. To break the seal of a letter and unfold it.

3. To separate parts that are close; as, to *open* the lips; to *open* the mouth or eyes or eyelids; to *open* a book.

4. To remove a covering from; as, to *open* a pit.

5. To cut through; to perforate; to lance; as, to *open* the skin; to *open* an abscess.

6. To break; to divide; to split or rend; as, the earth was *opened* in many places by an earthquake; a rock is *opened* by blasting.

7. To clear; to make by removing obstructions; as, to *open* a road; to *open* a passage; the heat of spring *opens* rivers bound with ice.

8. To spread; to expand; as, to *open* the hand.

9. To unstop; as, to *open* a bottle.

10. To begin; to make the first exhibition. The attorney general *opens* the cause on the part of the king or the state. Homer *opens* his poem with the utmost simplicity and modesty.

11. To show; to bring to view or knowledge.

The English did adventure far to *open* the north parts of America. *Abbot.*

12. To interpret; to explain.

—While he *opened* to us the Scriptures. Luke xxiv.

13. To reveal; to disclose. He *opened* his mind very freely.

14. To make liberal; as, to *open* the heart.

15. To make the first discharge of artillery; as, to *open* a heavy fire on the enemy.

16. To enter on or begin; as, to *open* a negotiation or correspondence; to *open* a trade with the Indies.

17. To begin to see by the removal of something that intercepted the view; as, we sailed round the point and *opened* the harbor.

OPEN, *v. i. o'pn.* To unclose itself; to be unclosed; to be parted.

The earth *opened* and swallowed up Dathan, and covered the company of Abiram. Ps. cvi.

2. To begin to appear. As we sailed round the point, the harbor *opened* to our view.

3. To commence; to begin. Sales of stock *opened* at par.

4. To bark; *a term in hunting.*

OPENED, *pp. o'pned.* Unclosed; unbarred; unsealed; uncovered; revealed; disclosed; made plain; freed from obstruction.

OPENER, *n. o'pner.* One that opens or removes any fastening or covering. *Milton.*

2. One that explains; an interpreter. *Shak.*

3. That which separates; that which rends. *Boyle.*

4. An aperient in medicine.

OPENEYED, *a. o'pneyed.* Watchful; vigilant. *Shak.*

OPENHANDED, *a. o'pnhanded.* Generous; liberal; munificent. *Rowe.*

OPENHE'ARTED, *a. o'pnhàrted.* Candid; frank; generous. *Dryden.*

OPENHE'ARTEDLY, *adv.* With frankness; without reserve. *Ch. Relig. Appeal.*

OPENHE'ARTEDNESS, *n.* Frankness; candor; sincerity; munificence; generosity. *Johnson.*

OPENING, *ppr. o'pning.* Unclosing; unsealing; uncovering; revealing; interpreting.

OPENING, *n. o'pning.* A breach; an aperture; a hole or perforation.

2. A place admitting entrance; as a bay or creek.

3. Dawn; first appearance or visibleness; beginning of exhibition or discovery.

The *opening* of your glory was like that of light. *Dryden.*

OPENLY, *adv. o'pnly.* Publicly; not in private; without secrecy; as, to avow our sins and follies *openly.*

How grossly and *openly* do many of us contradict the precepts of the gospel by our ungodliness and worldly lusts! *Tillotson.*

2. Plainly; evidently; without reserve or disguise.

OPENMOUTHED, *a. o'pnmouthed.* Greedy; ravenous; clamorous; as an *openmouthed* lion. *L'Estrange.*

OPENNESS, *n. o'pnness.* Freedom from covering or obstruction; as the *openness* of a country.

2. Plainness; clearness; freedom from obscurity or ambiguity; as, deliver your answers with more *openness.* *Shak.*

3. Freedom from disguise; unreservedness; plainness. *Felton.*

4. Expression of frankness or candor; as *openness* of countenance.

5. Unusual mildness; freedom from snow and frost; as the *openness* of a winter.

OP'ERA, *n.* [It. Sp. Fr. from L. *opera*, work, labor.]

A dramatic composition set to music and sung on the stage, accompanied with musical instruments and enriched with magnificent dresses, machines, dancing, &c. *Encyc.*

OP'ERABLE, *a.* Practicable. [*Not used.*] *Brown.*

OP'ERANT, *a.* [See *Operate.*] Having power to produce an effect. [Not used. We now use *operative.*] *Shak.*

OP'ERATE, *v. i.* [L. *operor*; Sp. *operar*; Fr. *operer*; Eth. ገበረ gabèr, to make, do, form or ordain; deriv. ተገበረ tagabar, to work, to operate, to labor, to till; W. *goberu*, to operate; Arm. *ober* or *gober*, to make; *ober* or *euffr*, work; Ir. *obair*; Sp. Port. *obra*; Fr. *œuvre*, *ouvrage.* The corresponding verb in Hebrew and Chaldee, גבר signifies to be strong, to prevail, and in Arabic, to bind fast, to consolidate, to repair. The primary sense is to strain or press, to exert force. Class Br. No. 14.]

1. To act; to exert power or strength, physical or mechanical. External bodies *operate* on animals by means of perception. Sound *operates* upon the auditory nerves through the medium of air. Medicines *operate* on the body by increasing or diminishing organic action.

2. To act or produce effect on the mind; to exert moral power or influence. Motives *operate* on the mind in determining the judgment. Examples *operate* in producing imitation.

The virtues of private persons *operate* but on a few— *Atterbury.*

A plain convincing reason *operates* on the mind both of a learned and an ignorant hearer as long as he lives. *Swift.*

3. In *surgery*, to perform some manual act in a methodical manner upon a human body, and usually with instruments, with a view to restore soundness or health; as in amputation, lithotomy and the like.

4. To act; to have agency; to produce any effect.

OP'ERATE, *v. t.* To effect; to produce by agency.

The same cause would *operate* a diminution of the value of stock— *Hamilton.*

[*This use is not frequent, and can hardly be said to be well authorized.*]

OPERAT'ICAL, *a.* Pertaining to the opera; *a word used by musicians.* *Busby.*

OP'ERATING, *ppr.* Acting; exerting agency or power; performing some manual act in surgery.

OPERA'TION, *n.* [L. *operatio.*] The act or process of operating; agency; the exertion of power, physical, mechanical or moral.

Speculative painting without the assistance of manual *operation*, can never attain to perfection. *Dryden.*

The pain and sickness caused by manna are the effects of its *operation* on the stomach. *Locke.*

So we speak of the *operation* of motives, reasons or arguments on the mind, the *operation* of causes, &c.

2. Action; effect.

Many medicinal drugs of rare *operation.* *Heylin.*

3. Process; manipulation; series of acts in experiments; as in chimistry or metallurgy.

4. In *surgery*, any methodical action of the hand, or of the hand with instruments, on the human body, with a view to heal a

part diseased, fractured or dislocated, as in amputation, &c.

5. Action or movements of an army or fleet; as military or naval *operations.*

6. Movements of machinery.

7. Movements of any physical body.

OP'ERATIVE, *a.* Having the power of acting; exerting force, physical or moral; having or exerting agency; active in the production of effects.

In actions of religion we should be zealous, active and *operative,* so far as prudence will permit. *Taylor.*

It holds in all *operative* principles, especially in morality. *South.*

2. Efficacious; producing the effect.

OP'ERATOR, *n.* He or that which operates; he or that which produces an effect.

2. In *surgery,* the person who performs some act upon the human body by means of the hand, or with instruments; as a skillful *operator.*

OPER'CULATE, } *a.* [L. *operculatus,* from OPER'CULATED, } *operio,* to cover.] In *botany,* having a lid or cover, as a capsule. *Martyn.*

OPER'CULIFORM, *a.* [L. *operculum,* a lid, and *form.*] Having the form of a lid or cover. *Say.*

OPERO'SE, *a.* [L. *operosus,* from *opera, operor.*]

Laborious; attended with labor; tedious. *Burnet.*

OPERO'SENESS, *n.* The state of being laborious. *More.*

O'PETIDE, *n.* [*ope* and *tide.*] The ancient time of marriage, from Epiphany to Ash-Wednesday. *Bp. Hall.*

OPHID'IAN, *a.* [Gr. οφις, a serpent.] Pertaining to serpents; designating an order of vertebral animals destitute of feet or fins.

OPHID'ION, *n.* [Gr. from οφις, a serpent.] A fish of the anguilliform kind, resembling the common eel, but shorter, more depressed and of a paler color; found in the Mediterranean. *Dict. Nat. Hist.*

ŌPHIOLOĠ'IC, } *a.* Pertaining to ophi-ŌPHIOLOĠ'ICAL, } ology.

ŌPHIOL'OĠIST, *n.* One versed in the natural history of serpents.

ŌPHIOL'OĠY, *n.* [Gr. οφις, serpent, and λογος, discourse.]

That part of natural history which treats of serpents, or which arranges and describes the several kinds. *Ed. Encyc.*

ŌPHIOM'ANCY, *n.* [Gr. οφις, a serpent, and μαντεια, divination.]

In *antiquity,* the art of divining or predicting events by serpents, as by their manner of eating or by their coils. *Encyc.*

ŌPHIOMORPH'OUS, *a.* [Gr. οφις and μορφη, form.] Having the form of a serpent. *Ray.*

ŌPHIOPH'AGOUS, *a.* [Gr. οφις, a serpent, and φαγω, to eat.] Eating or feeding on serpents. *Brown.*

O'PHITE, *n.* [Gr. οφις, a serpent.] Pertaining to a serpent. *Holwell.*

O'PHITE, *a.* [Gr. οφις, a serpent, whence οφιτης, a stone spotted like a serpent.]

Green porphyry, or serpentine; a variety of greenstone of a dusky green color of different shades, sprinkled with spots of a lighter green; in other words, containing greenish white crystals of feldspar. *Cleaveland.*

OPHIU'CHUS, *n.* [Gr. οφιουχος; οφις, a serpent, and εχω, to have.]

A constellation in the northern hemisphere. *Milton.*

OPHTHAL'MIC, *a.* [See *Ophthalmy.*] Pertaining to the eye.

OPHTHALMOS'COPY, *n.* [Gr. οφθαλμος, the eye, and σκοπεω, to view.]

A branch of physiognomy which deduces the knowledge of a man's temper and manner from the appearance of the eyes. *Encyc.*

OPH'THALMY, *n.* [Gr. οφθαλμια, from οφθαλμος, the eye.]

A disease of the eyes; an inflammation of the membranes which invest the eye. *Encyc.*

Inflammation of the eye or its appendages. *Good.*

O'PIATE, *n.* [from *opium.*] Primarily, a medicine of a thicker consistence than sirup, prepared with opium. *Encyc.*

A soft electuary.

Electuaries when soft are called *opiata.* *Parr.*

But in modern usage generally,

2. Any medicine that has the quality of inducing sleep or repose; a narcotic. *Encyc.*

3. That which induces rest or inaction; that which quiets uneasiness.

They chose atheism as an *opiate.* *Bentley.*

O'PIATE, *a.* Inducing sleep; soporiferous; somniferous; narcotic. *Bacon.*

2. Causing rest or inaction. *Milton.*

OPIF'ICER, *n.* [L. *opifex; opus,* work, and *facio,* to do.]

One who performs any work. [*Not used.*] *Bentley.*

OPI'NABLE, *a.* [L. *opinor.*] That may be thought. [*Not used.*] *Dict.*

OPINA'TION, *n.* Act of thinking; opinion. [*Not used.*] *Dict.*

OPIN'ATIVE, *a.* Stiff in opinion. [*Not used.*] *Burton.*

OPINA'TOR, *n.* One fond of his own opinions; one who holds an opinion. [*Not in use.*] *Glanville.*

OPI'NE, *v. i.* [L. *opinor.*] To think; to suppose. *Obs.* *South.*

OPI'NED, *pp.* Thought; conceived. *Obs.*

OPI'NER, *n.* One who thinks or holds an opinion. *Obs.* *Taylor.*

OPINIAS'TER, } [Fr. *opiniâtre.*] Un-OPINIAS'TROUS, } *a.* duly attached to OPINIA'TRE, } one's own opinion, or stiff in adhering to it. *Obs.* *Raleigh.*

OPIN'IATE, *v. t.* To maintain one's opinion with obstinacy. *Obs.* *Barrow.*

OPIN'IATED, *a.* Unduly attached to one's own opinions. *Shenstone.*

OPINIA'TER, *a.* Stiff in opinion; obstinate. *Obs.* *Barrow.*

OPIN'IATIVE, *a.* Very stiff in adherence to preconceived notions. *Sandys.*

2. Imagined; not proved. *Glanville.*

OPIN'IATIVENESS, *n.* Undue stiffness in opinion. *Raleigh.*

OPINIA'TOR, *n.* One unduly attached to his own opinion. *Obs.*

OPIN'IATRY, *n.* Unreasonable attachment to one's own notions; obstinacy in opinions. *Obs.* *Brown.*

OPI'NING, *ppr.* Thinking. *Obs.*

OPI'NING, *n.* Opinion; notion. *Obs.* *Taylor.*

OPINION, *n.* *opin'yon.* [Fr. *id.*; L. *opinio,* from *opinor,* to think, Gr. επινοεω; or Ar. أبن abana, to think, to suspect. The primary sense is to set, to fix in the mind, as in L. *suppono.*]

1. The judgment which the mind forms of any proposition, statement, theory or event, the truth or falsehood of which is supported by a degree of evidence that renders it probable, but does not produce absolute knowledge or certainty. It has been a received *opinion* that all matter is comprised in four elements. This *opinion* is proved by many discoveries to be false. From circumstances we form *opinions* respecting future events.

Opinion is when the assent of the understanding is so far gained by evidence of probability, that it rather inclines to one persuasion than to another, yet not without a mixture of uncertainty or doubting. *Hale.*

2. The judgment or sentiments which the mind forms of persons or their qualities. We speak of a good *opinion,* a favorable *opinion,* a bad *opinion,* a private *opinion,* and public or general *opinion,* &c.

Friendship gives a man a peculiar right and claim to the good *opinion* of his friend. *South.*

3. Settled judgment or persuasion; as religious *opinions;* political *opinion.*

4. Favorable judgment; estimation.

In actions of arms, small matters are of great moment, especially when they serve to raise an *opinion* of commanders. *Hayward.*

However, I have no *opinion* of these things— *Bacon.*

OPIN'ION, *v. t.* To think. [*Not used.*] *Brown.*

OPIN'IONATE, } *a.* Stiff in opinion; firm-OPIN'IONATED, } ly or unduly adhering to one's own opinion; obstinate in opinion. *Bedell.*

OPIN'IONATELY, *adv.* Obstinately; conceitedly. *Feltham.*

OPIN'IONATIVE, *a.* Fond of preconceived notions; unduly attached to one's own opinions. *Burnet.*

OPIN'IONATIVELY, *adv.* With undue fondness for one's own opinions; stubbornly.

OPIN'IONATIVENESS, *n.* Excessive attachment to one's own opinions; obstinacy in opinion.

OPIN'IONED, *a.* Attached to particular opinions; conceited. *South.*

OPIN'IONIST, *n.* One fond of his own notions, or one unduly attached to his own opinions. *Glanville.*

OPIS'THODOME, *n.* [Gr. οπισθιος, that is behind, and δομος, house.]

In *Greece,* a part or place in the back part of a house. *Mitford.*

O'PIUM, *n.* [L. *opium;* Gr. οπιον, from οπος, juice.]

Opium is the inspissated juice of the capsules of the papaver somniferum, or somniferous white poppy with which the fields in Asia Minor are sown, as ours are with wheat and rye. It flows from incisions made in the heads of the plant, and the best flows from the first incision. It is imported into Europe and America from the Levant and the East Indies. It is brought in cakes or masses weighing from eight ounces to a pound. It is heavy, of a dense texture, of a brownish yellow color, not perfectly dry, but easily receiving an impression from the finger; it has a dead and faint smell, and its taste is bitter and acrid. Opium is of great use as a medicine. *Hill. Encyc.*

O'PLE-TREE, *n.* [L. *opulus.*] The witch-hazel. *Obs.* *Ainsworth.*

OPOBAL'SAM, *n.* [L. Gr. οπος, juice, and *balsamum.*]

The balm or balsam of Gilead. It has a yellowish or greenish yellow color, a warm bitterish aromatic taste, and an acidulous fragrant smell. It is held in esteem as a medicine and as an odoriferous unguent and cosmetic. The shrub or tree producing this balsam is of the genus Amyris, and grows spontaneously in Arabia Felix. *Encyc.*

OPODEL'DOC, *n.* The name of a plaster, said to have been invented by Mindererus; but in modern usage,

2. A saponaceous camphorated liniment; a solution of soap in ardent spirits, with the addition of camphor and essential oils. *Nicholson.*

OPO'PANAX, *n.* [L.; Gr. οπος, juice, and πanaξ, a plant.]

A gum-resin of a tolerably firm texture, brought in loose granules or drops, sometimes in larger masses. This substance on the outside is of a brownish red color, with specks of white, and within of a dusky yellow or whitish color. It has a strong smell and an acrid taste. It is obtained from the roots of an umbelliferous plant of the genus Pastinaca or parsnep, and is brought from Turkey and the East Indies. *Encyc. Parr.*

OPOS'SUM, *n.* A quadruped of the genus Didelphis. It has a prehensile tail, like some of the monkeys, and is distinguished by a pouch or false belly, in which it protects and carries its young. The name is also given to other species of the genus, some of which want the pouch. *Encyc. Cuvier.*

OP'PIDAN, *n.* [L. *oppidanus*, from *oppidum*, a city or town.] An inhabitant of a town. [*Not used.*] *Wood.*

2. An appellation given to the students of Eton school in England. *Mason.*

OP'PIDAN, *a.* Pertaining to a town. [*Not used.*] *Howell.*

OPPIG'NERATE, *v. t.* [L. *oppignero; ob* and *pignero*, to pledge, from *pignus*, pledge.] To pledge; to pawn. [*Not in use.*] *Bacon.*

OP'PILATE, *v. t.* [L. *oppilo; ob* and *pilo*, to drive.]

To crowd together; to fill with obstructions.

OPPILA'TION, *n.* The act of filling or crowding together; a stopping by redundant matter; obstructions, particularly in the lower intestines. *Encyc. Harvey.*

OP'PILATIVE, *a.* [Fr. *oppilatif.*] Obstructive. *Sherwood.*

OPPLE'TED, *a.* [L. *oppletus.*] Filled; crowded. [*Not in use.*]

OPPO'NE, *v. t.* [L. *oppono; ob* and *pono*, to put.] To oppose. [*Not used.*] *B. Jonson.*

OPPO'NENCY, *n.* [See *Opponent.*] The opening of an academical disputation; the proposition of objections to a tenet; an exercise for a degree. [*I believe not used in America.*] *Todd.*

OPPO'NENT, *a.* [L. *opponens, oppono; ob* and *pono*, to set, put or lay, that is, to thrust against; Heb. Syr. Ch. Ar. בנה to build, that is, to set, to *found*, L. *fundo.*] That opposes; opposite; adverse. *Prior.*

OPPO'NENT, *n.* One that opposes; particularly, one that opposes in controversy, disputation or argument. It is sometimes applied to the person that begins a dispute by raising objections to a tenet or doctrine, and is correlative to *defendant* or *respondent.* In common usage, however, it is applicable to either party in a controversy, denoting any person who opposes another or his cause. Opponent may sometimes be used for *adversary*, and for *antagonist*, but not with strict propriety, as the word does not necessarily imply enmity nor bodily strife. Nor is it well used in the sense of rival or competitor.

OPPORTU'NE, *a.* [L. *opportunus; ob* and *porto*, to bear or bring; probably from the root of *fero* or *porto*, to bear. The sense of the verb *opporto*, would be to bring to or upon. See *Import, Importune.* In this and all words of like signification, the primary sense is to fall, come or bring to. See *Luck, Fortune, Season.*]

Properly, having come or being present at a proper time; hence, seasonable; timely; well timed. It agrees with *seasonable* rather than with *convenient*, though the sense of the latter may be included in it.

> Perhaps in view
> Of those bright confines, whence with neighboring arms,
> And *opportune* excursion, we may chance
> Re-enter heaven. *Milton.*

OPPORTU'NELY, *adv.* Seasonably; at a time favorable for the purpose. It has been applied to *place*, as well as to *time*, but its proper application is to *time*, and hence it accords with *seasonably*, rather than with *conveniently.*

OPPORTU'NITY, *n.* [L. *opportunitas.*] Fit or convenient time; a time favorable for the purpose; suitable time combined with other favorable circumstances. Suitableness of *time* is the predominant signification, but it includes generally circumstances of place and other conveniences adapted to the end desired.

> A wise man will make more *opportunities* than he finds. *Bacon.*

> I had an *opportunity* to see the cloud descend. *Brown.*

> Neglect no *opportunity* of doing good. *Atterbury.*

2. Convenient means. I had an *opportunity* of sending the letter, or no *opportunity* to send it. *Opportunities* rarely occur or frequently offer.

OPPO'SAL, *n.* *s* as *z.* Opposition. [*Not used.*] *Herbert.*

OPPO'SE, *v. t.* *s* as z. [Fr. *opposer; ob* and *poser*, to set; L. *oppono, opposui.* It is doubtful whether Fr. *poser*, and the preterit and participle passive of the Latin verb belong to *pono.* The change of *n* into *s* is unusual. Two different verbs may be used, as in L. *fero, tuli.* See *Pose.*]

1. To set against; to put in oppposition, with a view to counterbalance or countervail, and thus to hinder, defeat, destroy or prevent effect; as, to *oppose* one argument to another.

> I may without presumption *oppose* my single opinion to his. *Locke.*

2. To act against; to resist, either by physical means, by arguments or other means. The army *opposed* the progress of the enemy, but without success. Several members of the house strenuously *opposed* the bill, but it passed.

3. To check; to resist effectually. The army was not able to *oppose* the progress of the enemy.

4. To place in front; to set opposite. *Shak.*

5. To act against, as a competitor.

OPPO'SE, *v. i.* *s* as *z.* To act adversely; with *against;* as, a servant *opposed against* the act. [*Not used.*] *Shak.*

2. To object or act against in controversy. *Johnson.*

OPPO'SED, *pp.* Set in opposition; resisted.

2. *a.* Being in opposition in principle or in act; adverse.

> Certain characters were formerly *opposed* to it. *Federalist, Jay.*

OPPO'SELESS, *a.* Not to be opposed; irresistible. [*Not in use.*] *Shak.*

OPPO'SER, *n.* One that opposes; an opponent in party, in principle, in controversy or argument. We speak of the *opposers* of public measures; the *opposers* of ecclesiastical discipline; an *opposer* of christianity or of orthodoxy.

2. One who acts in opposition; one who resists; as an *opposer* of law or of the execution of law.

3. An antagonist; an adversary; an enemy; a rival.

OP'POSITE, *a.* [Fr. from L. *oppositus.*]

1. Standing or situated in front; facing; as an edifice *opposite* to the Exchange. Brooklyn lies *opposite* to New York, or on the *opposite* side of the river.

2. Adverse; repugnant.

> —Novels, by which the reader is misled into another sort of pleasure *opposite* to that designed in an epic poem. *Dryden.*

3. Contrary; as words of *opposite* significations; *opposite* terms. The medicine had an effect *opposite* to what was expected.

4. In *botany*, growing in pairs, each pair decussated or crossing that above and below it; as *opposite* leaves or branches. *Martyn.*

OP'POSITE, *n.* An opponent; an adversary; an enemy; an antagonist. *Shak. Dryden.*

2. That which is opposed or contrary.

OP'POSITELY, *adv.* In front; in a situation to face each other. *Grew.*

2. Adversely; against each other.

> Winds from all quarters *oppositely* blow. *May.*

OP'POSITENESS, *n.* The state of being opposite or contrary.

OPPOSITIFO'LIOUS, *a.* [L. *oppositus* and *folium*, a leaf.]

In *botany*, opposite to the leaf; as an *oppositifolious* peduncle. *Lee.*

OPPOSI''TION, *n.* [L. *oppositio.*] Situation so as to front something else; a standing over against; as the *opposition* of two mountains or buildings.

2. The act of opposing; attempt to check, restrain or defeat. He makes *opposition* to the measure; the bill passed without *opposition*. Will any *opposition* be made to the suit, to the claim or demand?

3. Obstacle. The river meets with no *opposition* in its course to the ocean.

4. Resistance; as the *opposition* of enemies. Virtue will break through all *opposition*.

5. Contrariety; repugnance in principle; as the *opposition* of the heart to the laws of God.

6. Contrariety of interests, measures or designs. The two parties are in *opposition* to each other.

7. Contrariety or diversity of meaning; as one term used in *opposition* to another.

8. Contradiction; inconsistency. *Locke.*

9. The collective body of opposers; in England, the party in Parliament which opposes the ministry; in America, the party that opposes the existing administration.

10. In *astronomy*, the situation of two heavenly bodies, when distant from each other 180 degrees.

OPPOSI′′TIONIST, *n.* One that belongs to the party opposing the administration.

OPPOS′ITIVE, *a.* That may be put in opposition. *Hall.*

OPPRESS′, *v. t.* [Fr. *oppresser*; L. *oppressus*, from *opprimo*; *ob* and *premo*, to press.]

1. To load or burden with unreasonable impositions; to treat with unjust severity, rigor or hardship; as, to *oppress* a nation with taxes or contributions; to *oppress* one by compelling him to perform unreasonable service.

2. To overpower; to overburden; as, to be *oppressed* with grief.

3. To sit or lie heavy on; as, excess of food *oppresses* the stomach.

OPPRESS′ED, *pp.* Burdened with unreasonable impositions; overpowered; overburdened; depressed.

OPPRESS′ING, *ppr.* Overburdening.

OPPRES′SION, *n.* The act of oppressing; the imposition of unreasonable burdens, either in taxes or services; cruelty; severity.

2. The state of being oppressed or overburdened; misery. *Shak.*

> The Lord—saw the *oppression* of Israel. 2 Kings xiii.

3. Hardship; calamity. *Addison.*

4. Depression; dullness of spirits; lassitude of body. *Arbuthnot.*

5. A sense of heaviness or weight in the breast, &c.

OPPRESS′IVE, *a.* Unreasonably burdensome; unjustly severe; as *oppressive* taxes; *oppressive* exactions of service.

2. Tyrannical; as an *oppressive* government.

3. Heavy; overpowering; overwhelming; as *oppressive* grief or wo.

OPPRESS′IVELY, *adv.* In a manner to oppress; with unreasonable severity. *Burke.*

OPPRESS′IVENESS, *n.* The quality of being oppressive.

OPPRESS′OR, *n.* One that oppresses; one that imposes unjust burdens on others; one that harasses others with unjust laws or unreasonable severity.

> Power when employed to relieve the oppressed and to punish the *oppressor*, becomes a great blessing. *Swift.*

OPPRO′BRIOUS, *a.* [See *Opprobrium.*]

1. Reproachful and contemptuous; scurrilous; as *opprobrious* language; *opprobrious* words or terms.

2. Blasted with infamy; despised; rendered hateful; as an *opprobrious* name. *Milton. Daniel.*

OPPRO′BRIOUSLY, *adv.* With reproach mingled with contempt; scurrilously. *Shak.*

OPPRO′BRIOUSNESS, *n.* Reproachfulness mingled with contempt; scurrility.

OPPRO′BRIUM, *n.* [L. *ob* and *probrum*, disgrace.]

Reproach mingled with contempt or disdain.

OPPUGN, *v. t.* *oppu′ne.* [L. *oppugno*; *ob* and *pugno*, to fight, from *pugnus*, the fist, Sp. *puño*, Fr. *poing*.]

To attack; to oppose; to resist.

> They said the manner of their impeachment they could not but conceive did *oppugn* the rights of parliament. *Clarendon.*

[It is never used in the literal sense, to *fight*.]

OPPUG′NANCY, *n.* Opposition; resistance. *Shak.*

OPPUGNA′TION, *n.* Opposition; resistance. *Hall.*

OPPUGNED, *pp.* *oppu′ned.* Opposed; resisted.

OPPUGNER, *n.* *oppu′ner.* One who opposes or attacks; that which opposes. *Boyle.*

OPPUGNING, *ppr.* *oppu′ning.* Attacking; opposing.

OPSIM′ATHY, *n.* [Gr. ὀψιμαθεια; ὀψε, late, and μανθανω, to learn.] Late education; education late in life. [*Little used.*] *Hales.*

OPSONA′TION, *n.* [L. *obsono*, to cater.] A catering; a buying of provisions. [*Not used.*] *Dict.*

OP′TABLE, *a.* [L. *optabilis*, from *opto*, to desire.] Desirable. [*Not used.*]

OPTA′TION, *n.* [L. *optatio.*] A desiring; the expression of a wish. *Peacham.*

OP′TATIVE, *a.* [L. *optativus*, from *opto*, to desire or wish.]

Expressing desire or wish. The *optative* mode, in grammar, is that form of the verb in which wish or desire is expressed.

OP′TATIVE, *n.* Something to be desired. [*Little used.*] *Bacon.*

OP′TIC, OP′TICAL, *a.* [Gr. οπτικος, from οπτομαι, to see; ωψ, the eye.] Relating or pertaining to vision or sight.

2. Relating to the science of optics.

Optic angle, is that which the optic axes of the eyes make with one another, as they tend to meet at some distance before the eyes.

Optic axis, is the axis of the eye, or a line going through the middle of the pupil and the center of the eye. *Encyc.*

OP′TIC, *n.* An organ of sight. *Trumbull.*

OPTI′′CIAN, *n.* A person skilled in the science of optics. *Smith.*

2. One who makes or sells optic glasses and instruments. *Adams.*

OP′TICS, *n.* The science which treats of light and the phenomena of vision. *Encyc.*

OP′TIMACY, *n.* [L. *optimates*, grandees, from *optimus*, best.] The body of nobles; the nobility. *Howell.*

OP′TIMISM, *n.* [L. *optimus*, best.] The opinion or doctrine that every thing in nature is ordered for the best; or the order of things in the universe that is adapted to produce the most good.

> The true and amiable philosophy of *optimism*. *Walsh.*

> A system of strict *optimism* may be the real system in both cases. *Paley.*

OPTIM′ITY, *n.* The state of being best.

OP′TION, *n.* [L. *optio*, from *opto*, to wish or desire.]

1. The power of choosing; the right of choice or election; as the archbishop's *option* in collating to a vacant benefice.

> There is an *option* left to the U. States of America, whether they will be respectable and prosperous, or contemptible and miserable, as a nation. *Washington.*

2. The power of wishing; wish.

3. Choice; election; preference. He ought not to complain of his lot; it was his own *option*. We leave this to your own *option*.

OP′TIONAL, *a.* Left to one's wish or choice; depending on choice or preference. It is *optional* with you to go or stay.

2. Leaving something to choice.

> Original writs are either *optional* or peremptory. *Blackstone.*

OP′ULENCE, *n.* [L. *opulentia*, from *opes*, wealth.] Wealth; riches; affluence. [*Opulency is little used.*] *Swift.*

OP′ULENT, *a.* [L. *opulentus.*] Wealthy; rich; affluent; having a large estate or property. *Bacon. South.*

OP′ULENTLY, *adv.* Richly; with abundance or splendor.

OPUS′CULE, *n.* [L. *opusculum.*] A small work. *Jones.*

OR, a termination of Latin nouns, is a contraction of *vir*, a man, or from the same radix. The same word *vir*, is in our mother tongue, *wer*, and from this we have the English termination *er*.

It denotes an agent, as in *actor*, *creditor*. We annex it to many words of English origin, as in *lessor*, as we do *er* to words of Latin and Greek origin, as in *astronomer*, *laborer*. In general, *or* is annexed to words of Latin, and *er* to those of English origin.

OR, *conj.* [Sax. *other*; G. *oder*. It seems that *or* is a mere contraction of *other*.]

A connective that marks an alternative. "You may read *or* may write;" that is, you may do one of the things at your pleasure, but not both. It corresponds to *either*. You may *either* ride to London, *or* to Windsor. It often connects a series of words or propositions, presenting a choice of either. He may study law *or* medicine *or* divinity, *or* he may enter into trade. *Or* sometimes begins a sentence, but in this case it expresses an alternative with the foregoing sentence. Matt. vii. and ix.

In poetry, *or* is sometimes used for *either*.

> For thy vast bounties are so numberless,
> That them *or* to conceal or else to tell
> Is equally impossible. *Cowley.*

Or is often used to express an alternative of terms, definitions or explanations of the same thing in different words. Thus we say, a thing is a square, *or* a figure under four equal sides and angles.

Or ever. In this phrase, *or* is supposed to be a corruption of *ere*, Sax. *ære*, before; that is, *before ever.*

OR, in heraldry, gold. [Fr. *or*, L. *aurum.*]

OR'AƇH, OR'RAƇH, } *n.* A plant of the genus Atriplex, used as a substitute for spinage. *Encyc.*

Wild orach is of the genus Chenopodium.

OR'AƇLE, *n.* [Fr. from L. *oraculum*, from *oro*, to utter; Sp. *oraculo;* Ir. *oracolo.*]

1. Among *pagans*, the answer of a god or some person reputed to be a god, to an inquiry made respecting some affair of importance, usually respecting some future event, as the success of an enterprise or battle.
2. The deity who gave or was supposed to give answers to inquiries; as the Delphic *oracle.*
3. The place where the answers were given. *Encyc.*
4. Among christians, *oracles*, in the plural, denotes the communications, revelations or messages delivered by God to prophets. In this sense it is rarely used in the singular; but we say, the *oracles* of God, divine *oracles*, meaning the Scriptures.
5. The sanctuary or most holy place in the temple, in which was deposited the ark of the covenant. 1 Kings vi.
6. Any person or place where certain decisions are obtained. *Pope.*
7. Any person reputed uncommonly wise, whose determinations are not disputed, or whose opinions are of great authority.
8. A wise sentence or decision of great authority.

OR'AƇLE, *v. i.* To utter oracles. *Milton.*

ORAƇ'ULAR, ORAƇ'ULOUS, } *a.* Uttering oracles; as an *oracular* tongue.

The *oraculous* seer. *Pope.*

2. Grave; venerable; like an oracle; as an *oracular* shade.

They have something venerable and *oracular* in that unadorned gravity and shortness in the expression. *Pope.*

3. Positive; authoritative; magisterial; as *oraculous* expressions of sentiments. *Glanville.*
4. Obscure; ambiguous, like the oracles of pagan deities. *King.*

ORAƇ'ULARLY, ORAƇ'ULOUSLY, } *adv.* In the manner of an oracle. *Brown.*

2. Authoritatively; positively. *Burke.*

ORAƇ'ULOUSNESS, *n.* The state of being oracular.

OR'AISON, *n.* [Fr. *oraison;* L. *oratio.*] Prayer; verbal supplication or oral worship; now written *orison.* *Shak. Dryden.*

O'RAL, *a.* [Fr. from L. *os*, *oris*, the mouth.] Uttered by the mouth or in words; spoken, not written; as *oral* traditions; *oral* testimony; *oral* law. *Addison.*

O'RALLY, *adv.* By mouth; in words, without writing; as traditions derived *orally* from ancestors.

OR'ANĠE, *n.* [Fr. from L. *aurantium;* so named from *aurum*, gold, which the orange resembles in color; It. *arancio;* Sp. *naranjo;* Port. *laranja;* D. *oranje;* G. *orange.*]

The fruit of a species of Citrus which grows in warm climates. The fruit is round and depressed; it has a rough rind, which when ripe is yellow. This contains a vesicular pulp inclosed in nine cells for seeds. The tree producing oranges grows to the highth of ten or twelve feet and bears the same name.

OR'ANĠE-MUSK, *n.* A species of pear.

OR'ANĠE-PEEL, *n.* The rind of an orange separated from the fruit.

OR'ANĠERY, *n.* [Fr. *orangerie.*] A plantation of orange trees. *Johnson.*

OR'ANĠE-TAWNY, *a.* Of the color of an orange. *Bacon.*

OR'ANĠE-WIFE, *n.* A woman that sells oranges.

ŌRANG-OU'TANG, *n.* The satyr or great ape (*Simia satyrus,*) an animal with a flat face and deformed resemblance of the human form. These animals walk erect like man, feed on fruits, sleep on trees, and make a shelter against inclemencies of the weather. They grow to the highth of six feet, are remarkably strong, and wield weapons with the hand. They are solitary animals, inhabiting the interior of Africa and the isles of Sumatra, Borneo and Java. *Encyc.*

The orang-outang is found only in S. Eastern Asia. The African animal resembling it, is the chimpanzee (*Simia troglodytes.*) *Cuvier.*

ORA'TION, *n.* [L. *oratio*, from *oro*, to pray, to utter.]

1. A speech or discourse composed according to the rules of oratory, and spoken in public. Orations may be reduced to three kinds; demonstrative, deliberative, and judicial. *Encyc.*
2. In *modern usage*, an oration differs from a sermon, from an argument at the bar, and from a speech before a deliberative assembly. The word is now applied chiefly to discourses pronounced on special occasions, as a funeral *oration*, an *oration* on some anniversary, &c. and to academic declamations.
3. A harangue; a public speech or address.

OR'ATOR, *n.* [L.] A public speaker. In *ancient Rome*, orators were advocates for clients in the forum and before the senate and people. They were employed in causes of importance instead of the common patron. *Encyc.*

2. In *modern usage*, a person who pronounces a discourse publicly on some special occasion, as on the celebration of some memorable event.
3. An eloquent public speaker; a speaker, by way of eminence. We say, a man writes and reasons well, but is no *orator.* Lord Chatham was an *orator.*
4. In *France*, a speaker in debate in a legislative body.
5. In *chancery*, a petitioner.
6. An officer in the universities in England.

ORATO'RIAL, ORATOR'IƇAL, } *a.* Pertaining to an orator or to oratory; rhetorical; becoming an orator. We say, a man has many *oratorical* flourishes, or he speaks in an *oratorical* way. *Watts.*

ORATO'RIALLY, ORATOR'IƇALLY, } *adv.* In a rhetorical manner. *Taylor.*

ORATO'RIO, *n.* [It.] In *Italian music*, a sacred drama of dialogues, containing recitatives, duets, trios, ritornellos, choruses, &c. The subjects are mostly taken from the Scriptures. *Encyc.*

2. A place of worship; a chapel.

OR'ATORY, *n.* [Low L. *oratoria*, from *orator.*]

1. The art of speaking well, or of speaking according to the rules of rhetoric, in order to persuade. To constitute *oratory*, the speaking must be just and pertinent to the subject; it must be methodical, all parts of the discourse being disposed in due order and connection; and it must be embellished with the beauties of language and pronounced with eloquence. Oratory consists of four parts, *invention, disposition, elocution*, and *pronunciation.* *Encyc. Cyc.*
2. Exercise of eloquence. *Arbuthnot.*
3. Among *the Romanists*, a close apartment near a bed-chamber, furnished with an altar, a crucifix, &c. for private devotions.
4. A place allotted for prayer, or a place for public worship. *Hooker. Taylor.*

OR'ATRESS, OR'ATRIX, } *n.* A female orator. *Warner.*

ORB, *n.* [L. *orbis;* Fr. It. Sp. *orbe.*] A spherical body; as the celestial *orbs.*

2. In *astronomy*, a hollow globe or sphere. *Encyc.*
3. A wheel; a circular body that revolves or rolls; as the *orbs* of a chariot. *Milton.*
4. A circle; a sphere defined by a line; as, he moves in a larger *orb.* *Holiday. Shak.*
5. A circle described by any mundane sphere; an orbit. *Dryden.*
6. Period; revolution of time. *Shak.*
7. The eye. *Milton.*
8. In *tactics*, the circular form of a body of troops, or a circular body of troops. *Encyc.*

The ancient astronomers conceived the heavens as consisting of several vast azure transparent orbs or spheres inclosing one another, and including the bodies of the planets. *Hutton.*

ORB, *v. t.* To form into a circle. *Milton.*

ORB'ATE, *a.* [L. *orbatus.*] Bereaved; fatherless; childless.

ORBA'TION, *n.* [L. *orbatio*, from *orbo*, to bereave.]

Privation of parents or children, or privation in general. [*Not used.*]

ORB'ED, *a.* Round; circular; orbicular. *Shak.*

2. Formed into a circle or round shape. *Milton.*
3. Rounded or covered on the exterior.

The wheels were *orbed* with gold. *Addison.*

ORB'IƇ, *a.* Spherical. *Bacon.*

ORBIƇ'ULAR, *a.* [Fr. *orbiculaire*, from L. *orbiculus.*] Spherical; circular; in the form of an orb. *Milton. Addison.*

ORBIƇ'ULARLY, *adv.* Spherically.

ORBIƇ'ULARNESS, *n.* Sphericity; the state of being orbicular.

ORBIƇ'ULATE, ORBIƇ'ULATED, } *a.* [L. *orbiculatus.*] Made or being in the form of an orb. In *botany*, an *orbicu-*

late or *orbicular* leaf is one that has the periphery of a circle, or both its longitudinal and transverse diameters equal. *Martyn.*

ORBICULA'TION, *n.* The state of being made in the form of an orb. *More.*

ORB'IS, ORB'-FISH, *n.* A fish of a circular form. It is covered with a firm hard skin full of small prickles, but is destitute of scales. It is unfit for food. *Dict. Nat. Hist.*

ORB'IT, *n.* [Fr. *orbite*; L. *orbita*, a trace or track, from *orbis*, a wheel.]

1. In *astronomy*, the path of a planet or comet; the curve line which a planet describes in its periodical revolution round its central body; as the *orbit* of Jupiter or Mercury. The *orbit* of the earth is nearly one hundred and ninety millions of miles in diameter. The *orbit* of the moon is 480,000 miles in diameter. The *orbits* of the planets are elliptical.
2. A small orb. [*Not proper.*] *Young.*
3. In *anatomy*, the cavity in which the eye is situated.

ORB'ITAL, ORBIT'UAL, *a.* Pertaining to the orbit. *Med. Repos. Hooper.*

[*Orbital* is the preferable word.]

ORB'ITUDE, ORB'ITY, *n.* [L. *orbitas.*] Bereavement by loss of parents or children. [*Little used.*] *Hall.*

ORB'Y, *a.* [from *orb.*] Resembling an orb. *Chapman.*

ORC, *n.* [L. *orca*; Gr. ορυγα.] A sea-fish, a species of whale. *Drayton.*

The Delphinus orca is the grampus.

ORCHAL, ORCHEL, ORCHIL. [See *Archil.*]

OR'CHANET, *n.* A plant, [*Anchusa tinctoria.*] *Ainsworth.*

OR'CHARD, *n.* [Sax. *ortgeard*; Goth. *aurtigards*; Dan. *urtegaard*; Sw. *örtegård*; that is, *wort-yard*, a yard for herbs. The Germans call it *baumgarten*, tree-garden, and the Dutch *boomgaard*, tree-yard. See *Yard.*]

An inclosure for fruit trees. In Great Britain, a department of the garden appropriated to fruit trees of all kinds, but chiefly to apple trees. In America, any piece of land set with apple trees, is called an orchard; and orchards are usually cultivated land, being either grounds for mowing or tillage. In some parts of the country, a piece of ground planted with peach trees is called a peach-orchard. But in most cases, I believe the orchard in both countries is distinct from the garden.

OR'CHARDING, *n.* The cultivation of orchards. *Evelyn.*

2. Orchards in general. *U. States.*

OR'CHARDIST, *n.* One that cultivates orchards.

OR'CHESTER, OR'CHESTRA, *n.* [L. *orchestra*; Gr. ορχησρα, from ορχησηρ, a dancer, from ορχεομαι, to dance; originally, the place for the chorus of dancers.]

1. The part of a theater or other public place appropriated to the musicians. In the Grecian theaters, the orchester was a part of the stage; it was of a semicircular form and surrounded with seats. In the Roman theaters, it was no part of the scena, but answered nearly to the pit in modern play houses, and was occupied by senators and other persons of distinction. *Encyc.*
2. The body of performers in the orchester. *Busby.*

OR'CHESTRAL, *a.* [supra.] Pertaining to an orchester; suitable for or performed in the orchester. *Busby.*

OR'CHIS, *n.* [L. *orchis*; Gr. ορχις.] A genus of plants, called fool-stones. *Encyc.*

ORD, *n.* [Sax.] An edge or point; as in *ordhelm.*

Ord signifies beginning; as in *ords and ends.*

ORDA'IN, *v. t.* [L. *ordino*, from *ordo*, order; Fr. *ordonner*; It. *ordinare*; Sp. *ordenar*; Ir. *orduighim.*]

1. Properly, to set; to establish in a particular office or order; hence, to invest with a ministerial function or sacerdotal power; to introduce and establish or settle in the pastoral office with the customary forms and solemnities; as, to *ordain* a minister of the gospel. In America, men are *ordained* over a particular church and congregation, or as evangelists without the charge of a particular church, or as deacons in the episcopal church.
2. To appoint; to decree.

   Jeroboam *ordained* a feast in the eighth month. 1 Kings xii.

   As many as were *ordained* to eternal life, believed. Acts xiii.

   The fatal tent,
   The scene of death and place *ordained* for punishment. *Dryden.*
3. To set; to establish; to institute; to constitute.

   Mulmutius
   Ordained our laws. *Shak.*
4. To set apart for an office; to appoint.

   Jesus *ordained* twelve that they should be with him. Mark iii.
5. To appoint; to prepare.

   For Tophet is *ordained* of old. Is. xxx.

ORDA'INABLE, *a.* That may be appointed. *Hall.*

ORDA'INED, *pp.* Appointed; instituted; established; invested with ministerial or pastoral functions; settled.

ORDA'INER, *n.* One who ordains, appoints or invests with sacerdotal powers.

ORDA'INING, *ppr.* Appointing; establishing; investing with sacerdotal or pastoral functions.

OR'DEAL, *n.* [Sax. *ordal* or *ordæl*; G. *urtheil*; D. *ordeel.* The last syllable is *deal*, to divide or distribute. The sense of the prefix is less obvious. Wilkins supposes *or* to signify *without*, as in some Saxon words it has that sense, and *ordeal* to signify without difference or distinction of persons, entire judgment. In Saxon, *ord* signifies origin, cause, beginning, prime. In G. *ur* signifies prime, very, original; *urwort*, primitive word. In Dutch, *oor* is the *ear*; *oorlog*, war. But this prefix would seem to be the same as in *furlow* [furlough]; for in G. *urlaub*, D. *oorlof*, Dan. *orlov*, Sw. *orlof*, is a furlow, and this indicates that *or* is a corruption of *far* or *for*. In Welsh, this word is *gordal*, which Owen compounds of *gor*, high, superior, extreme, above, and *tâl*, reward, requital; and *gordal* signifies not only *ordeal*, but an over-payment, a making satisfaction over and above. *Or* then may signify *out, away*, and in *ordeal* may denote *ultimate, final.* But the real sense is not obvious. The practice of ordeal however seems to have had its origin in the belief that the substances used had each its particular presiding deity that had perfect control over it.]

1. An ancient form of trial to determine guilt or innocence, practiced by the rude nations of Europe, and still practiced in the East Indies. In England, the ordeal was of two sorts, *fire-ordeal* and *water-ordeal*; the former being confined to persons of higher rank, the latter to the common people. Both might be performed by deputy, but the principal was to answer for the success of the trial.

   Fire-ordeal was performed either by taking in the hand a piece of red hot iron, or by walking barefoot and blindfold over nine red hot plowshares laid lengthwise at unequal distances; and if the person escaped unhurt, he was adjudged innocent, otherwise he was condemned as guilty.

   Water-ordeal was performed, either by plunging the bare arm to the elbow in boiling water, or by casting the person suspected into a river or pond of cold water, and if he floated without an effort to swim, it was an evidence of guilt, but if he sunk he was acquitted.

   Both in England and Sweden, the clergy presided at this trial. It was at last condemned as unlawful by the canon law, and in England it was abolished by an order in council of Henry III. *Blackstone.*

   It is probable our proverbial phrase, to *go through fire and water*, denoting severe trial or danger, is derived from the ordeal; as also the trial of witches by water.
2. Severe trial; accurate scrutiny.

OR'DER, *n.* [L. *ordo*; [qu. Pers. رَدَه radah, order, series;] Fr. *ordre*; It. *ordine*; Sp. *orden*; Sw. Dan. G. Russ. *id.*; Ir. *ord*; but all from the Latin except the Persian.]

1. Regular disposition or methodical arrangement of things; *a word of extensive application*; as the *order* of troops on parade; the *order* of books in a library; the *order* of proceedings in a legislative assembly. *Order* is the life of business.

   Good *order* is the foundation of all good things. *Burke.*
2. Proper state; as the muskets are all in good *order.* When the bodily organs are in *order*, a person is in health; when they are out of *order*, he is indisposed.
3. Adherence to the point in discussion, according to established rules of debate; as, the member is not in *order*, that is, he wanders from the question.
4. Established mode of proceeding. The motion is not in *order.*
5. Regularity; settled mode of operation. This fact could not occur in the *order* of nature; it is against the natural *order* of things.
6. Mandate; precept; command; authoritative direction. I have received an *order* from the commander in chief. The general gave *orders* to march. There is an *order* of council to issue letters of marque.
7. Rule; regulation; as the rules and *orders* of a legislative house.

8. Regular government or discipline. It is necessary for society that good *order* should be observed. The meeting was turbulent; it was impossible to keep *order*.
9. Rank; class; division of men; as the *order* of nobles; the *order* of priests; the higher *orders* of society; men of the lowest *order*; *order* of knights; military *orders*, &c.
10. A religious fraternity; as the *order* of Benedictines.
11. A division of natural objects, generally intermediate between class and genus. The classes, in the Linnean artificial system, are divided into *orders*, which include one or more genera. Linne also arranged vegetables, in his natural system, into groups of genera, called *orders*. In the natural system of Jussieu, *orders* are subdivisions of classes.
12. Measures; care. Take some *order* for the safety and support of the soldiers.

Provide me soldiers
Whilst I take *order* for my own affairs. *Shak.*

13. In *rhetoric*, the placing of words and members in a sentence in such a manner as to contribute to force and beauty of expression, or to the clear illustration of the subject. *Encyc.*
14. The title of certain ancient books containing the divine office and manner of its performance. *Encyc.*
15. In *architecture*, a system of several members, ornaments and proportions of columns and pilasters; or a regular arrangement of the projecting parts of a building, especially of the columns, so as to form one beautiful whole. The orders are five, the Tuscan, Doric, Ionic, Corinthian, and Composite. The order consists of two principal members, the *column*, and the *entablature*, each of which is composed of three principal parts. Those of the column are the base, the shaft, and the capital; those of the entablature are the architrave, the frize, and the cornice. The highth of the Tuscan column is 14 modules or semidiameters of the shaft at the bottom, and that of the entablature 3½. The highth of the Doric order is 16 modules and that of the entablature 4; that of the Ionic is 18 modules, and that of the entablature 4½, that of the Corinthian order is 20 modules, and that of the entablature 5. The highth of the Composite order agrees with that of the Corinthian. *Encyc.*

In orders, set apart for the performance of divine service; ordained to the work of the gospel ministry.

In order, for the purpose; to the end; as means to an end. The best knowledge is that which is of the greatest use *in order* to our eternal happiness.

General orders, the commands or notices which a military commander in chief issues to the troops under his command.

OR'DER, *v. t.* To regulate; to methodize; to systemize; to adjust; to subject to system in management and execution; as, to *order* domestic affairs with prudence.
2. To lead; to conduct; to subject to rules or laws.

To him that *ordereth* his conversation aright, will I show the salvation of God. Ps. l.

3. To direct; to command. The general *ordered* his troops to advance.
4. To manage; to treat.

How shall we *order* the child? Judges xiii.

5. To ordain. [*Not used.*] *Whitgifte.*
6. To direct; to dispose in any particular manner.

Order my steps in thy word. Ps. cxix.

OR'DER, *v. i.* To give command or direction. *Milton.*

OR'DERED, *pp.* Regulated; methodized; disposed; commanded; managed.

OR'DERER, *n.* One that gives orders.
2. One that methodizes or regulates.

OR'DERING, *ppr.* Regulating; systemizing; commanding; disposing.

OR'DERING, *n.* Disposition; distribution. 2 Chron. xxiv.

OR'DERLESS, *a.* Without regularity; disorderly; out of rule. *Shak.*

OR'DERLINESS, *n.* [from *orderly*.] Regularity; a state of being methodical.
2. The state of being orderly.

OR'DERLY, *a.* Methodical; regular. *Hooker.*
2. Observant of order or method. *Chapman.*
3. Well regulated; performed in good order; not tumultuous; as an *orderly* march. *Clarendon.*
4. According to established method. *Hooker.*
5. Not unruly; not inclined to break from inclosures; peaceable. We say, cattle are *orderly*.

Orderly book, in military affairs, a book for every company, in which the sergeants write general and regimental orders. *Cyc.*

Orderly sergeant, a military officer who attends on a superior officer.

OR'DERLY, *adv.* Methodically; according to due order; regularly; according to rule. *Shak.*

ORDINABIL'ITY, *n.* Capability of being appointed. [*Not used.*] *Bull.*

OR'DINABLE, *a.* Such as may be appointed. [*Not used.*] *Hammond.*

OR'DINAL, *a.* [L. *ordinalis*; Fr. *ordinal*.] Noting order; as the *ordinal* numbers, first, second, third, &c.

OR'DINAL, *n.* A number noting order.
2. A book containing the order of divine service; a ritual. *Encyc.*

OR'DINANCE, *n.* [It. *ordinanza*; Fr. *ordonnance*.]
1. A rule established by authority; a permanent rule of action. An ordinance may be a law or statute of sovereign power. In this sense it is often used in the Scriptures. Ex. xv. Num. x. Ezra iii. It may also signify a decree, edict or rescript, and the word has sometimes been applied to the statutes of Parliament, but these are usually called acts or laws. In the United States, it is never applied to the acts of Congress, or of a state legislature.
2. Observance commanded. *Taylor.*
3. Appointment. *Shak.*
4. Established rite or ceremony. Heb. ix. In this sense, baptism and the Lord's supper are denominated *ordinances*.

OR'DINANT, *a.* [L. *ordinans*.] Ordaining; decreeing. [*Not used.*] *Shak.*

OR'DINARILY, *adv.* Primarily, according to established rules or settled method; hence, commonly; usually; in most cases as a winter more than *ordinarily* severe. *Glanville.*

OR'DINARY, *a.* [L. *ordinarius*.] According to established order; methodical; regular; customary; as the *ordinary* forms of law or justice. *Addison.*
2. Common; usual.

Method is not less requisite in *ordinary* conversation than in writing. *Addison.*

3. Of common rank; not distinguished by superior excellence; as an *ordinary* reader; men of *ordinary* judgment. *Hooker.*
4. Plain; not handsome; as an *ordinary* woman; a person of an *ordinary* form; an *ordinary* face.
5. Inferior; of little merit; as, the book is an *ordinary* performance.
6. An *ordinary* seaman is one not expert or fully skilled.

OR'DINARY, *n.* In *the common* and *canon law*, one who has ordinary or immediate jurisdiction in matters ecclesiastical; an ecclesiastical judge. In England, the bishop of the diocese is commonly the *ordinary*, and the archbishop is the *ordinary* of the whole province. The *ordinary* of assizes and sessions was formerly a deputy of the bishop, appointed to give malefactors their neck-verses. The *ordinary* of Newgate is one who attends on condemned malefactors to prepare them for death. *Encyc.*
2. Settled establishment. *Bacon.*
3. Regular price of a meal. *Shak.*
4. A place of eating where the prices are settled. *Swift.*
5. The establishment of persons employed by government to take charge of ships of war laid up in harbors. Hence a ship *in ordinary* is one laid up under the direction of the master attendant.

In ordinary, in actual and constant service; statedly attending and serving; as a physician or chaplain *in ordinary*. An embassador *in ordinary*, is one constantly resident at a foreign court.

OR'DINATE, *v. t.* To appoint. [*Not used.*]

OR'DINATE, *a.* [L. *ordinatus*.] Regular; methodical. An *ordinate* figure is one whose sides and angles are equal. *Ray.*

OR'DINATE, *n.* In *geometry* and *conic sections*, a line drawn from any point of the circumference of an ellipsis or other conic section, perpendicularly across the axis to the other side. *Encyc.*

An *ordinate* is a line drawn perpendicular to the axis of a curve and terminating the curvilinear space. *Bp. Berkley. Todd.*

Ordinates of a curve, right lines parallel to one another, terminated by the curve, and bisected by a right line called the diameter. *Cyc.*

OR'DINATELY, *adv.* In a regular methodical manner. *Skelton.*

ORDINA'TION, *n.* [L. *ordinatio*.] The state of being ordained or appointed; established order or tendency consequent on a decree.

Virtue and vice have a natural *ordination* to the happiness and misery of life respectively. *Norris.*

2. The act of conferring holy orders or sacerdotal power; called also consecration. *Encyc.*

3. In *the presbyterian* and *congregational churches*, the act of settling or establishing a licensed clergyman over a church and congregation with pastoral charge and authority; also, the act of conferring on a clergyman the powers of a settled minister of the gospel, without the charge or oversight of a particular church, but with the general powers of an evangelist, who is authorized to form churches and administer the sacraments of baptism and the Lord's supper, wherever he may be called to officiate.

OR'DINATIVE, *a.* Directing; giving order. *Cotgrave.*

ORD'NANCE, *n.* [from *ordinance.*] Cannon or great guns, mortars and howitzers; artillery.

OR'DONNANCE, *n.* [Fr.] In *painting*, the disposition of the parts of a picture, either in regard to the whole piece or to the several parts. *Cyc.*

OR'DURE, *n.* [Fr.] Dung; excrements. *Shak.*

ORE, *n.* [Sax. *ore, ora*; D. *erts*; G. *erz.* Qu. L. *æs, æris*, brass; Rabbinic, עור a mineral.]

1. The compound of a metal and some other substance, as oxygen, sulphur or carbon, called its mineralizer, by which its properties are disguised or lost. Metals found free from such combination and exhibiting naturally their appropriate character, are not called ores, but native metals. *D. Olmsted.*

2. Metal; as the liquid *ore*. *Milton.*

O'READ, *n.* [from Gr. ορος, mountain.] A mountain nymph. *Milton.*

OR'E-WEED, OR'E-WOOD, *n.* Sea weed. [*Not used.*] *Carew.*

ORF'GILD, *n.* [Sax. *orf*, cattle, and *geld*, payment.]

The restitution of goods or money stolen, if taken in the day time. *Ainsworth.*

OR'FRAYS, *n.* [Fr. *orfroi.*] Fringe of gold; gold embroidery. *Chaucer.*

OR'GAL, *n.* Argal; lees of wine dried; tartar. *Encyc.*

OR'GAN, *n.* [L. *organum*; Gr. οργανον; Sp. It. *organo*; Fr. *organe*; D. G. *orgel*; Pers. Ar. *arganon.*]

1. A natural instrument of action or operation, or by which some process is carried on. Thus the arteries and veins of animal bodies are *organs* of circulation; the lungs are *organs* of respiration; the nerves are *organs* of perception and sensation; the muscles are *organs* of motion; the ears are *organs* of hearing; the tongue is the *organ* of speech.

2. The instrument or means of conveyance or communication. A secretary of state is the *organ* of communication between the government and a foreign power.

3. The largest and most harmonious of wind instruments of music, consisting of pipes which are filled with wind, and stops touched by the fingers. It is blown by a bellows. *Johnson. Encyc.*

OR'GAN-BUILDER, *n.* An artist whose occupation is to construct organs.

ORGAN'IC, ORGAN'ICAL, *a.* [L. *organicus.*] Pertaining to an organ or to organs; consisting of organs or containing them; as the *organic* structure of the human body or of plants.

2. Produced by the organs; as *organic* pleasure. *Kames.*

3. Instrumental; acting as instruments of nature or art to a certain end; as *organic* arts. *Milton.*

Organic bodies, are such as possess organs, on the action of which depend their growth and perfection; as animals and plants.

ORGAN'ICALLY, *adv.* With organs; with organical structure or disposition of parts. The bodies of animals and plants are *organically* framed.

2. By means of organs.

ORGAN'ICALNESS, *n.* The state of being organical. *Johnson.*

OR'GANISM, *n.* Organical structure; as the *organism* of bodies. *Grew.*

OR'GANIST, *n.* One who plays on the organ. *Boyle.*

2. One who sung in parts; *an old musical use of the word.*

ORGANIZA'TION, *n.* The act or process of forming organs or instruments of action.

2. The act of forming or arranging the parts of a compound or complex body in a suitable manner for use or service; the act of distributing into suitable divisions and appointing the proper officers, as an army or a government.

> The first *organization* of the general government. *Pickering.*

3. Structure; form; suitable disposition of parts which are to act together in a compound body. *Locke.*

OR'GANIZE, *v. t.* [Fr. *organiser*; It. *organizzare*; Sp. *organizar.*]

1. To form with suitable organs; to construct so that one part may cooperate with another.

> Those nobler faculties of the soul *organized* matter could never produce. *Ray.*

2. To sing in parts; as, to *organize* the halleluiah. *Busby.*

3. To distribute into suitable parts and appoint proper officers, that the whole may act as one body; as, to *organize* an army. So we say, to *organize* the house of representatives, which is done by the appointment of officers and verification of the powers of the several members. So we say, a club, a party or a faction is *organized*, when it takes a systemized form.

> This original and supreme will *organizes* the government. *W. Cranch.*

OR'GANIZED, *pp.* Formed with organs; constructed organically; systemized; reduced to a form in which all the parts may act together to one end. Animals and plants are *organized* bodies. Minerals are not *organized* bodies.

OR'GANIZING, *ppr.* Constructing with suitable organs; reducing to system in order to produce united action to one end.

OR'GAN-LOFT, *n.* The loft where an organ stands. *Tatler.*

ORGANOGRAPH'IC, ORGANOGRAPH'ICAL, *a.* Pertaining to organography.

ORGANOG'RAPHY, *n.* [Gr. οργανον and γραφω.] In *botany*, a description of the organs of plants, or of the names and kinds of their organs. *Decandolle.*

OR'GAN-PIPE, *n.* The pipe of a musical organ. *Shak.*

OR'GAN-STOP, *n.* The stop of an organ, or any collection of pipes under one general name. *Busby.*

ORGANY. [See *Origan.*]

ORGAN'ZINE, *n.* Silk twisted into threads; thrown silk. *Aikin.*

OR'GASM, *n.* [Gr. οργασμος, from οργαω, to swell; οργαζω, to irritate.]

Immoderate excitement or action; as the *orgasm* of the blood or spirits. *Blackmore. Derham.*

OR'GEAT, *n.* [Fr. from *orge*, barley.] A liquor extracted from barley and sweet almonds. *Mason.*

OR'GEIS, *n.* A fish, called also *organ-ling*; supposed to be from *Orkneys*, on the coast of which it is taken. *Johnson.*

OR'GIES, *n. plu.* [Gr. οργια, from οργαω, to swell; οργη, fury; L. *orgia*; Fr. *orgies.*]

Frantic revels at the feast in honor of Bacchus, or the feast itself. This feast was held in the night; hence nocturnal *orgies*. *Dryden. Encyc.*

ORGIL'LOUS, *a.* [Fr. *orgueilleux*, from *orgueil*, Sax. *orgel*, pride, haughtiness; Gr. οργαω, to swell.] Proud; haughty. [*Not used.*] *Shak.*

OR'GUES, *n.* [Fr.] In *the military art*, long thick pieces of timber, pointed and shod with iron and hung over a gateway, to be let down in case of attack. *Encyc.*

2. A machine composed of several musket barrels united, by means of which several explosions are made at once to defend breaches. *Cyc.*

OR'ICHALCH, ORICHAL'CUM, *n.* [L. *orichalcum*, mountain brass; Gr. ορος and χαλκος; or *aurichalcum*, gold-brass.]

A metallic substance resembling gold in color, but inferior in value; the brass of the ancients. *Spenser. Encyc. Ure.*

O'RIEL, O'RIOL, *n.* [Old Fr. *oriol.*] A small apartment next a hall, where particular persons dine; a sort of recess. *Obs.* *Cowel.*

O'RIENCY, *n.* [See *Orient.*] Brightness or strength of color. [*Little used.*] *Waterhouse.*

O'RIENT, *a.* [L. *oriens*, from *orior*, to arise.]

1. Rising, as the sun.

> —Moon, that now meet'st the *orient* sun. *Milton.*

> The *orient* morn. *Milton.*

2. Eastern; oriental.

3. Bright; shining; glittering; as *orient* pearls. *Dryden.*

O'RIENT, *n.* The east; the part of the horizon where the sun first appears in the morning.

ORIENT'AL, *a.* Eastern; situated in the east; as *oriental* seas or countries.

2. Proceeding from the east; as the *oriental* radiations of the sun. *Brown.*

ORIENT'AL, *n.* A native or inhabitant of some eastern part of the world. We give the appellation to the inhabitants of Asia from the Hellespont and Mediterranean to Japan.

ORIENT'ALISM, *n.* An eastern mode of speech; an idiom of the eastern languages. *Warton.*

ORIENT'ALIST, *n.* An inhabitant of the eastern parts of the world. *Peters.*

2. One versed in the eastern languages and literature. *Ouseley.*

ORIENTAL'ITY, *n.* The state of being oriental or eastern. [*Not used.*] *Brown.*

OR'IFICE, *n.* [Fr. from L. *orificium* ; *os, oris*, mouth, and *facio*, to make.]

The mouth or aperture of a tube, pipe or other cavity ; as the *orifice* of an artery or vein ; the *orifice* of a wound.

The *orifice* of Etna. *Addison.*

OR'IFLAMB, *n.* [Fr. *oriflamme.*] The ancient royal standard of France. *Ainsworth.*

OR'IGAN, } *n.* [L. from Gr. οριγανον.]
ORIGA'NUM, } Marjoram, a genus of plants. One species of this genus is a rich aromatic, excellent for culinary purposes.

OR'IGENISM, *n.* The doctrines or tenets of Origen, who united Platonism with christianity. *Milner.*

OR'IGENIST, *n.* A follower of Origen of Alexandria, a celebrated christian father. The Origenists held that the souls of men have a pre-existent state; that they are holy intelligences, and sin before they are united to the body; that Christ will be crucified hereafter for the salvation of devils, &c. *Encyc.*

OR'IGIN, *n.* [Fr. It. *origine* ; Sp. *origen* ; L. *origo.*]

1. The first existence or beginning of any thing ; as the *origin* of Rome. In history it is necessary, if practicable, to trace all events to their *origin.*

2. Fountain ; source ; cause ; that from which any thing primarily proceeds ; that which gives existence or beginning. The apostasy is believed to have been the *origin* of moral evil. The *origin* of many of our customs is lost in antiquity. Nations, like individuals, are ambitious to trace their descent from an honorable *origin.*

ORIG'INAL, *n.* Origin. [See *Origin*, with which it accords in signification.]

2. First copy ; archetype ; that from which any thing is transcribed or translated, or from which a likeness is made by the pencil, press or otherwise. Thus we say, the translation is not equal to the *original.* If the *original* cannot be produced, we are permitted to offer an authenticated copy.

ORIG'INAL, *a.* [Fr. *originel* ; L. *originalis.*]

1. First in order ; preceding all others ; as the *original* state of man ; the *original* laws of a country ; *original* rights or powers ; the *original* question in debate.

2. Primitive ; pristine ; as the *original* perfection of Adam.

Original sin, as applied to Adam, was his first act of disobedience in eating the forbidden fruit ; as applied to his posterity, it is understood to mean either the sin of Adam imputed to his posterity, or that corruption of nature, or total depravity, which has been derived from him in consequence of his apostasy. On this subject divines are not agreed.

In strictness, *original sin* is an improper use of words, as sin, *ex vi termini*, implies volition and the transgression of a known rule of duty by a moral agent. But this application of the words has been established by long use, and it serves to express ideas which many wise and good men entertain on this subject.

3. Having the power to originate new thoughts or combinations of thought ; as an *original* genius.

ORIGINAL'ITY, *n.* The quality or state of being original.

2. The power of originating or producing new thoughts, or uncommon combinations of thought ; as *originality* of genius.

ORIG'INALLY, *adv.* Primarily ; from the beginning or origin.

God is *originally* holy in himself. *Pearson.*

2. At first ; at the origin. *Woodward.*

3. By the first author ; as a book *originally* written by another hand. *Roscommon.*

ORIG'INALNESS, *n.* The quality or state of being original.

ORIG'INARY, *a.* [Fr. *originaire.*] Productive ; causing existence.

The production of animals in the *originary* way, requires a certain degree of warmth. *Cheyne.*

2. Primitive ; original. *Sandys.*
[*This word is little used.*]

ORIG'INATE, *v. t.* To cause to be ; to bring into existence ; to produce what is new.

The change is to be effected without a decomposition of the whole civil and political mass, for the purpose of *originating* a new civil order out of the elements of society. *Burke.*

That matter which cannot think, will, or *originate* motion, should communicate thought, volition and motivity, is plainly impossible. *Dwight.*

ORIG'INATE, *v. i.* To take first existence ; to have origin ; to be begun. The scheme *originated* with the governor and council. It *originated* in pure benevolence.

ORIG'INATED, *pp.* Brought into existence.

ORIG'INATING, *ppr.* Bringing into existence.

ORIGINA'TION, *n.* The act of bringing or coming into existence ; first production.

Descartes first introduced the fancy of making a world, and deducing the *origination* of the universe from mechanical principles. *Keil.*

2. Mode of production or bringing into being.

This eruca is propagated by animal parents, to wit, butterflies, after the common *origination* of all caterpillars. *Ray.*

ORIL'LON, *n.* [Fr.] In *fortification*, a rounding of earth, faced with a wall, raised on the shoulder of those bastions that have casemates, to cover the cannon in the retired flank, and prevent their being dismounted. *Encyc. Cyc.*

O'RIOLE, *n.* A genus of birds of the order of picæ.

ORI'ON, *n.* [Gr. ωριων ; unfortunately accented by the poets on the second syllable.]

A constellation in the southern hemisphere, containing seventy eight stars. *Encyc.*

OR'ISON, *n.* [Fr. *oraison*, from L. *oratio*, from, *oro.*]

A prayer or supplication.

Lowly they bowed adoring, and began
Their *orisons*, each morning duly paid. *Milton.*

ORK, *n.* [L. *orca.*] A fish.

ORLE, *n.* [infra.] In *heraldry*, an ordinary in the form of a fillet, round the shield.

OR'LET, } *n.* [Fr. *ourlet*, It. *orlo*, a hem. Qu.
OR'LO, } Heb. עלה, and Ch. Syr.] In *architecture*, a fillet under the ovolo of a capital.

OR'LOP, *n.* [D. *overloop*, a running over or overflowing, an orlop, that is, a spreading over.]

In *a ship of war*, a platform of planks laid over the beams in the hold, on which the cables are usually coiled. It contains also sail-rooms, carpenters' cabins and other apartments. *Mar. Dict.*

Also, a tier of beams below the lower deck for a like purpose. *Cyc.*

OR'NAMENT, *n.* [L. *ornamentum*, from *orno*, to adorn. Varro informs us that this was primitively *osnamentum* ; but this is improbable. See *Adorn.*]

1. That which embellishes ; something which, added to another thing, renders it more beautiful to the eye.

The chains, and the bracelets, and the mufflers, the bonnets and the *ornaments* of the legs— Is. iii.

2. In *architecture*, ornaments are sculpture or carved work.

3. Embellishment ; decoration ; additional beauty.

—The *ornament* of a meek and quiet spirit, which is in the sight of God of great price. 1 Pet. iii.

OR'NAMENT, *v. t.* To adorn ; to deck ; to embellish. *Warburton.*

ORNAMENT'AL, *a.* Serving to decorate ; giving additional beauty ; embellishing.

Some think it most *ornamental* to wear their bracelets on their wrists ; others about their ankles. *Brown.*

ORNAMENT'ALLY, *adv.* In such a manner as to add embellishment.

OR'NAMENTED, *pp.* Decorated ; embellished ; beautified. *Shenstone.*

OR'NAMENTING, *ppr.* Decorating ; embellishing.

OR'NATE, *a.* [L. *ornatus.*] Adorned ; decorated ; beautiful. *Milton.*

OR'NATELY, *adv.* With decoration. *Skelton.*

OR'NATENESS, *n.* State of being adorned.

OR'NATURE, *n.* Decoration. [*Little used.*]

ORNISCOP'ICS, *n.* Divination by the observation of fowls. *Bailey.*

ORNIS'COPIST, *n.* [Gr. ορνις, a bird, and σκοπεω, to view.]

One who views the flight of fowls in order to foretell future events by their manner of flight. [*Little used.*] *Johnson.*

ORNITH'OLITE, *n.* A petrified bird.

ORNITHOLOG'ICAL, *a.* Pertaining to ornithology.

ORNITHOL'OGIST, *n.* [See *Ornithology.*] A person who is skilled in the natural history of fowls, who understands their form, structure, habits and uses ; one who describes birds.

ORNITHOL'OGY, *n.* [Gr. ορνις, a fowl, and λογος, discourse.]

The science of fowls, which comprises a knowledge of their form, structure, habits and uses.

ORNITH'OMANCY, *n.* [Gr. ορνις, a fowl, and μαντεια, divination.]

Augury, a species of divination by means of fowls, their flight, &c. *Encyc.*

OROLOĠ'IEAL, *a.* [See *Orology.*] Pertaining to a description of mountains.

OROL'OĠIST, *n.* A describer of mountains.

OROL'OĠY, *n.* [Gr. ορος, a mountain, and λογος, discourse.] The science or description of mountains.

OR'PHAN, *n.* [Gr. ορφανος; It. *orfano*; Fr. *orphelin.*]
A child who is bereaved of father or mother or of both.

OR'PHAN, *a.* Bereaved of parents. *Sidney.*

OR'PHANAĠE, } *n.* The state of an orphan.
OR'PHANISM, } *Sherwood.*

OR'PHANED, *a.* Bereft of parents or friends. *Young.*

ORPHANOT'ROPHY, *n.* [Gr. ορφανος, orphan, and τροφη, food.] A hospital for orphans. *Todd.*

OR'PHEAN, } *a.* Pertaining to Orpheus, the
OR'PHIE, } poet and musician; as *Orphic* hymns. *Bryant.*

OR'PHEUS, *n.* A fish found in the Mediterranean, broad, flat and thick, and sometimes weighing twenty pounds. The orpheus of the Greeks is said to have been a different fish. *Dict. Nat. Hist. Encyc.*

OR'PIMENT, *n.* [L. *auripigmentum; aurum*, gold, and *pigmentum.*]
Sulphuret of arsenic, found native and then an ore of arsenic, or artificially composed. The native orpiment appears in yellow, brilliant and seemingly talcky masses of various sizes. The red orpiment is called *realgar.* It is more or less lively and transparent, and often crystalized in bright needles. In this form it is called *ruby of arsenic.*
Fourcroy. Nicholson. Encyc. Ure.

OR'PINE, *n.* [Fr. *orpin.*] A plant of the genus Sedum, lesser houseleek or livelong. The *bastard orpine* is of the genus Andrachne; the *lesser orpine* of the genus Crassula.

ORRACH. [See *Orach.*]

OR'RERY, *n.* A machine so constructed as to represent by the movements of its parts, the motions and phases of the planets in their orbits. This machine was invented by George Graham, but Rowley, a workman, borrowed one from him, and made a copy for the earl of Orrery, after whom it was named by Sir Richard Steele. Similar machines are called also planetariums. *Cyc.*

OR'RIS, *n.* The plant *iris*, of which *orris* seems to be a corruption; fleur de lis or flag-flower. *Encyc.*
2. A sort of gold or silver lace. Qu. *orfrais.* *Johnson.*

ORT, *n.* A fragment; refuse. *Shak.*

OR'TALON, *n.* A small bird of the genus Alauda. *Encyc.*

OR'THITE, *n.* [Gr. ορθος, straight.] A mineral occurring in straight layers in felspath rock with albite, &c. It is of a blackish brown color, resembling gadolinite, but differs from it in fusibility.
Dict. Nat. Hist. Ure. Cleaveland.

ORTHOCER'ATITE, *n.* [Gr. ορθος, straight, and κερας, a horn.]
The name of certain fossil univalve shells, straight or but slightly curved, arranged by Cuvier in the genus Nautilus.

OR'THODOX, *a.* [See *Orthodoxy.*] Sound in the christian faith; believing the genuine doctrines taught in the Scriptures; opposed to *heretical;* as an *orthodox* christian.
2. According with the doctrines of Scripture; as an *orthodox* creed or faith.

OR'THODOXLY, *adv.* With soundness of faith. *Bacon.*

OR'THODOXNESS, *n.* The state of being sound in the faith, or of according with the doctrines of Scripture.

OR'THODOXY, *n.* [Gr. ορθοδοξια; ορθος, right, true, and δοξα, opinion, from δοκεω, to think.]
1. Soundness of faith; a belief in the genuine doctrines taught in the Scriptures.

Basil bears full and clear testimony to Gregory's *orthodoxy.* *Waterland.*

2. Consonance to genuine scriptural doctrines; as the *orthodoxy* of a creed.

ORTHODROM'IE, *a.* [See *Orthodromy.*] Pertaining to orthodromy.

ORTHODROM'IES, *n.* The art of sailing in the arc of a great circle, which is the shortest distance between any two points on the surface of the globe. *Harris.*

OR'THODROMY, *n.* [Gr. ορθος, right, and δρομος, course.] The sailing in a straight course.

OR'THOEPIST, *n.* [See *Orthoepy.*] One who pronounces words correctly, or who is well skilled in pronunciation.

OR'THOEPY, *n.* [Gr. ορθοεπεια; ορθος, right, and επος, word, or επω, to speak.]
The art of uttering words with propriety; a correct pronunciation of words. *Nares.*

OR'THOGON, *n.* [Gr. ορθος, right, and γωνια, angle.] A rectangular figure. *Peacham.*

ORTHOG'ONAL, *a.* Right angled; rectangular. *Selden.*

ORTHOG'RAPHER, *n.* [See *Orthography.*] One that spells words correctly, according to common usage. *Shak.*

ORTHOGRAPH'IE, } *a.* Correctly spell-
ORTHOGRAPH'IEAL, } ed; written with the proper letters.
2. Pertaining to the spelling of words; as, to make an *orthographical* mistake.

Orthographic projection of the sphere, a delineation of the sphere upon a plane that cuts it in the middle, the eye being supposed to be placed at an infinite distance from it. *Bailey.*

A projection in which the eye is supposed to be at an infinite distance; so called because the perpendiculars from any point of the sphere will all fall in the common intersection of the sphere with the plane of the projection. *Encyc.*

ORTHOGRAPH'IEALLY, *adv.* According to the rules of proper spelling.
2. In the manner of orthographic projection.

ORTHOG'RAPHY, *n.* [Gr. ορθογραφια; ορθος, right, and γραφη, writing.]
1. The art of writing words with the proper letters, according to common usage.
2. The part of grammar which treats of the nature and properties of letters, and of the art of writing words correctly. *Encyc.*
3. The practice of spelling or writing words with the proper letters. *Swift.*
4. In *geometry*, the art of delineating the fore right plane or side of any object, and of expressing the elevations of each part; so called because it determines things by perpendicular lines falling on the geometrical plane. *Encyc.*
5. In *architecture*, the elevation of a building, showing all the parts in their true proportion. *Encyc.*
6. In *perspective*, the fore right side of any plane, that is, the side or plane that lies parallel to a straight line that may be imagined to pass through the outward convex points of the eyes, continued to a convenient length. *Encyc.*
7. In *fortification*, the profile or representation of a work in all its parts, as they would appear if perpendicularly cut from top to bottom. *Cyc.*

ORTHOL'OĠY, *n.* [Gr. ορθος, right, and λογος, discourse.] The right description of things. *Fotherby.*

ORTHOM'ETRY, *n.* [Gr. ορθος, right, and μετρον, measure.]
The art or practice of constructing verse correctly; the laws of correct versification. *S. Jones.*

ORTHOP'NY, *n.* [Gr. ορθοπνοια; ορθος, right, erect, and πνοη, breath; πνεω, to breathe.]
1. A species of asthma in which respiration can be performed only in an erect posture. *Harvey.*
2. Any difficulty of breathing. *Parr.*

OR'TIVE, *a.* [L. *ortivus*, from *ortus*, *orior*, to rise.]
Rising, or eastern. The *ortive* amplitude of a planet is an arc of the horizon intercepted between the point where a star rises, and the east point of the horizon, the point where the horizon and equator intersect. *Encyc.*

OR'TOLAN, *n.* [It. *ortolano*, a gardener, an ortolan, L. *hortulanus*, from *hortus*, a garden.]
A bird of the genus Emberiza, about the size of the lark, with black wings. It is found in France and Italy, feeds on panic grass, and is delicious food. *Encyc.*

ORTS, *n.* Fragments; pieces; refuse.

OR'VAL, *n.* [Fr. *orvale.*] The herb clary. *Dict.*

ORVIE'TAN, *n.* [It. *orvietano*, so named from a mountebank at Orvieto.] An antidote or counter poison. [*Not used.*] *Bailey.*

ORYETOGNOS'TIE, *a.* Pertaining to oryctognosy. *Kirwan.*

ORYETOG'NOSY, *n.* [Gr. ορυκτος, fossil, and γνωσις, knowledge.]
That branch of mineralogy which has for its object the classification of minerals, according to well ascertained characters, and under appropriate denominations. *Cyc.*

Oryctognosy consists in the description of minerals, the determination of their nomenclature, and the systematic arrangement of their different species. It coincides nearly with *mineralogy*, in its modern acceptation. *Cleaveland.*

ORYETOG'RAPHY, *n.* [Gr. ορυκτος, fossil, and γραφω, to describe.]
That part of natural history in which fossils are described. *Cyc.*

ORYCTOL'OĠY, *n.* [Gr. ορυκτος, fossil, and λογος, discourse.] That part of physics which treats of fossils. *Cyc.*

OS'CHEOCELE, *n.* [Gr. οσχεον, the scrotum, and κηλη, a tumor.] A rupture in the scrotum; scrotal hernia. *Cyc. Coxe.*

OS'CILLATE, *v. i.* [L. *oscillo*, from ant. *cillo*, Gr. κελλω, to move.]

To swing; to move backward and forward; to vibrate. *Chambers.*

OSCILLA'TION, *n.* [L. *oscillatio.*] Vibration; a moving backward and forward, or swinging like a pendulum.

OS'CILLATORY, *a.* Moving backward and forward like a pendulum; swinging; as an *oscillatory* motion. *Arbuthnot.*

OS'CITANCY, *n.* [L. *oscito*, to yawn, from *os*, the mouth.] The act of gaping or yawning.

2. Unusual sleepiness; drowsiness; dullness.

It might proceed from the *oscitancy* of transcribers. *Addison.*

OS'CITANT, *a.* Yawning; gaping.

2. Sleepy; drowsy; dull; sluggish. *Decay of Piety.*

OS'CITANTLY, *adv.* Carelessly. *More.*

OSCITA'TION, *n.* The act of yawning or gaping from sleepiness.

OSCULA'TION, *n.* [L. *osculatio*, a kissing.] In *geometry*, the contact between any given curve and its osculatory circle, that is, a circle of the same curvature with the given curve. *Cyc.*

OS'CULATORY, *a.* An *osculatory circle*, in geometry, is a circle having the same curvature with any curve at any given point. *Cyc.*

OS'CULATORY, *n.* In *church history*, a tablet or board, with the picture of Christ or the virgin, &c. which is kissed by the priest and then delivered to the people for the same purpose. *Cyc.*

OSIER, *n.* *o'zher.* [Fr. *osier*; Sax. *hos.* Qu.] A willow or water willow, or the twig of the willow, used in making baskets. *Pope.*

OS'MAZOME, *n.* [Gr. οσμη, odor, and ζωμος, juice.]

A substance of an aromatic flavor, obtained from the flesh of the ox. *Thenard.*

OS'MIUM, *n.* [Gr. οσμη, odor.] A metal recently discovered, and contained in the ore of platinum. A native alloy of this metal with iridium is found in grains along the rivers in South America. Osmium has a dark gray color; it is not volatile when heated in close vessels, but heated in the open air, it absorbs oxygen and forms a volatile oxyd. It is insoluble in the acids, readily soluble in potassa and very volatile. It takes its name from the singular smell of its oxyd. *Cyc. Webster's Manual.*

OS'MUND, *n.* A plant, or a genus of plants, osmunda, moonwort. The most remarkable species is the osmund royal or flowering fern, growing in marshes, the root of which boiled, is very slimy, and is used in stiffening linen. *Encyc.*

OSNABURG, *n.* *oz'nburg.* A species of coarse linen imported from Osnaburg, in Germany.

OS'PRAY, *n.* [L. *ossifraga*; *os*, a bone, and *frango*, to break; the bone-breaker.]

The sea-eagle, a fowl of the genus Falco or hawk, of the size of a peacock. This is our fish hawk. It feeds on fish, which it takes by suddenly darting upon them, when near the surface of the water. *Encyc.*

OS'SELET, *n.* [Fr. from L. *os*, *ossis*, a bone.]

A hard substance growing on the inside of a horse's knee, among the small bones. *Far. Dict.*

OS'SEOUS, *a.* [L. *osseus*, from *os*, a bone.] Bony; resembling bone. *Parkhurst.*

OS'SICLE, *n.* [L. *ossiculum.*] A small bone. *Holder.*

OSSIF'EROUS, *a.* [L. *os*, a bone, and *fero*, to produce.] Producing or furnishing bones. *Buckland.*

OSSIF'IC, *a.* [L. *os*, a bone, and *facio*, to make.]

Having power to ossify or change carneous and membranous substances to bone. *Wiseman.*

OSSIFICA'TION, *n.* [from *ossify.*] The change or process of changing from flesh or other matter of animal bodies into a bony substance; as the *ossification* of an artery. *Sharp.*

2. The formation of bones in animals.

OS'SIFIED, *pp.* Converted into bone, or a hard substance like bone.

OS'SIFRAĠE, *n.* [L. *ossifraga.* See *Ospray.*]

The ospray or sea-eagle. In Leviticus xi. 13, it denotes a different fowl.

OS'SIFȲ, *v. t.* [L. *os*, bone, and *facio*, to form.]

To form bone; to change from a soft animal substance into bone, or convert into a substance of the hardness of bones. This is done by the deposition of calcarious phosphate or carbonate on the part. *Sharp. Ure.*

OS'SIFȲ, *v. i.* To become bone; to change from soft matter into a substance of bony hardness.

OSSIV'OROUS, *a.* [L. *os*, bone, and *voro*, to eat.]

Feeding on bones; eating bones; as *ossivorous* quadrupeds. *Derham.*

OS'SUARY, *n.* [L. *ossuarium.*] A charnel house; a place where the bones of the dead are deposited. *Dict.*

OST, } *n.* A kiln for dying hops or malt.
OUST, } *Dict. Eng.*

OSTENSIBIL'ITY, *n.* [See *Ostensible.*] The quality or state of appearing or being shown.

OSTEN'SIBLE, *a.* [It. *ostensibile*, from L. *ostendo*, to show.]

1. That may be shown; proper or intended to be shown. *Warton.*

2. Plausible; colorable. *Pownall.*

3. Appearing; seeming; shown, declared or avowed. We say, the *ostensible* reason or motive for a measure may be the real one, or very different from the real one. This is the common, and I believe the only sense in which the word is used in America.

One of the *ostensible* grounds on which the proprietors had obtained their charter— *Ramsay.*

OSTEN'SIBLY, *adv.* In appearance; in a manner that is declared or pretended.

An embargo and non-intercourse which totally defeat the interests they are *ostensibly* destined to promote. *Walsh.*

OSTEN'SIVE, *a.* [Fr. from L. *ostendo.*] Showing; exhibiting. *Ostensive demonstration*, is one which plainly and directly demonstrates the truth of a proposition. *Cyc.*

OS'TENT, *n.* [L. *ostentum*, from *ostendo.*]

1. Appearance; air; manner; mien. [*Little used.*] *Shak.*

2. Show; manifestation; token. [*Little used.*] *Shak.*

3. A prodigy; a portent; any thing ominous. [*Little used.*] *Chapman. Dryden.*

OS'TENTATE, *v. t.* [L. *ostento.*] To make an ambitious display of; to show or exhibit boastingly. [*Not used.*] *Taylor.*

OSTENTA'TION, *n.* [L. *ostentatio.*] Outward show or appearance. *Shak.*

2. Ambitious display; vain show; display of any thing dictated by vanity, or intended to invite praise or flattery. *Ostentation* of endowments is made by boasting or self-commendation. *Ostentation* often appears in works of art and sometimes in acts of charity.

He knew that good and bountiful minds are sometimes inclined to *ostentation.* *Atterbury.*

The painter is to make no *ostentation* of the means by which he strikes the imagination. *Reynolds.*

3. A show or spectacle. [*Not used.*] *Shak.*

OSTENTA'TIOUS, *a.* Making a display from vanity; boastful; fond of presenting one's endowments or works to others in an advantageous light.

Your modesty is so far from being *ostentatious* of the good you do— *Dryden.*

2. Showy; gaudy; intended for vain display; as *ostentatious* ornaments.

OSTENTA'TIOUSLY, *adv.* With vain display; boastfully.

OSTENTA'TIOUSNESS, *n.* Vain display; vanity; boastfulness.

OSTENTA'TOR, *n.* [L.] One who makes a vain show; a boaster. [*Little used.*] *Sherwood.*

OSTENT'OUS, *a.* Fond of making a show. [*Little used.*] *Feltham.*

OS'TEOCOL, } *n.* [Gr. οςεον, a bone, and
OSTEOCOL'LA, } κολλα, glue.] A carbonate of lime, a fossil formed by incrustation on the stem of a plant. It is found in long, thick, and irregular cylindric pieces, generally hollow, sometimes filled with calcarious earth, and in size, from that of a crow's quill to that of a man's arm. It is always found in sand. *Nicholson. Encyc. Cleaveland.*

This word takes its name from an opinion that it has the quality of uniting fractured bones.

OS'TEOCOPE, *n.* [Gr. οςεον, a bone, and κοπος, labor, uneasiness.]

Pain in the bones; a violent fixed pain in any part of a bone. *Quincy. Coxe.*

OSTEOL'OĠER, } *n.* [See *Osteology.*] One
OSTEOL'OĠIST, } who describes the bones of animals. *Smith.*

OSTEOLOĠ'IC, } *a.* Pertaining to a de-
OSTEOLOĠ'ICAL, } scription of the bones.

OSTEOLOĠ'ICALLY, *adv.* According to osteology. *Lawrence, Lect.*

OSTEOL'OĠY, *n.* [Gr. οςεον, a bone, and λογος, discourse.]

1. A description of the bones; that part of anatomy which treats of the bones. *Encyc.*

2. The system of animal bones.

OS'TIARY, *n.* [L. *ostium*, mouth.] The mouth or opening by which a river discharges its waters into the sea, or into a lake. *Brown.*

OSTLER. [See *Hostler.*]

OSTLERY. [See *Hostlery.*]

OST'MEN, *n. plu.* East men; Danish settlers in Ireland, so called. *Lyttleton.*

OS'TRACISM, *n.* [Gr. οϛρακισμος, from οϛρακον, a shell, or potter's ware.]

1. In *Grecian antiquity*, banishment by the people of Athens, of a person whose merit and influence gave umbrage to them. It takes this name from the shell on which the name or the note of acquittal or condemnation was written. It is however most probable that this shell was a piece of baked earth, rendered by the Latins *testa*. *Encyc.*

2. Banishment; expulsion; separation.

Sentenced to a perpetual *ostracism* from the esteem and confidence, and honors and emoluments of his country. *Federalist, Hamilton.*

OS'TRACITE, *n.* [Gr. οϛρακιτης, from οϛρακον, a shell.]

An oyster shell in its fossil state, or a stone formed in the shell, the latter being dissolved. This stone is found in many parts of England, and has been in repute for its efficacy in cases of the gravel. *Encyc.*

OS'TRACIZE, *v. t.* [See *Ostracism.*] To banish by the popular voice, particularly a person eminent for public services, but who has lost his popularity. *Marvel.*

OS'TRICH, *n.* [Fr. *autruche*; Sp. *avestruz*; Port. *abestruz*; It. *struzzo*; G. *strauss*; D. *struis* or *struis-vogel*; Dan. *struds*; Sw. *struss*; L. *struthio-camelus*; Gr. ϛρουθος, a sparrow, and an ostrich. The meaning of this name is not obvious. The word *strauss* in German, signifies a bush, a tuft, a bunch; but the latter part of this name *struz, struds, strauss*, coincides also with the Eng. *strut*, Dan. *strutter*, G. *strotzen*; and this is the L. *struthio*, Gr. ϛρουθος. The first part of the word in Fr. Sp. and Port. is from L. *avis*. The primary sense of *struz, struthio*, &c. is to reach, stretch, extend or erect; but whether this name was given to the fowl from its stately walk or appearance, or from some part of its plumage, let the reader judge.]

A fowl now considered as constituting a distinct genus, the Struthio. This is the largest of all fowls, being four feet high from the ground to the top of the back, and seven, eight, and it is said even ten to the top of the head, when standing erect. Its thighs and the sides of the body are naked, and the wings are so short as to be unfit for flying. The plumage is elegant, and much used in ornamental and showy dress. The speed of this fowl in running exceeds that of the fleetest horse. *Encyc.*

OTACOUS'TIC, *a.* [Gr. ωτα, ears, and ακουω, to hear.] Assisting the sense of hearing; as an *otacoustic* instrument.

OTACOUS'TIC, *n.* An instrument to facilitate hearing. *Grew.*

ŎTH'ER, *a.* [Sax. *other*; G. *oder*; Gr. ετερος. Qu. Sp. *otro*. If the radical letters are *tr*, qu. Heb. and Ch. יתר, residue. The French *autre* is from the Latin *alter.*]

1. Not the same; different; not this or these.

Then the *other* company which is left shall escape. Gen. xxxii.

Behold, it was turned again as his *other* flesh. Ex. iv.

Other lords besides thee have had dominion over us. Is. xxvi.

There is one God, and there is none *other* but he. Mark xii.

2. Not this, but the contrary; as, on this side of the river stands Troy, on the *other* side stands Albany.

Whosoever shall smite thee on thy right cheek, turn to him the *other* also. Matt. v.

3. Noting something besides. To the knowledge of the Latin and Greek, join as much *other* learning as you can.

4. Correlative to *each*, and applicable to any number of individuals.

They asked *each other* of their welfare. Ex. xviii.

5. Opposed to *some*; as, "*some* fell among thorns—but *other* fell into good ground." Matt. xiii.

6. The next. *Shak.*

7. The third part. *B. Jonson.*

Other is used as a substitute for a noun, and in this use has the plural number, and the sign of the possessive case.

—The fool and the brutish person die, and leave their wealth to *others*. Ps. xlix.

What do ye more than *others?* Matt. v.

We were children of wrath even as *others*. Eph. ii.

The confusion arises, when the one will put their sickle into the *other's* harvest. *Lesley.*

With the sign of the possessive, *other* is preceded by *the*, as in the last example.

Other is sometimes put elliptically for *other thing*. From such a man, we can expect no *other*.

The other day, at a certain time past, not distant but indefinite; not long ago.

ŎTH'ERGATES, *adv.* [*other* and *gate*, for way, manner.] In another manner. *Obs.* *Shak.*

ŎTH'ERGUISE, *adv.* [*other* and *guise*, manner.] Of another kind. [corruptly pronounced *otherguess.*]

ŎTH'ERWHERE, *adv.* [*other* and *where.*] In some other place; or in other places. *Milton.*

ŎTH'ERWHILE, } *adv.* [*other and while.*]
ŎTH'ERWHILES, } At other times.

ŎTH'ERWISE, *adv.* [*other* and *wise*, manner.] In a different manner.

Thy father was a worthy prince,
And merited, alas! a better fate;
But heaven thought *otherwise*. *Addison.*

2. By other causes.

Sir John Norris failed in the attempt of Lisborn, and returned with the loss, by sickness and *otherwise*, of 8000 men. *Raleigh.*

3. In other respects.

It is said truly, that the best men *otherwise*, are not always the best in regard to society. *Hooker.*

OT'OMO, *n.* A fowl of the Lagopus kind, about the size of a tame pigeon, a native of Germany, and highly esteemed for food. *Dict. Nat. Hist.*

OT'TER, } *n.* The essential oil or essence
AT'TAR, } of roses. *Asiat. Res.*

OT'TER, *n.* [Sax. *oter*, *otor* or *otter*; G. *otter*, an otter, an *adder* or viper; D. *otter*; Sw. *utter*. The Latin *lutra*, Fr. *loutre*, It. *lontra*, Sp. *nutria*, may possibly be the same word varied in dialect.]

A quadruped of the genus Mustela, nearly two feet in length, of a brown color, with short legs, amphibious and feeding on fish. It burrows in the banks of rivers and ponds, and its toes being webbed, it swims with great rapidity. There are several other species, of which the sea otter is the largest, being about three feet in length.

OT'TER, *n.* The name of a coloring substance.

OT'TOMAN, *a.* Designating something that pertains to the Turks or to their government; as the *Ottoman* power or empire. The word originated in Othman or Osman, the name of a sultan who assumed the government about the year 1300. *Eton.*

OUCH, *n.* A bezil or socket in which a precious stone or seal is set. Ex. xxxix.

2. The blow given by a boar's tusk. *Obs.* *Ainsworth.*

OUGHT. [See *Aught*, the true orthography.]

OUGHT, *v. imperfect. aut.* [This word seems to be the preterit tense of the original verb to owe, that is, Sax. *agan*, Goth. *aigan*, Sw. *åga*, to have or possess, the radical sense being to hold, to restrain or stop; hence the passive participle would signify held, bound. In this sense it was used by Spelman and Dryden. But *ought* as used, is irregular, being used in all persons both in the present and past tenses; as, *I ought, thou oughtest, he ought; we, ye, they ought.*]

1. To be held or bound in duty or moral obligation.

These *ought* ye to have done, and not to leave the other undone. Matt. xxiii.

We that are strong *ought* to bear the infirmities of the weak. Rom. xv.

Thou *oughtest* therefore to have put my money to the exchangers. Matt. xxv.

2. To be necessary; to behoove.

Ought not Christ to have suffered these things and to enter into glory? Luke xxiv.

3. To be fit or expedient in a moral view.

My brethren, these things *ought* not so to be. James iii.

4. As a participle, owed; been indebted to.

The love and duty I long have *ought* you. *Spelman.*

That followed, sir, which to myself I *ought*. *Dryden.*

[*In this sense, obsolete.*]

5. In Chaucer's time, it was used impersonally. "Wel *ought* us werke," that is, well it behooveth us to work.

OUNCE, *n.* ouns. [L. *uncia*, the twelfth part of any thing; Gr. ουγγια; but the Greek is from the Latin; Fr. *once*; It. *oncia*, an ounce, and an inch; Sp. *onza*; D. *once*; G. *unze*. *Inch* is from the same root, being the twelfth part of a foot.]

1. A weight, the twelfth part of a pound troy, and the sixteenth of a pound avoirdupois. In troy weight, the ounce is 20 pennyweights, each of 24 grains.

2. An animal of the genus Felis. [See *Once.*]

OUND'ED, } *a.* Waving. [Fr. *onde*, L.
OUND'ING, } *unda.*] [*Not used.*] *Chaucer.*

OUPHE, *n.* oof'y. [Teutonic, *auff*; but probably contracted from *elf*, G. *alp.*] A fairy; a goblin; an elf. *Obs.* *Shak.*

OUPHEN, *n.* oof'en. Elfish. *Obs.* *Shak.*

OUR, *a.* [Sax. *ure;* in the oblique cases, *urum, urne,* whence our vulgar *ourn;* Sw. *vår;* Dan. *vor;* Ir. *ar;* Basque, *gure.*]

1. Pertaining or belonging to us; as *our* country; *our* rights; *our* troops.
2. *Ours,* which is primarily the possessive case of *our,* is never used as an adjective, but as a substitute for the adjective and the noun to which it belongs. Your house is on a plain; *ours* is on a hill. This is good English, but certainly *ours* must be the nominative to *is,* or it has none.

Their organs are better disposed than *ours* for receiving grateful impressions from sensible objects. *Atterbury.*

Here *ours* stands in the place of *our organs,* and cannot, in conformity with any rule of construction, be in the possessive case.

The same thing was done by them in suing in their courts, which is now done by us in suing in *ours.* *Kettleworth.*

OURANOG'RAPHY, *n.* [Gr. ουρανος, heaven, and γραφω, to describe.] A description of the heavens. *Hist. Roy. Society.*

OURSELF', *pron. reciprocal.* [*our* and *self.*] This is added after *we* and *us,* and sometimes is used without either for *myself,* in the regal style only; as, we *ourself* will follow. *Shak.*

—Unless we would denude *ourself* of all force to defend us. *Clarendon.*

OURSELVES, *plu.* of *ourself.* We or us, not others; added to *we,* by way of emphasis or opposition.

We *ourselves* might distinctly number in words a great deal farther than we usually do. *Locke.*

Safe in *ourselves,* while on *ourselves* we stand. *Dryden.*

OUSE, *n. ooz.* [for *ooze.*] Tanner's bark. *Ainsworth.*

OUSEL, *n. oo'zl.* [Sax. *osle.*] The blackbird, a species of the genus Turdus. *Shak.*

OUST, *v. t.* [Fr. *ôter,* for *ouster.* It seems to be a contracted word, for in Norman, *oghsta* is ousted. I take this to be our vulgar *oost,* used in the sense of *lift.* The usual signification then will be that of the Latin *tollo, sustuli.*]

1. To take away; to remove.

Multiplications of actions upon the case were rare formerly, and thereby wager of law *ousted.* *Hall.*

2. To eject; to disseize.

Afterward the lessor, reversioner or remainder-man or any stranger doth eject or *oust* the lessee of his term. *Blackstone.*

OUST'ED, *pp.* Taken away; removed; ejected.

OUST'ER, *n.* Amotion of possession; disseizin; dispossession; ejection. *Blackstone.*

Ouster of the freehold is effected by abatement, intrusion, disseizin, discontinuance or deforcement. *Ib.*

Ouster le main, [*ouster* and Fr. *le main,* the hand.]

A delivery of lands out of the hands of a guardian, or out of the king's hands; or a judgment given for that purpose. *Blackstone. Encyc.*

OUST'ING, *ppr.* Taking away; removing; ejecting.

OUT, *adv.* [Sax. *ut;* D. *uit;* G. *aus;* Dan. *ud;* Sw. *ut.* In Scotland, it is used as a verb, to lay out. The primary sense of the verb must be to issue forth, to depart. In Russ. *ot* signifies *from.*]

1. Without; on the outside; not within; on the exterior or beyond the limits of any inclosed place or given line; opposed to *in* or *within;* as, to go *out* and come *in;* to rush *out.*
2. Abroad; not at home. The master of the house is *out;* a colloquial phrase for *gone out.*
3. In a state of disclosure or discovery. The secret is *out,* that is, has come *out,* is disclosed. We shall find *out* the rogue.
4. Not concealed.

When these are gone,
The woman will be *out.* *Shak.*

5. In a state of extinction. The candle or the fire is *out.*
6. In a state of being exhausted. The wine is *out.*
7. In a state of destitution. We are *out* of bread corn.
8. Not in office or employment. I care not who is in or who is *out.* He is *out* of business.
9. Abroad or from home, in a party, at church, in a parade, &c. He was not *out* to-day. The militia companies are *out.* The man was *out* in a frolick last night.
10. To the end.

Hear me *out.* *Dryden.*

11. Loudly; without restraint; as, to laugh *out.*
12. Not in the hands of the owner. The land is *out* upon a lease.
13. In an error.

As a musician that will always play,
And yet is always *out* at the same note. *Roscommon.*

14. At a loss; in a puzzle.

I have forgot my part, and I am *out.* *Shak.*

15. Uncovered; with clothes torn; as, to be *out* at the knees or elbows.
16. Away, so as to consume; as, to sleep *out* the best time in the morning.
17. Deficient; having expended. He was *out* of pocket. He was *out* fifty pounds. *Fell.*
18. It is used as an exclamation with the force of command, away; begone; as, *out* with the dog. *Shak.*

Out upon you, out upon it, expressions of dislike or contempt.

Out is much used as a modifier of verbs; as, to come *out,* to go *out,* to lead *out,* to run *out,* to leak *out,* to creep *out,* to flow *out,* to pass *out,* to look *out.* to burn *out,* to cut *out,* to saw *out,* to grow *out,* to spin *out,* to write *out,* to boil *out,* to beat *out,* &c. bearing the sense of issuing, extending, drawing from, separating, bringing to open view, or in short, the passing of a limit that incloses or restrains; or bearing the metaphorical sense of vanishing, coming to an end.

Out of. In this connection, *out* may be considered as an adverb, and *of* as a preposition.

1. Proceeding from; as produce. Plants grow *out of* the earth. He paid me *out of* his own funds.

Keep thy heart with all diligence, for *out of* it are the issues of life. Prov. iv.

Out of the same mouth proceedeth blessing and cursing. James iii.

2. From or proceeding from a place, or the interior of a place; as, to take any thing *out of* the house. Mark xiii.
3. Beyond; as *out of* the power of fortune.

They were astonished *out of* measure. Mark x.

4. From, noting taking or derivation.

To whom he expounded and testified the kingdom of God, persuading them concerning Jesus, both *out of* the law of Moses, and *out of* the prophets. Acts xxviii.

5. Not in, noting extraordinary exertion.

Be instant in season, *out of* season. 2 Tim. iv.

6. Not in, noting exclusion, dismission, departure, absence or dereliction; as *out of* favor; *out of* use; *out of* place; *out of* fashion.
7. Not in, noting unfitness or impropriety. He is witty *out of* season. The seed was sown *out of* season.
8. Not within, noting extraordinary delay; as, a ship is *out of* time.
9. Not within; abroad; as *out of* the door or house.
10. From, noting copy from an original; as, to cite or copy *out of* Horace.
11. From, noting rescue or liberation; as, to be delivered *out of* afflictions.

Christianity recovered the law of nature *out of* all those errors. *Addison.*

12. Not in, noting deviation, exorbitance or irregularity. This is *out of* all method; *out of* all rule. He goes *out of* his way to find cause of censure. He is *out of* order.
13. From, noting dereliction or departure. He will not be flattered or frightened *out of* his duty. He attempted to laugh men *out of* virtue.
14. From, noting loss or change of state. The mouth is *out of* taste; the instrument is *out of* tune. *Bacon.*
15. Not according to, noting deviation; as, he acts or speaks *out of* character.
16. Beyond; not within the limits of; as, to be *out of* hearing, *out of* sight, *out of* reach. Time *out of* mind, is time beyond the reach of memory.
17. Noting loss or exhaustion; as, to be *out of* breath.
18. Noting loss; as *out of* hope.
19. By means of.

Out of that will I cause those of Cyprus to mutiny. *Shak.*

20. In consequence of, noting the motive, source or reason.

What they do not grant *out of* the generosity of their nature, they may grant *out of* mere impatience. *Smalridge.*

So we say, a thing is done *out of* envy, spite or ambition.

Out of hand, immediately, as that is easily used which is ready in the hand.

Gather we our forces *out of* hand. *Shak.*

Out of print, denotes that a book is not in market, or to be purchased; the copies printed having been all sold.

OUT, *v. t.* To eject; to expel; to deprive by expulsion.

The French having been *outed* of their holds. *Heylin.*

In composition, *out* signifies beyond, more, ejection or extension.

For the participles of the following compounds, see the simple verbs.

OUTACT′, *v. t.* To do beyond; to exceed in act.

He has made me heir to treasures,
Would make me *outact* a real widow's whining. *Otway.*

OUTBAL′ANCE, *v. t.* To outweigh; to exceed in weight or effect.

Let dull Ajax bear away my right,
When all his days *outbalance* this one night. *Dryden.*

OUTBAR, *v. t.* To shut out by bars or fortification.

These to *outbar* with painful pionings. *Spenser.*

OUTBID′, *v. t.* To bid more than another; to offer a higher price.

For Indian spices, for Peruvian gold,
Prevent the greedy and *outbid* the bold. *Pope.*

OUTBID′, **OUTBID′DEN**, *pp.* Exceeded in the price offered.

OUTBID′DER, *n.* One that outbids.

OUTBID′DING, *ppr.* Bidding a price beyond another.

OUTBLOWN, *pp.* Inflated; swelled with wind. *Dryden.*

OUTBLUSH′, *v. t.* To exceed in rosy color. *Shipman.*

OUT′BORN, *a.* Foreign; not native. [*Little used.*]

OUT′BOUND, *a.* Destined or proceeding from a country or harbor to a distant country or port; as an *outbound* ship. *Dryden.*

[The usual phrase among seamen is *outward bound.*]

OUTBRA′VE, *v. t.* To bear down by more daring or insolent conduct.

I would outstare the sternest eyes that look,
Outbrave the heart most daring on the earth,
To win thee, lady. *Shak.*

2. To exceed in splendid appearance.

The towers as well as men *outbrave* the sky. *Cowley.*

OUTBRA′ZEN, *v. t.* To bear down with a brazen face or impudence.

OUT′BREAK, *n.* A bursting forth; eruption.

The flash and *outbreak* of a fiery mind. *Shak.*

OUT′BREAKING, *n.* That which bursts forth. *Herbert.*

OUTBRE′ATHE, *v. t.* To weary by having better breath. *Shak.*

2. To expire. *Spenser.*

OUTBUD′, *v. i.* To sprout forth. *Spenser.*

OUTBUILD, *v. t. outbild′.* To exceed in building, or in durability of building.

OUTCANT′, *v. t.* To surpass in canting. *Pope.*

OUT′CAST, *pp.* or *a.* Cast out; thrown away; rejected as useless. *Spenser.*

OUT′CAST, *n.* One who is cast out or expelled; an exile; one driven from home or country. Is. xvi.

OUTCEPT, for *except*, is not in use. *B. Jonson.*

OUTCLIMB, *v. t.* To climb beyond. *Davenant.*

OUTCOM′PASS, *v. t.* To exceed due bounds. *Bacon.*

OUTCRAFT, *v. t.* To exceed in cunning. *Shak.*

OUT′CRY, *n.* A vehement or loud cry; cry of distress. *Denham.*

2. Clamor; noisy opposition or detestation. *South.*

3. Sale at public auction. *Ainsworth.*

OUTDA′RE, *v. t.* To dare or venture beyond. *Shak.*

OUTDA′TE, *v. t.* To antiquate; as *outdated* ceremonies. [*Not used.*] *Hammond.*

OUTDÖ, *v. t.* pret. *outdid;* pp. *outdone.* [See *Do.*]

To excel; to surpass; to perform beyond another.

An imposture *outdoes* the original. *L'Estrange.*

I grieve to be *outdone* by Gay. *Swift.*

OUTDÖING, *ppr.* Excelling; surpassing in performance.

OUTDÖING, *n.* Excess in performance. *Pope.*

OUTDONE, *pp.* of *outdo.*

OUTDRINK′, *v. t.* [See *Drink.*] To exceed in drinking. *Donne.*

OUTDWELL′, *v. t.* To dwell or stay beyond. *Shak.*

OUT′ER, *a.* [*comp.* of *out.*] Being on the outside; external; opposed to *inner;* as the *outer* wall; the *outer* part of a thing; the *outer* court or gate.

OUT′ERLY, *adv.* Towards the outside. *Grew.*

OUT′ERMOST, *a.* [*superl.* from *outer.*] Being on the extreme external part; remotest from the midst; as the *outermost* row. *Boyle.*

OUTFA′CE, *v. t.* To brave; to bear down with an imposing front or with impudence; to stare down. *Shak. Raleigh.*

OUT′FALL, *n.* A fall of water; a canal.

OUTFAWN, *v. t.* To exceed in fawning or adulation. *Hudibras.*

OUTFE′AST, *v. t.* To exceed in feasting. *Taylor.*

OUT′FIT, *n.* A fitting out, as of a ship for a voyage; usually in the plural, *outfits*, the expenses of equipping and furnishing a ship for a voyage.

OUTFLANK′, *v. t.* To extend the flank of one army beyond that of another.

OUTFLY, *v. t.* To fly faster than another; to advance before in flight or progress. *Garth.*

OUTFOOL′, *v. t.* To exceed in folly. *Young.*

OUT′FORM, *n.* External appearance. *B. Jonson.*

OUTFROWN′, *v. t.* To frown down; to overbear by frowning. *Shak.*

OUT′GATE, *n.* An outlet; a passage outward. *Spenser.*

OUTGEN′ERAL, *v. t.* To exceed in generalship; to gain advantage over by superior military skill. *Chesterfield.*

OUTGIVE, *v. t. outgiv′.* To surpass in giving. *Dryden.*

OUTGO′, *v. t.* [See *Go.*] To go beyond; to advance before in going; to go faster.

2. To surpass; to excel. *Carew. Dryden.*

3. To circumvent; to overreach. *Denham.*

OUTGO′ING, *ppr.* Going beyond.

OUT′GOING, *n.* The act of going out.

2. The state of going out. Ps. lxv.

3. Utmost border; extreme limit. Josh. xvii.

OUTGRIN′, *v. t.* To surpass in grinning. *Addison.*

OUTGROW, *v. t.* To surpass in growth.

2. To grow too great or too old for any thing. Children *outgrow* their garments, and men *outgrow* their usefulness.

OUTGROWN, *pp.* of *outgrow.*

OUT′GUARD, *n.* A guard at a distance from the main body of an army; or a guard at the farthest distance; any thing for defense placed at a distance from the thing to be defended. *Dryden. South.*

OUTHER′OD, *v. t.* To surpass in enormity, absurdity or cruelty. *Beddoes.*

OUT′HOUSE, *n.* A small house or building at a little distance from the main house.

OUTJEST′, *v. t.* To overpower by jesting. *Shak.*

OUTJUG′GLE, *v. t.* To surpass in juggling. *Hall.*

OUTKNAVE, *v. t. outna′ve.* To surpass in knavery. *L'Estrange.*

OUT′LAND, *a.* [Sax. *utlænde*, a foreigner.] Foreign. *Obs.* *Strutt.*

OUT′LANDER, *n.* A foreigner; not a native. *Obs.* *Wood.*

OUTLAND′ISH, *a.* [Sax. *utlændisc; out* and *land.*]

1. Foreign; not native. *Donne.*

Nevertheless, even him did *outlandish* women cause to sin. Neh. xiii.

2. Born or produced in the interior country, or among rude people; hence, vulgar; rustic; rude; clownish. [*This is the sense in which the word is among us most generally used.*]

OUTLAST, *v. t.* To last longer than something else; to exceed in duration. Candles laid in bran will *outlast* others of the same stuff. *Bacon.*

OUT′LAW, *n.* [Sax. *ullaga; out* and *law.*] A person excluded from the benefit of the law, or deprived of its protection. Formerly any person might kill an outlaw; but it is now held unlawful for any person to put to death an outlaw, except the sheriff, who has a warrant for that purpose. *Blackstone.*

OUT′LAW, *v. t.* [Sax. *utlagian.*] To deprive of the benefit and protection of law; to proscribe. *Blackstone.*

OUT′LAWED, *pp.* Excluded from the benefit of law.

OUT′LAWING, *ppr.* Depriving of the benefit of law.

OUT′LAWRY, *n.* The putting a man out of the protection of law, or the process by which a man is deprived of that protection; the punishment of a man who when called into court, contemptuously refuses to appear. *Blackstone.*

OUT′LAY, *n.* A laying out or expending; expenditure.

OUTLE′AP, *v. t.* To leap beyond; to pass by leaping.

OUT′LEAP, *n.* Sally; flight; escape. *Locke.*

OUT′LET, *n.* Passage outward; the place or the means by which any thing escapes or is discharged. A gate is the *outlet* of a city or fort. The mouth of a river is its *outlet*. Colonies are the *outlets* of a populous nation. *Bacon.*

OUT′LICKER, *n.* In ships, a small piece of timber fastened to the top of the poop.

OUTLI′E, *v. t.* To exceed in lying. *Hall.*

OUT′LIER, *n.* One who does not reside in the place with which his office or duty connects him. *Frewen.*

OUT′LINE, *n.* Contour; the line by which a figure is defined; the exterior line.

2. The first sketch of a figure.
3. First general sketch of any scheme or design.
OUT'LINE, *v. t.* To draw the exterior line; to delineate; to sketch.
OUTLIVE, *v. t. outliv'.* To live beyond; to survive; to live after something has ceased; as, a man may *outlive* his children; a person may *outlive* his estate, his fame and his usefulness.
They live too long who happiness *outlive.* *Dryden.*
2. To live better or to better purpose. *Scott.*
OUTLIV'ER, *n.* A survivor.
OUTLOOK', *v. t.* To face down; to browbeat. *Shak.*
2. To select. [*Not in use.*]
OUT'LOOK, *n.* Vigilant watch; foresight. *Young.*
[But *look-out* is generally used.]
OUT'LOPE, *n.* [See *Lope* and *Leap.*] An excursion. [*Not used.*] *Florio.*
OUTLUS'TER, } *v. t.* To excel in brightness.
OUTLUS'TRE, } *Shak.*
OUTLY'ING, *a.* Lying or being at a distance from the main body or design. *Temple. Addison.*
2. Being on the exterior or frontier. *Gibbon.*
OUTM'ARCH, *v. t.* To march faster than; to march so as to leave behind.
The horse *outmarched* the foot. *Clarendon.*
OUTMEASURE, *v. t. outmezh'ur.* To exceed in measure or extent. *Brown.*
OUT'MOST, *a.* Farthest outward; most remote from the middle. *Milton.*
OUTNUM'BER, *v. t.* To exceed in number. The troops *outnumbered* those of the enemy.
OUTPA'CE, *v. t.* To outgo; to leave behind. *Chapman.*
OUTPAR'AMOUR, *v. t.* [See *Paramour.*] To exceed in keeping mistresses. *Shak.*
OUT'PARISH, *n.* A parish lying without the walls, or on the border. *Graunt.*
OUT'PART, *n.* A part remote from the center or main part. *Ayliffe.*
OUTP'ASS, *v. t.* To pass beyond; to exceed in progress. *Kirwan.*
OUTPOISE, *v. t. outpoiz'.* To outweigh. *Howell.*
OUT'PORCH, *n.* An entrance. *Milton.*
OUT'POST, *n.* A post or station without the limits of a camp, or at a distance from the main body of an army.
2. The troops placed at such a station. *Marshall.*
OUTPOUR, *v. t.* To pour out; to send forth in a stream. *Milton.*
2. To effuse.
OUT'POURING, *n.* A pouring out; effusion. *Milner. Bogue.*
OUTPRA'Y, *v. t.* To exceed in prayer or in earnestness of entreaty. *Scott.*
OUTPRE'ACH, *v. t.* To surpass in preaching; to produce more effect in inculcating lessons or truth.
And for a villain's quick conversion
A pill'ry can *outpreach* a parson. *J. Trumbull.*
OUTPRI'ZE, *v. t.* To exceed in value or estimated worth. *Shak.*
OUT'RAGE, *v. t.* [Fr. *outrager*; Arm. *outrachi, outragi*; It. *oltraggiare*; Sp. Port. *ultrajar*; from the L. *ultra*, beyond, It. *oltre*, with the common termination *age*; or more probably it is a compound of *ultra, oltra, outre*, with the Sp. *ajar*, to spoil, to mar, to abuse with injurious language.]
To treat with violence and wrong; to abuse by rude or insolent language; to injure by rough, rude treatment of any kind.
Base and insolent minds *outrage* men, when they have hopes of doing it without a return. *Atterbury.*
This interview *outrages* all decency. *Broome.*
OUT'RAGE, *v. i.* To commit exorbitances; to be guilty of violent rudeness. *Ascham.*
OUT'RAGE, *n.* [Fr. *id*; It. *oltraggio*; Sp. Port. *ultraje.*]
Injurious violence offered to persons or things; excessive abuse; wanton mischief. Rude abusive language, scurrility, or opprobrious and contemptuous words, may be an *outrage* to persons, or to decency and civility. A violent attack upon person or property is an *outrage.*
He wrought great *outrages*, wasting all the country where he went. *Spenser.*
OUTRA'GEOUS, *a.* [It. *oltraggioso*; Fr. *outrageux.*]
1. Violent; furious; exorbitant; exceeding all bounds of moderation; as *outrageous* villainies; *outrageous* talk; *outrageous* abuse. *Sidney. Spenser.*
2. Excessive; exceeding reason or decency; as *outrageous* panegyric. *Dryden.*
3. Enormous; atrocious; as *outrageous* crimes. *Shak.*
4. Tumultuous; turbulent.
OUTRA'GEOUSLY, *adv.* With great violence; furiously; excessively. *Spenser. South.*
OUTRA'GEOUSNESS, *n.* Fury; violence; enormity. *Dryden.*
OUTRA'ZE, *v. t.* To raze to extermination. *Sandys.*
OUTRE, *a. ootra'y.* [Fr.] Being out of the common course or limits; extravagant. *Geddes.*
OUTRE'ACH, *v. t.* To go or extend beyond. *Brown.*
OUTRE'ASON, *v. t.* To excel or surpass in reasoning. *South.*
OUTRECK'ON, *v. t.* To exceed in assumed computation. *Pearson.*
OUTREIGN, *v. t.* To reign through the whole of. *Spenser.*
OUTRI'DE, *v. t.* To pass by riding; to ride faster than. *Hall.*
OUTRI'DE, *v. i.* To travel about on horseback, or in a vehicle. *Addison.*
OUT'RIDER, *n.* A summoner whose office is to cite men before the sheriff. [*Not used.*] *Dict.*
2. One who travels about on horseback.
3. An attending servant.
OUT'RIGGER, *n.* In *seamen's language*, a strong beam fixed on the side of a ship and projecting from it, in order to secure the masts in the operation of careening, by counteracting the strain it suffers from the effort of the careening tackle; also, a boom occasionally used in the tops to thrust out the breast back-stays to windward, to increase the angle of tension, and give additional security to the topmast. [See *Prow.*] *Mar. Dict.*
OUT'RIGHT, *adv.* Immediately; without delay; at once. *Arbuthnot.*
2. Completely. *Addison.*
OUTRI'VAL, *v. t.* To surpass in excellence. *Addison.*
OUTROAR, *v. t.* To exceed in roaring. *Shak.*
OUT'RODE, *n.* An excursion. 1 Macc. xv.
OUTROOT', *v. t.* To eradicate; to extirpate. *Rowe.*
OUTRUN', *v. t.* To exceed in running; to leave behind in running. *Dryden.*
2. To exceed; as, to *outrun* one's income. *Addison.*
OUTSA'IL, *v. t.* To sail faster than; to leave behind in sailing. *Broome.*
OUTSCA'PE, *n.* Power of escaping. [*Not used.*] *Chapman.*
OUTSCORN', *v. t.* To bear down or confront by contempt; to despise.
OUTSCOUR'INGS, *n.* [*out* and *scour.*] Substances washed or scoured out. *Buckland.*
OUTSELL', *v. t.* To exceed in amount of sales.
2. To exceed in the prices of things sold.
3. To gain a higher price. *Shak.*
OUT'SET, *n.* Beginning; first entrance on any business. *Mason. Smith.*
Every thing almost depends upon giving a proper direction to this *outset* of life. *J. Hawes.*
OUTSHI'NE, *v. t.* To send forth brightness or luster. *Shak.*
2. To excel in luster or excellence; as, Homer *outshines* all other poets. *Addison.*
OUTSHOOT', *v. t.* To exceed in shooting. *Dryden.*
2. To shoot beyond. *Norris.*
OUTSHUT', *v. t.* To shut out or exclude. *Donne.*
OUTSI'DE, *n.* The external part of a thing; the part, end or side which forms the surface or superficies. *Bacon. Dryden.*
2. Superficial appearance; exterior; as the *outside* of a man or of manners.
Created beings see nothing but our *outside.* *Addison.*
3. Person; external man. *Shak. Bacon.*
4. The part or place that lies without or beyond an inclosure.
I threw open the door of my chamber and found the family standing on the *outside.* *Spectator.*
5. The utmost. *Mortimer.*
OUTSIT', *v. t.* To sit beyond the time of any thing. *South.*
OUTSKIP', *v. t.* To avoid by flight. *B. Jonson.*
OUT'SKIRT, *n.* Border; outpost; suburb. *Clarendon.*
OUTSLEE'P, *v. t.* To sleep beyond. *Shak.*
OUTSOAR, *v. t.* To soar beyond. *Gov. of the Tongue.*
OUTSOUND', *v. t.* To surpass in sound. *Hammond.*
OUTSPE'AK, *v. t.* To speak something beyond; to exceed. *Shak.*
OUTSPORT, *v. t.* To sport beyond; to outdo in sporting. *Shak.*
OUTSPREAD', *v. t.* To extend; to spread; to diffuse. *Pope.*

OUTSTAND′, *v. t.* To resist effectually; to withstand; to sustain without yielding. [*Little used.*] *Woodward.*

2. To stand beyond the proper time. *Shak.*

OUTSTAND′, *v. i.* To project outwards from the main body.

OUTSTAND′ING, *ppr.* Resisting effectually. [*Little used.*]

2. Projecting outward.

3. Not collected; unpaid; as *outstanding* debts.

The whole amount of revenues—as well *outstanding* as collected. *Hamilton.*

OUTSTA′RE, *v. t.* To face down; to browbeat; to outface with effrontery; as we say, to *stare out* of countenance. *Shak.*

OUTSTEP′, *v. t.* To step or go beyond; to exceed. *Cumberland.*

OUTSTORM′, *v. t.* To overbear by storming.

Insults the tempest and *outstorms* the skies. *J. Barlow.*

OUT′STREET, *n.* A street in the extremities of a town.

OUTSTRETCH′, *v. t.* To extend; to stretch or spread out; to expand. *Milton.*

OUTSTRI′DE, *v. t.* To surpass in striding. *B. Jonson.*

OUTSTRIP′, *v. t.* To outgo; to outrun; to advance beyond. *South. Dryden.*

OUTSWEAR, *v. t.* To exceed in swearing; to overpower by swearing. *Shak.*

OUTSWEE′TEN, *v. t.* To exceed in sweetness. *Shak.*

OUTSWELL′, *v. t.* To overflow; to exceed in swelling.

OUTTALK, *v. t.* *outtauk′*. To overpower by talking; to exceed in talking. *Shak.*

OUTTHRŌW, *v. t.* To throw out or beyond. *Swift.*

OUTTŎNGUE, *v. t.* *outtung′*. To bear down by talk, clamor or noise. *Shak.*

OUTTOP′, *v. t.* To overtop. [*Not used.*] *Williams.*

OUTVAL′UE, *v. t.* To exceed in price or value. *Boyle.*

OUTVEN′OM, *v. t.* To exceed in poison. *Shak.*

OUTVI′E, *v. t.* To exceed; to surpass. *Dryden. Addison.*

OUTVIL′LAIN, *v. t.* To exceed in villainy. *Shak.*

OUTVOICE, *v. t.* *outvois′*. To exceed in roaring or clamor. [*Not used.*] *Shak.*

OUTVO′TE, *v. t.* To exceed in the number of votes given; to defeat by plurality of suffrages. *South.*

OUTWALK, *v. t.* *outwauk′*. To walk faster than; to leave behind in walking.

2. To exceed the walking of a specter. *B. Jonson.*

OUT′WALL, *n.* The exterior wall of a building or fortress.

2. Superficial appearance. [*Unusual.*] *Shak.*

OUT′WARD, *a.* [Sax. *utweard* or *uteweard*; *ut*, out, and *weard*, L. *versus*.]

1. External; exterior; forming the superficial part; as the *outward* coat of an onion; an *outward* garment.

2. External; visible; opposed to *inward*; as *outward* hate.

3. Extrinsic; adventitious.

And *outward* honor for an inward toil. *Shak.*

4. Foreign; not intestine; as an *outward* war. [*Not now used.* We now say, *external* or *foreign* war.] *Hayward.*

5. Tending to the exterior part.

The fire will force its *outward* way. *Dryden.*

6. In *Scripture*, civil; public; as opposed to *religious.* 1 Chron. xxvi.

7. In *theology*, carnal; fleshly; corporeal; not spiritual; as the *outward* man.

OUT′WARD, *n.* External form. *Shak.*

OUT′WARD, OUT′WARDS, } *adv.* To the outer parts; tending or directed towards the exterior.

The light falling on them [black bodies] is not reflected *outwards.* *Newton.*

2. From a port or country; as a ship bound *outwards.*

OUTWARD-BOUND′, *a.* Proceeding from a port or country.

OUT′WARDLY, *adv.* Externally; opposed to *inwardly*; as *outwardly* content, but *inwardly* uneasy.

2. In appearance; not sincerely. Many may inwardly reverence the goodness which they *outwardly* seem to despise.

OUTWAȘH′, *v. t.* To wash out; to cleanse from. [*Little used.*] *Donne.*

OUTWAȚCH′, *v. t.* To surpass in watching. *B. Jonson.*

OUTWEAR, *v. t.* To wear out. [*Not used.*] *Donne.*

2. To pass tediously to the end.

By the stream, if I the night *outwear*— *Pope.*

3. To last longer than something else. [*This is the common signification.*]

OUTWEE′D, *v. t.* To weed out; to extirpate, as a weed. *Spenser.*

OUTWEE′P, *v. t.* To exceed in weeping. *Dryden.*

OUTWEIGH, *v. t.* *outwa′y.* [See *Weigh.*]

1. To exceed in weight. *Wilkins.*

2. To exceed in value, influence or importance.

One self-approving hour whole years *outweighs*
Of stupid starers and of loud huzzas. *Pope.*

OUTWELL′, *v. t.* or *i.* To pour out. [*Not used.*] *Spenser.*

OUTWENT′, *pret.* of *outgo.*

OUTWHO′RE, *v. t.* To exceed in lewdness. *Pope.*

OUTWIN′, *v. t.* To get out of. [*Not used.*] *Spenser.*

OUTWIND, *v. t.* To extricate by winding; to unloose. *More.*

OUTWING′, *v. t.* To move faster on the wing; to outstrip. *Garth.*

OUTWIT′, *v. t.* To surpass in design or stratagem; to overreach; to defeat or frustrate by superior ingenuity. *Dryden.*

OUT′WŎRK, *n.* The part of a fortification most remote from the main fortress or citadel. *Bacon.*

OUTWŎRN, *pp.* [See *Wear.*] Worn out; consumed by use. *Milton.*

OUTWŎRTH, *v. t.* To exceed in value. *Shak.*

OUTWREST, *v. t.* *outrest′.* To extort; to draw from or forth by violence. *Spenser.*

OUTWRITE, *v. t.* *outri′te.* To surpass in writing. *Addison.*

OUTWROUGHT, *pp.* *outraut′.* [See *Work.*] Outdone; exceeded in act or efficacy.

OUTZA′NY, *v. t.* [See *Zany.*] To exceed in buffoonery.

O′VAL, *a.* [Fr. *ovale*, from L. *ovum*, an egg.]

1. Of the shape or figure of an egg; oblong; curvilinear; resembling the longitudinal section of an egg. It is sometimes synonymous with *elliptical;* but an ellipsis is equally broad at both ends, and is not strictly egg-shaped. *Encyc.*

2. Pertaining to eggs; done in the egg; as *oval* conceptions. *Brown.*

O′VAL, *n.* A body or figure in the shape of an egg. *Watts.*

OVA′RIOUS, *a.* Consisting of eggs; as *ovarious* food. *Thomson.*

O′VARY, *n.* [Fr. *ovaire;* L. *ovarium*, from *ovum*, an egg.]

The part of a female animal in which the eggs are formed or lodged; or the part in which the fetus is supposed to be formed. *Encyc. Coxe.*

O′VATE, O′VATED, } *a.* [L. *ovatus*, from *ovum*, an egg.] Egg-shaped; as an *ovate* leaf.

ŎVATE-LAN′CEOLATE, *a.* Having something of the form of an egg and a lance, inclining to the latter. *Martyn.*

ŎVATE-SUB′ULATE, *a.* Having something of the form of an egg and an awl, but most tending to the latter. *Martyn.*

OVA′TION, *n.* [L. *ovatio.*] In *Roman antiquity*, a lesser triumph allowed to commanders who had conquered without blood, or defeated an inconsiderable enemy. *Encyc.*

ŎVATO-OB′LONG, *a.* Oblong in the shape of an egg, or with the end lengthened. *Martyn.*

ŎVEN, *n.* *uv′n.* [Sax. G. *ofen;* D. *oven;* Dan. *ovn.* Qu. Gr. ιπνος, Sw. *ugn.* In Russ. *ovini* are small wooden kilns for drying corn. *Tooke.*]

An arch of brick or stone work, for baking bread and other things for food. *Ovens* are made in chimneys or set in the open air.

O′VER, *prep.* [Sax. *ober*, *ofer;* Goth. *ufar;* G. *über;* D. Dan. *over;* Sw. *ofver;* Gr. υπερ, whence probably L. *super;* Arm. *uvar, var, oar, ar;* Ir. *ar*, formerly *fair* or *fer;* W. *ar;* Corn. *uar.* Qu. Gr. παρα. This word corresponds in sense with עבר in the Shemitic dialects, signifying to pass, in almost any manner; to pass over, as a river, to pass beyond, to pass away, to pass by; in short, to move, depart or go, Sax. *faran*, to *fare.* Hence the derivative sense of beyond, either on the other side or above; hence the sense of excess, which supposes the passing of a limit; hence the sense of *opposite* or *against*, in the Gr. υπερ, for the further side of a river is the opposite side. We do not use the word in this sense, except with *against.* See Class Br. No. 23. The Persian corresponding word is فرا fara, which coincides nearly with the Greek παρα, and both seem to be more directly from the Ar. افر to go beyond. Class Br. No. 37.]

1. Across; from side to side; implying a passing or moving either above the sub-

stance or thing, or on the surface of it. Thus we say, a dog leaps *over* a stream, or *over* a table; a boat sails *over* a lake.

2. Above in place or position; opposed to *below*; as the clouds *over* our heads. The smoke rises *over* the city.

The mercy-seat that is *over* the testimony. Ex. xxx.

3. Above, denoting superiority in excellence, dignity or value; as the advantages which the christian world has *over* the heathen. *Swift.*

Young Pallas shone conspicuous *o'er* the rest. *Dryden.*

4. Above in authority, implying the right or power of superintending or governing; opposed to *under*.

Thou shalt be *over* my house. Gen. xli.
I will make thee ruler *over* many things. Matt. xxv.

5. Upon the surface or whole surface; through the whole extent; as, to wander *over* the earth; to walk *over* a field, or *over* a city.

6. Upon. Watch *over* your children.

Dost thou not watch *over* my sin? Job xiv.
His tender mercies are *over* all his works. Ps. cxlv.

7. During the whole time; from beginning to end; as, to keep any thing *over* night; to keep corn *over* winter.

8. Above the top; covering; immersing; as, the water is *over* the shoes or boots.

Over night. In this phrase, *over* sometimes signifies *before*; as, when preparing for a journey, we provide things necessary *over night.*

Over, in poetry, is often contracted into *o'er.*

O'VER, *adv.* From side to side; as a board a foot *over*; a tree a foot *over*, a foot in diameter.

2. On the opposite side. The boat is safe *over.*

3. From one to another by passing; as, to deliver *over* goods to another.

4. From one country to another by passing; as, to carry any thing *over* to France, or to bring any thing *over* to England. *Bacon.*

5. On the surface.

6. Above the top.

Good measure, pressed down and shaken together, and running *over*, shall men give into your bosom. Luke vi.

7. More than the quantity assigned; beyond a limit.

He that gathered much had nothing *over*. Ex. xvi.

8. Throughout; from beginning to end; completely; as, to read *over* a book; to argue a question *over* again.

Over and over, repeatedly; once and again.

And every night review'd it *o'er and o'er*. *Harte.*

Over again, once more; with repetition.

O kill not all my kindred *o'er again*. *Dryden.*

Over and above, besides; beyond what is supposed or limited.

He gained, *over and above*, the good will of the people. *L'Estrange.*

Over against, opposite; in front.

Over against this church stands a large hospital. *Addison.*

Over is used with rolling or turning from side to side; as, to turn *over*; to roll *over*.

To give over, to cease from; as, to *give over* an enterprize.

2. To consider as in a hopeless state; as, the physicians have *given over* their patient.

Over, in composition, denotes spreading, covering above; as in *overcast, overflow*; or across, as to *overhear*; or above, as to *overhang*; or turning, changing sides, as in *overturn*; or more generally beyond, implying excess or superiority, as in *overact, overcome.*

O'VER, *a.* Past.

The Olympic games were *over*. *Milner.*

2. Upper; covering; as *over*-shoes; *over*-lether.

OVERABOUND', *v. i.* To abound more than enough; to be superabundant. *Pope.*

OVERACT', *v. t.* To act or perform to excess; as, he *overacted* his part. *Atterbury.*

OVERACT', *v. i.* To act more than is necessary. *B. Jonson.*

OVERAG'ITATE, *v. t.* To agitate or discuss beyond what is expedient. *Hall.*

O'VERALLS, *n.* A kind of trowsers.

OVERANX'IOUS, *a.* Anxious to excess.

OVER'ARCH, *v. t.* To arch over; to cover with an arch.

Brown with *o'erarching* shades. *Pope.*

OVERAWE, *v. t. overaw'.* To restrain by awe, fear or superior influence.

The king was present in person to overlook the magistrates and *overawe* the subjects with the terror of his sword. *Spenser.*

OVERBAL'ANCE, *v. t.* To weigh down; to exceed in weight, value or importance. The evils which spring from vice *overbalance* all its pleasures.

OVERBAL'ANCE, *n.* Excess of weight or value; something more than an equivalent; as an *overbalance* of exports; an *overbalance* of probabilities. *Temple. Locke.*

OVERBAT'TLE, *a.* [qu. from the root of *batten*, to fatten.]
Too fruitful; exuberant. [*Not used.*] *Hooker.*

OVERBEAR, *v. t.* [See *Bear.*] To bear down; to repress; to subdue.

The point of reputation, when the news first came of the battle lost, did *overbear* the reason of war. *Bacon.*

Yet fortune, valor, all is *overborne*
By numbers. *Derham.*
Till *overborne* with weight the Cyprians fell. *Dryden.*

OVERBEARING, *ppr.* Bearing down; repressing.

2. *a.* Haughty and dogmatical; disposed or tending to repress or subdue by insolence or effrontery.

OVERBEND', *v. t.* To bend or stretch to excess. *Donne.*

OVERBID', *v. t.* To bid or offer beyond.

2. To bid or offer more than an equivalent.

OVERBLOW, *v. i.* To blow with too much violence; *a seaman's phrase.*

2. To blow over, or be past its violence. [*Not used.*]

OVERBLOW, *v. t.* To blow away; to dissipate by wind. *Waller.*

OVERBLOWN, *pp.* Blown by and gone; blown away; driven by; past. *Dryden.*

And when this cloud of sorrow's *overblown.* *Waller.*

OVERBOARD, *adv.* [*over* and Fr. *bord*, side.] Literally, over the side of a ship; hence, out of a ship or from on board; as, to fall *overboard*; which of course is to fall into the water. *Mar. Dict.*

OVERBROW', *v. t.* To hang over. *Collins.*

OVERBUILT, *pp. overbilt'.* Built over. *Milton.*

OVERBULK', *v. t.* To oppress by bulk. [*Not used.*] *Shak.*

OVERBUR'DEN, *v. t.* To load with too great weight. *Sidney.*

OVERBUR'DENED, *pp.* Overloaded.

OVERBURN', *v. t.* To burn too much. *Mortimer.*

OVERBUSY, *a. overbiz'zy.* Too busy; officious. *Decay of Piety.*

OVERBUY', *v. t.* To buy at too dear a rate. *Dryden.*

OVERCAN'OPY, *v. t.* To cover as with a canopy. *Shak.*

OVERCA'RE, *n.* Excessive care or anxiety. *Dryden.*

OVERCA'REFUL, *a.* Careful to excess.

OVERCAR'RY, *v. t.* To carry too far; to carry or urge beyond the proper point. *Hayward.*

OVERC'AST, *v. t.* To cloud; to darken; to cover with gloom.

The clouds that *overcast* our morn shall fly. *Dryden.*

2. To cast or compute at too high a rate; to rate too high.

The king in his account of peace and calms did much *overcast* his fortunes— *Bacon.*

3. To sew over.

OVERC'AST, *pp.* Clouded; overspread with clouds or gloom.

The dawn is *overcast*. *Addison.*
Our days of age are sad and *overcast*. *Raleigh.*

OVERCAU'TIOUS, *a.* Cautious or prudent to excess. *Addison.*

OVERCH'ARGE, *v. t.* To charge or load to excess; to cloy; to oppress.

The heavy load of abundance with which we *overcharge* nature— *Raleigh.*

2. To crowd too much.

Our language is *overcharged* with consonants. *Addison.*

3. To burden. *Shak.*

4. To fill to excess; to surcharge; as, to *overcharge* the memory. *Locke.*

5. To load with too great a charge, as a gun. *Denham.*

6. To charge too much; to enter in an account more than is just.

O'VERCHARGE, *n.* An excessive load or burden.

2. A charge in an account of more than is just.

3. A charge beyond what is proper.

OVERCLIMB, *v. t.* To climb over. *Surrey.*

OVERCLOUD', *v. t.* To cover or overspread with clouds. *Tickel.*

OVERCLOY', *v. t.* To fill beyond satiety. *Shak.*

OVERCOLD, *a.* Cold to excess. *Wiseman.*

OVERCOME, *v. t.* [See *Come.*] To conquer; to vanquish; to subdue; as, to *overcome* enemies in battle.

2. To surmount; to get the better of; as, to *overcome* difficulties or obstacles.

3. To overflow; to surcharge. [*Not used.*] *Philips.*

4. To come upon; to invade. [*Not used.*]

OVERCOME, *v. i.* To gain the superiority; to be victorious. Rom. iii.

ŌVERCŌMER, *n.* One who vanquishes or surmounts.

ŌVERCŌMINGLY, *adv.* With superiority. *More.*

ŌVERCON′FIDENCE, *n.* Excessive confidence.

ŌVERCORN′, *v. t.* To corn to excess. *Addison.*

ŌVERCOUNT′, *v. t.* To rate above the true value. *Shak.*

ŌVERCŌV′ER, *v. t.* To cover completely. *Shak.*

ŌVERCRED′ULOUS, *a.* Too apt to believe. *Shak.*

ŌVERCROW, *v. t.* To crow as in triumph. [*Not used.*] *Spenser.*

ŌVERCU′RIOUS, *a.* Curious or nice to excess. *Bacon.*

ŌVERDA′TE, *v. t.* To date beyond the proper period. *Milton.*

ŌVERDI′GHT, *a.* Covered over. *Obs.* *Spenser.*

ŌVERDIL′IGENT, *a.* Diligent to excess.

ŌVERDÖ, *v. t.* To do or perform too much. *Shak.*

2. To harass; to fatigue; to oppress by too much action or labor.

3. To boil, bake or roast too much. *Swift.*

ŌVERDÖ, *v. i.* To labor too hard; to do too much. *Grew.*

ŌVERDŌNE, *pp.* Overacted; acted to excess.

2. Wearied or oppressed by too much labor.

3. Boiled, baked or roasted too much. *Swift.*

ŌVERDOSE, *n.* Too great a dose.

ŌVERDRESS′, *v. t.* To dress to excess; to adorn too much. *Pope.*

ŌVERDRINK′, *v. t.* To drink to excess.

ŌVERDRI′VE, *v. t.* To drive too hard, or beyond strength. Gen. xxxiii.

ŌVERDRY′, *v. t.* To dry too much. *Burton.*

ŌVERE′AGER, *a.* Too eager; too vehement in desire. *Goodman.*

ŌVERE′AGERLY, *adv.* With excessive eagerness.

ŌVERE′AGERNESS, *n.* Excess of earnestness.

ŌVERE′AT, *v. t.* To eat to excess.

ŌVEREL′EGANT, *a.* Elegant to excess. *Johnson.*

ŌVEREMP′TY, *v. t.* To make too empty. *Carew.*

ŌVEREYE, *v. t.* To superintend; to inspect. [*Little used.*]

2. To observe; to remark. *Shak.*

O′VERFALL, *n.* A cataract; the fall of a river. *Raleigh.*

ŌVERFATIGUE, *n.* *overfatee′g.* Excessive fatigue.

ŌVERFATIGUE, *v. t.* *overfatee′g.* To fatigue to excess. *Watts.*

ŌVERFEE′D, *v. t.* To feed to excess. *Dryden.*

ŌVERFILL′, *v. t.* To fill to excess; to surcharge. *Dryden.*

ŌVERFLŌAT, *v. t.* To overflow; to inundate. *Dryden.*

ŌVERFLOURISH, *v. t.* *overflur′ish.* To make excessive display or flourish. *Collier.*

ŌVERFLŌW, *v. t.* To spread over, as water; to inundate; to cover with water or other fluid.

2. To fill beyond the brim.

3. To deluge; to overwhelm; to cover, as with numbers.

The northern nations *overflowed* all christendom. *Spenser.*

ŌVERFLŌW, *v. i.* To run over; to swell and run over the brim or banks. *Dryden.*

2. To be abundant; to abound; to exuberate; as *overflowing* plenty. *Rogers.*

O′VERFLŌW, *n.* An inundation; also, superabundance. *Bacon.*

ŌVERFLŌWING, *ppr.* Spreading over, as a fluid; inundating; running over the brim or banks.

ŌVERFLŌWING, *a.* Abundant; copious; exuberant.

ŌVERFLŌWING, *n.* Exuberance; copiousness. *Denham.*

ŌVERFLŌWINGLY, *adv.* Exuberantly; in great abundance. *Boyle.*

ŌVERFLUSH′, *v. t.* To flush to excess.

ŌVERFLUSH′ED, *pp.* Flushed to excess; reddened to excess.

2. Elated to excess. *Addison.*

ŌVERFLY′, *v. t.* To pass over or cross by flight. *Dryden.*

ŌVERFOR′WARD, *a.* Forward to excess.

ŌVERFOR′WARDNESS, *a.* Too great forwardness or readiness; officiousness. *Hale.*

ŌVERFREIGHT, *v. t.* *overfra′te.* [See *Freight.*] To load too heavily; to fill with too great quantity or numbers; as, to *overfreight* a boat.

ŌVERFRU′ITFUL, *a.* Too rich; producing superabundant crops. *Dryden.*

ŌVERGET′, *v. t.* To reach; to overtake. [*Not used.*] *Sidney.*

ŌVERGILD′, *v. t.* To gild over; to varnish.

ŌVERGIRD′, *v. t.* To gird or bind too closely. *Milton.*

ŌVERGL′ANCE, *v. t.* To glance over; to run over with the eye. *Shak.*

ŌVERGO,′ *v. t.* To exceed; to surpass. *Sidney.*

2. To cover. [*Not used.*] *Chapman.*

ŌVERGONE, *pp.* *overgawn′.* Injured; ruined. *Shak.*

ŌVERGORGE, *v. t.* *overgorj′.* To gorge to excess. *Shak.*

ŌVERGR′ASSED, *pp.* Overstocked with grass; overgrown with grass. *Spenser.*

ŌVERGREAT, *a.* Too great. *Locke.*

ŌVERGRŌW, *v. t.* To cover with growth or herbage. *Spenser.*

2. To grow beyond; to rise above. *Mortimer.*

ŌVERGRŌW, *v. i.* To grow beyond the fit or natural size; as a huge *overgrown* ox. *L′Estrange.*

ŌVERGRŌWTH, *n.* Exuberant or excessive growth. *Bacon.*

OVERHALE. [See *Overhaul.*]

ŌVERHAND′LE, *v. t.* To handle too much; to mention too often. *Shak.*

ŌVERHANG′, *v. t.* To impend or hang over.

2. To jut or project over. *Milton.*

ŌVERHANG′, *v. i.* To jut over. *Milton.*

ŌVERH′ARDEN, *v. t.* To harden too much; to make too hard. *Boyle.*

ŌVERHĀSTILY, *adv.* In too much haste. *Hales.*

ŌVERHĀSTINESS, *n.* Too much haste; precipitation. *Reresby.*

ŌVERHĀSTY, *a.* Too hasty; precipitate. *Hammond.*

ŌVERHAUL′, *v. t.* To spread over. *Spenser.*

2. To turn over for examination; to separate and inspect.

3. To draw over.

4. To examine again.

5. To gain upon in a chase; to overtake.

ŌVERHEAD, *adv.* *overhed′.* Aloft; above; in the zenith or cieling. *Milton. Addison.*

ŌVERHE′AR, *v. t.* To hear by accident; to hear what is not addressed to the hearer, or not intended to be heard by him. *Wotton. Milton.*

ŌVERHE′ARD, *pp.* Heard by accident.

ŌVERHE′AT, *v. t.* To heat to excess. *Addison.*

ŌVERHE′LE, *v. t.* To cover over. [*Not used.*] *B. Jonson.*

ŌVERHEND′, *v. t.* To overtake. [*Not used.*] *Spenser.*

ŌVERJOY′, *v. t.* To give great joy to; to transport with gladness. *Taylor.*

O′VERJOY, *n.* Joy to excess; transport.

ŌVERLA′BOR, *v. t.* To harass with toil. *Dryden.*

2. To execute with too much care.

ŌVERLA′DE, *v. t.* To load with too great a cargo or other burden.

ŌVERLA′DEN, *pp.* Overburdened; loaded to excess.

ŌVERLA′ID, *pp.* [See *Overlay.*] Oppressed with weight; smothered; covered over.

ŌVERL′ARGE, *a.* Too large; too great. *Collier.*

ŌVERL′ARGENESS, *n.* Excess of size.

ŌVERLASH′, *v. i.* To exaggerate. [*Little used.*] *Barrow.*

2. To proceed to excess. [*Little used.*] *Boyle.*

ŌVERLA′Y, *v. t.* To lay too much upon; to oppress with incumbent weight; as a country *overlaid* with inhabitants. *Raleigh.*

Our sins have *overlaid* our hopes. *K. Charles.*

2. To cover or spread over the surface; as, to *overlay* capitals of columns with silver; cedar *overlaid* with gold.

3. To smother with close covering; as, to *overlay* an infant. *Milton.*

4. To overwhelm; to smother.

A heap of ashes that *o′erlays* your fire. *Dryden.*

5. To cloud; to overcast.

—As when a cloud his beam doth *overlay.* *Spenser.*

6. To cover; to join two opposite sides by a cover.

And *overlay*
With this portentous bridge the dark abyss. *Milton.*

ŌVERLA′YING, *n.* A superficial covering. Ex. xxxviii.

ŌVERLE′AP, *v. t.* To leap over; to pass or move from side to side by leaping; as, to *overleap* a ditch or a fence. *Dryden.*

O′VERLEATHER, } *n.* The lether which
O′VERLETHER, } forms or is intended to form the upper part of a shoe; that which is over the foot. [With us, this is called *upper lether.*] *Shak.*

ŌVERLEAVEN, *v. t. overlev'n.* To leaven too much; to cause to rise and swell too much. *B. Jonson.*
2. To mix too much with; to corrupt. *Shak.*

ŌVERLIB'ERAL, *a.* Too liberal; too free; abundant to excess; as *overliberal* diet. *Bacon.*

ŌVERLIGHT, *n.* Too strong a light. *Bacon.*

ŌVERLIVE, *v. t. overliv'.* To outlive; to live longer than another; to survive. [We generally use *outlive.*] *Sidney.*

ŌVERLIVE, *v. i. overliv'.* To live too long. *Milton.*

ŌVERLIV'ER, *n.* One that lives longest; a survivor. *Bacon.*

ŌVERLŌAD, *v. t.* To load with too heavy a burden or cargo; to fill to excess; as, to *overload* the stomach or a vehicle.

ŌVERLONG', *a.* Too long. *Boyle.*

ŌVERLOOK', *v. t.* To view from a higher place; *applied to persons;* as, to stand on a hill and *overlook* a city.
2. To stand in a more elevated place, or to rise so high as to afford the means of looking down on; *applied to things.* The tower *overlooked* the town.
3. To see from behind or over the shoulder of another; to see from a higher position; as, to *overlook* a paper when one is writing. *Dryden.*
4. To view fully; to peruse. *Shak.*
5. To inspect; to superintend; to oversee; implying care and watchfulness.

He was present in person to *overlook* the magistrates. *Spenser.*

6. To review; to examine a second time or with care.

The time and care that are required
To *overlook*, and file and polish well. *Roscommon.*

7. To pass by indulgently; to excuse; not to punish or censure; as, to *overlook* faults. *Addison.*
8. To neglect; to slight.

They *overlook* truth in the judgment they pass on adversity and prosperity. *Atterbury.*

ŌVERLOOK'ER, *n.* One that overlooks.

ŌVERLOOP, now written *orlop,* which see.

ŌVERLŌVE, *v. t.* To love to excess; to prize or value too much. *Hall.*

O'VERLY, *a.* [Sax. *oferlice.*] Careless; negligent; inattentive. [*Not used.*] *Hall.*

ŌVERM'AST, *v. t.* To furnish with a mast or with masts that are too long or too heavy for the weight of keel.

ŌVERM'ASTED, *pp.* Having masts too long or too heavy for the ship. *Mar. Dict.*

ŌVERM'ASTER, *v. t.* To overpower; to subdue; to vanquish; to govern. *Milton.*

ŌVERMATCH', *v. t.* To be too powerful for; to conquer; to subdue; to oppress by superior force. *Dryden.*

ŌVERMATCH', *n.* One superior in power; one able to overcome. *Milton. Addison.*

ŌVERMEASURE, *v. t. overmezh'ur.* To measure or estimate too largely. *Bacon.*

ŌVERMEASURE, *n. overmezh'ur.* Excess of measure; something that exceeds the measure proposed.

ŌVERMIX', *v. t.* To mix with too much. *Creech.*

ŌVERMOD'EST, *a.* Modest to excess; bashful. *Hales.*

O'VERMŌST, *a.* Highest; over the rest in authority. *Ainsworth.*

ŌVERMUCH', *a.* Too much; exceeding what is necessary or proper. *Locke.*

ŌVERMUCH', *adv.* In too great a degree. *Hooker.*

ŌVERMUCH', *n.* More than sufficient. *Milton.*

ŌVERMUCH'NESS, *n.* Superabundance. [*Not used and barbarous.*] *B. Jonson.*

ŌVERMUL'TITUDE, *v. t.* To exceed in number. [*Not used.*] *Milton.*

ŌVERNA'ME, *v. t.* To name over or in a series. [*Not used.*] *Shak.*

ŌVERNE'AT, *a.* Excessively neat. *Spectator.*

ŌVERNIGHT, *n.* Night before bed-time. [See *Over,* prep.] *Shak.*

ŌVERNOISE, *v. t. overnoiz'.* To overpower by noise. *Cowley.*

ŌVEROFFEND'ED, *a.* Offended to excess. *Steele.*

ŌVEROF'FICE, *v. t.* To lord by virtue of an office. [*Not used.*] *Shak.*

ŌVEROFFI''CIOUS, *a.* Too busy; too ready to intermeddle; too importunate. *Collier.*

ŌVERPA'INT, *v. t.* To color or describe too strongly. *Hill.*

ŌVERP'ASS, *v. t.* To cross; to go over. *Dryden.*
2. To overlook; to pass without regard. *Milton. Hooker.*
3. To omit, as in reckoning. *Raleigh.*
4. To omit; not to receive or include. *Hooker.*

ŌVERP'ASSED, } *pp.* Passed by; passed
ŌVERP'AST, } away; gone; past. *Shak.*

ŌVERPA'Y, *v. t.* To pay too much or more than is due.
2. To reward beyond the price or merit. *Prior.*

ŌVERPEE'R, *v. t.* To overlook; to hover over. [*Not used.*] *Shak.*

ŌVERPE'OPLE, *v. t.* To overstock with inhabitants. *Johnson.*

ŌVERPERCH', *v. t.* To perch over or above; to fly over. *Shak.*

ŌVERPERSUA'DE, *v. t.* To persuade or influence against one's inclination or opinion. *Pope.*

ŌVERPIC'TURE, *v. t.* To exceed the representation or picture. *Shak.*

O'VERPLUS, *n.* [*over* and L. *plus,* more, or perhaps G. *überfluss,* overflow.] Surplus; that which remains after a supply, or beyond a quantity proposed. Take what is wanted and return the *overplus.*

It would look like a fable to report that this gentleman gives away all which is the *overplus* of a great fortune. *Addison.*

ŌVERPLY', *v. t.* To ply to excess; to exert with too much vigor. *Milton.*

ŌVERPOISE, *v. t. overpoiz'.* To outweigh. *Brown.*

ŌVERPOISE, *n. overpoiz'.* Preponderant weight. *Dryden.*

ŌVERPOL'ISH, *v. t.* To polish too much. *Blackwall.*

ŌVERPON'DEROUS, *a.* Too heavy; too depressing. *Milton.*

ŌVERPŌST, *v. t.* To hasten over quickly. *Shak.*

ŌVERPOW'ER, *v. t.* To affect with a power or force that cannot be borne; as, the light *overpowers* the eyes.
2. To vanquish by force; to subdue; to reduce to silence in action or submission; to defeat. *Dryden. Watts.*

ŌVERPRESS', *v. t.* To bear upon with irresistible force; to crush; to overwhelm. *Sidney. Swift.*
2. To overcome by importunity.

ŌVERPRI'ZE, *v. t.* To value or prize at too high a rate. *Wotton.*

ŌVERPROMPT', *a.* Too prompt; too ready or eager.

ŌVERPROMPT'NESS, *n.* Excessive promptness; precipitation.

ŌVERPROPO'RTION, *v. t.* To make of too great proportion.

ŌVERQUI'ETNESS, *n.* Too much quietness. *Brown.*

ŌVERRA'KE, *v. t.* To break in upon a ship. When the waves break in upon a ship riding at anchor, it is said, they *overrake* her, or she is *overraked.* *Mar. Dict.*

ŌVERRANK', *a.* Too rank or luxuriant. *Mortimer.*

ŌVERRA'TE, *v. t.* To rate at too much; to estimate at a value or amount beyond the truth. *Dryden.*

ŌVERRE'ACH, *v. t.* To reach beyond in any direction; to rise above; to extend beyond. *Burnet.*
2. To deceive by cunning, artifice or sagacity; to cheat. *Tillotson.*

ŌVERRE'ACH, *v. i.* Applied to *horses,* to strike the toe of the hind foot against the heel or shoe of the fore foot.

ŌVERRE'ACH, *n.* The act of striking the heel of the fore foot with the toe of the hind foot. *Encyc.*

ŌVERRE'ACHER, *n.* One that overreaches; one that deceives.

ŌVERRE'ACHING, *n.* The act of deceiving; a reaching too far.

ŌVERRE'AD, *v. t.* To read over; to peruse. [*Not used.*] *Shak.*

ŌVERRED', *v. t.* To smear with a red color. [*Not used.*] *Shak.*

ŌVERRI'DE, *v. t.* To ride over. [*Not used.*] *Chaucer.*
2. To ride too much; to ride beyond the strength of the horse.

ŌVERRID', } *pp.* Rid to excess.
ŌVERRID'DEN, }

ŌVERRI'PEN, *v. t.* To make too ripe. *Shak.*

ŌVERRŌAST, *v. t.* To roast too much. *Shak.*

ŌVERRU'LE, *v. t.* To influence or control by predominant power; to subject to superior authority. The law must *overrule* all private opinions of right and wrong.

His passion and animosity *overruled* his conscience. *Clarendon.*

2. To govern with high authority. *Hayward.*
3. In *law,* to supersede or reject; as, the plea was *overruled* by the court.

ŌVERRU'LER, *n.* One who controls, directs or governs. *Sidney.*

ŌVERRU'LING, *ppr.* Controlling; subjecting to authority.
2. *a.* Exerting superior and controlling power; as an *overruling* Providence.

ŌVERRUN', *v. t.* To run or spread over; to grow over; to cover all over. The sluggard's farm is *overrun* with weeds.

Some plants unchecked will soon *overrun* a field. The Canada thistle is *overrunning* the northern parts of New England, as it has *overrun* Normandy.

2. To march or rove over; to harass by hostile incursions; to ravage. The south of Europe was formerly *overrun* by the Goths, Vandals and other barbarians.

3. To outrun; to run faster than another and leave him behind.

Ahimaaz ran by the way of the plain, and *overran* Cushi. 2 Sam. xviii.

4. To overspread with numbers. Were it not for the ibis, it has been supposed Egypt would be *overrun* with crocodiles.

5. To injure by treading down.

6. Among *printers*, to change the disposition of types and carry those of one line into another, either in correction, or in the contraction or extension of columns.

ŌVERRUN′, *v. i.* To overflow; to run over. *Smith.*

ŌVERRUN′NER, *n.* One that overruns.

ŌVERRUN′NING, *ppr.* Spreading over; ravaging; changing the disposition of types.

ŌVERSAT′URATE, *v. t.* To saturate to excess.

ŌVERSAT′URATED, *pp.* More than saturated.

ŌVERSAT′URATING, *ppr.* Saturating to excess.

ŌVERSCRU′PULOUS, *a.* Scrupulous to excess. *Mitford.*

ŌVERSEA, *a.* Foreign; from beyond sea. *Wilson.*

ŌVERSEE′, *v. t.* To superintend; to overlook, implying care.

2. To pass unheeded; to omit; to neglect. [*Not used.*] *Hudibras.*

ŌVERSEE′N, *pp.* Superintended.

2. Mistaken; deceived. [*Not used.*] *Hooker.*

ŌVERSEE′R, *n.* One who overlooks; a superintendent; a supervisor.

2. An officer who has the care of the poor or of an idiot, &c.

ŌVERSET′, *v. t.* To turn from the proper position or basis; to turn upon the side, or to turn bottom upwards; as, to *overset* a coach, a ship or a building.

2. To subvert; to overthrow; as, to *overset* the constitution of a state; to *overset* a scheme of policy.

3. To throw off the proper foundation. *Dryden.*

ŌVERSET′, *v. i.* To turn or be turned over; to turn or fall off the basis or bottom. A crank vessel is liable to *overset.*

ŌVERSHA′DE, *v. t.* To cover with shade; to cover with any thing that causes darkness; to render dark or gloomy. *Bacon. Dryden.*

ŌVERSHAD′ŌW, *v. t.* To throw a shadow over; to overshade. *Milton.*

2. To shelter; to protect; to cover with protecting influence. *Milton.*

ŌVERSHAD′ŌWER, *n.* One that throws a shade over any thing. *Bacon.*

ŌVERSHAD′ŌWING, *ppr.* Throwing a shade over; protecting.

ŌVERSHOOT′, *v. t.* To shoot beyond the mark. *Tillotson.*

2. To pass swiftly over. *Harte.*

To overshoot one's self, to venture too far; to assert too much. *Hooker.*

ŌVERSHOOT′, *v. i.* To fly beyond the mark. *Collier.*

ŌVERSHOT′, *pp.* Shot beyond.

O′VERSHOT, *a.* An *overshot* wheel is one that receives the water, *shot over* the top, on the descent. An *overshot* wheel is moved by less water than an undershot wheel.

O′VERSIGHT, *n.* Superintendence; watchful care. 1 Pet. v.

2. Mistake; an overlooking; omission; error. *Pope.*

ŌVERSI′ZE, *v. t.* To surpass in bulk or size. [*Not much used.*] *Sandys.*

2. To cover with viscid matter. *Shak.*

ŌVERSKIP′, *v. t.* To skip or leap over; to pass by leaping. *Hooker.*

2. To pass over. *Donne.*

3. To escape. *Shak.*

ŌVERSLEE′P, *v. t.* To sleep too long; as, to *oversleep* the usual hour of rising.

ŌVERSLIP′, *v. t.* To slip or pass without notice; to pass undone, unnoticed or unused; to omit; to neglect; as, to *overslip* time or opportunity. *Hammond.*

ŌVERSLŌW, *v. t.* To render slow; to check; to curb. [*Not used.*] *Hammond.*

ŌVERSNŌW, *v. t.* To cover with snow. [*Not much used.*] *Dryden.*

ŌVERSOLD, *pp.* Sold at too high a price. *Dryden.*

ŌVERSOON′, *adv.* Too soon. *Sidney.*

ŌVERSOR′ROW, *v. t.* To grieve or afflict to excess. *Milton.*

ŌVERSPAN′, *v. t.* To reach or extend over.

ŌVERSPE′AK, *v. t.* To speak too much; to use too many words. *Hales.*

ŌVERSPENT′, *pp.* [See *Spend.*] Harassed or fatigued to an extreme degree. *Dryden.*

ŌVERSPREAD, *v. t. overspred′.* To spread over; to cover over. The deluge *overspread* the earth.

2. To scatter over.

ŌVERSPREAD, *v. i. overspred′.* To be spread or scattered over; as, weeds *overspread* the ground.

ŌVERSTAND′, *v. t.* To stand too much on price or conditions; to lose a sale by holding the price too high. *Dryden.*

ŌVERSTA′RE, *v. t.* To stare wildly. [*Not used.*] *Ascham.*

ŌVERSTEP′, *v. t.* To step over or beyond; to exceed. *Shak.*

ŌVERSTOCK′, *n.* Superabundance; more than is sufficient. *Tatler.*

ŌVERSTOCK′, *v. t.* To fill too full; to crowd; to supply with more than is wanted. The world may be *overstocked* with inhabitants. The market is often *overstocked* with goods.

2. To furnish with more cattle than are wanted; as, to *overstock* a farm.

3. To supply with more seed than is wanted; as, to *overstock* land with clover.

ŌVERSTO′RE, *v. t.* To store with too much; to supply or fill with superabundance. *Hale.*

ŌVERSTRA′IN, *v. i.* To strain to excess; to make too violent efforts. *Dryden.*

ŌVERSTRA′IN, *v. t.* To stretch too far. *Ayliffe.*

ŌVERSTREW′, } *v. t.* To spread or scatter over. *Shak.*
ŌVERSTRŌW, }

ŌVERSTRI′KE, *v. t.* To strike beyond. *Spenser.*

ŌVERSTRŌWN, *pp.* Spread or scattered over. *J. Barlow.*

ŌVERSUPPLY′, *v. t.* To furnish more than is sufficient. *Melmoth.*

ŌVERSWA′Y, *v. t.* To overrule; to bear down; to control. *Hooker.*

ŌVERSWELL′, *v. t.* To swell or rise above; to overflow. *Shak.*

O′VERT, *a.* [Fr. *ouvert*, from *ouvrir*, to open, It. *aprire*, L. *aperio.*] Open to view; public; apparent; as *overt* virtues; an *overt* essay. But the word is now used chiefly in law. Thus an *overt* act of treason is distinguished from secret design or intention not carried into effect, and even from words spoken. A market *overt*, is a place where goods are publicly exposed to sale. A pound *overt*, is one open overhead, as distinguished from a pound *covert* or close. *Blackstone.*

ŌVERTA′KE, *v. t.* To come up with in a course, pursuit, progress or motion; to catch.

The enemy said, I will pursue, I will *overtake.* Ex. xv.

2. To come upon; to fall on afterwards. Vengeance shall *overtake* the wicked.

3. To take by surprise.

Brethren, if a man be *overtaken* in a fault, ye who are spiritual, restore such one in the spirit of meekness. Gal. vi.

ŌVERT′ASK, *v. t.* To impose too heavy a task or injunction on. *Harvey.*

ŌVERTAX′, *v. t.* To tax too heavily.

ŌVERTHRŌW, *v. t.* [See *Throw.*] To turn upside down.

His wife *overthrew* the table. *Taylor.*

2. To throw down.

3. To ruin; to demolish.

When the walls of Thebes he *overthrew.* *Dryden.*

4. To defeat; to conquer; to vanquish; as, to *overthrow* an army or an enemy.

5. To subvert; to destroy; as, to *overthrow* the constitution or state; to *overthrow* religion.

O′VERTHRŌW, *n.* The state of being overturned or turned off the basis.

2. Ruin; destruction; as the *overthrow* of the state.

3. Defeat; discomfiture; as the *overthrow* of enemies. *Dryden.*

4. Degradation. *Shak.*

ŌVERTHRŌWER, *n.* One that overthrows, defeats or destroys.

ŌVERTHWART′, *a.* Opposite; being over the way or street. *Shak.*

2. Crossing at right angles.

3. Cross; perverse; adverse; contradictious. *Clarendon.*

ŌVERTHWART′, *prep.* Across; from side to side.

ŌVERTHWART′LY, *adv.* Across; transversely. *Peacham.*

2. Perversely.

ŌVERTHWART′NESS, *n.* The state of being athwart or lying across.

2. Perverseness; pervicacity. *Johnson.*

ŌVERTI′RE, *v. t.* To tire to excess; to subdue by fatigue. *Milton.*

ŌVERTI′TLE, *v. t.* To give too high a title to. *Fuller.*

O′VERTLY, *adv.* Openly; in open view; publicly.

ŎVERTỌOK′, *pret.* of *overtake.*
ŎVERTOP′, *v. t.* To rise above the top. *Shak.*
2. To excel; to surpass. *Harvey.*
3. To obscure; to make of less importance by superior excellence. *Swift.*
ŎVERTOW′ER, *v. t.* To soar too high. *Fuller.*
ŎVERTRIP′, *v. t.* To trip over; to walk nimbly over. *Shak.*
ŎVERTRUST′, *v. t.* To trust with too much confidence. *Hall.*
O′VERTURE, *n.* [Fr. *ouverture.* See *Overt.*]
1. Opening; disclosure; discovery. [*In this literal sense, little used.*] *Shak.*
2. Proposal; something offered for consideration, acceptance or rejection. The prince made *overtures* of peace, which were accepted.
3. The opening piece, prelude or symphony of some public act, ceremony or entertainment. The *overture* in theatrical entertainments, is a piece of music usually ending in a fugue. The *overture* of a jubilee is a general procession, &c. *Encyc.*
ŎVERTURN′, *v. t.* To overset; to turn or throw from a basis or foundation; as, to *overturn* a carriage or a building.
2. To subvert; to ruin; to destroy. *Locke. Atterbury.*
3. To overpower; to conquer. *Milton.*
O′VERTURN, *n.* State of being overturned or subverted; overthrow.
ŎVERTURN′ABLE, *a.* That may be overturned. [*Not much used.*]
ŎVERTURN′ED, *pp.* Overset; overthrown.
ŎVERTURN′ER, *n.* One that overturns or subverts. *Swift.*
ŎVERTURN′ING, *ppr.* Oversetting; overthrowing; subverting.
ŎVERTURN′ING, *n.* An oversetting; subversion; change; revolution.
ŎVERVAL′UE, *v. t.* To rate at too high a price. *Hooker.*
ŎVERVA′IL, ŎVERVẸIL, } *v. t.* To cover; to spread over. *Shak.*
ŎVERVO′TE, *v. t.* To outvote; to outnumber in votes given. *K. Charles.*
ŎVERWẠTCH′, *v. t.* To watch to excess; to subdue by long want of rest. *Dryden.*
ŎVERWẠTCH′ED, *a.* Tired by too much watching. *Sidney.*
ŎVERWE′AK, *a.* Too weak; too feeble. *Raleigh.*
ŎVERWE′ARY, *v. t.* To subdue with fatigue. *Dryden.*
ŎVERWEATHER, *v. t.* *overweth′er.* [See *Weather.*] To bruise or batter by violence of weather.
ŎVERWEE′N, *v. i.* [*ween* is obsolete, except in composition. See the word.]
1. To think too highly; to think arrogantly or conceitedly.
2. To reach beyond the truth in thought; to think too favorably. *Shak. Milton.*
ŎVERWEE′NING, *ppr.* Thinking too highly or conceitedly.
2. *a.* That thinks too highly, particularly of one's self; conceited; vain; as *overweening* pride; an *overweening* brain. *Locke.*
ŎVERWEE′NINGLY, *adv.* With too much vanity or conceit.
ŎVERWẸIGH, *v. t.* To exceed in weight; to cause to preponderate; to outweigh; to overbalance. *Hooker.*
ŎVERWẸIGHT, *n.* Greater weight; preponderance. *Bacon.*
ŎVERWHELM′, *v. t.* To overspread or crush beneath something violent and weighty, that covers or encompasses the whole; as, to *overwhelm* with waves.
2. To immerse and bear down; in a figurative sense; as, to be *overwhelmed* with cares, afflictions or business.
3. To overlook gloomily. *Shak.*
4. To put over. [*Not used.*]
O′VERWHELM, *n.* The act of overwhelming. *Young.*
ŎVERWHELM′ING, *ppr.* Crushing with weight or numbers.
ŎVERWHELM′INGLY, *adv.* In a manner to overwhelm.
ŎVERWING′, *v. t.* To outflank; to extend beyond the wing of an army. *Milton.*
ŎVERWI′SE, *a.* *s* as *z.* Wise to affectation. *Ecclus.*
ŎVERWI′SENESS, *n.* Pretended or affected wisdom. *Raleigh.*
ŎVERWŎRD′, *v. t.* To say too much.
ŎVERWŎRK′, *v. t.* To work beyond the strength; to cause to labor too much; to tire. *South.*
ŎVERWŎRN, *a.* Worn out; subdued by toil. *Dryden.*
2. Spoiled by time. *Shak.*
ŎVERWRESTLE, *v. t.* *overres′l.* To subdue by wrestling. *Spenser.*
ŎVERWROUGHT, *pp.* *overraut′.* Labored to excess. *Dryden.*
2. Worked all over; as *overwrought* with ornaments. *Pope.*
ŎVERYE′ARED, *a.* Too old. [*Not used.*] *Fairfax.*
ŎVERZE′ALED, *a.* Too much excited with zeal; ruled by too much zeal. *Fuller.*
ŎVERZEALOUS, *a.* *overzel′ous.* Too zealous; eager to excess. *Locke.*
ŎVIC′ULAR, *a.* [from L. *ovum,* an egg.] Pertaining to an egg. *Bryant.*
O′VIDUCT, *n.* [L. *ovum,* an egg, and *ductus,* a duct.]
In animals, a passage for the egg from the ovary to the womb, or a passage which conveys the egg from the ovary. *Hist. Roy. Soc.*
O′VIFORM, *a.* [L. *ovum,* egg, and *forma,* form.] Having the form or figure of an egg. *Burnet.*
O′VINE, *a.* [L. *ovinus,* from *ovis,* sheep.] Pertaining to sheep; consisting of sheep.
ŎVIP′AROUS, *a.* [L. *ovum,* egg, and *pario,* to produce.]
Producing eggs, or producing young from eggs. Fowls and reptiles are *oviparous* animals.
O′VOID, *a.* [L. *ovum,* egg, and Gr. ειδος, form.] Having the shape of an egg.
O′VOLO, *n.* In *architecture,* a round molding, the quarter of a circle; called also the *quarter round.* *Encyc.*
OWE, *v. t.* *o.* [a regular verb, pret. and pp. *owed;* used with the auxiliary *have, had,* but not with the substantive verb to *be.* This verb is doubtless the Sax. *agan,* Goth. *aigan,* Sw. *åga,* Ice. *eg,* to have or possess, that is, to hold or retain, coinciding with the Gr. εχω. The Saxon participle *agen,* Dan. *egen,* is the English *own. Ought* is a derivative tense, and was formerly used in the sense of *owed.* The proper sense of *owe,* is to be held or bound to pay; nearly as we now use *have* in the phrases, "I *have* to pay a sum of money to-morrow," "I *have* to go to town to-day."]
1. To be indebted; to be obliged or bound to pay. The merchants *owe* a large sum to foreigners.

> A son *owes* help and honor to his father. *Holyday.*
>
> One was brought to him who *owed* him ten thousand talents. Matt. xviii.
>
> *Owe* no man any thing, but to love one another. Rom. xiii.

2. To be obliged to ascribe to; to be obliged for; as, that he may *owe* to me all his deliverance. *Milton.*
3. To possess; to have; to be the owner of. [This is the original sense, but now obsolete. In place of it, we use *own,* from the participle. See *Own.*]

> Thou dost here usurp
> The name thou *owest* not. *Shak.*

4. To be due or owing.

> O deem thy fall not *ow'd* to man's decree. *Pope.*

[*This passive form is not now used.*]
OWE, *v. i.* To be bound or obliged. *Bp. Fisher.*
ŎWING, *ppr.* [This is used in a passive form, contrary to analogy, for *owen* or *owed.* But the use is inveterately established.]
1. Due; that moral obligation requires to be paid; as the money *owing* to a laborer for services, or to another country for goods.
2. Consequential; ascribable to, as the cause. Misfortunes are often *owing* to vices or miscalculations.
3. Imputable to as an agent. His recovery from sickness is *owing* less to his physician, than to the strength of his constitution.
OWL, *n.* [Sax. *ula, ule;* D. *uil;* G. *eule;* Sw. *ugla* or *uggla;* L. *ulula.* The orthography, except in the Swedish, coincides with *howl,* L. *ululo;* but the radical letters are not obvious.]
A fowl of the genus Strix, that flies chiefly in the night.
OWL′ER, *n.* [qu. from *owl,* or from *wool.*] One that conveys contraband goods. *Swift.*
OWL′ET, *n.* [Fr. *hulotte.*] An owl, which see.
OWL′ING, *n.* The offense of transporting wool or sheep out of England, contrary to the statute. *Blackstone.*
[This explanation of *owling* favors the derivation of the word from *wool.*]
OWL′-LIGHT, *n.* Glimmering or imperfect light. *Warburton.*
OWL′-LIKE, *a.* Like an owl in look and habits. *Donne.*
ŎWN, *a.* [Sax. *agen;* Sw. Dan. *egen;* D. G. *eigen;* the participle of Sax. *agan,* to possess. See *Owe* and *Ought.*]
1. Belonging to; possessed; peculiar; usually expressing property with emphasis, or in express exclusion of others. It follows *my, your, his, their, thy, her.* God created man in *his own* image. Adam begat a son in *his own* likeness. Let them fall by *their own* counsel. He washed us from our sins in *his own* blood. *Scripture.*
In the phrases, his *own* nation, his *own*

country, the word *own* denotes that the person belongs to the nation or country.

2. *Own* often follows a verb; as, the book is not my *own*, that is, my *own book.*

3. It is used as a substitute.

That they may dwell in a place of their *own.* 2 Sam. vii.

In this use, a noun cannot follow *own.*

4. "He came to his *own*, and his *own* received him not," that is, his *own* nation or people; *own* being here used as a substitute, like many other adjectives.

ŌWN, *v. t* [from the adjective.] To have the legal or rightful title to; to have the exclusive right of possession and use. A freeholder in the United States *owns* his farm. Men often *own* land or goods which are not in their possession.

2. To have the legal right to, without the exclusive right to use; as, a man *owns* the land in front of his farm to the middle of the highway.

3. To acknowledge to belong to; to avow or admit that the property belongs to.

When you come, find me out
And *own* me for your son. *Dryden.*

4. To avow; to confess, as a fault, crime or other act; that is, to acknowledge that one has done the act; as, to *own* the faults of youth; to *own* our guilt. The man is charged with theft, but he has not *owned* it.

5. In general, to acknowledge; to confess; to avow; to admit to be true; not to deny; as, to *own* our weakness and frailty.

Many *own* the gospel of salvation more from custom than conviction. *J. M. Mason.*

ŌWNED, *pp.* The legal title being vested in; as, the property is *owned* by a company.

2. Acknowledged; avowed; confessed.

ŌWNER, *n.* The rightful proprietor; one who has the legal or rightful title, whether he is the possessor or not.

The ox knoweth his *owner.* Is. i.

The centurion believed the master and *owner* of the ship. Acts xxvii.

ŌWNERSHIP, *n.* Property; exclusive right of possession; legal or just claim or title. The *ownership* of the estate is in A; the possession is in B.

ŌWNING, *ppr.* Having the legal or just title to.

2. Acknowledging; avowing; confessing.

OWRE, *n.* [L. *urus.*] A beast. [*Not used.*] *Ainsworth.*

OWSE, *n.* Bark of oak beaten or ground to small pieces. *Ash.*

OW'SER, *n.* Bark and water mixed in a tan-pit. *Ash.*

OX, *n.* plu. *oxen.* pron. *ox'n.* [Sax. *oxa*; G. *ochs, ochse*; D. *os*; Sw. Dan. *oxe*; Sans. *uksha*; Armen. *os.*]

The male of the bovine genus of quadrupeds, castrated and grown to his size or nearly so. The young male is called in America a *steer.* The same animal not castrated is called a *bull.* These distinctions are well established with us in regard to domestic animals of this genus. When we speak of wild animals of this kind, *ox* is sometimes applied both to the male and female, and in zoology, the same practice exists in regard to the domestic animals. So in common usage, a pair of bulls yoked may be sometimes called *oxen.* We never apply the name *ox* to the *cow* or female of the domestic kind. *Oxen* in the plural may comprehend both the male and female.

OX'ALATE, *n.* [See *Oxalic.*] In chimistry, a salt formed by a combination of the oxalic acid with a base.

OXAL'IC, *a.* [Gr. οξαλις, sorrel, from οξυς, acid.]

Pertaining to sorrel. The *oxalic* acid is the acid of sorrel.

OX'BANE, *n.* A plant, buphonos. *Ainsworth.*

OX'-EYE, *n.* [*ox* and *eye.*] A plant of the genus Buphthalmum; another of the genus Anthemis; also, the ox-eye daisy or Chrysanthemum. *Fam. of Plants.*

OX'EYED, *a.* Having large full eyes, like those of an ox. *Burton.*

OX'FLY, *n.* A fly hatched under the skin of cattle.

OX'GANG, *n.* [*ox* and *gang*, going.] In *ancient laws*, as much land as an ox can plow in a year; said to be fifteen acres, or as others alledge, twenty acres.

OX'HEAL, *n.* A plant. *Ainsworth.*

OXIOD'IC, *a.* Pertaining to or consisting of the compound of oxygen and iodine. *Webster's Manual.*

OX'LIKE, *a.* [*ox* and *like.*] Resembling an ox. *Sandys.*

OX'LIP, *n.* A plant, the cowslip.

OX'STALL, *n.* A stall or stand for oxen.

OXTŎNGUE, *n.* *ox'tung.* A plant of the genus Picris.

OX'YCRATE, *n.* [Gr. οξυς, acid, and κεραω, to mix.]

A mixture of water and vinegar. [*Little used.*] *Wiseman.*

OX'YD, *n.* [Gr. οξυς, acid, sharp; οξος, vinegar. The true orthography of this word is *oxyd*, as originally written by Lavoisier and his associates. No analogy in the language is better established than the uniform translation of the Greek υ into the English *y*, as in Latin, and it is very absurd to preserve this analogy in *oxygen, oxymuriate* and *hydrogen*, and depart from it in *oxyd.*]

In *chimistry*, a substance formed by the combination of a portion of oxygen with some base; or a substance combined with oxygen, without being in the state of an acid. *Dict. Nat. Hist. Ure.*

OXYDABIL'ITY, *n.* The capacity of being converted into an oxyd. *Med. Repos.*

OX'YDABLE, *a.* Capable of being converted into an oxyd.

OX'YDATE, *v. t.* To convert into an oxyd, as metals and other substances, by combination with oxygen. It differs from *acidify*, to make acid, or to convert into an acid, as in oxydation the acid that enters into combination is not sufficient to form an acid.

OX'YDATED, *pp.* Converted into an oxyd.

OX'YDATING, *ppr.* Converting into an oxyd.

OXYDA'TION, *n.* The operation or process of converting into an oxyd, as metals or other substances, by combining with them a certain portion of oxygen. *Lavoisier. Ure.*

OX'YDIZE, *v. t.* To oxydate, which see.

OX'YDIZED, *pp.* Oxydated.

OX'YDIZEMENT, *n.* Oxydation.

OX'YDIZING, *ppr.* Oxydating.

[*Oxydize* and its derivatives are now more generally used than *oxydate*, though there seems to be no ground for the preference.]

OX'YGEN, *n.* [Gr. οξυς, acid, and γενναω, to generate.]

In *chimistry*, oxygen or oxygen gas is an element or substance so named from its property of generating acids; it is the respirable part of air, vital air, or the basis of it; it is called the acidifying principle, and the principle or support of combustion. Modern experiments, however, prove that it is not necessary in all cases to combustion or to acidity. Oxygen is a permanently elastic fluid, invisible, inodorous, and a little heavier than atmospheric air. In union with azote or nitrogen, it forms atmospheric air, of which it constitutes about a fifth part. Water contains about 85 per cent. of it, and it exists in most vegetable and animal products, acids, salts and oxyds. It forms 50 per cent. of silex, 47 of alumin, 28 of lime, 40 of magnesia, 17 of potash, and 25 of soda. *Dict. Nat. Hist. Cyc. Ure. Phillips.*

OX'YGENATE, *v. t.* To unite or cause to combine with oxygen, without the evolution of heat or light; to acidify by oxygen.

OX'YGENATED, *pp.* United with oxygen.

OX'YGENATING, *ppr.* Uniting with oxygen.

OXYGENA'TION, *n.* The act, operation or process of combining with oxygen.

OX'YGENIZABLE, *a.* Capable of being oxygenized.

OX'YGENIZE, *v. t.* To oxygenate, which see.

OX'YGENIZED, *pp.* Oxygenated.

OX'YGENIZEMENT, *n.* Oxygenation.

OX'YGENIZING, *ppr.* Oxygenating.

OXYG'ENOUS, *a.* Pertaining to oxygen, or obtained from it.

OX'YGON, *n.* [Gr. οξυς, sharp, and γωνια, an angle.]

A triangle having three acute angles. *Dict.*

OXY-I'ODINE, *n.* In *chimistry*, a compound of the chloriodic and oxiodic acids. *Davy.*

OX'YMEL, *n.* [Gr. οξυς, acid, and μελι, honey.]

A mixture of vinegar and honey. *Arbuthnot.*

OXYMO'RON, *n.* [Gr. οξυμωρον, a smart saying which at first view appears foolish.]

A rhetorical figure, in which an epithet of a quite contrary signification is added to a word; as *cruel kindness.*

Oxyprussic acid, chloroprussic acid.

OXYR'RHODINE, *n.* [compounded of Gr. οξυς, acid, and ροδον, rose.]

A mixture of two parts of the oil of roses with one of the vinegar of roses. *Floyer.*

OX'YTONE, *a.* [Gr. οξυς, sharp, and τονος, tone.]

Having an acute sound. *Walker.*

OX'YTONE, *n.* An acute sound.

OY'ER, *n.* [Norm. *oyer*, hearing; Fr. *ouir*, to hear.]

In *law*, a hearing or trial of causes. A court of oyer and terminer is constituted by a commission to inquire, hear and determine all treasons, felonies and misdemeanors. *Blackstone.*

2. The hearing, as of a writ, bond, note or other specialty; as when a defendant in court prays *oyer* of a writing. *Blackstone.*

OYES, [Fr. *oyez*, hear ye.] This word is used by the sheriff or his substitute in making proclamation in court, requiring silence and attention. It is thrice repeated, and most absurdly pronounced, *O yes.*

OYLET-HOLE. [See *Eyelet-hole.*]

OYS'TER, *n.* [G. *auster*; D. *oester*; Sw. *ostra*; Dan. *öster*; Fr. *huitre*; Arm. *histrenn* or *eistren*; Russ. *ystritz*; Corn. *estren*; L. *ostrea*; Gr. οςρεον; probably connected in origin with οςεον, bone, and named from its hardness.]

A bivalvular testaceous animal, found adhering to rocks or other fixed substances in salt water which is shallow, or in the mouths of rivers. *Oysters* are deemed nourishing and delicious food.

OYS'TER-SHELL, *n.* The hard covering or shell of the oyster.

OYS'TER-WENCH, } A woman whose
OYS'TER-WIFE, } *n.* occupation is to
OYS'TER-WÖMAN, } sell oysters; a low woman. *Shak.*

P.

P is the sixteenth letter of the English Alphabet, and a labial articulation formed by a close compression of the anterior part of the lips, as in *ep*. It is convertible into *b* and *f*, sometimes into *v*, and in Greek, into φ. This letter is found in the oriental languages, from which it was received into the Greek and Latin; except however the Arabic, which has not this letter, and the Arabians cannot easily pronounce it. In some words which we have borrowed from the Greek, *p* is mute, as in *psalm*, *ptisan*; but is not silent in English words, unless it may be in *receipt*, and a few irregular words. P aspirated or followed by *h*, represents the Greek φ, which answers to the English *f*, as in *philosophy*.

As an abbreviation, P. stands for *Publius*, *pondo*, &c.; P. A. DIG. for *patricia dignitas*; P. C. for *Patres Conscripti*; P. F. for *Publius Fabius*; P. P. for *propositum publice*; P. R. for *populus Romanus*; P. R. S. for *prætoris sententia*; P. R. S. P. for *præses provinciæ*.

P. M. stands for *post meridiem*, afternoon.

As a numeral, P, like G, stands for one hundred, and with a dash over it, P̄, for four hundred thousand.

Among physicians, P. stands for *pugil*, or the eighth part of a handful; P. Æ. for *partes æquales*, equal parts of the ingredients; P. P. for *pulvis patrum*, or the Jesuits' bark in powder; and *ppt.* for *præparatus*, prepared. *Encyc.*

PA'AGE, *n.* [Norm. *paage*, payment. See *Pay.*]

A toll for passage over another person's grounds. [*Not used.*] *Burke.*

PAB'ULAR, *a.* [L. *pabulum*, food.] Pertaining to food; affording food or aliment.

PABULA'TION, *n.* [L. *pabulatio*, from *pabulor*, to feed.]

The act of feeding or procuring provender. *Cockeram.*

PAB'ULOUS, *a.* [L. *pabulum*, food.] Affording aliment or food; alimental. *Brown.*

PAB'ULUM, *n.* [L.] Food; aliment; that which feeds.

2. Fuel; that which supplies the means of combustion. *Encyc.*

PA'CA, *n.* A small animal of America, bearing some resemblance to a hare and a pig. It is a species of cavy; called also the *spotted cavy.* *Dict. Nat. Hist.* *Ed. Encyc.*

PA'CATE, *a.* [L. *pacatus.*] Peaceful; tranquil. [*Not used.*]

PA'CATED, *a.* Appeased. [*Little used.*] *Bailey.*

PACA'TION, *n.* [L. *paco*, to calm or appease.] The act of appeasing.

PACCAN', *n.* An American tree and its nut.

PACE, *n.* [Fr. *pas*; It. *passo*; Sp. *paso*; L. *passus*, from *pando*, to open, or Gr. πατεω, to tread. See *Pass.*]

1. A step.
2. The space between the two feet in walking, estimated at two feet and a half. But the geometrical pace is five feet, or the whole space passed over by the same foot from one step to another. Sixty thousand such paces make one degree on the equator. *Encyc.*
3. Manner of walking; gait; as a languishing *pace*; a heavy *pace*; a quick or slow *pace*. *Addison.*
4. Step; gradation in business. [*Little used.*] *Temple.*
5. A mode of stepping among horses, in which the legs on the same side are lifted together. In a general sense, the word may be applied to any other mode of stepping.
6. Degree of celerity. Let him mend his *pace*.

> To-morrow, and to-morrow, and to-morrow,
> Creeps in this petty *pace* from day to day— *Shak.*

To keep or *hold pace*, to keep up; to go or move as fast as something else.

PACE, *v. i.* To go; to walk; to move. *Spenser.* *Shak.*

2. To go, move or walk slowly.
3. To move by lifting the legs on the same side together, as a horse.

PACE, *v. t.* To measure by steps; as, to *pace* a piece of ground.

2. To regulate in motion.

> If you can, *pace* your wisdom
> In that good path that I would wish it go— *Shak.*

PA'CED, *a.* Having a particular gait; used chiefly in composition; as slow-*paced*.

2. In composition, going all lengths; as a thorough-*paced* intriguer.

PA'CER, *n.* One that paces; a horse that paces.

PACHYDERM'ATOUS, *a.* [Gr. παχυς, thick, and δερμα, skin.]

Having a thick skin; an epithet applied to an order of animals, called *Pachydermata*, embracing all the hoofed quadrupeds which do not ruminate, as the elephant, mastodon or N. American mammoth, hippopotamus, sus or hog, rhinoceros, tapir, and horse. *Cuvier.*

The horse constitutes a separate order, (*Solipeda.*) *Ed. Encyc.*

PACIF'IC, *a.* [L. *pacificus*, from *pacifico*, to make peace. See *Peace.*]

1. Peace-making; conciliatory; suited to make or restore peace; adapted to reconcile differences; mild; appeasing; as, to offer *pacific* propositions to a belligerent power. The measures proposed are in their nature *pacific*.
2. Calm; tranquil; as a *pacific* state of things.

PACIF'IC, *n.* The appellation given to the ocean situated between America on the west, and Asia; so called on account of its exemption from violent tempests.

PACIFICA'TION, *n.* [L. *pacificatio.* See *Pacify.*]

1. The act of making peace between nations or parties at variance. *Bacon.* *South.*
2. The act of appeasing or pacifying wrath. *Hooker.*

PACIFICA'TOR, *n.* [L.] A peace-maker; one that restores amity between contending parties or nations. *Bacon.*

PACIF'ICATORY, *a.* Tending to make peace; conciliatory. *Barrow.*

PAC'IFIED, *pp.* Appeased; tranquilized.

PAC'IFIER, *n.* One who pacifies.

PAC'IFY, *v. t.* [Fr. *pacifier*; Sp. *pacificar*; It. *pacificare*; L. *pacifico*; *pax*, *pacis*, peace, and *facio*, to make.]

1. To appease, as wrath or other violent passion or appetite; to calm; to still; to quiet; to allay agitation or excitement; as, to *pacify* a man when angry, or to *pacify* his wrath or rage; the word being applied both to the person and to the passion. So we say, to *pacify* hunger, to *pacify* importunate demands.
2. To restore peace to; to tranquilize; as, to *pacify* countries in contention. *Bacon.*

PAC'IFYING, *ppr.* Appeasing; tranquilizing.

PACK, *n.* [D. *pak*; G. Sw. *pack*. See the Verb.]

1. A bundle of any thing inclosed in a cover or bound fast with cords; a bale; as a *pack* of goods or cloth. The soldier bears a *pack* on his back.

2. A burden or load; as a *pack* of sorrows. *Shak.*

3. A number of cards, or the number used in games; so called from being inclosed together. *Addison.*

4. A number of hounds or dogs, hunting or kept together, that is, a crowd or assemblage united. *Dryden.*

5. A number of persons united in a bad design or practice; as a *pack* of thieves or knaves. *Swift.*

6. A great number crowded together; as a *pack* of troubles. [*Not used.*] *Ainsworth.*

7. A loose or lewd person. [Sax. *pæcan*, to deceive.] [*Not used.*] *Skelton.*

PACK, *v. t.* [D. *pakken*; G. *packen*; Sw. *packa*; L. *pango, pactum, pactus*; *impingo, compingo*; Gr. πηγνυω, παχυς, πηγος; Dan. *pagt*, a covenant, a farm; hence *dispatch*, to send away. The sense is to *send*, to drive, whence to press, to make *compact*. Hence we say, to *pack* off, Sw. *packa*, that is, to depart with speed; Ar. بَكَّ bakka, to be compressed, to press, Ch. אבק. Class Bg. No. 18. See also No. 33. 66. 32.]

1. To place and press together; to place in close order; as, to *pack* goods in a box or chest.

2. To put together and bind fast; as, to *pack* any thing for carriage with cords or straps.

3. To put in close order with salt intermixed; as, to *pack* meat or fish in barrels.

4. To send in haste. *Shak.*

5. To put together, as cards, in such a manner as to secure the game; to put together in sorts with a fraudulent design, as cards; hence, to unite persons iniquitously, with a view to some private interest; as, to *pack* a jury, that is, to select persons for a jury who may favor a party; to *pack* a parliament; to *pack* an assembly of bishops. *Pope. Butler. Atterbury.*

PACK, *v. i.* To be pressed or close; as, the goods *pack* well.

2. To close; to shut. *Cleaveland.*

3. To depart in haste; with *off*.

> Poor Stella must *pack off* to town. *Swift.*

4. To unite in bad measures; to confederate for ill purposes; to join in collusion.

> Go, *pack* with him. *Shak.*

PACK'AGE, *n.* A bundle or bale; a quantity pressed or bound together; as a *package* of cloth.

2. A charge made for packing goods.

PACK'CLOTH, *n.* A cloth for packing goods, or in which they are tied.

PACK'ED, *pp.* Put together and pressed; tied or bound in a bundle; put down and salted, as meat; sent off; united iniquitously.

PACK'ER, *n.* One that packs; an officer appointed to pack meat, as beef, pork, fish, &c. *Stat. of Conn.*

PACK'ET, *n.* [Fr. *paquet*; Sp. Port. *paquete*; from *pack*.]

1. A small pack or package; a little bundle or parcel; as a *packet* of letters. *Bacon.*

2. A dispatch-vessel; a ship or other vessel employed by government to convey letters from country to country or from port to port. [Originally *packet-boat*, Sp. *paquebote*, Fr. *paquebot*.]

3. A vessel employed in conveying dispatches and passengers from place to place, or to carry passengers and goods coastwise. *U. States.*

PACK'ET, *v. i.* To ply with a packet or dispatch-vessel. *U. States.*

PACKET-BOAT. [See *Packet*.]

PACK'ET-SHIP, *n.* A ship that sails regularly between distant countries for the conveyance of dispatches, letters, passengers, &c.

PACK'HORSE, *n.* A horse employed in carrying packs or goods and baggage. *Locke.*

2. A beast of burden.

PACK'ING, *ppr.* Laying together in close order; binding in a bundle; putting in barrels with salt, &c.; uniting, as men for a fraudulent purpose.

PACK'ING, *n.* A trick; collusion. *Bale.*

PACK'SADDLE, *n.* A saddle on which packs or burdens are laid for conveyance.

PACK'STAFF, *n.* A staff on which a traveler occasionally supports his pack. *Bp. Hall.*

PACK'THREAD, *n.* Strong thread or twine used in tying up parcels.

PACK'-WAX, *n.* A tendinous substance of the neck of an animal. *Ray.*

PA'CO, **PA'COS**, *n.* An animal of South America, resembling the camel in shape, but much smaller. It is sometimes called the ***Peruvian sheep***, on account of its long thick hair. *Encyc.*

PACT, *n.* [Fr.; L. *pactum*, from *pango*. See *Pack*.]

A contract; an agreement or covenant. *Bacon.*

PAC'TION, *n.* [L. *pactio*. See *Pack*.] An agreement or contract. *Hayward.*

PAC'TIONAL, *a.* By way of agreement. *Sanderson.*

PACTI''TIOUS, *a.* Settled by agreement or stipulation.

PAD, *n.* [Sax. *paad*, for *path*. See *Path*.]

1. A foot path; a road. [*Not now used.*] *Prior.*

2. An easy paced horse. *Addison. Pope.*

3. A robber that infests the road on foot; usually called a foot-pad.

PAD, *n.* A soft saddle, cushion or bolster stuffed with straw, hair or other soft substance. *Camden.*

PAD, *v. i.* [Gr. πατεω. See *Path*.] To travel slowly.

2. To rob on foot.

3. To beat a way smooth and level.

PAD'AR, *n.* Grouts; coarse flour or meal. [*Not used in U. States.*] *Wotton.*

PAD'DER, *n.* A robber on foot; a highwayman. *Dryden.*

PAD'DLE, *v. i.* [The French *patrouiller* signifies to *paw*, to paddle, and hence the English *patrol*. This word seems to be from *patte*, a paw, allied perhaps to L. *pes, pedis*, the foot, and this is allied to the Gr. πατεω, to tread. To paddle, then, is to use the paw. But perhaps it is from the noun, which see.]

1. To row; to beat the water, as with oars. *Gay.*

2. To play in the water with the hands, as children; or with the feet, as fowls or other animals.

3. To finger. *Shak.*

PAD'DLE, *v. t.* To propel by an oar or paddle.

PAD'DLE, *n.* [In L. *batillus* is a paddle-staff; in Gr. παττaλος is a pole; in W. *padell* is a pan. The latter would express the broad part of an oar; but it may have no connection with *paddle*.]

1. An oar, but not a large oar. It is now applied to a sort of short oar used in propelling and steering canoes and boats.

2. The blade or the broad part of an oar or weapon.

> Thou shalt have a *paddle* on thy weapon. Deut. xxiii.

PAD'DLER, *n.* One that paddles.

PAD'DLE-STAFF, *n.* A staff headed with broad iron. *Hall.*

PAD'DOCK, *n.* [Sax. *pada* or *pad*; D. *pad, padder*.] A toad or frog. *Walton. Dryden.*

PAD'DOCK, *n.* [said to be corrupted from Sax. *parruc*, park.]

1. A small inclosure for deer or other animals. *Johnson.*

2. An inclosure for races with hounds, &c. *Encyc.*

PAD'DOCK-PIPE, *n.* A plant of the genus Equisetum.

PAD'DOCK-STOOL, *n.* A plant of the genus Agaricus; a mushroom, vulgarly *toadstool*.

PADELI'ON, *n.* [Fr. *pas de lion*, lion's foot.] A plant. *Ainsworth.*

PAD'LOCK, *n.* [qu. D. *padde*, a toad, from its shape.]

A lock to be hung on a staple and held by a link. *Prior.*

PAD'LOCK, *v. t.* To fasten with a padlock; to stop; to shut; to confine. *Bull. Milton.*

PAD'NAG, *n.* An ambling nag. *Dr. Pope.*

PAD'OW-PIPE, *n.* A plant. [See *Paddock-pipe*.]

PADUASOY', *n.* [from *Padua*, in Italy, and Fr. *soie*, silk.] A particular kind of silk stuff.

PÆ'AN, **PE'AN**, *n.* Among the ancients, a song of rejoicing in honor of Apollo; hence, a song of triumph. *Pope.*

2. In *ancient poetry*, a foot of four syllables; written also *pæon*. Of this there are four kinds; the first consisting of one long and three short syllables, or a trochee and a pyrrhic, as *tēmpŏrĭbŭs*; the second of a short syllable, a long and two short, or an iambus and a pyrrhic, as *pŏtēntĭă*; the third of two short syllables, a long and a short one, or a pyrrhic and a trochee, as *ănĭmātŭs*; the fourth of three short syllables and a long one, or a pyrrhic and iambus, as *cĕlĕrĭtās*. *Encyc.*

PA'GAN, *n.* [L. *paganus*, a peasant or countryman, from *pagus*, a village.]

A heathen; a Gentile; an idolater; one who worships false gods. This word was originally applied to the inhabitants of the country, who on the first propagation of the christian religion adhered to the worship of false gods, or refused to receive christianity, after it had been received by the inhabitants of the cities. In like manner, *heathen* signifies an inhabitant of the *heath* or woods, and *caffer*, in Arabic, signifies the inhabitant of a hut or cottage, and one that does not receive the religion of Mohammed. Pagan is used to distinguish one from a Christian and a Mohammedan.

PA'GAN, *a.* Heathen; heathenish; Gentile; noting a person who worships false gods.

2. Pertaining to the worship of false gods.

PA'GANISH, *a.* [Sax. *paganisc.*] Heathenish; pertaining to pagans. *King.*

PA'GANISM, *n.* [Fr. *paganisme;* It. *paganesimo.*]

Heathenism; the worship of false gods, or the system of religious opinions and worship maintained by pagans. *Addison. Hooker.*

Men instructed from their infancy in the principles and duties of christianity, never sink to the degradation of *paganism.* *G. Spring.*

PA'GANIZE, *v. t.* To render heathenish; to convert to heathenism. *Ch. Obs.*

PA'GANIZE, *v. i.* To behave like pagans. *Milton.*

PA'GANIZED, *pp.* Rendered heathenish.

PA'GANIZING, *ppr.* Rendering heathenish; behaving like pagans; adopting heathen principles and practice.

PAĠE, *n.* [Fr. Sp. *page;* It. *paggio;* Port. *pagem;* Arm. *paich;* Sw. *poike;* Dan. *pog;* Russ. *paj,* a boy, a page. The Gr. παις, a boy, is undoubtedly a contracted form of the same word; for παιζω, from παις, forms παιξω, παιχθεις; hence it may be inferred that παις was originally παιχις. The Eng. *boy* is a contraction of this word; W. *baçgen,* a boy, a child, from *baç,* small; Pers. فيج faige, a footman or lackey.]

1. A boy attending on a great person, rather for formality or show, than for servitude.

He had two *pages* of honor, on either hand one. *Bacon.*

2. A boy or man that attends on a legislative body. In Massachusetts, the page is a boy that conveys papers from the members of the house of representatives to the speaker, and from the speaker or clerk to the members.

PAĠE, *n.* [L. *pagina;* Fr. *page.*] One side of a leaf of a book. *Watts.*

2. A book or writing or writings; as the *page* of history.

3. *Pages,* in the plural, signifies also books or writings; as the sacred *pages.*

PAĠE, *v. t.* To mark or number the pages of a book or manuscript.

2. To attend, as a page. *Shak.*

PAĠEANT, *n. pa'jent.* [L. *pegma;* Gr. πηγμα, something showy carried in triumph.]

1. A statue in show, or a triumphal car, chariot, arch or other pompous thing, decorated with flags, &c. and carried in public shows and processions. *Cyc.*

2. A show; a spectacle of entertainment; something intended for pomp.

I'll play my part in fortune's *pageant.* *Shak.*

3. Any thing showy, without stability or duration.

Thus unlamented pass the proud away,
The gaze of fools, and *pageant* of a day. *Pope.*

PA'ĠEANT, *a.* Showy; pompous; ostentatious. *Dryden.*

PA'ĠEANT, *v. t.* To exhibit in show; to represent. *Shak.*

PA'ĠEANTRY, *n.* Show; pompous exhibition or spectacle.

Such *pageantry* be to the people shown. *Dryden.*

PAĠ'INAL, *a.* Consisting of pages. *Brown.*

PA'GOD, PAGO'DA, *n.* [Pers. *pout ghod,* or *boot khoda,* a house of idols, or abode of God; Hind. *boot kuda. Thomson. Fryer.*]

1. A temple in the East Indies in which idols are worshiped. *Pope.*

2. An idol; an image of some supposed deity. *Stillingfleet.*

PAGO'DA, *n.* A gold or silver coin current in Hindoostan, of different values in different parts of India, from $1 75 cts. to $2, or from 8 to 9s. sterling.

PA'GODITE, *n.* A name given to the mineral of which the Chinese make their pagodas. It is called also lardite, koreite, and agalmatolite.

PAID, *pret.* and *pp.* of *pay; paid* for *payed.*

PA'IGLE, PA'ĠIL, *n.* A plant and flower of the genus Primula or primrose; cowslip-primrose. *Fam. of Plants.*

PAIL, *n.* [W. *paeol;* Gr. πελλα.] An open wooden vessel used in families for carrying liquids, as water and milk, usually containing from eight to twelve quarts.

PA'IL-FUL̤L, *n.* The quantity that a pail will hold.

PAILMAIL. [See *Pallmall.*]

PAIN, *n.* [W. *poen;* Corn. Arm. *poan;* Ir. *pian;* Fr. *peine;* Norm. *pene, peine;* D. *pyn;* Sax. *pin* or *pine;* G. *pei.*; Dan. *pine;* Sw. *pina;* It. Sp. Port. *pena;* L. *pœna;* Gr. ποινη, penalty, and πονος, pain, labor; Sans. *pana;* Ar. فن fanna, to drive, afflict, distress. Class Bn. No. 22. 23. 26. See the Verb.]

1. An uneasy sensation in animal bodies, of any degree from slight uneasiness to extreme distress or torture, proceeding from pressure, tension or spasm, separation of parts by violence, or any derangement of functions. Thus violent pressure or stretching of a limb gives *pain;* inflammation produces *pain;* wounds, bruises and incisions give *pain.*

2. Labor; work; toil; laborious effort. In this sense, the plural only is used; as, to take *pains;* to be at the *pains.*

High without taking *pains* to rise. *Waller.*

The same with *pains* we gain, but lose with ease. *Pope.*

3. Labor; toilsome effort; task; in the singular. [*Not now used.*] *Spenser. Waller.*

4. Uneasiness of mind; disquietude; anxiety; solicitude for the future; grief, sorrow for the past. We suffer *pain* when we fear or expect evil; we feel *pain* at the loss of friends or property.

5. The throws or distress of travail or childbirth.

She bowed herself and travailed, for her *pains* came upon her. 1 Sam. iv.

6. Penalty; punishment suffered or denounced; suffering or evil inflicted as a punishment for a crime, or annexed to the commission of a crime.

None shall presume to fly under *pain* of death. *Addison.*

Interpose, on *pain* of my displeasure,
Betwixt their swords. *Dryden.*

PAIN, *v. t.* [W. *poeni;* Norm. *painer;* Fr. *peiner;* Sp. *penar;* It. *penare;* D. *pynen;* Dan. *piner;* Sw. *pina;* Sax. *pinan;* Gr. πονεω. The primary sense is to strain, urge, press. See the Noun.]

1. To make uneasy or to disquiet; to cause uneasy sensations in the body, of any degree of intensity; to make simply uneasy, or to distress, to torment. The pressure of fetters may *pain* a limb; the rack *pains* the body.

2. To afflict; to render uneasy in mind; to disquiet; to distress. We are *pained* at the death of a friend; grief *pains* the heart; we are often *pained* with fear or solicitude.

I am *pained* at my very heart. Jer. iv.

3. Reciprocally, to *pain one's self,* to labor; to make toilsome efforts. [*Little used.*] *Spenser.*

PA'INFUL̤, *a.* Giving pain, uneasiness or distress to the body; as a *painful* operation in surgery.

2. Giving pain to the mind; afflictive; disquieting; distressing.

Evils have been more *painful* to us in the prospect, than in the actual pressure. *Addison.*

3. Full of pain; producing misery or affliction. *Milton.*

4. Requiring labor or toil; difficult; executed with laborious effort; as a *painful* service. The army had a *painful* march.

5. Laborious; exercising labor; undergoing toil; industrious.

Nor must the *painful* husbandman be tired. *Dryden.*

PA'INFUL̤LY, *adv.* With suffering of body; with affliction, uneasiness or distress of mind.

2. Laboriously; with toil; with laborious effort or diligence. *Raleigh.*

PA'INFUL̤NESS, *n.* Uneasiness or distress of body. *South.*

2. Affliction; sorrow; grief; disquietude or distress of mind.

3. Laborious effort or diligence; toil. *Hooker.*

PA'INIM, *n.* [Norm. *paynim;* Fr. *païen;* contracted from *pagan.*] A pagan. [*Not used.*] *Peacham.*

PA'INIM, *a.* Pagan; infidel. [*Not used.*] *Milton.*

PA'INLESS, *a.* Free from pain. *Fell.*

2. Free from trouble. *Dryden.*

PA'INSTAKER, *n.* A laborious person. *Gay.*

PA'INSTAKING, *a.* Laborious; industrious. *Harris.*

PA'INSTAKING, *n.* Labor; great industry.

PA'INT, *v. t.* [Fr. *peindre, peignant, peint;* L. *pingo, pictus;* Sp. *pintar;* It. *pignere* or *pingere,* to throw, to push, to paint. The elements are probably *Pg* or *Pk,* as in *fingo, fictus.*]

1. To form a figure or likeness in colors; as, to *paint* a hero or a landscape.

2. To cover or besmear with color or colors, either with or without figures; as, to *paint* a cloth; to *paint* a house.

3. To represent by colors or images; to exhibit in form.

When folly grows romantic, we must *paint* it. *Pope.*

4. To represent or exhibit to the mind; to present in form or likeness to the intellectual view; to describe.

Disloyal!
—The word is too good to *paint* out her wickedness. *Shak.*

5. To color; to diversify with colors. *Spenser.*

6. To lay on artificial color for ornament.

Jezebel *painted* her face and tired her head. 2 Kings ix.

PAINT, *v. i.* To lay colors on the face. It is said the ladies in France *paint.*

2. To practice painting. The artist *paints* well.

PAINT, *n.* A coloring substance; a substance used in painting, either simple or compound; as a white *paint*, or red *paint.*

2. Color laid on canvas or other material; color representing any thing. *Pope. Addison.*

3. Color laid on the face; rouge. *Young.*

PA'INTED, *pp.* Colored; rubbed over with paint; as a *painted* house or cloth.

2. Represented in form by colors.

3. Described.

PA'INTER, *n.* One whose occupation is to paint; one skilled in representing things in colors.

PA'INTER, *n.* [qu. Ir. *painter*, a snare, that which holds.]

A rope used to fasten a boat to a ship or other object. *Mar. Dict.*

PA'INTING, *ppr.* Representing in colors; laying on colors.

PA'INTING, *n.* The art of forming figures or resembling objects in colors on canvas or other material, or the art of representing to the eye by means of figures and colors, any object of sight, and sometimes the emotions of the mind. *Encyc.*

2. A picture; a likeness or resemblance in colors. *Shak.*

3. Colors laid on. *Shak.*

PA'INTURE, *n.* [Fr. *peinture.*] The art of painting. *Dryden.*

PAIR, *n.* [Fr. *pair*; L. Sp. Port. *par*; It. *pari*; Arm. *par*; D. *paar*; G. *par, paar*; Sw. *par*; Norm. *par* or *peir*; Ir. *peire*; Sax. *gefera*, with a prefix. In W. *par* signifies what is contiguous or in continuity, a state of readiness or *preparedness*, a *pair*, fellow, match or couple, and *para* signifies to endure, to continue, to persevere; *paru*, to couple or join. In this language, as in Spanish, *par*, pair, is shown to be connected with the L. *paro*, to prepare. Now in Heb. Ch. Syr. Eth. חבר signifies to join, couple or associate, and the noun, an associate, evidently this very word, which goes far to prove that חבר is a derivative of the root ברא, from which the Latins probably have *paro*. See Class Br. No. 19. The primary sense of the root is to throw, strain and extend, and hence *par*, equal, is extended to, near, contiguous, or equally extended.]

1. Two things of a kind, similar in form, applied to the same purpose, and suited to each other or used together; as a *pair* of gloves or stockings; a *pair* of shoes; a *pair* of oxen or horses.

2. Two of a sort; a couple; a brace; as a *pair* of nerves; a *pair* of doves. Luke ii.

PAIR, *v. i.* To be joined in pairs; to couple; as, birds *pair* in summer.

2. To suit; to fit; as a counterpart.

Ethelinda,
My heart was made to fit and *pair* with thine. *Rowe.*

PAIR, *v. t.* To unite in couples; as minds *paired* in heaven. *Dryden.*

2. To unite as correspondent, or rather to contrast.

Glossy jet is *paired* with shining white. *Pope.*

PAIR, *v. t.* To impair. [See *Impair.*]

PA'IRED, *pp.* Joined in couples; fitted; suited.

PA'IRING, *ppr.* Uniting in pairs; fitting.

PAL'ACE, *n.* [Fr. *palais*; L. *palatium*; It. *palazzo*; Sp. *palacio*; G. *pfalz*, whence *pfalzgraf*, palsgrave; W. *plâs*; Russ. *palata.*]

1. A magnificent house in which an emperor, a king or other distinguished person resides; as an imperial *palace*; a royal *palace*; a pontifical *palace*; a ducal *palace.*

2. A splendid place of residence; as the sun's bright *palace.* *Addison.*

PAL'ACE-COURT, *n.* The domestic court of the kings of Great Britain, which administers justice between the king's domestic servants. It is held once a week before the steward of the household and knight marshal; its jurisdiction extending twelve miles in circuit from his majesty's palace. *Blackstone.*

PALA'CIOUS, *a.* [from *palace.*] Royal; noble; magnificent. [*Not used.*] *Graunt.*

PALANKEE'N, PALAN'QUIN, } *n.* [In Hindoo, *palkee*, apparently from Sans. *paluk*, a couch. But it accords better with Sp. It. *palanca*, a pole, Port. *palanque.*]

A covered carriage used in India, China, &c. borne on the shoulders of men, and in which a single person is conveyed from place to place.

PAL'ATABLE, *a.* [from *palate.*] Agreeable to the taste; savory. *Addison.*

2. That is relished.

PAL'ATABLENESS, *n.* The quality of being agreeable to the taste; relish. *Aikin.*

PAL'ATAL, *a.* Pertaining to the palate; uttered by the aid of the palate.

PAL'ATAL, *n.* A letter pronounced by the aid of the palate, or an articulation of the root of the tongue with the roof of the mouth; as *g* hard and *k*, in *eg, ek.*

PAL'ATE, *n.* [L. *palatum*, properly the arch or cope of heaven.]

1. The roof or upper part of the mouth. The glands in this part of the mouth secrete a mucous fluid, which lubricates the mouth and throat, and facilitates deglutition. *Encyc.*

2. Taste.

Hard task to hit the *palates* of such guests. *Pope.*

[This signification of the word originated in the opinion that the palate is the instrument of taste. This is a mistake. In itself it has no power of taste.]

3. Mental relish; intellectual taste.

Men of nice *palates* could not relish Aristotle, as dressed up by the schoolmen. *Baker.*

PAL'ATE, *v. t.* To perceive by the taste. [*Not used.*] *Shak.*

PALA'TIAL, *a.* [from *palate.*] Pertaining to the palate; as the *palatial* retraction of the tongue. *Barrow.*

PALA'TIAL, *a.* [from L. *palatium*, palace.] Pertaining to a palace; becoming a palace; magnificent. *Drummond.*

PAL'ATIC, *a.* Belonging to the palate. [*Not used.*] *Holder.*

PALAT'INATE, *n.* [It. *palatinato*, from L. *palatinus.* See *Palatine.*]

The province or seignory of a palatine; as the *Palatinate* of the Rhine in Germany, called the upper and lower *Palatinate.* *Encyc.*

PAL'ATINE, *a.* [Fr. *palatin*; It. *palatino*; from L. *palatinus*, from *palatium*, palace.]

Pertaining to a palace; an epithet applied originally to persons holding an office or employment in the king's palace; hence it imports possessing royal privileges; as a count *palatine.*

In England, formerly, were three counties *palatine*, Chester, Durham and Lancaster; the two former by prescription, the latter by grant of Edward III. They were so called, because the proprietors, the earl of Chester, the bishop of Durham and the duke of Lancaster, possessed royal rights, as fully as the king in his palace. Of these, the county of Durham is the only one now remaining in the hands of a subject. *Blackstone.*

PAL'ATINE, *n.* One invested with royal privileges and rights. A palatine or count palatine, on the continent of Europe, is one delegated by a prince to hold courts of justice in a province, or one who has a palace and a court of justice in his own house. In Poland, a palatine may be regarded as the governor of a province. *Encyc.*

PAL'ATIVE, *a.* Pleasing to the taste. [*Not used.*] *Brown.*

PAL'AVER, *n.* [Sp. *palabra*, Port. *palavra*, a word. Qu. W. *llavar*, utterance; with a prefix.]

1. Idle talk.

2. Flattery; adulation. [*This is used with us in the vulgar dialect.*]

3. Talk; conversation; conference; *a sense used in Africa, as appears by the relations of missionaries.*

PAL'AVER, *v. t.* To flatter. [*In vulgar use.*]

PALE, *a.* [Fr. *pale, palir*; L. *palleo, pallidus*; Russ. *bielie*, white; *bieliju*, to whiten. It is probably allied to Sax. *falewe*, *fealo*, fallow, pale red or yellow, D. *vaal*, from the sense of *failing*, withering; W. *pallu*, to fail. See Class Bl. No. 6. 7. 13. 18.]

1. White or whitish; wan; deficient in color; not ruddy or fresh of color; as a *pale* face or skin; *pale* cheeks. We say also, a *pale* red, a *pale* blue, that is, a whitish red or blue. *Pale* is not precisely synonymous with white, as it usually denotes what we call *wan*, a darkish dun white.

2. Not bright; not shining; of a faint luster; dim; as the *pale* light of the moon.

The night, methinks, is but the daylight sick;
It looks a little *paler.* *Shak.*

PALE, *v. t.* To make pale. *Shak. Prior.*

PALE, *n.* [Sax. *pal*; G. *pfahl*; D. *paal*; Sw. *påle*; Dan. *pæl*; W. *pawl*; L. *palus*; coinciding with Eng. *pole*, as well as *pale*; Russ. *palitz*, a stick or club. It has the elements of L. *pala*, a spade or shovel, and the radical sense is probably an extended thing, or a shoot. Qu. Ar. نبل nabala, to dart. Class Bl. No. 18.]

1. A narrow board pointed or sharpened at one end, used in fencing or inclosing. This is with us more generally called a *picket*.
2. A pointed stake; hence to *empale*, which see.
3. An inclosure; properly, that which incloses, like *fence*, *limit*; hence, the space inclosed. He was born within the *pale* of the church; within the *pale* of christianity. *Atterbury.*
4. District; limited territory. *Clarendon.*
5. In *heraldry*, an ordinary, consisting of two perpendicular lines drawn from the top to the base of the escutcheon, and containing the third middle part of the field. *Encyc.*

PALE, *v. t.* [D. *paalen*; G. *pfählen*.] To inclose with pales or stakes. *Mortimer.*

2. To inclose; to encompass. *Shak.*

PALEA'CEOUS, *a.* [L. *palea*, straw, chaff.]

1. Chaffy; resembling chaff, or consisting of it; as a *paleaceous* pappus. *Lee.*
2. Chaffy; furnished with chaff; as a *paleaceous* receptacle. *Martyn.*

PA'LED, *pp.* Inclosed with pales or pickets.

2. Striped.

PA'LE-EYED, *a.* Having eyes dimmed. *Milton.*

PA'LE-FACED, *a.* Having a pale or wan face. *Shak.*

2. Causing paleness of face; as *pale-faced* fear. *Shak.*

PA'LE-HE'ARTED, *a.* Dispirited. *Shak.*

PA'LELY, *adv.* Wanly; not freshly or ruddily.

PAL'ENDAR, *n.* A kind of coasting vessel. *Obs.* *Knolles.*

PA'LENESS, *n.* Wanness; defect of color; want of freshness or ruddiness; a sickly whiteness of look.

> The blood the virgin's cheek forsook,
> A livid *paleness* spreads o'er all her look. *Pope.*

2. Want of color or luster; as the *paleness* of a flower. *Shak.*

PALEOG'RAPHY, *n.* [Gr. παλαιος, ancient, and γραφη, writing.]

1. The art of explaining ancient writings. More correctly,
2. An ancient manner of writing; as Punic *paleography*. *E. Stiles.*

PALEOL'OGIST, *n.* One who writes on antiquity, or one conversant with antiquity. *Good.*

PALEOL'OGY, *n.* [Gr. παλαιος, ancient, and λογος, discourse.]

A discourse or treatise on antiquities, or the knowledge of ancient things.

PA'LEOUS, *a.* [L. *palea*, chaff.] Chaffy; like chaff. *Brown.*

PALES'TRIAN, PALES'TRIC, } *a.* [Gr. παλαιςρικος, from παλη, a struggling or wrestling; παλαιω, to wrestle, to strive.] Pertaining to the exercise of wrestling. *Bryant.*

PAL'ET, *n.* [Fr. *pelote*, a ball.] The crown of the head. [*Not used.*] *Skelton.*

PALETTE. [See *Pallet.*]

PAL'FREY, *n.* [Fr. *palefroi*; It. *palafreno*; Sp. *palafren*; Port. *palafrem*; W. *palvre*. Ainsworth gives for the original word, in Low Latin, *paraveredi*, [plu. of *veredus*,] horses of a large size, used for carrying the baggage of an army.]

1. A horse used by noblemen and others for state, distinguished from a war horse. *Encyc.*
2. A small horse fit for ladies. *Johnson. Spectator.*

PAL'FREYED, *a.* Riding on a palfrey.

PALIFICA'TION, *n.* [from L. *palus*, a stake or post.]

The act or practice of driving piles or posts into the ground for making it firm. *Wotton.*

PAL'INDROME, *n.* [Gr. παλινδρομια; παλιν, again, and δρομεω or δρεμω, to run, *disused*.]

A word, verse or sentence that is the same when read backwards or forwards; as *madam*, or "Roma tibi subito motibus ibit amor." *Encyc.*

PA'LING, *ppr.* Inclosing with pales.

PA'LING, *n.* A fence formed with pales.

PAL'INODE, PAL'INODY, } *n.* [Gr. παλινωδια; παλιν, again, and ωδη, a song.]

A recantation, or declaration contrary to a former one. *Encyc. Sandys.*

PALISA'DE, *n.* [Fr. *palissade*; Sp. *palizada*; It. *palizzata*; from *pale*, or the same root. The Welsh has *palis*, a thin partition of boards or laths, a wainscot; *palisaw*, to wainscot.]

A fence or fortification consisting of a row of stakes or posts sharpened and set firmly in the ground. In fortification, the posts are set two or three inches apart, parallel to the parapet in the covered way, to prevent a surprise. Palisades serve also to fortify the avenues of open forts, gorges, half-moons, the bottom of ditches, &c. *Encyc.*

PALISA'DE, *v. t.* To surround, inclose or fortify with stakes or posts.

PA'LISH, *a.* [from *pale*.] Somewhat pale or wan; as a *palish* blue. *Arbuthnot.*

PALL, *n.* [L. *pallium*; Sax. *pælle*; It. *pallio*; Arm. *pallen*; Ir. *peall*.]

1. A cloke; a mantle of state. *Milton.*
2. The mantle of an archbishop. *Ayliffe.*
3. The cloth thrown over a dead body at funerals. *Dryden.*

PALL, *n.* In *heraldry*, a figure like the Greek Υ. *Encyc.*

PALL, *v. t.* To cloke; to cover or invest. *Shak.*

PALL, *v. i.* [W. *pallu*, to fail; allied to *pale*, and to Gr. παλαιος, old; Heb. Ch. Ar. כלה; Heb. נבל. See *Fail*. Class Bl. No. 6. 18. 21.]

1. To become vapid; to lose strength, life, spirit or taste; to become insipid; as, the liquor *palls*.

> Beauty soon grows familiar to the lover,
> Fades in the eye and *palls* upon the sense. *Addison.*

PALL, *v. t.* To make vapid or insipid.

> Reason and reflection—blunt the edge of the keenest desires, and *pall* all his enjoyments. *Atterbury.*

2. To make spiritless; to dispirit; to depress.

> The more we raise our love,
> The more we *pall* and cool and kill his ardor. *Dryden.*

3. To weaken; to impair; as, to *pall* fortune. *Shak.*
4. To cloy; as the *palled* appetite. *Tatler.*

PALLA'DIUM, *n.* [Gr. παλλαδιον, from Pallas, the goddess.]

1. Primarily, a statue of the goddess Pallas, which represented her as sitting with a pike in her right hand, and in her left a distaff and spindle. On the preservation of this statue depended the safety of Troy. Hence,
2. Something that affords effectual defense, protection and safety; as when we say, the trial by jury is the *palladium* of our civil rights. *Blackstone.*
3. A metal found in very small grains, of a steel gray color and fibrous structure, in auriferous and platiniferous sand. It is infusible by ordinary heat, and when native, is alloyed with a little platina and iridium. *Dict. Nat. Hist.*

PAL'LET, *n.* [Fr. *palette*; It. *paletta*, a fire-shovel; Sp. *paleta*; from L. *pala*, W. *pâl*, a shovel, a *peel*.]

1. Among *painters*, a little oval table or board, or piece of ivory, on which the painter places the colors to be used. On the middle the colors are mixed to obtain the tints required. *Encyc.*
2. Among *potters*, *crucible makers*, &c. a wooden instrument for forming, heating and rounding their works. It is oval, round, &c. *Encyc.*
3. In *gilding*, an instrument made of a squirrel's tail, to take up the gold leaves from the pillow, and to apply and extend them. *Encyc.*
4. In *heraldry*, a small *pale*. [See *Pale*.]
5. A small part belonging to the balance of a watch; the nut of a watch. It is sometimes written *pallat*.
6. A measure formerly used by surgeons, containing three ounces. *Hakewill.*

PAL'LET, *n.* [*paillet*, Chaucer; Fr. *paille*, L. *palea*, straw; Ir. *peall*, a couch.] A small bed. *Milton.*

PAL'LIAMENT, *n.* [L. *pallium*, a cloke.] A dress; a robe. [*Not used.*] *Shak.*

PAL'LIARD, *n.* [Fr.] A lecher; a lewd person. [*Not used nor English.*]

PAL'LIARDISE, *n.* Fornication. [*Not used.*] *Buck.*

PAL'LIATE, *v. t.* [Fr. *pallier*; Sp. *paliar*; It. *palliare*; from Low L. *pallio*, from *pallium*, a cloke or robe.]

1. To clothe. *Obs.*
2. To cover with excuse; to conceal the enormity of offenses by excuses and apologies; hence, to extenuate; to lessen; to soften by favorable representations; as, to *palliate* faults, offenses, crimes or vices. *Dryden.*
3. To reduce in violence; to mitigate; to lessen or abate; as, to *palliate* a disease.

PAL'LIATE, *a.* Eased; mitigated. [*Not used.*]

PAL'LIATED, *pp.* Covered by excuses; extenuated; softened.

PAL'LIATING, *ppr.* Concealing the enormity or most censurable part of conduct; extenuating; softening.

PALLIA'TION, *n.* The act of palliating; concealment of the most flagrant circumstances of an offense; extenuation by favorable representation; as the *palliation* of faults, offenses, vices or crimes.

2. Mitigation; alleviation; abatement; as of a disease.

PAL'LIATIVE, *a.* [Fr. *palliatif.*] Extenuating; serving to extenuate by excuses or favorable representation. *Warton.*

2. Mitigating; alleviating; as pain or disease. *Arbuthnot.*

PAL'LIATIVE, *n.* That which extenuates.

2. That which mitigates, alleviates or abates the violence of pain, disease or other evil. *Swift.*

PAL'LID, *a.* [L. *pallidus*, from *palleo*, to become pale. See *Pale.*]

Pale; wan; deficient in color; not high colored; as a *pallid* countenance; *pallid* blue. *Spenser. Thomson. Harte.*

PAL'LIDLY, *adv.* Palely; wanly. *Taylor.*

PAL'LIDNESS, *n.* Paleness; wanness.

PALL'MALL, *n.* [L. *pila*, a ball, and *malleus*, mallet; It. *palla*, a ball, and *malleo*, a hammer.]

A play in which a ball is driven through an iron ring by a mallet; also, the mallet. *Johnson.*

PAL'LOR, *n.* [L.] Paleness. *Taylor.*

PALM, *n.* *p'am.* [L. *palma*; W. *palv*; from spreading.]

1. The inner part of the hand.

2. A hand or hand's breadth; a lineal measure of three inches. *Holder. Bacon.*

3. The broad triangular part of an anchor at the end of the arms.

4. The name of many species of plants, but particularly of the date-tree or great palm, a native of Asia and Africa.

The *palms* constitute a natural order of monocotyledonous plants, with a simple cylindric stem, terminating in a crown of leaves or fronds, within which rises a tuft of flowers and fruits; all natives of warm climates. They vary in size from 2 to more than 100 feet in highth. *Jussieu. Linne.*

5. Branches of the palm being worn in token of victory, hence the word signifies superiority, victory, triumph. The palm was adopted as an emblem of victory, it is said, because the tree is so elastic as when pressed, to rise and recover its correct position. *Encyc.*

Namur subdued is England's *palm* alone. *Dryden.*

6. Among *seamen*, an instrument used in sewing canvas instead of a thimble.

PALM, *v. t.* *p'am.* To conceal in the palm of the hand.

They *palmed* the trick that lost the game. *Prior.*

2. To impose by fraud.

For you may *palm* upon us new for old. *Dryden.*

3. To handle. *Prior.*

4. To stroke with the hand. *Ainsworth.*

PALM-SUNDAY, *n.* *p'am-sunday.* The Sunday next before Easter; so called in commemoration of our Savior's triumphal entry into Jerusalem, when the multitude strewed palm branches in the way.

PALM-TREE, *n.* *p'am-tree.* The date tree, or *Phœnix Lactylifera*, a native of Asia and Africa, which grows to the highth of 60 and even of 100 feet, with an upright stem, crowned with a cluster of leaves or branches eight or nine feet long, extending all around like an umbrella. The fruit is in shape somewhat like an acorn. This tree transplanted will grow in Europe, but the fruit never ripens. *Encyc.*

This name is applied to other species of palms.

PAL'MAR, *a.* [L. *palmaris.*] Of the breadth of the hand. *Lee.*

PAL'MATED, *a.* [L. *palmatus*, from *palma*, palm.]

1. Having the shape of a hand; resembling a hand with the fingers spread; as *palmated* leaves or stones. *Encyc.*

2. Entirely webbed; as the *palmated* feet of aquatic fowls.

PALMER, *n.* *p'amer.* One that returned from the Holy Land bearing branches of palm; a pilgrim or crusader. *Pope.*

PALMER-WORM, *n.* *p'amer-worm.* A worm covered with hair; supposed to be so called because he wanders over all plants. Joel i. *Johnson.*

PALMET'TO, *n.* A species of palm-tree, growing in the West Indies, of the genus Chamærops. *Thomson.*

PALMIF'EROUS, *a.* [L. *palma* and *fero*, to bear.] Bearing palms. *Dict.*

PAL'MIPED, *a.* [L. *palma* and *pes*, foot.] Web-footed; having the toes connected by a membrane; as a water fowl.

PAL'MIPED, *n.* A fowl that has webbed feet, or the toes connected by a membrane. *Encyc.*

PAL'MISTER, *n.* [L. *palma.*] One who deals in palmistry, or pretends to tell fortunes by the palm of the hand.

PAL'MISTRY, *n.* [L. *palma*, palm.] The art or practice of divining or telling fortunes by the lines and marks in the palm of the hand; a trick of imposture, much practiced by gipseys.

2. Addison uses it humorously for the action of the hand. *Spectator.*

PALMY, *a.* *p'amy.* Bearing palms. *Shak.*

PALP, *v. t.* To feel. [*Not authorized.*]

PALPABIL'ITY, *n.* [from *palpable.*] The quality of being perceptible by the touch. *Arbuthnot.*

PAL'PABLE, *a.* [Fr. from L. *palpor*, to feel; It. *palpabile.*]

1. Perceptible by the touch; that may be felt; as a *palpable* substance; *palpable* darkness. *Shak.*

2. Gross; coarse; easily perceived and detected; as a *palpable* absurdity. *Tillotson.*

3. Plain; obvious; easily perceptible; as *palpable* phenomena; *palpable* proof. *Hooker. Glanville.*

PAL'PABLENESS, *n.* The quality of being palpable; plainness; obviousness; grossness.

PAL'PABLY, *adv.* In such a manner as to be perceived by the touch.

2. Grossly; plainly; obviously.

Clodius was acquitted by a corrupt jury that had *palpably* taken shares of money. *Bacon.*

PALPA'TION, *n.* [L. *palpatio*, from *palpo*, to feel, to stroke, from the root of *feel*, and Gr. παλλω, to shake. Probably the primary sense is to beat or strike gently, or to touch, or to spring, to leap, allied to Gr. βαλλω, Fr. *baller.*] The act of feeling.

PAL'PITATE, *v. i.* [L. *palpito*, from *palpo. Palpito* illustrates the primary sense of *palpo.*]

To beat gently; to beat, as the heart; to flutter, that is, to move with little throws; as we say, to go *pit a pat*; applied particularly to a preternatural or excited movement of the heart.

PALPITA'TION, *n.* [L. *palpitatio.*] A beating of the heart; particularly, a preternatural beating or pulsation excited by violent action of the heart, by fear, fright or disease. *Harvey. Arbuthnot.*

2. A violent, irregular motion of the heart. *Cullen. Parr.*

PALS'GRAVE, *n.* *pawlzgrave.* [G. *pfalzgraf*, from *pfalz*, contracted from L. *palatium*, palace, and *graf*, an earl; D. *paltsgraaf*; Sax. *gerefa*, a *reeve*, whence *sheriff.*]

A count or earl who has the superintendence of the king's palace. *Dict.*

PAL'SICAL, *a.* *s* as *z.* [from *palsy.*] Affected with palsy; paralytic.

PAL'SIED, *a.* [from *palsy.*] Affected with palsy.

PAL'SY, *n.* *s* as *z.* [supposed to be contracted from Gr. παραλυσις, relaxation; παραλυω, to loosen or relax.]

The loss or defect of the power of voluntary muscular motion in the whole body, or in a particular part; paralysis. When one side only of the body is affected, it is called *hemiplegy*. When the lower part of the body is paralytic, it is called *paraplegy*. Palsy may be a loss of the power of motion without a loss of sensation, or a loss of sensation without loss of motion, or a loss of both. *Encyc. Good. Quincy.*

PAL'TER, *v. i.* [probably allied to *faulter* or *falter*, W. *pallu*, Eng. *fail*; Sp. Port. *faltar*, to want, to fail, to miss, to balk, to come short. See *Fail* and *Pall.*]

To shift; to dodge; to play tricks. *Johnson.*

Rather, to fail; to come short; to balk.

Romans, that have spoke the word
And will not *palter*. *Shak.*

PAL'TER, *v. t.* To squander. Qu. [*Not used.*] *Ainsworth.*

PAL'TERER, *n.* One that palters, fails or falls short.

PAL'TRINESS, *n.* [from *paltry.*] The state of being paltry, vile or worthless.

PAL'TRY, *a.* [Sw. *palta*, plu. *paltor*, rags; Dan. *pialt*, a rag; *pialted*, ragged; Scot. *paltrie* or *peltrie*, vile trash; It. *paltone*, a vagabond. It may be allied to Gr. φαυλος, vile, and to *fail*. Qu. Fr. *piètre*, a contracted word.]

Ragged; mean; vile; worthless; despicable; as a *paltry* boy; a *paltry* slave; a *paltry* trifle. *Shak. Addison.*

PA'LY, *a.* [from *pale.*] Pale; wanting color; *used only in poetry.* *Shak. Gay.*

2. In *heraldry*, divided by pales into four equal parts. *Encyc.*

PAM, *n.* [supposed to be from *palm*, victory.] The knave of clubs. *Pope.*

PAM'PER, *v. t.* [from It. *pambere*, bread and drink; *pamberato*, pampered, well fed; *pane*, bread, and *bere*, to drink, L. *bibo.*]

1. To feed to the full; to glut; to saginate; to feed luxuriously; as, to *pamper* the body or the appetite. *Spenser.*

We are proud of a body fattening for worms and *pampered* for corruption and the grave. *Dwight.*

2. To gratify to the full; to furnish with that which delights; as, to *pamper* the imagination.

PAM'PERED, *pp.* Fed high; glutted or gratified to the full.

PAM'PERING, *ppr.* Glutting; feeding luxuriously; gratifying to the full.

PAM'PERING, *n.* Luxuriancy. *Fulke.*

PAM'PHLET, *n.* [Sp. *papelon*, from *papel*, paper. The word signifies both a pamphlet and a bill posted. Sp. *papeleta*, a slip of paper on which any thing is written; *papel volante*, a small pamphlet. It has also been deduced from *paunflet*, *pagina filata*, a word said to have been used by Caxton.]

A small book consisting of a sheet of paper, or of sheets stitched together but not bound.

PAM'PHLET, *v. t.* To write a pamphlet or pamphlets. *Howell.*

PAMPHLETEE'R, *n.* A writer of pamphlets; a scribbler. *Tatler.*

PAN, *n.* [Sax. Sw. *panna*; G. *pfanne*; D. *pan*; W. *id.*]

1. A vessel broad and somewhat hollow or depressed in the middle, or with a raised border; used for setting milk and other domestic purposes. *Dryden.*

2. The part of a gun-lock or other fire-arms which holds the priming that communicates with the charge.

3. Something hollow; as the brain *pan*.

4. Among *farmers*, the hard stratum of earth that lies below the soil; called the *hard pan*.

5. The top of the head. *Chaucer.*

PAN, *v. t.* To join; to close together. [*Local.*] *Bailey.*

PANACE'A, *n.* [L. from Gr. πανακεια; παν, all, and ακεομαι, to cure.]

1. A remedy for all diseases; a universal medicine. *Warton.*

2. An herb. *Ainsworth.*

PANA'DA, PANA'DO, *n.* [Fr. *panade*, from L. *panis*, Sp. *pan*, It. *pane*, bread.]

A kind of food made by boiling bread in water to the consistence of pulp and sweetened. *Wiseman.*

PAN'CAKE, *n.* A thin cake fried in a pan.

Some folks think it will never be good times, till houses are tiled with *pancakes*. *Franklin.*

PANCH, *n.* [W. *panu*, to form a texture, to full.]

Among *seamen*, a thick and strong mat, to be fastened on yards to prevent friction.

PANCRAT'IC, PANCRAT'ICAL, *a.* [Gr. παν, all, and κρατος, strength.]

Excelling in all gymnastic exercises; very strong or robust. *Brown.*

PAN'CREAS, *n.* [Gr. παν, all, and κρεας, flesh.]

A gland of the body situated between the bottom of the stomach and the vertebers of the loins, reaching from the liver to the spleen, and attached to the peritonæum. It is two fingers in breadth, and six in length, soft and supple. It secretes a kind of saliva and pours it into the duodenum. *Quincy. Coxe.*

PANCREAT'IC, *a.* Pertaining to the pancreas; as *pancreatic* juice. *Arbuthnot.*

PANCY. [See *Pansy.*]

PAN'DECT, *n.* [L. *pandectæ*, from Gr. πανδεκτης; παν, all, and δεχομαι, to contain, to *take*.]

1. A treatise which contains the whole of any science. *Swift.*

2. *Pandects*, in the plural, the digest or collection of civil or Roman law, made by order of the emperor Justinian, and containing 534 decisions or judgments of lawyers, to which the emperor gave the force and authority of law. This compilation consists of fifty books, forming the first part of the civil law.

PANDEM'IC, *a.* [Gr. παν, all, and δημος, people.]

Incident to a whole people; epidemic; as a *pandemic* disease. *Harvey. Parr.*

PAN'DER, *n.* [qu. It. *pandere*, to set abroad, or *Pandarus*, in Chaucer. In Pers. بُنْدار bondar, is the keeper of a warehouse or granary, a forestaller who buys and hoards goods to enhance the price; answering to L. *mango*. But the real origin of the word is not obvious.]

A pimp; a procurer; a male bawd; a mean profligate wretch who caters for the lust of others. *Dryden. Shak.*

PAN'DER, *v. t.* To pimp; to procure lewd women for others. *Shak.*

PAN'DER, *v. i.* To act as agent for the lusts of others.

2. To be subservient to lust or passion.

PAN'DERAGE, *n.* A procuring of sexual connection. *Ch. Relig. Appeal.*

PAN'DERISM, *n.* The employment or vices of a pander; a pimping. *Swift.*

PAN'DERLY, *a.* Pimping; acting the pander. *Shak.*

PANDICULA'TION, *n.* [L. *pandiculor*, to yawn, to stretch.]

A yawning; a stretching; the tension of the solids that accompanies yawning, or that restlessness and stretching that accompanies the cold fit of an intermittent. *Encyc. Floyer.*

PAN'DIT, PUN'DIT, *n.* In Hindoostan, a learned man.

PAN'DORE, PAN'DORAN, *n.* [Gr. πανδουρα.] An instrument of music of the lute kind; a bandore. *Drayton.*

PANE, *n.* [Fr. *pan*, from extending, whence *panneau*, a panel; Arm. *panell*; Sp. *entrepaño*; D. *paneel*.] A square of glass.

2. A piece of any thing in variegated works. *Donne.*

PANEGYR'IC, *n.* [Fr. *panegyrique*; It. Sp. *panegirico*; L. *panegyricus*, from the Gr. πανηγυρις, a public meeting or celebration; πας, παν, all, and αγυρις, an assembly.]

1. An oration or eulogy in praise of some distinguished person or achievment; a formal or elaborate encomium. *Stillingfleet.*

2. An encomium; praise bestowed on some eminent person, action or virtue. *Dryden.*

PANEGYR'IC, *a.* Containing praise or eulogy; encomiastic.

PANEGY'RIS, *n.* A festival; a public meeting. *Milton.*

PANEGYR'IST, *n.* One who bestows praise; an eulogist; an encomiast, either by writing or speaking. *Camden.*

PAN'EGYRIZE, *v. t.* To praise highly; to write or pronounce an eulogy on. *Ch. Obs.*

PAN'EGYRIZE, *v. i.* To bestow praises. *Mitford.*

PAN'EGYRIZED, *pp.* Highly praised or eulogized.

PAN'EGYRIZING, *ppr.* Praising highly; eulogizing.

PAN'EL, *n.* [Fr. *panneau*; Sw. *panna*, pan; *pannela*, to wainscot; Russ. *panel*, ceiling or wainscot; probably named from breadth, extension.]

1. A square piece of board, or other piece somewhat similar inserted between other pieces; as the *panel* of a door. *Addison. Swift.*

2. A piece of parchment or schedule, containing the names of persons summoned by the sheriff. Hence more generally,

3. The whole jury.

PAN'EL, *v. t.* To form with panels; as, to *panel* a wainscot. *Pennant.*

PA'NELESS, *a.* Without panes of glass. *Shenstone.*

PANG, *n.* [D. *pynigen*, G. *peinigen*, to torture, from *pyn*, *pein*, pain; Sax. *pinan*. See *Pain*.]

Extreme pain; anguish; agony of body; particularly, a sudden paroxysm of extreme pain, as in spasm, or childbirth. Is. xxi.

I saw the hoary traitor,
Grin in the *pangs* of death, and bite the ground. *Addison.*

PANG, *v. t.* To torture; to give extreme pain to. *Shak.*

PAN'GOLIN, *n.* A species of Manis or scaly lizard, found only in Hindoostan. *Encyc.*

PAN'IC, *n.* [Sp. It. *panico*; Fr. *panique*; Gr. πανικος; W. *pannu*, to cause to sink, to depress or hollow, to cause a panic. The primary sense is intransitive, to shrink, or transitive, to cause to shrink; hence the fabled *Pan*, the frightful deity of the woods or shepherds.]

A sudden fright; particularly, a sudden fright without real cause, or terror inspired by a trifling cause or misapprehension of danger; as, the troops were seized with a *panic*; they fled in a *panic*.

PAN'IC, *a.* Extreme or sudden; applied to fright; as *panic* fear.

PAN'IC, *n.* [L. *panicum*.] A plant and its grain, of the genus Panicum. The grain or seed is like millet, and it is cultivated in some parts of Europe for bread.

PAN'IC-GRASS, *n.* A plant of the genus Panicum.

PAN'ICLE, *n.* [L. *panicula*, down upon reeds, cat's tail, allied to L. *pannus*, cloth; W. *pân*, nap, down, the fulling of cloth; *panu*, to cover with nap, to full or mill cloth, to beat, to bang. The primary sense is to drive, strike or press, hence to full or make thick.]

In *botany*, a species of inflorescence, in which the flowers or fruits are scattered on peduncles variously subdivided, as in oats and some of the grasses. The panicle is of various kinds, as the dense or close, the spiked, the squeezed, the spreading, the diffused, the divaricating. *Martyn.*

PAN'ICLED, *a.* Furnished with panicles. *Eaton.*

PANIC'ULATE, PANIC'ULATED, *a.* Having branches variously subdivided; as a *paniculate* stem.

2\. Having the flowers in panicles; as a *paniculate* inflorescence. *Lee.*

PAN'NADE, *n.* The curvet of a horse. [See *Panic.*] *Ainsworth.*

PAN'NAGE, *n.* [from L. *panis.*] The food of swine in the woods; as beach nuts, acorns, &c. called also pawns; also, the money taken by agistors for the mast of the king's forest. *Cowel.*

PAN'NEL, *n.* [W. *panel*, something plaited or matted; L. *pannus*, cloth.] A kind of rustic saddle. *Tusser.*

2\. The stomach of a hawk. *Ainsworth.*

PANNELLA'TION, *n.* The act of impaneling a jury. [*Not used.*] *Wood.*

PANNIER, *n.* pan'yer. [Fr. *panier*; It. *paniera*; Sp. *panera*, a pannier, and a granary; from L. *panis*, bread.]

A wicker basket; primarily, a bread-basket, but used for carrying fruit or other things on a horse. *Addison.*

PAN'NIKEL, *n.* The brain pan or skull. [*Not in use.*] *Spenser.*

PAN'OPLY, *n.* [Gr. πανοπλια; παν, all, and οπλα, arms.]

Complete armor or defense.

> We had need to take the christian *panoply*, to put on the whole armor of God. *Ray.*

PANOR'AMA, *n.* [Gr. παν, all, and οραμα, view, from οραω, to see.]

Complete or entire view; a circular painting having apparently no beginning or end, from the center of which the spectator may have a complete view of the objects presented.

PANSOPH'ICAL, *a.* [See *Pansophy.*] Pretending to have a knowledge of every thing. *Worthington.*

PAN'SOPHY, *n.* [Gr. παν, all, and σοφια, wisdom.] Universal wisdom or knowledge. [*Little used.*] *Hartlib.*

PAN'SY, *n.* [Fr *pensée*, fancy or thought, from *penser*, to think.]

A plant and flower of the genus Viola; the *viola tricolor*, or garden violet. *Fam. of Plants.*

P'ANT, *v. i.* [Fr. *panteler*, probably from the root of W. *panu*, to beat. See *Panicle*, and qu. G. πνεω.]

1\. To palpitate; to beat with preternatural violence or rapidity, as the heart in terror, or after hard labor, or in anxious desire or suspense.

> Yet might her piteous heart be seen to *pant* and quake. *Spenser.*

2\. To have the breast heaving, as in short respiration or want of breath.

> Pluto *pants* for breath from out his cell. *Dryden.*

3\. To play with intermission or declining strength.

> The whispering breeze
> *Pants* on the leaves and dies upon the trees. *Pope.*

4\. To long; to desire ardently.

> Who *pants* for glory, finds but short repose. *Pope.*

> As the hart *panteth* after the water brooks, so *panteth* my soul after thee, O God. Ps. xlii.

P'ANT, *n.* Palpitation of the heart. *Shak.*

PANTALOON', *n.* [Fr. *pantalon.* Qu. W. *pannu*, to involve, or *panu*, to cover, and Fr. *talon*, the heel.]

1\. A garment for males in which breeches and stockings are in a piece; a species of close long trowsers extending to the heels.

2\. A character in the Italian comedy, and a buffoon in pantomimes; so called from his close dress. *Addison.*

P'ANTER, *n.* One that pants.

PANT'ER, *n.* [Ir. *painter*, a snare.] A net. *Chaucer.*

P'ANTESS, *n.* [from *pant.*] The difficulty of breathing in a hawk. *Ainsworth.*

PAN'THEISM, *n.* [Gr. παν, all, and θεος, God, whence *theism.*]

The doctrine that the universe is God, or the system of theology in which it is maintained that the universe is the supreme God. *Encyc. Asiat. Res.*

PANTHE'IST, *n.* One that believes the universe to be God; a name given to the followers of Spinosa.

> The earliest Grecian *pantheist* of whom we read is Orpheus. *Encyc.*

PANTHEIS'TIC, PANTHEIS'TICAL, *n.* Pertaining to pantheism; confounding God with the universe. *Enfield. Waterland.*

PANTHE'ON, *n.* [Gr. πας, παν, all, and θεος, God.]

A temple or magnificent edifice at Rome, dedicated to all the gods. It is now converted into a church. It was built or embellished by Agrippa, son-in-law to Augustus, is of a round or cylindrical form, with a spherical dome, and 144 feet in diameter. *Encyc.*

PAN'THER, *n.* [L. from Gr. πανθηρ. Qu. θηρ, a wild beast.]

A fierce, ferocious quadruped of the genus Felis, of the size of a large dog, with short hair, of a yellow color, diversified with roundish black spots. This animal is carnivorous, and will climb trees in pursuit of small animals. It is a native of Africa. The name is also applied to other species of the genus.

PAN'TILE, *n.* [qu. W. *pantu*, to dimple, to sink in, to become hollow; *pan*, a bowl, a *pan*; or Fr. *pente*, a bending.] A gutter tile. But qu. *pentile.*

P'ANTING, *ppr.* [See *Pant.*] Palpitating; breathing with a rapid succession of inspirations and expirations; longing.

P'ANTING, *n.* Palpitation; rapid breathing; longing.

P'ANTINGLY, *adv.* With palpitation or rapid breathing.

PANT'LER, *n.* [Fr. *panetier*, from *pain*, L. *panis*, bread.]

The officer in a great family who has charge of the bread. *Shak.*

PAN'TOFLE, *n.* [Fr. *pantoufle*; It. *pantofola*, a slipper; Sp. *pantuflo*; Sw. *toffla*, *toffel*, a slipper or sandal; Dan. *töfel*; Russ. *tufel.*] A slipper for the foot.

PAN'TOGRAPH, *n.* [Gr. παντα, all, and γραφω, to describe.]

A mathematical instrument so formed as to copy any sort of drawing or design.

PANTOGRAPH'IC, PANTOGRAPH'ICAL, *a.* Pertaining to a pantograph; performed by a pantograph.

PANTOG'RAPHY, *n.* General description; view of an entire thing.

PANTOM'ETER, *n.* [Gr. παντα, all, and μετρεω, to measure.]

An instrument for measuring all sorts of elevations, angles and distances. *Bailey.*

PANTOMET'RIC, PANTOMET'RICAL, *a.* Pertaining to a pantometer; performed by a pantometer.

PAN'TOMIME, *n.* [L. *pantomimus*; Gr. παντομιμος; πας, παν, all, and μιμος, a mimic.]

1\. One that imitates all sorts of actions and characters without speaking; one that expresses his meaning by mute action. The pantomimes of antiquity used to express in gestures and action, whatever the chorus sung, changing their countenance and behavior as the subject of the song varied. *Encyc.*

2\. A scene or representation in dumb show.

3\. A species of musical entertainment. *Busby.*

PAN'TOMIME, *a.* Representing only in mute action. *Smith.*

PANTOMIM'IC, PANTOMIM'ICAL, *a.* Pertaining to the pantomime; representing characters and actions by dumb show.

PAN'TON, PAN'TON-SHOE, *n.* [qu. L. *pando*, to open.] A horse shoe contrived to recover a narrow and hoof-bound heel. *Far. Dict.*

PAN'TRY, *n.* [Fr. *panetière*, a shepherd's scrip; L. *panarium*, from *panis*, bread.]

An apartment or closet in which provisions are kept.

PAN'URGY, *n.* [Gr. πανουργια; παν, all, and εργον, work.] Skill in all kinds of work or business; craft. *Bailey.*

PAP, *n.* [L. *papilla.*] A nipple of the breast; a teat. *Dryden.*

PAP, *n.* [Low L. *papa*; It. *pappa*; D. *pap*; Pers. *bob*, food.]

1\. A soft food for infants, made with bread boiled or softened with water. *Boyle.*

2\. The pulp of fruit. *Ainsworth.*

PAP, *v. t.* To feed with pap.

PAP'A, *n.* [L. Fr. *papa*; D. G. *id.*; Gr. παππας; It. Sp. *papa*, the *pope*; a word used by the ancient Scythians, as also in the Syriac and Chaldaic.] Father; a word with us used by children. *Swift.*

PA'PACY, *n.* [Fr. *papauté*; It. *papato*; from *papa*, the pope.]

1\. The office and dignity of the pope or bishop of Rome; popedom. *Bacon.*

2\. Papal authority. *Milner.*

PA'PAL, *a.* [Fr. from *pape*, the pope.] Belonging to the pope or pontiff of Rome; popish; as *papal* authority; the *papal* chair.

2\. Proceeding from the pope; as a *papal* license or indulgence; a *papal* edict.

3\. Annexed to the bishopric of Rome.

PA'PALIN, *n.* A papist. [*Not used.*] *Herbert.*

PAPAV'EROUS, *a.* [L. *papavereus*, from *papaver*, a poppy.]

Resembling the poppy; of the nature or qualities of poppies. *Brown.*

PAPAW', *n.* [Fr. *papayer.*] The *carica papaya*, a tree growing in warm climates to the highth of eighteen or twenty feet, with a soft herbaceous stem, naked nearly to the top, where the leaves issue on every side on long foot-stalks. Between the leaves grow the flower and the fruit, which is of the size of a melon. The juice is acrid and milky, but the fruit when boiled is eaten with meat, like other vegetables. *Encyc.*

2. The papaw of North America belongs to the genus Annona or custard apple.

PAPE, *n.* The pope.

PA'PER, *n.* [Fr. *papier*; It. *papiro*; Port. Sp. *papel*; D. G. *papier*; W. *papyr*; Gr. παπυρος; L. *papyrus*, the name of an Egyptian plant, from which was made a kind of paper.]

1. A substance formed into thin sheets on which letters and figures are written or printed. Paper is made of different materials; but among us it is usually made of linen or cotton rags. A fine paper is made of silk, particularly for bank-notes, which require to be very thin.

2. A piece of paper. *Locke.*

3. A single sheet printed or written; as a daily *paper*; a weekly *paper*; a periodical *paper*; referring to essays, journals, newspapers, &c.

4. Any written instrument, whether note, receipt, bill, invoice, bond, memorial, deed, and the like. The *papers* lie on the speaker's table.

They brought a *paper* to me to be signed. *Dryden.*

5. A promissory note or notes or a bill of exchange; as negotiable *paper*. *Kent.*

6. Hangings printed or stamped; paper for covering the walls of rooms.

PA'PER, *a.* Made of paper; consisting of paper.

2. Thin; slight; as a *paper* wall. *Burnet.*

PA'PER, *v. t.* To cover with paper; to furnish with paper hangings; as, to *paper* a room or a house.

2. To register. [*Not used.*] *Shak.*

3. To fold or inclose in paper.

PAPER-CRED'IT, *n.* Evidences of debt; promissory notes, &c. passing current in commercial transactions.

3. Notes or bills emitted by public authority, promising the payment of money. The revolution in N. America was carried on by means of *paper-credit*.

PA'PER-FACED, *a.* Having a face as white as paper. *Shak.*

PA'PER-KITE, *n.* A light frame covered with paper for flying in the air like a kite. *Warton.*

PA'PER-MAKER, *n.* One that manufactures paper.

PA'PER-MILL, *n.* A mill in which paper is manufactured.

PAPER-MŎNEY, *n.* Notes or bills issued by authority, and promising the payment of money, circulated as the representative of coin. We apply the word to notes or bills issued by a state or by a banking corporation; rarely or never to private notes or bills of exchange, though the latter may be included.

PA'PER-STAINER, *n.* One that stains, colors or stamps paper for hangings.

PAPES'CENT, *a.* [from *pap.*] Containing pap; having the qualities of pap. *Arbuthnot.*

PA'PESS, *n.* A female pope. *Hall.*

PAP'IL, *n.* [L. *papilla.*] A small pap or nipple.

PAPIL'IO, *n.* [L.] A butterfly. In *zoology*, a genus of insects of numerous species. These insects are produced from the caterpillar. The chrysalis is the tomb of the caterpillar and the cradle of the butterfly. *Barbut.*

PAPILIONA'CEOUS, *a.* Resembling the butterfly; a term in botany, used to describe the corols of plants which have the shape of a butterfly, such as that of the pea. The *papilionaceous* plants are of the leguminous kind. *Encyc. Quincy.*

The papilionaceous corol is usually four-petaled, having an upper spreading petal, called the *banner*, two side petals called *wings*, and a lower petal called the *keel*. *Martyn.*

PAP'ILLARY, } *a.* Pertaining to the pap or
PAP'ILLOUS, } nipple; resembling the nipple; covered with papils. *Derham.*

PAP'ILLATE, *v. i.* To grow into a nipple. *Fleming.*

PAP'ILLOSE, *a.* Nipply; covered with fleshy dots or points; verrucose; warty; as a *papillose* leaf. *Martyn.*

Covered with soft tubercles, as the ice-plant. *Smith.*

PA'PISM, *n.* [from Fr. *pape*, pope.] Popery. *Bedell.*

PA'PIST, *n.* [Fr. *papiste*; It. *papista*; from Fr. *pape*, pope.]

A Roman catholic; one that adheres to the church of Rome and the authority of the pope. *Clarendon.*

PAPIS'TIC, } *a.* Popish; pertaining to
PAPIS'TICAL, } popery; adherent to the church of Rome and its doctrines and ceremonies. *Whitgifte.*

PA'PISTRY, *n.* Popery; the doctrines and ceremonies of the church of Rome. *Ascham. Whitgifte.*

PA'PIZED, *a.* Conformed to popery. *Fuller.*

PAP'POUS, *a.* [from L. *pappus*; Gr. παππος.] Downy; furnished with a pappus, as the seeds of certain plants, such as thistles, dandelions, &c. *Ray.*

PAP'PUS, *n.* [L. from Gr. παππος, an old man or grandfather, hence a substance resembling gray hairs.]

The soft downy substance that grows on the seeds of certain plants, as on those of the thistle. *Encyc.*

PAP'PY, *a.* [from *pap.*] Like pap; soft; succulent. *Burnet.*

PAP'ULÆ, *n.* [L.] Pimples; blisters; eruptions on the skin.

PAP'ULOSE, *a.* Covered with vesicular points or with little blisters; as a *papulose* leaf. *Martyn.*

PAP'ULOUS, *a.* Full of pimples or pustules.

PAPY'RUS, *n.* [L.] An Egyptian plant, a kind of reed, of which the ancients made paper.

P'AR, *n.* [L. *par*, equal; W. *par*, that is upon or contiguous, that is in continuity, a state of readiness or preparedness, a *pair*, a fellow, Eng. *peer.* The word seems to be formed on the root of L. *paro*, and the Shemitic ברא, and the primary sense, to extend or reach.]

1. State of equality; equal value; equivalence without discount or premium. Bills of exchange are at *par*, above *par*, or below *par*. Bills are at *par*, when they are sold at their nominal amount for coin or its equivalent.

2. Equality in condition.

PAR'ABLE, *a.* [L. *parabilis.*] Easily procured. [*Not used.*] *Brown.*

PAR'ABLE, *n.* [Fr. *parabole*, from L. *parabola*; Gr. παραβολη, from παραβαλλω, to throw forward or against, to compare; παρα, to or against, and βαλλω, to throw; as in *confero*, *collatum*, to set together, or one thing with another.]

A fable or allegorical relation or representation of something real in life or nature, from which a moral is drawn for instruction; such as the *parable* of the trees choosing a king, Judges ix.; the *parable* of the poor man and his lamb, 2 Sam. xii.; the *parable* of the ten virgins, Matt. xxv.

PAR'ABLE, *v. t.* To represent by fiction or fable. *Milton.*

PARAB'OLA, *n.* [L. See *Parable.*] A conic section arising from cutting a cone by a plane parallel to one of its sides, or parallel to a plane that touches one of its sides. *Harris.*

PARABOLE, *n.* *parab'oly.* [See *Parable.*] In oratory, similitude; comparison. *Encyc.*

PARABOL'IC, } *a.* Expressed by para-
PARABOL'ICAL, } ble or allegorical representation; as *parabolical* instruction or description. *Brown.*

2. [from *parabola.*] Having the form of a parabola; as a *parabolic* curve. *Cheyne.*

PARABOL'ICALLY, *adv.* By way of parable. *Brown.*

2. In the form of a parabola.

PARABOL'IFORM, *a.* Having the form of a parabola.

PARAB'OLISM, *n.* [from *parabola.*] In *algebra*, the division of the terms of an equation by a known quantity that is involved or multiplied in the first term. *Dict.*

PARAB'OLOID, *n.* [Gr. παραβολη and ειδος, form.]

In *geometry*, a paraboliform curve whose ordinates are supposed to be in the subtriplicate, subquadruplicate, &c. ratio of their respective abscissæ. Another species is when the parameter multiplied into the square of the abscissæ, is equal to the cube of the ordinate. The curve is then called a semi-cubical paraboloid. *Harris.*

A *parabolic conoid.* [See *Conoid.*] *Encyc.*

PARACEL'SIAN, *n.* A physician who follows the practice of Paracelsus, a Swiss physician of celebrity, who lived at the close of the fifteenth century. *Ferrand.*

PARACEL'SIAN, *a.* Denoting the medical practice of Paracelsus. *Hakewill.*

PARACENTE'SIS, } *n.* [Gr. παρακεντησις;
PARACEN'TESY, } παρα, through, and κεντεω, to pierce.]

The operation in surgery called *tapping*. *Encyc.*

PARACEN'TRIC, } *a.* [Gr. παρα, be-
PARACEN'TRICAL, } yond, and κεντρον, center.]

Deviating from circularity. *Cheyne.*

PARACH'RONISM, *n.* [Gr. παρα, beyond, and χρονος, time.]

An error in chronology; a mistake in regard to the true date of an event. *Encyc.*

PAR'ACHUTE, *n.* [Gr. παρα, against, and Fr. *chute*, a fall.]
In *aerostation*, an instrument to prevent the rapidity of descent.

PAR'ACLETE, *n.* [Gr. παρακλητος, from παρακαλεω; παρα, to, and καλεω, to call.]
Properly, an advocate; one called to aid or support; hence, the consoler, comforter or intercessor, a term applied to the Holy Spirit. *Pearson. Bale.*

PARA'DE, *n.* [Fr. *parade*, parade, and a parrying; It. *parata;* Sp. *parada*, a stop or stopping, halt, end of a course, a fold for cattle, a relay of horses, a dam or bank, a stake, bet or wager, a parade. This is from the root of L. *paro*, Sp. *parar*, to prepare.]
1. In *military affairs*, the place where troops assemble for exercise, mounting guard or other purpose. *Encyc.*
2. Show; ostentation; display.

Be rich, but of your wealth make no *parade*. *Swift.*

3. Pompous procession.

The rites performed, the parson paid,
In state return'd the grand *parade*. *Swift.*

4. Military order; array; as warlike *parade*. *Milton.*
5. State of preparation or defense. *Locke.*
6. The action of parrying a thrust. [Fr.] *Encyc.*

PARA'DE, *v. t.* To assemble and array or marshal in military order. The general gave orders to *parade* the troops. The troops were *paraded* at the usual hour.
2. To exhibit in a showy or ostentatious manner.

PARA'DE, *v. i.* To assemble and be marshaled in military order.
2. To go about in military procession. *Scott.*
3. To walk about for show.

PARA'DED, *pp.* Assembled and arrayed.

PARADIGM, *n. par'adim.* [Gr. παραδειγμα; παρα and δειγμα, example, from δεικνυμι, to show.]
An example; a model. In *grammar*, an example of a verb conjugated in the several modes, tenses and persons.

PARADIGMAT'IC, **PARADIGMAT'ICAL**, *a.* Exemplary. [*Little used.*] *More.*

PARADIG'MATIZE, *v. t.* To set forth as a model or example. [*Little used.*] *Hammond.*

PARA'DING, *ppr.* Assembling and arraying in due order; making an ostentatious show.

PAR'ADISE, *n.* [Gr. παραδεισος.] The garden of Eden, in which Adam and Eve were placed immediately after their creation. *Encyc. Milton.*
2. A place of bliss; a region of supreme felicity or delight.

The earth
Shall all be *paradise*— *Milton.*

3. Heaven, the blissful seat of sanctified souls after death.

This day shalt thou be with me in *paradise*. Luke xxiii.

4. Primarily, in Persia, a pleasure-garden with parks and other appendages. *Mitford.*

PARADIS'EA, *n.* Bird of Paradise, a genus of fowls, natives of the isles in the East Indies and of New Guinea. *Encyc.*

PARADIS'EAN, **PARADISI'ACAL**, *a.* Pertaining to Eden or Paradise, or to a place of felicity.
2. Suiting paradise; like paradise.

PAR'ADOX, *n.* [Fr. *paradoxe;* It. *paradosso;* Gr. παραδοξια; παρα, beyond, and δοξα, opinion; δοκεω, to think or suppose.]
A tenet or proposition contrary to received opinion, or seemingly absurd, yet true in fact.

A gloss there is to color that *paradox*, and make it appear in show not to be altogether unreasonable. *Hooker.*

PARADOX'ICAL, *a.* Having the nature of a paradox. *Brown. Norris.*
2. Inclined to tenets or notions contrary to received opinions; *applied to persons.*

PARADOX'ICALLY, *adv.* In a paradoxical manner, or in a manner seemingly absurd. *Collier.*

PARADOX'ICALNESS, *n.* State of being paradoxical.

PARADOXOL'OGY, *n.* [*paradox* and Gr. λογος, discourse.]
The use of paradoxes. [*Not used.*] *Brown.*

PARAGOGE, *n. par'agojy.* [Gr. παραγωγη, a drawing out; παρα and αγω.]
The addition of a letter or syllable to the end of a word; as *dicier* for *dici.* This is called a figure in grammar. *Encyc.*

PARAGOG'IC, **PARAGOG'ICAL**, *a.* Pertaining to a paragoge; lengthening a word by the addition of a letter or syllable. *Parkhurst. Milton.*

PAR'AGON, *n.* [Fr. *parangon*, comparison, a pattern; It. *paragone*, from *paraggio*, comparison; Sp. *paragon*, model; from L. *par*, equal.]
1. A model or pattern; a model by way of distinction, implying superior excellence or perfection; as a *paragon* of beauty or eloquence.
2. A companion; a fellow. *Obs. Spenser.*
3. Emulation; a match for trial. *Obs. Spenser.*

PAR'AGON, *v. t.* [Sp. *paragonar;* It. *paragonare*, to compare, to equal; Fr. *parangonner.*]
1. To compare; to parallel.

The picture of Pamela, in little form, he wore in a tablet, purposing to *paragon* the little one with Artesia's length. [*Little used.*] *Sidney.*

2. To equal. [*Little used.*] *Shak.*

PAR'AGON, *v. i.* To pretend comparison or equality. [*Little used.*] *Scott.*

PAR'AGRAM, *n.* [Gr. παραγραμμα.] A play upon words or a pun. *Addison.*

PARAGRAM'MATIST, *n.* A punster. *Addison.*

PAR'AGRAPH, *n.* [It. *paragrafo;* Fr. *paragraphe;* Gr. παραγραφη, a marginal note; παραγραφω, to write near or beyond the text; παρα, beyond, and γραφω, to write.]
A distinct part of a discourse or writing; any portion or section of a writing or chapter which relates to a particular point, whether consisting of one sentence or many sentences. A paragraph is sometimes marked thus, ¶. But more generally, a paragraph is distinguished only by a break in the composition or lines.

PAR'AGRAPH, *v. t.* To form or write paragraphs.

PARAGRAPH'IC, *a.* Consisting of paragraphs or short divisions, with breaks.

PARAGRAPH'ICALLY, *adv.* By paragraphs; with distinct breaks or divisions.

PARALEP'SIS, **PAR'ALEPSY**, *n.* [Gr. παραλειψις, omission; παρα, beyond or by, and λειπω, to leave.]
In *rhetoric*, a pretended or apparent omission; a figure by which a speaker pretends to pass by what at the same time he really mentions. *Encyc.*

PARALIPOM'ENA, *n.* [Gr. παραλειπω, to omit; παρα, beyond, and λειπω, to leave.]
Things omitted; a supplement containing things omitted in the preceding work. The books of Chronicles are so called. *Encyc. Bailey.*

PAR'ALIZE, *v. t.* [Gr. παραλυω, παραλυσις.] To affect as with palsy; to check action, or destroy the power of action.

PARALLAC'TIC, **PARALLAC'TICAL**, *a.* [See *Parallax.*] Pertaining to the parallax of a heavenly body.

PAR'ALLAX, *n.* [Gr. παραλλαξις, from παραλλασσω, to vary, to decline or wander; παρα, beyond, and αλλασσω, to change.]
In *astronomy*, the change of place in a heavenly body in consequence of being viewed from different points.

Diurnal parallax, the difference between the place of a celestial body, as seen from the surface, and from the center of the earth, at the same instant.

Annual parallax, the change of place in a heavenly body, in consequence of being viewed at opposite extremities of the earth's orbit.

PAR'ALLEL, *a.* [Gr. παραλληλος; παρα, against or opposite, and αλληλων, one the other.]
1. In *geometry*, extended in the same direction, and in all parts equally distant. One body or line is *parallel* to another, when the surfaces of the bodies or the lines are at an equal distance throughout the whole length.
2. Having the same direction or tendency; running in accordance with something.

When honor runs *parallel* with the laws of God and our country, it cannot be too much cherished. *Addison.*

3. Continuing a resemblance through many particulars; like; similar; equal in all essential parts; as a *parallel* case; a *parallel* passage in the evangelists. *Watts.*

PAR'ALLEL, *n.* A line which throughout its whole extent is equidistant from another line; as *parallels* of latitude.

Who made the spider *parallels* design,
Sure as De Moivre without rule or line? *Pope.*

2. A line on the globe marking the latitude.
3. Direction conformable to that of another line. *Garth.*
4. Conformity continued through many particulars or in all essential points; resemblance; likeness.

'Twixt earthly females and the moon,
All *parallels* exactly run. *Swift.*

5. Comparison made; as, to draw a *parallel* between two characters. *Addison.*
6. Any thing equal to or resembling another in all essential particulars.

None but thyself can be thy *parallel*. *Pope.*

PAR'ALLEL, *v. t.* To place so as to keep the same direction, and at an equal distance from something else. *Brown.*
2. To level; to equal. *Fell. Shak.*
3. To correspond to. *Burnet.*
4. To be equal to; to resemble in all essential points. *Dryden.*
5. To compare. *Locke.*

PAR'ALLELABLE, *a.* That may be equaled. [*Not much used.*] *Hall.*

PAR'ALLELISM, *n.* State of being parallel. *More.*
2. Resemblance; equality of state; comparison. *Warton.*

PAR'ALLELLY, *adv.* In a parallel manner; with parallelism. *Scott.*

PARALLEL'OGRAM, *n.* [Gr. παραλληλος and γραμμα.]
1. In *geometry*, a right lined quadrilateral figure, whose opposite sides are parallel and equal. *Harris.*
2. In *common use*, this word is applied to quadrilateral figures of more length than breadth, and this is its sense in the passage cited by Johnson from Brown.

PARALLELOGRAM'IC, PARALLELOGRAM'ICAL, *a.* Having the properties of a parallelogram.

PARALLELOPIP'ED, *n.* [*parallel* and Gr. επι, on, and πεδον, a plain.]
In *geometry*, a regular solid comprehended under six parallelograms, the opposite ones of which are similar, parallel and equal to each other, or it is a prism whose base is a parallelogram. It is always triple to a pyramid of the same base and highth. Or a parallelopiped is a solid figure bounded by six faces, parallel to each other two and two. *Harris. Encyc.*

PARALLELOPIPE'DIA, *n.* A genus of spars, externally of a determinate and regular figure, always found loose and separate from other bodies, and in the form of an oblique parallelopiped, with six parallelogramic sides and eight solid angles. *Encyc.*

PARAL'OGISM, *n.* [Gr. παραλογισμος; παρα, beyond, and λογισμος, reasoning; λογος, discourse, reason.]
In *logic*, a fallacious argument or false reasoning; an error committed in demonstration, when a consequence is drawn from principles which are false, or though true, are not proved; or when a proposition is passed over that should have been proved by the way. *Encyc.*

PARAL'OGIZE, *v. i.* To reason falsely. *Ash.*

PARAL'OGY, *n.* False reasoning. [supra.] *Brown.*

PARAL'YSIS, *n.* [Gr. παραλυσις, from παραλυω, to loosen, dissolve or weaken; παρα and λυω.]
Palsy; the loss of the power of muscular motion, or of the command of the muscles.

PARALYT'IC, PARALYT'ICAL, *a.* Affected with palsy; deprived of the power of muscular motion; sometimes, weak; trembling; subject to an involuntary shaking; as a *paralytic* arm.
2. Inclined or tending to palsy.

PARALYT'IC, *n.* A person affected with palsy. *Hall.*

PARAM'ETER, *n.* [from Gr. παραμετρεω.]
1. The latus rectum of a parabola. It is a third proportional to the abscissa and any ordinate, so that the square of the ordinate is always equal to the rectangle under the parameter and abscissa; but in the ellipsis and hyperbola it has a different proportion. *Harris.*
2. In *conic sections*, a third proportional to any diameter and its conjugate. In the parabola, a third proportional to any abscissa and its ordinate.

PAR'AMOUNT, *a.* [Norm. *peramont; per* and *mount, amont* or *monter*, to ascend.]
1. Superior to all others; possessing the highest title or jurisdiction; as lord *paramount*, the chief lord of the fee, or of lands, tenements and hereditaments. In England, the king is lord paramount, of whom all the land in the kingdom is supposed to be held. But in some cases the lord of several manors is called the lord paramount. *Blackstone.*
2. Eminent; of the highest order. *Bacon.*
3. Superior to all others; as, private interest is usually *paramount* to all other considerations.

PAR'AMOUNT, *n.* The chief; the highest in rank or order. *Milton.*

PAR'AMÖUR, *n.* [Fr. *par*, L. *per*, and *amour;* Norm. *paraimer*, to love affectionately.]
1. A lover; a wooer. *Milton.*
2. A mistress. *Shak.*

PARANTHINE. [See *Scapolite.*]

PAR'ANYMPH, *n.* [Gr. παρα, by, and νυμφη, a bride or spouse.]
1. A brideman; one who leads the bride to her marriage. *Milton.*
2. One who countenances and supports another. *Taylor.*

PARAPEGM, *n. par'apem.* [Gr. παραπηγμα.]
A brazen table fixed to a pillar, on which laws and proclamations were anciently engraved; also, a table set in a public place, containing an account of the rising and setting of the stars, eclipses, seasons, &c. *Phillips.*

PAR'APET, *n.* [Fr.; Sp. *parapeto;* It. *parapetto; para*, for, and *petto*, breast, L. *pectus.*]
Literally, a wall or rampart to the breast or breast high; but in practice, a wall, rampart or elevation of earth for covering soldiers from an enemy's shot. *Encyc.*

PARAPHER'NA, PARAPHERNA'LIA, *n.* [Gr. παραφερνα; παρα, beyond, and φερνη, dower.]
The goods which a wife brings with her at her marriage, or which she possesses beyond her dower or jointure, and which remain at her disposal after her husband's death. Such are her apparel and her ornaments, over which the executors have no control, unless when the assets are insufficient to pay the debts. *Blackstone.*

PAR'APHRASE, *n. s* as *z.* [Gr. παραφρασις; παρα, beyond, and φρασις, phrase.]
An explanation of some text or passage in a book, in a more clear and ample manner than is expressed in the words of the author. Such as the *paraphrase* of the New Testament by Erasmus.

In *paraphrase*, or translation with latitude, the author's words are not so strictly followed as his sense. *Dryden.*

PAR'APHRASE, *v. t.* To explain, interpret or translate with latitude; to unfold the sense of an author with more clearness and particularity than it is expressed in his own words.

PAR'APHRASE, *v. i.* To interpret or explain amply; to make a paraphrase.

Where translation is impracticable, they may *paraphrase.* *Felton.*

PAR'APHRASED, *pp.* Amply explained or translated.

PAR'APHRASING, *ppr.* Explaining or translating amply and freely.

PAR'APHRAST, *n.* [Gr. παραφραςης.] One that paraphrases; one that explains or translates in words more ample and clear than the words of the author. *Hooker.*

PARAPHRAS'TIC, PARAPHRAS'TICAL, *a.* Free, clear and ample in explanation; explaining or translating in words more clear and ample than those of the author; not verbal or literal.

PARAPHRAS'TICALLY, *adv.* In a paraphrastic manner. *Howell.*

PARAPHREN'ITIS, *n.* [Gr. παρα and φρενιτις, delirium.]
An inflammation of the diaphragm. *Arbuthnot.*

PAR'APLEGY, *n.* [Gr. παρα, beyond, and πληγη, stroke; πλησσω, to smite.]
That kind of palsy which affects the lower part of the body. *Good.*

PARAQUET', *n.* A little parrot. *Shak.*

PAR'ASANG, *n.* A Persian measure of length, which Herodotus states to be thirty stadia, nearly four English miles; but in different times and places, it has been 30, 40 or 50 stadia. *Herod. Euterp. Encyc.*

PARASCEUAS'TIC, *a.* Preparatory.

PARASCE'VE, *n.* [Gr. παρασκευη, preparation.]
Preparation; the sabbath-eve of the Jews. *Todd.*

PARASELE'NE, *n.* [Gr. παρα, about or near, and σεληνη, the moon.]
A mock moon; a luminous ring or circle encompassing the moon, in which sometimes are other bright spots bearing some resemblance to the moon. *Encyc.*

PAR'ASITE, *n.* [Fr. *parasite;* It. *parassito;* Sp. *parasito;* L. *parasita;* from Gr. παρασιτος; παρα, by, and σιτος, corn.]
1. In *ancient Greece*, a priest or minister of the gods whose office was to gather of the husbandman the corn allotted for public sacrifices. The public store-house in which this corn was deposited was called παρασιτον. The parasites also superintended the sacrifices. *Potter's Antiq.*
2. In *modern usage*, a trencher friend; one that frequents the tables of the rich and earns his welcome by flattery; a hanger on; a fawning flatterer. *Milton. Dryden.*
3. In *botany*, a plant growing on the stem or branch of another plant and receiving its nourishment from it, as the misletoe. *Encyc.*

PARASIT'IC, PARASIT'ICAL, *a.* Flattering; wheedling; fawning for bread or favors.
2. Growing on the stem or branch of another plant; as a *parasitic* plant.

PARASIT'ICALLY, *adv.* In a flattering or wheedling manner; by dependence on another.

PAR'ASITISM, *n.* The behavior or manners of a parasite. *Milton.*

PAR'ASOL, *n.* [Fr. Sp.; It. *parasole*; Gr. παρα, against, or It. *parare*, to parry, and L. *sol*, Fr. *soleil*, It. *sole*, the sun.]
A small umbrella used by ladies to defend themselves from rain, or their faces from the sun's rays.

PAR'AT, *n.* A fish of the mullet kind, found in Brazil.

PARATH'ESIS, *n.* [Gr. παραθεσις; παρα, and θεσις.]
In *grammar*, apposition, or the placing of two or more nouns in the same case. *Jones.*

PARAVA'IL, *a.* [Norm. *par*, by, and *availe*, profit.]
In *feudal law*, the tenant *paravail*, is the lowest tenant holding under a mean or mediate lord, as distinguished from a tenant *in capite*, who holds immediately of the king. *Blackstone.*

PAR'AVANT, } *adv.* [Fr. *par* and *avant*,
PAR'AVAUNT, } before.] In front; publicly. [*Not English nor used.*] *Spenser.*

P'ARBOIL, *v. t.* [Fr. *parbouillir*. *Bouillir* is to boil, and in Arm. *porbollen* is a pustule or little push.]
1. To boil in part; to boil in a moderate degree.
2. To cause little pustules or pushes on the skin by means of heat; as *parboiled* wretches. *Donne.*

P'ARBREAK, *v. i.* [See *Break*.] To vomit. *Obs.* *Skelton.*

P'ARBUCKLE, *n.* Among seamen, a rope like a pair of slings for hoisting casks, &c.

P'ARCEL, *n.* [Fr. *parcelle*, contracted probably from L. *particula*, particle, from *pars*, part.]
1. A part; a portion of any thing taken separately.

The same experiments succeed on two *parcels* of the white of an egg. *Arbuthnot.*

2. A quantity; any mass. *Newton.*
3. A part belonging to a whole; as in law, one piece of ground is part and *parcel* of a greater piece.
4. A small bundle or package of goods.
5. A number of persons; in contempt. *Shak.*
6. A number or quantity; in contempt; as a *parcel* of fair words. *L'Estrange.*

P'ARCEL, *v. t.* To divide into parts or portions; as, to *parcel* an estate among heirs.

These ghostly kings would *parcel* out my power. *Dryden.*

2. To make up into a mass. [*Little used.*] *Shak.*

To parcel a seam, in seamen's language, to lay canvas over it and daub it with pitch. *Mar. Dict.*

P'ARCELED, *pp.* Divided into portions.

P'ARCELING, *ppr.* Dividing into portions.

P'ARCELING, *n.* Among *seamen*, long narrow slips of canvas daubed with tar and bound about a rope like a bandage, before it is sewed. It is used also to raise a mouse on the stays, &c. *Mar. Dict.*

P'ARCENARY, *n.* [Norm. *parcenier.*] Co-heirship; the holding or occupation of lands of inheritance by two or more persons. It differs from *joint-tenancy*, which is created by deed or devise; whereas *parcenary*, or co-parcenary, is created by the descent of lands from an ancestor. *Blackstone.*

P'ARCENER, *n.* [Scot. *parsenere*; Norm. *parcunnier*; from *part*, L. *pars.*]
Parcener or co-parcener is a co-heir, or one who holds lands by descent from an ancestor in common with another or with others; as when land descends to a man's daughters, sisters, aunts, cousins, or their representatives. In this case, all the heirs inherit as *parceners* or co-heirs. *Blackstone.*

P'ARCH, *v. t.* [I know not from what source we have received this word. It corresponds in elements with the Italian *bruciare*, to burn or roast. Qu. L. *peraresco.*]
1. To burn the surface of a thing; to scorch; as, to *parch* the skin; to *parch* corn.
2. To dry to extremity; as, the heat of the sun's rays *parches* the ground; the mouth is *parched* with thirst. *Milton. Dryden.*

P'ARCH, *v. i.* To be scorched or superficially burnt; as, corn will dry and *parch* into barley. *Mortimer.*
2. To become very dry.

P'ARCHED, *pp.* Scorched; dried to extremity.

P'ARCHEDNESS, *n.* The state of being scorched or dried to extremity.

P'ARCHING, *ppr.* Scorching; drying to extremity.
2. *a.* Having the quality of burning or drying; as the *parching* heat of African sands.

P'ARCHMENT, *n.* [Fr. *parchemin*; It. *pargameno*; Sp. *pargamino*; Arm. *parich* or *parichemin*; D. *parkement*; G. *pergament*; L. *pergamena*; supposed to be from *Pergamus*, to whose king Eumenes, the invention has been ascribed. This is probably a mere conjecture, originating in a resemblance of orthography; such conjectures being very common. In Spanish, *parche* is *parchment*, and a piece of linen covered with ointment or plaster. It is more probable that the first syllable is from some root that signifies to cleanse, purify or make clear, perhaps the root of L. *purgo*, or the oriental ברק or פרג. See *Membrane*. See Class Br. No. 9. and Class Brg. No. 4. 5.]
The skin of a sheep or goat dressed or prepared and rendered fit for writing on. This is done by separating all the flesh and hair, rubbing the skin with pumice stone, and reducing its thickness with a sharp instrument. Vellum is made of the skins of abortive or very young calves. *Encyc.*

P'ARCHMENT-MAKER, *n.* One who dresses skins for parchment.

P'ARD, *n.* [L. *pardus*; Gr. παρδος; Syr. *bardona*. The word signifies spotted, from ברד to hail, properly to scatter or sprinkle, as with hail.]
The leopard; or in poetry, any spotted beast. Instead of *pard*, we generally use *leopard*, the lion-pard. *Pardale*, from the Latin *pardalis*, is not used.

P'ARDON, *v. t.* [Fr. *pardonner*; It. *perdonare*; Sp. *perdonar*; Port. *perdoar*; L. *per* and *dono*, to give; *per* having the sense of the English *for* in *forgive*, and *re* in L. *remitto*, properly to give back or away.]
1. To forgive; to remit; as an offense or crime. *Guilt* implies a being bound or subjected to censure, penalty or punishment. To *pardon*, is to *give up* this obligation, and release the offender. We apply the word to the crime or to the person. We *pardon* an offense, when we remove it from the offender and consider him as not guilty; we *pardon* the offender, when we release or absolve him from his liability to suffer punishment.

I pray thee, *pardon* my sin. 1 Sam. xv.

2. To remit, as a penalty.

I *pardon* thee thy life before thou ask it. *Shak.*

3. To excuse, as for a fault. *Dryden.*
4. *Pardon me*, is a phrase used when one asks for excuse, or makes an apology, and it is often used in this sense, when a person means civilly to deny or contradict what another affirms.

P'ARDON, *n.* Forgiveness; the release of an offense or of the obligation of the offender to suffer a penalty, or to bear the displeasure of the offended party. We seek the *pardon* of sins, transgressions and offenses.
2. Remission of a penalty. An amnesty is a general *pardon*.
3. Forgiveness received. *South.*

P'ARDONABLE, *a.* That may be pardoned; *applied to persons.* The offender is *pardonable.*
2. Venial; excusable; that may be forgiven, overlooked or passed by; *applied to things*; as a *pardonable* offense.

P'ARDONABLENESS, *n.* The quality of being pardonable; venialness; susceptibility of forgiveness; as the *pardonableness* of sin. *Hall.*

P'ARDONABLY, *adv.* In a manner admitting of pardon; venially; excusably. *Dryden.*

P'ARDONED, *pp.* Forgiven; excused.

P'ARDONER, *n.* One that forgives; one that absolves an offender.
2. One that sells the pope's indulgences. *Cowell.*

P'ARDONING, *ppr.* Forgiving; remitting an offense or crime; absolving from punishment.

PARE, *v. t.* [Fr. *parer*; Arm. *para*, to dress, to trim, to *parry* or ward off, to stop; Sp. Port. *parar*, to *parry*, to stop, to *prepare*; Port. *aparar*, to *pare*, and to *parry*; L. *paro*; W. *par*, a state of readiness, also a *pair*; *para*, to continue, to persevere, to last, to endure; Fr. *parer des cuirs*, to dress or curry lether; *parer le pied d'un cheval*, to pare a horse's foot or hoof; Pers. پريدن poridan, to *pare* or cut off; [qu. Gr. πηρος, lame; πηροω, to mutilate;] Ar. برا to be free, to free, liberate or absolve, to dismiss, to remit, to create; Heb. Ch. Syr. Sam. ברא to create; Heb. Ch. *id.* to cut off. The primary sense is to thrust or drive, hence to drive off, to separate, to stop by setting or repelling, as in *parry*, or to drive off or out, as in separating or producing. In Portuguese and Welsh, it has the sense of stretching, extending, and the Welsh unites *par*, equal, a pair, with the root of this word; *par*, a pair, what is continued to or contiguous. See ברר and ברא. Class Br. No. 6. 7. 8. and 10.]

1. To cut off, as the superficial substance or extremities of a thing; to shave off with a sharp instrument; as, to *pare* an apple or an orange; to *pare* the nails; to *pare* a horse's hoof; to *pare* land in agriculture.
2. To diminish by little and little.

The king began to *pare* a little the privilege of clergy. *Bacon.*

When *pare* is followed by the thing diminished, the noun is in the objective case; as, to *pare* the nails. When the thing separated is the object, *pare* is followed by *off* or *away*; as, to *pare off* the rind of fruit; to *pare away* redundances.

PA'RED, *pp.* Freed from any thing superfluous on the surface or at the extremities.

PAREGOR'IC, *a.* [Gr. παρηγορικος, from παρηγορεω, to mitigate.]

Mitigating; assuaging pain; as *paregoric* elixir.

PAREGOR'IC, *n.* A medicine that mitigates pain; an anodyne. *Encyc.*

PAREL'CON, *n.* [Gr. παρελκω, to draw out.]

In *grammar*, the addition of a word or syllable to the end of another. *Encyc.*

PAREMBOLE, *n. parem'boly.* [Gr. παρεμβολη, insertion.]

In *rhetoric*, the insertion of something relating to the subject in the middle of a period. It differs from the *parenthesis* only in this; the *parembole* relates to the subject, the *parenthesis* is foreign from it. *Encyc. Vossius.*

PAREN'CHYMA, *n.* [Gr. παρεγχυμα, from παρεγχυω, to suffuse.]

1. In *anatomy*, the solid and interior part of the viscera, or the substance contained in the interstices between the blood vessels of the viscera; a spungy substance. *Coxe. Encyc.*

Parenchyma is the substance or basis of the glands. *Cyc.*

2. In *botany*, the pith or pulp of plants. *Encyc.*

PARENCHYM'ATOUS, PAREN'CHYMOUS, } *a.* [See the Noun.]

Pertaining to parenchyma; spungy; soft; porous. *Grew. Cheyne.*

PAREN'ESIS, *n.* [Gr. παραινεσις; παραινεω, to exhort.]

Persuasion; exhortation. [*Little used.*] *Dict.*

PARENET'IC, PARENET'ICAL, } *a.* Hortatory; encouraging. *Potter.*

PA'RENT, *n.* [L. *parens*, from *pario*, to produce or bring forth. The regular participle of *pario* is *pariens*, and *parens* is the regular participle of *pareo*, to appear. But both verbs probably belong to one family; Eth. ፈረየ fari or feri, to *bear*. Class Br. No. 35. Heb. פרה farah, id. No. 33.]

1. A father or mother; he or she that produces young. The duties of *parents* to their children are to maintain, protect and educate them.

When *parents* are wanting in authority, children are wanting in duty. *Ames.*

2. That which produces; cause; source. Idleness is the *parent* of vice.

Regular industry is the *parent* of sobriety. *Channing.*

PAR'ENTAGE, *n.* [Fr.] Extraction; birth; condition with respect to the rank of parents; as a man of mean *parentage*; a gentleman of noble *parentage*. *Shak.*

PARENT'AL, *a.* [It. *parentale.*] Pertaining to parents; as *parental* government.

2. Becoming parents; tender; affectionate; as *parental* care or solicitude.

PARENTA'TION, *n.* [from L. *parento.*] Something done or said in honor of the dead. *Potter. Johnson.*

PAREN'THESIS, *n.* [Gr. παρενθεσις; παρα and εντιθημι, to insert.]

A sentence, or certain words inserted in a sentence, which interrupt the sense or natural connection of words, but serve to explain or qualify the sense of the principal sentence. The parenthesis is usually included in hooks or curved lines, thus, ().

These officers, whom they still call bishops, are to be elected to a provision comparatively mean, through the same arts, *(that is, electioneering arts,)* by men of all religious tenets that are known or can be invented. *Burke.*

Do not suffer every occasional thought to carry you away into a long *parenthesis*. *Watts.*

PARENTHET'IC, PARENTHET'ICAL, } *a.* Pertaining to a parenthesis; expressed in a parenthesis. *Hales.*

2. Using parentheses.

PARENT'ICIDE, *n.* [L. *parens* and *cædo.*] One who kills a parent. *Bailey.*

PA'RENTLESS, *a.* Deprived of parents.

PA'RER, *n.* [from *pare.*] He or that which pares; an instrument for paring. *Tusser.*

PAR'ERGY, *n.* [Gr. παρα, beyond, and εργον, work.]

Something unimportant, or done by the by. [*Not used.*] *Brown.*

P'ARGASITE, *n.* [from the isle *Pargas*, in Finland.]

A mineral of a grayish or bluish green, in rounded grains, with a dull, dun surface, rarely bright; or in crystals in carbonate of lime, in little plates mixed with lamellar mica; a variety of actinolite. *Dict.*

P'ARGET, *n.* [Sp. *parche*, a plaster; *emparchar*, to plaster. Qu.] Gypsum or plaster stone. *Encyc.*

2. Plaster laid on roofs or walls. *Spenser.*
3. Paint. *Drayton.*

Parget is applied to the several kinds of gypsum, which when slightly calcined, is called *plaster of Paris*, and is used in casting statues, in stucco for floors, cielings, &c. *Cyc.*

PAR'GET, *v. t.* To plaster walls.

2. To paint; to cover with paint. *B. Jonson.*

P'ARGETED, *pp.* Plastered; stuccoed.

P'ARGETER, *n.* A plasterer.

P'ARGETING, *ppr.* Plastering; as a noun, plaster or stucco.

PARHE'LION, *n.* [Gr. παρα, near, and ηλιος, the sun.]

A mock sun or meteor, appearing in the form of a bright light near the sun; sometimes tinged with colors like the rainbow, with a luminous train.

PA'RIAL, PAIR-ROYAL, } *n.* Three of a sort in certain games of cards. *Butler.*

PA'RIAN, *a.* Pertaining to Paros, an isle in the Egean sea; as *Parian* marble.

Parian chronicle, a chronicle of the city of Athens, engraven on marble in capital letters in the isle of Paros. It contains a chronological account of events from Cecrops, 1582 years before Christ, to the archonship of Diognetus, 264 years before that era; but the chronicle of the last 90 years is lost. This marble was procured from Asia Minor in 1627, by the earl of Arundel, and being broken, the pieces are called *Arundelian marbles*. They are now deposited in the university of Oxford. The antiquity of the inscription has been disputed. *Cyc. Encyc.*

PARIE'TAL, *a.* [from L. *paries*, a wall, properly a partition wall, from the root of *part* or *pare.*] Pertaining to a wall.

2. The *parietal* bones form the sides and upper part of the skull. They are so called because they defend the brain like walls. *Parr.*

PARI'ETARY, *n.* [Fr. *parietaire*, from L. *paries*, a wall.]

A plant, the pellitory of the wall, of the genus Parietaria.

PAR'IETINE, *n.* [L. *paries*, wall.] A piece of a wall. [*Not used.*] *Burton.*

PA'RING, *ppr.* Cutting or shaving off the extremities.

PA'RING, *n.* That which is pared off; rind separated from fruit; a piece clipped off. *Mortimer. Pope.*

2. The act or practice of cutting off the surface of grass land, for tillage.

PAR'IS, *n.* A plant, herb Paris or true-love, or rather a genus of plants of one species. *Encyc.*

PAR'ISH, *n.* [Fr. *paroisse*; It. *parrocchia*; Sp. *parroquia*; Arm. *parres*; Ir. *parraiste*; usually deduced from the Low L. *parochia*, Gr. παροικια, a dwelling or near residence; παρα, near, and οικος, house, or οικεω, to dwell; or more probably from the Greek παροχη, a salary or largess, an allowance for support, from παρεχω, to afford, yield or supply, whence L. *parocha*, entertainment given to embassadors at the public expense; whence It. *parrocchii*. If *parish* is to be deduced from either of these sources, it is probably from the latter, and *parish* is equivalent to benefice, living, as prebend, from L. *præbeo*. In German, *pfarre* signifies a benefice or parish; *pfarrer* or *pfarrherr*, a parson, the lord of a living or parish, and this is evidently from the same root as *parson*. I know not the origin of *pfarre*, but it coincides in elements with the W. *pori*, to graze, Corn. *peuri*, L. *voro*, Gr. βορα. The Italian and Spanish words are undoubtedly from the Latin and Greek, and the French *paroisse* may be from the same source.]

1. The precinct or territorial jurisdiction of a secular priest, or the precinct, the inhabitants of which belong to the same church.
2. In some of the American states, *parish* is an ecclesiastical society not bounded by territorial limits; but the inhabitants of a

town belonging to one church, though residing promiscuously among the people belonging to another church, are called a *parish*. This is particularly the case in Massachusetts. In Connecticut, the legal appellation of such a society is ecclesiastical society.

PAR'ISH, *a.* Belonging to a parish; having the spiritual charge of the inhabitants belonging to the same church; as a *parish* priest. *Dryden.*

2. Belonging to a parish; as a *parish* church; *parish* records.

3. Maintained by the parish; as *parish* poor. *Gay.*

PARISH'IONER, *n.* One that belongs to a parish. *Addison.*

PARISYLLAB'IC, PARISYLLAB'ICAL, } *a.* [L. *par*, equal, and *syllaba*, syllable.] Having equal or like syllables.

PAR'ITOR, *n.* [for *apparitor.*] A beadle; a summoner of the courts of civil law. *Dryden.*

PAR'ITY, *n.* [Fr. *parité*; It. *parità*; from L. *par*, equal. See *Pair* and *Peer.*]

1. Equality; as *parity* of reason. *South.*

2. Equality; like state or degree; as a *parity* of orders or persons.

P'ARK, *n.* [Sax. *parruc*, *pearruc*; Scot. *parrok*; W. *parc*; Fr. *id.*; It. *parco*; Sp. *parque*; Ir. *pairc*; G. Sw. *park*; D. *perk*. It may be from the root of *bar*, but it coincides in elements with L. *parcus*, saving, and the Teutonic *bergen*, to keep.]

A large piece of ground inclosed and privileged for wild beasts of chase, in England, by the king's grant or by prescription. To constitute a park, three things are required; a royal grant or license; inclosure by pales, a wall or hedge; and beasts of chase, as deer, &c. *Encyc.*

Park of artillery, or *artillery park*, a place in the rear of both lines of an army for encamping the artillery, which is formed in lines, the guns in front, the ammunition-wagons behind the guns, and the pontoons and tumbrils forming the third line. The whole is surrounded with a rope. The gunners and matrosses encamp on the flanks; the bombardiers, pontoon-men and artificers in the rear. *Encyc.*

Also, the whole train of artillery belonging to an army or division of troops.

Park of provisions, the place where the sutlers pitch their tents and sell provisions, and that where the bread wagons are stationed.

P'ARK, *v. t.* To inclose in a park. *Shak.*

P'ARKER, *n.* The keeper of a park.

P'ARKLEAVES, *n.* A plant of the genus Hypericum. *Ainsworth. Lee.*

P'ARLANCE, *n.* [Norm. from Fr. *parler*, to speak; part. *parlant*, It. *parlante.*] Conversation; discourse; talk. *Woodeson.*

PARLE, *n.* p'arl. Conversation; talk; oral treaty or discussion. [*Not used.*] [See *Parley.*] *Shak.*

P'ARLEY, *v. i.* [Fr. *parler*, It. *parlare*, Sp. *parlar*, W. *parliaw*, to speak; Ir. *bearla*, language, from *bearadh* or *beirim*, to speak, to tell, relate, narrate, to *bear*, to carry; Goth. *bairan*, Sax. *bæran*, to bear, L. *fero*, or *pario*. So we have *report*, from L. *porto.*]

In a general sense, to speak with another; to discourse; but appropriately, to confer with on some point of mutual concern; to discuss orally; hence, to confer with an enemy; to treat with by words; as on an exchange of prisoners, on a cessation of arms, or the subject of peace. *Knolles. Broome.*

P'ARLEY, *n.* Mutual discourse or conversation; discussion; but appropriately, a conference with an enemy in war.

We yield on *parley*, but are storm'd in vain. *Dryden.*

To beat a parley, in military language, to beat a drum or sound a trumpet, as a signal for holding a conference with the enemy.

P'ARLIAMENT, *n.* [Fr. *parlement*; Sp. It. Port. *parlamento*; Arm. *parlamand*; composed of Fr. *parler*, Sp. *parlar*, to speak, and the termination *ment*, as in *complement*, &c. noting state. See *Parley.*] Literally, a speaking, conference, mutual discourse or consultation; hence,

1. In *Great Britain*, the grand assembly of the three estates, the lords spiritual, lords temporal, and the commons; the general council of the nation constituting the legislature, summoned by the king's authority to consult on the affairs of the nation, and to enact and repeal laws. Primarily, the king may be considered as a constituent branch of parliament; but the word is generally used to denote the three estates above named, consisting of two distinct branches, the house of lords and house of commons.

The word *parliament* was introduced into England under the Norman kings. The supreme council of the nation was called under the Saxon kings, *wittenagemote*, the meeting of wise men or sages.

2. The supreme council of Sweden, consisting of four estates; the nobility and representatives of the gentry; the clergy, one of which body is elected from every rural deanery of ten parishes; the burghers, elected by the magistrates and council of every corporation; and the peasants, elected by persons of their own order.

3. In France, before the revolution, a council or court consisting of certain noblemen.

PARLIAMENTA'RIAN, PARLIAMENTEE'R, } *n.* One of those who adhered to the parliament in the time of Charles I. *Aubrey.*

PARLIAMENTA'RIAN, *a.* Serving the parliament in opposition to king Charles I. *Wood.*

PARLIAMENT'ARY, *a.* Pertaining to parliament; as *parliamentary* authority.

2. Enacted or done by parliament; as a *parliamentary* act.

3. According to the rules and usages of parliament, or to the rules and customs of legislative bodies.

P'ARLOR, *n.* [Fr. *parloir*; It. Sp. *parlatorio*; W. *parlawr*; from Fr. *parler*, Sp. *parlar*, to speak.]

Primarily, the apartment in a nunnery where the nuns are permitted to meet and converse with each other; hence with us, the room in a house which the family usually occupy when they have no company, as distinguished from a drawing room intended for the reception of company, or from a dining room, when a distinct apartment is allotted for that purpose. In most houses, the parlor is also the dining room.

P'ARLOUS, *a.* [from Fr. *parler*, to speak.] Keen; sprightly; waggish. [*Not used.*] *Dryden.*

PARO'CHIAL, *a.* [from L. *parochia.*] Belonging to a parish; as *parochial* clergy; *parochial* duties. *Atterbury.*

PAROCHIAL'ITY, *n.* The state of being parochial. *Mariot.*

PARO'CHIAN, *a.* Pertaining to a parish. *Bacon.*

PARO'CHIAN, *n.* [supra.] A parishioner. *Burghley.*

PAROD'IC, PAROD'ICAL, } *a.* [See *Parody.*] Copying after the manner of parody. *Warton.*

PAR'ODY, *n.* [Fr. *parodie*; Gr. παρωδια; παρα and ωδη, ode.]

1. A kind of writing in which the words of an author or his thoughts are, by some slight alterations, adapted to a different purpose; a kind of poetical pleasantry, in which verses written on one subject, are altered and applied to another by way of burlesque. *Johnson. Encyc.*

2. A popular maxim, adage or proverb. *Encyc.*

PAR'ODY, *v. t.* To alter, as verses or words, and apply to a purpose different from that of the original.

I have translated, or rather *parodied* a poem of Horace. *Pope.*

PARŎL, PARO'LE, } *n.* [W. *paryl*; It. *parola*; Fr. *parole*, from *parler*, to speak; or contracted from L. *parabola.*]

1. Properly, a word; hence, in a legal sense, words or oral declaration; word of mouth. Formerly, conveyances were made by *parol* or word of mouth only. *Blackstone.*

2. Pleadings in a suit; as anciently all pleadings were *viva voce* or *ore tenus*.

The *parol* may demur. *Blackstone.*

PARŎL, PARO'LE, } *a.* Given by word of mouth; oral; not written; as *parol* evidence. *Blackstone.*

[It would be well to write this word *parole*, in uniformity with the following, there being no good reason for a distinction.]

PARO'LE, *n.* [See *Parol.*] Word of mouth. In *military affairs*, a promise given by a prisoner of war, when he has leave to depart from custody, that he will return at the time appointed, unless discharged. A *parole* is properly a verbal or unwritten promise, but I believe it is customary to take a promise in writing.

2. A word given out every day in orders by a commanding officer, in camp or garrison, by which friends may be distinguished from enemies. *Encyc.*

PARONOMA'SIA, PARONOM'ASY, } *n.* [from Gr. παρα-νομεω, to transgress law or rule.]

A rhetorical figure, by which words nearly alike in sound, but of different meanings, are affectedly or designedly used; a play upon words; a pun. [See *Pun.*] *Encyc.*

PARONOMAS'TIC, PARONOMAS'TICAL, } *a.* Pertaining to paronomasy; consisting in a play upon words. *More.*

PARONYCHIA, *n.* [Gr. παρωνυχια; παρα, by, and ονυξ, the nail.] In surgery, a whitlow or felon. *Encyc.*

PARON'YMOUS, *a.* [Gr. παρωνυμος; παρα and ονομα, name.] Resembling another word. *Watts.*

PAR'OQUET, } *n.* A small species of parrot. *Grew.*
PAR'OKET, }

[More properly *perroquet*, which see.]

PAROT'ID, *a.* [Gr. παρα, near, and ους, ωτα, ear.]

Pertaining to or denoting certain glands below and before the ears, or near the articulation of the lower jaw. The parotid glands secrete a portion of the saliva. *Parr. Coxe. Grew.*

PARO'TIS, *n.* [Gr. παρωτις. See *Parotid.*]

1. The parotid gland; a secreting salivary conglomerate gland below and before the ear. *Parr.*

2. An inflammation or abscess of the parotid gland. *Quincy.*

PAR'OXYSM, *n.* [Gr. παροξυσμος, from παροξυνω, to excite or sharpen; παρα and οξυς, sharp.]

An exasperation or exacerbation of a disease; a fit of higher excitement or violence in a disease that has remissions or intermissions; as the *paroxysm* of a fever or gout. *Encyc.*

PAROXYS'MAL, *a.* Pertaining to paroxysm; as a *paroxysmal* disposition. *Asiat. Res.*

PAR'REL, *n.* [Port. *aparelho*, from *aparelhar*, to prepare; Sp. *aparejo*, tackle and rigging, from *aparejar*, to prepare, L. *paro*. It coincides with *apparel*, which see.]

Among seamen, an apparatus or frame made of ropes, trucks and ribs, so contrived as to go round the mast, and being fastened at both ends to a yard, serves to hoist it. *Encyc.*

PARRICI'DAL, } *a.* [See *Parricide.*] Pertaining to parricide; containing the crime of murdering a parent or child.
PARRICID'IOUS, }

2. Committing parricide.

PAR'RICIDE, *n.* [Fr. from L. *paricida*, from *pater*, father, and *cædo*, to kill.]

1. A person who murders his father or mother.

2. One who murders an ancestor, or any one to whom he owes reverence. Blackstone applies the word to one who kills his child.

3. The murder of a parent or one to whom reverence is due. *Bacon.*

4. One who invades or destroys any to whom he owes particular reverence, as his country or patron.

PAR'RIED, *pp.* [See *Parry.*] Warded off; driven aside. *Johnson.*

PAR'ROT, *n.* [supposed to be contracted from Fr. *perroquet.*]

1. The name of fowls of the genus Psittacus, of numerous species. The bill is hooked and the upper mandible movable. The hooked bill of the parrot is used in climbing. These fowls are found almost every where in tropical climates. They breed in hollow trees and subsist on fruits and seeds. They are also remarkable for the faculty of making indistinct articulations of words in imitation of the human voice.

2. A fish found among the Bahama isles, esteemed to be delicate food and remarkable for the richness of its colors. *Pennant.*

PAR'RY, *v. t.* [Fr. *parer;* It. *parare*, to adorn, to parry; Sp. *parar*, to stop; Port. *id.* to stop, to *parry;* from the root of *pare*, to cut off, to separate. See *Pare.*]

1. In fencing, to ward off; to stop or to put or turn by; as, to *parry* a thrust.

2. To ward off; to turn aside; to prevent a blow from taking effect.

3. To avoid; to shift off.

> The French government has *parried* the payment of our claims. *E. Everett.*

PAR'RY, *v. i.* To ward off; to put by thrusts or strokes; to fence. *Locke.*

PAR'RYING, *ppr.* Warding off, as a thrust or blow.

PARSE, *v. t.* *p'ars.* [from L. *pars*, part, or one of the Shemitic roots, פרס to divide, or פרש to spread.]

In *grammar*, to resolve a sentence into its elements, or to show the several parts of speech composing a sentence, and their relation to each other by government or agreement.

PARSIMO'NIOUS, *a.* [See *Parsimony.*] Sparing in the use or expenditure of money; covetous; near; close. It differs from *frugal*, in implying more closeness or narrowness of mind, or an attachment to property somewhat excessive, or a disposition to spend less money than is necessary or honorable.

> Extraordinary funds for one campaign may spare us the expense of many years; whereas a long *parsimonious* war will drain us of more men and money. *Addison.*

[It is sometimes used in a good sense for *frugal.*]

PARSIMO'NIOUSLY, *adv.* With a very sparing use of money; covetously.

PARSIMO'NIOUSNESS, *n.* A very sparing use of money, or a disposition to save expense.

P'ARSIMONY, *n.* [L. *parsimonia*, from *parcus*, saving, literally close. *Parcus* seems to be from the root of the G. D. *bergen*, Sax. *beorgan*, to save or keep, Eng. *park.* So in Russ. *beregu* is to keep or save, whence *berejlivei*, parsimonious. And this seems to be the root of *burg*, a borough, originally a fortified hill or castle.]

Closeness or sparingness in the use or expenditure of money; sometimes used perhaps in a good sense, implying due or justifiable caution in expenditure, in which sense it differs little from *frugality* and *economy.* More generally, it denotes an excessive caution or closeness; in which case, it is allied to *covetousness*, but it implies less meanness than *niggardliness.* It generally implies some want of honorable liberality.

> The ways to enrich are many; *parsimony* is one of the best, and yet is not innocent, for it withholdeth men from works of liberality. *Bacon.*

P'ARSLEY, *n.* [Fr. *persil;* Sp. *perexil;* Port. *perrexil;* It. *petroselino*, corrupted to *petrosemolo;* Sax. *peterselige;* G. *petersilie;* D. *pieterselie;* Sw. *persilia;* Dan. *petersille, persille;* Ir. *peirsil;* W. *perllys;* L. *petroselinon;* Gr. πετροσελινον; πετρος, a stone, and σελινον, parsley; stone-parsley, a plant growing among rocks.]

A plant of the genus Apium. The leaves of parsley are used in cookery, and the root is an aperient medicine.

P'ARSNEP, *n.* [The last syllable of this word is the Sax. *næpe*, L. *napus*, which occurs also in *turnep.*]

A plant of the genus Pastinaca. The root of the garden parsnep is deemed a valuable esculent.

PARSON, *n.* *p'arsn.* [G. *pfarrherr*, *pfarrer*, lord of the *pfarre*, benefice or living. I know not from what root *pfarre* is derived. See *Parish.*]

1. The priest of a parish or ecclesiastical society; the rector or incumbent of a parish, who has the parochial charge or cure of souls. It is used in this sense by all denominations of christians; but among independents or congregationalists it is merely a colloquial word.

2. A clergyman; a man that is in orders or has been licensed to preach. *Shak.*

P'ARSONAGE, *n.* In *America*, the glebe and house belonging to a parish or ecclesiastical society, and appropriated to the maintenance of the incumbent or settled pastor of a church.

2. In *England*, the benefice of a parish, or the house appropriated to the residence of the incumbent. *Addison. Gray.*

Parsonically, in Chesterfield, is not an authorized word.

P'ART, *n.* [L. *pars, partis;* Fr. *part;* Sp. It. *parte;* W. *parth;* from פרד, or פרס, or פרץ, which in the Shemitic languages signify to separate, to break.]

1. A portion, piece or fragment separated from a whole thing; as, to divide an orange into five *parts.*

2. A portion or quantity of a thing not separated in fact, but considered or mentioned by itself. In what *part* of England is Oxford situated? So we say, the upper *part* or lower *part*, the fore *part*, a remote *part*, a small *part*, or a great *part.*

> The people stood at the nether *part* of the mount. Ex. xix.

3. A portion of number, separated or considered by itself; as a *part* of the nation or congregation.

4. A portion or component particle; as the component *parts* of a fossil or metal.

5. A portion of man; as the material *part* or body, or the intellectual *part*, the soul or understanding; the perishable *part;* the immortal *part.*

6. A member.

> All the *parts* were formed in his mind into one harmonious body. *Locke.*

7. Particular division; distinct species or sort belonging to a whole; as all the *parts* of domestic business or of a manufacture.

8. Ingredient in a mingled mass; a portion in a compound.

9. That which falls to each in division; share; as, let me bear my *part* of the danger. *Dryden.*

10. Proportional quantity; as four *parts* of lime with three of sand.

11. Share; concern; interest.

> Sheba said, we have no *part* in David. 2 Sam. xx.

12. Side; party; interest; faction.

> And make whole kingdoms take her brother's *part.* *Waller.*

13. Something relating or belonging to; that which concerns; as for your *part*; for his *part*; for her *part*.

For my *part*, I have no servile end in my labor. *Wotton.*

14. Share of labor, action or influence; particular office or business.

Accuse not nature, she hath done her *part*,
Do thou but thine. *Milton.*

15. Character appropriated in a play. The *parts* of the comedy were judiciously cast and admirably performed.

16. Action; conduct. *Shak.*

17. In *mathematics*, such a portion of any quantity, as when taken a certain number of times, will exactly make that quantity. Thus 3 is a *part* of 12. It is the opposite of *multiple*.

Parts, in the plural, qualities; powers; faculties; accomplishments.

Such licentious *parts* tend for the most part to the hurt of the English— *Spenser.*

Parts, applied to place, signifies quarters, regions, districts.

When he had gone over those *parts*, and had given them much exhortation, he came into Greece. Acts xx.

All *parts* resound with tumults, plaints and fears. *Dryden.*

In general, *parts* is used for excellent or superior endowments, or more than ordinary talents. This is what we understand by the phrase, a *man of parts*.

In good part, as well done; favorably; acceptably; in a friendly manner; not in displeasure.

God accepteth it *in good part* at the hands of faithful man. *Hooker.*

In ill part, as ill done; unfavorably; with displeasure.

For the most part, commonly; oftener than otherwise. *Heylin.*

In part, in some degree or extent; partly.

Logical part, among schoolmen, a division of some universal as its whole; in which sense, species are *parts* of a genus, and individuals are *parts* of a species. *Encyc.*

Physical parts, are of two kinds, homogeneous and heterogeneous; the first is of the same denomination; the second of different ones.

Aliquot part, is a quantity which being repeated any number of times, becomes equal to an integer. Thus 6 is an *aliquot part* of 24.

Aliquant part, is a quantity which being repeated any number of times, becomes greater or less than the whole, as 5 is an *aliquant part* of 17.

Part of speech, in grammar, a sort or class of words of a particular character. Thus the noun is a *part of speech*, denoting the names of things, or those vocal sounds which usage has attached to things. The verb is a *part of speech* expressing motion, action or being.

P'ART, *v. t.* [L. *partio*; Fr. *partir*; W. *parthu*.]

1. To divide, separate or break; to sever into two or more pieces.

2. To divide into shares; to distribute. Acts ii.

3. To separate or disunite, as things which are near each other. Ruth i.

4. To keep asunder; to separate. A narrow sea *parts* England from France.

5. To separate, as combatants. Night *parted* the armies.

6. To secern; to secrete.

The liver minds his own affair,
And *parts* and strains the vital juices. *Prior.*

7. In *seamen's language*, to break; as, the ship *parted* her cables.

8. To separate metals.

P'ART, *v. i.* To be separated, removed or detached.

Powerful hands will not *part*
Easily from possession won with arms. *Milton.*

2. To quit each other.

He wrung Bassanio's hand, and so they *parted*. *Shak.*

3. To take or bid farewell. *Swift.*

4. To have a share.

They shall *part* alike. 1 Sam. xxx.

5. [Fr. *partir*.] To go away; to depart.

Thy father
Embraced me, *parting* for th' Etrurian land. *Dryden.*

6. To break; to be torn asunder. The cable *parted*.

To part with, to quit; to resign; to lose; to be separated from; as, to *part with* near friends.

Celia, for thy sake I *part*
With all that grew so near my heart. *Waller.*

PARTABLE. [See *Partible*.]

P'ARTAGE, *n.* Division; severance; the act of dividing or sharing; *a French word*. [*Little used.*] *Locke.*

PARTA'KE, *v. i.* pret. *partook*; pp. *partaken*. [*part* and *take*.]

1. To take a part, portion or share in common with others; to have a share or part; to participate; usually followed by *of*, sometimes less properly by *in*. All men *partake of* the common bounties of Providence. Clodius was at the feast, but could not *partake of* the enjoyments.

2. To have something of the property, nature, claim or right.

The attorney of the duchy of Lancaster *partakes* partly *of* a judge, and partly *of* an attorney general. *Bacon.*

3. To be admitted; not to be excluded. *Shak.*

PARTA'KE, *v. t.* To have a part in; to share.

My royal father lives;
Let every one *partake* the general joy. *Dryden.*

[This is probably elliptical, *of* being omitted.]

2. To admit to a part. [*Not used.*] *Shak.*

PARTA'KEN, *pp.* Shared with others; participated.

PARTA'KER, *n.* One who has or takes a part, share or portion in common with others; a sharer; a participator; usually followed by *of*.

If the Gentiles have been made *partakers of* their spiritual things— Rom. xv.

Sometimes followed by *in*.

Wish me *partaker in* thy happiness— *Shak.*

If we had been in the days of our fathers, we would not have been *partakers* with them *in* the blood of the prophets. Matt. xxiii.

2. An accomplice; an associate.

When thou sawest a thief, thou consentedst with him, and hast been *partaker* with adulterers. Ps. l.

PARTA'KING, *ppr.* Sharing with others; participating.

PARTA'KING, *n.* An associating; combination in an evil design. *Hale.*

P'ARTED, *pp.* Separated; divided; severed. *Sidney.*

P'ARTER, *n.* One that parts or separates.

PARTERRE, *n.* *parta're.* [Fr.] In *gardening*, a level division of ground furnished with evergreens and flowers; sometimes cut into shell and scroll work with alleys. *Encyc.*

P'ARTIAL, *a.* [Fr. from L. *pars*; It. *parziale*.]

1. Biased to one party; inclined to favor one party in a cause, or one side of a question, more than the other; not indifferent. It is important to justice that a judge should not be *partial*.

Self-love will make men *partial* to themselves and friends. *Locke.*

2. Inclined to favor without reason. Authors are *partial* to their wit, and critics to their judgment.

3. Affecting a part only; not general or universal; not total. It has been much disputed whether the deluge was *partial* or total.

All *partial* evil, universal good. *Pope.*

4. More strongly inclined to one thing than to others. [*Colloquial.*]

5. In *botany*, subordinate; *applied to subdivisions*; as a *partial* umbel or umbellicle; a *partial* peduncle. A *partial* involucre is placed at the foot of a *partial* umbel.

P'ARTIALIST, *n.* One who is partial. [*Unusual.*] *Bp. Morton.*

PARTIALITY, *n.* *parshal'ity.* Inclination to favor one party or one side of a question more than the other; an undue bias of mind towards one party or side, which is apt to warp the judgment. *Partiality* springs from the will and affections, rather than from a love of truth and justice.

2. A stronger inclination to one thing than to others; as a *partiality* for poetry or painting; *a colloquial use*.

P'ARTIALIZE, *v. t.* To render partial. [*Not used.*] *Shak.*

P'ARTIALLY, *adv.* With undue bias of mind to one party or side; with unjust favor or dislike; as, to judge *partially*.

2. In part; not totally; as, the story may be *partially* true; the body may be *partially* affected with disease; the sun and moon are often *partially* eclipsed.

PARTIBIL'ITY, *n.* [See *Partible*.] Susceptibility of division, partition or severance; separability; as the *partibility* of an inheritance.

P'ARTIBLE, *a.* [It. *partibile*, *partire*, to part.]

Divisible; separable; susceptible of severance or partition; as, an estate of inheritance may be *partible*. *Blackstone.*

PARTIC'IPABLE, *a.* [See *Participate*.] That may be participated or shared. *Norris.*

PARTIC'IPANT, *a.* [See *Participate*.] Sharing; having a share or part; followed by *of*.

The prince saw he should confer with one *participant of* more than monkish speculations. *Wotton.*

PARTIC'IPANT, *n.* A partaker; one having a share or part. *Bacon.*

PARTIC'IPATE, *v. i.* [L. *participo; pars*, part, and *capio*, to take.]

1. To partake; to have a share in common with others. The heart of sensibility *participates* in the sufferings of a friend. It is sometimes followed by *of*.

He would *participate of* their wants. *Hayward.*

2. To have part of more things than one.

Few creatures *participate* of the nature of plants and metals both. *Bacon.*

PARTIC'IPATE, *v. t.* To partake; to share; to receive a part of.

Fellowship
Such as I seek, fit to *participate*
All rational delight— *Milton.*

PARTIC'IPATED, *pp.* Shared in common with others; partaken.

PARTIC'IPATING, *ppr.* Having a part or share; partaking.

PARTICIPA'TION, *n.* The state of sharing in common with others; as a *participation* of joys or sorrows.

2. The act or state of receiving or having part of something.

Those deities are so by *participation*, and subordinate to the Supreme. *Stillingfleet.*

3. Distribution; division into shares. *Raleigh.*

PARTIC'IPATIVE, *a.* Capable of participating.

PARTICIP'IAL, *a.* [L. *participialis*. See *Participle.*]

1. Having the nature and use of a participle.
2. Formed from a participle; as a *participial* noun.

PARTICIP'IALLY, *adv.* In the sense or manner of a participle.

P'ARTICIPLE, *n.* [L. *participium*, from *participo; pars*, part, and *capio*, to take.]

1. In *grammar*, a word so called because it partakes of the properties of a noun and of a verb; as *having, making*, in English; *habens, faciens*, in Latin. The English participles *having, making*, become nouns by prefixing *the* to them; as *the having* of property; *the making* of instruments. But all participles do not partake of the properties of a noun, as the passive participles for example, *had, made.*

Participles sometimes lose the properties of a verb and become adjectives, as *willing*, in the phrase, a *willing* heart; *engaging*, as *engaging* manners; *accomplished*, as an *accomplished* orator.

2. Any thing that participates of different things. [*Not used.*] *Bacon.*

P'ARTICLE, *n.* [It. *particola*; Fr. *particule*; L. *particula*, from *pars*, part.]

1. A minute part or portion of matter; as a *particle* of sand, of lime or of light.
2. In *physics*, a minute part of a body, an aggregation or collection of which constitutes the whole body or mass. The word is sometimes used in the same sense as atom, in the ancient Epicurean philosophy, and corpuscle in the latter. In this sense, *particles* are the elements or constituent parts of bodies. *Encyc.*
3. Any very small portion or part; as, he has not a *particle* of patriotism or virtue; he would not resign a *particle* of his property.
4. In *the Latin church*, a crumb or little piece of consecrated bread. *Encyc.*
5. In *grammar*, a word that is not varied or inflected; as a preposition.

Organic particles, very minute moving bodies, perceptible only by the help of the microscope, discovered in the semen of animals. *Encyc.*

PARTIC'ULAR, *a.* [Sp. Port. *id.*; It. *particolare*; Fr. *particulier*; Low L. *particularis*, from *particula.*]

1. Pertaining to a single person or thing; not general; as, this remark has a *particular* application.
2. Individual; noting or designating a single thing by way of distinction. Each plant has its *particular* nutriment. Most persons have a *particular* trait of character. He alludes to a *particular* person.
3. Noting some property or thing peculiar.

Of this prince there is little *particular* memory. *Bacon.*

4. Attentive to things single or distinct; minute. I have been *particular* in examining the reasons of this law.
5. Single; not general.
6. Odd; singular; having something that eminently distinguishes one from others.
7. Singularly nice in taste; as a man very *particular* in his diet or dress.
8. Special; more than ordinary. He has brought no *particular* news.
9. Containing a part only; as a *particular* estate, precedent to the estate in remainder. *Blackstone.*
10. Holding a particular estate; as a *particular* tenant. *Blackstone.*

PARTIC'ULAR, *n.* A single instance; a single point.

I must reserve some *particulars*, which it is not lawful for me to reveal. *Bacon.*

2. A distinct, separate or minute part; as, he told me all the *particulars* of the story. *Addison.*
3. An individual; a private person. *L'Estrange.*
4. Private interest; as, they apply their minds to those branches of public prayer, wherein their own *particular* is moved. [*Not in use.*] *Hooker.*
5. Private character; state of an individual.

For his *particular*, I will receive him gladly. [*Not in use.*] *Shak.*

6. A minute detail of things singly enumerated.

The reader has a *particular* of the books wherein this law was written. [*Not in use.*] *Ayliffe.*

In particular, specially; peculiarly; distinctly.

This, *in particular*, happens to the lungs. *Blackmore.*

PARTICULAR'ITY, *n.* Distinct notice or specification of particulars.

—Even descending to *particularities*, what kingdoms he should overcome. *Sidney.*

2. Singleness; individuality; single act; single case. *Hooker.*
3. Petty account; minute incident.

To see the titles that were most agreeable to such an emperor—with the like *particularities*— *Addison.*

4. Something belonging to single persons. *Shak.*
5. Something peculiar or singular.

I saw an old heathen altar with this *particularity*, that it was hollowed like a dish at one end, but not the end on which the sacrifice was laid. *Addison.*

6. Minuteness in detail. He related the story with great *particularity.*

PARTIC'ULARIZE, *v. t.* To mention distinctly or in particulars; to enumerate or specify in detail.

He not only boasts of his parentage as an Israelite, but *particularizes* his descent from Benjamin. *Atterbury.*

PARTIC'ULARIZE, *v. i.* To be attentive to single things. *Herbert.*

PARTIC'ULARLY, *adv.* Distinctly; singly. *South.*

2. In an especial manner.

This exact propriety of Virgil I *particularly* regarded as a great part of his character. *Dryden.*

PARTICULATE, to mention, is not in use.

P'ARTING, *ppr.* [from *part.*] Dividing; separating; breaking in pieces.

2. *a.* Given at separation; as a *parting* kiss or look.
3. Departing; declining; as the *parting* day. *Pope.*

P'ARTING, *n.* Division; separation. Ezek. xxi.

2. In *chimistry*, an operation by which gold and silver are separated from each other by different menstruums.
3. In *seamen's language*, the breaking of a cable by violence.

P'ARTISAN, *n.* *s* as *z*. [Fr. from *parti*, *partir.*]

1. An adherent to a party or faction. *Addison.*
2. In *war*, the commander of a party or detachment of troops, sent on a special enterprise; hence,
3. By way of distinction, a person able in commanding a party, or dextrous in obtaining intelligence, intercepting convoys or otherwise annoying an enemy.
4. A commander's leading staff. *Ainsworth.*
5. A kind of halbert. [Fr. *pertuisane*; It. *partigiano.*]

P'ARTITE, *a.* [L. *partitus*, from *partio*, to divide. See *Part.*]

In *botany*, divided. A *partite* leaf is a simple leaf separated down to the base. *Lee.*

PARTI''TION, *n.* [L. *partitio*, from *partio*, to divide.]

1. The act of dividing, or state of being divided.
2. Division; separation; distinction.

And good from bad find no *partition*. *Shak.*

3. Separate part; as lodged in a small *partition*. *Milton.*
4. That by which different parts are separated; as a *partition* of wood or stone in a building.
5. Part where separation is made.

No sight could pass
Betwixt the nice *partitions* of the grass. *Dryden.*

6. Division of an estate into severalty, which is done by deed of partition. *Blackstone.*

PARTI''TION, *v. t.* To divide into distinct parts; as, to *partition* the floor of a house.

2. To divide into shares; as, to *partition* an estate.

P'ARTITIVE, *a.* In *grammar*, distributive; as a noun *partitive.*

P'ARTITIVELY, *adv.* In a partitive manner; distributively. *Lilly.*

P'ARTLET, *n.* [from *part.*] A ruff; a band or collar for the neck. *Obs.* *Hall.*

2. A hen. *Obs.* *Shak.*

P'ARTLY, *adv.* In part; in some measure or degree; not wholly.

P'ARTNER, *n.* [from *part.*] One who partakes or shares with another; a partaker; an associate; as, she is *partner* of my life, of my joys, of my griefs.

Those of the race of Shem were no *partners* in the unbelieving work of the tower. *Raleigh.*

2. An associate in any business or occupation; a joint owner of stock or capital, employed in commerce, manufactures or other business. Men are sometimes *partners* in a single voyage or adventure, sometimes in a firm or standing company.

3. One who dances with another, either male or female, as in a contra dance.

4. A husband or wife.

P'ARTNER, *v. t.* To join; to associate with a partner. [*Little used.*] *Shak.*

Partners, in a ship, pieces of plank nailed round the scuttles in a deck where the masts are placed; also, the scuttles themselves. *Mar. Dict.*

P'ARTNERSHIP, *n.* The association of two or more persons for the purpose of undertaking and prosecuting any business, particularly trade or manufactures, at their joint expense. In this case, the connection is formed by contract; each partner furnishing a part of the capital stock and being entitled to a proportional share of profit, or subject to a proportional share of loss; or one or more of the partners may furnish money or stock, and the other or others contribute their services. The duration of the partnership may be limited by the contract, or it may be left indefinite, subject to be dissolved by mutual agreement. A partnership or association of this kind is a standing or permanent company, and is denominated a *firm* or *house.* We say, A and B entered into *partnership* for the importation and sale of goods, or for manufacturing cotton or glass.

Partnerships may be and usually are associations of private persons, not incorporated. In other cases, the company is incorporated. Banking companies in the United States are usually incorporated, and are essentially partnerships, but do not bear that name. Manufacturing companies are also frequently incorporated.

2. Joint interest or property. *Dryden.*

PARTOOK', *pret.* of *partake.*

P'ARTRIDGE, *n.* [Fr. *perdrix*; It. *pernice*; Sp. *perdiz*; L. *perdix*; Gr. περδιξ; D. *patrys*; Ir. *patrisg.*]

A wild fowl of the genus Tetrao. (Linn.) Latham arranges the partridge and quail in a genus under the name of *Perdix*, and assigns the grous to the genus *Tetrao.* The partridge is esteemed a great delicacy at the table.

The term *partridge* is applied in Pennsylvania to the bird called quail in New England, a peculiar species of Perdix; in New England it is applied to the ruffed grous, a species of Tetrao.

PARTU'RIATE, *v. i.* [L. *parturio*, from *partus*, birth, from *pario*, to *bear.*] To bring forth young. [*Little used.*]

PARTU'RIENT, *a.* [L. *parturiens.*] Bringing forth or about to bring forth young.

PARTURI''TION, *n.* [L. *parturio.*] The act of bringing forth or being delivered of young. *Encyc.*

P'ARTY, *n.* [Fr. *partie*, from L. *pars.* See *Part.*]

1. A number of persons united in opinion or design, in opposition to others in the community. It differs from *faction*, in implying a less dishonorable association, or more justifiable designs. *Parties* exist in all governments; and free governments are the hot-beds of *party.* Formerly, the political *parties* in England were called whigs and tories.

2. One of two litigants; the plaintiff or defendant in a lawsuit.

The cause of both *parties* shall come before the judges. Ex. xxii.

3. One concerned or interested in an affair. This man was not a *party* to the trespass or affray. He is not a *party* to the contract or agreement.

4. Side; persons engaged against each other.

The peace both *parties* want, is like to last. *Dryden.*

Small *parties* make up in diligence what they want in numbers. *Johnson.*

5. Cause; side.

Ægle came in to make their *party* good. *Dryden.*

6. A select company invited to an entertainment; as a dining *party*, a tea *party*, an evening *party.*

7. A single person distinct from or opposed to another.

If the jury found that the *party* slain was of English race, it had been adjudged felony. *Davies.*

8. In *military affairs*, a detachment or small number of troops sent on a particular duty, as to intercept the enemy's convoy, to reconnoiter, to seek forage, to flank the enemy, &c.

Party is used to qualify other words and may be considered either as part of a compound word, or as an adjective; as *party* man, *party* rage, *party* disputes, &c.

P'ARTY-COLORED, *a.* Having divers colors; as a *party-colored* plume; a *party-colored* flower.

P'ARTY-JURY, *n.* A jury consisting of half natives and half foreigners.

P'ARTY-MAN, *n.* One of a party; usually, a factious man; a man of violent party principles; an abettor of a party.

P'ARTY-SPIRIT, *n.* The spirit that supports a party.

P'ARTY-WALL, *n.* A wall that separates one house from the next. *Moxon.*

PAR'U, *n.* A singular American fish.

P'ARVIS, *n.* [Fr.] A church or church porch. [*Not used.*] *Chaucer.*

P'ARVITUDE, } *n.* Littleness. [*Not used.*]
P'ARVITY, }

PAS, *n.* [Fr. *pas*, a step.] Right of going foremost; precedence. [*Not used.*] *Arbuthnot.*

PASCH, *n.* [See *Paschal.*] The passover; the feast of Easter. [*Not used.*]

PAS'CHAL, *a.* [L. *pascha*; Gr. πασχα; from the Heb.]

Pertaining to the passover, or to Easter.

PASCH-EGG, *n.* An egg stained and presented to young persons, about the time of Easter. [*Local.*]

PASH, *n.* [Sp. *faz*, L. *facies*, face.] A face. [*Not used.*] *Hanmer.*

2. A blow. [*Not used.*]

PASH, *v. t.* To strike; to strike down. [*Not used.*] *Dryden.*

PASHAW', *n.* [Pers. پاشا pashaw.] In *the Turkish dominions*, a viceroy, governor or commander; a bashaw. *Castle. Eaton.*

PASHAW'LIC, *n.* The jurisdiction of a pashaw.

PASIG'RAPHY, *n.* [Gr. πας, all, and γραφη, writing.]

A system of universal writing, or a manner of writing that may be understood and used by all nations. *Good.*

PASQUE-FLOWER, *n.* *pask'-flower.* A flower, a species of anemone. *Fam. of Plants.*

PAS'QUIL, } *n.* A mutilated statue at
PAS'QUIN, } Rome, in a corner of the palace of Ursini, so called from a cobbler of that name who was remarkable for his sneers and gibes. On this statue it has been customary to paste satiric papers. Hence, a lampoon. *Encyc. Cyc.*

PAS'QUIL, }
PAS'QUIN, } *v. t.* To lampoon; to satirize.
PASQUINA'DE, } *Burton.*

PAS'QUILER, *n.* A lampooner. *Burton.*

PASQUINA'DE, *n.* A lampoon or satirical writing. *Tatler.*

P'ASS, *v. i.* [Fr. *passer*, It. *passare*, Sp. *pasar*, Port. *passar*, to pass; G. *pass*, fit, which is the Eng. *pat*, and as a noun, a *pass*, a defile, an ambling, *pace*; *passen*, to be fit, to suit; D. *pas*, a *pace*, a step, a *pass*, a passage, a defile, time, season; *van pas*, fit, convenient, *pat* in time; *passen*, to fit, to try, to mind, tend, or wait on, to make ready, to *pass*; Dan. *pas*, a *pass* or passport, a mode or medium; *passer*, to be fit, to suit, to be applicable; *passerer*, to pass, to come or go over; Sw. *pass*, a pass or passage, a passport; *passa*, to fit, to suit, to adapt, to become; *passera*, to pass; W. *pâs*, that is expulsive, that causes to pass, a *pass*, an exit, a cough, hooping-cough; *pasiaw*, to pass, to cause an exit, to expel; Sp. *pasar*, to pass, go or travel, to bring or convey, to penetrate, to exceed or surpass, to depart, to suffer, bear, undergo, [L. *patior*, whence *passion*,] to happen or come to pass; *pasear*, to walk; *paseo*, a walking, a gait; *paso*, a *pace*, a step, gait, [Gr. πατεω]; It. *passare*, to pass; *passo*, a pace, a step; *passabile*, tolerable; *passibile*, suffering. We observe that this word unites *pass*, the L. *patior*, to suffer, and *peto*, *competo*, in the sense of *fit.* The Gr. πατεω, to walk or step, and πασχω, to suffer, are from the same root. The word *pass* coincides with L. *passus*, a step, and this is from *pando*, to extend; *n* being casual, the original word was *pado.* The radical sense is to stretch, reach, extend, to open; a *pace* is the reach of the foot, and *fitness* is from reaching or coming to, like *convenient.* We learn from this word that the sense of *suffering* is from *extending*, *holding on*, or *continuing*. See ברא in the introduction. Ar. فَاتَ to pass; Heb. פסח, פשע, Ch. פסע. Class Bd. No. 45. 64. and Bs or Bz. No. 52. 53. 70.]

1. To move, in almost any manner; to go; to proceed from one place to another. A man may *pass* on foot, on horseback or in a carriage; a bird and a meteor *pass* through the air; a ship *passes* on or through the water; light *passes* from the sun to the planets; it *passes* from the sun to the earth in about eight minutes.

2. To move from one state to another; to alter or change, or to be changed in condition; as, to *pass* from health to sickness; to *pass* from just to unjust. *Temple.*

3. To vanish; to disappear; to be lost. In this sense, we usually say, to *pass away*.

> Beauty is a charm, but soon the charm will *pass*. *Dryden.*

4. To be spent; to go on or away progressively.

> The time when the thing existed, is the idea of that space of duration which *passed* between some fixed period and the being of that thing. *Locke.*

5. To die; to depart from life. [*Little used.*] *Shak.*

6. To be in any state; to undergo; with *under*; as, to *pass under* the rod.

7. To be enacted; to receive the sanction of a legislative house or body by a majority of votes.

> Neither of these bills has yet *passed* the house of commons. *Swift.*

8. To be current; to gain reception or to be generally received. Bank bills *pass* as a substitute for coin.

> False eloquence *passeth* only where true is not understood. *Felton.*

9. To be regarded; to be received in opinion or estimation.

> This will not *pass* for a fault in him, till it is proved to be one in us. *Atterbury.*

10. To occur; to be present; to take place; as, to notice what *passes* in the mind. *Watts.*

11. To be done.

> Provided no indirect act *pass* upon our prayers to defile them. *Taylor.*

12. To determine; to give judgment or sentence.

> Though well we may not *pass* upon his life. *Shak.*

13. To thrust; to make a push in fencing or fighting. *Shak.*

14. To omit; to suffer to go unheeded or neglected. We saw the act, but let it *pass*.

15. To move through any duct or opening; as, substances in the stomach that will not *pass*, nor be converted into aliment. *Arbuthnot.*

16. To percolate; to be secreted; as juices that *pass* from the glands into the mouth.

17. To be in a tolerable state.

> A middling sort of man was left well enough by his father to *pass*, but he could never think he had enough, so long as any had more. *L'Estrange.*

18. To be transferred from one owner to another. The land article *passed* by livery and seizin.

19. To go beyond bounds. *Obs.* For this we generally use *surpass*. *Shak.*

20. To run or extend; as a line or other thing. The north limit of Massachusetts *passes* three miles north of the Merrimac.

To come to pass, to happen; to arrive; to come; to be; to exist; *a phrase much used in the Scriptures.*

To pass away, to move from sight; to vanish.

2. To be spent; to be lost.

> A good part of their lives *passes away* without thinking. *Locke.*

To pass by, to move near and beyond. He *passed by* as we stood in the road.

To pass on, to proceed.

To pass over, to go or move from side to side; to cross; as, to *pass over* to the other side.

To pass into, to unite and blend, as two substances or colors, in such a manner that it is impossible to tell where one ends and the other begins.

P'ASS, *v. t.* To go beyond. The sun has *passed* the meridian. The young man has not *passed* the age of frivolousness.

2. To go through or over; as, to *pass* a river.

3. To spend; to live through; as, to *pass* time; to *pass* the night in revelry, and the day in sleep.

4. To cause to move; to send; as, to *pass* the bottle from one guest to another; to *pass* a pauper from one town to another; to *pass* a rope round a yard; to *pass* the blood from the right to the left ventricle of the heart. *Derham.*

5. To cause to move hastily.

> I had only time to *pass* my eye over the medals, which are in great number. *Addison.*

6. To transfer from one owner to another; to sell or assign; as, to *pass* land from A to B by deed; to *pass* a note or bill.

7. To strain; to cause to percolate; as, to *pass* wine through a filter. *Bacon.*

8. To utter; to pronounce; as, to *pass* compliments; to *pass* sentence or judgment; to *pass* censure on another's works. *Watts.*

9. To procure or cause to go.

> Waller *passed* over five thousand horse and foot by Newbridge. *Clarendon.*

10. To put an end to.

> This night
> We'll *pass* the business privately and well. *Shak.*

11. To omit; to neglect either to do or to mention.

> I *pass* their warlike pomp, their proud array. *Dryden.*

12. To transcend; to transgress or go beyond; as, to *pass* the bounds of moderation.

13. To admit; to allow; to approve and receive as valid or just; as, to *pass* an account at the war-office.

14. To approve or sanction by a constitutional or legal majority of votes; as, the house of representatives *passed* the bill. Hence,

15. To enact; to carry through all the forms necessary to give validity; as, the legislature *passed* the bill into a law.

16. To impose fraudulently; as, she *passed* the child on her husband for a boy. *Dryden.*

17. To practice artfully; to cause to succeed; as, to *pass* a trick on one.

18. To surpass; to excel; to exceed.

19. To thrust; to make a push in fencing.

> To see thee fight, to see thee *pass* thy puncto. *Shak.*

To pass away, to spend; to waste; as, to *pass away* the flower of life in idleness.

To pass by, to pass near and beyond.

2. To overlook; to excuse; to forgive; not to censure or punish; as, to *pass by* a crime or fault.

3. To neglect; to disregard.

> Certain passages of Scripture we cannot *pass by* without injury to truth. *Burnet.*

To pass over, to move from side to side; to cross; as, to *pass over* a river or mountain.

2. To omit; to overlook or disregard. He *passed over* one charge without a reply.

P'ASS, *n.* [W. *pâs.*] A narrow passage, entrance or avenue; a narrow or difficult place of entrance and exit; as a *pass* between mountains. *Encyc. Clarendon.*

2. A passage; a road. *Raleigh.*

3. Permission to pass, to go or to come; a license to pass; a passport.

> A gentleman had a *pass* to go beyond the seas. *Clarendon.*
>
> A ship sailing under the flag and *pass* of an enemy. *Kent.*

4. An order for sending vagrants or impotent persons to their place of abode. *Johnson.*

5. In fencing and fighting, a thrust; a push; attempt to stab or strike; as, to make a *pass* at an antagonist.

6. State; condition or extreme case; extremity.

> To what a *pass* are our minds brought. *Sidney.*
>
> Matters have been brought to this *pass*— *South.*

P'ASS-PAROLE, *n.* [*pass* and *parole.*] In *military affairs*, a command given at the head of an army and communicated by word of mouth to the rear. *Encyc.*

P'ASSABLE, *a.* [It. *passabile.*] That may be passed, traveled or navigated. The roads are not *passable*. The stream is *passable* in boats.

2. That may be penetrated; as a substance *passable* by a fluid.

3. Current; receivable; that may be or is transferred from hand to hand; as bills *passable* in lieu of coin. False coin is not *passable*.

4. Popular; well received. *Bacon.*

5. Supportable. [This should be *passible.*] *Dryden.*

P'ASSABLY, *adv.* Tolerably. [See *Passibly.*]

PASSA'DE, PASSA'DO, } *n.* A push or thrust.

PASSA'DE, *n.* [Fr.] In *the menage*, a turn or course of a horse backwards or forwards on the same spot of ground. *Encyc.*

P'ASSAGE, *n.* [Fr. *passage*; Sp. *pasage*; It. *passaggio.*]

1. The act of passing or moving by land or water, or through the air or other substance; as the *passage* of a man or a carriage; the *passage* of a ship or a fowl; the *passage* of light or a meteor; the *passage* of fluids through the pores of the body, or from the glands. Clouds intercept the *passage* of solar rays.

2. The time of passing from one place to another. What *passage* had you? We

had a *passage* of twenty five days to Havre de Grace, and of thirty eight days from England.

3. Road; way; avenue; a place where men or things may pass or be conveyed. *Temple.*

And with his pointed dart,
Explores the nearest *passage* to his heart. *Dryden.*

4. Entrance or exit.

What! are my doors opposed against my *passage?* *Shak.*

5. Right of passing; as, to engage a *passage* on board a ship bound to India.

6. Occurrence; event; incident; that which happens; as a remarkable *passage* in the life of Newton. [See the Spanish verb, supra. This sense is obsolescent.]

7. A passing away; decay. [*Little used.*] *Shak.*

8. Intellectual admittance; mental reception.

Among whom I expect this treatise will have a fairer *passage* than among those deeply imbued with other principles. *Digby.*

9. Manner of being conducted; management.

On consideration of the conduct and *passage* of affairs in former times— *Davies.*

10. Part of a book or writing; a single clause, place or part of indefinite extent.

How commentators each dark *passage* shun. *Young.*

11. Enactment; the act of carrying through all the regular forms necessary to give validity; as the *passage* of a law, or of a bill into a law, by a legislative body. *Hopkinson. Wheaton's Rep.*

Bird of passage, a fowl that passes at certain seasons from one climate to another, as in autumn to the south to avoid the winter's cold, and in spring to the north for breeding. Hence the phrase is sometimes applied to a man who has no fixed residence.

P'ASSAGER, *n.* [Fr. from *passage*; It. *passaggiere.*]

A traveler or voyager; one who passes or journeys on foot, in a vehicle, or in a ship or boat. This word is usually written corruptly *passenger*, and the first vowel is often short.

P'ASSED, } *pp.* Gone by; done; accomplished; ended.
P'AST, }

2. Enacted; having received all the formalities necessary to constitute a law.

P'ASSENGER, *n.* One who is traveling, as in a public coach, or in a ship, or on foot. This is the usual, though corrupt orthography.

Passenger falcon, a kind of migratory hawk. *Ainsworth.*

P'ASSER, *n.* One that passes; a passenger. *Rowe.*

P'ASSERINE, *a.* [L. *passer*, a sparrow.] Pertaining to sparrows, or to the order of birds to which sparrows belong, the *Passeres.*

PASSIBIL'ITY, *n.* [Fr. *passibilité*, from *passible.* See *Passion.*]

The quality or capacity of receiving impressions from external agents; aptness to feel or suffer. *Hakewill.*

PAS'SIBLE, *a.* [Fr. *passible*; It. *passibile.* See *Passion.*]

Susceptible of feeling or of impressions from external agents.

Apollinarius held even Deity to be *passible.* *Hooker.*

PASSIBLENESS, the same as *passibility.*

P'ASSING, *ppr.* Moving; proceeding.

2. *a.* Exceeding; surpassing; eminent. *Fairfax.*

3. Adverbially used to enforce or enhance the meaning of another word; exceedingly; as *passing* fair; *passing* strange.

P'ASSING-BELL, *n.* The bell that rings at the hour of death to obtain prayers for the *passing* soul. It is also used for the bell that rings immediately after death. *Swift.*

P'ASSINGLY, *adv.* Exceedingly. *Obs.* *Wickliffe.*

P'ASSING-NOTE, *n.* In *music*, a note introduced between two others for the purpose of softening a distance or melodizing a passage. *Busby.*

PAS'SION, *n.* [L. *passio*, from *patior*, to suffer.]

1. The impression or effect of an external agent upon a body; that which is suffered or received.

A body at rest affords us no idea of any active power to move, and when set in motion, it is rather a *passion* than an action in it. *Locke.*

2. Susceptibility of impressions from external agents.

The differences of moldable and not moldable, &c., and many other *passions* of matter, are plebeian notions. [*Little used.*] *Bacon.*

3. Suffering; emphatically, the last suffering of the Savior.

To whom also he showed himself alive after his *passion*, by many infallible proofs. Acts i.

4. The feeling of the mind, or the sensible effect of impression; excitement, perturbation or agitation of mind; as desire, fear, hope, joy, grief, love, hatred. The eloquence of the orator is employed to move the *passions.*

5. Violent agitation or excitement of mind, particularly such as is occasioned by an offense, injury or insult; hence, violent anger. *Watts.*

6. Zeal; ardor; vehement desire.

When statesmen are ruled by faction and interest, they can have no *passion* for the glory of their country. *Addison.*

7. Love.

He owned his *passion* for Amestris. *Rowe.*

8. Eager desire; as a violent *passion* for fine clothes. *Swift.*

PAS'SION, *v. i.* To be extremely agitated. [*Not used.*] *Shak.*

PAS'SION-FLOWER, *n.* A flower and plant of the genus Passiflora.

PAS'SION-WEEK, *n.* The week immediately preceding the festival of Easter; so called because in that week our Savior's passion and death took place.

PAS'SIONARY, *n.* A book in which are described the sufferings of saints and martyrs. *Warton.*

PAS'SIONATE, *a.* [It. *passionato*; Fr. *passionné.*]

1. Easily moved to anger; easily excited or agitated by injury or insult; *applied to persons.*

Homer's Achilles is haughty and *passionate.* *Prior.*

2. Highly excited; vehement; warm; *applied to things*; as *passionate* affection; *passionate* desire; *passionate* concern.

3. Expressing strong emotion; animated; as *passionate* eloquence.

PAS'SIONATE, *v. t.* To affect with passion; to express passionately. [*Not used.*] *Spenser. Shak.*

PAS'SIONATELY, *adv.* With passion; with strong feeling; ardently; vehemently; as, to covet any thing *passionately*; to be *passionately* fond.

2. Angrily; with vehement resentment; as, to speak *passionately.*

PAS'SIONATENESS, *n.* State of being subject to passion or anger.

2. Vehemence of mind. *Boyle.*

PAS'SIONED, *a.* Disordered; violently affected. *Spenser.*

2. Expressing passion. *Spenser.*

PAS'SIONLESS, *a.* Not easily excited to anger; of a calm temper. *Shelton.*

2. Void of passion.

P'ASSIVE, *a.* [It. *passivo*; Sp. *pasivo*; Fr. *passif*; L. *passivus*, from *passus*, *patior*, to suffer.]

1. Suffering; not acting, receiving or capable of receiving impressions from external agents. We were *passive* spectators, not actors in the scene.

The mind is wholly *passive* in the reception of all its simple ideas. *Locke.*

God is not in any respect *passive.* *Bradwardine.*

2. Unresisting; not opposing; receiving or suffering without resistance; as *passive* obedience; *passive* submission to the laws.

Passive verb, in grammar, is a verb which expresses passion, or the effect of an action of some agent; as in L. *doceor*, I am taught; in English, she *is loved* and *admired* by her friends; he *is assailed* by slander.

Passive obedience, as used by writers on government, denotes not only quiet unresisting submission to power, but implies the denial of the right of resistance, or the recognition of the duty to submit in all cases to the existing government.

Passive prayer, among mystic divines, is a suspension of the activity of the soul or intellectual faculties, the soul remaining quiet and yielding only to the impulses of grace. *Encyc.*

Passive commerce, trade in which the productions of a country are carried by foreigners in their own bottoms. [See *Active commerce.*]

P'ASSIVELY, *adv.* With a passive nature or temper; with a temper disposed to submit to the acts of external agents, without resistance. *Dryden.*

2. Without agency. *Pearson.*

3. According to the form of the passive verb. *Lilly.*

P'ASSIVENESS, *n.* Quality of receiving impressions from external agents or causes; as the *passiveness* of matter.

2. Passibility; capacity of suffering.

We shall lose our *passiveness* with our being. *Decay of Piety.*

3. Patience; calmness; unresisting submission. *Fell.*

PASSIV'ITY, *n.* Passiveness, which see. [*Little used.*] *Cheyne.*

2. The tendency of a body to persevere in a given state, either of motion or rest, till disturbed by another body. *Good.*

P'ASSLESS, *a.* Having no passage. *Cowley.*

P'ASSOVER, *n.* [*pass* and *over.*] A feast of the Jews, instituted to commemorate the providential escape of the Hebrews, in Egypt, when God smiting the first-born of the Egyptians, *passed over* the houses of the Israelites, which were marked with the blood of the paschal lamb.

2. The sacrifice offered at the feast of the passover.

P'ASSPŌRT, *n.* [Fr. *passeport; passer*, to pass, and *porter*, to carry; It. *passaporto;* Sp. *pasaporte.*]

1. A written license from a king or other proper authority, granting permission or safe conduct for one to pass through his territories, or to pass from one country to another, or to navigate a particular sea without hindrance or molestation.

2. A license for importing or exporting contraband goods or movables without paying the usual duties.

3. That which enables one to pass with safety or certainty.

His *passport* is his innocence and grace. *Dryden.*

PAS'SY-MEASURE, *n.* [It. *pasamezzo*, middle pace or step.]

An old stately kind of dance; a cinque-pace. *Obs.* *Shak.*

P'AST, *pp.* of *pass.* Gone by or beyond; not present; not future.

2. Spent; ended; accomplished.

P'AST, *n.* Elliptically, past time; as indemnity for the *past.* *Fenton.*

P'AST, *prep.* Beyond in time. Heb. xi.

2. Having lost; not possessing; as, he was *past* sense of feeling.

3. Beyond; out of reach of; as, he was *past* cure or help.

Love, when once *past* government, is consequently *past* shame. *L'Estrange.*

4. Beyond; further than; as *past* the boundary.

5. Above; more than.

The northern Irish Scots have bows not *past* three quarters of a yard long. *Spenser.*

[*Not now used.*]

6. After; beyond in time. The company assembled at half *past* seven, that is, at half an hour after seven.

PĀSTE, *n.* [Fr. *pâte*, for *paste;* It. Sp. *pasta.* Qu. L. *pistus*, or Gr. *πασσω*, to sprinkle, or some root which signifies to mix and knead.]

1. A soft composition of substances, as flour moistened with water or milk and kneaded, or any kind of earth moistened and formed to the consistence of dough. *Paste* made of flour is used in cookery; *paste* made of flour or earth, is used in various arts and manufactures, as a cement.

2. An artificial mixture in imitation of precious stones or gems, used in the glass trade. *Encyc.*

3. In *mineralogy*, the mineral substance in which other minerals are imbedded.

PĀSTE, *v. t.* To unite or cement with paste; to fasten with paste. *Watts.*

PĀSTEBŌARD, *n.* A species of thick paper formed of several single sheets pasted one upon another, or by macerating paper and casting it in molds, &c. It is used for the covering of books, for bonnets, &c.

PAS'TEL, *n.* A plant, the woad, of the genus Isatis. *Ed. Encyc.* *Ainsworth.*

2. A coloring substance. [Sp.]

PAS'TERN, *n.* [Fr. *pâturon.*] The part of a horse's leg between the joint next the foot and the coronet of the hoof. *Encyc.*

2. The human leg; in contempt. *Dryden.*

PAS'TERN-JOINT, *n.* The joint in a horse's leg next the foot.

PASTIC'CIO, *n.* [It.] A medley; an olio. *Swinburne.*

PAS'TIL, *n.* [L. *pastillus;* It. *pastiglia;* Fr. *pastille.* See *Paste.*]

1. A roll of paste, or a kind of paste made of different colors ground with gum-water in order to make crayons. *Encyc.*

2. In *pharmacy*, a dry composition of sweet smelling resins, aromatic woods, &c. burnt to clear and scent the air of a room. *Encyc.*

P'ASTIME, *n.* [*pass* and *time.*] Sport; amusement; diversion; that which amuses and serves to make time pass agreeably. *Milton.* *Watts.*

P'ASTIME, *v. i.* To sport; to use diversion. [*Little used.*]

P'ASTOR, *n.* [L. from *pasco, pastum*, to feed, Gr. *βοσκω*, W. *pesgi*, Arm. *pasqa*, Fr. *paître*, for *paistre*, like *naître*, from L. *nasco;* Russ. *pastovuyu, pasu.* It seems to be allied to *bush*, D. *bosch*, G. *busch*, Sw. *buska*, Dan. *busk*, as *browse* is to *brush;* It. *brusca;* Gr. *βρωσκω.*]

1. A shepherd; one that has the care of flocks and herds. *Dryden.*

2. A minister of the gospel who has the charge of a church and congregation, whose duty is to watch over the people of his charge, and instruct them in the sacred doctrines of the christian religion. *South.* *Swift.*

P'ASTORAL, *a.* [L. *pastoralis.*] Pertaining to shepherds; as a *pastoral* life; *pastoral* manners.

2. Descriptive of the life of shepherds; as a *pastoral* poem.

3. Relating to the care of souls, or to the pastor of a church; as *pastoral* care or duties; a *pastoral* letter. *Hooker.* *Dryden.*

Piety is the life and soul of *pastoral* fidelity. *H. Humphrey.*

P'ASTORAL, *n.* A poem describing the life and manners of shepherds, or a poem in imitation of the action of a shepherd, and in which the speakers take upon themselves the character of shepherds; an idyl; a bucolic. *Pope.*

A *pastoral* is a poem in which any action or passion is represented by its effects on a country life. *Rambler.*

P'ASTORATE, *n.* The office, state or jurisdiction of a spiritual pastor. *President Stiles.* *Tooke.*

P'ASTORLIKE, } *a.* Becoming a pastor.
P'ASTORLY, } *Milton.*

P'ASTORSHIP, *n.* The office or rank of pastor. *Bull.*

PĀSTRY, *n.* [from *paste.*] Things in general which are made of paste, or of which paste constitutes a principal ingredient, as pies, tarts, cake and the like.

2. The place where pastry is made. *Shak.*

PĀSTRY-COOK, *n.* One whose occupation is to make and sell articles made of paste. *Arbuthnot.*

P'ASTURABLE, *a.* [from *pasture.*] Fit for pasture.

P'ASTURAGE, *n.* [Fr. *pâturage.* See *Pasture.*]

1. The business of feeding or grazing cattle. *Spenser.*

2. Grazing ground; land appropriated to grazing. *Addison.*

3. Grass for feed. *Arbuthnot.*

P'ASTURE, *n.* [Fr. *pâture*, for *pasture*, from L. *pasco, pastum*, to feed, Gr. *βοσκω.*]

1. Grass for the food of cattle; the food of cattle taken by grazing. *Brown.*

2. Ground covered with grass appropriated for the food of cattle. The farmer has a hundred acres of *pasture.* It is sometimes called *pasture-land.*

3. Human culture; education. [*Not used.*] *Dryden.*

Common of pasture, is the right of feeding cattle on another's ground.

P'ASTURE, *v. t.* To feed on grass or to supply grass for food. We apply the word to *persons*, as the farmer *pastures* fifty oxen; or to *ground*, as the land will *pasture* fifty oxen.

P'ASTURE, *v. i.* To graze; to take food by eating grass from the ground. *Milton.*

PĀSTY, *a.* Like paste; of the consistence of paste. *Cooper.*

PĀSTY, *n.* [from *paste.*] A pie made of paste and baked without a dish. *Pope.* *King.*

PAT, *a.* [G. *pass;* D. *pas.* See *Fit* and *Pass.*] Fit; convenient; exactly suitable either as to time or place. [Not an elegant word, but admissible in burlesque.] *Atterbury.* *Swift.*

PAT, *adv.* Fitly; conveniently. *Shak.*

PAT, *n.* [W. *fat*, a blow; *fatiaw*, to strike lightly, to *pat.* Qu. Fr. *patte.*]

A light quick blow or stroke with the fingers or hand.

PAT, *v. t.* To strike gently with the fingers or hand; to tap.

Gay *pats* my shoulder and you vanish quite. *Pope.*

PATA'CA, } *n.* [from the Sp.] A Span-
PATACOON', } ish coin of the value of 4s. 8d. sterling, or about $1,04 cents. *Sp. Dict.*

PATA'CHE, *n.* [Sp.] A tender or small vessel employed in conveying men or orders from one ship or place to another. *Sp. Dict.*

PATAVIN'ITY, *n.* The use of local words, or the peculiar style or diction of Livy, the Roman historian; so denominated from *Patavium* or *Padua*, the place of his nativity. *Encyc.* *Lempriere.*

PATCH, *n.* [It. *pezza*, a piece, Fr. *pièce*, Arm. *pez*, Sp. *pieza.* Qu.]

1. A piece of cloth sewed on a garment to repair it. *Dryden.*

2. A small piece of any thing used to repair a breach.

3. A small piece of silk used to cover a defect on the face, or to add a charm.

4. A piece inserted in mosaic or variegated work. *Locke.*

5. A small piece of ground, or a small detached piece. *Shak.*

6. A paltry fellow. This use is sometimes heard in vulgar language; as a *cross-patch.*

PATCH, *v. t.* To mend by sewing on a piece or pieces; as, to *patch* a coat.

2. To adorn with a patch or with patches.

In the middle boxes were several ladies who *patched* both sides of their faces. *Spectator.*

3. To mend with pieces; to repair clumsily. *Shak.*

4. To repair with pieces fastened on; as, to *patch* the roof of a house.

5. To make up of pieces and shreds. *Raleigh.*

6. To dress in a party-colored coat. *Shak.*

7. To make suddenly or hastily; to make without regard to forms; as, to *patch* up a peace.

PATCH'ED, *pp.* Mended with a patch or patches; mended clumsily.

PATCH'ER, *n.* One that patches or botches.

PATCH'ERY, *n.* Bungling work; botchery; forgery. *Shak.*

PATCH'ING, *ppr.* Mending with a piece or pieces; botching.

PATCH'WŎRK, *n.* Work composed of pieces of various figures sewed together. *Swift.*

2. Work composed of pieces clumsily put together. *Swift.*

PATE, *n.* [Qu. Ir. *bathas*, a top; or Sp. It. *patena.*]

1. The head, or rather the top of the head; *applied to persons, it is now used in contempt or ridicule.*

2. The skin of a calf's head.

3. In *fortification*, a kind of platform resembling what is called a horse shoe. *Encyc.*

PA'TED, *a.* In *composition*, having a pate; as long-*pated*, cunning; shallow-*pated*, having weak intellect.

PATEE', } *n.* In *heraldry*, a cross small
PATTEE', } in the center, and widening to the extremities which are broad. *Encyc.*

PATEFAC'TION, *n.* [L. *patefactio*; *pateo*, to open, and *facio*, to make.]

The act of opening or manifesting; open declaration. *Pearson.*

PATEL'LIFORM, *a.* [L. *patella*, a dish, and *form*] Of the form of a dish or saucer. *Barton.*

PAT'ELLITE, *n.* Fossil remains of the patella, a shell.

PAT'EN, } *n.* [L. *patina.*] A plate. [*Not*
PAT'IN, } *used.*] *Shak.*

2. In *the Romish church*, the cover of the chalice, used for holding particles of the host. *Bp. Bedell.*

PAT'ENT, *a.* [Fr. from L. *patens*, from *pateo*, to open; Gr. πεταω, Ch. פתח to open, dilate or expand; Syr. Sam. id. Class Bd. No. 63. 64. 65.] Open; spread; expanded.

1. In *botany*, spreading; forming an acute angle with the stem or branch; as a *patent* leaf. *Martyn.*

2. Open to the perusal of all; as letters *patent.* [See *Letter.*]

3. Appropriated by letters patent.

Madder—in the time of Charles the first, was made a *patent* commodity. *Mortimer.*

4. Apparent; conspicuous. *Horseley.*

PAT'ENT, *n.* A writing given by the proper authority and duly authenticated, granting a privilege to some person or persons. By *patent*, or letters *patent*, that is, open letters, the king of Great Britain grants lands, honors and franchises.

PAT'ENT, *v. t.* To grant by patent.

2. To secure the exclusive right of a thing to a person; as, to *patent* an invention or an original work to the author.

PAT'ENTED, *pp.* Granted by patent; secured by patent or by law as an exclusive privilege.

PATENTEE', *n.* One to whom a grant is made or a privilege secured by patent or by law.

PAT'ENTING, *ppr.* Granting by patent; securing as a privilege.

PATENT-RŎLLS, *n.* The records or registers of patents.

PATERN'AL, *a.* [Fr. *paternel*; L. *paternus*, from *pater*, father.]

1. Pertaining to a father; fatherly; as *paternal* care or affection; *paternal* favor or admonition.

2. Derived from the father; hereditary; as a *paternal* estate. *Dryden. Addison.*

PATERN'ITY, *n.* [Fr. *paternité*; It. *paternità.*] Fathership; the relation of a father.

The world, while it had scarcity of people, underwent no other dominion than *paternity* and eldership. *Raleigh.*

PA'TERNOSTER, *n.* [L. our father.] The Lord's prayer.

P'ATH, *n.* plu. *paths.* [Sax. *path*, *pæth*, or *paad*, *paat*; D. *pad*; G. *pfad*; Sans. *patha*; Gr. πατος, from πατεω, to tread. The sense of *path* is beaten, trod; but the primary sense of treading, stepping, is probably to open, stretch, extend.]

1. A way beaten or trodden by the feet of man or beast, or made hard by wheels; that part of a highway on which animals or carriages ordinarily pass; *applied to the ground only, and never to a paved street in a city.*

2. Any narrow way beaten by the foot.

3. The way, course or track where a body moves in the atmosphere or in space; as the *path* of a planet or comet; the *path* of a meteor.

4. A way or passage.

5. Course of life.

He marketh all my *paths.* Job xxxiii.

6. Precepts; rules prescribed.

Uphold my goings in thy *paths.* Ps. xvii.

7. Course of providential dealings; moral government.

All the *paths* of the Lord are mercy and truth to such as keep his covenant. Ps. xxv.

P'ATH, *v. t.* [Sax. *peththian.*] To make a path by treading; to beat a path, as in snow. *U. States.*

2. To push forward; to cause to go; to make way for. *Shak.*

P'ATH, *v. i.* To walk abroad. *Shak.*

PATHET'IC, } *a.* [Gr. παθητικος, from
PATHET'ICAL, } παθος, passion; πασχω, to suffer.]

Affecting or moving the passions, particularly pity, sorrow, grief or other tender emotion; as a *pathetic* song or discourse; *pathetic* expostulation. *Spectator.*

No theory of the passions can teach a man to be *pathetic.* *E. Porter.*

PATHET'IC, *n.* Style or manner adapted to awaken the passions, especially tender emotions.

A musician at Venice is said to have so excelled in the *pathetic*, as to be able to play any of his auditors into distraction. *Encyc.*

PATHET'ICALLY, *adv.* In such a manner as to excite the tender passions.

PATHET'ICALNESS, *n.* The quality of moving the tender passions.

P'ATHFLY, *n.* A fly found in foot-paths.

PATH'IC, *n.* [from the Gr. παθος.] A catamite; a male that submits to the crime against nature. *Gillies.*

P'ATHLESS, *a.* Having no beaten way; untrodden; as a *pathless* forest; a *pathless* coast. *Prior.*

PATHOGNOMON'IC, *a.* [Gr. παθογνωμονικος; παθος, passion or suffering, and γνωμων, from γινωσκω, to know.]

Indicating that which is inseparable from a disease, being found in that and in no other; hence, indicating that by which a disease may be certainly known; characteristic; as *pathognomonic* symptoms.

PATHOG'NOMY, *n.* [Gr. παθος and γνωμη, signification.]

Expression of the passions; the science of the signs by which human passions are indicated. *Good.*

PATHOLOG'IC, } *a.* [See *Pathology.*]
PATHOLOG'ICAL, } Pertaining to pathology.

PATHOLOG'ICALLY, *adv.* In the manner of pathology.

PATHOL'OGIST, *n.* One who treats of pathology.

PATHOL'OGY, *n.* [Gr. παθος, passion, suffering, and λογος, discourse.]

That part of medicine which explains the nature of diseases, their causes and symptoms; or the doctrine of the causes and nature of diseases, comprehending nosology, etiology, symptomatology, and therapeutics. *Encyc. Coxe.*

PA'THOS, *n.* [Gr. from πασχω, to suffer.] Passion; warmth or vehemence, in a speaker; or in language, that which excites emotions and passions. *Mason.*

P'ATHWAY, *n.* A path; usually, a narrow way to be passed on foot. *Gay.*

2. A way; a course of life. Prov. xii.

PAT'IBLE, *a.* [L. *patibilis*, from *patior*, to suffer.]

Sufferable; tolerable; that may be endured. [*Not used.*] *Dict.*

PATIB'ULARY, *a.* [Fr. *patibulaire*, from L. *patibulum*, a gallows.]

Belonging to the gallows, or to execution on the cross. *Dict.*

PATIENCE, *n.* *pa'shens.* [Fr. from L. *patientia*, from *patior*, to suffer; It. *pazienza*; Sp. Port. *paciencia.* The primary sense is continuance, holding out, from extending. Hence we see the connection between *pass*, and L. *pando*, *passus*, and Gr. πατεω. See *Pass.*]

1. The suffering of afflictions, pain, toil, calamity, provocation or other evil, with a calm, unruffled temper; endurance without murmuring or fretfulness. *Patience* may spring from constitutional fortitude, from a kind of heroic pride, or from christian submission to the divine will.

2. A calm temper which bears evils without murmuring or discontent.

3. The act or quality of waiting long for justice or expected good without discontent.

Have *patience* with me, and I will pay thee all. Matt. xviii.

4. Perseverance; constancy in labor or exertion.

He learnt with *patience*, and with meekness taught. *Harte.*

5. The quality of bearing offenses and injuries without anger or revenge.

His rage was kindled and his *patience* gone. *Harte.*

6. Sufferance; permission. [*Not used.*] *Hooker.*

7. A plant, a species of rumex or dock. *Mortimer.*

PATIENT, *a. pa'shent.* [Fr. from L. *patiens.*]

1. Having the quality of enduring evils without murmuring or fretfulness; sustaining afflictions of body or mind with fortitude, calmness or christian submission to the divine will; as a *patient* person, or a person of *patient* temper. It is followed by *of* before the evil endured; as *patient of* labor or pain; *patient of* heat or cold. *Ray.*

2. Not easily provoked; calm under the sufferance of injuries or offenses; not revengeful.

Be *patient* towards all men. 1 Thess. v.

3. Persevering; constant in pursuit or exertion; calmly diligent.

Whatever I have done is due to *patient* thought. *Newton.*

4. Not hasty; not over eager or impetuous; waiting or expecting with calmness or without discontent.

Not *patient* to expect the turns of fate. *Prior.*

PA'TIENT, *n.* A person or thing that receives impressions from external agents; he or that which is passively affected.

Malice is a passion so impetuous and precipitate, that it often involves the agent and the *patient.* *Gov. of the Tongue.*

2. A person diseased or suffering bodily indisposition. It is used in relation to the physician; as, the physician visits his *patient* morning and evening.

3. It is sometimes used absolutely for a sick person.

It is wonderful to observe how inapprehensive these *patients* are of their disease. *Blackmore.*

PA'TIENT, *v. t.* To compose one's self. [*Not used.*] *Shak.*

PA'TIENTLY, *adv.* With calmness or composure; without discontent or murmuring. Submit *patiently* to the unavoidable evils of life.

2. With calm and constant diligence; as, to examine a subject *patiently.*

3. Without agitation, uneasiness or discontent; without undue haste or eagerness; as, to wait *patiently* for more favorable events.

PATIN. [See *Paten.*]

PAT'LY, *adv.* [from *pat.*] Fitly; conveniently.

PAT'NESS, *n.* [from *pat.*] Fitness; suitableness; convenience. *Barrow.*

PA'TRIARCH, *n.* [L. *patriarcha;* Gr. πατριαρχης; πατρια, a family, from πατηρ, father, and αρχος, a chief.]

1. The father and ruler of a family; one who governs by paternal right. It is usually applied to the progenitors of the Israelites, Abraham, Isaac, Jacob and the sons of Jacob, or to the heads of families before the flood; as the antediluvian *patriarchs.*

2. A learned and distinguished character among the Jews.

3. In *the christian church,* a dignitary superior to the order of archbishops; as the *patriarch* of Constantinople, of Alexandria, or of Ephesus.

PATRIARCH'AL, } *a.* Belonging to patriarchs; possessed by patriarchs; as *patriarchal* power or jurisdiction; a *patriarchal* see.
PATRIARCH'IC, }

2. Subject to a patriarch; as a *patriarchal* church.

Patriarchal cross, in heraldry, is that where the shaft is twice crossed, the lower arms being longer than the upper ones. *Encyc.*

PA'TRIARCHATE, } *n.* The office, dignity or jurisdiction of a patriarch or ecclesiastical superior. *Selden. Ayliffe.*
PA'TRIARCHSHIP, }

PA'TRIARCHY, *n.* The jurisdiction of a patriarch; a patriarchate. *Brerewood.*

PATRI"CIAN, *a.* [Fr. *patricien;* L. *patricius,* from *pater,* father.]

Senatorial; noble; not plebeian. This epithet is derived from the Roman *patres,* fathers, the title of Roman senators; as *patrician* birth or blood; *patrician* families. *Addison.*

PATRI"CIAN, *n.* A nobleman. In the Roman state, the patricians were the descendants of the first Roman senators.

PATRIMO'NIAL, *a.* [Fr. See *Patrimony.*] Pertaining to a patrimony; inherited from ancestors; as a *patrimonial* estate.

PATRIMO'NIALLY, *adv.* By inheritance. *Davenant.*

PAT'RIMONY, *n.* [L. *patrimonium,* from *pater,* father.]

1. A right or estate inherited from one's ancestors. *Dryden.*

2. A church estate or revenue; as St. Peter's *patrimony.*

PAT'RIOT, *n.* [Fr. *patriote,* from L. *patria,* one's native country, from *pater,* father.]

A person who loves his country, and zealously supports and defends it and its interests.

Such tears as *patriots* shed for dying laws. *Pope.*

PAT'RIOT, *a.* Patriotic; devoted to the welfare of one's country; as *patriot* zeal.

PATRIOT'IC, *a.* Full of patriotism; actuated by the love of one's country; as a *patriotic* hero or statesman.

2. Inspired by the love of one's country; directed to the public safety and welfare; as *patriotic* zeal.

PAT'RIOTISM, *n.* Love of one's country; the passion which aims to serve one's country, either in defending it from invasion, or protecting its rights and maintaining its laws and institutions in vigor and purity. *Patriotism* is the characteristic of a good citizen, the noblest passion that animates a man in the character of a citizen.

PATRIS'TIC, } *a.* [from L. *pater, patres,* fathers.]
PATRIS'TICAL, }

Pertaining to the ancient fathers of the christian church. *M. Stuart.*

PATROC'INATE, *v. t.* To patronize. [*Not used.*]

PATROCINA'TION, *n.* Countenance; support. [*Not used.*] *Hall.*

PATRŌL, } *n.* [Fr. *patrouille;* Sp. *patrulla;* Port. *patrulha.* See the Verb.]
PATRŌLL, }

1. In *war,* a round; a walking or marching round by a guard in the night, to watch and observe what passes, and to secure the peace and safety of a camp or other place.

2. The guard or persons who go the rounds for observation; a detachment whose duty is to patroll.

In France, there is an army of *patrols* to secure her fiscal regulations. *Hamilton.*

PATRŌLL, *v. i.* [Fr. *patrouiller,* to paddle or puddle, to patroll, to fumble; Sp. *patrullar.* Hence the word seems to be formed from the name of the foot, *pad* or *ped, paw.* In our vulgar dialect, *pad* is used in the sense of walking or stepping about. It seems to be allied to Gr. πατεω.]

To go the rounds in a camp or garrison; to march about and observe what passes; as a guard. *Encyc.*

PATRŌLLING, *ppr.* Going the rounds, as a guard.

PAT'RON, *n.* [L. *patronus;* Gr. πατρων, from πατηρ, father.]

1. Among the Romans, a master who had freed his slave, and retained some rights over him after his emancipation; also, a man of distinction under whose protection another placed himself. Hence,

2. One who countenances, supports and protects either a person or a work. *Prior.*

3. In *the church of Rome,* a guardian or saint, whose name a person bears, or under whose special care he is placed and whom he invokes; or a saint in whose name a church or order is founded. *Encyc.*

4. In *the canon* or *common law,* one who has the gift and disposition of a benefice. *Encyc.*

5. An advocate; a defender; one that specially countenances and supports, or lends aid to advance; as *patrons* of the arts; a *patron* of useful undertakings; the *patrons* of virtue. *Locke.*

6. In *seamen's language,* the commander of a small vessel or passage-boat; also, one who steers a ship's long boat.

PAT'RONAǴE, *n.* Special countenance or support; favor or aid afforded to second the views of a person or to promote a design. *Sidney.*

2. Guardianship, as of a saint. *Addison.*

3. Advowson; the right of presentation to a church or ecclesiastical benefice. *Encyc.*

PAT'RONAǴE, *v. t.* To patronize or support. [*Not used.*] *Shak.*

PAT'RONAL, *a.* Doing the office of a patron; protecting; supporting; favoring; defending. [*Little used.*] *Brown.*

PAT'RONESS, *n.* A female that favors, countenances or supports.

Now night came down, and rose full soon
That *patroness* of rogues, the moon. *Trumbull's M'Fingal.*

2. A female guardian saint.

3. A female that has the right of presenting to a church living.

PAT'RONIZE, *v. t.* To support; to countenance; to defend; as a patron his client.

2. To favor; to lend aid to promote; as an undertaking. *Dryden.*

3. To maintain; to defend; to support.

This idea has been *patronized* by two states only. *Hamilton.*

PAT'RONIZED, *pp.* Defended; supported; favored; promoted.

PAT'RONIZER, *n.* One that supports, countenances or favors.

PAT′RONIZING, *ppr.* Defending; supporting; favoring; promoting.

PAT′RONLESS, *a.* Destitute of a patron. *Shaftsbury.*

PATRONYM′IC, *n.* [Gr. πατρωνυμικος; L. *patronymicus*; from Gr. πατηρ, father, and ονομα, name.]

A name of men or women derived from that of their parents or ancestors; as *Tydides*, the son of Tydeus; *Pelides*, the son of Peleus, that is, Achilles. *Encyc.*

PAT′TEN, *n.* [Fr. *patin*, probably from the name of the foot.]

1. The base of a column or pillar. *Ainsworth.*

2. A wooden shoe with an iron ring, worn to keep the shoes from the dirt or mud. *Camden. Gay.*

PAT′TEN-MAKER, *n.* One that makes pattens.

PAT′TER, *v. i.* [from *pat*, to strike gently; or Fr. *patte*, the foot.]

To strike, as falling drops of water or hail, with a quick succession of small sounds; as *pattering* hail. *Dryden.*

The stealing shower is scarce to *patter* heard. *Thomson.*

PAT′TERING, *ppr.* Striking with a quick succession of small sounds.

PAT′TERN, *n.* [Fr. *patron*; Arm. *patroum*; D. *patroon*. See *Patron*.]

1. An original or model proposed for imitation; the archetype; an exemplar; that which is to be copied or imitated, either in things or in actions; as the *pattern* of a machine; a *pattern* of patience. Christ was the most perfect *pattern* of rectitude, patience and submission ever exhibited on earth.

2. A specimen; a sample; a part showing the figure or quality of the whole; as a *pattern* of silk cloth.

3. An instance; an example. *Hooker.*

4. Any thing cut or formed into the shape of something to be made after it.

PAT′TERN, *v. t.* To make in imitation of some model; to copy. *Shak.*

2. To serve as an example to be followed. *Shak.*

To pattern after, to imitate; to follow.

PAT′TY, *n.* [Fr. *pâte*, paste.] A little pie.

PAT′TY-PAN, *n.* A pan to bake a little pie in.

PAT′ULOUS, *a.* [L. *patulus*, from *pateo*, to be open.]

Spreading, as a *patulous* calyx; bearing the flowers loose or dispersed, as a *patulous* peduncle. *Lee. Martyn.*

PAUCIL′OQUY, *n.* [L. *paucus*, few, and *loquor*, to speak.]

The utterance of few words. [*Little used.*]

PAU′CITY, *n.* [L. *paucitas*, from *paucus*, few.]

1. Fewness; smallness of number; as the *paucity* of schools. *Hooker.*

2. Smallness of quantity; as *paucity* of blood. *Brown.*

PAUM, *v. t.* To impose by fraud; a corruption of *palm.* *Swift.*

PAUNCH, *n.* [Fr. *panse*; It. Sp. *panza*; Port. *pança*; D. *pens*; Basque, *pantza*; L. *pantex*. Qu. G. *wanst.*] The belly and its contents.

The *paunch*, in ruminating quadrupeds, is the first and largest stomach, into which the food is received before rumination. *Monro.*

PAUNCH, *v. t.* To pierce or rip the belly; to eviscerate; to take out the contents of the belly. *Shak. Garth.*

PAUP′ER, *n.* [L. *pauper*; Fr. *pauvre*; Sp. *pobre*; It. *povero.*]

A poor person; particularly, one so indigent as to depend on the parish or town for maintenance.

PAUP′ERISM, *n.* The state of being poor or destitute of the means of support; the state of indigent persons requiring support from the community. The increase of *pauperism* is an alarming evil.

PAUSE, *n.* *pauz.* [L. Sp. It. *pausa*; Fr. *pause*; D. *poos*; Sw. *paus*; G. Dan. *pause*; Gr. παυσις, from παυω, to cease, or cause to rest.]

1. A stop; a cessation or intermission of action, of speaking, singing, playing or the like; a temporary stop or rest. *Hooker. Locke.*

2. Cessation proceeding from doubt; suspense.

I stand in *pause* where I shall first begin. *Shak.*

3. Break or paragraph in writing. *Locke.*

4. A temporary cessation in reading. The use of punctuation is to mark the *pauses* in writing. In verse, there are two kinds of *pauses*, the cesural and the final. The cesural *pause* divides the verse; the final *pause* closes it. The *pauses* which mark the sense, and which may be called *sentential*, are the same in prose and verse.

5. A mark of cessation or intermission of the voice; a point.

PAUSE, *v. i.* *pauz.* To make a short stop; to cease to speak for a time; to intermit speaking or action.

Pausing a while, thus to herself she mused. *Milton.*

2. To stop; to wait; to forbear for a time.

Tarry, *pause* a day or two,
Before you hazard. *Shak.*

3. To be intermitted. The music *pauses*.

To pause upon, to deliberate. *Shak. Knolles.*

PAUS′ER, *n.* *s* as *z*. One who pauses; one who deliberates. *Shak.*

PAUS′ING, *ppr.* Stopping for a time; ceasing to speak or act; deliberating.

PAUS′INGLY, *adv.* After a pause; by breaks. *Shak.*

PAVAN′, *n.* [Sp. *pavana*, from *pavon*, L. *pavo*, a peacock.]

A grave dance among the Spaniards. In this dance, the performers make a kind of wheel before each other, the gentlemen dancing with cap and sword, princes with long robes, and the ladies with long trails; the motions resembling the stately steps of the peacock. *Encyc. Sp. Dict. Shak.*

PAVE, *v. t.* [Fr. *paver*; L. *pavio*, Gr. παιω, to beat, to strike.]

1. To lay or cover with stone or brick so as to make a level or convenient surface for horses, carriages or foot passengers; to floor with brick or stone; as, to *pave* a street; to *pave* a side-walk; to *pave* a court or stable.

2. To prepare a passage; to facilitate the introduction of. The invention of printing *paved* the way for intellectual improvement.

PA′VED, *pp.* Laid over with stones or bricks; prepared; as a way.

PA′VEMENT, *n.* [L. *pavimentum.*] A floor or covering consisting of stones or bricks, laid on the earth in such a manner as to make a hard and convenient passage; as a *pavement* of pebbles, of bricks, or of marble.

PA′VEMENT, *v. t.* To pave; to floor with stone or brick. [*Unusual.*] *Bp. Hall.*

PA′VER, PA′VIER, *n.* One who lays stones for a floor, or whose occupation is to pave. *Gay.*

PAVILION, *n.* *pavil′yun.* [Fr. *pavillon*; Sp. *pabellon*; Port. *pavilham*; Arm. *pavilhon*; W. *pabell*; It. *paviglione* and *padiglione*; L. *papilio*, a butterfly, and a pavilion. According to Owen, the Welsh *pabell* signifies a moving habitation.]

1. A tent; a temporary movable habitation.

2. In *architecture*, a kind of turret or building, usually insulated and contained under a single roof; sometimes square and sometimes in the form of a dome. Sometimes a pavilion is a projecting part in the front of a building; sometimes it flanks a corner. *Encyc.*

3. In *military affairs*, a tent raised on posts. The word is sometimes used for a flag, colors, ensign or banner.

4. In *heraldry*, a covering in form of a tent, investing the armories of kings.

5. Among *jewelers*, the under side and corner of brilliants, lying between the girdle and collet.

PAVIL′ION, *v. t.* To furnish with tents. *Milton.*

2. To shelter with a tent. *Pope.*

PAVIL′IONED, *pp.* Furnished with pavilions; sheltered by a tent.

PA′VING, *ppr.* Flooring with stones or bricks.

PA′VING, *n.* Pavement; a floor of stones or bricks.

PA′VO, *n.* [L. a peacock; W. *paw*, spreading.]

A constellation in the southern hemisphere, consisting of fourteen stars; also, a fish.

PAVO′NE, *n.* [L. *pavo.*] A peacock. [*Not used.*] *Spenser.*

PAV′ONINE, *a.* [L. *pavoninus*, from *pavo*, a peacock.]

Resembling the tail of a peacock; iridescent. *Cleaveland.*

PAW, *n.* [W. *pawen*, a paw, a hoof; Arm. *pau*; Hindoo, *pauw*; Pers. پای pai, the foot; perhaps contracted from *pad* or *pat*, as the Dutch have *poot*, and the Fr. *patte*. If so, the word coincides in elements with L. *pes*, *pedis*, Gr. πους, Eng. *foot*, Gr. πατεω.]

1. The foot of beasts of prey having claws, as the lion, the tiger, the dog, cat, &c. Lev. xi.

2. The hand; in contempt. *Dryden.*

PAW, *v. i.* To draw the fore foot along the ground; to scrape with the fore foot; as a fiery horse, *pawing* with his hoof. *Swift.*

He *paweth* in the valley. Job xxxix.

PAW, *v. t.* To scrape with the fore foot.

His hot courser *paw'd* th' Hungarian plain. *Tickel.*

2. To handle roughly; to scratch.
3. To fawn; to flatter. *Ainsworth.*
PAW'ED, *a.* Having paws.
2. Broad footed. *Johnson.*
PAWK'Y, *a.* [from Sax. *pæcan*, to deceive.] Arch; cunning. [*Local.*] *Grose.*
PAWL, *n.* [W. *pawl*, Eng. *pole*, L. *palus.* See *Pole.*]
Among *seamen*, a short bar of wood or iron fixed close to the capstan or windlass of a ship to prevent it from rolling back or giving way. *Mar. Dict.*
PAWN, *n.* [D. *pand;* G. *pfand;* Sw. *pant;* Port. *penhor;* It. *pegno;* Sp. *empeño;* L. *pignus.* The sense may be that which is laid down or deposited.]
1. Something given or deposited as security for the payment of money borrowed; a pledge. *Pawn* is applied only to goods, chattels or money, and not to real estate.

Men will not take *pawns* without use. *Bacon.*

2. A pledge for the fulfillment of a promise. *Shak.*
3. A common man at chess. [See *Peon.*] *Cowley.*
In pawn, at pawn, the state of being pledged.

Sweet wife, my honor is *at pawn.* *Shak.*

PAWN, *v. t.* [D. *panden;* Sp. *empeñar;* Port. *empenhar;* It. *impegnare;* L. *pignero.*]
1. To give or deposit in pledge, or as security for the payment of money borrowed; to pledge; as, she *pawned* the last piece of plate.
2. To pledge for the fulfillment of a promise; as, to *pawn* one's word or honor that an agreement shall be fulfilled.
PAWN'-BROKER, *n.* One who lends money on pledge or the deposit of goods. *Arbuthnot.*
PAWN'ED, *pp.* Pledged; given in security.
PAWNEE', *n.* The person to whom a pawn is delivered as security; one that takes any thing in pawn.

If the pawn is laid up and the *pawnee* robbed, he is not answerable. *Encyc.*

PAWN'ER, *n.* One that pledges any thing as security for the payment of borrowed money.
PAWN'ING, *ppr.* Pledging, as goods; giving as security.
PAX, *n.* [L. *pax*, peace.] A little image or piece of board with the image of Christ upon the cross on it, which people before the reformation, used to kiss after the service; the ceremony being considered as the kiss of *peace.* *Todd.*
PAY, *v. t.* pret. and pp. *paid.* [Fr. *payer*, Norm. *pair*, contracted from It. *pagare*, Port. Sp. *pagar*, Arm. *paca.* Class Bg. From the different applications of *pay*, the sense appears to be to send or send to, for in our vulgar language, to *pay on*, is to strike, to beat; and to *pay* with pitch, is to *put on* or rub over. In the sense of strike, this coincides with the Greek παιω, εμπαιω, W. *pwyaw.* In another seamen's phrase, the word signifies to loosen or slacken, as to *pay out* cable, that is, to send or extend. But this word cannot belong to the root of the Greek and Welsh words, unless these are contracted from *Pg* or *Pk.*]
1. To discharge a debt; to deliver to a creditor the value of the debt, either in money or goods, to his acceptance or satisfaction, by which the obligation of the debtor is discharged.
2. To discharge a duty created by promise or by custom or by the moral law; as, to *pay* a debt of honor or of kindness.

You have *paid* down
More penitence, than done trespass. *Shak.*

3. To fulfill; to perform what is promised; as, to *pay* one's vows. *Scripture.*
4. To render what is due to a superior, or demanded by civility or courtesy; as, to *pay* respect to a magistrate; to *pay* due honor to parents.
5. To beat.

For which, or *pay* me quickly, or I'll *pay* you. *B. Jonson.*

6. To reward; to recompense; as, to *pay* for kindness with neglect. *Dryden.*
To pay for, to make amends; to atone by suffering. Men often *pay for* their mistakes with loss of property or reputation, sometimes with life.
2. To give an equivalent for any thing purchased.
To pay, or *pay over*, in seamen's language, to daub or besmear the surface of any body, to preserve it from injury by water or weather.
To pay the bottom of a vessel, to cover it with a composition of tallow, sulphur, rosin, &c.; to bream.
To pay a mast or *yard*, to besmear it with tar, turpentine, rosin, tallow or varnish.
To pay a seam, to pour melted pitch along it, so as to defend the oakum.
To pay off, to make compensation to and discharge; as, to *pay off* the crew of a ship.
To pay out, to slacken, extend or cause to run out; as, to *pay out* more cable. *Mar. Dict.*
PAY, *v. i.* To *pay off*, in seamen's language, is to fall to leeward, as the head of a ship. *Mar. Dict.*
To pay on, to beat with vigor; to redouble blows. [*Colloquial.*]
PAY, *n.* Compensation; recompense; an equivalent given for money due, goods purchased or services performed; salary or wages for services; hire. The merchant receives *pay* for goods sold; the soldier receives *pay* for his services, but the soldiers of the American revolution never received full *pay.*
2. Compensation; reward.

Here only merit constant *pay* receives— *Pope.*

PA'YABLE, *a.* [Fr.] That may or ought to be paid. In general, money is *payable* as soon as it is due, or at the time payment is stipulated, or at the expiration of the credit; but by the usage of merchants, three or more days of grace are allowed to the debtor, and a note *due* at the day when payment is promised, is not *payable* till the expiration of the days of grace.
2. That can be paid; that there is power to pay.

Thanks are a tribute *payable* by the poorest. *South.*

PA'Y-BILL, *n.* A bill of money to be paid to the soldiers of a company.
PA'Y-DAY, *n.* The day when payment is to be made or debts discharged; the day on which wages or money is stipulated to be paid. *Locke.*
PAYEE', *n.* The person to whom money is to be paid; the person named in a bill or note to whom the amount is promised or directed to be paid.
PAY'ER, *n.* One that pays. In bills of exchange, the person on whom the bill is drawn, and who is directed to pay the money to the holder.
PA'YMASTER, *n.* One who is to pay; one from whom wages or reward is received. *Taylor.*
2. In *the army*, an officer whose duty is to pay the officers and soldiers their wages, and who is entrusted with money for this purpose.
PA'YMENT, *n.* The act of paying, or giving compensation. *Bacon.*
2. The thing given in discharge of a debt or fulfillment of a promise. *Shak.*
3. Reward; recompense. *South.*
4. Chastisement; sound beating. [*Not used.*] *Ainsworth.*
PAYNIM. [See *Painim.*]
PA'Y-OFFICE, *n.* A place or office where payment is made of public debts.
PAYSE, PAYSER, for *poise*, *poiser*, not used. *Spenser.*
PEA, *n.* [Sax. *pisa;* Fr. *pois;* It. *pisello;* L. *pisum;* Gr. πισον; W. *pys*, *pysen;* Ir. *pis.*]
A plant and its fruit of the genus Pisum, of many varieties. This plant has a papilionaceous flower, and the pericarp is a legume, called in popular language a *pod.* In the plural, we write *peas*, for two or more individual seeds, but *pease*, for an indefinite number in quantity or bulk. We write two, three or four *peas*, but a bushel of *pease.* [*This practice is arbitrary.*]
PEACE, *n.* [Sax. Norm. *pais;* Fr. *paix;* It. *pace;* Sp. Port. *paz;* Arm. *peoch*, from *peoh;* L. *pax.* Qu. Russ. *pokoi.* The elements are *Pg*, or their cognates, for the L. has *paco*, to appease, coinciding with the root of *pack*, and signifying to press or to stop.]
1. In *a general sense*, a state of quiet or tranquillity; freedom from disturbance or agitation; applicable to society, to individuals, or to the temper of the mind.
2. Freedom from war with a foreign nation; public quiet.
3. Freedom from internal commotion or civil war.
4. Freedom from private quarrels, suits or disturbance.
5. Freedom from agitation or disturbance by the passions, as from fear, terror, anger, anxiety or the like; quietness of mind; tranquillity; calmness; quiet of conscience.

Great *peace* have they that love thy law. Ps. cxix.

6. Heavenly rest; the happiness of heaven. Is. lvii.
7. Harmony; concord; a state of reconciliation between parties at variance.
8. Public tranquillity; that quiet, order and security which is guaranteed by the laws; as, to keep the *peace;* to break the *peace.*

This word is used in commanding silence or quiet; as, *peace* to this troubled soul.

Peace, the lovers are asleep. *Crashaw.*

To be at peace, to be reconciled; to live in harmony.
To make peace, to reconcile, as parties at variance.
To hold the peace, to be silent; to suppress one's thoughts; not to speak.

PE'ACEABLE, *a.* Free from war, tumult or public commotion. We live in *peaceable* times. The reformation was introduced in a *peaceable* manner.
2. Free from private feuds or quarrels. The neighbors are *peaceable*. These men are *peaceable*.
3. Quiet; undisturbed; not agitated with passion. His mind is very *peaceable*.
4. Not violent, bloody or unnatural; as, to die a *peaceable* death.

PE'ACEABLENESS, *n.* The state of being peaceable; quietness.
2. Disposition to peace. *Hammond.*

PE'ACEABLY, *adv.* Without war; without tumult or commotion; without private feuds and quarrels.
2. Without disturbance; quietly; without agitation; without interruption.

PE'ACEBREAKER, *n.* One that violates or disturbs public peace.

PE'ACEFUL, *a.* Quiet; undisturbed; not in a state of war or commotion; as a *peaceful* time; a *peaceful* country.
2. Pacific; mild; calm; as *peaceful* words; a *peaceful* temper.
3. Removed from noise or tumult; still; undisturbed; as the *peaceful* cottage; the *peaceful* scenes of rural life.

PE'ACEFULLY, *adv.* Without war or commotion.
2. Quietly; without disturbance.

Our loved earth, where *peacefully* we slept. *Dryden.*

3. Mildly; gently.

PE'ACEFULNESS, *n.* Quiet; freedom from war, tumult, disturbance or discord.
2. Freedom from mental perturbation; as *peacefulness* of mind.

PE'ACELESS, *a.* Without peace; disturbed. *Sandys.*

PE'ACEMAKER, *n.* One who makes peace by reconciling parties that are at variance.

Blessed are the *peacemakers*, for they shall be called the children of God. Matt. v.

PE'ACE-OFFERING, *n.* An offering that procures peace. Among the Jews, an offering or sacrifice to God for atonement and reconciliation for a crime or offense. *Leviticus.*

PE'ACE-OFFICER, *n.* A civil officer whose duty is to preserve the public peace, to prevent or punish riots, &c.; as a sheriff, or constable.

PE'ACE-PARTED, *a.* Dismissed from the world in peace. *Shak.*

PEACH, *n.* [Fr. *pêche*; It. *pesca*; Arm. *pechesen.*]
A tree and its fruit, of the genus Amygdalus, of many varieties. This is a delicious fruit, the produce of warm or temperate climates. In America, the *peach* thrives and comes to perfection in the neighborhood of Boston, northward of which it usually fails.

PEACH, for *impeach*, not used. *Dryden.*

PE'ACH-COLOR, *n.* The pale red color of the peach blossom.

PE'ACH-COLORED, *a.* Of the color of a peach blossom. *Shak.*

PE'ACHER, *n.* An accuser. [*Not used.*] *Fox.*

PE'ACHICK, *n.* The chicken or young of the peacock. *Southern.*

PE'ACH-TREE, *n.* The tree that produces the peach.

PE'ACOCK, *n.* [*Pea*, in this word, is from L. *pavo.* Sax. *pawa*; Fr. *paon*, contracted from *pavonis*; It. *pavone*; Sp. *pavon*; D. *paauw*; G. *pfau*; W. *pawan*, from *paw*, spreading, extending.]
A large and beautiful fowl of the genus Pavo, properly the male of the species, but in usage the name is applied to the species in general. The fethers of this fowl's tail are very long, and variegated with rich and elegant colors. The peacock is a native of India.

PE'ACOCK-FISH, *n.* A fish of the Indian seas, having streaks of beautiful colors.

PE'AHEN, *n.* [G. *pfauhenne* or *pfauen*; D. *paauwin.*] The hen or female of the peacock.

PEAK, *n.* [Sax. *peac*; W. *pig*; Ir. *peac*; Eng. *pike, beak*; Fr. *pique*; It. *becco*; Sp. *pico.* These are of one family, signifying a point, from shooting or thrusting.]
1. The top of a hill or mountain, ending in a point; as the *peak* of Teneriffe.
2. A point; the end of any thing that terminates in a point.
3. The upper corner of a sail which is extended by a gaff or yard; also, the extremity of the yard or gaff. *Mar. Dict.*

PEAK, *v. i.* To look sickly or thin. [*Not used.*] *Shak.*
2. To make a mean figure; to sneak. [*Not used.*] *Shak.*

PEAK, *v. t.* To raise a gaff or yard more obliquely to the mast. *Mar. Dict.*

PE'AKING, *a.* Mean; sneaking; poor. [*Vulgar.*]

PE'AKISH, *a.* Denoting or belonging to an acuminated situation. *Drayton.*

PEAL, *n.* [from L. *pello*, whence *appello*, to *appeal.* The sense is to drive; a *peal* is a driving of sound. This word seems to belong to the family of L. *balo*, and Eng. to *bawl, jubilee, bell*, &c.]
A loud sound, usually a succession of loud sounds, as of bells, thunder, cannon, shouts of a multitude, &c. *Bacon. Milton. Addison.*

PEAL, *v. i.* To utter loud and solemn sounds; as the *pealing* organ. *Milton.*

PEAL, *v. t.* To assail with noise.

Nor was his ear less *pealed.* *Milton.*

2. To cause to ring or sound; to celebrate.

The warrior's name
Though *pealed* and chimed on all the tongues of fame. *J. Barlow.*

3. To stir or agitate. [*Not used.*] *Ainsworth.*

PE'ALED, *pp.* Assailed with sound; resounded; celebrated.

PE'ALING, *ppr.* Uttering a loud sound or successive sounds; resounding.

PE'AN, *n.* [L. *pœan*; Gr. παιαν.] A song of praise or triumph.

PE'ANISM, *n.* The song or shouts of praise or of battle; shouts of triumph. *Mitford.*

PEAR, *n.* [Sax. Sp. Port. It. *pera*; D. *peer*; G. *birn*; Sw. *påron*; Dan. *pære*; Arm. *peren*; W. *pêr*; L. *pyrum.*]
The fruit of the *Pyrus communis*, of many varieties, some of which are delicious to the taste.

PEARCH. [See *Perch.*]

PEARL, *n. perl.* [Fr. *perle*; It. Sp. *perla*; Ir. *pearla*; Sax. *pearl*; Sw. *pärla*; D. *paarl*; G. *perle*; W. *perlyn.* This may be radically the same word as *beryl*, and so named from its clearness.]
1. A white, hard, smooth, shining body, usually roundish, found in a testaceous fish of the oyster kind. The pearl-shell is called *matrix perlarum*, mother of pearl, and the pearl is found only in the softer part of the animal. It is found in the Persian seas and in many parts of the ocean which washes the shores of Arabia and the continent and isles of Asia, and is taken by divers. Pearls are of different sizes and colors; the larger ones approach to the figure of a pear; some have been found more than an inch in length. They are valued according to their size, their roundness, and their luster or purity, which appears in a silvery brightness. *Cyc. Nicholson. Encyc.*
2. Poetically, something round and clear, as a drop of water or dew. *Drayton.*
3. A white speck or film growing on the eye. *Ainsworth.*

PEARL, *v. t. perl.* To set or adorn with pearls.

PEARL, *v. i. perl.* To resemble pearls. *Spenser.*

PEARLASH, *n. perl'ash.* An alkali obtained from the ashes of wood; refined potash.

PEARLED, *a. perl'ed.* Set or adorned with pearls. *Milton.*

PEARL-EYED, *a. perl'-eyed.* Having a speck in the eye. *Johnson.*

PEARL-SINTER, *n.* Fiorite; a variety of silicious sinter, the color gray and white. *Ure.*

PEARL-SPAR, *n. perl'-spar.* Brown spar.

PEARL-STONE, *n.* A mineral regarded as a volcanic production. It occurs in basaltic and porphyritic rocks, and is classed with pitch stone. *Dict.*
Pearl-stone is a subspecies of indivisible quartz. *Jameson.*

PEARL-WORT, } *n.* A plant of the genus
PEARL-GRASS, } Sagina. *Fam. of Plants.*

PEARLY, *a. perl'y.* Containing pearls; abounding with pearls; as *pearly* shells; a *pearly* shore.
2. Resembling pearls; clear; pure; transparent; as the *pearly* flood; *pearly* dew. *Drayton. Dryden.*

PEARMAIN, *n.* A variety of the apple.

PEAR-TREE, *n.* The tree that produces pears.

PEASANT, *n. pez'ant.* [Fr. *paysan*; Sp. Port. *paisano*; from the name of country, Fr. *pais* or *pays*, Sp. Port. *pais*, It. *paese*; W. *peues*, a place of rest, a country, from *pau*, coinciding with Gr. παυω, to rest.]
A countryman; one whose business is rural labor.

PEASANT, *a. pez'ant.* Rustic; rural. *Spenser.*

PEAS'ANTLIKE, } *a.* Rude; clownish;
PEAS'ANTLY, } illiterate; resembling peasants. *Milton.*

PEASANTRY, *n.* *pez'antry.* Peasants; rustics; the body of country people. *Locke.*
2. Rusticity. [*Not used.*] *Butler.*

PE'AS-COD, } *n.* The legume or pericarp
PE'A-SHELL, } of the pea. *Walton. Gay.*

PE'ASTONE, *n.* A subspecies of limestone.

PEASE, *n.* Peas collectively, or used as food. [See *Pea.*] *Arbuthnot.*

PEAT. *n.* [G. *pfütze*, a bog.] A substance resembling turf, used as fuel. It is found in low grounds or moorish lands, and is of several species; one is of a brown or yellowish brown color, and when first cut has a viscid consistence, but hardens when exposed to the air; another consists chiefly of vegetable substances, as branches of trees, roots, grass, &c. *Bacon. Nicholson. Encyc.*

PEAT. [Fr. *petit.* See *Pet.*]

PEAT-MOSS, *n.* [*peat* and *moss.*] An earthy material used as fuel.
2. A fen producing peat.

PEB'BLE, } *n.* [Sax. *pabob, papol-*
PEB'BLESTONE, } *stana.*] In *popular usage*, a roundish stone of any kind from the size of a nut to that of a man's head. In *a philosophical sense*, minerals distinguished from flints by their variety of colors, consisting of crystaline matter debased by earths of various kinds, with veins, clouds and other variegations, formed by incrustation round a central nucleus, but sometimes the effect of a simple concretion. Pebbles are much used in the pavement of streets. *Encyc.*

A general term for water-worn minerals. *D. Olmsted.*

PEB'BLE-CRYSTAL, *n.* A crystal in form of nodules, found in earthy stratums and irregular in shape. *Woodward.*

PEB'BLED, *a.* Abounding with pebbles. *Thomson.*

PEB'BLY, *a.* Full of pebbles; abounding with small roundish stones.

PEC'ARY, } *n.* A quadruped of Mexico,
PEC'CARY, } in general appearance resembling a hog, but its body is less bulky, its legs shorter, and its bristles thicker and stronger, like the quills of the porcupine. Its color is black and white, and it has on the hind part of the back a protuberance like the navel of other animals, with an orifice from which issues a liquor of a very strong scent. *Dict. Nat. Hist.*

PECCABIL'ITY, *n.* [from *peccable.*] State of being subject to sin; capacity of sinning. *Decay of Piety.*

PEC'CABLE, *a.* [from L. *pecco*, Ir. *peachadh*; W. *pec, pecawd*, sin; *pecu*, to sin, Fr. *pecher*, It. *peccare*, Sp. *pecar.*]
Liable to sin; subject to transgress the divine law. *Priestley.*

PECCADIL'LO, *n.* [Sp. *dim.* from *pecado*, L. *peccatum*; Fr. *peccadille.* See *Peccable.*]
1. A slight trespass or offense; a petty crime or fault. *Dryden.*
2. A sort of stiff ruff. *B. Taylor.*

PEC'CANCY, *n.* [from *peccant.*] Bad quality; as the *peccancy* of the humors. *Wiseman.*
2. Offense. *Mountague.*

PEC'CANT, *a.* [L. *peccans*; Fr. *peccant.* See *Peccable.*]
1. Sinning; guilty of sin or transgression; criminal; as *peccant* angels. *Milton.*
2. Morbid; bad; corrupt; not healthy; as *peccant* humors. *Arbuthnot.*
3. Wrong; bad; defective; informal; as a *peccant* citation. [*Not used.*] *Ayliffe.*

PEC'CANT, *n.* An offender. [*Not used.*] *Whitlock.*

PECCA'VI. [L. I have offended.] A colloquial word used to express confession or acknowledgment of an offense. *Aubrey.*

PECH'BLEND, *n.* [G. *pech*, pitch, and *blende*, blend.]
Pitchblend, an ore of uranium; a metallic substance found in masses, or stratified with earths or with other minerals, in Swedish and Saxon mines. It is of a blackish color, inclining to a deep steel gray, and one kind has a mixture of spots of red. *Nicholson.*

PECK, *n.* [Arm. *pech*, a fourth; Fr. *picotin.*]
1. The fourth part of a bushel; a dry measure of eight quarts; as a *peck* of wheat or oats.
2. In *low language*, a great deal; as, to be in a *peck* of troubles. Qu. *pack.*

PECK, *v. t.* [It. *beccare*; Sp. *picar*; Fr. *becqueter*; D. *piken*; G. *picken*; Dan. *pikker.* This verb is connected with the nouns *beak* and *pike.*]
1. To strike with the beak; to thrust the beak into, as a bird that *pecks* a hole in a tree.
2. To strike with a pointed instrument, or to delve or dig with any thing pointed, as with a pick-ax. *Carew.*
3. To pick up food with the beak. *Dryden.*
4. To strike with small and repeated blows; to strike in a manner to make small impressions. In this sense, the verb is generally intransitive. We say, to *peck at.* *South.*

[This verb and *pick* are radically the same.]

PECK'ED, *pp.* Struck or penetrated with a beak or pointed instrument.

PECK'ER, *n.* One that pecks; a bird that pecks holes in trees; a woodpecker. *Dryden.*

PECK'ING, *ppr.* Striking with the bill; thrusting the beak into; thrusting into with a pointed instrument; taking up food with the beak.

PECKLED, for *speckled*, not used. *Walton.*

PEC'TINAL, *a.* [L. *pecten*, a comb; *pecto*, to comb, Gr. πεκτεω, from πεκω.] Pertaining to a comb; resembling a comb.

PEC'TINAL, *n.* A fish whose bones resemble the teeth of a comb. *Brown.*

PEC'TINATE, } *a.* [from L. *pecten*, a
PEC'TINATED, } comb.] Having resemblance to the teeth of a comb. In *botany*, a pectinate leaf is a sort of pinnate leaf, in which the leaflets are toothed like a comb. *Martyn.*

A mineral is *pectinated*, when it presents short filaments, crystals or branches, nearly parallel and equidistant. *Phillips.*

PECTINA'TION, *n.* The state of being pectinated.
2. A combing; the combing of the head. *Cyc.*

PEC'TINITE, *n.* [L. *pecten*, a comb.] A fossil pecten or scallop, or scallop petrified. *Kirwan.*

PEC'TORAL, *a.* [L. *pectoralis*, from *pectus*, breast.]
Pertaining to the breast; as the *pectoral* muscles; *pectoral* medicines. *Milton.*
The *pectoral* fins of a fish are situated on the sides of the fish, behind the gills.

PEC'TORAL, *n.* A breastplate. *Encyc. Johnson.*
2. A sacerdotal habit or vestment worn by the Jewish high priest, called in our version of the Bible, a breastplate. *Encyc.*
3. A medicine adapted to cure or relieve complaints of the breast and lungs.

PEC'ULATE, *v. i.* [L. *peculatus, peculor*, from *peculium*, private property, from *pecus*, cattle.]
1. To defraud the public of money or goods entrusted to one's care, by appropriating the property to one's own use; to defraud by embezzlement.
2. Among civilians, to steal. *Encyc.*

PECULA'TION, *n.* The act, practice or crime of defrauding the public by appropriating to one's own use the money or goods entrusted to one's care for management or disbursement; embezzlement of public money or goods.

PEC'ULATOR, *n.* [L.] One that defrauds the public by appropriating to his own use money entrusted to his care.

PECU'LIAR, *a.* [L. *peculiaris*, from *peculium*, one's own property, from *pecus*, cattle.]
1. Appropriate; belonging to a person and to him only. Almost every writer has a *peculiar* style. Most men have manners *peculiar* to themselves.
2. Singular; particular. The man has something *peculiar* in his deportment.
3. Particular; special.

My fate is Juno's most *peculiar* care. *Dryden.*

[*Most* cannot, in strict propriety, be prefixed to *peculiar*, but it is used to give emphasis to the word.]
4. Belonging to a nation, system or other thing, and not to others.

PECU'LIAR, *n.* Exclusive property; that which belongs to a person in exclusion of others. *Milton.*
2. In *the canon law*, a particular parish or church which has the probate of wills within itself, exempt from the jurisdiction of the ordinary or bishop's court. *Encyc.*

Court of peculiars, in England, is a branch of the court of arches. It has jurisdiction over all the parishes dispersed through the province of Canterbury, in the midst of other dioceses, which are exempt from the ordinary jurisdiction, and subject to the metropolitan only. *Blackstone.*

PECULIAR'ITY, *n.* Something peculiar to a person or thing; that which belongs to or is found in one person or thing and in no other; as a *peculiarity* of style or manner of thinking; *peculiarity* in dress.

PECU'LIARIZE, *v. t.* To appropriate; to make peculiar. *Smith.*

PECU'LIARLY, *adv.* Particularly; singly. *Woodward.*
2. In a manner not common to others. *Drayton.*

PEC'ULIARNESS, *n.* The state of being peculiar; appropriation. [*Little used.*] *Mede.*

PEC'U'NIARY, *a.* [Fr. *pecuniaire;* It. *pecuniale;* L. *pecuniarius*, from *pecunia*, money, from *pecus*, cattle.]
1. Relating to money; as *pecuniary* affairs or losses.
2. Consisting of money; as a *pecuniary* mulct or penalty. *Bacon.*

PEC'U'NIOUS, *a.* Full of money. [*Not used.*] *Sherwood.*

PED, *n.* [for *pad.*] A small pack-saddle. *Tusser.*
2. A basket; a hamper. *Spenser.*

PEDAGOG'IC, } *a.* [from *pedagogue.*]
PEDAGOG'ICAL, } Suiting or belonging to a teacher of children or to a pedagogue.

PED'AGOGISM, *n.* The business, character or manners of a pedagogue.

PEDAGOGUE, *n.* *ped'agog.* [Gr. παιδαγωγος; παις, a child, and αγω, to lead.]
1. A teacher of children; one whose occupation is to instruct young children; a schoolmaster.
2. A pedant.

PED'AGOGUE, *v. t.* To teach with the air of a pedagogue; to instruct superciliously. *Prior.*

PED'AGOGY, *n.* Instruction in the first rudiments; preparatory discipline. *South.*

PE'DAL, *a.* [L. *pedalis*, from *pes*, *pedis*, foot.] Pertaining to a foot.

PED'AL, *n.* One of the large pipes of an organ, so called because played and stopped with the foot. *Encyc.*
2. A fixed or stationary base. *Busby.*

PED'AL-NOTE, *n.* In music, a holding-note. *Busby.*

PEDA'NEOUS, *a.* [L. *pedaneus*, from *pes*, the foot.] Going on foot; walking. *Dict.*

PED'ANT, *n.* [Fr. *pedant;* It. Sp. Port. *pedante.* See *Pedagogue.*]
1. A schoolmaster. *Shak.*
2. A person who makes a vain display of his learning. *Addison.*

PEDANT'IC, } *a.* Ostentatious of learn-
PEDANT'ICAL, } ing; vainly displaying or making a show of knowledge; *applied to persons or things;* as a *pedantic* writer or scholar; a *pedantic* description or expression.

PEDANT'ICALLY, *adv.* With a vain or boastful display of learning.

PED'ANTIZE, *v. i.* To play the pedant; to domineer over lads; to use pedantic expressions. *Cotgrave.*

PED'ANTRY, *n.* [Fr. *pedanterie.*] Vain ostentation of learning; a boastful display of knowledge of any kind.

> Horace has enticed me into this *pedantry* of quotation. *Cowley.*

> *Pedantry* is the unseasonable ostentation of learning. *Rambler.*

PEDA'RIAN, *n.* A Roman senator who gave his vote by the feet, that is, by walking over to the side he espoused, in divisions of the senate. *Encyc.*

PED'ATE, *a.* [L. *pedatus*, from *pes*, the foot.]
In *botany*, divided like the toes. A *pedate* leaf is one in which a bifid petiole connects several leaflets on the inside only. *Martyn.*

PED'ATIFID, *a.* [L. *pes*, foot, and *findo*, to divide.]
A *pedatifid* leaf, in botany, is one whose parts are not entirely separate, but connected like the toes of a water-fowl. *Martyn.*

PED'DLE, *v. i.* [perhaps from the root of *petty*, W. *pitw*, Fr. *petit*, small.] To be busy about trifles.
2. To travel about the country and retail goods. He *peddles* for a living.

PED'DLE, *v. t.* To sell or retail, usually by traveling about the country.

PED'DLING, *ppr.* Traveling about and selling small wares.
2. *a.* Trifling; unimportant.

PED'ERAST, *n.* [Gr. παιδεραςης, from παις, a boy, and ερως, love.] A sodomite. *Encyc.*

PEDERAS'TIC, *a.* Pertaining to pederasty.

PED'ERASTY, *n.* Sodomy; the crime against nature.

PEDERE'RO, *n.* [Sp. *pedrero*, from *piedra*, a stone, L. *petra*, Gr. πετρος; so named from the use of stones in the charge, before the invention of iron balls.] A swivel gun; sometimes written *paterero.*

PED'ESTAL, *n.* [Sp. *pedestal;* It. *piedestallo;* Fr. *piedestal;* L. *pes*, the foot, and Teut. *stall;* G. *stellen*, to set.]
In *architecture*, the lowest part of a column or pillar; the part which sustains a column or serves as its foot. It consists of three parts, the base, the die and the cornice. *Addison. Encyc.*

PEDES'TRIAL, *a.* [L. *pedestris.*] Pertaining to the foot. *Moseley.*

PEDES'TRIAN, *a.* [L. *pedestris*, from *pes*, the foot.]
Going on foot; walking; made on foot; as a *pedestrian* journey.

PEDES'TRIAN, *n.* One that walks or journeys on foot.
2. One that walks for a wager; a remarkable walker.

PEDES'TRIOUS, *a.* Going on foot; not winged. *Brown.*

PED'ICEL, } *n.* [L. *pediculus*, from *pes*, the
PED'ICLE, } foot.] In *botany*, the ultimate division of a common peduncle; the stalk that supports one flower only when there are several on a peduncle. *Martyn.*

PED'ICELLATE, *a.* Having a pedicel, or supported by a pedicel.

PEDIC'ULAR, } *a.* [L. *pedicularis*, from
PEDIC'ULOUS, } *pediculus*, a louse.] Lousy; having the lousy distemper.

PED'IGREE, *n.* [probably from L. *pes*, *pedis*, foot, like D. *stam*, G. *stamm*, stem, stock, degree.]
1. Lineage; line of ancestors from which a person or tribe descends; genealogy.

> Alterations of surnames—have obscured the truth of our *pedigrees.* *Camden.*

2. An account or register of a line of ancestors.

> The Jews preserved the *pedigrees* of their several tribes. *Atterbury.*

PED'ILUVY, *n.* [L. *pes*, foot, and *lavo*, to wash.] The bathing of the feet; a bath for the feet.

PED'IMENT, *n.* [from L. *pes*, the foot.] In *architecture*, an ornament that crowns the ordonances, finishes the fronts of buildings and serves as a decoration over gates, windows and niches. It is of two forms, triangular and circular. A pediment is properly the representation of the roof. *Encyc.*

PED'LER, *n.* [from *peddle*, to sell by traveling; or from L. *pes*, *pedis*, the foot.]
A traveling foot-trader; one that carries about small commodities on his back, or in a cart or wagon, and sells them. *Spenser. Swift.*

PED'LERESS, *n.* A female pedler. *Overbury.*

PED'LERY, *n.* Small wares sold or carried about for sale by pedlers.

PEDOBAP'TISM, *n.* [Gr. παις, παιδος, a child, and βαπτισμα, baptism.] The baptism of infants or of children.

PEDOBAP'TIST, *n.* One that holds to infant baptism; one that practices the baptism of children. Most denominations of christians are *pedobaptists.*

PEDOM'ETER, *n.* [L. *pes*, the foot, and Gr. μετρον, measure.]
An instrument by which paces are numbered as a person walks, and the distance from place to place ascertained. It also marks the revolutions of wheels. This is done by means of wheels with teeth and a chain or string fastened to the foot or to the wheel of a carriage; the wheels advancing a notch at every step or at every revolution of the carriage wheel. *Encyc.*

PEDOMET'RICAL, *a.* Pertaining to or measured by a pedometer.

PEDUN'CLE, *n.* [L. *pes*, the foot.] In *botany*, the stem or stalk that supports the fructification of a plant, and of course the fruit. *Martyn.*

PEDUN'CULAR, *a.* Pertaining to a peduncle; growing from a peduncle; as a *peduncular* tendril. *Martyn.*

PEDUN'CULATE, *a.* Growing on a peduncle; as a *pedunculate* flower.

PEE, *v. i.* To look with one eye. [*Not used.*] *Ray.*

PEED, *a.* Blind of one eye. [*Not used.*] *Ray.*

PEEK, in our popular dialect, is the same as *peep*, to look through a crevice.

PEEL, *v. t.* [Fr. *peler*, *piller;* Sp. *pelar*, *pillar;* Port. *pelar*, *pilhar;* It. *pigliare;* L. *pilo*, to pull off hair and to pillage; Arm. *pilha;* W. *piliaw*, to take off the surface or rind. The first verb *peler*, *pelar*, seems to be formed from L. *pilus*, the hair. The Eng. *peel* is therefore from the other verb. See *Pill.* Class Bl. No. 32. 44. 51.]
1. To strip off skin, bark or rind without a cutting instrument; to strip by drawing or tearing off the skin; to bark; to flay; to decorticate. When a knife is used, we call it *paring.* Thus we say, to *peel* a tree, to *peel* an orange; but we say, to *pare* an apple, to *pare* land.
2. In *a general sense*, to remove the skin, bark or rind, even with an instrument.
3. To strip; to plunder; to pillage; as, to *peel* a province or conquered people. *Milton. Dryden.*

PEEL, *n.* [L. *pellis*, Fr. *peau*, G. *fell*, D. *vel*, skin; from *peeling.*]
The skin or rind of any thing; as the *peel* of an orange.

PEEL, *n.* [Fr. *pelle*; L. Sp. It. *pala*; W. *pal*; probably from thrusting, throwing, L. *pello*, Gr. βαλλω, like Eng. *shovel*, from *shove*; or from spreading.]
A kind of wooden shovel used by bakers, with a broad palm and long handle; hence, in popular use in America, any large fire-shovel.

PEE'LED, *pp.* Stripped of skin, bark or rind; plundered; pillaged.

PEE'LER, *n.* One that peels, strips or flays.
2. A plunderer; a pillager.

PEE'LING, *ppr.* Stripping off skin or bark; plundering.

PEEP, *v. i.* [Ir. *piobam*, to pipe, to peep; D. *piepen*, to pipe, to chirp; G. *pfeifen*; Sw. *pipa*; Dan. *piper*, *pipper*; L. *pipio*. The primary sense is to open or to shoot, to thrust out or forth; Dan. *pipper frem*, to sprout, to bud. This coincides with *pipe*, *fife*, &c., Heb. יבב to cry out, *Abib*, &c.]
1. To begin to appear; to make the first appearance; to issue or come forth from concealment, as through a narrow avenue.

I can see his pride
Peep through each part of him. *Shak.*
When flowers first *peeped*— *Dryden.*

2. To look through a crevice; to look narrowly, closely or slyly.

A fool will *peep* in at the door. *Ecclus.*
Thou art a maid and must not *peep*. *Prior.*

3. To cry, as chickens; to utter a fine shrill sound, as through a crevice; usually written *pip*, but without reason, as it is the same word as is here defined, and in America is usually pronounced *peep*.

PEEP, *n.* First appearance; as the *peep* of day.
2. A sly look, or a look through a crevice. *Swift.*
3. The cry of a chicken.

PEE'PER, *n.* A chicken just breaking the shell. *Bramston.*
2. In *familiar language*, the eye.

PEE'P-HOLE, } *n.* A hole or crevice
PEE'PING-HOLE, } through which one may peep or look without being discovered.

PEER, *n.* [Fr. *pair*; L. *par*; It. *pari*; Sp. *par*. See *Pair*.]
1. An equal; one of the same rank. A man may be familiar with his *peers*.
2. An equal in excellence or endowments.

In song he never had his *peer*. *Dryden.*

3. A companion; a fellow; an associate.

He all his *peers* in beauty did surpass. *Spenser.*

4. A nobleman; as a *peer* of the realm; the house of *peers*, so called because noblemen and barons were originally considered as the companions of the king, like L. *comes*, count. In England, persons belonging to the five degrees of nobility are all peers.

PEER, *v. i.* [L. *pareo*; Norm. *perer*. See *Appear*.]
1. To come just in sight; to appear; *a poetic word.*

So honor *peereth* in the meanest habit. *Shak.*
See how his gorget *peers* above his gown. *B. Jonson.*

2. To look narrowly; to peep; as the *peering* day. *Milton.*

Peering in maps for ports and piers and roads. *Shak.*

PEE'RAGE, *n.* [See *Peer*, an equal.] The rank or dignity of a peer or nobleman. *Blackstone.*
2. The body of peers. *Dryden.*

PEE'RDOM, *n.* Peerage. [*Not used.*]

PEE'RESS, *n.* The consort of a peer; a noble lady. *Pope.*

PEE'RLESS, *a.* Unequaled; having no peer or equal; as *peerless* beauty or majesty. *Dryden.*

PEE'RLESSLY, *adv.* Without an equal.

PEE'RLESSNESS, *n.* The state of having no equal.

PEE'VISH, *a.* [In Scot. *pew* is to complain or mutter. It is probably a contracted word, and perhaps from the root of *pet*, *petulant*.]
1. Fretful; petulant; apt to mutter and complain; easily vexed or fretted; querulous; hard to please.

She is *peevish*, sullen, froward. *Shak.*

2. Expressing discontent and fretfulness.

I will not presume
To send such *peevish* tokens to a king. *Shak.*

3. Silly; childish. *Shak.*

PEE'VISHLY, *adv.* Fretfully; petulantly; with discontent and murmuring. *Hayward.*

PEE'VISHNESS, *n.* Fretfulness; petulance; disposition to murmur; sourness of temper; as childish *peevishness*.

When *peevishness* and spleen succeed. *Swift.*

PEG, *n.* [This is probably from the root of L. *pango*, *pactus*, Gr. πηγνυμι; denoting that which fastens, or allied to *beak* and *picket*.]
1. A small pointed piece of wood used in fastening boards or other work of wood, &c. It does the office of a nail. The word is applied only to small pieces of wood pointed; to the larger pieces thus pointed we give the name of *pins*, and pins in ship carpentry are called *tree-nails* or *trenails*. Coxe, in his travels in Russia, speaks of poles or beams fastened into the ground with *pegs*.
2. The pins of an instrument on which the strings are strained. *Shak.*
3. A nickname for Margaret.
To take a peg lower, to depress; to lower. *Hudibras.*

PEG, *v. t.* To fasten with pegs. *Evelyn.*

PEG'GER, *n.* One that fastens with pegs. *Sherwood.*

PEGM, *n. pem.* [Gr. πηγμα.] A sort of moving machine in the old pageants. *B. Jonson.*

PEG'MATITE, *n.* Primitive granitic rock, composed essentially of lamellar feldspar and quartz; frequently with a mixture of mica. In it are found kaolin, tin tourmalin, beryl, aqua marina, tantale, scheelin and other valuable minerals. *Dict.*

PEIRAS'TIC, *a.* [Gr. πειραςικος, from πειραω, to strain, to attempt.] Attempting; making trial.
2. Treating of or representing trials or attempts; as the *peirastic* dialogues of Plato. *Enfield.*

PEISE. [See *Poise*.]

PEK'AN, *n.* A species of weasel. *Buffon. Pennant.*

PEL'AGE, *n.* [Fr. from L. *pilus*, hair.] The vesture or covering of wild beasts, consisting of hair, fur or wool. *Bacon.*

PELA'GIAN, } *a.* [L. *pelagus*, the sea.]
PEL'AGIC, } Pertaining to the sea; as *pelagian* shells. *Journ. of Science.*

PELA'GIAN, *n.* [from *Pelagius*, a native of Great Britain, who lived in the fourth century.]
A follower of Pelagius, a monk of Banchor or Bangor, who denied original sin, and asserted the doctrine of free will and the merit of good works. *Bp. Hall.*

PELA'GIAN, *a.* Pertaining to Pelagius and his doctrines. *South.*

PELA'GIANISM, *n.* The doctrines of Pelagius. *South.*

PELF, *n.* [probably allied to *pilfer*.] Money; riches; but it often conveys the idea of something ill gotten or worthless. It has no plural.

PEL'ICAN, *n.* [Low L. *pelicanus*; Gr. πελεκαν; Fr. *pelican*.]
1. A fowl of the genus Pelicanus. It is larger than the swan, and remarkable for its enormous bill, to the lower edges of the under chop of which is attached a pouch or bag, capable of being distended so as to hold many quarts of water. In this bag the fowl deposits the fish it takes for food. *Encyc.*
2. A chimical glass vessel or alembic with a tubulated capital, from which two opposite and crooked beaks pass out and enter again at the belly of the cucurbit. It is designed for continued distillation and cohobation; the volatile parts of the substance distilling, rising into the capital and returning through the beaks into the cucurbit. *Nicholson.*

PE'LIOM, *n.* [Gr. πελιωμα, black color.] A mineral, a variety of iolite. *Cleaveland.*

PELÏSSE, *n. pelee's.* [Fr. from L. *pellis*, skin.]
Originally, a furred robe or coat. But the name is now given to a silk coat or habit worn by ladies.

PELL, *n.* [L. *pellis*, It. *pelle*, a skin.] A skin or hide.
Clerk of the pells, in England, an officer of the exchequer, who enters every teller's bill on the parchment rolls, the roll of receipts and the roll of disbursements.

PEL'LET, *n.* [Fr. *pelote*; W. *pellen*, from L. *pila*, a ball, It. *palla*.] A little ball; as a *pellet* of wax or lint. *Bacon. Wiseman.*
2. A bullet; a ball for fire-arms. [*Not now used.*] *Bacon. Ray.*

PEL'LETED, *a.* Consisting of bullets. *Shak.*

PEL'LICLE, *n.* [L. *pellicula*, dim. of *pellis*, skin.] A thin skin or film. *Sharp. Encyc.*
2. Among *chimists*, a thin saline crust formed on the surface of a solution of salt evaporated to a certain degree. This pellicle consists of saline particles crystalized. *Encyc. Nicholson.*

PEL'LITORY, *n.* [Sp. *pelitre*; corrupted perhaps from L. *parietaria*, the wall plant, from *paries*.]
The name of several plants of different genera. The *pellitory of the wall* or *common pellitory* is of the genus Parietaria; the *bastard pellitory* of the genus Achillea; and the *pellitory of Spain* is the Anthemis pyrethrum. *Lee. Parr.*

PELL'-MELL, *adv.* With confused violence. *Shak. Hudibras.*

PELLU'CID, *a.* [L. *pellucidus ; per* and *lucidus ;* very bright. See *Light.*]
Perfectly clear; transparent; not opake; as a body as *pellucid* as crystal. *Woodward.*

PELLUCID'ITY, } *n.* Perfect clearness;
PELLU'CIDNESS, } transparency; as the *pellucidity* of the air; the *pellucidness* of a gem. *Locke. Keil.*

PELT, *n.* [G. *pelz ;* Sp. *pelada ;* L. *pellis.* See *Fell.*]
1. The skin of a beast with the hair on it; a raw hide. *Brown.*
2. The quarry of a hawk all torn. *Ainsworth.*
3. A blow or stroke from something thrown. [infra.]

PELT, *v. t.* [Fr. *peloter*, from *pelote*, a ball; or contracted from *pellet.* In Sw. *bulta* is to beat. The word is from Fr. *pelote*, a little ball, or from L. *pello*, Gr. βαλλω.]
1. Properly, to strike with something thrown, driven or falling; as, to *pelt* with stones; *pelted* with hail.
The chiding billows seem to *pelt* the clouds. *Shak.*
2. To drive by throwing something. *Atterbury.*

PELT'ATE, } *a.* [L. *pelta*, a target.] In
PELT'ATED, } *botany*, having the shape of a target or round shield, as a *peltate* stigma; having the petiole inserted in the disk, as a *peltate* leaf. *Martyn.*

PELT'ATELY, *adv.* In the form of a target. *Eaton.*

PELT'ED, *pp.* Struck with something thrown or driven.

PELT'ER, *n.* One that pelts; also, a pinch-penny; a mean, sordid person. *Huloet.*

PELT'ING, *ppr.* Striking with something thrown or driven.

PELT'ING, *n.* An assault with any thing thrown. *Shak.*

PELT'ING, *a.* In Shakspeare, mean; paltry. [*Improper.*]

PELT'-MONGER, *n.* A dealer in pelts or raw hides.

PEL'TRY, *n.* [from *pelt*, a skin.] The skins of animals producing fur; skins in general, with the fur on them; furs in general. *Smollett.*

PELVIM'ETER, *n.* [L. *pelvis* and Gr. μετρον, measure.]
An instrument to measure the dimensions of the female pelvis. *Coxe.*

PEL'VIS, *n.* [L. *pelvis*, a bason.] The cavity of the body formed by the os sacrum, os coccyx, and ossa innominata, forming the lower part of the abdomen.

PEN, *n.* [L. *penna ;* Sax. *pinn ;* D. *pen ;* It. *penna*, a fether, a pen, and a top; W. *pen*, top, summit, head; Ir. *beann, beinn*, written also *ben.* The Celtic nations called the peak of a mountain, *ben* or *pen.* Hence the name *Apennine*, applied to the mountains of Italy. It may belong to the same root as L. *pinna*, a *fin*, that is, a shoot or point.]
1. An instrument used for writing, usually made of the quill of some large fowl, but it may be of any other material.
2. A fether; a wing. [*Not used.*] *Spenser.*

PEN, *v. t.* pret. and pp. *penned.* To write; to compose and commit to paper. *Addison.*

PEN, *n.* [Sax. *pinan*, to press, or *pyndan*, to pound or shut up; both probably from one root.]
A small inclosure for beasts, as for cows or sheep.

PEN, *v. t.* pret. and pp. *penned* or *pent.* To shut in a pen; to confine in a small inclosure; to coop; to confine in a narrow place; usually followed by *up*, which is redundant. *Boyle. Milton.*

PE'NAL, *a.* [Fr. Sp. *id. ;* It. *penale ;* from L. *pœna*, Gr. ποινη, pain, punishment. See *Pain.*]
1. Enacting punishment; denouncing the punishment of offenses; as a *penal* law or statute; the *penal* code. *Penal* statutes must be construed strictly. *Blackstone.*
2. Inflicting punishment.
Adamantine chains and *penal* fire. *Milton.*
3. Incurring punishment; subject to a penalty; as a *penal* act or offense.

PENAL'ITY, *n.* Liableness or condemnation to punishment. [*Not used.*] *Brown.*

PEN'ALTY, *n.* [It. *penalità ;* Sp. *penalidad.* See *Penal.*]
1. The suffering in person or property which is annexed by law or judicial decision to the commission of a crime, offense or trespass, as a punishment. A fine is a pecuniary *penalty.* The usual *penalties* inflicted on the person, are whipping, cropping, branding, imprisonment, hard labor, transportation or death.
2. The suffering to which a person subjects himself by covenant or agreement, in case of non-fulfillment of his stipulations; the forfeiture or sum to be forfeited for non-payment, or for non-compliance with an agreement; as the *penalty* of a bond.

PEN'ANCE, *n.* [Sp. *penante*, from *penar*, It. *penare*, to suffer pain. See *Pain.*]
1. The suffering, labor or pain to which a person voluntarily subjects himself, or which is imposed on him by authority as a punishment for his faults, or as an expression of penitence; such as fasting, flagellation, wearing chains, &c. *Penance* is one of the seven sacraments of the Romish church. *Encyc.*
2. Repentance.

PENCE, *n. pens.* The plural of *penny*, when used of a sum of money or value. When pieces of coin are mentioned, we use *pennies.*

PEN'CIL, *n.* [Fr. *pinceau ;* Sp. *pincel ;* L. *penicillus.*]
1. A small brush used by painters for laying on colors. The proper pencils are made of fine hair or bristles, as of camels, badgers or squirrels, or of the down of swans, inclosed in a quill. The larger pencils, made of swine's bristles, are called *brushes.* *Encyc.*
2. A pen formed of carburet of iron or plumbago, black lead or red chalk, with a point at one end, used for writing and drawing. *Encyc.*
3. Any instrument of writing without ink. *Johnson.*
4. An aggregate or collection of rays of light.

PEN'CIL, *v. t.* To paint or draw; to write or mark with a pencil. *Shak. Harte.*

PEN'CILED, *pp.* Painted, drawn or marked with a pencil.
2. Radiated; having pencils of rays.

PEN'CILING, *ppr.* Painting, drawing or marking with a pencil.

PEN'CIL-SHAPED, *a.* Having the shape of a pencil.

PEND'ANT, *n.* [Fr. from L. *pendeo*, to hang, or Sp. *pendon.* See *Pennon.*]
1. An ornament or jewel hanging at the ear, usually composed of pearl or some precious stone. *Pope.*
2. Any thing hanging by way of ornament. *Waller.*
3. In *heraldry*, a part hanging from the label, resembling the drops in the Doric frieze. *Encyc.*
4. A streamer; a small flag or long narrow banner displayed from a ship's mast head, usually terminating in two points called the swallow's tail. It denotes that a ship is in actual service. The broad pendant is used to distinguish the chief of a squadron. *Mar. Dict.*
5. A short piece of rope fixed on each side under the shrouds, on the heads of the main and fore-mast, having an iron thimble to receive the hooks of the tackle. *Mar. Dict.*
There are many other pendants consisting of a rope or ropes, to whose lower extremity is attached a block or tackle. The rudder-pendant is a rope made fast to the rudder by a chain, to prevent the loss of the rudder when unshipped. *Mar. Dict.*
6. A pendulum. [*Not used.*] *Digby.*

PEND'ENCE, *n.* [L. *pendens, pendeo*, to hang.] Slope; inclination. *Wotton.*

PEND'ENCY, *n.* [L. *pendens, pendeo*, supra.]
Suspense; the state of being undecided; as, to wait during the *pendency* of a suit or petition.

PEND'ENT, *a.* [L. *pendens.*] Hanging; fastened at one end, the other being loose.
With ribbons *pendent*, flaring about her head. *Shak.*
2. Jutting over; projecting; as a *pendant* rock. *Shak.*
3. Supported above the ground. *Milton.*

PEND'ING, *a.* [L. *pendeo*, to hang; *pendente lite.*]
Depending; remaining undecided; not terminated. This was done, *pending* the suit.

PENDULOS'ITY, } *n.* [See *Pendulous.*]
PEND'ULOUSNESS, } The state of hanging; suspension. [*The latter is the preferable word.*]

PEND'ULOUS, *a.* [L. *pendulus*, from *pendeo*, to hang.]
Hanging; swinging; fastened at one end, the other being movable. The dewlap of an animal is *pendulous.*

PEND'ULUM, *n.* [L. *pendulus, pendulum.*]
A vibrating body suspended from a fixed point; as the *pendulum* of a clock. The oscillations of a pendulum depend on gravity, and are always performed in nearly equal times, supposing the length of the pendulum and the gravity to remain the same.

PENETRABIL'ITY, *n.* [from *penetrable.*]
Susceptibility of being penetrated, or of being entered or passed through by another body.

There being no mean between *penetrability* and impenetrability. *Cheyne.*

PEN'ETRABLE, *a.* [Fr. from L. *penetrabilis.* See *Penetrate.*]

1. That may be penetrated, entered or pierced by another body.

Let him try thy dart,
And pierce his only *penetrable* part. *Dryden.*

2. Susceptible of moral or intellectual impression.

I am not made of stone,
But *penetrable* to your kind entreaties. *Shak.*

PEN'ETRAIL, *n.* [L. *penetralia.*] Interior parts. [*Not used.*] *Harvey.*

PEN'ETRANCY, *n.* [L. *penetrans.*] Power of entering or piercing; as the *penetrancy* of subtil effluvia. *Ray.*

PEN'ETRANT, *a.* [L. *penetrans.*] Having the power to enter or pierce; sharp; subtil; as *penetrant* spirit; food subtilized and rendered fluid and *penetrant.* *Boyle. Ray.*

PEN'ETRATE, *v. t.* [L. *penetro,* from the root of *pen,* a point.]

1. To enter or pierce; to make way into another body; as, a sword or dart *penetrates* the body; oil *penetrates* wood; marrow, the most *penetrating* of oily substances. *Arbuthnot.*

2. To affect the mind; to cause to feel. I am *penetrated* with a lively sense of your generosity.

3. To reach by the intellect; to understand; as, to *penetrate* the meaning or design of any thing.

4. To enter; to pass into the interior; as, to *penetrate* a country.

PEN'ETRATE, *v. i.* To pass; to make way.

Born where heaven's influence scarce can *penetrate.* *Pope.*

2. To make way intellectually. He had not *penetrated* into the designs of the prince.

PEN'ETRATED, *pp.* Entered; pierced; understood; fathomed.

PEN'ETRATING, *ppr.* Entering; piercing; understanding.

2. *a.* Having the power of entering or piercing another body; sharp; subtil. Oil is a *penetrating* substance.

3. Acute; discerning; quick to understand; as a *penetrating* mind.

PENETRA'TION, *n.* The act of entering a body. *Milton.*

2. Mental entrance into any thing abstruse; as a *penetration* into the abstruse difficulties of algebra. *Watts.*

3. Acuteness; sagacity; as a man of great or nice *penetration.*

PEN'ETRATIVE, *a.* Piercing; sharp; subtil.

Let not air be too gross nor too *penetrative.* *Wotton.*

2. Acute; sagacious; discerning; as *penetrative* wisdom. *Swift.*

3. Having the power to affect or impress the mind; as *penetrative* shame. *Shak.*

PEN'ETRATIVENESS, *n.* The quality of being penetrative.

PEN'FISH, *n.* A kind of eelpout with a smooth skin. *Dict. Nat. Hist.*

PEN'GUIN, *n.* [W. *pen,* head, and *gwyn,* white; or L. *pinguidine,* with fatness.]

1. A genus of fowls of the order of Palmipeds. The penguin is an aquatic fowl with very short legs, with four toes, three of which are webbed; the body is clothed with short fethers, set as compactly as the scales of a fish; the wings are small like fins, and covered with short scale-like fethers, so that they are useless in flight. Penguins seldom go on shore, except in the season of breeding, when they burrow like rabbits. On land they stand erect; they are tame and may be driven like a flock of sheep. In water they swim with rapidity, being assisted by their wings. These fowls are found only in the southern latitudes. *Encyc.*

2. A species of fruit. *Miller.*

PEN'ICIL, *n.* [L. *penicillus.* See *Pencil.*]

1. Among physicians, a tent or pledget for wounds or ulcers.

2. A species of shell.

PENIN'SULA, *n.* [L. *pene,* almost, and *insula,* an isle; It. *penesolo.*]

1. A portion of land, connected with a continent by a narrow neck or isthmus, but nearly surrounded with water. Thus Boston stands on a *peninsula.*

2. A large extent of country joining the main land by a part narrower than the tract itself. Thus Spain and Portugal are said to be situated on a *peninsula.*

PENIN'SULAR, *a.* In the form or state of a peninsula; pertaining to a peninsula.

PENIN'SULATE, *v. t.* To encompass almost with water; to form a peninsula.

South river *peninsulates* Castle hill farm, and at high tides, surrounds it. *Bentley's Hist. Coll.*

PENIN'SULATED, *pp.* Almost surrounded with water.

PENIN'SULATING, *ppr.* Nearly surrounding with water.

PEN'ITENCE, } *n.* [Fr. *penitence,* from L.
PEN'ITENCY, } *pœnitentia,* from *pœniteo,* from *pœna,* pain, punishment. See *Pain.*]

Repentance; pain; sorrow or grief of heart for sins or offenses; contrition. Real *penitence* springs from a conviction of guilt and ingratitude to God, and is followed by amendment of life.

PEN'ITENT, *a.* [Fr. from L. *pœnitens.*] Suffering pain or sorrow of heart on account of sins, crimes or offenses; contrite; sincerely affected by a sense of guilt and resolving on amendment of life.

The proud he tam'd, the *penitent* he cheer'd. *Dryden.*

PEN'ITENT, *n.* One that repents of sin; one sorrowful on account of his transgressions.

2. One under church censure, but admitted to penance. *Stillingfleet.*

3. One under the direction of a confessor.

Penitents is an appellation given to certain fraternities in catholic countries, distinguished by their habits and employed in charitable acts. *Encyc.*

Order of penitents, a religious order established by one Bernard of Marseilles, about the year 1272, for the reception of reformed courtezans. The *congregation of penitents* at Paris, was founded with a similar view. *Encyc.*

PENITEN'TIAL, *a.* [Fr. *penitentiel;* It. *penitenziale.*] Proceeding from or expressing penitence or contrition of heart; as *penitential* sorrow or tears. *South.*

PENITEN'TIAL, *n.* Among the Romanists, a book containing the rules which relate to penance and the reconciliation of penitents. *Encyc.*

PENITEN'TIARY, *a.* Relating to penance, or to the rules and measures of penance. *Bramhall.*

PENITEN'TIARY, *n.* One that prescribes the rules and measures of penance. *Bacon. Ayliffe.*

2. A penitent; one that does penance. *Hammond.*

3. At *the court of Rome,* an office in which are examined and delivered out the secret bulls, graces or dispensations relating to cases of conscience, confession, &c. *Encyc.*

4. An officer in some cathedrals, vested with power from the bishop to absolve in cases reserved to him. The pope has a grand penitentiary, who is a cardinal and is chief of the other penitentiaries. *Encyc.*

5. A house of correction in which offenders are confined for punishment and reformation, and compelled to labor; a workhouse. A state prison is a *penitentiary.*

PEN'ITENTLY, *adv.* With penitence; with repentance, sorrow or contrition for sin.

PEN'KNIFE, *n.* [See *Pen* and *Knife.*] A small knife used for making and mending pens.

PEN'MAN, *n.* plu. *penmen.* [See *Pen* and *Man.*]

1. A man that professes or teaches the art of writing. More generally,

2. One that writes a good hand.

3. An author; a writer; as the sacred *penmen.* *Addison.*

PEN'MANSHIP, *n.* The use of the pen in writing; the art of writing.

2. Manner of writing; as good or bad *penmanship.*

PEN'NACHED, *a.* [Fr. *pennaché* or *panaché,* from *panache,* a plume or bunch of fethers.]

Radiated; diversified with natural stripes of various colors; as a flower. [*Little used.*] *Evelyn.*

PEN'NANT, } *n.* [Fr. *fanion, pennon;* It.
PEN'NON, } *pennone;* Sp. *pendon;* W. *penwn;* Goth. *fana;* L. *pannus,* a cloth.]

1. A small flag; a banner. [See *Pendant.*]

2. A tackle for hoisting things on board a ship. *Ainsworth.*

PEN'NATE, } *a.* [L. *pennatus,* winged,
PEN'NATED, } from *penna,* a quill or wing.]

1. Winged.

2. In *botany,* a pennate leaf is a compound leaf in which a simple petiole has several leaflets attached to each side of it. [See *Pinnate.*]

PEN'NED, *pp.* Written.

PEN'NED, *a.* Winged; having plumes. *Huloet.*

PEN'NER, *n.* A writer.

2. A pen-case. [*Local.*] *Ainsworth.*

PEN'NIFORM, *a.* [L. *penna,* a fether or quill, and *form.*]

Having the form of a quill or fether. *Encyc.*

PEN'NILESS, *a.* [from *penny.*] Moneyless; destitute of money; poor. *Arbuthnot.*

PEN'NING, *ppr.* Committing to writing.

PENNON. [See *Pennant.*]

PEN'NY, *n.* plu. *pennies* or *pence.* *Pennies* denotes the number of coins; *pence* the amount of pennies in value. [Sax. *penig*; D. Sw. *penning*; G. *pfennig*; Dan. *penge*, money.]

1. An ancient English silver coin; but now an imaginary money of account, twelve of which are equal to a shilling. It is the radical denomination from which English coin is numbered. *Johnson.*

2. In ancient English statutes, any or all silver money.

3. Proverbially, a small sum. He will not lend a *penny.*

4. Money in general.

Be sure to turn the *penny.* *Dryden.*

PEN'NYPOST, *n.* One that carries letters from the post office and delivers them to the proper persons for a penny or other small compensation.

PENNYROY'AL, *n.* A plant of the genus Mentha. *Fam. of Plants.*

The English pennyroyal is the *Mentha pulegium*; the N. American pennyroyal is the *Cunila pulegioides.* *Parr. Bigelow.*

PEN'NYWEIGHT, *n.* A troy weight containing twenty four grains, each grain being equal in weight to a grain of wheat from the middle of the ear, well dried. It was anciently the weight of a silver penny, whence the name. Twenty pennyweights make an ounce troy.

PEN'NYWISE, *a.* Saving small sums at the hazard of larger; niggardly on improper occasions. *Bacon.*

PEN'NYWORTH, *n.* As much as is bought for a penny.

2. Any purchase; any thing bought or sold for money; that which is worth the money given. *South.*

3. A good bargain; something advantageously purchased, or for less than it is worth. *Dryden.*

4. A small quantity. *Swift.*

PEN'SILE, *a.* [L. *pensilis*, from *pendeo*, to hang.]

1. Hanging; suspended; as a *pensile* bell. *Bacon. Prior.*

2. Supported above the ground; as a *pensile* garden. *Prior.*

PEN'SILENESS, *n.* The state of hanging. *Bacon.*

PEN'SION, *n.* [Fr. Sp. *id.*; It. *pensione*; from L. *pensio*, from *pendo*, *pensum*, to pay.]

1. An annual allowance of a sum of money to a person by government in consideration of past services, civil or military. Men often receive *pensions* for eminent services on retiring from office. But in particular, officers, soldiers and seamen receive *pensions* when they are disabled for further services.

2. An annual payment by an individual to an old or disabled servant.

3. In *Great Britain*, an annual allowance made by government to indigent widows of officers killed or dying in public service.

4. Payment of money; rent. 1 Esdras.

5. A yearly payment in the inns of court. *Eng.*

6. A certain sum of money paid to a clergyman in lieu of tithes. *Cyc.*

7. An allowance or annual payment, considered in the light of a bribe.

PEN'SION, *v. t.* To grant a pension to; to grant an annual allowance from the public treasury to a person for past services, or on account of disability incurred in public service, or of old age.

PEN'SIONARY, *a.* Maintained by a pension; receiving a pension; as *pensionary* spies. *Donne.*

2. Consisting in a pension; as a *pensionary* provision for maintenance.

PEN'SIONARY, *n.* A person who receives a pension from government for past services, or a yearly allowance from some prince, company or individual.

2. The first minister of the states of the province of Holland; also, the first minister of the regency of a city in Holland. *Encyc.*

PEN'SIONED, *pp.* Having a pension.

PEN'SIONER, *n.* One to whom an annual sum of money is paid by government in consideration of past services.

2. One who receives an annual allowance for services.

3. A dependant.

4. In the university of Cambridge, and in that of Dublin, an undergraduate or bachelor of arts who lives at his own expense. *Encyc.*

5. One of an honorable band of gentlemen who attend on the king of England, and receive a pension or an annual allowance of a hundred pounds. This band was instituted by Henry VII. Their duty is to guard the king's person in his own house. *Encyc. Cyc.*

PEN'SIONING, *ppr.* Granting an annual allowance for past services.

PEN'SIVE, *a.* [It. *pensivo*, *pensieroso*; Sp. *pensativo*; Fr. *pensif*, from *penser*, to think or reflect; L. *penso*, to weigh, to consider; *pendo*, to weigh.]

1. Literally, thoughtful; employed in serious study or reflection; but it often implies some degree of sorrow, anxiety, depression or gloom of mind; thoughtful and sad, or sorrowful.

Anxious cares the *pensive* nymph oppress'd. *Pope.*

2. Expressing thoughtfulness with sadness; as *pensive* numbers; *pensive* strains. *Prior.*

PEN'SIVELY, *adv.* With thoughtfulness; with gloomy seriousness or some degree of melancholy. *Spenser.*

PEN'SIVENESS, *n.* Gloomy thoughtfulness; melancholy; seriousness from depressed spirits. *Hooker.*

PEN'STOCK, *n.* [*pen* and *stock.*] A narrow or confined place formed by a frame of timber planked or boarded, for holding or conducting the water of a mill-pond to a wheel, and furnished with a flood gate which may be shut or opened at pleasure.

PENT, *pp.* of *pen.* Shut up; closely confined.

PENTACAP'SULAR, *a.* [Gr. πεντε, five, and *capsular.*] In *botany*, having five capsules.

PEN'TACHORD, *n.* [Gr. πεντε, five, and *chord.*]

1. An instrument of music with five strings.

2. An order or system of five sounds. *Busby.*

PEN'TACOCCOUS, *a.* [Gr. πεντε, five, and L. *coccus*, a berry.]

Having or containing five grains or seeds, or having five united cells with one seed in each. *Martyn.*

PEN'TACOSTER, *n.* [Gr.] In *ancient Greece*, a military officer commanding fifty men; but the number varied. *Mitford.*

PEN'TACOSTYS, *n.* [Gr.] A body of fifty soldiers; but the number varied. *Mitford.*

PENTAC'RINITE, *n.* The fossil remains of a zoophyte.

PENTACROS'TIC, *a.* [Gr. πεντε, five, and *acrostic.*]

Containing five acrostics of the same name in five divisions of each verse.

PENTACROS'TIC, *n.* A set of verses so disposed as to have five acrostics of the same name in five divisions of each verse. *Encyc.*

PENTADAC'TYL, *n.* [Gr. πεντε, five, and δακτυλος, finger.]

1. In *botany*, a plant called *five fingers*; a name given to the Ricinus or Palma Christi, from the shape of its leaf. *Encyc.*

2. In *ichthyology*, the five fingered fish; a name given to a fish common in the East Indian seas, which has five black strokes on each side resembling the prints of five fingers. *Encyc.*

PEN'TAGON, *n.* [Gr. πεντε, five, and γωνια, a corner.]

1. In *geometry*, a figure of five sides and five angles. *Encyc.*

2. In *fortification*, a fort with five bastions. *Encyc.*

PENTAG'ONAL, PENTAG'ONOUS, *a.* Having five corners or angles. *Woodward. Lee. Martyn.*

PEN'TAGRAPH, *n.* [Gr. πεντε, five, and γραφω, to write.]

An instrument for drawing figures in any proportion at pleasure, or for copying or reducing a figure, plan, print, &c. to any desired size.

PENTAGRAPH'IC, PENTAGRAPH'ICAL, *a.* Pertaining to a pentagraph; performed by a pentagraph.

PEN'TAGYN, *n.* [Gr. πεντε, five, and γυνη, a female.] In *botany*, a plant having five pistils.

PENTAGYN'IAN, *a.* Having five pistils.

PENTAHE'DRAL, PENTAHE'DROUS, *a.* Having five equal sides.

PENTAHE'DRON, *n.* [Gr. πεντε, five, and εδρα, a side or base.] A figure having five equal sides.

PENTAHEXAHE'DRAL, *a.* [Gr. πεντε, five, and *hexahedral.*]

In *crystalography*, exhibiting five ranges of faces one above another, each range containing six faces. *Cleaveland.*

PENTAM'ETER, *n.* [Gr. πεντε, five, and μετρον, measure.]

In *ancient poetry*, a verse of five feet. The two first feet may be either dactyls or spondees; the third is always a spondee, and the two last anapests. A pentameter verse subjoined to a hexameter, constitutes what is called elegiac. *Encyc.*

PENTAM'ETER, *a.* Having five metrical feet. *Warton.*

PENTAN'DER, *n.* [Gr. πεντε, five, and ανηρ, a male.]
In *botany*, a plant having five stamens.

PENTAN'DRIAN, *a.* Having five stamens.

PENTAN'GULAR, *a.* [Gr. πεντε, five, and *angular.*] Having five corners or angles. *Grew.*

PENTAPET'ALOUS, *a.* [Gr. πεντε, five, and πεταλον, a petal.]
Having five petals or flower leaves. *Encyc.*

PENTAPH'YLLOUS, *a.* [Gr. πεντε, five, and φυλλον, a leaf.] Having five leaves.

PEN'TARCHY, *n.* [Gr. πεντε, five, and αρχη, rule.]
A government in the hands of five persons. *Brewer.*

PEN'TASPAST, *n.* [Gr. πεντε, five, and σπαω, to draw.]
An engine with five pulleys. *Dict.*

PENTASPERM'OUS, *a.* [Gr. πεντε, five, and σπερμα, seed.] Containing five seeds. *Encyc.*

PEN'TASTICH, *n.* [Gr. πεντε, five, and ςιχος, verse.]
A composition consisting of five verses. *Dict.*

PEN'TASTYLE, *n.* [Gr. πεντε, five, and ςυλος, a column.]
In *architecture*, a work containing five rows of columns.

PEN'TATEUCH, *n.* [Gr. πεντε, five, and τευχος, a book or composition.]
The first five books of the Old Testament.

PEN'TECONTER, *n.* [from the Greek.] A Grecian vessel of fifty oars, smaller than a trireme. *Mitford.*

PEN'TECOST, *n.* [Gr. πεντεκοςη, πεντεκοςος, fiftieth.]
1. A solemn festival of the Jews, so called because celebrated on the fiftieth day after the sixteenth of Nisan, which was the second day of the passover. It was called the *feast* of weeks, because it was celebrated seven weeks after the passover. It was instituted to oblige the people to repair to the temple of the Lord, there to acknowledge his absolute dominion over the country, and offer him the first fruits of their harvest; also that they might call to mind and give thanks to God for the law which he had given them at Sinai on the fiftieth day from their departure from Egypt. *Calmet. Encyc.*
2. Whitsuntide, a solemn feast of the church, held in commemoration of the descent of the Holy Spirit on the apostles. Acts ii.

PEN'TECOSTAL, *a.* Pertaining to Whitsuntide. *Sanderson.*

PENTECOS'TALS, *n.* Oblations formerly made by parishioners to the parish priest at the feast of Pentecost, and sometimes by inferior churches to the mother church. *Cowel.*

PENT'HOUSE, *n.* [Fr. *pente*, a slope, and *house.* In Welsh, *penty.*]
A shed standing aslope from the main wall or building.

PEN'TICE, *n.* [It. *pendice*, a declivity, from L. *pendo*, to bend.]
A sloping roof. [*Little used.*] *Wotton.*

PEN'TILE, *n.* [Fr. *pente*, a bending, and *tile.*]
A tile for covering the sloping part of a roof. [Qu. *pantile.*] *Johnson.*

PEN'TREMITE, *n.* A genus of zoophytes or fossil shells.

PENULT', *n.* [L. *penultimus*; *pene*, almost, and *ultimus*, last.]
The last syllable of a word except one.

PENULT'IMATE, *a.* [supra.] The last but one; a word used of the last syllable of a word except one. It may be sometimes used as a noun.

PENUM'BRA, *n.* [L. *pene*, almost, and *umbra*, shade.]
In *astronomy*, a partial shade or obscurity on the margin of the perfect shade in an eclipse, or between the perfect shade, where the light is entirely intercepted, and the full light. *Cyc.*

PENU'RIOUS, *a.* [It. *penurioso*, from L. *penuria*, scarcity, want; Gr. πενης, poor; σπανος, rare.]
1. Excessively saving or sparing in the use of money; parsimonious to a fault; sordid; as a *penurious* man. It expresses somewhat less than *niggardly.*
2. Scanty; affording little; as a *penurious* spring. *Addison.*

PENU'RIOUSLY, *adv.* In a saving or parsimonious manner; with scanty supply.

PENU'RIOUSNESS, *n.* Parsimony; a sordid disposition to save money. *Addison.*
2. Scantiness; not plenty.

PEN'URY, *n.* [L. *penuria*, from Gr. πενης, needy.]
Want of property; indigence; extreme poverty.

> All innocent they were exposed to hardship and *penury.* *Sprat.*

PE'ON, *n.* In Hindoostan, a foot soldier, or a footman armed with sword and target; said to be corrupted from *piadah.* [Qu. L. *pes, pedis.*] Hence,
2. In *France*, a common man in chess; usually written and called *pawn.*

PE'ONY, *n.* [L. *pæonia*; Gr. παιωνια, from παιων, Apollo.]
A plant and flower of the genus Pæonia. It is written also *piony.*

PEOPLE, *n.* [Fr. *peuple*; L. *populus*; W. *pawb, pob*, each, every one; *poblac*, common people; G. *pobel*; Ir. *pupal, pobal*; Sp. *pueblo*; Russ. *bobiel*, a peasant. This word coincides in elements with *babe* and *pupil*, and perhaps originally signified the children of a family, like *gens.*]
1. The body of persons who compose a community, town, city or nation. We say, the *people* of a town; the *people* of London or Paris; the English *people.* In this sense, the word is not used in the plural, but it comprehends all classes of inhabitants, considered as a collective body, or any portion of the inhabitants of a city or country.
2. The vulgar; the mass of illiterate persons.

> The knowing artist may judge better than the *people.* *Waller.*

3. The commonalty, as distinct from men of rank.

> Myself shall mount the rostrum in his favor,
> And strive to gain his pardon from the *people.* *Addison.*

4. Persons of a particular class; a part of a nation or community; as country *people.*
5. Persons in general; any persons indefinitely; like *on* in French, and *man* in Saxon.

> *People* were tempted to lend by great premiums and large interest. *Swift.*

6. A collection or community of animals.

> The ants are a *people* not strong, yet they prepare their meat in the summer. Prov. xxx.

7. When *people* signifies a separate nation or tribe, it has the plural number.

> Thou must prophesy again before many *peoples.* Rev. x.

8. In *Scripture*, fathers or kindred. Gen. xxv.
9. The Gentiles.

> —To him shall the gathering of the *people* be. Gen. xlix.

PEOPLE, *v. t.* [Fr. *peupler.*] To stock with inhabitants. Emigrants from Europe have *peopled* the United States.

PEOPLED, *pp.* Stocked or furnished with inhabitants.

PEOPLING, *ppr.* Stocking with inhabitants.

PEOPLISH, *a.* Vulgar. *Chaucer.*

PEPAS'TIC, *n.* [Gr. πεπαινω, to concoct or mature.]
A medicine that serves to help digestion; applied particularly to such medicines as tend to promote the digestion of wounds. *Coxe.*

PEP'PER, *n.* [L. *piper*; Sax. *peppor*; D. *peper*; Sw. *peppar*; G. *pfeffer*; Dan. *peber*; Fr. *poivre*; It. *pepe*; Gr. πεπερι; Hindoo, *pipel*; Sanscrit, *pipali*; Pers. *pilpil.*]
A plant and its seed or grain, of the genus Piper. The stem of the plant is a vine requiring a prop, which is usually a tree. The leaves are oval and the flower white. We have three kinds of pepper, the black, the white, and the long. The black pepper is the produce of Java, Sumatra, Ceylon, and other Asiatic countries; the white pepper is the black pepper decorticated; the long pepper is the fruit of a different species, also from the E. Indies. It consists of numerous grains attached to a common footstalk. Pepper has a strong aromatic smell and a pungent taste. *Asiat. Res. Encyc.*

PEP'PER, *v. t.* To sprinkle with pepper.
2. To beat; to pelt with shot; to mangle with blows. *Shak.*

PEP'PER-BOX, *n.* A small box with a perforated lid, used for sprinkling pulverized pepper on food.

PEP'PER-CAKE, *n.* A kind of spiced cake or gingerbread.

PEP'PER-CORN, *n.* The berry or seed of the pepper-plant.
2. Something of inconsiderable value; as lands held at the rent of a *pepper-corn.*

PEP'PERED, *pp.* Sprinkled with pepper; pelted; spotted.

PEPPER-GIN'GERBREAD, *n.* A kind of cake made in England.

PEP'PERGRASS, *n.* A plant of the genus Pilularia; also, a plant of the genus Lepidium.

PEP'PERING, *ppr.* Sprinkling with pepper; pelting.
2. *a.* Hot; pungent; angry. *Swift.*

PEP'PERMINT, *n.* A plant of the genus Mentha. It is aromatic and pungent. Also, a liquor distilled from the plant.

PEP'PERMINT-TREE, *n.* The Eucalyptus piperita, a native of New South Wales. *Encyc.*

PEP'PER-POT, *n.* A plant of the genus Capsicum.

PEP'PER-TREE, *n.* A plant of the genus Vitis.

PEP'PER-WATER, *n.* A liquor prepared from powdered black pepper; used in microscopical observations. *Encyc.*

PEP'PER-WŎRT, *n.* A plant of the genus Lepidium.

PEP'TIC, *a.* [Gr. πεπτικος, from πεπτω, to digest.]

Promoting digestion; dietetic, as *peptic* precepts. *Kitchener.*

PER, a Latin preposition, denoting through, passing, or over the whole extent, as in *perambulo.* Hence it is sometimes equivalent to *very* in English, as in *peracutus*, very sharp. As a prefix, in English, it retains these significations, and in chimistry it is used to denote *very* or *fully, to the utmost extent*, as in *peroxyd*, a substance oxydated to the utmost degree.

Per is used also for *by*, as *per* bearer, *by* the bearer.

Per annum, [L.] by the year; in each year successively.

Per se, [L.] by himself; by itself; by themselves.

PERACU'TE, *a.* [L. *peracutus; per*, through, and *acutus*, sharp.]

Very sharp; very violent; as a *peracute* fever. [*Little used.*] *Harvey.*

PERADVENT'URE, *adv.* [Fr. *par aventure; par*, by, and *aventure*, from L. *venio*, to come.]

By chance; perhaps; it may be. *Hooker.*

It has been used as a noun for doubt or question, but rather improperly. The word is obsolescent and inelegant.

PER'AGRATE, *v. i.* [L. *peragro; per*, through, over, and *ager*, a field.]

To travel over or through; to wander; to ramble. [*Little used.*]

PERAGRA'TION, *n.* The act of passing through any space; as the *peragration* of the moon in her monthly revolution. [*Little used.*] *Brown. Holder.*

PERAM'BULATE, *v. t.* [L. *perambulo; per* and *ambulo*, to walk.]

To walk through or over; properly and technically, to pass through or over for the purpose of surveying or examining something; to visit as overseers: as, to *perambulate* a parish. So in New England, the laws require the selectmen of towns to appoint suitable persons annually to *perambulate* the borders or bounds of the township, and renew the boundaries, or see that the old ones are in a good state.

PERAM'BULATED, *pp.* Passed over; inspected.

PERAM'BULATING, *ppr.* Passing over or through for the purpose of inspection.

PERAMBULA'TION, *n.* The act of passing or walking through or over. *Bacon.*

2. A traveling survey or inspection. *Howell.*

3. A district within which a person has the right of inspection; jurisdiction. *Holiday.*

4. Annual survey of the bounds of a parish in England, or of a township in America.

PERAM'BULATOR, *n.* An instrument or wheel for measuring distances, to be used in surveying or traveling; called also a *pedometer.* *Encyc.*

PERBISUL'PHATE, *n.* A sulphate with two proportions of sulphuric acid, and combined with an oxyd at the maximum of oxydation. *Silliman.*

PERC'ARBURETED, *a.* The percarbureted hydrogen of the French chimists is said to be the only definite compound of these two elements. *Ure.*

PERCA'SE, *adv.* [*per* and *case*, by case.] Perhaps; perchance. [*Not used.*] *Bacon.*

PER'CEANT, *a.* [Fr. *perçant.*] Piercing; penetrating. [*Not used.*] *Spĕnser.*

PERCE'IVABLE, *a.* [See *Perceive.*] Perceptible; that may be perceived; that may fall under perception or the cognizance of the senses; that may be felt, seen, heard, smelt or tasted. We say, the roughness of cloth is *perceivable;* the dawn of the morning is *perceivable;* the sound of a bell is *perceivable;* the scent of an orange is *perceivable;* the difference of taste in an apple and an orange is *perceivable.*

2. That may be known, understood or conceived. [*Less proper.*]

PERCE'IVABLY, *adv.* In such a manner as to be perceived.

PERCE'IVANCE, *n.* Power of perceiving. [*Not in use.*] *Milton.*

PERCE'IVE, *v. t.* [L. *percipio; per* and *capio*, to take.]

1. To have knowledge or receive impressions of external objects through the medium or instrumentality of the senses or bodily organs; as, to *perceive* light or color; to *perceive* the cold of ice or the taste of honey.

2. To know; to understand; to observe.

Till we ourselves see it with our own eyes, and *perceive* it by our own understanding, we are in the dark. *Locke.*

3. To be affected by; to receive impressions from.

The upper regions of the air *perceive* the collection of the matter of tempests before the air below. *Bacon.*

PERCE'IVED, *pp.* Known by the senses; felt; understood; observed.

PERCE'IVER, *n.* One who perceives, feels or observes.

PERCEPTIBIL'ITY, *n.* The state or quality of being perceptible; as the *perceptibility* of light or color.

2. Perception. [*Less proper.*] *More.*

PERCEP'TIBLE, *a.* [Fr.; from L. *percipio, perceptus.*]

1. That may be perceived; that may impress the bodily organs; that may come under the cognizance of the senses; as a *perceptible* degree of heat or cold; a *perceptible* odor; a *perceptible* sound. A thing may be too minute to be *perceptible* to the touch.

2. That may be known or conceived of.

PERCEP'TIBLY, *adv.* In a manner to be perceived.

The woman decays *perceptibly* every week. *Pope.*

PERCEP'TION, *n.* [L. *perceptio.* See *Perceive.*]

1. The act of perceiving or of receiving impressions by the senses; or that act or process of the mind which makes known an external object. In other words, the notice which the mind takes of external objects. We gain a knowledge of the coldness and smoothness of marble by *perception.*

2. In *philosophy*, the faculty of perceiving; the faculty or peculiar part of man's constitution, by which he has knowledge through the medium or instrumentality of the bodily organs. *Reid. Encyc.*

3. Notion; idea. *Hall.*

4. The state of being affected or capable of being affected by something external.

This experiment discovers *perception* in plants. *Bacon.*

PERCEP'TIVE, *a.* Having the faculty of perceiving. *Glanville.*

PERCEPTIV'ITY, *n.* The power of perception or thinking. *Locke.*

PERCH, *n.* [Fr. *perche;* L. *perca;* G. *bars*, a perch, and *barsch*, sharp, keen, pungent; D. *baars;* Sw. *abbore;* Dan. *aborre.* It would seem from the German, that this fish is named from its prickly spines, and the name allied to *perk.*]

A fish of the genus Perca. This fish has a deep body, very rough scales, an arched back, and prickly dorsal fins.

PERCH, *n.* [Fr. *perche;* L. *pertica;* W. *perc;* Arm. *perchen;* probably allied to the former word in the sense of sharpness, shooting or extending. See *Perk.*]

1. A pole; hence, a roost for fowls, which is often a pole; also, any thing on which they light.

2. A measure of length containing five yards and a half; a rod. In the popular language of America, *rod* is chiefly used; but *rod, pole* and *perch*, all signifying the same thing, may be used indifferently.

PERCH, *v. i.* To sit or roost; as a bird.

2. To light or settle on a fixed body; as a bird.

PERCH, *v. t.* To place on a fixed object or perch. *More.*

PERCH'ANCE, *adv.* [*per* and *chance.*] By chance; perhaps. *Wotton.*

PERCH'ERS, *n.* Paris candles anciently used in England; also, a larger sort of wax candles which were usually set on the altar. *Bailey.*

PERCHLO'RATE, *n.* A compound of perchloric acid with a base.

PERCHLO'RIC, *a.* Perchloric acid is chlorine converted into an acid by combining with a maximum of oxygen. *Silliman.*

PERCIP'IENT, *a.* [L. *percipiens.*] Perceiving; having the faculty of perception. Animals are *percipient* beings; mere matter is not *percipient.* *Bentley.*

PERCIP'IENT, *n.* One that perceives or has the faculty of perception. *More.*

PERCLO'SE, *n.* s as z. Conclusion. [*Not used.*] *Raleigh.*

PER'COLATE, *v. t.* [L. *percolo; per* and *colo*, to strain; Fr. *couler*, to flow or run.]

To strain through; to cause to pass through small interstices, as a liquor; to filter. *Hale.*

PER'COLATE, *v. i.* To pass through small interstices; to filter; as, water *percolates* through a porous stone.

PER'COLATED, *pp.* Filtered; passed through small interstices.

PER'COLATING, *ppr.* Filtering.

PERCOLA'TION, *n.* The act of straining or filtering; filtration; the act of passing through small interstices, as liquor through felt or a porous stone.

Percolation is intended for the purification of liquors. *Bacon.*

PERCUSS', *v. t.* [L. *percussus*, from *percutio*, to strike.] To strike. [*Little used.*] *Bacon.*

PERCUS'SION, *n.* [L. *percussio.*] The act of striking one body against another, with some violence; as the vibrations excited in the air by *percussion.* *Newton.*

2. The impression one body makes on another by falling on it or striking it. *Encyc.*

3. The impression or effect of sound on the ear. *Rymer.*

PERCU'TIENT, *n.* [L. *percutiens.*] That which strikes, or has power to strike. *Bacon.*

PER'DIFOIL, *n.* [L. *perdo*, to lose, and *folium*, leaf.]

A plant that annually loses or drops its leaves; opposed to *evergreen.*

The passion flower of America and the jasmine of Malabar, which are evergreens in their native climates, become *perdifoils* when transplanted into Britain. *Barton.*

PERDI''TION, *n.* [L. *perditio*, from *perdo*, to lose, to ruin. Qu. *per* and *do*, or Gr. *περθω.*]

1. Entire loss or ruin; utter destruction; as the *perdition* of the Turkish fleet. *Shak.* [In this sense, the word is now nearly or wholly obsolete.]

2. The utter loss of the soul or of final happiness in a future state; future misery or eternal death. The impenitent sinner is condemned to final *perdition.*

If we reject the truth, we seal our own *perdition.* *J. M. Mason.*

3. Loss. [*Not used.*] *Shak.*

PERDU', PERDU'E, *adv.* [Fr. *perdu*, lost, from *perdre*, to lose, L. *perdo.*]

Close; in concealment.

The moderator, out of view,
Beneath the desk had lain *perdue.*
Trumbull's M'Fingal.

PERDU', *n.* One that is placed on the watch or in ambush. *Shak.*

PERDU', *a.* Abandoned; employed on desperate purposes; accustomed to desperate purposes or enterprises. *Beaum. and Fletcher.*

PER'DULOUS, *a.* [Fr. *perdu*, from L. *perdo.*] Lost; thrown away. [*Not used.*] *Bramhall.*

PERDU'RABLE, *a.* [Fr. from L. *perduro*; *per* and *duro*, to last.]

Very durable; lasting; continuing long. [*Not used.*] *Shak. Drayton.*

PERDU'RABLY, *adv.* Very durably. [*Not used.*] *Shak.*

PERDURA'TION, *n.* Long continuance. [*Not used.*] *Ainsworth.*

PER'DY, *adv.* [Fr. *par Dieu.*] Certainly; verily; in truth. *Obs.* *Spenser.*

PER'EGAL, *a.* [Fr. *per* and *egal*, equal.] Equal. [*Not used.*] *Spenser.*

PER'EGRINATE, *v. i.* [L. *peregrinor*, from *peregrinus*, a traveler or stranger; *peragro*, to wander; *per* and *ager.*]

To travel from place to place or from one country to another; to live in a foreign country. *Dict.*

PEREGRINA'TION, *n.* A traveling from one country to another; a wandering; abode in foreign countries. *Hammond. Bentley.*

PER'EGRINATOR, *n.* A traveler into foreign countries. *Casaubon.*

PER'EGRINE, *a.* [L. *peregrinus.*] Foreign; not native. [*Little used.*] *Bacon.*

Peregrine falcon, a species of hawk, the black hawk or falcon, found in America and in Asia, and which wanders in summer to the Arctic circle. *Pennant.*

PEREMPT', *v. t.* [L. *peremptus*, *perimo*, to kill.]

In *law*, to kill; to crush or destroy. [*Not used.*] *Ayliffe.*

PEREMP'TION, *n.* [L. *peremptio.*] A killing; a quashing; nonsuit. [*Not used.*] *Ayliffe.*

PER'EMPTORILY, *adv.* [from *peremptory.*] Absolutely; positively; in a decisive manner; so as to preclude further debate.

Never judge *peremptorily* on first appearances. *Clarissa.*

PER'EMPTORINESS, *n.* Positiveness; absolute decision; dogmatism.

Peremptoriness is of two sorts; one, a magisterialness in matters of opinion; the other, a positiveness in matters of fact.
Gov. of the Tongue.

PER'EMPTORY, *a.* [Fr. *peremptoire*; It. *perentorio*; L. *peremptorius*, from *peremptus*, taken away, killed.]

1. Express; positive; absolute; decisive; authoritative; in a manner to preclude debate or expostulation. The orders of the commander are *peremptory.*

2. Positive in opinion or judgment. The genuine effect of sound learning is to make men less *peremptory* in their determinations.

3. Final; determinate.

4. *Peremptory* challenge, in law, a challenge or right of challenging jurors without showing cause.

PEREN'NIAL, *a.* [L. *perennis*; *per* and *annus*, a year.]

1. Lasting or continuing without cessation through the year. *Cheyne.*

2. Perpetual; unceasing; never failing. *Harvey.*

3. In *botany*, continuing more than two years; as a *perennial* stem or root. *Martyn.*

4. Continuing without intermission; as a fever. *Coxe.*

PEREN'NIAL, *n.* In *botany*, a plant which lives or continues more than two years, whether it retains its leaves or not. That which retains its leaves during winter is called an *evergreen*; that which casts its leaves, *deciduous*, or a *perdifoil.*

PEREN'NIALLY, *adv.* Continually; without ceasing.

PEREN'NITY, *n.* [L. *perennitas.*] An enduring or continuing through the whole year without ceasing. *Derham.*

PERERRA'TION, *n.* [L. *pererro*; *per* and *erro*, to wander.]

A wandering or rambling through various places. *Howell.*

PER'FECT, *a.* [L. *perfectus*, *perficio*, to complete; *per* and *facio*, to do or make through, to carry to the end.]

1. Finished; complete; consummate; not defective; having all that is requisite to its nature and kind; as a *perfect* statue; a *perfect* likeness; a *perfect* work; a *perfect* system.

As full, as *perfect* in a hair as heart. *Pope.*

2. Fully informed; completely skilled; as men *perfect* in the use of arms; *perfect* in discipline.

3. Complete in moral excellencies.

Be ye therefore *perfect*, even as your Father who is in heaven is *perfect.* Matt. v.

4. Manifesting perfection.

My strength is made *perfect* in weakness. 2 Cor. xii.

Perfect chord, in music, a concord or union of sounds which is perfectly coalescent and agreeable to the ear, as the fifth and the octave; a perfect consonance.

A perfect flower, in botany, has both stamen and pistil, or at least anther and stigma. *Martyn.*

Perfect tense, in grammar, the preterit tense; a tense which expresses an act completed.

PER'FECT, *v. t.* [L. *perfectus*, *perficio.*] To finish or complete so as to leave nothing wanting; to give to any thing all that is requisite to its nature and kind; as, to *perfect* a picture or statue. 2 Chron. viii.

—Inquire into the nature and properties of things, and thereby *perfect* our ideas of distinct species. *Locke.*

If we love one another, God dwelleth in us, and his love is *perfected* in us. 1 John iv.

2. To instruct fully; to make fully skillful; as, to *perfect* one's self in the rules of music or architecture; to *perfect* soldiers in discipline.

PER'FECTED, *pp.* Finished; completed.

PER'FECTER, *n.* One that makes perfect. *Broome.*

PERFECTIBIL'ITY, *n.* [from *perfectible.*] The capacity of becoming or being made perfect.

PERFECT'IBLE, *a.* Capable of becoming or being made perfect, or of arriving at the utmost perfection of the species.

PER'FECTING, *ppr.* Finishing; completing; consummating.

PERFEC'TION, *n.* [L. *perfectio.*] The state of being perfect or complete, so that nothing requisite is wanting; as *perfection* in an art or science; *perfection* in a system of morals.

2. *Physical perfection*, is when a natural object has all its powers, faculties or qualities entire and in full vigor, and all its parts in due proportion. *Encyc.*

3. *Metaphysical* or *transcendental perfection*, is the possession of all the essential attributes or all the parts necessary to the integrity of a substance. This is absolute, where all defect is precluded, such as the *perfection* of God; or according to its kind, as in created things. *Encyc.*

4. *Moral perfection*, is the complete possession of all moral excellence, as in the Supreme Being; or the possession of such moral qualities and virtues as a thing is capable of.

5. A quality, endowment or acquirement completely excellent, or of great worth. In this sense, the word has a plural.

What tongue can her *perfections* tell? *Sidney.*

6. An inherent or essential attribute of supreme or infinite excellence; or one perfect

in its kind; as the *perfections* of God. The infinite power, holiness, justice, benevolence and wisdom of God are denominated his *perfections*.

7. Exactness; as, to imitate a model to *perfection*.

PERFEC'TIONAL, *a.* Made complete. *Pearson.*

PERFEC'TIONATE, used by Dryden and Tooke, in lieu of the verb to *perfect*, is a useless word.

PERFEC'TIONIST, *n.* One pretending to perfection; an enthusiast in religion. *South.*

PERFECT'IVE, *a.* Conducing to make perfect or bring to perfection; followed by *of*.

Praise and adoration are actions *perfective of* the soul. *More.*

PERFECT'IVELY, *adv.* In a manner that brings to perfection. *Grew.*

PER'FECTLY, *adv.* In the highest degree of excellence.

2. Totally; completely; as work *perfectly* executed or performed; a thing *perfectly* new.

3. Exactly; accurately; as a proposition *perfectly* understood.

PER'FECTNESS, *n.* Completeness; consummate excellence; perfection.

2. The highest degree of goodness or holiness of which man is capable in this life.

And above all things put on charity, which is the bond of *perfectness*. Col. iii.

3. Accurate skill. *Shak.*

PERFI"CIENT, *n.* [L. *perficiens.*] One who endows a charity.

PERFID'IOUS, *a.* [L. *perfidus*; *per* and *fidus*, faithful. *Per* in this word signifies *through*, *beyond*, or *by*, *aside*.]

1. Violating good faith or vows; false to trust or confidence reposed; treacherous; as a *perfidious* agent; a *perfidious* friend. [See *Perfidy*.]

2. Proceeding from treachery, or consisting in breach of faith; as a *perfidious* act.

3. Guilty of violated allegiance; as a *perfidious* citizen; a man *perfidious* to his country.

PERFID'IOUSLY, *adv.* Treacherously; traitorously; by breach of faith or allegiance. *Swift.*

PERFID'IOUSNESS, *n.* The quality of being perfidious; treachery; traitorousness; breach of faith, of vows or allegiance.

PER'FIDY, *n.* [L. *perfidia*; *per* and *fides*, faith.]

The act of violating faith, a promise, vow or allegiance; treachery; the violation of a trust reposed. Perfidy is not applied to violations of contracts in ordinary pecuniary transactions, but to violations of faith or trust in friendship, in agency and office, in allegiance, in connubial engagements, and in the transactions of kings.

PERFLA'TE, *v. t.* [L. *perflo*; *per* and *flo*, to blow.] To blow through. *Harvey.*

PERFLA'TION, *n.* The act of blowing through. *Woodward.*

PERFO'LIATE, *a.* [L. *per* and *folium*, a leaf.]

In *botany*, a *perfoliate* or perforated leaf, is one that has the base entirely surrounding the stem transversely. *Martyn.*

PER'FORATE, *v. t.* [L. *perforo*; *per* and *foro*, Eng. to *bore*.]

1. To bore through.

2. To pierce with a pointed instrument; to make a hole or holes through any thing by boring or driving; as, to *perforate* the bottom of a vessel.

PER'FORATED, *pp.* Bored or pierced through; pierced.

PER'FORATING, *ppr.* Boring or piercing through; piercing.

PERFORA'TION, *n.* The act of boring or piercing through.

2. A hole or aperture passing through any thing, or into the interior of a substance, whether natural or made by an instrument.

PER'FORATIVE, *a.* Having power to pierce; as an instrument.

PER'FORATOR, *n.* An instrument that bores or perforates. *Sharp.*

PERFORCE, *adv.* [*per* and *force*.] By force or violence. *Shak.*

PERFORM', *v. t.* [L. *per* and *formo*, to make.]

1. To do; to execute; to accomplish; as, to *perform* two days' labor in one day; to *perform* a noble deed or achievment.

2. To execute; to discharge; as, to *perform* a duty or office.

3. To fulfill; as, to *perform* a covenant, promise or contract; to *perform* a vow.

PERFORM', *v. i.* To do; to act a part. The player *performs* well in different characters. The musician *performs* well on the organ.

PERFORM'ABLE, *a.* That may be done, executed or fulfilled; practicable. *Brown.*

PERFORM'ANCE, *n.* Execution or completion of any thing; a doing; as the *performance* of work or of an undertaking; the *performance* of duty.

2. Action; deed; thing done. *Shak.*

3. The acting or exhibition of character on the stage. Garrick was celebrated for his theatrical *performances*.

4. Composition; work written.

Few of our comic *performances* give good examples. *Clarissa.*

5. The acting or exhibition of feats; as *performances* of horsemanship.

PERFORM'ED, *pp.* Done; executed; discharged.

PERFORM'ER, *n.* One that performs any thing, particularly in an art; as a good *performer* on the violin or organ; a celebrated *performer* in comedy or tragedy, or in the circus.

PERFORM'ING, *ppr.* Doing; executing; accomplishing.

PERFORM'ING, *n.* Act done; deed; act of executing. *Swift.*

PERFU'MATORY, *a.* [from *perfume*.] That perfumes. *Leigh.*

PERFU'ME, *n.* [Fr. *parfum*; It. *profumo*; Sp. *perfume*; L. *per* and *fumus*, smoke, or *fumo*, to fumigate.]

1. A substance that emits a scent or odor which affects agreeably the organs of smelling, as musk, civet, spices or aromatics of any kind; or any composition of aromatic substances.

2. The scent, odor or volatile particles emitted from sweet smelling substances.

No rich *perfumes* refresh the fruitful field. *Pope.*

PERFU'ME, *v. t.* To scent; to fill or impregnate with a grateful odor; as, to *perfume* an apartment; to *perfume* a garment.

And Carmel's flowery top *perfumes* the skies. *Pope.*

PERFU'MED, *pp.* Scented; impregnated with fragrant odors.

PERFU'MER, *n.* He or that which perfumes.

2. One whose trade is to sell perfumes. *Bacon.*

PERFU'MERY, *n.* Perfumes in general.

PERFU'MING, *ppr.* Scenting; impregnating with sweet odors.

PERFUNC'TORILY, *adv.* [L. *perfunctorie*, from *perfungor*; *per* and *fungor*, to do or execute.]

Carelessly; negligently; in a manner to satisfy external form. *Clarendon.*

PERFUNC'TORINESS, *n.* Negligent performance; carelessness. *Whitlock.*

PERFUNC'TORY, *a.* [supra.] Slight; careless; negligent. *Woodward.*

2. Done only for the sake of getting rid of the duty. *Bickersteth.*

PERFU'SE, *v. t.* *s* as *z*. [L. *perfusus*, *perfundo*; *per* and *fundo*, to pour.] To sprinkle, pour or spread over. *Harvey.*

PER'GOLA, *n.* [It.] A kind of arbor. *Finett.*

PERHAPS', *adv.* [*per* and *hap*. See *Happen*.] By chance; it may be.

Perhaps her love, *perhaps* her kingdom charmed him. *Smith.*

PER'IANTH, *n.* [Gr. περι, about, and ανθος, flower.]

The calyx of a flower when contiguous to the other parts of fructification. *Martyn.*

PER'IAPT, *n.* [Gr. περιαπτω, to fit or tie to.]

An amulet; a charm worn to defend against disease or mischief. [*Not used.*] *Hanmer. Shak.*

PERIAUGER, } [See *Pirogue*.]
PERIAGUA. }

PERICARD'IUM, *n.* [Gr. περι, around, and καρδια, the heart.]

A membrane that incloses the heart. It contains a liquor which prevents the surface of the heart from becoming dry by its continual motion. *Quincy.*

PER'ICARP, *n.* [Gr. περι, about, and καρπος, fruit.]

The seed-vessel of a plant; a general name including the capsule, legume, silique, follicle, drupe, pome, berry and strobile. *Martyn.*

PERICRA'NIUM, *n.* [Gr. περι, about, and κρανιον, the skull.]

The periosteum or membrane that invests the skull. *Coxe.*

PERIC'ULOUS, *a.* [L. *periculosus*. See *Peril*.] Dangerous; hazardous. *Brown.*

PERIDODECAHE'DRAL, *a.* [Gr. περι, and *dodecahedral*.]

Designating a crystal whose primitive form is a four sided prism, and in its secondary form is converted into a prism of twelve sides. *Cleaveland.*

PER'IDOT, *n.* [Fr.] Another name of the chrysolite. It may be known by its leek or olive green color of various shades, and by its infusibility. It is found in grains, granular masses, and rounded crystals. *Dict. Nat. Hist.*

PERIE'CIAN, *n.* [Gr. περιοικος.] An inhabitant of the opposite side of the globe, in the same parallel of latitude.

PER'IGEE, } *n.* [Gr. περι, about, and γη,
PERIGE'UM, } the earth.]
That point in the orbit of the sun or moon in which it is at the least distance from the earth; opposed to *apogee*. *Encyc.*

PER'IGORD-STONE, *n.* An ore of manganese of a dark gray color, like basalt or trap; so called from Perigord, in France. *Encyc.*

PER'IGRAPH, *n.* [Gr. περι, about, and γραφη, a writing.]
1. A careless or inaccurate delineation of any thing.
2. The white lines or impressions that appear on the musculus rectus of the abdomen. *Encyc.*

PERIG'YNOUS, *a.* [Gr. περι, about, and γυνη, female.]
In *botany*, inserted around the pistil, as the corol or stamens; having the corol or stamens inserted around the pistil, as a flower or plant. *Jussieu. Smith.*

PERIHE'LION, } *n.* [Gr. περι, about, and
PERIHE'LIUM, } ηλιος, the sun.]
That part of the orbit of a planet or comet, in which it is at its least distance from the sun; opposed to *aphelion*. *Encyc.*

PERIHEXAHE'DRAL, *a.* [Gr. περι, and *hexahedral*.]
Designating a crystal whose primitive form is a four sided prism, and in the secondary form is converted into a prism of six sides. *Cleaveland.*

PER'IL, *n.* [Fr.; It. *periglio*; Sp. *peligro*; Port. *perigo*; from L. *periculum*, from Gr. πειραω, to try, to attempt, that is, to strain; πειρα, an attempt, danger, hazard; allied to πειρω, to pass, to thrust in or transfix. πειρα is also the point or edge of a sword, coinciding with W. *ber* and *pêr*, a spit, a *spear* or pike. Hence L. *experior*, Eng. *experience*. The Greek πειραω is expressed in Dutch by *vaaren*, to go, to sail, to *fare*; *gevaar*, danger, peril; G. *gefahr*, from *fahren*. These words are all of one family. See *Pirate*. The primary sense of *peril* is an advance, a pushing or going forward; the radical sense of boldness. The Welsh has *perig*, perilous, from *pêr*, and *peri*, to bid or command, the root of L. *impero*, from the same root.]
1. Danger; risk; hazard; jeopardy; particular exposure of person or property to injury, loss or destruction from any cause whatever.

In *perils* of waters; in *perils* of robbers. 2 Cor. xi.

2. Danger denounced; particular exposure. You do it at your *peril*, or at the *peril* of your father's displeasure.

PER'IL, *v. i.* To be in danger. [*Not used.*] *Milton.*

PER'ILOUS, *a.* [Fr. *perileux*.] Dangerous; hazardous; full of risk; as a *perilous* undertaking; a *perilous* situation.
2. Vulgarly used for *very*, like mighty; as *perilous* shrewd. *Obs.* *Hudibras.*
3. Smart; witty; as a *perilous* [parlous] boy. [*Vulgar and obsolete.*]

PER'ILOUSLY, *adv.* Dangerously; with hazard.

PER'ILOUSNESS, *n.* Dangerousness; danger; hazard.

PERIM'ETER, *n.* [Gr. περι, about, and μετρον, measure.]
In *geometry*, the bounds and limits of a body or figure. The *perimeters* of surfaces or figures are lines; those of bodies are surfaces. In circular figures, instead of *perimeter*, we use *circumference* or *periphery*. *Encyc.*

PERIOCTAHE'DRAL, *a.* [Gr. περι and *octahedral*.]
Designating a crystal whose primitive form is a four sided prism, and in its secondary form is converted into a prism of eight sides.

PE'RIOD, *n.* [L. *periodus*; Fr. *periode*; It. Sp. Port. *periodo*; Gr. περιοδος; περι, about, and οδος, way.]
1. Properly, a circuit; hence, the time which is taken up by a planet in making its revolution round the sun, or the duration of its course till it returns to the point of its orbit where it began. Thus the period of the earth or its annual revolution is 365 days, 6 hours, 9 minutes, and 30 seconds. *Encyc.*
2. In *chronology*, a stated number of years; a revolution or series of years by which time is measured; as the Calippic *period*; the Dionysian *period*; the Julian *period*.
3. Any series of years or of days in which a revolution is completed, and the same course is to be begun.
4. Any specified portion of time, designated by years, months, days or hours complete; as a *period* of a thousand years; the *period* of a year; the *period* of a day.
5. End; conclusion. Death puts a *period* to a state of probation.
6. An indefinite portion of any continued state, existence or series of events; as the first *period* of life; the last *period* of a king's reign; the early *periods* of history.
7. State at which any thing terminates; limit.
8. Length or usual length of duration.

Some experiments would be made how by art to make plants more lasting than their ordinary *period*. *Bacon.*

9. A complete sentence from one full stop to another.

Periods are beautiful when they are not too long. *B. Jonson.*

10. The point that marks the end of a complete sentence; a full stop, thus, (.)
11. In *numbers*, a distinction made by a point or comma after every sixth place or figure. *Encyc.*
12. In *medicine*, the time of intension and remission of a disease, or of the paroxysm and remission. *Encyc.*

Julian period, in chronology, a period of 7980 years; a number produced by multiplying 28, the years of the solar cycle, into 19, the years of the lunar cycle, and their product by 15, the years of the Roman indiction.

PE'RIOD, *v. t.* To put an end to. [*Not used.*] *Shak.*

PERIOD'IC, } *a.* [It. *periodico*; Fr. *pe-*
PERIOD'ICAL, } *riodique*.]
1. Performed in a circuit, or in a regular revolution in a certain time, or in a series of successive circuits; as the *periodical* motion of the planets round the sun; the *periodical* motion of the moon round the earth. *Watts.*
2. Happening by revolution, at a stated time; as, the conjunction of the sun and moon is *periodical*.
3. Happening or returning regularly in a certain period of time. The Olympiads among the Greeks were *periodical*, as was the jubilee of the Jews.
4. Performing some action at a stated time; as the *periodical* fountains in Switzerland, which issue only at a particular hour of the day. *Addison.*
5. Pertaining to a period; constituting a complete sentence. *Adam's Lect.*
6. Pertaining to a revolution or regular circuit. *Brown.*

PERIOD'ICALLY, *adv.* At stated periods; as a festival celebrated *periodically*.

PERIOS'TEUM, *n.* [Gr. περι, about, and οςεον, bone.]
A nervous vascular membrane endued with quick sensibility, immediately investing the bones of animals. *Encyc. Coxe.*

The periosteum has very little sensibility in a sound state, but in some cases of disease it appears to be very sensible. *Wistar.*

PERIPATET'IC, *a.* [Gr. περιπατητικος, from περιπατεω, to walk about; περι and πατεω.]
Pertaining to Aristotle's system of philosophy, or to the sect of his followers.

PERIPATET'IC, *n.* A follower of Aristotle, so called because the founders of his philosophy taught, or his followers disputed questions, *walking* in the Lyceum at Athens. *Encyc.*
2. It is ludicrously applied to one who is obliged to walk, or cannot afford to ride. *Tatler.*

PERIPATET'ICISM, *n.* The notions or philosophical system of Aristotle and his followers. *Barrow.*

PERIPH'ERAL, *a.* Peripheric. *Fleming.*

PERIPHER'IC, } *a.* Pertaining to a pe-
PERIPHER'ICAL, } riphery; constituting a periphery.

PERIPH'ERY, *n.* [Gr. περι, around, and φερω, to bear.]
The circumference of a circle, ellipsis, or other regular curvilinear figure. *Encyc.*

PER'IPHRASE, *n.* *s* as *z*. [Gr. περιφρασις; περι, about, and φραζω, to speak.]
Circumlocution; a circuit of words; the use of more words than are necessary to express the idea; a figure of rhetoric employed to avoid a common and trite manner of expression. *Encyc.*

PER'IPHRASE, *v. t.* To express by circumlocution.

PER'IPHRASE, *v. i.* To use circumlocution.

PERIPHRASIS. [See *Periphrase*.]

PERIPHRAS'TIC, } *a.* Circumlocutory;
PERIPHRAS'TICAL, } expressing or expressed in more words than are necessary; expressing the sense of one word in many.

PERIPHRAS'TICALLY, *adv.* With circumlocution. *Boswell.*

PER'IPLUS, *n.* [Gr. περιπλους; περι, about, and πλεω, to sail.]

Circumnavigation; a voyage round a certain sea or sea coast. *Vincent.*

PERIPNEUMON'IC, *a.* Pertaining to peripneumony; consisting in an inflammation of the lungs.

PERIPNEU'MONY, *n.* [Gr. περι, about, and πνευμων, the lungs.]

An inflammation of the lungs, or of some part of the thorax, attended with acute fever and difficult respiration. *Encyc.*

PERIPOLYG'ONAL, *a.* [Gr. περι and *polygon.*]

In *crystalography*, having a great number of sides.

PERIS'CIAN, *n.* [Gr. περισκιοι; περι, around, and σκια, shadow.]

An inhabitant of a frigid zone or within a polar circle, whose shadow moves round, and in the course of the day falls in every point of compass. The Greek word *periscii*, in the plural, is generally used in geographies; but the English word is preferable.

PER'ISH, *v. i.* [Fr. *perir, perissant*; It. *perire*; Sp. *perecer*; from L. *pereo*, supposed to be compounded of *per* and *eo*, to go; literally, to depart wholly.]

1. To die; to lose life in any manner; *applied to animals.* Men *perish* by disease or decay, by the sword, by drowning, by hunger or famine, &c.
2. To die; to wither and decay; *applied to plants.*
3. To waste away; as, a leg or an arm has *perished.*
4. To be in a state of decay or passing away.

Duration, and time which is a part of it, is the idea we have of *perishing* distance. *Locke.*

5. To be destroyed; to come to nothing.

Perish the lore that deadens young desire.

6. To fail entirely or to be extirpated. 2 Kings ix.
7. To be burst or ruined; as, the bottles shall *perish.* Luke v.
8. To be wasted or rendered useless. Jer. ix.
9. To be injured or tormented. 1 Cor. viii.
10. To be lost eternally; to be sentenced to endless misery. 2 Pet. ii.

PER'ISH, *v. t.* To destroy. [*Not legitimate.*]

PER'ISHABLE, *a.* Liable to perish; subject to decay and destruction. The bodies of animals and plants are *perishable.* The souls of men are not *perishable.*

2. Subject to speedy decay.

Property of a *perishable* nature, saved from a wreck, may be sold within a year and a day. *Stat. of Conn.*

PER'ISHABLENESS, *n.* Liableness to decay or destruction. *Locke.*

PER'ISPERM, *n.* [Gr. περι, around, and σπερμα, seed.]

A thick, farinaceous, fleshy, horny or woody part of the seed of plants, either entirely or only partially surrounding the embryo, and inclosed within the investing membrane. It corresponds to the *albumen* of Gærtner. *Jussieu. Smith.*

PERISPHER'IC, *a.* [Gr. περι and σφαιρα.] Globular; having the form of a ball. *Journ. of Science.*

PERISSOLOG'ICAL, *a.* Redundant in words.

PERISSOL'OGY, *n.* [Gr. περισσολογια; περισσος, redundant, and λογος, discourse.]

Superfluous words; much talk to little purpose. [*Little used.*] *Campbell.*

PERISTAL'TIC, *a.* [Gr. περιςαλτικος, from περιςελλω, to involve.]

Spiral; vermicular or worm-like. The *peristaltic* motion of the intestines is performed by the contraction of the circular and longitudinal fibres composing their fleshy coats, by which the chyle is driven into the orifices of the lacteals, and the excrements are protruded towards the anus. *Encyc.*

PERISTE'RION, *n.* [Gr.] The herb vervain. *Dict.*

PER'ISTYLE, *n.* [Gr. περιςυλον; περι, about, and ςυλος, a column.]

A circular range of columns, or a building encompassed with a row of columns on the outside. *Johnson. Encyc.*

PERISYSTOLE, *n.* *perisys'toly.* [Gr. περι, about, and συςολη, contraction.]

The pause or interval between the systole or contraction, and the diastole or dilatation of the heart. *Quincy.*

PERI'TE, *a.* [L. *peritus.*] Skillful. [*Little used.*] *Whitaker.*

PERITO'NEAL, *a.* Pertaining to the peritoneum.

PERITONE'UM, *n.* [Gr. περιτοναιον; περι, about, and τονοω, to stretch.]

A thin, smooth, lubricous membrane investing the whole internal surface of the abdomen, and more or less completely, all the viscera contained in it. *Encyc. Parr.*

PER'IWIG, *n.* [Ir. *pereabhic.* Qu. D. *paruik*; G. *perrücke*; Dan. *perryk*; Fr. *perruque*; It. *parrucca.*]

A small wig; a kind of close cap formed by an intertexture of false hair, worn by men for ornament or to conceal baldness. *Periwigs* were in fashion in the days of Addison.

PER'IWIG, *v. t.* To dress with a periwig, or with false hair, or with any thing in like form. *Swift.*

PER'IWINKLE, *n.* [Sax. *peruince*; It. *pervinca*; Fr. *pervenche*; L. *vinca*; Sax. *wincle*, a shell fish. If *n* is casual, *vinca* may be and probably is the W. *gwic*, for *wic*, a squeak, whence *gwiciad*, a periwinkle.]

1. A sea snail, or small shell fish.
2. A plant of the genus Vinca.

PERJURE, *v. t.* *per'jur.* [L. *perjuro*; *per* and *juro*, to swear; that is, to swear aside or beyond.]

Willfully to make a false oath when administered by lawful authority or in a court of justice; to forswear; as, the witness *perjured* himself.

PER'JURE, *n.* A perjured person. [*Not used.*] *Shak.*

PER'JURED, *pp.* Guilty of perjury; having sworn falsely.

PER'JURER, *n.* One that willfully takes a false oath lawfully administered.

PER'JURING, *ppr.* Taking a false oath lawfully administered.

PERJU'RIOUS, *a.* Guilty of perjury; containing perjury. *Coke.*

PER'JURY, *n.* [L. *perjurium.*] The act or crime of willfully making a false oath, when lawfully administered; or a crime committed when a lawful oath is administered in some judicial proceeding, to a person who swears willfully, absolutely and falsely in a matter material to the issue. *Coke.*

PERK, *a.* [W. *perc*, compact, trim, perk; as a noun, something that is close, compact, trim, and a *perch.*] Properly, erect; hence, smart; trim.

PERK, *v. i.* [W. *percu*, to trim, to make smart.]

To hold up the head with affected smartness. *Pope.*

PERK, *v. t.* To dress; to make trim or smart; to prank. *Shak.*

PERK'IN, *n.* Cyderkin; a kind of cyder made by steeping the murk in water. *Encyc.*

Perlate acid, the acidulous phosphate of soda. *Chimistry. Nicholson.*

Perlated acid, or *ouretic*, biphosphate of soda.

PER'LOUS, for *perilous*, is not used. *Spenser.*

PERLUSTRA'TION, *n.* [L. *perlustro*; *per* and *lustro*, to survey.] The act of viewing all over. *Howell.*

PER'MAGY, *n.* A little Turkish boat. *Dict.*

PER'MANENCE, } *n.* [See *Permanent.*]
PER'MANENCY, } Continuance in the same state, or without a change that destroys the form or nature of a thing; duration; fixedness; as the *permanence* of a government or state; the *permanence* of institutions or of a system of principles.

2. Continuance in the same place or at rest.

PER'MANENT, *a.* [L. *permanens*, *permaneo*; *per* and *maneo*, to remain. Class Mn.]

Durable; lasting; continuing in the same state, or without any change that destroys the form or nature of the thing. The laws, like the character of God, are unalterably *permanent.* Human laws and institutions may be to a degree *permanent*, but they are subject to change and overthrow. We speak of a *permanent* wall or building, a *permanent* bridge, when they are so constructed as to endure long; in which examples, *permanent* is equivalent to *durable* or *lasting*, but not to *undecaying* or *unalterable.* So we say, a *permanent* residence, a *permanent* intercourse, *permanent* friendship, when it continues a long time without interruption.

PER'MANENTLY, *adv.* With long continuance; durably; in a fixed state or place; as a government *permanently* established.

PERMAN'SION, *n.* [L. *permansio.*] Continuance. [*Not used.*] *Brown.*

PERMEABIL'ITY, *n.* [infra.] The quality or state of being permeable. *Journ. of Science.*

PER'MEABLE, *a.* [L. *permeo*; *per* and *meo*, to pass or glide.]

That may be passed through without rupture or displacement of its parts, as solid matter; applied particularly to substances that admit the passage of fluids. Thus cloth, lether, wood are *permeable* to water and oil; glass is *permeable* to light, but not to water.

PER'MEANT, *a.* [supra.] Passing through. [*Not used.*] *Brown.*

PER'MEATE, *v. t.* [L. *permeo*; *per* and *meo*, to glide, flow or pass.]

To pass through the pores or interstices of a body; to penetrate and pass through a substance without rupture or displacement of its parts; applied particularly to fluids which pass through substances of loose texture; as, water *permeates* sand or a filtering stone; light *permeates* glass.

PER′MEATED, *pp.* Passed through, as by a fluid.

PER′MEATING, *ppr.* Passing through the pores or interstices of a substance.

PERMEA′TION, *n.* The act of passing through the pores or interstices of a body.

PERMIS′CIBLE, *a.* [L. *permisceo; per* and *misceo,* to mix.] That may be mixed. [*Little used.*]

PERMIS′SIBLE, *a.* [See *Permit.*] That may be permitted or allowed.

PERMIS′SION, *n.* [L. *permissio,* from *permitto,* to permit.]
1. The act of permitting or allowing.
2. Allowance; license or liberty granted.

You have given me your *permission* for this address. *Dryden.*

PERMIS′SIVE, *a.* Granting liberty; allowing. *Milton.*
2. Granted; suffered without hinderance.

Thus I emboldened spake, and freedom used *Permissive,* and acceptance found. *Milton.*

PERMIS′SIVELY, *adv.* By allowance; without prohibition or hinderance.

PERMIS′′TION, } *n.* [L. *permistio, permixtio.*] The act of mixing; the state of being mingled.
PERMIX′TION,

PERMIT′, *v. t.* [L. *permitto; per* and *mitto,* to send; Fr. *permettre;* It. *permettere;* Sp. *permitir.*]
1. To allow; to grant leave or liberty to by express consent. He asked my leave and I *permitted* him.
2. To allow by silent consent or by not prohibiting; to suffer without giving express authority. The laws *permit* us to do what is not expressly or impliedly forbid.

What God neither commands nor forbids, he *permits* with approbation to be done or left undone. *Hooker.*

3. To afford ability or means. Old age does not *permit* us to retain the vigor of youth. The man's indigence does not *permit* him to indulge in luxuries.
4. To leave; to give or resign.

Let us not aggravate our sorrows,
But to the gods *permit* the event of things. *Addison.*

[The latter sense is obsolete or obsolescent.]

PERMIT′, *n.* A written license or permission from the custom house officer or other proper authority, to export or transport goods or to land goods or persons.
2. Warrant; leave; permission.

PERMIT′TANCE, *n.* Allowance; forbearance of prohibition; permission. *Derham.*

PERMIXTION. [See *Permistion.*]

PERMUTA′TION, *n.* [L. *permutatio, permuto; per* and *muto,* to change.]
1. In *commerce,* exchange of one thing for another; barter. *Bacon.*
2. In *the canon law,* the exchange of one benefice for another. *Encyc.*
3. In *algebra,* change or different combination of any number of quantities. *Wallis.*

PERMU′TE, *v. t.* [L. *permuto; per* and *muto,* to change.] To exchange; to barter. [*Not used.*]

PERMU′TER, *n.* One that exchanges. [*Not used.*]

PER′NANCY, *n.* [Norm. *perner,* to take.] A taking or reception, as the receiving of rents or tithes in kind. *Blackstone.*

PERNI′′CIOUS, *a.* [L. *perniciosus,* from *pernicies; perneco,* to kill; *per* and *nex, necis,* death.]
1. Destructive; having the quality of killing, destroying or injuring; very injurious or mischievous. Food, drink or air may be *pernicious* to life or health.
2. Destructive; tending to injure or destroy. Evil examples are *pernicious* to morals. Intemperance is a *pernicious* vice.
3. [L. *pernix.*] Quick. [*Not used.*] *Milton.*

PERNI′′CIOUSLY, *adv.* Destructively; with ruinous tendency or effects. *Ascham.*

PERNI′′CIOUSNESS, *n.* The quality of being very injurious, mischievous or destructive.

PERNIC′ITY, *n.* [L. *pernicitas,* from *pernix.*] Swiftness of motion; celerity. [*Little used.*] *Ray.*

PERNOCTA′TION, *n.* [L. *pernocto; per* and *nox,* night.]
The act of passing the whole night; a remaining all night. *Taylor.*

PEROGUE. [See *Pirogue.*]

PERORA′TION, *n.* [L. *peroratio,* from *peroro; per* and *oro,* to pray.]
The concluding part of an oration, in which the speaker recapitulates the principal points of his discourse or argument, and urges them with greater earnestness and force, with a view to make a deep impression on his hearers. *Encyc.*

PEROX′YD, *n.* [*per* and *oxyd.*] A substance containing an unusual quantity of oxygen. *Davy.*

PEROX′YDIZE, *v. t.* To oxydize to the utmost degree. *Cutbush.*

PERPEND′, *v. t.* [L. *perpendo; per* and *pendo,* to weigh.] To weigh in the mind; to consider attentively. [*Little used.*] *Shak. Brown.*

PERPEND′ER, *n.* [Fr. *parpaing.*] A coping stone. *Johnson.*

PERPEND′ICLE, *n.* [Fr. *perpendicule,* from L. *perpendiculum.*]
Something hanging down in a direct line; a plumb line. *Dict.*

PERPENDIC′ULAR, *a.* [L. *perpendicularis,* from *perpendiculum,* a plumb line; *perpendeo; per* and *pendeo,* to hang.]
1. Hanging or extending in a right line from any point towards the center of the earth or of gravity, or at right angles with the plane of the horizon.
2. In *geometry,* falling directly on another line at right angles. The line A is *perpendicular* to the line B.

PERPENDIC′ULAR, *n.* A line falling at right angles on the plane of the horizon, that is, extending from some point in a right line towards the center of the earth or center of gravity, or any body standing in that direction.
2. In *geometry,* a line falling at right angles on another line, or making equal angles with it on each side. *Encyc.*

PERPENDICULAR′ITY, *n.* The state of being perpendicular. *Watts.*

PERPENDIC′ULARLY, *adv.* In a manner to fall on another line at right angles.
2. So as to fall on the plane of the horizon at right angles; in a direction towards the center of the earth or of gravity.

PERPEN′SION, *n.* [L. *perpendo.*] Consideration. [*Not used.*] *Brown.*

PERPES′SION, *n.* [L. *perpessio, perpetior,* to suffer; *per* and *patior.*] Suffering; endurance. [*Not used.*] *Pearson.*

PER′PETRATE, *v. t.* [L. *perpetro; per* and *patro,* to go through, to finish.]
To do; to commit; to perform; in an ill sense, that is, always used to express an evil act; as, to *perpetrate* a crime or an evil design. *Dryden.*

PER′PETRATED, *pp.* Done; committed; as an evil act.

PER′PETRATING, *ppr.* Committing; as a crime or evil act.

PERPETRA′TION, *n.* The act of committing a crime. *Wotton.*
2. An evil action. *K. Charles.*

PER′PETRATOR, *n.* One that commits a crime.

PERPET′UAL, *a.* [Fr. *perpetuel;* L. *perpetuus,* from *perpes, perpetis; per* and *pes,* from a root signifying to pass.]
1. Never ceasing; continuing forever in future time; destined to be eternal; as a *perpetual* covenant; a *perpetual* statute. [Literally true with respect to the decrees of the Supreme Being.]
2. Continuing or continued without intermission; uninterrupted; as a *perpetual* stream; the *perpetual* action of the heart and arteries.
3. Permanent; fixed; not temporary; as a *perpetual* law or edict; *perpetual* love or amity; *perpetual* incense. Ex. xxx.
4. Everlasting; endless.

Destructions are come to a *perpetual* end. Ps. ix.

5. During the legal dispensation. Ex. xxix.

Perpetual curacy, is where all the tithes are appropriated and no vicarage is endowed. *Blackstone.*

Perpetual motion, motion that generates a power of continuing itself forever or indefinitely, by means of mechanism or some application of the force of gravity; not yet discovered, and probably impossible.

Perpetual screw, a screw that acts against the teeth of a wheel and continues its action without end. *Wilkins.*

PERPET′UALLY, *adv.* Constantly; continually; applied to things which proceed without intermission, or which occur frequently or at intervals, without limitation. A perennial spring flows *perpetually;* the weather varies *perpetually.*

The Bible and common prayer book in the vulgar tongue, being *perpetually* read in churches, have proved a kind of standard for language. *Swift.*

PERPET′UATE, *v. t.* [L. *perpetuo.*] To make perpetual; to eternize.
2. To cause to endure or to be continued indefinitely; to preserve from extinction or oblivion; as, to *perpetuate* the remembrance of a great event or of an illustrious character. The monument in London *perpetuates* the remembrance of the conflagration in 1666. Medals may *perpetuate* the glories of a prince. *Addison.*
3. To continue by repetition without limitation.

PERPET'UATED, *pp.* Made perpetual; continued through eternity, or for an indefinite time.

PERPET'UATING, *ppr.* Continuing forever or indefinitely.

PERPETUA'TION, *n.* The act of making perpetual, or of preserving from extinction or oblivion through an endless existence, or for an indefinite period of time. *Brown.*

PERPETU'ITY, *n.* [L. *perpetuitas.*] Endless duration; continuance to eternity.

2. Continued uninterrupted existence, or duration for an indefinite period of time; as the *perpetuity* of laws and institutions; the *perpetuity* of fame.

3. Something of which there will be no end. *South.*

PERPHOS'PHATE, *n.* A phosphate in which the phosphoric acid is combined with an oxyd at the maximum of oxydation.

PERPLEX', *v. t.* [L. *perplexus, perplexor; per* and *plector,* to twist, from the root of Gr. πλεκω, L. *plico,* to fold.]

1. To make intricate; to involve; to entangle; to make complicated and difficult to be understood or unraveled.

What was thought obscure, *perplexed* and too hard for our weak parts, will lie open to the understanding in a fair view. *Locke.*

2. To embarrass; to puzzle; to distract; to tease with suspense, anxiety or ambiguity.

We can distinguish no general truths, or at least shall be apt to *perplex* the mind. *Locke.*

We are *perplexed,* but not in despair. 2 Cor. iv.

3. To plague; to vex. *Glanville.*

PERPLEX', *a.* Intricate; difficult. [*Not used.*] *Glanville.*

PERPLEX'ED, *pp.* Made intricate; embarrassed; puzzled.

PERPLEX'EDLY, *adv.* Intricately; with involution.

PERPLEX'EDNESS, *n.* Intricacy; difficulty from want of order or precision.

2. Embarrassment of mind from doubt or uncertainty.

PERPLEX'ITY, *n.* Intricacy; entanglement. The jury were embarrassed by the *perplexity* of the case.

2. Embarrassment of mind; disturbance from doubt, confusion, difficulty or anxiety.

Perplexity not suffering them to be idle, they think and do, as it were, in a frenzy. *Hooker.*

PERQUADRISUL'PHATE, *n.* A sulphate with four proportions of sulphuric acid combined with a maximum oxyd. *Silliman.*

PER'QUISITE, *n.* *s* as *z.* [L. *perquisitus, perquiro; per* and *quæro,* to seek.]

A fee or pecuniary allowance to an officer for services, beyond his ordinary salary or settled wages; or a fee allowed by law to an officer for a specific service, in lieu of an annual salary. [*The latter is the common acceptation of the word in America.*]

PER'QUISITED, *a.* Supplied with perquisites. [*A bad word and not used.*] *Savage.*

PERQUISI''TION, *n.* *s* as *z.* [L. *perquisitus.*] An accurate inquiry or search. *Ainsworth.*

PERROQUET', *n.* [Fr.] A species of parrot; also, the Alca Psittacula, an aquatic fowl inhabiting the isles of Japan and the western shores of America. *Pennant.*

PER'RY, *n.* [Fr. *poiré,* from *poire,* W. *pêr,* a pear.]

The juice of pears, which being clarified by fermentation, is a pleasant drink.

PERSCRUTA'TION, *n.* [L. *perscrutatio, perscrutor.*] A searching thoroughly; minute search or inquiry.

PER'SECUTE, *v. t.* [Fr. *persecuter;* It. *perseguitare;* Sp. *perseguir;* L. *persequor; per* and *sequor,* to pursue. See *Seek* and *Essay.*]

1. In *a general sense,* to pursue in a manner to injure, vex or afflict; to harass with unjust punishment or penalties for supposed offenses; to inflict pain from hatred or malignity.

2. Appropriately, to afflict, harass or destroy for adherence to a particular creed or system of religious principles, or to a mode of worship. Thus Nero *persecuted* the Christians by crucifying some, burning others, and condemning others to be worried by dogs. See Acts xxii.

3. To harass with solicitations or importunity.

PER'SECUTED, *pp.* Harassed by troubles or punishments unjustly inflicted, particularly for religious opinions.

PER'SECUTING, *ppr.* Pursuing with enmity or vengeance, particularly for adhering to a particular religion.

PERSECU'TION, *n.* The act or practice of persecuting; the infliction of pain, punishment or death upon others unjustly, particularly for adhering to a religious creed or mode of worship, either by way of penalty or for compelling them to renounce their principles. Historians enumerate ten *persecutions* suffered by the Christians, beginning with that of Nero, A. D. 31, and ending with that of Diocletian, A. D. 303 to 313.

2. The state of being persecuted.

Our necks are under *persecution;* we labor and have no rest. Lam. v.

PER'SECUTOR, *n.* One that persecutes; one that pursues another unjustly and vexatiously, particularly on account of religious principles.

Henry rejected the pope's supremacy, but retained every corruption beside, and became a cruel *persecutor.* *Swift.*

PERSEVE'RANCE, *n.* [Fr. from L. *perseverantia.* See *Persevere.*]

1. Persistence in any thing undertaken; continued pursuit or prosecution of any business or enterprise begun; *applied alike to good or evil.*

Perseverance keeps honor bright. *Shak.*

Patience and *perseverance* overcome the greatest difficulties. *Clarissa.*

2. In *theology,* continuance in a state of grace to a state of glory; sometimes called *final perseverance.* *Hammond.*

PERSEVE'RANT, *a.* Constant in pursuit of an undertaking. [*Not used.*] *Ainsworth.*

PERSEVE'RE, *v. i.* [L. *persevero.* The last component part of this word, *severo,* must be the same as in *assevero,* with the radical sense of *set, fixed* or *continued.* So *persist* is formed with *per* and *sisto,* to stand. *Constant* and *continue* have a like primary sense. So we say, to *hold on.*]

To persist in any business or enterprise undertaken; to pursue steadily any design or course commenced; not to give over or abandon what is undertaken; *applied alike to good and evil.*

Thrice happy, if they know
Their happiness, and *persevere* upright! *Milton.*

To *persevere* in any evil course, makes you unhappy in this life. *Wake.*

PERSEVE'RING, *ppr.* Persisting in any business or course begun.

2. *a.* Constant in the execution of a purpose or enterprise; as a *persevering* student.

PERSEVE'RINGLY, *adv.* With perseverance or continued pursuit of what is undertaken.

PER'SIFLAGE, *n.* [Fr. from *persifler;* L. *sibilo,* to hiss.] A jeering; ridicule. *H. More.*

PERSIM'MON, *n.* A tree and its fruit, a species of Diospyros, a native of the states south of New York. The fruit is like a plum, and when not ripe, very astringent. *Mease.*

PERSIST', *v. i.* [L. *persisto; per* and *sisto,* to stand or be fixed.]

To continue steadily and firmly in the pursuit of any business or course commenced; to persevere. [*Persist* is nearly synonymous with *persevere;* but *persist* frequently implies more obstinacy than *persevere,* particularly in that which is evil or injurious to others.]

If they *persist* in pointing their batteries against particular persons, no laws of war forbid the making reprisals. *Addison.*

PERSIST'ENCE, *n.* The state of persisting; steady pursuit of what is undertaken; perseverance in a good or evil course, more generally in that which is evil and injurious to others, or unadvisable.

2. Obstinacy; contumacy. *Shak.*

PERSIST'ENT, } *a.* In *botany,* continuing
PERSIST'ING, } without withering; opposed to *marcescent;* as a *persisting* stigma: continuing after the corol is withered, as a *persistent* calyx; continuing after the leaves drop off, as a *persistent* stipule; remaining on the plant till the fruit is ripe, or till after the summer is over, as a *persistent* leaf. *Lee. Martyn.*

PERSIST'ING, *ppr.* Continuing in the prosecution of an undertaking; persevering.

PERSIST'IVE, *a.* Steady in pursuit; not receding from a purpose or undertaking; persevering. *Shak.*

PERSON, *n.* *per'sn.* [L. *persona;* said to be compounded of *per,* through or by, and *sonus,* sound; a Latin word signifying primarily a mask used by actors on the stage.]

1. An individual human being consisting of body and soul. We apply the word to *living* beings only, possessed of a rational nature; the body when dead is not called a *person.* It is applied alike to a man, woman or child.

A *person* is a thinking intelligent being. *Locke.*

2. A man, woman or child, considered as opposed to things, or distinct from them.

A zeal for *persons* is far more easy to be perverted, than a zeal for things. *Sprat.*

3. A human being, considered with respect

to the living body or corporeal existence only. The form of her *person* is elegant.

You'll find her *person* difficult to gain. *Dryden.*

The rebels maintained the fight for a small time, and for their *persons* showed no want of courage. *Bacon.*

4. A human being, indefinitely; one; a man. Let a *person's* attainments be never so great, he should remember he is frail and imperfect.

5. A human being represented in dialogue, fiction, or on the stage; character. A player appears in the *person* of king Lear.

These tables, Cicero pronounced under the *person* of Crassus, were of more use and authority than all the books of the philosophers. *Baker.*

6. Character of office.

How different is the same man from himself, as he sustains the *person* of a magistrate and that of a friend. *South.*

7. In *grammar*, the nominative to a verb; the agent that performs or the patient that suffers any thing affirmed by a verb; as, *I* write; *he* is smitten; *she* is beloved; the *rain* descends in torrents. I, thou or you, he, she or it, are called the first, second and third *persons*. Hence we apply the word *person* to the termination or modified form of the verb used in connection with the persons; as the first or the third *person* of the verb; the verb is in the second *person*.

8. In *law*, an *artificial person*, is a corporation or body politic. *Blackstone.*

In person, by one's self; with bodily presence; not by representative.

The king *in person* visits all around. *Dryden.*

PER'SON, *v. t.* To represent as a person; to make to resemble; to image. [*Not in use.*] *Milton.*

PER'SONABLE, *a.* Having a well formed body or person; graceful; of good appearance; as a *personable* man or woman. *Raleigh.*

2. In *law*, enabled to maintain pleas in court. *Cowel.*

3. Having capacity to take any thing granted or given. *Plowden.*

[*The two latter senses, I believe, are little used.*]

PER'SONAGE, *n.* [F. *personnage.*] A man or woman of distinction; as an illustrious *personage*.

2. Exterior appearance; stature; air; as a tall *personage*; a stately *personage*. *Shak. Hayward.*

3. Character assumed.

The Venetians, naturally grave, love to give in to the follies of such seasons, when disguised in a false *personage*. *Addison.*

4. Character represented.

Some persons must be found, already known in history, whom we may make the actors and *personages* of this fable. *Broome.*

PER'SONAL, *a.* [L. *personalis.*] Belonging to men or women, not to things; not real.

Every man so termed by way of *personal* difference only. *Hooker.*

2. Relating to an individual; affecting individuals; peculiar or proper to him or her, or to private actions or character.

The words are conditional; if thou doest well; and so *personal* to Cain. *Locke.*

Character and success depend more on *personal* effort than on any external advantages. *J. Hawes.*

So we speak of *personal* pride, *personal* reflections.

3. Pertaining to the corporal nature; exterior; corporal; as *personal* charms or accomplishments. *Addison.*

4. Present in person; not acting by representative; as a *personal* interview.

The immediate and *personal* speaking of God almighty to Abraham, Job and Moses. *White.*

Personal estate, in law, movables; chattels; things belonging to the person; as money, jewels, furniture, &c. as distinguished from *real* estate in land and houses.

Personal action, in law, a suit or action by which a man claims a debt or personal duty, or damages in lieu of it; or wherein he claims satisfaction in damages for an injury to his person or property; an action founded on contract or on tort or wrong; as an action on a debt or promise, or an action for a trespass, assault or defamatory words; opposed to *real* actions, or such as concern real property. *Blackstone.*

Personal identity, in metaphysics, sameness of being, of which consciousness is the evidence.

Personal verb, in grammar, a verb conjugated in the three persons; thus called in distinction from an impersonal verb, which has the third person only. *Encyc.*

PER'SONAL, *n.* A movable. [*Not in use.*]

PERSONAL'ITY, *n.* That which constitutes an individual a distinct pe son, or that which constitutes individuality.

The *personality* of an intelligent being extends itself beyond present existence to what is past, only by conciousness— *Locke.*

2. Direct application or applicability to a person; as the *personality* of a remark.

PER'SONALLY, *adv.* In person; by bodily presence; not by representative or substitute; as, to be *personally* present; to deliver a letter *personally*. They *personally* declared their assent to the measure.

2. With respect to an individual; particularly.

She bore a mortal hatred to the house of Lancaster, and *personally* to the king. *Bacon.*

3. With regard to numerical existence.

The converted man is *personally* the same he was before. *Rogers.*

PER'SONATE, *v. t.* To represent by a fictitious or assumed character so as to pass for the person represented. *Bacon.*

2. To represent by action or appearance; to assume the character and act the part of another.

3. To pretend hypocritically. [*Little used.*] *Swift.*

4. To counterfeit; to feign; as a *personated* devotion. *Hammond.*

5. To resemble.

The lofty cedar *personates* thee. *Shak.*

6. To make a representation of, as in picture. *Obs.* *Shak.*

7. To describe. *Obs.* *Shak.*

8. To celebrate loudly. [L. *persono.*] [*Not used.*] *Milton.*

PER'SONATE, *a.* [L. *persona*, a mask.] Masked. A *personate* corol is irregular and closed by a kind of palate; or ringent, but closed between the lips by the palate. *Smith. Linne.*

PERSONA'TION, *n.* The counterfeiting of the person and character of another. *Bacon.*

PER'SONATOR, *n.* One who assumes the character of another. *B. Jonson.*

2. One that acts or performs. *B. Jonson.*

PERSONIFICA'TION, *n.* [from *personify.*] The giving to an inanimate being the figure or the sentiments and language of a rational being; prosopopœia; as, "*confusion* heard his voice." *Milton.*

PERSON'IFIED, *pp.* Represented with the attributes of a person.

PERSON'IFY, *v. t.* [L. *persona* and *facio.*] To give animation to inanimate objects; to ascribe to an inanimate being the sentiments, actions or language of a rational being or person, or to represent an inanimate being with the affections and actions of a person. Thus we say, the plants *thirst* for rain.

The trees *said* to the fig-tree, come thou, and reign over us. Judges ix.

PERSON'IFYING, *ppr.* Giving to an inanimate being the attributes of a person.

PER'SONIZE, *v. t.* To personify. [*Not much used.*] *Richardson.*

PERSPEC'TIVE, *a.* [infra.] Pertaining to the science of optics; optical. *Bacon.*

2. Pertaining to the art of perspective. *Encyc.*

PERSPEC'TIVE, *n.* [Fr.; It. *perspettiva*; Sp. *perspectiva*; from L. *perspicio*; *per* and *specio*, to see.]

1. A glass through which objects are viewed. *Temple.*

2. The art of drawing on a plane surface true resemblances or pictures of objects, as the objects appear to the eye from any distance and situation, real and imaginary; as the rules of *perspective*. *Encyc.*

3. A representation of objects in perspective. *Encyc.*

4. View; vista; as *perspectives* of pleasant shades. *Dryden.*

5. A kind of painting, often seen in gardens and at the end of a gallery, designed expressly to deceive the sight by representing the continuation of an alley, a building, a landscape or the like.

Aerial perspective, the art of giving due diminution to the strength of light, shade and colors of objects, according to their distances and the quantity of light falling on them, and to the medium through which they are seen. *Encyc.*

PERSPEC'TIVELY, *adv.* Optically; through a glass; by representation. *Shak.*

PER'SPICABLE, *a.* Discernible. *Herbert.*

PERSPICA'CIOUS, *a.* [L. *perspicax*, from *perspicio.*]

1. Quick sighted; sharp of sight.

2. Of acute discernment. *South.*

PERSPICA'CIOUSNESS, *n.* Acuteness of sight.

PERSPICAC'ITY, *n.* [L. *perspicacitas.*]

1. Acuteness of sight; quickness of sight.

2. Acuteness of discernment or understanding.

PER'SPICACY, *n.* Acuteness of sight or discernment. *B. Jonson.*

PER'SPICIL, *n.* [L. *per* and *speculum*, a glass.] An optic glass. [*Little used.*] *Crashaw. Glanville.*

PERSPICU'ITY, *n.* [Fr. *perspicuité*; L. *perspicuitas*, from *perspicio*.]

1. Transparency; clearness; that quality of a substance which renders objects visible through it. [*Little used.*] *Brown.*

2. Clearness to mental vision; easiness to be understood; freedom from obscurity or ambiguity; that quality of writing or language which readily presents to the mind of another the precise ideas of the author. *Perspicuity* is the first excellence of writing or speaking.

PERSPIC'UOUS, *a.* [L. *perspicuus*.] Transparent; translucent. [*Little used.*] *Peacham.*

2. Clear to the understanding; that may be clearly understood; not obscure or ambiguous. Language is *perspicuous* when it readily presents to the reader or hearer the precise ideas which are intended to be expressed. Meaning, sense or signification is *perspicuous*, when it is clearly and easily comprehended.

PERSPIC'UOUSLY, *adv.* Clearly; plainly; in a manner to be easily understood. *Bacon.*

PERSPIC'UOUSNESS, *n.* Clearness to intellectual vision; plainness; freedom from obscurity.

[We generally apply *perspicuous* to objects of intellect, and *conspicuous* to objects of ocular sight.]

PERSPIRABIL'ITY, *n.* [from *perspirable*.] The quality of being perspirable.

PER'SPIRABLE, *a.* [from L. *perspiro*. See *Perspire*.]

1. That may be perspired; that may be evacuated through the pores of the skin. *Arbuthnot.*

2. Emitting perspiration. [*Not proper.*] *Bacon.*

PERSPIRA'TION, *n.* [L. *perspiro*. See *Perspire*.]

1. The act of perspiring; excretion by the cuticular pores; evacuation of the fluids of the body through the pores of the skin. *Encyc. Arbuthnot.*

2. Matter perspired.

PER'SPIRATIVE, *a.* Performing the act of perspiration.

PER'SPIRATORY, *a.* Perspirative. *Berkeley.*

PERSPI'RE, *v. i.* [L. *per* and *spiro*, to breathe.]

1. To evacuate the fluids of the body through the pores of the skin; as, a person *perspires* freely.

2. To be evacuated or excreted through the pores of the skin; as, a fluid *perspires*.

PERSPI'RE, *v. t.* To emit or evacuate through the pores of the skin. *Smollett.*

PERSTRINGE, *v. t.* *perstrinj'*. [L. *perstringo*; *per* and *stringo*, to graze or brush.] To graze; to glance on. *Burton.*

PERSUA'DABLE, *a.* [See *Persuade*.] That may be persuaded.

PERSUA'DABLY, *adv.* So as to be persuaded.

PERSUA'DE, *v. t.* [L. *persuadeo*; *per* and *suadeo*, to urge or incite.]

1. To influence by argument, advice, intreaty or expostulation; to draw or incline the will to a determination by presenting motives to the mind.

> I should be glad, if I could *persuade* him to write such another critick on any thing of mine. *Dryden.*

> Almost thou *persuadest* me to be a christian. Acts xxvi.

2. To convince by argument, or reasons offered; or to convince by reasons suggested by reflection or deliberation, or by evidence presented in any manner to the mind.

> Beloved, we are *persuaded* better things of you. Heb. vi.

3. To inculcate by argument or expostulation. [*Little used.*] *Taylor.*

4. To treat by persuasion. [*Not in use.*] *Shak.*

PERSUA'DED, *pp.* Influenced or drawn to an opinion or determination by argument, advice or reasons suggested; convinced; induced.

PERSUA'DER, *n.* One that persuades or influences another. *Bacon.*

2. That which incites.

> Hunger and thirst at once,
> Powerful *persuaders!* *Milton.*

PERSUA'DING, *ppr.* Influencing by motives presented.

PERSUASIBIL'ITY, *n.* Capability of being persuaded. *Hallywell.*

PERSUA'SIBLE, *a.* [L. *persuasibilis*.] That may be persuaded or influenced by reasons offered.

PERSUA'SIBLENESS, *n.* The quality of being influenced by persuasion.

PERSUA'SION, *n.* *s* as *z*. [Fr. from L. *persuasio*.]

1. The act of persuading; the act of influencing the mind by arguments or reasons offered, or by any thing that moves the mind or passions, or inclines the will to a determination.

> For thou hast all the arts of fine *persuasion*. *Otway.*

2. The state of being persuaded or convinced; settled opinion or conviction proceeding from arguments and reasons offered by others, or suggested by one's own reflections.

> When we have no other certainty of being in the right, but our own *persuasion* that we are so— *Gov. of the Tongue.*

3. A creed or belief; or a sect or party adhering to a creed or system of opinions; as men of the same *persuasion*; all *persuasions* concur in the measure.

PERSUA'SIVE, *a.* Having the power of persuading; influencing the mind or passions; as *persuasive* eloquence; *persuasive* evidence. *Hooker. South.*

PERSUA'SIVELY, *adv.* In such a manner as to persuade or convince. *Milton.*

PERSUA'SIVENESS, *n.* The quality of having influence on the mind or passions. *Taylor.*

PERSUA'SORY, *a.* Having power or tendency to persuade. *Brown.*

PERSUL'PHATE, *n.* A combination of sulphuric acid with the peroxyd of iron. *Webster's Manual.*

PERT, *a.* [W. *pert*, smart, spruce; probably allied to *perk*, primarily erect, from shooting up or forward.]

1. Lively; brisk; smart.

> Awake the *pert* and nimble spirit of mirth. *Shak.*

> On the lawny sands and shelves,
> Trip the *pert* fairies, and the dapper elves. *Milton.*

2. Forward; saucy; bold; indecorously free.

> A lady bids me in a very *pert* manner mind my own affairs— *Addison.*

PERTA'IN, *v. i.* [L. *pertineo*; *per* and *teneo*, to hold; It. *pertenere*.]

1. To belong; to be the property, right or duty of.

> Men hate those who affect honor by ambition, which *pertaineth* not to them. *Hayward.*

> He took the fortified cities which *pertained* to Judah. 2 Kings xii.

> It *pertains* to the governor to open the ports by proclamation. *Anon.*

2. To have relation to. Acts i.

PERTEREBRA'TION, *n.* [L. *per* and *terebratio*.] The act of boring through. *Ainsworth.*

PERTINA'CIOUS, *a.* [L. *pertinax*; *per* and *teneo*, to hold.]

1. Holding or adhering to any opinion, purpose or design with obstinacy; obstinate; perversely resolute or persistent; as *pertinacious* in opinion; a man of *pertinacious* confidence. *Walton.*

2. Resolute; firm; constant; steady.

> Diligence is a steady, constant, *pertinacious* study— *South.*

[This word often implies a censurable degree of firmness or constancy, like *obstinacy*.]

PERTINA'CIOUSLY, *adv.* Obstinately; with firm or perverse adherence to opinion or purpose. He *pertinaciously* maintains his first opinions.

PERTINA'CIOUSNESS, **PERTINAC'ITY**, } *n.* [L. *pertinacia*.] Firm or unyielding adherence to opinion or purpose; obstinacy. He pursues his scheme with *pertinacity*.

2. Resolution; constancy.

PER'TINACY, *n.* [supra.] Obstinacy; stubbornness; persistency; resolution; steadiness. [*Little used.*] *Taylor.*

PER'TINENCE, **PER'TINENCY**, } *n.* [L. *pertinens*, *pertineo*; *per* and *teneo*, to hold.] Justness of relation to the subject or matter in hand; fitness; appositeness; suitableness.

> I have shown the fitness and *pertinency* of the apostle's discourse to the persons he addressed. *Bentley.*

PER'TINENT, *a.* [L. *pertinens*.] Related to the subject or matter in hand; just to the purpose; adapted to the end proposed; apposite; not foreign to the thing intended. We say, he used an argument not *pertinent* to his subject or design. The discourse abounds with *pertinent* remarks. He gave *pertinent* answers to the questions.

2. Regarding; concerning; belonging. [*Little used.*] *Hooker.*

PER'TINENTLY, *adv.* Appositely; to the purpose. He answered *pertinently*.

PER'TINENTNESS, *n.* Appositeness.

PERTIN'GENT, *a.* [L. *pertingens*.] Reaching to.

PERT'LY, *adv.* Briskly; smartly; with prompt boldness.

2. Saucily; with indecorous confidence or boldness. *Swift.*

PERT'NESS, *n.* Briskness; smartness.

2. Sauciness; forward promptness or boldness; implying less than *effrontery* or *impudence*.

Pertness and ignorance may ask a question in three lines, which it will cost learning and ingenuity thirty pages to answer. *G. Spring.*

3. Petty liveliness; sprightliness without force, dignity or solidity.

There is in Shaftsbury's works a lively *pertness* and a parade of literature. *Watts.*

PERTURB′, PER′TURBATE, *v. t.* [L. *perturbo; per* and *turbo*, properly to turn, or to stir by turning.]

1. To disturb; to agitate; to disquiet.
2. To disorder; to confuse. *Brown.*

[This verb is little used. The participle is in use.]

PERTURBA′TION, *n.* [L. *perturbatio.*]

1. Disquiet or agitation of mind. *Milton.*
2. Restlessness of passions; great uneasiness.
3. Disturbance; disorder; commotion in public affairs. *Bacon.*
4. Disturbance of passions; commotion of spirit. *B. Jonson.*
5. Cause of disquiet.

O polished *perturbation*, golden care! *Shak.*

PERTURBA′TOR, PERTURB′ER, *n.* One that disturbs or raises commotion. [*Little used.*]

PERTURB′ED, *pp.* Disturbed; agitated; disquieted.

Rest, rest, *perturbed* spirit. *Shak.*

PERTU′SE, PERTU′SED, *a.* [L. *pertusus, pertundo; per* and *tundo*, to beat.]

1. Punched; pierced with holes.
2. In *botany*, full of hollow dots on the surface, as a leaf.

PERTU′SION, *n. s* as *z.* [L. *pertusus, pertundo.*]

1. The act of punching, piercing or thrusting through with a pointed instrument.

The manner of opening a vein in Hippocrates's time, was by stabbing or *pertusion.* *Arbuthnot.*

2. A little hole made by punching; a perforation. *Bacon.*

PERU′KE, *n.* [Fr. *perruque;* It. *perrucca;* Sp. *peluca;* D. *paruik;* G. *perrücke;* Sw. *peruk.*]

An artificial cap of hair; a periwig. *Wiseman.*

PERU′KE-MAKER, *n.* A maker of perukes; a wig-maker.

PERU′SAL, *n. s* as *z.* [from *peruse.*] The act of reading.

This treatise requires application in the *perusal.* *Woodward.*

2. Careful view or examination. [*Unusual.*] *Tatler.*

PERU′SE, *v. t. s* as *z.* [Some of the senses of this word would lead to the inference that it is from the Latin *perviso.* If not, I know not its origin.]

1. To read, or to read with attention. *Addison.*
2. To observe; to examine with careful survey. *Obs.*

I have *perus'd* her well. *Shak.*
Myself I then *perus'd*, and limb by limb
Survey'd. *Milton.*

PERU′SED, *pp.* Read; observed; examined.

PERU′SER, *n.* One that reads or examines. *Woodward.*

PERU′SING, *ppr.* Reading; examining.

PERU′VIAN, *a.* Pertaining to Peru, in South America.

Peruvian bark, the bark of the Cinchona, a tree of Peru; called also *Jesuits' bark.* The taste is bitter and pungent, and it is used as an astringent and tonic, in cases of debility, and particularly as a febrifuge in intermittents.

PERVA′DE, *v. t.* [L. *pervado; per* and *vado*, to go, Eng. to *wade.*]

1. To pass through an aperture, pore or interstice; to permeate; as liquors that *pervade* the pores. *Newton.*
2. To pass or spread through the whole extent of a thing and into every minute part.

What but God
Pervades, adjusts and agitates the whole? *Thomson.*

3. We use this verb in a transitive form to express a passive or an intransitive signification. Thus when we say, "the electric fluid *pervades* the earth," or "ether *pervades* the universe," we mean only that the fluid is diffused through the earth or universe, or exists in all parts of them. So when we say, "a spirit of conciliation *pervades* all classes of men," we may mean that such a spirit *passes through* all classes, or it exists among all classes.

PERVA′DED, *pp.* Passed through; permeated; penetrated in every part.

PERVA′DING, *ppr.* Passing through or extending to every part of a thing.

PERVA′SION, *n. s* as *z.* The act of pervading or passing through the whole extent of a thing. *Boyle.*

PERVERSE, *a. pervers′.* [L. *perversus.* See *Pervert.*]

1. Literally, turned aside; hence, distorted from the right. *Milton.*
2. Obstinate in the wrong; disposed to be contrary; stubborn; untractable.

To so *perverse* a sex all grace is vain. *Dryden.*

3. Cross; petulant; peevish; disposed to cross and vex.

I'll frown and be *perverse*, and say thee nay. *Shak.*

PERVERSELY, *adv. pervers′ly.* With intent to vex; crossly; peevishly; obstinately in the wrong. *Locke. Swift.*

PERVERSENESS, *n. pervers′ness.* Disposition to cross or vex; untractableness; crossness of temper; a disposition uncomplying, unaccommodating or acting in opposition to what is proper or what is desired by others.

Her whom he wishes most, shall seldom gain
Through her *perverseness.* *Milton.*

2. Perversion. [*Not used.*] *Bacon.*

PERVER′SION, *n.* [Fr. from L. *perversus.*] The act of perverting; a turning from truth or propriety; a diverting from the true intent or object; change to something worse. We speak of the *perversion* of the laws, when they are misinterpreted or misapplied; a *perversion* of reason, when it is misemployed; a *perversion* of Scripture, when it is willfully misinterpreted or misapplied, &c.

PERVERS′ITY, *n.* Perverseness; crossness; disposition to thwart or cross. *Norris.*

PERVERS′IVE, *a.* Tending to pervert or corrupt.

PERVERT′, *v. t.* [L. *perverto; per* and *verto*, to turn.]

1. To turn from truth, propriety, or from its proper purpose; to distort from its true use or end; as, to *pervert* reason by misdirecting it; to *pervert* the laws by misinterpreting and misapplying them; to *pervert* justice; to *pervert* the meaning of an author; to *pervert* nature; to *pervert* truth. *Milton. Dryden.*
2. To turn from the right; to corrupt.

He in the serpent had *perverted* Eve. *Milton.*

PERVERT′ED, *pp.* Turned from right to wrong; distorted; corrupted; misinterpreted; misemployed.

PERVERT′ER, *n.* One that perverts or turns from right to wrong; one that distorts, misinterprets or misapplies.

PERVERT′IBLE, *a.* That may be perverted. *Ainsworth.*

PERVERT′ING, *ppr.* Turning from right to wrong; distorting; misinterpreting; misapplying; corrupting.

[*Pervert*, when used of persons, usually implies evil design.]

PERVES′TIGATE, *v. t.* [L. *pervestigo; per* and *vestigo*, to trace; *vestigium*, a track.]

To find out by research. *Cockeram.*

PERVESTIGA′TION, *n.* Diligent inquiry; thorough research. *Chillingworth.*

PERVICA′CIOUS, *a.* [L. *pervicax;* composed perhaps of *per* and Teutonic *wigan*, to strive or contend.]

Very obstinate; stubborn; willfully contrary or refractory. *Denham.*

PERVICA′CIOUSLY, *adv.* With willful obstinacy.

PERVICA′CIOUSNESS, PERVICAC′ITY, *n.* Stubbornness; willful obstinacy. [*Little used.*]

PER′VIOUS, *a.* [L. *pervius; per* and *via*, way, or from the root of that word.]

1. Admitting passage; that may be penetrated by another body or substance; permeable; penetrable. We say, glass is *pervious* to light; a porous stone is *pervious* to water; a wood is *pervious* or not *pervious* to a body of troops.

A country *pervious* to the arms and authority of the conqueror. *Gibbon.*

2. That may be penetrated by the mental sight.

By darkness they mean God, whose secrets are *pervious* to no eye. *Taylor.*

3. Pervading; permeating; as *pervious* fire. [*Not proper.*] *Prior.*

PER′VIOUSNESS, *n.* The quality of admitting passage or of being penetrated; as the *perviousness* of glass to light. *Boyle.*

PESA′DE, *n.* [Fr. *passade.* See *Pass.*] The motion of a horse when he raises his fore quarters, keeping his hind feet on the ground without advancing. *Far. Dict.*

PE′SO, *n.* [supra.] A Spanish coin weighing an ounce; a piaster; a piece of eight. *Sp. Dict.*

PES′SARY, *n.* [Fr. *pessaire;* It. *pessario;* L. *pessus.*]

A solid substance composed of wool, lint or linen, mixed with powder, oil, wax, &c. made round and long like a finger, to be introduced into the neck of the matrix for the cure of some disorder. *Encyc.*

An instrument that is introduced into the vagina to support the uterus. It is made of wood, elastic gum, waxed linen, &c. *Hooper. Cooper.*

PEST, *n.* [Fr. *peste;* L. *pestis;* It. *peste,* whence *appestare,* to infect or corrupt, Sp. *apestar.* These words may be allied to the Heb. Ch. Syr. Eth. באש to be fetid, Ar. to beat or throw down, or to a verb of that family. The primary sense is probably to strike or beat, hence a stroke. See Class Bs. No. 25. 39. 48.]

1. Plague; pestilence; a fatal epidemic disease.

> Let fierce Achilles
> The god propitiate, and the *pest* assuage. *Pope.*

2. Any thing very noxious, mischievous or destructive. The talebearer, the gambler, the libertine, the drunkard, are *pests* to society.

> Of all virtues justice is the best;
> Valor without it is a common *pest.* *Waller.*

PEST'ER, *v. t.* [Fr. *pester.*] To trouble; to disturb; to annoy; to harass with little vexations.

> We are *pestered* with mice and rats. *More.*

> A multitude of scribblers daily *pester* the world with their insufferable stuff. *Dryden.*

2. To encumber. *Milton.*

PEST'ERED, *pp.* Troubled; disturbed; annoyed.

PEST'ERER, *n.* One that troubles or harasses with vexation.

PEST'ERING, *ppr.* Troubling; disturbing.

PEST'EROUS, *a.* Encumbering; burdensome. [*Little used.*] *Bacon.*

PEST'HOUSE, *n.* A house or hospital for persons infected with any contagious and mortal disease.

PESTIF'EROUS, *a.* [L. *pestis,* plague, and *fero,* to produce.]

1. Pestilential; noxious to health; malignant; infectious; contagious. *Arbuthnot.*

2. Noxious to peace, to morals or to society; mischievous; destructive.

3. Troublesome; vexatious. *Shak.*

PEST'ILENCE, *n.* [L. *pestilentia,* from *pestilens; pestis,* plague.]

1. Plague, appropriately so called; but in a general sense, any contagious or infectious disease that is epidemic and mortal. *Shak.*

2. Corruption or moral disease destructive to happiness.

> Profligate habits carry *pestilence* into the bosom of domestic society. *J. M. Mason.*

PEST'ILENT, *a.* [L. *pestilens,* from *pestis,* plague.]

1. Producing the plague, or other malignant, contagious disease; noxious to health and life; as a *pestilent* air or climate. *Bacon.*

2. Mischievous; noxious to morals or society; destructive; in a general sense; as *pestilent* books.

3. Troublesome; mischievous; making disturbance; corrupt; as a *pestilent* fellow. Acts xxiv.

PESTILEN'TIAL, *a.* Partaking of the nature of the plague or other infectious disease; as a *pestilential* fever.

2. Producing or tending to produce infectious disease; as *pestilential* vapors.

3. Mischievous; destructive; pernicious. *South.*

PEST'ILENTLY, *adv.* Mischievously; destructively.

PESTILLA'TION, *n.* [from L. *pistillum,* Eng. *pestle.*]

The act of pounding and bruising in a mortar. [*Little used.*] *Brown.*

PESTLE, *n. pes'l.* [L. *pistillum,* and probably *pinso,* for *piso,* to pound or beat; Sw. *piska,* to strike. See *Pest.*]

An instrument for pounding and breaking substances in a mortar. *Locke.*

Pestle of pork, a gammon of bacon. *Ainsworth.*

PET, *n.* [This word may be contracted from *petulant,* or belong to the root of that word. *Peevish,* which is evidently a contracted word, may be from the same root.]

A slight fit of peevishness or fretful discontent.

> Life given for noble purposes must not be thrown away in a *pet,* nor whined away in love. *Collier.*

PET, *n.* [formerly *peat.* Qu. W. *pêth,* a little; *pêthan,* a babe or little thing; D. *bout,* a duck or dear; Ir. *baidh,* love; L. *peto,* or Gr. ποθος, ποθεω. In Pers. بُت bat is an idol, a dear friend, a mistress. In Russ. *pitayu* signifies to feed, nourish or bring up. The real origin of the word is doubtful.]

1. A cade lamb; a lamb brought up by hand.

2. A fondling; any little animal fondled and indulged. *Tatler.*

PET, *v. t.* To treat as a pet; to fondle; to indulge.

PE'TAL, *n.* [Fr. *petale;* Gr. πεταλον, from πεταω, to expand, L. *pateo.* Class Bd. No. 65. &c.]

In *botany,* a flower leaf. In flowers of one *petal,* the corol and *petal* are the same. In flowers of several *petals,* the corol is the whole, and the *petals* are the parts, or the *petal* is one of the leaves of which the whole corol is composed. *Martyn.*

PET'ALED, } *a.* Having petals; as a *petaled* flower; opposed to
PET'ALOUS, }
apetalous. This word is much used in compounds; as one-*petaled;* three-*petaled.*

PET'ALINE, *a.* Pertaining to a petal; attached to a petal; as a *petaline* nectary. *Barton.*

PET'ALISM, *n.* [Gr. πεταλισμος. See *Petal.*] A form of sentence among the ancient Syracusans, by which they proscribed a citizen whose wealth or popularity alarmed their jealousy, or who was suspected of aspiring to sovereign power; temporary proscription, or banishment for five years. The mode was to give their votes by writing his name on a leaf. *Petalism* in Syracuse answered to *ostracism* in Athens. *Encyc. Cyc.*

PET'ALITE, *n.* [Gr. πεταλον, a leaf.] A rare mineral occurring in masses, having a foliated structure; its color milk white or shaded with gray, red or green. The new alkali, lithia, was first discovered in this mineral. *Cleaveland.*

PET'ALOID, *a.* [*petal* and Gr. ειδος, form.] Having the form of petals. *Barton. Rafinesque.*

PET'AL-SHAPED, *a.* Having the shape of a petal.

PET'ARD, *n.* [It. Sp. *petardo;* Fr. *petard.*]

An engine of war made of metal, nearly in the shape of a hat, to be loaded with powder and fixed on a madrier or plank, and used to break gates, barricades, drawbridges and the like, by explosion. *Encyc.*

PETE'CHIÆ, *n.* [Sp. *petequia;* It. *petecchia.*]

Purple spots which appear on the skin in malignant fevers.

PETE'CHIAL, *a.* [Sp. *petequial;* It. *petecchiale.*]

Spotted. A *petechial* fever is a malignant fever accompanied with purple spots on the skin.

PETER, } [See *Saltpeter.*]
PETRE. }

PET'EREL, } *n.* An aquatic fowl of the genus Procellaria.
PET'REL, }

PE'TERPENCE, *n.* A tax or tribute formerly paid by the English people to the pope; being a penny for every house, payable at Lammas day. It was called also Romescot. *Hall.*

PE'TERWŎRT, *n.* A plant.

PET'IOLAR, } *a.* Pertaining to a petiole, or proceeding from it;
PET'IOLARY, }
as a *petiolar* tendril.

2. Formed from a petiole; as a *petiolar* bud.

3. Growing on a petiole; as a *petiolar* gland. *Martyn.*

PET'IOLATE, } *a.* Growing on a petiole; as a *petiolate* leaf.
PET'IOLED, }
Martyn.

PET'IOLE, *n.* [L. *petiolus,* probably a diminutive from *pes, pedis.*]

In *botany,* a leaf-stalk; the foot-stalk of a leaf. *Martyn.*

PETIT, *a. pet'ty.* [Fr. See *Petty.*] Small; little; mean. *South.*

This word *petit* is now generally written *petty.*

Petit constable, an inferior civil officer subordinate to the high constable.

Petit jury, a jury of twelve freeholders who are empanneled to try causes at the bar of a court; so called in distinction from the grand jury, which tries the truth of indictments.

Petit larceny, the stealing of goods of the value of twelve pence, or under that amount; opposed to *grand larceny.*

Petit serjeanty, in English law, the tenure of lands of the king, by the service of rendering to him annually some implement of war, as a bow, an arrow, a sword, lance, &c.

Petit treason, the crime of killing a person, to whom the offender owes duty or subjection. Thus it is *petit treason* for a wife to kill her husband, or a servant his lord or master. *Blackstone.*

PETIT-MAITRE, *n. pet'ty-maitre.* [Fr. a little master.]

A spruce fellow that dangles about females; a fop; a coxcomb. *Addison.*

PETI''TION, *n.* [L. *petitio,* from *peto,* to ask, properly to urge or press, Sax. *biddan,* Goth. *bidyan,* G. *bitten,* D. *bidden,* Sw. *bedia,* Dan. *beder,* Sp. *pedir,* Arm. *pidi,* Ir. *impidhim,* Corn. *pidzha.* Qu.

Ch. פיט to supplicate. See Class Bd. No. 57. 63. 64.]

1. In *a general sense*, a request, supplication or prayer; but chiefly and appropriately, a solemn or formal supplication; a prayer addressed by a person to the Supreme Being, for something needed or desired, or a branch or particular article of prayer. *Law.*

2. A formal request or supplication, verbal or written; particularly, a written supplication from an inferior to a superior, either to a single person clothed with power, or to a legislative or other body, soliciting some favor, grant, right or mercy.

3. The paper containing a supplication or solicitation. Much of the time of our legislative bodies is consumed in attending to private *petitions*. The speaker's table is often loaded with *petitions*. *Petitions* to the king of Great Britain must contain nothing reflecting on the administration. *Encyc.*

PETI″TION, *v. t.* To make a request to; to ask from; to solicit; particularly, to make supplication to a superior for some favor or right; as, to *petition* the legislature; to *petition* a court of chancery.

> The mother *petitioned* her goddess to bestow on them the greatest gift that could be given. *Addison.*

PETI″TIONARILY, *adv.* By way of begging the question. *Brown.*

PETI″TIONARY, *a.* Supplicatory; coming with a petition.

> Pardon thy *petitionary* countrymen. *Shak.*

2. Containing a petition or request; as a *petitionary* prayer; a *petitionary* epistle. *Hooker. Swift.*

PETI″TIONER, *n.* One that presents a petition, either verbal or written.

PETI″TIONING, *ppr.* Asking as a favor, grant, right or mercy; supplicating.

PETI″TIONING, *n.* The act of asking or soliciting; solicitation; supplication. Tumultuous *petitioning* is made penal by statute.

PET′ITORY, *a.* Petitioning; soliciting. [*Not used.*] *Brewer.*

PETONG′, *n.* The Chinese name of a species of copper of a white color. It is sometimes confounded with tutenag. *Pinkerton.*

PETRE′AN, *a.* [L. *petra*, a rock.] Pertaining to rock or stone. *Faber.*

PETRES′CENCE, *n.* The process of changing into stone. *Kirwan.*

PETRES′CENT, *a.* [Gr. πετρος, a stone, L. *petra.*]
Converting into stone; changing into stony hardness. *Boyle.*

PETRIFAC′TION, *n.* [See *Petrify.*] The process of changing into stone; the conversion of wood or any animal or vegetable substance into stone or a body of stony hardness.

> When the water in which wood is lodged is slightly impregnated with petrescent particles, the *petrifaction* very slowly takes place. *Kirwan.*

2. That which is converted from animal or vegetable substance into stone.

> —The calcarious *petrifaction* called osteocolla. *Kirwan.*

An organized body rendered hard by depositions of stony matter in its cavities. *Ure.*

3. In *popular usage*, a body incrusted with stony matter; an incrustation. *Ed. Encyc.*

PETRIFAC′TIVE, *a.* Pertaining to petrifaction.

2. Having power to convert vegetable or animal substances into stone. *Brown.*

PETRIF′IC, *a.* Having power to convert into stone. *Milton.*

> The cold, dry, *petrific* mace of a false and unfeeling philosophy. *Burke.*

PET′RIFICATE, *v. t.* To petrify. [*Not used.*] *Hall.*

PETRIFICA′TION, *n.* The process of petrifying.

2. That which is petrified; a petrifaction. [The latter word is generally used.]

3. Obduracy; callousness. *Hallywell.*

PET′RIFIED, *pp.* Changed into stone.

2. Fixed in amazement.

PET′RIFY, *v. t.* [L. *petra*, Gr. πετρος, a stone or rock, and *facio*, to make.]

1. To convert to stone or stony substance; as an animal or vegetable substance.

> North of Quito, there is a river that *petrifies* any sort of wood or leaves. *Kirwan.*

2. To make callous or obdurate; as, to *petrify* the heart.

> And *petrify* a genius to a dunce. *Pope.*

3. To fix; as, to *petrify* one with astonishment.

PET′RIFY, *v. i.* To become stone, or of a stony hardness, as animal or vegetable substances by means of calcarious or other depositions in their cavities.

PET′RIFYING, *ppr.* Converting into stone; as *petrifying* operation. *Kirwan.*

PE′TROL, } *n.* [Fr. *petrole*, from Gr. πετρος, a stone, and
PETRO′LEUM, } ελαιον, oil; quasi *petrolaion.*]
Rock oil, a liquid inflammable substance or bitumen exsuding from the earth and collected on the surface of the water in wells, in various parts of the world, or oozing from cavities in rocks. This is essentially composed of carbon and hydrogen. *Fourcroy. Kirwan. Cyc.*

PET′RONEL, *n.* A horseman's pistol.

PET′ROSILEX, *n.* [L. *petra*, Gr. πετρος, a stone, and *silex*, flint.]
Rock stone; rock flint, or compact feldspar.

PETROSILI″CIOUS, *a.* Consisting of petrosilex; as *petrosilicious* breccias. *Kirwan.*

PE′TROUS, *a.* [L. *petra*, a stone.] Like stone; hard; stony. *Hooper.*

PET′TICOAT, *n.* [Fr. *petit*, petty, and *coat.*] A garment worn by females and covering the lower limbs.

PET′TIFOG, *v. i.* [Fr. *petit*, small, and *voguer*, to row. But in Norman, *voguer* is rendered to call again, to return, as if from L. *voco*, like *advocate.*]
To do small business; as a lawyer. [*Vulgar.*]

PET′TIFOGGER, *n.* An inferior attorney or lawyer who is employed in small or mean business.

PET′TIFOGGERY, *n.* The practice of a pettifogger; tricks; quibbles. *Milton.*

PET′TINESS, *n.* [from *petty.*] Smallness; littleness. *Shak.*

PET′TISH, *a.* [from *pet.*] Fretful; peevish; subject to freaks of ill temper. *Creech.*

PET′TISHLY, *adv.* In a pet; with a freak of ill temper.

PET′TISHNESS, *n.* Fretfulness; petulance; peevishness. *Collier.*

PET′TITOES, *n.* [*petty* and *toes.*] The toes or feet of a pig; sometimes used for the human feet in contempt. *Shak.*

PET′TO, *n.* [It. from L. *pectus*, the breast.] The breast; hence, *in petto*, in secrecy; in reserve. *Chesterfield.*

PET′TY, *a.* [Fr. *petit.*] Small; little; trifling; inconsiderable; as a *petty* trespass; a *petty* crime. *Milton.*

2. Inferior; as a *petty* prince. *Denham.*

We usually write *petty* constable, *petty* jury, *petty* larceny, *petty* treason. [See *Petit.*]

PET′TYCHAPS, *n.* A small bird of the genus Motacilla, called also *beambird;* found in the north of Europe. *Pennant.*

> The beambird is the spotted fly-catcher, of the genus Muscicapa. *Ed. Encyc.*

PET′TYCOY, *n.* An herb. *Ainsworth.*

PET′ULANCE, } *n.* [L. *petulantia;* Fr. *pet-*
PET′ULANCY, } *ulance.*]
Freakish passion; peevishness; pettishness; sauciness. *Peevishness* is not precisely synonymous with *petulance;* the former implying more permanence of a sour, fretful temper; the latter more temporary or capricious irritation.

> That which looked like pride in some, and *petulance* in others. *Clarendon.*

> The pride and *petulance* of youth. *Watts.*

PET′ULANT, *a.* [L. *petulans.*] Saucy; pert or forward with fretfulness or sourness of temper; as a *petulant* youth.

2. Manifesting petulance; proceeding from pettishness; as a *petulant* demand; a *petulant* answer.

3. Wanton; freakish in passion.

PET′ULANTLY, *adv.* With petulance; with saucy pertness.

PETUNSE, }
PETUNTSE, } *n. petuns′.* Porcelain clay so called, used by the Chinese
PETUNTZE, }
in the manufacture of porcelain or china-ware. It is a variety of feldspar. *Encyc. Cleaveland.*

PEW, *n.* [D. *puye;* L. *podium.*] An inclosed seat in a church. Pews were formerly made square; in modern churches in America they are generally long and narrow, and sometimes called *slips.*

PEW, *v. t.* To furnish with pews. [*Little used.*] *Ash.*

PE′WET, *n.* An aquatic fowl, the sea crow or mire crow, of the genus Larus. *Encyc.*

2. The lapwing. *Ainsworth.*

PEW′-FELLOW, *n.* A companion. *Bp. Hall.*

PEW′TER, *n.* [It. *peltro;* Sp. *peltre*, from which *pewter* is formed by a change of *l* into *w*, as the French change *belle* into *beau*. We receive the word from the Norm. *peautre.*]

1. A composition or factitious metal, consisting of tin and lead, or tin, lead and brass, in the proportions of a hundred pounds of tin to fifteen of lead, and six of brass. This was formerly in extensive use in domestic utensils or vessels; but being a soft composition and easily melted, is now less used.

2. Vessels or utensils made of pewter; as plates, dishes, porringers and the like. *Addison.*

PEW'TERER, *n.* One whose occupation is to make vessels and utensils of pewter. *Boyle.*

PHA'ETON, *n.* [Gr. from φαινω, to shine.]

1. In *mythology*, the son of Phœbus and Clymene, or of Cephalus and Aurora, that is, the son of light or of the sun. This aspiring youth begged of Phœbus that he would permit him to guide the chariot of the sun, in doing which he manifested want of skill, and being struck with a thunderbolt by Jupiter, he was hurled headlong into the river Po. This fable probably originated in the appearance of a comet with a splendid train, which passed from the sight in the northwest of Italy and Greece.
2. An open carriage like a chaise, on four wheels, and drawn by two horses.
3. In *ornithology*, a genus of fowls, the tropic bird.

PHAGEDEN'IC, *a.* [Gr. φαγεδαινικος, from φαγω, to eat.]

Eating or corroding flesh; as a *phagedenic* ulcer or medicine.

Phagedenic water, is made from quick lime and corrosive sublimate.

PHAGEDEN'IC, *n.* A medicine or application that eats away proud or fungous flesh. *Encyc. Hooper.*

PHALAN'GIOUS, *a.* [Gr. φαλαγγιον, a kind of spider, from φαλαγξ.]

Pertaining to the genus of spiders denominated φαλαγγιον, phalangium. *Brown.*

PHAL'ANGITE, *n.* [Gr. φαλαγγιτης, a legionary soldier.]

A soldier belonging to a phalanx. *Mitford.*

PHAL'ANX, *n.* [L.; Gr. φαλαγξ.] In *Grecian antiquity*, a square battalion or body of soldiers, formed in ranks and files close and deep, with their shields joined and pikes crossing each other, so as to render it almost impossible to break it. The Macedonian *phalanx*, celebrated for its force, consisted of 8000 men; but smaller bodies of soldiers were called by the same name. *Encyc. Mitford.*

2. Any body of troops or men formed in close array, or any combination of people distinguished for firmness and solidity of union.
3. In *anatomy*, the three rows of small bones forming the fingers.
4. In *natural history*, a term used to express the arrangement of the columns of a sort of fossil corolloid, called *lithostrotion*, found in Wales. *Woodward.*

PHAL'AROPE, *n.* The name of several species of water fowls inhabiting the northern latitudes of Europe and America. *Pennant.*

PHAN'TASM, *n.* [Gr. φαντασμα, from φανταζω, to show, from the root of φαινω, to shine; φαινομαι, to appear.]

That which appears to the mind; the image of an external object; hence, an idea or notion. It usually denotes a vain or airy appearance; something imagined.

All the interim is
Like a *phantasm* or a hideous dream. *Shak.*

PHANTAS'TIC, **PHAN'TASY.** [See *Fantastic* and *Fancy.*]

PHAN'TOM, *n.* [Fr. *fantôme*, corrupted from L. *phantasma.*]

1. Something that appears; an apparition; a specter.

Strange *phantoms* rising as the mists arise. *Pope.*

2. A fancied vision. *Pope.*

PHA'RAON, *n.* The name of a game of chance.

PHARAON'IC, *a.* Pertaining to the Pharaohs or kings of Egypt, or to the old Egyptians. *Niebuhr.*

PHARISA'IC, **PHARISA'ICAL**, *a.* [from *Pharisee.*] Pertaining to the Pharisees; resembling the Pharisees, a sect among the Jews, distinguished by their zeal for the traditions of the elders, and by their exact observance of these traditions and the ritual law. Hence *pharisaic* denotes addicted to external forms and ceremonies; making a show of religion without the spirit of it; as *pharisaic* holiness. *Bacon.*

PHARISA'ICALNESS, *n.* Devotion to external rites and ceremonies; external show of religion without the spirit of it.

PHAR'ISAISM, *n.* The notions, doctrines and conduct of the Pharisees, as a sect.

2. Rigid observance of external forms of religion without genuine piety; hypocrisy in religion. *Encyc. Milner.*

PHARISE'AN, *a.* Following the practice of the Pharisees. *Milton.*

PHAR'ISEE, *n.* [Heb. פרש, to separate.] One of a sect among the Jews, whose religion consisted in a strict observance of rites and ceremonies and of the traditions of the elders, and whose pretended holiness led them to separate themselves as a sect, considering themselves as more righteous than other Jews.

PHARMACEU'TIC, **PHARMACEU'TICAL**, *a.* [Gr φαρμακευτικος, from φαρμακευω, to practice witchcraft or use medicine; φαρμακον, poison or medicine.]

Pertaining to the knowledge or art of pharmacy, or to the art of preparing medicines.

PHARMACEU'TICALLY, *adv.* In the manner of pharmacy.

PHARMACEU'TICS, *n.* The science of preparing and exhibiting medicines. *Parr.*

PHAR'MACOLITE, *n.* Arseniate of lime, snow white or milk white, inclining to reddish or yellowish white. It occurs in small reniform, botryoidal and globular masses, and has a silky luster. *Dict.*

PHARMACOL'OGIST, *n.* [Gr. φαρμακον and λεγω.]

One that writes on drugs, or the composition and preparation of medicines. *Woodward.*

PHARMACOL'OGY, *n.* [supra.] The science or knowledge of drugs, or the art of preparing medicines.

2. A treatise on the art of preparing medicines. *Encyc.*

PHARMACOPÆ'IA, **PHAR'MACOPY**, *n.* [Gr. φαρμακον and ποιεω, to make.]

A dispensatory; a book or treatise describing the preparations of the several kinds of medicines, with their uses and manner of application.

PHARMACOP'OLIST, *n.* [Gr. φαρμακον and πωλεω, to sell.] One that sells medicines; an apothecary.

PHAR'MACY, *n.* [Gr. φαρμακεια, a medicament, whether salutary or poisonous.] The art or practice of preparing, preserving and compounding substances, whether vegetable, mineral or animal, for the purposes of medicine; the occupation of an apothecary. *Encyc.*

PHA'ROS, *n.* [Gr. φαρος. This word is generally supposed to be taken from the name of a small isle, near Alexandria, in Egypt. But qu. is not the word from the root of *fire*, or from the Celtic *fairim*, to watch, and the isle so called from the tower upon it?]

1. A light-house or tower which anciently stood on a small isle of that name, adjoining the Egyptian shore, over against Alexandria. It consisted of several stories and galleries, with a lantern on the top, which was kept burning at night as a guide to seamen. *Encyc. Cyc.*
2. Any light-house for the direction of seamen; a watch-tower; a beacon.

PHARYNGOT'OMY, *n.* [Gr. φαρυγξ, the muscular and glandular bag that leads to the esophagus, and τεμνω, to cut.]

The operation of making an incision into the pharynx to remove a tumor or any thing that obstructs the passage. *Coxe.*

PHASE, **PHA'SIS**, *n.* plu. *phases.* [Gr. φασις, from φαινω, φαω, to shine.]

1. In *a general sense*, an appearance; that which is exhibited to the eye; appropriately, any appearance or quantity of illumination of the moon or other planet. The moon presents different *phases* at the full and the quadratures.
2. In *mineralogy*, transparent green quartz. *Cyc.*

PHAS'EL, *n.* [Gr. φασηλος or φασιολος.] The French bean or kidney bean.

PHASM, **PHAS'MA**, *n.* [Gr. from φαινω, φαω, supra.] Appearance; fancied apparition; phantom. [*Little used.*] *Hammond.*

PHAS'SACHATE, *n.* The lead colored agate. [See *Agate.*] *Encyc.*

PHEASANT, *n.* *phez'ant.* [Fr. *faisan*; It. *fagiano*; Sp. *faysan*; L. *phasianus*; Gr. φασιανος; Russ. *phazan*; supposed to be so named from the river Phasis, in Asia. But is it not from some root signifying to be *spotted*? See Class Bs. No. 34.]

A fowl of the genus Phasianus, of beautiful plumage, and its flesh delicate food.

PHEER, *n.* A companion. [Sax. *gefera.*] [See *Peer.*]

PHEESE, *v. t.* To comb. [See *Fease.*]

PHEN'GITE, *n.* [Gr. φεγγιτης, from φεγγω, to shine.]

A beautiful species of alabaster, superior in brightness to most species of marbles. *Encyc.*

PHEN'ICOPTER, *n.* [Gr. φοινικοπτερος, red winged; φοινικος, red, and πτερον, wing.]

A fowl of the genus Phænicopterus, the flamingo, inhabiting the warm latitudes of both continents. *Hakewill.*

PHE'NIX, *n.* [Gr. φοινιξ; L. *phœnix*, the palm or date tree, and a fowl.]

1. The fowl which is said to exist single, and to rise again from its own ashes. *Locke.*
2. A person of singular distinction.

PHENOGAM'IAN, *a.* [Gr. φαινω and γαμος.]

In *botany*, having the essential organs of fructification visible.

PHENOMENOL'OGY, *n.* [*phenomenon* and Gr. λογος, discourse.] A description or history of phenomena. *Encyc.*

PHENOM'ENON, *n.* plu. *phenomena.* [Gr. φαινομενον, from φαινομαι, to appear.]
In *a general sense*, an appearance; any thing visible; whatever is presented to the eye by observation or experiment, or whatever is discovered to exist; as the *phenomena* of the natural world; the *phenomena* of heavenly bodies, or of terrestrial substances; the *phenomena* of heat or of color. It sometimes denotes a remarkable or unusual appearance.

PHE'ON, *n.* In *heraldry*, the barbed iron head of a dart.

PHI'AL, *n.* [L. *phiala*; Gr. φιαλη; Pers. *pialah*; It. *fiale*; Fr. *fiole*.]
1. A glass vessel or bottle; in common usage, a small glass vessel used for holding liquors, and particularly liquid medicines. It is often written and pronounced *vial.*
2. A large vessel or bottle made of glass; as the *Leyden phial*, which is a glass vessel partly coated with tinfoil, to be used in electrical experiments.

PHI'AL, *v. t.* To put or keep in a phial. *Shenstone.*

PHILADELPH'IAN, *a.* [Gr. φιλος and αδελφος.]
Pertaining to Philadelphia, or to Ptolemy Philadelphus.

PHILADELPH'IAN, *n.* One of the family of love. *Tatler.*

PHILANTHROP'IC, PHILANTHROP'ICAL, *a.* [See *Philanthropy.*] Possessing general benevolence; entertaining good will towards all men; loving mankind.
2. Directed to the general good.

PHILAN'THROPIST, *n.* A person of general benevolence; one who loves or wishes well to his fellow men, and who exerts himself in doing them good.

PHILAN'THROPY, *n.* [Gr. φιλεω, to love, or φιλος, a friend, and ανθρωπος, man.]
The love of mankind; benevolence towards the whole human family; universal good will. It differs from *friendship*, as the latter is an affection for individuals. *Encyc. Addison.*

PHILIP'PIC, *n.* An oration of Demosthenes, the Grecian orator, against Philip, king of Macedon, in which the orator inveighs against the indolence of the Athenians. Hence the word is used to denote any discourse or declamation full of acrimonious invective. The fourteen orations of Cicero against Mark Anthony are also called *Philippics.*

PHIL'IPPIZE, *v. i.* To write or utter invective; to declaim against. [*Unusual.*] *Burke.*
2. To side with Philip; to support or advocate Philip. *Swift.*

PHILLYRE'A, *n.* A genus of plants, Mock-privet. *Encyc.*

PHILOL'OGER, PHILOL'OGIST, *n.* One versed in the history and construction of language. *Philologist* is generally used.

PHILOLOG'IC, PHILOLOG'ICAL, *a.* [See *Philology.*] Pertaining to philology, or to the study and knowledge of language. *Watts.*

PHILOL'OGIZE, *v. i.* To offer criticisms. [*Little used.*] *Evelyn.*

PHILOL'OGY, *n.* [Gr. φιλολογια; φιλεω, to love, and λογος, a word.]
1. Primarily, a love of words, or a desire to know the origin and construction of language. In a more general sense,
2. That branch of literature which comprehends a knowledge of the etymology or origin and combination of words; grammar, the construction of sentences or use of words in language; criticism, the interpretation of authors, the affinities of different languages, and whatever relates to the history or present state of languages. It sometimes includes rhetoric, poetry, history and antiquities.

PHI'LOMATH, *n.* [Gr. φιλομαθης; φιλος, a lover, and μανθανω, to learn.] A lover of learning.

PHILOMATH'IC, *a.* Pertaining to the love of learning.
2. Having a love of letters. *Med. Repos.*

PHIL'OMATHY, *n.* The love of learning.

PHI'LOMEL, PHILOME'LA, *n.* [from *Philomela*, daughter of Pandion, king of Athens, who was changed into a nightingale.] The nightingale. *Pope.*

PHIL'OMOT, *a.* [corrupted from Fr. *feuille morte*, a dead leaf.] Of the color of a dead leaf. *Addison.*

PHILOMU'SICAL, *a.* Loving music. *Busby.*

PHILOPOLEM'IC, *a.* [Gr. φιλος, a lover, and πολεμικος, warlike.]
Ruling over opposite or contending natures; an epithet of Minerva. *Pausanias, Trans.*

PHILOS'OPHATE, *v. i.* [L. *philosophor*, *philosophatus.*] To play the philosopher; to moralize. [*Not used.*] *Barrow.*

PHILOSOPHA'TION, *n.* Philosophical discussion. [*Not used.*] *Petty.*

PHILOS'OPHEME, *n.* [Gr. φιλοσοφημα.] Principle of reasoning; a theorem. [*Little used.*]

PHILOS'OPHER, *n.* [See *Philosophy.*] A person versed in philosophy, or in the principles of nature and morality; one who devotes himself to the study of physics, or of moral or intellectual science.
2. In *a general sense*, one who is profoundly versed in any science.
Philosopher's stone, a stone or preparation which the alchimists formerly sought, as the instrument of converting the baser metals into pure gold.

PHILOSOPH'IC, PHILOSOPH'ICAL, *a.* Pertaining to philosophy; as a *philosophical* experiment or problem.
2. Proceeding from philosophy; as *philosophic* pride.
3. Suitable to philosophy; according to philosophy; as *philosophical* reasoning or arguments.
4. Skilled in philosophy; as a *philosophical* historian.
5. Given to philosophy; as a *philosophical* mind.
6. Regulated by philosophy or the rules of reason; as *philosophic* fare. *Dryden.*
7. Calm; cool; temperate; rational; such as characterizes a philosopher.

PHILOSOPH'ICALLY, *adv.* In a philosophical manner; according to the rules or principles of philosophy; as, to argue *philosophically.*
2. Calmly; wisely; rationally.

PHILOS'OPHISM, *n.* [Gr. φιλος, a lover, and σοφισμα, sophism.]
1. The love of fallacious arguments or false reasoning.
2. The practice of sophistry. *Ch. Obs.*

PHILOS'OPHIST, *n.* A lover of sophistry; one who practices sophistry. *Porteus.*

PHILOSOPHIS'TIC, PHILOSOPHIS'TICAL, *a.* Pertaining to the love or practice of sophistry.

PHILOS'OPHIZE, *v. i.* [from *philosophy.*] To reason like a philosopher; to search into the reason and nature of things; to investigate phenomena and assign rational causes for their existence. Sir Isaac Newton lays down four rules of *philosophizing.*

> Two doctors of the schools were *philosophizing* on the advantages of mankind above all other creatures. *L'Estrange.*

PHILOS'OPHIZING, *ppr.* Searching into the reasons of things; assigning reasons for phenomena.

PHILOS'OPHY, *n.* [L. *philosophia*; Gr. φιλοσοφια; φιλια, love; φιλεω, to love, and σοφια, wisdom.]
1. Literally, the love of wisdom. But in modern acceptation, *philosophy* is a general term denoting an explanation of the reasons of things; or an investigation of the causes of all phenomena both of mind and of matter. When applied to any particular department of knowledge, it denotes the collection of general laws or principles under which all the subordinate phenomena or facts relating to that subject, are comprehended. Thus, that branch of *philosophy* which treats of God, &c. is called *theology*; that which treats of nature, is called *physics* or *natural philosophy*; that which treats of man is called *logic* and *ethics*, or *moral philosophy*; that which treats of the mind is called *intellectual* or *mental philosophy*, or *metaphysics.*
The objects of philosophy are to ascertain facts or truth, and the causes of things or their phenomena; to enlarge our views of God and his works, and to render our knowledge of both practically useful and subservient to human happiness.

> True religion and true *philosophy* must ultimately arrive at the same principle. *S. S. Smith.*

2. Hypothesis or system on which natural effects are explained.

> We shall in vain interpret their words by the notions of our *philosophy* and the doctrines in our schools. *Locke.*

3. Reasoning; argumentation. *Milton.*
4. Course of sciences read in the schools. *Johnson.*

PHIL'TER, *n.* [Fr. *philtre*; L. *philtra*; Gr. φιλτρον, from φιλεω, to love, or φιλος.]
1. A potion intended or adapted to excite love. *Addison.*
2. A charm to excite love.

PHIL'TER, *v. t.* To impregnate with a love-potion; as, to *philter* a draught.

2. To charm to love; to excite to love or animal desire by a potion.

PHIZ, *n.* [supposed to be a contraction of *physiognomy.*] The face or visage; in contempt. *Stepney.*

PHLEBOT'OMIST, *n.* [See *Phlebotomy.*] One that opens a vein for letting blood; a blood-letter.

PHLEBOT'OMIZE, *v. t.* To let blood from a vein. *Howell.*

PHLEBOT'OMY, *n.* [Gr. φλεβοτομια; φλεψ, a vein, and τεμνω, to cut.]
The act or practice of opening a vein for letting blood for the cure of diseases or preserving health.

PHLEGM, PHLEM, *n.* [Gr. φλεγμα, inflammation, and pituitous matter, from φλεγω, to burn; hence the word must have originally expressed the matter formed by suppuration.]
1. Cold animal fluid; watery matter; one of the four humors of which the ancients supposed the blood to be composed. *Coxe. Encyc.*
2. In *common usage*, bronchial mucus; the thick viscid matter secreted in the throat.
3. Among *chimists*, water, or the water of distillation. *Coxe.*
4. Dullness; coldness; sluggishness; indifference.

PHLEGMAGOGUE, *n. phleg'magog.* [Gr. φλεγμα, phlegm, and αγω, to drive.]
A term anciently used to denote a medicine supposed to possess the property of expelling phlegm. *Obs. Encyc. Floyer.*

PHLEGMAT'IC, *a.* [Gr. φλεγματικος.]
1. Abounding in phlegm; as *phlegmatic* humors; a *phlegmatic* constitution. *Harvey.*
2. Generating phlegm; as *phlegmatic* meat. *Shak.*
3. Watery. *Newton.*
4. Cold; dull; sluggish; heavy; not easily excited into action or passion; as a *phlegmatic* temper or temperament. *Addison.*

PHLEGMAT'ICALLY, *adv.* Coldly; heavily. *Warburton.*

PHLEG'MON, *n.* [Gr. φλεγμονη, from φλεγω, to burn.]
An external inflammation and tumor, attended with burning heat.

PHLEG'MONOUS, *a.* Having the nature or properties of a phlegmon; inflammatory; burning; as a *phlegmonous* tumor. *Harvey.*

PHLEME, *n.* [Arm. *flemm*, a sharp point.] [See *Fleam.*]

PHLOGIS'TIAN, *n.* A believer in the existence of phlogiston.

PHLOGIS'TIC, *a.* [See *Phlogiston.*] Partaking of phlogiston; inflaming. *Adams.*

PHLOGIS'TICATE, *v. t.* To combine phlogiston with.

PHLOGISTICA'TION, *n.* The act or process of combining with phlogiston.

PHLOGIS'TON, *n.* [Gr. φλογιςος, from φλογιζω, to burn or inflame; φλεγω, to burn.]
The principle of inflammability; the matter of fire in composition with other bodies. Stahl gave this name to an element which he supposed to be pure fire fixed in combustible bodies, in order to distinguish it from fire in action or in a state of liberty. But the theory has been proved to be false and is generally abandoned. *Bartram.*

PHO'LADITE, *n.* A petrified shell of the genus Pholas. *Jameson.*

PHON'ICS, *n.* [Gr. φωνη, sound.] The doctrine or science of sounds; otherwise called *acoustics.* *Encyc.*
2. The art of combining musical sounds. *Busby.*

PHONOCAMP'TIC, *a.* [Gr. φωνη, sound, and καμπτω, to inflect.]
Having the power to inflect sound, or turn it from its direction, and thus to alter it. *Derham.*

PHON'OLITE, *n.* [Gr. φωνη, sound, and λιθος, stone.]
Sounding stone; a name proposed as a substitute for *klingstein* [jingling stone.]

PHONOLOG'ICAL, *a.* Pertaining to phonology.

PHONOL'OGY, *n.* [Gr. φωνη, sound, voice, and λογος, discourse.]
A treatise on sounds, or the science or doctrine of the elementary sounds uttered by the human voice in speech, including its various distinctions or subdivisions of tones. *Du Ponceau.*

PHOS'GENE, *a.* [Gr. φως, light, and γενναω, to generate.]
Generating light. Phosgene gas is generated by the action of light on chlorin and carbonic oxyd gas. *Silliman.*

PHOS'PHATE, *n.* [See *Phosphor* and *Phosphorus.*]
1. A salt formed by a combination of phosphoric acid with a base of earth, alkali or metal. *Lavoisier.*
2. A mineral found in Estremadura, &c.

PHOS'PHITE, *n.* A salt formed by a combination of phosphorous acid with a salifiable base. *Lavoisier.*

PHOS'PHOLITE, *n.* [*phosphor* and Gr. λιθος, a stone.] An earth united with phosphoric acid. *Kirwan.*

PHOS'PHOR, *n.* [Gr. φωσφορος; φως, light, from φαω, to shine, and φερω, to bring. See *Phosphorus.*]
The morning star or Lucifer; Venus, when it precedes the sun and shines in the morning. In this sense, it is also written *Phosphorus.* *Pope.*

PHOS'PHORATE, *v. t.* To combine or impregnate with phosphorus.

PHOS'PHORATED, *pp.* Combined or impregnated with phosphorus.

PHOS'PHORATING, *ppr.* Combining with phosphorus.

PHOSPHORESCE, *v. i. phosphoress'.* [See *Phosphorus.*]
To shine, as phosphorus, by exhibiting a faint light without sensible heat.

> Arenaceous limestone *phosphoresces* in the dark, when scraped with a knife. *Kirwan.*

PHOSPHORES'CENCE, *n.* A faint light or luminousness of a body, unaccompanied with sensible heat. It is exhibited by certain animals, as well as by vegetable and mineral substances.

PHOSPHORES'CENT, *a.* Shining with a faint light; luminous without sensible heat.

PHOSPHORES'CING, *ppr.* Exhibiting light without sensible heat. *Cleaveland.*

PHOS'PHORIC, *a.* Pertaining to or obtained from phosphorus. The phosphoric acid is formed by a saturated combination of phosphorus and oxygen.

PHOS'PHORITE, *n.* A species of calcarious earth; a subspecies of apatite. *Ure.*

PHOSPHORIT'IC, *a.* Pertaining to phosphorite, or of the nature of phosphorite. *Spallanzani.*

PHOS'PHOROUS, *a.* The phosphorous acid is formed by a combination of phosphorus with oxygen.

PHOS'PHORUS, PHOS'PHOR, *n.* [L. from the Greek. See *Phosphor.*]
1. The morning star.
2. *Phosphorus*, in *chimistry*, a combustible substance, hitherto undecomposed. It is of a yellowish color and semi-transparent, resembling fine wax. It burns in common air with great rapidity; and in oxygen gas, with the greatest vehemence. Even at the common temperature, it combines with oxygen, undergoing a slow combustion and emitting a luminous vapor. It is originally obtained from *urine;* but it is now manufactured from *bones*, which consist of phosphate of lime. *D. Olmsted.*

PHOS'PHURET, *n.* A combination of phosphorus not oxygenated, with a base; as *phosphuret* of iron or copper. *Hooper.*

PHOS'PHURETED, *a.* Combined with a phosphuret.

PHO'TIZITE, *n.* A mineral, an oxyd of manganese. *Phillips.*

PHOTOLOG'IC, PHOTOLOG'ICAL, *a.* [See *Photology.*] Pertaining to photology, or the doctrine of light.

PHOTOL'OGY, *n.* [Gr. φως, light, and λογος, discourse.]
The doctrine or science of light, explaining its nature and phenomena. *Mitchill.*

PHOTOM'ETER, *n.* [Gr. φως, light, and μετρον, measure.]
An instrument for measuring the relative intensities of light. *Rumford. Leslie.*

PHOTOMET'RIC, PHOTOMET'RICAL, *a.* Pertaining to or made by a photometer.

PHRASE, *n. s* as *z.* [Gr. φρασις, from φραζω, to speak.]
1. A short sentence or expression. A phrase may be *complete*, as when it conveys complete sense, as *humanum est errare*, to err is human; or it may be *incomplete*, as when it consists of several words without affirming any thing, or when the noun and the verb do the office of a noun only; as, *that which is true*, that is, *truth*, satisfies the mind. *Encyc.*
2. A particular mode of speech; a peculiar sentence or short idiomatic expression; as a Hebrew *phrase;* an Italian *phrase.*
3. Style; expression.

> Thou speak'st
> In better *phrase.* *Shak.*

4. In *music*, any regular symmetrical course of notes which begin and complete the intended expression. *Busby.*

PHRASE, *v. t.* To call; to style; to express in words or in peculiar words.

> These suns,
> For so they *phrase* them. *Shak.*

PHRA'SELESS, *a.* Not to be expressed or described.

PHRASEOLOǴIC, } *a.* Peculiar in ex-
PHRASEOLOǴICAL, } pression; consisting of a peculiar form of words.

PHRASEOL'OǴY, *n.* [Gr. φρασις, phrase, and λεγω, to speak.]
1. Manner of expression; peculiar words used in a sentence; diction.
2. A collection of phrases in a language. *Encyc.*

PHRENET'IC, *a.* [Gr. φρενετικος. See *Phrensy.*]
Subject to strong or violent sallies of imagination or excitement, which in some measure pervert the judgment and cause the person to act in a manner different from the more rational part of mankind; wild and erratic; partially mad. [It has been sometimes written *phrentic*, but is now generally written *frantic.*]

PHRENET'IC, *n.* A person who is wild and erratic in his imagination. *Woodward.*

PHREN'IC, *a.* [from Gr. φρενες, the diaphragm.]
Belonging to the diaphragm; as a *phrenic* vein.

PHREN'ITIS, *n.* [Gr. φρενιτις, from φρην, the mind. The primary sense of the root of this word is to move, advance or rush forward; as in L. *animus*, *animosus*, and the Teutonic *mod*, Eng. *mood.*]
1. In *medicine*, an inflammation of the brain, or of the meninges of the brain, attended with acute fever and delirium. *Encyc.*
2. Madness, or partial madness; delirium; phrenzy. [It is generally written in English, *phrensy* or *frenzy.*]

PHRENOL'OǴY, *n.* [Gr. φρην, the mind, and λογος, discourse.]
The science of the human mind and its various properties. *Ch. Obs.*
Phrenology is now applied to the science of the mind as connected with the supposed organs of thought and passion in the brain, broached by Gall.

PHREN'SY, *n. s.* as z. [supra.] Madness; delirium, or that partial madness which manifests itself in wild and erratic sallies of the imagination. It is written also *frenzy.*

Demoniac *phrensy;* moping melancholy. *Milton.*

PHRON'TISTERY, *n.* [Gr. φροντιστηριον, from φρονεω, to think; φρην, mind.]
A school or seminary of learning. [*Not used.*]

PHRYǴ'IAN, *a.* [from *Phrygia*, in Asia Minor.]
Pertaining to Phrygia; an epithet applied to a sprightly animating kind of music. *Arbuthnot.*
Phrygian stone, a stone described by the ancients, used in dyeing; a light spungy stone resembling a pumice, said to be drying and astringent. *Pliny. Dioscorides.*

PHTHIS'IC, *n. tiz'zic.* A consumption. [*Little used.*]

PHTHISICAL, *a. tiz'zical.* [Gr. φθισικος. See *Phthisis.*]
Wasting the flesh; as a *phthisical* consumption. *Harvey.*

PHTHISIS, *n. the'sis* or *thi'sis.* [Gr. φθισις, from φθιω, φθεω, to consume.]
A consumption occasioned by ulcerated lungs. *Encyc. Coxe.*

PHYLAC'TER, } *n.* [Gr. φυλακτηριον, from
PHYLAC'TERY, } φυλασσω, to defend or guard.]
1 In *a general sense*, any charm, spell or amulet worn as a preservative from danger or disease.
2. Among *the Jews*, a slip of parchment on which was written some text of Scripture, particularly of the decalogue, worn by devout persons on the forehead, breast or neck as a mark of their religion. *Encyc.*
3. Among *the primitive christians*, a case in which they inclosed the relics of the dead. *Encyc.*

PHYLAC'TERED, *a.* Wearing a phylactery; dressed like the Pharisees. *Green.*

PHYLAC'TERIC, } *a.* Pertaining to
PHYLACTER'ICAL, } phylacteries. *Addison.*

PHYL'LITE, *n.* [Gr. φυλλον, a leaf, and λιθος, a stone.]
A petrified leaf, or a mineral having the figure of a leaf. *Lunier.*

PHYLLOPH'OROUS, *a.* [Gr. φυλλον, a leaf, and φερω, to bear.] Leaf-bearing; producing leaves.

PHYS'ALITE, *n.* [Gr. φυσαω, to swell or inflate, and λιθος, a stone.]
A mineral of a greenish white color, a subspecies of prismatic topaz; called also pyrophysalite, as it intumesces in heat. *Jameson. Phillips.*

PHYSETER. [See *Cachalot.*]

PHYSIAN'THROPY, *n.* [Gr. φυσις, nature, and ανθρωπος, man.]
The philosophy of human life, or the doctrine of the constitution and diseases of man, and the remedies. *Med. Repos.*

PHYS'IC, *n. s* as z. [Gr. φυσικη, from φυσις, nature; φυω, to produce.]
1. The art of healing diseases. This is now generally called *medicine.* *Encyc.*
2. Medicines; remedies for diseases. We desire *physic* only for the sake of health. *Hooker.*
3. In *popular language*, a medicine that purges; a purge; a cathartic. [In technical and elegant language this sense is not used.]

PHYS'IC, *v. t.* To treat with physic; to evacuate the bowels with a cathartic; to purge. *Shak.*
2. To cure. *Shak.*

PHYS'ICAL, *a.* Pertaining to nature or natural productions, or to material things, as opposed to things moral or imaginary. We speak of *physical* force or power, with reference to material things; as, muscular strength is *physical* force; armies and navies are the *physical* force of a nation; whereas wisdom, knowledge, skill, &c. constitute *moral* force. A *physical* point is a real point, in distinction from a mathematical or imaginary point. A *physical* body or substance is a material body or substance, in distinction from spirit or metaphysical substance.
2. External; perceptible to the senses; as the *physical* characters of a mineral; opposed to *chimical.* *Phillips.*
3. Relating to the art of healing; as a *physical* treatise.
4. Having the property of evacuating the bowels; as *physical* herbs.
5. Medicinal; promoting the cure of diseases.
6. Resembling physic; as a *physical* taste. *Johnson.*

[In the three latter senses, nearly obsolete among professional men.]

Physical education, the education which is directed to the object of giving strength, health and vigor to the bodily organs and powers.

PHYS'ICALLY, *adv.* According to nature; by natural power or the operation of natural laws in the material system of things, as distinguished from *moral* power or influence. We suppose perpetual motion to be *physically* impossible.

I am not now treating *physically* of light or colors. *Locke.*

2. According to the art or rules of medicine. *Obs.*

He that lives *physically*, must live miserably. *Cheyne.*

PHYSI''CIAN, *n.* A person skilled in the art of healing; one whose profession is to prescribe remedies for diseases.
2. In *a spiritual sense*, one that heals moral diseases; as a *physician* of the soul.

PHYSICO-LOǴ'IC, *n.* Logic illustrated by natural philosophy.

PHYSICO-LOǴ'ICAL, *a.* Pertaining to physico-logic. [*Little used.*] *Swift.*

PHYSICO-THEOL'OǴY, *n.* [*physic* or *physical* and *theology.*]
Theology or divinity illustrated or enforced by physics or natural philosophy.

PHYS'ICS, *n. s* as z. In *its most extensive sense*, the science of nature or of natural objects, comprehending the study or knowledge of whatever exists.
2. In *the usual and more limited sense*, the science of the material system, including natural history and philosophy. This science is of vast extent, comprehending whatever can be discovered of the nature and properties of bodies, their causes, effects, affections, operations, phenomena and laws.

PHYSIOGNOMER. [See *Physiognomist.*]

PHYSIOGNOM'IC, } *a.* *s* as z. [See
PHYSIOGNOM'ICAL, } *Physiognomy.*]
Pertaining to physiognomy; expressing the temper, disposition or other qualities of the mind by signs in the countenance; or drawing a knowledge of the state of the mind from the features of the face.

PHYSIOGNOM'ICS, *n.* Among *physicians*, signs in the countenance which indicate the state, temperament or constitution of the body and mind. *Encyc.*

PHYSIOG'NOMIST, *n.* One that is skilled in physiognomy; one that is able to judge of the particular temper or other qualities of the mind, by signs in the countenance. *Dryden.*

PHYSIOG'NOMY, *n.* [Gr. φυσιογνωμονια; φυσις, nature, and γνωμονικος, knowing; γινωσκω, to know.]
1. The art or science of discerning the character of the mind from the features of the face; or the art of discovering the predominant temper or other characteristic qualities of the mind by the form of the body, but especially by the external signs of the countenance, or the combination of the features. *Bacon. Lavater.*
2. The face or countenance with respect to the temper of the mind; particular configuration, cast or expression of countenance. *Dryden.*

[*This word formerly comprehended the art of foretelling the future fortunes of persons by indications of the countenance.*]

PHYSIOG'RAPHY, *n.* [Gr. φυσις, nature, and γραφω, to describe.]

A description of nature, or the science of natural objects. *Journ. of Science.*

PHYSIOL'OĠER, *n.* A physiologist. [*The latter is generally used.*]

PHYSIOLOĠ'IC, PHYSIOLOĠ'ICAL, *a.* [See *Physiology.*] Pertaining to physiology; relating to the science of the properties and functions of living beings.

PHYSIOLOĠ'ICALLY, *adv.* According to the principles of physiology. *Lawrence's Lect.*

PHYSIOL'OĠIST, *n.* One who is versed in the science of living beings, or in the properties and functions of animals and plants.

2. One that treats of physiology.

PHYSIOL'OĠY, *n.* [Gr. φυσιολογια; φυσις, nature, and λεγω, to discourse.]

1. According to the Greek, this word signifies a discourse or treatise of nature, but the moderns use the word in a more limited sense, for the science of the properties and functions of animals and plants, comprehending what is common to all animals and plants, and what is peculiar to individuals and species.

2. The science of the mind, of its various phenomena, affections and powers. *Brown.*

PHYSY, for *fusee.* [*Not used.*] *Locke.*

PHYTIV'OROUS, *a.* [Gr. φυτον, a plant, and L. *voro*, to eat.]

Feeding on plants or herbage; as *phytivorous* animals. *Ray.*

PHYTOGRAPH'ICAL, *a.* Pertaining to the description of plants.

PHYTOG'RAPHY, *n.* [Gr. φυτον, a plant, and γραφη, description.] A description of plants.

PHYT'OLITE, *n.* [Gr. φυτον, a plant, and λιθος, a stone.] A plant petrified, or fossil vegetable.

PHYTOL'OĠIST, *n.* [See *Phytology.*] One versed in plants, or skilled in phytology; a botanist. *Evelyn.*

PHYTOL'OĠY, *n.* [Gr. φυτον, a plant, and λογος, discourse.]

A discourse or treatise of plants, or the doctrine of plants; description of the kinds and properties of plants.

Pia mater, [L.] in *anatomy*, a thin membrane immediately investing the brain. *Coxe.*

PIABA, *n.* A small fresh water fish of Brazil, about the size of the minnow, much esteemed for food. *Encyc.*

PI'ACLE, *n.* [L. *piaculum.*] An enormous crime. [*Not used.*] *Howell.*

PIAC'ULAR, PIAC'ULOUS, *a.* [L. *piacularis*, from *pio*, to expiate.]

1. Expiatory; having power to atone.
2. Requiring expiation. *Brown.*
3. Criminal; atrociously bad. *Glanville.*

[*These words are little used.*]

PI'ANET, *n.* [L. *pica* or *picus.*] A bird, the lesser woodpecker. *Bailey.*

2. The magpie.

PI'ANIST, *n.* A performer on the forte-piano, or one well skilled in it. *Busby.*

PIANO-FORTE, *n.* [It. *piano*, from L. *planus*, plain, smooth, and It. *forte*, L. *fortis*, strong.]

A keyed musical instrument of German origin and of the harpsichord kind, but smaller; so called from its softer notes or expressions. Its tones are produced by hammers instead of quills, like the virginal and spinet. *Encyc. Cyc.*

PIAS'TER, *n.* [It. *piastra*, a thin plate of metal, or a dollar. See *Plate.*]

An Italian coin of about 80 cents value, or 3s. 7d. sterling. But the value is different in different states or countries. It is called also, a *piece of eight.*

PIAZ'ZA, *n.* [It. for *plazza*; Sp. *plaza*; Port. *praça*, for *plaça*; Fr. *place*; Eng. *id.*; D. *plaats*; G. *platz*; Dan. *plads*; Sw. *plats.*]

In *building*, a portico or covered walk supported by arches or columns. *Encyc.*

PIB'-CORN, *n.* [W. pipe-horn.] Among the Welsh, a wind instrument or pipe with a horn at each end.

PI'BROCH, *n.* [Gael. *piobaireachd*, pipe-music; Celtic *pib, piob*, a pipe.]

A wild irregular species of music, peculiar to the Highlands of Scotland. It is performed on a bagpipe, and adapted to excite or assuage passion, and particularly to rouse a martial spirit among troops going to battle. *Encyc. Jamieson.*

PI'CA, *n.* In *ornithology*, the pie or magpie, a species of Corvus.

2. In *medicine*, a vitiated appetite which makes the patient crave what is unfit for food, as chalk, ashes, coal, &c.

3. A printing type of a large size; probably named from *litera picata*, a great black letter at the beginning of some new order in the liturgy; hence,

4. *Pica, pye* or *pie*, formerly an ordinary, a table or directory for devotional services; also, an alphabetical catalogue of names and things in rolls and records. *Encyc.*

Pica marina, the sea-pye, ostralegus, or oyster-catcher; an aquatic fowl of the genus Hæmatopus. This fowl feeds on oysters, limpets and marine insects.

PICAROON', *n.* [Fr. *picoreur*, from *picorer*, to plunder; Scot. *pikary*, rapine; from the root of *pick, peck*, Sp. *picar.*]

A plunderer; a pirate. This word is not applied to a highway robber, but to pirates and plunderers of wrecks.

> In all wars, Corsica and Majorca have been nests of *picaroons*. *Temple.*

PIC'CADIL, PICCADIL'LY, PICK'ARDIL, *n.* [probably from the root of *pike, peak.*] A high collar or a kind of ruff. *Wilson.*

PIC'CAĠE, *n.* [Norm. *pecker*, to break open; from the root of *pick, peck.*]

Money paid at fairs for breaking ground for booths. *Ainsworth.*

PICK, *v. t.* [Sax. *pycan*; D. *pikken*; G. *picken*; Dan. *pikker*; Sw. *picka*; W. *pigaw*, to *pick* or *peck*; Sp. *picar*; Fr. *piquer*; Gr. πεκω or πεικω; L. *pecto.* The verb may be radical, [see Class Bg. No. 61. 62. 65.] or derived from the use of the *beak* or any pointed instrument. It belongs to a numerous family of words, at least if connected with *beak, pike*, &c.]

1. To pull off or pluck with the fingers something that grows or adheres to another thing; to separate by the hand, as fruit from trees; as, to *pick* apples or oranges; to *pick* strawberries.

2. To pull off or separate with the teeth, beak or claws; as, to *pick* flesh from a bone; hence,

3. To clean by the teeth, fingers or claws, or by a small instrument, by separating something that adheres; as, to *pick* a bone; to *pick* the ears.

4. To take up; to cause or seek industriously; as, to *pick* a quarrel.

5. To separate or pull asunder; to pull into small parcels by the fingers; to separate locks for loosening and cleaning; as, to *pick* wool.

6. To pierce; to strike with a pointed instrument; as, to *pick* an apple with a pin. *Bacon.*

7. To strike with the bill or beak; to puncture. In this sense, we generally use *peck.*

8. To steal by taking out with the fingers or hands; as, to *pick* the pocket. *South.*

9. To open by a pointed instrument; as, to *pick* a lock.

10. To select; to cull; to separate particular things from others; as, to *pick* the best men from a company. In this sense, the word is often followed by *out.*

To pick off, to separate by the fingers or by a small pointed instrument.

To pick out, to select; to separate individuals from numbers.

To pick up, to take up with the fingers or beak; also, to take particular things here and there; to gather; to glean.

To pick a hole in one's coat, to find fault.

PICK, *v. i.* To eat slowly or by morsels; to nibble. *Dryden.*

2. To do any thing nicely or by attending to small things. *Dryden.*

PICK, *n.* [Fr. *pique*; D. *pik.*] A sharp pointed tool for digging or removing in small quantities.

> What the miners call chert and whern—is so hard that the *picks* will not touch it. *Woodward.*

2. Choice; right of selection. You may have your *pick.*

3. Among *printers*, foul matter which collects on printing types from the balls, bad ink, or from the paper impressed.

PICKAPACK, *adv.* In manner of a pack. [*Vulgar.*] *L'Estrange.*

PICK'AX, *n.* [*pick* and *ax.*] An ax with a sharp point at one end and a broad blade at the other. *Milton.*

PICK'BACK, *a.* On the back. *Hudibras.*

PICK'ED, *pp.* Plucked off by the fingers, teeth or claws; cleaned by picking; opened by an instrument; selected.

PICK'ED, PIK'ED, *a.* Pointed; sharp.

> Let the stake be made *picked* at the top. *Mortimer.*

PICK'EDNESS, *n.* State of being pointed at the end; sharpness.

2. Foppery; spruceness. *Johnson.*

PICKEE'R, *v. t.* [Fr. *picorer*; from *pick.*]

1. To pillage; to pirate. *Hudibras.*

2. To skirmish, as soldiers on the outposts of an army, or in pillaging parties.

PICK'ER, *n.* One that picks or culls. *Mortimer.*

2. A pickax or instrument for picking or separating. *Mortimer.*

3. One that excites a quarrel between himself and another.

PICK'EREL, *n.* [from *pike.*] A small pike, a fish of the genus Esox.

PICK'EREL-WEED, *n.* A plant supposed to breed pickerels. *Walton.*

PICK'ET, *n.* [Fr. *piquet;* Russ. *beket.*] A stake sharpened or pointed; used in fortification and encampments.

2. A narrow board pointed; used in making fence.

3. A guard posted in front of an army to give notice of the approach of the enemy. *Marshall.*

4. A game at cards. [See *Piquet.*]

5. A punishment which consists in making the offender stand with one foot on a pointed stake.

PICK'ET, *v. t.* To fortify with pointed stakes.

2. To inclose or fence with narrow pointed boards.

3. To fasten to a picket. *Moore.*

PICK'ETED, *pp.* Fortified or inclosed with pickets.

PICK'ETING, *ppr.* Inclosing or fortifying with pickets.

PICK'ING, *ppr.* Pulling off with the fingers or teeth; selecting.

PICK'ING, *n.* The act of plucking; selection; gathering; gleaning.

PICK'LE, *n.* [D. *pekel;* G. *pökel.*] Brine; a solution of salt and water, sometimes impregnated with spices, in which flesh, fish or other substance is preserved; as *pickle* for beef; *pickle* for capers or for cucumbers; *pickle* for herring.

2. A thing preserved in pickle.

3. A state or condition of difficulty or disorder; *a word used in ridicule or contempt.* You are in a fine *pickle.*

> How cam'st thou in this *pickle?* *Shak.*

4. A parcel of land inclosed with a hedge. [*Local.*]

PICK'LE, *v. t.* To preserve in brine or pickle; as, to *pickle* herring.

2. To season in pickle.

3. To imbue highly with any thing bad; as a *pickled* rogue.

PICKLE-HER'RING, *n.* A merry Andrew; a zany; a buffoon. *Spectator.*

PICK'LOCK, *n.* [*pick* and *lock.*] An instrument for opening locks without the key. *L'Estrange. Arbuthnot.*

2. A person who picks locks.

PICK'NICK, *n.* An assembly where each person contributes to the entertainment. *Todd.*

PICK'POCKET, *n.* One who steals from the pocket of another. *Arbuthnot.*

PICK'PURSE, *n.* One that steals from the purse of another. *Swift.*

PICK'THANK, *n.* An officious fellow who does what he is not desired to do, for the sake of gaining favor; a whispering parasite. *South.*

PICK'TOOTH, *n.* An instrument for picking or cleaning the teeth. [But *toothpick* is more generally used.]

PĬCO, *n.* [Sp. See *Peak.*] A peak; the pointed head of a mountain.

PIC'ROLITE, *n.* A mineral composed chiefly of the carbonate of magnesia, of a green color. [See *Pikrolite.*]

PIC'ROMEL, *n.* [Gr. πικρος, bitter.] The characteristic principle of bile. *Ure.*

PICROTOX'IN, *n.* [Gr. πικρος, bitter, and L. *toxicum.*] The bitter and poisonous principle of the Cocculus Indicus. *Ure.*

PICT, *n.* [L. *pictus, pingo.*] A person whose body is painted.

PICTO'RIAL, *a.* [L. *pictor,* a painter.] Pertaining to a painter; produced by a painter. *Brown.*

PIC'TURAL, *n.* A representation. [*Not in use.*] *Spenser.*

PIC'TURE, *n.* [L. *pictura,* from *pingo,* to *paint;* It. *pittura.*]

1. A painting exhibiting the resemblance of any thing; a likeness drawn in colors.

> *Pictures* and shapes are but secondary objects. *Bacon.*

2. The works of painters; painting.

> Quintilian, when he saw any well expressed image of grief, either in *picture* or sculpture, would usually weep. *Wotton.*

3. Any resemblance or representation, either to the eye or to the understanding. Thus we say, a child is the *picture* of his father; the poet has drawn an exquisite *picture* of grief.

PIC'TURE, *v. t.* To paint a resemblance.

> Love is like a painter, who, in drawing the picture of a friend having a blemish in one eye, would *picture* only the other side of the face. *South.*

2. To represent; to form or present an ideal likeness.

> I do *picture* it in my mind. *Spenser.*

PIC'TURED, *pp.* Painted in resemblance; drawn in colors; represented.

PICTURESQUE, PICTURESK', } *a.* [Fr. *pittoresque;* It. *pittoresco;* from the L. *pictura,* or *pictor.* In English, this would be *picturish.*] Expressing that peculiar kind of beauty which is agreeable in a picture, natural or artificial; striking the mind with great power or pleasure in representing objects of vision, and in painting to the imagination any circumstance or event as clearly as if delineated in a picture. *Gray.*

PICTURESQUELY, PICTURESK'LY, } *adv.* In a picturesque manner. *Montgomery.*

PICTURESQUENESS, PICTURESK'NESS, } *n.* The state of being picturesque. *Price.*

PID'DLE, *v. i.* [This is a different spelling of *peddle,* or from the same source.]

1. To deal in trifles; to spend time in trifling objects; to attend to trivial concerns or the small parts rather than to the main. *Ainsworth.*

2. To pick at table; to eat squeamishly or without appetite. *Swift.*

PID'DLER, *n.* One who busies himself about little things.

2. One that eats squeamishly or without appetite.

PIE, *n.* [Ir. *pighe,* perhaps from the paste; Gr. παχυς, thick; or from mixing.] An article of food consisting of paste baked with something in it or under it, as apple, minced meat, &c.

PIE, *n.* [L. *pica;* W. *piog.*] The magpie, a party-colored bird of the genus Corvus. It is sometimes written *pye.*

2. The old popish service book, supposed to be so called from the different color of the text and rubric, or from *litera picata,* a large black letter, used at the beginning of each order.

3. Printers' types mixed or unsorted.

Cock and pie, an adjuration by the pie or service book, and by the sacred name of the Deity corrupted. *Shak.*

PI'EBALD, *a.* [Sp. *pio,* of various colors.] Of various colors; diversified in color; as a *piebald* horse. *Pope.*

PIECE, *n.* [Fr. *pièce;* It. *pezzo;* Sp. *pieza;* Port. *peça;* Ir. *piosa;* Arm. *pez.* If the elements of this word are *Bz,* it may be from the Heb. Ch. Syr. Ar. בצע, to cut off or clip.]

1. A fragment or part of any thing separated from the whole, in any manner, by cutting, splitting, breaking or tearing; as, to cut in *pieces,* break in *pieces,* tear in *pieces,* pull in *pieces,* &c.; a *piece* of a rock; a *piece* of paper.

2. A part of any thing, though not separated, or separated only in idea; not the whole; a portion; as a *piece* of excellent knowledge. *Tillotson.*

3. A distinct part or quantity; a part considered by itself, or separated from the rest only by a boundary or divisional line; as a *piece* of land in the meadow or on the mountain.

4. A separate part; a thing or portion distinct from others of a like kind; as a *piece* of timber; a *piece* of cloth; a *piece* of paper hangings.

5. A composition, essay or writing of no great length; as a *piece* of poetry or prose; a *piece* of music.

6. A separate performance; a distinct portion of labor; as a *piece* of work.

7. A picture or painting.

> If unnatural, the finest colors are but daubing, and the *piece* is a beautiful monster at the best. *Dryden.*

8. A coin; as a *piece* of eight.

9. A gun or single part of ordnance. We apply the word to a cannon, a mortar, or a musket. Large guns are called battering *pieces;* smaller guns are called field *pieces.*

10. In *heraldry,* an ordinary or charge. The fess, the bend, the pale, the bar, the cross, the saltier, the chevron are called honorable *pieces.*

11. In ridicule or contempt. A *piece* of a lawyer is a smatterer.

12. A castle; a building. [*Not in use.*] *Spenser.*

A-piece, to each; as, he paid the men a dollar *a-piece.*

Of a piece, like; of the same sort, as if taken from the same whole. They seemed all *of a piece.* Sometimes followed by *with.*

> The poet must be *of a piece with* the spectators to gain reputation. *Dryden.*

PIECE, *v. t.* To enlarge or mend by the addition of a piece; to patch; as, to *piece* a garment; to *piece* the time. *Shak.*

To piece out, to extend or enlarge by addition of a piece or pieces. *Temple.*

PIECE, *v. i.* To unite by coalescence of parts; to be compacted, as parts into a whole. *Bacon.*

PIE'CED, *pp.* Mended or enlarged by a piece or pieces.

PIE'CELESS, *a.* Not made of pieces; consisting of an entire thing. *Donne.*

PIE'CEMEAL, *adv.* [*piece* and Sax. *mel*, time. Qu.]
1. In pieces; in fragments.
On which it *piecemeal* broke. *Chapman.*
2. By pieces; by little and little in succession.
Piecemeal they win this acre first, then that. *Pope.*

PIE'CEMEAL, *a.* Single; separate; made of parts or pieces. *South.*

PIE'CEMEALED, *a.* Divided into small pieces. *Cotgrave.*

PIE'CER, *n.* One that pieces; a patcher.

PI'ED, *a.* [allied probably to *pie*, in *piebald*, and a contracted word, perhaps from the root of L. *pictus.*]
Variegated with spots of different colors; spotted. We now apply the word chiefly or wholly to animals which are marked with large spots of different colors. If the spots are small, we use *speckled.* This distinction was not formerly observed, and in some cases, *pied* is elegantly used to express a diversity of colors in small spots.
Meadows trim with daisies *pied.* *Milton.*

PI'EDNESS, *n.* Diversity of colors in spots. *Shak.*

PIE'LED, *a.* [See *Peel.*] Bald; bare.

PIE'POUDRE, *n.* [Fr. *pied*, foot, and *poudreux*, dusty, from *poudre*, dust; or *pied puldreaux*, a pedlar.]
An ancient court of record in England, incident to every fair and market, of which the steward of him who owns or has the toll, is the judge. It had jurisdiction of all causes arising in the fair or market. *Blackstone.*

PIER, *n.* [Sax. *per*, *pere*; D. *beer*, *steene beer.* If this word is from the French *pierre*, it is a contraction of L. *petra.* But more probably it is not from the French.]
1. A mass of solid stone work for supporting an arch or the timbers of a bridge or other building.
2. A mass of stone work or a mole projecting into the sea, for breaking the force of the waves and making a safe harbor.

PIERCE, *v. t. pers.* [Fr. *percer*; Gr. πειρω. The primary sense is probably to thrust or drive, and the word may be connected in origin with the W. *ber* or *pêr*, a spit, a *spear*, Ir. *bior.*]
1. To thrust into with a pointed instrument; as, to *pierce* the body with a sword or spear; to *pierce* the side with a thorn.
2. To penetrate; to enter; to force a way into; as, a column of troops *pierced* the main body of the enemy; a shot *pierced* the ship.
3. To penetrate the heart deeply; to touch the passions; to excite or affect the passions. 1 Tim. vi.
4. To dive or penetrate into, as a secret or purpose.

PIERCE, *v. i. pers.* To enter; as a pointed instrument.
2. To penetrate; to force a way into or through any thing. The shot *pierced* through the side of the ship.
Her tears will *pierce* into a marble heart. *Shak.*
3. To enter; to dive or penetrate, as into a secret.
She would not *pierce* further into his meaning than himself should declare. *Sidney.*
4. To affect deeply.

PIERCEABLE, *a. pers'able.* That may be pierced. *Spenser.*

PIERCED, *pp. pers'ed.* Penetrated; entered by force; transfixed.

PIERCER, *n. pers'er.* An instrument that pierces, penetrates or bores.
2. One that pierces or perforates.

PIERCING, *ppr. pers'ing.* Penetrating; entering, as a pointed instrument; making a way by force into another body.
2. Affecting deeply; as eloquence *piercing* the heart.
3. *a.* Affecting; cutting; keen.

PIERCINGLY, *adv. pers'ingly.* With penetrating force or effect; sharply.

PIERCINGNESS, *n. pers'ingness.* The power of piercing or penetrating; sharpness; keenness. *Derham.*

PI'ETISM, *n.* [See *Piety.*] Extremely strict devotion, or affectation of piety. *Frey.*

PI'ETIST, *n.* One of a sect professing great strictness and purity of life, despising learning, school theology and ecclesiastical polity, as also forms and ceremonies in religion, and giving themselves up to mystic theology. This sect sprung up among the protestants of Germany, in the latter part of the seventeenth century. *Encyc. Burnet.*

PI'ETY, *n.* [L. *pietas*, from *pius*, or its root, probably a contracted word; Fr. *pieté*; It. *pietà*, piety, and pity; Sp. *piedad*, piety, pity, charity.]
1. Piety in *principle*, is a compound of veneration or reverence of the Supreme Being and love of his character, or veneration accompanied with love; and piety in *practice*, is the exercise of these affections in obedience to his will and devotion to his service.
Piety is the only proper and adequate relief of decaying man. *Rambler.*
2. Reverence of parents or friends, accompanied with affection and devotion to their honor and happiness.

PIEZOM'ETER, *n.* [Gr. πιεζω, to press, and μετρον, measure.]
An instrument for ascertaining the compressibility of water, and the degree of such compressibility under any given weight. *Perkins.*

PIG, *n.* [D. *big.* In Sax. *piga*, Dan. *pige*, is a little girl; Sw. *piga*, a maid-servant. The word signifies a little one, or issue.]
1. The young of swine, male or female.
2. An oblong mass of unforged iron, lead or other metal. A pig of lead is the eighth of a fother, or 250 pounds. *Encyc.*

PIG, *v. t.* or *i.* To bring forth pigs.

PIĠ'EON, *n.* [Fr. *id.*; It. *piccione.* This word seems to belong to the family of *pick*, *peck*, *pie*, *pica.*]
A fowl of the genus Columba, of several species, as the stock dove, the ring dove, the turtle dove, and the migratory or wild pigeon of America. The domestic pigeon breeds in a box, often attached to a building, called a *dovecot* or *pigeon-house.* The wild pigeon builds a nest on a tree in the forest.

PIĠ'EON-FOOT, *n.* A plant. *Ainsworth.*

PIĠ'EON-HE'ARTED, *a.* Timid; easily frightened. *Beaum.*

PIĠ'EON-HOLE, *n.* A little apartment or division in a case for papers.

PIĠ'EON-HOLES, *n.* An old English game in which balls were rolled through little cavities or arches. *Steevens.*

PIĠ'EON-LIVERED, *a.* Mild in temper; soft; gentle. *Shak.*

PIĠ'EON-PEA, *n.* A plant of the genus Cytisus.

PIG'GIN, *n.* [Scot. a milking pail.] A small wooden vessel with an erect handle, used as a dipper.

PIG'HEADED, *a.* Having a large head; stupid. *B. Jonson.*

PIGHT, *pp. pite.* [Scot. *pight* or *picht*; from *pitch*, W. *piciaw.*] Pitched; fixed; determined. *Obs.* *Shak.*

PIGHT, *v. t.* [W. *pigaw.*] To pierce. *Obs.* *Wickliffe.*

PIGHTEL, *n.* A little inclosure. [*Local.*]

PIGME'AN, *a.* [from *pigmy.*] Very small; like a pigmy; as an image of *pigmean* size. *Parkhurst.*

PIG'MENT, *n.* [L. *pigmentum*, from the root of *pingo*, to paint.]
Paint; a preparation used by painters, dyers, &c. to impart colors to bodies. *Encyc.*

PIG'MY, *n.* [It. Sp. Port. *pigmeo*; L. *pygmæus*; Gr. πυγμαιος, from πυγμη, the fist.]
A dwarf; a person of very small stature; a name applied to a fabled nation said to have been devoured by cranes.

PIG'MY, *a.* Very small in size; mean; feeble; inconsiderable.

PIGNORA'TION, *n.* [L. *pignero*, to pledge.] The act of pledging or pawning.

PIG'NORATIVE, *a.* Pledging; pawning. [*Little used.*] *Dict.*

PIG'NUT, *n.* [*pig* and *nut.*] The ground nut, a plant of the genus Bunium; also, a tree and its fruit of the genus Juglans.

PIG'SNEY, *n.* [Sax. *piga*, a little girl.] A word of endearment to a girl. [*Little used.*] *Hudibras.*

PIG'TAIL, *n.* [*pig* and *tail.*] A cue; the hair of the head tied in the form of a pig's tail.
2. A small roll of tobacco.

PIGWID'ĠEON, *n.* [*pig* and *widgeon.*] A fairy; a cant word for any thing very small. *Cleaveland.*

PIKE, *n.* [This word belongs to a numerous family of words expressing something pointed, or a sharp point, or as verbs, to dart, to thrust, to prick; Sax. *piic*, a small needle; W. *pig*, a point, a pike; *pigaw*, to prick; *piciaw*, to dart; It. *pica*, a pike; *piccare*, to prick or sting; Sp. *pica*, *picar*; Fr. *pique*, *piquer*; Arm. *picq*, *picqat*; D. *piek*; G. *pieke*; Sw. Dan. *pik*; Eng. *peak*, *beak*, &c. Class Bg.]
1. A military weapon consisting of a long wooden shaft or staff, with a flat steel head pointed; called the spear. This weapon was formerly used by infantry, but its use is now limited to officers, and it is called a *sponton* or *spontoon.* Its use among soldiers is superseded by the bayonet.
2. A fork used in husbandry; but we now use *fork* or *pitchfork.* *Tusser.*
3. Among *turners*, the iron sprigs used to fasten any thing to be turned. *Moxon.*
4. In *ichthyology*, a fish of the genus Esox, so named from its long shape or from the form of its snout. It is a fresh water fish,

living in deep water and very voracious, but very palatable food.

The *pike*, the tyrant of the flood. *Pope.*

PIK'ED, *a.* Ending in a point; acuminated. *Camden.*

PI'KEMAN, *n.* A soldier armed with a pike. *Knolles.*

PI'KESTAFF, *n.* The staff or shaft of a pike. *Tatler.*

PIK'ROLITE, *n.* [qu. Gr. πικρος, bitter, and λιθος, a stone.]

A mineral found at Taberg, in Sweden, supposed to be a variety of serpentine. *Cleaveland.*

PILAS'TER, *n.* [It. *pilastro*; Fr. *pilastre*; Sp. *pilastra*, from *pila*, a pile, whence *pillar.*]

A square column, sometimes insulated; but usually pilasters are set within a wall, projecting only one quarter of their diameter. Their bases, capitals and entablatures have the same parts as those of columns. *Encyc.*

PILCH, *n.* [It. *pelliccia*; Fr. *pelisse*; Sax. *pylca*, *pylece*; L. *pellis*, a skin.]

A furred gown or case; something lined with fur. [*Not used.*] *Chaucer. Shak.*

PIL'CHARD, *n.* [Ir. *pilseir.*] A fish resembling the herring, but thicker and rounder; the nose is shorter and turns up; the under jaw is shorter; the back more elevated, and the belly less sharp. These fishes appear on the Cornish coast in England, about the middle of July, in immense numbers, and furnish a considerable article of commerce. *Encyc.*

PILE, *n.* [Sp. It. *pila*; Port. *pilha*; Fr. *pile*; from L. *pila*; Gr. πιλος. The *bolei* mentioned by Pausanias, were heaps of stones.]

1. A heap; a mass or collection of things in a roundish or elevated form; as a *pile* of stones; a *pile* of bricks; a *pile* of wood or timber; a *pile* of ruins.
2. A collection of combustibles for burning a dead body; as a funeral *pile*.
3. A large building or mass of buildings; an edifice.

The *pile* o'erlook'd the town and drew the sight. *Dryden.*

4. A heap of balls or shot laid in horizontal courses, rising into a pyramidical form.

PILE, *n.* [D. *paal*; G. *pfahl*; Sw. Dan. *pol*, a pole; L. *palus*; D. *pyl*, an arrow or dart; Sw. Dan. *pil*, id.; W. *pill*, a stem. These have the same elements and the like radical meaning, that of a shoot or extended thing.]

1. A large stake or piece of timber, pointed and driven into the earth, as at the bottom of a river, or in a harbor where the ground is soft, for the support of a building or other superstructure. The stadthouse in Amsterdam is supported by *piles*.
2. One side of a coin; originally, a punch or puncheon used in stamping figures on coins, and containing the figures to be impressed. Hence the arms-side of a coin is called the *pile*, and the head the *cross*, which was formerly in the place of the head. Hence *cross and pile*. *Encyc.*
3. In *heraldry*, an ordinary in form of a point inverted or a stake sharpened.

PILE, *n.* [D. *pyl*; Dan. Sw. *pil*; L. *pilum.*] The head of an arrow.

PILE, *n.* [L. *pilus*; G. *boll*; Hindoo, *bal*; Gipsey, *ballow.*] Properly, a hair; hence, the fiber of wool, cotton and the like; hence, the nap, the fine hairy substance of the surface of cloth.

PILE, *v. t.* To lay or throw into a heap; to collect many things into a mass; as, to *pile* wood or stones.

2. To bring into an aggregate; to accumulate; as, to *pile* quotations or comments. *Atterbury. Felton.*
3. To fill with something heaped. *Abbot.*
4. To fill above the brim or top.
5. To break off the awns of threshed barley. [*Local.*]

PIL'EATE, PIL'EATED, *a.* [L. *pileus*, a cap.] Having the form of a cap or cover for the head. *Woodward.*

PI'LEMENT, *n.* An accumulation. [*Not used.*] *Hall.*

PI'LER, *n.* [from *pile*, a heap.] One who piles or forms a heap.

PILES, *n. plu.* The hemorrhoids, a disease.

PI'LEWŎRM, *n.* A worm found in piles in Holland.

PI'LEWŎRT, *n.* A plant of the genus Ranunculus.

PIL'FER, *v. i.* [W. *yspeiliata*, to pilfer; *yspeiliaw*, to *spoil*, to ravage; Sp. *pellizcar*, to pinch, to pilfer, to take little food. It seems to be allied to *peel*, *pillage.*]

To steal in small quantities; to practice petty theft; as a boy accustomed to *pilfer*.

A *pilfering* hand. *Dryden.*

PIL'FER, *v. t.* To steal or gain by petty theft; to filch.

He would not *pilfer* the victory, and the defeat was easy. *Bacon.*

PIL'FERED, *pp.* Stolen in small parcels.

PIL'FERER, *n.* One that pilfers or practices petty theft. *Young.*

PIL'FERING, *pp.* Stealing; practicing petty thefts.

PIL'FERING, *n.* Petty theft.

Pilfering was so universal in all the South sea islands, that it was hardly recognized in the moral code of the natives as an offense, much less a crime. *J. Sparks.*

PIL'FERINGLY, *adv.* With petty theft; filchingly.

PIL-G'ARLICK, PILL'ED-G'ARLICK, *n.* [*pilled*, *peeled*, and *garlick.*]

One who has lost his hair by disease; a poor forsaken wretch. *Stevens.*

PIL'GRIM, *n.* [G. *pilger*; Fr. *pelerin*; It. *pellegrino*; Sp. Port. *peregrino*; L. *peregrinus*. Qu. L. *peragro*, to wander. In W. *pererin* is a pilgrim, and *pellynig* is wandering, far-roaming, from *pellau*, to remove far, coinciding with the L. *palor*. The Corn. *pirgrin* and Arm. *pirchirin*, seem to be the L. *peregrinus*. The D. *palsrok*, a pilgrim's coat, and *palsterstok*, a pilgrim's staff, indicate that the first syllable is from the root of L. *palor*, to wander. The uncertainty of the true original orthography renders the derivation uncertain.]

1. A wanderer; a traveler; particularly, one that travels to a distance from his own country to visit a holy place, or to pay his devotion to the remains of dead saints. [See *Pilgrimage.*]
2. In *Scripture*, one that has only a temporary residence on earth. Heb. xi.

PIL'GRIM, *v. i.* To wander or ramble. [*Not used.*] *Grew.*

PIL'GRIMAĠE, *n.* A long journey, particularly a journey to some place deemed sacred and venerable, in order to pay devotion to the relics of some deceased saint. Thus in the middle ages, kings, princes, bishops and others made *pilgrimages* to Jerusalem, in pious devotion to the Savior. Pilgrims now resort to Loretto, in Italy, to visit the chamber of the blessed virgin, and the Mohammedans make pilgrimages to Mecca, where their prophet was buried.

2. In *Scripture*, the journey of human life. Gen. xlvii.
3. Time irksomely spent. *Shak.*

PIL'GRIMIZE, *v. i.* To wander about as a pilgrim. [*Not used.*] *B. Jonson.*

PILL, *n.* [L. *pila*, a ball; *pilula*, a little ball; W. *pel*, a ball; Ir. *pillim*, to roll. It is probable that this word and *ball* are of the same family.]

1. In *pharmacy*, a medicine in the form of a little ball or small round mass, to be swallowed whole. *Bacon.*
2. Any thing nauseous. *Young.*

PILL, *v. t.* [Fr. *piller*; It. *pigliare*; Sp. *pillar.*]

To rob; to plunder; to pillage, that is, to *peel*, to strip. [See *Peel*, the same word in the proper English orthography.]

PILL, *v. i.* To be peeled; to come off in flakes. *Shak. Dryden.*

2. To rob. [See *Peel.*]

PILL'AĠE, *n.* [Fr. from *piller*, to strip or peel.]

1. Plunder; spoil; that which is taken from another by open force, particularly and chiefly from enemies in war.
2. The act of plundering.
3. In *architecture*, a square pillar behind a column to bear up the arches. *Cyc.*

PILL'AĠE, *v. t.* To strip of money or goods by open violence; as, troops *pillage* the camp or towns of an enemy; to plunder; to spoil. It differs from stealing, as it implies open violence, and from robbery, which may be committed by one individual on another; whereas *pillaging* is usually the act of bands or numbers. To *pillage* and to *rob* are however sometimes used synonymously.

PILL'AĠED, *pp.* Plundered by open force.

PILL'AĠER, *n.* One that plunders by open violence; a plunderer.

PILL'AĠING, *ppr.* Plundering; stripping.

PIL'LAR, *n.* [Fr. *pilier*; Sp. Port. *pilar*; It. *pila* or *piliere*; L. *pila*, a *pile*, a *pillar*, a mortar and pestle. The L. *pila* denotes a heap, or things thrown, put or driven together; W. *piler*; Ir. *pileir*; Sw. *pelare*; Dan. *pille*; D. *pylaar*; G. *pfeiler.*]

Literally, a pile or heap; hence,

1. A kind of irregular column round an insulate, but deviating from the proportions of a just column. Pillars are either too massive or too slender for regular architecture; they are not restricted to any rules, and their parts and proportions are arbitrary. A square pillar is a massive work, called also a *pier* or *piedroit*, serving to support arches, &c. *Cyc.*
2. A supporter; that which sustains or upholds; that on which some superstructure rests. Gal. ii. *Shak.*

3. A monument raised to commemorate any person or remarkable transaction.

And Jacob set a *pillar* on her grave. Gen. xxxv. 2 Sam. xviii.

4. Something resembling a pillar; as a *pillar* of salt. Gen. xix.

So a *pillar* of a cloud, a *pillar* of fire. Ex. xiii.

5. Foundation; support. Job ix.

6. In *ships*, a square or round timber fixed perpendicularly under the middle of the beams for supporting the decks. *Cyc.*

7. In *the manege*, the center of the volta, ring or manege ground, around which a horse turns. There are also pillars on the circumference or side, placed at certain distances by two and two.

PIL'LARED, *a.* Supported by pillars. *Milton.*

2. Having the form of a pillar. *Thomson.*

PILL'ER, *n.* One that pills or plunders. [*Not used.*] *Chaucer.*

PILL'ERY, *n.* Plunder; pillage; rapine. [*Not in use.*] *Huloet.*

PILLION, *n.* *pil'yun.* [Ir. *pillin;* from *pile*, L. *pilus*, hair, or from stuffing. See *Pillow.*]

1. A cushion for a woman to ride on behind a person on horseback. *Swift.*

2. A pad; a pannel; a low saddle. *Spenser.*

3. The pad of a saddle that rests on the horse's back.

PIL'LORIED, *a.* Put in a pillory.

PIL'LORY, *n.* [Ir. *pilori, pioloir;* Fr. *pilori;* Arm. *bouilhour;* from the root of L. *palus*, a stake, a pile, G. *pfahl. An den pfahl stellen*, to put in the *pillory.*]

A frame of wood erected on posts, with movable boards and holes, through which are put the head and hands of a criminal for punishment.

PIL'LORY, *v. t.* To punish with the pillory. *Gov. of the Tongue.*

PIL'LŌW, *n.* [Sax. *pile* or *pyle;* Ir. *pilliur;* L. *pulvinar;* from L. *pilus*, hair, or from stuffing.]

1. A long cushion to support the head of a person when reposing on a bed; a sack or case filled with fethers, down or other soft material.

2. In *a ship*, the block on which the inner end of a bowsprit is supported. *Mar. Dict.*

The *pillow of a plow*, is a cross piece of wood which serves to raise or lower the beam. *Cyc.*

PIL'LŌW, *v. t.* To rest or lay on for support. *Milton.*

PIL'LŌW-BIER, } *n.* The case or sack of
PIL'LŌW-ĈASE, } a pillow which contains the fethers. Pillow-*bier* is the pillow-*bearer.*

PIL'LŌWED, *pp.* or *a.* Supported by a pillow.

PIL'LŌWING, *ppr.* Resting or laying on a pillow.

PILO'SE, } *a.* [L. *pilosus*, from *pilus*, hair.]
PI'LOUS, } Hairy. A *pilose* leaf, in botany, is one covered with long distinct hairs. A *pilose* receptacle has hairs between the florets. *Martyn.*

PILOS'ITY, *n.* [supra.] Hairiness. *Bacon.*

PI'LOT, *n.* [Fr. *pilote;* It. Sp. Port. *piloto.* The French word *piloter* signifies to drive in piles, as well as to *pilot*, and *pilotage* is a piling, pile-work, a foundation of piles; Arm. *pilocha*, to drive piles. The D. *loots*, G. *lothse*, and Dan. *lods*, are from *lead;* the pilot then is the *lead-man*, he that throws the lead.]

1. One who steers a ship in a dangerous navigation, or rather one whose office or occupation is to steer ships, particularly along a coast, or into and out of a harbor, bay or river, where navigation is dangerous.

2. A guide; a director of the course of another person. [*In colloquial use.*]

PI'LOT, *v. t.* To direct the course of a ship in any place where navigation is dangerous.

PI'LOTAĜE, *n.* The compensation made or allowed to one who directs the course of a ship.

2. The pilot's skill or knowledge of coasts, rocks, bars and channels. [*Not now used.*] *Raleigh.*

PI'LOT-FISH, *n.* A fish, a species of Gasterosteus, called also rudder-fish, of an oblong shape; so named because it often accompanies ships. *Encyc.*

PI'LOTING, *ppr.* Steering; as a ship in dangerous navigation.

PI'LOTING, *n.* The act of steering a ship.

PI'LOTISM, } *n.* Pilotage; skill in piloting.
PI'LOTRY, } [*Not used.*]

PI'LOUS, *a.* [L. *pilosus.* See *Pilose.*] Hairy; abounding with hair. *Robinson.*

2. Consisting of hair.

PIL'SER, *n.* The moth or fly that runs into a flame. *Ainsworth.*

PIM'ELITE, *n.* [Gr. πιμελη, fat, and λιθος, stone.]

A terrene substance of an apple green color, fat and unctuous to the touch, tender and not fusible by the blowpipe. It is supposed to be colored by nickel. It is a variety of steatite. *Dict. Nat. Hist. Ure.*

PI'MENT, *n.* Wine with a mixture of spice or honey. *Chaucer.*

PIMEN'TO, *n.* [Sp. *pimienta.*] Jamaica pepper, popularly called *allspice.* The tree producing this spice is of the genus Myrtus, and grows spontaneously in Jamaica in great abundance. *Encyc.*

PIMP, *n.* A man who provides gratifications for the lust of others; a procurer; a pander. *Addison.*

PIMP, *v. i.* To pander; to procure lewd women for the gratification of others.

PIM'PERNEL, } *n.* [L. *pimpinella;* Fr. *pimprenelle.*]
PIM'PINEL, }

The name of several plants of different genera. The *scarlet pimpernel* is of the genus Anagallis, the *water pimpernel* of the genus Veronica, and the *yellow pimpernel* of the genus Lysimachia. *Lee.*

PIM'PILLO, *n.* A plant of the genus Cactus.

PIMPINEL'LA, *n.* A genus of plants, including the burnet saxifrage and the anise. *Encyc.*

PIMP'ING, *ppr.* Pandering; procuring lewd women for others.

PIMP'ING, *a.* Little; petty. *Skinner.*

PIM'PLE, *n.* [Sax. *pinpel;* probably from *pin*, or its root.]

A small pustule on the face or other part of the body, usually a red pustule.

PIM'PLED, *a.* Having red pustules on the skin; full of pimples.

PIMP'LIKE, *a.* Like a pimp; vile; infamous; mean.

PIN, *n.* [W. *pin*, a pin or *pen;* *piner, piniaw*, to *pin;* Ir. *pion;* Sw. *pinne*, whence *pinnsuin*, pin-swine, the porcupine; Dan. *pind*, a sprig; *pindsviin*, the porcupine; Port. *pino*, a peg; D. *pen, penne*, a *pin* or peg; G. *pinne*, a pin; *pinsel*, a pencil; Fr. *epine*, a *spine*, and qu. *epingle*, a pin; L. *penna, pinna;* W. *pen*, a summit; Sax. *pinn*, a pen, and *pinn-treow*, the pine-tree. See *Pine, Fin*, and *Porcupine.* This word denotes a sharp point or end, or that which fastens; Sax. *pinan, pyndan.* If the sense is a point, it is a shoot. From this is formed *spine*, W. *yspin.*]

1. A small pointed instrument made of brass wire and headed; used chiefly by females for fastening their clothes.

2. A piece of wood or metal sharpened or pointed, used to fasten together boards, plank or other timber. The larger pins of metal are usually called *bolts*, and the wooden pins used in ship building are called *treenails* [trunnels.] A small wooden pin is called a *peg.*

3. A thing of little value. It is not a *pin's* matter. I care not a *pin.*

4. A linchpin.

5. The central part. *Shak.*

6. A peg used in musical instruments in straining and relaxing the strings.

7. A note or strain. [*Vulgar and not used.*] *L'Estrange.*

8. A horny induration of the membranes of the eye. *Hanmer.*

9. A cylindrical roller made of wood. *Corbet.*

10. A noxious humor in a hawk's foot. *Ainsworth.*

11. The pin of a block is the axis of the sheave.

PIN, *v. t.* [W. *piniaw.*] To fasten with a pin or with pins of any kind; as, to *pin* the clothes; to *pin* boards or timbers.

2. To fasten; to make fast; or to join and fasten together.

Our gates—we have but *pinned* with rushes. *Shak.*

She lifted the princess from the earth, and so locks her in embracing, as if she would *pin* her to her heart. *Shak.*

3. To inclose; to confine. [See the verbs *Pen* and *Pound.*] *Hooker.*

PINAS'TER, *n.* [L. See *Pine.*] The wild pine.

PIN'ĈASE, *n.* A case for holding pins.

PINCERS, an erroneous orthography of *pinchers*, which see.

PINCH, *v. t.* [Fr. *pincer*, formerly *pinser;* Arm. *pinça;* Sp. *pizcar;* It. *pizzare, pizzicare.* These are evidently from the root of It. *piccare*, to prick, smart, itch, to peck, to provoke, Sp. Port. *picar*, to sting or prick, to peck, to dig, to bite or pinch, as cold. The root then is that of *peck, pick, pike;* and *pinch* is primarily to press between two sharp points, or to prick. Hence its peculiar application to pressure between the fingers.]

1. To press hard or squeeze between the ends of the fingers, the teeth, claws, or with an instrument, &c.

2. To squeeze or compress between any two hard bodies.
3. To squeeze the flesh till it is pained or livid.
4. To gripe; to straiten; to oppress with want; as, to *pinch* a nation; to *pinch* the belly; to be *pinched* for want of food.
5. To pain by constriction; to distress; as *pinching* cold. The winter *pinches*.
6. To press; to straiten by difficulties; as, the argument *pinches* the objector.

The respondent is *pinched* with a strong objection. *Watts.*

7. To press hard; to try thoroughly. *Collier.*

PINCH, *v. i.* To act with pressing force; to bear hard; to be puzzling. You see where the reasons *pinch*. *Dryden.*

2. To spare; to be straitened; to be covetous.

The wretch whom avarice bids to *pinch* and spare,
Starve, steal and pilfer to enrich an heir. *Franklin.*

PINCH, *n.* A close compression with the ends of the fingers. *Dryden.*

2. A gripe; a pang. *Shak.*
3. Distress inflicted or suffered; pressure; oppression; as necessity's sharp *pinch*. *Shak.*
4. Straits; difficulty; time of distress from want. *Bacon.*

PINCH'BECK, *n.* [said to be from the name of the inventor.]

An alloy of copper; a mixture of copper and zink, consisting of three or four parts of copper with one of zink. *Encyc.*

PINCH'ER, *n.* He or that which pinches.

PINCH'ERS, *n. plu.* [from *pinch*, not from the French *pincette*.]

An instrument for drawing nails from boards and the like, or for griping things to be held fast.

PINCH'FIST, } *n.* A miser; a niggard.
PINCH'PENNY, }

PIN'CUSHION, *n.* A small case stuffed with some soft material, in which females stick pins for safety and preservation.

PINDAR'IC, *a.* After the style and manner of Pindar.

PINDAR'IC, *n.* An ode in imitation of the odes of Pindar the Grecian, and prince of the lyric poets; an irregular ode. *Addison.*

PIN'DUST, *n.* Small particles of metal made by pointing pins. *Digby.*

PINE, *n.* [Fr. *pin*; Sp. It. *pino*; L. *pinus*; Sax. *pinn-treow*, pin-tree; D. *pyn-boom*; W. *pin-bren*, pin-tree, and *pin-gwyz*, pin-wood. These words indicate that this name is from the leaves of the pine, which resemble *pins*. But the Welsh has also *feinid-wyz*, from *feinid*, a rising to a point, from *fain*, a cone, and *gwyz*, wood. The latter name is from the cones.]

A tree of the genus Pinus, of many species, some of which furnish timber of the most valuable kind. The species which usually bear this name in the United States, are the *white pine*, Pinus strobus, the prince of our forests; the *yellow pine*, Pinus resinosa; and the *pitch pine*, Pinus rigida. The other species of this genus are called by other names, as fir, hemlock, larch, spruce, &c.

PINE, *v. i.* [Sax. *pinan*, to pain or torture, and to pine or languish. This verb in the sense of *pain*, is found in the other Teutonic dialects, but not in the sense of languishing. The latter sense is found in the Gr. πεινάω, πένω. See Ar. فَنَّ fanna, Class Bn. No. 22. and فَنِيَ No. 25. and أَفَنَ, No. 29.]

1. To languish; to lose flesh or wear away under any distress or anxiety of mind; to grow lean; followed sometimes by *away*.

Ye shall not mourn nor weep, but ye shall *pine away* for your iniquities. Ezek. xxiv.

2. To languish with desire; to waste away with longing for something; usually followed by *for*.

Unknowing that she *pin'd for* your return. *Dryden.*

PINE, *v. t.* To wear out; to make to languish.

Where shivering cold and sickness *pines* the clime. *Shak.*

Beroe *pined* with pain. *Dryden.*

2. To grieve for; to bemoan in silence.

Abashed the devil stood—
Virtue in her own shape how lovely, saw,
And *pined* his loss. *Milton.*

[In the transitive sense, this verb is now seldom used, and this use is improper, except by ellipsis.]

PINE, *n.* [Sax. *pin*, D. *pyn*, pain; Gr. πενομαι, πονος.] Woe; want; penury; misery. *Spenser.*

[This is obsolete. See *Pain*.]

PIN'EAL, *a.* [Fr. *pineale*, from L. *pinus*.] The *pineal* gland is a part of the brain, about the bigness of a pea, situated in the third ventricle; so called from its shape. It was considered by Descartes as the seat of the soul.

PINE-APPLE, *n.* The ananas, a species of Bromelia, so called from its resemblance to the cone of the pine tree. *Miller. Locke.*

PI'NEFUL, *a.* Full of woe. [*Not used.*] *Hall.*

PI'NERY, *n.* A place where pine-apples are raised. *Todd.*

PIN'-FETHER, *n.* A small or short fether.

PIN'-FETHERED, *a.* Having the fethers only beginning to shoot; not fully fledged. *Dryden.*

PIN'FOLD, *n.* [*pin* or *pen* and *fold*; Dan. *pindan*, Eng. to *pound*.]

A place in which beasts are confined. We now call it a *pound*.

PIN'GLE, *n.* A small close. [*Not used.*] *Ainsworth.*

PIN'GUID, *a.* [L. *pinguis*; Gr. παχυς, compact, L. *pactus*, Eng. *pack*.]

Fat; unctuous. [*Not used.*] *Mortimer.*

PIN'HOLE, *n.* A small hole made by the puncture or perforation of a pin; a very small aperture. *Wiseman.*

PI'NING, *ppr.* Languishing; wasting away.

PINION, *n. pin'yon.* [Fr. *pignon*, the cope of the ridge of a house; Norm. *id.* a pen; Sp. *piñon*, pinion; from Celtic *pen*, top, summit.]

1. The joint of a fowl's wing, remotest from the body.
2. A fether; a quill. *Shak.*
3. A wing.

Hope humbly then, on trembling *pinions* soar. *Pope.*

4. The tooth of a smaller wheel, answering to that of a larger.
5. Fetters or bands for the arms. *Ainsworth.*

PINION, *v. t. pin'yon.* To bind or confine the wings. *Bacon.*

2. To confine by binding the wings.
3. To cut off the first joint of the wing.
4. To bind or confine the arm or arms to the body. *Dryden.*
5. To confine; to shackle; to chain; as, to be *pinioned* by formal rules of state. *Norris.*
6. To bind; to fasten to. *Pope.*

PIN'IONED, *pp.* Confined by the wings; shackled.

2. *a.* Furnished with wings. *Dryden.*

PIN'IONIST, *n.* A winged animal; a fowl. [*Not used.*] *Brown.*

PINIRO'LO, *n.* A bird resembling the sandpiper, but larger; found in Italy. *Dict. Nat. Hist.*

PIN'ITE, *n.* [from *Pini*, a mine in Saxony.]

A mineral holding a middle place between steatite and mica; the micarel of Kirwan. It is found in prismatic crystals of a greenish white color, brown or deep red. It occurs also massive. *Dict. Nat. Hist.*

PINK, *n.* [In Welsh, *pinc* signifies smart, fine, gay, and a *finch*, and *pinciaw*, to sprig. This is by Owen formed from *pin*, a pen or pin. But in Portuguese, *picar*, to sting, to prick, to *peck*, to nip, to *pinch*, to dig, to spur, and *picado*, pricked, *pinked*, as cloth, are from the root of *peck*, *pick*, *pico*, *beak*, *pike*, Sp. *picar*, It. *piccare*. The latter would, with *n* casual, give *pink*, a little eye or perforation, and the sense of pink, in *pink-sterned*. The Welsh gives *pink*, a flower.]

1. An eye, or a small eye; but now disused except in composition, as in *pink-eyed*, *pink-eye*. *Shak.*
2. A plant and flower of the genus Dianthus, common in our gardens.
3. A color used by painters; from the color of the flower. *Dryden.*
4. Any thing supremely excellent.
5. A ship with a very narrow stern. [Fr. *pinque*, D. *pink*, that is, *piked*, *n* being casual; hence *pink-sterned*.]
6. A fish, the minnow. *Ainsworth.*

PINK, *v. t.* To work in eyelet-holes; to pierce with small holes. *Carew. Prior.*

2. To stab; to pierce. *Addison.*

PINK, *v. i.* [D. *pinken*.] To wink. [*Not used.*] *L'Estrange.*

PINK'-EYED, *a.* Having small eyes. *Holland.*

PINK'-NEEDLE, *n.* A shepherd's bodkin. *Sherwood.*

PINK'-STERNED, *a.* Having a very narrow stern; as a ship. *Mar. Dict.*

PIN'-MAKER, *n.* One whose occupation is to make pins.

PIN'-MONEY, *n.* A sum of money allowed or settled on a wife for her private expenses. *Addison.*

PIN'NACE, *n.* [Sp. *pinaza*; Fr. *pinasse*; Port. *pinaça*.]

A small vessel navigated with oars and sails, and having generally two masts rigged like those of a schooner; also, a boat usually rowed with eight oars. *Mar. Dict.*

PIN'NACLE, *n.* [Fr. *pinacle;* It. *pinacolo;* W. *pinygyl,* from Celtic *pen,* summit, L. *pinna.*]

1. A turret, or part of a building elevated above the main building.

Some metropolis
With glistering spires and *pinnacles* adorn'd. *Milton.*

2. A high spiring point; summit. *Cowley.*

PIN'NACLE, *v. t.* To build or furnish with pinnacles. *Warton.*

PIN'NACLED, *pp.* Furnished with pinnacles.

PIN'NAGE, *n.* Poundage of cattle. [*Not used.*] [See *Pound.*]

PIN'NATE, PIN'NATED, *a.* [L. *pinnatus,* from *pinna,* a fether or fin.]

In *botany,* a *pinnate* leaf is a species of compound leaf wherein a simple petiole has several leaflets attached to each side of it. *Martyn.*

PIN'NATIFID, *a.* [L. *pinna,* a fether, and *findo,* to cleave.]

In *botany,* fether-cleft. A *pinnatifid* leaf is a species of simple leaf, divided transversely by oblong horizontal segments or jags, not extending to the mid rib. *Martyn.*

PIN'NATIPED, *a.* [L. *pinna* and *pes,* foot.] Fin-footed; having the toes bordered by membranes. *Latham.*

PIN'NED, *pp.* Fastened with pins; confined.

PIN'NER, *n.* One that pins or fastens; also, a pounder of cattle, or the pound-keeper.

2. A pin-maker.

3. The lappet of a head which flies loose. *Gay.*

PIN'NITE, *n.* Fossil remains of the Pinna, a genus of shells. *Jameson.*

PIN'NOCK, *n.* A small bird, the tomtit. *Ainsworth.*

PIN'NULATE, *a.* A *pinnulate* leaf is one in which each pinna is subdivided. *Martyn.*

PINT, *n.* [D. *pint;* Fr. *pinte;* Sp. *pinta.*]

Half a quart, or four gills. In *medicine,* twelve ounces. It is applied both to liquid and dry measure.

PIN'TLE, *n.* A little pin. In *artillery,* a long iron bolt.

PIN'ULES, *n. plu.* In *astronomy,* the sights of an astrolabe. *Dict.*

PIONEE'R, *n.* [Fr. *pionnier,* contracted from *piochnier,* from *pioche,* a *pickax; piocher,* to dig, that is, to *peck,* W. *pigaw,* Sp. Port. *picar.* The Italians use *guastatore,* Sp. *gastador,* from *guastare, gastar,* to waste, to wear away. The Germans use *schanzgräber,* D. *schansgraaver,* a trench-digger.]

1. In *the art and practice of war,* one whose business is to march with or before an army, to repair the road or clear it of obstructions, work at intrenchments, or form mines for destroying an enemy's works. *Bacon.*

2. One that goes before to remove obstructions or prepare the way for another.

PI'ONING, *n.* The work of pioneers. [*Not used.*] *Spenser.*

PI'ONY, PE'ONY, *n.* [Sax. *pionie,* from L. *pæonia;* Gr. παιωνια, from παιων, Apollo, a physician, and a hymn.]

An herbaceous perennial plant of the genus Pæonia, with tuberous roots, and bearing large beautiful red flowers. *Encyc.*

PI'OUS, *a.* [L. *pius;* Fr. *pieux;* Sp. It. Port. *pio.* In Sp. and It. the word signifies not only *pious,* but mild and compassionate, and *pity* and *piety* are expressed by one and the same word. See *Pity.*]

1. Godly; reverencing and honoring the Supreme Being in heart and in the practice of the duties he has enjoined; having due veneration and affection for the character of God, and habitually obeying his commands; religious; devoted to the service of God; *applied to persons.*

2. Dictated by reverence to God; proceeding from piety; *applied to things;* as *pious* awe; *pious* services or affections; *pious* sorrow.

3. Having due respect and affection for parents or other relatives; practicing the duties of respect and affection towards parents or other near relatives. *Taylor. Pope.*

4. Practiced under the pretense of religion; as *pious* frauds.

PI'OUSLY, *adv.* In a pious manner; with reverence and affection for God; religiously; with due regard to sacred things or to the duties God has enjoined. *Hammond.*

2. With due regard to natural or civil relations and to the duties which spring from them. *Addison.*

PIP, *n.* [D. *pip;* Fr. *pepie.*] A disease of fowls; a horny pellicle that grows on the tip of their tongue. *Johnson. Hudibras.*

2. A spot on cards. *Addison.*

PIP, *v. i.* [L. *pipio;* W. *pipian;* Dan. *piper.*] To cry or chirp, as a chicken; commonly pronounced *peep.* *Boyle.*

PIPE, *n.* [Sax. *pipe;* W. *pib;* Ir. *pib, piob;* Sw. *pip, pipa;* D. *pyp;* G. *pfeife,* whence Eng. *fife;* Dan. *pibe;* Port. It. Sp. *pipa;* Fr. *pipe;* Arm. *pip* or *pimp.*]

1. A wind instrument of music, consisting of a long tube of wood or metal; as a rural *pipe.* The word, I believe, is not now the proper technical name of any particular instrument, but is applicable to any tubular wind instrument, and it occurs in *bagpipe.*

2. A long tube or hollow body; applied to the veins and arteries of the body, and to many hollow bodies, particularly such as are used for conductors of water or other fluids.

3. A tube of clay with a bowl at one end; used in smoking tobacco.

4. The organs of voice and respiration; as in *windpipe.* *Peacham.*

5. The key or sound of the voice. *Shak.*

6. In *England,* a roll in the exchequer, or the exchequer itself. Hence, *pipe-office* is an office in which the clerk of the pipe makes out leases of crown lands, accounts of sheriffs, &c.

7. A cask containing two hogsheads or 120 gallons, used for wine; or the quantity which it contains.

8. In *mining,* a pipe is where the ore runs forward endwise in a hole, and does not sink downwards or in a vein. *Encyc.*

PIPE, *v. i.* To play on a pipe, fife, flute or other tubular wind instrument of music. *Dryden. Swift.*

We have *piped* to you, and ye have not danced. Matt. xi.

2. To have a shrill sound; to whistle. *Shak.*

PIPE, *v. t.* To play on a wind instrument. 1 Cor. xiv.

PI'PED, *a.* Formed with a tube; tubular. *Encyc.*

PI'PE-FISH, *n.* A fish of the genus Syngnathus. *Encyc.*

PI'PER, *n.* One who plays on a pipe or wind instrument.

PIP'ERIDGE, *n.* A shrub, the berberis, or barberry. *Fam. of Plants.*

The *piperidge* of New England is the *nyssa villosa,* a large tree with very tough wood.

PIP'ERIN, *n.* A concretion of volcanic ashes. *De Costa. Kirwan.*

2. A peculiar crystaline substance extracted from black pepper. The crystals of piperin are transparent, of a straw color, and they assume the tetrahedral prismatic form with oblique summits. *Carpenter.*

PIPE-TREE, *n.* The lilac.

PI'PING, *ppr.* Playing on a pipe.

2. *a.* Weak; feeble; sickly. [Vulgar and not in use in America.]

3. Very hot; boiling; from the sound of boiling fluids. [Used in vulgar language.]

PIPIS'TREL, *n.* A species of bat, the smallest of the kind.

PIP'KIN, *n.* [*dim.* of *pipe.*] A small earthen boiler. *Pope.*

PIP'PIN, *n.* [D. *pippeling.*] A kind of apple; a tart apple. This name in America is given to several kinds of apples, as to the Newtown pippin, an excellent winter apple, and the summer pippin, a large apple, but more perishable than the Newtown pippin.

PIQUANCY, *n. pik'ancy.* [infra.] Sharpness; pungency; tartness; severity. *Barrow.*

PIQUANT, *a. pik'ant.* [Fr. from *piquer,* to prick or sting, It. *piccare,* Sp. Port. *picar,* from the root of *pike, peak.*]

1. Pricking; stimulating to the tongue; as rock as *piquant* to the tongue as salt. *Addison.*

2. Sharp; tart; pungent; severe; as *piquant* railleries. *Gov. of the Tongue.*

PIQUANTLY, *adv. pik'antly.* With sharpness or pungency; tartly. *Locke.*

PÏQUE, *n. peek.* [Fr. See *Piquant.*] An offense taken; usually, slight anger, irritation or displeasure at persons, rather temporary than permanent, and distinguished either in degree or temporariness from settled enmity or malevolence.

Out of personal *pique* to those in service, he stands as a looker on, when the government is attacked. *Addison.*

2. A strong passion. *Hudibras.*

3. Point; nicety; punctilio.

Add long prescription of established laws,
And *pique* of honor to maintain a cause. *Dryden.*

PÏQUE, *v. t. peek.* [Fr. *piquer.* See *Piquant.*]

1. To offend; to nettle; to irritate; to sting; to fret; to excite a degree of anger. It expresses less than *exasperate.*

The lady was *piqued* by her indifference. *Female Quixote.*

2. To stimulate; to excite to action; to touch with envy, jealousy or other passion.

Piqu'd by Protogenes' fame,
From Co to Rhodes Apelles came— *Prior.*

3. With the reciprocal pronoun, to pride or value one's self.

Men *pique themselves* on their skill in the learned languages. *Locke.*

PÏQUED, *pp. pee'ked.* Irritated; nettled; offended; excited.

PIQUEER. [See *Pickeer.*]

PIQUEE'RER, *n.* A plunderer; a freebooter. [See *Pickeerer.*] *Swift.*

PIQUET. [See *Picket.*]

PIQUET, *n. piket'.* [Fr.] A game at cards played between two persons, with only thirty two cards; all the deuces, threes, fours, fives and sixes being set aside. *Encyc.*

PÏQUING, *ppr. pee'king.* Irritating; offending; priding.

PI'RACY, *n.* [Fr. *piraterie*; L. *piratica*, from Gr. πειρατεια, from πειραω, to attempt, to dare, to enterprise, whence L. *periculum*, *experior*. The primary sense of the root is to run, rush or drive forward; allied to Sax. *faran*, Eng. to *fare* Class Br.]

1. The act, practice or crime of robbing on the high seas; the taking of property from others by open violence and without authority, on the sea; a crime that answers to robbery on land. *Waller. Arbuthnot.*

Other acts than robbery on the high seas, are declared by statute to be *piracy*. See Act of Congress, April 30, 1790.

2. The robbing of another by taking his writings.

PI'RATE, *n.* [It. *pirato*; L. Sp. *pirata*; Gr. πειρατης, from πειραω. See *Piracy*. Formerly this word signified a ship or sea soldier, answering to the marine of the present day.]

1. A robber on the high seas; one that by open violence takes the property of another on the high seas. In strictness, the word pirate is one who makes it his business to cruise for robbery or plunder; a freebooter on the seas.

2. An armed ship or vessel which sails without a legal commission, for the purpose of plundering other vessels indiscriminately on the high seas.

3. A bookseller that seizes the copies or writings of other men without permission. *Johnson.*

PI'RATE, *v. i.* To rob on the high seas. *Arbuthnot.*

PI'RATE, *v. t.* To take by theft or without right or permission, as books or writings.

They advertised they would *pirate* his edition. *Pope.*

PI'RATED, *pp.* Taken by theft or without right.

PI'RATING, *ppr.* Robbing on the high seas; taking without right, as a book or writing.

2. *a.* Undertaken for the sake of piracy; as a *pirating* expedition. *Mitford.*

PIRAT'ICAL, *a.* [L. *piraticus.*] Robbing or plundering by open violence on the high seas; as a *piratical* commander or ship.

2. Consisting in piracy; predatory; robbing; as a *piratical* trade or occupation.

3. Practicing literary theft.

The errors of the press were multiplied by *piratical* printers. *Pope.*

PIRAT'ICALLY, *adv.* By piracy. *Bryant.*

PIROGUE, } *n.* { *piro'ge*, [Sp. *piragua*.
PIRAGUA, } { *pirau'gua*. This word is variously written, *periagua* or *pirogue*. The former is the spelling of Washington and Jefferson; the latter of Charlevoix.]

1. A canoe formed out of the trunk of a tree, or two canoes united. *Charlevoix.*

2. In *modern usage in America*, a narrow ferry boat carrying two masts and a lee-board.

PIR'RY, *n.* A rough gale of wind; a storm. [*Not used.*] *Elyot.*

PIS'CARY, *n.* [It. *pescheria*, from *pescare*, to fish, Sp. *pescar*; Fr. *pêcherie*, from *pêcher*, to fish; L. *piscis*, a fish; *piscor*, to fish.]

In *law*, the right or privilege of fishing in another man's waters. *Blackstone.*

PISCA'TION, *n.* [L. *piscatio*. See *Piscary* and *Fish*.] The act or practice of fishing. *Brown.*

PIS'CATORY, *a.* [L. *piscatorius*.] Relating to fishes or to fishing; as a *piscatory* eclogue. *Addison.*

PIS'CES, *n. plu.* [L. *piscis*.] In *astronomy*, the Fishes, the twelfth sign or constellation in the zodiac.

PIS'CINE, *a.* [L. *piscis*, a fish.] Pertaining to fish or fishes; as *piscine* remains. *Kirwan.*

PISCIV'OROUS, *a.* [L. *piscis*, a fish, and *voro*, to eat.]

Feeding or subsisting on fishes. Many species of aquatic fowls are *piscivorous*.

PISH, *exclam.* [perhaps the oriental בוש or בזה. Class Bs. No. 2. 3.]

A word expressing contempt; sometimes spoken and written *pshaw*.

PISH, *v. i.* To express contempt. *Pope.*

PIS'IFORM, *a.* [L. *pisum*, a pea, and *forma*, form.] Having the form of a pea.

Masses of *pisiform* argillaceous iron ore. *Kirwan.*

PIS'MIRE, *n.* [The last syllable is the Sw. *myra*, Dan. *myre*, D. *mier*, an ant; Sax. *myra*, tender. I know not the origin or meaning of the first syllable.] The insect called the ant or emmet. *Prior. Mortimer.*

PIS'OLITE, *n.* [Gr. πισον, a pea, and λιθος, a stone.]

Peastone, a carbonate of lime, slightly colored by the oxyd of iron. It occurs in little globular concretions of the size of a pea or larger, which usually contain each a grain of sand as a nucleus. These concretions in union sometimes compose entire beds of secondary mountains. It is sometimes called calcarious tufa. *Dict. Nat. Hist. Cleaveland.*

PIS'OPHALT, *n.* Pea-mineral or mineral-pea; a soft bitumen, black and of a strong pungent smell. It appears to be petrol passing to asphalt. It holds a middle place between petrol, which is liquid, and asphalt, which is dry and brittle. *Dict. Nat. Hist.*

PISS, *v. t.* [D. G. *pissen*; Dan. *pisser*; Sw. *pissa*; Fr. *pisser*; W. *pisaw*; Basque, *pisye*; It. *pisciare*; Pers. پیشار pishar, urine. Class Br. No. 61. 69.]

To discharge the liquor secreted by the kidneys and lodged in the urinary bladder.

PISS, *n.* Urine; the liquor secreted by the kidneys into the bladder of an animal and discharged through the proper channel.

PISS'ABED, *n.* The vulgar name of a yellow flower, growing among grass.

PIS'SASPHALT, *n.* [Gr. πισσα, pitch, and ασφαλτος, asphalt; Sp. *pisasfalto*.]

Earth-pitch; pitch mixed with bitumen, natural or artificial; a fluid opake mineral substance, thick and inflammable, but leaving a residuum after burning. *Encyc.*

PISS'BURNT, *a.* Stained with urine.

PIST, } *n.* [Fr. *piste*, from Sp. Port. *pista*,
PISTE, } from Sp. *pistar*, to beat, or *pisonar*, to ram or drive.]

The track or foot-print of a horseman on the ground he goes over. *Johnson.*

PISTA'CHIO, *n.* [Fr. *pistache*; It. *pistacchio*; L. *pistachia*; Gr. πιςακια; Pers. فستق; Ar. فستق.]

The nut of the *Pistacia terebinthus* or turpentine tree, containing a kernel of a pale greenish color, of a pleasant taste, resembling that of the almond, and yielding a well tasted oil. It is wholesome and nutritive. The tree grows in Syria, Arabia and Persia. *Encyc.*

PIS'TACITE, }
PIS'TAZITE. } [See *Epidote*.]

PISTAREE'N, *n.* A silver coin of the value of 17 or 18 cents, or 9d. sterling.

PIS'TIL, *n.* [L. *pistillum*, a pestle.] In *botany*, the pointal, an organ of female flowers adhering to the fruit for the reception of the pollen, supposed to be a continuation of the pith, and when perfect, consisting of three parts, the germ or ovary, the style, and the stigma. *Martyn.*

PISTILLA'CEOUS, *a.* Growing on the germ or seed bud of a flower. *Barton.*

PIS'TILLATE, *a.* Having or consisting in a pistil.

PISTILLA'TION, *n.* [L. *pistillum*, a pestle, that is, a beater or driver.] The act of pounding in a mortar. [*Little used.*]

PISTILLIF'EROUS, *a.* [*pistil* and L. *fero*, to bear.]

Having a pistil without stamens; as a female flower.

PIS'TOL, *n.* [Fr. *pistole*, *pistolet*; It. Sp. *pistola*, a pistol. This word, like *piston* and *pestle*, signifies a driver, or a canal or spout, from the same root. Class Bs.]

A small fire-arm, or the smallest fire-arm used, differing from a musket chiefly in size. Pistols are of different lengths, and borne by horsemen in cases at the saddle bow, or by a girdle. Small pistols are carried in the pocket.

PIS'TOL, *v. t.* [Fr. *pistoler*.] To shoot with a pistol.

PISTO'LE, *n.* [Fr.] A gold coin of Spain, but current in the neighboring countries.

PIS'TOLET, *n.* [Fr.] A little pistol.

PIS'TON, *n.* [Fr. Sp. *piston*, from the root of Sp. *pisar*, *pistar*, L. *pinso*, the primary sense of which is to press, send, drive, thrust or strike, like *embolus*, from Gr. εμβαλλω, βαλλω.]

A short cylinder of metal or other solid substance, used in pumps and other engines or machines for various purposes. It is fitted exactly to the bore of another body so as to prevent the entrance or escape of air, and is usually applied to the purpose of forcing some fluid into or out of the canal or tube which it fills, as in pumps, fire-engines and the like.

PIT, *n.* [Sax. *pit* or *pyt*; D. *put*; W. *pyd*; Ir. *pit*; L. *puteus*; Sans. *put*, *puttu*; W. *pydaw*, a well or spring, an oozing fluid. It is uncertain whether this word originally signified a hollow place dug in the earth, or a natural spring of water and its bason.

See Ar. نَبَطَ to spring, and Class Bd. No. 58. 59. 63.]

1. An artificial cavity made in the earth by digging; a deep hole in the earth. *Bacon. Shak.*
2. A deep place; an abyss; profundity.

> Into what *pit* thou seest
> From what height fallen. *Milton.*

3. The grave. Ps. xxviii. and xxx.
4. The area for cock-fighting; whence the phrase, to *fly the pit*. *Locke. Hudibras.*
5. The middle part of a theater. *Dryden.*
6. The hollow of the body at the stomach. We say, the *pit* of the stomach.
7. The cavity under the shoulder; as the *arm-pit*.
8. A dint made by impression on a soft substance, as by the finger, &c.
9. A little hollow in the flesh, made by a pustule, as in the small pocks.
10. A hollow place in the earth excavated for catching wild beasts; hence in Scripture, whatever ensnares and brings into calamity or misery, from which it is difficult to escape. Ps. vii. Prov. xxii. and xxiii.
11. Great distress and misery, temporal, spiritual or eternal. Is. xxxviii. Ps. xl.
12. Hell; as the bottomless *pit*. Rev. xx.

PIT, *v. t.* To indent; to press into hollows.
2. To mark with little hollows, as by variolous pustules; as the face *pitted* by the small pocks.
3. To set in competition, as in combat. *Federalist, Madison.*

PITAHA'YA, *n.* A shrub of California, which yields a delicious fruit, the *Cactus Pitajaya*. *Encyc.*

PIT'APAT, *adv.* [probably allied to *beat*.] In a flutter; with palpitation or quick succession of beats; as, his heart went *pitapat*.

PIT'APAT, *n.* A light quick step.

> Now I hear the *pitapat* of a pretty foot, through the dark alley. *Dryden.*

PITCH, *n.* [Sax. *pic*; D. *pik*; G. *pech*; Sw. *beck*; Dan. *beg* or *beeg*; Ir. *pic* or *pech*; W. *pyg*; Sp. *pez*; It. *pece*; Ir. *poix*; L. *pix*; Gr. *πισσα* or *πιττα*; most probably named from its thickness or inspissation, from the root of *πηγω*, *πηγνυω*, *πησσω*, L. *figo*. See Class Bg. No. 23. 24. 33. 66.]

1. A thick tenacious substance, the juice of a species of pine or fir called *abies picea*, obtained by incision from the bark of the tree. When melted and pressed in bags of cloth, it is received into barrels. This is white or Burgundy pitch; by mixture with lampblack it is converted into black pitch. When kept long in fusion with vinegar, it becomes dry and brown, and forms *colophony*. The smoke of pitch condensed forms lampblack. *Fourcroy.*
2. The resin of pine, or turpentine, inspissated; used in calking ships and paying the sides and bottom.

PITCH, *n.* [from the root of *pike*, *peak*, W. *pig*. See the Verb.]

1. Literally, a point; hence, any point or degree of elevation; as a high *pitch*; lowest *pitch*.

> How high a *pitch* his resolution soars. *Shak.*

> Alcibiades was one of the best orators of his age, notwithstanding he lived when learning was at its highest *pitch*. *Addison.*

2. Highest rise. *Shak.*
3. Size; stature.

> So like in person, garb and *pitch*. *Hudibras.*

4. Degree; rate.

> No *pitch* of glory from the grave is free. *Waller.*

5. The point where a declivity begins, or the declivity itself; descent; slope; as the *pitch* of a hill.
6. The degree of descent or declivity.
7. A descent; a fall; a thrusting down.
8. Degree of elevation of the key-note of a tune or of any note.

PITCH, *v. t.* [formerly *pight*; W. *piciaw*, to dart, from *pig*, a point, a pike; D. *pikken*, to *peck*, to *pick*, to pitch; G. *pichen*; Fr. *ficher*; Arm. *ficha*; coinciding with L. *figo*, to *fix*, and uniting *pike*, *pique* with *fix*, Sp. *picar*, It. *piccare*, to prick or sting.]

1. To throw or thrust, and primarily, to thrust a long or pointed object; hence, to fix; to plant; to set; as, to *pitch* a tent or pavilion, that is, to set the stakes. *Dryden.*
2. To throw at a point; as, to *pitch* quoits.
3. To throw headlong; as, to *pitch* one in the mire or down a precipice.
4. To throw with a fork; as, to *pitch* hay or sheaves of corn.
5. To regulate or set the key-note of a tune in music.
6. To set in array; to marshal or arrange in order; used chiefly in the participle; as a *pitched* battle.
7. [from *pitch*.] To smear or pay over with pitch; as, to *pitch* the seams of a ship.

PITCH, *v. i.* To light; to settle; to come to rest from flight.

> Take a branch of the tree on which the bees *pitch*, and wipe the hive. *Mortimer.*

2. To fall headlong; as, to *pitch* from a precipice; to *pitch* on the head. *Dryden.*
3. To plunge; as, to *pitch* into a river.
4. To fall; to fix choice; with *on* or *upon*.

> *Pitch upon* the best course of life, and custom will render it the most easy. *Tillotson.*

5. To fix a tent or temporary habitation; to encamp.

> Laban with his brethren *pitched* in the mount of Gilead. Gen. xxxi.

6. In *navigation*, to rise and fall, as the head and stern of a ship passing over waves.
7. To flow or fall precipitously, as a river.

> Over this rock, the river *pitches* in one entire sheet. *B. Trumbull.*

PITCH'ED, *pp.* Set; planted; fixed; thrown headlong; set in array; smeared with pitch.

PITCH'ER, *n.* [Arm. *picher*; Basque, *pegar*; from its spout, or from throwing.]

1. An earthen vessel with a spout for pouring out liquors. This is its present signification. It seems formerly to have signified a water pot, jug or jar with ears. *Shak.*
2. An instrument for piercing the ground. *Mortimer.*

PITCH-FARTHING, *n.* A play in which copper coin is pitched into a hole; called also chuck-farthing, from the root of *choke*.

PITCH'FORK, *n.* [W. *picforç*.] A fork or farming utensil used in throwing hay or sheaves of grain, in loading or unloading carts and wagons.

PITCH'INESS, *n.* [from *pitch*.] Blackness; darkness. [*Little used.*]

PITCH'ING, *ppr.* Setting; planting or fixing; throwing headlong; plunging; daubing with pitch; setting, as a tune.
2. *a.* Declivous; descending; sloping; as a hill.

PITCH'ING, *n.* In *navigation*, the rising and falling of the head and stern of a ship, as she moves over waves; or the vertical vibration of a ship about her center of gravity. *Mar. Dict.*

PITCH'-ORE, *n.* Pitch-blend, an ore of uranium.

PITCH'PIPE, *n.* An instrument used by choristers in regulating the *pitch* or elevation of the key or leading note of a tune. *Spectator.*

PITCH'-STONE, *n.* A mineral, a subspecies of quartz, which in luster and texture resembles pitch, whence its name. It is sometimes called *resinite*. Its colors are, several shades of green; black with green, brown or gray; brown, tinged with red, green or yellow; sometimes yellowish or blue. It occurs in large beds and sometimes forms whole mountains. *Cleaveland.*

PITCH'Y, *a.* Partaking of the qualities of pitch; like pitch. *Woodward.*
2. Smeared with pitch. *Dryden.*
3. Black; dark; dismal; as the *pitchy* mantle of night. *Shak.*

PIT'COAL, *n.* Fossil coal; coal dug from the earth.

PIT'EOUS, *a.* [See *Pity*.] Sorrowful; mournful; that may excite pity; as a *piteous* look.
2. Wretched; miserable; deserving compassion; as a *piteous* condition.
3. Compassionate; affected by pity. *Prior. Pope.*
4. Pitiful; paltry; poor; as *piteous* amends. *Milton.*

PIT'EOUSLY, *adv.* In a piteous manner; with compassion. *Shak.*
2. Sorrowfully; mournfully.

PIT'EOUSNESS, *n.* Sorrowfulness.
2. Tenderness; compassion.

PIT'FALL, *n.* A pit slightly covered for concealment, and intended to catch wild beasts or men.

PIT'FALL, *v. t.* To lead into a pitfall. *Milton.*

PIT-FISH, *n.* A small fish of the Indian seas, about the size of a smelt, of a green and yellow color. It has the power of protruding or retracting its eyes at pleasure. *Dict. Nat. Hist.*

PITH, *n.* [Sax. *pitha*; D. *pit*, pith, kernel.]
1. The soft spungy substance in the center of plants and trees. *Bacon. Encyc.*

2. In *animals*, the spinal marrow. *Ray.*
3. Strength or force. *Shak.*
4. Energy; cogency; concentrated force; closeness and vigor of thought and style.
5. Condensed substance or matter; quintessence. The summary contains the *pith* of the original.
6. Weight; moment; importance.

Enterprises of great *pith* and moment. *Shak.*

PITH'ILY, *adv.* With strength; with close or concentrated force; cogently; with energy.

PITH'INESS, *n.* Strength; concentrated force; as the *pithiness* of a reply. *Spenser.*

PITH'LESS, *a.* Destitute of pith; wanting strength.
2. Wanting cogency or concentrated force.

PIT'HOLE, *n.* A mark made by disease. *Obs. Beaum.*

PITH'Y, *a.* Consisting of pith; containing pith; abounding with pith; as a *pithy* substance; a *pithy* stem.
2. Containing concentrated force; forcible; energetic; as a *pithy* word or expression.

This *pithy* speech prevailed and all agreed. *Dryden.*

3. Uttering energetic words or expressions.

In all these, Goodman Fact was very short, but *pithy*. *Addison.*

PIT'IABLE, *a.* [Fr. *pitoyable;* from *pity.*] Deserving pity; worthy of compassion; miserable; as *pitiable* persons; a *pitiable* condition. *Atterbury.*

PIT'IABLENESS, *n.* State of deserving compassion. *Kettlewell.*

PIT'IED, *pp.* Compassionated. [See the verb, to *pity.*]

PIT'IFUL, *a.* [See *Pity.*] Full of pity; tender; compassionate; having a heart to feel sorrow and sympathy for the distressed. James v. 1 Pet. iii. [*This is the proper sense of the word.*]
2. Miserable; moving compassion; as a sight most *pitiful;* a *pitiful* condition. *Shak. Ray.*

This is a very improper use of *pitiful* for *pitiable.*

3. To be pitied for its littleness or meanness; paltry; contemptible; despicable.

That's villainous, and shows a most *pitiful* ambition in the fool that uses it. *Shak.*

4. Very small; insignificant.

PIT'IFULLY, *adv.* With pity; compassionately.

Pitifully behold the sorrows of our hearts. *Com. Prayer.*

2. In a manner to excite pity.

They would sigh and groan as *pitifully* as other men. *Tillotson.*

3. Contemptibly; with meanness. *Richardson.*

PIT'IFULNESS, *n.* Tenderness of heart that disposes to pity; mercy; compassion. *Sidney.*
2. Contemptibleness.

PIT'ILESS, *a.* Destitute of pity; hard-hearted; *applied to persons;* as a *pitiless* master.
2. Exciting no pity; as a *pitiless* state.

PIT'ILESSLY, *adv.* Without mercy or compassion. *Sherwood.*

PIT'ILESSNESS, *n.* Unmercifulness; insensibility to the distresses of others.

PIT'MAN, *n.* The man that stands in a pit when sawing timber with another man who stands above. *Moxon.*

PIT'-SAW, *n.* A large saw used in dividing timber, and used by two men, one of whom stands in a pit below. *Moxon.*

PIT'TANCE, *n.* [Fr. *pitance;* It. *pietanza;* Port. *pitânça.* The word signifies primarily, a portion of food allowed to a monk. The Spanish has *pitar*, to distribute allowances of meat, and *pitancero*, a person who distributes allowances, or a friar who lives on charity.]
1. An allowance of meat in a monastery.
2. A very small portion allowed or assigned. *Shak.*
3. A very small quantity. *Arbuthnot.*

PITU'ITARY, *a.* [L. *pituita*, phlegm, rheum; Gr. πτνω, to spit.]
That secretes phlegm or mucus; as the *pituitary* membrane. *Med. Repos.*

The *pituitary gland* is a small oval body on the lower side of the brain, supposed by the ancients to secrete the mucus of the nostrils. *Parr. Quincy.*

PIT'UITE, *n.* [Fr. from L. *pituita.*] Mucus.

PITU'ITOUS, *a.* [L. *pituitosus.*] Consisting of mucus, or resembling it in qualities.

PIT'Y, *n.* [Fr. *pitié;* It. *pietà*, pity and piety; Sp. *pietad*, pity and piety; Port. *piedade*, id. The Latin, Italian, Spanish and Portuguese languages unite *pity* and *piety* in the same word, and the word may be from the root of *compassion;* L. *patior*, to suffer; It. *compatire*, Sp. Port. *compadecerse*, to pity.]
1. The feeling or suffering of one person, excited by the distresses of another; sympathy with the grief or misery of another; compassion or fellow-suffering.

He that hath *pity* upon the poor lendeth to the Lord. Prov. xix.

In Scripture however, the word *pity* usually includes compassion accompanied with some act of charity or benevolence, and not simply a fellow feeling of distress.

Pity is always painful, yet always agreeable. *Kames.*

2. The ground or subject of pity; cause of grief; thing to be regretted.

What *pity* is it
That we can die but once to serve our country! *Addison.*

That he is old, the more is the *pity*, his white hairs do witness it. *Shak.*

In this sense, the word has a plural. It is a thousand *pities* he should waste his estate in prodigality.

PIT'Y, *v. t.* [Fr. *pitoyer.*] To feel pain or grief for one in distress; to have sympathy for; to compassionate; to have tender feelings for one, excited by his unhappiness.

Like as a father pitieth his children, so the Lord *pitieth* them that fear him. Ps. ciii.

Taught by that power who *pities* me,
I learn to *pity* them. *Goldsmith.*

PIT'Y, *v. i.* To be compassionate; to exercise pity.

I will not *pity* nor spare, nor have mercy. Jer. xiii.

[*But this may be considered as an elliptical phrase.*]

PIV'OT, *n.* [Fr. In Italian, *pivolo* or *piuolo* is a peg or pin.] A pin on which any thing turns. *Dryden.*

PIX, *n.* [L. *pyxis.*] A little box or chest in which the consecrated host is kept in Roman catholic countries. *Hanmer.*
2. A box used for the trial of gold and silver coin. *Leake.*

PIZ'ZLE, *n.* [D. *pees*, a tendon or string.] In certain quadrupeds, the part which is official to generation and the discharge of urine. *Brown.*

PLACABIL'ITY, **PLA'CABLENESS**, *n.* [from *placable.*] The quality of being appeasable; susceptibility of being pacified.

PLA'CABLE, *a.* [It. *placabile;* Sp. *placable;* L. *placabilis*, from *placo*, to pacify; probably formed on the root of *lay.* See *Please.*]
That may be appeased or pacified; appeasable; admitting its passions or irritations to be allayed; willing to forgive.

Methought I saw him *placable* and mild. *Milton.*

PLAC'ARD, *n* [Fr. *placard;* Sp. *placarte;* D. *plakaat; plakken*, to paste or stick; G. Dan. *placat;* Fr. *plaquer*, to clap on, Arm. *placqa.* According to the French orthography, this word is composed of *plaquer*, to lay or clap on, and *carte*, card.]
Properly, a written or printed paper posted in a public place. It seems to have been formerly the name of an edict, proclamation or manifesto issued by authority, but this sense is, I believe, seldom or never annexed to the word. A *placard* now is an advertisement, or a libel, or a paper intended to censure public or private characters or public measures, posted in a public place. In the case of libels or papers intended to censure public or private characters, or the measures of government, these papers are usually pasted up at night for secrecy.

PLA'CATE, *v. t.* [L. *placo*, to appease.] To appease or pacify; to conciliate. *Forbes.*

PLACE, *n.* [Fr. *id.;* Sp. *plaza;* Port. *praça;* It. *piazza*, for *plazza;* Arm. *plaçz;* D. *plaats;* G. *platz;* Sw. *plats;* Dan. *plads.* Words of this signification have for their radical sense, to *lay.*]
1. A particular portion of space of indefinite extent, occupied by any person or thing, and considered as the space where a person or thing does or may rest or has rested, as distinct from space in general.

Look from the *place* where thou art. Gen. xiii.

The *place* where thou standest is holy ground. Ex. iii.

Every *place* whereon the soles of your feet shall tread shall be yours. Deut. xi.

David's *place* was empty. 1 Sam. xx.

2. Any portion of space, as distinct from space in general.

Enlargement and deliverance shall arise to the Jews from another *place.* Esth. iv.

3. Local existence.

From whose face the earth and the heaven fled away, and there was found no *place* for them. Rev. xx.

4. Separate room or apartment.

His catalogue had an especial *place* for sequestered divines. *Fell.*

5. Seat; residence; mansion.

The Romans shall come and take away both our *place* and nation. John xi.

6. A portion or passage of writing or of a book.

The *place* of the Scripture which he read was this. Acts viii.

7. Point or degree in order of proceeding; as in the first *place*; in the second *place*; in the last *place*. Hence,

8. Rank; order of priority, dignity or importance. He holds the first *place* in society, or in the affections of the people.

9. Office; employment; official station. The man has a *place* under the government.

Do you your office, or give up your *place*. *Shak.*

10. Ground; room.

There is no *place* of doubting but that it is the very same. *Hammond.*

11. Station in life; calling; occupation; condition. All, in their several *places*, perform their duty.

12. A city; a town; a village. In what *place* does he reside? He arrived at this *place* in the mail coach. Gen. xviii.

13. In *military affairs*, a fortified town or post; a fortress; a fort; as a strong *place*; a *place* easily defended. The *place* was taken by assault.

14. A country; a kingdom. England is the *place* of his birth.

15. Space in general.

But she all *place* within herself confines. *Davies.*

16. Room; stead; with the sense of substitution.

And Joseph said unto them, fear not; for am I in the *place* of God? Gen. l.

17. Room; kind reception.

My word hath no *place* in you. John viii.

18. The *place* of the moon, in astronomy, is the part of its orbit where it is found at any given time. The *place* of the sun or a star, is the sign and degree of the zodiac, in which it is at any given time, or the degree of the ecliptic, reckoning from the beginning of Aries, which the star's circle of longitude cuts, and therefore coincides with the longitude of the sun or star. *Encyc.*

To take place, to come; to happen; to come into actual existence or operation; as when we say, this or that event will or will not *take place*. The perfect exemption of man from calamity can never *take place* in this state of existence.

2. To take the precedence or priority. *Addison. Locke.*

To take the place, but sometimes to *take place*, omitting the article, is to occupy the place or station of another.

To have place, to have a station, room or seat. Such desires can *have* no *place* in a good heart.

2. To have actual existence.

To give place, to make room or way. *Give place* to your superiors.

2. To give room; to give advantage; to yield to the influence of; to listen to.

Neither *give place* to the devil. Eph. iv.

3. To give way; to yield to and suffer to pass away.

High place, in Scripture, a mount on which sacrifices were offered.

PLACE, *v. t.* [Fr. *placer.*] To put or set in a particular part of space, or in a particular part of the earth, or in something on its surface; to locate; as, to *place* a house by the side of a stream; to *place* a book on a shelf; to *place* a body of cavalry on each flank of an army.

2. To appoint, set, induct or establish in an office.

Thou shalt provide out of all the people able men, such as fear God, men of truth, hating covetousness; and *place* such over them to be rulers of thousands, &c. Ex. xviii.

It is a high moral duty of sovereigns and supreme magistrates and councils, to *place* in office men of unquestionable virtue and talents. *Anon.*

3. To put or set in any particular rank, state or condition. Some men are *placed* in a condition of rank and opulence, others are *placed* in low or narrow circumstances; but in whatever sphere men are *placed*, contentment will insure to them a large portion of happiness.

4. To set; to fix; as, to *place* one's affections on an object; to *place* confidence in a friend.

5. To put; to invest; as, to *place* money in the funds or in a bank.

6. To put out at interest; to lend; as, to *place* money in good hands or in good security.

PLA'CED, *pp.* Set; fixed; located; established.

PLA'CE-MAN, *n.* One that has an office under a government.

PLACEN'TA, *n.* [L.; probably from the root of D. *plakken*, Fr. *plaquer*, to stick or clap together.]

1. In *anatomy*, the substance that connects the fetus to the womb, a soft roundish mass or cake by which the circulation is carried on between the parent and the fetus. *Coxe. Quincy.*

2. The part of a plant or fruit to which the seeds are attached. *Coxe. Parr.*

PLACEN'TAL, *a.* Pertaining to the placenta. *Waterhouse.*

PLACENTA'TION, *n.* In *botany*, the disposition of the cotyledons or lobes in the vegetation or germination of seeds. *Martyn.*

PLA'CER, *n.* One who places, locates or sets. *Spenser.*

PLAC'ID, *a.* [L. *placidus*, from *placo*, to appease.]

1. Gentle; quiet; undisturbed; equable; as a *placid* motion of the spirits. *Bacon.*

2. Serene; mild; unruffled; indicating peace of mind; as a *placid* countenance or smile.

3. Calm; tranquil; serene; not stormy; as a *placid* sky.

4. Calm; quiet; unruffled; as a *placid* stream.

PLAC'IDLY, *adv.* Mildly; calmly; quietly; without disturbance or passion.

PLAC'IDNESS, *n.* Calmness; quiet; tranquillity; unruffled state.

2. Mildness; gentleness; sweetness of disposition. *Chandler.*

PLAC'IT, *n.* [L. *placitum*, that which pleases, a decree, from *placeo*, to please.] A decree or determination. [*Not in use.*] *Glanville.*

PLACK'ET, *n.* [from the Fr. *plaquer*, to clap on. See *Placard.*]

A petticoat. If this is the sense of the word in Shakspeare, it is a derivative. The word signifies the opening of the garment; but it is nearly or wholly obsolete.

PLA'ǴIARISM, *n.* [from *plagiary.*] The act of purloining another man's literary works, or introducing passages from another man's writings and putting them off as one's own; literary theft. *Swift.*

PLA'ǴIARIST, *n.* One that purloins the writings of another and puts them off as his own.

PLA'ǴIARY, *n.* [L. *plagium*, a kidnapping, probably from *plagæ*, nets, toils, that which is layed or spread, from the root of Eng. *lay*. The L. *plaga*, a stroke, is the same word differently applied, a *laying on.*]

1. A thief in literature; one that purloins another's writings and offers them to the public as his own. *South. Dryden.*

2. The crime of literary theft. [*Not used.*] *Brown.*

PLA'ǴIARY, *a.* Stealing men; kidnapping. [*Not used.*] *Brown.*

2. Practicing literary theft. *Hall.*

PLAGUE, *n.* *plāg.* [Sp. *plaga* or *llaga*, a wound, a plague; It. *piaga*, for *plaga*; G. Dan. *plage*; Sw. *plåga*; W. *pla*, plague; *llac*, a slap; *llaciaw*, to strike, to lick, to cudgel; Ir. *plaig*; L. *plaga*, a stroke, Gr. πληγη. See *Lick* and *Lay*. The primary sense is a stroke or striking. So *afflict* is from the root of *flog*, and probably of the same family as *plague.*]

1. Any thing troublesome or vexatious; but in this sense, applied to the vexations we suffer from men, and not to the unavoidable evils inflicted on us by Divine Providence. The application of the word to the latter, would now be irreverent and reproachful.

2. A pestilential disease; an acute, malignant and contagious disease that often prevails in Egypt, Syria and Turkey, and has at times infected the large cities of Europe with frightful mortality.

3. A state of misery. Ps. xxxviii.

4. Any great natural evil or calamity; as the ten *plagues* of Egypt.

PLAGUE, *v. t.* *plāg.* [Sp. *plagar*; W. *placaw*; It. *piagare*; G. *plagen*; Dan. *plager*; Sw. *plåga*; from the noun.]

1. To infest with disease, calamity or natural evil of any kind.

Thus were they *plagued*
And worn with famine. *Milton.*

2. To vex; to tease; to harass; to trouble; to embarrass; *a very general and indefinite signification.*

If her nature be so,
That she will *plague* the man that loves her most— *Spenser.*

PLAGUEFUL, *a.* Abounding with plagues; infected with plagues.

PLAGUILY, *adv.* Vexatiously; in a manner to vex, harass or embarrass; greatly; horribly. [*In vulgar use.*] *Swift. Dryden.*

PLAGUY, *a.* Vexatious; troublesome; tormenting. [*Vulgar.*] *Hudibras.*

PLAICE, PLAISE, } *n.* [Fr. *plie*; Sp. *platija*; G. *platteise*; Dan. *plat-fisk*, flat-fish; from *plat*, flat.]

A fish of the genus Pleuronectes, growing to the size of eight or ten pounds or more. This fish is more flat and square than the halibut.

PLAID, } *n.* [qu. W. *plaid*, a partition; di-
PLAD, } versity of colors being often named from dividing.]

A striped or variegated cloth worn by the highlanders in Scotland. It is a narrow woolen stuff worn round the waist or on the shoulders, reaching to the knees, and in cold weather to the feet. It is worn by both sexes. *Pennant.*

PLAIN, *a.* [Fr. *plain;* It. *piano;* Sp. *plano, llano;* Port. *plano;* from L. *planus;* G. Sw. *plan;* D. *plein;* Sw. Dan. D. G. *plan,* a plan or scheme; W. *plan,* a plane, a plantation, a shoot or cion, a ray of light, whence *plant,* children, issue; *pleiniaw,* to radiate; *plenig,* radiant, splendid, whence *ysplan,* clear, bright, splendid, and *ysplander,* L. *splendor.* The Gr. πλαναω, to wander, is from the same root. Here we have decisive evidence, that *plain, plan, plant,* and *splendor* are from the same radix. See *Plant.* Class Ln. No. 4. 6. 7.]

1. Smooth; even; level; flat; without elevations and depressions; not rough; as *plain* ground or land; a *plain* surface. In this sense, in philosophical writings, it is written *plane.*

2. Open; clear.

Our troops beat an army in *plain* fight and open field. *Felton.*

3. Void of ornament; simple; as a *plain* dress.

Plain without pomp, and rich without a show. *Dryden.*

4. Artless; simple; unlearned; without disguise, cunning or affectation; without refinement; as men of the *plainer* sort. Gen. xxv. *Bacon.*

Plain but pious christians— *Hammond.*

5. Artless; simple; unaffected; unembellished; as a *plain* tale or narration.

6. Honestly undisguised; open; frank; sincere; unreserved. I will tell you the *plain* truth.

Give me leave to be *plain* with you. *Bacon.*

7. Mere; bare; as a *plain* knave or fool. *Shak. Pope.*

8. Evident to the understanding; clear; manifest; not obscure; as *plain* words or language; a *plain* difference; a *plain* argument.

It is *plain* in the history, that Esau was never subject to Jacob. *Locke.*

9. Not much varied by modulations; as a *plain* song or tune.

10. Not high seasoned; not rich; not luxuriously dressed; as a *plain* diet.

11. Not ornamented with figures; as *plain* muslin.

12. Not dyed.

13. Not difficult; not embarrassing; as a *plain* case in law.

14. Easily seen or discovered; not obscure or difficult to be found; as a *plain* road or path. Our course is very *plain.* Ps. xxvii.

A *plain* or *plane figure,* in geometry, is a uniform surface, from every point of whose perimeter right lines may be drawn to every other point in the same. *Encyc.*

A *plain figure,* in geometry, is a surface in which, if any two points are taken, the straight line which joins them lies wholly in that surface.

A *plain angle,* is one contained under two lines or surfaces, in contradistinction to a solid angle. *Encyc.*

PLAIN, *adv.* Not obscurely; in a manner to be easily understood.

2. Distinctly; articulately; as, to speak *plain.* Mark vii.

3. With simplicity; artlessly; bluntly.

PLAIN, *n.* [Ir. *cluain;* W. *llan;* Fr. *plaine.* See the Adjective.]

1. Level land; usually, an open field with an even surface, or a surface little varied by inequalities; as all the *plain* of Jordan. Gen. xiii.

2. Field of battle. *Arbuthnot.*

PLAIN, *v. t.* To level; to make plain or even on the surface. *Hayward.*

PLAIN, *v. i.* [Fr. *plaindre;* L. *plango.*] To lament or wail. [*Not used.*] [See *Complain.*] *Spenser.*

PLAIN-DE'ALING, *a.* [*plain* and *deal.*] Dealing or communicating with frankness and sincerity; honest; open; speaking and acting without art; as a *plain-dealing* man. *Shak. L'Estrange.*

PLAIN DE'ALING, *n.* A speaking or communicating with openness and sincerity; management without art, stratagem or disguise; sincerity. *Dryden.*

PLA'IN-HE'ARTED, *a.* Having a sincere heart; communicating without art, reserve or hypocrisy; of a frank disposition. *Milton.*

PLAIN-HE'ARTEDNESS, *n.* Frankness of disposition; sincerity. *Hallywell.*

PLA'INLY, *adv.* With a level surface. [*Little used.*]

2. Without cunning or disguise.

3. Without ornament or artificial embellishment; as, to be *plainly* clad.

4. Frankly; honestly; sincerely; as, deal *plainly* with me. *Pope.*

5. In earnest; fairly. *Clarendon.*

6. In a manner to be easily seen or comprehended.

Thou shalt write on the stones all the words of this law very *plainly.* Deut. xxvii.

7. Evidently; clearly; not obscurely. The doctrines of grace are *plainly* taught in the Scriptures.

PLA'INNESS, *n.* Levelness; evenness or surface.

2. Want of ornament; want of artificial show.

So modest *plainness* sets off sprightly wit. *Pope.*

3. Openness; rough, blunt or unrefined frankness.

Your *plainness* and your shortness please me well. *Shak.*

4. Artlessness; simplicity; candor; as unthinking *plainness.* *Dryden.*

5. Clearness; openness; sincerity.

Seeing then we have such hope, we use great *plainness* of speech. 2 Cor. iii.

PLA'IN-SONG, *n.* The plain, unvaried chant of churches; so called in contradistinction from the prick-song, or variegated music sung by note. *Shak.*

PLA'IN-SPOKEN, *a.* Speaking with plain, unreserved sincerity. *Dryden.*

PLAINT, *n.* [Fr. *plainte,* from *plaindre,* to lament, from L. *plango,* to strike, to beat, to lament, whence *complaint;* Gr. πλησσω, πλήττω, to strike, from the root πληγω, *disused,* whence πληγη, a stroke, L. *plaga,* Eng. *plague;* Goth. *flekan,* to lament; Sp. *planir,* from the Latin. The primary sense is to strike, that is, to drive or thrust, applied to the hand or to the voice; or the sense of complaint and lamentation is from beating the breast, as in violent grief; Sw. *plagga,* to beat.]

1. Lamentation; complaint; audible expression of sorrow.

From inward grief
His bursting passion into *plaints* thus pour'd. *Milton.*

2. Complaint; representation made of injury or wrong done.

There are three just grounds of war with Spain; one of *plaints;* two upon defense. *Bacon.*

3. In *law,* a private memorial tendered to a court, in which the person sets forth his cause of action. *Blackstone.*

4. In *law,* a complaint; a formal accusation exhibited by a private person against an offender for a breach of law or a public offense. *Laws of N. York and Conn.*

PLA'INTFUL, *a.* Complaining; expressing sorrow with an audible voice; as my *plaintful* tongue. *Sidney.*

PLA'INTIF, *n.* [Fr. *plaintif,* mournful, making complaint.]

In *law,* the person who commences a suit before a tribunal, for the recovery of a claim; opposed to *defendant.*

[Prior uses this word as an adjective, in the French sense, for *plaintive,* but the use is not authorized.]

PLA'INTIVE, *a.* [Fr. *plaintif.*] Lamenting; complaining; expressive of sorrow; as a *plaintive* sound or song. *Dryden.*

2. Complaining; expressing sorrow or grief; repining.

To sooth the sorrows of her *plaintive* son. *Dryden.*

PLA'INTIVELY, *adv.* In a manner expressive of grief.

PLA'INTIVENESS, *n.* The quality or state of expressing grief.

PLA'INTLESS, *a.* Without complaint; unrepining.

PLA'IN-WORK, *n.* Plain needlework, as distinguished from embroidery. *Pope.*

PLAIT, *n.* [W. *pleth,* a plait or fold; *plethu,* to plait or braid, from *lleth;* Sw. *flåta,* Dan. *fletter,* to plait, braid, twist, Russ. *pletu, opletayu,* Fr. *plisser,* with a dialectical change of *t* to *s.* Qu. Gr. πλωθω, to twist.]

1. A fold; a doubling; as of cloth.

It is very difficult to trace out the figure of a vest through all the *plaits* and folding of the drapery. *Addison.*

2. A braid of hair; a tress.

PLAIT, *v. t.* To fold; to double in narrow streaks; as, to *plait* a gown or a sleeve. *Gay.*

2. To braid; to interweave strands; as, to *plait* the hair.

3. To entangle; to involve. *Shak.*

PLA'ITED, *pp.* Folded; braided; interwoven.

PLA'ITER, *n.* One that plaits or braids.

PLA'ITING, *ppr.* Folding; doubling; braiding.

PLAN, *n.* [Fr. G. D. Dan. Sw. Russ. *plan.* The Italian has *pianta,* a *plant,* and a *plan,* and in Welsh, *plan* is a shoot, cion, plantation or planting, and a *plane.* Hence *plan, plain, plane* and *plant* are from one root. The primary sense of the verb is to extend.]

1. A draught or form; properly, the representation of any thing drawn on a *plane,* as a map or chart, which is a representa-

tion of some portion of land or water. But the word is applied particularly to the model of a building, showing the form, extent and divisions in miniature, and it may be applied to the draught or representation of any projected work on paper or on a plain surface; as the *plan* of a town or city, or of a harbor or fort. The form of a machine in miniature, is called a *model.*

2. A scheme devised; a project; the form of something to be done existing in the mind, with the several parts adjusted in idea, expressed in words or committed to writing; as the *plan* of a constitution of government; the *plan* of a treaty; the *plan* of an expedition.

PLAN, *v. t.* To form a draught or representation of any intended work.

2. To scheme; to devise; to form in design; as, to *plan* the conquest of a country; to *plan* a reduction of taxes or of the national debt.

PLA'NARY, *a.* Pertaining to a plane. *Dict.*

PLANCH, *v. t.* [Fr. *planche,* a plank. See *Plank.*]

To plank; to cover with planks or boards. *Gorges.*

PLANCH'ED, *pp.* Covered or made of planks or boards.

PLANCH'ER, *n.* A floor. *Bacon.*

PLANCH'ET, *n.* [Fr. *planchette.* See *Plank.*] A flat piece of metal or coin. *Encyc.*

PLANCH'ING, *n.* The laying of floors in a building; also, a floor of boards or planks. *Carew.*

PLANE, *n.* [from L. *planus.* See *Plain.*] In *geometry,* an even or level surface, like *plain* in popular language.

2. In *astronomy,* an imaginary surface supposed to pass through any of the curves described on the celestial sphere; as the *plane* of the ecliptic; the *plane* of a planet's orbit; the *plane* of a great circle.

3. In *mechanics.* [See *Plain figure.*]

4. In *joinery* and *cabinet work,* an instrument consisting of a smooth piece of wood, with an aperture, through which passes obliquely a piece of edged steel or chisel, used in paring or smoothing boards or wood of any kind.

PLANE, *v. t.* To make smooth; to pare off the inequalities of the surface of a board or other piece of wood by the use of a plane.

2. To free from inequalities of surface. *Arbuthnot.*

PLA'NED, *pp.* Made smooth with a plane; leveled.

PLAN'ET, *n.* [Fr. *planete;* It. *pianeta;* L. Sp. Port. *planeta;* W. *planed;* Gr. πλανητης, wandering, from πλαναω, to wander, allied to L. *planus,* Fr. *loin.* See *Plant.*]

A celestial body which revolves about the sun or other center, or a body revolving about another planet as its center. The planets which revolve about the sun as their center, are called *primary* planets; those which revolve about other planets as their center, and with them revolve about the sun, are called *secondary* planets, satellites or moons. The primary planets are named Mercury, Venus, Earth, Mars, Jupiter, Saturn and Herschell. Four smaller planets, denominated by some, *asteroids,* namely, Ceres, Pallas, Juno and Vesta, have recently been discovered between the orbits of Mars and Jupiter. Mars, Jupiter, Saturn and Herschell, being without the earth's orbit, are sometimes called the *superior* planets; Venus and Mercury, being within the earth's orbit, are called *inferior* planets. The planets are opake bodies which receive their light from the sun. They are so named from their *motion* or *revolution,* in distinction from the *fixed* stars, and are distinguished from the latter by their not twinkling.

PLANETA'RIUM, *n.* An astronomical machine which, by the movement of its parts, represents the motions and orbits of the planets, agreeable to the Copernican system. *Encyc.*

PLAN'ETARY, *a.* [Fr. *planetaire.*] Pertaining to the planets; as *planetary* inhabitants; *planetary* motions.

2. Consisting of planets; as a *planetary* system.

3. Under the dominion or influence of a planet; as a *planetary* hour. [*Astrology.*] *Dryden.*

4. Produced by planets; as *planetary* plague or influence. *Shak.*

5. Having the nature of a planet; erratic or revolving. *Blackmore.*

Planetary days, the days of the week as shared among the planets, each having its day, as we name the days of the week after the planets.

PLAN'ETED, *a.* Belonging to planets. *Young.*

PLANET'ICAL, *a.* Pertaining to planets. [*Not used.*] *Brown.*

PLA'NE-TREE, *n.* [L. *platanus;* Fr. *plane, platane.*]

A tree of the genus Platanus. The oriental plane-tree is a native of Asia; it rises with a straight smooth branching stem to a great highth, with palmated leaves and long pendulous peduncles, sustaining several heads of small close sitting flowers. The seeds are downy, and collected into round, rough, hard balls. The occidental plane-tree, which grows to a great highth, is a native of N. America; it is called also *button-wood.*

PLAN'ET-STRUCK, *a.* Affected by the influence of planets; blasted. *Suckling.*

PLANIFO'LIOUS, *a.* [L. *planus,* plain, and *folium,* leaf.]

In *botany,* a *planifolious* flower is one made up of plain leaves, set together in circular rows round the center. [See *Planipetalous.*] *Dict.*

PLANIMET'RIC, PLANIMET'RICAL, *a.* Pertaining to the mensuration of plain surfaces.

PLANIM'ETRY, *n.* [L. *planus,* plain, and Gr. μετρεω, to measure.]

The mensuration of plain surfaces, or that part of geometry which regards lines and plain figures, without considering their highth or depth. *Encyc.*

PLANIPET'ALOUS, *a.* [L. *planus,* plain, and Gr. πεταλον, a petal.]

In *botany,* flat-leafed, as when the small flowers are hollow only at the bottom, but flat upwards, as in dandelion and succory. *Dict.*

PLAN'ISH, *v. t.* [from *plane.*] To make smooth or plain; to polish; used by manufacturers. *Henry's Chim.*

PLAN'ISHED, *pp.* Made smooth.

PLAN'ISHING, *ppr.* Making smooth; polishing.

PLAN'ISPHERE, *n.* [L. *planus,* plain, and *sphere.*]

A sphere projected on a plane, in which sense, maps in which are exhibited the meridians and other circles, are *planispheres.* *Encyc.*

PLANK, *n.* [Fr. *planche;* Arm. *plancquenn,* plu. *plench;* W. *planc;* D. *plank;* G. Dan. *planke;* Sw. *planka;* Russ. *placha,* a board or plank. Probably *n* is casual and the word belongs to Class Lg.]

A broad piece of sawed timber, differing from a board only in being thicker. In America, broad pieces of sawed timber which are not more than an inch or an inch and a quarter thick, are called *boards;* like pieces from an inch and a half to three or four inches thick, are called *planks.* Sometimes pieces more than four inches thick are called *planks.*

PLANK, *v. t.* To cover or lay with planks; as, to *plank* a floor or a ship.

PLAN'NED, *pp.* Devised; schemed.

PLAN'NER, *n.* One who plans or forms a plan; a projector.

PLAN'NING, *ppr.* Scheming; devising; making a plan.

PLANO-CON'ICAL, *a.* [*plain* and *conical.*] Plain or level on one side and conical on the other. *Grew.*

PLANO-CON'VEX, *a.* [*plain* and *convex.*] Plain or flat on one side and convex on the other; as a *plano-convex* lens. *Newton.*

PLANO-HORIZON'TAL, *a.* Having a level horizontal surface or position. *Lee.*

PLANO-SUB'ULATE, *a.* [See *Subulate.*] Smooth and awl-shaped. *Lee.*

PLANT, *n.* [Fr. *plante;* It. *pianta;* L. Sp. Port. Sw. *planta;* Ir. *plaunda;* D. *plant;* G. *pflanze;* Dan. *plante;* Arm. *plantenn;* W. *plant,* issue, offspring, children, from *plan,* a ray, a shoot, a plantation or planting, a plane; *planed,* a shooting body, a *planet; pleiniaw,* to radiate; *plenig,* radiant, *splendid; plent,* that is rayed; *plentyn,* a child; *planta,* to beget or to bear children. In It. Sp. and Port. *planta* signifies a *plant* and a *plan.* Here we find *plan, plane, plant, planet,* all from one stock, and the Welsh *pleiniaw,* to radiate, shows that the L. *splendeo, splendor,* are of the same family. The Celtic *clan* is probably the Welsh *plan, plant,* with a different prefix. The radical sense is obvious, to shoot, to extend.]

1. A vegetable; an organic body, destitute of sense and spontaneous motion, adhering to another body in such a manner as to draw from it its nourishment, and having the power of propagating itself by seeds; "whose seed is in itself." Gen. i. This definition may not be perfectly correct, as it respects all plants, for some marine plants grow without being attached to any fixed body.

The woody or dicotyledonous plants consist of three parts; the bark or exterior coat, which covers the wood; the wood which is hard and constitutes the principal part; and the pith or center of the stem. In monocotyledonous plants, the ligneous or fibrous parts, and the pithy or parenchymatous, are equally distributed through the whole internal substance; and in the lower plants, funguses, sea weed, &c. the substance is altogether parenchymatous. By means of proper vessels, the nourishing juices are distributed to every part of the plant. In its most general sense, *plant* comprehends all vegetables, trees, shrubs, herbs, grasses, &c. In popular language, the word is generally applied to the smaller species of vegetables.

2. A sapling. *Dryden.*

3. In *Scripture*, a child; a descendant; the inhabitant of a country. Ps. cxliv. Jer. xlviii.

4. The sole of the foot. [*Little used.*]

Sea-plant, a plant that grows in the sea or in salt water; sea weed.

Sensitive plant, a plant that shrinks on being touched, the mimosa.

PLANT, *v. t.* To put in the ground and cover, as seed for growth; as, to *plant* maiz.

2. To set in the ground for growth, as a young tree or a vegetable with roots.

3. To engender; to set the germ of any thing that may increase.

> It engenders choler, *planteth* anger. *Shak.*

4. To set; to fix.

> His standard *planted* on Laurentum's towers. *Dryden.*

5. To settle; to fix the first inhabitants; to establish; as, to *plant* a colony.

6. To furnish with plants; to lay out and prepare with plants; as, to *plant* a garden or an orchard.

7. To set and direct or point; as, to *plant* cannon against a fort.

8. To introduce and establish; as, to *plant* christianity among the heathen.

> I have *planted*, Apollos watered, but God gave the increase. 1 Cor. iii.

9. To unite to Christ and fix in a state of fellowship with him. Ps. xcii.

PLANT, *v. i.* To perform the act of planting. *Pope.*

PLANT'ABLE, *a.* Capable of being planted. *Edwards, W. Indies.*

PLANT'AGE, *n.* [L. *plantago.*] An herb, or herbs in general. [*Not in use.*] *Shak.*

PLANT'AIN, *n.* [Fr.; from L. *plantago*; It. *piantaggine.*]

A plant of the genus Plantago, of several species. The *water plantain* is of the genus Alisma. *Encyc.*

PLANT'AIN, PLANT'AIN-TREE, } *n.* [Sp. *platano.*] A tree of the genus Musa, the most remarkable species of which are, the *paradisiaca* or plantain, and the *sapientum* or banana tree. The plantain rises with a soft stem fifteen or twenty feet high, and the fruit is a substitute for bread. *Encyc.*

PLANT'AL, *a.* Belonging to plants. [*Not used.*] *Glanville.*

PLANTA'TION, *n.* [L. *plantatio*, from *planto*, to plant.]

1. The act of planting or setting in the earth for growth.

2. The place planted; applied to ground planted with trees, as an orchard or the like. *Addison.*

3. In *the United States* and *the West Indies*, a cultivated estate; a farm. In *the United States*, this word is applied to an estate, a tract of land occupied and cultivated, in those states only where the labor is performed by slaves, and where the land is more or less appropriated to the culture of tobacco, rice, indigo and cotton, that is, from Maryland to Georgia inclusive, on the Atlantic, and in the western states where the land is appropriated to the same articles or to the culture of the sugar cane. From Maryland, northward and eastward, estates in land are called *farms.*

4. An original settlement in a new country; a town or village planted.

> While these *plantations* were forming in Connecticut— *B. Trumbull.*

5. A colony. *Bacon.*

6. A first planting; introduction; establishment; as the *plantation* of christianity in England. *K. Charles.*

PLANT'-CANE, *n.* In *the West Indies*, the original plants of the sugar cane, produced from germs placed in the ground; or canes of the first growth, in distinction from the ratoons, or sprouts from the roots of canes which have been cut. *Edwards, W. Indies.*

PLANT'ED, *pp.* Set in the earth for propagation; set; fixed; introduced; established.

2. Furnished with seeds or plants for growth; as a *planted* field.

3. Furnished with the first inhabitants; settled; as territory *planted* with colonists.

4. Filled or furnished with what is new.

> A man in all the world's new fashion *planted.* [See Def. 3.] *Shak.*

PLANT'ER, *n.* One that plants, sets, introduces or establishes; as a *planter* of maiz; a *planter* of vines; the *planters* of a colony.

2. One that settles in a new or uncultivated territory; as the first *planters* in Virginia.

3. One who owns a plantation; used in the West Indies and southern states of America.

4. One that introduces and establishes.

> The apostles were the first *planters* of christianity. *Nelson. Addison.*

PLANT'ERSHIP, *n.* The business of a planter, or the management of a plantation, as in the West Indies. *Encyc.*

PLANT'ICLE, *n.* A young plant or plant in embryo. *Darwin.*

PLANT'ING, *ppr.* Setting in the earth for propagation; setting; settling; introducing; establishing.

PLANT'ING, *n.* The act or operation of setting in the ground for propagation, as seeds, trees, shrubs, &c.

PLANT'-LOUSE, *n.* An insect that infests plants; a vine fretter; the puceron.

PLASH, *n.* [D. *plas*, a puddle; G. *plätschern*, to plash, to dabble; Dan. *plasker*, to plash; Gr. πλαδος, superabundant moisture. Qu. παλασσω.]

1. A small collection of standing water; a puddle. *Bacon. Pope.*

2. The branch of a tree partly cut or lopped and bound to other branches. *Mortimer.*

PLASH, *v. i.* To dabble in water; usually *splash.*

PLASH, *v. t.* [Fr. *plisser.* See *Plait.* But perhaps originally *pleach*, from L. *plico*, to fold.]

To interweave branches; as, to *plash* a hedge or quicksets. [In New England, to *splice.*]

PLASH'ING, *ppr.* Cutting and interweaving, as branches in a hedge.

PLASH'ING, *n.* The act or operation of cutting and lopping small trees and interweaving them, as in hedges. *Encyc.*

PLASH'Y, *a.* Watery; abounding with puddles. *Sandys.*

PLASM, *n.* [Gr. πλασμα, from πλασσω, to form.]

A mold or matrix in which any thing is cast or formed to a particular shape. [*Little used.*] *Woodward.*

PLAS'MA, *n.* A silicious mineral of a color between grass green and leek green, occurring in angular pieces in beds, associated with common chalcedony, and among the ruins of Rome. *Ure.*

PLASMAT'IC, PLASMAT'ICAL, } *a.* Giving shape; having the power of giving form. *More.*

PL'ASTER, *n.* [G. *pflaster*; D. *pleistre*; Sw. *plåster*; Dan. *plaster*; Fr. *plâtre*; Arm. *plastr*; W. *plastyr*: Ir. *plastar*, *plastrail*; Sp. *emplasto*; Port. *id.* or *emprasto*; It. *impiastro*; L. *emplastrum*; Gr. εμπλαςρον, from εμπλασσω, to daub or smear, properly to lay or spread on; πλασσω, to daub or to fashion, mold or shape.]

1. A composition of lime, water and sand, well mixed into a kind of paste and used for coating walls and partitions of houses. This composition when dry becomes hard, but still retains the name of plaster. Plaster is sometimes made of different materials, as chalk, gypsum, &c. and is sometimes used to parget the whole surface of a building.

2. In *pharmacy*, an external application of a harder consistence than an ointment, to be spread, according to different circumstances, either on linen or lether. *Encyc.*

Plaster of Paris, a composition of several species of gypsum dug near Montmartre, near Paris in France, used in building and in casting busts and statues. In popular language, this name is applied improperly to plaster-stone, or to any species of gypsum.

PL'ASTER, *v. t.* To overlay with plaster, as the partitions of a house, walls, &c.

2. To cover with plaster, as a wound.

3. In *popular language*, to smooth over; to cover or conceal defects or irregularities.

PL'ASTERED, *pp.* Overlaid with plaster.

PL'ASTERER, *n.* One that overlays with plaster.

2. One that makes figures in plaster. *Wotton.*

PL'ASTERING, *ppr.* Covering with or laying on plaster.

PL'ASTERING, *n.* The act or operation of overlaying with plaster.

2. The plaster-work of a building; a covering of plaster.

PL'ASTER-STONE, *n.* Gypsum, which see. This when pulverized is extensively used as a manure.

PLAS'TIC, *a.* [Gr. πλαςικος, from πλασσω, to form.]

Having the power to give form or fashion to a mass of matter; as the *plastic* hand of the Creator; the *plastic* virtue of nature. *Prior. Woodward.*

PLASTIC'ITY, *n.* The quality of giving form or shape to matter. *Encyc.*

PLAS'TRON, *n.* [See *Plaster.*] A piece of lether stuffed; used by fencers to defend the body against pushes. *Dryden.*

PLAT, *v. t.* [from *plait*, or *plat*, flat.] To weave; to form by texture. Matt. xxvii. *Ray. Spectator.*

PLAT', **PLAT'TING**, *n.* Work done by platting or interweaving.

PLAT, *n.* [Dan. D. *plat*, flat; Fr. *id.*; G. *platt*; W. *plad*, *plâs*; Gr. πλατυς, broad, L. *latus*; or from the root of *place*, G. *platz*. See *Plot*, the same word differently written. But probably these are all of one family. The sense is *laid, spread.*]

A small piece of ground, usually a portion of flat even ground; as a flowery *plat*; a *plat* of willows. *Milton. Spectator.*

PLAT, *a.* Plain; flat. [*Not used.*] *Chaucer.*

PLAT, *adv.* Plainly; flatly; downright. [*Not used.*] *Chaucer.*

2. Smoothly; evenly. [*Not used.*] *Drant.*

PLA'TANE, *n.* [L. *platanus.*] The plane-tree, which see. *Milton.*

PLAT'BAND, *n.* A border of flowers in a garden, along a wall or the side of a parterre.

2. In *architecture*, a flat square molding whose highth much exceeds its projecture, such as the faces of an architrave.

3. The lintel of a door or window.

4. A list or fillet between the flutings of a column. *Cyc.*

PLATE, *n.* [D. *plaat*, G. *platte*, plate; Sw. *platt*; Dan. D. *plat*, G. *platt*, flat; It. *piatto*, flat, and *piastra*; Sp. *plata*; Ir. *id.*; W. *plâd*, a plate; probably allied to Gr. πλατυς, L. *latus*, with the radical sense of *laid, spread.*]

1. A piece of metal, flat or extended in breadth. *Bacon. South.*

2. Armor of plate, composed of broad pieces, and thus distinguished from *mail.* *Spenser.*

3. A piece of wrought silver, as a dish or other shallow vessel; hence, vessels of silver; wrought silver in general. *Plate*, by the laws of some states, is subject to a tax by the ounce.

4. A small shallow vessel, made of silver or other metal, or of earth glazed and baked, from which provisions are eaten at table. A wooden plate is called a *trencher.*

5. The prize given for the best horse in a race.

6. In *architecture*, the piece of timber which supports the ends of the rafters. [See *Platform.*]

PLATE, *v. t.* To cover or overlay with plate or with metal; used particularly of silver; as *plated* vessels.

2. To arm with plate or metal for defense; as, to *plate* sin with gold. *Shak.*

> Why *plated* in habiliments of war? *Shak.*

3. To adorn with plate; as a *plated* harness.

4. To beat into thin flat pieces or lamens. *Dryden. Newton.*

PLA'TED, *pp.* Covered or adorned with plate; armed with plate; beaten into plates.

PLAT'EN, *n.* [from its *flatness.*] Among printers, the flat part of a press by which the impression is made.

PLA'TEY, *a.* Like a plate; flat. *Gregory.*

PLAT'FORM, *n.* [*plat*, flat, and *form.*] The sketch of any thing horizontally delineated; the ichnography. *Sandys.*

2. A place laid out after any model. *Pope.*

3. In *the military art*, an elevation of earth or a floor of wood or stone, on which cannons are mounted to fire on an enemy. *Encyc.*

4. In *architecture*, a row of beams or a piece of timber which supports the timber-work of a roof, and lying on the top of the wall. *Encyc.*

This in New England is called the *plate.*

5. A kind of terrace or broad smooth open walk on the top of a building, as in the oriental houses. *Encyc.*

6. In *ships*, the orlop. [See *Orlop.*]

7. Any number of planks or other materials forming a floor for any purpose. *Mar. Dict.*

8. A plan; a scheme; ground-work. *Bacon.*

9. In *some of the New England states*, an ecclesiastical constitution, or a plan for the government of churches; as the Cambridge or Saybrook *platform.*

Platic aspect, in astrology, a ray cast from one planet to another, not exactly, but within the orbit of its own light. *Bailey.*

PLATI'NA, **PLATI'NUM**, *n.* [Sp. *platina*, from *plata*, silver.]

A metal discovered in the mines of Choco in Peru, nearly of the color of silver, but less bright, and the heaviest of the metals. Its specific gravity is to that of water as 23 to 1. It is harder than iron, undergoes no alteration in air, resists the action of acids and alkalies, is very ductile and capable of being rolled into thin plates. *Encyc.*

PLA'TING, *ppr.* Overlaying with plate or with a metal; beating into thin lamens.

PLA'TING, *n.* The art or operation of covering any thing with plate or with a metal, particularly of overlaying a baser metal with a thin plate of silver. The coating of silver is soddered to the metal with tin or a mixture of three parts of silver with one of brass.

PLATINIF'EROUS, *a.* [*platina* and *fero*, to produce.]

Producing platina; as *platiniferous* sand. *Dict. Nat. Hist.*

PLATON'IC, *a.* Pertaining to Plato the philosopher, or to his philosophy, his school or his opinions.

Platonic love, is a pure spiritual affection subsisting between the sexes, unmixed with carnal desires, and regarding the mind only and its excellencies; a species of love for which Plato was a warm advocate.

Platonic year, the *great year*, or a period of time determined by the revolution of the equinoxes, or the space of time in which the stars and constellations return to their former places in respect to the equinoxes. This revolution, which is calculated by the precession of the equinoxes, is accomplished in about 25,000 years. *Encyc.*

PLATON'ICALLY, *adv.* After the manner of Plato. *Wotton.*

PLA'TONISM, *n.* The philosophy of Plato, consisting of three branches, *theology, physics* and *mathematics.* Under theology is included moral philosophy. The foundation of Plato's theology is the opinion that there are two eternal, primary, independent and incorruptible principles or causes of all things, which are *God*, the maker of all things, and *matter*, from which all things are made. It was a fundamental maxim with him that from nothing, nothing can proceed. While therefore he held God to be the maker of the universe, he held matter, the substance of which the universe was made, to be eternal. *Enfield.*

PLA'TONIST, **PLA'TONIZER**, *n.* One that adheres to the philosophy of Plato; a follower of Plato. *Hammond.*

PLA'TONIZE, *v. i.* To adopt the opinions or philosophy of Plato. *Milner.*

PLA'TONIZE, *v. t.* To explain on the principles of the Platonic school, or to accommodate to those principles. *Enfield.*

PLA'TONIZED, *pp.* Accommodated to the philosophy of Plato. *Enfield.*

PLA'TONIZING, *ppr.* Adopting the principles of Plato; accommodating to the principles of the Platonic school. *Enfield.*

PLATOON', *n.* [Fr. *peloton*, a ball of thread, a knot of men, from *pelote*, a ball; Sp. *peloton.* See *Ball.*]

A small square body of soldiers or musketeers, drawn out of a battalion of foot when they form a hollow square, to strengthen the angles; or a small body acting together, but separate from the main body; as, to fire by *platoons.*

PLAT'TER, *n.* [from *plate.*] A large shallow dish for holding the provisions of a table. *Dryden.*

2. One that plats or forms by weaving. [See *Plat.*]

PLAT'TER-FACED, *a.* Having a broad face.

PLAT'TING, *ppr.* Weaving; forming by texture.

PLAT'YPUS, *n.* A quadruped of New Holland, whose jaws are elongated into the shape of a duck's bill. The body is covered with thick hair and the feet are webbed.

This animal has been arranged with the *Mammalia*, but it is now presumed to be oviparous; at least its breasts have not hitherto been observed. *Ed. Encyc. Cuvier.*

PLAUD'IT, *n.* [L. *plaudo*, to praise, said to be taken from *plaudite*, a demand of applause by players when they left the stage.]

Applause; praise bestowed. *Denham.*

PLAUSIBIL'ITY, *n.* *s* as *z.* [See *Plausible.*]

Speciousness; superficial appearance of right. *Swift.*

PLAUS'IBLE, *a.* *s* as *z.* [L. *plausibilis*, from *plaudo*, to clap hands in token of approbation; W. *bloez*, an outcry; *bloeziaw*, to shout; *blozest*, applause, acclamation; Ir. *bladh*, *bladhh*; from the root of Gr. χλειω, L. *laus*, *laudo*, Eng. *loud.*]

1. That may be applauded; that may gain favor or approbation; hence, superficially pleasing; apparently right; specious; popular; as a *plausible* argument; a *plausible* pretext; a *plausible* doctrine.
2. Using specious arguments or discourse; as a *plausible* man.

PLAUS'IBLENESS, *n.* Speciousness; show of right or propriety; as the *plausibleness* of Arminianism. *Sanderson.*

PLAUS'IBLY, *adv.* With fair show; speciously; in a manner adapted to gain favor or approbation.

They could talk *plausibly* about what they did not understand. *Collier.*

PLAUS'IVE, *a.* Applauding; manifesting praise.
2. Plausible. *Shak.*

PLAY, *v. i.* [Sax. *plegan, plegian*, to play, to joke, to perform on an instrument of music, to move or vibrate, to clap or applaud, to deride or make sport of; *plegan*, to ply or bend to, or to lean or lie on; *ge-plægan*, to play, and to dance or leap. The Sw. *leka*, Dan. *leger*, to play, are the same word without a prefix, and in the northern counties of England, *leka* is used as it is in Sweden. This word seems to be formed on the same root as *lay*.]
1. To use any exercise for pleasure or recreation; to do something not as a task or for profit, but for amusement; as, to *play* at cricket.

The people sat down to eat and to drink, and rose up to *play*. Ex. xxxii.

2. To sport; to frolick; to frisk.

The lamb thy riot dooms to bleed to day,
Had he thy reason, would he skip and *play?* *Pope.*

3. To toy; to act with levity. *Milton.*
4. To trifle; to act wantonly and thoughtlessly.

Men are apt to *play* with their healths and their lives as they do with their clothes. *Temple.*

5. To do something fanciful; to give a fanciful turn to; as, to *play* upon words. *Shak.*
6. To make sport, or practice sarcastic merriment.

I would make use of it rather to *play* upon those I despise, than trifle with those I love. *Pope.*

7. To mock; to practice illusion.

Art thou alive,
Or is it fancy *plays* upon our eyesight? *Shak.*

8. To contend in a game; as, to *play* at cards or dice; to *play* for diversion; to *play* for money.
9. To practice a trick or deception.

His mother *played* false with a smith. *Shak.*

10. To perform on an instrument of music; as, to *play* on a flute, a violin or a harpsichord.

Play, my friend, and charm the charmer. *Granville.*

11. To move, or to move with alternate dilatation and contraction.

The heart beats, the blood circulates, the lungs *play*. *Cheyne.*

12. To operate; to act. The engines *play* against a fire. *Dryden.*
13. To move irregularly; to wanton.

Ev'n as the waving sedges *play* with wind. *Shak.*

The setting sun
Plays on their shining arms and burnish'd helmets. *Addison.*

All fame is foreign, but of true desert,
Plays round the head, but comes not to the heart. *Pope.*

14. To act a part on the stage; to personate a character.

A lord will hear you *play* to-night. *Shak.*

15. To represent a standing character.

Courts are theaters where some men *play*. *Donne.*

16. To act in any particular character; as, to *play* the fool; to *play* the woman; to *play* the man. *Shak.*
17. To move in any manner; to move one way and another; as any part of a machine.

PLAY, *v. t.* To put in action or motion; as, to *play* cannon or a fire-engine.
2. To use an instrument of music; as, to *play* the flute or the organ. [*Elliptical.*] *Gay.*
3. To act a sportive part or character.

Nature here
Wanton'd as in her prime, and *play'd* at will
Her virgin fancies. *Milton.*

4. To act or perform by representing a character; as, to *play* a comedy; to *play* the part of king Lear.
5. To act; to perform; as, to *play* our parts well on the stage of life.
6. To perform in contest for amusement or for a prize; as, to *play* a game at whist.

To play off, to display; to show; to put in exercise; as, to *play off* tricks.

To play on or *upon*, to deceive; to mock or to trifle with.
2. To give a fanciful turn to.

PLAY, *n.* Any exercise or series of actions intended for pleasure, amusement or diversion, as at cricket or quoit, or at blind man's buff.
2. Amusement; sport; frolick; gambols. *Spenser.*

Two gentle fawns at *play*. *Milton.*

3. Game; gaming; practice of contending for victory, for amusement or for a prize, as at dice, cards or billiards.
4. Practice in any contest; as sword-*play*.

He was resolved not to speak distinctly, knowing his best *play* to be in the dark. *Tillotson.*

John naturally loved rough *play*. *Arbuthnot.*

5. Action; use; employment; office.

—But justifies the next who comes in *play*. *Dryden.*

6. Practice; action; manner of acting in contest or negotiation; as fair *play*; foul *play*.
7. A dramatic composition; a comedy or tragedy; a composition in which characters are represented by dialogue and action.

A *play* ought to be a just image of human nature. *Dryden.*

8. Representation or exhibition of a comedy or tragedy; as, to be at the *play*. He attends every *play*.
9. Performance on an instrument of music.
10. Motion; movement, regular or irregular; as the *play* of a wheel or piston.
11. State of agitation or discussion.

Many have been sav'd, and many may,
Who never heard this question brought in *play*. *Dryden.*

12. Room for motion.

The joints are let exactly into one another, that they have no *play* between them. *Moxon.*

13. Liberty of acting; room for enlargement or display; scope; as, to give full *play* to mirth. Let the genius have free *play*.

PLA'YBILL, *n.* A printed advertisement of a play, with the parts assigned to the actors.

PLA'YBOOK, *n.* A book of dramatic compositions.

PLA'Y-DAY, PLA'YING-DAY, } *n.* A day given to play or diversion; a day exempt from work. *Swift.*

PLA'YDEBT, *n.* A debt contracted by gaming. *Arbuthnot.*

PLA'YED, *pp.* Acted; performed; put in motion.

PLA'YER, *n.* One who plays in any game or sport.
2. An idler. *Shak.*
3. An actor of dramatic scenes; one whose occupation is to imitate characters on the stage. *Bacon.*
4. A mimic. *Dryden.*
5. One who performs on an instrument of music.
6. A gamester.
7. One that acts a part in a certain manner. *Carew.*

PLA'YFELLOW, *n.* A companion in amusements or sports. *Sidney.*

PLA'YFUL, *a.* Sportive; given to levity; as a *playful* child. *Spectator.*
2. Indulging a sportive fancy; as a *playful* genius.

PLA'YFULLY, *adv.* In a sportive manner.

PLA'YFULNESS, *n.* Sportiveness.

PLA'YGAME, *n.* Play of children. *Locke.*

PLA'YHOUSE, *n.* A house appropriated to the exhibition of dramatic compositions; a theater. *Pope. Dryden.*

PLA'YMATE, *n.* A playfellow; a companion in diversions. *More.*

PLA'Y-PLEASURE, *n.* Idle amusement. [*Not used.*] *Bacon.*

PLA'YSOME, *a.* Playful; wanton. *Shelton.*

PLA'YSOMENESS, *n.* Playfulness; wantonness.

PLA'YTHING, *n.* A toy; any thing that serves to amuse.

A child knows his nurse, and by degrees the *playthings* of a little more advanced age. *Locke.*

PLA'YWRIGHT, *n.* A maker of plays. *Pope.*

PLEA, *n.* [Norm. *plait, plet, plaid, ple*; plu. *pliz, pleytz*; Fr. *plaider*, to plead; *plaidoyer*, a plea; It. *piato*, a plea; *piatire*, to plead; Sp. *pleyto*, dispute; *pleytear*, to plead; *pleyteador*, a pleader; Port. *pleito, pleitear*; D. *pleit, pleiten*. The Spanish word *pleyto* signifies a dispute, contest, debate, lawsuit, and a covenant, contract or bargain, and *pleyta* is a *plaited* strand of brass. The Portuguese verb *pleitear* signifies to plead, to go to law, to strive or vie. The elements of this word are probably *Ld* or *Pld*. In the sense of pleading, the word accords with the Gr. λιτη, and in that of striving, with the L. *lis, litis.*]
1. In *law*, that which is alledged by a party in support of his demand; but in a more limited and technical sense, the answer of

the defendant to the plaintif's declaration and demand. That which the plaintif alledges in his declaration is answered and repelled or justified by the defendant's *plea*. Pleas are *dilatory*, or pleas *to the action*. *Dilatory* pleas, are to the jurisdiction of the court, to the disability of the plaintif, or in abatement. Pleas *to the action* are an answer to the merits of the complaint, which confesses or denies it. Pleas that deny the plaintif's complaint or demand, are the general issue, which denies the whole declaration; or special pleas in bar, which state something which precludes the plaintif's right of recovery.

2. A cause in court; a lawsuit, or a criminal process; as the *pleas* of the crown; the court of common *pleas*.

The supreme judicial court shall have cognizance of *pleas* real, personal and mixed. *Laws of Mass.*

3. That which is alledged in defense or justification; an excuse; an apology; as the tyrant's *plea*.

When such occasions are,
No *plea* must serve; 'tis cruelty to spare. *Denham.*

4. Urgent prayer or entreaty.

PLEACH, *v. t.* [Fr. *plisser*, or from the root of L. *plico*, Gr. πλεκω.] To bend; to interweave. [*Not in use.*] *Shak.*

PLEAD, *v. i.* [See *Plea.*] In *a general sense*, to argue in support of a claim, or in defense against the claim of another.

2. In *law*, to present an answer to the declaration of a plaintif; to deny the plaintif's declaration and demand, or to alledge facts which show that he ought not to recover in the suit. The plaintif declares or alledges; the defendant *pleads* to his declaration. The king or the state prosecutes an offender, and the offender *pleads* not guilty, or confesses the charge.

3. To urge reasons for or against; to attempt to persuade one by argument or supplication; as, to *plead* for the life of a criminal; to *plead* in his favor; to *plead* with a judge or with a father.

O that one might *plead* for a man with God, as a man *pleadeth* for his neighbor! Job xvi.

4. To supplicate with earnestness.

5. To urge; to press by operating on the passions.

Since you can love, and yet your error see,
The same resistless power may *plead* for me. *Dryden.*

PLEAD, *v. t.* To discuss, defend and attempt to maintain by arguments or reasons offered to the tribunal or person who has the power of determining; as, to *plead* a cause before a court or jury. In this sense, *argue* is more generally used by lawyers.

2. To alledge or adduce in proof, support or vindication. The law of nations may be *pleaded* in favor of the rights of embassadors.

3. To offer in excuse.

I will neither *plead* my age nor sickness in excuse of faults. *Dryden.*

4. To alledge and offer in a legal plea or defense, or for repelling a demand in law; as, to *plead* usury; to *plead* a statute of limitations. *Ch. Kent.*

5. In *Scripture*, to plead the cause of the righteous, as God, is to avenge or vindicate them against enemies, or to redress their grievances. Is. li.

PLE'ADABLE, *a.* That may be pleaded; that may be alledged in proof, defense or vindication; as a right or privilege *pleadable* at law. *Dryden.*

PLE'ADED, *pp.* Offered or urged in defense; alledged in proof or support.

PLE'ADER, *n.* [Fr. *plaideur.*] One who argues in a court of justice. *Swift.*

2. One that forms pleas or pleadings; as a special *pleader*.

3. One that offers reasons for or against; one that attempts to maintain by arguments.

So fair a *pleader* any cause may gain. *Dryden.*

PLE'ADING, *ppr.* Offering in defense; supporting by arguments or reasons; supplicating.

PLE'ADING, *n.* The art of supporting by arguments, or of reasoning to persuade.

PLE'ADINGS, *n.* In *law*, the mutual altercations between the plaintif and defendant, or written statements of the parties in support of their claims, comprehending the declaration, count or narration of the plaintif, the plea of the defendant in reply, the replication of the plaintif to the defendant's plea, the defendant's rejoinder, the plaintif's sur-rejoinder, the defendant's rebutter, the plaintif's sur-rebutter, &c. till the question is brought to issue, that is, to rest on a single point.

PLEASANCE, *n. plez'ance.* [Fr. *plaisance.* See *Please.*] Gayety; pleasantry; merriment. *Obs.* *Spenser. Shak.*

PLEASANT, *a. plez'ant.* [Fr. *plaisant.* See *Please.*]

1. Pleasing; agreeable; grateful to the mind or to the senses; as a *pleasant* ride; a *pleasant* voyage; a *pleasant* view. Light is *pleasant* to the eye; an orange is *pleasant* to the taste; harmony is *pleasant* to the ear; a rose is *pleasant* to the smell.

How good and how *pleasant* it is for brethren to dwell together in unity! Ps. cxxxiii.

2. Cheerful; enlivening; as *pleasant* society or company.

3. Gay; lively; humorous; sportive; as a *pleasant* companion.

4. Trifling; adapted rather to mirth than use. *Locke.*

5. Giving pleasure; gratifying.

This word expresses less than *delightful*, to the mind, and *delicious*, to the taste.

PLEASANTLY, *adv. plez'antly.* In such a manner as to please or gratify.

2. Gayly; merrily; in good humor. *Clarendon.*

3. Lightly; ludicrously. *Broome.*

PLEASANTNESS, *n. plez'antness.* State of being pleasant or agreeable; as the *pleasantness* of a situation. *Sidney.*

2. Cheerfulness; gayety; merriment; as the *pleasantness* of youth.

PLEASANTRY, *n. plez'antry.* [Fr. *plaisanterie.*] Gayety; merriment.

The harshness of reasoning is not a little softened and smoothed by the infusions of mirth and *pleasantry*. *Addison*

2. Sprightly saying; lively talk; effusion of humor.

The grave abound in *pleasantries*, the dull in repartees and points of wit. *Addison.*

PLEASE, *v. t. s* as *z.* [Fr. *plaire, plaisant*, from L. *placere, placeo*; Arm. *pligea, pligeout*; It. *piacere*; Sp. *placer*; Corn. *plezia*; formed perhaps on the root of *like.* Class Lg.]

1. To excite agreeable sensations or emotions in; to gratify; as, to *please* the taste; to *please* the mind.

Their words *pleased* Hamor, and Shechem, Hamor's son. Gen. xxxiv.

Leave such to trifle with more grace than ease,
Whom folly *pleases*, and whose follies *please*. *Pope.*

2. To satisfy; to content.

What next I bring shall *please*
Thy wish exactly to thy heart's desire. *Milton.*

3. To prefer; to have satisfaction in; to like; to choose.

Many of our most skilful painters were *pleased* to recommend this author to me. *Dryden.*

To be pleased in or *with*, to approve; to have complacency in. Matt. iii.

To please God, is to love his character and law and perform his will, so as to become the object of his approbation.

They that are in the flesh cannot *please God*. Rom. viii.

PLEASE, *v. i. s* as *z.* To like; to choose; to prefer.

Spirits, freed from mortal laws, with ease
Assume what sexes and what shapes they *please*. *Pope.*

2. To condescend; to comply; to be pleased; a word of ceremony.

Please you, lords,
In sight of both our battles we may meet. *Shak.*

The first words that I learnt were, to express my desire that he would *please* to give me my liberty. *Swift.*

Please expresses less gratification than *delight.*

PLE'ASED, *pp.* Gratified; affected with agreeable sensations or emotions.

PLE'ASEMAN, *n.* An officious person who courts favor servilely; a pickthank. *Shak.*

PLE'ASER, *n.* One that pleases or gratifies; one that courts favor by humoring or flattering compliances or a show of obedience; as *men-pleasers.* Eph. vi. Col. iii.

PLE'ASING, *ppr.* Gratifying; exciting agreeable sensations or emotions in.

PLE'ASING, *a.* Giving pleasure or satisfaction; agreeable to the senses or to the mind; as a *pleasing* prospect; a *pleasing* reflection; *pleasing* manners.

2. Gaining approbation. 1 John iii.

PLE'ASING, *n.* The act of gratifying.

PLE'ASINGLY, *adv.* In such a manner as to give pleasure. *Dryden.*

PLE'ASINGNESS, *n.* The quality of giving pleasure.

PLEASURABLE, *a. plezh'urable.* [from *pleasure.*] Pleasing; giving pleasure; affording gratification.

Planting of orchards is very profitable as well as *pleasurable*. *Bacon.*

PLEAS'URABLY, *adv.* With pleasure; with gratification of the senses or the mind. *Harris.*

PLEAS'URABLENESS, *n.* The quality of giving pleasure. *Feltham.*

PLEASURE, *n. plezh'ur.* [Fr. *plaisir*; Arm. *pligeadur*; It. *piacere*; Sp. *placer*; Port. *prazer.* See *Please.*]

1. The gratification of the senses or of the mind; agreeable sensations or emotions; the excitement, relish or happiness produced by enjoyment or the expectation of of good; opposed to *pain*. We receive *pleasure* from the indulgence of appetite; from the view of a beautiful landscape; from the harmony of sounds; from agreeable society; from the expectation of seeing an absent friend; from the prospect of gain or success of any kind. *Pleasure*, bodily and mental, carnal and spiritual, constitutes the whole of positive happiness, as *pain* constitutes the whole of misery.

Pleasure is properly positive excitement of the passions or the mind; but we give the name also to the absence of excitement, when that excitement is painful; as when we cease to labor, or repose after fatigue, or when the mind is tranquilized after anxiety or agitation.

Pleasure is susceptible of increase to any degree; but the word when unqualified, expresses less excitement or happiness than *delight* or *joy*.

2. Sensual or sexual gratification.
3. Approbation.

The Lord taketh *pleasure* in his people. Ps. cxlvii. and cxlix.

4. What the will dictates or prefers; will; choice; purpose; intention; command; as, use your *pleasure*. *Shak.*

Cyrus, he is my shepherd and shall perform all my *pleasure*. Is. xliv.

My counsel shall stand and I will do all my *pleasure*. Is. xlvi.

5. A favor; that which pleases.

Festus, willing to do the Jews a *pleasure*, answered Paul. Acts xxv.

6. Arbitrary will or choice. He can vary his scheme at *pleasure*.

PLEAS′URE, *v. t. plezh′ur.* To give or afford pleasure to; to please; to gratify. [*A word authorized by some good writers, but superfluous and not much used.*] *Bacon. Shak.*

PLEAS′URE-BOAT, *n.* A boat appropriated to sailing for amusement.

PLEAS′URE-CARRIAGE, *n.* A carriage for pleasure.

PLEAS′UREFUL, *a.* Pleasant; agreeable. [*Little used.*] *Abbot.*

PLEAS′URE-GROUND, *n.* Ground laid out in an ornamental manner and appropriated to pleasure or amusement. *Graves.*

PLEAS′URIST, *n.* A person devoted to worldly pleasure. [*Little used.*] *Brown.*

PLEBE′IAN, *a.* [It. *plebeio*; Sp. *plebeyo*; L. *plebeius*, from *plebs*, the common people.]

1. Pertaining to the common people; vulgar; as *plebeian* minds; *plebeian* sports.
2. Consisting of common people; as a *plebeian* throng.

PLEBE′IAN, *n.* One of the common people or lower ranks of men. [Usually applied to the common people of ancient Rome.] *Swift.*

PLEBE′IANCE, *n.* The common people. [*Not in use.*]

PLEDGE, *n.* [Fr. *pleige*; It. *pieggeria*; Norm. *plegg*. This is evidently the Celtic form of the Teutonic *plight*, Sax. *pliht*, *plihtan*. See *Plight*. It coincides with L. *plico*, Gr. πλεκω, W. *plygu*, to fold, properly to *lay to*, to put or throw to or on. A *pledge* is that which is laid or deposited.]

1. Something put in pawn; that which is deposited with another as security for the repayment of money borrowed, or for the performance of some agreement or obligation; a pawn. A borrows ten pounds of B, and deposits his watch as a *pledge* that the money shall be repaid; and by repayment of the money, A redeems the *pledge*.
2. Any thing given or considered as a security for the performance of an act. Thus a man gives his word or makes a promise to another, which is received as a *pledge* for fulfillment. The mutual affection of husband and wife is a *pledge* for the faithful performance of the marriage covenant. Mutual interest is the best *pledge* for the performance of treaties.
3. A surety; a hostage. *Raleigh. Dryden.*
4. In *law*, a gage or security real or personal, given for the repayment of money. It is of two kinds; *vadium vivum*, a living pledge, as when a man borrows money and grants an estate to be held by the pledgee, till the rents and profits shall refund the money, in which case the land or pledge is said to be *living*; or it is *vadium mortuum*, a *dead pledge*, called a *mortgage*. [See *Mortgage*.] *Blackstone.*
5. In *law*, bail; surety given for the prosecution of a suit, or for the appearance of a defendant, or for restoring goods taken in distress and replevied. The distress itself is also called a *pledge*, and the glove formerly thrown down by a champion in trial by battel, was a *pledge* by which the champion stipulated to encounter his antagonist in that trial. *Blackstone.*
6. A warrant to secure a person from injury in drinking.

To put in pledge, to pawn.

To hold in pledge, to keep as security.

PLEDGE, *v. t.* [Fr. *pleiger*. See *Plight*.]

1. To deposit in pawn; to deposit or leave in possession of a person something which is to secure the repayment of money borrowed, or the performance of some act. [This word is applied chiefly to the depositing of goods or personal property. When real estate is given as security we usually apply the word *mortgage*.]
2. To give as a warrant or security; as, to *pledge* one's word or honor; to *pledge* one's veracity.
3. To secure by a pledge.

I accept her,
And here to *pledge* my vow I give my hand.
[*Unusual.*] *Shak.*

4. To invite to drink by accepting the cup or health after another. *Johnson.* Or to warrant or be surety for a person that he shall receive no harm while drinking, or from the draught; a practice which originated among our ancestors in their rude state, and which was intended to secure the person from being stabbed while drinking, or from being poisoned by the liquor. In the first case, a by-stander *pledges* the person drinking; in the latter, the person drinking *pledges* his guest by drinking first, and then handing the cup to his guest. The latter practice is frequent among the common people in America to this day; the owner of the liquor taking the cup says to his friend, *I pledge you*, and drinks, then hands the cup to his guest; a remarkable instance of the power of habit, as the reason of the custom has long since ceased.

PLEDG′ED, *pp.* Deposited as security; given in warrant.

PLEDGEE′, *n.* The person to whom any thing is pledged.

PLEDG′ER, *n.* One that pledges or pawns any thing; one that warrants or secures. [*Pledgor*, in Blackstone, is not to be countenanced.]

2. One that accepts the invitation to drink after another, or that secures another by drinking.

PLEDG′ERY, *n.* A pledging; suretiship. [*Not in use.*] *Encyc.*

PLEDG′ET, *n.* [from *folding* or *laying*.] In *surgery*, a compress or small flat tent of lint, laid over a wound to imbibe the matter discharged and keep it clean. *Encyc.*

PLEDG′ING, *ppr.* Depositing in pawn or as security; giving warrant for security or safety.

PLEIADS, *n. ple′yads.* [L. *Pleiades*; Gr. πλειαδες, supposed to be formed from πλεω, to sail, as the rising of the seven stars indicated the time of safe navigation.]

In *astronomy*, a cluster of seven stars in the neck of the constellation Taurus. The Latins called them *Vergiliæ*, from *ver*, spring, because of their rising about the vernal equinox. *Encyc. Ainsworth.*

PLE′NAL, *a.* [See *Plenary*.] Full. [*Not used.*] *Beaumont.*

PLE′NARILY, *adv.* [from *plenary*.] Fully; completely. *Ayliffe.*

PLE′NARINESS, *n.* Fullness; completeness.

PLEN′ARTY, *n.* The state of a benefice when occupied. *Blackstone.*

PLE′NARY, *a.* [L. *plenus*; Fr. *plein*; It. *plenario*, *pieno*; Sp. *pleno*, *lleno*; W. *llawn*; Ir. *lain*, *lan*; Arm. *leun*. The Russ. has *polnei* and *polon*, full, and with a prefix, *napolniayu*, to fill. Qu. the radical letters, and the identity of the Russ. with the others.]

Full; entire; complete; as a *plenary* license; *plenary* consent; *plenary* indulgence. The *plenary* indulgence of the pope is an entire remission of penalties due to all sins. *Encyc.*

PLE′NARY, *n.* Decisive procedure. [*Not used.*] *Ayliffe.*

PLENILU′NARY, *a.* Relating to the full moon. *Brown.*

PLEN′ILUNE, *n.* [L. *plenilunium*; *plenus*, full, and *luna*, moon.] The full moon. [*Not used.*] *B. Jonson.*

PLENIP′OTENCE, *n.* [L. *plenus*, full, and *potentia*, power.] Fullness or completeness of power. *Milton.*

PLENIP′OTENT, *a.* [L. *plenipotens*, supra.] Possessing full power. *Milton.*

PLENIPOTEN′TIARY, *n.* [Fr. *plenipotentiaire*. See *Plenipotence*.]

A person invested with full power to transact any business; usually, an embassador or envoy to a foreign court, furnished with full power to negotiate a treaty or to transact other business.

PLENIPOTEN′TIARY, *a.* Containing full power; as *plenipotentiary* license or authority.

PLENISH, for *replenish*, not used.

PLE'NIST, *n.* [L. *plenus.*] One who maintains that all space is full of matter. *Boyle.*

PLEN'ITUDE, *n.* [L. *plenitudo*, from *plenus*, full.] Fullness; as the *plenitude* of space. *Bentley.*

2. Repletion; animal fullness; plethora; redundancy of blood and humors in the animal body. *Encyc.*

3. Fullness; complete competence; as the *plenitude* of the pope's power. *Bacon.*

4. Completeness; as the *plenitude* of a man's fame. *Prior.*

PLEN'TEOUS, *a.* [from *plenty.*] Abundant; copious; plentiful; sufficient for every purpose; as a *plenteous* supply of provisions; a *plenteous* crop. *Milton.*

2. Yielding abundance; as a *plenteous* fountain.

The seven *plenteous* years. Gen. xli.

3. Having an abundance.

The Lord shall make thee *plenteous* in goods. Deut. xxviii.

4. Possessing in abundance and ready to bestow liberally. Ps. lxxxvi.

[This word is less used than *plentiful.*]

PLEN'TEOUSLY, *adv.* In abundance; copiously; plentifully. *Milton.*

PLEN'TEOUSNESS, *n.* Abundance; copious supply; plenty; as the seven years of *plenteousness* in Egypt.

PLEN'TIFUL, *a.* [from *plenty.*] Copious; abundant; adequate to every purpose; as a *plentiful* crop of grain; a *plentiful* harvest; a *plentiful* supply of water; a *plentiful* fortune.

2. Yielding abundant crops; affording ample supply; fruitful; as a *plentiful* year. *Bacon.*

PLEN'TIFULLY, *adv.* Copiously; abundantly; with ample supply. *Addison.*

PLEN'TIFULNESS, *n.* The state of being plentiful; abundance.

2. The quality of affording full supply.

PLEN'TY, *n.* [from L. *plenus.*] Abundance; copiousness; full or adequate supply; as, we have a *plenty* of corn for bread; the garrison has a *plenty* of provisions. Its application to persons, as a *plenty* of buyers or sellers, is inelegant.

2. Fruitfulness; *a poetic use.*

The teeming clouds
Descend in gladsome *plenty* o'er the world. *Thomson.*

PLEN'TY, *a.* Plentiful; being in abundance.

Where water is *plenty*— *Tusser.*

If reasons were as *plenty* as blackberries. *Shak.*

In every country where liquors are *plenty.* *Hist. Collections.*

The common sorts of fowls and the several gallinaceous species are *plenty.* *Tooke, Russ. Emp.*

A variety of other herbs and roots which are *plenty.* *Adair.*

They seem formed for those countries where shrubs are *plenty* and water scarce. *Goldsmith.*

When laborers are *plenty*, their wages will be low. *Franklin.*

In the country, where wood is more *plenty*, they make their beams stronger. *Encyc.*

[The use of this word as an adjective seems too well authorized to be rejected. It is universal in common parlance in the United States.]

PLE'NUM, *n.* [L.] Fullness of matter in space. *Descartes.*

PLE'ONASM, *n.* [L. *pleonasmus*; Gr. πλεονασμος, from the root of πλεος, full, πλειον, more, L. *pleo*, in *impleo*, to *fill.*]

Redundancy of words in speaking or writing; the use of more words to express ideas, than are necessary. This may be justifiable when we intend to present thoughts with particular perspicuity or force.

PLE'ONASTE, *n.* [Gr. πλεοναςος, abundant; from its four facets, sometimes found on each solid angle of the octahedron.]

A mineral, commonly considered as a variety of the spinelle ruby. [See *Ceylonite.*]

PLEONAS'TI€, } *a.* Pertaining to pleonasm; partaking of pleonasm; redundant. *Blackwall.*
PLEONAS'TI€AL, }

PLEONAS'TI€ALLY, *adv.* With redundancy of words.

PLEROPH'ORY, *n.* [Gr. πληροφορια; πληρης, full, and φερω, to bear.]

Full persuasion or confidence. [*Little used.*] *Hall.*

PLESH, for *plash*, not used. *Spenser.*

PLETH'ORA, *n.* [Gr. πληθωρα, from πληθος, fullness.] Literally, fullness.

In *medicine*, fullness of blood; excess of blood; repletion; the state of the vessels of the human body, when they are too full or overloaded with fluids. *Coxe. Parr. Encyc.*

PLETH'ORI€, *a.* Having a full habit of body, or the vessels overcharged with fluids. *Arbuthnot.*

PLETH'ORY. [See *Plethora.*]

PLETH'RON, } *n.* [Gr. πλεθρον.] A square measure used in Greece, but the contents are not certainly known. Some authors suppose it to correspond with the Roman juger, or 240 feet; others alledge it to be double the Egyptian aroura, which was the square of a hundred cubits.
PLETH'RUM, }

PLEU'RA, *n.* [Gr. the side.] In *anatomy*, a thin membrane which covers the inside of the thorax.

PLEU'RISY, *n.* [Gr. πλευριτις, from πλευρα, the side; Fr. *pleuresie*; It. *pleurisia.*]

An inflammation of the pleura or membrane that covers the inside of the thorax. It is accompanied with fever, pain, difficult respiration and cough. The usual remedies are venesection, other evacuations, diluents, &c. *Encyc.*

PLEURIT'I€, } *a.* Pertaining to pleurisy; as *pleuritic* symptoms or affections.
PLEURIT'I€AL, }

2. Diseased with pleurisy. *Arbuthnot.*

PLEV'IN, *n.* [Old Fr.] A warrant of assurance. *Obs.*

PLEX'IFORM, *a.* [L. *plexus*, a fold, and *form.*]

In the form of net-work; complicated. *Quincy.*

PLEX'US, *n.* [L.] Any union of vessels, nerves or fibers, in the form of net-work. *Coxe.*

PLIABIL'ITY, *n.* [from *pliable.*] The quality of bending or yielding to pressure or force without rupture; flexibility; pliableness.

PLI'ABLE, *a.* [Fr. from *plier*, to bend, to fold; L. *plico*, Gr. πλεκω, W. *plygu*, It. *piegare*, to fold; *pieghevole*, pliable.]

1. Easy to be bent; that readily yields to pressure without rupture; flexible; as, willow is a *pliable* plant.

2. Flexible in disposition; readily yielding to moral influence, arguments, persuasion or discipline; as a *pliable* youth.

PLI'ABLENESS, *n.* Flexibility; the quality of yielding to force or to moral influence; pliability; as the *pliableness* of a plant or of the disposition. *Hammond.*

PLI'ANCY, *n.* [from *pliant.*] Easiness to be bent; in a physical sense; as the *pliancy* of a rod, of cordage or of limbs. *Addison.*

2. Readiness to yield to moral influence; as *pliancy* of temper.

PLI'ANT, *a.* [Fr.] That may be easily bent; readily yielding to force or pressure without breaking; flexible; flexile; lithe; limber; as a *pliant* thread. *Spectator.*

2. That may be easily formed or molded to a different shape; as *pliant* wax.

3. Easily yielding to moral influence; easy to be persuaded; ductile.

The will was then more ductile and *pliant* to right reason. *South.*

PLI'ANTNESS, *n.* Flexibility. *Bacon.*

PLI'€A, *n.* [L. a fold.] The *plica polonica* is a disease of the hair, peculiar to Poland and the neighboring countries. In this disease, the hair of the head is matted or clotted by means of an acrid viscid humor which exsudes from the hair. *Coxe.*

PLI'€ATE, } *a.* [L. *plicatus*, *plico*, to fold.] Plaited; folded like a fan; as a *plicate* leaf. *Lee. Martyn.*
PLI'€ATED, }

PLI€A'TION, *n.* [from L. *plico.*] A folding or fold.

PLI€'ATURE, *n.* [L. *plicatura*; *plico*, to fold.] A fold; a doubling.

PLI'ERS, *n. plu.* [Fr. *plier*, to fold. See *Ply.*]

An instrument by which any small thing is seized and bent. *Moxon.*

PLI'FORM, *a.* [Fr. *pli*, a fold, and *form.*] In the form of a fold or doubling. *Pennant.*

PLIGHT, *v. t. plite.* [Sax. *plihtan*, to pledge, and to expose to danger or rather perhaps to perplexity; Sw. *beplichta*, to bind; D. *pligt*, duty, mortgage; G. *pflicht*, duty, pledge; Dan. *pligt*, duty, obligation; *pligtig*, bound, obliged; Sw. *plicht.* This seems to be the Teutonic form of the Celtic *pledge*, Fr. *pleige*, *pleiger*, L. *plico*, Gr. πλεκω, It. *piegare*, Sp. *plegar*, Fr. *plier*, Arm. *plega*, W. *plygu*, to fold; Sp. *pleyto*, a covenant or contract; and the G. *flechten*, to braid, coinciding with the L. *flecto*, to bend, appears to be of the same family. If the elements are *Lg*, as I suspect, *pledge* and *plight* are formed on the root of *lay*, Arm. *lacqaat.* To *pledge* or *plight* is to lay down, throw down, set or deposit. *Plight* may however be more directly from the root of L. *ligo*, but this is of the same family. See *Alloy* and *Ply.*]

1. To pledge; to give as security for the performance of some act; *but never applied to property or goods.* We say, he *plight-*

ed his hand, his faith, his vows, his honor, his truth or troth. *Pledge* is applied to property as well as to word, faith, truth, honor, &c. To *plight* faith is, as it were, to *deposit it in pledge* for the performance of an act, on the non-performance of which, the pledge is forfeited.

2. To weave; to braid. *Spenser. Milton.*

[This is the primary sense of the word, L. *plico*, but now obsolete.]

PLIGHT, *n. plite.* Literally, a state of being involved, [L. *plicatus, implicatus, implicitus;*] hence, perplexity, distress, or a distressed state or condition; as a miserable *plight.* But the word by itself does not ordinarily imply distress. Hence,

2. Condition; state; and sometimes good case; as, to keep cattle in *plight.*

In most cases, this word is now accompanied with an adjective which determines its signification; as *bad plight; miserable* or *wretched plight; good plight.*

3. Pledge; gage.

The Lord, whose hand must take my *plight.* *Shak.*

4. A fold [L. *plica;*] a double; a plait.

All in a silken Camus, lily white,
Purfled upon with many a folded *plight. Obs.* *Spenser.*

5. A garment. [*Not used.*] *Chapman.*

PLIGHTED, *pp. pli'ted.* Pledged.

PLIGHTER, *n. pli'ter.* One that pledges; that which plights.

PLIGHTING, *ppr. pli'ting.* Pledging.

PLIM, *v. i.* To swell. [*Not in use.*] *Grose.*

PLINTH, *n.* [Gr. πλινθος, a brick or tile; L. *plinthus.*]

In *architecture,* a flat square member in form of a brick, which serves as the foundation of a column; being the flat square table under the molding of the base and pedestal, at the bottom of the order. Vitruvius gives the name to the abacus or upper part of the Tuscan order, from its resemblance to the plinth.

Plinth of a statue, is a base, flat, round or square. *Encyc.*

Plinth of a wall, two or three rows of bricks advanced from the wall in form of a platband; and in general, any flat high molding that serves in a front wall to mark the floors, to sustain the eaves of a wall or the larmier of a chimney. *Encyc.*

PLOD, *v. i.* [D. *plots,* dull, heavy. Qu.] To travel or work slowly or with steady laborious diligence.

A *plodding* diligence brings us sooner to our journey's end, than a fluttering way of advancing by starts. *L'Estrange.*

Some stupid, *plodding,* money-loving wight. *Young.*

2. To study heavily with steady diligence. *Shak. Swift.*

3. To toil; to drudge.

PLOD'DER, *n.* A dull, heavy, laborious person. *Shak.*

PLOD'DING, *ppr.* Traveling or laboring with slow movement and steady diligence; studying closely but heavily.

2. *a.* Industrious; diligent, but slow in contrivance or execution.

PLOD'DING, *n.* Slow movement or study with steadiness or persevering industry. *Prideaux.*

PLOT, *n.* [a different orthography of *plat.*]

1. A plat or small extent of ground; as a garden *plot.* *Locke.*

It was a chosen *plot* of fertile land. *Spenser.*

When we mean to build,
We first survey the *plot.* *Shak.*

2. A plantation laid out. *Sidney.*

3. A plan or scheme. [Qu. the next word.] *Spenser.*

4. In *surveying,* a plan or draught of a field, farm or manor surveyed and delineated on paper.

PLOT, *v. t.* To make a plan of; to delineate. *Carew.*

PLOT, *n.* [The French retain this word in the compounds *complot, comploter;* Arm. *complod, complodi.* It may be from the root of *plait,* to weave, Russ. *pletu,* whence *opletayu,* to plait, to twist, to deceive; *oplot,* a hedge. See *Plait.*]

1. Any scheme, stratagem or plan of a complicated nature, or consisting of many parts, adapted to the accomplishment of some purpose, usually a mischievous one. A *plot* may be formed by a single person or by numbers. In the latter case, it is a conspiracy or an intrigue. The latter word more generally denotes a scheme directed against individuals; the former against the government. But this distinction is not always observed.

O think what anxious moments pass between
The birth of *plots,* and their last fatal periods! *Addison.*

2. In *dramatic writings,* the knot or intrigue; the story of a play, comprising a complication of incidents which are at last unfolded by unexpected means.

If the *plot* or intrigue must be natural, and such as springs from the subject, the winding up of the *plot* must be a probable consequence of all that went before. *Pope.*

3. Contrivance; deep reach of thought; ability to plot.

A man of much *plot.* *Denham.*

PLOT, *v. i.* To form a scheme of mischief against another, or against a government or those who administer it. A traitor *plots* against his king.

The wicked *plotteth* against the just. Ps. xxxvii.

2. To contrive a plan; to scheme.

The prince did *plot* to be secretly gone. *Wotton.*

PLOT, *v. t.* To plan; to devise; to contrive; as, to *plot* an unprofitable crime. *Dryden.*

PLOT'TED, *pp.* Contrived; planned.

PLOT'TER, *n.* One that plots or contrives; a contriver. *Shak.*

2. A conspirator. *Dryden.*

PLOT'TING, *ppr.* Contriving; planning; forming an evil design.

PLOUGH. [See *Plow.*]

PLOV'ER, *n.* [Fr. *pluvier,* the water bird, from L. *pluvialis,* rainy; *pluo,* to rain.]

The common name of several species of birds that frequent the banks of rivers and the sea shore, belonging to the genus Charadrius. *Encyc.*

PLOW, *n.* [Norm. Sax. *ploge;* D. *ploeg;* G. *pflug;* Dan. *ploug, plov;* Ice. *plog;* Sw. *id.;* Russ. *plug;* Polish, *plug;* Scot. *pleuch, pleugh.* It corresponds in elements with *plug,* and both perhaps from thrusting.]

1. In *agriculture,* an instrument for turning up, breaking and preparing the ground for receiving the seed. It is drawn by oxen or horses and saves the labor of digging; it is therefore the most useful instrument in agriculture.

The emperor lays hold of the *plow* and turns up several furrows. *Grosier, Trans.*

Where fern succeeds, ungrateful to the *plow.* *Dryden.*

2. Figuratively, tillage; culture of the earth; agriculture.

3. A joiner's instrument for grooving.

PLOW, *v. t.* To trench and turn up with a plow; as, to *plow* the ground for wheat; to *plow* it into ridges.

2. To furrow; to divide; to run through in sailing.

With speed we *plow* the watery wave. *Pope.*

3. To tear; to furrow. *Shak.*

4. In *Scripture,* to labor in any calling.

He that *ploweth* should *plow* in hope. 1 Cor. ix.

To plow on the back, to scourge; to mangle, or to persecute and torment. Ps. cxxix.

To plow with one's heifer, to deal with the wife to obtain something from the husband. Judges xiv.

To plow iniquity or *wickedness, and reap it,* to devise and practice it, and at last suffer the punishment of it. Job xiv. Hos. x.

To plow in, to cover by plowing; as, to *plow in* wheat.

To plow up or *out,* to turn out of the ground by plowing.

To put one's hand to the plow and look back, is to enter on the service of Christ and afterwards abandon it. Luke ix.

[The difference of orthography often made between the noun and verb is wholly unwarrantable, and contrary to settled analogy in our language. Such a difference is never made in changing into verbs, *plot, harrow, notice, question,* and most other words. See *Practice.*]

PLOW'-ALMS, *n.* A penny formerly paid by every plow-land to the church. *Cowel.*

PLOW'-BOTE, *n.* In *English law,* wood or timber allowed to a tenant for the repair of instruments of husbandry.

PLOW'BOY, *n.* A boy that drives or guides a team in plowing; a rustic boy. *Watts.*

PLOW'ED, *pp.* Turned up with a plow; furrowed.

PLOW'ER, *n.* One that plows land; a cultivator. *Spenser.*

PLOW'ING, *ppr.* Turning up with a plow; furrowing.

PLOW'ING, *n.* The operation of turning up ground with a plow; as the first and second *plowing;* three *plowings.*

PLOW'-LAND, *n.* Land that is plowed, or suitable for tillage.

PLOW'MAN, *n.* One that plows or holds a plow.

At last the robber binds the *plowman* and carries him off with the oxen. *Spelman.*

2. A cultivator of grain; a husbandman. *Temple.*

3. A rustic; a countryman; a hardy laborer. *Shak. Arbuthnot.*

PLOW'-MONDAY, *n.* The Monday after twelfth-day. *Tusser.*

PLOW'SHARE, *n.* [See *Shear.*] The part of a plow which cuts the ground at the bottom of the furrow, and raises the slice to the mold-board, which turns it over.

PLUCK, *v. t.* [Sax. *pluccian*, which seems to be the same word, with a prefix, as *lyccan* or *alucan*, *aluccan*, to pull off or out; G. *pflücken;* D. *plukken;* Dan. *plukker;* Sw. *plocka;* Fr. *eplucher;* W. *pliciaw*, to pluck, to peel; *plig*, a peel.]

1. To pull with sudden force or effort, or to pull off, out or from, with a twitch. Thus we say, to *pluck* fethers from a fowl; to *pluck* hair or wool from a skin; to *pluck* grapes or other fruit.

They *pluck* the fatherless from the breast. Job xxiv.

2. To strip by plucking; as, to *pluck* a fowl.

They that pass by do *pluck* her. Ps. lxxx.

The sense of this verb is modified by particles.

To pluck away, to pull away, or to separate by pulling; to tear away.

He shall *pluck away* his crop with his fethers. Lev. i.

To pluck down, to pull down; to demolish; or to reduce to a lower state. *Shak.*

To pluck off, is to pull or tear off; as, to *pluck off* the skin. Mic. iii.

To pluck on, to pull or draw on. *Obs.* *Shak.*

To pluck up, to tear up by the roots or from the foundation; to eradicate; to exterminate; to destroy; as, to *pluck up* a plant; to *pluck up* a nation. Jer. xii.

To pluck out, to draw out suddenly or to tear out; as, to *pluck out* the eyes; to *pluck out* the hand from the bosom. Ps. lxxiv.

To pluck up, to resume courage; properly, to pluck up the heart. [*Not elegant.*] *Knolles.*

PLUCK, *n.* The heart, liver and lights of an animal.

PLUCK'ED, *pp.* Pulled off; stripped of fethers or hair.

PLUCK'ER, *n.* One that plucks. *Mortimer.*

PLUCK'ING, *ppr.* Pulling off; stripping.

PLUG, *n.* [D. *plug;* Dan. *plyg;* Sw. *pligg;* G. *pflock;* W. *ploc*, a block; *plociaw*, to block, to *plug*. It seems to be the same word radically as *block*, W. *lloc.*]

A stopple; any piece of pointed wood or other substance used to stop a hole, but larger than a peg or spile. *Boyle.* *Swift.*

Hawse-plug, in marine affairs, a plug to stop a hawse-hole.

Shot-plug, a plug to stop a breach made by a cannon ball in the side of a ship. *Mar. Dict.*

PLUG, *v. t.* To stop with a plug; to make tight by stopping a hole.

PLUM, *n.* [Sax. *plume;* G. *pflaume;* Dan. *blomme;* Sw. *plommon;* Corn. *pluman;* Ir. *pluma.*]

1. The fruit of a tree belonging to the genus Prunus. The fruit is a drupe, containing a nut or stone with prominent sutures and inclosing a kernel. The varieties of the plum are numerous and well known.
2. A grape dried in the sun; a raisin.
3. The sum of £100,000 sterling. *London.*
4. A kind of play. *Ainsworth.*

[Dr. Johnson remarks that this word is often written improperly *plumb*. This is true, not only of this word, but of all words in which *b* follows *m*, as in *thumb*, *dumb*, &c.]

PLU'MAGE, *n.* [Fr. from *plume.*] The fethers that cover a fowl.

Smit with her varying *plumage*, spare the dove. *Pope.*

PLUMB, *n.* *plum.* [Fr. *plomb;* Sp. *plomo;* It. *piombo;* W. *plwm;* L. *plumbum*, lead; probably a *clump* or *lump.*]

A mass of lead attached to a line, and used to ascertain a perpendicular position of buildings and the like. But the word as a noun is seldom used, except in composition. [See *Plumb-line.*]

PLUMB, *a.* Perpendicular, that is, standing according to a plumb-line. The post of the house or the wall is *plumb.* [*This is the common language of our mechanics.*]

PLUMB, *adv.* In a perpendicular direction; in a line perpendicular to the plane of the horizon. The wall stands *plumb.*

Plumb down he falls. *Milton.*

2. Directly; suddenly; at once; as a falling mass; usually pronounced *plump.* He fell *plumb* into the water.

PLUMB, *v. t.* To adjust by a plumb-line; to set in a perpendicular direction; as, to *plumb* a building or a wall.

2. [W. *plymiaw.*] To sound with a plummet, as the depth of water. [*Little used.*] *Swift.*

PLUMBAG'INOUS, *a.* Resembling plumbago; consisting of plumbago, or partaking of its properties.

PLUMBA'GO, *n.* [L.] A mineral consisting of carbon and iron; used for pencils, &c.

PLUM'BEAN, } *a.* Consisting of lead; re-
PLUM'BEOUS, } sembling lead. *Ellis.*

2. Dull; heavy; stupid. *J. P. Smith.*

PLUMBED, *pp.* *plum'med.* Adjusted by a plumb-line.

PLUMBER, *n.* *plum'mer.* One who works in lead.

PLUMBERY, *n.* *plum'mery.* Works in lead; manufactures of lead; the place where lead is wrought.

2. The art of casting and working lead, or of making sheets and pipes of lead.

PLUMBIF'EROUS, *a.* [L. *plumbum*, lead, and *fero*, to produce.] Producing lead. *Kirwan.*

PLUMB-LINE, *n.* *plum'-line.* A line perpendicular to the plane of the horizon; or a line directed to the center of gravity in the earth.

PLUM-CAKE, *n.* Cake containing raisins or currants.

PLUME, *n.* [Fr. *plume;* L. Sp. *pluma;* It. *piuma;* W. *plu, pluv.*]

1. The fether of a fowl, particularly a large fether. *Shak.*
2. A fether worn as an ornament, particularly an ostrich's fether.

And his high *plume* that nodded o'er his head. *Dryden.*

3. Pride; towering mien. *Shak.*
4. Token of honor; prize of contest.

Ambitious to win from me some *plume.* *Milton.*

PLUME, } *n.* In *botany*, the ascending
PLU'MULE, } scaly part of the corculum or heart of a seed; the scaly part of the embryo plant within the seed, which rises and becomes the stem or body. It extends itself into the cavity of the lobes, and is terminated by a small branch resembling a fether, from which it derives its name. *Martyn.* *Milne.*

PLUME, *v. t.* To pick and adjust plumes or fethers.

Swans must be kept in some inclosed pond, where they may have room to come on shore and *plume* themselves. *Mortimer.*

2. To strip of fethers. Carnivorous animals will not take pains to *plume* the birds they devour.
3. To strip; to peel. *Bacon.*
4. To set as a plume; to set erect.

His stature reach'd the sky, and on his crest
Sat honor *plum'd.* *Milton.*

5. To adorn with fethers or plumes. *Shak.*
6. To pride; to value; to boast. He *plumes* himself on his skill or his prowess.

PLUME-AL'UM, *n.* A kind of asbestus. *Wilkins.*

PLU'MELESS, *a.* Without fethers or plumes. *Eusden.*

PLUMIG'EROUS, *a.* [L. *pluma*, a fether, and *gero*, to wear.] Fethered; having fethers. *Dict.*

PLU'MIPED, *a.* [infra.] Having feet covered with fethers.

PLU'MIPED, *n.* [L. *pluma*, fether, and *pes*, foot.]

A fowl that has fethers on its feet. *Dict.*

PLUM'MET, *n.* [Sp. *plomada.* See *Plumb.*]

1. A long piece of lead attached to a line, used in sounding the depth of water.
2. An instrument used by carpenters, masons, &c. in adjusting erections to a perpendicular line, and with a square, to determine a horizontal line. It consists of a piece of lead fastened to a line.
3. Any weight. *Wilkins.*
4. A piece of lead used by school boys to rule their paper for writing.

PLUM'MING, *n.* Among miners, the operation of finding by means of a mine dial the place where to sink an air shaft, or to bring an adit to the work, or to find which way the lode inclines. *Encyc.*

PLU'MOSE, } *a.* [L. *plumosus.*] Fethery;
PLU'MOUS, } resembling fethers.

2. In *botany*, a *plumose bristle* is one that has hairs growing on the sides of the main bristle. *Plumose pappus* or down is a flying crown to some seeds, composed of fethery hairs. *Martyn.*

PLUMOS'ITY, *n.* The state of having fethers.

PLUMP, *a.* [Dan. *plomp*, plump, blunt, unhandy, clownish, rude; Sw. *plump;* D. *plomp;* G. *plump.* The primary sense seems to be thick, as if allied to *lump* and *clump.* See the Noun.]

1. Full; swelled with fat or flesh to the full size; fat; having a full skin; round; as a *plump* boy; a *plump* habit of body.

The famish'd crow grows *plump* and round. *Swift.*

2. Full; blunt; unreserved; unqualified; as a *plump* lie.

PLUMP, *n.* A knot; a cluster; a clump; a number of things closely united or standing together; as a *plump* of trees; a *plump* of fowls; a *plump* of horsemen. *Bacon.* *Hayward.* *Dryden.*

[This word is not now used in this sense, but the use of it formerly, is good evidence that *plump* is *clump*, with a different prefix, and both are radically one word with *lump*. *Plumb*, L. *plumbum*, is the same word, a *lump* or mass.]

PLUMP, *v. t.* [from the adjective.] To swell; to extend to fullness; to dilate; to fatten.

The particles of air expanding themselves, *plump* out the sides of the bladder. *Boyle.*

A wedding at our house will *plump* me up with good cheer. [*Colloquial.*] *L'Estrange.*

PLUMP, *v. i.* [from the noun; G. *plumpen*, D. *plompen*, Dan. *plomper*, to plunge.]

1. To plunge or fall like a heavy mass or lump of dead matter; to fall suddenly or at once.

2. To enlarge to fullness; to be swelled. *Ainsworth.*

PLUMP, *adv.* Suddenly; heavily; at once, or with a sudden heavy fall. *B. Jonson.*

PLUMP'ER, *n.* Something carried in the mouth to dilate the cheeks; any thing intended to swell out something else. *Swift.*

2. A full unqualified lie. [*In vulgar use.*]

PLUMP'LY, *adv.* Fully; roundly; without reserve; as, to assert a thing *plumply; a word in common popular use.*

PLUMP'NESS, *n.* Fullness of skin; distention to roundness; as the *plumpness* of a boy; *plumpness* of the eye or cheek. *Newton.*

PLUM-POR'RIDGE, *n.* Porridge with plums. *Addison.*

PLUM-PUD'DING, *n.* Pudding containing raisins or currants.

PLUMP'Y, *a.* Plump; fat; jolly. [*Not elegant.*] *Shak.*

PLUM-TREE, *n.* [Sax. *plum-treow.*] A tree that produces plums.

PLU'MULE, *n.* [L. *plumula.*] The ascending scaly part of the embryo plant, which becomes the stem. [See *Plume.*]

PLU'MY, *a.* [from *plume.*] Fethered; covered with fethers. *Milton.*

2. Adorned with plumes; as a *plumy* crest. *Addison.*

PLUN'DER, *v. t.* [G. *plündern; D. plunderen;* Sw. *plundra;* Dan. *plyndrer.* Qu. the root of *eloign.*]

1. To pillage; to spoil; to strip; to take the goods of an enemy by open force. Nebuchadnezzar *plundered* the temple of the Jews.

2. To take by pillage or open force. The enemy *plundered* all the goods they found. We say, he *plundered* the tent, or he *plundered* the goods of the tent. The first is the proper use of the word.

3. To rob, as a thief; to take from; to strip; as, the thief *plundered* the house; the robber *plundered* a man of his money and watch; pirates *plunder* ships and men.

PLUN'DER, *n.* That which is taken from an enemy by force; pillage; prey; spoil.

2. That which is taken by theft, robbery or fraud.

PLUN'DERED, *pp.* Pillaged; robbed.

PLUN'DERER, *n.* A hostile pillager; a spoiler.

2. A thief; a robber. *Addison.*

PLUN'DERING, *ppr.* Pillaging; robbing.

PLUNǴE, *v. t.* [Fr. *plonger;* Arm. *plungea* or *plugein;* W. *plwng*, a plunge, from the same root as *llwnc* or *llwng*, the gullet, a gulp or swallow; probably connected with *luncheon.*]

1. To thrust into water or other fluid substance, or into any substance that is penetrable; to immerse in a fluid; to drive into flesh, mire or earth, &c.; as, to *plunge* the body in water; to *plunge* the arm into fire or flame; to *plunge* a dagger into the breast. *Milton. Dryden.*

2. To thrust or drive into any state in which the thing is considered as enveloped or surrounded; as, to *plunge* one's self into difficulties or distress; to *plunge* a nation into war.

3. To baptize by immersion.

PLUNǴE, *v. i.* To pitch; to thrust or drive one's self into water or a fluid; to dive or to rush in. He *plunged* into the river. The troops *plunged* into the stream.

His courser *plung'd*,
And threw him off; the waves whelm'd over him. *Dryden.*

2. To fall or rush into distress or any state or circumstances in which the person or thing is enveloped, inclosed or overwhelmed; as, to *plunge* into a gulf; to *plunge* into debt or embarrassments; to *plunge* into war; a body of cavalry *plunged* into the midst of the enemy.

3. To pitch or throw one's self headlong.

PLUNǴE, *n.* The act of thrusting into water or any penetrable substance.

2. Difficulty; strait; distress; a state of being surrounded or overwhelmed with difficulties.

People when put to a *plunge*, cry out to heaven for help. *L'Estrange.*

And wilt thou not reach out a friendly arm,
To raise me from amidst this *plunge* of sorrow? *Addison.*

[*In this sense, the word is now little used.*]

PLUNǴ'ED, *pp.* Thrust into a fluid or other penetrable substance; immersed; involved in straits.

PLUN'ǴEON, *n.* A sea fowl. *Ainsworth.*

PLUNǴ'ER, *n.* One that plunges; a diver.

2. A cylinder used as a forcer in pumps.

PLUNǴ'ING, *ppr.* Immersing; diving; rushing headlong.

PLUNǴ'Y, *a.* Wet. [*Not used.*] *Chaucer.*

PLUNK'ET, *n.* A kind of blue color. *Ainsworth.*

PLU'RAL, *a.* [L. *pluralis*, ftom *plus, pluris*, more.]

1. Containing more than one; consisting of two or more, or designating two or more; as a *plural* word.

2. In *grammar*, the *plural* number is that which designates more than one, that is, any number except one. Thus in most languages, a word in the *plural* number expresses two or more. But the Greek has a *dual* number to express *two;* and the *plural* expresses more than two.

PLU'RALIST, *n.* A clerk or clergyman who holds more ecclesiastical benefices than one, with cure of souls. *Johnson.*

PLURAL'ITY, *n.* [Fr. *pluralité*, from L. *pluralis.*]

1. A number consisting of two or more of the same kind; as a *plurality* of gods; a *plurality* of worlds. *Encyc.*

2. A state of being or having a greater number.

3. In elections, a *plurality of votes* is when one candidate has more votes than any other, but *less than half* of the whole number of votes given. It is thus distinguished from a *majority*, which is *more than half* of the whole number.

4. *Plurality of benefices*, is where the same clerk is possessed of more benefices than one, with cure of souls. In this case, each benefice thus held is called a *plurality.*

PLU'RALLY, *adv.* In a sense implying more than one.

PLŪRILIT'ERAL, *a.* [L. *plus* and *litera*, letter.] Containing more letters than three.

PLŪRILIT'ERAL, *n.* A word consisting of more letters than three.

PLU'RISY, *n.* [L. *plus, pluris.*] Superabundance. [*Not used.*] *Shak.*

PLUS, [L. more,] in *algebra*, a character marked thus, +, used as the sign of addition.

PLUSH, *n.* [G. *plüsch*, shag; D. *pluis*, flock, nap, plush; *pluizen*, to fray, pick, carp, *fleece.* Qu. Fr. *peluche.* The Italian *peluzzo* signifies a little hair or down, from *pelo*, hair, L. *pilus.*]

Shag; a species of shaggy cloth or stuff with a velvet nap on one side, composed regularly of a woof of a single thread and a double warp; the one, wool of two threads twisted, the other of goat's or camel's hair. But some plushes are made wholly of worsted; others wholly of hair. *Encyc.*

PLUSH'ER, *n.* A marine fish. *Carew.*

PLUTO'NIAN, *a.* Plutonic, which see.

PLUTO'NIAN, *n.* One who maintains the origin of mountains, &c. to be from fire. *Journ. of Science.*

The *Plutonian* theory of the formation of rocks and mountains is opposed to the *Neptunian.*

PLUTON'IC, *a.* [from *Pluto*, in mythology, the king of the infernal regions.]

Pertaining to or designating the system of the Plutonists; as the *Plutonic* theory. *Kirwan.*

PLU'TONIST, *n.* One who adopts the theory of the formation of the world in its present state from igneous fusion. *Good.*

PLU'VIAL, PLU'VIOUS, *a.* [L. *pluvialis*, from *pluvia*, rain; Fr. It. *pluviale;* Sp. *pluvial.*]

Rainy; humid. *Brown.*

PLU'VIAL, *n.* [Fr. *pluvial.*] A priest's cope. *Ainsworth.*

PLŪVIAM'ETER, *n.* [L. *pluvia*, rain, and Gr. μετρον, measure.]

A rain gage, an instrument for ascertaining the quantity of water that falls in rain, or in rain and snow, in any particular climate or place.

PLUVIAMET'RICAL, *a.* Pertaining to a pluviameter; made or ascertained by a pluviameter. *Journ. of Science.*

PLȲ, *v. t.* [Fr. *plier*, to bend or fold, formerly written *ployer*, whence *employ;* Arm. *plega*, W. *plygu*, It. *piegare*, Sp. *plegar*, Port. *pregar*, L. *plico*, Gr. πλεκω, to fold; Sax. *pleggan*, to play and to lie on; D. *pleegen*, to use, to exercise; Dan. *plejer*, to exercise, to perform an office, to tend, to nurse; G. *pflegen*, id.; Sw. *plāga.* That these words are from the root of *lie, lay*, is obvious, for in G. *liegen*, to *lie*, signifies also to *ply*, to *apply*. The prefix *p* may be used for the Teutonic *be*; *be-liegen*, to lie close, to bend to. See *Lay* and *Lie*.]

1. To *lay on*, to put to or on with force and repetition; to *apply* to closely, with continuation of efforts or urgency.

And *plies* him with redoubled strokes. *Dryden.*

The hero from afar
Plies him with darts and stones. *Dryden.*

We retain the precise sense in the phrase to *lay on*, to put it on him.

2. To employ with diligence; to apply closely and steadily; to keep busy.

Her gentle wit she *plies*. *Spenser.*

The wearied Trojans *ply* their shattered oars. *Dryden.*

3. To practice or perform with diligence.

Their bloody task, unweari'd, still they *ply*. *Waller.*

4. To urge; to solicit with pressing or persevering importunity.

He *plies* the duke at morning and at night. *Shak.*

5. To urge; to press; to strain; to force.

PLY, *v. i.* To bend; to yield.

The willow *plied* and gave way to the gust. *L'Estrange.*

2. To work steadily.

He was forced to *ply* in the streets. *Spectator.*

3. To go in haste.

Thither he *plies* undaunted. *Milton.*

4. To busy one's self; to be steadily employed. *Dryden.*

5. To endeavor to make way against the wind. *Mar. Dict.*

PLȲ, *n.* A fold; a plait. *Arbuthnot.*

2. Bent; turn; direction; bias.

The late learners cannot so well take the *ply*. *Bacon.*

PLY'ER, *n.* He or that which plies. In fortification, *plyers* denotes a kind of balance used in raising and letting down a drawbridge, consisting of timbers joined in the form of St. Andrew's cross.

PLY'ING, *ppr.* Laying on with steadiness or repetition; applying closely; employing; performing; urging; pressing or attempting to make way against the wind.

PLY'ING, *n.* Urgent solicitation. *Hammond.*

2. Effort to make way against the wind.

PNEUMATIC, PNEUMATICAL, *a.* numat'ic. [Gr. πνευματικος, from πνευμα, breath, spirit; πνεω, to breathe or blow.]

1. Consisting of air, as a thin compressible substance; opposed to *dense* or *solid* substances.

The *pneumatic* substance being, in some bodies, the native spirit of the body. *Bacon.*

2. Pertaining to air, or to the philosophy of its properties; as *pneumatic* experiments; a *pneumatic* engine. *Locke. Encyc.*

3. Moved or played by means of air; as a *pneumatic* instrument of music.

PNEUMAT'ICS, *n.* In *natural philosophy*, that branch which treats of air. In *chimistry*, that branch which treats of the gases.

2. In *the schools*, the doctrine of spiritual substances, as God, angels, and the souls of men. *Dict.*

PNEUMAT'OCELE, *n.* [Gr. πνευμα, air, and κηλη, a tumor.] In *surgery*, a distension of the scrotum by air. *Coxe.*

PNEUMATOLOĠ'ICAL, *a.* Pertaining to pneumatology. *Davy.*

PNEUMATOL'OĠIST, *n.* One versed in pneumatology.

PNEUMATOL'OĠY, *n.* [Gr. πνευμα, air, and λογος, discourse.]

1. The doctrine of the properties of elastic fluids, or of spiritual substances.

2. A treatise on elastic fluids, or on spiritual substances.

PNEUMO'NIA, PNEU'MONY, *n.* [Gr. πνευμων, the lungs, from πνεω, to breathe.] In *medicine*, an inflammation of the lungs.

PNEUMON'IC, *a.* Pertaining to the lungs; pulmonic.

PNEUMON'IC, *n.* A medicine for affections of the lungs. *Coxe.*

PŌACH, *v. t.* [Fr. *pocher*. In Fr. *poche* is a pocket, a bag or purse net; *pocheter des fruits*, to mellow fruit in the pocket; Ir. *boucquaat* is to soften; Sax. *pocca*, a pouch.]

1. To boil slightly. *Johnson.*

2. To dress by boiling slightly and mixing in a soft mass.

3. To begin and not complete. *Bacon.*

4. To tread soft ground, or snow and water, as cattle, whose feet penetrate the soil or soft substance and leave deep tracks. [*New England.*]

5. To steal game; properly, to pocket game, or steal it and convey it away in a bag. *England.*

6. To steal; to plunder by stealth.

They *poach* Parnassus, and lay claim for praise. *Garth.*

PŌACH, *v. t.* [Corn. *pokkia*, to thrust; perhaps Fr. *pocher*. It seems to be allied to Eng. *poke*, *poker*, Norm. *pouchon*, a puncheon. If so, it is from the root of L. *pungo*, Eng. to *punch*; G. *pochen*, to knock.]

To stab; to pierce; to spear; as, to *poach* fish. *England.*

PŌACH, *v. i.* To be trodden with deep tracks, as soft ground. We say, the ground is soft in spring, and *poaches* badly.

Chalky and clay lands burn in hot weather, chap in summer, and *poach* in winter. *Mortimer.*

PŌACHARD, PŌCHARD, *n.* [from *poach*.] A fresh water duck of an excellent taste, weighing a pound and twelve ounces. It is the red headed duck of Lawson; found in America and in the north of Europe. *Pennant.*

PŌACHED, *pp.* Slightly boiled or softened; trodden with deep footsteps; stolen.

PŌACHER, *n.* One that steals game. *More.*

PŌACHINESS, *n.* Wetness and softness; the state of being easily penetrable by the feet of beasts; *applied to land.*

PŌACHY, *a.* Wet and soft; such as the feet of cattle will penetrate to some depth; *applied to land or ground of any kind.*

PŎCK, *n.* [Sax. *poc* or *pocc*; D. *pok*; G. *pocke*; Dan. *pukkel*; W. *pwg*, that swells out; Ir. *bocam*, to swell, coinciding with G. *bauch*, D. *buik*, Dan. *bug*, the belly, Eng. *big*, &c.; probably all of one family.]

A pustule raised on the surface of the body in the variolous and vaccine diseases, named from the pustules, *small pox*, or as it ought to be written, *small pocks*.

POCK'ET, *n.* [Fr. *pochette*, from *poche*, pocket, *pouch*; Sax. *pocca*.]

1. A small bag inserted in a garment for carrying small articles.

2. A small bag or net to receive the balls in billiards.

3. A certain quantity; as a *pocket* of hops, as in other cases we use *sack*. [*Not used in America.*] *Johnson.*

POCK'ET, *v. t.* To put or conceal in the pocket; as, to *pocket* a penknife.

2. To take clandestinely.

To pocket an insult or *affront*, to receive it without resenting it, or at least without seeking redress. [*In popular use.*]

POCK'ET-BOOK, *n.* A small book of paper covered with lether; used for carrying papers in the pocket.

POCK'ET-GLASS, *n.* A portable looking glass.

POCK'ET-HOLE, *n.* The opening into a pocket.

POCK'ET-LID, *n.* The flap over the pocket-hole.

POCK'ET-MŎNEY, *n.* Money for the pocket or for occasional expenses.

POCK'-HOLE, *n.* The pit or scar made by a pock.

POCK'INESS, *n.* The state of being pocky.

POCK'WOOD, *n.* Lignum vitæ, a very hard wood.

POCK'Y, *a.* [from *pock*.] Infected with the small pocks; full of pocks.

2. Vile; rascally; mischievous; contemptible. [*In vulgar use.*]

PO'CULENT, *a.* [L. *poculentus*, from *poculum*, a cup.] Fit for drink. [*Not used.*]

POD, *n.* [In W. *podi* signifies to take in or comprehend; but I know not from what source we have this word.]

The pericarp, capsule or seed vessel of certain plants. The silique or *pod* is an oblong, membranaceous, two valved pericarp, having the seeds fixed along both sutures. A legume is a pericarp of two valves, in which the seeds are fixed along one suture only. *Martyn.*

According to these descriptions, the seed vessels of peas and beans are legumes, and not pods; but in popular language, *pod* is used for the legume as well as for the silique or siliqua. In New England, it is the only word in popular use.

POD, *v. i.* To swell; to fill; also, to produce pods.

PODAG'RIC, PODAG'RICAL, *a.* [L. *podagra*; Gr. ποδαγρα; πους, the foot, and αγρα, a seizure.]

1. Pertaining to the gout; gouty; partaking of the gout.

2. Afflicted with the gout. *Brown.*

POD'DED, *a.* Having its pods formed; furnished with pods.

POD'DER, *n.* A gatherer of pods.

PODĠE, *n.* A puddle; a plash. *Skinner.*

PO'EM, *n.* [L. *poema*; Gr. ποιημα, from ποιεω, to make, to compose songs. In Russ. *poyu* signifies to sing. The radical sense is the same, to strain.]

1. A metrical composition; a composition in which the verses consist of certain measures, whether in blank verse or in rhyme; as the *poems* of Homer or of Milton; opposed to *prose*. *Dryden.*

2. This term is also applied to some compositions in which the language is that of excited imagination; as the *poems* of Ossian.

PO'ESY, *n.* [Fr. *poesie;* L. *poesis:* Gr. ποιησις, from ποιεω, to make.]

1. The art or skill of composing poems; as, the heavenly gift of *poesy.* *Dryden.*

2. Poetry; metrical composition.

Music and *poesy* used to quicken you. *Shak.*

3. A short conceit engraved on a ring or other thing. *Shak.*

PO'ET, *n.* [Fr. *poete;* L. Sp. It. *poeta;* Gr. ποιητης. See *Poem.*]

1. The author of a poem; the inventor or maker of a metrical composition.

A *poet* is a maker, as the word signifies; and he who cannot make, that is, invent, hath his name for nothing. *Dryden.*

2. One skilled in making poetry, or who has a particular genius for metrical composition; one distinguished for poetic talents. Many write verses who cannot be called *poets.*

PO'ETASTER, *n.* A petty poet; a pitiful rhymer or writer of verses. *Roscommon.*

PO'ETESS, *n.* A female poet. *Hall.*

POET'IC, POET'ICAL, *a.* [Gr. ποιητικος; L. *poeticus;* Fr. *poetique.*]

1. Pertaining to poetry; suitable to poetry; as a *poetical* genius; *poetic* turn or talent; *poetic* license.

2. Expressed in poetry or measure; as a *poetical* composition.

3. Possessing the peculiar beauties of poetry; sublime; as a composition or passage highly *poetical.*

POET'ICALLY, *adv.* With the qualities of poetry; by the art of poetry; by fiction. *Dryden.*

POET'ICS, *n.* The doctrine of poetry. *Warton.*

PO'ETIZE, *v. i.* [Fr. *poetiser.*] To write as a poet; to compose verse. *Donne.*

POET-LAUREAT, *n.* A poet employed to compose poems for the birth days of a prince or other special occasion.

POET-MUSI''CIAN, *n.* An appellation given to the bard and lyrist of former ages, as uniting the professions of poetry and music. *Busby.*

PO'ETRESS, *n.* A female poet.

PO'ETRY, *n.* [Gr. ποιητρια.] Metrical composition; verse; as heroic *poetry;* dramatic *poetry;* lyric or Pindaric *poetry.*

2. The art or practice of composing in verse. He excels in *poetry.*

3. Poems; poetical composition. We take pleasure in reading *poetry.*

4. This term is also applied to the language of excited imagination and feeling.

POIGNANCY, *n. poin'ancy.* [See *Poignant.*]

1. Sharpness; the power of stimulating the organs of taste. *Swift.*

2. Point; sharpness; keenness; the power of irritation; asperity; as the *poignancy* of wit or sarcasm.

3. Severity; acuteness.

POIGNANT, *a. poin'ant.* [Fr. *poignant,* participle of *poindre,* from L. *pungere, pungo,* to prick.]

1. Sharp; stimulating the organs of taste; as *poignant* sauce. *Dryden.*

2. Pointed; keen; bitter; irritating; satirical; as *poignant* wit.

3. Severe; piercing; very painful or acute; as *poignant* pain or grief. *Norris. South.*

POIGNANTLY, *adv. poin'antly.* In a stimulating, piercing or irritating manner; with keenness or point.

POINT, *n.* [Fr. from *poinct;* Sp. It. *punto, punta;* W. *pwnc;* from L. *punctum,* from *pungo,* to prick, properly to thrust, pret. *pepugi,* showing that *n* is not radical. Hence it accords with Norm. *pouchon,* a *puncheon,* Fr. *poinçon,* Eng. to *punch,* and with *poke, poker,* Gr. πηγνυω, &c.]

1. The sharp end of any instrument or body; as the *point* of a knife, of a sword or of a thorn.

2. A string with a tag; as a silken *point.* *Shak.*

3. A small cape, headland or promontory; a tract of land extending into the sea, a lake or river, beyond the line of the shore, and becoming narrow at the end; as *point* Judith; Montauk *point.* It is smaller than a cape.

4. The sting of an epigram; a lively turn of thought or expression that strikes with force and agreeable surprise.

With periods, *points* and tropes he slurs his crimes. *Dryden.*

5. An indivisible part of time or space. We say, a *point* of time, a *point* of space. *Locke. Davies.*

6. A small space; as a small *point* of land. *Prior.*

7. Punctilio; nicety; exactness of ceremony; as *points* of precedence.

8. Place near, next or contiguous to; verge; eve. He is on the *point* of departure, or at the *point* of death.

9. Exact place. He left off at the *point* where he began.

10. Degree; state of elevation, depression or extension; as, he has reached an extraordinary *point* of excellence. He has fallen to the lowest *point* of degradation.

11. A character used to mark the divisions of writing, or the pauses to be observed in reading or speaking; as the comma, semicolon, colon and period. The period is called a *full stop,* as it marks the close of a sentence.

12. A spot; a part of a surface divided by spots or lines; as the ace or sise *point.*

13. In *geometry,* that which has neither parts nor magnitude. *Euclid.*

A *point* is that which has position but not magnitude. *Playfair.*

A *point* is a limit terminating a line. *Legendre.*

14. In *music,* a mark or note anciently used to distinguish tones or sounds. Hence, *simple counterpoint* is when a note of the lower part answers exactly to that of the upper, and *figurative counterpoint,* is when a note is syncopated and one of the parts makes several notes or inflections of the voice while the other holds on one. *Encyc.*

15. In *modern music,* a dot placed by a note to raise its value or prolong its time by one half, so as to make a semibreve equal to three minims; a minim equal to three quavers, &c.

16. In *astronomy,* a division of the great circles of the horizon, and of the mariner's compass. The four *cardinal points,* are the east, west, north and south. On the space between two of these points, making a quadrant or quarter of a circle, the compass is marked with subordinate divisions, the whole number being thirty two points.

17. In *astronomy,* a certain place marked in the heavens, or distinguished for its importance in astronomical calculations. The zenith and nadir are called *vertical points;* the nodes are the *points* where the orbits of the planets intersect the plane of the ecliptic; the place where the equator and ecliptic intersect are called *equinoctial points;* the points of the ecliptic at which the departure of the sun from the equator, north and south, is terminated, are called *solstitial points.*

18. In *perspective,* a certain pole or place with regard to the perspective plane. *Encyc.*

19. In *manufactories,* a lace or work wrought by the needle; as *point le Venice, point de Genoa,* &c. Sometimes the word is used for lace woven with bobbins. *Point devise* is used for needle work, or for nice work.

20. The place to which any thing is directed, or the direction in which an object is presented to the eye. We say, in this *point* of view, an object appears to advantage. In this or that *point* of view, the evidence is important.

21. Particular; single thing or subject. In what *point* do we differ? All *points* of controversy between the parties are adjusted. We say, in *point* of antiquity, in *point* of fact, in *point* of excellence. The letter in every *point* is admirable. The treaty is executed in every *point.*

22. Aim; purpose; thing to be reached or accomplished; as, to gain one's *point.*

23. The act of aiming or striking.

What a *point* your falcon made. *Shak.*

24. A single position; a single assertion; a single part of a complicated question or of a whole.

These arguments are not sufficient to prove the *point.*

Strange *point* and new!
Doctrine which we would know whence learned. *Milton.*

25. A note or tune.

Turning your tongue divine
To a loud trumpet, and a *point* of war. *Shak.*

26. In *heraldry,* points are the several different parts of the escutcheon, denoting the local positions of figures. *Encyc.*

27. In *electricity,* the acute termination of a body which facilitates the passage of the fluid to or from the body. *Encyc.*

28. In *gunnery,* point-blank denotes the shot of a gun leveled horizontally. The *point-blank range* is the extent of the apparent right line of a ball discharged. In shooting point-blank, the ball is supposed to move directly to the object, without a curve. Hence adverbially, the word is equivalent to *directly.*

29. In *marine language,* points are flat pieces of braided cordage, tapering from the middle towards each end; used in reefing the courses and top-sails of square-rigged vessels. *Mar. Dict.*

Point de vise, [Fr.] exactly in the point of view. *Shak.*

Vowel-points, in the Hebrew and other eastern languages, are certain marks placed above or below the consonants, or attached to them, as in the Ethiopic, representing the vocal sounds or vowels, which precede or follow the articulations.

The point, the subject; the main question; the precise thing to be considered, determined or accomplished. This argument may be true, but it is not to *the point*.

POINT, *v. t.* To sharpen; to cut, forge, grind or file to an acute end; as, to *point* a dart or a pin; also, to taper, as a rope.

2. To direct towards an object or place, to show its position, or excite attention to it; as, to *point* the finger at an object; to *point* the finger of scorn at one. *Shak.*

3. To direct the eye or notice.

Whosoever should be guided through his battles by Minerva, and *pointed* to every scene of them, would see nothing but subjects of surprise. *Pope.*

4. To aim; to direct towards an object; as, to *point* a musket at a wolf; to *point* a cannon at a gate.

5. To mark with characters for the purpose of distinguishing the members of a sentence, and designating the pauses; as, to *point* a written composition.

6. To mark with vowel-points.

7. To appoint. [*Not in use.*] *Spenser.*

8. To fill the joints of with mortar, and smooth them with the point of a trowel; as, to *point* a wall.

To point out, to show by the finger or by other means.

To point a sail, to affix points through the eyelet-holes of the reefs.

POINT, *v. i.* To direct the finger for designating an object, and exciting attention to it; with *at*.

Now must the world *point at* poor Catherine. *Shak.*

Point at the tatter'd coat and ragged shoe. *Dryden.*

2. To indicate, as dogs do to sportsmen.

He treads with caution, and he *points* with fear. *Gay.*

3. To show distinctly by any means.

To *point* at what time the balance of power was most equally held between the lords and commons at Rome, would perhaps admit a controversy. *Swift.*

4. To fill the joints or crevices of a wall with mortar.

5. In *the rigging of a ship*, to taper the end of a rope or splice, and work over the reduced part a small close netting, with an even number of knittles twisted from the same. *Cyc.*

To point at, to treat with scorn or contempt by pointing or directing attention to.

POINT'AL, *n.* In *botany*, the pistil of a plant: an organ or viscus adhering to the fruit for the reception of the pollen. Its appearance is that of a column or set of columns in the center of the flower. *Martyn.*

POINT'ED, *pp.* Sharpened; formed to a point; directed; aimed.

2. Aimed at a particular person or transaction.

3. *a.* Sharp; having a sharp point; as a *pointed* rock.

4. Epigrammatical; abounding in conceits or lively turns; as *pointed* wit. *Pope.*

POINT'EDLY, *adv.* In a pointed manner; with lively turns of thought or expression.

He often wrote too *pointedly* for his subject. *Dryden.*

2. With direct assertion; with direct reference to a subject; with explicitness; as, he declared *pointedly* he would accede to the proposition.

POINT'EDNESS, *n.* Sharpness; pickedness with asperity. *Johnson.*

2. Epigrammatical keenness or smartness.

In this you excel Horace, that you add *pointedness* of thought. *Dryden.*

POINT'EL, *n.* Something on a point.

These poises or *pointels* are, for the most part, little balls set at the top of a slender stalk, which they can move every way at pleasure. *Derham.*

2. A kind of pencil or style. *Wickliffe.*

POINT'ER, *n.* Any thing that points.

2. The hand of a time-piece. *Watts.*

3. A dog that points out the game to sportsmen. *Gay.*

POINT'ING, *ppr.* Directing the finger; showing; directing.

2. Marking with points; as a writing.

3. Filling the joints and crevices of a wall with mortar or cement.

POINT'ING, *n.* The art of making the divisions of a writing; punctuation.

2. The state of being pointed with marks or points.

POINT'ING-STOCK, *n.* An object of ridicule or scorn. *Shak.*

POINT'LESS, *a.* Having no point; blunt; obtuse; as a *pointless* sword.

2. Having no smartness or keenness.

POISE, *n. poiz.* [W. *pwys*, weight; Arm. *poes*; Fr. *poids*. See the Verb.]

1. Weight; gravity; that which causes a body to descend or tend to the center. *Spenser.*

2. The weight or mass of metal used in weighing with steelyards, to balance the substance weighed.

3. Balance; equilibrium; a state in which things are balanced by equal weight or power; equipoise. The mind may rest in a *poise* between two opinions.

The particles forming the earth, must convene from all quarters towards the middle, which would make the whole compound rest in a *poise*. *Bentley.*

4. A regulating power; that which balances.

Men of an unbounded imagination often want the *poise* of judgment. *Dryden.*

POISE, *v. t. poiz.* [W. *pwysaw*, to throw down, to press, to lean or incline, to weigh; Arm. *poesa*; It. *pesare*; Sp. Port. *pesar*; Corn. *puza*; Fr. *peser.*]

1. To balance in weight; to make of equal weight; as, to *poise* the scales of a balance.

2. To hold or place in equilibrium or equiponderance.

Our nation with united interest blest,
Not now content to *poise*, shall sway the rest. *Dryden.*

3. To load with weight for balancing.

Where could they find another form so fit,
To *poise* with solid sense a sprightly wit? *Dryden.*

4. To examine or ascertain, as by the balance; to weigh.

He cannot consider the strength, *poise* the weight, and discern the evidence of the clearest argumentations, where they would conclude against his desires. *South.*

5. To oppress; to weigh down.

Lest leaden slumber *poise* me down to-morrow,
When I should mount on wings of victory. *Shak.*

POIS'ED, *pp.* Balanced; made equal in weight; resting in equilibrium.

POIS'ING, *ppr.* Balancing.

POISON, *n. poiz'n.* [Fr. *poison*; Arm. *empoesoun, pouison*; Sp. *ponzoña*; Port. *peçonha*. Qu. its alliance to L. *pus*. See Class Bs. No. 25.]

1. A substance which, when taken into the stomach, mixed with the blood or applied to the skin or flesh, proves fatal or deleterious by an action not mechanical; venom. The more active and virulent poisons destroy life in a short time; others are slow in their operation, others produce inflammation without proving fatal. In the application of poison, much depends on the quantity.

2. Any thing infectious, malignant, or noxious to health; as the *poison* of pestilential diseases.

3. That which taints or destroys moral purity or health; as the *poison* of evil example; the *poison* of sin. *South.*

POIS'ON, *v. t.* To infect with any thing fatal to life; as, to *poison* an arrow.

2. To attack, injure or kill by poison.

He was so discouraged that he *poisoned* himself and died. 2 Macc.

3. To taint; to mar; to impair; as, discontent *poisons* the happiness of life.

Hast thou not
With thy false arts *poison'd* his people's loyalty? *Rowe.*

4. To corrupt. Our youth are *poisoned* with false notions of honor, or with pernicious maxims of government.

To suffer the thoughts to be vitiated, is to *poison* the fountains of morality. *Rambler.*

POIS'ONED, *pp.* Infected or destroyed by poison.

POIS'ONER, *n.* One who poisons or corrupts; that which corrupts.

POIS'ONING, *ppr.* Infecting with poison; corrupting.

POIS'ONOUS, *a.* Venomous; having the qualities of poison; corrupting; impairing soundness or purity.

POIS'ONOUSLY, *adv.* With fatal or injurious effects; venomously.

POIS'ONOUSNESS, *n.* The quality of being fatal or injurious to health and soundness; venomousness.

POIS'ON-TREE, *n.* A tree that poisons the flesh. This name is given to a species of Rhus or sumac, the *Rhus vernix* or *poison ash*, a native of America; also to the *bohun upas* of Java. *Encyc.*

POI'TREL, *n.* [Fr. *poitrail*, from L. *pectorale*, from *pectus*, the breast.]

1. Armor for the breast. *Skinner.*

2. A graving tool. [Qu. *pointel.*] *Ainsworth.*

POIZE, a common spelling of *poise*. [See *Poise.*]

POKE, *n.* [Sax. *pocca*, *poha*; Fr. *poche*, a pouch or bag.]

A pocket; a small bag; as a pig in a *poke*. *Camden. Spectator.*

POKE, PO'KE-WEED, } *n.* The popular name of a plant of the genus Phytolacca, otherwise called *cocum* and *garget*; a native of N. America. As a medicine, it has emetic and cathartic qualities, and has had some reputation as a remedy for rheumatism. It was formerly called in Virginia, *pocan*. *Bigelow.*

POKE, *v. t.* [Corn. *pokkia*, to thrust or push. In Armoric, *pochan* is one that dives or plunges.]

1. Properly, to thrust; hence, to feel or search for with a long instrument. *Brown.*

2. To thrust at with the horns, as an ox; *a popular use of the word in New England.* And intransitively, to *poke at*, is to thrust the horns at.

POKE, *n.* In *New England*, a machine to prevent unruly beasts from leaping fences, consisting of a yoke with a pole inserted, pointing forward.

POKE, *v. t.* To put a poke on; as, to *poke* an ox. *New England.*

PO'KER, *n.* [from *poke.*] An iron bar used in stirring the fire when coal is used for fuel. *Swift.*

PO'KER, *n.* [Dan. *pokker*, the duse; W. *pwca*, a hobgoblin; *bwg*, id.; *bwgan*, a bugbear; *bw*, terror, fright. These words seem to be allied to *buw*, *buwc*, an ox or cow, L. *bos*, *bovis*, and all perhaps from the bellowing of bulls.]

Any frightful object, especially in the dark; a bugbear; a word in common popular use in America.

PO'KING, *ppr.* Feeling in the dark; stirring with a poker; thrusting at with the horns; putting a poke on.

PO'KING, *a.* Drudging; servile. [*Colloquial.*] *Gray.*

PO'KING-STICK, *n.* An instrument formerly used in adjusting the plaits of ruffs then worn. *Middleton. Shak.*

POLA'CRE, *n.* [Sp. *id.*; Port. *polaca*, *polhacra*; Fr. *polacre*, *polaque.*]

A vessel with three masts, used in the Mediterranean. The masts are usually of one piece, so that they have neither tops, caps nor cross-trees, nor horses to their upper yards. *Mar. Dict. Encyc.*

PO'LAR, *a.* [Fr. *polaire*; It. *polare*; Sp. *polar.* See *Pole.*]

1. Pertaining to the poles of the earth, north or south, or to the poles of artificial globes; situated near one of the poles; as *polar* regions; *polar* seas; *polar* ice or climates.

2. Proceeding from one of the regions near the poles; as *polar* winds.

3. Pertaining to the magnetic pole, or to the point to which the magnetic needle is directed.

POLAR'ITY, *n.* That quality of a body in virtue of which peculiar properties reside in certain points; usually, as in electrified or magnetized bodies, properties of attraction or repulsion, or the power of taking a certain direction. Thus we speak of the polarity of the magnet or magnetic needle, whose *pole* is not always that of the earth, but a point somewhat easterly or westerly; and the deviation of the needle from a north and south line is called its variation. A mineral is said to possess *polarity*, when it attracts one pole of a magnetic needle and repels the other.

POLARIZA'TION, *n.* The act of giving polarity to a body.

Polarization of light, a change produced upon light by the action of certain media, by which it exhibits the appearance of having *polarity*, or poles possessing different properties. This property of light was first discovered by Huygens in his investigation of the cause of double refraction. as seen in the Iceland crystal. The attention of opticians was more particularly directed towards it by the discoveries of Malus, in 1810. The knowledge of this singular property of light, has afforded an explanation of several very intricate phenomena in optics.

PO'LARIZE, *v. t.* To communicate polarity to.

PO'LARIZED, *pp.* Having polarity communicated to.

PO'LARIZING, *ppr.* Giving polarity to.

PO'LARY, *a.* [See *Polar.*] Tending to a pole; having a direction to a pole. *Brown.*

POLE, *n.* [Sax. *pol*, *pal*; G. *pfahl*; D. *paal*; Sw. *påle*; Dan. *pæl*; W. *pawl*; L. *palus.* See *Pale.*]

1. A long slender piece of wood, or the stem of a small tree deprived of its branches. Thus seamen use *poles* for setting or driving boats in shallow water; the stems of small trees are used for hoops and called *hoop-poles*; the stems of small, but tall straight trees, are used as *poles* for supporting the scaffolding in building.

2. A rod; a perch; a measure of length of five yards and a half.

[In New England, *rod* is generally used.]

3. An instrument for measuring. *Bacon.*

Bare poles. A ship is under *bare poles*, when her sails are all furled. *Mar. Dict.*

POLE, *n.* [Fr. *pole*; It. Sp. *polo*; G. Dan. Sw. *pol*; D. *pool*; L. *polus*; Gr. πολος, from πολεω, to turn.]

1. In *astronomy*, one of the extremities of the axis on which the sphere revolves. These two points are called the *poles* of the world.

2. In *spherics*, a point equally distant from every part of the circumference of a great circle of the sphere; or it is a point 90° distant from the plane of a circle, and in a line passing perpendicularly through the center, called the axis. Thus the zenith and nadir are the *poles* of the horizon.

3. In *geography*, the extremity of the earth's axis, or one of the points on the surface of our globe through which the axis passes.

4. The star which is vertical to the pole of the earth; the *pole*-star.

Poles of the ecliptic, are two points on the surface of the sphere, 23° 30′ distant from the poles of the world.

Magnetic poles, two points in a lodestone, corresponding to the poles of the world; the one pointing to the north, the other to the south.

POLE, *n.* [from *Poland.*] A native of Poland.

POLE, *v. t.* To furnish with poles for support; as, to *pole* beans.

2. To bear or convey on poles; as, to *pole* hay into a barn.

3. To impel by poles, as a boat; to push forward by the use of poles.

PO'LE-AX, PO'LE-AXE, } *n.* An ax fixed to a pole or handle; or rather a sort of hatchet with a handle about fifteen inches in length, and a point or claw bending downward from the back of its head. It is principally used in actions at sea, to cut away the rigging of the enemy attempting to board; sometimes it is thrust into the side of a ship to assist in mounting the enemy's ship, and it is sometimes called a *boarding-ax*. *Mar. Dict. Encyc.*

PO'LECAT, *n.* [Qu. foul cat, or Gr. φαυλος.] A quadruped of the genus Mustela; the fitchew or fitchet. *Encyc.*

PO'LE-DAVY, *n.* A sort of coarse cloth. *Ainsworth.*

POL'EMARCH, *n.* [Gr. πολεμαρχος; πολεμος, war, and αρχη, rule, or αρχος, chief.]

1. Anciently, a magistrate of Athens and Thebes, who had under his care all strangers and sojourners in the city, and all children of parents who had lost their lives in the service of their country. *Encyc. Mitford.*

2. A military officer in Lacedæmon.

POLEM'IC, POLEM'ICAL, } *a.* [Gr. πολεμικος, from πολεμος, war.]

1. Controversial; disputative; intended to maintain an opinion or system in opposition to others; as a *polemic* treatise, discourse, essay or book; *polemic* divinity.

2. Engaged in supporting an opinion or system by controversy; as a *polemic* writer. *South.*

POLEM'IC, *n.* A disputant; a controvertist; one who writes in support of an opinion or system in opposition to another. *Pope.*

POLEM'OSCOPE, *n.* [Gr. πολεμος, war, and σκοπεω, to view.]

An oblique perspective glass contrived for seeing objects that do not lie directly before the eye. It consists of a concave glass placed near a plane mirror in the end of a short round tube, and a convex glass in a hole in the side of the tube. It is called *opera-glass*, or *diagonal opera-glass*. *Encyc.*

PO'LE-STAR, *n.* A star which is vertical, or nearly so, to the pole of the earth; a lodestar. The northern pole-star is of great use to navigators in the northern hemisphere.

2. That which serves as a guide or director. *Burton.*

PO'LEY-GRASS, *n.* A plant of the genus Lythrum. *Fam. of Plants.*

PO'LEY-MOUNTAIN, *n.* A plant of the genus Teucrium. *Ib.*

POLI'CE, *n.* [Fr. from L. *politia*; Gr. πολιτεια, from πολις, city.]

1. The government of a city or town; the administration of the laws and regulations of a city or incorporated town or borough; as the *police* of London, of New York or Boston. The word is applied also to the government of all towns in New England which are made corporations by a general statute, for certain purposes.

2. The internal regulation and government of a kingdom or state. *Blackstone.*

3. The corporation or body of men governing a city. *Jamieson.*

4. In Scottish, the pleasure-ground about a gentleman's seat.

POL'ICED, *a.* Regulated by laws; furnished with a regular system of laws and administration. *Bacon.*

POLĬCE-OFFICER, *n.* An officer entrusted with the execution of the laws of a city.

POL'ICY, *n.* [Fr. *police;* L. *politia;* Gr. πολιτεια, from πολις, city, Sans. *palya.*]

1. *Policy,* in its primary signification, is the same as *polity,* comprehending the fundamental constitution or frame of civil government in a state or kingdom. But by usage, *policy* is now more generally used to denote what is included under *legislation* and *administration,* and may be defined, the art or manner of governing a nation; or that system of measures which the sovereign of a country adopts and pursues, as best adapted to the interests of the nation. Thus we speak of *domestic policy,* or the system of internal regulations in a nation; *foreign policy,* or the measures which respect foreign nations; *commercial policy,* or the measures which respect commerce.

2. Art, prudence, wisdom or dexterity in the management of public affairs; *applied to persons governing.* It has been the *policy* of France to preclude females from the throne. It has been the *policy* of Great Britain to encourage her navy, by keeping her carrying trade in her own hands. In this she manifests sound *policy.* Formerly, England permitted wool to be exported and manufactured in the Low Countries, which was very bad *policy.*

> The *policy* of all laws has made some forms necessary in the wording of last wills and testaments. *Blackstone.*

> All violent *policy* defeats itself. *Hamilton.*

3. In *common usage,* the art, prudence or wisdom of individuals in the management of their private or social concerns.

4. Stratagem; cunning; dexterity of management.

5. A ticket or warrant for money in the public funds. [It. *polizza.*]

6. [Sp. *poliza.*] *Policy,* in commerce, the writing or instrument by which a contract of indemnity is effected between the insurer and the insured; or the instrument containing the terms or conditions on which a person or company undertakes to indemnify another person or company against losses of property exposed to peculiar hazards, as houses or goods exposed to fire, or ships and goods exposed to destruction on the high seas. This writing is subscribed by the insurer, who is called the underwriter. The terms *policy of insurance,* or *assurance,* are also used for the contract between the insured and the underwriter.

Policies are *valued* or *open; valued,* when the property or goods insured are valued at prime cost; *open,* when the goods are not valued, but if lost, their value must be proved. *Park. Blackstone.*

Wagering policies, which insure sums of money, interest or no interest, are illegal.

> All insurances, interest or no interest, or without further proof of interest than the *policy* itself, are null and void. *Blackstone.*

The word *policy* is used also for the writing which insures against other events, as well as against loss of property.

PO'LING, *n.* In *gardening,* the operation of dispersing the worm-casts all over the walks, with long ash poles. This destroys the worm-casts and is beneficial to the walks. *Cyc.*

PO'LING, *ppr.* Furnishing with poles for support.

2. Bearing on poles.

3. Pushing forward with poles, as a boat.

PO'LISH, *a.* [from Slav. *pole,* a plain, whence *Poland.* See the Verb.]

Pertaining to Poland, a level country on the south of Russia and the Baltic.

POL'ISH, *v. t.* [Fr. *polir, polissant;* Arm. *pouliçza;* It. *polire* or *pulire;* Sp. *polir, pulir;* L. *polio;* Dan. *polerer;* Sw. *polera;* Russ. *poliruyu;* W. *caboli,* with a prefix; Ar. خفل chafala, to polish. Qu. its alliance to *file.*]

1. To make smooth and glossy, usually by friction; as, to *polish* glass, marble, metals and the like.

2. To refine; to wear off rudeness, rusticity and coarseness; to make elegant and polite; as, to *polish* life or manners. *Milton.*

> The Greeks were *polished* by the Asiatics and Egyptians. *S. S. Smith.*

POL'ISH, *v. i.* To become smooth; to receive a gloss; to take a smooth and glossy surface.

> Steel will *polish* almost as white and bright as silver. *Bacon.*

POL'ISH, *n.* A smooth glossy surface produced by friction.

> Another prism of clearer glass and better *polish* seemed free from veins. *Newton.*

2. Refinement; elegance of manners.

> What are these wond'rous civilizing arts,
> This Roman *polish?* *Addison.*

POL'ISHABLE, *a.* Capable of being polished.

POL'ISHED, *pp.* Made smooth and glossy; refined.

POL'ISHER, *n.* The person or instrument that polishes. *Addison.*

POL'ISHING, *ppr.* Making smooth and glossy; refining.

POL'ISHING, *n.* Smoothness; glossiness; refinement. *Goldsmith.*

POLI'TE, *a.* [L. *politus,* polished, from *polio,* supra.]

1. Literally, smooth, glossy, and used in this sense till within a century.

> Rays of light falling on a *polite* surface. *Newton.*

[This application of the word is, I believe, entirely obsolete.]

2. Being polished or elegant in manners; refined in behavior; well bred.

> He marries, bows at court and grows *polite.* *Pope.*

3. Courteous; complaisant; obliging.

> His manners were warm without insincerity, and *polite* without pomp. t.

POLI'TELY, *adv.* With elegance of manners; genteelly; courteously.

POLI'TENESS, *n.* Polish or elegance of manners; gentility; good breeding; ease and gracefulness of manners, united with a desire to please others and a careful attention to their wants and wishes.

2. Courteousness; complaisance; obliging attentions.

POL'ITIC, *a.* [L. *politicus;* Gr. πολιτικος, from πολιτεια, from πολις, a city. This word in its origin is the same as *political,* and was formerly used as synonymous with it. It is so still in the phrase, *body politic.* Burke used *politic* distinction for *political* distinction, but present usage does not warrant this application.]

1. Wise; prudent and sagacious in devising and pursuing measures adapted to promote the public welfare; *applied to persons;* as a *politic* prince.

2. Well devised and adapted to the public prosperity; *applied to things.*

> This land was famously enriched
> With *politic* grave counsel. *Shak.*

3. Ingenious in devising and pursuing any scheme of personal or national aggrandizement, without regard to the morality of the measure; cunning; artful; sagacious in adapting means to the end, whether good or evil.

> I have been *politic* with my friend, smooth with my enemy. *Shak. Pope.*

4. Well devised; adapted to its end, right or wrong.

POLIT'ICAL, *a.* [supra.] Pertaining to policy, or to civil government and its administration. *Political* measures or affairs are measures that respect the government of a nation or state. So we say, *political* power or authority; *political* wisdom; a *political* scheme; *political* opinions. A good prince is the *political* father of his people. The founders of a state and wise senators are also called *political* fathers.

2. Pertaining to a nation or state, or to nations or states, as distinguished from *civil* or *municipal;* as in the phrase, *political* and *civil* rights, the former comprehending rights that belong to a nation, or perhaps to a citizen as an individual of a nation; and the latter comprehending the local rights of a corporation or any member of it.

> Speaking of the *political* state of Europe, we are accustomed to say of Sweden, she lost her liberty by the revolution. *Paley.*

3. Public; derived from office or connection with government; as *political* character.

4. Artful; skillful. [See *Politic.*]

5. Treating of politics or government; as a *political* writer. *Paley.*

Political arithmetic, the art of reasoning by figures, or of making arithmetical calculations on matters relating to a nation, its revenues, value of lands and effects, produce of lands or manufactures, population, &c.

Political economy, the administration of the revenues of a nation; or the management and regulation of its resources and productive property and labor. Political economy comprehends all the measures by which the property and labor of citizens are directed in the best manner to the success of individual industry and enterprise, and to the public prosperity. Political economy is now considered as a *science.*

POLIT'ICALLY, *adv.* With relation to the government of a nation or state.

2. Artfully; with address. *Obs. Knolles.*

POLIT'ICASTER, *n.* A petty politician; a pretender to politics. *L'Estrange.*

POLITI′′CIAN, *a.* Cunning; using artifice. *Obs.*

POLITI′′CIAN, *n.* [Fr. *politicien.*] One versed in the science of government and the art of governing; one skilled in politics. *Dryden. Pope.*

2. A man of artifice or deep contrivance. *South.*

POL′ITICS, *n.* [Fr. *politique ;* Gr. πολιτικη. See *Policy.*]

The science of government; that part of ethics which consists in the regulation and government of a nation or state, for the preservation of its safety, peace and prosperity; comprehending the defense of its existence and rights against foreign control or conquest, the augmentation of its strength and resources, and the protection of its citizens in their rights, with the preservation and improvement of their morals. *Politics*, as a science or an art, is a subject of vast extent and importance.

POL′ITIZE, *v. i.* To play the politician. [*Not in use.*] *Milton.*

POL′ITURE, *n.* [See *Polish.*] Polish; the gloss given by polishing. [*Not used.*] *Donne.*

POL′ITY, *n.* [Gr. πολιτεια.] The form or constitution of civil government of a nation or state; and in free states, the frame or fundamental system by which the several branches of government are established, and the powers and duties of each designated and defined.

Every branch of our civil *polity* supports and is supported, regulates and is regulated by the rest. *Blackstone.*

With respect to their interior *polity*, our colonies are properly of three sorts; provincial establishments, proprietary governments, and charter governments. *Blackstone.*

The word seems also to embrace legislation and administration of government.

2. The constitution or general fundamental principles of government of any class of citizens, considered in an appropriate character, or as a subordinate state.

Were the whole christian world to revert back to the original model, how far more simple, uniform and beautiful would the church appear, and how far more agreeable to the ecclesiastical *polity* instituted by the holy apostles. *President Stiles.*

PŌLL, *n.* [D. *bol*, a ball, bowl, crown, poll, pate, bulb.]

1. The head of a person, or the back part of the head, and in composition, applied to the head of a beast, as in *poll-evil.*

2. A register of heads, that is, of persons. *Shak.*

3. The entry of the names of electors who vote for civil officers. Hence,

4. An election of civil officers, or the place of election.

Our citizens say, at the opening or close of the *poll*, that is, at the beginning of the register of voters and reception of votes, or the close of the same. They say also, we are going to the *poll;* many voters appeared at the *poll.* *New York.*

5. A fish called a chub or chevin. [See *Pollard.*]

PŌLL, *v. t.* To lop the tops of trees. *Bacon.*

2. To clip; to cut off the ends; to cut off hair or wool; to shear. The phrases, to *poll the hair*, and to *poll the head*, have been used. The latter is used in 2 Sam. xiv. 26. To *poll a deed*, is a phrase still used in law language. *Z. Swift.*

3. To mow; to crop. [*Not used.*] *Shak.*

4. To peel; to strip; to plunder. *Obs.* *Bacon. Spenser.*

5. To take a list or register of persons; to enter names in a list.

6. To enter one's name in a list or register. *Dryden.*

7. To insert into a number as a voter. *Tickel.*

POL′LARD, *n.* [from *poll.*] A tree lopped. *Bacon.*

2. A clipped coin. *Camden.*

3. The chub fish. *Ainsworth.*

4. A stag that has cast his horns.

5. A mixture of bran and meal. *Ainsworth.*

POL′LARD, *v. t.* To lop the tops of trees; to poll. *Evelyn.*

POL′LEN, *n.* [L. *pollen, pollis*, fine flour; Russ. *pil, piel*, dust, L. *pulvis.*]

1. The fecundating dust or fine substance like flour or meal, contained in the anther of flowers, which is dispersed on the pistil for impregnation; farin or farina. *Encyc. Milne. Martyn.*

2. Fine bran. *Bailey.*

POL′LENGER, *n.* Brushwood. *Obs.* *Tusser.*

POL′LENIN, *n.* [from *pollen.*] A substance prepared from the pollen of tulips, highly inflammable, and insoluble in agents which dissolve other vegetable products. Exposed to the air, it soon undergoes putrefaction. *Webster's Manual.*

PŌLLER, *n.* [from *poll.*] One that shaves persons; a barber. [*Not used.*]

2. One that lops or polls trees.

3. A pillager; a plunderer; one that fleeces by exaction. [*Not used.*] *Bacon.*

4. One that registers voters, or one that enters his name as a voter.

PŌLL-EVIL, *n.* [*poll* and *evil.*] A swelling or impostem on a horse's head, or on the nape of the neck between the ears. *Far. Dict.*

POLLICITA′TION, *n.* [L. *pollicitatio.*] A promise; a voluntary engagement, or a paper containing it. *Henry's Britain.*

POLLINC′TOR, *n.* [L.] One that prepares materials for embalming the dead; a kind of undertaker. *Greenhill.*

POLLINIF′EROUS, *a.* [L. *pollen* and *fero*, to produce.] Producing pollen.

POL′LOCK, } *n.* A fish, a species of Gadus
POL′LACK, } or cod.

POLLU′TE, *v. t.* [L. *polluo ;* Fr. *polluer.* If this word is compound, as I suspect, it seems to be composed of the preposition *po*, which is in the Russian language and retained in the L. *polluceo* and *possideo*, and according to Ainsworth, of *lavo.* But this combination would not naturally give the signification. If the word is simple, the first syllable coincides with *foul.* But neither is this etymology satisfactory.]

1. To defile; to make foul or unclean; in a general sense. But appropriately, among the Jews, to make unclean or impure, in a legal or ceremonial sense, so as to disqualify a person for sacred services, or to render things unfit for sacred uses. Num. xviii. Ex. xx. 2 Kings xxiii. 2 Chron. xxxvi.

2. To taint with guilt.

Ye *pollute* yourselves with all your idols. Ezek. xx.

3. To profane; to use for carnal or idolatrous purposes.

My sabbaths they greatly *polluted.* Ezek. xx.

4. To corrupt or impair by mixture of ill, moral or physical.

Envy you my praise, and would destroy
With grief my pleasures, and *pollute* my joy? *Dryden.*

5. To violate by illegal sexual commerce.

POLLU′TE, *a.* Polluted; defiled. *Milton.*

PLLLU′TED, *pp.* Defiled; rendered unclean; tainted with guilt; impaired; profaned.

POLLU′TEDNESS, *n.* The state of being polluted; defilement.

POLLU′TER, *n.* A defiler; one that pollutes or profanes.

POLLU′TING, *ppr.* Defiling; rendering unclean; corrupting; profaning.

POLLU′TION, *n.* [L. *pollutio ;* Fr. *pollution ;* Sp. *polucion ;* It. *polluzione.*]

1. The act of polluting.

2. Defilement; uncleanness; impurity; the state of being polluted.

3. In *the Jewish economy*, legal or ceremonial uncleanness, which disqualified a person for sacred services or for common intercourse with the people, or rendered any thing unfit for sacred use.

4. In *medicine*, the involuntary emission of semen in sleep.

5. In *a religious sense*, guilt, the effect of sin; idolatry, &c.

POL′LUX, *n.* A fixed star of the second magnitude, in the constellation Gemini or the Twins. *Encyc.*

2. [See *Castor.*]

POLONA′ISE, } *n.* A robe or dress adopt-
POLONE′SE, } ed from the fashion of the Poles; sometimes worn by ladies.

POLONE′SE, *n.* The Polish language. *Encyc.*

POLONOISE, *n.* In *music*, a movement of three crotchets in a bar, with the rhythmical cesure on the last. *Busby.*

PŌLT, *n.* [Sw. *bulta*, to beat.] A blow, stroke or striking; *a word in common popular use in N. England.*

PŌLT-FOOT, *n.* A distorted foot. [*Not in use.*] *Herbert.*

PŌLT-FOOT, } *a.* Having distorted feet.
PŌLT-FOOTED, } [*Not in use.*] *B. Jonson.*

POLTROON′, *n.* [Fr. *poltron ;* It. *poltrone*, an idle fellow, a coward; *poltrire*, to sleep, to be idle, to loiter; Sp. *poltron*, idle, lazy, easy, commodious; Port. *poltram*, an idler; *poltram, poltrona*, lazy, cowardly; Arm. *poultroun ;* certainly not from *pollice truncato.* The primary sense is idle, at ease, whence lazy; perhaps from the root of *fail*, W. *pallu.*]

An arrant coward; a dastard; a wretch without spirit or courage. *Dryden.*

POLTROON′ERY, *n.* Cowardice; baseness of mind; want of spirit.

POL′VERIN, } *n.* [L. *pulvis*, dust; It. *pol-*
POL′VERINE, } *verino.*] The calcined ashes of a plant, of the nature of pot and pearl ashes, brought from the Levant and Syria. In the manufacture of glass, it is preferred to other ashes, as the glass made with it is perfectly white. *Encyc.*

POLY, POLEY, n. [L. *polium*; Gr. πολιον, from πολιος, white.] A plant. The *poley grass* is of the genus Lythrum.

POLY, in compound words, is from the Greek πολυς, and signifies *many*; as in *polygon*, a figure of many angles.

POLYACOUS'TIC, a. [Gr. πολυς, many, and ακουω, to hear.]
That multiplies or magnifies sound; as a noun, an instrument to multiply sounds.

POL'YADELPH, n. [Gr. πολυς, many, and αδελφος, brother.]
In *botany*, a plant having its stamens united in three or more bodies or bundles by the filaments.

POLYADELPH'IAN, a. Having its stamens united in three or more bundles.

POLYAN'DER, n. [Gr. πολυς, many, and ανηρ, a male.]
In *botany*, a plant having many stamens, or any number above twenty, inserted in the receptacle.

POLYAN'DRIAN, a. Having many stamens, that is, any number above twenty, inserted in the receptacle.

POLYAN'DRY, n. [supra.] The practice of females' having more husbands than one at the same time; plurality of husbands. *Forster's Obs.*

POL'YANTH, POLYANTH'OS, n. [Gr. πολυς, many, and ανθος, a flower.] A plant of the genus Primula or primrose, whose flower stalks produce flowers in clusters. *Encyc.*

POLYAUTOG'RAPHY, n. [Gr. πολυς, many, αυτος, he himself, and γραφω, to write.]
The act or practice of multiplying copies of one's own handwriting or of manuscripts, by engraving on stone; a species of lithography. *Delasteyrie. Med. Repos.*

POL'YCHORD, a. [Gr. πολυς, many, and *chord.*]
Having many chords or strings. *Ch. Relig. Appeal.*

POL'YCHREST, n. [Gr. πολυς, many, and χρησος, useful.]
In *pharmacy*, a medicine that serves for many uses, or that cures many diseases. *Obs.*

POL'YCHROITE, n. [Gr. πολυς, many, and χροιζω, to color.] The coloring matter of saffron. *Ure.*

POLYCOTYL'EDON, n. [Gr. πολυς, many, and κοτυληδων, a cavity.]
In *botany*, a plant that has many or more than two cotyledons or lobes to the seed. *Martyn.*

POLYCOTYLED'ONOUS, a. Having more than two lobes to the seed.

POLYEDRIC, POLYEDROUS. [See *Polyhedron* and *Polyhedral.*]

POL'YGAM, POLYGAM'IAN, n. [Gr. πολυς, many, and γαμος, marriage.] In *botany*, a plant which bears hermaphrodite flowers, with male or female flowers, or both, not inclosed in the same common calyx, but scattered either on the same plant, or on two or three distinct individuals. *Martyn.*

POLYGAM'IAN, a. Producing hermaphrodite flowers, with male or female flowers, or both.

POLYG'AMIST, n. [See *Polygamy.*] A person who maintains the lawfulness of polygamy.

POLYG'AMOUS, a. Consisting of polygamy. *Encyc.*
2. Inclined to polygamy; having a plurality of wives.

POLYG'AMY, n. [Gr. πολυς, many, and γαμος, marriage.]
A plurality of wives or husbands at the same time; or the having of such plurality. When a man has more wives than one, or a woman more husbands than one, at the same time, the offender is punishable for *polygamy.* Such is the fact in christian countries. But *polygamy* is allowed in some countries, as in Turkey.

POL'YGAR, n. In Hindoostan, an inhabitant of the woods.

POLYG'ENOUS, a. [Gr. πολυς, many, and γενος, kind.]
Consisting of many kinds; as a *polygenous* mountain, which is composed of strata of different species of stone. *Kirwan.*

POL'YGLOT, a. [Gr. πολυς, many, and γλωττα, tongue.]
Having or containing many languages; as a *polyglot* lexicon or Bible.

POL'YGLOT, n. A book containing many languages, particularly the Bible containing the Scriptures in several languages.
2. One who understands many languages. [*Not in use.*] *Howell.*

POL'YGON, n. [Gr. πολυς, many, and γωνια, an angle.]
In *geometry*, a figure of many angles and sides, and whose perimeter consists at least of more than four sides. *Encyc.*

POLYG'ONAL, POLYG'ONOUS, a. Having many angles. *Lee.*

POLYG'ONUM, POL'YGON, n. [Gr. πολυς, many, and γονυ, knee or knot.] Knotgrass, a genus of plants so named from the numerous joints in the stem.

POL'YGRAM, n. [Gr. πολυς, many, and γραμμα, a writing.] A figure consisting of many lines. *Dict.*

POL'YGRAPH, n. [See *Polygraphy.*] An instrument for multiplying copies of a writing with ease and expedition.

POLYGRAPH'IC, POLYGRAPH'ICAL, a. Pertaining to polygraphy; as a *polygraphic* instrument.
2. Done with a polygraph; as a *polygraphic* copy or writing.

POLYG'RAPHY, n. [Gr. πολυς, many, and γραφη, a writing; γραφω, to write.]
The art of writing in various ciphers, and of deciphering the same. *Dict. Encyc.*

POL'YGYN, n. [Gr. πολυς, many, and γυνη, a female.] In *botany*, a plant having many pistils.

POLYGYN'IAN, a. Having many pistils.

POLYG'YNY, n. [Gr. πολυς, many, and γυνη, a female.]
The practice of having more wives than one at the same time. *Forster's Obs.*

POLYHA'LITE, n. [Gr. πολυς, many, and αλς, salt.]
A mineral or salt occurring in masses of a fibrous structure, of a brick red color, being tinged with iron. It contains sulphates of lime, of magnesia, of potash and of soda. *Cleaveland.*

POLYHE'DRAL, POLYHE'DROUS, a. [See *Polyhedron.*] Having many sides; as a solid body.

POLYHE'DRON, n. [Gr. πολυς, many, and εδρα, side.]
1. In *geometry*, a body or solid contained under many sides or planes.
2. In *optics*, a multiplying glass or lens consisting of several plane surfaces disposed in a convex form. *Encyc.*

POLYL'OGY, n. [Gr. πολυς, many, and λογος, discourse.]
A talking much; talkativeness; garrulity. [*Not in use.*] *Granger.*

POLYMATH'IC, a. [See *Polymathy.*] Pertaining to polymathy.

POLYM'ATHY, n. [Gr. πολυς, many, and μαθησις, learning; μανθανω, to learn.]
The knowledge of many arts and sciences; acquaintance with many branches of learning or with various subjects. *Johnson. Encyc.*

POL'YMNITE, n. [stone of many marshes.] A stone marked with dendrites and black lines, and so disposed as to represent rivers, marshes and ponds. *Dict. Nat. Hist.*

POL'YMORPH, n. [Gr. πολυς, many, and μορφη, form.]
A name given by Soldani to a numerous tribe or series of shells, which are very small, irregular and singular in form, and which cannot be referred to any known genus. *Dict. Nat. Hist.*

POLYMORPH'OUS, a. [supra.] Having many forms. *Bigelow.*

POL'YNEME, n. A fish having a scaly compressed head, with a blunt prominent nose, and pliform appendages to the pectoral fins. *Pennant.*

POLYNE'SIA, n. s as z. [Gr. πολυς, many, and νησος, isle.]
A new term in geography, used to designate a great number of isles in the Pacific ocean, as the Pelew isles, the Ladrones, the Carolines, the Sandwich isles, the Marquesas, the Society isles and the Friendly isles. *De Brosses. Pinkerton.*

POLYNE'SIAN, a. Pertaining to Polynesia.

POL'YNOME, n. [Gr. πολυς, many, and ονομα, name.]
In *algebra*, a quantity consisting of many terms.

POLYNO'MIAL, a. Containing many names or terms.

POLYON'OMOUS, a. [Gr. πολυς, many, and ονομα, name.]
Having many names or titles; many-titled. *Sir W. Jones.*

POLYON'OMY, n. [supra.] Variety of different names. *Faber.*

POLYOP'TRUM, n. [Gr. πολυς, many, and οπτομαι, to see.]
A glass through which objects appear multiplied.

POL'YPE, POL'YPUS, n. [Gr. πολυπους; πολυς, many, and πους, foot.]
1. Something that has many feet or roots.
2. In *zoology*, a species of fresh water insect, belonging to the genus Hydra and order of zoophytes. Of this animal it is remarkable, that if cut into pieces, each part will shoot out a new head and tail and become a distinct animal. The general character of this animal is, it fixes itself by its base, is gelatinous, linear, naked, contractile, and capable of changing place. *Encyc.*

The common name of all those small gelatinous animals, whose mouth is surrounded by *tentacula* or feelers, (whence the name,) and conducts to a simple stomach, or one followed by intestines in the form of vessels. They constitute a distinct class or order of zoophytes, and include those compound animals, with a fixed and solid stem, which were formerly regarded as marine plants *(Lithophytes.)* *Cuvier.*

3. A concretion of blood in the heart and blood vessels. *Parr.*

4. A tumor with a narrow base, somewhat resembling a pear; found in the nose, uterus, &c. *Cooper.*

POLYPET'ALOUS, *a.* [Gr. πολυς, many, and πεταλον, a petal.]

In *botany*, having many petals; as a *polypetalous* corol. *Martyn.*

POLYPHON'IC, *a.* [infra.] Having or consisting of many voices or sounds. *Busby.*

POLYPH'ONISM, POLYPH'ONY, *n.* [Gr. πολυς, many, and φωνη, sound.] Multiplicity of sounds, as in the reverberations of an echo. *Derham.*

POLYPH'YLLOUS, *a.* [Gr. πολυς, many, and φυλλον, leaf.]

In *botany*, many-leafed; as a *polyphyllous* calyx or perianth.

POL'YPIER, *n.* The name given to the habitations of polypes, or to the common part of those compound animals called polypes. *Dict. Nat. Hist.* *Cuvier.*

POL'YPITE, *n.* Fossil polype.

POL'YPODE, *n.* [Gr. πολυς and πους.] An animal having many feet; the milleped or wood-louse. *Coxe.*

POLYP'ODY, *n.* [L. *polypodium*, from the Greek. See *Polype.*]

A plant of the genus Polypodium, of the order of Filices or ferns. The fructifications are in roundish points, scattered over the inferior disk of the frons or leaf. There are numerous species, of which the most remarkable is the common male fern. *Encyc.*

POL'YPOUS, *a.* [from *polypus.*] Having the nature of the polypus; having many feet or roots, like the polypus; as a *polypous* concretion. *Arbuthnot.*

POL'YSCOPE, *n.* [Gr. πολυς, many, and σκοπεω, to view.]

A glass which makes a single object appear as many. *Dict.*

POL'YSPAST, *n.* [Sp. *polispastos*; Gr. πολυς, many, and σπαω, to draw.]

A machine consisting of many pulleys. *Dict.*

POL'YSPERM, *n.* [Gr. πολυς, many, and σπερμα, seed.]

A tree whose fruit contains many seeds. *Evelyn.*

POLYSPERM'OUS, *a.* Containing many seeds; as a *polyspermous* capsule or berry. *Martyn.*

POLYSYLLAB'IC, POLYSYLLAB'ICAL, *a.* [from *polysyllable.*] Pertaining to a polysyllable; consisting of many syllables, or of more than three.

POL'YSYLLABLE, *n.* [Gr. πολυς, many, and συλλαβη, a syllable.]

A word of many syllables, that is, consisting of more syllables than three, for words of a less number than four are called monosyllables, dissyllables and trisyllables. *Encyc.*

POLYSYN'DETON, *n.* [Gr. πολυσυνδετος; πολυς, many, and συνδετος, connecting.]

A figure of rhetoric by which the copulative is often repeated; as, "we have ships and men and money and stores."

POLYTECH'NIC, *a.* [Gr. πολυς, many, and τεχνη, art.]

Denoting or comprehending many arts; as a *polytechnic* school.

POL'YTHEISM, *n.* [Fr. *polytheisme*; Gr. πολυς, many, and θεος, God.]

The doctrine of a plurality of gods or invisible beings superior to man, and having an agency in the government of the world. *Stillingfleet.*

POL'YTHEIST, *n.* A person who believes in or maintains the doctrine of a plurality of gods.

POLYTHEIS'TIC, POLYTHEIS'TICAL, *a.* Pertaining to polytheism; as *polytheistic* belief or worship.

2. Holding a plurality of gods; as a *polytheistic* writer. *Milner.* *Encyc.*

PŎMACE, *n.* [from L. *pomum*, an apple, It. *pome*, Sp. *pomo*, Fr. *pomme.*]

The substance of apples or of similar fruit crushed by grinding. In America, it is so called before and after being pressed. [See *Pomp* and *Pommel.*]

POMA'CEOUS, *a.* Consisting of apples; as *pomaceous* harvests. *Philips.*

2. Like pomace.

POMA'DE, *n.* [Fr. *pommade*; It. *pomata*; Sp. *pomada*, either from *pomo*, fruit, or from perfuming; *poma* signifying in Spanish, a perfume-box.] Perfumed ointment. [*Little used.*]

PO'MANDER, *n.* [Fr. *pomme d'ambre*. *Johnson.*]

A sweet ball; a perfumed ball or powder. *Bacon.* *Shak.*

POMA'TUM, *n.* [Fr. *pommade*; It. *pomata*; Sp. *pomada*. See *Pomade.*]

An unguent or composition used in dressing the hair. It is also used in medicine. *Encyc.*

POMA'TUM, *v. t.* To apply pomatum to the hair. *Dict.*

POME, *n.* [L. *pomum.*] In *botany*, a pulpy pericarp without valves, containing a capsule or core, as the apple, pear, &c. *Martyn.*

POME, *v. i.* [Fr. *pommer.*] To grow to a head, or form a head in growing. [*Not used.*] *Dict.*

POMECIT'RON, *n.* A citron apple. *B. Jonson.*

PŎMEGRAN'ATE, *n.* [L. *pomum*, an apple, and *granatum*, grained. See *Grain* and *Granate.*]

1. The fruit of a tree belonging to the genus Punica. This fruit is as large as an orange, having a hard rind filled with a soft pulp and numerous seeds. It is of a reddish color.

2. The tree that produces pomegranates.

3. An ornament resembling a pomegranate, on the robe and ephod of the Jewish high priest.

PŎMEGRANATE-TREE, *n.* The tree which produces pomegranates.

PO'MEROY, POMEROY'AL, *n.* Royal apple; a particular sort of apple. *Ainsworth.*

PO'ME-WATER, *n.* A sort of apple. *Shak.*

POMIF'EROUS, *a.* [L. *pomum*, an apple, and *fero*, to produce.]

Apple-bearing; an epithet applied to plants which bear the larger fruits, such as melons, gourds, pumpkins, cucumbers, &c. in distinction from the bacciferous or berry-bearing plants. *Ray.* *Arbuthnot.*

POMME, POMMETTE, *n.* In *heraldry*, a cross with one or more knobs at each of the ends. *Encyc.*

PŎMMEL, *n.* [Fr. *pommeau*; It. *pomo*, an apple; *pomo della spada*, the pommel of a hilt; Sp. *pomo*, L. *pomum*, an apple, or a similar fruit; W. *pwmp*, a round mass or lump.]

1. A knob or ball. 2 Chron. iv.

2. The knob on the hilt of a sword; the protuberant part of a saddle-bow; the round knob on the frame of a chair, &c.

PŎMMEL, *v. t.* [from the noun.] To beat as with a pommel, that is, with something thick or bulky; to bruise.

[The French *se pommeler*, to grow dapple, to curdle, is from the same source; but the sense is to make knobs or lumps, and hence to variegate, or make spots like knobs. The Welsh have from the same root, or *pwmp*, a mass, *pwmpiaw*, to form a round mass, and to thump, to bang, Eng. to *bump.*]

PŎMMELED, *pp.* Beaten; bruised.

2. In *heraldry*, having pommels; as a sword or dagger.

POMME'LION, *n.* [from *pommel.*] The cascabel or hindmost knob of a cannon. *Mar. Dict.*

POMP, *n.* [L. *pompa*; Fr. *pompe*; Arm. *pomp*; *pompadi*, to boast; It. Sp. *pompa*; Sw. *pomp*; D. *pomp*, a pump, and *pompoen*, a gourd, a pumpkin; G. *pomp*, show, and *pumpe*, a pump. These words appear to be all of one family, coinciding with L. *bombus*, Sp. *bomba*, Eng. *bomb*, *bombast*. The radical sense is to swell or dilate; Gr. πομπη, πομπεια, πομπευω.]

1. A procession distinguished by ostentation of grandeur and splendor; as the *pomp* of a Roman triumph.

2. Show of magnificence; parade; splendor.

> Hearts formed for love, but doom'd in vain to glow
> In prison'd *pomp*, and weep in splendid woe.
> *D. Humphreys.*

POMPAT'IC, *a.* [Low L. *pompaticus*, *pompatus.*]

Pompous; splendid; ostentatious. [*Not in use.*] *Barrow.*

POMP'ET, *n.* The ball which printers use to black the types. *Cotgrave.*

POM'PHOLYX, *n.* [L. from Gr. πομφολυξ; πομφος, a tumor; πεμφιξ, a blast, a puff, a bubble, a pustule. See *Pomp.*]

The white oxyd which sublimes during the combustion of zink; called flowers of zink. It rises and adheres to the dome of the furnace and the covers of crucibles. *Hill.* *Nicholson.* *Ure.*

POMP'ION, *n.* [D. *pompoen*, a pumpkin, a gourd; Sw. *pumpa*. See *Pomp* and *Pomace.*]

A pumpkin; a plant and its fruit of the genus Cucurbita.

POM'PIRE, *n.* [L. *pomum*, apple, and *pyrus*, pear.] A sort of pearmain. *Ainsworth.*

POMPOS'ITY, *n.* [It. *pomposità.*] Pompousness; ostentation; boasting. *Aikin.*

POMP'OUS, *a.* [Fr. *pompeux*; It. *pomposo.*]

1. Displaying pomp; showy with grandeur; splendid; magnificent; as a *pompous* procession; a *pompous* triumph.
2. Ostentatious; boastful; as a *pompous* account of private adventures.

POMP'OUSLY, *adv.* With great parade or display; magnificently; splendidly; ostentatiously. *Dryden.*

POMP'OUSNESS, *n.* The state of being pompous; magnificence; splendor; great display of show; ostentatiousness. *Addison.*

POM'-WATER, *n.* The name of a large apple. *Dict.*

POND, *n.* [Sp. Port. It. *pantano*, a pool of stagnant water, also in Sp. hinderance, obstacle, difficulty. The name imports standing water, from setting or confining. It may be allied to L. *pono*; Sax. *pyndan*, to pound, to pen, to restrain, and L. *pontus*, the sea, may be of the same family.]

1. A body of stagnant water without an outlet, larger than a puddle, and smaller than a lake; or a like body of water with a small outlet. In the United States, we give this name to collections of water in the interior country, which are fed by springs, and from which issues a small stream. These ponds are often a mile or two or even more in length, and the current issuing from them is used to drive the wheels of mills and furnaces.
2. A collection of water raised in a river by a dam, for the purpose of propelling millwheels. These artificial ponds are called *mill-ponds.*

Pond for fish. [See *Fish-pond.*]

POND, *v. t.* [from the noun.] To make a pond; to collect in a pond by stopping the current of a river.

POND, *v. t.* To ponder. [*Not in use.*] *Spenser.*

PON'DER, *v. t.* [L. *pondero*, from *pondo*, *pondus*, a pound; *pendeo*, *pendo*, to weigh; Pers. پنداشتن pindashatan, and بندازیدن bandazidan, to think, to consider.]

1. To weigh in the mind; to consider and compare the circumstances or consequences of an event, or the importance of the reasons for or against a decision.

   Mary kept all these things, and *pondered* them in her heart. Luke ii.

2. To view with deliberation; to examine.

   Ponder the path of thy feet. Prov. iv.
   The Lord *pondereth* the hearts. Prov. xxi.

To ponder on, is sometimes used, but is not to be countenanced.

PON'DERABLE, *a.* That may be weighed; capable of being weighed. *Brown.*

PON'DERAL, *a.* [from L. *pondus*, weight.] Estimated or ascertained by weight, as distinguished from *numeral*; as a *ponderal* drachma. *Arbuthnot.*

PON'DERANCE, *n.* Weight; gravity. *Gregory.*

PON'DERATE, *v. t.* To weigh in the mind; to consider. [*Not in use.*] *Ch. Relig. Appeal.*

PONDERA'TION, *n.* The act of weighing. [*Little used.*] *Arbuthnot.*

PON'DERED, *pp.* Weighed in the mind; considered; examined by intellectual operation.

PON'DERER, *n.* One that weighs in his mind. *Whitlock.*

PON'DERING, *ppr.* Weighing intellectually; considering; deliberating on.

PON'DERINGLY, *adv.* With consideration or deliberation. *Hammond.*

PONDEROS'ITY, *n.* Weight; gravity; heaviness. *Brown. Ray.*

PON'DEROUS, *a.* [L. *ponderosus*; It. Sp. Port. *ponderoso.*]

1. Very heavy; weighty; as a *ponderous* shield; a *ponderous* load.
2. Important; momentous; as a *ponderous* project. [*This application of the word is unusual.*]
3. Forcible; strongly impulsive; as a motion vehement or *ponderous*; a *ponderous* blow. *Bacon. Dryden.*

Ponderous spar, heavy spar, or baryte.

PON'DEROUSLY, *adv.* With great weight.

PON'DEROUSNESS, *n.* Weight; heaviness; gravity. *Boyle.*

POND'-WEED, *n.* [*pond* and *weed.*] A plant of the genus Potamogeton. The *triple-headed pond-weed* is of the genus Zannichellia.

PO'NENT, *a.* [It. *ponente*, the west; L. *ponens*, from *pono*, to set.]

Western; as the *ponent* winds. [*Little used.*] *Milton.*

PON'GO, *n.* A name of the orang outang. *Dict. Nat. Hist.*

The name *pongo* was applied by Buffon to a large species of orang outang, which is now ascertained to have been an imaginary animal. It is applied by Cuvier to the largest species of ape known, which inhabits Borneo, and resembles the true orang outang in its general form and erect position, but has the cheek pouches and lengthened muzzle of the baboon. It has also been applied (*Ed. Encyc.*) to the *Simia troglodytes* or chimpanzee of Cuvier, a native of W. Africa. *Cuvier. Ed. Encyc.*

PONIARD, *n.* *pon'yard.* [Fr. *poignard*; It. *pugnale*; Sp. *puñal*; Port. *punhal.* There is an appearance of the formation of this word from the name of the fist, Fr. *poing*, Sp. *puño*, It. *pugno*, L. *pugnus*; but this is not obvious.]

A small dagger; a pointed instrument for stabbing, borne in the hand or at the girdle, or in the pocket. *Encyc.*

PONIARD, *v. t.* *pon'yard.* To pierce with a poniard; to stab.

PONK, *n.* [qu. W. *pwca*, *bwg*, a hobgoblin; Ice. *puke.*]

A nocturnal spirit; a hag. [*Not in use.*] *Shak.*

PONT'AGE, *n.* [L. *pons*, *pontis*, a bridge, Sp. *puente*, W. *pont.*]

A duty paid for repairing bridges. *Ayliffe.*

PONTEE', *n.* In *glass works*, an iron instrument used to stick the glass at the bottom, for the more convenient fashioning the neck of it. *Cyc.*

PONT'IC, *a.* [L. *Pontus*, the Euxine sea, Gr. πόντος.]

Pertaining to the Pontus, Euxine, or Black Sea. *J. Barlow.*

PONT'IF, *n.* [Fr. *pontife*; L. *pontifex*; said to be from *pons*, a bridge, and *facio*, to make.]

A high priest. The Romans had a college of *pontifs*; the Jews had their *pontifs*; and in modern times, the pope is called *pontif* or sovereign *pontif.* *Encyc.*

PONTIF'IC, *a.* Relating to priests; popish. *Milton. Shenstone.*

PONTIF'ICAL, *a.* [L. *pontificalis.*] Belonging to a high priest; as *pontifical* authority; hence, belonging to the pope; popish. *Raleigh.*

2. Splendid; magnificent. *Shak.*
3. Bridge-building. [*Not used.*] *Milton.*

PONTIF'ICAL, *n.* A book containing rites and ceremonies ecclesiastical. *South. Stillingfleet.*

2. The dress and ornaments of a priest or bishop. *Lowth.*

PONTIFICAL'ITY, *n.* The state and government of the pope; the papacy. [*Not used.*] *Usher.*

PONTIF'ICALLY, *adv.* In a pontifical manner.

PONTIF'ICATE, *n.* [L. *pontificatus.*] The state or dignity of a high priest; particularly, the office or dignity of the pope.

   He turned hermit in the view of being advanced to the *pontificate.* *Addison.*

2. The reign of a pope.

   Painting, sculpture and architecture may all recover themselves under the present *pontificate.* *Addison.*

PONT'IFICE, *n.* Bridge-work; structure or edifice of a bridge. [*Little used.*] *Milton.*

PONTIFI''CIAL, *a.* Popish. *Burton.*

PONTIFI''CIAN, *a.* Popish; papistical. *Hall.*

PONTIFI''CIAN, *n.* One that adheres to the pope; a papist. *Mountague.*

PON'TINE, } *a.* [L. *pontina*, a lake.] Designating a large marsh between Rome and Naples.
POMP'TINE, }

PONT'LEVIS, *n.* In *horsemanship*, a disorderly resisting of a horse by rearing repeatedly on his hind legs, so as to be in danger of coming over. *Bailey.*

PONTOON', *n.* [Fr. Sp. *ponton*, from Fr. *pont*, L. *pons*, a bridge, probably from the root of *pono*, to lay.]

1. A flat-bottomed boat, whose frame of wood is covered and lined with tin, or covered with copper; used in forming bridges over rivers for armies. *Encyc.*
2. A lighter; a low flat vessel resembling a barge, furnished with cranes, capstans and other machinery; used in careening ships, chiefly in the Mediterranean. *Mar. Dict.*

Pontoon-bridge, is a bridge formed with pontoons, anchored or made fast in two lines, about five feet asunder. *Cyc.*

Pontoon-carriage, is made with two wheels only, and two long side pieces, whose fore ends are supported by timbers. *Cyc.*

PO'NY, *n.* A small horse.

POOD, *n.* A Russian weight, equal to 40 Russian or 36 English pounds.

POOL, *n.* [Sax. *pol*, *pul*; D. *poel*; G. *pfuhl*; Dan. *pöl*; W. *pwll*, a pool or pit; Arm.

poul; L. *palus*; Gr. πηλος; probably from setting, standing, like L. *stagnum*, or from issuing, as a spring.]

A small collection of water in a hollow place, supplied by a spring, and discharging its surplus water by an outlet. It is smaller than a lake, and in New England is never confounded with *pond* or *lake*. It signifies with us, a spring with a small bason or reservoir on the surface of the earth. It is used by writers with more latitude, and sometimes signifies a body of stagnant water. *Milton. Encyc. Bacon.*

POOL, } *n.* [Fr. *poule*.] The stakes played
POULE, } for in certain games of cards. *Southern.*

POOP, *n.* [Fr. *poupe*; It. *poppa*; Sp. *popa*; L. *puppis*; probably a projection.]

The highest and aftmost part of a ship's deck. *Mar. Dict.*

POOP, *v. t.* To strike upon the stern, as a heavy sea.

2. To strike the stern, as one vessel that runs her stem against another's stern. *Mar. Dict.*

POOP'ING, *n.* The shock of a heavy sea on the stern or quarter of a ship, when scudding in a tempest; also, the action of one ship's running her stem against another's stern. *Mar. Dict.*

POOR, *a.* [L. *pauper*; Fr. *pauvre*; Sp. *pobre*; It. *povero*; Arm. *paour*; Norm. *pour, power*.]

1. Wholly destitute of property, or not having property sufficient for a comfortable subsistence; needy. It is often synonymous with *indigent*, and with *necessitous*, denoting extreme want; it is also applied to persons who are not entirely destitute of property, but are not rich; as a *poor* man or woman; *poor* people.

2. In *law*, so destitute of property as to be entitled to maintenance from the public.

3. Destitute of strength, beauty or dignity; barren; mean; jejune; as a *poor* composition; a *poor* essay; a *poor* discourse.

4. Destitute of value, worth or importance; of little use; trifling.

> That I have wronged no man, will be a *poor* plea or apology at the last day. *Calamy.*

5. Paltry; mean; of little value; as a *poor* coat; a *poor* house.

6. Destitute of fertility; barren; exhausted; as *poor* land. The ground is become *poor*.

7. Of little worth; unimportant; as in my *poor* opinion. *Swift.*

8. Unhappy; pitiable.

> Vex'd sailors curse the rain
> For which *poor* shepherds pray'd in vain. *Waller.*

9. Mean; depressed; low; dejected; destitute of spirit.

> A soothsayer made Antonius believe that his genius, which was otherwise brave, was, in the presence of Octavianus, *poor* and cowardly. *Bacon.*

10. Lean; emaciated; as a *poor* horse. The ox is *poor*.

11. Small, or of a bad quality; as a *poor* crop; a *poor* harvest.

12. Uncomfortable; restless; ill. The patient has had a *poor* night.

13. Destitute of saving grace. Rev. iii.

14. In general, wanting good qualities, or the qualities which render a thing valuable, excellent, proper, or sufficient for its purpose; as a *poor* pen; a *poor* ship; a *poor* carriage; *poor* fruit; *poor* bread; *poor* wine, &c.

15. A word of tenderness or pity; dear.

> *Poor*, little, pretty, fluttering thing. *Prior.*

16. A word of slight contempt; wretched.

> The *poor* monk never saw many of the decrees and councils he had occasion to use. *Baker.*

17. *The poor*, collectively, used as a noun; those who are destitute of property; the indigent; the needy; in a legal sense, those who depend on charity or maintenance by the public.

> I have observed the more public provisions are made for the *poor*, the less they provide for themselves. *Franklin.*

Poor in spirit, in a Scriptural sense, humble; contrite; abased in one's own sight by a sense of guilt. Matt. v.

POOR'JOHN, *n.* A sort of fish [*callarius*] of the genus Gadus. *Ainsworth.*

POOR'LY, *adv.* Without wealth; in indigence or want of the conveniences and comforts of life; as, to live *poorly*. *Sidney.*

2. With little or no success; with little growth, profit or advantage; as, wheat grows *poorly* on the Atlantic borders of New England; these men have succeeded *poorly* in business.

3. Meanly; without spirit.

> Nor is their courage or their wealth so low,
> That from his wars they *poorly* would retire. *Dryden.*

4. Without excellence or dignity. He performs *poorly* in elevated characters.

POOR'LY, *a.* Somewhat ill; indisposed; not in health; *a common use of the word in America.*

> For three or four weeks past I have lost ground, having been *poorly* in health. *Th. Scott.*

POOR'NESS, *n.* Destitution of property; indigence; poverty; want; as the *poorness* of the exchequer.

> No less I hate him than the gates of hell,
> That *poorness* can force an untruth to tell. *Chapman.*

[In this sense, we generally use *poverty*.]

2. Meanness; lowness; want of dignity; as the *poorness* of language.

3. Want of spirit; as *poorness* and degeneracy of spirit. *Addison.*

4. Barrenness; sterility; as the *poorness* of land or soil.

3. Unproductiveness; want of the metallic substance; as the *poorness* of ore.

6. Smallness or bad quality; as the *poorness* of crops or of grain.

7. Want of value or importance; as the *poorness* of a plea.

8. Want of good qualities, or the proper qualities which constitute a thing good in its kind; as the *poorness* of a ship or of cloth.

9. Narrowness; barrenness; want of capacity. *Spectator.*

Poorness of spirit, in a theological sense, true humility or contrition of heart on account of sin.

POOR-SPIR'ITED, *a.* Of a mean spirit; cowardly; base. *Denham.*

POOR-SPIR'ITEDNESS, *n.* Meanness or baseness of spirit; cowardice. *South.*

POP, *n.* [D. *poep*. The primary sense is to drive or thrust.]

A small smart quick sound or report. *Spectator.*

POP, *v. i.* To enter or issue forth with a quick, sudden motion.

> I startled at his *popping* upon me unexpectedly. *Addison.*

2. To dart; to start from place to place suddenly. *Swift.*

POP, *v. t.* To thrust or push suddenly with a quick motion.

> He *popp'd* a paper into his hand. *Milton.*
> Did'st thou never *pop*
> Thy head into a tinman's shop? *Prior.*

To pop off, to thrust away; to shift off. *Locke.*

POP, *adv.* Suddenly; with sudden entrance or appearance.

POPE, *n.* [Gr. παπα, παππας, παππος; Low L. *papa*; Hindoo, *bab*; Turkish, *baba*; Bythinian, *pappas*; Sp. It. Port. *papa*; Fr. *pape*; Scythian, *papa*. The word denotes father, and is among the first words articulated by children.]

1. The bishop of Rome, the head of the catholic church. *Encyc.*

2. A small fish, called also a ruff. *Walton.*

PO'PEDOM, *n.* The place, office or dignity of the pope; papal dignity. *Shak.*

2. The jurisdiction of the pope.

PO'PE-JOAN, *n.* A game of cards. *Jenner.*

PO'PELING, *n.* An adherent of the pope.

PO'PERY, *n.* The religion of the church of Rome, comprehending doctrines and practices. *Swift. Encyc.*

PO'PE'S-EYE, *n.* [*pope* and *eye*.] The gland surrounded with fat in the middle of the thigh. *Johnson.*

POP'GUN, *n.* A small gun or tube used by children to shoot wads and make a noise. *Cheyne.*

POP'INJAY, *n.* [Sp. *papagayo*; *papa* and *gayo*; Port. *id.*; It. *pappagallo*.]

1. A parrot. *Grew.*

2. A woodpecker, a bird with a gay head. *Peacham.*

The green woodpecker, with a scarlet crown, a native of Europe. *Ed. Encyc.*

3. A gay, trifling young man; a fop or coxcomb. *Shak.*

PO'PISH, *a.* Relating to the pope; taught by the pope; pertaining to the pope or to the church of Rome; as *popish* tenets or ceremonies.

PO'PISHLY, *adv.* In a popish manner; with a tendency to popery; as, to be *popishly* affected or inclined.

POP'LAR, *n.* [L. *populus*; Fr. *peuplier*; It. *pioppo*; D. *populier*; G. *pappel*, poplar and mallows; Sw. *poppel-träd*; Ir. *pobhlar*.]

A tree of the genus Populus, of several species, as the abele, the white poplar, the black poplar, the aspen-tree, &c. It is numbered among the aquatic trees. *Encyc.*

POP'LIN, *n.* A stuff made of silk and worsted.

POPLIT'EAL, } *a.* [from L. *poples*, the
POPLIT'IC, } ham.]

Pertaining to the ham or knee joint. *Med. Repos.*

POPPET. [See *Puppet*.]

POP'PY, *n.* [Sax. *popeg*; W. *pabi*; Fr. *pavot*; L. *papaver*; It. *papavero*.]

A plant of the genus Papaver, of several species, from one of which, the *somniferum* or white poppy, is collected opium. This is the milky juice of the capsule when half grown, which exsudes from incisions in the cortical part of the capsule, is scraped off, and worked in an iron pot in the sun's heat, till it is of a consistence to form cakes. *Encyc.*

POP'ULACE, *n.* [Fr. from the It. *popolaccio*, from L. *populus*. See *People*.]

The common people; the vulgar; the multitude, comprehending all persons not distinguished by rank, education, office, profession or erudition. *Pope. Swift.*

POP'ULACY, *n.* The populace or common people. *K. Charles.*

POP'ULAR, *a.* [Fr. *populaire*; It. *popolare*; Sp. *popular*; L. *popularis*. See *People*.]

1. Pertaining to the common people; as the *popular* voice; *popular* elections.

So the *popular* vote inclines. *Milton.*

2. Suitable to common people; familiar; plain; easy to be comprehended; not critical or abstruse.

Homilies are plain and *popular* instructions. *Hooker.*

3. Beloved by the people; enjoying the favor of the people; pleasing to people in general; as a *popular* governor; a *popular* preacher; a *popular* ministry; a *popular* discourse; a *popular* administration; a *popular* war or peace. Suspect the man who endeavors to make that *popular* which is wrong.

4. Ambitious; studious of the favor of the people.

A *popular* man is in truth no better than a prostitute to common fame and to the people. *Dryden.*

[*This sense is not usual. It is more customary to apply this epithet to a person who has already gained the favor of the people.*]

5. Prevailing among the people; extensively prevalent; as a *popular* disease.

6. In *law*, a *popular* action is one which gives a penalty to the person that sues for the same. *Blackstone.*

[Note. *Popular*, at least in the United States, is not synonymous with *vulgar*; the latter being applied to the lower classes of people, the illiterate and low bred; the former is applied to all classes, or to the body of the people, including a great portion at least of well educated citizens.]

POPULAR'ITY, *n.* [L. *popularitas*.] Favor of the people; the state of possessing the affections and confidence of the people in general; as the *popularity* of the ministry; the *popularity* of a public officer or of a preacher. It is applied also to things; as the *popularity* of a law or public measure; the *popularity* of a book or poem. The most valuable trait in a patriot's character is to forbear all improper compliances for gaining *popularity*.

I have long since learned the little value which is to be placed in *popularity*, acquired by any other way than virtue; I have also learned that it is often obtained by other means. *P. Henry, Wirt's Sketches.*

The man whose ruling principle is duty—is never perplexed with anxious corroding calculations of interest and *popularity*. *J. Hawes.*

2. Representation suited to vulgar or common conception; that which is intended or adapted to procure the favor of the people. [*Little used.*] *Bacon.*

POP'ULARIZE, *v. t.* To make popular or common; to spread among the people; as, to *popularize* philosophy or physics; to *popularize* a knowledge of chemical principles. *Beddoes. Ure.*

POP'ULARIZED, *pp.* Made popular, or introduced among the people.

POP'ULARIZING, *ppr.* Making popular, or introducing among the people.

POP'ULARLY, *adv.* In a popular manner; so as to please the populace.

The victor knight,
Bareheaded, *popularly* low had bow'd. *Dryden.*

2. According to the conceptions of the common people. *Brown.*

POP'ULATE, *v. i.* [It. *popolare*, from L. *populus*.]

To breed people; to propagate.

When there be great shoals of people which go on to *populate*. *Bacon.*

POP'ULATE, *v. t.* To people; to furnish with inhabitants, either by natural increase, or by immigration or colonization.

POPULATE, for *populous*, is not now in use.

POP'ULATED, *pp.* Furnished with inhabitants; peopled.

POP'ULATING, *ppr.* Peopling.

POPULA'TION, *n.* The act or operation of peopling or furnishing with inhabitants; multiplication of inhabitants. The value of our western lands is annually enhanced by *population*. *U. States.*

2. The whole number of people or inhabitants in a country. The *population* of England is estimated at ten millions of souls; that of the United States in 1823, was ten millions.

A country may have a great *population*, and yet not be populous. *Tooke.*

3. The state of a country with regard to its number of inhabitants, or rather with regard to its numbers compared with their expenses, consumption of goods and productions, and earnings.

Neither is the *population* to be reckoned only by number; for a smaller number that spend more and earn less, do wear out an estate sooner than a greater number that live lower and gather more. *Bacon.*

POPULOS'ITY, *n.* Populousness. [*Not used.*] *Brown.*

POP'ULOUS, *a.* [L. *populosus*.] Full of inhabitants; containing many inhabitants in proportion to the extent of the country. A territory containing fifteen or twenty inhabitants to a square mile is not a *populous* country. The Netherlands, and some parts of Italy, containing a hundred and fifty inhabitants to a square mile, are deemed *populous*.

POP'ULOUSLY, *adv.* With many inhabitants in proportion to the extent of country.

POP'ULOUSNESS, *n.* The state of having many inhabitants in proportion to the extent of country.

By *populousness*, in contradistinction to *population*, is understood the proportion the number bears to the surface of the ground they live on. *Tooke.*

POR'CATED, *a.* [L. *porca*, a ridge.] Ridged; formed in ridges. *Asiat. Res.*

POR'CELAIN, *n.* [Sp. Port. *porcelana*; It. *porcellana*, signifying *porcelain* and *purslain*, a plant; Fr. *porcelaine*, porcelain, the sea-snail, the purple fish, and purslain; Arm. *pourcelinnen*. Our *purslain* is doubtless from the Latin *portulaca*, as Pliny writes it, or *porculata*, as others write it. But I know not the reason of the name.]

1. The finest species of earthern ware, originally manufactured in China and Japan, but now made in several European countries. All earthern wares which are white and semi-transparent, are called porcelains, but they differ much in their fineness and beauty. The porcelain of China is said to be made of two species of earth, the petuntse, which is fusible, and the kaolin, which is not fusible, or not with the degree of heat which fuses the petuntse, and that in porcelain the substances are only semi-vitrified, or one substance only is vitrified, the other not. Hence it is concluded that porcelain is an intermediate substance between earth and glass. Hence the second degree of fusibility, of which *emollescence* is the first, is called by Kirwan the *porcelain state*. *Dict. Nat. Hist. Nicholson. Kirwan. Encyc.*

2. The plant called purslain, which see. *Ainsworth.*

PORCELLA'NEOUS, *a.* [from *porcelain*.] Pertaining to or resembling porcelain; as *porcellaneous* shells. *Hatchett.*

POR'CELLANITE, *n.* A silicious mineral, a species of jasper, of various colors. It seems to be formed accidentally in coal mines which have indurated and semi-vitrified beds of coal-shale or slate-clay. It is sometimes marked with vegetable impressions of a brick red color. *Kirwan, from Peithner. Cyc. Cleaveland.*

PORCH, *n.* [Fr. *porche*, from L. *porticus*, from *porta*, a gate, entrance or passage, or from *portus*, a shelter.]

1. In *architecture*, a kind of vestibule supported by columns at the entrance of temples, halls, churches or other buildings. *Encyc.*

2. A portico; a covered walk.

3. By way of distinction, *the porch*, was a public portico in Athens, where Zeno, the philosopher, taught his disciples. It was called ποικιλη, the painted porch, from the pictures of Polygnotus and other eminent painters, with which it was adorned. Hence, *the Porch* is equivalent to the *school of the Stoics*. *Enfield.*

POR'CINE, *a.* [L. *porcinus*, from *porcus*. See *Pork*.]

Pertaining to swine; as the *porcine* species of animals. *Gregory.*

POR'CUPINE, *n.* [It. *porco-spinoso*, the spinous hog or spine-hog; L. *porcus*, W. *porc*, a pig, and L. *spina*, a spine or thorn. So in French, *porc-epic*, the *spike-hog*; Sp. *puerco-espin*; Port. *porco-espinho*; D. *yzervarken*, iron-hog; G. *stachelschwein*, thorn-swine; Sw. *pinsvin*, Dan. *pindsviin*, pin-swine.]

In *zoology*, a quadruped of the genus Hystrix. The crested porcupine has a body about two feet in length, four toes on each of the fore feet, and five on each of the hind feet, a crested head, a short tail, and the upper lip divided like that of the hare. The body is covered with prickles which are very sharp, and some of them nine or ten inches long; these he can erect at pleasure. When attacked, he rolls his body into a round form, in which position the prickles are presented in every direction to the enemy. This species is a native of Africa and Asia. *Encyc.*

POR'CUPINE-FISH, *n.* A fish which is covered with spines or prickles. It is of the diodon kind, and about fourteen inches in length. *Dict. Nat. Hist.*

PORE, *n.* [Fr. *pore*; Sp. It. *poro*; Gr. πορος, from the root of πορευομαι, to go, to pass, Sax. *faran*, Eng. to *fare*. See *Fare*. The word then signifies a *passage*.]

1. In *anatomy*, a minute interstice in the skin of an animal, through which the perspirable matter passes to the surface or is excreted.
2. A small spiracle, opening or passage in other substances; as the *pores* of plants or of stones. *Quincy. Dryden.*

PORE, *v. i.* [Qu. Gr. εφορω, εφοραω, to inspect. In Sp. *porrear* is to dwell long on, to persist importunately; *porro*, dull; W. *para*, to continue, to persevere.]

To look with steady continued attention or application. To *pore on*, is to read or examine with steady perseverance, to dwell on; and the word seems to be limited in its application to the slow patient reading or examination of books, or something written or engraved.

Painfully to *pore* upon a book. *Shak.*

With sharpened sight pale antiquaries *pore*. *Pope.*

PO'RE-BLIND, } *a.* [Qu. Gr. πωρος.] Near-
PUR'BLIND, } sighted; short-sighted. *Bacon.*

PO'RER, *n.* One who pores or studies diligently. *Temple.*

POR'GY, *n.* A fish of the gilt-head kind.

PO'RINESS, *n.* [from *pory*.] The state of being pory or having numerous pores. *Wiseman.*

PO'RISM, *n.* [Gr. πορισμος, acquisition, from ποριζω, to gain, from πορος, a passing; πορευομαι, to pass.]

In *geometry*, a name given by ancient geometers to two classes of propositions. Euclid gave this name to propositions involved in others which he was investigating, and obtained without a direct view to their discovery. These he called *acquisitions*, but such propositions are now called *corollaries*. A porism is defined, "a proposition affirming the possibility of finding such conditions as will render a certain problem indeterminate or capable of innumerable solutions." It is not a theorem, nor a problem, or rather it includes both. It asserts that a certain problem may become indeterminate, and so far it partakes of the nature of a theorem, and in seeking to discover the conditions by which this may be effected, it partakes of the nature of a problem. *Encyc.*

PORIS'TIC, } *a.* Pertaining to a po-
PORIS'TICAL, } rism; seeking to determine by what means and in how many ways a problem may be solved.

PO'RITE, *n.* plu. *porites*. A petrified madrepore. *Dict. Nat. Hist.*

PORK, *n.* [L. *porcus*, a hog or pig; Fr. *porc*; W. *porç*; Arm. *porcq*, *porchell*. Qu. from the shape of his back, L. *porca*, a ridge; or from his snout and rooting. In Sax. *berga* is a barrow.]

The flesh of swine, fresh or salted, used for food.

PORK-EATER, *n.* One that feeds on swine's flesh. *Shak.*

PORKER, *n.* A hog; a pig. [*Not used in America.*] *Pope.*

PORKET, *n.* A young hog. *Dryden.*

PORKLING, *n.* A pig. *Tusser.*

POROS'ITY, *n.* [from *porous*.] The quality or state of having pores or interstices. *Bacon.*

PO'ROUS, *a.* [from *pore*.] Having interstices in the skin or substance of the body; having spiracles or passages for fluids; as a *porous* skin; *porous* wood; *porous* earth. *Milton. Chapman.*

PO'ROUSNESS, *n.* The quality of having pores; porosity; as the *porousness* of the skin of an animal, or of wood, or of fossils.

2. The porous parts. [*Not authorized.*] *Digby.*

POR'PESS, *n.* [It. *porco*, a hog, and *pesce*, fish; hog-fish, called by other nations, sea-hog, G. *meerschwein*, Fr. *marsouin*, Dan. Sw. Norwegian, *marsvin*, Sw. *hafssvin*. In W. *morhwc*, sea-hog, is the name of the dolphin and grampus, from the resemblance of these animals to the hog, probably from the roundness of the back, as they appear in the water.]

In *zoology*, a cetaceous fish of the genus Delphinus, whose back is usually blackish or brown, whence it is called in Dutch, *bruinvisch*, brown fish; the body is thick towards the head, but more slender towards the tail, which is semi-lunar. This fish preys on other fish, and seeks food not only by swimming, but by rooting like a hog in the sand and mud, whence some persons suppose the name has been given to it.

Of cetaceous fish, we met with *porpesses*, or as some sailors call them, sea-hogs. *Kalm's Travels.*

PORPHYRIT'IC, } *a.* [See *Porphyry*.]
PORPHYRA'CEOUS, } Pertaining to porphyry; resembling porphyry.

2. Containing or composed of porphyry; as *porphyraceous* mountains. *Kirwan.*

POR'PHYRIZE, *v. t.* To cause to resemble porphyry; to make spotted in its composition. *Cooper.*

POR'PHYRY, *n.* [Gr. πορφυρα, purple; L. *porphyrites*; Fr. *porphyre*; It. Sp. *porfido*.]

A mineral consisting of a homogeneous ground with crystals of some other mineral imbedded, giving to the mass a speckled complexion. One variety of Egyptian porphyry has a *purple* ground, whence the name of the species; but the homogeneous ground with imbedded crystals, being all that is essential to porphyry, its composition and colors are consequently various. *D. Olmsted.*

Porphyry is very hard, and susceptible of a fine polish.

Porphyry is composed of paste in which are disseminated a multitude of little angular and granuliform parts, of a color different from the ground. *Dict. Nat. Hist.*

PORPHYRY-SHELL, *n.* An animal or shell of the genus Murex. It is of the snail kind, the shell consisting of one spiral valve. From one species of this genus was formerly obtained a liquor that produced the Tyrian purple.

POR'PITE, } *n.* The hair-button-stone, a
POR'PITES, } small species of fossil coral of a roundish figure, flattened and striated from the center to the circumference; found immersed in stone. *Encyc.*

PORRA'CEOUS, *a.* [L. *porraceus*, from *porrum*, a leek or onion.] Greenish; resembling the leek in color. *Wiseman.*

PORREC'TION, *n.* [L. *porrectio*, *porrigo*; *per* or *por*, Eng. *for*, *fore*, and *rego*, Eng. to *reach*.] The act of stretching forth. [*Not used.*]

POR'RET, *n.* [L. *porrum*; It. *porro*, *porretta*, a leek.] A scallion; a leek or small onion. *Brown.*

POR'RIDGE, *n.* [Qu. *pottage*, by corruption, or L. *farrago*, or from *porrum*, a leek.]

A kind of food made by boiling meat in water; broth. *Johnson.*

This mixture is usually called in America, broth or soup, but not *porridge*. With us, *porridge* is a mixture of meal or flour, boiled with water. Perhaps this distinction is not always observed.

POR'RIDGE-POT, *n.* The pot in which flesh, or flesh and vegetables are boiled for food.

POR'RINGER, *n.* [Qu. *porridge*, or Fr. *potager*; Corn. *podzher*.]

1. A small metal vessel in which children eat porridge or milk, or used in the nursery for warming liquors.
2. A head-dress in the shape of a porringer; in contempt. *Shak.*

PORT, *n.* [Fr. from L. *portus*; Sp. *puerto*; It. *porto*; Arm. *porz*; W. *porth*; from L. *porto*, to carry, Gr. φορεω, L. *fero*, Eng. to *bear*. The Welsh *porth* unites the significations of L. *porta* and *portus*, and the Gr. φορεω and πορευομαι are probably of one family. The primary sense of L. *portus*, Eng. *port*, is probably an entrance, place of entrance or passage.]

1. A harbor; a haven; any bay, cove, inlet or recess of the sea or of a lake or the mouth of a river, which ships or vessels can enter, and where they can lie safe from injury by storms. Ports may be *natural* or *artificial*, and sometimes works of art, as piers and moles, are added to the natural shores of a place to render a harbor more safe. The word *port* is generally applied to spacious harbors much resorted to by ships, as the *port* of London or of Boston, and not to small bays or coves which are entered occasionally, or in stress of weather only. *Harbor* includes all places of safety for shipping.
2. A gate. [L. *porta*.]

   From their ivory *port* the cherubim
   Forth issued. *Milton.*
3. An embrasure or opening in the side of a ship of war, through which cannon are discharged; a port-hole. *Raleigh.*
4. The lid which shuts a port-hole. *Mar. Dict.*
5. Carriage; air; mien; manner of movement or walk; demeanor; external ap-

pearance; as a *proud* port; the *port* of a gentleman.

Their *port* was more than human. *Milton.*

With more terrific *port*
Thou walkest. *Philips.*

6. In *seamen's language*, the larboard or left side of a ship; as in the phrase, "the ship heels to *port*." "*Port* the helm," is an order to put the helm to the larboard side.

7. A kind of wine made in Portugal; so called from *Oporto*. *Encyc.*

Port of the voice, in music, the faculty or habit of making the shakes, passages and diminutions, in which the beauty of a song consists. *Encyc.*

PŌRT, *v. t.* To carry in form; as *ported* spears. *Milton.*

2. To turn or put to the left or larboard side of a ship. See the noun, No. 6. It is used in the imperative.

PŌRTABLE, *a.* [It. *portabile*, from L. *porto*, to carry.]

1. That may be carried by the hand or about the person, on horseback, or in a traveling vehicle; not bulky or heavy; that may be easily conveyed from place to place with one's traveling baggage; as a *portable* bureau or secretary.

2. That may be carried from place to place.

3. That may be borne along with one.

The pleasure of the religious man is an easy and *portable* pleasure. *South.*

4. Sufferable; supportable. [*Not in use.*] *Shak.*

PŌRTABLENESS, *n.* The quality of being portable.

PŌRTAĠE, *n.* [Fr. See *Port.*] The act of carrying.

2. The price of carriage. *Fell.*

3. A port-hole. [*Unusual.*] *Shak.*

4. A carrying place over land between navigable waters. *Jefferson. Gallatin.*

PŌRTAL, *n.* [It. *portella*; Fr. *portail.*] In *architecture*, a little gate, where there are two gates of different dimensions. *Encyc.*

2. A little square corner of a room, separated from the rest by a wainscot, and forming a short passage into a room. *Encyc.*

3. A kind of arch of joiner's work before a door. *Encyc.*

4. A gate; an opening for entrance; as the *portals* of heaven.

PŌRTANCE, *n.* [from Fr. *porter*, to carry.] Air; mien; carriage; port; demeanor. [*Obs.*] *Spenser. Shak.*

PŌRTASS, *n.* A breviary; a prayer book. [*portuis, porthose.*] [*Not used.*] *Spenser. Camden. Chaucer.*

PŌRTATIVE, *a.* [Fr. *portatif.*] Portable. [*Not used.*] *Chaucer.*

PŌRT-BAR, *n.* A bar to secure the ports of a ship in a gale of wind.

Port-charges, in commerce, charges to which a ship or its cargo is subjected in a harbor, as wharfage, &c.

PŌRT-€RAYON, *n.* A pencil-case. *Encyc.*

PŌRT€UL'LIS, *n.* [*coulisse*, in French, is from *couler*, to flow or slip down. It signifies a groove or gutter. I think it cannot be from L. *clausus.*]

In *fortification*, an assemblage of timbers joined across one another, like those of a harrow, and each pointed with iron; hung over the gateway of a fortified town, to be let down in case of surprise, to prevent the entrance of an enemy. *Encyc.*

PŌRT€UL'LIS, *v. t.* To shut; to bar; to obstruct. *Shak.*

PŌRT€UL'LISED, *a.* Having a portcullis. *Shenstone.*

PŌRTE, *n.* The Ottoman court, so called from the gate of the Sultan's palace where justice is administered; as the Sublime *Porte.*

PŌRTED, *a.* Having gates. [*Not used.*] *B. Jonson.*

2. Borne in a certain or regular order. *Jones.*

PORTEND', *v. t.* [L. *portendo*; *por*, Eng. *fore*, and *tendo*, to stretch.]

To foreshow; to foretoken; to indicate something future by previous signs.

A moist and cool summer *portends* a hard winter. *Bacon.*

PORTEND'ED, *pp.* Foreshown; previously indicated by signs.

PORTEND'ING, *ppr.* Foreshowing.

PORTEN'SION, *n.* The act of foreshowing. [*Not in use.*] *Brown.*

PORTENT', *n.* [L. *portentum.*] An omen of ill; any previous sign or prodigy indicating the approach of evil or calamity.

My loss by dire *portents* the god foretold. *Dryden.*

PORTENT'OUS, *a.* [L. *portentosus.*] Ominous; foreshowing ill. Ignorance and superstition hold meteors to be *portentous.*

2. Monstrous; prodigious; wonderful; *in an ill sense.*

No beast of more *portentous* size,
In the Hercynian forest lies. *Roscommon.*

PŌRTER, *n.* [It. *portiere*; Fr. *portier*; Sp. *portero*; from L. *porta*, a gate.]

1. A man that has the charge of a door or gate; a door-keeper. *Arbuthnot.*

2. One that waits at the door to receive messages. *Pope.*

3. [Fr. *porteur*, from *porter*, to carry, L. *porto.*] A carrier; a person who carries or conveys burdens for hire. *Howell. Watts.*

4. A malt liquor which differs from ale and pale beer, in being made with high dried malt.

PŌRTERAĠE, *n.* Money charged or paid for the carriage of burdens by a porter. *Tooke.*

2. The business of a porter or door-keeper. *Churchill.*

PŌRTERLY, *a.* Coarse; vulgar. [*Little used.*] *Bray.*

PORTESSE. [See *Portass.*]

PŌRT-FIRE, *n.* A composition for setting fire to powder, &c. frequently used in preference to a match. It is wet or dry. The wet is composed of saltpeter, four parts, of sulphur one, and of mealed powder four; mixed and sifted, moistened with a little lintseed oil, and well rubbed. The dry is composed of saltpeter, four parts, sulphur one, mealed powder two, and antimony one. These compositions are driven into small papers for use. *Encyc.*

PORTFOLIO, *n.* [Fr. *porte-feuille*; *porter*, to carry, and *feuille*, a leaf, L. *folium.*]

A case of the size of a large book, to keep loose papers in.

To have or *hold the portfolio*, is to hold the office of minister of foreign affairs. *E. Everett.*

PORTGLAVE, *n.* [Fr. *porter*, to carry, and W. *glaiv*, a crooked sword; *llaiv*, a shave, Celtic.] A sword-bearer. [*Not in use.*] *Ainsworth.*

PŌRTGRAVE, PŌRTGREVE, PŌRTREEVE, } *n.* [L. *portus*, a port, and G. *graf*, D. *graaf*, Sax. *gerefa*, a count, an earl.]

Formerly, the chief magistrate of a port or maritime town. This officer is now called mayor or bailif.

PŌRT-HOLE, *n.* [*port* and *hole.*] The embrasure of a ship of war. [See *Port.*]

PŌRTI€O, *n.* [It. *portico*; L. *porticus*, from *porta* or *portus.*]

In *architecture*, a kind of gallery on the ground, or a piazza encompassed with arches supported by columns; a covered walk. The roof is sometimes flat; sometimes vaulted. *Encyc.*

PŌRTION, *n.* [L. *portio*, from *partio*, to divide, from *pars*, part. See *Part.*]

1. In *general*, a part of any thing separated from it. Hence,

2. A part, though not actually divided, but considered by itself.

These are parts of his ways, but how little a *portion* is heard of him. Job xxvi.

3. A part assigned; an allotment; a dividend.

How small
A *portion* to your share would fall. *Waller.*

The priests had a *portion* assigned them of Pharaoh. Gen. xlvii.

4. The part of an estate given to a child or heir, or descending to him by law, and distributed to him in the settlement of the estate.

5. A wife's fortune.

PŌRTION, *v. t.* To divide; to parcel; to allot a share or shares.

And *portion* to his tribes the wide domain. *Pope.*

2. To endow.

Him *portion'd* maids, apprentic'd orphans blest. *Pope.*

PŌRTIONED, *pp.* Divided into shares or parts.

2. Endowed; furnished with a portion.

PŌRTIONER, *n.* One who divides or assigns in shares.

PŌRTIONING, *ppr.* Dividing; endowing.

PŌRTIONIST, *n.* One who has a certain academical allowance or portion.

2. The incumbent of a benefice which has more rectors or vicars than one. *Life of A. Wood.*

PŌRTLAND-STONE, *n.* A compact sandstone from the isle of Portland in England, which forms a calcarious cement. *Nicholson.*

PŌRTLAST, PŌRTOISE, } *n.* The gunwale of a ship.

To lower the yards a portlast, is to lower them to the gunwale.

To ride a portoise, is to have the lower yards and top-masts struck or lowered down, when at anchor in a gale of wind. *Mar. Dict.*

PŌRTLID, *n.* The lid that closes a port-hole. *Mar. Dict.*

PŌRTLINESS, *n.* [from *portly.*] Dignity of mien or of personal appearance, consisting in size and symmetry of body, with dignified manners and demeanor. *Camden.*

PŌRTLY, *a.* [from *port.*] Grand or dignified in mien; of a noble appearance and carriage. *Shak.*

2. Bulky; corpulent. *Shak.*

PŌRT-MAN, *n.* [*port* and *man.*] An inhabitant or burgess, as of a cinque port.

PŌRTMAN'TEAU, *n.* [Fr. *porte-manteau*, from *porter*, to carry, and *manteau*, a a cloke, L. *mantele*, It. *mantello.* It is often pronounced *portmantle.*]
A bag usually made of lether, for carrying apparel and other furniture on journeys, particularly on horseback.

PŌRT-MOTE, *n.* [*port* and Sax. *mot*, a meeting.] Anciently, a court held in a port town. *Blackstone.*

PORTOISE. [See *Portlast.*]

PŌRTRAIT, *n.* [Fr. *portrait*, from *portraire*, to draw, Eng. to *portray*; *pour*, Eng. *for*, *fore*, and *traire*, L. *trahere*, Eng. to *draw*; Arm. *pourtrezi.* The Italian is *ritratto*, Sp. Port. *retrato*, from L. *re* and *tracto.*]
A picture or representation of a person, and especially of a face, drawn from the life.

In *portraits*, the grace, and we may add, the likeness, consist more in the general air than in the exact similitude of every feature. *Reynolds.*

PŌRTRAIT, *v. t.* To portray; to draw. [*Not used.*] *Spenser.*

PŌRTRAITURE, *n.* [Fr.] A portrait; painted resemblance. *Milton. Pope.*

PŌRTRA'Y, *v. t.* [Fr. *portraire.* See *Portrait.*]
1. To paint or draw the likeness of any thing in colors; as, to *portray* a king on horseback; to *portray* a city or temple with a pencil or with chalk.
2. To describe in words. It belongs to the historian to *portray* the character of Alexander of Russia. Homer *portrays* the character and achievments of his heroes in glowing colors.
3. To adorn with pictures; as shields *portrayed.* *Milton.*

PŌRTRA'YED, *pp.* Painted or drawn to the life; described.

PŌRTRA'YER, *n.* One who paints, draws to the life or describes.

PŌRTRA'YING, *ppr.* Painting or drawing the likeness of; describing.

PŌRTRESS, } *n.* [from *porter.*] A female
PŌRTERESS, } guardian of a gate. *Milton.*

PŌRTREVE, *n.* [The modern orthography of *portgreve*, which see.]
The chief magistrate of a port or maritime town.

PŌRT-ROPE, *n.* A rope to draw up a portlid. *Mar. Dict.*

POR'WIGLE, *n.* A tadpole; a young frog. [*Not used.*] *Brown.*

PŌRY, *a.* [from *pore.*] Full of pores or small interstices. *Dryden.*

POSE, *n.* *s* as z. [See the Verb.] In *heraldry*, a lion, horse or other beast standing still, with all his feet on the ground. *Encyc.*

POSE, *n.* *s* as z. [Sax. *gepose.*] A stuffing of the head; catarrh. *Obs.* *Chaucer.*

POSE, *v.t.* *s* as z. [W. *posiaw*, to pose, to make an increment, to gather knowledge, to investigate, to interrogate; *pos*, a heap, increment, growth, increase; *posel*, curdled milk, *posset*; Sax. *gepose*, heaviness, stuffing of the head. The primary sense is to set or fix, from thrusting or pressing, L. *posui*, Sp. *posar*, Fr. *poser*; hence the sense of collecting into a lump or fixed mass, Ch. and Syr. חבץ to press, compress, collect, coagulate. Class Bs. No. 24. See also Ar. No. 21. 31. and No. 32. 33. 35. and others in that class.]
1. To puzzle, [a word of the same origin;] to set; to put to a stand or stop; to gravel.

Learning was *pos'd*, philosophy was set. *Herbert.*

I design not to *pose* them with those common enigmas of magnetism. *Glanville.*

2. To puzzle or put to a stand by asking difficult questions; to set by questions; hence, to interrogate closely, or with a view to scrutiny. *Bacon.*

PO'SED, *pp.* Puzzled; put to a stand; interrogated closely.

PO'SER, *n.* One that puzzles by asking difficult questions; a close examiner.

PO'SING, *ppr.* Puzzling; putting to a stand; questioning closely.

POS'ITED, *a.* [L. *positus*, from *pono*, to put; probably however, *pono* is a different root, and *positus* from the root of *pose.*] Put; set; placed. *Hale.*

POSI''TION, *n.* [L. *positio*, from *positus.* See *Pose* and *Posited.*]
1. State of being placed; situation; often with reference to other objects, or to different parts of the same object.

We have different prospects of the same thing according to our different *positions* to it. *Locke.*

2. Manner of standing or being placed; attitude; as an inclining *position.*
3. Principle laid down; proposition advanced or affirmed as a fixed principle, or stated as the ground of reasoning, or to be proved.

Let not the proof of any *position* depend on the *positions* that follow, but always on those which precede. *Watts.*

4. The advancement of any principle. *Brown.*
5. State; condition.

Great Britain, at the peace of 1763, stood in a *position* to prescribe her own terms. *Ames.*

6. In *grammar*, the state of a vowel placed between two consonants, as in *pompous*, or before a double consonant, as in *axle.* In prosody, vowels are said to be long or short by *position.*

POSI''TIONAL, *a.* Respecting position. [*Not used.*] *Brown.*

POS'ITIVE, *a.* [It. *positivo*; Fr. *positif*; Low L. *positivus.*]
1. Properly, set; laid down; expressed; direct; explicit; opposed to *implied*; as, he told us in *positive* words; we have his *positive* declaration to the fact; the testimony is *positive.*
2. Absolute; express; not admitting any condition or discretion. The commands of the admiral are *positive.*
3. Absolute; real; existing in fact; opposed to *negative*, as *positive* good, which exists by itself, whereas *negative* good is merely the absence of evil; or opposed to *relative* or *arbitrary*, as beauty is not a *positive* thing, but depends on the different tastes of people. *Locke. Encyc.*
4. Direct; express; opposed to *circumstantial*; as *positive* proof. *Blackstone.*
5. Confident; fully assured; *applied to persons.* The witness is very *positive* that he is correct in his testimony.
6. Dogmatic; over-confident in opinion or assertion.

Some *positive* persisting fops we know,
That, if once wrong, will needs be always so. *Pope.*

7. Settled by arbitrary appointment; opposed to *natural* or *inbred.*

In laws, that which is natural, bindeth universally; that which is *positive*, not so. *Hooker.*

Although no laws but *positive* are mutable, yet all are not mutable which are *positive.* *Hooker.*

8. Having power to act directly; as a *positive* voice in legislation. *Swift.*

Positive degree, in grammar, is the state of an adjective which denotes simple or absolute quality, without comparison or relation to increase or diminution; as *wise*, *noble.*

Positive electricity, according to Dr. Franklin, consists in a superabundance of the fluid in a substance. Others suppose it to consist in a tendency of the fluid outwards. It is not certain in what consists the difference between *positive* and *negative* electricity. *Positive* electricity being produced by rubbing glass, is called the *vitreous*; *negative* electricity, produced by rubbing amber or resin, is called the *resinous.* *Encyc.*

POS'ITIVE, *n.* What is capable of being affirmed; reality. *South.*
2. That which settles by absolute appointment. *Waterland.*
3. In *grammar*, a word that affirms or asserts existence. *Harris.*

POS'ITIVELY, *adv.* Absolutely; by itself, independent of any thing else; not comparatively.

Good and evil removed may be esteemed good or evil comparatively, and not *positively* or simply. *Bacon.*

2. Not negatively; really; in its own nature; directly; inherently. A thing is *positively* good, when it produces happiness by its own qualities or operation. It is *negatively* good, when it prevents an evil, or does not produce it.
3. Certainly; indubitably. This is *positively* your handwriting.
4. Directly; explicitly; expressly. The witness testified *positively* to the fact.
5. Peremptorily; in strong terms.

The divine law *positively* requires humility and meekness. *Sprat.*

6. With full confidence or assurance. I cannot speak *positively* in regard to the fact.

Positively electrified, in the science of electricity. A body is said to be *positively* electrified or charged with electric matter, when it contains a superabundance of the fluid, and *negatively* electrified or charged, when some part of the fluid which it naturally contains, has been taken from it. *Franklin.*

According to other theorists, when the electric fluid is directed outwards from a body, the substance is electrified *positively*; but when it is entering or has a tendency to enter another substance, the body is supposed to be *negatively* electrified. The two species of electricity attract each other, and each repels its own kind.

POS'ITIVENESS, *n.* Actualness; reality of existence; not mere negation.

The *positiveness* of sins of commission lies both in the habitude of the will and in the executed act too; the *positiveness* of sins of omission is in the habitude of the will only. *Norris.*

2. Undoubting assurance; full confidence; peremptoriness; as, the man related the facts with *positiveness.* In matters of opinion, *positiveness* is not an indication of prudence.

POSITIV'ITY, *n.* Peremptoriness. [*Not used.*] *Watts.*

POSITURE, for *posture*, is not in use. [See *Posture.*]

POS'NET, *n.* [W. *posned*, from *posiaw.* See *Pose.*]

A little basin; a porringer, skillet or saucepan. *Owen.*

POSOLOG'ICAL, *a.* Pertaining to posology.

POSOL'OGY, *n.* [Gr. ποσος, how much, and λογος, discourse.]

In *medicine*, the science or doctrine of doses. *Amer. Dispensatory.*

POS'POLITE, *n.* A kind of militia in Poland, consisting of the gentry, who in case of invasion, are summoned to arms for the defense of the country. *Coxe.*

Posse comitatus, in law, the power of the country, or the citizens, who are summoned to assist an officer in suppressing a riot, or executing any legal precept which is forcibly opposed. The word *comitatus* is often omitted, and *posse* alone is used in the same sense. *Blackstone.*

2. In *low language*, a number or crowd of people; a rabble.

POSSESS', *v. t.* [L. *possessus, possideo*, a compound of *po*, a Russian preposition, perhaps *by*, and *sedeo*, to sit; to *sit in* or *on.* We have this word from the Latin, but the same compound is in our mother tongue, Sax. *besittan*, to possess; *be*, by, and *sittan*, to sit; *gesittan, besettan, gesettan*, are also used; D. *bezitten*; G. *besitzen*; Dan. *besidder*; Sw. *besitta*; Fr. *posseder*; Arm. *poçzedi*; Sp. *poseer*; It. *possedere.*]

1. To have the just and legal title, ownership or property of a thing; to own; to hold the title of, as the rightful proprietor, or to hold both the title and the thing. A man may *possess* the farm which he cultivates, or he may *possess* an estate in a foreign country, not in his own occupation. He may *possess* many farms which are occupied by tenants. In this as in other cases, the original sense of the word is enlarged, the holding or tenure being applied to the *title* or *right*, as well as to the thing itself.

2. To hold; to occupy without title or ownership.

I raise up the Chaldeans, to *possess* the dwelling-places that are not theirs. Hab. i.

Neither said any of them that aught of the things which he *possessed* was his own. Acts iv.

3. To have; to occupy. The love of the world usually *possesses* the heart.

4. To seize; to gain; to obtain the occupation of.

The English marched towards the river Eske, intending to *possess* a hill called Under-Eske. *Hayward.*

5. To have power over; as an invisible agent or spirit. Luke viii.

Beware what spirit rages in your breast;
For ten inspired, ten thousand are *possess'd.* *Roscommon.*

6. To affect by some power.

Let not your ears despise my tongue,
Which shall *possess* them with the heaviest sound
That ever yet they heard. *Swift.*

To possess of, or *with*, more properly to *possess of*, is to give possession, command or occupancy.

Of fortune's favor long *possess'd.* *Dryden.*

This *possesses* us *of* the most valuable blessing of human life, friendship. *Gov. of the Tongue.*

To possess one's self of, to take or gain possession or command; to make one's self master of.

We *possessed ourselves of* the kingdom of Naples. *Addison.*

To possess with, to furnish or fill with something permanent; or to be retained.

It is of unspeakable advantage to *possess* our minds *with* an habitual good intention. *Addison.*

If they are *possessed with* honest minds. *Addison.*

POSSESS'ED, *pp.* Held by lawful title; occupied; enjoyed; affected by demons or invisible agents.

POSSESS'ING, *ppr.* Having or holding by absolute right or title; occupying; enjoying.

POSSES'SION, *n.* The having, holding or detention of property in one's power or command; actual seizin or occupancy, either rightful or wrongful. One man may have the *possession* of a thing, and another may have the right of possession or property.

If the *possession* is severed from the property; if A has the right of property, and B by unlawful means has gained *possession*, this is an injury to A. This is a bare or naked *possession.* *Blackstone.*

In *bailment*, the bailee, who receives goods to convey, or to keep for a time, has the *possession* of the goods, and a temporary right over them, but not the property. *Property in possession*, includes both the right and the occupation. Long undisturbed *possession* is presumptive proof of right or property in the possessor.

2. The thing possessed; land, estate or goods owned; as foreign *possessions.*

The house of Jacob shall possess their *possessions.* Obad. 17.

When the young man heard that saying, he went away sorrowful, for he had great *possessions.* Matt. xix.

3. Any thing valuable possessed or enjoyed. Christian peace of mind is the best *possession* of life.

4. The state of being under the power of demons or invisible beings; madness; lunacy; as demoniacal *possession.*

Writ of possession, a precept directing a sherif to put a person in peaceable possession of property recovered in ejectment. *Blackstone.*

To take possession, to enter on, or to bring within one's power or occupancy.

To give possession, to put in another's power or occupancy.

POSSES'SION, *v. t.* To invest with property. [*Not used.*] *Carew.*

POSSES'SIONER, *n.* One that has possession of a thing, or power over it. [*Little used.*] *Sidney.*

POSSESS'IVE, *a.* [L. *possessivus.*] Pertaining to possession; having possession.

Possessive case, in English grammar, is the genitive case, or case of nouns and pronouns, which expresses, 1st, possession, ownership, as *John's* book; or 2dly, some relation of one thing to another, as *Homer's* admirers.

POSSESS'OR, *n.* An occupant; one that has possession; a person who holds in his hands or power any species of property, real or personal. The owner or proprietor of property is the permanent *possessor* by legal right; the lessee of land and the bailee of goods are temporary *possessors* by right; the disseizor of land and the thief are wrongful *possessors.*

2. One that has, holds or enjoys any good or other thing.

Think of the happiness of the prophets and apostles, saints and martyrs, *possessors* of eternal glory. *Law.*

POSSESS'ORY, *a.* Having possession; as a *possessory* lord. *Howell.*

Possessory action, in law, an action or suit in which the right of possession only, and not that of property, is contested. *Blackstone.*

POS'SET, *n.* [W. *posel*, from the root of *pose*, W. *posiaw*, to gather. The L. *posca* may have the same origin.]

Milk curdled with wine or other liquor. *Dryden. Arbuthnot.*

POS'SET, *v. t.* To curdle; to turn. *Shak.*

POSSIBIL'ITY, *n.* [from *possible*; Fr. *possibilité.*]

The power of being or existing; the power of happening; the state of being possible. It often implies improbability or great uncertainty. There is a *possibility* that a new star may appear this night. There is a *possibility* of a hard frost in July in our latitude. It is not expedient to hazard much on the bare *possibility* of success. It is prudent to reduce contracts to writing, and to render them so explicit as to preclude the *possibility* of mistake or controversy.

POS'SIBLE, *a.* [Fr.; It. *possibile*; Sp. *posible*; from L. *possibilis*, from *posse.* See *Power.*]

That may be or exist; that may be now, or may happen or come to pass; that may be done; not contrary to the nature of things. It is *possible* that the Greeks and Turks may now be engaged in battle. It is *possible* the peace of Europe may continue a century. It is not physically *possible* that a stream should ascend a mountain, but it is *possible* that the Supreme Being may suspend a law of nature, that is, his usual course of proceeding. It is not *possible* that 2 and 3 should be 7, or that the same action should be morally right and morally wrong.

This word when pronounced with a certain emphasis, implies improbability. A thing is *possible*, but very improbable.

POS'SIBLY, *adv.* By any power, moral or physical, really existing. Learn all that can *possibly* be known.

Can we *possibly* his love desert? *Milton.*

2. Perhaps; without absurdity.

Arbitrary power tends to make a man a bad sovereign, who might *possibly* have been a good one, had he been invested with authority circumscribed by laws. *Addison.*

PŌST, *a.* [from Fr. *aposter.*] Suborned; hired to do what is wrong. [*Not in use.*] *Sandys.*

PŌST, *n.* [W. *pôst*; D. Dan. Sw. *post*; G. *pfoste, posten*, and *post*; Fr. *poste*; Sp. *poste, posta*; It. *posta, posto*; L. *postis*, from *positus*, the given participle of *pono*, to place, but coinciding with Sp. *posar*, It. *posare*, to put or set.]

1. A piece of timber set upright, usually larger than a stake, and intended to support something else; as the *posts* of a house; the *posts* of a door; the *posts* of a gate; the *posts* of a fence.
2. A military station; the place where a single soldier or a body of troops is stationed. The sentinel must not desert his *post.* The troops are ordered to defend the *post.* Hence,
3. The troops stationed in a particular place, or the ground they occupy. *Marshall. Encyc.*
4. A public office or employment, that is, a fixed place or station.

When vice prevails and impious men bear sway,
The *post* of honor is a private station. *Addison.*

5. A messenger or a carrier of letters and papers; one that goes at stated times to convey the mail or dispatches. This sense also denotes fixedness, either from the practice of using relays of horses stationed at particular places, or of stationing men for carrying dispatches, or from the fixed stages where they were to be supplied with refreshment. [See *Stage.*] Xenophon informs us that Cyrus, king of Persia, established such stations or houses.
6. A seat or situation. *Burnet.*
7. A sort of writing paper, such as is used for letters; letter paper.
8. An old game at cards.

To ride post, to be employed to carry dispatches and papers, and as such carriers rode in haste, hence the phrase signifies to ride in haste, to pass with expedition. *Post* is used also adverbially, for swiftly, expeditiously, or expressly.

Sent from Media *post* to Egypt. *Milton.*

Hence, to *travel post*, is to travel expeditiously by the use of fresh horses taken at certain stations.

Knight of the post, a fellow suborned or hired to do a bad action.

PŌST, *v. i.* [Fr. *poster*; Sp. *postear.*] To travel with speed.

And *post* o'er land and ocean without rest. *Milton.*

PŌST, *v. t.* To fix to a post; as, to *post* a notification.

2. To expose to public reproach by fixing the name to a post; to expose to opprobrium by some public action; as, to *post* a coward.
3. To advertise on a post or in a public place; as, to *post* a stray horse. *Laws of New England.*
4. To set; to place; to station; as, to *post* troops on a hill, or in front or on the flank of an army.
5. In *book-keeping*, to carry accounts from the waste-book or journal to the ledger.

To post off, to put off; to delay. [*Not used.*] *Shak.*

PŌST, a Latin preposition, signifying *after.* It is used in this sense in composition in many English words.

PŌSTABLE, *a.* That may be carried. [*Not used.*] *Mountague.*

PŌSTAĠE, *n.* The price established by law to be paid for the conveyance of a letter in a public mail.

2. A portage. [*Not used.*] *Smollet.*

PŌSTBOY, *n.* A boy that rides as post; a courier. *Tatler.*

PŌST-CHAISE, *n.* [See *Chaise.*] A carriage with four wheels for the conveyance of travelers.

PŌSTDA'TE, *v. t.* [L. *post*, after, and *date*, L. *datum.*]

To date after the real time; as, to *postdate* a contract, that is, to date it after the true time of making the contract.

PŌSTDILU'VIAL, **PŌSTDILU'VIAN**, *a.* [L. *post*, after, and *diluvium*, the deluge.]

Being or happening posterior to the flood in Noah's days. *Woodward. Buckland.*

PŌSTDILU'VIAN, *n.* A person who lived after the flood, or who has lived since that event. *Grew.*

PŌST-DISSE'IZIN, *n.* A subsequent disseizin. A writ of *post-disseizin* is intended to put in possession a person who has been disseized after a judgment to recover the same lands of the same person, under the statute of Merton. *Blackstone.*

PŌST-DISSE'IZOR, *n.* A person who disseizes another of lands which he had before recovered of the same person. *Blackstone.*

PŌSTEA, *n.* [L.] The record of what is done in a cause subsequent to the joining of issue and awarding of trial. *Blackstone.*

PŌSTED, *pp.* Placed; stationed.

2. Exposed on a post or by public notice.
3. Carried to a ledger, as accounts.

PŌSTER, *n.* One who posts; also, a courier; one that travels expeditiously.

POSTE'RIOR, *a.* [from L. *posterus*, from *post*, after; Fr. *posterieur.*]

1. Later or subsequent in time.

Hesiod was *posterior* to Homer. *Broome.*

2. Later in the order of proceeding or moving; coming after. [*Unfrequent.*]

POSTERIOR'ITY, *n.* [Fr. *posteriorité.*]

The state of being later or subsequent; as *posteriority* of time or of an event; opposed to *priority.* *Hale.*

POSTE'RIORS, *n. plu.* The hinder parts of an animal body. *Swift.*

POSTER'ITY, *n.* [Fr. *posterité*; L. *posteritas*, from *posterus*, from *post*, after.]

1. Descendants; children, children's children, &c. indefinitely; the race that proceeds from a progenitor. The whole human race are the *posterity* of Adam.
2. In *a general sense*, succeeding generations; opposed to *ancestors.*

To the unhappy that unjustly bleed,
Heav'n gives *posterity* t' avenge the deed. *Pope.*

PŌSTERN, *n.* [Fr. *pôterne*, for *posterne*, from L. *post*, behind.]

1. Primarily, a back door or gate; a private entrance; hence, any small door or gate. *Dryden. Locke.*
2. In *fortification*, a small gate, usually in the angle of the flank of a bastion, or in that of the curtain or near the orillon, descending into the ditch. *Encyc.*

PŌSTERN, *a.* Back; being behind; private. *Dryden.*

PŌST-EXIST'ENCE, *n.* Subsequent or future existence. *Addison.*

PŌST-FINE, *n.* In *English law*, a fine due to the king by prerogative, after a licentia concordandi given in a fine of lands and tenements; called also the king's silver. *Blackstone.*

PŌSTFIX, *n.* [L. *post*, after, and *fix.*] In *grammar*, a letter, syllable or word added to the end of another word; a suffix. *Parkhurst.*

PŌSTFIX', *v. t.* To add or annex a letter, syllable or word, to the end of another or principal word. *Parkhurst.*

PŌSTFIX'ED, *pp.* Added to the end of a word.

PŌSTFIX'ING, *ppr.* Adding to the end of a word.

PŌST-HACK'NEY, *n.* [*post* and *hackney.*] A hired posthorse. *Wotton.*

PŌST-HĀSTE, *n.* Haste or speed in traveling, like that of a post or courier. *Shak.*

PŌST-HĀSTE, *adv.* With speed or expedition. He traveled *post-haste*, that is, by an ellipsis, *with post-haste.*

PŌST-HORSE, *n.* A horse stationed for the use of couriers. *Sidney.*

PŌST-HOUSE, *n.* A house where a post-office is kept for receiving and dispatching letters by public mails; a post-office. [*The latter word is now in general use.*]

POST'HUME, *a.* Posthumous. [*Not used.*] *Watts.*

POST'HUMOUS, *a.* [L. *post*, after, and *humus*, earth; *humatus*, buried.]

1. Born after the death of the father, or taken from the dead body of the mother; as a *posthumous* son or daughter. *Blackstone.*
2. Published after the death of the author; as *posthumous* works.
3. Being after one's decease; as a *posthumous* character. *Addison.*

POST'HUMOUSLY, *adv.* After one's decease.

PŌSTIC, *a.* [L. *posticus.*] Backward. [*Not used.*] *Brown.*

POS'TIL, *n.* [It. *postilla*; Sp. *postila*; from L. *post.*]

A marginal note; originally, a note in the margin of the Bible, so called because written after the text. *Encyc.*

POS'TIL, *v. t.* [It. *postillare.*] To write marginal notes; to gloss; to illustrate with marginal notes. *Bacon.*

POS'TILER, *n.* One who writes marginal notes; one who illustrates the text of a book by notes in the margin.

PŌSTILLION, *n. postil'yon.* [Fr. *postillon*, a postboy, from *poste.*]

One that rides and guides the first pair of horses in a coach or other carriage; also, one that rides one of the horses, when one pair only is used, either in a coach or post-chaise.

PŌSTING, *ppr.* Setting up on a post; exposing the name or character to reproach by public advertisement.
2. Placing; stationing.
3. Transferring accounts to a ledger.

PŌSTLIMIN'IAR, PŌSTLIMIN'IOUS, *a.* [See *Postliminium.*] Contrived, done or existing subsequently; as a *postliminious* application.

PŌSTLIMIN'IUM, PŌSTLIM'INY, *n.* [L. *post*, after, and *limen*, end, limit.]
Postliminium, among the Romans, was the return of a person to his own country who had gone to sojourn in a foreign country, or had been banished or taken by an enemy.
In the modern law of nations, the right of *postliminy* is that by virtue of which, persons and things taken by an enemy in war, are restored to their former state, when coming again under the power of the nation to which they belonged. The sovereign of a country is bound to protect the person and the property of his subjects; and a subject who has suffered the loss of his property by the violence of war, on being restored to his country, can claim to be re-established in all his rights, and to recover his property. But this right does not extend, in all cases, to personal effects or movables, on account of the difficulty of ascertaining their identity. *Vattel. Du Ponceau.*

PŌSTMAN, *n.* A post or courier; a letter-carrier. *Granger.*

PŌSTMARK, *n.* The mark or stamp of a post-office on a letter.

PŌSTMASTER, *n.* The officer who has the superintendence and direction of a post-office.
Postmaster-general, is the chief officer of the post-office department, whose duty is to make contracts for the conveyance of the public mails and see that they are executed, and who receives the moneys arising from the postage of letters, pays the expenses, keeps the accounts of the office, and superintends the whole department.

PŌSTMERID'IAN, *a.* [L. *postmeridianus.* See *Meridian.*]
Being or belonging to the afternoon; as *postmeridian* sleep. *Bacon.*

PŌSTNATE, *a.* [L. *post*, after, and *natus*, born.] Subsequent. [*Little used.*] *Taylor.*

PŌST-NOTE, *n.* [*post* and *note.*] In *commerce*, a bank note intended to be transmitted to a distant place by the public mail, and made payable to *order.* In this it differs from a common bank note, which is payable to the *bearer.*

PŌST-OFFICE, *n.* An office or house where letters are received for delivery to the persons to whom they are addressed, or to be transmitted to other places in the public mails; a post-house.

PŌST-PAID, *a.* Having the postage paid on; as a letter.

PŌSTPO'NE, *v. t.* [L. *postpono; post*, after, and *pono*, to put.]
1. To put off; to defer to a future or later time; to delay; as, to *postpone* the consideration of a bill or question to the afternoon, or to the following day.
2. To set below something else in value or importance.
All other considerations should give way and be *postponed* to this. *Locke.*

PŌSTPO'NED, *pp.* Delayed; deferred to a future time; set below in value.

PŌSTPO'NEMENT, *n.* The act of deferring to a future time; temporary delay of business. *T. Pickering. Kent.*

PŌSTPO'NENCE, *n.* Dislike. [*Not in use.*] *Johnson.*

PŌSTPO'NING, *ppr.* Deferring to a future time.

POSTPOSI''TION, *n.* [*post* and *position.*] The state of being put back or out of the regular place. *Mede.*

PŌSTREMO'TE, *a.* [*post* and *remote.*] More remote in subsequent time or order. *Darwin.*

PŌSTSCRIPT, *n.* [L. *post*, after, and *scriptum*, written.]
A paragraph added to a letter after it is concluded and signed by the writer; or any addition made to a book or composition after it had been supposed to be finished, containing something omitted, or something new occurring to the writer. *Locke. Addison.*

PŌST-TOWN, *n.* A town in which a post-office is established by law.
2. A town in which post-horses are kept.

POS'TULANT, *n.* [See *Postulate.*] One who makes demand.

POS'TULATE, *n.* [L. *postulatum*, from *postulo*, to demand, from the root of *posco*, to ask or demand. The sense is to urge or push.]
A position or supposition assumed without proof, or one which is considered as self-evident, or too plain to require illustration. *Encyc.*
A self-evident problem, answering to axiom, which is a self-evident theorem. *D. Olmsted.*

POS'TULATE, *v. t.* [supra.] To beg or assume without proof. [*Little used.*] *Brown.*
2. To invite; to solicit; to require by entreaty. *Burnet.*
3. To assume; to take without positive consent.
The Byzantine emperors appear to have exercised, or at least to have *postulated* a sort of paramount supremacy over this nation. *Tooke.*

POSTULA'TION, *n.* [L. *postulatio.*] The act of supposing without proof; gratuitous assumption. *Hale.*
2. Supplication; intercession; also, suit; cause. *Pearson. Burnet.*

POS'TULATORY, *a.* Assuming without proof.
2. Assumed without proof. *Brown.*

POSTULA'TUM, *n.* [L.] A postulate, which see. *Addison.*

POS'TURE, *n.* [Fr. from L. *positura; pono, positus.*]
1. In *painting* and *sculpture*, attitude; the situation of a figure with regard to the eye, and of the several principal members with regard to each other, by which action is expressed. *Postures* should be accommodated to the character of the figure, and the *posture* of each member to its office. *Postures* are natural or artificial. *Natural* postures are such as our ordinary actions and the occasions of life lead us to exhibit; *artificial* postures are such as are assumed or learnt for particular purposes, or in particular occupations, as in dancing, fencing, &c. *Addison. Encyc.*
2. Situation; condition; particular state with regard to something else; as the *posture* of public affairs before or after a war.
3. Situation of the body; as an abject *posture.* *Milton.*
4. State; condition. The fort is in a *posture* of defense.
5. The situation or disposition of the several parts of the body with respect to each other, or with respect to a particular purpose.

He casts
His eyes against the moon in most strange *postures.* *Shak.*

The *posture* of a poetic figure is the description of the heroes in the performance of such or such an action. *Dryden.*

6. Disposition; frame; as the *posture* of the soul. *Bailey.*

POS'TURE, *v. t.* To place in a particular manner; to dispose the parts of a body for a particular purpose.
He was raw with *posturing* himself according to the direction of the chirurgeons. *Brook.*

POS'TURE-MASTER, *n.* One that teaches or practices artificial postures of the body. *Spectator.*

PO'SY, *n.* *s* as *z.* [Qu. *poesy;* or a collection, a cluster, from the W. *posiaw*, to collect. See *Pose.*]
1. A motto inscribed on a ring, &c. *Addison.*
2. A bunch of flowers. *Spenser.*

POT, *n.* [Fr. *pot;* Arm. *pod;* Ir. *pota;* Sw. *potta;* Dan. *potte;* W. *pot*, a pot, and *potel*, a bottle; *poten*, a pudding, the paunch, something bulging; D. *pot*, a pot, a stake, a hoard; *potten*, to hoard.]
1. A vessel more deep than broad, made of earth, or iron or other metal, used for several domestic purposes; as an iron *pot*, for boiling meat or vegetables; a *pot* for holding liquors; a cup, as a *pot* of ale; an earthern *pot* for plants, called a *flower pot*, &c.
2. A sort of paper of small sized sheets.
To go to pot, to be destroyed, ruined, wasted or expended. [*A low phrase.*]

POT, *v. t.* To preserve seasoned in pots; as *potted* fowl and fish. *Dryden.*
2. To inclose or cover in pots of earth. *Mortimer.*
3. To put in casks for draining; as, to *pot* sugar, by taking it from the cooler and placing it in hogsheads with perforated heads, from which the melasses percolates through the spungy stalk of a plantain leaf. *Edwards, W. Indies.*

PO'TABLE, *a.* [Fr.; Low L. *potabilis;* It. *potabile;* from L. *poto*, to drink; *potus*, drink, Gr. ποτος, from πινω, πιομαι, to drink.]
Drinkable; that may be drank; as water fresh and *potable.* *Bacon.*
Rivers run *potable* gold. *Milton.*

PO'TABLE, *n.* Something that may be drank. *Philips.*

PO'TABLENESS, *n.* The quality of being drinkable.

POT'AGE, *n.* [from *pot;* Fr. *id.;* It. *potaggio;* Port. *potagem;* W. *potes;* Arm.

podaich. This is a more correct orthography than *pottage.*]
A species of food made of meat boiled to softness in water, usually with some vegetables or sweet herbs.
POT'AGER, *n.* [from *potage.*] A porringer. *Grew.*
POTAG'RO, POTAR'GO, *n.* A kind of pickle imported from the West Indies. *King.*
PO'TANCE, *n.* With *watchmakers,* the stud in which the lower pivot of the verge is placed. *Ash. Scott.*
POT'ASH, *n.* [*pot* and *ashes; D. potasch; G. pottasche; Dan. potaske;* Fr. *potasse.*]
The popular name of vegetable fixed alkali in an impure state, procured from the ashes of plants by lixiviation and evaporation. The matter remaining after evaporation is refined in a crucible or furnace, and the extractive substance burnt off or dissipated. Refined potash is called *pearlash.* The plants which yield the greatest quantity of potash are wormwood and fumitory. *Kirwan. Nicholson. Encyc.*
By recent discoveries of Sir H. Davy, it appears that potash is a metallic oxyd; the metal is called *potassium,* and the alkali, in books of science, is called *potassa.*
POTAS'SA, *n.* The scientific name of vegetable alkali or potash.
POTAS'SIUM, *n.* A name given to the metallic basis of vegetable alkali. According to Dr. Davy, 100 parts of potash consist of 86.1 parts of the basis, and 13.9 of oxygen. *Med. Repos.*
Potassium has the most powerful affinity for oxygen of all substances known; it takes it from every other compound, and hence is a most important agent in chimical analysis.
POTA'TION, *n.* [L. *potatio.* See *Potable.*]
1. A drinking or drinking bout.
2. A draught. *Shak.*
3. A species of drink. *Shak.*
POTA'TO, *n.* [Ind. *batatas.*] A plant and esculent root of the genus Solanum, a native of America. The root of this plant, which is usually called *potatoe,* constitutes one of the cheapest and most nourishing species of vegetable food; it is the principal food of the poor in some countries, and has often contributed to prevent famine. It was introduced into the British dominions by Sir Walter Raleigh or other adventurers in the 16th century; but it came slowly into use, and at this day is not much cultivated and used in some countries of Europe. In the British dominions and in the United States, it has proved one of the greatest blessings bestowed on man by the Creator.
POT'-BELLIED, *a.* Having a prominent belly.
POT'-BELLY, *n.* A protuberant belly.
POTCH, *v. t.* [Fr. *pocher,* Eng. to *poke.*] To thrust; to push. [*Not used.*] *Shak.*
2. To poach; to boil slightly. [*Not used.*] *Wiseman.*
POT-COMPAN'ION, *n.* An associate or companion in drinking; *applied generally to habitual hard drinkers.*
PO'TELOT, *n.* [Qu. G. *pottloth,* D. *potlood,* black lead.]
The sulphuret of molybden. *Fourcroy.*

PO'TENCE, *n.* In *heraldry,* a cross whose ends resemble the head of a crutch. *Encyc.*
PO'TENCY, *n.* [L. *potentia,* from *potens; possum, posse.* See *Power.*]
1. Power; physical power, energy or efficacy; strength. *Shak.*
2. Moral power; influence; authority.

Now arriving
At place of *potency* and sway o' th' state. *Shak.*

PO'TENT, *a.* [L. *potens.*] Powerful; physically strong; forcible; efficacious; as a *potent* medicine.

Moses once more his *potent* rod extends. *Milton.*

2. Powerful, in a moral sense; having great influence; as *potent* interest; a *potent* argument. *Decay of Piety.*
3. Having great authority, control or dominion; as a *potent* prince. *Shak.*
PO'TENT, *n.* A prince; a potentate. [*Not in use.*] *Shak.*
2. A walking staff or crutch. [*Not used.*] *Chaucer.*
PO'TENTACY, *n.* Sovereignty. [*Not used.*] *Barrow.*
PO'TENTATE, *n.* [Fr. *potentat;* It. *potentato.*]
A person who possesses great power or sway; a prince; a sovereign; an emperor, king or monarch.

Exalting him not only above earthly princes and *potentates,* but above the highest of the celestial hierarchy. *Boyle.*

POTEN'TIAL, *a.* [L. *potentialis.*] Having power to impress on us the ideas of certain qualities, though the qualities are not inherent in the thing; as *potential* heat or cold. *Encyc.*
2. Existing in possibility, not in act.

This *potential* and imaginary materia prima, cannot exist without form. *Raleigh.*

3. Efficacious; powerful. [*Not in use.*] *Shak.*
Potential cautery, in medicine, is the consuming or reducing to an eschar, any part of the body by a caustic alkaline or metallic salt, &c. instead of a red hot iron, the use of which is called *actual cautery. Encyc.*
Potential mode, in grammar, is that form of the verb which is used to express the power, possibility, liberty or necessity of an action or of being; as, I *may go;* he *can write.* This, in English, is not strictly a distinct mode, but the indicative or declarative mode, affirming the *power* to act, instead of the act itself. I *may go* or *can go,* are equivalent to, I *have power to go.*
POTEN'TIAL, *n.* Any thing that may be possible. *Bacon.*
POTENTIAL'ITY, *n.* Possibility; not actuality. *Taylor. Bentley.*
POTEN'TIALLY, *adv.* In possibility; not in act; not positively.

This duration of human souls is only *potentially* infinite. *Bentley.*

2. In efficacy, not in actuality; as *potentially* cold. *Boyle.*
PO'TENTLY, *adv.* Powerfully; with great force or energy.

You are *potently* opposed. *Shak.*

PO'TENTNESS, *n.* Powerfulness; strength; might. [*Little used.*]
PO'TESTATIVE, *a.* [from L. *potestas.*] Authoritative. [*Not used.*] *Pearson.*

POTGUN, for *popgun.* [*Not used.*] *Swift.*
POT'-HANGER, *n.* [*pot* and *hanger.*] A pot-hook.
POTH'ECARY, contracted from *apothecary,* and very vulgar. [See the latter.]
POTH'ER, *n.* [This word is vulgarly pronounced *bother.* Its origin and affinities are not ascertained.]
1. Bustle; confusion; tumult; flutter. [*Low.*] *Shak. Swift.*
2. A suffocating cloud. *Drayton.*
POTH'ER, *v. i.* To make a blustering ineffectual effort; to make a stir.
POTH'ER, *v. t.* To harass and perplex; to puzzle. *Locke.*
POT'HERB, *n.* An herb for the pot or for cookery; a culinary plant. *Arbuthnot.*
POT'-HOOK, *n.* A hook on which pots and kettles are hung over the fire.
2. A letter or character like a pot-hook; a scrawled letter. *Dryden.*
PO'TION, *n.* [Fr. from L. *potio; poto,* to drink.]
A draught; usually, a liquid medicine; a dose. *Bacon. Milton.*
POT'LID, *n.* The lid or cover of a pot. *Derham.*
POT'-MAN, *n.* A pot companion.
POT'SHERD, *n.* [*pot* and Sax. *sceard,* a fragment, from *scearan,* to *shear;* D. *potscherf;* G. *scherbe.*]
A piece or fragment of a broken pot. Job ii.
POT'STONE, *n.* Potstone appears to be indurated black talck, passing into serpentine. It has a curved and undulatingly lamellar structure, passing into slaty. *Cyc.*
Potstone is of a greenish gray color. It occurs massive, or in granular concretions. *Ure.*
Potstone is a variety of steatite. *Cleaveland.*
POT'TAGE, *n.* Broth; soup. [See *Potage,* the more correct orthography.]
POT'TED, *pp.* Preserved or inclosed in a pot; drained in a cask. *Edwards.*
POT'TER, *n.* [from *pot.*] One whose occupation is to make earthern vessels. *Dryden. Mortimer.*
POT'TERN-ORE, *n.* A species of ore, which, from its aptness to vitrify like the glazing of potter's ware, the miners call by this name. *Boyle.*
POT'TERY, *n.* [Fr. *poterie;* from *pot.*] The vessels or ware made by potters; earthern ware, glazed and baked.
2. The place where earthern vessels are manufactured.
POT'TING, *n.* [from *pot.*] Drinking; tippling. *Shak.*
2. In the W. Indies, the process of putting sugar in casks for draining. *Edwards.*
POT'TING, *ppr.* Preserving in a pot; draining, as above; drinking.
POT'TLE, *n.* [W. *potel,* a bottle; from *pot.*]
1. A liquid measure of four pints.
2. A vessel; a pot or tankard.
POT-VAL'IANT, *a.* [*pot* and *valiant.*] Courageous over the cup; heated to valor by strong drink. *Addison.*
POUCH, *n.* [Fr. *poche,* a pocket or *bag,* a purse-net, the paunch; Ir. *pucan;* G. *bauch,* D. *buik,* Sw. *buk,* Dan. *bug,* the belly, from bulging and extending.]
1. A small bag; usually, a lethern bag to be carried in the pocket. *Swift.*
2. A protuberant belly.

3. The bag or sack of a fowl, as that of the pelican.

POUCH, *v. t.* To pocket; to save. *Tusser.*

2. To swallow; used of fowls, whose crop is called in French, *poche*. *Derham.*

3. To pout. [*Not used.*] *Ainsworth.*

POUCH'-MOUTHED, *a.* Blubber-lipped. [*Not used.*] *Ainsworth.*

POUL'-DAVIS, *n.* A sort of sail cloth. [*Not used.*] *Ainsworth.*

POULE. [See *Pool.*]

POULT, *n.* [Fr. *poulet.* See *Poultry.*] A young chicken. [*Little used.*] *King.*

POULTERER, *n.* [Norm. *poltaire.* See *Poultry.*]

1. One who makes it his business to sell fowls for the table.

2. Formerly, in England, an officer of the king's household, who had the charge of the poultry.

POULTICE, *n.* [It. *polta*, pap, L. *puls, pultis*, Gr. *πολτος.*]

A cataplasm; a soft composition of meal, bran, or the like substance, to be applied to sores, inflamed parts of the body, &c. *Bacon.*

POULTICE, *v. t.* To apply a cataplasm to.

POULTIVE, for *poultice*, is not used. *Temple.*

POULTRY, *n.* [from Fr. *poule*, a hen, dim. *poulet*; It. *pollo*, a chicken, *pollame*, poultry; Sp. *polla*; L. *pullus*, a chicken, or other young animal; allied to Eng. *foal*; W. *ebawl, eboles*, a filly or colt; It. *pollare*, to sprout, L. *pullulo.*]

Domestic fowls which are propagated and fed for the table, such as cocks and hens, capons, turkies, ducks and geese.

POULTRY-YARD, *n.* A yard or place where fowls are kept for the use of the table.

POUNCE, *n.* pouns. [Fr. *pierre-ponce*, pumice-stone; *poncer*, to rub with pumice-stone; Arm. *maen-puncz*, pumice-stone.]

1. Gum-sandarach pulverized, a fine powder used to prevent ink from spreading on paper.

2. Charcoal dust inclosed in some open stuff, as muslin, &c. to be passed over holes pricked in the work, to mark the lines or designs on a paper underneath. This kind of pounce is used by embroiderers to transfer their patterns upon their stuffs; also by lace-makers, and sometimes by engravers. It is also used in varnishing. *Cyc.*

3. Cloth worked in eyelet-holes. *Todd.*

POUNCE, *v. t.* To sprinkle or rub with pounce.

POUNCE, *n.* [This word seems to be connected with the It. *punzone*, a bodkin, a punch, a push, which is from the L. *pungo*, whence Sp. *punzar.*]

The claw or talon of a bird of prey.

POUNCE, *v. i.* To fall on suddenly; to fall on and seize with the claws; as, a rapacious fowl *pounces* on a chicken.

POUNCE-BOX, } *n.* A small box with a
POUN'CET-BOX, } perforated lid, used for sprinkling pounce on paper. *Shak.*

POUN'CED, *pp.* Furnished with claws or talons. *Thomson.*

POUND, *n.* [Sax. Goth. Sw. Dan. *pund*; D. *pond*; G. *pfund*; L. *pondo, pondus*, weight, a pound; *pendo*, to weigh, to *bend.*]

1. A standard weight consisting of twelve ounces troy or sixteen ounces avoirdupois.

2. A money of account consisting of twenty shillings, the value of which is different in different countries. The pound sterling is equivalent to $4 44. 44 cts. money of the United States. In New England and Virginia, the pound is equal to $3⅓; in New York to $2½.

POUND, *n.* [Sax. *pyndan, pindan*, to confine.]

An inclosure erected by authority, in which cattle or other beasts are confined when taken in trespassing, or going at large in violation of law; a pin-fold.

POUND, *v. t.* To confine in a public pound.

POUND, *v. t.* [Sax. *punian*; W. *pwniaw*, to beat and to load.]

1. To beat; to strike with some heavy instrument, and with repeated blows, so as to make an impression.

> With cruel blows she *pounds* her blubber'd cheeks. *Dryden.*

2. To comminute and pulverize by beating; to bruise or break into fine parts by a heavy instrument; as, to *pound* spice or salt.

> Loud strokes with *pounding* spice the fabric rend. *Garth.*

POUND'AGE, *n.* [from *pound.*] A sum deducted from a pound, or a certain sum paid for each pound. *Swift.*

2. In *England*, a subsidy of 12d. in the pound, granted to the crown on all goods exported or imported, and if by aliens, more. *Blackstone.*

POUND'BREACH, *n.* The breaking of a public pound for releasing beasts confined in it. *Blackstone.*

POUND'ED, *pp.* Beaten or bruised with a heavy instrument; pulverized or broken by pounding.

2. Confined in a pound; impounded.

POUND'ER, *n.* A pestle; the instrument of pounding.

2. A person or thing denominated from a certain number of pounds; as a cannon is called a twelve-*pounder*; a person of ten pounds annual income is called a ten-*pounder*; a note or bill is called a ten-*pounder*. *Johnson.*

3. A large pear. *Dryden.*

Pound foolish. The phrase, *penny wise and pound foolish*, signifies negligent in the care of large sums, but careful to save small sums.

POUND'ING, *ppr.* Beating; bruising; pulverizing; impounding.

POUPETON, *n.* [Fr. *poupee.*] A puppet or little baby.

POUPIES, *n.* In *cookery*, a mess of victuals made of veal steaks and slices of bacon. *Bailey.*

POUR, *v. t.* [W. *bwrw*, to cast, send, throw, thrust.]

1. To throw, as a fluid in a stream, either out of a vessel or into it; as, to *pour* water *from* a pail, or *out of* a pail; to *pour* wine *into* a decanter. *Pour* is appropriately but not exclusively applied to fluids, and signifies merely to cast or throw, and this sense is modified by *out, from, in, into, against, on, upon, under*, &c. It is applied not only to liquors, but to other fluids, and to substances consisting of fine particles; as, to *pour* a stream of gas or air upon a fire; to *pour* out sand. It expresses particularly the bestowing or sending forth in copious abundance.

> I will *pour out* my Spirit upon all flesh. Joel ii.

> To *pour out* dust. Lev. xiv.

2. To emit; to send forth in a stream or continued succession.

> London doth *pour out* her citizens. *Shak.*

3. To send forth; as, to *pour out* words, prayers or sighs; to *pour out* the heart or soul. Ps. lxii. xlii.

4. To throw in profusion or with overwhelming force.

> I will shortly *pour out* my fury on thee. Ezek. vii.

POUR, *v. i.* To flow; to issue forth in a stream, or continued succession of parts; to move or rush, as a current. The torrent *pours* down from the mountain, or along the steep descent.

2. To rush in a crowd or continued procession.

> A ghastly band of giants,
> All *pouring* down the mountain, crowd the shore. *Pope.*

POURED, *pp.* Sent forth; thrown; as a fluid.

POURER, *n.* One that pours.

POURING, *ppr.* Sending, as a fluid; driving in a current or continued stream.

POURLIEU. [See *Purlieu.*]

POURPRES'TURE, *n.* [Fr. *pour*, for, and *pris*, taken.]

In *law*, a wrongful inclosure or encroachment on another's property. *Encyc. Cowel.*

POURSUIVANT. [See *Pursuivant.*]

POURVEYANCE. [See *Purveyance.*]

POUSSE, corrupted from *pulse*, peas. *Spenser.*

POUT, *n.* A fish of the genus Gadus, about an inch in length; the whiting pout. *Dict. Nat. Hist.*

2. A bird. *Carew.*

3. A fit of sullenness. [*Colloquial.*]

POUT, *v. i.* [Fr. *bouder*; allied probably to *bud, pudding*, Gr. *βοτανη*, W. *poten*; from the sense of bulging or pushing out.]

1. To thrust out the lips, as in sullenness, contempt or displeasure; hence, to look sullen. *Shak.*

2. To shoot out; to be prominent; as *pouting* lips. *Dryden.*

POUT'ING, *ppr.* Shooting out, as the lips.

2. Looking sullen.

POV'ERTY, *n.* [Norm. *pouerti*; Fr. *pauvreté*; It. *povertà*; Sp. Port. *pobreza*; L. *paupertas.* See *Poor.*]

1. Destitution of property; indigence; want of convenient means of subsistence. The consequence of *poverty* is dependence.

> The drunkard and the glutton shall come to *poverty*. Prov. xxiii.

2. Barrenness of sentiment or ornament; defect; as the *poverty* of a composition.

3. Want; defect of words; as the *poverty* of language.

POW'DER, *n.* [Fr. *poudre*, contracted from *pouldre*; Arm. *poultra*; It. *polvere*; Sp. *polvo*; L. *pulvis.* The G. has *puder*, and the D. *poeder*, but whether from the same source I know not. *Pulvis* is probably from *pulso, pulto*, to beat.]

1. Any dry substance composed of minute

particles, whether natural or artificial; more generally, a substance comminuted or triturated to fine particles. Thus dust is the *powder* of earth; flour is the *powder* of grain. But the word is particularly applied to substances reduced to fine particles for medicinal purposes.

2. A composition of saltpeter, sulphur and charcoal, mixed and granulated; gunpowder.

3. Hair powder; pulverized starch.

POW'DER, *v. t.* To reduce to fine particles; to comminute; to pulverize; to triturate; to pound, grind or rub into fine particles.

2. To sprinkle with powder; as, to *powder* the hair.

3. To sprinkle with salt; to corn; as meat. *Bacon.*

POW'DER, *v. i.* To come violently. [*Not in use.*] *L'Estrange.*

POW'DER-BOX, *n.* A box in which hair-powder is kept. *Gay.*

POW'DER-CART, *n.* A cart that carries powder and shot for artillery.

POW'DER-CHEST, *n.* A small box or case charged with powder, old nails, &c. fastened to the side of a ship, to be discharged at an enemy attempting to board. *Mar. Dict.*

POW'DERED, *pp.* Reduced to powder; sprinkled with powder; corned; salted.

POW'DER-FLASK, *n.* A flask in which gunpowder is carried.

POW'DER-HORN, *n.* A horn in which gunpowder is carried by sportsmen. *Swift.*

POW'DERING, *ppr.* Pulverizing; sprinkling with powder; corning; salting.

POW'DERING-TUB, *n.* A tub or vessel in which meat is corned or salted.

2. The place where an infected lecher is cured. *Shak.*

POW'DER-MILL, *n.* A mill in which gunpowder is made. *Arbuthnot.*

POW'DER-ROOM, *n.* The apartment in a ship where gunpowder is kept. *Waller.*

POW'DERY, *a.* Friable; easily crumbling to pieces.

2. Dusty; sprinkled with powder.

3. Resembling powder.

POW'DIKE, *n.* A marsh or fen dike. [*Local.*]

POW'ER, *n.* [Fr. *pouvoir;* Norm. *povare;* from the root of Sp. Port. *poder*, It. *podere;* or rather the same word varied in orthography. The Latin has *posse, possum, potes, potentia.* The primary sense of the verb is to strain, to exert force.]

1. In *a philosophical sense*, the faculty of doing or performing any thing; the faculty of moving or of producing a change in something; ability or strength. A man raises his hand by his own *power*, or by *power* moves another body. The exertion of *power* proceeds from the will, and in strictness, no being destitute of will or intelligence, can exert *power.* Power in man is *active* or *speculative.* *Active power* is that which moves the body; *speculative power* is that by which we see, judge, remember, or in general, by which we *think.*

Power may exist without exertion. We have *power* to speak when we are silent. *Locke. Reid.*

Power has been distinguished also into *active* and *passive*, the power of *doing* or *moving*, and the power of *receiving* impressions or of *suffering.* In strictness, *passive* power is an absurdity in terms. To say that gold has a *power* to be melted, is improper language, yet for want of a more appropriate word, *power* is often used in a passive sense, and is considered as two-fold; viz. as able to *make* or able to *receive* any change. *Cyc.*

2. Force; animal strength; as the *power* of the arm, exerted in lifting, throwing or holding.

3. Force; strength; energy; as the *power* of the mind, of the imagination, of the fancy. He has not *powers* of genius adequate to the work.

4. Faculty of the mind, as manifested by a particular mode of operation; as the *power* of thinking, comparing and judging; the reasoning *powers.*

5. Ability, natural or moral. We say, a man has the *power* of doing good; his property gives him the *power* of relieving the distressed; or he has the *power* to persuade others to do good; or it is not in his *power* to pay his debts. The moral *power* of man is also his *power* of judging or discerning in moral subjects.

6. In *mechanics*, that which produces motion or force, or which may be applied to produce it. Thus the inclined plane is called a mechanical *power*, as it produces motion, although this in reality depends on gravity. The wheel and axle, and the lever, are mechanical *powers*, as they may be applied to produce force. These *powers* are also called *forces*, and they are of two kinds, *moving* power, and *sustaining* power.

7. Force. The great *power* of the screw is of extensive use in compression. The *power* of steam is immense.

8. That quality in any natural body which produces a change or makes an impression on another body; as the *power* of medicine; the *power* of heat; the *power* of sound.

9. Force; strength; momentum; as the *power* of the wind, which propels a ship or overturns a building.

10. Influence; that which may move the mind; as the *power* of arguments or of persuasion.

11. Command; the right of governing, or actual government; dominion; rule; sway; authority. A large portion of Asia is under the *power* of the Russian emperor. The *power* of the British monarch is limited by law. The *powers* of government are legislative, executive, judicial, and ministerial.

> *Power* is no blessing in itself, but when it is employed to protect the innocent. *Swift.*

Under this sense may be comprehended civil, political, ecclesiastical, and military *power.*

12. A sovereign, whether emperor, king or governing prince or the legislature of a state; as the *powers* of Europe; the great *powers;* the smaller *powers.* In this sense, the state or nation governed seems to be included in the word *power.* Great Britain is a great naval *power.*

13. One invested with authority; a ruler; a civil magistrate. Rom. xiii.

14. Divinity; a celestial or invisible being or agent supposed to have dominion over some part of creation; as celestial *powers;* the *powers* of darkness.

15. That which has physical power; an army; a navy; a host; a military force.

> Never such a *power*—
> Was levied in the body of a land. *Shak.*

16. Legal authority; warrant; as a *power* of attorney; an agent invested with ample *power.* The envoy has full *powers* to negotiate a treaty.

17. In *arithmetic* and *algebra*, the product arising from the multiplication of a number or quantity into itself; as, a cube is the third *power;* the biquadrate is the fourth *power.*

18. In Scripture, right; privilege. John i. 1 Cor. ix.

19. Angels, good or bad. Col. i. Eph. vi.

20. Violence; force; compulsion. Ezek. iv.

21. Christ is called the *power of God*, as through him and his gospel, God displays his power and authority in ransoming and saving sinners. 1 Cor. i.

22. The *powers of heaven* may denote the celestial luminaries. Matt. xxiv.

23. Satan is said to have the *power of death*, as he introduced sin, the cause of death, temporal and eternal, and torments men with the fear of death and future misery.

24. In *vulgar language*, a large quantity; a great number; as a *power* of good things. [This is, I believe, obsolete, even among our common people.]

Power of attorney, authority given to a person to act for another.

POW'ERFUL, *a.* Having great physical or mechanical power; strong; forcible; mighty; as a *powerful* army or navy; a *powerful* engine.

2. Having great moral power; forcible to persuade or convince the mind; as a *powerful* reason or argument.

3. Possessing great political and military power; strong in extent of dominion or national resources; potent; as a *powerful* monarch or prince; a *powerful* nation.

4. Efficacious; possessing or exerting great force or producing great effects; as a *powerful* medicine.

5. In *general*, able to produce great effects; exerting great force or energy; as *powerful* eloquence.

> The word of God is quick and *powerful.* Heb. iv.

6. Strong; intense; as a *powerful* heat or light.

POW'ERFULLY, *adv.* With great force or energy; potently; mightily; with great effect; forcibly; either in a physical or moral sense. Certain medicines operate *powerfully* on the stomach; the practice of virtue is *powerfully* recommended by its utility.

POW'ERFULNESS, *n.* The quality of having or exerting great power; force; power; might. *Hakewill.*

POW'ERLESS, *a.* Destitute of power, force or energy; weak; impotent; not able to produce any effect. *Shak.*

POWL'DRON, *n.* [Qu. Fr. *epaule*, the shoulder.]

In *heraldry*, that part of armor which covers the shoulders. *Sandys.*

POW'TER, } *n.* A variety of the common POU'TER, } domestic pigeon, with an inflated breast. *Ed. Encyc.*

POX, *n.* [a corruption of *pocks*, Sax. *poc* or *pocc*, D. *pok*, that is, a *push*, eruption or pustule. It is properly a plural word, but by usage is singular.]

Strictly, pustules or eruptions of any kind, but chiefly or wholly restricted to three or four diseases, the small pox, chicken pox, the vaccine and the venereal diseases. *Pox*, when used without an epithet, signifies the latter, *lues venerea*.

POY, *n.* [Sp. *apoyo*, a prop or stay, Fr. *appui*. The verb signifies to bear or lean upon, from the root of *poize*.] A rope dancer's pole.

POZE, for *pose*, to puzzle. [See *Pose*.]

PRA€'TI€, for *practical*, is not in use. It was formerly used for *practical*, and Spenser uses it in the sense of *artful*.

PRA€TI€ABIL'ITY, } *n.* [from *prac-* PRA€'TI€ABLENESS, } *ticable*.] The quality or state of being practicable; feasibility.

PRA€'TI€ABLE, *a.* [Fr. *praticable*; It. *praticabile*; Sp. *practicable*. See *Practice*.]

1. That may be done, effected or performed by human means, or by powers that can be applied. It is sometimes synonymous with *possible*, but the words differ in this: *possible* is applied to that which might be performed, if the necessary powers or means could be obtained; *practicable* is limited in its application to things which are to be performed by the means given, or which may be applied. It was *possible* for Archimedes to lift the world, but it was not *practicable*.

2. That may be practiced; as a *practicable* virtue. *Dryden.*

3. That admits of use, or that may be passed or traveled; as a *practicable* road. In *military affairs*, a *practicable* breach is one that can be entered by troops. *Mitford.*

PRA€'TI€ABLY, *adv.* In such a manner as may be performed. "A rule *practicably* applied before his eyes," is not correct language. It is probably a mistake for *practically*. *Rogers.*

PRA€'TI€AL, *a.* [L. *practicus*; It. *pratico*; Fr. *pratique*; Sp. *practico*. See *Practice*.] Pertaining to practice or action.

2. Capable of practice or active use; opposed to *speculative*; as a *practical* understanding. *South.*

3. That may be used in practice; that may be applied to use; as *practical* knowledge. *Tillotson.*

4. That reduces his knowledge or theories to actual use; as a *practical* man.

5. Derived from practice or experience; as *practical* skill or knowledge.

PRA€'TI€ALLY, *adv.* In relation to practice.

2. By means of practice or use; by experiment; as *practically* wise or skillful.

3. In practice or use; as a medicine *practically* safe; theoretically wrong, but *practically* right.

PRA€'TI€ALNESS, *n.* The quality of being practical.

PRA€'TICE, *n.* [Sp. *practica*; It. *pratica*; Fr. *pratique*; Gr. πρακτικη, from the root of πρασσω, πραττω, to act, to do, to make. The root of this verb is πραγ or πραχ, as appears by the derivatives πραγμα, πρακτικη, and from the same root, in other languages, are formed G. *brauchen*, to use; *brauch*, use, practice; D. *gebruiken*, to use, employ, enjoy; *bruiker*, a tenant, one that occupies a farm; Sax. *brucan*, to use, to enjoy, to eat, whence Eng. to *brook*, and *broker*; Dan. *bruger*, to use or employ; *brug*, use, practice; Sw. *bruka*; L. *fruor*, for *frugor* or *frucor*, whence *fructus*, contracted into *fruit*; Ir. *freacair*, use, *practice*, *frequency*, L. *frequens*. The W. *praith*, practice, *preithiaw*, to practice, may be the same word, with the loss of the palatal letter *c* or *g*.]

1. Frequent or customary actions; a succession of acts of a similar kind or in a like employment; as the *practice* of rising early or of dining late; the *practice* of reading a portion of Scripture morning and evening; the *practice* of making regular entries of accounts; the *practice* of virtue or vice. *Habit* is the effect of *practice*.

2. Use; customary use.

> Obsolete words may be revived when they are more sounding or significant than those in *practice*. *Dryden.*

3. Dexterity acquired by use. [*Unusual.*] *Shak.*

4. Actual performance; distinguished from *theory*.

> There are two functions of the soul, contemplation and *practice*, according to the general division of objects, some of which only entertain our speculations, others employ our actions. *South.*

5. Application of remedies; medical treatment of diseases. Two physicians may differ widely in their *practice*.

6. Exercise of any profession; as the *practice* of law or of medicine; the *practice* of arms.

7. Frequent use; exercise for instruction or discipline. The troops are daily called out for *practice*.

8. Skillful or artful management; dexterity in contrivance or the use of means; art; stratagem; artifice; usually in a bad sense.

> He sought to have that by *practice* which he could not by prayer. *Sidney.*

[This use of the word is genuine; Sp. *practico*, skillful, It. *pratico*; like *expert*, from L. *experior*. It is not a mistake as Johnson supposes. See the Verb.]

9. A rule in arithmetic, by which the operations of the general rules are abridged in use.

PRA€'TICE, *v. t.* [From the noun. The orthography of the verb ought to be the same as of the noun; as in *notice* and *to notice*.]

1. To do or perform frequently, customarily or habitually; to perform by a succession of acts; as, to *practice* gaming; to *practice* fraud or deception; to *practice* the virtues of charity and beneficence; to *practice* hypocrisy. Is. xxxii.

> Many praise virtue who do not *practice* it. *Anon.*

2. To use or exercise any profession or art; as, to *practice* law or medicine; to *practice* gunnery or surveying.

3. To use or exercise for instruction, discipline or dexterity. [*In this sense, the verb is usually intransitive.*]

4. To commit; to perpetrate; as the horrors *practiced* at Wyoming. *Marshall.*

5. To use; as a *practiced* road. [*Unusual.*] *Milford.*

PRA€'TICE, *v. i.* To perform certain acts frequently or customarily, either for instruction, profit or amusement; as, to *practice* with the broad sword; to *practice* with the rifle.

2. To form a habit of acting in any manner.

> They shall *practice* how to live secure. *Milton.*

3. To transact or negotiate secretly.

> I have *practic'd* with him,
> And found means to let the victor know
> That Syphax and Sempronius are his friends. *Addison.*

4. To try artifices.

> Others, by guilty artifice and arts
> Of promis'd kindness, *practic'd* on our hearts. *Granville.*

5. To use evil arts or stratagems.

> If you there
> Did *practice* on my state— *Shak.*

6. To use medical methods or experiments.

> I am little inclined to *practice* on others, and as little that others should *practice* on me. *Temple.*

7. To exercise any employment or profession. A physician has *practiced* many years with success.

PRA€'TICED, *pp.* Done by a repetition of acts; customarily performed or used.

PRA€'TICER, *n.* One that practices; one that customarily performs certain acts.

2. One who exercises a profession. In this sense, *practitioner* is generally used.

PRA€'TICING, *ppr.* Performing or using customarily; exercising, as an art or profession.

PRA€'TISANT, *n.* An agent. [*Not used.*] *Shak.*

PRA€TI''TIONER, *n.* One who is engaged in the actual use or exercise of any art or profession, particularly in law or medicine.

2. One who does any thing customarily or habitually. *Whitgifte.*

3. One that practices sly or dangerous arts. *South.*

PRÆ€OG'NITA, *n. plu.* [L. before known.] Things previously known in order to understand something else. Thus a knowledge of the structure of the human body is one of the *præcognita* of medical science and skill.

PRÆMUNI'RE, *n.* [a corruption of the L. *præmonere*, to pre-admonish.]

1. A writ, or the offense for which it is granted. The offense consists in introducing a foreign authority or power into England, that is, introducing and maintaining the papal power, creating imperium in imperio, and yielding that obedience to the mandates of the pope, which constitutionally belongs to the king. Both the offense and the writ are so denominated from the words used in the writ, *præmunine facias*, cause A B to be forewarn-

ed to appear before us to answer the contempt wherewith he stands charged. *Blackstone. Encyc.*

2. The penalty incurred by infringing a statute. *South.*

PRAGMAT'IC, } *a.* [L. *pragmaticus*; Gr. πραγματικος,
PRAGMAT'ICAL, } from πραγμα, business; πρασσω, to do. See *Practice.*]

Forward to intermeddle; meddling; impertinently busy or officious in the concerns of others, without leave or invitation.

The fellow grew so *pragmatical*, that he took upon him the government of my whole family. *Arbuthnot.*

Pragmatic sanction, in the German empire, the settlement made by Charles VI. the emperor, who in 1722, having no sons, settled his hereditary dominions on his eldest daughter, the archduchess Maria Theresa, which settlement was confirmed by most of the powers of Europe.

In the civil law, *pragmatic sanction* may be defined, a rescript or answer of the sovereign, delivered by advice of his council to some college, order, or body of people, who consult him in relation to the affairs of their community. The like answer given to a particular person, is called simply a rescript. *Hottoman. Encyc.*

PRAGMAT'ICALLY, *adv.* In a meddling manner; impertinently.

PRAGMAT'ICALNESS, *n.* The quality of intermeddling without right or invitation.

PRAG'MATIST, *n.* One who is impertinently busy or meddling. *Reynolds.*

PRA'ISABLE, *a.* That may be praised. [*Not used.*] *Wickliffe.*

PRAISE, *n.* *s* as *z.* [D. *prys*, praise and price; G. *preis*, praise, price, prize, value; Dan. *priis*, Sw. *pris*, id.; W. *prîs*, price, value; Fr. *prix*; It. *prezzo*; Sp. *precio*, price, value; *presa*, a prize; W. *prid*; L. *pretium*; Sp. *prez*, glory, *praise*; Scot. *prys*, praise and prize. See the Verb.]

1. Commendation bestowed on a person for his personal virtues or worthy actions, on meritorious actions themselves, or on any thing valuable; approbation expressed in words or song. *Praise* may be expressed by an individual, and in this circumstance differs from *fame*, *renown*, and *celebrity*, which are the expression of the approbation of numbers, or public commendation. When *praise* is applied to the expression of public approbation, it may be synonymous with *renown*, or nearly so. A man may deserve the *praise* of an individual, or of a nation.

There are men who always confound the *praise* of goodness with the practice. *Rambler.*

2. The expression of gratitude for personal favors conferred; a glorifying or extolling.

He hath put a new song into my mouth, even *praise* to our God. Ps. xl.

3. The object, ground or reason of praise.

He is thy *praise*, and he is thy God. Deut. x.

PRAISE, *v. t.* [D. *pryzen*, to praise; *pryzeeren*, to estimate or value; G. *preisen*, to praise; Dan. *priser*, to praise, extol or lift up; Sw. *prisa*; W. *prisiaw*; Arm. *presa*; Fr. *priser*, to prize, to value; It. *prezzare*; Sp. *preciar*; Port. *prezar*, to estimate; *prezarse*, to boast or glory. It appears that *praise*, *price*, *prize*, are all from one root, the primary sense of which is to lift, to raise, or rather to strain. So from L. *tollo*, *extollo*, we have *extol*. Now in Dan. *roser*, Sw. *rosa*, signifies to praise, and it may be questioned whether this is *praise* without a prefix. The Latin *pretium*, W. *prid*, is probably from the same root, denoting that which is *taken* for a thing sold, or the *rising* or amount, as we use *high*; a *high* value or price; corn is *high*. In Pers. افراز afaraz, is high, lofty; افرازيدن afrazidan, to extol. Qu. Fr. *prôner*, for *prosner*.]

1. To commend; to applaud; to express approbation of personal worth or actions.

We *praise* not Hector, though his name we know
Is great in arms; 'tis hard to *praise* a foe. *Dryden.*

2. To extol in words or song; to magnify; to glorify on account of perfections or excellent works.

Praise him, all his angels, *praise* ye him, all his hosts. Ps. cxlviii.

3. To express gratitude for personal favors. Ps. cxxxviii.

4. To do honor to; to display the excellence of.

All thy works shall *praise* thee, O Lord. Ps. cxlv.

PRA'ISED, *pp.* Commended; extolled.

PRA'ISEFUL, *a.* Laudable; commendable. [*Not used.*] *Sidney.*

PRA'ISER, *n.* One who praises, commends or extols; an applauder; a commender. *Sidney. Donne.*

PRA'ISELESS, *a.* Without praise or commendation. *Sidney.*

PRAISEWÖRTHILY, *adv.* In a manner deserving of commendation. *Spenser.*

PRAISEWÖRTHINESS, *n.* The quality of deserving commendation. *Smith.*

PRAISEWÖRTHY, *a.* Deserving of praise or applause; commendable; as a *praiseworthy* action. *Arbuthnot.*

PRA'ISING, *ppr.* Commending; extolling in words or song.

PRAM, } *n.* [D. *praam.*] A flat-bottomed
PRAME, } boat or lighter; used in Holland for conveying goods to or from a ship in loading or unloading. *Encyc.*

2. In *military affairs*, a kind of floating battery or flat-bottomed vessel, mounting several cannon; used in covering the disembarkation of troops. *Encyc.*

PR'ANCE, *v. i.* *pràns.* [W. *pranciaw*, to frolick, to play a prank, from *rhanc*, a reaching or craving, the same as *rank*; Ir. *rincim*, to dance; Port. *brincar*, to sport; Sp. *brincar*, to leap. It is allied to *prank*, which see.]

1. To spring or bound, as a horse in high mettle.

Now rule thy *prancing* steed. *Gay.*

2. To ride with bounding movements; to ride ostentatiously.

Th' insulting tyrant *prancing* o'er the field. *Addison.*

3. To walk or strut about in a showy manner or with warlike parade. *Swift.*

PR'ANCING, *ppr.* Springing; bounding; riding with gallant show.

PR'ANCING, *n.* A springing or bounding, as of a high spirited horse. Judg. v.

PRANK, *v. t.* [If *n* is not radical, this word coincides with G. *pracht*, D. Dan. *pragt*, Sw. *prackt*, pomp, magnificence; also with G. *prangen*, to shine, to make a show; D. *pronken*, to shine or make a show, to be adorned, to strut; Dan. *pranger*, to prance, to make a show, to sell by retail; the latter sense perhaps from *breaking*; Sw. *prunka*. So in Port. *brincar*, to sport; Sp. *id.* to leap. These are evidently the Ar. برق to adorn, to lighten. *Prink* is probably from the same root.]

To adorn in a showy manner; to dress or adjust to ostentation.

In sumptuous tire she joyed herself to *prank*. *Milton.*

It is often followed by *up*.

—And me, poor lowly maid,
Most goddess-like *prankt up*. *Shak.*

PRANK, *n.* [W. *pranc.*] Properly, a sudden start or sally. [See *Prance.*] Hence, a wild flight; a capering; a gambol.

2. A capricious action; a ludicrous or merry trick, or a mischievous act, rather for sport than injury. Children often play their *pranks* on each other.

—In came the harpies and played their accustomed *pranks*. *Raleigh.*

PRANK, *a.* Frolicksome; full of gambols or tricks. *Brewer.*

PRANK'ED, } *pp.* Adorned in a showy
PRANKT, } manner.

PRANK'ER, *n.* One that dresses ostentatiously.

PRANK'ING, *ppr.* Setting off or adorning for display.

PRANK'ING, *n.* Ostentatious display of dress. *More.*

PRASE, *n.* *s* as *z.* A silicious mineral; a subspecies of quartz of a leek green color. *Cleaveland.*

PRASON, *n.* *pra'sn.* [Gr. πρασον.] A leek; also, a sea weed green as a leek. *Bailey.*

PRATE, *v. i.* [D. *praaten*, to prate; Sw. *prata*, to tattle; Gr. φραδαω. Qu. allied perhaps to Sax. *ræd*, speech.]

To talk much and without weight, or to little purpose; to be loquacious; as the vulgar express it, to *run on.*

To *prate* and talk for life and honor. *Shak.*
And made a fool presume to *prate* of love. *Dryden.*

PRATE, *v. t.* To utter foolishly.

What nonsense would the fool, thy master, *prate*,
When thou, his knave, canst talk at such a rate? *Dryden.*

PRATE, *n.* Continued talk to little purpose; trifling talk; unmeaning loquacity. *Shak. Denham.*

PRA'TER, *n.* One that talks much to little purpose, or on trifling subjects. *Southern.*

PRAT'IC, } *n.* [It. *pratica*; Sp. *practica*;
PRATÏQUE, } Fr. *pratique.* See *Practice.*]

In *commerce*, primarily, converse; intercourse; the communication between a ship and the port in which she arrives.

Hence, a license or permission to hold intercourse and trade with the inhabitants of a place, after having performed quarantine, or upon a certificate that the ship did not come from an infected place; a term used particularly in the south of Europe, where vessels coming from countries infected with contagious diseases, are subjected to quarantine.

PRA'TING, *ppr.* Talking much on a trifling subject; talking idly.

PRA'TINGLY, *adv.* With much idle talk; with loquacity.

PRAT'TLE, *v. i.* [*dim.* of *prate.*] To talk much and idly; to be loquacious on trifling subjects. *Locke. Addison.*

This word is particularly applied to the talk of children.

PRAT'TLE, *n.* Trifling talk; loquacity on trivial subjects.

Mere *prattle* without practice,
Is all his soldiership. *Shak.*

PRAT'TLEMENT, *n.* Prattle. *Hayley.*

PRAT'TLER, *n.* An idle talker. *Herbert.*

PRAT'TLING, *ppr.* Talking much on trivial affairs.

PRAV'ITY, *n.* [L. *pravitas*, from *pravus*, crooked, evil.]
Deviation from right; moral perversion; want of rectitude; corrupt state; as the *pravity* of human nature; the *pravity* of the will. *Milton. South.*

PRAWN, *n.* A small crustaceous fish of the genus Cancer, with a serrated snout bending upwards. *Encyc.*

PRAX'IS, *n.* [L. from the Gr. See *Practice.*] Use; practice. *Coventry.*

2. An example or form to teach practice. *Lowth.*

PRAY, *v. i.* [Fr. *prier;* It. *pregare;* L. *precor;* Russ. *prochu;* allied perhaps to the Sax. *frægnan*, G. *fragen*, D. *vraagen*, Sw. *fråga*, to ask, L. *proco.* This word belongs to the same family as *preach* and *reproach*, Heb. Ch. Syr. Eth. Ar. ברך to bless, to *reproach;* rendered in Job ii. 9, to curse; properly, to reproach, to rail at or upbraid, W. *rhegu.* The primary sense is to throw, to pour forth sounds or words; for the same word in Arabic, بَرَكَ baraka, signifies to pour out water, as in violent rain, Gr. βρεχω. See *Rain.* As the oriental word signifies to bless, and to reproach or curse, so in Latin the same word *precor* signifies to supplicate good or evil, and *precis* signifies a prayer and a curse. See *Imprecate.* Class Brg. No. 3. and see No. 4. 6. 7. 8.]

1. To ask with earnestness or zeal, as for a favor, or for something desirable; to entreat; to supplicate.

Pray for them who despitefully use you and persecute you. Matt. v.

2. To petition; to ask, as for a favor; as in application to a legislative body.

3. In *worship*, to address the Supreme Being with solemnity and reverence, with adoration, confession of sins, supplication for mercy, and thanksgiving for blessings received.

When thou *prayest*, enter into thy closet, and when thou hast shut thy door, *pray* to thy Father who is in secret, and thy Father who seeth in secret, shall reward thee openly. Matt. vi.

4. I *pray*, that is, I *pray you tell me*, or *let me know*, is a common mode of introducing a question.

PRAY, *v. t.* To supplicate; to entreat; to urge.

We *pray* you in Christ's stead, be ye reconciled to God. 2 Cor. v.

2. In *worship*, to supplicate; to implore; to ask with reverence and humility.

Repent therefore of this thy wickedness, and *pray* God, if perhaps the thought of thy heart may be forgiven thee. Acts viii.

3. To petition. The plaintif *prays* judgment of the court.

He that will have the benefit of this act, must *pray* a prohibition before a sentence in the ecclesiastical court. *Ayliffe.*

4. To ask or intreat in ceremony or form.

Pray my colleague Antonius I may speak with him. *B. Jonson.*

[In most instances, this verb is transitive only by ellipsis. To *pray God*, is used for to *pray to God;* to *pray a prohibition*, is to *pray for a prohibition*, &c.]

To pray in aid, in law, is to call in for help one who has interest in the cause.

PRA'YER, *n.* In *a general sense*, the act of asking for a favor, and particularly with earnestness.

2. In *worship*, a solemn address to the Supreme Being, consisting of *adoration*, or an expression of our sense of God's glorious perfections, *confession* of our sins, *supplication* for mercy and forgiveness, *intercession* for blessings on others, and *thanksgiving*, or an expression of gratitude to God for his mercies and benefits. A *prayer* however may consist of a single petition, and it may be extemporaneous, written or printed.

3. A formula of church service, or of worship, public or private.

4. Practice of supplication.

As he is famed for mildness, peace and *prayer*. *Shak.*

5. That part of a memorial or petition to a public body, which specifies the request or thing desired to be done or granted, as distinct from the recital of facts or reasons for the grant. We say, the *prayer* of the petition is that the petitioner may be discharged from arrest.

PRA'YER-BOOK, *n.* A book containing prayers or the forms of devotion, public or private. *Swift.*

PRA'YERFUL, *a.* Devotional; given to prayer; as a *prayerful* frame of mind.

2. Using much prayer.

PRA'YERFULLY, *adv.* With much prayer.

PRA'YERLESS, *a.* Not using prayer; habitually neglecting the duty of prayer to God; as a *prayerless* family.

PRA'YERLESSNESS, *n.* Total or habitual neglect of prayer. *T. H. Skinner.*

PRA'YING, *ppr.* Asking; supplicating.

PRA'YINGLY, *adv.* With supplication to God.

PRE, an English prefix, is the L. *præ*, before, probably a contracted word; Russ. *pred.* It expresses priority of time or rank. It may be radically the same as the Italian *proda*, the *prow* of a ship; *prode*, profit, also valiant, whence *prowess*, from some root signifying to *advance.* It sometimes signifies *beyond*, and may be rendered *very*, as in *prepotent.*

PREACH, *v. i.* [D. *preeken;* Fr. *prêcher*, for *prescher;* Arm. *pregnein* or *prezecq;* W. *preg*, a greeting; *pregeth*, a sermon; *pregethu*, to preach, derived from the noun, and the noun from *rheg*, a sending out, utterance, a gift, a curse, imprecation; *rhegu*, to send out, to give or consign, to curse; Heb. Ch. Ar. ברך; L. *præco*, a crier, Sax. *fricca* or *fryccea*, a crier. This is from the same root as *pray*, L. *precor*, and with *s* prefixed, gives the G. *sprechen*, D. *spreeken*, Sw. *språka*, to speak; Dan. *sprog*, speech. Class Brg. No. 2. 3. 4. 5.]

1. To pronounce a public discourse on a religious subject, or from a text of Scripture. The word is usually applied to such discourses as are formed from a text of Scripture. This is the modern sense of *preach.*

2. To discourse on the gospel way of salvation and exhort to repentance; to discourse on evangelical truths and exhort to a belief of them and acceptance of the terms of salvation. This was the extemporaneous manner of preaching pursued by Christ and his apostles. Matt. iv. x. Acts x. xiv.

PREACH, *v. t.* To proclaim; to publish in religious discourses.

What ye hear in the ear, that *preach* ye on the house-tops. Matt. x.

The Lord hath anointed me to *preach* good tidings to the meek. Is. lxi.

2. To inculcate in public discourses.

I have *preached* righteousness in the great congregation. Ps. xl.

He oft to them *preach'd*
Conversion and repentance. *Milton.*

To preach Christ or *Christ crucified*, to announce Christ as the only Savior, and his atonement as the only ground of acceptance with God. 1 Cor. i.

To preach up, to discourse in favor of.

Can they *preach up* equality of birth? *Dryden.*

PREACH, *n.* A religious discourse. [*Not used.*] *Hooker.*

PRE'ACHED, *pp.* Proclaimed; announced in public discourse; inculcated.

PRE'ACHER, *n.* One who discourses publicly on religious subjects. *Bacon.*

2. One that inculcates any thing with earnestness.

No *preacher* is listened to but time. *Swift.*

PRE'ACHERSHIP, *n.* The office of a preacher. [*Not used.*] *Hall.*

PRE'ACHING, *ppr.* Proclaiming; publishing in discourse; inculcating.

PRE'ACHING, *n.* The act of preaching; a public religious discourse. *Milner.*

PRE'ACHMAN, *n.* A preacher; in contempt. *Howell.*

PRE'ACHMENT, *n.* A discourse or sermon; in contempt; a discourse affectedly solemn. *Shak.*

PREA€QUA'INTANCE, *n.* Previous acquaintance or knowledge. *Harris.*

PREA€QUA'INTED, *a.* Previously acquainted. *Sheridan.*

PREAD'AMITE, *n.* [*pre*, before, and *Adam.*]
An inhabitant of the earth that lived before Adam. *Pereyra.*

PREADAMIT'I€, *a.* Designating what existed before Adam; as fictitious *preadamitic* periods. *Kirwan.*

PREADMINISTRA'TION, *n.* Previous administration. *Pearson.*

PREADMON'ISH, *v. t.* To admonish previously.

PREADMONI''TION, *n.* Previous warning or admonition.

PRE'AMBLE, *n.* [It. *preambolo*; Sp. *preambulo*; Fr. *préambule*; L. *præ*, before, and *ambulo*, to go.]

1. Something previous; introduction to a discourse or writing.
2. The introductory part of a statute, which states the reasons and intent of the law. *Encyc. Dryden.*

PRE'AMBLE, *v. t.* To preface; to introduce with previous remarks. *Feltham.*

PREAM'BULARY, } *a.* Previous; intro-
PREAM'BULOUS, } ductory. [*Not used.*] *Brown.*

PREAM'BULATE, *v. i.* [L. *præ*, before, and *ambulo*, to walk.] To walk or go before. *Jordan.*

PREAMBULA'TION, *n.* A preamble. [*Not in use.*] *Chaucer.*

2. A walking or going before.

PREAM'BULATORY, *a.* Going before; preceding. *Taylor.*

PREAPPREHEN'SION, *n.* [See *Apprehend.*] An opinion formed before examination. *Brown.*

PREASE, *n.* Press; crowd. [*Not used.* See *Press.*] *Chapman.*

PRE'ASING, *ppr.* or *a.* Crowding. [*Not used.*] *Spenser.*

PREAU'DIENCE, *n.* [See *Audience.*] Precedence or rank at the bar among lawyers; right of previous audience. *Blackstone.*

PREB'END, *n.* [It. *prebenda*, prebend, provision; Sp. *prebenda*; Fr. *prebende*, from L. *præbeo*, to afford, to allow.]

1. The stipend or maintenance granted out of the estate of a cathedral or collegiate church. Prebends are *simple* or *dignitary*; *simple*, when they are restricted to the revenue only, and *dignitary*, when they have jurisdiction annexed to them. *Encyc.*
2. A prebendary. [*Not in use.*] *Bacon.*

PREBEND'AL, *a.* Pertaining to a prebend. *Chesterfield.*

PREB'ENDARY, *n.* [Fr. *prebendier.*] An ecclesiastic who enjoys a prebend; the stipendiary of a cathedral church. *Swift.*

A prebendary differs from a canon in this; the prebendary receives his prebend in consideration of his officiating in the church; the canon merely in consequence of his being received into the cathedral or college. *Encyc.*

PREB'ENDARYSHIP, *n.* The office of a prebendary; a canonry. *Wotton.*

PRECA'RIOUS, *a.* [L. *precarius*, from *precor*, to pray or entreat; primarily, depending on request, or on the will of another.]

1. Depending on the will or pleasure of another; held by courtesy; liable to be changed or lost at the pleasure of another. A privilege depending on another's will is *precarious*, or held by a *precarious* tenure. *Addison.*
2. Uncertain; held by a doubtful tenure; depending on unknown or unforeseen causes or events. Temporal prosperity is *precarious*; personal advantages, health, strength and beauty are all *precarious*, depending on a thousand accidents. *Rogers.*

We say also, the weather is *precarious*; a phrase in which we depart not more from the primary sense of the word, than we do in a large part of all the words in the language.

PRECA'RIOUSLY, *adv.* At the will or pleasure of others; dependently; by an uncertain tenure; as, he subsists *precariously*. *Lesley. Pope.*

PRECA'RIOUSNESS, *n.* Uncertainty; dependence on the will or pleasure of others, or on unknown events; as the *precariousness* of life or health.

PRE'CATIVE, } *a.* [L. *precor*, to pray.]
PRE'CATORY, } Suppliant; beseeching. *Harris. Hopkins.*

PRECAU'TION, *n.* [Fr. from L. *precautus*, *præcaveo*; *præ*, before, and *caveo*, to take care.]

Previous caution or care; caution previously employed to prevent mischief or secure good in possession. *Addison.*

PRECAU'TION, *v. t.* To warn or advise beforehand for preventing mischief or securing good. *Locke.*

PRECAU'TIONAL, *a.* Preventive of mischief. *Montague.*

PRECAU'TIONARY, *a.* Containing previous caution; as *precautionary* advice or admonition.

2. Proceeding from previous caution; adapted to prevent mischief or secure good; as *precautionary* measures.

PRECEDA'NEOUS, *a.* [from *precede*, L. *præcedo.*]

Preceding; antecedent; anterior. [*Not used.*] *Hale.*

PRECE'DE, *v. t.* [L. *præcedo*; *præ*, before, and *cedo*, to move.]

1. To go before in the order of time. The corruption of morals *precedes* the ruin of a state.
2. To go before in rank or importance.
3. To cause something to go before; to make to take place in prior time.

It is usual to *precede* hostilities by a public declaration. [*Unusual.*] *Kent.*

PRECE'DED, *pp.* Being gone before.

PRECE'DENCE, } *n.* The act or state of
PRECE'DENCY, } going before; priority in time; as the *precedence* of one event to another.

2. The state of going or being before in rank or dignity or the place of honor; the right to a more honorable place in public processions, in seats or in the civilities of life. *Precedence* depends on the order of nature or rank established by God himself, as that due to age; or on courtesy, custom or political distinction, as that due to a governor or senator, who, though younger in years, takes rank of a subordinate officer, though older; or it is settled by authority, as in Great Britain. In the latter case, a violation of the right of *precedence* is actionable.

Precedence went in truck,
And he was competent whose purse was so. *Cowper.*

3. The foremost in ceremony. *Milton.*
4. Superiority; superior importance or influence.

Which of the different desires has *precedency* in determining the will to the next action. *Locke.*

PRECE'DENT, *a.* Going before in time; anterior; antecedent; as *precedent* services; a *precedent* fault of the will.

The world, or any part thereof, could not be *precedent* to the creation of man. *Hale.*

A precedent condition, in law, is a condition which must happen or be performed before an estate or some right can vest, and on failure of which the estate or right is defeated. *Blackstone.*

PREC'EDENT, *n.* Something done or said, that may serve or be adduced as an example to authorize a subsequent act of the like kind.

Examples for cases can but direct as *precedents* only. *Hooker.*

2. In *law*, a judicial decision, interlocutory or final, which serves as a rule for future determinations in similar or analogous cases; or any proceeding or course of proceedings which may serve for a rule in subsequent cases of a like nature.

PREC'EDENTED, *a.* Having a precedent; authorized by an example of a like kind.

PRECE'DENTLY, *adv.* Beforehand; antecedently.

PRECEL'LENCE, *n.* Excellence. [*Not in use.*] *Sheldon.*

PRECEN'TOR, *n.* [Low L. *præcentor*; Fr. *precenteur*; It. *precentore*; L. *præ*, before, and *canto*, to sing.]

The leader of the choir in a cathedral; called also the chanter or master of the choir. *Encyc.*

PRE'CEPT, *n.* [Fr. *precepte*; Sp. *precepto*; It. *precetto*; L. *præceptum*, from *præcipio*, to command; *præ*, before, and *capio*, to take.]

1. In *a general sense*, any commandment or order intended as an authoritative rule of action; but applied particularly to commands respecting moral conduct. The ten commandments are so many *precepts* for the regulation of our moral conduct.

No arts are without their *precepts*. *Dryden.*

2. In *law*, a command or mandate in writing. *Encyc.*

PRECEP'TIAL, *a.* Consisting of precepts. [*Not in use.*] *Shak.*

PRECEP'TION, *n.* A precept. [*Not in use.*] *Hall.*

PRECEP'TIVE, *a.* [L. *præceptivus.*] Giving precepts or commands for the regulation of moral conduct; containing precepts; as the *preceptive* parts of the Scriptures.

2. Directing in moral conduct; giving rules or directions; didactic.

The lesson given us here is *preceptive* to us. *L'Estrange.*

Preceptive poetry. *Encyc.*

PRECEP'TOR, *n.* [L. *præceptor*. See *Precept.*]

1. In *a general sense*, a teacher; an instructor.
2. In *a restricted sense*, the teacher of a school; sometimes, the principal teacher of an academy or other seminary.

PRECEPTO'RIAL, *a.* Pertaining to a preceptor. *Lit. Magazine.*

PRECEP'TORY, *a.* Giving precepts. *Anderson.*

PRECEP'TORY, *n.* A subordinate religious house where instruction was given

PRECES'SION, *n.* [Fr. *precession ;* It. *precessione ;* from the L. *præcessus, præcedo,* to go before.]

1. Literally, the act of going before, but in this sense rarely or never used.
2. In *astronomy*, the *precession of the equinox*, is an annual motion of the ecliptic of the equinox, or point when the ecliptic intersects the equator, to the westward, amounting to 50¼″. This precession was discovered by Hipparchus, a century and a half before the christian era, though it is alledged that the astronomers of India had discovered it long before. At that time, the point of the autumnal equinox was about six degrees to the eastward of the star called *spica virginis*. In 1750, that is, about nineteen hundred years after, this point was observed to be about 20° 21′ westward of that star. Hence it appears that the equinoctial points will make an entire revolution in about 25,745 years. *Encyc.*

PRE'CINCT, *n.* [L. *præcinctus, præcingo,* to encompass ; *præ* and *cingo,* to surround or gird.]

1. The limit, bound or exterior line encompassing a place ; as the *precincts* of light. *Milton.*
2. Bounds of jurisdiction, or the whole territory comprehended within the limits of authority.

   Take the body of A B, if to be found within your *precincts*. *Technical Law.*
3. A territorial district or division.

   It is to be observed that this word is generally used in the plural, except in the third sense.

   In case of non-acceptance [of the collector] the parish or *precinct* shall proceed to a new choice. *Law of Massachusetts.*

PRECIOSITY, for *preciousness* or value, not used. *Brown. More.*

PRE''CIOUS, *a.* [Fr. *precieux ;* L. *pretiosus,* from *pretium,* price. See *Praise.*]

1. Of great price ; costly ; as a *precious* stone.
2. Of great value or worth ; very valuable.

   She is more *precious* than rubies. Prov. iii.
3. Highly valued ; much esteemed.

   The word of the Lord was *precious* in those days ; there was no open vision. 1 Sam. iii.
4. Worthless ; in irony and contempt. *Locke.*

Precious metals, gold and silver, so called on account of their value.

PRE''CIOUSLY, *adv.* Valuably ; to a great price.

2. Contemptibly ; in irony.

PRE''CIOUSNESS, *n.* Valuableness ; great value ; high price. *Wilkins.*

PRECIPE, *n.* *pres'ipy.* [L. *præcipio.* See *Precept.*]

In *law*, a writ commanding the defendant to do a certain thing, or to show cause to the contrary ; giving him his choice to redress the injury or to stand the suit. *Blackstone.*

PREC'IPICE, *n.* [Fr. from L. *præcipitium,* from *præceps,* headlong ; *præ,* forward, and *ceps,* for *caput,* head. See *Chief.*]

1. Strictly, a falling headlong ; hence, a steep descent of land ; a fall or descent of land, perpendicular or nearly so.

   Where wealth, like fruit, on *precipices* grew. *Dryden.*
2. A steep descent, in general.

   In the breaking of the waves there is ever a *precipice*. *Bacon.*

   Swift down the *precipice* of time it goes. *Dryden.*

PRECIP'IENT, *a.* [L. *præcipiens.* See *Precept.*] Commanding ; directing.

PRECIPITABIL'ITY, *n.* [from *precipitable.*] The quality or state of being precipitable.

PRECIP'ITABLE, *a.* [from L. *præcipito,* from *præceps,* headlong.]

That may be precipitated or cast to the bottom, as a substance in solution.

PRECIP'ITANCE, PRECIP'ITANCY, *n.* [from *precipitant.*] Headlong hurry ; rash haste ; haste in resolving, forming an opinion or executing a purpose without due deliberation.

Hurried on by the *precipitance* of youth. *Swift.*

Rashness and *precipitance* of judgment. *Watts.*

2. Hurry ; great haste in going. *Milton.*

PRECIP'ITANT, *a.* [L. *præcipitans, præcipito,* from *præceps,* headlong.]

1. Falling or rushing headlong ; rushing down with velocity.

   They leave their little lives
Above the clouds, *precipitant* to earth. *Philips.*
2. Hasty ; urged with violent haste.

   Should he return, that troop so blithe and bold,
Precipitant in fear, would wing their flight. *Pope.*
3. Rashly hurried or hasty ; as *precipitant* rebellion. *K. Charles.*
4. Unexpectedly brought on or hastened. *Taylor.*

PRECIP'ITANT, *n.* In *chimistry*, a liquor, which when poured on a solution, separates what is dissolved and makes it precipitate, or fall to the bottom in a concrete state. *Encyc.*

PRECIP'ITANTLY, *adv.* With great haste ; with rash unadvised haste ; with tumultuous hurry. *Milton.*

PRECIP'ITATE, *v. t.* [L. *præcipito,* from *præceps,* headlong. See *Precipice.*]

1. To throw headlong ; as, he *precipitated* himself from a rock. *Milton. Dryden.*
2. To urge or press with eagerness or violence ; as, to *precipitate* a flight. *Dryden.*
3. To hasten.

   Short intermittent and swift recurrent pains do *precipitate* patients into consumptions. *Harvey.*
4. To hurry blindly or rashly.

   If they be daring, it may *precipitate* their designs and prove dangerous. *Bacon.*
5. To throw to the bottom of a vessel ; as a substance in solution.

   All metals may be *precipitated* by alkaline salts. *Encyc.*

PRECIP'ITATE, *v. i.* To fall headlong. *Shak.*

2. To fall to the bottom of a vessel, as sediment, or any substance in solution. *Bacon.*
3. To hasten without preparation. *Bacon.*

PRECIP'ITATE, *a.* Falling, flowing or rushing with steep descent.

Precipitate the furious torrent flows. *Prior.*

2. Headlong ; over hasty ; rashly hasty ; as, the king was too *precipitate* in declaring war.
3. Adopted with haste or without due deliberation ; hasty ; as a *precipitate* measure.
4. Hasty ; violent ; terminating speedily in death ; as a *precipitate* case of disease. *Arbuthnot.*

PRECIP'ITATE, *n.* A substance which, having been dissolved, is again separated from its solvent and thrown to the bottom of the vessel by pouring another liquor upon it.

Precipitate per se, Red precipitate, the red oxyd or peroxyd of mercury. *Thomson.*

PRECIP'ITATED, *pp.* Hurried ; hastened rashly ; thrown headlong.

PRECIP'ITATELY, *adv.* Headlong ; with steep descent.

2. Hastily ; with rash haste ; without due caution. Neither praise nor censure *precipitately.*

PRECIP'ITATING, *ppr.* Thowing headlong ; hurrying ; hastening rashly.

PRECIPITA'TION, *n.* [L. *præcipitatio.*]

1. The act of throwing headlong. *Shak.*
2. A falling, flowing or rushing down with violence and rapidity.

   The hurry, *precipitation* and rapid motion of the water. *Woodward.*
3. Great hurry ; rash, tumultuous haste ; rapid movement.

   The *precipitation* of inexperience is often restrained by shame. *Rambler.*
4. The act or operation of throwing to the bottom of a vessel any substance held in solution by its menstruum. *Precipitation* is often effected by a double elective attraction. *Encyc.*

PRECIP'ITATOR, *n.* One that urges on with vehemence or rashness. *Hammond.*

PRECIP'ITOUS, *a.* [L. *præceps.*] Very steep ; as a *precipitous* cliff or mountain.

2. Headlong ; directly or rapidly descending ; as a *precipitous* fall. *K. Charles.*
3. Hasty ; rash ; heady.

   Advice unsafe, *precipitous* and bold. *Dryden.*

PRECIP'ITOUSLY, *adv.* With steep descent ; in violent haste.

PRECIP'ITOUSNESS, *n.* Steepness of descent.

2. Rash haste. *Hammond.*

PRECI'SE, *a.* [L. *præcisus,* from *præcido,* to cut off ; *præ* and *cædo ;* literally, cut or pared away, that is, pared to smoothness or exactness.]

1. Exact ; nice ; definite ; having determinate limitations ; not loose, vague, uncertain or equivocal ; as *precise* rules of morality ; *precise* directions for life and conduct.

   The law in this point is *precise*. *Bacon.*

   For the hour *precise*
Exacts our parting. *Milton.*
2. Formal ; superstitiously exact ; excessively nice ; punctilious in conduct or ceremony. *Addison.*

PRECI'SELY, *adv.* Exactly ; nicely ; accurately ; in exact conformity to truth or to a model. The ideas are *precisely* expressed. The time of an eclipse may be *precisely* determined by calculation.

When more of these orders than one are to be set in several stories, there must be an exquisite care to place the columns *precisely* one over another. *Wotton.*

2. With excess of formality; with scrupulous exactness or punctiliousness in behavior or ceremony.

PRECI'SENESS, *n.* Exactness; rigid nicety; as the *preciseness* of words or expressions.

I will distinguish the cases; though give me leave, in handling them, not to sever them with too much *preciseness*. *Bacon.*

2. Excessive regard to forms or rules; rigid formality.

PRECI''SIAN, *n.* *s* as *z.* One that limits or restrains. *Shak.*

2. One who is rigidly or ceremoniously exact in the observance of rules. *Drayton. Watts.*

PRECI''SIANISM, *n.* Excessive exactness; superstitious rigor. *Milton.*

[These two words are, I believe, little used, or not at all.]

PRECI''SION, *n.* *s* as *z.* [Fr. from L. *præcisio.*] Exact limitation; exactness; accuracy. *Precision* in the use of words is a prime excellence in discourse; it is indispensable in controversy, in legal instruments and in mathematical calculations. Neither perspicuity nor *precision* should be sacrificed to ornament.

PRECI'SIVE, *a.* Exactly limiting by separating what is not relative to the purpose; as *precisive* abstraction. *Watts.*

PRECLU'DE, *v. t.* [L. *præcludo; præ*, before, and *cludo, claudo*, to shut.]

1. To prevent from entering by previously shutting the passage, or by any previous measures; hence, to hinder from access, possession or enjoyment. Sin, by its very nature, *precludes* the sinner from heaven; it *precludes* the enjoyment of God's favor; or it *precludes* the favor of God.

The valves *preclude* the blood from entering the veins. *Darwin.*

2. To prevent from happening or taking place.

PRECLU'DED, *pp.* Hindered from entering or enjoyment; debarred from something by previous obstacles.

PRECLU'DING, *ppr.* Shutting out; preventing from access or possession or from having place.

PRECLU'SION, *n.* *s* as *z.* The act of shutting out or preventing from access or possession; the state of being prevented from entering, possession or enjoyment. *Rambler.*

PRECLU'SIVE, *a.* Shutting out, or tending to preclude; hindering by previous obstacles. *Burke.*

PRECLU'SIVELY, *adv.* With hinderance by anticipation.

PRECO'CIOUS, *a.* [L. *præcox; præ*, before, and *coquo*, to cook or prepare.]

1. Ripe before the proper or natural time; as *precocious* trees. *Brown.*

2. Premature.

PRECO'CIOUSNESS, } *n.* Rapid growth
PRECOC'ITY, } and ripeness before the usual time; prematureness. *Howell.*

I cannot learn that he gave, in his youth, any evidence of that *precocity* which sometimes distinguishes uncommon genius. *Wirt's Life of P. Henry.*

PRECOG'ITATE, *v. t.* [L. *præcogito; præ* and *cogito.*] To consider or contrive beforehand. [*Little used.*] *Sherwood.*

PRECOGITA'TION, *n.* Previous thought or consideration. *Dict.*

PRECOGNITA. [See *Præcognita.*]

PRECOGNI''TION, *n.* [L. *præ*, before, and *cognitio*, knowledge.]

1. Previous knowledge; antecedent examination. *Fotherby.*

2. In *Scots law*, an examination of witnesses to a criminal act, before a judge, justice of the peace or sherif, before the prosecution of the offender, in order to know whether there is ground of trial, and to enable the prosecutor to set forth the facts in the libel. *Encyc.*

PRECOMPO'SE, *v. t.* [See *Compose.*] To compose beforehand. *Johnson.*

PRECOMPO'SED, *pp.* Composed beforehand.

PRECOMPO'SING, *ppr.* Composing beforehand.

PRECONCE'IT, *n.* [See *Preconceive.*] An opinion or notion previously formed. *Hooker.*

PRECONCE'IVE, *v. t.* [L. *præ*, before, and *concipio*, to conceive.]

To form a conception or opinion beforehand; to form a previous notion or idea.

In a dead plain, the way seems the longer, because the eye has *preconceived* it shorter than the truth. *Bacon.*

PRECONCE'IVED, *pp.* Conceived beforehand; previously formed; as *preconceived* opinions; *preconceived* ends or purposes. *South.*

PRECONCE'IVING, *ppr.* Conceiving or forming beforehand.

PRECONCEP'TION, *n.* Conception or opinion previously formed. *Hakewill.*

PRECONCERT', *v. t.* [*pre* and *concert.*] To concert beforehand; to settle by previous agreement.

PRECONCERT'ED, *pp.* Previously concerted or settled. *Warton.*

PRECONCERT'ING, *ppr.* Contriving and settling beforehand.

PRECONIZA'TION, *n.* [L. *præconium*, from *præco*, a crier.]

A publishing by proclamation, or a proclamation. [*Not used.*] *Hall.*

PRECONSIGN, *v. t.* [*pre* and *consign.*] To consign beforehand; to make a previous consignment of.

PRECON'STITUTE, *v. t.* [*pre* and *constitute.*]

To constitute or establish beforehand.

PRECON'STITUTED, *pp.* Previously established. *Paley.*

PRECON'STITUTING, *ppr.* Constituting beforehand.

PRECON'TRACT, *n.* [*pre* and *contract.*] A contract previous to another. *Shak.*

PRECONTRACT', *v. t.* To contract or stipulate previously.

PRECONTRACT', *v. i.* To make a previous contract or agreement.

PRECONTRACT'ED, *pp.* Previously contracted or stipulated; previously engaged by contract; as a woman *precontracted* to another man. *Ayliffe.*

PRECONTRACT'ING, *ppr.* Stipulating or covenanting beforehand.

PRECURSE, *n.* *precurs'.* [L. *præcursus, præcurro; præ* and *curro*, to run.]

A forerunning. [*Not used.*] *Shak.*

PRECURS'OR, *n.* [L. *præcursor*, supra.] A forerunner; a harbinger; he or that which precedes an event and indicates its approach; as Jove's lightnings, the *precursors* of thunder. *Shak.*

A cloud in the southwest, in winter, is often the *precursor* of a snow storm. A hazy atmosphere in the west, at sunset, is often the *precursor* of a cloudy or of a rainy day. *U. States.*

Evil thoughts are the invisible, airy *precursors* of all the storms and tempests of the soul. *Buckminster.*

PRECURS'ORY, *a.* Preceding as the harbinger; indicating something to follow; as *precursory* symptoms of a fever. *Med. Repos.*

PRECURS'ORY, *n.* An introduction. [*Not used.*] *Hammond.*

PREDA'CEOUS, *a.* [L. *prædaceus*, from *præda*, prey, spoil.]

Living by prey. *Derham.*

PRE'DAL, *a.* [L. *præda*, prey.] Pertaining to prey.

2. Practicing plunder. *Boyle.*

PRED'ATORY, *a.* [L. *prædatorius*, from *præda*, prey.]

1. Plundering; pillaging; characterized by plundering; practicing rapine; as a *predatory* war; a *predatory* excursion; a *predatory* party.

2. Hungry; ravenous; as *predatory* spirits or appetite. [*Hardly allowable.*] *Bacon.*

PREDECE'ASE, *v. i.* [*pre* and *decease.*] To die before. *Shak.*

PREDECE'ASED, *a.* Dead before. *Shak.*

PREDECES'SOR, *n.* [Fr. *prédécesseur*; L. *præ* and *decedo*, to depart.]

A person who has preceded another in the same office. The king, the president, the judge, or the magistrate, follows the steps of his *predecessor*, or he does not imitate the example of his *predecessors*. It is distinguished from *ancestor*, who is of the same blood; but it may perhaps be sometimes used for it. *Hooker. Addison.*

PREDESIGN, *v. t.* To design or purpose beforehand; to predetermine.

PREDESIGNED, *pp.* Purposed or determined previously. *Mitford.*

PREDESIGNING, *ppr.* Designing previously.

PREDESTINA'RIAN, *n.* [See *Predestinate.*]

One that believes in the doctrine of predestination. *Walton.*

PREDES'TINATE, *a.* Predestinated; foreordained. *Burnet.*

PREDES'TINATE, *v. t.* [It. *predestinare*; Fr. *predestiner*; L. *prædestino; præ* and *destino*, to appoint.]

To predetermine or foreordain; to appoint or ordain beforehand by an unchangeable purpose.

Whom he did foreknow, he also did *predestinate* to be conformed to the image of his Son. Rom. viii.

Having *predestinated* us unto the adoption of children by Jesus Christ to himself. Eph. i.

PREDES'TINATED, *pp.* Predetermined; foreordained; decreed.

PREDES'TINATING, *ppr.* Foreordaining; decreeing; appointing beforehand by an unchangeable purpose.

2. Holding predestination.

And pricks up his *predestinating* ears. *Dryden.*

PREDESTINA'TION, *n.* The act of decreeing or foreordaining events; the decree of God by which he hath, from eternity, unchangeably appointed or determined whatever comes to pass. It is used particularly in theology to denote the preordination of men to everlasting happiness or misery. *Encyc.*

Predestination is a part of the unchangeable plan of the divine government; or in other words, the unchangeable purpose of an unchangeable God.

PREDES'TINATOR, *n.* Properly, one that foreordains.

2. One that holds to predestination. *Cowley.*

PREDES'TINE, *v. t.* To decree beforehand; to foreordain.

And bid *predestined* empires rise and fall. *Prior.*

PREDETERM'INATE, *a.* Determined beforehand; as the *predeterminate* counsel of God. *Parkhurst.*

PREDETERMINA'TION, *n.* [See *Predetermine.*]

1. Previous determination; purpose formed beforehand; as the *predetermination* of God's will. *Hammond.*

2. Premotion; that concurrence of God which determines men in their actions. *Encyc.*

PREDETERM'INE, *v. t.* [*pre* and *determine.*]

1. To determine beforehand; to settle in purpose or counsel.

If God foresees events, he must have *predetermined* them. *Hale.*

2. To doom by previous decree.

PRE'DIAL, *a.* [Sp. *predial*, from L. *prædium*, a farm or estate.]

1. Consisting of land or farms; real estate. *Ayliffe.*

2. Attached to land or farms; as *predial* slaves. *Encyc.*

3. Growing or issuing from land; as *predial* tithes.

PREDICABIL'ITY, *n.* [from *predicable.*] The quality of being predicable, or capable of being affirmed of something, or attributed to something. *Reid.*

PRED'ICABLE, *a.* [L. *prædicabilis*, from *prædico*, to affirm; *præ* and *dico*, to say.]

That may be affirmed of something; that may be attributed to. Animal is *predicable* of man. Intelligence is not *predicable* of plants. More or less is not *predicable* of a circle or of a square. Whiteness is not *predicable* of time.

PRED'ICABLE, *n.* One of the five things which can be affirmed of any thing. Genus, species, difference, property, and accident are the five *predicables.* *Watts.*

PREDIC'AMENT, *n.* [Fr. from L. *prædicamentum*, from *prædico*, to affirm.]

1. In *logic*, a category; a series or order of all the predicates or attributes contained under any genus. The school philosophers distribute all the objects of our thoughts and ideas into genera or classes, which the Greeks call *categories*, and the Latins *predicaments.* Aristotle made ten categories, viz. substance, quantity, quality, relation, action, passion, time, place, situation and habit. *Encyc.*

2. Class or kind described by any definite marks; hence, condition; particular situation or state. *Shak.*

We say, the country is in a singular *predicament.*

PREDICAMENT'AL, *a.* Pertaining to a predicament. *Hale.*

PRED'ICANT, *n.* [L. *prædicans, prædico.*] One that affirms any thing.

PRED'ICATE, *v. t.* [L. *prædico; præ* and *dico*, to say.]

To affirm one thing of another; as, to *predicate* whiteness of snow. Reason may be *predicated* of man.

PRED'ICATE, *v. i.* To affirm; to comprise an affirmation. *Hale.*

PRED'ICATE, *n.* In *logic*, that which, in a proposition, is affirmed or denied of the subject. In these propositions, "*paper is white*," "*ink is not white*," whiteness is the *predicate* affirmed of paper, and denied of ink. *Watts.*

PREDICA'TION, *n.* [L. *prædicatio.*] Affirmation of something, or the act of affirming one thing of another. *Locke.*

PRED'ICATORY, *a.* Affirmative; positive. *Bp. Hall.*

PREDICT', *v. t.* [L. *prædictus, prædico; præ*, before, and *dico*, to tell.]

To foretell; to tell beforehand something that is to happen. Moses *predicted* the dispersion of the Israelites. Christ *predicted* the destruction of Jerusalem.

PREDICT'ED, *pp.* Foretold; told before the event.

PREDICT'ING, *ppr.* Foretelling.

PREDIC'TION, *n.* [L. *prædictio.*] A foretelling; a previous declaration of a future event; prophecy. The fulfillment of the *predictions* of the prophets is considered to be a strong argument in favor of the divine origin of the Scriptures.

PREDICT'IVE, *a.* Foretelling; prophetic. *More.*

PREDICT'OR, *n.* A foreteller; one who prophesies. *Swift.*

PREDIGES'TION, *n.* [*pre* and *digestion.*] Too hasty digestion.

Predigestion fills the body with crudities. *Bacon.*

PREDILEC'TION, *n.* [Fr.; It. *predilezione*; L. *præ*, before, and *dilectus, diligo*, to love.]

A previous liking; a prepossession of mind in favor of something. *Warton.*

PREDISPO'NENT, *n.* That which predisposes.

PREDISPO'SE, *v. t. s* as *z.* [*pre* and *dispose.*]

1. To incline beforehand; to give a previous disposition to; as, to *predispose* the mind or temper to friendship. *South.*

2. To fit or adapt previously; as, debility *predisposes* the body to disease.

PREDISPO'SED, *pp.* Previously inclined or adapted.

PREDISPO'SING, *ppr.* Inclining or adapting beforehand.

2. *a.* Tending or able to give predisposition or liableness; as the *predisposing* causes of disease.

PREDISPOSI''TION, *n.* Previous inclination or propensity to any thing; *applied to the mind.*

2. Previous fitness or adaptation to any change, impression or purpose; *applied to matter;* as the *predisposition* of the body to disease; the *predisposition* of the seasons to generate diseases. *Wiseman. Bacon.*

PREDOM'INANCE, **PREDOM'INANCY**, } *n.* [See *Predominant.*]

1. Prevalence over others; superiority in strength, power, influence or authority; ascendancy; as the *predominance* of a red color in a body of various colors; the *predominance* of love or anger among the passions; the *predominance* of self-interest over all other considerations; the *predominance* of imperial authority in the confederacy.

2. In *astrology*, the superior influence of a planet.

PREDOM'INANT, *a.* [Fr. *predominant*; It. *predominante*; L. *præ* and *dominans, dominor*, to rule.]

Prevalent over others; superior in strength, influence or authority; ascendant; ruling; controlling; as a *predominant* color; *predominant* beauty or excellence; a *predominant* passion.

Those helps—were *predominant* in the king's mind. *Bacon.*

Foul subornation is *predominant.* *Shak.*

PREDOM'INANTLY, *adv.* With superior strength or influence. *Brown.*

PREDOM'INATE, *v. i.* [Fr. *predominer*; Sp. *predominar*; It. *predominare*; L. *præ*, before, and *dominor*, to rule, from *dominus*, lord.]

To prevail; to surpass in strength, influence or authority; to be superior; to have controlling influence. In some persons, the love of money *predominates* over all other passions; in others, ambition or the love of fame *predominates;* in most men, self-interest *predominates* over patriotism and philanthropy.

So much did love t' her executed lord
Predominate in this fair lady's heart. *Daniel.*

The rays reflected least obliquely may *predominate* over the rest. *Newton.*

PREDOM'INATE, *v. t.* To rule over.

PREDOM'INATING, *ppr.* Having superior strength or influence; ruling; controlling.

PREDOMINA'TION, *n.* Superior strength or influence. *Browne.*

PRE-ELECT', *v. t.* [*pre* and *elect.*] To choose or elect beforehand. *Dict.*

PRE-ELEC'TION, *n.* Choice or election by previous determination of the will. *Prideaux.*

PRE-EM'INENCE, *n.* [Fr.; It. *preeminenza*; *pre* and *eminence.*]

1. Superiority in excellence; distinction in something commendable; as *pre-eminence* in honor or virtue; *pre-eminence* in eloquence, in legal attainments or in medical skill.

The *preeminence* of christianity to any other religious scheme— *Addison.*

2. Precedence; priority of place; superiority in rank or dignity.

That in all things he might have the *preeminence.* Col. i.

Painful *preeminence!* yourself to view
Above life's weakness and its comforts too. *Pope.*

3. Superiority of power or influence. *Hooker.*

4. Sometimes in a bad sense; as *pre-eminence* in guilt or crime.

PRE-EM'INENT, *a.* [Fr.; *pre* and *eminent*; L. *præ*, before, and *eminens, emineo.* See *Menace.*]

1. Superior in excellence; distinguished for something commendable or honorable.

In goodness and in power *preeminent*. *Milton.*

2. Surpassing others in evil or bad qualities; as *pre-eminent* in crime or guilt.

PRE-EM'INENTLY, *adv.* In a preeminent degree; with superiority or distinction above others; as *pre-eminently* wise or good.

2. In a bad sense; as *pre-eminently* guilty.

PRE-EMP'TION, *n.* [L. *præ*, before, and *emptio*, a buying; *emo*, to buy.] The act of purchasing before others.

2. The right of purchasing before others. Prior discovery of unoccupied land gives the discoverer the prior right of occupancy. Prior discovery of land inhabited by savages is held to give the discoverer the *pre-emption*, or right of purchase before others.

3. Formerly, in *England*, the privilege or prerogative enjoyed by the king, of buying provisions for his household in preference to others, abolished by statute 19. Charles II.

PREEN, *n.* [Scot. *prein*, *prin*, a pen; Dan. *preen*, the point of a graving tool, a bodkin; D. *priem*, a pin, a spike; G. *pfrieme*, a punch. These are probably the same word, a little varied.]

A forked instrument used by clothiers in dressing cloth.

PREEN, *v. t.* [Scot. *proyne*, *prunyie*; Chaucer, *proine*. This word is probably the same as the foregoing, denoting the use of the beak in cleaning and composing the fethers. So *pikith*, in Chaucer, is from *pike*, *pick*.

He kembith him; he *proinith* him and pikith. *Cant. Tales*, 9885.

If not, the word may be contracted from the Fr. *provigner*, to propagate vines by laying cuttings in the ground.]

To clean, compose and dress the fethers, as fowls, to enable them to glide more easily through the air or water. For this purpose they are furnished with two glands on their rump, which secrete an oily substance into a bag, from which they draw it with the bill and spread it over their fethers. *Bailey. Encyc.*

PRE-ENGA'GE, *v. t.* [*pre* and *engage.*] To engage by previous contract.

To Cipseus by his friends his suit he mov'd,
But he was *pre-engag'd* by former ties. *Dryden.*

2. To engage or attach by previous influence.

The world has the unhappy advantage of *pre-engaging* our passions. *Rogers.*

3. To engage beforehand.

PRE-ENGA'GED, *pp.* Previously engaged by contract or influence.

PRE-ENGA'GEMENT, *n.* Prior engagement; as by stipulation or promise. A would accept my invitation, but for his *pre-engagement* to B.

2. Any previous attachment binding the will or affections.

My *pre-engagements* to other themes were not unknown to those for whom I was to write. *Boyle.*

PRE-ENGA'GING, *ppr.* Previously engaging.

PREE'NING, *ppr.* Cleaning and composing the fethers, as fowls.

PRE-ESTAB'LISH, *v. t.* [*pre* and *establish.*] To establish or settle beforehand. *Coventry.*

PRE-ESTAB'LISHED, *pp.* Previously established.

PRE-ESTAB'LISHING, *ppr.* Settling or ordaining beforehand.

PRE-ESTAB'LISHMENT, *n.* Settlement beforehand.

PRE-EXAMINA'TION, *n.* Previous examination.

PRE-EXAM'INE, *v. t.* To examine beforehand.

PRE-EXIST', *v. i.* [*pre* and *exist.*] To exist beforehand or before something else. It has been believed by many philosophers that the souls of men *pre-exist*, that is, exist before the formation of the body.

PRE-EXIST'ENCE, *n.* Existence previous to something else.

Wisdom declares her antiquity and *pre-existence* to all the works of this earth. *Burnet.*

2. Existence of the soul before its union with the body, or before the body is formed; *a tenet of eastern sages.* *Addison.*

PRE-EXIST'ENT, *a.* Existing beforehand; preceding in existence.

What mortal knows his *pre-existent* state? *Pope.*

PRE-EXISTIMA'TION, *n.* Previous esteem. [*Not in use.*] *Brown.*

PRE-EXIST'ING, *ppr.* Previously existing.

PRE-EXPECTA'TION, *n.* Previous expectation. [Qu. is not this tautology?] *Gerard.*

PREF'ACE, *n.* [Fr. from L. *præfatio*; *præ*, before, and *for*, *fari*, *fatus*, to speak.]

Something spoken as introductory to a discourse, or written as introductory to a book or essay, intended to inform the hearer or reader of the main design, or in general, of whatever is necessary to the understanding of the discourse, book or essay; a proem; an introduction or series of preliminary remarks. *Milton.*

PREF'ACE, *v. t.* To introduce by preliminary remarks; as, to *preface* a book or discourse. The advocate *prefaced* his argument with a history of the case.

2. To face; to cover; *a ludicrous sense.*

Not *prefacing* old rags with plush. *Cleaveland.*

PREF'ACE, *v. i.* To say something introductory. *Spectator.*

PREF'ACED, *pp.* Introduced with preliminary observations.

PREF'ACER, *n.* The writer of a preface. *Dryden.*

PREF'ACING, *ppr.* Introducing with preliminary remarks.

PREF'ATORY, *a.* Pertaining to a preface; introductory to a book, essay or discourse. *Dryden.*

PRE'FECT, *n.* [L. *præfectus*; *præ*, before, and *factus*, made; but directly from *præficior*, *præfectus.*]

1. In *ancient Rome*, a chief magistrate who governed a city or province in the absence of the king, consuls or emperor. *Encyc.*

2. A governor, commander, chief magistrate or superintendent. *Hammond. Addison.*

PRE'FECTSHIP, **PRE'FECTURE**, *n.* The office of a chief magistrate, commander or viceroy.

2. Jurisdiction of a prefect.

PREFER', *v. t.* [L. *præfero*; *præ*, before, and *fero*, to bear or carry; Fr. *preferer*; It. *preferire*; Sp. *preferir.*]

1. Literally, to bear or carry in advance, in the mind, affections or choice; hence, to regard more than another; to honor or esteem above another.

It is sometimes followed by *above*, *before*, or *to*.

If I *prefer* not Jerusalem *above* my chief joy. Ps. cxxxvii.

He that cometh after me, is *preferred before* me. John i.

2. To advance, as to an office or dignity; to raise; to exalt; as, to *prefer* one to a bishopric; to *prefer* an officer to the rank of general.

3. To offer; to present; to exhibit; usually with solemnity, or to a public body. It is our privilege to enjoy the right of *preferring* petitions to rulers for redress of wrongs.

My vows and prayers to thee *preferred*. *Sandys.*

Prefer a bill against all kings and parliaments since the conquest. *Collier.*

4. To offer or present ceremoniously, or in ordinary familiar language.

He spake, and to her hand *preferr'd* the bowl. *Pope.*

[*This is allowable, at least in poetry, though not usual.*]

PREF'ERABLE, *a.* [Fr.] Worthy to be preferred or chosen before something else; more eligible; more desirable. Virtue is far *preferable* to vice, even for its pleasures in this life.

2. More excellent; of better quality; as, Madeira wine is *preferable* to claret.

PREF'ERABLENESS, *n.* The quality or state of being preferable. *Mountague.*

PREF'ERABLY, *adv.* In preference; in such a manner as to prefer one thing to another.

How comes he to choose Plautus *preferably* to Terence? *Dennis.*

PREF'ERENCE, *n.* The act of preferring one thing before another; estimation of one thing above another; choice of one thing rather than another.

Leave the critics on either side to contend about the *preference* due to this or that sort of poetry. *Dryden.*

It has *to*, *above*, *before*, or *over*, before the thing postponed. All men give the *preference to* Homer as an epic poet. The human body has the *preference above* or *before* those of brutes.

The knowledge of things alone gives a value to our reasonings, and *preference* of one man's knowledge *over* another's. *Locke.*

PREFER'MENT, *n.* [It. *preferimento.*] Advancement to a higher office, dignity or station. Change of manners and even of character often follows *preferment*. A profligate life should be considered a disqualification for *preferment*, no less than want of ability.

2. Superior place or office. All *preferments* should be given to competent men.

3. Preference. [*Not used.*] *Brown.*

PREFER'RED, *pp.* Regarded above others; elevated in station.

PREFER'RER, *n.* One who prefers.

PREFER'RING, *ppr.* Regarding above others; advancing to a higher station; offering; presenting.

PREFIG'URATE, *v. t.* [See *Prefigure.*] To show by antecedent representation. [*Little used.*]

PREFIGURA'TION, *n.* Antecedent representation by similitude.

A variety of prophecies and *prefigurations* had their punctual accomplishment in the author of this institution. *Norris.*

PREFIG'URATIVE, *a.* Showing by previous figures, types or similitude. The sacrifice of the paschal lamb was *prefigurative* of the death of Christ.

PREFIG'URE, *v. t.* [L. *præ*, before, and *figuro*, to fashion.]

To exhibit by antecedent representation, or by types and similitude.

In the Old Testament, things are *prefigured*, which are performed in the New. *Hooker.*

PREFIG'URED, *pp.* Exhibited by antecedent signs, types or similitude.

PREFIG'URING, *ppr.* Showing antecedently by similitude.

PREFI'NE, *v. t.* [L. *præfinio; præ*, before, and *finio*, to limit; *finis*, limit.] To limit beforehand. [*Little used.*] *Knolles.*

PREFINI''TION, *n.* Previous limitation. [*Little used.*] *Fotherby.*

PREFIX', *v. t.* [L. *præfigo; præ*, before, and *figo*, to fix.]

1. To put or fix before, or at the beginning of another thing; as, to *prefix* a syllable to a word; to *prefix* an advertisement to a book.

2. To set or appoint beforehand; as, to *prefix* the hour of meeting.

A time *prefix*, and think of me at last. *Sandys.*

3. To settle; to establish.

I would *prefix* some certain boundary between the old statutes and the new. *Hale.*

PRE'FIX, *n.* A letter, syllable or word put to the beginning of a word, usually to vary its signification. A *prefix* is united with the word, forming a part of it; hence it is distinguished from a preposition; as *pre*, in *prefix; con*, in *conjure; with*, in *withstand. Prefixes* are sometimes called particles, or inseparable prepositions.

PREFIX'ED, *pp.* Set before; appointed beforehand; settled.

PREFIX'ING, *ppr.* Putting before; previously appointing; establishing.

PREFIX'ION, *n.* The act of prefixing.

PREFORM', *v. t.* [*pre* and *form.*] To form beforehand. *Shak.*

PREFORM'ATIVE, *n.* [L. *præ*, before, and *formative.*]

A formative letter at the beginning of a word. *M. Stuart.*

PREFUL'GENCY, *n.* [L. *præfulgens; præ*, before, and *fulgeo*, to shine.]

Superior brightness or effulgency. *Barrow.*

PREG'NABLE, *a.* [Fr. *prenable.*] That may be taken or won by force; expugnable. [*Little used.*] *Cotgrave.*

PREG'NANCY, *n.* [See *Pregnant.*] The state of a female who has conceived, or is with child. *Ray.*

2. Fertility; fruitfulness; inventive power; as the *pregnancy* of wit or invention. *Prior.*

Pregnance, in a like sense, is not used.

PREG'NANT, *a.* [L. *prægnans;* supposed to be compounded of *præ*, before, and *geno*, Gr. γεννάω, to beget; It. *pregnante;* Sp. *preñado.*]

1. Being with young, as a female; breeding; teeming.

2. Fruitful; fertile; impregnating; as *pregnant* streams. *Dryden.*

3. Full of consequence; as a *pregnant* instance of infatuation.

An egregious and *pregnant* instance how far virtue surpasses ingenuity. *Woodward.*

4. Easy to admit or receive.

I am *pregnant* to good pity. [*Not proper.*] *Shak.*

5. Free; kind; ready; witty; apt. [*Not proper.*] *Shak.*

6. Plain; clear; evident; full. [*Not in use.*] *Shak.*

PREG'NANTLY, *adv.* Fruitfully.

2. Fully; plainly; clearly. [*Not used.*] *Shak. South.*

PRE'GRAVATE, *v. t.* [L. *prægravo.*] To bear down; to depress. [*Not in use.*] *Hall.*

PREGRAV'ITATE, *v. i.* To descend by gravity. *Boyle.*

PREGUSTA'TION, *n.* [L. *præ* and *gusto*, to taste.] The act of tasting before another. *Dict.*

PREHEN'SILE, *a.* [L. *prehendo*, to take or seize; *prehensus.*]

Seizing; grasping; adapted to seize or grasp. The tails of some monkeys are *prehensile. Nat. Hist. Encyc.*

PREHEN'SION, *n.* A taking hold; a seizing; as with the hand or other limb. *Lawrence.*

PREHN'ITE, *n.* [from *Prehn*, the name of the person who first brought this stone from the Cape of Good Hope.]

A mineral of the silicious kind, of an apple green or greenish gray color. It has been called shorl, emerald, chrysoprase, felspath, chrysolite, and zeolite. It has some resemblance to zeolite, but differs from it in several particulars, and is therefore considered to be a particular species. *Kirwan.*

Prehnite is near to stilbite, and is classed by the French with the family of zeolites.

It is massive or crystalized, but the form of its crystals cannot be determined in consequence of their aggregation. *Cleaveland.*

PREINSTRUCT', *v. t.* [*pre* and *instruct.*] To instruct previously. *More.*

PREINSTRUCT'ED, *pp.* Previously instructed or directed.

PREINSTRUCT'ING, *ppr.* Previously instructing.

PREINTIMA'TION, *n.* [*pre* and *intimation.*]

Previous intimation; a suggestion beforehand. *T. Scott.*

PREJUDGE, *v. t.* *prejudj'.* [Fr. *prejuger;* L. *præ* and *judico*, to judge.]

1. To judge in a cause before it is heard, or before the arguments and facts in the case are fully known.

The committee of council hath *prejudged* the whole case, by calling the united sense of both houses of parliament an universal clamor. *Swift.*

2. To judge and determine before the cause is heard; hence sometimes, to condemn beforehand or unheard. *Milton.*

PREJUDG'ED, *pp.* Judged beforehand; determined unheard.

PREJUDG'ING, *ppr.* Judging or determining without a hearing or before the case is fully understood.

PREJUDG'MENT, *n.* Judgment in a case without a hearing or full examination. *Knox.*

PREJU'DICACY, *n.* Prejudice; prepossession. [*Not used.*] *Blount.*

PREJU'DICATE, *v. t.* [L. *præ*, before, and *judico*, to judge.]

To prejudge; to determine beforehand to disadvantage.

Our dearest friend
Prejudicates the business. *Shak.*

PREJU'DICATE, *v. i.* To form a judgment without due examination of the facts and arguments in the case. *Sidney.*

PREJU'DICATE, *a.* Formed before due examination. *Watts.*

2. Prejudiced; biased by opinions formed prematurely; as a *prejudicate* reader. [*Little used.*] *Brown.*

PREJU'DICATED, *pp.* Prejudged.

PREJU'DICATING, *ppr.* Prejudging.

PREJUDICA'TION, *n.* The act of judging without due examination of facts and evidence. *Sherwood.*

2. In *Roman oratory*, prejudications were of three kinds; first, precedents or adjudged cases, involving the same points of law; second, previous decisions on the same question between other parties; third, decisions of the same cause and between the same parties, before tribunals of inferior jurisdiction. *Adams' Lect.*

PREJU'DICATIVE, *a.* Forming an opinion or judgment without examination. *More.*

PREJ'UDICE, *n.* [Fr. from L. *prejudicium; præ* and *judico.*]

1. Prejudgment; an opinion or decision of mind, formed without due examination of the facts or arguments which are necessary to a just and impartial determination. It is used in a good or bad sense. Innumerable are the *prejudices* of education; we are accustomed to believe what we are taught, and to receive opinions from others without examining the grounds by which they can be supported. A man has strong *prejudices* in favor of his country or his party, or the church in which he has been educated; and often our *prejudices* are unreasonable. A judge should disabuse himself of *prejudice* in favor of either party in a suit.

My comfort is that their manifest *prejudice* to my cause will render their judgment of less authority. *Dryden.*

2. A previous bent or bias of mind for or against any person or thing; prepossession.

There is an unaccountable *prejudice* to projectors of all kinds. *Addison.*

3. Mischief; hurt; damage; injury. Violent factions are a *prejudice* to the authority of the sovereign.

How plain this abuse is, and what *prejudice* it does to the understanding of the sacred Scriptures. *Locke.*

[*This is a sense of the word too well established to be condemned.*]

PREJ'UDICE, *v. t.* To prepossess with unexamined opinions, or opinions formed without due knowledge of the facts and circumstances attending the question; to bias the mind by hasty and incorrect notions, and give it an unreasonable bent to one side or other of a cause.

Suffer not any beloved study to *prejudice* your mind so far as to despise all other learning. *Watts.*

2. To obstruct or injure by prejudices, or an undue previous bias of the mind; or to hurt; to damage; to diminish; to impair; in a very general sense. The advocate who attempts to prove too much, may *prejudice* his cause.

I am not to *prejudice* the cause of my fellow poets, though I abandon my own defense. *Dryden.*

PREJ'UDICED, *pp.* or *a.* Prepossessed by unexamined opinions; biased.

PREJUDI''CIAL, *a.* Biased or blinded by prejudices; as a *prejudicial* eye. [*Not in use.*] *Hooker.*

2. Hurtful; mischievous; injurious; disadvantageous; detrimental; tending to obstruct or impair. A high rate of interest is *prejudicial* to trade and manufactures. Intemperance is *prejudicial* to health.

His going away the next morning with all his troops, was most *prejudicial* to the king's affairs. *Clarendon.*

One of the young ladies reads while the others are at work; so that the learning of the family is not at all *prejudicial* to its manufactures. *Addison.*

PREJUDI''CIALNESS, *n.* The state of being prejudicial; injuriousness.

PRE'LACY, *n.* [from *prelate.*] The office or dignity of a prelate.

Prelacies may be termed the greater benefices. *Ayliffe.*

2. Episcopacy; the order of bishops.

How many are there that call themselves protestants, who put *prelacy* and popery together as terms convertible? *Swift.*

3. Bishops, collectively.

Divers of the reverend *prelacy.* *Hooker.*

PRE'LATE, *n.* [Fr. *prelat*; It. *prelato*; from L. *prælatus, præfero.*]

An ecclesiastic of the higher order, as an archbishop, bishop or patriarch; a dignitary of the church. *Bacon.*

PRE'LATESHIP, *n.* The office of a prelate. *Harmar.*

PRELAT'IC, } *a.* Pertaining to prelates
PRELAT'ICAL, } or prelacy; as *prelatical* authority.

PRELAT'ICALLY, *adv.* With reference to prelates. *Morton.*

PRELA'TION, *n.* [L. *prælatio, præfero.*] Preference; the setting of one above another. [*Little used.*] *Hale.*

PRE'LATISM, *n.* Prelacy; episcopacy. *Milton.*

PRE'LATIST, *n.* [from *prelate.*] An advocate for prelacy or the government of the church by bishops; a high churchman.

I am an episcopalian, but not a *prelatist.* *T. Scott.*

PRE'LATURE, } *n.* [Fr. *prelature.*]
PRE'LATURESHIP, } The state or dignity of a prelate. *Dict.*

PRE'LATY, *n.* Episcopacy; prelacy. [*Not in use.*] *Milton.*

PRELECT', *v. t.* [L. *prælectus, prælego*; *præ*, before, and *lego*, to read.]

To read a lecture or public discourse. *Horsley.*

PRELEC'TION, *n.* [L. *prælectio.*] A lecture or discourse read in public or to a select company. *Hale.*

PRELEC'TOR, *n.* A reader of discourses; a lecturer. *Sheldon.*

PRELIBA'TION, *n.* [from L. *prælibo*; *præ*, before, and *libo*, to taste.]

1. Foretaste; a tasting beforehand or by anticipation.

The joy that proceeds from a belief of pardon is a *prelibation* of heavenly bliss.

2. An effusion previous to tasting. Qu. *Johnson.*

PRELIM'INARY, *a.* [Fr. *preliminaire*; It. *preliminare*; Sp. *preliminar*; L. *præ*, before, and *limen*, threshhold or limit.]

Introductory; previous; proemial; that precedes the main discourse or business; as *preliminary* observations to a discourse or book; *preliminary* articles to a treaty; *preliminary* measures.

PRELIM'INARY, *n.* That which precedes the main discourse, work, design or business; something previous or preparatory; as the *preliminaries* to a negotiation or treaty; the *preliminaries* to a combat. The parties met to settle the *preliminaries.*

PRE'LUDE, *n.* [Fr. *id.*; It. Sp. *preludio*; Low L. *præludium*, from *præludo*; *præ*, before, and *ludo*, to play.]

1. A short flight of music, or irregular air played by a musician before he begins the piece to be played, or before a full concert. *Encyc. Young.*

2. Something introductory or that shows what is to follow; something preceding which bears some relation or resemblance to that which is to follow.

The last Georgic was a good *prelude* to the Æneis. *Addison.*

3. A forerunner; something which indicates a future event.

PRELU'DE, *v. t.* To introduce with a previous performance; to play before; as, to *prelude* a concert with a lively air.

2. To precede, as an introductory piece; as, a lively air *preludes* the concert.

PRELU'DE, *v. i.* To serve as an introduction to. *Dryden.*

PRELU'DED, *pp.* Preceded by an introductory performance; preceded.

PRE'LUDER, *n.* One that plays a prelude, or introduces by a previous irregular piece of music.

PRELU'DING, *ppr.* Playing an introductory air; preceding.

PRELU'DIOUS, *a.* Previous; introductory. *Cleaveland.*

PRELU'DIUM, *n.* [Low L.] A prelude. *Dryden.*

PRELU'SIVE, *a.* Previous; introductory; indicating that something of a like kind is to follow; as *prelusive* drops. *Thomson.*

PRELU'SORY, *a.* Previous; introductory; prelusive. *Bacon.*

PREMATU'RE, *a.* [Fr. *prématuré*, from L. *præmaturus*; *præ*, before, and *maturus*, ripe.]

1. Ripe before the natural or proper time; as the *premature* fruits of a hot bed.

2. Happening, arriving, performed or adopted before the proper time; as a *premature* fall of snow in autumn; a *premature* birth; a *premature* opinion; a *premature* measure.

3. Arriving or received without due authentication or evidence; as *premature* report, news or intelligence.

PREMATU'RELY, *adv.* Too soon; too early; before the proper time; as fruits *prematurely* ripened; opinions *prematurely* formed; measures *prematurely* taken.

2. Without due evidence or authentication; as intelligence *prematurely* received.

PREMATU'RENESS, } *n.* Ripeness be-
PREMATU'RITY, } fore the natural or proper time.

2. Too great haste; unseasonable earliness. *Warton.*

PREMED'ITATE, *v. t.* [Fr. *premediter*; It. *premeditare*; L. *præmeditor*; *præ*, before, and *meditor*, to meditate.]

To think on and revolve in the mind beforehand; to contrive and design previously; as, to *premeditate* theft or robbery.

With words *premeditated* thus he said. *Dryden.*

PREMED'ITATE, *v. i.* To think, consider or revolve in the mind beforehand; to deliberate; to have formed in the mind by previous thought or meditation. *Hooker.*

PREMED'ITATE, *a.* Contrived by previous meditation. *Burnet.*

PREMED'ITATED, *pp.* Previously considered or meditated.

2. Previously contrived, designed or intended; deliberate; willful; as *premeditated* murder.

PREMED'ITATELY, *adv.* With previous meditation. *Feltham.*

PREMED'ITATING, *ppr.* Previously meditating; contriving or intending beforehand.

PREMEDITA'TION, *n.* [L. *præmeditatio.*]

1. The act of meditating beforehand; previous deliberation.

A sudden thought may be higher than nature can raise without *premeditation.* *Dryden.*

2. Previous contrivance or design formed; as the *premeditation* of a crime.

PREMER'IT, *v. t.* [*pre* and *merit.*] To merit or deserve beforehand. [*Little used.*] *K. Charles.*

PREM'ICES, *n.* [Fr. from L. *primitiæ. primus.*] First fruits. [*Not used.*] *Dryden.*

PRE'MIER, *a.* [Fr. from L. *primus*, first.]

First; chief; principal; as the *premier* place; *premier* minister. *Camden. Swift.*

PRE'MIER, *n.* The first minister of state; the prime minister.

PRE'MIERSHIP, *n.* The office or dignity of the first minister of state.

PREMI'SE, *v. t.* *s* as *z.* [L. *præmissus, præmitto*, to send before.]

1. To speak or write before, or as introductory to the main subject; to offer previously, as something to explain or aid in understanding what follows.

I *premise* these particulars that the reader may know that I enter upon it as a very ungrateful task. *Addison.*

2. To send before the time. [*Not in use.*] *Shak.*

3. To lay down premises or first propositions, on which rest the subsequent reasonings. *Burnet.*

4. To use or apply previously.

If venesection and a cathartic be *premised.* *Darwin.*

PREMI'SE, *v. i.* To state antecedent propositions. *Swift.*

PREM'ISE, *n. prem'is.* A first or antecedent proposition. Hence,

PREM'ISES, *n.* [Fr. *premisses*; L. *præmissa.*]

1. In *logic*, the two first propositions of a syllogism, from which the inference or conclusion is drawn; as,

All sinners deserve punishment;
A B is a sinner.

These propositions, which are the *premises*, being true or admitted, the conclusion follows, that A B deserves punishment.

2. Propositions antecedently supposed or proved.

While the *premises* stand firm, it is impossible to shake the conclusion. *Decay of Piety.*

3. In *law*, land or other things mentioned in the preceding part of a deed.

PREM'ISS, *n.* Antecedent proposition. [*Rarely used.*] *Watts.*

PRE'MIUM, *n.* [L.] Properly, a reward or recompense; a prize to be won by competition; the reward or prize to be adjudged to the best performance or production.

2. The recompense or prize offered for a specific discovery or for success in an enterprise; as for the discovery of the longitude, or of a northwest passage to the Pacific Ocean.

3. A bounty; something offered or given for the loan of money, usually a sum beyond the interest.

4. The recompense to underwriters for insurance, or for undertaking to indemnify for losses of any kind.

5. It is sometimes synonymous with interest, but generally in obtaining loans, it is a sum per cent. distinct from the interest. The bank lends money to government at a *premium* of 2 per cent.

6. A bounty.

The law that obliges parishes to support the poor, offers a *premium* for the encouragement of idleness. *Franklin.*

PREMON'ISH, *v. t.* [L. *præmoneo*; *præ* and *moneo*, to warn.] To forewarn; to admonish beforehand.

PREMON'ISHED, *pp.* Forewarned.

PREMON'ISHING, *ppr.* Admonishing beforehand.

PREMON'ISHMENT, *n.* Previous warning or admonition; previous information.

PREMONI''TION, *n.* Previous warning, notice or information. Christ gave to his disciples *premonitions* of their sufferings.

PREMON'ITORY, *a.* Giving previous warning or notice.

PREMON'STRANTS, *n.* [L. *præmonstrans.*]

A religious order of regular canons or monks of Premontre, in the isle of France; instituted by Norbert, in 1120. They are called also white canons. These monks were poor at first, but within 30 years they had more than 100 abbeys in France and Germany, and in time they were established in all parts of christendom. *Encyc.*

PREMON'STRATE, *v. t.* [L. *præmonstro*; *præ*, before, and *monstro*, to show.] To show beforehand. [*Little used.*] *Herbert.*

PREMONSTRA'TION, *n.* A showing beforehand. [*Little used.*] *Shelford.*

PREMORSE, *a. premors'.* [L. *præmordeo*, *præmorsus*; *præ* and *mordeo*, to gnaw.] Bitten off.

Premorse roots, in *botany*, are such as are not tapering, but blunt at the end, as if bitten off short.

Premorse leaves, are such as end very obtusely with unequal notches. *Martyn.*

PREMO'TION, *n.* [*pre* and *motion.*] Previous motion or excitement to action. *Encyc.*

PREMUNI'RE, *n.* [See *Præmunire.* If really anglicized, *premunire* is the regular orthography. But this is not yet settled.]

1. In *law*, the offense of introducing foreign authority into England, and the writ which is grounded on the offense.

2. The penalty incurred by the offense above described.

Woolsey incurred a *premunire*, and forfeited his honor, estate and life. *South.*

PREMUNI''TION, *n.* [L. *præmunitio*, from *præmunio.*] An anticipation of objections. *Dict.*

PRENO'MEN, *n.* [L. *prænomen.*] Among the Romans, a name prefixed to the family name, answering to our christian name; as Caius, Lucius, Marcus, &c.

PRENOM'INATE, *v. t.* [L. *præ* and *nomino*, to name.] To forename.

PRENOM'INATE, *a.* Forenamed. *Shak.*

PRENOMINA'TION, *n.* The privilege of being named first. *Brown.*

PRENO'TION, *n.* [L. *prænotio*; *præ* and *nosco*, to know.]

A notice or notion which precedes something else in time; previous notion or thought; foreknowledge. *Bacon. Brown.*

PRENSA'TION, *n.* [L. *prensatio*, from *prenso*, to seize.]

The act of seizing with violence. [*Little used.*] *Barrow.*

PRENTICE, a colloquial contraction of *apprentice*, which see.

PRENTICESHIP, a contraction of *apprenticeship*, which see. *Pope.*

PRENUNCIA'TION, *n.* [L. *prænuncio*; *præ* and *nuncio*, to tell.] The act of telling before. [*Not used.*] *Dict.*

PREOBTA'IN, *v. t.* To obtain beforehand.

PREOBTA'INED, *pp.* Previously obtained

PREOC'CUPANCY, *n.* [L. *præoccupans.*]

1. The act of taking possession before another. The property of unoccupied land is vested by *preoccupancy.*

2. The right of taking possession before others. The first discoverer of unoccupied land has the *preoccupancy* of it, by the law of nature and nations.

PREOC'CUPATE, *v. t.* [L. *præoccupo*; *præ* and *occupo*, to seize.]

1. To anticipate; to take before. *Bacon.*

2. To prepossess; to fill with prejudices. *Wotton.*

[Instead of this, *preoccupy* is used.]

PREOCCUPA'TION, *n.* A taking possession before another; prior occupation.

2. Anticipation.

3. Prepossession. *Barrington.*

4. Anticipation of objections. *South.*

PREOC'CUPY, *v. t.* [L. *præoccupo*; *præ*, before, and *occupo*, to seize.]

1. To take possession before another; as, to *preoccupy* a country or land not before occupied.

2. To prepossess; to occupy by anticipation or prejudices.

I think it more respectful to the reader to leave something to reflections, than to *preoccupy* his judgment. *Arbuthnot.*

PREOM'INATE, *v. t.* [L. *præ* and *ominor*, to prognosticate.]

To prognosticate; to gather from omens any future event. *Brown.*

PREOPIN'ION, *n.* [*pre* and *opinion.*] Opinion previously formed; prepossession. *Brown.*

PREOP'TION, *n.* [*pre* and *option.*] The right of first choice. *Stackhouse.*

PREORDA'IN, *v. t.* [*pre* and *ordain.* To ordain or appoint beforehand; to predetermine. All things are supposed to be *preordained* by God.

PREORDA'INED, *pp.* Antecedently ordained or determined.

PREORDA'INING, *ppr.* Ordaining beforehand.

PREOR'DINANCE, *n.* [*pre* and *ordinance.*] Antecedent decree or determination. *Shak.*

PREOR'DINATE, *a.* Foreordained. [*Little used.*]

PREORDINA'TION, *n.* The act of foreordaining; previous determination. *Fotherby.*

PREPA'RABLE, *a.* [See *Prepare.*] That may be prepared. *Boyle.*

PREPARA'TION, *n.* [L. *præparatio.* See *Prepare.*]

1. The act or operation of preparing or fitting for a particular purpose, use, service or condition; as the *preparation* of land for a crop of wheat; the *preparation* of troops for a campaign; the *preparation* of a nation for war; the *preparation* of men for future happiness. *Preparation* is intended to prevent evil or secure good.

2. Previous measures of adaptation.

I will show what *preparations* there were in nature for this dissolution. *Burnet.*

3. Ceremonious introduction. [*Unusual.*] *Shak.*

4. That which is prepared, made or compounded for a particular purpose.

I wish the chimists had been more sparing, who magnify their *preparations.* *Brown.*

5. The state of being prepared or in readiness; as a nation in good *preparation* for attack or defense.

6. Accomplishment; qualification. [*Not in use.*] *Shak.*

7. In *pharmacy*, any medicinal substance fitted for the use of the patient. *Encyc.*

8. In *anatomy*, the parts of animal bodies

prepared and preserved for anatomical uses. *Encyc.*

Preparation of dissonances, in music, is their disposition in harmony in such a manner that by something congenial in what precedes, they may be rendered less harsh to the ear than they would be without such preparation. *Encyc.*

Preparation of medicines, the process of fitting any substance for use in the art of healing.

PREPAR'ATIVE, *a.* [It. *preparativo;* Fr. *preparatif.*]

Tending to prepare or make ready; having the power of preparing, qualifying or fitting for any thing; preparatory.

He spent much time in quest of knowledge *preparative* to this work. *South.*

PREPAR'ATIVE, *n.* That which has the power of preparing or previously fitting for a purpose; that which prepares.

Resolvedness in sin can with no reason be imagined a *preparative* to remission. *Decay of Piety.*

2. That which is done to prevent an evil or secure some good.

The miseries we suffer may be *preparative* of future blessings. *K. Charles.*

3. Preparation; as, to make the necessary *preparatives* for a voyage. *Dryden.*

PREPAR'ATIVELY, *adv.* By way of preparation. *Hale.*

PREPAR'ATORY, *a.* [It. Sp. *preparatorio;* Fr. *preparatoire.*]

1. Previously necessary; useful or qualifying; preparing the way for any thing by previous measures of adaptation. The practice of virtue and piety is *preparatory* to the happiness of heaven.

2. Introductory; previous; antecedent and adapted to what follows. *Hale.*

PREPA'RE, *v. t.* [Fr. *preparer;* It. *preparare;* Sp. Port. *preparar;* from L. *præparo; præ* and *paro;* Russ. *ubirayu;* W. *parodi.* The L. *paro* is probably the Shemitic ברא, برا to create or bring forth, coinciding with English *bear;* and from the L. are derived Fr. *parer*, Sp. Port. *parar*, It. *parare.* The sense of *prepare* is derived from many kinds of actions. See ברא in the introduction.]

1. In *a general sense*, to fit, adapt or qualify for a particular purpose, end, use, service or state, by any means whatever. We *prepare* ground for seed by tillage; we *prepare* cloth for use by dressing; we *prepare* medicines by pulverization, mixture, &c.; we *prepare* young men for college by previous instruction; men are *prepared* for professions by suitable study; holiness of heart is necessary to *prepare* men for the enjoyment of happiness with holy beings.

2. To make ready; as, to *prepare* the table for entertaining company.

3. To provide; to procure as suitable; as, to *prepare* arms, ammunition and provisions for troops; to *prepare* ships for defense.

Absalom *prepared* him chariots and horses, and fifty men to run before him. 2 Sam. xv.

4. To set; to establish.

The Lord hath *prepared* his throne in the heavens. Ps. ciii.

5. To appoint.

It shall be given to them for whom it is *prepared.* Matt. xx.

6. To guide, direct or establish. 1 Chron. xxix.

PREPA'RE, *v. i.* To make all things ready; to put things in suitable order; as, *prepare* for dinner. *Shak.*

2. To take the necessary previous measures.

Dido *preparing* to kill herself. *Peacham.*

3. To make one's self ready.

Prepare to meet thy God, O Israel. Amos iv.

PREPA'RE, *n.* Preparation. [*Not in use.*] *Shak.*

PREPA'RED, *pp.* Fitted; adapted; made suitable; made ready; provided.

PREPA'REDLY, *adv.* With suitable previous measures. *Shak.*

PREPA'REDNESS, *n.* The state of being prepared or in readiness. *South.*

PREPA'RER, *n.* One that prepares, fits or makes ready.

2. One that provides.

3. That which fits or makes suitable; as, certain manures are *preparers* of land for particular crops. *Mortimer.*

PREPA'RING, *ppr.* Fitting; adapting; making ready; providing.

PREPENSE, *a. prepens'.* [L. *præpensus, præpendeo; præ* and *pendeo*, to incline or hang down.] Preconceived; premeditated; aforethought.

Malice *prepense* is necessary to constitute murder. *Blackstone.*

PREPENSE, *v. t. prepens'.* [supra.] To weigh or consider beforehand. [*Not used.*] *Elyot.*

PREPENSE, *v. i. prepens'.* To deliberate beforehand. [*Not used.*] *Spenser.*

PREPENS'ED, *pp.* or *a.* Previously conceived; premeditated. [*Little used.*] [See *Prepense.*]

PREPOL'LENCE, } *n.* [L. *præpollens, præpolleo; præ* and *polleo.*] Prevalence; superiority of power.
PREPOL'LENCY, } *Coventry.*

PREPOL'LENT, *a.* Having superior gravity or power; prevailing. *Boyle.*

PREPOND'ER, *v. t.* [See *Preponderate.*] To outweigh. [*Not used.*] *Wolton.*

PREPOND'ERANCE, } *n.* [See *Preponderate.*]
PREPOND'ERANCY, }

1. An outweighing; superiority of weight. The least *preponderance* of weight on one side of a ship or boat will make it incline or heel.

2. Superiority of power, force or weight; in a figurative sense; as a *preponderance* of evidence. *Locke.*

PREPOND'ERANT, *a.* Outweighing. *Reid.*

PREPOND'ERATE, *v. t.* [L. *præpondero; præ*, before, and *pondero*, to weigh.]

1. To outweigh; to overpower by weight.

An inconsiderable weight, by distance from the center of the balance, will *preponderate* greater magnitudes. *Glanville.*

2. To overpower by stronger influence or moral power.

PREPOND'ERATE, *v. i.* To exceed in weight; hence, to incline or descend, as the scale of a balance.

That is no just balance in which the heaviest side will not *preponderate.* *Wilkins.*

2. To exceed in influence or power; hence, to incline to one side.

By putting every argument on one side and the other, into the balance, we must form a judgment which side *preponderates.* *Watts.*

PREPOND'ERATING, *ppr.* Outweighing; inclining to one side.

PREPONDERA'TION, *n.* The act or state of outweighing any thing, or of inclining to one side. *Watts.*

PREPO'SE, *v. t. s* as *z.* [Fr. *preposer; pre* and *poser*, to put.] To put before. [*Not much used.*] *Focaloir.*

PREPOSI''TION, *n. s* as *z.* [Fr. from L. *præpositio; præpono, præpositus; præ* and *pono*, to put.]

In *grammar*, a word usually put before another to express some relation or quality, action or motion to or from the thing specified; as medicines salutary *to* health; music agreeable *to* the ear; virtue is valued *for* its excellence; a man is riding *to* Oxford *from* London. Prepositions govern cases of nouns, and in English are sometimes placed *after* the word governed; as, *which person* do you speak *to?* for, *to which person* do you speak? This separation of the preposition from the governed word is sometimes allowable in colloquial use, but is generally inelegant.

PREPOSI''TIONAL, *a.* Pertaining to a preposition, or to preceding position. *Encyc.*

PREPOS'ITIVE, *a.* Put before; as a *prepositive* particle. *Jones.*

PREPOS'ITIVE, *n.* [supra.] A word or particle put before another word. *Jones.*

PREPOS'ITOR, *n.* [L. *præpositor.*] A scholar appointed by the instructor to inspect other scholars. *Todd.*

PREPOS'ITURE, *n.* The office or place of a provost; a provostship.

PREPOSSESS', *v. t.* [*pre* and *possess.*] To preoccupy, as ground or land; to take previous possession of. *Dryden.*

2. To preoccupy the mind or heart so as to preclude other things; hence, to bias or prejudice. A mind *prepossessed* with opinions favorable to a person or cause, will not readily admit unfavorable opinions to take possession, nor yield to reasons that disturb the possessors. When a lady has *prepossessed* the heart or affections of a man, he does not readily listen to suggestions that tend to remove the prepossession. *Prepossess* is more frequently used in a good sense than *prejudice.*

PREPOSSESS'ED, *pp.* Preoccupied; inclined previously to favor or disfavor.

PREPOSSESS'ING, *ppr.* Taking previous possession.

2. *a.* Tending to invite favor; having power to secure the possession of favor, esteem or love. The countenance, address and manners of a person are sometimes *prepossessing* on a first acquaintance.

PREPOSSES'SION, *n.* Preoccupation; prior possession. *Hammond.*

2. Preconceived opinion; the effect of previous impressions on the mind or heart, in favor or against any person or thing. It is often used in a good sense; sometimes it is equivalent to *prejudice*, and sometimes a softer name for it. In general, it conveys an idea less odious than *prejudice;* as the *prepossessions* of education. *South.*

PREPOS'TEROUS, *a.* [L. *præposterus; præ*, before, and *posterus*, latter.]

1. Literally, having that first which ought to be last; inverted in order.

The method I take may be censured as *preposterous*, because I treat last of the antediluvian earth, which was first in the order of nature. *Woodward.*

2. Perverted; wrong; absurd; contrary to nature or reason; not adapted to the end; as, a republican government in the hands of females, is *preposterous*. To draw general conclusions from particular facts, is *preposterous* reasoning. *Bacon. Woodward.*

3. Foolish; absurd; *applied to persons.* *Shak.*

PREPOS'TEROUSLY, *adv.* In a wrong or inverted order; absurdly; foolishly. *Shak. Bentley.*

PREPOS'TEROUSNESS, *n.* Wrong order or method; absurdity; inconsistency with nature or reason. *Feltham.*

PREPO'TENCY, *n.* [L. *præpotentia; præ* and *potentia*, power.] Superior power; predominance. [*Little used.*] *Brown.*

PREPO'TENT, *a.* [L. *præpotens.*] Very powerful. [*Little used.*] *Plaifere.*

PRE'PUCE, *n.* [Fr. from L. *præputium.*] The foreskin; a prolongation of the cutis of the penis, covering the glans. *Encyc.*

PREREMO'TE, *a.* [*pre* and *remote.*] More remote in previous time or prior order.

In some cases, two more links of causation may be introduced; one of them may be termed the *preremote* cause, the other the postremote effect. *Darwin.*

PREREQUI'RE, *v. t.* [*pre* and *require.*] To require previously. *Hammond.*

PREREQ'UISITE, *a. s* as *z.* [*pre* and *requisite.*] Previously required or necessary to something subsequent; as, certain attainments are *prerequisite* to an admission to orders.

PREREQ'UISITE, *n.* Something that is previously required or necessary to the end proposed. An acquaintance with Latin and Greek is a *prerequisite* to the admission of a young man into a college.

PRERESOLVE, *v. t. s* as *z.* [*pre* and *resolve.*] To resolve previously. *Dering.*

PRERESOLV'ED, *pp.* Resolved beforehand; previously determined.

PRERESOLV'ING, *ppr.* Resolving beforehand.

PREROG'ATIVE, *n.* [Fr. *id.*; It. *prerogativo*; Sp. *prerogativa*; L. *prærogativa*, precedence in voting; *præ*, before, and *rogo*, to ask or demand.] An exclusive or peculiar privilege. A *royal prerogative*, is that special pre-eminence which a king has over all other persons, and out of the course of the common law, in right of his regal dignity. It consists in the possession of certain rights which the king may exercise to the exclusion of all participation of his subjects; for when a right or privilege is held in common with the subject, it ceases to be a *prerogative*. Thus the right of appointing embassadors, and of making peace and war, are, in Great Britain, *royal prerogatives*. The right of governing created beings is the *prerogative* of the Creator.

It is the *prerogative* of the house of peers in Great Britain to decide legal questions in the last resort. It is the *prerogative* of the house of commons to determine the validity of all elections of their own members. It is the *prerogative* of a father to govern his children. It is the *prerogative* of the understanding to judge and compare.

In the United States, it is the *prerogative* of the president, with the advice of the senate, to ratify treaties.

PREROG'ATIVE-COURT, *n.* In *Great Britain*, a court for the trial of all testamentary causes, where the deceased has left *bona notabilia*, or effects of the value of five pounds, in two different dioceses. In this case, the probate of the will belongs to the metropolitan or archbishop of the province, and the court where such will is proved is called the *prerogative-court*, as it is held by virtue of the special prerogative of the metropolitan, who appoints the judge. *Blackstone.*

PREROG'ATIVED, *a.* Having prerogative. [*Little used.*] *Shak.*

PREROG'ATIVE-OFFICE, *n.* The office in which the wills proved in the prerogative court, are registered. *Blackstone.*

PRE'SAGE, *n.* [Fr.; Sp. It. *presagio*; from L. *præsagium*; *præ*, before, and *sagio*, to perceive or foretell.] Something which foreshows a future event; a prognostic; a present fact indicating something to come.

Joy and shout, *presage* of victory. *Milton*

PRESA'GE, *v. t.* To forebode; to foreshow; to indicate by some present fact what is to follow or come to pass. A fog rising from a river in an autumnal morning *presages* a pleasant day. A physical phenomenon cannot be considered as *presaging* an event, unless it has some connection with it in cause. Hence the error of vulgar superstition, which *presages* good or evil from facts which can have no relation to the future event.

2. To foretell; to predict; to prophesy.

Wish'd freedom I *presage* you soon will find. *Dryden.*

PRESA'GE, *v. i.* To form or utter a prediction; with *of.* We may *presage of* heats and rains. [*Not common nor elegant.*] *Dryden.*

PRESA'GED, *pp.* Foreboded; foreshown; foretold.

PRESA'GEFUL, *a.* Full of presages; containing presages. *Thomson.*

PRESA'GEMENT, *n.* A foreboding; foretoken. *Wotton.*

2. A foretelling; prediction.

PRESA'GER, *n.* A foreteller; a foreshower. *Shak.*

PRESA'GING, *ppr.* Foreshowing; foretelling.

PRES'BYTER, *n.* [Gr. πρεσβυτερος, from πρεσβυς, old, elder.]

1. In *the primitive christian church*, an elder; a person somewhat advanced in age, who had authority in the church, and whose duty was to feed the flock over which the Holy Spirit had made him overseer.

2. A priest; a person who has the pastoral charge of a particular church and congregation; called in the Saxon laws, *mass-priest.* *Hooker.*

3. A presbyterian. *Butler.*

PRESBYTE'RIAL, PRESBYTE'RIAN, *a.* Pertaining to a presbyter, or to ecclesiastical government by presbyters.

2. Consisting of presbyters; as *presbyterian* government. The government of the church of Scotland is *presbyterian.*

PRESBYTE'RIAN, *n.* One that maintains the validity of ordination and government by presbyters.

2. One that belongs to a church governed by presbyters.

PRESBYTE'RIANISM, *n.* The doctrines, principles and discipline or government of presbyterians. *Addison.*

PRES'BYTERY, *n.* A body of elders in the christian church.

Neglect not the gift that is in thee, which was given thee by prophecy, with the laying on of the hands of the *presbytery.* 1 Tim. iv.

2. In *ecclesiastical government*, a judicatory consisting of all the pastors of churches within a certain district, and one ruling elder, a layman, from each parish, commissioned to represent the parish in conjunction with the minister. This body receives appeals from the kirk-session, and appeals from the presbytery may be carried to the provincial synod. *Encyc. Scotland.*

The presbytery of the churches in the United States is composed in a manner nearly similar.

3. The presbyterian religion. *Tatler.*

PRESCIENCE, *n. presi'ence* or *pre'shens.* [Low L. *præscientia*; *præ*, before, and *scientia*, knowledge; Fr. *prescience*; It. *prescienza.* The common pronunciation of this word, *pre'shens*, obscures the sense.] Foreknowledge; knowledge of events before they take place. Absolute *prescience* belongs to God only.

Of things of the most accidental and mutable nature, God's *prescience* is certain. *South.*

PRESCIENT, *a. presi'ent* or *pre'shent.* Foreknowing; having knowledge of events before they take place.

Who taught the nations of the field and wood, *Prescient*, the tides or tempests to withstand? *Pope.*

PRESCIND', *v. t.* [L. *præscindo*; *præ* and *scindo*, to cut.] To cut off; to abstract. [*Little used.*] *Norris.*

PRESCIND'ENT, *a.* Cutting off; abstracting. *Cheyne.*

PRE'SCIOUS, *a.* [L. *præscius*; *præ* and *scio*, to know.] Foreknowing; having foreknowledge; as *prescious* of ills. *Dryden.*

PRESCRI'BE, *v. t.* [L. *præscribo*, to write before.]

1. In *medicine*, to direct, as a remedy to be used or applied to a diseased patient. Be not offended with the physician who *prescribes* harsh remedies.

2. To set or lay down authoritatively for direction; to give as a rule of conduct; as, to *prescribe* laws or rules.

There's joy, when to wild will you laws *prescribe.* *Dryden.*

3. To direct.

Let streams *prescribe* their fountains where to run. *Dryden.*

PRESCRI'BE, *v. i.* To write or give medical directions; to direct what remedies are to be used; as, to *prescribe* for a patient in a fever.

2. To give law; to influence arbitrarily.

A forwardness to *prescribe* to the opinions of others. *Locke.*

3. In *law*, to claim by prescription; to claim a title to a thing by immemorial use and enjoyment; with *for.* A man may be allowed to *prescribe for* a right of way, a common or the like; a man cannot *prescribe for* a castle; he can *prescribe* only *for* incorporeal hereditaments. *Blackstone.*

4. To influence by long use. [*Not in use.*] *Brown.*

PRESCRI'BED, *pp.* Directed; ordered.

PRESCRI'BER, *n.* One that prescribes.

PRESCRI'BING, *ppr.* Directing; giving as a rule of conduct or treatment.

PRE'SCRIPT, *a.* [L. *præscriptus.*] Directed; prescribed. *Hooker.*

PRE'SCRIPT, *n.* [L. *præscriptum.*] A direction; a medical order for the use of medicines. [But *prescription* is chiefly used.]

2. Direction; precept; model prescribed.

PRESCRIP'TIBLE, *a.* That may be prescribed for.

PRESCRIP'TION, *n.* [L. *præscriptio.* See *Prescribe.*]

1. The act of prescribing or directing by rules; or that which is prescribed; particularly, a medical direction of remedies for a disease and the manner of using them; a recipe.

2. In *law*, a prescribing for title; the claim of title to a thing by virtue of immemorial use and enjoyment; or the right to a thing derived from such use. *Prescription* differs from *custom*, which is a local usage. *Prescription* is a *personal* usage, usage annexed to the person. Nothing but incorporeal hereditaments can be claimed by *prescription.* *Blackstone.*

The use and enjoyment of navigation and fishery in the sea, for any length of time, does not create a title by *prescription.* The common right of nations to the use and enjoyment of the sea is *imprescriptible;* it cannot be lost by a particular nation for want of use. *Vattel.*

3. In *Scots law*, the title to lands acquired by uninterrupted possession for the time which the law declares to be sufficient, or 40 years. This is *positive* prescription. *Negative* prescription is the loss or omission of a right by neglecting to use it during the time limited by law. This term is also used for *limitation*, in the recovery of money due by bond, &c. Obligations are lost by *prescription*, or neglect of prosecution for the time designated by law. *Encyc.*

PRESCRIP'TIVE, *a.* Consisting in or acquired by immemorial use and enjoyment; as a *prescriptive* right or title.

The right to be drowsy in protracted toil, has become *prescriptive.* *J. M. Mason.*

2. Pleading the continuance and authority of custom. *Hurd.*

PRES'EANCE, *n.* [Fr.] Priority of place in sitting. [*Not in use.*] *Carew.*

PRES'ENCE, *n.* *s* as *z.* [Fr. from L. *præsentia; præ*, before, and *esse*, to be.]

The existence of a person or thing in a certain place; opposed to *absence.* This event happened during the king's *presence* at the theater. In examining the patient, the *presence* of fever was not observed. The *presence* of God is not limited to any place.

2. A being in company near or before the face of another. We were gratified with the *presence* of a person so much respected.

3. Approach face to face or nearness of a great personage.

Men that very *presence* fear,
Which once they knew authority did bear. *Daniel.*

4. State of being in view; sight. An accident happened in the *presence* of the court.

5. *By way of distinction*, state of being in view of a superior.

I know not by what pow'r I am made bold,
In such a *presence* here to plead my thoughts. *Shak.*

6. A number assembled before a great person.

Odmar, of all this *presence* does contain,
Give her your wreath whom you esteem most fair. *Dryden.*

7. Port; mien; air; personal appearance; demeanor.

Virtue is best in a body that is comely, and that has rather dignity of *presence*, than beauty of aspect. *Bacon.*

A graceful *presence* bespeaks acceptance. *Collier.*

8. The apartment in which a prince shows himself to his court.

An't please your grace, the two great cardinals
Wait in the *presence.* *Shak.*

9. The person of a superior. *Milton.*

Presence of mind, a calm, collected state of the mind with its faculties at command; undisturbed state of the thoughts, which enables a person to speak or act without disorder or embarrassment in unexpected difficulties.

Errors, not to be recalled, do find
Their best redress from *presence of the mind.* *Waller.*

PRES'ENCE-CHAMBER, } *n.* The room
PRES'ENCE-ROOM, } in which a great personage receives company. *Addison.*

PRESENSA'TION, *n.* [*pre* and *sensation.*] Previous notion or idea. *More.*

PRESEN'SION, *n.* [L. *præsensio, præsentio; præ* and *sentio*, to perceive.] Previous perception. [*Little used.*] *Brown.*

PRES'ENT, *a.* *s* as *z.* [Fr. *present;* L. *præsens; præ* and *sum, esse*, to be.]

1. Being in a certain place; opposed to *absent.*

2. Being before the face or near; being in company. Inquire of some of the gentlemen *present.*

These things have I spoken unto you, being yet *present* with you. John xiv.

3. Being now in view or under consideration. In the *present* instance, facts will not warrant the conclusion. The *present* question must be decided on different principles.

4. Now existing, or being at this time; not past or future; as the *present* session of congress. The court is in session at the *present* time. We say, a *present* good, the *present* year or age.

5. Ready at hand; quick in emergency; as *present* wit.

'Tis a high point of philosophy and virtue for a man to be *present* to himself. *L'Estrange.*

6. Favorably attentive; not heedless; propitious.

Nor could I hope in any place but there
To find a god so *present* to my prayer. *Dryden.*

7. Not absent of mind; not abstracted; attentive.

The present, an elliptical expression for *the present time.* *Milton.*

At present, elliptically for, *at the present time.*

Present tense, in grammar, the tense or form of a verb which expresses action or being in the present time, as I *am writing;* or something that exists at all times, as virtue *is* always to be preferred to vice; or it expresses habits or general truths, as plants *spring* from the earth; fishes *swim;* reptiles *creep;* birds *fly;* some animals *subsist* on herbage, others *are* carnivorous.

PRES'ENT, *n.* [Fr. *id.* See the Verb.] That which is presented or given; a gift; a donative; something given or offered to another gratuitously; *a word of general application.* Gen. xxxii.

Presents, in *the plural*, is used in law for a deed of conveyance, a lease, letter of attorney or other writing; as in the phrase, "Know all men by these *presents*," that is, by the writing itself, *per presentes.* In this sense, it is rarely used in the singular.

PRESENT', *v. t.* [Low L. *præsento;* Fr. *presenter;* It. *presentare;* Sp. *presentar;* L. *præsens; præ*, before, and *sum, esse*, to be.]

1. To set, place or introduce into the presence or before the face of a superior, as to *present* an envoy to the king; and with the reciprocal pronoun, to come into the presence of a superior.

Now there was a day when the sons of God came to *present themselves* before the Lord. Job i.

2. To exhibit to view or notice. The top of Mount Holyoke, in Hampshire county, in Massachusetts, *presents* one of the finest prospects in America.

3. To offer; to exhibit.

O hear what to my mind first thoughts *present.* *Milton.*

He is ever ready to *present* to us the thoughts or observations of others. *Watts.*

4. To give; to offer gratuitously for reception. The first President of the American Bible Society, *presented* to that institution ten thousand dollars.

5. To put into the hands of another in ceremony.

So ladies in romance assist their knight,
Present the spear, and arm him for the fight. *Pope.*

6. To favor with a gift; as, we *present* a man *with* a suit of clothes. Formerly the phrase was, to *present a person.*

Octavia *presented* the poet, for his admirable elegy on her son Marcellus. *Dryden.*

[*This use is obsolete.*]

7. To nominate to an ecclesiastical benefice; to offer to the bishop or ordinary as a candidate for institution.

The patron of a church may *present* his clerk to a parsonage or vicarage; that is, may offer him to the bishop of the diocese to be instituted. *Blackstone.*

8. To offer.

He—*presented* battle to the French navy, which was refused. *Hayward.*

9. To lay before a public body for consideration, as before a legislature, a court of judicature, a corporation, &c.; as, to *present* a memorial, petition, remonstrance or indictment.

10. To lay before a court of judicature as an object of inquiry; to give notice officially of a crime or offense. It is the duty of grand juries to *present* all breaches of law within their knowledge. In America, grand juries *present* whatever they think to be public injuries, by notifying them to the public with their censure.

11. To point a weapon, particularly some species of fire-arms; as, to *present* a musket to the breast of another; in manual exercise, to *present* arms.

12. To indict; *a customary use of the word in the United States.*

PRESENT'ABLE, *a.* That may be presented; that may be exhibited or represented. *Burke.*

2. That may be offered to a church living; as a *presentable* clerk.

3. That admits of the presentation of a clerk; as a church *presentable.* [*Unusual.*] *Ayliffe.*

PRESENTA'NEOUS, *a.* [L. *præsentaneus.*] Ready; quick; immediate; as *presentaneous* poison. *Harvey.*

PRESENTA'TION, *n.* [Fr.] The act of presenting.

Prayers are sometimes a *presentation* of mere desires. *Hooker.*

2. Exhibition; representation; display; as the *presentation* of fighting on the stage. *Dryden.*

3. In *ecclesiastical law*, the act of offering a clerk to the bishop or ordinary for institution in a benefice. An advowson is he right of *presentation.*

If the bishop admits the patron's *presentation*, the clerk so admitted is next to be instituted by him. *Blackstone.*

4. The right of presenting a clerk. The patron has the *presentation* of the benefice.

PRESENT'ATIVE, *a.* In *ecclesiastical affairs*, that has the right of presentation, or offering a clerk to the bishop for institution. Advowsons are *presentative*, collative or donative.

An advowson *presentative* is where the patron hath a right of presentation to the bishop or ordinary. *Blackstone.*

2. That admits the presentation of a clerk; as a *presentative* parsonage. *Spelman.*

PRESENT'ED, *pp.* Offered; given; exhibited to view; accused.

PRES'ENTEE, *n.* One presented to a benefice. *Ayliffe.*

PRESENT'ER, *n.* One that presents.

PRESEN'TIAL, *a.* Supposing actual presence. [*Little used.*] *Norris.*

PRESENTIAL'ITY, *n.* The state of being present. [*Little used.*] *South.*

PRESEN'TIATE, *v. t.* To make present. [*Little used.*] *Grew.*

PRESENTIF'IC, **PRESENTIF'ICAL**, *a.* Making present. [*Not in use.*]

PRESENTIF'ICLY, *adv.* In such a manner as to make present. [*Not in use.*] *More.*

PRESENT'IMENT, *n.* [*pre* and *sentiment*, or Fr. *pressentiment.*] Previous conception, sentiment or opinion; previous apprehension of something future. *Butler.*

PRES'ENTLY, *adv.* *s* as *z.* At present; at this time.

The towns and forts you *presently* have. *Obs.* *Sidney.*

2. In a short time after; soon after.

Him therefore I hope to send *presently*, so soon as I shall see how it will go with me. Phil. ii.

3. Immediately.

And *presently* the fig-tree withered away. Matt. xxi.

PRESENT'MENT, *n.* *s* as *z.* The act of presenting. *Shak.*

2. Appearance to the view; representation. *Milton.*

3. In *law*, a presentment, properly speaking, is the notice taken by a grand jury of any offense from their own knowledge or observation, without any bill of indictment laid before them at the suit of the king; as the *presentment* of a nuisance, a libel or the like, on which the officer of the court must afterwards frame an indictment, before the party presented can be put to answer it. *Blackstone.*

4. In *a more general sense*, presentment comprehends inquisitions of office and indictments. *Blackstone.*

In the United States, a *presentment* is an official accusation presented to a tribunal by the grand jury in an indictment; or it is the act of offering an indictment. It is also used for the indictment itself. The grand jury are charged to inquire and due *presentment* make of all crimes, &c. The use of the word is limited to accusations by grand jurors.

5. The official notice in court which the jury or homage gives of the surrender of a copyhold estate. *Blackstone.*

PRES'ENTNESS, *n.* *s* as *z.* Presence; as *presentness* of mind. [*Not used.*] *Clarendon.*

PRESERV'ABLE, *a.* [See *Preserve.*] That may be preserved.

PRESERVA'TION, *n.* [from *preserve;* It. *preservazione;* Sp. *preservacion.*] The act of preserving or keeping safe; the act of keeping from injury, destruction or decay; as the *preservation* of life or health; the preservation of buildings from fire or decay; the *preservation* of grain from insects; the *preservation* of fruit or plants. When a thing is kept entirely from decay, or nearly in its original state, we say it is in a high state of *preservation.*

PRESERV'ATIVE, *a.* [It. *preservativo;* Fr. *preservatif.*] Having the power or quality of keeping safe from injury, destruction or decay; tending to preserve.

PRESERV'ATIVE, *n.* That which preserves or has the power of preserving; something that tends to secure a person or thing in a sound state, or prevent it from injury, destruction, decay or corruption; a preventive of injury or decay. Persons formerly wore tablets of arsenic, as *preservatives* against the plague. Clothing is a *preservative* against cold. Temperance and exercise are the best *preservatives* of health. Habitual reverence of the Supreme Being is an excellent *preservative* against sin and the influence of evil examples.

PRESERV'ATORY, *a.* That tends to preserve. *Hall.*

PRESERV'ATORY, *n.* That which has the power of preserving; a preservative. *Whitlock.*

PRESERVE, *v. t.* *prezerv'.* [Fr. *preserver;* It. *preservare;* Sp. *preservar;* Low L. *præservo;* *præ* and *servo*, to keep.]

1. To keep or save from injury or destruction; to defend from evil.

God did send me before you to *preserve* life. Gen. xlv.

O Lord, *preserve* me from the violent man. Ps. cxl.

2. To uphold; to sustain.

O Lord, thou *preservest* man and beast. Ps. xxxvi.

3. To save from decay; to keep in a sound state; as, to *preserve* fruit in winter. Salt is used to *preserve* meat.

4. To season with sugar or other substances for preservation; as, to *preserve* plums, quinces or other fruit.

5. To keep or defend from corruption; as, to *preserve* youth from vice.

PRESERVE, *n.* *prezerv'.* Fruit or a vegetable seasoned and kept in sugar or sirup. *Mortimer.*

PRESERV'ED, *pp.* Saved from injury, destruction or decay; kept or defended from evil; seasoned with sugar for preservation.

PRESERV'ER, *n.* The person or thing that preserves; one that saves or defends from destruction or evil.

What shall I do to thee, O thou *preserver* of men? Job vii.

2. One that makes preserves of fruits.

PRESERV'ING, *ppr.* Keeping safe from injury, destruction or decay; defending from evil.

PRESI'DE, *v. i.* *s* as *z.* [L. *præsideo;* *præ*, before, and *sedeo*, to sit; It. *presidere;* Fr. *presider;* Sp. *presidir.*]

1. To be set over for the exercise of authority; to direct, control and govern, as the chief officer. A man may *preside* over a nation or province; or he may *preside* over a senate, or a meeting of citizens. The word is used chiefly in the latter sense. We say, a man *presides* over the senate with dignity. Hence it usually denotes temporary superintendence and government.

2. To exercise superintendence; to watch over as inspector.

Some o'er the public magazines *preside.* *Dryden.*

PRES'IDENCY, *n.* Superintendence; inspection and care. *Ray.*

2. The office of president. Washington was elected to the *presidency* of the United States by a unanimous vote of the electors.

3. The term during which a president holds his office. President J. Adams died during the *presidency* of his son.

4. The jurisdiction of a president; as in the British dominions in the East Indies.

5. The family or suit of a president.

A worthy clergyman belonging to the *presidency* of Fort St. George. Qu. *Buchanan*, 251.

PRES'IDENT, *n.* [Fr. from L. *præsidens.*]
1. An officer elected or appointed to preside over a corporation, company or assembly of men, to keep order, manage their concerns or govern their proceedings; as the *president* of a banking company; the *president* of a senate, &c.
2. An officer appointed or elected to govern a province or territory, or to administer the government of a nation. The *president* of the United States is the chief executive magistrate.
3. The chief officer of a college or university. *U. States.*
4. A tutelar power.
Just Apollo, *president* of verse. *Waller.*
Vice-president, one who is second in authority to the president. The vice-president of the United States is president of the senate *ex officio*, and performs the duties of president when the latter is removed or disabled.

PRESIDEN'TIAL, *a.* Pertaining to a president; as the *presidential* chair. *Walsh.*
2. Presiding over. *Glanville.*

PRES'IDENTSHIP, *n.* The office and place of president. *Hooker.*
2. The term for which a president holds his office.

PRESID'IAL, PRESID'IARY, *a.* [L. *præsidium*, a garrison; *præ* and *sedeo.*] Pertaining to a garrison; having a garrison. *Howell.*

PRESIGNIFICA'TION, *n.* [from *presignify.*] The act of signifying or showing beforehand. *Barrow.*

PRESIG'NIFY, *v. t.* [*pre* and *signify.*] To intimate or signify beforehand; to show previously. *Pearson.*

PRESS, *v. t.* [Fr. *presser*; It. *pressare*, to press, crowd, urge, hurry; D. G. *pressen*; Sw. *prässa*; Dan. *presser*; W. *brysiaw*, to hurry, formed from *rhys*, extreme ardency, a *rushing*. Here we have proof that *press* is formed from the root of *rush*, with a prefix. The Spanish has *apretar*, *prensar* and *aprensar*. The L. *pressus* is from the same root.]
1. To urge with force or weight; a word of extensive use, denoting the application of any power, physical or moral, to something that is to be moved or affected. We *press* the ground with the feet when we walk; we *press* the couch on which we repose; we *press* substances with the hands, fingers or arms; the smith *presses* iron with his vise; we are *pressed* with the weight of arguments or of cares, troubles and business.
2. To squeeze; to crush; as, to *press* grapes. Gen. xl.
3. To drive with violence; to hurry; as, to *press* a horse in motion, or in a race.
4. To urge; to enforce; to inculcate with earnestness; as, to *press* divine truth on an audience.
5. To embrace closely; to hug.
Leucothoe shook
And *press'd* Palemon closer in her arms. *Pope.*
6. To force into service, particularly into naval service; to impress. *Clarendon. Dryden.*
7. To straiten; to distress; as, to be *pressed* with want or with difficulties.
8. To constrain; to compel; to urge by authority or necessity.
The posts that rode on mules and camels went out, being hastened and *pressed* on by the king's commandment. Esth. viii.
9. To urge; to impose by importunity.
He *pressed* a letter upon me, within this hour, to deliver to you. *Dryden.*
10. To urge or solicit with earnestness or importunity. He *pressed* me to accept of his offer.
11. To urge; to constrain.
Paul was *pressed* in spirit, and testified to the Jews that Jesus was Christ. Acts xviii.
Wickedness *pressed* with conscience, forecasteth grievous things. *Wisdom.*
12. To squeeze for making smooth; as cloth or paper.
Press differs from *drive* and *strike*, in usually denoting a slow or continued application of force; whereas *drive* and *strike* denote a sudden impulse of force.

PRESS, *v. i.* To urge or strain in motion; to urge forward with force.
I *press* towards the mark for the prize of the high calling of God in Christ Jesus. Phil. iii.
Th' insulting victor *presses* on the more. *Dryden.*
2. To bear on with force; to encroach.
On superior powers
Were we to *press*, inferior might on ours. *Pope.*
3. To bear on with force; to crowd; to throng.
Thronging crowds *press* on you as you pass. *Dryden.*
4. To approach unseasonably or importunately.
Nor *press* too near the throne. *Dryden.*
5. To urge with vehemence and importunity.
He *pressed* upon them greatly, and they turned in to him. Gen. xix.
6. To urge by influence or moral force.
When arguments *press* equally in matters indifferent, the safest method is to give up ourselves to neither. *Addison.*
7. To push with force; as, to *press* against the door.

PRESS, *n.* [It. *pressa*, haste, hurry, a crowd; Sp. *prensa*; Fr. *presse*, *pressoir*; Sw. *präss*; Dan. G. *presse.*]
1. An instrument or machine by which any body is squeezed, crushed or forced into a more compact form; as a *wine-press*, *cider-press* or *cheese-press*.
2. A machine for printing; a printing-press. Great improvements have been lately made in the construction of *presses*.
3. The art or business of printing and publishing. A free *press* is a great blessing to a free people; a licentious *press* is a curse to society.
4. A crowd; a throng; a multitude of individuals crowded together.
And when they could not come nigh to him for the *press*— Mark ii.
5. The act of urging or pushing forward.
Which in their throng and *press* to the last hold,
Confound themselves. *Shak.*
6. A wine-vat or cistern. Hag. ii.
7. A case or closet for the safe keeping of garments. *Shak.*
8. Urgency; urgent demands of affairs; as a *press* of business.
9. A commission to force men into public service, particularly into the navy; for *impress*. *Raleigh.*
Press of sail, in navigation, is as much sail as the state of the wind will permit. *Mar. Dict.*
Liberty of the press, in civil policy, is the free right of publishing books, pamphlets or papers without previous restraint; or the unrestrained right which every citizen enjoys of publishing his thoughts and opinions, subject only to punishment for publishing what is pernicious to morals or to the peace of the state.

PRESS'-BED, *n.* A bed that may be raised and inclosed in a case.

PRESS'ED, *pp.* Urged by force or weight; constrained; distressed; crowded; embraced; made smooth and glossy by pressure, as cloth.

PRESS'ER, *n.* One that presses.

PRESS'-GANG, *n.* [*press* and *gang.*] A detachment of seamen under the command of an officer, empowered to impress men into the naval service.

PRESS'ING, *ppr.* Urging with force or weight; squeezing; constraining; crowding; embracing; distressing; forcing into service; rolling in a press.
2. *a.* Urgent; distressing.

PRESS'ING, *n.* The act or operation of applying force to bodies. The *pressing* of cloth is performed by means of the screw, or by a calendar.

PRESS'INGLY, *adv.* With force or urgency; closely. *Howell.*

PRES'SION, *n.* [It. *pressione.*] The act of pressing. But *pressure* is more generally used. *Newton.*
2. In *the Cartesian philosophy*, an endeavor to move.

PRESS'ITANT, *a.* Gravitating; heavy. [*Not in use.*] *More.*

PRESS'MAN, *n.* In *printing*, the man who manages the press and impresses the sheets.
2. One of a press-gang, who aids in forcing men into the naval service. *Chapman.*

PRESS'-MONEY, *n.* Money paid to a man impressed into public service. [See *Prest-money.*] *Gay.*

PRESS'URE, *n.* [It. L. *pressura.*] The act of pressing or urging with force.
2. The act of squeezing or crushing. Wine is obtained by the *pressure* of grapes.
3. The state of being squeezed or crushed.
4. The force of one body acting on another by weight or the continued application of power. *Pressure* is occasioned by weight or gravity, by the motion of bodies, by the expansion of fluids, by elasticity, &c. *Mutual pressure* may be caused by the meeting of moving bodies, or by the motion of one body against another at rest, and the resistance or elastic force of the latter. The degree of *pressure* is in proportion to the weight of the pressing body, or to the power applied, or to the elastic force of resisting bodies. The screw is a most powerful instrument of *pressure*. The *pressure* of wind on the sails of a ship is in proportion to its velocity.
5. A constraining force or impulse; that which urges or compels the intellectual or moral faculties; as the *pressure* of motives on the mind, or of fear on the conscience.

6. That which afflicts the body or depresses the spirits; any severe affliction, distress, calamity or grievance; straits, difficulties, embarrassments, or the distress they occasion. We speak of the *pressure* of poverty or want, the *pressure* of debts, the *pressure* of taxes, the *pressure* of afflictions or sorrow.

My own and my people's *pressures* are grievous. *K. Charles.*

To this consideration he retreats with comfort in all his *pressures.* *Atterbury.*

We observe that *pressure* is used both for trouble or calamity, and for the distress it produces.

7. Urgency; as the *pressure* of business.

8. Impression; stamp; character impressed.

All laws of books, all forms, all *pressures* past. *Shak.*

PREST, sometimes used for *pressed.* [See *Press.*]

PREST, *a.* [Old Fr. *prest* or *preste*, now *prêt, prét* or *preste;* Sp. It. *presto*, from L. *præsto*, to stand before or forward; *præ* and *sto.*]

1. Ready; prompt. *Obs.* *Fairfax.*
2. Neat; tight. *Obs.* *Tusser.*

PREST, *n.* [Fr. *prêt*, supra.] A loan. *Obs.* *Bacon.*

2. Formerly, a duty in money, to be paid by the sherif on his account in the exchequer, or for money left or remaining in his hands. 2 and 3 Edw. 6.

PREST'-MŎNEY, *n.* Money paid to men impressed into the service. *Encyc.*

PRESTA'TION, *n.* [L. *præstatio.*] Formerly, a payment of money; sometimes used for purveyance. *Encyc.*

PRESTA'TION-MŎNEY, *n.* A sum of money paid yearly by archdeacons and other dignitaries to their bishop, *pro exteriore jurisdictione.* *Encyc.*

PRES'TER, *n.* [Gr. πρηςηρ, from πρηθω, to kindle or inflame.]

1. A meteor thrown from the clouds with such violence, that by collision it is set on fire. *Encyc.*
2. The external part of the neck, which swells when a person is angry. *Encyc.*

PRES'TIĠES, *n.* [L. *præstigiæ.*] Juggling tricks; impostures. *Dict.*

PRESTIĠIA'TION, *n.* [L. *præstigiæ*, tricks.]

The playing of legerdemain tricks; a juggling. *Dict.*

PRESTIĠIA'TOR, *n.* A juggler; a cheat. *More.*

PRESTIĠ'IATORY, *a.* Juggling; consisting of impostures.

PRESTIĠ'IOUS, *a.* Practicing tricks; juggling. *Bale.*

PRES'TIMONY, *n.* [Port. Sp. *prestimonio;* L. *præsto*, to supply; *præ* and *sto.*] In *canon law*, a fund for the support of a priest, appropriated by the founder, but not erected into any title of benefice, and not subject to the pope or the ordinary, but of which the patron is the collator. *Port. Dict.* *Encyc.*

But in a Spanish Dictionary thus defined, "a prebend for the maintenance of poor clergymen, on condition of their saying prayers at certain stated times."

PRES'TO, *adv.* [Sp. It. *presto*, quick or quickly; L. *præsto.*]

1. In *music*, a direction for a quick lively movement or performance.
2. Quickly; immediately; in haste. *Swift.*

PRESTRIC'TION, *n.* [L. *præstringo, præstrictus.*] Dimness. *Milton.*

PRESU'MABLE, *a.* *s* as *z.* [from *presume.*] That may be presumed; that may be supposed to be true or entitled to belief, without examination or direct evidence, or on probable evidence.

PRESU'MABLY, *adv.* By presuming or supposing something to be true, without direct proof. *Brown.*

PRESU'ME, *v. t.* *s* as *z.* [Fr. *presumer;* It. *presumere;* Sp. *presumir;* from L. *præsumo; præ*, before, and *sumo*, to take.]

To take or suppose to be true or entitled to belief, without examination or positive proof, or on the strength of probability. We *presume* that a man is honest, who has not been known to cheat or deceive; but in this we are sometimes mistaken. In many cases, the law *presumes* full payment where positive evidence of it cannot be produced.

We not only *presume* it may be so, but we actually find it so. *Gov. of the Tongue.*

In cases of implied contracts, the law *presumes* that a man has covenanted or contracted to do what reason and justice dictate. *Blackstone.*

PRESU'ME, *v. i.* To venture without positive permission; as, we may *presume* too far. *Bacon.*

2. To form confident or arrogant opinions; with *on* or *upon*, before the cause of confidence.

This man *presumes upon* his parts. *Locke.*
I will not *presume* so far *upon* myself. *Dryden.*

3. To make confident or arrogant attempts.

In that we *presume* to see what is meet and convenient, better than God himself. *Hooker.*

4. It has *on* or *upon* sometimes before the thing supposed.

Luther *presumes upon* the gift of continency. *Atterbury.*

It is sometimes followed by *of*, but improperly.

PRESU'MED, *pp.* Supposed or taken to be true, or entitled to belief, without positive proof.

PRESU'MER, *n.* One that presumes; also, an arrogant person. *Wotton.*

PRESU'MING, *ppr.* Taking as true, or supposing to be entitled to belief, on probable evidence.

2. *a.* Venturing without positive permission; too confident; arrogant; unreasonably bold.

PRESUMP'TION, *n.* [Fr. *presomption;* L. *præsumptio.*]

1. Supposition of the truth or real existence of something without direct or positive proof of the fact, but grounded on circumstantial or probable evidence which entitles it to belief. Presumption in law is of three sorts, *violent* or *strong*, *probable*, and *light.*

Next to positive proof, circumstantial evidence or the doctrine of *presumptions* must take place; for when the fact cannot be demonstratively evinced, that which comes nearest to the proof of the fact is the proof of such circumstances as either necessarily or usually attend such facts. These are called *presumptions. Violent* presumption is many times equal to full proof. *Blackstone.*

2. Strong probability; as in the common phrase, the *presumption* is that an event has taken place, or will take place.
3. Blind or headstrong confidence; unreasonable adventurousness; a venturing to undertake something without reasonable prospect of success, or against the usual probabilities of safety; presumptuousness.

Let my *presumption* not provoke thy wrath. *Shak.*

I had the *presumption* to dedicate to you a very unfinished piece. *Dryden.*

4. Arrogance. He had the *presumption* to attempt to dictate to the council.
5. Unreasonable confidence in divine favor.

The awe of his majesty will keep us from *presumption.* *Rogers.*

PRESUMP'TIVE, *a.* Taken by previous supposition; grounded on probable evidence.

2. Unreasonably confident; adventuring without reasonable ground to expect success; presumptuous; arrogant. *Brown.*

Presumptive evidence, in *law*, is that which is derived from circumstances which necessarily or usually attend a fact, as distinct from direct evidence or positive proof.

Presumptive evidence of felony should be cautiously admitted. *Blackstone.*

Presumptive heir, one who would inherit an estate if the ancestor should die with things in their present state, but whose right of inheritance may be defeated by the birth of a nearer heir before the death of the ancestor. Thus the *presumptive* succession of a brother or nephew may be destroyed by the birth of a child. *Presumptive heir* is distinguished from *heir apparent*, whose right of inheritance is indefeasible, provided he outlives the ancestor. *Blackstone.*

PRESUMP'TIVELY, *adv.* By presumption, or supposition grounded on probability. *Burke.*

PRESUMP'TUOUS, *a.* [Fr. *presomptueux;* It. Sp. *presuntuoso.*]

1. Bold and confident to excess; adventuring without reasonable ground of success; hazarding safety on too slight grounds; rash; *applied to persons;* as a *presumptuous* commander.

There is a class of *presumptuous* men whom age has not made cautious, nor adversity wise. *Buckminster.*

2. Founded on presumption; proceeding from excess of confidence; *applied to things;* as *presumptuous* hope. *Milton.*
3. Arrogant; insolent; as a *presumptuous* priest. *Shak.*

Presumptuous pride. *Dryden.*

4. Unduly confident; irreverent with respect to sacred things.
5. Willful; done with bold design, rash confidence or in violation of known duty; as a *presumptuous* sin.

PRESUMP'TUOUSLY, *adv.* With rash confidence.

2. Arrogantly; insolently.
3. Willfully; in bold defiance of conscience or violation of known duty; as, to sin *presumptuously.* Num. xv.
4. With groundless and vain confidence in the divine favor. *Hammond.*

PRESUMP'TUOUSNESS, *n.* The quality of being presumptuous or rashly confident; groundless confidence; arrogance; irreverent boldness or forwardness.

PRESUPPOSAL, *n.* *presuppo'zal.* [*pre* and *supposal.*]

Supposal previously formed; presupposition. *Hooker.*

PRESUPPO'SE, *v. t.* *presuppo'ze.* [Fr. *presupposer*; It. *presupporre*; Eng. *pre* and *suppose.*]

To suppose as previous; to imply as antecedent. The existence of created things *presupposes* the existence of a Creator.

Each kind of knowledge *presupposes* many necessary things learned in other sciences and known beforehand. *Hooker.*

PRESUPPO'SED, *pp.* Supposed to be antecedent.

PRESUPPO'SING, *ppr.* Supposing to be previous.

PRESUPPOSI''TION, *n.* Supposition previously formed.

2. Supposition of something antecedent.

PRESURMISE, *n.* *presurmi'ze.* [*pre* and *surmise.*]

A surmise previously formed. *Shak.*

PRETEND', *v. t.* [L. *prætendo*; *præ*, before, and *tendo*, to tend, to reach or stretch; Fr. *pretendre*; It. *pretendere*; Sp. *pretender.*]

1. Literally, to reach or stretch forward; used by Dryden, but this use is not well authorized.

2. To hold out, as a false appearance; to offer something feigned instead of that which is real; to simulate, in words or actions.

This let him know,
Lest willfully transgressing, he *pretend*
Surprisal. *Milton.*

3. To show hypocritically; as, to *pretend* great zeal when the heart is not engaged; to *pretend* patriotism for the sake of gaining popular applause or obtaining an office.

4. To exhibit as a cover for something hidden.

Lest that too heavenly form, *pretended*
To hellish falsehood, snare them. *Milton.*
[*Not in use.*]

5. To claim.

Chiefs shall be grudg'd the part which they *pretend.* *Dryden.*

In this sense, we generally use *pretend to.*

6. To intend; to design. [*Not used.*] *Spenser.*

PRETEND', *v. t.* To put in a claim, truly or falsely; to hold out the appearance of being, possessing or performing. A man may *pretend* to be a physician, and *pretend* to perform great cures. Bad men often *pretend* to be patriots.

PRETEND'ED, *pp.* Held out, as a false appearance; feigned; simulated.

2. *a.* Ostensible; hypocritical; as a *pretended* reason or motive; *pretended* zeal.

PRETEND'EDLY, *adv.* By false appearance or representation. *Hammond.*

PRETEND'ER, *n.* One who makes a show of something not real; one who lays claim to any thing.

2. In *English history*, the heir of the royal family of Stuart, who lays claim to the crown of Great Britain, but is excluded by law. *Burnet.*

PRETEND'ERSHIP, *n.* The right or claim of the Pretender. *Swift.*

PRETEND'ING, *ppr.* Holding out a false appearance; laying claim to, or attempting to make others believe one is what in truth he is not, or that he has or does something which he has or does not; making hypocritical professions.

PRETEND'INGLY, *adv.* Arrogantly; presumptuously.

PRETENSE, *n.* *pretens'.* [L. *prætensus*, *prætendo.*]

1. A holding out or offering to others something false or feigned; a presenting to others, either in words or actions, a false or hypocritical appearance, usually with a view to conceal what is real, and thus to deceive. Under *pretense* of giving liberty to nations, the prince conquered and enslaved them. Under *pretense* of patriotism, ambitious men serve their own selfish purposes.

Let not Trojans, with a feigned *pretense*
Of proffer'd peace, delude the Latian prince. *Dryden.*

It is sometimes preceded by *on*; as *on pretense* of revenging Cesar's death. *Middleton.*

2. Assumption; claim to notice.

Never was any thing of this *pretense* more ingeniously imparted. *Evelyn.*

3. Claim, true or false.

Primogeniture cannot have any *pretense* to a right of solely inheriting property or power. *Locke.*

4. Something held out to terrify or for other purpose; as a *pretense* of danger. *Shak.*

PRETENS'ED, *a.* Pretended; feigned; as a *pretensed* right to land. [*Little used.*] *Encyc.*

PRETEN'SION, *n.* [It. *pretensione*; Fr. *pretention.*]

1. Claim, true or false; a holding out the appearance of right or possession of a thing, with a view to make others believe what is not real, or what, if true, is not yet known or admitted. A man may make *pretensions* to rights which he cannot maintain; he may make *pretensions* to skill which he does not possess; and he may make *pretensions* to skill or acquirements which he really possesses, but which he is not known to possess. Hence we speak of ill founded *pretensions*, and well founded *pretensions.*

2. Claim to something to be obtained, or a desire to obtain something, manifested by words or actions. Any citizen may have *pretensions* to the honor of representing the state in the senate or house of representatives.

The commons demand that the consulship should lie in common to the *pretensions* of any Roman. *Swift.*

Men indulge those opinions and practices that favor their *pretensions.* *L'Estrange.*

3. Fictitious appearance; *a Latin phrase, not now used.*

This was but an invention and *pretension* given out by the Spaniards. *Bacon.*

PRETENT'ATIVE, *a.* [L. *præ* and *tento*, to try.]

That may be previously tried or attempted. [*Little used.*] *Wotton.*

PRETER, a Latin preposition, [*præter*,] is used in some English words as a prefix. Its proper signification is *beyond*, hence *beside*, *more.*

PRETERIMPER'FECT, *a.* [beyond or beside unfinished.]

In *grammar*, designating the tense which expresses action or being not perfectly past; *an awkward epithet, very ill applied.*

PRE'TERIT, *a.* [L. *præteritus*, *prætereo*; *præter*, beyond, and *eo*, to go.]

Past; applied to the tense in grammar which expresses an action or being perfectly past or finished, often that which is just past or completed, but without a specification of time. It is called also the *perfect* tense; as, *scripsi*, I *have written.* We say, "I *have written* a letter to my correspondent;" in which sentence, the time is supposed to be not distant and not specified. But when the time is mentioned, we use the imperfect tense so called; as, "I *wrote* to my correspondent yesterday." In this use of the *preterit* or perfect tense, the English differs from the French, in which *j'ai ecrit hier*, is correct; but I *have written yesterday*, would be very bad English.

PRETERI''TION, *n.* [Fr. from L. *prætereo*, to pass by.]

1. The act of going past; the state of being past. *Hall.*

2. In *rhetoric*, a figure by which, in pretending to pass over any thing, we make a summary mention of it; as, "I will not say, he is valiant, he is learned, he is just," &c. The most artful praises are those bestowed by way of *preterition.* *Encyc.*

PRE'TERITNESS, *n.* [from *preterit.*] The state of being past. [*Little used.*] *Bentley.*

PRETERLAPS'ED, *a.* [L. *præterlapsus*, *præterlabor*; *præter* and *labor*, to glide.]

Past; gone by; as *preterlapsed* ages. *Walker.*

PRETERLE'GAL, *a.* [L. *præter* and *legal.*] Exceeding the limits of law; not legal. [*Little used.*] *K. Charles.*

PRETERMIS'SION, *n.* [L. *prætermissio*, from *prætermitto.*] A passing by; omission.

2. In *rhetoric*, the same as *preterition.*

PRETERMIT', *v. t.* [L. *prætermitto*; *præter*, beyond, and *mitto*, to send.]

To pass by; to omit. *Bacon.*

PRETERNAT'URAL, *a.* [L. *præter* and *natural.*]

Beyond what is natural, or different from what is natural; irregular. We call those events in the physical world *preternatural*, which are extraordinary, which are deemed to be *beyond* or without the ordinary course of things, and yet are not deemed miraculous; in distinction from events which are *supernatural*, which cannot be produced by physical laws or powers, and must therefore be produced by a direct exertion of omnipotence. We also apply the epithet to things uncommon or irregular; as a *preternatural* swelling; a *preternatural* pulse; a *preternatural* excitement or temper.

PRETERNATURAL'ITY, *n.* Preternaturalness. [*Little used.*] *Smith.*

PRETERNAT'URALLY, *adv.* In a manner beyond or aside from the common order of nature; as vessels of the body *preternaturally* distended.

PRETERNAT'URALNESS, *n.* A state or manner different from the common order of nature.

PRETERPER'FECT, *a.* [L. *præter* and *perfectus.*]

Literally, *more than complete* or *finished*; an epithet equivalent to *preterit*, applied to the tense of verbs which expresses action or being absolutely past. [*Grammar.*] *Spectator.*

PRETERPLUPER'FECT, *a.* [L. *præter*, beyond, *plus*, more, and *perfectus*, perfect.]

Literally, *beyond more than perfect*; an epithet designating the tense of verbs which expresses action or being past prior to another past event or time; better denominated the *prior past* tense, that is, past prior to another event.

PRETEX', *v. t.* [L. *prætexo*; *præ* and *texo*, or *tego*, *texui.*]

To cloak; to conceal. [*Not used.*] *Edwards.*

PRETEXT', *n.* [L. *prætextus*; Fr. *pretexte*; It. *pretesto*; Sp. *pretexto.*]

Pretense; false appearance; ostensible reason or motive assigned or assumed as a color or cover for the real reason or motive. He gave plausible reasons for his conduct, but these were only a *pretext* to conceal his real motives.

He made *pretext* that I should only go
And help convey his freight; but thought not so. *Chapman.*

They suck the blood of those they depend on, under a *pretext* of service and kindness. *L'Estrange.*

PRE'TOR, *n.* [L. *prætor*, from the root of *præ*, before.]

Among *the ancient Romans*, a judge; an officer answering to the modern chief justice or chancellor, or to both. In later times, subordinate judges appointed to distribute justice in the provinces, were created and called *pretors* or *provincial pretors*. These assisted the consuls in the government of the provinces. *Encyc.*

In modern times, the word is sometimes used for a mayor or magistrate. *Dryden. Spectator.*

PRETO'RIAL, *a.* Pertaining to a pretor or judge; judicial. *Burke.*

PRETO'RIAN, *a.* Belonging to a pretor or judge; judicial; exercised by the pretor; as *pretorian* power or authority. *Bacon.*

Pretorian bands or *guards*, in Roman history, were the emperor's guards. Their number was ultimately increased to ten thousand men. *Encyc.*

PRE'TORSHIP, *n.* The office of pretor. *Warton.*

PRETTILY, *adv. prit'tily.* [from *pretty.*] In a pretty manner; with neatness and taste; pleasingly; without magnificence or splendor; as a woman *prettily* dressed; a parterre *prettily* ornamented with flowers.

2. With decency, good manners and decorum without dignity.

Children kept out of ill company, take a pride to behave themselves *prettily*. *Locke.*

PRETTINESS, *n. prit'tiness.* [from *pretty.*]

1. Diminutive beauty; a pleasing form without stateliness or dignity; as the *prettiness* of the face; the *prettiness* of a bird or other small animal; the *prettiness* of dress. *More.*

2. Neatness and taste displayed on small objects; as the *prettiness* of a flower bed.

3. Decency of manners; pleasing propriety without dignity or elevation; as the *prettiness* of a child's behavior.

PRETTY, *a. prit'ty.* [Sax. *præte*, adorned; *prætig*, sly, crafty; Dan. *prydet*, adorned; Sw. *prydd*, id.; W. *pryd*, comeliness, beauty, also that is present, stated time, hour or season, visage, aspect; *prydain*, exhibiting presence or an open countenance, beautiful; *prydiaw*, to represent an object, to record an event, to render seasonable, to set apart a time, to become seasonable. This word seems to be connected with *priawd*, appropriate, proper, fitting, whence *priodi*, to render appropriate, to espouse or marry, and *priodverç*, a *bride*. Hence it is evident, the radical sense is set, or as we say, *set off*, implying enlargement.]

1. Having diminutive beauty; of a pleasing form without the strong lines of beauty, or without gracefulness and dignity; as a *pretty* face; a *pretty* person; a *pretty* flower.

The *pretty* gentleman is the most complaisant creature in the world. *Spectator.*

That which is little can be but *pretty*, and by claiming dignity becomes ridiculous. *Johnson.*

2. Neat and appropriate without magnificence or splendor; as a *pretty* dress.

3. Handsome; neatly arranged or ornamented; as a *pretty* flower bed.

4. Neat; elegant without elevation or grandeur; as a *pretty* tale or story; a *pretty* song or composition.

5. Sly; crafty; as, he has played his friend a *pretty* trick. This seems to be the sense of the word in this phrase, according with the Saxon *prætig*. And hence perhaps the phrase, a *pretty* fellow.

6. Small; diminutive; in contempt. He will make a *pretty* figure in a triumph.

7. Not very small; moderately large; as a *pretty* way off.

Cut off the stalks of cucumbers immediately after their bearing, close by the earth, and then cast a *pretty* quantity of earth upon the plant, and they will bear next year before the ordinary time. [*Not in use.*] *Bacon.*

PRETTY, *adv. prit'ty.* In some degree; tolerably; moderately; as a farm *pretty* well stocked; the colors became *pretty* vivid; I am *pretty* sure of the fact; the wind is *pretty* fair. The English farthing is *pretty* near the value of the American cent. In these and similar phrases, *pretty* expresses less than *very.*

The writer *pretty* plainly professes himself a sincere christian. *Atterbury.*

PRETYP'IFIED, *pp.* [from *pretypify.*] Antecedently represented by type; prefigured.

PRETYP'IFY, *v. t.* [*pre* and *typify.*] To prefigure; to exhibit previously in a type. *Pearson.*

PRETYP'IFYING, *ppr.* Prefiguring.

PREVA'IL, *v. i.* [Fr. *prevaloir*; It. *prevalere*; Sp. *prevalecer*; L. *prævaleo*; *præ*, before, and *valeo*, to be strong or well. *Valeo* seems to be from the same root as the Eng. *well.* The primary sense is to stretch or strain forward, to advance.]

1. To overcome; to gain the victory or superiority; to gain the advantage.

When Moses held up his hand, Israel *prevailed*; when he let down his hand, Amalek *prevailed.* Ex. xvii.

With *over* or *against.*

David *prevailed over* the Philistine with a sling and with a stone. 1 Sam. xvii.

This kingdom could never *prevail against* the united power of England. *Swift.*

2. To be in force; to have effect, power or influence.

This custom makes the short-sighted bigots and the warier sceptics, as far as it *prevails.* *Locke.*

3. To be predominant; to extend over with force or effect. The fever *prevailed* in a great part of the city.

4. To gain or have predominant influence; to operate with effect. These reasons, arguments or motives ought to *prevail* with all candid men. In this sense, it is followed by *with.*

5. To persuade or induce; with *on* or *upon.* They *prevailed on* the president to ratify the treaty. It is also followed by *with.* They could not *prevail with* the king to pardon the offender. But *on* is more common in modern practice.

6. To succeed. The general attempted to take the fort by assault, but did not *prevail.* The most powerful arguments were employed, but they did not *prevail.*

PREVA'ILING, *ppr.* Gaining advantage, superiority or victory; having effect; persuading; succeeding.

2. *a.* Predominant; having more influence; prevalent; superior in power. The love of money and the love of power are the *prevailing* passions of men.

3. Efficacious.

Saints shall assist thee with *prevailing* prayers. *Rowe.*

4. Predominant; most general; as the *prevailing* disease of a climate; a *prevailing* opinion. Intemperance is the *prevailing* vice of many countries.

PREVA'ILMENT, *n.* Prevalence. [*Little used.*] *Shak.*

PREV'ALENCE, } *n.* Superior strength, in-
PREV'ALENCY, } fluence or efficacy; most efficacious force in producing an effect.

The duke better knew what kind of arguments were of *prevalence* with him. *Clarendon.*

2. Predominance; most general reception or practice; as the *prevalence* of vice, or of corrupt maxims; the *prevalence* of opinion or fashion.

3. Most general existence or extension; as the *prevalence* of a disease.

4. Success; as the *prevalence* of prayer.

PREV'ALENT, *a.* Gaining advantage or superiority; victorious.

Brennus told the Roman embassadors, that *prevalent* arms were as good as any title. *Raleigh.*

2. Powerful; efficacious; successful; as *prevalent* supplications.

3. Predominant; most generally received or current; as a *prevalent* opinion. *Woodward.*

4. Predominant; most general; extensively existing; as a *prevalent* disease.

PREV'ALENTLY, *adv.* With predominance or superiority; powerfully.

The evening star so falls into the main
To rise at morn more *prevalently* bright. *Prior.*

PREVAR'I€ATE, *v. i.* [It. *prevaricare*; Sp. *prevaricar*; Fr. *prevariquer*; L. *prævaricor*; *præ* and *varico*, *varicor*, to straddle.]
1. To shuffle; to quibble; to shift or turn from one side to the other, from the direct course or from truth; to play foul play

I would think better of himself, than that he would wilfully *prevaricate*. *Stillingfleet.*

2. In *the civil law*, to collude; as where an informer colludes with the defendant, and makes a sham prosecution. *Encyc.*
3. In *English law*, to undertake a thing falsely and deceitfully, with the purpose of defeating or destroying it. *Cowel.*

PREVAR'I€ATE, *v. t.* To pervert; to corrupt; to evade by a quibble. [*But in a transitive sense, this word is seldom or never used.*]

PREVARI€A'TION, *n.* A shuffling or quibbling to evade the truth or the disclosure of truth; the practice of some trick for evading what is just or honorable; a deviation from the plain path of truth and fair dealing. *Addison.*
2. In *the civil law*, the collusion of an informer with the defendant, for the purpose of making a sham prosecution. *Encyc.*
3. In *common law*, a seeming to undertake a thing falsely or deceitfully, for the purpose of defeating or destroying it. *Cowel.*
4. A secret abuse in the exercise of a public office or commission. *Encyc.*

PREVAR'I€ATOR, *n.* One that prevaricates; a shuffler; a quibbler.
2. A sham dealer; one who colludes with a defendant in a sham prosecution. *Civil Law.*
3. One who abuses his trust.

PREVE'NE, *v. t.* [L. *prævenio*; *præ*, before, and *venio*, to come.]
Literally, to come before; hence, to hinder. [*Not used.*] *Philips.*

PREVE'NIENT, *a.* [L. *præveniens.*] Going before; preceding; hence, preventive; as *prevenient* grace. *Milton.*

PREVENT', *v. t.* [It. *prevenire*; Sp. Fr. *prevenir*; L. *prævenio*, supra.]
1. To go before; to precede.

I *prevented* the dawning of the morning, and cried. Ps. cxix.

2. To precede, as something unexpected or unsought.

The days of my affliction *prevented* me. Job xxx. 2 Sam. xxii.

3. To go before; to precede; to favor by anticipation or by hindering distress or evil.

The God of my mercy shall *prevent* me. Ps. lix.

Prevent us, O Lord, in all our doings, with thy most gracious favor. *Common Prayer.*

4. To anticipate.

Their ready guilt *preventing* thy commands. *Pope.*

5. To preoccupy; to pre-engage; to attempt first.

Thou hast *prevented* us with overtures of love. *K. Charles.*

[*In all the preceding senses, the word is obsolete.*]

6. To hinder; to obstruct; to intercept the approach or access of. *This is now the only sense.* No foresight or care will *prevent* every misfortune. Religion supplies consolation under afflictions which cannot be *prevented*. It is easier to *prevent* an evil than to remedy it.

Too great confidence in success, is the likeliest to *prevent* it. *Atterbury.*

PREVENT', *v. i.* To come before the usual time. [*Not in use.*] *Bacon.*

PREVENT'ABLE, *a.* That may be prevented or hindered. *Reynolds.*

PREVENT'ED, *pp.* Hindered from happening or taking effect.

PREVENT'ER, *n.* One that goes before. [*Not in use.*] *Bacon.*
2. One that hinders; a hinderer; that which hinders; as a *preventer* of evils or of disease.

PREVENT'ING, *ppr.* Going before. *Obs.*
2. Hindering; obviating.

PREVENT'INGLY, *adv.* In such a manner or way as to hinder. *Dr. Walker.*

PREVEN'TION, *n.* [Fr.] The act of going before. *Obs.* *Bacon.*
2. Preoccupation; anticipation. [*Little used.*] *Hammond.*
3. The act of hindering; hinderance; obstruction of access or approach.

Prevention of sin is one of the greatest mercies God can vouchsafe. *South.*

4. Prejudice; prepossession; *a French sense, but not in use in English.* *Dryden.*

PREVEN'TIONAL, *a.* Tending to prevent. *Dict.*

PREVENT'IVE, *a.* Tending to hinder; hindering the access of; as a medicine *preventive* of disease. *Brown.*

PREVENT'IVE, *n.* That which prevents; that which intercepts the access or approach of. Temperance and exercise are excellent *preventives* of debility and languor.
2. An antidote previously taken. A medicine may be taken as a *preventive* of disease.

PREVENT'IVELY, *adv.* By way of prevention; in a manner that tends to hinder.

PRE'VIOUS, *a.* [L. *prævius*; *præ*, before, and *via*, way, that is, a going, Sax. *wæg.*]
Going before in time; being or happening before something else; antecedent; prior; as a *previous* intimation of a design; a *previous* notion; a *previous* event.

Sound from the mountain, *previous* to the storm,
Rolls o'er the muttering earth. *Thomson.*

PRE'VIOUSLY, *adv.* In time preceding; beforehand; antecedently; as a plan *previously* formed.

PRE'VIOUSNESS, *n.* Antecedence; priority in time.

PREVI''SION, *n.* s as z. [L. *prævisus*, *prævideo*; *præ*, before, and *video*, to see.]
Foresight; foreknowledge; prescience. *Encyc.*

PREWARN', *v. t.* [See *Warn.*] To warn beforehand; to give previous notice of. *Beaum.*

PREY, *n.* [L. *præda*; It. *preda*; Fr. *proie*; Arm. *preyz* or *preih*; D. *prooi*. In Welsh, *praiz*, Ir. *preit*, signifies booty or spoil of cattle taken in war, also a flock or herd; *preiziaw*, to herd, to collect a herd, to drive off or make booty of cattle.]
1. Spoil; booty; plunder; goods taken by force from an enemy in war.

And they brought the captives and the *prey* and the spoil to Moses and Eleazar the priest. Num. xxxi.

In this passage, the captives are distinguished from *prey*. But sometimes *persons* are included.

They [Judah] shall become a *prey* and a spoil to all their enemies. 2 Kings xxi.

2. That which is seized or may be seized by violence to be devoured; ravine. The eagle and the hawk dart upon their *prey*.

She sees herself the monster's *prey*. *Dryden.*

The old lion perisheth for lack of *prey*. Job iv.

3. Ravage; depredation.

Hog in sloth, fox in stealth, lion in *prey*. *Shak.*

Animal or *beast of prey*, is a carnivorous animal; one that feeds on the flesh of other animals. The word is applied to the larger animals, as lions, tigers, hawks, vultures, &c. rather than to insects; yet an insect feeding on other insects may be called an *animal of prey*.

PREY, *v. i.* To *prey on* or *upon*, is to rob; to plunder; to pillage.
2. To feed by violence, or to seize and devour. The wolf *preys on* sheep; the hawk *preys on* chickens.
3. To corrode; to waste gradually; to cause to pine away. Grief *preys on* the body and spirits; envy and jealousy *prey on* the health.

Language is too faint to show
His rage of love; it *preys upon* his life;
He pines, he sickens, he despairs, he dies. *Addison.*

PREYER, *n.* He or that which preys; a plunderer; a waster; a devourer.

PREYING, *ppr.* Plundering; corroding; wasting gradually.

PRICE, *n.* [Fr. *prix*; It. *prezzo*; Sp. *precio*; Arm. *pris*; D. *prys*; G. *preis*; Dan. *priis*; W. *pris* or *prid*; *prisiaw*, to value, to apprize; *pridiaw*, to give a price, value or equivalent, to pawn, to ransom; L. *pretium*. See *Praise.*]
1. The sum or amount of money at which a thing is valued, or the value which a seller sets on his goods in market. A man often sets a *price* on goods which he cannot obtain, and often takes less than the *price* set.
2. The sum or equivalent given for an article sold; as the *price* paid for a house, an ox or a watch.
3. The current value or rate paid for any species of goods; as the market *price* of wheat.
4. Value; estimation; excellence; worth.

Who can find a virtuous woman? for her *price* is far above rubies. Prov. xxxi.

5. Reward; recompense.

That vice may merit; 'tis the *price* of toil;
The knave deserves it when he tills the soil. *Pope.*

The price of redemption, is the atonement of Jesus Christ. 1 Cor. vi.

A price in the hands of a fool, the valuable offers of salvation, which he neglects. Prov. xvii.

PRICE, *v. t.* To pay for. [*Not in use.*] *Spenser.*
2. To set a price on. [See *Prize.*]

PRI'CELESS, *a.* Invaluable; too valuable to admit of a price. *Shak.*
2. Without value; worthless or unsalable. *J. Barlow.*

PRICK, *v. t.* [Sax. *priccian*; D. *prikken*; Dan. *prikker*; Sw. *pricka*; Ir. *priocam.*]

1. To pierce with a sharp pointed instrument or substance; as, to *prick* one with a pin, a needle, a thorn or the like.
2. To erect a pointed thing, or with an acuminated point; applied chiefly to the ears, and primarily to the pointed ears of an animal. The horse *pricks* his ears, or *pricks up* his ears.
3. To fix by the point; as, to *prick* a knife into a board. *Newton.*
4. To hang on a point.

The cooks *prick* a slice on a prong of iron. *Sandys.*

5. To designate by a puncture or mark.

Some who are *pricked* for sherifs, and are fit, set out of the bill. *Bacon.*

6. To spur; to goad; to incite; sometimes with *on* or *off*.

My duty *pricks* me *on* to utter that
Which no worldly good should draw from me. *Shak.*

But how if honor *prick* me *off*. *Shak.*

7. To affect with sharp pain; to sting with remorse.

When they heard this, they were *pricked* in their hearts. Acts ii. Ps. lxxiii.

8. To make acid or pungent to the taste; as, wine is *pricked*. *Hudibras.*
9. To write a musical composition with the proper notes on a scale.
10. In *seamen's language*, to run a middle seam through the cloth of a sail. *Mar. Dict.*

To prick a chart, is to trace a ship's course on a chart. *Mar. Dict.*

PRICK, *v. i.* To become acid; as, cider *pricks* in the rays of the sun.
2. To dress one's self for show.
3. To come upon the spur; to shoot along.

Before each van
Prick forth the airy knights. *Milton.*

4. To aim at a point, mark or place. *Hawkins.*

PRICK, *n.* [Sax. *pricca;* Sw. *prick* or *preka; tand-preka*, a tooth pick; Ir. *prioca.*]
1. A slender pointed instrument or substance, which is hard enough to pierce the skin; a goad; a spur.

It is hard for thee to kick against the *pricks*. Acts ix.

2. Sharp stinging pain; remorse. *Shak.*
3. A spot or mark at which archers aim. *Carew.*
4. A point; a fixed place. *Spenser.*
5. A puncture or place entered by a point. *Brown.*
6. The print of a hare on the ground.
7. In *seamen's language*, a small roll; as a *prick* of spun yarn; a *prick* of tobacco.

PRICK'ED, *pp.* Pierced with a sharp point; spurred; goaded; stung with pain; rendered acid or pungent; marked; designated.

PRICK'ER, *n.* A sharp pointed instrument. *Moxon.*
2. In *colloquial use*, a prickle.
3. A light horseman. [*Not in use.*] *Hayward.*

PRICK'ET, *n.* A buck in his second year. *Manwood.*

PRICK'ING, *ppr.* Piercing with a sharp point; goading; affecting with pungent pain; making or becoming acid.

PRICK'ING, *n.* A sensation of sharp pain, or of being pricked.

PRICK'LE, *n.* In *botany*, a small pointed shoot or sharp process, growing from the *bark* only, and thus distinguished from the *thorn*, which grows from the *wood* of a plant. Thus the rose, the bramble, the gooseberry and the barberry are armed with *prickles*. *Martyn.*
2. A sharp pointed process of an animal.

PRICK'LE-BACK, *n.* A small fish, so named from the prickles on its back; the stickle-back. *Dict. Nat. Hist.*

PRICK'LINESS, *n.* [from *prickly.*] The state of having many prickles.

PRICK'LOUSE, *n.* A low word in contempt for a taylor. *L'Estrange.*

PRICK'LY, *a.* Full of sharp points or prickles; armed with prickles; as a *prickly* shrub. *Martyn. Swift.*

PRICK'MADAM, *n.* A species of houseleek. *Johnson.*

PRICK'PUNCH, *n.* A piece of tempered steel with a round point, to prick a round mark on cold iron. *Moxon.*

PRICK'SONG, *n.* A song set to music, or a variegated song; in distinction from a plain song. *Shak. Bale.*

PRICK'WOOD, *n.* A tree of the genus Euonymus. *Fam. of Plants.*

PRIDE, *n.* [Sax. *pryt, pryde;* D. *prat*, proud.]
1. Inordinate self-esteem; an unreasonable conceit of one's own superiority in talents, beauty, wealth, accomplishments, rank or elevation in office, which manifests itself in lofty airs, distance, reserve, and often in contempt of others.

Martial *pride* looks down on industry. *T. Dawes.*

Pride goeth before destruction. Prov. xvi.
Pride that dines on vanity, sups on contempt. *Franklin.*

All *pride* is abject and mean. *Johnson.*

Those that walk in *pride* he is able to abase. Dan. iv.

2. Insolence; rude treatment of others; insolent exultation.

That hardly we escap'd the *pride* of France. *Shak.*

3. Generous elation of heart; a noble self-esteem springing from a consciousness of worth.

The honest *pride* of conscious virtue. *Smith.*

4. Elevation; loftiness.

A falcon tow'ring in her *pride* of place. *Shak.*

5. Decoration; ornament; beauty displayed.

Whose lofty trees, yclad with summer's *pride*. *Spenser.*

Be his this sword
Whose ivory sheath, inwrought with curious *pride*,
Adds graceful terror to the wearer's side. *Pope.*

6. Splendid show; ostentation.

In this array, the war of either side
Through Athens pass'd with military *pride*. *Dryden.*

7. That of which men are proud; that which excites boasting.

I will cut off the *pride* of the Philistines. Zech. ix. Zeph. iii.

8. Excitement of the sexual appetite in a female beast. *Shak.*
9. Proud persons. Ps. xxxvi.

PRIDE, *v. t.* With the reciprocal pronoun, to *pride one's self*, to indulge pride; to take pride; to value one's self; to gratify self-esteem. They *pride themselves* in their wealth, dress or equipage. He *prides himself* in his achievments.

PRI'DEFUL, *a.* Full of pride; insolent; scornful. *Richardson.*

PRI'DELESS, *a.* Destitute of pride; without pride. *Chaucer.*

PRI'DING, *ppr.* Indulging pride or self-esteem; taking pride; valuing one's self.

PRI'DINGLY, *adv.* With pride; in pride of heart. *Barrow.*

PRIE, supposed to be so written for *privet*. *Tusser.*

PRIE, for *pry*. *Chaucer.*

PRIEF, for *proof*, obsolete. *Chaucer.*

PRI'ER, *n.* [from *pry.*] One who inquires narrowly; one who searches and scrutinizes.

PRIEST, *n.* [Sax. *preost;* D. G. *priester;* Dan. *præst;* Fr. *prêtre;* It. *prete;* from L. *præstes*, a chief, one that presides; *præ*, before, and *sto*, to stand, or *sisto*, or Gr. ιςημι. This is probably the origin of the word. In Persic, پَرَسْتِش parastash is worship; پَرَسْتِيدَن parastidan, to worship, to adore.]
1. A man who officiates in sacred offices. Among *pagans*, priests were persons whose appropriate business was to offer sacrifices and perform other sacred rites of religion. In primitive ages, the fathers of families, princes and kings were priests. Thus Cain and Abel, Noah, Abraham, Melchizedeck, Job, Isaac and Jacob offered their own sacrifices. In the days of Moses, the office of priest was restricted to the tribe of Levi, and the priesthood consisted of three orders, the high priest, the priests, and the Levites, and the office was made hereditary in the family of Aaron.

Every *priest* taken from among men is ordained for men in things pertaining to God, that he may offer both gifts and sacrifices for sins. Heb. v.

2. In *the modern church*, a person who is set apart or consecrated to the ministry of the gospel; a man in orders or licensed to preach the gospel; a presbyter. In its most general sense, the word includes archbishops, bishops, patriarchs, and all subordinate orders of the clergy, duly approved and licensed according to the forms and rules of each respective denomination of christians; as all these orders "are ordained for men in things pertaining to God." But in Great Britain, the word is understood to denote the subordinate orders of the clergy, above a deacon and below a bishop. In the United States, the word denotes any licensed minister of the gospel.

PRIE'STCRAFT, *n.* [*priest* and *craft.*] The stratagems and frauds of priests; fraud or imposition in religious concerns; management of selfish and ambitious priests to gain wealth and power, or to impose on the credulity of others. *Pope. Spectator.*

PRIE'STESS, *n.* A female among pagans, who officiated in sacred things. *Addison. Swift.*

PRIE'STHOOD, *n.* The office or character of a priest. *Whitgifte.*
2. The order of men set apart for sacred offices; the order composed of priests. *Dryden.*

PRIE'STLIKE, *a.* Resembling a priest, or that which belongs to priests. *Shak.*

PRIE'STLINESS, *n.* The appearance and manner of a priest.

PRIE'STLY, *a.* Pertaining to a priest or to priests; sacerdotal; as the *priestly* office.

2. Becoming a priest; as *priestly* sobriety and purity of life.

PRIE'STRIDDEN, *a.* [*priest* and *ridden.* See *Ride.*] Managed or governed by priests. *Swift.*

PRIEVE, for *prove.* *Spenser.*

PRIG, *n.* [G. *frech*, bold, saucy, impudent.]

1. A pert, conceited, saucy, pragmatical fellow. *Addison. Swift.*

2. A thief.

PRIG, *v. i.* To haggle about the price of a commodity. *Obs.* *Ramsay's Poems.*

PRIG, *v. t.* To filch or steal.

PRILL, *n.* A birt or turbot. *Ainsworth.*

PRIM, *a.* [Russ. *primo* or *priamo*, in a right line, directly; *priamei*, straight, direct, true, just. See *Prime.*]

Properly, straight; erect; hence, formal; precise; affectedly nice. *Swift.*

PRIM, *v.t.* To deck with great nicety; to form with affected preciseness.

PRI'MACY, *n.* [It. *primazia*; Fr. *primatie*; Sp. *primacia*; from L. *primatus*, from *primus*, first. See *Prime.*]

1. The chief ecclesiastical station or dignity; the office or dignity of an archbishop. *Clarendon.*

2. Excellency; supremacy. *Barrow.*

PRI'MAGE, *n.* In *commerce*, a small duty payable to the master and mariners of a ship. *Encyc.*

PRI'MAL, *a.* [See *Prime.*] First. [*Not in use.*] *Shak.*

PRI'MARILY, *adv.* [from *primary.*] In the first place; originally; in the first intention. The word emperor *primarily* signifies a general or military commander in chief. In diseases, the physician is to attend to the part *primarily* affected.

PRI'MARINESS, *n.* The state of being first in time, in act or intention. *Norris.*

PRI'MARY, *a.* [L. *primarius.* See *Prime.*]

1. First in order of time; original; as the church of Christ in its *primary* institution. *Pearson.*

These I call original or *primary* qualities of body. *Locke.*

2. First in dignity or importance; chief; principal. Our ancestors considered the education of youth of *primary* importance.

3. Elemental; intended to teach youth the first rudiments; as *primary* schools.

4. Radical; original; as the *primary* sense of a word.

Primary planets, are those which revolve about the sun, in distinction from the *secondary planets*, which revolve about the primary.

Primary qualities of bodies, are such as are original and inseparable from them.

PRI'MATE, *n.* [It. *primato*; Fr. *primat*; Low L. *primas.* See *Prime.*]

The chief ecclesiastic in the church; an archbishop. *Encyc. Swift.*

PRI'MATESHIP, *n.* The office or dignity of an archbishop.

PRIMA'TIAL, *a.* Pertaining to a primate. *D'Anville, Trans.*

PRIMAT'ICAL, *a.* Pertaining to a primate. *Barrow.*

PRIME, *a.* [L. *primus*; Sax. Goth. *frum*, beginning, origin; Goth. *frumist*, first; Dan. *frem*, forward, straight on; *fremmer*, to forward or promote; Sw. *fram*, *frâmja*; W. *priv*, first; *priviaw*, to grow up, to increase, to prosper; Ir. *priomh*, first, and *reamain*, beginning. See Class Rm. No. 3. 7. 9.]

1. First in order of time; original; as *prime* fathers; *prime* creation. *Shak.*

In this sense, the use of the word is nearly superseded by *primitive*, except in the phrase, *prime* cost.

2. First in rank, degree or dignity; as *prime* minister.

3. First in excellence; as *prime* wheat; cloth of a *prime* quality. Humility and resignation are *prime* virtues. *Dryden.*

4. Early; blooming.

His starry helm unbuckl'd, showed him *prime*
In manhood, where youth ended. *Milton.*

5. First in value or importance.

Prime number, in arithmetic, a number which is divisible only by unity, as 5. 7. 11. *Encyc.*

Prime figure, in geometry, a figure which cannot be divided into any other figure more simple than itself, as a triangle, a pyramid, &c.

PRIME, *n.* The first opening of day; the dawn; the morning.

Early and late it rung, at evening and at *prime.* *Spenser.*

The sweet hour of *prime.* *Milton.*

2. The beginning; the early days.

In the very *prime* of the world. *Hooker.*

3. The spring of the year.

Hope waits upon the flowery *prime.* *Waller.*

4. The spring of life; youth; hence, full health, strength or beauty.

That crop the golden *prime* of this sweet prince. *Shak.*

The *prime* of youth. *Dryden.*

5. The best part.

Give him always of the *prime.* *Swift.*

6. The utmost perfection.

The plants—would have been all in *prime.* *Woodward.*

7. In *the Romish church*, the first canonical hour, succeeding to lauds. *Encyc.*

8. In *fencing*, the first of the chief guards. *Encyc.*

9. In *chimistry*, primes are numbers employed, in conformity with the doctrine of definite proportions, to express the ratios in which bodies enter into combination. Primes duly arranged in a table, constitute a scale of chimical equivalents. They also express the ratios of the weights of atoms, according to the atomic theory.

Prime of the moon, the new moon, when it first appears after the change. *Encyc.*

Prime vertical, the vertical circle which passes through the poles of the meridian, or the east and west points of the horizon. Dials projected on the plane of this circle, are called prime vertical or north and south dials. *Encyc.*

PRIME, *v. t.* To put powder in the pan of a musket or other fire-arm; or to lay a train of powder for communicating fire to a charge. *Encyc.*

2. To lay on the first color in painting. *Encyc.*

PRIME, *v. i.* To serve for the charge of a gun. *Beaum.*

PRI'MED, *pp.* Having powder in the pan; having the first color in painting.

PRI'MELY, *adv.* At first; originally; primarily. *South.*

2. Most excellently.

PRI'MENESS, *n.* The state of being first.

2. Supreme excellence. [*Little used in either sense.*]

PRI'MER, *a.* First; original. [*Not in use.*] *Drayton.*

PRIM'ER, *n.* A small prayer book for church service, or an office of the virgin Mary.

2. A small elementary book for teaching children to read.

PRIMER-FI'NE, *n.* In *England*, a fine due to the king on the writ or commencement of a suit by fine. *Blackstone.*

PRIMER'O, *n.* A game at cards. [Sp.]

PRIMER-SE'IZIN, *n.* [*prime* and *seizin.*]

In *feudal law*, the right of the king, when a tenant *in capite* died seized of a knight's fee, to receive of the heir, if of full age, one year's profits of the land if in possession, and half a year's profits if the land was in reversion expectant on an estate for life; abolished by 12 Car. 2. *Encyc.*

PRIME'VAL, *a.* [L. *primus*, first, and *ævum*, age; *primævus.*]

Original; primitive; as the *primeval* innocence of man; *primeval* day. *Blackmore.*

PRIME'VOUS, *a.* Primeval.

PRIMIGE'NIAL, *a.* [L. *primigenius*; *primus*, first, and *genus*, kind, or *gignor*, to beget.] First born; original; primary. *Bp. Hall.*

PRIMIG'ENOUS, *a.* [supra.] First formed or generated; original; as semi-*primigenous* strata. *Kirwan.*

PRI'MING, *ppr.* Putting powder in the pan of a fire-arm.

2. Laying on the first color.

PRI'MING, *n.* The powder in the pan of a gun, or laid along the channel of a cannon for conveying fire to the charge.

2. Among *painters*, the first color laid on canvas or on a building, &c.

PRI'MING-WIRE, *n.* A pointed wire, used to penetrate the vent of a piece, for examining the powder of the charge or for piercing the cartridge. *Encyc.*

PRIMIP'ILAR, *a.* [L. *primipilus*, the centurion of the first cohort of a Roman legion.]

Pertaining to the captain of the vanguard. *Barrow.*

PRIMI''TIAL, *a.* Being of the first production. *Ainsworth.*

PRIM'ITIVE, *a.* [It. *primitivo*; Fr. *primitif*; L. *primitivus*; from *primus*, first.]

1. Pertaining to the beginning or origin; original; first; as the *primitive* state of Adam; *primitive* innocence; *primitive* ages; the *primitive* church; the *primitive* christian church or institutions; the *primitive* fathers. *White. Tillotson.*

2. Formal; affectedly solemn; imitating the supposed gravity of old times. *Johnson.*

3. Original; primary; radical; not derived; as a *primitive* verb in grammar.

Primitive rocks, in geology, rocks supposed to be first formed, being irregularly crystalized, and aggregated without a cement, and containing no organic remains; as granite, gneiss, &c.

PRIM'ITIVE, *n.* An original word; a word not derived from another.

PRIM'ITIVELY, *adv.* Originally; at first. *Brown.*

2. Primarily; not derivatively.

3. According to the original rule or ancient practice. *South.*

PRIM'ITIVENESS, *n.* State of being original; antiquity; conformity to antiquity. *Johnson.*

PRIM'ITY, *n.* The state of being original. [*Not used.*] *Pearson.*

PRIM'NESS, *n.* [from *prim.*] Affected formality or niceness; stiffness; preciseness.

PRIMOGE'NIAL, *a.* [L. *primigenius.* See *Primigenial.*]

First born, made or generated; original; primary; constituent; elemental; as *primogenial* light; *primogenial* bodies. *Boyle.*

PRIMOGEN'ITOR, *n.* [L. *primus*, first, and *genitor*, father.] The first father or forefather. *Gayton.*

PRIMOGEN'ITURE, *n.* [L. *primus*, first, and *genitus*, begotten.]

1. The state of being born first of the same parents; seniority by birth among children.

2. In *law*, the right which belongs to the eldest son or daughter. Thus in Great Britain, the right of inheriting the estate of the father belongs to the eldest son, and in the royal family, the eldest son of the king is entitled to the throne by *primogeniture.* Among the females, the crown descends by right of *primogeniture* to the eldest daughter only and her issue. *Blackstone.*

Before the revolution, *primogeniture*, in some of the American colonies, entitled the eldest son to a double portion of his father's estate, but this right has been abolished.

PRIMOGEN'ITURESHIP, *n.* The right of eldership.

PRIMOR'DIAL, *a.* [Fr. from L. *primordialis, primordium*; *primus*, first, and *ordo*, order.]

First in order; original; existing from the beginning. *Boyle.*

PRIMOR'DIAL, *n.* Origin; first principle or element. *More.*

PRIMOR'DIAN, *n.* A kind of plum.

PRIMOR'DIATE, *a.* [See *Primordial.*] Original; existing from the first. *Boyle.*

PRIMP, *v. i.* To be formal or affected. [*Not English, or local.*]

PRIM'ROSE, *n.* *s* as *z.* [L. *primula veris*; *primus*, first, and *rose*; literally, the first or an early rose in spring.]

A plant of the genus Primula, of several varieties, as the white, the red, the yellow flowered, the cowslip, &c. Shakspeare uses the word for gay or flowery; as the *primrose* way.

PRI'MY, *a.* Blooming. [*Not used.*] *Shak.*

PRINCE, *n. prins.* [Fr. *id.*; It. Sp. *principe*; L. *princeps*; D. *prins*; G. *prinz*; Arm. *prinç.* This word is probably compounded of *primus*, corrupted, as the Gr. *πρων*, and *ceps*, head, Fr. *chef*; or perhaps of the Celtic *breen*, summit, whence W. *brenin*, king, an exalted one, and *ceps.* Hence *Brennus*, the name of a celebrated Gaulish commander. In Pers. بَرِين barin signifies lofty, or one elevated in place or office.]

1. In *a general sense*, a sovereign; the chief and independent ruler of a nation or state. Thus when we speak of the *princes* of Europe, we include emperors and kings. Hence, a chief in general; as a *prince* of the celestial host. *Milton.*

2. A sovereign in a certain territory; one who has the government of a particular state or territory, but holds of a superior to whom he owes certain services; as the *princes* of the German states.

3. The son of a king or emperor, or the issue of a royal family; as *princes* of the blood. In England, the eldest son of the king is created *prince* of Wales. *Encyc.*

4. The chief of any body of men. *Peacham.*

5. A chief or ruler of either sex. Queen Elizabeth is called by Camden *prince*, but this application is unusual and harsh.

Prince of the senate, in ancient Rome, was the person first called in the roll of senators. He was always of consular and censorian dignity. *Encyc.*

In *Scripture*, this name *prince* is given to God, Dan. viii; to Christ, who is called the *prince* of peace, Is. ix. and the *prince* of life, Acts iii.; to the chief of the priests, the *prince* of the sanctuary, Is. xliii.; to the Roman emperor, Dan. ix.; to men of superior worth and excellence, Eccles. x.; to nobles, counselors and officers of a kingdom, Is. x.; to the chief men of families or tribes, Num. xvii.; to Satan, who is called the *prince* of this world, John xii. and *prince* of the power of the air, Eph. ii.

PRINCE, *v. i.* To play the prince; to take state. *Shak.*

PRINCEDOM, *n. prins'dom.* The jurisdiction, sovereignty, rank or estate of a prince.

> Under thee, as head supreme,
> Thrones, *princedoms*, powers, dominions, I reduce. *Milton.*

PRINCELIKE, *a. prins'like.* Becoming a prince. *Shak.*

PRINCELINESS, *n. prins'liness.* [from *princely.*]

The state, manner or dignity of a prince. *Sherwood.*

PRINCELY, *a. prins'ly.* Resembling a prince; having the appearance of one high born; stately; dignified; as a *princely* gentleman; a *princely* youth. *Shak.*

2. Having the rank of princes; as a man of *princely* birth; a *princely* dame. *Sidney. Waller.*

3. Becoming a prince; royal; grand; august; as a *princely* gift; *princely* virtues. *Shak. Waller.*

4. Very large; as a *princely* fortune.

5. Magnificent; rich; as a *princely* entertainment.

PRINCELY, *adv. prins'ly.* In a princelike manner. *Johnson.*

PRINCES'-FETHER, *n.* A plant of the genus Amaranthus. *Fam. of Plants.*

Prince's metal, a mixture of copper and zink, in imitation of gold. *Encyc.*

PRIN'CESS, *n.* A female sovereign, as an empress or queen. *Dryden.*

2. A sovereign lady of rank next to that of a queen. *Johnson.*

3. The daughter of a king. *Shak.*

4. The consort of a prince; as the *princess* of Wales.

PRIN'CIPAL, *a.* [Fr. from L. *principalis*, from *princeps.*]

1. Chief; highest in rank, character or respectability; as the *principal* officers of a government; the *principal* men of a city, town or state. Acts xxv. 1 Chron. xxiv.

2. Chief; most important or considerable; as the *principal* topics of debate; the *principal* arguments in a case; the *principal* points of law; the *principal* beams of a building; the *principal* productions of a country.

> Wisdom is the *principal* thing. Prov. iv.

3. In *law*, a *principal challenge*, is where the cause assigned carries with it *prima facie* evidence of partiality, favor or malice. *Blackstone.*

4. In *music*, fundamental.

PRIN'CIPAL, *n.* A chief or head; one who takes the lead; as the *principal* of a faction, an insurrection or mutiny.

2. The president, governor, or chief in authority. We apply the word to the chief instructor of an academy or seminary of learning.

3. In *law*, the actor or absolute perpetrator of a crime, or an abettor. A *principal* in the first degree, is the absolute perpetrator of the crime; a *principal* in the second degree, is one who is present, aiding and abetting the fact to be done; distinguished from an *accessory.* In treason, all persons concerned are *principals.* *Blackstone.*

4. In *commerce*, a capital sum lent on interest, due as a debt or used as a fund; so called in distinction from *interest* or *profits.*

> Taxes must be continued, because we have no other means for paying off the *principal.* *Swift.*

5. One primarily engaged; a chief party; in distinction from an *auxiliary.*

> We were not *principals*, but auxiliaries in the war. *Swift.*

PRINCIPAL'ITY, *n.* [Fr. *principalité.*]

1. Sovereignty; supreme power. *Sidney. Spenser.*

2. A prince; one invested with sovereignty. Tit. iii. *Milton.*

3. The territory of a prince; or the country which gives title to a prince; as the *principality* of Wales.

4. Superiority; predominance. [*Little used.*] *Taylor.*

5. In *Scripture*, royal state or attire. Jer. xiii.

PRIN'CIPALLY, *adv.* Chiefly; above all.

> They mistake the nature of criticism, who think its business is *principally* to find fault. *Dryden.*

PRIN'CIPALNESS, *n.* The state of being principal or chief.

PRIN'CIPATE, *n.* Principality; supreme rule. *Barrow.*

PRINCIP'IA, *n. plu.* [L. *principium.*] First principles. *Ash.*

PRINCIPIA'TION, *n.* [from L. *principium.*] Analysis into constituent or elemental parts. [*Not used.*] *Bacon.*

PRIN'CIPLE, *n.* [It. *principio;* Fr. *principe;* L. *principium*, beginning.]

1. In *a general sense*, the cause, source or origin of any thing; that from which a thing proceeds; as the *principle* of motion; the *principles* of action. *Dryden.*

2. Element; constituent part; primordial substance.

Modern philosophers suppose matter to be one simple *principle*, or solid extension diversified by its various shapes. *Watts.*

3. Being that produces any thing; operative cause.

The soul of man is an active *principle.* *Tillotson.*

4. In *science*, a truth admitted either without proof, or considered as having been before proved. In the former sense, it is synonymous with *axiom;* in the latter, with the phrase, *established principle.*

5. Ground; foundation; that which supports an assertion, an action, or a series of actions or of reasoning. On what *principle* can this be affirmed or denied? He justifies his proceedings on the *principle* of expedience or necessity. He reasons on sound *principles.*

6. A general truth; a law comprehending many subordinate truths; as the *principles* of morality, of law, of government, &c.

7. Tenet; that which is believed, whether truth or not, but which serves as a rule of action or the basis of a system; as the *principles* of the Stoics, or of the Epicureans.

8. A *principle of human nature*, is a law of action in human beings; a constitutional propensity common to the human species. Thus it is a *principle of human nature* to resent injuries and repel insults.

PRIN'CIPLE, *v. t.* To establish or fix in tenets; to impress with any tenet, good or ill; *chiefly used in the participle.*

Men have been *principled* with an opinion, that they must not consult reason in things of religion. *Locke.*

2. To establish firmly in the mind. *Locke.*

PRIN'CIPLED, *pp.* Established in opinion or in tenets; firmly fixed in the mind.

PRIN'€OCK, } *n.* [Qu. *prink* or *prim* and
PRIN'€OX, } *cock.*] A coxcomb; a conceited person; a pert young rogue; a ludicrous word. [*Little used.*] *Shak.*

PRINK, *v. i.* [D. *pronken*, to shine, to make a show, to strut; G. *prangen*, to shine, to make a show; *prunken*, id.; Dan. *prunker*, to make a show, to strut; Sw. *prunka*, to make a figure. If *n* is casual, these words are radically the same as Sw. *prackt*, Dan. D. *pragt*, G. *pracht*, pomp, show, and all coinciding in origin with Ar. برق baraka, to shine, to adorn. See *Prance* and *Prank.*]

1. To prank; to dress for show.

2. To strut; to put on stately airs.

PRINT, *v. t.* [W. *printiaw*, to print; Fr. *imprimer, empreinte;* Sp. *imprimir;* It. *imprimere;* from L. *imprimo;* *in* and *premo*, to press; It. *improntare*, to print, to importune, and this from *prontare*, to importune, [that is, to press,] from *pronto*, ready, bold, L. *promptus*, that is, pressed or pressing forward. In W. *print* is said by Owen to be from *rhint*, a groove or notch, and if this is the original word, *print* must be a different word from the Fr. *imprimer.* The Italian unites the L. *premo* and *promo.*]

1. In *general*, to take or form letters, characters or figures on paper, cloth or other material by impression. Thus letters are taken on paper by impressing it on types blackened with ink. Figures are *printed* on cloth by means of blocks or a cylinder. The rolling press is employed to take prints on impressions from copper-plates. Thus we say, to *print* books, to *print* calico, to *print* tunes, music, likenesses, &c.

2. To mark by pressing one thing on another.

On his fiery steed betimes he rode,
That scarcely *prints* the turf on which he trod. *Dryden.*

3. To impress any thing so as to leave its form.

Perhaps some footsteps *printed* in the clay— *Roscommon.*

4. To form by impression.

Ye shall not make any cuttings in your flesh, nor *print* any marks upon you. Lev. xix.

PRINT, *v. i.* To use or practice the art of typography, or of taking impressions of letters, figures and the like.

2. To publish a book. [*Elliptical.*]

From the moment he *prints*, he must expect to hear no more of truth. *Pope.*

PRINT, *n.* A mark made by impression; any line, character, figure or indentation of any form, made by the pressure of one body or thing on another; as the *print* of the tooth or of the nails in flesh; the *print* of the foot in sand or snow; the *print* of a wheel; the *print* of types on paper. Hence,

2. The impressions of types in general, as to form, size, &c.; as a small *print;* a large *print;* a fair *print.*

3. That which impresses its form on any thing; as a butter *print;* a wooden *print.*

4. The representation or figure of any thing made by impression; as the *print* of the face; the *print* of a temple; *prints* of antiquities. *Dryden.*

5. The state of being printed and published. Diffidence sometimes prevents a man from suffering his works to appear in *print.*

I love a ballad in *print.* *Shak.*

6. A single sheet printed for sale; a newspaper.

The *prints*, about three days after, were filled with the same terms. *Addison.*

7. Formal method. [*Not in use.*] *Locke.*

Out of print, a phrase which signifies that, of a printed and published work, there are no copies for sale, or none for sale by the publisher.

PRINT'ED, *pp.* Impressed; indented.

PRINT'ER, *n.* One that prints books, pamphlets or papers.

3. One that stains or prints cloth with figures, as calico.

3. One that impresses letters or figures with copper-plates.

PRINT'ING, *ppr.* Impressing letters, characters or figures on any thing; making marks or indentations.

PRINT'ING, *n.* The art or practice of impressing letters, characters or figures on paper, cloth or other material; the business of a printer; typography.

PRINT'ING-INK, *n.* Ink used by printers of books.

PRINT'ING-PAPER, *n.* Paper to be used in the printing of books, pamphlets, &c.; as distinguished from writing-paper, press-paper, wrapping-paper, &c.

PRINT'ING-PRESS, *n.* A press for the printing of books, &c.

PRINT'LESS, *a.* That leaves no print or impression; as *printless* feet. *Milton.*

PRI'OR, *a.* [L. comp. Probably the first syllable is contracted from *pris, prid*, or some other word, for the Latin has *prisce, pristinus.*]

Preceding in the order of time; former; antecedent; anterior; as a *prior* discovery; *prior* obligation. The discovery of the continent of America by Cabot was six or seven weeks *prior* to the discovery of it by Columbus. The discovery of the Labrador coast by Cabot was on the 11th of June, 1499; that of the continent by Columbus, was on the first of August of the same year.

PRI'OR, *n.* [Fr. *prieur;* It. *priore;* L. *prior.*]

1. The superior of a convent of monks, or one next in dignity to an abbot. Priors are *claustral* or *conventical.* The *conventical* are the same as abbots. A *claustral* prior is one that governs the religious of an abbey or priory *in commendam*, having his jurisdiction wholly from the abbot. *Encyc.*

2. In some churches, one who presides over others in the same churches. *Ayliffe.*

PRI'ORATE, *n.* Government by a prior. *Warton.*

PRI'ORESS, *n.* A female superior of a convent of nuns. *Dryden.*

PRIOR'ITY, *n.* The state of being antecedent in time, or of preceding something else; as *priority* of birth. The *priority* of Homer or Hesiod has been a subject of dispute.

2. Precedence in place or rank. *Shak.*

Priority of debts, is a superior claim to payment, or to payment before others.

PRI'ORLY, *adv.* Antecedently. [*A bad word and not used.*] *Geddes.*

PRI'ORSHIP, *n.* The state or office of prior.

PRI'ORY, *n.* A convent of which a prior is the superior; in dignity below an abbey. *Shak.*

2. *Priories* are the churches given to priors *in titulum*, or by way of title. *Ayliffe.*

PRI'SAGE, *n.* [Fr. *prise*, from *priser*, to prize or value.]

A right belonging to the crown of England, of taking two tons of wine from every ship importing twenty tons or more; one before and one behind the mast. This by charter of Edward I. was exchanged into a duty of two shillings for every tun imported by merchant strangers, and called butlerage, because paid to the king's butler. *Blackstone.*

PRISCIL'LIANIST, *n.* In church history, one of a sect so denominated from Priscillian, a Spaniard, bishop of Avila, who practiced magic, maintained the errors of the Manichees, and held it to be lawful to make false oaths in the support of one's cause and interest. *Encyc.*

PRISM, *n.* [Fr. *prisme;* Low L. Sp. It. *prisma;* Gr. πρισμα, from πριω, to cut with a saw, to press or strain, Russ. *pru.*]

A solid whose bases or ends are any similar, equal and parallel plane figures, and whose sides are parallelograms. *D. Olmsted.*

A prism of glass is one bounded by two equal and parallel triangular ends and three plain and well polished sides which meet in three parallel lines, running from the three angles of one end to the three angles of the other end. *Newton.*

PRISMAT'IC, PRISMAT'ICAL, *a.* Resembling a prism; as a *prismatic* form.

2. Separated or distributed by a prism; formed by a prism; as *prismatic* colors.

3. Pertaining to a prism.

PRISMAT'ICALLY, *adv.* In the form or manner of a prism. *Boyle.*

PRISMATOID'AL, *a.* [L. *prisma* and Gr. ειδος.] Having a prismatic form. *Ure.*

PRIS'MOID, *n.* [L. *prisma* and Gr. ειδος, form.]

A body that approaches to the form of a prism. *Johnson.*

PRIS'MY, *a.* Pertaining to or like a prism. *Am. Review.*

PRISON, *n.* priz'n. [Fr. from *pris*, taken, from *prendre*, to take, L. *prendo*; Sp. *prision;* Arm. *prisoun.*]

1. In *a general sense*, any place of confinement or involuntary restraint; but appropriately, a public building for the confinement or safe custody of debtors and criminals committed by process of law; a jail. Originally, a prison, as Lord Coke observes, was only a place of safe custody; but it is now employed as a place of punishment. We have *state-prisons*, for the confinement of criminals by way of punishment.

2. Any place of confinement or restraint.

> The tyrant Æolus,
> With power imperial curbs the struggling winds,
> And sounding tempests in dark *prisons* binds. *Dryden.*

3. In *Scripture*, a low, obscure, afflicted condition. Eccles. iv.

4. The cave where David was confined. Ps. cxlii.

5. A state of spiritual bondage. Is. xlii.

PRIS'ON, *v. t.* To shut up in a prison; to confine; to restrain from liberty.

2. To confine in any manner. *Shak.*

3. To captivate; to enchain. *Milton.*

[This word is proper, but *imprison* is more commonly used.]

PRIS'ON-BASE, *n.* A kind of rural sports; commonly called *prison-bars. Sandys.*

PRIS'ONED, *pp.* Imprisoned; confined; restrained.

PRIS'ONER, *n.* One who is confined in a prison by legal arrest or warrant.

2. A person under arrest or in custody of the sherif, whether in prison or not; as a *prisoner* at the bar of a court.

3. A captive; one taken by an enemy in war.

4. One whose liberty is restrained, as a bird in a cage.

PRIS'ON-HOUSE, *n.* A house in which prisoners are confined; a jail. Judges xvi. *Shak.*

PRIS'ONING, *ppr.* Confining; imprisoning.

PRIS'ONMENT, *n.* Confinement in a prison; imprisonment.

[*The latter is commonly used.*] *Shak.*

PRIS'TINE, *a.* [L. *pristinus*. See *Prior* and *Præ.*]

First; original; primitive; as the *pristine* state of innocence; the *pristine* manners of a people; the *pristine* constitution of things. *Newton.*

PRITH'EE, a corruption of *pray thee*, as I *prithee;* but it is generally used without the pronoun, *prithee.*

PRI'VACY, *n.* [from *private.*] A state of being in retirement from the company or observation of others; secrecy.

2. A place of seclusion from company or observation; retreat; solitude; retirement.

> Her sacred *privacies* all open lie. *Rowe.*

3. Privity. [*Not used.*] [See *Privity.*] *Arbuthnot.*

4. Taciturnity. [*Not used.*] *Ainsworth.*

5. Secrecy; concealment of what is said or done.

PRIVA'DO, *n.* [Sp.] A secret friend. [*Not used.*] *Bacon.*

PRI'VATE, *a.* [L. *privatus*, from *privo*, to bereave, properly to strip or separate; *privus*, singular, several, peculiar to one's self, that is, separate; It. *privare*, Sp. *privar*, Fr. *priver*, to deprive. *Privo* is probably from the root of *bereave*, Sax. *bereafian* or *gereafian*, from *reafian*, to strip, to spoil, L. *rapio, diripio, eripio; privo* for *perivo* or *berivo;* W. *rhaib*, a snatching; *rheibiaw*, to snatch. See *Rip, Reap* and *Strip.*]

1. Properly, separate; unconnected with others; hence, peculiar to one's self; belonging to or concerning an individual only; as a man's *private* opinion, business or concerns; *private* property; the king's *private* purse; a man's *private* expenses. Charge the money to my *private* account in the company's books.

2. Peculiar to a number in a joint concern, to a company or body politic; as the *private* interest of a family, of a company or of a state; opposed to *public*, or to the general interest of nations.

3. Sequestered from company or observation; secret; secluded; as a *private cell;* a *private* room or apartment; *private* prayer.

4. Not publicly known; not open; as a *private* negotiation.

5. Not invested with public office or employment; as a *private* man or citizen; *private* life. *Shak.*

> A *private* person may arrest a felon. *Blackstone.*

6. Individual; personal; in contradistinction from *public* or *national;* as *private* interest.

Private way, in law, is a way or passage in which a man has an interest and right, though the ground may belong to another person. In common language, a *private* way may be a secret way, one not known or public.

A *private act* or *statute*, is one which operates on an individual or company only; opposed to a *general law*, which operates on the whole community.

A *private nusance* or *wrong*, is one which affects an individual. *Blackstone.*

In private, secretly; not openly or publicly. *Scripture.*

PRI'VATE, *n.* A secret message; particular business. [*Unusual.*] *Shak. B. Jonson.*

2. A common soldier.

PRIVATEE'R, *n.* [from *private.*] A ship or vessel of war owned and equipped by a private man or by individuals, at their own expense, to seize or plunder the ships of an enemy in war. Such a ship must be licensed or commissioned by government, or it is a pirate.

PRIVATEE'R, *v. i.* To cruise in a commissioned private ship against an enemy, for seizing their ships or annoying their commerce.

PRI'VATELY, *adv.* In a secret manner; not openly or publicly.

2. In a manner affecting an individual or company. He is not *privately* benefited.

PRI'VATENESS, *n.* Secrecy; privacy. *Bacon.*

2. Retirement; seclusion from company or society. *Wotton.*

3. The state of an individual in the rank of common citizens, or not invested with office.

PRIVA'TION, *n.* [Fr. from L. *privatio*, from *privo*. See *Private.*]

1. The state of being deprived; particularly, deprivation or absence of what is necessary for comfort. He endures his *privations* with wonderful fortitude.

2. The act of removing something possessed; the removal or destruction of any thing or quality. The garrison was compelled by *privation* to surrender.

> For what is this contagious sin of kind
> But a *privation* of that grace within? *Davies.*

3. Absence, in general. Darkness is a *privation* of light. *Encyc.*

4. The act of the mind in separating a thing from something appendant. *Johnson.*

5. The act of degrading from rank or office. *Bacon.*

[But in this sense, *deprivation* is now used. See *Deprivation.*]

PRIV'ATIVE, *a.* Causing privation.

2. Consisting in the absence of something; not positive. *Privative* is in *things*, what *negative* is in *propositions;* as *privative* blessings, safeguard, liberty and integrity. *Taylor.*

PRIV'ATIVE, *n.* That of which the essence is the absence of something. Blackness and darkness are *privatives. Bacon.*

2. In *grammar*, a prefix to a word which changes its signification and gives it a contrary sense, as α, in Greek; αδικος, unjust; α and δικη; *un* and *in* in English, as *unwise, inhuman.* The word may also be applied to suffixes, as *less*, in *harmless.*

PRIV'ATIVELY, *adv.* By the absence of something.

2. Negatively.

> The duty of the new covenant is set down first *privatively.* [*Unusual.*] *Hammond.*

PRIV'ATIVENESS, *n.* Notation of the absence of something. [*Little used.*]

PRIV'ET, *n.* A plant of the genus Ligustrum. The *evergreen privet* is of the genus Rhamnus. *Mock privet* is of the genus Phillyrea. *Fam. of Plants.*

PRIV'ILEGE, *n.* [Fr. from L. *privilegium*; *privus*, separate, private, and *lex*, law; originally a private law, some public act that regarded an individual.]

1. A particular and peculiar benefit or advantage enjoyed by a person, company or society, beyond the common advantages of other citizens. A privilege may be a particular right granted by law or held by custom, or it may be an exemption from some burden to which others are subject. The nobles of Great Britain have the *privilege* of being triable by their peers only. Members of parliament and of our legislatures have the *privilege* of exemption from arrests in certain cases. The powers of a banking company are *privileges* granted by the legislature.

He pleads the legal *privilege* of a Roman. *Kettlewell.*

The *privilege* of birthright was a double portion. *Locke.*

2. Any peculiar benefit or advantage, right or immunity, not common to others of the human race. Thus we speak of national *privileges*, and civil and political *privileges*, which we enjoy above other nations. We have ecclesiastical and religious *privileges* secured to us by our constitutions of government. *Personal privileges* are attached to the person; as those of embassadors, peers, members of legislatures, &c. *Real privileges* are attached to place; as the *privileges* of the king's palace in England.

3. Advantage; favor; benefit.

A nation despicable by its weakness, forfeits even the *privilege* of being neutral. *Federalist, Hamilton.*

Writ of privilege, is a writ to deliver a privileged person from custody when arrested in a civil suit. *Blackstone.*

PRIV'ILEGE, *v. t.* To grant some particular right or exemption to; to invest with a peculiar right or immunity; as, to *privilege* representatives from arrest; to *privilege* the officers and students of a college from military duty.

2. To exempt from censure or danger.

This place doth *privilege* me. *Daniel.*

PRIV'ILEGED, *pp.* Invested with a privilege; enjoying a peculiar right or immunity. The clergy in Great Britain were formerly a *privileged* body of men. No person is *privileged* from arrest for indictable crimes.

PRIV'ILEGING, *ppr.* Investing with a peculiar right or immunity.

PRIV'ILY, *adv.* [from *privy*.] Privately; secretly.

—False teachers among you, who shall *privily* bring in damnable heresies. 2 Pet. ii.

PRIV'ITY, *n.* [Fr. *privauté*. See *Private* and *Privy*.] Privacy; secrecy; confidence.

I will to you, in *privity*, discover the drift of my purpose. [*Little used.*] *Spenser.*

2. Private knowledge; joint knowledge with another of a private concern, which is often supposed to imply consent or concurrence.

All the doors were laid open for his departure, not without the *privity* of the prince of Orange. *Swift.*

But it is usual to say, "a thing is done with his *privity* and consent;" in which phrase, *privity* signifies merely private knowledge.

3. *Privities*, in the plural, secret parts; the parts which modesty requires to be concealed.

PRIV'Y, *a.* [Fr. *privé*; L. *privus*. See *Private*.]

1. Private; pertaining to some person exclusively; assigned to private uses; not public; as the *privy* purse; the *privy* coffer of a king. *Blackstone.*

2. Secret; clandestine; not open or public; as a *privy* attempt to kill one.

3. Private; appropriated to retirement; not shown; not open for the admission of company; as a *privy* chamber. Ezek. xxi.

4. Privately knowing; admitted to the participation of knowledge with another of a secret transaction.

He would rather lose half of his kingdom than be *privy* to such a secret. *Swift.*

Myself am one made *privy* to the plot. *Shak.*

His wife also being *privy* to it. Acts v.

5. Admitted to secrets of state. The *privy council* of a king consists of a number of distinguished persons selected by him to advise him in the administration of the government. *Blackstone.*

A *privy verdict*, is one given to the judge out of court, which is of no force unless afterward affirmed by a public verdict in court. *Blackstone.*

PRIV'Y, *n.* In *law*, a partaker; a person having an interest in any action or thing; as a *privy* in blood. Privies are of four kinds; privies in blood, as the heir to his father; privies in representation, as executors and administrators to the deceased; privies in estate, as he in reversion and he in remainder; donor and donee; lessor and lessee; privy in tenure, as the lord in escheat. *Encyc.*

2. A necessary house.

Privy chamber, in Great Britain, the private apartment in a royal residence or mansion. Gentlemen of the *privy chamber* are servants of the king, who are to wait and attend on him and the queen at court, in their diversions, &c. They are forty eight in number, under the lord chamberlain. *Encyc.*

PRIVY-COUN'SELOR, *n.* A member of the privy council.

Privy-counselors are made by the king's nomination without patent or grant. *Blackstone.*

PRIV'Y-SEAL, **PRIVY-SIG'NET**, } *n.* In *England*, the seal which the king uses previously in grants, &c. which are to pass the great seal, or which he uses in matters of subordinate consequence, which do not require the great seal.

2. *Privy-seal*, is used elliptically for the principal secretary of state, or person entrusted with the privy-seal.

The king's sign manual is the warrant to the *privy-seal*, who makes out a writ or warrant thereon to the chancery. The sign manual is the warrant to the *privy-seal*, and the *privy-seal* is the warrant to the great seal. *Blackstone.*

PRIZE, *n.* [Fr. *prise*, from *pris*, taken; Sp. Port. *presa*; G. *preis*; D. *prys*; Dan. *priis*; Sw. *pris*. See *Praise* and *Price*.] Literally, that which is taken; hence,

1. That which is taken from an enemy in war; any species of goods or property seized by force as spoil or plunder; or that which is taken in combat, particularly a ship. A privateer takes an enemy's ship as a *prize*. They make *prize* of all the property of the enemy.

2. That which is taken from another; that which is deemed a valuable acquisition.

Then prostrate falls, and begs with ardent eyes,
Soon to obtain and long possess the *prize*. *Pope.*

3. That which is obtained or offered as the reward of contest.

—I will never wrestle for *prize*. *Shak.*

I fought and conquer'd, yet have lost the *prize*. *Dryden.*

4. The reward gained by any performance. *Dryden.*

5. In *colloquial language*, any valuable thing gained.

6. The money drawn by a lottery ticket; opposed to *blank*.

PRIZE, *v. t.* [Fr. *priser*, from *prix*, price, L. *pretium*; It. *apprezzare*; Fr. *apprecier*. English analogy requires that the compound should be conformed to the orthography of this word, and written *apprize*.]

1. To set or estimate the value of; to rate; as, to *prize* the goods specified in an invoice.

Life I *prize* not a straw. *Shak.*

2. To value highly; to estimate to be of great worth; to esteem.

I *prize* your person, but your crown disdain. *Dryden.*

PRI'ZED, *pp.* Rated; valued; esteemed.

PRI'ZE-FIGHTER, *n.* One that fights publicly for a reward. *Pope.*

PRI'ZER, *n.* One that estimates or sets the value of a thing. *Shak.*

PRI'ZING, *ppr.* Rating; valuing; esteeming.

PRO, a Latin and Greek preposition, signifying *for*, *before*, *forth*, is probably contracted from *prod*, coinciding with It. *proda*, a prow, *prode*, brave; having the primary sense of moving forward. See *Prodigal*. In the phrase, *pro* and *con*, that is, *pro* and *contra*, it answers to the English *for*; *for* and *against*. *Prior.*

In composition, *pro* denotes *fore*, *forth*, *forward*.

PRO'A, *n.* Flying proa, a vessel used in the south seas, with the head and stern exactly alike, but with the sides differently formed. That which is intended for the lee side is flat, the other rounding. To prevent oversetting, the vessel is furnished with a frame extended from the windward side, called an out-rigger. *Encyc.*

PROBABIL'ITY, *n.* [Fr. *probabilité*; L. *probabilitas*. See *Probable*.]

1. Likelihood; appearance of truth; that state of a case or question of fact which results from superior evidence or preponderation of argument on one side, inclining the mind to receive it as the truth, but leaving some room for doubt. It therefore falls short of moral certainty, but produces what is called *opinion*.

Probability is the appearance of the agreement or disagreement of two ideas, by the intervention of proofs whose connection is not constant, but appears for the most part to be so. *Locke.*

Demonstration produces science or certain knowledge; proof produces belief, and *probability* opinion. *Encyc.*

2. Any thing that has the appearance of reality or truth. In this sense, the word admits of the plural number.

The whole life of man is a perpetual comparison of evidence and balancing of *probabilities*. *Buckminster.*

PROB'ABLE, *a.* [Fr. from L. *probabilis*, from *probo*, to prove. See *Prove.*]

1. Likely; having more evidence than the contrary, or evidence which inclines the mind to belief, but leaves some room for doubt.

That is accounted *probable*, which has better arguments producible for it than can be brought against it. *South.*

I do not say that the principles of religion are merely *probable*; I have before asserted them to be morally certain. *Wilkins.*

2. That renders something probable; as *probable* evidence, or *probable* presumption. *Blackstone.*

3. That may be proved. [*Not in use.*] *Milton.*

PROB'ABLY, *adv.* Likely; in likelihood; with the appearance of truth or reality; as, the story is *probably* true; the account is *probably* correct.

Distinguish between what may possibly, and what will *probably* be done. *L'Estrange.*

PRO'BANG, *n.* [See *Probe.*] In *surgery*, an instrument of whalebone and spunge, for removing obstructions in the throat or esophagus. *Coxe.*

A flexible piece of whalebone, with spunge fixed to the end. *Parr.*

PRO'BATE, *n.* [L. *probatus, probo*, to prove.]

1. The *probate* of a will or testament is the proving of its genuineness and validity, or the exhibition of the will to the proper officer, with the witnesses if necessary, and the process of determining its validity, and the registry of it, and such other proceedings as the laws prescribe, as preliminary to the execution of it by the executor.

2. The right or jurisdiction of proving wills. In England, the spiritual court has the *probate* of wills. In the United States, the *probate* of wills belongs to a court of civil jurisdiction established by law, usually to a single judge, called a judge of probate, or a surrogate.

3. Proof. [*Not used.*] *Skelton.*

PROBA'TION, *n.* [L. *probatio.*] The act of proving; proof. *Wilkins. Locke.*

2. Trial; examination; any proceeding designed to ascertain truth; in universities, the examination of a student, as to his qualifications for a degree.

3. In *a monastic sense*, trial or the year of novitiate, which a person must pass in a convent, to prove his virtue and his ability to bear the severities of the rule. *Encyc.*

4. Moral trial; the state of man in the present life, in which he has the opportunity of proving his character and being qualified for a happier state.

Probation will end with the present life. *Nelson.*

5. In *America*, the trial of a clergyman's qualifications as a minister of the gospel, preparatory to his settlement. We say, a man is preaching on *probation.*

6. In *general*, trial for proof, or satisfactory evidence, or the time of trial.

PROBA'TIONAL, *a.* Serving for trial. *Bp. Richardson.*

PROBA'TIONARY, *a.* Serving for trial.

All the *probationary* work of man is ended when death arrives. *Dwight.*

PROBA'TIONER, *n.* One who is on trial, or in a state to give proof of certain qualifications for a place or state.

While yet a young *probationer*,
And candidate for heaven. *Dryden.*

2. A novice. *Decay of Piety.*

3. In *Scotland*, a student in divinity, who, producing a certificate of a professor in an university of his good morals and qualifications, is admitted to several trials, and on acquitting himself well, is licensed to preach. *Encyc.*

PROBA'TIONERSHIP, *n.* The state of being a probationer; novitiate. [*Little used.*] *Locke.*

PROBA'TIONSHIP, *n.* A state of probation; novitiate; probation. [*Little used and unnecessary.*]

PRO'BATIVE, *a.* Serving for trial or proof. *South.*

PROBA'TOR, *n.* [L.] An examiner; an approver. *Maydman.*

2. In *law*, an accuser. *Cowel.*

PRO'BATORY, *a.* Serving for trial. *Bramhall.*

2. Serving for proof. *Bp. Taylor.*

3. Relating to proof. *Quintilian, Trans.*

Probatum est, [L. it is proved,] an expression subjoined to a receipt for the cure of a disease, denoting that it has been tried or proved.

PROBE, *n.* [from L. *probo*; Fr. *eprouvette*, a probe; G. *probe*, proof; Russ. *probivayu*, to pierce. The primary sense is to thrust, to drive, from straining, exertion of force.]

A surgeon's instrument for examining the depth or other circumstances of a wound, ulcer or cavity, or the direction of a sinus, or for searching for stones in the bladder and the like. *Encyc. Parr.*

PROBE, *v. t.* To examine a wound, ulcer or some cavity of the body, by the use of an instrument thrust into the part. *South.*

2. To search to the bottom; to scrutinize; to examine thoroughly into causes and circumstances.

PRO'BE-SCISSORS, *n.* Scissors used to open wounds, the blade of which, to be thrust into the orifice, has a button at the end. *Wiseman.*

PROB'ITY, *n.* [L. *probitas*, from *probo*, to prove; It. *probità*; Fr. *probité.*]

Primarily, tried virtue or integrity, or approved actions; but in general, strict honesty; sincerity; veracity; integrity in principle, or strict conformity of actions to the laws of justice. *Probity* of mind or principle is best evinced by *probity* of conduct in social dealings, particularly in adhering to strict integrity in the observance and performance of rights called *imperfect*, which public laws do not reach and cannot enforce.

PROB'LEM, *n.* [Fr. *probleme*; L. It. Sp. *problema*; Gr. προβλημα, from προβαλλω, to throw forward; προ and βαλλω, to throw, L. *pello.*] A question proposed.

1. In *logic*, a proposition that appears neither absolutely true nor false, and consequently may be asserted either in the affirmative or negative.

2. In *geometry*, a proposition in which some operation or construction is required, as to divide a line or an angle, to let fall a perpendicular, &c. *Encyc.*

3. In *general*, any question involving doubt or uncertainty, and requiring some operation, experiment or further evidence for its solution.

The *problem* is, whether a strong and constant belief that a thing will be, helps any thing to the effecting of the thing. *Bacon.*

PROBLEMAT'ICAL, *a.* Questionable; uncertain; unsettled; disputable; doubtful.

Diligent inquiries into *problematical* guilt, leave a gate wide open to informers. *Swift.*

PROBLEMAT'ICALLY, *adv.* Doubtfully; dubiously; uncertainly.

PROB'LEMATIZE, *v. t.* To propose problems. [*Ill formed and not used.*] *B. Jonson.*

PROBOS'CIS, *n.* [L. from the Gr. προβοσκις; προ, before, and βοσκω, to feed or graze.]

The snout or trunk of an elephant and of other animals, particularly of insects. The proboscis of an elephant is a flexible muscular pipe or canal of about 8 feet in length, and is properly the extension of the nose. This is the instrument with which he takes food and carries it to his mouth. The proboscis of insects is used to suck blood from animals, or juice from plants.

PROCA'CIOUS, *a.* [L. *procax*; *pro*, forward, and perhaps the root of It. *cacciare*, Sp. *cazar*, to chase, that is, to push forward.] Pert; petulant; saucy. [*Little used.*] *Barrow.*

PROCAC'ITY, *n.* [L. *procacitas.*] Impudence; petulance. [*Little used.*] *Burton.*

PROCATARC'TIC, *a.* [Gr. προκαταρκτικος; προ, κατα and αρχω, to begin.]

In *medicine*, pre-existing or predisposing; remote; as *procatarctic* causes of a disease, in distinction from *immediate* or *exciting* causes. Thus heat may be the *procatarctic*, and extreme fatigue the immediate or exciting cause of a fever.

PROCATARX'IS, *n.* [Gr. supra.] The predisposing cause of a disease. *Quincy.*

PROCE'DURE, *n.* [Fr. See *Proceed.*] The act of proceeding or moving forward; progress; process; operation; series of actions; as the *procedure* of the soul in certain actions. But it is more generally applied to persons; as, this is a strange *procedure* in a public body. The motions of physical causes are more generally denominated *operations.*

2. Manner of proceeding; management; conduct. *South.*

3. That which proceeds from something; produce. [*Not in use.*] *Bacon.*

PROCEE'D, PROCE'DE, *v. i.* [Fr. Sp. Port. *proceder*; It. *procedere*; from L. *procedo*; *pro*, forward, and *cedo*, to move. The more correct orthography is *procede*, in analogy with *precede, concede, recede, procedure.*]

1. To move, pass or go forward from one place to another; *applied to persons or things.* A man *proceeds* on his journey; a ship *proceeds* on her voyage.

This word thus used implies that the motion, journey or voyage had been previously commenced, and to *proceed* is then to *renew* or *continue* the motion or progress.

2. To pass from one point, stage or topic to another. The preacher *proceeds* from one division of his subject, and the advocate from one argument, to another.

3. To issue or come as from a source or fountain. Light *proceeds* from the sun; vice *proceeds* from a depraved heart; virtuous affections *proceed* from God.

4. To come from a person or place. Christ says, "I *proceeded* forth and came from God." John viii.

5. To prosecute any design.

He that *proceeds* on other principles in his inquiry into any sciences, posts himself in a party. *Locke.*

6. To be transacted or carried on.

He will, after his sour fashion, tell you,
What hath *proceeded* worthy note to-day.
[*Not now in use.*] *Shak.*

7. To make progress; to advance. *Milton.*

8. To begin and carry on a series of actions or measures. The attorney was at a loss in what manner to *proceed* against the offender. In this sense, the word is often followed by *against.*

9. To transact; to act; to carry on methodically.

From them I will not hide
My judgments, how with mankind I *proceed.* *Milton.*

10. To have a course.

This rule only *proceeds* and takes place, when a person cannot of common law condemn another by his sentence. *Ayliffe.*

11. To issue; to be produced or propagated.

From my loins thou shalt *proceed.* *Milton.*

12. To be produced by an effectual cause. All created things *proceed* from God. *Milton.*

PROCEE'DER, *n.* One who goes forward, or who makes a progress. *Bacon.*

PROCEE'DING, *ppr.* Moving forward; passing on; issuing; transacting; carrying on.

PROCEE'DING, *n.* Process or movement from one thing to another; a measure or step taken in business; transaction; in the plural, a course of measures or conduct; course of dealing with others. We speak of a legal or an illegal *proceeding,* a cautious *proceeding,* a violent *proceeding.* In *the plural,* the *proceedings* of the legislature have been wise and salutary. It is our duty to acquiesce cheerfully in all God's *proceedings* towards us.

2. In *law,* the course of steps or measures in the prosecution of an action is denominated *proceedings.* [See *Process.*]

PROCEE'DS, *n. plu.* Issue; rent; produce; as the *proceeds* of an estate.

2. In *commerce,* the sum, amount or value of goods sold or converted into money. The consignee was directed to sell the cargo and vest the *proceeds* in coffee. The *proceeds* of the goods sold amounted to little more than the prime cost and charges.

PROCELEUSMAT'I€, *a.* [Gr. προκελευσματικος; προ and κελευσμα, mandate, incitement.]

Inciting; animating; encouraging. This epithet is given to a metrical foot in poetry, consisting of four short syllables. *Johnson.*

PROCEP'TION, *n.* Preoccupation. [*Ill formed and not in use.*] *K. Charles.*

PROCER'ITY, *n.* [L. *proceritas,* from *procerus,* tall.] Tallness; highth of stature. [*Little used.*] *Addison.*

PROC'ESS, *n.* [Fr. *procès;* L. *processus,* from *procedo.* See *Proceed.*]

1. A proceeding or moving forward; progressive course; tendency; as the *process* of man's desire. *Hooker.*

2. Proceedings; gradual progress; course; as the *process* of a war. *Dryden.*

3. Operations; experiment; series of actions or experiments; as a chimical *process.*

4. Series of motions or changes in growth, decay, &c. in physical bodies; as the *process* of vegetation or of mineralization; the *process* of decomposition.

5. Course; continual flux or passage; as the *process* of time. *Milton. Boyle.*

6. Methodical management; series of measures or proceedings.

The *process* of the great day—is described by our Savior. *Nelson.*

7. In *law,* the whole course of proceedings, in a cause, real or personal, civil or criminal, from the original writ to the end of the suit. *Original process* is the means taken to compel the defendant to appear in court. *Mesne process* is that which issues, pending the suit, upon some collateral or interlocutory matter. *Final process* is the process of execution. *Blackstone.*

8. In *anatomy,* any protuberance, eminence or projecting part of a bone. *Encyc. Coxe.*

PROCES'SION, *n.* [Fr. from L. *processio.* See *Proceed.*]

1. The act of proceeding or issuing. *Pearson.*

2. A train of persons walking, or riding on horseback or in vehicles, in a formal march, or moving with ceremonious solemnity; as a *procession* of clergy and people in the Romish church; a triumphal *procession;* a funeral *procession.*

Him all his train
Follow'd in bright *procession.* *Milton.*

PROCES'SIONAL, *a.* Pertaining to a procession; consisting in a procession. *Saurin, Trans.*

PROCES'SIONAL, *n.* A book relating to processions of the Romish church. *Gregory.*

PROCES'SIONARY, *a.* Consisting in procession; as *processionary* service. *Hooker.*

PROCHEIN, *a. pro'shen.* [Fr. *prochain;* L. *proximus.*]

Next; nearest; used in the law phrase, *prochein amy,* the next friend, any person who undertakes to assist an infant or minor in prosecuting his rights. *Blackstone.*

PRO'€HRONISM, *n.* [Gr. προχρονεω, to precede in time; προ, before, and χρονος, time.]

An antedating; the dating of an event before the time it happened; hence, an error in chronology. *Gregory.*

PRO'CIDENCE, *n.* [L. *procidentia; procido,* to fall down.]

A falling down; a prolapsus; as of the intestinum rectum. *Coxe. Parr.*

PROCID'UOUS, *a.* That falls from its place. *Jones.*

PROCIN€T', *n.* [L. *procinctus; procingo,* to prepare, that is, to gird.]

Complete preparation for action. [*Little used.*] *Milton.*

PRO€LA'IM, *v. t.* [L. *proclamo; pro* and *clamo,* to cry out. See *Claim.*]

1. To promulgate; to announce; to publish; as, to *proclaim* a fast; to *proclaim* a feast. Lev. xxiii. 1 Kings xxi.

He hath sent me to *proclaim* liberty to the captives. Is. lxi.

2. To denounce; to give official notice of. Heralds were formerly employed to *proclaim* war.

3. To declare with honor; as, to *proclaim* the name of the Lord, that is, to declare his perfections. Ex. xxxiii.

4. To utter openly; to make public. Some profligate wretches openly *proclaim* their atheism.

Most men will *proclaim* every one his own goodness. Prov. xx.

5. To outlaw by public denunciation.

I heard myself *proclaimed.* *Shak.*

PRO€LA'IMED, *pp.* Published officially; promulgated; made publicly known.

PRO€LA'IMER, *n.* One who publishes by authority; one that announces or makes publicly known. *Milton.*

PRO€LA'IMING, *ppr.* Publishing officially; denouncing; promulgating; making publicly known.

PRO€LAMA'TION, *n.* [Fr. from L. *proclamatio,* from *proclamo.*]

1. Publication by authority; official notice given to the public.

King Asa made a *proclamation* throughout all Judah. 1 Kings xv.

2. In England, a declaration of the king's will, openly published.

Proclamations are a branch of the king's prerogative, and are binding on the subject. *Encyc.*

3. The declaration of any supreme magistrate publicly made known; as the *proclamation* of the governor appointing a day of thanksgiving.

4. The paper containing an official notice to a people. The sherif receives and distributes the governor's *proclamations.* *New England.*

PRO€LI'VE, *a.* Proclivous. [*Not used.*]

PRO€LIV'ITY, *n.* [L. *proclivitas, proclivis; pro* and *clivus,* a cliff.]

1. Inclination; propensity; proneness; tendency.

The sensitive appetite may engender a *proclivity* to steal, but not a necessity to steal. *Bp. Hall.*

2. Readiness; facility of learning.

He had such a dextrous *proclivity,* that his teachers were fain to restrain his forwardness. *Wotton.*

PRO€LI'VOUS, *a.* [L. *proclivus, proclivis,* supra.]

Inclined; tending by nature. *Dict.*

PRO€ON'SUL, *n.* [L. *pro,* for, and *consul.*]

A Roman magistrate sent to govern a

province with consular authority. The proconsuls were appointed from the body of the senate, and their authority expired at the end of a year from their appointment. *Encyc.*

PROCON'SULAR, *a.* Pertaining to a proconsul; as *proconsular* powers.

2. Under the government of a proconsul; as a *proconsular* province.

PROCON'SULSHIP, *n.* The office of a proconsul, or the term of his office.

PROCRAS'TINATE, *v. t.* [L. *procrastinor; pro* and *crastinus; cras,* to-morrow.]

To put off from day to day; to delay; to defer to a future time; as, to *procrastinate* repentance.

PROCRAS'TINATE, *v. i.* To delay; to be dilatory.

I *procrastinate* more than I did twenty years ago. *Swift.*

PROCRAS'TINATED, *pp.* Delayed; deferred.

PROCRAS'TINATING, *ppr.* Delaying; putting off to a future time.

PROCRASTINA'TION, *n.* [L. *procrastinatio.*]

A putting off to a future time; delay; dilatoriness.

PROCRAS'TINATOR, *n.* One that defers the performance of any thing to a future time.

PRO'CREANT, *a.* [L. *procreans.* See *Procreate.*]

Generating; producing; productive; fruitful. *Shak.*

PRO'CREATE, *v. t.* [L. *procreo; pro* and *creo,* to create.]

1. To beget; to generate and produce; to engender; *used properly of animals.* *Bentley.*

2. To produce; *used of plants, but hardly allowable.* *Blackmore.*

PRO'CREATED, *pp.* Begotten; generated.

PRO'CREATING, *ppr.* Begetting; generating; as young.

PROCREA'TION, *n.* [Fr. from L. *procreatio.*]

The act of begetting; generation and production of young. *South.*

PRO'CREATIVE, *a.* Generative; having the power to beget. *Hale.*

PRO'CREATIVENESS, *n.* The power of generating. *Decay of Piety.*

PRO'CREATOR, *n.* One that begets; a generator; a father or sire.

PROC'TOR, *n.* [contracted from L. *procurator,* from *procuro; pro* and *curo.*]

1. In *a general sense,* one who is employed to manage the affairs of another. *Hooker.*

2. *Appropriately,* a person employed to manage another's cause in a court of civil or ecclesiastical law, as in the court of admiralty, or in a spiritual court. *Swift.*

3. The magistrate of a university. *Walter.*

PROC'TOR, *v. i.* To manage; *a cant word.* *Shak.*

PROC'TORAGE, *n.* Management; in contempt. *Milton.*

PROCTOR'ICAL, *a.* Belonging to the academical proctor; magisterial. *Prideaux.*

PROC'TORSHIP, *n.* The office or dignity of the proctor of a university. *Clarendon.*

PROCUM'BENT, *a.* [L. *procumbens, procumbo; pro* and *cubo,* to lie down.] Lying down or on the face; prone.

2. In *botany,* trailing; prostrate; unable to support itself, and therefore lying on the ground, but without putting forth roots; as a *procumbent* stem. *Martyn.*

PROCU'RABLE, *a.* [from *procure.*] That may be procured; obtainable. *Boyle.*

PRO'CURACY, *n.* [from L. *procuro.*] The management of any thing. [*Not used.*]

PROCURA'TION, *n.* [L. *procuratio.* See *Procure.*]

1. The act of procuring. [*Procurement* is generally used.]

2. The management of another's affairs.

3. The instrument by which a person is empowered to transact the affairs of another. *Encyc.*

4. A sum of money paid to the bishop or archdeacon by incumbents, on account of visitations; called also *proxy.* *Todd.*

PROC'URATOR, *n.* The manager of another's affairs. [See *Proctor.*] *Shak. Taylor.*

PROCURATO'RIAL, *a.* Pertaining to a procurator or proctor; made by a proctor. *Ayliffe.*

PROCURA'TORSHIP, *n.* The office of a procurator. *Pearson.*

PROCU'RATORY, *a.* Tending to procuration.

PROCU'RE, *v. t.* [Fr. *procurer;* It. *procurare;* Sp. *procurar;* L. *procuro; pro* and *curo,* to take care. But the French only has the sense of the English word. In the sense of *manage,* it is never used.]

1. To get; to gain; to obtain; as by request, loan, effort, labor or purchase. We *procure* favors by request; we *procure* money by borrowing; we *procure* food by cultivating the earth; offices are *procured* by solicitation or favor; we *procure* titles to estate by purchase. It is used of things of temporary possession more generally than *acquire.* We do not say, we *acquired* favor, we *acquired* money by borrowing, but we *procured.*

2. To persuade; to prevail on.

What unaccustom'd cause *procures* her hither? [*Unusual.*] *Shak.*

3. To cause; to bring about; to effect; to contrive and effect.

Proceed, Salinus, to *procure* my fall. *Shak.*

4. To cause to come on; to bring on.

We no other pains endure
Than those that we ourselves *procure.* *Dryden.*

5. To draw to; to attract; to gain. Modesty *procures* love and respect.

PROCU'RE, *v. i.* To pimp. *Dryden.*

PROCU'RED, *pp.* Obtained; caused to be done; effected; brought on.

PROCU'REMENT, *n.* The act of procuring or obtaining; obtainment.

2. A causing to be effected.

They think it done
By her *procurement.* *Dryden.*

PROCU'RER, *n.* One that procures or obtains; that which brings on or causes to be done. *Walton.*

2. A pimp; a pander. *South.*

PROCU'RESS, *n.* A bawd. *Spectator.*

PROCU'RING, *ppr.* Getting; gaining; obtaining.

2. Causing to come or to be done.

3. *a.* That causes to come; bringing on. Sin is the *procuring* cause of all our woes.

PROD'IGAL, *a.* [Fr. *prodigue;* Sp. It. *prodigo;* from L. *prodigus,* from *prodigo,* to drive forth, to lavish. The last component part of the word is *ago,* to drive; the first I suppose to be *prod,* the original word, afterward contracted to *pro.* See *Pro.* The Welsh *bradyn,* a prodigal, if from the Latin, is doubtless of the same origin; but Owen deduces this from *brad,* a breaking, treachery, treason, and this coincides with Dan. *bryder,* to break. See *Brittle.*]

1. Given to extravagant expenditures; expending money or other things without necessity; profuse; lavish; wasteful; not frugal or economical; as a *prodigal* man; the *prodigal* son. A man may be *prodigal* of his strength, of his health, of his life or blood, as well as of his money.

2. Profuse; lavish; expended to excess or without necessity; as *prodigal* expenses.

3. Very liberal; profuse. Nature is *prodigal* of her bounties.

PROD'IGAL, *n.* One that expends money extravagantly or without necessity; one that is profuse or lavish; a waster; a spendthrift. *Dryden.*

PRODIGAL'ITY, *n.* [Fr. *prodigalité;* It. *prodigalità;* Sp. *prodigalidad.*]

1. Extravagance in the expenditure of what one possesses, particularly of money; profusion; waste; excessive liberality. It is opposed to *frugality, economy,* and *parsimony.*

By the Roman law a man of notorious *prodigality* was treated as non compos. *Encyc.*

The most severe censor cannot but be pleased with the *prodigality* of his wit. *Dryden.*

2. Profuse liberality.

PROD'IGALIZE, *v. i.* To be extravagant in expenditures. [*Not used.*] *Sherwood.*

PROD'IGALLY, *adv.* With profusion of expenses; extravagantly; lavishly; wastefully; as an estate *prodigally* dissipated.

2. With liberal abundance; profusely.

Nature not bounteous now, but lavish grows,
Our paths with flow'rs she *prodigally* strows. *Dryden.*

PRODIG'IOUS, *a.* [Sp. It. *prodigioso;* Fr. *prodigieux;* L. *prodigiosus.* See *Prodigy.*]

1. Very great; huge; enormous in size, quantity, extent, &c.; as a mountain of *prodigious* size or altitude; a *prodigious* mass or quantity of water; an ocean or plain of *prodigious* extent. Hence,

2. Wonderful; astonishing; such as may seem a prodigy; monstrous; portentous.

It is *prodigious* to have thunder in a clear sky. *Brown.*

Prodigious to relate. *Dryden.*

PRODIG'IOUSLY, *adv.* Enormously; wonderfully; astonishingly; as a number *prodigiously* great. *Ray.*

2. Very much; extremely; *in familiar language.* He was *prodigiously* pleased.

PRODIG'IOUSNESS, *n.* Enormousness of size; the state of having qualities that excite wonder or astonishment. *Hall.*

PROD'IGY, *n.* [L. *prodigium,* from *prodigo,* to shoot out, drive out, properly to spread to a great extent.]

1. Any thing out of the ordinary process of

nature, and so extraordinary as to excite wonder or astonishment; as a *prodigy* of learning. *Spectator.*

2. Something extraordinary from which omens are drawn; portent. Thus eclipses and meteors were anciently deemed *prodigies.*

3. A monster; an animal or other production out of the ordinary course of nature. *B. Jonson.*

PRODI''TION, *n.* [L. *proditio*, from *prodo*, to betray; supposed to be compounded of *pro* and *do*, to give. But in W. *bradu* is to betray.]

Treachery; treason. *Ainsworth.*

PROD'ITOR, *n.* [L.] A traitor. [*Not in use.*] *Shak.*

PRODITO'RIOUS, *a.* Treacherous; perfidious; traitorous. [*Not in use.*] *Daniel.*

2. Apt to make discoveries or disclosures. [*Not in use.*] *Wotton.*

PROD'ITORY, *a.* Treacherous; perfidious. *Milton.*

PRO'DROME, *n.* [Gr. προδρομος; προ and τρεχω, to run.]

A forerunner. [*Not in use.*] *Coles.*

PRODU'CE, *v. t.* [L. *produco*; *pro* and *duco*, to lead or draw; Sax. *teogan*, *teon*, to tug; It. *producere*, *produrre*; Sp. *producir*; Fr. *produire*.]

1. To bring forward; to bring or offer to view or notice; as, to *produce* a witness or evidence in court.

> *Produce* your cause. Is. xli.

2. To exhibit to the public.

> Your parents did not *produce* you much into the world. *Swift.*

3. To bring forth; to bear; as plants or the soil. Trees *produce* fruit; the earth *produces* trees and grass; wheat *produces* an abundance of food.

4. To bear; to generate and bring forth; as young. The seas *produce* fish in abundance.

> They—
> *Produce* prodigious births of body or mind. *Milton.*

5. To cause; to effect; to bring into existence. Small causes sometimes *produce* great effects. The clouds *produce* rain. The painter *produces* a picture or a landscape. The sculptor *produces* a statue. Vice *produces* misery.

6. To raise; to bring into being. The farmer *produces* grain enough for his family.

7. To make; to bring into being or form. The manufacturer *produces* excellent wares.

8. To yield or furnish. Money *produces* interest; capital *produces* profit. The commerce of the country *produces* a revenue to government.

9. In *general*, to bring into existence or into view.

10. To draw out in length; to extend; as a line *produced* from A to B. *Geometry.*

PROD'UCE, *n.* That which is produced, brought forth or yielded; product; as the *produce* of a farm; the *produce* of trees; the *produce* of a country; the *produce* of a manufacture; the *produce* of the sea; the *produce* of a tax; the *produce* of a mine. But when we speak of something formed by an individual artisan or genius, we call it a *production.*

PRODU'CED, *pp.* Brought into life, being or view; yielded.

PRODU'CEMENT, *n.* Production. [*Not used.*] *Milton.*

PRODU'CENT, *n.* One that exhibits or offers to view or notice. [*Not much used.*] *Ayliffe.*

PRODU'CER, *n.* One that generates; one that produces. *Locke. Suckling.*

PRODUCIBIL'ITY, *n.* The power of producing. [*Not used.*] *Barrow.*

PRODU'CIBLE, *a.* [It. *producibile*, *produttibile*.]

1. That may be brought into being; that may be generated or made; as *producible* salts. *Boyle.*

2. That may be brought into view or notice; that may be exhibited. *Hammond.*

PRODU'CIBLENESS, *n.* The state or quality of being producible; as the *producibleness* of salts. *Boyle.*

PRODU'CING, *ppr.* Generating; bringing into existence or notice.

PROD'UCT, *n.* [L. *productus*, from *produco*; Fr. *produit*.]

1. That which is produced by nature, as fruits, grain, metals; as the *product* of land; the *products* of the season.

2. That which is formed or produced by labor or by mental application; as the *products* of manufactures, of commerce or of art; the *products* of great and wise men. In the latter sense, *production* is now generally used.

In general, *products* comprehends whatever is produced or made; as when we speak of the *products* of a country exported.

> The *product* of the impost and excise. *Belknap, N. Hamp.*

3. Effect; result; something consequential.

> These are the *product*
> Of those ill mated marriages. *Milton.*

4. In *arithmetic*, the amount of two or more numbers multiplied. Thus $5\times7=35$, the product. *Product* results from *multiplication*, as *sum* does from *addition.*

5. In *geometry*, the factum of two or more lines.

PRODUC'TILE, *a.* That may be extended in length.

PRODUC'TION, *n.* [Fr. from L. *productio*.]

1. The act or process of producing, bringing forth or exhibiting to view.

2. That which is produced or made; as the *productions* of the earth, comprehending all vegetables and fruits; the *productions* of art, as manufactures of every kind, paintings, sculpture, &c.; the *productions* of intellect or genius, as poems and prose compositions.

PRODUC'TIVE, *a.* [It. *produttivo*; Sp. *productivo*.]

1. Having the power of producing; as, *productive* labor is that which increases the number or amount of products; opposed to *unproductive* labor. The labor of the farmer and mechanic is *productive*; the labor of officers and professional men is *unproductive* to the state. A tree which bears fruit, and the land which bears grass or grain, is *productive.*

2. Fertile; producing good crops. We often denote by this word that land or plants yield large *products.*

3. Producing; bringing into being; causing to exist; efficient; as an age *productive* of great men; a spirit *productive* of heroic achievments.

> This is turning nobility into a principle of virtue, and making it *productive* of merit. *Spectator.*

> And kindle with thy own *productive* fire. *Dryden.*

PRODUC'TIVENESS, *n.* The quality of being productive; as the *productiveness* of land or labor.

PRO'EM, *n.* [Fr. *proeme*; It. Sp. *proemio*; L. *prœmium*; Gr. προοιμιον; προ, before, and οιμη, οιμος, way.]

Preface; introduction; preliminary observations to a book or writing. *Swift. Milton.*

PRO'EM, *v. t.* To preface. [*Not used.*] *South.*

PROE'MIAL, *a.* Introductory; prefatory; preliminary. *Hammond. Johnson.*

PROEMP'TOSIS, *n.* [Gr. from προεμπιπτω, to fall before.]

In *chronology*, the lunar equation or addition of a day, necessary to prevent the new moon from happening a day too soon. *Cyc.*

PROFANA'TION, *n.* [Fr.; It. *profanazione*; Sp. *profanacion*; from L. *profano.* See *Profane.*]

1. The act of violating sacred things, or of treating them with contempt or irreverence; as the *profanation* of the sabbath by sports, amusements or unnecessary labor; the *profanation* of a sanctuary; the *profanation* of the name of God by swearing, jesting, &c.

2. The act of treating with abuse or disrespect.

> 'Twere *profanation* of our joys
> To tell the laity our love. *Donne.*

PROFA'NE, *a.* [L. *profanus*; *pro* and *fanum*, a temple; It. Sp. *profano*; Fr. *profane*.]

1. Irreverent to any thing sacred; *applied to persons.* A man is *profane* when he takes the name of God in vain, or treats sacred things with abuse and irreverence.

2. Irreverent; proceeding from a contempt of sacred things, or implying it; as *profane* words or language; *profane* swearing.

3. Not sacred; secular; relating to secular things; as *profane* history.

4. Polluted; not pure.

> Nothing is *profane* that serveth to holy things. *Raleigh.*

5. Not purified or holy; allowed for common use; as a *profane* place. Ezek. xlii. and xlviii.

6. Obscene; heathenish; tending to bring reproach on religion; as *profane* fables. 1 Tim. iv.

Profane is used chiefly in Scripture in opposition to *holy*, or qualified ceremonially for sacred services.

PROFA'NE, *v. t.* To violate any thing sacred, or treat it with abuse, irreverence, obloquy or contempt; as, to *profane* the name of God; to *profane* the sabbath; to *profane* the Scriptures or the ordinances of God. *Dwight.*

2. To pollute; to defile; to apply to temporal uses; to use as base or common. Ezek. xxiv.

3. To violate. Mal. ii.

4. To pollute; to debase. Lev. xxi.
5. To put to a wrong use. *Shak.*

PROFA'NED, *pp.* Violated; treated with irreverence or abuse; applied to common uses; polluted.

PROFA'NELY, *adv.* With irreverence to sacred things or names.

The character of God *profanely* impeached. *Dwight.*

2. With abuse or contempt for any thing venerable.

That proud scholar—speaks of Homer too *profanely*. *Broome.*

PROFA'NENESS, *n.* Irreverence of sacred things; particularly, the use of language which implies irreverence towards God; the taking of God's name in vain. *Dryden. Atterbury. Dwight.*

Profaneness in men is vulgar and odious; in females, is shocking and detestable.

PROFA'NER, *n.* One who by words or actions, treats sacred things with irreverence; one who uses profane language.

2. A polluter; a defiler; as a *profaner* of the temple. *Hooker.*

PROFA'NING, *ppr.* Violating; treating with irreverence; polluting.

PROFAN'ITY, *n.* Profaneness, which see.

In a revel of debauchery, amid the brisk interchange of *profanity* and folly, religion might appear a dumb, unsocial intruder. *Buckminster.*

PROFEC'TION, *n.* [L. *profectio.*] A going forward; advance; progression. [*Not in use.*] *Brown.*

PRO'FERT, *n.* [L. 3d. person of *profero.*] In *law*, the exhibition of a record or paper in open court.

PROFESS', *v. t.* [It. *professare*; Sp. *profesar*; Fr. *professer*; L. *professus*, *profiteor*; *pro* and *fateor.*]

1. To make open declaration of; to avow or acknowledge.

Let no man who *professes* himself a christian, keep so heathenish a family as not to see God be daily worshipped in it. *Decay of Piety.*

They *profess* that they know God, but in works they deny him. Tit. i.

2. To declare in strong terms.

Then will I *profess* to them, I never knew you. Matt. vii.

3. To make a show of any sentiments by loud declaration.

To your *professing* bosoms I commit him. *Shak.*

4. To declare publicly one's skill in any art or science, for inviting employment; as, to *profess* one's self a physician; he *professes* surgery.

PROFESS', *v. i.* To declare friendship. [*Not in use.*] *Shak.*

PROFESS'ED, **PROFEST'**, } *pp.* Openly declared, avowed or acknowledged; as a *professed* foe; a *professed* tyrant; a *professed* christian; a *professed* atheist.

PROFESS'EDLY, *adv.* By profession; by open declaration or avowal.

I could not grant too much to men—*professedly* my subjects. *K. Charles.*

England I traveled over, *professedly* searching all places as I passed along. *Woodward.*

PROFESS'ING, *ppr.* Openly declaring; avowing; acknowledging.

PROFES'SION, *n.* [Fr. from L. *professio.*]

1. Open declaration; public avowal or acknowledgment of one's sentiments or belief; as *professions* of friendship or sincerity; a *profession* of faith or religion.

The *professions* of princes, when a crown is the bait, are a slender security. *Lesley.*

The Indians quickly perceive the coincidence or the contradiction between *professions* and conduct, and their confidence or distrust follows of course. *J. Morse.*

2. The business which one professes to understand and to follow for subsistence; calling; vocation; employment; as the learned *professions.* We speak of the *profession* of a clergyman, of a lawyer, and of a physician or surgeon; the *profession* of lecturer on chimistry or mineralogy. But the word is not applied to an occupation merely mechanical.

3. The collective body of persons engaged in a calling. We speak of practices honorable or disgraceful to a *profession.*

4. Among the Romanists, the entering into a religious order, by which a person offers himself to God by a vow of inviolable obedience, chastity and poverty. *Encyc.*

PROFES'SIONAL, *a.* Pertaining to a profession or to a calling; as *professional* studies, pursuits, duties, engagements; *professional* character or skill.

PROFES'SIONALLY, *adv.* By profession or declaration. He is *professionally* a friend to religion.

2. By calling; as one employed *professionally.*

PROFESS'OR, *n.* [L.] One who makes open declaration of his sentiments or opinions, particularly, one who makes a public avowal of his belief in the Scriptures and his faith in Christ, and thus unites himself to the visible church. *Bacon. Hammond.*

2. One that publicly teaches any science or branch of learning; particularly, an officer in a university, college or other seminary, whose business is to read lectures or instruct students in a particular branch of learning; as a *professor* of theology or mathematics.

PROFESSO'RIAL, *a.* [L. *professorius.*] Pertaining to a professor; as the *professorial* chair. *Enfield.*

PROFESS'ORSHIP, *n.* The office of a professor or public teacher of the sciences. *Walton.*

PROFESS'ORY, *a.* Pertaining to a professor.

PROF'FER, *v. t.* [L. *profero*; *pro* and *fero*, to bear; It. *profferere*, *profferire*; Sp. *proferir*; Fr. *proferer.*]

1. To offer for acceptance; as, to *proffer* a gift; to *proffer* services; to *proffer* friendship.

2. To essay or attempt of one's own accord.

None
So hardy as to *proffer* or accept
Alone the dreadful voyage. *Milton.*

PROF'FER, *n.* An offer made; something proposed for acceptance by another; as *proffers* of peace or friendship.

He made a *proffer* to lay down his commission of command in the army. *Clarendon.*

2. Essay; attempt. *Bacon.*

PROF'FERED, *pp.* Offered for acceptance.

PROF'FERER, *n.* One who offers any thing for acceptance.

PROF'FERING, *ppr.* Offering for acceptance.

PROFI''CIENCE, **PROFI''CIENCY**, } *n.* [from L. *proficiens.* from *proficio*, to advance forward; *pro* and *facio*, to make.] Advance in the acquisition of any art, science or knowledge; improvement; progression in knowledge. Students are examined that they may manifest their *proficiency* in their studies or in knowledge.

PROFI''CIENT, *n.* One who has made considerable advances in any business, art, science or branch of learning; as a *proficient* in a trade or occupation; a *proficient* in mathematics, in anatomy, in music, &c.

PROFIC'UOUS, *a.* [L. *proficuus*, *proficio*, supra.]

Profitable; advantageous; useful. [*Little used.*] *Harvey.*

PROFILE, *n. pro'fil.* [Fr. *profil*; *pro* and *fil*; It. *profilo*; Sp. Port. *perfil*; *per* and *fil*, L. *filum*, a thread or line.]

1. Primarily, an outline or contour; hence, in sculpture and painting, a head or portrait represented sidewise or in a side view; the side face or half face; as, to draw or appear in *profile*; the *profile* of Pope or Addison.

2. In *architecture*, the contour or outline of a figure, building or member; also, the draught of a building, representing it as if cut down perpendicularly from the roof to the foundation. *Encyc.*

PRO'FILE, *v. t.* [Fr. *profiler*; It. *profilare*; Sp. *perfilar.*]

To draw the outline of a head sidewise; to draw in profile; as a building.

PRO'FILED, *pp.* Drawn so as to present a side view.

PRO'FILING, *ppr.* Drawing a portrait so as to represent a side view; drawing an outline. *Encyc.*

PROF'IT, *n.* [Fr. *profit*; It. *profitto*; from L. *profectus*, *proficio*, to profit, literally to proceed forward, to advance; *pro* and *facio.* The primary sense of *facio* is to urge or drive.]

1. In *commerce*, the advance in the price of goods sold beyond the cost of purchase. *Net profit* is the gain made by selling goods at an advanced price, or a price beyond what they had cost the seller, and beyond all costs and charges. The *profit* of the farmer and the manufacturer is the gain made by the sale of produce or manufactures, after deducting the value of the labor, materials, rents and all expenses, together with the interest of the capital employed, whether land, machinery, buildings, instruments or money.

Let no man anticipate uncertain *profits*. *Rambler.*

2. Any gain or pecuniary advantage; as an office of *profit* or honor.

3. Any advantage; any accession of good from labor or exertion; an extensive signification, comprehending the acquisition of any thing valuable, corporeal or intellectual, temporal or spiritual. A person may derive *profit* from exercise, amusements, reading, study, meditation, social intercourse, religious instruction, &c. Every improvement or advance in knowledge is *profit* to a wise man.

PROF'IT, *v. t.* [It. *profittare*; Fr. *profiter.*]

1. To benefit; to advantage; *applied to one's self*, to derive some pecuniary interest or some accession of good from any thing; as, to *profit one's self* by a commercial undertaking, or by reading or instruction. In this sense, the verb is generally used

intransitively. *Applied to others,* to communicate good to; to advance the interest of.

Brethren, if I come to you speaking with tongues, what shall I *profit you?* 1 Cor. xiv.
Whereto might the strength of their hands *profit me?* Job xxx.

2. To improve; to advance.

It is a great means of *profiting* yourself, to copy diligently excellent pieces and beautiful designs. *Dryden.*

PROF'IT, *v. i.* To gain advantage in pecuniary interest; as, to *profit* by trade or manufactures.

2. To make improvement; to improve; to grow wiser or better; to advance in any thing useful; as, to *profit* by reading or by experience.

She has *profited* by your counsel. *Dryden.*

3. To be of use or advantage; to bring good to.

Riches *profit* not in the day of wrath. Prov. xi.

PROF'ITABLE, *a.* [Fr.] Yielding or bringing profit or gain; gainful; lucrative; as a *profitable* trade; *profitable* business; a *profitable* study or profession.

2. Useful; advantageous.

What was so *profitable* to the empire, became fatal to the emperor. *Arbuthnot.*

PROF'ITABLENESS, *n.* Gainfulness; as the *profitableness* of trade.

2. Usefulness; advantageousness. *More. Calamy.*

PROF'ITABLY, *adv.* With gain; gainfully. Our ships are *profitably* employed.

2. Usefully; advantageously; with improvement. Our time may be *profitably* occupied in reading.

PROF'ITED, *pp.* Benefited; advanced in interest or happiness; improved.

What is a man *profited,* if he shall gain the whole world and lose his own soul? Matt. xvi.

PROF'ITING, *ppr.* Gaining interest or advantage; improving.

PROF'ITING, *n.* Gain; advantage; improvement.

That thy *profiting* may appear to all. 1 Tim. iv.

PROF'ITLESS, *a.* Void of profit, gain or advantage. *Shak.*

PROF'LIGACY, *n.* [See *Profligate.*] A profligate or very vicious course of life; a state of being abandoned in moral principle and in vice. *Barrington.*

PROF'LIGATE, *a.* [L. *profligatus, profligo,* to rout, to ruin; *pro* and *fligo,* to drive or dash. The word then signifies dashed, broken or ruined in morals. See *Flog* and *Afflict.*]

Abandoned to vice; lost to principle, virtue or decency; extremely vicious; shameless in wickedness; as a *profligate* man or wretch.

Next age will see
A race more *profligate* than we. *Roscommon.*
Made prostitute and *profligate* the muse,
Debas'd to each obscene and impious use. *Dryden.*

PROF'LIGATE, *n.* An abandoned man; a wretch who has lost all regard to good principles, virtue or decency.

How could such a *profligate* as Antony, or a boy of eighteen like Octavius, ever dare to dream of giving law to such an empire? *Swift.*

PROF'LIGATE, *v. t.* To drive away; *a Latin signification.* [*Not used.*]

2. To overcome. [*Not used.*] *Harvey.*

PROF'LIGATELY, *adv.* Without principle or shame. *Swift.*

2. In a course of extreme viciousness; as, to spend life *profligately.*

PROF'LIGATENESS, *n.* The quality or state of being lost to virtue and decency. *Butler.*

2. An abandoned course of life: extreme viciousness; profligacy.

PROFLIGA'TION, *n.* Defeat; rout. [*Not used.*] *Bacon.*

PROF'LUENCE, *n.* [L. *profluens, profluo; pro* and *fluo,* to flow.]

A progress or course. [*Not used.*] *Wotton.*

PROF'LUENT, *a.* Flowing forward; as a *profluent* stream. *Milton.*

PROFOUND', *a.* [Fr. *profond;* It. *profondo;* Sp. *profundo;* L. *profundus; pro* and *fundus,* bottom. See *Found.*]

1. Deep; descending or being far below the surface, or far below the adjacent places; as a gulf *profound.* *Milton.*

2. Intellectually deep; that enters deeply into subjects; not superficial or obvious to the mind; as a *profound* investigation; *profound* reasoning; a *profound* treatise.

3. Humble; very lowly; submissive; as a *profound* reverence for the Supreme Being. *Duppa.*

4. Penetrating deeply into science or any branch of learning; as a *profound* scholor; a *profound* mathematician; a *profound* historian.

5. Deep in skill or contrivance.

The revolters are *profound* to make slaughter. Hos. v.

6. Having hidden qualities.

Upon the corner of the moon
There hangs a vap'rous drop *profound.* *Shak.*

PROFOUND', *n.* The deep; the sea; the ocean; as the vast *profound.* *Dryden.*

2. The abyss.

I travel this *profound.* *Milton.*

PROFOUND', *v. i.* To dive; to penetrate. [*Not in use.*] *Glanville.*

PROFOUND'LY, *adv.* Deeply; with deep concern.

Why sigh you so *profoundly?* *Shak.*

2. With deep penetration into science or learning; with deep knowledge or insight; as *profoundly* wise; *profoundly* skilled in music or painting. *Dryden.*

PROFOUND'NESS, *n.* Depth of place.

2. Depth of knowledge or of science. *Hooker.*

PROFUND'ITY, *n.* [It. *profondità;* Sp. *profundidad;* from L. *profundus.*]

Depth of place, of knowledge or of science. *Milton.*

PROFU'SE, *a.* [L. *profusus, profundo,* to pour out; *pro* and *fundo.*]

1. Lavish; liberal to excess; prodigal; as a *profuse* government; a *profuse* administration. Henry the eighth, a *profuse* king, dissipated the treasures which the parsimony of his father had amassed. A man's friends are generally too *profuse* of praise, and his enemies too sparing.

2. Extravagant; lavish; as *profuse* expenditures.

3. Overabounding; exuberant.

On a green shady bank, *profuse* of flowers— *Milton.*
O liberty! thou goddess heavenly bright,
Profuse of bliss— *Addison.*
Profuse ornament in painting, architecture or gardening, as well as in dress or in language, shows a mean or corrupted taste. *Kames.*

PROFU'SE, *v. t. s* as *z.* To pour out. [*Little used.*] *Armstrong.*

2. To squander. [*Little used.*] *Steele.*

PROFU'SELY, *adv.* Lavishly; prodigally; as an income *profusely* expended.

2. With exuberance; with rich abundance. The earth is *profusely* adorned with flowers; ornaments may be too *profusely* scattered over a building.

PROFU'SENESS, *n.* Lavishness; prodigality; extravagant expenditures.

Hospitality sometimes degenerates into *profuseness.* *Atterbury.*

2. Great abundance; profusion; as *profuseness* of ornaments.

PROFU'SION, *n. s* as *z.* [L. *profusio.*]

1. Lavishness; prodigality; extravagance of expenditures; as, to waste an estate by *profusion.*

What meant thy pompous progress through the empire,
Thy vast *profusion* to the factious nobles? *Rowe.*

2. Lavish effusion.

He was desirous to avoid not only *profusion,* but the least effusion of christian blood. *Hayward.*

3. Rich abundance; exuberant plenty. The table contained a *profusion* of dainties. Our country has a *profusion* of food for man and beast.

The raptur'd eye
The fair *profusion,* yellow autumn, spies. *Thomson.*

PROG, *v. i.* [D. *prachgen,* to beg; Dan. *prakker,* id.; Sw. *pracka,* to make use of shifts; L. *proco, procor.*]

1. To shift meanly for provisions; to wander about and seek provisions where they are to be found; to live by beggarly tricks. [*A low word.*]

You are the lion; I have been endeavoring to *prog* for you. *Burke.*

PROG, *n.* Victuals or provisions sought by begging or found by wandering about.

2. Victuals of any kind. [*A low word.*] *Swift.*

PROG, *n.* One that seeks his victuals by wandering and begging.

PROĠEN'ERATE, *v. t.* [L. *progenero.*] To beget. [*Not in use.*]

PROĠENERA'TION, *n.* The act of begetting; propagation. [*Not used.*]

PROĠEN'ITOR, *n.* [L. from *progigno; pro* and *gigno,* to beget, Gr. γειναω.]

An ancestor in the direct line; a forefather. Adam was the *progenitor* of the human race.

PROĠEN'ITURE, *n.* A begetting or birth. [*Little used.*]

PROĠ'ENY, *n.* [It. *progenie;* L. *progenies,* from *progignor.*]

Offspring; race; children; descendants of the human kind, or offspring of other animals; as the *progeny* of a king; the *progeny* of Adam; the *progeny* of beasts or fowls; *a word of general application.*

PROGNO'SIS, *n.* [Gr. προγνωσις, from προγινωσκω, to know before; προ and γινωσκω.]

In *medicine*, the art of foretelling the event of a disease; the judgment of the event of a disease by particular symptoms. *Coxe. Hooper.*

PROGNOS'TI€, *a.* Foreshowing; indicating something future by signs or symptoms; as the *prognostic* symptoms of a disease; *prognostic* signs.

PROGNOS'TI€, *n.* In *medicine*, the judgment formed concerning the event of a disease by means of the symptoms. *Encyc.*

2. Something which foreshows; a sign by which a future event may be known or foretold.

In *medicine*, a sign or symptom indicating the event of a disease. The appearance of the tongue—is of considerable importance as a *prognostic*. *Parr.*

3. A foretelling; prediction. *Swift.*

PROGNOS'TI€ABLE, *a.* That may be foreknown or foretold. *Brown.*

PROGNOS'TI€ATE, *v. t.* [from *prognostic*; It. *prognosticare.*]

1. To foreshow; to indicate a future event by present signs. A clear sky at sunset *prognosticates* a fair day.

2. To foretell by means of present signs; to predict.

> I neither will nor can *prognosticate*
> To the young gaping heir his father's fate.
> *Dryden.*

PROGNOS'TI€ATED, *pp.* Foreshown; foretold.

PROGNOS'TI€ATING, *ppr.* Foreshowing; foretelling.

PROGNOSTI€A'TION, *n.* The act of foreshowing a future event by present signs.

2. The act of foretelling an event by present signs. *Burnet.*

3. A foretoken; previous sign. *Shak.*

PROGNOS'TI€ATOR, *n.* A foreknower or foreteller of a future event by present signs.

PROGRAM'MA, *n.* [Gr. from προγραφω, to write previously; προ and γραφω, to write.]

1. Anciently, a letter sealed with the king's seal. *Encyc.*

2. In *a university*, a billet or advertisement to invite persons to an oration. *Encyc.*

3. A proclamation or edict posted in a public place. *Life of A. Wood.*

4. That which is written before something else; a preface. *Warton.*

PROG'RESS, *n.* [Fr. *progrès*; Sp. *progreso*; L. *progressus, progredior*; *pro* and *gradior*, to step or go. See *Grade* and *Degree.*]

1. A moving or going forward; a proceeding onward. A man makes a slow *progress* or a rapid *progress* on a journey; a ship makes slow *progress* against the tide. He watched the *progress* of the army on its march, or the *progress* of a star or comet.

2. A moving forward in growth; increase; as the *progress* of a plant or animal.

3. Advance in business of any kind; as the *progress* of a negotiation; the *progress* of arts.

4. Advance in knowledge; intellectual or moral improvement; proficiency. The student is commended for his *progress* in learning; the christian for his *progress* in virtue and piety.

5. Removal; passage from place to place.

> From Egypt arts their *progress* made to Greece. *Denham.*

6. A journey of state; a circuit. *Blackstone. Addison.*

PROGRESS', *v. i.* To move forward in space; to pass; to proceed.

> Let me wipe off this honorable dew
> That silverly doth *progress* on thy cheeks.
> *Shak.*
>
> —Although the popular blast
> Hath rear'd thy name up to bestride a cloud,
> Or *progress* in the chariot of the sun.
> *Broken Heart, by Ford, vol. 1. p.* 303, *Gifford's Ed. Lond.* 1827.

[These authors accent the first syllable, but the accent is now on the second.]

2. To proceed; to continue onward in course.

> After the war had *progressed* for some time. *Marshall.*

3. To advance; to make improvement. *Du Ponceau. Bayard.*

PROGRES'SION, *n.* [Fr. from L. *progressio, progredior.*]

1. The act of moving forward; a proceeding in a course; motion onwards. *Locke.*

2. Intellectual advance; as the *progression* of thought. *Locke.*

3. Course; passage. *Shak.*

4. In *mathematics*, regular or proportional advance in increase or decrease of numbers; continued proportion, arithmetical or geometrical. Continued arithmetical proportion, is when the terms increase or decrease by equal differences. Thus,

2. 4. 6. 8. 10. } by the difference 2.
10. 8. 6. 4. 2. }

Geometrical proportion or progression, is when the terms increase or decrease by equal ratios. Thus,

2. 4. 8. 16. 32. 64. } by a con-
64. 32. 16. 8. 4. 2. } tinual multiplication or division by 2. *Encyc.*

PROGRES'SIONAL, *a.* That advances; that is in a state of advance. *Brown.*

PROGRESS'IVE, *a.* Moving forward; proceeding onward; advancing; as *progressive* motion or course; opposed to *retrograde.* *Bacon. Ray.*

2. Improving. The arts are in a *progressive* state.

PROGRESS'IVELY, *adv.* By motion onward; by regular advances. *Hooker.*

PROGRESS'IVENESS, *n.* The state of moving forward; an advancing; state of improvement; as the *progressiveness* of science, arts or taste.

PROHIB'IT, *v. t.* [L. *prohibeo*; *pro* and *habeo*, to hold; Fr. *prohiber*; It. *proibire*; Sp. *prohibir.*]

1. To forbid; to interdict by authority; *applicable to persons or things, but implying authority or right.* God *prohibited* Adam to eat of the fruit of a certain tree. The moral law *prohibits* what is wrong and commands what is right. We *prohibit* a person to do a thing, and we *prohibit* the thing to be done.

2. To hinder; to debar; to prevent; to preclude.

> Gates of burning adamant,
> Barr'd over us, *prohibit* all egress. *Milton.*

PROHIB'ITED, *pp.* Forbid; interdicted; hindered.

PROHIB'ITER, *n.* One who prohibits or forbids; a forbidder; an interdicter.

PROHIB'ITING, *ppr.* Forbidding; interdicting; debarring.

PROHIBI''TION, *n.* [Fr. from L. *prohibitio.*]

1. The act of forbidding or interdicting; a declaration to hinder some action; interdict.

> The law of God in the ten commandments consists mostly of *prohibitions*; "thou shalt not do such a thing." *Tillotson.*

2. In *law*, a *writ of prohibition*, is a writ issuing from a superior tribunal, directed to the judges of an inferior court, commanding them to cease from the prosecution of a suit. By ellipsis, *prohibition* is used for the writ itself. *Blackstone.*

PROHIB'ITIVE, } *a.* Forbidding; implying prohibition.
PROHIB'ITORY, } *Barrow. Ayliffe.*

PROIN, *v. t.* [Fr. *provigner*; *pro* and *vigne*, vine.] To lop; to trim; to prune. *Obs.* [See *Prune.*] *B. Jonson.*

PROIN, *v. i.* To be employed in pruning. *Obs.* *Bacon.*

PROJE€T', *v. t.* [L. *projicio*; *pro*, forward, and *jacio*, to throw; It. *progettare*; Fr. *projeter*; Sp. *proyectar.*]

1. To throw out; to cast or shoot forward.

> Th' ascending villas
> *Project* long shadows o'er the crystal tide.
> *Pope.*

2. To cast forward in the mind; to scheme; to contrive; to devise something to be done; as, to *project* a plan for paying off the national debt; to *project* an expedition to South America; to *project* peace or war. *Milton.*

3. To draw or exhibit, as the form of any thing; to delineate.

PROJE€T', *v. i.* To shoot forward; to extend beyond something else; to jut; to be prominent; as, the cornice *projects.*

PROJ'E€T, *n.* [Fr. *projet.*] A scheme; a design; something intended or devised; contrivance; as the *project* of a canal from the Hudson to the lakes; all our *projects* of happiness are liable to be frustrated.

2. An idle scheme; a design not practicable; as a man given to *projects.*

PROJE€T'ED, *pp.* Cast out or forward; schemed; devised; delineated.

PROJE€T'ILE, *a.* Impelling forward; as a *projectile* force.

2. Given by impulse; impelled forward; as *projectile* motion. *Arbuthnot.*

PROJE€T'ILE, *n.* A body projected, or impelled forward by force, particularly through the air.

2. *Projectiles*, in mechanical philosophy, is that part which treats of the motion of bodies thrown or driven by an impelling force from the surface of the earth, and affected by gravity and the resistance of the air.

PROJE€T'ING, *ppr.* Throwing out or forward; shooting out; jutting; scheming; contriving.

PROJE€'TION, *n.* [L. *projectio.*] The act of throwing or shooting forward. *Brown.*

2. A jutting out; extension beyond something else.

3. The act of scheming; plan; scheme; design of something to be executed.

4. Plan; delineation; the representation of something; as the *projection* of the sphere, is a representation of the circles on the surface of the sphere. There are three principal points of *projection*; the *stereographic*, in which the eye is supposed to be placed on the surface of the sphere; the *orthographic*, in which the eye is supposed to be at an infinite distance; and the *gnomonic*, in which the eye is placed in the center of the sphere. *Encyc.*

In perspective, *projection* denotes the appearance or representation of an object on the perspective plane. *Encyc.*

5. In *alchimy*, the casting of a certain powder, called *powder of projection*, into a crucible or other vessel full of some prepared metal or other matter, which is to be thereby transmuted into gold. *Encyc.*

PROJECT'MENT, *n.* Design; contrivance. [*Little used.*] *Clarendon.*

PROJECT'OR, *n.* One who forms a scheme or design. *Addison.*

2. One who forms wild or impracticable schemes. *Pope.*

PROJECT'URE, *n.* A jutting or standing out beyond the line or surface of something else. *Encyc.*

PROLAPSE, *n.* *prolaps'.* [L. *prolapsus*, *prolabor.*]

A falling down or falling out of some part of the body, as of the uterus or intestines. *Encyc.*

PROLAPSE, *v. i.* *prolaps'.* To fall down or out: to project too much.

PROLAP'SION, **PROLAP'SUS.** [See *Prolapse.*]

PROLA'TE, *v. t.* [L. *prolatum*, *profero.*] To utter; to pronounce. [*Not used.*] *Howell.*

PRO'LATE, *a.* [supra.] Extended beyond the line of an exact sphere. A prolate spheriod is produced by the revolution of a semi-ellipsis about its larger diameter. *Encyc.*

PROLA'TION, *n.* [L. *prolatio*, from *profero.*] Utterance; pronunciation. [*Little used.*] *Ray.*

2. Delay; act of deferring. [*Not used.*] *Ainsworth.*

3. A method in music of determining the power of semibreves and minims. *Busby.*

PROLEGOM'ENA, *n. plu.* [Gr. προλεγομενα; προ and λεγω, to speak.]

Preliminary observations; introductory remarks or discourses prefixed to a book or treatise. *Walton.*

PROLEP'SIS, **PROLEP'SY**, *n.* [Gr. προληψις, from προλαμβανω; προ and λαμβανω, to take.]

1. Anticipation; a figure in rhetoric by which objections are anticipated or prevented. *Bramhall.*

2. An error in chronology, when an event is dated before the actual time; an anachronism. *Theobald.*

PROLEP'TIC, **PROLEP'TICAL**, *a.* Pertaining to prolepsis or anticipation.

2. Previous; antecedent. *Glanville.*

3. In *medicine*, anticipating the usual time; applied to a periodical disease, whose paroxysm returns at an earlier hour at every repetition. *Encyc.*

PROLEP'TICALLY, *adv.* By way of anticipation.

PROLETA'RIAN, *a.* [L. *proletarius*, from *proles*, offspring.] Mean; vile; vulgar. [*Not used.*] *Hudibras.*

PRO'LETARY, *n.* A common person. [*Not used.*] *Burton.*

PROLIF'EROUS, *a.* [infra.] In *botany*, prolific; as a *proliferous* flower. *Lee. Martyn.*

A *proliferous* stem is one which puts forth branches only from the center of the top, or which shoots out new branches from the summits of the former ones, as the pine and fir. *Martyn. Smith.*

A *proliferous* umbel is a compound umbel which has the umbellicle subdivided. *Martyn.*

PROLIF'IC, **PROLIF'ICAL**, *a.* [It. Sp. *prolifico*; Fr. *prolifique*; L. *proles*, offspring, and *facio*, to make.]

1. Producing young or fruit; fruitful; generative; productive; *applied to animals and plants*; as a *prolific* female; a *prolific* tree.

2. Productive; having the quality of generating; as a controversy *prolific* of evil consequences; a *prolific* brain.

3. A *prolific* flower, [*prolifer*,] in botany, is one which produces a second flower from its own substance, or which has smaller flowers growing out of the principal one. But *proliferous* is commonly used. *Encyc. Martyn.*

PROLIF'ICACY, *n.* Fruitfulness; great productiveness. *Encyc.*

PROLIF'ICALLY, *adv.* Fruitfully; with great increase.

PROLIFICA'TION, *n.* [See *Prolific.*] The generation of young or of plants.

2. In *botany*, the production of a second flower from the substance of the first. This is either from the center of a simple flower, or from the side of an aggregate flower. *Lee.*

PROLIF'ICNESS, *n.* The state of being prolific. *Scott.*

PRO'LIX, *a.* [L. *prolixus*; *pro* and *laxus*, literally drawn out.]

1. Long; extended to a great length; minute in narration or argument; *applied only to discourses, speeches and writings*; as a *prolix* oration; a *prolix* poem; a *prolix* sermon.

2. Of long duration. [*Not in use.*]

PROLIX'ITY, **PROLIX'NESS**, *n.* Great length; minute detail; *applied only to discourses and writings.* *Prolixity* is not always tedious.

PROLIX'LY, *adv.* At great length. *Dryden.*

PROLOC'UTOR, *n.* [L. *proloquor*; *pro* and *loquor*, to speak.] The speaker or chairman of a convocation. *Swift.*

PROLOC'UTORSHIP, *n.* The office or station of a prolocutor.

PRO'LOGIZE, *v. i.* To deliver a prologue. [*Not in use.*]

PROLOGUE, *n.* *pro'log.* [Fr. from L. *prologus*; Gr. προλογος; προ and λογος, discourse.]

The preface or introduction to a discourse or performance, chiefly the discourse or poem spoken before a dramatic performance or play begins. *Encyc.*

PROLOGUE, *v. t.* *pro'log.* [It. *prologare.*] To introduce with a formal preface. *Shak.*

PROLONG', *v. t.* [Fr. *prolonger*; It. *prolungare*; Sp. *prolongar*; L. *pro* and *longus*. See *Long.*]

1. To lengthen in time; to extend the duration of. Temperate habits tend to *prolong* life.

2. To lengthen; to draw out in time by delay; to continue.

> Th' unhappy queen with talk *prolong'd* the night. *Dryden.*

3. To put off to a distant time.

> For I myself am not so well provided
> As else I would be, were the day *prolong'd*. *Shak.*

4. To extend in space or length.

PROLON'GATE, *v. t.* To extend or lengthen in space; as, to *prolongate* a line.

2. To extend in time. [*Little used.*]

PROLON'GATED, *pp.* Extended in space; continued in length.

PROLON'GATING, *ppr.* Lengthening in space.

PROLONGA'TION, *n.* [Fr.] The act of lengthening in time or space; as the *prolongation* of life. *Bacon.*

> The *prolongation* of a line. *Lavoisier, Trans.*

2. Extension of time by delay or postponement; as the *prolongation* of days for payment. *Bacon.*

PROLONG'ED, *pp.* Lengthened in duration or space.

PROLONG'ER, *n.* He or that which lengthens in time or space.

PROLONG'ING, *ppr.* Extending in time; continuing in length.

PROLU'SION, *n.* *s* as *z.* [L. *prolusio*, *proludo*; *pro* and *ludo*, to play.]

A prelude; entertainment; diverting performance. [*Little used.*] *Hakewill.*

PROMENA'DE, *n.* [Fr. from *promener*; *pro* and *mener*, to lead.]

1. A walk for amusement or exercise.

2. A place for walking.

PROMER'IT, *v. t.* [L. *promereo*, *promeritum*; *pro* and *mereo*, to merit.]

1. To oblige; to confer a favor on. *Hall.*

2. To deserve; to procure by merit. *Pearson.* [*This word is little used or not at all.*]

PROMETHE'AN, *a.* Pertaining to Prometheus, who stole fire from heaven.

PROM'INENCE, **PROM'INENCY**, *n.* [L. *prominentia*, from *promineo*; *pro* and *minor*, to menace, that is, to shoot forward.]

A standing out from the surface of something, or that which juts out; protuberance; as the *prominence* of a joint; the *prominence* of a rock or cliff; the *prominence* of the nose. Small hills and knolls are *prominences* on the surface of the earth.

PROM'INENT, *a.* [L. *prominens.*] Standing out beyond the line or surface of something; jutting; protuberant; in high relief; as a *prominent* figure on a vase.

2. Full; large; as a *prominent* eye.

3. Eminent; distinguished above others; as a *prominent* character.

4. Principal; most visible or striking to the eye; conspicuous. The figure of a man

or of a building holds a *prominent* place in a picture.

PROM'INENTLY, *adv.* In a prominent manner; so as to stand out beyond the other parts; eminently; in a striking manner; conspicuously.

PROMIS'€UOUS, *a.* [L. *promiscuus; pro* and *misceo*, to mix.]

1. Mingled; consisting of individuals united in a body or mass without order; confused; undistinguished; as a *promiscuous* crowd or mass.

A wild where weeds and flow'rs *promiscuous* shoot. *Pope.*

2. Common; indiscriminate; not restricted to an individual; as *promiscuous* love or intercourse.

PROMIS'€UOUSLY, *adv.* In a crowd or mass without order; with confused mixture; indiscriminately; as men of all classes *promiscuously* assembled; particles of different earths *promiscuously* united.

2. Without distinction of kinds.

Like beasts and birds *promiscuously* they join. *Pope.*

PROMIS'€UOUSNESS, *n.* A state of being mixed without order or distinction. *Ash.*

PROM'ISE, *n.* [L *promissum*, from *promitto*, to send before or forward; *pro* and *mitto*, to send; Fr. *promettre, promis, promesse;* It. *promettere, promessa;* Sp. *prometer, promesa.*]

1. In *a general sense*, a declaration, written or verbal, made by one person to another, which binds the person who makes it, either in honor, conscience or law, to do or forbear a certain act specified; a declaration which gives to the person to whom it is made, a right to expect or to claim the performance or forbearance of the act. The promise of a visit to my neighbor, gives him a right to expect it, and I am bound in honor and civility to perform the *promise.* Of such a *promise* human laws have no cognizance; but the fulfillment of it is one of the minor moralities, which civility, kindness and strict integrity require to be observed.

2. In *law*, a declaration, verbal or written, made by one person to another for a good or valuable consideration, in the nature of a covenant, by which the promiser binds *himself*, and as the case may be, his *legal representatives*, to do or forbear some act; and gives to the promisee a legal right to demand and enforce a fulfillment.

3. A binding declaration of something to be done or given for another's benefit; as the *promise* of a grant of land. A promise may be *absolute* or *conditional; lawful* or *unlawful; express* or *implied.* An *absolute promise* must be fulfilled at all events. The obligation to fulfill a *conditional promise* depends on the performance of the condition. An *unlawful promise* is not binding, because it is void; for it is incompatible with a prior paramount obligation of obedience to the laws. An *express promise*, is one expressed in words or writing. An *implied promise*, is one which reason and justice dictate. If I hire a man to perform a day's labor, without any declaration that I will pay him, the law presumes a *promise* on my part that I will give him a reasonable reward, and will enforce such *implied promise.*

4. Hopes; expectation, or that which affords expectation of future distinction; as a youth of great *promise.*

My native country was full of youthful *promise.* *Irving.*

5. That which is promised; fulfillment or grant of what is promised.

He commanded them that they should not depart from Jerusalem, but wait for the *promise* of the Father. Acts i.

6. In *Scripture*, the *promise* of God is the declaration or assurance which God has given in his word of bestowing blessings on his people. Such assurance resting on the perfect justice, power, benevolence and immutable veracity of God, cannot fail of performance.

The Lord is not slack concerning his *promises.* 2 Pet. iii.

PROM'ISE, *v. t.* To make a declaration to another, which binds the promiser in honor, conscience or law, to do or forbear some act; as, to *promise* a visit to a friend; to *promise* a cessation of hostilities; to *promise* the payment of money.

2. To afford reason to expect; as, the year *promises* a good harvest.

3. To make declaration or give assurance of some benefit to be conferred; to pledge or engage to bestow.

The proprietors *promised* large tracts of land. *Charter of Dartmouth College.*

PROM'ISE, *v. i.* To assure one by a promise or binding declaration. The man *promises* fair; let us forgive him.

2. To afford hopes or expectations; to give ground to expect good. The youth *promises* to be an eminent man; the wheat *promises* to be a good crop; the weather *promises* to be pleasant.

3. In *popular use*, this verb sometimes threatens or assures of evil. The rogue shall be punished, I *promise* you.

Will not the ladies be afraid of the lion?
—I fear it, I *promise* you. *Shak.*

In the latter example, *promise* is equivalent to *declare;* "I *declare* to you."

4. To *promise one's self*, to be assured or to have strong confidence.

I dare *promise myself* you will attest the truth of all I have advanced. *Rambler.*

PROM'ISE-BREACH, *n.* Violation of promise. *Shak.*

PROM'ISE-BREAKER, *n.* A violator of promises. *Shak.*

PROM'ISED, *pp.* Engaged by word or writing; stipulated.

PROMISEE', *n.* The person to whom a promise is made. *Encyc.*

PROM'ISER, *n.* One who promises; one who engages, assures, stipulates or covenants. Fear, says Dryden, is a great *promiser.* We may say that hope is a very liberal *promiser.*

The import of a promise, when disputed, is not to be determined by the sense of the *promiser*, nor by the expectations of the *promisee.* *Paley. Encyc*

[*Note.* In law language, *promisor* is used, but without necessity or advantage.]

PROM'ISING, *ppr.* Engaging by words or writing; stipulating; assuring.

2. Affording just expectations of good or reasonable ground of hope; as a *promising* youth; a *promising* prospect. [*In this sense, the word may be a participle or an adjective.*]

PROM'ISSORILY, *adv.* By way of promise.

PROM'ISSORY, *a.* Containing a promise or binding declaration of something to be done or forborne. *Arbuthnot.*

2. In *law*, a promissory note is a writing which contains a promise of the payment of money or the delivery of property to another, at or before a time specified, in consideration of value received by the promiser. In England, *promissory* notes and bills of exchange, being negotiable for the payment of a less sum than twenty shillings, are declared to be void by Stat 15. Geo. III. *Blackstone.*

PROM'ONTORY, *n.* [L. *promontorium; pro*, forward, and *mons*, a mountain; Fr. *promontoire;* It. Sp. *promontorio.*]

In *geography*, a high point of land or rock, projecting into the sea beyond the line of the coast; a head land. It differs from a cape in denoting high land; a cape may be a similar projection of land high or low.

Like one that stands upon a *promontory.* *Shak.*

If you drink tea on a *promontory* that overhangs the sea, it is preferable to an assembly. *Pope.*

PROMO'TE, *v. t.* [L. *promotus, promoveo*, to move forward; *pro* and *moveo*, to move; It. *promovere;* Sp. *promover;* Fr. *promouvoir.*]

1. To forward; to advance; to contribute to the growth, enlargement or excellence of any thing valuable, or to the increase of any thing evil; as, to *promote* learning, knowledge, virtue or religion; to *promote* the interests of commerce or agriculture; to *promote* the arts; to *promote* civilization or refinement; to *promote* the propagation of the gospel; to *promote* vice and disorder.

2. To excite; as, to *promote* mutiny.

3. To exalt; to elevate; to raise; to prefer in rank or honor.

I will *promote* thee to very great honors. Num. xxii.

Exalt her, and she shall *promote* thee. Prov. iv.

PROMO'TED, *pp.* Advanced; exalted.

PROMO'TER, *n.* He or that which forwards, advances or promotes; an encourager; as a *promoter* of charity. *Atterbury.*

2. One that excites; as a *promoter* of sedition.

3. An informer; a make-bate. *Obs.*

PROMO'TING, *ppr.* Forwarding; advancing; exciting; exalting.

PROMO'TION, *n.* [Fr.; from *promote.*]

1. The act of promoting; advancement; encouragement; as the *promotion* of virtue or morals; the *promotion* of peace or of discord.

2. Exaltation in rank or honor; preferment.

My *promotion* will be thy destruction. *Milton.*

Promotion cometh neither from the east nor from the west, nor from the south. Ps. lxxv.

PROMO'TIVE, *a.* Tending to advance or promote; tending to encourage. *Hume.*

PROMÖVE, *v. t.* To advance. [*Not used.*] *Fell. Suckling.*

PROMPT, *a.* [Fr. *prompt;* It. Sp. *pronto;* L. *promptus*, from *promo.*]

1. Ready and quick to act as occasion demands.

Very discerning and *prompt* in giving orders. *Clarendon.*

2. Of a ready disposition; acting with cheerful alacrity; as *prompt* in obedience or compliance.

Tell him
I'm *prompt* to lay my crown at's feet. *Shak.*

3. Quick; ready; not dilatory; *applied to things;* as, he manifested a *prompt* obedience; he yielded *prompt* assistance.

When Washington heard the voice of his country in distress, his obedience was *prompt.* *Ames.*

4. Quick; hasty; indicating boldness or forwardness.

And you perhaps too *prompt* in your replies. *Dryden.*

5. Ready; present; told down; as *prompt* payment.

6. Easy; unobstructed. *Wotton.*

PROMPT, *v. t.* To incite; to move or excite to action or exertion; to instigate. Insults *prompt* anger or revenge; love *prompts* desire; benevolence *prompts* men to devote their time and services to spread the gospel. Ambition *prompted* Alexander to wish for more worlds to conquer.

2. To assist a speaker when at a loss, by pronouncing the words forgotten or next in order, as to *prompt* an actor; or to assist a learner, by suggesting something forgotten or not understood. *Ascham. Shak. Bacon.*

3. To dictate; to suggest to the mind.

And whisp'ring angels *prompt* her golden dreams. *Pope.*

4. To remind. [*Not used.*] *Brown.*

PROMPT'ED, *pp.* Incited; moved to action; instigated; assisted in speaking or learning.

PROMPT'ER, *n.* One that prompts; one that admonishes or incites to action.

2. One that is placed behind the scenes in a play-house, whose business is to assist the speakers when at a loss, by uttering the first words of a sentence or words forgotten; or any person who aids a public speaker when at a loss, by suggesting the next words of his piece. *Pope.*

PROMPT'ING, *ppr.* Inciting; moving to action; aiding a speaker when at a loss for the words of his piece.

PROMPT'ITUDE, *n.* [Fr. from L. *promptus;* It. *prontitudine;* Sp. *prontitud.*]

1. Readiness; quickness of decision and action when occasion demands. In the sudden vicissitudes of a battle, *promptitude* in a commander is one of the most essential qualifications.

2. Readiness of will; cheerful alacrity; as *promptitude* in obedience or compliance.

PROMPT'LY, *adv.* Readily; quickly; expeditiously; cheerfully. *Taylor.*

PROMPT'NESS, *n.* Readiness; quickness of decision or action. The young man answered questions with great *promptness.*

2. Cheerful willingness; alacrity.

3. Activity; briskness; as the *promptness* of animal actions. *Arbuthnot.*

PROMPT'UARY, *n.* [Fr. *promptuaire;* L. *promptuarium.*] That from which supplies are drawn; a storehouse; a magazine; a repository. *Woodward.*

PROMPT'URE, *n.* Suggestion; incitement. [*Not used.*] *Shak.*

PROMUL'GATE, *v. t.* [L. *promulgo.*] To publish; to make known by open declaration; as, to *promulgate* the secrets of a council. It is particularly applied to the publication of laws and the gospel. The moral law was *promulgated* at mount Sinai. The apostles *promulgated* the gospel. Edicts, laws and orders are *promulgated* by circular letters, or through the medium of the public prints.

PROMUL'GATED, *pp.* Published; made publicly known.

PROMUL'GATING, *ppr.* Publishing.

PROMUL'GATION, *n.* The act of promulgating; publication; open declaration; as the *promulgation* of the law or of the gospel.

PROMUL'GATOR, *n.* A publisher; one who makes known or teaches publicly what was before unknown.

PROMULĠE, *v. t.* *promulj'.* To promulgate; to publish or teach. [Less used than *promulgate.*]

PROMULĠ'ED, *pp.* Published.

PROMULĠ'ER, *n.* One who publishes or teaches what was before unknown. *Atterbury.*

PROMULĠ'ING, *ppr.* Publishing.

PRONA'TION, *n.* [from L. *pronus*, having the face downwards.]

1. Among *anatomists*, that motion of the radius whereby the palm of the hand is turned downwards; the act of turning the palm downwards; opposed to *supination.* *Encyc. Coxe.*

2. That position of the hand, when the thumb is turned towards the body, and the palm downwards. *Parr.*

PRONA'TOR, *n.* A muscle of the fore arm which serves to turn the palm of the hand downward; opposed to *supinator.* *Encyc.*

PRONE, *a.* [L. *pronus.*] Bending forward; inclined; not erect. *Milton.*

2. Lying with the face downward; contrary to *supine.* *Brown.*

3. Headlong; precipitous; inclining in descent.

Down thither *prone* in flight. *Milton.*

4. Sloping; declivous; inclined.

Since the floods demand
For their descent, a *prone* and sinking land. *Blackmore.*

5. Inclined; propense; disposed; *applied to the mind or affections, usually in an ill sense;* as men *prone* to evil, *prone* to strife, *prone* to intemperance, *prone* to deny the truth, *prone* to change.

PRO'NENESS, *n.* The state of bending downward; as the *proneness* of beasts that look downwards; opposed to the *erectness* of man. *Brown.*

2. The state of lying with the face downwards; contrary to *supineness.*

3. Descent; declivity; as the *proneness* of a hill.

4. Inclination of mind, heart or temper; propension; disposition; as the *proneness* of the Israelites to idolatry; *proneness* to self-gratification or to self-justification; *proneness* to comply with temptation; sometimes in a good sense; as the *proneness* of good men to commiserate want. *Atterbury.*

PRONG, *n.* [Possibly it is formed with *n* casual, from the W. *prociaw*, to stab, or Scot. *prog, brog*, a sharp point.]

1. A sharp pointed instrument.

Prick it on a *prong* of iron. *Sandys.*

2. The tine of a fork or of a similar instrument; as a fork of two or three *prongs.* [*This is the sense in which it is used in America.*]

PRONG'HOE, *n.* A hoe with prongs to break the earth. *Encyc.*

PRONITY, for *proneness*, is not used. *More.*

PRONOM'INAL, *a.* [L. *pronomen.* See *Pronoun.*] Belonging to or of the nature of a pronoun. *Lowth.*

PRO'NOUN, *n.* [Fr. *pronom;* It. *pronome;* Sp. *pronombre;* L. *pronomen; pro*, for, and *nomen*, name.]

In *grammar*, a word used instead of a noun or name, to prevent the repetition of it. The personal pronouns in English, are *I, thou* or *you, he, she, we, ye* and *they.* The last is used for the name of things, as well as for that of persons. Other words are used for the names of persons, things, sentences, phrases and for adjectives; and when they stand for sentences, phrases and adjectives, they are not strictly *pronouns*, but relatives, substitutes or representatives of such sentences. Thus we say, "the jury found the prisoner guilty, and the court pronounced sentence on him. *This* or *that* gave great joy to the spectators." In these sentences, *this* or *that* represents the whole preceding sentence, which is the proper antecedent. We also say, "the jury pronounced the man *guilty, this* or *that* or *which* he could not be, for he proved an alibi." In which sentence, *this* or *that* or *which* refers immediately to *guilty*, as its antecedent.

PRONOUNCE, *v. t.* *pronouns'.* [Fr. *prononcer;* It. *pronunziare;* Sp. *pronunciar;* L. *pronuncio; pro* and *nuncio.*]

1. To speak; to utter articulately. The child is not able to *pronounce* words composed of difficult combinations of letters. Adults rarely learn to *pronounce* correctly a foreign language.

2. To utter formally, officially or solemnly. The court *pronounced* sentence of death on the criminal.

Then Baruch answered them, he *pronounced* all these words to me with his mouth. Jer. xxxvi.

Sternly he *pronounc'd*
The rigid interdiction. *Milton.*

3. To speak or utter rhetorically; to deliver; as, to *pronounce* an oration.

4. To speak; to utter, in almost any manner.

5. To declare or affirm. He *pronounced* the book to be a libel; he *pronounced* the act to be a fraud.

PRONOUNCE, *v. i.* *pronouns'.* To speak; to make declaration; to utter an opinion.

How confidently soever men *pronounce* of themselves— *Decay of Piety.*

PRONOUNCEABLE, *a.* *pronouns'able.* That may be pronounced or uttered. *Pinkerton.*

PRONOUN'CED, *pp.* Spoken; uttered; declared solemnly.

PRONOUN'CER, *n.* One who utters or declares.

PRONOUN'CING, *ppr.* Speaking; uttering; declaring.

2. *a.* Teaching pronunciation.

PRONUNCIA'TION, *n.* [Fr. *prononciation*, from L. *pronunciatio.*]

1. The act of uttering with articulation; utterance; as the *pronunciation* of syllables or words; distinct or indistinct *pronunciation.*

2. The mode of uttering words or sentences; particularly, the art or manner of uttering a discourse publicly with propriety and gracefulness; now called *delivery.* *J. Q. Adams.*

PRONUN'CIATIVE, *a.* Uttering confidently; dogmatical. *Bacon.*

PROOF, *n.* [Sax. *profian*, to prove; Sw. *prof*, proof; Dan. *pröve;* D. *proef;* G. *probe;* W. *praw;* Fr. *preuve;* It. *prova;* Sp. *prueba;* Russ. *proba.* See *Prove.*]

1. Trial; essay; experiment; any effort, process or operation that ascertains truth or fact. Thus the quality of spirit is ascertained by *proof;* the strength of gunpowder, of fire arms and of cannon is determined by *proof;* the correctness of operations in arithmetic is ascertained by *proof.*

2. In *law* and *logic*, that degree of evidence which convinces the mind of the certainty of truth or fact, and produces belief. *Proof* is derived from personal knowledge, or from the testimony of others, or from conclusive reasoning. *Proof* differs from *demonstration*, which is applicable only to those truths of which the contrary is inconceivable.

This has neither evidence of truth, nor *proof* sufficient to give it warrant. *Hooker.*

3. Firmness or hardness that resists impression, or yields not to force; impenetrability of physical bodies; as a wall that is of *proof* against shot.

See arms of *proof.* *Dryden.*

4. Firmness of mind; stability not to be shaken; as a mind or virtue that is *proof* against the arts of seduction and the assaults of temptation.

5. The *proof of spirits* consists in little bubbles which appear on the top of the liquor after agitation, called the *bead*, and by the French, *chapelet.* Hence,

6. The degree of strength in spirit; as high *proof;* first *proof;* second, third or fourth *proof.*

7. In *printing* and *engraving*, a rough impression of a sheet, taken for correction; plu. *proofs*, not *proves.*

8. Armor sufficiently firm to resist impression. [*Not used.*] *Shak.*

Proof is used elliptically for *of proof.*

I have found thee
Proof against all temptation. *Milton.*

It is sometimes followed by *to*, more generally by *against.*

PROOF'LESS, *a.* Wanting sufficient evidence to induce belief; not proved. *Boyle.*

PROP, *v. t.* [D. Dan. *prop*, a stopple, Sw. *propp;* G. *pfropf*, id.; D. *proppen;* G. *pfropfen*, to stuff or thrust; Dan. *propper.* These are probably the same word differently applied.]

1. To support or prevent from falling by placing something under or against; as, to *prop* a fence or an old building.

2. To support by standing under or against.

Till the bright mountains *prop* th' incumbent sky. *Pope.*

3. To support; to sustain; in a general sense; as, to *prop* a declining state.

I *prop* myself upon the few supports that are left me. *Pope.*

PROP, *n.* That which sustains an incumbent weight; that on which any thing rests for support; a support; a stay; as a *prop* for vines; a *prop* for an old building. An affectionate child is the *prop* of declining age.

PROP'AGABLE, *a.* [See *Propagate.*] That may be continued or multiplied by natural generation or production; *applied to animals and vegetables.*

2. That may be spread or extended by any means, as tenets, doctrines or principles.

PROP'AGANDISM, *n.* [See *Propagate.*] The art or practice of propagating tenets or principles. *Dwight.*

PROPAGAND'IST, *n.* A person who devotes himself to the spread of any system of principles.

Bonaparte selected a body to compose his Sanhedrim of political *propagandists.* *Walsh.*

PROP'AGATE, *v. t.* [L. *propago;* It. *propaggine;* G. *pfropf*, a stopple; *pfropfen*, to thrust, also to graft. See *Prop.* The Latin noun *propago*, is the English *prop*, and the termination *ago*, as in *cartilago*, &c. The sense of the noun is that which is set or thrust in.]

1. To continue or multiply the kind by generation or successive production; *applied to animals and plants;* as, to *propagate* a breed of horses or sheep; to *propagate* any species of fruit tree.

2. To spread; to extend; to impel or continue forward in space; as, to *propagate* sound or light.

3. To spread from person to person; to extend; to give birth to, or originate and spread; as, to *propagate* a story or report.

4. To carry from place to place; to extend by planting and establishing in places before destitute; as, to *propagate* the christian religion.

5. To extend; to increase.

Griefs of my own lie heavy in my breast,
Which thou wilt *propagate.* *Shak.*

6. To generate; to produce.

Superstitious notions, *propagated* in fancy, are hardly ever totally eradicated. *Richardson.*

PROP'AGATE, *v. i.* To have young or issue; to be produced or multiplied by generation, or by new shoots or plants. Wild horses *propagate* in the forests of S. America.

PROP'AGATED, *pp.* Continued or multiplied by generation or production of the same kind; spread; extended.

PROP'AGATING, *ppr.* Continuing or multiplying the kind by generation or production; spreading and establishing.

PROPAGA'TION, *n.* [Fr. from L. *propagatio.*]

1. The act of propagating; the continuance or multiplication of the kind by generation or successive production; as the *propagation* of animals or plants.

There is not in nature any spontaneous generation, but all come by *propagation.* *Ray.*

2. The spreading or extension of any thing; as the *propagation* of sound or of reports.

3. The spreading of any thing by planting and establishing in places before destitute; as the *propagation* of the gospel among pagans.

4. A forwarding or promotion.

PROP'AGATOR, *n.* One that continues or multiplies his own species by generation.

2. One that continues or multiplies any species of animals or plants.

3. One that spreads or causes to circulate, as a report.

4. One that plants and establishes in a country destitute; as a *propagator* of the gospel.

5. One that plants, originates or extends; one that promotes.

PROPEL', *v. t.* [L. *propello; pro*, forward, and *pello*, to drive.]

To drive forward; to urge or press onward by force. The wind or steam *propels* ships; balls are *propelled* by the force of gunpowder; mill wheels are *propelled* by water or steam; the blood is *propelled* through the arteries and veins by the action of the heart. [*This word is commonly applied to material bodies.*]

PROPEL'LED, *pp.* Driven forward.

PROPEL'LING, *ppr.* Driving forward.

PROPEND', *v. i.* [L. *propendeo; pro*, forward, and *pendeo*, to hang.]

To lean towards; to incline; to be disposed in favor of any thing. [*Little used.*] *Shak.*

PROPEND'ENCY, *n.* [L. *propendens.*] A leaning towards; inclination; tendency of desire to any thing.

2. Preconsideration; attentive deliberation. [*Little used.*] *Hale.*

PROPEND'ING, *ppr.* Inclining towards.

PROPENSE, *a.* *propens'.* [L. *propensus.*] Leaning towards, in a moral sense; inclined; disposed, either to good or evil; as women *propense* to holiness. *Hooker.*

PROPEN'SION, } *n.* [Fr. *propension;* L. *propensio.*]
PROPENS'ITY, }

1. Bent of mind, natural or acquired; inclination; *in a moral sense;* disposition to any thing good or evil, particularly to evil; as a *propensity* to sin; the corrupt *propensity* of the will. *Rogers.*

It requires critical nicety to find out the genius or *propensions* of a child. *L'Estrange.*

2. Natural tendency; as the *propension* of bodies to a particular place. *Digby.*

[In a moral sense, *propensity* is now chiefly used.]

PROP'ER, *a.* [Fr. *propre;* It. *proprio* or *propio;* Sp. *propio;* L. *proprius*, supposed to be allied to *prope*, near; W. *priawd*, proper, appropriate.]

1. Peculiar; naturally or essentially belonging to a person or thing; not common. That is not *proper*, which is common to many. Every animal has his *proper* instincts and inclinations, appetites and habits. Every muscle and vessel of the body has its *proper* office. Every art has its *proper* rules. Creation is the *proper* work of an Almighty Being.

2. Particularly suited to. Every animal lives in his *proper* element.
3. One's own. It may be joined with any possessive pronoun; as *our proper* son. *Shak.*

Our proper conceptions. *Glanville.*
Now learn the difference at *your proper* cost. *Dryden.*

[NOTE. *Own* is often used in such phrases; "at *your own proper* cost." This is really tautological, but sanctioned by usage, and expressive of emphasis.]

4. Noting an individual; pertaining to one of a species, but not common to the whole; as a *proper* name. *Dublin* is the *proper* name of a city.
5. Fit; suitable; adapted; accommodated. A thin dress is not *proper* for clothing in a cold climate. Stimulants are *proper* remedies for debility. Gravity of manners is very *proper* for persons of advanced age.

In Athens, all was pleasure, mirth and play,
All *proper* to the spring and sprightly May. *Dryden.*

6. Correct; just; as a *proper* word; a *proper* expression.
7. Not figurative. *Burnet.*
8. Well formed; handsome.

Moses was a *proper* child. Heb. xi.

9. Tall; lusty; handsome with bulk. [*Low and not used.*] *Shak.*
10. In *vulgar language*, very; as *proper* good; *proper* sweet. [This is very improper, as well as vulgar.]

Proper receptacle, in *botany*, that which supports only a single flower or fructification; *proper perianth* or *involucre*, that which incloses only a single flower; *proper flower* or *corol*, one of the single florets or corollets in an aggregate or compound flower; *proper nectary*, separate from the petals and other parts of the flower. *Martyn.*

PROP'ERLY, *adv.* Fitly; suitably; in a proper manner; as a word *properly* applied; a dress *properly* adjusted.

2. In a strict sense.

The miseries of life are not *properly* owing to the unequal distribution of things. *Swift.*

PROP'ERNESS, *n.* The quality of being proper. [*Little used.*]

2. Tallness. [*Not in use.*]
3. Perfect form; handsomeness.

PROP'ERTY, *n.* [This seems to be formed directly from *proper*; if not, it is contracted. The Latin is *proprietas*, Fr. *proprieté*, from which we have *propriety*.]

1. A peculiar quality of any thing; that which is inherent in a subject, or naturally essential to it; called by logicians an *essential mode.* Thus color is a *property* of light; extension and figure are *properties* of bodies.
2. An acquired or artificial quality; that which is given by art or bestowed by man. The poem has the *properties* which constitute excellence.
3. Quality; disposition.

It is the *property* of an old sinner to find delight in reviewing his own villainies in others. *South.*

4. The exclusive right of possessing, enjoying and disposing of a thing; ownership. In the beginning of the world, the Creator gave to man dominion over the earth, over the fish of the sea and the fowls of the air, and over every living thing. This is the foundation of man's *property* in the earth and in all its productions. Prior occupancy of land and of wild animals gives to the possessor the *property* of them. The labor of inventing, making or producing any thing constitutes one of the highest and most indefeasible titles to *property*. *Property* is also acquired by inheritance, by gift or by purchase. *Property* is sometimes held in common, yet each man's right to his share in common land or stock is exclusively his own. One man may have the *property* of the soil, and another the right of use, by prescription or by purchase.
5. Possession held in one's own right. *Dryden.*
6. The thing owned; that to which a person has the legal title, whether in his possession or not. It is one of the greatest blessings of civil society that the *property* of citizens is well secured.
7. An estate, whether in lands, goods or money; as a man of large *property* or small *property.*
8. An estate; a farm; a plantation. In this sense, which is common in the United States and in the West Indies, the word has a plural.

The still-houses on the sugar plantations, vary in size, according to the fancy of the proprietor or the magnitude of the *property*. *Edwards, W. Indies.*

I shall confine myself to such *properties* as fall within the reach of daily observation. *ib.*

9. Nearness or right.

Here I disclaim all my paternal care,
Propinquity and *property* of blood. *Shak.*

10. Something useful; an appendage; a theatrical term.

I will draw a bill of *properties*. *Shak.*
High pomp and state are useful *properties*. *Dryden.*

11. Propriety. [*Not in use.*] *Camden.*

Literary property, the exclusive right of printing, publishing and making profit by one's own writings. No right or title to a thing can be so perfect as that which is created by a man's own labor and invention. The exclusive right of a man to his literary productions, and to the use of them for his own profit, is entire and perfect, as the faculties employed and labor bestowed are entirely and perfectly his own. On what principle then can a legislature or a court determine that an author can enjoy only a *temporary property* in his own productions? If a man's right to his own *productions in writing* is as perfect as to the *productions* of his farm or his shop, how can the former be abridged or limited, while the latter is held without limitation? Why do the *productions* of *manual labor* rank higher in the scale of rights or *property*, than the *productions* of the *intellect?*

PROP'ERTY, *v. t.* To invest with qualities, or to take as one's own; to appropriate. [*An awkward word and not used.*] *Shak.*

PROPHANE. [See *Profane.*]

PRO'PHASIS, *n.* [Gr. προφασις, from προφημι, to foretell.]

In *medicine*, prognosis; foreknowledge of a disease.

PROPH'ECY, *n.* [Gr. προφητεια, from προφημι, to foretell; προ, before, and φημι, to tell. This ought to be written prophesy.]

1. A foretelling; prediction; a declaration of something to come. As God only knows future events with certainty, no being but God or some person informed by him, can utter a real *prophecy*. The *prophecies* recorded in Scripture, when fulfilled, afford most convincing evidence of the divine original of the Scriptures, as those who uttered the *prophecies* could not have foreknown the events predicted without supernatural instruction. 2 Pet. i.
2. In *Scripture*, a book of prophecies; a history; as the *prophecy* of Ahijah. 2 Chron. ix.
3. Preaching; public interpretation of Scripture; exhortation or instruction. Prov. xxxi.

PROPH'ESIED, *pp.* Foretold; predicted.

PROPH'ESIER, *n.* One who predicts events.

PROPH'ESY, *v. t.* To foretell future events; to predict.

I hate him, for he doth not *prophesy* good concerning me, but evil. 1 Kings xxii.

2. To foreshow. [*Little used.*] *Shak.*

PROPH'ESY, *v. i.* To utter predictions; to make declaration of events to come. Jer. xi.

2. In *Scripture*, to preach; to instruct in religious doctrines; to interpret or explain Scripture or religious subjects; to exhort. 1 Cor. xiii. Ezek. xxxvii.

PROPH'ESYING, *ppr.* Foretelling events.

PROPH'ESYING, *n.* The act of foretelling or of preaching.

PROPH'ET, *n.* [Gr. προφητης; L. *propheta*; Fr. *prophète.*]

1. One that foretells future events; a predicter; a foreteller.
2. In *Scripture*, a person illuminated, inspired or instructed by God to announce future events; as Moses, Elijah, David, Isaiah, &c.
3. An interpreter; one that explains or communicates sentiments. Ex. vii.
4. One who pretends to foretell; an impostor; as a false *prophet.* Acts xiii.

School of the prophets, among the Israelites, a school or college in which young men were educated and qualified for public teachers. These students were called *sons of the prophets.*

PROPH'ETESS, *n.* A female prophet; a woman who foretells future events, as Miriam, Huldah, Anna, &c. Ex. xv. Judg. iv. Luke ii.

PROPHET'IC, PROPHET'ICAL, } *a.* Containing prophecy; foretelling future events; as *prophetic* writings.

2. Unfolding future events; as *prophetic* dreams.

It has *of* before the thing foretold.
And fears are oft *prophetic of* th' event. *Dryden.*

PROPHET'ICALLY, *adv.* By way of prediction; in the manner of prophecy. *Dryden.*

PROPH'ETIZE, *v. i.* To give prediction. [*Not used.*]

PROPHYLAC'TIC, PROPHYLAC'TICAL, } *a.* [Gr. προφυλακτικος, from προφυλασσω, to prevent, to guard against; προ and φυλασσω, to preserve.]

In *medicine*, preventive; defending from disease. *Coxe.*

PROPHYLAC'TIC, *n.* A medicine which preserves or defends against disease; a preventive. *Coxe.*

PROPINA'TION, *n.* [L. *propinatio*, *propino*; Gr. προ and πινω, to drink.]

The act of pledging, or drinking first and then offering the cup to another. *Potter.*

PROPI'NE, *v. t.* [L. *propino*, supra.] To pledge; to drink first and then offer the cup to another. [*Not used.*]

2. To expose. [*Not used.*]

PROPIN'QUITY, *n.* [L. *propinquitas*, from *propinquus*, near.]

1. Nearness in place; neighborhood. *Ray.*
2. Nearness in time. *Brown.*
3. Nearness of blood; kindred. *Shak.*

PROPI''TIABLE, *a.* [See *Propitiate.*] That may be induced to favor, or that may be made propitious.

PROPI''TIATE, *v. t.* [L. *propitio*. Qu. *pro*, and the root of L. *pio*, Eng. *pity.*]

To conciliate; to appease one offended and render him favorable; to make propitious.

> Let fierce Achilles, dreadful in his rage,
> The god *propitiate* and the pest assuage. *Pope.*

PROPI''TIATED, *pp.* Appeased and rendered favorable; conciliated.

PROPI''TIATING, *ppr.* Conciliating; appeasing the wrath of and rendering favorable.

PROPITIATION, *n.* *propisia'shon.* [Fr.; from *propitiate.*]

1. The act of appeasing wrath and conciliating the favor of an offended person; the act of making propitious.
2. In *theology*, the atonement or atoning sacrifice offered to God to assuage his wrath and render him propitious to sinners. Christ is the *propitiation* for the sins of men. Rom. iii. 1 John ii.

PROPITIA'TOR, *n.* One who propitiates. *Sherwood.*

PROPI''TIATORY, *a.* Having the power to make propitious; as a *propitiatory* sacrifice. *Stillingfleet.*

PROPI''TIATORY, *n.* Among the Jews, the mercy-seat; the lid or cover of the ark of the covenant, lined within and without with plates of gold. This was a type of Christ. *Encyc.*

PROPI''TIOUS, *a.* [L. *propitius.*] Favorable; kind; *applied to men.*

2. Disposed to be gracious or merciful; ready to forgive sins and bestow blessings; *applied to God.*
3. Favorable; as a *propitious* season.

PROPI''TIOUSLY, *adv.* Favorably; kindly. *Roscommon.*

PROPI''TIOUSNESS, *n.* Kindness; disposition to treat another kindly; disposition to forgive.

2. Favorableness; as the *propitiousness* of the season or climate. *Temple.*

PRO'PLASM, *n.* [Gr. προ and πλασμα, a device.] A mold; a matrix. *Woodward.*

PROPLAS'TICE, *n.* [supra.] The art of making molds for castings.

PRO'POLIS, *n.* [Gr. before the city, or the front of the city.]

A thick odorous substance having some resemblance to wax and smelling like storax; used by bees to stop the holes and crevices in their hives to prevent the entrance of cold air, &c. Pliny represents it as the third coat; the first he calls *commosis*; the second *pissoceros*; the third, more solid than the others, he calls *propolis*. *Plin. Nat. Hist.*

This account of the propolis may not be perfectly correct, as authors do not agree in their descriptions of it.

PROPO'NENT, *n.* [L. *proponens*; *pro* and *pono*, to place.]

One that makes a proposal, or lays down a proposition. *Dryden.*

PROPŌRTION, *n.* [L. *proportio*; *pro* and *portio*, part or share. See *Portion.*]

1. The comparative relation of any one thing to another. Let a man's exertions be in *proportion* to his strength.
2. The identity or similitude of two ratios. *Proportion* differs from *ratio*. *Ratio* is the relation which determines the quantity of one thing from the quantity of another, without the intervention of a third. Thus the ratio of 5 and 10 is 2; the ratio of 8 and 16 is 2. *Proportion* is the sameness or likeness of two such relations. Thus 5 is to 10, as 8 to 16, or A is to B, as C is to D; that is, 5 bears the same relation to 10, as 8 does to 16. Hence we say, such numbers are in *proportion*. *Encyc.*

Proportion, in *mathematics*, an equality of ratios. *Day.*

The term proportion is sometimes improperly used for ratio. The ratio between two quantities, is expressed by the quotient of one divided by the other: thus, the ratio of 10 to 5 is 2, and the ratio of 16 to 8 is 2. These two equal ratios constitute a proportion, which is expressed by saying, 10 is to 5 as 16 is to 8; or more concisely, 10 : 5 : : 16 : 8. [See *Ratio.*] *D. Olmsted.*

3. In *arithmetic*, a rule by which, when three numbers are given, a fourth number is found, which bears the same relation to the third as the second does to the first; or a fourth number is found, bearing the same relation to the second as the first does to the third. The former is called *direct*, and the latter, *inverse proportion.*
4. Symmetry; suitable adaptation of one part or thing to another; as the *proportion* of one limb to another in the human body; the *proportion* of the length and breadth of a room to its highth.

> Harmony, with every grace,
> Plays in the fair *proportions* of her face. *Mrs. Carter.*

5. Equal or just share; as, to ascertain the *proportion* of profit to which each partner in a company is entitled.
6. Form; size. [*Little used.*] *Davies.*
7. The relation between unequal things of the same kind, by which their several parts correspond to each other with an equal augmentation and diminution, as in reducing and enlarging figures. *Encyc.*

[This more properly belongs to *ratio.*]

Harmonical or *musical proportion*, is when, of three numbers, the first is to the third as the difference of the first and second to the difference of the second and third. Thus 2. 3. 6. are in harmonical proportion; for 2 is to 6 as 1 to 3. So also four numbers are harmonical, when the first is to the fourth, as the difference of the first and second is to the difference of the third and fourth. Thus, 24. 16. 12. 9. are harmonical, for 24 : 9 : : 8 : 3. *Encyc.*

Arithmetical and *geometrical proportion.* [See *Progression*, No. 4.]

Reciprocal proportion, an equality between a direct and a reciprocal ratio. Thus, 4 : 2 : : $\frac{1}{3}$: $\frac{1}{6}$. [See *Reciprocals*, and *Reciprocal ratio.*]

PROPORTION, *v. t.* To adjust the comparative relation of one thing or one part to another; as, to *proportion* the size of a building to its highth, or the thickness of a thing to its length; to *proportion* our expenditures to our income.

> In the loss of an object, we do not *proportion* our grief to its real value, but to the value our fancies set upon it. *Addison.*

2. To form with symmetry or suitableness, as the parts of the body.

PROPŌRTIONABLE, *a.* That may be proportioned or made proportional. This is the true sense of the word; but it is erroneously used in the sense of *proportional*, being in proportion; having a due comparative relation; as infantry with a *proportionable* number of horse.

PROPŌRTIONABLY, *adv.* According to proportion or comparative relation; as a large body, with limbs *proportionably* large.

PROPŌRTIONAL, *a.* [It. *proporzionale*; Fr. *proportionnel.*]

Having a due comparative relation; being in suitable proportion or degree; as, the parts of an edifice are *proportional*. In *pharmacy*, medicines are compounded of certain *proportional* quantities of ingredients. The velocity of a moving body is *proportional* to the impelling force, when the quantity of matter is given; its momentum is *proportional* to the quantity of matter it contains, when its velocity is given.

Proportional, in *chimistry*, a term employed in the theory of definite proportions, to denote the same as the weight of an atom or a prime. [See *Prime.*]

Proportionals, in *geometry*, are quantities, either linear or numeral, which bear the same ratio or relation to each other. *Encyc.*

PROPŌRTIONAL'ITY, *n.* The quality of being in proportion. *Grew.*

PROPŌRTIONALLY, *adv.* In proportion; in due degree; with suitable comparative relation; as all parts of a building being *proportionally* large.

PROPŌRTIONATE, *a.* Adjusted to something else according to a certain rate or comparative relation; proportional.

> The connection between the end and means is *proportionate*. *Grew.*
>
> Punishment should be *proportionate* to the transgression. *Locke.*

PROPŌRTIONATE, *v. t.* To proportion; to make proportional; to adjust according to a settled rate or to due comparative relation; as, to *proportionate* punishments to crimes. [This verb is less used than *proportion.*]

PROPŌRTIONATELY, *adv.* With due proportion; according to a settled or suitable rate or degree. *Pearson.*

PROPŌRTIONATENESS, *n.* The state of being adjusted by due or settled proportion or comparative relation; suitableness of proportions. *Hale.*

PROPORTIONED, *pp.* Made or adjusted with due proportion or with symmetry of parts.

PROPORTIONING, *ppr.* Making proportional.

PROPORTIONLESS, *a.* Without proportion; without symmetry of parts.

PROPO'SAL, *n. s* as *z.* [from *propose.*]

1. That which is offered or propounded for consideration or acceptance; a scheme or design, terms or conditions proposed; as, to make *proposals* for a treaty of peace; to offer *proposals* for erecting a building; to make *proposals* of marriage; *proposals* for subscription to a loan or to a literary work.

2. Offer to the mind; as the *proposal* of an agreeable object. *South.*

PROPO'SE, *v. t. s* as *z.* [Fr. *proposer;* L. *propono, proposui;* W. *posiaw,* to pose, that is, to set; literally to put or throw forward.]

1. To offer for consideration, discussion, acceptance or adoption; as, to *propose* a bill or resolve to a legislative body; to *propose* terms of peace; to *propose* a question or subject for discussion; to *propose* an alliance by treaty or marriage; to *propose* alterations or amendments in a law.

2. To offer or present for consideration.

In learning any thing, as little as possible should be *proposed* to the mind at first. *Watts.*

To propose to one's self, to intend; to design; to form a design in the mind.

PROPO'SE, *v. i.* To lay schemes. [*Not in use.*] *Shak.*

[*Propose* is often used for *purpose;* as, I *propose* to ride to New York to-morrow. *Purpose* and *propose* are different forms of the same word.]

PROPO'SED, *pp.* Offered or presented for consideration, discussion, acceptance or adoption.

PROPO'SER, *n.* One that offers any thing for consideration or adoption. *Locke.*

PROPO'SING, *ppr.* Offering for consideration, acceptance or adoption.

PROPOSI''TION, *n. s* as *z.* [Fr. from L. *propositio,* from *propositus, propono.*]

1. That which is proposed; that which is offered for consideration, acceptance or adoption; a proposal; offer of terms. The enemy made *propositions* of peace; the *propositions* were not accepted.

2. In *logic,* one of the three parts of a regular argument; the part of an argument in which some quality, negative or positive, is attributed to a subject; as, "snow is white;" "water is fluid;" "vice is not commendable."

3. In *mathematics,* a statement in terms of either a truth to be demonstrated, or an operation to be performed. It is called a *theorem,* when it is something to be proved; and a *problem,* when it is something to be done. *D. Olmsted.*

4. In *oratory,* that which is offered or affirmed as the subject of the discourse; any thing stated or affirmed for discussion or illustration.

5. In *poetry,* the first part of a poem, in which the author states the subject or matter of it. Horace recommends modesty and simplicity in the *proposition* of a poem.

PROPOSI''TIONAL, *a.* Pertaining to a proposition; considered as a proposition; as a *propositional* sense. *Watts.*

PROPOUND', *v. t.* [L. *propono; pro* and *pono,* to set, put or place.]

1. To propose; to offer for consideration; as, to *propound* a rule of action. *Wotton.*

The existence of the church hath been *propounded* as an object of faith. *Pearson.*

2. To offer; to exhibit; to propose; as, to *propound* a question. *Shak.*

3. In *congregational churches,* to propose or name as a candidate for admission to communion with a church. Persons intending to make public profession of their faith, and thus unite with the church, are *propounded* before the church and congregation; that is, their intention is notified some days previous, for the purpose of giving opportunity to members of the church to object to their admission to such communion, if they see cause.

PROPOUND'ED, *pp.* Proposed; offered for consideration.

PROPOUND'ER, *n.* One that proposes or offers for consideration.

PROPOUND'ING, *ppr.* Proposing; offering for consideration.

PROP'PED, *pp.* [from *prop.*] Supported; sustained by something placed under.

PROP'PING, *ppr.* Supporting by something beneath.

PROPRE'FECT, *n.* Among *the Romans,* a prefect's lieutenant commissioned to do a part of the duty of the prefect. *Encyc.*

PROPRE'TOR, *n.* [L. *proprætor.*] Among *the Romans,* a magistrate who, having discharged the office of pretor at home, was sent into a province to command there with his former pretorial authority; also, an officer sent extraordinarily into the provinces to administer justice with the authority of pretor. *Encyc.*

PROPRI'ETARY, *n.* [Fr. *proprietaire,* from *proprieté.*]

1. A proprietor or owner; one who has the exclusive title to a thing; one who possesses or holds the title to a thing in his own right. The grantees of Pennsylvania and Maryland and their heirs were called the *proprietaries* of those provinces.

2. In *monasteries,* such monks were called *proprietaries,* as had reserved goods and effects to themselves, notwithstanding their renunciation of all at the time of their profession. *Encyc.*

PROPRI'ETARY, *a.* Belonging to a proprietor or owner, or to a proprietary. The governments of Pennsylvania and Maryland were formerly *proprietary.*

PROPRI'ETOR, *n.* [from L. *proprietas, proprius.*]

An owner; the person who has the legal right or exclusive title to any thing whether in possession or not; as the *proprietor* of a farm or of a mill. By the gift of God, man is constituted the *proprietor* of the earth.

PROPRI'ETRESS, *n.* A female who has the exclusive legal right to a thing. *L'Estrange.*

PROPRI'ETY, *n.* [Fr. *proprieté;* L. *proprietas,* from *proprius.*]

1. Property; peculiar or exclusive right of possession; ownership. [This primary sense of the word, as used by Locke, Milton, Dryden, &c. seems now to be nearly or wholly obsolete. See *Property.*]

2. Fitness; suitableness; appropriateness; consonance with established principles, rules or customs; justness; accuracy. *Propriety* of conduct, in a moral sense, consists in its conformity to the moral law; *propriety* of behavior, consists in conformity to the established rules of decorum; *propriety* in language, is correctness in the use of words and phrases, according to established usage, which constitutes the rule of speaking and writing.

3. Proper state. *Shak.*

PROPT. [See *Propped.*]

PROPUGN, *v. t.* *propu'ne.* [L. *propugno; pro* and *pugno,* to fight.]

To contend for; to defend; to vindicate. [*Little used.*] *Hammond.*

PROPUG'NACLE, *n.* [L. *propugnaculum.*] A fortress. [*Not used.*] *Howell.*

PROPUGNA'TION, *n.* [L. *propugnatio.*] Defense. [*Not used.*] *Shak.*

PROPUGNER, *n.* *propu'ner.* A defender; a vindicator.

PROPULSA'TION, *n.* [L. *propulsatio, propulso.* See *Propel.*]

The act of driving away or repelling; the keeping at a distance. *Hall.*

PROPULSE, *v. t.* *propuls'.* [L. *propulso; pro* and *pulso,* to strike. See *Propel.*]

To repel; to drive off. [*Little used.*] *Cotgrave.*

PROPUL'SION, *n.* [L. *propulsus, propello.* See *Propel.*] The act of driving forward. *Bacon.*

Pro rata, [L.] in proportion.

PRORE, *n.* [L. *prora.*] The prow or fore part of a ship. [*Not in use, except in poetry.*] *Pope.*

Pro re nata, [L.] according to exigences or circumstances.

PROROGA'TION, *n.* [L. *prorogatio.* See *Prorogue.*]

1. Continuance in time or duration; a lengthening or prolongation of time; as the *prorogation* of something already possessed. [*This use is uncommon.*] *South.*

2. In England, the continuance of parliament from one session to another, as an adjournment is a continuance of the session from day to day. This is the established language with respect to the parliament of Great Britain. In the United States, the word is, I believe, rarely or never used; *adjournment* being used not only in its etymological sense, but for *prorogation* also.

PROROGUE, *v. t.* *prorōg.* [Fr. *proroger;* L. *prorogo; pro* and *rogo.* The latter word signifies to ask, or to propose; but the primary sense is to *reach,* to stretch forward; and this is its import in the derivative *prorogo.*]

1. To protract; to prolong.

He *prorogued* his government. *Dryden.*

2 To defer; to delay; as, to *prorogue* death. *Shak.*

[*In the foregoing senses, the word is now rarely used.*]

3. To continue the parliament from one session to another. Parliament is *prorogued* by the king's authority, either by the lord chancellor in his majesty's presence, or by commission, or by proclamation. *Blackstone.*

PRORUP'TION, *n.* [L. *proruptus, prorumpo; pro* and *rumpo*, to burst.]
The act of bursting forth; a bursting out. *Brown.*

PROSA'IC, *a.* *s* as *z*. [L. *prosaicus*, from *prosa*, prose; Fr. *prosaique.*]
Pertaining to prose; resembling prose; not restricted by numbers; *applied to writings;* as a *prosaic* composition.

PRO'SAL, *a.* Prosaic. [*Not used.*] *Brown.*

PROSCRI'BE, *v. t.* [L. *proscribo; pro* and *scribo*, to write. The sense of this word originated in the Roman practice of writing the names of persons doomed to death, and posting the list in public.]
1. To doom to destruction; to put one out of the protection of law, and promise a reward for his head. Sylla and Marius *proscribed* each other's adherents.
2. To put out of the protection of the law.
Robert Vere, earl of Oxford, was banished the realm and *proscribed.* *Spenser.*
3. To denounce and condemn as dangerous and not worthy of reception; to reject utterly.
In the year 325, the Arian doctrines were *proscribed* and anathematized by the council of Nice. *Waterland.*
4. To censure and condemn as utterly unworthy of reception. *South.*
5. To interdict; as, to *proscribe* the use of ardent spirits.

PROSCRI'BED, *pp.* Doomed to destruction; denounced as dangerous, or as unworthy of reception; condemned; banished.

PROSCRI'BER, *n.* One that dooms to destruction; one that denounces as dangerous, or as utterly unworthy of reception.

PROSCRI'BING, *ppr.* Dooming to destruction; denouncing as unworthy of protection or reception; condemning; banishing.

PROSCRIP'TION, *n.* [L. *proscriptio.*] The act of proscribing or dooming to death; among *the Romans*, the public offer of a reward for the head of a political enemy. Such were the *proscriptions* of Sylla and Marius. Under the triumvirate, many of the best Roman citizens fell by *proscription.*
2. A putting out of the protection of law; condemning to exile.
3. Censure and condemnation; utter rejection.

PROSCRIP'TIVE, *a.* Pertaining to or consisting in proscription; proscribing. *Burke.*

PROSE, *n.* *s* as *z*. [L. It. Sp. *prosa;* Fr. *prose.* Qu. orient. פרס, פרץ or פרש.]
1. The natural language of man; language loose and unconfined to poetical measure, as opposed to *verse* or *metrical composition.*
Things unattempted yet in *prose* or rhyme. *Milton.*
2. A prayer used in the Romish church on particular days. *Harmar.*

PROSE, *v. t.* To write in prose. *Milton.*
2. To make a tedious relation. *Mason.*

PROS'ECUTE, *v. t.* [L. *prosecutus, prosequor; pro* and *sequor*, to follow, Eng. to *seek.* See *Essay.*]
1. To follow or pursue with a view to reach, execute or accomplish; to continue endeavors to obtain or complete; to continue efforts already begun; as, to *prosecute* a scheme; to *prosecute* an undertaking. The great canal in the state of New York has been *prosecuted* with success.
That which is morally good is to be desired and *prosecuted.* *Wilkins.*
This word signifies either to *begin* and *carry on*, or simply to *continue* what has been begun. When I say, "I have devised a plan which I have not the courage or means to *prosecute*," the word signifies to *begin to execute.* When we say, "the nation began a war which it had not means to *prosecute*," it signifies to *continue to carry on.* The latter is the genuine sense of the word, but both are well authorized. We *prosecute* any work of the hands or of the head. We *prosecute* a purpose, an enterprise, a work, studies, inquiries, &c.
2. To seek to obtain by legal process; as, to *prosecute* a right in a court of law.
3. To accuse of some crime or breach of law, or to pursue for redress or punishment, before a legal tribunal; as, to *prosecute* a man for trespass or for a riot. It is applied to civil suits for damages, as well as to criminal suits, but not to suits for debt. We never say, a man *prosecutes* another on a bond or note, or in assumpsit; but he *prosecutes* his right or claim in an action of debt, detinue, trover or assumpsit. So we say, a man *prosecutes* another for assault and battery, for a libel or for slander, or for breaking his close. In these cases, *prosecute* signifies to *begin* and to *continue* a suit. The attorney general *prosecutes* offenders in the name of the king or of the state, by information or indictment.
Prosecute differs from *persecute*, as in law it is applied to legal proceedings only, whereas *persecute* implies cruelty, injustice or oppression.

PROS'ECUTED, *pp.* Pursued, or begun and carried on for execution or accomplishment, as a scheme; pursued for redress or punishment in a court of law, as a person; demanded in law, as a right or claim.

PROS'ECUTING, *ppr.* Pursuing, or beginning and carrying on for accomplishment; pursuing for redress or punishment; suing for, as a right or claim.

PROSECU'TION, *n.* The act or process of endeavoring to gain or accomplish something; pursuit by efforts of body or mind; as the *prosecution* of a scheme, plan, design or undertaking; the *prosecution* of war or of commerce; the *prosecution* of a work, study, argument or inquiry.
2. The institution and carrying on of a suit in a court of law or equity, to obtain some right, or to redress and punish some wrong. The *prosecution* of a claim in chancery is very expensive. Malicious *prosecutions* subject the offender to punishment.
3. The institution or commencement and continuance of a criminal suit; the process of exhibiting formal charges against an offender before a legal tribunal, and pursuing them to final judgment; as *prosecutions* of the crown or of the state by the attorney or solicitor general. *Prosecutions* may be by presentment, information or indictment. *Blackstone.*

PROS'ECUTOR, *n.* One who pursues or carries on any purpose, plan or business.
2. The person who institutes and carries on a criminal suit in a legal tribunal, or one who exhibits criminal charges against an offender. The attorney general is the *prosecutor* for the king or state. *Blackstone.*

PROS'ELYTE, *n.* [Fr. *proselyte;* It. *prosolita;* Gr. προσηλυτος; προς and ερχομαι, to come; ηλυθον, ηλθον.]
A new convert to some religion or religious sect, or to some particular opinion, system or party. Thus a Gentile converted to Judaism is a *proselyte;* a pagan converted to christianity is a *proselyte;* and we speak familiarly of *proselytes* to the theories of Brown, of Black, or of Lavoisier. The word primarily refers to converts to some religious creed.

PROS'ELYTE, *v. t.* To make a convert to some religion, or to some opinion or system. *Macknight.*

PROS'ELYTISM, *n.* The making of converts to a religion or religious sect, or to any opinion, system or party.
They were possessed with a spirit of *proselytism* in the most fanatical degree. *Burke.*
2. Conversion to a system or creed.

PROS'ELYTIZE, to make converts, or to convert, is not well authorized, or not in common use, and is wholly unnecessary.

PROSEMINA'TION, *n.* [L. *proseminatus; pro* and *semino*, to sow.]
Propagation by seed. [*Not used.*] *Hale.*

PROSENNEAHE'DRAL, *a.* [Gr. προς, εννεα and εδρα.]
In *crystalography*, having nine faces on two adjacent parts of the crystal.

PRO'SER, *n.* *s* as *z*. [from *prose.*] A writer of prose. *Drayton.*
2. In *cant language*, one who makes a tedious narration of uninteresting matters.

PROSO'DIAL, } *a.* [from *prosody.*] Pertaining to prosody or
PROSOD'ICAL, } the quantity and accents of syllables; according to the rules of prosody. *Warton. Ed. Dispens.*

PROSO'DIAN, *n.* [from *prosody.*] One skilled in prosody or in the rules of pronunciation and metrical composition.

PROS'ODIST, *n.* [from *prosody.*] One who understands prosody. *Walker.*

PROS'ODY, *n.* [Fr. *prosodie;* L. *prosodia;* Gr. προσωδια; προς and ωδη, an ode.]
That part of grammar which treats of the quantity of syllables, of accent, and of the laws of versification. It includes also the art of adjusting the accent and metrical arrangement of syllables in compositions for the lyre.

PROSOPOLEP'SY, *n.* [Gr. προσωποληψια.] Respect of persons; more particularly, a premature opinion or prejudice against a person, formed by a view of his external appearance. *Moore. Addison.*

PROSOPOPE'IA, } *n.* [Gr. προσωποποιια; προσωπον, person,
PROS'OPOPY, } and ποιεω, to make.]
A figure in rhetoric by which things are represented as persons, or by which things inanimate are spoken of as animated beings, or by which an absent person is introduced as speaking, or a deceased person is

represented as alive and present. It includes *personification*, but is more extensive in its signification. *Encyc.*

PROS′PECT, *n.* [L. *prospectus, prospicio*, to look forward; *pro* and *specio*, to see.]

1. View of things within the reach of the eye.

Eden and all the coast in *prospect* lay. *Milton.*

2. View of things to come; intellectual sight; expectation. The good man enjoys the *prospect* of future felicity.

3. That which is presented to the eye; the place and the objects seen. There is a noble *prospect* from the dome of the state house in Boston, a *prospect* diversified with land and water, and every thing that can please the eye.

4. Object of view.

Man to himself
Is a large *prospect*. *Denham.*

5. View delineated or painted; picturesque representation of a landscape. *Reynolds.*

6. Place which affords an extended view. *Milton.*

7. Position of the front of a building; as a *prospect* towards the south or north. Ezek. xl.

8. Expectation, or ground of expectation. There is a *prospect* of a good harvest. A man has a *prospect* of preferment; or he has little *prospect* of success. *Washington.*

9. A looking forward; a regard to something future.

Is he a prudent man as to his temporal estate, who lays designs only for a day, without any *prospect* to or provision for the remaining part of life? [*Little used.*] *Tillotson.*

PROSPEC′TION, *n.* The act of looking forward, or of providing for future wants. *Paley.*

PROSPEC′TIVE, *a.* Looking forward in time; regarding the future; opposed to *retrospective.*

The supporting of Bible societies is one of the points on which the promises, at the time of ordination, had no *prospective* bearing. *W. Jay.*

2. Acting with foresight.

The French king and king of Sweden, are circumspect, industrious and *prospective* in this affair. *Child.*

3. Pertaining to a prospect; viewing at a distance. *Milton.*

4. Furnishing an extensive prospect. *Dwight.*

PROSPEC′TIVELY, *adv.* With reference to the future.

PROSPEC′TUS, *n.* [L.] The plan of a literary work, containing the general subject or design, with the manner and terms of publication, and sometimes a specimen of it.

PROS′PER, *v. t.* [L. *prospero*, from *prosperus*, from the Gr. προσφερω, to carry to or toward; προς and φερω, to bear.]

To favor; to render successful.

All things concur to *prosper* our design. *Dryden.*

PROS′PER, *v. i.* To be successful; to succeed.

The Lord made all that he did to *prosper* in his hand. Gen. xxxix.

He that covereth his sins, shall not *prosper.* Prov. xxviii.

2. To grow or increase; to thrive; to make gain; as, to *prosper* in business. Our agriculture, commerce and manufactures now *prosper.*

PROS′PERED, *pp.* Having success; favored.

PROS′PERING, *ppr.* Rendering successful; advancing in growth, wealth or any good.

PROSPER′ITY, *n.* [L. *prosperitas.*] Advance or gain in any thing good or desirable; successful progress in any business or enterprise; success; attainment of the object desired; as the *prosperity* of arts; agricultural or commercial *prosperity; national prosperity.* Our disposition to abuse the blessings of providence renders *prosperity* dangerous.

The *prosperity* of fools shall destroy them. Prov. i.

PROS′PEROUS, *a.* [L. *prosperus.*] Advancing in the pursuit of any thing desirable; making gain or increase; thriving; successful; as a *prosperous* trade; a *prosperous* voyage; a *prosperous* expedition or undertaking; a *prosperous* man, family or nation; a *prosperous* war.

The seed shall be *prosperous;* the vine shall give her fruit. Zech. viii.

2. Favorable; favoring success; as a *prosperous* wind. *Denham.*

PROS′PEROUSLY, *adv.* With gain or increase; successfully. *Bacon.*

PROS′PEROUSNESS, *n.* The state of being successful; prosperity.

PROSPI″CIENCE, *n.* [L. *prospiciens.*] The act of looking forward. *Dict.*

PROS′TATE, *a.* [from Gr. προιςημι, to set before.]

In *anatomy*, the *prostate gland* is a gland situated just before the neck of the bladder in males, and surrounding the beginning of the urethra. It is situated on the under and posterior part of the neck of the bladder, so as to surround the lower side of the urethra. *Encyc. Wistar.*

PROSTERNA′TION, *n.* [L. *prosterno*, to prostrate; *pro* and *sterno.*]

A state of being cast down; dejection; depression. [*Little used.*] *Wiseman.*

PROS′THESIS, PROTH′ESIS, *n.* [Gr.] In *surgery*, the addition of an artificial part to supply a defect of the body; as a wooden leg, &c. *Quincy. Coxe.*

PROSTHET′IC, *a.* [Gr. προσθετος.] Prefixed, as a letter to a word.

PROS′TITUTE, *v. t.* [L. *prostituo; pro* and *statuo*, to set.]

1. To offer freely to a lewd use, or to indiscriminate lewdness.

Do not *prostitute* thy daughter. Lev. xix.

2. To give up to any vile or infamous purpose; to devote to any thing base; to sell to wickedness; as, to *prostitute* talents to the propagation of infidel principles; to *prostitute* the press to the publication of blasphemy.

3. To offer or expose upon vile terms or to unworthy persons. *Tillotson.*

PROS′TITUTE, *a.* Openly devoted to lewdness; sold to wickedness or to infamous purposes.

Made bold by want and *prostitute* for bread. *Prior.*

PROS′TITUTE, *n.* A female given to indiscriminate lewdness; a strumpet. *Dryden.*

2. A base hireling; a mercenary; one who offers himself to infamous employments for hire.

No hireling she, no *prostitute* to praise. *Pope.*

PROS′TITUTED, *pp.* Offered to common lewdness; devoted to base purposes.

PROS′TITUTING, *ppr.* Offering to indiscriminate lewdness; devoting to infamous uses.

PROSTITU′TION, *n.* [Fr. from L. *prostituo.*]

1. The act or practice of offering the body to an indiscriminate intercourse with men; common lewdness of a female. *Spectator.*

2. The act of setting one's self to sale, or offering one's self to infamous employments; as the *prostitution* of talents or abilities.

PROS′TITUTOR, *n.* One who prostitutes; one who submits himself or offers another to vile purposes.

PROS′TRATE, *a.* [L. *prostratus*, from *prosterno*, to lay flat; *pro* and *sterno.*]

1. Lying at length, or with the body extended on the ground or other surface.

Groveling and *prostrate* on yon lake of fire. *Milton.*

2. Lying at mercy, as a supplicant. *Shak. Chapman.*

3. Lying in the posture of humility or adoration. *Milton. Pope.*

PROS′TRATE, *v. t.* To lay flat; to throw down; as, to *prostrate* the body; to *prostrate* trees or plants.

2. To throw down; to overthrow; to demolish; to ruin; as, to *prostrate* a village; to *prostrate* a government; to *prostrate* law or justice; to *prostrate* the honor of a nation.

3. To *prostrate one's self*, to throw one's self down or to fall in humility or adoration. *Duppa.*

4. To bow in humble reverence.

5. To sink totally; to reduce; as, to *prostrate* strength.

PROS′TRATED, *pp.* Laid at length; laid flat; thrown down; destroyed.

PROS′TRATING, *ppr.* Laying flat; throwing down; destroying.

PROSTRA′TION, *n.* The act of throwing down or laying flat; as the *prostration* of the body, of trees or of corn.

2. The act of falling down, or the act of bowing in humility or adoration; primarily. the act of falling on the face, but it is now used for kneeling or bowing in reverence and worship.

3. Great depression; dejection; as a *prostration* of spirits.

4. Great loss of natural strength and vigor; that state of the body in disease in which the system is passive and requires powerful stimulants to excite it into action. *Coxe.*

PRO′STȲLE, *n.* [Gr. προςυλος; προ and ςυλος, a column.]

In *architecture*, a range of columns in the front of a temple. *Encyc.*

PROSYL′LOGISM, *n.* [*pro* and *syllogism.*] A prosyllogism is when two or more syllogisms are so connected that the conclusion of the former is the major or minor of the following. *Watts.*

PRO′TASIS, *n.* [Gr. προτασις, from προτεινω, to present.]

1. A proposition; a maxim. *Johnson.*
2. In *the ancient drama*, the first part of a comic or tragic piece, in which the several persons are shown, their characters intimated, and the subject proposed and entered on. The protasis might extend to two acts, where it ended, and the epitasis commenced. *Encyc.*

PROTAT′IC, *a.* [Gr. προτατικος.] Being placed in the beginning; previous. *Dryden.*

PRO′TEAN, *a.* Pertaining to Proteus; readily assuming different shapes. [See *Proteus.*]

PROTECT′, *v. t.* [L. *protectus, protego; pro* and *tego*, to cover; Gr. ςεγω, with a prefix; Eng. *deck.* See *Deck.*]

To cover or shield from danger or injury; to defend; to guard; to preserve in safety; *a word of general import both in a literal and figurative sense.* Walls *protect* a city or garrison; clothing is designed to *protect* the body from cold; arms may *protect* one from an assault; our houses *protect* us from the inclemencies of the weather; the law *protects* our persons and property; the father *protects* his children, and the guardian his ward; a shade *protects* us from extreme heat; a navy *protects* our commerce and our shores; embassadors are *protected* from arrest.

PROTECT′ED, *pp.* Covered or defended from injury; preserved in safety.

PROTECT′ING, *ppr.* Shielding from injury; defending; preserving in safety.

PROTEC′TION, *n.* The act of protecting; defense; shelter from evil; preservation from loss, injury or annoyance. We find *protection* under good laws and an upright administration. How little are men disposed to acknowledge divine *protection!*

2. That which protects or preserves from injury.

> Let them rise up and help you, and be your *protection.* Deut. xxxii.

3. A writing that protects; a passport or other writing which secures from molestation.
4. Exemption. Embassadors at foreign courts are entitled to *protection* from arrest. Members of parliament, representatives and senators, are entitled to *protection* from arrest during their attendance on the legislature, as are suitors and witnesses attending a court.

Writ of protection, a writ by which the king of Great Britain exempts a person from arrest. *Blackstone.*

PROTECT′IVE, *a.* Affording protection; sheltering; defensive. *Thomson.*

PROTECT′OR, *n.* [Fr. *protecteur.*] One that defends or shields from injury, evil or oppression; a defender; a guardian. The king or sovereign is, or ought to be, the *protector* of the nation; the husband is the *protector* of his wife, and the father of his children.

2. In *England*, one who formerly had the care of the kingdom during the king's minority; a regent. Cromwell assumed the title of *lord Protector.*
3. In catholic countries, every nation and every religious order has a *protector* residing at Rome. He is a cardinal, and called *cardinal protector.*

PROTECT′ORATE, *n.* Government by a protector. *Walpole.*

PROTECT′ORSHIP, *n.* The office of a protector or regent. *Burnet.*

PROTECT′RESS, *n.* A woman or female that protects. *Bacon. Addison.*

PROTEND′, *v. t.* [L. *protendo; pro* and *tendo*, to stretch.]

To hold out; to stretch forth.

> With his *protended* lance he makes defense. *Dryden.*

PROTEND′ED, *pp.* Reached or stretched forth. *Mitford.*

PROTEND′ING, *ppr.* Stretching forth.

PROTENSE, *n. protens′.* Extension. [*Not used.*] *Spenser.*

PROTERV′ITY, *n.* [L. *protervitas*, from *protervus; pro* and *torvus*, crabbed.] Peevishness; petulance. [*Little used.*]

PROTEST′, *v. i.* [L. *protestor; pro* and *testor*, to affirm; It. *protestare;* Fr. *protester;* Sp. *protestar.*]

1. To affirm with solemnity; to make a solemn declaration of a fact or opinion; as, I *protest* to you, I have no knowledge of the transaction.
2. To make a solemn declaration expressive of opposition; with *against;* as, he *protests against* your votes. *Denham.*

> The conscience has power to *protest against* the exorbitancies of the passions. *South.*

3. To make a formal declaration in writing against a public law or measure. It is the privilege of any lord in parliament to *protest against* a law or resolution.

PROTEST′, *v. t.* To call as a witness in affirming or denying, or to prove an affirmation.

> Fiercely they oppos'd
> My journey strange, with clamorous uproar
> *Protesting* fate supreme. *Milton.*

2. To prove; to show; to give evidence of. [*Not in use.*] *Shak.*
3. In *commerce*, to *protest a bill of exchange*, is for a notary public, at the request of the payee, to make a formal declaration under hand and seal, against the drawer of the bill, on account of non-acceptance or non-payment, for exchange, cost, commissions, damages and interest; of which act the indorser must be notified within such time as the law or custom prescribes. In like manner, notes of hand given to a banking corporation are *protested* for non-payment.

PRO′TEST, *n.* A solemn declaration of opinion, commonly against some act; appropriately, a formal and solemn declaration in writing of dissent from the proceedings of a legislative body; as the *protest* of lords in parliament, or a like declaration of dissent of any minority against the proceedings of a majority of a body of men.

2. In *commerce*, a formal declaration made by a notary public, under hand and seal, at the request of the payee or holder of a bill of exchange, for non-acceptance or non-payment of the same, protesting against the drawer and others concerned, for the exchange, charges, damages and interest. This *protest* is written on a copy of the bill, and notice given to the indorser of the same, by which he becomes liable to pay the amount of the bill, with charges, damages and interest; also, a like declaration against the drawer of a note of hand for non-payment to a banking corporation, and of the master of a vessel against seizure, &c. A *protest* is also a writing attested by a justice of the peace or consul, drawn by the master of a vessel, stating the severity of the voyage by which the ship has suffered, and showing that the damage suffered was not owing to the neglect or misconduct of the master.

PROT′ESTANT, *a.* Pertaining to those who, at the reformation of religion, protested against a decree of Charles V. and the diet of Spires; pertaining to the adherents of Luther, or others of the reformed churches; as the *protestant* religion. *Addison. Milner.*

PROT′ESTANT, *n.* One of the party who adhered to Luther at the reformation in 1529, and protested, or made a solemn declaration of dissent from a decree of the emperor Charles V. and the diet of Spires, and appealed to a general council. This name was afterwards extended to the followers of Calvin, and *Protestants* is the denomination now given to all who belong to the reformed churches. The king of Prussia has, however, interdicted the use of this name in his dominions.

PROT′ESTANTISM, *n.* The protestant religion. *South.*

PROT′ESTANTLY, *adv.* In conformity to the protestants. [*A very bad word and not used.*] *Milton.*

PROTESTA′TION, *n.* [Fr.; from *protest.*]

1. A solemn declaration of a fact, opinion or resolution. *Hooker.*
2. A solemn declaration of dissent; a protest; as the *protestation* of certain noblemen against an order of council. *Clarendon.*
3. In *law*, a declaration in pleading, by which the party interposes an oblique allegation or denial of some fact, protesting that it does or does not exist. The lord may alledge the villenage of the plaintif by way of *protestation*, and thus deny the demand. *Blackstone.*

PROTEST′ED, *pp.* Solemnly declared or alledged: declared against for non-acceptance or non-payment.

PROTEST′ER, *n.* One who protests; one who utters a solemn declaration.

2. One who protests a bill of exchange.

PROTEST′ING, *ppr.* Solemnly declaring or affirming; declaring against for non-acceptance or non-payment.

PRO′TEUS, *n.* [L. from Gr. Πρωτευς.] In *mythology*, a marine deity, the son of Oceanus and Tethys, whose distinguishing characteristic was the faculty of assuming different shapes. Hence we denominate one who easily changes his form or principles, a *Proteus.*

PROTHON′OTARISHIP, *n.* The office of a prothonotary. [*An awkward, harsh word and little used.*] *Carew.*

PROTHON′OTARY, *n.* [Low L. *protonotarius;* Gr. πρωτος, first, and L. *notarius*, a scribe.]

1. Originally, the chief notary; and anciently, the title of the principal notaries of the emperors of Constantinople. Hence,

2. In *England*, an officer in the court of king's bench and common pleas. The prothonotary of the king's bench records all civil actions. In the common pleas, the prothonotaries, of which there are three, enter and enroll all declarations, pleadings, judgments, &c., make out judicial writs and exemplifications of records, enter recognizances, &c. *Encyc.*

3. In *the United States*, a register or clerk of a court. The word however is not applied to any officer, except in particular states.

Apostolical prothonotaries, in the court of Rome, are twelve persons constituting a college, who receive the last wills of cardinals, make informations and proceedings necessary for the canonization of saints, &c. *Encyc.*

PRO'TOCOL, *n.* [Low L. *protocollum*; Gr. πρωτος, first, and κολλα, glue; so called perhaps from the gluing together of pieces of paper, or from the spreading of it on tablets. It was formerly the upper part of a leaf of a book on which the title or name was written.]

1. The original copy of any writing. [*Not now used.*] *Ayliffe.*

2. A record or registry.

PRO'TOCOLIST, *n.* In Russia, a register or clerk. *Tooke.*

PRO'TOM'ARTYR, *n.* [Gr. πρωτος, first, and μαρτυρ, martyr.]

1. The first martyr; *a term applied to Stephen, the first christian martyr.*

2. The first who suffers or is sacrificed in any cause. *Dryden.*

PRO'TOPLAST, *n.* [Gr. πρωτος, first, and πλαςος, formed.]

The original; the thing first formed, as a copy to be imitated. Thus Adam has been called our *protoplast*. *Bryant. Harvey.*

PROTOPLAS'TIC, *a.* First formed. *Howell.*

PRO'TOPOPE, *n.* [Gr. πρωτος, first, and *pope.*]

Chief pope or imperial confessor, an officer of the holy directing synod, the supreme spiritual court of the Greek church in Russia. *Tooke, Russ.*

PROTOSUL'PHATE, *n.* In *chimistry*, the combination of sulphuric acid with a protoxyd.

PRO'TOTYPE, *n.* [Fr. from Gr. πρωτοτυπος; πρωτος, first, and τυπος, type, form, model.]

An original or model after which any thing is formed; the pattern of any thing to be engraved, cast, &c.; exemplar; archetype. *Wotton. Encyc.*

PROTOX'YD, *n.* [Gr. πρωτος, first, and οξυς, acid.]

A substance combined with oxygen in the first degree, or an oxyd formed by the first degree of oxydizement. *Thomson.*

PROTOX'YDIZE, *v. t.* To oxydize in the first degree.

PROTRACT', *v. t.* [L. *protractus*, from *protraho*; *pro* and *traho*, to draw.]

1. To draw out or lengthen in time; to continue; to prolong; as, to *protract* an argument; to *protract* a discussion; to *protract* a war or a negotiation.

2. To delay; to defer; to put off to a distant time; as, to *protract* the decision of a question; to *protract* the final issue.

PROTRACT', *n.* Tedious continuance. [*Not used.*] *Spenser.*

PROTRACT'ED, *pp.* Drawn out in time; delayed.

PROTRACT'ER, *n.* One who protracts or lengthens in time.

PROTRACT'ING, *ppr.* Drawing out or continuing in time; delaying.

PROTRAC'TION, *n.* The act of drawing out or continuing in time; the act of delaying the termination of a thing; as the *protraction* of a debate.

PROTRACT'IVE, *a.* Drawing out or lengthening in time; prolonging; continuing; delaying.

> He suffered their *protractive* arts. *Dryden.*

PROTRACT'OR, *n.* An instrument for laying down and measuring angles on paper with accuracy and dispatch, and by which the use of the line of chords is superseded. It is of various forms, semicircular, rectangular or circular. *Encyc.*

PROTREP'TICAL, *a.* [Gr. προτρεπτικος, from προτρεπω, προτρεπομαι, to exhort; προ and τρεπω, to turn.]

Hortatory; suasory; intended or adapted to persuade. [*Little used.*] *Ward.*

PROTRU'DE, *v. t.* [L. *protrudo*; *pro* and *trudo*, to *thrust*. See *Thrust.*]

1. To thrust forward; to drive or force along; as food *protruded* from the stomach into the intestine. *Locke.*

2. To thrust out, as from confinement. The contents of the abdomen are *protruded* in hernia.

PROTRU'DE, *v. i.* To shoot forward; to be thrust forward.

> The parts *protrude* beyond the skin. *Bacon.*

PROTRU'DED, *pp.* Thrust forward or out.

PROTRU'DING, *ppr.* Thrusting forward or out.

PROTRU'SION, *n.* *s* as *z.* The act of thrusting forward or beyond the usual limit; a thrusting or driving; a push. *Locke.*

PROTRU'SIVE, *a.* Thrusting or impelling forward; as *protrusive* motion. *Darwin.*

PROTU'BERANCE, *n.* [L. *protuberans*, *protubero*; *pro* and *tuber*, a puff, bunch or knob.]

A swelling or tumor on the body; a prominence; a bunch or knob; any thing swelled or pushed beyond the surrounding or adjacent surface; on the surface of the earth, a hill, knoll or other elevation. *Hale. More.*

Protuberance differs from *projection*, being applied to parts that rise from the surface with a gradual ascent or small angle; whereas a *projection* may be at a right angle with the surface.

PROTU'BERANT, *a.* Swelling; prominent beyond the surrounding surface; as a *protuberant* joint; a *protuberant* eye.

PROTU'BERATE, *v. i.* [L. *protubero*, supra.]

To swell or be prominent beyond the adjacent surface; to bulge out.

> If the navel *protuberates*, make a small puncture with a lancet through the skin. *Sharp.*

PROTUBERA'TION, *n.* The act of swelling beyond the surrounding surface. *Cooke.*

PROTU'BEROUS, *a.* Protuberant. *Smith.*

PROUD, *a.* [Sax. *prut*; D. *preutsch*, proud, prudish, also *prat*, proud, and *pratten*, to fret. We find in the Italian, *prode* is valiant, brave; *proda*, the *prow* of a ship; *prodezza*, prowess; probably of the same family, with the radical sense of swelling, stretching or erecting. See *Prude.*]

1. Having inordinate self-esteem; possessing a high or unreasonable conceit of one's own excellence, either of body or mind. A man may be *proud of* his person, *of* his talents, *of* his accomplishments or *of* his achievments. He may be *proud of* any thing to which he bears some relation. He may be *proud of* his country, his government, his equipage, or of whatever may, by association, gratify his esteem of himself. He may even be *proud of* his religion or *of* his church. He conceives that any thing excellent or valuable, in which he has a share, or to which he stands related, contributes to his own importance, and this conception exalts his opinion of himself. *Proud* is followed by *of*, before the object, supra.

2. Arrogant; haughty; supercilious.

> A foe so *proud* will not the weaker seek. *Milton.*

3. Daring; presumptuous.

> By his understanding he smiteth through the *proud*. Job xxvi.

4. Lofty of mien; grand of person; as a *proud* steed. *Milton.*

5. Grand; lofty; splendid; magnificent.

> Storms of stones from the *proud* temple's height. *Dryden.*

6. Ostentatious; grand; as *proud* titles. *Shak.*

7. Splendid; exhibiting grandeur and distinction; exciting pride; as a *proud* day for Rome.

8. Excited by the animal appetite; *applied particularly to the female of the canine species.*

9. Fungous; as *proud* flesh. *Sharp.*

PROUD'LY, *adv.* With an inordinate self-esteem; in a proud manner; haughtily; ostentatiously; with lofty airs or mien.

> *Proudly* he marches on and void of fear. *Pope.*

PRÖVABLE, *a.* [See *Prove.*] That may be proved.

PRÖVABLY, *adv.* In a manner capable of proof. *Huloet.*

PRO'VAND, *n.* Provender. [*Not in use.*]

PRÖVE, *v. t.* *pröv.* [Sax. *profian*; D. *proeven*; G. *probiren*; Dan. *pröver*; Sw. *profva*; W. *provi*; Arm. *proui*, *prouein*; L. *probo*; It. *provare*; Sp. *probar*, to try; Fr. *eprouver*; Russ. *probuyu*, to prove; *probevayu*, to pierce, to penetrate, to send by force. The primary sense is to strain, to urge by force, or rather to thrust or drive. The word *brow* may be of the same family, from its projection. See *Probe.*]

1. To try; to ascertain some unknown quality or truth by an experiment, or by a test or standard. Thus we *prove* the strength of gunpowder by experiment; we *prove* the strength or solidity of cannon by experiment. We *prove* the contents of a

vessel by comparing it with a standard measure.

2. To evince, establish or ascertain as truth, reality or fact, by testimony or other evidence. The plaintif in a suit, must *prove* the truth of his declaration; the prosecutor must *prove* his charges against the accused.

3. To evince truth by argument, induction or reasoning; to deduce certain conclusions from propositions that are true or admitted. If it is admitted that every immoral act is dishonorable to a rational being, and that dueling is an immoral act; then it is *proved* by necessary inference, that dueling is dishonorable to a rational being.

4. To ascertain the genuineness or validity of; to verify; as, to *prove* a will.

5. To experience; to try by suffering or encountering; to gain certain knowledge by the operation of something on ourselves, or by some act of our own.

Let him in arms the power of Turnus *prove*. *Dryden.*

6. In *arithmetic*, to show, evince or ascertain the correctness of any operation or result. Thus in subtraction, if the difference between two numbers, added to the lesser number, makes a sum equal to the greater, the correctness of the subtraction is *proved*. In other words, if the sum of the remainder and of the subtrahend, is equal to the minuend, the operation of subtraction is *proved* to be correct.

7. To try; to examine.

Prove your own selves. 2 Cor. xiii.

8. Men *prove God*, when by their provocations they put his patience to trial, Ps. xcv.; or when by obedience they make trial how much he will countenance such conduct, Mal. iii.

PRÖVE, *v. i.* To make trial; to essay.

The sons prepare—
To *prove* by arms whose fate it was to reign. *Dryden.*

2. To be found or to have its qualities ascertained by experience or trial; as, a plant or medicine *proves* salutary.

3. To be ascertained by the event or something subsequent; as the report *proves* to be true, or *proves* to be false.

When the inflammation ends in a gangrene, the case *proves* mortal. *Arbuthnot.*

4. To be found true or correct by the result.

5. To make certain; to show; to evince. This argument *proves* how erroneous is the common opinion.

6. To succeed.

If the experiment *proved* not— *Bacon.*
[*Not in use.*]

PROVED, *pp.* Tried; evinced; experienced.

PROVED'ITOR, } *n.* [It. *proveditore*, from PROVEDO'RE, } *provedere*, to provide. See *Provide.*]

A purveyor; one employed to procure supplies for an army.

Proveditor, in Venice and other parts of Italy, is an officer who superintends matters of policy. *Encyc.*

PROVEN'CIAL, *a.* [Fr. *provençal.*] Pertaining to Provence, in France.

PROV'ENDER, *n.* [Fr. *provende*, provender; Norm. *provender*, a prebendary; *provendre*, a prebend; D. *prove*, a *prebend*; [qu. G. D. Sw. *proviant*, provisions;] It. *provianda*, victuals; Ir. *proantain*, provender. The Italian *provianda* is probably composed of *pro* and *vivanda*, victuals, from *vivere*, L. *vivo*, to live, and from *vivanda* the French have *viande*, Eng. *viand*. Whether the French *provende* and Norm. *provender* are from the same source, may be doubted. The German *proviant* may be formed from the L. *provideo*, Sp. *proveer*, Port. *provêr*. Qu. L. *proventus*. It is said that *provend*, *provender*, originally signified a vessel containing a measure of corn daily given to a horse or other beast. But qu. *N* may be casual in *provender*, as in *messenger*, and the word may be from *provideo.*]

1. Dry food for beasts, usually meal, or a mixture of meal and cut straw or hay. In a more general sense, it may signify dry food of any kind. *Swift. Mortimer.*

2. Provisions; meat; food. *Coxe.*

[*Not used of food for man in New England.*]

PRÖVER, *n.* One that proves or tries; that which proves.

PROV'ERB, *n.* [Fr. *proverbe*; It. *proverbio*; L. *proverbium*; *pro* and *verbum*, a word.]

1. A short sentence often repeated, expressing a well known truth or common fact, ascertained by experience or observation; a maxim of wisdom.

The *proverb* is true, that light gains make heavy purses, for light gains come often, great gains now and then. *Bacon.*

2. A by-word; a name often repeated; and hence frequently, a reproach or object of contempt. Jer. xxiv.

3. In *Scripture*, it sometimes signifies a moral sentence or maxim that is enigmatical; a dark saying of the wise that requires interpretation. Prov. i.

4. *Proverbs*, a canonical book of the Old Testament, containing a great variety of wise maxims, rich in practical truths and excellent rules for the conduct of all classes of men.

PROV'ERB, *v. t.* To mention in a proverb. [*Not in use.*] *Milton.*

2. To provide with a proverb. [*Not in use.*] *Shak.*

PROVERB'IAL, *a.* Mentioned in a proverb; as a *proverbial* cure or remedy.

In case of excesses, I take the German *proverbial* cure, by a hair of the same beast, to be the worst in the world. *Temple.*

2. Comprised in a proverb; used or current as a proverb; as a *proverbial* saying or speech. *Pope.*

3. Pertaining to proverbs; resembling a proverb; suitable to a proverb; as a *proverbial* obscurity. *Brown.*

PROVERB'IALIST, *n.* One who speaks proverbs. *Langhorne.*

PROVERB'IALIZE, *v. t.* To make a proverb; to turn into a proverb, or to use proverbially. [*Unusual.*] *Good.*

PROVERB'IALLY, *adv.* In a proverb; as, it is *proverbially* said. *Brown.*

PROVI'DE, *v. t.* [L. *provideo*, literally to see before; *pro* and *video*, to see; Fr. *pourvoir*; It. *provvedere*; Sp. *proveer*; Port. *provêr.*]

1. To procure beforehand; to get, collect or make ready for future use; to prepare.

Abraham said, God will *provide* himself a lamb for a burnt-offering. Gen. xxii.

Provide neither gold nor silver nor brass in your purses. Matt. x.

Provide things honest in the sight of all men. Rom. xii.

2. To furnish; to supply; followed by *with*.

Rome, by the care of the magistrates, was well *provided with* corn. *Arbuthnot.*

Provided of is now obsolete.

3. To stipulate previously. The agreement *provides* that the party shall incur no loss.

4. To make a previous conditional stipulation. [See *Provided.*]

5. To foresee; *a Latinism.* [*Not in use.*] *B. Jonson.*

6. *Provide*, in a transitive sense, is followed by *against* or *for*. We *provide* warm clothing *against* the inclemencies of the weather; we *provide* necessaries *against* a time of need; or we *provide* warm clothing *for* winter, &c.

PROVI'DE, *v. i.* To procure supplies or means of defense; or to take measures for counteracting or escaping an evil. The sagacity of brutes in *providing against* the inclemencies of the weather is wonderful.

Government is a contrivance of human wisdom to *provide for* human wants. *Burke.*

PROVI'DED, *pp.* Procured beforehand; made ready for future use; supplied; furnished; stipulated.

2. Stipulated as a condition, which condition is expressed in the following sentence or words; as, "*provided* that nothing in this act shall prejudice the rights of any person whatever." This sentence is in the nature of the case absolute, the clause or sentence independent; "*this* or *that being provided*, which follows;" "*this condition being provided.*" The word *being* is understood, and the participle *provided* agrees with the whole sentence absolute. "*This condition being previously stipulated* or *established.*" *This* and *that* here refer to the whole member of the sentence.

PROV'IDENCE, *n.* [Fr. from L. *providentia.*]

1. The act of providing or preparing for future use or application.

Providence for war is the best prevention of it. [*Now little used.*] *Bacon.*

2. Foresight; timely care; particularly, active foresight, or foresight accompanied with the procurement of what is necessary for future use, or with suitable preparation. How many of the troubles and perplexities of life proceed from want of *providence!*

3. In *theology*, the care and superintendence which God exercises over his creatures. He that acknowledges a creation and denies a *providence*, involves himself in a palpable contradiction; for the same power which caused a thing to exist is necessary to continue its existence. Some persons admit a *general providence*, but deny a *particular providence*, not considering that a *general providence* consists of *particulars*. A belief in divine *providence*, is a source of great consolation to good men. By *divine providence* is often understood God himself.

4. Prudence in the management of one's concerns or in private economy.

PROV'IDENT, *a.* Foreseeing wants and making provision to supply them; forecasting; cautious; prudent in preparing for future exigences; as a *provident* man; a *provident* animal.

The parsimonious emmet, *provident*
Of future. *Milton.*

Orange is what Augustus was,
Brave, wary, *provident* and bold. *Waller.*

PROVIDEN'TIAL, *a.* Effected by the providence of God; referable to divine providence; proceeding from divine direction or superintendence; as the *providential* contrivance of things; a *providential* escape from danger. How much are we indebted to God's unceasing *providential* care! *Woodward.*

PROVIDEN'TIALLY, *adv.* By means of God's providence.

Every animal is *providentially* directed to the use of its proper weapons. *Ray.*

PROV'IDENTLY, *adv.* With prudent foresight; with wise precaution in preparing for the future.

PROVI'DER, *n.* One who provides, furnishes or supplies; one that procures what is wanted. *Shak.*

PROV'INCE, *n.* [Fr. from L. *provincia*; usually supposed to be formed from *pro* and *vinco*, to conquer. This is very doubtful, as *provinco* was not used by the Romans.]

1. Among *the Romans*, a country of considerable extent, which being reduced under their dominion, was new-modeled, subjected to the command of an annual governor sent from Rome, and to such taxes and contributions as the Romans saw fit to impose. That part of France next to the Alps, was a Roman *province*, and still bears the name *Provence*. *Encyc.*
2. Among *the moderns*, a country belonging to a kingdom or state, either by conquest or colonization, usually situated at a distance from the kingdom or state, but more or less dependent on it or subject to it. Thus formerly, the English colonies in North America were *provinces* of Great Britain, as Nova Scotia and Canada still are. The *provinces* of the Netherlands formerly belonged to the house of Austria and to Spain.
3. A division of a kingdom or state, of considerable extent. In *England*, a division of the ecclesiastical state under the jurisdiction of an archbishop, of which there are two, the *province* of Canterbury and that of York.
4. A region of country; *in a general sense;* a tract; a large extent.

Over many a tract
Of heaven they march'd, and many a *province* wide. *Milton.*

They never look abroad into the *provinces* of the intellectual world. *Watts.*

5. The proper office or business of a person. It is the *province* of the judge to decide causes between individuals.

The woman's *province* is to be careful in her economy, and chaste in her affection. *Tatler.*

PROVIN'CIAL, *a.* Pertaining to a province or relating to it; as a *provincial* government; a *provincial* dialect.

2. Appendant to the principal kingdom or state; as *provincial* dominion; *provincial* territory. *Brown.*
3. Not polished; rude; as *provincial* accent or manners. *Dryden.*
4. Pertaining to an ecclesiastical province, or to the jurisdiction of an archbishop; not ecumenical; as a *provincial* synod. *Ayliffe.*

PROVIN'CIAL, *n.* A spiritual governor. In *catholic countries*, one who has the direction of the several convents of a province. *Encyc.*

2. A person belonging to a province. *Burke.*

PROVIN'CIALISM, *n.* A peculiar word or manner of speaking in a province or district of country remote from the principal country or from the metropolis. *Marsh.*

PROVINCIAL'ITY, *n.* Peculiarity of language in a province. *Warton.*

PROVIN'CIATE, *v. t.* To convert into a province. [*Unusual.*] *Howell.*

PROVI'NE, *v. i.* [Fr. *provigner; pro* and *vigne*, a vine.]

To lay a stock or branch of a vine in the ground for propagation. *Johnson.*

PRÖVING, *ppr.* Trying; ascertaining; evincing; experiencing.

PROVI''SION, *n. s* as *z.* [Fr. from L. *provisio, provideo.* See *Provide.*]

1. The act of providing or making previous preparation.
2. Things provided; preparation; measures taken beforehand, either for security, defense or attack, or for the supply of wants. We make *provision* to defend ourselves from enemies; we make *provision* for war; we make *provision* for a voyage or for erecting a building; we make *provision* for the support of the poor. Government makes *provision* for its friends.
3. Stores provided; stock; as *provision* of victuals; *provision* of materials. *Knolles. South.*
4. Victuals; food; provender; all manner of eatables for man and beast; as *provisions* for the table or for the family; *provisions* for an army. *Milton. Encyc.*
5. Previous stipulation; terms or agreement made, or measures taken for a future exigency.

In the law, no *provision* was made to abolish the barbarous customs of the Irish. *Davies.*

Papal provision, a previous nomination by the pope to a benefice before it became vacant, by which practice the rightful patron was deprived of his presentation. *Blackstone.*

PROVI''SION, *v. t.* To supply with victuals or food. The ship was *provisioned* for a voyage of six months. The garrison was well *provisioned.*

PROVI''SIONAL, *a.* [Fr. *provisionnel.*] Provided for present need or for the occasion; temporarily established; temporary; as a *provisional* government or regulation; a *provisional* treaty.

PROVI''SIONALLY, *adv.* By way of provision; temporarily; for the present exigency. *Locke.*

PROVI''SIONARY, *a.* Provisional; provided for the occasion; not permanent. *Burke.*

PROVI'SO, *n. s* as *z.* [L. *provisus*, ablative *proviso*, it being provided.]

An article or clause in any statute, agreement, contract, grant or other writing, by which a condition is introduced; a conditional stipulation that affects an agreement, contract, law, grant, &c. The charter of the bank contains a *proviso* that the legislature may repeal it at their pleasure.

PROVI'SOR, *n.* [Fr. *proviseur.*] In *church affairs*, a person appointed by the pope to a benefice before the death of the incumbent, and to the prejudice of the rightful patron. Formerly the pope usurped the right of presenting to church livings, and it was his practice to nominate persons to benefices by anticipation, or before they became vacant; the person thus nominated was called a *provisor.* In England, this practice was restrained by statutes of Richard II. and Henry IV.

More sharp and penal laws were devised against *provisors;* it being enacted that whoever disturbs any patron in the presentation to a living by virtue of any papal provision, such *provisor* shall pay fine and ransom to the king at his will, and be imprisoned till he renounces such provision. *Blackstone.*

2. The purveyor, steward or treasurer of a religious house. *Cowel.*

PROVI'SORY, *a.* Making temporary provision; temporary. *State Papers.*

2. Containing a proviso or condition; conditional.

PROVOCA'TION, *n.* [Fr. from L. *provocatio.* See *Provoke.*]

1. Any thing that excites anger; the cause of resentment. 1 Kings xxi.

Harden not your hearts, as in the *provocation.* Ps. xcv.

2. The act of exciting anger.
3. An appeal to a court or judge. [*A Latinism, not now used.*] *Ayliffe.*
4. Incitement. [*Not used.*] *Hooker.*

PROVO'CATIVE, *a.* Exciting; stimulating; tending to awaken or incite appetite or passion.

PROVO'CATIVE, *n.* Any thing that tends to excite appetite or passion; a stimulant; as a *provocative* of hunger or of lust. *Addison.*

PROVO'CATIVENESS, *n.* The quality of being provocative or stimulating.

PROVO'KE, *v. t.* [L. *provoco*, to call forth; *pro* and *voco*, to call; Fr. *provoquer;* It. *provocare;* Sp. *provocar.*]

1. To call into action; to arouse; to excite; as, to *provoke* anger or wrath by offensive words or by injury; to *provoke* war.
2. To make angry; to offend; to incense; to enrage.

Ye fathers, *provoke* not your children to wrath. Eph. vi.

Often *provoked* by the insolence of some of the bishops— *Clarendon.*

3. To excite; to cause; as, to *provoke* perspiration; to *provoke* a smile. *Arbuthnot.*
4. To excite; to stimulate; to increase.

The taste of pleasure *provokes* the appetite, and every successive indulgence of vice which is to form a habit, is easier than the last. *Buckminster.*

5. To challenge.

He now *provokes* the sea-gods from the shore. *Dryden.*

6. To move; to incite; to stir up; to induce by motives. Rom. x. *Bacon.*

Let us consider one another to *provoke* to love and to good works. Heb. x.

7. To incite; to rouse; as, to *provoke* one to anger. Deut. xxxii.

PROVO'KE, *v. i.* To appeal. [*A Latinism, not used.*] *Dryden.*

PROVO'KED, *pp.* Excited; roused; incited; made angry; incensed.

PROVO'KER, *n.* One that excites anger or other passion; one that excites war or sedition.

2. That which excites, causes or promotes. *Shak.*

PROVO'KING, *ppr.* Exciting into action; inciting; inducing by motives; making angry.

2. *a.* Having the power or quality of exciting resentment; tending to awaken passion; as *provoking* words; *provoking* treatment.

PROVO'KINGLY, *adv.* In such a manner as to excite anger.

PRO'VOST, *n.* [Sax. *profost, profast*; Dan. *provst*; G. *probst, propst*; Arm. *provost*; Fr. *prevôt*; Port. Sp. *preboste*; It. *proposto*; from the L. *præpositus*, placed before, from *præpono*; *præ* and *pono*, to set or place.]

In *a general sense*, a person who is appointed to superintend or preside over something; the chief magistrate of a city or town; as the *provost* of Edinburgh or of Glasgow, answering to the *mayor* of other cities; the *provost* of a college, answering to *president*. In France, formerly, a *provost* was an inferior judge who had cognizance of civil causes.

The grand provost of France, or *of the household*, had jurisdiction in the king's house and over its officers.

The provost marshal of an army, is an officer appointed to arrest and secure deserters and other criminals, to hinder the soldiers from pillaging, to indict offenders and see sentence passed on them and executed. He also regulates weights and measures. He has under him a lieutenant and a clerk, an executioner, &c. *Encyc.*

The provost marshal in the navy, has charge of prisoners, &c.

The provost of the mint, is a particular judge appointed to apprehend and prosecute false coiners. *Encyc.*

Provost of the king's stables, is an officer who attends at court and holds the king's stirrup when he mounts his horse. *Encyc.*

PRO'VOSTSHIP, *n.* The office of a provost. *Hakewill.*

PROW, *n.* [Fr. *proue*; It. *prua* and *proda*; Sp. *proa*. These may be from the L. *prora*; but qu. is not *proda* the original word, and *prora* a contraction of *prodera*? The primary sense is that which projects or stretches forward.]

1. The forepart of a ship. *Dryden.*

2. In *seamen's language*, the beak or pointed cutwater of a xebec or galley. The upper part is usually furnished with a grating platform. *Mar. Dict.*

3. The name of a particular kind of vessel used in the East Indian seas.

PROW, *a.* Valiant. [*Not in use.*] *Spenser.*

PROW'ESS, *n.* [Fr. *prouesse*; It. *prodezza*, from *prode*, brave, and as a noun, profit, benefit; Sp. *proeza*. The primary sense of the root is to stretch, shoot or advance forward, and hence the sense of profit.]

Bravery; valor; particularly, military bravery; gallantry; intrepidity in war; fearlessness of danger.

> Men of such *prowess* as not to know fear in themselves. *Sidney.*

PROW'EST, *a.* [*superl.* of *prow.*] Bravest. [*Not in use.*] *Spenser.*

PROWL, *v. t.* [I know not the origin of this word, nor from what source it is derived. It may be derived from the root of *stroll, troll*, with a different prefix.] To rove over.

> He *prowls* each place, still in new colors deck'd. *Sidney.*

PROWL, *v. i.* To rove or wander, particularly for prey, as a wild beast; as a *prowling* wolf. *Milton.*

2. To rove and plunder; to prey; to plunder. *Tusser.*

PROWL, *n.* A roving for prey; colloquially, something to be seized and devoured.

PROWL'ER, *n.* One that roves about for prey. *Thomson.*

PROWL'ING, *ppr.* Wandering about in search of prey or plunder.

PROX'IMAL. [See *Proximate.*]

PROX'IMATE, *a.* [L. superl. *proximus*; Fr. *proche*; *approcher*, to *approach*; *reprocher*, to *reproach*. The primary sense of the root is to drive or press. See Class Brg.]

Nearest; next. A *proximate* cause is that which immediately precedes and produces the effect, as distinguished from the *remote, mediate* or *predisposing* cause. *Watts.*

PROX'IMATELY, *adv.* Immediately; by immediate relation to or effect on. *Bentley.*

PROX'IME, *a.* Next; immediately. [*Not used.*] *Watts.*

PROXIM'ITY, *n.* [Fr. *proximité*; L. *proximitas.*]

The state of being next; immediate nearness either in place, blood or alliance. The succession to the throne and to estates is usually regulated by *proximity* of blood. *Dryden. Swift.*

PROX'Y, *n.* [contracted from *procuracy*, or some word from the root of *procure, proctor.*]

1. The agency of another who acts as a substitute for his principal; agency of a substitute; appearance of a representative. None can be familiar by *proxy*. None can be virtuous or wise by *proxy*.

2. The person who is substituted or deputed to act for another. A wise man will not commit important business to a *proxy*, when he can transact it in person. In England, any peer may make another lord of parliament his *proxy* to vote for him in his absence. *Blackstone.*

3. In *popular use*, an election or day of voting for officers of government.

PROX'YSHIP, *n.* The office or agency of a proxy.

PRUCE, *n.* [from *Prussia.*] Prussian lether. [*Not in use.*] *Dryden.*

PRUDE, *n.* [Fr. *prude*, wise, discrete, sober, formal, precise; D. *preutsch*, prudish, and proud; G. *spröde*, a prude, and shy, cold, reserved, coy, demure, and applied to metals, brittle, friable; Dan. *sprödig*, eager, brittle, harsh, dry, rugged; W. *pruz*, [*prudh*,] prudent, discrete, serious, sad, sorrowful; Goth. *frods*, prudent; Gr. φραδη, prudence; Goth. *frathi*, mind, intellect; *frathyan*, to be wise, to understand. The Goth. *frod* signifies both wise, prudent, and broken; D. *vroed*, prudent. We see that *prude, prudent*, and *proud* are from the same root. The sense of *brittle* would indicate that these words belong to the same family with the Dan. *bryder*, to break; and the radical elements are the same. The Welsh *pruz* is from tending out or reaching, hence *pryder*, anxiety, a stretching of the mind. The sense of *prude* is probably from stretching, straitness, stiffness; and the sense of *wise* is derivative. *Prudence* is from the same root, implying care, a tension of mind.]

A woman of great reserve, coyness, affected stiffness of manners and scrupulous nicety.

> Less modest than the speech of *prudes*. *Swift.*

PRU'DENCE, *n.* [Fr. from L. *prudentia*; It. *prudenza*; Sp. *prudencia*. See *Prude.*]

Wisdom applied to practice. *Johnson.*

Prudence implies caution in deliberating and consulting on the most suitable means to accomplish valuable purposes, and the exercise of sagacity in discerning and selecting them. Prudence differs from wisdom in this, that prudence implies more caution and reserve than wisdom, or is exercised more in foreseeing and avoiding evil, than in devising and executing that which is good. It is sometimes mere caution or circumspection.

> *Prudence* is principally in reference to actions to be done, and due means, order, season and method of doing or not doing. *Hale.*

PRU'DENT, *a.* Cautious; circumspect; practically wise; careful of the consequences of enterprises, measures or actions; cautious not to act when the end is of doubtful utility, or probably impracticable.

> The *prudent* man looketh well to his going. Prov. xiv.
>
> A *prudent* man foreseeth the evil and hideth himself. Prov. xxii.

2. Dictated or directed by prudence; as *prudent* behavior.

3. Foreseeing by instinct; as the *prudent* crane. *Milton.*

4. Frugal; economical; as a *prudent* woman; *prudent* expenditure of money.

5. Wise; intelligent.

PRUDEN'TIAL, *a.* Proceeding from prudence; dictated or prescribed by prudence; as *prudential* motives; *prudential* rules.

2. Superintending the discretionary concerns of a society; as a *prudential* committee. *N. England.*

PRUDENTIAL'ITY, *n.* The quality of being prudential; eligibility on principles of prudence. [*Not used.*] *Brown.*

PRUDEN'TIALLY, *adv.* In conformity with prudence; prudently. *South.*

PRUDEN'TIALS, *n. plu.* Maxims of prudence or practical wisdom.

> Many stanzas in poetic measures contain rules relating to common *prudentials*, as well as to religion. *Watts.*

2. The subordinate discretionary concerns

and economy of a company, society or corporation. The board of trustees appoint annually a committee to manage the *prudentials* of the corporation. *N. England.*

PRU'DENTLY, *adv.* With prudence; with due caution or circumspection; discretely; wisely; as domestic affairs *prudently* managed; laws *prudently* framed or executed.

2. With frugality; economically; as income *prudently* expended.

PRU'DERY, *n.* [from *prude.*] Affected scrupulousness; excessive nicety in conduct; stiffness; affected reserve or gravity; coyness. *Tatler.*

PRU'DISH, *a.* [from *prude.*] Affectedly grave; very formal, precise or reserved; as a *prudish* woman; *prudish* manners.

> A formal lecture, spoke with *prudish* face. *Garrick.*

PRU'NE, *v. t.* [perhaps from Fr. *provigner,* to lay down vine stocks for propagation. If not, I know not its origin.]

1. To lop or cut off the superfluous branches of trees, to make them bear better fruit or grow higher, or to give them a more handsome and regular appearance. *Encyc. Milton.*

2. To clear from any thing superfluous; to dress; to trim.

> His royal bird
> *Prunes* the immortal wing, and cloys his beak. *Shak.*

PRUNE, *v. i.* To dress; to prink; *a ludicrous word.* *Dryden.*

PRUNE, *n.* [Fr. *prune;* It. Sp. *pruna;* L. *prunum;* D. *pruim.* In Latin, *prunus* is a plum tree, Gr. προυνη, and *prunum,* the fruit.]

A plum, or a dried plum. *Bacon.*

PRU'NED, *pp.* Divested of superfluous branches; trimmed.

2. Cleared of what is unsuitable or superfluous.

PRU'NEL, *n.* A plant. *Ainsworth.*

PRUNEL'LO, *n.* A kind of stuff of which clergymen's gowns are made. *Pope.*

PRUNEL'LO, *n.* [Fr. *prunelle,* from *prune.*] A kind of plum. *Ainsworth.*

PRU'NER, *n.* One that prunes trees or removes what is superfluous.

PRUNIF'EROUS, *a.* [L. *prunum,* a plum, and *fero,* to bear.] Bearing plums.

PRU'NING, *ppr.* Lopping off superfluous branches; trimming; clearing of what is superfluous.

PRU'NING, *n.* In *gardening* and *agriculture,* the lopping off the superfluous branches of trees, either for improving the trees or their fruit.

PRU'NING-HOOK, } *n.* An instrument used in pruning
PRU'NING-KNIFE, } trees. It is of various forms. *Dryden. Philips.*

PRU'RIENCE, } *n.* [L. *pruriens, prurio,* to
PRU'RIENCY, } itch.]

An itching, longing desire or appetite for any thing. *Swift.*

PRU'RIENT, *a.* Itching; uneasy with desire. *Warton.*

PRURIG'INOUS, *a.* [L. *pruriginosus,* from *prurigo,* an itching, from *prurio,* to itch.]

Tending to an itch. *Greenhill.*

PRUSSIAN, *a.* [from *Prussia.*] Pertaining to Prussia.

Prussian blue, a combination of iron with ferrocyanic acid. This is used as a pigment of a beautiful blue color.

PRUSSIATE, *n.* A salt formed by the union of the prussic acid, or coloring matter of prussian blue, with a salifiable base; as the *prussiate* of alumin. *Lavoisier. Fourcroy.*

PRUSSIC, *a.* The *prussic acid* is a compound of kyanogen or cyanogen, prussic gas and hydrogen, and hence called hydrocyanic acid. It is one of the strongest poisons known.

PRY, *v. i.* [a contracted word, the origin of which is not obvious.]

To peep narrowly; to inspect closely; to attempt to discover something with scrutinizing curiosity, whether impertinently or not; as, to *pry* into the mysteries of nature, or into the secrets of state.

> Nor need we with a *prying* eye survey
> The distant skies to find the milky way. *Creech.*

PRY, *n.* Narrow inspection; impertinent peeping. *Smart.*

PRY, *v. t.* To raise or attempt to raise with a lever. This is the common popular pronunciation of *prize,* in America. The lever used is also called a *pry.*

PRY'ING, *ppr.* Inspecting closely; looking into with curiosity.

PRY'INGLY, *adv.* With close inspection or impertinent curiosity.

PRY'TANE, } *n.* [Gr. πρυτανις.] In *ancient*
PRYT'ANIS, } *Greece,* a president of the senate of five hundred. *Encyc. Anacharsis.*

[It is to be noted that in words beginning with *Ps* and *Pt,* the letter *p* has no sound.]

PSALM, *n.* s'am. [L. *psalmus;* Gr. ψαλμος, from ψαλλω, to touch or beat, to sing; Fr. *psaume;* It. Sp. *salmo.*]

A sacred song or hymn; a song composed on a divine subject and in praise of God. The most remarkable psalms are those composed by David and other Jewish saints, a collection of one hundred and fifty of which constitutes a canonical book of the Old Testament, called *Psalms,* or the *book of Psalms.* The word is also applied to sacred songs composed by modern poets, being versifications of the scriptural psalms, or of these with other parts of Scripture, composed for the use of churches; as the *Psalms* of Tate and Brady, of Watts, &c.

PS'ALMIST, *n.* A writer or composer of sacred songs; a title particularly applied to David and the other authors of the scriptural psalms.

2. In *the church of Rome,* a clerk, precentor, singer or leader of music in the church.

PS'ALMODY, *n.* The act, practice or art of singing sacred songs. *Psalmody* has always been considered an important part of public worship.

PSALMOG'RAPHER, } *n.* [See *Psalmog-*
PSALMOG'RAPHIST, } *raphy.*]

A writer of psalms or divine songs and hymns.

PSALMOG'RAPHY, *n.* [Gr. ψαλμος, psalm, and γραφω, to write.]

The act or practice of writing psalms or sacred songs and hymns.

PSAL'TER, *n.* [L. *psalterium;* Gr. ψαλτηριον; It. Sp. *salterio;* Fr. *psautier.*]

1. The book of Psalms; often applied to a book containing the Psalms separately printed.

2. In *Romish countries,* a large chaplet or rosary, consisting of a hundred and fifty beads, according to the number of the psalms.

PSAL'TERY, *n.* [Gr. ψαλτηριον.] An instrument of music used by the Hebrews, the form of which is not now known. That which is now used is a flat instrument in form of a trapezium or triangle truncated at the top, strung with thirteen chords of wire, mounted on two bridges at the sides, and struck with a plectrum or crooked stick. *Encyc.*

> Praise the Lord with harp; sing to him with the *psaltery,* and an instrument of ten strings. Ps. xxxiii.

PSAM'MITE, *n.* [Gr. ψαμμος, sand.] A species of micaceous sandstone. *Brongniart.*

PSEUDO, Gr. ψευδος, false, a prefix signifying false, counterfeit or spurious.

PSEUDO-APOS'TLE, *n.* A false apostle; one who falsely pretends to be an apostle.

PSEUDO-CHI'NA, *n.* The false China root, a plant of the genus Smilax, found in America. *Encyc.*

PSEUDO-GALE'NA, *n.* False galena or black jack.

PSEU'DOGRAPH, } *n.* [Gr. ψευδος, false,
PSEUDOG'RAPHY, } and γραφη, writing.]

False writing. *Holder.*

PSEUDOL'OGY, *n.* [Gr. ψευδολογια; ψευδος, false, and λογος, discourse.]

Falsehood of speech. *Arbuthnot.*

PSEUDO-METAL'LIC, *a.* *Pseudo-metallic* luster is that which is perceptible only when held towards the light; as in minerals. *Phillips.*

PSEUDOMORPH'OUS, *a.* [*pseudo* and Gr. μορφη, form.]

Not having the true form. A *pseudomorphous* mineral is one which has received its form from some extraneous cause, not from natural crystalization.

PSEUDO-TINEA, *n.* In *natural history,* the name of a remarkable species of insect or larva, resembling a moth. It feeds on wax, and is a terrible enemy to bees, as it enters the hive and sometimes compels the bees to abandon it, being covered with a coat that is impervious to their stings. *Encyc.*

PSEUDO-VOLCAN'IC, *a.* Pertaining to or produced by a pseudo-volcano. *Cleaveland.*

PSEUDO-VOLCA'NO, *n.* A volcano that emits smoke and sometimes flame, but no lava; also, a burning mine of coal. *Kirwan.*

PSHAW, *exclam.* An expression of contempt, disdain or dislike.

PSO'AS, *n.* [Gr.] The name of two inside muscles of the loins.

PSO'RA, *n.* [Gr.] The itch.

PSYCHOLOG'IC, } *a.* Pertaining to a
PSYCHOLOG'ICAL, } treatise on the soul, or to the study of the soul of man. *Literary Mag.*

PSYCHOL'OGY, *n.* [Gr. ψυχη, soul, and λογος, discourse.]

A discourse or treatise on the human soul;

or the doctrine of the nature and properties of the soul. *Campbell.*

PT'ARMIGAN, *n.* A fowl of the genus Tetrao, the lagopus or white game. The color of the plumage is a pale brown or ash, elegantly crossed or mottled with dusky spots and minute bars; the belly and wings are white. This fowl is seen on the summits of mountains in the north of England and of Scotland. *Encyc.*

PTISAN, *n. tiz'an.* [L. *ptisana;* Gr. πτισανη, from πτισσω, to pound.]

A decoction of barley with other ingredients. *Encyc. Arbuthnot.*

PTOLEMA'I€, *a.* [from *Ptolemy,* the geographer and astrologer.]

Pertaining to Ptolemy. The *Ptolemaic* system, in astronomy, is that maintained by Ptolemy, who supposed the earth to be fixed in the center of the universe, and that the sun and stars revolve around it. This theory was received for ages, but has been rejected for the Copernican system.

PTY'ALISM, *n.* [Gr. πτυαλισμος, a spitting, from πτυαλιζω, to spit often.]

In *medicine,* salivation; an unnatural or copious flow of saliva. *Coxe. Encyc.*

PTYS'MAGOGUE, *n.* [Gr. πτυσμα, saliva, and αγω, to drive.]

A medicine that promotes discharges of saliva. *Dict.*

PU'BERTY, *n.* [L. *pubertas,* from *pubes.*] The age at which persons are capable of procreating and bearing children. This age is different in different climates, but is with us considered to be at fourteen years in males, and twelve in females.

PU'BES, *n.* [L.] In *botany,* the hairiness of plants; a downy or villous substance which grows on plants; pubescence. *Martyn.*

PUBES'CENCE, *n.* [L. *pubescens, pubesco,* to shoot, to grow mossy or hairy.]

1. The state of a youth who has arrived at puberty; or the state of puberty. *Brown.*

2. In *botany,* hairiness; shagginess; the hairy or downy substance on plants.

PUBES'CENT, *a.* Arriving at puberty. *Brown.*

2. In *botany,* covered with pubescence, such as hair, bristles, beard, down, &c.; as the leaves of plants.

PUB'LI€, *a.* [L. *publicus,* from the root of *populus,* people; that is, *people-like;* Sp. *publico;* It. *pubblico;* Fr. *publique;* W. *pobyl,* people; *pob, pawb,* each, every, every body.]

1. Pertaining to a nation, state or community; extending to a whole people; as a *public* law, which binds the people of a nation or state, as opposed to a *private* statute or resolve, which respects an individual or a corporation only. Thus we say, *public* welfare, *public* good, *public* calamity, *public* service, *public* property.

2. Common to many; current or circulated among people of all classes; general; as *public* report; *public* scandal.

3. Open; notorious; exposed to all persons without restriction.

> Joseph her husband being a just man, and not willing to make her a *public* example, was minded to put her away privily. Matt. i.

4. Regarding the community; directed to the interest of a nation, state or community; as *public* spirit; *public* mindedness; opposed to *private* or *selfish.* *South.*

5. Open for general entertainment; as a *public* house.

6. Open to common use; as a *public* road.

7. In general, *public* expresses something common to mankind at large, to a nation, state, city or town, and is opposed to *private,* which denotes what belongs to an individual, to a family, to a company or corporation.

Public law, is often synonymous with the *law of nations.*

PUB'LI€, *n.* The general body of mankind or of a nation, state or community; the people, indefinitely.

> The *public* is more disposed to censure than to praise. *Addison.*

In this passage, *public* is followed by a verb in the singular number; but being a noun of multitude, it is more generally followed by a plural verb; the *public are.*

In public, in open view; before the people at large; not in private or secresy.

> In private grieve, but with a careless scorn,
> *In public* seem to triumph, not to mourn. *Granville.*

PUB'LI€AN, *n.* [L. *publicanus,* from *publicus.*]

1. A collector of toll or tribute. Among *the Romans,* a *publican* was a farmer of the taxes and public revenues, and the inferior officers of this class were deemed oppressive.

> As Jesus sat at meat in the house, behold, many *publicans* and sinners came and sat down with him and his disciples. Matt. ix.

2. The keeper of a public house; an inn-keeper.

PUBLI€A'TION, *n.* [L. *publicatio,* from *publico,* from *publicus.*]

1. The act of publishing or offering to public notice; notification to a people at large, either by words, writing or printing; proclamation; divulgation; promulgation; as the *publication* of the law at mount Sinai; the *publication* of the gospel; the *publication* of statutes or edicts.

2. The act of offering a book or writing to the public by sale or by gratuitous distribution. The author consented to the *publication* of his manuscripts.

3. A work printed and published; any pamphlet or book offered for sale or to public notice; as a new *publication;* a monthly *publication.*

PUB'LI€-HE'ARTED, *a.* Public-spirited. [*Not used.*] *Clarendon.*

PUB'LICIST, *n.* A writer on the laws of nature and nations; one who treats of the rights of nations. *Kent. Du Ponceau.*

PUBLIC'ITY, *n.* [Fr. *publicité.*] The state of being public or open to the knowledge of a community; notoriety.

PUB'LI€LY, *adv.* Openly; with exposure to popular view or notice; without concealment; as property *publicly* offered for sale; an opinion *publicly* avowed; a declaration *publicly* made.

2. In the name of the community. A reward is *publicly* offered for the discovery of the longitude, or for finding a northwestern passage to Asia.

PUB'LI€-MINDED, *a.* Disposed to promote the public interest. [*Little used.*]

PUB'LI€-MINDEDNESS, *n.* A disposition to promote the public weal or advantage. [*Little used.*] *South.*

PUB'LI€NESS, *n.* The state of being public, or open to the view or notice of people at large; as the *publicness* of a sale.

2. State of belonging to the community; as the *publicness* of property. *Boyle.*

PUBLI€-SPIR'ITED, *a.* Having or exercising a disposition to advance the interest of the community; disposed to make private sacrifices for the public good; as *public-spirited* men. *Dryden.*

2. Dictated by a regard to public good; as a *public-spirited* project or measure. *Addison.*

PUBLI€-SPIR'ITEDNESS, *n.* A disposition to advance the public good, or a willingness to make sacrifices of private interest to promote the common weal. *Whitlock.*

PUB'LISH, *v. t.* [Fr. *publier;* Sp. *publicar;* It. *pubblicare;* L. *publico.* See *Public.*]

1. To discover or make known to mankind or to people in general what before was private or unknown; to divulge, as a private transaction; to promulgate or proclaim, as a law or edict. We *publish* a secret, by telling it to people without reserve. Laws are *published* by printing or by proclamation. Christ and his apostles *published* the glad tidings of salvation.

> Th' unwearied sun, from day to day,
> Does his Creator's power display;
> And *publishes* to every land
> The work of an Almighty hand. *Spectator.*

2. To send a book into the world; or to sell or offer for sale a book, map or print.

3. To utter; to put off or into circulation; as, to *publish* a forged or counterfeit paper. *Laws of Mass. and Conn.*

4. To make known by posting, or by reading in a church; as, to *publish* banns of matrimony. We say also, the persons intending marriage are *published;* that is, their intention of marriage is published.

PUB'LISHED, *pp.* Made known to the community; divulged; promulgated; proclaimed.

PUB'LISHER, *n.* One who makes known what was before private or unknown; one that divulges, promulgates or proclaims. *Atterbury.*

2. One who sends a book or writing into the world for common use; one that offers a book, pamphlet, &c., for sale.

3. One who utters, passes or puts into circulation a counterfeit paper.

PUB'LISHING, *ppr.* Making known; divulging; promulgating; proclaiming; selling or offering publicly for sale; uttering.

PUB'LISHMENT, *n.* In *popular usage in New England,* a notice of intended marriage.

PU€€OON', *n.* A plant, a species of Sanguinaria; the blood-root. *Fam. of Plants.*

PUCE, *a.* Of a dark brown color. Qu.

PU'CELAGE, *n.* [Fr.] A state of virginity. [*Little used.*] *Robinson.*

PU'CERON, *n.* [Fr. from *puce,* a flea.] The name of a tribe of small insects which are found in great numbers on the bark and leaves of plants, and live by sucking the sap; the Aphis, vine fretter, or plant louse. *Encyc.*

PUCK, *n.* [Ice. Sw. *puke*, a demon; Scot. *puck.*]
A demon; a mischievous spirit. *Shak.*

PUCK′-BALL, } *n.* [from *puck.*] A kind of
PUCK′-FIST, } mushroom full of dust. *Dict.*

PUCK′ER, *v. t.* [Sp. *buche*, a purse, rumple or pucker; *bucle*, a *buckle*; *buchar*, to hide. *Buche* signifies also a crop or craw, and the breast; hence perhaps L. *pectus*; Port. *bucho*, the crop, the stomach. Qu. Ir. *fighim*, to weave; G. *fach.* In Gr. πυκα signifies closely, densely; πυκαζω, to cover. Class Bg. The primary sense is probably to draw, to wrinkle.]
To gather into small folds or wrinkles; to contract into ridges and furrows; to corrugate.

His face pale and withered, and his skin *puckered* in wrinkles. *Spectator.*

It is usually followed by *up*; as, to *pucker up* cloth; but *up* is superfluous. It is a popular word, but not elegant.

PUCK′ER, *n.* A fold or wrinkle, or a collection of folds.

PUCK′ERED, *pp.* Gathered in folds; wrinkled.

PUCK′ERING, *ppr.* Wrinkling.

PUD′DER, *n.* [This is supposed to be the same as *pother.*]
A tumult; a confused noise; a bustle. [*Vulgar.*] *Shak. Locke.*

PUD′DER, *v. i.* To make a tumult or bustle. *Locke.*

PUD′DER, *v. t.* To perplex; to embarrass; to confuse; vulgarly to *bother.* *Locke.*

PUD′DING, *n.* [W *poten*, what bulges out, a paunch, a pudding; Fr. *boudin*, a pudding, from *bouder*, to *pout*; Ir. *boideal*; G. Dan. *pudding*; Sw. *puding.* Class Bd.]

1. A species of food of a soft or moderately hard consistence, variously made, but usually a compound of flour, or meal of maiz, with milk and eggs, sometimes enriched with raisins and called *plum-pudding.*
2. An intestine. *Shak.*
3. An intestine stuffed with meat, &c. now called a sausage.
4. Proverbially, food or victuals.

Eat your *pudding*, slave, and hold your tongue. *Prior.*

PUD′DING, } *n.* In *seamen's language,*
PUD′DENING, } a thick wreath or circle of cordage, tapering from the middle towards the ends, and fastened about the mast below the trusses, to prevent the yards from falling down when the ropes sustaining them are shot away.

PUD′DING-GRASS, *n.* A plant of the genus Mentha. *Fam. of Plants.*

PUD′DING-GROSS, *n.* A plant. Qu. *Johnson.*

PUD′DING-PIE, *n.* A pudding with meat baked in it. *Hudibras.*

PUDDING PIPE-TREE, *n.* A plant of the genus Cassia. *Fam. of Plants.*

PUD′DING-SLEEVE, *n.* A sleeve of the full dress clerical gown. *Swift.*

PUD′DING-STONE, *n.* Conglomerate; a coarse sandstone composed of silicious pebbles, flint, &c. united by a cement. *Cleaveland.*

PUD′DING-TIME, *n.* The time of dinner, pudding being formerly the first dish set on the table, or rather first eaten; a practice not yet obsolete among the common people of New England.
2. The nick of time; critical time. *Hudibras.*

PUD′DLE, *n.* [Ir. *boidhlia*; G. *pfütze.*] A small stand of dirty water; a muddy plash. *Dryden. Addison.*

PUD′DLE, *v. t.* To made foul or muddy; to pollute with dirt; to mix dirt and water. *Shak. Dryden.*
2. To make thick or close.

PUD′DLED, *pp.* Made muddy or foul.

PUD′DLING, *ppr.* Making muddy or dirty.

PUD′DLY, *a.* Muddy; foul; dirty. *Carew.*

PUD′DOCK, } *n.* [for *paddock* or *parrock*,
PUR′ROCK, } park.] A small enclosure. [*Provincial in England.*]

PU′DENCY, *n.* [L. *pudens, pudeo*, to blush or be ashamed; Ar. عبد abada, to worship, to prostrate one's self, to cast down, to subdue, to be ashamed, or Ch. בהת to blush. Qu. Heb. בוש in a different dialect. The first is the more probable affinity. Class Bd. No. 11. 26.]
Modesty; shamefacedness. *Shak.*

PUDEN′DA, *n. plu.* [L.] The parts of generation.

PU′DIC, } *a.* [L. *pudicus*, modest.] Per-
PU′DICAL, } taining to the parts which modesty requires to be concealed; as the *pudic* artery. *Quincy.*

PUDIC′ITY, *n.* [Fr. *pudicité*; L. *pudicitia.*] Modesty; chastity. *Howell.*

PUE-FELLOW. [See *Pew-fellow.*]

PU′ERILE, *a.* [Fr. from L. *puerilis*, from *puer*, a boy.]
Boyish; childish; trifling; as a *puerile* amusement. *Pope.*

PUERIL′ITY, *n.* [Fr. *puerilité*; L. *puerilitas*, from *puer*, a boy.]
1. Childishness; boyishness; the manners or actions of a boy; that which is trifling. *Brown. Dryden.*
2. In *discourse*, a thought or expression which is flat, insipid or childish. *Encyc.*

PUER′PERAL, *a.* [L. *puerpera*, a lying-in-woman; *puer*, a boy, and *pario*, to bear.]
Pertaining to childbirth; as a *puerperal* fever.

PUER′PEROUS, *a.* [L. *puerperus*, supra.] Bearing children; lying in.

PUET. [See *Pewet.*]

PUFF, *n.* [D. *pof*; G. *puff*, a puff, a thump; *puffen*, to cuff, to thump, to *buffet*; Dan. *puff*, a puff, blast, buffet; *puffer*, to crack; W. *pwf* and *pif.* This is only a dialectical variation of *buff, buffet*; It. *buffo, buffa, buffetto, beffa*, whence *buffoon*; Sp. *bufar*, to puff. The radical sense is to drive, to thrust, hence to swell. See *Buffet* and *Buffoon.* The Dutch orthography is precisely the Pers. پف pof, a puff.]
1. A sudden and single emission of breath from the mouth; a quick forcible blast; a whiff. *Philips.*
2. A sudden and short blast of wind. *Raleigh.*
3. A fungous ball filled with dust.
4. Any thing light and porous, or something swelled and light; as *puff*-paste. *Tatler.*
5. A substance of loose texture, used to sprinkle powder on the hair. *Ainsworth.*
6. A tumid or exaggerated statement or commendation. *Cibber.*

PUFF, *v. i.* [G. *puffen*, to puff, to thump, to buffet; *verpuffen*, to detonize; D. *poffen*; W. *pifiaw, pwfiaw*, to puff; Fr. *bouffer*, to puff, to swell. See the Noun.]
1. To drive air from the mouth in a single and quick blast. *Shak.*
2. To swell the cheeks with air.
3. To blow as an expression of scorn or contempt.

It is really to defy heaven, to *puff* at damnation. *South.*

4. To breathe with vehemence, as after violent exertion.

The ass comes back again, *puffing* and blowing from the chase. *L'Estrange.*

5. To do or move with hurry, agitation and a tumid, bustling appearance.

Then came brave glory *puffing* by. *Herbert.*

6. To swell with air; to dilate or inflate. *Boyle.*

PUFF, *v. t.* To drive with a blast of wind or air; as, the north wind *puffs* away the clouds. *Dryden.*
2. To swell; to inflate; to dilate with air; as a bladder *puffed* with air.

The sea *puffed* up with winds. *Shak.*

3. To swell; to inflate; to blow up; as *puffed* up with pride, vanity or conceit; to *puff* up with praise or flattery. *Denham. Bacon.*
4. To drive with a blast in scorn or contempt.

I *puff* the prostitute away. *Dryden.*

5. To praise with exaggeration; as, to *puff* a pamphlet.

PUFF-BALL, *n.* A fungus or mushroom full of dust, of the genus Lycoperdon. *Lee.*

PUFF′ED, *pp.* Driven out suddenly, as air or breath; blown up; swelled with air; inflated with vanity or pride; praised.

PUFF′ER, *n.* One that puffs; one that praises with noisy commendation.

PUFF′IN, *n.* A water fowl of the genus Alca or auk.
2. A kind of fish.
3. A kind of fungus with dust; a fuzzball.

PUFF′IN-APPLE, *n.* A sort of apple so called. *Ainsworth.*

PUFF′ING, *ppr.* Driving out the breath with a single, sudden blast; blowing up; inflating; praising pompously.

PUFF′INGLY, *adv.* Tumidly; with swell.
2. With vehement breathing or shortness of breath.

PUFF′Y, *a.* Swelled with air or any soft matter; tumid with a soft substance; as a *puffy* tumor. *Wiseman.*
2. Tumid; turgid; bombastic; as a *puffy* style. *Dryden.*

PUG, *n.* [Sax. Sw. *piga*, a little girl; Dan. *pige*; W. *baç, byçan*; Sp. *poco* or *pequeño*, little; Ir. *beag*, from the root of *pig*, that is, a shoot, as we use *imp.* See *Beagle.*]
The name given to a little animal treated with familiarity, as a monkey, a little dog, &c. *Spectator.*

PUGGERED, for *puckered*, is not in use. *More.*

PUGH, *exclam.* A word used in contempt or disdain.

PU'GIL, *n.* [It. *pugillo*, a handful; Fr. *pugile*; L. *pugillum*, from the root of *pugnus*, the fist; probably coinciding with the Greek πυκνοω, to make thick, that is, to close or press.]
As much as is taken up between the thumb and two first fingers. *Bacon.*

PU'GILISM, *n.* [L. Sp. *pugil*, a champion or prize-fighter, from the Gr. πυκτης, id.; πυγμη, the fist; πυξ, with the fist; πυκνοω, to close or make fast; allied probably to *pack*, L. *pango*. Class Bg.]
The practice of boxing or fighting with the fist.

PU'GILIST, *n.* A boxer; one who fights with his fists.

PUGILIS'TIC, *a.* Pertaining to boxing or fighting with the fist.

PUGNA'CIOUS, *a.* [L. *pugnax*, from *pugna*, a fight; from *pugnus*, the fist. See *Pugil.*]
Disposed to fight; inclined to fighting; quarrelsome; fighting. *More.*

PUGNAC'ITY, *n.* Inclination to fight; quarrelsomeness. [*Little used.*] *Bacon.*

PUISNE, *a. pu'ny.* [Fr. *puis*, since, afterwards, and *né*, born.]
1. In *law*, younger or inferior in rank; as a chief justice and three *puisne* justices of the court of common pleas; the *puisne* barons of the court of exchequer. *Blackstone.*
2. Later in date. [*Not used.*] *Hale.*

PU'ISSANCE, *n.* [Fr. from *pouvoir*, to be able; L. *posse*, *possum*, *potes*, *potest*; Sp. *poder*, power, It. *podere.*] Power; strength; might; force. *Milton. Shak.*

PU'ISSANT, *a.* Powerful; strong; mighty; forcible; as a *puissant* prince or empire. *Milton. Raleigh.*

PU'ISSANTLY, *adv.* Powerfully; with great strength.

PUKE, *v. i.* [Heb. בק to evacuate, to empty, L. *vacuo*; or בקע to burst forth; Ch. id., and פקע. Qu. W. *cyvogi*, to vomit; *cy* is a prefix. *Spew* is probably from the same source; L. *spuo*, for *spuco*, with a prefix. The radical sense is to throw or drive.] To vomit; to eject from the stomach. *Shak.*

PUKE, *n.* A vomit; a medicine which excites vomiting.

PUKE, *a.* Of a color between black and russet. *Shak.*

PU'KED, *pp.* Vomited.

PU'KER, *n.* A medicine causing vomiting.

PU'KING, *ppr.* Vomiting.

PUL'CHRITUDE, *n.* [L. *pulchritudo*, from *pulcher*, beautiful.]
1. Beauty; handsomeness; grace; comeliness; that quality of form which pleases the eye. *Brown. More.*
2. Moral beauty; those qualities of the mind which good men love and approve. *South.*

PULE, *v. i.* [Fr. *piauler.* This word belongs probably to the root of *bawl*, *bellow*, L. *pello.*]
1. To cry like a chicken. *Bacon.*
2. To whine; to cry as a complaining child; to whimper.

> To speak *puling* like a beggar at halimass. *Shak.*

PU'LIC, *n.* A plant. *Ainsworth.*

PU'LICOSE, } *a.* [L. *pulicosus*, from *pulex*,
PU'LICOUS, } a flea.] Abounding with fleas. [*Not used.*] *Dict.*

PU'LING, *ppr.* Crying like a chicken; whining.

PU'LING, *n.* A cry, as of a chicken; a whining. *Bacon.*

PU'LINGLY, *adv.* With whining or complaint.

PU'LIOL, *n.* A plant. *Ainsworth.*

PULK'HA, *n.* A Laplander's traveling sled or sleigh.

PULL, *v. t.* [Sax. *pullian*; L. *vello.* Qu. Eth. በለሐ baleach. Class Bl. No. 7.]
1. To draw; to draw towards one or to make an effort to draw. *Pull* differs from *draw*; we use *draw* when motion follows the effort, and *pull* is used in the same sense; but we may also *pull* forever without drawing or moving the thing. This distinction may not be universal. *Pull* is opposed to *push.*

> Then he put forth his hand and took her and *pulled* her in to him into the ark. Gen. viii.

2. To pluck; to gather by drawing or forcing off or out; as, to *pull* fruit; to *pull* flax.
3. To tear; to rend; but in this sense followed by some qualifying word or phrase; as, to *pull in pieces*; to *pull asunder* or *apart.* To *pull in two*, is to separate or tear by violence into two parts.
To pull down, to demolish or to take in pieces by separating the parts; as, to *pull down* a house.
2. To demolish; to subvert; to destroy.

> In political affairs, as well as mechanical, it is easier to *pull down* than to build up. *Howell.*

3. To bring down; to degrade; to humble.

> To raise the wretched and *pull down* the proud. *Roscommon.*

To pull off, to separate by pulling; to pluck; also, to take off without force; as, to *pull off* a coat or hat.
To pull out, to draw out; to extract.
To pull up, to pluck up; to tear up by the roots; hence, to extirpate; to eradicate; to destroy.

PULL, *n.* The act of pulling or drawing with force; an effort to move by drawing towards one. *Swift.*
2. A contest; a struggle. *Carew.*
3. Pluck; violence suffered. *Shak.*

PULL'BACK, *n.* That which keeps back, or restrains from proceeding.

PULL'ED, *pp.* Drawn towards one; plucked.

PULL'EN, *n.* [Fr. *poule*, a hen, L. *pullus.* See *Pullet* and *Foal.*] Poultry. [*Not used.*] *Bailey.*

PULL'ER, *n.* One that pulls. *Shak.*

PULL'ET, *n.* [Fr. *poulet*, dim. from *poule*, a hen; It. *pollo*; L. *pullus*; Gr. πωλος; coinciding with Eng. *foal.*]
A young hen or female of the gallinaceous kind of fowls. *Wiseman.*

PULL'EY, *n.* plu. *pulleys.* [Fr. *poulie*; Sp. *polla*; L. *polus*; Gr. πολος, from πολεω, to turn.]
A small wheel turning on a pin in a block, with a furrow or groove in which runs the rope that turns it.
The pulley is one of the mechanical powers. The word is used also in the general sense of tackle, to denote all parts of the machine for raising weights, of which the pulley forms a part.

PUL'LICAT, *n.* A kind of silk handkerchief.

PULL'ING, *ppr.* Drawing; making an effort to draw; plucking.

PUL'LULATE, *v. i.* [L. *pullulo*, from *pullus*, a shoot.] To germinate; to bud. *Granger.*

PULLULA'TION, *n.* A germinating or budding; the first shooting of a bud. *More.*

PUL'MONARY, *a.* [L. *pulmonarius*, from *pulmo*, the lungs, from *pello*, *pulsus*, *pulso*, to drive or beat.]
Pertaining to the lungs; affecting the lungs; as a *pulmonary* disease or consumption; the *pulmonary* artery.

PUL'MONARY, *n.* [L. *pulmonaria.*] A plant, lungwort. *Ainsworth.*

PULMON'IC, *a.* [Fr. *pulmonique*, from L. *pulmo*, the lungs.]
Pertaining to the lungs; affecting the lungs; as a *pulmonic* disease; *pulmonic* consumption.

PULMON'IC, *n.* A medicine for diseases of the lungs.
2. One affected by a disease of the lungs. *Arbuthnot.*

PULP, *n.* [Fr. *pulpe*; L. *pulpa.* This is probably allied to L. *puls*, *pulmentum*, Gr. πολτος, from softness. Qu. from *pulsus*, beaten.]
1. A soft mass; *in general.*
2. The soft substance within a bone; marrow. *Bacon.*
3. The soft, succulent part of fruit; as the *pulp* of an orange.
4. The aril or exterior covering of a coffee-berry. *Edwards, W. Ind.*

PULP, *v. t.* To deprive of the pulp or integument, as the coffee-berry.

> The other mode is to *pulp* the coffee immediately as it comes from the tree. By a simple machine, a man will *pulp* a bushel in a minute. *Edwards, W. Ind.*

PUL'PIT, *n.* [L. *pulpitum*, a stage, scaffold, or higher part of a stage; It. Sp. *pulpito*; Fr. *pupitre.*]
1. An elevated place or inclosed stage in a church, in which the preacher stands. It is called also a *desk.*
2. In *the Roman theater*, the pulpitum was the place where the players performed their parts, lower than the scena and higher than the orchestra. *Encyc.*
3. A movable desk, from which disputants pronounced their dissertations, and authors recited their works. *Encyc.*

PULPIT-EL'OQUENCE, } *n.* Eloquence
PULPIT-OR'ATORY, } or oratory in delivering sermons.

Pulpitically, in Chesterfield, is not an authorized word.

PULPIT-OR'ATOR, *n.* An eloquent preacher.

PULP'OUS, *a.* [from *pulp.*] Consisting of pulp or resembling it; soft like pap. *Philips.*

PULP'OUSNESS, *n.* Softness; the quality of being pulpous.

PULP'Y, *a.* Like pulp; soft; fleshy; succulent; as the *pulpy* covering of a nut; the *pulpy* substance of a peach or cherry. *Ray. Arbuthnot.*

PULS′ATE, *v. i.* [L. *pulsatus*, *pulso*, to beat, from the root of *pello*, to drive.] To beat or throb.

The heart of a viper or frog will continue to *pulsate* long after it is taken from the body. *Darwin.*

PULS′ATILE, *a.* [L. *pulsatilis*, from *pulso*, to beat.]

That is or may be struck or beaten; played by beating; as a *pulsatile* instrument of music. *Mus. Dict.*

PULSA′TION, *n.* [L. *pulsatio*, supra.] The beating or throbbing of the heart or of an artery, in the process of carrying on the circulation of the blood. The blood being propelled by the contraction of the heart, causes the arteries to dilate, so as to render each dilatation perceptible to the touch in certain parts of the body, as in the radial artery, &c.

2. In *law*, any touching of another's body willfully or in anger. This constitutes *battery*.

By the Cornelian law, *pulsation* as well as verberation is prohibited. *Blackstone.*

PULS′ATIVE, *a.* Beating; throbbing. *Encyc.*

PULSA′TOR, *n.* A beater; a striker. *Dict.*

PULS′ATORY, *a.* Beating; throbbing; as the heart and arteries. *Wotton.*

PULSE, *n.* *puls.* [L. *pulsus*, from *pello*, to drive; Fr. *pouls*.]

1. In *animals*, the beating or throbbing of the heart and arteries; more particularly, the sudden dilatation of an artery, caused by the projectile force of the blood, which is perceptible to the touch. Hence we say, to *feel the pulse*. The *pulse* is frequent or rare, quick or slow, equal or unequal, regular or intermitting, hard or soft, strong or weak, &c. The *pulses* of an adult in health, are little more than one pulse to a second; in certain fevers, the number is increased to 90, 100, or even to 140 in a minute.

2. The stroke with which a medium is affected by the motion of light, sound, &c.; oscillation; vibration.

Sir Isaac Newton demonstrates that the velocities of the *pulses* of an elastic fluid medium are in a ratio compounded of half the ratio of the elastic force directly, and half the ratio of the density inversely. *Encyc.*

To feel one's pulse, metaphorically, to sound one's opinion; to try or to know one's mind.

PULSE, *v. i.* To beat, as the arteries. [*Little used.*] *Ray.*

PULSE, *v. t.* [L. *pulso.*] To drive, as the pulse. [*Little used.*]

PULSE, *n.* [Qu. from L. *pulsus*, beaten out, as seeds; or Heb. Ch. פול a bean, from פלה to separate.]

Leguminous plants or their seeds; the plants whose pericarp is a legume or pod, as beans, peas, &c. *Milton. Dryden.*

PULSIF′IC, *a.* [*pulse* and L. *facio*, to make.] Exciting the pulse; causing pulsation. *Smith.*

PUL′SION, *n.* [from L. *pulsus.*] The act of driving forward; in opposition to *suction* or *traction*. [*Little used.*] *More. Bentley.*

PULTA′CEOUS, *a.* [from Gr. πολτος, L. *puls*. See *Pulp*.] Macerated; softened; nearly fluid. *Beddoes.*

PUL′VERABLE, *a.* [from L. *pulvis*, dust, probably from *pello*, *pulso*, or its root, that which is beaten fine, or that which is driven. See *Powder*.]

That may be reduced to fine powder; capable of being pulverized. *Boyle.*

PUL′VERATE, *v. t.* To beat or reduce to powder or dust.

[But *pulverize* is generally used.]

PUL′VERIN, } *n.* Ashes of barilla.
PUL′VERINE, }

PULVERIZA′TION, *n.* [from *pulverize*.] The act of reducing to dust or powder.

PUL′VERIZE, *v. t.* [It. *polverizzare*; Fr. *pulveriser*.]

To reduce to fine powder, as by beating, grinding, &c. Friable substances may be *pulverized* by grinding or beating; but to *pulverize* malleable bodies, other methods must be pursued. *Encyc.*

PUL′VERIZED, *pp.* Reduced to fine powder.

PUL′VERIZING, *ppr.* Reducing to fine powder.

PUL′VEROUS, *a.* Consisting of dust or powder; like powder.

PULVER′ULENCE, *n.* Dustiness; abundance of dust or powder.

PULVER′ULENT, *a.* Dusty; consisting of fine powder; powdery.

2. Addicted to lying and rolling in the dust, as fowls.

PUL′VIL, *n.* A sweet scented powder. [*Little used.*] *Gay.*

PUL′VIL, *v. t.* To sprinkle with a perfumed powder. [*Not used.*] *Congreve.*

PU′MA, *n.* A rapacious quadruped of America, of the genus Felis.

PUM′ICE, *n.* [L. *pumex*, supposed to be from the root of *spuma*, foam; G. *bimstein*; D. *puimsteen*.]

A substance frequently ejected from volcanoes, of various colors, gray, white, reddish brown or black; hard, rough and porous; specifically lighter than water, and resembling the slag produced in an iron furnace. It consists of parallel fibers, and is supposed to be asbestos decomposed by the action of fire. *Encyc. Nicholson.*

Pumice is of three kinds, glassy, common, and porphyritic. *Ure.*

PUM′ICE-STONE, *n.* The same as *pumice*.

PUMI″CEOUS, *a.* Pertaining to pumice; consisting of pumice or resembling it.

PUMMEL. [See *Pommel*.]

PUMP, *n.* [Fr. *pompe*, a *pump* and *pomp*; D. *pomp*; Dan. *pompe*; Sp. *bomba*, a *pump* and a *bomb*. We see that *pump*, *pomp*, and *bomb* are the same word, differently applied by different nations. The L. *bombus* is of the same family, as is the Eng. *bombast*; Ir. *buimpis*, a *pump*; W. *pwmp*, a round mass. The primary sense of the root seems to be to swell.]

1. A hydraulic engine for raising water, by exhausting the incumbent air of a tube or pipe, in consequence of which the water rises in the tube by means of the pressure of the air on the surrounding water. There is however a forcing pump in which the water is raised in the tube by a force applied to a lateral tube, near the bottom of the pump.

2. A shoe with a thin sole. *Swift.*

PUMP, *v. i.* To work a pump; to raise water with a pump.

PUMP, *v. t.* To raise with a pump; as, to *pump* water.

2. To draw out by artful interrogatories; as, to *pump* out secrets.

3. To examine by artful questions for the purpose of drawing out secrets.

But *pump* not me for politics. *Otway.*

Chain-pump, is a chain equipped with a sufficient number of valves at proper distances, which working on two wheels, passes down through one tube and returns through another. *Mar. Dict.*

PUMP′-BOLTS, *n.* Two pieces of iron, one used to fasten the pump-spear to the brake, the other as a fulcrum for the brake to work upon. *Mar. Dict.*

PUMP′-BRAKE, *n.* The arm or handle of a pump. *Mar. Dict.*

PUMP′-DALE, *n.* A long wooden tube, used to convey the water from a chain-pump across the ship and through the side. *Mar. Dict.*

PUMP′ER, *n.* The person or the instrument that pumps.

PUMP′-GEAR, *n.* The materials for fitting and repairing pumps. *Mar. Dict.*

PUMP′-HOOD, *n.* A semi-cylindrical frame of wood, covering the upper wheel of a chain-pump.

PUMP′ION, *n.* [D. *pompoen*, Sw. *pomp*, a gourd.]

A plant and its fruit, of the genus Cucurbita.

PUMP′KIN, *n.* A pompion. [*This is the common orthography of the word in the United States.*]

PUMP′-SPEAR, *n.* The bar to which the upper box of a pump is fastened, and which is attached to the brake or handle. *Mar. Dict.*

PUN, *n.* [Qu. W. *pun*, equal.] An expression in which a word has at once different meanings; an expression in which two different applications of a word present an odd or ludicrous idea; a kind of quibble or equivocation; *a low species of wit*. Thus a man who had a tall wife named *Experience*, observed that he had, by *long experience*, proved the blessings of a married life.

A *pun* can be no more engraven, than it can be translated. *Addison.*

PUN, *v. i.* To quibble; to use the same word at once in different senses. *Dryden.*

PUN, *v. t.* To persuade by a pun. *Addison.*

PUNCH, *n.* [W. *pwnc*, a point; Arm. *poençonn*; Fr. *poinçon*; Sp. *punzon*; L. *punctum*, *pungo*.]

An instrument of iron or steel, used in several arts for perforating holes in plates of metal, and so contrived as to cut out a piece.

PUNCH, *n.* [Sp. *ponche*; D. *pons*; G. *punsch*; Dan. *pons*, *ponsh*.]

A drink composed of water sweetened with sugar, with a mixture of lemon juice and spirit. *Encyc. Swift.*

PUNCH, *n.* The buffoon or harlequin of a puppet show. [See *Punchinello.*]

PUNCH, *n.* A well set horse with a short back, thin shoulders, broad neck, and well covered with flesh. *Far. Dict.*

2. A short fat fellow.

PUNCH, *v. t.* [Sp. *punzar;* W. *pynciaw;* L. *pungo.* In this word, *n* is probably casual, and the root is *Pg*, of the same family as *peg*, *pack*, or *pike*, with the primary sense of driving or thrusting, a point.]

1. To perforate with an iron instrument, either pointed or not; as, to *punch* a hole in a plate of metal. *Wiseman.*

2. In *popular usage*, to thrust against with something obtuse; as, to *punch* one with the elbow.

PUNCH'BOWL, *n.* A bowl in which punch is made, or from which it is drank.

PUNCH'ED, *pp.* Perforated with a punch.

PUNCH'EON, *n.* [Fr. *poinçon*, a bodkin, a puncheon.]

1. A small piece of steel, on the end o which is engraved a figure or letter, in creux or relievo, with which impressions are stamped on metal or other substance; used in coinage, in forming the matrices of types, and in various arts. *Encyc.*

2. In *carpentry*, a piece of timber placed upright between two posts, whose bearing is too great; also, a piece of timber set upright under the ridge of a building, wherein the legs of a couple, &c. are jointed. *Encyc.*

3. A measure of liquids, or a cask containing usually 120 gallons. Rum or spirits is imported from the West Indies in *puncheons*, but these are often called also *hogsheads.*

PUNCH'ER, *n.* One that punches.

2. A punch or perforating instrument.

PUNCHINEL'LO, *n.* A punch; a buffoon. *Tatler.*

PUNCH'ING, *ppr.* Perforating with a punch; driving against.

PUNCH'Y, *a.* Short and thick, or fat.

PUNC'TATE, PUNC'TATED, *a.* [L. *punctus*, *pungo.*] Pointed.

2. In *botany*, perforated; full of small holes; having hollow dots scattered over the surface. *Martyn.*

PUNC'TIFORM, *a.* [L. *punctum*, point, and *form.*] Having the form of a point. *Ed. Encyc.*

PUNCTIL'IO, *n.* [Sp. *puntilla;* It. *puntiglio;* from L. *punctum*, a point.]

A nice point of exactness in conduct, ceremony or proceeding; particularity or exactness in forms; as the *punctilios* of a public ceremony. *Addison.*

PUNCTIL'IOUS, *a.* Very nice or exact in the forms of behavior, ceremony or mutual intercourse; very exact in the observance of rules prescribed by law or custom; sometimes, exact to excess. *Rogers.*

PUNCTIL'IOUSLY, *adv.* With exactness or great nicety.

PUNCTIL'IOUSNESS, *n.* Exactness in the observance of forms or rules; attentive to nice points of behavior or ceremony.

PUNC'TO, *n.* [Sp. It. *punto;* L. *punctum*, from *pungo*, to prick.]

1. Nice point of form or ceremony. *Bacon.*

2. The point in fencing. *Shak.*

PUNC'TUAL, *a.* [Fr. *ponctuel;* It. *puntuale;* Sp. *puntual;* from L. *punctum*, a point.]

1. Consisting in a point; as this *punctual* spot. [*Little used.*] *Milton.*

2. Exact; observant of nice points; punctilious, particularly in observing time, appointments or promises. It is honorable in a man to be *punctual* to appointments, or to appointed hours; it is just to be *punctual* in paying debts.

3. Exact; as a *punctual* correspondence between a prediction and an event.

4. Done at the exact time; as *punctual* payment.

PUNC'TUALIST, *n.* One that is very exact in observing forms and ceremonies. *Milton.*

PUNCTUAL'ITY, *n.* Nicety; scrupulous exactness. He served his prince with *punctuality.* *Howell.*

2. It is now used chiefly in regard to time. He pays his debts with *punctuality.* He is remarkable for the *punctuality* of his attendance.

PUNC'TUALLY, *adv.* Nicely; exactly; with scrupulous regard to time, appointments, promises or rules; as, to attend a meeting *punctually;* to pay debts or rent *punctually;* to observe *punctually* one's engagements.

PUNC'TUALNESS, *n.* Exactness; punctuality. *Felton.*

PUNC'TUATE, *v. t.* [Fr. *ponctuer*, from L. *punctum*, a point.]

To mark with points; to designate sentences, clauses or other divisions of a writing by points, which mark the proper pauses. *M. Stuart.*

PUNC'TUATED, *pp.* Pointed. *Fourcroy.*

2. Having the divisions marked with points.

PUNC'TUATING, *ppr.* Marking with points.

PUNCTUA'TION, *n.* In *grammar*, the act or art of pointing a writing or discourse, or the act or art of marking with points the divisions of a discourse into sentences and clauses or members of a sentence. Punctuation is performed by four points, the period (.); the colon (:); the semicolon (;); and the comma (,). The ancients were unacquainted with *punctuation;* they wrote without any distinction of members, periods or words.

PUNC'TULATE, *v. t.* [L. *punctulum.*] To mark with small spots. [*Not used.*] *Woodward.*

PUNC'TURE, *n.* [L. *punctura;* It. *puntura.*]

The act of perforating with a pointed instrument; or a small hole made by it; as the *puncture* of a nail, needle or pin.

> A lion may perish by the *puncture* of an asp. *Rambler.*

PUNC'TURE, *v. t.* To prick; to pierce with a small pointed instrument; as, to *puncture* the skin.

PUNC'TURED, *pp.* Pricked; pierced with a sharp point.

PUNC'TURING, *ppr.* Piercing with a sharp point.

PUN'DIT, *n.* [In Persic, پند pand, learning.] In Hindoostan, a learned Bramin; one versed in the Sanscrit language, and in the science, laws and religion of that country.

PUN'DLE, *n.* A short and fat woman. [*Not used.*] *Ainsworth.*

PUN'GAR, *n.* A fish. *Ainsworth.*

PUN'GENCY, *n.* [L. *pungens*, *pungo*, to prick.]

1. The power of pricking or piercing; as the *pungency* of a substance. *Arbuthnot.*

2. That quality of a substance which produces the sensation of pricking, or affecting the taste like minute sharp points; sharpness; acridness.

3. Power to pierce the mind or excite keen reflections or remorse; as the *pungency* of a discourse.

4. Acrimoniousness; keenness; as the *pungency* of wit or of expressions. *Stillingfleet.*

PUN'GENT, *a.* [L. *pungens*, *pungo.*] Pricking; stimulating; as *pungent* snuff.

> The *pungent* grains of titillating dust. *Pope.*

2. Acrid; affecting the tongue like small sharp points; as the sharp and *pungent* taste of acids. *Newton.*

3. Piercing; sharp; as *pungent* pains; *pungent* grief. *Swift.*

4. Acrimonious; biting. *Fell.*

PU'NIC, *a.* [L. *punicus*, pertaining to Carthago or its inhabitants, from *Pœni*, the Carthaginians; qu. from *Phœni*, as Carthage was settled by Phenicians.]

Pertaining to the Carthaginians; faithless; treacherous; deceitful; as *punic* faith.

PU'NIC, *n.* The ancient language of the Carthaginians, of which Plautus has left a specimen. *Asiat. Res.*

PU'NICE, *n.* A wall-louse; a bug. [*Not in use.*] *Ainsworth.*

PUNI''CEOUS, *a.* [L. *puniceus.* See *Punic.*] Purple. *Dict.*

PU'NINESS, *n.* [from *puny.*] Littleness; pettiness; smallness with feebleness.

PUN'ISH, *v. t.* [Arm. *puniçza;* Fr. *punir*, *punissant;* It. *punire;* Sp. *punir;* from L. *punio*, from the root of *pœna*, pain. The primary sense is to press or strain.]

1. To pain; to afflict with pain, loss or calamity for a crime or fault; primarily, to afflict with bodily pain, as to *punish* a thief with pillory or stripes; but the word is applied also to affliction by loss of property, by transportation, banishment, seclusion from society, &c. The laws require murderers to be *punished* with death. Other offenders are to be *punished* with fines, imprisonment, hard labor, &c. God *punishes* men for their sins with calamities personal and national.

2. To chastise; as, a father *punishes* his child for disobedience.

3. To reward with pain or suffering inflicted on the offender; *applied to the crime;* as, to *punish* murder or theft.

PUN'ISHABLE, *a.* Worthy of punishment.

2. Liable to punishment; capable of being punished by law or right; *applied to persons or offenses;* as, a man is *punishable* for robbery or for trespass; a crime is *punishable* by law.

PUN'ISHABLENESS, *n.* The quality of deserving or being liable to punishment.

PUN'ISHED, *pp.* Afflicted with pain or evil as the retribution of a crime or offense; chastised.

PUN'ISHER, *n.* One that inflicts pain, loss or other evil for a crime or offense. *Milton.*

PUN'ISHING, *ppr.* Afflicting with pain, penalty or suffering of any kind, as the retribution of a crime or offense.

PUN'ISHMENT, *n.* Any pain or suffering inflicted on a person for a crime or offense, by the authority to which the offender is subject, either by the constitution of God or of civil society. The *punishment* of the faults and offenses of children by the parent, is by virtue of the right of government with which the parent is invested by God himself. This species of punishment is *chastisement* or *correction.* The *punishment* of crimes against the laws is inflicted by the supreme power of the state in virtue of the right of government, vested in the prince or legislature. The right of *punishment* belongs only to persons clothed with authority. Pain, loss or evil willfully inflicted on another for his crimes or offenses by a private unauthorized person, is *revenge* rather than *punishment.*

Some *punishments* consist in exile or transportation, others in loss of liberty by imprisonment; some extend to confiscation by forfeiture of lands and goods, others induce a disability of holding offices, of being heirs and the like. *Blackstone.*

Divine *punishments* are doubtless designed to secure obedience to divine laws, and uphold the moral order of created intelligent beings.

The rewards and *punishments* of another life, which the Almighty has established as the enforcements of his law, are of weight enough to determine the choice against whatever pleasure or pain this life can show. *Locke.*

PUNI''TION, *n.* [Fr. from L. *punitio*, from *punio.*] Punishment. [*Little used.*]

PU'NITIVE, *a.* [It. *punitivo.*] Awarding or inflicting punishment; that punishes; as *punitive* law or justice. *Hammond.*

PU'NITORY, *a.* Punishing or tending to punishment.

PUNK, *n.* A prostitute; a strumpet. *Shak.*

PUN'NER, *n.* A punster, which see. *Steele.*

PUN'NING, *ppr.* [from *pun.*] Using a word at once in different senses.

PUN'NING, *n.* The art or practice of using puns; a playing on words. *Addison.*

PUN'STER, *n.* One that puns or is skilled in punning; a quibbler; a low wit. *Arbuthnot.*

PUNT, *v. i.* To play at basset and omber. *Addison.*

PUNT, *n.* [Sax. *punt*, L. *pons*, a bridge.] A flat-bottomed boat used in calking and repairing ships. *Mar. Dict.*

PUNT'ER, *n.* One that plays in basset against the banker or dealer. *Encyc.*

PU'NY, *a.* [contracted from Fr. *puisné*, which see.]

1. Properly, young or younger; but in this sense not used.
2. Inferior; petty; of an under rate; small and feeble. This word generally includes the signification of both smallness and feebleness; as a *puny* animal; a *puny* subject; a *puny* power; a *puny* mind. *Milton. South. Dryden.*

PU'NY, *n.* A young inexperienced person; a novice. *South.*

PUP, *v. i.* [This word appears to be radically the same as the L. *pupa*, Eng. *babe*, W. *pob*, the root of *populus.*]

To bring forth whelps or young, as the female of the canine species.

PUP, *n.* A puppy.

PU'PA, *n.* [L. supra.] In *natural history*, an insect in that state in which it resembles an infant in swaddling clothes. As some insects in this state have a bright exterior, as if gilded, it has been called *chrysalis* or *aurelia*, from the Gr. χρυσος, and L. *aurum*, gold; but as this gilded appearance belongs to few insects, the term *pupa* is now more generally used.

PU'PIL, *n.* [L. *pupilla*, dim. of *pupa, pupus.* See *Pup.*]

The apple of the eye; a little aperture in the middle of the iris and uvea of the eye, through which the rays of light pass to the crystaline humor, to be painted on the retina. *Encyc.*

PU'PIL, *n.* [Fr. *pupille*; L. *pupillus*, dim. of *pupa, pupus.* See *Pup.*]

1. A youth or scholar of either sex under the care of an instructor or tutor. *Locke.*
2. A ward; a youth or person under the care of a guardian. *Dryden.*
3. In *the civil law*, a boy or girl under the age of puberty, that is, under 14 if a male, and under 12 if a female. *Encyc.*

PU'PILAGE, *n.* The state of being a scholar, or under the care of an instructor for education and discipline. *Locke.*

2. Wardship; minority. *Spenser.*

In this latter sense, the Scots use *pupilarity.* *Beattie.*

PU'PILARY, *a.* [Fr. *pupillaire*; L. *pupillaris.*] Pertaining to a pupil or ward. *Johnson.*

PUPIV'OROUS, *a.* [*pupa* and L. *voro.*] Feeding on the larvas and crysalids of insects. *S. L. Mitchill.*

PUP'PET, *n.* [Fr. *poupée*; L. *pupus.* See *Pup.*]

1. A small image in the human form, moved by a wire in a mock drama; a wooden tragedian. *Pope.*
2. A doll.
3. A word of contempt. *Shak.*

PUP'PETMAN, } *n.* The master of a
PUP'PETM'ASTER, } puppet-show. *Swift.*

PUP'PET-PLAYER, *n.* One that manages the motions of puppets. *Hales.*

PUP'PETRY, *n.* Affectation. *Marston.*

PUP'PET-SHOW, *n.* A mock drama performed by wooden images moved by wires. *Swift. Pope.*

PUP'PY, *n.* [See *Pup.*] A whelp; the young progeny of a bitch or female of the canine species.

2. *Applied to persons*, a name expressing extreme contempt. *Addison.*

PUP'PY, *v. t.* To bring forth whelps.

PUP'PYISM, *n.* Extreme meanness.

2. Extreme affectation. *Todd.*

PUR, *v. i.* To utter a low murmuring continued sound, as a cat.

PUR, *v. t.* To signify by purring. *Gray.*

PUR, *n.* The low murmuring continued sound of a cat.

PURANA, *n.* Among the Hindoos, a sacred poem or book. *Asiat. Res.*

PURAN'IC, *a.* Pertaining to the sacred poems of the Hindoos. *Asiat. Res.*

PURBECK-STONE, *n.* A hard sandstone, the cement of which is calcarious. *Nicholson.*

PUR'BLIND, *a.* [said to be from *pore* and *blind.*]

Near sighted or dim sighted; seeing obscurely; as a *purblind* eye; a *purblind* mole. *Shak. Drummond.*

PUR'BLINDNESS, *n.* Shortness of sight; near sightedness; dimness of vision.

PUR'CHASABLE, *a.* [from *purchase.*] That may be bought, purchased or obtained for a consideration.

PUR'CHASE, *v. t.* [Fr. *pourchasser*, to seek, to pursue; *pour* and *chasser*, to chase, It. *cacciare*, Sp. *cazar.* This word seems to be considered by Blackstone as formed from the L. *perquisitio.* This is an error. The word is from the root of *chase*; *pourchasser* is to pursue to the end or object, and hence to obtain. In law Latin, *purchase*, the noun, was written *purchacium.* The legal use of the word in obtaining writs, shows best its true origin; to *purchase* a writ, is to *sue out* a writ, that is, to seek it out; for *sue, seek*, and L. *sequor*, are all of one origin, and synonymous with *chase.* See Blackstone, B. 3. Ch. 18. Spelman *ad voc.*]

1. In *its primary and legal sense*, to gain, obtain or acquire by any means, except by descent or hereditary right. *Blackstone.*
2. In *common usage*, to buy; to obtain property by paying an equivalent in money. It differs from *barter* only in the circumstance, that in *purchasing*, the price or equivalent given or secured is money; in *bartering*, the equivalent is given in goods. We *purchase* lands or goods for ready money or on credit.
3. To obtain by an expense of labor, danger or other sacrifice; as, to *purchase* favor with flattery.

A world who would not *purchase* with a bruise? *Milton.*

4. To expiate or recompense by a fine or forfeit; as, to *purchase* out abuses with tears and prayer. *Shak.*
5. To sue out or procure, as a writ.

PUR'CHASE, *v. i.* In *seaman's language*, to draw in; as, the capstern *purchases* apace, that is, it draws in the cable apace, it gains it. *Encyc.*

PUR'CHASE, *n.* [Norm. Fr. *pourchas* or *purchas.*]

1. In *law*, the act of obtaining or acquiring the title to lands and tenements by money, deed, gift or any means, except by descent; the acquisition of lands and tenements by a man's own act or agreement. *Littleton. Blackstone.*
2. In *law*, the suing out and obtaining a writ.
3. In *common usage*, the acquisition of the title or property of any thing by rendering an equivalent in money.

It is foolish to lay out money in the *purchase* of repentance. *Franklin.*

4. That which is purchased; any thing of which the property is obtained by giving an equivalent price in money.

The scrip was complete evidence of his right in the *purchase*. *Wheaton.*

5. That which is obtained by labor, danger, art, &c.

A beauty waning and distressed widow
Made prize and *purchase* of his wanton eye—
Shak.

6. Formerly, robbery, and the thing stolen. *Chaucer.*

7. Any mechanical power or force applied to the raising or removing of heavy bodies.

PUR'CHASED, *pp.* Obtained or acquired by one's own act or agreement.

2. Obtained by paying an equivalent in money.

3. Obtained by labor, danger, art, &c.

PUR'CHASE-MŎNEY, *n.* The money paid for any thing bought. *Berkeley.*

PUR'CHASER, *n.* In *law*, one who acquires or obtains by conquest or by deed or gift, or in any manner other than by descent or inheritance. In this sense, the word is by some authors written *purchasor.* *Blackstone.*

2. One who obtains or acquires the property of any thing by paying an equivalent in money.

PUR'CHASING, *ppr.* Buying; obtaining by one's own act or for a price.

PURE, *a.* [L. *purus*; It. Sp. *puro*; Fr. *pur*; W. *pûr*; Sax. *pur*; Heb. בר. The verb ברר signifies to separate, free, clear; a sense taken from driving off. The word varied in orthography, occurs in Ch. Syr. and Ar. See ברא in the Introduction. Class Br. No. 7. and 6. 8. 9. 10.]

1. Separate from all heterogeneous or extraneous matter; clear; free from mixture; as *pure* water; *pure* clay; *pure* sand; *pure* air; *pure* silver or gold. *Pure* wine is very scarce.

2. Free from moral defilement; without spot; not sullied or tarnished; incorrupt; undebased by moral turpitude; holy.

Thou art of *purer* eyes than to behold evil. Hab. i. Prov. xx.

3. Genuine; real; true; incorrupt; unadulterated; as *pure* religion. James i.

4. Unmixed; separate from any other subject or from every thing foreign; as *pure* mathematics.

5. Free from guilt; guiltless; innocent.

No hand of strife is *pure*, but that which wins. *Daniel.*

6. Not vitiated with improper or corrupt words or phrases; as a *pure* style of discourse or composition.

7. Disinterested; as *pure* benevolence.

8. Chaste; as a *pure* virgin.

9. Free from vice or moral turpitude. Tit. i.

10. Ceremonially clean; unpolluted. Ezra vi.

11. Free from any thing improper; as, his motives are *pure*.

12. Mere; absolute; that and that only; unconnected with any thing else; as a *pure* villain. He did that from *pure* compassion, or *pure* good nature.

PURE, *v. t.* To purify; to cleanse. [*Not in use.*] *Chaucer.*

PU'RELY, *adv.* In a pure manner; with an entire separation of heterogeneous or foul matter. Is. i.

2. Without any mixture of improper or vicious words or phrases.

3. Innocently; without guilt.

4. Merely; absolutely; without connection with any thing else; completely; totally. The meeting was *purely* accidental.

PU'RENESS, *n.* Clearness; an unmixed state; separation or freedom from any heterogeneous or foreign matter; as the *pureness* of water or other liquor; the *pureness* of a metal; the *pureness* of marl or clay; the *pureness* of air.

2. Freedom from moral turpitude or guilt.

May we evermore serve thee in holiness and *pureness* of living. *Com. Prayer.*

3. Simplicity; freedom from mixture or composition.

An essence eternal and spiritual, of absolute *pureness* and simplicity. *Raleigh.*

4. Freedom from vicious or improper words, phrases or modes of speech; as *pureness* of style. *Ascham.*

Pure villenage, in the feudal law, is a tenure of lands by uncertain services at the will of the lord; opposed to *privileged villenage.* *Blackstone.*

PUR'FILE, *n.* [Fr. *pourfilée*; *pour* and *file.*]

A sort of ancient trimming for women's gowns, made of tinsel and thread, called also bobbin work. *Bailey.*

[*The thing and the name are obsolete.*]

PUR'FLE, *v. t.* [Fr. *pourfiler*; It. *profilare.* See *Profile.*]

To decorate with a wrought or flowered border; to embroider; as, to *purfle* with blue and white, or with gold and pearl. *Obs.* *Spenser. Shak. Milton.*

PUR'FLE, } *n.* A border of embroidered
PUR'FLEW, } work.

2. In *heraldry*, ermins, peans or furs which compose a bordure. *Encyc.*

PURG'AMENT, *n.* [L. *purgamen.*] A cathartic. *Bacon.*

PURGA'TION, *n.* [Fr. from L. *purgatio.* See *Purge.*]

1. The act or operation of cleansing or purifying by separating and carrying off impurities or whatever is superfluous; *applied to the body*; as, the bowels are cleansed by *purgation.* So also in *pharmacy* and in *chimistry*, medicines, metals and minerals are purified by *purgation.* *Encyc.*

2. In *law*, the act of cleansing from a crime, accusation or suspicion of guilt. This was *canonical* or *vulgar. Canonical purgation*, prescribed by the canon law, was performed before the bishop or his deputy, and by a jury of twelve clerks. The party accused first made oath to his own innocence, and then the twelve clerks or compurgators swore that they believed he spoke the truth; after which, other witnesses were examined upon oath, on behalf of the prisoner only. *Vulgar purgation* was performed by the ordeal of fire or water, or by combat. [See *Ordeal.*] *Blackstone.*

PURG'ATIVE, *a.* [It. *purgativo*; Fr. *purgatif.*]

Having the power of cleansing; usually, having the power of evacuating the bowels; cathartic.

PURG'ATIVE, *n.* A medicine that evacuates the bowels; a cathartic.

PURGATO'RIAL, } *a.* Pertaining to purg-
PURGATO'RIAN, } atory. *Mede.*

PURG'ATORY, *a.* [L. *purgatorius*, from *purgo*, to purge.]

Tending to cleanse; cleansing; expiatory. *Burke.*

PURG'ATORY, *n.* [Fr. *purgatoire.*] Among catholics, a supposed place or state after death, in which the souls of persons are purified, or in which they expiate such offenses committed in this life, as do not merit eternal damnation. After this purgation from the impurities of sin, the souls are supposed to be received into heaven. *Encyc. Stillingfleet.*

PURĠE, *v. t.* *purj.* [L. *purgo*; Fr. *purger*; Sp. *purgar*; It. *purgare*; probably a derivative from the root of *pure.*]

1. To cleanse or purify by separating and carrying off whatever is impure, heterogeneous, foreign or superfluous; as, to *purge* the body by evacuation; to *purge* the Augean stable. It is followed by *away*, *of*, or *off.* We say, to *purge away* or to *purge off* filth, and to *purge* a liquor *of* its scum.

2. To clear from guilt or moral defilement; as, to *purge* one *of* guilt or crime; to *purge away* sin.

Purge away our sins, for thy name's sake. Ps. lxxix.

Purge me with hyssop and I shall be clean. Ps. li.

3. To clear from accusation or the charge of a crime, as in ordeal.

4. To remove what is offensive; to sweep away impurities. Ezek. xx.

5. To clarify; to defecate; as liquors.

PURĠE, *v. i.* To become pure by clarification.

2. To have frequent or preternatural evacuations by stool.

PURĠE, *n.* A medicine that evacuates the body by stool; a cathartic. *Arbuthnot.*

PURĠ'ED, *pp.* Purified; cleansed; evacuated.

PURĠ'ER, *n.* A person or thing that purges or cleanses.

2. A cathartic.

PURĠ'ING, *ppr.* Cleansing; purifying; carrying off impurities or superfluous matter.

PURĠ'ING, *n.* A diarrhea or dysentery; preternatural evacuation by stool; looseness of bowels.

PURIFI€A'TION, *n.* [Fr. from L. *purificatio.* See *Purify.*]

1. The act of purifying; the act or operation of separating and removing from any thing that which is heterogeneous or foreign to it; as the *purification* of liquors or of metals. *Boyle.*

2. In *religion*, the act or operation of cleansing ceremonially, by removing any pollution or defilement. *Purification* by washing or by other means, was common to the Hebrews and to pagans. The Mohammedans use *purification* as a preparation for devotion. 2 Chron. xxx. Esth. ii. Luke ii. *Encyc.*

3. A cleansing from guilt or the pollution of sin; the extinction of sinful desires, appetites and inclinations.

PURIF'I€ATIVE, } *a.* Having power to
PURIF'I€ATORY, } purify; tending to cleanse.

PU'RIFIER, *n.* [from *purify.*] That which purifies or cleanses; a cleanser; a refiner. Fire was held by the ancients to be an excellent *purifier.*

PU'RIFORM, *a.* [L. *pus*, *puris* and *form.*] Like pus; in the form of pus. *Med. Repos.*

PU'RIFY, *v. t.* [Fr. *purifier;* L. *purifico; purus*, pure, and *facio*, to make.]

1. To make pure or clear; to free from extraneous admixture; as, to *purify* liquors or metals; to *purify* the blood; to *purify* the air.

2. To free from pollution ceremonially; to remove whatever renders unclean and unfit for sacred services.

Purify yourselves and your captives on the third day, and on the seventh day *purify* all your raiment. Num. xxxi.

3. To free from guilt or the defilement of sin; as, to *purify* the heart.

Who gave himself for us, that he might redeem us from all iniquity, and *purify* to himself a peculiar people, zealous of good works. Tit. ii.

4. To clear from improprieties or barbarisms; as, to *purify* a language. *Sprat.*

PU'RIFY, *v. i.* To grow or become pure or clear. Liquors will gradually *purify.* *Burnet.*

PU'RIFYING, *ppr.* Removing foreign or heterogeneous matter; cleansing from pollution; fining; making clear.

PU'RIFYING, *n.* The act or operation of making pure, or of cleansing from extraneous matter or from pollution.

PU'RIM, *n.* Among the Jews, the feast of lots, instituted to commemorate their deliverance from the machinations of Haman. Esth. ix.

PU'RIST, *n.* [Fr. *puriste.*] One excessively nice in the use of words. *Chesterfield. Johnson.*

PU'RITAN, *n.* [from *pure.*] A dissenter from the church of England. The *puritans* were so called in derision, on account of their professing to follow the *pure* word of God, in opposition to all traditions and human constitutions. *Encyc.*

Hume gives this name to three parties; the *political puritans*, who maintained the highest principles of civil liberty; the *puritans in discipline*, who were averse to the ceremonies and government of the episcopal church; and the *doctrinal puritans*, who rigidly defended the speculative system of the first reformers.

PU'RITAN, *a.* Pertaining to the puritans, or dissenters from the church of England. *Sanderson.*

PURITAN'I€, } *a.* Pertaining to the pu-
PURITAN'I€AL, } ritans or their doctrines and practice; exact; rigid; as *puritanical* notions or opinions; *puritanical* manners.

PU'RITANISM, *n.* The notions or practice of puritans. *Mountague.*

PU'RITANIZE, *v. i.* To deliver the notions of puritans. *Mountague.*

PU'RITY, *n.* [Fr. *pureté;* L. *puritas*, from *purus.*]

1. Freedom from foreign admixture or heterogeneous matter; as the *purity* of water, of wine, of spirit; the *purity* of drugs; the *purity* of metals.

2. Cleanness; freedom from foulness or dirt; as the *purity* of a garment.

The *purity* of a linen vesture. *Holyday.*

3. Freedom from guilt or the defilement of sin; innocence; as *purity* of heart or life.

4. Chastity; freedom from contamination by illicit sexual connection. *Shak.*

5. Freedom from any sinister or improper views; as the *purity* of motives or designs.

6. Freedom from foreign idioms, from barbarous or improper words or phrases; as *purity* of style or language.

PURL, *n.* [supposed to be contracted from *purfle.* Qu.]

1. An embroidered and puckered border. *Johnson. Bacon.*

2. A kind of edging for bone-lace. *Bailey.*

PURL, *n.* A species of malt liquor; ale or beer medicated with wormwood or aromatic herbs. *Bailey. Johnson.*

PURL, *n.* Two rounds in knitting.

PURL, *v. i.* [Sw. *porla;* W. *freulaw*, to purl, to ripple; *fraul*, a rippling. It may be allied to G. *brüllen*, D. *brullen*, Dan. *broler*, to roar, and to Eng. *frill*, *trill* and *roll.*]

1. To murmur, as a small stream flowing among stones or other obstructions, which occasion a continued series of broken sounds. It is applied only to small streams. Large streams running in like manner, are said to *roar.* In descriptions of rural scenery, the poets seldom omit a *purling* brook or stream.

My flowery theme,
A painted mistress or a *purling* stream. *Pope.*

2. To flow or run with a murmuring sound.

Around th' adjoining brook that *purls* along
The vocal grove, now fretting o'er a rock. *Thomson.*

PURL, *v. t.* To decorate with fringe or embroidery. *B. Jonson.*

PURL, *n.* A gentle continued murmur of a small stream of rippling water.

PURLIEU, *n. pur'lu.* [Fr. *pur*, pure, and *lieu*, place.]

A border; a limit; a certain limited extent or district; originally, the ground near a royal forest, which being severed from it, was made *purlieu*, that is, pure or free from the forest laws. *Encyc.*

PUR'LIN, *n.* In *architecture*, a piece of timber extending from end to end of a building or roof, across and under the rafters, to support them in the middle. *Encyc.*

PURL'ING, *ppr.* [from *purl.*] Murmuring or gurgling, as a brook.

PURL'ING, *n.* The continued gentle murmur of a small stream.

PURLOIN', *v. t.* [Fr. *pour* and *loin*, far off. See *Eloign.*]

1. Literally, to take or carry away for one's self; hence, to steal; to take by theft.

Your butler *purloins* your liquor. *Arbuthnot.*

2. To take by plagiarism; to steal from books or manuscripts. *Dryden.*

PURLOIN'ED, *pp.* Stolen; taken by plagiarism.

PURLOIN'ER, *n.* A thief; a plagiary.

PURLOIN'ING, *ppr.* Stealing; committing literary theft.

PURLOIN'ING, *n.* Theft; plagiarism.

PUR'PARTY, *n.* [Fr. *pour* and *partie*, part.] In *law*, a share, part or portion of an estate, which is allotted to a co-parcener by partition. *Cowel.*

PUR'PLE, *a.* [Fr. *pourpré;* L. *purpureus;* Sp. *purpureo;* It. *porporino;* Gr. πορφυρεος, from πορφυρα, L. *purpura*, a shell from which the color was obtained.]

1. Designating a color composed of red and blue blended, much admired, and formerly the Roman emperors wore robes of this color.

2. In *poetry*, red or livid; dyed with blood.

I view a field of blood,
And Tyber rolling with a *purple* flood. *Dryden.*

PUR'PLE, *n.* A purple color or dress; hence, imperial government in the Roman empire, as a *purple* robe was the distinguishing dress of the emperors. *Gibbon.*

2. A cardinalate. *Addison. Hume.*

PUR'PLE, *v. t.* [L. *purpuro.*] To make purple, or to dye of a red color; as hands *purpled* with blood.

When morn
Purples the east. *Milton.*
Reclining soft in blissful bowers,
Purpled sweet with springing flowers. *Fenton.*

PUR'PLES, *n. plu.* Spots of a livid red on the body; livid eruptions which appear in certain malignant diseases; a purple fever.

PUR'PLISH, *a.* Somewhat purple. *Boyle.*

PUR'PORT, *n.* [Fr. *pour*, for, and *porter*, to bear.]

1. Design or tendency; as the *purport* of Plato's dialogue. *Norris.*

2. Meaning; import; as the *purport* of a word or phrase.

PUR'PORT, *v. t.* To intend; to intend to show. *Bacon.*

2. To mean; to signify.

PUR'PORTED, *pp.* Designed; intended; meant.

PUR'PORTING, *ppr.* Designing; intending; importing.

PUR'POSE, *n.* [Fr. *propos;* Sp. It. *proposito;* L. *propositum*, *propono;* *pro*, before, and *pono*, to set or place.]

1. That which a person sets before himself as an object to be reached or accomplished; the end or aim to which the view is directed in any plan, measure or exertion. We believe the Supreme Being created intelligent beings for some benevolent and glorious *purpose*, and if so, how glorious and benevolent must be his *purpose* in the plan of redemption! The ambition of men is generally directed to one of two *purposes*, or to both; the acquisition of wealth or of power. We build houses for the *purpose* of shelter; we labor for the *purpose* of subsistence.

2. Intention; design. This sense, however, is hardly to be distinguished from the former; as *purpose* always includes the end in view.

Every *purpose* is established by counsel. Prov. xx.

Being predestinated according to the *purpose* of him who worketh all things after the counsel of his own will. Eph. i.

3. End; effect; consequence, good or bad. What good *purpose* will this answer? We sometimes labor to no *purpose*. Men often employ their time, talents and money for very evil *purposes*.

To what *purpose* is this waste? Matt. xxvi.

4. Instance; example. [*Not in use.*]

5. Conversation. [*Not in use.*] *Spenser.*

Of purpose, on purpose, with previous design; with the mind directed to that object. *On purpose* is more generally used, but the true phrase is *of purpose*.

PUR'POSE, *v. t.* To intend; to design; to resolve; to determine on some end or object to be accomplished.

I have *purposed* it, I will also do it. Is. xlvi. Eph. iii.

Paul *purposed* in the spirit, when he had passed through Macedonia and Achaia, to go to Jerusalem. Acts xix.

PUR'POSED, *pp.* Intended; designed; *applied to things.*

2. Resolved; having formed a design or resolution; *applied to persons.*

I am *purposed* that my mouth shall not transgress. Ps. xvii.

PUR'POSELESS, *a.* Having no effect. [*Little used.*] *Hall.*

PUR'POSELY, *adv.* By design; intentionally; with predetermination.

In composing this discourse, I *purposely* declined all offensive and displeasing truths. *Atterbury.*

So much they scorn the crowd, that if the throng
By chance go right, they *purposely* go wrong. *Pope.*

PUR'PRESTURE, *n.* [from Fr. *pour* and *prendre, pris*, to take.]

In *law*, a nuisance, consisting in an inclosure of or encroachment on something that belongs to the public; as a house erected or inclosure made on the king's demesnes, or of a highway, &c. *Blackstone.*

PUR'PRISE, *n.* [Fr. *pourpris*, supra.] A close or inclosure; also, the whole compass of a manor. *Bacon.*

PUR'PURATE, *n.* A compound of purpuric acid and a salifiable base. *Ure.*

PUR'PURE, *n.* In *heraldry*, purple, represented in engraving by diagonal lines. *Encyc.*

PUR'PURIC, *a.* Purpuric acid is produced by the action of nitric acid upon the lithic or uric acid. *Dr. Prout.*

PURR, *v. i.* To murmur as a cat. [See *Pur.*]

PURR, *n.* A sea lark. *Ainsworth.*

PURRE, *n.* Cyderkin or perkin; the liquor made by steeping the gross matter of pressed apples. *Encyc.*

PUR'RING, *ppr.* Murmuring as a cat.

PURSE, *n. purs.* [Fr. *bourse;* It. *borsa;* Sp. Port. *bolsa;* D. *beurs;* G. *börse;* Dan. *börs;* L. *byrsa*, an ox hide; Gr. *βυρσα*, id. Qu.]

1. A small bag in which money is contained or carried in the pocket. It was formerly made of lether, and is still made of this material by common people. It is usually of silk net-work.

2. A sum of money offered as the prize of winning in a horse race.

3. In *Turkey*, a sum of money, about £50 sterling, or $222.

4. The public coffers; the treasury; as, to exhaust a nation's *purse*, or the public *purse*.

Long purse, or *heavy purse*, wealth; riches.

Light purse, or *empty purse*, poverty, or want of resources.

Sword and purse, the military power and wealth of a nation.

PURSE, *v. t.* To put in a purse. *Dryden. Milton.*

2. To contract into folds or wrinkles.

Thou didst contract and *purse* thy brow. *Shak.*

PURS'ED, *pp.* Put in a purse.

2. Contracted into folds or wrinkles.

PURSENET, *n. purs'net.* A net, the mouth of which may be closed or drawn together like a purse. *Mortimer.*

PURSE-PRIDE, *n.* Pride of money; insolence proceeding from the possession of wealth. *Hall.*

PURSE-PROUD, *a.* Proud of wealth; puffed up with the possession of money or riches.

PURS'ER, *n.* In *the navy*, an officer who has charge of the provisions of a ship of war, and attends to their preservation and distribution among the officers and crew. *Mar. Dict.*

PURSINESS, a mistake for *pussiness.* [See *Pussy.*]

PURS'LAIN, *n.* [It. *porcellana*, porcelain and purslain; Sp. *verdolaga*, purslain, which seems to be green leek, green plant. The Portuguese write very corruptly *beldroega.* The Latin is *portulaca.* See *Leek.*]

A plant of the genus Portulaca. The *sea purslain* is of the genus Atriplex. The *tree sea purslain* is the *Atriplex halimus.* (See *Purslain tree.*) The *water purslain* is of the genus Peplis. *Lee.*

PURS'LAIN-TREE, *n.* [L. *halimus.*] A shrub proper for hedges.

PURSU'ABLE, *a.* [from *pursue.*] That may be pursued, followed or prosecuted. *Sherwood.*

PURSU'ANCE, *n.* [from *pursue.*] A following; prosecution, process or continued exertion to reach or accomplish something; as in *pursuance* of the main design.

2. Consequence; as in *pursuance* of an order from the commander in chief.

PURSU'ANT, *a.* [from *pursue*, or rather from Fr. *poursuivant.*]

Done in consequence or prosecution of any thing; hence, agreeable; conformable. *Pursuant* to a former resolution, the house proceeded to appoint the standing committees. This measure was adopted *pursuant* to a former order.

PURSUE, *v. t.* [Fr. *poursuivre; pour* and *suivre*, to follow, L. *sequor; prosequor*, or *persequor.* See *Seek.*]

1. To follow; to go or proceed after or in a like direction. The captain *pursued* the same course as former navigators have taken. A subsequent legislature *pursued* the course of their predecessors.

2. To take and proceed in, without following another. Captain Cook *pursued* a new and unexplored course. New circumstances often compel us to *pursue* new expedients and untried courses. What course shall we *pursue*?

3. To follow with a view to overtake; to follow with haste; to chase; as, to *pursue* a hare; to *pursue* an enemy.

4. To seek; to use measures to obtain; as, to *pursue* a remedy at law.

5. To prosecute; to continue. A stream proceeds from a lake and *pursues* a southerly course to the ocean.

He that *pursueth* evil, *pursueth* it to his own death. Prov. xi.

6. To follow as an example; to imitate.

The fame of ancient matrons you *pursue*. *Dryden.*

7. To endeavor to attain to; to strive to reach or gain.

We happiness *pursue;* we fly from pain. *Prior.*

8. To follow with enmity; to persecute.

This verb is frequently followed by *after.* Gen. xxxv.

PURSUE, *v. i.* To go on; to proceed; to continue; *a Gallicism.*

I have, *pursues* Carneades, wondered chimists should not consider— *Boyle.*

PURSU'ED, *pp.* Followed; chased; prosecuted; continued.

PURSU'ER, *n.* One that follows; one that chases; one that follows in haste with a view to overtake. *Shak. Milton.*

PURSU'ING, *ppr.* Following; chasing; hastening after to overtake; prosecuting; proceeding in; continuing.

PURSUIT, *n.* [Fr. *poursuite.*] The act of following with a view to overtake; a following with haste, either for sport or in hostility; as the *pursuit* of game; the *pursuit* of an enemy.

2. A following with a view to reach, accomplish or obtain; endeavor to attain to or gain; as the *pursuit* of knowledge; the *pursuit* of happiness or pleasure; the *pursuit* of power, of honor, of distinction, of a phantom.

3. Proceeding; course of business or occupation; continued employment with a view to some end; as mercantile *pursuits;* literary *pursuits.*

4. Prosecution; continuance of endeavor. *Clarendon.*

PUR'SUIVANT, *n.* [Fr. *poursuivant.*] A state messenger; an attendant on the heralds. *Spenser. Camden.*

PURS'Y, a corrupt orthography. [See *Pussy.*]

PUR'TENANCE, *n.* [from the L. *pertinens, pertineo.* See *Appurtenance.*]

Appurtenance; but applied to the pluck of an animal, Ex. xii.

PU'RULENCE, } *n.* [L. *purulentus*, from
PU'RULENCY, } *pus, puris*, matter.]

The generation of pus or matter; pus. *Arbuthnot.*

PU'RULENT, *a.* Consisting of pus or matter; partaking of the nature of pus. *Bacon.*

PURVEY, *v. t.* [Fr. *pourvoir; pour* and *voir*, to see; L. *provideo;* It. *provedere;* Sp. *proveer.*]

1. To provide; to provide with conveniences. *Dryden.*

2. To procure. *Thomson.*

PURVEY, *v. i.* To purchase provisions; to provide. *Milton.*

PURVEYANCE, *n.* Procurement of provisions or victuals.

2. Provision; victuals provided. *Spenser.*

3. In *English laws*, the royal prerogative or right of pre-emption, by which the king was authorized to buy provisions and ne-

cessaries for the use of his household at an apprized value, in preference to all his subjects, and even without the consent of the owner; also, the right of impressing horses and carriages, &c.; a right abolished by Stat. 12. Charles II. 24.

PURVEYOR, *n.* One who provides victuals, or whose business is to make provision for the table; a victualer. *Raleigh.*

2. An officer who formerly provided or exacted provision for the king's household. *England.*

3. One who provides the means of gratifying lust; a procurer; a pimp; a bawd. *Dryden. Addison.*

PUR'VIEW, *n.* [Norm. Fr. *pourveu, purvieu,* purvey; Fr. *pourvu,* provided, from *pourvoir.* See *Purvey.*]

1. Primarily, a condition or proviso; *but in this sense not used.*

2. The body of a statute, or that part which begins with "*Be it enacted,*" as distinguished from the *preamble.* *Cowel. Encyc.*

3. In *modern usage,* the limit or scope of a statute; the whole extent of its intention or provisions. *Marshall.*

4. Superintendence.

The federal power—is confined to objects of a general nature, more within the *purview* of the United States, than of any particular one. [*Unusual.*] *Ramsay.*

5. Limit or sphere intended; scope; extent.

In determining the extent of information required in the exercise of a particular authority, recourse must be had to the objects within the *purview* of that authority. *Federalist, Madison.*

PUS, *n.* [L.] The white or yellowish matter generated in ulcers and wounds in the process of healing. *Encyc.*

PUSH, *v. t.* [Fr. *pousser;* D. *puis,* a push; Sw. *pösa,* to swell; W. *pos,* growth, increase; *posiaw,* to increase, or *pwysaw,* to press, to weigh. The sense is to thrust, press or urge. See Class Bz.]

1. To press against with force; to drive or impel by pressure; or to endeavor to drive by steady pressure, without striking; opposed to *draw.* We *push* a thing forward by force applied behind it; we *draw* by applying force before it. We may *push* without moving the object.

2. To butt; to strike with the end of the horns; to thrust the points of horns against.

If the ox shall *push* a man-servant or maid-servant—he shall be stoned. Ex. xxi.

3. To press or urge forward; as, to *push* an objection too far.

He forewarns his care
With rules to *push* his fortune or to bear. *Dryden.*

4. To urge; to drive.

Ambition *pushes* the soul to such actions as are apt to procure honor to the actor. *Spectator.*

5. To enforce; to press; to drive to a conclusion.

We are *pushed* for an answer. *Swift.*

6. To importune; to press with solicitation; to tease.

To push down, to overthrow by pushing or impulse.

PUSH, *v. i.* To make a thrust; as, to *push* with the horns or with a sword. *Dryden. Addison.*

2. To make an effort.

At length
Both sides resolv'd to *push,* we tried our strength. *Dryden.*

3. To make an attack.

The king of the south shall *push* at him. Dan. xi.

4. To burst out.

To push on, to drive or urge forward; to hasten. *Push on,* brave men.

PUSH, *n.* A thrust with a pointed instrument, or with the end of a thing. *Spenser.*

2. Any pressure, impulse or force applied; as, to give the ball the first *push.* *Addison.*

3. An assault or attack. *Watts.*

4. A forcible onset; a vigorous effort. *Addison.*

5. Exigence; trial; extremity.

When it comes to the *push,* it is no more than talk. *L'Estrange.*

6. A sudden emergence. *Shak.*

7. A little swelling or pustule; a wheal; a pimple; an eruption. *Bacon.*

PUSHED, *pp.* Pressed; urged; driven.

PUSHER, *n.* One that drives forward.

PUSHING, *ppr.* Pressing; driving; urging forward.

2. *a.* Pressing forward in business; enterprising; driving; vigorous.

PUSHPIN, *n.* A child's play in which pins are pushed alternately. *L'Estrange.*

PUSILLANIM'ITY, *n.* [Fr. *pusillanimité;* L. *pusillanimitas; pusillus,* small, weak, and *animus,* courage.]

Want of that firmness and strength of mind which constitutes courage or fortitude; weakness of spirit; cowardliness; that feebleness of mind which shrinks from trifling or imaginary dangers.

It is obvious to distinguish between an act of *pusillanimity* and an act of great modesty or humility. *South.*

PUSILLAN'IMOUS, *a.* [Fr. *pusillanime;* It. *pusillanimo,* supra.]

1. Destitute of that strength and firmness of mind which constitutes courage, bravery and fortitude; being of weak courage; mean spirited; cowardly; *applied to persons;* as a *pusillanimous* prince.

2. Proceeding from weakness of mind or want of courage; feeble; as *pusillanimous* counsels. *Bacon.*

PUSILLAN'IMOUSLY, *adv.* With want of courage.

PUSILLAN'IMOUSNESS, *n.* Pusillanimity; want of courage.

PUSS, *n.* [D. *poes,* puss, a fur tippet, and a kiss; Ir. *pus,* a cat, and the lip.]

1. The fondling name of a cat. *Watts.*

2. The sportsman's name for a hare. *Gay.*

PUS'SINESS, *n.* [from *pussy.*] A state of being swelled or bloated; inflation; hence, shortness of breath.

PUS'SY, *a.* [Fr. *poussif,* from *pousser,* to push; Sw. *pösa,* to swell or inflate; Ir. *baois,* lust, vanity; allied to *boast.* This word has been written *pursy,* evidently by mistake. We have the word probably from the French *poussif,* from *pousser,* to *push.*]

Properly, inflated, swelled; hence, fat, short and thick; and as persons of this make labor in respiration, the word is used for short breathed.

PUS'TULATE, *v. t.* [L. *pustulatus.* See *Pustule.*]

To form into pustules or blisters. *Stackhouse.*

PUSTULE, *n.* *pus'l* or *pus'tul;* the former is the usual pronunciation in America. [Fr. *pustule;* L. *pustula;* from the root of *push.*]

A pimple or wheal; a small push or eruption on the skin. *Arbuthnot.*

PUS'TULOUS, *a.* [L. *pustulosus.*] Full of pustules or pimples.

PUT, *v. t.* pret. and pp. *put.* [D. *pooten,* to set or plant; *poot,* the foot; Dan. *poder,* to graft; *pode,* a cion; Gr. φυω, contracted from φυδω or φυτω, whence φυτον, a germ, shoot or twig. We find the same word in the L. *puto,* to prune, that is, to thrust off, also to think or consider, that is, to set in the mind, as we use *suppose,* L. *suppono.* But we see the English sense more distinctly in the compounds, *imputo,* to *impute,* that is, to *put to* or *on; computo,* to *compute,* to *put together.* The Welsh *pwtian,* to poke, to thrust, and *pwtiaw,* to butt, are doubtless the same word. The L. *posui,* from *pono,* is probably a dialectical orthography of the same root. See Class Bd. and Bs. The primary sense is to thrust, throw, drive or send.]

1. To set, lay or place; *in a general sense.* Thus we say, to *put* the hand to the face; to *put* a book on the shelf; to *put* a horse in the stable; to *put* fire to the fuel; to *put* clothes on the body. God planted a garden and there he *put* Adam.

2. *Put* is applicable to *state* or *condition,* as well as to *place.* *Put* him in a condition to help himself. *Put* the fortress in a state of defense. The apostles were *put* in trust with the gospel. We are often *put* in jeopardy by our own ignorance or rashness. We do not always *put* the best men in office.

3. To repose.

How wilt thou—*put* thy trust on Egypt for chariots? 2 Kings xviii.

4. To push into action.

Thank him who *puts* me, loth, to this revenge. *Milton.*

5. To apply; to set to employment.

No man having *put* his hand to the plow, and looking back, is fit for the kingdom of God. Luke ix.

6. To throw or introduce suddenly. He had no time to *put* in a word.

7. To consign to letters.

He made a proclamation—and *put* it also in writing. 2 Chron. xxxvi.

8. To oblige; to require.

We are *put* to prove things which can hardly be made plainer. *Tillotson.*

9. To incite; to instigate; to urge by influence. The appearance of a formidable enemy *put* the king on making vigorous preparations for defense.

This *put* me upon observing the thickness of the glass. *Newton.*

These wretches *put* us upon all mischief, to feed their lusts and extravagances. *Swift.*

10. To propose; as, to *put* a question to the witness; to *put* a case in point.

11. To reach to another. Hab. ii.

12. To bring into a state of mind or temper.

Solyman, to *put* the Rhodians out of all suspicion of invasion— *Knolles.*

13. To offer; to advance.

I am ashamed to *put* a loose indigested play upon the public— *Dryden.*

14. To cause.

The natural constitutions of men *put* a wide difference between them. *Locke.*

To put about, to turn; to change the course; to gibe ship.

To put by, to turn away; to divert.

The design of the evil one is to *put* thee *by* from thy spiritual employment. *Taylor.*

A fright hath *put by* an ague fit. *Grew.*

2. To thrust aside.

Jonathan had died for being so,
Had not just God *put by* th' unnatural blow. *Cowley.*

To put down, to baffle; to repress; to crush; as, to *put down* a party.

2. To degrade; to deprive of authority, power or place.

3. To bring into disuse.

Sugar hath *put down* the use of honey. *Obs. Bacon.*

4. To confute; to silence.

Mark now how a plain tale shall *put* you *down.* *Shak.*

To put forth, to propose; to offer to notice.

Sampson said, I will now *put forth* a riddle to you. Judges xiv.

2. To extend; to reach; as, to *put forth* the hand.

3. To shoot out; to send out, as a sprout; as, to *put forth* leaves.

4. To exert; to bring into action; as, to *put forth* strength.

5. To publish, as a book.

To put in, to introduce among others; as, to *put in* a word while others are discoursing.

2. To insert; as, to *put in* a passage or clause; to *put in* a cion.

3. To conduct into a harbor.

To put in fear, to affright; to make fearful.

To put in mind, to remind; to call to remembrance.

To put in practice, to use; to exercise; as, to *put in practice* the maxims of the wise man.

To put into another's hands, to trust; to commit to the care of.

To put off, to divest; to lay aside; as, to *put off* a robe; to *put off* mortality or the mortal body; to *put off* haughty airs.

2. To turn aside from a purpose or demand; to defeat or delay by artifice.

I hoped for a demonstration, but Themistices hopes to *put* me *off* with a harangue. *Boyle.*

This is an unreasonable demand, and we might *put* him *off* with this answer. *Bentley.*

3. To delay; to defer; to postpone. How generally do men *put off* the care of their salvation to future opportunities!

4. To pass fallaciously; to cause to be circulated or received; as, to *put off* upon the world some plausible reports or ingenious theory.

5. To discard.

The clothiers all *put off*
The spinsters, carders, fullers, weavers— *Shak.*

6. To recommend; to vend; to obtrude. *Bacon.*

7. To vend; to sell.

8. To pass into other hands; as, to *put off* a counterfeit coin or note.

9. To push from land; as, to *put off* the boat.

To put on or *upon*, to impute; to charge; as, to *put* one's own crime or blame *on* another.

2. To invest with, as clothes or covering; as, to *put on* a cloke.

3. To assume; as, to *put on* a grave countenance; to *put on* a counterfeit appearance.

Mercury—*put on* the shape of a man. *L'Estrange.*

4. To forward; to promote.

This came handsomely to *put on* the peace. *Obs.* *Bacon.*

5. To impose; to inflict.

That which thou *puttest on* me, I will bear. 2 Kings xviii.

To be put upon, to be imposed on; to be deceived; *used chiefly in the passive form.*

To put over, to refer; to send.

For the certain knowledge of that truth,
I *put* you o'er to heaven and to my mother. *Shak.*

2. To defer; to postpone. The court *put over* the cause to the next term.

To put out, to place at interest; to lend at use. Money *put out* at compound interest, nearly doubles in eleven years.

2. To extinguish; as, to *put out* a candle, lamp or fire; to *put out* the remains of affection. *Addison.*

3. To send; to emit; to shoot; as a bud or sprout; as, to *put out* leaves.

4. To extend; to reach out; to protrude; as, to *put out* the hand.

5. To drive out; to expel; to dismiss.

When I am *put out* of the stewardship. Luke xvi.

6. To publish; to make public; as, to *put out* a pamphlet. [*Now vulgar.*]

7. To confuse; to disconcert; to interrupt; as, to *put* one *out* in reading or speaking.

To put out the eyes, to destroy the power of sight; to render blind.

To put to, to add; to unite; as, to *put* one sum *to* another.

2. To refer to; to expose; as, to *put* the fate of the army or nation *to* a battle; to *put* the safety of the state *to* hazard.

3. To punish by; to distress by; as, to *put* a man *to* the rack or torture.

To put to it, to distress; to press hard; to perplex; to give difficulty to.

O gentle lady, do not *put* me *to* 't. *Shak.*

To be put to it, *in the passive form*, to have difficulty.

I shall be hard *put to it* to bring myself off. *Addison.*

To put the hand to, to apply; to take hold; to begin; to undertake; as, *to put the hand to* the plow. See Deut. xii. 7.

2. To take by theft or wrong; to embezzle.

Then shall an oath of the Lord be between them both, that he hath not *put his hand to* his neighbor's goods. Ex. xxii.

To put to the sword, to kill; to slay. *Bacon.*

To put to death, to kill.

To put to a stand, to stop; to arrest by obstacles or difficulties.

To put to trial, or *on trial*, to bring before a court and jury for examination and decision.

2. To bring to a test; to try.

To put together, to unite in a sum, mass or compound; to add; as, *to put* two sums *together*; *put together* the ingredients.

2. To unite; to connect. *Put* the two chains *together.*

3. To place in company or in one society.

To put trust in, to confide in; to repose confidence in.

To put up, to pass unavenged; to overlook; not to punish or resent; as, to *put up* injuries; to *put up* indignities.

Such national injuries are not to be *put up*, but when the offender is below resentment. *Addison.*

[I have never heard this phrase used in America. We always say, to *put up with*; we cannot *put up with* such injuries.]

2. To send forth or shoot up, as plants; as, to *put up* mushrooms. *Obs.* *Bacon.*

3. To expose; to offer publicly; as, to *put up* goods to sale or auction.

4. To start from a cover. *Obs.* *Spectator.*

5. To hoard.

Himself never *put up* any of the rent. *Spelman.*

6. To reposit for preservation; as, to *put up* apples for winter.

7. To pack; to reposit in casks with salt for preservation; as, to *put up* pork, beef or fish.

8. To hide or lay aside. *Put up* that letter. *Shak.*

9. To put in a trunk or box; to pack; as, to *put up* clothing for a journey.

PUT, *v. i.* To go or move; as, when the air first *puts* up. *Obs.* *Bacon.*

2. To steer.

His fury thus appeas'd, he *puts* to land. *Dryden.*

3. To shoot; to germinate.

The sap *puts* downward. *Bacon.*

To put forth, to shoot; to bud; to germinate.

Take earth from under walls where nettles *put forth.* *Bacon.*

2. To leave a port or haven. *Shak.*

To put in, to enter a harbor; to sail into port.

2. To offer a claim. A *puts in* for a share of profits.

To put in for, to offer one's self; to stand as a candidate for. *Locke.*

To put off, to leave land.

To put on, to urge motion; to drive vehemently.

To put over, to sail over or across. *Abbot.*

To put to sea, to set sail; to begin a voyage; to advance into the ocean. *Dryden.*

To put up, to take lodgings; to lodge. We *put up* at the Golden Ball.

2. To offer one's self as a candidate. *L'Estrange.*

To put up to, to advance to. [*Little used.*] *Swift.*

To put up with, to overlook or suffer without recompense, punishment or resentment; as, to *put up with* an injury or affront.

2. To take without opposition or dissatisfaction; as, to *put up with* bad fare.

This verb, in all its uses, retains its primary sense, to *set*, *throw*, *thrust*, *send*, &c.; but its signification is modified in a great variety of ways, by other words standing in connection with it.

PUT, *n.* An action of distress; as a forced *put.* *L'Estrange.*

2. A game at cards.

PUT, *n.* [Qu. W. *pwt*, a short thick person.] A rustic; a clown.

PUT, *n.* [Fr. *putain*; W. *putan*; It. *putta*, *puttano*; Sp. *puta.*] A strumpet; a prostitute.

Put case, for *put the case*, suppose the case to be so; a vulgar or at least inelegant phrase. *Burton.*

PU'TAGE, *n.* [See *Put*, a prostitute.] In *law*, prostitution or fornication on the part of a female. *Cowel.*

PU'TANISM, *n.* [Fr. *putanisme.*] Customary lewdness or prostitution of a female.

PU'TATIVE, *a.* [Fr. *putatif; It. putativo;* from L. *puto*, to suppose.]
Supposed; reputed; commonly thought or deemed; as the *putative* father of a child.

PU'TID, *a.* [L. *putidus*, from *puteo*, to have an ill smell; W. *pwd.*] Mean; base; worthless. *L'Estrange. Taylor.*

PU'TIDNESS, *n.* Meanness; vileness.

PUT'LOG, *n.* A short piece of timber used in scaffolds. *Moxon.*

PUT-OFF, *n.* An excuse; a shift for evasion or delay. *L'Estrange.*

PUTRED'INOUS, *a.* [from L. *putredo*, from *putreo, putris.*]
Proceeding from putrefaction, or partaking of the putrefactive process; having an offensive smell. *Floyer.*

PUTREFAC'TION, *n.* [Fr. from L. *putrefacio; putris*, putrid, and *facio*, to make.]
A natural process by which animal and vegetable bodies are disorganized and dissolved, or reduced to their original separate elements. *Putrefaction* is greatly accelerated by heat and moisture.

PUTREFAC'TIVE, *a.* Pertaining to putrefaction; as the *putrefactive* smell or process.
2. Tending to promote putrefaction; causing putrefaction. *Brown.*

PU'TREFIED, *pp.* Dissolved; rotten.

PU'TREFY, *v. t.* [F. *putrefier;* L. *putrefacio; putris*, putrid, and *facio*, to make.]
1. To cause to dissolve; to disorganize and reduce to the simple constituent elements, as animal or vegetable bodies; to cause to rot. Heat and moisture soon *putrefy* dead flesh or vegetables.
2. To corrupt; to make foul; as, to *putrefy* the air. [*Little used.*] *Shak.*
3. To make morbid, carious or gangrenous; as, to *putrefy* an ulcer or wound. *Wiseman. Temple.*

PU'TREFY, *v. i.* To dissolve and return to the original distinct elements, as animal and vegetable substances deprived of the living principle; to rot.

PUTRES'CENCE, *n.* [from L. *putrescens, putresco.*]
The state of dissolving, as an animal or vegetable substance; a putrid state. *Brown.*

PUTRES'CENT, *a.* Becoming putrid; passing from an organized state into the constituent elements. *Brown.*
2. Pertaining to the process of putrefaction; as a *putrescent* smell.

PUTRES'CIBLE, *a.* That may be putrefied; liable to become putrid; as *putrescible* substances. *Ramsay, Hist.*

PU'TRID, *a.* [Fr. *putride;* L. *putridus*, from *putris, putreo.*]
1. In a state of dissolution or disorganization, as animal and vegetable bodies; corrupt; rotten; as *putrid* flesh.
Indicating a state of dissolution; tending to disorganize the substances composing the body; malignant; as a *putrid* fever.
3. Proceeding from putrefaction or pertaining to it; as a *putrid* scent.

PU'TRIDNESS, PUTRID'ITY, *n.* The state of being putrid; corruption. *Floyer.*

PU'TRY, *a.* Rotten. [*Not used.*] *Marston.*

PUT'TER, *n.* [from *put.*] One who puts or places. *L'Estrange.*

PUT'TER-ON, *n.* An inciter or instigator. *Shak.*

PUT'TING, *ppr.* [from *put.*] Setting; placing; laying.

PUT'TING-STONE, *n.* In *Scotland*, a stone laid at the gates of great houses for trials of strength. *Johnson. Pope.*

PUT'TOC, *n.* A kite. *Spenser.*

Puttoc-shrouds, probably a mistake for *futtoc-shrouds.*

PUT'TY, *n.* [Sp. Port. *potea.*] A kind of paste or cement compounded of whiting and lintseed oil, beaten or kneaded to the consistence of dough; used in fastening glass in sashes and in stopping crevices.
2. A powder of calcined tin, used in polishing glass and steel. *Encyc.*

PUZ'ZLE, *v. t.* [from the root of *pose*, which see.]
1. To perplex; to embarrass; to put to a stand; to gravel.

> A shrewd disputant in those points, is dexterous in *puzzling* others. *More.*
>
> He is perpetually *puzzled* and perplexed amidst his own blunders. *Addison.*

2. To make intricate; to entangle.

> The ways of heaven are dark and intricate,
> *Puzzl'd* in mazes and perplex'd with error. *Addison.*

PUZ'ZLE, *v. i.* To be bewildered; to be awkward. *L'Estrange.*

PUZ'ZLE, *n.* Perplexity; embarrassment. *Bacon.*

PUZ'ZLED, *pp.* Perplexed; intricate; put to a stand.

PUZ'ZLE-HEADED, *a.* Having the head full of confused notions. *Johnson.*

PUZ'ZLER, *n.* One that perplexes.

PUZ'ZLING, *ppr.* Perplexing; embarrassing; bewildering.

PUZ'ZOLAN, PUZZOLA'NA, *n.* A loose porous volcanic substance or stone.

PYC'NITE, *n.* [Qu. Gr. πυκνος, compact.]
A mineral, the shorlite of Kirwan, or shorlous topaz of Jameson. It usually appears in long irregular prisms or cylinders, longitudinally striated, and united in bundles. *Werner. Cleaveland.*

PYC'NOSTYLE, *n.* [Gr. πυκνος, thick, and ϛυλος, column.]
In *ancient architecture*, a building where the columns stand very close to each other; only one diameter and a half of the column being allowed to each intercolumniation. *Encyc.*

PYE, *n.* [probably a contracted word, and the same as *pie*, a mass.]
A confused mass; the state of printing types when the sorts are mixed.

PYE, *n.* A bird. [See *Pie.*]

PY'GARG, PYG'ARGUS, *n.* [Gr. πυγαργος.] A fowl of the genus Falco, the female of the hen harrier. *Ed. Encyc.*

PYGME'AN, *a.* Pertaining to a pygmy or dwarf; very small; dwarfish. *Milton.*

PYG'MY, *n.* [Fr. *pygmée;* It. *pigmeo;* L. *pygmæus;* Gr. πυγμαιος, from πυγμη, the fist; as big as the fist.]
A dwarf; a person not exceeding a cubit in highth. This appellation was given by the ancients to a fabulous race of beings inhabiting Thrace, who waged war with the cranes and were destroyed. *Encyc.*

PYL'AGORE, *n.* [Gr. πυλαγορας.] In *ancient Greece*, a delegate or representative of a city, sent to the Amphictyonic council. *Mitford.*

PYLOR'IC, *a.* Pertaining to the pylorus; as the *pyloric* artery.

PYLO'RUS, *n.* [Gr. πυλωρος, from πυλη, a gate.]
The lower and right orifice of the stomach. *Coxe.*

PYR'ACANTH, *n.* [Gr. πυραχανθα, fiery thorn.]
A plant; a kind of thorn of the genus Mespilus. *Mason. Lee.*

PYRAL'LOLITE, *n.* [Gr. πυρ, fire, αλλος and λιθος; alluding to its changes of color before the blowpipe.]
A new mineral found in Finland, massive and in crystals, friable and yielding to the knife. Its color is greenish. *Cleaveland.*

PYR'AMID, *n.* [Fr. *pyramide;* It. *piramide;* L. *pyramis;* Gr. πυραμις. The origin and composition of this word are not ascertained. It is supposed that the Gr. πυρ, fire, forms one of its component parts; but W. *bera* is a pyramid, and a stack of corn.]
A solid body standing on a triangular, square or polygonal base, and terminating in a point at the top; or in geometry, a solid figure consisting of several triangles, whose bases are all in the same plane, and which have one common vertex. *Encyc.*

The *pyramids* of Egypt may have been erected to the sun, during the prevalence of Sabianism.

A *pyramid* is formed by the meeting of three or more planes at a point termed the apex. *Phillips.*

PYRAM'IDAL, *a.* [Fr. *pyramidale;* It. *piramidale.*] Pyramidical.

PYRAMID'ICAL, *a.* Having the form of a pyramid.

> The particles of earth being cubical, those of fire, *pyramidical.* *Enfield on Plato.*
>
> A *pyramidical* rock. *Goldsmith.*

PYRAMID'ICALLY, *adv.* In the form of a pyramid. *Bacon.*

PYRAM'IDOID, PYR'AMOID, *n.* [*pyramid* and Gr. ειδος, form.]
A solid figure, formed by the rotation of a semi-parabola about its base or greatest ordinate.

PYR'AMIS, *n.* [L.] A pyramid. *Bacon.*

PYRE, *n.* [L. *pyra.*] A funeral pile; a pile to be burnt. *Pope.*

PYR'ENITE, *n.* A mineral of a grayish black color, found in the Pyrenees, and considered as a variety of garnet. It occurs in minute rhombic dodecahedrons. *Cleaveland.*

PYRETOL'OGY, *n.* [Gr. πυρετος, fever, from πυρ, fire, and λογος, discourse.]
A discourse or treatise on fevers, or the doctrine of fevers. *Hooper.*

PYR'GOM, *n.* A mineral, called also fassaite.

PYR'IFORM, *a.* [L. *pyrum*, a pear, and *form.*] Having the form of a pear. *Gregory.*

PYRITA'CEOUS, *a.* Pertaining to pyrite. [See *Pyritic.*] *Lavoisier.*

PYR'ITE, *n.* plu. *pyrites.* [Gr. πυριτης, from πυρ, fire.]
Fire-stone; a genus of inflammable substances composed of sulphur and iron or other metal; a sulphuret of iron or other metal.

Hence sable coal his massy couch extends,
And stars of gold the sparkling *pyrite* blends. *Darwin.*

[I have anglicized this word, according to Darwin and the French mineralogists; making *pyrites* a regular plural.]

PYRIT'IC, PYRIT'ICAL, PYR'ITOUS, *a.* Pertaining to pyrite; consisting of or resembling pyrite.

PYRITIF'EROUS, *a.* [*pyrite* and L. *fero*, to produce.] Containing or producing pyrite.

PYR'ITIZE, *v. t.* To convert into pyrite. *Ed. Encyc.*

PYRITOL'OGY, *n.* [*pyrite* and Gr. λογος, discourse.] A discourse or treatise on pyrites. *Fourcroy.*

PYR'OGOM, *n.* A variety of diopside. *Ure.*

PYROL'ATRY, *n.* [Gr. πυρ, fire, and λατρεια, worship.] The worship of fire. *Young.*

PYROLIG'NEOUS, PYROLIG'NIC, PYROLIG'NOUS, *a.* [Gr. πυρ, fire, and L. *ligneus*, from *lignum*, wood.]
Generated or procured by the distillation of wood; a term applied to the acid obtained by the distillation of wood. *Chimistry.*

PYROLIG'NITE, *n.* [supra.] A salt formed by the combination of pyrolignous acid with another substance.

PYROLITH'IC, *a.* [Gr. πυρ, fire, and λιθος, stone.]
The pyrolithic acid is an acid of recent discovery. It is obtained from the silvery white plates which sublime from uric acid concretions, when distilled in a retort.

PYROL'OGIST, *n.* [See *Pyrology.*] A believer in the doctrine of latent heat. *Black.*

PYROL'OGY, *n.* [Gr. πυρ, fire, and λογος, discourse.]
A treatise on heat; or the natural history of heat, latent and sensible. *Mitchill.*

PYROM'ALATE, *n.* [See *Pyromalic.*] A compound of malic acid and a salifiable base. *Ure.*

PYROMA'LIC, *a.* [Gr. πυρ, fire, and L. *malum*, an apple.]
The pyromalic acid is a substance obtained by distillation from the malic acid.

PYR'OMANCY, *n.* [Gr. πυρ, fire, and μαντεια, divination.] Divination by fire. *Encyc.*

PYROMAN'TIC, *a.* Pertaining to pyromancy.

PYROMAN'TIC, *n.* One who pretends to divine by fire. *Herbert.*

PYROM'ETER, *n.* [Gr. πυρ, fire, and μετρον, measure.]
1. An instrument for measuring the expansion of bodies by heat.
2. An instrument for measuring degrees of heat above those indicated by the mercurial thermometer; as the *pyrometer* of Wedgewood.

PYROMU'CITE, *n.* A combination of pyromucous acid with another substance.

PYROMU'COUS, *a.* [Gr. πυρ, fire, and L. *mucus.*]
The pyromucous acid is obtained by the distillation of sugar or other saccharine substance.

PYR'OPE, *n.* [Gr. πυρωπος; πυρ, fire, and ωψ, face.]
A mineral regarded as a variety of garnet, occurring in small masses or grains, never in crystals. Its color is a poppy or blood red, frequently with a tinge of orange. *Brochant. Cleaveland.*

PYR'OPHANE, *n.* [Gr. πυρ, fire, and φανος, clear.]
A mineral which in its natural state is opake, but rendered transparent by heat. *Kirwan.*

PYROPH'ANOUS, *a.* Rendered transparent by heat.

PYROPH'OROUS, *a.* Pertaining to or resembling pyrophorus.

PYROPH'ORUS, *n.* [Gr. πυρ, fire, and φορος, bearing.]
A substance which takes fire on exposure to air, or which maintains or retains light. *Thomson.*

PYROPHYS'ALITE. [See *Topaz* and *Physalite.*]

PYROR'THITE, *n.* A mineral little known, resembling orthite, but very different from it, for it burns in the flame of the blowpipe like charcoal; whereas orthite melts. Pyrorthite is in black plates, thin and almost parallel. *Dict. Nat. Hist.*

PYR'OSCOPE, *n.* [Gr. πυρ, fire, and σκοπεω, to view.]
An instrument for measuring the pulsatory motion of the air, or the intensity of heat radiating from a fire. *Leslie.*

PYROS'MALITE, *n.* A mineral of a liver brown color, or pistachio green, occurring in six sided prisms, of a lamellar structure, found in Sweden. *Phillips.*

PYROT'ARTARIC, PYROT'ARTAROUS, *a.* [Gr. πυρ, fire, and *tartar.*]
Denoting an acid obtained by distilling pure tartrite of potash.

PYROT'ARTRITE, *n.* A salt formed by the combination of pyrotartarous acid with another substance. *Hooper.*

PYROTECH'NIC, PYROTECH'NICAL, *a.* [Gr. πυρ, fire, and τεχνη, art.]
Pertaining to fire works or the art of forming them.

PYROTECH'NICS, PYR'OTECHNY, *n.* [supra.] The art of making fire works; or the science which teaches the management and application of fire in its various operations, in gunnery, rockets, &c.

PYROTECH'NIST, *n.* One skilled in pyrotechny. *Stevens.*

PYROT'IC, *a.* [Gr. πυροω, to burn.] Caustic. [See *Caustic.*]

PYROT'IC, *n.* A caustic medicine.

PYR'OXENE, *n.* [Gr. πυρ, fire, and ξενος, a stranger; a guest in fire, unaltered.]
Augite. *Ure.*
A species of minerals of the class of stones, which has been named volcanic shorl; but it is a family which comprehends many substances of different appearances. It is almost always crystalized, but in complicated forms. *Dict. Nat. Hist.*

PYROXEN'IC, *a.* Pertaining to pyroxene, or partaking of its qualities. *Humboldt.*

PYR'RHIC, *n.* [L. *pyrrhichius*; Gr. πυρριχιος, from πυρριχη, a nimble dance.]
1. In poetry, a foot consisting of two short syllables.
2. An ancient military dance.

PYRRHON'IC, *a.* Pertaining to Pyrrhonism.

PYR'RHONISM, *n.* [from *Pyrrho*, the founder of the sceptics.] Scepticism; universal doubt.

PYR'RHONIST, *n.* A sceptic; one who doubts of every thing.

PYTHAGO'REAN, *n.* A follower of Pythagoras, the founder of the Italic sect of philosophers.

PYTHAGO'REAN, PYTHAGOR'IC, PYTHAGOR'ICAL, *a.* Belonging to the philosophy of Pythagoras.

PYTHAG'ORISM, *n.* The doctrines of Pythagoras. *More.*

PYTH'IAN, *a.* [from *Pythia*, the priestess of Apollo.]
Pertaining to the priestess of Apollo, who delivered oracles.

PYTH'ONESS, *n.* [from L. *Pytho*, Gr. πυθων, a dragon or serpent.]
A sort of witch; also, the female or priestess who gave oracular answers at Delphi, in Greece. *Mitford.*

PYTHON'IC, *a.* Pretending to foretell future events.

PYTH'ONIST, *n.* A conjurer.

PYX, *n.* [L. *pyxis*; Gr. πυξις.] The box in which the catholics keep the host. *Cranmer.*

Q.

Q is the seventeenth letter of the English Alphabet; an articulation borrowed from the oriental *koph* or *qoph*, Ch. and Heb. ק, Samaritan ࠒ, Syriac ܩ, Arabic ق Kaf.

It is supposed to be an articulation more deeply guttural than that of K; indeed it might have been pronounced as we pronounce *qu;* for we observe that in the Latin language, from which the moderns have borrowed the letter, it is always followed by *u,* as it is in English. This letter is not in the Greek alphabet. In our mother tongue, the Anglo Saxon, this letter is not used; but in the place of *qu, cu,* or more generally, *cw* is used; as in *cwic,* quick; *cwen,* queen. This letter is superfluous; for *ku* or *koo,* in English, have precisely the same sounds as *qu.* It is alledged that in expressing *q,* the cheeks are contracted, and the lips put into a canular form, for the passage of the breath; circumstances which distinguish it from *k.* This appears to be a mistake. This position of the organs is entirely owing to the following letter *u;* and *kuestion* and *question* are pronounced precisely alike, and with the same configuration of the organs. For *qu* in English, the Dutch use *kw,* the Germans *qu,* the Swedes and the Danes *qv,* which answer to our *kw.* The Gothic has a character which answers to *qu.* It appears then that *q* is precisely *k,* with this difference in use, that *q* is always followed by *u* in English, and *k* is not. Q never ends an English word. Its name *cue,* is said to be from the French *queue,* a tail.

As a numeral, Q stands for 500, and with a dash, Q̄, for 500,000.

Used as an abbreviation, Q. stands for *quantity,* or *quantum;* as among *physicians, q. pl. quantum placet,* as much as you please; *q. s. quantum sufficit,* as much as is required, or as is sufficient.

Among *mathematicians,* Q. E. D. stands for *quod erat demonstrandum,* which was to be demonstrated; Q. E. F. *quod erat faciendum,* which was to be done.

In the notes of the ancients, Q. stands for *Quintus,* or *Quintius; Quint.* for *Quintilius;* and *Quæs.* for *quæstor.*

In English, Q. is an abbreviation for *question.*

QUAB, *n.* [G. *quappe;* D. *kwab;* Dan. *qvabbe.*]

A fish of Russian rivers, which delights in clear water. *Dict. Nat. Hist.*

QUACHIL'TO, *n.* A Brazilian fowl of the moor-hen kind, of a fine black color variegated with white. Its voice resembles the crowing of a cock. *Dict. Nat. Hist.*

QUACK, *v. i.* [D. *kwaaken,* G. *quaken,* Dan. *qvakker,* to croak.]

1. To cry like a duck or goose. *King.*

2. To boast; to bounce; to talk noisily and ostentatiously; as, pretenders to medical skill *quack* of their cures. *Hudibras.*

QUACK, *n.* [from the verb.] A boaster; one who pretends to skill or knowledge which he does not possess. *Felton.*

2. A boastful pretender to medical skill which he does not possess; an empiric; an ignorant practitioner. *Addison.*

QUACK'ERY, *n.* The boastful pretensions or mean practice of an ignoramus, particularly in medicine; empiricism.

QUACK'ISH, *a.* Like a quack; boasting of skill not possessed; trickish. *Burke.*

QUACK'ISM, *n.* The practice of quackery. *Ash.*

QUACK'LED, } *a.* Almost choked or suf-
QUACK'ENED, } focated.

QUACK'SALVER, *n.* [Sw. *qvacksalfvare; quack* and *salve.*]

One who boasts of his skill in medicines and salves, or of the efficacy of his prescriptions; a charlatan. *Brown. Burton.*

QUAD, *a.* [D. *kwaad.*] Evil; bad. [*Not used.*] *Gower.*

QUAD'RAGENE, *n.* [L. *quadrageni.*] A papal indulgence multiplying remissions by forties. *Taylor.*

QUADRAGES'IMA, *n.* [L. *quadragesimus,* fortieth, from *quatuor,* four.]

Lent; so called because it consists of forty days. *Encyc.*

QUADRAGES'IMAL, *a.* [supra.] Belonging to Lent; used in Lent. *Sanderson.*

QUADRAGES'IMALS, *n. plu.* [supra.] Offerings formerly made to the mother church on mid-lent Sunday.

QUAD'RANGLE, *n.* [L. *quadratus,* square, from *quatuor,* four, and *angulus,* angle.]

In *geometry,* a quadrilateral figure; a square; a figure consisting of four sides and four angles. *Encyc.*

QUADRAN'GULAR, *a.* [supra.] Square; having four sides and four angles. *Woodward.*

2. In *botany,* having four prominent angles, as a stem or leaf. *Martyn.*

QUAD'RANT, *n.* [L. *quadrans,* a fourth.]

1. The fourth part; the quarter. *Brown.*

2. In *geometry,* the quarter of a circle; the arc of a circle containing ninety degrees; also, the space or area included between this arc and two radii drawn from the center to each extremity. *Encyc.*

3. An instrument for taking the altitudes of the sun or stars, of great use in astronomy and navigation. Quadrants are variously made, but they all consist of the quarter of a circle whose limb is divided into ninety degrees; or, as in Hadley's reflecting quadrant, an arc of forty five degrees is made to serve the same purpose as an arc of ninety degrees.

Quadrant of altitude, an appendage of the artificial globe, consisting of a slip of brass of the length of a quadrant of one of the great circles of the globe, and graduated. It is filled to the meridian and movable round to all points of the horizon. It serves as a scale in measuring altitudes, azimuths, &c. *Encyc.*

QUADRANT'AL, *a.* [supra.] Pertaining to a quadrant; also, included in the fourth part of a circle; as *quadrantal* space. *Derham.*

QUADRANT'AL, *n.* [supra.] A vessel used by the Romans; originally called *amphora.* It was square and contained 80 pounds of water. *Encyc.*

QUAD'RAT, *n.* [L. *quadratus,* squared.]

1. In *printing,* a piece of metal used to fill the void spaces between words, &c. Quadrats are of different sizes; as m-*quadrats,* &c.

2. A mathematical instrument, called also a *geometrical* square, and *line of shadows.* *Encyc.*

QUAD'RATE, *a.* Square; having four equal and parallel sides.

2. Divisible into four equal parts. *Brown.*

3. Square; equal; exact. *Howell.*

4. Suited; fitted; applicable; correspondent. *Harvey.*

QUAD'RATE, *n.* A square; a surface with four equal and parallel sides. *Wotton. Milton.*

2. In *astrology,* an aspect of the heavenly bodies, in which they are distant from each other ninety degrees, or the quarter of a circle; the same as *quartile.* *Dict.*

QUAD'RATE, *v. i.* [L. *quadro;* Fr. *quadrer, cadrer.*]

To suit; to correspond; to agree with; to be accommodated; followed by *with.*

> Aristotle's rules for epic poetry—cannot be supposed to *quadrate* exactly *with* modern heroic poems. *Addison.*

QUADRAT'IC, *a.* Square; denoting a square or pertaining to it.

Quadratic equation, in algebra, an equation in which the unknown quantity is of two dimensions, or raised to the second power; or one in which the highest power of the unknown quantity is a square. *Encyc. Bailey.*

QUAD'RATRIX, *n.* A square or squared figure. *Bailey.*

2. In *geometry,* a mechanical line by means of which we can find right lines equal to the circumference of circles or other curves and their several parts. *Encyc.*

QUAD'RATURE, *n.* [L. *quadratura.*] The act of squaring; the reducing of a figure to a square. Thus the finding of a square which shall contain just as much area as a circle or a triangle, is the *quadrature* of that circle or triangle. *Encyc.*

2. A quadrate; a square. *Milton.*

3. In *astronomy,* the aspect of the moon when distant from the sun 90 degrees or a quarter of the circle; or when the moon is at an equal distance from the points of conjunction and opposition.

Quadrature of curves, in mathematics, the finding of rectilineal figures containing the same areas as figures bounded by curved lines. *D. Olmsted.*

QUAD′REL, *n.* [It. *quadrello.*] In *architecture*, a kind of artificial stone made of chalky earth and dried in the shade for two years; so called from being square. *Encyc.*

QUADREN′NIAL, *a.* [L. *quadriennium; quadra* or *quadrans*, from *quatuor*, four, and *annus*, year.]

1. Comprising four years; as a *quadrennial* period.

2. Occurring once in four years; as *quadrennial* games.

QUADREN′NIALLY, *adv.* Once in four years.

QUAD′RIBLE, *a.* [L. *quadro*, to square.] That may be squared. *Derham.*

QUADRICAP′SULAR, *a.* [L. *quadra* and *capsula.*]

In *botany*, having four capsules to a flower; as a *quadricapsular* pericarp. *Martyn.*

QUADRIDEC′IMAL, *a.* [L. *quadra* and *decem.*]

In *crystalography*, designating a crystal whose prism or the middle part has four faces and two summits, containing together ten faces.

QUADRIDEN′TATE, *a.* [L. *quadra* and *dentatus*, toothed.]

In *botany*, having four teeth on the edge. *Martyn.*

QUAD′RIFID, *a.* [L. *quadrifidus; quadra* and *findo*, to divide.]

In *botany*, four-cleft, as a *quadrifid* perianth; cut into four segments, with linear sinuses and straight margins, as a *quadrifid* leaf. *Martyn.*

QUADRIJU′GOUS, *a.* [L. *quadra* and *jugum*, yoke.]

In *botany*, pinnate, with four pairs of leaflets; as a *quadrijugous* leaf.

QUADRILAT′ERAL, *a.* [L. *quadra*, or *quatuor*, four, and *latus*, side.] Having four sides and four angles.

QUADRILAT′ERAL, *n.* A figure having four sides and four angles; a quadrangular figure. *Encyc.*

QUADRILAT′ERALNESS, *n.* The property of having four right lined sides, forming as many right angles. *Dict.*

QUADRILIT′ERAL, *a.* [L. *quadra*, or *quatuor*, four, and *litera*, letter.]

Consisting of four letters. *Parkhurst. Asiat. Res.*

QUADRILLE, *n.* *quadril′*, or *cadril′*. [Fr.]

1. A game played by four persons with 40 cards, being the remainder of the pack after the four tens, nines and eights are discarded. *Encyc.*

2. A kind of dance.

QUAD′RILOBATE, } *a.* [L. *quadra*, or *quatuor*, four, and
QUAD′RILOBED, } *lobe*, Gr. λοβος.]

In *botany*, having four lobes; as a *quadrilobed* leaf. *Martyn.*

QUADRILOC′ULAR, *a.* [L. *quadra*, *quatuor*, and *loculus*, a cell.]

Having four cells; four-celled; as a *quadrilocular* pericarp. *Martyn.*

QUAD′RIN, *n.* [L. *quadrinus.*] A mite; a small piece of money, in value about a farthing. [*Not in use.*] *Bailey.*

QUADRINO′MIAL, *a.* [L. *quadra*, *quatuor*, and *nomen*, name.]

Consisting of four denominations or terms. *Dict.*

QUADRIP′ARTITE, *a.* [L. *quadra*, *quatuor*, and *partitus*, divided.]

Divided into four parts, or consisting of four corresponding parts.

QUADRIP′ARTITELY, *adv.* In four divisions; in a quadripartite distribution.

QUADRIPARTI′′TION, *n.* A division by four or into four parts; or the taking the fourth part of any quantity or number. *Dict.*

QUADRIPH′YLLOUS, *a.* [L. *quadra*, *quatuor*, four, and Gr. φυλλον, leaf.] Having four leaves.

QUAD′RIREME, *n.* [L. *quadriremis; quatuor*, four, and *remus*, oar.]

A galley with four benches of oars or rowers. *Mitford.*

QUADRISYL′LABLE, *n.* [L. *quadra*, *quatuor*, and *syllable.*] A word consisting of four syllables.

QUAD′RIVALVE, } *a.* In *botany*, having four valves;
QUADRIVALV′ULAR, } four-valved; as a *quadrivalve* pericarp. *Martyn.*

QUAD′RIVALVES, *n. plu.* [L. *quadra*, *quatuor*, and *valva*, valve.] A door with four folds or leaves.

QUADRIV′IAL, *a.* [L. *quadrivium; quatuor*, four, and *via*, way.] Having four ways meeting in a point.

QUADROON′, *n.* [L. *quadra*, *quatuor.*] In Spanish America, the offspring of a mulatto woman by a white man; a person quarter-blooded. *Clavigero.*

QUAD′RUMAN, *n.* [L. *quadra* and *manus*, hand.]

An animal having four hands or limbs that correspond to the hands of a man, as a monkey. *Lawrence, Lect.*

QUAD′RUMANOUS, *a.* Having four hands; four-handed. *Lawrence, Lect.*

QUAD′RUNE, *n.* A gritstone with a calcarious cement.

QUAD′RUPED, *a.* [L. *quadrupes; quadra*, *quatuor*, four, and *pes*, foot.] Having four legs and feet.

QUAD′RUPED, *n.* An animal having four legs and feet, as a horse, an ox, a lion, &c.

QUAD′RUPLE, *a.* [L. *quadruplus; quadra*, *quatuor*, and *plico*, to fold.]

Fourfold; four times told; as, to make *quadruple* restitution for trespass or theft.

QUAD′RUPLE, *n.* Four times the sum or number; as, to receive *quadruple* the amount in damages or profits.

QUADRU′PLICATE, *a.* Fourfold; four times repeated; as a *quadruplicate* ratio or proportion.

QUADRU′PLICATE, *v. t.* [L. *quadruplico; quatuor* and *plico*, to fold.] To make fourfold; to double twice.

QUADRUPLICA′TION, *n.* The act of making fourfold and taking four times the simple sum or amount.

QUAD′RUPLY, *adv.* To a fourfold quantity; as, to be *quadruply* recompensed. *Swift.*

QUÆRE, [L.] inquire; better written *query*, which see.

QUÆSTOR. [See *Questor.*]

QU′AFF, *v. t.* [Fr. *coiffer*, to cap or hood; *se coiffer*, to fuddle, or be fuddled, from *coiffe*, a hood. But qu. In the Ethiopic, ኰወፈ quaf or kwof, is to draw, to draw out. Ludolf, 407. In Arabic, قَابَ is to drink largely, or to devour, as food.] To drink; to swallow in large draughts.

He *quaffs* the muscadel. *Shak.*

They in communion sweet
Quaff immortality and joy. *Milton.*

QU′AFF, *v. i.* To drink largely or luxuriously. *South. Dryden.*

QU′AFFED, *pp.* Drank; swallowed in large draughts.

QU′AFFER, *n.* One that quaffs or drinks largely.

QU′AFFER, *v. t.* To feel out. [*Not in use.*] *Derham.*

QU′AFFING, *ppr.* Drinking; swallowing draughts.

QUAG′GY, *a.* [supposed to be from the root of *quake.*]

Yielding to the feet or trembling under the foot, as soft wet earth.

QUAG′MIRE, *n.* [that is, *quake-mire.*] Soft wet land, which has a surface firm enough to bear a person, but which shakes or yields under the feet. *Tusser. Shak. More.*

QUAHAUG, *n.* *quaw′hog.* In New England, the popular name of a large species of clams or bivalvular shells.

[*This name is probably derived from the natives.*]

QUAID, *a.* or *pp.* [for *quailed.*] Crushed, subdued, or depressed. [*Not used.*] *Spenser.*

QUAIL, *v. i.* [*Quail*, in English, signifies to sink or languish, to curdle, and to crush or quell. The Italian has *quagliare*, to curdle, and the Sax. *cwellan*, to quell, and the D. *kwaal* is disease. If these are of one family, the primary sense is to shrink, to withdraw, and transitively, to beat down. In W. *cwl* signifies a flagging or drooping; *cwla*, faint, languid.]

1. To sink into dejection; to languish; to fail in spirits. [*Little used.*] *Shak. Knolles.*

2. To fade; to wither. *Obs.* *Hakewill.*

QUAIL, *v. i.* [Fr. *cailler;* Sp. *cuajar;* Port. *coalhar;* It. *quagliare*, to curdle; W. *caul*, a calf's maw, rennet, chyle, a curd; *ceulaw*, to curdle. The sense is to contract.] To curdle; to coagulate; as milk. *Bailey.*

QUAIL, *v. t.* [Sax. *cwellan.*] To crush; to depress; to sink; to subdue. [This orthography is obsolete. The word is now written *quell.*] *Spenser.*

QUAIL, *n.* [It. *quaglia;* Fr. *caille;* Arm. *coaill.*]

A bird of the genus Tetrao or grous kind, or according to Latham's arrangement, of the genus Perdix, in which he comprehends the partridge and quail. In *New England*, the name is applied to a peculiar species of the perdix, which is called *partridge* in the middle states, but it is neither the partridge nor quail of Europe.

QUA′ILING, *ppr.* Failing; languishing. *Obs.*

QUA′ILING, *n.* The act of failing in spirit or resolution; decay. *Obs.* *Shak.*

QUA'IL-PIPE, *n.* A pipe or call for alluring quails into a net; a kind of lethern purse in the shape of a pear, partly filled with horse hair, with a whistle at the end. *Encyc.*

QUAINT, *a.* [Old Fr. *coint*, Arm. *coent*, *coant*, pretty. In Norman French, *coint* is familiar, affable, and *accoinet*, is very necessary or familiar. The latter word would lead us to refer *quaint* to the Latin *accinctus*, ready, but Skinner thinks it more probably from *comptus*, neat, well dressed.]

1. Nice; scrupulously and superfluously exact; having petty elegance; as a *quaint* phrase; a *quaint* fashion. *Sidney. Shak.*

To show how *quaint* an orator you are. *Shak.*

2. Subtil; artful. *Obs.* *Chaucer.*
3. Fine-spun; artfully framed. *Shak. Milton.*
4. Affected; as *quaint* fopperies. *Swift.*
5. In *common use*, odd; fanciful; singular; and so used by Chaucer.

QUA'INTLY, *adv.* Nicely; exactly; with petty neatness or spruceness; as hair more *quaintly* curled. *B. Jonson.*

2. Artfully.

Breathe his faults so *quaintly*. *Shak.*

3. Ingeniously; with dexterity.

I *quaintly* stole a kiss. *Gay.*

QUA'INTNESS, *n.* Niceness; petty neatness or elegance.

There is a majesty in simplicity, which is far above the *quaintness* of wit. *Pope.*

2. Oddness; peculiarity.

QUAKE, *v. i.* [Sax. *cwacian*; G. *quackeln*; Eth. ሀወከ hwyk, to shake, to agitate.]

1. To shake; to tremble; to be agitated with quick but short motions continually repeated; to shudder. Thus we say, a person *quakes* with fear or terror, or with cold. Heb. xii.
2. To shake with violent convulsions, as well as with trembling; as, the earth *quakes*; the mountains *quake*. Neh. i.
3. To shake, tremble or move, as the earth under the feet; as the *quaking* mud. *Pope.*

QUAKE, *v. t.* To frighten; to throw into agitation. [*Not used.*] *Shak.*

QUAKE, *n.* A shake; a trembling; a shudder; a tremulous agitation. *Suckling.*

QUA'KER, *n.* One that quakes; but usually, one of the religious sect called *friends*. This name, *quakers*, is said to have been given to the sect in reproach, on account of some agitations which distinguished them; but it is no longer appropriated to them by way of reproach.

QUA'KERISM, *n.* The peculiar manners, tenets or worship of the quakers. *Milner. Boswell.*

QUA'KERLY, *a.* Resembling quakers. *Goodman.*

QUA'KERY, *n.* Quakerism.

QUA'KING, *ppr.* Shaking; trembling.

QUA'KING, *n.* A shaking; tremulous agitation; trepidation. Dan. x.

QUA'KING-GRASS, *n.* An herb. *Ainsworth.*

QUAL'IFIABLE, *a.* [from *qualify*.] That may be qualified; that may be abated or modified. *Barrow.*

QUALIFICA'TION, *n.* [Fr. See *Qualify*.]

1. Any natural endowment or any acquirement which fits a person for a place, office or employment, or enables him to sustain any character with success. Integrity and talents should be considered as indispensable *qualifications* for men entrusted with public affairs; but private interest and party-spirit will often dispense with these and all other *qualifications*.

There is no *qualification* for government but virtue and wisdom, actual or presumptive. *Burke.*

2. Legal power or requisite; as the *qualifications* of electors.
3. Abatement; diminution. *Raleigh.*
4. Modification; restriction; limitation. Words or expressions may be used in a general sense, without any *qualification*.

QUAL'IFIED, *pp.* Fitted by accomplishments or endowments; modified.

Qualified fee, in *law*, a base fee, or an estate which has a qualification annexed to it, and which ceases with the qualification, as a grant to A and his heirs, *tenants of the manor of Dale*.

Qualified negative, in legislation, the power of negativing bills which have passed the two houses of the legislature; a power vested in the president, governor or other officer, but subject to be overruled and defeated by a subsequent vote of the two houses, passed in conformity with the provisions of the constitution. *U. States. W. Smith.*

Qualified property, is that which depends on temporary possession, as that in wild animals reclaimed.

QUAL'IFIEDNESS, *n.* The state of being qualified or fitted.

QUAL'IFIER, *n.* He or that which qualifies; that which modifies, reduces, tempers or restrains. *Junius.*

QUAL'IFY, *v. t.* [Fr. *qualifier*; It. *qualificare*; Sp. *calificar*; L. *qualis*, such, and *facio*, to make.]

1. To fit for any place, office, occupation or character; to furnish with the knowledge, skill or other accomplishment necessary for a purpose; as, to *qualify* a man for a judge, for a minister of state or of the gospel, for a general or admiral. Holiness alone can *qualify* men for the society of holy beings.
2. To make capable of any employment or privilege; to furnish with legal power or capacity; as, in England, to *qualify* a man to kill game.
3. To abate; to soften; to diminish; as, to *qualify* the rigor of a statute.

I do not seek to quench your love's hot fire,
But *qualify* the fire's extreme rage. *Shak.*

4. To ease; to assuage. *Spenser.*
5. To modify; to restrain; to limit by exceptions; as, to *qualify* words or expressions, or to *qualify* the sense of words or phrases.
6. To modify; to regulate; to vary; as, to *qualify* sounds.

QUAL'IFYING, *ppr.* Furnishing with the necessary qualities, properties or accomplishments for a place, station or business; furnishing with legal power; abating; tempering; modifying; restraining.

QUAL'ITY, *n.* [L. *qualitas*, from *qualis*, such; Fr. *qualité*; Sp. *calidad*; It. *qualità*; Ir. *cail*.]

1. Property; that which belongs to a body or substance, or can be predicated of it. Qualities are *natural* or *accidental*. Thus whiteness is a *natural quality* of snow; softness is a *natural quality* of wool and fur; hardness is a *natural quality* of metals and wood; figure and dimension are the *natural qualities* of solids; but a particular figure, as a cube, a square or a sphere, is an *accidental* or *adventitious quality*. The fluidity of metals is an *accidental quality*. *Essential* qualities are such as are necessary to constitute a thing what it is. *Sensible* qualities are such as are perceptible to the senses, as the light of the sun, the color of cloth, the taste of salt or sugar, &c.
2. Nature, relatively considered; as the *quality* of an action, in regard to right and wrong.

Other creatures have not judgment to examine the *quality* of that which is done by them. *Hooker.*

3. Virtue or particular power of producing certain effects; as the *qualities* of plants or medicines.
4. Disposition; temper.

To-night we'll wander through the streets, and note
The *qualities* of people. *Shak.*

5. Virtue or vice; as good *qualities*, or bad *qualities*. *Dryden.*
6. Acquirement; accomplishment; as the *qualities* of horsemanship, dancing and fencing. *Clarendon.*
7. Character.

The attorney partakes of both *qualities*, that of a judge of the court, and that of attorney general. *Bacon.*

8. Comparative rank; condition in relation to others; as people of every *quality*.

We obtained acquaintance with many citizens, not of the meanest *quality*. *Bacon.*

9. Superior rank; superiority of birth or station; as persons of *quality*; ladies of *quality*.
10. Persons of high rank, collectively.

I shall appear at the masquerade dressed up in my fethers, that the *quality* may see how pretty they will look in their traveling habits. *Addison.*

QU'ALM, *n.* quàm. [D. *kwaal*, disease; *kwaalyk*, sick; G. *quälen*, to pain or vex. In G. *qualm* is steam, vapor, exhalation; D. *kwalm*, id. The Danish *qvalm* signifies vapor, steam, fume, exhalation; *qvalmer*, to ramble; *det giver qvalme*, it rises in the stomach. The latter is the English word.]

1. A rising in the stomach, as it is commonly called; a fit of nausea, or a disposition or effort of the stomach to eject its contents.
2. A sudden fit or seizure of sickness at the stomach; a sensation of nausea; as *qualms* of heart-sickagony. *Milton.*

For who, without a *qualm*, hath ever look'd
On holy garbage, though by Homer cook'd? *Roscommon.*

3. A scruple of conscience, or uneasiness of conscience.

QU'ALMISH, *a.* *quàmish.* [supra.] Sick at the stomach; inclined to vomit; affected with nausea or sickly languor. *Dryden.*

QU'ALMISHNESS, *n.* Nausea.

QUAM'OCLIT, *n.* A plant of the genus Ipomoea. *Fam. of Plants.*

QUAN'DARY, *n.* Doubt; uncertainty; a state of difficulty or perplexity.

QUAN'DARY, *v. t.* To bring into a state of uncertainty or difficulty. [*Not used.*] *Otway.*

QUAN'TITATIVE, *a.* [See *Quantity.*] Estimable according to quantity. *Taylor.*

QUAN'TITIVE, *a.* [See *Quantity.*] Estimable according to quantity. *Digby.*

QUAN'TITY, *n.* [Fr. *quantité*; It. *quantità*; Sp. *cantitad*; from L. *quantitas*, from *quantus*, how much, or as much as; Pers. چند chand, how much; چندي chandi, quantity.]

1. That property of any thing which may be increased or diminished. *Cheyne. Johnson.*

This definition is defective, and as applicable to many other properties as to quantity. A definition strictly philosophical cannot be given. In common usage, *quantity* is a mass or collection of matter of indeterminate dimensions, but consisting of particles which cannot be distinguished, or which are not customarily distinguished, or which are considered in the aggregate. Thus we say, a *quantity* of earth, a *quantity* of water, a *quantity* of air, of light, of heat, of iron, of wood, of timber, of corn, of paper. But we do not say, a *quantity* of men, or of horses, or of houses; for as these are considered as separate individuals or beings, we call an assemblage of them, a *number* or *multitude.*

2. An indefinite extent of space.

3. A portion or part.

> If I were sawed into *quantities.* [*Not in use.*] *Shak.*

4. A large portion; as a medicine taken in *quantities*, that is, in *large quantities.* *Arbuthnot.*

5. In *mathematics*, any thing which can be multiplied, divided or measured. *Day.*

Thus mathematics is called the science of quantity. In algebra, quantities are *known* and *unknown. Known quantities* are usually represented by the first letters of the alphabet, as *a*, *b*, *c*, and *unknown quantities* are expressed by the last letters, *x*, *y*, *z*, &c. Letters thus used to represent quantities are themselves called quantities. A simple quantity is expressed by one term, as $+a$, or $-abc$; a compound is expressed by more terms than one, connected by the signs, + plus, or — minus, as $a+b$, or $a-b+c$. Quantities which have the sign + prefixed, are called *positive* or *affirmative*; those which have the sign — prefixed are called *negative.* *Day's Algebra.*

6. In *grammar*, the measure of a syllable; that which determines the time in which it is pronounced. *Holder. Encyc.*

7. In *logic*, a category, universal, or predicament; a general conception. *Bailey. Encyc.*

8. In *music*, the relative duration of a note or syllable. *Busby.*

Quantity of matter, in a body, is the measure arising from the joint consideration of its magnitude and density. *Bailey.*

Quantity of motion, in a body, is the measure arising from the joint consideration of its quantity of matter and its velocity. *Bailey.*

QUAN'TUM, *n.* [L.] The quantity; the amount.

Quantum meruit, in law, an action grounded on a promise that the defendant would pay to the plaintif for his service as much as he should deserve.

Quantum valebat, an action to recover of the defendant for goods sold, as much as they were worth. *Blackstone.*

QUAR'ANTINE, *n.* [It. *quarantina*, forty; Sp. *quarentena*; Fr. *quarantaine*; from the root of L. *quartus*, fourth, Fr. *carreau*, a square, *carrer*, to square, Arm. *carrea*, to square, W. *cwar*, square, Eng. *quart.* See *Quart* and *Square.*]

1. Properly, the space of forty days; appropriately, the term of forty days during which a ship arriving in port and suspected of being infected with a malignant, contagious disease, is obliged to forbear all intercourse with the city or place. Hence,

2. Restraint of intercourse to which a ship is subjected on the presumption that she may be infected, either for forty days or for any other limited term. It is customary for the proper officers to determine the period of restraint at their discretion, according to circumstances. Hence we hear of a *quarantine* of five days, of ten, of thirty, &c. as well as of forty. We say, a ship performs *quarantine*, or rides at *quarantine.* We also apply the word to persons. The passengers and crew perform *quarantine.*

3. In *law*, the period of forty days, during which the widow of a man dying seized of land, has the privilege of remaining in the mansion house.

QUARANTÏNE, *v. t.* To prohibit from intercourse with a city or its inhabitants; to compel to remain at a distance from shore for forty days, or for other limited period, on account of real or supposed infection; applied to ships, or to persons and goods.

QUARANTÏNED, *pp.* Restrained from communication with the shore for a limited period; as a ship or its crew and passengers.

QUARANTÏNING, *ppr.* Prohibiting from intercourse with the port; as a ship or its crew and passengers.

QUARRE, for *quarry*, not in use.

QUAR'REL, *n.* [W. *cweryl*; Fr. *querelle*; L. It. *querela*; Sp. *querella* or *queja*; Arm. *qarell*; L. *queror*, to complain, that is, to cry out with a loud voice. Hence we see the primary sense is the same as *brawl.* The L. *queror* coincides in elements with the Ir. *gairim*, to call, to bawl, to shout, and *gearan*, a complaint; Sax. *ceorian*, to complain or murmur; G. *girren* and *kirren*; D. *kirren* and *korren*; Dan. *kerrer.* The latter signifies to complain, to expostulate, and *kerrer sig efter*, to *care*, or take heed of, a sense which would unite the word with the L. *curo*, *cura*; and in Saxon, *cearig* signifies complaining, and careful, solicitous; Heb. Ch. Syr. Ar. קרא. Class Gr. No. 49. and see No. 1. 2. 14. 15. 19. 23.]

1. A brawl; a petty fight or scuffle; from its noise and uproar. *Shak.*

2. A dispute; a contest.

> On open seas their *quarrels* they debate. *Dryden.*

3. A breach of friendship or concord; open variance between parties. *Hammond.*

4. Cause of dispute.

> The king's *quarrel* is honorable. *Shak.*

5. Something that gives a right to mischief, reprisal or action.

> He thought he had a good *quarrel* to attack him. [*Not used.*] *Holingshed.*

6. Objection; ill will, or reason to complain; ground of objection or dispute.

> Herodias had a *quarrel* against him. Mark vi.

7. Something peevish, malicious, or disposed to make trouble. [*Not used.*] *Shak.*

QUAR'REL, *n.* [W. *çwarel*, a dart or javelin, a kernel; *çwarelu*, to dart, to kern, to curdle; from *çwar*, a quick rise, a puff; Fr. *carreau*, a bolt. The primary sense is to shoot, throw or drive.]

1. An arrow with a square head. [*Not used unless in poetry.*] *Camden.*

2. A pane of glass; a square. [See *Quarry* and *Square.*]

QUAR'REL, *v. i.* [Fr. *quereller.* See the Noun.]

1. To dispute violently or with loud and angry words; to wrangle; to scold. How odious to see husband and wife *quarrel!*

2. To fight; to scuffle; to contend; to squabble; used of two persons or of a small number. It is never used of armies and navies in combat. Children and servants often *quarrel* about trifles. Tavern-haunters sometimes *quarrel* over their cups.

3. To fall into variance.

> Our people *quarrel* with obedience. *Shak.*

4. To find fault; to cavil.

> I will not *quarrel* with a slight mistake. *Roscommon.*

> Men at enmity with their God, *quarreling* with his attributes—*quarreling* with the being that made them, and who is constantly doing them good. *Eliph. Steele.*

5. To disagree; to be at variance; not to be in accordance in form or essence.

> Some things arise of strange and *quarr'ling* kind,
> The forepart lion, and a snake behind. *Cowley.*

QUAR'REL, *v. t.* To quarrel with. *B. Jonson.*

2. To compel by a quarrel; as, to *quarrel* a man out of his estate or rights.

QUAR'RELER, *n.* One who quarrels, wrangles or fights.

QUAR'RELING, *ppr.* Disputing with vehemence or loud angry words; scolding; wrangling; fighting; finding fault; disagreeing.

QUAR'RELING, *n.* [supra.] Contention; dispute in angry words; breach of concord; a caviling or finding fault; disagreement.

QUAR'RELOUS, *a.* Apt or disposed to quarrel; petulant; easily provoked to enmity or contention. [*Little used.*] *Shak.*

QUAR'RELSOME, *a.* Apt to quarrel; given to brawls and contention; inclined to petty fighting; easily irritated or provoked to contest; irascible; choleric; petulant. *Bacon.*

QUAR'RELSOMELY, *adv.* In a quarrelsome manner; with a quarrelsome temper; petulantly. *Hall.*

QUAR'RELSOMENESS, *n.* Disposition to engage in contention and brawls; petulance.

QUAR'RIED, *pp.* Dug from a pit or cavern.

QUAR'RY, *n.* [Fr. *carré*, for *quarré*; Arm. id. See *Quarantine.*]

1. A square; as a *quarry* of glass. [*Not in use.*] *Mortimer.*
2. An arrow with a square head. [See *Quarrel.*] [*Not in use.*] *Fairfax.*
3. In *falconry*, the game which a hawk is pursuing or has killed. [Perhaps from L. *quæro*, Fr. *querir*, to seek.]
4. Among *hunters*, a part of the entrails of the beast taken, given to the hounds. *Encyc.*

QUAR'RY, *n.* [Fr. *carriere*, formerly Norm. *quarrier*. I know not whether the original sense of this word was a pit or mine, from *digging*, or whether the sense was a place for *squaring* stone. The Fr. *carriere* signifies not only a quarry, but a *career*, *course*, race, from the L. *curro*, which cannot be from squaring. If the sense was a pit, it may be referred to the Heb. Ch. Eth. כרה, to dig; Ar. كَرَا to dig, to run violently, to leap. If the sense is from *squaring*, see *Square*. See Class Gr. No. 35. 36. 52. 57. 63.]

1. A place, cavern or pit where stones are dug from the earth, or separated from a large mass of rocks. We generally apply the word *mine* to the pit from which are taken metals and coal; from *quarries* are taken stones for building, as marble, freestone, slate, &c.
2. In *Paris*, the *quarries* are a vast cavern under the city, several miles in extent.

QUAR'RY, *v. i.* To prey upon, as a vulture or harpy. [*A low word and not much used.*] *L'Estrange.*

QUAR'RY, *v. t.* To dig or take from a quarry; as, to *quarry* marble.

QUAR'RYING, *ppr.* Digging stones from a quarry.

QUAR'RYMAN, *n.* A man who is occupied in quarrying stones.

QUART, *n. quort.* [It. *quarta*; Fr. *quarte*, from *quart*, a fourth, L. *quartus*; D. *kwart*; G. *quart*; from W. *cwar*, the root of *square*, or from the root of G. αρω, to fit or suit, to square. We see in the Amharic, the ancient dialect of the Ethiopic, *art* is four, and *arten* is fourth, L. *quartus*. Ludolf, Amh. 57. This with the Celtic pronunciation, as *guerre* for *war*, becomes *quart.*]

1. The fourth part; a quarter. [*Not in use.*] *Spenser.*
2. The fourth part of a gallon; two pints.
3. A vessel containing the fourth of a gallon.
4. A sequence of four cards in the game of picket.

QUARTAN, *a. quort'an.* [L. *quartanus*, the fourth.] Designating the fourth; occurring every fourth day; as a *quartan* ague or fever.

QUART'AN, *n.* An intermitting ague that occurs every fourth day, or with intermissions of seventy two hours.

2. A measure containing the fourth part of some other measure.

QUARTA'TION, *n.* In *chimistry* and *metallurgy*, the operation by which the quantity of one thing is made equal to the fourth part of another thing. *Encyc.*

QUARTER, *n. quort'er.* [Fr. *quart*, *quartier*; It. *quartiere*; Sp. *quartel*; D. *kwartier*; G. *quartier*; Sw. *qvart*, *qvartal*; Dan. *qvart*, *qvartal*, *qvarteer*; L. *quartus*, the fourth part; from W. *cwar*, a square.]

1. The fourth part; as the *quarter* of an hour or of a mile; one *quarter* of the expense. Living is a *quarter* dearer in the city than in the country.
2. In *weight*, the fourth part of a hundred pounds avoirdupois, or of 112lb., that is, 28lb.; as a *quarter* of sugar.
3. In *dry measure*, the fourth of a tun in weight, or eight bushels; as a *quarter* of wheat.
4. In *astronomy*, the fourth part of the moon's period or monthly revolution; as the first *quarter* after the change or full.
5. A region in the hemisphere or great circle; primarily, one of the four cardinal points; as the four *quarters* of the globe; but used indifferently for any region or point of compass. From what *quarter* does the wind blow? Hence,
6. A particular region of a town, city or country; as all *quarters* of the city; in every *quarter* of the country or of the continent. Hence,
7. Usually in the plural, *quarters*, the place of lodging or temporary residence; appropriately, the place where officers and soldiers lodge, but applied to the lodgings of any temporary resident. He called on the general at his *quarters*; the place furnished good winter *quarters* for the troops. I saw the stranger at his *quarters*.
8. Proper station.

> Swift to their several *quarters* hasten then— *Milton.*

Bacon uses the word in the singular. "Make love keep *quarter*."

9. On board of ships, *quarters* signifies the stations or places where the officers and men are posted in action. Pipe all hands to *quarters*.
10. In *military affairs*, the remission or sparing of the life of a captive or an enemy when in one's power; mercy granted by a conqueror to his enemy, when no longer able to defend himself. In desperate encounters, men will sometimes neither ask nor give *quarter*. The barbarous practice of giving no *quarter* to soldiers in a fortress taken by assault, is nearly obsolete.

> He magnified his own clemency, now they were at his mercy, to offer them *quarter* for their lives, if they would give up the castle. *Clarendon.*

> Lambs at the mercy of wolves must expect no *quarter*. *L'Estrange.*

11. Treatment shown to an enemy; indulgence.

> To the young, if you give tolerable *quarter*, you indulge them in idleness and ruin them. [*Rarely used.*] *Collier.*

12. Friendship; amity; concord. [*Not in use.*] *Shak.*
13. In *the slaughter house*, one limb of a quadruped with the adjoining parts; or one fourth part of the carcase of a quadruped, including a limb; as a fore *quarter*, or hind *quarter*.
14. In *the menage*, the *quarters* of a horse's foot are the sides of the coffin, between the toe and the heel. *False quarters* are a cleft in the horn of the hoof, extending from the coronet to the shoe, or from top to bottom. When for any disorder, one of the quarters is cut, the horse is said to be *quarter-cast*. *Encyc.*
15. In a siege, *quarters* are the encampment on one of the principal passages round the place besieged, to prevent relief and intercept convoys. *Encyc.*
16. In *seminaries of learning*, a fourth part of the year, or three months. Tuition and board at twenty five dollars the *quarter*. This is a moderate *quarter* bill.
17. The *quarter of a ship*, is the part of a ship's side which lies towards the stern, or the part between the aftmost end of the main-chains and the sides of the stern, where it is terminated by the quarter-pieces. *Mar. Dict.*
18. In *heraldry*, one of the parts or members of the first division of a coat that is divided into four parts.

On the quarter, in seamen's language, is a point in the horizon considerably abaft the beam, but not in the direction of the stern.

Quarter-bill, among seamen, is a list containing the different stations where the officers and crew are to take post in time of action, and the names of the men assigned to each.

Quarter-cloths, long pieces of painted canvas, extended on the outside of the quarter-netting from the upper part of the gallery to the gangway.

Quarter-deck, that part of the deck of a ship which extends from the stern to the mainmast. But in some kinds of vessels, the quarter-deck does not extend to the mainmast, but is raised above the main deck.

Quarter-gallery, a sort of balcony on the quarters of a ship.

Quarter-railing, narrow molded planks, reaching from the top of the stern to the gangway, serving as a fence to the quarter-deck.

Quarter-master, in an army, an officer whose business is to attend to the quarters for the soldiers, their provisions, fuel, forage, &c.; in the navy, an officer who assists the mates in their duties, in stowing the hold, coiling the cables, attending the steerage, and keeping time by the watch glasses.

Quarter-master-general, in military affairs, is an officer whose duty is to mark the marches and encampments of an army, the head-quarters, the place for the artillery, and procure supplies of provisions and forage, &c.

Quarter-staff, a long staff borne by foresters and park-keepers, as a badge of office and a weapon. *Encyc.*

2. A staff of defense. *Dryden.*

Quarter-sessions, in England, a general court held quarterly by the justices of peace of each county, with jurisdiction to try and determine felonies and trespasses; but capital offenses are seldom or never tried in this court. *Blackstone.*

Quarter-round, in architecture, the echinus or ovolo.

Head-quarters, the tent or mansion of the commander in chief of an army.

QUART'ER, *v. t.* To divide into four equal parts.

2. To divide; to separate into parts. *Shak.*

3. To divide into distinct regions or compartments.

The sailors *quarter'd* heaven. *Dryden.*

4. To station soldiers for lodging; as, to *quarter* troops in the city or among the inhabitants, or on the inhabitants.

5. To lodge; to fix on a temporary dwelling.

They mean this night in Sardis to be *quarter'd.* *Shak.*

6. To diet. [*Not in use.*] *Hudibras.*

7. To bear as an appendage to the hereditary arms.

The coat of Beauchamp—*quartered* by the earl of Hertford. *Peacham.*

QUART'ER, *v. i.* To lodge; to have a temporary residence. The general *quarters* at a hotel in Church street.

QUART'ERAGE, *n.* A quarterly allowance. *Hudibras.*

QUART'ER-DAY, *n.* The day that completes three months, the quarter of a year; the day when quarterly payments are made of rent or interest. *Spectator.*

QUART'ERED, *pp.* Divided into four equal parts or quarters; separated into distinct parts; lodged; stationed for lodging.

QUART'ERING, *ppr.* Dividing into quarters or into distinct parts; stationing for lodgings.

QUART'ERING, *n.* A station. *Mountagu.*

2. Assignment of quarters for soldiers.

3. The division of a shield containing many coats. *Ashmole.*

QUART'ERLY, *a.* Containing or consisting of a fourth part; as *quarterly* seasons.

2. Recurring at the end of each quarter of the year; as *quarterly* payments of rent; a *quarterly* visitation or examination. The secretary requires *quarterly* returns from his officers.

QUART'ERLY, *adv.* Once in a quarter of a year. The returns are made *quarterly.*

QUART'ERN, *n.* The fourth part of a pint; a gill.

QUART'ILE, *n.* An aspect of the planets, when they are distant from each other a quarter of the circle, ninety degrees, or three signs. *Harris. Dryden.*

QUART'O, *n.* [L. *quartus.*] A book of the size of the fourth of a sheet; a size made by twice folding a sheet, which then makes four leaves.

QUART'O, *a.* Denoting the size of a book, in which a sheet makes four leaves.

QUARTZ, *n. quortz.* [G. *quartz.*] A species of silicious minerals, of various colors, white, gray, reddish, yellowish or brownish; commonly amorphous, and frequently crystalized. The subspecies and varieties are numerous. *Kirwan. Cleaveland.*

QUARTZ'Y, *a.* Pertaining to quartz; partaking of the nature or qualities of quartz; resembling quartz. [*Quartzy* is the regular adjective, and *quartzose* and *quartzous* may be dispensed with.]

QUAS, *n.* In *Russia*, a drink of common domestic use; being a liquor prepared from pollard, meal and bread, or from meal and malt, by an acid fermentation. *Tooke.*

QUASH, *v. t.* [Sax. *cwysan;* D. *kwetsen;* G. *quetschen;* Fr. *casser;* It. *squassare;* L. *quasso, quatio.* Class Gs. No. 17. 28. 60. 68. and Class Gd. No. 38. 76. See *Squeeze.*]

1. Properly, to beat down or beat in pieces; to crush.

The whales
Against sharp rocks, like reeling vessels, *quash'd.* *Waller.*

2. To crush; to subdue; as, to *quash* a rebellion. *Addison.*

3. In *law*, to abate, annul, overthrow or make void; as, to *quash* an indictment. He prays judgment of the writ or declaration that the same may be *quashed.* *Blackstone.*

QUASH, *v. i.* To be shaken with a noise. *Sharp.*

QUASH, *n.* A species of cucurbita; but in America pronounced *squash;* so called probably from its softness. [See the Verb.]

QUASH'ED, *pp.* Crushed; subdued; abated.

QUASH'ING, *ppr.* Crushing; subduing; abating.

QUASSA'TION, *n.* [L. *quassatio.*] The act of shaking; concussion; the state of being shaken. *Gayton.*

QUAS'SIA, *n.* A plant, or rather a genus of plants of three species, the *amara, simaruba,* and *excelsa* or *polygama,* natives of South America and of some of the isles of the West Indies, and possessing valuable medicinal qualities. *Encyc.*

QUAT, *n.* A pustule or pimple. [*Not used.*] *Shak.*

QUATER-COUSINS, *n. ka'ter-cuzns.* [L. *quatuor*, four, and *cousin.*]

Those within the first four degrees of kindred. *Skinner.*

QUAT'ERN, *a.* [L. *quaterni*, four, from *quatuor*, four.]

Consisting of four; fourfold; growing by fours; as *quatern* leaves. *Martyn.*

QUATERN'ARY, *n.* [L. *quaternarius*, from *quatuor*, four.]

The number four. *Boyle.*

QUATERN'ARY, *a.* Consisting of four. *Gregory.*

QUATERN'ION, *n.* [L. *quaternio*, from *quatuor*, four.]

1. The number four. *Milton.*

2. A file of four soldiers. Acts xii.

QUATERN'ION, *v. t.* To divide into files or companies. *Milton.*

QUATERN'ITY, *n.* [supra.] The number four. *Brown.*

QUAT'RAIN, *n.* [Fr. from *quatre*, L. *quatuor*, four.]

A stanza of four lines rhyming alternately. *Dryden.*

QUAVE, for *quaver*, is not used.

QUAVEMIRE, for *quagmire*, is not used.

QUA'VER, *v. i.* [W. *cwibiaw*, to quaver, to trill; Sp. *quiebro*, a musical shake or trill; *quiebra*, a break, fracture, failure. It coincides in elements with *quibble, quiver, whiffle, wabble.* The primary sense is to move, hence to break, applied to motion and sound. See *Quiver* and *Vibrate.*]

1. To shake the voice; to utter or form sound with rapid vibrations, as in singing; to sing with tremulous modulations of voice. *Bacon.*

2. To tremble; to vibrate.

The finger—moved with a *quavering* motion. *Newton.*

QUA'VER, *n.* A shake or rapid vibration of the voice, or a shake on an instrument of music. *Addison.*

2. A note and measure of time in music, equal to half a crotchet or the eighth of a semibreve.

QUA'VERED, *a.* or *pp.* Distributed into quavers. *Harmar.*

QUA'VERER, *n.* A warbler.

QUA'VERING, *ppr.* Shaking the voice or the sound of an instrument.

QUA'VERING, *n.* The act of shaking the voice, or of making rapid vibrations of sound on an instrument of music.

QUAY, *n. ke.* [Fr. *quai;* D. *kaai;* Arm. *qae;* Ir. *ceigh.* If this word is radically the same as *key*, the sense is that which fastens or secures. Class Cg or Gk.]

A key; a mole or wharf, constructed in harbors for securing vessels and receiving goods unladen or to be shipped on board.

QUAY, *v. t.* To furnish with quays. *J. Barlow.*

QUEACH, *n.* A thick bushy plot. *Obs.* *Chapman.*

QUEACH, *v. i.* To stir; to move. *Obs.* [See *Quick.*]

QUE'ACHY, *a.* [from *queach.*] Shaking; moving, yielding or trembling under the feet, as moist or boggy ground.

The *queachy* fens. *Drayton.*
Godwin's *queachy* sands. *Ib.*

[This word is still in use in New England, and if the word is from the root of *quick*, we recognize the application of it in *quicksand.*]

2. Thick; bushy. [*Not in use.*] *Cockeram.*

QUEAN, *n.* [Sax. *cwæn* or *cwen*, a woman. See *Queen.*]

A worthless woman; a slut; a strumpet. [*Not in common use.*] *Dryden. Swift.*

QUE'ASINESS, *n. s* as *z.* [from *queasy.*] Nausea; qualmishness; inclination to vomit.

QUE'ASY, *a. s* as *z.* [allied perhaps to the W. *chudy*, [Lhuyd,] Corn. *huedzha*, Arm. *chueda* or *huyda*, to vomit. Class Gs. No. 19. Class Gd. No. 54.]

1. Sick at the stomach; affected with nausea; inclined to vomit. *Shak.*

2. Fastidious; squeamish; delicate. *Shak. Dryden.*

3. Causing nausea; as a *queasy* question. *Shak.*

QUECK, *v. i.* [G. *quackeln*, to quake, to be unsettled, to flinch.]

To shrink; to flinch. *Obs.* *Bacon.*

QUEEN, *n.* [Sax. *cwæn* or *cwen*, Goth. *queins, quens*, Dan. *qvinde*, Sw. *qvinna*, a woman; Sans. *kanya.* Qu. Ir. *coinne* and Gr. γυνη.]

1. The consort of a king; a *queen consort.*

2. A woman who is the sovereign of a kingdom; a *queen-regent;* as Elizabeth, *queen* of England; Mary, *queen* of Scotland.

3. The sovereign of a swarm of bees, or the female of the hive.

> A hive of bees cannot subsist without a *queen.* *Encyc.*

Queen of the meadows, meadow sweet, a plant of the genus Spiræa. *Lee.*

QUEEN, *v. i.* To play the queen; to act the part or character of a queen. *Shak.*

QUEE'N-APPLE, *n.* A kind of apple, so called. *Mortimer.*

QUEEN-DOW'AĠER, *n.* The widow of a king.

QUEE'N-GŌLD, *n.* A royal duty or revenue belonging to every queen of England during her marriage to the king.

QUEE'NING, *n.* An apple. *Mortimer.*

QUEE'NLIKE, *a.* Resembling a queen. *Drayton.*

QUEE'NLY, *a.* Like a queen; becoming a queen; suitable to a queen.

QUEER, *a.* [G. *quer,* cross, oblique, traverse; *querkopf,* a *queer* fellow; *querlen,* to twirl. The primary sense is probably to turn.]

Odd; singular; hence, whimsical. *Spectator.*

QUEE'RLY, *adv.* In an odd or singular manner.

QUEE'RNESS, *n.* Oddity; singularity; particularity. [*A familiar, not an elegant word.*]

QUEEST, *n.* A ring dove, a species of pigeon. *Todd.*

QUEINT, *pret.* and *pp.* of *quench.* *Gower.*

QUELL, *v. t.* [Sax. *cwellan,* to kill; Dan. *qvæler,* to stifle, suffocate, choke, stop, quell, gall, tease, torment, vex; Sw. *qväl-ja,* id.; G. *quälen.* The primary sense is to stop, to press or force down, and thus cause action or motion to cease.]

1. To crush; to subdue; to cause to cease; as, to *quell* an insurrection or sedition.

2. To quiet; to allay; to reduce to peace; as, to *quell* the tumult of the soul.

3. To subdue; to reduce.

> This *quell'd* her pride. *Dryden.*

QUELL, *v. i.* To die; to abate. *Spenser.*

QUELL, *n.* Murder. [*Not in use.*] *Shak.*

QUELL'ED, *pp.* Crushed; subdued; quieted.

QUELL'ER, *n.* One that crushes or subdues. *Shak.*

QUELL'ING, *ppr.* Crushing; subduing; reducing to peace.

QUELQUE-CHOSE, *n.* *keck-shows.* [Fr. something.]

A trifle; a kickshaw. *Donne.*

QUEME, *v. t.* [Sax. *cweman.*] To please. [*Obs.*] *Spenser.*

QUENCH, *v. t.* [Sax. *cwencan.*] To extinguish; to put out; as, to *quench* flame.

2. To still; to quiet; to repress; as, to *quench* a passion or emotion. *Shak.*

3. To allay or extinguish; as, to *quench* thirst.

4. To destroy. *Davies.*

5. To check; to stifle; as, to *quench* the Spirit. 1 Thess. v.

QUENCH, *v. i.* To cool; to become cool.

> Dost thou think, in time
> She will not *quench?* *Shak.*

[*Not in use.*]

QUENCH'ABLE, *a.* That may be quenched or extinguished. *Sherwood.*

QUENCH'ED, *pp.* Extinguished; allayed; repressed.

QUENCH'ER, *n.* He or that which extinguishes.

QUENCH'ING, *ppr.* Extinguishing; quieting; stifling; repressing.

QUENCH'LESS, *a.* That cannot be quenched or repressed; inextinguishable; as *quenchless* fire or fury. *Shak. Crashaw.*

QUER'CITRON, *n.* [L. *quercus,* an oak.] The bark of the yellow oak, used in dyeing. *Bancroft.*

QUER'ELE, *n.* [L. *querela;* Fr. *querelle.*] A complaint to a court. [*Not in use.* See *Audita querela.*] *Ayliffe.*

QUE'RENT, *n.* [L. *querens, queror,* to complain.]

The complainant; the plaintif. [*Not in use.*]

QUE'RENT, *n.* [L. *quærens, quæro,* to inquire.]

An inquirer. [*Not much used.*] *Aubrey.*

QUERIMO'NIOUS, *a.* [L. *querimonia,* complaint, from *queror.*]

Complaining; querulous; apt to complain.

QUERIMO'NIOUSLY, *adv.* With complaint; querulously.

QUERIMO'NIOUSNESS, *n.* Disposition to complain; a complaining temper.

QUE'RIST, *n.* [from L. *quæro,* to inquire.] One who inquires or asks questions. *Swift.*

QUERK. [See *Quirk.*]

QUERK'ENED, *a.* Choked. [*Illegitimate and obsolete.*]

QUERL, *v. t.* [G. *querlen.*] To twirl; to turn or wind round; to coil; as, to *querl* a cord, thread or rope. [This is a legitimate English word, in common use in New England. It may be a dialectical variation of *whirl,* Dan. *hvirvler,* and *twirl.*]

QUERN, *n.* [Sax. *cwyrn, cweorn;* Goth. *quairn;* D. *kweern;* Dan. *qvern;* Sw. *qvarn.* Qu. W. *cwyrn,* a quick motion, a whirl.]

A hand-mill for grinding grain; a mill, the stone of which was turned by hand, used before the invention of windmills and watermills. *Shak.*

QUERP'O, *n.* [Sp. *cuerpo,* the body, L. *corpus;* Sp. *en cuerpo de camisa,* half dressed, having on a shirt only.]

A waistcoat or garment close to the body. *Dryden.*

QUER'QUEDULE, *n.* [L. *querquedula.*] An aquatic fowl, a species of teal of the genus Anas. *Encyc.*

QUER'RY, *n.* A groom. [See *Equerry.*]

QUER'ULOUS, *a.* [L. *querulus,* from *queror,* to complain. See *Quarrel.*]

1. Complaining, or habitually complaining; disposed to murmur; as a *querulous* man or people. *Hooker.*

2. Expressing complaint; as a *querulous* tone of voice.

QUER'ULOUSLY, *adv.* In a complaining manner. *Young.*

QUER'ULOUSNESS, *n.* Disposition to complain, or the habit or practice of murmuring.

QUE'RY, *n.* [from L. *quære,* imperative of *quæro;* perhaps Ch. Heb. חקר to seek, to search, to inquire; בקר id.; Ar. قرا karau, to follow, to seek. Class Gr. No. 51. 53. 55. The sense is to press on, to follow, to urge.]

A question; an inquiry to be answered or resolved.

> I will conclude by proposing some *queries.* *Newton.*

QUE'RY, *v. i.* To ask a question or questions.

> Three Cambridge sophs
> Each prompt to *query,* answer and debate. *Pope.*

QUE'RY, *v. t.* To seek; to inquire; as, *query* the sum or amount; *query* the motive or the fact.

2. To examine by questions. *Gayton.*

3. To doubt of.

QUEST, *n.* [Fr. *quête,* for *queste;* L. *quæro, quæstus.* As the letter *r* is rarely changed into *s,* perhaps the L. *quæsivi, quæstus,* may be from the root of *quæso,* W. *ceis-iaw,* to seek, to endeavor, *cais,* effort. See Class Gs. No. 35.]

1. The act of seeking; search; as, to rove in *quest* of game; to go in *quest* of a lost child; in *quest* of property, &c. *Addison. Milton.*

2. Inquest; a jury. [*Not used.*] *Shak.*

3. Searchers, collectively. [*Not used.*] *Shak.*

4. Inquiry; examination. [*Not used.*] *Shak.*

5. Request; desire; solicitation.

> Gad not abroad at every *quest* and call
> Of an untrain'd hope or passion. *Herbert.*

QUEST, *v. i.* To go in search. [*Not used.*]

QUEST, *v. t.* To search or seek for. *Herbert.*

QUEST'ANT, *n.* [supra.] A seeker. [*Not used.*] *Shak.*

QUESTION, *n.* *ques'chun.* [Fr. Sp. *question;* L. *quæstio.* See *Quest.*]

1. The act of asking; an interrogatory; as, to examine by *question* and answer.

2. That which is asked; something proposed which is to be solved by answer. What is the *question?*

3. Inquiry; disquisition; discussion.

> It is to be put to *question,* whether it is lawful for christian princes to make an invasive war, simply for the propagation of the faith. *Bacon.*

4. Dispute or subject of debate.

> There arose a *question* between some of John's disciples and the Jews, about purifying. John iii.

5. Doubt; controversy; dispute. The story is true beyond all *question.*

> This does not bring their truth in *question.* *Locke.*

6. Trial; examination; judicial trial or inquiry.

> Of the hope and the resurrection of the dead I am called in *question.* Acts xxiii. xxiv.

7. Examination by torture. *Blackstone. Ayliffe.*

8. Endeavor; effort; act of seeking. [*Not in use.*] *Shak.*

9. In *logic,* a proposition stated by way of interrogation.

In question, in debate; in the course of examination or discussion; as, the matter or point *in question.*

QUES'TION, *v. i.* To ask a question or questions; to inquire by interrogatory or proposition to be answered.

> He that *questioneth* much, shall learn much. *Bacon

2. To debate by interrogatories. *Shak.*

QUES'TION, *v. t.* To inquire of by asking questions; to examine by interrogatories; as, to *question* a witness.

2. To doubt of; to be uncertain of.

And most we *question* what we most desire. *Prior.*

3. To have no confidence in; to treat as doubtful. If a man is frustrated in his designs, his prudence is *questioned.*

QUES'TIONABLE, *a.* That may be questioned; doubtful; uncertain; disputable. The deed is of *questionable* authority.

It is *questionable* whether Galen ever saw the dissection of a human body. *Baker.*

2. Suspicious; liable to be doubted or disputed; liable to suspicion. His veracity is *questionable.*

Thou com'st in such a *questionable* shape,
That I will speak to thee. *Shak.*

QUES'TIONABLENESS, *n.* The quality or state of being doubtful, questionable or suspicious.

QUES'TIONARY, *a.* Inquiring; asking questions; as *questionary* epistles. *Pope.*

QUES'TIONED, *pp.* Interrogated; examined by questions.

2. Doubted; disputed.

QUES'TIONER, *n.* One that asks questions; an inquirer.

QUES'TIONING, *ppr.* Interrogating; calling in question; doubting.

QUES'TIONIST, *n.* A questioner; an inquirer. *Hall.*

QUES'TIONLESS, *adv.* Beyond a question or doubt; doubtless; certainly. *Raleigh. South.*

QUEST'MAN, } *n.* A starter of law-
QUEST'MŎNGER, } suits or prosecutions. [*Not used.*] *Bacon.*

QUES'TOR, *n.* [L. *quæstor.* See *Quest* and *Query.*]
In Roman antiquity, an officer who had the management of the public treasure; the receiver of taxes, tribute, &c.

QUES'TORSHIP, *n.* The office of a questor or Roman treasurer.

2. The term of a questor's office.

QUES'TRIST, *n.* A seeker; a pursuer. [*Not in use.*] *Shak.*

QUES'TUARY, *a.* Studious of profit. *Brown.*

QUES'TUARY, *n.* One employed to collect profits. *Taylor.*

QUEUE. [See *Cue.*]

QUIB, *n.* [W. *cwip*, a flirt, a quirk, or *gwib*, a quick course or turn; *cwipiaw*, to move quickly, to whip; as we say, he *whipped* round the corner.]
A sarcasm; a bitter taunt; a quip; a gibe.

QUIB'BLE, *n.* [It seems to be from the root of *quib*, supra, W. *cwipiaw*, to turn or move rapidly, or *gwibiaw*, to wander. See *Wabble.*]

1. A start or turn from the point in question, or from plain truth; an evasion; a cavil; a pretense; as, to answer a sound argument by *quibbles.*

Quirks and *quibbles* have no place in the search after truth. *Watts.*

2. A pun; a low conceit. *Addison.*

QUIB'BLE, *v. i.* To evade the point in question, or plain truth, by artifice, play upon words, caviling or any conceit; to trifle in argument or discourse. *L'Estrange.*

2. To pun.

QUIB'BLER, *n.* One who evades plain truth by trifling artifices, play upon words, or cavils.

2. A punster.

QUICK, *v. i.* [Sax. *cwic*, alive; *cwiccian*, to vivify.]
To stir; to move. [*Not in use.*] *Spenser.*

QUICK, *a.* [Sax. *cwic*, living, alive; D. *kwik*; G. *quick*; Dan. *qvik*; Sw. *qvick*. Qu. W. *cig*, Arm. *qicq*, flesh. If *q* is a dialectical prefix, as I suppose, this word coincides with the L. *vigeo*, *vegeo*, and *vig*, *veg*, radical, coincide with *wag*. Now the Dutch call a wagtail, *kwikstaart.*]

1. Primarily, alive; living; opposed to *dead* or *unanimated;* as *quick* flesh. Lev. xiii.

The Lord Jesus Christ, who shall judge the *quick* and the dead. 2 Tim. iv.

[In this sense, the word is obsolete, except in some compounds or in particular phrases.]

2. Swift; hasty; done with celerity; as *quick* dispatch.

3. Speedy; done or occurring in a short time; as a *quick* return of profits.

Oft he to her his charge of *quick* return
Repeated. *Milton.*

4. Active; brisk; nimble; prompt; ready. He is remarkably *quick* in his motions. He is a man of *quick* parts.

5. Moving with rapidity or celerity; as *quick* time in music.

Quick with child, pregnant with a living child. *Blackstone.*

QUICK, *adv.* Nimbly; with celerity; rapidly; with haste; speedily; without delay; as, run *quick; be quick.*

If we consider how very *quick* the actions of the mind are performed. *Locke.*

2. Soon; in a short time; without delay. Go, and return *quick.*

QUICK, *n.* [Sw. *qviga*, a heifer; Dan. *qvæg*, cattle; that is, living.]

1. A living animal. *Obs.* *Spenser.*

2. The living flesh; sensible parts; as penetrating to the *quick;* stung to the *quick;* cut to the *quick.* *Bacon. Dryden.*

3. Living shrubs or trees; as a ditch or bank set with *quick.* *Mortimer.*

QUICK, *v. t.* [Sax. *cwiccian.*] To revive; to make alive. *Obs.* *Chaucer.*

QUICK, *v. i.* To become alive. *Obs.* *Chaucer.*

QUICK'-BEAM, } *n.* A tree, the wild
QUICK'EN-TREE, } sorb, a species of wild ash. *Mortimer.*

The *Sorbus aucuparia*, or mountain ash, a species of service tree. *Lee.*

QUICKEN, *v. t. quik'n.* [Sax. *cwiccian;* Dan. *qvæger.*]

1. Primarily, to make alive; to vivify; to revive or resuscitate, as from death or an inanimate state. Rom. iv.

Hence flocks and herds, and men and beasts
and fowls,
With breath are *quicken'd*, and attract their
souls. *Dryden.*

2. To make alive in a spiritual sense; to communicate a principle of grace to.

You hath he *quickened*, who were dead in trespasses and sins. Eph. ii.

3. To hasten; to accelerate; as, to *quicken* motion, speed or flight.

4. To sharpen; to give keener perception to; to stimulate; to incite; as, to *quicken* the appetite or taste; to *quicken* desires. *South. Tatler.*

5. To revive; to cheer; to reinvigorate; to refresh by new supplies of comfort or grace. Ps. cxix.

QUICKEN, *v. i. quik'n.* To become alive.

The heart is the first part that *quickens*, and the last that dies. *Ray.*

2. To move with rapidity or activity.

And keener lightning *quickens* in her eye. *Pope.*

QUICK'ENED, *pp.* Made alive; revived; vivified; reinvigorated.

2. Accelerated; hastened.

3. Stimulated; incited.

QUICK'ENER, *n.* One who revives, vivifies, or communicates life.

2. That which reinvigorates.

3. That which accelerates motion or increases activity. *More.*

QUICK'ENING, *ppr.* Giving life; accelerating; inciting.

QUICK'-EYED, *a.* Having acute sight; of keen and ready perception.

QUICK-GRASS. [See *Quitch-grass.*]

QUICK'LIME, *n.* [See *Lime.*] Any calcarious substance deprived of its fixed or carbonic air, or an earthy substance calcined; as chalk, limestone, oyster-shells, &c.; unslacked lime. Calcarious stones and shells are reduced to quicklime by being subjected for a considerable time to intense heat, which expels the carbonic and aqueous matter.

QUICK'LY, *adv.* Speedily; with haste or celerity.

2. Soon; without delay.

QUICK-MATCH, *n.* [See *Match.*] A combustible preparation formed of cotton strands dipped in a boiling composition of white vinegar, saltpeter and mealed powder; used by artillerymen. *Encyc.*

QUICK'NESS, *n.* Speed; velocity; celerity; rapidity; as the *quickness* of motion.

2. Activity; briskness; promptness; as the *quickness* of the imagination or wit. *Wotton. Dryden.*

3. Acuteness of perception; keen sensibility; as *quickness* of sensation. *Locke.*

4. Sharpness; pungency. *Mortimer.*

QUICK'SAND, *n.* Sand easily moved or readily yielding to pressure, loose sand abounding with water. *Dryden.*

2. Unsolid ground. *Addison.*

QUICK'SCENTED, *a.* Having an acute perception by the nose; of an acute smell.

QUICK'SET, *n.* A living plant set to grow, particularly for a hedge. *Evelyn.*

QUICK'SET, *v. t.* To plant with living shrubs or trees for a hedge or fence; as, to *quickset* a ditch. *Mortimer.*

QUICK'SIGHTED, *a.* Having quick sight or acute discernment; quick to see or discern. *Locke. Bentley.*

QUICK'SIGHTEDNESS, *n.* Quickness of sight or discernment; readiness to see or discern. *Locke.*

QUICK'SILVER, *n.* [that is, living silver, *argentum vivum*, so called from its fluidity.]
Mercury, a metal found both native and in the state of ore, in mines, in various parts of the world, and so remarkably fusible as to be congealable only with the intense cold indicated by 39° or 40° below zero, on Fahrenheit's thermometer. It is the heaviest of the metals, next to platina and gold. It is used in various arts and in medicine.

QUICK'SILVERED, *a.* Overlaid with quicksilver. *Newton.*

QUICK'-WITTED, *a.* Having ready wit. *Shak.*

QUID, *n.* A vulgar pronunciation of *cud*; as a *quid* of tobacco.

QUI'DAM, *n.* [L.] Somebody. [*Not in use.*] *Spenser.*

QUID'DANY, *n.* [G. *quitte*, a quince; L. *cydonium.*]
Marmalade; a confection of quinces prepared with sugar.

QUID'DATIVE, *a.* Constituting the essence of a thing. *Encyc.*

QUID'DIT, *n.* [L. *quidlibet*, or Fr. *que dit.*] A subtilty; an equivocation. [*Not in use.*] *Shak.*

QUID'DITY, *n.* [L. *quid*, what.] A barbarous term used in school philosophy for *essence*, that unknown and undefinable something which constitutes its peculiar nature, or answers the question, *quid est?* The essence of a thing constitutes it *tale quid*, such a thing as it is, and not another. *Encyc.*

2. A trifling nicety; a cavil; a captious question. *Camden.*

QUID'NUNC, *n.* [L. what now.] One who is curious to know every thing that passes; one who knows or pretends to know all occurrences. *Tatler.*

Quid pro quo, [L.] in *law*, an equivalent; something given or done for another thing; mutual consideration and performance.

QUIESCE, *v. i.* *quiess'*. [L. *quiesco.*] To be silent, as a letter; to have no sound. *M. Stuart.*

QUIES'CENCE, } *n.* [L. *quiescens*, *quiesco.*
QUIES'CENCY, } See *Quiet.*]

1. Rest; repose; state of a thing without motion. *Glanville.*

2. Rest of the mind; a state of the mind free from agitation or emotion.

3. Silence; the having no sound; as of a letter.

QUIES'CENT, *a.* [L. *quiescens.*] Resting; being in a state of repose; still: not moving; as a *quiescent* body or fluid. *Newton.*

2. Not ruffled with passion; unagitated; as the mind.

3. Silent; not sounded; having no sound; as a *quiescent* letter. Sow, mow, with *w quiescent;* say, day, with *y quiescent.* *M. Stuart, Heb. Gram.*

QUIES'CENT, *n.* A silent letter. *M. Stuart.*

QUI'ET, *a.* [Fr. *quiet*, L. *quietus*, It. *quieto*, quiet; *quietare*, to pacify, and *quetare*, to quiet, and to acquit, to quit; Sp. *quieto*, quiet; *quietar*, to appease; *quedo*, quiet, and *quedar*, to stop, to leave, to quit; Port. *quieto*, quiet; *queda*, a fall, declivity; *quedo*, quiet. *Quiet* and *quit* seem to belong to one radix.]

1. Still; being in a state of rest; not moving. Judg. xvi.

2. Still; free from alarm or disturbance; unmolested; as a *quiet* life. *Shak.*

> In his days the land was *quiet* ten years. 2 Chron. xiv.

3. Peaceable; not turbulent; not giving offense; not exciting controversy, disorder or trouble; mild; meek; contented.

> The ornament of a meek and *quiet* spirit. 1 Pet. iii. 1 Thess. iv.

4. Calm; not agitated by wind; as a *quiet* sea or atmosphere.

5. Smooth; unruffled. *Shak.*

6. Undisturbed; unmolested; as the *quiet* possession or enjoyment of an estate. *Blackstone.*

7. Not crying; not restless; as a *quiet* child.

QUI'ET, *n.* [L. *quies.*] Rest; repose; stillness; the state of a thing not in motion.

2. Tranquility; freedom from disturbance or alarm; civil or political repose. Our country enjoys *quiet.*

3. Peace; security. Judg. xviii.

QUI'ET, *v. t.* To stop motion; to still; to reduce to a state of rest; as, to *quiet* corporeal motion. *Locke.*

2. To calm; to appease; to pacify; to lull; to tranquilize; as, to *quiet* the soul when agitated; to *quiet* the passions; to *quiet* the clamors of a nation; to *quiet* the disorders of a city or town.

3. To allay; to suppress; as, to *quiet* pain or grief.

QUI'ETED, *pp.* Made still; calmed; pacified.

QUI'ETER, *n.* The person or thing that quiets.

QUI'ETING, *ppr.* Reducing to rest or stillness; appeasing; tranquilizing.

QUI'ETISM, *n.* Peace or tranquility of mind; apathy; dispassion; indisturbance; inaction. In history, *quietism* is the system of the quietists, who maintained that religion consists in the internal rest or recollection of the mind, employed in contemplating God and submitting to his will.

QUI'ETIST, *n.* One of a sect of mystics, originated by Molino, a Spanish priest, who maintained the principles of quietism. *Encyc.*

QUI'ETLY, *adv.* In a quiet state; without motion; in a state of rest; as, to lie or sit *quietly.*

2. Without tumult, alarm, dispute or disturbance; peaceably; as, to live *quietly.*

3. Calmly; without agitation or violent emotion; patiently. Submit *quietly* to unavoidable evils.

QUI'ETNESS, *n.* A state of rest; stillness.

2. Calm; tranquility; as the *quietness* of the ocean or atmosphere.

3. Freedom from agitation or emotion; calmness; coolness; as the *quietness* of the mind.

4. Freedom from disturbance, disorder or commotion; peace; tranquility; as the *quietness* of a city or state.

QUI'ETSŎME, *a.* Calm; still; undisturbed. [*Not in use.*] *Spenser.*

QUI'ETUDE, *n.* [Fr.] Rest; repose; quiet; tranquility. *Wotton.*

QUIE'TUS, *n.* [L.] Rest; repose; death; hence, a final discharge or acquittance; that which silences claims. *Shak.*

QUILL, *n.* [Ir. *cuille*, a reed or quill; Corn. *cuilan;* L. *calamus;* W. *calav;* probably a shoot.]

1. The large strong fether of a goose or other large fowl; used much for writing-pens. Hence,

2. The instrument of writing; as the proper subject of his *quill.* *Wotton.*

3. The spine or prickle of a porcupine. *Encyc.*

4. A piece of small reed or other hollow plant, on which weavers wind the thread which forms the woof of cloth. *Spenser.*

5. The instrument with which musicians strike the strings of certain instruments. *Dryden.*

To carry a good quill, to write well.

QUILL, *v. t.* To plait, or to form with small ridges like quills or reeds; as a woolen stuff *quilled.*

[In the United States, this word is generally, if not universally, pronounced *twilled.*]

QUIL'LET, *n.* [L. *quidlibet*, what you please.]
Subtilty; nicety; fraudulent distinction; petty cant. [*Not much used.*] *Shak.*

QUILT, *n.* [It. *coltre;* L. *culcita;* Ir. *cuilt*, a bed-tick, a bed; Port. Sp. *colcha;* Sp. *colchar*, *acolchar*, to quilt; perhaps from uniting, gathering or holding.]
A cover or garment made by putting wool, cotton or other substance between two cloths and sewing them together; as beds covered with magnificent *quilts.* *Arbuthnot.*

QUILT, *v. t.* To stitch together two pieces of cloth with some soft and warm substance between them; as a *quilted* bedcover; a *quilted* coat. *Dryden.*

2. To sew in the manner of a quilt.

QUILT'ED, *pp.* Stitched together, as two pieces of cloth, with a soft substance between them.

QUILT'ING, *ppr.* Stitching together, as two cloths, with some soft substance between them.

QUILT'ING, *n.* The act of forming a quilt.

2. In *New England*, the act of quilting by a collection of females who bestow their labor gratuitously to aid a female friend, and conclude with an entertainment.

QUI'NARY, *a.* [L. *quinarius*, from *quinque*, five.] Consisting of five; as a *quinary* number. *Boyle.*

QUI'NATE, *a.* [from L. *quinque.*] In *botany*, a *quinate* leaf is a sort of digitate leaf having five leaflets on a petiole. *Martyn. Lee.*

QUINCE, *n.* *quins.* [Fr. *coin* or *coing;* Arm. *aval-couign*, the cornered apple or wedge-apple; G. *quitte* or *quittenapfel*, which seems to be a different word, and rather allied to the L. *cydonius.*]
The fruit of the *Pyrus cydonia*, so named from *Cydonia*, a town of Crete, famous for abounding with this fruit. One species of this fruit is of an oblong shape, from which probably it has its French name.

QUINCE, } *n.* The tree which pro-
QUINCE-TREE, } duces the quince.

QUINCH, *v. i.* [probably a vulgar pronunciation of *wince* or *winch.*] To stir, wince or flounce. [*Not in use.*] *Spenser.*

QUINCUN'CIAL, *a.* [from L. *quincunx.*] Having the form of a quincunx. *Ray.*

QUIN'CUNX, *n.* [L. composed of *quinque*, five, and *uncia*, ounce.]
In *gardening*, the *quincunx* order is a plantation of trees disposed in a square, consisting of five trees, one at each corner and a fifth in the middle, thus ∴̇∴ ; which order repeated indefinitely, forms a regular grove or wood, which viewed by an

angle of the square or parallelogram, presents equal or parallel alleys.

QUINDEC'AGON, *n.* [L. *quinque*, five, Gr. δεκα, ten, and γωνια, angle.]

In *geometry*, a plain figure with fifteen sides and fifteen angles. *Encyc.*

QUINDEC'EMVIR, *n.* [L. *quinque*, five, *decem*, ten, and *vir*, man.]

In *Roman history*, one of a collection or body of fifteen magistrates, whose business was to preside over the sacrifices. *Encyc.*

QUINDECEM'VIRATE, *n.* The body of fifteen magistrates, or their office.

QUIN'IA, } *n.* In *pharmacy*, a substance
QUIN'INE, } prepared from yellow bark (cinchona cordifolia,) possessing in a concentrated form, the tonic virtues of the bark, and capable of forming salts with acids. One of these, the sulphate of quinine, is much employed in intermittent fevers and other diseases, where powerful tonics are required.

QUINQUAGES'IMA, *n.* [L. fifty.] Quinquagesima Sunday, so called as being about the fiftieth day before Easter; Shrove Sunday. *Encyc.*

QUINQUAN'GULAR, *a.* [L. *quinque*, five, and *angulus*, angle.] Having five angles or corners. *Woodward.*

QUINQUARTIC'ULAR, *a.* [L. *quinque*, five, and *articulus*, article.] Consisting of five articles. [*Little used.*] *Sanderson.*

QUINQUECAP'SULAR, *a.* [L. *quinque*, five, and *capsula*, a little chest.]

In *botany*, having five capsules to a flower; as a *quinquecapsular* pericarp. *Martyn.*

QUINQUEDEN'TATE, *a.* [L. *quinque*, five, and *dentatus*, toothed; *dens*, tooth.] In *botany*, five-toothed.

QUINQUEFA'RIOUS, *a.* [L. *quinque*, five, and probably Sax. *faran*, to go, Eng. to *fare*, or from the root of *vary.*] In *botany*, opening into five parts. *Lee.*

QUIN'QUEFID, *a.* [L. *quinque*, five, and *findo*, to split.]

In *botany*, five-cleft; cut into five segments with linear sinuses and straight margins; as a leaf. *Martyn.*

QUINQUEFO'LIATED, *a.* [L. *quinque*, five, and *folium*, leaf.] Having five leaves. *Johnson.*

QUINQUELIT'ERAL, *a.* [L. *quinque*, five, and *litera*, letter.] Consisting of five letters. *M. Stuart.*

QUIN'QUELOBATE, } *a.* [L. *quinque*, five,
QUIN'QUELOBED, } and *lobus*, lobe.]

Five-lobed; divided to the middle into five distinct parts with convex margins. *Martyn.*

QUINQUELOC'ULAR, *a.* [L. *quinque*, five, and *loculus*, a cell.]

Five-celled; having five cells; as a pericarp. *Martyn.*

QUINQUEN'NIAL, *a.* [L. *quinquennalis*, *quinquennis*; *quinque*, five, and *annus*, year.] Occurring once in five years, or lasting five years. *Potter.*

QUINQUEP'ARTITE, *a.* [L. *quinque*, five, and *partitus*, divided.]

1. Divided into five parts almost to the base. *Martyn.*
2. Consisting of two parts.

QUIN'QUEREME, *n.* [L. *quinque*, five, and *remus*, oar.]

A galley having five seats or rows of oars.

QUIN'QUEVALVE, } *a.* [L. *quinque*,
QUINQUEVALV'ULAR, } five, and *valvæ*, valves.] Having five valves, as a pericarp.

QUIN'QUEVIR, *n.* [L. *quinque*, five, and *vir*, man.] One of an order of five priests in Rome.

QUIN'SY, *n.* *s* as *z*. [corrupted from Fr. *esquinancie*, *squinancie*; It. *squinanzia*; Sp. *esquinancia.*]

1. An inflammation of the throat; a species of angina which renders respiration difficult, or intercepts it.
2. An inflammation of the fauces, particularly of the tonsils. *Hooper.*

QUINT, *n.* [from L. *quintus*, fifth, Fr. *quinte.*] A set or sequence of five; as in piquet.

QUINT'AIN, *n.* [Fr. *quintaine.*] A post with a turning top. *Shak.*

QUINT'AL, *n.* [Fr. *quintal*; It. *quintale*; from the root of L. *centum*, a hundred.]

A hundred pounds in weight; or a weight of that number of pounds; sometimes written and pronounced *kentle.*

QUINTES'SENCE, *n.* [L. *quinta essentia*, fifth essence.]

1. In *alchimy*, the fifth or last and highest essence of power in a natural body. Hence,
2. An extract from any thing, containing its virtues or most essential part in a small quantity.

> Let there be light, said God; and forthwith light
> Etherial, first of things, *quintessence* pure,
> Sprung from the deep. *Milton.*

3. In *chimistry*, a preparation consisting of the essential oil of a vegetable substance, mixed and incorporated with spirit of wine.
4. The pure essential part of a thing. *Hakewill.*

[I have followed Bailey and Ash and our general usage in the accentuation of this word. Jameson has done the same. The accent on the first syllable is very unnatural.]

QUINTESSEN'TIAL, *a.* Consisting of quintessence.

QUINT'ILE, *n.* [L. *quintus*, fifth.] The aspect of planets when distant from each other the fifth part of the zodiac, or 72 degrees.

QUINT'IN, *n.* [Fr. *quintaine*, W. *çwintan*, a hymeneal game.]

An upright post on the top of which turned a cross piece, on one end of which was fixed a broad board, and on the other a sand bag. The play was to tilt or ride against the broad end with a lance, and pass without being struck by the sand bag behind. *B. Jonson.*

QUINT'UPLE, *a.* [L. *quintuplus*, fivefold; *quintus* and *plico.*]

Fivefold; containing five times the amount. *Graunt.*

QUIP, *n.* [W. *çwip*, a quick flirt or turn; *çwipiaw*, to move briskly, to *whip*; as we say, to *whip* round a corner in running.]

A smart sarcastic turn; a taunt; a severe retort. *Milton. Shak.*

QUIP, *v. t.* To taunt; to treat with a sarcastic retort. *Ainsworth.*

QUIP, *v. i.* To scoff. *Sidney.*

QUIRE, *n.* [Fr. *choeur*; It. *coro*; L. *chorus*; Gr. χορος.]

1. A body of singers; a chorus. [See *Chorus* and *Choir.*] *Milton.*
2. The part of a church where the service is sung.

QUIRE, *n.* [Qu. from the root of *chorus*, or from Fr. *cahier*, a sheet of paper, or rather a book of loose sheets.]

A collection of paper consisting of twenty four sheets, each having a single fold.

QUIRE, *v. i.* To sing in concert or chorus. *Shak.*

QUIR'ISTER, *n.* One that sings in concert; more generally, the leader of a quire, particularly in divine service; a chorister. But in America, this word is little used and vulgar. The word used is *chorister.*

QUIRITA'TION, *n.* [L. *quiritatio*, from *quirito*, from *queror.*] A crying for help. [*Not used.*] *Bp. Hall.*

QUIRK, *n.* *quurk.* [from the root of W. *çwired*, a sudden start or turn, craft, deceit; *çwyrn*, a *whirl.*]

1. Literally, a turn; a starting from the point or line; hence, an artful turn for evasion or subterfuge; a shift; a quibble; as the *quirks* of a pettifogger. *L'Estrange.*
2. A fit or turn; a short paroxysm; as a *quirk* of joy or grief. *Shak.*
3. A smart taunt or retort.

> I may chance to have some odd *quirks* and remnants of wit broken on me. *Shak.*

4. A slight conceit or quibble. *Watts.*
5. A flight of fancy. [*Not in use.*] *Shak.*
6. An irregular air; as light *quirks* of music. *Pope.*
7. In *building*, a piece of ground taken out of any regular ground-plot or floor, as to make a court or yard, &c. *Encyc.*

QUIRK'ISH, *a.* Consisting of quirks, turns, quibbles or artful evasions. *Barrow.*

2. Resembling a quirk.

QUIRP'ELE, *n.* The Indian ferret, an animal of the weasel kind. *Dict. Nat. Hist.*

QUIT, *v. t.* pret. and pp. *quit* or *quitted.* [Fr. *quitter*; It. *quitare* and *chitare*; Port. Sp. *quitar*; D. *kwyten*; G. *quittiren*; Dan. *quitterer*; Sw. *quitta*; W. *gadu* and *gadaw*, to quit; Ir. *cead*, leave; *cuitighim*, to requite. This is the L. *cedo.* The sense of *quit* is to leave, to withdraw from; but the primary sense of the root must have been to move or to send; for to *requite* is to send back. See Class Cd. and Cs.]

1. To leave; to depart from, either temporarily or forever. It does not necessarily include the idea of *abandoning*, without a qualifying word. A man *quits* his house for an hour, or for a month. He *quits* his native country on a voyage, or he *quits* it forever; he *quits* an employment with the intention of resuming it.
2. To free; to clear; to liberate; to discharge from.

> To *quit* you of this fear, you have already looked death in the face. [*Nearly obsolete.*] *Wake.*

3. To carry through; to do or perform something to the end, so that nothing remains; to discharge or perform completely.

> Never a worthy prince a day did *quit*
> With greater hazard and with more renown. *Daniel.*

4. To *quit one's self*, reciprocally, to clear one's self of incumbent duties by full performance.

Samson hath *quit himself*
Like Samson. *Milton.*

In this sense, *acquit* is generally used.

5. To repay; to requite. *Spenser.*

—Enkindle all the sparks of nature
To *quit* this horrid act. *Shak.*

In this sense, *quit* is now rarely used. We use *requite.*

6. To vacate obligation; to release; to free from.

Dangers of law,
Actions, decrees, judgments against us *quitted.* *B. Jonson.*

7. To pay; to discharge; hence, to free from; as, to *quit* the debt of gratitude. *Milton.*

8. To set free; to release; to absolve; to acquit.

Guiltless I *quit*, guilty I set them free. *Fairfax.*

In this sense, *acquit* is now used.

9. To leave; to give up; to resign; to relinquish; as, to *quit* an office.

10. To pay.

Before that judge that *quits* each soul his hire. [*Not used.*] *Fairfax.*

11. To forsake; to abandon.

Such a superficial way of examining is to *quit* truth for appearance. *Locke.*

To quit cost, to pay; to free from by an equivalent; to reimburse; as, the cultivation of barren land will not always *quit cost.*

To quit scores, to make even; to clear mutually from demands by mutual equivalents given. We will *quit scores* [marks of charges] before we part.

Does not the earth *quit scores* with all the elements in her noble fruits? *South.*

QUIT, *a.* Free; clear; discharged from; absolved.

The owner of the ox shall be *quit.* Ex. xxi.

[This word, though primarily a participle, and never placed before its noun, has properly the sense of an adjective.]

Qui tam, [L.] A *qui tam* action, in law, is a popular action, in which a man prosecutes an offender for the king or state, as well as for himself.

QUITCH'-GRASS, *n.* [properly *quick-grass*, probably from its vigorous growth, or the difficulty of eradicating it.]

Dog-grass; a species of grass which roots deeply and is not easily killed.

QUIT'CLAIM, *v. t.* [*quit* and *claim.*] To release a claim by deed without covenants of warranty; to convey to another who hath some right in lands or tenements, all one's right, title and interest in the estate, by relinquishing all claim to them. The words used in the instrument are, "A hath remised, released and forever *quitclaimed* all his right, title and interest to a certain estate." *Blackstone.*

QUIT'CLAIM, *n.* A deed of release; an instrument by which all claims to an estate are relinquished to another without any covenant or warranty, express or implied. *Z. Swift.*

QUIT'CLAIMED, *pp.* Released by deed.

QUIT'CLAIMING, *ppr.* Conveying by deed of release.

QUITE, *adv.* [from *quit*; that is, primarily, free or clear by complete performance.]

Completely; wholly; entirely; totally; perfectly. The work is not *quite* done; the object is *quite* accomplished.

He hath sold us and *quite* devoured also our money. Gen. xxxi.

The same actions may be aimed at different ends, and arise from *quite* contrary principles. *Spectator.*

QUIT'-RENT, *n.* [L. *quietus reditus.*] A rent reserved in grants of land, by the payment of which the tenant is quieted or quit from all other service. *Blackstone.*

QUITS, *adv.* [from *quit.*] An exclamation used when mutual demands are adjusted and the parties are even, each quit of the other.

QUIT'TAL, *n.* Return; repayment. *Shak.*

QUIT'TANCE, *n.* [Fr.] Discharge from a debt or obligation; an acquittance. [See *Acquittance*, which is chiefly used.] *Shak.*

2. Recompense; return; repayment. *Shak.*

QUIT'TANCE, *v. t.* To repay. [*Not in use.*] *Shak.*

QUIT'TED, *pp.* Left; relinquished; acquitted.

QUIT'TER, *n.* One who quits.

2. A deliverer. [*Not in use.*] *Ainsworth.*

3. Scoria of tin. *Ainsworth.*

QUIT'TER-BONE, *n.* In *farriery*, a hard round swelling on the coronet, between the heel and the quarter, usually on the inside of the foot. *Far. Dict.*

QUIV'ER, *n.* [Qu. Fr. *couvrir*, to cover.]

A case or sheath for arrows.

Take thy *quiver* and thy bow. Gen. xxvii.

QUIV'ER, *a.* Nimble; active. [*Not in use.*] *Shak.*

QUIV'ER, *v. i.* [D. *huiveren*, to shiver. This word seems to belong to the family of *quaver*, W. *çwibiaw*, to trill, to quiver, *çwiv*, a whirl or turn, *çwiviaw*, to fly about, to wander, *çwipiaw*, to move briskly, *çwyvaw*, to stir, move, agitate.]

1. To shake or tremble; to quake; to shudder; to shiver. This word expresses that tremulous motion of the body which proceeds from loss of heat or vigor. Thus persons *quiver* with fear or with cold.

He *quiver'd* with his feet and lay for dead. *Dryden.*

And left the limbs still *quiv'ring* on the ground. *Addison.*

2. To play or be agitated with a tremulous motion.

The green leaves *quiver* with the cooling wind. *Shak.*

The lakes that *quiver* to the curling breeze. *Pope.*

QUIV'ERED, *a.* [from the noun *quiver.*]

1. Furnished with a quiver; as the *quivered* nymph. *Milton.*

2. Sheathed as in a quiver.

—Whose quills stand *quivered* at his ear. *Pope.*

QUIV'ERING, *ppr.* Trembling, as with cold or fear; moving with a tremulous agitation.

QUIV'ERING, *n.* The act of shaking or trembling; agitation; as, to be seized with a *quivering.* *Sidney.*

QUIXOT'IC, *a.* Like Don Quixote; romantic to extravagance.

QUIX'OTISM, *n.* Romantic and absurd notions; schemes or actions like those of Don Quixote, the hero of Cervantes.

QUIZ, *n.* [Norm. *quis, quiz*, sought; Sp. *quisicosa*; from the root of *question.*] An enigma; a riddle or obscure question.

QUIZ, *v. t.* To puzzle. [A popular, but not an elegant word.]

Quo warranto, in Law Latin, a writ brought before a proper tribunal, to inquire by what warrant a person or corporation exercises certain powers. *Blackstone.*

QUOB, *v. i.* [W. *çwapiaw*, to strike.] To move, as the fetus in utero; to throb. [*Local, vulgar, and little used.*]

QUOD'LIBET, *n.* [L. what you please.]

A nice point; a subtilty. *Prior.*

QUODLIBETA'RIAN, *n.* One who talks and disputes on any subject at pleasure.

QUODLIBET'ICAL, *a.* Not restrained to a particular subject; moved or discussed at pleasure for curiosity or entertainment.

QUODLIBET'ICALLY, *adv.* At pleasure; for curiosity; so as to be debated for entertainment. *Brown. Dict.*

QUOIF, *n.* [Fr. *coiffe.*] A cap or hood. [See *Coif.*] *Shak.*

QUOIF, *v. t.* To cover or dress with a coif. [See *Coif.*] *Addison.*

[*This word may be discarded with advantage.*]

QUOIF'FURE, *n.* A head dress. *Addison.*

QUOIL. [See *Coil*, the better word.]

QUOIN, *n.* [Fr. *coin*, a corner; Sp. *cuña.* See *Coin.*]

1. A corner. *Mortimer.*

2. An instrument to raise any thing; a wedge employed to raise cannon to a proper level, and for other purposes. *Mar. Dict.*

3. In *architecture*, the corner of a brick or stone wall. *Encyc.*

QUOIT, *n.* [D. *coite.*] A kind of horse shoe to be pitched or thrown at a fixed object in play. In *common practice*, a plain flat stone is used for this purpose.

2. In some authors, the discus of the ancients, thrown in trials of strength. *Dryden.*

QUOIT, *v. i.* To throw quoits; to play at quoits. *Dryden.*

QUOIT, *v. t.* To throw. [*Not used.*] *Shak.*

QUOLL, *n.* An animal of New Holland, resembling the polecat. *Dict. Nat. Hist.*

QUON'DAM, *used adjectively.* [L.] Having been formerly; former; as a *quondam* king or friend. *Shak.*

QUOOK, *pret.* of *quake.* *Obs.* *Spenser.*

QUO'RUM, *n.* [L. *gen. plu.* of *qui*, who.]

1. A bench of justices, or such a number of officers or members as is competent by law or constitution to transact business; as a *quorum* of the house of representatives. A constitutional *quorum* was not present.

2. A special commission of justices.

QUO'TA, *n.* [L. *quotus*; It. Sp. *quota*; Ir. *cod, cota*, a part.]

A just part or share; or the share, part or proportion assigned to each. Each state was ordered to furnish its *quota* of troops.

QUOTA'TION, *n.* [from *quote.*] The act of quoting or citing.

2. The passage quoted or cited; the part of a book or writing named, repeated or adduced as evidence or illustration. *Locke.*

3. In *mercantile language*, the naming of the price of commodities; or the price specified to a correspondent.

4. Quota; share. [*Not used.*]

QUOTE, *v. t.* [Fr. *quoter*, now *coter;* connected with *quoth.*]

1. To cite, as a passage from some author; to name, repeat or adduce a passage from an author or speaker, by way of authority or illustration; as, to *quote* a passage from Homer; to *quote* the words of Peter, or a passage of Paul's writings; to *quote* chapter and verse. *Atterbury. Swift.*

2. In *commerce*, to name, as the price of an article.

3. To note. *Shak.*

QUOTE, *n.* A note upon an author. *Obs. Cotgrave.*

QUO'TED, *pp.* Cited; adduced; named.

QUO'TER, *n.* One that cites the words of an author or speaker.

QUOTH, *v. i.* [Sax. *cwythan, cythan,* Goth. *quithan,* to say, to tell; W. *gwed, gwedyd;* Ir. *ceadach.* Qu. L. *inquio,* contracted.]

To say; to speak. This verb is defective, being used only in the first and third persons in the present and past tenses, as *quoth I, quoth he,* and the nominative always follows the verb. It is used only in ludicrous language, and has no variation for person, number or tense.

QUOTID'IAN, *a.* [L. *quotidianus; quotus* and *dies.*] Daily; occurring or returning daily; as a *quotidian* fever.

QUOTID'IAN, *n.* A fever whose paroxysms return every day.

2. Any thing returning daily. *Milton.*

QUO'TIENT, *n.* [Fr. from L. *quoties,* how often.]

In *arithmetic*, the number resulting from the division of one number by another, and showing how often a less number is contained in a greater. Thus 3)12(4. Here 4 is the *quotient*, showing that 3 is contained 4 times in 12. Or *quotient* is an expression denoting a certain part of a unit; as $\frac{3}{4}$.

R.

R is the eighteenth letter of the English Alphabet, and an articulation *sui generis*, having little or no resemblance in pronunciation to any other letter. But from the position of the tongue in uttering it, it is commutable with *l*, into which letter it is changed in many words by the Spaniards and Portuguese, and some other nations; as *l* is also changed into *r*. It is numbered among the liquids and semi-vowels, and is sometimes called the canine letter. It is uttered with a guttural extrusion of the breath, and in some words, particularly at the end or after a labial and a dental letter, with a sort of quivering motion or slight jar of the tongue. Its English uses, which are uniform, may be understood by the customary pronunciation of *rod, room, rose, bar, bare, barren, disturb, catarrh, free, brad, pride, drip, drag, drown.*

In words which we have received from the Greek language, we follow the Latins, who wrote *h* after *r*, as the representative of the aspirated sound with which this letter was pronounced by the Greeks. It is the same in the Welsh language. But as the letter is not aspirated in English, *h* is entirely superfluous; *rhapsody, rheum, rhetoric* being pronounced *rapsody, reum, retoric.*

As an abbreviation, R. in English, stands for *rex*, king, as George R.

In the notes of the ancients, R. or RO. stands for *Roma;* R. C. for *Romana civitas;* R. G. C. for *rei gerendæ causa;* R. F. E. D. for *recte factum et dictum;* R. G. F. for *regis filius;* R. P. *respublica*, or *Romani principes.*

As a numeral, R, in Roman authors, stands for 80, and with a dash over it, R̄, for 80,000. But in Greek, ρ, with a small mark over it, thus, ρ́, signifies 100, and with the same mark under it, it denoted 1000×100, or 100,000. In Hebrew, ר denoted 200, and with two horizontal points over it, ר̈, 1000×200, or 200,000.

Among physicians, R. stands for *recipe*, take.

RA, as an inseparable prefix or preposition, is the Latin *re*, coming to us through the Italian and French, and primarily signifying *again, repetition.* [See *Re.*]

RABA'TE, *v. t.* [Fr. *rabattre;* It. *rabbattere; ra* and *battre, battere,* to *beat.* See *Beat* and *Abate.*]

In *falconry*, to recover a hawk to the fist. *Ainsworth.*

RABA'TO, *n.* [Fr. *rabat.*] A neckband or ruff. [*Not in use.*]

RAB'BET, *v. t.* [Fr. *raboter.*] To pare down the edge of a board or other piece of timber, for the purpose of receiving the edge of another piece by lapping and thus uniting the two. *Moxon.*

2. To lap and unite the edges of boards, &c. In ship carpentry, to let the edge of a plank into the keel. *Mar. Dict.*

RAB'BET, *n.* A cut on the side of a board, &c. to fit it to another by lapping; a joint made by lapping boards, &c.

RAB'BETED, *pp.* Pared down at the edge; united by a rabbet joint.

RAB'BETING, *ppr.* Paring down the edge of a board; uniting by a rabbet joint.

RAB'BET-PLANE, *n.* A joiner's plane for paring or cutting square down the edge of a board, &c. *Moxon.*

RAB'BI, RAB'BIN, } *n.* [Ch. רבא, Ar. رَبّ, lord, master.]

A title assumed by the Jewish doctors, signifying master or lord. This title is not conferred by authority, but assumed or allowed by courtesy to learned men. *Encyc.*

RABBIN'IC, RABBIN'ICAL, } *a.* Pertaining to the Rabbins, or to their opinions, learning and language.

RABBIN'IC, *n.* The language or dialect of the Rabbins; the later Hebrew.

RAB'BINISM, *n.* A Rabbinic expression or phraseology; a peculiarity of the language of the Rabbins. *Encyc.*

RAB'BINIST, *n.* Among the Jews, one who adhered to the Talmud and the traditions of the Rabbins, in opposition to the Caraites, who rejected the traditions.

RAB'BINITE, *n.* The same as *rabbinist.*

RAB'BIT, *n.* [said to be from the Belgic *robbe, robbeken.*]

A small quadruped of the genus Lepus, which feeds on grass or other herbage, and burrows in the earth. The rabbit is said to be less sagacious than the hare. It is a very prolific animal, and is kept in warrens for the sake of its flesh.

RAB'BLE, *n.* [L. *rabula*, a brawler, from *rabo*, to *rave;* Dan. *raaber;* D. *rabbelen;* connected with a great family of words with these elements, *Rb, Rp.* Qu. Sp. *rabel*, the tail.]

1. A tumultuous crowd of vulgar, noisy people; the mob; a confused disorderly crowd. *Shak.*

2. The lower class of people, without refference to an assembly; the dregs of the people. *Addison.*

RAB'BLE-CHARMING, *a.* Charming or delighting the rabble. *South.*

RAB'BLEMENT, *n.* A tumultuous crowd of low people. [*Not in use.*] *Spenser. Shak.*

RABDOL'OGY, *n.* [Gr. ῥαβδος, a rod, and λογος, discourse.]

A method of performing mathematical operations by little square rods. *Ash.*

RAB'ID, *a.* [L. *rabidus*, from *rabio, rabo*, to rage; W. *rhaib.*]

Furious; raging; mad; as a *rabid* dog or wolf. It is particularly applied to animals of the canine genus, affected with the distemper called *rabies*, and whose bite communicates hydrophobia.

RAB'IDNESS, *n.* Furiousness; madness.

RAB'INET, *n.* A kind of smaller ordnance. *Ainsworth.*

R'ACA, *n.* A Syriac word signifying empty, beggarly, foolish; a term of extreme contempt. Matt. v.

RACE, *n.* [Fr. *race*, from the It. *razza;* Sp. *raza*, a race, a ray, and *raiz*, a root, L. *radix;* Russ. *rod*, a generation, race; *roju*, to beget. The primary sense of the root is to thrust or shoot; the L. *radix* and *radius* having the same original. This word coincides in origin with *rod, ray, radiate,* &c. Class Rd.]

1. The lineage of a family, or continued series of descendants from a parent who is called the stock. A race is the series of descendants indefinitely. Thus all mankind are called the *race* of Adam; the Israelites are of the *race* of Abraham and Jacob. Thus we speak of a *race* of kings, the *race* of Clovis or Charlemagne; a *race* of nobles, &c.

Hence the long *race* of Alban fathers come. *Dryden.*

2. A generation; a family of descendants.

A *race* of youthful and unhandled colts. *Shak.*

3. A particular breed; as a *race* of mules; a *race* of horses; a *race* of sheep. *Chapman.*

Of such a *race* no matter who is king. *Murphy.*

4. A root; as *race*-ginger, ginger in the root or not pulverized.

5. A particular strength or taste of wine; a kind of tartness. [Query, does this belong to this root or to the following?] *Temple. Massenger.*

RACE, *n.* [D. *ras;* Sw. *resa,* to go; Dan. *rejse,* a going or course; L. *gradior, gressus,* with the prefix *g;* Ir. *ratha,* a running; *reatham,* to run; W. *graz,* a step, from *rhaz,* a going; allied to W. *rhêd,* a race; *rhedu,* to run, to race; allied to Eng. *ride.* See Class Rd. No 5. and 9.]

1. A running; a rapid course or motion, either on the feet, on horseback or in a carriage, &c.; particularly, a contest in running; a running in competition for a prize.

The *race* was one of the exercises of the Grecian games. *Encyc.*

I wield the gauntlet and I run the *race.* *Pope.*

2. Any running with speed.

The flight of many birds is swifter than the *race* of any beast. *Bacon.*

3. A progress; a course; a movement or progression of any kind.

My *race* of glory run. *Pope.*

Let us run with patience the *race* that is set before us. Heb. xii.

4. Course; train; process; as the prosecution and *race* of the war. [*Not now used.*] *Bacon.*

5. A strong or rapid current of water, or the channel or passage for such a current; as a mill-*race.*

6. *By way of distinction,* a contest in the running of horses; generally in the plural. The *races* commence in October.

RACE, *v. i.* To run swiftly; to run or contend in running. The animals *raced* over the ground.

RACE-GIN′GER, *n.* Ginger in the root or not pulverized.

RA′CE-HORSE, *n.* A horse bred or kept for running in contest; a horse that runs in competition. *Addison.*

RACEMA′TION, *n.* [L. *racemus,* a cluster.]

1. A cluster, as of grapes. *Brown.*

2. The cultivation of clusters of grapes. *Burnet.*

RAC′EME, *n.* [L. *racemus,* a bunch of berries.]

In *botany,* a species of inflorescence, consisting of a peduncle with short lateral branches. It is simple or compound, naked or leafy, &c. *Martyn.*

RACEMIF′EROUS, *a.* [L. *racemus,* a cluster, and *fero,* to bear.]

Bearing racemes or clusters; as the *racemiferous* fig-tree. *Asiat. Res.*

RAC′EMOUS, *a.* Growing in racemes or clusters. *Encyc.*

RA′CER, *n.* [from *race.*] A runner; one that contends in a race.

And bade the nimblest *racer* seize the prize. *Pope.*

RACH, *n.* [Sax. *ræcc;* D. *brak;* Fr. *braque.*] A setting dog.

RA′CINESS, *n.* [See *Racy.*] The quality of being racy.

RACK, *n.* [D. *rek,* rack, stretch; *rekker,* to stretch; Sax. *racan, ræcan,* Eng. to *reach;* G. *recken,* to stretch; *reckbank,* a rack. See *Reach* and *Break.* Class Rg. No. 18. 21. 33.]

1. An engine of torture, used for extorting confessions from criminals or suspected persons. The *rack* is entirely unknown in free countries.

2. Torture; extreme pain; anguish.

A fit of the stone puts a king to the *rack* and makes him as miserable as it does the meanest subject. *Temple.*

3. Any instrument for stretching or extending any thing; as a *rack* for bending a bow. *Temple.*

4. A grate on which bacon is laid.

5. A wooden frame of open work in which hay is laid for horses and cattle for feeding.

6. The frame of bones of an animal; a skeleton. We say, a *rack* of bones.

7. A frame of timber on a ship's bowsprit. *Mar. Dict.*

RACK, *n.* [Sax. *hracca,* the neck; Gr. ῥαχις, the spine; W. *rhac;* D. *kraag,* G. *kragen,* Sw. Dan. *krage,* a collar; Old Eng. *crag.*]

The neck and spine of a fore quarter of veal or mutton.

[*The two foregoing words are doubtless from one original.*]

RACK, *n.* [Sax. *rec,* steam; *recan,* to exhale; D. *rook, rooken;* G. *rauch, rauchen;* Sw. *rök, röka;* Dan. *rog, roger.* See *Reek.*]

Properly, vapor; hence, thin flying broken clouds, or any portion of floating vapor in the sky.

The winds in the upper region, which move the clouds above, which we call the *rack*— *Bacon.*

The great globe itself,
Yea, all which it inherit, shall dissolve,
And, like this unsubstantial pageant, faded,
Leave not a *rack* behind. *Shak.*

It is disputed however, whether *rack* in this passage should not be *wreck.*

RACK, *n.* [for *arrack.* See *Arrack.*] Among the Tartars, a spirituous liquor made of mare's milk which has become sour and is then distilled. *Encyc.*

RACK, *v. i.* [Sax. *recan.* See the Noun.]

1. Properly, to steam; to rise, as vapor. [See *Reek,* which is the word used.]

2. To fly, as vapor or broken clouds. *Shak.*

RACK, *v. t.* [from the noun.] To torture; to stretch or strain on the rack or wheel; as, to *rack* a criminal or suspected person, to extort a confession of his guilt, or compel him to betray his accomplices. *Dryden.*

2. To torment; to torture; to affect with extreme pain or anguish; as *racked* with deep despair. *Milton.*

3. To harass by exaction.

The landlords there shamefully *rack* their tenants. *Spenser.*

4. To stretch; to strain vehemently; to wrest; as, to *rack* and stretch Scripture; to *rack* invention. *Hooker. Waterland.*

The wisest among the heathens *racked* their wits— *Tillotson.*

5. To stretch; to extend. *Shak.*

RACK, *v. t.* [Ar. راق rauka, to clear, to strain. Class Rg. No. 8.]

To draw off from the lees; to draw off, as pure liquor from its sediment; as, to *rack* cider or wine; to *rack* off liquor. *Bacon.*

RACK′ED, *pp.* Tortured; tormented; strained to the utmost.

2. Drawn off, as liquor.

RACK′ER, *n.* One that tortures or torments; one that racks.

RACK′ET, *n.* [This word belongs to the root of *crack,* Fr. *craquer.* See *Rocket.*]

1. A confused, clattering noise, less loud than *uproar;* applied to the confused sounds of animal voices, or such voices mixed with other sound. We say, the children make a *racket;* the *racket* of a flock of fowls.

2. Clamor; noisy talk. *Swift.*

RACK′ET, *v. i.* To make a confused noise or clamor; to frolick. *Gray.*

RACK′ET, *n.* [Fr. *raquette;* Sp. *raqueta;* G. *racket;* D. *raket.*]

The instrument with which players at tennis strike the ball. *Shak. Digby.*

RACK′ET, *v. t.* To strike as with a racket. *Hewyt.*

RACK′ETY, *a.* Making a tumultuous noise.

RACK′ING, *ppr.* Torturing; tormenting; straining; drawing off.

2. *a.* Tormenting; excruciating; as a *racking* pain.

RACK′ING, *n.* Torture; a stretching on the rack.

2. Torment of the mind; anguish; as the *rackings* of conscience.

3. The act of stretching cloth on a frame for drying.

4. The act of drawing from the sediment, as liquors.

RACK′ING-PACE, *n.* The racking-pace of a horse is an amble, but with a quicker and shorter tread. *Far. Dict.*

RACK′-RENT, *n.* An annual rent of the full value of the tenement or near it. *Blackstone.*

RACK′-RENTED, *a.* Subjected to the payment of rack-rent. *Franklin.*

RACK′-RENTER, *n.* One that is subjected to pay rack-rent. *Locke.*

RACOON′, *n.* An American quadruped of the genus Ursus. It is somewhat larger than a fox, and its fur is deemed valuable, next to that of the beaver. This animal lodges in a hollow tree, feeds on vegetables, and its flesh is palatable food. It inhabits North America from Canada to the tropics. *Belknap. Dict. Nat. Hist.*

RA′CY, *a.* [This word, if the sense of it is strong, vigorous, would seem to belong to

the family of Sax. *hrœs*, force; *rœsan*, to *rush*. But the application of it by Cowley in the passage below, seems to indicate its connection with the Sp. Port. *raiz*, root, L. *radix*.]
Strong; flavorous; tasting of the soil; as *racy* cider; *racy* wine. *Johnson.*

Rich *racy* verses, in which we
The soil from which they come, taste, smell
and see. *Cowley.*

RAD, the *old pret.* of *read*. *Spenser.*

RAD, RED, ROD, an initial or terminating syllable in names, is the D. *raad*, G. *rath*, counsel; as in *Conrad*, powerful in counsel; *Ethelred*, noble counsel.

RAD'DLE, *v. t.* [probably from Sax. *wræd*, *wrad* or *wræth*, a band or wreath, or from the same root.]
To twist; to wind together. [*Not in use.*] *Defoe.*

RAD'DLE, *n.* [supra.] A long stick used in hedging; also, a hedge formed by interweaving the shoots and branches of trees or shrubs. *Todd.*

[I believe the two foregoing words are not used in the United States, and probably they are local.]

RAD'DOCK, RUD'DOCK, *n.* [from *red*, *ruddy*, which see.] A bird, the redbreast. *Shak.*

RA'DIAL, *a.* [from L. *radius*, a ray, a *rod*, a spoke. See *Radius* and *Ray*.]
Pertaining to the radius or to the fore arm of the human body; as the *radial* artery or nerve. *Rush.*

The *radial muscles* are two muscles of the fore arm, one of which bends the wrist, the other extends it. *Encyc. Parr.*

Radial curves, in geometry, curves of the spiral kind, whose ordinates all terminate in the center of the including circle, and appear like so many semidiameters. *Bailey.*

RA'DIANCE, RA'DIANCY, *n.* [L. *radians*, *radio*, to beam or shoot rays. See *Radius* and *Ray*.]
Properly, brightness shooting in rays or beams; hence in general, brilliant or sparkling luster; vivid brightness; as the *radiance* of the sun.

The Son
Girt with omnipotence, with *radiance* crown'd
Of majesty divine. *Milton.*

RA'DIANT, *a.* Shooting or darting rays of light; beaming with brightness; emitting a vivid light or splendor; as the *radiant* sun.

Mark what *radiant* state she spreads. *Milton.*

Radiant in glittering arms and beamy pride. *Milton.*

RA'DIANT, *n.* In *optics*, the luminous point or object from which light emanates, that falls on a mirror or lens.

RA'DIANTLY, *adv.* With beaming brightness; with glittering splendor.

RA'DIATE, *v. i.* [L. *radio*. See *Ray*.] To issue in rays, as light; to dart, as beams of brightness; to shine.

Light *radiates* from luminous bodies directly to our eyes. *Locke.*

2. To issue and proceed in direct lines from a point.

RA'DIATE, *v. t.* To enlighten; to illuminate; to shed light or brightness on. [Usually *irradiate*.] *Hewyt.*

RA'DIATE, *a.* In *botany*, a *rayed* or *radiate* corol or flower, is a compound flower consisting of a disk, in which the corollets or florets are tubular and regular, and of a ray, in which the florets are irregular. *Martyn.*

Or a flower with several semiflosculous florets set round a disk in form of a radiant star. *Encyc.*

RA'DIATED, *pp.* Adorned with rays of light. *Addison.*

2. Having crystals diverging from a center. *Mineralogy.*

RA'DIATING, *ppr.* Darting rays of light; enlightening; as the *radiating* point in optics.

RADIA'TION, *n.* [L. *radiatio*.] The emission and diffusion of rays of light; beamy brightness. *Bacon.*

2. The shooting of any thing from a center, like the diverging rays of light.

RAD'ICAL, *a.* [Fr. from L. *radicalis*, from *radix*, root. See *Race* and *Ray*.]

1. Pertaining to the root or origin; original; fundamental; as a *radical* truth or error; a *radical* evil; a *radical* difference of opinions or systems.

2. Implanted by nature; native; constitutional; as the *radical* moisture of a body. *Bacon.*

3. Primitive; original; underived; uncompounded; as a *radical* word.

4. Serving to origination.

5. In *botany*, proceeding immediately from the root; as a *radical* leaf or peduncle. *Martyn.*

RAD'ICAL, *n.* In *philology*, a primitive word; a radix, root, or simple underived uncompounded word.

2. A primitive letter; a letter that belongs to the radix.

3. In *chimistry*, an element, or a simple constituent part of a substance, which is incapable of decomposition. *Parke.*

That which constitutes the distinguishing part of an acid, by its union with oxygen. *Ure.*

Compound radical, is the base of an acid composed of two or more substances. Thus a vegetable acid having a radical composed of hydrogen and carbon, is said to be an acid with a *compound radical*.

Radical quantities, in algebra, quantities whose roots may be accurately expressed in numbers. The term is sometimes extended to all quantities under the radical sign.

Radical sign, the sign $\surd$ placed before any quantity, denoting that its root is to be extracted; thus, $\sqrt{a}$ or $\sqrt{a+b}$. *Encyc. Bailey.*

RADICAL'ITY, *n.* Origination. *Brown.*

2. A being radical; a quantity which has relation to a root. *Bailey.*

RAD'ICALLY, *adv.* Originally; at the origin or root; fundamentally; as a scheme or system *radically* wrong or defective.

2. Primitively; essentially; originally; without derivation.

These great orbs thus *radically* bright. *Prior.*

RAD'ICALNESS, *n.* The state of being radical or fundamental.

RAD'ICANT, *a.* [L. *radicans*.] In *botany*, rooting; as a *radicant* stem or leaf. *Lee. Martyn.*

RAD'ICATE, *v. t.* [L. *radicatus*, *radicor*, from *radix*, root.]
To root; to plant deeply and firmly; as *radicated* opinions; *radicated* knowledge. *Glanville.*

Meditation will *radicate* these seeds— *Hammond.*

RAD'ICATE, RAD'ICATED, *pp.* or *a.* Deeply planted.

—Prejudices of a whole race of people *radicated* by a succession of ages. *Burke.*

RADICA'TION, *n.* [from *radicate*.] The process of taking root deeply; as the *radication* of habits.

2. In *botany*, the disposition of the root of a plant with respect to the ascending and descending caudex and the radicles. *Lee.*

RAD'ICLE, *n.* [L. *radicula*, from *radix*.]

1. That part of the seed of a plant which upon vegetating becomes the root. *Encyc.*

2. The fibrous part of a root, by which the stock or main body of it is terminated. *Martyn.*

RADIOM'ETER, *n.* [L. *radius*, rod, and Gr. μετρον, measure.]
The forestaff, an instrument for taking the altitudes of celestial bodies. *Ash.*

RAD'ISH, *n.* [Sax. *rædic*; D. *radys*; G. *radiess*; Corn. *rydhik*; Ir. *raidis*; W. *rhuzygyl*, from *rhuzyg*, red. See *Ruddy*.]
A plant of the genus Raphanus, the root of which is eaten raw. *Horse-radish* is of the genus Cochlearia. *Water-radish* is of the genus Sisymbrium.

RA'DIUS, *n.* [L. *id.* a *ray*, a *rod*, a beam, a spoke, that is, a shoot; *radio*, to shine, that is, to dart beams. See *Ray*.]

1. In *geometry*, a right line drawn or extending from the center of a circle to the periphery, and hence the semidiameter of the circle. In trigonometry, the radius is the whole sine, or sine of 90°.

2. In *anatomy*, the exterior bone of the fore arm, descending along with the ulna from the elbow to the wrist.

3. In *botany*, a ray; the outer part or circumference of a compound radiate flower, or radiated discous flower. *Martyn.*

RA'DIX, *n.* [L. a root.] In etymology, a primitive word from which spring other words.

2. In *logarithms*, the base of any system of logarithms, or that number whose logarithm is unity. Thus in Briggs', or the common system of logarithms, the radix is 10; in Napier's, it is 2.7182818284. All other numbers are considered as some powers or roots of the radix, the exponents of which powers or roots, constitute the logarithms of those numbers respectively.

3. In *algebra*, radix sometimes denotes the root of a finite expression, from which a series is derived. *Hutton.*

R'AFF, *v. t.* [G. *raffen*, to sweep, to seize or snatch. It seems to be from the root of

Sax. *reafian*, L. *rapio*; Ch. Syr. Heb. גרף, Ar. جرف jarafa, to sweep away; Persic روفتن roftan, id.]

To sweep; to snatch, draw or huddle together; to take by a promiscuous sweep. *Obs.*

Their causes and effects I thus *raff* up together. *Carew.*

R'AFF, *n.* The sweepings of society; the rabble; the mob [*colluvies.*] This is used chiefly in the compound or duplicate, *riff-raff.* [Pers. روفته roftah, L. *quisquiliæ*, sweepings.]

2. A promiscuous heap or collection; a jumble. *Barrow.*

RAF'FLE, *v. i.* [Fr. *rafler*, to sweep away, to sweep stakes; D. *ryffelen*; Sp. *rifar*, to *raffle*, and to *strive*, to quarrel, to dispute, and to *rive*, to split a sail; Port. *rifa*, a set of cards of the same color, and a raffle or raffling, also a craggy or steep place; *rifar*, to neigh, as a mettlesome horse; probably from *riving*, opening with a burst of sound, or as we say, to *rip out* (an oath.) The Sp. *rifar*, to strive, is precisely the Heb. רוב, to strive; Syr. to make a tumult or clamor; all from driving or violence. See Class Rb. No. 4. 12. 19. Pers. روفتن roftan, to sweep, to clean the teeth. See *Raff.*]

To cast dice for a prize, for which each person concerned in the game lays down a stake, or hazards a part of the value; as, to *raffle* for a watch.

RAF'FLE, *n.* A game of chance, or lottery in which several persons deposit a part of the value of the thing, in consideration of the chance of gaining it. The successful thrower of the dice takes or sweeps the whole.

RAF'FLER, *n.* One who raffles.

RAF'FLING, *ppr.* The act of throwing dice for a prize staked by a number.

R'AFT, *n.* [In Dan. *raft* is a rack for hay; in Sax. *reafian* is the L. *rapio*; qu. from floating, sweeping along, or Gr. ῥαπτω, to sew, that is, to fasten together, and allied to *reeve*; or Gr. ερεφω, whence οροφη, a flooring. [See *Rafter* and *Roof.*]

An assemblage of boards, planks or pieces of timber fastened together horizontally and floated down a stream; a float. *Shak. Pope.*

R'AFT, *pp.* [Sax. *reafian*, to seize, L. *rapio*; *bereafian*, to snatch away, to bereave.]

Torn; rent; severed. *Obs.* *Spenser.*

R'AFTER, *n.* [Sax. *ræfter*; Gr. ερεφω, to cover; οροφη, a roof; Russ. *strop*, a roof.]

A roof timber; a piece of timber that extends from the plate of a building to the ridge and serves to support the covering of the roof. *Milton. Pope.*

R'AFTERED, *a.* Built or furnished with rafters.

R'AFTY, *a.* Damp; musty. [*Local.*] *Robinson.*

RAG, *n.* [Sax. *hracod*, torn, *ragged*; *racian*, to rake; Dan. *rager*, to rake; *ragerie*, old clothes; Sw. *raka*, to shave; *ragg*, rough hair; Gr. ῥακος, a torn garment; ῥακοω, to tear; ῥαγας, a rupture, a rock, a *crag*; ῥαγοω, to tear asunder; W. *rhwygaw*, to rend; Arm. *roga*, id. The Spanish has the word in the compounds *andrajo*, a rag, *andrajoso*, ragged; It. *straccio*, a rent, a rag; *stracciare*, to tear; Ar. خرق charaka or garaka, to tear. Class Rg. No. 34.]

1. Any piece of cloth torn from the rest; a tattered cloth, torn or worn till its texture is destroyed. Linen and cotton *rags* are the chief materials of paper.

2. Garments worn out; proverbially, mean dress.

Drowsiness shall clothe a man with *rags*. Prov. xxiii.

And virtue, though in *rags*, will keep me warm. *Dryden.*

3. A fragment of dress. *Hudibras.*

RAG, *v. t.* [Qu. Sax. *wregian*, to accuse; or from the root of *rage*. The sense is to break or burst forth.]

To scold; to rail. [*Local.*] *Pegge.*

RAGAMUF'FIN, *n.* [Qu. *rag* and Sp. *mofar*, to mock, or It. *muffo*, musty.]

A paltry fellow; a mean wretch. *Swift.*

RAG'-BOLT, *n.* An iron pin with barbs on its shank to retain it in its place. *Mar. Dict.*

RAĠE, *n.* [Fr. *rage*, whence *enrager*, to enrage; Corn. *arraich*; Arm. *arragi*, *arragein*, to enrage. This belongs to the family of *Rg*, to break or burst forth. See *Rag.* Perhaps Heb. Ch. Syr. חרק, to grind or gnash the teeth; in Ar. to burn, to break, to *crack*, to grind the teeth, to be angry. The radical sense of *burn* is in many cases to rage or be violent. Class Rg. No. 34.]

1. Violent anger accompanied with furious words, gestures or agitation; anger excited to fury. Passion sometimes rises to *rage*.

Torment and loud lament and furious *rage*. *Milton.*

2. Vehemence or violent exacerbation of any thing painful; as the *rage* of pain; the *rage* of a fever; the *rage* of hunger or thirst. *Pope.*

3. Fury; extreme violence; as the *rage* of a tempest.

4. Enthusiasm; rapture.

Who brought green poesy to her perfect age,
And made that art which was a *rage*. *Cowley.*

5. Extreme eagerness or passion directed to some object; as the *rage* for money.

You purchase pain with all that joy can give,
And die of nothing but a *rage* to live. *Pope.*

RAĠE, *v. i.* To be furious with anger; to be exasperated to fury; to be violently agitated with passion.

At this he inly *rag'd*. *Milton.*

2. To be violent and tumultuous.

Why do the heathen *rage*? Ps. ii.

3. To be violently driven or agitated; as the *raging* sea or winds.

4. To ravage; to prevail without restraint, or with fatal effect; as, the plague *rages* in Cairo.

5. To be driven with impetuosity; to act or move furiously.

The chariots shall *rage* in the streets. Nah. ii.

The madding wheels of brazen chariots *rag'd*. *Milton.*

6. To toy wantonly; to sport. [*Not in use.*] *Gower.*

RA'ĠEFUL, *a.* Full of rage; violent; furious. *Sidney. Hammond.*

RA'ĠERY, *n.* Wantonness. [*Not used.*] *Chaucer.*

RAGG, *n.* Rowley ragg, a species of silicious stone, of a dusky or dark gray color, with shining crystals, of a granular texture, and by exposure to the air acquiring an ochery crust. *Encyc.*

RAG'GED, *a.* [from *rag.*] Rent or worn into tatters, or till its texture is broken; as a *ragged* coat; a *ragged* sail. *Arbuthnot.*

2. Broken with rough edges; uneven; as a *ragged* rock.

3. Having the appearance of being broken or torn; jagged; rough with sharp or irregular points.

The moon appears, when looked upon through a good glass, rude and *ragged*. *Burnet.*

4. Wearing tattered clothes; as a *ragged* fellow.

5. Rough; rugged.

What shepherd owns those *ragged* sheep? *Dryden.*

RAG'GEDNESS, *n.* The state of being dressed in tattered clothes.

2. The state of being rough or broken irregularly; as the *raggedness* of a cliff.

RA'ĠING, *ppr.* [from *rage.*] Acting with violence or fury.

2. *a.* Furious; impetuous; vehemently driven or agitated; as the *raging* sea or tempest.

RA'ĠING, *n.* Fury; violence; impetuosity. Jonah i.

RA'ĠINGLY, *adv.* With fury; with violent impetuosity. *Hall.*

RAG'MAN, *n.* A man who collects or deals in rags, the materials of paper. *Rawlinson.*

RAGMAN'S-ROLL, *n.* A roll or register of the value of benefices in Scotland, made by Ragimund, a legate of the pope, according to which the clergy were afterwards taxed by the court of Rome. [See *Rigmarole.*] *Encyc.*

RAGOO', **RAGOUT**, *n.* [Fr. *ragout*; Arm. *ragoud.*] A sauce or seasoning for exciting a languid appetite; or a high seasoned dish, prepared with fish, flesh, greens and the like, stewed with salt, pepper, cloves, &c. *Encyc.*

RAG'STONE, *n.* A stone of the silicious kind, so named from its rough fracture. It is of a gray color, the texture obscurely laminar or rather fibrous, the lamins consisting of a congeries of grains of a quartzy appearance, coarse and rough. It effervesces with acids, and gives fire with steel. It is used for a whetstone without oil or water, for sharpening coarse cutting tools. *Encyc. Nicholson.*

RAG'WŎRT, *n.* A plant of the genus Senecio.

RAIL, *n.* [G. *riegel*, rail, bolt or bar; W. *rhail.*]

1. A cross beam fixed at the ends in two upright posts. *Moxon.*

[In New England, this is never called a *beam*; pieces of timber of the proper size for rails are called *scantling*.]

2. In *the United States*, a piece of timber cleft, hewed or sawed, rough or smooth, inserted in upright posts for fencing. The common *rails* among farmers, are rough, being used as they are split from the chestnut or other trees. The *rails* used in fences of boards or pickets round gentlemen's houses and gardens, are usually sawed scantling and often dressed with the plane.

3. A bar of wood or iron used for inclosing any place; the piece into which ballusters are inserted.

4. A series of posts connected with cross beams, by which a place is inclosed. *Johnson.*

In New England we never call this series a *rail*, but by the general term *railing*. In a picket fence, the pales or pickets rise above the rails; in a ballustrade, or fence resembling it, the ballusters usually terminate in the rails.

5. In *a ship*, a narrow plank nailed for ornament or security on a ship's upper works; also, a curved piece of timber extending from the bows of a ship to the continuation of its stern, to support the knee of the head, &c. *Mar. Dict.*

RAIL, *n.* A bird of the genus Rallus, consisting of many species. The water rail has a long slender body with short concave wings. The birds of this genus inhabit the slimy margins of rivers and ponds covered with marsh plants. *Encyc.*

RAIL, *n.* [Sax. *hrægle*, *rægle*, from *wrigan*, to put on or cover, to *rig*.]

A woman's upper garment; retained in the word *nightrail*, but not used in the United States.

RAIL, *v. t.* To inclose with rails. *Carew. Spectator.*

2. To range in a line. *Bacon.*

RAIL, *v. i.* [D. *rallen*, to jabber; Sp. *rallar*, to grate, to molest; Port. *ralhar*, to swagger, to hector, to huff, to scold. This corresponds nearly with the G. *prahlen*, which may be the same word with a prefix, Eng. to *brawl*, Fr. *brailler*; Sw. *ralla*, to prate; Fr. *railler*, to rally. In Dan. *driller* signifies to drill and to banter.]

To utter reproaches; to scoff; to use insolent and reproachful language; to reproach or censure in opprobrious terms; followed by *at* or *against*, formerly by *on*. *Shak.*

And *rail at* arts he did not understand. *Dryden.*

Lesbia forever *on* me *rails*. *Swift.*

RAIL-BIRD, *n.* A bird of the genus Cuculus. *Encyc.*

RA'ILER, *n.* One who scoffs, insults, censures or reproaches with opprobrious language. *South. Thomson.*

RA'ILING, *ppr.* Clamoring with insulting language; uttering reproachful words.

2. *a.* Expressing reproach; insulting; as a *railing* accusation. 2 Pet. ii.

RA'ILING, *n.* Reproachful or insolent language. 1 Pet. iii.

RA'ILING, *ppr.* Inclosing with rails.

RA'ILING, *n.* A series of rails; a fence.

2. Rails in general; or the scantling for rails.

RA'ILINGLY, *adv.* With scoffing or insulting language.

RA'ILLERY, *n.* [Fr. *raillerie.*] Banter; jesting language; good humored pleasantry or slight satire; satirical merriment.

Let *raillery* be without malice or heat. *B. Jonson.*

—Studies employed on low objects; the very naming of them is sufficient to turn them into *raillery*. *Addison.*

RA'ILLEUR, *n.* [Fr.] A banterer; a jester; a mocker. [*Not English nor in use.*] *Sprat.*

RA'IMENT, *n.* [for *arrayment*; Norm. *araer*, to *array*; *araies*, array, apparel. See *Array* and *Ray*.]

1. Clothing in general; vestments; vesture; garments. Gen. xxiv. Deut. viii.

Living, both food and *raiment* she supplies. *Dryden.*

2. A single garment. *Sidney.*

[*In this sense it is rarely used, and indeed is improper.*]

RAIN, *v. i.* [Sax. *hregnan*, *regnan*, *renian*, *rinan*, to rain; Goth. *rign*, rain; Sax. *racu*, Cimbric, *raekia*, rain; D. G. *regen*, rain; D. *regenen*, to rain; Sw. *regn*, rain; *regna*, to rain; Dan. *regn*, rain; *regner*, to rain; G. *beregnen*, to rain on. It seems that *rain* is contracted from *regen*. It is the Gr. βρεχω, to rain, to water, which we retain in *brook*, and the Latins, by dropping the prefix, in *rigo*, *irrigo*, to *irrigate*. The primary sense is to pour out, to drive forth, Ar. بَرَكَ baraka, coinciding with Heb. Ch. Syr. ברך. Class Brg. No. 3.]

1. To fall in drops from the clouds, as water; used mostly with *it* for a nominative; as, *it rains*; *it* will *rain*; *it rained*, or *it* has *rained*.

2. To fall or drop like rain; as, tears *rained* at their eyes. *Milton.*

RAIN, *v. t.* To pour or shower down from the upper regions, like rain from the clouds.

Then said the Lord to Moses, behold, I will *rain* bread from heaven for you. Ex. xvi.

God shall cast the fury of his wrath upon him, and shall *rain* it upon him while he is eating. Job xx.

Upon the wicked he shall *rain* snares, fire and brimstone, and a horrible tempest. Ps. xi.

RAIN, *n.* [Sax. *rægn*, *regn*, *ren.*] The descent of water in drops from the clouds; or the water thus falling. *Rain* is distinguished from *mist*, by the size of the drops, which are distinctly visible. When water falls in very small drops or particles, we call it *mist*, and *fog* is composed of particles so fine as to be not only indistinguishable, but to float or be suspended in the air.

RA'INBAT, *a.* Beaten or injured by the rain. [*Not used.*] *Hall.*

RA'INBOW, *n.* A bow, or an arch of a circle, consisting of all the colors formed by the refraction and reflection of rays of light from drops of rain or vapor, appearing in the part of the hemisphere opposite to the sun. When the sun is at the horizon, the rainbow is a semicircle. The rainbow is called also *iris*. *Newton.*

The moon sometimes forms a bow or arch of light, more faint than that formed by the sun, and called *lunar rainbow*. Similar bows at sea are called *marine rainbows* or *sea bows*. *Encyc.*

RA'IN-DEER, *n.* [Sax. *hrana*; Basque, *orena* or *orina*.]

The rane, a species of the cervine genus; thus written Spect. No. 406. [See *Rane*.]

RA'ININESS, *n.* [from *rainy*.] The state of being rainy.

RA'IN-WATER, *n.* Water that has fallen from the clouds. *Boyle.*

RA'INY, *a.* Abounding with rain; wet; showery; as *rainy* weather; a *rainy* day or season.

RAISE, *v. t. raze.* [Goth. *raisyan*, *ur-raisyan*, to raise, to rouse, to excite; *ur-reisan*, to rise. This word occurs often in the Gothic version of the gospels, Luke iii. 8. John vi. 40. 44. In Sw. *resa* signifies to go, walk or travel, and to *raise*; Dan. *rejser*, the same. These verbs appear to be the L. *gradior*, *gressus*, without the prefix; and *gradior* is the Shemitic רדה, which has a variety of significations, but in Syriac, to go, to walk, to pass, as in Latin. Whether the Swedish and Danish verbs are from different roots, blended by usage or accident, or whether the different senses have proceeded from one common signification, to move, to open, to stretch, let the reader judge.]

1. To lift; to take up; to heave; to lift from a low or reclining posture; as, to *raise* a stone or weight; to *raise* the body in bed.

The angel smote Peter on the side and *raised* him up. Acts xii.

2. To set upright; as, to *raise* a mast.

3. To set up; to erect; to set on its foundations and put together; as, to *raise* the frame of a house.

4. To build; as, to *raise* a city, a fort, a wall, &c.

I will *raise* forts against thee. Is. xxix. Amos ix.

5. To rebuild.

They shall *raise* up the former desolations. Is. lxi.

6. To form to some highth by accumulation; as, to *raise* a heap of stones. Josh. viii.

7. To make; to produce; to amass; as, to *raise* a great estate out of small profits.

8. To enlarge; to amplify. *Shak.*

9. To exalt; to elevate in condition; as, to *raise* one from a low estate.

10. To exalt; to advance; to promote in rank or honor; as, to *raise* one to an office of distinction.

This gentleman came to be *raised* to great titles. *Clarendon.*

11. To enhance; to increase; as, to *raise* the value of coin; to *raise* the price of goods.

12. To increase in current value.

The plate pieces of eight were *raised* three pence in the piece. *Temple.*

13. To excite; to put in motion or action; as, to *raise* a tempest or tumult.

He commandeth and *raiseth* the stormy wind. Ps. cvii.

14. To excite to sedition, insurrection, war or tumult; to stir up. Acts xxiv.

Æneas then employs his pains
In parts remote to *raise* the Tuscan swains. *Dryden.*

15. To rouse; to awake; to stir up.

They shall not awake, nor be *raised* out of their sleep. Job xiv.

16. To increase in strength; to excite from languor or weakness. The pulse is *raised* by stimulants, sometimes by venesection.

17. To give beginning of importance to; to elevate into reputation; as, to *raise* a family.

18. To bring into being.

God vouchsafes to *raise* another world
From him. *Milton.*

19. To bring from a state of death to life.

He was delivered for our offenses, and *raised* again for our justification. Rom. iv. 1 Cor. xv.

20. To call into view from the state of separate spirits; as, to *raise* a spirit by spells and incantations. *Sandys.*

21. To invent and propagate; to originate; to occasion; as, to *raise* a report or story.

22. To set up; to excite; to begin by loud utterance; as, to *raise* a shout or cry. *Dryden.*

23. To utter loudly; to begin to sound or clamor. He *raised* his voice against the measures of administration.

24. To utter with more strength or elevation; to swell. Let the speaker *raise* his voice.

25. To collect; to obtain; to bring into a sum or fund. Government *raises* money by taxes, excise and imposts. Private persons and companies *raise* money for their enterprises.

26. To levy; to collect; to bring into service; as, to *raise* troops; to *raise* an army. *Milton.*

27. To give rise to. *Milton.*

28. To cause to grow; to procure to be produced, bred or propagated; as, to *raise* wheat, barley, hops, &c.; to *raise* horses, oxen or sheep. *New England.*

[The English now use *grow* in regard to crops; as, to *grow* wheat. This verb intransitive has never been used in New England in a transitive sense, until recently some persons have adopted it from the English books. We always use *raise*, but in New England it is never applied to the breeding of the human race, as it is in the southern states.]

29. To cause to swell, heave and become light; as, to *raise* dough or paste by yeast or leaven.

Miss Liddy can dance a jig and *raise* paste. *Spectator.*

30. To excite; to animate with fresh vigor; as, to *raise* the spirits or courage.

31. To ordain; to appoint; or to call to and prepare; to furnish with gifts and qualification suited to a purpose; *a Scriptural sense.*

I will *raise* them up a prophet from among their brethren. Deut. xviii.

For this cause have I *raised* thee up, to show in thee my power. Ex. ix. Judg. ii.

32. To keep in remembrance. Ruth iv.

33. To cause to exist by propagation. Matt. xxii.

34. To incite; to prompt. Ezra i.

35. To increase in intensity or strength; as, to *raise* the heat of a furnace.

36. In *seamen's language,* to elevate, as an object by a gradual approach to it; to bring to be seen at a greater angle; opposed to *laying;* as, to *raise* the land; to *raise* a point. *Mar. Dict.*

To raise a purchase, in seamen's language, is to dispose instruments or machines in such a manner as to exert any mechanical force required. *Mar. Dict.*

To raise a siege, is to remove a besieging army and relinquish an attempt to take the place by that mode of attack, or to cause the attempt to be relinquished.

RA'ISED, *pp.* Lifted; elevated; exalted; promoted; set upright; built; made or enlarged; produced; enhanced; excited; restored to life; levied; collected; roused; invented and propagated; increased.

RA'ISER, *n.* One who raises; that which raises; one that builds; one that levies or collects; one that begins, produces or propagates. *Bacon. Taylor.*

RAISIN, *n.* *răzn.* [Fr. Ir. *id.;* Arm. *ræsin, resin;* D. *rozyn;* G. *rosine,* a raisin, and *rosinfarbe,* crimson, [raisin-color;] Dan. *rosin.* In Dan. and Sw. *rosen* signifies the erysipelas. It is evident that the word is from the same root as *red* and *rose,* being named from the color. See *Red* and *Rose.* This word is in some places pronounced corruptly *reezn.* The pronunciation of Sheridan, Perry and Jameson accords with that which prevails in the eastern states, which is regular, and which I have followed.]

A dried grape. Grapes are suffered to remain on the vines till they are perfectly ripe, and then dried in an oven, or by exposure to the heat of the sun. Those dried in the sun are the sweetest. *Hill.*

RA'ISING, *ppr.* Lifting; elevating; setting upright; exalting; producing; enhancing; restoring to life; collecting; levying; propagating, &c.

RA'ISING, *n.* The act of lifting, setting up, elevating, exalting, producing, or restoring to life.

2. In New England, the operation or work of setting up the frame of a building.

RA'JAH, RA'JA, *n.* [L. *rex, regis.*] In India, a prince. Some of the rajahs are said to be independent princes; others are tributary to the Mogul. *Encyc.*

RA'JAHSHIP, *n.* The dignity or principality of a rajah. *Asiat. Res.*

RAKE, *n.* [Sax. *raca, race;* G. *rechen;* Ir. *raca;* W. *rhacai, rhacan.* See the Verb.]

An instrument consisting of a head-piece in which teeth are inserted, and a long handle; used for collecting hay or other light things which are spread over a large surface, or in gardens for breaking and smoothing the earth.

RAKE, *n.* [Dan. *rækel;* probably from the root of *break.*]

A loose, disorderly, vicious man; a man addicted to lewdness and other scandalous vices. *Addison. Pope.*

RAKE, *n.* [Sax. *racan,* to *reach.*] The projection of the upper parts of a ship, at the highth of the stem and stern, beyond the extremities of the keel. The distance between a perpendicular line from the extremity of stem or stern to the end of the keel, is the length of the rake; one the *fore-rake,* the other the *rake-aft.*

2. The inclination of a mast from a perpendicular direction. *Mar. Dict.*

RAKE, *v. t.* [Sax. *racian;* Sw. *raka;* Dan. *rager,* to shave, to rake; Corn. *rackan;* W. *rhacanu;* Ir. *racam;* G. *rechen;* Fr. *racler;* Arm. *racla.* The D. *hark, harken,* is our *harrow,* but of the same family, the great family of *break, crack,* L. *frico.* Class Rg. No. 34. 38. 47.]

1. Properly, to scrape; to rub or scratch with something rough; as, to *rake* the ground.

2. To gather with a rake; as, to *rake* hay or barley.

3. To clear with a rake; to smooth with a rake; as, to *rake* a bed in a garden; to *rake* land.

4. To collect or draw together something scattered; to gather by violence; as, to *rake* together wealth; to *rake* together slanderous tales; to *rake* together the rabble of a town.

5. To scour; to search with eagerness all corners of a place.

The statesman *rakes* the town to find a plot. *Swift.*

6. In *the military art,* to enfilade; to fire in a direction with the length of any thing; particularly in naval engagements, to *rake* is to cannonade a ship on the stern or head, so that the balls range the whole length of the deck. Hence the phrase, to *rake* a ship fore and aft.

To rake up, applied to fire, is to cover the fire with ashes.

RAKE, *v. i.* To scrape; to scratch into for finding something; to search minutely and meanly; as, to *rake* into a dunghill. *South.*

2. To search with minute inspection into every part.

One is for *raking* in Chaucer for antiquated words. *Dryden.*

3. To pass with violence or rapidity.

Pas could not stay, but over him did *rake.* *Sidney.*

4. To seek by raking; as, to *rake* for oysters.

5. To lead a dissolute, debauched life. *Shenstone.*

6. To incline from a perpendicular direction; as, a mast *rakes* aft.

RA'KED, *pp.* Scraped; gathered with a rake; cleaned with a rake; cannonaded fore and aft.

RA'KEHELL, *n.* [Dan. *rækel;* now contracted into *rake;* properly *rakel.*]

A lewd, dissolute fellow; a debauchee; a rake.

RA'KEHELLY, *a.* Dissolute; wild. *B. Jonson.*

RA'KER, *n.* One that rakes.

RA'KESHAME, *n.* A vile dissolute wretch. *Milton.*

RA'KING, *ppr.* Scraping; gathering with a rake; cleaning and smoothing with a rake; cannonading in the direction of the length; inclining.

And *raking* chase-guns through our sterns they send. *Dryden.*

2. *a.* That rakes; as a *raking* fire or shot.

RA'KING, *n.* The act of using a rake; the act or operation of collecting with a rake, or of cleaning and smoothing with a rake.

2. The space of ground raked at once; or the quantity of hay, &c. collected by once passing the rake.

RA'KISH, *a.* Given to a dissolute life; lewd; debauched. *Richardson.*

RA'KISHNESS, *n.* Dissolute practices.

RAL'LY, *v. t.* [Fr. *rallier.* This seems to be a compound of *re, ra,* and *lier,* L. *ligo,* to unite.]

1. To reunite; to collect and reduce to order troops dispersed or thrown into confusion.
2. To collect; to unite; as things scattered. *Atterbury.*

RAL'LY, *v. t.* [Fr. *railler.* See *Raillery.*] To treat with good humor and pleasantry, or with slight contempt or satire, according to the nature of the case.

> Honeycomb *rallies* me upon a country life. *Addison.*

> Strephon had long confess'd his am'rous pain,
> Which gay Corinna *rallied* with disdain. *Gay.*

RAL'LY, *v. i.* To assemble; to unite.

> Innumerable parts of matter chanced then to *rally* together and to form themselves into this new world. *Tillotson.*

2. To come back to order.

> The Grecians *rally* and their pow'rs unite. *Dryden.*

3. To use pleasantry or satirical merriment. *Johnson.*

RAL'LY, *n.* The act of bringing disordered troops to their ranks.

2. Exercise of good humor or satirical merriment.

RAM, *n.* [Sax. D. *ram;* G. *ramm,* but *rammbock,* ram-buck, is used. See the Verb.]

1. The male of the sheep or ovine genus; in some parts of England called a *tup.* In the United States, the word is applied, I believe, to no other male, except in the compound *ram-cat.*
2. In *astronomy,* Aries, the sign of the zodiac which the sun enters on the 21st of March, or a constellation of fixed stars in the figure of a ram. It is considered the first of the twelve signs.
3. An engine of war, used formerly for battering and demolishing the walls of cities; called a *battering-ram.* [See *Battering-ram.*]

RAM, *v. t.* [G. *rammen;* D. *rammeijen;* Dan. *ramler,* to ram or drive; *rammer,* to strike, to hit, to touch; W. *rham, rhum,* a thrusting, a projection forward. To the same family belong L. *ramus,* a branch, that is, a shoot or thrust, Heb. Ch. Syr. רמה ramah, to throw, to project, Eth. ረመየ rami, to strike; Ar. رمي ramai, to shoot, to throw or dart. Class Rm. No. 7. 8. 9. See *Cram.*]

1. To thrust or drive with violence; to force in; to drive down or together; as, to *ram* down a cartridge; to *ram* piles into the earth.
2. To drive, as with a battering ram.
3. To stuff; to cram.

RAM'ADAN, *n.* Among the Mohammedans, a solemn season of fasting.

RAM'AĠE, *n.* [L. *ramus,* a branch, whence Fr. *ramage.*]

1. Branches of trees. [*Not in use.*]
2. The warbling of birds sitting on boughs. *Drummond.*
3. [See *Rummage.*]

RAM'BLE, *v. i.* [It. *ramengare,* to ramble, to rove; Arm. *rambreal,* to rave; W. *rhempiaw,* to run to an extreme, to be infatuated, and *rhamu,* to rise or reach over, to soar. These seem to be allied to *roam, romp, rampant;* Ar. رام to exceed or go beyond, to depart. Class Rm. No. 5.]

1. To rove; to wander; to walk, ride or sail from place to place, without any determinate object in view; or to visit many places; to rove carelessly or irregularly; as, to *ramble* about the city; to *ramble* over the country.

> Never ask leave to go abroad, for you will be thought an idle *rambling* fellow. *Swift.*

2. To go at large without restraint and without direction.
3. To move without certain direction.

> O'er his ample sides, the *rambling* sprays
> Luxuriant shoot. *Thomson.*

RAM'BLE, *n.* A roving; a wandering; a going or moving from place to place without any determinate business or object; an irregular excursion.

> Coming home after a short christmas *ramble,* I found a letter upon my table. *Swift.*

RAM'BLER, *n.* One that rambles; a rover; a wanderer.

RAM'BLING, *ppr.* Roving; wandering; moving or going irregularly.

RAM'BLING, *n.* A roving; irregular excursion. *South.*

RAM'BOOZE, RAM'BUSE, } *n.* A drink made of wine, ale, eggs and sugar in winter, or of wine, milk, sugar and rose water in summer. *Bailey.*

RAM'EKIN, RAM'EQUINS, } *n.* [Fr. *ramequin.*] In *cookery,* small slices of bread covered with a farce of cheese and eggs. *Bailey.*

RAM'ENTS, *n.* [L. *ramenta,* a chip.] Scrapings; shavings. [*Not used.*] *Dict.*

2. In *botany,* loose scales on the stems of plants. *Linne.*

RA'MEOUS, *a.* [L. *ramus,* a branch.] In *botany,* belonging to a branch; growing on or shooting from a branch. *Lee.*

RAMIFICA'TION, *n.* [Fr. from L. *ramus,* a branch.]

1. The process of branching or shooting branches from a stem.
2. A branch; a small division proceeding from a main stock or channel; as the *ramifications* of a family; the *ramifications* of an artery. *Arbuthnot.*
3. A division or subdivision; as the *ramifications* of a subject or scheme.
4. In *botany,* the manner in which a tree produces its branches or boughs. *Lee.*
5. The production of figures resembling branches. *Encyc.*

RAM'IFIED, *pp.* Divided into branches.

RAM'IFȲ, *v. t.* [Fr. *ramifier;* L. *ramus,* a branch, and *facio,* to make.] To divide into branches or parts; as, to *ramify* an art, a subject or scheme. *Boyle.*

RAM'IFȲ, *v. i.* To shoot into branches, as the stem of a plant.

> When the asparagus begins to *ramify*— *Arbuthnot.*

2. To be divided or subdivided; as a main subject or scheme.

RAM'IFȲING, *ppr.* Shooting into branches or divisions.

RAM'ISH, *a.* [Dan. *ram,* bitter, strong scented.] Rank; strong scented. *Chaucer.*

RAM'ISHNESS, *n.* [from *ram.*] Rankness; a strong scent.

RAM'MED, *pp.* [See *Ram.*] Driven forcibly.

RAM'MER, *n.* One that rams or drives.

2. An instrument for driving any thing with force; as a *rammer* for driving stones or piles, or for beating the earth to more solidity.
3. A gun-stick; a ramrod; a rod for forcing down the charge of a gun.

RAM'MING, *ppr.* Driving with force.

RAMOON', *n.* A tree of America.

RA'MOUS, *a.* [L. *ramosus,* from *ramus,* a branch.]

1. In *botany,* branched, as a stem or root; having lateral divisions. *Martyn.*
2. Branchy; consisting of branches; full of branches. *Newton. Woodward.*

RAMP, *v. i.* [Fr. *ramper,* to creep; It. *rampa,* a paw; *rampare,* to paw; *rampicare,* to creep; W. *rhamp,* a rise or reach over; *rhamant,* a rising up, a vaulting or springing; *rhamu,* to reach over, to soar, to vault. See *Ramble* and *Romance.*]

1. To climb, as a plant; to creep up.

> Plants furnished with tendrils catch hold, and so *ramping* on trees, they mount to a great highth. *Ray.*

2. To spring; to leap; to bound; to prance; to frolick.

> Their bridles they would champ—
> And trampling the fine element, would fiercely *ramp.* *Spenser.*

> Sporting the lion *ramp'd.* *Milton.*

[In the latter sense, the word is usually written and pronounced *romp;* the word being originally pronounced with *a* broad.]

RAMP, *n.* A leap; a spring; a bound. *Milton.*

RAMPAL'LIAN, *n.* A mean wretch. [*Not in use.*] *Shak.*

RAMP'ANCY, *n.* [from *rampant.*] Excessive growth or practice; excessive prevalence; exuberance; extravagance; as the *rampancy* of vice. *South.*

RAMP'ANT, *a.* [Fr. from *ramper;* Sax. *rempend,* headlong. See *Ramp* and *Ramble.*]

1. Overgrowing the usual bounds; rank in growth; exuberant; as *rampant* weeds. *Clarissa.*
2. Overleaping restraint; as *rampant* vice. *South.*
3. In *heraldry,* applied to the lion, leopard or other beast, *rampant* denotes the animal reared and standing on his hind legs, in the posture of climbing. It differs from *saliant,* which indicates the posture of springing or making a sally. *Encyc.*

> The lion *rampant* shakes his brinded mane. *Milton.*

RAM'PART, *n.* [Fr. *rempart;* Arm. *ramparz, ramparzi;* Fr. *se remparer,* to fence or intrench one's self; It. *riparamento,* from *riparare,* to repair, to defend, to stop; Port. *reparo; reparar,* to repair, to *parry* in defense. Hence we see *rampart* is from L. *reparo; re* and *paro.* See *Parry* and *Repair.*]

1. In *fortification,* an elevation or mound of earth round a place, capable of resisting cannon shot, and formed into bastions, curtains, &c. *Encyc.*

> No standards from the hostile *ramparts* torn. *Prior.*

2. That which fortifies and defends from assault; that which secures safety.

RAM'PART, *v. t.* To fortify with ramparts. [*Not in use.*] *Shak.*

RAM'PION, *n.* [from *ramp.*] The name of several plants; as the *common esculent rampion*, a species of Campanula; the *crested rampion*, a species of Lobelia; the *horned rampion*, a species of Phyteuma. *Fam. of Plants.*

RAMP'IRE, *n.* The same as *rampart;* but obsolete.

RAM'SONS, *n.* A plant, a species of Allium. *Fam. of Plants.*

RAN, the *pret.* of *run.* In old writers, open robbery. *Lambard.*

RANCES'CENT, *a.* [L. *ranceo*, to be rank.] Becoming rancid or sour. *Encyc.*

RANCH, *v. t.* [corrupted from *wrench.*] To sprain; to injure by violent straining or contortion. [*Not used.*] *Dryden. Garth.*

RAN'CID, *a.* [L. *rancidus*, from *ranceo*, to be rank. This is the Eng. *rank*, luxuriant in growth.]

Having a rank smell; strong scented; sour; musty; as *rancid* oil. *Arbuthnot.*

RANCID'ITY, **RAN'CIDNESS**, *n.* The quality of being rancid; a strong, sour scent, as of old oil.

> The *rancidity* of oils may be analogous to the oxydation of metals. *Ure.*

RAN'COR, *n.* [L. from *ranceo*, to be *rank.*]

1. The deepest malignity or spite; deep seated and implacable malice; inveterate enmity. [*This is the strongest term for enmity which the English language supplies.*]

> It issues from the *rancor* of a villain. *Shak.*

2. Virulence; corruption. *Shak.*

RAN'COROUS, *a.* Deeply malignant; implacably spiteful or malicious; intensely virulent.

> So flam'd his eyes with rage and *ranc'rous* ire. *Spenser.*
>
> *Rancorous* opposition to the gospel of Christ. *West.*

RAN'COROUSLY, *adv.* With deep malignity or spiteful malice.

RAND, *n.* [G. D. Dan. *rand*, a border, edge, margin, brink; from shooting out, extending.]

A border; edge; margin; as the *rand* of a shoe.

RAN'DOM, *n.* [Norm. Sax. *randun;* Fr. *randonnée*, a rapid course of water; *randon*, a gushing.]

1. A roving motion or course without direction; hence, want of direction, rule or method; hazard; chance; used in the phrase, *at random*, that is, without a settled point of direction; at hazard.

2. Course; motion; progression; distance of a body thrown; as the furthest *random* of a missile weapon. *Digby.*

RAN'DOM, *a.* Done at hazard or without settled aim or purpose; left to chance; as a *random* blow.

2. Uttered or done without previous calculation; as a *random* guess.

RAN'DOM-SHOT, *n.* A shot not directed to a point, or a shot with the muzzle of the gun elevated above a horizontal line. *Mar. Dict.*

RAN'DY, *a.* Disorderly; riotous. [*Not used or local.*] *Grose.*

RANE, **RANEDEER**, *n.* [Sax. *hrana;* Fr. *renne;* D. *rendier;* G. *rennthier;* Basque, *oreña* or *orina;* so named probably from *running.* The true spelling is *rane.*]

A species of deer found in the northern parts of Europe and Asia. He has large branched palmated horns, and travels with great speed. Among the Laplanders, he is a substitute for the horse, the cow, the goat and the sheep, as he furnishes food, clothing and the means of conveyance. This animal will draw a sled on the snow more than a hundred miles in a day. *Encyc.*

RAN'FŌRCE, *n.* The ring of a gun next to the vent. *Bailey.*

[I do not find this word in modern books.]

RANG, the old *pret.* of *ring.* [*Nearly obsolete.*]

RĀNĠE, *v. t.* [Fr. *ranger;* Arm. *rencqa*, *ranqein;* W. *rhenciaw*, from *rhenc*, *reng*, rank, which see.]

1. To set in a row or in rows; to place in a regular line, lines or ranks; to dispose in the proper order; as, to *range* troops in a body; to *range* men or ships in the order of battle.

2. To dispose in proper classes, orders or divisions; as, to *range* plants and animals in genera and species.

3. To dispose in a proper manner; to place in regular method; *in a general sense. Range* and *arrange* are used indifferently in the same sense.

4. To rove over; to pass over.

> Teach him to *range* the ditch and force the brake. *Gay.*

[This use is elliptical, *over* being omitted.]

5. To sail or pass in a direction parallel to or near; as, to *range the coast*, that is, *along the coast.*

RĀNĠE, *v. i.* To rove at large; to wander without restraint or direction.

> As a roaring lion and a *ranging* bear. Prov. xxviii.

2. To be placed in order; to be ranked.

> 'Tis better to be lowly born,
> And *range* with humble livers in content— *Shak.*

[In this sense, *rank* is now used.]

3. To lie in a particular direction.

> Which way thy forests *range*— *Dryden.*

We say, the front of a house *ranges* with the line of the street.

4. To sail or pass near or in the direction of; as, to *range* along the coast.

RĀNĠE, *n.* [Fr. *rangée.* See *Rank.*] A row; a rank; things in a line; as a *range* of buildings; a *range* of mountains; *ranges* of colors. *Newton.*

2. A class; an order.

> The next *range* of beings above him are the immaterial intelligences— *Hale.*

3. A wandering or roving; excursion.

> He may take a *range* all the world over. *South.*

4. Space or room for excursion.

> A man has not enough *range* of thought— *Addison.*

5. Compass or extent of excursion; space taken in by any thing extended or ranked in order; as the *range* of Newton's thought. No philosopher has embraced a wider *range.*

> Far as creation's ample *range* extends. *Pope.*

6. The step of a ladder. [Corrupted in popular language to *rung.*] *Clarendon.*

7. A kitchen grate. *Bacon. Wotton.*

8. A bolting sieve to sift meal.

9. In *gunnery*, the path of a bullet or bomb, or the line it describes from the mouth of the piece to the point where it lodges; or the whole distance which it passes. When a cannon lies horizontally, it is called the right level, or point blank range; when the muzzle is elevated to 45 degrees, it is called the utmost range. To this may be added the ricochet, the rolling or bounding shot, with the piece elevated from three to six degrees. *Encyc. Mar. Dict.*

RĀNĠED, *pp.* Disposed in a row or line; placed in order; passed in roving; placed in a particular direction.

RĀNĠER, *n.* One that ranges; a rover; a robber. [*Now little used.*] *Spenser.*

2. A dog that beats the ground. *Gay.*

3. In *England*, a sworn officer of a forest, appointed by the king's letters patent, whose business is to walk through the forest, watch the deer, present trespasses, &c. *Encyc*

RĀNĠERSHIP, *n.* The office of the keeper of a forest or park.

RĀNĠING, *ppr.* Placing in a row or line; disposing in order, method or classes; roving; passing near and in the direction of.

RĀNĠING, *n.* The act of placing in lines or in order; a roving, &c.

RANK, *n.* [Ir. *ranc;* W. *rhenc;* Arm. *rencq;* Fr. *rang*, a row or line; It. *rango*, rank, condition; Port. Sp. *rancho*, a mess or set of persons; D. Dan. G. *rang.* In these words, *n* is probably casual; Ar. رَكَّا to set in order; Heb. Ch. ערך id. Class Rg. No. 13. 47. See also No. 18. 20. 21. 27. 46. The primary sense is probably to *reach*, to *stretch*, or to pass, to stretch along. Hence *rank* and *grade* are often synonymous.]

1. A row or line, applied to troops; a line of men standing abreast or side by side, and as opposed to *file*, a line running the length of a company, battalion or regiment. Keep your *ranks;* dress your *ranks.*

> Fierce fiery warriors fight upon the clouds
> In *ranks* and squadrons and right form of war. *Shak.*

2. *Ranks*, in the plural, the order of common soldiers; as, to reduce an officer to the *ranks.*

3. A row; a line of things, or things in a line; as a *rank* of osiers. *Shak.*

4. Degree; grade; *in military affairs;* as the *rank* of captain, colonel or general; the *rank* of vice-admiral.

5. Degree of elevation in civil life or station; the order of elevation or of subordination. We say, all *ranks* and orders of men; every man's dress and behavior should correspond with his *rank;* the highest and the lowest *ranks* of men or of other intelligent beings.

6. Class; order; division; any portion or number of things to which place, degree or order is assigned. Profligate men, by

their vices, sometimes degrade themselves to the *rank* of brutes.

7. Degree of dignity, eminence or excellence; as a writer of the first *rank*; a lawyer of high *rank*.

These are all virtues of a meaner *rank*. *Addison.*

8. Dignity; high place or degree in the orders of men; as a man of *rank*.

Rank and file, the order of common soldiers. Ten officers and three hundred *rank and file* fell in the action.

To fill the ranks, to supply the whole number, or a competent number.

To take rank, to enjoy precedence, or to have the right of taking a higher place. In G. Britain, the king's sons *take rank* of all the other nobles.

RANK, *a.* [Sax. *ranc*, proud, haughty; Sp. It. *rancio*; L. *rancidus*, from *ranceo*, to smell strong. The primary sense of the root is to advance, to shoot forward, to grow luxuriantly, whence the sense of strong, vigorous; W. *rhac*, *rhag*, before; *rhacu*, *rhaciaw*, to advance, to put forward. This word belongs probably to the same family as the preceding.]

1. Luxuriant in growth; being of vigorous growth; as *rank* grass; *rank* weeds.

Seven ears came up upon one stalk, *rank* and good. Gen. xli.

2. Causing vigorous growth; producing luxuriantly; very rich and fertile; as, land is *rank*. *Mortimer.*

3. Strong scented; as *rank* smelling rue. *Spenser.*

4. Rancid; musty; as oil of a *rank* smell.

5. Inflamed with venereal appetite. *Shak.*

6. Strong to the taste; high tasted.

Divers sea fowls taste *rank* of the fish on which they feed. *Boyle.*

7. Rampant; high grown; raised to a high degree; excessive; as *rank* pride; *rank* idolatry.

I do forgive
Thy *rankest* faults. *Shak.*

8. Gross; coarse. *Shak.*

9. Strong; clinching. Take *rank* hold. Hence,

10. Excessive; exceeding the actual value; as a *rank* modus in law. *Blackstone.*

To set rank, as the iron of a plane, to set it so as to take off a thick shaving. *Moxon.*

RANK, *v. t.* To place abreast or in a line. *Milton.*

2. To place in a particular class, order or division.

Poets were *ranked* in the class of philosophers. *Broome.*

Heresy is *ranked* with idolatry and witchcraft. *Decay of Piety.*

3. To dispose methodically; to place in suitable order.

Who now shall rear you to the sun, or *rank* your tribes? *Milton.*

Ranking all things under general and special heads. *Watts.*

RANK, *v. i.* To be ranged; to be set or disposed; as in a particular degree, class, order or division.

Let that one article *rank* with the rest. *Shak.*

2. To be placed in a rank or ranks.

Go, *rank* in tribes, and quit the savage wood. *Tate.*

3. To have a certain grade or degree of elevation in the orders of civil or military life. He *ranks* with a major. He *ranks* with the first class of poets. He *ranks* high in public estimation.

RANK'ED, *pp.* Placed in a line; disposed in an order or class; arranged methodically.

RANK'ER, *n.* One that disposes in ranks; one that arranges.

RANK'ING, *ppr.* Placing in ranks or lines; arranging; disposing in orders or classes; having a certain rank or grade.

RANK'LE, *v. i.* [from *rank*.] To grow more rank or strong; to be inflamed; to fester; as a *rankling* wound.

A malady that burns and *rankles* inward. *Rowe.*

2. To become more violent; to be inflamed; to rage; as *rankling* malice; *rankling* envy. Jealousy *rankles* in the breast.

RANK'LY, *adv.* With vigorous growth; as, grass or weeds grow *rankly*.

2. Coarsely; grossly. *Shak.*

RANK'NESS, *n.* Vigorous growth; luxuriance; exuberance; as the *rankness* of plants or herbage.

2. Exuberance; excess; extravagance; as the *rankness* of pride; the *rankness* of joy. *Shak.*

3. Extraordinary strength.

The crane's pride is in the *rankness* of her wing. *L'Estrange.*

4. Strong taste; as the *rankness* of flesh or fish.

5. Rancidness; rank smell; as the *rankness* of oil.

6. Excessiveness; as the *rankness* of a composition or modus. *Blackstone.*

RAN'NY, *n.* The shrew-mouse. *Brown.*

RAN'SACK, *v. t.* [Dan. *randsager*; Sw. *ransaka*; Gaelic, *ransuchadh*. *Rand*, in Danish, is edge, margin, Eng. *rand*, and *ran* is rapine. The last syllable coincides with the English verb to *sack*, to pillage, and in Spanish, this verb which is written *saquear*, signifies to ransack.]

1. To plunder; to pillage completely; to strip by plundering; as, to *ransack* a house or city. *Dryden.*

Their vow is made to *ransack* Troy. *Shak.*

2. To search thoroughly; to enter and search every place or part. It seems often to convey the sense of opening doors and parcels, and turning over things in search; as, to *ransack* files of papers.

I *ransack* the several caverns. *Woodward.*

3. To violate; to ravish; to deflour; as *ransacked* chastity. [*Not in use.*] *Spenser.*

RAN'SACKED, *pp.* Pillaged; searched narrowly.

RAN'SACKING, *ppr.* Pillaging; searching narrowly.

RAN'SŎM, *n.* [Dan. *ranzon*; Sw. *ranson*; G. *ranzion*; Norm. *raancon*; Fr. *rançon*; Arm. *rançzon*. In French, the word implies not only redemption, but exaction; but I know not the component parts of the word. Qu. G. *sühne*, atonement.]

1. The money or price paid for the redemption of a prisoner or slave, or for goods captured by an enemy; that which procures the release of a prisoner or captive, or of captured property, and restores the one to liberty and the other to the original owner.

By his captivity in Austria, and the heavy *ransom* he paid for his liberty, Richard was hindered from pursuing the conquest of Ireland. *Davies.*

2. Release from captivity, bondage or the possession of an enemy. They were unable to procure the *ransom* of the prisoners.

3. In *law*, a sum paid for the pardon of some great offense and the discharge of the offender; or a fine paid in lieu of corporal punishment. *Encyc. Blackstone.*

4. In *Scripture*, the price paid for a forfeited life, or for delivery or release from capital punishment.

Then he shall give for the *ransom* of his life, whatever is laid upon him. Ex. xxi.

5. The price paid for procuring the pardon of sins and the redemption of the sinner from punishment.

Deliver him from going down to the pit; I have found a *ransom*. Job xxxiii.

The Son of man came—to give his life a *ransom* for many. Matt. xx. Mark x.

RAN'SŎM, *v. t.* [Sw. *ransonera*; Dan. *ranzonerer*; Fr. *rançonner*; Arm. *rançzouna*.]

1. To redeem from captivity or punishment by paying an equivalent; *applied to persons*; as, to *ransom* prisoners from an enemy.

2. To redeem from the possession of an enemy by paying a price deemed equivalent; *applied to goods or property*.

3. In *Scripture*, to redeem from the bondage of sin, and from the punishment to which sinners are subjected by the divine law.

The *ransomed* of the Lord shall return. Is. xxxv.

4. To rescue; to deliver. Hos. xiii.

RAN'SŎMED, *pp.* Redeemed or rescued from captivity, bondage or punishment by the payment of an equivalent.

RAN'SŎMER, *n.* One that redeems.

RAN'SŎMING, *ppr.* Redeeming from captivity, bondage or punishment by giving satisfaction to the possessor; rescuing; liberating.

RAN'SŎMLESS, *a.* Free from ransom. *Shak.*

RANT, *v. i.* [Heb. Ch. רנן, Ar. رنّ ranna, to cry out, to shout, to sound, groan, murmur; W. *rhonta*, to frisk, to gambol, a sense of the Hebrew also.]

To rave in violent, high sounding or extravagant language, without correspondent dignity of thought; to be noisy and boisterous in words or declamation; as a *ranting* preacher.

Look where my *ranting* host of the garter comes. *Shak.*

RANT, *n.* High sounding language without dignity of thought; boisterous, empty declamation; as the *rant* of fanatics.

This is stoical *rant*, without any foundation in the nature of man, or reason of things. *Atterbury.*

RANT'ER, *n.* A noisy talker; a boisterous preacher.

RANT'ING, *ppr.* Uttering high sounding words without solid sense; declaiming or preaching with boisterous empty words.

RANT'IPOLE, *a.* [from *rant.*] Wild; roving; rakish. [*A low word.*] *Congreve.*

RANT'IPOLE, *v. i.* To run about wildly. [*Low.*] *Arbuthnot.*

RANT'ISM, *n.* The practice or tenets of ranters. *Bp. Rust.*

RANT'Y, *a.* Wild; noisy; boisterous.

RAN'ULA, *n.* [L. *rana*, a frog; *dim.* a little frog.]

A swelling under the tongue, similar to the encysted tumors in different parts of the body. *Coxe.*

RANUN'CULUS, *n.* [L. from *rana*, a frog.]

In *botany*, crowfoot, a genus of plants of many species, some of them beautiful flowering plants, particularly the Asiatic, or Turkey and Persian ranunculus, which is diversified with many rich colors. *Encyc.*

RAP, *v. i.* [Sax. *hrepan*, *hreppan*, to touch; *repan*, to touch, to seize, L. *rapio*; Sw. *rappa*; Dan. *rapper*, to snatch away, and *rapper sig*, to hasten; *rap*, a stroke, Sw. *rapp*; Fr. *frapper*, to strike. The primary sense of the root is to rush, to drive forward, to fall on, hence both to strike and to seize. That the sense is to drive or rush forward, is evident from L. *rapidus*, rapid, from *rapio*. See Class Rb. No. 26. 27. 28. 29.]

To strike with a quick sharp blow; to knock; as, to *rap* on the door.

RAP, *v. t.* To strike with a quick blow; to knock.

> With one great peal they *rap* the door. *Prior.*

To rap out, to utter with sudden violence; as, to *rap out* an oath. *Addison.* [Sax. *hreopan*, to cry out, that is, to drive out the voice. This is probably of the same family as the preceding word. In the popular language of the U. States, it is often pronounced *rip*, to *rip out an oath*; L. *crepo*, Fr. *crever.*]

RAP, *v. t.* To seize and bear away, as the mind or thoughts; to transport out of one's self; to affect with ecstasy or rapture; as *rapt* into admiration.

> I'm *rapt* with joy to see my Marcia's tears. *Addison.*
>
> *Rapt* into future times the bard begun. *Pope.*

2. To snatch or hurry away.

> And *rapt* with whirling wheels. *Spenser.*
>
> *Rapt* in a chariot drawn by fiery steeds. *Milton.*

3. To seize by violence. *Drayton.*

4. To exchange; to truck. [*Low and not used.*]

To rap and rend, to seize and tear or strip; to fall on and plunder; to snatch by violence. They brought off all they could *rap and rend.* [See *Rend.*]

RAP, *n.* A quick smart blow; as a *rap* on the knuckles.

RAPA'CIOUS, *a.* [L. *rapax*, from *rapio*, to seize. See *Rap.*]

1. Given to plunder; disposed or accustomed to seize by violence; seizing by force; as a *rapacious* enemy.

> Well may thy lord, appeas'd,
> Redeem thee quite from death's *rapacious* claim. *Milton.*

2. Accustomed to seize for food; subsisting on prey or animals seized by violence; as a *rapacious* tiger; a *rapacious* fowl.

RAPA'CIOUSLY, *adv.* By rapine; by violent robbery or seizure.

RAPA'CIOUSNESS, *n.* The quality of being rapacious; disposition to plunder or to exact by oppression.

RAPAC'ITY, *n.* [Fr. *rapacité*; L. *rapacitas*, from *rapax*, *rapio.*]

1. Addictedness to plunder; the exercise of plunder; the act or practice of seizing by force; as the *rapacity* of a conquering army; the *rapacity* of pirates; the *rapacity* of a Turkish pashaw; the *rapacity* of extortioners.

2. Ravenousness; as the *rapacity* of animals.

3. The act or practice of extorting or exacting by oppressive injustice.

RAPE, *n.* [L. *rapio*, *raptus*; It. *ratto*; Fr. *rapt*; W. *rhaib*, a snatching; *rheibiaw*, to snatch. See *Rap.*]

1. In *a general sense*, a seizing by violence; also, a seizing and carrying away by force, as females. *Milford.*

2. In *law*, the carnal knowledge of a woman forcibly and against her will. *Blackstone.*

3. Privation; the act of seizing or taking away. *Chapman.*

> And ruin'd orphans of thy *rapes* complain. *Sandys.*

4. Something taken or seized and carried away.

> Where now are all my hopes? oh, never more
> Shall they revive, nor death her *rapes* restore. *Sandys.*

5. Fruit plucked from the cluster. *Ray.*

6. A division of a county in Sussex, in England; or an intermediate division between a hundred and a shire, and containing three or four hundreds. *Blackstone.*

RAPE, *n.* [Ir. *raib*; L. *rapa*, *rapum*; Gr. ῥαπυς; D. *raap*; G. *rübe*; Sw. *rofva.*]

A plant of the genus Brassica, called also cole-rape and cole-seed, and of which the navew or French turnip is a variety. *Lee. Ed. Encyc.*

The *broom-rape* is of the genus Orobanche.

RA'PEROOT. [See *Rape.*]

RA'PESEED, *n.* The seed of the rape, from which oil is expressed.

RAP'ID, *a.* [L. *rapidus*, from *rapio*, the primary sense of which is to *rush.*]

1. Very swift or quick; moving with celerity; as a *rapid* stream; a *rapid* flight; a *rapid* motion.

> Part shun the goal with *rapid* wheels. *Milton.*

2. Advancing with haste or speed; speedy in progression; as *rapid* growth; *rapid* improvement.

3. Of quick utterance of words; as a *rapid* speaker.

RAPID'ITY, *n.* [L. *rapiditas*; Fr. *rapidité*, supra.]

1. Swiftness; celerity; velocity; as the *rapidity* of a current; the *rapidity* of motion of any kind.

2. Haste in utterance; as the *rapidity* of speech or pronunciation.

3. Quickness of progression or advance; as *rapidity* of growth or improvement.

RAP'IDLY, *adv.* With great speed, celerity or velocity; swiftly; with quick progression; as, to run *rapidly*; to grow or improve *rapidly.*

2. With quick utterance; as, to speak *rapidly.*

RAP'IDNESS, *n.* Swiftness; speed; celerity; rapidity.

RAP'IDS, *n. plu.* The part of a river where the current moves with more celerity than the common current. Rapids imply a considerable descent of the earth, but not sufficient to occasion a fall of the water, or what is called a cascade or cataract.

RA'PIER, *n.* [Fr. *rapière*; Ir. *roipeir*; from thrusting, driving, or quick motion.] A small sword used only in thrusting. *Shak. Pope.*

RA'PIER-FISH, *n.* The sword-fish. *Grew.*

RAP'IL, } *n.* Pulverized volcanic sub-
RAPIL'LO, } stances.

RAP'INE, *n.* [Fr. from L. *rapina*; *rapio*, to seize.]

1. The act of plundering; the seizing and carrying away of things by force.

2. Violence; force. *Milton.*

RAP'INE, *v. t.* To plunder. *Buck.*

RAPPAREE', *n.* A wild Irish plunderer; so called from *rapery*, a half pike that he carries. *Todd.*

RAPPEE', *n.* A coarse kind of snuff.

RAP'PER, *n.* [from *rap.*] One that raps or knocks.

2. The knocker of a door. [*Not in common use.*]

3. An oath or a lie. [*Not in use.*] *Parker.*

RAP'PORT, *n.* [Fr. from *re* and *porter*, to bear.] Relation; proportion. [*Not in use.*] *Temple.*

RAPT, *pp.* [from *rap.*] Transported; ravished.

RAPT, *v. t.* To transport or ravish. [*Not legitimate or in use.*] *Chapman.*

RAPT, *n.* An ecstasy; a trance. *Morton.*

2. Rapidity. [*Not in use.*]

RAP'TER, } *n.* [L. *raptor.*] A ravisher; a
RAP'TOR, } plunderer. *Drayton.*

RAP'TURE, *n.* [L. *raptus*, *rapio.*] A seizing by violence. [*Little used.*] *Chapman.*

2. Transport; ecstasy; violence of a pleasing passion; extreme joy or pleasure.

> Music when thus applied, raises in the mind of the hearer great conceptions; it strengthens devotion and advances praise into *rapture.* *Spectator.*

3. Rapidity with violence; a hurrying along with velocity; as rolling with torrent *rapture.* *Milton.*

4. Enthusiasm; uncommon heat of imagination.

> You grow correct, that once with *rapture* writ. *Pope.*

RAP'TURED, *a.* Ravished; transported. *Thomson.*

[But *enraptured* is generally used.]

RAP'TURIST, *n.* An enthusiast. *Spenser.*

RAP'TUROUS, *a.* Ecstatic; transporting; ravishing; as *rapturous* joy, pleasure or delight. *Collier.*

RARE, *a.* [L. *rarus*, thin; Sp. Port. It. *raro*; Fr. *rare*; D. *raar*; G. Dan. *rar.*]

1. Uncommon; not frequent; as a *rare* event; a *rare* phenomenon.

2. Unusually excellent; valuable to a degree seldom found.

> *Rare* work, all fill'd with terror and delight. *Cowley.*
>
> Above the rest I judge one beauty *rare.* *Dryden.*

3. Thinly scattered.

Those *rare* and solitary, these in flocks— *Milton.*

4. Thin; porous; not dense; as a *rare* and attenuate substance.

Water is nineteen times lighter and by consequence nineteen times *rarer* than gold. *Newton.*

5. [Sax. *hrere.*] Nearly raw; imperfectly roasted or boiled; as *rare* beef or mutton; eggs roasted *rare.* *Dryden.*

RA'REESHOW, *n.* [*rare* and *show.*] A show carried in a box. *Pope.*

RAREFAC'TION, *n.* [Fr. See *Rarefy.*] The act or process of expanding or distending bodies, by separating the parts and rendering the bodies more rare or porous, by which operation they appear under a larger bulk, or require more room, without an accession of new matter; opposed to *condensation;* as the *rarefaction* of air. *Encyc.*

RAR'EFIABLE, *a.* Capable of being rarefied.

RAR'EFY, *v. t.* [Fr. *rarefier;* L. *rarefacio; rarus,* rare, and *facio,* to make.] To make thin and porous or less dense; to expand or enlarge a body without adding to it any new portion of its own matter; opposed to *condense.* *Encyc. Thomson.*

RAR'EFY, *v. i.* To become thin and porous. *Dryden.*

RAR'EFYING, *ppr.* Making thin or less dense.

RA'RELY, *adv.* Seldom; not often; as things *rarely* seen.

2. Finely; nicely. [*Little used.*] *Shak.*

RA'RENESS, *n.* The state of being uncommon; uncommonness; infrequency.

And let the *rareness* the small gift commend. *Dryden.*

2. Value arising from scarcity. *Bacon.*

3. Thinness; tenuity; as the *rareness* of air or vapor.

4. Distance from each other; thinness. *Johnson.*

RA'RERIPE, *a.* [Sax. *arœran,* to excite, to hasten.] Early ripe; ripe before others, or before the usual season.

RA'RERIPE, *n.* An early fruit, particularly a kind of peach which ripens early.

RAR'ITY, *n.* [Fr. *rareté;* L. *raritas.*] Uncommonness; infrequency.

Far from being fond of a flower for its *rarity*— *Spectator.*

2. A thing valued for its scarcity.

I saw three *rarities* of different kinds, which pleased me more than any other shows in the place. *Addison.*

3. Thinness; tenuity; opposed to *density;* as the *rarity* of air. *Digby.*

RAS'CAL, *n.* [Sax. *id.* This word is said to signify a lean beast.] A mean fellow; a scoundrel; in *modern usage,* a trickish dishonest fellow; a rogue; particularly applied to men and boys guilty of the lesser crimes, and indicating less enormity or guilt than *villain.*

I have sense to serve my turn in store,
And he's a *rascal* who pretends to more. *Dryden.*

RAS'CAL, *a.* Lean; as a *rascal* deer.

2. Mean; low. *Spenser.*

RASCAL'ION, *n.* [from *rascal.*] A low mean wretch. *Hudibras.*

RASCAL'ITY, *n.* The low mean people. *South.*

2. Mean trickishness or dishonesty; base fraud. [*This is its sense in present usage in America.*]

RAS'CALLY, *a.* Meanly trickish or dishonest; vile.

2. Mean; vile; base; worthless; as a *rascally* porter. *Swift.*

RASE, *v. t. s* as z. [Fr. *raser;* Sp. Port. *rasar;* It. *rasare* and *raschiare;* Arm. *raza;* L. *rasus, rado.* With these words accord the W. *rhathu,* to rub off, *rhathell,* a rasp, Eth. ረወተ to rub or wipe. See the verb to *row,* which is radically the same word. If g in *grate* is a prefix, the word is formed on the same radix. Class Rd. No. 10. 13. 17. 25. 35. 38. 42. 56. 58. 61. 62. 64. 81.]

1. To pass along the surface of a thing, with striking or rubbing it at the same time; to *graze.*

Might not the bullet which *rased* his cheek, have gone into his head? *Obs.* *South.*

2. To erase; to scratch or rub out; or to blot out; to cancel. *Milton.*

[In this sense, *erase* is generally used.]

3. To level with the ground; to overthrow; to destroy; as, to *rase* a city. *Milton.*

[In this sense, *raze* is generally used. This orthography, *rase,* may therefore be considered as nearly obsolete; *graze, erase* and *raze* having superseded it.]

RASE, *n.* A cancel; erasure. [*Not in use.*]

2. A slight wound. [*Not in use.*]

RASH, *a.* [D. G. *rasch,* quick; Sw. Dan. *rask,* id.; Sax. *hrad, hræd, hræth,* quick, hasty, *ready,* and *hræs, ræs,* impetus, force, and *hreosan, reosan, ræsan,* to *rush.* See *Ready* and *Rush.* The sense is advancing, pushing forward. Class Rd. No. 5. 9.]

1. Hasty in council or action; precipitate; resolving or entering on a project or measure without due deliberation and caution, and thus encountering unnecessary hazard; *applied to persons;* as a *rash* statesman or minister; a *rash* commander.

2. Uttered or undertaken with too much haste or too little reflection; as *rash* words; *rash* measures.

3. Requiring haste; urgent.

I have scarce leisure to salute you,
My matter is so *rash.* *Shak.*

4. Quick; sudden; as *rash* gunpowder. [*Not in use.*]

RASH, *n.* Corn so dry as to fall out with handling. [*Local.*] *Grose.*

RASH, *n.* [It. *rascia.*] Satin.

2. An eruption or efflorescence on the body. [In Italian, *raschia* is the itch.]

RASH, *v. t.* [It. *raschiare,* to scrape or grate; W. *rhâsg, rhasgyl, rhasgliaw;* from the root of *rase, graze.*] To slice; to cut into pieces; to divide. *Spenser.*

RASH'ER, *n.* A thin slice of bacon; a thin cut. *Shak.*

RASH'LY, *adv.* With precipitation; hastily; without due deliberation.

He that doth any thing *rashly,* must do it willingly. *L'Estrange.*

So *rashly* brave, to dare the sword of Theseus. *Smith.*

RASH'NESS, *n.* Too much haste in resolving or in undertaking a measure; precipitation; inconsiderate readiness or promptness to decide or act, implying disregard of consequences or contempt of danger; *applied to persons.* The failure of enterprises is often owing to *rashness.*

We offend by *rashness,* which is an affirming or denying before we have sufficiently informed ourselves. *South.*

2. The quality of being uttered or done without due deliberation; as the *rashness* of words or of undertakings.

R'ASP, *n.* [Sw. D. *rasp;* G. *raspel;* Dan. *raspe;* Fr. *râpe,* for *raspe;* It. Sp. *raspa.* See *Rase.*]

1. A large rough file; a grater.

2. A raspberry, which see. *Bacon.*

R'ASP, *v. t.* [D. *raspen;* Dan. *rasper;* Sw. *raspa;* It. *raspare;* Sp. *raspar;* Fr. *râper;* W. *rhathell,* in a different dialect. See *Rase.*] To rub or file with a rasp; to rub or grate with a rough file; as, to *rasp* wood to make it smooth; to *rasp* bones to powder. *Wiseman. Moxon.*

R'ASPATORY, *n.* A surgeon's rasp. *Wiseman.*

R'ASPBERRY, *n.* [from *rasp,* so named from the roughness of the brambles; G. *kratzbeere,* from *kratzen,* to *scratch.*] The fruit of a bramble or species of rubus; a berry growing on a prickly plant; as the black *raspberry;* the red and the white *raspberry.*

R'ASPBERRY-BUSH, *n.* The bramble producing raspberries.

RA'SURE, *n. s* as z. [L. *rasura,* from *rado, rasus.* See *Rase.*]

1. The act of scraping or shaving; the act of erasing.

2. The mark by which a letter, word or any part of a writing is erased, effaced or obliterated; an erasure. *Ayliffe.*

RAT, *n.* [Sax. *ræt;* D. *rat;* G. *ratze;* Fr. *rat;* Arm. *raz;* Sp. *rato;* Port. *id.* a rat, and *ratos,* sharp stones in the sea that wear cables; probably named from gnawing, and from the root of L. *rodo.*] A small quadruped of the genus Mus, which infests houses, stores and ships; a troublesome race of animals.

To smell a rat, to be suspicious, to be on the watch from suspicion; as a cat by the scent or noise of a rat.

RA'TABLE, *a.* [from *rate.*] That may be rated, or set at a certain value; as a Danish ore *ratable* at two marks. *Camden.*

2. Liable or subjected by law to taxation; as *ratable* estate. *Stat. of Conn.*

RA'TABLY, *adv.* By rate or proportion; proportionally. *Raleigh.*

RATAFIA, *n. ratafee'.* [Sp.] A fine spirituous liquor, prepared from the kernels of several kinds of fruits, particularly of cherries, apricots and peaches. *Sp. Dict. Encyc.*

RATAN', *n.* [Malay, *rotan;* Java, *rottang.*] A small cane, the growth of India.

RAT'-CATCHER, *n.* One who makes it his business to catch rats.

RATCH, *n.* In *clock work,* a sort of wheel having twelve fangs, which serve to lift the detents every hour and thereby cause the clock to strike. *Encyc.*

RATCH'ET, *n.* In *a watch,* a small tooth at the bottom of the fusee or barrel, which stops it in winding up. *Encyc.*

RATCH'IL, *n.* Among *miners,* fragments of stone. *Kirwan.*

RATE, *n.* [Norm. *rate;* L. *ratus, reor,* contracted from *retor, redor* or *resor.* See *Ratio* and *Reason.*]

1. The proportion or standard by which quantity or value is adjusted; as silver valued at the *rate* of six shillings and eight pence the ounce.

The *rate* and standard of wit was different then from what it is in these days. *South.*

2. Price or amount stated or fixed on any thing. A king may purchase territory at too dear a *rate*. The *rate* of interest is prescribed by law.
3. Settled allowance; as a daily *rate* of provisions. 2 Kings xxv.
4. Degree; comparative highth or value.

I am a spirit of no common *rate*. *Shak.*

In this did his holiness and godliness appear above the *rate* and pitch of other men's, in that he was so infinitely merciful. *Calamy.*

5. Degree in which any thing is done. The ship sails at the *rate* of seven knots an hour.

Many of the horse could not march at that *rate*, nor come up soon enough. *Clarendon.*

6. Degree of value; price. Wheat in England is often sold at the *rate* of fifty shillings the quarter. Wit may be purchased at too dear a *rate*.
7. A tax or sum assessed by authority on property for public use, according to its income or value; as parish *rates;* town *rates*; highway *rates*.
8. In *the navy*, the order or class of a ship, according to its magnitude or force. Ships of the first *rate* mount a hundred guns or upwards; those of the second *rate* carry from 90 to 98 guns; those of the third *rate* carry from 64 to 80 guns; those of the fourth *rate* from 50 to 60 guns; those of the fifth *rate* from 32 to 44 guns; those of the sixth *rate* from 20 to 30 guns. Those of the two latter *rates* are called *frigates*. *Mar. Dict.*

RATE, *v. t.* To set a certain value on; to value at a certain price or degree of excellence.

You seem not high enough your joys to *rate*. *Dryden.*

Instead of *rating* the man by his performances, we too frequently *rate* the performance by the man. *Rambler.*

2. To fix the magnitude, force or order, as of ships. A ship is *rated* in the first class, or as a ship of the line.

RATE, *v. i.* To be set or considered in a class, as a ship. The ship *rates* as a ship of the line.

2. To make an estimate.

RATE, *v. t.* [Sw. *rata*, to refuse, to find fault; *ryta*, to roar, to huff; Ice. *reita*, or G. *bereden*, from *reden*, to speak, Sax. *rædan*. See *Read*. It is probably allied to *rattle*, and perhaps to L. *rudo*. See Class Rd. No. 71. 76. Ar.]

To chide with vehemence; to reprove; to scold; to censure violently.

Go, *rate* thy minions, proud insulting boy. *Shak.*

An old lord of the council *rated* me the other day in the street about you, sir. *Shak.*

RA'TED, *pp.* Set at a certain value; estimated; set in a certain order or rank.

2. Chid; reproved.

RA'TER, *n.* One who sets a value on or makes an estimate.

RATH, *n.* [Ir. *rath*, a hill, mount or fortress.] A hill. *Obs.* *Spenser.*

RATH, *a.* [Sax. *rath, ræthe, hræth, hrathe, hræd* or *hrad*, quick, hasty; Ir. *ratham*, to grow or be prosperous; from the same root as *ready* and *rash*, from the sense of shooting forward. See *Ready.*]

Early; coming before others, or before the usual time.

Bring the *rath* primrose, that forsaken dies. *Milton.*

We sometimes see the word *rath-ripe*, early ripe, Sax. *ræd-ripe;* but it is obsolete or nearly so. In the United States, I believe it is not used at all.

RATH'ER, *adv.* [Sax. *rathor, hrathor; comp.* of *rath*, quick, prompt, hasty, *ready*. So we use *sooner* in an equivalent sense. I would *rather* go, or *sooner* go. The use is taken from pushing or moving forward. So the Italians use *anzi*, [L. *ante*, before.] "Ma egli disse, anzi, beati coloro ch'odono la parola di Dio, e l'osservano." But he said, yea *rather*, happy are they that hear the word of God and keep it. Luke xi.]

1. More readily or willingly; with better liking; with preference or choice.

My soul chooseth strangling and death *rather* than life. Job vii.

Light is come into the world, and men loved darkness *rather* than light, because their deeds were evil. John iii. Ps. lxxxiv.

2. In preference; preferably; with better reason. Good is *rather* to be chosen than evil. See Acts v.
3. In a greater degree than otherwise.

He sought throughout the world, but sought in vain,
And no where finding, *rather* fear'd her slain. *Dryden.*

4. More properly; more correctly speaking.

This is an art
Which does mend nature, change it *rather;* but
The art itself is nature. *Shak.*

5. Noting some degree of contrariety in fact.

She was nothing better, but *rather* grew worse. Mark v. Matt. xxvii.

The rather, especially; for better reason; for particular cause.

You are come to me in a happy time,
The rather for I have some sport in hand. *Shak.*

Had rather, is supposed to be a corruption of *would rather*.

I *had rather* speak five words with my understanding— 1 Cor. xiv.

This phrase may have been originally, 'I'd rather," for *I would rather*, and the contraction afterwards mistaken for *had*. Correct speakers and writers generally use *would* in all such phrases; I *would rather*, I prefer; I desire in preference.

RATH'OFFITE, *n.* A mineral brought from Sweden, of the garnet kind. Its color is a dingy brownish black, and it is accompanied with calcarious spar and small crystals of hornblend. *Phillips.*

RATIFICA'TION, *n.* [Fr.; from *ratify.*]

1. The act of ratifying; confirmation.
2. The act of giving sanction and validity to something done by another; as the *ratification* of a treaty by the senate of the United States.

RAT'IFIED, *pp.* Confirmed; sanctioned; made valid.

RAT'IFIER, *n.* He or that which ratifies or sanctions.

RAT'IFY, *v. t.* [Fr. *ratifier;* L. *ratum facio*, to make firm.] To confirm; to establish; to settle.

We have *ratified* to them the borders of Judea. 1 Macc.

2. To approve and sanction; to make valid; as, to *ratify* an agreement or treaty.

RAT'IFYING, *ppr.* Confirming; establishing; approving and sanctioning.

RA'TING, *ppr.* [from *rate.*] Setting at a certain value; assigning rank to; estimating.

2. Chiding; reproving.

RA'TIO, *n. ra'sho.* [L. from *ratus, reor*, to think or suppose, to set, confirm or establish. *Reor* is contracted from *redor* or *retor*, and primarily signifies to throw, to thrust, hence to speak, to set in the mind, to think, like L. *suppono;* and *setting* gives the sense of a fixed *rate* or rule. See *Reason.*]

Proportion, or the relation of homogeneous things which determines the quantity of one from the quantity of another, without the intervention of a third. *Encyc.*

The relation which one quantity has to another of the same kind, as expressed by the quotient of the one divided by the other. Thus the ratio of 4 to 2 is $\frac{4}{2}$, or 2; and the ratio of 5 to 6 is $\frac{5}{6}$. This is *geometrical* ratio, which is that signified when the term is used without distinction; but *arithmetical* ratio is the *difference* between two quantities. Thus the arithmetical ratio of 2 to 6 is 4.

Ratio respects magnitudes of the same kind only. One line may be compared with another line, but a line cannot be compared with a superficies, and hence between a line and a superficies there can be no *ratio*. *Encyc.*

RA'TIOCINATE, *v. i.* [L. *ratiocinor*, from *ratio*, reason.] To reason; to argue. [*Little used.*]

RATIOCINA'TION, *n.* [L. *ratiocinatio.*] The act or process of reasoning, or of deducing consequences from premises. [See *Reasoning.*] *Brown. South.*

RATIOC'INATIVE, *a.* Argumentative; consisting in the comparison of propositions or facts, and the deduction of inferences from the comparison; as a *ratiocinative* process. [*A bad word and little used.*] *Hale.*

RA'TION, *n.* [Fr. from L. *ratio*, proportion.]

A portion or fixed allowance of provisions, drink and forage, assigned to each soldier in an army for his daily subsistence and for the subsistence of horses. Officers have several *rations* according to their rank or number of attendants. Seamen in the navy also have *rations* of certain articles. *Encyc.*

RA'TIONAL, *a.* [Fr. *rationnel;* It. *razionale;* L. *rationalis.*]

1. Having reason or the faculty of reasoning; endowed with reason; opposed to *irrational;* as, man is a *rational* being; brutes are not *rational* animals.

It is our glory and happiness to have a *rational* nature. *Law.*

2. Agreeable to reason; opposed to *absurd;* as a *rational* conclusion or inference; *rational* conduct.

3. Agreeable to reason; not extravagant.
4. Acting in conformity to reason; wise; judicious; as a *rational* man.

RA'TIONAL, *n.* A rational being. *Young.*

RATIONA'LE, *n.* A detail with reasons; a series of reasons assigned; as Dr. Sparrow's *rationale* of the Common Prayer.
2. An account or solution of the principles of some opinion, action, hypothesis, phenomenon, &c. *Encyc.*

RA'TIONALIST, *n.* One who proceeds in his disquisitions and practice wholly upon reason. *Bacon.*

RATIONAL'ITY, *n.* The power of reasoning.

God has made *rationality* the common portion of mankind. *Gov. of the Tongue.*

2. Reasonableness.

Well directed intentions, whose *rationalities* will not bear a rigid examination. *Brown.*

RA'TIONALLY, *adv.* In consistency with reason; reasonably. We *rationally* expect every man will pursue his own happiness.

RA'TIONALNESS, *n.* The state of being rational or consistent with reason.

RAT'LIN, } *n.* A small line traversing
RAT'LINE, } the shrouds of a ship, making the step of a ladder for ascending to the mast-heads. *Mar. Dict.*

RATOON', *n.* [Sp. *retono*; *retoñar*, to sprout again.]
A sprout from the root of the sugar cane, which has been cut. *Edwards, W. Ind.*

RATS'BANE, *n.* [*rat* and *bane.*] Poison for rats; arsenic. *Swift.*

RATS'BANED, *a.* Poisoned by ratsbane. *Junius.*

RAT'-TAIL, *n.* In farriery, an excrescence growing from the pastern to the middle of the shank of a horse. *Encyc.*

RATTEEN', *n.* [Sp. *ratina*, ratteen, and a musk mouse.] A thick woolen stuff quilled or twilled.

RATTINET', *n.* A woolen stuff thinner than ratteen.

RAT'TLE, *v. i.* [D. *ratelen*, *reutelen*; G. *rasseln*; Dan. *rasler*; Sw. *rassla*; Gr. *κροτεω*, *κροταλον*, with a prefix. Qu. *rate.*]
1. To make a quick sharp noise rapidly repeated, by the collision of bodies not very sonorous. When bodies are sonorous, it is called *jingling*. We say, the wheels *rattle* over the pavement.

And the rude hail in *rattling* tempest forms. *Addison.*

He fagoted his notions as they fell,
And if they rhym'd and *rattl'd*, all was well. *Dryden.*

2. To speak eagerly and noisily; to utter words in a clattering manner.

Thus turbulent in *rattling* tone she spoke. *Dryden.*

He *rattles* it out against popery. *Swift.*

RAT'TLE, *v. t.* To cause to make a rattling sound or a rapid succession of sharp sounds; as, to *rattle* a chain. *Dryden.*
2. To stun with noise; to drive with sharp sounds rapidly repeated.

Sound but another, and another shall,
As loud as thine, *rattle* the welkin's ear. *Shak.*

3. To scold; to rail at clamorously; as, to *rattle* off servants sharply. *Arbuthnot.*

RAT'TLE, *n.* A rapid succession of sharp clattering sounds; as the *rattle* of a drum. *Prior.*
2. A rapid succession of words sharply uttered; loud rapid talk; clamorous chiding.
3. An instrument with which a clattering sound is made.

The *rattles* of Isis and the cymbals of Brasilea nearly enough resemble each other. *Raleigh.*

The rhymes and *rattles* of the man or boy. *Pope.*

4. A plant of the genus Pedicularis, lousewort. *Fam. of Plants.*
Yellow rattle, a plant of the genus Rhinanthus. *Ibm.*

RAT'TLE-HEADED, *a.* Noisy; giddy; unsteady.

RAT'TLESNAKE, *n.* A snake that has rattles at the tail, of the genus Crotalus. The rattles consist of articulated horny cells, which the animal vibrates in such a manner as to make a rattling sound. The poison of the rattlesnake is deadly.

RATTLESNAKE-ROOT, *n.* A plant or root of the genus Polygala, and another of the genus Prenanthes.

RATTLESNAKE-WEED, *n.* A plant of the genus Eryngium. *Fam. of Plants.*

RAT'TLING, *ppr.* Making a quick succession of sharp sounds.

RAT'TLING, *n.* A rapid succession of sharp sounds. Nah. iii.

RAU'CITY, *n.* [L. *raucus*, hoarse. *Raucus* is the Eng. *rough*, which see.]
1. Hoarseness; a loud rough sound; as the *raucity* of a trumpet. *Bacon.*
2. Among physicians, hoarseness of the human voice.

RAU'COUS, *a.* Hoarse; harsh. [*Not in use.*]

RAUGHT, the old participle of *reach.* *Obs.*

RAUNCH. [See *Wrench.*]

RAV'AGE, *n.* [Fr. from *ravir*, to rob or spoil, L. *rapio*. See Class Rb. No. 18. 19. 26. 27.]
1. Spoil; ruin; waste; destruction by violence, either by men, beasts or physical causes; as the *ravage* of a lion; the *ravages* of fire or tempest; the ravages of an army.

Would one think 'twere possible for love
To make such *ravage* in a noble soul. *Addison.*

2. Waste; ruin; destruction by decay; as the *ravages* of time.

RAV'AGE, *v. t.* [Fr. *ravager.*] To spoil; to plunder; to pillage; to sack.

Already Cesar
Has *ravag'd* more than half the globe! *Addison.*

2. To lay waste by any violent force; as, a flood or inundation *ravages* the meadows.

The shatter'd forest and the *ravag'd* vale. *Thomson.*

3. To waste or destroy by eating; as fields *ravaged* by swarms of locusts.

RAV'AGED, *pp.* Wasted; destroyed; pillaged.

RAV'AGER, *n.* A plunderer; a spoiler; he or that which lays waste. *Swift.*

RAV'AGING, *ppr.* Plundering; pillaging; laying waste.

RAVE, *v. i.* [D. *revelen*, to rave, Eng. to *revel*; Sp. *rabiar*; Port. *raivar*; L. *rabio*, to rave, to rage or be furious; *rabies*, rage; It. *rabbia*, whence *arrabbiare*, to enrage; Fr. *rêver*, if not a contracted word; Dan. *raver*, to reel. See Class Rb. No. 27. 34.]
1. To wander in mind or intellect; to be delirious; to talk irrationally; to be wild.

When men thus *rave*, we may conclude their brains are turned. *Gov. of the Tongue.*

2. To utter furious exclamations; to be furious or raging; as a madman.

Have I not cause to *rave* and beat my breast? *Addison.*

3. To dote; to be unreasonably fond; followed by *upon*; as, to *rave upon* antiquity. [*Hardly proper.*] *Locke.*

RAVE, *n.* The upper side-piece of timber of the body of a cart. *New England.*

RAVEL, *v. t.* *rav'l.* [D. *raaffelen* and *ravelen.* See Class Rb. No. 3. 4. 34. This word is used in opposite senses.]
1. To entangle; to entwist together; to make intricate; to involve; to perplex.

What glory's due to him that could divide
Such *ravel'd* int'rests, has the knot unty'd? *Waller.*

2. To untwist; to unweave or unknot; to disentangle; as, to *ravel* out a twist; to *ravel* out a stocking.

Sleep, that knits up the *ravel'd* sleeve of care. *Shak.*

3. To hurry or run over in confusion. [*Not in use.*] *Digby.*

RAVEL, *v. i.* *rav'l.* To fall into perplexity and confusion.

Till by their own perplexities involv'd,
They *ravel* more, still less resolv'd. *Milton.*

2. To work in perplexities; to busy one's self with intricacies; to enter by winding and turning.

It will be needless to *ravel* far into the records of elder times. *Decay of Piety.*

The humor of *raveling* into all these mystical or entangled matters—produced infinite disputes. *Temple.*

3. To be unwoven. *Spenser.*
[As far as my observation extends, *ravel*, in the United States, is used only in the second sense above, viz. to *unweave*, to separate the texture of that which is woven or knit; so that *ravel* and *unravel* are with us always synonymous. Etymology proves this to be the true sense of the word *ravel.*]

RAV'ELED, *pp.* Twisted together; made intricate; disentangled.

RAV'ELIN, *n.* [Fr. *id.*; Sp. *rebellin*; Port. *rebelim*; It. *ravellino.*]
In *fortification*, a detached work with two faces which make a salient angle, without any flanks, and raised before the counterscarp of the place. In this it differs from a half moon, which is placed before an angle. *Encyc. Dict.*

RAV'ELING, *ppr.* Twisting or weaving; untwisting; disentangling.

RAVEN, *n.* *ra'vn.* [Sax. *hræfn*, *hrefn* or *ræfn*; G. *rabe*; D. *raaf.* Qu. Heb. ערב, from its color. But this may be L. *corvus.* The Saxon orthography would indicate that this fowl is named from pilfering; *hreafian*, *reafian*, to plunder, to rob, L. *rapio.*]
A large fowl of a black color, of the genus Corvus. *Encyc.*

RAVEN, *v. t.* *rav'n.* [G. *rauben*; Dan. *röver*; Sw. *roffa*, *rofva*, to rob; Sax. *reafian*, *hreafian.* But it is more nearly allied to Ar. رفّ raffa, to eat much, to pluck off in feeding. Class Rb. No. 12. See No. 18. 19. 34.]

1. To devour with great eagerness; to eat with voracity.

Our natures do pursue,
Like rats that *raven* down their proper bane,
A thirsty evil, and when we drink, we die. *Shak.*

Like a roaring lion, *ravening* the prey. Ezek. xxii.

2. To obtain by violence. *Hakewill.*

RAVEN, *v. i. rav'n.* To prey with rapacity.

Benjamin shall *raven* as a wolf. Gen. xlix.

RAVEN, *n. rav'n.* Prey; plunder; food obtained by violence. Nah. ii.

2. Rapine; rapacity. *Ray.*

RAV'ENED, *pp.* Devoured with voracity.

RAV'ENER, *n.* One that ravens or plunders. *Gower.*

RAV'ENING, *ppr.* Preying with rapacity; voraciously devouring; as a *ravening* wolf.

RAV'ENING, *n.* Eagerness for plunder. Luke xi.

RAV'ENOUS, *a.* Furiously voracious; hungry even to rage; devouring with rapacious eagerness; as a *ravenous* wolf, lion or vulture. *Milton.*

2. Eager for prey or gratification; as *ravenous* appetite or desire. *Shak.*

RAV'ENOUSLY, *adv.* With raging voracity. *Burnet.*

RAV'ENOUSNESS, *n.* Extreme voracity; rage for prey; as the *ravenousness* of a lion. *Hale.*

RAVEN'S DUCK, *n.* [G. *ravenstuch.*] A species of sail cloth. *Tooke.*

RA'VER, *n.* [from *rave.*] One that raves or is furious.

RAV'ET, *n.* An insect shaped like a cockchaffer, which infests the West Indies. *Encyc.*

RAVIN. [See *Raven.*]

RAV'IN, *a.* Ravenous. [*Not in use.*] *Shak.*

RAV'IN, RAVİNE, *n.* [Fr. *ravin*, from *ravir*, to snatch or tear away.] A long deep hollow worn by a stream or torrent of water; hence, any long deep hollow or pass through mountains, &c.

RA'VING, *ppr.* or *a.* Furious with delirium; mad; distracted.

RA'VINGLY, *adv.* With furious wildness or frenzy; with distraction. *Sidney.*

RAV'ISH, *v. t.* [Fr. *ravir;* Arm. *raviçza;* Sax. *hreafian;* W. *rheibiaw;* L. *rapio.* See Class Rb. No. 18. 19. 26. 27.]

1. To seize and carry away by violence.

These hairs which thou dost *ravish* from my chin,
Will quicken and accuse thee. *Shak.*

This hand shall *ravish* thy pretended right. *Dryden.*

2. To have carnal knowledge of a woman by force and against her consent. Is. xiii. Zech. xiv.

3. To bear away with joy or delight; to delight to ecstasy; to transport.

Thou hast *ravished* my heart. Cant. iv. Prov. v.

RAV'ISHED, *pp.* Snatched away by violence; forced to submit to carnal embrace; delighted to ecstasy.

RAV'ISHER, *n.* One that takes by violence. *Pope.*

2. One that forces a woman to his carnal embrace.

3. One that transports with delight.

RAV'ISHING, *ppr.* Snatching or taking by violence; compelling to submit to carnal intercourse; delighting to ecstasy.

2. *a.* Delighting to rapture; transporting.

RAV'ISHING, *n.* A seizing and carrying away by violence.

2. Carnal knowledge by force against consent.

3. Ecstatic delight; transport.

RAV'ISHINGLY, *adv.* To extremity of delight. *Chapman.*

RAV'ISHMENT, *n.* The act of forcing a woman to carnal connection; forcible violation of chastity. *Taylor. Dryden.*

2. Rapture; transport of delight; ecstasy; pleasing violence on the mind or senses.

All things joy with *ravishment*
Attracted by thy beauty still to gaze. *Milton.*

3. The act of carrying away; abduction; as the *ravishment* of children from their parents, of a ward from his guardian, or of a wife from her husband. *Blackstone.*

RAW, *a.* [Sax. *hreaw, reaw;* D. *raauw;* G. *roh;* Dan. *raa;* Sw. *rå;* L. *crudus;* Sp. It. *crudo;* Fr. *cru;* Arm. *criz* or *crih;* W. *crau*, blood; *cri*, raw. In the Teutonic dialects, the last radical is lost or sunk to *w* or *h*, but the Saxon initial *h* represents the L. *c.* Ar. أَرَضَ aradza, to eat or corrode, L. *rodo*, also to become *raw.* Class Rd. No. 35.]

1. Not altered from its natural state; not roasted, boiled or cooked; not subdued by heat; as *raw* meat. *Spenser.*

2. Not covered with skin; bare, as flesh.

If there is quick *raw* flesh in the risings, it is an old leprosy. Lev. xiii.

3. Sore.

And all his sinews waxen weak and *raw*
Through long imprisonment. *Spenser.*

4. Immature; unripe; not concocted. *Johnson.*

5. Not altered by heat; not cooked or dressed; being in its natural state; as *raw* fruit.

6. Unseasoned; unexperienced; unripe in skill; as people while young and *raw.* *South.*

So we say, *raw* troops; and new seamen are called *raw* hands.

7. New; untried; as a *raw* trick. *Shak.*

8. Bleak; chilly; cold, or rather cold and damp; as a *raw* day; a *raw* cold climate. *Spenser.*

Once upon a *raw* and gusty day— *Shak.*

9. Not distilled; as *raw* water. [*Not used.*] *Bacon.*

10. Not spun or twisted; as *raw* silk.

11. Not mixed or adulterated; as *raw* spirits.

12. Bare of flesh. *Spenser.*

13. Not tried or melted and strained; as *raw* tallow.

14. Not tanned; as *raw* hides.

RAW'-BŌNED, *a.* Having little flesh on the bones. *Shak.*

RAW'HEAD, *n.* The name of a specter, mentioned to frighten children; as *rawhead* and bloody bones. *Dryden.*

RAW'ISH, *a.* Somewhat raw; cool and damp. [*Not much used.*] *Marston.*

RAW'LY, *adv.* In a raw manner.

2. Unskillfully; without experience.

3. Newly. *Shak.*

RAW'NESS, *n.* The state of being raw; uncooked; unaltered by heat; as the *rawness* of flesh.

2. Unskillfulness; state of being inexperienced; as the *rawness* of seamen or troops.

3. Hasty manner. [*Not legitimate.*] *Shak.*

4. Chilliness with dampness.

RAY, *n.* [Fr. *raie, rayon;* It. *razzo, raggio, radio;* Sp. Port. *rayo;* from L. *radius;* W. *rhaiz;* Ir. *riodh;* Arm. *rea, roudenn;* Sans. *radina.* It coincides with *rod* and *row*, from shooting, extending. Hence in W. *rhaiz* is a spear, as well as a ray.]

1. A line of light, or the right line supposed to be described by a particle of light. A collection of parallel rays constitutes a *beam;* a collection of diverging or converging rays, a *pencil.* *D. Olmsted.*

The mixed solar beam contains, 1st. *calorific rays*, producing heat aud expansion, but not vision and color; 2d. *colorific rays*, producing vision and color, but not heat nor expansion; 3d. *chimical rays*, producing certain effects on the composition of bodies, but neither heat, expansion, vision or color; 4th. a power producing magnetism, but whether a distinct or associated power, is not determined. It seems to be associated with the *violet*, more than with the other rays. *Silliman.*

2. Figuratively, a beam of intellectual light.

3. Light; luster.

The air sharpen'd his visual *ray.* *Milton.*

4. In *botany*, the outer part or circumference of a compound radiate flower. *Martyn.*

5. In *ichthyology*, a bony or cartilaginous ossicle in the fins of fishes, serving to support the membrane.

6. A plant, [*lolium.*] *Ainsworth.*

7. Ray, for *array.* [*Not in use.*] *Spenser. B. Jonson.*

Pencil of rays, a number of rays of light issuing from a point and diverging. *Encyc.*

RAY, *n.* [Fr. *raie;* Sp. *raya;* G. *roche.*] A fish; a common name for the species of the genus Raia, including the skate, thornback, torpedo, stingray, &c.

RAY, *v. t.* To streak; to mark with long lines. *Spenser. Shak.*

2. To foul; to beray. [*Not in use.*] *Spenser.*

3. To array. [*Not in use.*]

4. To shoot forth. *Thomson.*

RA'YLESS, *a.* Destitute of light; dark; not illuminated. *Young.*

RAZE, *n.* A root. [See *Race-ginger*, under *Race.*]

RAZE, *v. t.* [Fr. *raser;* L. *rasus, rado;* Sp. *arrasar.* See *Rase* and *Erase.*]

1. To subvert from the foundation; to overthrow; to destroy; to demolish; as, to *raze* a city to the ground.

The royal hand that *raz'd* unhappy Troy. *Dryden.*

2. To erase; to efface; to obliterate.

Razing the characters of your renown. *Shak.*

[In this sense, *rase* and *erase* are now used.]

3. To extirpate.

And *raze* their factions and their family. *Shak.*

RA'ZED, *pp.* Subverted; overthrown; wholly ruined; erased; extirpated.

RAZEE', *n.* A ship of war cut down to a smaller size.

RA'ZING, *ppr.* Subverting; destroying; erasing; extirpating.

RA'ZOR, *n.* [Fr. *rasoir;* It. *rasoio;* from Fr. *raser*, L. *rasus, rado*, to scrape.]

An instrument for shaving off beard or hair.

Razors of a boar, a boar's tusks.

RA'ZORABLE, *a.* Fit to be shaved. [*Not in use.*] *Shak.*

RA'ZOR-BILL, *n.* An aquatic fowl, the *Alca torda;* also, the *Rhynchops nigra* or cut-water. *Ed. Encyc.*

RA'ZOR-FISH, *n.* A species of fish with a compressed body.

RA'ZURE, *n.* [Fr. *rasure;* L. *rasura*, from *rado.*]

The act of erasing or effacing; obliteration. [See *Rasure.*]

RE, a prefix or inseparable particle in the composition of words, denotes return, repetition, iteration. It is contracted from *red*, which the Latins retained in words beginning with a vowel, as in *redamo, redeo, redintegro;* Ar. رَدَّ radda, to return, restore, bring back, repel, to answer. Class Rd. No. 1. From the Latin or the original Celtic, the Italians, Spanish and French have their *re, ra*, as prefixes. In a few English words, all or most of which, I believe, we receive from the French, it has lost its appropriate signification, as in *rejoice, recommend, receive.*

REABSORB', *v. t.* [*re* and *absorb.*] To draw in or imbibe again what has been effused, extravasated or thrown off; used of fluids; as, to *reabsorb* chyle, lymph, blood, gas, &c.

2. To swallow up again.

REABSORB'ED, *pp.* Imbibed again.

REABSORB'ING, *ppr.* Reimbibing.

REABSORP'TION, *n.* The act or process of imbibing what has been previously thrown off, effused or extravasated; the swallowing a second time. *Lavoisier.*

REACCESS', *n.* [*re* and *access.*] A second access or approach; a visit renewed. *Hakewill.*

REACH, *v. t.* *Raught*, the ancient preterit, is obsolete. The verb is now regular; pp. *reached.* [Sax. *racan, recan, ræcan* or *hræcan;* Goth. *rakyan;* Ir. *righim, roichim;* Dan. *rekker;* D. *reiken, rekken;* G. *reichen, recken;* Sw. *räcka;* Gr. ορεγω; It. *recere*, to reach, retch or vomit; L. *rego*, to rule or govern, to make *right* or straight, that is, to strain or stretch, the radical sense. The English sense of *reach* appears in L. *porrigo* and *porricio.* We find in the Shemitic languages, Ch. רגג to desire, to long for, Syr. ܪܓ and ܐܪܓ to desire. This is the Greek ορεγω, to reach, to stretch, the radical sense of desiring. The latter Syriac word is the Hebrew ארג to weave; but the primary sense is to stretch or strain. This verb in Arabic أَرِجَ signifies to send forth a grateful smell, to breathe fragrance, the root of the L. *fragro.* But the primary sense is the same, to reach, to extend, to shoot forth. The same word in Ethiopic ረገዐ signifies to congeal or condense, to make stiff or *rigid.* This is the L. *rigeo*, Gr. ριγοω, and hence L. *frigeo*, whence *frigid.* This sense also is from stretching or drawing, making tense or rigid. The radical sense of רקע is the same, whence *region*, and the Heb. רקיע the expanse of heaven or the firmament. The L. *rogo* has the same radical sense, to reach, to urge. See Class Rg. No. 1. 8. 15. 18. 21.]

1. To extend; to stretch; *in a general sense;* sometimes followed by *out* and *forth;* as, to *reach out* the arm. Hence,

2. To extend to; to touch by extending, either the arm alone, or with an instrument in the hand; as, to *reach* a book on the shelf; I cannot *reach* the object with my cane; the seaman *reaches* the bottom of the river with a pole or a line.

3. To strike from a distance.

O patron power, thy present aid afford,
That I may *reach* the beast. *Dryden.*

4. To deliver with the hand by extending the arm; to hand. He *reached* [to] me an orange.

He *reached* me a full cup. 2 *Esdras.*

5. To extend or stretch from a distance.

Reach hither thy finger—*reach* hither thy hand. John xx.

6. To arrive at; to come to. The ship *reached* her port in safety. We *reached* New York on Thursday. The letter *reached* me at seven o'clock.

7. To attain to or arrive at, by effort, labor or study; hence, to gain or obtain. Every artist should attempt to *reach* the point of excellence.

The best accounts of the appearances of nature which human penetration can *reach*, come short of its reality. *Cheyne.*

8. To penetrate to.

Whatever alterations are made in the body, if they *reach* not the mind, there is no perception. *Locke.*

9. To extend to so as to include or comprehend in fact or principle.

The law *reached* the intention of the promoters, and this act fixed the natural price of money. *Locke.*

If these examples of grown men *reach* not the case of children, let them examine. *Locke.*

10. To extend to.

Thy desire leads to no excess that *reaches* blame. *Milton.*

11. To extend; to spread abroad.

Trees *reach'd* too far their pampered boughs. *Milton.*

12. To take with the hand.

Lest therefore now his bolder hand
Reach also of the tree of life and eat. [*Unusual.*] *Milton.*

13. To overreach; to deceive. *South.*

REACH, *v. i.* To be extended.

The new world *reaches* quite across the torrid zone. *Boyle.*

The border shall descend, and shall *reach* to the side of the sea of Chinnereth eastward. Num. xxxiv.

And behold, a ladder set on the earth, and the top of it *reached* to heaven. Gen. xxviii.

2. To penetrate.

Ye have slain them in a rage that *reacheth* to heaven. 2 Chron. xxviii.

3. To make efforts to vomit. [See *Retch.*] *Cheyne.*

To reach after, to make efforts to attain to or obtain.

He would be in a posture of mind, *reaching after* a positive idea of infinity. *Locke.*

REACH, *n.* In *a general sense*, extension; a stretching; extent.

2. The power of extending to, or of taking by the hand, or by any instrument managed by the hand. The book is not within my *reach.* The bottom of the sea is not within the *reach* of a line or cable.

3. Power of attainment or management, or the limit of power, physical or moral. He used all the means within his *reach.* The causes of phenomena are often beyond the *reach* of human intellect.

Be sure yourself and your own *reach* to know. *Pope.*

4. Effort of the mind in contrivance or research; contrivance; scheme.

—Drawn by others who had deeper *reaches* than themselves to matters which they least intended. *Hayward.*

5. A fetch; an artifice to obtain an advantage.

The duke of Parma had particular *reaches* and ends of his own underhand, to cross the design. *Bacon.*

6. Tendency to distant consequences.

Strain not my speech
To grosser issues, nor to larger *reach*
Than to suspicion. *Shak.*

7. Extent.

And on the left hand, hell
With long *reach* interpos'd. *Milton.*

8. Among *seamen*, the distance between two points on the banks of a river, in which the current flows in a straight course. *Mar. Dict.*

9. An effort to vomit.

RE'ACHED, *pp.* Stretched out; extended; touched by extending the arm; attained to; obtained.

RE'ACHER, *n.* One that reaches or extends; one that delivers by extending the arm.

RE'ACHING, *ppr.* Stretching out; extending; touching by extension of the arm; attaining to; gaining; making efforts to vomit.

REACT', *v. t.* [*re* and *act.*] To act or perform a second time; as, to *react* a play. The same scenes were *reacted* at Rome.

REACT', *v. i.* To return an impulse or impression; to resist the action of another body by an opposite force. Every elastic body *reacts* on the body that impels it from its natural state.

2. To act in opposition; to resist any influence or power.

REACT'ED, *pp.* Acted or performed a second time.

REACT'ING, *ppr.* Acting again; in *physics*, resisting the impulse of another body.

REAC'TION, *n.* In *physics*, counteraction; the resistance made by a body to the action or impulse of another body, which endeavors to change its state, either of motion or rest. Action and *reaction* are equal. *Newton. Arbuthnot.*

2. Any action in resisting other action or power.

READ, *n.* [Sax. *ræd.* See the Verb.]
1. Counsel. [*Obs.*] *Sternhold.*
2. Saying; sentence. *Obs.* *Spenser.*

READ, *v. t.* The preterite and pp. *read*, is pronounced *red.* [Sax. *ræd*, *rad*, *red*, speech, discourse, counsel, advice, knowledge, benefit, *reason; rædan*, *redan*, to read, to decree, to appoint, to command, to rule or govern, to conjecture, to give or take counsel; *arædan*, to read, to tell, to narrate; *gerædan*, to read, to consult; *gerad*, mode, condition or state, reason, ratio or account, knowledge, instruction or learning, and as an adjective or participle, knowing, instructed, *ready*, suited; *gerad beon*, to be *ready*, to accord or agree; *geradod*, excited, quick. These significations unite this word with *ready*, which see. G. *rede*, speech, talk, account; *reden*, to speak; D. *rede*, speech; *reden*, reason; Dan. *rede*, account, and *ready;* G. *bereden*, to *berate;* *rath*, advice, counsel, a council or senate; *rathen*, to advise, to conjecture or guess, to solve a *riddle;* D. *raad*, counsel, advice; *raaden*, to counsel; Sw. *råd*, Dan. *raad*, counsel; *råda*, *raader*, to counsel, to instruct; W. *rhaith*, straight, right, that is, set right, decision, verdict; *rheitheg*, rhetoric, from *rhaith;* Dan. *ret*, law, justice, right, *reason;* Sw. *rätt*, *rätta*, id.; Ir. *radh*, a saying; *radham*, to say, tell, relate; W. *adrawz*, to tell or rehearse; Gr. ρεω, for ρεθω, to say or tell, to flow; ρητωρ, a speaker, a *rhetorician;* Goth. *rodyan*, to speak. The primary sense of *read* is to speak, to utter, that is, to push, drive or advance. This is also the primary sense of *ready*, that is, prompt or advancing, quick. The Sax. *gerad*, ready, accords also in elements with the W. *rhâd*, L. *gratia*, the primary sense of which is prompt to favor, advancing towards, free. The elements of these words are the same as those of *ride* and L. *gradior*, &c. The sense of *reason* is secondary, that which is uttered, said or set forth; hence counsel also. The Sw. *rätta*, Dan. *ret*, if not contracted words, are from the same root. See *Ready.* Class Rd. No. 1. 3. 5. 9. 26.]

1. To utter or pronounce written or printed words, letters or characters in the proper order; to repeat the names or utter the sounds customarily annexed to words, letters or characters; as, to *read* a written or printed discourse; to *read* the letters of an alphabet; to *read* figures; to *read* the notes of music, or to *read* music.

2. To inspect and understand words or characters; to peruse silently; as, to *read* a paper or letter without uttering the words; to *read* to one's self.

3. To discover or understand by characters, marks or features; as, to *read* a man's thoughts in his countenance.

> To *read* the interior structure of the globe. *Journ. of Science.*

> An armed corse did lie,
> In whose dead face he *read* great magnanimity. *Spenser.*

4. To learn by observation.

> Those about her
> From her shall *read* the perfect ways of honor. *Shak.*

5. To know fully.

> Who is't can *read* a woman? *Shak.*

6. To suppose; to guess. *Obs.* *Spenser.*
7. To advise. *Obs.* *Spenser.*

READ, *v. i.* To perform the act of reading.

> So they *read* in the book of the law of God distinctly, and gave the sense. Neh. viii.

2. To be studious; to practice much reading.

> It is sure that Fleury *reads.* *Taylor.*

3. To learn by reading.

> I have *read* of an eastern king who put a judge to death for an iniquitous sentence. *Swift.*

4. To tell; to declare. [*Not in use.*] *Spenser.*

READ, *pp. red.* Uttered; pronounced, as written words in the proper order; as, the letter was *read* to the family.

2. Silently perused.

READ, *a. red.* Instructed or knowing by reading; versed in books; learned. *Well read* is the phrase commonly used; as *well read* in history; *well read* in the classics.

> A poet *well read* in Longinus— *Addison.*

RE'ADABLE, *a.* That may be read; fit to be read. *Hurd.*

READEP'TION, *n.* [from L. *re* and *adeptus*, obtained.] A regaining; recovery of something lost. [*Not much used.*] *Bacon.*

RE'ADER, *n.* One that reads; any person who pronounces written words; particularly, one whose office is to read prayers in a church.

2. By way of distinction, one that reads much; one studious in books.

RE'ADERSHIP, *n.* [See *Read.*] The office of reading prayers in a church. *Swift.*

READILY, *adv. red'ily.* [See *Ready.*] Quickly; promptly; easily. I *readily* perceive the distinction you make.

2. Cheerfully; without delay or objection; without reluctance. He *readily* granted my request.

READINESS, *n. red'iness.* [from *ready.*]
1. Quickness; promptness; promptitude; facility; freedom from hinderance or obstruction; as *readiness* of speech; *readiness* of thought; *readiness* of mind in suggesting an answer; *readiness* of reply.

2. Promptitude; cheerfulness; willingness; alacrity; freedom from reluctance; as, to grant a request or assistance with *readiness.*

> They received the word with all *readiness* of mind. Acts xvii.

3. A state of preparation; fitness of condition. The troops are in *readiness.*

RE'ADING, *ppr.* Pronouncing or perusing written or printed words or characters of a book or writing.

2. Discovering by marks; understanding.

RE'ADING, *n.* The act of reading; perusal.

2. Study of books; as a man of extensive *reading.*

3. A lecture or prelection.

4. Public recital.

> The Jews had their weekly *readings* of the law. *Hooker.*

5. In *criticism*, the manner of reading the manuscripts of ancient authors, where the words or letters are obscure. No small part of the business of critics is to settle the true *reading*, or real words used by the author; and the various *readings* of different critics are often perplexing.

6. A commentary or gloss on a law, text or passage. *Encyc.*

7. In *legislation*, the formal recital of a bill by the proper officer, before the house which is to consider it. In Congress and in the state legislatures, a bill must usually have three several *readings* on different days, before it can be passed into a law.

READJOURN', *v. t.* [*re* and *adjourn.*] To adjourn a second time.

2. To cite or summon again. [*Not used.*] *Colgrave.*

READJUST', *v. t.* [*re* and *adjust.*] To settle again; to put in order again what had been discomposed. *Fielding.*

READJUST'ED, *pp.* Adjusted again; resettled.

READJUST'ING, *ppr.* Adjusting again.

READJUST'MENT, *n.* A second adjustment.

READMIS'SION, *n.* [*re* and *admission.*] The act of admitting again what had been excluded; as the *readmission* of fresh air into an exhausted receiver; the *readmission* of a student into a seminary. *Arbuthnot.*

READMIT', *v. t.* [*re* and *admit.*] To admit again.

> Whose ear is ever open and his eye
> Gracious to *readmit* the suppliant. *Milton.*

READMIT'TANCE, *n.* A second admittance; allowance to enter again.

READOPT', *v. t.* [*re* and *adopt.*] To adopt again. *Young.*

READORN', *v. t.* To adorn anew; to decorate a second time. *Blackmore.*

READVERT'ENCY, *n.* [*re* and *advertency.*] The act of reviewing. *Norris.*

READY, *a. red'y.* [Sax. *ræd*, *hrad*, *hræd*, quick, brisk, prompt, ready; *gerad*, prepared, ready, prudent, learned; *hradian*, *gehradian*, to hasten, to accelerate; *gerædian*, to make ready; D. *reeden*, to prepare; *reed*, pret. of *ryden*, to ride; *reede*, a road; *bereid*, ready; *bereiden*, to prepare; *gereed*, ready; G. *bereit*, id.; *bereiten*, to prepare, and to *ride; reede*, a road; Dan. *rede*, ready; *reder*, to make the bed, to *rid; rede*, an account; Sax. *ræd*, from the root of *read; bereder*, to prepare; *rider*, *berider*, to ride; Sw. *reda*, to make ready, to clear or disentangle, Eng. to *rid; redo*, ready; *rida*, to ride; *bereda*, to prepare; Ir. *reidh*, ready; *reidhim*, to prepare, to agree; Gr. ραδιος, easy; W. *rhedu*, to run. The primary sense is to go, move, or advance forward, and it seems to be clear that *ready*, *ride*, *read*, *riddle*, are all of one family, and probably from the root of L. *gradior.* See *Read* and *Red.* Class Rd. No. 23.]

1. Quick; prompt; not hesitating; as *ready* wit; a *ready* consent.

2. Quick to receive or comprehend; not slow or dull; as a *ready* apprehension.

3. Quick in action or execution; dextrous; as an artist *ready* in his business; a *ready* writer. Ps. xlv.

4. Prompt; not delayed; present in hand. He makes *ready* payment; he pays *ready* money for every thing he buys.

5. Prepared; fitted; furnished with what is necessary, or disposed in a manner suited to the purpose; as a ship *ready* for sea.

My oxen and fatlings are killed, and all things are *ready*. Matt. xxii.

6. Willing; free; cheerful to do or suffer; not backward or reluctant; as a prince always *ready* to grant the reasonable requests of his subjects.

The spirit is *ready*, but the flesh is weak. Mark xiv.

I am *ready* not to be bound only, but also to die at Jerusalem for the name of the Lord Jesus. Acts xxi.

7. Willing; disposed. Men are generally *ready* to impute blame to others. They are more *ready* to give than to take reproof.

8. Being at the point; near; not distant; about to do or suffer.

A Syrian *ready* to perish was my father. Deut. xxvi. Job xxix. Ps. lxxxviii.

9. Being nearest or at hand.

A sapling pine he wrench'd from out the ground,
The *readiest* weapon that his fury found. *Dryden.*

10. Easy; facile; opportune; short; near, or most convenient; the Greek sense, ῥαδιος.

Sometimes the *readiest* way which a wise man has to conquer, is to flee. *Hooker.*

Through the wild desert, not the *readiest* way. *Milton.*

The *ready* way to be thought mad, is to contend you are not so. *Spectator.*

To make ready, to prepare; to provide and put in order.

2. An elliptical phrase, for *make things ready*; to make preparations; to prepare.

READY, *adv.* *red'y.* In a state of preparation, so as to need no delay.

We ourselves will go *ready* armed before the house of Israel. Num. xxxii.

READY, *n.* *red'y.* For *ready money.*

Lord Strut was not flush in *ready*, either to go to law, or to clear old debts. [*A low word.*] *Arbuthnot.*

READY, *v. t.* *red'y.* To dispose in order; to prepare. [*Not in use.*] *Brooke.*

REAFFIRM', *v. t.* [*re* and *affirm.*] To affirm a second time.

REAFFIRM'ANCE, *n.* A second confirmation. *Ayliffe.*

REA'GENT, *n.* [*re* and *agent.*] In *chimistry*, a substance employed to precipitate another in solution, or to detect the ingredients of a mixture.

Bergman reckons barytic muriate to be one of the most sensible *reagents*. *Fourcroy.*

REAGGRAVA'TION, *n.* [*re* and *aggravation.*]

In the Romish ecclesiastical law, the last monitory, published after three admonitions and before the last excommunication. Before they proceed to fulminate the last excommunication, they publish an aggravation and a reaggravation. *Encyc.*

REAK, *n.* A rush. [*Not in use.*]

RE'AL, *a.* [Low L. *realis*; It. *reale*; Sp. *real*; Fr. *reel*; from L. *res, rei*, Ir. *raod, red, rod.* *Res* is of the Class Rd. from the root of *read, ready*, from rushing, driving or falling. *Res*, like *thing*, is primarily that which comes, falls out or happens, corresponding with *event*, from L. *evenio.* *Res* then denotes that which actually exists. The L. *res* and Eng. *thing* coincide exactly with the Heb. דבר, a word, a thing, an event. See *Read* and *Thing.*]

1. Actually being or existing; not fictitious or imaginary; as a description of *real* life. The author describes a *real* scene or transaction.

2. True; genuine; not artificial, counterfeit or factitious; as *real* Madeira wine; *real* ginger.

3. True; genuine; not affected; not assumed. The woman appears in her *real* character.

4. Relating to things, not to persons; not personal.

Many are perfect in men's humors, that are not greatly capable of the *real* part of business. [*Little used or obsolete.*] *Bacon.*

5. In *law*, pertaining to things fixed, permanent or immovable, as to lands and tenements; as *real* estate, opposed to *personal* or *movable* property. *Blackstone.*

Real action, in *law*, is an action which concerns real property.

Real assets, assets consisting in real estate, or lands and tenements descending to an heir, sufficient to answer the charges upon the estate created by the ancestor.

Chattels real, are such chattels as concern or savor of the reality; as a term for years of land, wardships in chivalry, the next presentation to a church, estate by statute-merchant, elegit, &c.

Real composition, is when an agreement is made between the owner of lands and the parson or vicar, with consent of the ordinary, that such lands shall be discharged from payment of tithes, in consequence of other land or recompense given to the parson in lieu and satisfaction thereof. *Blackstone.*

Real presence, in the Romish church, the actual presence of the body and blood of Christ in the eucharist, or the conversion of the substance of the bread and wine into the real body and blood of Christ. *Encyc.*

RE'AL, } *n.* A scholastic philosopher,
RE'ALIST, } who maintains that things and not words, are the objects of dialectics; opposed to *nominal* or *nominalist.* *Encyc.*

RE'AL, *n.* [Sp.] A small Spanish coin of the value of forty maravedis; but its value is different in different provinces, being from five or six to ten cents, or six pence sterling. It is sometimes written *rial.*

RE'ALGAR, *n.* [Fr. *reagal* or *realgal*; Port. *rosalgar*, red algar.]

A combination of sulphur and arsenic; red sulphuret of arsenic. Realgar differs from orpiment in having undergone a greater degree of heat. *Chaptal. Nicholson.*

REAL'ITY, *n.* [Fr. *realité.*] Actual being or existence of any thing; truth; fact; in distinction from mere appearance.

A man may fancy he understands a critic, when in *reality* he does not comprehend his meaning. *Addison.*

2. Something intrinsically important, not merely matter of show.

And to *realities* yield all her shows. *Milton.*

3. In *the schools*, that may exist of itself, or which has a full and absolute being of itself, and is not considered as a part of any thing else. *Encyc.*

4. In *law*, immobility, or the fixed, permanent nature of property; as chattels which savor of the *realty.* [This word is so written in law, for *reality.*] *Blackstone.*

REALIZA'TION, *n.* [from *realize.*] The act of realizing or making real. *Beddoes.*

2. The act of converting money into land.

3. The act of believing or considering as real.

4. The act of bringing into being or act. *Glanville.*

RE'ALIZE, *v. t.* [Sp. *realizar*; Fr. *realiser.*]

1. To bring into being or act; as, to *realize* a scheme or project.

We *realize* what Archimedes had only in hypothesis, weighing a single grain of sand against the globe of earth. *Glanville.*

2. To convert money into land, or personal into real estate.

3. To impress on the mind as a reality; to believe, consider or treat as real. How little do men in full health *realize* their frailty and mortality.

Let the sincere christian *realize* the closing sentiment. *T. Scott.*

4. To bring home to one's own case or experience; to consider as one's own; to feel in all its force. Who, at his fire side, can *realize* the distress of shipwrecked mariners?

This allusion must have had enhanced strength and beauty to the eye of a nation extensively devoted to a pastoral life, and therefore *realizing* all its fine scenes and the tender emotions to which they gave birth. *Dwight.*

5. To bring into actual existence and possession; to render tangible or effective. He never *realized* much profit from his trade or speculations.

RE'ALIZED, *pp.* Brought into actual being; converted into real estate; impressed, received or treated as a reality; felt in its true force; rendered actual, tangible or effective.

RE'ALIZING, *ppr.* Bringing into actual being; converting into real estate; impressing as a reality; feeling as one's own or in its real force; rendering tangible or effective.

2. *a.* That makes real, or that brings home as a reality; as a *realizing* view of eternity.

REALLEDGE, *v. t.* *reallej'.* [*re* and *alledge.*] To alledge again. *Cotgrave.*

RE'ALLY, *adv.* With actual existence. *Pearson.*

2. In truth; in fact; not in appearance only; as things *really* evil.

The anger of the people is *really* a short fit of madness. *Swift.*

In this sense, it is used familiarly as a slight corroboration of an opinion or declaration.

Why *really*, sixty five is somewhat old. *Young.*

REALM, *n.* *relm.* [Fr. *royaume*; It. *reame*; from Fr. *roi*, It. *re*, L. *rex*, king, whence *regalis*, royal.]

1. A royal jurisdiction or extent of government; a kingdom; a king's dominions; as the *realm* of England.

2. Kingly government; as the *realm* of bees. [*Unusual.*] *Milton.*

RE'ALTY, *n.* [It. *realtà*, from *re*, king, L. *rex.*]

1. Loyalty. [*Not in use.*] *Milton.*
2. Reality. [*Not in use.*] *More.*
3. In *law*, immobility. [See *Reality.*]

REAM, *n.* [Sax. *ream*, a band; D. *riem;* Dan. *rem* or *reem;* Sw. *rem;* W. *rhwym*, a bond or tie. The Dutch word signifies a strap, thong or girdle, and an oar, L. *remus.* In Fr. *rame* is a ream and an oar, and if the English *ream* and the L. *remus* are the same word, the primary sense is a shoot, L. *ramus*, a branch, for the shoots of trees or shrubs were the first bands used by men. See *Gird* and *Withe.* The Italian has *risma*, and the Sp. Port. *resma*, a ream, G. *riess.* See Class Rm. No. 7. 9.]

A bundle or package of paper, consisting of twenty quires. *Pope.*

REAN'IMATE, *v. t.* [*re* and *animate.*] To revive; to resuscitate; to restore to life; as a person dead or apparently dead; as, to *reanimate* a drowned person.

2. To revive the spirits when dull or languid; to invigorate; to infuse new life or courage into; as, to *reanimate* disheartened troops; to *reanimate* drowsy senses or languid spirits.

REAN'IMATED, *pp.* Restored to life or action.

REAN'IMATING, *ppr.* Restoring life to; invigorating with new life and courage.

REANIMA'TION, *n.* The act or operation of reviving from apparent death; the act or operation of giving fresh spirits, courage or vigor.

REANNEX', *v. t.* [*re* and *annex.*] To annex again; to reunite; to annex what has been separated. *Bacon.*

REANNEXA'TION, *n.* The act of annexing again. *Marshall.*

REANNEX'ED, *pp.* Annexed or united again.

REANNEX'ING, *ppr.* Annexing again; reuniting.

REAP, *v. t.* [Sax. *rip, hrippe, gerip*, harvest; *ripan*, to reap; *ripe*, ripe; *rypan*, to *rip;* allied probably to *reafian*, to seize, spoil, lay waste, L. *rapio*, G. *reif*, ripe, D. *raapen*, to reap, *ryp*, ripe, Gr. αρπη, a sickle, αρπαω, to reap, L. *carpo*, Eng. *crop.* See Class Rb. No. 18. 26. 27.]

1. To cut grain with a sickle; as, to *reap* wheat or rye.

> When ye *reap* the harvest, thou shalt not wholly *reap* the corners of thy field. Lev. xix.

2. To clear of a crop by reaping; as, to *reap* a field.
3. To gather; to obtain; to receive as a reward, or as the fruit of labor or of works; *in a good or bad sense;* as, to *reap* a benefit from exertions.

> He that soweth to the flesh, shall of the flesh *reap* corruption. Gal. vi.
>
> Ye have plowed wickedness; ye have *reaped* iniquity. Hos. x.

REAP, *v. i.* To perform the act or operation of reaping. In New England, farmers *reap* in July and August.

2. To receive the fruit of labor or works.

> They that sow in tears, shall *reap* in joy. Ps. cxxvi.

RE'APED, *pp.* Cut with a sickle; received as the fruit of labor or works.

RE'APER, *n.* One that cuts grain with a sickle.

RE'APING, *ppr.* Cutting grain with a sickle; receiving as the fruit of labor or the reward of works.

RE'APING-HOOK, *n.* An instrument used in reaping; a sickle.

REAPPAR'EL, *v. t.* [*re* and *apparel.*] To clothe again. *Donne.*

REAPPAR'ELED, *pp.* Clothed again.

REAPPAR'ELING, *ppr.* Clothing again.

REAPPE'AR, *v. i.* [*re* and *appear.*] To appear a second time.

REAPPE'ARANCE, *n.* A second appearance.

REAPPE'ARING, *ppr.* Appearing again.

REAPPLICA'TION, *n.* [See *Reapply.*] A second application.

REAPPLY', *v. t.* or *i.* [*re* and *apply.*] To apply again.

REAPPLY'ING, *ppr.* Applying again.

REAPPOINT', *v. t.* To appoint again.

REAPPOINT'MENT, *n.* A second appointment.

REAPPORTION, *v. t.* To apportion again.

REAPPORTIONED, *pp.* Apportioned again.

REAPPORTIONING, *ppr.* Apportioning again.

REAPPORTIONMENT, *n.* A second apportionment. *Madison.*

REAR, *n.* [Fr. *arriere;* but this is compound; Arm. *refr, rever, reor*, the seat, the fundament; W. *rhêv*, something thick, a bundle; *rhevyr*, the fundament. *Rear* is contracted from *rever.* Class Rb.]

1. In *a general sense*, that which is behind or backwards; *appropriately*, the part of an army which is behind the other, either when standing on parade or when marching; also, the part of a fleet which is behind the other. It is opposed to *front* or *van.* Bring up the *rear.*
2. The last class; the last in order.

> Coins I place in the *rear.* *Peacham.*

In the rear, behind the rest; backward, or in the last class. In this phrase, *rear* signifies the part or place behind.

REAR, *a.* [Sax. *hrere.*] Raw; rare; not well roasted or boiled.

2. [Sax. *aræran*, to hasten; *hreran*, to excite.] Early. [*A provincial word.*]

REAR, *v. t.* [Sax. *ræran, reran, aræran*, to erect, to excite, to hasten; *hreran*, to excite; Sw. *röra*, to move; Dan. *rörer*, to move, stir, shake; *rörig*, quick, lively, rising in the stomach.]

1. To raise.

> Who now shall *rear* you to the sun, or rank
> Your tribes? *Milton.*

2. To lift after a fall.

> In adoration at his feet I fell
> Submiss; he *rear'd* me. *Milton.*

3. To bring up or to raise to maturity, as young; as, to *rear* a numerous offspring. *Thomson.*
4. To educate; to instruct.

> He wants a father to protect his youth,
> And *rear* him up to virtue. *Southern.*

5. To exalt; to elevate.

> Charity, decent, modest, easy, kind,
> Softens the high, and *rears* the abject mind. *Prior.*

6. To rouse; to stir up.

> And seeks the tusky boar to *rear.* *Dryden.*

7. To raise; to breed; as cattle. *Harte.*
8. To achieve; to obtain. *Spenser.*

To rear the steps, to ascend; to move upward. *Milton.*

REAR-ADMIRAL. [See *Admiral.*]

RE'ARED, *pp.* Raised; lifted; brought up; educated; elevated.

RE'AR-GU'ARD, *n.* The body of an army that marches in the rear of the main body to protect it.

RE'ARING, *ppr.* Raising; educating; elevating.

REAR-LINE, *n.* The line in the rear of an army.

RE'AR-MOUSE, *n.* [Sax. *hrere-mus.*] The lether-winged bat. *Shak. Abbot.*

REAR-RANK, *n.* The rank of a body of troops which is in the rear.

RE'ARWARD, *n.* [from *rear.* See *Rereward.*]

1. The last troop; the rear-guard.
2. The end; the tail; the train behind. *Shak.*
3. The latter part. *Shak.*

REASCEND', *v. i.* [*re* and *ascend.*] To rise, mount or climb again. *Milton. Spenser.*

REASCEND', *v. t.* To mount or ascend again.

> He mounts aloft and *reascends* the skies. *Addison.*

REASCEND'ED, *pp.* Ascended again.

REASCEND'ING, *ppr.* Ascending again.

REASCEN'SION, *n.* The act of reascending; a remounting.

REASCENT', *n.* A returning ascent; acclivity. *Cowper.*

REASON, *n.* re'zn. [Ir. *reasun;* W. *rheswm;* Arm. *resoun;* Fr. *raison;* Sp. *razon;* Port. *razam;* It. *ragione;* L. *ratio;* Russ. *razum;* Goth. *rathyo*, an account, number, ratio; *rathyan*, to number; *garathyan*, to number or count; *rodyan*, to speak; D. *rede*, speech; *reden*, reason, argument; *redenkunst*, rhetoric; G. *rede, reden;* Sax. *ræd, ræda*, speech, reason; *ræswian*, to reason. We find united the Sax. *ræd*, speech, *rædan, redan*, to *read*, the Greek ρεω, to say or speak, whence *rhetoric*, and the L. *ratio*, which is from *ratus*, and which proves *reor* to be contracted from *redo, redor*, and all unite with *rod*, L. *radius*, &c. Primarily, *reason* is that which is uttered. See *Read.* So Gr. λογος, from λεγω.]

1. That which is thought or which is alledged in words, as the ground or cause of opinion, conclusion or determination. I have *reasons* which I may choose not to disclose. You ask me my *reasons.* I freely give my *reasons.* The judge assigns good *reasons* for his opinion, *reasons* which justify his decision. Hence in general,
2. The cause, ground, principle or motive of any thing said or done; that which supports or justifies a determination, plan or measure.

> Virtue and vice are not arbitrary things; but there is a natural and eternal *reason* for that goodness and virtue, and against vice and wickedness. 1 Pet. iii. *Tillotson.*

3. Efficient cause. He is detained by *reason* of sickness.

> Spain is thin sown of people, partly by *reason* of its sterility of soil. *Bacon.*
>
> The *reason* of the motion of the balance in a wheel-watch is by motion of the next wheel. *Hale.*

4. Final cause.

Reason, in the English language, is sometimes taken for true and clear principles; sometimes for clear and fair deductions; sometimes for the cause, particularly the final cause. *Locke.*

5. A faculty of the mind by which it distinguishes truth from falsehood, and good from evil, and which enables the possessor to deduce inferences from facts or from propositions. *Encyc.*

Self-love, the spring of motion, acts the soul,
Reason's comparing balance rules the whole—
That sees immediate good by present sense,
Reason the future and the consequence. *Pope.*

Reason is the director of man's will. *Hooker.*

6. Ratiocination; the exercise of reason.

But when by *reason* she the truth has found— *Davies.*

7. Right; justice; that which is dictated or supported by reason. Every man claims to have *reason* on his side.

I was promised on a time
To have *reason* for my rhyme. *Spenser.*

8. Reasonable claim; justice.

God brings good out of evil, and therefore it were but *reason* we should trust God to govern his own world. *Taylor.*

9. Rationale; just account.

This *reason* did the ancient fathers render, why the church was called catholic. *Pearson.* [See No. 1. and 2.]

10. Moderation; moderate demands; claims which reason and justice admit or prescribe.

The most probable way of bringing France to *reason*, would be by the making an attempt on the Spanish West Indies— *Addison.*

In reason, in all reason, in justice; with rational ground.

When any thing is proved by as good arguments as a thing of that kind is capable of, we ought not *in reason* to doubt of its existence. *Tillotson.*

RE'ASON, *v. i.* [Fr. *raisonner;* Sax. *ræswian.*]

1. To exercise the faculty of reason; to deduce inferences justly from premises. Brutes do not *reason;* children *reason* imperfectly.

2. To argue; to infer conclusions from premises, or to deduce new or unknown propositions from previous propositions which are known or evident. To *reason* justly is to infer from propositions which are known, admitted or evident, the conclusions which are natural, or which necessarily result from them. Men may *reason* within themselves; they may *reason* before a court or legislature; they may *reason* wrong as well as right.

3. To debate; to confer or inquire by discussion or mutual communication of thoughts, arguments or reasons.

And they *reasoned* among themselves. Matt. xvi.

To reason with, to argue with; to endeavor to inform, convince or persuade by argument. *Reason with* a profligate son, and if possible, persuade him of his errors.

2. To discourse; to talk; to take or give an account.

Stand still, that I may *reason with* you before the Lord, of all the righteous acts of the Lord. *Obs.* 1 Sam. xii.

RE'ASON, *v. t.* To examine or discuss by arguments; to debate or discuss. I *reasoned* the matter with my friend.

When they are clearly discovered, well digested and well *reasoned* in every part, there is beauty in such a theory. *Burnet.*

2. To persuade by reasoning or argument; as, to *reason* one into a belief of truth; to *reason* one out of his plan; to *reason* down a passion.

RE'ASONABLE, *a.* Having the faculty of reason; endued with reason; as a *reasonable* being. [In this sense, *rational* is now generally used.]

2. Governed by reason; being under the influence of reason; thinking, speaking or acting rationally or according to the dictates of reason; as, the measure must satisfy all *reasonable* men.

3. Conformable or agreeable to reason; just; rational.

By indubitable certainty, I mean that which does not admit of any *reasonable* cause of doubting. *Wilkins.*

A law may be *reasonable* in itself, though a man does not allow it. *Swift.*

4. Not immoderate.

Let all things be thought upon,
That may with *reasonable* swiftness add
More feathers to our wings. *Shak.*

5. Tolerable; being in mediocrity; moderate; as a *reasonable* quantity. *Abbot.*

6. Not excessive; not unjust; as a *reasonable* fine; a *reasonable* sum in damages.

RE'ASONABLENESS, *n.* The faculty of reason. [*In this sense, little used.*]

2. Agreeableness to reason; that state or quality of a thing which reason supports or justifies; as the *reasonableness* of our wishes, demands or expectations.

The *reasonableness* and excellency of charity. *Law.*

3. Conformity to rational principles.

The whole frame and contexture of a watch carries in it a *reasonableness*—the passive impression of the reason or intellectual idea that was in the artist. [*Unusual.*] *Hale.*

4. Moderation; as the *reasonableness* of a demand.

RE'ASONABLY, *adv.* In a manner or degree agreeable to reason; in consistency with reason. We may *reasonably* suppose self interest to be the governing principle of men.

2. Moderately; in a moderate degree; not fully; in a degree reaching to mediocrity.

If we can by industry make our deaf and dumb persons *reasonably* perfect in the language— *Holder.*

RE'ASONER, *n.* One who reasons or argues; as a fair *reasoner;* a close *reasoner;* a logical *reasoner.*

RE'ASONING, *ppr.* Arguing; deducing inferences from premises; debating; discussing.

RE'ASONING, *n.* The act or process of exercising the faculty of reason; that act or operation of the mind by which new or unknown propositions are deduced from previous ones which are known and evident, or which are admitted or supposed for the sake of argument; argumentation; ratiocination; as fair *reasoning;* false *reasoning;* absurd *reasoning;* strong or weak *reasoning.* The *reasonings* of the advocate appeared to the court conclusive.

RE'ASONLESS, *a.* Destitute of reason; as a *reasonless* man or mind. *Shak. Raleigh.*

2. Void of reason; not warranted or supported by reason.

This proffer is absurd and *reasonless.* *Shak.*

REASSEM'BLAGE, *n.* Assemblage a second time.

REASSEM'BLE, *v. t.* [*re* and *assemble.*] To collect again. *Milton.*

REASSEM'BLE, *v. i.* To assemble or convene again.

REASSEM'BLED, *pp.* Assembled again.

REASSEM'BLING, *ppr.* Assembling again.

REASSERT', *v. t.* [*re* and *assert.*] To assert again; to maintain after suspension or cessation.

Let us hope—we may have a body of authors who will *reassert* our claim to respectability in literature. *Walsh.*

REASSERT'ED, *pp.* Asserted or maintained anew.

REASSERT'ING, *ppr.* Asserting again; vindicating anew.

REASSIGN, *v. t.* [*re* and *assign.*] To assign back; to transfer back what has been assigned.

REASSIM'ILATE, *v. t.* [*re* and *assimilate.*] To assimilate or cause to resemble anew; to change again into a like or suitable substance. *Encyc.*

REASSIM'ILATED, *pp.* Assimilated anew; changed again to a like substance.

REASSIM'ILATING, *ppr.* Assimilating again.

REASSIMILA'TION, *n.* A second or renewed assimilation. *Encyc.*

REASSU'ME, *v. t.* [*re* and *assume.*] To resume; to take again. *Milton.*

REASSU'MED, *pp.* Resumed; assumed again.

REASSU'MING, *ppr.* Assuming or taking again.

REASSUMP'TION, *n.* A resuming; a second assumption.

REASSU'RANCE, *n.* [See *Sure* and *Assurance.*]

A second assurance against loss; or the assurance of property by an underwriter, to relieve himself from a risk he has taken. *Blackstone. Park.*

REASSURE, *v. t.* *reasshu're.* [*re* and *assure;* Fr. *rassurer.*]

1. To restore courage to; to free from fear or terror.

They rose with fear,
Till dauntless Pallas *reassur'd* the rest. *Dryden.*

2. To insure a second time against loss, or rather to insure by another what one has already insured; to insure against loss that may be incurred by taking a risk.

REASSU'RED, *pp.* Restored from fear; re-encouraged.

2. Insured against loss by risk taken, as an underwriter.

REASSU'RER, *n.* One who insures the first underwriter.

REASSU'RING, *ppr.* Restoring from fear, terror or depression of courage.

2. Insuring against loss by insurance.

RE'ASTINESS, *n.* Rancidness. [*Not in use or local.*] *Cotgrave.*

RE'ASTY, *a.* [Qu. *rusty.*] Covered with a kind of rust and having a rancid taste; *applied to dried meat.* [*Not in use or local.*] *Skelton.*

RE'ATE, *n.* A kind of long small grass that grows in water and complicates itself. [*Not in use or local.*] *Walton.*

REATTACH', *v. t.* [*re* and *attach.*] To attach a second time.

REATTACH'MENT, *n.* A second attachment.

REATTEMPT', *v. t.* [*re* and *attempt.*] To attempt again.

REAVE, *v. t.* [Sax. *reafian.*] To take away by stealth or violence; to bereave. *Obs.* [See *Bereave.*] *Shak. Spenser.*

REBAP'TISM, *n.* A second baptism.

REBAPTIZA'TION, *n.* [from *rebaptize.*] A second baptism. *Hooker.*

REBAPTI'ZE, *v. t.* [*re* and *baptize.*] To baptize a second time. *Ayliffe.*

REBAPTI'ZED, *pp.* Baptized again.

REBAPTI'ZING, *ppr.* Baptizing a second time.

REBA'TE, *v. t.* [Fr. *rebattre; re* and *battre;* It. *ribattere.*]

To blunt; to beat to obtuseness; to deprive of keenness.

> He doth *rebate* and blunt his natural edge. *Shak.*
>
> The keener edge of battle to *rebate.* *Dryden.*

REBA'TE, } *n.* Diminution.
REBA'TEMENT, }

2. In *commerce,* abatement in price; deduction. *Encyc.*

3. In *heraldry,* a diminution or abatement of the bearings in a coat of arms. *Encyc.*

REBA'TO, *n.* A sort of ruff. [See *Rabato.*]

RE'BECK, *n.* [Fr. *rebec;* It. *ribecca.*] A three stringed fiddle. [*Not much used.*] *Milton.*

REB'EL, *n.* [Fr. *rebelle,* from L. *rebellis,* making war again.]

1. One who revolts from the government to which he owes allegiance, either by openly renouncing the authority of that government, or by taking arms and openly opposing it. A *rebel* differs from an *enemy,* as the latter is one who does not owe allegiance to the government which he attacks. Num. xvii.

2. One who willfully violates a law. *Encyc.*

3. One who disobeys the king's proclamation; a contemner of the king's laws. *British Laws. Blackstone.*

4. A villain who disobeys his lord. *Encyc.*

REB'EL, *a.* Rebellious; acting in revolt. *Milton.*

REBEL', *v. i.* [L. *rebello,* to make war again; *re* and *bello;* W. *rhyvela,* to make war; *rhy* and *bel,* war.]

1. To revolt; to renounce the authority of the laws and government to which one owes allegiance. Subjects may *rebel* by an open renunciation of the authority of the government, without taking arms; but ordinarily, rebellion is accompanied by resistance in arms.

> Ye have built you an altar, that ye might *rebel* this day against the Lord. Josh. xxii. Is. i.

2. To rise in violent opposition against lawful authority.

> How could my hand *rebel* against my heart?
> How could your heart *rebel* against your reason? *Dryden.*

REBEL'LED, *pp.* or *a.* Rebellious; guilty of rebellion. *Milton.*

REBEL'LER, *n.* One that rebels. *Dict.*

REBEL'LING, *ppr.* Renouncing the authority of the government to which one owes allegiance; rising in opposition to lawful authority.

REBEL'LION, *n.* [Fr. from L. *rebellio.* Among the Romans, rebellion was originally a revolt or open resistance to their government by nations that had been subdued in war. It was a renewed war.]

1. An open and avowed renunciation of the authority of the government to which one owes allegiance; or the taking of arms traitorously to resist the authority of lawful government; revolt. *Rebellion* differs from *insurrection* and from *mutiny. Insurrection* may be a rising in opposition to a particular act or law, without a design to renounce wholly all subjection to the government. *Insurrection* may be, but is not necessarily, rebellion. *Mutiny* is an insurrection of soldiers or seamen against the authority of their officers.

> No sooner is the standard of *rebellion* displayed, than men of desperate principles resort to it. *Ames.*

2. Open resistance to lawful authority.

Commission of rebellion, in *law,* a commission awarded against a person who treats the king's authority with contempt, in not obeying his proclamation according to his allegiance, and refusing to attend his sovereign when required; in which case, four commissioners are ordered to attach him wherever he may be found. *Blackstone.*

REBEL'LIOUS, *a.* Engaged in rebellion; renouncing the authority and dominion of the government to which allegiance is due; traitorously resisting government or lawful authority. Deut. ix. xxi.

REBEL'LIOUSLY, *adv.* With design to throw off the authority of legitimate government; in opposition to the government to which one is bound by allegiance; with violent or obstinate disobedience to lawful authority. *Camden.*

REBEL'LIOUSNESS, *n.* The quality or state of being rebellious.

REBEL'LOW, *v. i.* [*re* and *bellow.*] To bellow in return; to echo back a loud roaring noise.

> The cave *rebellow'd* and the temple shook. *Dryden.*

REBEL'LOWING, *ppr.* Bellowing in return or in echo.

REBLOS'SOM, *v. i.* [*re* and *blossom.*] To blossom again.

REBOA'TION, *n.* [L. *reboo; re* and *boo.*] The return of a loud bellowing sound. [*Not used.*] *Patrick.*

REBOIL', *v. i.* [L. *re* and *bullio.*] To take fire; to be hot. *Elyot.*

REBOUND', *v. i.* [Fr. *rebondir; re* and *bondir.*]

To spring back; to start back; to be reverberated by an elastic power resisting force or impulse impressed; as a *rebounding* echo.

> Bodies absolutely hard, or so soft as to be void of elasticity, will not *rebound* from one another. *Newton.*

REBOUND', *v. t.* To drive back; to reverberate.

> Silenus sung; the vales his voice *rebound.* *Dryden.*

REBOUND', *n.* The act of flying back in resistance of the impulse of another body; resilience.

> Put back as from a rock with swift *rebound.* *Dryden.*

REBOUND'ING, *ppr.* Springing or flying back; reverberating.

REBRA'CE, *v. t.* [*re* and *brace.*] To brace again. *Gray.*

REBRE'ATHE, *v. i.* [*re* and *breathe.*] To breathe again.

REBUFF', *n.* [It. *rabbuffo;* Fr. *rebuffade: re* and It. *buffa, buffare,* Fr. *bouffer.*]

1. Repercussion, or beating back; a quick and sudden resistance.

> The strong *rebuff* of some tumultuous cloud. *Milton.*

2. Sudden check; defeat.

3. Refusal; rejection of solicitation.

REBUFF', *v. t.* To beat back; to offer sudden resistance to; to check.

REBUILD', } *v. t.* [*re* and *build.*] To build again; to renew a structure; to build or construct what has been demolished; as, to *rebuild* a house, a wall, a wharf or a city.
REBILD', }

REBUILD'ING, } *ppr.* Building again.
REBILD'ING, }

REBUILT', } *pp.* Built again; reconstructed.
REBILT', }

REBU'KABLE, *a.* [from *rebuke.*] Worthy of reprehension. *Shak.*

REBU'KE, *v. t.* [Norm. *rebuquer;* Arm. *rebechat,* to reproach. Qu. Fr. *reboucher,* to stop; *re* and *boucher,* to stop. The Italian has *rimbeccare,* to repulse or drive back, to *peck,* from *becco,* the beak. The word is a compound of *re* and a root in *Bg,* signifying to drive. See *Pack* and *Impeach.* Class Bg. No. 20.]

1. To chide; to reprove; to reprehend for a fault; to check by reproof.

> The proud he tam'd, the penitent he cheer'd,
> Nor to *rebuke* the rich offender fear'd. *Dryden.*
>
> Thou shalt in any wise *rebuke* thy neighbor. Lev. xix.

2. To check or restrain.

> The Lord *rebuke* thee, O Satan. Zech. iii. Is. xvii.

3. To chasten; to punish; to afflict for correction.

> O Lord, *rebuke* me not in thine anger. Ps. vi.

4. To check; to silence.

> Master, *rebuke* thy disciples. Luke xix.

5. To check; to heal.

> And he stood over her and *rebuked* the fever. Luke iv.

6. To restrain; to calm.

> He arose and *rebuked* the winds and the sea. Matt. viii.

REBU'KE, *n.* A chiding; reproof for faults; reprehension.

> Why bear you these *rebukes* and answer not? *Shak.*

2. In *Scripture,* chastisement; punishment; affliction for the purpose of restraint and correction. Ezek. v. Hos. v.

3. In *low language,* any kind of check. *L'Estrange.*

To suffer rebuke, to endure the reproach and persecution of men. Jer. xv.

To be without rebuke, to live without giving cause of reproof or censure; to be blameless.

REBU'KED, *pp.* Reproved; reprehended; checked; restrained; punished for faults.

REBU'KEFUL, *a.* Containing or abounding with rebukes.

REBU'KEFULLY, *adv.* With reproof or reprehension.

REBU'KER, *n.* One that rebukes; a chider; one that chastises or restrains.

REBU'KING, *ppr.* Chiding; reproving; checking; punishing.

REBULLI′′TION, *n.* [See *Ebullition* and *Boil.*] Act of boiling or effervescing. [*Little used.*] *Wotton.*

REBURY, *v. t.* *reber′ry.* [*re* and *bury.*] To inter again. *Ashmole.*

RE′BUS, *n.* [L. from *res*, which is of the class *Rd*, *Rs*, and of the same family as *riddle.* See *Riddle*, *Read* and *Real.*]

1. An enigmatical representation of some name, &c. by using figures or pictures instead of words. A gallant in love with a woman named *Rose Hill*, painted on the border of his gown, a rose, a hill, an eye, a loaf and a well, which reads, *Rose Hill I love well.* *Encyc.*

2. A sort of riddle.

3. In *some chemical writers*, sour milk; sometimes, the ultimate matter of which all bodies are composed. *Encyc.*

4. In *heraldry*, a coat of arms which bears an allusion to the name of the person; as three cups, for Butler. *Encyc.*

REBUT′, *v. t.* [Fr. *rebuter*; Norm. *rebutter*; from the root of *but*, Fr. *bout*, end; *bouter*, to put; *bouder*, to *pout*; It. *ributtare*, to drive back, also to vomit. See *Butt* and *Pout.* Class Bd.]

To repel; to oppose by argument, plea or countervailing proof. [*It is used by lawyers in a general sense.*]

REBUT′, *v. i.* To retire back. *Obs.* *Spenser.*

2. To answer, as a plaintif's sur-rejoinder.

The plaintif may answer the rejoinder by a sur-rejoinder; on which the defendant may *rebut.* *Blackstone.*

REBUT′TED, *pp.* Repelled; answered.

REBUT′TER, *n.* In *law pleadings*, the answer of a defendant to a plaintif's sur-rejoinder. *Blackstone.*

If I grant to a tenant to hold without impeachment of waste, and afterward implead him for waste done, he may debar me of this action by showing my grant, which is a *rebutter.* *Encyc.*

REBUT′TING, *ppr.* Repelling; opposing by argument, countervailing allegation or evidence.

RE€ALL′, *v. t.* [*re* and *call.*] To call back; to take back; as, to *recall* words or declarations.

2. To revoke; to annul by a subsequent act; as, to *recall* a decree.

3. To call back; to revive in memory; as, to *recall* to mind what has been forgotten. *Broome.*

4. To call back from a place or mission; as, to *recall* a minister from a foreign court; to *recall* troops from India.

RE€ALL′, *n.* A calling back; revocation.

2. The power of calling back or revoking.

'Tis done, and since 'tis done, 'tis past *recall.* *Dryden.*

RE€ALL′ABLE, *a.* That may be recalled. *Ramsay.*

Delegates *recallable* at pleasure. *Madison.*

RE€ALL′ED, *pp.* Called back; revoked.

RE€ALL′ING, *ppr.* Calling back; revoking.

RE€ANT′, *v. t.* [L. *recanto*; *re* and *canto.* See *Cant.*]

To retract; to recall; to contradict a former declaration.

How soon would ease *recant*
Vows made in pain, as violent as void. *Milton.*

RE€ANT′, *v. i.* To recall words; to revoke a declaration or proposition; to unsay what has been said. Convince me I am wrong, and I will *recant.*

RE€ANTA′TION, *n.* The act of recalling; retraction; a declaration that contradicts a former one. *Sidney.*

RE€ANT′ED, *pp.* Recalled; retracted.

RE€ANT′ER, *n.* One that recants. *Shak.*

RE€ANT′ING, *ppr.* Recalling; retracting.

RE€APAC′ITATE, *v. t.* [*re* and *capacitate.*] To qualify again; to confer capacity on again. *Atterbury.*

RE€APAC′ITATED, *pp.* Capacitated again.

RE€APAC′ITATING, *ppr.* Conferring capacity again.

RE€APIT′ULATE, *v. t.* [Fr. *recapituler*; It. *raccapitolare*; *re* and L. *capitulum.* See *Capitulate.*]

To repeat the principal things mentioned in a preceding discourse, argument or essay; to give a summary of the principal facts, points or arguments. *Dryden.*

RE€APIT′ULATED, *pp.* Repeated in a summary.

RE€APIT′ULATING, *ppr.* Repeating the principal things in a discourse or argument.

RE€APITULA′TION, *n.* The act of recapitulating.

2. A summary or concise statement or enumeration of the principal points or facts in a preceding discourse, argument or essay. *South.*

RE€APIT′ULATORY, *a.* Repeating again; containing recapitulation. *Garretson.*

RE€AP′TION, *n.* [L. *re* and *captio*; *capio*, to take.]

The act of retaking; reprisal; the retaking of one's own goods, chattels, wife or children from one who has taken them and wrongfully detains them. *Blackstone.*

Writ of recaption, a writ to recover property taken by a second distress, pending a replevin for a former distress for the same rent or service. *Blackstone.*

RE€AP′TOR, *n.* [*re* and *captor.*] One who retakes; one that takes a prize which had been previously taken.

RE€AP′TURE, *n.* [*re* and *capture.*] The act of retaking; particularly, the retaking of a prize or goods from a captor.

2. A prize retaken.

RE€AP′TURE, *v. t.* To retake; particularly, to retake a prize which had been previously taken. *Du Ponceau.*

RE€AP′TURED, *pp.* Retaken.

RE€AP′TURING, *ppr.* Retaking, as a prize from the captor.

RE€′ARNIFȲ, *v. t.* [*re* and *carnify*, from L. *caro*, flesh.]

To convert again into flesh. [*Not much used.*] *Howell.*

RE€AR′RIED, *pp.* Carried back or again.

RE€AR′RY, *v. t.* [*re* and *carry.*] To carry back. *Walton.*

RE€AR′RYING, *ppr.* Carrying back.

RE€′AST, *v. t.* [*re* and *cast.*] To cast again; as, to *recast* cannon.

2. To throw again. *Florio.*

3. To mold anew. *Burgess.*

4. To compute a second time.

RE€′AST, *pp.* Cast again; molded anew.

RE€′ASTING, *ppr.* Casting again; molding anew.

RECE′DE, *v. i.* [L. *recedo*; *re* and *cedo.*]

1. To move back; to retreat; to withdraw.

Like the hollow roar
Of tides *receding* from th' insulted shore. *Dryden.*

All bodies moved circularly, endeavor to *recede* from the center. *Bentley.*

2. To withdraw a claim or pretension; to desist from; to relinquish what had been proposed or asserted; as, to *recede* from a demand; to *recede* from terms or propositions.

RECE′DE, *v. t.* [*re* and *cede.*] To cede back; to grant or yield to a former possessor; as, to *recede* conquered territory.

RECE′DED, *pp.* Ceded back; regranted.

RECE′DING, *ppr.* Withdrawing; retreating; moving back.

2. Ceding back; regranting.

RECE′IPT, } *n.* *recee′t.* [It. *ricetta*, from the
RECE′IT, } L. *receptus.* This word ought to follow the analogy of *conceit*, *deceit*, from L. *conceptus*, *deceptus*, and be written without *p*, *receit.*]

1. The act of receiving; as the *receit* of a letter.

2. The place of receiving; as the *receit* of custom. Matt. ix.

3. Reception; as the *receit* of blessings or mercies.

4. Reception; welcome; as the kind *receit* of a friend. *Obs.*

[In this sense, *reception* is now used.]

5. Recipe; prescription of ingredients for any composition, as of medicines, &c. *Dryden. Arbuthnot.*

6. In *commerce*, a writing acknowledging the taking of money or goods. A receit of money may be in part or in full payment of a debt, and it operates as an acquittance or discharge of the debt either in part or in full. A receit of goods makes the receiver liable to account for the same, according to the nature of the transaction, or the tenor of the writing. It is customary for sherifs to deliver goods taken in execution, to some person who gives his *receit* for them, with a promise to redeliver them to the sherif at or before the time of sale.

RECEIPT, } *v. t.* *recee′t.* To give a receit
RECEIT, } for; as, to *receit* goods delivered by a sherif.

RECE′IVABLE, *a.* That may be received.

RECE′IVABLENESS, *n.* Capability of being received. *Whitlock.*

RECE′IVE, *v. t.* [Fr. *recevoir*; Arm. *receff*, *recevi*; It. *ricevere*; Sp. *recibir*; Port. *receber*; L. *recipio*; *re* and *capio*, to take.]

1. To take, as a thing offered or sent; to accept. He had the offer of a donation, but he would not *receive* it.

2. To take as due or as a reward. He *received* the money on the day it was payable. He *received* ample compensation.

3. To take or obtain from another in any manner, and either good or evil.

Shall we *receive* good at the hand of God, and shall we not *receive* evil? Job ii.

4. To take, as a thing communicated; as, to *receive* a wound by a shot; to *receive* a disease by contagion.

The idea of solidity we *receive* by our touch. *Locke.*

5. To take or obtain intellectually; as, to *receive* an opinion or notion from others.
6. To embrace.
Receive with meekness the engrafted word. James i.
7. To allow; to hold; to retain; as a custom long *received.*
8. To admit.
Thou shalt guide me with thy counsel, and afterward *receive* me to glory. Ps. lxxiii.
9. To welcome; to lodge and entertain; as a guest.
They kindled a fire and *received* us every one, because of the present rain and because of the cold. Acts xxviii.
10. To admit into membership or fellowship.
Him that is weak in the faith, *receive* ye. Rom. xiv.
11. To take in or on; to hold; to contain.
The brazen altar was too little to *receive* the burnt-offering. 1 Kings viii.
12. To be endowed with.
Ye shall *receive* power after that the Holy Spirit has come upon you. Acts i.
13. To take into a place or state.
After the Lord had spoken to them, he was *received* up into heaven. Mark xvi.
14. To take or have as something ascribed; as, to *receive* praise or blame. Rev. iv. v.
15. To bear with or suffer. 2 Cor. xi.
16. To believe in. John i.
17. To accept or admit officially or in an official character. The minister was *received* by the emperor or court.
18. To take stolen goods from a thief, knowing them to be stolen. *Blackstone.*

RECE'IVED, *pp.* Taken; accepted; admitted; embraced; entertained; believed.

RECE'IVEDNESS, *n.* General allowance or belief; as the *receivedness* of an opinion. *Boyle.*

RECE'IVER, *n.* One who takes or receives in any manner.
2. An officer appointed to receive public money; a treasurer. *Bacon.*
3. One who takes stolen goods from a thief, knowing them to be stolen, and incurs the guilt of partaking in the crime. *Blackstone.*
4. A vessel for receiving and containing the product of distillation.
5. The vessel of an air pump, for containing the thing on which an experiment is to be made.
6. One who partakes of the sacrament. *Taylor.*

RECE'IVING, *ppr.* Taking; accepting; admitting; embracing; believing; entertaining.

RECEL'EBRATE, *v. t.* [*re* and *celebrate.*] To celebrate again. *B. Jonson.*

RECEL'EBRATED, *pp.* Celebrated anew.

RECEL'EBRATING, *ppr.* Celebrating anew.

RECELEBRA'TION, *n.* A renewed celebration.

RE'CENCY, *n.* [L. *recens.*] Newness; new state; late origin; as the *recency* of a wound or tumor.
2. Lateness in time; freshness; as the *recency* of a transaction.

RECENSE, *v. t. recens'.* [L. *recenseo; re* and *censeo.*]
To review; to revise. *Bentley.*

RECEN'SION, *n.* [L. *recensio.*] Review; examination; enumeration. *Evelyn.*

RE'CENT, *a.* [L. *recens.*] New; being of late origin or existence.
The ancients believed some parts of Egypt to be *recent,* and formed by the mud discharged into the sea by the Nile. *Woodward.*
2. Late; modern; as great and worthy men ancient or *recent.* [*Modern* is now used.] *Bacon.*
3. Fresh; lately received; as *recent* news or intelligence.
4. Late; of late occurrence; as a *recent* event or transaction.
5. Fresh; not long dismissed, released or parted from; as Ulysses, *recent* from the storms. *Pope.*

RE'CENTLY, *adv.* Newly; lately; freshly; not long since; as advices *recently* received; a town *recently* built or repaired; an isle *recently* discovered.

RE'CENTNESS, *n.* Newness; freshness; lateness of origin or occurrence; as the *recentness* of alluvial land; the *recentness* of news or of events.

RECEP'TACLE, *n.* [L. *receptaculum,* from *receptus, recipio.*]
1. A place or vessel into which something is received or in which it is contained, as a vat, a tun, a hollow in the earth, &c. The grave is the common *receptacle* of the dead.
2. In *botany,* one of the parts of the fructification; the base by which the other parts of the fructification are connected. A *proper receptacle* belongs to one fructification only; a *common receptacle* connects several florets or distinct fructifications. The receptacle of the fructification is common both to the flower and the fruit, or it embraces the corol and germ. The receptacle of the flower, is the base to which the parts of the flower, exclusive of the germ, are fixed. The receptacle of the fruit, is the base of the fruit only. The receptacle of the seeds, is the base to which the seeds are fixed. *Martyn.*
3. In *anatomy,* the receptacle of the chyle is situated on the left side of the upper verteber of the loins, under the aorta and the vessels of the left kidney. *Encyc.*

RECEPTAC'ULAR, *a.* In *botany,* pertaining to the receptacle or growing on it, as the nectary.

REC'EPTARY, *n.* Thing received. [*Not in use.*] *Brown.*

RECEPTIBIL'ITY, *n.* The possibility of receiving. *Glanville.*
[Qu. The possibility of being received.]

RECEP'TION, *n.* [Fr.; L. *receptio.*] The act of receiving; *in a general sense;* as the *reception* of food into the stomach, or of air into the lungs.
2. The state of being received. *Milton.*
3. Admission of any thing sent or communicated; as the *reception* of a letter; the *reception* of sensation or ideas.
4. Readmission.
All hope is lost
Of my *reception* into grace. *Milton.*
5. Admission of entrance for holding or containing; as a sheath fitted for the *reception* of a sword; a channel for the *reception* of water.
6. A receiving or manner of receiving for entertainment; entertainment. The guests were well pleased with their *reception.* Nothing displeases more than a cold *reception.*
7. A receiving officially; as the *reception* of an envoy by a foreign court.
8. Opinion generally admitted.
Philosophers who have quitted the popular doctrines of their countries, have fallen into as extravagant opinions, as even common *reception* countenanced. [*Not in use.*] *Locke.*
9. Recovery. [*Not in use.*] *Bacon.*

RECEP'TIVE, *a.* Having the quality of receiving or admitting what is communicated.
Imaginary space is *receptive* of all bodies. *Glanville.*

RECEPTIV'ITY, *n.* The state or quality of being receptive. *Fotherby.*

RECEP'TORY, *a.* Generally or popularly admitted or received. [*Not in use.*] *Brown.*

RECESS', *n.* [L. *recessus,* from *recedo.* See *Recede.*]
1. A withdrawing or retiring; a moving back; as the *recess* of the tides.
2. A withdrawing from public business or notice; retreat; retirement.
My *recess* hath given them confidence that I may be conquered. *K. Charles.*
And every neighbouring grove
Sacred to soft *recess* and gentle love. *Prior.*
3. Departure. *Glanville.*
4. Place of retirement or secrecy; private abode.
This happy place, our sweet
Recess. *Milton.*
5. State of retirement; as lords in close *recess.* *Milton.*
In the *recess* of the jury, they are to consider their evidence. *Hale.*
6. Remission or suspension of business or procedure; as, the house of representatives had a *recess* of half an hour.
7. Privacy; seclusion from the world or from company.
Good verse *recess* and solitude requires. *Dryden.*
8. Secret or abstruse part; as the difficulties and *recesses* of science. *Watts.*
9. A withdrawing from any point; removal to a distance. *Brown.*
10. [Fr. *recez.*] An abstract or registry of the resolutions of the imperial diet. [*Not in use.*] *Ayliffe.*
11. The retiring of the shore of the sea or of a lake from the general line of the shore, forming a bay.

RECES'SION, *n.* [L. *recessio.*] The act of withdrawing, retiring or retreating.
2. The act of receding from a claim, or of relaxing a demand. *South.*
3. A cession or granting back; as the *recession* of conquered territory to its former sovereign.

RECHANGE, *v. t.* [Fr. *rechanger; re* and *change.*] To change again.

RECHANGED, *pp.* Changed again.

RECHANGING, *ppr.* Changing again.

RECH'ARGE, *v. t.* [Fr. *recharger; re* and *charge.*]
1. To charge or accuse in return. *Hooker.*
2. To attack again; to attack anew. *Dryden.*

RECH'ARGED, *pp.* Accused in return; attacked anew.

RECH'ARGING, *ppr.* Accusing in return; attacking anew.

RECHE'AT, *n.* [said to be from Old French.]

Among *hunters*, a lesson which the huntsman winds on the horn when the hounds have lost the game, to call them back from pursuing a counter scent. *Bailey. Shak.*

RECHE'AT, *v. t.* To blow the recheat. *Drayton.*

RECHOOSE, *v. t.* *rechooz'.* To choose a second time.

RECHOSEN, *pp.* or *a.* *recho'zn.* Re-elected; chosen again.

RECIDIVA'TION, *n.* [L. *recidivus*, from *recido*, to fall back; *re* and *cado*, to fall.]

A falling back; a backsliding. [*Not much used.*] *Hammond.*

RECID'IVOUS, *a.* [L. *recidivus.*] Subject to backslide. [*Little used.*]

RECIPE, *n.* *res'ipy.* [L. imperative of *recipio*, to take.]

A medical prescription; a direction of medicines to be taken by a patient. *Encyc.*

RECIP'IENT, *n.* [L. *recipiens*, *recipio.*] A receiver; the person or thing that receives; he or that to which any thing is communicated. *Glanville.*

2. The receiver of a still. *Decay of Piety.*

RECIP'ROCAL, *a.* [L. *reciprocus*; Sp. It. *reciproco*; Fr. *reciproque.*]

1. Acting in vicissitude or return; alternate.

> Corruption is *reciprocal* to generation. *Bacon.*

2. Mutual; done by each to the other; as *reciprocal* love; *reciprocal* benefits or favors; *reciprocal* duties; *reciprocal* aid.

3. Mutually interchangeable.

> These two rules will render a definition *reciprocal* with the thing defined. *Watts.*

Reciprocal terms, in logic, those terms that have the same signification, and consequently are convertible and may be used for each other. *Encyc.*

Reciprocal quantities, in mathematics, are those which, multiplied together, produce unity. *Encyc.*

Reciprocal figures, in geometry, are those which have the antecedents and consequents of the same ratio in both figures. *Encyc.*

Reciprocal ratio, is the ratio between the reciprocals of two quantities; as, the reciprocal ratio of 4 to 9, is that of $\frac{1}{4}$ to $\frac{1}{9}$.

RECIP'ROCAL, *n.* The *reciprocal* of any quantity, is unity divided by that quantity. Thus the *reciprocal* of 4 is $\frac{1}{4}$.

RECIP'ROCALLY, *adv.* Mutually; interchangeably; in such a manner that each affects the other and is equally affected by it.

> These two particles do *reciprocally* affect each other with the same force. *Bentley.*

RECIP'ROCALNESS, *n.* Mutual return; alternateness. *Decay of Piety.*

RECIP'ROCATE, *v. i.* [L. *reciproco*; Fr. *reciproquer.*] To act interchangeably; to alternate.

> One brawny smith the puffing bellows plies,
> And draws and blows *reciprocating* air. *Dryden.*

RECIP'ROCATE, *v. t.* To exchange; to interchange; to give and return mutually; as, to *reciprocate* favors.

RECIP'ROCATED, *pp.* Mutually given and returned; interchanged.

RECIP'ROCATING, *ppr.* Interchanging; each giving or doing to the other the same thing.

RECIPROCA'TION, *n.* [L. *reciprocatio.*]

1. Interchange of acts; a mutual giving and returning; as the *reciprocation* of kindnesses.

2. Alternation; as the *reciprocation* of the sea in the flow and ebb of tides. *Brown.*

3. Regular return or alternation of two symptoms or diseases. *Coxe.*

RECIPROC'ITY, *n.* [Fr. *reciprocité.*] Reciprocal obligation or right; equal mutual rights or benefits to be yielded or enjoyed. The commissioners offered to negotiate a treaty on principles of *reciprocity.*

RECI''SION, *n.* *s* as *z.* [L. *recisio*, from *recido*, to cut off; *re* and *cædo.*]

The act of cutting off. *Sherwood.*

RECI'TAL, *n.* [from *recite.*] Rehearsal; the repetition of the words of another or of a writing; as the *recital* of a deed; the *recital* of testimony. *Encyc.*

2. Narration; a telling of the particulars of an adventure or of a series of events. *Addison.*

3. Enumeration. *Prior.*

RECITA'TION, *n.* [L. *recitatio.*] Rehearsal; repetition of words. *Hammond. Temple.*

2. In *colleges* and *schools*, the rehearsal of a lesson by pupils before their instructor.

RECIT'ATIVE, *a.* [Fr. *recitatif*; It. *recitativo.* See *Recite.*]

Reciting; rehearsing; pertaining to musical pronunciation. *Dryden.*

RECIT'ATIVE, *n.* A kind of musical pronunciation, such as that in which the several parts of the liturgy are rehearsed in churches, or that of actors on the stage, when they express some action or passion, relate some event or reveal some design. *Encyc.*

In *recitative*, the composer and the performer endeavor to imitate the inflections, accent and emphasis of natural speech. *Busby.*

[Note. The natural and proper English accent of this word is on the second syllable. The foreign accent may well be discarded.]

RECIT'ATIVELY, *adv.* In the manner of recitative.

RECI'TE, *v. t.* [L. *recito*; *re* and *cito*, to call or name.]

1. To rehearse; to repeat the words of another or of a writing; as, to *recite* the words of an author or of a deed or covenant.

2. In *writing*, to copy; as, the words of a deed are *recited* in the pleading.

3. To tell over; to relate; to narrate; as, to *recite* past events; to *recite* the particulars of a voyage.

4. To rehearse, as a lesson to an instructor.

5. To enumerate.

RECI'TE, *v. i.* To rehearse a lesson. The class will *recite* at eleven o'clock. *American Seminaries.*

RECITE, for *recital.* [*Not in use.*]

RECI'TED, *pp.* Rehearsed; told; repeated; narrated.

RECI'TER, *n.* One that recites or rehearses; a narrator.

RECI'TING, *ppr.* Rehearsing; telling; repeating; narrating.

RECK, *v. i.* [Sax. *recan*, *reccan*, to say, to tell, to narrate, to *reckon*, to care, to rule or govern, L. *rego.* The primary sense is to strain. *Care* is a straining of the mind. See *Rack* and *Reckon.*]

To care; to mind; to rate at much; as we say, to *reckon* much of; followed by *of.* *Obs.*

> Thou's but a lazy loorde,
> And *recks* much *of* thy swinke. *Spenser.*
> I *reck* as little what betideth me,
> As much I wish all good befortune you. *Shak.*
> Of night or loneliness it *recks* me not. *Milton.*

RECK, *v. t.* To heed; to regard; to care for.

> This son of mine not *recking* danger. *Sidney.*

[This verb is obsolete unless in poetry. We observe the primary sense and application in the phrase, "it *recks* me not," that is, it does not strain or distress me; it does not *rack* my mind. To *reck* danger is a derivative form of expression, and a deviation from the proper sense of the verb.]

RECK'LESS, *a.* Careless; heedless; mindless.

> I made the king as *reckless*, as them diligent. *Sidney.*

RECK'LESSNESS, *n.* Heedlessness; carelessness; negligence. *Sidney.*

[*These words, formerly disused, have been recently revived.*]

RECKON, *v. t.* *rek'n.* [Sax. *recan*, *reccan*, to tell, to relate, to *reck* or care, to rule, to *reckon*; D. *reckenen*, to count or compute; G. *rechnen*, to count, to reckon, to esteem, and *recken*, to stretch, to strain, to *rack*; Sw. *råkna*, to count, to tell; Dan. *regner*, to *reckon*, to count, to rain. The Saxon word signifies not only to tell or count, but to *reck* or care, and to rule or govern; and the latter signification proves it to be the L. *rego*, *rectus*, whence *regnum*, *regno*, Eng. to *reign*, and hence Sax. *reht*, *riht*, Eng. *right*, G. *recht*, &c. The primary sense of the root is to strain, and *right* is strained, stretched to a straight line; hence we see that these words all coincide with *reach*, *stretch* and *rack*, and we say, we are *racked* with care. It is probable that *wreck* and *wretched* are from the same root. Class Rg. No. 18. 21.]

1. To count; to number; that is, to tell the particulars.

> The priest shall *reckon* to him the money, according to the years that remain, even to the year of jubilee, and it shall be abated. Lev. xxvii.
>
> I *reckoned* above two hundred and fifty on the outside of the church. *Addison.*

2. To esteem; to account; to repute. Rom. viii.

> For him I *reckon* not in high estate. *Milton.*

3. To repute; to set in the number or rank of.

> He was *reckoned* among the transgressors. Luke xxii.

4. To assign in an account. Rom. iv.

5. To compute; to calculate. *Addison.*

RECK'ON, *v. i.* To reason with one's self and conclude from arguments.

> I *reckoned* till morning, that as a lion, so will he break all my bones. Is. xxxviii.

2. To charge to account; with *on.*

I call posterity
Into the debt, and *reckon on* her head.
B. Jonson.

3. To pay a penalty; to be answerable; with *for*.

If they fail in their bounden duty, they shall *reckon for* it one day. *Sanderson.*

To reckon with, to state an account with another, compare it with his account, ascertain the amount of each and the balance which one owes to the other. In this manner the countrymen of New England who have mutual dealings, *reckon with* each other at the end of each year, or as often as they think fit.

After a long time the lord of those servants cometh, and *reckoneth with* them. Matt. xxv.

2. To call to punishment.

God suffers the most grievous sins of particular persons to go unpunished in this world, because his justice will have another opportunity to meet and *reckon with* them. *Tillotson.*

To reckon on or *upon*, to lay stress or dependence on. He *reckons on* the support of his friends.

RECKONED, *pp.* *rek'nd.* Counted; numbered; esteemed; reputed; computed; set or assigned to in account.

RECKONER, *n.* *rek'ner.* One who reckons or computes.

Reckoners without their host must reckon twice. *Camden.*

RECKONING, *ppr.* *rek'ning.* Counting; computing; esteeming; reputing; stating an account mutually.

RECK'ONING, *n.* The act of counting or computing; calculation.

2. An account of time. *Sandys.*

3. A statement of accounts with another; a statement and comparison of accounts mutually for adjustment; as in the proverb, "short *reckonings* make long friends."

The way to make *reckonings* even, is to make them often. *South.*

4. The charges or account made by a host.

A coin would have a nobler use than to pay a *reckoning.* *Addison.*

5. Account taken. 2 Kings xxii.

6. Esteem; account; estimation.

You make no further *reckoning* of beauty, than of an outward fading benefit nature bestowed. *Sidney.*

7. In *navigation*, an account of the ship's course and distance calculated from the log-board without the aid of celestial observation. This account from the log-board, is called the *dead reckoning*.
Mar. Dict.

RECK'ONING-BOOK, *n.* A book in which money received and expended is entered.
Johnson.

RECLA'IM, *v. t.* [Fr. *reclamer*; L. *reclamo*; *re* and *clamo*, to call. See *Claim*.]

1. To claim back; to demand to have returned. The vender may *reclaim* the goods.
Z. Swift.

2. To call back from error, wandering or transgression, to the observance of moral rectitude; to reform; to bring back to correct deportment or course of life.

It is the intention of Providence in its various expressions of goodness, to *reclaim* mankind.
Rogers.

3. To reduce to the state desired.

Much labor is requir'd in trees, to tame
Their wild disorder, and in ranks *reclaim.*
Dryden.

4. To call back; to restrain.

Or is her tow'ring flight *reclaim'd*
By seas from Icarus' downfall nam'd?
Prior.

5. To recall; to cry out against.

The headstrong horses hurried Octavius along, and were deaf to his *reclaiming* them. [*Unusual.*] *Dryden.*

6. To reduce from a wild to a tame or domestic state; to tame; to make gentle; as, to *reclaim* a hawk, an eagle or a wild beast. *Dryden.*

7. To demand or challenge; to make a claim; *a French use.*

8. To recover. *Spenser.*

9. In *ancient customs*, to pursue and recall, as a vassal. *Encyc.*

10. To encroach on what has been taken from one; to attempt to recover possession.

A tract of land [Holland] snatched from an element perpetually *reclaiming* its prior occupancy. *Coxe, Switz.*

RECLA'IM, *v. i.* To cry out; to exclaim.
Pope.

RECLA'IMABLE, *a.* That may be reclaimed, reformed or tamed.

RECLA'IMANT, *n.* One that opposes, contradicts or remonstrates against.
Waterland.

RECLA'IMED, *pp.* Recalled from a vicious life; reformed; tamed; domesticated; recovered.

RECLA'IMING, *ppr.* Recalling to a regular course of life; reforming; recovering; taking; demanding.

RECLAMA'TION, *n.* Recovery.

2. Demand; challenge of something to be restored; claim made. *Gallatin.*

REC'LINATE, *a.* [L. *reclinatus.* See *Recline.*]

In *botany*, reclined, as a leaf; bent downwards, so that the point of the leaf is lower than the base. *Martyn.*

A *reclinate* stem is one that bends in an arch towards the earth. *Lee.*

RECLINA'TION, *n.* The act of leaning or reclining.

RECLI'NE, *v. t.* [L. *reclino*; *re* and *clino*, to lean.]

To lean back; to lean to one side or sidewise; as, to *recline* the head on a pillow, or on the bosom of another, or on the arm.

The mother
Reclin'd her dying head upon his breast.
Dryden.

RECLI'NE, *v. i.* To lean; to rest or repose; as, to *recline* on a couch.

RECLI'NE, *a.* [L. *reclinis.*] Leaning; being in a leaning posture.

They sat *recline*
On the soft downy bank damask'd with flowers. [*Little used.*] *Milton.*

RECLI'NED, *pp.* Inclined back or sidewise.

RECLI'NING, *ppr.* Leaning back or sidewise; resting; lying.

RECLO'SE, *v. t.* *s* as *z.* [*re* and *close.*] To close or shut again. *Pope.*

RECLO'SED, *pp.* Closed again.

RECLO'SING, *ppr.* Closing again.

RECLU'DE, *v. t.* [L. *recludo*; *re* and *claudo*, *cludo.*] To open. [*Little used.*] *Harvey.*

RECLU'SE, *a.* [Fr. *reclus*, from L. *reclusus*, *recludo*, but with a signification directly opposite.]

Shut up; sequestered; retired from the world or from public notice; solitary; as a *recluse* monk or hermit; a *recluse* life.

I all the live-long day
Consume in meditation deep, *recluse*
From human converse. *Philips.*

RECLU'SE, *n.* A person who live in retirement or seclusion from intercourse with the world; as a hermit or monk.

2. A person who confines himself to a cell in a monastery.

RECLU'SELY, *adv.* In retirement or seclusion from society.

RECLU'SENESS, *n.* Retirement; seclusion from society.

RECLU'SION, *n.* *s* as *z.* A state of retirement from the world; seclusion.

RECLU'SIVE, *a.* Affording retirement from society. *Shak.*

RECOAGULA'TION, *n.* [*re* and *coagulation.*] A second coagulation. *Boyle.*

RECOCT', *a.* [L. *recoctus*, *recoquo.*] New vamped. [*Not used.*] *Taylor.*

RECOGNITION, *n.* *reconish'on* or *recognish'on.* [L. *recognitio.*]

1. Acknowledgment; formal avowal; as the *recognition* of a final concord on a writ of covenant. *Bacon.*

2. Acknowledgment; memorial. *White.*

3. Acknowledgment; solemn avowal by which a thing is owned or declared to belong to. or by which the remembrance of it is revived.

The lives of such saints had, at the time of their yearly memorials, solemn *recognition* in the church of God. *Hooker.*

4. Knowledge confessed or avowed; as the *recognition* of a thing present; memory of it as passed. *Grew.*

RECOGNITOR, *n.* *recon'itor.* One of a jury upon assize. *Blackstone.*

RECOGNIZABLE, *a.* *recon'izable.* [from *recognize.*] That may be recognized or acknowledged. *Orient. Collections.*

RECOGNIZANCE, *n.* *recon'izance.* [Fr. *reconnoisance.*]

1. Acknowledgment of a person or thing; avowal; profession; as the *recognizance* of christians, by which they avow their belief in their religion. *Hooker.*

2. In *law*, an obligation of record which a man enters into before some court of record or magistrate duly authorized, with condition to do some particular act, as to appear at the assizes, to keep the peace or pay a debt. This *recognizance* differs from a bond, as it does not create a new debt, but it is the acknowledgment of a former debt on record. This is witnessed by the record only, and not by the party's seal. There is also a *recognizance* in the nature of a statute staple, acknowledged before either of the chief justices or their substitutes, the mayor of the staple at Westminster and the recorder of London, which is to be enrolled and certified into chancery. *Blackstone.*

3. The verdict of a jury impanneled upon assize. *Cowell.*

RECOGNIZE, *v. t.* *rec'onize.* [It. *riconoscere*; Sp. *reconocer*; Fr. *reconnoitre*; L. *recognosco*; *re* and *cognosco*, to know. The *g* in these words has properly no sound in English. It is not a part of the root of the word, being written merely to give to *con* the French sound of *gn*, or that of the

Spanish ñ, and this sound does not properly belong to our language.]

2. To recollect or recover the knowledge of, either with an avowal of that knowledge or not. We *recognize* a person at a distance, when we recollect that we have seen him before, or that we have formerly known him. We *recognize* his features or his voice.

Speak, vassal; *recognize* thy sovereign queen. *Harte.*

2. To review; to re-examine. *South.*

REC'OGNIZE, *v. i.* To enter an obligation of record before a proper tribunal. A B *recognized* in the sum of twenty pounds.

REC'OGNIZED, *pp.* Acknowledged; recollected as known; bound by recognizance.

RECOGNIZEE, *n. reconizee'.* The person to whom a recognizance is made. *Blackstone.*

REC'OGNIZING, *ppr.* Acknowledging; recollecting as known; entering a recognizance.

RECOGNIZOR, *n. reconizor'.* One who enters into a recognizance. *Blackstone.*

RECOIL', *v. i.* [Fr. *reculer*, to draw back; *recul*, a *recoil*; Arm. *arguila*; Fr. *cul*, Sp. *culo*, Arm. *gil*, *guil*, the back part; W. *ciliaw*, to recede; It. *rinculare*; Sp. *recular.*]

1. To move or start back; to roll back; as, a cannon *recoils* when fired; waves *recoil* from the shore.
2. To fall back; to retire. *Milton.*
3. To rebound; as, the blow *recoils*. *Dryden.*
4. To retire; to flow back; as, the blood *recoils* with horror at the sight.
5. To start back; to shrink. Nature *recoils* at the bloody deed.
6. To return. The evil will *recoil* upon his own head.

RECOIL', *v. t.* To drive back. [*Not used.*] *Spenser.*

RECOIL', *n.* A starting or falling back; as the *recoil* of fire-arms; the *recoil* of nature or the blood.

RECOIL'ING, *ppr.* Starting or falling back; retiring; shrinking.

RECOIL'ING, *n.* The act of starting or falling back; a shrinking; revolt. *South.*

RECOIL'INGLY, *adv.* With starting back or retrocession.

RECOIN', *v. t.* [*re* and *coin.*] To coin again; as, to *recoin* gold or silver.

RECOIN'AGE, *n.* The act of coining anew.
2. That which is coined anew.

RECOIN'ED, *pp.* Coined again.

RECOIN'ING, *ppr.* Coining anew.

RECOLLECT', *v. t.* [*re* and *collect*; L. *recolligo*, *recollectus.*]

1. To collect again; *applied to ideas that have escaped from the memory*; to recover or call back ideas to the memory. I *recollect* what was said at a former interview; or I cannot *recollect* what was said.
2. To recover or recall the knowledge of; to bring back to the mind or memory. I met a man whom I thought I had seen before, but I could not *recollect* his name, or the place where I had seen him. I do not *recollect* you, sir.
3. To recover resolution or composure of mind.

The Tyrian queen
Admir'd his fortunes, more admir'd the man,
Then *recollected* stood. *Dryden.*

[In this sense, *collected* is more generally used.]

RE-COLLECT', *v. t.* To gather again; to collect what has been scattered; as, to *re-collect* routed troops.

RECOLLECT'ED, *pp.* Recalled to the memory.

RECOLLECT'ING, *ppr.* Recovering to the memory.

RECOLLEC'TION, *n.* The act of recalling to the memory, as ideas that have escaped; or the operation by which ideas are recalled to the memory or revived in the mind. *Recollection* differs from *remembrance*, as it is the consequence of volition, or an effort of the mind to revive ideas; whereas *remembrance* implies no such volition. We often *remember* things without any voluntary effort. *Recollection* is called also *reminiscence.*

2. The power of recalling ideas to the mind, or the period within which things can be recollected; remembrance. The events mentioned are not within my *recollection.*
3. In popular language, *recollection* is used as synonymous with *remembrance.*

RECOLLECT'IVE, *a.* Having the power of recollecting. *Foster.*

REC'OLLET, *n.* [Sp. Port. *recoleto.*] A monk of a reformed order of Franciscans.

RECOMBINA'TION, *n.* Combination a second time.

RECOMBI'NE, *v. t.* [*re* and *combine.*] To combine again.

If we *recombine* these two elastic fluids. *Lavoisier.*

RECOMBI'NED, *pp.* Combined anew.

RECOMBI'NING, *ppr.* Combining again.

RECŎMFORT, *v. t.* [*re* and *comfort.*] To comfort again; to console anew. *Sidney.*
2. To give new strength. *Bacon.*

RECŎMFORTED, *pp.* Comforted again.

RECŎMFORTING, *ppr.* Comforting again.

RECŎMFORTLESS, *a.* Without comfort. [*Not used.*] *Spenser.*

RECOMMENCE, *v. t. recommens'.* [*re* and *commence.*] To commence again; to begin anew.

RECOMMEN'CED, *pp.* Commenced anew.

RECOMMEN'CING, *ppr.* Beginning again.

RECOMMEND', *v. t.* [*re* and *commend*; Fr. *recommander.*]

1. To praise to another; to offer or commend to another's notice, confidence or kindness by favorable representations.

Mæcenas *recommended* Virgil and Horace to Augustus. *Dryden.*

[In this sense, *commend*, though less common, is the preferable word.]

2. To make acceptable.

A decent boldness ever meets with friends,
Succeeds, and ev'n a stranger *recommends.* *Pope.*

3. To commit with prayers.

Paul chose Silas and departed, being *recommended* by the brethren to the grace of God. Acts xv.

[*Commend* here is much to be preferred.]

RECOMMEND'ABLE, *a.* That may be recommended; worthy of recommendation or praise. *Glanville.*

RECOMMENDA'TION, *n.* The act of recommending or of commending; the act of representing in a favorable manner for the purpose of procuring the notice, confidence or civilities of another. We introduce a friend to a stranger by a *recommendation* of his virtues or accomplishments.

2. That which procures a kind or favorable reception. The best *recommendation* of a man to favor is politeness. Misfortune is a *recommendation* to our pity.

RECOMMEND'ATORY, *a.* That commends to another; that recommends. *Madison. Swift.*

RECOMMEND'ED, *pp.* Praised; commended to another.

RECOMMEND'ER, *n.* One who commends.

RECOMMEND'ING, *ppr.* Praising to another; commending.

RECOMMIS'SION, *v. t.* [*re* and *commission.*] To commission again.

Officers whose time of service had expired, were to be *recommissioned.* *Marshall.*

RECOMMIS'SIONED, *pp.* Commissioned again.

RECOMMIS'SIONING, *ppr.* Commissioning again.

RECOMMIT', *v. t.* [*re* and *commit.*] To commit again; as, to *recommit* persons to prison. *Clarendon.*
2. To refer again to a committee; as, to *recommit* a bill to the same committee.

RECOMMIT'MENT, *n.* A second or renewed commitment; a renewed reference to a committee.

RECOMMIT'TED, *pp.* Committed anew; referred again.

RECOMMIT'TING, *ppr.* Committing again; referring again to a committee.

RECOMMU'NICATE, *v. i.* [*re* and *communicate.*] To communicate again.

RECOMPACT', *v. t.* [*re* and *compact.*] To join anew.

Repair
And *recompact* my scatter'd body. *Donne.*

RECOMPENSA'TION, *n.* Recompense. [*Not used.*]

REC'OMPENSE, *v. t.* [Fr. *recompenser*; *re* and *compenser.*]

1. To compensate; to make return of an equivalent for any thing given, done or suffered; as, to *recompense* a person for services, for fidelity or for sacrifices of time, for loss or damages.

The word is followed by the *person* or the *service*. We *recompense* a *person* for his services, or we *recompense* his *kindness*. It is usually found more easy to neglect than to *recompense* a favor.

2. To requite; to repay; to return an equivalent; *in a bad sense.*

Recompense to no man evil for evil. Rom. xii.

3. To make an equivalent return in profit or produce. The labor of man is *recompensed* by the fruits of the earth.
4. To compensate; to make amends by any thing equivalent.

Solyman—said he would find occasion for them to *recompense* that disgrace. *Knolles.*

5. To make restitution or an equivalent return for. Num. v.

REC'OMPENSE, *n.* An equivalent returned for any thing given, done or suffered;

compensation; reward; amends; as a *recompense* for services, for damages, for loss, &c.

2. Requital; return of evil or suffering or other equivalent; as a punishment.

To me belongeth vengeance and *recompense*. Deut. xxxii.

And every transgression and disobedience received a just *recompense* of reward. Heb. ii.

REC'OMPENSED, *pp.* Rewarded; requited.

REC'OMPENSING, *ppr.* Rewarding; compensating; requiting.

RECOMPI'LEMENT, *n.* [*re* and *compilement.*] New compilation or digest; as a *recompilement* of laws. *Bacon.*

RECOMPO'SE, *v. t. s* as *z.* [*re* and *compose.*]

1. To quiet anew; to compose or tranquilize that which is ruffled or disturbed; as, to *recompose* the mind. *Taylor.*

2. To compose anew; to form or adjust again.

We produced a lovely purple which we can destroy or *recompose* at pleasure. *Boyle.*

RECOMPO'SED, *pp.* Quieted again after agitation; formed anew; composed a second time.

RECOMPO'SING, *ppr.* Rendering tranquil after agitation; forming or adjusting anew.

RECOMPOSI''TION, *n.* Composition renewed.

RECONCI'LABLE, *a.* Capable of being reconciled; capable of renewed friendship. The parties are not *reconcilable.*

2. That may be made to agree or be consistent; consistent.

The different accounts of the numbers of ships are *reconcilable.* *Arbuthnot.*

3. Capable of being adjusted; as, the difference between the parties is *reconcilable.*

RECONCI'LABLENESS, *n.* The quality of being reconcilable; consistency; as the *reconcilableness* of parts of Scripture which apparently disagree.

2. Possibility of being restored to friendship and harmony.

RECONCI'LE, *v. t.* [Fr. *reconcilier*; L. *reconcilio*; *re* and *concilio*; *con* and *calo*, to *call*, Gr. *χαλεω*. The literal sense is to call back into union.]

1. To conciliate anew; to call back into union and friendship the affections which have been alienated; to restore to friendship or favor after estrangement; as, to *reconcile* men or parties that have been at variance.

Go thy way; first be *reconciled* to thy brother— Matt. v.

We pray you in Christ's stead, be ye *reconciled* to God. 2 Cor. v. Eph. ii. Col. i.

2. To bring to acquiescence, content or quiet submission; with *to*; as, to *reconcile* one's self *to* afflictions. It is our duty to be *reconciled to* the dispensations of Providence.

3. To make consistent or congruous; to bring to agreement or suitableness; followed by *with* or *to.*

The great men among the ancients understood how to *reconcile* manual labor *with* affairs of state. *Locke.*

Some figures monstrous and misshap'd appear,
Considered singly, or beheld too near;
Which but proportion'd to their light and place,
Due distance *reconciles to* form and grace. *Pope.*

4. To adjust; to settle; as, to *reconcile* differences or quarrels.

RECONCI'LED, *pp.* Brought into friendship from a state of disagreement or enmity; made consistent; adjusted.

RECONCI'LEMENT, *n.* Reconciliation; renewal of friendship. Animosities sometimes make *reconcilement* impracticable.

2. Friendship renewed.

No cloud
Of anger shall remain, but peace assured
And *reconcilement.* *Milton.*

RECONCI'LER, *n.* One who reconciles; one who brings parties at variance into renewed friendship. *Fell.*

2. One who discovers the consistence of propositions. *Norris.*

RECONCILIA'TION, *n.* [Fr. from L. *reconciliatio.*]

1. The act of reconciling parties at variance; renewal of friendship after disagreement or enmity.

Reconciliation and friendship with God, really form the basis of all rational and true enjoyment. *S. Miller.*

2. In *Scripture*, the means by which sinners are reconciled and brought into a state of favor with God, after natural estrangement or enmity; the atonement; expiation.

Seventy weeks are determined upon thy people and upon thy holy city, to finish the transgression and to make an end of sin, and to make *reconciliation* for iniquity. Dan. ix. Heb. ii.

3. Agreement of things seemingly opposite, different or inconsistent. *Rogers.*

RECONCIL'IATORY, *a.* Able or tending to reconcile. *Hall.*

RECONCI'LING, *ppr.* Bringing into favor and friendship after variance; bringing to content or satisfaction; showing to be consistent; adjusting; making to agree.

RECONDENSA'TION, *n.* The act of recondensing.

RECONDENSE, *v. t.* *recondens'.* [*re* and *condense.*] To condense again. *Boyle.*

RECONDENS'ED, *pp.* Condensed anew.

RECONDENS'ING, *ppr.* Condensing again.

REC'ONDITE, *a.* [L. *reconditus*, *recondo*; *re* and *condo*, to conceal.]

1. Secret; hidden from the view or intellect; abstruse; as *recondite* causes of things.

2. Profound; dealing in things abstruse; as *recondite* studies.

RECOND'ITORY, *n.* [supra.] A repository; a store-house or magazine. [*Little used.*] *Ash.*

RECONDUCT', *v. t.* [*re* and *conduct.*] To conduct back or again. *Dryden.*

RECONDUCT'ED, *pp.* Conducted back or again.

RECONDUCT'ING, *ppr.* Conducting back or again.

RECONFIRM', *v. t.* [*re* and *confirm.*] To confirm anew. *Clarendon.*

RECONJOIN', *v. t.* [*re* and *conjoin.*] To join or conjoin anew. *Boyle.*

RECONJOIN'ED, *pp.* Joined again.

RECONJOIN'ING, *ppr.* Joining anew.

RECONNOIT'ER, *v. t.* [Fr. *reconnoitre*; *re* and *connoitre*, to know.]

To view; to survey; to examine by the eye; particularly in military affairs, to examine the state of an enemy's army or camp, or the ground for military operations.

RECONNOIT'ERED, *pp.* Viewed; examined by personal observation.

RECONNOIT'ERING, *ppr.* Viewing; examining by personal observation.

RECONQUER, *v. t.* *recon'ker.* [*re* and *conquer*; Fr. *reconquérir.*]

1. To conquer again; to recover by conquest. *Davies.*

2. To recover; to regain. [*A French use.*]

RECON'QUERED, *pp.* Conquered again; regained.

RECON'QUERING, *ppr.* Conquering again; recovering.

RECON'SECRATE, *v. t.* [*re* and *consecrate.*] To consecrate anew.

RECON'SECRATED, *pp.* Consecrated again.

RECON'SECRATING, *ppr.* Consecrating again.

RECONSECRA'TION, *n.* A renewed consecration.

RECONSID'ER, *v. t.* [*re* and *consider.*] To consider again; to turn in the mind again; to review.

2. To annul; to take into consideration a second time and rescind; as, to *reconsider* a motion in a legislative body; to *reconsider* a vote. The vote has been *reconsidered*, that is, rescinded.

RECONSIDERA'TION, *n.* A renewed consideration or review in the mind.

2. A second consideration; annulment; rescision.

RECONSID'ERED, *pp.* Considered again; rescinded.

RECONSID'ERING, *ppr.* Considering again; rescinding.

RECON'SOLATE, *v. t.* To console or comfort again. [*Not in use.*] *Wotton.*

RECONVE'NE, *v. t.* [*re* and *convene.*] To convene or call together again.

RECONVE'NE, *v. i.* To assemble or come together again.

RECONVE'NED, *pp.* Assembled anew.

RECONVE'NING, *ppr.* Assembling anew.

RECONVER'SION, *n.* [*re* and *conversion.*] A second conversion. *Weever.*

RECONVERT', *v. t.* [*re* and *convert.*] To convert again.

RECONVERT'ED, *pp.* Converted again.

RECONVERT'ING, *ppr.* Converting again.

RECONVEY, *v. t.* [*re* and *convey.*] To convey back or to its former place; as, to *reconvey* goods.

2. To transfer back to a former owner; as, to *reconvey* an estate.

RECONVEYED, *pp.* Conveyed back; transferred to a former owner.

RECONVEYING, *ppr.* Conveying back; transferring to a former owner.

RECORD', *v. t.* [L. *recordor*, to call to mind, to remember, from *re* and *cor*, *cordis*, the heart or mind; Sp. *recordar*, to remind, also to awake from sleep; Port. to remind, to con a lesson, or get by heart; Fr. *recorder*, to con a lesson, also to *record.*]

1. To register; to enroll; to write or enter in a book or on parchment, for the purpose of preserving authentic or correct evidence of a thing; as, to *record* the proceedings of a court; to *record* a deed or lease; to *record* historical events.
2. To imprint deeply on the mind or memory; as, to *record* the sayings of another in the heart. *Locke.*
3. To cause to be remembered.

So ev'n and morn *recorded* the third day. *Milton.*

4. To recite; to repeat. [*Not in use.*] *Fairfax.*
5. To call to mind. [*Not in use.*] *Spenser.*

RE€ORD′, *v. i.* To sing or repeat a tune. [*Not in use.*] *Shak.*

RE€′ORD, *n.* A register; an authentic or official copy of any writing, or account of any facts and proceedings, entered in a book for preservation; or the book containing such copy or account; as the *records* of statutes or of judicial courts; the *records* of a town or parish. *Records* are properly the registers of official transactions, made by officers appointed for the purpose, or by the officer whose proceedings are directed by law to be recorded.
2. Authentic memorial; as the *records* of past ages.

Court of record, is a court whose acts and judicial proceedings are enrolled on parchment or in books for a perpetual memorial; and their records are the highest evidence of facts, and their truth cannot be called in question.

Debt of record, is a debt which appears to be due by the evidence of a court of record, as upon a judgment or a recognizance. *Blackstone.*

Trial by record, is where a matter of record is pleaded, and the opposite party pleads that there is no such record. In this case, the trial is by inspection of the record itself, no other evidence being admissible. *Blackstone.*

RE€ORDA′TION, *n.* [L. *recordatio.*] Remembrance. [*Not in use.*] *Shak. Wotton.*

RE€ORD′ED, *pp.* Registered; officially entered in a book or on parchment; imprinted on the memory.

RE€ORD′ER, *n.* A person whose official duty is to register writings or transactions; one who enrolls or records.
2. An officer of a city who is keeper of the rolls or records, or who is invested with judicial powers.
3. Formerly, a kind of flute, flageolet or wind instrument.

The figures of *recorders*, flutes and pipes are straight; but the *recorder* hath a less bore and a greater above and below. *Bacon.*

RE€ORD′ING, *ppr.* Registering; enrolling; imprinting on the memory.

RE€OUCH′, *v. i.* [*re* and *couch.*] To retire again to a lodge, as lions. *Wotton.*

RE€OUNT′, *v. t.* [Fr. *reconter;* Sp. *recontar;* It. *raccontare; re* and *count.*]

To relate in detail; to recite; to tell or narrate the particulars; to rehearse.

Say from these glorious seeds what harvest flows,
Recount our blessings, and compare our woes. *Dryden.*

RE€OUNT′ED, *pp.* Related or told in detail; recited.

RE€OUNT′ING, *ppr.* Relating in a series; narrating.

RE€OUNT′MENT, *n.* Relation in detail; recital. [*Little used.*] *Shak.*

RE€OURED, for *recovered* or *recured.* [*Not used.*] *Spenser.*

RE€OURSE, *n.* [Fr. *recours;* It. *ricorso;* Sp. *recurso;* L. *recursus; re* and *cursus, curro,* to run.] Literally, a running back; a return.

1. Return; new attack. [*Not in use.*] *Brown.*
2. A going to with a request or application, as for aid or protection. Children have *recourse* to their parents for assistance.
3. Application of efforts, art or labor. The general had *recourse* to stratagem to effect his purpose.

Our last *recourse* is therefore to our art. *Dryden.*

4. Access. [*Little used.*]
5. Frequent passage. *Shak.*

RE€OURSE, *v. i.* To return. [*Not used.*] *Fox.*

RE€OURSEFUL, *a.* Moving alternately. [*Not in use.*] *Drayton.*

RE€ŎVER, *v. t.* [Fr. *recouvrer;* It. *ricoverare* or *ricuperare;* Sp. Port. *recobrar;* L. *recupero; re* and *capio,* to take.]

1. To regain; to get or obtain that which was lost; as, to *recover* stolen goods; to recover a town or territory which an enemy had taken; to *recover* sight or senses; to *recover* health or strength after sickness.

David *recovered* all that the Amalekites had carried away. 1 Sam. xxx.

2. To restore from sickness; as, to *recover* one from leprosy. 2 Kings v.
3. To revive from apparent death; as, to *recover* a drowned man.
4. To regain by reparation; to repair the loss of, or to repair an injury done by neglect; as, to *recover* lost time.

Good men have lapses and failings to lament and *recover*. *Rogers.*

5. To regain a former state by liberation from capture or possession.

That they may *recover* themselves out of the snare of the devil. 2 Tim. ii.

6. To gain as a compensation; to obtain in return for injury or debt; as, to *recover* damages in trespass; to *recover* debt and cost in a suit at law.
7. To reach; to come to.

The forest is not three leagues off;
If we *recover* that, we're sure enough. *Shak.*

8. To obtain title to by judgment in a court of law; as, to *recover* lands in ejectment or common recovery.

RE€ŎVER, *v. i.* To regain health after sickness; to grow well; followed by *of* or *from.*

Go, inquire of Baalzebub, the god of Ekron, whether I shall *recover of* this disease. 2 Kings i.

2. To regain a former state or condition after misfortune; as, to *recover* from a state of poverty or depression.
3. To obtain a judgment in law; to succeed in a lawsuit. The plaintif has *recovered* in his suit.

RE€ŎVERABLE, *a.* That may be regained or recovered. Goods lost or sunk in the ocean are not *recoverable.*

2. That may be restored from sickness.
3. That may be brought back to a former condition.

A prodigal course
Is like the sun's, but not like his *recoverable.* *Shak.*

4. That may be obtained from a debtor or possessor. The debt is *recoverable.*

RE€ŎVERED, *pp.* Regained; restored obtained by judicial decision.

RE€OVEREE′, *n.* In *law,* the tenant or person against whom a judgment is obtained in common recovery. *Blackstone.*

RE€ŎVERING, *ppr.* Regaining; obtaining in return or by judgment in law; regaining health.

RE€ŎVEROR, *n.* In *law,* the demandant or person who obtains a judgment in his favor in common recovery. *Blackstone.*

RE€ŎVERY, *n.* The act of regaining, retaking or obtaining possession of any thing lost. The crusades were intended for the *recovery* of the holy land from the Saracens. We offer a reward for the *recovery* of stolen goods.

2. Restoration from sickness or apparent death. The patient has a slow *recovery* from a fever. *Recovery* from a pulmonary affection is seldom to be expected. Directions are given for the *recovery* of drowned persons.
3. The capacity of being restored to health. The patient is past *recovery.*
4. The obtaining of right to something by a verdict and judgment of court from an opposing party in a suit; as the *recovery* of debt, damages and costs by a plaintif; the *recovery* of cost by a defendant; the *recovery* of land in ejectment.

Common recovery, in law, is a species of assurance by matter of record, or a suit or action, actual or fictitious, by which lands are recovered against the tenant of the freehold; which recovery binds all persons, and vests an absolute fee simple in the recoveror. *Blackstone.*

RE€′REANT, *a.* [Norm. *recreant,* cowardly, properly crying out, from *recrier;* that is, begging. See *Craven.*]

1. Crying for mercy, as a combatant in the trial by battel; yielding; hence, cowardly; mean spirited. *Blackstone.*
2. Apostate; false.

Who for so many benefits receiv'd,
Turn'd *recreant* to God, ingrate and false. *Milton.*

RE€′REANT, *n.* One who yields in combat and cries craven; one who begs for mercy; hence, a mean spirited, cowardly wretch. *Blackstone.*

RE€′REATE, *v. t.* [L. *recreo; re* and *creo,* to create; Fr. *recreer;* It. *ricreare;* Sp. *recrear.*]

1. To refresh after toil; to reanimate, as languid spirits or exhausted strength; to amuse or divert in weariness.

Painters when they work on white grounds, place before them colors mixed with blue and green, to *recreate* their eyes. *Dryden.*

St. John is said to have *recreated* himself with sporting with a tame partridge. *Taylor.*

2. To gratify; to delight.

These ripe fruits *recreate* the nostrils with their aromatic scent. *More.*

3. To relieve; to revive; as, to *recreate* the lungs with fresh air. *Harvey.*

REC'REATE, *v. i.* To take recreation. *Addison.*

RE-CREA'TE, *v. t.* To create or form anew.

On opening the campaign of 1776, instead of reinforcing, it was necessary to *re-create* the army. *Marshall.*

REC'REATED, *pp.* Refreshed; diverted; amused; gratified.

RE-CREA'TED, *pp.* Created or formed anew.

REC'REATING, *ppr.* Refreshing after toil; reanimating the spirits or strength; diverting; amusing.

RE-CREA'TING, *ppr.* Creating or forming anew.

RECREA'TION, *n.* Refreshment of the strength and spirits after toil; amusement; diversion. *South.*

2. Relief from toil or pain; amusement in sorrow or distress. *Sidney.*

RE-CREA'TION, *n.* A forming anew.

REC'REATIVE, *a.* Refreshing; giving new vigor or animation; giving relief after labor or pain; amusing; diverting. Choose such sports as are *recreative* and healthful.

Let the music be *recreative.* *Bacon.*

REC'REATIVELY, *adv.* With recreation or diversion. *Sherwood.*

REC'REATIVENESS, *n.* The quality of being refreshing or diverting.

REC'REMENT, *n.* [L. *recrementum*; probably *re* and *cerno*, to secrete.] Superfluous matter separated from that which is useful; dross; scoria; spume; as the *recrement* of ore or of the blood.

RECREMENT'AL, RECREMENTI''TIAL, RECREMENTI''TIOUS, *a.* Drossy; consisting of superfluous matter separated from that which is valuable. *Fourcroy.*

RECRIM'INATE, *v. i.* [Fr. *recriminer*; L. *re* and *criminor*, to accuse.]

1. To return one accusation with another.

It is not my business to *recriminate.* *Stillingfleet.*

2. To charge an accuser with the like crime.

RECRIM'INATE, *v. t.* To accuse in return. *South.*

RECRIM'INATING, *ppr.* Returning one accusation with another.

RECRIMINA'TION, *n.* The return of one accusation with another.

2. In *law*, an accusation brought by the accused against the accuser upon the same fact. *Encyc.*

RECRIM'INATOR, *n.* He that accuses the accuser of a like crime.

RECRIM'INATORY, *a.* Retorting accusation. *Burke.*

RECROSS', *v. t.* To cross a second time. *Washington.*

RECROSS'ED, *pp.* Crossed a second time.

RECROSS'ING, *ppr.* Crossing a second time.

RECRUDES'CENCE, RECRUDES'CENCY, *n.* [from L. *recrudescens*; *re* and *crudesco*, to grow raw; *crudus*, raw.] The state of becoming sore again. *Bacon.*

RECRUDES'CENT, *a.* Growing raw, sore or painful again.

RECRUIT, *v. t.* [Fr. *recruter*; It. *reclutare*; Sp. *reclutar*; Port. *reclutar* or *recrutar*; from the root of Fr. *recroître*; *re* and *croître*, to grow, L. *cresco*; It. *ricrescere*, to *increase.*]

1. To repair by fresh supplies any thing wasted. We say, food *recruits* the flesh; fresh air and exercise *recruit* the spirits.

Her cheeks glow the brighter, *recruiting* their color. *Granville.*

2. To supply with new men any deficiency of troops; as, to *recruit* an army.

RECRUIT, *v. i.* To gain new supplies of any thing wasted; to gain flesh, health, spirits, &c.; as, lean cattle *recruit* in fresh pastures.

2. To gain new supplies of men; to raise new soldiers. *Addison.*

RECRUIT, *n.* The supply of any thing wasted; chiefly, a new raised soldier to supply the deficiency of an army.

RECRUITED, *pp.* Furnished with new supplies of what is wasted.

RECRUITING, *ppr.* Furnishing with fresh supplies; raising new soldiers for an army.

RECRUITING, *n.* The business of raising new soldiers to supply the loss of men in an army.

RECRUITMENT, *n.* The act or business of raising new supplies of men for an army. *Walsh.*

RECRYS'TALIZE, *v. i.* To crystalize a second time. *Henry.*

RECT'ANGLE, *n.* [Fr. from L. *rectangulus*; *rectus*, right, and *angulus*, angle.]

1. A right angled parallelogram.

2. In *arithmetic*, the product of two lines multiplied into each other. *Bailey.*

RECT'ANGLED, *a.* Having right angles, or angles of ninety degrees.

RECTAN'GULAR, *a.* Right angled; having angles of ninety degrees. *Wotton.*

RECTAN'GULARLY, *adv.* With or at right angles. *Brown.*

RECTIFIABLE, *a.* [from *rectify.*] That may be rectified; capable of being corrected or set right; as a *rectifiable* mistake.

RECTIFICA'TION, *n.* [Fr. See *Rectify.*]

1. The act or operation of correcting, amending or setting right that which is wrong or erroneous; as the *rectification* of errors, mistakes or abuses. *Forbes.*

2. In *chimistry*, the process of refining or purifying any substance by repeated distillation, which separates the grosser parts; as the *rectification* of spirits or sulphuric acid. *Nicholson. Encyc.*

REC'TIFIED, *pp.* Corrected; set or made right; refined by repeated distillation or sublimation.

REC'TIFIER, *n.* One that corrects or amends. *Bailey.*

2. One who refines a substance by repeated distillations.

3. An instrument that shows the variations of the compass, and rectifies the course of a ship. *Encyc.*

REC'TIFY, *v. t.* [Fr. *rectifier*; It. *rettificare*; Sp. *rectificar*; L. *rectus*, right, and *facio*, to make.]

1. To make right; to correct that which is wrong, erroneous or false; to amend; as, to *rectify* errors, mistakes or abuses; to *rectify* the will, the judgment, opinions; to *rectify* disorders. *Hooker. Addison.*

2. In *chimistry*, to refine by repeated distillation or sublimation, by which the fine parts of a substance are separated from the grosser; as, to *rectify* spirit or wine. *Encyc.*

3. To *rectify the globe*, is to bring the sun's place in the ecliptic on the globe to the brass meridian. *Bailey.*

REC'TIFYING, *ppr.* Correcting; amending; refining by repeated distillation or sublimation.

RECTILIN'EAL, RECTILIN'EAR, *a.* [L. *rectus*, right, and *linea*, line.] Right lined; consisting of a right line or of right lines; straight; as a *rectilinear* figure or course; a *rectilinear* side or way. *Newton.*

RECTILIN'EOUS, *a.* Rectilinear. *Obs.* *Ray.*

REC'TITUDE, *n.* [Fr. from L. *rectus*, right, straight; It. *rettitudine*; Sp. *rectitud*; literally straightness, but not applied to material things.]

In *morality*, rightness of principle or practice; uprightness of mind; exact conformity to truth, or to the rules prescribed for moral conduct, either by divine or human laws. Rectitude of *mind* is the disposition to act in conformity to any known standard of right, truth or justice; rectitude of *conduct* is the actual conformity to such standard. *Perfect rectitude* belongs only to the Supreme Being. The more nearly the *rectitude* of men approaches to the standard of the divine law, the more exalted and dignified is their character. Want of *rectitude* is not only sinful, but debasing.

There is a sublimity in conscious *rectitude*—in comparison with which the treasures of earth are not worth naming. *J. Hawes.*

REC'TOR, *n.* [L. *rector*, from *rego*, *rectum*, to rule; Fr. *recteur*; It. *rettore.*]

1. A ruler or governor.

God is the supreme *rector* of the world. *Hale.*

[*This application of the word is unusual.*]

2. A clergyman who has the charge and cure of a parish, and has the tithes, &c.; or the parson of an unimpropriated parish. *Blackstone.*

3. The chief elective officer of some universities, as in France and Scotland. The same title was formerly given to the president of a college in New England, but it is now in disuse. In Scotland, it is still the title of the head master of a principal school.

4. The superior officer or chief of a convent or religious house; and among the Jesuits, the superior of a house that is a seminary or college. *Encyc.*

REC'TORAL, RECTO'RIAL, *a.* Pertaining to a rector. *Blackstone.*

REC'TORSHIP, *n.* The office or rank of a rector. *Shak.*

REC'TORY, *n.* A parish church, parsonage or spiritual living, with all its rights, tithes and glebes. *Encyc.*

2. A rector's mansion or parsonage house. *Encyc.*

REC'TRESS, REC'TRIX, *n.* [L. *rectrix.*] A governess. *B. Jonson.*

REC'TUM, *n.* [L.] In *anatomy*, the third and last of the large intestines. *Encyc.*

RECUBA'TION, *n.* [L. *recubo*; *re* and *cubo*, to lie down.] The act of lying or leaning. [*Little used.*] *Brown.*

RECU'LE, *v. i.* To recoil. [*Not used.* See *Recoil.*] *Barret.*

RECUMB′, *v. i.* [L. *recumbo; re* and *cumbo*, to lie down.] To lean; to recline; to repose. *Allen.*

RECUMB′ENCE, *n.* [from L. *recumbens.*] The act of reposing or resting in confidence. *Ld. North.*

RECUMB′ENCY, *n.* The posture of leaning, reclining or lying. *Brown.*

2. Rest; repose; idle state. *Locke.*

RECUMB′ENT, *a.* [L. *recumbens.*] Leaning; reclining; as the *recumbent* posture of the Romans at their meals.

2. Reposing; inactive; idle. *Young.*

RECUPERA′TION, *n.* [L. *recuperatio.*] Recovery, as of any thing lost.

RECU′PERATIVE, } *a.* Tending to recov-
RECU′PERATORY, } ery; pertaining to recovery.

RECUR′, *v. i.* [L. *recurro; re* and *curro*, to run; Fr. *recourir.*]

1. To return to the thought or mind.

> When any word has been used to signify an idea, the old idea will *recur* in the mind, when the word is heard. *Watts.*

2. To resort; to have recourse.

> If to avoid succession in eternal existence, they *recur* to the punctum stans of the schools, they will very little help us to a more positive idea of infinite duration. *Locke.*

RECU′RE, *v. t.* [*re* and *cure.*] To cure; to recover. [*Not in use.*] *Spenser.*

RECU′RE, *n.* Cure; recovery. [*Not in use.*] *Knolles.*

RECU′RELESS, *a.* Incapable of cure or remedy. [*Not in use.*] *Bp. Hall.*

RECUR′RENCE, } *n.* [See *Recur.*] Re-
RECUR′RENCY, } turn; as the *recurrence* of error. *Brown.*

2. Resort; the having recourse.

RECUR′RENT, *a.* [L. *recurrens.*] Returning from time to time; as *recurrent* pains of a disease. *Harvey.*

2. In *crystalography*, a recurrent crystal is one whose faces, being counted in annular ranges from one extremity to the other, furnish two different numbers which succeed each other several times, as 4, 8, 4, 8, 4.

3. In *anatomy*, the *recurrent nerve* is a branch of the par vagum, given off in the upper part of the thorax, which is reflected and runs up along the trachea to the larynx. *Wistar.*

RECUR′SION, *n.* [L. *recursus, recurro; re* and *curro*, to run.] Return. [*Little used.*] *Boyle.*

RECURV′ATE, *v. t.* [L. *recurvo; re* and *curvo*, to bend.] To bend back. *Pennant.*

RECURV′ATE, *a.* In *botany*, bent, bowed or curved downwards; as a *recurvate* leaf. *Martyn.*

2. Bent outwards; as a *recurvate* prickle, awn, petiole, calyx or corol. *Martyn.*

RECURVA′TION, } *n.* A bending or flex-
RECURV′ITY, } ure backwards. *Brown.*

RECURVE, *v. t.* *recurv′.* [L. *recurvo*, supra.] To bend back.

RECURV′ED, *pp.* Bent back or downwards; as a *recurved* leaf. *Martyn.*

RECURV′IROSTER, *n.* [L. *recurvus*, bent back, and *rostrum*, a beak.]

A fowl whose beak or bill bends upwards, as the avoset.

RECURV′OUS, *a.* [L. *recurvus.*] Bent backwards. *Derham.*

RECU′SANCY, *n.* Non-conformity. [See *Recusant.*] *Coke.*

RECU′SANT, *a.* *s* as *z.* [L. *recusans, recuso*, to refuse; *re* and the root of *causa*, signifying to drive. The primary sense is to repel or drive back.]

Refusing to acknowledge the supremacy of the king, or to conform to the established rites of the church; as a *recusant* lord. *Clarendon.*

RECU′SANT, *n.* [supra.] In English history, a person who refuses to acknowledge the supremacy of the king in matters of religion; as a popish *recusant*, who acknowledges the supremacy of the pope. *Encyc.*

2. One who refuses communion with the church of England; a non-conformist.

> All that are *recusants* of holy rites. *Holyday.*

RECUSA′TION, *n.* [L. *recusatio.*] Refusal.

2. In *law*, the act of refusing a judge, or challenging that he shall not try the cause, on account of his supposed partiality. [*This practice is now obsolete.*] *Blackstone.*

RECU′SE, *v. t.* *s* as *z.* [L. *recuso.*] To refuse or reject, as a judge; to challenge that the judge shall not try the cause. [*The practice and the word are obsolete.*] *Digby.*

RED, *a.* [Sax. *red, read*, and *reod, rude*, red, ruddy; D. *rood;* G. *roth;* Sw. *röd;* Dan. *röd;* Corn. *rydh;* Ir. *ruadh;* Arm. *ruydh;* W. *rhuz*, red, ruddy; Sans. *rohida;* Russ. *rdeyu*, to redden; Gr. ερυθρος, red, and ροδον, a rose, from its color; Ar. ورد warada, to be present, to enter, to descend, to come, to invade, to blossom, to stain with a rose color, to bring to be of a red color; deriv. ورد a rose, the Gr. ροδον; Ch. ורד a rose; Syr. nearly the same; Eth. ወረደ warad, to descend, to bring down. These Arabic and Ethiopic words are the Heb. Ch. ירד to descend, to bring down, and this is radically the same as רדה which is rendered in Hebrew, to descend or come down, to decline, to bring down, to subdue, to have dominion; Ch. like senses, and to correct, to chastise, to expand or open, to flow, to plow; Syr. to go, to walk, to journey, L. *gradior*, also to correct, to teach; [qu. L. *erudio.*] The Arabic gives the sense of *rose*, which may be from opening, as blossoms, a sense coinciding with the Chaldee; and *red* from the same sense, or from the color of the rose. The Greeks called the Arabian gulf the *Erythrean* or *Red* sea, probably from Edom or Idumea; improperly applying the meaning of Edom, *red*, to the sea, and this improper application has come down to the present time.]

Of a bright color, resembling blood. Red is a simple or primary color, but of several different shades or hues, as scarlet, crimson, vermilion, orange red, &c. We say, *red* color, *red* cloth, *red* flame, *red* eyes, *red* cheeks, *red* lead, &c.

Red book of the exchequer, an ancient English record or manuscript containing various treatises relating to the times before the conquest. *Encyc.*

Red men, red people, red children, the aboriginals of America, as distinguished from the *whites.* *Rawle.*

RED, *n.* A red color; as a brighter color, the best of all the *reds.* *Newton.*

REDACT′, *v. t.* [L. *redactus, redigo; red, re*, and *ago.*]

To force; to reduce to form. [*Not used.*] *Drummond.*

RED′AN, *n.* [written sometimes *redent* and *redens;* said to be contracted from L. *recedens.* Lunier.]

In *fortification*, a work indented, or formed with salient and re-entering angles, so that one part may flank and defend another. *Lunier. Encyc.*

RED′ARGUE, *v. t.* [L. *redarguo; red, re*, and *arguo.*] To refute. [*Not in use.*] *Hakewill.*

REDARGU′TION, *n.* [supra.] Refutation; conviction. [*Not in use.*] *Bacon.*

RED′-BERRIED, *a.* Having or bearing red berries; as *red-berried* shrub cassia. *Miller.*

RED-BIRD, *n.* The popular name of several birds in the U. States, as the *Tanagra æstiva* or summer red-bird, the *Tanagra rubra*, and the Baltimore oriole or hang-nest.

RED′BREAST, *n.* A bird so called from the color of its breast, a species of Motacilla. In America, this name is given to the robin, so called, a species of Turdus.

RED′BUD, *n.* A plant or tree of the genus Cercis. *Fam. of Plants.*

RED-CHALK, *n.* A kind of clay ironstone; reddle. *Ure.*

RED′-COAT, *n.* A name given to a soldier who wears a red coat. *Dryden.*

REDDEN, *v. t.* *red′n.* [from *red.*] To make red. *Dryden.*

REDDEN, *v. i.* *red′n.* To grow or become red.

> —The coral *redden* and the ruby glow. *Pope.*

2. To blush.

> Appius *reddens* at each word you speak. *Pope.*

REDDEND′UM, *n.* In *law*, the clause by which rent is reserved in a lease.

RED′DISH, *a.* Somewhat red; moderately red. Lev. xiii.

RED′DISHNESS, *n.* Redness in a moderate degree. *Boyle.*

REDDI″TION, *n.* [L. *reddo*, to return.] A returning of any thing; restitution; surrender. *Howell.*

2. Explanation; representation. *Milton.*

RED′DITIVE, *a.* [L. *redditivus*, from *reddo.*]

Returning; answering to an interrogative; *a term of grammar.* *Johnson.*

RED′DLE, *n.* [from *red.*] Red chalk, commonly used as a pigment. It is a mineral of a florid color, but not of a deep red. *Nicholson. Hill.*

REDE, *n.* [Sax. *ræd.*] Counsel; advice. *Obs.* *Shak.*

REDE, *v. t.* To counsel or advise. *Obs.* *Spenser.*

REDEE′M, *v. t.* [L. *redimo; red, re*, and *emo*, to obtain or purchase.]

1. To purchase back; to ransom; to liberate or rescue from captivity or bondage, or from any obligation or liability to suffer or to be forfeited, by paying an equivalent; as, to *redeem* prisoners or captured goods; to *redeem* a pledge.

2. To repurchase what has been sold; to regain possession of a thing alienated, by repaying the value of it to the possessor.

If a man [shall] sell a dwelling house in a walled city, then he may *redeem* it within a whole year after it is sold. Lev. xxv.

3. To rescue; to recover; to deliver from.

Th' Almighty from the grave
Hath me *redeem'd*. *Sandys.*

Redeem Israel, O God, out of all his troubles. Ps. xxv. Deut. vii.

The mass of earth not yet *redeemed* from chaos. *S. S. Smith.*

4. To compensate; to make amends for.

It is a chance which does *redeem* all sorrows. *Shak.*

By lesser ills the greater to *redeem*. *Dryden.*

5. To free by making atonement.

Thou hast one daughter
Who *redeems* nature from the general curse. *Shak.*

6. To pay the penalty of.

Which of you will be mortal to *redeem*
Man's mortal crime? *Milton.*

7. To save.

He could not have *redeemed* a portion of his time for contemplating the powers of nature. *S. S. Smith.*

8. To perform what has been promised; to make good by performance. He has *redeemed* his pledge or promise.

9. In *law*, to recall an estate, or to obtain the right to re-enter upon a mortgaged estate by paying to the mortgagee his principal, interest, and expenses or costs. *Blackstone.*

10. In *theology*, to rescue and deliver from the bondage of sin and the penalties of God's violated law, by obedience and suffering in the place of the sinner, or by doing and suffering that which is accepted in lieu of the sinner's obedience.

Christ hath *redeemed* us from the curse of the law, being made a curse for us. Gal. iii. Tit. ii.

11. In *commerce*, to purchase or pay the value in specie, of any promissory note, bill or other evidence of debt, given by the state, by a company or corporation, or by an individual. The credit of a state, a banking company or individuals, is good when they can *redeem* all their stock, notes or bills, at par.

To redeem time, is to use more diligence in the improvement of it; to be diligent and active in duty and preparation. Eph. v.

REDEE'MABLE, *a.* That may be redeemed; capable of redemption.

2. That may be purchased or paid for in gold and silver, and brought into the possession of government or the original promiser.

The capital of the debt of the United States may be considered in the light of an annuity *redeemable* at the pleasure of the government. *Hamilton.*

REDEE'MABLENESS, *n.* The state of being reedeemable.

REDEE'MED, *pp.* Ransomed; delivered from bondage, distress, penalty, liability, or from the possession of another, by paying an equivalent.

REDEE'MER, *n.* One who redeems or ransoms.

2. The Savior of the world, Jesus Christ.

REDEE'MING, *ppr.* Ransoming; procuring deliverance from captivity, capture, bondage, sin, distress or liability to suffer, by the payment of an equivalent.

REDELIB'ERATE, *v. i.* [*re* and *deliberate.*] To deliberate again.

REDELIB'ERATE, *v. t.* To reconsider. [*Not in use.*]

REDELIV'ER, *v. t.* [*re* and *deliver.*] To deliver back. *Ayliffe.*

2. To deliver again; to liberate a second time.

REDELIV'ERANCE, *n.* A second deliverance.

REDELIV'ERED, *pp.* Delivered back; liberated again.

REDELIV'ERING, *ppr.* Delivering back; liberating again.

REDELIV'ERY, *n.* The act of delivering back; also, a second delivery or liberation.

REDEM'AND, *v. t.* [*re* and *demand*; Fr. *redemander.*]

To demand back; to demand again. *Addison.*

REDEM'AND, *n.* A demanding back again.

REDEM'ANDABLE, *a.* That may be demanded back.

REDEM'ANDED, *pp.* Demanded back or again.

REDEM'ANDING, *ppr.* Demanding back or again.

REDEMI'SE, *v. t. s* as *z.* [*re* and *demise.*] To convey or transfer back, as an estate in fee simple, fee tail, for life or a term of years. *Encyc.*

REDEMI'SE, *n.* Reconveyance; the transfer of an estate back to the person who has demised it; as the demise and *redemise* of an estate in fee simple, fee tail, or for life or years, by mutual leases. *Encyc.*

REDEMI'SED, *pp.* Reconveyed, as an estate.

REDEMI'SING, *ppr.* Reconveying.

REDEMP'TION, *n.* [Fr.; It. *redenzione*; Sp. *redencion*; from L. *redemptio.* See *Redeem.*]

1. Repurchase of captured goods or prisoners; the act of procuring the deliverance of persons or things from the possession and power of captors by the payment of an equivalent; ransom; release; as the *redemption* of prisoners taken in war; the *redemption* of a ship and cargo.

2. Deliverance from bondage, distress, or from liability to any evil or forfeiture, either by money, labor or other means.

3. Repurchase, as of lands alienated. Lev. xxv. Jer. xxxii.

4. The liberation of an estate from a mortgage; or the purchase of the right to reenter upon it by paying the principal sum for which it was mortgaged, with interest and cost; also, the right of redeeming and re-entering.

5. Repurchase of notes, bills or other evidence of debt by paying their value in specie to their holders.

6. In *theology*, the purchase of God's favor by the death and sufferings of Christ; the ransom or deliverance of sinners from the bondage of sin and the penalties of God's violated law by the atonement of Christ. *Dryden. Nelson.*

In whom we have *redemption* through his blood. Eph. i. Col. i.

REDEMP'TIONER, *n.* One who redeems himself, or purchases his release from debt or obligation to the master of a ship by his services; or one whose services are sold to pay the expenses of his passage to America.

REDEMP'TORY, *a.* Paid for ransom; as Hector's *redemptory* price. *Chapman.*

REDENT'ED, *a.* Formed like the teeth of a saw; indented.

REDESCEND', *v. i.* [*re* and *descend.*] To descend again. *Howell.*

REDESCEND'ING, *ppr.* Descending again.

RED'EYE, *n.* [*red* and *eye.*] A fish of a red color, particularly the iris.

RED'GUM, *n.* A disease of new born infants; an eruption of red pimples in early infancy. *Good.*

RED'-HAIRED, *a.* Having hair of a red or sandy color.

RED'-HOT, *n.* Red with heat; heated to redness; as *red-hot* iron; *red-hot* balls.

RED'IENT, *a.* [L. *rediens*, *redeo*, to return.] Returning. *E. H. Smith.*

REDIGEST', *v. t.* To digest or reduce to form a second time. *Kent.*

REDIGEST'ED, *pp.* Digested again.

REDIGEST'ING, *ppr.* Digesting a second time; reducing again to order.

REDIN'TEGRATE, *v. t.* [L. *redintegro*; *red*, *re*, and *integro*, from *integer*, whole.] To make whole again; to renew; to restore to a perfect state. *B. Jonson.*

REDIN'TEGRATE, *a.* Renewed; restored to wholeness or a perfect state. *Bacon.*

REDIN'TEGRATED, *pp.* Renewed; restored to entireness.

REDIN'TEGRATING, *ppr.* Restoring to a perfect state.

REDINTEGRA'TION, *n.* Renovation; restoration to a whole or sound state. *Decay of Piety.*

2. In *chimistry*, the restoration of any mixed body or matter to its former nature and constitution. *Coxe.*

REDISBURSE, *v. t. redisburs'.* [*re* and *disburse.*] To repay or refund. *Spenser.*

REDISPOSE, *v. t. s* as *z.* [*re* and *dispose.*] To dispose or adjust again. *Baxter.*

REDISPO'SED, *pp.* Disposed anew.

REDISPO'SING, *ppr.* Disposing or adjusting anew.

REDISSE'IZIN, *n.* [*re* and *disseizin.*] In *law*, a *writ of redisseizin*, is a writ to recover seizin of lands or tenements against a redisseizor.

REDISSE'IZOR, *n.* [*re* and *disseizor.*] A person who disseizes lands or tenements a second time, or after a recovery of the same from him in an action of novel disseizin. *Blackstone.*

REDISSOLVE, *v. t. redizolv'.* [*re* and *dissolve.*] To dissolve again.

REDISSOLV'ED, *pp.* Dissolved a second time.

REDISSOLV'ING, *ppr.* Dissolving again.

REDISTRIB'UTE, *v. t.* [*re* and *distribute.*] To distribute again; to deal back again. *Cotgrave.*

REDISTRIB'UTED, *pp.* Distributed again or back.

REDISTRIB'UTING, *ppr.* Distributing again or back.

REDISTRIBU'TION, *n.* A dealing back, or a second distribution.

RED'-LEAD, *n. red-led.* [*red* and *lead.*] Minium, or red oxyd of lead, composed of 88 parts of lead and 12 of oxygen.

RED'LY, *adv.* With redness. *Cotgrave.*

RED'NESS, *n.* [Sax. *readnesse.* See *Red.*] The quality of being red; red color. *Spectator.*

RED'OLENCE, }
RED'OLENCY, } *n.* [from *redolent.*] Sweet scent. *Boyle. Mortimer.*

RED'OLENT, *a.* [L. *redolens, redoleo; red, re,* and *oleo,* to smell.]
Having or diffusing a sweet scent. *Sandys.*

REDOUBLE, *v. t. redub'l.* [*re* and *double.*]
1. To repeat in return. *Spenser.*
2. To repeat often; as, to *redouble* blows. *Shak.*
3. To increase by repeated or continued additions.

And Ætna rages with *redoubl'd* heat. *Addison.*

REDOUBLE, *v. i. redub'l.* To become twice as much.

The argument *redoubles* upon us. *Spectator.*

REDOUBLED, *pp. redub'ld.* Repeated in return; repeated over and over; increased by repeated or continued additions.

REDOUBLING, *ppr. redub'ling.* Repeating in return; repeating again and again; increasing by repeated or continued additions.

REDOUND', *v. i.* [It. *ridondare;* L. *redundo; red, re,* and *undo,* to rise or swell, as waves.]
1. To be sent, rolled or driven back.

The evil, soon
Driven back, *redounded* as a flood on those
From whom it sprung. *Milton.*

2. To conduce in the consequence; to contribute; to result.

The honor done to our religion ultimately *redounds* to God, the author of it. *Rogers.*

3. To proceed in the consequence or effect; to result.

There will no small use *redound* from them to that manufacture. *Addison.*

REDOUND'ING, *ppr.* Conducing; contributing; resulting.

REDOUT', *n.* [It. *ridotto,* a shelter, a retreat; Sp. *reducto;* Port. *reduto, reducto* or *redutto;* Fr. *redoute, reduit;* L. *reductus, reduco,* to bring back; literally a retreat. The usual orthography, *redoubt,* is egregiously erroneous.]
In *fortification,* an outwork; a small square fort without any defense, except in front; used in trenches, lines of circumvallation, contravallation and approach, to defend passages, &c. *Encyc.*

REDOUT'ABLE, *a.* [Fr. from *redouter,* to fear or dread, Arm. *dougea, dougein.* The common orthography of this word is incorrect.]
Formidable; that is to be dreaded; terrible to foes; as a *redoubtable* hero. Hence the implied sense is valiant. *Pope.*

REDOUT'ED, *a.* Formidable. [*Not in use.*] *Spenser. Shak.*

RED'POLE, *n.* A bird with a red head or poll, of the genus Fringilla.

REDR'AFT, *v. t.* [*re* and *draft.*] To draw or draft anew.

REDR'AFT, *n.* A second draft or copy.
2. In *the French commercial code,* a new bill of exchange which the holder of a protested bill draws on the drawer or indorsers, by which he reimburses to himself the amount of the protested bill with costs and charges. *Walsh.*

REDR'AFTED, *pp.* Drafted again; transcribed into a new copy.

REDR'AFTING, *ppr.* Redrawing; drafting or transcribing again.

REDRAW', *v. t.* [*re* and *draw.*] To draw again. In *commerce,* to draw a new bill of exchange, as the holder of a protested bill, on the drawer or indorsers. *Walsh.*
2. To draw a second draft or copy.

REDRESS', *v. t.* [Fr. *redresser; re* and *dress.*]
1. To set right; to amend.

In yonder spring of roses,
Find what to *redress* till noon. *Milton.*

[*In this sense, as applied to material things, rarely used.*]
2. To remedy; to repair; to relieve from, and sometimes to indemnify for; as, to *redress* wrongs; to *redress* injuries; to *redress* grievances. Sovereigns are bound to protect their subjects, and *redress* their grievances.
3. To ease; to relieve; as, she labored to *redress* my pain. *Sidney.*
[We use this verb before the person or the thing. We say, to *redress* an injured *person,* or to *redress* the *injury.* The latter is most common.]

REDRESS', *n.* Reformation; amendment.

For us the more necessary is a speedy *redress* of ourselves. *Hooker.*

[*This sense is now unusual.*]
2. Relief; remedy; deliverance from wrong, injury or oppression; as the *redress* of grievances. We applied to government, but could obtain no *redress.*

There is occasion for *redress* when the cry is universal. *Davenant.*

3. Reparation; indemnification. [This sense is often directly intended or implied in *redress.*]
4. One who gives relief.

Fair majesty, the refuge and *redress*
Of those whom fate pursues and wants oppress. *Dryden.*

REDRESS'ED, *pp.* Remedied; set right; relieved; indemnified.

REDRESS'ER, *n.* One who gives redress.

REDRESS'ING, *ppr.* Setting right; relieving; indemnifying.

REDRESS'IVE, *a.* Affording relief. *Thomson.*

REDRESS'LESS, *a.* Without amendment; without relief. *Sherwood.*

REDSE'AR, *v. i.* [*red* and *sear.*] To break or crack when too hot, as iron under the hammer; *a term of workmen.* *Moxon.*

RED'SHANK, *n.* A bird of the genus Scolopax.
2. A contemptuous appellation for bare legged persons. *Spenser.*

RED'SHORT, *a.* [*red* and *short.*] Brittle, or breaking short when red hot, as a metal; *a term of workmen.*

RED'START, }
RED'TAIL, } *n.* [*red* and *start,* Sax. *steort,* a tail.] A bird of the genus Motacilla.

RED'STREAK, *n.* [*red* and *streak.*] A sort of apple, so called from its red streaks. *Mortimer.*
2. Cider pressed from the red streak apples. *Smith.*

REDU'CE, *v. t.* [L. *reduco; re* and *duco,* to lead or bring; Fr. *reduire;* It. *ridicere* or *ridurre;* Sp. *reducir.*]
1. Literally, to bring back; as, to *reduce* these bloody days again. *Shak.*
[*In this sense, not in use.*]
2. To bring to a former state.

It were but just
And equal to *reduce* me to my dust. *Milton.*

3. To bring to any state or condition, good or bad; as, to *reduce* civil or ecclesiastical affairs to order; to *reduce* a man to poverty; to *reduce* a state to distress; to *reduce* a substance to powder; to *reduce* a sum to fractions; to *reduce* one to despair.
4. To diminish in length, breadth, thickness, size, quantity or value; as, to *reduce* expenses; to *reduce* the quantity of any thing; to *reduce* the intensity of heat; to *reduce* the brightness of color or light; to *reduce* a sum or amount; to *reduce* the price of goods.
5. To lower; to degrade; to impair in dignity or excellence.

Nothing so excellent but a man may fasten on something belonging to it, to *reduce* it. *Tillotson.*

6. To subdue; to bring into subjection. The Romans *reduced* Spain, Gaul and Britain by their arms.
7. To reclaim to order. *Milton.*
8. To bring, as into a class, order, genus or species; to bring under rules or within certain limits of description; as, to *reduce* animals or vegetables to a class or classes; to *reduce* men to tribes; to *reduce* language to rules.
9. In *arithmetic,* to change numbers from one denomination into another without altering their value; or to change numbers of one denomination into others of the same value; as, to *reduce* a dollar to a hundred cents, or a hundred cents to a dollar.
10. In *algebra,* to *reduce equations,* is to clear them of all superfluous quantities, bring them to their lowest terms, and separate the known from the unknown, till at length the unknown quantity only is found on one side and the known ones on the other. *Encyc.*
11. In *metallurgy,* to bring back metallic substances which have been divested of their form, into their original state of metals. *Encyc.*
12. In *surgery,* to restore to its proper place or state a dislocated or fractured bone.
To reduce a figure, design or *draught,* to make a copy of it larger or smaller than the original, but preserving the form and proportion. *Encyc.*

REDU'CED, *pp.* Brought back; brought to a former state; brought into any state or condition; diminished; subdued; impoverished.

REDU'CEMENT, *n.* The act of bringing back; the act of diminishing; the act of subduing; reduction. *Bacon.*
[This word is superseded by *reduction.*]

REDU'CER, *n.* One that reduces. *Sidney.*

REDU'CIBLE, *a.* That may be reduced.
All the parts of painting are *reducible* into these mentioned by the author. *Dryden.*

REDU'CIBLENESS, *n.* The quality of being reducible.

REDU'CING, *ppr.* Bringing back; bringing to a former state, or to a different state or form; diminishing; subduing; impoverishing.

REDUCT', *v. t.* [L. *reductus, reduco.*] To reduce. [*Not in use.*] *Warde.*

REDUCT', *n.* In *building*, a little place taken out of a larger to make it more regular and uniform, or for some other convenience. *Chambers.*

REDUC'TION, *n.* [Fr. from L. *reductio.*]
1. The act of reducing, or state of being reduced; as the *reduction* of a body to powder; the *reduction* of things to order.
2. Diminution; as the *reduction* of the expenses of government; the *reduction* of the national debt.
3. Conquest; subjugation; as the *reduction* of a province to the power of a foreign nation.
4. In *arithmetic*, the bringing of numbers of different denominations into one denomination; as the *reduction* of pounds, ounces, pennyweights and grains to grains, or the *reduction* of grains to pounds; the *reduction* of days and hours to minutes, or of minutes to hours and days. The change of numbers of a higher denomination into a lower, as of pounds into pence or farthings, is called *reduction descending*; the change of numbers of a lower denomination into a higher, as of cents into dimes, dollars or eagles, is called *reduction ascending*. Hence the rule for bringing sums of different denominations into one denomination, is called *reduction.*
5. In *algebra*, reduction of equations is the clearing of them of all superfluous quantities, bringing them to their lowest terms, and separating the known from the unknown, till the unknown quantity alone is found on one side, and the known ones on the other. *Encyc.*
6. *Reduction of a figure, map, &c.* is the making of a copy of it on a smaller or larger scale, preserving the form and proportions. *Encyc.*
7. In *surgery*, the operation of restoring a dislocated or fractured bone to its former place.
8. In *metallurgy*, the operation of bringing metallic substances which have been changed, or divested of their metallic form, into their natural and original state of metals. This is called also *revivification.* *Nicholson. Encyc.*

REDUC'TIVE, *a.* [Fr. *reductif.*] Having the power of reducing. *Brevint.*

REDUC'TIVE, *n.* That which has the power of reducing. *Hale.*

REDUC'TIVELY, *adv.* By reduction; by consequence. *Hammond.*

REDUND'ANCE, REDUND'ANCY, *n.* [L. *redundantia, redundo.* See *Redound.*]
1. Excess or superfluous quantity; superfluity; superabundance; as a *redundancy* of bile.
Labor throws off *redundancies.* *Addison.*
2. In discourse, superfluity of words. *Encyc.*

REDUND'ANT, *a.* Superfluous; exceeding what is natural or necessary; superabundant; exuberant; as a *redundant* quantity of bile or food.
Notwithstanding the *redundant* oil in fishes, they do not encrease fat so much as flesh. *Arbuthnot.*
Redundant words, in writing or discourse, are such as are synonymous with others used, or such as add nothing to the sense or force of the expression.
2. Using more words or images than are necessary or useful.
Where an author is *redundant*, mark those paragraphs to be retrenched. *Watts.*
3. In *music*, a *redundant* chord is one which contains a greater number of tones, semitones or lesser intervals, than it does in its natural state, as from *fa* to *sol* sharp. It is called by some authors, a chord extremely sharp. *Encyc.*

REDUND'ANTLY, *adv.* With superfluity or excess; superfluously; superabundantly.

REDU'PLICATE, *v. t.* [L. *reduplico*; *re* and *duplico.* See *Duplicate.*]
To double. *Pearson.*

REDUPLICATE, *a.* Double.

REDUPLICA'TION, *n.* The act of doubling. *Digby.*

REDU'PLICATIVE, *a.* Double. *Watts.*

RED'WING, *n.* [*red* and *wing.*] A bird of the genus Turdus.

REE, RE, *n.* A small Portuguese coin or money of account, value about one mill and a fourth, American money.

REE, *v. t.* [This belongs to the root of *rid*, *riddle*, which see.]
To riddle; to sift; that is, to separate or throw off. [*Not in use or local.*] *Mortimer.*

RE-ECH'O, *v. t.* [*re* and *echo.*] To echo back; to reverberate again; as, the hills *re-echo* the roar of cannon.

RE-ECH'O, *v. i.* [supra.] To echo back; to return back or be reverberated; as an echo.
And a loud groan *re-echoes* from the main. *Pope.*

RE-ECH'O, *n.* The echo of an echo.

RE-ECH'OED, *pp.* [supra.] Returned, as sound; reverberated again.

RE-ECH'OING, *ppr.* Returning or reverberating an echo.

REECH'Y, *a.* [a mis-spelling of *reeky.* See *Reek.*]
Tarnished with smoke; sooty; foul; as a *reechy* neck. *Shak.*

REED, *n.* [Sax. *hreod, reod*; G. *rieth*; D. *riet*; Goth. *raus*; Fr. *roseau*; Ir. *readan*; probably allied to *rod.*]
1. The common name of many aquatic plants; most of them large grasses, with hollow jointed stems, such as the common reed of the genus Arundo, the bamboo, &c. The *bur-reed* is of the genus Sparganium; the *Indian flowering reed* of the genus Canna.
2. A musical pipe; reeds being anciently used for instruments of music. *Milton.*
3. A little tube through which a hautboy, bassoon or clarinet is blown.
4. An arrow, as made of a reed headed. *Prior.*
5. Thatch. *West of England.*

REE'DED, *a.* Covered with reeds. *Tusser.*
2. Formed with channels and ridges like reeds.

REEDEN, *a.* *ree'dn.* Consisting of a reed or reeds; as *reeden* pipes. *Dryden.*

REE'DGRASS, *n.* A plant, bur-reed, of the genus Sparganium.

RE-EDIFICA'TION, *n.* [from *re-edify.*] Act or operation of rebuilding; state of being rebuilt. *D'Anville, Trans.*

RE-ED'IFIED, *pp.* Rebuilt.

RE-ED'IFY, *v. t.* [Fr. *réédifier*; *re* and *edify.*]
To rebuild; to build again after destruction. *Milton.*

RE-ED'IFYING, *ppr.* Rebuilding.

REE'DLESS, *a.* Destitute of reeds; as *reedless* banks. *May.*

REE'DMACE, *n.* A plant of the genus Typha. *Lee.*

REE'DY, *a.* Abounding with reeds; as a *reedy* pool. *Thomson.*

REEF, *n.* [D. *reef*; Dan. *riv* or *rift*; Sw. *ref.* These words coincide in orthography with the verb to *rive*, and if from this root, the primary sense is a division. W. *rhiv* and *rhif.* But in Welsh, *rhêv* signifies a collection or bundle, and thick; *rhevu*, to thicken in compass; and if from this root, a *reef* is a fold, and to *reef* is to fold.]
A certain portion of a sail between the top or bottom and a row of eyelet holes, which is folded or rolled up to contract the sail, when the violence of the wind renders it necessary. *Mar. Dict.*

REEF, *n.* [G. *riff*; D. *rif*, a reef or sand bank, a carcass, a skeleton. Qu. W. *rhevu*, to thicken.]
A chain or range of rocks lying at or near the surface of the water. *Mar. Dict.*

REEF, *v. t.* [from the noun.] To contract or reduce the extent of a sail by rolling or folding a certain portion of it and making it fast to the yard. *Mar. Dict.*

REE'F-BAND, *n.* A piece of canvas sewed across a sail, to strengthen it in the part where the eyelet holes are formed.

REE'FED, *pp.* Having a portion of the top or bottom folded and made fast to the yard.

REE'FING, *ppr.* Folding and making fast to the yard, as a portion of a sail.

REE'F-LINE, *n.* A small rope formerly used to reef the courses by being passed through the holes of the reef spirally. *Mar. Dict.*

REE'F-TACKLE, *n.* A tackle upon deck, communicating with its pendant, and passing through a block at the top-mast head, and through a hole in the top-sail-yard-arm, is attached to a cringle below the lowest reef; used to pull the skirts of the top-sails close to the extremities of the yards to lighten the labor of reefing. *Mar. Dict.*

REEK, *n.* [Sax. *rec*; D. *rook*; G. *rauch*; Sw. *rök*; Dan. *rög.*]
1. Vapor; steam.
2. A rick, which see. *Shak.*

REEK, *v. i.* [Sax. *recan, reocan*; D. *rooken, ruiken*; G. *rauchen*; Sw. *rôka*; Dan. *röger, ryger*, to reek, to smoke; W. *rhogli*, to smell. This may be from the same root as the L. *fragro*, and all coinciding with the Ar. أرج to diffuse odor. The primary sense is to send out or emit, to extend, to *reach*. Class Rg.]

To steam; to exhale; to emit vapor; *applied especially to the vapor of certain moist substances*, rather than to the smoke of burning bodies.

> I found me laid
> In balmy sweat, which with his beams the sun
> Soon dry'd, and on the *reeking* moisture fed. *Milton.*

> Whose blood yet *reeks* on my avenging sword. *Smith.*

REE'KING, *ppr.* Steaming; emitting vapor.

REE'KY, *a.* Smoky; soiled with smoke or steam; foul. *Shak.*

REEL, *n.* [Sax. *hreol, reol*. See *Reel*, to stagger.]

1. A frame or machine turning on an axis, and on which yarn is extended for winding, either into skains, or from skains on to spools and quills. On a reel also seamen wind their log-lines, &c.

2. A kind of dance.

REEL, *v. t.* To gather yarn from the spindle. *Wilkins.*

REEL, *v. i.* [Sw. *ragla*. Qu. Class Rg, or Ar. رغل ragala, to lean. Class Rl. No. 4.]

To stagger; to incline or move in walking, first to one side and then to the other; to vacillate.

> He with heavy fumes opprest,
> *Reel'd* from the palace and retir'd to rest. *Pope.*

> They *reel* to and fro, and stagger like a drunken man. Ps. cvii.

RE-ELECT', *v. t.* [*re* and *elect*.] To elect again; as, to *re-elect* the former governor.

RE-ELECT'ED, *pp.* Elected again; rechosen.

RE-ELECT'ING, *ppr.* Electing again.

RE-ELEC'TION, *n.* Election a second time, or repeated election; as the *re-election* of a former representative. *Swift.*

RE-ELIGIBIL'ITY, *n.* The capacity of being re-elected to the same office.

RE-EL'IGIBLE, *a.* [*re* and *eligible*.] Capable of being elected again to the same office.

RE-EMB'ARK, *v.t.* [*re* and *embark*.] To embark or put on board again.

RE-EMB'ARK, *v. i.* To embark or go on board again.

RE-EMBARKA'TION, *n.* A putting on board or a going on board again.

RE-EMBAT'TLE, *v. t.* [*re* and *embattle*.] To array again for battle; to arrange again in the order of battle.

RE-EMBAT'TLED, *pp.* Arrayed again for battle.

RE-EMBAT'TLING, *ppr.* Arranging again in battle array.

RE-EMBOD'Y, *v. t.* [*re* and *embody*.] To embody again.

RE-ENACT', *v. t.* [*re* and *enact*.] To enact again. *Arbuthnot.*

RE-ENACT'ED, *pp.* Enacted again.

RE-ENACT'ING, *ppr.* Enacting anew; passing again into a law.

RE-ENAC'TION, *n.* The passing into a law again.

RE-ENACT'MENT, *n.* The enacting or passing of a law a second time; the renewal of a law. *Key. Wheaton's Rep.*

RE-ENFORCE, *v. t.* [*re* and *enforce*.] To strengthen with new force, assistance or support, as to *re-enforce* an argument; but particularly, to strengthen an army or a fort with additional troops, or a navy with additional ships.

RE-ENFORCED, *pp.* Strengthened by additional force, troops or ships.

RE-ENFORCEMENT, *n.* The act of re-enforcing.

2. Additional force; fresh assistance; particularly, additional troops or force to augment the strength of an army or of ships.

3. Any augmentation of strength or force by something added.

RE-ENFORCING, *ppr.* Strengthening by additional force.

RE-ENGA'GE, *v. t.* To engage a second time.

RE-ENGA'GE, *v. i.* To engage again; to enlist a second time; to covenant again. *Mitford.*

RE-ENJOY', *v. t.* [*re* and *enjoy*.] To enjoy anew or a second time. *Pope.*

RE-ENJOY'ED, *pp.* Enjoyed again.

RE-ENJOY'ING, *ppr.* Enjoying anew.

RE-ENJOY'MENT, *n.* A second or repeated enjoyment.

RE-ENKIN'DLE, *v. t.* [*re* and *enkindle*.] To enkindle again; to rekindle. *Taylor.*

RE-ENKIN'DLED, *pp.* Enkindled again.

RE-ENKIN'DLING, *ppr.* Enkindling anew.

RE-ENLIST', *v. t.* To enlist a second time. [See *Re-inlist*.]

RE-EN'TER, *v. t.* [*re* and *enter*.] To enter again or anew.

RE-EN'TER, *v. i.* To enter anew.

RE-EN'TERED, *pp.* Entered again.

RE-EN'TERING, *ppr.* Entering anew.

2. Entering in return; as salient and *re-entering* angles. *Encyc.*

RE-ENTHRO'NE, *v. t.* [*re* and *enthrone*.] To enthrone again; to replace on a throne. *Southern.*

RE-ENTHRO'NED, *pp.* Raised again to a throne.

RE-ENTHRO'NING, *ppr.* Replacing on a throne.

RE-EN'TRANCE, *n.* [*re* and *entrance*.] The act of entering again. *Hooker.*

RE'ERMOUSE, *n.* [Sax. *hreremus*.] A rear-mouse; a bat.

RE-ESTAB'LISH, *v. t.* [*re* and *establish*.] To establish anew; to fix or confirm again; as, to *re-establish* a covenant; to *re-establish* health.

RE-ESTAB'LISHED, *pp.* Established or confirmed again.

RE-ESTAB'LISHER, *n.* One who establishes again.

RE-ESTAB'LISHING, *ppr.* Establishing anew; confirming again.

RE-ESTAB'LISHMENT, *n.* The act of establishing again; the state of being re-established; renewed confirmation; restoration. *Addison.*

RE-ESTA'TE, *v. t.* [*re* and *estate*.] To re-establish. [*Not used*.] *Waller.*

REEVE, *n.* [Sax. *gerefa*; G. *graf*.] A steward. *Obs.* *Dryden.*

REEVE, *n.* A bird, the female of the ruff.

REEVE, *v. t.* In *seamen's language*, to pass the end of a rope through any hole in a block, thimble, cleat, ring-bolt, cringle, &c. *Mar. Dict.*

RE-EXAMINA'TION, *n.* A renewed or repeated examination.

RE-EXAM'INE, *v. t.* [*re* and *examine*.] To examine anew. *Hooker.*

RE-EXAM'INED, *pp.* Examined again.

RE-EXAM'INING, *ppr.* Examining anew.

RE-EXCHANGE, *n.* [*re* and *exchange*.] A renewed exchange.

2. In *commerce*, the exchange chargeable on the redraft of a bill of exchange.

> The rate of *re-exchange* is regulated with respect to the drawer, at the course of exchange between the place where the bill of exchange was payable, and the place where it was drawn. *Re-exchanges* cannot be cumulated. *Walsh.*

RE-EXPORT, *v. t.* [*re* and *export*.] To export again; to export what has been imported. In the United States, a drawback is allowed on commodities *re-exported*.

RE-EX'PORT, *n.* Any commodity re-exported.

RE-EXPORTA'TION, *n.* The act of exporting what has been imported.

RE-EXPORTED, *pp.* Exported after being imported.

RE-EXPORTING, *ppr.* Exporting what has been imported.

REFECT', *v. t.* [L. *refectus, reficio*; *re* and *facio*, to make.]

To refresh; to restore after hunger or fatigue. [*Not in use*.] *Brown.*

REFEC'TION, *n.* [Fr. from L. *refectio*.]

1. Refreshment after hunger or fatigue. *South. Pope.*

2. A spare meal or repast. *Encyc.*

REFECT'IVE, *a.* Refreshing; restoring.

REFECT'IVE, *n.* That which refreshes.

REFECT'ORY, *n.* [Fr. *refectoire*.] A room of refreshment; properly, a hall or apartment in convents and monasteries, where a moderate repast is taken. *Encyc.*

REFEL', *v. t.* [L. *refello*.] To refute; to disprove; to repress; as, to *refel* the tricks of a sophister. [*Little used*.] *Shak.*

REFER', *v. t.* [L. *refero*; *re* and *fero*, to bear; Fr. *referrer*; It. *referire*; Sp. Port. *referir*.]

1. To direct, leave or deliver over to another person or tribunal for information or decision; as when parties to a suit *refer* their cause to another court; or the court *refers* a cause to individuals for examination and report. A person whose opinion is requested, sometimes *refers* the inquirer to another person or other source of information.

2. To reduce as to the ultimate end.

> You profess and practice to *refer* all things to yourself. *Bacon.*

3. To reduce; to assign; as to an order, genus or class. Naturalists are sometimes at a loss to know to what class or genus an animal or plant is to be *referred*.

To refer one's self, to betake; to apply. [*Little used.*] *Shak.*

REFER', *v. i.* To respect; to have relation. Many passages of Scripture *refer* to the peculiar customs of the orientals.

2. To appeal; to have recourse; to apply.

In suits it is good to *refer* to some friend of trust. *Bacon.*

3. To allude; to have respect to by intimation without naming. I *refer* to a well known fact.

REF'ERABLE, *a.* That may be referred; capable of being considered in relation to something else. *More.*

2. That may be assigned; that may be considered as belonging to or related to.

It is a question among philosophers, whether all the attractions which obtain between bodies, are *referable* to one general cause. *Nicholson.*

REFEREE', *n.* One to whom a thing is referred; particularly, a person appointed by a court to hear, examine and decide a cause between parties, pending before the court, and make report to the court. In New England, a *referee* differs from an *arbitrator*, in being appointed by the court to decide in a cause which is depending before that court. An *arbitrator* is chosen by parties to decide a cause between them.

REF'ERENCE, *n.* A sending, dismission or direction to another for information. *Swift.*

2. Relation; respect; view towards.

The christian religion commands sobriety, temperance and moderation, in *reference* to our appetites and passions. *Tillotson.*

3. Allusion to. In his observations he had no *reference* to the case which has been stated.

4. In *law*, the process of assigning a cause depending in court, for a hearing and decision, to persons appointed by the court.

REFEREND'ARY, *n.* One to whose decision a cause is referred. [*Not in use.*] *Bacon.*

2. An officer who delivered the royal answer to petitions. *Harmar.*

REFER'MENT, *n.* Reference for decision. [*Not used.*] *Laud.*

RE-FERMENT', *v. t.* [*re* and *ferment.*] To ferment again. *Blackmore.*

REFER'RED, *pp.* Dismissed or directed to another; assigned, as to a class, order or cause; assigned by a court to persons appointed to decide.

REFER'RIBLE, *a.* That may be referred; referable. *Brown.*

REFER'RING, *ppr.* Dismissing or directing to another for information; alluding; assigning, as to a class, order, cause, &c.; or assigning to private persons for decision.

RE-FIND, *v. t.* [*re* and *find.*] To find again; to experience anew. *Sandys.*

REFI'NE, *v. t.* [Fr. *raffiner;* It. *raffinare;* Sp. Port. *refinar; re* and *fine.*]

1. To purify; *in a general sense;* applied to liquors, to depurate; to defecate; to clarify; to separate, as liquor, from all extraneous matter. In this sense, the verb is used with propriety, but it is customary to use *fine.*

2. *Applied to metals,* to separate the metallic substance from all other matter, whether another metal or alloy, or any earthy substance; in short, to detach the pure metal from all extraneous matter.

I will bring the third part through the fire, and will *refine* them as silver is *refined.* Zech. xiii.

3. To purify, as manners, from what is gross, clownish or vulgar; to polish; to make elegant. We expect to see *refined* manners in courts.

4. To purify, as language, by removing vulgar words and barbarisms.

5. To purify, as taste; to give a nice and delicate perception of beauty and propriety in literature and the arts.

6. To purify, as the mind or moral principles; to give or implant in the mind a nice perception of truth, justice and propriety in commerce and social intercourse. This nice perception of what is right constitutes rectitude of principle, or moral refinement of mind; and a correspondent practice of social duties, constitutes rectitude of conduct or purity of morals. Hence we speak of a *refined* mind, *refined* morals, *refined* principles.

To refine the heart or *soul,* to cleanse it from all carnal or evil affections and desires, and implant in it holy or heavenly affections.

REFI'NE, *v. i.* To improve in accuracy, delicacy, or in any thing that constitutes excellence.

Chaucer *refined* on Boccace and mended his stories. *Dryden.*

Let a lord but own the happy lines,
How the wit brightens, how the sense *refines!* *Pope.*

2. To become pure; to be cleared of feculent matter.

So the pure limpid stream, when foul with stains,
Works itself clear, and as it runs, *refines.* *Addison.*

3. To affect nicety. Men sometimes *refine* in speculation beyond the limits of practical truth.

He makes another paragraph about our *refining* in controversy. *Atterbury.*

REFI'NED, *pp.* Purified; separated from extraneous matter; assayed, as metals; clarified, as liquors; polished; separated from what is coarse, rude or improper.

REFI'NEDLY, *adv.* With affected nicety or elegance. *Dryden.*

REFI'NEDNESS, *n.* State of being refined; purity; refinement; also, affected purity. *Barrow.*

REFI'NEMENT, *n.* The act of purifying by separating from a substance all extraneous matter; a clearing from dross, dregs or recrement; as the *refinement* of metals or liquors.

2. The state of being pure.

The more bodies are of a kin to spirit in subtilty and *refinement,* the more diffusive are they. *Norris.*

3. Polish of language; elegance; purity.

From the civil war to this time, I doubt whether the corruptions in our language have not equaled its *refinements.* *Swift.*

4. Polish of manners; elegance; nice observance of the civilities of social intercourse and of graceful decorum. *Refinement* of manners is often found in persons of corrupt morals.

5. Purity of taste; nice perception of beauty and propriety in literature and the arts.

6. Purity of mind and morals; nice perception and observance of rectitude in moral principles and practice.

7. Purity of heart; the state of the heart purified from sensual and evil affections. This *refinement* is the effect of christian principles.

8. Artificial practice; subtilty; as the *refinements* of cunning. *Rogers.*

9. Affectation of nicety, or of elegant improvement; as the *refinements* of reasoning or philosophy.

REFI'NER, *n.* One that refines metals or other things. *Bacon.*

2. An improver in purity and elegance; as a *refiner* of language. *Swift.*

3. An inventor of superfluous subtilties; one is who over nice in discrimination, in argument, reasoning, philosophy, &c.

REFI'NERY, *n.* The place and apparatus for refining metals.

REFI'NING, *ppr.* Purifying; separating from alloy or any extraneous matter; polishing; improving in accuracy, delicacy or purity.

REFIT', *v. t.* [*re* and *fit.*] To fit or prepare again; to repair; to restore after damage or decay; as, to *refit* ships of war.

REFIT'TED, *pp.* Prepared again; repaired.

REFIT'TING, *ppr.* Repairing after damage or decay.

REFLECT', *v. t.* [L. *reflecto; re* and *flecto,* to bend; Fr. *reflechir;* It. *riflettere.*]

To throw back; to return. In the rainbow, the rays of light are *reflected* as well as refracted.

Bodies close together *reflect* their own color. *Dryden.*

REFLECT', *v. i.* To throw back light; to return rays or beams; as a *reflecting* mirror or gem. *Shak.*

2. To bend back. *Bentley.*

3. To throw or turn back the thoughts upon the past operations of the mind or upon past events. We *reflect* with pleasure on a generous or heroic action; we *reflect* with pain on our follies and vices; we *reflect* on our former thoughts, meditations and opinions.

4. To consider attentively; to revolve in the mind; to contemplate; as, I will *reflect* on this subject.

And as I much *reflected,* much I mourn'd. *Prior.*

In every action, *reflect* upon the end. *Taylor.*

[To *reflect* on things *future,* is not strictly possible, yet the word is often used as synonymous with *meditate* and *contemplate.*]

5. To bring reproach.

Errors of wives *reflect* on husband still. *Dryden.*

To reflect on, to cast censure or reproach.

I do not *reflect* in the least *on* the memory of his late majesty. *Swift.*

REFLECT'ED, *pp.* Thrown back; returned; as *reflected* light.

REFLECT'ENT, *a.* Bending or flying back; as the ray descendent, and ray *reflectent.* *Digby.*

REFLECT'IBLE, *a.* That may be reflected or thrown back. *Gregory.*

REFLECT'ING, *ppr.* Throwing back.

2. Turning back, as thoughts upon themselves or upon past events.

3. *Reflecting on*, casting censure or reproach.

REFLECT'INGLY, *adv.* With reflection; with censure. *Swift.*

REFLEC'TION, *n.* [from *reflect.*] The act of throwing back; as the *reflection* of light or colors. The angle of incidence and the angle of *reflection* are always equal.

2. The act of bending back. *Bentley.*

3. That which is reflected.

As the sun in water we can bear,
Yet not the sun, but his *reflection* there. *Dryden.*

4. The operation of the mind by which it turns its views back upon itself and its operations; the review or reconsideration of past thoughts, opinions or decisions of the mind, or of past events. *Encyc.*

5. Thought thrown back on itself, on the past or on the absent; as melancholy *reflections*; delightful *reflections*.

Job's *reflections* on his once flourishing estate, at the same time afflicted and encouraged him. *Atterbury.*

6. The expression of thought.

7. Attentive consideration; meditation; contemplation.

This delight grows and improves under thought and *reflection*. *South.*

8. Censure; reproach cast.

He died, and oh! may no *reflection* shed
Its pois'nous venom on the royal dead. *Prior.*

REFLECT'IVE, *a.* Throwing back images; as a *reflective* mirror.

In the *reflective* stream the sighing bride,
Viewing her charms impair'd— *Prior.*

2. Considering the operations of the mind, or things past; as *reflective* reason. *Prior.*

REFLECT'OR, *n.* One who reflects or considers. *Boyle.*

2. That which reflects.

RE'FLEX, *a.* [L. *reflexus.*] Directed back; as a *reflex* act of the soul, the turning of the intellectual eye inward upon its own actions. *Hale.*

2. Designating the parts of a painting illuminated by light reflected from another part of the same picture. *Encyc.*

3. In *botany*, bent back; reflected.

REFLEX', *n.* Reflection. [*Not used.*] *Hooker.*

REFLEX', *v. t.* To reflect. *Shak.*

2. To bend back; to turn back. [*Little used.*] *Gregory.*

REFLEXIBIL'ITY, *n.* The quality of being reflexible or capable of being reflected; as the *reflexibility* of the rays of light. *Newton.*

REFLEX'IBLE, *a.* Capable of being reflected or thrown back.

The light of the sun consists of rays differently refrangible and *reflexible*. *Cheyne.*

REFLEX'ION. [See *Reflection.*]

REFLEX'ITY, *n.* Capacity of being reflected.

REFLEX'IVE, *a.* Having respect to something past.

Assurance *reflexive* cannot be a divine faith. *Hammond.*

REFLEX'IVELY, *adv.* In a direction backward. *Gov. of the Tongue.*

RE'FLOAT, *n.* [*re* and *float.*] Reflux; ebb; a flowing back. [*Little used.*] *Bacon.*

REFLORES'CENCE, *n.* [*re* and *florescence.*] A blossoming anew.

REFLOURISH, *v. i.* *reflur'ish.* [*re* and *flourish.*] To flourish anew. *Milton.*

REFLOUR'ISHING, *ppr.* Flourishing again.

REFLOW, *v. i.* [*re* and *flow.*] To flow back; to ebb.

REFLOWING, *ppr.* Flowing back; ebbing. *Darwin.*

REFLUCTUA'TION, *n.* A flowing back.

REF'LUENCE, REF'LUENCY, *n.* [from *refluent.*] A flowing back. *Mountague.*

REF'LUENT, *a.* [L. *refluens*; *re* and *fluo.*]

1. Flowing back; ebbing; as the *refluent* tide.

2. Flowing back; returning, as a fluid; as *refluent* blood. *Arbuthnot.*

RE'FLUX, *n.* [Fr. from L. *refluxus.*] A flowing back; the returning of a fluid; as the flux and *reflux* of the tides; the flux and *reflux* of Euripus. *Brown.*

REFO'CILLATE, *v. t.* [It. *refocillare*; Sp. *refocilar*; L. *refocillo*; *re* and the root of *focus.*] To refresh; to revive; to give new vigor to. [*Little used.*] *Aubrey.*

REFOCILLA'TION, *n.* The act of refreshing or giving new vigor; restoration of strength by refreshment. [*Little used.*] *Middleton.*

REFOMENT', *v. t.* [*re* and *foment.*] To foment anew; to warm or cherish again. *Colgrave.*

2. To excite anew.

REFOMENT'ED, *pp.* Fomented or excited anew.

REFOMENT'ING, *ppr.* Fomenting anew; exciting again.

REFORM', *v. t.* [Fr. *reformer*; L. *reformo*; *re* and *formo*, to form.]

1. To change from worse to better; to amend; to correct; to restore to a former good state, or to bring from a bad to a good state; as, to *reform* a profligate man; to *reform* corrupt manners or morals.

The example alone of a vicious prince will corrupt an age, but that of a good one will not *reform* it. *Swift.*

2. To change from bad to good; to remove that which is bad or corrupt; as, to *reform* abuses; to *reform* the vices of the age.

REFORM', *v. i.* To abandon that which is evil or corrupt, and return to a good state; to be amended or corrected. A man of settled habits of vice will seldom *reform*.

RE'-FORM, *v. t.* [*re* and *form*; *with the accent on the first syllable.*] To form again; to create or shape anew.

REFORM', *n.* Reformation; amendment of what is defective, vicious, corrupt or depraved; as the *reform* of parliamentary elections; *reform* of government.

REF'ORMATION, *n.* The act of reforming; correction or amendment of life, manners, or of any thing vicious or corrupt; as the *reformation* of manners; *reformation* of the age; *reformation* of abuses.

Satire lashes vice into *reformation*. *Dryden.*

2. *By way of eminence*, the change of religion from the corruptions of popery to its primitive purity, begun by Luther, A. D. 1517.

RE-FORMA'TION, *n.* The act of forming anew; a second forming in order; as the *re-formation* of a column of troops into a hollow square. *Mitford.*

REFORM'ED, *pp.* Corrected; amended; restored to a good state; as a *reformed* profligate; the *reformed* church.

RE'-FORMED, *pp.* Formed anew.

REFORM'ER, *n.* One who effects a reformation or amendment; as a *reformer* of manners or of abuses.

2. One of those who commenced the reformation of religion from popish corruption; as Luther, Melancthon, Zuinglius and Calvin.

REFORM'ING, *ppr.* Correcting what is wrong; amending; restoring to a good state.

RE'-FORMING, *ppr.* Forming anew.

REFORM'IST, *n.* One who is of the reformed religion. *Howell.*

2. One who proposes or favors a political reform.

REFORTIFICA'TION, *n.* A fortifying a second time. *Mitford.*

REFOR'TIFY, *v. t.* [*re* and *fortify.*] To fortify anew.

REFOS'SION, *n.* The act of digging up. *Bp. Hall.*

REFOUND', *v. t.* [*re* and *found.*] To found or cast anew. *Warton.*

REFRACT', *v. t.* [L. *refractus*, *refringo*; *re* and *frango*, to break.]

To break the natural course of the rays of light; to cause to deviate from a direct course. A dense medium *refracts* the rays of light, as they pass into it from a rare medium.

REFRACTA'RIAS, *n.* A mineral.

REFRACT'ED, *pp.* Turned from a direct course, as rays of light.

2. *a.* In *botany*, bent back at an acute angle; as a *refracted* corol. *Martyn.*

REFRACT'ING, *ppr.* Turning from a direct course.

2. *a.* That turns rays from a direct course; as a *refracting* medium.

REFRAC'TION, *n.* The deviation of a moving body, chiefly rays of light, from a direct course. This is occasioned by the different densities of the mediums through which light passes.

Refraction out of a rarer medium into a denser, is made towards the perpendicular. *Newton.*

Refraction may be caused by a body's falling obliquely out of one medium into another. *Encyc.*

Refraction double, the separation of a ray of light into two separate parts, by passing through certain transparent mediums, as the Iceland crystal. All crystals, except those whose primitive form is either a cube or a regular octahedron, exhibit double refraction.

REFRACT'IVE, *a.* That refracts or has power to refract or turn from a direct course; as *refractive* densities. *Newton.*

REFRACT'ORINESS, *n.* [from *refractory.*] Perverse or sullen obstinacy in opposition or disobedience.

I never allowed any man's *refractoriness* against the privileges and orders of the house. *K. Charles.*

REFRACT'ORY, *a.* [Fr. *refractaire*; L. *refractarius*, from *refragor*, to resist; *re* and *fragor*, from *frango.*]

1. Sullen or perverse in opposition or disobedience; obstinate in non-compliance;

as a *refractory* child; a *refractory* servant.

Raging appetites that are
Most disobedient and *refractory*. *Shak.*

2. Unmanageable; obstinately unyielding; as a *refractory* beast.
3. *Applied to metals*, difficult of fusion; not easily yielding to the force of heat.

REFRACT'ORY, *n.* A person obstinate in opposition or disobedience. *Hall.*

2. Obstinate opposition. [*Not used.*] *Taylor.*

REFRA'GABLE, *a.* [L. *refragor; re* and *frango.*]
That may be refuted, that is, broken.

REFRA'IN, *v. t.* [Fr. *refrener*; It. *rinfrenare*; L. *refrœno*; *re* and *frœno*, to curb; *frœnum*, a rein. See *Rein.*]
To hold back; to restrain; to keep from action.

My son—*refrain* thy foot from their path. Prov. i.

Then Joseph could not *refrain* himself before all them that stood by. Gen. xlv.

REFRA'IN, *v. i.* To forbear; to abstain; to keep one's self from action or interference.

Refrain from these men and let them alone. Acts v.

REFRA'IN, *n.* [Fr. *refrein.*] The burden of a song; a kind of musical repetition. *Mason.*

REFRA'INED, *pp.* Held back; restrained.

REFRA'INING, *ppr.* Holding back; forbearing.

REFRA'ME, *v. t.* [*re* and *frame.*] To frame again. *Hakewill.*

REFRANGIBIL'ITY, *n.* [from *refrangible.*]
The disposition of rays of light to be refracted or turned out of a direct course, in passing out of one transparent body or medium into another. *Newton.*

REFRAN'GIBLE, *a.* [L. *re* and *frango*, to break.]
Capable of being refracted or turned out of a direct course in passing from one medium to another; as rays of light. *Locke.*

REFRENA'TION, *n.* [See *Refrain.*] The act of restraining. [*Not used.*]

REFRESH', *v. t.* [Fr. *rafraichir*; *re* and *fraichir*, from *fraiche*, fresh; It. *rinfrescare*; Sp. Port. *refrescar*. See *Fresh.*]

1. To cool; to allay heat.

A dew coming after a heat *refresheth*. *Ecclus.*

2. To give new strength to; to invigorate; to relieve after fatigue; as, to *refresh* the body. A man or a beast is *refreshed* by food and rest. Ex. xxiii.
3. To revive; to reanimate after depression; to cheer; to enliven.

For they have *refreshed* my spirit and yours. 1 Cor. xvi.

4. To improve by new touches any thing impaired.

The rest *refresh* the scaly snakes. *Dryden.*

5. To revive what is drooping; as, rain *refreshes* the plants.

REFRESH', *n.* Act of refreshing. [*Not used.*] *Daniel.*

REFRESH'ED, *pp.* Cooled; invigorated; revived; cheered.

REFRESH'ER, *n.* He or that which refreshes, revives or invigorates. *Thomson.*

REFRESH'ING, *ppr.* or *a.* Cooling; invigorating; reviving; reanimating.

REFRESH'ING, *n.* Refreshment; relief after fatigue or suffering. *Mortimer.*

REFRESH'MENT, *n.* Act of refreshing; or new strength or vigor received after fatigue; relief after suffering; *applied to the body.*

2. New life or animation after depression; *applied to the mind or spirits.*
3. That which gives fresh strength or vigor, as food or rest. *South. Sprat.*

REFRET', *n.* The burden of a song. *Dict.*

REFRIG'ERANT, *a.* [Fr. See *Refrigerate.*] Cooling; allaying heat. *Bacon.*

REFRIG'ERANT, *n.* Among *physicians*, a medicine which abates heat and refreshes the patient.

REFRIG'ERATE, *v. t.* [L. *refrigero*; *re* and *frigus*, cold.] To cool; to allay the heat of; to refresh. *Bacon.*

REFRIG'ERATED, *pp.* Cooled.

REFRIG'ERATING, *ppr.* Allaying heat; cooling.

REFRIGERA'TION, *n.* The act of cooling; the abatement of heat; state of being cooled. *Bacon.*

REFRIG'ERATIVE, *a.* Cooling.

REFRIG'ERATIVE, *n.* A remedy that allays heat.

REFRIG'ERATORY, *a.* Cooling; mitigating heat.

REFRIG'ERATORY, *n.* In *distillation*, a vessel filled with cold water, through which the worm passes; by which means the vapors are condensed as they pass through the worm.

2. Any thing internally cooling. *Mortimer.*

REFRIGE'RIUM, *n.* [L.] Cooling refreshment; refrigeration. [*Not in use.*] *South.*

REFT, *pp.* of *reave*. Deprived; bereft. [*Not in use.*] *Shak.*

2. *pret.* of *reave*. Took away. [*Not in use.*] *Spenser.*

REFT, *n.* A chink. [See *Rift.*]

REF'UGE, *n.* [Fr. from L. *refugium*, *refugio*; *re* and *fugio*, to flee.]

1. Shelter or protection from danger or distress.

—Rocks, dens and caves, but I in none of these
Find place or *refuge*. *Milton.*

We have made lies our *refuge*. Is. xxviii.

—We might have strong consolation, who have fled for *refuge* to lay hold on the hope set before us. Heb. vi.

2. That which shelters or protects from danger, distress or calamity; a strong hold which protects by its strength, or a sanctuary which secures safety by its sacredness; any place inaccessible to an enemy.

The high hills are a *refuge* for the wild goats. Ps. civ.

The Lord also will be a *refuge* for the oppressed. Ps. ix.

3. An expedient to secure protection or defense.

This last old man—
Their latest *refuge* was to send to him. *Shak.*

4. Expedient, in general.

Light must be supplied, among graceful *refuges*, by terracing any story in danger of darkness. *Wotton.*

Cities of refuge, among *the Israelites*, certain cities appointed to secure the safety of such persons as might commit homicide without design. Of these there were three on each side of Jordan. Josh. xx.

REF'UGE, *v. t.* To shelter; to protect.

REFUGEE', *n.* [Fr. *refugié.*] One who flies to a shelter or place of safety. *Dryden.*

2. One who, in times of persecution or political commotion, flees to a foreign country for safety; as the French *refugees*, who left France after the revocation of the edict of Nantz, and settled in Flanders and America; the *refugees* from Hispaniola, in 1792; and the American *refugees*, who left their country at the revolution.

REFUL'GENCE, } *n.* [L. *refulgens*, *refulgeo*; *re* and *fulgeo*,
REFUL'GENCY, }
to shine.] A flood of light; splendor.

REFUL'GENT, *a.* Casting a bright light; shining; splendid; as *refulgent* beams; *refulgent* light; *refulgent* arms.

A conspicuous and *refulgent* truth. *Boyle.*

REFUL'GENTLY, *adv.* With a flood of light; with great brightness.

REFUND', *v. t.* [L. *refundo*; *re* and *fundo*, to pour.] To pour back.

Were the humors of the eye tinctured with any color, they would *refund* that color upon the object. [*Unusual or obsolete.*] *Ray.*

2. To repay; to return in payment or compensation for what has been taken; to restore; as, to *refund* money taken wrongfully; to *refund* money advanced with interest; to *refund* the amount advanced.

REFUND'ED, *pp.* Poured back; repaid.

REFUND'ING, *ppr.* Pouring back; returning by payment or compensation.

REFU'SABLE, *a.* *s* as *z.* [from *refuse.*] That may be refused. *Young.*

REFU'SAL, *n.* *s* as *z.* The act of refusing; denial of any thing demanded, solicited or offered for acceptance. The first *refusal* is not always proof that the request will not be ultimately granted.

2. The right of taking in preference to others; the choice of taking or refusing: option; pre-emption. We say, a man has the *refusal* of a farm or a horse, or the *refusal* of an employment.

REFU'SE, *v. t.* *s* as *z.* [Fr. *refuser*; Arm. *reusi*, *reusein*; It. *rifiutare*, *rifusare*; Sp. *rehusar*; Port. *refusar*; L. *recuso*; *re* and the root of *causor*, to accuse; *causa*, cause. The primary sense of *causor* is to drive, to throw or thrust at, and *recuso* is to drive back, to repel or repulse, the sense of *refuse.*]

1. To deny a request, demand, invitation or command; to decline to do or grant what is solicited, claimed or commanded.

Thus Edom *refused* to give Israel passage through his border. Num. xx.

2. To decline to accept what is offered; as, to *refuse* an office; to *refuse* an offer.

If they *refuse* to take the cup at thy hand— Jer. xxv.

3. To reject; as, to *refuse* instruction or reproof. Prov. x.

The stone which the builders *refused* is become the head of the corner. Ps. cxviii.

[NOTE.—*Refuse* expresses rejection more strongly than *decline.*]

REFU'SE, *v. i.* *s* as *z.* To decline to accept; not to comply.

Too proud to ask, to humble too *refuse*. *Garth.*

REF'USE, *a.* [Fr. *refus*, refusal, denial, and that which is denied.]
Literally, refused; rejected; hence, worthless; of no value; left as unworthy of re-

ception; as the *refuse* parts of stone or timber.

Please to bestow on him the *refuse* letters. *Spectator.*

REF'USE, *n.* That which is refused or rejected as useless; waste matter. *Hooker. Bacon. Addison.*

REFU'SE, *n.* Refusal. *Obs.* *Fairfax.*

REFU'SED, *pp.* Denied; rejected; not accepted.

REFU'SER, *n.* One that refuses or rejects. *Taylor.*

REFU'SING, *ppr.* Denying; declining to accept; rejecting.

REFU'TABLE, *a.* [from *refute.*] That may be refuted or disproved; that may be proved false or erroneous.

REFU'TAL, *n.* Refutation. [*Not used.*]

REFUTA'TION, *n.* [L. *refutatio.* See *Refute.*]

The act or process of refuting or disproving; the act of proving to be false or erroneous; the overthrowing of an argument, opinion, testimony, doctrine or theory, by argument or countervailing proof. *Bentley.*

REFU'TE, *v. t.* [Fr. *refuter;* L. *refuto; re* and *futo*, obs. The primary sense of *futo*, is to drive or thrust, to beat back. Class Bd.]

To disprove and overthrow by argument, evidence or countervailing proof; to prove to be false or erroneous; to confute. We say, to *refute* arguments, to *refute* testimony, to *refute* opinions or theories, to *refute* a disputant.

There were so many witnesses to these two miracles, that it is impossible to *refute* such multitudes. *Addison.*

REFU'TED, *pp.* Disproved; proved to be false or erroneous.

REFU'TER, *n.* One that refutes.

REFU'TING, *ppr.* Proving to be false or erroneous; confuting.

REGA'IN, *v. t.* [*re* and *gain;* Fr. *regagner.*]

To gain anew; to recover what has escaped or been lost. *Milton.*

REGA'INED, *pp.* Recovered; gained anew.

REGA'INING, *ppr.* Gaining anew; recovering.

RE'GAL, *a.* [Fr. from L. *regalis*, from *rex*, Sans. *raja*, connected with *rego*, to govern; Sax. *recan* or *reccan*, to say, to *reck*, to *reckon*, to rule, to *direct;* the root of *right*, L. *rectus*, Sax. *reht.* See *Reck* and *Reckon.*]

Pertaining to a king; kingly; royal; as a *regal* title; *regal* authority; *regal* state, pomp or splendor; *regal* power or sway. But we say, a *royal* or *kingly* government, not a *regal* one. We never say, a *regal* territory, *regal* dominions, *regal* army, or *regal* navy. *Regal* expresses what is more personal.

RE'GAL, *n.* [Fr. *régale.*] A musical instrument. *Bacon.*

REGA'LE, *n.* [Fr. *régale.*] The prerogative of monarchy. *Johnson.*

REGA'LE, *n.* [See the verb, below.] A magnificent entertainment or treat given to embassadors and other persons of distinction. *Encyc.*

REGA'LE, *v. t.* [Fr. *regaler;* Sp. *regalar*, to regale, to refresh, entertain, caress, cajole, delight, cherish; *regalarse*, to entertain one's self, to take pleasure, also to melt, to be dissolved; Port. *regalar*, to regale, to treat daintily, to delight; It. *regalare*, to present with gifts, to regale, to season. This word is probably a compound of *re* and the root of It. *galloria*, a transport of joy, *gallare*, to exult, *gala*, ornament, Port. *galhofa*, mirth, good cheer, Sp. *gallardo*, gay, Fr. *gaillard*, &c. In Russ. *jaluyu* signifies to regale, to gratify with presents, to visit, &c. The primary sense is to excite, to rouse and be brisk, or to shoot, leap, dart or rush. We probably see the same root in the Eng. *gale, gallant*, Gr. αγαλλιαω, Fr. *joli*, Eng. *jolly*, and in many other words.]

To refresh; to entertain with something that delights; to gratify, as the senses; as, to *regale* the taste, the eye or the ear. The birds of the forest *regale* us with their songs.

REGA'LE, *v. t.* To feast; to fare sumptuously.

REGA'LED, *pp.* Refreshed; entertained; gratified.

REGA'LEMENT, *n.* Refreshment; entertainment; gratification.

REGA'LIA, *n.* [L. from *rex*, king.] Ensigns of royalty; the apparatus of a coronation; as the crown, scepter, &c.

2. In *law*, the rights and prerogatives of a king. *Blackstone.*

REGA'LING, *ppr.* Refreshing; entertaining; gratifying.

REGAL'ITY, *n.* [from L. *regalis;* It. *realtà;* Fr. *royauté.*] Royalty; sovereignty; kingship.

He came partly in by the sword and had high courage in all points of *regality.* *Bacon.*

RE'GALLY, *adv.* In a royal manner. *Milton.*

REG'ARD, *v. t.* [Fr. *regarder;* It. *riguardare;* from Fr. *garder*, to guard, keep, defend; It. *guardare*, to guard, to look, view, behold, to beware, to take heed, to discern. The primary sense of *guard* is to drive off or repel, and thus to protect, or to hold, keep, retain; probably the former. To *regard* is to extend or direct the eye to an object, or to hold it in view. We observe a somewhat similar process of deriving the sense of *looking*, in the It. *scorto*, seen, perceived, prudent, guided, convoyed, wary, crafty, discerning, and as a noun, an abridgment; *scorta*, a guide, an *escort*, a guard.]

1. To look towards; to point or be directed.

It is a peninsula which *regardeth* the main land. *Sandys.*

2. To observe; to notice with some particularity.

If much you note him,
You offend him; feed and *regard* him not. *Shak.*

3. To attend to with respect and estimation; to value.

This aspect of mine,
The best *regarded* virgins of your clime
Have lov'd. *Shak.*

4. To attend to as a thing that affects our interest or happiness; to fix the mind on as a matter of importance. He does not *regard* the pain he feels. He does not *regard* the loss he has suffered. He *regards* only the interest of the community.

5. To esteem; to hold in respect and affection. The people *regard* their pastor, and treat him with great kindness. 2 Kings iii.

6. To keep; to observe with religious or solemn attention.

He that *regardeth* the day, *regardeth* it to the Lord. Rom. xiv.

7. To attend to as something to influence our conduct.

He that *regardeth* the clouds shall not reap. Eccles. xi.

8. To consider seriously; to lay to heart.

They *regard* not the work of the Lord. Is. v.

9. To notice with pity or concern. Deut. xxviii.

10. To notice favorably or with acceptance; to hear and answer.

He will *regard* the prayer of the destitute. Ps. cii.

11. To love and esteem; to practice; as, to *regard* iniquity in the heart. Ps. lxvi.

12. To respect; to have relation to. The argument does not *regard* the question.

To regard the person, to value for outward honor, wealth or power. Matt. xxii.

REG'ARD, *n.* [Fr. *regard;* It. *riguardo.*]

1. Look; aspect directed to another.

But her with stern *regard* he thus repell'd.
[*Nearly or quite obsolete.*] *Milton.*

2. Attention of the mind; respect in relation to something. He has no *regard* to the interest of society; his motives are wholly selfish.

3. Respect; esteem; reverence; that view of the mind which springs from value, estimable qualities, or any thing that excites admiration.

With some *regard* to what is just and right
They'll lead their lives. *Milton.*

To him they had *regard*, because of long time he had bewitched them with sorceries. Acts viii.

4. Respect; account.

Change was thought necessary, in *regard* of the injury the church received by a number of things then in use. *Hooker.*

5. Relation; reference.

To persuade them to pursue and persevere in virtue, in *regard* to themselves; in justice and goodness, in *regard* to their neighbors; and piety towards God. *Watts.*

6. Note; eminence; account.

Mac Ferlagh was a man of meanest *regard* among them. *Spenser.*

7. Matter demanding notice. *Spenser.*

8. Prospect; object of sight. [*Not proper nor in use.*] *Shak.*

9. In *the forest laws*, view; inspection.

Court of regard, or *survey of dogs*, a forest court in England, held every third year for the lawing or expeditation of mastiffs, that is, for cutting off the claws and ball of the fore feet, to prevent them from running after deer. *Blackstone.*

REG'ARDABLE, *a.* Observable; worthy of notice. *Brown. Carew.*

REG'ARDANT, *a.* In *law*, a villain regardant is one annexed to the manor or land. *Blackstone.*

2. In *heraldry*, looking behind, as a lion or other beast. *Encyc.*

REG'ARDED, *pp.* Noticed; observed; esteemed; respected.

REG'ARDER, *n.* One that regards.

2. In *law*, the regarder of the forest is an officer whose business is to view the forest, inspect the officers, and inquire of all offenses and defaults. *Eng.*

REG'ARDFUL, *a.* Taking notice; heedful; observing with care; attentive.

Let a man be very tender and *regardful* of every pious motion made by the Spirit of God on his heart. *South.*

REG'ARDFULLY, *adv.* Attentively; heedfully.

2. Respectfully. *Shak.*

REG'ARDING, *ppr.* Noticing; considering with care; attending to; observing; esteeming; caring for.

2. Respecting; concerning; relating to.

REG'ARDLESS, *a.* Not looking or attending to; heedless; negligent; careless; as *regardless* of life or of health; *regardless* of danger; *regardless* of consequences.

Regardless of the bliss wherein he sat. *Milton.*

2. Not regarded; slighted. *Spectator.*

REG'ARDLESSLY, *adv.* Heedlessly; carelessly; negligently.

REG'ARDLESSNESS, *n.* Heedlessness; inattention; negligence. *Whitlock.*

REGA'TA, REGAT'TA, *n.* [It. *regatta.*] In Venice, a grand rowing match in which many boats are rowed for a prize.

REGATH'ER, *v. t.* To gather or collect a second time. *B. Trumbull.*

REGATH'ERED, *pp.* Collected again.

REGATH'ERING, *ppr.* Gathering a second time.

REG'EL, REG'IL, *n.* A fixed star of the first magnitude in Orion's left foot.

RE'GENCY, *n.* [L. *regens*, from *rego*, to govern.]

1. Rule; authority; government. *Hooker.*
2. Vicarious government. *Temple.*
3. The district under the jurisdiction of a vicegerent. *Milton.*
4. The body of men entrusted with vicarious government; as a *regency* constituted during a king's minority, insanity, or absence from the kingdom.

REGEN'ERACY, *n.* [See *Regenerate.*] The state of being regenerated. *Hammond.*

REGEN'ERATE, *v. t.* [L. *regenero; re* and *genero*. See *Generate.*]

1. To generate or produce anew; to reproduce.

Through all the soil a genial ferment spreads,
Regenerates the plants and new adorns the meads. *Blackmore.*

2. In *theology*, to renew the heart by a change of affections; to change the heart and affections from natural holy enmity to the love of God; to implant holy affections in the heart. *Scott. Addison.*

REGEN'ERATE, *a.* [L. *regeneratus.*] Reproduced. *Shak.*

2. Born anew; renovated in heart; changed from a natural to a spiritual state. *Milton. Wake.*

REGEN'ERATED, *pp.* Reproduced.

2. Renewed; born again.

REGEN'ERATENESS, *n.* The state of being regenerated.

REGEN'ERATING, *ppr.* Reproducing.

2. Renovating the nature by the implantation of holy affections in the heart.

REGENERA'TION, *n.* Reproduction; the act of producing anew.

2. In *theology*, new birth by the grace of God; that change by which the will and natural enmity of man to God and his law are subdued, and a principle of supreme love to God and his law, or holy affections, are implanted in the heart.

He saved us by the washing of *regeneration* and renewing of the Holy Spirit. Tit. iii.

REGEN'ERATORY, *a.* Renewing; having the power to renew; tending to reproduce or renovate. *Faber.*

RE'GENT, *a.* [L. *regens*, from *rego*, to rule.]

1. Ruling; governing; as a *regent* principle. *Hale.*
2. Exercising vicarious authority. *Milton.*

Queen regent, a queen who governs; opposed to *queen consort.*

RE'GENT, *n.* A governor; a ruler; *in a general sense;* as Uriel, *regent* of the sun. *Milton.*

2. One invested with vicarious authority; one who governs a kingdom in the minority, absence or disability of the king. *Encyc.*
3. In *colleges*, a teacher of arts and sciences, having pupils under his care, generally of the lower classes; those who instruct the higher classes being called *professors.* *Encyc.*
4. In *English universities*, a master of arts under five years standing, and a doctor under two. *Encyc.*
5. In *the state of New York*, the member of a corporate body which is invested with the superintendence of all the colleges, academies and schools in the state. This board consists of twenty one members, who are called "the regents of the university of the state of New York." They are appointed and removable by the legislature. They have power to grant acts of incorporation for colleges, to visit and inspect all colleges, academies and schools, and to make regulations for governing the same. *Stat. N. York.*

RE'GENTESS, *n.* A protectress of a kingdom. *Cotgrave.*

RE'GENTSHIP, *n.* The power of governing, or the office of a regent.

2. Deputed authority. *Shak.*

REGERM'INATE, *v. i.* [*re* and *germinate.*] To germinate again.

Perennial plants *regerminate* several years successively. *Lee.*

REGERM'INATING, *ppr.* Germinating anew.

REGERMINA'TION, *n.* A sprouting or germination anew.

REGEST', *n.* A register. [*Not in use.*] *Milton.*

REG'IBLE, *a.* Governable. [*Not in use.*] *Dict.*

REG'ICIDE, *n.* [It. Sp. *regicida;* Fr. *regicide;* L. *rex*, king, and *cædo*, to slay.]

1. A king-killer; one who murders a king. *Dryden.*
2. The killing or murder of a king. *Pope.*

REG'IMEN, *n.* [L. from *rego*, to govern.]

1. In *medicine*, the regulation of diet with a view to the preservation or restoration of health; or in a more general sense, the regulation of all the non-naturals for the same purposes. *Encyc.*
2. Any regulation or remedy which is intended to produce beneficial effects by gradual operation. *Hume.*
3. In *grammar*, government; that part of syntax or construction, which regulates the dependency of words, and the alterations which one occasions or requires in another in connection with it; the words governed.
4. Orderly government; system of order.

REG'IMENT, *n.* [L. *regimen.*] In *military affairs*, a body of men, either horse, foot or artillery, commanded by a colonel or lieutenant colonel and major, and consisting of a number of companies, usually from eight to ten.

2. Government; mode of ruling; rule; authority; as used by Hooker, Hale and others. [*Wholly obsolete.*]

REG'IMENT, *v. t.* To form into a regiment or into regiments with proper officers. [*A military use of the word.*] *Washington. Smollet.*

REGIMENT'AL, *a.* Belonging to a regiment; as *regimental* officers; *regimental* clothing.

REGIMENT'ALS, *n. plu.* The uniform worn by the troops of a regiment.

REG'IMENTED, *pp.* Formed into a regiment; incorporated with a regiment. *Washington.*

REGION, *n. re'jun.* [Fr. Sp. *region;* It. *regione;* L. *regio;* Ir. *crioch*, with a prefix; from the root of *reach, reck*, L. *rego.*]

1. A tract of land or space of indefinite extent, usually a tract of considerable extent. It is sometimes nearly synonymous with *country;* as all the *region* of Argob. Deut. iii.

He had dominion over all the *region* on this side the river. 1 Kings iv.

So we speak of the airy *region*, the etherial *regions*, the upper *regions*, the lower *regions.*

2. The inhabitants of a region or district of country. Matt. iii.
3. A part of the body; as the *region* of the heart or liver.
4. Place; rank.

He is of too high a *region*. [*Unusual.*] *Shak.*

REG'ISTER, *n.* [Fr. *registre, regitre;* Low L. *registrum*, from *regero*, to set down in writing; *re* and *gero*, to carry. But Spelman considers the word as formed of *re* and Norm. *gister* or *giser*, to lay, and equivalent to *repository.*]

1. A written account or entry of acts, judgments or proceedings, for preserving and conveying to future times an exact knowledge of transactions. The word appropriately denotes an official account of the proceedings of a public body, a prince, a legislature, a court, an incorporated company and the like, and in this use it is synonymous with *record.* But in a lax sense, it signifies any account entered on paper to preserve the remembrance of what is done.
2. The book in which a register or record is kept, as a parish *register;* also, a list, as the *register* of seamen.
3. [Low L. *registrarius.*] The officer or person whose business is to write or enter in a book accounts of transactions, particularly of the acts and proceedings of courts or other public bodies; as the *register* of a court of probate; a *register* of deeds.
4. In *chimistry* and *the arts*, an aperture with a lid, stopper or sliding plate, in a furnace.

stove, &c. for regulating the admission of air and the heat of the fire.

5. The inner part of the mold in which types are cast.

6. In *printing*, the correspondence of columns on the opposite sides of the sheet.

7. A sliding piece of wood, used as a stop in an organ.

Parish register, a book in which are recorded the baptisms of children and the marriages and burials of the parish.

Register ship, a ship which obtains permission to trade to the Spanish West Indies and is registered before sailing. *Encyc.*

REG'ISTER, *v. t.* To record; to write in a book for preserving an exact account of facts and proceedings. The Greeks and Romans *registered* the names of all children born.

2. To enroll; to enter in a list. *Milton.*

REG'ISTERSHIP, *n.* The office of register.

REG'ISTRAR, *n.* An officer in the English universities, who has the keeping of all the public records. *Encyc.*

REGISTRA'TION, *n.* The act of inserting in a register. *Walsh.*

REG'ISTRY, *n.* The act of recording or writing in a register.

2. The place where a register is kept.

3. A series of facts recorded. *Temple.*

REG'LEMENT, *n.* [Fr.] Regulation. [*Not used.*] *Bacon.*

REG'LET, *n.* [Fr. from *règle*, rule, L. *regula, rego.*]

A ledge of wood exactly planed, used by printers to separate lines and make the work more open.

REG'NANT, *a.* [Fr. from *regner*, L. *regno*, to reign.]

1. Reigning; exercising regal authority; as a queen *regnant*. The modern phrase is queen *regent*. *Wotton.*

2. Ruling; predominant; prevalent; having the chief power; as vices *regnant*. We now say, *reigning* vices. *Swift.*

REGORGE, *v. t.* *regorj'.* [Fr. *regorger*; *re* and *gorge.*]

1. To vomit up; to eject from the stomach; to throw back or out again. *Hayward.*

2. To swallow again. *Dryden.*

3. To swallow eagerly. *Milton.*

REGRA'DE, *v. i.* [L. *regredior*; *re* and *gradior*, to go.] To retire; to go back. [*Not used.*] *Hales.*

REGR'AFT, *v. t.* [*re* and *graft.*] To graft again. *Bacon.*

REGR'AFTED, *pp.* Grafted again.

REGR'AFTING, *ppr.* Grafting anew.

REGR'ANT, *v. t.* [*re* and *grant.*] To grant back. *Ayliffe.*

REGR'ANT, *n.* The act of granting back to a former proprietor.

REGR'ANTED, *pp.* Granted back.

REGR'ANTING, *ppr.* Granting back.

REGRA'TE, *v. t.* [Fr. *regratter*, to scratch again, to new-vamp, to *regrate*, or drive a huckster's trade; *re* and *gratter*, to *grate*, to scratch, to rake.]

1. To offend; to shock. [*Little used.*]

2. To buy provisions and sell them again in the same market or fair; a practice which, by raising the price, is a public offense and punishable. *Regrating* differs from *engrossing* and *monopolizing*, which signify the buying the whole of certain articles, or large quantities, and from *forestalling*, which signifies the purchase of provisions on the way, before they reach the market. *Blackstone.*

REGRA'TER, *n.* One who buys provisions and sells them in the same market or fair.

REGRA'TING, *ppr.* Purchasing provisions and selling them in the same market.

REGREE'T, *v. t.* [*re* and *greet.*] To greet again; to resalute. *Shak.*

REGREE'T, *n.* A return or exchange of salutation. *Shak.*

REGREE'TED, *pp.* Greeted again or in return.

REGREE'TING, *ppr.* Greeting again; resaluting.

RE'GRESS, *n.* [Fr. *regrès*; L. *regressus*, *regredior.*]

1. Passage back; return; as ingress and *regress*.

2. The power of returning or passing back.

REGRESS', *v. i.* To go back; to return to a former place or state. *Brown.*

REGRES'SION, *n.* The act of passing back or returning. *Brown.*

REGRESS'IVE, *a.* Passing back; returning.

REGRESS'IVELY, *adv.* In a backward way or manner; by return. *Johnson.*

REGRET', *n.* [Fr. *regret*; either from the root of *grate*, or more directly from the root of Sp. Port. *gritar*, It. *gridare*, Sw. *gråta*, Ice. *groet*, Dan. *græder*, Goth. *grietan*, W. *grydiaw*, to scream or cry out, to utter a rough sound; in some dialects, to weep or lament. But *grate* and Sp. *gritar* are probably of the same family.]

1. Grief; sorrow; pain of mind. We feel *regret* at the loss of friends, *regret* for our own misfortunes, or for the misfortunes of others.

> Never any prince expressed a more lively *regret* for the loss of a servant. *Clarendon.*
>
> Her piety itself would blame,
> If her *regrets* should waken thine. *Prior.*

2. Pain of conscience; remorse; as a passionate *regret* at sin. *Decay of Piety.*

3. Dislike; aversion. [*Not proper nor in use.*] *Decay of Piety.*

REGRET', *v. t.* [Fr. *regretter.*] To grieve at; to lament; to be sorry for; to repent.

> Calmly he look'd on either life, and here
> Saw nothing to *regret*, or there to fear. *Pope.*

2. To be uneasy at. [*Not proper nor in use.*] *Glanville.*

REGRET'FUL, *a.* Full of regret. *Fanshaw.*

REGRET'FULLY, *adv.* With regret. *Greenhill.*

REGRET'TED, *pp.* Lamented.

REGRET'TING, *ppr.* Lamenting; grieving at; repenting.

REGUERDON, *n.* *regerd'on.* [*re* and Fr. *guerdon*, a reward. See *Reward.*]

A reward; a recompense. [*Not in use.*] *Shak.*

REGUERDON, *v. t.* *regerd'on.* To reward. [*Not in use.*] *Shak.*

REG'ULAR, *a.* [Sp. id.; Fr. *regulier*; L. *regularis*, from *regula*, a rule, from *rego*, to rule.]

1. Conformed to a rule; agreeable to an established rule, law or principle, to a prescribed mode or to established customary forms; as a *regular* epic poem; a *regular* verse in poetry; a *regular* piece of music; *regular* practice of law or medicine; a *regular* plan; a *regular* building.

2. Governed by rule or rules; steady or uniform in a course or practice; as *regular* in diet; *regular* in attending on divine worship.

3. In *geometry*, a regular figure is one whose sides and angles are equal, as a square, a cube, or an equilateral triangle. Regular figures of more than three or four sides are usually called regular polygons. *Encyc.*

4. Instituted or initiated according to established forms or discipline; as a *regular* physician.

5. Methodical; orderly; as a *regular* kind of sensuality or indulgence. *Law.*

6. Periodical; as the *regular* return of day and night; a *regular* trade wind or monsoon.

7. Pursued with uniformity or steadiness; as a *regular* trade.

8. Belonging to a monastic order; as *regular* clergy, in distinction from the *secular* clergy.

Regular troops, troops of a permanent army; opposed to *militia*.

REG'ULAR, *n.* In *a monastery*, one who has taken the vows, and who is bound to follow the rules of the order. *Encyc.*

2. A soldier belonging to a permanent army.

REGULAR'ITY, *n.* Agreeableness to a rule or to established order; as the *regularity* of legal proceedings.

2. Method; certain order. *Regularity* is the life of business.

3. Conformity to certain principles; as the *regularity* of a figure.

4. Steadiness or uniformity in a course; as the *regularity* of the motion of a heavenly body. There is no *regularity* in the vicissitudes of the weather.

REG'ULARLY, *adv.* In a manner accordant to a rule or established mode; as a physician or lawyer *regularly* admitted to practice; a verse *regularly* formed.

2. In uniform order; at certain intervals or periods; as day and night *regularly* returning.

3. Methodically; in due order; as affairs *regularly* performed.

REG'ULATE, *v. t.* To adjust by rule, method or established mode; as, to *regulate* weights and measures; to *regulate* the assize of bread; to *regulate* our moral conduct by the laws of God and of society; to *regulate* our manners by the customary forms.

2. To put in good order; as, to *regulate* the disordered state of a nation or its finances.

3. To subject to rules or restrictions; as, to *regulate* trade; to *regulate* diet.

REG'ULATED, *pp.* Adjusted by rule, method or forms; put in good order; subjected to rules or restrictions.

REG'ULATING, *ppr.* Adjusting by rule, method or forms; reducing to order; subjecting to rules or restrictions.

REGULA'TION, *n.* The act of regulating or reducing to order. *Ray.*

2. A rule or order prescribed by a superior for the management of some business, or for the government of a company or society.

REG'ULATOR, *n.* One who regulates.
2. The small spring of a watch, which regulates its motions by retarding or accelerating them.
3. Any part of a machine which regulates its movements.

REG'ULINE, *a.* [See *Regulus.*] Pertaining to regulus or pure metal.
Bodies which we can reduce to the metallic or *reguline* state. *Lavoisier.*

REG'ULIZE, *v. t.* To reduce to regulus or pure metal; to separate pure metal from extraneous matter.

REG'ULUS, *n.* [L. a petty king; Fr. *regule.* For the plural, some authors write *reguli,* and others *reguluses.*]
In *chimistry,* the finer or pure part of a metallic substance, which, in the melting of ores, falls to the bottom of the crucible. *Encyc. Lavoisier.*

REGURG'ITATE, *v. t.* [Fr. *regorger;* L. *re* and *gurges.*]
To throw or pour back, as from a deep or hollow place; to pour or throw back in great quantity. *Graunt. Bentley.*

REGURG'ITATE, *v. i.* To be thrown or poured back. *Harvey.*

REGURG'ITATED, *pp.* Thrown or poured back.

REGURG'ITATING, *ppr.* Throwing or pouring back.

REGURGITA'TION, *n.* The act of pouring back.
2. The act of swallowing again; reabsorption. *Sharp.*

REHABIL'ITATE, *v. t.* [Fr. *rehabiliter; re* and *habiliter.*]
To restore to a former capacity; to reinstate; to qualify again; to restore, as a delinquent to a former right, rank or privilege lost or forfeited; *a term of the civil and canon law.* *Chambers.*

REHABIL'ITATED, *pp.* Restored to a former rank, right, privilege or capacity; reinstated.

REHABIL'ITATING, *ppr.* Restoring to a former right, rank, privilege or capacity; reinstating.

REHABILITA'TION, *n.* The act of reinstating in a former rank or capacity; restoration to former rights. *Walsh.*

REHE'AR, *v. t.* pret. and pp. *reheard.* [*re* and *hear.*]
To hear again; to try a second time; as, to *rehear* a cause in the court of king's bench.

REHE'ARD, *pp.* Heard again.

REHE'ARING, *ppr.* Hearing a second time.

REHE'ARING, *n.* A second hearing. *Addison.*
2. In *law,* a second hearing or trial.

REHEARSAL, *n.* *rehers'al.* [from *rehearse.*]
1. Recital; repetition of the words of another or of a written work; as the *rehearsal* of the Lord's prayer. *Hooker.*
2. Narration; a telling or recounting, as of particulars in detail; as the *rehearsal* of a soldier's adventures.
3. The recital of a piece before the public exhibition of it; as the *rehearsal* of a comedy. *Dryden.*

REHEARSE, *v. t.* *rehers'.* To recite; to repeat the words of a passage or composition; to repeat the words of another.
When the words were heard which David spoke, they *rehearsed* them before Saul. 1 Sam. xvii.
2. To narrate or recount events or transactions.
There shall they *rehearse* the righteous acts of the Lord. Judg. v. Acts xi.
3. To recite or repeat in private for experiment and improvement, before a public representation; as, to *rehearse* a tragedy.

REHEARSED, *pp.* *rehers'ed.* Recited; repeated; as words; narrated.

REHEARSER, *n.* *rehers'er.* One who recites or narrates.

REHEARSING, *ppr.* *rehers'ing.* Reciting; repeating words; recounting; telling; narrating.

RE'IGLE, *n.* [Fr. *règle,* rule.] A hollow cut or channel for guiding any thing; as the *reigle* of a side post for a flood gate. *Carew.*

REIGN, *v. i.* *rane.* [L. *regno,* a derivative of *rego, regnum;* Fr. *regner;* It. *regnare;* Sp. *reynar.*]
1. To possess or exercise sovereign power or authority; to rule; to exercise government, as a king or emperor; or to hold the supreme power. George the third *reigned* over Great Britain more than fifty years.
Behold, a king shall *reign* in righteousness. Is. xxxii.
2. To be predominant; to prevail.
Pestilent diseases which commonly *reign* in summer or autumn. *Bacon.*
3. To rule; to have superior or uncontrolled dominion. Rom. vi.
[This word is never applied to the exercise of supreme power by a legislative body or the executive administration, in the U. States.]

REIGN, *n.* *rane.* [Fr. *regne;* L. *regnum.*]
1. Royal authority; supreme power; sovereignty.
He who like a father held his *reign.* *Pope.*
2. The time during which a king, queen or emperor possesses the supreme authority. The Spanish armada was equipped to invade England in the *reign* of queen Elizabeth. Magna Charta was obtained in the *reign* of king John.
3. Kingdom; dominion.
Saturn's sons received the threefold *reign*
Of heav'n, of ocean, and deep hell beneath. *Prior.*
4. Power; influence. *Chapman.*
5. Prevalence.

REIGNING, *ppr.* *ra'ning.* Holding or exercising supreme power; ruling; governing as king, queen or emperor.
2. *a.* Predominating; prevailing; as a *reigning* vice or disease.

REIMBARK. [See *Re-embark.*]

REIMBOD'Y, *v. i.* [*re* and *imbody* or *embody.*]
To imbody again; to be formed into a body anew. *Boyle.*

REIMBURS'ABLE, *a.* That may be repaid.
A loan has been made of two millions of dollars, *reimbursable* in ten years. *Hamilton.*

REIMBURSE, *v. t.* *reimburs'.* [Fr. *rembourser; re* and *embourser; en,* in, and *bourse,* a purse; It. *rimborsare;* Sp. *re-embolsar.*]
To refund; to replace in a treasury or in a private coffer, an equivalent to the sum taken from it, lost or expended; as, to *reimburse* the expenses of a war or a canal. The word is used before the person expending, or the treasury from which the advances are made, or before the expenses. We say, to *reimburse* the individual, to *reimburse* the treasury, or to *reimburse* the expenses. To *reimburse* the person, is to repay to him his losses, expenses or advances; to *reimburse* the treasury, is to refund to it the sum drawn from it; to *reimburse* losses or expenses, is to repay them or make them good.

REIMBURS'ED, *pp.* Repaid; refunded; made good, as loss or expense.

REIMBURSEMENT, *n.* *reimburs'ment.* The act of repaying or refunding; repayment; as the *reimbursement* of principal and interest. *Hamilton.*

REIMBURS'ER, *n.* One who repays or refunds what has been lost or expended.

REIMBURS'ING, *ppr.* Repaying; refunding; making good, as loss or expense.

REIMPLANT', *v. t.* [*re* and *implant.*] To implant again. *Taylor.*

REIMPLANT'ED, *pp.* Implanted anew.

REIMPLANT'ING, *ppr.* Implanting again.

REIMPORTU'NE, *v. t.* [*re* and *importune.*] To importune again.

REIMPORTU'NED, *pp.* Importuned again.

REIMPORTU'NING, *ppr.* Importuning again.

REIMPREG'NATE, *v. t.* [*re* and *impregnate.*]
To impregnate again. *Brown.*

REIMPREG'NATED, *pp.* Impregnated again.

REIMPREG'NATING, *ppr.* Impregnating again.

REIMPRESS', *v. t.* [*re* and *impress.*] To impress anew. *Buckminster.*

REIMPRESS'ED, *pp.* Impressed again.

REIMPRESS'ING, *ppr.* Impressing again.

REIMPRES'SION, *n.* A second or repeated impression.

REIMPRINT', *v. t.* [*re* and *imprint.*] To imprint again.

REIMPRINT'ED, *pp.* Imprinted again.

REIMPRINT'ING, *ppr.* Imprinting anew.

REIN, *n.* [Fr. *rêne,* from *resne.* The It. *redine* is evidently from the L. *retina, retinaculum,* Sp. *rienda.* If contracted from the Latin, it is from *retineo,* otherwise from the root of *arrest.*]
1. The strap of a bridle, fastened to the curb or snaffle on each side, by which the rider of a horse restrains and governs him.
2. The instrument of curbing, restraining or governing; government. *Shak.*
To give the reins, to give license; to leave without restraint. *Pope.*
To take the reins, to take the guidance or government.

REIN, *v. t.* To govern by a bridle. *Milton.*
2. To restrain; to control. *Shak.*

REINDEER, *n.* [Sax. *hrana.* See *Rane.*]
A species of the cervine genus; more correctly written *ranedeer,* or rather *rane,* which is the true name.

REINFECT', *v. t.* [*re* and *infect.*] To infect again.

REINFECT'ED, *pp.* Infected again.

REINFECT'ING, *ppr.* Infecting again.

REINFEC'TIOUS, *a.* Capable of infecting again. *Vaughan. Med. Repos.*

REINFORCE, *v. t.* [*re* and *enforce.*] To give new force to; to strengthen by new assistance or support. [It is written also *re-enforce*; but *reinforce* seems now to be the most common.]

REINFORCED, *pp.* Strengthened by additional force.

REINFORCEMENT, *n.* New force added; fresh supplies of strength; particularly, additional troops or ships.

REINFORCING, *ppr.* Adding fresh force to.

REINGRA'TIATE, *v. t.* To ingratiate again. *Mitford.*

REINGRA'TIATE, *v. t.* [*re* and *ingratiate.*] To ingratiate again; to recommend again to favor. *Herbert.*

REINGRA'TIATED, *pp.* Reinstated in favor.

REINGRA'TIATING, *ppr.* Ingratiating again.

REINHAB'IT, *v. t.* [*re* and *inhabit.*] To inhabit again. *Mede.*

REINHAB'ITED, *pp.* Inhabited again.

REINHAB'ITING, *ppr.* Inhabiting a second time.

REINLESS, *a.* Without rein; without restraint; unchecked.

REINLIST', *v. t.* or *i.* [*re* and *inlist.*] To inlist again. *Marshall.*

[It is written also *re-enlist.*]

REINLIST'ED, *pp.* Inlisted anew.

REINLIST'ING, *ppr.* Inlisting anew.

REINLIST'MENT, *n.* The act of inlisting anew; the act of engaging again in military service.

REINQUI'RE, *v. t.* To inquire a second time. *Brown.*

REINS, *n. plu.* [Fr. *rein, rognon*; L. *ren, renes*; It. *rene, arnione*; Sp. *riñones.*]

1. The kidneys; the lower part of the back.

2. In *Scripture*, the inward parts; the heart, or seat of the affections and passions. Ps. lxxiii.

REINSERT', *v. t.* [*re* and *insert.*] To insert a second time.

REINSERT'ED, *pp.* Inserted again.

REINSERT'ING, *ppr.* Inserting again.

REINSER'TION, *n.* A second insertion.

REINSPECT', *v. t.* [*re* and *inspect.*] To inspect again, as provisions.

REINSPEC'TION, *n.* The act of inspecting a second time. *Laws of Conn.*

REINSPI'RE, *v. t.* [*re* and *inspire.*] To inspire anew. *Milton.*

REINSPI'RED, *pp.* Inspired again. *Dryden.*

REINSPI'RING, *ppr.* Inspiring again.

REINSTALL', *v. t.* [*re* and *install.*] To install again; to seat anew. *Milton.*

REINSTALL'ED, *pp.* Installed anew.

REINSTALL'ING, *ppr.* Installing again.

REINSTALL'MENT, *n.* A second installment.

REINSTA'TE, *v. t.* [*re* and *instate.*] To place again in possession or in a former state; to restore to a state from which one had been removed; as, to *reinstate* a king in the possession of the kingdom; to *reinstate* one in the affections of his family.

REINSTA'TED, *pp.* Replaced in possession or in a former state.

REINSTA'TEMENT, *n.* The act of putting in a former state; re-establishment. *Marshall.*

REINSTA'TING, *ppr.* Replacing in a former state; putting again in possession.

REINSU'RANCE, *n.* [*re* and *insurance.* See *Sure.*]

An insurance of property already insured; a second insurance of the same property. Such *reinsurance* is permitted by the French commercial code; but in England is prohibited by statute, except when the first underwriter is insolvent. *Walsh.*

REINSU'RE, *v. t.* [*re* and *insure.*] To insure the same property a second time by other underwriters.

The insurer may cause the property insured to be *reinsured* by other persons. *Walsh. French Com. Code.*

REINSU'RED, *pp.* Insured a second time by other persons.

REINSU'RING, *ppr.* Insuring a second time by other persons.

REIN'TEGRATE, *v. t.* [Fr. *reintegrer*; L. *redintegro*; *red, re*, and *integro*, from *integer.*]

To renew with regard to any state or quality; to restore. [*Little used.*] *Bacon.*

REINTER'ROGATE, *v. t.* [*re* and *interrogate.*]

To interrogate again; to question repeatedly. *Cotgrave.*

REINTHRO'NE, *v. t.* [*re* and *inthrone.* See *Enthrone.*]

To replace on the throne. *Herbert.*

REINTHRO'NED, *pp.* Placed again on the throne.

REINTHRO'NING, *ppr.* Replacing on the throne.

REINTHRO'NIZE, *v. t.* To reinthrone. [*Not in use.*]

REINVEST', *v. t.* [*re* and *invest.*] To invest anew.

REINVEST'ED, *pp.* Invested again.

REINVEST'ING, *ppr.* Investing anew.

REINVEST'MENT, *n.* The act of investing anew; a second or repeated investment.

REINVIG'ORATE, *v. t.* To revive vigor in; to reanimate.

REIT, *n.* Sedge; sea weed. *Bailey.*

REIT'ERATE, *v. t.* [Fr. *reiterer*; L. *re* and *itero.*]

To repeat; to repeat again and again; as *reiterated* crimes; to *reiterate* requests. *Milton.*

REIT'ERATED, *pp.* Repeated again and again.

REIT'ERATING, *ppr.* Repeating again and again.

REITERA'TION, *n.* Repetition. *Boyle.*

REJECT', *v. t.* [L. *rejicio, rejectus*; *re* and *jacio*, to throw.]

1. To throw away, as any thing useless or vile.

2. To cast off.

Have I *rejected* those that me ador'd? *Brown.*

3. To cast off; to forsake. Jer. vii.

4. To refuse to receive; to slight; to despise.

Because thou hast *rejected* knowledge, I will *reject* thee. Hos. iv. 1 Sam. xv.

5. To refuse to grant; as, to *reject* a prayer or request.

6. To refuse to accept; as, to *reject* an offer.

REJECT'ABLE, *a.* That may be rejected.

REJECTAMENT'A, *n.* [from L. *rejecto.*] Things thrown out or away. [*Ill formed.*] *Fleming.*

REJECTA'NEOUS, *a.* [from the L.] Not chosen or received; rejected. *More.*

REJECT'ED, *pp.* Thrown away; cast off; refused; slighted.

REJECT'ER, *n.* One that rejects or refuses. *Clarke.*

REJECT'ING, *ppr.* Throwing away; casting off; refusing to grant or accept; slighting.

REJEC'TION, *n.* [L. *rejectio.*] The act of throwing away; the act of casting off or forsaking; refusal to accept or grant. *Bacon.*

REJECT'IVE, *a.* That rejects, or tends to cast off.

REJECT'MENT, *n.* Matter thrown away. *Eaton.*

REJOICE, *v. i.* *rejois'.* [Fr. *rejouir, rejouissant*; *re* and *jouir*, to enjoy; Arm. *joauçzaat*; It. *gioire*; Sp. *regocijar*, to rejoice; Sp. Port. *gozar*, to enjoy; *gozo*, joy. In most of the dialects, the last radical of *joy* is lost; but the Spanish and Portuguese retain it in *z*, which is a palatal letter. Hence this word seems to be the D. *juichen*, to rejoice, to shout; G. *jauchzen.* Qu. the Dan. *hujer*, to rejoice; *huj*, a shout, joy, rejoicing, which is the English *hue*, in *hue and cry*; Fr. *huer* and *hucher.* Amidst such changes of letters, it is not easy to ascertain the primary elements. But it is easy to see that the primary sense is to *shout*, or to be animated or excited.]

To experience joy and gladness in a high degree; to be exhilarated with lively and pleasurable sensations; to exult.

When the righteous are in authority, the people *rejoice*; but when the wicked beareth rule, the people mourn. Prov. xxix.

I will *rejoice* in thy salvation. Ps. ix.

REJOICE, *v. t.* *rejois'.* To make joyful; to gladden; to animate with lively pleasurable sensations; to exhilarate.

Whoso loveth wisdom *rejoiceth* his father. Prov. xxix.

While she, great saint, *rejoices* heaven. *Prior.*

REJOIC'ED, *pp.* Made glad; exhilarated.

REJOIC'ER, *n.* One that rejoices. *Taylor.*

REJOIC'ING, *ppr.* Animating with gladness; exhilarating; feeling joy.

REJOIC'ING, *n.* The act of expressing joy and gladness.

The voice of *rejoicing* and salvation is in the tabernacles of the righteous. Ps. cxviii.

2. The subject of joy.

Thy testimonies have I taken as an heritage forever, for they are the *rejoicing* of my heart. Ps. cxix.

3. The experience of joy. Gal. vi.

REJOIC'INGLY, *adv.* With joy or exultation. *Sheldon.*

REJOIN', *v. t.* [*re* and *join*; Fr. *rejoindre.*]

1. To join again; to unite after separation. *Brown.*

2. To meet one again. *Pope.*

REJOIN', *v. i.* To answer to a reply. *Dryden.*

2. In *law pleadings*, to answer, as the defendant to the plaintiff's replication.

REJOIND'ER, *n.* An answer to a reply; or in general, an answer.

2. In *law pleadings*, the defendant's answer to the plaintiff's replication.

REJOIN'ED, *pp.* Joined again; reunited.

REJOIN'ING, *ppr.* Joining again; answering a plaintif's replication.

REJOINT', *v. t.* [*re* and *joint.*] To reunite joints. *Barrow.*

REJOLT, *n.* [*re* and *jolt.*] A reacting jolt or shock. [*Not used.*] *South.*

REJOURN, *v. t. rejurn'.* [Fr. *reajourner.* See *Adjourn.*]
To adjourn to another hearing or inquiry. [*Not used.*] *Burton.*

REJUDGE, *v. t. rejuj'.* [*re* and *judge.*] To judge again; to re-examine; to review; to call to a new trial and decision.

> *Rejudge* his acts, and dignify disgrace. *Pope.*

REJUDG'ED, *pp.* Reviewed; judged again.

REJUDG'ING, *ppr.* Judging again.

REJUVENES'CENCE, REJUVENES'CENCY, *n.* [L. *re* and *juvenescens; juvenis*, a youth.]
A renewing of youth; the state of being young again. *Paus. Trans.*

REKIN'DLE, *v. t.* [*re* and *kindle.*] To kindle again; to set on fire anew. *Cheyne.*
2. To inflame again; to rouse anew. *Pope.*

REKIN'DLED, *pp.* Kindled again; inflamed anew.

REKIN'DLING, *ppr.* Kindling again; inflaming anew.

RELA'ID, *pp.* Laid a second time.

RELAND', *v. t.* [*re* and *land.*] To land again; to put on land what had been shipped or embarked. *Judge Sewall.*

RELAND', *v. i.* To go on shore after having embarked.

RELAND'ED, *pp.* Put on shore again.

RELAND'ING, *ppr.* Landing again.

RELAPSE, *v. i. relaps'.* [L. *relapsus, relabor*, to slide back; *re* and *labor*, to slide.]
1. To slip or slide back; to return.
2. To fall back; to return to a former state or practice; as, to *relapse* into vice or error after amendment.
3. To fall back or return from recovery or a convalescent state; as, to *relapse* into a fever.

RELAPSE, *n. relaps'.* A sliding or falling back, particularly into a former bad state, either of body or of morals; as a *relapse* into a disease from a convalescent state; a *relapse* into a vicious course of life. [In the sense of a person relapsing, not used.]

RELAPS'ER, *n.* One that relapses into vice or error.

RELAPS'ING, *ppr.* Sliding or falling back, as into disease or vice.

RELA'TE, *v. t.* [L. *relatus, refero; re* and *fero*, to produce.]
1. To tell; to recite; to narrate the particulars of an event; as, to *relate* the story of Priam; to *relate* the adventures of Don Quixote.
2. To bring back; to restore. [*Not in use.*]
3. To ally by connection or kindred.
To relate one's self, to vent thoughts in words. [*Ill.*]

RELA'TE, *v. i.* To have reference or respect; to regard.

> All negative words *relate* to positive ideas. *Locke.*

RELA'TED, *pp.* Recited; narrated.
2. *a.* Allied by kindred; connected by blood or alliance, particularly by consanguinity; as a person *related* in the first or second degree.

RELA'TER, *n.* One who tells, recites or narrates; a historian. *Milton. Swift.*

RELA'TING, *ppr.* Telling; reciting; narrating.
2. *a.* Having relation or reference; concerning.

RELA'TION, *n.* [Fr. from L. *relatio, refero.*]
1. The act of telling; recital; account; narration; narrative of facts; as a historical *relation.* We listened to the *relation* of his adventures.
2. Respect; reference; regard.

> I have been importuned to make some observations on this art, in *relation* to its agreement with poetry. *Dryden.*

3. Connection between things; mutual respect, or what one thing is with regard to another; as the *relation* of a citizen to the state; the *relation* of a subject to the supreme authority; the *relation* of husband and wife, or of master and servant; the *relation* of a state of probation to a state of retribution.
4. Kindred; alliance; as the *relation* of parents and children.

> Relations dear, and all the charities
> Of father, son and brother, first were known. *Milton.*

5. A person connected by consanguinity or affinity; a kinsman or kinswoman. He passed a month with his *relations* in the country.
6. Resemblance of phenomena; analogy.
7. In *geometry*, ratio; proportion.

RELA'TIONAL, *a.* Having relation or kindred.

> We might be tempted to take these two nations for *relational* stems *Tooke.*

RELA'TIONSHIP, *n.* The state of being related by kindred, affinity or other alliance. *Mason.*
[*This word is generally tautological and useless.*]

REL'ATIVE, *a.* [Fr. *relatif;* L. *relativus.*]
1. Having relation; respecting. The arguments may be good, but they are not *relative* to the subject.
2. Not absolute or existing by itself; considered as belonging to or respecting something else.

> Every thing sustains both an absolute and a *relative* capacity; an absolute, as it is such a thing, endued with such a nature; and a *relative*, as it is a part of the universe, and so stands in such a relation to the whole. *South.*

3. Incident to man in society; as *relative* rights and duties.
4. Particular; positive. [*Not in use.*] *Shak.*
Relative mode, in music, the mode which the composer interweaves with the principal mode in the flow of the harmony. *Encyc.*
Relative terms, in logic, terms which imply relation, as guardian and ward; master and servant; husband and wife.
Relative word, in grammar, a word which relates to another word, called its antecedent, or to a sentence or member of a sentence, or to a series of sentences.

REL'ATIVE, *n.* A person connected by blood or affinity; strictly, one allied by blood; a relation; a kinsman or kinswoman.

> Confining our care either to ourselves and *relatives.* *Fell.*

2. That which has relation to something else. *Locke.*
3. In *grammar*, a word which relates to or represents another word, called its antecedent, or to a sentence or member of a sentence, or to a series of sentences, which constitutes its antecedent. "He seldom lives frugally, *who* lives by chance." Here *who* is the relative, which represents *he*, the antecedent.
"Judas declared him innocent, *which* he could not be, had he deceived his disciples." *Porteus.* Here *which* refers to *innocent*, an adjective, as its antecedent.
"Another reason that makes me doubt of any innate practical principles, is, that I think there cannot any one moral rule be proposed, whereof a man may not justly demand a reason; *which* would be perfectly ridiculous and absurd, if they were innate, or so much as self-evident, *which* every innate principle must needs be." *Locke.*
If we ask the question, what would be ridiculous and absurd, the answer must be, *whereof a man may justly demand a reason*, and this part of the sentence is the antecedent to *which. Self-evident* is the antecedent to *which*, near the close of the sentence.

REL'ATIVELY, *adv.* In relation or respect to something else; not absolutely.

> Consider the absolute affections of any being as it is in itself, before you consider it *relatively.* *Watts.*

REL'ATIVENESS, *n.* The state of having relation.

RELA'TOR, *n.* In *law*, one who brings an information in the nature of a *quo warranto.* *Blackstone.*

RELAX', *v. t.* [L. *relaxo; re* and *laxo*, to slacken; Fr. *relâcher, relascher;* It. *rilassare;* Sp. *relaxar.* See *Lax.*]
1. To slacken; to make less tense or rigid; as, to *relax* a rope or cord; to *relax* the muscles or sinews; to *relax* the reins in riding.
2. To loosen; to make less close or firm; as, to *relax* the joints. *Milton.*
3. To make less severe or rigorous; to remit or abate in strictness; as, to *relax* a law or rule of justice; to *relax* a demand. *Swift.*
4. To remit or abate in attention, assiduity or labor; as, to *relax* study; to *relax* exertions or efforts.
5. To unbend; to ease; to relieve from close attention; as, conversation *relaxes* the student or the mind.
6. To relieve from constipation; to loosen; to open; as, medicines *relax* the bowels.
7. To open; to loose. *Milton.*
8. To make languid.

RELAX', *v. i.* To abate in severity; to become more mild or less rigorous.

> In others she *relax'd* again,
> And govern'd with a looser rein. *Prior.*

2. To remit in close attention. It is useful for the student to *relax* often, and give himself to exercise and amusements.

RELAX', *n.* Relaxation. [*Not used.*] *Feltham.*

RELAX'ABLE, *a.* That may be remitted. *Barrow.*

RELAXA'TION, *n.* [Fr. from L. *relaxatio.*] 1. The act of slackening or remitting tension; as a *relaxation* of the muscles, fibers or nerves; a *relaxation* of the whole system. *Bacon. Encyc.*

2. Cessation of restraint. *Burnet.*

3. Remission or abatement of rigor; as a *relaxation* of the law. *Swift.*

4. Remission of attention or application; as a *relaxation* of mind, study or business.

5. An opening or loosening.

RELAX'ATIVE, *a.* Having the quality of relaxing. [See *Laxative.*] *B. Jonson.*

RELAX'ED, *pp.* Slackened; loosened; remitted or abated in rigor or in closeness; made less vigorous; languid.

RELAX'ING, *ppr.* Slackening; loosening; remitting or abating in rigor, severity or attention; rendering languid.

RELA'Y, *n.* [Fr. *relais.*] A supply of horses placed on the road to be in readiness to relieve others, that a traveler may proceed without delay.

2. Hunting dogs kept in readiness at certain places to pursue the game, when the dogs that have been in pursuit are weary.

RELA'Y, *v. t.* [*re* and *lay.*] To lay again; to lay a second time; as, to *relay* a pavement. *Smollett.*

RELA'YING, *ppr.* Laying a second time.

RELE'ASE, *v. t.* [This is usually derived from Fr. *relâcher*, to slacken, to *relax*, It. *rilassare* and *rilasciare*, and these words have the sense of *release;* but the English word has not the sense of *relax*, but of *re* and *lease*, from Fr. *laisser*, Eng. *let*, a word that has no connection with *relax.* So in G. *freilassen*, D. *vrylaaten; free* and *let.* If it is from *relâcher*, it has undergone a strange alteration.]

1. To set free from restraint of any kind, either physical or moral; to liberate from prison, confinement or servitude. Matt. xv. Mark xv.

2. To free from pain, care, trouble, grief, &c.

3. To free from obligation or penalty; as, to *release* one from debt, from a promise or covenant.

4. To quit; to let go, as a legal claim; as, to *release* a debt or forfeiture. Deut. xv.

5. To discharge or relinquish a right to lands or tenements, by conveying it to another that has some right or estate in possession, as when the person in remainder *releases* his right to the tenant in possession; when one co-parcener *releases* his right to the other; or the mortgagee *releases* his claim to the mortgager.

6. To relax. [*Not in use.*] *Hooker.*

RELE'ASE, *n.* Liberation or discharge from restraint of any kind, as from confinement or bondage.

2. Liberation from care, pain or any burden.

3. Discharge from obligation or responsibility, as from debt, penalty or claim of any kind; acquittance.

4. In *law*, a release or deed of release is a conveyance of a man's right in lands or tenements to another who has some estate in possession; a quitclaim. The efficient words in such an instrument are, "remised, *released*, and forever quitclaimed." *Blackstone.*

RELE'ASED, *pp.* Set free from confinement; freed from obligation or liability; freed from pain; quitclaimed.

RELE'ASEMENT, *n.* The act of releasing from confinement or obligation. *Milton.*

RELE'ASER, *n.* One who releases.

RELE'ASING, *ppr.* Liberating from confinement or restraint; freeing from obligation or responsibility, or from pain or other evil; quitclaiming.

REL'EGATE, *v. t.* [L. *relego; re* and *lego*, to send.] To banish; to send into exile.

REL'EGATED, *pp.* Sent into exile.

REL'EGATING, *ppr.* Banishing.

RELEGA'TION, *n.* [L. *relegatio.*] The act of banishment; exile. *Ayliffe.*

RELENT', *v. i.* [Fr. *ralentir;* Sp. *relenter;* It. *rallentare;* Sp. *ablandar;* Port. *abrandar;* the two latter from *blando*, L. *blandus*, which unites the L. *blandus* with *lentus.* The English is from *re* and L. *lentus*, gentle, pliant, slow, the primary sense of which is soft or yielding. The L. *lenis* is probably of the same family. See *Blund.*]

1. To soften; to become less rigid or hard; to give.

> In some houses, sweetmeats will *relent* more than in others. *Bacon.*
>
> When op'ning buds salute the welcome day,
> And earth *relenting* feels the genial ray. *Pope.*

[*This sense of the word is admissible in poetry, but is not in common use.*]

2. To grow moist; to deliquesce; applied to salts; as the *relenting* of the air. *Bacon.*

> Salt of tartar—placed in a cellar, will begin to *relent.* *Boyle.*

[*This sense is not in use.*]

3. To become less intense. [*Little used.*] *Sidney.*

4. To soften in temper; to become more mild and tender; to feel compassion. [*This is the usual sense of the word.*]

> Can you behold
> My tears, and not once *relent?* *Shak.*

RELENT', *v. t.* To slacken.

> And oftentimes he would *relent* his pace *Obs.* *Spenser.*

2. To soften; to mollify. *Obs.* *Spenser.*

RELENT', *pp.* Dissolved. *Obs.*

RELENT', *n.* Remission; stay. *Obs.* *Spenser.*

RELENT'ING, *ppr.* Softening in temper; becoming more mild or compassionate.

RELENT'ING, *n.* The act of becoming more mild or compassionate.

RELENT'LESS, *a.* Unmoved by pity; unpitying; insensible to the distresses of others; destitute of tenderness; as a prey to *relentless* despotism.

> For this th' avenging pow'r employs his darts,
> Thus will persist, *relentless* in his ire. *Dryden.*

Relentless thoughts, in Milton, may signify unremitted, intently fixed on disquieting objects. *Johnson.*

[*This sense of the word is unusual and not to be countenanced.*]

RELESSEE', *n.* [See *Release.*] The person to whom a release is executed.

RELESSOR', *n.* The person who executes a release.

> There must be a privity of estate between the *relessor* and *relessee.* *Blackstone.*

REL'EVANCE, **REL'EVANCY**, *n.* [See *Relevant.*] The state of being relevant, or of affording relief or aid.

2. Pertinence; applicableness.

3. In *Scots law*, sufficiency to infer the conclusion.

REL'EVANT, *a.* [Fr. from L. *relever*, to relieve, to advance, to raise; *re* and *lever*, to raise.]

1. Relieving; lending aid or support. *Pownall.*

2. Pertinent; applicable. The testimony is not *relevant* to the case. The argument is not *relevant* to the question. [*This is the sense in which the word is now generally used.*]

3. Sufficient to support the cause. *Scots Law.*

RELEVA'TION, *n.* A raising or lifting up. [*Not in use.*]

RELI'ANCE, *n.* [from *rely.*] Rest or repose of mind, resulting from a full belief of the veracity or integrity of a person, or of the certainty of a fact; trust; confidence; dependence. We may have perfect *reliance* on the promises of God; we have *reliance* on the testimony of witnesses; we place *reliance* on men of known integrity, or on the strength and stability of government.

REL'IC, *n.* [Fr. *relique;* L. *reliquiæ*, from *relinquo*, to *leave; re* and *linquo.*]

1. That which remains; that which is left after the loss or decay of the rest; as the *relics* of a town; the *relics* of magnificence; the *relics* of antiquity. The *relics* of saints, real or pretended, are held in great veneration by the catholics.

2. The body of a deceased person; a corpse. [*Usually in the plural.*] *Dryden. Pope.*

REL'ICT, *n.* [L. *relictus, relicta*, from *relinquo*, to leave.] A widow; a woman whose husband is dead. *Sprat. Garth.*

RELIE'F, *n.* [Fr. *relief;* It. *rilevo, rilievo*, from *rilevare*, to raise, to lift, to remove; Sp. *relieve, relevar; re* and *llevar*, to raise.]

1. The removal, in whole or in part, of any evil that afflicts the body or mind; the removal or alleviation of pain, grief, want, care, anxiety, toil or distress, or of any thing oppressive or burdensome, by which some ease is obtained. Rest gives *relief* to the body when weary; an anodyne gives *relief* from pain; the sympathy of friends affords some *relief* to the distressed; a loan of money to a man embarrassed may afford him a temporary *relief;* medicines which will not cure a disease, sometimes give a partial *relief.* A complete *relief* from the troubles of life is never to be expected.

2. That which mitigates or removes pain, grief or other evil. *Dryden.*

3. The dismission of a sentinel from his post, whose place is supplied by another soldier; also, the person who takes his place.

4. In *sculpture*, &c. the projecture or prominence of a figure above or beyond the ground or plane on which it is formed. Relief is of three kinds; high relief [*alto relievo;*] low relief [*basso relievo;*] and demi relief [*demi relievo.*] The difference is in the degree of projecture. *High relief*

is formed from nature, as when a figure projects as much as the life. *Low relief* is when the figure projects but little, as in medals, festoons, foliages and other ornaments. *Demi relief* is when one half of the figure rises from the plane. *Encyc.*

5. In *painting*, the appearance of projection, or the degree of boldness which a figure exhibits to the eye at a distance.
6. In *feudal law*, a fine or composition which the heir of a tenant, holding by knight's service or other tenure, paid to the lord at the death of the ancestor, for the privilege of taking up the estate which, on strict feudal principles, had lapsed or fallen to the lord on the death of the tenant. This relief consisted of horses, arms, money and the like, the amount of which was originally arbitrary, but afterwards fixed at a certain rate by law. It is not payable, unless the heir at the death of his ancestor had attained to the age of twenty one years. *Blackstone. Encyc.*
7. A remedy, partial or total, for any wrong suffered; redress; indemnification. He applied to chancery, but could get no *relief.* He petitioned the legislature and obtained *relief.*
8. The exposure of any thing by the proximity of something else. *Johnson.*

RELI'ER, *n.* [from *rely.*] One who relies, or places full confidence in.

RELIE'VABLE, *a.* Capable of being relieved; that may receive relief. *Hale.*

RELIE'VE, *v. t.* [Fr. *relever;* L. *relevo.* See *Relief.*]

1. To free, wholly or partially, from pain, grief, want, anxiety, care, toil, trouble, burden, oppression, or any thing that is considered to be an evil; to ease of any thing that pains the body or distresses the mind. Repose *relieves* the wearied body; a supply of provisions *relieves* a family in want; medicines may *relieve* the sick man, even when they do not cure him. We all desire to be *relieved* from anxiety and from heavy taxes. Law or duty, or both, require that we should *relieve* the poor and destitute.
2. To alleviate or remove; as when we say, to *relieve* pain or distress; to *relieve* the wants of the poor.
3. To dismiss from a post or station, as sentinels, a guard or ships, and station others in their place. Sentinels are generally *relieved* every two hours; a guard is usually *relieved* once in twenty four hours.
4. To right; to ease of any burden, wrong or oppression by judicial or legislative interposition, by the removal of a grievance, by indemnification for losses and the like.
5. To abate the inconvenience of any thing by change, or by the interposition of something dissimilar. The moon *relieves* the luster of the sun with a milder light.

> The poet must not encumber his poem with too much business, but sometimes *relieve* the subject with a moral reflection. *Addison.*

6. To assist; to support.

> Parallels or like relations alternately *relieve* each other; when neither will pass asunder, yet are they plausible together. *Brown.*

RELIE'VED, *pp.* Freed from pain or other evil; eased or cured; aided; succored; dismissed from watching.

2. Alleviated or removed; as pain or distress.

RELIE'VER, *n.* One that relieves; he or that which gives ease.

RELIE'VING, *ppr.* Removing pain or distress, or abating the violence of it; easing; curing; assisting; dismissing from a post, as a sentinel; supporting.

RELIE'VO, *n.* [It.] Relief; prominence of figures in statuary, architecture, &c.; apparent prominence of figures in painting.

RELIGHT, *v. t.* *reli'te.* [*re* and *light.*] To light anew; to illuminate again.

2. To rekindle; to set on fire again.

RELIGHTED, *pp.* Lighted anew; rekindled.

RELIGHTING, *ppr.* Lighting again; rekindling.

RELIG'ION, *n.* *relij'on.* [Fr. Sp. *religion;* It. *religione;* L. *religio,* from *religo,* to bind anew; *re* and *ligo,* to bind. This word seems originally to have signified an oath or vow to the gods, or the obligation of such an oath or vow, which was held very sacred by the Romans.]

1. Religion, in its most comprehensive sense, includes a belief in the being and perfections of God, in the revelation of his will to man, in man's obligation to obey his commands, in a state of reward and punishment, and in man's accountableness to God; and also true godliness or piety of life, with the practice of all moral duties. It therefore comprehends theology, as a system of doctrines or principles, as well as practical piety; for the practice of moral duties without a belief in a divine lawgiver, and without reference to his will or commands, is not religion.
2. *Religion,* as distinct from *theology,* is godliness or real piety in practice, consisting in the performance of all known duties to God and our fellow men, in obedience to divine command, or from love to God and his law. James i.

> *Religion* will attend you—as a pleasant and useful companion, in every proper place and every temperate occupation of life. *Buckminster.*

3. *Religion,* as distinct from *virtue,* or *morality,* consists in the performance of the duties we owe directly to God, from a principle of obedience to his will. Hence we often speak of *religion* and *virtue,* as different branches of one system, or the duties of the first and second tables of the law.

> Let us with caution indulge the supposition, that morality can be maintained without *religion.* *Washington.*

4. Any system of faith and worship. In this sense, religion comprehends the belief and worship of pagans and Mohammedans, as well as of christians; any religion consisting in the belief of a superior power or powers governing the world, and in the worship of such power or powers. Thus we speak of the *religion* of the Turks, of the Hindoos, of the Indians, &c. as well as of the christian *religion.* We speak of *false religion,* as well as of *true religion.*
5. The rites of religion; in the plural. *Milton.*

RELIG'IONARY, *a.* Relating to religion; pious. [*Not used.*] *Bp. Barlow.*

RELIG'IONIST, *n.* A bigot to any religious persuasion. *Swift.*

RELIG'IOUS, *a.* [Fr. *religieux;* L. *religiosus.*]

1. Pertaining or relating to religion; as a *religious* society; a *religious* sect; a *religious* place; *religious* subjects.
2. Pious; godly; loving and reverencing the Supreme Being and obeying his precepts; as a *religious* man.
3. Devoted to the practice of religion; as a *religious* life.
4. Teaching religion; containing religious subjects or the doctrines and precepts of religion, or the discussion of topics of religion; as a *religious* book.
5. Exact; strict; such as religion requires; as a *religious* observance of vows or promises.
6. Engaged by vows to a monastic life; as a *religious* order or fraternity.
7. Appropriated to the performance of sacred or religious duties; as a *religious* house. *Law.*

RELIG'IOUS, *n.* A person bound by monastic vows, or sequestered from secular concerns and devoted to a life of piety and devotion; a monk or friar; a nun.

RELIG'IOUSLY, *adv.* Piously; with love and reverence to the Supreme Being; in obedience to the divine commands. *Drayton.*

2. According to the rites of religion. *Shak.*
3. Reverently; with veneration. *Duppa.*
4. Exactly; strictly; conscientiously; as a vow or promise *religiously* observed.

RELIG'IOUSNESS, *n.* The quality or state of being religious.

RELIN'QUISH, *v. t.* [L. *relinquo;* *re* and *linquo,* to leave, to fail or faint; from the same root as *liqueo, liquo,* to melt or dissolve, *deliquium,* a fainting, Ir. *leagham,* to melt. Hence the sense is to withdraw or give way; to relinquish is to recede from. It is probably allied to *flag* and *slack;* W. *llac, llaciaw,* to *slacken; llegu,* to flag. Class Lg.]

1. To withdraw from; to leave; to quit. It may be to forsake or abandon, but it does not necessarily express the sense of the latter. A man may *relinquish* an enterprise for a time, or with a design never to resume it. In general, to *relinquish* is to leave without the intention of resuming, and equivalent to *forsake,* but is less emphatical than *abandon* and *desert.*

> They placed Irish tenants on the lands *relinquished* by the English. *Davies.*

2. To forbear; to withdraw from; as, to *relinquish* the practice of intemperance; to *relinquish* the rites of a church. *Hooker.*
3. To give up; to renounce a claim to; as, to *relinquish* a debt.

To relinquish back, or *to,* to give up; to release; to surrender; as, to *relinquish* a claim *to* another.

RELIN'QUISHED, *pp.* Left; quitted; given up.

RELIN'QUISHER, *n.* One who leaves or quits.

RELIN'QUISHING, *ppr.* Quitting; leaving; giving up.

RELIN'QUISHMENT, *n.* The act of leaving or quitting; a forsaking; the renouncing a claim to.

REL'IQUARY, *n.* [Fr. *reliquaire*, from L. *relinquo.*]
A depository for relics; a casket in which relics are kept. *Encyc.*

RELIQ'UIDATE, *v. t.* [*re* and *liquidate.*] To liquidate anew; to adjust a second time.

RELIQ'UIDATED, *pp.* Liquidated again.

RELIQ'UIDATING, *ppr.* Liquidating again.

RELIQUIDA'TION, *n.* A second or renewed liquidation; a renewed adjustment. *Hamilton.*

REL'ISH, *n.* Taste; or rather, a pleasing taste; that sensation of the organs which is experienced when we take food or drink of an agreeable flavor. Different persons have different *relishes*. *Relish* is often natural, and often the effect of habit.

2. Liking; delight; appetite.

> We have such a *relish* for faction, as to have lost that of wit. *Addison.*

3. Sense; the faculty of perceiving excellence; taste; as a *relish for* fine writing, or a *relish of* fine writing. Addison uses both *of* and *for* after *relish.*

4. That which gives pleasure; the power of pleasing.

> When liberty is gone,
> Life grows insipid and has lost its *relish*. *Addison.*

5. Cast; manner.

> It preserves some *relish* of old writing. *Pope.*

6. Taste; a small quantity just perceptible.

> Devotion, patience, courage, fortitude,
> I have no *relish* of them. *Shak.*

REL'ISH, *v. t.* To give an agreeable taste to.

> A sav'ry bit that serv'd to *relish* wine. *Dryden.*

2. To like the taste of; as, to *relish* venison.

3. To be gratified with the enjoyment or use of.

> He knows how to prize his advantages and to *relish* the honors which he enjoys. *Atterbury.*

> Men of nice palates would not *relish* Aristotle, as dressed up by the schoolmen. *Baker.*

REL'ISH, *v. i.* To have a pleasing taste. The greatest dainties do not always *relish.*

2. To give pleasure.

> Had I been the finder-out of this secret, it would not have *relished* among my other discredits. *Shak.*

3. To have a flavor.

> A theory which, how much soever it may *relish* of wit and invention, hath no foundation in nature. *Woodward.*

REL'ISHABLE, *a.* Gustable; having an agreeable taste.

REL'ISHED, *pp.* Giving an agreeable taste; received with pleasure.

RELIVE, *v. i.* *reliv'.* [*re* and *live.*] To live again; to revive. *Spenser.*

RELIVE, *v. t.* *reliv'.* To recall to life. [*Not in use.*] *Spenser.*

RELŎAN, *v. t.* [*re* and *loan.*] To loan again; to lend what has been lent and repaid.

RELŎAN, *n.* A second lending of the same money. *President's Message.*

RELŎANED, *pp.* Loaned again.

RELŎANING, *ppr.* Loaning again.

RELŎVE, *v. t.* [*re* and *love.*] To love in return. [*Not in use.*] *Boyle.*

RELU'CENT, *a.* [L. *relucens, reluceo; re* and *luceo*, to shine.]
Shining; transparent; clear; pellucid; as a *relucent* stream. *Thomson.*

RELUCT', *v. i.* [L. *reluctor; re* and *luctor*, to struggle.] To strive or struggle against. [*Little used.*]

RELUCT'ANCE, } *n.* [literally a straining
RELUCT'ANCY, } or striving against.]
Unwillingness; great opposition of mind; repugnance; with *to* or *against;* as, to undertake a war with *reluctance.* He has a great *reluctance* to this measure.

> Bear witness, heav'n, with what *reluctancy*
> Her helpless innocence I doom to die. *Dryden.*

RELUCT'ANT, *a.* Striving against; unwilling; much opposed in heart.

> *Reluctant* now I touch'd the trembling string. *Tickell.*

2. Unwilling; acting with slight repugnance; coy. *Milton.*

3. Proceeding from an unwilling mind; granted with reluctance; as *reluctant* obedience. *Mitford.*

RELUCT'ANTLY, *adv.* With opposition of heart; unwillingly. What is undertaken *reluctantly* is seldom well performed.

RELUCT'ATE, *v. t.* To resist; to struggle against. *Decay of Piety.*

RELUCTA'TION, *n.* Repugnance; resistance. *Bacon.*

RELUCT'ING, *ppr.* Striving to resist.

2. *a.* Averse; unwilling.

RELU'ME, *v. t.* [Fr. *rallumer;* L. *re* and *lumen*, light.] To rekindle; to light again. *Pope.*

RELU'MED, *pp.* Rekindled; lighted again.

RELU'MINE, *v. t.* [It. *ralluminare;* L. *relumino; re* and *lumen*, light, from *luceo*, to shine.]

1. To light anew; to rekindle. *Shak.*

2. To illuminate again.

RELU'MINED, *pp.* Rekindled; illuminated anew.

RELU'MING, *ppr.* Kindling or lighting anew.

RELU'MINING, *ppr.* Rekindling; enlightening anew.

RELY', *v. i.* [*re* and *lie*, or from the root of *lie, lay.*]
To rest on something, as the mind when satisfied of the veracity, integrity or ability of persons, or of the certainty of facts or of evidence; to have confidence in; to trust in; to depend; with *on.* We *rely on* the promise of a man who is known to be upright; we *rely on* the veracity or fidelity of a tried friend; a prince *relies on* the affections of his subjects for support, and *on* the strength of his army for success in war; above all things, we *rely on* the mercy and promises of God. That which is the ground of confidence, is a certainty or full conviction that satisfies the mind and leaves it at rest, or undisturbed by doubt.

> Because thou hast *relied on* the king of Syria, and not *relied on* the Lord thy God— 2 Chron. xvi.

RELY'ING, *ppr.* Reposing on something, as the mind; confiding in; trusting in; depending.

REMA'DE, *pret.* and *pp.* of *remake.*

REMA'IN, *v. i.* [L. *remaneo; re* and *maneo*, Gr. *μενω, μενεω;* Pers. ماندن mandan, and مانیدن manidan, to remain, to be left, to delay, to be like, to dismiss, to leave. The sense seems to be to draw out in time, or to be fixed, or to continue. See analogies in *leave.* The sense of likeness may be a drawing.]

1. To continue; to rest or abide in a place for a time indefinite. They *remained* a month in Rome. We *remain* at an inn for a night, for a week, or a longer time.

> *Remain* a widow at thy father's house, till Shelah my son be grown. Gen. xxxviii.

2. To be left after others have withdrawn; to rest or abide in the same place when others remove, or are lost, destroyed or taken away.

> Noah only *remained* alive, and they that were with him in the ark. Gen. vii.

3. To be left after a part or others have past. Let our *remaining* time or years be employed in active duties.

4. To continue unchanged, or in a particular state. He *remains* stupid; he *remains* in a low state of health.

5. Not to be lost; not to escape; not to be forgotten.

> All my wisdom *remained* with me. *Ecclus.*

6. To be left, out of a greater number or quantity. Part of the debt is paid, that which *remains* will be on interest.

> That which *remaineth* over, lay up for you to be kept till the morning. Ex. xvi.

7. To be left as not included or comprised. There *remains* one argument which has not been considered.

> That an elder brother has power over his brethren, *remains* to be proved. *Locke.*

8. To continue in the same state.

> Childless thou art, childless *remain.* *Milton.*

REMA'IN, *v. t.* To await; to be left to; as, the easier conquest now *remains* thee. [This is elliptical for *remains to* thee. *Remain* is not properly a transitive verb.]

REMA'IN, *n.* That which is left; a corpse; also, abode. [*Not used.*]

REMA'INDER, *n.* Any thing left after the separation and removal of a part.

> If these decoctions be repeated till the water comes off clear, the *remainder* yields no salt. *Arbuthnot.*

> The last *remainders* of unhappy Troy. *Dryden.*

2. Relics; remains; the corpse of a human being. [*Not now used.*] *Shak.*

3. That which is left after a part is past; as the *remainder* of the day or week; the *remainder* of the year; the *remainder* of life.

4. The sum that is left after subtraction or after any deduction.

5. In *law*, an estate limited to take effect and be enjoyed after another estate is determined. A grants land to B for twenty years; *remainder* to D in fee. If a man by deed or will limits his books or furniture to A for life, with *remainder* to B, this *remainder* is good. *Blackstone.*

A writ of formedon in remainder, is a writ which lies where a man gives lands to another for life or in tail, with remainder to a third person in tail or in fee, and he who has the particular estate dies without issue heritable, and a stranger intrudes upon him in remainder and keeps him out of possession; in this case, the remainder-man shall have his writ of formedon in the remainder. *Blackstone.*

REMA'INDER, *a.* Remaining; refuse; left; as the *remainder* biscuit; the *remainder* viands. *Obs.* *Shak.*

REMA'INDER-MAN, *n.* In *law*, he who has an estate after a particular estate is determined. *Blackstone.*

REMA'INING, *ppr.* Continuing; resting; abiding for an indefinite time; being left after separation and removal of a part, or after loss or destruction, or after a part is passed, as of time.

REMA'INS, *n. plu.* That which is left after a part is separated, taken away or destroyed; as the *remains* of a city or house demolished.

2. A dead body; a corpse. *Pope.*

The singular, *remain*, in the like sense, and in the sense of *abode*, is entirely obsolete. *Shak.*

REMA'KE, *v. t.* pret. and pp. *remade.* [*re* and *make.*] To make anew.

REM'AND, *v. t.* [Fr. *remander;* L. *re* and *mando.*]

To call or send back him or that which is ordered to a place; as, to *remand* an officer from a distant place; to *remand* an envoy from a foreign court.

REM'ANDED, *pp.* Called or sent back.

REM'ANDING, *ppr.* Calling or sending back.

REM'ANENT, *n.* [L. *remanens.*] The part remaining. [*Little used.* It is contracted into *remnant.*]

REM'ANENT, *a.* Remaining. [*Little used.*] *Taylor.*

REM'ARK, *n.* [Fr. *remarque; re* and *mark.*] Notice or observation, particularly notice or observation expressed in words or writing; as the *remarks* of an advocate; the *remarks* made in conversation; the judicious or the uncandid *remarks* of a critic. A *remark* is not always expressed, for we say, a man makes his *remarks* on a preacher's sermon while he is listening to it. In this case the notice is silent, a mere act of the mind.

REM'ARK, *v. t.* [Fr. *remarquer.*] To observe; to note in the mind; to take notice of without expression. I *remarked* the manner of the speaker; I *remarked* his elegant expressions.

2. To express in words or writing what one thinks or sees; to express observations; as, it is necessary to repeat what has been before *remarked.*

3. To mark; to point out; to distinguish. [*Not in use.*]

His manacles *remark* him. *Milton.*

REM'ARKABLE, *a.* [Fr. *remarquable.*] Observable; worthy of notice.

'Tis *remarkable* that they
Talk most, who have the least to say. *Prior.*

2. Extraordinary; unusual; that deserves particular notice, or that may excite admiration or wonder; as the *remarkable* preservation of lives in shipwreck. The dark day in May, 1790, was a *remarkable* phenomenon.

REM'ARKABLENESS, *n.* Observableness; worthiness of remark; the quality of deserving particular notice. *Hammond.*

REM'ARKABLY, *adv.* In a manner or degree worthy of notice; as, the winters of 1825, 1826 and 1828 were *remarkably* free from snow. The winter of 1827 was *remarkable* for a great quantity of snow.

2. In an extraordinary manner.

REM'ARKED, *pp.* Noticed; observed; expressed in words or writing.

REM'ARKER, *n.* An observer; one who makes remarks. *Watts.*

REM'ARKING, *ppr.* Observing; taking notice of; expressing in words or writing.

REMAR'RIED, *pp.* Married again or a second time.

REMAR'RY, *v. t.* [*re* and *marry.*] To marry again or a second time. *Tindal.*

REMAR'RYING, *ppr.* Marrying again or a second time.

REMAS'TICATE, *v. t.* [*re* and *masticate.*] To chew or masticate again; to chew over and over, as in chewing the cud.

REMAS'TICATED, *pp.* Chewed again or repeatedly.

REMAS'TICATING, *ppr.* Chewing again or over and over.

REMASTICA'TION, *n.* The act of masticating again or repeatedly.

REME'DIABLE, *a.* [from *remedy.*] That may be remedied or cured. The evil is believed to be *remediable.*

REME'DIAL, *a.* [L. *remedialis.*] Affording a remedy; intended for a remedy, or for the removal of an evil.

The *remedial* part of law is so necessary a consequence of the declaratory and directory, that laws without it must be very vague and imperfect. Statutes are declaratory or *remedial.* *Blackstone.*

REME'DIATE, in the sense of *remedial*, is not in use.

REM'EDIED, *pp.* [from *remedy.*] Cured; healed; repaired.

REMED'ILESS, *a.* [In modern books, the accent is placed on the first syllable, which would be well if there were no derivatives; but *remedilessly, remedilessness*, require the accent on the second syllable.]

1. Not admitting a remedy; incurable; desperate; as a *remediless* disease.

2. Irreparable; as, a loss or damage is *remediless.*

3. Not admitting change or reversal; as a *remediless* doom. *Milton.*

4. Not admitting recovery; as a *remediless* delusion. *South.*

REMED'ILESSLY, *adv.* In a manner or degree that precludes a remedy. *Clarendon.*

REMED'ILESSNESS, *n.* Incurableness.

REM'EDY, *n.* [L. *remedium; re* and *medeor*, to heal; Fr. *remède.*]

1. That which cures a disease; any medicine or application which puts an end to disease and restores health; with *for;* as a *remedy for* the gout.

2. That which counteracts an evil of any kind; with *for, to* or *against;* usually with *for.* Civil government is the *remedy for* the evils of natural liberty. What *remedy* can be provided *for* extravagance in dress? The man who shall invent an effectual *remedy for* intemperance, will deserve every thing from his fellow men.

3. That which cures uneasiness.

Our griefs how swift, our *remedies* how slow. *Prior.*

4. That which repairs loss or disaster; reparation.

In the death of a man there is no *remedy.* *Wisdom.*

REM'EDY, *v. t.* [Fr. *remedier.*] To cure; to heal; as, to *remedy* a disease.

2. To cure; to remove, as an evil; as, to *remedy* grief; to *remedy* the evils of a war.

3. To repair; to remove mischief; *in a very general sense.*

REM'EDYING, *ppr.* Curing; healing; removing; restoring from a bad to a good state.

REMELT', *v. t.* [*re* and *melt.*] To melt a second time.

REMELT'ED, *pp.* Melted again.

REMELT'ING, *ppr.* Melting again.

REMEM'BER, *v. t.* [Norm. *remembre;* Low L. *rememoror; re* and *memoror.* See *Memory.*]

1. To have in the mind an idea which had been in the mind before, and which recurs to the mind without effort.

We are said to *remember* any thing, when the idea of it arises in the mind with the consciousness that we have had this idea before. *Watts.*

2. When we use effort to recall an idea, we are said to *recollect* it. This distinction is not always observed. Hence *remember* is often used as synonymous with *recollect*, that is, to call to mind. We say, we cannot *remember* a fact, when we mean, we cannot *recollect* it.

Remember the days of old. Deut. xxxii.

3. To bear or keep in mind; to attend to.

Remember what I warn thee; shun to taste. *Milton.*

4. To preserve the memory of; to preserve from being forgotten.

Let them have their wages duly paid,
And something over to *remember* me. *Shak.*

5. To mention. [*Not in use.*] *Ayliffe.*

6. To put in mind; to remind; as, to *remember* one of his duty. [*Not in use.*] *Clarendon.*

7. To think of and consider; to meditate. Ps. lxiii.

8. To bear in mind with esteem; or to reward. Eccles. ix.

9. To bear in mind with praise or admiration; to celebrate. 1 Chron. xvi.

10. To bear in mind with favor, care, and regard for the safety or deliverance of any one. Ps. lxxiv. Gen. viii. Gen. xix.

11. To bear in mind with intent to reward or punish. 3 John 10. Jer. xxxi.

12. To bear in mind with confidence; to trust in. Ps. xx.

13. To bear in mind with the purpose of assisting or relieving. Gal. ii.

14. To bear in mind with reverence; to obey.

Remember thy Creator in the days of thy youth. Eccles. xii.

15. To bear in mind with regard; to keep as sacred; to observe.

Remember the sabbath day, to keep it holy. Ex. xx.

To remember mercy, is to exercise it. Hab. iii.

REMEM'BERED, *pp.* Kept in mind; recollected.

REMEM'BERER, *n.* One that remembers. *Wotton.*

REMEM'BERING, *ppr.* Having in mind.

REMEM'BRANCE, *n.* [Fr.] The retaining or having in mind an idea which had been present before, or an idea which had been previously received from an object when present, and which recurs to the mind afterwards without the presence of its object. Technically, *remembrance* differs from *reminiscence* and *recollection*, as the former implies that an idea occurs to the mind spontaneously, or without much mental exertion. The latter imply the power or the act of recalling ideas which do not spontaneously recur to the mind.

The righteous shall be in everlasting *remembrance.* Ps. cxii.

Remembrance is when the same idea recurs, without the operation of the like object on the external sensory. *Locke.*

2. Transmission of a fact from one to another.

Titan
Among the heav'ns th' immortal fact display'd,
Lest the *remembrance* of his grief should fail. *Addison.*

3. Account preserved; something to assist the memory.

Those proceedings and *remembrances* are in the Tower. *Hale.*

4. Memorial.

But in *remembrance* of so brave a deed,
A tomb and funeral honors I decreed. *Dryden.*

5. A token by which one is kept in the memory.

Keep this *remembrance* for thy Julia's sake. *Shak.*

6. Notice of something absent.

Let your *remembrance* still apply to Banquo. *Shak.*

7. Power of remembering; limit of time within which a fact can be remembered; as when we say, an event took place before our *remembrance*, or since our *remembrance.*

8. Honorable memory. [*Not in use.*] *Shak.*

9. Admonition. *Shak.*

10. Memorandum; a note to help the memory. *Chillingworth.*

REMEM'BRANCER, *n.* One that reminds, or revives the remembrance of any thing.

God is present in the consciences of good and bad; he is there a *remembrancer* to call our actions to mind. *Taylor.*

2. An officer in the exchequer of England, whose business is to record certain papers and proceedings, make out processes, &c.; a recorder. The officers bearing this name were formerly called *clerks of the remembrance.* *Encyc.*

REMEM'ORATE, *v.t.* [L. *rememoratus, rememoror.*]
To remember; to revive in the memory. [*Not in use.*]

REMEMORA'TION, *n.* Remembrance. [*Not in use.*]

REMER'CIE, } *v. t.* [Fr. *remercier.*] To
REMER'CY, } thank. [*Not in use.*] *Spenser.*

REM'IGRATE, *v. i.* [L. *remigro; re* and *migro*, to migrate.]
To remove back again to a former place or state; to return. [See *Migrate.*] *Boyle.*

REMIGRA'TION, *n.* Removal back again; a migration to a former place. *Hale.*

REMIND, *v. t.* [*re* and *mind.*] To put in mind; to bring to the remembrance of; as, to *remind* a person of his promise.

2. To bring to notice or consideration. The infirmities of old age *remind* us of our mortality.

REMINDED, *pp.* Put in mind.

REMINDING, *ppr.* Putting in mind; calling attention to.

REMINIS'CENCE, *n.* [Fr. from L. *reminiscens, reminiscor*, Gr. *μναομαι.* See *Memory.*]

1. That faculty of the mind by which ideas formerly received into it, but forgotten, are recalled or revived in the memory. *Encyc.*

2. Recollection; recovery of ideas that had escaped from the memory. *Hale.*

REMINISCEN'TIAL, *a.* Pertaining to reminiscence or recollection. *Brown.*

REMI'SE, *v. t.* *s* as *z.* [Fr. *remise*, from *remettre;* L. *remissus, remitto; re* and *mitto*, to send.]
To give or grant back; to release a claim; to resign or surrender by deed. A B hath *remised*, released, and forever quitclaimed to B C, all his right to the manor of Dale. *Blackstone.*

REMI'SED, *pp.* Released.

REMI'SING, *ppr.* Surrendering by deed.

REMISS', *a.* [Fr. *remis;* L. *remissus*, supra.]

1. Slack; dilatory; negligent; not performing duty or business; not complying with engagements at all, or not in due time; as to be *remiss* in attendance on official duties; *remiss* in payment of debts.

2. Slow; slack; languid. *Woodward.*

3. Not intense.

These nervous, bold; those languid and *remiss.* *Roscommon.*

REMISS'IBLE, *a.* That may be remitted or forgiven. *Feltham.*

REMIS'SION, *n.* [Fr. from L. *remissio*, from *remitto*, to send back.]

1. Abatement; relaxation; moderation; as the *remission* of extreme rigor. *Bacon.*

2. Abatement; diminution of intensity; as the *remission* of the sun's heat; the *remission* of cold; the *remission* of close study or of labor. *Woodward. Locke.*

3. Release; discharge or relinquishment of a claim or right; as the *remission* of a tax or duty. *Addison.*

4. In *medicine*, abatement; a temporary subsidence of the force or violence of a disease or of pain, as distinguished from *intermission*, in which the disease leaves the patient entirely for a time.

5. Forgiveness; pardon; that is, the giving up of the punishment due to a crime; as the *remission* of sins. Matt. xxvi. Heb. ix.

6. The act of sending back. [*Not in use.*]

REMISS'LY, *adv.* Carelessly; negligently; without close attention. *Hooker.*

2. Slowly; slackly; not vigorously; not with ardor. *Clarendon.*

REMISS'NESS, *n.* Slackness; slowness; carelessness; negligence; want of ardor or vigor; coldness; want of ardor; want of punctuality; want of attention to any business, duty or engagement in the proper time or with the requisite industry. *Denham. Arbuthnot.*

REMIT', *v. t.* [L. *remitto*, to send back; *re* and *mitto*, to send; Fr. *remettre;* It. *rimettere;* Sp. *remitir.*]

1. To relax, as intensity; to make less tense or violent.

So willingly doth God *remit* his ire. *Milton.*

2. To forgive; to surrender the right of punishing a crime; as, to *remit* punishment. *Dryden.*

3. To pardon, as a fault or crime.

Whose soever sins ye *remit*, they are *remitted* to them. John xx.

4. To give up; to resign.

In grievous and inhuman crimes, offenders should be *remitted* to their prince. *Hayward.*

5. To refer; as a clause that *remitted* all to the bishop's discretion. *Bacon.*

6. To send back.

The pris'ner was *remitted* to the guard. *Dryden.*

7. To transmit money, bills or other thing in payment for goods received. American merchants *remit* money, bills of exchange or some species of stock, in payment for British goods.

8. To restore.

In this case, the law *remits* him to his ancient and more certain right. *Blackstone.*

REMIT', *v. i.* To slacken; to become less intense or rigorous.

When our passions *remit*, the vehemence of our speech *remits* too. *Broome.*

So we say, cold or heat *remits.*

2. To abate in violence for a time, without intermission; as, a fever *remits* at a certain hour every day.

REMIT'MENT, *n.* The act of remitting to custody.

2. Forgiveness; pardon. *Milton.*

REMIT'TAL, *n.* A remitting; a giving up; surrender; as the *remittal* of the first fruits. *Swift.*

REMIT'TANCE, *n.* In *commerce*, the act of transmitting money, bills or the like, to a distant place, in return or payment for goods purchased.

2. The sum or thing remitted in payment. *Addison.*

REMIT'TED, *pp.* Relaxed; forgiven; pardoned; sent back; referred; given up; transmitted in payment.

REMIT'TER, *n.* One who remits, or makes remittance for payment.

2. In *law*, the restitution of a more ancient and certain right to a person who has right to lands, but is out of possession and hath afterwards the freehold cast upon him by some subsequent defective title, by virtue of which he enters. *Blackstone.*

3. One that pardons.

REM'NANT, *n.* [contracted from *remanent.* See *Remain.*]

1. Residue; that which is left after the separation, removal or destruction of a part.

The *remnant* that are left of the captivity. Neh. i.

2. That which remains after a part is done, performed, told or passed.

The *remnant* of my tale is of a length
To tire your patience. *Dryden.*

Where I may think the *remnant* of my thoughts. *Shak.*

REM'NANT, *a.* Remaining; yet left.

And quiet dedicate her *remnant* life
To the just duties of a humble wife. [*Little used.*] *Prior.*

REMOD'EL, *v. t.* [*re* and *model.*] To model or fashion anew.

REMOD'ELED, *pp.* Modeled anew.

REMOD'ELING, *ppr.* Modeling again.

REMŌLD, *v. t.* [*re* and *mold.*] To mold or shape anew.

REMŌLDED, *pp.* Molded again. *J. Barlow.*

REMŌLDING, *ppr.* Molding anew.

REMŌLTEN, *a.* or *pp.* [*re* and *molten*, from *melt.*] Melted again. *Bacon.*

REMON'STRANCE, *n.* [Fr. *remontrance.* See *Remonstrate.*]

1. Show; discovery. [*Not in use.*] *Shak.*
2. Expostulation; strong representation of reasons against a measure, either public or private, and when addressed to a public body, a prince or magistrate, it may be accompanied with a petition or supplication for the removal or prevention of some evil or inconvenience. A party aggrieved presents a *remonstrance* to the legislature.
3. Pressing suggestions in opposition to a measure or act; as the *remonstrances* of conscience or of justice. *Rogers.*
4. Expostulatory counsel or advice; reproof. *Encyc.*

REMON'STRANT, *a.* Expostulatory; urging strong reasons against an act.

REMON'STRANT, *n.* One who remonstrates. The appellation of *remonstrants* is given to the Arminians who remonstrated against the decisions of the Synod of Dort, in 1618. *Encyc.*

REMON'STRATE, *v. i.* [L. *remonstro; re* and *monstro*, to show; Fr. *remontrer.* See *Muster.*]

1. To exhibit or present strong reasons against an act, measure or any course of proceedings; to expostulate. Men *remonstrate* by verbal argument, or by a written exposition of reasons.
2. To suggest urgent reasons in opposition to a measure. Conscience *remonstrates* against a profligate life.

REMON'STRATE, *v. t.* To show by a strong representation of reasons.

REMON'STRATING, *ppr.* Urging strong reasons against a measure.

REMONSTRA'TION, *n.* The act of remonstrating. [*Little used.*]

REMON'STRATOR, *n.* One who remonstrates.

REM'ORA, *n.* [L. from *re* and *moror*, to delay.]

1. Delay; obstacle; hinderance. [*Not in use.*]
2. The sucking fish, a species of Echeneis, which is said to attach itself to the bottom or side of a ship and retard its motion.

REM'ORATE, *v. t.* [L. *remoror.*] To hinder; to delay. [*Not in use.*]

REMORD', *v. t.* [L. *remordeo; re* and *mordeo*, to gnaw.]

To rebuke; to excite to remorse. [*Not in use.*] *Skelton.*

REMORD', *v. i.* To feel remorse. [*Not in use.*] *Elyot.*

REMORD'ENCY, *n.* Compunction; remorse. *Killingbeck*

REMORSE, *n. remors'.* [L. *remorsus*, from *remordeo.*]

1. The keen pain or anguish excited by a sense of guilt; compunction of conscience for a crime committed. *Clarendon.*
2. Sympathetic sorrow; pity; compassion.

Curse on th' unpard'ning prince, whom tears can draw
To no *remorse.* *Dryden.*

[*This sense is nearly or quite obsolete.*]

REMORS'ED, *a.* Feeling remorse or compunction. [*Not used.*] *Bp. Hall.*

REMORSEFUL, *a. remors'ful.* Full of remorse. *Bp. Hall.*

2. Compassionate; feeling tenderly. [*Not in use.*] *Shak.*
3. Pitiable. [*Not in use.*] *Chapman.*

REMORSELESS, *a. remors'less.* Unpitying; cruel; insensible to distress; as the *remorseless* deep. *Milton.*

Remorseless adversaries. *South.*

REMORSELESSLY, *adv. remors'lessly.* Without remorse. *South.*

REMORSELESSNESS, *n. remors'lessness.* Savage cruelty; insensibility to distress. *Beaum.*

REMO'TE, *a.* [L. *remotus, removeo; re* and *moveo*, to move.]

1. Distant in place; not near; as a *remote* country; a *remote* people.

Give me a life *remote* from guilty courts. *Granville.*

2. Distant in time, past or future; as *remote* antiquity. Every man is apt to think the time of his dissolution to be *remote.*
3. Distant; not immediate.

It is not all *remote* and even apparent good that affects us. *Locke.*

4. Distant; primary; not proximate; as the *remote* causes of a disease.
5. Alien; foreign; not agreeing with; as a proposition *remote* from reason. *Locke.*
6. Abstracted; as the mind placed by thought amongst or *remote* from all bodies. *Locke.*
7. Distant in consanguinity or affinity; as a *remote* kinsman.
8. Slight; inconsiderable; as a *remote* analogy between cases; a *remote* resemblance in form or color.

REMO'TELY, *adv.* At a distance in space or time; not nearly.

2. At a distance in consanguinity or affinity.
3. Slightly; in a small degree; as, to be *remotely* affected by an event.

REMO'TENESS, *n.* State of being distant in space or time; distance; as the *remoteness* of a kingdom or of a star; the *remoteness* of the deluge from our age; the *remoteness* of a future event, of an evil or of success.

2. Distance in consanguinity or affinity.
3. Distance in operation or efficiency; as the *remoteness* of causes.
4. Slightness; smallness; as *remoteness* of resemblance.

REMO'TION, *n.* The act of removing; the state of being removed to a distance. [*Little used.*] *Shak. Brown.*

REMOUNT', *v. t.* [Fr. *remonter; re* and *monter.*] To mount again; as, to *remount* a horse.

REMOUNT', *v. i.* To mount again; to reascend. *Woodward.*

REMÖVABIL'ITY, *n.* The capacity of being removable from an office or station; capacity of being displaced.

REMÖVABLE, *a.* [from *remove.*] That may be removed from an office or station.

Such curate is *removable* at the pleasure of the rector of the mother church. *Ayliffe.*

2. That may be removed from one place to another.

REMÖVAL, *n.* The act of moving from one place to another for residence; as the *removal* of a family.

2. The act of displacing from an office or post.
3. The act of curing or putting away; as the *removal* of a disease.
4. The state of being removed; change of place. *Locke.*
5. The act of putting an end to; as the *removal* of a grievance.

REMÖVE, *v. t.* [L. *removeo; re* and *moveo*, to move; Fr. *remuer;* It. *rimuovere;* Sp. *remover.*]

1. To cause to change place; to put from its place in any manner; as, to *remove* a building.

Thou shalt not *remove* thy neighbor's landmark. Deut. xix.

2. To displace from an office.
3. To take or put away in any manner; to cause to leave a person or thing; to banish or destroy; as, to *remove* a disease or complaint.

Remove sorrow from thine heart. Eccles. xi.

4. To carry from one court to another; as, to *remove* a cause or suit by appeal.
5. To take from the present state of being; as, to *remove* one by death.

REMÖVE, *v. i.* To change place in any manner.

2. To go from one place to another. *Prior.*
3. To change the place of residence; as, to *remove* from New York to Philadelphia.

[*Note.* The verb *remove*, in most of its applications, is synonymous with *move*, but not in all. Thus we do not apply *remove* to a mere change of posture, without a change of place or the seat of a thing. A man *moves* his head when he turns it, or his finger when he bends it, but he does not *remove* it. *Remove* usually or always denotes a change of place in a body, but we never apply it to a regular continued course or motion. We never say, the wind or water or a ship *removes* at a certain rate by the hour; but we say, a ship *was removed* from one place in a harbor to another. *Move* is a generic term, including the sense of *remove*, which is more generally applied to a change from one station or permanent position, stand or seat, to another station.]

REMÖVE, *n.* Change of place. *Chapman.*

2. Translation of one to the place of another. *Shak.*
3. State of being removed. *Locke.*
4. Act of moving a man in chess or other game.
5. Departure; a going away. *Waller.*
6. The act of changing place; removal. *Bacon.*
7. A step in any scale of gradation.

A freeholder is but one *remove* from a legislator. *Addison.*

8. Any indefinite distance; as a small or great *remove.* *Rogers.*
9. The act of putting a horse's shoes on different feet. *Swift.*
10. A dish to be changed while the rest of the course remains. *Johnson.*

11. Susceptibility of being removed. [*Not in use.*] *Glanville.*

REMÖVED, *pp.* Changed in place; carried to a distance; displaced from office; placed far off.

2. *a.* Remote; separate from others. *Shak.*

REMÖVEDNESS, *n.* State of being removed; remoteness. *Shak.*

REMÖVER, *n.* One that removes; as a *remover* of landmarks. *Bacon.*

REMÖVING, *ppr.* Changing place; carrying or going from one place to another; displacing; banishing.

REMUNERABIL′ITY, *n.* The capacity of being rewarded.

REMU′NERABLE, *a.* [from *remunerate.*] That may be rewarded; fit or proper to be recompensed.

REMU′NERATE, *v. t.* [L. *remunero; re* and *munero*, from *munus*, a gift.]
To reward; to recompense; to requite; in a good sense; to pay an equivalent to for any service, loss, expense or other sacrifice; as, to *remunerate* the troops of an army for their services and sufferings; to *remunerate* men for labor. The pious sufferer in this life will be *remunerated* in the life to come.

REMU′NERATED, *pp.* Rewarded; compensated.

REMU′NERATING, *ppr.* Rewarding; recompensing.

REMUNERA′TION, *n.* Reward; recompense; the act of paying an equivalent for services, loss or sacrifices. *Shak.*

2. The equivalent given for services, loss or sufferings.

REMU′NERATIVE, *a.* Exercised in rewarding; that bestows rewards; as *remunerative* justice. *Boyle.*

REMU′NERATORY, *a.* Affording recompense; rewarding. *Johnson.*

REMUR′MUR, *v. t.* [L. *remurmuro; re* and *murmuro.*]
To utter back in murmurs; to return in murmurs; to repeat in low hoarse sounds. *Dryden.*

> The trembling trees in every plain and wood,
> Her fate *remurmur* to the silver flood. *Pope.*

REMUR′MUR, *v. i.* To murmur back; to return or echo in low rumbling sounds.

> The realms of Mars *remurmur'd* all around. *Dryden.*

REMUR′MURED, *pp.* Uttered back in murmurs.

REMUR′MURING, *ppr.* Uttering back in low sounds.

RE′NAL, *a.* [L. *renalis*, from *renes*, the kidneys.]
Pertaining to the kidneys or reins; as the *renal* arteries.

REN′ARD, *n.* [Fr.; G. *reineke.*] A fox; a name used in fables, but not in common discourse. *Dryden.*

RENAS′CENCY, *n.* The state of springing or being produced again. *Brown.*

RENAS′CENT, *a.* [L. *renascens, renascor; re* and *nascor*, to be born.]
Springing or rising into being again; reproduced.

RENAS′CIBLE, *a.* That may be reproduced; that may spring again into being.

RENAV′IGATE, *v. t.* [*re* and *navigate.*] To navigate again; as, to *renavigate* the Pacific ocean.

RENAV′IGATED, *pp.* Navigated again; sailed over anew.

RENAV′IGATING, *ppr.* Navigating again.

RENCOUN′TER, *n.* [Fr. *rencontre; re* and *encontre; en* and *contre*, against.] Literally, a meeting of two bodies. Hence,

1. A meeting in opposition or contest.

> The jostling chiefs in rude *rencounter* join. *Glanville.*

2. A casual combat; a sudden contest or fight without premeditation; as between individuals or small parties.

3. A casual action; an engagement between armies or fleets.

> The confederates should—outnumber the enemy in all *rencounters* and engagements. *Addison.*

4. Any combat, action or engagement.

RENCOUN′TER, *v. t.* To meet unexpectedly without enmity or hostility. [This use is found in some recent publications, but is not common.]

2. To attack hand to hand. *Spenser.*

RENCOUN′TER, *v. i.* To meet an enemy unexpectedly.

2. To clash; to come in collision.

3. To skirmish with another.

4. To fight hand to hand. *Johnson.*

REND, *v. t.* pret. and pp. *rent.* [Sax. *rendan, hrendan;* Ir. *rannam, rannaim;* W. *rhanu;* Arm. *ranna*, to divide, and *crenna*, to abridge, whence Eng. *cranny*, L. *crena.* Qu. L. *cerno*, Gr. κρινω. Class Rn. No. 4. 8. 13. 16.]

1. To separate any substance into parts with force or sudden violence; to tear asunder; to split; as, powder *rends* a rock in blasting; lightning *rends* an oak.

> An empire from its old foundation *rent.* *Dryden.*

> I *rend* my tresses, and my breast I wound. *Pope.*

> Neither *rend* your clothes, lest ye die. Lev. x.

2. To separate or part with violence.

> I will surely *rend* the kingdom from thee. 1 Kings xi.

To rend the heart, in Scripture, to have bitter sorrow for sin. Joel ii.

To rend the heavens, to appear in majesty. Is. lxiv.

Rend differs somewhat from *lacerate.* We never say, to *lacerate* a rock or a kingdom, when we mean to express splitting or division. *Lacerate* is properly applicable to the tearing off of small pieces of a thing, as to *lacerate* the body with a whip or scourge; or to the tearing of the flesh or other thing without entire separation.

REND′ER, *n.* [from *rend.*] One that tears by violence.

REN′DER, *v. t.* [Fr. *rendre;* It. *rendere;* Sp. *rendir;* Port. *render.* This is probably the L. *reddo*, with *n* casually inserted.]

1. To return; to pay back.

> See that none *render* evil for evil to any man. 1 Thess. v.

2. To inflict, as a retribution.

> I will *render* vengeance to my enemies. Deut. xxxii.

3. To give on demand; to give; to assign.

> The sluggard is wiser in his own conceit, than seven men that can *render* a reason. Prov. xxvi.

4. To make or cause to be, by some influence upon a thing, or by some change; as, to *render* a person more safe or more unsafe; to *render* him solicitous or cautious; to *render* a fortress more secure or impregnable; to *render* a ferocious animal more mild and tractable.

5. To translate, as from one language into another; as, to *render* Latin into English. We say, to *render* a word, a sentence, a book, or an author into a different language. *Locke.*

6. To surrender; to yield or give up the command or possession of; as, to *render* one's self to his enemies. *K. Charles. Clarendon.*
[Less used than *surrender.*]

7. To afford; to give for use or benefit. Washington *rendered* great service to his country.

8. To represent; to exhibit.

> He did *render* him the most unnatural
> That liv'd amongst men. [*Not in use.*] *Shak.*

To render back, to return; to restore.

REN′DER, *n.* A surrender; a giving up. *Shak.*

2. A return; a payment of rent.

> In those early times, the king's household was supported by specific *renders* of corn and other victuals from the tenants of the demains. *Blackstone.*

3. An account given. *Shak.*

REN′DERABLE, *a.* That may be rendered. *Sherwood.*

REN′DERED, *pp.* Returned; paid back; given; assigned; made; translated; surrendered; afforded.

REN′DERING, *ppr.* Returning; giving back; assigning; making; translating; surrendering; affording.

REN′DERING, *n.* Version; translation. *Lowth.*

REN′DEZVOUS, *n.* [Fr. *rendez vous*, render yourselves, repair to a place. This word is anglicized, and may well be pronounced as an English word.]

1. A place appointed for the assembling of troops, or the place where they assemble; or the port or place where ships are ordered to join company.

2. A place of meeting, or a sign that draws men together. [*Rarely used.*] *Bacon.*

3. An assembly; a meeting. [*Rarely used.*]

REN′DEZVOUS, *v. i.* To assemble at a particular place, as troops.

> The place where the Gauls and Bruti had *rendezvoused.* *Alfred's Orosius, Trans.* *B. Trumbull. Hook, Rom. Hist.*

REN′DEZVOUS, *v. t.* To assemble or bring together at a certain place. *Echard.*

REN′DEZVOUSING, *ppr.* Assembling at a particular place.

REN′DIBLE, *a.* That may be yielded or surrendered.

2. That may be translated. [*Little used in either sense.*] *Howell.*

RENDI′′TION, *n.* [from *render.*] The act of yielding possession; surrender. *Fairfax.*

2. Translation. *South.*

REN′EGADE, RENEGA′DO, } *n.* [Sp. Port. *renegado*, from *renegar*, to deny; L. *re* and *nego*, to deny; It. *rinegato;* Fr. *renégat;* primarily an *apostate.*]

1. An apostate from the faith. *Addison.*

2. One who deserts to an enemy; a deserter. *Arbuthnot.*

3. A vagabond. [*This is the sense in which this word is mostly used in popular language.*]

RENE'GE, *v. t.* [L. *renego.*] To deny; to disown. *Obs.* *Shak.*

RENE'GE, *v. i.* To deny. *Obs.* *Shak.*

RENERVE, *v. t. renerv'.* [*re* and *nerve.*] To nerve again; to give new vigor to. *J. Barlow.*

RENERV'ED, *pp.* Nerved anew.

RENERV'ING, *ppr.* Giving new vigor to.

RENEW', *v. t.* [L. *renovo; re* and *novo*, or *re* and *new.*]

1. To renovate; to restore to a former state, or to a good state, after decay or depravation; to rebuild; to repair.

Asa *renewed* the altar of the Lord. 2 Chron. xv.

2. To re-establish; to confirm.

Let us go to Gilgal and *renew* the kingdom there. 1 Sam. xi.

3. To make again; as, to *renew* a treaty or covenant.

4. To repeat; as, to *renew* expressions of friendship; to *renew* a promise; to *renew* an attempt.

5. To revive; as, to *renew* the glories of an ancestor or of a former age. *Shak.*

6. To begin again.

The last great age *renews* its finish'd course. *Dryden.*

7. To make new; to make fresh or vigorous; as, to *renew* youth; to *renew* strength; to *renew* the face of the earth. Ps. ciii. Is. xl. Ps. civ.

8. In *theology*, to make new; to renovate; to transform; to change from natural enmity to the love of God and his law; to implant holy affections in the heart; to regenerate.

Be ye transformed by the *renewing* of your mind. Rom. xii. Eph. iv.

RENEW'ABLE, *a.* That may be renewed; as a lease *renewable* at pleasure. *Swift.*

RENEW'AL, *n.* The act of renewing; the act of forming anew; as the *renewal* of a treaty.

2. Renovation; regeneration.

3. Revival; restoration to a former or to a good state.

RENEW'ED, *pp.* Made new again; repaired; re-established; repeated; revived; renovated; regenerated.

RENEW'EDNESS, *n.* State of being renewed. *Hammond.*

RENEW'ER, *n.* One who renews. *Sherwood.*

RENEW'ING, *ppr.* Making new again; repairing; re-establishing; repeating; reviving; renovating.

2. *a.* Tending or adapted to renovate.

RENEW'ING, *n.* The act of making new; renewal.

REN'IFORM, *a.* [L. *renes*, the kidneys, and *form.*]

Having the form or shape of the kidneys. *Kirwan.*

REN'ITENCE, } *n.* [L. *renitens, renitor*, to
REN'ITENCY, } resist; *re* and *nitor*, to struggle or strive.]

1. The resistance of a body to pressure; the effort of matter to resume the place or form from which it has been driven by the impulse of other matter; the effect of elasticity. *Quincy.*

2. Moral resistance; reluctance.

We find a *renitency* in ourselves to ascribe life and irritability to the cold and motionless fibers of plants. *Darwin.*

REN'ITENT, *a.* Resisting pressure or the effect of it; acting against impulse by elastic force. *Ray.*

REN'NET, *n.* [G. *rinnen*, to run, to curdle; D. *runnen, ronnen*, to curdle or coagulate; Sax. *gerunnen*, coagulated.]

The concreted milk found in the stomach of a sucking quadruped, particularly of the calf. It is also written *runnet*, and this is the preferable orthography. *Encyc.*

REN'NET, } *n.* A kind of apple.
REN'NETING, } *Mortimer.*

RENOUNCE, *v. t. renouns'.* [Fr. *renoncer;* L. *renuncio; re* and *nuncio*, to declare, from the root of *nomen*, name.]

1. To disown; to disclaim; to reject; as a title or claim; to refuse to own or acknowledge as belonging to; as, to *renounce* a title to land or a claim to reward; to *renounce* all pretensions to applause.

2. To deny; to cast off; to reject; to disclaim; as an obligation or duty; as, to *renounce* allegiance.

3. To cast off or reject, as a connection or possession; to forsake; as, to *renounce* the world and all its cares. *Shak.*

We have *renounced* the hidden things of dishonesty. 2 Cor. iv.

RENOUNCE, *v. i. renouns'.* To declare a renunciation.

He of my sons who fails to make it good,
By one rebellious act *renounces* to my blood.
[*Not in use.*] *Dryden.*

2. In cards, not to follow suit, when the person has a card of the same sort.

RENOUNCE, *n. renouns'.* The declining to follow suit, when it can be done.

RENOUN'CED, *pp.* Disowned; denied; rejected; disclaimed.

RENOUNCEMENT, *n. renouns'ment.* The act of disclaiming or rejecting; renunciation. *Shak.*

RENOUN'CER, *n.* One who disowns or disclaims.

RENOUN'CING, *ppr.* Disowning; disclaiming; rejecting.

RENOUN'CING, *n.* The act of disowning, disclaiming, denying or rejecting.

REN'OVATE, *v. t.* [L. *renovo; re* and *novo*, to make new; *novus*, new.]

To renew; to restore to the first state, or to a good state, after decay, destruction or depravation. It is synonymous with *renew*, except in its fourth definition, supra.

REN'OVATED, *pp.* Renewed; made new, fresh or vigorous.

REN'OVATING, *ppr.* Renewing.

RENOVA'TION, *n.* [Fr. from L. *renovatio.*]

1. The act of renewing; a making new after decay, destruction or depravation; renewal; as the *renovation* of the heart by grace.

There is something inexpressibly pleasing in the annual *renovation* of the world. *Rambler.*

2. A state of being renewed. *Bacon.* *Milton.*

RENOWN', *n.* [Fr. *renommée; re* and *nommer*, to name.]

Fame; celebrity; exalted reputation derived from the extensive praise of great achievments or accomplishments.

Giants of old, men of *renown.* Gen. vi. Num. xvi.

RENOWN', *v. t.* To make famous.

Soft elocution does thy style *renown.* *Dryden.*

A bard whom pilfer'd pastorals *renown.* *Pope.*

[*This verb is nearly or quite obsolete.*]

RENOWN'ED, *a.* Famous; celebrated for great and heroic achievments, for distinguished qualities or for grandeur; eminent; as *renowned* men; a *renowned* king; a *renowned* city. *Milton.* *Dryden.*

RENOWN'EDLY, *adv.* With fame or celebrity.

RENOWN'LESS, *a.* Without renown; inglorious.

RENT, *pp.* of *rend.* Torn asunder; split or burst by violence; torn.

RENT, *n.* [from *rend.*] A fissure; a break or breach made by force; as a *rent* made in the earth, in a rock or in a garment.

2. A schism; a separation; as a *rent* in the church. *White.*

RENT, *v. t.* To tear. [See *Rend.*]

RENT, *v. i.* To rant. [*Not in use.*] *Hudibras.*

RENT, *n.* [Fr. *rente*, from *rendre;* It. *rendita;* Sp. *renta;* D. Dan. G. *rente;* Sw. *rånta.*]

A sum of money, or a certain amount of other valuable thing, issuing yearly from lands or tenements; a compensation or return, in the nature of an acknowledgment, for the possession of a corporeal inheritance. *Blackstone.*

Rents, at common law, are of three kinds; *rent-service*, *rent-charge*, and *rent-seck.* *Rent-service* is when some corporal service is incident to it, as by fealty and a sum of money; *rent-charge* is when the owner of the rent has no future interest or reversion expectant in the land, but the rent is reserved in the deed by a clause of distress for rent in arrear; *rent-seck*, dry rent, is rent reserved by deed, but without any clause of distress. There are also *rents of assize*, certain established rents of freeholders and copy-holders of manors, which cannot be varied; called also *quit-rents.* These when payable in silver, are called *white rents*, in contradistinction to rents reserved in work or the baser metals, called *black rents*, or *black mail.* *Rack-rent* is a rent of the full value of the tenement, or near it. A *fee farm rent* is a rent-charge issuing out of an estate in fee, of at least one fourth of the value of the lands at the time of its reservation. *Blackstone.*

RENT, *v. t.* To lease; to grant the possession and enjoyment of lands or tenements for a consideration in the nature of rent. The owner of an estate or house *rents* it to a tenant for a term of years.

2. To take and hold by lease the possession of land or a tenement, for a consideration in the nature of rent. The tenant *rents* his estate for a year.

RENT, *v. i.* To be leased, or let for rent; as, an estate or a tenement *rents* for five hundred dollars a year.

RENT'ABLE, *a.* That may be rented.

RENT'AGE, *n.* Rent. [*Not used.*]

RENT'AL, *n.* A schedule or account of rents.

RENT'ED, *pp.* Leased on rent.

RENT'ER, *n.* One who leases an estate; more generally, the lessee or tenant who takes an estate or tenement on rent.

RENT'ER, *v. t.* [Fr. *rentraire; L. retraho, retrahere; re* and *traho*, to draw.]

1. To fine-draw; to sew together the edges of two pieces of cloth without doubling them, so that the seam is scarcely visible.
2. In *tapestry*, to work new warp into a piece of damaged tapestry, and on this to restore the original pattern or design. *Encyc.*
3. To sew up artfully, as a rent.

REN'TERED, *pp.* Fine-drawn; sewed artfully together.

REN'TERER, *n.* A fine-drawer.

REN'TERING, *ppr.* Fine-drawing; sewing artfully together.

RENT'ING, *ppr.* Leasing on rent; taking on rent.

RENT-ROLL, *n.* [*rent* and *roll.*] A rental; a list or account of rents or income.

RENUNCIA'TION, *n.* [L. *renunciatio.*] The act of renouncing; a disowning; rejection. [See *Renounce.*] *Taylor.*

RENVERSE, *v. t. renvers'.* [Fr. *renverser.*] To reverse. [*Not used.*] *Spenser.*

RENVERSE, *a. renvers'.* In *heraldry*, inverted; set with the head downward or contrary to the natural posture. *Encyc.*

RENVERSEMENT, *n. renvers'ment.* The act of reversing. [*Not in use.*] *Stukely.*

REOBTA'IN, *v. t.* [*re* and *obtain.*] To obtain again.

REOBTA'INABLE, *a.* That may be obtained again. *Sherwood.*

REOBTA'INED, *pp.* Obtained again.

REOBTA'INING, *ppr.* Obtaining again.

REOPPO'SE, *v. t. s* as *z.* To oppose again.

REORDA'IN, *v. t.* [*re* and *ordain; Fr. reordonner.*]

To ordain again, as when the first ordination is defective.

REORDA'INED, *pp.* Ordained again.

REORDA'INING, *ppr.* Ordaining again.

REORDINA'TION, *n.* A second ordination. *Atterbury.*

REORGANIZA'TION, *n.* The act of organizing anew; as repeated *reorganization* of the troops. *Marshall.*

REOR'GANIZE, *v. t.* [*re* and *organize.*] To organize anew; to reduce again to a regular body, or to a system; as, to *reorganize* a society or an army.

REOR'GANIZED, *pp.* Organized anew.

REOR'GANIZING, *ppr.* Organizing anew.

REPAC'IFIED, *pp.* Pacified or appeased again.

REPAC'IFY, *v. t.* [*re* and *pacify.*] To pacify again.

REPAC'IFYING, *ppr.* Pacifying again.

REPACK', *v. t.* [*re* and *pack.*] To pack a second time; as, to *repack* beef or pork.

REPACK'ED, *pp.* Packed again.

REPACK'ER, *n.* One that repacks.

REPACK'ING, *ppr.* Packing anew.

REPA'ID, *pp.* of *repay.* Paid back.

REPA'IR, *v. t.* [Fr. *reparer; L. reparo; re* and *paro*, to prepare. See *Pare.*]

1. To restore to a sound or good state after decay, injury, dilapidation or partial destruction; as, to *repair* a house, a wall or a ship; to *repair* roads and bridges. Temperance and diet may *repair* a broken or enfeebled constitution. Food *repairs* the daily waste of the body.
2. To rebuild a part decayed or destroyed; to fill up; as, to *repair* a breach.
3. To make amends, as for an injury, by an equivalent; to indemnify for; as, to *repair* a loss or damage.

REPA'IR, *n.* Restoration to a sound or good state after decay, waste, injury or partial destruction; supply of loss; reparation; as, materials are collected for the *repair* of a church or a city.

REPA'IR, *v. i.* [Fr. *repairer.*] To go to; to betake one's self; to resort; as, to *repair* to a sanctuary for safety.

> Go, mount the winds and to the shades *repair.* *Pope.*

REPA'IR, *n.* The act of betaking one's self to any place; a resorting; abode. *Dryden.*

REPA'IRABLE, *a.* That may be repaired; reparable.

REPA'IRED, *pp.* Restored to a good or sound state; rebuilt; made good.

REPA'IRER, *n.* One who repairs, restores or makes amends; as the *repairer* of decay. *Dryden.*

REPA'IRING, *ppr.* Restoring to a sound state; rebuilding; making amends for loss or injury.

REPAND', *a.* [L. *repandus.*] In *botany*, a repand leaf is one, the rim of which is terminated by angles having sinuses between them, inscribed in the segment of a circle; or which has a bending or waved margin, without any angles; or which is bordered with numerous minute angles and small segments of circles alternately. *Martyn. Lee. Smith.*

REPAND'OUS, *a.* [supra.] Bent upwards; convexedly crooked. *Brown.*

REP'ARABLE, *a.* [Fr. from L. *reparabilis.* See *Repair.*]

1. That may be repaired or restored to a sound or good state; as, a house or wall is not *reparable.*
2. That may be retrieved or made good; as, the loss is *reparable.*
3. That may be supplied by an equivalent; as a *reparable* injury.

REP'ARABLY, *adv.* In a manner admitting of restoration to a good state, or of amends, supply or indemnification.

REPARA'TION, *n.* The act of repairing; restoration to soundness or a good state; as the *reparation* of a bridge or of a highway.

2. Supply of what is wasted; as the *reparation* of decaying health or strength after disease or exhaustion.
3. Amends; indemnification for loss or damage. A loss may be too great for *reparation.*
4. Amends; satisfaction for injury.

> I am sensible of the scandal I have given by my loose writings, and make what *reparation* I am able. *Dryden.*

REPAR'ATIVE, *a.* That repairs; restoring to a sound or good state; that amends defect or makes good. *Taylor.*

REPAR'ATIVE, *n.* That which restores to a good state; that which makes amends. *Wotton. Kettlewell.*

REPARTEE', *n.* [Fr. *repartie*, from *repartir*, to divide, to share, to reply; *re* and *partir*, to divide.]

A smart, ready and witty reply.

> Cupid was as bad as he;
> Hear but the youngster's *repartee.* *Prior.*

REPARTEE', *v. i.* To make smart and witty replies. *Prior.*

REP'ASS, *v. t.* [Fr. *repasser;* It. *ripassare; re* and *pass.*]

To pass again; to pass or travel back; as, to *repass* a bridge or a river; to *repass* the sea. *Pope.*

REP'ASS, *v. i.* To pass or go back; to move back; as troops passing and *repassing* before our eyes.

REP'ASSED, *pp.* Passed or traveled back.

REP'ASSING, *ppr.* Passing back.

REP'AST, *n.* [Fr. *repas*, from *repaître;* L. *re* and *pasco*, to feed.]

1. The act of taking food; or the food taken; a meal.

> From dance to sweet *repast* they turn. *Milton.*
>
> A *repast* without luxury. *Johnson.*

2. Food; victuals.

> Go, and get me some *repast.* *Shak.*

REP'AST, *v. t.* To feed; to feast. *Shak.*

REP'ASTURE, *n.* Food; entertainment. [*Not in use.*] *Shak.*

REPA'Y, *v. t.* [Fr. *repayer; re* and *pay.*]

1. To pay back; to refund; as, to *repay* money borrowed or advanced.
2. To make return or requital; in a good or bad sense; as, to *repay* kindness; to *repay* an injury.

> Benefits which cannot be *repaid*—are not commonly found to increase affection. *Rambler.*

3. To recompense, as for a loss. *Milton.*
4. To compensate; as false honor *repaid* in contempt. *Bacon.*

REPA'YABLE, *a.* That is to be repaid or refunded; as money lent, *repayable* at the end of sixty days.

REPA'YING, *ppr.* Paying back; compensating; requiting.

REPA'YMENT, *n.* The act of paying back; reimbursement.

2. The money or other thing repaid.

REPE'AL, *v. t.* [Fr. *rappeler*, to recall; *re* and *appeler*, L. *appello; ad* and *pello.*]

1. To recall. [*Obsolete as it respects persons.*] *Shak.*
2. To recall, as a deed, will, law or statute; to revoke; to abrogate by an authoritative act, or by the same power that made or enacted; as, the legislature may *repeal* at one session, a law enacted at a preceding one.

REPE'AL, *n.* Recall from exile. [*Not in use.*] *Shak.*

2. Revocation; abrogation; as the *repeal* of a statute.

REPEALABIL'ITY, *n.* The quality of being repealable.

REPEA'LABLE, *a.* Capable of being repealed; revocable by the same power that enacted. It is held as a sound principle, that charters or grants which vest rights in individuals or corporations, are not *repealable* without the consent of the grantees, unless a clause reserving the right is inserted in the act.

REPE'ALED, *pp.* Revoked; abrogated.

REPE'ALER, *n.* One that repeals.

REPE'ALING, *ppr.* Revoking; abrogating.

REPE'AT, *v. t.* [Fr. *repeter;* It. *ripetere;* Sp. *repetir;* L. *repeto; re* and *peto,* to make at or drive towards. This verb ought to be written *repete,* in analogy with *compete,* and with *repetition.*]

1. To do, make, attempt or utter again; to iterate; as, to *repeat* an action; to *repeat* an attempt or exertion; to *repeat* a word or discourse; to *repeat* a song; to *repeat* an argument.

2. To try again.

I the danger will *repeat.* *Dryden.*

3. To recite; to rehearse.

He *repeated* some lines of Virgil. *Waller.*

To repeat signals, in the navy, is to make the same signal which the admiral or commander has made, or to make a signal again. *Mar. Dict.*

REPE'AT, *n.* In *music,* a mark directing a part to be repeated in performance.

2. Repetition.

REPE'ATED, *pp.* Done, attempted or spoken again; recited.

REPE'ATEDLY, *adv.* More than once; again and again, indefinitely. He has been *repeatedly* warned of his danger.

REPE'ATER, *n.* One that repeats; one that recites or rehearses.

2. A watch that strikes the hours at will, by the compression of a spring.

REPE'ATING, *ppr.* Doing or uttering again.

REPEDA'TION, *n.* [Low L. *repedo; re* and *pes,* the foot.] A stepping or going back. [*Not in use.*] *More.*

REPEL', *v. t.* [L. *repello; re* and *pello,* to drive.]

1. To drive back; to force to return; to check advance; as, to *repel* an enemy or an assailant.

Hippomedon *repell'd* the hostile tide. *Pope.*
And virtue may *repel,* though not invade. *Dryden.*

2. To resist; to oppose; as, to *repel* an argument.

REPEL', *v. i.* To act with force in opposition to force impressed. Electricity sometimes attracts and sometimes *repels.*

2. In *medicine,* to check an afflux to a part of the body.

REPEL'LED, *pp.* Driven back; resisted.

REPEL'LENCY, *n.* The principle of repulsion; the quality of a substance which expands or separates particles and enlarges the volume; as the *repellency* of heat. *Black.*

2. The quality that repels, drives back or resists approach; as the *repellency* of the electric fluid.

3. Repulsive quality. *Forster.*

REPEL'LENT, *a.* Driving back; able or tending to repel.

REPEL'LENT, *n.* In *medicine,* a medicine which drives back morbid humors into the mass of the blood, from which they were unduly secreted; or which prevents such an afflux of fluid to a part, as would raise it to a tumor; a discutient. *Encyc. Quincy. Parr.*

REPEL'LER, *n.* He or that which repels.

REPEL'LING, *ppr.* Driving back; resisting advance or approach effectually.

RE'PENT, *a.* [L. *repo,* to creep.] Creeping; as a *repent* root.

REPENT', *v. i.* [Fr. *repentir;* It. *pentire, pentirsi;* Sp. *arrepentirse;* L. *re* and *pœniteo,* from *pœna,* pain, Gr. ποινη. See *Pain.*]

1. To feel pain, sorrow or regret for something done or spoken; as, to *repent* that we have lost much time in idleness or sensual pleasure; to *repent* that we have injured or wounded the feelings of a friend. A person *repents* only of what he himself has done or said.

2. To express sorrow for something past.

Enobarbus did before thy face *repent.* *Shak.*

3. To change the mind in consequence of the inconvenience or injury done by past conduct.

Lest peradventure the people *repent* when they see war, and they return. Ex. xiii.

4. *Applied to the Supreme Being,* to change the course of providential dealings. Gen. vi. Ps. cvi.

5. In *theology,* to sorrow or be pained for sin, as a violation of God's holy law, a dishonor to his character and government, and the foulest ingratitude to a Being of infinite benevolence.

Except ye *repent,* ye shall all likewise perish. Luke xiii. Acts iii.

REPENT', *v. t.* To remember with sorrow; as, to *repent* rash words; to *repent* an injury done to a neighbor; to *repent* follies and vices. [See *Repentance.*]

2. With the reciprocal pronoun. [Fr. *se repentir.*]

No man *repented him* of his wickedness. Jer. viii.

[*This form of expression is now obsolete.*]

REPENT'ANCE, *n.* [Fr.] Sorrow for any thing done or said; the pain or grief which a person experiences in consequence of the injury or inconvenience produced by his own conduct.

2. In *theology,* the pain, regret or affliction which a person feels on account of his past conduct, because it exposes him to punishment. This sorrow proceeding merely from the fear of punishment, is called *legal repentance,* as being excited by the terrors of legal penalties, and it may exist without an amendment of life.

3. Real penitence; sorrow or deep contrition for sin, as an offense and dishonor to God, a violation of his holy law, and the basest ingratitude towards a Being of infinite benevolence. This is called *evangelical repentance,* and is accompanied and followed by amendment of life.

Repentance is a change of mind, or a conversion from sin to God. *Hammond.*

Godly sorrow worketh *repentance* to salvation. 2 Cor. vii. Matt. iii.

Repentance is the relinquishment of any practice, from conviction that it has offended God. *Johnson.*

REPENT'ANT, *a.* [Fr.] Sorrowful for past conduct or words.

2. Sorrowful for sin. *Milton.*

3. Expressing or showing sorrow for sin; as *repentant* tears; *repentant* ashes; *repentant* sighs. *Shak. Pope.*

REPENT'ANT, *n.* One who repents; a penitent.

2. One that expresses sorrow for sin. *Lightfoot.*

REPENT'ER, *n.* One that repents.

REPENT'ING, *ppr.* Grieving for what is past; feeling pain or contrition for sin.

REPENT'ING, *n.* Act of repenting. Hos. xi.

REPENT'INGLY, *adv.* With repentance.

REPEOPLE, *v. t.* [*re* and *people;* Fr. *repeupler.*] To people anew; to furnish again with a stock of people. The world after the flood was *repeopled* by the descendants of one family.

REPEOPLED, *pp.* Stocked anew with inhabitants.

REPEOPLING, *ppr.* Furnishing again with a stock of inhabitants.

REPEOPLING, *n.* [supra.] The act of furnishing again with inhabitants. *Hale.*

REPERCUSS', *v. t.* [L. *repercutio; re* and *percutio; per* and *quatio,* to shake, to beat.] To beat back. *Bacon.*

REPERCUS'SION, *n.* [L. *repercussio.*]

1. The act of driving back; reverberation; as the *repercussion* of sound.

2. In *music,* frequent repetition of the same sound. *Encyc.*

REPERCUSS'IVE, *a.* Driving back; having the power of sending back; causing to reverberate; as *repercussive* rocks. *Pattison.*

2. Repellent; as a *repercussive* medicine. [*Not in use.*] *Bacon.*

3. Driven back; reverberated. *Thomson.*

REPERCUSS'IVE, *n.* A repellent. *Obs.* *Bacon.*

REPERTI''TIOUS, *a.* [from L. *repertus, reperio.*] Found; gained by finding. [*Not in use.*] *Dict.*

REP'ERTORY, *n.* [Fr. *repertoire;* L. *repertorium,* from *reperio,* to find again; *re* and *aperio,* to uncover.]

1. A place in which things are disposed in an orderly manner, so that they can be easily found, as the index of a book, a common-place book, &c.

2. A treasury; a magazine.

REPETEND', *n.* [L. *repetendus, repeto.*] The parts of decimals continually repeated.

REPETI''TION, *n.* [L. *repetitio.* See *Repeat.*]

1. The act of doing or uttering a second time; iteration of the same act, or of the same words or sounds. *Hooker.*

2. The act of reciting or rehearsing; the act of reading over. *Shak.*

3. Recital. *Chapman.*

4. Recital from memory, as distinct from *reading.*

5. In *music,* the art of repeating, singing or playing the same part a second time. *Encyc.*

6. In *rhetoric,* reiteration, or a repeating the same word, or the same sense in different words, for the purpose of making a deeper impression on the audience.

REPETI''TIONAL, REPETI''TIONARY, } *a.* Containing repetition. [*Little used.*]

REPI'NE, *v. i.* [*re* and *pine.*] To fret one's self; to be discontented; to feel inward discontent which preys on the spirits; with *at* or *against.* It is our duty never to *repine at* the allotments of Providence.

2. To complain discontentedly; to murmur.

Multitudes *repine* at the want of that which nothing but idleness hinders them from enjoying. *Rambler.*

3. To envy. *Johnson.*

REPI'NER, *n.* One that repines or murmurs.

REPI'NING, *ppr.* Fretting one's self; feeling discontent that preys on the spirits; complaining; murmuring.

2. *a.* Disposed to murmur or complain; as a *repining* temper.

REPI'NING, *n.* The act of fretting or feeling discontent or of murmuring. *Burnet.*

REPI'NINGLY, *adv.* With murmuring or complaint. *Hall.*

REPLA'CE, *v. t.* [Fr. *replacer; re* and *place.*]

1. To put again in the former place; as, to *replace* a book.

The earl—was *replaced* in his government. *Bacon.*

2. To put in a new place. *Dryden.*

3. To repay; to refund; as, to *replace* a sum of money borrowed.

4. To put a competent substitute in the place of another displaced or of something lost. The paper is lost and cannot be *replaced.*

REPLA'CED, *pp.* Put again in a former place; supplied by a substitute. Thus in petrifaction, the animal or vegetable substance gradually wastes away, and is *replaced* by silex.

REPLA'CEMENT, *n.* The act of replacing.

REPLA'CING, *ppr.* Putting again in a former place; supplying the place of with a substitute.

REPLA'IT, *v. t.* [*re* and *plait.*] To plait or fold again; to fold one part over another again and again. *Dryden.*

REPLA'ITED, *pp.* Folded again or often.

REPLA'ITING, *ppr.* Folding again or often.

REPLANT', *v. t.* [Fr. *replanter; re* and *plant.*] To plant again. *Bacon.*

REPLANT'ABLE, *a.* That may be planted again. *Cotgrave.*

REPLANTA'TION, *n.* The act of planting again.

REPLANT'ED, *pp.* Planted anew.

REPLANT'ING, *ppr.* Planting again.

REPLE'AD, *v. t.* [*re* and *plead.*] To plead again.

REPLE'ADER, *n.* In *law*, a second pleading or course of pleadings; or the power of pleading again.

Whenever a *repleader* is granted, the pleadings must begin *de novo.* *Blackstone.*

REPLEN'ISH, *v. t.* [Norm. *replener*, to fill; It. *riempire*; L. *re* and *plenus*, full.]

1. To fill; to stock with numbers or abundance. The magazines are *replenished* with corn. The springs are *replenished* with water.

Multiply and *replenish* the earth. Gen. i.

2. To finish; to complete. [*Not in use.*] *Shak.*

REPLEN'ISH, *v. i.* To recover former fullness. *Bacon.*

REPLEN'ISHED, *pp.* Filled; abundantly supplied.

REPLEN'ISHING, *ppr.* Filling; supplying with abundance.

REPLE'TE, *a.* [L. *repletus; re* and *pleo*, to fill.] Completely filled; full.

His words *replete* with guile. *Milton.*

REPLE'TION, *n.* [Fr. from L. *repletio.*]

1. The state of being completely filled; or superabundant fullness. *Bacon.*

2. In *medicine*, fullness of blood; plethora. *Coxe.*

REPLE'TIVE, *a.* Filling; replenishing. *Cotgrave.*

REPLEV'IABLE, *a.* [See *Replevy.*] In *law*, that may be replevied.

REPLEV'IED, *pp.* Taken by a writ of replevin.

REPLEV'IN, *n.* [See *Replevy.*] An action or remedy granted on a distress, by which a person whose cattle or goods are distrained, has them returned to his own possession upon giving security to try the right of taking in a suit at law, and if that should be determined against him, to return the cattle or goods into the possession of the distrainor. *Blackstone.*

2. The writ by which a distress is replevied.

REPLEV'ISABLE, *a.* That may be replevied; but little used, being superseded by *repleviable.*

REPLEV'Y, *v. t.* [*re* and *pledge*, Norm. *plegg* or *plevy*, whence in Law L. *replegiabilis* and *replegiare.*]

1. To take back, by a writ for that purpose, cattle or goods that have been distrained, upon giving security to try the right of distraining in a suit at law, and if that should be determined against the plaintif, to return the cattle or goods into the hands of the distrainor. In this case, the person whose goods are distrained becomes the plaintif, and the person distraining the defendant or avowant. *Blackstone.*

2. To bail.

REPLEV'YING, *ppr.* Retaking a distress. [See *Replevy.*]

REPLICA'TION, *n.* [L. *replicatio.* See *Reply.*] An answer; a reply. Particularly,

2. In *law pleadings*, the reply of the plaintif to the defendant's plea.

3. Return or repercussion of sound. [*Not used.*] *Shak.*

REPLI'ER, *n.* One who answers; he that speaks or writes in return to something spoken or written.

REPLY', *v. i.* [Fr. *repliquer*; L. *replico; re* and *plico*, to fold, that is, to turn or send to; It. *replicare*; Sp. *replicar.* See *Apply*, *Employ* and *Ply.*]

1. To answer; to make a return in words or writing to something said or written by another.

O man, who art thou that *repliest* against God? Rom. ix.

2. In *law*, to answer a defendant's plea. The defendant pleads in bar to the plaintif's declaration; the plaintif *replies* to the defendant's plea in bar.

REPLY', *v. t.* To return for an answer. He knows not what to *reply.*

REPLY', *n.* [Fr. *replique*; It. *replica.*] An answer; that which is said or written in answer to what is said or written by another.

2. A book or pamphlet written in answer to another.

REPLY'ING, *ppr.* Answering either in words or writing.

REPOL'ISH, *v. t.* [Fr. *repolir; re* and *polish.*] To polish again. *Donne.*

REPOL'ISHED, *pp.* Polished again.

REPOL'ISHING, *ppr.* Polishing anew.

REPORT, *v. t.* [Fr. *rapporter*; L. *reporto*, to carry back; *re* and *porto*, to bear.]

1. To bear or bring back an answer, or to relate what has been discovered by a person sent to examine, explore or investigate; as, a messenger *reports* to his employer what he has seen or ascertained. The committee *reported* the whole number of votes.

2. To give an account of; to relate; to tell.

They *reported* his good deeds before me. Neh. vi. Acts iv.

3. To tell or relate from one to another; to circulate publicly, as a story; as in the common phrase, it is *reported.*

It is *reported* among the heathen, and Gashmu saith it, that thou and the Jews think to rebel. Neh. vi.

In this form of expression, *it* refers to the subsequent clause of the sentence; "that thou and the Jews think to rebel, is *reported.*"

4. To give an official account or statement; as, the secretary of the treasury *reports* to congress annually the amount of revenue and expenditure.

5. To give an account or statement of cases and decisions in a court of law or chancery.

6. To return, as sound; to give back. *Bacon.*

To be reported, or usually, *to be reported of*, to be well or ill spoken of; to be mentioned with respect or reproach. Acts xvi. Rom. iii.

REPORT, *v. i.* To make a statement of facts. The committee will *report* at twelve o'clock.

REPORT, *n.* An account returned; a statement or relation of facts given in reply to inquiry, or by a person authorized to examine and make return to his employer.

From Thetis sent as spies to make *report.* *Waller.*

2. Rumor; common fame; story circulated. *Report*, though often originating in fact, soon becomes incorrect, and is seldom deserving of credit. When we have no evidence but popular *report*, it is prudent to suspend our opinions in regard to the facts.

3. Repute; public character; as evil *report* and good *report.* 2 Cor. vi.

Cornelius was of good *report* among the Jews. Acts x.

4. Account; story; relation.

It was a true *report* that I heard in my own land of thy acts and of thy wisdom. 1 Kings x.

5. Sound; noise; as the *report* of a pistol or cannon. *Bacon.*

6. An account or statement of a judicial opinion or decision, or of a case argued and determined in a court of law, chancery, &c. The books containing such statements are also called *reports.*

7. An official statement of facts, verbal or written; particularly, a statement in writing of proceedings and facts exhibited by an officer to his superiors; as the *reports* of the heads of departments to congress,

of a master in chancery to the court, of committees to a legislative body and the like.

REPORTED, *pp.* Told, related or stated in answer to inquiry or direction; circulated in popular rumors; reputed; stated officially.

REPORTER, *n.* One that gives an account, verbal or written, official or unofficial.

2. An officer or person who makes statements of law proceedings and decisions, or of legislative debates.

REPORTING, *ppr.* Giving account; relating; presenting statements of facts or of adjudged cases in law.

REPORTINGLY, *adv.* By report or common fame.

REPO'SAL, *n.* *s* as *z.* [from *repose.*] The act of reposing or resting. *Shak.*

REPO'SE, *v. t.* *s* as *z.* [Fr. *reposer; re* and *poser,* to put; It. *riposare;* Sp. *reposar;* L. *repono, reposui.*]

1. To lay at rest.

—After the toil of battle, to *repose*
Your wearied virtue. *Milton.*

2. To lay; to rest, as the mind, in confidence or trust; as, to *repose* trust or confidence in a person's veracity.

3. To lay up; to deposit; to lodge; as pebbles *reposed* in cliffs. *Woodward.*

4. To place in confidence.

REPO'SE, *v. i.* To lie at rest; to sleep.

Within a thicket I *repos'd.* *Chapman.*

2. To rest in confidence. I *repose* on the faith and honor of a friend.

3. To lie; to rest; as trap *reposing* on sand.

REPO'SE, *n.* [Fr. *repos.*] A lying at rest.

2. Sleep; rest; quiet. *Milton. Shak.*

3. Rest of mind; tranquillity; freedom from uneasiness.

4. Cause of rest.

After great lights must be great shadows, which we call *reposes.* *Dryden.*

5. In *poetry,* a rest; a pause. *Encyc.*

6. In *painting,* harmony of colors, as when nothing glaring appears. *Gilpin.*

REPO'SED, *pp.* Laid at rest; placed in confidence.

REPO'SEDNESS, *n.* State of being at rest.

REPO'SING, *ppr.* Laying at rest; placing in confidence; lying at rest; sleeping.

REPOS'IT, *v. t.* [L. *repositus, repono.*] To lay up; to lodge, as for safety or preservation.

Others *reposit* their young in holes. *Derham.*

REPOS'ITED, *pp.* Laid up; deposited for safety or preservation.

REPOS'ITING, *ppr.* Laying up or lodging for safety or preservation.

REPOSI''TION, *n.* The act of replacing; as the *reposition* of a bone. *Wiseman.*

REPOS'ITORY, *n.* [L. *repositorium,* from *repono.*]

A place where things are or may be deposited for safety or preservation. A granary is a *repository* for corn, an arsenal for arms. The mind or memory is called the *repository* of ideas. *Locke.*

REPOSSESS', *v. t.* [*re* and *possess.*] To possess again.

Nor shall my father *repossess* the land. *Pope.*

To repossess one's self, to obtain possession again.

REPOSSESS'ED, *pp.* Possessed again.

REPOSSESS'ING, *ppr.* Possessing again; obtaining possession again.

REPOSSES'SION, *n.* The act of possessing again; the state of possessing again.

REPOUR, *v. t.* [*re* and *pour.*] To pour again.

REPREHEND', *v. t.* [L. *reprehendo; re* and *prehendo,* to seize; Fr. *reprendre.*]

1. To chide; to reprove.

Pardon me for *reprehending* thee. *Shak.*

2. To blame; to censure.

I nor advise, nor *reprehend* the choice. *Philips.*

3. To detect of fallacy.

This color will be *reprehended* or encountered, by imputing to all excellencies in compositions a kind of poverty. [*Not in use.*] *Bacon.*

4. To accuse; to charge with a fault; with *of;* as Aristippus, being *reprehended of* luxury. *Bacon.*

REPREHEND'ED, *pp.* Reproved; blamed.

REPREHEND'ER, *n.* One that reprehends; one that blames or reproves. *Hooker.*

REPREHEND'ING, *ppr.* Reproving; blaming.

REPREHEN'SIBLE, *a.* [Fr. from L. *reprehensus.*]

Blamable; culpable; censurable; deserving reproof; *applied to persons or things;* as a *reprehensible* person; *reprehensible* conduct.

REPREHEN'SIBLENESS, *n.* Blamableness; culpableness.

REPREHEN'SIBLY, *adv.* Culpably; in a manner to deserve censure or reproof.

REPREHEN'SION, *n.* [Fr. from L. *reprehensio.*]

Reproof; censure; open blame. Faults not punishable, may deserve *reprehension.*

REPREHEN'SIVE, *a.* Containing reproof. *South.*

REPREHEN'SORY, *a.* Containing reproof. *Boswell.*

REPRESENT', *v. t.* *s* as *z.* [Fr. *representer;* L. *repræsento; re* and Low L. *præsento,* from *præsens,* present.]

1. To show or exhibit by resemblance.

Before him burn
Seven lamps, as in a zodiac, *representing*
The heavenly fires. *Milton.*

2. To describe; to exhibit to the mind in words.

The managers of the bank at Genoa have been *represented* as a second kind of senate. *Addison.*

3. To exhibit; to show by action; as a tragedy well *represented.* *Johnson.*

4. To personate; to act the character or to fill the place of another in a play; as, to *represent* the character of king Richard.

5. To supply the place of; to act as a substitute for another. The parliament of Great Britain *represents* the nation. The congress of the United States *represents* the people or nation. The senate is considered as *representing* the states in their corporate capacity.

6. To show by arguments, reasoning or statement of facts. The memorial *represents* the situation of the petitioner. *Represent* to your son the danger of an idle life or profligate company.

7. To stand in the place of, in the right of inheritance.

All the branches inherit the same share that their root, whom they *represent,* would have done. *Blackstone.*

REPRESENT'ANCE, *n.* Representation; likeness. [*Not used.*] *Donne.*

REPRESENT'ANT, *n.* A representative. [*Not in use.*] *Wotton.*

REPRESENTA'TION, *n.* The act of representing, describing or showing.

2. That which exhibits by resemblance; image, likeness, picture or statue; as *representations* of God. *Stillingfleet.*

3. Any exhibition of the form or operations of a thing by something resembling it. A map is a *representation* of the world or a part of it. The terrestrial globe is a *representation* of the earth. An orrery is a *representation* of the planets and their revolutions.

4. Exhibition, as of a play on the stage.

5. Exhibition of a character in theatrical performance.

6. Verbal description; statement of arguments or facts in narration, oratory, debate, petition, admonition, &c.; as the *representation* of a historian, of a witness or an advocate.

7. The business of acting as a substitute for another; as the *representation* of a nation in a legislative body.

8. Representatives, as a collective body. It is expedient to have an able *representation* in both houses of congress.

9. Public exhibition.

10. The standing in the place of another, as an heir, or in the right of taking by inheritance. *Blackstone.*

REPRESENT'ATIVE, *a.* [Fr. *representatif.*]

1. Exhibiting a similitude.

They own the legal sacrifices, though *representative,* to be proper and real. *Atterbury.*

2. Bearing the character or power of another; as a council *representative* of the people. *Swift.*

REPRESENT'ATIVE, *n.* One that exhibits the likeness of another.

A statue of Rumor, whispering an idiot in the ear, who was the *representative* of credulity. *Addison.*

2. In *legislative* or *other business,* an agent, deputy or substitute who supplies the place of another or others, being invested with his or their authority. An attorney is the *representative* of his client or employer. A member of the house of commons is the *representative* of his constituents and of the nation. In matters concerning his constituents only, he is supposed to be bound by their instructions, but in the enacting of laws for the nation, he is supposed not to be bound by their instructions, as he acts for the whole nation.

3. In *law,* one that stands in the place of another as heir, or in the right of succeeding to an estate of inheritance, or to a crown.

4. That by which any thing is exhibited or shown.

This doctrine supposes the perfections of God to be the *representatives* to us of whatever we perceive in the creatures. *Locke.*

REPRESENT'ATIVELY, *adv.* In the character of another; by a representative. *Barrow.*

2. By substitution; by delegation of power. *Sandys.*

REPRESENT'ATIVENESS, *n.* The state or quality of being representative.

Dr. Burnet observes that every thought is attended with consciousness and *representativeness.* *Spectator.*

REPRESENT'ED, *pp.* Shown; exhibited; personated; described; stated; having substitutes.

REPRESENT'ER, *n.* One who shows, exhibits or describes.

2. A representative; one that acts by deputation. [*Little used.*] *Swift.*

REPRESENT'ING, *ppr.* Showing; exhibiting; describing; acting in another's character; acting in the place of another.

REPRESENT'MENT, *n.* Representation; image; an idea proposed as exhibiting the likeness of something. *Taylor. Brown.*

REPRESS', *v. t.* [L. *repressus, reprimo; re* and *premo,* to press.]

1. To crush; to quell; to put down; to subdue; to suppress; as, to *repress* sedition or rebellion; to *repress* the first risings of discontent.

2. To check; to restrain.

Such kings
Favor the innocent, *repress* the bold. *Waller.*

REPRESS', *n.* The act of subduing. [*Not in use.*]

REPRESS'ED, *pp.* Crushed; subdued.

REPRESS'ER, *n.* One that crushes or subdues.

REPRESS'ING, *ppr.* Crushing; subduing; checking.

REPRES'SION, *n.* The act of subduing; as the *repression* of tumults. *K. Charles.*

2. Check; restraint.

REPRESS'IVE, *a.* Having power to crush; tending to subdue or restrain.

REPRIE'VAL, *n.* Respit; reprieve. [*Not in use.*] *Overbury.*

REPRIE'VE, *v. t.* [I know not the origin of this word, unless it is the French *reprendre, repris.* In Norm. *repriont* is rendered *reprieved deductions,* and *reprises,* deductions and duties yearly paid out of lands.]

1. To respit after sentence of death; to suspend or delay the execution of for a time; as, to *reprieve* a criminal for thirty days.

He *reprieves* the sinner from time to time. *Rogers.*

2. To grant a respit to; to relieve for a time from any suffering.

Company, though it may *reprieve* a man from his melancholy, yet cannot secure a man from his conscience. *South.*

REPRIE'VE, *n.* The temporary suspension of the execution of sentence of death on a criminal. *Clarendon.*

2. Respit; interval of ease or relief.

All that I ask is but a short *reprieve,*
Till I forget to love, and learn to grieve. *Denham.*

REPRIE'VED, *pp.* Respited; allowed a longer time to live than the sentence of death permits.

REPRIE'VING, *ppr.* Respiting; suspending the execution of for a time.

REP'RIMAND, *v. t.* [Fr. *reprimander.* If this word is from L. *reprimo,* it must be formed from the participle *reprimendus.*]

1. To reprove severely; to reprehend; to chide for a fault.

Germanicus was severely *reprimanded* by Tiberius, for traveling into Egypt without his permission. *Arbuthnot.*

2. To reprove publicly and officially, in execution of a sentence. The court ordered the officer to be *reprimanded.*

REP'RIMAND, *n.* Severe reproof for a fault; reprehension, private or public. *Spectator.*

REP'RIMANDED, *pp.* Severely reproved.

REP'RIMANDING, *ppr.* Reproving severely.

REPRINT', *v. t.* [*re* and *print.*] To print again; to print a second or any new edition. *Pope.*

2. To renew the impression of any thing.

The business of redemption is—to *reprint* God's image on the soul. *South.*

RE'PRINT, *n.* A second or a new edition of a book. *Review of Griesbach.*

REPRINT'ED, *pp.* Printed anew; impressed again.

REPRINT'ING, *ppr.* Printing again; renewing an impression.

REPRI'SAL, *n.* *s* as *z.* [Fr. *represailles;* It. *ripresaglia;* Sp. *represalra;* Fr. *reprendre, repris,* to retake; *re* and *prendre,* L. *prendo.*]

1. The seizure or taking of any thing from an enemy by way of retaliation or indemnification for something taken or detained by him.

2. That which is taken from an enemy to indemnify an owner for something of his which the enemy has seized. Reprisals may consist of persons or of goods. Letters of marque and reprisal may be obtained in order to seize the bodies or goods of the subjects of an offending state, until satisfaction shall be made. *Blackstone.*

3. Recaption; a retaking of a man's own goods or any of his family, wife, child or servant, wrongfully taken from him or detained by another. In this case, the owner may retake the goods or persons wherever he finds them. *Blackstone.*

Letters of marque and reprisal, a commission granted by the supreme authority of a state to a subject, empowering him to pass the frontiers [*marque,*] that is, enter an enemy's territories and capture the goods and persons of the enemy, in return for goods or persons taken by him.

4. The act of retorting on an enemy by inflicting suffering or death on a prisoner taken from him, in retaliation of an act of inhumanity. *Vattel.*

REPRI'SE, *n.* *s* as *z.* [Fr.] A taking by way of retaliation. *Obs.* *Dryden.*

REPRI'SE, *v. t.* *s* as *z.* To take again. *Obs.* *Spenser.*

2. To recompense; to pay. *Obs.* *Grant.*

REPRI'ZES, *n. plu.* In *law,* yearly deductions out of a manor, as rent-charge, rent-seck, &c. *Jones.*

REPRÖACH, *v. t.* [Fr. *reprocher;* It. *rimprocciare;* from the same root as *approach,* and Fr. *proche,* near, L. *prox,* in *proximus,* from a root in Class *Brg,* signifying to thrust or drive; probably ברך.]

1. To censure in terms of opprobrium or contempt.

Mezentius with his ardor warm'd
His fainting friends, *reproach'd* their shameful flight,
Repell'd the victors. *Dryden.*

2. To charge with a fault in severe language.

That shame
There sit not, and *reproach* us as unclean. *Milton.*

3. To upbraid; to suggest blame for any thing. A man's conscience will *reproach* him for a criminal, mean or unworthy action.

4. To treat with scorn or contempt. Luke vi.

REPRÖACH, *n.* Censure mingled with contempt or derision; contumelious or opprobrious language towards any person; abusive reflections; as foul-mouthed *reproach.* *Shak.*

2. Shame; infamy; disgrace.

Give not thine heritage to *reproach.* Joel ii. Is. iv.

3. Object of contempt, scorn or derision.

Come, and let us build up the wall of Jerusalem, that we may be no more a *reproach.* Neh. ii.

4. That which is the cause of shame or disgrace. Gen. xxx.

REPRÖACHABLE, *a.* Deserving reproach.

2. Opprobrious; scurrilous. [*Not proper.*] *Elyot.*

REPRÖACHED, *pp.* Censured in terms of contempt; upbraided.

REPRÖACHFUL, *a.* Expressing censure with contempt; scurrilous; opprobrious; as *reproachful* words. *Shak.*

2. Shameful; bringing or casting reproach; infamous; base; vile; as *reproachful* conduct; a *reproachful* life.

REPRÖACHFULLY, *adv.* In terms of reproach; opprobriously; scurrilously. 1 Tim. v.

2. Shamefully; disgracefully; contemptuously.

REP'ROBATE, *a.* [L. *reprobatus, reprobo,* to disallow; *re* and *probo,* to prove.]

1. Not enduring proof or trial; not of standard purity or fineness; disallowed; rejected.

Reprobate silver shall men call them, because the Lord hath rejected them. Jer. vi.

2. Abandoned in sin; lost to virtue or grace.

They profess that they know God, but in works deny him, being abominable and disobedient, and to every good work *reprobate.* Tit. i.

3. Abandoned to error, or in apostasy. 2 Tim. iii.

REP'ROBATE, *n.* A person abandoned to sin; one lost to virtue and religion.

I acknowledge myself a *reprobate,* a villain, a traitor to the king. *Raleigh.*

REP'ROBATE, *v. t.* To disapprove with detestation or marks of extreme dislike; to disallow; to reject. It expresses more than *disapprove* or *disallow.* We *disapprove* of slight faults and improprieties; we *reprobate* what is mean or criminal.

2. In a milder sense, to disallow.

Such an answer as this, is *reprobated* and disallowed of in law. *Ayliffe.*

3. To abandon to wickedness and eternal destruction. *Hammond.*
4. To abandon to his sentence, without hope of pardon.

Drive him out
To *reprobated* exile. *Southern.*

REP'ROBATED, *pp.* Disapproved with abhorrence; rejected; abandoned to wickedness or to destruction.

REP'ROBATENESS, *n.* The state of being reprobate.

REP'ROBATER, *n.* One that reprobates.

REP'ROBATING, *ppr.* Disapproving with extreme dislike; rejecting; abandoning to wickedness or to destruction.

REPROBA'TION, *n.* [Fr. from L. *reprobatio.*]
1. The act of disallowing with detestation, or of expressing extreme dislike.
2. The act of abandoning or state of being abandoned to eternal destruction.

When a sinner is so hardened as to feel no remorse or misgiving of conscience, it is considered as a sign of *reprobation.* *Encyc.*

3. A condemnatory sentence; rejection.

Set a brand of *reprobation* on clipt poetry and false coin. *Dryden.*

REPROBA'TIONER, *n.* One who abandons others to eternal destruction. *South.*

REPRODU'CE, *v. t.* [*re* and *produce.*] To produce again; to renew the production of a thing destroyed. Trees are *reproduced* by new shoots from the roots or stump; and certain animals, as the polype, are *reproduced* from cuttings. *Encyc.*

REPRODU'CED, *pp.* Produced anew.

REPRODU'CER, *n.* One or that which reproduces. *Burke.*

REPRODU'CING, *ppr.* Producing anew.

REPRODUC'TION, *n.* The act or process of reproducing that which has been destroyed; as the *reproduction* of plants or animals from cuttings or slips. The *reproduction* of several parts of lobsters and crabs is one of the greatest curiosities in natural history. *Encyc.*

REPROOF', *n.* [from *reprove.*] Blame expressed to the face; censure for a fault; reprehension.

Those best can bear *reproof,* who merit praise. *Pope.*

He that hateth *reproof* is brutish. Prov. xii.

2. Blame cast; censure directed to a person.

REPRÖVABLE, *a.* [from *reprove.*] Worthy of reproof; deserving censure; blamable. *Taylor.*

REPRÖVE, *v. t.* [Fr. *reprouver;* L. *reprobo; re* and *probo,* to prove.]
1. To blame; to censure.

I will not *reprove* thee for thy sacrifices—Ps. l.

2. To charge with a fault to the face; to chide; to reprehend. Luke iii.
3. To blame for; with *of;* as, to *reprove* one *of* laziness. *Carew.*
4. To convince of a fault, or to make it manifest. John xvi.
5. To refute; to disprove. [*Not in use.*] *Shak.*
6. To excite a sense of guilt. The heart or conscience *reproves* us.
7. To manifest silent disapprobation or blame.

The vicious cannot bear the presence of the good, whose very looks *reprove* them, and whose life is a severe, though silent admonition. *Buckminster.*

REPRÖVED, *pp.* Blamed; reprehended; convinced of a fault.

REPRÖVER, *n.* One that reproves; he or that which blames. Conscience is a bold *reprover.* *South.*

REPRÖVING, *ppr.* Blaming; censuring.

REPRU'NE, *v. t.* [*re* and *prune.*] To prune a second time. *Evelyn.*

REPRU'NED, *pp.* Pruned a second time.

REPRU'NING, *ppr.* Pruning a second time.

REP'TILE, *a.* [Fr. from L. *reptilis,* from *repo,* to creep, Gr. ερπω; It. *rettile;* Sp. *reptil.* See *Creep.* The primary sense is probably to *rub* or scrape, or to seize.]
1. Creeping; moving on the belly, or with many small feet.
2. Groveling; low; vulgar; as a *reptile* race or crew; *reptile* vices. *Burke.*

REP'TILE, *n.* An animal that moves on its belly, or by means of small short legs, as earth-worms, caterpillars, snakes and the like.

In *zoology,* the *reptiles* constitute an order of the class Amphibia, including all such as are furnished with limbs or articulated extremities, as tortoises, lizards and frogs. *Linne.*

2. A groveling or very mean person; a term of contempt.

REPUB'LIC, *n.* [L. *respublica; res* and *publica;* public affairs.]
1. A commonwealth; a state in which the exercise of the sovereign power is lodged in representatives elected by the people. In modern usage, it differs from a democracy or democratic state, in which the people exercise the powers of sovereignty in person. Yet the democracies of Greece are often called *republics.*
2. Common interest; the public. [*Not in use.*] *B. Jonson.*

Republic of letters, the collective body of learned men.

REPUB'LICAN, *a.* Pertaining to a republic; consisting of a commonwealth; as a *republican* constitution or government.
2. Consonant to the principles of a republic; as *republican* sentiments or opinions; *republican* manners.

REPUB'LICAN, *n.* One who favors or prefers a republican form of government.

REPUB'LICANISM, *n.* A republican form or system of government.
2. Attachment to a republican form of government. *Burke.*

REPUB'LICANIZE, *v. t.* To convert to republican principles; as, to *republicanize* the rising generation. *Ramsay.*

REPUBLICA'TION, *n.* [*re* and *publication.*]
1. A second publication, or a new publication of something before published.
2. A second publication, as of a former will, renewal.

If there be many testaments, the last overthrows all the former; but the *republication* of a former will, revokes one of a later date, and establishes the first. *Blackstone.*

REPUB'LISH, *v. t.* [*re* and *publish.*] To publish a second time, or to publish a new edition of a work before published.
2. To publish anew.

Unless, subsequent to the purchase or contract, the devisor *republishes* his will. *Blackstone.*

REPUB'LISHED, *pp.* Published anew.

REPUB'LISHER, *n.* One who republishes.

REPUB'LISHING, *ppr.* Publishing again.

REPU'DIABLE, *a.* [from *repudiate.*] That may be rejected; fit or proper to be put away.

REPU'DIATE, *v. t.* [Fr. *repudier;* L. *repudio; re* and one of the roots in class *Bd,* which signifies to send or thrust.] To cast away; to reject; to discard.

Atheists—*repudiate* all title to the kingdom of heaven. *Bentley.*

2. Appropriately, to put away; to divorce; as a wife.

REPU'DIATED, *pp.* Cast off; rejected; discarded; divorced.

REPU'DIATING, *ppr.* Casting off; rejecting; divorcing.

REPUDIA'TION, *n.* [Fr. from L. *repudiatio.*] Rejection.
2. Divorce; as the *repudiation* of a wife. *Arbuthnot.*

REPUGN, *n.* *repu'ne.* [L. *repugno; re* and *pugno.*]
To oppose; to resist. [*Not used.*] *Elyot.*

REPUG'NANCE, } *n.* [Fr. *repugnance;* It.
REPUG'NANCY, } *ripugnanza;* L. *repugnantia,* from *repugno,* to resist; *re* and *pugno,* to fight.]
1. Opposition of mind; reluctance; unwillingness. *Shak. Dryden.*
2. Opposition or struggle of passions; resistance. *South.*
3. Opposition of principles or qualities; inconsistency; contrariety.

But where difference is without *repugnancy,* that which hath been can be no prejudice to that which is. *Hooker.*

REPUG'NANT, *a.* [Fr. from L. *repugnans.*]
1. Opposite; contrary; inconsistent; properly followed by *to.* Every sin is *repugnant to* the will of God. Every thing morally wrong, is *repugnant* both *to* the honor, as well as *to* the interest of the offender.
2. Disobedient; not obsequious. [*Not in use.*] *Shak.*

REPUG'NANTLY, *adv.* With opposition; in contradiction. *Brown.*

REPUL'LULATE, *v. i.* [L. *re* and *pullulo,* to bud.] To bud again. *Howell.*

REPULLULA'TION, *n.* The act of budding again.

REPULSE, *n.* *repuls'.* [L. *repulsa,* from *repello; re* and *pello,* to drive.]
1. A being checked in advancing, or driven back by force. The enemy met with a *repulse* and retreated.
2. Refusal; denial. *Bailey.*

REPULSE, *v. t.* *repuls'.* [L. *repulsus, repello.*]
To repel; to beat or drive back; as, to *repulse* an assailant or advancing enemy. *Knolles. Milton.*

REPULS'ED, *pp.* Repelled; driven back.

REPULS'ER, *n.* One that repulses or drives back. *Sherwood.*

REPULS'ING, *ppr.* Driving back.

REPUL'SION, *n.* In *physics,* the power of repelling or driving off; that property of bodies which causes them to recede from each other or avoid coming in contact. *Encyc.*

2. The act of repelling.

REPULS'IVE, *a.* Repelling; driving off, or keeping from approach. The *repulsive* power of the electric fluid is remarkable.

2. Cold; reserved; forbidding; as *repulsive* manners.

REPULS'IVENESS, *n.* The quality of being repulsive or forbidding.

REPULS'ORY, *a.* Repulsive; driving back.

REPUR'CHASE, *v. t.* [*re* and *purchase.*] To buy again; to buy back; to regain by purchase or expense. *Hale.*

REPUR'CHASE, *n.* The act of buying again; the purchase again of what has been sold.

REPUR'CHASED, *pp.* Bought back or again; regained by expense; as a throne *repurchased* with the blood of enemies. *Shak.*

REPUR'CHASING, *ppr.* Buying back or again; regaining by the payment of a price.

REP'UTABLE, *a.* [from *repute.*] Being in good repute; held in esteem; as a *reputable* man or character; *reputable* conduct. It expresses less than *respectable* and *honorable*, denoting the good opinion of men, without distinction or great qualities.

2. Consistent with reputation; not mean or disgraceful. It is evidence of extreme depravity that vice is in any case *reputable.*

In the article of danger, it is as *reputable* to elude an enemy as to defeat one. *Broome.*

REP'UTABLENESS, *n.* The quality of being reputable.

REP'UTABLY, *adv.* With reputation; without disgrace or discredit; as, to fill an office *reputably.*

REPUTA'TION, *n.* [Fr. from L. *reputatio.*]

1. Good name; the credit, honor or character which is derived from a favorable public opinion or esteem. *Reputation* is a valuable species of property or right, which should never be violated. With the loss of *reputation*, a man and especially a woman, loses most of the enjoyments of life.

The best evidence of *reputation* is a man's whole life. *Ames.*

2. Character by report; in a good or bad sense; as, a man has the *reputation* of being rich or poor, or of being a thief. *Addison.*

REPU'TE, *v. t.* [L. *reputo*; *re* and *puto*, to think; Fr. *reputer.*]

To think; to account; to hold; to reckon.

The king was *reputed* a prince most prudent. *Shak.*

Wherefore are we counted as beasts, and *reputed* vile in your sight? Job xviii.

REPU'TE, *n.* Reputation; good character; the credit or honor derived from common or public opinion; as men of *repute.*

2. Character; in a bad sense; as a man held in bad *repute.*

3. Established opinion; as upheld by old *repute.* *Milton.*

REPU'TED, *pp.* Reckoned; accounted.

REPU'TEDLY, *adv.* In common opinion or estimation. *Barrow.*

REPU'TELESS, *a.* Disreputable; disgraceful. *Shak.*

REPU'TING, *ppr.* Thinking; reckoning; accounting.

REQUEST', *n.* [Fr. *requête*; L. *requisitus*, *requiro*; *re* and *quæro*, to seek; It. *richiesta*; Sp. *requesta.* See *Quest*, *Question.*]

1. The expression of desire to some person for something to be granted or done; an asking; a petition.

Haman stood up to make *request* for his life to Esther the queen. Esth. vii.

2. Prayer; the expression of desire to a superior or to the Almighty. Phil. iv.

3. The thing asked for or requested.

I will both hear and grant you your *requests.* *Shak.*

He gave them their *request*; but sent leanness into their soul. Ps. cvi.

4. A state of being desired or held in such estimation as to be sought after or pursued.

Knowledge and fame were in as great *request* as wealth among us now. *Temple.*

In request, in demand; in credit or reputation.

Coriolanus being now *in no request.* *Shak.*

Request expresses less earnestness than *entreaty* and *supplication*, and supposes a right in the person requested to deny or refuse to grant. In this it differs from *demand.*

REQUEST', *v. t.* [Fr. *requêter.*] To ask; to solicit; to express desire for.

The weight of the golden ear-rings which he *requested*, was a thousand and seven hundred shekels of gold. Judges viii.

2. To express desire to; to ask. We *requested* a friend to accompany us.

Court of requests, in England, a court of equity for the relief of such persons as addressed his majesty by supplication; abolished by Stat. 16 and 17 Ca. 1. *Encyc.*

2. A court of conscience for the recovery of small debts, held by two aldermen and four commoners, who try causes by the oath of parties and of other witnesses. *Blackstone.*

REQUEST'ED, *pp.* Asked; desired; solicited.

REQUEST'ER, *n.* One who requests; a petitioner.

REQUEST'ING, *ppr.* Asking; petitioning.

REQUICK'EN, *v. t.* [*re* and *quicken.*] To reanimate; to give new life to. *Shak.*

REQUICK'ENED, *pp.* Reanimated.

REQUICK'ENING, *ppr.* Reanimating; invigorating.

RE'QUIEM, *n.* [L.] In *the Romish church*, a hymn or mass sung for the dead, for the rest of his soul; so called from the first word. *Encyc.*

2. Rest; quiet; peace. [*Not in use.*] *Sandys.*

REQUI'ETORY, *n.* [Low L. *requietorium.*] A sepulcher. [*Not in use.*] *Weever.*

REQUI'RABLE, *a.* [from *require.*] That may be required; fit or proper to be demanded. *Hale.*

REQUI'RE, *v. t.* [L. *requiro*; *re* and *quæro*, to seek; Fr. Sp. *requerir.* See *Query.*]

1. To demand; to ask, as of right and by authority. We *require* a person to do a thing, and we *require* a thing to be done.

Why then doth my lord *require* this thing? 1 Chron. xxi.

2. To claim; to render necessary; as a duty or any thing indispensable; as, the law of God *requires* strict obedience.

3. To ask as a favor; to request.

I was ashamed to *require* of the king a band of soldiers and horsemen to help us against the enemy in the way. Ezra viii.

[*In this sense, the word is rarely used.*]

4. To call to account for.

I will *require* my flock at their hand. Ezek. xxxiv.

5. To make necessary; to need; to demand.

The king's business *required* haste. 1 Sam. xxi.

6. To avenge; to take satisfaction for. 1 Sam. xx.

REQUI'RED, *pp.* Demanded; needed; necessary.

REQUI'REMENT, *n.* Demand; requisition. *Scott. Chalmers.*

This ruler was one of those who believe that they can fill up every *requirement* contained in the rule of righteousness. *J. M. Mason.*

The Bristol water is of service where the secretions exceed the *requirements* of health. *Encyc.*

REQUI'RER, *n.* One who requires.

REQUI'RING, *ppr.* Demanding; needing.

REQ'UISITE, *a.* *s* as *z.* [L. *requisitus*, from *requiro.*]

Required by the nature of things or by circumstances; necessary; so needful that it cannot be dispensed with. Repentance and faith are *requisite* to salvation. Air is *requisite* to support life. Heat is *requisite* to vegetation.

REQ'UISITE, *n.* That which is necessary; something indispensable. Contentment is a *requisite* to a happy life.

God on his part has declared the *requisites* on ours; what we must do to obtain blessings, is the great business of us all to know. *Wake.*

REQ'UISITELY, *adv.* Necessarily; in a requisite manner. *Boyle.*

REQ'UISITENESS, *n.* The state of being requisite or necessary; necessity. *Boyle.*

REQUISI''TION, *n.* [Fr.; It. *requisizione.* See *Require.*]

Demand; application made as of right. Under the old confederation of the American states, congress often made *requisitions* on the states for money to supply the treasury; but they had no power to enforce their *requisitions*, and the states neglected or partially complied with them. *Hamilton.*

REQUIS'ITIVE, *a.* Expressing or implying demand. *Harris.*

REQUIS'ITORY, *a.* Sought for; demanded. [*Little used.*]

REQUI'TAL, *n.* [from *requite.*] Return for any office, good or bad; in a good sense, compensation; recompense; as the *requital* of services; in a bad sense, retaliation or punishment, as the *requital* of evil deeds.

2. Return; reciprocal action.

No merit their aversion can remove,
Nor ill *requital* can efface their love.
Waller.

REQUI'TE, *v. t.* [from *quit*, L. *cedo*; Ir. *cuitighim*, to *requite*; *cuiteach*, recompense.]

1. To repay either good or evil; in a good sense, to recompense; to return an equivalent in good; to reward.

I also will *requite* you this kindness. 2 Sam. ii. 1 Tim. v.

In a bad sense, to retaliate; to return evil for evil; to punish.

Joseph will certainly *requite* us all the evil which we did to him. Gen. l.

2. To do or give in return.

He hath *requited* me evil for good. 1 Sam. xxv.

REQUI'TED, *pp.* Repaid; recompensed; rewarded.

REQUI'TER, *n.* One who requites.

REQUI'TING, *ppr.* Recompensing; rewarding; giving in return.

RE'RE-MOUSE, *n.* [Sax. *hreremus.*] A bat. [See *Rear-mouse.*]

RE-RESOLVE, *v. t. re-rezolv'.* To resolve a second time.

RE'RE-WARD, *n.* [*rear* and *ward.*] The part of an army that marches in the rear, as the guard; the rear guard. [*The latter orthography is to be preferred.*] Num. x. Is. lii.

RESA'IL, *v.* . or *i.* [*re* and *sail.*] To sail back. *Pope.*

RESA'LE, *n.* [*re* and *sale.*] A sale at second hand. *Bacon.*

2. A second sale; a sale of what was before sold to the possessor.

RESALU'TE, *v. t.* [L. *resaluto; re* and *saluto*, to salute; Fr. *resaluer.*]

1. To salute or greet anew. *Milton.*

2. To return a salutation.

RESALU'TED, *pp.* Saluted again.

RESALU'TING, *ppr.* Saluting anew.

RESCIND', *v. t.* [L. *rescindo; re* and *scindo*, to cut; Fr. *rescinder.*]

1. To abrogate; to revoke; to annul; to vacate an act by the enacting authority or by superior authority; as, to *rescind* a law, a resolution or a vote; to *rescind* an edict or decree; to *rescind* a judgment.

2. To cut off. [*Not used.*]

RESCISSION, *n. resizh'on.* [Fr. *rescision*, from L. *rescissus.*]

1. The act of abrogating, annulling or vacating; as the *rescission* of a law, decree or judgment.

2. A cutting off.

RESCIS'SORY, *a.* [Fr. *rescisoire.*] Having power to cut off or to abrogate. *Selden.*

RES'COUS, in law. [See *Rescue.*]

RESCRI'BE, *v. t.* [L. *rescribo; re* and *scribo*, to write.]

1. To write back. *Ayliffe.*

2. To write over again. *Howell.*

RE'SCRIPT, *n.* [L. *rescriptum, rescribo.*] The answer of an emperor, when consulted by particular persons on some difficult question. This answer serves as a decision of the question, and is therefore equivalent to an edict or decree. *Encyc.*

RESCRIP'TIVELY, *adv.* By rescript. [*Unusual.*] *Burke.*

RES'CUABLE, *a.* That may be rescued. *Gayton.*

RESCUE, *v. t. res'cu.* [Norm. *rescure*, to *rescue; rescous*, retaken, rescued, relieved; Fr. *recourre, recous;* qu. from *recouvrer*, to recover. The Italian *riscattare*, Sp. *rescatar*, Port. *resgatar*, to redeem, to *rescue*, is compounded of *re* and *cattare*, to *get.* The Fr. *recous* is evidently the It. *riscossa*, recovery, *riscosso*, recovered, from *riscuotere*, to redeem, ransom, regain, escape, exact, or recover, contracted in Fr. *recourre*, from *ri* or *re* and It. *scuotere*, to shake; *scossa*, a shaking; L. *re* and *quatio.*]

To free or deliver from any confinement, violence, danger or evil; to liberate from actual restraint, or to remove or withdraw from a state of exposure to evil; as, to *rescue* a prisoner from an officer; to *rescue* seamen from destruction by shipwreck.

So the people *rescued* Jonathan that he died not. 1 Sam. xiv. xxx. Ps. xxxv.

Cattle taken by distress contrary to law, may be *rescued* by the owner, while on their way to the pound. *Blackstone.*

Estimate the value of one soul *rescued* from eternal guilt and agony, and destined to grow forever in the knowledge and likeness of God. *A. Dickinson.*

RES'CUE, *n.* [See the Verb.] Deliverance from restraint, violence or danger, by force or by the interference of an agent.

2. In *law*, rescue or rescous, the forcible retaking of a lawful distress from the distrainor, or from the custody of the law; also, the forcible liberation of a defendant from the custody of the officer, in which cases, the remedy is by *writ of rescous.* But when the distress is unlawfully taken, the owner may lawfully make rescue.

The *rescue* of a prisoner from the court, is punished with perpetual imprisonment and forfeiture of goods. *Blackstone.*

RES'CUED, *pp.* Delivered from confinement or danger; or forcibly taken from the custody of the law.

RES'CUER, *n.* One that rescues or retakes. *Kent.*

RES'CUING, *ppr.* Liberating from restraint or danger; forcibly taking from the custody of the law.

RESEARCH, *n. reserch'.* [Fr. *recherche.*] Diligent inquiry or examination in seeking facts or principles; laborious or continued search after truth; as *researches* of human wisdom. *Rogers.*

RESEARCH, *v. t. reserch'.* [Fr. *rechercher; re* and *chercher.*]

1. To search or examine with continued care; to seek diligently for the truth.

It is not easy to *research* with due distinction, in the actions of eminent personages, both how much may have been blemished by the envy of others, and what was corrupted by their own felicity. [*Unusual.*] *Wotton.*

2. To search again; to examine anew.

RESEARCHER, *n. reserch'er.* One who diligently inquires or examines.

RESE'AT, *v. t.* [*re* and *seat.*] To seat or set again. *Dryden.*

RESE'ATED, *pp.* Seated again.

RESE'ATING, *ppr.* Seating again.

RESEC'TION, *n.* [L. *resectio, reseco.*] The act of cutting or paring off. *Cotgrave.*

RESEE'K, *v. t.* pret. and pp. *resought.* [*re* and *seek.*]

To seek again. *J. Barlow.*

RESE'IZE, *v. t.* [*re* and *seize.*] To seize again; to seize a second time. *Spenser.*

2. In *law*, to take possession of lands and tenements which have been disseized.

Whereupon the sherif is commanded to *reseize* the land and all the chattels thereon, and keep the same in his custody till the arrival of the justices of assize. *Blackstone.*

RESE'IZED, *pp.* Seized again.

RESE'IZER, *n.* One who seizes again.

RESE'IZING, *ppr.* Seizing again.

RESEIZURE, *n. rese'zhur.* A second seizure; the act of seizing again. *Bacon.*

RESELL', *v. t.* To sell again; to sell what has been bought or sold. *Wheaton*, v. 4.

RESEM'BLABLE, *a.* [See *Resemble.*] That may be compared. [*Not in use.*] *Gower.*

RESEM'BLANCE, *n.* [Fr. *ressemblance.* See *Resemble.*]

1. Likeness; similitude, either of external form or of qualities. We observe a *resemblance* between persons, a *resemblance* in shape, a *resemblance* in manners, a *resemblance* in dispositions. Painting and poetry bear a great *resemblance* to each other, as one object of both is to please. *Dryden.*

2. Something similar; similitude; representation.

These sensible things which religion hath allowed, are *resemblances* formed according to things spiritual. *Hooker.*

Fairest *resemblance* of thy Maker fair— *Milton.*

RESEM'BLE, *v. t. s* as *z.* [Fr. *ressembler;* It. *rassembrare;* Sp. *asemejar;* Port. *assemelhar.* See *Similar.*]

1. To have the likeness of; to bear the similitude of something, either in form, figure or qualities. One man may *resemble* another in features; he may *resemble* a third person in temper or deportment.

Each one *resembled* the children of a king. Judges viii.

2. To liken; to compare; to represent as like something else.

The torrid parts of Africa are *resembled* to a libbard's skin, the distance of whose spots represents the dispersed situation of the habitations. *Brerewood.*

RESEM'BLED, *pp.* Likened; compared.

RESEM'BLING, *ppr.* Having the likeness of; likening; comparing.

RESEND', *v. t.* pret. and pp. *resent.* [*re* and *send.*]

To send again; to send back. [*Not in use.*] *Shak.*

RESENT', *v. t. s* as *z.* [Fr. *ressentir*, to perceive again, to have a deep sense of; *re* and *sentir*, to perceive, L. *sentio;* It. *risentire*, to resent, to hear again, to resound; Sp. *resentirse*, to resent, also to begin to give way or to fail; *resentimiento*, resentment, a flaw or crack.]

1. To take well; to receive with satisfaction. *Obs.* *Bacon.*

2. To take ill; to consider as an injury or affront; to be in some degree angry or provoked at.

Thou with scorn
And anger would'st *resent* the offer'd wrong. *Milton.*

RESENT'ED, *pp.* Taken ill; being in some measure angry at.

RESENT'ER, *n.* One who resents; one that feels an injury deeply. *Wotton.*

2. In the sense of one that takes a thing well. *Obs.*

RESENT'FUL, *a.* Easily provoked to anger; of an irritable temper.

RESENT'ING, *ppr.* Taking ill; feeling angry at.

RESENT'INGLY, *adv.* With a sense of wrong or affront; with a degree of anger.

2. With deep sense or strong perception. *Obs.* *More.*

RESENT'IVE, *a.* Easily provoked or irritated; quick to feel an injury or affront. *Thomson.*

RESENT'MENT, *n.* [Fr. *ressentiment*; It. *risentimento*; Sp. *resentimiento.*]

1. The excitement of passion which proceeds from a sense of wrong offered to ourselves, or to those who are connected with us; anger. This word usually expresses less excitement than *anger*, though it is often synonymous with it. It expresses much less than *wrath, exasperation*, and *indignation*. In this use, *resentment* is not the sense or perception of injury, but the excitement which is the effect of it.

Can heavenly minds such high *resentment* show? *Dryden.*

2. Strong perception of good. [*Not in use.*] *More.*

RESERVA'TION, *n.* *s* as *z.* [Fr. from L. *reservo.*]

1. The act of reserving or keeping back or in the mind; reserve; concealment or withholding from disclosure; as mental *reservation.*

2. Something withheld, either not expressed or disclosed, or not given up or brought forward.

With *reservation* of a hundred knights. *Shak.*

In the United States, a tract of land not sold with the rest, is called a *reservation.*

3. Custody; state of being treasured up or kept in store. *Shak.*

4. In *law*, a clause or part of an instrument by which something is reserved, not conceded or granted; also, a proviso.

Mental reservation is the withholding of expression or disclosure of something that affects a proposition or statement, and which if disclosed, would materially vary its import.

Mental reservations are the refuge of hypocrites. *Encyc.*

RESERV'ATIVE, *a.* Keeping; reserving.

RESERV'ATORY, *n.* [from *reserve.*] A place in which things are reserved or kept. *Woodward.*

RESERVE, *v. t.* *rezerv'.* [Fr. *reserver*; L. *reservo*; *re* and *servo*, to keep.]

1. To keep in store for future or other use; to withhold from present use for another purpose. The farmer sells his corn, *reserving* only what is necessary for his family.

Hast thou seen the treasures of hail, which I have *reserved* against the day of trouble? Job xxxviii.

2. To keep; to hold; to retain.

Will he *reserve* his anger for ever? Jer. iii.

3. To lay up and keep for a future time. 2 Pet. ii.

Reserve your kind looks and language for private hours. *Swift.*

RESERVE, *n.* *rezerv'.* That which is kept for other or future use; that which is retained from present use or disposal.

The virgins, besides the oil in their lamps, carried likewise a *reserve* in some other vessel for a continual supply. *Tillotson.*

2. Something in the mind withheld from disclosure.

However any one may concur in the general scheme, it is still with certain *reserves* and deviations. *Addison.*

3. Exception; something withheld.

Is knowledge so despis'd?
Or envy, or what *reserve* forbids to taste? *Milton.*

4. Exception in favor.

Each has some darling lust, which pleads for a *reserve.* *Rogers.*

5. Restraint of freedom in words or actions; backwardness; caution in personal behavior. *Reserve* may proceed from modesty, bashfulness, prudence, prudery or sullenness.

My soul surpris'd, and from her sex disjoin'd,
Left all *reserve*, and all the sex behind. *Prior.*

6. In *law*, reservation.

In reserve, in store; in keeping for other or future use. He has large quantities of wheat *in reserve.* He has evidence or arguments *in reserve.*

Body of reserve, in military affairs, the third or last line of an army drawn up for battle, reserved to sustain the other lines as occasion may require; a body of troops kept for an exigency.

RESERV'ED, *pp.* Kept for another or future use; retained.

2. *a.* Restrained from freedom in words or actions; backward in conversation; not free or frank.

To all obliging, yet *reserv'd* to all. *Walsh.*
Nothing *reserv'd* or sullen was to see. *Dryden.*

RESERV'EDLY, *adv.* With reserve; with backwardness; not with openness or frankness. *Woodward.*

2. Scrupulously; cautiously; coldly. *Pope.*

RESERV'EDNESS, *n.* Closeness; want of frankness, openness or freedom. A man may guard himself by that silence and *reservedness* which every one may innocently practice. *South.*

RESERV'ER, *n.* One that reserves.

RESERV'ING, *ppr.* Keeping back; keeping for other use or for use at a future time; retaining.

RESERVOIR', *n.* [Fr.] A place where any thing is kept in store, particularly a place where water is collected and kept for use when wanted, as to supply a fountain, a canal or a city by means of aqueducts, or to drive a mill-wheel and the like; a cistern; a mill-pond; a bason.

RE'SET, *n.* In *Scots law*, the receiving and harboring of an outlaw or a criminal. *Encyc.*

RESET'TLE, *v. t.* [*re* and *settle.*] To settle again. *Swift.*

2. To install, as a minister of the gospel.

RESET'TLE, *v. i.* To settle in the ministry a second time; to be installed.

RESET'TLED, *pp.* Settled again; installed.

RESET'TLEMENT, *n.* The act of settling or composing again.

The *resettlement* of my discomposed soul. *Norris.*

2. The state of settling or subsiding again; as the *resettlement* of lees. *Mortimer.*

3. A second settlement in the ministry.

RESET'TLING, *ppr.* Settling again; installing.

RESHIP', *v. t.* [*re* and *ship.*] To ship again; to ship what has been conveyed by water or imported; as coffee and sugar imported into New York, and *reshipped* for Hamburg.

RESHIP'MENT, *n.* The act of shipping or loading on board of a ship a second time; the shipping for exportation what has been imported.

2. That which is reshipped.

RESHIP'PED, *pp.* Shipped again.

RESHIP'PING, *ppr.* Shipping again.

RE'SIANCE, *n.* [See *Resiant.*] Residence; abode. *Obs.* *Bacon.*

RE'SIANT, *a.* [Norm. *resiant, resseant*, from the L. *resideo.* See *Reside.*] Resident; dwelling; present in a place. *Obs.* *Knolles.*

RESI'DE, *v. i.* *s* as *z.* [Fr. *resider*; L. *resideo, resido*; *re* and *sedeo*, to sit, to settle.]

1. To dwell permanently or for a length of time; to have a settled abode for a time. The peculiar uses of this word are to be noticed. When the word is applied to the natives of a state, or others who dwell in it as permanent citizens, we use it only with reference to the *part* of a city or country in which a man dwells. We do not say generally, that Englishmen *reside* in England, but a particular citizen *resides* in London or York, or at such a house in such a street, in the Strand, &c.

When the word is applied to strangers or travelers, we do not say, a man *resides* in an inn for a night, but he *resided* in London or Oxford a month or a year; or he may *reside* in a foreign country a great part of his life. A man lodges, stays, remains, abides, for a day or very short time, but *reside* implies a longer time, though not definite.

2. To sink to the bottom of liquors; to settle. *Obs.* *Boyle.*

[In this sense, *subside* is now used.]

RES'IDENCE, *n.* [Fr.] The act of abiding or dwelling in a place for some continuance of time; as the *residence* of an American in France or Italy for a year.

The confessor had often made considerable *residences* in Normandy. *Hale.*

2. The place of abode; a dwelling; a habitation.

Caprea had been—the *residence* of Tiberius for several years.

3. That which falls to the bottom of liquors. *Obs.* *Bacon.*

4. In *the canon* and *common law*, the abode of a parson or incumbent on his benefice; opposed to *non-residence.* *Blackstone.*

RES'IDENT, *a.* [L. *residens*; Fr. *resident.*] Dwelling or having an abode in a place for a continuance of time, but not definite; as a minister *resident* at the court of St. James. A B is now *resident* in South America.

RES'IDENT, *n.* One who resides or dwells in a place for some time. A B is now a *resident* in London.

2. A public minister who resides at a foreign court. It is usually applied to ministers of a rank inferior to that of embassadors. *Encyc.*

RESIDEN'TIARY, *a.* Having residence. *More.*

RESIDEN'TIARY, *n.* An ecclesiastic who keeps a certain residence. *Eccles. Canons.*

RESI'DER, *n.* One who resides in a particular place. *Swift.*

RESI'DING, *ppr.* Dwelling in a place for some continuance of time.

RESID'UAL, *a.* Remaining after a part is taken. *Davy.*

RESID'UARY, *a.* [L. *residuus.* See *Reside.*]

Pertaining to the residue or part remaining; as the *residuary* advantage of an estate. *Ayliffe.*

Residuary legatee, in law, the legatee to whom is bequeathed the part of goods and estate which remains after deducting all the debts and specific legacies. *Blackstone.*

RES'IDUE, *n.* [Fr. *residu*; L. *residuus.*]

1. That which remains after a part is taken, separated, removed or designated.

The locusts shall eat the *residue* of that which has escaped. Ex. x.

The *residue* of them will I deliver to the sword. Jer. xv.

2. The balance or remainder of a debt or account.

RESID'UUM, *n.* [L.] Residue; that which is left after any process of separation or purification. *Chimistry. Metallurgy.*

2. In *law*, the part of an estate or of goods and chattels remaining after the payment of debts and legacies. *Blackstone.*

RESIE'GE, *v. t.* [*re* and *siege.*] To seat again; to reinstate. *Obs.* *Spenser.*

RESIGN, *v. t.* *rezi'ne.* [Fr. *resigner*; L. *resigno*; *re* and *signo*, to sign. The radical sense of *sign* is to send, to drive, hence to set. To *resign* is to send back or send away.]

1. To give up; to give back, as an office or commission, to the person or authority that conferred it; hence, to surrender an office or charge in a formal manner; as, a military officer *resigns* his commission; a prince *resigns* his crown.

Phœbus *resigns* his darts, and Jove
His thunder, to the god of love. *Denham.*

2. To withdraw, as a claim. He *resigns* all pretensions to skill.

3. To yield; as, to *resign* the judgment to the direction of others. *Locke.*

4. To yield or give up in confidence.

What more reasonable, than that we should in all things *resign* ourselves to the will of God? *Tillotson.*

5. To submit, particularly to Providence.

A firm, yet cautious mind;
Sincere, though prudent; constant, yet *resign'd.* *Pope.*

6. To submit without resistance or murmur. *Shak.*

RE'SIGN, *v.t.* To sign again.

RESIGN, *n.* Resignation. *Obs.*

RESIGNA'TION, *n.* [Fr.] The act of resigning or giving up, as a claim or possession; as the *resignation* of a crown or commission.

2. Submission; unresisting acquiescence; as a blind *resignation* to the authority of other men's opinions. *Locke.*

3. Quiet submission to the will of Providence; submission without discontent, and with entire acquiescence in the divine dispensations. This is christian *resignation.*

RESIGNED, *pp.* Given up; surrendered; yielded.

2. *a.* Submissive to the will of God.

RESIGNEDLY, *adv.* With submission.

RESIGNER, *n.* One that resigns.

RESIGNING, *ppr.* Giving up; surrendering; submitting.

RESIGNMENT, *n.* The act of resigning. *Obs.*

RES'ILAH, *n.* An ancient patriarchal coin.

RESIL'IENCE, } *n.* *s* as *z.* [L. *resiliens*, *resilio*; *re* and *salio*, to spring.]
RESIL'IENCY,

The act of leaping or springing back, or the act of rebounding; as the *resilience* of a ball or of sound. *Bacon.*

RESIL'IENT, *a.* [L. *resiliens.*] Leaping or starting back; rebounding.

RESILI''TION, *n.* [L. *resilio.*] The act of springing back; resilience.

RES'IN, *n.* *s* as *z.* [Fr. *resine*; L. It. Sp. *resina*; Ir. *roisin*; Gr. ῥητίνη, probably from ῥεω, to flow.]

An inflammable substance, hard when cool, but viscid when heated, exsuding in a fluid state from certain kinds of trees, as pine, either spontaneously or by incision. *Resins* are soluble in oils and alcohol, and are said to be nothing but oils concreted by combination with oxygen. *Resins* differ from *gums*, which are vegetable mucilage; and they are less sweet and odorous than balsams. *Encyc. Nicholson. Fourcroy.*

RESINIF'EROUS, *a.* [L. *resina* and *fero*, to produce.]

Yielding resin; as a *resiniferous* tree or vessels. *Gregory.*

RES'INIFORM, *a.* Having the form of resin. *Cyc.*

RESINO-ELEC'TRIC, *a.* Containing or exhibiting negative electricity, or that kind which is produced by the friction of resinous substances. *Ure.*

RES'INO-EXTRAC'TIVE, *a.* Designating extractive matter in which resin predominates.

RES'INOUS, *a.* Partaking of the qualities of resin; like resin. *Resinous* substances are combustible.

Resinous electricity, is that electricity which is excited by rubbing bodies of the resinous kind. This is generally negative.

RES'INOUSLY, *adv.* By means of resin; as *resinously* electrified. *Gregory.*

RES'INOUSNESS, *n.* The quality of being resinous.

RESIPIS'CENCE, *n.* [Fr. from L. *resipisco*, from *resipio*; *re* and *sapio*, to taste.]

Properly, wisdom derived from severe experience; hence, repentance. [*Little used.*]

RESIST, *v. t.* *rezist'.* [L. *resisto*; *re* and *sisto*, to stand; Fr. *resister*; Sp. *resistir*; It. *resistere.*]

1. Literally, to stand against; to withstand; hence, to act in opposition, or to oppose. A dam or mound *resists* a current of water *passively*, by standing unmoved and interrupting its progress. An army *resists* the progress of an enemy *actively*, by encountering and defeating it. We *resist* measures by argument or remonstrance.

Why doth he yet find fault? for who hath *resisted* his will? Rom. ix.

2. To strive against; to endeavor to counteract, defeat or frustrate.

Ye do always *resist* the Holy Spirit. Acts vii.

3. To baffle; to disappoint.

God *resisteth* the proud, but giveth grace to the humble. James iv.

RESIST', *v. i.* To make opposition. *Shak.*

RESIST'ANCE, *n.* The act of resisting; opposition. Resistance is *passive*, as that of a fixed body which interrupts the passage of a moving body; or *active*, as in the exertion of force to stop, repel or defeat progress or designs.

2. The quality of not yielding to force or external impression; that power of a body which acts in opposition to the impulse or pressure of another, or which prevents the effect of another power; as the *resistance* of a ball which receives the force of another; the *resistance* of wood to a cutting instrument; the *resistance* of air to the motion of a cannon ball, or of water to the motion of a ship.

RESIST'ANT, *n.* He or that which resists. *Pearson.*

RESIST'ED, *pp.* Opposed; counteracted; withstood.

RESIST'ER, *n.* One that opposes or withstands.

RESISTIBIL'ITY, *n.* The quality of resisting.

The name body, being the complex idea of extension and *resistibility* together in the same subject— *Locke.*

2. Quality of being resistible; as the *resistibility* of grace. *Hammond.*

RESIST'IBLE, *a.* That may be resisted; as a *resistible* force; *resistible* grace. *Hale.*

RESIST'ING, *ppr.* Withstanding; opposing.

Resisting medium, a substance which opposes the passage of a body through it.

RESIST'IVE, *a.* Having the power to resist. *B. Jonson.*

RESIST'LESS, *a.* That cannot be effectually opposed or withstood; irresistible.

Resistless in her love as in her hate. *Dryden.*

2. That cannot resist; helpless. *Spenser.*

RESIST'LESSLY, *adv.* So as not to be opposed or denied. *Blackwall.*

RESOLD, *pp.* of *resell.* Sold a second time, or sold after being bought.

RES'OLUBLE, *a.* *s* as *z.* [*re* and L. *solubilis.* See *Resolve.*]

That may be melted or dissolved; as bodies *resoluble* by fire. *Boyle.*

RES'OLUTE, *a.* [Fr. *resolu*; It. *resoluto.* The Latin *resolutus* has a different signification. See *Resolve.*]

Having a fixed purpose; determined; hence, bold; firm; steady; constant in pursuing a purpose.

Edward is at hand,
Ready to fight; therefore be *resolute.* *Shak.*

RES'OLUTELY, *adv.* With fixed purpose; firmly; steadily; with steady perseverance. Persist *resolutely* in a course of virtue.

2. Boldly; firmly.

Some of these facts he examines, some he *resolutely* denies. *Swift.*

RES'OLUTENESS, *n.* Fixed purpose; firm determination; unshaken firmness.

RESOLU'TION, *n.* [Fr. from L. *resolutio.* See *Resolve.*]

1. The act, operation or process of separating the parts which compose a complex idea or a mixed body; the act of reducing any compound or combination to its component parts; analysis; as the *resolution*

of complex ideas; the *resolution* of any material substance by chemical operations.

2. The act or process of unraveling or disentangling perplexities, or of dissipating obscurity in moral subjects; as the *resolution* of difficult questions in moral science.

3. Dissolution; the natural process of separating the component parts of bodies. *Digby.*

4. In *music*, the resolution of a dissonance, is the carrying of it, according to rule, into a consonance in the subsequent chord. *Encyc.*

5. In *medicine*, the disappearing of any tumor without coming to suppuration; the dispersing of inflammation. *Encyc. Coxe.*

6. Fixed purpose or determination of mind; as a *resolution* to reform our lives; a *resolution* to undertake an expedition. *Locke.*

7. The effect of fixed purpose; firmness, steadiness or constancy in execution, implying courage.

They who governed the parliament, had the *resolution* to act those monstrous things. *Clarendon.*

8. Determination of a cause in a court of justice; as a judicial *resolution.* *Hale.*

[But this word is now seldom used to express the decision of a judicial tribunal. We use *judgment, decision* or *decree.*]

9. The determination or decision of a legislative body, or a formal proposition offered for legislative determination. We call that a *resolution*, which is reduced to form and offered to a legislative house for consideration, and we call it a *resolution* when adopted. We say, a member moved certain *resolutions;* the house proceeded to consider the *resolutions* offered; they adopted or rejected the *resolutions.*

10. The formal determination of any corporate body, or of any association of individuals; as the *resolutions* of a town or other meeting.

11. In *algebra*, the resolution of an equation, is the same as reduction; the bringing of the unknown quantity by itself on one side, and all the known quantities on the other, without destroying the equation, by which is found the value of the unknown quantity. *Day's Algebra.*

12. Relaxation; a weakening. *Obs. Brown.*

RESOLU'TIONER, *n.* One who joins in the declaration of others. [*Not in use.*] *Burnet.*

RES'OLUTIVE, *a.* Having the power to dissolve or relax. [*Not much used.*] *Johnson.*

RESOLV'ABLE, *a.* That may be resolved or reduced to first principles.

RESOLVE, *v. t. rezolv'.* [L. *resolvo; re* and *solvo*, to loose; Fr. *resoudre;* It. *risolvere;* Sp. *resolver.*]

1. To separate the component parts of a compound substance; to reduce to first principles; as, to *resolve* a body into its component or constituent parts; to *resolve* a body into its elements.

2. To separate the parts of a complex idea; to reduce to simple parts; to analyze.

3. To separate the parts of a complicated question; to unravel; to disentangle of perplexities; to remove obscurity by analysis; to clear of difficulties; to explain; as, to *resolve* questions in moral science; to *resolve* doubts; to *resolve* a riddle.

4. To inform; to free from doubt or perplexity; as, to *resolve* the conscience.

Resolve me, strangers, whence and what you are? *Dryden.*

5. To settle in an opinion; to make certain.

Long since we were *resolv'd* of your truth,
Your faithful service and your toil in war. *Shak.*

6. To confirm; to fix in constancy.

Quit presently the chapel, or *resolve* you
For more amazement. [*Unusual.*] *Shak.*

7. To melt; to dissolve. *Arbuthnot.*

8. To form or constitute by resolution, vote or determination; as, the house *resolved* itself into a committee of the whole.

9. In *music*, to resolve a discord or dissonance, is to carry it, according to rule, into a consonance in the subsequent chord. *Rousseau. Encyc.*

10. In *medicine*, to disperse or scatter; to discuss; as inflammation or a tumor.

11. To relax; to lay at ease. *Spenser.*

12. In *algebra*, to resolve an equation, is to bring all the known quantities to one side of the equation, and the unknown quantity to the other.

RESOLVE, *v. i. rezolv'.* To fix in opinion or purpose; to determine in mind. He *resolved* to abandon his vicious course of life.

2. To determine by vote. The legislature *resolved* to receive no petitions after a certain day.

3. To melt; to dissolve; to become fluid.

When the blood stagnates in any part, it first coagulates, then *resolves* and turns alkaline. *Arbuthnot.*

4. To separate into its component parts, or into distinct principles; as, water *resolves* into vapor; a substance *resolves* into gas.

5. To be settled in opinion.

Let men *resolve* of that as they please. [*Unusual.*] *Locke.*

RESOLVE, *n. rezolv'.* Fixed purpose of mind; settled determination; resolution.

He strait revokes his bold *resolve.* *Denham.*

2. Legal or official determination; legislative act concerning a private person or corporation, or concerning some private business. Public acts of a legislature respect the state, and to give them validity, the bills for such acts must pass through all the legislative forms. Resolves are usually private acts, and are often passed with less formality. Resolves may also be the acts of a single branch of the legislature; whereas public acts must be passed by a majority of both branches. *Am. Legislatures.*

3. The determination of any corporation or association; resolution.

RESOLV'ED, *pp.* Separated into its component parts; analyzed.

2. Determined in purpose; as, I am *resolved* not to keep company with gamesters. This phrase is properly, "*I have resolved;*" as we say, a person *is* deceased, for *has* deceased; he *is* retired, for *has* retired. In these phrases, the participle is rather an adjective.

3. Determined officially or by vote.

RESOLV'EDLY, *adv.* With firmness of purpose. *Grew.*

RESOLV'EDNESS, *n.* Fixedness of purpose; firmness; resolution. *Decay of Piety.*

RESOLV'ENT, *n.* That which has the power of causing solution. In *medicine*, that which has power to disperse inflammation and prevent the suppuration of tumors; a discutient. *Coxe. Encyc.*

RESOLV'ER, *n.* One that resolves or forms a firm purpose.

RESOLV'ING, *ppr.* Separating into component parts; analyzing; removing perplexities or obscurity; discussing, as tumors; determining.

RESOLV'ING, *n.* The act of determining or forming a fixed purpose; a resolution. *Clarendon.*

RES'ONANCE, *n. s* as *z.* [L. *resonans.*] A resounding; a sound returned from the sides of a hollow instrument of music; reverberated sound or sounds. *Encyc.*

2. A sound returned.

RES'ONANT, *a.* [L. *resonans; re* and *sono*, to sound.] Resounding; returning sound; echoing back. *Milton.*

RESORB', *v. t.* [L. *resorbeo; re* and *sorbeo*, to drink in.] To swallow up. *Young.*

RESORB'ENT, *a.* Swallowing up. *Woodhull.*

RESORT', *v. i. s* as *z.* [Fr. *ressortir; re* and *sortir*, to go or come out.]

1. To have recourse; to apply; to betake.

The king thought it time to *resort* to other counsels. *Clarendon.*

2. To go; to repair.

The people *resort* to him again. Mark x. John xviii.

3. To fall back.

The inheritance of the son never *resorted* to the mother. *Obs.* *Hale.*

RESORT', *n.* The act of going to or making application; a betaking one's self; as a *resort* to other means of defense; a *resort* to subterfuges for evasion.

2. Act of visiting.

Join with me to forbid him her *resort.* *Shak.*

3. Assembly; meeting. *Dryden.*

4. Concourse; frequent assembling; as a place of *resort.* *Swift.*

5. The place frequented; as, alehouses are the *resorts* of the idle and dissolute.

6. Spring; active power or movement; *a Gallicism.* [*Not in use.*] *Bacon.*

Last resort, ultimate means of relief; also, final tribunal; that from which there is no appeal.

RESORT'ER, *n.* One that resorts or frequents.

RESORT'ING, *ppr.* Going; having recourse; betaking; frequenting.

RESOUND', *v. t. s* as *z.* [L. *resono; re* and *sono*, to sound; Fr. *resonner;* It. *risuonare;* Sp. *resonar.*] To send back sound; to echo.

And Albion's cliffs *resound* the rural lay. *Pope.*

2. To sound; to praise or celebrate with the voice or the sound of instruments. *Milton.*

3. To praise; to extol with sounds; to spread the fame of.

The man for wisdom's various arts renown'd,
Long exercis'd in woes, O muse, *resound.* *Pope.*

RESOUND', *v. i.* To be echoed; to be sent back, as sound; as, common fame *resounds* back to them. *South.*

2. To be much and loudly mentioned. *Milton.*

RE'SOUND, *v. t.* [*re* and *sound; with the accent on the first syllable.*] To sound again. *Jones.*

RESOUND', *n. s* as *z.* Return of sound; echo. *Beaum.*

RESOUND'ED, *pp.* Echoed; returned, as sound; celebrated.

RESOUND'ING, *ppr.* Echoing; returning, as sound.

RESOURCE, *n.* [Fr. *ressource; re* and *source.*]

1. Any source of aid or support; an expedient to which a person may resort for assistance, safety or supply; means yet untried; resort. An enterprising man finds *resources* in his own mind.

Pallas view'd
His foes pursuing and his friends pursu'd,
Used threat'nings mix'd with prayers, his last *resource.* *Dryden.*

2. *Resources,* in the plural, pecuniary means; funds; money or any property that can be converted into supplies; means of raising money or supplies. Our national *resources* for carrying on war are abundant. Commerce and manufactures furnish ample *resources.*

RESOURCELESS, *a.* Destitute of resources. [*A word not to be countenanced.*] *Burke.*

RESOW, *v. t.* pret. *resowed*; pp. *resowed* or *resown.* [*re* and *sow.*] To sow again. *Bacon.*

RESOWED, RESOWN, } *pp.* Sown anew.

RESPE'AK, *v. t.* pret. *respoke*; pp. *respoken, respoke.* [*re* and *speak.*]

1. To answer; to speak in return; to reply. [*Little used.*] *Shak.*
2. To speak again; to repeat.

RESPECT', *v. t.* [L. *respecto*, or *respectus*, from *respicio*; *re* and *specio*, to view; Fr. *respecter*; It. *rispettare*; Sp. *respetar.*]

1. To regard; to have regard to in design or purpose.

In orchards and gardens, we do not so much *respect* beauty, as variety of ground for fruits, trees and herbs. *Bacon.*

2. To have regard to, in relation or connection; to relate to. The treaty particularly *respects* our commerce.
3. To view or consider with some degree of reverence; to esteem as possessed of real worth.

I always loved and *respected* Sir William. *Swift.*

4. To look towards.

Palladius adviseth the front of his house should so *respect* the south. [*Not in use.*] *Brown.*

To respect the person, to suffer the opinion or judgment to be influenced or biased by a regard to the outward circumstances of a person, to the prejudice of right and equity.

Thou shalt not *respect the person* of the poor. Lev. xix.

Neither doth God *respect* any *person.* 2 Sam. xiv.

RESPECT', *n.* [L. *respectus*; Fr. *respect.*]

1. Regard; attention. *Shak.*
2. That estimation or honor in which men hold the distinguished worth or substantial good qualities of others. It expresses less than *reverence* and *veneration*, which regard elders and superiors; whereas *respect* may regard juniors and inferiors. *Respect* regards the qualities of the mind, or the actions which characterize those qualities.

Seen without awe, and serv'd without *respect.* *Prior.*

3. That deportment or course of action which proceeds from esteem; regard; due attention; as, to treat a person with *respect.*

These same men treat the sabbath with little *respect.* *Nelson.*

4. Good will; favor.

The Lord had *respect* to Abel and his offering. Gen. iv.

5. Partial regard; undue bias to the prejudice of justice; as the phrase, *respect of persons.* 1 Pet. i. James ii. Prov. xxiv.
6. Respected character; as persons of the best *respect* in Rome. *Shak.*
7. Consideration; motive in reference to something.

Whatever secret *respects* were likely to move them— *Hooker.*

8. Relation; regard; reference; followed by *of*, but more properly by *to.*

They believed but one Supreme Deity, which, with *respect to* the benefits men received from him, had several titles. *Tillotson.*

RESPECTABIL'ITY, *n.* State or quality of being respectable; the state or qualities which deserve or command respect. *Cumberland. Kett.*

RESPECT'ABLE, *a.* [Fr.; It. *rispettabile*; Sp. *respetable.*]

1. Possessing the worth or qualities which deserve or command respect; worthy of esteem and honor; as a *respectable* citizen; *respectable* company.

No government, any more than an individual, will long be respected, without being truly *respectable.* *Federalist, Madison.*

2. In *popular language*, this word is much used to express what is moderate in degree of excellence or in number, but not despicable. We say, a *respectable* discourse or performance, a *respectable* audience, a *respectable* number of citizens convened.

RESPECT'ABLENESS, *n.* Respectability.

RESPECT'ABLY, *adv.* With respect; more generally, in a manner to merit respect.

2. Moderately, but in a manner not to be despised.

RESPECT'ED, *pp.* Held in honorable estimation.

RESPECT'ER, *n.* One that respects; chiefly used in the phrase, *respecter of persons*, which signifies a person who regards the external circumstances of others in his judgment, and suffers his opinion to be biased by them, to the prejudice of candor, justice and equity.

I perceive that God is no *respecter of persons.* Acts x.

RESPECT'FUL, *a.* Marked or characterized by respect; as *respectful* deportment.

With humble joy and with *respectful* fear. *Prior.*

RESPECT'FULLY, *adv.* With respect; in a manner comporting with due estimation. *Dryden.*

RESPECT'FULNESS, *n.* The quality of being respectful.

RESPECT'ING, *ppr.* Regarding; having regard to; relating to. This word, like *concerning*, has reference to a single word or to a sentence. In the sentence, "his conduct *respecting* us is commendable," *respecting* has reference to *conduct.* But when we say, "*respecting* a further appropriation of money, it is to be observed, that the resources of the country are inadequate," *respecting* has reference to the whole subsequent clause or sentence.

RESPECT'IVE, *a.* [Fr. *respectif*; It. *rispettivo.*]

1. Relative; having relation to something else; not absolute; as the *respective* connections of society.
2. Particular; relating to a particular person or thing. Let each man retire to his *respective* place of abode. The officers were found in their *respective* quarters; they appeared at the head of their *respective* regiments. Let each give according to his *respective* proportion.
3. Worthy of respect. [*Not in use.*] *Shak.*
4. Careful; circumspect; cautious; attentive to consequences; as *respective* and wary men. [*Not in use.*] *Hooker.*

RESPECT'IVELY, *adv.* As relating to each; particularly; as each belongs to each. Let each man *respectively* perform his duty.

The impressions from the objects of the senses do mingle *respectively* every one with its kind. *Bacon.*

2. Relatively; not absolutely. *Raleigh.*
3. Partially; with respect to private views. *Obs.*
4. With respect. *Obs.* *Shak.*

RESPECT'LESS, *a.* Having no respect; without regard; without reference. [*Little used.*] *Drayton.*

RESPECT'LESSNESS, *n.* The state of having no respect or regard; regardlessness. [*Little used.*] *Shelton.*

RESPERSE, *v. t.* *respers'.* [L. *respersus*, *respergo*; *re* and *spargo*, to sprinkle.] To sprinkle. [*Rarely used.*] *Taylor.*

RESPER'SION, *n.* [L. *respersio.*] The act of sprinkling. *Johnson.*

RES'PIRABLE, *a.* [from *respire.*] That may be breathed; fit for respiration or for the support of animal life; as *respirable* air. Azotic gas is not *respirable.*

RESPIRA'TION, *n.* [Fr. from L. *respiratio.*]

1. The act of breathing; the act of inhaling air into the lungs and again exhaling or expelling it, by which animal life is supported. The *respiration* of fishes, [for these cannot live long without air,] appears to be performed by the air contained in the water acting on the gills.
2. Relief from toil. *Milton.*

RES'PIRATORY, *a.* Serving for respiration; as *respiratory* organs. *Asiat. Res.*

RESPI'RE, *v. i.* [Fr. *respirer*; L. *respiro*; *re* and *spiro*, to breathe.]

1. To breathe; to inhale air into the lungs and exhale it, for the purpose of maintaining animal life.
2. To catch breath. *Spenser.*
3. To rest; to take rest from toil. *Milton.*

RESPI'RE, *v. t.* To exhale; to breathe out; to send out in exhalations. *B. Jonson.*

RESPI'RED, *pp.* Breathed; inhaled and exhaled.

RESPI'RING, *ppr.* Breathing; taking breath.

RES'PIT, *n.* [Fr. *repit.*] Pause; temporary intermission of labor, or of any process or operation; interval of rest.

Some pause and *respit* only I require. *Denham.*

2. In *law*, reprieve; temporary suspension of the execution of a capital offender. *Milton. Prior.*

3. Delay; forbearance; prolongation of time for the payment of a debt beyond the legal time.

4. The delay of appearance at court granted to a jury, beyond the proper term. *Blackstone.*

RES'PIT, *v. t.* To relieve by a pause or interval of rest.

To *respit* his day-labor with repast. *Milton.*

2. To suspend the execution of a criminal beyond the time limited by the sentence; to delay for a time. *Clarendon.*

3. To give delay of appearance at court; as, to *respit* a jury. *Blackstone.*

RES'PITED, *pp.* Relieved from labor; allowed a temporary suspension of execution.

RES'PITING, *ppr.* Relieving from labor; suspending the execution of a capital offender.

RESPLEN'DENCE, RESPLEN'DENCY, *n.* [L. *resplendens, resplendeo; re* and *splendeo*, to shine.] Brilliant luster; vivid brightness; splendor.

Son! thou in whom my glory I behold
In full *resplendence*, heir of all my might. *Milton.*

RESPLEN'DENT, *a.* [supra.] Very bright; shining with brilliant luster.

With royal arras and *resplendent* gold. *Spenser.*

RESPLEN'DENTLY, *adv.* With brilliant luster; with great brightness.

RESPLIT', *v. t.* [*re* and *split.*] To split again.

RESPOND', *v. i.* [Fr. *repondre;* It. *rispondere;* Sp. *responder;* L. *respondeo; re* and *spondeo*, to promise, that is, to send to. Hence *respondeo* is to send back.]

1. To answer; to reply.

A new affliction strings a new chord in the heart, which *responds* to some new note of complaint within the wide scale of human woe. *Buckminster.*

2. To correspond; to suit.

To every theme *responds* thy various lay. *Broome.*

3. To be answerable; to be liable to make payment; as, the defendant is held to *respond* in damages.

RESPOND', *v. t.* To answer; to satisfy by payment. The surety was held to *respond* the judgment of court. The goods attached shall be held to *respond* the judgment. *Sedgwick, Mass. Rep.*

RESPOND', *n.* A short anthem interrupting the middle of a chapter, which is not to proceed till the anthem is ended. *Wheatly.*

2. An answer. [*Not in use.*] *Ch. Relig. Appeal.*

RESPOND'ED, *pp.* Answered; satisfied by payment.

RESPOND'ENT, *a.* Answering; that answers to demand or expectation.

—Wealth *respondent* to payment and contributions. *Bacon.*

RESPOND'ENT, *n.* One that answers in a suit, particularly a chancery suit.

2. In *the schools*, one who maintains a thesis in reply, and whose province is to refute objections or overthrow arguments. *Watts.*

RESPOND'ING, *ppr.* Answering; corresponding.

RESPONS'AL, *a.* Answerable; responsible. [*Not in use.*] *Heylin.*

RESPONS'AL, *n.* Response; answer. *Brevint.*

2. One who is responsible. [*Not in use.*] *Barrow.*

RESPONSE, *n.* *respons'.* [L. *responsum.*]

1. An answer or reply; particularly, an oracular answer.

2. The answer of the people or congregation to the priest, in the litany and other parts of divine service. *Addison.*

3. Reply to an objection in a formal disputation. *Watts.*

4. In *the Romish church*, a kind of anthem sung after the morning lesson.

5. In *a fugue*, a repetition of the given subject by another part. *Busby.*

RESPONSIBIL'ITY, *n.* [from *responsible.*]

1. The state of being accountable or answerable, as for a trust or office, or for a debt. *Burke. Paley.*

It is used in the plural; as heavy *responsibilities.* *Johnson's Rep.*

2. Ability to answer in payment; means of paying contracts.

RESPONS'IBLE, *a.* [from L. *responsus, respondeo.*]

1. Liable to account; accountable; answerable; as for a trust reposed, or for a debt. We are all *responsible* for the talents entrusted to us by our Creator. A guardian is *responsible* for the faithful discharge of his duty to his ward. The surety is *responsible* for the debt of his principal.

2. Able to discharge an obligation; or having estate adequate to the payment of a debt. In taking bail, the officer will ascertain whether the proposed surety is a *responsible* man.

RESPONS'IBLENESS, *n.* State of being liable to answer, repay or account; responsibility.

2. Ability to make payment of an obligation or demand.

RESPON'SION, *n.* [L. *responsio.*] The act of answering. [*Not used.*]

RESPONS'IVE, *a.* Answering; making reply.

2. Correspondent; suited to something else.

The vocal lay *responsive* to the strings. *Pope.*

RESPONS'ORY, *a.* Containing answer.

RESPONS'ORY, *n.* A response; the answer of the people to the priest in the alternate speaking, in church service.

REST, *n.* [Sax. *rest, ræst*, quiet or a lying down; Dan. G. Sw. *rast;* D. *rust.* The German has also *ruhe*, Sw. *ro*, Dan. *roe*, rest, repose. In W. *araws*, and *arosi*, signify to stay, stop, wait. This Teutonic word cannot be the L. *resto*, if the latter is a compound of *re* and *sto;* but is an original word of the Class Rd, Rs. See the Verb.]

1. Cessation of motion or action of any kind, and applicable to any body or being; as *rest* from labor; *rest* from mental exertion; *rest* of body or mind. A body is at *rest*, when it ceases to move; the mind is at *rest*, when it ceases to be disturbed or agitated; the sea is never at *rest*. Hence,

2. Quiet; repose; a state free from motion or disturbance; a state of reconciliation to God.

Learn of me, for I am meek and lowly in heart; and ye shall find *rest* to your souls. Matt. xi.

3. Sleep; as, retire to *rest.*

4. Peace; national quiet.

The land had *rest* eighty years. Judg. iii. Deut. xii.

5. The final sleep, death. *Dryden.*

6. A place of quiet; permanent habitation.

Ye are not as yet come to the *rest*, and to the inheritance which the Lord your God giveth you. Deut. xii.

7. Any place of repose.

In dust, our final *rest*, and native home. *Milton.*

8. That on which any thing leans or lies for support. 1 Kings vi.

Their vizors clos'd, their lances in the *rest*. *Dryden.*

9. In *poetry*, a short pause of the voice in reading; a cesura.

10. In *philosophy*, the continuance of a body in the same place.

11. Final hope.

Sea fights have been final to the war; but this is, when princes set up their *rest* upon the battle. *Obs.* *Bacon.*

12. Cessation from tillage. Lev. xxv.

13. The gospel church or new covenant state in which the people of God enjoy repose, and Christ shall be glorified. Is. xi.

14. In *music*, a pause; an interval during which the voice is intermitted; also, the mark of such intermission.

REST, *n.* [Fr. *reste*, from *rester*, to remain, L. *resto.*]

1. That which is left, or which remains after the separation of a part, either in fact or in contemplation; remainder.

Religion gives part of its reward in hand, the present comfort of having done our duty, and for the *rest*, it offers us the best security that heaven can give. *Tillotson.*

2. Others; those not included in a proposition or description. [In this sense, *rest* is a noun, but with a singular termination expressing plurality.]

Plato and the *rest* of the philosophers— *Stillingfleet.*

Arm'd like the *rest*, the Trojan prince appears. *Dryden.*

The election hath obtained it and the *rest* were blinded. Rom. xi.

REST, *v. i.* [Sax. *restan, hrestan*, to pause, to cease, to be quiet; D. *rusten;* G. *rasten;* Sw. *rasta.* See Class Rd. No. 81. 82.]

1. To cease from action or motion of any kind; to stop; a word applicable to any body or being, and to any kind of motion.

2. To cease from labor, work or performance.

God *rested* on the seventh day from all his work which he had made. Gen. ii.

So the people *rested* on the seventh day. Ex. xvi.

3. To be quiet or still; to be undisturbed.

There *rest*, if any rest can harbor there. *Milton.*

4. To cease from war; to be at peace.

And the land *rested* from war. Josh. xi.

5. To be quiet or tranquil, as the mind; not to be agitated by fear, anxiety or other passion.
6. To lie; to repose; as, to *rest* on a bed.
7. To sleep; to slumber.

Fancy then retires
Into her private cell, when nature *rests*. *Milton.*

8. To sleep the final sleep; to die or be dead.

Glad I'd lay me down,
As in my mother's lap; there I should *rest*,
And sleep secure. *Milton.*

9. To lean; to recline for support; as, to *rest* the arm on a table. The truth of religion *rests* on divine testimony.
10. To stand on; to be supported by; as, a column *rests* on its pedestal.
11. To be satisfied; to acquiesce; as, to *rest* on heaven's determination. *Addison.*
12. To lean; to trust; to rely; as, to *rest* on a man's promise.
13. To continue fixed. Is. li.
14. To terminate; to come to an end. Ezek. xvi.
15. To hang, lie or be fixed.

Over a tent a cloud shall *rest* by day. *Milton.*

16. To abide; to remain with.

They said, the spirit of Elijah doth *rest* on Elisha. 2 Kings ii. Eccles. vii.

17. To be calm or composed in mind; to enjoy peace of conscience.

REST, *v. i.* [Fr. *rester.*] To be left; to remain. *Obs.* *Milton.*

REST, *v. t.* To lay at rest; to quiet.

Your piety has paid
All needful rites, to *rest* my wandering shade. *Dryden.*

2. To place, as on a support. We *rest* our cause on the truth of the Scripture.

Her weary head upon your bosom *rest*. *Waller.*

RESTAG'NANT, *a.* [L. *restagnans.*] Stagnant; remaining without a flow or current. [*Not much used.*] *Boyle.*

RESTAG'NATE, *v. i.* [L. *restagno*; *re* and *stagno*, to stagnate.]
To stand or remain without flowing. *Wiseman.*
[This word is superseded by *stagnate.*]

RESTAGNA'TION, *n.* Stagnation, which see.

REST'ANT, *a.* [L. *restans*, *resto.*] In *botany*, remaining, as footstalks after the fructification has fallen off. *Lee.*

RESTAURA'TION, *n.* [L *restauro.*] Restoration to a former good state.
[The present orthography is *restoration*, which see.]

REST'ED, *pp.* Laid on for support.

RESTEM', *v. t.* [*re* and *stem.*] To force back against the current. *Shak.*

REST'FUL, *a.* [from *rest.*] Quiet; being at rest. *Shak.*

REST'FULLY, *adv.* In a state of rest or quiet. *Herbert.*

REST-HARROW, *n.* A plant of the genus Ononis.

REST'IF, *a.* [Fr. *retif*; It. *restivo*, *restio*; from L. *resto.*]
1. Unwilling to go, or only running back; obstinate in refusing to move forward; stubborn; as a *restif* steed. It seems originally to have been used of horses that would not be driven forward. It is sometimes written *restive*.

All who before him did ascend the throne,
Labor'd to draw three *restive* nations on. *Roscommon.*

2. Unyielding; as *restif* stubbornness. *L'Estrange.*
3. Being at rest, or less in action. [*Not in use.*] *Brown.*

REST'IF, *n.* A stubborn horse.

REST'IFNESS, *n.* Obstinate reluctance or indisposition to move.
2. Obstinate unwillingness. *Bacon.*

RESTINC'TION, *n.* [L. *restinctio*, *restinguo*; *re* and *extinguo.*] The act of quenching or extinguishing.

REST'ING, *ppr.* Ceasing to move or act; ceasing to be moved or agitated; lying; leaning; standing; depending or relying.

REST'ING-PLACE, *n.* A place for rest.

RESTIN'GUISH, *v. t.* [L. *restinguo*; *re* and *extinguo.*] To quench or extinguish. *Field.*

RES'TITUTE, *v. t.* [L. *restituo*; *re* and *statuo*, to set.]
To restore to a former state. [*Not used.*] *Dyer.*

RESTITU'TION, *n.* [L. *restitutio.*] The act of returning or restoring to a person some thing or right of which he has been unjustly deprived; as the *restitution* of ancient rights to the crown. *Spenser.*
Restitution is made by restoring a specific thing taken away or lost.
2. The act of making good, or of giving an equivalent for any loss, damage or injury; indemnification.

He *restitution* to the value makes. *Sandys.*

3. The act of recovering a former state or posture. [*Unusual.*] *Grew.*
Restitution of all things, the putting the world in a holy and happy state. Acts iii.

RES'TITUTOR, *n.* One who makes restitution. [*Little used.*]

RESTIVE, RESTIVENESS. [See *Restif.*]

REST'LESS, *a.* [from *rest*; Sax. *restleas.*]
1. Unquiet; uneasy; continually moving; as a *restless* child.
2. Being without sleep; uneasy.

Restless he pass'd the remnant of the night. *Dryden.*

3. Passed in unquietness; as, the patient has had a *restless* night.
4. Uneasy; unquiet; not satisfied to be at rest or in peace; as a *restless* prince; *restless* ambition; *restless* passions.
5. Uneasy; turbulent; as *restless* subjects.
6. Unsettled; disposed to wander or to change place or condition.

—*Restless* at home, and ever prone to range. *Dryden.*

REST'LESSLY, *adv.* Without rest; unquietly.

When the mind casts and turns itself *restlessly* from one thing to another. *South.*

REST'LESSNESS, *n.* Uneasiness; unquietness; a state of disturbance or agitation, either of body or mind.
2. Want of sleep or rest; uneasiness. *Harvey.*
3. Motion; agitation; as the *restlessness* of the magnetic needle. *Boyle.*

RESTO'RABLE, *a.* [from *restore.*] That may be restored to a former good condition; as *restorable* land. *Swift.*

RESTO'RAL, *n.* Restitution. [*Not in use.*] *Barrow.*

RESTORA'TION, *n.* [Fr. *restauration*; L. *restauro.*]
1. The act of replacing in a former state.

Behold the different climes agree,
Rejoicing in thy *restoration*. *Dryden.*

So we speak of the *restoration* of a man to his office, or to a good standing in society.
2. Renewal; revival; re-establishment; as the *restoration* of friendship between enemies; the *restoration* of peace after war; the *restoration* of a declining commerce.
3. Recovery; renewal of health and soundness; as *restoration* from sickness or from insanity.
4. Recovery from a lapse or any bad state; as the *restoration* of man from apostasy.
5. In *theology*, universal restoration, the final recovery of all men from sin and alienation from God, to a state of happiness; universal salvation.
6. In *England*, the return of king Charles II. in 1660, and the re-establishment of monarchy.

RESTO'RATIVE, *a.* That has power to renew strength and vigor. *Encyc.*

RESTO'RATIVE, *n.* A medicine efficacious in restoring strength and vigor, or in recruiting the vital powers. *Arbuthnot.*

RESTO'RE, *v. t.* [Fr. *restaurer*; It. *restaurare*; Sp. Port. *restaurar*; L. *restauro.* This is a compound of *re* and the root of *store, story, history.* The primary sense is to *set*, to lay or to throw, as in Gr. ϛερεος, solid.]
1. To return to a person, as a specific thing which he has lost, or which has been taken from him and unjustly detained. We *restore* lost or stolen goods to the owner.

Now therefore *restore* to the man his wife. Gen. xx.

2. To replace; to return; as a person or thing to a former place.

Pharaoh shall *restore* thee to thy place. Gen. xl.

3. To bring back.

The father banish'd virtue shall *restore*. *Dryden.*

4. To bring back or recover from lapse, degeneracy, declension or ruin to its former state.

—Loss of Eden, till one greater man
Restore it, and regain the blissful seat. *Milton.*

—Our fortune *restored* after the severest afflictions. *Prior.*

5. To heal; to cure; to recover from disease.

His hand was *restored* whole like as the other. Matt. xii.

6. To make restitution or satisfaction for a thing taken, by returning something else, or something of different value.

He shall *restore* five oxen for an ox, and four sheep for a sheep. Ex. xxii.

7. To give for satisfaction for pretended wrongs something not taken. Ps. lxix.
8. To repair; to rebuild; as, to *restore* and to build Jerusalem. Dan. ix.
9. To revive; to resuscitate; to bring back to life.

Whose son he had *restored* to life. 2 Kings viii.

10. To return or bring back after absence. Heb. xiii.

11. To bring to a sense of sin and amendment of life. Gal. vi.
12. To renew or re-establish after interruption; as, peace is *restored.* Friendship between the parties is *restored.*
13. To recover or renew, as passages of an author obscured or corrupted; as, to *restore* the true reading.

RE'-STORE, *v. t.* [*re* and *store.*] To store again. The goods taken out were *restored.*

RESTO'RED, *pp.* Returned; brought back; retrieved; recovered; cured; renewed; re-established.

RESTO'REMENT, *n.* The act of restoring; restoration. [*Not used.*] *Brown.*

RESTO'RER, *n.* One that restores; one that returns what is lost or unjustly detained; one who repairs or re-establishes.

RESTO'RING, *ppr.* Returning what is lost or taken; bringing back; recovering; curing; renewing; repairing; re-establishing.

RESTRA'IN, *v. t.* [Fr. *restraindre;* It. *ristrignere, restringere;* Sp. *restriñir, restringer;* L. *restringo; re* and *stringo,* to *strain.* The letter *g* appears from the participle to be casual; *stringo,* for *strigo.* Hence *strictus, strict, stricture.* If the two letters *st* are removed, the word *rigo* coincides exactly, in primary sense, with L. *rego, rectus, right,* and the root of *reach, stretch, straight.*]
1. To hold back; to check; to hold from action, proceeding or advancing, either by physical or moral force, or by any interposing obstacle. Thus we *restrain* a horse by a bridle; we *restrain* cattle from wandering by fences; we *restrain* water by dams and dikes; we *restrain* men from crimes and trespasses by laws; we *restrain* young people, when we can, by arguments or counsel; we *restrain* men and their passions; we *restrain* the elements; we attempt to *restrain* vice, but not always with success.
2. To repress; to keep in awe; as, to *restrain* offenders.
3. To suppress; to hinder or repress; as, to *restrain* excess.
4. To abridge; to hinder from unlimited enjoyment; as, to *restrain* one of his pleasure or of his liberty. *Clarendon. Shak.*
5. To limit; to confine.

> Not only a metaphysical or natural, but a moral universality is also to be *restrained* by a part of the predicate. *Watts.*

6. To withhold; to forbear.

> Thou *restrainest* prayer before God. Job xv.

RESTRA'INABLE, *a.* Capable of being restrained. *Brown.*

RESTRA'INED, *pp.* Held back from advancing or wandering; withheld; repressed; suppressed; abridged; confined.

RESTRA'INEDLY, *adv.* With restraint; with limitation. *Hammond.*

RESTRA'INER, *n.* He or that which restrains. *Brown.*

RESTRA'INING, *ppr.* Holding back from proceeding; checking; repressing; hindering from motion or action; suppressing.
2. *a.* Abridging; limiting; as a *restraining* statute.

RESTRA'INT, *n.* [from Fr. *restreint.*]
1. The act or operation of holding back or hindering from motion, in any manner; hinderance of the will, or of any action, physical, moral or mental.
2. Abridgment of liberty; as the *restraint* of a man by imprisonment or by duress.
3. Prohibition. The commands of God should be effectual *restraints* upon our evil passions.
4. Limitation; restriction.

> If all were granted, yet it must be maintained, within any bold *restraints,* far otherwise than it is received. *Brown.*

5. That which restrains, hinders or represses. The laws are *restraints* upon injustice.

RESTRI€T', *v. t.* [L. *restrictus,* from *restringo.* See *Restrain.*] To limit; to confine; to restrain within bounds; as, to *restrict* words to a particular meaning; to *restrict* a patient to a certain diet.

RESTRI€T'ED, *pp.* Limited; confined to bounds.

RESTRI€T'ING, *ppr.* Confining to limits.

RESTRI€'TION, *n.* [Fr. from L. *restrictus.*]
1. Limitation; confinement within bounds.

> This is to have the same *restriction* as all other recreations. *Gov. of the Tongue.*

Restriction of words, is the limitation of their signification in a particular manner or degree.
2. Restraint; as *restrictions* on trade.

RESTRI€T'IVE, *a.* [Fr. *restrictif.*] Having the quality of limiting or of expressing limitation; as a *restrictive* particle.
2. Imposing restraint; as *restrictive* laws of trade.
3. Styptic. [*Not used.*] *Wiseman.*

RESTRI€T'IVELY, *adv.* With limitation. *Gov. of the Tongue.*

RESTRINĠE, *v. t. restrinj'.* [L. *restringo,* supra.] To confine; to contract; to astringe.

RESTRIN'ĠENCY, *n.* The quality or power of contracting. *Petty.*

RESTRIN'ĠENT, *a.* Astringent; styptic.

RESTRIN'ĠENT, *n.* A medicine that operates as an astringent or styptic. *Harvey.*

RESTRI'VE, *v. i.* [*re* and *strive.*] To strive anew. *Sackville.*

REST'Y, *a.* The same as *restive* or *restif,* of which it is a contraction.

RESUBJE€'TION, *n.* [*re* and *subjection.*] A second subjection. *Bp. Hall.*

RESUBLIMA'TION, *n.* A second sublimation.

RESUBLI'ME, *v. t.* [*re* and *sublime.*] To sublime again; as, to *resublime* mercurial sublimate. *Newton.*

RESUBLI'MED, *pp.* Sublimed a second time.

RESUBLI'MING, *ppr.* Subliming again.

RESUDA'TION, *n.* [L. *resudatus, resudo; re* and *sudo,* to sweat.] The act of sweating again.

RESULT', *v. i. s* as *z.* [Fr. *resulter;* L. *resulto, resilio; re* and *salio,* to leap.] To leap back; to rebound.

> The huge round stone, *resulting* with a bound— *Pope.*

2. To proceed, spring or rise, as a consequence, from facts, arguments, premises, combination of circumstances, consultation or meditation. Evidence *results* from testimony, or from a variety of concurring circumstances; pleasure *results* from friendship; harmony *results* from certain accordances of sounds.

> Pleasure and peace naturally *result* from a holy and good life. *Tillotson.*

3. To come to a conclusion or determination. The council *resulted* in recommending harmony and peace to the parties.

RESULT', *n.* Resilience; act of flying back.

> Sound is produced between the string and the air, by the return of the *result* of the string. *Bacon.*

2. Consequence; conclusion; inference; effect; that which proceeds naturally or logically from facts, premises or the state of things; as the *result* of reasoning; the *result* of reflection; the *result* of a consultation or council; the *result* of a legislative debate.
3. Consequence or effect.

> The misery of sinners will be the natural *result* of their vile affections and criminal indulgences. *J. Lathrop.*

4. The decision or determination of a council or deliberative assembly; as the *result* of an ecclesiastical council. *New England.*

RESULT'ANCE, *n.* The act of resulting.

RESULT'ANT, *n.* In *mechanics,* a force which is the combined effect of two or more forces, acting in different directions.

RESULT'ING, *ppr.* Proceeding as a consequence, effect or conclusion of something; coming to a determination.
2. In law, *resulting use,* is a use which returns to him who raised it, after its expiration or during the impossibility of vesting in the person intended.

RESU'MABLE, *a. s* as *z.* [from *resume.*] That may be taken back, or that may be taken up again.

RESU'ME, *v. t. s* as *z.* [L. *resumo; re* and *sumo,* to take.]
1. To take back what has been given.

> The sun, like this from which our sight we have,
> Gaz'd on too long, *resumes* the light he gave. *Denham.*

2. To take back what has been taken away.

> They *resume* what has been obtained fraudulently. *Davenant.*

3. To take again after absence; as, to *resume* a seat.

> Reason *resum'd* her place, and passion fled. *Dryden.*

4. To take up again after interruption; to begin again; as, to *resume* an argument or discourse. [*This is now its most frequent use.*]

RESU'MED, *pp.* Taken back; taken again; begun again after interruption.

RESU'MING, *ppr.* Taking back; taking again; beginning again after interruption.

RESUM'MON, *v. t.* To summon or call again.
2. To recall; to recover. *Bacon.*

RESUM'MONED, *pp.* Summoned again; recovered.

RESUM'MONING, *ppr.* Recalling; recovering.

RESUMP'TION, *n.* [Fr. from L. *resumptus.*]

The act of resuming, taking back or taking again; as the *resumption* of a grant.

RESUMP'TIVE, *a.* Taking back or again.

RESU'PINATE, *a.* [L. *resupinatus, resupino*; *re* and *supino, supinus*, lying on the back.]

In *botany*, reversed; turned upside down. A *resupinate* corol is when the upper lip faces the ground, and the lower lip the sky. A *resupinate* leaf is when the upper surface becomes the lower, and the contrary; or when the lower disk looks upward. *Martyn. Lee.*

RESUPINA'TION, *n.* [supra.] The state of lying on the back; the state of being resupinate or reversed, as a corol.

RESU'PINE, *a.* Lying on the back.

RESURREC'TION, *n. s* as *z.* [Fr. from L. *resurrectus, resurgo*; *re* and *surgo*, to rise.]

A rising again; chiefly, the revival of the dead of the human race, or their return from the grave, particularly at the general judgment. By the *resurrection* of Christ we have assurance of the future *resurrection* of men. 1 Pet. i.

In the *resurrection*, they neither marry, nor are given in marriage. Matt. xxii.

RESURVEY, *v. t.* [*re* and *survey.*] To survey again or anew; to review. *Shak.*

RESUR'VEY, *n.* A second survey.

RESURVEYED, *pp.* Surveyed again.

RESURVEYING, *ppr.* Surveying anew; reviewing.

RESUS'CITATE, *v.t.* [L. *resuscito*; *re* and *suscito*, to raise.]

1. To revivify; to revive; particularly, to recover from apparent death; as, to *resuscitate* a drowned person; to *resuscitate* withered plants.

2. To reproduce, as a mixed body from its ashes. *Chimistry.*

RESUS'CITATED, *pp.* Revived; revivified; reproduced.

RESUS'CITATING, *ppr.* Reviving; revivifying; reproducing.

RESUSCITA'TION, *n.* The act of reviving from a state of apparent death; the state of being revivified. *Pope.*

2. The reproducing of a mixed body from its ashes. *Chimistry.*

RESUS'CITATIVE, *a.* Reviving; revivifying; raising from apparent death; reproducing.

RETA'IL, RE'TAIL, *v. t.* [Fr. *retailler*; *re* and *tailler*, to cut; It. *ritagliare.*]

1. To sell in small quantities or parcels, from the sense of cutting or dividing; *opposed to selling by wholesale*; as, to *retail* cloth or groceries.

2. To sell at second hand. *Pope.*

3. To tell in broken parts; to tell to many; as, to *retail* slander or idle reports.

RE'TAIL, *n.* The sale of commodities in small quantities or parcels, or at second hand. *Addison.*

RETA'ILED, *pp.* Sold in small quantities.

RETA'ILER, RE'TAILER, *n.* [This word, like the noun *retail*, is often, perhaps generally accented on the first syllable in America.]

One who sells goods by small quantities or parcels.

RETA'ILING, *ppr.* Selling in small quantities.

RETA'IN, *v. t.* [Fr. *retenir*; It. *ritenere*; Sp. *retener*; L. *retineo*; *re* and *teneo*, to hold.]

1. To hold or keep in possession; not to lose or part with or dismiss. The memory *retains* ideas which facts or arguments have suggested to the mind.

They did not like to *retain* God in their knowledge. Rom. i.

2. To keep, as an associate; to keep from departure.

Whom I would have *retained* with me. Phil. 13.

3. To keep back; to hold.

An executor may *retain* a debt due to him from the testator. *Blackstone.*

4. To hold from escape. Some substances *retain* heat much longer than others. Metals readily receive and transmit heat, but do not long *retain* it. Seek cloths that *retain* their color.

5. To keep in pay; to hire.

A Benedictine convent has now *retained* the most learned father of their order to write in its defense. *Addison.*

6. To engage; to employ by a fee paid; as, to *retain* a counselor.

RETA'IN, *v. i.* To belong to; to depend on; as coldness mixed with a somewhat languid relish *retaining* to bitterness. *Boyle.*

[Not in use. We now use *pertain.*]

2. To keep; to continue. [*Not in use.*]

RETA'INED, *pp.* Held; kept in possession; kept as an associate; kept in pay; kept from escape.

RETA'INER, *n.* One who retains; as an executor, who retains a debt due from the testator. *Blackstone.*

2. One who is kept in service; an attendant; as the *retainers* of the ancient princes and nobility.

3. An adherent; a dependant; a hanger on. *Shak.*

4. A servant, not a domestic, but occasionally attending and wearing his master's livery. *Encyc. Cowel.*

5. Among *lawyers*, a fee paid to engage a lawyer or counselor to maintain a cause.

6. The act of keeping dependants, or being in dependence. *Bacon.*

RETA'INING, *ppr.* Keeping in possession; keeping as an associate; keeping from escape; hiring; engaging by a fee.

RETA'KE, *v. t.* pret. *retook*; pp. *retaken.* [*re* and *take.*] To take again. *Clarendon.*

2. To take from a captor; to recapture; as, to *retake* a ship or prisoners.

RETA'KER, *n.* One who takes again what has been taken; a recaptor. *Kent.*

RETA'KING, *ppr.* Taking again; taking from a captor.

RETA'KING, *n.* A taking again; recapture.

RETAL'IATE, *v. t.* [Low L. *retalio*; *re* and *talio*, from *talis*, like.]

To return like for like; to repay or requite by an act of the same kind as has been received. It is now seldom used except in a bad sense, that is, to return evil for evil; as, to *retaliate* injuries. In war, enemies often *retaliate* the death or inhuman treatment of prisoners, the burning of towns or the plunder of goods.

It is unlucky to be obliged to *retaliate* the injuries of authors, whose works are so soon forgotten that we are in danger of appearing the first aggressors. *Swift.*

RETAL'IATE, *v. i.* To return like for like; as, to *retaliate* upon an enemy.

RETAL'IATED, *pp.* Returned, as like for like.

RETAL'IATING, *ppr.* Returning, like for like.

RETALIA'TION, *n.* The return of like for like; the doing that to another which he has done to us; requital of evil. *South.*

2. In *a good sense*, return of good for good.

God takes what is done to others as done to himself, and by promise obliges himself to full *retaliation.* *Calamy.*

[This, according to modern usage, is harsh.]

RETAL'IATORY, *a.* Returning like for like; as *retaliatory* measures; *retaliatory* edicts. *Canning. Walsh.*

RET'ARD, *v. t.* [Fr. *retarder*; L. *retardo*; *re* and *tardo*, to delay; *tardus*, slow, late. See *Target.*]

1. To diminish the velocity of motion; to hinder; to render more slow in progress; as, to *retard* the march of an army; to *retard* the motion of a ship. The resistance of air *retards* the velocity of a cannon ball. It is opposed to *accelerate.*

2. To delay; to put off; to render more late; as, to *retard* the attacks of old age; to *retard* a rupture between nations. My visit was *retarded* by business.

RET'ARD, *v. i.* To stay back. [*Not in use.*] *Brown.*

RETARDA'TION, *n.* The act of abating the velocity of motion; hinderance; the act of delaying; as the *retardation* of the motion of a ship; the *retardation* of hoary hairs. *Bacon.*

RET'ARDED, *pp.* Hindered in motion; delayed.

RET'ARDER, *n.* One that retards, hinders or delays.

RET'ARDING, *ppr.* Abating the velocity of motion; hindering; delaying.

RET'ARDMENT, *n.* The act of retarding or delaying. *Cowley.*

RETCH, *v. i.* [Sax. *hræcan*; Dan. *rekker*, to *reach*, to stretch, to *retch*, to vomit; the same word as *reach*; the present orthography, *retch*, being wholly arbitrary. See *Reach.*]

To make an effort to vomit; to heave; as the stomach; to strain, as in vomiting; properly to *reach.*

RETCHLESS, careless, is not in use. [See *Reckless.*] *Dryden.*

RETEC'TION, *n.* [L. *retectus*, from *retego*, to uncover; *re* and *tego*, to cover.]

The act of disclosing or producing to view something concealed; as the *retection* of the native color of the body. *Boyle.*

RETENT', *n.* That which is retained. *Kirwan.*

RETEN'TION, *n.* [Fr. from L. *retentio, retineo*; *re* and *teneo*, to hold.] The act of retaining or keeping.

2. The power of retaining; the faculty of the mind by which it retains ideas. *Locke.*

3. In *medicine*, the power of retaining, or that state of contraction in the solid or vascular parts of the body, by which they hold their proper contents and prevent in-

voluntary evacuations; undue retention of some natural discharge. *Encyc. Coxe.*

4. The act of withholding; restraint. *Shak.*

5. Custody; confinement. [*Not in use.*] *Shak.*

RETEN'TIVE, *a.* [Fr. *retentif.*] Having the power to retain; as a *retentive* memory; the *retentive* faculty; the *retentive* force of the stomach; a body *retentive* of heat or moisture.

RETEN'TIVENESS, *n.* The quality of retention; as *retentiveness* of memory.

RET'ICENCE, } *n.* [Fr. *reticence*, from L.
RET'ICENCY, } *reticentia, reticeo; re* and *taceo*, to be silent.]
Concealment by silence. In *rhetoric*, aposiopesis or suppression; a figure by which a person really speaks of a thing, while he makes a show as if he would say nothing on the subject. *Encyc.*

RET'ICLE, *n.* [L. *reticulum*, from *rete*, a net.] A small net.

2. A contrivance to measure the quantity of an eclipse; a kind of micrometer. *Ash.*

RETIC'ULAR, *a.* [supra.] Having the form of a net or of net-work; formed with interstices; as a *reticular* body or membrane. *Encyc.*

In *anatomy*, the *reticular body*, or *rete mucosum*, is the layer of the skin, intermediate between the cutis and the cuticle, the principal seat of color in man; the *reticular membrane* is the same as the cellular membrane. *Parr.*

RETIC'ULATE, } *a.* [L. *reticulatus*, from
RETIC'ULATED, } *rete*, a net.] Netted; resembling net-work; having distinct veins crossing like net-work; as a *reticulate* corol or petal. *Martyn.*

RETICULA'TION, *n.* Net-work; organization of substances resembling a net. *Darwin.*

RET'IFORM, *a.* [L. *retiformis; rete*, a net, and *forma*, form.]
Having the form of a net in texture; composed of crossing lines and interstices; as the *retiform* coat of the eye. *Ray.*

RET'INA, *n.* [L. from *rete*, a net.] In *anatomy*, one of the coats of the eye, being an expansion of the optic nerve over the bottom of the eye, where the sense of vision is first received. *Encyc.*

RETINASPHALT', *n.* A bituminous or resinous substance of a yellowish or reddish brown color, found in irregular pieces very light and shining. [See *Retinite.*]

RET'INITE, *n.* [Gr. ῥητινη, resin.] Pitchstone; stone of fusible pitch, of a resinous appearance, compact, brown, reddish, gray, yellowish, blackish or bluish, rarely homogeneous, and often containing crystals of feldspar and scales of mica. It is the pechstein porphyry or obsidian of the Germans. It is called also retinasphalt. *Ure. Cyc.*

RET'INUE, *n.* [Fr. *retenue*, from *retenir*, to retain, L. *retineo; re* and *teneo*, to hold.]
The attendants of a prince or distinguished personage, chiefly on a journey or an excursion; a train of persons. *Dryden.*

RETIRA'DE, *n.* [Fr. from *retirer*, to withdraw; Sp. *retirada*, a retreat.]
In *fortification*, a kind of retrenchment in the body of a bastion or other work, which is to be disputed inch by inch, after the defenses are dismantled. It usually consists of two faces, which make a re-entering angle. *Encyc.*

RETI'RE, *v. i.* [Fr. *retirer; re* and *tirer*, to draw; It. *ritirare;* Sp. *retirar.*]

1. To withdraw; to retreat; to go from company or from a public place into privacy; as, to *retire* from the world; to *retire* from notice.

2. To retreat from action or danger; as, to *retire* from battle.

3. To withdraw from a public station. Gen. Washington, in 1796, *retired* to private life.

4. To break up, as a company or assembly. The company *retired* at eleven o'clock.

5. To depart or withdraw for safety or for pleasure. Men *retire* from the town in summer for health and pleasure. But in South Carolina, the planters *retire* from their estates to Charleston, or to an isle near the town.

6. To recede; to fall back. The shore of the sea *retires* in bays and gulfs.

RETI'RE, *v. t.* To withdraw; to take away.

> He *retired* himself, his wife and children into a forest. *Sidney.*
>
> As when the sun is present all the year,
> And never doth *retire* his golden ray. *Davies.*

[This transitive use of *retire* is now obsolete.]

RETI'RE, *n.* Retreat; recession; a withdrawing. *Obs. Shak. Bacon.*

2. Retirement; place of privacy. *Obs. Milton.*

RETI'RED, *a.* Secluded from much society or from public notice; private. He lives a *retired* life; he has a *retired* situation.

2. Secret; private; as *retired* speculations.

3. Withdrawn. *Locke.*

RETI'REDLY, *adv.* In solitude or privacy. *Sherwood.*

RETI'REDNESS, *n.* A state of retirement; solitude; privacy or secrecy. *Atterbury.*

RETI'REMENT, *n.* The act of withdrawing from company or from public notice or station. *Milton.*

2. The state of being withdrawn; as the *retirement* of the mind from the senses. *Locke.*

3. Private abode; habitation secluded from much society or from public life.

> Caprea had been the *retirement* of Augustus. *Addison.*
>
> *Retirement* is as necessary to me as it will be welcome. *Washington.*

4. Private way of life.

> *Retirement*, rural quiet, friendship, books,
> Progressive virtue and approving heaven. *Thomson.*

RETI'RING, *ppr.* Withdrawing; retreating; going into seclusion or solitude.

2. *a.* Reserved; not forward or obtrusive; as *retiring* modesty; *retiring* manners.

RETOLD, *pret.* and *pp.* of *retell;* as a story *retold.*

RETORT', *v. t.* [L. *retortus, retorqueo; re* and *torqueo*, to throw.]

1. To throw back; to reverberate.

> And they *retort* that heat again
> To the first giver. *Shak.*

2. To return an argument, accusation, censure or incivility; as, to *retort* the charge of vanity.

> He pass'd through hostile scorn;
> And with *retorted* scorn, his back he turn'd. *Milton.*

3. To bend or curve back; as a *retorted* line. *Bacon.*

RETORT', *v. i.* To return an argument or charge; to make a severe reply. He *retorted* upon his adversary with severity.

RETORT', *n.* The return of an argument, charge or incivility in reply; as the *retort* courteous. *Shak.*

2. In *chimistry*, a spherical vessel with its neck bent, to which the receiver is fitted; *used in distillation. Encyc.*

RETORT'ED, *pp.* Returned; thrown back; bent back.

RETORT'ER, *n.* One that retorts.

RETORT'ING, *ppr.* Returning; throwing back.

RETOR'TION, *n.* The act of retorting. *Spenser.*

RETOSS', *v. t.* [*re* and *toss.*] To toss back. *Pope.*

RETOSS'ED, *pp.* Tossed back.

RETOSS'ING, *ppr.* Tossing back.

RETOUCH, *v. t. retuch'.* [*re* and *touch.*] To improve by new touches; as, to *retouch* a picture or an essay. *Dryden. Pope.*

RETOUCHED, *pp. retuch'ed.* Touched again; improved by new touches.

RETOUCHING, *ppr. retuch'ing.* Improving by new touches.

RETRA'CE, *v. t.* [Fr. *retracer; re* and *tracer*, to trace.]

1. To trace back; to go back in the same path or course; as, to *retrace* one's steps; to *retrace* one's proceedings.

2. To trace back, as a line.

> Then if the line of Turnus you *retrace*,
> He springs from Inachus of Argive race. *Dryden.*

RETRA'CED, *pp.* Traced back.

RETRA'CING, *ppr.* Tracing back.

RETRACT', *v. t.* [Fr. *retracter;* Norm. *retraicter;* L. *retractus, retraho; re* and *traho*, to draw.]

1. To recall, as a declaration, words or saying; to disavow; to recant; as, to *retract* an accusation, charge or assertion.

> I would as freely have *retracted* the charge of idolatry, as I ever made it. *Stillingfleet.*

2. To take back; to rescind. [*Little used.*] *Woodward.*

3. To draw back, as claws.

RETRACT', *v. i.* To take back; to unsay; to withdraw concession or declaration.

> She will, and she will not; she grants, denies,
> Consents, *retracts*, advances, and then flies. *Granville.*

RETRACT', *n.* Among *horsemen*, the prick of a horse's foot in nailing a shoe.

RETRACT'ABLE, *a.* That may be retracted or recalled.

RETRACTA'TION, *n.* [Fr. from L. *retractatio.*]
The recalling of what has been said; recantation; change of opinion declared. *South.*

RETRACT'ED, *pp.* Recalled; recanted; disavowed.

RETRACT'IBLE, *a.* That may be drawn back; retractile. *Journ. of Science.*

RETRACT'ILE, *a.* Capable of being drawn back.

A walrus with fiery eyes—*retractile* from external injuries. *Pennant.*

RETRACT'ING, *ppr.* Recalling; disavowing; recanting.

RETRAC'TION, *n.* [from *retract.*] The act of withdrawing something advanced, or changing something done. *Woodward.*

2. Recantation; disavowal of the truth of what has been said; declaration of change of opinion. *Sidney.*

3. Act of withdrawing a claim.

Other men's insatiable desire of revenge, hath beguiled church and state of the benefit of my *retractions* or concessions. *K. Charles.*

RETRACT'IVE, *a.* Withdrawing; taking from.

RETRACT'IVE, *n.* That which withdraws or takes from.

RETRA'ICT, *n.* Retreat. *Obs.* [See *Retreat.*] *Bacon.*

RETRA'IT, *n.* [It. *ritratto*, from *ritrarre*, to draw.] A cast of countenance; a picture. *Obs.* *Spenser.*

RETRAX'IT, *n.* [L. *retraho, retraxi.*] In *law*, the withdrawing or open renunciation of a suit in court, by which the plaintif loses his action. *Blackstone.*

RETRE'AT, *n.* [Fr. *retraite*, from *retraire*; *re* and *traire*, to draw; L. *retractus*, *retraho*; *re* and *traho*; It. *ritratta.*]

1. The act of retiring; a withdrawing of one's self from any place.

But beauty's triumph is well tim'd *retreat.* *Pope.*

2. Retirement; state of privacy or seclusion from noise, bustle or company.

Here in the calm still mirror of *retreat.* *Pope.*

3. Place of retirement or privacy.

He built his son a house of pleasure—and spared no cost to make it a delicious *retreat.* *L'Estrange.*

4. Place of safety or security.

That pleasing shade they sought, a soft *retreat*
From sudden April show'rs, a shelter from the heat. *Dryden.*

5. In *military affairs*, the retiring of an army or body of men from the face of an enemy or from any ground occupied to a greater distance from the enemy, or from an advanced position. A *retreat* is properly an orderly march, in which circumstance it differs from a *flight.* *Encyc.*

6. The withdrawing of a ship or fleet from an enemy; or the order and disposition of ships declining an engagement.

7. The beat of the drum at the firing of the evening gun, to warn soldiers to forbear firing and the sentinels to challenge. *Encyc.*

RETRE'AT, *v. i.* To retire from any position or place.

2. To withdraw to a private abode or to any secluded situation. *Milton.*

3. To retire to a place of safety or security; as, to *retreat* into a den or into a fort.

4. To move back to a place before occupied; to retire.

The rapid currents drive,
Towards the *retreating* sea, their furious tide. *Milton.*

5. To retire from an enemy or from any advanced position.

RETRE'ATED, as a passive participle, though used by Milton, is not good English.

RETRENCH', *v. t.* [Fr. *retrancher*; *re* and *trancher*, to cut; It. *trincea*, a trench; *trincerare*, to intrench; *trinciare*, to carve; W. *trycu*, to cut.]

1. To cut off; to pare away.

And thy exuberant parts *retrench.* *Denham.*

2. To lessen; to abridge; to curtail; as, to *retrench* superfluities or expenses. *Atterbury.*

3. To confine; to limit. [*Not proper.*] *Addison.*

RETRENCH', *v. i.* To live at less expense. It is more reputable to *retrench* than to live embarrassed.

RETRENCH'ED, *pp.* Cut off; curtailed; diminished.

RETRENCH'ING, *ppr.* Cutting off; curtailing.

RETRENCH'MENT, *n.* [Fr. *retranchement*; Sp. *atrincheramiento.*]

1. The act of lopping off; the act of removing what is superfluous; as the *retrenchment* of words or lines in a writing. *Dryden. Addison.*

2. The act of curtailing, lessening or abridging; diminution; as the *retrenchment* of expenses.

3. In *military affairs*, any work raised to cover a post and fortify it against an enemy; such as fascines, gabions, sandbags and the like. *Encyc.*

Numerous remains of Roman *retren ments*, constructed to cover the country— *D'Anville, Trans.*

RETRIB'UTE, *v. t.* [Fr. *retribuer*; L. *retribuo*; *re* and *tribuo*, to give or bestow.]

To pay back; to make payment, compensation or reward in return; as, to *retribute* one for his kindness; to *retribute* to a criminal what is proportionate to his offense. *Locke.*

RETRIB'UTED, *pp.* Paid back; given in return; rewarded.

RETRIB'UTER, *n.* One that makes retribution.

RETRIB'UTING, *ppr.* Requiting; making repayment; rewarding

RETRIBU'TION, *n.* [Fr.] Repayment; return accommodated to the action; reward; compensation.

In good offices and due *retributions*, we may not be pinching and niggardly. *Hall.*

2. A gratuity or present given for services in the place of a salary. *Encyc.*

3. The distribution of rewards and punishments at the general judgment.

It is a strong argument for a state of *retribution* hereafter, that in this world virtuous persons are very often unfortunate, and vicious persons prosperous. *Spectator.*

RETRIB'UTIVE, } *a.* Repaying; rewarding for good deeds,
RETRIB'UTORY, } and punishing for offenses; as *retributive* justice.

RETRIE'VABLE, *a.* [from *retrieve.*] That may be retrieved or recovered. *Gray.*

RETRIE'VE, *v. t.* [Fr. *retrouver*, to find again; It. *ritrovare.* See *Trover.*]

1. To recover; to restore from loss or injury to a former good state; as, to *retrieve* the credit of a nation; to *retrieve* one's character; to *retrieve* a decayed fortune.

2. To repair.

Accept my sorrow, and *retrieve* my fall. *Prior*

3. To regain.

With late repentance now they would *retrieve*
The bodies they forsook, and wish to live. *Dryden.*

4. To recall; to bring back; as, to *retrieve* men from their cold trivial conceits. *Berkeley.*

RETRIE'VE, *n.* A seeking again; a discovery. [*Not in use.*] *B. Jonson*

RETRIE'VED, *pp.* Recovered; repaired; regained; recalled.

RETRIE'VING, *ppr.* Recovering; repairing; recalling.

RETROAC'TION, *n.* [L. *retro*, backward, and *action.*]

1. Action returned, or action backwards.

2. Operation on something past or preceding.

RETROAC'TIVE, *a.* [Fr. *retroactif*; L. *retro*, backward, and *active.*]

Operating by returned action; affecting what is past; retrospective. *Beddoes.*

A *retroactive law* or *statute*, is one which operates to affect, make criminal or punishable, acts done prior to the passing of the law.

RETROAC'TIVELY, *adv.* By returned action or operation; by operating on something past. *Wheaton.*

RETROCE'DE, *v. t.* [L. *retro*, back, and *cedo*, to give; Fr. *retroceder.*]

To cede or grant back; as, to *retrocede* a territory to a former proprietor.

RETROCE'DED, *pp.* Granted back.

RETROCE'DING, *ppr.* Ceding back.

RETROCES'SION, *n.* A ceding or granting back to a former proprietor. *Am. State Papers.*

2. The act of going back. *More.*

RETRODUC'TION, *n.* [L. *retroduco*; *retro*, back, and *duco*, to lead.] A leading or bringing back.

RET'ROFLEX, *a.* [L. *retro*, back, and *flexus*, bent.]

In *botany*, bent this way and that, or in different directions, usually in a distorted manner; as a *retroflex* branch. *Martyn.*

RET'ROFRACT, } *a.* [L. *retro*, back, and *fractus*, broken.]
RETROFRACT'ED, }

Reduced to hang down as it were by force so as to appear as if broken; as a *retrofract* peduncle. *Martyn.*

Bent back towards its insertion, as if it were broken. *Lee.*

RETROGRADA'TION, *n.* [Fr. See *Retrograde.*]

1. The act of moving backwards; applied to the apparent motion of the planets. *Ray.*

2. A moving backwards; decline in excellence. *N. Chipman.*

RET'ROGRADE, *a.* [Fr. from L. *retrogradior*; *retro*, backwards, and *gradior*, to go.]

1. Going or moving backwards. *Bacon.*

2. In *astronomy*, apparently moving backward and contrary to the succession of the signs, as a planet. *Harris.*

3. Declining from a better to a worse state.

RET'ROGRADE, *v. i.* [Fr. *retrograder*; L. *retrogradior*; *retro* and *gradior*, to go.] To go or move backward. *Bacon.*

RETROGRES'SION, *n.* The act of going backward. *Brown.*

RETROGRESS'IVE, *a.* Going or moving backward; declining from a more perfect to a less perfect state.

Geography is at times *retrogressive.* *Pinkerton.*

RETROMIN'GENCY, *n.* [L. *retro*, backward, and *mingo*, to discharge urine.]

The act of quality of discharging the contents of the bladder backwards. *Brown.*

RETROMIN'GENT, *a.* Discharging the urine backwards.

RETROMIN'GENT, *n.* In *zoology*, an animal that discharges its urine backwards. The *retromingents* are a division of animals whose characteristic is that they discharge their urine backwards, both male and female. *Encyc.*

RETROPUL'SIVE, *a.* [L. *retro*, back, and *pulsus, pello*, to drive.] Driving back; repelling. *Med. Repos.*

RETRORSELY, *adv. retrors'ly.* [L. *retrorsum*, backward.] In a backward direction; as a stem *retrorsely* aculeate. *Eaton.*

RET'ROSPECT, *n.* [L. *retro*, back, and *specio*, to look.]

A looking back on things past; view or contemplation of something past. The *retrospect* of a life well spent affords peace of mind in old age.

RETROSPEC'TION, *n.* The act of looking back on things past.

2. The faculty of looking back on past things. *Swift.*

RETROSPECT'IVE, *a.* Looking back on past events; as a *retrospective* view.

2. Having reference to what is past; affecting things past. A penal statute can have no *retrospective* effect or operation.

RETROSPECT'IVELY, *adv.* By way of retrospect.

RETROVER'SION, *n.* A turning or falling backwards; as the *retroversion* of the uterus.

RET'ROVERT, *v. t.* To turn back.

RET'ROVERTED, *a.* [L. *retro*, back, and *verto*, to turn.] Turned back. *Lawrence, Lect. Med. Repos.*

RETRU'DE, *v t.* [L. *retrudo*; *re* and *trudo*, to thrust.] To thrust back. *More.*

RETUND', *v. t.* [L. *retundo*; *re* and *tundo*, to beat.]

To blunt; to turn; as an edge; to dull; as, to *retund* the edge of a weapon. *Ray.*

RETURN, *v. i.* [Fr. *retourner*; *re* and *tourner*, to turn, L. *torno*; It. *ritornare*; Sp. *retornar.*]

1. To come or go back to the same place. The gentleman goes from the country to London and *returns*, or the citizen of London rides into the country and *returns*. The blood propelled from the heart, passes through the arteries to the extremities of the body, and *returns* through the veins. Some servants are good to go on errands, but not good to *return*.

2. To come to the same state; as, to *return* from bondage to a state of freedom. *Locke.*

3. To answer.

He said, and thus the queen of heaven *return'd.* *Pope.*

4. To come again; to revisit.

Thou to mankind
Be good and friendly still, and oft *return*. *Milton.*

5. To appear or begin again after a periodical revolution.

With the year
Seasons *return*, but not to me *returns*
Day— *Milton.*

6. To show fresh signs of mercy.

Return, O Lord, deliver my soul. Ps. vi.

To return to God, to return from wickedness, to repent of sin or wandering from duty. *Scripture.*

RETURN', *v. t.* To bring, carry or send back; as, to *return* a borrowed book; to *return* a hired horse.

2. To repay; as, to *return* borrowed money.

3. To give in recompense or requital.

In any wise, *return* him a trespass-offering. 1 Sam. vi.

The Lord shall *return* thy wickedness upon thy own head. 1 Kings ii.

4. To give back in reply; as, to *return* an answer.

5. To tell, relate or communicate.

And Moses *returned* the words of the people to the Lord. Ex. xix.

6. To retort; to recriminate.

If you are a malicious reader, you *return* upon me, that I affect to be thought more impartial than I am. *Dryden.*

7. To render an account, usually an official account to a superior. Officers of the army and navy *return* to the commander the number of men in companies, regiments, &c.; they *return* the number of men sick or capable of duty; they *return* the quantity of ammunition, provisions, &c.

8. To render back to a tribunal or to an office; as, to *return* a writ or an execution.

9. To report officially; as, an officer *returns* his proceedings on the back of a writ or precept.

10. To send; to transmit; to convey.

Instead of a ship, he should levy money and *return* the same to the treasurer for his majesty's use. *Clarendon.*

RETURN', *n.* The act of coming or going back to the same place.

Takes little journeys and makes quick *returns*. *Dryden.*

2. The act of sending back; as the *return* of a borrowed book or of money lent.

3. The act of putting in the former place.

4. Retrogression; the act of moving back.

5. The act or process of coming back to a former state; as the *return* of health.

6. Revolution; a periodical coming to the same point; as the *return* of the sun to the tropic of Cancer.

7. Periodical renewal; as the *return* of the seasons or of the year.

8. Repayment; reimbursement in kind or in something equivalent, for money expended or advanced, or for labor. One occupation gives quick *returns*; in others, the *returns* are slow. The *returns* of the cargo were in gold. The farmer has *returns* in his crops.

9. Profit; advantage.

From these few hours we spend in prayer, the *return* is great. *Taylor.*

10. Remittance; payment from a distant place. *Shak.*

11. Repayment; retribution; requital.

Is no *return* due from a grateful breast? *Dryden.*

12. Act of restoring or giving back; restitution. *South.*

13. Either of the adjoining sides of the front of a house or ground-plot, is called a *return* side. *Moxon.*

14. In *law*, the rendering back or delivery of a writ, precept or execution, to the proper officer or court; or the certificate of the officer executing it, indorsed. We call the transmission of the writ to the proper officer or court, a *return*; and we give the same name to the certificate or official account of the officer's service or proceedings. The sherif or his subordinate officers make *return* of all writs and precepts. We use the same language for the sending back of a commission with the certificate of the commissioners.

15. A day in bank. The day on which the defendant is ordered to appear in court, and the sherif is to bring in the writ and report his proceedings, is called the *return* of the writ. *Blackstone.*

16. In *military* and *naval affairs*, an official account, report or statement rendered to the commander; as the *return* of men fit for duty; the *return* of the number of the sick; the *return* of provisions, ammunition, &c.

RETURN'ABLE, *a.* That may be returned or restored.

2. In *law*, that is legally to be returned, delivered, given or rendered; as a writ or precept *returnable* at a certain day; a verdict *returnable* to the court; an attachment *returnable* to the king's bench.

RETURN'-DAY, *n.* The day when the defendant is to appear in court and the sherif is to return the writ and his proceedings.

RETURN'ED, *pp.* Restored; given or sent back; repaid; brought or rendered to the proper court or officer.

RETURN'ER, *n.* One who returns; one that repays or remits money.

RETURN'ING, *ppr.* Giving, carrying or sending back; coming or going back; making report.

RETURN'ING-OFFICER, *n.* The officer whose duty it is to make returns of writs, precepts, juries, &c.

RETURN'LESS, *a.* Admitting no return. [*Little used.*] *Chapman.*

RETU'SE, *a.* [L. *retusus, retundo.*] In *botany*, a *retuse* leaf is one ending in a blunt sinus, or whose apex is blunt. This term is applied also to the seed. *Martyn. Lee.*

REUN'ION, *n.* A second union; union formed anew after separation or discord; as a *reunion* of parts or particles of matter; a *reunion* of parties or sects.

2. In *medicine*, union of parts separated by wounds or accidents. *Parr.*

REUNI'TE, *v. t.* [*re* and *unite.*] To unite again; to join after separation. *Shak.*

2. To reconcile after variance.

REUNI'TE, *v. i.* To be united again; to join and cohere again.

REUNI'TED, *pp.* United or joined again; reconciled.

REUNI'TING, *ppr.* Uniting again; reconciling.

REUS'SITE, *n.* [from *Reuss*, the place where it is found.]

A salt found in the form of a mealy efflorescence, or crystalized in flat six sided prisms, and in acicular crystals. *Cyc.*

REVE, *n.* [Sax. *gerefa.*] The bailif of a franchise or manor. It is usually written *reeve.*

REVE'AL, *v. t.* [Fr. *reveler*; L. *revelo*; *re* and *velo*, to veil.]

1. To disclose; to discover; to show; to make known something before unknown or concealed; as, to *reveal* secrets.

2. To disclose, discover or make known from heaven. God has been pleased to *reveal* his will to man.

The wrath of God is *revealed* from heaven against all ungodliness and unrighteousness of men. Rom. i.

REVE'AL, *n.* A revealing; disclosure. [*Not in use.*] *Brown.*

REVE'ALED, *pp.* Disclosed; discovered; made known; laid open.

REVE'ALER, *n.* One that discloses or makes known.

2. One that brings to view. *Dryden.*

REVE'ALING, *ppr.* Disclosing; discovering; making known.

REVE'ALMENT, *n.* The act of revealing. [*Little used.*] *South.*

REVEILLE, REVEILLE', REV'ELLY, *n.* [Fr. *reveiller*, to awake; *re* and *veiller*, to watch; contracted from L. *vigilo.* See *Watch.*]

In *military affairs*, the beat of drum about break of day, to give notice that it is time for the soldiers to rise and for the sentinels to forbear challenging. *Encyc.*

[This word might well be anglicised *rev'elly.*]

REV'EL, *v. i.* [D. *revelen*, to rave; from the root of L. *rabo*, *rabio*, to rage, whence *rabies*, *rabid*; Dan. *raaben*, to bawl, to clamor; Sw. *ropa*; allied to *rove*, *rapio*; Ir. *rioboid*, a spendthrift; *rioboidim*, to riot or revel.]

1. To feast with loose and clamorous merriment; to carouse; to act the bacchanalian.

Antony, that *revels* long o'nights. *Shak.*

2. To move playfully or without regularity.

REV'EL, *n.* A feast with loose and noisy jollity. *Shak.*

Some men ruin the fabric of their bodies by incessant *revels.* *Rambler.*

REVEL', *v. t.* [L. *revello*; *re* and *vello*, to pull.]

To draw back; to retract; to make a revulsion. *Harvey. Friend.*

REVELA'TION, *n.* [Fr. from L. *revelatus*, *revelo.* See *Reveal.*]

1. The act of disclosing or discovering to others what was before unknown to them; appropriately, the disclosure or communication of truth to men by God himself, or by his authorized agents, the prophets and apostles.

How that by *revelation* he made known to me the mystery, as I wrote before in few words. Eph. iii. 2 Cor. xii.

2. That which is revealed; appropriately, the sacred truths which God has communicated to man for his instruction and direction. The *revelations* of God are contained in the Old and New Testament.

3. The Apocalypse; the last book of the sacred canon, containing the prophecies of St. John.

REV'ELER, *n.* [See *Revel.*] One who feasts with noisy merriment. *Pope.*

REV'ELING, *ppr.* Feasting with noisy merriment; carousing.

REV'ELING, *n.* A feasting with noisy merriment; revelry. Gal. v. 1 Pet. iv.

REV'EL-ROUT, *n.* [See *Rout.*] Tumultuous festivity. *Rowe.*

2. A mob; a rabble tumultuously assembled; an unlawful assembly. *Ainsworth.*

REV'ELRY, *n.* Noisy festivity; clamorous jollity. *Milton.*

REVEN'DICATE, *v. t.* [Fr. *revendiquer*; *re* and *vendiquer*, to claim or challenge, L. *vindico.* See *Vindicate.*]

To reclaim what has been taken away; to claim to have restored what has been seized.

Should some subsequent fortunate revolution deliver it from the conqueror's yoke, it can *revendicate* them. *Vattel, Trans.*

REVEN'DICATED, *pp.* Reclaimed; regained; recovered.

REVEN'DICATING, *ppr.* Reclaiming; redemanding; recovering.

REVENDICA'TION, *n.* [Fr.] The act of reclaiming or demanding the restoration of any thing taken by an enemy; as by right of postliminium.

The endless disputes which would spring from the *revendication* of them, have introduced a contrary practice. *Vattel, Trans.*

REVENGE, *v. t.* *revenj'.* [Fr. *revancher*, *venger*; Sp. *vengar*; Port. *vingar*; L. *vindex*, *vindico*; It. *vendicare.* See *Vindicate.*]

1. To inflict pain or injury in return for an injury received.

[*Note.* This word and *avenge* were formerly used as synonymous, and it is so used in the common version of the Scripture, and applied to the Supreme Being. "O Lord—*revenge* me of my persecutors." Jer. xv. In consequence of a distinction between *avenge* and *revenge*, which modern usage has introduced, the application of this word to the Supreme Being appears extremely harsh, irreverent and offensive. *Revenge* is now used in an ill sense, for the infliction of pain maliciously or illegally; *avenge* for inflicting just punishment.]

2. According to *modern usage*, to inflict pain deliberately and maliciously, contrary to the laws of justice and humanity, in return for injury, pain or evil received; to wreak vengeance spitefully on one who injures or offends. We say, to *revenge* an injury or insult, or with the reciprocal pronoun, to *revenge ourselves* on an enemy or for an injury, that is, to take vengeance or satisfaction.

3. To vindicate by punishment of an enemy.

The gods are just and will *revenge* our cause. *Dryden.*

[According to modern usage, *avenge* should here be substituted for *revenge.*]

REVENGE, *n.* *revenj'.* [Fr. *revanche*; Arm. *revanch.*]

1. Return of an injury; the deliberate infliction of pain or injury on a person in return for an injury received from him. *Milton. Dryden.*

2. According to *modern usage*, a malicious or spiteful infliction of pain or injury, contrary to the laws of justice and christianity, in return for an injury or offense. *Revenge* is dictated by *passion*; *vengeance* by *justice.*

3. The passion which is excited by an injury done or an affront given; the desire of inflicting pain on one who has done an injury; as, to glut *revenge.*

Revenge, as the word is now understood, is always contrary to the precepts of Christ.

The indulgence of *revenge* tends to make men more savage and cruel. *Kames.*

REVENG'ED, *pp.* Punished in return for an injury; spitefully punished. The injury is *revenged.*

REVENGEFUL, *a.* *revenj'ful.* Full of revenge or a desire to inflict pain or evil for injury received; spiteful; malicious; wreaking revenge.

If thy *revengeful* heart cannot forgive. *Shak.*

2. Vindictive; inflicting punishment.

May my hands
Never brandish more *revengeful* steel. *Shak.*

REVENGEFULLY, *adv.* *revenj'fully.* By way of revenge; vindictively; with the spirit of revenge. *Dryden.*

REVENGEFULNESS, *n.* *revenj'fulness.* Vindictiveness. *More.*

REVENGELESS, *a.* *revenj'less.* Unrevenged. *Marston.*

REVENGEMENT, *n.* *revenj'ment.* Revenge; return of an injury. [*Little used.*] *Spenser.*

REVENG'ER, *n.* One who revenges; one who inflicts pain on another spitefully in return for an injury. *Spenser.*

2. One who inflicts just punishment for injuries. [*Less proper.*] *Bentley.*

REVENG'ING, *ppr.* Inflicting pain or evil spitefully for injury or affront received.

2. Vindicating; punishing.

REVENG'INGLY, *adv.* With revenge; with the spirit of revenge; vindictively. *Shak.*

REV'ENUE, *n.* [Fr. *revenu*, from *revenir*, to return, L. *revenio*; *re* and *venio*, to come.]

1. In *a general sense*, the annual rents, profits, interest or issues of any species of property, real or personal, belonging to an individual or to the public. When used of individuals, it is equivalent to *income.* In modern usage, *income* is applied more generally to the rents and profits of individuals, and *revenue* to those of the state. In the latter case, *revenue* is

2. The annual produce of taxes, excise, customs, duties, rents, &c. which a nation or state collects and receives into the treasury for public use.

3. Return; reward; as a rich *revenue* of praise.

4. A fleshy lump on the head of a deer. *Encyc.*

REVERB', *v. t.* To reverberate. [*Not in use.*] *Shak.*

REVERB'ERANT, *a.* [L. *reverberans.* See *Reverberate.*]

Returning sound; resounding; driving back. *Shak.*

REVERB'ERATE, *v. t.* [L. *reverbero*; *re* and *verbero*, to beat.]

1. To return, as sound; to send back; to echo; as, an arch *reverberates* the voice. *Shak.*

2. To send or beat back; to repel; to reflect; as, to *reverberate* rays of light. *Swift.*

3. To send or drive back; to repel from side to side; as flame *reverberated* in a furnace.

REVERB'ERATE, *v. i.* To be driven back; to be repelled, as rays of light, or sound. *Howell.*

2. To resound.

And even at hand, a drum is ready brac'd,
That shall *reverberate* all as well as thine. *Shak.*

REVERB'ERATE, *a.* Reverberant. *Shak.*

REVERB'ERATED, *pp.* Driven back; sent back; driven from side to side.

REVERB'ERATING, *ppr.* Driving or sending back; reflecting, as light; echoing, as sound.

REVERBERA'TION, *n.* [Fr.; from *reverberate.*]

The act of driving or sending back; particularly, the act of reflecting light and heat or repelling sound. Thus we speak of the *reverberation* of the rays of light from an object, the *reverberation* of sound in echoes, or the *reverberation* of heat or flame in a furnace.

REVERB'ERATORY, *a.* Returning or driving back; as a *reverberatory* furnace or kiln. *Moxon.*

REVERB'ERATORY, *n.* A furnace with a kind of dome that reflects the flame upon a vessel placed within it, so as to surround it. *Nicholson.*

REVE'RE, *v. t.* [Fr. *reverer*; It. *reverire*; L. *revereor*; *re* and *vereor*, to fear.]

To regard with fear mingled with respect and affection; to venerate; to reverence; to honor in estimation.

Marcus Aurelius, whom he rather *revered* as his father, than treated as his partner in the empire— *Addison.*

REVE'RED, *pp.* Regarded with fear mingled with respect and affection.

REV'ERENCE, *n.* [Fr. from L. *reverentia.*]

1. Fear mingled with respect and esteem; veneration.

When quarrels and factions are carried openly, it is a sign that the *reverence* of government is lost. *Bacon.*

The fear acceptable to God, is a filial fear, an awful *reverence* of the divine nature, proceeding from a just esteem of his perfections, which produces in us an inclination to his service and an unwillingness to offend him. *Rogers.*

Reverence is nearly equivalent to *veneration*, but expresses something less of the same emotion. It differs from *awe*, which is an emotion compounded of fear, dread or terror, with admiration of something great, but not necessarily implying love or affection. We feel *reverence* for a parent, and for an upright magistrate, but we stand in *awe* of a tyrant. This distinction may not always be observed.

2. An act of respect or obeisance; a bow or courtesy. 2 Sam. ix. *Dryden. Fairfax.*

3. A title of the clergy. *Shak.*

4. A poetical title of a father. *Shak.*

REV'ERENCE, *v. t.* To regard with reverence; to regard with fear mingled with respect and affection. We *reverence* superiors for their age, their authority and their virtues. We ought to *reverence* parents and upright judges and magistrates. We ought to *reverence* the Supreme Being, his word and his ordinances.

Those that I *reverence*, those I fear, the wise. *Shak.*

They will *reverence* my son. Matt. xxi.

Let the wife see that she *reverence* her husband. Eph. v.

REV'ERENCED, *pp.* Regarded with fear mingled with respect and affection.

REV'ERENCER, *n.* One that regards with reverence. *Swift.*

REV'ERENCING, *ppr.* Regarding with fear mixed with respect and affection.

REV'EREND, *a.* [Fr. from L. *reverendus.*]

1. Worthy of reverence; entitled to respect mingled with fear and affection; as *reverend* and gracious senators. *Shak.*

A *reverend* sire among them came. *Milton.*

[This epithet is, I believe, never applied to the Supreme Being, or to his laws or institutions. In lieu of it we use *venerable.*]

2. A title of respect given to the clergy or ecclesiastics. We style a clergyman *reverend*; a bishop is styled *right reverend*; an archbishop *most reverend.* The religious in catholic countries, are styled *reverend fathers*; abbesses, prioresses, &c. *reverend mothers.* In Scotland, as in the United States, the clergy are individually styled *reverend.* A synod is styled *very reverend*, and the general assembly *venerable.* *Encyc.*

REV'ERENT, *a.* Expressing reverence, veneration or submission; as *reverent* words or terms; a *reverent* posture in prayer; *reverent* behavior.

2. Submissive; humble; impressed with reverence.

They prostrate fell before him *reverent.* *Milton.*

REVEREN'TIAL, *a.* [from *reverence.*] Proceeding from reverence, or expressing it; as *reverential* fear or awe; *reverential* gratitude or esteem.

Religion—consisting in a *reverential* esteem of things sacred. *South.*

REVEREN'TIALLY, *adv.* With reverence, or show of reverence. *Brown.*

REV'ERENTLY, *adv.* With reverence; with respectful regard.

Chide him for faults, and do it *reverently.* *Shak.*

2. With veneration; with fear of what is great or terrifying.

So *reverently* men quit the open air,
When thunder speaks the angry Gods abroad. *Dryden.*

REVE'RER, *n.* One who reveres or venerates.

REVERIE. [See *Revery.*]

REVE'RING, *ppr.* Regarding with fear mixed with respect and affection; venerating.

REVERS'AL, *a.* [See *Reverse.*] Intended to reverse; implying reverse. *Burnet.*

REVERS'AL, *n.* [from *reverse.*] A change or overthrowing; as the *reversal* of a judgment, which amounts to an official declaration that it is false. So we speak of the *reversal* of an attainder or of an outlawry, by which the sentence is rendered void. *Blackstone.*

REVERSE, *v. t. revers'.* [L. *reversus*, *reverto*; *re* and *verto*, to turn.]

1. To turn upside down; as, to *reverse* a pyramid or cone. *Temple.*

2. To overturn; to subvert; as, to *reverse* the state. *Pope.*

3. To turn back; as with swift wheel *reverse.* *Milton.*

4. To turn to the contrary; as, to *reverse* the scene.

—Or affectations quite *reverse* the soul. *Pope.*

5. To put each in the place of the other; as, to *reverse* the distinctions of good and evil. *Rogers.*

6. In *law*, to overthrow by a contrary decision; to make void; to annul; as, to *reverse* a judgment, sentence or decree. Judgments are *reversed* by writs of error; and for certain causes, may be *reversed* without such writs.

7. To recall. [*Not in use.*] *Spenser.*

REVERSE, *v. i. revers'.* To return. [*Not in use.*] *Spenser.*

REVERSE, *n. revers'.* Change; vicissitude; a turn of affairs; *in a good sense.*

By a strange *reverse* of things, Justinian's law, which for many ages was neglected, now obtains— *Baker.*

2. Change for the worse; misfortune. By an unexpected *reverse* of circumstances, an affluent man is reduced to poverty.

3. A contrary; an opposite.

The performances to which God has annexed the promises of eternity, are just the *reverse* of all the pursuits of sense. *Rogers.*

4. [Fr. *revers.*] The *reverse* of a medal or coin is the second or back side, opposite to that on which the head or principal figure is impressed. *Encyc.*

REVERS'ED, *pp.* Turned side for side or end for end; changed to the contrary.

2. In *law*, overthrown or annulled.

3. *a.* In *botany*, resupinate; having the upper lip larger and more expanded than the lower; as a *reversed* corol. *Bigelow.*

REVERS'EDLY, *adv.* In a reversed manner. *South.*

REVERSELESS, *a. revers'less.* Not to be reversed; irreversible. *Seward.*

REVERSELY, *adv. revers'ly.* On the other hand; on the opposite. *Pearson.*

REVERS'IBLE, *a.* That may be reversed; as a *reversible* judgment or sentence.

REVERS'ING, *ppr.* Turning upside down; subverting; turning the contrary way; annulling.

REVER'SION, *n.* [Fr. from L. *reversio.*]

1. In *a general sense*, a returning; *appropriately*, in law, the returning of an estate to the grantor or his heirs, after a particular estate is ended. Hence,

2. The residue of an estate left in the grantor, to commence in possession after the determination of the particular estate granted. Thus when there is a gift in tail, the *reversion* of the fee is, without any special reservation, vested in the donor by act of law. *Blackstone.*

3. Succession; right to future possession or enjoyment.

4. In *algebra*, reversion of series, a kind of reversed operation of an infinite series. *Encyc.*

REVER'SIONARY, *a.* Pertaining to a reversion, that is, to be enjoyed in succession, or after the determination of a particular estate; as a *reversionary* interest or right.

REVER'SIONER, *n.* The person who has a reversion, or who is entitled to lands or tenements, after a particular estate granted is determined. *Blackstone.*

REVERT', *v. t.* [L. *reverto; re* and *verto,* to turn.]

1. To turn back; to turn to the contrary; to reverse.

Till happy chance *revert* the cruel scene. *Prior.*

[Instead of *revert,* in this sense, *reverse* is generally used.]

2. To drive or turn back; to reverberate; as a stream *reverted.* *Thomson.*

REVERT', *v. i.* To return; to fall back.

2. In *law,* to return to the proprietor, after the determination of a particular estate. A feud granted to a man for life, or to him and his issue male, on his death or failure of issue male, *reverted* to the lord or proprietor.

REVERT', *n.* In *music,* return; recurrence; antistrophy. *Peacham.*

REVERT'ED, *pp.* Reversed; turned back.

REVERT'ENT, *n.* A medicine which restores the natural order of the inverted irritative motions in the animal system. *Darwin.*

REVERT'IBLE, *a.* That may revert or return.

REVERT'ING, *ppr.* Turning back; returning.

REVERT'IVE, *a.* Changing; reversing. *Thomson.*

REV'ERY, *n.* [Fr. *rêverie,* from *rêver,* to dream, to rave, to be light headed. It is often written in English as in French.]

1. Properly, a raving or delirium; but its sense, as generally used, is a loose or irregular train of thoughts, occurring in musing or meditation; wild, extravagant conceit of the fancy or imagination. There are *reveries* and extravagancies which pass through the minds of wise men as well as fools. *Addison.*

2. A chimera; a vision.

REVEST', *v. t.* [Fr. *revêtir;* Low L. *revestio; re* and *vestio,* to clothe.]

1. To clothe again. *Wotton.*

2. To reinvest; to vest again with possession or office; as, to *revest* a magistrate with authority.

3. To lay out in something less fleeting than money; as, to *revest* money in stocks.

REVEST', *v. i.* To take effect again, as a title; to return to a former owner; as, the title or right *revests* in A, after alienation.

REVEST'ED, *pp.* Clothed again; invested anew.

REVEST'IARY, *n.* [Fr. *revestiaire,* from L. *revestio.*]

The place or apartment in a church or temple where the dresses are deposited; now contracted into *vestry.* *Camden.*

REVET'MENT, *n.* [Fr. *revêtement,* the lining of a ditch, from *revêtir,* supra.]

In *fortification,* a strong wall on the outside of a rampart, intended to support the earth.

REVI'BRATE, *v. i.* [*re* and *vibrate.*] To vibrate back or in return.

REVIBRA'TION, *n.* The act of vibrating back.

REVIC'TION, *n.* [L. *re* and *vivo, victum,* to live.] Return to life. [*Not used.*] *Brown.*

REVICTUAL, *v. t.* *revit'l.* [*re* and *victual.*] To furnish again with provisions. *Raleigh.*

REVICTUALED, *pp.* *revit'ld.* Furnished with victuals again.

REVICTUALING, *ppr.* *revit'ling.* Supplying again with provisions.

REVI'E, *v. t.* [*re* and *vie.*] To accede to the proposal of a stake and to overtop it; *an old phrase at cards. Obs.* *B. Jonson.*

REVI'E, *v. i.* To return the challenge of a wager at cards; to make a retort. *Obs.* *Trial of the seven Bishops.*

REVIEW, *v. t.* *revu'.* [*re* and *view;* or Fr. *revoir, revu.*]

1. To look back on. *Denham.*

2. To see again.

I shall *review* Sicilia. *Shak.*

3. To view and examine again; to reconsider; to revise; as, to *review* a manuscript. It is said that Virgil was prevented by death from *reviewing* the Æneis.

4. To retrace.

Shall I the long laborious scene *review?* *Pope.*

5. To survey; to inspect; to examine the state of any thing, particularly of troops; as, to *review* a regiment.

REVIEW, *n.* *revu'.* [Fr. *revue,* from *revoir; re* and *voir,* from L. *video,* to see.]

1. A second or repeated view; a re-examination; resurvey; as a *review* of the works of nature; a *review* of life.

2. Revision; a second examination with a view to amendment or improvement; as an author's *review* of his works.

3. In *military affairs,* an examination or inspection of troops under arms, by a general or commander, for the purpose of ascertaining the state of their discipline, equipments, &c.

4. In *literature,* a critical examination of a new publication, with remarks.

5. A periodical pamphlet containing examinations or analyses of new publications; as the Critical *Review.*

Commission of review, a commission granted by the British king to revise the sentence of the court of delegates. *Encyc.*

REVIEW'ED, *pp.* Resurveyed; re-examined; inspected; critically analysed.

REVIEW'ER, *n.* One that reviews or re-examines; an inspector; one that critically examines a new publication, and communicates his opinion upon its merits.

REVIEW'ING, *ppr.* Looking back on; seeing again; revising; re-examining; inspecting, as an army; critically examining and remarking on.

REVIG'ORATE, *v. t.* [*re* and *vigor.*] To give new vigor to. [*Not in use.*]

REVI'LE, *v. t.* [*re* and *vile. Rivilant* is found in the Norman.]

To reproach; to treat with opprobrious and contemptuous language.

She *revileth* him to his face. *Swift.*

Thou shalt not *revile* the gods. Ex. xxii.

Blessed are ye when men shall *revile* you. Matt. v.

REVI'LE, *n.* Reproach; contumely; contemptuous language. [*Not in use.*] *Milton.*

REVI'LED, *pp.* Reproached; treated with opprobrious or contemptuous language.

REVI'LEMENT, *n.* Reproach; contemptuous language. *More.*

REVI'LER, *n.* One who reviles another; one who treats another with contemptuous language.

REVI'LING, *ppr.* Reproaching; treating with language of contempt.

REVI'LING, *n.* The act of reviling or treating with reproachful words. Is. li.

REVI'LINGLY, *adv.* With reproachful or contemptuous language; with opprobrium.

REVIN'DICATE, *v. t.* To vindicate again; to reclaim; to demand and take back what has been lost. *Milford.*

REVI'SAL, *n.* [from *revise.*] Revision; the act of reviewing and re-examining for correction and improvement; as the *revisal* of a manuscript; the *revisal* of a proof sheet.

REVI'SE, *v. t.* *s* as *z.* [L. *revisus, reviso,* to revisit; *re* and *viso,* to see, to visit.]

1. To review; to re-examine; to look over with care for correction; as, to *revise* a writing; to *revise* a proof sheet. *Pope.*

2. To review, alter and amend; as, to *revise* statutes.

REVI'SE, *n.* Review; re-examination. *Boyle.*

2. Among printers, a second proof sheet; a proof sheet taken after the first correction.

REVI'SED, *pp.* Reviewed; re-examined for correction.

REVI'SER, *n.* One that revises or re-examines for correction.

REVI'SING, *ppr.* Reviewing; re-examining for correction.

REVI''SION, *n.* [Fr.] The act of reviewing; review; re-examination for correction; as the *revision* of a book or writing or of a proof sheet; a *revision* of statutes.

2. Enumeration of inhabitants. *Tooke.*

REVI''SIONAL, } *a.* Pertaining to revision.
REVI''SIONARY, }

REVIS'IT, *v. t.* *s* as *z.* [Fr. *revisiter;* L. *revisito; re* and *visito,* from *viso,* to see or *visit.*] To visit again.

Let the pale sire *revisit* Thebes. *Pope.*

REVISITA'TION, *n.* The act of revisiting.

REVIS'ITED, *pp.* Visited again.

REVIS'ITING, *ppr.* Visiting again.

REVI'SOR, *n.* In *Russia,* one who has taken the number of inhabitants. *Tooke.*

REVI'VAL, *n.* [from *revive.*] Return, recall or recovery to life from death or apparent death; as the *revival* of a drowned person.

2. Return or recall to activity from a state of languor; as the *revival* of spirits.

3. Recall, return or recovery from a state of neglect, oblivion, obscurity or depression; as the *revival* of letters or learning.

4. Renewed and more active attention to religion; an awakening of men to their spiritual concerns.

REVI'VE, *v. i.* [Fr. *revivre;* L. *revivisco; re* and *vivo,* to live.]

1. To return to life; to recover life.

The soul of the child came into him again, and he *revived.* 1 Kings xvii. Rom. xiv.

2. To recover new life or vigor; to be reanimated after depression.

When he saw the wagons which Joseph had sent to carry him, the spirit of Jacob their father *revived.* Gen. xlv.

3. To recover from a state of neglect, oblivion, obscurity or depression. Learning *revived* in Europe after the middle ages.

4. In *chimistry,* to recover its natural state, as a metal.

Sin revives, when the conscience is awakened by a conviction of guilt. Rom. vii.

REVI'VE, *v. t.* To bring again to life; to reanimate. *Milton.*

2. To raise from languor, depression or discouragement; to rouse; as, to *revive* the spirits or courage.

3. To renew; to bring into action after a suspension; as, to *revive* a project or scheme that had been laid aside.

4. To renew in the mind or memory; to recall.

The mind has the power in many cases to *revive* ideas or perceptions, which it has once had. *Locke.*

5. To recover from a state of neglect or depression; as, to *revive* letters or learning.

6. To recomfort; to quicken; to refresh with joy or hope.

Wilt thou not *revive* us again? Ps. lxxxv.

7. To bring again into notice.

Revive the libels born to die. *Swift.*

8. In *chimistry*, to restore or reduce to its natural state or to its metallic state; as, to *revive* a metal after calcination.

REVI'VED, *pp.* Brought to life; reanimated; renewed; recovered; quickened; cheered; reduced to a metallic state.

REVI'VER, *n.* That which revives; that which invigorates or refreshes; one that redeems from neglect or depression.

REVIV'IFICATE, *v. t.* [Fr. *revivifier*; L. *re* and *vivifico*; *vivus*, alive, and *facio*, to make.]

To revive; to recall or restore to life. [*Little used.*]

REVIVIFICA'TION, *n.* Renewal of life; restoration of life; or the act of recalling to life. *Spectator.*

2. In *chimistry*, the reduction of a metal to its metallic state.

REVIV'IFY, *v. t.* [Fr. *revivifier.*] To recall to life; to reanimate. *Stackhouse.*

2. To give new life or vigor to.

REVI'VING, *ppr.* Bringing to life again; reanimating; renewing; recalling to the memory; recovering from neglect or depression; refreshing with joy or hope; reducing to a metallic state.

REVIVIS'CENCE, REVIVIS'CENCY, *n.* Renewal of life; return to life. *Burnet.*

REVIVIS'CENT, *a.* Reviving; regaining or restoring life or action. *Darwin.*

REVI'VOR, *n.* In *law*, the reviving of a suit which is abated by the death of any of the parties. This is done by a bill of *revivor*. *Blackstone.*

REV'OCABLE, *a.* [Fr. from L. *revocabilis*. See *Revoke.*]

That may be recalled or revoked; that may be repealed or annulled; as a *revocable* edict or grant.

REV'OCABLENESS, *n.* The quality of being revocable.

REV'OCATE, *v. t.* [L. *revoco*; *re* and *voco*, to call.] To recall; to call back. [*Not in use.* See *Revoke.*]

REVOCA'TION, *n.* [Fr. from L. *revocatio.*]

1. The act of recalling or calling back; as the *revocation* of Calvin. *Hooker.*

2. State of being recalled. *Howell.*

3. Repeal; reversal; as the *revocation* of the edict of Nantz. A law may cease to operate without an express *revocation*. So we speak of the *revocation* of a will, of a use, of a devise, &c.

REVO'KE, *v. t.* [Fr. *revoquer*; L. *revoco*; *re* and *voco*, to call.]

1. To recall; to repeal; to reverse. A law, decree or sentence is *revoked* by the same authority which enacted or passed it. A charter or grant which vests rights in a corporation, cannot be legally *revoked* without the consent of the corporation. A devise may be *revoked* by the devisor, a use by the grantor, and a will by the testator.

2. To check; to repress; as, to *revoke* rage. [*Not in use.*] *Spenser.*

3. To draw back.

Seas are troubled when they do *revoke*
Their flowing waves into themselves again.
[*Unusual.*] *Davies.*

REVO'KE, *v. i.* To renounce at cards.

REVO'KE, *n.* The act of renouncing at cards.

REVO'KED, *pp.* Repealed; reversed.

REVO'KEMENT, *n.* Revocation; reversal. [*Little used.*] *Shak.*

REVO'KING, *ppr.* Reversing; repealing.

REVOLT', *v. i.* [Fr. *revolter*; It. *rivoltare*; *ri* and *voltare*, to turn; from L. *revolvo*; *re* and *volvo*, to turn, Eng. *wallow.*]

1. To fall off or turn from one to another. *Shak.*

2. To renounce allegiance and subjection to one's prince or state; to reject the authority of a sovereign; as a province or a number of people. *It is not applied to individuals.*

The Edomites *revolted* from under the hand of Judah. 2 Chron. xxi.

3. To change. [*Not in use.*] *Shak.*

4. In *Scripture*, to disclaim allegiance and subjection to God; to reject the government of the King of kings. Is. xxxi.

REVOLT', *v. t.* To turn; to put to flight; to overturn. *Burke.*

2. To shock; to do violence to; to cause to shrink or turn away with abhorrence; as, to *revolt* the mind or the feelings.

Their honest pride of their purer religion had *revolted* the Babylonians. *Mitford.*

REVOLT', *n.* Desertion; change of sides; more correctly, a renunciation of allegiance and subjection to one's prince or government; as the *revolt* of a province of the Roman empire.

2. Gross departure from duty. *Shak.*

3. In *Scripture*, a rejection of divine government; departure from God; disobedience. Is. lix.

4. A revolter. [*Not in use.*] *Shak.*

REVOLT'ED, *pp.* Having swerved from allegiance or duty. *Milton.*

2. Shocked; grossly offended.

REVOLT'ER, *n.* One who changes sides; a deserter. *Atterbury.*

2. One who renounces allegiance and subjection to his prince or state.

3. In *Scripture*, one who renounces the authority and laws of God. Jer. vi. Hos. ix.

REVOLT'ING, *ppr.* Changing sides; deserting.

2. Disclaiming allegiance and subjection to a prince or state.

3. Rejecting the authority of God.

4. *a.* Doing violence, as to the feelings; exciting abhorrence.

REV'OLUTE, *a.* [L. *revolutus*, from *revolvo.*] In *botany*, rolled back or downwards; as *revolute* foliation or leafing, when the sides of the leaves in the bud are rolled spirally back or towards the lower surface; a *revolute* leaf or tendril; a *revolute* corol or valve. *Martyn. Lee.*

REVOLU'TION, *n.* [Fr. from L. *revolutus*, *revolvo.*]

1. In *physics*, rotation; the circular motion of a body on its axis; a course or motion which brings every point of the surface or periphery of a body back to the place at which it began to move; as the *revolution* of a wheel; the diurnal *revolution* of the earth.

2. The motion of a body round any fixed point or center; as the annual *revolution* of the earth or other planet in its orbit round the center of the system.

3. Motion of any thing which brings it to the same point or state; as the *revolution* of day and night or of the seasons.

4. Continued course marked by the regular return of years; as the *revolution* of ages.

5. Space measured by some regular return of a revolving body or of a state of things; as the *revolution* of a day. *Dryden.*

6. In *politics*, a material or entire change in the constitution of government. Thus the *revolution* in England, in 1688, was produced by the abdication of king James II. the establishment of the house of Orange upon the throne, and the restoration of the constitution to its primitive state. So the *revolutions* in Poland, in the United States of America, and in France, consisted in a change of constitution. We shall rejoice to hear that the Greeks have effected a *revolution*.

7. Motion backward. *Milton.*

This word is used adjectively, as in the phrase, *revolution principles*. *Addison. Smollet.*

REVOLU'TIONARY, *a.* Pertaining to a revolution in government; as a *revolutionary* war; *revolutionary* crimes or disasters. *Burke.*

2. Tending to produce a revolution; as *revolutionary* measures.

REVOLU'TIONER, *n.* One who is engaged in effecting a revolution; a revolutionist. *Ramsay.*

2. In England, one who favored the revolution in 1688. *Smollet.*

REVOLU'TIONIST, *n.* One engaged in effecting a change of government; the favorer of a revolution. *Burke. S. S. Smith.*

REVOLU'TIONIZE, *v. t.* To effect a change in the form of a political constitution; as, to *revolutionize* a government. *Ames.*

2. To effect an entire change of principles in.

The gospel, if received in truth, has *revolutionized* his soul. *J. M. Mason.*

REVOLU'TIONIZED, *pp.* Changed in constitutional form and principles.

REVOLU'TIONIZING, *ppr.* Changing the form and principles of a constitution.

REVOLV'ENCY, *n.* State, act or principle of revolving; revolution.

Its own *revolvency* upholds the world. *Cowper.*

REVOM'IT, *v. t.* [*re* and *vomit*; Fr. *revomir.*]

To vomit or pour forth again; to reject from the stomach. *Hakewill.*

REVOM'ITED, *pp.* Vomited again.

REVOM'ITING, *ppr.* Vomiting again.

REVUL'SION, *n.* [Fr. from L. *revulsus*, *revello; re* and *vello*, to pull.]

1. In *medicine*, the act of turning or diverting a flux of humors or any cause of disease, from one part of the body to another. *Encyc.*

2. The act of holding or drawing back. *Brown.*

REVUL'SIVE, *a.* Having the power of revulsion.

REVUL'SIVE, *n.* That which has the power of diverting humors from one part to another.

2. That which has the power of withdrawing. *Fell.*

REW, *n.* A row. [*Not in use. Spenser.*

REWARD', *v. t. a* as *aw.* [Norm. *regarder*, to allow; *regardes*, fees, allowances, perquisites, rewards; *regardez*, awarded. In these words there appears to be an alliance with *regard*. But in the Fr. and Norm. *guerdon*, a reward, and *guerdonner*, to reward, this alliance does not appear. So the Italian *guiderdonare*, to reward, is evidently a compound of the L. *dono* with another word, and apparently with the Sax. *wither*, G. *wider* and *wieder*, D. *weder*, answering to L. *re*, denoting return. The Spanish and Portuguese have the Latin word with a different prefix; Sp. *galardon*, a reward; *galardonar*, to reward; Port. *galardam*, *galadoar*. The Armoric has *garredon*, *garredoner*. *Reward* appears to be from the Norman.]

To give in return, either good or evil.

Thou hast *rewarded* me good, whereas I have *rewarded* thee evil. 1 Sam. xxiv.

Hence, when good is returned for good, *reward* signifies to repay, to recompense, to compensate. When evil or suffering is returned for injury or wickedness, *reward* signifies to punish with just retribution, to take vengeance on, according to the nature of the case.

I will render vengeance to my enemies; and will *reward* them that hate me. Deut. xxxii.

The Son of man shall come in the glory of his Father, with his angels, and then he shall *reward* every man according to his works. Matt. xvi.

In the latter passage, *reward* signifies to render both good and evil.

REWARD', *n.* Recompense, or equivalent return for good done, for kindness, for services and the like. *Rewards* may consist of money, goods or any return of kindness or happiness.

The laborer is worthy of his *reward.* 1 Tim. v.

Great is your *reward* in heaven. Matt. v.

Rewards and punishments presuppose moral agency, and something voluntarily done, well or ill; without which respect, though we may receive good, it is only a benefit and not a *reward.*

2. The fruit of men's labor or works.

The dead know not any thing, neither have they any more a *reward.* Eccles. ix.

3. A bribe; a gift to pervert justice. Deut. xxvii.

4. A sum of money offered for taking or detecting a criminal, or for recovery of any thing lost.

5. Punishment; a just return of evil or suffering for wickedness.

Only with thine eyes shalt thou behold and see the *reward* of the wicked. Ps. xci.

6. Return in human applause. Matt. vi.

7. Return in joy and comfort. Ps. xix.

REWARD'ABLE, *a.* That may be rewarded; worthy of recompense. *Hooker. Taylor.*

REWARD'ABLENESS, *n.* The state of being worthy of reward. *Goodman.*

REWARD'ED, *pp.* Requited; recompensed or punished.

REWARD'ER, *n.* One who rewards; one that requites or recompenses. Heb. xi. *Addison. Swift.*

REWARD'ING, *ppr.* Making an equivalent return for good or evil; requiting; recompensing or punishing.

REWŎRD, *v. t.* [*re* and *word.*] To repeat in the same words. [*Not in use.*] *Shak.*

REWRI'TE. *v. t.* To write a second time.

REWRIT'TEN, *pp.* Written again. *Kent.*

REYS, *n.* The master of an Egyptian bark or ship.

RHAB'ARBARATE, *a.* [See *Rhubarb.*] Impregnated or tinctured with rhubarb. *Floyer.*

RHABDOL'OĠY, *n.* [Gr. ῥαβδος, a staff or wand, and λογος, discourse.]

The act or art of computing or numbering by Napier's rods or Napier's bones. *Jones.*

RHAB'DOMANCY, *n.* [Gr. ῥαβδος, a rod, and μαντεια, divination.]

Divination by a rod or wand. *Brown.*

RHAPSOD'IЄ, **RHAPSOD'IЄAL**, *a.* [from *rhapsody.*] Pertaining to or consisting of rhapsody; unconnected. *Mason. Martin.*

RHAP'SODIST, *n.* [from *rhapsody.*] One that writes or speaks without regular dependence of one part of his discourse on another. *Watts.*

2. One who recites or sings rhapsodies for a livelihood; or one who makes and repeats verses extempore.

3. Anciently, one whose profession was to recite the verses of Homer and other poets.

RHAP'SODY, *n.* [Gr. ῥαψωδια; ῥαπτω, to sew or unite, and ωδη, a song.]

Originally, a discourse in verse, sung or rehearsed by a rhapsodist; or a collection of verses, particularly those of Homer. In modern usage, a collection of passages, thoughts or authorities, composing a new piece, but without necessary dependence or natural connection. *Locke. Watts.*

RHEIN-BERRY, *n.* Buckthorn, a plant. *Johnson.*

RHE'NISH, *a.* Pertaining to the river Rhine, or to Rheims in France; as *Rhenish* wine; as a noun, the wine produced on the hills about Rheims, which is remarkable as a solvent of iron. *Encyc.*

RHE'TIAN, *a.* Pertaining to the ancient Rhæti, or to Rhætia, their country; as the *Rhetian* Alps, now the country of Tyrol and the Grisons.

RHE'TOR, *n.* [L. from Gr. ῥητωρ, an orator or speaker.]

A rhetorician. [*Little used.*] *Hammond.*

RHET'ORIЄ, *n.* [Gr. ῥητορικη, from ῥεω, to speak, to flow, contracted from ῥετω or ῥεθω, Eng. to *read.* The primary sense is to drive or send. See *Read.*]

1. The art of speaking with propriety, elegance and force. *Locke. Dryden. Encyc.*

2. The power of persuasion or attraction; that which allures or charms. We speak of the *rhetoric* of the tongue, and the *rhetoric* of the heart or eyes.

Sweet silent *rhetoric* of persuading eyes. *Daniel.*

RHETOR'IЄAL, *a.* Pertaining to rhetoric; as the *rhetorical* art.

2. Containing the rules of rhetoric; as a *rhetorical* treatise.

3. Oratorial; as a *rhetorical* flourish. *More.*

RHETOR'IЄALLY, *adv.* In the manner of rhetoric; according to the rules of rhetoric; as, to treat a subject *rhetorically*; a discourse *rhetorically* delivered.

RHETOR'IЄATE, *v. i.* To play the orator. [*Not in use.*] *Decay of Piety.*

RHETORIЄA'TION, *n.* Rhetorical amplification. [*Not in use.*] *Waterland.*

RHETORI''CIAN, *n.* [Fr. *rhetoricien.*] One who teaches the art of rhetoric, or the principles and rules of correct and elegant speaking.

The ancient sophists and *rhetoricians*, who had young auditors, lived till they were a hundred years old. *Bacon.*

2. One well versed in the rules and principles of rhetoric.

3. An orator. [*Less proper.*] *Dryden.*

RHETORI''CIAN, *a.* [See the Noun.] Suiting a master of rhetoric. [*Not in use.*] *Blackmore.*

RHET'ORIZE, *v. i.* To play the orator. *Cotgrave.*

RHET'ORIZE, *v. t.* To represent by a figure of oratory. *Milton.*

RHEUM, *n.* [Gr. ῥευμα, from ῥεω, to flow.]

1. An increased and often inflammatory action of the vessels of any organ; but generally applied to the inflammatory action of the mucous glands, attended with increased discharge and an altered state of their excreted fluids. *Parr.*

2. A thin serous fluid, secreted by the mucous glands, &c.; as in catarrh. *Shak.*

RHEUMAT'IЄ, *a.* [L. *rheumaticus;* Gr. ῥευματικος, from ῥευμα, rheum, which see.]

Pertaining to rheumatism, or partaking of its nature; as *rheumatic* pains or affections.

RHEU'MATISM, *n.* [L. *rheumatismus;* Gr. ῥευματισμος, from ῥευμα, a watery humor, from ῥεω, to flow; the ancients supposing the disease to proceed from a defluxion of humors.]

A painful disease affecting muscles and joints of the human body, chiefly the larger joints, as the hips, knees, shoulders, &c. *Encyc. Parr.*

RHEU'MY, *a.* [from *rheum.*] Full of rheum or watery matter; consisting of rheum or partaking of its nature.

2. Affected with rheum. *Dryden.*

3. Abounding with sharp moisture; causing rheum. *Shak.*

RHIME. [See *Rhyme.*]

RHI'NO, *n.* A cant word for gold and silver, or money. *Wagstaffe.*

RHINOCE'RIAL, *a.* [from *rhinoceros.*] Pertaining to the rhinoceros; resembling the rhinoceros. *Tatler.*

RHINOC'EROS, *n.* [Fr. *rhinoceros* or *rhinocerot;* It. Sp. *rinoceronte;* L. *rhinoceros;* Gr. ρινοκερως, nose-horn; ριν, the nose, W. *rhyn*, a point, and κερας, a horn.]

A genus of quadrupeds of two species, one of which, the *unicorn*, has a single horn growing almost erect from the nose. This animal when full grown, is said to be 12 feet in length. There is another species with two horns, the *bicornis*. They are natives of Asia and Africa. *Encyc.*

RHINOCEROS-BIRD, *n.* A bird of the genus Buceros, having a crooked horn on the forehead, joined to the upper mandible.

RHO'DIAN, *a.* Pertaining to Rhodes, an isle of the Mediterranean; as *Rhodian* laws.

RHO'DIUM, *n.* A metal recently discovered among grains of crude platinum.

RHODODEN'DRON, *n.* [Gr. ροδον, a rose, and δενδρον, a tree.]

The dwarf rosebay. *Evelyn.*

RHO'DONITE, *n.* A mineral of a red, reddish, or yellowish white color, and splintery fracture, occurring compact or fibrous in the Hartz, at Strahlberg, &c. *Phillips.*

RHOE'TIZITE, } *n.* A mineral occurring
RHET'IZITE, } in masses or in radiated concretions, and of a white color.

RHOMB, *n.* [Fr. *rhombe;* L. *rhombus;* Gr. ρομβος, from ρεμβω, to turn or whirl round, to wander, to *roam* or *rove;* literally, a deviating square.]

In *geometry*, an oblique angled parallelogram, or a quadrilateral figure whose sides are equal and parallel, but the angles unequal, two of the angles being obtuse and two acute. It consists of two equal and right cones united at the base. *Encyc. Harris.*

RHOMB'IC, *a.* Having the figure of a rhomb. *Grew.*

RHOM'BO, *n.* A fish of the turbot kind. *Dict. Nat. Hist.*

RHOM'BOID, *n.* [Gr. ρομβος, rhomb, and ειδος, form.]

1. In *geometry*, a figure having some resemblance to a rhomb; or a quadrilateral figure whose opposite sides and angles are equal, but which is neither equilateral nor equiangular. *Encyc.*

2. *a.* In *anatomy*, the *rhomboid muscle* is a thin, broad and obliquely square fleshy muscle, between the basis of the scapula and the spina dorsi. *Encyc.*

RHOMBOID'AL, *a.* Having the shape of a rhomboid, or a shape approaching it. *Woodward.*

RHOMB-SPAR, *n.* A mineral of a grayish white, occurring massive, disseminated and crystalized in rhomboids, imbedded in chlorite slate, limestone, &c. It consists chiefly of carbonates of lime and magnesia. *Ure.*

RHU'BARB, *n.* [Pers. راوند rawand.

In Syr. *raiborig.* It seems to be a compound word, latinized *rhabarbarum.*]

A plant of the genus Rheum, of several species; as the rhapontic, or common rhubard; the palmated, or true Chinese rhubarb; the compact or Tartarian; the undulated, or waved-leafed Chinese rhubarb; and the ribes, or currant rhubarb of mount Libanus. The root is medicinal and much used as a moderate cathartic.

RHUB'ARBARINE, *n.* A vegetable substance obtained from rhubarb. *Journ. of Science.*

RHUMB, *n.* [from *rhomb.*] In *navigation*, a vertical circle of any given place, or the intersection of such a circle with the horizon; in which last sense, rhumb is the same as a point of the compass.

RHUMB-LINE, *n.* In *navigation*, a line prolonged from any point of the compass on a nautical chart, except from the four cardinal points.

RHYME, } *n.* [Sax. *rim* and *gerim*, number;
RIME, } *riman*, to number; *ge-riman*, id.; *riman* and *ryman*, to give place, to open a way, to make *room;* Sw. Dan. *rim;* D. *rym;* G. *reim;* W. *rhiv;* Ir. *rimh* or *reomh.* The Welsh word is rendered also, that divides or separates, and the Sax. *rim* seems to be connected with *room*, from opening, spreading. The deduction of this word from the Greek ρυθμος, is a palpable error. The true orthography is *rime* or *ryme;* but as *rime* is hoar frost, and *rhyme* gives the true pronunciation, it may be convenient to continue the present orthography.]

1. In *poetry*, the correspondence of sounds in the terminating words or syllables of two verses, one of which succeeds the other immediately, or at no great distance.

For *rhyme* with reason may dispense,
And sound has right to govern sense. *Prior.*

To constitute this correspondence in single words or in syllables, it is necessary that the *vowel*, and the *final* articulations or consonants, should be the same, or have nearly the same sound. The initial consonants may be different, as in *find* and *mind*, *new* and *drew*, *cause* and *laws.*

2. A harmonical succession of sounds.

The youth with songs and *rhymes*,
Some dance, some haul the rope. *Denham.*

3. Poetry; a poem.

He knew
Himself to sing, and build the lofty *rhyme.* *Milton.*

4. A word of sound to answer to another word. *Young.*

Rhyme or reason, number or sense.

But from that time unto this season,
I had neither *rhyme nor reason.* *Spenser.*

RHYME, *v. i.* To accord in sound.

But fagoted his notions as they fell,
And if they *rhym'd* and rattl'd, all was well. *Dryden.*

2. To make verses.

There march'd the bard and blockhead side by side,
Who *rhym'd* for hire, and patroniz'd for pride. *Pope.*

RHYME, *v. t.* To put into rhyme. *Wilson.*

RHY'MELESS, *a.* Destitute of rhyme; not having consonance of sound. *Hall.*

RHY'MER, } One who makes rhymes;
RHY'MIST, } *n.* a versifier; a poor poet.
RHY'MSTER, } *Johnson. Dryden.*

RHY'MIC, *a.* Pertaining to rhyme.

RHYTHM, } *n.* [Gr. ρυθμος.] In *music*,
RHYTH'MUS, } variety in the movement as to quickness or slowness, or length and shortness of the notes; or rather the proportion which the parts of the motion have to each other. *Encyc.*

2. Meter; verse; number. *Howell.*

RHYTH'MICAL, *a.* [Gr. ρυθμικος; L. *rhythmicus.*]

Having proportion of sound, or one sound proportioned to another; harmonical. *Johnson.*

Duly regulated by cadences, accents and quantities. *Busby.*

RIAL, *n.* A Spanish coin. [See *Real.*]

RI'AL, *n.* [from *royal.*] A royal; a gold coin of the value of ten shillings sterling, formerly current in Britain. *Encyc.*

RI'ANT, *a.* [Fr. from *rire*, to laugh.] Laughing; exciting laughter. [*Not anglicized.*] *Buck.*

RIB, *n.* [Sax. *rib* or *ribb;* Ice. *rif;* G. *rippe;* D. *rib*, a rib or rafter; Sw. *refben*, rib or side bone; Dan. *ribbe* or *ribbeen*, ribbone; Russ. *rebro*, a rib or side. This word, like the L. *costa*, signifies side, border, extremity, whence the compound in Sw. Dan. *rib-bone*, that is, side-bone. It may be allied to the L. *ripa.* The sense of *side* is generally from extending.]

1. A bone of animal bodies which forms a part of the frame of the thorax. The ribs in the human body are twelve on each side, proceeding from the spine to the sternum, or towards it, and serving to inclose and protect the heart and lungs.

2. In *ship building*, a piece of timber which forms or strengthens the side of a ship.

Ribs of a parrel, are short pieces of plank, having holes through which are reeved the two parts of the parrel-rope. *Mar. Dict.*

3. In *botany*, the continuation of the petiole along the middle of a leaf, and from which the veins take their rise. *Martyn.*

4. In *cloth*, a prominent line or rising, like a rib.

5. Something long, thin and narrow; a strip. [W. *rhib.*]

RIB, *v. t.* To furnish with ribs. In *manufactures*, to form with rising lines and channels; as, to *rib* cloth; whence we say, *ribbed* cloth.

2. To inclose with ribs. *Shak.*

RIB'ALD, *n.* [Fr. *ribaud;* It. *ribaldo*, a rogue, and as an adjective, poor, beggarly; Arm. *ribaud*, a fornicator. Qu. D. *rabout*, *rabauw*, a rogue or rascal. According to the Italian, this word is a compound of *ri* or *re*, and *baldo*, bold, or Sp. *baldio*, idle, lazy, vagrant, untilled. But the real composition of the word is not ascertained.]

A low, vulgar, brutal wretch; a lewd fellow. *Shak. Spenser. Pope.*

RIB'ALD, *a.* Low; base; mean. *Shak.*

RIB'ALDISH, *a.* Disposed to ribaldry. *Hall.*

RIB'ALDRY, *n.* [It. *ribalderia.*] Mean, vulgar language; chiefly, obscene language. *Dryden. Swift.*

RIB'AN, *n.* In *heraldry*, the eighth part of a bend. *Encyc.*

RIB'BED, *pp.* or *a.* Furnished with ribs; as *ribbed* with steel. *Sandys.*

2. Inclosed as with ribs. *Shak.*

3. Marked or formed with rising lines and channels; as *ribbed* cloth.

RIB'IN, *n.* [W. *rhibin*, a row or streak, a dribblet; *rhib*, id.; Ir. *ruibin*; Fr. *ruban*; Arm. *rubanou*. This word has no connection with *band*, and the common orthography is grossly erroneous.]

1. A fillet of silk; a narrow web of silk used for an ornament, as a badge, or for fastening some part of female dress. *Dryden.*

2. In *naval architecture*, a long narrow flexible piece of timber, nailed upon the outside of the ribs from the stem to the sternpost, so as to encompass the ship lengthwise; the principal are the floor-ribin and the breadth-ribin. *Mar. Dict.*

RIB'IN, *v. t.* To adorn with ribins. *Beaum.*

RIB'RŌAST, *v. t.* [*rib* and *roast*.] To beat soundly; *a burlesque word*. *Butler.*

RIB'RŌASTED, *pp.* Soundly beaten.

RIB'RŌASTING, *ppr.* Beating soundly.

RIB'WŎRT, *n.* A plant of the genus Plantago.

RIC, } as a termination, denotes jurisdic-
RICK, } tion, or a district over which government is exercised, as in *bishoprick*; Sax. *cyne-ric*, king-ric. It is the Gothic *reiki*, dominion, Sax. *rice* or *ric*; from the same root as L. *rego*, to rule, and *region*.

RIC, as a termination of names, denotes rich or powerful, as in *Alfric*, *Frederick*, like the Greek *Polycrates* and *Plutarchus*. It is the first syllable of *Richard*; Sax. *ric*, *rice*. [See *Rich*.]

RICE, *n.* [Fr. *riz* or *ris*; It. *riso*; Sp. Port. *arroz*; G. *reis* or *reiss*; D. *ryst*; Dan. *ris*; L. *oryza*; Gr. *ορυζα*; Eth. *rez*; Ar. ارز arozon, from the verb ارز araza, to be contracted, or to be firmly fixed. The word is common to most of the Asiatics, Persians, Turks, Armenians and Tartars.]

A plant of the genus Oryza, and its seed. The calyx is a bivalvular uniflorous glume; the corol bivalvular, nearly equal, and adhering to the seed. There is only one species. This plant is cultivated in all warm climates, and the grain forms a large portion of the food of the inhabitants. In America, it grows chiefly on low moist land, which can be overflowed. It is a light food, and said to be little apt to produce acidity in the stomach. Indeed it seems intended by the wise and benevolent Creator to be the proper food of men in warm climates.

RICE-BIRD, } *n.* A bird of the United
RICE-BUNTING, } States, the *Emberiza oryzivora*; so named from its feeding on rice in the S. States. In New England, it is called *bob-lincoln*. *Wilson.*

RICH, *a.* [Fr. *riche*; Sp. *rico*; It. *ricco*; Sax. *ric*, *rice*, *ricca*; D. *ryk*; G. *reich*; Sw. *rik*; Dan. *rig*, *riig*. This word in Saxon signifies great, noble, powerful, as well as rich. It is probable therefore it is connected with *ric*, dominion, L. *rego*, *regnum*, Eng. *reach*, *region*, from *extending*.]

1. Wealthy; opulent; possessing a large portion of land, goods or money, or a larger portion than is common to other men or to men of like rank. A farmer may be *rich* with property which would not make a nobleman *rich*. An annual income of £500 sterling would make a *rich* vicar, but not a *rich* bishop. Men more willingly acknowledge others to be *richer*, than to be wiser than themselves.

> Abram was very *rich* in cattle, in silver and in gold. Gen. xiii.

2. Splendid; costly; valuable; precious; sumptuous; as a *rich* dress; a *rich* border; a *rich* silk; *rich* furniture; a *rich* present.

3. Abundant in materials; yielding great quantities of any thing valuable; as a *rich* mine; *rich* ore.

4. Abounding in valuable ingredients or qualities; as a *rich* odor or flavor; *rich* spices. *Waller. Baker.*

So we say, a *rich* description; a discourse *rich* in ideas.

5. Full of valuable achievments or works.

> Each minute shall be *rich* in some great action. *Rowe.*

6. Fertile; fruitful; capable of producing large crops or quantities; as a *rich* soil; *rich* land; *rich* mold. *Philips.*

7. Abundant; large; as a *rich* crop.

8. Abundant; affording abundance; plentiful.

> The gorgeous East with *richest* hand
> Pours on her sons barbaric pearl and gold. *Milton.*

9. Full of beautiful scenery; as a *rich* landscape; a *rich* prospect.

10. Abounding with elegant colors; as a *rich* picture.

11. Plentifully stocked; as pastures *rich* in flocks.

12. Strong; vivid; perfect; as a *rich* color.

13. Having something precious; as a grove of *rich* trees. *Milton.*

14. Abounding with nutritious qualities; as a *rich* diet.

15. Highly seasoned; as *rich* paste; a *rich* dish of food.

16. Abounding with a variety of delicious food; as a *rich* table or entertainment.

17. Containing abundance beyond wants; as a *rich* treasury.

18. In *music*, full of sweet or harmonious sounds.

19. In *Scripture*, abounding; highly endowed with spiritual gifts; as *rich* in faith. James ii.

20. Placing confidence in outward prosperity. Matt. xix.

21. Self-righteous; abounding, in one's own opinion, with spiritual graces. Rev. iii.

Rich in mercy, spoken of God, full of mercy, and ready to bestow good things on sinful men. Eph. ii. Rom. x.

The rich, used as a noun, denotes a rich man or person, or more frequently in the plural, rich men or persons.

> The *rich* hath many friends. Prov. xiv.

RICH, *v. t.* To enrich. [*Not used.* See *Enrich.*] *Gower.*

RICH'ED, *pp.* Enriched. [*Not used.*] *Shak.*

RICH'ES, *n.* [Fr. *richesse*; It. *ricchezza*; Sp. *riqueza*. This is in the singular number in fact, but treated as the plural.]

1. Wealth; opulence; affluence; possessions of land, goods or money in abundance.

> *Riches* do not consist in having more gold and silver, but in having more in proportion than our neighbors. *Locke.*

2. Splendid sumptuous appearance.

> The *riches* of heav'n's pavement, trodden gold. *Milton.*

3. In *Scripture*, an abundance of spiritual blessings. Luke xvi.

The riches of God, his fullness of wisdom, power, mercy, grace and glory, Eph. i. ii.; or the abundance supplied by his works. Ps. civ.

The riches of Christ, his abundant fullness of spiritual and eternal blessings for men. Eph. iii.

The riches of a state or *kingdom*, consist less in a full treasury than in the productiveness of its soil and manufactures, and in the industry of its inhabitants.

RICH'LY, *adv.* With riches; with opulence; with abundance of goods or estate; with ample funds; as a hospital *richly* endowed.

> In Belmont is a lady *richly* left. *Shak.*

2. Gayly; splendidly; magnificently; as *richly* dressed; *richly* ornamented.

3. Plenteously; abundantly; amply; as, to be *richly* paid for services. The reading of ancient authors will *richly* reward us for the perusal.

4. Truly; really; abundantly; fully; as a chastisement *richly* deserved. *Addison.*

RICH'NESS, *n.* Opulence; wealth. *Sidney.*

2. Finery; splendor. *Johnson.*

3. Fertility; fecundity; fruitfulness; the qualities which render productive; as the *richness* of a soil. *Addison.*

4. Fullness; abundance; as the *richness* of a treasury.

5. Quality of abounding with something valuable; as the *richness* of a mine or an ore; the *richness* of milk or of cane-juice.

6. Abundance of any ingredient or quality; as the *richness* of spices or of fragrance.

7. Abundance of beautiful scenery; as the *richness* of a landscape or prospect.

8. Abundance of nutritious qualities; as the *richness* of diet.

9. Abundance of high seasoning; as the *richness* of cake.

10. Strength; vividness; or whatever constitutes perfection; as the *richness* of color or coloring.

11. Abundance of imagery or of striking ideas; as *richness* of description.

RICK, *n.* [Sax. *hreac* or *hrig*; Ir. *cruach*; W. *crug*, a *rick*, an impostem, a heap, a stack, a hillock; *crugaw*, to heap or pile, to swell, to grow into an impostem. It coincides with the G. *rücken*, D. *rug*, the back, Eng. *ridge*.]

A heap or pile of grain or hay in the field or open air, but sheltered with a kind of roof. In America, we usually give this name to a long pile; the round and conical pile being called *stack*. In the north of England, it is said this name is given to small piles of corn in the field. *Mortimer.*

RICK'ETS, *n.* [In technical language, *rachitis*, Gr. *ραχιτις*, from *ραχις*, back or spine, Eng. *rack*, applied to the neck piece of meat; Sp. *raquitio*, the *rickets*. See *Rack* and *Ridge*.]

A disease which affects children, and in which the joints become knotted, and the legs and spine grow crooked. As the child advances in life, the head is enlarged, the thorax is compressed on the sides, and the sternum rises. *Encyc.*

RICK'ETY, *a.* Affected with rickets. *Arbuthnot.*

2. Weak; feeble in the joints; imperfect.

RIC'OCHET, *n.* [Fr. duck and drake.] In *gunnery*, the firing of guns, mortars or howitzers with small charges, and elevated a few degrees, so as to carry the balls or shells just over the parapet, and cause them to roll along the opposite rampart. This is called ricochet-firing, and the batteries are called ricochet-batteries. *Encyc.*

RID, *pret.* of *ride.*

RID, *v. t.* pret. *rid*; pp. *id.* [Sax. *ahreddan* or *hreddan*; D. *redden*; G. *retten* or *erretten*; Dan. *redder*; allied probably to W. *rhidiaw*, to secrete, to drain, that is, to separate or drive off, whence *riddle.* See Class Rd. No. 63. 69.]

1. To free; to deliver; properly, to separate, and thus to deliver or save.

That he might *rid* him out of their hands. Gen. xxxvii.

I will *rid* you out of their bondage. Ex. vi.

2. To separate; to drive away.

I will *rid* evil beasts out of the land. Lev. xxvi.

[*This use is not common.*]

3. To free; to clear; to disencumber; as, to *rid* one of his care. It is not easy to *rid* the sea of pirates. *B. Jonson.*

Resolv'd at once to *rid* himself of pain. *Dryden.*

4. To dispatch.

For willingness *rids* away. *Shak.*

5. To drive away; to remove by violence; to destroy.

Ah death's men! you have *rid* this sweet young prince. *Shak.*

RID, *pp.* or *a.* Free; clear; as, to be *rid* of trouble.

To get rid of, to free one's self. *Addison.*

RID'DANCE, *n.* Deliverance; a setting free; as *riddance* from all adversity. *Hooker.*

2. Disencumbrance. *Shak.*

3. The act of clearing away. *Milton.*

Thou shalt not make clean *riddance* of the corners of thy field. Lev. xxiii.

RID'DEN, RID, } *pp.* of *ride.*

RID'DING, *ppr.* Freeing; clearing; disencumbering.

RID'DLE, *n.* [Sax. *hriddel*; W. *rhidyll*, from *rhidiaw*, to secrete, to separate; Corn. *ridar* or *krodar*; Arm. *ridell* or *croezr*; Ir. *criathar*, a riddle; *cratham*, to shake; G. *rütteln*, to shake, to riddle; W. *crydu*, to shake; allied to *rid* and to *cradle*, from driving. See *Cradle.*]

An instrument for cleaning grain, being a large sieve with a perforated bottom, which permits the grain to pass through it, but retains the chaff.

RID'DLE, *v. t.* To separate, as grain from the chaff with a riddle; as, to *riddle* wheat. [*Note.* The machines now used have nearly superseded the riddle.]

RID'DLE, *n.* [Sax. *rædelse*; D. *raadzel*; G. *räthsel*; from Sax. *ræden*, D. *raaden*, G. *rathen*, to counsel or advise, also to guess. See *Read.*]

1. An enigma; something proposed for conjecture, or that is to be solved by conjecture; a puzzling question; an ambiguous proposition. Judges xiv. *Milton.*

2. Any thing ambiguous or puzzling. *Hudibras.*

RID'DLE, *v. t.* To solve; to explain; but we generally use *unriddle*, which is more proper.

Riddle me this, and guess him if you can. *Dryden.*

RID'DLE, *v. i.* To speak ambiguously, obscurely or enigmatically. *Shak.*

RID'DLER, *n.* One who speaks ambiguously or obscurely. *Horne.*

RID'DLINGLY, *adv.* In the manner of a riddle; secretly. *Donne.*

RIDE, *v. i.* pret. *rode* or *rid*; pp. *rid*, *ridden.* [Sax. *ridan*; G. *reiten*; D. *ryden*; Sw. *rida*; Dan. *rider*; W. *rhedu*, to run; L. *rheda*, a chariot or vehicle; Hindoo, *ratha*, id.; Sax. *rad*, a riding or a *road*; Ir. *ratha*, *riadh*, a running; *reatham*, to run; *ridire*, a knight; allied to *ready*, G. *bereit*; *bereiten*, to ride, and to get *ready.* See *Ready.* Class Rd. No. 5. and 9.]

1. To be carried on horseback, or on any beast, or in any vehicle. We *ride* on a horse, on a camel, in a coach, chariot, wagon, &c.

2. To be borne on or in a fluid. A ship *rides* at anchor; the ark *rode* on the flood; a balloon *rides* in the air.

He *rode* on a cherub and did fly; yea, he did fly on the wings of the wind. Ps. xviii.

3. To be supported in motion.

Strong as the axle-tree
On which heaven *rides.* *Shak.*

4. To practice riding. He *rides* often for his health.

5. To manage a horse well.

He *rode*, he fenc'd, he mov'd with graceful ease. *Dryden.*

6. To be supported by something subservient; to sit.

On whose foolish honesty
My practices *rid* easy. *Shak.*

To ride easy, in *seaman's language*, is when a ship does not labor or feel a great strain on her cables.

To ride hard, is when a ship pitches violently, so as to strain her cables, masts and hull.

To ride out, as a gale, signifies that a ship does not drive during a storm.

RIDE, *v. t.* To sit on, so as to be carried; as, to *ride* a horse.

They *ride* the air in whirlwind. *Milton.*

2. To manage insolently at will; as in priest-*ridden.*

The nobility could no longer endure to be *ridden* by bakers, coblers and brewers. *Swift.*

3. To carry. [*Local.*]

RIDE, *n.* An excursion on horseback or in a vehicle.

2. A saddle horse. [*Local.*] *Grose.*

3. A road cut in a wood or through a ground for the amusement of riding; a riding.

RI'DER, *n.* One who is borne on a horse or other beast, or in a vehicle.

2. One who breaks or manages a horse. *Shak.*

3. The matrix of an ore. *Gregory.*

4. An inserted leaf or an additional clause, as to a bill in parliament.

5. In *ship building*, a sort of interior rib fixed occasionally in a ship's hold, opposite to some of the timbers to which they are bolted, and reaching from the keelson to the beams of the lower deck, to strengthen her frame. *Mar. Dict.*

RIDGE, *n.* [Sax. *rig*, *ricg*, *hric*, *hricg*, the back; Sw. *rygg*; D. *rug*; G. *rücken*; Ice. *hriggur.* The Welsh have *rhig*, a notch or groove, and *rhyç*, a trench or furrow between ridges. The Dutch has *reeks*, a ridge, chain or series, and the Dan. *rekke* is a row, rank, range, a file, and a *ridge*, from the root of *rekker*, to reach. If connected with the latter word, the primary sense is to draw or stretch, L. *rugo.*]

1. The back or top of the back. *Hudibras.*

2. A long or continued range of hills or mountains; or the upper part of such a range. We say, a long *ridge* of hills, or the highest *ridge.* *Milton.* *Ray.*

3. A steep elevation, eminence or protuberance.

Part rise in crystal wall, or *ridge* direct. *Milton.*

4. A long rising land, or a strip of ground thrown up by a plow or left between furrows. Ps. lxv. *Mortimer.*

5. The top of the roof of a building. *Moxon.*

6. Any long elevation of land.

7. *Ridges* of a horse's mouth, are wrinkles or risings of flesh in the roof of the mouth. *Far. Dict.*

RIDGE, *v. t.* To form a ridge; as bristles that *ridge* the back of a boar. *Milton.*

2. In *tillage*, to form into ridges with the plow. The farmers in Connecticut *ridge* their land for maiz, leaving a balk between two ridges.

3. To wrinkle. *Cowper.*

RIDG'IL, RIDG'LING, } *n.* The male of any beast half gelt. *Encyc.*

RIDG'Y, *a.* Having a ridge or ridges; rising in a ridge. *Dryden.*

RID'ICULE, *n.* [Fr. from L. *ridiculum*, from *rideo*, to laugh or laugh at; Fr. *rider*, to wrinkle, to bend the brow; Arm. *redenna.*]

1. Contemptuous laughter; laughter with some degree of contempt; derision. It expresses less than *scorn.* Ridicule is aimed at what is not only laughable, but improper, absurd or despicable. Sacred subjects should never be treated with *ridicule.* [See *Ludicrous.*]

Ridicule is too rough an entertainment for the polished and refined. It is banished from France, and is losing ground in England. *Kames.*

2. That species of writing which excites contempt with laughter. It differs from *burlesque*, which may excite laughter without contempt, or it may provoke derision. *Ibid.*

Ridicule and *derision* are not exactly the same, as *derision* is applied to persons only, and *ridicule* to persons or things. We *deride* the man, but *ridicule* the man or his performances.

RID'ICULE, *v. t.* To laugh at with expressions of contempt; to deride.

2. To treat with contemptuous merriment; to expose to contempt or derision by writing.

RID'ICULE, *a.* Ridiculous. [*Not in use.*]

RID'ICULED, *pp.* Treated with laughter and contempt; derided.

RID'IЄULER, *n.* One that ridicules. *Chesterfield.*

RID'IЄULING, *ppr.* Laughing at in contempt; exposing to contempt and derision.

RIDIЄ'ULOUS, *a.* [L. *ridiculus;* It. *ridicoloso.*]
That may justly excite laughter with contempt; as a *ridiculous* dress; *ridiculous* behavior. A fop and a dandy are *ridiculous* in their dress.

RIDIЄ'ULOUSLY, *adv.* In a manner worthy of contemptuous merriment; as a man *ridiculously* vain.

RIDIЄ'ULOUSNESS, *n.* The quality of being ridiculous; as the *ridiculousness* of worshiping idols.

RI'DING, *ppr.* [from *ride.*] Passing or traveling on a beast or in a vehicle; floating.

2. *a.* Employed to travel on any occasion.

> No suffragan bishop shall have more than one *riding* apparitor. *Ayliffe.*

RI'DING, *n.* A road cut in a wood or through a ground, for the diversion of riding therein. *Sidney. Encyc.*

2. [corrupted from *trithing,* third.] One of the three intermediate jurisdictions between a three and a hundred, into which the county of York, in England, is divided, anciently under the government of a reeve. *Blackstone.*

RI'DING-ЄLERK, *n.* In *England,* one of the six clerks in chancery. *Ash.*

RI'DING-ЄOAT, *n.* A coat for riding on a journey. *Swift.*

RI'DING-HABIT, *n.* A garment worn by females when they ride or travel. *Guardian.*

RI'DING-HOOD, *n.* A hood used by females when they ride; a kind of cloke with a hood.

RI'DING-SЄHOOL, *n.* A school or place where the art of riding is taught. It may in some places be called a *riding-house.*

RIDOT'TO, *n.* [It. from L. *reductus.*] A public assembly.

2. A musical entertainment consisting of singing and dancing, in the latter of which the whole company join. *Busby.*

RIE. [See *Rye.*]

RIFE, *a.* [Sax. *ryfe.* Qu. Heb. רבה to multiply.]
Prevailing; prevalent. It is used of epidemic diseases.

> The plague was then *rife* in Hungary. *Knolles.*

RI'FELY, *adv.* Prevalently; frequently.

> It was *rifely* reported that the Turks were coming in a great fleet. *Knolles.*

RI'FENESS, *n.* Frequency; prevalence. *Arbuthnot.*

RIFF'RAFF, *n.* [Fr. *rifler;* G. *raffen,* to sweep; Dan. *rips, raps.*] Sweepings; refuse. *Hall.*

RI'FLE, *v. t.* [Fr. *rifler,* to *rifle,* to sweep away; allied probably to *friper* and *griveler;* G. *raffen,* to sweep; *riffeln,* to hatchel. This is one of the family of *rip, rive, reap, raffle,* L. *rapio,* W. *rheibiaw,* D. *ryven,* to grate, Eng. *rub,* &c.]

1. To seize and bear away by force; to snatch away.

> Till time shall *rifle* ev'ry youthful grace. *Pope.*

2. To strip; to rob; to pillage; to plunder.

> You have *rifled* my master. *L'Estrange.*

RI'FLE, *n.* [Dan. *rifle* or *riffle,* the *rifle* of a gun; *riffelbösse,* a rifle gun; G. *reifeln,* to chamfer, to *rifle.* This word belongs to the family of *rip, rive,* L. *rapio,* &c. supra. The word means primarily a channel or groove.]
A gun about the usual length and size of a musket, the inside of whose barrel is *rifled,* that is, grooved, or formed with spiral channels.

RI'FLE, *v. t.* To groove; to channel.

RI'FLED, *pp.* Seized and carried away by violence; pillaged; channeled.

RI'FLEMAN, *n.* A man armed with a rifle.

RI'FLER, *n.* A robber; one that seizes and bears away by violence.

RI'FLING, *ppr.* Plundering; seizing and carrying away by violence; grooving.

RIFT, *n.* [from *rive.*] A cleft; a fissure; an opening made by riving or splitting. *Milton. Dryden.*

RIFT, *v. t.* To cleave; to rive; to split; as, to *rift* an oak or a rock. *Milton. Pope.*

RIFT, *v. i.* To burst open; to split.

> Timber—not apt to *rift* with ordnance. *Bacon.*

2. To belch; to break wind.. [*Local.*]

RIFT'ED, *pp.* Split; rent; cleft.

RIFT'ING, *ppr.* Splitting; cleaving; bursting.

RIG, *n.* [Sax.] A ridge, which see.

RIG, *v. t.* [Sax. *wrigan,* to put on, to cover, whence Sax. *hrægle,* a garment, contracted into *rail,* in *night-rail.*]

1. To dress; to put on; when applied to persons, not elegant, but rather a ludicrous word, to express the putting on of a gay, flaunting or unusual dress.

> Jack was *rigged* out in his gold and silver lace, with a fether in his cap. *L'Estrange.*

2. To furnish with apparatus or gear; to fit with tackling.

3. To *rig a ship,* in *seamen's language,* is to fit the shrouds, stays, braces, &c. to their respective masts and yards. *Mar. Dict.*

RIG, *n.* [See the Verb.] Dress; also, bluster.

2. A romp; a wanton; a strumpet.

To run the rig, to play a wanton trick.

To run the rig upon, to practice a sportive trick on.

RIG, *v. i.* To play the wanton.

RIGADOON', *n.* [Fr. *rigodon.*] A gay brisk dance performed by one couple, and said to have been borrowed from Provence in France. *Encyc.*

RIGA'TION, *n.* [L. *rigatio,* from *rigo,* Gr. βρεχω. See *Rain.*]
The act of watering; but *irrigation* is generally used.

RIG'GED, *pp.* Dressed; furnished with shrouds, stays, &c. as a ship.

RIG'GER, *n.* One that rigs or dresses; one whose occupation is to fit the rigging of a ship.

RIG'GING, *ppr.* Dressing; fitting with shrouds, braces, &c.

RIG'GING, *n.* Dress; tackle; particularly, the ropes which support the masts, extend and contract the sails, &c. of a ship. This is of two kinds, *standing* rigging, as the shrouds and stays, and *running* rigging, such as braces, sheets, halliards, clewlines, &c. *Mar. Dict.*

RIG'GISH, *a.* Wanton; lewd. [*Not in use.*] *Shak.*

RIG'GLE, *v. i.* To move one way and the other. [See *Wriggle.*]

RIGHT, *a.* *rite.* [Sax. *riht, reht;* D. *regt;* G. *recht;* Dan. *rigtig;* Sw. *ricktig;* It. *retto;* Sp. *recto;* L. *rectus,* from the root of *rego,* properly to strain or stretch, whence *straight;* Sax. *recan.* See Class Rg. No. 18. 46. 47.]
Properly, strained; stretched to straightness; hence,

1. Straight. A *right* line in geometry is the shortest line that can be drawn or imagined between two points. A *right* line may be horizontal, perpendicular, or inclined to the plane of the horizon.

2. In *morals* and *religion,* just; equitable; accordant to the standard of truth and justice or the will of God. That alone is *right* in the sight of God, which is consonant to his will or law; this being the only perfect standard of truth and justice. In social and political affairs, that is *right* which is consonant to the laws and customs of a country, provided these laws and customs are not repugnant to the laws of God. A man's intentions may be *right,* though his actions may be wrong in consequence of a defect in judgment.

3. Fit; suitable; proper; becoming. In things indifferent, or which are regulated by no positive law, that is *right* which is best suited to the character, occasion or purpose, or which is fitted to produce some good effect. It is *right* for a rich man to dress himself and his family in expensive clothing, which it would not be *right* for a poor man to purchase. It is *right* for every man to choose his own time for eating or exercise.
Right is a relative term; what may be *right* for one end, may be *wrong* for another.

4. Lawful; as the *right* heir of an estate.

5. True; not erroneous or wrong; according to fact.

> If there be no prospect beyond the grave, the inference is certainly *right,* "let us eat and drink, for to-morrow we die." *Locke.*

6. Correct; passing a true judgment; not mistaken or wrong.

> You are *right,* justice, and you weigh this well. *Shak.*

7. Not left; most convenient or dextrous; as the *right* hand, which is generally most strong or most convenient in use.

8. Most favorable or convenient.

> The lady has been disappointed on the *right* side. *Spectator.*

9. Properly placed, disposed or adjusted; orderly; well regulated.

10. Well performed, as an art or act.

11. Most direct; as the *right* way from London to Oxford.

12. Being on the same side as the right hand; as the *right* side.

13. Being on the right hand of a person whose face is towards the mouth of a river; as the *right* bank of the Hudson.

RIGHT, *adv.* In a right or straight line; directly.

> Let thine eyes look *right* on. Prov. iv.

2. According to the law or will of God, or to the standard of truth and justice; as, to judge *right.*

3. According to any rule of art.

You with strict discipline instructed *right*. *Roscommon.*

4. According to fact or truth; as, to tell a story *right*.
5. In a great degree; very; as *right* humble; *right* noble; *right* valiant. [*Obsolescent or inelegant.*]
6. It is prefixed to titles; as in *right* honorable; *right* reverend.

RIGHT, is used elliptically for *it is right, what you say is right, it is true*, &c.

Right, cries his lordship. *Pope.*

On the right, on the side with the right hand.

RIGHT, *n.* Conformity to the will of God, or to his law, the perfect standard of truth and justice. In the literal sense, *right* is a straight line of conduct, and *wrong* a crooked one. *Right* therefore is rectitude or straightness, and perfect rectitude is found only in an infinite Being and his will.

2. Conformity to human laws, or to other human standard of truth, propriety or justice. When laws are definite, *right* and wrong are easily ascertained and understood. In arts, there are some principles and rules which determine what is *right*. In many things indifferent, or left without positive law, we are to judge what is *right* by fitness or propriety, by custom, civility or other circumstances.
3. Justice; that which is due or proper; as, to do *right* to every man.

Long love to her has borne the faithful knight,
And well deserv'd, had fortune done him *right*. *Dryden.*

4. Freedom from error; conformity with truth or fact.

Seldom your opinions err,
Your eyes are always in the *right*. *Prior.*

5. Just claim; legal title; ownership; the legal power of exclusive possession and enjoyment. In hereditary monarchies, a *right* to the throne vests in the heir on the decease of the king. A deed vests the *right* of possession in the purchaser of land. Right and possession are very different things. We often have occasion to demand and sue for *rights* not in *possession*.
6. Just claim by courtesy, customs, or the principles of civility and decorum. Every man has a *right* to civil treatment. The magistrate has a *right* to respect.
7. Just claim by sovereignty; prerogative. God, as the author of all things, has a *right* to govern and dispose of them at his pleasure.
8. That which justly belongs to one.

Born free, he sought his *right*. *Dryden.*

9. Property; interest.

A subject in his prince may claim a *right*. *Dryden.*

10. Just claim; immunity; privilege. All men have a *right* to the secure enjoyment of life, personal safety, liberty and property. We deem the *right* of trial by jury invaluable, particularly in the case of crimes. *Rights* are natural, civil, political, religious, personal, and public.
11. Authority; legal power. We have no *right* to disturb others in the enjoyment of their religious opinions.
12. In *the United States*, a tract of land; or a share or proportion of property, as in a mine or manufactory.
13. The side opposite to the left; as on the *right*. Look to the *right*.

To rights, in a direct line; straight. [*Unusual.*] *Woodward.*

2. Directly; soon.

To set to rights, } to put into good order; to
To put to rights, } adjust; to regulate what is out of order.

Bill of rights, a list of rights; a paper containing a declaration of rights, or the declaration itself.

Writ of right, a writ which lies to recover lands in fee simple, unjustly withheld from the true owner. *Blackstone.*

RIGHT, *v. t.* To do justice to; to relieve from wrong; as, to *right* an injured person. *Taylor.*

2. In *seamen's language*, to *right a ship*, is to restore her to an upright position from a careen.

To right the helm, to place it in the middle of the ship.

RIGHT, *v. i.* To rise with the masts erect, as a ship.

RIGHTED, *pp.* Relieved from injustice; set upright.

RIGHTEN, *v. t.* [Sax. *gerihtan.*] To do justice to. *Obs.*

RIGHTEOUS, *a.* *ri'chus.* [Sax. *rihtwise*; *right* and *wise*, manner, as in *otherwise, lengthwise.*]

1. Just; accordant to the divine law. *Applied to persons*, it denotes one who is holy in heart, and observant of the divine commands in practice; as a *righteous* man. *Applied to things*, it denotes consonant to the divine will or to justice; as a *righteous* act. It is used chiefly in theology, and applied to God, to his testimonies and to his saints.

The righteous, in Scripture, denote the servants of God, the saints.

2. Just; equitable; merited.

And I thy *righteous* doom will bless. *Dryden.*

RIGHTEOUSLY, *adv.* *ri'chusly.* Justly; in accordance with the laws of justice; equitably; as a criminal *righteously* condemned.

Thou shalt judge the people *righteously*. Ps. lxvii.

RIGHTEOUSNESS, *n.* *ri'chusness.* Purity of heart and rectitude of life; conformity of heart and life to the divine law. *Righteousness*, as used in Scripture and theology, in which it is chiefly used, is nearly equivalent to holiness, comprehending holy principles and affections of heart, and conformity of life to the divine law. It includes all we call justice, honesty and virtue, with holy affections; in short, it is true religion.

2. *Applied to God*, the perfection or holiness of his nature; exact rectitude; faithfulness.
3. The active and passive obedience of Christ, by which the law of God is fulfilled. Dan. ix.
4. Justice; equity between man and man. Luke i.
5. The cause of our justification.

The Lord our *righteousness*. Jer. xxiii.

RIGHTER, *n.* One who sets right; one who does justice or redresses wrong.

RIGHTFUL, *a.* Having the right or just claim according to established laws; as the *rightful* heir to a throne or an estate.

2. Being by right, or by just claim; as a *rightful* lord; *rightful* property; *rightful* judge.
3. Just; consonant to justice; as a *rightful* cause; a *rightful* war. *Prior.*

RIGHTFULLY, *adv.* According to right, law or justice; as a title *rightfully* vested.

RIGHTFULNESS, *n.* Justice; accordance with the rules of right; as the *rightfulness* of a claim to lands or tenements.

2. Moral rectitude.

But still although we fail of perfect *rightfulness*. [*Not usual.*] *Sidney.*

RIGHT-HAND, *n.* The hand opposite to the left, usually the strongest, most convenient or dextrous hand, and hence its name in other languages, as well as in ours.

RIGHTING, *ppr.* Doing justice to; setting upright.

RIGHTLY, *adv.* According to justice; according to the divine will or moral rectitude; as duty *rightly* performed.

2. Properly; fitly; suitably; as a person *rightly* named.
3. According to truth or fact; not erroneously. He has *rightly* conjectured.
4. Honestly; uprightly. *Shak.*
5. Exactly.

Thou didst not *rightly* see. *Dryden.*

6. Straightly; directly. [*Not in use.*] *Ascham.*

RIGHTNESS, *n.* Correctness; conformity to truth or to the divine will, which is the standard of moral rectitude. It is important that a man should have such persuasion of the *rightness* of his conscience as to exclude rational doubt. *South.*

2. Straightness; as the *rightness* of a line. *Bacon.*

RIG'ID, *a.* [Fr. *rigide*; It. Sp. *rigido*; L. *rigidus*, from *rigeo*; Gr. ρυγοω, to be stiff; ρυγιος, stiff, whence L. *frigeo, frigidus*; Eth. ረገዐ, Heb. רגע to be still, to be stiff or rigid. Class Rg. No. 3. 27. The primary sense is probably to strain or extend.]

1. Stiff; not pliant; not easily bent. It is applied to bodies or substances that are naturally soft or flexible, but not fluid. We never say, a *rigid* stone or *rigid* iron, nor do we say, *rigid* ice; but we say, an animal body or limb, when cold, is *rigid*. *Rigid* is then opposed to *flexible*, but expresses less than *inflexible*.
2. Strict in opinion, practice or discipline; severe in temper; opposed to *lax* or *indulgent*; as a *rigid* father or master; a *rigid* officer.
3. Strict; exact; as a *rigid* law or rule; *rigid* discipline; *rigid* criticism.
4. Severely just; as a *rigid* sentence or judgment.
5. Exactly according to the sentence or law; as *rigid* execution.

RIGID'ITY, *n.* [Fr. *rigidité*; L. *rigiditas.*]

1. Stiffness; want of pliability; the quality of not being easily bent. *Arbuthnot.*
2. A brittle hardness, as opposed to *ductility, malleability* and *softness*. *Encyc.*
3. Stiffness of appearance or manner; want of ease or airy elegance. *Wotton.*

RIG'IDLY, *adv.* Stiffly; unpliantly.

2. Severely; strictly; exactly; without laxity, indulgence or abatement; as, to judge *rigidly*; to criticize *rigidly*; to execute a law *rigidly*.

RIG'IDNESS, *n.* Stiffness of a body; the quality of not being easily bent; as the *rigidness* of a limb or of flesh.

2. Severity of temper; strictness in opinion or practice; but expressing less than *inflexibility*.

RIG'LET, *n.* [Fr. from L. *regula*, *rego*.] A flat thin piece of wood, used for picture frames; also used in printing, to regulate the margin, &c.

RIG'MAROLE, *n.* A repetition of stories; a succession of stories. *Goldsmith.*

RIG'OL, *n.* A circle; a diadem. *Shak.*

RIG'OLL, *n.* A musical instrument consisting of several sticks bound together, but separated by beads. *Encyc.*

RIG'OR, *n.* [L. from *rigeo*, to be stiff; Fr. *rigueur*.]

1. Stiffness; rigidness; as Gorgonian *rigor*. *Milton.*

2. In *medicine*, a sense of chilliness, with contraction of the skin; a convulsive shuddering or slight tremor, as in the cold fit of a fever. *Coxe. Encyc. Parr.*

3. Stiffness of opinion or temper; severity; sternness.

> All his *rigor* is turned to grief and pity. *Denham.*

4. Severity of life; austerity; voluntary submission to pain, abstinence or mortification. *Fell.*

5. Strictness; exactness without allowance, latitude or indulgence; as the *rigor* of criticism; to execute a law with *rigor*; to enforce moral duties with *rigor*.

6. Violence; fury. [*Not in use.*] *Spenser.*

7. Hardness; solidity. [*Unusual.*] *Dryden.*

8. Severity; asperity; as the *rigors* of a cold winter.

RIG'OROUS, *a.* [Fr. *rigoureux*.] Severe; allowing no abatement or mitigation; as a *rigorous* officer of justice.

2. Severe; exact; strict; without abatement or relaxation; as a *rigorous* execution of law; an enforcement of *rigorous* discipline.

3. Exact; strict; scrupulously accurate; as a *rigorous* definition or demonstration.

4. Severe; very cold; as a *rigorous* winter.

RIG'OROUSLY, *adv.* Severely; without relaxation, abatement or mitigation; as a sentence *rigorously* executed.

2. Strictly; exactly; with scrupulous nicety; rigidly.

> The people would examine his works more *rigorously* than himself. *Dryden.*

RIG'OROUSNESS, *n.* Severity without relaxation or mitigation; exactness. *Ash.*

2. Severity.

RILL, *n.* [In G. *rille*, W. *rhill*, is a groove, trench, channel, the root of *drill*. In Sw. *strila* is to run or glide; Dan. *ryller*, to ramble.]

A small brook; a rivulet; a streamlet. *Milton.*

RILL, *v. i.* To run in a small stream, or in streamlets. *Prior.*

RILL'ET, *n.* A small stream; a rivulet. *Drayton.*

RIM, *n.* [Sax. *rima* and *reoma*, a rim, a ream; W. *rhim* and *rhimp*, a rim, edge, termination; hence *crimp*, a sharp ridge; *crimpiaw*, to form into a ridge, also to pinch. *Rim*, like *ramp*, *ramble*, is from extending; the extremity. In Russ. *kroma* is a border.]

1. The border, edge or margin of a thing; as the *rim* of a kettle or bason; usually applied to things circular or curving.

2. The lower part of the belly or abdomen. *Brown.*

RIM, *v. t.* To put on a rim or hoop at the border.

RIME, *n.* [Sax. *rim*, number; W. *rhiv*. This is the more correct orthography, but *rhyme* is commonly used, which see.]

RIME, *n.* [Sax. *hrim*; Ice. *hrym*; D. *rym*. The French write this *frimas*, Arm. *frim*; probably allied to *cream*. In G. it is *reif*, D. *ryp*.]

White or hoar frost; congealed dew or vapor. *Bacon.*

RIME, *n.* [L. *rima*; Sw. *remna*, whence *remna*, to split; perhaps from the root of *rive*.]

A chink; a fissure; a rent or long aperture. [*Not in use.*]

RIME, *v. i.* To freeze or congeal into hoar frost.

RI'MOSE, } *a.* [L. *rimosus*, from *rima*.] In
RI'MOUS, } *botany*, chinky; abounding with clefts, cracks or chinks; as the bark of trees.

RIM'PLE, *n.* [Sax. *hrympelli*.] A fold or wrinkle. [See *Rumple*.]

RIM'PLE, *v. t.* To rumple; to wrinkle.

RIM'PLING, *n.* Undulation.

RI'MY, *a.* [from *rime*.] Abounding with rime; frosty. *Harvey.*

RIND, *n.* [Sax. *rind* or *hrind*; G. *rinde*; Gr. ῥινος; W. *croen*, skin.]

The bark of a plant; the skin or coat of fruit that may be pared or peeled off; also, the inner bark of trees. *Dryden. Milton. Encyc.*

RIND, *v. t.* To bark; to decorticate. [*Not in use.*]

RIN'DLE, *n.* [from the root of *run*; Dan. *rinder*, to flow.] A small water course or gutter. *Ash.*

RING, *n.* [Sax. *ring* or *hring*; D. *ring* or *kring*; G. D. Sw. *ring*, a circle; Sw. *kring*, about, around. This coincides with *ring*, to sound, and with *wring*, to twist; G. *ringen*, to ring or sound, and to wrestle. The sense is to strain or stretch, and *n* is probably not radical. The root then belongs to Class Rg.]

1. A circle, or a circular line, or any thing in the form of a circular line or hoop. Thus we say of men, they formed themselves into a *ring*, to see a wrestling match. *Rings* of gold were made for the ark. Ex. xxv. *Rings* of gold or other material are worn on the fingers and sometimes in the ears, as ornaments.

2. A circular course.

> Place me, O place me in the dusty *ring*,
> Where youthful charioteers contend for glory. *Smith.*

RING, *n.* [from the verb.] A sound; particularly, the sound of metals; as the *ring* of a bell.

2. Any loud sound, or the sounds of numerous voices; or sound continued, repeated or reverberated; as the *ring* of acclamations. *Bacon.*

3. A chime, or set of bells harmonically tuned. *Prior.*

RING, *v. t.* pret. and pp. *rung*. [Sax. *ringan*, *hringan*; G. D. *ringen*; Sw. *ringa*; Dan. *ringer*.]

To cause to sound, particularly by striking a metallic body; as, to *ring* a bell. This word expresses appropriately the sounding of metals.

RING, *v. t.* [from the noun.] To encircle. *Shak.*

2. To fit with rings, as the fingers, or as a swine's snout. Farmers *ring* swine to prevent their rooting.

> And *ring* these fingers with thy household worms. *Shak.*

RING, *v. i.* To sound, as a bell or other sonorous body, particularly a metallic one. *Dryden.*

2. To practice the art of making music with bells. *Holder.*

3. To sound; to resound.

> With sweeter notes each rising temple *rung*. *Pope.*

4. To utter, as a bell; to sound.

> The shardborn beetle with his drowsy hums,
> Hath *rung* night's yawning peal. *Shak.*

5. To tinkle; to have the sensation of sound continued.

> My ears still *ring* with noise. *Dryden.*

6. To be filled with report or talk. The whole town *rings* with his fame.

RING'-BOLT, *n.* An iron bolt with an eye to which is fitted a ring of iron. *Mar. Dict.*

RING'-BONE, *n.* A callus growing in the hollow circle of the little pastern of a horse, just above the coronet. *Far. Dict.*

RING'DÖVE, *n.* [G. *ringeltaube*.] A species of pigeon, the *Columba palumbus*, the largest of the European species. *Encyc.*

RING'ENT, *a.* [L. *ringor*, to make wry faces, that is, to wring or twist.]

In *botany*, a ringent or labiate corol is one which is irregular, monopetalous, with the border usually divided into two parts, called the upper and lower lip; or irregular and gaping, like the mouth of an animal. *Martyn. Smith.*

RING'ER, *n.* One who rings. [In the sense of *wringer*, not used.]

RING'ING, *ppr.* Causing to sound, as a bell; sounding; fitting with rings.

RING'ING, *n.* The act of sounding or of causing to sound.

RING'LEAD, *v. t.* To conduct. [*Little used.*]

RING'LEADER, *n.* [*ring* and *leader*.] The leader of any association of men engaged in violation of law or an illegal enterprise, as rioters, mutineers and the like. This name is derived from the practice which men associating to oppose law have sometimes adopted, of signing their names to articles of agreement in a *ring*, that no one of their number might be distinguished as the leader.

RING'LET, *n.* [*dim.* of *ring*.] A small ring. *Pope.*

2. A curl; particularly, a curl of hair.

> Her golden tresses in wanton *ringlets* wav'd. *Milton.*

3. A circle.

To dance our *ringlets* in the whistling wind. *Shak.*

RING'-OUSEL, *n.* A bird of the genus Turdus, *(T. torquatus,)* inhabiting the hilly and mountainous parts of G. Britain. *Ed. Encyc.*

RING'-STREAKED, *a.* [*ring* and *streak.*] Having circular streaks or lines on the body; as *ring-streaked* goats. Gen. xxx.

RING'-TAIL, *n.* [*ring* and *tail.*] A kind of kite with a whitish tail. *Bailey.*

2. A small quadrilateral sail, set on a small mast on a ship's tafferel.

RING'-WORM, *n.* [*ring* and *worm.*] A circular eruption on the skin; a kind of tetter. [*Herpes serpigo.* Sauvages.] *Wiseman. Parr.*

RINSE, *v. t. rins.* [Sw. *rensa* or *rena*, to cleanse or purify; Dan. *renser*, to clean, to purge, to purify, to scour; Sax. D. G. *rein*, clean; Fr. *rincer;* Arm. *rinsa, rinsein.* Our common people pronounce this word *rens*, retaining their native pronunciation. This is one of a thousand instances in which the purity of our vernacular language has been corrupted by those who have understood French better than their mother tongue.]

1. To wash; to cleanse by washing. But in present usage,

2. To cleanse with a second or repeated application of water, after washing. We distinguish *washing* from *rinsing. Washing* is performed by rubbing, or with the use of soap; *rinsing* is performed with clean water, without much rubbing or the use of soap. Clothes are *rinsed* by dipping and dashing; and vessels are *rinsed* by dashing water on them, or by slight rubbing. A close barrel may be *rinsed*, but cannot well be *washed.*

RINS'ED, *pp.* Cleansed with a second water; cleaned.

RINS'ER, *n.* One that rinses.

RINS'ING, *ppr.* Cleansing with a second water.

RI'OT, *n.* [Norm. *riotti;* It. *riotta;* Fr. *riote*, a brawl or tumult. The W. *broth, brwth*, commotion, may be from the same root with a prefix, which would connect this word with *brydian, brydiaw*, to heat, to boil. The Spanish has *alboroto*, and Port. *alvoroto*, in a like sense. In Danish, *rutter* is to drink hard, to *riot.* The primary sense is probably noise or agitation.]

1. In *a general sense*, tumult; uproar; hence technically, in *law*, a riotous assembling of twelve persons or more, and not dispersing upon proclamation. *Blackstone.*

The definition of *riot* must depend on the laws. In Connecticut, the assembling of *three* persons or more, to do an unlawful act by violence against the person or property of another, and not dispersing upon proclamation, is declared to be a riot. In Massachusetts and New Hampshire, the number necessary to constitute a riot is twelve.

2. Uproar; wild and noisy festivity. *Milton.*

3. Excessive and expensive feasting. 2 Pet. ii.

4. Luxury.

> The lamb thy *riot* dooms to bleed to-day. *Pope.*

To run riot, to act or move without control or restraint. *Swift.*

RI'OT, *v. i.* [Fr. *rioter;* It. *riottare.*] To revel; to run to excess in feasting, drinking or other sensual indulgences.

2. To luxuriate; to be highly excited.

> No pulse that *riots*, and no blood that glows. *Pope.*

3. To banquet; to live in luxury; to enjoy.

> How base is the ingratitude which forgets the benefactor, while it is *rioting* on the benefit! *Dwight.*

4. To raise an uproar or sedition. *Johnson.*

RI'OTER, *n.* One who indulges in loose festivity or excessive feasting.

2. In *law*, one guilty of meeting with others to do an unlawful act, and declining to retire upon proclamation.

RI'OTING, *ppr.* Reveling; indulging in excessive feasting.

RI'OTING, *n.* A reveling.

RI'OTISE, *n.* Dissoluteness; luxury. [*Not in use.*] *Spenser.*

RI'OTOUS, *a.* [It. *riottoso.*] Luxurious; wanton or licentious in festive indulgencies; as *riotous* eaters of flesh. Prov. xxiii.

2. Consisting of riot; tumultuous; partaking of the nature of an unlawful assembly; seditious.

3. Guilty of riot; *applied to persons.*

RI'OTOUSLY, *adv.* With excessive or licentious luxury. *Ecclus.*

2. In the manner of an unlawful assembly; tumultuously; seditiously.

RI'OTOUSNESS, *n.* The state or quality of being riotous.

RIP, *v. t.* [Sax. *rypan, ryppan, hrypan;* Sw. *rifva;* Dan. *river.* This belongs to the great family of Sax. *reafian*, L. *rapio*, Ir. *reabam*, Eng. *reap* and *rive;* allied perhaps to the L. *crepo*, Fr. *crever.*]

1. To separate by cutting or tearing; to tear or cut open or off; to tear off or out by violence; as, to *rip* open a garment by cutting the stitches; to *rip* off the skin of a beast; to *rip* open a sack; to *rip* off the shingles or clapboards of a house; to *rip* up a floor. We never use *lacerate* in these senses, but apply it to a partial tearing of the skin and flesh.

2. To take out or away by cutting or tearing. *Otway.*

> He'll *rip* the fatal secret from her heart. *Granville.*

3. To tear up for search or disclosure or for alteration; to search to the bottom; with *up.*

> You *rip up* the original of Scotland. *Spenser.*

> They *ripped up* all that had been done from the beginning of the rebellion. *Clarendon.*

4. To rip out, as an oath. [This seems to be the D. *roepen*, Sax. *hreopan*, to cry out; allied to L. *crepo*, Fr. *crever.*]

RIP, *n.* A tearing; a place torn; laceration. *Addison.*

2. A wicker basket to carry fish in. *Cowel.*

3. Refuse. [*Not in use or local.*]

RIPE, *a.* [Sax. *ripe, gerip;* D. *ryp;* G. *reif.* The Saxon word signifies harvest, a *reap* or *reaping; ripa*, a handful of corn; *ripan*, to reap; *ripian*, to *ripen.*]

1. Brought to perfection in growth or to the best state; mature; fit for use; as *ripe* fruit; *ripe* corn.

2. Advanced to perfection; matured; as *ripe* judgment, or *ripe* in judgment.

3. Finished; consummate; as a *ripe* scholar.

4. Brought to the point of taking effect; matured; ready; prepared; as things just *ripe* for war. *Addison.*

5. Fully qualified by improvement; prepared; as a student *ripe* for the university; a saint *ripe* for heaven. *Fell. Dryden.*

6. Resembling the ripeness of fruit; as a *ripe* lip. *Shak.*

7. Complete; proper for use.

> When time is *ripe.* *Shak.*

8. Maturated; suppurated; as an abscess or tumor.

RIPE, *v. i.* To ripen; to grow ripe; to be matured. [*Not used.* See *Ripen.*] *Shak.*

RIPE, *v. t.* To mature; to ripen. [*Not used.*] *Shak.*

RI'PELY, *adv.* Maturely; at the fit time. *Shak.*

RIPEN, *v. i. ri'pn.* [Sax. *ripian;* D. *rypen;* G. *reifen.*]

1. To grow ripe; to be matured; as grain or fruit. Grain *ripens* best in dry weather.

2. To approach or come to perfection; to be fitted or prepared; as, a project is *ripening* for execution.

RIPEN, *v. t. ri'pn.* To mature; to make ripe; as grain or fruit.

2. To mature; to fit or prepare; as, to *ripen* one for heaven.

3. To bring to perfection; as, to *ripen* the judgment.

RI'PENESS, *n.* The state of being ripe or brought to that state of perfection which fits for use; maturity; as the *ripeness* of grain.

2. Full growth.

> Time which made them their fame outlive,
> To Cowley scarce did *ripeness* give. *Denham.*

3. Perfection; completeness; as the *ripeness* of virtue, wisdom or judgment.

4. Fitness; qualification. *Shak.*

5. Complete maturation or suppuration, as of an ulcer or abscess.

6. A state of preparation; as the *ripeness* of a project for execution.

RIPHE'AN, *a.* An epithet given to certain mountains in the north of Asia, probably signifying snowy mountains.

RIP'IER, } *n.* In *old laws*, one who brings
RIP'PER, } fish to market in the inland country. *Cowel.*

RIP'PED, *pp.* Torn or cut off or out; torn open.

RIP'PER, *n.* One who tears or cuts open.

RIP'PING, *ppr.* Cutting or tearing off or open; tearing up.

RIP'PING, *n.* A tearing.

2. A discovery. *Obs.* *Spenser.*

RIP'PLE, *v. i.* [In Dan. *ripper* is to stir or agitate; in G. *riffe* is a hatchel; and *riffeln*, to hatchel; in Sax. *gerifled* is wrinkled. *Ripple* is probably allied to *rip.*]

To fret on the surface; as water when agitated or running over a rough bottom, appears rough and broken, or as if *ripped* or torn.

RIP'PLE, *v. t.* [G. *riffeln*, to hatchel.] To clean, as flax. *Ray.*

2. To agitate the surface of water.

RIP'PLE, *n.* The fretting of the surface of water; little curling waves.

2. A large comb or hatchel for cleaning flax.

RIP'PLING, *ppr.* Fretting on the surface.

RIP'PLING, *n.* The ripple dashing on the shore, or the noise of it. *Pennant.*

2. The act or method of cleaning flax; a hatcheling.

RIPT, *pp.* for *ripped.*

RIP'TOWELL, *n.* A gratuity given to tenants after they had reaped their lord's corn. *Bailey. Todd.*

RISE, *v. i. rize.* pret. *rose*; pp. *risen*; pron. *roze, rizn.* [Sax. *arisan*; D. *ryzen*; Goth. *reisan*, in *ur-reisan*, to rise, and *ur-raisyan*, to raise. See *Raise.*]

1. To move or pass upward in any manner; to ascend; as, a fog *rises* from a river or from low ground; a fish *rises* in water; fowls *rise* in the air; clouds *rise* from the horizon towards the meridian; a balloon *rises* above the clouds.

2. To get up; to leave the place of sleep or rest; as, to *rise* from bed.

3. To get up or move from any recumbent to an erect posture; as, to *rise* after a fall.

4. To get up from a seat; to leave a sitting posture; as, to *rise* from a sofa or chair.

5. To spring; to grow; as a plant; hence, to be high or tall. A tree *rises* to the highth of 60 feet.

6. To swell in quantity or extent; to be more elevated; as, a river *rises* after a rain.

7. To break forth; to appear; as, a boil *rises* on the skin.

8. To appear above the horizon; to shine; as, the sun or a star *rises*.

He maketh his sun to *rise* on the evil and on the good. Matt. v.

9. To begin to exist; to originate; to come into being or notice. Great evils sometimes *rise* from small imprudences.

10. To be excited; to begin to move or act; as, the wind *rose* at 12 o'clock.

11. To increase in violence. The wind continued to *rise* till 3 o'clock.

12. To appear in view; as, to *rise* up to the reader's view. *Addison.*

13. To appear in sight; also, to appear more elevated; as in sailing towards a shore, the land *rises*.

14. To change a station; to leave a place; as, to *rise* from a siege. *Knolles.*

15. To spring; to be excited or produced. A thought now *rises* in my mind.

16. To gain elevation in rank, fortune or public estimation; to be promoted. Men may *rise* by industry, by merit, by favor, or by intrigue.

Some *rise* by sin, and some by virtue fall. *Shak.*

When the wicked *rise*, men hide themselves. Prov. xxviii.

17. To break forth into public commotions; to make open opposition to government; or to assemble and oppose government; or to assemble in arms for attacking another nation. The Greeks have *risen* against their oppressors.

No more shall nation against nation *rise*. *Pope.*

18. To be excited or roused into action.

Rise up to the battle. Jer. xlix.

19. To make a hostile attack; as when a man *riseth* against his neighbor. Deut. xxii.

Also, to rebel. 2 Sam. xviii.

20. To increase; to swell; to grow more or greater. A voice, feeble at first, *rises* to thunder. The price of goods *rises*. The heat *rises* to intensity.

21. To be improved; to recover from depression; as, a family may *rise* after misfortune to opulence and splendor.

22. To elevate the style or manner; as, to *rise* in force of expression; to *rise* in eloquence.

23. To be revived from death.

The dead in Christ shall *rise* first. 1 Thess. iv.

24. To come by chance. *Spenser.*

25. To ascend; to be elevated above the level or surface; as, the ground *rises* gradually one hundred yards. The Andes *rise* more than 20,000 feet above the level of the ocean; a mountain in Asia is said to *rise* still higher.

26. To proceed from.

A scepter shall *rise* out of Israel. Num. xxiv.

27. To have its sources in. Rivers *rise* in lakes, ponds and springs.

28. To be moved, roused, excited, kindled or inflamed, as passion. His wrath *rose* to rage.

29. To ascend in the diatonic scale; as, to *rise* a tone or semitone.

30. To amount. The public debt *rises* to a hundred millions.

31. To close a session. We say, congress will *rise* on the 4th of March; the legislature or the court will *rise* on a certain day.

This verb is written also *arise*, which see. In general, it is indifferent which orthography is used; but custom has, in some cases, established one to the exclusion of the other. Thus we never say, the price of goods *arises*, when we mean *advances*, but we always say, the price *rises*. We never say, the ground *arises* to a certain altitude, and rarely, a man *arises* into an office or station. It is hardly possible to class or define the cases in which usage has established a difference in the orthography of this verb. A knowledge of these cases must be acquired by observation.

RISE, *n. rise.* The act of rising, either in a literal or figurative sense; ascent; as the *rise* of vapor in the air; the *rise* of mercury in the barometer; the *rise* of water in a river.

2. The act of springing or mounting from the ground; as the *rise* of the feet in leaping.

3. Ascent; elevation, or degree of ascent; as the *rise* of a hill or mountain.

4. Spring; source; origin; as the *rise* of a stream in a mountain. All sin has its *rise* in the heart.

5. Any place elevated above the common level; as a *rise* of land.

6. Appearance above the horizon; as the *rise* of the sun or a star.

7. Increase; advance; as a *rise* in the price of wheat.

8. Advance in rank, honor, property or fame. Observe a man after his *rise* to office, or a family after its *rise* from obscurity.

9. Increase of sound on the same key; a swelling of the voice.

10. Elevation or ascent of the voice in the diatonic scale; as a *rise* of a tone or semitone.

11. Increase; augmentation.

12. [D. *rys*; from the verb.] A bough or branch. [*Not in use.*] *Chaucer.*

RIS'EN, *pp.* [See *Rise.*]

RI'SER, *n.* One that rises; as an early *riser.*

2. Among *joiners*, the upright board of a stair.

RISIBIL'ITY, *n.* [from *risible.*] The quality of laughing, or of being capable of laughter. *Risibility* is peculiar to the human species.

2. Proneness to laugh.

RI'SIBLE, *a.* [Fr. *risible*; L. *risibilis*, from *rideo, risi*, to laugh. See *Ridiculous.*]

1. Having the faculty or power of laughing. Man is a *risible* animal.

2. Laughable; capable of exciting laughter. The description of Falstaff in Shakspeare, exhibits a *risible* scene. *Risible* differs from *ludicrous*, as species from genus; *ludicrous* expressing that which is playful and sportive; *risible*, that which may excite laughter. *Risible* differs from *ridiculous*, as the latter implies something mean or contemptible, and *risible* does not.

RI'SING, *ppr.* Getting up; ascending; mounting; springing; proceeding from; advancing; swelling; increasing; appearing above the horizon; reviving from death, &c.

2. Increasing in wealth, power or distinction; as a *rising* state; a *rising* character.

RI'SING, *n.* The act of getting up from any recumbent or sitting posture.

2. The act of ascending; as the *rising* of vapor.

3. The act of closing a session, as of a public body; as the *rising* of the legislature.

4. The appearance of the sun or a star above the horizon.

5. The act of reviving from the dead; resurrection. Mark ix.

6. A tumor on the body. Lev. xiii.

7. An assembling in opposition to government; insurrection; sedition or mutiny.

RISK, *n.* [Fr. *risque*; Arm. *risql*; Sp. *riesgo*; Port. *risco*; It. *rischio*, risk, danger, peril; Fr. *risquer*, Arm. *risqla*, Sp. *arriesgar*, Port. *arriscar*, to *risk*. The sense is a pushing forward, a *rushing*, as in *rash.* Qu. Dan. *dristig*, bold, rash; *drister*, to dare; Sw. *drista*, to *trust*, to be bold, hardy or *rash.* In Portuguese, *risco* signifies not only hazard, but a stroke, a dash, and with painters, delineation; *riscar* signifies to dash or strike out with a pen, to erase. The primary sense then is to throw or dash, or to rush, to drive forward. See *Peril, Rash* and *Rush.*]

1. Hazard; danger; peril; exposure to harm. He, at the *risk* of his life, saved a drowning man.

2. In *commerce*, the hazard of loss, either of ship, goods or other property. Hence, *risk* signifies also the degree of hazard or danger; for the premiums of insurance are calculated upon the *risk*. The underwriters now take *risks* at a low premium.

To run a risk, is to incur hazard; to encounter danger.

RISK, *v. t.* To hazard; to endanger; to expose to injury or loss; as, to *risk* goods on board of a ship; to *risk* one's person in battle; to *risk* one's fame by a publication; to *risk* life in defense of rights.

2. To venture; to dare to undertake; as, to *risk* a battle or combat.

RISK'ED, *pp.* Hazarded; exposed to injury or loss.

RISK'ER, *n.* One who hazards.

RISK'ING, *ppr.* Hazarding; exposing to injury or loss.

RISSE, obsolete *pret.* of *rise*. *B. Jonson.*

RITE, *n.* [Fr. *rit, rite*; L. *ritus*; It. Sp. *rito*; Sans. *riti*, service.]

The manner of performing divine or solemn service as established by law, precept or custom; formal act of religion, or other solemn duty. The *rites* of the Israelites were numerous and expensive; the *rites* of modern churches are more simple. Funeral *rites* are very different in different countries. The sacrament is a holy *rite*. *Hammond.*

RITORNEL'LO, *n.* [It. from *ritorno*, return, or *ritornare*, to return.]

In *music*, a repeat; the burden of a song, or the repetition of a verse or strain.

RIT'UAL, *a.* [It. *rituale.*] Pertaining to rites; consisting of rites; as *ritual* service or sacrifices. *Prior.*

2. Prescribing rites; as the *ritual* law.

RIT'UAL, *n.* A book containing the rites to be observed, or the manner of performing divine service in a particular church, diocese or the like. *Encyc.*

RIT'UALIST, *n.* One skilled in the ritual. *Gregory.*

RIT'UALLY, *adv.* By rites; or by a particular rite. *Selden.*

RIV'AGE, *n.* [Fr. from *rive*, bank.] A bank, shore or coast. [*Not in use.*] *Spenser.*

RI'VAL, *n.* [L. *rivalis*; Fr. Sp. *rival*; It. *rivale*; Ir. *rioblach*; Heb. ריב to contend, to strive; Dan. *rives*, to strive; Sp. *rifa*, strife, raffle; *rifar*, to dispute, quarrel or *raffle*, and to split a sail. Qu. to *rive* or *rip*. See *Raffle.*]

1. One who is in pursuit of the same object as another; one striving to reach or obtain something which another is attempting to obtain, and which one only can possess; a competitor; as *rivals* in love; *rivals* for a crown. Love will not patiently bear a *rival*.

2. One striving to equal or exceed another in excellence; as two *rivals* in eloquence.

3. An antagonist; a competitor in any pursuit or strife.

RI'VAL, *a.* Having the same pretensions or claims; standing in competition for superiority; as *rival* lovers; *rival* claims or pretensions.

> Equal in years and *rival* in renown. *Dryden.*

RI'VAL, *v. t.* To stand in competition with; to strive to gain the object which another is contending for; as, to *rival* one in love.

2. To strive to equal or excel; to emulate.

> To *rival* thunder in its rapid course. *Dryden.*

RI'VAL, *v. i.* To be competitors. [*Not in use.*] *Shak.*

RIVAL'ITY, *n.* Rivalry. [*Not in use.*] *Shak.*

RI'VALRY, *n.* [from *rival.*] Competition; a strife or effort to obtain an object which another is pursuing; as *rivalry* in love; or an endeavor to equal or surpass another in some excellence; emulation; as *rivalry* for superiority at the bar or in the senate.

RI'VALSHIP, *n.* The state or character of a rival. *B. Jonson.*

2. Strife; contention for superiority; emulation; rivalry.

RIVE, *v. t.* pret. *rived;* pp. *rived* or *riven.* [Dan. *revner*, to split; *river*, to pluck off or away, to rake; Sw. *rifva*, to pull asunder, to burst or rend, to rake, to tear; Ice. *rifa*, Sw. *refva*, a chink or crevice; Fr. *crever*, whence *crevasse*, crevice; Russ. *rvu*; allied to L. *rumpo, rupi*. It may be allied to the family of L. *rapio, reap, rip.*]

To split; to cleave; to rend asunder by force; as, to *rive* timber for rails or shingles with wedges; the *riven* oak; the *riven* clouds. *Dryden. Milton.*

> The scolding winds
> Have riv'd the knotty oaks. *Shak.*

RIVE, *v. i.* To be split or rent asunder.

> Freestone *rives*, splits and breaks in any direction. *Woodward.*

RIV'EL, *v. t.* [Sax. *gerifled*, wrinkled; from the root of Dan. *river*, to draw, to wrest, Sw. *rifva* This word is obsolete, but *shrivel*, from the same root, is in use. It may be allied to *ruffle.*]

To contract into wrinkles; to shrink; as *riveled* fruits; *riveled* flowers. *Dryden. Pope.*

RIV'EN, *pp.* of *rive*. Split; rent or burst asunder.

RI'VER, *n.* One who rives or splits.

RIV'ER, *n.* [Fr. *rivière*; Arm. *rifyer*; Corn. *ryvier*; It. *riviera*; from L. *rivus, rivulus*; D. *rivier*. The Italian word signifies a river, and a bank or shore, L. *ripa*, Sp. *ribera.*]

1. A large stream of water flowing in a channel on land towards the ocean, a lake or another river. It is larger than a rivulet or brook; but is applied to any stream from the size of a mill-stream to that of the Danube, Maranon and Mississippi. We give this name to large streams which admit the tide and mingle salt water with fresh, as the *rivers* Hudson, Delaware and St. Lawrence.

2. A large stream; copious flow; abundance; as *rivers* of blood; *rivers* of oil.

RIV'ER-DRAGON, *n.* A crocodile; a name given by Milton to the king of Egypt.

RIV'ERET, *n.* A small river. [*Not in use.*]

RIV'ER-GOD, *n.* A deity supposed to preside over a river, as its tutelary divinity; a naiad. *Lempriere.*

RIV'ER-HORSE, *n.* The hippopotamus, an animal inhabiting rivers. *Milton.*

RIV'ER-WATER, *n.* The water of a river, as distinguished from *rain-water*.

RIV'ET, *v. t.* [It. *ribadire*; Port. *rebitar*. These are compounds of a verb with *re* for a prefix. The Spanish has *roblar*. The French *river*, and Arm. *riva* or *rinva*, would seem to be the Heb. ריב to drive.]

1. To fasten with a rivet or with rivets; as, to *rivet* two pieces of iron.

2. To clinch; as, to *rivet* a pin or bolt. *Moxon.*

3. To fasten firmly; to make firm, strong or immovable; as, to *rivet* friendship or affection. *Atterbury.*

> *Rivet* and nail me where I stand, ye pow'rs. *Congreve.*

RIV'ET, *n.* A pin of iron or other metal with a head, driven through a piece of timber or metal, and the point bent or spread and beat down fast, to prevent its being drawn out; or a pin or bolt clinched at both ends.

RIV'ETED, *pp.* Clinched; made fast.

RIV'ETING, *ppr.* Clinching; fastening firmly.

RIV'ULET, *n.* [L. *rivulus.*] A small stream or brook; a streamlet.

> By fountain or by shady *rivulet*,
> He sought them. *Milton.*

RIXA'TION, *n.* [L. *rixatio*, from *rixor*, to brawl or quarrel.]

A brawl or quarrel. [*Not in use.*]

RIX-DOL'LAR, *n.* [G. *reichsthaler*; D. *ryksdaalder*; Sw. *riksdaler*; Dan. *rigsdaler*; the dollar of the realm.]

A silver coin of Germany, Denmark and Sweden, of different value in different places. In Hamburg and some other parts of Germany, its value is the same as the American dollar, or 4-6*d.* sterling. In other parts of Germany, its value is 3-6*d.* sterling, or about 78 cents.

ROACH, *n.* [Sax. *reohche, hreoce*; G. *roche*; Dan. *rokke*; Sw. *rocka*; Fr. *rouget*, from the root of *rouge*, red.]

A fish of the genus Cyprinus, found in fresh water, easily caught and tolerably good for food.

As sound as a roach, is a phrase supposed to have been originally, as sound as a *rock*, (Fr. *roche.)*

ROAD, *n.* [Sax. *rad, rade*, a ride, a passing or traveling on horseback, a way, a *road*, corresponding with the G. *reise*, D. *reis*, Dan. *rejse*, Sw. *resa*; but in the sense of a place for anchoring ships, the Fr. has *rade*, Sp. *rada*, G. D. *reede*, Sw. *redd*, Dan. *rede*, *reed*. In the sense of way, the Spanish has *rauta*, W. *rhawd*, all connected with *ride*, W. *rhedu*, to run, and L. *gradior*, W. *rhodiaw*, to walk or go. The Slavonic has *brud*, and the Bohemian *brod*, a way. See *Grade.*]

1. An open way or public passage; ground appropriated for travel, forming a communication between one city, town or place and another. The word is generally applied to highways, and as a generic term it includes highway, street and lane. The military *roads* of the Romans were paved with stone, or formed of gravel or pebbles, and some of them remain to this day entire.

2. A place where ships may ride at anchor at some distance from the shore; sometimes called *roadstead*, that is, a place for *riding*, meaning at anchor.

3. A journey. [Not used, but we still use *ride* as a noun; as a long *ride*; a short *ride*; the same word differently written.] *Milton.*

4. An inroad; incursion of an enemy. [*Not in use.*] *Shak.*

On the road, passing; traveling. *Law.*

ROADER, } *n.* Among seamen, a vessel riding at anchor in a road
ROADSTER, } or bay. *Mar. Dict.*

RŌADSTEAD. [See *Road.*]

RŌADWAY, *n.* A highway. [*Tautological.*] *Shak.*

RŌAM, *v. i.* [If *m* is radical, this word seems to be connected with *ramble*, L. *ramus.* In W. *rhamu* is to rise over, to soar, to vault; whence *rhamant*, a rising boldly, *romance*; *rhem*, *rhum*, something projecting; *rhim*, rim, the exterior part of a thing; Ar. رام to exceed, to depart. Class Rm. No. 5. See also No. 9. and 23.]

To wander; to ramble; to rove; to walk or move about from place to place without any certain purpose or direction. The wolf and the savage *roam* in the forest.

Daphne *roaming* through a thorny wood. *Shak.*

RŌAM, *v. t.* To range; to wander over; as, to *roam* the woods; but the phrase is elliptical. *Milton.*

RŌAMER, *n.* A wanderer; a rover; a rambler; a vagrant.

RŌAMING, *ppr.* Wandering; roving.

RŌAMING, *n.* The act of wandering.

RŌAN, *a.* [Fr. *rouan.*] A roan horse is one that is of a bay, sorrel or dark color, with spots of gray or white thickly interspersed. *Far. Dict.*

RŌAN-TREE, *n.* A tree of the genus Sorbus; the mountain ash. *Lee.*

RŌAR, *v. i.* [Sax. *rarian*, to roar; W. *rhawr*, the roaring of the sea.]

1. To cry with a full, loud, continued sound; to bellow, as a beast; as a *roaring* bull; a *roaring* lion. *Shak. Dryden.*

2. To cry aloud, as in distress.

The suff'ring chief
Roar'd out for anguish. *Dryden.*

3. To cry aloud; to bawl; as a child.

4. To cause a loud continued sound. We say, the sea or the wind *roars*; a company *roar* in acclamation.

5. To make a loud noise.

The brazen throat of war had ceas'd to *roar.* *Milton.*

RŌAR, *n.* A full loud sound of some continuance; the cry of a beast; as the *roar* of a lion or bull.

2. The loud cry of a child or person in distress.

3. Clamor; outcry of joy or mirth; as a *roar* of laughter. He set the company in a *roar.*

4. The loud continued sound of the sea in a storm, or the howling of a tempest. *Philips.*

5. Any loud sound of some continuance; as the *roar* of cannon.

RŌARER, *n.* One that roars, man or beast.

RŌARING, *ppr.* Crying like a bull or lion; uttering a deep loud sound.

RŌARING, *n.* The cry of a lion or other beast; outcry of distress, Job iii.; loud continued sound of the billows of the sea or of a tempest. Is. v.

RŌARY, *a.* Dewy; more properly *rory.*

RŌAST, *v. t.* [W. *rhostiaw*; Ir. *rostam*; Arm. *rosta*; Fr. *rôtir*; It. *arrostire*; D. *roosten*; G. *rösten*; Sw. *rosta*; Dan. *rister*, to roast, and *rist*, a gridiron, G. *rost.* If the verb is from the noun, the sense is to dress or cook on a gridiron or grate, and *rist*, *rost*, coincide in elements with L. *rastellum*, a rake. If the verb is the root, the sense probably is to contract or *crisp*, or to throw or agitate, hence to make rough. The Welsh has also *crasu*, to roast, from *crâs.* This coincides with *crisp.*]

1. To cook, dress or prepare meat for the table by exposing it to heat, as on a spit, in a bake-pan, in an oven or the like. We now say, to *roast* meat on a spit, in a pan, or in a tin oven, &c.; to *bake* meat in an oven; to *broil* meat on a gridiron.

2. To prepare for food by exposure to heat; as, to *roast* apples or potatoes; to *roast* eggs.

3. To heat to excess; to heat violently.

Roasted in wrath and fire. *Shak.*

4. To dry and parch by exposure to heat; as, to *roast* coffee.

5. In *metallurgy*, to dissipate the volatile parts of ore by heat.

6. In *common discourse*, to jeer; to banter severely. *Scott.*

RŌAST, *n.* That which is roasted.

RŌAST, *a.* [for *roasted.*] Roasted; as *roast* beef.

RŌAST, *n.* In the phrase, to *rule the roast*, this word is a corrupt pronunciation of the G. *rath*, counsel, Dan. D. *raad*, Sw. *råd.*

RŌASTED, *pp.* Dressed by exposure to heat on a spit.

RŌASTER, *n.* One that roasts meat; also, a gridiron.

2. A pig for roasting.

RŌASTING, *ppr.* Preparing for the table by exposure to heat on a spit; drying and parching.

2. Bantering with severity.

RŌASTING, *n.* A severe teasing or bantering.

ROB, *n.* [Sp. *rob*; Ar. راب rauba, to be thick.]

The inspissated juice of ripe fruit, mixed with honey or sugar to the consistence of a conserve. *Sp. Dict.*

ROB, *v. t.* [G. *rauben*; D. *rooven*; Sw. *roffa* and *rôfva*; Dan. *röver*; It. *rubare*; Sp. *robar*; Port. *roubar*; Pers. ربودن robodan. This word has the elements of W. *rhaib*, a snatching, Sax. *reafian*, L. *rapio*, Fr. *ravir.* Class Rb. No. 26. 27. 29. 30.]

1. In *law*, to take from the person of another feloniously, forcibly and by putting him in fear; as, to *rob* a passenger on the road. *Blackstone.*

2. To seize and carry from any thing by violence and with felonious intent; as, to *rob* a coach; to *rob* the mail.

3. To plunder; to strip unlawfully; as, to *rob* an orchard; to *rob* a man of his just praise.

4. To take away by oppression or by violence.

Rob not the poor because he is poor. Prov. xxii.

5. To take from; to deprive. A large tree *robs* smaller plants near it of their nourishment.

6. In a loose sense, to steal; to take privately without permission of the owner. *Tooke.*

7. To withhold what is due. Mal. iii.

ROBAL'LO, *n.* A fish found in Mexico, which affords a most delicate food. *Clavigero.*

ROB'BE, *n.* [G.] The sea dog or seal.

ROB'BED, *pp.* Deprived feloniously and by violence; plundered; seized and carried away by violence.

ROB'BER, *n.* In *law*, one that takes goods or money from the person of another by force or menaces, and with a felonious intent. *Blackstone.*

2. In *a looser sense*, one who takes that to which he has no right; one who steals, plunders or strips by violence and wrong.

ROB'BERY, *n.* In *law*, the forcible and felonious taking from the person of another any money or goods, putting him in fear, that is, by violence or by menaces of death or personal injury. *Robbery* differs from *theft*, as it is a violent felonious taking from the person or presence of another; whereas *theft* is a felonious taking of goods privately from the person, dwelling, &c. of another. These words should not be confounded.

2. A plundering; a pillaging; a taking away by violence, wrong or oppression.

ROB'BING, *ppr.* Feloniously taking from the person of another; putting him in fear; stripping; plundering; taking from another unlawfully or by wrong or oppression.

ROB'BINS, } *n.* [*rope* and *bands.*] Short
ROPE-BANDS, } flat plaited pieces of rope with an eye in one end, used in pairs to tie the upper edges of square sails to their yards. *Mar. Dict.*

ROBE, *n.* [Fr. *robe*; Sp. *ropa*; Port. *roupa*; Ir. *roba*; It. *roba*, a robe, and goods or estate; *far roba*, to get money; *robone*, a long gown; *robbiccia*, trifles, idle stuff. The Spanish and Portuguese words signify clothing in general, cloth, stuff, wearing apparel, also a loose garment worn over the rest, a gown; Sp. *ropage* is wearing apparel, *drapery*; *roperia*, the trade of dealers in clothes. In Sp. and Port. then the word coincides with the Fr. *drap*, Eng. *drapery* and *frippery.* In Sax. *reaf* is clothing in general, and spoil, plunder, from *reafian*, to *rob.* From these facts, let the reader judge whether this word had its origin in *rubbing*, like *wearing* apparel, or from *stripping*, the name being originally given to skins, the primitive clothing of rude nations.]

1. A kind of gown or long loose garment worn over other dress, particularly by persons in elevated stations. The robe is properly a dress of state or dignity, as of princes, judges, priests, &c. See Ex. xxix. 55. 1 Sam. xxiv. 4. Matt. xxvii. 28.

2. A splendid female gown or garment. 2 Sam. xiii.

3. An elegant dress; splendid attire.

4. In *Scripture*, the vesture of purity or righteousness, and of happiness. Job xxix. Luke xv.

ROBE, *v. t.* To put on a robe; or to dress with magnificence; to array. *Pope. Thomson.*

2. To dress; to invest, as with beauty or elegance; as fields *robed* with green.

Such was his power over the expression of his countenance, that he could in an instant shake off the sternness of winter, and *robe* it in the brightest smiles of spring. *Wirt.*

ROʹBED, *pp.* Dressed with a robe; arrayed with elegance.

ROBʹERSMAN, } *n.* In *the old statutes*
ROBʹERTSMAN, } *of England*, a bold stout robber or night thief, said to be so called from *Robinhood*, a famous robber. *Johnson.*

ROBʹERT, } *n.* A plant of the genus
HERB-ROBERT, } Geranium; stork's bill. *Fam. of Plants. Ainsworth.*

ROBʹERTINE, *n.* One of an order of monks, so called from Robert Flower, the founder, A. D. 1187.

ROBʹIN, *n.* [L. *rubecula*, from *rubeo*, to be red.]

1. A bird of the genus Motacilla, called also *redbreast*. This is the English application of the word.

2. In *the United States*, a bird with a red breast, a species of Turdus.

ROBIN-GOODFELLOW, *n.* An old domestic goblin. *Dering.*

ROBʹORANT, *a.* [L. *roborans*, *roboro.*] Strengthening.

ROBʹORANT, *n.* A medicine that strengthens; but *corroborant* is generally used.

ROBORAʹTION, *n.* [from L. *roboro*, from *robur*, strength.]

A strengthening. [*Little used.*] *Coles.*

ROBOʹREOUS, *a.* [L. *roboreus*, from *robur*, strength, and an oak.]

Made of oak. *Dict.*

ROBUSTʹ, *a.* [L. *robustus*, from *robur*, strength.]

1. Strong; lusty; sinewy; muscular; vigorous; forceful; as a *robust* body; *robust* youth. It implies full flesh and sound health.

2. Sound; vigorous; as *robust* health.

3. Violent; rough; rude.

> Romp loving miss
> Is haul'd about in gallantry *robust*. *Thomson.*

4. Requiring strength; as *robust* employment. *Locke.*

[NOTE. This is one of the words in which we observe a strong tendency in practice to accentuate the first syllable, as in *access;* and there are many situations of the word in which this is the preferable pronunciation. *Robustious* is extremely vulgar, and in the U. States nearly obsolete.]

ROBUSTʹNESS, *n.* Strength; vigor, or the condition of the body when it has full firm flesh and sound health. *Arbuthnot.*

ROCʹAMBOLE, } *n.* [from the French.]
ROKʹAMBOLE, } A sort of wild garlic, the *Allium scorodoprasum*, growing naturally in Denmark and Sweden. It has a heart-shaped root at the side of the stalk. *Encyc.*

ROCHE-ALUM, *n.* [Fr. *roche*, a rock. It ought to be written and called *rock-alum.*]

Rock-alum, a purer kind of alum. *Mortimer.*

Rochelle salt, tartrate of potash and soda.

ROCHʹET, *n.* [Fr. *rochet;* It. *roccetto*, *rocchetto;* Sax. *rocc;* G. *rock;* D. *rok.* This coincides in origin with *frock.*]

A surplice; the white upper garment of a priest worn while officiating. *Cleaveland.*

ROCHʹET, *n.* A fish, the *roach*, which see.

ROCK, *n.* [Fr. *roc* or *roche;* It. *rocca*, a rock, and a distaff; Sp. *roca;* Port. *roca*, *rocha;* Arm. *roch;* Basque, *arroca.* Dropping the first letter of *crag*, rock would seem to be the same word, and so named from breaking and the consequent roughness, corresponding with Gr. ραχια, as *crag* does with *crack;* Ar. خرق garaka, to burst, crack, tear, *rake.* So L. *rupes*, from the root of *rumpo*, to break or burst. If this is not the origin of *rock*, I know not to what root to assign it. See Class Rg. No. 34.]

1. A large mass of stony matter, usually compounded of two or more simple minerals, either bedded in the earth or resting on its surface. Sometimes *rocks* compose the principal part of huge mountains; sometimes huge *rocks* lie on the surface of the earth, in detached blocks or masses. Under this term, mineralogists class all mineral substances, coal, gypsum, salt, &c.

2. In *Scripture*, figuratively, defense; means of safety; protection; strength; asylum.

> The Lord is my *rock.* 2 Sam. xxii.

3. Firmness; a firm or immovable foundation. Ps. xxvii. Matt. vii. and xvi.

4. A species of vultur or condor. *Encyc.*

5. A fabulous bird in the Eastern tales.

ROCK, *n.* [Dan. *rok;* Sw. *rock;* D. *rokken;* G. *rocken;* It. *rocca;* Sp. *rueca.* The latter is rendered a distaff, a winding or twisting, and the fish of a mast or yard. The sense is probably a *rack* or frame.]

A distaff used in spinning; the staff or frame about which flax is arranged, from which the thread is drawn in spinning.

ROCK, *v. t.* [Dan. *rokker*, to move, stir, wag, rack, advance; G. *rücken;* Old Fr. *rocquer* or *roquer;* Sw. *ragla*, to reel; W. *rhocian*, to rock; *rhoc*, a shooting or moving different ways; Ar. رج to shake, to tremble, to agitate. This latter verb in Ch. Syr. signifies to desire, to long for, that is, to *reach* or *stretch*, Gr. ορεγω; and it may be a different word.]

1. To move backward and forward, as a body resting on a foundation; as, to *rock* a cradle; to *rock* a chair; to *rock* a mountain. It differs from *shake*, as denoting a slower and more uniform motion, or larger movements. It differs from *swing*, which expresses a vibratory motion of something suspended.

> A rising earthquake *rock'd* the ground. *Dryden.*

2. To move backwards and forwards in a cradle, chair, &c.; as, to *rock* a child to sleep. *Dryden.*

3. To lull to quiet.

> Sleep *rock* thy brain. [*Unusual.*] *Shak.*

ROCK, *v. i.* To be moved backwards and forwards; to reel.

> The *rocking* town
> Supplants their footsteps. *Philips.*

ROCKʹ-ALUM, *n.* The purest kind of alum. [See *Roche-alum.*]

ROCKʹ-BASON, *n.* A cavity or artificial bason cut in a rock for the purpose, as is supposed, of collecting the dew or rain for ablutions and purifications prescribed by the druidical religion. *Grosier. Encyc.*

ROCK-BUTTER, *n.* A subsulphite of alumin, oozing from aluminous rocks. *Cyc.*

ROCK-CRYSʹTAL, *n.* The most perfect variety of silicious earth or quartz; limpid quartz. When purest it is white or colorless, but it is found of a grayish or yellowish white, pale yellow or citrine. Its most usual form is that of hexagonal prisms, surmounted by hexagonal pyramids. *Kirwan. Cleaveland.*

ROCKʹ-DOE, *n.* A species of deer. *Grew.*

ROCKʹED, *pp.* [from *rock*, the verb.] Moved one way and the other.

ROCKʹER, *n.* One who rocks the cradle; also, the curving piece of wood on which a cradle or chair rocks.

ROCKʹET, *n.* [Dan. *raket*, *rakette*, a rocket, cracker or squib; G. *rackete;* probably from the root of *crack* and *racket*, Fr. *craquer*, *craqueter.*]

An artificial fire-work, consisting of a cylindrical case of paper, filled with a composition of combustible ingredients, as niter, charcoal and sulphur. This being tied to a stick and fired, ascends into the air and bursts. *Encyc.*

ROCKʹET, *n.* [L. *eruca.*] A plant of the genus Brassica. There is also the *bastard rocket*, of the genus Reseda; the *corn rocket* and the *sea rocket*, of the genus Bunias; the *marsh rocket*, the *water rocket*, and the *winter rocket*, of the genus Sisymbrium; and the *dame's violet rocket*, of the genus Hesperis. *Fam. of Plants.*

ROCKʹ-FISH, *n.* A species of Gobius.

ROCKʹINESS, *n.* [from *rocky.*] State of abounding with rocks.

ROCKʹING, *ppr.* Moving backwards and forwards.

ROCKʹLESS, *a.* Being without rocks. *Dryden.*

ROCKʹ-OIL, *n.* Another name for petrol or petroleum.

ROCKʹ-PIGEON, *n.* A pigeon that builds her nest on a rock. *Mortimer.*

ROCKʹ-ROSE, *n.* A plant of the genus Cistus.

ROCK-RUBY, *n.* A name sometimes given to the garnet, when it is of a strong, but not a deep red, and has a cast of blue. *Hill.*

ROCKʹ-SALT, *n.* Fossil or mineral salt; salt dug from the earth; muriate of soda. But in America, this name is sometimes given to salt that comes in large crystals from the West Indies, which salt is formed by evaporation from sea water, in large basons or cavities, on the isles. Hexahedral rock-salt occurs foliated and fibrous. *Ure.*

ROCKʹ-WOOD, *n.* Ligniform asbestus. *Cyc.*

ROCKʹ-WORK, *n.* Stones fixed in mortar in imitation of the asperities of rocks, forming a wall.

2. A natural wall of rock. *Addison.*

ROCKʹY, *a.* [from *rock.*] Full of rocks; as a *rocky* mountain; a *rocky* shore.

2. Resembling a rock; as the *rocky* orb of a shield. *Milton.*

3. Very hard; stony; obdurate; insusceptible of impression; as a *rocky* bosom. *Shak.*

ROD, *n.* [Sax. *rod;* Dan. *rode;* D. *roede*, *roe;* G. *ruthe* and *reis.* In Danish, *rod* is a *root;* and I suppose *rod*, *root*, L. *radius*, ray, *radix*, root, and Dan. Sw. *rad*, to be of one family. The sense is a shoot, from extending. The Russ. *prut*, a rod, is probably the same word with a prefix.]

1. The shoot or long twig of any woody plant; a branch, or the stem of a shrub; as a *rod* of hazle, of birch, of oak or hickory. Hence,

2. An instrument of punishment or correction; chastisement.

I will chasten him with the *rod* of men. 2 Sam. vii. Prov. x.

3. Discipline; ecclesiastical censures. 1 Cor. iv.

4. A kind of scepter.

The *rod* and bird of peace. *Shak.*

5. A pole for angling; something long and slender. *Gay.*

6. An instrument for measuring; but more generally, a measure of length containing five yards, or sixteen feet and a half; a pole; a perch. In many parts of the United States, *rod* is universally used for *pole* or *perch.*

7. In *Scripture*, a staff or wand. 1 Sam. xiv.

8. Support.

Thy *rod* and thy staff, they comfort me. Ps. xxiii.

9. A shepherd's crook. Lev. xxvii.

10. An instrument for threshing. Is. xxviii.

11. Power; authority. Ps. cxxv.

12. A tribe or race. Ps. lxxiv.

Rod of iron, the mighty power of Christ. Rev. xix. Ps. ii.

RODE, *pret.* of *ride*; also, a cross. [See *Rood.*]

ROD'OMONT, *n.* [Fr. *id.*; It. *rodomonte*, a bully; Ir. *raidhmeis*, silly stories, rodomontade; *roithre*, a babbler, a *prating* fellow; *roithreacht*, silly talk, loquacity, *rhetoric*; from *radham*, to say, tell, relate, W. *adrawz*. The Ir. *radh, radham*, are the Sax. *ræd*, speech, and *rædan*, to read. See *Read*. The last syllable may be the Fr. *monter*, to *mount*, and the word then signifies one that speaks loftily. Hence the name of Ariosto's hero.]

A vain boaster. *Herbert.*

ROD'OMONT, *a.* Bragging; vainly boasting.

RODOMONTA'DE, *n.* [Fr. *id.*; It. *rodomontata*. See *Rodomont.*]

Vain boasting; empty bluster or vaunting; rant.

I could show that the *rodomontades* of Almanzor are neither so irrational nor impossible. *Dryden.*

RODOMONTA'DE, *v. i.* To boast; to brag; to bluster; to rant.

RODOMONT'ADIST, RODOMONTA'DOR, *n.* A blustering boaster; one that brags or vaunts. *Terry. Todd.*

RŌE, RŌEBUCK, *n.* [Sax. *ra* or *raa*, *ræge* or *hræge*; G. *reh* and *rehbock*; Dan. *raa* or *raabuk*; Sw. *råbock.*]

1. A species of deer, the *Cervus capreolus*, with erect cylindrical branched horns, forked at the summit. This is one of the smallest of the cervine genus, but of elegant shape and remarkably nimble. It prefers a mountainous country, and herds in families. *Encyc.*

2. *Roe*, the female of the hart. *Sandys.*

RŌE, *n.* [G. *rogen*; Dan. *rogn, ravn*; that which is ejected. So in Dan. *roge* is spittle.]

The seed or spawn of fishes. The roe of the male is called *soft roe* or *milt*; that of the female, *hard roe* or *spawn*. *Encyc.*

RO'E-STONE, *n.* Called also oolite, which see.

ROGA'TION, *n.* [Fr. from L. *rogatio*; *rogo*, to ask.]

1. Litany; supplication.

He perfecteth the *rogations* or litanies before in use. *Hooker.*

2. In *Roman jurisprudence*, the demand by the consuls or tribunes, of a law to be passed by the people.

ROGA'TION-WEEK, *n.* The second week before Whitsunday, thus called from the three fasts observed therein; viz., on Monday, Tuesday, and Wednesday, called rogation-days, because of the extraordinary prayers then made for the fruits of the earth, or as a preparation for the devotion of the Holy Thursday. *Dict.*

RŌGUE, *n. rōg.* [Sax. *earg, arg*, idle, stupid, mean; *eargian*, to become dull or torpid; D. G. Sw. Dan. *arg*, evil, crafty, wicked; Gr. αργος. Hence Cimbric *argur*, and Eng. *rogue*, by transposition of letters. The word *arga*, in the laws of the Longobards, denotes a cuckold. Spel. voc. *Arga.*]

1. In *law*, a vagrant; a sturdy beggar; a vagabond. Persons of this character were, by the ancient laws of England, to be punished by whipping and having the ear bored with a hot iron. *Encyc. Spenser.*

2. A knave; a dishonest person; applied now, I believe, exclusively to males. This word comprehends thieves and robbers, but is generally applied to such as cheat and defraud in mutual dealings, or to counterfeiters.

The *rogue* and fool by fits is fair and wise. *Pope.*

3. A name of slight tenderness and endearment.

Alas, poor *rogue*, I think indeed she loves. *Shak.*

4. A wag. *Shak.*

RŌGUE, *v. i. rōg.* To wander; to play the vagabond. [*Little used.*] *Spenser.*

2. To play knavish tricks. [*Little used.*] *Johnson.*

RŌGUERY, *n.* The life of a vagrant. [*Now little used.*] *Donne.*

2. Knavish tricks; cheating; fraud; dishonest practices.

'Tis no scandal grown,
For debt and *roguery* to quit the town. *Dryden.*

3. Waggery; arch tricks; mischievousness.

RŌGUESHIP, *n.* The qualities or personage of a rogue. *Dryden.*

RŌGUISH, *a.* Vagrant; vagabond. [*Nearly obsolete.*] *Spenser.*

2. Knavish; fraudulent; dishonest. [*This is the present sense of the word.*] *Swift.*

3. Waggish; wanton; slightly mischievous. *Addison.*

RŌGUISHLY, *adv.* Like a rogue; knavishly; wantonly.

RŌGUISHNESS, *n.* The qualities of a rogue; knavery; mischievousness.

2. Archness; sly cunning; as the *roguishness* of a look.

RŌGUY, *a.* Knavish; wanton. [*Not in use.*] *L'Estrange.*

ROIL, *v. t.* [This is the Arm. *brella*, Fr. *brouiller, embrouiller*, It. *brogliare, imbrogliare*, Sp. *embrollar*, Port. *embrulhar*; primarily to turn or stir, to make intricate, to twist, wrap, involve, hence to mix, confound, perplex, whence Eng. *broil*, Fr. *brouillard*, mist, fog. In English, the prefix or first letter is lost.]

1. To render turbid by stirring up the dregs or sediment; as, to *roil* wine, cider or other liquor in casks or bottles.

2. To excite some degree of anger; to disturb the passion of resentment. [*These senses are in common use in New England, and locally in England.*]

3. To perplex. [*Local in England.*]

ROIL'ED, *pp.* Rendered turbid or foul by disturbing the lees or sediment; angered slightly; disturbed in mind by an offense.

ROIL'ING, *ppr.* Rendering turbid; or exciting the passion of anger.

[*Note.* This word is as legitimate as any in the language.]

ROINT. [See *Aroynt.*]

ROIST, ROIST'ER, *v. i.* [Arm. *reustla*, to embroil. This word belongs to the root of *rustle, brustle*, Sax. *brysan*, to shake, to rush, W. *rhysiaw*, to *rush*, to straiten, to entangle, *rhysu*, id.]

To bluster; to swagger; to bully; to be bold, noisy, vaunting or turbulent. [*Not in use.*] *Shak. Swift.*

ROIST'ER, ROIST'ERER, *n.* A bold, blustering, turbulent fellow. [*Not in use.*]

RO'KY, *a.* [See *Reek.*] Misty; foggy; cloudy. [*Not in use.*] *Ray.*

RŌLL, *v. t.* [D. G. *rollen*; Sw. *rulla*; Dan. *ruller*; W. *rholiaw*; Fr. *rouler*; Arm. *ruilha* and *rolla*; It. *rullare*; Ir. *rolam*. It is usual to consider this word as formed by contraction from the Latin *rotula*, a little wheel, from *rota*, W. *rhod*, a wheel. But it is against all probability that all the nations of Europe have fallen into such a contraction. *Roll* is undoubtedly a primitive root, on which have been formed *troll* and *stroll.*]

1. To move by turning on the surface, or with a circular motion in which all parts of the surface are successively applied to a plane; as, to *roll* a barrel or puncheon; to *roll* a stone or ball. Sisyphus was condemned to *roll* a stone to the top of a hill, which, when he had done so, *rolled* down again, and thus his punishment was eternal.

2. To revolve; to turn on its axis; as, to *roll* a wheel or a planet.

3. To move in a circular direction.

To dress, to troll the tongue and *roll* the eye. *Milton.*

4. To wrap round on itself; to form into a circular or cylindrical body; as, to *roll* a piece of cloth; to *roll* a sheet of paper; to *roll* parchment; to *roll* tobacco.

5. To enwrap; to bind or involve in a bandage or the like. *Wiseman.*

6. To form by rolling into round masses. *Peacham.*

7. To drive or impel any body with a circular motion, or to drive forward with violence or in a stream. The ocean *rolls* its billows to the shore. A river *rolls* its waters to the ocean.

8. To spread with a roller or rolling pin; as to *roll* paste.

9. To produce a periodical revolution.

Heav'n shone and *roll'd* her motions. *Milton.*

10. To press or level with a roller; as, to *roll* a field.

To roll one's self, to wallow. Mic. i.

RÔLL, *v. i.* To move by turning on the surface, or with the successive application of all parts of the surface to a plane; as, a ball or a wheel *rolls* on the earth; a body *rolls* on an inclined plane.

2. To move, turn or run on an axis; as a wheel. [In this sense, *revolve* is more generally used.]

3. To run on wheels.

And to the *rolling* chair is bound. *Dryden.*

4. To revolve; to perform a periodical revolution; as the *rolling* year. Ages *roll* away.

5. To turn; to move circularly.

And his red eyeballs *roll* with living fire. *Dryden.*

6. To float in rough water; to be tossed about.

Twice ten tempestuous nights I *roll'd*— *Pope.*

7. To move, as waves or billows, with alternate swells and depressions. Waves *roll* on waves.

8. To fluctuate; to move tumultuously.

What diff'rent sorrows did within thee *roll*. *Prior.*

9. To be moved with violence; to be hurled.

Down they fell
By thousands, angel on archangel *roll'd*. *Milton.*

10. To be formed into a cylinder or ball; as, the cloth *rolls* well.

11. To spread under a roller or rolling pin. The paste *rolls* well.

12. To wallow; to tumble; as, a horse *rolls*.

13. To rock or move from side; as, a ship *rolls* in a calm.

14. To beat a drum with strokes so rapid that they can scarcely be distinguished by the ear.

RÔLL, *n.* The act of rolling, or state of being rolled; as the *roll* of a ball.

2. The thing rolling. *Thomson.*

3. A mass made round; something like a ball or cylinder; as a *roll* of fat; a *roll* of wool. *Addison. Mortimer.*

4. A roller; a cylinder of wood, iron or stone; as a *roll* to break clods. *Mortimer.*

5. A quantity of cloth wound into a cylindrical form: as a *roll* of woolen or satin; a *roll* of lace.

6. A cylindrical twist of tobacco.

7. An official writing; a list; a register; a catalogue; as a muster-*roll*; a court-*roll*.

8. The beating of a drum with strokes so rapid as scarcely to be distinguished by the ear.

9. *Rolls* of court, of parliament, or of any public body, are the parchments on which are engrossed, by the proper officer, the acts and proceedings of that body, and which being kept in rolls, constitute the records of such public body.

10. In *antiquity*, a volume: a book consisting of leaf, bark, paper, skin or other material on which the ancients wrote, and which being kept *rolled* or folded, was called in Latin *volumen*, from *volvo*, to roll. Hence,

11. A chronicle; history; annals.

Nor names more noble graced the *rolls* of fame. *B. Trumbull.*

12. Part; office; that is, round of duty, like *turn*. *Obs.*

RÔLLED, *pp.* Moved by turning; formed into a round or cylindrical body; leveled with a roller, as land.

RÔLLER, *n.* That which rolls; that which turns on its own axis; particularly, a cylinder of wood, stone or metal, used in husbandry and the arts. *Rollers* are of various kinds and used for various purposes.

2. A bandage; a fillet; properly, a long and broad bandage used in surgery.

3. A bird of the magpye kind, about the size of a jay. *Dict. N. Hist.*

A bird of the genus Coracias, found in Europe; called also the *German parrot*. *Ed. Encyc.*

RÔLLING, *ppr.* Turning over; revolving; forming into a cylinder or round mass; leveling, as land.

RÔLLING, *n.* The motion of a ship from side to side.

RÔLLING-PIN, *n.* A round piece of wood, tapering at each end, with which paste is molded and reduced to a proper thickness. *Wiseman.*

RÔLLING-PRESS, *n.* An engine consisting of two cylinders, by which cloth is calendered, waved and tabbled; also, an engine for taking impressions from copper plates; also, a like engine for drawing plates of metal, &c.

RÔLLY-POOLY, *n.* [said to be *roll* and *pool*, or *roll*, *ball* and *pool*.]

A game in which a ball, rolling into a certain place, wins. *Arbuthnot.*

RÔMAĜE, *n.* Bustle; tumultuous search. [See *Rummage*.] *Shak.*

RÔMAL, *n. romaul'.* A species of silk handkerchief.

RO'MAN, *a.* [L. *Romanus*, from *Roma*, the principal city of the Romans in Italy. *Rome* is the oriental name *Ramah*, elevated, that is, a hill; for fortresses and towns were often placed on hills for security; Heb. Ch. רום to be high, to raise. Class Rm. No. 3.]

1. Pertaining to Rome, or to the Roman people.

2. Romish; popish; professing the religion of the pope.

Roman catholic, as an adjective, denoting the religion professed by the people of Rome and of Italy, at the head of which is the pope or bishop of Rome; as a noun, one who adheres to the papal religion.

RO'MAN, *n.* A native of Rome.

2. A citizen of Rome; one enjoying the privileges of a Roman citizen.

3. One of the christian church at Rome to which Paul addressed an epistle, consisting of converts from Judaism or paganism.

ROMANCE, *n. romans', ro'mans.* [Fr. *roman*; It. *romanzo*; Sp. *romance*, the common vulgar language of Spain, and *romance*; Port. *id.* any vulgar tongue, and a species of poetry; W. *rham*, a rising over; *rhamant*, a rising over, a vaulting or springing, an omen, a figurative expression, *romance*, as an adjective, rising boldly, *romantic*; *rhamanta*, to rise over, to soar, to reach to a distance, to divine, to romance, to allegorize; *rhamantu*, to use figurative or high flown language, &c. The Welsh retains the signification of the oriental word from which *Rome* is derived, and indeed the sense of *romance* is evidently from the primitive sense of the root, rather than from the use of the Roman language. The Welsh use of the word proves also the correctness of the foregoing derivation of *Roma*, and overthrows the fabulous account of the origin of the word from Romulus or Remus. It is probable that this word is allied to *ramble*.]

1. A fabulous relation or story of adventures and incidents, designed for the entertainment of readers; a tale of extraordinary adventures, fictitious and often extravagant, usually a tale of love or war, subjects interesting the sensibilities of the heart, or the passions of wonder and curiosity. *Romance* differs from the *novel*, as it treats of great actions and extraordinary adventures; that is, according to the Welsh signification, it vaults or soars beyond the limits of fact and real life, and often of probability.

The first *romances* were a monstrous assemblage of histories, in which truth and fiction were blended without probability; a composition of amorous adventures and the extravagant ideas of chivalry. *Encyc.*

2. A fiction. *Prior.*

ROMANCE, *v. i. romans', ro'mans.* To forge and tell fictitious stories; to deal in extravagant stories. *Richardson.*

ROMAN'CER, } *n.* One who invents fictitious stories.
RO'MANCER, } *L'Estrange.*

2. A writer of romance. *Aubrey.*

ROMAN'CING, } *ppr.* Inventing and telling fictitious tales; building castles in the air.
RO'MANCING, }

ROMAN'CY, *a.* Romantic. [*Not proper.*]

RO'MANISM, *n.* The tenets of the church of Rome. *Brevint.*

RO'MANIST, *n.* An adherent to the papal religion; a Roman catholic. *Encyc.*

RO'MANIZE, *v. t.* To latinize; to fill with Latin words or modes of speech. *Dryden.*

2. To convert to the Roman catholic religion, or to papistical opinions.

RO'MANIZE, *v. i.* To conform to Romish opinions, customs or modes of speech.

RO'MANIZED, *pp.* Latinized.

ROMANSH', *n.* The language of the Grisons in Switzerland, a corruption of the Latin.

ROMAN'TIC, *a.* Pertaining to romance, or resembling it; wild; fanciful; extravagant; as a *romantic* taste; *romantic* notions; *romantic* expectations; *romantic* zeal.

2. Improbable or chimerical; fictitious; as a *romantic* tale.

3. Fanciful; wild; full of wild or fantastic scenery; as a *romantic* prospect or landscape; a *romantic* situation.

ROMAN'TICALLY, *adv.* Wildly; extravagantly. *Pope.*

ROMAN'TICNESS, *n.* Wildness; extravagance; fancifulness.

2. Wildness of scenery.

ROMAN'ZOVITE, *n.* A recently discovered mineral of the garnet kind, of a brown or brownish yellow color; named from count Romanzoff. *Cleaveland.*

ROMEPENNY, } *n.* [*Rome*, and Sax. *pen-*
ROMESCOT, } *nig* or *sceat.*] A tax of a penny on a house, formerly paid by the people of England to the church of Rome.

RO'MISH, *a.* [from *Rome.*] Belonging or relating to Rome, or to the religion professed by the people of Rome and of the western empire, of which Rome was the metropolis; catholic; popish; as the *Romish* church; the *Romish* religion, ritual or ceremonies.

RO'MIST, *n.* A papist. *South.*

ROMP, *n.* [a different spelling of *ramp;* W. *rham*, a rising over; *rhamu*, to reach over, to soar, to vault. See *Ramp* and *Romance.*]

1. A rude girl who indulges in boisterous play. *Addison.*

2. Rude play or frolick.

> *Romp* loving miss
> Is haul'd about in gallantry robust. *Thomson.*

ROMP, *v. i.* To play rudely and boisterously; to leap and frisk about in play. *Richardson.*

ROMP'ING, *ppr.* Playing rudely; as a noun, rude boisterous play.

ROMP'ISH, *a.* Given to rude play; inclined to romp. *Ash.*

ROMP'ISHNESS, *n.* Disposition to rude boisterous play; or the practice of romping. *Steele.*

ROM'PU, } *n.* [L. *rumpo*, to break.] In
ROMPEE', } *heraldry*, an ordinary that is broken, or a chevron, a bend or the like, whose upper points are cut off. *Encyc.*

RONDEAU, } *n.* [Fr. *rondeau*, from *rond*,
RON'DO, } round.] A kind of poetry, commonly consisting of thirteen verses, of which eight have one rhyme, and five another. It is divided into three couplets, and at the end of the second and third, the beginning of the rondeau is repeated in an equivocal sense, if possible. *Warton. Trevoux.*

2. In *music*, the rondo, vocal or instrumental, generally consists of three strains, the first of which closes in the original key, while each of the others is so constructed in modulation as to reconduct the ear in an easy and natural manner to the first strain. *Busby.*

3. A kind of jig or lively tune that ends with the first strain repeated. *Todd.*

RON'DLE, *n.* [from *round.*] A round mass. [*Not in use.*] *Peacham.*

RON'DURE, *n.* [Fr. *rondeur.*] A round; a circle. [*Not in use.*] *Shak.*

RONG, the old *pret.* and *pp.* of *ring*, now *rung.* *Chaucer.*

RONION, *n.* run'yon. [Fr. *rognon*, kidney.] A fat bulky woman. [*Not in use.*] *Shak.*

RONT, *n.* An animal stinted in its growth. [Now written and pronounced *runt.*] *Spenser.*

ROOD, *n.* [a different orthography of *rod*, which see.]

1. The fourth part of an acre, or forty square rods. [See *Acre.*]

2. A pole; a measure of five yards; a rod or perch. [*Not used in America, and probably local in England.*]

ROOD, *n.* [Sax. *rode* or *rod.*] The cross; or an image of Christ, of the virgin Mary and a saint or St. John, on each side of it. *Shak.*

ROOD'LOFT, *n.* A loft or gallery in a church on which relics and images were set to view. *Johnson.*

ROOF, *n.* [Sax. *rof, hrof;* Gr. ὀροφη, ὀροφος, from ἐρεφω, to cover. Qu. Russ. *krov*, Slav. *strop.* See the Ar. Class Rb. No. 12. and Syr. No. 40.]

1. The cover or upper part of a house or other building, consisting of rafters covered with boards, shingles or tiles, with a side or sides sloping from the ridge, for the purpose of carrying off the water that falls in rain or snow. In Asia, the *roofs* of houses are flat or horizontal. The same name, *roof*, is given to the sloping covers of huts, cabins and ricks; to the arches of ovens, furnaces, &c.

2. A vault; an arch; or the interior of a vault; as the *roof* of heaven.

3. The vault of the mouth; the upper part of the mouth; the palate.

> If I do not remember thee, let my tongue cleave to the *roof* of my mouth. Ps. cxxxvii.

ROOF, *v. t.* To cover with a roof.

> I have not seen the remains of any Roman buildings, that have not been *roofed* with vaults or arches. *Addison.*

2. To inclose in a house; to shelter.

> Here had we now our country's honor *roof'd.* *Shak.*

ROOF'ED, *pp.* Furnished or covered with a roof or arch.

ROOF'ING, *ppr.* Covering with a roof.

ROOF'ING, *n.* The materials of which a roof is composed; or materials for a roof. *Encyc.*

ROOF'LESS, *a.* [Sax. *roflease.*] Having no roof; as a *roofless* house.

2. Having no house or home; unsheltered.

ROOF'Y, *a.* Having roofs. *Dryden.*

ROOK, *n.* [Sax. *hroc;* G. *roche;* Dan. *roge, raage*, a rook, and *krage*, a crow. This word belongs to the root of *crow*, or is rather the same word dialectically varied; Dan. *krage;* Sw. *kraka;* G. *krähe;* D. *kraai;* L. *graculus;* probably from its voice; Ir. *grag, gragam.* See *Crow* and *Croak.*]

1. A fowl of the genus Corvus, the fowl mentioned by Virgil under this name. This fowl resembles the crow, but differs from it in not feeding on carrion, but on insects and grain. In crows also the nostrils and root of the bill are clothed with fethers, but in rooks the same parts are naked, or have only a few bristly hairs. The rook is gregarious. *Encyc.*

2. A cheat; a trickish, rapacious fellow. *Wycherley.*

ROOK, *n.* [It. *rocco*, a bishop's staff, a crosier, a rook at chess.] A common man at chess. *Encyc.*

ROOK, *v. i.* To cheat; to defraud. *Locke.*

ROOK, *v. t.* To cheat; to defraud by cheating. *Aubrey.*

ROOK, *v. i.* To squat. [See *Ruck.*]

ROOK'ERY, *n.* A nursery of rooks. *Pope.*

2. In *low language*, a brothel.

ROOK'Y, *a.* Inhabited by rooks; as the *rooky* wood. *Shak.*

ROOM, *n.* [Sax. Dan. Sw. *rum;* D. *ruim;* G. *raum;* Goth. *rumis*, room, place; Ir. *rum*, a floor or room; G. *räumen*, Sax. *rumian, ryman*, to give place, to amplify, to enlarge; Sax. *rum-gifa*, liberal. It may be allied to *roam, ramble.* Class Rm. No. 4. 9.]

1. Space; compass; extent of place, great or small. Let the words occupy as little *room* as possible.

2. Space or place unoccupied.

> Lord, it is done as thou hast commanded, and yet there is *room.* Luke xiv.

3. Place for reception or admission of any thing. In this case, there is no *room* for doubt or for argument.

4. Place of another; stead; as in succession or substitution. One magistrate or king comes in the *room* of a former one. We often place one thing in the *room* of another. 1 Kings xx.

5. Unoccupied opportunity. The eager pursuit of wealth leaves little *room* for serious reflection.

6. An apartment in a house; any division separated from the rest by a partition; as a parlor, drawing *room* or bed-*room;* also, an apartment in a ship, as the cook-*room*, bread-*room*, gun-*room*, &c.

7. A seat. Luke xiv.

To make room, to open a way or passage; to free from obstructions.

To make room, to open a space or place for any thing.

To give room, to withdraw; to leave space unoccupied for others to pass or to be seated.

ROOM, *v. i.* To occupy an apartment; to lodge; *an academic use of the word.* A B *rooms* at No. 7.

ROOM'AGE, *n.* [from *room.*] Space; place. [*Not used.*] *Wotton.*

ROOM'FUL, *a.* Abounding with rooms. *Donne.*

ROOM'INESS, *n.* Space; spaciousness; large extent of space.

Roomth, space, and *roomthy*, spacious, are ill formed words and not used in the United States.

ROOM'Y, *a.* Spacious; wide; large; having ample room; as a *roomy* mansion; a *roomy* deck. *Dryden.*

ROOST, *n.* [Sax. *hrost;* D. *roest*, roost; *roesten*, to roost.]

The pole or other support on which fowls rest at night.

> He clapp'd his wings upon his *roost.* *Dryden.*

At roost, in a state for rest and sleep.

ROOST, *v. i.* To sit, rest or sleep, as fowls on a pole, tree or other thing at night.

2. To lodge, in burlesque.

ROOST'ING, *ppr.* Sitting for rest and sleep at night.

ROOT, *n.* [Dan. *rod;* Sw. *rot;* L. *radix;* It. *radice;* Sp. *raiz;* Ir. *raidis;* W. *rhaiz*, a ray or spear, whence *gwraiz*, a root. A root is a shoot, and only a different application of *rod*, L. *radius.*]

1. That part of a plant which enters and fixes itself in the earth, and serves to support the plant in an erect position, while by means of its fibrils it imbibes nutriment for the stem, branches and fruit.

2. The part of any thing that resembles the

roots of a plant in manner of growth; as the *roots* of a cancer, of teeth, &c.
3. The bottom or lower part of any thing.

Deep to the *roots* of hell— *Milton.*

Burnet uses *root* of a mountain, but we now say, *base, foot* or *bottom.* See Job xxviii. 9.
4. A plant whose root is esculent or the most useful part; as beets, carrots, &c.
5. The original or cause of any thing.

The love of money is the *root* of all evil. 1 Tim. vi.
6. The first ancestor.

They were the *roots* out of which sprung two distinct people— *Locke.*
7. In *arithmetic* and *algebra,* the root of any quantity is such a quantity as, when multiplied into itself a certain number of times, will exactly produce that quantity. Thus 2 is a root of 4, because when multiplied into itself, it exactly produces 4.
8. Means of growth. "He hath no *root* in himself;" that is, no soil in which grace can grow and flourish. Matt. xiii.
9. In *music,* the fundamental note of any chord. *Busby.*

Root of bitterness, in Scripture, any error, sin or evil that produces discord or immorality.

To take root, to become planted or fixed; or to be established; to increase and spread.

To take deep root, to be firmly planted or established; to be deeply impressed. *Dryden.*

ROOT, *v. i.* To fix the root; to enter the earth, as roots.

In deep grounds, the weeds *root* deeper. *Mortimer.*

2. To be firmly fixed; to be established.

The multiplying brood of the ungodly shall not take deep *rooting.* *Wisdom.*

3. To sink deep.

If any error chanced—to cause misapprehensions, he gave them not leave to *root* and fasten by concealment. *Fell.*

ROOT, *v. t.* To plant and fix deep in the earth; used chiefly in the participle; as *rooted* trees or forests. *Dryden.*
2. To plant deeply; to impress deeply and durably. Let the leading truths of the gospel be *deeply rooted* in the mind; let holy affections be well *rooted* in the heart.
3. In *Scripture,* to be *rooted* and grounded in Christ, is to be firmly united to him by faith and love, and well established in the belief of his character and doctrines. Eph. iii.

ROOT, *v. i.* or *t.* [Sax. *wrot,* a snout or proboscis; *wrotan,* to dig or root; D. *wroeten,* G. *reuten,* Dan. *roder,* Sw. *rota,* to root. This seems to be of the same family as the former word and *rod,* from the use of the snout.]

To turn up the earth with the snout, as swine. Swine *root* to find worms; they *root* the ground wherever they come.

To root up or *out,* to eradicate; to extirpate; to remove or destroy root and branch; to exterminate. Deut. xxix. Job xxxi.

ROOT'-BOUND, *a.* Fixed to the earth by roots. *Milton.*

ROOT'-BUILT, *a.* Built of roots. *Shenstone.*

ROOT'ED, *pp.* Having its roots planted or fixed in the earth; hence, fixed; deep; radical; as *rooted* sorrow; *rooted* aversion; *rooted* prejudices.

ROOT'EDLY, *adv.* Deeply; from the heart. *Shak.*

ROOT'ER, *n.* One that roots; or one that tears up by the roots.

ROOT'-HOUSE, *n.* A house made of roots. *Dodsley.*

ROOT'ING, *ppr.* Striking or taking root; turning up with the snout.

ROOT'-LEAF, *n.* A leaf growing immediately from the root. *Martyn.*

ROOT'LET, *n.* A radicle; the fibrous part of a root. *Martyn.*

ROOT'Y, *a.* Full of roots; as *rooty* ground. *Adams.*

ROPAL'IC, *a.* [Gr. ῥοπαλον, a club.] Club-formed; increasing or swelling towards the end.

ROPE, *n.* [Sax. *rap;* Sw. *rep;* Dan. *reeb;* W. *rhaf;* Ir. *ropa, roibin.*]
1. A large string or line composed of several strands twisted together. It differs from *cord, line* and *string,* only in its size; being the name given to all sorts of cordage above an inch in circumference. Indeed the smaller *ropes,* when used for certain purposes, are called *lines.*

Ropes are by seamen ranked under two descriptions, *cable-laid,* and *hawser-laid;* the former composed of nine strands, or three great strands, each consisting of three small ones; the latter made with three strands, each composed of a certain number of rope-yarns. *Mar. Dict.*
2. A row or string consisting of a number of things united; as a *rope* of onions.
3. *Ropes,* [Sax. *roppas,*] the intestines of birds. *Lye.*

Rope of sand, proverbially, feeble union or tie; a band easily broken. *Locke.*

ROPE, *v. i.* To draw out or extend into a filament or thread, by means of any glutinous or adhesive quality. Any glutinous substance will *rope* considerably before it will part.

RO'PE-BAND. [See *Robbin.*]

RO'PE-DANCER, *n.* [*rope* and *dancer.*] One that walks on a rope suspended. *Addison.*

RO'PE-LADDER, *n.* A ladder made of ropes.

RO'PE-MAKER, *n.* One whose occupation is to make ropes or cordage. [I do not know that *roper* is ever used.]

RO'PE-MAKING, *n.* The art or business of manufacturing ropes or cordage.

RO'PERY, *n.* A place where ropes are made. [*Not used in the United States.*]
2. A trick that deserves the halter. *Shak.*

RO'PE-TRICK, *n.* A trick that deserves the halter. *Shak.*

RO'PE-WALK, *n.* A long covered walk, or a long building over smooth ground, where ropes are manufactured.

RO'PE-YARN, *n.* Yarn for ropes, consisting of a single thread. The threads are twisted into strands, and the strands into ropes.

RO'PINESS, *n.* [from *ropy.*] Stringiness, or aptness to draw out in a string or thread without breaking, as of glutinous substances; viscosity; adhesiveness.

RO'PY, *a.* [from *rope.*] Stringy; adhesive; that may be drawn into a thread; as a glutinous substance; viscous; tenacious; glutinous; as *ropy* wine; *ropy* lees. *Dryden. Philips.*

ROQ'UELAUR, *n.* [from Fr.; Dan. *rokkelor;* G. *rock,* a coat, D. *rok,* Sax. *rocc,* whence *frock,* Sp. *roclo.* Qu. the last syllable, or is the word derived from a duke of this name?] A cloke for men. *Gay.*

RO'RAL, *a.* [L. *roralis,* from *ros,* dew.] Pertaining to dew or consisting of dew; dewy. *Green.*

RORA'TION, *n.* [L. *roratio.*] A falling of dew. [*Not used.*] *Dict.*

RO'RID, *a.* [L. *roridus.*] Dewy. *Granger.*

RORIF'EROUS, *a.* [L. *ros,* dew, and *fero,* to produce.] Generating or producing dew. *Dict.*

RORIF'LUENT, *a.* [L. *ros,* dew, and *fluo,* to flow.] Flowing with dew. [*Not used.*] *Dict.*

ROSA'CEOUS, *a.* *s* as *z.* [L. *rosaceus.* See *Rose.*]

Rose-like; composed of several petals, arranged in a circular form; as a *rosaceous* corol. *Martyn. Encyc.*

RO'SARY, *n.* *s* as *z.* [L. *rosarium.* See *Rose.*]
1. A bed of roses, or place where roses grow.
2. A chaplet. *Taylor.*
3. A string of beads used by Roman catholics, on which they count their prayers.

ROSAS'IC, *a.* The rosasic acid is obtained from the urine of persons affected with intermitting and nervous fevers. *Ure.*

ROS'CID, *a.* [L. *roscidus,* from *ros,* dew.] Dewy; containing dew, or consisting of dew. [*Not used.*] *Bacon.*

ROSE, *n.* *s* as *z.* [Fr. *rose;* L. It. Sp. *rosa;* G. Dan. *rose;* D. *roos, rooze;* Sw. *ros;* Arm. *rosen;* Ir. *ros* or *rosa;* W. *rhôs;* Gr. ῥοδον; from the root of *red, ruddy,* W. *rhuz.* See *Red.*]
1. A plant and flower of the genus Rosa, of many species and varieties, as the wild, canine or dog-rose, the white rose, the red rose, the cinnamon rose, the eglantine or sweet briar, &c. There are five petals; the calyx is urceolate, quinquefid, and corneous; the seeds are numerous, hispid, and fixed to the inside of the calyx. *Encyc.*
2. A knot of ribin in the form of a rose, used as an ornamental tie of a shoe.

Under the rose, in secret; privately; in a manner that forbids disclosure.

Rose of Jericho, a plant growing on the plain of Jericho, the *Anastatica hierochuntica.*

ROSE, *pret.* of *rise.*

RO'SEAL, *a.* [L. *roseus.*] Like a rose in smell or color. *Elyot.*

RO'SEATE, *a.* [Fr. *rosat.*] Rosy; full of roses; as *roseate* bowers. *Pope.*
2. Blooming; of a rose color; as *roseate* beauty. *Boyle.*

RO'SEBAY, *n.* A plant, the *Nerium oleander.* The *dwarf rosebay* is the Rhododendron. *Lee.*

RO'SED, *a.* Crimsoned; flushed. *Shak.*

RO'SE-GALL, *n.* An excrescence on the dog-rose. *Dict.*

ROSE-MALLOW, *n.* A plant of the genus Alcea, larger than the common mallow. *Miller.*

RO'SEMARY, *n.* [L. *rosmarinus*, sea-rose; *rosa* and *marinus*. So in W. *rhos-mari*, and in Ir. *bath-ros*, sea-rose.]
A verticillate plant of the genus Rosmarinus, growing naturally in the southern part of France, Spain and Italy. It has a fragrant smell and a warm pungent bitterish taste. *Encyc.*

RO'SE-NOBLE, *n.* A ancient English gold coin, stamped with the figure of a rose, first struck in the reign of Edward III. and current at 6s. 8d. or according to Johnson, at 16 shillings.

RO'SE-QUARTZ, *n.* A subspecies of quartz, rose red or milk white.

RO'SE-ROOT, *n.* A plant of the genus Rhodiola.

RO'SET, *n.* [Fr. *rosette*, from *rose.*] A red color used by painters. *Peacham.*

RO'SE-WATER, *n.* Water tinctured with roses by distillation. *Encyc.*

RO'SE-WOOD, *n.* A plant or tree of the genus Aspalathus, growing in warm climates, from which is obtained the *oleum rhodii*, an agreeable perfume, used in scenting pomatum and liniments. *Encyc.*

ROSICRU'CIAN, *n.* [L. *ros*, dew, and *crux*, cross; *dew*, the most powerful dissolvent of gold, according to these fanatics, and *cross*, the emblem of light.]
The Rosicrucians were a sect or cabal of hermetical philosophers, or rather fanatics, who sprung up in Germany in the fourteenth century, and made great pretensions to science; and among other things, pretended to be masters of the secret of the philosopher's stone. *Encyc.*

ROSICRU'CIAN, *a.* Pertaining to the Rosicrucians, or their arts. *Hudibras.*

ROSIER, *n. ro'zhur.* [Fr.] A rose bush. [*Not in use.*] *Spenser.*

ROS'IN, *n. s* as *z.* [This is only a different orthography of *resin*; Ir. *roisin*; Fr. *resine*; L. *resina.* See *Resin.*]
1. Inspissated turpentine, a juice of the pine. *Garth.*
2. Any inspissated matter of vegetables that dissolves in spirit of wine. *Arbuthnot.*

ROS'IN, *v. t.* To rub with rosin. *Gay.*

RO'SINESS, *n. s* as *z.* The quality of being rosy, or of resembling the color of the rose. *Davenant.*

ROS'INY, *a.* Like rosin, or partaking of its qualities. *Temple.*

ROS'LAND, *n.* [W. *rhos*, peat, or a moor.] Heathy land; land full of ling; moorish or watery land.

ROS'PO, *n.* A fish of Mexico, perfectly round, without scales, and good for food. *Clavigero.*

ROSS, *n.* [Qu. G. *graus*, rubbish.] The rough scaly matter on the surface of the bark of certain trees. *New England.*

ROSS'EL, *n.* Light land. [*Not used in America.*] *Mortimer.*

ROSS'ELLY, *a.* Loose; light. [*Not in use.*] *Mortimer.*

ROS'SET, *n.* The large ternate bat.

ROS'SIGNOL, *n.* [Fr. *id.*; It. *rosignuolo.*] The nightingale. *Asiat. Res.*

ROS'TEL, *n.* [L. *rostellum*, *dim.* of *rostrum*, a beak.]
In *botany*, the descending plane part of the corcle or heart, in the first vegetation of a seed. *Martyn.*

ROS'TER, *n.* In *military affairs*, a plan or table by which the duty of officers is regulated. *Brit. Mil. Journal.*
In *Massachusetts*, a list of the officers of a division, brigade, regiment or battalion, containing under several heads their names, rank, the corps to which they belong, date of commission and place of abode. These are called division rosters, brigade rosters, regimental or battalion rosters.
The word is also used frequently instead of *register*, which comprehends a general list of all the officers of the state, from the commander in chief to the lowest in commission, under the same appropriate heads, with an additional column for noting the alterations which take place. *W. H. Sumner.*

ROS'TRAL, *a.* [from L. *rostrum*, beak.]
1. Resembling the beak of a ship. *Tatler.*
2. Pertaining to the beak.

ROS'TRATE, ROS'TRATED, } *a.* [L. *rostratus.*] In *botany*, beaked; having a process resembling the beak of a bird. *Martyn.*
2. Furnished or adorned with beaks; as *rostrated* galleys.

ROS'TRUM, *n.* [L.; W. *rhetgyr*, a snout, or *rhethren*, a pike.]
1. The beak or bill of a bird.
2. The beak or head of a ship.
3. In *ancient Rome*, a scaffold or elevated place in the forum, where orations, pleadings, funeral harangues, &c., were delivered.
4. The pipe which conveys the distilling liquor into its receiver, in the common alembic.
5. A crooked pair of scissors, used by surgeons for dilating wounds. *Coxe. Quincy.*

RO'SY, *a.* [from *rose.*] Resembling a rose in color or qualities; blooming; red; blushing; charming.

> While blooming youth and gay delight
> Sit on thy *rosy* cheeks confest. *Prior.*
>
> The *rosy* morn resigns her light. *Waller.*

2. Made in the form of a rose. *B. Jonson.*

ROT, *v.i.* [Sax. *rotian*; D. *rotten*; Sw. *rôta*; Dan. *raadner.*]
To lose the natural cohesion and organization of parts, as animal and vegetable substances; to be decomposed and resolved into its original component parts by the natural process, or the gradual operation of heat and air; to putrefy.

ROT, *v. t.* To make putrid; to cause to be decomposed by the natural operation of air and heat; to bring to corruption.

ROT, *n.* A fatal distemper incident to sheep, usually supposed to be owing to wet seasons and moist pastures. The immediate cause of the mortality of sheep, in this disease, is found to be a great number of small animals, called flukes, (*Fasciola,*) found in the liver, and supposed to be produced from eggs swallowed with their food. *Encyc.*
2. Putrefaction; putrid decay. *Philips.*
3. *Dry rot*, in timber, the decay of the wood without the access of water.

RO'TA, *n.* [L. *rota*, W. *rhod*, a wheel; allied to *rhedu*, to run. See *Rotary.*]
1. An ecclesiastical court of Rome, composed of twelve prelates, of whom one must be a German, another a Frenchman, and two Spaniards; the other eight are Italians. This is one of the most august tribunals in Rome, taking cognizance of all suits in the territory of the church by appeal, and of all matters beneficiary and patrimonial. *Encyc.*
2. In *English history*, a club of politicians, who, in the time of Charles I. contemplated an equal government by rotation. *Hudibras.*

RO'TALITE, *n.* A genus of fossil shells.

RO'TARY, *a.* [L. *rota*, a wheel, W. *rhod*, Sp. *rueda*, Port. *roda*, Arm. *rod*, Fr. *roue*, G. D. *rad*; Malayan, *rata*, a chariot; allied to W. *rhedu*, to run. So *car* is allied to L. *curro.*]
Turning, as a wheel on its axis; as *rotary* motion.

RO'TATE, *a.* In *botany*, wheel-shaped; monopetalous, spreading flat, without any tube, or expanding into a flat border, with scarcely any tube; as a *rotate* corol. *Martyn. Smith.*

RO'TATED, *a.* [L. *rotatus.*] Turned round, as a wheel.

ROTA'TION, *n.* [L. *rotatio*, from *roto*, to turn; *rota*, a wheel.]
1. The act of turning, as a wheel or solid body on its axis, as distinguished from the progressive motion of a body revolving round another body or a distant point. Thus the daily turning of the earth on its axis, is a *rotation*; its annual motion round the sun is a *revolution.*
2. Vicissitude of succession; the course by which officers or others leave their places at certain times and are succeeded by others; applied also to a change of crops.

RO'TATIVE, *a.* Turning, as a wheel; rotary. [*Little used.*]

ROTA'TO-PLANE, *a.* In *botany*, wheel-shaped and flat, without a tube; as a *rotato-plane* corol. *Lee.*

ROTA'TOR, *n.* [L.] That which gives a circular or rolling motion; a muscle producing a rolling motion. *Coxe.*

RO'TATORY, *a.* [from *rotator.*] Turning on an axis, as a wheel; rotary.
2. Going in a circle; following in succession; as *rotatory* assemblies. *Burke.*
[This word is often used, probably by mistake, for *rotary.* It may be regularly formed from *rotator*, but not with the exact sense in which it is used. With *rotator* for its original, it would signify *causing* rather than *being* in a circular motion. The true word is *rotary.*]

ROTE, *n.* [a contraction of *crowd*, W. *crwth*, Ir. *cruit.*] A kind of violin or harp. *Obs.*

ROTE, *n.* [L. *rota*, a wheel, whence Fr. *routine.*]
Properly, a round of words; frequent repetition of words or sounds, without attending to the signification, or to principles and rules; a practice that impresses words in the memory without an effort of the understanding, and without the aid of

rules. Thus children learn to speak by *rote;* they often repeat what they hear, till it becomes familiar to them. So we learn to sing by *rote,* as we hear notes repeated, and soon learn to repeat them ourselves.

ROTE, *v. t.* To fix in the memory by means of frequent repetition ourselves, or by hearing the repetition of others, without an effort of the understanding to comprehend what is repeated, and without the aid of rules or principles. [*Little used.*] *Shak.*

ROTE, *v. i.* To go out by rotation or succession. [*Little used.*] *Grey.*

ROTH'ER-BEASTS, *n.* [Sax. *hryther,* a quadruped.]
Cattle of the bovine genus; called in England *black cattle.* [*Not used in America.*] *Golding.*

ROTH'ER-NAILS, *n.* [corrupted from *rudder-nails.*]
Among shipwrights, nails with very full heads, used for fastening the rudder irons of ships. *Bailey.*

ROTH'OFFITE, *n.* A variety of grenate, brown or black, found in Sweden. It has a resemblance to melanite, another variety, but differs from it in having a small portion of alumin. *Cyc.*

RO'TOCO, *n.* An eastern weight of 5lbs. *Entick.*

ROTTEN, *a. rot'n.* [Sw. *rutten.*] Putrid; carious; decomposed by the natural process of decay; as a *rotten* plank.
2. Not firm or trusty; unsound; defective in principle; treacherous; deceitful.
3. Defective in substance; not sound or hard. *Knolles.*
4. Fetid; ill smelling. *Shak.*

ROT'TENNESS, *n.* State of being decayed or putrid; cariousness; putrefaction; unsoundness.

ROT'TEN-STONE, *n.* A soft stone or mineral, called also Tripoli, terra Tripolitana, from the country from which it was formerly brought. It is used in all sorts of finer grinding and polishing in the arts, and for cleaning furniture of metallic substances. The rotten-stone of Derbyshire, in England, is a Tripoli mixed with calcarious earth. *Nicholson. Encyc.*

ROTUND', *a.* [L. *rotundus,* probably formed on *rota,* a wheel, as *jocundus* on *jocus.*]
1. Round; circular; spherical. *Addison.*
2. In *botany,* circumscribed by one unbroken curve, or without angles; as a *rotund* leaf. *Linne.*

ROTUNDIFO'LIOUS, *a.* [L. *rotundus,* round, and *folium,* a leaf.] Having round leaves.

ROTUND'ITY, *n.* Roundness; sphericity; circularity; as the *rotundity* of a globe. *Bentley.*

ROTUND'O, *n.* [It. *rotondo,* round.] A round building; any building that is round both on the outside and inside. The most celebrated edifice of this kind is the Pantheon at Rome. *Encyc.*

ROUCOU, *n. roo'coo.* A substance used in dyeing; the same as anotta.

ROUGE, *a. roozh.* [Fr.] Red. *Davies.*

ROUGE, *n. roozh.* Red paint; a substance used for painting the cheeks.

ROUGE, *v. i.* [supra.] To paint the face, or rather the cheeks.

ROUGE, *v. t.* [supra.] To paint, or tinge with red paint.

ROUGH, *a. ruf.* [Sax. *hreog, hreoh, hrug, reoh, rug, ruh, href, hreof;* D. *ruig,* rough, shaggy, whence our *rug, rugged;* G. *rauh,* rough, and *rauch,* hoarse, L. *raucus,* It. *rauco;* Sw. *rugg,* entangled hair; *ruggig,* rugged, shaggy; Dan. *rog, rug,* rye; W. *crec* and *cryg,* rough, rugged, hoarse, curling, and *crecian,* to creak, to scream, Eng. *shriek; creg,* hoarse, from *cryg,* or the same word varied. *Cryg* is from *rhyg,* Eng. *rye,* that is, rough; [*crwca,* crooked, is probably from the same source;] Sax. *raca, hraca,* a cough; L. *ruga,* a wrinkle; W. *rhoçi,* to grunt or growl; *rhwc,* what is *rough,* irregular, a grunt; *rhwçiaw,* to grunt; *rhuwc,* a rug, a rough garment, an exterior coat; *rhuc,* a coat, husk or shell; *rhwnc,* a snoring, snorting, or rattling noise. The latter is probably from the same root, from roughness, and this is the Gr. ρεγχω, to snore; Arm. *rochat* or *dirochat,* to snore; *diroch,* snoring. The Welsh unites *rough* with *creak, shriek;* and *shrug* is formed on the root of L. *ruga,* a wrinkle, a *ridge.* See *Ridge.* The primary sense is to stretch or strain; but applied to roughness or wrinkling, it is to draw or contract, a straining together.]
1. Having inequalities, small ridges or points on the surface; not smooth or plane; as a *rough* board; a *rough* stone; *rough* cloth.
2. Stony; abounding with stones and stumps; as *rough* land; or simply with stones; as a *rough* road.
3. Not wrought or polished; as a *rough* diamond.
4. Thrown into huge waves; violently agitated; as a *rough* sea.
5. Tempestuous; stormy; boisterous; as *rough* weather.
6. Austere to the taste; harsh; as *rough* wine.
7. Harsh to the ear; grating; jarring; unharmonious; as *rough* sounds; *rough* numbers. *Pope.*
8. Rugged of temper; severe; austere; rude; not mild or courteous.

> A fiend, a fury, pitiless and *rough.* *Shak.*

9. Coarse in manners; rude.

> A surly boatman, *rough* as seas and wind. *Prior.*

10. Harsh; violent; not easy; as a *rough* remedy. *Clarendon.*
11. Harsh; severe; uncivil; as *rough* usage. *Locke.*
12. Hard featured; not delicate; as a *rough* visage. *Dryden.*
13. Terrible; dreadful.

> On the *rough* edge of battle, ere it join'd,
> Satan advanc'd. *Milton.*

14. Rugged; disordered in appearance; coarse.

> *Rough* from the tossing surge Ulysses moves. *Pope.*

15. Hairy; shaggy; covered with hairs, bristles and the like.

ROUGH-CAST, *v. t. ruf'-cast.* [*rough* and *cast.*]
1. To form in its first rudiments, without revision, correction and polish. *Dryden.*
2. To mold without nicety or elegance, or to form with asperities. *Cleaveland.*
3. To cover with a mixture of plaster and shells or pebbles; as, to *rough-cast* a building.

ROUGH-CAST, *n. ruf'-cast.* A rude model; the form of a thing in its first rudiments, unfinished. *Digby.*
2. A plaster with a mixture of shells or pebbles, used for covering buildings.

ROUGH-DRAUGHT, *n. ruf'-draft.* A draught in its rudiments; a draught not perfected; a sketch. *Dryden.*

ROUGH-DRAW, *v. t. ruf'-draw.* To draw or delineate coarsely. *Dryden.*

ROUGH-DRAWN, *pp. ruf'-drawn.* Coarsely drawn.

ROUGHEN, *v. t. ruf'n.* [from *rough.*] To make rough. *Swift.*

ROUGHEN, *v. i. ruf'n.* To grow or become rough. *Thomson.*

ROUGH-FOOTED, *a. ruf'-footed.* Fether-footed; as a *rough-footed* dove. *Sherwood.*

ROUGH-HEW, *v. t. ruf'-hew.* [*rough* and *hew.*]
1. To hew coarsely without smoothing; as, to *rough-hew* timber.
2. To give the first form or shape to a thing.

> There's a divinity that shapes our ends,
> *Rough-hew* them how we will. *Shak.*

ROUGH-HEWN, *pp.* or *a. ruf'-hewn.* Hewn coarsely without smoothing.
2. Rugged; unpolished; of coarse manners; rude.

> A *rough-hewn* seaman. *Bacon.*

3. Unpolished; not nicely finished. *Howell.*

ROUGHINGS, *n. ruf'ings.* Grass after mowing or reaping. [*Local.*]

ROUGHLY, *adv. ruf'ly.* With uneven surface; with asperities on the surface.
2. Harshly; uncivilly; rudely; as, to be treated *roughly.*
3. Severely; without tenderness; as, to blame too *roughly.* *Dryden.*
4. Austerely to the taste.
5. Boisterously; tempestuously.
6. Harshly to the ear.
7. Violently; not gently.

ROUGHNESS, *n. ruf'ness.* Unevenness of surface, occasioned by small prominences; asperity of surface; as the *roughness* of a board, of a floor, or of a rock.
2. Austereness to the taste; as the *roughness* of sloes. *Brown.*
3. Taste of astringency. *Spectator.*
4. Harshness to the ear; as the *roughness* of sounds. *Swift.*
5. Ruggedness of temper; harshness; austerity. *Addison.*
6. Coarseness of manners or behavior; rudeness.

> Severity breedeth fear; but *roughness* breedeth hate. *Bacon.*

7. Want of delicacy or refinement; as military *roughness.*
8. Severity; harshness or violence of discipline.
9. Violence of operation in medicines.
10. Unpolished or unfinished state; as the *roughness* of a gem or a draught.
11. Inelegance of dress or appearance.
12. Tempestuousness; boisterousness; as of winds or weather.
13. Violent agitation by wind; as the *roughness* of the sea in a storm.
14. Coarseness of features.

ROUGH-SHOD, *a. ruf'-shod.* Shod with shoes armed with points; as a *rough-shod* horse. [This word is not generally used in America. In New-England, instead of rough-shod, *calked* is used.]

ROUGHT, for *raught;* pret. of *reach.* *Obs.* *Shak.*

ROUGH-WORK, *v. t. ruf'-work.* [*rough* and *work.*]

To work over coarsely, without regard to nicety, smoothness or finish. *Moxon.*

ROUGH-WROUGHT, *a. ruf'-raut.* Wrought or done coarsely.

ROULEAU, *n. roolo'.* [Fr.] A little roll; a roll of guineas in paper. *Pope.*

ROUN, *v. i.* [G. *raunen;* Sax. *runian,* from *run, runa,* mystery; whence *runic.*]

To whisper. *Obs.* *Gower.*

ROUN, *v. t.* To address in a whisper. *Obs.* *Bret.*

ROUNCE, *n. rouns'.* The handle of a printing press.

ROUN'CEVAL, *n.* [from Sp. *Roncesvalles,* a town at the foot of the Pyrenees.]

A variety of pea, so called. *Tusser.*

ROUND, *a.* [Fr. *rond;* It. Sp. Port. *ronda,* a round; Arm. *roundt;* G. Dan. Sw. *rund;* D. *rond.* Qu. W. *crwn,* Ir. *cruin,* Arm. *cren.*]

1. Cylindrical; circular; spherical or globular. *Round* is applicable to a cylinder as well as to a globe or sphere. We say, the barrel of a musket is *round;* a ball is *round;* a circle is *round.*

2. Full; large; as a *round* sum or price. *Addison.*

3. Full; smooth; flowing; not defective or abrupt.

In his satires, Horace is quick, *round* and pleasant. *Peacham.*

His style, though *round* and comprehensive— *Fell.*

4. Plain; open; candid; fair.

Round dealing is the honor of man's nature. *Bacon.*

Let her be *round* with him. *Shak.*

5. Full; quick; brisk; as a *round* trot. *Addison.*

6. Full; plump; bold; positive; as a *round* assertion.

A round number, is a number that ends with a cypher, and may be divided by 10 without a remainder; a complete or full number. It is remarkable that the W. *cant,* a hundred, the L. *centum,* and Sax. *hund,* signify properly a circle, and this use of *round* may have originated in a like idea.

ROUND, *n.* A circle; a circular thing, or a circle in motion.

With *rounds* of waxen tapers on their heads. *Shak.*

Knit your hands, and beat the ground
In a light fantastic *round.* *Milton.*

2. Action or performance in a circle, or passing through a series of hands or things, and coming to the point of beginning; or the time of such action.

Women to cards may be compared; we play
A *round* or two; when used, we throw away. *Granville.*

The feast was serv'd; the bowl was crown'd;
To the king's pleasure went the mirthful *round.* *Prior.*

So we say, a *round* of labors or duties. We run the daily *round.* *Addison.*

3. Rotation in office; succession in vicissitude. *Holyday.*

4. A rundle; the step of a ladder.

All the *rounds* like Jacob's ladder rise. *Dryden.*

5. A walk performed by a guard or an officer round the rampart of a garrison, or among sentinels, to see that the sentinels are faithful and all things safe. Hence the officer and men who perform this duty are called the *rounds.* *Encyc.*

6. A dance; a song; a roundelay, or a species of fugue. *Davies.*

7. A general discharge of fire-arms by a body of troops, in which each soldier fires once. In volleys, it is usual for a company or regiment to fire three *rounds.*

A round of cartridges and balls, one cartridge to each man; as, to supply a regiment with a single *round* or with twelve *rounds* of cartridges.

ROUND, *adv.* On all sides.

Thine enemies shall cast a trench about thee, and compass thee *round.* Luke xix.

2. Circularly; in a circular form; as, a wheel turns *round.*

3. From one side or party to another; as, to come or turn *round.* Hence these expressions signify to *change sides* or *opinions.*

4. Not in a direct line; by a course longer than the direct course. The shortest course is not the best; let us go *round.*

All round, in common speech, denotes over the whole place, or in every direction.

Round about is tautological.

ROUND, *prep.* On every side of; as, the people stood *round* him; the sun sheds light *round* the earth. In this sense, *around* is much used, and *all* is often used to modify the word. They stood *all round* or *around* him.

2. About; in a circular course, or in all parts; as, to go *round* the city. He led his guest *round* his fields and garden. He wanders *round* the world.

3. Circularly; about; as, to wind a cable *round* the windlass.

To come or *get round one,* in popular language, is to gain advantage over one by flattery or deception; to circumvent.

ROUND, *v. t.* To make circular, spherical or cylindrical; as, to *round* a silver coin; to *round* the edges of any thing.

Worms with many feet, that *round* themselves into balls, are bred chiefly under logs of timber. *Bacon.*

2. To surround; to encircle; to encompass.

Th' inclusive verge
Of golden metal that must *round* my brow. *Shak.*

Our little life is *rounded* with a sleep. *Shak.*

3. To form to the arch or figure of the section of a circle.

The figures on our modern medals are raised and *rounded* to very great perfection. *Addison.*

4. To move about any thing; as, the sun, in polar regions, *rounds* the horizon. *Milton.*

5. To make full, smooth and flowing; as, to *round* periods in writing. *Swift.*

To round in, among seamen, to pull upon a slack rope, which passes through one or more blocks in a direction nearly horizontal. *Mar. Dict.*

ROUND, *v. i.* To grow or become round.

The queen, your mother, *rounds* apace. *Shak.*

2. To go round, as a guard.

—They nightly *rounding* walk. *Milton.*

To round to, in sailing, is to turn the head of the ship towards the wind.

ROUND, *v. i.* [a corruption of *roun;* Sax. *runian;* G. *raunen.*]

To whisper; as, to *round* in the ear. *Obs.* *Bacon.*

ROUND'ABOUT, *a.* [*round* and *about.*] Indirect; going round; loose.

Paraphrase is a *roundabout* way of translating. *Felton.*

2. Ample; extensive; as *roundabout* sense. *Locke.*

3. Encircling; encompassing. *Tatler.*

[In any sense, this word is inelegant.]

ROUND'ABOUT, *n.* A large strait coat.

ROUND'EL, ROUND'ELAY, ROUND'O, } *n.* [Fr. *rondelet,* from *rond,* round.]

1. A sort of ancient poem, consisting of thirteen verses, of which eight are in one kind of rhyme, and five in another. It is divided into couplets; at the end of the second and third of which, the beginning of the poem is repeated, and that, if possible, in an equivocal or punning sense. *Trevoux. Encyc.*

2. [Fr. *rondelle,* a little shield.] A round form or figure. [*Not used.*] *Bacon.*

ROUND'ER, *n.* [See *Rondure.*] Circumference; inclosure. [*Not in use.*] *Shak.*

ROUND'HEAD, *n.* [*round* and *head.*] A name formerly given to a puritan, from the practice which prevailed among the puritans of cropping the hair round. *Spectator.*

ROUND'HEADED, *a.* Having a round head or top. *Lowth.*

ROUND'HOUSE, *n.* A constable's prison; the prison to secure persons taken up by the night-watch, till they can be examined by a magistrate. *Encyc.*

2. In *a ship of war,* a certain necessary near the head, for the use of particular officers.

3. In *large merchantmen* and *ships of war,* a cabin or apartment in the after part of the quarter-deck, having the poop for its roof; sometimes called the coach. It is the master's lodging room. *Mar. Dict. Encyc.*

ROUND'ING, *ppr.* Making round or circular.

2. Making full, flowing and smooth.

ROUND'ING, *a.* Round or roundish; nearly round.

ROUND'ING, *n.* Among *seamen,* old ropes wound about the part of the cable which lies in the hawse, or athwart the stem, to prevent its chafing.

Rounding in, a pulling upon a slack rope, which passes through one or more blocks in a direction nearly horizontal. *Rounding up* is a pulling in like manner, when a tackle hangs in a perpendicular direction. *Mar. Dict.*

ROUND'ISH, *a.* Somewhat round; nearly round; as a *roundish* seed; a *roundish* figure. *Boyle.*

ROUND'ISHNESS, *n.* The state of being roundish.

ROUND'LET, *n.* A little circle. *Gregory.*

ROUND'LY, *adv.* In a round form or manner.

2. Openly; boldly; without reserve; peremptorily.

He affirms every thing *roundly*. *Addison.*

3. Plainly; fully. He gives them *roundly* to understand that their duty is submission.

4. Briskly; with speed.

When the mind has brought itself to attention, it will be able to cope with difficulties and master them, and then it may go on *roundly*. *Locke.*

5. Completely; to the purpose; vigorously; in earnest. *Shak. Davies.*

ROUND'NESS, *n.* The quality of being round, circular, spherical, globular or cylindrical; circularity; sphericity; cylindrical form; rotundity; as the *roundness* of the globe, of the orb of the sun, of a ball, of a bowl, &c. *Watts.*

2. Fullness; smoothness of flow; as the *roundness* of a period.

3. Openness; plainness; boldness; positiveness; as the *roundness* of an assertion.

ROUND'RIDǴE, *v. t.* [*round* and *ridge.*] In *tillage*, to form round ridges by plowing. *Edwards, W. Ind.*

ROUND'ROBIN, *n.* [Fr. *rond* and *ruban. Todd.*]

A written petition, memorial or remonstrance signed by names in a ring or circle. *Forbes.*

ROUNDS, *n. plu.* [See *Round, n.* No. 5.]

2. Round-top. [See *Top.*]

ROUSE, *v. t.* *rouz.* [This word, written also *arouse*, seems to belong to the family of *raise* or *rush*. See *Raise*. In Sax. *hrysan*, to shake and to rush; Goth. *hrisyan*, to shake.]

1. To wake from sleep or repose. Gen. xlix.

2. To excite to thought or action from a state of idleness, languor, stupidity or inattention. *Addison. Atterbury.*

3. To put into action; to agitate.

Blust'ring winds that *rous'd* the sea. *Milton.*

4. To drive a beast from his den or place of rest. *Denham. Pope.*

ROUSE, *v. i.* To awake from sleep or repose.

Morpheus *rouses* from his bed. *Pope.*

2. To be excited to thought or action from a state of indolence, sluggishness, languor or inattention.

ROUSE, *v. i.* In *seamen's language*, to pull together upon a cable, &c. without the assistance of tackles or other mechanical power. *Mar. Dict.*

ROUSE, *n.* *rouz.* [D. *roes*, a bumper; G. *rausch*, drunkenness; *rauschen*, to *rush*, to rustle.]

A full glass of liquor; a bumper in honor of a health. *Obs.* *Shak.*

ROUS'ED, *pp.* Awakened from sleep; excited to thought or action.

ROUS'ER, *n.* One that rouses or excites.

ROUS'ING, *ppr.* Awaking from sleep; exciting; calling into action.

2. *a.* Having power to awaken or excite.

3. Great; violent; as a *rousing* fire. [*Vulgar.*]

ROUT, *n.* [G. *rotte*, D. *rot*, Dan. *rode*, a set, gang, rabble; Dan. *rotter*, G. *rotten*, to combine together, to plot; D. *rotten*, to assemble, and to *rot*; W. *rhawter*, a crowd; Fr. *ruta*, a herd. Qu. from the root of *crowd*, or from breaking, bursting, noise.]

1. A rabble; a clamorous multitude; a tumultuous crowd; as a *rout* of people assembled.

The endless *routs* of wretched thralls. *Spenser.*

2. In *law*, a rout is where three persons or more meet to do an unlawful act upon a common quarrel, as forcibly to break down fences on a right claimed of common or of way, and make some advances towards it. *Blackstone.*

3. A select company; a party for gaming.

ROUT, *n.* [Fr. *deroute*; It. *rotta*, a breaking, a defeat, a rout; *rotto*, broken, defeated; *rottura*, a *rupture*; Sp. *rota*, *roto*. This is a corruption of the L. *ruptus*, from *rumpo*, to break. Class Rb.]

The breaking or defeat of an army or band of troops, or the disorder and confusion of troops thus defeated and put to flight. *Milton.*

ROUT, *v. t.* To break the ranks of troops and put them to flight in disorder; to defeat and throw into confusion.

The king's horse—*routed* and defeated the whole army. *Clarendon.*

ROUT, *v. i.* To assemble in a clamorous and tumultuous crowd. [*Not in use.*] *Bacon.*

ROUT, *n.* [Fr. *route*; Sp. *rauta*; Arm. *roud*; W. *rhawd*, a rout or way; *rhodiaw*, to walk about; Eng. *road*. See *Road*. It belongs to the family of *ride* and L. *gradior*; properly a going or passing.]

The course or way which is traveled or passed, or to be passed; a passing; a course; a march.

Wide through the furzy field their *rout* they take. *Gay.*

Rout and *road* are not synonymous. We say, to mend or repair a *road*, but not to mend a *rout*. We use *rout* for a course of passing, and not without reference to the passing of some person or body of men; but *rout* is not the road itself.

ROUT, *v. i.* [Sax. *hrutan.*] To snore. *Obs.* *Chaucer.*

ROUT, *v. t.* [for *root.*] To turn up the ground with the snout; to search. [*Not in use.*]

ROUTĪNE, *n.* *rootee'n.* [Fr. from L. *rota*, a wheel.]

1. A round of business, amusements or pleasure, daily or frequently pursued; particularly, a course of business or official duties, regularly or frequently returning.

2. Any regular habit or practice not accommodated to circumstances.

ROVE, *v. i.* [Dan. *röver*, to rob; Sw. *röfva*. This corresponds with the Sax. *reafian* and L. *rapio*, Fr. *ravir*. In Sw. *ströfva*, to *rove* or wander, appears to be formed on this root. In D. *rooven*, G. *rauben*, signify to *rob.*]

To wander; to ramble; to range; to go, move or pass without certain direction in any manner, by walking, riding, flying or otherwise.

For who has power to walk, has power to *rove*. *Arbuthnot.*

ROVE, *v. t.* To wander over; as *roving* a field; *roving* the town. This is an elliptical form of expression, for roving *over*, *through* or *about* the town.

ROVE, *v. t.* [Qu. *reeve.*] To draw a thread, string or cord through an eye or aperture.

RO'VER, *n.* A wanderer; one who rambles about.

2. A fickle or inconstant person.

3. A robber or pirate; a freebooter. [So *corsair* is from L. *cursus*, *curro*, to run.] *Bacon.*

At rovers, without any particular aim; at random; as shooting *at rovers*. *South. Addison.*

[I never heard this expression in the U. States.]

RO'VING, *ppr.* Rambling; wandering; passing a cord through an eye.

RŌW, *n.* [Sax. *rawa*; G. *reihe*; D. *rei*. The Welsh has *rhes*. It is a contracted word, and probably the elements are *Rg*; the same as of *rank*. The primary sense is probably to stretch, to reach. If the elements are *Rd*, it coincides with *rod*; Sw. *rad*, a row.]

A series of persons or things arranged in a continued line; a line; a rank; a file; as a *row* of trees; a *row* of gems or pearls; a *row* of houses or columns.

Where the bright Seraphim in burning *row*. *Milton.*

RŌW, *v. t.* [Sax. *rowan*, *reowan*; Sw. *ro*; Dan. *roer*; D. *roeijen*; the latter signifies to *row* and to guage; G. *ruder*, an oar; *rudern*, to row; Sax. *rother*, an oar; Gr. ερεττω, ερεσσω, to row; ερετμος, an oar. If the noun is the primary word, *ruder* and *rother*, an oar, may be from the root of *rod*, L. *radius*, or from the root of *rado*, to rub, grate, sweep. If the verb is the primary word, the sense is to sweep, to urge, drive, impel. Class Rd. See *Rudder.*]

1. To impel, as a boat or vessel along the surface of water by oars; as, to *row* a boat.

2. To transport by rowing; as, to *row* the captain ashore in his barge.

RŌW, *v. i.* To labor with the oar; as, to *row* well; to *row* with oars muffled.

RŌWABLE, *a.* Capable of being rowed or rowed upon. [*Not in use.*] *B. Jonson.*

RŌWED, *pp.* Driven by oars.

ROW'EL, *n.* [Old Fr. *rouelle*; G. *rädel*; Sp. *rodaja*, a small wheel, a rowel; *rueda*, a wheel, L. *rota*, W. *rhod*. The French *rouelle* is a diminutive of *roue*, contracted from *rota.*]

1. The little wheel of a spur, formed with sharp points.

2. Among *farriers*, a roll of hair or silk, used as an issue on horses, answering to a seton in surgery. *Encyc.*

3. A little flat ring or wheel of plate or iron on horses' bits. *Spenser.*

ROW'EL, *v. t.* To insert a rowel in; to pierce the skin and keep open the wound by a rowel. *Mortimer.*

ROW'EN, *n.* [Qu. Heb. רען, to be green, to thrive.]

Rowen is a field kept up till after Michaelmas, that the corn left on the ground may sprout into green. *Notes on Tusser.*

Turn your cows that give milk into your *rowens*, till snow comes. *Mortimer.*

2. In *New England*, the second growth of grass in a season. We never apply the

word to a field, nor to a growth of corn, after harvest, nor is the word ever used in the plural. The first growth of grass for mowing is called the *first crop*, and the second *rowen*.

RŌWER, *n.* One that rows or manages an oar in rowing.

RŌWING, *ppr.* Impelling, as a boat by oars.

ROWLEY-RAGG. [See *Ragg*.]

ROW-LOCK, *n.* That part of a boat's gunwale on which the oar rests in rowing. *Mar. Dict.*

ROW-PORT, *n.* A little square hole in the side of small vessels of war, near the surface of the water, for the use of an oar for rowing in a calm. *Mar. Dict.*

ROY'AL, *a.* [Fr. *royal*; It. *reale*; Sp. Port. *real*; contracted from L. *regalis*, from *rex*, king. See *Reck* and *Right*.]

1. Kingly; pertaining to a king; regal; as *royal* power or prerogative; a *royal* garden; *royal* domains; the *royal* family.
2. Becoming a king; magnificent; as *royal* state.
3. Noble; illustrious.

> How doth that *royal* merchant, good Antonio? *Shak.*

ROY'AL, *n.* A large kind of paper. It is used as a noun or an adjective.

2. Among *seamen*, a small sail spread immediately above the top-gallant-sail; sometimes termed the top-gallant-royal. *Mar. Dict.*
3. One of the shoots of a stag's head. *Bailey.*
4. In *artillery*, a small mortar.
5. In *England*, one of the soldiers of the first regiment of foot, called the *royals*, and supposed to be the oldest regular corps in Europe. *James.*

ROY'ALISM, *n.* Attachment to the principles or cause of royalty, or to a royal government. *Madison.*

ROY'ALIST, *n.* An adherent to a king, or one attached to a kingly government.

> Where Candish fought, the *royalists* prevail'd. *Waller.*

ROY'ALIZE, *v. t.* To make royal. *Shak.*

ROY'ALLY, *adv.* In a kingly manner; like a king; as becomes a king.

> His body shall be *royally* interr'd. *Dryden.*

ROY'ALTY, *n.* [Fr. *royauté*; It. *realtà*.]

1. Kingship; the character, state or office of a king.

> *Royalty* by birth was the sweetest way of majesty. *Holyday.*

2. *Royalties*, plu. emblems of royalty; regalia. *Milton.*
3. Rights of a king; prerogatives. *Encyc.*

ROYNE, *v. t.* [Fr. *rogner*.] To bite; to gnaw. [*Not in use.*] *Spenser.*

RŌYN'ISH, *a.* [Fr. *rogneux*, mangy; Sp. *roñoso*; It. *rognoso*.]

Mean; paltry; as the *roynish* clown. [*Not in use.*] *Shak.*

ROY'TELET, *n.* [Fr. *roitelet*, from *roi*, king.] A little king. [*Not in use.*] *Heylin.*

ROY'TISH, *a.* Wild; irregular. [*Not in use.*] *Beaum.*

RUB, *v. t.* [W. *rhwbiaw*; D. *wryven*; G. *reiben*, to rub, to grate, also to upbraid; *reibe*, a grater. Qu. L. *probrum*, *exprobro*; Gr. *τριβω*, to rub. We have the elements of the word in *scrape*, *scrub*, L. *scribo*, Gr. *γραφω*. Class Rb. No. 30.]

1. To move something along the surface of a body with pressure; as, to *rub* the face or arms with the hand; to *rub* the body with flannel. Vessels are scoured or cleaned by *rubbing* them.
2. To wipe; to clean; to scour; but *rub* is a generic term, applicable to friction for every purpose.
3. To touch so as to leave behind something which touches; to spread over; as to *rub* any thing with oil.
4. To polish; to retouch; with *over*.

> The whole business of our redemption is to *rub over* the defaced copy of the creation. *South.*

5. To obstruct by collision. [*Unusual.*] *Shak.*

In popular language, *rub* is used for teasing, fretting, upbraiding, reproaching or vexing with gibes or sarcasms.

To rub down, to clean by rubbing; to comb or curry, as a horse. *Dryden.*

To rub off, to clean any thing by rubbing; to separate by friction; as, to *rub off* rust.

To rub out, to erase; to obliterate; as, to *rub out* marks or letters.

2. To remove or separate by friction; as, to *rub out* a stain.

To rub upon, to touch hard. *Sidney.*

To rub up, to burnish; to polish; to clean.

2. To excite; to awaken; to rouse to action; as, to *rub up* the memory.

RUB, *v. i.* To move along the surface of a body with pressure; as, a wheel *rubs* against the gate-post.

2. To fret; to chafe; as, to *rub* upon a sore. *Dryden.*
3. To move or pass with difficulty; as, to *rub* through woods, as huntsmen; to *rub* through the world. *Chapman. L'Estrange.*

RUB, *n.* The act of rubbing; friction.

2. That which renders motion or progress difficult; collision; hinderance; obstruction.

> Now every *rub* is smoothed in our way. *Shak.*
>
> Upon this *rub* the English embassadors thought fit to demur. *Hayward.*
>
> All sort of *rubs* will be laid in the way. *Davenant.*

3. Inequality of ground that hinders the motion of a bowl. *Shak.*
4. Difficulty; cause of uneasiness; pinch.

> To sleep, perchance to dream; ay, there's the *rub*. *Shak.*

5. Sarcasm; joke; something grating to the feelings.

RUB, RUB'-STONE, *n.* [*rub* and *stone*.] A stone, usually some kind of sandstone, used to sharpen instruments; a whetstone.

RUBBAGE, RUBBIDGE, RUBBLE, for *rubbish*, vulgar and not used.

RUB'BER, *n.* One that rubs.

2. The instrument or thing used in rubbing or cleaning. *Swift.*
3. A coarse file, or the rough part of it. *Moxon.*
4. A whetstone; a rubstone.
5. In *gaming*, two games out of three; or the game that decides the contest; or a contest consisting of three games.

India rubber, elastic resin, or caoutchouc, a substance produced from the syringe tree of South America; a substance remarkably pliable and elastic. *Encyc.*

RUB'BISH, *n.* [from *rub*; properly, that which is rubbed off; but not now used in this limited sense.]

1. Fragments of buildings; broken or imperfect pieces of any structure; ruins.

> He saw the towns one half in *rubbish* lie. *Dryden.*

2. Waste or rejected matter; any thing worthless.
3. Mingled mass; confusion. *Arbuthnot.*

RUB'BLE-STONE, *n.* A stone, so called from its being rubbed and worn by water; graywacke. *Woodward.*

RU'BEFACIENT, *a.* [L. *rubefacio*, infra.] Making red.

RU'BEFACIENT, *n.* In *medicine*, a substance or external application which excites redness of the skin.

RU'BELLITE, *n.* [from L. *rubeus*, red.] A silicious mineral of a red color of various shades; the red shorl; siberite. It occurs in accumulated groups of a middle or large size, with straight tubular-like stria. In a red heat, it becomes snow-white and seems to phosphoresce. *Kirwan.*

> Rubellite is red tourmalin. *Ure. Cyc.*

RUBES'CENT, *a.* [L. *rubescens*, *rubesco*, from *rubeo*, to redden or to be red.]

Growing or becoming red; tending to a red color.

RU'BICAN, *a.* [Fr. from L. *rubeo*, to be red.]

Rubican color of a horse, is a bay, sorrel or black, with a light gray or white upon the flanks, but the gray or white not predominant there. *Far. Dict.*

RU'BICEL, *n.* [L. *rubeo*, to be red.] A gem or mineral, a variety of ruby of a reddish color, from Brazil. *Nicholson.*

RU'BICUND, *a.* [L. *rubicundus*.] Inclining to redness.

RU'BIED, *a.* Red as a ruby; as a *rubied* lip; *rubied* nectar. *Milton.*

RUBIF'IC, *a.* [L. *ruber* and *facio*.] Making red; as *rubific* rays.

RUBIFICA'TION, *n.* The act of making red. *Chimistry.*

RU'BIFORM, *a.* [L. *ruber*, red, and *form*.] Having the form of red; as, the *rubiform* rays of the sun are least refrangible. *Newton.*

RU'BIFY, *v. t.* [L. *ruber*, red, and *facio*, to make.] To make red. [*Little used.*] *Brown.*

RU'BIOUS, *a.* [L. *rubeus*.] Red; ruddy. [*Not in use.*] *Shak.*

RU'BLE, *n.* *roo'bl.* [Russ. from *rublyu*, to cut.]

A silver coin of Russia, of the value of about fifty seven cents, or two shillings and seven pence sterling; in Russia, a hundred kopecks; originally, the fourth part of a grivna or pound, which was cut into four equal parts. *Russ. Dict. Tooke.*

RU'BRIC, *n.* [Fr. *rubrique*; L. It. Sp. *rubrica*; from L. *rubeo*, to be red.]

1. In *the canon law*, a title or article in certain ancient law books; so called because written in red letters. *Encyc.*
2. Directions printed in prayer books.

The *rubric* and the rules relating to the liturgy are established by royal authority, as well as the liturgy itself. *Nelson.*

RU'BRIC, *v. t.* To adorn with red.

RU'BRIC, RU'BRICAL, } *a.* Red.

RU'BRICAL, *a.* Placed in rubrics.

RU'BRICATE, *v. t.* [L. *rubricatus.*] To mark or distinguish with red. *Herbert.*

RU'BRICATE, *a.* Marked with red. *Spelman.*

RU'BY, *n.* [Fr. *rubis;* Sp. *rubi;* Port. *rubi, rubim;* It. *rubino;* D. *robyn;* G. Dan. Sw. *rubin;* Ir. *id.;* from L. *rubeo,* to be red.]

1. A precious stone; a mineral of a carmine red color, sometimes verging to violet, or intermediate between carmine and hyacinth red; but its parts vary in color, and hence it is called sapphire ruby or orange red, and by some vermeille or rubicel. *Kirwan.*

There are two kinds of ruby, the oriental or corundum, and the spinelle. The latter is distinguishable from the former by its color and crystalization. *Phillips.*

The ruby is next in hardness and value to the diamond, and highly esteemed in jewelry.

2. Redness; red color. *Shak.*

3. Any thing red. *Milton.*

4. A blain; a blotch; a carbuncle. [The ruby is said to be the stone called by Pliny a *carbuncle.*]

Ruby of arsenic or *sulphur,* is the realgar, or red combination of arsenic and sulphur. *Encyc. Nicholson.*

Ruby of zink, is the red blend.

Rock ruby, the amethystizontes of the ancients, is the most valued species of garnet. *Encyc.*

RU'BY, *v. t.* To make red. *Pope.*

RU'BY, *a.* Of the color of the ruby; red; as *ruby* lips.

RUCK, *v. t.* [L. *rugo,* to wrinkle, to fold; *ruga,* a fold.]

1. To cower; to bend and set close. [*Not in use.*] *Gower.*

2. To wrinkle; as, to *ruck* up cloth or a garment.

[In this sense, the word is still used by the common people of New England.]

RUCK, *n.* A wrinkle; a fold; a plait.

RUCTA'TION, *n.* [L. *ructo,* to belch.] The act of belching wind from the stomach.

RUD, to make red, used by Spenser, is a different spelling of *red. Obs.* [See *Ruddy.*]

RUD, *n.* [Sax. *rude.* See *Red* and *Ruddy.*]

1. Redness; blush; also, red ocher.

2. The fish rudd.

RUDD, *n.* [probably from *red, ruddy.*] A fish of the genus Cyprinus, with a deep body like the bream, but thicker, a prominent back, and small head. The back is of an olive color; the sides and belly yellow, marked with red; the ventral and anal fins and tail of a deep red color. *Dict. N. Hist.*

RUD'DER, *n.* [G. *ruder,* an oar and a rudder; Sax. *rother,* an oar; D. *roer,* for *roeder;* Sw. *roder;* Dan. *roer.* See *Row.* The oar was the first rudder used by man, and is still the instrument of steering certain boats.]

1. In *navigation,* the instrument by which a ship is steered; that part of the helm which consists of a piece of timber, broad at the bottom, which enters the water and is attached to the stern-post by hinges, on which it turns. This timber is managed by means of the tiller or wheel. *Mar. Dict.*

2. That which guides or governs the course.

For rhyme the *rudder* is of verses. *Hudibras.*

3. A sieve. [*Local.* See *Riddle.*]

Rudder perch, a small fish with the upper part of the body brown, varied with large round spots of yellow, the belly and sides streaked with lines of white and yellow. This fish is said to follow the rudders of ships in the warm parts of the Atlantic. *Catesby. Pennant.*

RUD'DINESS, *n.* [from *ruddy.*] The state of being ruddy; redness, or rather a lively flesh color; that degree of redness which characterizes high health; applied chiefly to the complexion or color of the human skin; as the *ruddiness* of the cheeks or lips.

RUD'DLE, *n.* [W. *rhuzell;* from the root of *red, ruddy.*]

The name of a species of chalk or red earth, colored by iron. *Woodward.*

RUD'DLE-MAN, *n.* One who digs ruddle.

RUD'DOC, *n.* [Sax. *rudduc;* from the root of *red, ruddy.*]

A bird; otherwise called *red-breast.* *Carew.*

RUD'DY, *a.* [Sax. *rude, rudu, reod;* D. *rood;* G. *roth;* W. *rhuz;* Gr. ερυθρος; Sans. *rudhira,* blood. This seems to be a dialectical orthography of *red,* which see.]

1. Of a red color; of a lively flesh color, or the color of the human skin in high health. Thus we say, *ruddy* cheeks, *ruddy* lips, a *ruddy* face or skin, a *ruddy* youth; and in poetic language, *ruddy* fruit. But the word is chiefly applied to the human skin. *Dryden. Otway.*

2. Of a bright yellow color; as *ruddy* gold. [*Unusual.*] *Dryden.*

RUDE, *a.* [Fr. *rude;* It *rude* and *rozzo;* Sp. *rudo;* L. *rudis;* D. *ruw;* G. *roh,* raw, crude; Arm. *rust.* The sense is probably rough, broken, and this word may be allied to *raw* and *crude.* See Class Rd. No. 35. 38.]

1. Rough; uneven; rugged; unformed by art; as *rude* workmanship, that is, roughly finished; *rude* and unpolished stones. *Stillingfleet.*

2. Rough; of coarse manners; unpolished; uncivil; clownish; rustic; as a *rude* countryman; *rude* behavior; *rude* treatment; a *rude* attack.

Ruffian, let go that *rude* uncivil touch. *Shak.*

3. Violent; tumultuous; boisterous; turbulent; as *rude* winds; the *rude* agitation of the sea. *Boyle.*

4. Violent; fierce; impetuous; as the *rude* shock of armies.

5. Harsh; inclement; as the *rude* winter. *Waller.*

6. Ignorant; untaught; savage; barbarous; as the *rude* natives of America or of New Holland; the *rude* ancestors of the Greeks.

7. Raw; untaught; ignorant; not skilled or practiced; as *rude* in speech; *rude* in arms. *Wotton.*

8. Artless; inelegant; not polished; as a *rude* translation of Virgil. *Dryden.*

RU'DELY, *adv.* With roughness; as a mountain *rudely* formed.

2. Violently; fiercely; tumultuously. The door was *rudely* assaulted.

3. In a rude or uncivil manner; as, to be *rudely* accosted.

4. Without exactness or nicety; coarsely; as work *rudely* executed.

I that am *rudely* stamp'd, and want love's majesty
To strut before a wanton ambling nymph. *Shak.*

5. Unskillfully.

My muse, though *rudely,* has resign'd
Some faint resemblance of his godlike mind. *Dryden.*

6. Without elegance.

RU'DENESS, *n.* A rough broken state; unevenness; wildness; as the *rudeness* of a mountain, country or landscape.

2. Coarseness of manners; incivility; rusticity; vulgarity.

And kings the *rudeness* of their joy must bear. *Dryden.*

3. Ignorance; unskillfulness.

What he did amiss was rather through *rudeness* and want of judgment— *Hayward.*

4. Artlessness; coarseness; inelegance; as the *rudeness* of a painting or piece of sculpture.

5. Violence; impetuosity; as the *rudeness* of an attack or shock.

6. Violence; storminess; as the *rudeness* of winds or of the season.

RU'DENTURE, *n.* [Fr. from L. *rudens,* a rope.]

In *architecture,* the figure of a rope or staff, plain or carved, with which the flutings of columns are sometimes filled. *Bailey.*

RU'DERARY, *a.* [Low L. *ruderarius;* from the root of *rudis,* and indicating the primary sense of *rude* to be broken.] Belonging to rubbish. [*Not used.*] *Dict.*

RUDERA'TION, *n.* [L. *ruderatio,* from *rudero,* to pave with broken stones.]

The act of paving with pebbles or little stones. [*Not used.*] *Bailey.*

RU'DESBY, *n.* An uncivil turbulent fellow. [*Not in use.*] *Shak.*

RU'DIMENT, *n.* [Fr. from L. *rudimentum.* If connected with *erudio,* it denotes what is taught, and *erudio* may be connected with the Goth. *rodyan,* to speak, Sax. *rædan,* to read. But the real origin is not obvious. It may have been formed from some word in *Rd,* signifying to shoot or spring.]

1. A first principle or element; that which is to be first learnt; as the *rudiments* of learning or science. Articulate sounds are the *rudiments* of language; letters or characters are the *rudiments* of written language; the primary rules of any art or science are its *rudiments.* Hence instruction in the *rudiments* of any art or science, constitutes the beginning of education in that art or science.

2. The original of any thing in its first form. Thus in *botany,* the germen, ovary or seed-bud, is the *rudiment* of the fruit yet in embryo; and the seed is the *rudiment* of a new plant. *Martyn.*

Rudiment, in *natural history,* is also an imperfect organ; one which is never fully formed. Thus the flowers in the genus Pentstemon, have four stamens and a rudiment of a fifth, (a simple filament without an anther.)

God beholds the first imperfect *rudiments* of virtue in the soul. *Spectator.*

RU'DIMENT, *v. t.* To furnish with first principles or rules; to ground; to settle in first principles. *Gayton.*

RUDIMENT'AL, *a.* Initial; pertaining to rudiments, or consisting in first principles; as *rudimental* essays. *Spectator.*

RUE, *v. t. ru.* [Sax. *reowian, hreowian*; W. *rhuaw, rhuadu*; D. *rouwen*, G. *reuen*, to repent; Dan. Sw. *ruelse*, contrition. This is the L. *rudo*, to roar, to bray. Class Rd.]

To lament; to regret; to grieve for; as, to *rue* the commission of a crime; to *rue* the day.

Thy will
Chose freely what it now so justly *rues*. *Milton.*

RUE, *v. i.* To have compassion. [*Not in use.*] *Chaucer.*

RUE, *n.* Sorrow; repentance. [*Not in use.*] *Shak.*

RUE, *n. ru.* [Sax. *rude*; D. *ruit*; G. *raute*; Dan. *rude*; Gr. *ρυτη*; L. It. *ruta*; Sp. *ruda*; Fr. *rue*; Arm. *ry*; Ir. *ruith, raith*; Corn. *ryte*. *Rue* is a contracted word. Qu. from its bitter taste, *grating*, roughness.]

A plant of the genus Ruta, of several species. The common garden rue is medicinal, as a stimulant and detergent. *Encyc.*

RUEFUL, *a. ru'ful.* [*rue* and *full.*] Woful; mournful; sorrowful; to be lamented.

Spur them to *rueful* work. *Shak.*

2. Expressing sorrow.

He sigh'd and cast a *rueful* eye. *Dryden.*

RU'EFULLY, *adv.* Mournfully; sorrowfully. *More.*

RU'EFULNESS, *n.* Sorrowfulness; mournfulness.

RU'EING, *n.* Lamentation. *Smith.*

RUELLE, *n. ruel'.* [Fr. a narrow street, from *rue*, a street.]

A circle; a private circle or assembly at a private house. [*Not in use.*] *Dryden.*

RUFES'CENT, *a.* [L. *rufesco*, to grow red.] Reddish; tinged with red. *Ed. Encyc.*

RUFF, *n.* [Arm. *rouffenn*, a wrinkle; W. *rhevu*, to thicken.]

1. A piece of plaited linen worn by females around the neck. *Addison.*
2. Something puckered or plaited. *Pope.*
3. A small fish, a species of Perca. *Walton.*
4. A bird of the genus Tringa, with a tuft of fethers around the neck of the male, whence the name. The female is called *reeve*. *Ed. Encyc.*
5. A state of roughness. [Sax. *hreof.*] *Obs.* *Chapman.*
6. Pride; elevation; as princes in the *ruff* of all their glory. *L'Estrange.*
7. A particular species of pigeon.
8. At cards, the act of winning the trick by trumping the cards of another suit. [D. *troef, troeven.*]

RUFF, *v. t.* To ruffle; to disorder. *Spenser.*

2. To trump any other suit of cards at whist. [D. *troeven.*]

RUF'FIAN, *n.* [If this word signifies primarily a robber, it is from the root of *rob*, Sw. *röfva*, Dan. *röver*. In Scottish, *ruffie* is a worthless fellow. In It. *ruffiano* is a pimp, Sp. *rufian*, Port. *rufiam*; D. *roffiaan*, id.]

A boisterous, brutal fellow; a fellow ready for any desperate crime; a robber; a cut-throat; a murderer. *Addison.*

RUF'FIAN, *a.* Brutal; savagely boisterous; as *ruffian* rage. *Pope.*

RUF'FIAN, *v. i.* To play the ruffian; to rage; to raise tumult. *Shak.*

RUF'FIAN-LIKE, *a.* Like a ruffian; bold in crimes; violent; licentious. *Fulke.*

RUF'FLE, *v. t.* [Belgic, *ruyffelen*, to wrinkle. Chaucer has *riveling*, wrinkling, and Spelman cites *rifflura* or *rufflura* from Bracton, as signifying in law a breach or laceration of the skin, made by the stroke of a stick.]

1. Properly, to wrinkle; to draw or contract into wrinkles, open plaits or folds. *Addison.*
2. To disorder by disturbing a smooth surface; to make uneven by agitation; as, to *ruffle* the sea or a lake.

She smooth'd the *ruffl'd* seas. *Dryden.*

3. To discompose by disturbing a calm state of; to agitate; to disturb; as, to *ruffle* the mind; to *ruffle* the passions or the temper. It expresses less than *fret* and *vex*.
4. To throw into disorder or confusion.

—Where best
He might the *ruffl'd* foe invest. *Hudibras.*

5. To throw together in a disorderly manner.

I *ruffl'd* up fall'n leaves in heap. [*Unusual.*] *Chapman.*

6. To furnish with ruffles; as, to *ruffle* a shirt.

RUF'FLE, *v. i.* To grow rough or turbulent; as, the winds *ruffle*. *Shak.*

2. To play loosely; to flutter.

On his right shoulder his thick mane reclin'd,
Ruffles at speed and dances in the wind. *Dryden.*

3. To be rough; to jar; to be in contention.

They would *ruffle* with jurors. *Obs.* *Bacon.*

RUF'FLE, *n.* A strip of plaited cambric or other fine cloth attached to some border of a garment, as to the wristband or bosom. That at the bosom is sometimes called by the English, a *frill*.

2. Disturbance; agitation; commotion; as, to put the mind or temper in a *ruffle*.

RUF'FLE, RUFF, *n.* A particular beat or roll of the drum, used on certain occasions in military affairs, as a mark of respect. Lieutenant Generals have three *ruffles*, as they pass by the regiment, guard, &c. Major generals have two, brigadiers one, &c. *Encyc.*

RUF'FLE, RUFF, *v. t.* To beat the ruff or roll of the drum.

RUF'FLED, *pp.* Disturbed; agitated; furnished with ruffles.

RUF'FLER, *n.* A bully; a swaggerer. [*Not in use.*]

RUF'FLING, *ppr.* Disturbing; agitating; furnishing with ruffles.

RUF'FLING, *n.* Commotion; disturbance; agitation.

RUF'FLING, RUF'FING, *ppr.* Beating a roll of the drum.

RUF'FLING, RUF'FING, *n.* A particular beat or roll of the drum, used on certain occasions as a mark of respect.

RU'FOUS, *a.* [L. *rufus*; Sp. *rufo*; Port. *ruivo*; probably from the root of L. *rubeo.*] Reddish; of a reddish color, or rather of a yellowish red.

RUF'TER-HOOD, *n.* In *falconry*, a hood to be worn by a hawk when she is first drawn. *Bailey.*

RUG, *n.* [D. *ruig*, G. *rauch*, rough, hairy, shaggy; Sw. *rugg*, entangled hair; *ruggig*, rugged, shaggy. This coincides with Dan. *rug*, W. *rhyg*, rye, that is, *rough*; W. *rhug*, something abounding with points. In W. *brycan* is a *rug*, a clog, a brogue for the feet, a covering. This belongs to the great family of *rough*, L. *ruga*, *raucus.*]

1. A coarse nappy woolen cloth used for a bed cover, and in modern times particularly, for covering the carpet before a fire-place. This name was formerly given to a coarse kind of frieze used for winter garments, and it may be that the poor in some countries still wear it. But in America, I believe the name is applied only to a bed cover for ordinary beds, and to a covering before a fire-place.
2. A rough, woolly or shaggy dog.

RUG'GED, *a.* [from the root of *rug*, *rough*, which see.]

1. Rough; full of asperities on the surface; broken into sharp or irregular points or crags, or otherwise uneven; as a *rugged* mountain; a *rugged* road.
2. Uneven; not neat or regular.

His well proportion'd beard made rough and *rugged* *Shak.*

3. Rough in temper; harsh; hard; crabbed; austere. *South.*
4. Stormy; turbulent; tempestuous; as *rugged* weather; a *rugged* season.
5. Rough to the ear; harsh; grating; as a *rugged* verse in poetry; *rugged* prose. *Dryden.*
6. Sour; surly; frowning; wrinkled; as *rugged* looks.
7. Violent; rude; boisterous. *Hudibras.*
8. Rough; shaggy; as a *rugged* bear. *Fairfax.*
9. In *botany*, scabrous; rough with tubercles or stiff points; as a leaf or stem. *Martyn.*

RUG'GEDLY, *adv.* In a rough or rugged manner.

RUG'GEDNESS, *n.* The quality or state of being rugged; roughness; asperity of surface; as the *ruggedness* of land or of roads.

2. Roughness of temper; harshness; surliness.
3. Coarseness; rudeness of manners.
4. Storminess; boisterousness; as of a season.

RUG'-GOWNED, *a.* Wearing a coarse gown or rug. *Beaum.*

RUG'IN, *n.* A nappy cloth. [*Not used.*] *Wiseman.*

RU'GINE, *n.* [Fr.] A surgeon's rasp. *Sharp.*

RU'GOSE, RU'GOUS, *a.* [L. *rugosus*, from *ruga*, a wrinkle.] Wrinkled; full of wrinkles. *Wiseman.*

2. In *botany*, a rugose leaf is when the veins are more contracted than the disk, so that the latter rises into little inequalities, as in sage, primrose, cowslip, &c. *Martyn. Smith.*

RUGOS'ITY, *n.* A state of being wrinkled. [*Little used.*] *Smith.*

RU'IN, *n.* [Fr. *ruine*, from L. Sp. *ruina*; It. *ruina* and *rovina*; from L. *ruo*, to fall, to rush down; W. *rhewin*, a sudden glide, slip or fall, ruin; *rhew*, something slippery or smooth, ice, frost; *rheu*, to move or be active; *rhêb*, a running off; *rhêbyz*, a destroyer. Perhaps the latter words are of another family.]

1. Destruction; fall; overthrow; defeat; that change of any thing which destroys it, or entirely defeats its object, or unfits it for use; as the *ruin* of a house; the *ruin* of a ship or an army; the *ruin* of a constitution of government; the *ruin* of health; the *ruin* of commerce; the *ruin* of public or private happiness; the *ruin* of a project.

2. Mischief; bane; that which destroys.

The errors of young men are the *ruin* of business. *Bacon.*

3. *Ruin*, more generally *ruins*, the remains of a decayed or demolished city, house, fortress, or any work of art or other thing; as the *ruins* of Balbec, Palmyra or Persepolis; the *ruins* of a wall; a castle in *ruins*.

The labor of a day will not build up a virtuous habit on the *ruins* of an old and vicious character. *Buckminster.*

4. The decayed or enfeebled remains of a natural object; as, the venerable old man presents a great mind in *ruins*.

5. The cause of destruction.

They were the *ruin* of him and of all Israel. 2 Chron. xxviii.

RU'IN, *v. t.* [Fr. *ruiner.*] To demolish; to pull down, burn, or otherwise destroy; as, to *ruin* a city or an edifice.

2. To subvert; to destroy; as, to *ruin* a state or government.

3. To destroy; to bring to an end; as, to *ruin* commerce or manufactures.

4. To destroy in any manner; as, to *ruin* health or happiness; to *ruin* reputation.

5. To counteract; to defeat; as, to *ruin* a plan or project.

6. To deprive of felicity or fortune.

By thee rais'd I *ruin* all my foes. *Milton.*
Grace with a nod, and *ruin* with a frown. *Dryden.*

7. To impoverish; as, to be *ruined* by speculation.

The eyes of other people are the eyes that *ruin* us. *Franklin.*

8. To bring to everlasting misery; as, to *ruin* the soul.

RU'IN, *v. i.* To fall into ruins. *Milton.*

2. To run to ruin; to fall into decay or be dilapidated.

Though he his house of polish'd marble build,
Yet shall it *ruin* like the moth's frail cell. *Sandys.*

3. To be reduced; to be brought to poverty or misery.

If we are idle, and disturb the industrious in their business, we shall *ruin* the faster. *Locke.*

[*Note.* This intransitive use of the verb is now unusual.]

RU'INATE, *v. t.* To demolish; to subvert; to destroy; to reduce to poverty. [*This word is ill formed and happily is become obsolete.*]

RUINA'TION, *n.* Subversion; overthrow; demolition. [*Inelegant and obsolete.*]

RU'INED, *pp.* Demolished; destroyed; subverted; reduced to poverty; undone.

RU'INER, *n.* One that ruins or destroys. *Chapman.*

RU'INIFORM, *a.* [L. *ruina* and *form.*] Having the appearance of ruins, or the ruins of houses. Certain minerals are said to be *ruiniform*.

RU'INING, *ppr.* Demolishing; subverting; destroying; reducing to poverty; bringing to endless misery.

RU'INOUS, *a.* [L. *ruinosus*; Fr. *ruineux.*]

1. Fallen to ruin; entirely decayed; demolished; dilapidated; as an edifice, bridge or wall in a *ruinous* state.

2. Destructive; baneful; pernicious; bringing or tending to bring certain ruin. Who can describe the *ruinous* practice of intemperance?

3. Composed of ruins; consisting in ruins; as a *ruinous* heap. Is. xvii.

RU'INOUSLY, *adv.* In a ruinous manner; destructively.

RU'INOUSNESS, *n.* A ruinous state or quality.

RULE, *n.* [W. *rheol*; Arm. *rool*; Sax. *regol*, *reogol*; Sw. Dan. G. D. *regel*; Fr. *regle*; Sp. *regla*; Port. *regoa*, *regra*; It. *regola*; L. *regula*, from *rego*, to govern, that is, to stretch, strain or make straight. I suppose the Welsh *rheol* to be a contracted word.]

1. Government; sway; empire; control; supreme command or authority.

A wise servant shall have *rule* over a son that causeth shame. Prov. xvii.

And his stern *rule* the groaning land obey'd. *Pope.*

2. That which is established as a principle, standard or directory; that by which any thing is to be adjusted or regulated, or to which it is to be conformed; that which is settled by authority or custom for guidance and direction. Thus a statute or law is a *rule* of civil conduct; a canon is a *rule* of ecclesiastical government; the precept or command of a father is a *rule* of action or obedience to children; precedents in law are *rules* of decision to judges; maxims and customs furnish *rules* for regulating our social opinions and manners. The laws of God are *rules* for directing us in life, paramount to all others.

A *rule* which you do not apply, is no *rule* at all. *J. M. Mason.*

3. An instrument by which lines are drawn.

A judicious artist will use his eye, but he will trust only to his *rule*. *South.*

4. Established mode or course of proceeding prescribed in private life. Every man should have some fixed *rules* for managing his own affairs.

5. In *literature*, a maxim, canon or precept to be observed in any art or science. *Encyc.*

6. In *monasteries*, *corporations* or *societies*, a law or regulation to be observed by the society and its particular members.

7. In *courts*, rules are the determinations and orders of court, to be observed by its officers in conducting the business of the court.

8. In *arithmetic* and *algebra*, a determinate mode prescribed for performing any operation and producing a certain result.

9. In *grammar*, an established form of construction in a particular class of words; or the expression of that form in words. Thus it is a *rule* in English, that *s* or *es*, added to a noun in the singular number, forms the plural of that noun; but *man* forms its plural *men*, and is an exception to the *rule*.

Rule of three, is that rule of arithmetic which directs, when three terms are given, how to find a fourth, which shall have the same ratio to the third term, as the second has to the first.

RULE, *v. t.* To govern; to control the will and actions of others, either by arbitrary power and authority, or by established laws. The emperors of the east *rule* their subjects without the restraints of a constitution. In limited governments, men are *ruled* by known laws.

If a man know not how to *rule* his own house, how shall he take care of the church of God? 1 Tim. iii.

2. To govern the movements of things; to conduct; to manage; to control. That God *rules* the world he has created, is a fundamental article of belief.

3. To manage; to conduct, in almost any manner.

4. To settle as by a rule.

That's a *ruled* case with the schoolmen. *Atterbury.*

5. To mark with lines by a ruler; as, to *rule* a blank book.

6. To establish by decree or decision; to determine; as a court.

RULE, *v. i.* To have power or command; to exercise supreme authority.

By me princes *rule*. Prov. viii.

It is often followed by *over*.

They shall *rule over* their oppressors. Is. xiv.

We subdue and *rule over* all other creatures. *Ray.*

RU'LED, *pp.* Governed; controlled; conducted; managed; established by decision.

RU'LER, *n.* One that governs, whether emperor, king, pope or governor; any one that exercises supreme power over others.

2. One that makes or executes laws in a limited or free government. Thus legislators and magistrates are called *rulers*.

3. A rule; an instrument of wood or metal with straight edges or sides, by which lines are drawn on paper, parchment or other substance. When a ruler has the lines of chords, tangents, sines, &c. it is called a *plane scale*. *Encyc.*

RU'LING, *ppr.* Governing; controlling the will and actions of intelligent beings, or the movements of other physical bodies.

2. Marking by a ruler.

3. Deciding; determining.

4. *a.* Predominant; chief; controlling; as a *ruling* passion.

RU'LY, *a.* [from *rule.*] Orderly; easily restrained. [*Not in use.*] [See *Unruly.*]

RUM, *n.* Spirit distilled from cane juice; or the scummings of the juice from the boiling house, or from the treacle or melasses which drains from sugar, or from dunder, the lees of former distillations. *Edwards, W. Ind.*

In the United States, rum is distilled from melasses only.

2. A low cant word for a country parson. *Swift.*

RUM, *a.* Old fashioned; queer. [*Not in use.*]

RUM'BLE, *v. i.* [D. *rommelen*; G. *rummeln*; Dan. *rumler*; It. *rombare*. If *Rm* are the radical letters, this word may be referred to the Ch. Syr. Heb. Eth. רעם raam, Class Rm. No. 11. With a prefix, *grumble*, Gr. *βρεμω*, L. *fremo*, Ir. *cruim*, thunder, G. *brummen*, D. *brommen*, *bremmen*, &c.; Sw. *råma*, to bellow.]

To make a low, heavy, continued sound; as thunder *rumbles* at a distance, but when near, its sound is sharp and rattling. A heavy carriage *rumbles* on the pavement.

RUM'BLER, *n.* The person or thing that rumbles.

RUM'BLING, *ppr.* Making a low, heavy continued sound; as *rumbling* thunder. A *rumbling* noise is a low, heavy, continued noise.

RUM'BLING, *n.* A low, heavy, continued sound. Jer. xlvii.

RUM'BUD, *n.* A grog blossom; the popular name of a redness occasioned by the detestable practice of excessive drinking. Rumbuds usually appear first on the nose, and gradually extend over the face. *Rush.*

RU'MINANT, *a.* [Fr. from L. *rumino.*] Chewing the cud; having the property of chewing again what has been swallowed; as *ruminant* animals. *Ray.*

RU'MINANT, *n.* An animal that chews the cud. *Ruminants* are four footed, hairy and viviparous. *Encyc. Ray. Derham.*

RU'MINATE, *v. i.* [Fr. *ruminer*; L. *rumino*, from *rumen*, the cud; W. *rhum*, that swells out.]

1. To chew the cud; to chew again what has been slightly chewed and swallowed. Oxen, sheep, deer, goats, camels, hares and squirrels *ruminate* in fact; other animals, as moles, bees, crickets, beetles, crabs, &c. only appear to *ruminate*. *Peyer. Encyc.*

The only animals endowed with the genuine faculty of rumination, are the *Ruminantia*, or cloven-hoofed quadrupeds, (*Pecora*, Linne;) but the hare, although its stomach is differently organized, is an occasional and partial ruminant. *Ed. Encyc.*

2. To muse; to meditate; to think again and again; to ponder. It is natural to *ruminate* on misfortunes.

He practices a slow meditation, and *ruminates* on the subject. *Watts.*

RU'MINATE, *v. t.* To chew over again.

2. To muse on; to meditate over and over again.

Mad with desire, she *ruminates* her sin. *Dryden.*

RU'MINATED, *pp.* Chewed again; mused on.

RU'MINATING, *ppr.* Chewing the cud; musing.

RUMINA'TION, *n.* [L. *ruminatio.*] The act of chewing the cud.

2. The power or property of chewing the cud.

Rumination is given to animals, to enable them at once to lay up a great store of food, and afterwards to chew it. *Arbuthnot.*

3. A musing or continued thinking on a subject; deliberate meditation or reflection.

Retiring full of *rumination* sad. *Thomson.*

RU'MINATOR, *n.* One that ruminates or muses on any subject; one that pauses to deliberate and consider. *Cotgrave.*

RUM'MAĠE, *n.* A searching carefully by looking into every corner and by tumbling over things.

RUM'MAĠE, *v. t.* [Qu. L. *rimor*, or Fr. *remuer.*]

To search narrowly by looking into every corner and turning over or removing goods or other things.

Our greedy seamen *rummage* every hold. *Dryden.*

RUM'MAĠE, *v. i.* To search a place narrowly by looking among things.

I have often *rummaged* for old books in Little-Britain and Duck-Lane. *Swift.*

RUM'MAĠED, *pp.* Searched in every corner.

RUM'MAĠING, *ppr.* Searching in every corner.

RUM'MER, *n.* [D. *roemer*, a wine glass, from *roemen*, to vaunt, brag or praise.]

A glass or drinking cup. [*Not in use.*] *Philips.*

RU'MOR, *n.* [L.] Flying or popular report; a current story passing from one person to another, without any known authority for the truth of it.

Rumor next and chance
And tumult and confusion all imbroil'd. *Milton.*

When ye shall hear of wars and *rumors* of wars, be ye not troubled. Mark xiii.

2. Report of a fact; a story well authorized.

This *rumor* of him went forth throughout all Judea. Luke vii.

3. Fame; reported celebrity.

Great is the *rumor* of this dreadful knight. *Shak.*

RU'MOR, *v. t.* To report; to tell or circulate a report.

'Twas *rumor'd*
My father 'scap'd from out the citadel. *Dryden.*

RU'MORED, *pp.* Told among the people; reported.

RU'MORER, *n.* A reporter; a teller of news. *Shak.*

RU'MORING, *ppr.* Reporting; telling news.

RUMP, *n.* [G. *rumpf*; Sw. *rumpa*; Dan. *rumpe* or *rompe.*]

1. The end of the back bone of an animal with the parts adjacent. Among the Jews, the *rump* was esteemed the most delicate part of the animal. *Encyc.*

2. The buttocks. *Hudibras.*

RUM'PLE, *v. t.* [D. *rompelen*, to rumple; Sax. *hrympelle*, a fold; probably connected with *crumple*, W. *crwm*, *crom*, crooked, *crymu*, to bend.]

To wrinkle; to make uneven; to form into irregular inequalities; as, to *rumple* an apron or a cravat. *Swift.*

RUM'PLE, *n.* A fold or plait. *Dryden.*

RUM'PLED, *pp.* Formed into irregular wrinkles or folds.

RUMP'LESS, *a.* Destitute of a tail; as a *rumpless* fowl. *Lawrence.*

RUMP'LING, *ppr.* Making uneven.

RUN, *v. i.* pret. *ran* or *run*; pp. *run.* [Sax. *rennan*; and with a transposition of letters, *ærnan*, *arnian*, *yrnan*; Goth. *rinnan*; D. *rennen*; G. *rennen*, *rinnen*; Dan. *rinder*; Sw. *rånna*. The Welsh has *rhin*, a running, a channel, hence the *Rhine*.]

1. To move or pass in almost any manner, as on the feet or on wheels. Men and other animals *run* on their feet; carriages *run* on wheels, and wheels *run* on their axletrees.

2. To move or pass on the feet with celerity or rapidity, by leaps or long quick steps; as, men and quadrupeds *run* when in haste.

3. To use the legs in moving; to step; as, children *run* alone or *run* about. *Locke.*

4. To move in a hurry.

The priest and people *run* about. *B. Jonson.*

5. To proceed along the surface; to extend; to spread; as, the fire *runs* over a field or forest.

The fire *ran* along upon the ground. Ex. ix.

6. To rush with violence; as, a ship *runs* against a rock; or one ship *runs* against another.

7. To move or pass on the water; to sail; as, ships *run* regularly between New York and Liverpool. Before a storm, *run* into a harbor, or under the lee of the land. The ship has *run* ten knots an hour.

8. To contend in a race; as, men or horses *run* for a prize.

9. To flee for escape. When Gen. Wolfe was dying, an officer standing by him exclaimed, see how they *run*. Who *run*? said the dying hero. The enemy, said the officer. Then I die happy, said the general.

10. To depart privately; to steal away.

My conscience will serve me to *run* from this Jew, my master. *Shak.*

11. To flow in any manner, slowly or rapidly; to move or pass; as a fluid. Rivers *run* to the ocean or to lakes. The Connecticut *runs* on sand, and its water is remarkably pure. The tide *runs* two or three miles an hour. Tears *run* down the cheeks.

12. To emit; to let flow.

I command that the conduit *run* nothing but claret. *Shak.*

Rivers *run* potable gold. *Milton.*

But this form of expression is elliptical, *with* being omitted; "rivers *run with* potable gold."

13. To be liquid or fluid.

As wax dissolves, as ice begins to *run*— *Addison.*

14. To be fusible; to melt.

Sussex iron ores *run* freely in the fire. *Woodward.*

15. To fuse; to melt.

Your iron must not burn in the fire, that is, *run* or melt, for then it will be brittle. *Moxon.*

16. To turn; as, a wheel *runs* on an axis or on a pivot.

17. To pass; to proceed; as, to *run* through a course of business; to *run* through life; to *run* in a circle or a line; to *run* through all degrees of promotion.

18. To flow, as words, language or periods. The lines *run* smoothly.

19. To pass, as time.
As fast as our time *runs*, we should be glad in most part of our lives that it *ran* much faster. *Addison.*
20. To have a legal course; to be attached to; to have legal effect.
Customs *run* only upon our goods imported or exported, and that but once for all; whereas interest *runs* as well upon our ships as goods, and must be yearly paid. *Childs.*
21. To have a course or direction.
Where the generally allowed practice *runs* counter to it. *Locke.*
Little is the wisdom, where the flight
So *runs* against all reason. *Shak.*
22. To pass in thought, speech or practice; as, to *run* through a series of arguments; to *run* from one topic to another.
Virgil, in his first Georgic, has *run* into a set of precepts foreign to his subject. *Addison.*
23. To be mentioned cursorily or in few words.
The whole *runs* on short, like articles in an account. *Arbuthnot.*
24. To have a continued tenor or course. The conversation *ran* on the affairs of the Greeks.
The king's ordinary style *runneth*, "our sovereign lord the king." *Sanderson.*
25. To be in motion; to speak incessantly. Her tongue *runs* continually.
26. To be busied; to dwell.
When we desire any thing, our minds *run* wholly on the good circumstances of it; when it is obtained, our minds *run* wholly on the bad ones. *Swift.*
27. To be popularly known.
Men gave them their own names, by which they *run* a great while in Rome. *Temple.*
28. To be received; to have reception, success or continuance. The pamphlet *runs* well among a certain class of people.
29. To proceed in succession.
She saw with joy the line immortal *run*,
Each sire impress'd and glaring in his son. *Pope.*
30. To pass from one state or condition to another; as, to *run* into confusion or error; to *run* distracted. *Addison.*
31. To proceed in a train of conduct.
You should *run* a certain course. *Shak.*
32. To be in force.
The owner hath incurred the forfeiture of eight years profits of his lands, before he cometh to the knowledge of the process that *runneth* against him. *Bacon.*
33. To be generally received.
He was not ignorant what report *run* of himself. *Knolles.*
34. To be carried; to extend; to rise; as, debates *run* high.
In popish countries, the power of the clergy *runs* higher. *Ayliffe.*
35. To have a track or course.
Searching the ulcer with my probe, the sinus *run* up above the orifice. *Wiseman.*
36. To extend; to lie in continued length. Veins of silver *run* in different directions.
37. To have a certain direction. The line *runs* east and west.
38. To pass in an orbit of any figure. The planets *run* their periodical courses. The comets do not *run* lawless through the regions of space.
39. To tend in growth or progress. Pride is apt to *run* into a contempt of others.
40. To grow exuberantly. Young persons of 10 or 12 years old, soon *run* up to men and women.
If the richness of the ground cause turneps to *run* to leaves, treading down the leaves will help their rooting. *Mortimer.*
41. To discharge pus or other matter; as, an ulcer *runs*.
42. To reach; to extend to the remembrance of; as time out of mind, the memory of which *runneth* not to the contrary.
43. To continue in time, before it becomes due and payable; as, a note *runs* thirty days; a note of six months has ninety days to *run*.
44. To continue in effect, force or operation.
The statute may be prevented from *running*—by the act of the creditor.
Hopkinson. Wheaton's Rep.
45. To press with numerous demands of payment; as, to *run* upon a bank.
46. To pass or fall into fault, vice or misfortune; as, to *run* into vice; to *run* into evil practices; to *run* into debt; to *run* into mistakes.
47. To fall or pass by gradual changes; to make a transition; as, colors *run* one into another.
48. To have a general tendency.
Temperate climates *run* into moderate governments. *Swift.*
49. To proceed as on a ground or principle. *Obs.*
50. To pass or proceed in conduct or management.
Tarquin, *running* into all the methods of tyranny, after a cruel reign was expelled. *Swift.*
51. To creep; to move by creeping or crawling; as, serpents *run* on the ground.
52. To slide; as, a sled or sleigh *runs* on the snow.
53. To dart; to shoot; as a meteor in the sky.
54. To fly; to move in the air; as, the clouds *run* from N. E. to S. W.
55. In *Scripture*, to pursue or practice the duties of religion.
Ye did *run* well; who did hinder you? Gal. v.
56. In *elections*, to have interest or favor; to be supported by votes. The candidate will not *run*, or he will *run* well.
To run after, to pursue or follow.
2. To search for; to endeavor to find or obtain; as, to *run after* similes. *Locke.*
To run at, to attack with the horns, as a bull.
To run away, to flee; to escape.
To run away with, to hurry without deliberation. *Locke.*
2. To convey away; or to assist in escape or elopement.
To run in, to enter; to step in.
To run into, to enter; as, to *run into* danger.
To run in trust, to run in debt; to get credit. [*Not in use.*]
To run in with, to close; to comply; to agree with. [*Unusual.*] *Baker.*
2. To make towards; to near; to sail close to; as, to *run in with* the land; *a seaman's phrase.*
To run down a coast, to sail along it.
To run on, to be continued. Their accounts had *run on* for a year or two without a settlement.
2. To talk incessantly.
3. To continue a course. *Drayton.*
4. To press with jokes or ridicule; to abuse with sarcasms; to bear hard on.
To run over, to overflow; as, a cup *runs over;* or the liquor *runs over.*
To run out, to come to an end; to expire; as, a lease *runs out* at Michaelmas.
2. To spread exuberantly; as, insectile animals *run out* into legs. *Hammond.*
3. To expatiate; as, to *run out* into beautiful digressions. He *runs out* in praise of Milton. *Addison.*
4. To be wasted or exhausted; as, an estate managed without economy, will soon *run out.*
5. To become poor by extravagance.
And had her stock been less, no doubt
She must have long ago *run out.* *Dryden.*
To run up, to rise; to swell; to amount. Accounts of goods credited *run up* very fast.
RUN, *v. t.* To drive or push; *in a general sense.* Hence to *run* a sword through the body, is to stab or pierce it.
2. To drive; to force.
A talkative person *runs* himself upon great inconveniences, by blabbing out his own or others' secrets. *Ray.*
Others accustomed to retired speculations, *run* natural philosophy into metaphysical notions. *Locke.*
3. To cause to be driven.
They *ran* the ship aground. Acts xxvii.
4. To melt; to fuse.
The purest gold must be *run* and washed. *Felton.*
5. To incur; to encounter; to run the risk or hazard of losing one's property. To *run the danger*, is a phrase not now in use.
6. To venture; to hazard.
He would himself be in the Highlands to receive them, and *run* his fortune with them. *Clarendon.*
7. To smuggle; to import or export without paying the duties required by law; as, to *run* goods.
8. To pursue in thought; to carry in contemplation; as, to *run* the world back to its first original. *South.*
I would gladly understand the formation of a soul, and *run* it up to its *punctum saliens.* *Collier.*
9. To push; to thrust; as, to *run* the hand into the pocket or the bosom; to *run* a nail into the foot.
10. To ascertain and mark by metes and bounds; as, to *run* a line between towns or states.
11. To cause to ply; to maintain in running or passing; as, to *run* a stage coach from London to Bristol; to *run* a line of packets from New Haven to New York.
12. To cause to pass; as, to *run* a rope through a block.
13. To found; to shape, form or make in a mold; to cast; as, to *run* buttons or balls.
To run down, in hunting, to chase to weariness; as, to *run down* a stag.
2. In *navigation*, to *run down a vessel*, is to run against her, end on, and sink her. *Mar. Dict.*
3. To crush; to overthrow; to overbear.
Religion is *run down* by the license of these times. *Berkley.*
To run hard, to press with jokes, sarcasm or ridicule.
2. To urge or press importunately.

To run over, to recount in a cursory manner; to narrate hastily; as, to *run over* the particulars of a story.

2. To consider cursorily.

3. To pass the eye over hastily.

To run out, to thrust or push out; to extend.

2. To waste; to exhaust; as, to *run out* an estate.

To run through, to expend; to waste; as, to *run through* an estate.

To run up, to increase; to enlarge by additions. A man who takes goods on credit, is apt to *run up* his account to a large sum before he is aware of it.

2. To thrust up, as any thing long and slender.

RUN, *n.* The act of running.

2. Course; motion; as the *run* of humor. *Bacon.*

3. Flow; as a *run* of verses to please the ear. *Broome.*

4. Course; process; continued series; as the *run* of events.

5. Way; will; uncontrolled course.

Our family must have their *run*. *Arbuthnot.*

6. General reception; continued success.

It is impossible for detached papers to have a general *run* or long continuance, if not diversified with humor. *Addison.*

7. Modish or popular clamor; as a violent *run* against university education. *Swift.*

8. A general or uncommon pressure on a bank or treasury for payment of its notes.

9. The aftmost part of a ship's bottom. *Mar. Dict.*

10. The distance sailed by a ship; as, we had a good *run*.

11. A voyage; also, an agreement among sailors to work a passage from one place to another. *Mar. Dict.*

12. A pair of mill-stones. A mill has two, four or six *runs* of stones.

13. Prevalence; as, a disease, opinion or fashion has its *run*.

14. In the middle and southern states of America, a small stream; a brook.

In the long run, [*at the long run*, not so generally used,] signifies the whole process or course of things taken together; in the final result; in the conclusion or end.

The run of mankind, the generality of people.

RUN'AGATE, *n.* [Fr. *runagat.*] A fugitive; an apostate; a rebel; a vagabond. *Sidney. Shak.*

RUN'AWAY, *n.* [*run* and *away.*] One that flies from danger or restraint; one that deserts lawful service; a fugitive. *Shak.*

RUNCA'TION, *n.* [L. *runcatio.*] A weeding. [*Not in use.*] *Evelyn.*

RUN'CINATE, *a.* [L. *runcina*, a saw.] In *botany*, a *runcinate* leaf is a sort of pinnatifid leaf, with the lobes convex before and straight behind, like the teeth of a double saw, as in the dandelion. *Martyn.*

Lion toothed; cut into several transverse acute segments, pointing backwards. *Smith.*

RUND'LE, *n.* [from *round*, G. *rund.*] A round; a step of a ladder. *Duppa.*

2. Something put round an axis; a peritrochium; as a cylinder with a *rundle* about it. *Wilkins.*

RUND'LET, } *n.* [from *round.*] A small barrel of no certain dimensions. It may contain from 3 to 20 gallons. *Encyc.*
RUN'LET, }

RUNE, *n.* [See *Runic.*] The runic letter or character. *Temple.*

RU'NER, *n.* A bard or learned man among the ancient Goths. [See *Runic.*] *Temple.*

RU'NES, *n. plu.* Gothic poetry or rhymes. *Temple.*

RUNG, *pret.* and *pp.* of *ring*.

RUNG, *n.* A floor timber in a ship, whence the end is called a *rung-head*; more properly a *floor-head*. *Mar. Dict.*

RU'NIC, *a.* [W. *rhin*, Ir. *run*, Goth. *runa*, Sax. *run*, a secret or mystery, a letter.]

An epithet applied to the language and letters of the ancient Goths. [In Russ. *chronoyu* is to conceal.]

RUN'NEL, *n.* [from *run.*] A rivulet or small brook. [*Not in use.*] *Fairfax.*

RUN'NER, *n.* [from *run.*] One that runs; that which runs.

2. A racer. *Dryden.*

3. A messenger. *Swift.*

4. A shooting sprig.

In every root there will be one *runner*, with little buds on it. *Mortimer.*

5. One of the stones of a mill. *Ib.*

6. A bird. *Ainsworth.*

7. A thick rope used to increase the mechanical power of a tackle. *Mar. Dict.*

RUN'NET, *n.* [D. *runzel*, from *runnen*, *ronnen*, to curdle; G. *rinnen*, to curdle, and to *run* or flow; Sax. *gerunnen*, coagulated. It is sometimes written *rennet.*]

The concreted milk found in the stomachs of calves or other sucking quadrupeds. The same name is given to a liquor prepared by steeping the inner membrane of a calf's stomach in water, and to the membrane itself. This is used for coagulating milk, or converting it into curd in the making of cheese. *Encyc.*

RUN'NING, *ppr.* Moving or going with rapidity; flowing.

2. *a.* Kept for the race; as a *running* horse. *Law.*

3. In succession; without any intervening day, year, &c.; as, to visit two days *running*; to sow land two years *running*.

4. Discharging pus or other matter; as a *running* sore.

RUN'NING, *n.* The act of running, or passing with speed.

2. That which runs or flows; as the first *running* of a still or of cider at the mill.

3. The discharge of an ulcer or other sore.

RUN'NING-FIGHT, *n.* A battle in which one party flees and the other pursues, but the party fleeing keeps up the contest.

RUNNING-RIG'GING, *n.* That part of a ship's rigging or ropes which passes through blocks, &c.; in distinction from *standing-rigging*.

RUNNING-TITLE, *n.* In *printing*, the title of a book that is continued from page to page on the upper margin.

RUN'NION, *n.* [Fr. *rogner*, to cut, pare or shred.] A paltry scurvy wretch. *Shak.*

RUNT, *n.* [In D. *rund* is a bull or cow; in Scot. *runt* is the trunk of a tree, a hardened stem or stalk of a plant, an old withered woman It may be from D. *runnen*, to contract. See *Runnet.*]

Any animal small below the natural or usual size of the species.

Of tame pigeons, are croppers, carriers and *runts*. *Walton.*

RUPEE', *n.* [Pers. روپیه ropah, silver, and *ropiah* is a thick round piece of money in the Mogul's dominions, value 24 stivers. *Castle.*]

A silver coin of the East Indies, of the value of 2s. 4d. or 2s. 6d. sterling; about 52 or 56 cents.

RUP'TION, *n.* [L. *ruptio*, *rumpo*, to break.] Breach; a break or bursting open. *Wiseman.*

RUP'TURE, *n.* [Fr. from L. *ruptus*, *rumpo*, to break.]

1. The act of breaking or bursting; the state of being broken or violently parted; as the *rupture* of the skin; the *rupture* of a vessel or fiber. *Arbuthnot.*

2. Hernia; a preternatural protrusion of the contents of the abdomen.

3. Breach of peace or concord, either between individuals or nations; between nations, open hostility or war. We say, the parties or nations have come to an open *rupture*.

He knew that policy would disincline Napoleon from a *rupture* with his family. *E. Everett.*

RUP'TURE, *v. t.* To break; to burst; to part by violence; as, to *rupture* a blood vessel.

RUP'TURE, *v. i.* To suffer a breach or disruption.

RUP'TURED, *pp.* Broken; burst.

RUP'TURE-WORT, *n.* A plant of the genus Herniaria, and another of the genus Linum. *Fam. of Plants.*

RUP'TURING, *ppr.* Breaking; bursting.

RU'RAL, *a.* [Fr. from L. *ruralis*, from *rus*, the country.]

Pertaining to the country, as distinguished from a city or town; suiting the country, or resembling it; as *rural* scenes; a *rural* prospect; a *rural* situation; *rural* music. *Sidney. Thomson.*

RU'RALIST, *n.* One that leads a rural life. *Coventry.*

RU'RALLY, *adv.* As in the country. *Wakefield.*

RU'RALNESS, *n.* The quality of being rural. *Dict.*

RURIC'OLIST, *n.* [L. *ruricola*; *rus*, the country, and *colo*, to inhabit.]

An inhabitant of the country. [*Not in use.*] *Dict.*

RURIG'ENOUS, *a.* [L. *rus*, the country, and *gignor*, to be born.]

Born in the country. [*Not in use.*] *Dict.*

RUSE, *n.* [Fr.] Artifice; trick; stratagem; wile; fraud; deceit. [*Not English.*] *Ray.*

RUSH, *n.* [Sax. *rics* or *risc*; probably L. *ruscus*. The Swedish corresponding word is *säf*, the Hebrew סוף, usually rendered sea-weed, and applied to the Arabic gulf, Deut. i. 1. Numb. xxi. 14. This correspondence deserves notice, as illustrating certain passages in the Scriptures.]

1. A plant of the genus Juncus, of many species. The pith of the rush is used in some places for wicks to lamps and rush lights. *Encyc.*

2. Any thing proverbially worthless or of trivial value.

John Bull's friendship is not worth a *rush*. *Arbuthnot.*

RUSH, *v. i.* [Sax. *reosan, hreosan* or *ræsan*; Sw. *rusa*; G. *rauschen*; D. *ruischen*; Gr. ῥοθεω. The G. has also *brausen*, the Dutch *bruisschen*, to rush or roar; Dan. *brusen*, to rush. The Welsh has *brysiaw* and *crysiaw*, to hurry, to hasten; both from *rhys*, a rushing; *rhysiaw*, to rush. We have *rustle* and *brustle* probably from the same source. The Welsh *brysiaw* seems to be the English *press*. See Class Rd. No. 5. 9. &c.]

1. To move or drive forward with impetuosity, violence and tumultuous rapidity; as, armies *rush* to battle; waters *rush* down a precipice; winds *rush* through the forest. We ought never to *rush* into company, much less into a religious assembly.

2. To enter with undue eagerness, or without due deliberation and preparation; as, to *rush* into business or speculation; to *rush* into the ministry. *Sprat.*

RUSH, *v. t.* To push forward with violence. [*Not used.*]

RUSH, *n.* A driving forward with eagerness and haste; a violent motion or course; as a *rush* of troops; a *rush* of winds.

RUSH-CANDLE, *n.* A small blinking taper made by stripping a rush, except one small strip of the bark which holds the pith together, and dipping it in tallow. *Johnson. Milton.*

RUSH'ED, *a.* Abounding with rushes. *Warton.*

RUSH'ER, *n.* One who rushes forward. *Whitlock.*

2. One who formerly strewed rushes on the floor at dances. *B. Jonson.*

RUSH'INESS, *n.* [from *rushy.*] The state of abounding with rushes. *Scott.*

RUSH'ING, *ppr.* Moving forward with impetuosity.

RUSH'ING, *n.* A violent driving of any thing; rapid or tumultuous course. Is. xvii.

RUSH-LIGHT, *n.* The light of a rush-candle; a small feeble light.

2. A rush-candle. *Encyc.*

RUSH'-LIKE, *a.* Resembling a rush; weak.

RUSH'Y, *a.* Abounding with rushes. *Mortimer.*

2. Made of rushes. *Tickel.*

My *rushy* couch and frugal fare. *Goldsmith.*

RUSK, *n.* A kind of light cake.

2. Hard bread for stores. *Raleigh.*

RUS'MA, *n.* A brown and light iron substance, with half as much quicklime steeped in water, of which the Turkish women make their psilothron to take off their hair. *Grew.*

RUSS, *a. roos.* [Sw. *ryss.*] Pertaining to the Russ or Russians. [The native word is *Russ.* We have *Russia* from the south of Europe.]

RUSS, *n. roos.* The language of the Russ or Russians.

RUS'SET, *a.* [Fr. *roux, rousse*, red; It. *rosso*; Sp. *roso, roxo*; L. *russus.* See *Red* and *Ruddy.*]

1. Of a reddish brown color; as a *russet* mantle.

Our summer such a *russet* livery wears. *Dryden.*

2. Coarse; homespun; rustic. *Shak.*

RUS'SET, *n.* A country dress. *Dryden.*

RUS'SET, RUS'SETING, } *n.* A kind of apple of a russet color and rough skin. [I have never known a pear so called in America, though it seems that in England pears have this name.]

RUSSIAN, *a. roo'shan.* Pertaining to Russia.

RUSSIAN, *n. roo'shan.* A native of Russia.

RUST, *n.* [Sax. *rust*; D. *roest*; G. Sw. *rost*; Dan. *rust*; W. *rhwd*; Gr. ερυσιβη; probably from its color, and allied to *ruddy, red*, as L. *rubigo* is from *rubeo.* See *Ruddy.*]

1. The oxyd of a metal; a substance composed of oxygen combined with a metal, and forming a rough coat on its surface. All metals except gold are liable to *rust.*

2. Loss of power by inactivity, as metals lose their brightness and smoothness when not used.

3. Any foul matter contracted; as *rust* on corn or salted meat.

4. Foul extraneous matter; as sacred truths cleared from the *rust* of human mixtures.

5. A disease in grain, a kind of dust which gathers on the stalks and leaves. *Ed. Encyc.*

RUST, *v. i.* [Sax. *rustian*; W. *rhydu.*] To contract rust; to be oxydized and contract a roughness on the surface.

Our armors now may *rust.* *Dryden.*

2. To degenerate in idleness; to become dull by inaction.

Must I *rust* in Egypt? *Dryden.*

3. To gather dust or extraneous matter.

RUST, *v. t.* To cause to contract rust.

Keep up your bright swords, for the dew will *rust* them. *Shak.*

2. To impair by time and inactivity.

RUST'ED, *pp.* Affected with rust.

RUST'IC, RUST'ICAL, } *a.* [L. *rusticus*, from *rus*, the country.]

1. Pertaining to the country; rural; as the *rustic* gods of antiquity. *Encyc.*

2. Rude; unpolished; rough; awkward; as *rustic* manners or behavior.

3. Coarse; plain; simple; as *rustic* entertainment; *rustic* dress.

4. Simple; artless; unadorned. *Pope.*

Rustic work, in a building, is when the stones, &c. in the face of it, are hacked or pecked so as to be rough. *Encyc.*

RUST'IC, *n.* An inhabitant of the country; a clown.

RUST'ICALLY, *adv.* Rudely; coarsely; without refinement or elegance. *Dryden.*

RUST'ICALNESS, *n.* The quality of being rustical; rudeness; coarseness; want of refinement.

RUST'ICATE, *v. i.* [L. *rusticor*, from *rus.*] To dwell or reside in the country. *Pope.*

RUST'ICATE, *v. t.* To compel to reside in the country; to banish from a town or college for a time. *Spectator.*

RUST'ICATED, *pp.* Compelled to reside in the country.

RUST'ICATING, *ppr.* Compelling to reside in the country.

RUSTICA'TION, *n.* Residence in the country.

2. In *universities* and *colleges*, the punishment of a student for some offense, by compelling him to leave the institution and reside for a time in the country.

RUSTIC'ITY, *n.* [L. *rusticitas*; Fr. *rusticité.*]

The qualities of a countryman; rustic manners; rudeness; coarseness; simplicity; artlessness. *Addison. Woodward.*

RUST'ILY, *adv.* In a rusty state. *Sidney.*

RUST'INESS, *n.* [from *rusty.*] The state of being rusty.

RUST'ING, *ppr.* Contracting rust; causing to rust.

RUSTLE, *v. i. rus'l.* [Sax. *hristlan*; G. *rasseln*; Sw. *rossla*, to rattle.]

To make a quick succession of small sounds, like the rubbing of silk cloth or dry leaves; as a *rustling* silk; *rustling* leaves or trees; *rustling* wings. *Milton.*

He is coming; I hear the straw *rustle.* *Shak.*

RUS'TLING, *ppr.* Making the sound of silk cloth when rubbed.

RUS'TLING, *n.* A quick succession of small sounds, as a brushing among dry leaves or straw.

RUST'Y, *a.* Covered or affected with rust; as a *rusty* knife or sword.

2. Dull; impaired by inaction or neglect of use. *Shak.*

3. Surly; morose. *Guardian.*

4. Covered with foul or extraneous matter.

RUT, *n.* [Fr. *rut*; Arm. *rut*, the verb, *rudal, rutein*; probably allied to G. *reizen*, to excite, or Sw. *ryta*, to bellow.] The copulation of deer.

RUT, *v. i.* To lust, as deer.

RUT, *n.* [It. *rotaia*, from L. *rota*, a wheel.] The track of a wheel.

RUTA BAGA, *n.* The Swedish turnep.

RUTH, *n.* [from *rue.*] Mercy; pity; tenderness; sorrow for the misery of another. *Obs.* *Fairfax.*

2. Misery; sorrow. *Obs.* *Spenser.*

RUTHENUS, *n.* A fish of the genus Accipenser. *Encyc.*

RUTHFUL, *a.* Rueful; woful; sorrowful. *Obs.* *Carew.*

2. Merciful. *Obs.*

RUTHFULLY, *adv.* Wofully; sadly. *Obs.* *Knolles.*

2. Sorrowfully; mournfully. *Obs.* *Spenser.*

RUTHLESS, *a.* Cruel; pitiless; barbarous; insensible to the miseries of others.

Their rage the hostile bands restrain,
All but the *ruthless* monarch of the main. *Pope.*

RUTHLESSLY, *adv.* Without pity; cruelly; barbarously.

RUTHLESSNESS, *n.* Want of compassion; insensibility to the distresses of others.

RU'TIL, RU'TILE, } *n.* Sphene, an oxyd of titanium, of a dark red color, or of a light or brownish red. It occurs massive, disseminated, membranous, and in crystals. *Cyc.*

RU'TILANT, *a.* [L. *rutilans, rutilo*, to shine; perhaps from the root of *red, ruddy.*]

Shining. *Evelyn.*

RU'TILATE, *v. i.* [L. *rutilo.*] To shine; to emit rays of light. [*Not used.*] *Ure.*

RUT'TER, *n.* [G. *reiter*, D. *ruiter*, a *rider.* See *Ride.*]

A horseman or trooper. [*Not in use.*]

RUT'TERKIN, *n.* A word of contempt; an old crafty fox or beguiler. [*Not in use.*]

RUT'TIER, *n.* [Fr. *routier*, from *route.*] Direction of the road or course at sea; an old traveler acquainted with roads; an old soldier. [*Not in use.*] *Cotgrave.*

RUT'TISH, *a.* [from *rut.*] Lustful; libidinous. *Shak.*

RUT'TLE, for *rattle*, not much used. *Burnet.*

RY'AL, *n.* A coin. [See *Rial.*]

RY'DER, *n.* A clause added to a bill in parliament. [See *Rider* and *Ride.*]

RȲE, *n.* [Sax. *ryge*; D. *rogge*; G. *rocken*; Dan. *rog* or *rug*; Sw. *råg* or *rog*; W. *rhyg.* This word is the English *rough.*]

1. An esculent grain of the genus Secale, of a quality inferior to wheat, but a species of grain easily cultivated, and constituting a large portion of bread stuff.

2. A disease in a hawk. *Ainsworth.*

RȲE-GRASS, *n.* A species of strong grass, of the genus Hordeum. *Encyc.*

RY'OT, *n.* In Hindoostan, a renter of land by a lease which is considered as perpetual, and at a rate fixed by ancient surveys and valuations. *Asiat. Res. Encyc.*

S.

S, the nineteenth letter of the English Alphabet, is a sibilant articulation, and numbered among the semi-vowels. It represents the hissing made by driving the breath between the end of the tongue and the roof of the mouth, just above the upper teeth. It has two uses; one to express a mere hissing, as in *sabbath, sack, sin, this, thus*; the other a vocal hissing, precisely like that of *z*, as in *muse, wise*, pronounced *muze, wize.* It generally has its hissing sound at the beginning of all proper English words, but in the middle and end of words, its sound is to be known only by usage. In a few words it is silent, as in *isle* and *viscount.*

In abbreviations, S. stands for *societas*, society, or *socius*, fellow; as F. R. S. fellow of the Royal Society. In medical prescriptions, S. A. signifies *secundem artem*, according to the rules of art.

In the notes of the ancients, S. stands for *Sextus*; SP. for *Spurius*; S. C. for *senatus consultum*; S. P. Q. R. for *senatus populusque Romanus*; S. S. S. for *stratum super stratum*, one layer above another alternately; S. V. B. E. E. Q. V. for *si vales, bene est, ego quoque valeo.*

As a numeral, S. denoted *seven.* In the Italian music, S. signifies *solo.* In books of navigation and in common usage, S. stands for south; S. E. for south-east; S. W. for south-west; S. S. E. for south south-east; S. S. W. for south south-west, &c.

SAB'AOTH, *n.* [Heb. צבאות armies, from צבא to assemble, to fight. The primary sense is to drive, to urge or crowd.]

Armies; a word used, Rom. ix. 29., James v. 4, "the Lord of *Sabaoth.*"

SABBATA'RIAN, *n.* [from *sabbath.*] One who observes the seventh day of the week as the sabbath, instead of the first. A sect of baptists are called *sabbatarians.* They maintain that the Jewish sabbath has not been abrogated. *Encyc.*

SABBATA'RIAN, *a.* Pertaining to those who keep Saturday, or the seventh day of the week, as the sabbath. *Mountagu.*

SABBATA'RIANISM, *n.* The tenets of sabbatarians. *Bp. Ward.*

SAB'BATH, *n.* [Heb. שבת to cease, to rest, as a noun, cessation, rest, L. *sabbatum*; Ar. سبت.]

1. The day which God appointed to be observed by the Jews as a day of rest from all secular labor or employments, and to be kept holy and consecrated to his service and worship. This was originally the seventh day of the week, the day on which God rested from the work of creation; and this day is still observed by the Jews and some christians, as the sabbath. But the christian church very early begun and still continue to observe the first day of the week, in commemoration of the resurrection of Christ on that day, by which the work of redemption was completed. Hence it is often called the *Lord's day.* The heathen nations in the north of Europe dedicated this day to the *sun*, and hence their christian descendants continue to call the day *Sunday.* But in the United States, christians have to a great extent discarded the heathen name, and adopted the Jewish name *sabbath.*

2. Intermission of pain or sorrow; time of rest.

> Peaceful sleep out the *sabbath* of the tomb. *Pope.*

3. The sabbatical year among the Israelites. Lev. xxv.

SAB'BATH-BREAKER, *n.* [*sabbath* and *break.*]

One who profanes the sabbath by violating the laws of God or man which enjoin the religious observance of that day.

SAB'BATH-BREAKING, *n.* A profanation of the sabbath by violating the injunction of the fourth commandment, or the municipal laws of a state which require the observance of that day as holy time. All unnecessary secular labor, visiting, traveling, sports, amusements and the like are considered as *sabbath-breaking.*

SAB'BATHLESS, *a.* Without intermission of labor. *Bacon.*

SABBAT'IC, **SABBAT'ICAL**, *a.* [Fr. *sabbatique*; L. *sabbaticus.*] Pertaining to the sabbath.

2. Resembling the sabbath; enjoying or bringing an intermission of labor. *Gregory.*

Sabbatical year, in the Jewish economy, was every *seventh* year, in which the Israelites were commanded to suffer their fields and vineyards to *rest*, or lie without tillage, and the year next following every seventh sabbatical year in succession, that is, every fiftieth year, was the jubilee, which was also a year of rest to the lands, and a year of redemption or release. Lev. xxv.

SAB'BATISM, *n.* Rest; intermission of labor.

SABEAN. [See *Sabian.*]

SA'BEISM, *n.* The same as *Sabianism.* *D'Anville.*

SABEL'LIAN, *a.* Pertaining to the heresy of Sabellius.

SABEL'LIAN, *n.* A follower of Sabellius, a philosopher of Egypt in the third century, who openly taught that there is one person only in the Godhead, and that the Word and Holy Spirit are only virtues, emanations or functions of the Deity. *Encyc.*

SABEL'LIANISM, *n.* The doctrines or tenets of Sabellius. *Barrow.*

SA'BER, **SA'BRE**, *n.* [Fr. *sabre*; Arm. *sabrenn*, *sciabla*; Sp. *sable*; D. *sabel*; G. *säbel.* Qu. Ar. سب sabba, to cut.]

A sword or cimitar with a broad and heavy blade, thick at the back, and a little falcated or hooked at the point; a faulchion. *Encyc.*

SA'BER, *v. t.* To strike, cut or kill with a saber. A small party was surprised at night and almost every man *sabered.*

SA'BIAN, **SABE'AN**, *a.* Pertaining to Saba, in Arabia, celebrated for producing aromatic plants.

SA'BIAN, *a.* [Heb. צבא an army or host.] The Sabian worship or religion consisted in the worship of the sun and other heavenly bodies. *Encyc.*

SA'BIAN, *n.* A worshiper of the sun.

SA'BIANISM, *n.* That species of idolatry which consisted in worshiping the sun, moon and stars. This idolatry existed in Chaldea or Persia at an early period of the world, and was propagated by the inhabitants who migrated westward into Europe, and continued among our ancestors till they embraced the christian religion.

SAB'INE, *n.* A plant; usually written *savin*, which see.

SA'BLE, *n.* [Russ. *sobol*; G. *zobel*; Sw. Dan. D. *sabel*; Fr. *zibeline*; It. *zibellino*; Sp. *cebellina*; L. *zoboia* or *zobola*, an ermine. This word and the animal were probably not known to the Greeks and Romans till a late period. Jornandes mentions the sending to Rome, in the 6th century, *saphilinas pelles*, sable skins: and Marco Polo calls them *zibelines* and *zombolines.* Pennant, 1. 93.]

1. A small animal of the weasel kind, the *mustela zibellina*, found in the northern latitudes of America and Asia. It resembles the martin, but has a longer head and ears. Its hair is cinereous, but black at the tips. This animal burrows in the earth or under trees; in winter and summer subsisting on small animals, and in autumn on berries. The fur is very valuable. *Encyc.*

2. The fur of the sable.

SA'BLE, *a.* [Fr. Qu. Gr. ζοφος, darkness. See the Noun.]

Black; dark; used chiefly in poetry or in heraldry; as night with her *sable* mantle; the *sable* throne of night.

SAB'LIERE, *n.* [Fr. from *sable*, sand, L. *sabulum.*]

1. A sand pit. [*Not much used.*] *Bailey.*

2. In *carpentry*, a piece of timber as long, but not so thick as a beam. *Bailey.*

SABÔT, *n.* [Fr. *sabot;* Sp. *zapato.*] A wooden shoe. [*Not English.*] *Bramhall.*

SABULOS'ITY, *n.* [from *sabulous.*] Sandiness; grittiness.

SAB'ULOUS, *a.* [L. *sabulosus*, from *sabulum*, sand.] Sandy; gritty.

SAC, *n.* [Sax. *sac, saca, sace* or *sacu*, contention. This is the English *sake*, which see.]

In *English law*, the privilege enjoyed by the lord of a manor, of holding courts, trying causes and imposing fines. *Cowel.*

SACCA'DE, *n.* [Fr. a jerk.] A sudden violent check of a horse by drawing or twitching the reins on a sudden and with one pull; a correction used when the horse bears heavy on the hand. It should be used discretely. *Encyc.*

SACCHARIF'EROUS, *a.* [L. *saccharum*, sugar, and *fero*, to produce.]

Producing sugar; as *sacchariferous* canes. The maple is a *sacchariferous* tree.

SAC'CHARINE, *a.* [from Ar. Pers. *sakar*, L. *saccharum*, sugar.]

Pertaining to sugar; having the qualities of sugar; as a *saccharine* taste; the *saccharine* matter of the cane juice.

SACCHOLAC'TIC, *a.* [L. *saccharum*, sugar, and *lac*, milk.]

A term in the new chimistry, denoting an acid obtained from the sugar of milk; now called *mucic* acid. *Fourcroy. Ure.*

SAC'CHOLATE, *n.* In *chimistry*, a salt formed by the union of the saccholactic acid with a base. *Fourcroy.*

SACERDO'TAL, *a.* [L. *sacerdotalis*, from *sacerdos*, a priest. See *Sacred.*]

Pertaining to priests or the priesthood; priestly; as *sacerdotal* dignity; *sacerdotal* functions or garments; *sacerdotal* character. *Stillingfleet.*

SACH'EL, *n.* [L. *sacculus*, dim. of *saccus;* W. *saçell;* Fr. *sachet.*]

A small sack or bag; a bag in which lawyers and children carry papers and books.

SA'CHEM, *n.* In America, a chief among some of the native Indian tribes. [See *Sagamore.*]

SACK, *n.* [Sax. *sæc, sacc;* D. *zak, sek;* G. *sack;* Dan. *sæk;* Sw. *säck;* W. *saç;* Ir. *sac;* Corn. *zah;* Arm. *sach;* Fr. *sac;* It. *sacco;* Sp. *saco, saca;* Port. *saco, sacco;* L. *saccus;* G. σακκος; Hungarian, *saak;* Slav. *shakel;* Heb. שק. See the verb to *sack.*]

1. A bag, usually a large cloth bag, used for holding and conveying corn, small wares, wool, cotton, hops, and the like. Gen xlii.

Sack of wool, in England, is 22 stone of 14lb. each, or 308 pounds. In Scotland, it is 24 stone of 16 pounds each, or 384 pounds.

A sack of cotton, contains usually about 300lb. but it may be from 150 to 400 pounds.

Sack of earth, in fortification, is a canvas bag filled with earth, used in making retrenchments in haste. *Encyc.*

2. The measure of three bushels. *Johnson.*

SACK, *n.* [Fr. *sec, seche*, dry.] A species of sweet wine, brought chiefly from the Canary isles. *Encyc. Fr. Dict.*

SACK, *n.* [L. *sagum*, whence Gr. σαγος. But the word is Celtic or Teutonic; W. *segan*, a covering, a cloke.]

Among our rude ancestors, a kind of cloke of a square form, worn over the shoulders and body, and fastened in front by a clasp or thorn. It was originally made of skin, afterwards of wool. In modern times, this name has been given to a woman's garment, a gown with loose plaits on the back; but no garment of this kind is now worn, and the word is in disuse. [See *Varro, Strabo, Cluver, Bochart.*]

SACK, *v. t.* To put in a sack or in bags. *Betterton.*

SACK, *v. t.* [Arm. *sacqa;* Ir. *sacham*, to attack; Sp. Port. *saquear*, to plunder or pillage; Sp. to ransack; Sp. Port. *sacar*, to pull out, extort, dispossess; It. *saccheggiare*, to sack; Fr. *saccager*, to pillage; *saccade*, a jerk, a sudden pull. From comparing this word and *sack*, a bag, in several languages, it appears that they are both from one root, and that the primary sense is to strain, pull, draw; hence *sack*, a bag, is a tie, that which is tied or drawn together; and *sack*, to pillage, is to pull, to strip, that is, to take away by violence. See Class Sg. No. 5. 15. 16. 18. 30. 74. 77. &c.]

To plunder or pillage, as a town or city. Rome was twice taken and *sacked* in the reign of one pope. This word is never, I believe, applied to the robbing of persons, or pillaging of single houses, but to the pillaging of towns and cities; and as towns are usually or often *sacked*, when taken by assault, the word may sometimes include the sense of taking by storm.

The Romans lay under the apprehension of seeing their city *sacked* by a barbarous enemy. *Addison.*

SACK, *n.* The pillage or plunder of a town or city; or the storm and plunder of a town; as the *sack* of Troy. *Dryden.*

SACK'AGE, *n.* The act of taking by storm and pillaging. *Roscoe.*

SACK'BUT, *n.* [Sp. *sacabuche*, the tube or pipe of a pump, and a sackbut; Port. *sacabuxa* or *saquebuxo;* Fr. *saquebute.* The Dutch call it *schuif-trompet*, the *shove-trumpet*, the trumpet that may be drawn out or shortened. *Sack* then is of the same family as the preceding word, signifying to pull or draw. The last syllable is the L. *buxus.*]

A wind instrument of music; a kind of trumpet, so contrived that it can be lengthened or shortened according to the tone required. *Encyc.*

SACK'CLOTH, *n.* [*sack* and *cloth.*] Cloth of which sacks are made; coarse cloth. This word is chiefly used in Scripture to denote a cloth or garment worn in mourning, distress or mortification.

Gird you with *sackcloth* and mourn before Abner. 2 Sam. iii. Esth. iv. Job xvi.

SACK'CLOTHED, *a.* Clothed in sackcloth. *Hall.*

SACK'ED, *pp.* Pillaged; stormed and plundered.

SACK'ER, *n.* One that takes a town or plunders it.

SACK'FUL, *n.* A full sack or bag. *Swift.*

SACK'ING, *ppr.* Taking by assault and plundering or pillaging.

SACK'ING, *n.* The act of taking by storm and pillaging.

SACK'ING, *n.* [Sax. *sæccing*, from *sæc*, *sacc.*]

1. Cloth of which sacks or bags are made.

2. The coarse cloth or canvas fastened to a bedstead for supporting the bed.

SACK'LESS, *a.* [Sax. *sacleas*, from *sac*, contention, and *leas*, less.]

Quiet; peaceable; not quarrelsome; harmless; innocent. [*Local.*]

SACK-POS'SET, *n.* [*sack* and *posset.*] A posset made of sack, milk and some other ingredients. *Swift.*

SAC'RAMENT, *n.* [Fr. *sacrement;* It. Sp. *sacramento;* from L. *sacramentum*, an oath, from *sacer*, sacred.]

1. Among *ancient christian writers*, a mystery. [*Not in use.*]

2. An oath; a ceremony producing an obligation; *but not used in this general sense.*

3. In *present usage*, an outward and visible sign of inward and spiritual grace; or more particularly, a solemn religious ceremony enjoined by Christ, the head of the christian church, to be observed by his followers, by which their special relation to him is created, or their obligations to him renewed and ratified. Thus baptism is called a *sacrament*, for by it persons are separated from the world, brought into Christ's visible church, and laid under particular obligations to obey his precepts. The eucharist or communion of the Lord's supper, is also a *sacrament*, for by commemorating the death and dying love of Christ, christians avow their special relation to him, and renew their obligations to be faithful to their divine Master. When we use *sacrament* without any qualifying word, we mean by it,

4. The eucharist or Lord's supper. *Addison.*

SAC'RAMENT, *v. t.* To bind by an oath. [*Not used.*] *Laud.*

SACRAMENT'AL, *a.* Constituting a sacrament or pertaining to it; as *sacramental* rites or elements.

SACRAMENT'AL, *n.* That which relates to a sacrament. *Morton.*

SACRAMENT'ALLY, *adv.* After the manner of a sacrament. *Hall.*

SACRAMENTA'RIAN, *n.* One that differs from the Romish church in regard to the sacraments, or to the Lord's supper; *a word applied by the catholics to protestants.* *Encyc.*

SACRAMENT'ARY, *n.* An ancient book of the Romish church, written by pope Gelasius, and revised, corrected and abridged by St. Gregory, in which were contained all the prayers and ceremonies practiced in the celebration of the sacraments. *Encyc.*

2. A sacramentarian; a term of reproach applied by papists to protestants. *Stapleton.*

SACRAMENT'ARY, SACRAMENTA'RIAN, *a.* Pertaining to sacramentarians and to their controversy respecting the eucharist.

SACRE. [See *Saker.*]

SA'CRED, *a.* [Fr. *sacré*; Sp. It. Port. *sacro*; from L. *sacer*, sacred, holy, cursed, damnable; W. *segyr*, that keeps apart, from *sêg*, that is without access; *segru*, to secrete, to separate. We here see the connection between *sacredness* and *secrecy*. The sense is removed or separated from that which is common, vulgar, polluted, or open, public; and *accursed* is separated from society or the privileges of citizens, rejected, banished.]

1. Holy; pertaining to God or to his worship; separated from common secular uses and consecrated to God and his service; as a *sacred* place; a *sacred* day; a *sacred* feast; *sacred* service; *sacred* orders.

2. Proceeding from God and containing religious precepts; as the *sacred* books of the Old and New Testament.

3. Narrating or writing facts respecting God and holy things; as a *sacred* historian.

4. Relating to religion or the worship of God; used for religious purposes; as *sacred* songs; *sacred* music; *sacred* history.

5. Consecrated; dedicated; devoted; with *to.*

> A temple *sacred to* the queen of love. *Dryden.*

6. Entitled to reverence; venerable.

> Poet and saint to thee alone were given,
> The two most *sacred* names of earth and heav'n. *Cowley.*

7. Inviolable, as if appropriated to a superior being; as *sacred* honor or promise.

> Secrets of marriage still are *sacred* held. *Dryden.*

Sacred majesty. In this title, *sacred* has no definite meaning, or it is blasphemy.

Sacred place, in the civil law, is that where a deceased person is buried.

SA'CREDLY, *adv.* Religiously; with due reverence as of something holy or consecrated to God; as, to observe the sabbath *sacredly*; the day is *sacredly* kept.

2. Inviolably; strictly; as, to observe one's word *sacredly*; a secret to be *sacredly* kept.

SA'CREDNESS, *n.* The state of being sacred, or consecrated to God, to his worship or to religious uses; holiness; sanctity; as the *sacredness* of the sanctuary or its worship; the *sacredness* of the sabbath; the *sacredness* of the clerical office.

2. Inviolableness; as the *sacredness* of marriage vows or of a trust.

SACRIF'IC, SACRIF'ICAL, *a.* [L. *sacrificus*. See *Sacrifice.*] Employed in sacrifice. *Johnson.*

SACRIF'ICABLE, *a.* Capable of being offered in sacrifice. [*Ill formed, harsh and not used.*] *Brown.*

SACRIF'ICANT, *n.* [L. *sacrificans.*] One that offers a sacrifice. *Hallywell.*

SACRIFICA'TOR, *n.* [Fr. *sacrificateur.*] A sacrificer; one that offers a sacrifice. [*Not used.*] *Brown.*

SACRIF'ICATORY, *a.* Offering sacrifice. *Sherwood.*

SAC'RIFICE, *v. t.* *sac'rifize.* [L. *sacrifico*; Fr. *sacrifier*; Sp. *sacrificar*; It. *sacrificare*; L. *sacer*, sacred, and *facio*, to make.]

1. To offer to God in homage or worship, by killing and consuming, as victims on an altar; to immolate, either as an atonement for sin, or to procure favor, or to express thankfulness; as, to *sacrifice* an ox or a lamb. 2 Sam. vi.

2. To destroy, surrender or suffer to be lost for the sake of obtaining something; as, to *sacrifice* the peace of the church to a little vain curiosity. We should never *sacrifice* health to pleasure, nor integrity to fame.

3. To devote with loss.

> Condemn'd to *sacrifice* his childish years
> To babbling ignorance and to empty fears. *Prior.*

4. To destroy; to kill.

SAC'RIFICE, *v. i.* To make offerings to God by the slaughter and burning of victims, or of some part of them. Ex. iii.

SAC'RIFICE, *n.* [Fr. from L. *sacrificium.*]

1. An offering made to God by killing and burning some animal upon an altar, as an acknowledgment of his power and providence, or to make atonement for sin, appease his wrath or conciliate his favor, or to express thankfulness for his benefits. *Sacrifices* have been common to most nations, and have been offered to false gods, as well as by the Israelites to Jehovah. A *sacrifice* differs from an *oblation*; the latter being an offering of a thing entire or without change, as tithes or first fruits; whereas *sacrifice* implies a destruction or killing, as of a beast. Sacrifices are *expiatory, impetratory,* and *eucharistical*; that is, atoning for sin, seeking favor, or expressing thanks.

Human sacrifices, the killing and offering of human beings to deities, have been practiced by some barbarous nations.

2. The thing offered to God, or immolated by an act of religion.

> My life if thou preserv'st, my life
> Thy *sacrifice* shall be. *Addison.*

3. Destruction, surrender or loss made or incurred for gaining some object, or for obliging another; as the *sacrifice* of interest to pleasure, or of pleasure to interest.

4. Any thing destroyed.

SAC'RIFICED, *pp.* Offered to God upon an altar; destroyed, surrendered, or suffered to be lost.

SAC'RIFICER, *n.* One that sacrifices or immolates. *Dryden.*

SACRIFI''CIAL, *a.* Performing sacrifice; included in sacrifice; consisting in sacrifice. *Shak. Taylor.*

SAC'RILEGE, *n.* [Fr. from L. *sacrilegium*; *sacer*, sacred, and *lego*, to take or steal.]

The crime of violating or profaning sacred things; or the alienating to laymen or to common purposes what has been appropriated or consecrated to religious persons or uses.

> And the hid treasures in her sacred tomb
> With *sacrilege* to dig. *Spenser.*

SACRILE'GIOUS, *a.* [L. *sacrilegus.*] Violating sacred things; polluted with the crime of sacrilege.

> Above the reach of *sacrilegious* hands. *Pope.*

2. Containing sacrilege; as a *sacrilegious* attempt or act.

SACRILE'GIOUSLY, *adv.* With sacrilege; in violation of sacred things; as *sacrilegiously* invading the property of a church.

SACRILE'GIOUSNESS, *n.* The quality of being sacrilegious.

2. Disposition to sacrilege. *Scott.*

SAC'RILEGIST, *n.* One who is guilty of sacrilege. *Spelman.*

SA'CRING, *ppr.* [from Fr. *sacrer.*] Consecrating. [*Not in use.*] *Temple. Shak.*

SA'CRING-BELL, *n.* A bell rung before the host. *Dict.*

SA'CRIST, *n.* A sacristan; a person retained in a cathedral to copy out music for the choir, and take care of the books. *Busby.*

SAC'RISTAN, *n.* [Fr. *sacristain*; It. *sacristano*; Sp. *sacristan*; from L. *sacer*, sacred.]

An officer of the church who has the care of the utensils or movables of the church. It is now corrupted into *sexton.*

SAC'RISTY, *n.* [Fr. *sacristie*; Sp. It. *sacristia*; from L. *sacer*, sacred.]

An apartment in a church where the sacred utensils are kept; now called the *vestry.* *Dryden. Addison.*

SAC'ROSANCT, *a.* [L. *sacrosanctus*; *sacer* and *sanctus*, holy.] Sacred; inviolable. [*Not in use.*] *More.*

SAD, *a.* [In W. *sad* signifies wise, prudent, sober, permanent. It is probable this word is from the root of *set.* I have not found the word in the English sense, in any other language.]

1. Sorrowful; affected with grief; cast down with affliction.

> Th' angelic guards ascended, mute and *sad.* *Milton.*
>
> *Sad* for their loss, but joyful of our life. *Pope.*

2. Habitually melancholy; gloomy; not gay or cheerful.

> See in her cell *sad* Eloisa spread. *Pope.*

3. Downcast; gloomy; having the external appearance of sorrow; as a *sad* countenance. Matt. vi.

4. Serious; grave; not gay, light or volatile.

> Lady Catherine, a *sad* and religious woman. *Bacon.*

5. Afflictive; calamitous; causing sorrow; as a *sad* accident; a *sad* misfortune.

6. Dark colored.

> Woad or wade is used by the dyers to lay the foundation of all *sad* colors. *Mortimer.*

[*This sense is, I believe, entirely obsolete.*]

7. Bad; vexatious; as a *sad* husband. [*Colloquial.*] *Addison.*

8. Heavy; weighty; ponderous.

> With that his hand more *sad* than lump of lead. *Obs.* *Spenser.*

9. Close; firm; cohesive; opposed to *light* or *friable.*

> Chalky lands are naturally cold and *sad.* *Obs.* *Mortimer.*

[The two latter senses indicate that the primary sense is *set*, fixed; W. *sadiaw*, to make firm.]

SADDEN, *v. t.* *sad'n.* To make sad or sorrowful; also, to make melancholy or gloomy. *Pope.*

2. To make dark colored. *Obs.*

3. To make heavy, firm or cohesive.

Marl is binding, and *saddening* of land is the great prejudice it doth to clay lands. *Obs.* *Mortimer.*

SAD'DENED, *pp.* Made sad or gloomy.

SAD'DENING, *ppr.* Making sad or gloomy.

SADDLE, *n.* *sad'l.* [Sax. *sadel, sadl*; D. *zadel*; G. *sattel*; Dan. Sw. *sadel*; W. *sadell*; Ir. *sadhall*; Russ. *sedlo* or *siedlo*; from the root of *sit, set*, L. *sedeo, sedile.*]

1. A seat to be placed on a horse's back for the rider to sit on. Saddles are variously made, as the common saddle and the hunting saddle, and for females the side-saddle.

2. Among *seamen*, a cleat or block of wood nailed on the lower yard-arms to retain the studding sail-booms in their place. The name is given also to other circular pieces of wood; as the *saddle* of the bowsprit. *Mar. Dict.*

SAD'DLE, *v. t.* To put a saddle on.

Abraham rose early in the morning and *saddled* his ass. Gen. xxii.

2. To load; to fix a burden on; as, to be *saddled* with the expense of bridges and highways.

SAD'DLE-BACKED, *a.* Having a low back and an elevated neck and head, as a horse. *Far. Dict.*

SAD'DLE-BOW, *n.* [Sax. *sadl-boga.*] The bows of a saddle, or the pieces which form the front.

SAD'DLE-MAKER, } *n.* One whose occupation is to make
SAD'DLER, } saddles.

SADDUCE'AN, *a.* Pertaining to the Sadducees, a sect among the ancient Jews, who denied the resurrection, a future state, and the existence of angels. Acts xxiii.

SAD'DUCISM, *n.* The tenets of the Sadducees. *More.*

SAD'LY, *adv.* Sorrowfully; mournfully.

He *sadly* suffers in their grief. *Dryden.*

2. In a calamitous or miserable manner. The misfortunes which others experience we may one day *sadly* feel.

3. In a dark color. *Obs.* *B. Jonson.*

SAD'NESS, *n.* Sorrowfulness; mournfulness; dejection of mind; as grief and *sadness* at the memory of sin. *Decay of Piety.*

2. A melancholy look; gloom of countenance.

Dim *sadness* did not spare
Celestial visages. *Milton.*

3. Seriousness; sedate gravity. Let every thing in a mournful subject have an air of *sadness.*

SAFE, *a.* [Fr. *sauf, sauve*, contracted from L. *salvus*, from *salus*, safety, health.]

1. Free from danger of any kind; as *safe* from enemies; *safe* from disease; *safe* from storms; *safe* from the malice of foes.

2. Free from hurt, injury or damage; as, to walk *safe* over red hot plowshares. We brought the goods *safe* to land.

3. Conferring safety; securing from harm; as a *safe* guide; a *safe* harbor; a *safe* bridge.

4. Not exposing to danger. Phil. iii.

5. No longer dangerous; placed beyond the power of doing harm; *a ludicrous meaning.*

Banquo's *safe.*
—Aye, my good lord, *safe* in a ditch. *Shak.*

SAFE, *n.* A place of safety; a place for securing provisions from noxious animals.

SAFE, *v. t.* To render safe. [*Not in use.*] *Shak.*

SAFE-CON'DUCT, *n.* [*safe* and *conduct*; Fr. *sauf-conduit.*]

That which gives a safe passage, either a convoy or guard to protect a person in an enemy's country or in a foreign country, or a writing, a pass or warrant of security given to a person by the sovereign of a country to enable him to travel with safety.

SA'FEGU'ARD, *n.* [*safe* and *guard.*] He or that which defends or protects; defense; protection.

The sword, the *safeguard* of thy brother's throne. *Granville.*

2. A convoy or guard to protect a traveler.

3. A passport; a warrant of security given by a sovereign to protect a stranger within his territories; formerly, a protection granted to a stranger in prosecuting his rights in due course of law. *Encyc.*

4. An outer petticoat to save women's clothes on horseback. *Mason.*

SA'FEGU'ARD, *v. t.* To guard; to protect. [*Little used.*] *Shak.*

SAFE-KEE'PING, *n.* [*safe* and *keep.*] The act of keeping or preserving in safety from injury or from escape.

SA'FELY, *adv.* In a safe manner; without incurring danger or hazard of evil consequences. We may *safely* proceed, or *safely* conclude.

2. Without injury. We passed the river *safely.*

3. Without escape; in close custody; as, to keep a prisoner *safely.*

SA'FENESS, *n.* Freedom from danger; as the *safeness* of an experiment.

2. The state of being safe, or of conferring safety; as the *safeness* of a bridge or of a boat.

SA'FETY, *n.* Freedom from danger or hazard; as the *safety* of an electrical experiment; the *safety* of a voyage.

I was not in *safety*, nor had I rest. Job iii.

2. Exemption from hurt, injury or loss. We crossed the Atlantic in *safety.*

3. Preservation from escape; close custody; as, to keep a prisoner in *safety.*

4 Preservation from hurt. *Shak.*

SA'FETY-VALVE, *n.* A valve by means of which a boiler is preserved from bursting by the force of steam.

SAF'FLOW, } *n.* The plant, bastard saf-
SAF'FLOWER, } fron, of the genus Carthamus. *Petty.*

SAF'FLOWER, *n.* A deep red fecula separated from orange-colored flowers, particularly those of the *Carthamus tinctorius*; called also *Spanish red* and *China lake.* *Encyc. Ure.*

The dried flowers of the *Carthamus tinctorius.* *Thomson.*

SAF'FRON, *n.* [W. *safrwn, safyr*; Fr. *safran*; Arm. *zafron*; It. *zafferano*; Sp. *azafran*; Port. *açafram*; D. *saffraan*; G. Sw. Dan. *saffran*; Turk. *zafrani*; Ar. صفر to be yellow, to be empty; the root of *cipher.* The radical sense then is to fail, or to be hollow, or to be exhausted.]

1. A plant of the genus Crocus. The *bastard saffron* is of the genus Carthamus, and the *meadow saffron* of the genus Colchicum.

2. In *the materia medica*, saffron is formed of the stigmata of the *Crocus officinalis*, dried on a kiln and pressed into cakes. *Encyc.*

SAF'FRON, *a.* Having the color of saffron flowers; yellow; as a *saffron* face; a *saffron* streamer. *Shak. Dryden.*

SAF'FRON, *v. t.* To tinge with saffron; to make yellow; to gild. *Chaucer.*

SAG, *v. i.* [a different spelling of *swag*, which see.]

1. To yield; to give way; to lean or incline from an upright position, or to bend from a horizontal position. Our workmen say, a building *sags* to the north or south; or a beam *sags* by means of its weight.

2. In *sailing*, to incline to the leeward; to make lee way. *Mar. Dict.*

SAG, *v. t.* To cause to bend or give way; to load or burden.

SAGA'CIOUS, *a.* [L. *sagax*, from *sagus*, wise, foreseeing; *saga*, a wise woman; *sagio*, to perceive readily; Fr. *sage, sagesse*; Sp. *saga, sagaz*; It. *saggio.* The latter signifies wise, prudent, *sage*, and an *essay*, which unites this word with *seek*, and L. *sequor.*]

1. Quick of scent; as a *sagacious* hound; strictly perhaps, following by the scent, which sense is connected with L. *sequor*; with *of*; as *sagacious of* his quarry. *Milton.*

2. Quick of thought; acute in discernment or penetration; as a *sagacious* head; a *sagacious* mind. *Locke.*

I would give more for the criticisms of one *sagacious* enemy, than for those of a score of admirers. *H. Humphrey.*

SAGA'CIOUSLY, *adv.* With quick scent.

2. With quick discernment or penetration.

SAGA'CIOUSNESS, *n.* The quality of being sagacious; quickness of scent.

2. Quickness or acuteness of discernment.

SAGAC'ITY, *n.* [Fr. *sagacité*; L. *sagacitas.*]

1. Quickness or acuteness of scent; *applied to animals.*

2. Quickness or acuteness of discernment or penetration; readiness of apprehension; the faculty of readily discerning and distinguishing ideas, and of separating truth from falsehood.

Sagacity finds out the intermediate ideas, to discover what connection there is in each link of the chain. *Locke.*

SAG'AMORE, *n.* Among some tribes of American Indians, a king or chief. [In Sax. *sigora* is a conqueror.]

SAG'APEN, } *n.* In *pharmacy*, a gum-
SAGAPE'NUM, } resin, brought from Persia and the East in granules or in masses. It is a compact substance, heavy, of a reddish color, with small whitish or yellowish specks. It is an attenuant, aperient and discutient. *Encyc.*

SAG'ATHY, *n.* A kind of serge; a slight woolen stuff. *Tatler.*

SAGE, *n.* [Fr. *sauge*; Ar. *saoch.*] A plant of the genus Salvia, of several species; as the *officinalis*, or common large sage, of several varieties; the *tomentosa* or balsamic sage; the *auriculata*, or sage of virtue; and the *pomifera*. *Encyc.*

SAĠE, *a.* [Fr. *sage*; It. *saggio*; L. *saga*, *sagus*, *sagio*. See *Sagacious*.]

1. Wise; having nice discernment and powers of judging; prudent; grave; as a *sage* counselor.

2. Wise; judicious; proceeding from wisdom; well judged; well adapted to the purpose; as *sage* counsels.

SAĠE, *n.* A wise man; a man of gravity and wisdom; particularly, a man venerable for years, and known as a man of sound judgment and prudence; a grave philosopher.

> At his birth a star proclaims him come,
> And guides the eastern *sages*. *Milton.*
> Groves where immortal *sages* taught. *Pope.*

SA'ĠELY, *adv.* Wisely; with just discernment and prudence.

SAĠE'NE, *n.* A Russian measure of about seven English feet. [See *Sajene*.]

SA'ĠENESS, *n.* Wisdom; sagacity; prudence; gravity. *Ascham.*

SAĠ'ENITE, *n.* Acicular rutile. *Ure.*

SAĠ'ITTAL, *a.* [L. *sagittalis*, from *sagitta*, an arrow; that which is thrown or driven, probably from the root of *say* and *sing*.]

Pertaining to an arrow; resembling an arrow; as *sagittal* bars of yellow. *Pennant.*

In *anatomy*, the *sagittal suture* is the suture which unites the parietal bones of the skull. *Coxe.*

SAĠITTA'RIUS, *n.* [L. an archer.] One of the twelve signs of the zodiac, which the sun enters Nov. 22.

SAĠ'ITTARY, *n.* [supra.] A centaur, an animal half man, half horse, armed with a bow and quiver. *Shak.*

SAĠ'ITTATE, *a.* In *botany*, shaped like the head of an arrow; triangular, hollowed at the base, with angles at the hinder part; or with the hinder angles acute, divided by a sinus; applied to the leaf, stipula or anther. *Martyn.*

SA'GO, *n.* A dry mealy substance or granulated paste, imported from Java and the Philippine and Molucca isles. It is the pith or marrow of a species of palm tree, and much used in medicine as a restorative diet. *Fourcroy. Encyc.*

SAGOIN', *n.* The *Sagoins* form a division of the genus Simia, including such of the monkeys of America as have hairy tails, not prehensile. *Encyc.*

SA'ĠY, *a.* [from *sage*.] Full of sage; seasoned with sage.

SAH'LITE, *n.* A mineral named from the mountain *Sahla*, in Westermania, where it was discovered. It is of a light greenish gray color, occurs massive, and composed of coarse granular concretions. It is called also malacolite; a subspecies or variety of augite. *Thomson. Ure.*

SAIC, *n.* A Turkish or Grecian vessel, very common in the Levant, a kind of ketch which has no top-gallant-sail, nor mizen-top-sail. *Mar. Dict.*

SAID, *pret.* and *pp.* of *say*; so written for *sayed*. Declared; uttered; reported.

2. Aforesaid; before mentioned.

SAIL, *n.* [Sax. G. Sw. *segel*; Dan. *sejl*; D. *zeil*; W. *hwyl*, a sail, a course, order, state, journey; *hwyliaw*, to set in a course, train or order, to direct, to proceed, to sail, to attack, to butt. The Welsh appears to be the same word. So *hâl* is the L. *sal*, salt.]

1. In *navigation*, a spread of canvas, or an assemblage of several breadths of canvas, [or some substitute for it,] sewed together with a double seam at the borders, and edged with a cord called the bolt-rope, to be extended on the masts or yards for receiving the impulse of wind by which a ship is driven. The principal sails are the courses or lower sails, the top-sails and top-gallant-sails. *Mar. Dict.*

2. In poetry, wings. *Spenser.*

3. A ship or other vessel; used in the singular for a single ship, or as a collective name for many. We saw a *sail* at the leeward. We saw three *sail* on our starboard quarter. The fleet consists of twenty *sail*.

To loose sails, to unfurl them.

To make sail, to extend an additional quantity of sail.

To set sail, to expand or spread the sails; and hence, to begin a voyage.

To shorten sail, to reduce the extent of sail, or take in a part.

To strike sail, to lower the sails suddenly, as in saluting or in sudden gusts of wind.

2. To abate show or pomp. [*Colloquial.*] *Shak.*

SAIL, *v. i.* To be impelled or driven forward by the action of wind upon sails, as a ship on water. A ship *sails* from New-York for Liverpool. She *sails* ten knots an hour. She *sails* well close-hauled.

2. To be conveyed in a vessel on water; to pass by water. We *sailed* from London to Canton.

3. To swim.

> —Little dolphins, when they *sail*
> In the vast shadow of the British whale. *Dryden.*

4. To set sail; to begin a voyage. We *sailed* from New York for Havre, June 15, 1824. We *sailed* from Cowes for New York, May 10, 1825.

5. To be carried in the air, as a balloon.

6. To pass smoothly along.

> As is a wing'd messenger from heaven,
> When he bestrides the lazy pacing clouds,
> And *sails* upon the bosom of the air. *Shak.*

7. To fly without striking with the wings.

SAIL, *v. t.* To pass or move upon in a ship, by means of sails.

> A thousand ships were mann'd to *sail* the sea. *Dryden.*

[This use is elliptical, *on* or *over* being omitted.]

2. To fly through.

> Sublime she *sails*
> Th' aerial space, and mounts the winged gales. *Pope.*

SA'ILABLE, *a.* Navigable; that may be passed by ships. *Cotgrave.*

SA'IL-BORNE, *a.* Borne or conveyed by sails. *J. Barlow.*

SA'IL-BROAD, *a.* [See *Broad*.] Spreading like a sail. *Milton.*

SA'ILED, *pp.* Passed in ships or other water-craft.

SA'ILER, *n.* One that sails; a seaman; usually *sailor*.

2. A ship or other vessel, with reference to her manner of sailing. Thus we say, a heavy *sailer*; a fast *sailer*; a prime *sailer*.

SA'ILING, *ppr.* Moving on water or in air; passing in a ship or other vessel.

SA'ILING, *n.* The act of moving on water; or the movement of a ship or vessel impelled or wafted along the surface of water by the action of wind on her sails. *Mar. Dict.*

2. Movement through the air, as in a balloon.

3. The act of setting sail or beginning a voyage.

SA'IL-LOFT, *n.* A loft or apartment where sails are cut out and made.

SA'IL-MAKER, *n.* One whose occupation is to make sails.

2. An officer on board ships of war, whose business is to repair or alter sails. *Mar. Dict.*

SA'IL-MAKING, *n.* The art or business of making sails.

SA'ILOR, *n.* [a more common spelling than *sailer*.]

A mariner; a seaman; one who follows the business of navigating ships or other vessels, or one who understands the management of ships in navigation. This word however does not by itself express any particular skill in navigation. It denotes any person who follows the seas, and is chiefly or wholly applied to the common hands. [See *Seaman*.]

SA'IL-YARD, *n.* [Sax. *segl-gyrd*.] The yard or spar on which sails are extended. *Dryden.*

SAIM, *n.* [Sax. *seim*; W. *saim*; Fr. *saindoux*. Qu. L. *sebum*, contracted.] Lard. [*Local.*]

SAIN, for *sayen*, pp. of *say*. *Obs.* *Shak.*

SA'INFOIN, } *n.* [Fr. *sainfoin*; *saint*, sacred, and *foin*, hay.] A plant cultivated for fodder, of the genus Hedysarum.
SA'INTFOIN, }

SAINT, *n.* [Fr. from L. *sanctus*; It. Sp. *santo*.]

1. A person sanctified; a holy or godly person; one eminent for piety and virtue. It is particularly applied to the apostles and other holy persons mentioned in Scripture. A hypocrite may imitate a *saint*. Ps. xvi. *Addison.*

2. One of the blessed in heaven. Rev. xviii.

3. The holy angels are called saints, Deut. xxxiii, Jude 14.

4. One canonized by the church of Rome. *Encyc.*

SAINT, *v. t.* To number or enroll among saints by an official act of the pope; to canonize.

> Over against the church stands a large hospital, erected by a shoemaker who has been beatified, though never *sainted*. *Addison.*

SAINT, *v. i.* To act with a show of piety. *Pope.*

SA'INTED, *pp.* Canonized; enrolled among the saints.

2. *a.* Holy; pious; as, thy father was a most *sainted* king. *Shak.*

3. Sacred; as the gods on *sainted* hills. *Milton.*

SA'INTESS, *n.* A female saint. *Fisher.*

SAINT JOHN'S BREAD, *n.* A plant of the genus Ceratonia.

SAINT JOHN'S WÖRT, *n.* A plant of the genus Hypericum.

SA'INTLIKE, *a.* [*saint* and *like.*] Resembling a saint; as a *saintlike* prince. *Bacon.*

2. Suiting a saint; becoming a saint.

Gloss'd over only with a *saintlike* show. *Dryden.*

SA'INTLY, *a.* Like a saint; becoming a holy person; as wrongs with *saintly* patience borne. *Milton.*

SAINT PETER'S WŎRT, *n.* A plant of the genus Ascyrum, and another of the genus Hypericum.

SA'INT'S BELL, *n.* A small bell rung in churches when the priest repeats the words *sancte, sancte, sancte, Deus sabaoth,* that persons absent might fall on their knees in reverence of the holy office. *Bp. Hall.*

SA'INT-SEEMING, *a.* Having the appearance of a saint. *Mountagu.*

SA'INTSHIP, *n.* The character or qualities of a saint.

SAJE'NE, *n.* [written also *sagene.* Tooke writes it *sajene.*]

A Russian measure of length, equal to seven feet English measure.

SAKE, *n.* [Sax. *sac, saca, sace, sacu,* contention, discord, a suit or action at law, cause in court, hence the privilege which a lord had of taking cognizance of suits in his own manor; *sacan,* to contend, to strive; Goth. *sakan,* to rebuke, chide, upbraid; D. *zaak,* cause, case, thing, business, affair; G. *sache,* matter, thing; *eines sache führen,* to plead one's cause; *ursache,* cause, reason, motive; Sw. *sak* and *orsak,* id.; Dan. *sag,* cause, thing, affair, matter, case, suit, action; Ch. עסק to contend, to strive, to *seek;* Heb. עשק to press or oppress; Ch. to accuse, to criminate. Class Sg. No. 46. 92. The primary sense is to strain, urge, press or drive forward, and this is from the same root as *seek, essay* and L. *sequor,* whence we have *pursue* and *prosecute.* We have analagous words in *cause, thing,* and the L. *res.* Its Saxon sense is no longer in use, that is, cause, action, suit, a *seeking* or demand in court; but we use it in a sense nearly similar, though differently applied.]

1. Final cause; end; purpose; or rather the purpose of obtaining. I open a window for the *sake* of air, that is, to obtain it, for the purpose of obtaining air. I read for the *sake* of instruction, that is, to obtain it. *Sake* then signifies primarily *effort* to obtain, and secondarily *purpose* of obtaining. The hero fights for the *sake* of glory; men labor for the *sake* of subsistence or wealth.

2. Account; regard to any person or thing.

I will not again curse the ground any more for man's *sake.* Gen. viii.

Save me for thy mercies' *sake.* Ps. vi.

SA'KER, *n.* [Fr. *sacre.*] A hawk; a species of falcon.

2. A piece of artillery. *Hudibras.*

SAK'ERET, *n.* The male of the sakerhawk. *Bailey.*

SAL, *n.* [See *Salt.*] Salt; a word much used in chemistry and pharmacy.

SA'LABLE, *a.* [from *sale.*] That may be sold; that finds a ready market; being in good demand.

SA'LABLENESS, *n.* The state of being salable.

SA'LABLY, *adv.* In a salable manner.

SALA'CIOUS, *a.* [L. *salax,* from the root of *sal,* salt; the primary sense of which is shooting, penetrating, pungent, coinciding probably with L. *salio,* to leap. *Salacious* then is highly excited, or prompt to leap.] Lustful; lecherous. *Dryden.*

SALA'CIOUSLY, *adv.* Lustfully; with eager animal appetite.

SALA'CIOUSNESS, } *n.* Lust; lecherous-
SALAC'ITY, } ness; strong propensity to venery. *Brown.*

SAL'AD, *n.* [Fr. *salade;* Arm. *saladenn;* It. *insalata;* Sp. *ensalada,* that is literally, *salted;* D. *salaade;* G. Sw. *salat;* Dan. *salad.*]

Raw herbs, usually dressed with salt, vinegar, oil or spices, and eaten for giving a relish to other food.

Leaves eaten raw, are termed *salad.* *Watts.*

SAL'ADING, *n.* Vegetables for salads. *Cheyne.*

SAL-ALEMBROTH, *n.* A compound muriate of mercury and ammonia. *Ure.*

SALAM', *n.* [Oriental, peace or safety.] A salutation or compliment of ceremony or respect. [*Not in use.*] *Herbert.*

SAL'AMANDER, *n.* [L. Gr. *salamandra.*] An animal of the genus Lacerta or Lizard, one of the smaller species of the genus, not being more than six or seven inches in length. It has a short cylindrical tail, four toes on the four feet, and a naked body. The skin is furnished with small excresences like teats, which are full of holes from which oozes a milky liquor that spreads over the skin, forming a kind of transparent varnish. The eyes are placed in the upper part of the head. The color is dark, with a bluish cast on the belly, intermixed with irregular yellow spots. This animal is oviparous, inhabits cold damp places among trees or hedges, avoiding the heat of the sun. The vulgar story of its being able to endure fire, is a mistake. *Encyc.*

Salamander's hair or *wool,* a name given to a species of asbestos or mineral flax; I believe no longer used.

SALAMAN'DRINE, *a.* Pertaining to or resembling a salamander; enduring fire. *Spectator.*

Sal ammoniac, muriate of ammonia. The native sal ammoniac is of two kinds, volcanic and conchoidal. *Ure.*

SAL'ARIED, *a.* Enjoying a salary.

SAL'ARY, *n.* [Fr. *salaire;* It. Sp. *salario;* L. *salarium;* said to be from *sal,* salt, which was part of the pay of Roman soldiers.]

The recompense or consideration stipulated to be paid to a person for services, usually a fixed sum to be paid by the year, as to governors, magistrates, settled clergymen, instructors of seminaries, or other officers, civil or ecclesiastical. When wages are stated or stipulated by the month, week or day, we do not call the compensation *salary,* but *pay* or *wages;* as in the case of military men and laborers.

SALE, *n.* [W. *sal,* a pass, a cast or throw, a *sale;* Sax. *sal,* sale; *sellan, sylan, syllan, gesyllan,* to give, yield, grant, impart, deliver, also to *sell.* The primary sense of *sell,* is simply to deliver or cause to pass from one person to another; Sw. *sälja,* Dan. *sælger,* to sell.]

1. The act of selling; the exchange of a commodity for money of equivalent value. The exchange of one commodity for another is *barter* or *permutation,* and *sale* differs from *barter* only in the nature of the equivalent given.

2. Vent; power of selling; market. He went to market, but found no *sale* for his goods.

3. Auction; public sale to the highest bidder, or exposure of goods in market. [*Little used.*] *Temple.*

4. State of being venal, or of being offered to bribery; as, to set the liberty of a state to *sale.* *Addison.*

5. A wicker basket. [Qu. Sax. *sælan,* to bind.] *Spenser.*

SALE, *a.* Sold; bought; as opposed to *homemade.* [*Colloquial.*]

SALEBROS'ITY, *n.* [See *Salebrous.*] Roughness or ruggedness of a place or road. *Feltham.*

SAL'EBROUS, *a.* [L. *salebrosus,* from *salebra,* a rough place; probably allied to *salio,* to shoot out.] Rough; rugged; uneven. [*Little used.*]

SAL'EP, *n.* [said to be a Turkish word; written also *salop, saloop* and *saleb.*]

In *the materia medica,* the dried root of a species of orchis; also, a preparation of this root to be used as food. *Fourcroy. Parr.*

SA'LESMAN, *n.* [*sale* and *man.*] One that sells clothes ready made. *Swift.*

SA'LEWŎRK, *n.* Work or things made for sale; hence, work carelessly done.

This last sense is a satire on man. *Shak.*

SAL'IC, *a.* [The origin of this word is not ascertained.]

The Salic law of France is a fundamental law, by virtue of which males only can inherit the throne.

SA'LIENT, *a.* [L. *saliens, salio,* to leap.]

1. Leaping; an epithet in heraldry applied to a lion or other beast, represented in a leaping posture, with his right foot in the dexter point, and his hinder left foot in the sinister base of the escutcheon, by which it is distinguished from *rampant.* *Harris.*

2. In *fortification,* projecting; as a *salient* angle. A *salient* angle points outward, and is opposed to a *re-entering* angle, which points inward. *Encyc.*

SA'LIENT, *a.* [L. *saliens,* from *salio,* to leap or shoot out.]

1. Leaping; moving by leaps; as frogs. *Brown.*

2. Beating; throbbing; as the heart. *Blackmore.*

3. Shooting out or up; springing; darting; as a *salient* sprout. *Pope.*

SALIF'EROUS, *a.* [L. *sal,* salt, and *fero,* to produce.]

Producing or bearing salt; as *saliferous* rock. *Eaton.*

SAL'IFIABLE, *a.* [from *salify.*] Capable of becoming a salt, or of combining with an acid to form a neutral salt. *Salifiable* bases are alkalies, earths and metallic oxyds. *Lavoisier.*

SALIFICA'TION, *n.* The act of salifying.

SAL'IFIED, *pp.* Formed into a neutral salt by combination with an acid.

SAL'IFȲ, *v. t.* [L. *sal*, salt, and *facio*, to make.]

To form into a neutral salt, by combining an acid with an alkali, earth or metal.

SAL'IFȲING, *ppr.* Forming into a salt by combination with an acid.

SAL'IGOT, *n.* [Fr.] A plant, the water thistle.

SALINA'TION, *n.* [L. *sal*, salt; *salinator*, a salt maker; Fr. *salin*, salt, brinish.]

The act of washing with salt water. *Greenhill.*

SALI'NE, SALI'NOUS, *a.* [Fr. *salin*, from L. *sal*, salt.] Consisting of salt, or constituting salt; as *saline* particles; *saline* substances.

2. Partaking of the qualities of salt; as a *saline* taste.

SALI'NE, *n.* [Sp. It. *salina*; Fr. *saline.*] A salt spring, or a place where salt water is collected in the earth; a name given to the salt springs in the U. States.

SALINIF'EROUS, *a.* [L. *sal*, *salinum*, and *fero*, to produce.] Producing salt.

SALIN'IFORM, *a.* [L. *sal*, *salinum*, and *form.*] Having the form of salt.

SALINO-TERRENE, *a.* [L. *sal*, *salinum*, and *terrenus*, from *terra*, earth.] Denoting a compound of salt and earth.

SAL'ITE, *v. t.* [L. *salio*, from *sal*, salt.] To salt; to impregnate or season with salt. [*Little used.*]

SALI'VA, SAL'IVE, *n.* [L. *saliva*; Ir. *seile*; W. *haliw*, as if connected with *hâl*, salt. The Irish has *silim*, to drop or distill, and *sileadh*, saliva.]

The fluid which is secreted by the salivary glands, and which serves to moisten the mouth and tongue. It moistens our food also, and by being mixed with it in mastication, promotes digestion. When discharged from the mouth, it is called *spittle.*

SAL'IVAL, SAL'IVARY, *a.* [from *saliva.*] Pertaining to saliva; secreting or conveying saliva; as *salivary* glands; *salivary* ducts or canals. *Encyc. Arbuthnot.*

SAL'IVATE, *v. t.* [from *saliva*; Fr. *saliver.*]

To excite an unusual secretion and discharge of saliva in a person, usually by mercury; to produce ptyalism in a person. Physicians *salivate* their patients in diseases of the glands, of the liver, in the venereal disease, in yellow fever, &c.

SAL'IVATED, *pp.* Having an increased secretion of saliva from medicine.

SAL'IVATING, *ppr.* Exciting increased secretion of saliva.

SALIVA'TION, *n.* The act or process of promoting ptyalism, or of producing an increased secretion of saliva, for the cure of disease.

SALI'VOUS, *a.* Pertaining to saliva; partaking of the nature of saliva. *Wiseman.*

SAL'LET, *n.* [Fr. *salade.*] A head-piece or helmet. *Chaucer.*

SAL'LET, SAL'LETING, *n.* [corrupted from *salad. Not in use.*]

SAL'LIANCE, *n.* [from *sally.*] An issuing forth. [*Not in use.*] *Spenser.*

SAL'LOW, *n.* [Sax. *salh*, *salig*; Ir. *sail*; Fr. *saule*; It. *salcio*; Sp. *salce*; L. *salix*; W. *helig*. Qu. from its color, resembling brine.] A tree of the willow kind, or genus Salix.

SAL'LOW, *a.* [Sax. *salowig*, *sealwe*, from *salh*, L. *salix*, the tree, supra.]

Having a yellowish color; of a pale sickly color, tinged with a dark yellow; as a *sallow* skin.

SAL'LOWNESS, *n.* A yellowish color; paleness tinged with a dark yellow; as *sallowness* of complexion.

SAL'LY, *n.* [Fr. *saillie*; It. *salita*; Sp. *salida*; Port. *sahida*. See the Verb.] In *a general sense*, a spring; a darting or shooting. Hence,

1. An issue or rushing of troops from a besieged place to attack the besiegers. *Bacon.*

2. A spring or darting of intellect, fancy or imagination; flight; sprightly exertion. We say, *sallies* of wit, *sallies* of imagination.

3. Excursion from the usual track; range.

> He who often makes *sallies* into a country, and traverses it up and down, will know it better than one that goes always round in the same track. *Locke.*

4. Act of levity or extravagance; wild gayety; frolick; a bounding or darting beyond ordinary rules; as a *sally* of youth; a *sally* of levity. *Wotton. Swift.*

SAL'LY, *v. i.* [Fr. *saillir*; Arm. *sailha*; It *salire*; Sp. *salir*; Port. *sahir*, [*l* lost;] L. *salio*. Qu. Gr. αλλομαι, which is allied to the Ar. ال alla, or هل halla, both of which signify to impel, to shoot. See *Solar*, from L. *sol*, W. *haul*, Gr. ηλιος.]

1. To issue or rush out, as a body of troops from a fortified place to attack besiegers.

> They break the truce, and *sally* out by night. *Dryden.*

2. To issue suddenly; to make a sudden eruption.

SAL'LYING, *ppr.* Issuing or rushing out.

SAL'LY-PORT, *n.* In *fortification*, a postern gate, or a passage under ground from the inner to the outer works, such as from the higher flank to the lower, or to the tenailles, or to the communication from the middle of the curtain to the ravelin. *Encyc.*

2. A large port on each quarter of a fireship for the escape of the men into boats when the train is fired. *Mar. Dict.*

SALMAGUN'DI, *n.* [Sp. *salpicon*, corrupted. See *Salpicon.*]

A mixture of chopped meat and pickled herring with oil, vinegar, pepper and onions. *Johnson.*

Salmiac, a contraction of *sal ammoniac.*

SALMON, *n. sam'mon.* [L. *salmo*; Fr. *saumon.*]

A fish of the genus Salmo, found in all the northern climates of America, Europe and Asia, ascending the rivers for spawning in spring, and penetrating to their head streams. It is a remarkably strong fish, and will even leap over considerable falls which lie in the way of its progress. It has been known to grow to the weight of 75 pounds; more generally it is from 15 to 25 pounds. It furnishes a delicious dish for the table, and is an article of commerce.

SALMON-TROUT, *n. sam'mon-trout.* A species of trout resembling the salmon in color. *Walton.*

SALOON', *n.* [It. *salone*, from *sala*, hall; Sp. Fr. *salon*. See *Hall.*]

In *architecture*, a lofty spacious hall, vaulted at the top, and usually comprehending two stories, with two ranges of windows. It is a magnificent room in the middle of a building, or at the head of a gallery, &c. It is a state room much used in palaces in Italy for the reception of embassadors and other visitors. *Encyc.*

SALOOP, SALOP. [See *Salep.*]

SAL'PICON, *n.* [Sp. from *salpicar*, to besprinkle; Port. to corn, to powder, to spot; from *sal*, salt.]

Stuffing; farce; chopped meat or bread, &c. used to stuff legs of veal; called also *salmagundi*. [*I believe not used.*] *Bacon.*

SALSAMENTA'RIOUS, *a.* [L. *salsamentarius.*] Pertaining to salt things. [*Not in use.*] *Dict.*

SAL'SIFY, *n.* [Fr. *salsifis.*] Goat's beard, a plant of the genus Tragopogon. *Mortimer.*

SALSOAC'ID, *a.* [L. *salsus*, salt, and *acidus*, acid.]

Having a taste compounded of saltness and acidness. [*Little used.*] *Floyer.*

SALSU'GINOUS, *a.* [from L. *salsugo*, from *sal*, salt.] Saltish; somewhat salt. *Boyle.*

SALT, *n.* [Sax. *salt*, *sealt*; Goth. Sw. Dan. *salt*; G. *salz*; D. *sout*; Russ. *sol*; It. *sale*; Fr. *sel*; L. Sp. Port. *sal*; Gr. αλς; W. *halen*; Corn. Arm. *halinn*, from W. *hâl*, salt, a pervading substance. The radical sense is probably pungent, and if *s* is radical, the word belongs to the root of L. *salio*; but this is uncertain.]

1. Common salt is the muriate of soda, a substance used for seasoning certain kinds of food, and for the preservation of meat, &c. It is found native in the earth, or it is produced by evaporation and crystalization from water impregnated with saline particles.

2. In *chimistry*, a body compounded of an acid united to some base, which may be either an alkali, an earth, or a metallic oxyd. Accordingly, salts are alkaline, earthy, or metallic. Many compounds of this kind, of which common salt, (muriate of soda,) is the most distinguished, exist in nature; but most of these, together with many others not known in nature, have been formed by the artificial combination of their elements. Their entire number exceeds 2000. When the acid and base mutually saturate each other, so that the individual properties of each are lost, the compound is a *neutral* salt; when the acid predominates, it is a *super* salt; and when the base predominates, it is a *sub* salt. Thus we have a subcarbonate, a carbonate, and a supercarbonate of potash. *D. Olmsted.*

3. Taste; sapor; smack.

> We have some *salt* of our youth in us. *Shak.*

4. Wit; poignancy; as Attic *salt.*

SALT, *a.* Having the taste of salt; impregnated with salt; as *salt* beef; *salt* water.

2. Abounding with salt; as a *salt* land. Jer. xvii.
3. Overflowed with salt water, or impregnated with it; as a *salt* marsh.
4. Growing on salt marsh or meadows and having the taste of salt; as *salt* grass or hay.
5. Producing salt water; as a *salt* spring.
6. Lecherous; salacious. *Shak.*

SALT, *n.* The part of a river near the sea, where the water is salt. *Beverly.*
2. A vessel for holding salt.

SALT, *v. t.* To sprinkle, impregnate or season with salt; as, to *salt* fish, beef or pork.
2. To fill with salt between the timbers and planks, as a ship, for the preservation of the timber.

SALT, *v. i.* To deposit salt from a saline substance; as, the brine begins to *salt.* [*Used by manufacturers.*]

SALT, *n.* [Fr. *saut,* from *saillir,* to leap.] A leap; the act of jumping. [*Not in use.*] *B. Jonson.*

SALT'ANT, *a.* [L. *saltans,* from *salto,* to leap.] Leaping; jumping; dancing. *Dict.*

SALTA'TION, *n.* [L. *saltatio,* from *salto,* to leap.]
1. A leaping or jumping. *Brown.*
2. Beating or palpitation; as the *saltation* of the great artery. *Wiseman.*

SALT'CAT, *n.* A lump or heap of salt, made at the salt-works, which attracts pigeons. *Mortimer.*

SALT'-CELLAR, *n.* [*salt* and *cellar.*] A small vessel used for holding salt on the table. *Swift.*

SALT'ED, *pp.* Sprinkled, seasoned or impregnated with salt.

SALT'ER, *n.* One who salts; one who gives or applies salt.
2. One that sells salt. *Camden.*

SALT'ERN, *n.* A salt-work; a building in which salt is made by boiling or evaporation. *Encyc.*

SALT'IER, *n.* [Fr. *sautoir,* from *sauter,* L. *salto,* to leap.]
In *heraldry,* one of the honorable ordinaries, in the form of St. Andrew's cross. *Encyc.*

SALT'INBANCO, *n.* [Fr. *saltimbanque;* It. *saltare in banco,* to leap on the bench, to mount on the bench.] A mountebank; a quack. [*Not in use.*] *Brown.*

SALT'ING, *ppr.* Sprinkling, seasoning or impregnating with salt.

SALT'ING, *n.* The act of sprinkling or impregnating with salt.

SALT'ISH, *a.* Somewhat salt; tinctured or impregnated moderately with salt.

SALT'ISHLY, *adv.* With a moderate degree of saltness.

SALT'ISHNESS, *n.* A moderate degree of saltness.

SALT'LESS, *a.* Destitute of salt; insipid.

SALT'LY, *adv.* With taste of salt; in a salt manner.

SALT'-MINE, *n.* A mine where fossil salt is obtained.

SALT'NESS, *n.* The quality of being impregnated with salt; as the *saltness* of sea water or of provisions.
2. Taste of salt.

SALT'-PAN, } *n.* A pan, bason or pit where
SALT'-PIT, } salt is obtained or made. *Bacon. Woodward.*

SALTPE'TER, } *n.* [*salt* and Gr. πετρος, a
SALTPE'TRE, } stone.] A neutral salt formed by the nitric acid in combination with potash, and hence denominated nitrate of potash. It is found native in the East Indies, in Spain, in Naples and other places. It is also found on walls sheltered from rain, and it is extracted by lixiviation from the earths under cellars, stables and barns, &c. *Hooper. Lavoisier.*

SALTPE'TROUS, *a.* Pertaining to saltpeter, or partaking of its qualities; impregnated with saltpeter. *Med. Repos.*

SALTS, *n.* The salt water of rivers entering from the ocean. *S. Carolina.*

SALT'-WATER, *n.* Water impregnated with salt; sea water.

SALT'-WORK, *n.* A house or place where salt is made.

SALT'-WORT, *n.* A plant of the genus Salicornia; jointed glasswort.

SALU'BRIOUS, *a.* [L. *saluber, salubris,* from *salus.* See *Safe.*]
Favorable to health; healthful; promoting health; as *salubrious* air or water; a *salubrious* climate.

SALU'BRIOUSLY, *adv.* So as to promote health. *Burke.*

SALU'BRITY, *n.* [L. *salubritas.*] Wholesomeness; healthfulness; favorableness to the preservation of health; as the *salubrity* of air, of a country or climate.

SAL'UTARINESS, *n.* [See *Salutary.*]
1. Wholesomeness; the quality of contributing to health or safety.
2. The quality of promoting good or prosperity.

SAL'UTARY, *a.* [Fr. *salutaire;* L. *salutaris,* from *salus,* health.]
1. Wholesome; healthful; promoting health. Diet and exercise are *salutary* to men of sedentary habits.
2. Promotive of public safety; contributing to some beneficial purpose. The strict discipline of youth has a *salutary* effect on society.

SALUTA'TION, *n.* [Fr. from L. *salutatio.* See *Salute.*]
The act of saluting; a greeting; the act of paying respect or reverence by the customary words or actions; as in inquiring of persons their welfare, expressing to them kind wishes, bowing, &c. Luke i. Mark xii.

> In all public meetings and private addresses, use the forms of *salutation,* reverence and decency usual among the most sober people. *Taylor.*

SALU'TE, *v. t.* [L. *saluto;* It. *salutare;* Sp. *saludar;* Fr. *saluer;* from L. *salus* or *salvus.*]
1. To greet; to hail; to address with expressions of kind wishes.

> If ye *salute* your brethren only, what do ye more than others? Matt. v.

2. To please; to gratify. [*Unusual.*] *Shak.*
3. To kiss.
4. In *military* and *naval affairs,* to honor some person or nation by a discharge of cannon or small arms, by striking colors, by shouts, &c.

SALU'TE, *n.* The act of expressing kind wishes or respect; salutation; greeting. *South. Addison.*
2. A kiss. *Roscommon.*
3. In *military affairs,* a discharge of cannon or small arms in honor of some distinguished personage. A salute is sometimes performed by lowering the colors or beating the drums. The officers also salute each other by bowing their half pikes. *Encyc.*
4. In *the navy,* a testimony of respect or deference rendered by the ships of one nation to the ships of another, or by ships of the same nation to a superior or equal. This is performed by a discharge of cannon, volleys of small arms, striking the colors or top-sails, or by shouts of the seamen mounted on the masts or rigging. When two squadrons meet, the two chiefs only are to exchange *salutes.* *Encyc.*

SALU'TED, *pp.* Hailed; greeted.

SALU'TER, *n.* One who salutes.

SALUTIF'EROUS, *a.* [L. *salutifer; salus,* health, and *fero,* to bring.] Bringing health; healthy; as *salutiferous* air. *Dennis.*

SALVABIL'ITY, *n.* [from *salvable.*] The possibility of being saved or admitted to everlasting life. *Saunderson.*

SALV'ABLE, *a.* [L. *salvus,* safe; *salvo,* to save.]
That may be saved, or received to everlasting happiness.

SALV'AGE, *n.* [Fr. *salvage, sauvage,* from L. *salvus, salvo.*]
In *commerce,* a reward or recompense allowed by law for the saving of a ship or goods from loss at sea, either by shipwreck or other means, or by enemies or pirates. *Park.*

SALV'AGE, for *savage,* not used. [See *Savage.*]

SALVA'TION, *n.* [It. *salvazione;* Sp. *salvacion;* from L. *salvo,* to save.]
1. The act of saving; preservation from destruction, danger or great calamity.
2. Appropriately in theology, the redemption of man from the bondage of sin and liability to eternal death, and the conferring on him everlasting happiness. This is the *great salvation.*

> Godly sorrow worketh repentance to *salvation.* 2 Cor. vii.

3. Deliverance from enemies; victory. Ex. xiv.
4. Remission of sins, or saving graces. Luke xix.
5. The author of man's salvation. Ps. xxvii.
6. A term of praise or benediction. Rev. xix.

SALV'ATORY, *n.* [Fr. *salvatoire.*] A place where things are preserved; a repository. *Hale.*

SALVE, *n.* *sav.* [Sax. *sealfe;* from L. *salvus.*]
1. A glutinous composition or substance to be applied to wounds or sores; when spread on lether or cloth, it is called a *plaster.*
2. Help; remedy. *Hammond.*

SALVE, *v. t.* *sav.* To heal by applications or medicaments. [*Little used.*] *Spenser. Hooker.*
2. To help; to remedy. [*Little used.*] *Sidney.*

3. To help or remedy by a salvo, excuse or reservation. [*Little used.*] *Hooker. Bacon.*

4. To salute. [*Not in use.*] *Spenser.*

SAL'VER, *n.* A piece of plate with a foot; or a plate on which any thing is presented. *Addison. Pope.*

SALVIF'IC, *a.* [L. *salvus* and *facio.*] Tending to save or secure safety. [*A bad word and not used.*] *Ch. Relig. Appeal.*

SAL'VO, *n.* [from the L. *salvo jure*, an expression used in reserving rights.] An exception; a reservation; an excuse.

They admit many *salvos*, cautions and reservations. *K. Charles.*

SALV'OR, *n.* One who saves a ship or goods at sea. *Wheaton's Rep.*

SAMAR'ITAN, *a.* Pertaining to Samaria, the principal city of the ten tribes of Israel, belonging to the tribe of Ephraim, and after the captivity of those tribes, repeopled by Cuthites from Assyria or Chaldea.

2. Denoting the ancient characters and alphabet used by the Hebrews.

SAMAR'ITAN, *n.* An inhabitant of Samaria, or one that belonged to the sect which derived their appellation from that city. The Jews had no dealings with the *Samaritans.*

2. The language of Samaria, a dialect of the Chaldean.

SAM'BO, *n.* The offspring of a black person and a mulatto. *W. Indies.*

SAME, *a.* [Sax. *same;* Goth. *sama, samo;* Dan. *samme*, same, and *sammen*, together; Sw. *samme*, same; Dan. *samler, forsamler*, to collect, to *assemble;* Sw. *samla, forsmala*, id.; D. *zaam, zamen*, together; *zamelen*, to assemble; G. *sammeln*, id.; Sax. *samod*, L. *simul*, together; Sax. *samnian, semnian*, to assemble, to sum; W. *sum*, sum, amplitude; *swm*, the state of being together; *swmer*, that supports or keeps together, a beam, Eng. *summer*, in building. We observe that the Greek αμα agrees in signification with the L. *simul* and Sax. *samod*, Sans. *sam*, together. Shall we suppose then that *s* has passed into an aspirate in this word, as in *salt*, Gr. αλς, or has the Greek word lost *s*? The word *same* may be the L. *idem* or *dem*, dialectically varied. The primary sense is to set, to place, to put together. See Ar. ضم dhamma, to draw together, to set together, to join, to collect. Class Sm. No. 33. and see No. 43. 44.]

1. Identical; not different or other.

Thou art the *same*, and thy years shall have no end. Ps. cii.

The Lord Jesus, the *same* night in which he was betrayed, took bread. 1 Cor. xi.

2. Of the identical kind or species, though not the specific thing. We say, the horse of one country is the *same* animal as the horse of another country. The *same* plants and fruits are produced in the *same* latitudes. We see in men in all countries, the *same* passions and the *same* vices.

Th' etherial vigor is in all the *same.* *Dryden.*

3. That was mentioned before.

Do but think how well the *same* he spends,
Who spends his blood his country to relieve. *Daniel.*

4. Equal; exactly similar. One ship will not run the *same* distance as another in the *same* time, and with the *same* wind. Two balls of the *same* size have not always the *same* weight. Two instruments will not always make the *same* sound.

SAME, *adv.* [Sax. *sam.*] Together. *Obs.* *Spenser.*

SA'MENESS, *n.* Identity; the state of being not different or other; as the *sameness* of an unchangeable being.

2. Near resemblance; correspondence; similarity; as a *sameness* of manner; a sameness of sound; the *sameness* of objects in a landscape.

Samian earth. [Gr. *Samos*, the isle.] The name of a marl of two species, used in medicine as an astringent.

SA'MIEL, SIMOOM', *n.* [Ar. سموم samom. The Ar. سم signifies to be thin, or to become thin or pale, and to suffer the heat of the simoom, and سم signifies to poison. This word signifies probably that which is deleterious or destructive.]

A hot and destructive wind that sometimes blows in Arabia.

SAM'ITE, *n.* [Old Fr.] A species of silk stuff. *Obs.* *Chaucer.*

SAM'LET, *n.* A little salmon. *Walton.*

SAMP, *n.* A species of food composed of maiz broken or bruised, boiled and mixed with milk; a dish borrowed from the natives of America, but not much used. *New England.*

SAMP'ANE, *n.* A kind of vessel used by the Chinese. *Mar. Dict.*

SAM'PHIRE, *n.* [said to be a corruption of *Saint Pierre.*]

A plant of the genus Crithmum. The *golden samphire* is of the genus Inula. *Fam. of Plants.*

Samphire grows on rocks near the sea shore, where it is washed by the salt water. It is used for pickling. *Miller.*

SAM'PLE, *n.* [L. *exemplum;* Sp. Port. *exemplo;* It. *esempio;* Fr. *exemple;* Arm. *eçzempl;* Ir. *somplar, samhlachas*, from *samhail*, similar.]

1. A specimen; a part of any thing presented for inspection or intended to be shown, as evidence of the quality of the whole; as a *sample* of cloth or of wheat. Goods are often purchased in market by *samples.*

I design this as a *sample* of what I hope more fully to discuss. *Woodward.*

2. Example; instance. *Addison.*

SAM'PLE, *v. t.* To show something similar. *Ainsworth.*

SAM'PLER, *n.* [L. *exemplar*, supra.] A pattern of work; a specimen; particularly, a piece of needle work by young girls for improvement. *Shak. Pope.*

SAM'SON'S-POST, *n.* In *ships*, a notched post used instead of a ladder; also, a piece of timber that forms a return for a tackle fall. *Mar. Dict.*

SAN'ABLE, *a.* [L. *sanabilis*, from *sano*, to heal; *sanus*, sound. See *Sound.*]

That may be healed or cured; susceptible of remedy. *More.*

SANA'TION, *n.* [L. *sanatio*, from *sano*, to heal.] The act of healing or curing. [*Not used.*] *Wiseman.*

SAN'ATIVE, *a.* [L. *sano*, to heal.] Having the power to cure or heal; healing; tending to heal. *Bacon.*

SAN'ATIVENESS, *n.* The power of healing.

SANC'TIFICATE, *v. t.* To sanctify. [*Not in use.*] *Barrow.*

SANCTIFICA'TION, *n.* [Fr. from Low L. *sanctificatio*, from *sanctifico.* See *Sanctify.*]

1. The act of making holy. In an evangelical sense, the act of God's grace by which the affections of men are purified or alienated from sin and the world, and exalted to a supreme love to God.

God hath from the beginning chosen you to salvation, through *sanctification* of the Spirit and belief of the truth. 2 Thess. ii. 1 Pet. i.

2. The act of consecrating or of setting apart for a sacred purpose; consecration. *Stillingfleet.*

SANC'TIFIED, *pp.* Made holy; consecrated; set apart for sacred services.

2. Affectedly holy. *Hume.*

SANC'TIFIER, *n.* He that sanctifies or makes holy. In theology, the Holy Spirit is, by way of eminence, denominated the *Sanctifier.*

SANC'TIFY, *v. t.* [Fr. *sanctifier;* It. *santificare;* Sp. *santificar;* Low L. *sanctifico;* from *sanctus*, holy, and *facio*, to make.]

1. In *a general sense*, to cleanse, purify or make holy. *Addison.*

2. To separate, set apart or appoint to a holy, sacred or religious use.

God blessed the seventh day and *sanctified* it. Gen. ii.

So under the Jewish dispensation, to *sanctify* the altar, the temple, the priests, &c.

3. To purify; to prepare for divine service, and for partaking of holy things. Ex. xix.

4. To separate, ordain and appoint to the work of redemption and the government of the church. John x.

5. To cleanse from corruption; to purify from sin; to make holy by detaching the affections from the world and its defilements, and exalting them to a supreme love to God.

Sanctify them through thy truth; thy word is truth. John xvii. Eph. v.

6. To make the means of holiness; to render productive of holiness or piety.

Those judgments of God are the more welcome, as a means which his mercy hath *sanctified* so to me, as to make me repent of that unjust act. *K. Charles.*

7. To make free from guilt.

That holy man, amaz'd at what he saw,
Made haste to *sanctify* the bliss by law. *Dryden.*

8. To secure from violation.

Truth guards the poet, *sanctifies* the line. *Pope.*

To sanctify God, to praise and celebrate him as a holy being; to acknowledge and honor his holy majesty, and to reverence his character and laws. Is. viii.

God sanctifies himself or *his name*, by vindicating his honor from the reproaches of the wicked, and manifesting his glory. Ezek. xxxvi.

SANC'TIFYING, *ppr* Making holy; purifying from the defilements of sin; separating to a holy use.

2. *a.* Tending to sanctify; adapted to increase holiness.

SAN€TIMO'NIOUS, *a.* [L. *sanctimonia*, from *sanctus*, holy.]
Saintly; having the appearance of sanctity; as a *sanctimonious* pretense. *L'Estrange.*

SAN€TIMO'NIOUSLY, *adv.* With sanctimony.

SAN€TIMO'NIOUSNESS, *n.* State of being sanctimonious; sanctity, or the appearance of it; devoutness.

SAN€'TIMONY, *n.* [L. *sanctimonia.*] Holiness; devoutness; scrupulous austerity; sanctity, or the appearance of it. [*Little used.*] *Shak. Raleigh.*

SAN€'TION, *n.* [Fr. from L. *sanctio*, from *sanctus*, holy, solemn, established.]
1. Ratification; an official act of a superior by which he ratifies and gives validity to the act of some other person or body. A treaty is not valid without the *sanction* of the president and senate.
2. Authority; confirmation derived from testimony, character, influence or custom.
The strictest professors of reason have added the *sanction* of their testimony. *Watts.*
3. A law or decree. [*Improper.*] *Denham.*

SAN€'TION, *v. t.* To ratify; to confirm; to give validity or authority to. *Burke.*

SAN€'TIONED, *pp.* Ratified; confirmed; authorized.

SAN€'TIONING, *ppr.* Ratifying; authorizing.

SAN€'TITUDE, *n.* [L. *sanctus, sanctitudo.*] Holiness; sacredness. *Milton.*

SAN€'TITY, *n.* [L. *sanctitas.*] Holiness; state of being sacred or holy. God attributes no *sanctity* to place. *Milton.*
2. Goodness; purity; godliness; as the *sanctity* of love; *sanctity* of manners. *Shak. Addison.*
3. Sacredness; solemnity; as the *sanctity* of an oath.
4. A saint or holy being.
About him all the *sanctities* of heav'n— [*Unusual.*] *Milton.*

SAN€'TUARIZE, *v. t.* [from *sanctuary.*] To shelter by means of a sanctuary or sacred privileges. [*A bad word and not used.*] *Shak.*

SAN€'TUARY, *n.* [Fr. *sanctuaire*; It. Sp. *santuario*; L. *sanctuarium*, from *sanctus*, sacred.]
1. A sacred place; particularly among the Israelites, the most retired part of the temple at Jerusalem, called the *Holy of Holies*, in which was kept the ark of the covenant, and into which no person was permitted to enter except the high priest, and that only once a year to intercede for the people. The same name was given to the most sacred part of the tabernacle. Lev. iv. Heb. ix.
2. The temple at Jerusalem. 2 Chron. xx.
3. A house consecrated to the worship of God; a place where divine service is performed. Ps. lxxiii.
Hence *sanctuary* is used for a church.
4. In *catholic churches*, that part of a church where the altar is placed, encompassed with a ballustrade. *Encyc.*
5. A place of protection; a sacred asylum. Hence a *sanctuary-man* is one that resorts to a sanctuary for protection. *Bacon. Shak.*
6. Shelter; protection.
Some relics of painting took *sanctuary* under ground. *Dryden.*

SAND, *n.* [Sax. G. Sw. Dan. *sand*; D. *zand.*]
1. Any mass or collection of fine particles of stone, particularly of fine particles of silicious stone, but not strictly reduced to powder or dust.
That finer matter called *sand*, is no other than very small pebbles. *Woodward.*
2. *Sands*, in the plural, tracts of land consisting of sand, like the deserts of Arabia and Africa; as the Lybian *sands*. *Milton.*

SAND, *v. t.* To sprinkle with sand. It is customary among the common people in America, to *sand* their floors with white sand.
2. To drive upon the sand. *Burton.*

SAN'DAL, *n.* [Fr. *sandale*; It. *sandalo*; Sp. *sandalia*; L. *sandalium*; Gr. σανδαλιον. Qu. Syr. ܣܐܢ san, to shoe. Class Sn. No. 9.]
1. A kind of shoe, consisting of a sole fastened to the foot. The Greek and Roman ladies wore sandals made of a rich stuff, ornamented with gold or silver. *Pope. Encyc.*
2. A shoe or slipper worn by the pope and other Romish prelates when they officiate. A like sandal is worn by several congregations of monks. *Encyc.*

SAN'DAL, SAN'DAL-WOOD, SAN'DERS, *n.* [Ar. صَنْدَل; Pers. جُنْدُل jondul.]
A kind of wood which grows in the East Indies and on some of the isles of the Pacific. It is of three kinds, the white, the yellow, and the red. The tree which produces the two former is of the genus Santalum. It grows to the size of a walnut tree. Its wood has a bitter taste and an aromatic smell. The oriental nations burn it in their houses for the sake of its fragrant odor, and with the powder of it a paste is prepared, with which they anoint their bodies. The white and the yellow sandal-wood are different parts of the same tree; the white is the wood next to the bark; the yellow is the inner part of the tree. The red sandal-wood is obtained from a different tree, the *Pterocarpus santolinus*. It is of a dull red color, has little taste or smell, and is principally used as a coloring drug. *Encyc. Parr.*

SAN'DARA€, SAN'DARA€H, *n.* [L. *sandaraca*; Ar. سندروس sandros.]
1. A resin in white tears, more transparent than those of mastic; obtained from the juniper tree, in which it occupies the place between the bark and the wood. It is used in powder to prevent ink from sinking or spreading. This is the substance denoted by the Arabic word, and it is also called *varnish*, as it enters into the preparations of varnish. For distinction, this is called *gum sandarac* or *sandaric*. *Fourcroy.*
The sandarach is obtained from the *Thuya articulata*, (*Thomson*;) from the *Juniperus cedrus*, (*Parr.*)
2. A native fossil; also, a combination of arsenic and sulphur; orpiment. *Nicholson. Encyc.*

SAND'-BAG, *n.* A bag filled with sand; used in fortification.

SAND'-BATH, *n.* A bath made by warm sand, with which something is enveloped.

SAND'-BLIND, *a.* Having a defect of sight, by means of which small particles appear to fly before the eyes. *Shak.*

SAND'-BOX, *n.* A box with a perforated top or cover, for sprinkling paper with sand.
2. A tree or plant of the genus Hura. It is said that the pericarp of the fruit will burst in the heat of the day with a loud report, and throw the seeds to a distance. *Fam. of Plants. Miller.*

SAND'ED, *pp.* Sprinkled with sand; as a *sanded* floor.
2. *a.* Covered with sand; barren. *Mortimer.*
3. Marked with small spots; variegated with spots; speckled; of a sandy color, as a hound. *Shak.*
4. Short sighted. *Shak.*

SAND'-EEL, *n.* The ammodyte, a fish that resembles an eel. It seldom exceeds a foot in length; its head is compressed, the upper jaw larger than the under one, the body cylindrical, with scales hardly perceptible. There is one species only, a native of Europe. It coils with its head in the center, and penetrates into the sand; whence its name in Greek and English. It is delicate food. *Encyc.*

SAND'ERLING, *n.* A bird of the plover kind. *Carew.*

SANDERS. [See *Sandal.*]

SAN'DEVER, SAN'DIVER, *n.* [Fr. *sain de verre*, or *saint de verre*, dross or recrement of glass.]
Glass-gall; a whitish salt which is cast up from the materials of glass in fusion, and floating on the top, is skimmed off. A similar substance is thrown out in eruptions of volcanoes. It is used by gilders of iron, and in the fusion of certain ores. It is said to be good for cleansing the skin, and taken internally, is detergent. *Encyc.*

SAND'-FLOOD, *n.* A vast body of sand moving or borne along the deserts of Arabia. *Bruce.*

SAND'-HEAT, *n.* The heat of warm sand in chimical operations.

SAND'INESS, *n.* [from *sandy.*] The state of being sandy; as the *sandiness* of a road.
2. The state of being of a sandy color.

SAND'ISH, *a.* [from *sand.*] Approaching the nature of sand; loose; not compact. *Evelyn.*

SAND'IX, *n.* A kind of minium or red lead, made of ceruse, but inferior to the true minium. *Encyc.*

SAND'PIPER, *n.* A bird of the genus Tringa.

SAND'STONE, *n.* [*sand* and *stone.*] Sandstone is, in most cases, composed chiefly of grains of quartz united by a cement, calcarious, marly, argillaceous, or even silicious. The texture of some kinds is loose, of others close; the fracture is granular or earthy. *Cleaveland.*
Sandstones usually consist of the materials of older rocks, as granite, broken up

and comminuted, and afterwards deposited again. *D. Olmsted.*

SAND'-WÖRT, *n.* A plant.

SAND'Y, *a.* [Sax. *sandig.*] Abounding with sand; full of sand; covered or sprinkled with sand; as a *sandy* desert or plain; a *sandy* road or soil.

2. Consisting of sand; not firm or solid; as a *sandy* foundation.

3. Of the color of sand; of a yellowish red color; as *sandy* hair.

SANE, *a.* [L. *sanus*, Eng. *sound;* D. *gezond;* G. *gesund.* This is the Eng. *sound*, Sax. *sund.* See *Sound.*]

1. Sound; not disordered or shattered; healthy; as a *sane* body.

2. Sound; not disordered; having the regular exercise of reason and other faculties of the mind; as a *sane* person; a person of a *sane* mind.

SANG, *pret.* of *sing.*

SANG FROID, *n.* [Fr. cold blood.] Coolness; freedom from agitation or excitement of mind.

2. Indifference.

SAN'GIAC, *n.* A Turkish governor of a province.

SANGUIF'EROUS, *a.* [L. *sanguifer; sanguis*, blood, and *fero*, to carry.]

Conveying blood. The *sanguiferous* vessels are the arteries and veins.

SANGUIFICA'TION, *n.* [Fr. from L. *sanguis*, blood, and *facio*, to make.]

In *the animal economy*, the production of blood; the conversion of chyle into blood. *Arbuthnot.*

SAN'GUIFIER, *n.* A producer of blood. *Floyer.*

SANGUIF'LUOUS, *a.* [L. *sanguis*, blood, and *fluo*, to flow.] Floating or running with blood.

SAN'GUIFY, *v. i.* To produce blood. *Hale.*

SAN'GUIFYING, *ppr.* Producing blood.

SAN'GUINARY, *a.* [Fr. *sanguinaire;* L. *sanguinarius*, from *sanguis*, blood.]

1. Bloody; attended with much bloodshed; murderous; as a *sanguinary* war, contest or battle.

2. Blood thirsty; cruel; eager to shed blood.

> Passion—makes us brutal and *sanguinary.* *Broome.*

SAN'GUINARY, *n.* A plant. *Ainsworth.*

SAN'GUINE, } *a.* [Fr. *sanguin;* L. *san-*
SAN'GUIN, } *guineus*, from *sanguis*, blood.]

1. Red; having the color of blood; as a *sanguine* color or countenance. *Dryden. Milton.*

2. Abounding with blood; plethoric; as a *sanguine* habit of body.

3. Warm; ardent; as a *sanguine* temper.

4. Confident. He is *sanguine* in his expectations of success.

SAN'GUINE, *n.* Blood color. [*Not in use.*] *Spenser.*

SAN'GUINE, *v. t.* To stain with blood. [But *ensanguine* is generally used.]

2. To stain or varnish with a blood color.

SAN'GUINELESS, *a.* Destitute of blood; pale. [*A bad word and little used.*]

SAN'GUINELY, *adv.* Ardently; with confidence of success. *Chesterfield.*

SAN'GUINENESS, *n.* Redness; color of blood in the skin; as *sanguineness* of countenance.

2. Fullness of blood; plethory; as *sanguineness* of habit.

3. Ardor; heat of temper; confidence. *Decay of Piety.*

SANGUIN'EOUS, *a.* [L. *sanguineus.*]

1. Abounding with blood; plethoric. *Arbuthnot.*

2. Constituting blood. *Brown.*

SANGUIN'ITY, for *sanguineness*, is not in use. *Swift.*

SAN'GUISUGE, *n.* [L. *sanguisuga; sanguis*, blood, and *sugo*, to suck.]

The blood-sucker; a leech, or horse leech. *Encyc.*

SAN'HEDRIM, *n.* [Low L. *synedrium;* Gr. συνεδριον; συν, with, together, and εδρα, seat.]

The great council of seventy elders among the Jews, whose jurisdiction extended to all important affairs. They received appeals from inferior tribunals, and had power of life and death. *Encyc.*

SAN'ICLE, *n.* [from L. *sano*, to heal.] Self-heal, a plant or genus of plants, the Sanicula; also, a plant of the genus Saxifraga. The *American bastard sanicle* is of the genus Mitella, and the *bear's ear sanicle* of the genus Cortusa. *Fam. of Plants.*

SANID'IUM, *n.* A genus of fossils of the class of selenites, composed of plain flat plates. *Encyc.*

SA'NIES, *n.* [L.] A thin acrid discharge from wounds or sores; a serous matter, less thick and white than pus. *Coxe. Encyc.*

SA'NIOUS, *a.* [from *sanies.*] Pertaining to sanies, or partaking of its nature and appearance; thin; serous; as the *sanious* matter of an ulcer.

2. Running a thin serous matter; as a *sanious* ulcer. *Wiseman.*

SAN'ITY, *n.* [L. *sanitas.* See *Sane.*] Soundness; particularly, a sound state of mind; the state of a mind in the perfect exercise of reason. *Shak.*

SANK, *pret.* of *sink*, but nearly obsolete.

SAN'NAH, *n.* The name of certain kinds of India muslins.

SANS, *prep.* [Fr.] Without. *Shak.*

SAN'SCRIT, *n.* [According to H. T. Colebrooke, *Sanscrit* signifies the polished dialect. It is sometimes written *Shanscrit*, and in other ways. Asiat. Res. 7, 200.]

The ancient language of Hindoostan, from which are formed all the modern languages or dialects of the great peninsula of India. It is the language of the Bramins, and in this are written the ancient books of the country; but it is now obsolete. It is from the same stock as the ancient Persic, Greek and Latin, and all the present languages of Europe.

SANTER. [See *Saunter.*]

SANT'ON, *n.* A Turkish priest; a kind of dervis, regarded by the vulgar as a saint. *Herbert.*

SAP, *n.* [Sax. *sæp;* D. *zap;* G. *saft;* Sw. *saft, safve;* Dan. *saft, sæve;* Fr. *seve;* Arm. *sabr;* probably from softness or flowing. Qu. Pers. زبه zabah, a flowing.]

1. The juice of plants of any kind, which flows chiefly between the wood and the bark. From the *sap* of a species of maple, is made sugar of a good quality by evaporation.

2. The alburnum of a tree; the exterior part of the wood, next to the bark. [*A sense in general use in New England.*]

SAP, *v. t.* [Fr. *saper;* It. *zappare;* Arm. *sappa;* It. *zappa*, a spade; *zappone*, a mattoc. The primary sense is probably to dig or to thrust.]

1. To undermine; to subvert by digging or wearing away; to mine.

> Their dwellings were *sapp'd* by floods. *Dryden.*

2. To undermine; to subvert by removing the foundation of. Discontent *saps* the foundation of happiness. Intrigue and corruption *sap* the constitution of a free government.

SAP, *v. i.* To proceed by mining, or by secretly undermining.

> Both assaults are carried on by *sapping.* *Tatler.*

SAP, *n.* In *sieges*, a trench for undermining; or an approach made to a fortified place by digging or under cover. The single sap has only a single parapet; the double has one on each side, and the flying is made with gabions, &c. In all saps, traverses are left to cover the men. *Encyc.*

SAP'AJO, *n.* The sapajos form a division of the genus Simia, including such of the monkeys of America as have prehensile tails. *Encyc.*

SAP'-COLOR, *n.* An expressed vegetable juice inspissated by slow evaporation, for the use of painters, as sap-green, &c. *Parke.*

SAP'ID, *a.* [L. *sapidus*, from *sapio*, to taste.]

Tasteful; tastable; having the power of affecting the organs of taste; as *sapid* water. *Brown. Arbuthnot.*

SAPID'ITY, } *n.* Taste; tastefulness; sa-
SAP'IDNESS, } vor; the quality of affecting the organs of taste; as the *sapidness* of water or fruit. *Boyle.*

SA'PIENCE, *n.* [Fr. from L. *sapientia*, from *sapio*, to taste, to know.]

Wisdom; sageness; knowledge.

> —Still has gratitude and *sapience*
> To spare the folks that give him ha' pence. *Swift.*

SA'PIENT, *a.* Wise; sage; discerning.

> There the *sapient* king held dalliance. *Milton.*

SAPIEN'TIAL, *a.* Affording wisdom or instructions for wisdom. [*Not much used.*] *Bp. Richardson.*

SAP'LESS, *a.* [from *sap.*] Destitute of sap; as a *sapless* tree or branch. *Swift. Shak.*

2. Dry; old; husky; as a *sapless* usurer. *Dryden.*

SAP'LING, *n.* [from *sap.*] A young tree.

> Nurse the *saplings* tall. *Milton.*

SAPONA'CEOUS, *a.* [from L. *sapo*, soap.] Soapy; resembling soap; having the qualities of soap. *Saponaceous* bodies are often formed by oil and alkali.

SAP'ONARY, *a.* Saponaceous.

SAPONIFICA'TION, *n.* Conversion into soap.

SAPON'IFY, *v. t.* [L. *sapo*, soap, and *facio*, to make.]

To convert into soap by combination with an alkali. *Ure.*

SAP'ONULE, *n.* A combination of volatile or essential oil with some base.

SA'POR, *n.* [L.] Taste; savor; relish; the power of affecting the organs of taste.

There is some *sapor* in all aliments. *Brown.*

SAPORIF'IC, *a.* [Fr. *saporifique;* from L. *sapor* and *facio,* to make.]

Having the power to produce taste; producing taste. *Bailey. Johnson.*

SAPOROS'ITY, *n.* The quality of a body by which it excites the sensation of taste.

SA'POROUS, *a.* Having taste; yielding some kind of taste. *Bailey.*

SAPO'TA, *n.* In *botany,* a tree or plant of the genus Achras.

SAPPADIL'LO-TREE, SAPADIL'LO-TREE, *n.* A tree of the genus Sloanea. *Fam. of Plants. Lee.*

SAP'PARE, *n.* A mineral or species of earth, the kyanite; called by Haüy, disthene. *Ure.*

SAP'PED, *pp.* Undermined; subverted.

SAP'PER, *n.* One who saps. In an army, sappers and miners are employed in working at saps, to protect soldiers in their approach to a besieged place, or to undermine the works.

SAPPHIC, *a. saf'ic.* Pertaining to Sappho, a Grecian poetess; as *Sapphic* odes; *Sapphic* verse. The Sapphic verse consists of eleven syllables in five feet, of which the first, fourth and fifth are trochees, the second a spondee, and the third a dactyl, in the first three lines of each stanza, with a fourth consisting only of a dactyl and a spondee.

SAP'PHIRE, *n.* [L. *sapphirus;* Gr. σαπφειρος; from the Ar. سفر safara, to scrape, to shine, to be fair, open, beautiful; Ch. Syr. Sam. to scrape, to shave.]

A species of silicious gems or minerals, of several varieties. In hardness it is inferior to the diamond only. Its colors are blue, red, violet, yellow, green, white, or limpid, and one variety is chatoyant, and another asteriated or radiated. *Cleaveland.*

Sapphire is a subspecies of rhomboidal corundum. *Ure. Jameson.*

The oriental ruby and topaz are sapphires. *Ure.*

Sapphire is employed in jewelry and the arts.

SAP'PHIRINE, *a.* Resembling sapphire; made of sapphire; having the qualities of sapphire. *Boyle.*

SAP'PINESS, *n.* [from *sappy.*] The state or quality of being full of sap; succulence; juiciness.

SAP'PY, *a.* [Sax. *sæpig.*] Abounding with sap; juicy; succulent. *Mortimer.*

2. Young; not firm; weak.

When he had passed this weak and *sappy* age— *Hayward.*

3. Weak in intellect.

SAP'PY, *a.* [Qu. Gr. σηπω, to putrefy.] Musty; tainted. [*Not in use.*]

SAR'ABAND, *n.* [Sp. *zarabanda;* Port. It. *sarabanda;* Fr. *sarabande.*]

A dance and a tune used in Spain, said to be derived from the Saracens. *Sp. Dict. Encyc.*

SARACEN'IC, *a.* Pertaining to the Saracens, inhabitants of Arabia; so called from *sara,* a desert.

2. Denoting the architecture of the Saracens, the modern Gothic. *Johnson.*

SAR'AGOY, *n.* The opossum of the Molucca isles.

S'ARCASM, *n.* [L. *sarcasmus;* Gr. σαρκασμος, from σαρκαζω, to deride or sneer at, primarily to flay or pluck off the skin.]

A keen reproachful expression; a satirical remark or expression, uttered with some degree of scorn or contempt; a taunt; a gibe. Of this we have an example in the remark of the Jews respecting Christ, on the cross, "He saved others, himself he cannot save."

SARCAS'TIC, SARCAS'TICAL, *a.* Bitterly satirical; scornfully severe; taunting.

What a fierce and *sarcastic* reprehension would this have drawn from the friendship of the world! *South.*

SARCAS'TICALLY, *adv.* In a sarcastic manner; with scornful satire. *South.*

S'ARCENET, *n.* [Qu. *saracenicum* or *saracen,* silk.] A species of fine thin woven silk. *Dryden.*

S'ARCOCELE, *n.* [Gr. σαρξ, flesh, and κηλη, tumor.]

A spurious rupture or hernia, in which the testicle is swelled or indurated, like a scirrhus, or enlarged by a fleshy excrescence much beyond its natural size. *Encyc.*

S'ARCOCOL, S'ARCOCOL'LA, *n.* [Gr. compounded of σαρξ, flesh, and κολλα, glue.]

A semi-transparent solid substance, imported from Arabia and Persia in grains of a light yellow or red color. It is sometimes called a gum resin, as it partakes of the qualities of both gum and resin. It has its name from its use in healing wounds and ulcers. *Encyc.*

S'ARCOLITE, *n.* [flesh-stone.] A substance of a vitreous nature, and of a rose flesh color, found near Vesuvius. The French call it *hydrolite,* water stone. *Dict. Nat. Hist.*

Sarcolite is a variety of analcime. *Ure.*

SARCOLOG'ICAL, *a.* Pertaining to sarcology.

SARCOL'OGY, *n.* [Gr. σαρξ, flesh, and λογος, discourse.]

That part of anatomy which treats of the soft parts of the body, as the muscles, fat, intestines, vessels, &c. *Encyc.*

SARCO'MA, *n.* [Gr. from σαρξ, flesh.] Any fleshy excrescence on an animal body. *Encyc.*

SARCOPH'AGOUS, *a.* [See *Sarcophagus.*] Feeding on flesh; flesh-eating. *Dict.*

SARCOPH'AGUS, *n.* [L. from Gr. σαρκοφαγος; σαρξ, flesh, and φαγω, to eat.]

1. A species of stone used among the Greeks in their sculptures, which was so called because it consumed the flesh of bodies deposited in it within a few weeks. It is otherwise called *lapis Assius,* and said to be found at Assos, a city of Lycia. Hence,

2. A stone coffin or grave in which the ancients deposited bodies which they chose not to burn. *Encyc.*

SARCOPH'AGY, *n.* [supra.] The practice of eating flesh. *Brown.*

SARCOT'IC, *a.* [Gr. σαρξ, flesh.] In *surgery,* producing or generating flesh.

SARCOT'IC, *n.* A medicine or application which promotes the growth of flesh; an incarnative. *Coxe.*

S'ARDACHATE, *n.* The clouded and spotted agate, of a pale flesh color.

S'ARDAN, *n.* A fish resembling the herring. *Dict. Nat. Hist.*

S'ARDE, S'ARDOIN, *n.* A mineral, a variety of carnelian, which displays on its surface a rich reddish brown, but when held between the eye and the light, appears of a deep blood red. *Ure.*

S'ARDEL, S'ARDINE, S'ARDIUS, *n.* [L. *sardius;* Gr. σαρδιον; from *Sardis,* in Asia Minor, now *Sart.*] A precious stone. One of this kind was set in Aaron's breastplate. Ex. xxviii.

SARDO'NIAN, SARDON'IC, *a.* *Sardonian* or *sardonic laughter,* a convulsive involuntary laughter, so called from the *herba sardonia,* a species of ranunculus, which is said to produce such convulsive motions in the cheeks and lips as are observed during a fit of laughter. *Encyc.*

SARDON'IC, *a.* Denoting a kind of linen made at Colchis. *Bryant.*

S'ARDONYX, *n.* [L. *sardonyches,* from Gr. σαρδονυξ, from *Sardis,* a city of Asia Minor, and ονυξ, a nail; so named, according to Pliny, from the resemblance of its color to the flesh under the nail. Plin. Lib. 37. 6.]

A silicious stone or gem, nearly allied to carnelian. Its color is a reddish yellow, or nearly orange. We are informed that the yellow or orange colored agate, with an undulating surface, is now often called sardonyx. *Encyc. Cleaveland.*

S'ARGUS, *n.* A fish of the Mediterranean, whose body is variegated with brown transverse rings, resembling the variegations of the perch. This is also a name of the gardon. *Dict.*

S'ARK, *n.* [Sax. *syrc.*] In Scotland, a shirt.

2. A shark. [*Not used.*]

S'ARLAC, *n.* The grunting ox of Tartary.

SARMA'TIAN, SARMAT'IC, *a.* Pertaining to Sarmatia and its inhabitants, the ancestors of the Russians and Poles.

SARMENT'OUS, *a.* [L. *sarmentosus,* from *sarmentum,* a twig.]

A sarmentous stem, in *botany,* is one that is filiform and almost naked, or having only leaves in bunches at the joints or knots, where it strikes root. *Martyn.*

SARON'IC, *a.* Denoting a gulf of Greece between Attica and Sparta. *D'Anville.*

S'ARPLAR, *n.* A sarplar of wool is a sack containing 80 tod; a tod contains two stone of 14 pounds each. *Encyc.*

S'ARPLIER, *n.* [Fr. *serpillière.*] Canvas, or a packing cloth. *Bailey.*

SAR'ASIN, SAR'RASINE, *n.* A plant, a kind of birth wort. *Bailey.*

2. A portcullis or herse.

S'ARSA, S'ARSAPARIL'LA, *n.* A plant, a species of Smilax, valued in medicine for its mucilaginous and farinaceous or demulcent qualities. *Encyc.*

S'ARSE, *n.* [Qu. *sarcenet,* or Fr. *sas.*] A fine sieve; usually written *searce* or *searse.* [*Little used.*]

S'ARSE, *v. t.* [from the noun.] To sift through a sarse. [*Little used.*]

S'ART, *n.* A piece of woodland turned into arable. [*Not used in America.*] *Bailey.*

SASH, *n.* [an Arabic word signifying a band.]

1. A belt worn for ornament. Sashes are worn by military officers as badges of distinction, round the waist or over the shoulders. They are usually of silk, variously made and ornamented.

2. The frame of a window in which the lights or panes of glass are set.

> She ventures now to lift the *sash*. *Swift.*

SASH'OON, *n.* A kind of lether stuffing put into a boot for the wearer's ease. *Ainsworth.*

SAS'SAFRAS, *n.* [L. *saxifraga ; saxum*, a stone, and *frango*, to break.]

A tree of the genus Laurus, whose bark has an aromatic smell and taste.

SASSE, *n.* [D. *sas.*] A sluice, canal or lock on a navigable river; a word found in old British statutes. *Todd.*

SAS'SOLIN, } *n.* Native boracic acid,
SAS'SOLINE, } found in saline incrustations on the borders of hot springs near Sasso, in the territory of Florence. *Klaproth. Cyc.*

SAS'SOROL, } *n.* A species of pigeon,
SASSOROL'LA, } called rock pigeon. *Dict. Nat. Hist.*

SAS'TRA, *n.* Among the Hindoos, a sacred book; a book containing sacred ordinances. The six great *Sastras*, in the opinion of the Hindoos, contain all knowledge, human and divine. These are the Veda, Upaveda, Vedanga, Purana, Dherma, and Dersana. *Asiat. Res.*

SAT, *pret.* of *sit*.

SA'TAN, *n.* [Heb. an adversary.] The grand adversary of man; the devil or prince of darkness; the chief of the fallen angels.

SATAN'IC, } *a.* Having the qualities of
SATAN'ICAL, } Satan; resembling Satan; extremely malicious or wicked; devilish; infernal.

> Detest the slander which with a *satanic* smile, exults over the character it has ruined. *Dwight.*

SATAN'ICALLY, *adv.* With the wicked and malicious spirit of Satan; diabolically. *Hammond.*

SA'TANISM, *n.* The evil and malicious disposition of Satan; a diabolical spirit.

SA'TANIST, *n.* A very wicked person. [*Little used.*]

SATCH'EL, *n.* [See *Sachel.*] A little sack or bag.

SATE, *v. t.* [L. *satio ;* It. *saziare ;* Port. Sp. *saciar ;* Fr. *rassasier ;* allied to *set.* The primary sense is to stuff, to fill, from crowding, driving.]

To satiate; to satisfy appetite; to glut; to feed beyond natural desire.

> While the vultures *sate*
> Their maws with full repast. *Philips.*

SA'TED, *pp.* Filled; glutted; satiated.

SA'TELESS, *a.* Insatiable; not capable of being satisfied.

SAT'ELLITE, *n.* [Fr. It. *satellite ;* L. *satelles.* Qu. its alliance to *sit* or *side.*]

1. A secondary planet or moon; a small planet revolving round another. In the solar system, eighteen *satellites* have been discovered. The earth has *one*, called the moon, Jupiter *four*, Saturn *seven*, and Herschel *six*. *Morse.*

2. A follower; an obsequious attendant or dependant.

SATELLI"TIOUS, *a.* Consisting of satellites. *Cheyne.*

SATIATE, *v. t.* *sa'shate.* [L. *satiatus*, from *satio.* See *Sate.*]

1. To fill; to satisfy appetite or desire; to feed to the full, or to furnish enjoyment to the extent of desire; as, to *satiate* appetite or sense.

2. To fill to the extent of want; as, to *satiate* the earth or plants with water.

3. To glut; to fill beyond natural desire.

> He may be *satiated*, but not satisfied. *Norris.*

4. To gratify desire to the utmost.

> I may yet survive the malice of my enemies, although they should be *satiated* with my blood. *K. Charles.*

5. To saturate. [*Now unusual.* See *Saturate.*] *Newton.*

SA'TIATE, *a.* Filled to satiety; glutted; followed by *with* or *of*. The former is most common; as *satiate of* applause. [*Unusual.*] *Pope.*

SATIA'TION, *n.* The state of being filled. *Whitaker.*

SATI'ETY, *n.* [Fr. *satieté ;* L. *satietas.* See *Sate.*]

Properly, fullness of gratification, either of the appetite or any sensual desire; but it usually implies fullness beyond desire; an excess of gratification which excites wearisomeness or lothing; state of being glutted.

> In all pleasures there is *satiety*. *Hakewill.*
> —But thy words, with grace divine
> Imbu'd, bring to their sweetness no *satiety*. *Milton.*

SAT'IN, *n.* [Fr. *satin ;* W. *sidan*, satin or silk; Sw. *siden ;* Port. Sp. *seda ;* It. *seta ;* Gr. L. *sindon ;* Ch. Heb. סדין ; Ar. سندس.]

A species of glossy silk cloth, of a thick, close texture.

SATINET', *n.* A thin species of satin.

2. A particular kind of woolen cloth.

SAT'IN-FLOWER, *n.* A plant of the genus Lunaria.

SAT'IN-SPAR, *n.* A mineral, fibrous limestone. *Ure.*

SAT'IRE, *n.* [Fr. *satire ;* Sp. L. *satira ;* so named from sharpness, pungency. See *Satyriasis.*]

1. A discourse or poem in which wickedness or folly is exposed with severity. It differs from *lampoon* and *pasquinade*, in being general rather than personal. *Johnson.*

2. Severity of remark. It differs from *sarcasm*, in not expressing contempt or scorn.

SATIR'IC, } *a.* [L. *satiricus ;* Fr. *satir-*
SATIR'ICAL, } *ique.*] Belonging to satire; conveying satire; as a *satiric* style.

2. Censorious; severe in language. *Bacon.*

SATIR'ICALLY, *adv.* With severity of remark; with invective; with intention to censure.

SAT'IRIST, *n.* One who writes satire.

> Wycherly, in his writings, is the sharpest *satirist* of his time. *Granville.*

SAT'IRIZE, *v. t.* [Fr. *satiriser.*] To censure with keenness or severity.

> It is as hard to *satirize* well a man of distinguished vices, as to praise well a man of distinguished virtues. *Swift.*

SAT'IRIZED, *pp.* Severely censured.

SAT'IRIZING, *ppr.* Censuring with severity.

SATISFAC'TION, *n.* [Fr. from L. *satisfactio ;* It. *soddisfazione.* See *Satisfy.*]

1. That state of the mind which results from the full gratification of desire; repose of mind or contentment with present possession and enjoyment. Sensual pleasure affords no permanent *satisfaction.*

2. The act of pleasing or gratifying.

> The mind having a power to suspend the execution and *satisfaction* of its desires— *Locke.*

3. Repose of the mind on the certainty of any thing; that state which results from relief from suspense, doubt or uncertainty; conviction.

> What *satisfaction* can you have? *Shak.*

4. Gratification; that which pleases.

> Exchanging solid quiet to obtain
> The windy *satisfaction* of the brain. *Dryden.*

5. That which satisfies; amends; recompense; compensation; indemnification; atonement. *Satisfaction* for damages, must be an equivalent; but *satisfaction* in many cases, may consist in concession or apology.

6. Payment; discharge; as, to receive a sum in full *satisfaction* of a debt; to enter *satisfaction* on record.

SATISFAC'TIVE, *a.* Giving satisfaction. [*Little used or not at all.*] *Brown.*

SATISFAC'TORILY, *adv.* In a manner to give satisfaction or content.

2. In a manner to impress conviction or belief. The crime was *satisfactorily* proved.

SATISFAC'TORINESS, *n.* The power of satisfying or giving content; as the *satisfactoriness* of pleasure or enjoyment. *Boyle.*

SATISFAC'TORY, *a.* [Fr. *satisfactoire ;* Sp. *satisfactorio.*]

1. Giving or producing satisfaction; yielding content; particularly, relieving the mind from doubt or uncertainty and enabling it to rest with confidence; as, to give a *satisfactory* account of any remarkable transaction. A judge seeks for *satisfactory* evidence of guilt before he condemns.

2. Making amends, indemnification or recompense; causing to cease from claims and to rest content; atoning; as, to make *satisfactory* compensation, or a *satisfactory* apology for an offense.

> —A most wise and sufficient means of salvation by the *satisfactory* and meritorious death and obedience of the incarnate Son of God, Jesus Christ. *Sanderson.*

SAT'ISFIED, *pp.* Having the desires fully gratified; made content.

SAT'ISFIER, *n.* One that gives satisfaction.

SAT'ISFY, *v. t.* [L. *satisfacio ; satis*, enough, and *facio*, to make; Fr. *satisfaire ;* It. *soddisfare ;* Sp. *satisfacer ;* G. *satt*, D. *zat*, Dan. *sat*, filled, satisfied.]

1. To gratify wants, wishes or desires to the full extent; to supply possession or enjoyment till no more is desired. The de-

mands of hunger may be easily *satisfied*; but who can *satisfy* the passion for money or honor?

2. To supply fully what is necessary and demanded by natural laws; as, to *satisfy* with rain the desolate and waste ground. Job xxxviii.

3. To pay to content; to recompense or indemnify to the full extent of claims; as, to *satisfy* demands.

He is well paid, that is, well *satisfied*. *Shak.*

4. To appease by punishment; as, to *satisfy* rigor. *Milton.*

5. To free from doubt, suspense or uncertainty; to cause the mind to rest in confidence by ascertaining the truth; as, to *satisfy* one's self by inquiry.

6. To convince. A jury must be *satisfied* of the guilt of a man, before they can justly condemn him.

The standing evidences of the truth of the gospel are in themselves most firm, solid and *satisfying*. *Atterbury.*

7. To pay; to discharge; as, to *satisfy* an execution.

Debts due to the United States are to be first *satisfied*. *Wirt.*

SAT'ISFŸ, *v. i.* To give content. Earthly good never *satisfies*.

2. To feed or supply to the full.

3. To make payment. [But the intransitive use of this verb is generally elliptical.]

SAT'ISFŸING, *ppr.* Giving content; feeding or supplying to the full extent of desire; convincing; paying.

SA'TIVE, *a.* [L. *sativus*, from *sero*, *satum*, to sow.] Sown in gardens. *Evelyn.*

SAT'RAP, *n.* In Persia, an admiral; more generally, the governor of a province. *Encyc.*

SAT'RAPAL, *a.* Pertaining to a satrap or a satrapy. *Mitford.*

SAT'RAPESS, *n.* A female satrap. *Mitford.*

SAT'RAPY, *n.* The government or jurisdiction of a satrap. *D'Anville. Milton.*

SAT'URABLE, *a.* [See *Saturate*.] That may be saturated; capable of saturation. *Grew.*

SAT'URANT, *a.* [L. *saturans*.] Saturating; impregnating to the full.

SAT'URANT, *n.* In *medicine*, a substance which neutralizes the acid in the stomach; an absorbent. *Coxe.*

SAT'URATE, *v. t.* [L. *saturo*, from *satur*, filled; *satio*, to feed to the full. See *Sate*.]

1. To impregnate or unite with, till no more can be received. Thus an acid *saturates* an alkali, and an alkali *saturates* an acid, when the solvent can contain no more of the dissolving body.

2. To supply or fill to fullness. *Thomson.*

SAT'URATED, *pp.* Supplied to fullness.

SAT'URATING, *ppr.* Supplying to fullness.

SATURA'TION, *n.* In *a general sense*, a filling or supply to fullness. In *chimistry*, the union, combination or impregnation of one body with another by natural attraction, affinity or mixture, till the receiving body can contain no more; or solution continued till the solvent can contain no more. The *saturation* of an alkali by an acid, is by affinity; the *saturation* of water by salt, is by solution.

SAT'URDAY, *n.* [Sax. *Sæter-dæg*; D. *Saturdag*; Saturn's day.]

The last day of the week; the day next preceding the sabbath.

SATU'RITY, *n.* [L. *saturitas*. See *Saturate*.]

Fullness of supply; the state of being saturated. [*Little used.*]

SAT'URN, *n.* [L. *Saturnus*.] In *mythology*, one of the oldest and principal deities, the son of Cœlus and Terra, (heaven and earth,) and the father of Jupiter. He answers to the Greek Χρονος, Chronus or Time.

2. In *astronomy*, one of the planets of the solar system, less in magnitude than Jupiter, but more remote from the sun. Its diameter is seventy nine thousand miles, its mean distance from the sun somewhat more than nine hundred millions of miles, and its year, or periodical revolution round the sun, nearly twenty nine years and a half.

3. In *the old chimistry*, an appellation given to lead.

4. In *heraldry*, the black color in blazoning the arms of sovereign princes.

SATURNA'LIAN, *a.* [from L. *saturnalia*, feasts of Saturn.]

1. Pertaining to the festivals celebrated in honor of Saturn, Dec. 16, 17 or 18, in which men indulged in riot without restraint. Hence,

2. Loose; dissolute; sportive. *Burke.*

SATURN'IAN, *a.* In *fabulous history*, pertaining to Saturn, whose age or reign, from the mildness and wisdom of his government, is called the golden age; hence, golden; happy; distinguished for purity, integrity and simplicity.

Th' Augustus, born to bring *Saturnian* times. *Pope.*

SAT'URNINE, *a.* [Fr. *saturnien*, from L. *Saturnus*.]

1. Supposed to be under the influence of Saturn. Hence,

2. Dull; heavy; grave; not readily susceptible of excitement; phlegmatic; as a *saturnine* person or temper. *Addison.*

SAT'URNIST, *n.* A person of a dull, grave, gloomy temperament. *Browne.*

SAT'URNITE, *n.* A metallic substance of recent discovery, separated from lead in torrefaction, resembling lead in its color, weight, solubility in acids, &c. but more fusible and brittle; easily scorified and volatilized. *Kirwan. Nicholson. Encyc.*

SA'TYR, *n.* [L. *satyrus*; Gr. σατυρος, a monkey, a fawn.]

In *mythology*, a sylvan deity or demi-god, represented as a monster, half man and half goat, having horns on his head, a hairy body, with the feet and tail of a goat. Satyrs are usually found in the train of Bacchus, and have been distinguished for lasciviousness and riot. They have been represented as remarkable for their piercing eyes and keen raillery. *Encyc.*

SATYRI'ASIS, *n.* [Gr. σατυριασις. We observe in this word a connection with *satire*, in the sense of excitement, pungency.]

Immoderate venereal appetite. *Coxe.*

SATYR'ION, *n.* A plant. *Pope.*

SAUCE, *n.* [Fr. *sauce* or *sausse*, from L. *salsus*, salt, from *sal*; Arm. *saus*; It. Sp. *salsa*.]

1. A mixture or composition to be eaten with food for improving its relish.

High *sauces* and rich spices are brought from the Indies. *Baker.*

2. In New England, culinary vegetables and roots eaten with flesh. This application of the word falls in nearly with the definition.

Roots, herbs, vine-fruits, and sallad-flowers—they dish up various ways, and find them very delicious *sauce* to their meats, both roasted and boiled, fresh and salt. *Beverly, Hist. Virginia.*

Sauce consisting of stewed apples, is a great article in some parts of New England; but cranberries make the most delicious *sauce*.

To serve one the same sauce, is to retaliate one injury with another. [*Vulgar.*]

SAUCE, *v. t.* To accompany meat with something to give it a higher relish.

2. To gratify with rich tastes; as, to *sauce* the palate. *Shak.*

3. To intermix or accompany with any thing good, or ironically, with any thing bad.

Then fell she to *sauce* her desires with threatenings. *Sidney.*

Thou say'st his meat was *sauc'd* with thy upbraidings. *Shak.*

4. To treat with bitter, pert or tart language. [*Vulgar.*]

SAUCE-BOX, *n. saus'-box.* [from *saucy*.] A saucy impudent fellow. *Spectator.*

SAUCE-PAN, *n. saus'-pan.* A small pan for sauce, or a small skillet with a long handle, in which sauce or small things are boiled. *Swift.*

SAU'CER, *n.* [Fr. *sauciere* or *saussiere*.] A small pan in which sauce is set on a table. *Bacon.*

2. A piece of china or other ware, in which a tea cup or coffee cup is set.

SAU'CILY, *adv.* [from *saucy*.] Impudently; with impertinent boldness; petulantly. *Addison.*

SAU'CINESS, *n.* Impudence; impertinent boldness; petulance; contempt of superiors. *Bramhall. Dryden.*

SAU'CISSE, } *n.* [Fr. *saucisse*, a sausage;
SAU'CISSON, } from *sauce*.]

In *mining* or *gunnery*, a long pipe or bag, made of cloth well pitched, or of lether, filled with powder, and extending from the chamber of the mine to the entrance of the gallery. To preserve the powder from dampness, it is generally placed in a wooden pipe. It serves to communicate fire to mines, caissons, bomb-chests, &c. *Encyc.*

SAU'CY, *a.* [from *sauce*; L. *salsus*, salt or salted. The use of this word leads to the primary sense of salt, which must be shooting forward, penetrating, pungent, for *boldness* is a shooting forward.]

1. Impudent; bold to excess; rude; transgressing the rules of decorum; treating superiors with contempt. It expresses more than *pert*; as a *saucy* boy; a *saucy* fellow.

2. Expressive of impudence; as a *saucy* eye; *saucy* looks.

SAUL, an old spelling of *soul*.

SAUNDERS. [See *Sandal* and *Sanders*.]

SAUNTER, *v. i. s'anter.* To wander about idly; as *sauntering* from place to place. *Dryden.*

2. To loiter; to linger.

This must not run it into a lazy *sauntering* about ordinary things. *Locke.*

S'AUNTERER, *n.* One that wanders about idly.

S'AUNTERING, *ppr.* Wandering about lazily or idly; loitering.

SAU'RIAN, *a.* [Gr. σαυρος, a lizard.] Pertaining to lizards; designating an order of reptiles. *Ed. Encyc.*

SAUS'AĠE, *n.* [Fr. *saucisse;* from *sauce*, L. *salsus.*]
The intestine of an animal stuffed with minced meat seasoned.

SAUS'SURITE, *n.* A mineral so named from Saussure, the discoverer, of a white gray or green color, found at the foot of mount Rosa. It approaches andalusite. *Klaproth. Jameson.*

SA'VABLE, *a.* [from *save.*] Capable of being saved. *Chillingworth.*

SA'VABLENESS, *n.* Capability of being saved. *Ibm.*

SAV'AĠE, *a.* [Fr. *sauvage;* Arm. *savaich;* It. *selvaggio;* Sp. *salvage;* from L. *silva*, a wood, or *silvicola*, an inhabitant of a wood, or *silvaticus.*]
1. Pertaining to the forest; wild; remote from human residence and improvements; uncultivated; as a *savage* wilderness.

Cornels and *savage* berries of the wood. *Dryden.*

2. Wild; untamed; as *savage* beasts of prey.
3. Uncivilized; untaught; unpolished; rude; as *savage* life; *savage* manners. *Raleigh.*

What nation since the commencement of the christian era, ever rose from *savage* to civilized without christianity? *E. D. Griffin.*

4. Cruel; barbarous; fierce; ferocious; inhuman; brutal; as a *savage* spirit.

SAV'AĠE, *n.* A human being in his native state of rudeness; one who is untaught, uncivilized or without cultivation of mind or manners. The *savages* of America, when uncorrupted by the vices of civilized men, are remarkable for their hospitality to strangers, and for their truth, fidelity and gratitude to their friends, but implacably cruel and revengeful towards their enemies. From this last trait of the savage character, the word came to signify,
2. A man of extreme, unfeeling, brutal cruelty; a barbarian.
3. The name of a genus of fierce voracious flies. *Dict. Nat. Hist.*

SAV'AĠE, *v. t.* To make wild, barbarous or cruel. [*Not well authorized and little used.*] *Thomson.*

SAV'AĠELY, *adv.* In the manner of a savage; cruelly; inhumanly. *Shak.*

SAV'AĠENESS, *n.* Wildness; an untamed, uncultivated or uncivilized state; barbarism. Hence,
2. Cruelty; barbarousness.

Wolves and bears, they say,
Casting their *savageness* aside, have done
Like offices of pity. *Shak.*

SAV'AĠERY, *n.* Wild growth, as of plants. *Shak.*
2. Cruelty; barbarity. *Shak.*

SAV'AĠISM, *n.* The state of rude uncivilized men; the state of men in their native wildness and rudeness. *S. S. Smith. Walsh.*

The greater part of modern philosophers have declared for the original *savagism* of men. *Encyc.*

SAVAN'NA, *n.* [In Spanish, *sabana* is a sheet for a bed, or a large plain covered with snow.]
An extensive open plain or meadow, or a plain destitute of trees. *Locke.*

SAVE, *v. t.* [Fr. *sauver*, from L. *salvo*, It. *salvare*, Sp. *salvar*. As *salve* is used in Latin for salutation or wishing health, as *hail* is in English, I suspect this word to be from the root of *heal* or *hail*, the first letter being changed, as in Gr. αλς, W. *halen*, salt. See *Salt.*]
1. To preserve from injury, destruction or evil of any kind; to rescue from danger; as, to *save* a house from the flames; to *save* a man from drowning; to *save* a family from ruin; to *save* a state from war.

He cried, saying, Lord, *save* me. Matt. xiv. Gen. xlv.

2. To preserve from final and everlasting destruction; to rescue from eternal death.

Christ Jesus came into the world to *save* sinners. 1 Tim. i.

3. To deliver; to rescue from the power and pollution of sin.

He shall *save* his people from their sins. Matt. i.

4. To hinder from being spent or lost; as, to *save* the expense of a new garment. Order in all affairs *saves* time.
5. To prevent. Method in affairs *saves* much perplexity.
6. To reserve or lay by for preservation.

Now save a nation; and now *save* a groat. *Pope.*

7. To spare; to prevent; to hinder from occurrence.

Will you not speak to *save* a lady's blush? *Dryden.*

Silent and unobserv'd, to *save* his tears. *Dryden.*

8. To salve; as, to *save* appearances. *Milton.*
9. To take or use opportunely, so as not to lose. The ship sailed in time to *save* the tide.
10. To except; to reserve from a general admission or account.

Israel burned none of them, *save* Hazor only. Josh. xi.

Of the Jews five times received I forty stripes, *save* one. 2 Cor. xi.

[*Save* is here a verb followed by an object. It is the imperative used without a specific nominative; but it is now less frequently used than *except.*]

SAVE, *v. i.* To hinder expense.

Brass ordnance *saveth* in the quantity of the material. *Bacon.*

SA'VEALL, *n.* [*save* and *all.*] A small pan inserted in a candlestick to save the ends of candles. *Johnson.*

SA'VED, *pp.* Preserved from evil, injury or destruction; kept frugally; prevented; spared; taken in time.

SA'VELIN, *n.* A fish of the trout kind, having very small scales and a black back. *Dict. Nat. Hist.*

SA'VER, *n.* One that saves, preserves or rescues from evil or destruction; as the *saver* of the country. *Swift.*
2. One that escapes loss, but without gain. *Dryden.*
3. One that is frugal in expenses; an economist. *Wotton.*

SAV'IN, *n.* [Fr. *savinier;* L. Sp. *sabina.*]
A tree or shrub of the genus Juniperus. The savin of Europe resembles the red cedar of America, and the latter is sometimes called savin. *Bigelow.*

SA'VING, *ppr.* Preserving from evil or destruction; hindering from waste or loss; sparing; taking or using in time.
2. Excepting.
3. *a.* Frugal; not lavish; avoiding unnecessary expenses; economical; parsimonious. But it implies less rigorous economy than *parsimonious;* as a *saving* husbandman or housekeeper.
4. That saves in returns or receipts the principal or sum employed or expended; that incurs no loss, though not gainful; as a *saving* bargain. The ship has made a *saving* voyage.
5. That secures everlasting salvation; as *saving* grace.

SA'VING, *n.* Something kept from being expended or lost.

By reducing the interest of the debt, the nation makes a *saving*.

2. Exception; reservation.

Contend not with those that are too strong for us, but still with a *saving* to honesty. *L'Estrange.*

SA'VINGLY, *adv.* With frugality or parsimony.
2. So as to be finally saved from eternal death; as *savingly* converted.

SA'VINGNESS, *n.* Frugality; parsimony; caution not to expend money without necessity or use.
2. Tendency to promote eternal salvation. *Johnson.*

SA'VINGS-BANK, *n.* A bank in which the savings or earnings of the poor are deposited and put to interest for their benefit.

SĀVIOR, *n.* *sāvyur.* [Fr. *sauveur.*] One that saves or preserves; but properly applied only to Jesus Christ, the Redeemer, who has opened the way to everlasting salvation by his obedience and death, and who is therefore called *the Savior*, by way of distinction, the *Savior* of men, the *Savior* of the world. Gen. Washington may be called the *saver*, but not the *savior* of his country.

SA'VOR, *n.* [Fr. *saveur;* L. *sapor;* W. *sawyr;* Arm. *saour;* from L. *sapio*, to taste.]
1. Taste or odor; something that perceptibly affects the organs of taste and smell; as the *savor* of an orange or rose; an ill *savor;* a sweet *savor.*

I smell sweet *savors*— *Shak.*

In *Scripture*, it usually denotes smell, scent, odor. Lev. xxvi. Eccles. x.

2. The quality which renders a thing valuable; the quality which renders other bodies agreeable to the taste.

If the salt hath lost its *savor*— Matt. v.

3. In *Scripture*, character; reputation. Ex. v.
4. Cause; occasion. 2 Cor. ii.

Sweet savor, in Scripture, denotes that which renders a thing acceptable to God, or his acceptance. Hence, to *smell a sweet savor*, is to accept the offering or service. Gen. viii.

SA'VOR, *v. i.* To have a particular smell or taste.

2. To partake of the quality or nature of; or to have the appearance of. The answers *savor* of a humble spirit; or they *savor* of pride. *Wotton. Milton.*

I have rejected every thing that *savors* of party. *Addison.*

SA'VOR, *v. t.* To like; to taste or smell with pleasure. *Shak.*

2. To like; to delight in; to favor. Matt. xvi.

SA'VORILY, *adv.* [from *savory.*] With gust or appetite. *Dryden.*

2. With a pleasing relish. *Dryden.*

SA'VORINESS, *n.* Pleasing taste or smell; as the *savoriness* of a pine apple or a peach.

SA'VORLESS, *a.* Destitute of smell or taste; insipid. *Hall.*

SA'VORLY, *a.* Well seasoned; of good taste.

SA'VORLY, *adv.* With a pleasing relish. *Barrow.*

SA'VORY, *a.* [from *savor.*] Pleasing to the organs of smell or taste; as a *savory* odor. *Milton.*

Make me *savory* meat. Gen. xxvii.

SA'VORY, *n.* [Fr. *savorée.*] A plant of the genus Satureia.

SAVOY', *n.* A variety of the common cabbage, (*Brassica oleracea,*) much cultivated for winter use. *Ed. Encyc.*

SAW, *pret.* of *see.*

SAW, *n.* [Sax. *saga;* G. *säge;* D. *zaag;* Sw. *såga;* Dan. *saug;* Fr. *scie;* It. *sega.* See the Verb.]

1. A cutting instrument consisting of a blade or thin plate of iron or steel, with one edge dentated or toothed.

2. A saying; proverb; maxim; decree. *Obs.* [See *Say.*] *Shak.*

SAW, *v. t.* pret. *sawed;* pp. *sawed* or *sawn.* [G. *sägen;* D. *zaagen;* Sw. *såga;* Dan. *sauger;* Norm. *seguar;* It. *segare,* to saw, cut, reap; L. *seco;* Fr. *scier;* allied to *sickle.*]

1. To cut with a saw; to separate with a saw; as, to *saw* timber or marble.

2. To form by cutting with a saw; as, to *saw* boards or planks, that is, to *saw* timber into boards or planks.

SAW, *v. i.* To use a saw; to practice sawing; as, a man *saws* well.

2. To cut with a saw; as, the mill *saws* fast or well.

3. To be cut with a saw; as, the timber *saws* smooth.

SAW'-DUST, *n.* Dust or small fragments of wood or stone made by the attrition of a saw. *Mortimer.*

SAW'ED, *pp.* Cut, divided or formed with a saw.

SAW'ER, *n.* One that saws; corrupted into *sawyer.*

SAW'-FISH, *n.* A fish of the genus Pristis, which has a long beak or snout, with spines growing like teeth on both edges, and four or five spiracles or breathing holes in the sides of the neck. *Encyc.*

SAW'-FLY, *n.* A genus of flies, (*Tenthredo,*) having a serrated sting. *Encyc.*

SAW'-PIT, *n.* A pit over which timber is sawed by two men, one standing below the timber and the other above. *Mortimer.*

SAW'-WŎRT, *n.* A plant of the genus Serratula, so named from its serrated leaves.

SAW'-WREST, *n.* An instrument used to wrest or turn the teeth of saws a little outwards, that they may make a kerf somewhat wider than the thickness of the blade.

SAW'YER, *n.* One whose occupation is to saw timber into planks or boards, or to saw wood for fuel.

2. In *America,* a tree which, being undermined by a current of water, and falling into the stream, lies with its branches above water, which are continually raised and depressed by the force of the current, from which circumstance the name is derived. The *sawyers* in the Mississippi render the navigation dangerous, and frequently sink boats which run against them.

SAX'IFRAGE, *n.* [L. *saxifraga;* composed of *saxum,* a stone, and *frango,* to break.] A medicine that has the property of breaking or dissolving the stone in the bladder. But in *botany,* a genus of plants of many species. The *burnet saxifrage* is of the genus Pimpinella; the *golden saxifrage* is of the genus Chrysoplenium; the *meadow saxifrage* is of the genus Peucedanum. *Encyc.*

SAXIF'RAGOUS, *a.* Dissolving the stone. *Brown.*

SAX'ON, *n.* [Sax. *seax,* a knife, sword or dagger, a Saxon.]

1. One of the nation or people who formerly dwelt in the northern part of Germany, and who invaded and conquered England in the fifth and sixth centuries. The Welsh still call the English *Sæsons.*

2. The language of the Saxons.

SAX'ON, *a.* Pertaining to the Saxons, to their country, or to their language.

SAX'ONISM, *n.* An idiom of the Saxon language. *Warton.*

SAX'ONIST, *n.* One versed in the Saxon language.

SAY, *v. t.* pret. and pp. *said,* contracted from *sayed.* [Sax. *sægan, sacgan;* G. *sagen;* D. *zeggen;* Sw. *såga;* Dan. *siger;* Ch. סוח or סח to speak or say. The same verb in Arabic, سَاخَ signifies to *sink,* Goth. *sigcan.* The sense of the root is to throw or thrust. Class Sg. No. 28. Pers. *sachan,* a word, speech.]

1. To speak; to utter in words; as, he *said* nothing; he *said* many things; he *says* not a word. *Say* a good word for me.

It is observable that although this word is radically synonymous with *speak* and *tell,* yet the uses or applications of these words are different. Thus we say, to *speak* an oration, to *tell* a story; but in these phrases, *say* cannot be used. Yet to *say* a lesson is good English, though not very elegant. We never use the phrases, to *say* a sermon or discourse, to *say* an argument, to *say* a speech, to *say* testimony.

A very general use of *say* is to introduce a relation, narration or recital, either of the speaker himself or of something said or done or to be done by another. Thus Adam *said,* this is bone of my bone; Noah *said,* blessed be the Lord God of Shem. If we *say* we have no sin, we deceive ourselves. *Say* to the cities of Judah, behold your God. I cannot *say* what I should do in a similar case. *Say* thus precedes a sentence. But it is perhaps impracticable to reduce the peculiar and appropriate uses of *say, speak* and *tell,* to general rules. They can be learnt only by observation.

2. To declare. Gen. xxxvii.

3. To utter; to pronounce.

Say now Shibboleth. Judg. xii.

4. To utter, as a command.

God *said,* let there be light. Gen. i.

5. To utter, as a promise. Luke xxiii.

6. To utter, as a question or answer. Mark xi.

7. To affirm; to teach. Matt. xvii.

8. To confess. Luke xvii.

9. To testify. Acts xxiv.

10. To argue; to alledge by way of argument.

After all that can be *said* against a thing— *Tillotson.*

11. To repeat; to rehearse; to recite; as, to *say* a lesson.

12. To pronounce; to recite without singing. Then shall be *said* or sung as follows.

13. To report; as in the phrases, it is *said,* they *say.*

14. To answer; to utter by way of reply; to tell.

Say, Stella, feel you no content,
Reflecting on a life well spent? *Swift.*

[Note.—This verb is not properly intransitive. In the phrase, "as when we *say,* Plato is no fool," the last clause is the object after the verb; that is, "we *say* what follows." If this verb is properly intransitive in any case, it is in the phrase, "that is to *say,*" but in such cases, the subsequent clause is the object of the verb, being that which is said, uttered or related.]

SAY, *n.* [Sax. *saga, sagu.*] A speech; something said. [*In popular use, but not elegant.*]

SAY, *n.* [for *assay.*] A sample. *Obs.* *Sidney.*

2. Trial by sample. *Obs.* *Boyle.*

SAY, *n.* [Fr. *soie.*] A thin silk. *Obs.*

SAY, SAYE, *n.* In *commerce,* a kind of serge used for linings, shirts, aprons, &c. *Encyc.*

SA'YING, *ppr.* Uttering in articulate sounds or words; speaking; telling; relating; reciting.

SA'YING, *n.* An expression; a sentence uttered; a declaration.

Moses fled at this *saying.* Acts vii.
Cicero treasured up the *sayings* of Scævola. *Middleton.*

2. A proverbial expression. Many are the *sayings* of the wise. *Milton.*

SCAB, *n.* [Sax. *scæb, sceb;* G. *schabe;* Sw. *skabb;* Dan. *skab;* L. *scabies;* It. *scabbia.* It seems to be connected with L. *scabo,* to rub or scratch, G. *schaben,* to shave, W. *ysgubaw,* to sweep, L. *scaber,* rough, D. *schob,* a scale.]

1. An incrusted substance, dry and rough, formed over a sore in healing.

2. The itch or mange in horses; a disease of sheep.

3. A mean, dirty, paltry fellow. [*Low.*] *Shak.*

SCAB'BARD, *n.* The sheath of a sword. *Dryden.*

SCAB'BARD, *v. t.* To put in a sheath.

SCAB'BED, *a.* [from *scab.*] Abounding with scabs; diseased with scabs. *Bacon.*

2. Mean; paltry; vile; worthless. *Dryden.*

SCAB'BEDNESS, *n.* The state of being scabbed.

SCAB'BINESS, *n.* [from *scabby.*] The quality of being scabby.

SCAB'BY, *a.* [from *scab.*] Affected with scabs; full of scabs. *Dryden.*

2. Diseased with the scab or mange; mangy. *Swift.*

SCA'BIOUS, *a.* [L. *scabiosus*, from *scabies*, scab.]

Consisting of scabs; rough; itchy; leprous; as *scabious* eruptions. *Arbuthnot.*

SCA'BIOUS, *n.* A plant of the genus Scabiosa.

SCABRED'ITY, *n.* [L. *scabredo, scabrities.*] Roughness; ruggedness. [*Not in use.*] *Burton.*

SCA'BROUS, *a.* [L. *scabrosus, scaber*, from *scabies*, scab.]

1. Rough; rugged; having sharp points. *Arbuthnot.*

2. Harsh; unmusical. *B. Jonson.*

SCA'BROUSNESS, *n.* Roughness; ruggedness.

SCAB'WORT, *n.* A plant, a species of Helenium.

SCAD, *n.* A fish, the *shad*, which see. *Carew.*

2. A fish of the genus Caranx, (*Scomber trachurus*, Linne.) *Ed. Encyc.*

SCAF'FOLD, *n.* [Fr. *echafaud*; Arm. *chafod*; Ir. *scafal*; It. *scaffale*; D. *schavot*; G. *schafot*; Dan. *skafot*; perhaps from the root of *shape*, as *form* is used for *bench.* The last syllable is the L. *fala.* In Cornish, *skaval* is a bench or stool, and this word, *schavot*, in Dutch, signifies a tailor's bench, as well as a scaffold.]

1. Among *builders*, an assemblage or structure of timbers, boards or planks, erected by the wall of a building to support the workmen.

2. A temporary gallery or stage raised either for shows or spectators. *Milton.*

3. A stage or elevated platform for the execution of a criminal. *Sidney.*

SCAF'FOLD, *v. t.* To furnish with a scaffold; to sustain; to uphold.

SCAF'FOLDAGE, *n.* A gallery; a hollow floor. *Shak.*

SCAF'FOLDING, *n.* A frame or structure for support in an elevated place.

2. That which sustains; a frame; as the *scaffolding* of the body. *Pope.*

3. Temporary structure for support. *Prior.*

4. Materials for scaffolds.

SCA'LABLE, *a.* That may be scaled.

SCALA'DE, SCALA'DO, *n.* [Fr. *scalade*; Sp. *scalado*; from L. *scala*, a ladder. See *Scale.*]

A storm or assault on a fortified place, in which the soldiers enter the place by means of ladders. It is written also *escalade.*

SCA'LARY, *a.* Resembling a ladder; formed with steps. [*Little used.*] *Brown.*

SCALD, *v. t.* [It. *scaldare*; Sp. Port. *escaldar*; Fr. *echauder*, for *eschalder*; Sw. *skolla*; Dan. *skaalder*; Ir. *sgallaim*; from the root of L. *caleo, calda, calidus.* I suppose the primary sense of *caleo* is to contract, to draw, to make hard.]

1. To burn or painfully affect and injure by immersion in or contact with a liquor of a boiling heat, or a heat approaching it; as, to *scald* the hand or foot. We *scald* the part, when the heat of the liquor applied is so violent as to injure the skin and flesh. *Scald* is sometimes used to express the effect of the heat of other substances than liquids.

> Here the blue flames of *scalding* brimstone fall. *Cowley.*

2. To expose to a boiling or violent heat over a fire, or in water or other liquor; as, to *scald* meat or milk.

SCALD, *n.* [supra.] A burn, or injury to the skin and flesh by hot liquor.

SCALD, *n.* [Qu. Sax. *scyll*, a shell.] Scab; scurf on the head. *Spenser.*

SCALD, *a.* Scurvy; paltry; poor; as *scald* rhymers. *Shak.*

SCALD, *n.* [Dan. *skialdrer*, to make verses, also a poet. The primary sense is probably to *make* or to sing. If the latter, we find its affinities in G. *schallen*, D. *schellen*, Sw. *skalla.*]

Among the ancient Scandinavians, a poet; one whose occupation was to compose poems in honor of distinguished men and their achievments, and to recite and sing them on public occasions. The *scalds* of Denmark and Sweden answered to the bards of the Britons or Celts. *Mallet.*

SCALD'ED, *pp.* Injured by a hot liquor; exposed to boiling heat.

SCALD'ER, *n.* A scald; a Scandinavian poet.

SCALD'HEAD, *n.* [See *Scald.*] A lothesome affection of the head, in which it is covered with a continuous scab. *Johnson.*

SCALD'IC, *a.* Pertaining to the scalds or poets of antiquity; composed by scalds. *Warton.*

SCALD'ING, *ppr.* Burning or injuring by hot liquor.

2. Exposing to a boiling heat in liquor.

SCALD'ING-HOT, *a.* So hot as to scald the skin.

SCALE, *n.* [Sax. *scale, sceale*; D. *schaal*, a *scale*, a bowl, saucer or dish, and a *shell*, uniting the Sax. *scale* and *scell*; G. *schale*, a scale or balance, a dish, bowl, *shell*, peel or paring; Dan. *skal*, a shell; *skaler*, to shell, peel or pare; *skiel*, a fish scale; Sw. *skal*, a shell; Fr. *ecaille*; *ecailler*, to *scale* or peel; *ecale*, a *shell*; *ecaler*, to *shell*; *echelle*, a scale or ladder; It. *scaglia*, the scale of a fish; *scala*, a ladder; L. *id.*, Sp. *escala.* *Scale*, a shell and a dish, is probably from peeling or paring, that is, separating; but whether a simple or compound word, [*es-cal, ex-cal,*] I do not know. If the sense is to strip, it coincides with the Gr. σχυλαω, to spoil.]

1. The dish of a balance; and hence, the balance itself, or whole instrument; as, to turn the *scale.*

> Long time in even *scale*
> The battle hung. *Milton*

But in general, we use the plural, *scales*, for the whole instrument.

> The *scales* are turn'd; her kindness weighs no more
> Now than my vows. *Waller.*

2. The sign of the balance or Libra, in the zodiac. *Creech.*

3. The small shell or crust which composes a part of the covering of a fish; and hence, any thin layer or leaf exfoliated or separated; a thin lamin; as *scales* of iron or of bone. *Sharp.*

The *scales* of fish consist of alternate layers of membrane and phosphate of lime. The *scales* of serpents are composed of a horny membrane, without the calcarious phosphate. *Ure.*

4. A ladder; series of steps; means of ascending. [L. *scala.*] *Addison.*

5. The act of storming a place by mounting the wall on ladders; an escalade, or scalade. *Milton.*

6. A mathematical instrument of wood or metal, on which are marked lines and figures for the purpose of measuring distances, extent or proportions; as a plain *scale*; a diagonal *scale.*

7. Regular gradation; a series rising by steps or degrees like those of a ladder. Thus we speak of the *scale* of being, in which man occupies a higher rank than brutes, and angels a higher rank than man.

8. Any instrument, figure or scheme, graduated for the purpose of measuring extent or proportions; as a map drawn by a *scale* of half an inch to a league.

9. In *music*, a gamut; a diagram; or a series of lines and spaces rising one above another, on which notes are placed; or a scale consists of the regular gradations of sounds. A *scale* may be limited to an octave, called by the Greeks a tetrachord, or it may extend to the compass of any voice or instrument. *Encyc.*

10. Any thing graduated or marked with degrees at equal distances.

SCALE, *v. t.* [It. *scalare*, from *scala*, a ladder.]

1. To climb, as by a ladder; to ascend by steps; *and applied to the walls of a fortified place*, to mount in assault or storm.

> Oft have I *scal'd* the craggy oak. *Spenser.*

2. [from *scale*, a balance.] To measure; to compare; to weigh.

> *Scaling* his present bearing with his past. *Shak.*

3. [from *scale*, the covering of a fish.] To strip or clear of scales; as, to *scale* a fish.

4. To take off in thin lamins or scales.

5. To pare off a surface.

> If all the mountains were *scaled*, and the earth made even— *Burnet.*

6. In *the north of England*, to spread, as manure or loose substances; also, to disperse; to waste.

7. In *gunnery*, to clean the inside of a cannon by the explosion of a small quantity of powder. *Mar. Dict.*

SCALE, *v. i.* To separate and come off in thin layers or lamins.

> The old shells of the lobster *scale* off. *Bacon.*

SCA'LED, *pp.* Ascended by ladders or steps; cleared of scales; pared; scattered.

2. *a.* Having scales like a fish; squamous; as a *scaled* snake. *Shak.*

SCA'LELESS, *a.* Destitute of scales. *S. M. Mitchill.*

SCALE'NE, SCALE'NOUS, *a.* [Gr. σκαληνος, oblique, unequal, allied probably to σκολιος; G. *schel, schiel*, D. *scheel*, squinting; Dan. *skieler*, to squint.]

A *scalene triangle*, is one whose sides and angles are unequal.

SCALE'NE, *n.* A scalene triangle.

SCA'LINESS, *n.* [from *scaly.*] The state of being scaly; roughness.

SCA'LING, *ppr.* Ascending by ladders or steps; storming.
2. Stripping of scales.
3. Peeling; paring.

SCA'LING-LADDER, *n.* A ladder made for enabling troops to scale a wall.

SCALL, *n.* [See *Scald* and *Scaldhead.*] Scab; scabbiness; leprosy.

It is a dry *scall*, even a leprosy on the head. Lev. xiii.

SCAL'LION, *n.* [It. *scalogno*; L. *ascalonia*; Fr. *echalote*, whence our *shalot*; so named probably from its coats, *shell, scale.*]
A plant of the genus Allium; a variety of the common onion, which never forms a bulb at the root. *Encyc. Ed. Encyc.*

SCAL'LOP, *n.* [This is from the root of *shell, scale*; coinciding with *scalp*, D. *schulp*, a shell.]
1. A shell fish, or rather a genus of shell fish, called pecten. The shell is bivalvular, the hinge toothless, having a small ovated hollow. The great scallop is rugged and imbricated with scales, grows to a large size, and in some countries is taken and barreled for market. *Encyc.*
2. A recess or curving of the edge of any thing, like the segment of a circle; written also *scollop.*

SCAL'LOP, *v. t.* To mark or cut the edge or border of any thing into segments of circles. *Gray.*

SCALP, *n.* [D. *schelp* or *schulp*, a shell. The German has *hirnschale*, brain-shell. See *Scale.* But qu. the Ch. Syr. Ar. קלף to peel, to bark, and L. *scalpo.*]
1. The skin of the top of the head; as a hairless *scalp.* *Shak.*
2. The skin of the top of the head cut or torn off. A *scalp* among the Indians of America is a trophy of victory.

SCALP, *v. t.* To deprive of the scalp or integuments of the head. *Sharp.*

SCALP'ED, *pp.* Deprived of the skin of the head.

SCALP'EL, *n.* [L. *scalpellum*, from *scalpo*, to scrape.]
In *surgery*, a knife used in anatomical dissections and surgical operations. *Encyc.*

SCALP'ER, **SCALP'ING-IRON**, } *n.* An instrument of surgery, used in scraping foul and carious bones; a raspatory. *Encyc. Parr.*

SCALP'ING, *ppr.* Depriving of the skin of the top of the head.

SCA'LY, *a.* [from *scale.*] Covered or abounding with scales; rough; as a *scaly* fish; the *scaly* crocodile. *Milton.*
2. Resembling scales, lamina or layers.
3. In *botany*, composed of scales lying over each other, as a *scaly* bulb; having scales scattered over it, as a *scaly* stem. *Martyn.*

SCAM'BLE, *v. i.* [D. *schommelen*, to stir, to shake.]
1. To stir quick; to be busy; to scramble; to be bold or turbulent. *Shak.*
2. To shift awkwardly. *More.*

SCAM'BLE, *v. t.* To mangle; to maul. *Mortimer.*

SCAM'BLER, *n.* A bold intruder upon the generosity or hospitality of others. *Steevens.*

SCAM'BLING, *ppr.* Stirring; scrambling; intruding.

SCAM'BLINGLY, *adv.* With turbulence and noise; with bold intrusiveness.

SCAM'MEL, *n.* A bird.

SCAMMO'NIATE, *a.* [from *scammony.*] Made with scammony. [*Not used.*] *Wiseman.*

SCAM'MONY, *n.* [L. *scammonia*, from the Persian.] A plant of the genus Convolvulus.
2. A gum resin, obtained from the plant of that name, of a blackish gray color, a strong nauseous smell, and a bitter and very acrid taste. The best scammony comes from Aleppo, in light spungy masses, easily friable. That of Smyrna is black, ponderous, and mixed with extraneous matter. *Fourcroy. Encyc.*

SCAMP'ER, *v. i.* [D. *schampen*, to slip aside; Fr. *escamper*; It. *scampare*, to escape, to save one's self; *scampo*, safety; *campare*, to preserve, to fly, to escape; Sp. *escampar*, to clear out a place.]
To run with speed; to hasten escape. *Addison.*

SCAMP'ERING, *ppr.* Running with speed; hastening in flight.

SCAN, *v. t.* [Fr. *scander*; Sp. *escander*; It. *scandire, scandere*, to climb, to scan. The Italian is the L. *ascendo.* See *Ascend.*]
1. To examine with critical care; to scrutinize.

The actions of men in high stations are all conspicuous, and liable to be *scanned* and sifted. *Atterbury.*

2. To examine a verse by counting the feet; or according to modern usage, to recite or measure verse by distinguishing the feet in pronunciation. Thus in Latin and Greek, a hexameter verse is resolved into six feet by *scanning*, and the true quantities are determined.

SCAN'DAL, *n.* [Fr. *scandale*; It. *scandalo*; Sp. *escandalo*; L. *scandalum*; Gr. σκανδαλον; Ir. *scannail*, slander. In Greek, this word signifies a stumbling-block, something against which a person impinges, or which causes him to fall. In Sax. *scande, sconde*, signifies shame, confusion, dishonor, infamy; D. *schande*, id.; *schandaal*, reproach, *scandal*; G. *schande*, shame; *schänden*, to mar, disfigure, spoil, violate; Dan. *skiender*, to abuse, defame, &c.; Sans. *schiande* or *ishianda*, scandal. In Arm. *scandal* is a quarrel. The primary sense of the root must be to drive, to thrust, or to strike or cast down.]
1. Offense given by the faults of another.

His lustful orgies he enlarg'd
Even to the hill of *scandal.* *Milton.*

[In this sense, we now generally use *offense.*]
2. Reproachful aspersion; opprobrious censure; defamatory speech or report; something uttered which is false and injurious to reputation.

My known virtue is from *scandal* free. *Dryden.*

3. Shame; reproach; disgrace. Such is the perverted state of the human mind that some of the most hainous crimes bring little *scandal* upon the offender.

SCAN'DAL, *v. t.* To treat opprobriously; to defame; to asperse; to traduce; to blacken character.

I do fawn on men, and hug them hard,
And after *scandal* them. [*Little used.*] *Shak.*

2. To scandalize; to offend. [*Not used.*] *Bp. Story.*

SCAN'DALIZE, *v. t.* [Gr. σκανδαλιζω; L. *scandalizo*; Sp. *escandalizar*; It. *scandalezzare*; Fr. *scandaliser.*]
1. To offend by some action supposed criminal.

I demand who they are whom we *scandalize* by using harmless things? *Hooker.*

2. To reproach; to disgrace; to defame; as a *scandalizing* libeler. *Addison.*

SCAN'DALIZED, *pp.* Offended; defamed; disgraced.

SCAN'DALIZING, *ppr.* Giving offense to; disgracing.

SCAN'DALOUS, *a.* [It. *scandaloso*; Sp. *escandaloso*; Fr. *scandaleux*; Sw. *skåndelig.*] Giving offense.

Nothing *scandalous* or offensive to any. *Hooker.*

2. Opprobrious; disgraceful to reputation; that brings shame or infamy; as a *scandalous* crime or vice. How perverted must be the mind that considers seduction or dueling less *scandalous* than larceny!
3. Defamatory.

SCAN'DALOUSLY, *adv.* Shamefully; in a manner to give offense.

His discourse at table was *scandalously* unbecoming the dignity of his station. *Swift.*

2. Censoriously; with a disposition to find fault; as a critic *scandalously* nice. *Pope.*

SCAN'DALOUSNESS, *n.* The quality of being scandalous; the quality of giving offense, or of being disgraceful.

Scandalum magnatum, in law, a defamatory speech or writing made or published to the injury of a person of dignity. *Encyc.*

SCAND'ENT, *a.* [L. *scandens, scando*, to climb.]
Climbing, either with spiral tendrils for its support, or by adhesive fibers, as a stalk; climbing; performing the office of a tendril, as a petiole. *Smith. Bigelow.*

SCAN'NED, *pp.* Critically sifted or examined; resolved into feet in recital.

SCAN'NING, *ppr.* Critically examining; resolving into feet, as verse.

SCAN'SION, *n.* The act of scanning. *Percy.*

SCANT, *v. t.* [Dan. *skaanet*, from *skaaner*, to spare.]
To limit; to straiten; as, to *scant* one in provisions; to *scant* ourselves in the use of necessaries; to *scant* a garment in cloth.

I am *scanted* in the pleasure of dwelling on your actions. *Dryden.*

SCANT, *v. i.* To fail or become less; as, the wind *scants.*

SCANT, *a.* Not full, large or plentiful; scarcely sufficient; rather less than is wanted for the purpose; as a *scant* allowance of provisions or water; a *scant* pattern of cloth for a garment.
2. Sparing; parsimonious; cautiously affording.

Be somewhat *scanter* of your maiden presence. [*Not in use.*] *Shak.*

3. Not fair, free or favorable for a ship's course; as a *scant* wind. *Mar. Dict.*

SCANT, *adv.* Scarcely; hardly; not quite.

The people—received of the bankers *scant* twenty shillings for thirty. [*Obsolete or vulgar.*] *Camden.*

SCANT'ILY, *adv.* [from *scanty.*] Not fully; not plentifully. The troops were *scantily* supplied with flour.

2. Sparingly; niggardly; as, to speak *scantily* of one. [*Unusual.*] *Shak.*

SCANT'INESS, *n.* Narrowness; want of space or compass; as the *scantiness* of our heroic verse. *Dryden.*

2. Want of amplitude, greatness or abundance; limited extent.

Alexander was much troubled at the *scantiness* of nature itself. *South.*

3. Want of fullness; want of sufficiency; as the *scantiness* of supplies.

SCANT'LE, *v. t.* To be deficient; to fail. *Drayton.*

SCANT'LE, *v. i.* To divide into thin or small pieces; to shiver. *Chesterfield.*

SCANT'LET, *n.* [See *Scantling.*] A small pattern; a small quantity. [*Not in use.*] *Hale.*

SCANT'LING, *n.* [Fr. *echantillon*, a pattern; Sp. *escantillon*; Port. *escantilham.*]

1. A pattern; a quantity cut for a particular purpose. *L'Estrange.*

2. A small quantity; as a *scantling* of wit. *Dryden. Locke.*

3. A certain proportion or quantity. *Shak.*

4. In *the United States*, timber sawed or cut into pieces of a small size, as for studs, rails, &c. This seems to be allied to the L. *scandula*, and it is the sense in which I have ever heard it used in this country.

5. In *seamen's language*, the dimensions of a piece of timber, with regard to its breadth and thickness. *Mar. Dict.*

SCANT'LING, *a.* Not plentiful; small. [*Not in use.*] *Taylor.*

SCANT'LY, *adv.* Scarcely; hardly. *Obs.* *Camden.*

2. Not fully or sufficiently; narrowly; penuriously; without amplitude. *Dryden.*

SCANT'NESS, *n.* [from *scant.*] Narrowness; smallness; as the *scantness* of our capacities. *Glanville.*

SCANT'Y, *a.* [from *scant*, and having the same signification.]

1. Narrow; small; wanting amplitude or extent.

His dominions were very narrow and *scanty.* *Locke.*

Now *scantier* limits the proud arch confine. *Pope.*

2. Poor; not copious or full; not ample; hardly sufficient; as a *scanty* language; a *scanty* supply of words; a *scanty* supply of bread.

3. Sparing; niggardly; parsimonious.

In illustrating a point of difficulty, be not too *scanty* of words. *Watts.*

SCAP'AISM, *n.* [Gr. σκαπτω, to dig or make hollow.]

Among the Persians, a barbarous punishment inflicted on criminals by confining them in a hollow tree till they died. *Bailey.*

SCAPE, *v. t.* To escape; a contracted word, not now used except in poetry, and with a mark of elision. [See *Escape.*]

SCAPE, *n.* An escape. [See *Escape.*]

2. Means of escape; evasion. *Donne.*

3. Freak; aberration; deviation. *Shak.*

4. Loose act of vice or lewdness. *Shak.*

[*Obsolete in all its senses.*]

SCAPE, *n.* [L. *scapus*; probably allied to *scipio*, and the Gr. σκηπτρον, scepter.] In *botany*, a stem bearing the fructification without leaves, as in the narcissus and hyacinth. *Martyn.*

SCA'PE-GOAT, *n.* [*escape* and *goat.*] In *the Jewish ritual*, a goat which was brought to the door of the tabernacle, where the high priest laid his hands upon him, confessing the sins of the people, and putting them on the head of the goat; after which the goat was sent into the wilderness, bearing the iniquities of the people. Lev. xvi.

SCA'PELESS, *a.* [from *scape.*] In *botany*, destitute of a scape.

SCA'PEMENT, *n.* The method of communicating the impulse of the wheels to the pendulum of a clock. *Chambers.*

SCA'PHITE, *n.* [L. *scapha.*] Fossil remains of the scapha.

SCAP'OLITE, *n.* [Gr. σκαπος, a rod, and λιθος, a stone.]

A mineral which occurs massive, or more commonly in four or eight sided prisms, terminated by four sided pyramids. It takes its name from its long crystals, often marked with deep longitudinal channels, and collected in groups or masses of parallel, diverging or intermingled prisms. It is the radiated, foliated and compact scapolite of Jameson, and the paranthine and Wernerite of Haüy and Brongniart. *Cleaveland.*

SCAP'ULA, *n.* [L.] The shoulder blade. *Coxe.*

SCAP'ULAR, *a.* [L. *scapularis.*] Pertaining to the shoulder, or to the scapula; as the *scapular* arteries.

SCAP'ULAR, *n.* [supra.] In *anatomy*, the name of two pairs of arteries, and as many veins. *Encyc.*

2. In *ornithology*, a fether which springs from the shoulder of the wing, and lies along the side of the back. *Encyc.*

SCAP'ULAR, SCAP'ULARY, } *n.* A part of the habit of certain religious orders in the Romish church, consisting of two narrow slips of cloth worn over the gown, covering the back and breast, and extending to the feet. This is worn as a badge of peculiar veneration for the virgin Mary. *Encyc.*

SC'AR, *n.* [Fr. *escarre*; Arm. *scarr* or *yscar*; It. *escara*; Gr. εσχαρα; Dan. *skar*; probably from the root of *shear*, *share*, to cut, Sax. *sciran*, *scearan*, whence Dan. *skaar*, a notch.]

1. A mark in the skin or flesh of an animal, made by a wound or an ulcer, and remaining after the wound or ulcer is healed. The soldier is proud of his *scars.*

2. Any mark or injury; a blemish.

The earth had the beauty of youth—and not a wrinkle, *scar* or fracture on its body. *Burnet.*

3. [L. *scarus*; Gr. σκαρος.] A fish of the Labrus kind. *Dict. Nat. Hist.*

SC'AR, *v. t.* To mark with a scar. *Shak.*

SCAR'AB, SCAR'ABEE, } *n.* [L. *scarabæus*, from Gr. σκωρ, Sax. *scearn*, fimus.]

A beetle; an insect of the genus Scarabæus, whose wings are cased. [See *Beetle.*]

SCAR'AMOUCH, *n.* [Fr. *escarmouche*; It. *scaramuccio*; Sp. *escaramuza*, a skirmish.]

A buffoon in motley dress. *Collier.*

SCARCE, *a.* [It. *scarso*; D. *schaarsch.* In Arm. *scarz* is short, and perhaps the word is from the root of *shear*, to cut. The Spanish equivalent word is *escaso*, and it is observable that some of our common people pronounce this word *scase.*]

1. Not plentiful or abundant; being in small quantity in proportion to the demand. We say, water is *scarce*, wheat, rye, barley is *scarce*, money is *scarce*, when the quantity is not fully adequate to the demand.

2. Being few in number and scattered; rare; uncommon. Good horses are *scarce.*

The *scarcest* of all is a Pescennius Niger on a medallion well preserved. *Addison*

SCARCE, SCARCELY, } *adv.* Hardly; scantly.

We *scarcely* think our miseries our foes. *Shak.*

2. Hardly; with difficulty.

Slowly he sails, and *scarcely* stems the tides. *Dryden.*

SCARCENESS, SCARCITY, } *n.* Smallness of quantity, or smallness in proportion to the wants or demands; deficiency; defect of plenty; penury; as a *scarcity* of grain; a great *scarcity* of beauties; a *scarcity* of lovely women. *Dryden.*

Praise, like gold and diamonds, owes its value to its *scarcity.* *Rambler.*

A *scarcity* of snow would raise a mutiny at Naples. *Addison.*

2. Rareness; infrequency.

The value of an advantage is enhanced by its *scarceness.* *Collier.*

Root of scarcity, the mangold-wurzel, a variety of the white beet; G. *mangold-wurzel*, beet root, corrupted into *mangel-wurzel*; Fr. *racine de disette*, root of want or scarcity. *Ed. Encyc.*

SCARE, *v. t.* [In W. *esgar* is to separate; in It. *scorare* is to dishearten, from L. *ex* and *cor*, heart; but qu.]

To fright; to terrify suddenly; to strike with sudden terror.

The noise of thy cross-bow
Will *scare* the herd, and so my shot is lost. *Shak.*

To scare away, to drive away by frightening.

SCARECROW, *n.* [*scare* and *crow.*] Any frightful thing set up to frighten crows or other fowls from corn fields; hence, any thing terrifying without danger; a vain terror.

A *scarecrow* set to frighten fools away. *Dryden.*

2. A fowl of the sea gull kind; the black gull. *Dict. Nat. Hist. Pennant.*

SCARED, *pp.* Frightened; suddenly terrified.

SCAREFIRE, *n.* A fire breaking out so as to frighten people. [*Not used.*] *Holder.*

SC'ARF, *n.* plu. *scarfs.* [Fr. *echarpe*; It. *ciarpa*; Sax. *scearf*, a fragment or piece; from the root of *shear.*]

Something that hangs loose upon the shoulders; as a piece of cloth.

Put on your hood and *scarf.* *Swift.*

SC'ARF, *v. t.* To throw loosely on. *Shak.*

2. To dress in a loose vesture. *Shak.*

SC'ARF, *v. t.* [Sw. *skarfva*; Sp. *escarpar.*] To join; to piece; to unite two pieces of timber at the ends, by letting the end of one into the end of the other, or by laying the two ends together and fastening a third piece to both. *Mar. Dict.*

SC'ARFSKIN, *n.* [*scarf* and *skin.*] The cuticle; the epidermis; the outer thin integument of the body. *Cheyne.*

SCARIFICA'TION, *n.* [L. *scarificatio.* See *Scarify.*]
In *surgery*, the operation of making several incisions in the skin with a lancet or other cutting instrument, particularly the cupping instrument. *Encyc.*

SCARIFICA'TOR, *n.* An instrument used in scarification.

SCAR'IFIER, *n.* [from *scarify.*] The person who scarifies.
2. The instrument used for scarifying.

SCAR'IFY, *v. t.* [Fr. *scarifier*; L. *scarifico.* Qu. *scar*, Gr. εσχαρα, and L. *facio*, to make. But the Greek is σκαριφαομαι, from σκαριφος, a pointed instrument, or a sharp pointed piece of wood.]
To scratch or cut the skin of an animal, or to make small incisions by means of a lancet or cupping instrument, so as to draw blood from the smaller vessels without opening a large vein. *Encyc.*

SCAR'IFYING, *ppr.* Making small incisions in the skin with an instrument.

SCA'RIOUS, *a.* [Low L. *scarrosus*, rough.] In *botany*, tough, thin and semi-transparent, dry and sonorous to the touch; as a perianth. *Martyn.*

SCARLATI'NA, *n.* The scarlet fever; called in popular language, the *canker rash.*

SCARLAT'INOUS, *a.* Of a scarlet color; pertaining to the scarlet fever.

SC'ARLET, *n.* [Fr. *ecarlate*; Arm. *scarladd*; It. *scarlatto*; Sp. *escarlata*; Ir. *scarloid*; W. *ysgarlad*, the effusion of a wound, scarlet, from *ysgar*, to separate, [See *Shear*;] D. *scharlaken*; G. *scharlack*; Dan. *skarlagen.* Qu. Ch. סקר, to color, as a derivative, minium; Ar. شقر shakara, to be red.]
1. A beautiful bright red color, brighter than crimson. *Encyc.*
2. Cloth of a scarlet color.

All her household are clothed with *scarlet.* Prov. xxxi.

SC'ARLET, *a.* Of the color called scarlet; of a bright red color; as a *scarlet* cloth or thread; a *scarlet* lip. *Shak.*

SC'ARLET-BEAN, *n.* A plant; a red bean. *Mortimer.*

SC'ARLET-FE'VER, *n.* [*scarlatina.*] A disease in which the body is covered with an efflorescence or red color, first appearing about the neck and breast, and accompanied with a sore throat.

SC'ARLET-OAK, *n.* A species of oak, the *Quercus coccifera*, or kermes oak, producing small glandular excrescences, called *kermes* or *scarlet grain.* *Encyc.*

SC'ARMAGE, } peculiar modes of spelling
SC'ARMOGE, } *skirmish.* [*Not in use.*] *Spenser.*

SC'ARN, *n.* [Sax. *scearn.*] Dung. [*Not in use or local.*] *Ray.*

SC'ARN-BEE, *n.* A beetle. [*Not in use or local.*] *Ray.*

SC'ARP, *n.* [Fr. *escarpe*; It. *scarpa*, a scarp, a shoe, a slope; Sp. *escarpa.*]
In *fortification*, the interior talus or slope of the ditch next the place, at the foot of the rampart. *Encyc.*

SC'ARP, *n.* In *heraldry*, the scarf which military commanders wear for ornament; borne somewhat like a battoon sinister, but broader, and continued to the edges of the field. *Encyc.*

SCA'RUS, *n.* A fish. [See *Scar.*]

SCA'RY, *n.* Barren land having only a thin coat of grass upon it. [*Local.*]

SCATCH, *n.* [Fr. *escache.*] A kind of horse-bit for bridles. *Bailey.*

SCATCH'ES, *n. plu.* [Fr. *echasses.*] Stilts to put the feet in for walking in dirty places. *Bailey.*

SCATE, *n.* [D. *schaats*; Ice. *skid.* This word may belong to the root of *shoot*, and L. *scateo.*]
A wooden shoe furnished with a steel plate for sliding on ice.

SCATE, *v. i.* To slide or move on scates.

SCATE, *n.* [Sax. *sceadda*; L. *squatina*, *squatus.*] A fish, a species of ray.

SCA'TEBROUS, *a.* [L. *scatebra*, a spring; *scateo*, to overflow.] Abounding with springs. *Dict.*

SCATH, *v. t.* [Sax. *scathian*, *sceathian*, to injure, to damage, to steal; D. *schaaden*; G. *schaden*; Sw. *skada*; Dan. *skader.*] To damage; to waste; to destroy. [*Little used.*] *Milton.*

SCATH, *n.* Damage; injury; waste; harm. [*Little used.*] *Spenser.*

SCATH'FUL, *a.* Injurious; harmful; destructive. [*Little used.*] *Shak.*

SCATH'LESS, *a.* Without waste or damage. [*Little used.*] *Chaucer.*

SCAT'TER, *v. t.* [Sax. *scateran*, to pour out, to disperse; L. *scateo*; Gr. σκεδαω, to scatter, to discuss, L. *discutio.* This word may be formed on the root of *discutio.* The primary sense is to drive or throw.]
1. To disperse; to dissipate; to separate or remove things to a distance from each other.

From thence did the Lord *scatter* them abroad upon the face of all the earth. Gen. xi.

I will *scatter* you among the heathen. Lev. xxvi.

2. To throw loosely about; to sprinkle; as, to *scatter* seed in sowing.

Teach the glad hours to *scatter*, as they fly,
Soft quiet, gentle love and endless joy. *Prior.*

3. To spread or set thinly.

Why should my muse enlarge on Libyan swains,
Their *scatter'd* cottages, and ample plains. *Dryden.*

SCAT'TER, *v. i.* To be dispersed or dissipated. The clouds *scatter* after a storm.
2. To be liberal to the poor; to be charitable. Prov. xi.

SCAT'TERED, *pp.* Dispersed; dissipated; thinly spread; sprinkled or thinly spread over.
2. In *botany*, irregular in position; without any apparent regular order; as *scattered* branches.

SCAT'TEREDLY, *adv.* In a dispersed manner; separately. [*Not much used.*] *Clarke.*

SCAT'TERING, *ppr.* Dispersing; spreading thinly; sprinkling.
2. *a.* Not united; divided among many; as *scattering* votes.

SCAT'TERINGLY, *adv.* Loosely; in a dispersed manner; thinly; as habitations *scatteringly* placed over the country.

SCAT'TERLING, *n.* A vagabond; one that has no fixed habitation or residence. [*Little used.*]

SCATU'RIENT, *a.* [L. *scaturiens.*] Springing, as the water of a fountain. [*Not used.*] *Dict.*

SCATURIG'INOUS, *a.* [L. *scaturigo.*] Abounding with springs. [*Not used.*] *Dict.*

SCAUP, *n.* A fowl of the duck kind. *Encyc.*

SCAV'AGE, *n.* [Sax. *sceawian*, to show.]
In ancient customs, a toll or duty exacted of merchant-strangers by mayors, sherifs, &c. for goods shown or offered for sale within their precincts. *Cowel.*

SCAV'ENGER, *n.* [Sax. *scafan*, to scrape, to shave, G. *schaben*, Sw. *skafva*, Dan. *skaver*, L. *scabio.*]
A person whose employment is to clean the streets of a city, by scraping or sweeping and carrying off the filth.

SCEL'ERAT, *n.* [Fr. from L. *sceleratus.*] A villain; a criminal. [*Not in use.*] *Cheyne.*

SCENE, *n.* [Fr. *id.*; L. *scena*; Gr. σκηνη; Heb. שכן to dwell; Ch. to subside, to settle; Syr. to come or fall on; Ar. سكن sakana, to be firm, stable, quiet, to set or establish, to quiet or cause to rest. Class Gn. No. 43. 44. The Greek word signifies a tent, hut or cottage. In L. it is an arbor or stage. The primary sense is to set or throw down.]
1. A stage; the theater or place where dramatic pieces and other shows are exhibited. It does not appear that the ancients changed the *scenes* in different parts of the play. Indeed the original *scene* for acting was an open plat of ground, shaded or slightly covered. *Encyc.*
2. The whole series of actions and events connected and exhibited; or the whole assemblage of objects displayed at one view. Thus we say, the execution of a malefactor is a melancholy *scene.* The crucifixion of our Saviour was the most solemn *scene* ever presented to the view of man.

We say also, a *scene* of sorrow or of rejoicing, a noble *scene*, a sylvan *scene.*

A charming *scene* of nature is display'd. *Dryden.*

3. A part of a play; a division of an act. A play is divided into acts, and acts are divided into *scenes.*
4. So much of an act of a play as represents what passes between the same persons in the same place. *Dryden.*
5. The place represented by the stage. The *scene* was laid in the king's palace.
6. The curtain or hanging of a theater adapted to the play.
7. The place where any thing is exhibited.

The world is a vast *scene* of strife. *J. M. Mason.*

8. Any remarkable exhibition.

The shepherds, while watching their flocks upon the plains of Bethlehem, were suddenly interrupted by one of the most sublime and surprising *scenes* which have ever been exhibited on earth. *W. B. Sprague.*

SCE'NERY, *n.* The appearance of a place, or of the various objects presented to view; or the various objects themselves as seen together. Thus we may say, the *scenery* of the landscape presented to the view from mount Holyoke, in Hampshire county, Massachusetts, is highly picturesque, and exceeded only by the *scenery* of Boston and its vicinity, as seen from the State house.

Never need an American look beyond his own country for the sublime and beautiful of natural *scenery*. *Irving.*

2. The representation of the place in which an action is performed. *Pope.*
3. The disposition and consecution of the scenes of a play. *Dryden.*
4. The paintings representing the scenery of a play.

SCEN'IC, SCEN'ICAL, *a.* [L. *scenicus.*] Pertaining to scenery; dramatic; theatrical.

SCENOGRAPH'IC, SCENOGRAPH'ICAL, *a.* [See *Scenography.*] Pertaining to scenography; drawn in perspective.

SCENOGRAPH'ICALLY, *adv.* In perspective. *Mortimer.*

SCENOG'RAPHY, *n.* [Gr. σκηνη, scene, and γραφω, to describe.]
The representation of a body on a perspective plane; or a description of it in all its dimensions as it appears to the eye. *Encyc.*

SCENT, *n.* [Fr. *senteur*, from *sentir*, L. *sentio*, to perceive.]
1. Odor; smell; that substance which issuing from a body, affects the olfactory organs of animals; as the *scent* of an orange or an apple; the *scent* of musk. The word is applicable to any odor, agreeable or offensive.
2. The power of smelling; the smell; as a hound of nice *scent*.
3. Chase followed by the scent; course of pursuit; track.

He travelled upon the same *scent* into Ethiopia. *Temple.*

SCENT, *v. t.* To smell; to perceive by the olfactory organs; as, to *scent* game, as a hound.
2. To perfume; to imbue or fill with odor, good or bad. Aromatic plants *scent* the room. Some persons *scent* garments with musk; others *scent* their snuff.

SCENT'FUL, *a.* Odorous; yielding much smell. *Drayton.*
2. Of quick smell. *Browne.*

SCENT'LESS, *a.* Inodorous; destitute of smell.

SCEP'TER, *n.* [Fr. *sceptre;* L. *sceptrum;* Gr. σκηπτρον, from σκηπτω, to send or thrust; coinciding with L. *scipio*, that is, a shoot or rod.]
1. A staff or batoon borne by kings on solemn occasions, as a badge of authority. Hence,
2. The appropriate ensign of royalty; an ensign of higher antiquity than the crown. Hence,
3. Royal power or authority; as, to assume the *scepter.*

The *scepter* shall not depart from Judah, nor a lawgiver from between his feet, till Shiloh come. Gen. xlix.

4. A constellation.

SCEP'TER, *v. t.* To invest with royal authority, or with the ensign of authority. *Hall.*

SCEP'TERED, *a.* Bearing a scepter; as a *sceptered* prince.

To Britain's queen the *scepter'd* suppliant bends. *Tickel.*
Gold-*scepter'd* Juno. *Parnell.*

SCEP'TIC, *n.* [Gr. σκεπτικος, from σκεπτομαι, to look about, to consider, to speculate; Sax. *sceawian*, to look about, to see, also to show. See *Show.*]
1. One who doubts the truth and reality of any principle or system of principles or doctrines. In *philosophy*, a Pyrrhonist or follower of Pyrrho, the founder of a sect of sceptical philosophers, who maintained that no certain inferences can be drawn from the reports of the senses, and who therefore doubted of every thing. *Enfield.*
2. In *theology*, a person who doubts the existence and perfections of God, or the truth of revelation; one who disbelieves the divine original of the christian religion.

Suffer not your faith to be shaken by the sophistries of *sceptics.* *Clarke.*

SCEP'TIC, SCEP'TICAL, *a.* Doubting; hesitating to admit the certainty of doctrines or principles; doubting of every thing.
2. Doubting or denying the truth of revelation.

The *sceptical* system subverts the whole foundation of morals. *Rob. Hall.*

SCEP'TICALLY, *adv.* With doubt; in a doubting manner.

SCEP'TICISM, *n.* [Fr. *scepticisme.*] The doctrines and opinions of the Pyrrhonists or sceptical philosophers; universal doubt; the scheme of philosophy which denies the certainty of any knowledge respecting the phenomena of nature.
2. In *theology*, a doubting of the truth of revelation, or a denial of the divine origin of the christian religion, or of the being, perfections or truth of God.

Irreligious *scepticism* or atheistic profaneness. *Milner.*

Let no despondency or timidity or secret *scepticism* lead any one to doubt whether this blessed prospect will be realized. *S. Miller.*

SCEP'TICIZE, *v. i.* To doubt; to pretend to doubt of every thing. [*Little used.*] *Shaftesbury.*

SCHAALSTEIN, SCA'LE-STONE, *n.* A rare mineral, called also tafelspath and tabular spar, occurring in masses composed of thin lamins collected into large prismatic concretions or hexahedral prisms. Its color is grayish or pearly white, tinged with green, yellow or red. *Cleaveland.*

SCHED'ULE, *n.* [L. *schedula*, from *scheda*, a sheet or leaf of paper; Gr. σχεδη, from σχιζω, to cut or divide; L. *scindo*, for *scido.* The pronunciation ought to follow the analogy of *scheme*, &c.]
1. A small scroll or piece of paper or parchment, containing some writing. *Hooker.*
2. A piece of paper or parchment annexed to a larger writing, as to a will, a deed, a lease, &c. *Encyc.*
3. A piece of paper or parchment containing an inventory of goods. *Encyc.*

SCHEE'LIN, SCHE'LIUM, *n.* A different name of tungsten, a hard brittle metal of a grayish white color, and brilliant. *Dict.*

SCHE'MATISM, *n.* [Gr. σχηματισμος, from σχημα. See *Scheme.*]
1. Combination of the aspects of heavenly bodies.
2. Particular form or disposition of a thing. [*A word not much used.*] *Creech.*

SCHE'MATIST, *n.* A projector; one given to forming schemes. [*Schemer* is more generally used.]

SCHEME, *n.* [L. *schema;* Gr. σχημα, from σχεω, a contracted word, probably from σχεθω, to have or hold.]
1. A plan; a combination of things connected and adjusted by design; a system.

We shall never be able to give ourselves a satisfactory account of the divine conduct without forming such a *scheme* of things as shall take in time and eternity. *Atterbury.*

2. A project; a contrivance; a plan of something to be done; a design. Thus we say, to form a *scheme*, to lay a *scheme*, to contrive a *scheme.*

The stoical *scheme* of supplying our wants by lopping off our desires, is like cutting off our feet when we want shoes. *Swift.*

3. A representation of the aspects of the celestial bodies; any lineal or mathematical diagram. *Brown. Hudibras.*

SCHEME, *v. t.* To plan; to contrive.

SCHEME, *v. i.* To form a plan; to contrive.

SCHE'MER, *n.* One that contrives; a projector; a contriver.

SCHE'MING, *ppr.* Planning; contriving.
2. *a.* Given to forming schemes; artful.

SCHE'MIST, *n.* A schemer; a projector. *Coventry.*

SCHENE, *n.* [L. *schœnos;* Gr. σχοινος.] An Egyptian measure of length, equal to sixty stadia, or about 7½ miles. *Herodotus.*

SCHE'SIS, *n.* [Gr. σχεσις, from σχεω, σχεθω, to have or hold.]
Habitude; general state or disposition of the body or mind, or of one thing with regard to other things. *Norris.*

SCHILLER-SPAR, *n.* A mineral containing two subspecies, bronzite and common schiller-spar.

SCHISM, *n. sizm.* [L. *schisma;* Gr. σχισμα, from σχιζω, to divide, L. *scindo*, Sax. *sceadan*, D. *scheien*, *scheiden*, G. *scheiden*, to separate, to part.]
1. In *a general sense*, division or separation; but appropriately, a division or separation in a church or denomination of christians, occasioned by diversity of opinions; breach of unity among people of the same religious faith.

—Set bounds to our passions by reason, to our errors by truth, and to our *schisms* by charity. *K. Charles.*

In *Scripture*, the word seems to denote a breach of charity, rather than a difference of doctrine.

2. Separation; division among tribes or classes of people.

SCHISMAT'IC, SCHISMAT'ICAL, *a.* *sizmat'ic, sizmat'ical.* Pertaining to schism; implying schism; partaking of the nature of schism; tending to schism; as *schismatical* opinions or proposals. *K. Charles. South.*

SCHISMAT'IC, *n.* One who separates from an established church or religious faith, on account of a diversity of opinions. *Blackstone. Swift.*

SCHISMAT'ICALLY, *adv.* In a schismatical manner; by separation from a church on account of a diversity of opinions.

SCHISMAT'ICALNESS, *n.* The state of being schismatical.

SCHIS'MATIZE, *v. i.* To commit or practice schism; to make a breach of communion in the church. *Johnson.*

SCHISM'LESS, *a.* Free from schism; not affected by schism. [*Little used.*] *Milton.*

SCHIST. [See *Shist.*]

SCHOL'AR, *n.* [Low L. *scholaris*, from *schola*, a school; Gr. σχολη, leisure, a school; Fr. *ecolier*; D. *schoolier*; G. *schüler*; Dan. *skolelærd.* The Danish word signifies *school-learned.* See *School.*]

1. One who learns of a teacher; one who is under the tuition of a preceptor; a pupil; a disciple; hence, any member of a college, academy or school; applicable to the learner of any art, science or branch of literature.
2. A man of letters. *Locke.*
3. *Emphatically used*, a man eminent for erudition; a person of high attainments in science or literature.
4. One that learns any thing; as an apt *scholar* in the school of vice.
5. A pedant; a man of books. *Bacon.*

[But the word *scholar* seldom conveys the idea of a pedant.]

SCHOLAR'ITY, *n.* Scholarship. [*Not used.*] *B. Jonson.*

SCHOL'AR-LIKE, *a.* Like a scholar; becoming a scholar. *Bacon.*

SCHOL'ARSHIP, *n.* Learning; attainments in science or literature; as a man of great *scholarship.* *Pope.*

2. Literary education; as any other house of *scholarship.* [*Unusual.*] *Milton.*
3. Exhibition or maintenance for a scholar; foundation for the support of a student. *Ainsworth.*

SCHOLAS'TIC, SCHOLAS'TICAL, *a.* [L. *scholasticus.*] Pertaining to a scholar, to a school or to schools; as *scholastic* manners or pride; *scholastic* learning.

2. Scholar-like; becoming a scholar; suitable to schools; as *scholastic* precision.
3. Pedantic; formal.

Scholastic divinity, that species of divinity taught in some schools or colleges, which consists in discussing and settling points by reason and argument. It has now fallen into contempt, except in some universities, where the charters require it to be taught. *Encyc.*

SCHOLAS'TIC, *n.* One who adheres to the method or subtilties of the schools. *Milton.*

SCHOLAS'TICALLY, *adv.* In the manner of schools; according to the niceties or method of the schools.

SCHOLAS'TICISM, *n.* The method or subtilties of the schools. *Warton.*

The spirit of the old *scholasticism*, which spurned laborious investigation and slow induction— *J. P. Smith.*

SCHO'LIAST, *n.* [Gr. σχολιαστης. See *Scholium.*] A commentator or annotator; one who writes notes upon the works of another for illustrating his writings. *Dryden.*

SCHO'LIAZE, *v. i.* To write notes on an author's works. [*Not used.*] *Milton.*

SCHO'LICAL, *a.* Scholastic. [*Not in use.*] *Hales.*

SCHO'LIUM, *n.* plu. *scholia* or *scholiums.* [L. *scholion*; Gr. σχολιον, from σχολη, leisure, lucubration.]

In *mathematics*, a remark or observation subjoined to a demonstration.

SCHO'LY, *n.* A scholium. [*Not in use.*] *Hooker.*

SCHO'LY, *v. i.* To write comments. [*Not in use.*] *Hooker.*

SCHOOL, *n.* [L. *schola*; Gr. σχολη, leisure, vacation from business, lucubration at leisure, a place where leisure is enjoyed, a school. The adverb signifies at ease, leisurely, slowly, hardly, with labor or difficulty. In Sax. *sceol* is a crowd, a multitude, a school [shoal,] as of fishes, and a school for instruction. So also *scol*, *scolu*, a school; but the latter sense, I think, must have been derived from the Latin. D. *school*, an academy and a crowd; *schoolen*, to flock together; G. *schule*, a school for instruction; D. *skole*; Sw. *skola*; W. *ysgol*; Arm. *scol*; Fr. *ecole*; It. *scuola*; Sp. *escuela*; Port. *escola*; Sans. *schala.* This word seems originally to have denoted leisure, freedom from business, a time given to sports, games or exercises, and afterwards time given to literary studies. The sense of a crowd, collection or *shoal*, seems to be derivative.]

1. A place or house in which persons are instructed in arts, science, languages or any species of learning; or the pupils assembled for instruction. In American usage, *school* more generally denotes the collective body of pupils in any place of instruction, and under the direction and discipline of one or more teachers. Thus we say, a *school* consists of fifty pupils. The preceptor has a large *school*, or a small *school.* His discipline keeps the *school* well regulated and quiet.
2. The instruction or exercises of a collection of pupils or students, or the collective body of pupils while engaged in their studies. Thus we say, the *school* begins or opens at eight o'clock, that is, the pupils at that hour begin their studies. So we say, the teacher is now in *school*, the *school* hours are from nine to twelve, and from two to five.
3. The state of instruction.

Set him betimes to *school.* *Dryden.*

4. A place of education, or collection of pupils, of any kind; as the *schools* of the prophets. In modern usage, the word *school* comprehends every place of education, as university, college, academy, common or primary schools, dancing schools, riding schools, &c.; but ordinarily the word is applied to seminaries inferior to universities and colleges.

What is the great community of christians, but one of the innumerable *schools* in the vast plan, which God has instituted for the education of various intelligences? *Buckminster.*

5. Separate denomination or sect; or a system of doctrine taught by particular teachers, or peculiar to any denomination of christians or philosophers.

Let no man be less confident in his faith—by reason of any difference in the several *schools* of christians— *Taylor.*

Thus we say, the Socratic *school*, the Platonic *school*, the Peripatetic or Ionic *school*; by which we understand all those who adopted and adhered to a particular system of opinions.

6. The seminaries for teaching logic, metaphysics and theology, which were formed in the middle ages, and which were characterized by academical disputations and subtilties of reasoning; or the learned men who were engaged in discussing nice points in metaphysics or theology.

The supreme authority of Aristotle in the *schools* of theology as well as of philosophy— *Henry.*

Hence, *school divinity* is the divinity which discusses nice points, and proves every thing by argument.

7. Any place of improvement or learning. The world is an excellent *school* to wise men, but a *school* of vice to fools.

SCHOOL, *v. t.* To instruct; to train; to educate.

He's gentle, never *school'd*, yet learn'd. *Shak.*

2. To teach with superiority; to tutor; to chide and admonish; to reprove.

School your child,
And ask why God's anointed he revil'd. *Dryden.*

SCHOOL'-BOY, *n.* [See *Boy.*] A boy belonging to a school, or one who is learning rudiments. *Swift.*

SCHOOL'-DAME, *n.* [See *Dame.*] The female teacher of a school.

SCHOOL'-DAY, *n.* [See *Day.*] The age in which youth are sent to school. [*Not now used.*] *Shak.*

SCHOOL'-DISTRICT, *n.* A division of a town or city for establishing and conducting schools. [*U. States.*]

SCHOOL'ERY, *n.* Something taught; precepts. [*Not used.*] *Spenser.*

SCHOOL'-FELLOW, *n.* [See *Fellow.*] One bred at the same school; an associate in school. *Locke.*

SCHOOL'-HOUSE, *n.* [See *House.*] A house appropriated for the use of schools, or for instruction; but applied only to buildings for subordinate schools, not to colleges. In Connecticut and some other states, every town is divided into school-districts, and each district erects its own *school-house* by a tax on the inhabitants.

SCHOOL'ING, *ppr.* Instructing; teaching; reproving.

SCHOOL'ING, *n.* Instruction in school; tuition.

2. Compensation for instruction; price or reward paid to an instructor for teaching pupils.
3. Reproof; reprimand. He gave his son a good *schooling.*

SCHOOL'MAID, *n.* [See *Maid.*] A girl at school. *Shak.*

SCHOOL'MAN, *n.* [See *Man.*] A man versed in the niceties of academical disputation or of school divinity.

Unlearn'd, he knew no *schoolman's* subtil art. *Pope.*

2. A writer of scholastic divinity or philosophy.

Let subtil *schoolmen* teach these friends to fight. *Pope.*

SCHOOL'MASTER, *n.* [See *Master.*] The man who presides over and teaches a school; a teacher, instructor or preceptor of a school. [*Applied now only or chiefly to the teachers of primary schools.*]

Adrian VI. was sometime *schoolmaster* to Charles V. *Knolles.*

2. He or that which disciplines, instructs and leads.

The law was our *schoolmaster* to bring us to Christ. Gal. iii.

SCHOOL'MISTRESS, *n.* [See *Mistress.*] A woman who governs and teaches a school. *Gay.*

SCHOON'ER, *n.* [G. *schoner.*] A vessel with two masts, whose main-sail and fore-sail are suspended by gaffs, like a sloop's main-sail, and stretched below by booms. *Mar. Dict. Encyc.*

SCHORL. [See *Shorl.*]

SCIAGRAPH'ICAL, *a.* Pertaining to sciagraphy.

SCIAG'RAPHY, *n.* [Gr. σκιαγραφια; σκια, a shadow, and γραφω, to describe.] The art of sketching or delineating.

2. In *architecture*, the profile or section of a building to exhibit its interior structure. *Bailey.*

3. In *astronomy*, the art of finding the hour of the day or night by the shadows of objects, caused by the sun, moon or stars; the art of dialing. *Ash. Bailey.*

SCIATHER'IC, SCIATHER'ICAL, *a.* [Gr. σκια, a shadow, and θηρα, a catching.]

Belonging to a sun-dial. [*Little used.*] *Brown.*

SCIATHER'ICALLY, *adv.* After the manner of a sun-dial. *Gregory.*

SCIAT'IC, SCIAT'ICA, *n.* [L. *sciatica*, from Gr. ισχιαδικος, from ισχιας, a pain in the hips, from ισχιον, the hip, from ισχις, the loin.] Rheumatism in the hip. *Coxe.*

SCIAT'IC, SCIAT'ICAL, *a.* Pertaining to the hip; as the *sciatic* artery.

2. Affecting the hip; as *sciatic* pains.

SCI'ENCE, *n.* [Fr. from L. *scientia*, from *scio*, to know; Sp. *ciencia*; It. *scienza. Scio* is probably a contracted word.]

1. In *a general sense*, knowledge, or certain knowledge; the comprehension or understanding of truth or facts by the mind. The *science* of God must be perfect.

2. In *philosophy*, a collection of the general principles or leading truths relating to any subject. *Pure* science, as the mathematics, is built on self-evident truths; but the term science is also applied to other subjects founded on generally acknowledged truths, as *metaphysics*; or on experiment and observation, as *chimistry* and *natural philosophy*; or even to an assemblage of the general principles of an art, as the science of *agriculture*; the science of *navigation*. *Arts* relate to practice, as painting and sculpture.

A principle in *science* is a rule in art. *Playfair.*

3. Art derived from precepts or built on principles.

Science perfects genius. *Dryden.*

4. Any art or species of knowledge.

No *science* doth make known the first principles on which it buildeth. *Hooker.*

5. One of the seven liberal branches of knowledge, viz. grammar, logic, rhetoric, arithmetic, geometry, astronomy and music. *Bailey. Johnson.*

[*Note.*—Authors have not always been careful to use the terms *art* and *science* with due discrimination and precision. Music is an *art* as well as a *science*. In general, an *art* is that which depends on practice or performance, and *science* that which depends on abstract or speculative principles. The *theory* of music is a *science*; the *practice* of it an *art.*]

SCI'ENT, *a.* [L. *sciens.*] Skillful. [*Not used.*] *Cockeram.*

SCIEN'TIAL, *a.* Producing science. *Milton.*

SCIENTIF'IC, SCIENTIF'ICAL, *a.* [Fr. *scientifique*; It. *scientifico*; Sp. *cientifico*; L. *scientia* and *facio*, to make.]

1. Producing certain knowledge or demonstration; as *scientific* evidence. *South.*

2. According to the rules or principles of science; as a *scientific* arrangement of fossils.

3. Well versed in science; as a *scientific* physician.

SCIENTIF'ICALLY, *adv.* In such a manner as to produce knowledge.

It is easier to believe, than to be *scientifically* instructed. *Locke.*

2. According to the rules or principles of science.

SCIL'LITIN, *n.* [See *Squill.*] A white transparent acrid substance, extracted from squills by Vogel. *Ure.*

SCIM'ITAR. [See *Cimiter.*]

SCINK, *n.* A cast calf. [*Not in use or local.*] *Ainsworth.*

SCIN'TILLANT, *a.* [See *Scintillate.*] Emitting sparks or fine igneous particles; sparkling.

SCIN'TILLATE, *v. i.* [L. *scintillo.* This word seems to be a diminutive formed on the Teutonic *scinan*, Eng. to *shine.*]

1. To emit sparks or fine igneous particles.

Marbles do not *scintillate* with steel. *Fourcroy.*

2. To sparkle, as the fixed stars.

SCIN'TILLATING, *ppr.* Emitting sparks; sparkling.

SCINTILLA'TION, *n.* The act of emitting sparks or igneous particles; the act of sparkling. *Brown. Glanville.*

SCI'OLISM, *n.* [See *Sciolist.*] Superficial knowledge. *Brit. Critic.*

SCI'OLIST, *n.* [L. *sciolus*, a diminutive formed on *scio*, to know.]

One who knows little, or who knows many things superficially; a smatterer.

These passages in that book, were enough to humble the presumption of our modern *sciolists*, if their pride were not as great as their ignorance. *Temple.*

SCI'OLOUS, *a.* Superficially or imperfectly knowing.

SCIOM'ACHY, *n.* [Gr. σκια, a shadow, and μαχη, a battle.]

A battle with a shadow. [*Little used.*] *Cowley.*

SCION. [See *Cion.*]

SCIOP'TIC, *a.* [Gr. σκια, shadow, and οπτομαι, to see.]

Pertaining to the camera obscura, or to the art of exhibiting images through a hole in a darkened room. *Bailey.*

SCIOP'TIC, *n.* A sphere or globe with a lens made to turn like the eye; used in experiments with the camera obscura.

SCIOP'TICS, *n.* The science of exhibiting images of external objects, received through a double convex glass into a darkened room.

SCIRE FA'CIAS, *n.* [L.] In *law*, a judicial writ summoning a person to show cause to the court why something should not be done, as to require sureties to show cause why the plaintif should not have execution against them for debt and damages, or to require a third person to show cause why goods in his hands by replevin, should not be delivered to satisfy the execution, &c. *Blackstone.*

SCI'ROC, SCIROC'CO, *n.* [It. *scirocco.*] In Italy, a south-east wind; a hot suffocating wind, blowing from the burning deserts of Africa. This name is given also, in the north-east of Italy, to a cold bleak wind from the Alps. *Encyc.*

SCIRROS'ITY, *n.* [See *Scirrus.*] An induration of the glands. *Arbuthnot.*

SCIR'ROUS, *a.* Indurated; hard; knotty; as a gland.

2. Proceeding from scirrus; as *scirrous* affections; *scirrous* disease.

SCIR'RUS, *n.* [It. *scirro*; Sp. *escirro*; L. *scirrus*; Gr. σκιρρος.]

In *surgery* and *medicine*, a hard tumor on any part of the body, usually proceeding from the induration of a gland, and often terminating in a cancer. *Encyc. Coxe.*

SCISCITA'TION, *n.* [L. *sciscitor*, to inquire or demand.]

The act of inquiring; inquiry; demand. [*Little used.*] *Hall.*

SCIS'SIBLE, *a.* [L. *scissus*, *scindo*, to cut.] Capable of being cut or divided by a sharp instrument; as *scissible* matter or bodies. *Bacon.*

SCIS'SILE, *a.* [L. *scissilis*, from *scindo*, to cut.]

That may be cut or divided by a sharp instrument. *Arbuthnot.*

SCISSION, *n.* *sizh'on.* [Fr. from L. *scissio*, *scindo*, to cut.]

The act of cutting or dividing by an edged instrument. *Wiseman.*

SCISSORS, *n.* *siz'zors.* plu. [L. *scissor*, from *scindo*, to cut, Gr. σχιζω, Sax. *sceadan.*]

A cutting instrument resembling shears, but smaller, consisting of two cutting blades movable on a pin in the center, by which they are fastened. Hence we usually say, a *pair of scissors.*

SCIS'SURE, *n.* [L. *scissura*, from *scindo*, to cut.]

A longitudinal opening in a body, made by cutting. [This cannot legitimately be a crack, rent or fissure. In this use it may be an error of the press for *fissure. Decay of Piety.*]

SCITAMIN'EOUS, *a.* Belonging to the Scitamineæ, one of Linne's natural orders of plants. *Asiat. Res.*

SCLAVO'NIAN, SLAVON'IC, *a.* [from *Sclavi*, a people of the north of Europe.]

Pertaining to the Sclavi, a people that inhabited the country between the rivers Save and Drave, or to their language. Hence the word came to denote the language which is now spoken in Poland, Russia, Hungary, Bohemia, &c.

SCLEROT'IC, *a.* [Gr. σκληρος, hard; σκληροτης, hardness.]

Hard; firm; as the *sclerotic* coat or tunicle of the eye. *Ray.*

SCLEROT'IC, *n.* The firm white outer coat of the eye. *Coxe.*

2. A medicine which hardens and consolidates the parts to which it is applied. *Quincy. Coxe.*

SCOAT. [See *Scot.*]

SCOB'IFORM, *a.* [L. *scobs*, saw dust, and *form.*]

Having the form of saw dust or raspings.

SCOBS, *n.* [L. from *scabo*, to scrape.] Raspings of ivory, hartshorn or other hard substance; dross of metals, &c. *Chambers.*

SCOFF, *v. i.* [Gr. σκωπτω. The primary sense is probably to throw, in which sense it coincides with the D. *schoppen*, G. *schuppen*, to push, to shove. But I do not find the word in the English and Greek sense, in any modern language except the English.]

To treat with insolent ridicule, mockery or contumelious language; to manifest contempt by derision; with *at.* To *scoff at* religion and sacred things is evidence of extreme weakness and folly, as well as of wickedness.

They shall *scoff at* the kings. Hab. I.

SCOFF, *v. t.* To treat with derision or scorn. *Fotherby.*

SCOFF, *n.* Derision, ridicule, mockery or reproach, expressed in language of contempt; expression of scorn or contempt.

With *scoffs* and scorns and contumelious taunts. *Shak.*

SCOFF'ER, *n.* One who scoffs; one that mocks, derides or reproaches in the language of contempt; a scorner.

There shall come in the last days *scoffers*, walking after their own lusts, and saying, "Where is the promise of his coming?" 2 Pet. iii.

SCOFF'ING, *ppr.* Deriding or mocking; treating with reproachful language.

SCOFF'INGLY, *adv.* In mockery or contempt; by way of derision.

Aristotle applied this hemistich *scoffingly* to the sycophants at Athens. *Broome.*

SCOLD, *v. i.* [D. *schelden*; G. *schelten*; Dan. *skielder*, to rail, to scold; Sw. *skalla*, to sound or ring; *skallra*, to snap or crack; *skålla*, to bark, to scold. It seems to be formed on the root of G. *schelle*, a bell, a jingle, a box on the ear; *schellen*, *schallen*, to ring; D. *schel*, *schellen*. If *s* is a prefix, this word coincides with *call*, and Sax. *galan*, to sing, *gyllan*, *gielan*, to yell.]

To find fault or rail with rude clamor; to brawl; to utter railing or harsh, rude, boisterous rebuke; with *at*; as, to *scold at* a servant. A *scolding* tongue, a *scolding* wife, a *scolding* husband, a *scolding* master, who can endure?

Pardon me, 'tis the first time that ever
I'm forc'd to *scold*. *Shak.*

SCOLD, *v. t.* To chide with rudeness and boisterous clamor; to rate. *Boswell.*

[The transitive use of this word is of recent origin, at least within my knowledge.]

SCOLD, *n.* A rude, clamorous, foul-mouthed woman.

Scolds answer foul-mouth'd *scolds*. *Swift.*

2. A scolding; a brawl.

SCOLDER, *n.* One that scolds or rails.

SCOLDING, *ppr.* Railing with clamor; uttering rebuke in rude and boisterous language.

2. *a.* Given to scolding.

SCOLDING, *n.* The uttering of rude, clamorous language by way of rebuke or railing; railing language.

SCOLDINGLY, *adv.* With rude clamor or railing.

SCOL'LOP, *n.* A pectinated shell. [See *Scallop.*]

2. An indenting or cut like those of a shell.

SCOL'LOP, *v. t.* To form or cut with scollops.

SCOLOPEN'DRA, *n.* [Gr. σκολοπενδρα.] A venomous serpent. *Johnson.*

2. A genus of insects of the order of Apters, destitute of wings. These insects have as many feet on each side as there are segments in the body. There are several species. *Dict. Nat. Hist.*

3. A plant. [L. *scolopendrium.*] *Ainsworth.*

SCOMM, *n.* [L. *scomma*; Gr. σκωμμα, from σκωπτω. See *Scoff.*]

1. A buffoon. [*Not in use.*] *L'Estrange.*

2. A flout; a jeer. [*Not in use.*]

SCONCE, *n.* [D. *schans*; G. *schanze*; D. *skands*; Sw. *skans*, a fort or castle, a fortification.]

1. A fort or bulwark; a work for defense. *Obs.* *Shak.*

2. A hanging or projecting candlestick, generally with a mirror to reflect the light.

Golden *sconces* hang upon the walls. *Dryden.*

3. The circular tube with a brim in a candlestick, into which the candle is inserted, that is, the support, the holder of the candle; and from this sense the candlestick, in the preceding definition, has its name.

4. A fixed seat or shelf. [*Local.*]

SCONCE, *n.* [Dan. *skiönner*, to judge, to discern; *skiönsom*, judicious.]

1. Sense; judgment; discretion or understanding. This sense has been in vulgar use in New England within my memory.

2. The head; *a low word.* *Shak.*

3. A mulct or fine. [Qu. *poll-tax.*]

SCONCE, *v. t.* To mulct; to fine. [*A low word and not in use.*] *Warton.*

SCOOP, *n.* [D. *schop*, a scoop, and a shovel; G. *schüppe*; *schupp*, a shove; *schuppen*, to push or shove; Sw. *skuff*, a shove; Dan. *skuffe*, a *scoop*, a *shovel*, a box or drawer; D. *schuif*, *schuiven*, to *shove*; Fr. *ecope*; Arm. *esgop* or *scop.*]

1. A large ladle; a vessel with a long handle fastened to a dish, used for dipping liquors; also, a little hollow piece of wood for bailing boats.

2. An instrument of surgery. *Sharp.*

3. A sweep; a stroke; a swoop. *Shak.*

SCOOP, *v. t.* To lade out; properly, to take out with a scoop or with a sweeping motion.

He *scoop'd* the water from the crystal flood. *Dryden.*

2. To empty by lading; as, he *scooped* it dry. *Addison.*

3. To make hollow, as a scoop or dish; to excavate; as, the Indians *scoop* the trunk of a tree into a canoe.

Those carbuncles the Indians will *scoop*, so as to hold above a pint. *Arbuthnot.*

4. To remove, so as to leave a place hollow.

A spectator would think this circular mount had been actually *scooped* out of that hollow space. *Spectator.*

SCOOP'ED, *pp.* Taken out as with a scoop or ladle; hollowed; excavated; removed so as to leave a hollow.

SCOOP'ER, *n.* One that scoops; also, a water fowl.

SCOOP'ING, *ppr.* Lading out; making hollow; excavating; removing so as to leave a hollow.

SCOOP'-NET, *n.* A net so formed as to sweep the bottom of a river.

SCOPE, *n.* [L. *scopus*; Gr. σκοπος, from σκοπεω, to see or view; Heb. שקף to see, to behold; Ch. to drive or strike. Class Gb. No. 85. The primary sense is to stretch or extend, to reach; properly, the whole extent, space or reach, hence the whole space viewed, and hence the limit or ultimate end.]

1. Space; room; amplitude of intellectual view; as a free *scope* for inquiry; full *scope* for the fancy or imagination; ample *scope* for genius.

2. The limit of intellectual view; the end or thing to which the mind directs its view; that which is purposed to be reached or accomplished; hence, ultimate design, aim or purpose; intention; drift. It expresses both the purpose and thing purposed.

Your *scope* is as mine own,
So to enforce and qualify the laws,
As to your soul seems good. *Shak.*

The *scope* of all their pleading against man's authority, is to overthrow such laws and constitutions of the church— *Hooker.*

3. Liberty; freedom from restraint; room to move in. *Hooker.*

4. Liberty beyond just limits; license.

Give him line and *scope*. *Shak.*

5. Act of riot; sally; excess. *Obs.* *Shak.*

6. Extended quantity; as a *scope* of land. *Obs.* *Davies.*

7. Length; extent; sweep; as *scope* of cable. *Mar. Language.*

SCO'PIFORM, *a.* [L. *scopa*, a broom, and *form.*] Having the form of a broom or besom.

Zeolite, stelliform or *scopiform*. *Kirwan.*

SCOP'PET, *v. t.* To lade out. [*Not in use.*] *Bp. Hall.*

SCOP'TICAL, *a.* [Gr. σκωπτικος.] Scoffing. [*Not in use.*] *Hammond.*

SCOP'ULOUS, *a.* [L. *scopulosus.*] Full of rocks; rocky. [*Not in use.*] *Dict.*

SCORBUTE, *n.* [L. *scorbutus.*] Scurvy. [*Not in use.*] *Purchas.*

SCORBU'TIC, **SCORBU'TICAL**, } *a.* [Fr. *scorbutique*, from L. *scorbutus*, the scurvy. See *Scurf*, *Scurvy.*]

1. Affected or diseased with scurvy; as a *scorbutic* person.

2. Pertaining to scurvy, or partaking of its nature; as *scorbutic* complaints or symptoms.

3. Subject to scurvy; as a *scorbutic* habit.

SCORBU'TICALLY, *adv.* With the scurvy, or with a tendency to it; as a woman *scorbutically* affected. *Wiseman.*

SCORCE. [See *Scorse.*]

SCORCH, *v. t.* [D. *schroeijen*, *schrooken*, to scorch. If this is the same word, there has been a transposition of the vowel. The Saxon has *scorcned*, the participle. But it is probable the Dutch is the true orthography, and the word is to be referred to the Ch. חרך, Ar. حرق haraka or charaka, to burn, singe or roast. Class Rg. No. 33. 34.]

1. To burn superficially; to subject to a degree of heat that changes the color of a thing, or both the color and texture of the surface. Fire will *scorch* linen or cotton very speedily in extremely cold weather.
2. To burn; to affect painfully with heat. *Scorched* with the burning sun or burning sands of Africa.

SCORCH, *v. i.* To be burnt on the surface; to be parched; to be dried up.

> Scatter a little mungy straw and fern among your seedlings, to prevent the roots from *scorching*. *Mortimer.*

SCORCH'ED, *pp.* Burnt on the surface; pained by heat.

SCORCH'ING, *ppr.* Burning on the surface; paining by heat.

SCORCH'ING-FENNEL, *n.* A plant of the genus Thapsia; deadly carrot. *Lee.*

SCOR'DIUM, *n.* [L.] A plant, the water-germander, a species of Teucrium. *Encyc.*

SCORE, *n.* [Ir. *scor*, a notch; *sgoram*, to cut in pieces; Sax. *s or*, a score, twenty; Ice. *skora*, from the root of *shear*, *share*, *shire*.]

1. A notch or incision; hence, the number twenty. Our ancestors, before the knowledge of writing, numbered and kept accounts of numbers by cutting notches on a stick or tally, and making one notch the representative of twenty. A simple mark answered the same purpose.
2. A line drawn.
3. An account or reckoning; as, he paid his *score*. *Shak.*
4. An account kept of something past; an epoch; an era. *Tillotson.*
5. Debt, or account of debt. *Shak.*
6. Account; reason; motive.

> But left the trade, as many more
> Have lately done on the same *score*. *Hudibras.*

7. Account; sake.

> You act your kindness on Cydaria's *score*. *Dryden.*

8. In *music*, the original and entire draught of any composition, or its transcript. *Busby.*

To quit scores, to pay fully; to make even by giving an equivalent.

A song in score, the words with the musical notes of a song annexed. *Johnson.*

SCORE, *v. t.* To notch; to cut and chip for the purpose of preparing for hewing; as, to *score* timber.

2. To cut; to engrave. *Spenser.*
3. To mark by a line. *Sandys.*
4. To set down as a debt.

> Madam, I know when,
> Instead of five, you *scored* me ten. *Swift.*

5. To set down or take as an account; to charge; as, to *score* follies. *Dryden.*
6. To form a score in music. *Busby.*

SCO'RED, *pp.* Notched; set down; marked; prepared for hewing.

In *botany*, a *scored stem* is marked with parallel lines or grooves. *Martyn.*

SCO'RIA, *n.* [L. from the Gr. σκωρια, σκωρ, rejected matter, that which is thrown off. Class Gr.]

Dross; the recrement of metals in fusion, or the mass produced by melting metals and ores. *Newton. Encyc.*

SCORIA'CEOUS, *a.* Pertaining to dross; like dross or the recrement of metals; partaking of the nature of scoria.

SCORIFICA'TION, *n.* In *metallurgy*, the act or operation of reducing a body, either wholly or in part, into scoria. *Encyc.*

SCO'RIFIED, *pp.* Reduced to scoria.

SCO'RIFORM, *a.* [L. *scoria* and *form*.] Like scoria; in the form of dross. *Kirwan.*

SCO'RIFY, *v. t.* To reduce to scoria or drossy matter.

SCO'RIFYING, *ppr.* Reducing to scoria.

SCO'RING, *ppr.* Notching; marking; setting down as an account or debt; forming a score.

SCO'RIOUS, *a.* Drossy; recrementitious. *Brown.*

SCORN, *n.* [Sp. *escarnio*, scorn; *escarnecer*, to mock; Port. *escarneo*, *escarnecer*; It. *scherno*, *schernire*; W. *ysgorn*, *ysgorniaw*.]

1. Extreme contempt; that disdain which springs from a person's opinion of the meanness of an object, and a consciousness or belief of his own superiority or worth.

> He thought *scorn* to lay hands on Mordecai alone. Esth. iii.

> Every sullen frown and bitter *scorn*
> But fann'd the fuel that too fast did burn. *Dryden.*

2. A subject of extreme contempt, disdain or derision; that which is treated with contempt.

> Thou makest us a reproach to our neighbors, a *scorn* and a derision to them that are around us. Ps. xliv.

To think scorn, to disdain; to despise. *Obs. Sidney.*

To laugh to scorn, to deride; to make a mock of; to ridicule as contemptible.

> They *laughed* us *to scorn*. Neh. ii.

SCORN, *v. t.* To hold in extreme contempt; to despise; to contemn; to disdain. Job xvi.

> Surely he *scorneth* the scorner; but he giveth grace to the lowly. Prov. iii.

2. To think unworthy; to disdain.

> Fame that delights around the world to stray,
> *Scorns* not to take our Argos in her way *Pope.*

3. To slight; to disregard; to neglect.

> This my long suff'rance and my day of grace,
> Those who neglect and *scorn*, shall never taste. *Milton.*

SCORN, *v. i.* To *scorn at*, to scoff at; to treat with contumely, derision or reproach. *Obs. Shak.*

SCORN'ED, *pp.* Extremely contemned or despised; disdained.

SCORN'ER, *n.* One that scorns; a contemner; a despiser.

> They are great *scorners* of death. *Spenser.*

2. A scoffer; a derider; in Scripture, one who scoffs at religion, its ordinances and teachers, and who makes a mock of sin and the judgments and threatenings of God against sinners. Prov. i. xix.

SCORN'FUL, *a.* Contemptuous; disdainful; entertaining scorn; insolent.

> Th' enamor'd deity
> The *scornful* damsel shuns. *Dryden.*

2. Acting in defiance or disregard.

> *Scornful* of winter's frost and summer's sun. *Prior.*

3. In *Scripture*, holding religion in contempt; treating with disdain religion and the dispensations of God.

SCORN'FULLY, *adv.* With extreme contempt; contemptuously; insolently.

> The sacred rights of the christian church are *scornfully* trampled on in print— *Atterbury.*

SCORN'FULNESS, *n.* The quality of being scornful.

SCORN'ING, *ppr.* Holding in great contempt; despising; disdaining.

SCORN'ING, *n.* The act of contemning; a treating with contempt, slight or disdain.

> How long will the scorners delight in their *scorning?* Prov. i. Ps. cxxiii.

SCOR'PION, *n.* [Fr. from L. *scorpio*; Gr. σκορπιος; probably altered from the Oriental עקרב. The Arabic verb to which this word belongs, signifies to wound, to strike, &c.]

1. In *zoology*, an insect of the genus Scorpio, or rather the genus itself, containing several species, natives of southern or warm climates. This animal has eight feet, two claws in front, eight eyes, three on each side of the thorax and two on the back, and a long jointed tail ending in a pointed weapon or sting. It is found in the south of Europe, where it seldom exceeds four inches in length. In tropical climates, it grows to a foot in length, and resembles a lobster. The sting of this animal is sometimes fatal to life. *Encyc.*
2. In *Scripture*, a painful scourge; a kind of whip armed with points like a scorpion's tail. 1 Kings xii.

> Malicious and crafty men, who delight in injuring others, are compared to *scorpions*, Ezek. ii.

3. In *astronomy*, the eighth sign of the zodiac, which the sun enters, Oct. 23.
4. A sea fish. [L. *scorpius*.] *Ainsworth.*

Water scorpion, an aquatic insect of the genus Nepa.

SCOR'PION-FLY, *n.* An insect of the genus Panorna, having a tail which resembles that of a scorpion.

SCOR'PION-GRASS, } *n.* A plant of the **SCOR'PION'S TAIL**, } genus Scorpiurus, with trailing herbaceous stalks, and producing a pod resembling a caterpillar, whence it is called *caterpillars*. *Encyc.*

The *mouse-ear scorpion-grass*, is of the genus Myosotis.

SCOR'PION-SENNA, *n.* A plant of the genus Coronilla.

SCOR'PION'S-THORN, *n.* A plant of the genus Ulex.

SCOR'PION-WORT, *n.* A plant, the *Ornithopus scorpioides*. *Parr.*

SCORSE, *n.* [It. *scorsa*, a course; L. *ex* and *cursus*.] A course or dealing; barter. *Obs. Spenser.*

SCORSE, *v. t.* To chase. *Obs. Spenser.*

2. To barter or exchange. *Obs. Spenser.*

SCORSE, *v. i.* To deal for the purchase of a horse. *Obs. B. Jonson.*

SCORT'ATORY, *a.* [L. *scortator*, from *scortor*.] Pertaining to or consisting in lewdness.

SCOR'ZA, *n.* [Qu. It. *scorza*, bark; L. *ex* and *cortex*.] In *mineralogy*, a variety of epidote. *Ure.*

SCOT, } *v. t.* [Arm. *scoaz*, the shoulder,
SCOTCH, } whence *scoazya*, to shoulder up, to prop, to support; W. *ysgwyz*, a shoulder; *ysgwyzaw*, to shoulder, which is said to be from *cwyz*, a fall.]

To support, as a wheel, by placing some obstacle to prevent its rolling. Our wagoners and cartmen *scot* the wheels of their wagons and carts, when in ascending a hill they stop to give their team rest, or for other purpose. In Connecticut, I have generally heard this word pronounced *scot*, in Massachusetts, *scotch*.

SCOT, *n.* [Sax. *sceat*, a part, portion, angle or bay, a garment or vest, a towel, cloth or *sheet; sceat, sceata, sceatt*, money, tax, tribute, toll, price, gift; *sceta, scyta*, a sheet. This is the English *shot*, in the phrase, he paid his *shot;* and *scot*, in *scot and lot*. Ice. *skot*, D. *schot*, a wainscot, shot, scot; *schoot*, a sheet, a shoot, a shot, a sprig, a bolt, the lap, the womb; G. *schoss*, scot, a shoot, and *schooss*, lap, womb; Sw. *skatt*, tax, tribute, rent, Eng. *scot;* Dan. *skot, skat*, id.; *skiöd*, the lap, the bosom, the waist of a coat; Fr. *ecot*, shot, reckoning, It. *scotto;* Sp. *escote*, shot, reckoning, a tucker, or small piece of linen that shades a woman's breast, also the sloping of a garment; *escota*, a sheet, in seamen's language; Port. *escota ; escote*, shot, club. This word coincides in elements with *shade, scud, shoot, shed* and *sheet*, all of which convey the sense of driving, or of separating, cutting off.]

In *law* and *English history*, a portion of money, assessed or paid; a customary tax or contribution laid on subjects according to their ability; also, a tax or custom paid for the use of a sherif or bailif. Hence our modern *shot;* as, to pay one's *shot*.

Scot and lot, parish payments. When persons were taxed unequally, they were said to pay *scot and lot*. *Encyc.*

SCOT, *n.* [Sax. *scotta, scotte ;* W. *ysgotiad*, a woodsman, a *Scot*, from *ysgawd*, a shade; *ysgodi*, to shade, to shelter, Eng. *shade*, which see. This word signifies, according to the Welsh, an inhabitant of the woods, and from the same root probably as *Scythian, Scythia.*] A native of Scotland or North Britain.

SCOT'AL, } *n.* [*scot* and *ale*.] In *law*, the
SCOT'ALE, } keeping of an alehouse by the officer of a forest, and drawing people to spend their money for liquor, for fear of his displeasure.

SCOTCH, *a.* Pertaining to Scotland or its inhabitants. [See *Scotish*.]

SCOTCH. [See *Scot*, the verb.]

SCOTCH, *v. t.* [Qu. Arm. *sqeigea*, or Sax. *sceadan*. This cannot be from Fr. *ecorcher*, to flay or peel; *ecorce*, bark.]

To cut with shallow incisions. *Obs.* *Shak.*

SCOTCH, *n.* A slight cut or shallow incision. *Shak. Walton.*

SCOTCH-COLLOPS, } *n.* Veal cut into
SCOTCHED-COLLOPS, } small pieces.

SCOTCH-HOPPER, *n.* A play in which boys hop over scotches or lines in the ground. *Locke.*

SCO'TER, *n.* The black diver or duck, a species of Anas.

SCOT'FREE, *a.* Free from payment or scot; untaxed.

2. Unhurt; clear; safe.

SCO'TIA, *n.* In *architecture*, a semicircular cavity or channel between the tores in the bases of columns.

SCOT'ISH, } *a.* Pertaining to the inhabi-
SCOT'TISH, } tants of Scotland, or to their country or language; as *Scottish* industry or economy; a *Scottish* chief; the *Scottish* dialect.

SCO'TIST, *n.* [from Duns *Scotus*, a Scotish cordelier.]

One of the followers of Scotus, a sect of school divines who maintained the immaculate conception of the virgin, or that she was born without original sin; in opposition to the Thomists, or followers of Thomas Aquinas.

SCOT'OMY, *n.* [Gr. σκοτωμα, vertigo, from σκοτοω, to darken.]

Dizziness or swimming of the head, with dimness of sight.

SCOT'TERING, *n.* A provincial word in Herefordshire, England, denoting the burning of a wad of pease straw at the end of harvest. *Bailey. Johnson.*

SCOT'TICISM, *n.* An idiom or peculiar expression of the natives of Scotland. *Beattie.*

SCOTTISH. [See *Scotish*.]

SCOUN'DREL, *n.* [said to be from It. *scondaruole*, a lurker, one that sculks from the roll or muster, from L. *abscondo*. The Italian signifies properly the play hoodman-blind, or fox in the hole.]

A mean, worthless fellow; a rascal; a low petty villain; a man without honor or virtue.

> Go, if your ancient but ignoble blood
> Has crept through *scoundrels* ever since the flood. *Pope.*

SCOUN'DREL, *a.* Low; base; mean; unprincipled.

SCOUN'DRELISM, *n.* Baseness; turpitude; rascality. *Cotgrave.*

SCOUR, *v. t.* [Goth. *skauron*, to scour; Sax. *scur*, a scouring; D. *schuuren*; G. *scheuern ;* Dan. *skurer ;* Sw. *skura ;* Arm. *scarhein, scurhein* or *scurya ;* Fr. *ecurer*, to scour; Sp. *escurar*. See the roots גרר and גרע. Class Gr. No. 5. and 8.]

1. To rub hard with something rough, for the purpose of cleaning; as, to *scour* a kettle; to *scour* a musket; to *scour* armor.

2. To clean by friction; to make clean or bright.

3. To purge violently.

4. To remove by scouring.

> Never came reformation in a flood
> With such a heady current, *scouring* faults. *Shak.*

5. To range about for taking all that can be found; as, to *scour* the sea of pirates.

6. To pass swiftly over; to brush along; as, to *scour* the coast. *Milton.*

> Not so when swift Camilla *scours* the plain. *Pope.*

SCOUR, *v. i.* To perform the business of cleaning vessels by rubbing. *Shak.*

2. To clean.

> Warm water is softer than cold, for it *scoureth* better. *Bacon.*

3. To be purged to excess. *Bacon. Mortimer.*

4. To rove or range for sweeping or taking something.

> Barbarossa, thus *scouring* along the coast of Italy— *Knolles.*

5. To run with celerity; to scamper.

> So four fierce coursers, starting to the race,
> *Scour* through the plain, and lengthen every pace. *Dryden.*

SCOUR'ED, *pp.* Rubbed with something rough, or made clean by rubbing; severely purged; brushed along.

SCOUR'ER, *n.* One that scours or cleans by rubbing.

2. A drastic cathartic.

3. One that runs with speed.

SCOURĠE, *n.* *skurj.* [Fr. *escourgée ;* It. *scoreggia*, a lether thong; from L. *corrigia*, from *corrigo*, to straighten.]

1. A whip; a lash consisting of a strap or cord; an instrument of punishment or discipline.

> A *scourge* of small cords. John ii.

2. A punishment; vindictive affliction.

> Famine and plague are sent as *scourges* for amendment. 2 Esdras.

3. He or that which greatly afflicts, harasses or destroys; particularly, any continued evil or calamity. Attila was called the *scourge* of God, for the miseries he inflicted in his conquests. Slavery is a terrible *scourge*.

4. A whip for a top. *Locke.*

SCOURĠE, *v. t.* *skurj.* [It. *scoreggiare.*] To whip severely; to lash.

> Is it lawful for you to *scourge* a man that is a Roman? Acts xxii.

2. To punish with severity; to chastise; to afflict for sins or faults, and with the purpose of correction.

> He will *scourge* us for our iniquities, and will have mercy again. *Tobit.*
> Whom the Lord loveth he chasteneth, and *scourgeth* every son whom he receiveth. Heb. xii.

3. To afflict greatly; to harass, torment or injure.

SCOURĠ'ED, *pp.* Whipped; lashed; punished severely; harassed.

SCOURĠ'ER, *n.* One that scourges or punishes; one that afflicts severely.

SCOURĠ'ING, *ppr.* Whipping; lashing with severity; punishing or afflicting severely.

SCOUR'ING, *ppr.* Rubbing hard with something rough; cleaning by rubbing; cleansing with a drastic cathartic; ranging over for clearing.

SCOUR'ING, *n.* A rubbing hard for cleaning; a cleansing by a drastic purge; looseness; flux. *Bacon.*

SCOURSE. [See *Scorse.*]

SCOUT, *n.* [Fr. *ecout ; ecouter*, to hear, to listen; Norm. *escoult*, a hearing; It. *scolta*, a watch; *scoltare*, to listen; L. *ausculto ;* Gr. ους, the ear, and L. *culto, colo.*]

1. In *military affairs*, a person sent before an army, or to a distance, for the purpose of observing the motions of an enemy or discovering any danger, and giving notice to the general. Horsemen are generally employed as *scouts*. *Encyc.*

2. A high rock. [*Not in use.*]

SCOUT, *v. i.* To go on the business of watching the motions of an enemy; to act as a scout.

With obscure wing
Scout far and wide into the realm of night. *Milton.*

SCOUT, *v. t.* [perhaps Sw. *skiuta*, to shoot, to thrust, that is, to reject.]
To sneer at; to treat with disdain and contempt. [*This word is in good use in America.*]

SCO'VEL, *n.* [W *ysgubell*, from *ysgub*, a broom, L. *scopa.*]
A mop for sweeping ovens; a maulkin. *Ainsworth. Bailey.*

SCOW, *n.* [D. *schouw*; Dan. *skude*; Sw. *skuta.*]
A large flat bottomed boat; used as a ferry boat, or for loading and unloading vessels. [*A word in good use in New England.*]

SCOW, *v. t.* To transport in a scow.

SCOWL, *v. i.* [Sax. *scul*, in *scul-eaged*, scowl-eyed; probably from the root of G. *schel, schiel*, D. *scheel*, distorted; *schielen*, Dan. *skieler*, to squint; Gr. σχολιοω, to twist. See Class Gl. No. 59.]
1. To wrinkle the brows, as in frowning or displeasure; to put on a frowning look; to look sour, sullen, severe or angry.
She *scowl'd* and frown'd with froward countenance. *Spenser.*
2. To look gloomy, frowning, dark or tempestuous; as the *scowling* heavens. *Thomson.*

SCOWL, *v. t.* To drive with a scowl or frowns. *Milton.*

SCOWL, *n.* The wrinkling of the brows in frowning; the expression of displeasure, sullenness or discontent in the countenance.
2. Gloom; dark or rude aspect; as of the heavens. *Crashaw.*

SCOWL'ING, *ppr.* Contracting the brows into wrinkles; frowning; expressing displeasure or sullenness.

SCOWL'INGLY, *adv.* With a wrinkled, frowning aspect; with a sullen look.

SCRAB'BLE, *v. i.* [D. *krabbelen*, to *scrape, to scribble*; *krabben*, to scrape; G. *krabbeln, graben.* This word belongs to the root of *scrape*, L. *scribo*, Eng. *grave, engrave*, &c. See *Scrape.*]
1. To scrape, paw or scratch with the hands; to move along on the hands and knees by clawing with the hands; to scramble; as, to *scrabble* up a cliff or a tree. [*A word in common popular use in New England, but not elegant.*]
2. To make irregular or crooked marks; as, children *scrabble* when they begin to write; hence, to make irregular and unmeaning marks.
David—*scrabbled* on the doors of the gate. 1 Sam. xxi.

SCRAB'BLE, *v. t.* To mark with irregular lines or letters; as, to *scrabble* paper.

SCRAB'BLING, *ppr.* Scraping; scratching; scrambling; making irregular marks.

SCRAG, *n.* [This word is formed from the root of *rag, crag*, Gr. ῥαχια, ῥαχις, rack. Class Rg.]
Something thin or lean with roughness. A raw boned person is called a *scrag*, but the word is vulgar.

SCRAG'GED, SCRAG'GY, *a.* [supra.] Rough with irregular points or a broken surface; as a *scraggy* hill; a *scragged* back bone. *Bentley.*
2. Lean with roughness. *Arbuthnot.*

SCRAG'GEDNESS, SCRAG'GINESS, *n.* Leanness, or leanness with roughness; ruggedness; roughness occasioned by broken irregular points.

SCRAG'GILY, *adv.* With leanness and roughness.

SCRAM'BLE, *v. i.* [D. *schrammen*, to scratch. It is not improbable that this word is corrupted from the root of *scrape, scrabble.*]
1. To move or climb by seizing objects with the hand, and drawing the body forward; as, to *scramble* up a cliff.
2. To seize or catch eagerly at any thing that is desired; to catch with haste preventive of another; to catch at without ceremony. Man originally was obliged to *scramble* with wild beasts for nuts and acorns.
Of other care they little reck'ning make,
Than how to *scramble* at the shearer's feast. *Milton.*

SCRAM'BLE, *n.* An eager contest for something, in which one endeavors to get the thing before another.
The scarcity of money enhances the price and increases the *scramble*. *Locke.*
2. The act of climbing by the help of the hands.

SCRAM'BLER, *n.* One who scrambles; one who climbs by the help of the hands.

SCRAM'BLING, *ppr.* Climbing by the help of the hands.
2. Catching at eagerly and without ceremony.

SCRAM'BLING, *n.* The act of climbing by the help of the hands.
2. The act of seizing or catching at with eager haste and without ceremony.

SCR'ANCH, *v. t.* [D. *schranssen*; from *cranch, craunch*, by prefixing *s.*]
To grind with the teeth, and with a crackling sound; to craunch. [*This is in vulgar use in America.*]

SCRAN'NEL, *a.* [Qu. broken, split; from the root of *cranny.*] Slight; poor.
Grate on their *scrannel* pipes of wretched straw. [*Not in use.*] *Milton.*

SCRAP, *n.* [from *scrape.*] A small piece; properly something *scraped off*, but used for any thing cut off; a fragment; a crum; as *scraps* of meat. *Shak.*
2. A part; a detached piece; as *scraps* of history or poetry; *scraps* of antiquity; *scraps* of authors. *Locke. Pope.*
3. A small piece of paper. *Pope.*
[If used for *script*, it is improper.]

SCRAPE, *v. t.* [Sax. *screopan*; D. *schraapen, schrabben*; G. *schrapen*; Sw. *skrapa*; Dan. *skraber*; Ir. *scriobam, sgrabam*; Russ. *skrebu* and *ogrebayu*; L. *scribo*, Gr. γραφω, to write; W. *ysgravu*, to scrape, from *cravu*, to scrape, from *crav*, claws. Owen. But probably from the general root of *grave*. In Ch. and Syr. כרב signifies to plow; in Ar. to strain, distress, *gripe*. See *Grave.*]
1. To rub the surface of any thing with a sharp or rough instrument, or with something hard; as, to *scrape* the floor; to *scrape* a vessel for cleaning it; to *scrape* the earth; to *scrape* the body. Job ii.
2. To clean by scraping. Lev. xiv.
3. To remove or take off by rubbing.
I will also *scrape* her dust from her, and make her like the top of a rock. Ezek. xxvi.
4. To act upon the surface with a grating noise.
The chiming clocks to dinner call;
A hundred footsteps *scrape* the marble hall. *Pope.*

To scrape off, to remove by scraping; to clear away by rubbing.

To scrape together, to gather by close industry or small gains or savings; as, to *scrape together* a good estate.

SCRAPE, *v. i.* To make a harsh noise.
2. To play awkwardly on a violin.
3. To make an awkward bow.

To scrape acquaintance, to make one's self acquainted; to curry favor. [A low phrase introduced from the practice of *scraping* in bowing.]

SCRAPE, *n.* [Dan. *scrab*; Sw. *skrap.*] A rubbing.
2. The sound of the foot drawn over the floor.
3. A bow.
4. Difficulty; perplexity; distress; that which harasses. [*A low word.*]

SCRA'PED, *pp.* Rubbed on the surface with a sharp or rough instrument; cleaned by rubbing; cleared away by scraping.

SCRA'PER, *n.* An instrument with which any thing is scraped; as a *scraper* for shoes.
2. An instrument drawn by oxen or horses, and used for scraping earth in making or repairing roads, digging cellars, canals, &c.
3. An instrument having two or three sides or edges, for cleaning the planks, masts or decks of a ship, &c.
4. A miser; one who gathers property by penurious diligence and small savings; a scrape-penny.
5. An awkward fiddler.

SCRA'PING, *ppr.* Rubbing the surface with something sharp or hard; cleaning by a scraper; removing by rubbing; playing awkwardly on a violin.

SCRAT, *v. t.* [formed on the root of L. *rado.*] To scratch. [*Not in use.*] *Burton.*

SCRAT, *v. i.* To rake; to search. [*Not in use.*]

SCRAT, *n.* An hermaphrodite. [*Not in use*] *Skinner.*

SCRATCH, *v. t.* [G. *kratzen, ritzen, kritzeln*; D. *kratsen*; Sw. *kratsa*; Dan. *kradser*; probably from the root of *grate*, and L. *rado*. See Class Rd. No. 46. 49. 56. 58. 59.]
1. To rub and tear the surface of any thing with something sharp or ragged; as, to *scratch* the cheeks with the nails; to *scratch* the earth with a rake; to *scratch* the hands or face by riding or running among briers.
A sort of small sand-colored stones, so hard as to *scratch* glass. *Grew.*
2. To wound slightly.
3. To rub with the nails.
Be mindful, when invention fails,
To *scratch* your head and bite your nails. *Swift.*
4. To write or draw awkwardly; as, to *scratch* out a pamphlet. [*Not in use.*] *Swift.*
5. To dig or excavate with the claws. Some animals *scratch* holes in which they burrow.

To scratch out, to erase; to rub out; to obliterate.

SCRATCH, *v. i.* To use the claws in tearing the surface. The gallinaceous hen *scratches* for her chickens.

—Dull tame things that will neither bite nor *scratch*. *More.*

SCRATCH, *n.* A rent; a break in the surface of a thing made by scratching, or by rubbing with any thing pointed or ragged; as a *scratch* on timber or glass.

The coarse file—makes deep *scratches* in the work. *Moxon.*

These nails with *scratches* shall deform my breast. *Prior.*

2. A slight wound.

Heav'n forbid a shallow *scratch* should drive
The prince of Wales from such a field as this. *Shak.*

3. A kind of wig worn for covering baldness or gray hairs, or for other purpose. *Smollet.*

SCRATCH'ED, *pp.* Torn by the rubbing of something rough or pointed.

SCRATCH'ER, *n.* He or that which scratches.

SCRATCH'ES, *n. plu.* Cracked ulcers on a horse's foot, just above the hoof.

SCRATCH'ING, *ppr.* Rubbing with something pointed or rough; rubbing and tearing the surface.

SCRATCH'INGLY, *adv.* With the action of scratching. *Sidney.*

SCRAW, *n.* [Irish and Erse.] Surface; cut turf. [*Not in use.*] *Swift.*

SCRAWL, *v. t.* [Qu. from *crawl*, or its root, or from the D. *schravelen*, to scratch or scrape. Both may be from one root.]

1. To draw or mark awkwardly and irregularly. *Swift.*

2. To write awkwardly.

SCRAWL, *v. i.* To write unskillfully and inelegantly.

Though with a golden pen you *scrawl*. *Swift.*

2. To creep; to crawl. [This is from *crawl*, but I know not that it is in use.] *Ainsworth.*

SCRAWL, *n.* Unskillful or inelegant writing; or a piece of hasty bad writing. *Pope.*

2. In *New England*, a ragged, broken branch of a tree, or other brush wood.

SCRAWL'ER, *n.* One who scrawls; a hasty or awkward writer.

SCRAY, *n.* A fowl called the sea swallow, [*hirundo marina,*] of the genus Terna.

SCRE'ABLE, *a.* [L. *screabilis*, from *screo*, to spit out.] That may be spit out. *Obs.*

SCREAK, *v. i.* [Sw. *skrika*; Dan. *skriger*; W. *ysgreçian*, from *creçian*, to *creak*, to *shriek*, from *creç*, *cryç*, rough, roughness, or its root. This word is only a different orthography of *screech* and *shriek*, but is not elegant.]

To utter suddenly a sharp shrill sound or outcry; to scream; as in a sudden fright; also, to creak, as a door or wheel. [See *Screech.*]

[When applied to things, we use *creak*, and when to persons, *shriek*, both of which are elegant.]

SCREAK, *n.* A creaking; a screech.

SCREAM, *v. i.* [Sax. *reomian*, *hræman* or *hreman*; W. *ysgarmu*, to set up a scream or shout. It appears from the Welsh that this is also the English *skirmish*, Sp. *escaramuzar*, which in D. is *schermutselen*, from *scherm*, a fence or skreen; *schermen*, to fence. The primary sense is to thrust, drive or force out or away, to separate. See Class Rm. No. 11.]

1. To cry out with a shrill voice; to utter a sudden, sharp outcry, as in a fright or in extreme pain; to shriek.

The fearful matrons raise a *screaming* cry. *Dryden.*

2. To utter a shrill harsh cry; as the *screaming* owl.

SCREAM, *n.* A shriek or sharp shrill cry uttered suddenly, as in terror or in pain; or the shrill cry of a fowl; as *screams* of horror. *Pope.*

SCRE'AMER, *n.* A fowl, or genus of fowls, of the grallic order, of two species, natives of America.

SCRE'AMING, *ppr.* Uttering suddenly a sharp shrill cry; crying with a shrill voice.

SCRE'AMING, *n.* The act of crying out with a shriek of terror or agony.

SCREECH, *v. i.* [Sw. *skrika*; Dan. *skriger*; G. *schreien*; W. *ysgreçian*, from *creçian*, to creak; Ir. *screachaim.* See *Screak* and *Shriek*, and Class Rg. No. 1. 4. 49. 50.]

1. To cry out with a sharp shrill voice; to utter a sudden shrill cry, as in terror or acute pain; to scream; to shriek. *Bacon.*

2. To utter a sharp cry, as an owl; thence called *screech-owl.*

SCREECH, *n.* A sharp shrill cry uttered in acute pain, or in a sudden fright.

2. A harsh shrill cry, as of a fowl. *Pope.*

SCREE'CHING, *ppr.* Uttering a shrill or harsh cry.

SCREE'CH-OWL, *n.* An owl that utters a harsh disagreeable cry at night, no more ominous of evil than the notes of the nightingale.

SCREED, *n.* With *plasterers*, the floated work behind a cornice. *Encyc.*

SCREEN, *n.* [Fr. *ecran.* This word is evidently from the root of L. *cerno*, *excerno*, Gr. *κρινω*, to separate, to sift, to judge, to fight, contend, skirmish; Sp. *harnero*, a sieve. The primary sense of the root is to separate, to drive or force asunder, hence to sift, to discern, to judge, to separate or cut off danger.]

1. Any thing that separates or cuts off inconvenience, injury or danger; and hence, that which shelters or protects from danger, or prevents inconvenience. Thus a *screen* is used to intercept the sight, to intercept the heat of fire or the light of a candle.

Some ambitious men seem as *screens* to princes in matters of danger and envy. *Bacon.*

2. A riddle or sieve.

SCREEN, *v. t.* To separate or cut off from inconvenience, injury or danger; to shelter; to protect; to protect by hiding; to conceal; as fruits *screened* from cold winds by a forest or hill. Our houses and garments *screen* us from cold; an umbrella *screens* us from rain and the sun's rays. Neither rank nor money should *screen* from punishment the man who violates the laws.

2. To sift or riddle; to separate the coarse part of any thing from the fine, or the worthless from the valuable. *Evelyn.*

SCREE'NED, *pp.* Protected or sheltered from injury or danger; sifted.

SCREE'NING, *ppr.* Protecting from injury or danger.

SCREW, *n.* [D. *schroef*; G. *schraube*; Dan. *skruve* or *skrue*; Sw. *skruf.* The primary sense is probably to turn, or rather to strain. Class Rb.]

1. A cylinder of wood or metal, grooved spirally; or a cylinder with a spiral channel or thread cut in such a manner that it is equally inclined to the base of the cylinder throughout the whole length. A screw is male or female. In the male screw, the thread rises from the surface of the cylinder; in the female, the groove or channel is sunk below the surface to receive the thread of the male screw.

2. One of the six mechanical powers.

SCREW, *v. t.* To turn or apply a screw to; to press, fasten or make firm by a screw; as, to *screw* a lock on a door; to *screw* a press.

2. To force; to squeeze; to press.

3. To oppress by exactions. Landlords sometimes *screw* and rack their tenants without mercy.

4. To deform by contortions; to distort.

He *screw'd* his face into a harden'd smile. *Dryden.*

To screw out, to press out; to extort.

To screw up, to force; to bring by violent pressure; as, to *screw up* the pins of power too high. *Howell.*

To screw in, to force in by turning or twisting.

SCREW'ED, *pp.* Fastened with screws; pressed with screws; forced.

SCREW'ER, *n.* He or that which screws.

SCREW'ING, *ppr.* Turning a screw; fastening or pressing with a screw.

SCREW'-TREE, *n.* A plant of the genus Helicteres, of several species, natives of warm climates. They are shrubby plants, with yellow flowers, and capsules intorted or twisted inwards. *Encyc.*

SCRIB'BLE, *v. t.* [L. *scribillo*, dim. of *scribo*, to write, W. *ysgrivaw.* See *Scribe.*]

1. To write with haste, or without care or regard to correctness or elegance; as, to *scribble* a letter or pamphlet.

2. To fill with artless or worthless writing. *Milton.*

SCRIB'BLE, *v. i.* To write without care or beauty.

If Mævius *scribble* in Apollo's spite. *Pope.*

SCRIB'BLE, *n.* Hasty or careless writing; a writing of little value; as a hasty *scribble.* *Boyle.*

SCRIB'BLED, *pp.* Written hastily and without care.

SCRIB'BLER, *n.* A petty author; a writer of no reputation.

The *scribbler* pinch'd with hunger, writes to dine. *Granville.*

SCRIBE, *n.* [Fr. from L. *scriba*, from *scribo*, to write; formed probably on the root of *grave*, *scrape*, *scrub*; D. *schryven*; G. *schreiben*; Sw. *skrifva*; Dan. *skriver*; W. *ysgrivaw*, *ysgrivenu*, whence *scrivener*; It. *scrivere*; Sp. *escribir*; Port. *escrever*; Fr. *ecrire*, *ecrivant*; Arm. *scriva*, *scrifan*; Gr. *γραφω*; Ir. *grafadh*, to write, and *sgriobam*, *sgrabam*, to scrape, engrave or write; Russ. *skrebu*, *sgrebayu*, to *scrape*, *scrub*,

rake. Class Rb. The first writing was probably engraving on wood or stone.]
1. In a general sense, a writer. Hence,
2. A notary; a public writer.
3. In ecclesiastical meetings and associations in America, a secretary or clerk; one who records the transactions of an ecclesiastical body.
4. In *Scripture* and *the Jewish history*, a clerk or secretary to the king. Seraiah was *scribe* to king David. 2 Sam. viii.
5. An officer who enrolled or kept the rolls of the army, and called over the names and reviewed them. 2 Ch. xxvi. 2 Kings xxv.
6. A writer and a doctor of the law; a man of learning; one skilled in the law; one who read and explained the law to the people. Ezra vii.

SCRIBE, *v. t.* To mark by a model or rule; to mark so as to fit one piece to another; *a term used by carpenters and joiners.*

SCRI'MER, *n.* [Fr. *escrimeur.* See *Skirmish.*] A fencing-master. *Obs.* *Shak.*

SCRIMP, *v. t.* [Sw. *skrumpen*, shriveled; D. *krimpen*, to shrink, *crimp*, shrivel; G. *schrumpfen*; W. *crimpiaw*, to pinch.]
To contract; to shorten; to make too small or short; to limit or straiten; as, to *scrimp* the pattern of a coat. *New England.*

SCRIMP, *a.* Short; scanty.

SCRIMP, *n.* A pinching miser; a niggard; a close fisted person. *New England.*

SCRINE, *n.* [L. *scrinium*; Norm. *escrin*; probably from L. *cerno, secerno.*]
A shrine; a chest, book-case or other place where writings or curiosities are deposited. [See *Shrine*, which is generally used.]

SCRINGE, *v. i.* To cringe, of which this word is a corruption.

SCRIP, *n.* [W. *ysgrab, ysgrepan*, something puckered or drawn together, a wallet, a scrip; Sw. *skräppa.* This belongs to the root of *gripe*, our vulgar *grab*, that is, to seize or press.]
A small bag; a wallet; a satchel. David put five smooth stones in a *scrip.* 1 Sam. xvii. Matt. x.

SCRIP, *n.* [L. *scriptum, scriptio*, from *scribo*, to write.]
A small writing, certificate or schedule; a piece of paper containing a writing.

Bills of exchange cannot pay our debts abroad, till *scrips* of paper can be made current coin. *Locke.*

A certificate of stock subscribed to a bank or other company, or of a share of other joint property, is called in America a *scrip.*

SCRIP'PAGE, *n.* That which is contained in a scrip. [*Not in use.*] *Dict.*

SCRIPT, *n.* A scrip. [*Not in use.*] *Chaucer.*

SCRIP'TORY, *a.* [L. *scriptorius.* See *Scribe.*]
Written; expressed in writing; not verbal. [*Little used.*] *Swift.*

SCRIP'TURAL, *a.* [from *scripture.*] Contained in the Scriptures, so called by way of eminence, that is, in the Bible; as a *scriptural* word, expression or phrase.
2. According to the Scriptures or sacred oracles; as a *scriptural* doctrine.

SCRIP'TURALIST, *n.* One who adheres literally to the Scriptures and makes them the foundation of all philosophy.

SCRIP'TURE, *n.* [L. *scriptura*, from *scribo*, to write.]
1. In *its primary sense*, a writing; any thing written. *Raleigh.*
2. *Appropriately, and by way of distinction*, the books of the Old and New Testament; the Bible. The word is used either in the singular or plural number, to denote the sacred writings or divine oracles, called *sacred* or *holy*, as proceeding from God and containing sacred doctrines and precepts.

There is not any action that a man ought to do or forbear, but the *Scripture* will give him a clear precept or prohibition for it. *South.*

Compared with the knowledge which the *Scriptures* contain, every other subject of human inquiry is vanity and emptiness. *Buckminster.*

SCRIP'TURIST, *n.* One well versed in the Scriptures. *Newcombe.*

SCRIV'ENER, *n.* [W. *ysgrivenwr*, from *ysgrivenu*, to write; It. *scrivano*; Fr. *ecrivain.* See *Scribe.*]
1. A writer; one whose occupation is to draw contracts or other writings. *Encyc.*
2. One whose business is to place money at interest. *Dryden.*

SCROF'ULA, *n.* [L. In G. *kropf* is crop, craw, and scrofula. In D. it is *kropzeer*, neck-sore.]
A disease, called vulgarly the king's evil, characterized by hard, scirrous, and often indolent tumors in the glands of the neck, under the chin, in the arm-pits, &c. *Encyc.*

SCROF'ULOUS, *a.* Pertaining to scrofula, or partaking of its nature; as *scrofulous* tumors; a *scrofulous* habit of body.
2. Diseased or affected with scrofula.

Scrofulous persons can never be duly nourished. *Arbuthnot.*

SCROLL, *n.* [probably formed from *roll*, or its root; Fr. *ecroue*, a contracted word, whence *escrow.*]
A roll of paper or parchment; or a writing formed into a roll.

Here is the *scroll* of every man's name. *Shak.*

The heavens shall be rolled together as a *scroll.* Is. xxxiv.

SCRO'TUM, *n.* The bag which contains the testicles.

SCROYLE, *n.* [In Fr. *ecrouelles*, the king's evil; or D. *schraal*, thin, lean, meager.]
A mean fellow; a wretch. [*Not in use.*] *Shak.*

SCRUB, *v. t.* [Sw. *skrubba*, to *scrub*, to rebuke; Dan. *skrubber*; D. *schrobben*; G. *schrubben.* This word is probably formed on *rub*, or its root, and perhaps *scrape*, L. *scribo*, may be from the same radix; Ir. *scriobam.*]
To rub hard, either with the hand or with a cloth or an instrument; usually, to rub hard with a brush, or with something coarse or rough, for the purpose of cleaning, scouring or making bright; as, to *scrub* a floor; to *scrub* a deck; to *scrub* vessels of brass or other metal.

SCRUB, *v. i.* To be diligent and penurious; as, to *scrub* hard for a living.

SCRUB, *n.* A mean fellow; one that labors hard and lives meanly.
2. Something small and mean.

No little *scrub* joint shall come on my board. *Swift.*

3. A worn out brush. *Ainsworth.*

SCRUB'BED, **SCRUB'BY**, *a.* Small and mean; stunted in growth; as a *scrubbed* boy; a *scrubby* cur; a *scrubby* tree. *Shak.* *Swift.*

SCRUF, for *scurf*, not in use.

SCRU'PLE, *n.* [Fr. *scrupule*, from L. *scrupulus*, a doubt; *scrupulum*, the third part of a dram, from *scrupus*, a chess-man; probably a piece, a small thing, from *scraping*, like *scrap.* Qu. Gr. ακριβης. Is not the sense of doubt from being very nice?]
1. Doubt; hesitation from the difficulty of determining what is right or expedient; backwardness; reluctance to decide or to act. A man of fashionable honor makes no *scruple* to take another's life, or expose his own. He has no *scruples* of conscience, or he despises them.
2. A weight of twenty grains, the third part of a dram; among goldsmiths, the weight of 24 grains.
3. Proverbially, a very small quantity.
4. In *Chaldean chronology*, the $\frac{1}{1080}$ part of an hour; a division of time used by the Jews, Arabs, &c. *Encyc.*

Scruple of half duration, an arch of the moon's orbit, which the moon's center describes from the beginning of an eclipse to the middle.

Scruples of immersion or *incidence*, an arch of the moon's orbit, which her center describes from the beginning of the eclipse to the time when its center falls into the shadow.

Scruples of emersion, an arch of the moon's orbit, which her center describes in the time from the first emersion of the moon's limb to the end of the eclipse. *Encyc.*

SCRU'PLE, *v. i.* To doubt; to hesitate.

He *scrupl'd* not to eat,
Against his better knowledge. *Milton.*

SCRU'PLE, *v. t.* To doubt; to hesitate to believe; to question; as, to *scruple* the truth or accuracy of an account or calculation.

SCRU'PLED, *pp.* Doubted; questioned.

SCRU'PLER, *n.* A doubter; one who hesitates.

SCRU'PLING, *ppr.* Doubting; hesitating; questioning.

SCRUPULOS'ITY, *n.* [L. *scrupulositas.*]
1. The quality or state of being scrupulous; doubt; doubtfulness respecting some difficult point, or proceeding from the difficulty or delicacy of determining how to act; hence, the caution or tenderness arising from the fear of doing wrong or offending.

The first sacrilege is looked upon with some horror; but when they have once made the breach, their *scrupulosity* soon retires. *Decay of Piety.*

2. Nicety of doubt; or nice regard to exactness and propriety.

So careful, even to *scrupulosity*, were they to keep their sabbath. *South.*

3. Niceness; preciseness. *Johnson.*

SCRU'PULOUS, *a.* [L. *scrupulosus*; Fr. *scrupuleux.*]
1. Nicely doubtful; hesitating to determine or to act; cautious in decision from a fear of offending or doing wrong. Be careful in moral conduct, not to offend *scrupulous* brethren.

2. Given to making objections; captious.

Equality of two domestic pow'rs
Breeds *scrupulous* faction. *Shak.*

3. Nice; doubtful.

The justice of that cause ought to be evident; not obscure, not *scrupulous*. [*Not in use.*] *Bacon.*

4. Careful; cautious; exact in regarding facts. *Woodward.*

5. Nice; exact; as a *scrupulous* abstinence from labor. *Paley.*

SCRU'PULOUSLY, *adv.* With a nice regard to minute particulars or to exact propriety.

The duty consists not *scrupulously* in minutes and half hours. *Taylor.*

Henry was *scrupulously* careful not to ascribe the success to himself. *Addison.*

SCRU'PULOUSNESS, *n.* The state or quality of being scrupulous; niceness, exactness or caution in determining or in acting, from a regard to truth, propriety or expedience.

SCRU'TABLE, *a.* [See *Scrutiny.*] Discoverable by inquiry or critical examination. *Decay of Piety.*

SCRUTA'TION, *n.* Search; scrutiny. [*Not used.*]

SCRUTA'TOR, *n.* [L. from *scrutor.*] One that scrutinizes; a close examiner or inquirer. [*Little used.*] *Ayliffe.*

SCRU'TINIZE, *v. t.* [from *scrutiny.*] To search closely; to examine or inquire into critically; as, to *scrutinize* the measures of administration; to *scrutinize* the private conduct or motives of individuals.

SCRU'TINIZED, *pp.* Examined closely.

SCRU'TINIZING, *ppr.* Inquiring into with critical minuteness or exactness.

SCRU'TINIZER, *n.* One who examines with critical care.

SCRU'TINOUS, *a.* Closely inquiring or examining; captious. *Denham.*

SCRU'TINY, *n.* [Fr. *scrutin*; It. *scrutinio*; Sp. *escrutinio*; Low L. *scrutinium*, from *scrutor*, to search closely, to pry into; Sax. *scrudnian*; Ir. *scrudam.*]

1. Close search; minute inquiry; critical examination; as a *scrutiny* of votes; narrower *scrutiny*. In the heat of debate, observations may escape a prudent man which will not bear the test of *scrutiny*.

2. In *the primitive church*, an examination of catechumens in the last week of Lent, who were to receive baptism on Easter-day. This was performed with prayers, exorcisms and many other ceremonies. *Encyc.*

3. In *the canon law*, a ticket or little paper billet on which a vote is written. *Encyc.*

SCRUTO'IR, *n.* [Fr. *ecritoire*, from *ecrire*, to write. See *Scribe.*]

A kind of desk, case of drawers or cabinet, with a lid opening downward for the convenience of writing on it. *Prior.*

SCRÛZE, *v. t.* To crowd; to squeeze. [*A low word of local use.*] *Spenser.*

SCUD, *v. i.* [This is *shoot*, or from the same root; Dan. *skyder*, to shoot; *skud*, a shot; Sw. *skudda*, to throw or pour out; Sax. *sceotan*, to shoot, to flee or haste away; W. *ysgwdu*, to push or thrust; *ysgudaw*, *ysguthaw*, to whisk, to scud, to whirl about. See *Shoot.*]

1. In *a general sense*, to be driven or to flee or fly with haste. In seamen's language, to be driven with precipitation before a tempest. This is done with a sail extended on the foremast of the ship, or when the wind is too violent, without any sail set, which is called *scudding under bare poles*. *Mar. Dict.*

2. To run with precipitation; to fly. *Dryden.*

SCUD, *n.* A low thin cloud, or thin clouds driven by the wind. *Mar. Dict.*

2. A driving along; a rushing with precipitation. *Gay.*

SCUD'DING, *ppr.* Driving or being driven before a tempest; running with fleetness.

SCUD'DLE, *v. i.* To run with a kind of affected haste; commonly pronounced *scuttle*. [*A low word.*]

SCUF'FLE, *n.* [This is a different orthography of *shuffle*; from *shove*, or its root; Sw. *skuff*, a push; *skuffa*, to push, thrust, shove; Dan. *skuffe*, a drawer, a *scoop*, a *shovel*; *skuffer*, to *shuffle*, to cheat; D. *schuiven*, to shove, push or draw; G. *schieben.*]

1. A contention or trial of strength between two persons, who embrace each other's bodies; a struggle with close embrace, to decide which shall throw the other; in distinction from *wrestling*, which is a trial of strength and dexterity at arm's length. Among our common people, it is not unusual for two persons to commence a contest by wrestling, and at last *close in*, as it is called, and decide the contest by a *scuffle*.

2. A confused contest; a tumultuous struggle for victory or superiority; a fight.

The dog leaps upon the serpent and tears it to pieces; but in the *scuffle*, the cradle happened to be overturned. *L'Estrange.*

SCUF'FLE, *v. i.* To strive or struggle with close embrace, as two men or boys.

2. To strive or contend tumultuously, as small parties.

A gallant man prefers to fight to great disadvantages in the field, in an orderly way, rather than to *scuffle* with an undisciplined rabble. *K. Charles.*

SCUF'FLER, *n.* One who scuffles.

SCUF'FLING, *ppr.* Striving for superiority with close embrace; struggling or contending without order.

SCUG, *v. t.* [Dan. *skygger*, to shade; Sw. *skugga*, a shade.] To hide. [*Local.*] *Grose.*

SCULK, *v. i.* [Dan. *skiuler*; Sw. *skyla*; D. *schuilen*, to hide, shelter, sculk; the Eng. *shelter*. It is also written *skulk.*]

To retire into a close or covered place for concealment; to lurk; to lie close from shame, fear of injury or detection.

No news of Phyl! the bridegroom came,
And thought his bride had *sculk'd* for shame. *Swift.*

—And *sculk* behind the subterfuge of art. *Prior.*

SCULK'ER, *n.* A lurker; one that lies close for hiding.

SCULK'ING, *ppr.* Withdrawing into a close or covered place for concealment; lying close.

SCULL, *n.* The brain pan. [See *Skull.*]

2. A boat; a cock boat. [See *Sculler.*]

3. One who sculls a boat. But properly,

4. A short oar, whose loom is only equal in length to half the breadth of the boat to be rowed, so that one man can manage two, one on each side. *Mar. Dict.*

5. A shoal or multitude of fish. [Sax. *sceole.*] [*Not in use.*]

SCULL, *v. t.* To impel a boat by moving and turning an oar over the stern. *Mar. Dict.*

SCULL'-CAP. [See *Skull-cap.*]

SCULL'ER, *n.* A boat rowed by one man with two sculls or short oars.

2. One that sculls, or rows with sculls; one that impels a boat by an oar over the stern.

SCULL'ERY, *n.* [probably from the root of *shell*, *scale*, Fr. *ecuelle*; Scot. *skul*, *skoll*, a bowl; Dan. *skaal*, a drinking cup; *skal*, a *shell*, *skull*; G. *schale*, a *scale*, a *shell*, a dish or cup; D. *schall*, *schil*. *Skulls* and *shells* were the cups, bowls and dishes of rude men.]

A place where dishes, kettles and other culinary utensils are kept.

SCULL'ION, *n.* [Ir. *squille*, from the root of the preceding.]

A servant that cleans pots and kettles, and does other menial services in the kitchen.

SCULL'IONLY, *a.* Like a scullion; base; low; mean. [*Not used.*]

SCULP, *v. t.* [L. *sculpo*, *scalpo*. Qu. Gr. γλυφω; root גלף, Class Lb. No. 27; or *gall*, L. *calvus*, Class Gl. No. 8.]

To carve; to engrave. [*Not in use.*] *Sandys.*

SCULP'TILE, *a.* [L. *sculptilis.*] Formed by carving; as *sculptile* images. *Brown.*

SCULP'TOR, *n.* [L. See *Sculp.*] One whose occupation is to carve wood or stone into images; a carver. *Encyc.*

SCULP'TURE, *n.* [Fr.; L. *sculptura.*] The art of carving, cutting or hewing wood or stone into images of men, beasts or other things. *Sculpture* is a generic term, including carving or statuary and engraving.

2. Carved work.

There too, in living *sculpture*, might be seen
The mad affection of the Cretan queen. *Dryden.*

3. The art of engraving on copper.

SCULP'TURE, *v. t.* To carve; to engrave; to form images or figures with the chisel on wood, stone or metal.

SCULP'TURED, *pp.* Carved; engraved; as a *sculptured* vase; *sculptured* marble.

SCULP'TURING, *ppr.* Carving; engraving.

SCUM, *n.* [Fr. *ecume*; It. *schiuma*; Sw. Dan. *skum*; D. *schuim*; G. *schaum.*]

1. The extraneous matter or impurities which rise to the surface of liquors in boiling or fermentation, or which form on the surface by other means. The word is also applied to the scoria of metals. *Encyc.*

2. The refuse; the recrement; that which is vile or worthless.

The great and the innocent are insulted by the *scum* and refuse of the people. *Addison.*

SCUM, *v. t.* To take the scum from; to clear off the impure matter from the surface; to skim.

You that *scum* the molten lead. *Dryden.*

SCUM'BER, *n.* The dung of the fox. *Ainsworth.*

SCUM'MED, *pp.* Cleared of scum; skimmed.

SCUM'MER, *n.* [Fr. *ecumoire.*] An instrument used for taking off the scum of liquors; a skimmer.

SCUM'MING, *ppr.* Clearing of scum; skimming.

SCUM'MINGS, *n. plu.* The matter skimmed from boiling liquors; as the *scummings* of the boiling house. *Edwards, W. Indies.*

SCUP'PER, *n.* [Sp. *escupir*, to spit, to eject, to discharge.]
The scuppers or scupper holes of a ship, are channels cut through the water ways and sides of a ship at proper distances, and lined with lead for carrying off the water from the deck. *Mar. Dict.*

SCUP'PER-HOSE, *n.* A lethern pipe attached to the mouth of the scuppers of the lower deck of a ship, to prevent the water from entering. *Encyc.*

SCUP'PER-NAIL, *n.* A nail with a very broad head for covering a large surface of the hose. *Mar. Dict.*

SCUP'PER-PLUG, *n.* A plug to stop a scupper. *Mar. Dict.*

SCURF, *n.* [Sax. *scurf*; G. *schorf*; D. *schurft*; Dan. *skurv*; Sw. *skorf*; Ice. *skarfa*; L. *scorbutus.* In D. *scheuren* is to rend or crack, and *scheurbuik* is scurvy, Dan. *skiörbug*, from *skiör*, brittle. In Ir. *gearbh* is rough. It is named from breaking or roughness.]
1. A dry miliary scab or crust formed on the skin of an animal.
2. The soil or foul remains of any thing adherent; as the *scurf* of crimes. [*Not common nor elegant.*] *Dryden.*
3. Any thing adhering to the surface.

> There stood a hill, whose grisly top
> Shone with a glossy *scurf.* *Milton.*

SCURFF, *n.* Another name for the bull-trout. *Dict. Nat. Hist.*

SCURF'INESS, *n.* The state of being scurfy.

SCURF'Y, *a.* Having scurf; covered with scurf.
2. Resembling scurf.

SCUR'RIL, *a.* [L. *scurrilis*, from *scurra*, a buffoon; G. *scheren*, D. *scheeren*, to *jeer.*]
Such as befits a buffoon or vulgar jester; low; mean; grossly opprobrious in language; scurrilous; as *scurril* jests; *scurril* scoffing; *scurril* taunts. *Shak. Dryden.*

SCURRIL'ITY, *n.* [L. *scurrilitas*; Fr. *scurrilité.*]
Such low, vulgar, indecent or abusive language as is used by mean fellows, buffoons, jesters and the like; grossness of reproach or invective; obscene jests, &c.

> Banish *scurrility* and profaneness. *Dryden.*

SCUR'RILOUS, *a.* Using the low and indecent language of the meaner sort of people, or such as only the licence of buffoons can warrant; as a *scurrilous* fellow.
2. Containing low indecency or abuse; mean; foul; vile; obscenely jocular; as *scurrilous* language.

SCUR'RILOUSLY, *adv.* With gross reproach; with low indecent language.

> It is barbarous incivility, *scurrilously* to sport with what others count religion. *Tillotson.*

SCUR'RILOUSNESS, *n.* Indecency of language; vulgarity; baseness of manners.

SCUR'VILY, *adv.* [from *scurvy.*] Basely; meanly; with coarse and vulgar incivility.

> The clergy were never more learned, or so *scurvily* treated. *Swift.*

SCUR'VINESS, *n.* [from *scurvy.*] The state of being scurvy.

SCUR'VOGEL, *n.* A Brazilian fowl of the stork kind, the jabiru guacu. *Dict. Nat. Hist.*

SCUR'VY, *n.* [from *scurf; scurvy* for *scurfy*; Low L. *scorbutus.*]
A disease characterized by great debility, a pale bloated face, bleeding spongy gums, large livid tumors on the body, offensive breath, aversion to exercise, oppression at the breast or difficult respiration, a smooth, dry, shining skin, &c.; a disease most incident to persons who live confined, or on salted meats without fresh vegetables in cold climates. *Coxe. Encyc.*

SCUR'VY, *a.* Scurfy; covered or affected by scurf or scabs; scabby; diseased with scurvy. *Leviticus.*
2. Vile; mean; low; vulgar; worthless; contemptible; as a *scurvy* fellow.

> He spoke *scurvy* and provoking terms. *Shak.*

> That *scurvy* custom of taking tobacco. *Swift.*

SCUR'VY-GRASS, *n.* A plant of the genus Cochlearia; spoonwort. It grows on rocks near the sea, has an acrid, bitter taste, and is remarkable as a remedy for the scurvy. It is eaten raw as a salad. *Encyc.*

'SCUSES, for *excuses.* *Shak.*

SCUT, *n.* [Ice. *skott*; W. *cwt*, a tail or rump; *cwta*, short.]
The tail of a hare or other animal whose tail is short. *Brown. Swift.*

SCU'TAGE, *n.* [Law L. *scutagium*, from *scutum*, a shield.]
In *English history*, a tax or contribution levied upon those who held lands by knight service; originally, a composition for personal service which the tenant owed to his lord, but afterward levied as an assessment. *Blackstone.*

SCUTCHEON, a contraction of *escutcheon*, which see.

SCUTE, *n.* [L. *scutum*, a buckler.] A French gold coin of 3*s.* 4*d.* sterling. *Encyc.*

SCU'TELLATED, *a.* [L. *scutella*, a dish. See *Scuttle.*]
Formed like a pan; divided into small surfaces; as the *scutellated* bone of a sturgeon. *Woodward.*

SCU'TIFORM, *a.* [L. *scutum*, a buckler, and *form.*] Having the form of a buckler or shield.

SCUT'TLE, *n.* [L. *scutella*, a pan or saucer; W. *ysgudell*; Sax. *scutel, scuttel*, a dish.]
A broad shallow basket; so called from its resemblance to a dish.

SCUT'TLE, *n.* [Fr. *ecoutille*; Arm. *scoutilh*; Sp. *escotilla*; Sax. *scyttel*, a bolt or bar; *scyttan*, to bolt, to *shut.* See *Shut.*]
1. In ships, a small hatchway or opening in the deck, large enough to admit a man, and with a lid for covering it; also, a like hole in the side of a ship, and through the coverings of her hatchways, &c.
2. A square hole in the roof of a house, with a lid.
3. [from *scud*, and properly *scuddle.*] A quick pace; a short run. *Spectator.*

SCUT'TLE, *v. i.* To run with affected precipitation. *Arbuthnot.*

SCUT'TLE, *v. t.* [from the noun.] To cut large holes through the bottom or sides of a ship for any purpose.
2. To sink by making holes through the bottom; as, to *scuttle* a ship.

SCUT'TLE-BUTT, SCUT'TLE-CASK, *n.* A butt or cask having a square piece sawn out of its bilge, and lashed upon deck. *Mar. Dict.*

SCUT'TLED, *pp.* Having holes made in the bottom or sides; sunk by means of cutting holes in the bottom or side.

SCUT'TLE-FISH, *n.* The cuttle-fish, so called. [See *Cuttle-fish.*]

SCUT'TLING, *ppr.* Cutting holes in the bottom or sides; sinking by such holes.

SCYT'ALE, *n.* A species of serpent. *Dict. Nat. Hist.*

SCYTHE, a wrong spelling. [See *Sythe.*]

SCYTH'IAN, *a.* Pertaining to Scythia, a name given to the northern part of Asia, and Europe adjoining to Asia.

SCYTH'IAN, *n.* [See *Scot.*] A native of Scythia.

SDAIN, for *disdain.* [It. *sdegnare.*] [*Not in use.*] *Spenser.*

SDEINFUL, for *disdainful.* [*Not in use.*] *Spenser.*

SEA, *n. see.* [Sax. *sæ, secge*; G. *see*; D. *zee*; Sw. *siö*, the sea, a lake or pool; Basque, *sah*; contracted from *sæg, seeg.* Hence Sax. *garsege, garsecge, garsegg*, the ocean. This word, like *lake*, signifies primarily a seat, set or lay, a repository, a bason.]
1. A large bason, cistern or laver which Solomon made in the temple, so large as to contain more than six thousand gallons. This was called the *brazen sea*, and used to hold water for the priests to wash themselves. 1 Kings vii. 2 Chron. iv.
2. A large body of water, nearly inclosed by land, as the Baltic or the Mediterranean; as the *sea* of Azof. *Seas* are properly branches of the ocean, and upon the same level. Large bodies of water inland, and situated above the level of the ocean, are lakes. The appellation of *sea*, given to the Caspian lake, is an exception, and not very correct. So the lake of Galilee is called a *sea*, from the Greek.
3. The ocean; as, to go to *sea.* The fleet is at *sea*, or on the high *seas.*
4. A wave; a billow; a surge. The vessel shipped a *sea.*
5. The swell of the ocean in a tempest, or the direction of the waves; as, we head the *sea.*
6. Proverbially, a large quantity of liquor; as a *sea* of blood.
7. A rough or agitated place or element.

> In a troubled *sea* of passion tost. *Milton.*

Half seas over, half drunk. [*A low phrase.*] *Spectator.*

On the high seas, in the open sea, the common highway of nations.

SEA-ANEM'ONY, *n.* The animal flower, which see.

SE'A-APE, *n.* [*sea* and *ape.*] The name given to a marine animal which plays tricks like an ape. *Encyc.*

SE'A-BANK, *n.* [*sea* and *bank.*] The sea shore. *Shak.*
2. A bank or mole to defend against the sea.

SE'A-BAR, *n.* [*sea* and *bar.*] The sea-swallow, [*Hirundo piscis.*] *Johnson.*

SE'A-BAT, *n.* [*sea* and *bat.*] A sort of flying fish. *Cotgrave.*

SEA-BA'THED, *a.* [*sea* and *bathe.*] Bathed, dipped or washed in the sea. *Sandys.*

SE'A-BEAR, *n.* [*sea* and *bear.*] An animal of the bear kind that frequents the sea; the white or polar bear; also, the ursine seal.

SE'A-BEARD, *n.* [*sea* and *beard.*] A marine plant, *Conferva rupestris.* *Lee.*

SE'A-BEAST, *n.* [*sea* and *beast.*] A beast or monstrous animal of the sea. *Milton.*

SE'A-BEAT, } *a.* [*sea* and *beat.*] Beaten
SE'A-BEATEN, } by the sea; lashed by the waves.

Along the *sea-beat* shore. *Pope.*

SE'ABOARD, *n.* [*sea* and Fr. *bord*, side.] The sea shore.

SE'ABOARD, *adv.* Towards the sea.

SE'A-BOAT, *n.* [*sea* and *boat.*] A vessel that bears the sea firmly, without laboring or straining her masts and rigging. *Mar. Dict.*

SE'A-BORD, } *a.* [*sea* and Fr. *bord*,
SEA-BORD'ERING, } border.] Bordering on the sea or ocean.

SE'A-BORN, *a.* [*sea* and *born.*] Born of the sea; produced by the sea; as Neptune and his *sea-born* niece. *Waller.*

2. Born at sea.

SE'A-BOUND, } *a.* [*sea* and *bound.*]
SE'A-BOUNDED, } Bounded by the sea.

SE'A-BOY, *n.* [*sea* and *boy.*] A boy employed on shipboard.

SE'A-BREACH, *n.* [*sea* and *breach.*] Irruption of the sea by breaking the banks. *L'Estrange.*

SE'A-BREAM, *n.* [*sea* and *bream.*] A fish of the Sparus kind. *Dict. Nat. Hist.*

SE'A-BREEZE, *n.* [*sea* and *breeze.*] A wind or current of air blowing from the sea upon land; for the most part blowing during the day only, and subsiding at night.

SE'A-BUILT, *a.* [*sea* and *built.*] Built for the sea; as *sea-built* forts, [ships.] *Dryden.*

SEA-CAB'BAGE, } *n.* [*sea* and *cabbage.*]
SE'A-CALE, } Sea-colewort, a plant of the genus Crambe. *Encyc. Miller.*

SE'A-C'ALF, *n.* [*sea* and *calf.*] The common seal, a species of Phoca.

SE'A-CAP, *n.* [*sea* and *cap.*] A cap made to be worn at sea. *Shak.*

SE'A-C'ARD, *n.* [*sea* and *card.*] The mariner's card or compass.

SE'A-C'ARP, *n.* [*sea* and *carp.*] A spotted fish living among rocks and stones. *Johnson.*

SE'A-CHANGE, *n.* [*sea* and *change.*] A change wrought by the sea.

SE'A-CH'ART, *n.* [*sea* and *chart.*] A chart or map on which the line of the shore, isles, shoals, harbors, &c. are delineated.

[*Note.* This word has become useless, as we now use *chart* for a representation of the sea coast, and *map* for a representation of the land.]

SE'A-CIRCLED, *a.* [*sea* and *circle.*] Surrounded by the sea. *Sandys.*

SE'A-COAL, *n.* [*sea* and *coal.*] Coal brought by sea; a vulgar name for fossil coal, in distinction from *charcoal.*

SE'A-COAST, *n.* [*sea* and *coast.*] The shore or border of the land adjacent to the sea or ocean.

SE'A-COB, *n.* [*sea* and *cob.*] A fowl, called also sea-gull.

SE'A-COLEWORT, *n.* Sea-cale, which see.

SE'A-COMPASS, *n.* [*sea* and *compass.*] The mariner's card and needle; the compass constructed for use at sea. *Camden.*

SE'A-COOT, *n.* [*sea* and *coot.*] A sea fowl, [*Fulica marina.*]

SEA-COR'MORANT, *n.* [*sea* and *cormorant.*]

The sea-crow or sea-drake, [*Corvus marinus.*]

SE'A-COW, *n.* [*sea* and *cow.*] The *Trichechus manatus*, or *manati.* [See *Manati.*]

SE'A-CROW, *n.* [*sea* and *crow.*] A fowl of the gull kind; the mire-crow or pewet. *Encyc.*

SE'A-DEVIL, *n.* [*sea* and *devil.*] The fishing frog or toad-fish, of the genus Lophius; a fish of a deformed shape, resembling a tadpole, growing to a large size, with a head larger than the whole body. *Encyc.*

SE'A-DOG, *n.* [*sea* and *dog.*] A fish, perhaps the shark. *Pope. Roscommon.*

2. The sea-calf or common seal.

SE'A-DRAGON, *n.* [*sea* and *dragon.*] A marine monster caught in England in 1749, resembling in some degree an alligator, but having two large fins which served for swimming or flying. It had two legs terminating in hoofs, like those of an ass. Its body was covered with impenetrable scales, and it had five rows of teeth. Qu. *Gent. Magazine.*

SE'A-EAR, *n.* [*sea* and *ear.*] A sea plant, [*Auris marina.*] *Johnson.*

SE'A-EEL, *n.* [*sea* and *eel.*] An eel caught in salt water; the conger.

SEA-ENCIR'CLED, *a.* [*sea* and *encircled.*] Encompassed by the sea. *Thomson.*

SE'A-FARER, *n.* [*sea* and *fare.*] One that follows the seas; a mariner. *Pope.*

SE'A-FARING, *a.* [supra.] Following the business of a seaman; customarily employed in navigation. *Arbuthnot.*

SE'A-FENNEL, *n.* [*sea* and *fennel.*] The same as samphire.

SE'A-FIGHT, *n.* [*sea* and *fight.*] An engagement between ships at sea; a naval action. *Bacon.*

SE'A-FISH, *n.* [*sea* and *fish.*] Any marine fish; any fish that lives usually in salt water.

SE'A-FOWL, *n.* [*sea* and *fowl.*] A marine fowl; any fowl that lives by the sea, and procures its food from salt water. *Pope.*

SE'A-FOX, *n.* A species of squalus, having a tail longer than the body. *Dict. Nat. Hist.*

SE'A-GAGE, *n.* [*sea* and *gage.*] The depth that a vessel sinks in the water. *Encyc.*

SE'A-G'ARLAND, *n.* [*sea* and *garland.*] A plant.

SE'A-GIRDLES, *n.* [*sea* and *girdle.*] A sort of sea mushroom, [*Fungus phasganoides.*] *Johnson.*

SE'A-GIRT, *a.* [*sea* and *girt.*] Surrounded by the water of the sea or ocean; as a *sea-girt* isle. *Milton.*

SE'A-GOD, *n.* [*sea* and *god.*] A marine deity; a fabulous being supposed to preside over the ocean or sea; as Neptune.

SE'A-GOWN, *n.* [*sea* and *gown.*] A gown or garment with short sleeves, worn by mariners. *Shak.*

SE'A-GR'ASS, *n.* [*sea* and *grass.*] A plant growing on the sea shore; an aquatic plant of the genus Ruppia. *Lee.*

SE'A-GREEN, *a.* [*sea* and *green.*] Having the color of sea water; being of a faint green color. *Locke. Pope.*

SE'A-GREEN, *n.* The color of sea water.

2. A plant, the saxifrage.

SE'A-GULL, *n.* [*sea* and *gull.*] A fowl of the genus Larus; a species of gull; called also sea-crow.

SE'A-HARE, *n.* [*sea* and *hare.*] A marine animal of the genus Laplysia, whose body is covered with membranes reflected; it has a lateral pore on the right side, and four feelers resembling ears. The body is nearly oval, soft, gelatinous and punctated. Its juice is poisonous, and it is so fetid as to cause nausea. *Encyc.*

SEA-HEDGEHOG, *n.* A sea shell, a species of Echinus, so called from its prickles, which resemble in some measure those of the hedgehog or urchin. *Carew.*

SE'A-HEN, *n.* [*sea* and *hen.*] Another name of the guillemot.

SE'A-HOG, *n.* [*sea* and *hog.*] The porpess, which see.

SE'A-HOLLY, *n.* [*sea* and *holly.*] A plant of the genus Eryngium. *Lee.*

SE'A-HOLM, *n.* [*sea* and Dan. *holm*, an isle.] A small uninhabited isle.

2. Sea-holly. *Carew.*

SE'A-HORSE, *n.* [*sea* and *horse.*] In *ichthyology*, the morse, a species of Trichechus or walrus. *Woodward.*

2. The hippopotamus, or river-horse. *Dryden.*

3. A fish of the needle-fish kind, four or five inches in length, and half an inch in diameter. *Hill.*

A fish of the genus Syngnathus. (*S. hippocampus*, Linne.)

SE'A-LEGS, *n.* [*sea* and *leg.*] The ability to walk on a ship's deck when pitching or rolling. *Mar. Dict.*

SE'A-LEMON, *n.* [*sea* and *lemon.*] A marine animal of the genus Doris, having an oval body, convex, marked with numerous punctures, and of a lemon color. *Encyc.*

SE'A-LIKE, *a.* [*sea* and *like.*] Resembling the sea. *Thomson.*

SE'A-LION, *n.* [*sea* and *lion.*] An animal of the genus Phoca or seal, which has a mane like a lion, the *Phoca jubata.* *Encyc. Ed. Encyc.*

SE'A-MAID, *n.* [*sea* and *maid.*] The mermaid. [See *Mermaid.*] *Shak.*

2. A sea nymph.

SE'A-MALL, } *n.* A fowl, a species of gull
SE'A-MEW, } or Larus.

SE'AMAN, *n.* [*sea* and *man.*] A sailor; a mariner; a man whose occupation is to assist in the management of ships at sea.

2. By way of distinction, a skillful mariner; also, a man who is well versed in the art of navigating ships. In this sense, it is applied both to officers and common mariners.

3. Merman, the male of the mermaid. [*Little used.*] *Locke.*

SE'AMANSHIP, *n.* The skill of a good seaman; an acquaintance with the art of managing and navigating a ship; *applicable both to officers and to men.* *Naval skill*, is the art of managing a fleet, particularly in an engagement; a very different thing from *seamanship.*

SE'A-M'ARK, *n.* [*sea* and *mark.*] Any elevated object on land which serves for a direction to mariners in entering a harbor, or in sailing along or approaching a coast; a beacon; as a light-house, a mountain, &c. *Encyc.*

SE'A-MEW, *n.* A fowl, a species of gull or Larus.

SE'A-MONSTER, *n.* [*sea* and *monster.*] A huge marine animal. Lam. iv.

SE'A-MOSS, *n.* [*sea* and *moss.*] A name given to coral. [See *Coral.*]

SE'A-MOUSE, *n.* [*sea* and *mouse.*] A marine animal of the genus Aphrodita. *Encyc.*

SEA-NAVELWŎRT, *n.* [*sea, navel* and *wort.*] A plant growing in Syria, which is said to effect great cures. [L. *androsaces.*] *Johnson.*

SE'A-NEEDLE, *n.* [*sea* and *needle.*] A name of the gar or garfish, of the genus Esox. This fish has a slender body, with long pointed jaws and a forked tail. Its back is of a fine green color, and when in the water, its colors are extremely beautiful.

SE'A-NETTLE, *n.* [*sea* and *nettle.*] Another name of the animal flower, or sea-anemony. *Encyc.*

SE'A-NURSED, *a.* [*sea* and *nursed.*] Nursed by the sea. *J. Barlow.*

SE'A-NYMPH, *n.* [*sea* and *nymph.*] A nymph or goddess of the sea. *Broome.*

SE'A-ŎNION, *n.* [*sea* and *onion.*] A plant. *Ainsworth.*

SE'A-OOZE, *n.* [*sea* and *ooze.*] The soft mud on or near the sea shore. *Mortimer.*

SE'A-OTTER, *n.* [*sea* and *otter.*] A species of otter that has hind feet like those of a seal. It feeds on shell fish. *Dict. Nat. Hist.*

SE'A-OWL, *n.* [*sea* and *owl.*] Another name of the lump-fish. *Dict. Nat. Hist.*

SE'A-PAD, *n.* The star-fish. [*Stella marina.*] *Johnson.*

SE'A-PANTHER, *n.* [*sea* and *panther.*] A fish like a lamprey. *Johnson.*

SE'A-PHEASANT, *n.* [*sea* and *pheasant.*] The pin-tailed duck. *Dict. Nat. Hist.*

SE'A-PIE, } *n.* [*sea* and *pie*, pica.] A fowl
SE'A-PŸE, } of the genus Hæmatopus, and grallic order; called also the oyster-catcher, from its thrusting its beak into oysters when open, and taking out the animal.

SE'A-PIE, *n.* [*sea* and *pie.*] A dish of food consisting of paste and meat boiled together; so named because common at sea.

SE'A-PIECE, *n.* [*sea* and *piece.*] A picture representing a scene at sea. *Addison.*

SE'A-PLANT, *n.* [*sea* and *plant.*] A plant that grows in salt water, as the *fucus, conferva*, &c.

SE'A-POOL, *n.* [*sea* and *pool.*] A lake of salt water. *Spenser.*

SE'APŎRT, *n.* [*sea* and *port.*] A harbor near the sea, formed by an arm of the sea or by a bay.

2. A city or town situated on a harbor, on or near the sea. We call a town a *seaport*, instead of a *seaport town.*

SEA-RESEM'BLING, *a.* Like the sea; sea-like. *Sandys.*

SE'A-RISK, *n.* [*sea* and *risk.*] Hazard or risk at sea; danger of injury or destruction by the sea.

SE'A-ROBBER, *n.* [*sea* and *robber.*] A pirate; one that robs on the high seas.

SE'A-ROCKET, *n.* A plant of the genus Bunias. *Lee. Miller.*

SE'A-ROOM, *n.* [*sea* and *room.*] Ample space or distance from land, shoals or rocks, sufficient for a ship to drive or scud without danger of shipwreck. *Mar. Dict.*

SE'A-RŌVER, *n.* [*sea* and *rover.*] A pirate; one that cruizes for plunder.

2. A ship or vessel that is employed in cruizing for plunder.

SE'A-RUFF, *n.* A kind of sea fish. [L. *orphus.*] *Johnson.*

SEA-SCOR'PION, *n.* [*sea* and *scorpion.*] Another name for the fatherlasher. *Dict. Nat. Hist.*

SE'A-SERPENT, *n.* [*sea* and *serpent.*] A huge animal like a serpent inhabiting the sea. *Guthrie.*

SE'A-SERVICE, *n.* [*sea* and *service.*] Naval service; service in the navy or in ships of war.

SE'A-SH'ARK, *n.* [*sea* and *shark.*] A ravenous sea fish. *Shak.*

SE'A-SHELL, *n.* [*sea* and *shell.*] A marine shell; a shell that grows in the sea. *Mortimer.*

SEA-SHO'RE, *n.* [*sea* and *shore.*] The coast of the sea; the land that lies adjacent to the sea or ocean. *Locke.*

SE'A-SICK, *a.* [*sea* and *sick.*] Affected with sickness or nausea by means of the pitching or rolling of a vessel. *Dryden. Swift.*

SE'A-SICKNESS, *n.* The sickness or nausea occasioned by the pitching and rolling of a ship in an agitated sea.

SE'A-SIDE, *n.* [*sea* and *side.*] The land bordering on the sea; the country adjacent to the sea, or near it. *Scripture. Pope.*

SE'A-ST'AR, *n.* [*sea* and *star.*] The star-fish, a genus of marine animals, called technically Asterias.

SEA-SUR'GEON, *n.* [*sea* and *surgeon.*] A surgeon employed on shipboard. *Wiseman.*

SEA-SURROUND'ED, *a.* [*sea* and *surround.*] Encompassed by the sea.

SE'A-TERM, *n.* [*sea* and *term.*] A word or term used appropriately by seamen, or peculiar to the art of navigation.

SE'A-THIEF, *n.* [*sea* and *thief.*] A pirate. *Bp. of Chichester.*

SE'A-TŌAD, *n.* [*sea* and *toad.*] An ugly fish, so called. *Cotgrave.*

SE'A-TŌRN, *a.* [*sea* and *torn.*] Torn by or at sea. *Browne.*

SE'A-TOSSED, *a.* [*sea* and *tossed.*] Tossed by the sea. *Shak.*

SE'A-URCHIN, *n.* [*sea* and *urchin.*] A genus of marine animals, the Echinus, of many species. The body is roundish, covered with a bony crust, and often set with movable prickles. *Encyc.*

SE'A-WALLED, *a.* [*sea* and *walled.*] Surrounded or defended by the sea. *Shak.*

SE'AWARD, *a.* [*sea* and *ward.*] Directed towards the sea. *Donne.*

SE'AWARD, *adv.* Towards the sea. *Drayton.*

SE'A-WATER, *n.* [*sea* and *water.*] Water of the sea or ocean, which is salt. *Bacon.*

SE'A-WEED, *n.* [*sea* and *weed.*] A marine plant of the genus Fucus, used as manure, and for making glass and soap. A common name for the marine algæ, and some other plants growing in salt water.

SE'A-WITHWIND, *n.* Bindweed.

SE'A-WOLF, *n.* [*sea* and *wolf.* See *Wolf.*] A fish of the genus Anarrhicas, found in northern latitudes, about Greenland, Iceland, Norway, Scotland, England, &c. This fish is so named from its fierceness and ravenousness. It grows sometimes to the length of four and even seven feet, and feeds on crustaceous animals and shell fish. *Encyc.*

SEA-WŎRM'WQOD, *n.* A sort of wormwood growing in the sea, the *Artemisia maritima.* *Johnson. Lee.*

SE'AWŎRTHY, *a.* [*sea* and *worthy.*] Fit for a voyage; worthy of being trusted to transport a cargo with safety; as a *seaworthy* ship.

SEAL, *n.* [Sax. *seol, sele, syle;* Sw. *siäl.*] The common name for the species of the genus Phoca. These animals are amphibious, most of them inhabiting the sea coasts, particularly in the higher latitudes. They have six cutting teeth in the upper jaw, and four in the lower. Their hind feet are placed at the extremity of the body, in the same direction with it, and serve the purpose of a caudal fin; the fore feet are also adapted for swimming, and furnished each with five claws; the external ears are either very small or wanting. There are numerous species; as the *leonina*, sometimes 18 feet in length, and the *jubata*, sometimes 25 feet in length, with a mane like a lion, both called *sea-lion*, and found in the southern seas, and also in the N. Pacific; the *ursina*, or sea bear, 8 or 9 feet in length, and covered with long, thick and bristly hair, found in the N. Pacific; and the common seal *(P. vitulina,)* from 4 to 6 feet in length, found generally throughout the Atlantic and the seas and bays communicating with it, covered with short, stiff, glossy hair, with a smooth head without external ears, and with the fore legs deeply immersed in the skin. Seals are much sought after for their skins and fur. *Ed. Encyc. Encyc.*

SEAL, *n.* [Sax. *sigel, sigle;* G. *siegel;* D. *zegel;* Dan. *seigl, segl;* Fr. *sceau;* Arm. *syell;* L. *sigillum;* It. *sigillo;* Sp. *sigilo.* It is uncertain what was the original signification of *seal*, whether an image, or some ornament. In Saxon, the word signifies a necklace, or ornament for the neck, a stud or boss, a clasp, and a seal.]

1. A piece of metal or other hard substance, usually round or oval, on which is engraved some image or device, and sometimes a legend or inscription. This is used by individuals, corporate bodies and states, for making impressions on wax upon instruments of writing, as an evidence of their authenticity. The king of England has his great *seal* and his privy *seal.* *Seals* are sometimes worn in rings.

2. The wax set to an instrument, and impressed or stamped with a seal. Thus we give a deed under hand and *seal.* Wax is

generally used in sealing instruments, but other substances may be used.

3. The wax or wafer that makes fast a letter or other paper.

4. Any act of confirmation. *Milton.*

5. That which confirms, ratifies or makes stable; assurance. 2 Tim. ii.

6. That which effectually shuts, confines or secures; that which makes fast. Rev. xx.

SEAL, *v. t.* [Sw. *besegla, försegla;* Dan. *besegler, forsegler;* G. *siegeln;* D. *zegelen.* The root signifies probably to set, to fix, to impress, or to cut or engrave.]

1. To fasten with a seal; to attach together with a wafer or with wax; as, to *seal* a letter.

2. To set or affix a seal as a mark of authenticity; as, to *seal* a deed. Hence,

3. To confirm; to ratify; to establish.

And with my hand I *seal* our true hearts' love. *Shak.*

When therefore I have performed this, and have *sealed* to them this fruit, I will come by you into Spain. Rom. xv.

4. To shut or keep close; sometimes with *up.* *Seal* your lips; *seal up* your lips. *Shak.*

Open your ears, and *seal* your bosom upon the secret concerns of a friend. *Dwight.*

5. To make fast.

So they went and made the sepulcher sure, *sealing* the stone and setting a watch. Matt. xxvii.

6. To mark with a stamp, as an evidence of standard exactness, legal size, or merchantable quality. By our laws, weights and measures are to be *sealed* by an officer appointed and sworn for that purpose; and lether is to be *sealed* by a like officer, as evidence that it has been inspected and found to be of good quality. *Laws of Conn.*

7. To keep secret.

Shut up the words, and *seal* the book. Dan. xii. Is. viii.

8. To mark as one's property, and secure from danger. Cant. iv.

9. To close; to fulfill; to complete; with *up.* Dan. ix.

10. To imprint on the mind; as, to *seal* instruction. Job xxxiii.

11. To inclose; to hide; to conceal. Job xiv.

12. To confine; to restrain. Job xxxvii.

13. In *architecture,* to fix a piece of wood or iron in a wall with cement. *Encyc.*

SEAL, *v. i.* To fix a seal.

I will *seal* unto this bond. [*Unusual.*] *Shak.*

SE'ALED, *pp.* Furnished with a seal; fastened with a seal; confirmed; closed.

SE'ALER, *n.* One who seals; an officer in chancery who seals writs and instruments.

2. In *New England,* an officer appointed by the town or other proper authority, to examine and try weights and measures, and set a stamp on such as are according to the standards established by the state; also, an officer who inspects lether and stamps such as is good. These are called *sealers* of weights and measures, and *sealers* of lether.

SE'ALING, *ppr.* Fixing a seal; fastening with a seal; confirming; closing; keeping secret; fixing a piece of wood or iron in a wall with cement.

SE'ALING, *n.* [from *seal,* the animal.] The operation of taking seals and curing their skins.

SE'ALING-VOYAGE, *n.* A voyage for the purpose of killing seals and obtaining their skins.

SE'ALING-WAX, *n.* [*seal* and *wax.*] A compound of gum lac and the red oxyd of mercury; used for fastening a folded letter and thus concealing the writing, and for receiving impressions of seals set to instruments. Sealing wax is hard or soft, and may be of any color.

SEAM, *n.* [Sax. *seam;* D. *zoom;* G. *saum;* Dan. *söm;* Sw. *söm,* a seam, a suture; *söma,* to sew. The G. *saum* signifies a hem or border. The word probably signifies the *uniting by sewing.* In Danish, *sömmer* signifies to hem, and to *beseem,* to be seemly, to become, to be suitable. We see then that *seam* and *seem,* are from one root. The primary sense is to meet, to come or put together. See *Same* and *Assemble.* Class Sm. No. 33. 40.]

1. The suture or uniting of two edges of cloth by the needle. *Dryden.*

The coat was without *seam,* woven from the top throughout. John xix.

2. The joint or juncture of planks in a ship's side or deck; or rather the intervals between the edges of boards or planks in a floor, &c. The *seams* of ships are filled with oakum, and covered with pitch.

3. In *mines,* a vein or stratum of metal, ore, coal and the like. *Encyc. Kirwan.*

4. A cicatrix or scar.

5. A measure of eight bushels of corn; or the vessel that contains it. [*Not used in America.*]

A seam of glass, the quantity of 120 pounds, or 24 stone of five pounds each. [*Not used in America.*] *Encyc.*

SEAM, *n.* [Sax. *seim;* W. *saim.*] Tallow; grease; lard. [*Not in use.*] *Shak. Dryden.*

SEAM, *v. t.* To form a seam; to sew or otherwise unite.

2. To mark with a cicatrix; to scar; as *seamed* with wounds. *Pope.*

SEAMAN. [See under *Sea.*]

SE'AMED, *pp.* Marked with seams; having seams or scars.

SE'AMING, *ppr.* Marking with scars; making seams.

SE'AMLESS, *a.* Having no seam; as the *seamless* garment of Christ.

SE'AM-RENT, *n.* [*seam* and *rent.*] The rent of a seam; the separation of a suture.

SE'AMSTER, *n.* One that sews well, or whose occupation is to sew.

SE'AMSTRESS, *n.* [that is, *seamsteress;* Sax. *seamestre.*] A woman whose occupation is sewing.

SE'AMY, *a.* Having a seam; containing seams or showing them. *Shak.*

SEAN, *n.* A net. [See *Seine.*]

SE'APOY, } *n.* [Pers. *sipahi;* Hindoo, *sepahai.*] A native of India in the military service of an European power, and disciplined after the European manner.
SE'POY,

SEAR, *v. t.* [Sax. *searan;* Gr. αζηρεω, to dry; ξηραινω, to dry, to parch; ξηρος, dry; σειρ, the sun; σειρεω, to dry. Qu. L. *torreo,* in a different dialect.]

1. To burn to dryness and hardness the surface of any thing; to cauterize; to expose to a degree of heat that changes the color of the surface, or makes it hard; as, to *sear* the skin or flesh.

I'm *sear'd* with burning steel. *Rowe.*

Sear is allied to *scorch* in signification; but it is applied primarily to animal flesh, and has special reference to the effect of heat in making the surface *hard.* *Scorch* is applied to flesh, cloth or any other substance, and has no reference to the effect of hardness.

2. To wither; to dry. *Shak.*

3. To make callous or insensible.

Having their conscience *seared* with a hot iron. 1 Tim. iv.

To sear up, to close by searing or cauterizing; to stop.

Cherish veins of good humor, and *sear up* those of ill. *Temple.*

SEAR, *a.* Dry; withered. *Milton. Ray.*

SEARCE, *v. t. sers.* To sift; to bolt; to separate the fine part of meal from the coarse. [*Little used.*] *Mortimer.*

SEARCE, *n. sers.* A sieve; a bolter. [*Little used.*]

SEARCER, *n. sers'er.* One that sifts or bolts. [*Little used.*]

SEARCH, *v. t. serch.* [Fr. *chercher;* It. *cercare;* Arm. *kerchat,* to seek, to ramble.]

1. To look over or through for the purpose of finding something; to explore; to examine by inspection; as, to *search* the house for a book; to *search* the wood for a thief.

Send thou men, that they may *search* the land of Canaan. Num. xiii.

2. To inquire; to seek for.

Enough is left besides to *search* and know. *Milton.*

3. To probe; to seek the knowledge of by feeling with an instrument; as, to *search* a wound. *Shak.*

4. To examine; to try. Ps. cxxxix.

To search out, to seek till found, or to find by seeking; as, to *search out* truth. *Watts.*

SEARCH, *v. i. serch.* To seek; to look for; to make search.

Once more *search* with me. *Shak.*

2. To make inquiry; to inquire.

It suffices that they have once with care sifted the matter, and *searched* into all the particulars. *Locke.*

To search for, to look for; to seek; to try to find; as, to *search for* a gentleman now in the house. *Shak.*

SEARCH, *n. serch.* A seeking or looking for something that is lost, or the place of which is unknown; with *for* or *after;* as a *search for* lost money; a *search for* mines of gold and silver; a *search after* happiness or knowledge.

2. Inquiry; a seeking. He spent his life in *search* of truth.

3. Quest; pursuit for finding.

Nor did my *search* of liberty begin,
Till my black hairs were chang'd upon my chin. *Dryden.*

SEARCHABLE, *a. serch'able.* That may be searched or explored. *Cotgrave.*

SEARCHED, *pp. serch'ed.* Looked over carefully; explored; examined.

SEARCHER, *n. serch'er.* One who searches, explores or examines for the purpose of finding something.

2. A seeker; an inquirer. *Watts.*
3. An examiner; a trier; as the *Searcher* of hearts.
4. An officer in London, appointed to examine the bodies of the dead, and report the cause of their death. *Graunt.*
5. An officer of the customs, whose business is to search and examine ships outward bound, to ascertain whether they have prohibited goods on board, also baggage, goods, &c.
6. An inspector of lether. [*Local.*]
7. In *military affairs*, an instrument for examining ordnance, to ascertain whether guns have any cavities in them. *Encyc.*
8. An instrument used in the inspection of butter, &c. to ascertain the quality of that which is contained in firkins. [*Local.*] *Mass.*

SEARCHING, *ppr. serch'ing.* Looking into or over; exploring; examining; inquiring; seeking; investigating.
2. *a.* Penetrating; trying; close; as a *searching* discourse.

SEARCHING, *n. serch'ing.* Examination; severe inquisition. Judges v.

SEARCHLESS, *a. serch'less.* Inscrutable; eluding search or investigation.

SE'AR-CLOTH, *n.* [Sax. *sar-clath*, sorecloth.]
A cloth to cover a sore; a plaster. *Mortimer.*

SE'ARED, *pp.* [from *sear.*] Burnt on the surface; cauterized; hardened.

SE'AREDNESS, *n.* The state of being seared, cauterized or hardened; hardness; hence, insensibility. *Bp. Hall.*

SE'ASON, *n. se'zn.* [Fr. *saison;* Arm. *sæsonn, saçzun;* Port. *sazam, sezam*, season, proper time, state of being seasoned; *sazonar*, to season, ripen, temper, sweeten, bring to maturity; Sp. *sazon*, season, maturity, taste, relish; *sazonar*, to season. The primary sense, like that of time and opportunity, is to fall, to come, to arrive, and this word seems to be allied to *seize* and *assess;* to fall on, to set on.]
Season literally signifies that which comes or arrives; and in this general sense, is synonymous with *time.* Hence,
1. A fit or suitable time; the convenient time; the usual or appointed time; as, the messenger arrived in *season;* in good *season.* This fruit is out of *season.*
2. Any time, as distinguished from others.
   The *season* prime for sweetest scents and airs. *Milton.*
3. A time of some continuance, but not long.
   Thou shalt be blind, not seeing the sun for a *season.* Acts xiii.
4. One of the four divisions of the year, spring, summer, autumn, winter. The *season* is mild; it is cold for the *season.*
   We saw, in six days' traveling, the several *seasons* of the year in their beauty. *Addison.*
   We distinguish the season by prefixing its appropriate name, as the spring-season, summer-season, &c.
   To be in season, to be in good time, or sufficiently early for the purpose.
   To be out of season, to be too late, beyond the proper time, or beyond the usual or appointed time.
   From the sense of convenience, is derived the following.
5. That which matures or prepares for the taste; that which gives a relish.
   You lack the *season* of all nature, sleep. *Shak.*
   But in this sense, we now use *seasoning.*

SE'ASON, *v. t.* [Fr. *assaisonner;* Sp. Port. *sazonar.*]
1. To render palatable, or to give a higher relish to, by the addition or mixture of another substance more pungent or pleasant; as, to *season* meat with salt; to *season* any thing with spices. Lev. ii.
2. To render more agreeable, pleasant or delightful; to give a relish or zest to by something that excites, animates or exhilarates.
   You *season* still with sports your serious hours. *Dryden.*
   The proper use of wit is to *season* conversation. *Tillotson.*
3. To render more agreeable, or less rigorous and severe; to temper; to moderate; to qualify by admixture.
   When mercy *seasons* justice. *Shak.*
4. To imbue; to tinge or taint.
   Season their younger years with prudent and pious principles. *Taylor.*
5. To fit for any use by time or habit; to mature; to prepare.
   Who in want a hollow friend doth try,
   Directly *seasons* him an enemy. *Shak.*
6. To prepare for use by drying or hardening; to take out or suffer to escape the natural juices; as, to *season* timber.
7. To prepare or mature for a climate; to accustom to and enable to endure; as, to *season* the body to a particular climate. Long residence in the West Indies, or a fever, may *season* strangers.

SE'ASON, *v. i.* To become mature; to grow fit for use; to become adapted to a climate, as the human body.
2. To become dry and hard by the escape of the natural juices, or by being penetrated with other substance. Timber *seasons* well under cover in the air, and ship timber *seasons* in salt water.
3. To betoken; to savor. *Obs.* *Beaum.*

SE'ASONABLE, *a.* Opportune; that comes, happens or is done in good time, in due season or in proper time for the purpose; as a *seasonable* supply of rain.
   Mercy is *seasonable* in the time of affliction. *Ecclus.*

SE'ASONABLENESS, *n.* Opportuneness of time; the state of being in good time, or in time convenient for the purpose or sufficiently early. *Addison.*

SE'ASONABLY, *adv.* In due time; in time convenient; sufficiently early; as, to sow or plant *seasonably.*

SE'ASONAGE, *n.* Seasoning; sauce. [*Not used.*] *South.*

SE'ASONED, *pp.* Mixed or sprinkled with something that gives a relish; tempered; moderated; qualified; matured; dried and hardened.

SE'ASONER, *n.* He that seasons; that which seasons, matures or gives a relish.

SE'ASONING, *ppr.* Giving a relish by something added; moderating; qualifying; maturing; drying and hardening; fitting by habit.

SE'ASONING, *n.* That which is added to any species of food to give it a higher relish; usually, something pungent or aromatic; as salt, spices or other aromatic herbs, acids, sugar, or a mixture of several things. *Arbuthnot.*
2. Something added or mixed to enhance the pleasure of enjoyment; as, wit or humor may serve as a *seasoning* to eloquence.
   Political speculations are of so dry and austere a nature, that they will not go down with the public without frequent *seasonings.* *Addison.*

SEAT, *n.* [It. *sedia;* Sp. *sede, silio*, from L. *sedes, situs;* Sw. *säte;* Dan. *sæde;* G. *sitz;* D. *zetel, zitplaats;* W. *sêz;* Ir. *saidh;* W. with a prefix, *gosod*, whence *gosodi*, to *set.* See *Set* and *Sit.* The English *seat* retains the Roman pronunciation of *situs*, that is, *seetus.*]
1. That on which one sits; a chair, bench, stool or any other thing on which a person sits.
   Christ—overthrew the tables of the money changers and the *seats* of them that sold doves. Matt. xxi.
2. The place of sitting; throne; chair of state; tribunal; post of authority; as the *seat* of justice; judgment-*seat.*
3. Mansion; residence; dwelling; abode; as Italy the *seat* of empire. The Greeks sent colonies to seek a new *seat* in Gaul.
   In Alba he shall fix his royal *seat.* *Dryden.*
4. Site; situation. The *seat* of Eden has never been incontrovertibly ascertained.
5. That part of a saddle on which a person sits.
6. In *horsemanship*, the posture or situation of a person on horseback. *Encyc.*
7. A pew or slip in a church; a place to sit in.
8. The place where a thing is settled or established. London is the *seat* of business and opulence. So we say, the *seat* of the muses, the *seat* of arts, the *seat* of commerce.

SEAT, *v. t.* To place on a seat; to cause to sit down. We *seat* ourselves; we *seat* our guests.
   The guests were no sooner *seated* but they entered into a warm debate. *Arbuthnot.*
2. To place in a post of authority, in office or a place of distinction. He *seated* his son in the professor's chair.
   Then high was king Richard *seated.* *Shak.*
3. To settle; to fix in a particular place or country. A colony of Greeks *seated* themselves in the south of Italy; another at Massilia in Gaul.
4. To fix; to set firm.
   From their foundations, loosening to and fro,
   They pluck'd the *seated* hills. *Milton.*
5. To place in a church; to assign seats to. In New England, where the pews in churches are not private property, it is customary to *seat* families for a year or longer time; that is, assign and appropriate *seats* to their use.
6. To appropriate the pews in, to particular families; as, to *seat* a church.
7. To repair by making the seat new; as, to *seat* a garment.
8. To settle; to plant with inhabitants; as, to *seat* a country. [*Not much used.*] *Stith, Virg.*

SEAT, *v. i.* To rest; to lie down. [*Not in use.*] *Spenser.*

SE'ATED, *pp.* Placed in a chair or on a bench, &c.; set; fixed; settled; established; furnished with a seat.

SE'ATING, *ppr.* Placing on a seat; setting; settling; furnishing with a seat; having its seats assigned to individuals, as a church.

SEAVES, *n. plu.* [Sw. *s&f*; Dan. *siv*; Heb. סוף suf.] Rushes. [*Local.*]

SE'AVY, *a.* Overgrown with rushes. [*Local.*]

SEBA'CEOUS, *a.* [Low L. *sebaceus*, from *sebum*, *sevum*, tallow, W. *saim.* Qu. Eth. *sebach*, fat.] Made of tallow or fat; pertaining to fat.

Sebaceous humor, a suet-like or glutinous matter secreted by the sebaceous glands, which serves to defend the skin and keep it soft. *Coxe. Parr.*

Sebaceous glands, small glands seated in the cellular membrane under the skin, which secrete the sebaceous humor. *Parr.*

SEBAC'IC, *a.* [supra.] In *chimistry*, pertaining to fat; obtained from fat; as the *sebacic* acid. *Lavoisier.*

SE'BATE, *n.* [supra.] In *chimistry*, a salt formed by the sebacic acid and a base. *Hooper. Lavoisier.*

SEBES'TEN, *n.* The Assyrian plum, a plant of the genus Cordia, a species of jujube. *Lee. Coxe.*

SE'CANT, *a.* [L. *secans*, *seco*, to cut or cut off, coinciding with Eng. *saw.*] Cutting; dividing into two parts.

SE'CANT, *n.* [It. Fr. Sp. *secante*, supra.]

1. In *geometry*, a line that cuts another, or divides it into parts. The secant of a circle is a line drawn from the circumference on one side, to a point without the circumference on the other. In *trigonometry*, a secant is a right line drawn from the center of a circle, which, cutting the circumference, proceeds till it meets with a tangent to the same circle. *Encyc.*

2. In *trigonometry*, the secant of an arc is a right line drawn from the center through one end of the arc, and terminated by a tangent drawn through the other end.

SECE'DE, *v. i.* [L. *secedo*; *se*, from, and *cedo*, to move. *Se* is an inseparable preposition or prefix in Latin, but denoting departure or separation.]

To withdraw from fellowship, communion or association; to separate one's self; as, certain ministers *seceded* from the church of Scotland about the year 1733.

SECE'DER, *n.* One who secedes. In Scotland, the *seceders* are a numerous body of presbyterians who seceded from the communion of the established church, about the year 1733.

SECE'DING, *ppr.* Withdrawing from fellowship or communion.

SECERN', *v. t.* [L. *secerno*; *se* and *cerno*, to separate.] In *the animal economy*, to secrete.

> The mucus *secerned* in the nose—is a laudable humor. *Arbuthnot.*

SECERN'ED, *pp.* Separated; secreted.

SECERN'ENT, *n.* That which promotes secretion; that which increases the irritative motions, which constitute secretion. *Darwin.*

SECERN'ING, *ppr.* Separating; secreting; as *secerning* vessels.

SECES'SION, *n.* [L. *secessio.* See *Secede.*]

1. The act of withdrawing, particularly from fellowship and communion. *Encyc.*

2. The act of departing; departure. *Brown.*

SE'CLE, *n.* [Fr. *siècle*; L. *seculum.*] A century. [*Not in use.*] *Hammond.*

SECLU'DE, *v. t.* [L. *secludo*; *se* and *claudo*, *cludo*, to shut.]

1. To separate, as from company or society, and usually to keep apart for some length of time, or to confine in a separate state; as, persons in low spirits *seclude* themselves from society.

> Let eastern tyrants from the light of heav'n
> *Seclude* their bosom slaves. *Thomson.*

2. To shut out; to prevent from entering; to preclude.

> Inclose your tender plants in your conservatory, *secluding* all entrance of cold. *Evelyn.*

SECLU'DED, *pp.* Separated from others; living in retirement; shut out.

SECLU'DING, *ppr.* Separating from others; confining in solitude or in a separate state; preventing entrance.

SECLU'SION, *n.* *s* as *z.* The act of separating from society or connection; the state of being separate or apart; separation; a shutting out; as, to live in *seclusion.*

SECLU'SIVE, *a.* That secludes or sequesters; that keeps separate or in retirement.

SEC'OND, *a.* [Fr. from L. *secundus*; It. *secondo*; Sp. Port. *segundo*; from L. *sequor*, to follow. See *Seek.*]

1. That immediately follows the first; the next following the first in order of place or time; the ordinal of two. Take the *second* book from the shelf. Enter the *second* house.

> And he slept and dreamed the *second* time. Gen. xli.

2. Next in value, power, excellence, dignity or rank; inferior. The silks of China are *second* to none in quality. Lord Chatham was *second* to none in eloquence. Dr. Johnson was *second* to none in intellectual powers, but *second* to many in research and erudition.

Second terms, in *algebra*, those where the unknown quantity has a degree of power less than it has in the term where it is raised to the highest. *Encyc.*

At second-hand, in the second place of order; not in the first place, or by or from the first; by transmission; not primarily; not originally; as a report received *at second-hand.*

> In imitation of preachers *at second-hand*, I shall transcribe from Bruyere a piece of raillery. *Tatler.*

SEC'OND, *n.* One who attends another in a duel, to aid him, mark out the ground or distance, and see that all proceedings between the parties are fair. *Watts. Addison.*

2. One that supports or maintains another; that which supports.

> Being sure enough of *seconds* after the first onset. *Wotton.*

3. The sixtieth part of a minute of time or of a degree, that is, the *second* minúte or small division next to the hour. Sound moves above 1140 English feet in a *second.*

4. In *music*, an interval of a conjoint degree, being the difference between any sound and the next nearest sound above or below it. *Busby. Encyc.*

SEC'OND, *v. t.* [L. *secundo*; Fr. *seconder*; It. *secondare.*]

1. To follow in the next place.

> Sin is *seconded* with sin. [*Little used.*] *South.*

2. To support; to lend aid to the attempt of another; to assist; to forward; to promote; to encourage; to act as the maintainer.

> We have *supplies* to second our attempt. *Shak.*

> The attempts of Austria to circumscribe the conquests of Buonaparte, were *seconded* by Russia. *Anon.*

> In God's, one single can its ends produce,
> Yet serves to *second* too some other use. *Pope.*

3. In *legislation*, to support, as a motion or the mover. We say, to *second* a motion or proposition, or to *second* the mover.

SEC'ONDARILY, *adv.* [from *secondary.*] In the second degree or second order; not primarily or originally; not in the first intention. Duties on imports serve primarily to raise a revenue, and *secondarily* to encourage domestic manufactures and industry.

SEC'ONDARINESS, *n.* The state of being secondary. *Norris.*

SEC'ONDARY, *a.* [L. *secundarius*, from *secundus.*]

1. Succeeding next in order to the first; subordinate.

> Where there is moral right on the one hand, not *secondary* right can discharge it. *L'Estrange.*

2. Not primary; not of the first intention.

> Two are the radical differences; the *secondary* differences are as four. *Bacon.*

3. Not of the first order or rate; revolving about a primary planet. Primary planets revolve about the sun; *secondary* planets revolve about the primary.

4. Acting by deputation or delegated authority; as the work of *secondary* hands. *Milton.*

5. Acting in subordination, or as second to another; as a *secondary* officer. *Encyc.*

Secondary rocks, in geology, are those which were formed after the primary. They are always situated over or above the primitive and transition rocks; they abound with organic remains or petrifactions, and are supposed to be mechanical deposits from water. *Cleaveland.*

A secondary fever, is that which arises after a crisis, or the discharge of some morbid matter, as after the declension of the small pox or measles. *Quincy.*

Secondary circles, or *secondaries*, in astronomy, circles passing through the poles of any of the great circles of the sphere, perpendicular to the planes of those circles.

Secondary qualities, are the qualities of bodies which are not inseparable from them, but which proceed from casual circumstances, such as color, taste, odor, &c.

Secondary formations, in geology, formations of substances, subsequent to the primitive.

SEC'ONDARY, *n.* A delegate or deputy; one who acts in subordination to another; as the *secondaries* of the court of king's bench and of common pleas. *Encyc.*

2. A fether growing on the second bone of a fowl's wing.

SEC'ONDED, *pp.* Supported; aided.

SEC'ONDER, *n.* One that supports what another attempts, or what he affirms, or what he moves or proposes; as the *seconder* of an enterprise or of a motion.

SEC'OND-HAND, *n.* Possession received from the first possessor. *Johnson.*

SEC'OND-HAND, *a.* Not original or primary; received from another.

They have but a *second-hand* or implicit knowledge. *Locke.*

2. Not new; that has been used by another; as a *second-hand* book.

SEC'ONDLY, *adv.* In the second place. *Bacon.*

SEC'OND-RATE, *n.* [*second* and *rate.*] The second order in size, dignity or value.

They call it thunder of the *second-rate.* *Addison.*

So we say, a ship of the *second-rate.*

SEC'OND-RATE, *a.* Of the second size, rank, quality or value; as a *second-rate* ship; a *second-rate* cloth; a *second-rate* champion. *Dryden.*

SECOND-SIGHT, *n.* The power of seeing things future or distant; a power claimed by some of the highlanders in Scotland. *Addison.*

Nor less avail'd his optic sleight,
And Scottish gift of *second-sight.*
Trumbull's M'Fingal.

SEC'OND-SIGHTED, *a.* Having the power of second-sight. *Addison.*

SE'CRECY, *n.* [from *secret.*] Properly, a state of separation; hence, concealment from the observation of others, or from the notice of any persons not concerned; privacy; a state of being hid from view. When used of an individual, *secrecy* implies concealment from all others; when used of two or more, it implies concealment from all persons except those concerned. Thus a company of counterfeiters carry on their villainy in *secrecy.*

The lady Anne,
Whom the king hath in *secrecy* long married. *Shak.*

2. Solitude; retirement; seclusion from the view of others. *Milton.*

3. Forbearance of disclosure or discovery.

It is not with public as with private prayer; in this, rather *secrecy* is commanded than outward show. *Hooker.*

4. Fidelity to a secret; the act or habit of keeping secrets.

For *secrecy* no lady closer. *Shak.*

SE'CRET, *a.* [Fr. *secret;* It. Sp. Port. *secreto;* L. *secretus.* This is given as the participle of *secerno,* but it is radically a different word; W. *segyr,* that is apart, inclosed or *sacred; segru,* to secrete or put apart; *ség,* that is without access. The radical sense of *ség* is to separate, as in L. *seco,* to cut off; and not improbably this word is contracted into the Latin *se,* a prefix in *segrego, separo,* &c.]

1. Properly, separate; hence, hid; concealed from the notice or knowledge of all persons except the individual or individuals concerned.

I have a *secret* errand to thee, O king. Judges iii.

2. Unseen; private; secluded; being in retirement.

There *secret* in her sapphire cell,
He with the Naïs wont to dwell. *Fenton.*

3. Removed from sight; private; unknown.

Abide in a *secret* place, and hide thyself. 1 Sam. xix.

4. Keeping secrets; faithful to secrets entrusted; as *secret* Romans. *Shak.* [*Unusual.*]

5. Private; affording privacy. *Milton.*

6. Occult; not seen; not apparent; as the *secret* operations of physical causes.

7. Known to God only.

Secret things belong to the Lord our God. Deut. xxix.

8. Not proper to be seen; kept or such as ought to be kept from observation.

SE'CRET, *n.* [Fr. from L. *secretum.*] Something studiously concealed. A man who cannot keep his own *secrets,* will hardly keep the *secrets* of others.

To tell our own *secrets* is often folly; to communicate those of others is treachery. *Rambler.*

A talebearer revealeth *secrets.* Prov. xi.

2. A thing not discovered and therefore unknown.

All *secrets* of the deep, all nature's works. *Milton.*

Hast thou heard the *secret* of God? Job xv.

3. *Secrets,* plu., the parts which modesty and propriety require to be concealed.

In secret, in a private place; in privacy or secrecy; in a state or place not seen; privately.

Bread eaten *in secret* is pleasant. Prov. ix.

SE'CRET, *v. t.* To keep private. [*Not used.*] *Bacon.*

SEC'RETARISHIP, *n.* The office of a secretary. *Swift.*

SEC'RETARY, *n.* [Fr. *secrétaire;* Sp. It. *secretario;* from L. *secretus,* secret; originally a confident, one entrusted with secrets.]

1. A person employed by a public body, by a company or by an individual, to write orders, letters, dispatches, public or private papers, records and the like. Thus legislative bodies have *secretaries,* whose business is to record all their laws and resolves. Embassadors have *secretaries.*

2. An officer whose business is to superintend and manage the affairs of a particular department of government; as the *secretary* of state, who conducts the correspondence of a state with foreign courts; the *secretary* of the treasury, who manages the department of finance; the *secretary* of war, of the navy, &c.

SECRE'TE, *v. t.* To hide; to conceal; to remove from observation or the knowledge of others; as, to *secrete* stolen goods.

2. To secrete one's self; to retire from notice into a private place; to abscond.

3. In *the animal economy,* to secern; to produce from the blood substances different from the blood itself, or from any of its constituents; as the glands. The liver *secretes* bile; the salivary glands *secrete* saliva. *Ed. Encyc.*

SECRE'TED, *pp.* Concealed; secerned.

SECRE'TING, *ppr.* Hiding; secerning.

SECRE'TION, *n.* The act of secerning; the act of producing from the blood substances different from the blood itself, or from any of its constituents, as bile, saliva, mucus, urine, &c. This was considered by the older physiologists as merely a separation from the blood of certain substances previously contained in it; the literal meaning of *secretion.* But this opinion is now generally exploded. The organs of secretion are of very various form and structure, but the most general are those called *glands.* *Ed. Encyc.*

2. The matter secreted, as mucus, perspirable matter, &c.

SE'CRETIST, *n.* A dealer in secrets. [*Not in use.*] *Boyle.*

SECRETI"TIOUS, *a.* Parted by animal secretion. *Floyer.*

SE'CRETLY, *adv.* Privately; privily; not openly; without the knowledge of others; as, to dispatch a messenger *secretly.*

2. Inwardly; not apparently or visibly; latently.

Now *secretly* with inward grief she pin'd. *Addison.*

SE'CRETNESS, *n.* The state of being hid or concealed.

2. The quality of keeping a secret. *Donne.*

SE'CRETORY, *a.* Performing the office of secretion; as *secretory* vessels. *Ray.*

SECT, *n.* [Fr. *secte;* It. *setta;* L. Sp. *secta;* from L. *seco,* to cut off, to separate.]

1. A body or number of persons united in tenets, chiefly in philosophy or religion, but constituting a distinct party by holding sentiments different from those of other men. Most *sects* have originated in a particular person, who taught and propagated some peculiar notions in philosophy or religion, and who is considered to have been its founder. Among the Jews, the principal *sects* were the Pharisees, Sadducees, and Essenes. In Greece were the Cynic *sect,* founded by Antisthenes; and the Academic *sect,* by Plato. The Academic *sect* gave birth to the Peripatetic, and the Cynic to the Stoic. *Enfield.*

2. A cutting or cion. [*Not used.*] *Shak.*

SECTA'RIAN, *a.* [L. *sectarius.*] Pertaining to a sect or to sects; as *sectarian* principles or prejudices.

SECTA'RIAN, *n.* One of a sect; one of a party in religion which has separated itself from the established church, or which holds tenets different from those of the prevailing denomination in a kingdom or state.

SECTA'RIANISM, *n.* The disposition to dissent from the established church or predominant religion, and to form new sects.

SECT'ARISM, *n.* Sectarianism. [*Little used.*]

SECT'ARIST, *n.* A sectary. [*Not much used.*] *Warton.*

SECT'ARY, *n.* [Fr. *sectaire.*] A person who separates from an established church, or from the prevailing denomination of christians; one that belongs to a sect; a dissenter.

2. A follower; a pupil. [*Not in use.*] *Spenser.*

SECTA'TOR, *n.* [Fr. *sectateur.*] A follower; a disciple; an adherent to a sect. [*Not now used.*] *Raleigh.*

SECT'ILE, *a.* [L. *sectilis,* from *seco,* to cut.] A sectile mineral is one that is midway between the brittle and the malleable, as soapstone and plumbago. *Phillips*

SEC'TION, *n.* [Fr. from L. *sectio; seco*, to cut off.]

1. The act of cutting or of separating by cutting; as the *section* of bodies. *Wotton.*
2. A part separated from the rest; a division.
3. In *books* and *writings*, a distinct part or portion; the subdivision of a chapter; the division of a law or other writing or instrument. In laws, a *section* is sometimes called a paragraph or article. *Boyle. Locke.*
4. A distinct part of a city, town, country or people; a part of territory separated by geographical lines, or of a people considered as distinct. Thus we say, the northern or eastern *section* of the United States, the middle *section*, the southern or western *section.*
5. In *geometry*, a side or surface of a body or figure cut off by another; or the place where lines, planes, &c. cut each other. *Encyc.*

SEC'TIONAL, *a.* Pertaining to a section or distinct part of a larger body or territory.

SEC'TOR, *n.* [Fr. *secteur*, from L. *seco*, to cut.]

1. In *geometry*, a part of a circle comprehended between two radii and the arch; or a mixed triangle, formed by two radii and the arch of a circle. *Encyc.*
2. A mathematical instrument so marked with lines of sines, tangents, secants, chords, &c. as to fit all radii and scales, and useful in finding the proportion between quantities of the same kind. The sector is founded on the fourth proposition of the sixth book of Euclid, where it is proved that similar triangles have their homologous sides proportional. *Encyc.*

SEC'ULAR, *a.* [Fr. *seculaire;* It. *secolare;* Sp. *secular;* L. *secularis*, from *seculum*, the world or an age.]

1. Pertaining to this present world, or to things not spiritual or holy; relating to things not immediately or primarily respecting the soul, but the body; worldly. The *secular* concerns of life respect making provision for the support of life, the preservation of health, the temporal prosperity of men, of states, &c. *Secular* power is that which superintends and governs the temporal affairs of men, the civil or political power; and is contradistinguished from *spiritual* or *ecclesiastical* power.
2. Among *catholics*, not regular; not bound by monastic vows or rules; not confined to a monastery or subject to the rules of a religious community. Thus we say, the *secular* clergy, and the *regular* clergy. *Temple.*
3. Coming once in a century; as a *secular* year.

Secular games, in Rome, were games celebrated once in an age or century, which lasted three days and nights, with sacrifices, theatrical shows, combats, sports, &c. *Valerius Maximus.*

Secular music, any music or songs not adapted to sacred uses.

Secular song or *poem*, a song or poem composed for the secular games, or sung or rehearsed at those games.

SEC'ULAR, *n.* A church officer or officiate whose functions are confined to the vocal department of the choir. *Busby.*

SECULAR'ITY, *n.* Worldliness; supreme attention to the things of the present life. *Buchanan.*

SECULARIZA'TION, *n.* [from *secularize.*] The act of converting a regular person, place or benefice into a secular one. Most cathedral churches were formerly regular, that is, the canons were of religious or monastic orders; but they have since been secularized. For the *secularization* of a regular church, there is wanted the authority of the pope, that of the prince, the bishop of the place, the patron, and even the consent of the people. *Encyc.*

SEC'ULARIZE, *v. t.* [Fr. *seculariser;* from *secular.*]

1. To make secular; to convert from spiritual appropriation to secular or common use; or to convert that which is regular or monastic into secular; as, the ancient regular cathedral churches were *secularized.*

   At the reformation, the abbey was *secularized.* *Coxe, Switz.*

2. To make worldly.

SEC'ULARIZED, *pp.* Converted from regular to secular.

SEC'ULARIZING, *ppr.* Converting from regular or monastic to secular.

SEC'ULARLY, *adv.* In a worldly manner.

SEC'ULARNESS, *n.* A secular disposition; worldliness; worldly mindedness.

SEC'UNDINE, *n.* [Fr. *secondines;* from *second*, L. *secundus*, from *sequor*, to follow.]

Secundines, in the plural, as generally used, are the several coats or membranes in which the fetus is wrapped in the womb; the after-birth. *Coxe. Encyc.*

SECU'RE, *a.* [L. *securus;* It. *sicuro;* Sp. *seguro.* It coincides in elements with the oriental סגר and סכר to shut or inclose, to make fast.]

1. Free from danger of being taken by an enemy; that may resist assault or attack. The place is well fortified and very *secure.* Gibraltar is a *secure* fortress. In this sense, *secure* is followed by *against* or *from;* as *secure against* attack, or *from* an enemy.
2. Free from danger; safe; applied to persons; with *from.*
3. Free from fear or apprehension of danger; not alarmed; not disturbed by fear; confident of safety; hence, careless of the means of defense. Men are often most in danger when they feel most *secure.*

   Confidence then bore thee on, *secure*
   To meet no danger. *Milton.*

4. Confident; not distrustful; with *of.*

   But thou, *secure of* soul, unbent with woes. *Dryden.*

   It concerns the most *secure of* his strength, to pray to God not to expose him to an enemy. *Rogers.*

5. Careless; wanting caution. [See No. 3.]
6. Certain; very confident. He is *secure* of a welcome reception.

SECU'RE, *v. t.* To guard effectually from danger; to make safe. Fortifications may *secure* a city; ships of war may *secure* a harbor.

   I spread a cloud before the victor's sight,
   Sustain'd the vanquish'd, and *secur'd* his flight. *Dryden.*

2. To make certain; to put beyond hazard. Liberty and fixed laws *secure* to every citizen due protection of person and property. The first duty and the highest interest of men is to *secure* the favor of God by repentance and faith, and thus to *secure* to themselves future felicity.
3. To inclose or confine effectually; to guard effectually from escape; sometimes, to seize and confine; as, to *secure* a prisoner. The sherif pursued the thief with a warrant, and *secured* him.
4. To make certain of payment; as, to *secure* a debt by mortgage.
5. To make certain of receiving a precarious debt by giving bond, bail, surety or otherwise; as, to *secure* a creditor.
6. To insure, as property.
7. To make fast; as, to *secure* a door; to *secure* a rafter to a plate; to *secure* the hatches of a ship.

SECU'RED, *pp.* Effectually guarded or protected; made certain; put beyond hazard; effectually confined; made fast.

SECU'RELY, *adv.* Without danger; safely; as, to pass a river on ice *securely.* But *safely* is generally used.

2. Without fear or apprehension; carelessly; in an unguarded state; in confidence of safety.

   His daring foe *securely* him defy'd. *Milton.*

   Devise not evil against thy neighbor, seeing he dwelleth *securely* by thee. Prov. iii.

SECU'REMENT, *n.* Security; protection. [*Not used.*] *Brown.*

SECU'RENESS, *n.* Confidence of safety; exemption from fear; hence, want of vigilance or caution. *Bacon.*

SECU'RER, *n.* He or that which secures or protects.

SECU'RIFORM, *a.* [L. *securis*, an ax or hatchet, and *form.*] In *botany*, having the form of an ax or hatchet. *Lee.*

SECU'RITY, *n.* [Fr. *securité;* L. *securitas.*]

1. Protection; effectual defense or safety from danger of any kind; as a chain of forts erected for the *security* of the frontiers.
2. That which protects or guards from danger. A navy constitutes the *security* of Great Britain from invasion.
3. Freedom from fear or apprehension; confidence of safety; whence, negligence in providing means of defense. *Security* is dangerous, for it exposes men to attack when unprepared. *Security* in sin is the worst condition of the sinner.
4. Safety; certainty. We have no *security* for peace with Algiers, but the dread of our navy.
5. Any thing given or deposited to secure the payment of a debt, or the performance of a contract; as a bond with surety, a mortgage, the indorsement of a responsible man, a pledge, &c. *Blackstone.*
6. Something given or done to secure peace or good behavior. Violent and dangerous men are obliged to give *security* for their good behavior, or for keeping the peace. This *security* consists in being bound with one or more sureties in a recognizance to the king or state. *Blackstone.*

SEDAN', *n.* [Fr. from the L. *sedeo;* like L. *esseda.*] A portable chair or covered vehicle for carrying a single person. It is borne on poles by two men. *Dryden. Encyc.*

SEDA'TE, *a.* [L. *sedatus*, from *sedo*, to calm or appease, that is, to *set*, to cause to subside.]

Settled; composed; calm; quiet; tranquil; still; serene; unruffled by passion; undisturbed; as a *sedate* soul, mind or temper. So we say, a *sedate* look or countenance. *Dryden. Watts.*

SEDA'TELY, *adv.* Calmly; without agitation of mind. *Locke.*

SEDA'TENESS, *n.* Calmness of mind, manner or countenance; freedom from agitation; a settled state; composure; serenity; tranquillity; as *sedateness* of temper or soul; *sedateness* of countenance; *sedateness* of conversation. *Addison.*

SEDA'TION, *n.* The act of calming. [*Not in use.*] *Coles.*

SED'ATIVE, *a.* [Fr. *sedatif*, from L. *sedo*, to calm.]

In *medicine*, moderating muscular action or animal energy. *Quincy. Coxe.*

SED'ATIVE, *n.* A medicine that moderates muscular action or animal energy. *Quincy. Coxe.*

Se defendendo, in defending himself; the plea of a person charged with murder, who alledges that he committed the act in his own defense.

SED'ENTARILY, *adv.* [from *sedentary.*] The state of being sedentary, or living without much action.

SED'ENTARINESS, *n.* The state of being sedentary.

SED'ENTARY, *a.* [Fr. *sedentaire;* It. Sp. *sedentario;* L. *sedentarius*, from *sedens*, *sedeo*, to sit.]

1. Accustomed to sit much, or to pass most of the time in a sitting posture; as a *sedentary* man. Students, taylors and women are *sedentary* persons.

2. Requiring much sitting; as a *sedentary* occupation or employment.

3. Passed for the most part in sitting; as a *sedentary* life. *Arbuthnot.*

4. Inactive; motionless; sluggish; as the *sedentary* earth. *Milton.*

> The soul, considered abstractly from its passions, is of a remiss *sedentary* nature. *Spectator.*

SEDĠE, *n.* [Sax. *secg;* perhaps from the root of L. *seco*, to cut; that is, sword grass, like L. *gladiolus.*]

1. A narrow flag, or growth of such flags; called in the north of England, *seg* or *sag*. *Johnson. Barret.*

2. In *New England*, a species of very coarse grass growing in swamps, and forming bogs or clumps.

SEDĠ'ED, *a.* Composed of flags or sedge. *Shak.*

SEDĠ'Y, *a.* Overgrown with sedge.

> On the gentle Severn's *sedgy* bank. *Shak.*

SED'IMENT, *n.* [Fr. from L. *sedimentum*, from *sedeo*, to settle.]

The matter which subsides to the bottom of liquors; settlings; lees; dregs. *Bacon.*

SEDI''TION, *n.* [Fr. from L. *seditio.* The sense of this word is the contrary of that which is naturally deducible from *sedo*, or *sedeo*, denoting a rising or raging, rather than an appeasing. But to *set* is really to throw down, to drive, and *sedition* may be a setting or rushing together.]

A factious commotion of the people, or a tumultuous assembly of men rising in opposition to law or the administration of justice, and in disturbance of the public peace. Sedition is a rising or commotion of less extent than an *insurrection*, and both are less than *rebellion;* but some kinds of sedition, in Great Britain, amount to high treason. In general, sedition is a local or limited insurrection in opposition to *civil* authority, as mutiny is to *military*. Ezra iv. Luke xxiii. Acts xxiv. *Encyc.*

SEDI''TIONARY, *n.* An inciter or promoter of sedition. *Bp. Hall.*

SEDI''TIOUS, *a.* [Fr. *seditieux;* L. *seditiosus.*]

1. Pertaining to sedition; partaking of the nature of sedition; as *seditious* behavior; *seditious* strife.

2. Tending to excite sedition; as *seditious* words.

3. Disposed to excite violent or irregular opposition to law or lawful authority; turbulent; factious, or guilty of sedition; as *seditious* citizens.

SEDI''TIOUSLY, *adv.* With tumultuous opposition to law; in a manner to violate the public peace.

SEDI''TIOUSNESS, *n.* The disposition to excite popular commotion in opposition to law; or the act of exciting such commotion.

SEDU'CE, *v. t.* [L. *seduco;* *se*, from, and *duco*, to lead; Fr. *seduire;* It. *sedurre;* Sp. *seducir.*]

1. To draw aside or entice from the path of rectitude and duty in any manner, by flattery, promises, bribes or otherwise; to tempt and lead to iniquity; to corrupt; to deprave.

> Me the gold of France did not *seduce*. *Shak.*
>
> In the latter times, some shall depart from the faith, giving heed to *seducing* spirits. 1 Tim. iv.

2. To entice to a surrender of chastity. He that can *seduce* a female is base enough to betray her.

SEDU'CED, *pp.* Drawn or enticed from virtue; corrupted; depraved.

SEDU'CEMENT, *n.* The act of seducing; seduction.

2. The means employed to seduce; the arts of flattery, falsehood and deception. *Pope.*

SEDU'CER, *n.* One that seduces; one that by temptation or arts, entices another to depart from the path of rectitude and duty; pre-eminently, one that by flattery, promises or falsehood, persuades a female to surrender her chastity. The *seducer* of a female is little less criminal than the murderer.

2. That which leads astray; that which entices to evil.

> He whose firm faith no reason could remove,
> Will melt before that soft *seducer*, love. *Dryden.*

SEDU'CIBLE, *a.* Capable of being drawn aside from the path of rectitude; corruptible. *Brown.*

SEDU'CING, *ppr.* Enticing from the path of virtue or chastity.

SEDUC'TION, *n.* [Fr. from L. *seductio.*]

1. The act of seducing, or of enticing from the path of duty; *in a general sense.* *Hammond.*

2. *Appropriately*, the act or crime of persuading a female, by flattery or deception, to surrender her chastity. A woman who is above flattery, is least liable to *seduction;* but the best safeguard is principle, the love of purity and holiness, the fear of God and reverence for his commands.

SEDUC'TIVE, *a.* Tending to lead astray; apt to mislead by flattering appearances. *Stephens.*

SEDU'LITY, *n.* [L. *sedulitas;* It. *sedulità.* See *Sedulous.*]

Diligent and assiduous application to business; constant attention; unremitting industry in any pursuit. It denotes *constancy* and *perseverance* rather than *intenseness* of application.

> Let there be but the same propensity and bent of will to religion, and there will be the same *sedulity* and indefatigable industry in men's inquiries into it. *South.*

SED'ULOUS, *a.* [L. *sedulus*, from the root of *sedeo*, to sit; as *assiduous*, from *assideo.*]

Literally, sitting close to an employment; hence, assiduous; diligent in application or pursuit; constant, steady and persevering in business or in endeavors to effect an object; steadily industrious; as the *sedulous* bee. *Prior.*

> What signifies the sound of words in prayer, without the affection of the heart, and a *sedulous* application of the proper means that may lead to such an end? *L'Estrange.*

SED'ULOUSLY, *adv.* Assiduously; industriously; diligently; with constant or continued application.

SED'ULOUSNESS, *n.* Assiduity; assiduousness; steady diligence; continued industry or effort.

SEE, *n.* [Fr. *siége;* Scot. *sege;* Arm. *sich.*]

1. The seat of episcopal power; a diocese; the jurisdiction of a bishop. *Swift.*

2. The seat of an archbishop; a province or jurisdiction of an archbishop; as an archiepiscopal *see*. *Shak.*

3. The seat, place or office of the pope or Roman pontif; as the papal *see*.

4. The authority of the pope or court of Rome; as, to appeal to the *see* of Rome. *Addison.*

SEE, *v. t.* pret. *saw;* pp. *seen.* [Sax. *seon*, *seogan*, *geseon;* G. *sehen;* D. *zien*, pret. *zag*, saw; Dan. *seer;* Sw. *se.* This verb is contracted, as we know by the Eng. *sight*, Dan. *sigt*, G. *gesicht*, D. *zigt*, *gezigt*. Ch. סכא, סכה or סכי, to see. Class Sg. No. 34. In G. *besuchen* is to visit, to *see*, and this is from *suchen*, which is the Eng. to *seek*, and to *seek* is to look for. In G. *gesuch* is a *suit*, a seeking, demand, petition; and *versuchen* is to try, Eng. *essay*. We have then decisive evidence that *see*, *seek*, L. *sequor*, and Eng. *essay*, are all from the same radix. The primary sense of the root is to strain, stretch, extend; and as applied to *see*, the sense is to extend to, to reach, to strike with the eye or sight.]

1. To perceive by the eye; to have knowledge of the existence and apparent qualities of objects by the organs of sight; to behold.

> I will now turn aside and *see* this great sight. Ex. iii.
>
> We have *seen* the land, and behold, it is very good. Judges xviii.

2. To observe; to note or notice; to know; to regard or look to; to take care; to attend, as to the execution of some order, or to the performance of something.

Give them first one simple idea, and *see* that they fully comprehend before you go any farther. *Locke.*

See that ye fall not out by the way. Gen. xlv.

3. To discover; to descry; to understand. Who so dull as not to *see* the device or stratagem? Very noble actions often lose much of their excellence when the motives are *seen.*

4. To converse or have intercourse with. We improve by *seeing* men of different habits and tempers.

5. To visit; as, to call and *see* a friend. The physician *sees* his patient twice a day. 1 Sam. xv. 1 Cor. xvi.

6. To attend; to remark or notice.

I had a mind to *see* him out, and therefore did not care to contradict him. *Addison.*

7. To behold with patience or sufferance; to endure.

It was not meet for us to *see* the king's dishonor. Ezra iv.

8. In *Scripture*, to hear or attend to.

I turned to *see* the voice that spoke with me. Rev. i.

9. To feel; to suffer; to experience.

Make us glad according to the days wherein thou hast afflicted us, and the years in which we have *seen* evil. Ps. xc.

If a man shall keep my saying, he shall never *see* death. John viii. Luke ii.

10. To know; to learn.

Go, I pray thee, *see* whether it be well with thy brethren. Gen. xxxvii.

11. To perceive; to understand; to comprehend. I *see* the train of argument; I *see* his motives.

12. To perceive; to understand experimentally.

I *see* another law in my members. Rom. vii.

13. To beware.

See thou do it not. Rev. xix.

14. To know by revelation.

The word that Isaiah, the son of Amoz, *saw* concerning Judah and Jerusalem. Is. ii. xiii.

15. To have faith in and reliance on.

Seeing him who is invisible. Heb. xi.

16. To enjoy; to have fruition of.

Blessed are the pure in heart, for they shall *see* God. Matt. v.

SEE, *v. i.* To have the power of perceiving by the proper organs, or the power of sight. Some animals, it is said, are able to *see* best in the night.

2. To discern; to have intellectual sight; to penetrate; to understand; with *through* or *into;* as, to *see through* the plans or policy of another; to *see into* artful schemes and pretensions. *Tillotson.*

3. To examine or inquire. *See* whether the estimate is correct.

4. To be attentive. *Shak.*

5. To have full understanding.

But now ye say, we *see*, therefore your sin remaineth. John xix.

See to it, look well to it; attend; consider; take care.

Let me see, let us see, are used to express consideration, or to introduce the particular consideration of a subject, or some scheme or calculation.

See is used imperatively, to call the attention of others to an object or a subject. *See, see*, how the balloon ascends.

See what it is to have a poet in your house. *Pope.*

SEED, *n.* [Sax. *sæd;* G. *saat;* D. *zaad;* Dan. *sæd;* Sw. *såd;* from the verb *sow.* Qu. W. *hâd*, Arm. *had.*]

1. The substance, animal or vegetable, which nature prepares for the reproduction and conservation of the species. The seeds of plants are a deciduous part, containing the rudiments of a new vegetable. In some cases, the seeds constitute the fruit or valuable part of plants, as in the case of wheat and other esculent grain; sometimes the seeds are inclosed in the fruit, as in apples and melons. When applied to animal matter, it has no plural.

2. That from which any thing springs; first principle; original; as the *seeds* of virtue or vice. *Hooker.*

3. Principle of production.

Praise of great acts he scatters as a *seed.* *Waller.*

4. Progeny; offspring; children; descendants; as the *seed* of Abraham; the *seed* of David. In this sense, the word is applied to one person, or to any number collectively, and admits of the plural form; but rarely used in the plural.

5. Race; generation; birth.

Of mortal *seed* they were not held. *Waller.*

SEED, *v. i.* To grow to maturity, so as to produce seed. Maiz will not *seed* in a cool climate. *Swift.*

2. To shed the seed. *Mortimer.*

SEED, *v. t.* To sow; to sprinkle with seed, which germinates and takes root. *Belknap.*

SEE'D-BUD, *n.* [*seed* and *bud.*] The germ, germen or rudiment of the fruit in embryo.

SEE'D-CAKE, *n.* [*seed* and *cake.*] A sweet cake containing aromatic seeds. *Tusser.*

SEE'D-COAT, *n.* In *botany*, the aril or outer coat of a seed. *Martyn.*

SEE'D-LEAF, *n.* In *botany*, the primary leaf. The *seed-leaves* are the cotyledons or lobes of a seed expanded and in vegetation. *Martyn.*

SEE'DLING, *n.* A young plant or root just sprung from the seed. *Evelyn.*

SEE'D-LIP, SEE'D-LOP, } *n.* A vessel in which a sower carries the seed to be dispersed. *England.*

SEE'D-LOBE, *n.* The lobe of a seed; a cotyledon, which see.

SEE'DNESS, *n.* Seed-time. [*Not in use.*]

SEE'D-PEARL, *n.* [*seed* and *pearl.*] Small grains of pearl. *Boyle.*

SEE'D-PLAT, SEE'D-PLOT, } *n.* [*seed* and *plat.*] The ground on which seeds are sown to produce plants for transplanting; hence,

2. A nursery; a place where any thing is sown or planted for cultivation. *Hammond.*

SEE'DSMAN, *n.* [*seed* and *man.*] A person who deals in seeds; also, a sower. *Dict.*

SEE'D-TIME, *n.* [*seed* and *time.*] The season proper for sowing.

While the earth remaineth, *seed-time* and harvest, and cold and heat, and summer and winter, and day and night, shall not cease. Gen. viii.

SEE'D-VESSEL, *n.* In *botany*, the pericarp which contains the seeds.

SEE'DY, *a.* [from *seed.*] Abounding with seeds. *Dict.*

2. Having a peculiar flavor, supposed to be derived from the weeds growing among the vines; applied to French brandy. *Encyc.*

SEE'ING, *ppr.* [from *see.*] Perceiving by the eye; knowing; understanding; observing; beholding.

[*Note.* This participle appears to be used indefinitely, or without direct reference to a person or persons. "Wherefore come ye to me, *seeing* ye hate me?" Gen. xxvi. That is, since, or the fact being that or thus; because that. In this form of phraseology, *that* is understood or implied after *seeing;* why come ye to me, *seeing that*, ye hate me? The resolution of the phrase or sentence is, ye hate me; that fact being seen or known by you, why come ye to me? or, why come ye to me, ye seeing [knowing] that fact which follows, viz. ye hate me. In this case, *seeing* retains its participial character, although its relation to the pronoun is somewhat obscured. Originally, *seeing*, in this use, had direct relation to the speaker or to some other person. "Now I know that thou fearest God, *seeing* thou hast not withheld thy son." Gen. xxii. Here *seeing* refers to *I*, or according to the language of syntax, agrees or accords with *I.* I know thou fearest God, for I *see* thou hast not withheld thine only son; I know thou fearest God by *seeing*, in consequence of *seeing* this fact, thou hast not withheld thine only son. But the use of *seeing* is extended to cases in which it cannot be referred to a specific person or persons, in which cases it expresses the notoriety or admission of a fact in general, and is left, like the French *on*, in the phrases *on dit, on voit*, without application to any particular person.]

SEEK, *v. t.* pret. and pp. *sought*, pronounced *sawt.* [Sax. *secan, sæcan*, to seek, to come to; *asecan*, to require; *gesecan*, to seek, to come to; *forsacan, forsæcan*, to forsake; G. *suchen*, to seek; *absuchen*, to pick off; *besuchen*, to visit, to see; *gesuch*, suit, petition; *gesuche*, a continued seeking; *versuchen*, to try, prove, tempt, *essay*, strive; *versuch*, trial, *essay;* D. *zoeken*, to seek, to look for, to try or endeavor; *bezoeken*, to visit, to try; *gezoek*, a seeking; *opzoeken*, to seek; *verzoeken*, to request, desire, invite, try, tempt, to visit; Dan. *söger*, to seek, to endeavor; *besöger*, to visit; *forsöger*, to try, to *essay*, to experiment, to tempt; *opsöger*, to seek or search after; Sw. *sôka*, to seek, to sue, to court; *sôka en lagligen*, to sue one at law; *besôka*, to visit; *forsôka*, to try, to essay, to tempt. These words all accord with L. *sequor*, Ir. *seichim*, to follow; for to *seek* is to go after, and the primary sense is to advance, to press, to drive forward, as in the L. *peto.* See *Essay*, from the same root, through the Italian and French. Now in Sax. *forsacan, forsæcan*, is to *forsake; sacan* is to strive, contend, whence English *sake*, and *sæcan, secan*, is to seek. But in Swedish, *forsaka*, to forsake, to renounce, is from *sak*, thing, cause, suit, Sax. *saca*, English *sake;* in Danish, *forsager*, to renounce, is from *siger*, to say; *sag*, a thing, cause, matter, suit; *sagd*, a saying; G. *versagen*, to deny, to renounce, from *sagen*, to *say*, to tell; D. *verzaaken*, to deny, to *forsake*, to revoke, from *zaak*, thing, cause.

and *zeggen* is to say or tell, which is the Sax. *secgan*, to say. These close affinities prove that *seek*, *essay*, *say*, and L. *sequor*, are all from one radix, coinciding with Cr. עסק to seek, to strive. Class Sg. No. 46. and see No. 30. Ar. The English verb *see* seems to be from the same root.]

1. To go in search or quest of; to look for; to search for by going from place to place.

The man asked him, saying, what *seekest* thou? And he said, I *seek* my brethren. Gen. xxxvii.

2. To inquire for; to ask for; to solicit; to endeavor to find or gain by any means.

The young lions roar after their prey, and *seek* their meat from God. Ps. civ.

He found no place for repentance, though he *sought* it carefully with tears. Heb. xii.

Others tempting him, *sought* of him a sign. Luke xi.

3. *Seek* is followed sometimes by *out* or *after*. To *seek out*, properly implies to look for a specific thing among a number. But in general, the use of *out* and *after* with *seek*, is unnecessary and inelegant.

To seek God, his name, or *his face*, in Scripture, to ask for his favor, direction and assistance. Ps. lxiii. lxxxiii.

God seeks men, when he fixes his love on them, and by his word and Spirit, and the righteousness of Christ, reclaims and recovers them from their miserable condition as sinners. Ezek. xxxiv. Ps. cxix. Luke xv.

To seek after the life, or *soul*, to attempt by arts or machinations; or to attempt to destroy or ruin. Ps. xxxv.

To seek peace, or *judgment*, to endeavor to promote it; or to practice it. Ps. xxxiv. Is. i.

To seek an altar, temple, or *habitation*, to frequent it; to resort to it often. 2 Chron. i. Amos v.

To seek out God's works, to endeavor to understand them. Ps. cxi.

SEEK, *v. i.* To make search or inquiry; to endeavor to make discovery.

Seek ye out of the book of the Lord, and read. Is. xxxiv.

2. To endeavor.

Ask not what pains, nor further *seek* to know
Their process, or the forms of law below. *Dryden.*

To seek after, to make pursuit; to attempt to find or take. [See No. 3, supra.]

To seek for, to endeavor to find. *Knolles.*

To seek to, to apply to; to resort to. 1 Kings x.

To seek, at a loss; without knowledge, measures or experience.

Unpractic'd, unprepar'd and still *to seek*. *Milton.*

[This phrase, I believe, is wholly obsolete.]

SEE'KER, *n.* One that seeks; an inquirer; as a *seeker* of truth.

2. One of a sect that profess no determinate religion. *Johnson.*

SEE'K-SORROW, *n.* [*seek* and *sorrow*.] One that contrives to give himself vexation. [*Little used.*] *Sidney.*

SEEL, *v. t.* [Fr. *sceller*, to seal.] To close the eyes; a term of falconry, from the practice of closing the eyes of a wild hawk. *Bacon.*

SEEL, *v. i.* [Sax. *sylan*, to give. See *Sell*.] To lean; to incline to one side. *Obs.* *Bacon.*

SEEL, } *n.* The rolling or agitation of
SEE'LING, } a ship in a storm. *Obs.* *Ainsworth.*

SEEL, *n.* [Sax. *sæl.*] Time; opportunity; season. *Obs.* *Ray.*

SEE'LILY, *adv.* In a silly manner. *Obs.*

SEE'LY, *a.* [from *seel*.] Lucky; fortunate. *Obs.* *Spenser.*

2. Silly; foolish; simple. *Obs.* [See *Silly*.] *Tusser.*

SEEM, *v. i.* [G. *ziemen*, to become, to be fit or suitable; *geziemen*, to become, to *beseem*, to be meet, decent, *seemly*. In D. *zweemen* is to be like, to resemble, and *taamen* is to fit or suit, to become. In Dan. *söm* is a *seam*, and *sömmer*, signifies to hem, and also to become, to *beseem*, to be suitable, decent or *seemly*. This is certainly the G. *ziemen*; hence we see that *seam* and *seem* are radically the same word; It. *sembrare*, to seem; *sembiante*, like, similar, resembling; *rassembrare*, to resemble; Sp. *semejar*, to be like; Fr. *sembler*, to seem, to appear. These words seem to be of one family, having for their radical sense, to extend to, to meet, to unite, to come together, or to press together. If so, the Dutch *taamen* leads us to the oriental roots, Heb. Ch. Syr. דמה damah, to be like; Eth. አደመ adam, to please, to suit; Ar. أَدَمَ adama, to add, to unite, to agree, to suit, to conciliate, to confirm concord. Class Dm. No. 5 and 7. These verbs are radically one, and in these we find the primary sense of *Adam*; likeness, or form.]

1. To appear; to make or have a show or semblance.

Thou art not what thou *seem'st*. *Shak.*

All *seem'd* well pleas'd; all *seem'd*, but were not all. *Milton.*

2. To have the appearance of truth or fact; to be understood as true. It *seems* that the Turkish power is on the decline.

A prince of Italy, it *seems*, entertained his mistress on a great lake. *Addison.*

SEEM, *v. t.* To become; to befit. *Obs.* *Spenser.*

SEE'MER, *n.* One that carries an appearance or semblance.

Hence we shall see,
If pow'r change purpose, what our *seemers* be. *Shak.*

SEE'MING, *ppr.* Appearing; having the appearance or semblance, whether real or not.

2. *a.* Specious.

SEE'MING, *n.* Appearance; show; semblance.

2. Fair appearance.

These keep
Seeming and savor all the winter long. *Shak.*

3. Opinion or liking; favorable opinion.

Nothing more clear to their *seeming*. *Hooker.*

His persuasive words impregn'd
With reason to her *seeming*. *Obs.* *Milton.*

SEE'MINGLY, *adv.* In appearance; in show; in semblance.

This the father *seemingly* complied with. *Addison.*

They depend often on remote and *seemingly* disproportioned causes. *Atterbury.*

SEE'MINGNESS, *n.* Fair appearance; plausibility. *Digby.*

SEE'MLESS, *a.* Unseemly; unfit; indecorous. *Obs.* *Spenser.*

SEE'MLINESS, *n.* [from *seemly*.] Comeliness; grace; fitness; propriety; decency; decorum.

When *seemliness* combines with portliness. *Camden.*

SEE'MLY, *a.* [G. *ziemlich*; D. *taamelyk*; Dan. *sömmelig*.]

Becoming; fit; suited to the object, occasion, purpose or character; suitable.

Suspense of judgment and exercise of charity were safer and *seemlier* for christian men, than the hot pursuit of these controversies. *Hooker.*

Honor is not *seemly* for a fool. Prov. xxvi.

SEE'MLY, *adv.* In a decent or suitable manner. *Pope.*

SEE'MLYHED, *n.* [See *Head* and *Hood*.] Comely or decent appearance. *Obs.* *Chaucer.*

SEEN, *pp.* of *see*. Beheld; observed; understood.

2. *a.* Versed; skilled.

Noble Boyle, not less in nature *seen*— *Obs.* *Dryden.*

SEER, *n.* [from *see*.] One who sees; as a *seer* of visions. *Spectator.*

2. A prophet; a person who foresees future events. 1 Sam. ix.

SEER-WOOD. [See *Sear*, and *Sear-wood*, dry wood.]

SEE'-SAW, *n.* [Qu. *saw* and *saw*, or *sea* and *saw*.]

A vibratory or reciprocating motion. *Pope.*

SEE'-SAW, *v. i.* To move with a reciprocating motion; to move backward and forward, or upward and downward. *Arbuthnot.*

SEETHE, *v. t.* pret. *seethed*, *sod*; pp. *seethed*, *sodden*. [Sax. *seathan*, *seothan*, *sythan*; D. *zieden*; G. *sieden*; Sw. *siuda*; Dan. *syder*; Gr. ζεω, contracted from ζεθω; Heb. זוד to seethe, to boil, to swell, to be inflated. Class Sd. No. 4.]

To boil; to decoct or prepare for food in hot liquor; as, to *seethe* flesh.

Thou shalt not *seethe* a kid in its mother's milk. Ex. xxiii.

SEETHE, *v. i.* To be in a state of ebullition; to be hot. *Spenser.*

[*This word is rarely used in the common concerns of life.*]

SEE'THED, *pp.* Boiled; decocted.

SEE'THER, *n.* A boiler; a pot for boiling things. *Dryden.*

SEE'THING, *ppr.* Boiling; decocting.

SEG, *n.* Sedge. [*Not in use.*]

SEG'HOL, *n.* A Hebrew vowel-point, or short vowel, thus ∵, indicating the sound of the English *e*, in *men*. *M. Stuart.*

SEG'HOLATE, *a.* Marked with a seghol.

SEG'MENT, *n.* [Fr. from L. *segmentum*, from *seco*, to cut off. We observe here the Latin has *seg*, for *sec*, like the It. *segare*, Sp. *segar*, and like the Teutonic *sagen*, *zaagen*, to *saw*; properly, a piece cut off.]

1. In *geometry*, that part of the circle contained between a chord and an arch of that circle, or so much of the circle as is cut off by the chord. *Newton.*

2. In *general*, a part cut off or divided; as the *segments* of a calyx.

SEG'NITY, *n.* [from L. *segnis.*] Sluggishness; dullness; inactivity. [*Not used.*] *Dict.*

SEG'REGATE, *v. t.* [L. *segrego; se,* from, and *grex,* flock.]

To separate from others; to set apart. *Sherwood.*

SEG'REGATE, *a.* Select. [*Little used.*] *Wotton.*

Segregate polygamy, (*Polygamia segregata,* Linne,) a mode of inflorescence, when several florets comprehended within a common calyx, are furnished also with their proper perianths. *Martyn.*

SEG'REGATED, *pp.* Separated; parted from others.

SEG'REGATING, *ppr.* Separating.

SEGREGA'TION, *n.* [Fr.] Separation from others; a parting. *Shak.*

SEIGNEURIAL, *a.* *senu'rial.* [Fr. See *Seignior.*]

1. Pertaining to the lord of a manor; manorial.

2. Vested with large powers; independent. *Temple.*

SEIGNIOR, *n.* *see'nyor.* [Fr. *seigneur;* It. *signore;* Sp. *señor;* Port. *senhor;* from L. *senior,* elder; *senex,* old, Ir. *sean.*]

A lord; the lord of a manor; but used also in the south of Europe as a title of honor. The sultan of Turkey is called the *Grand Seignior.*

SEIGNIORAĠE, *n.* *see'nyorage.* A royal right or prerogative of the king of England, by which he claims an allowance of gold and silver brought in the mass to be exchanged for coin. *Encyc.*

SEIGNIO'RIAL, the same as *seigneurial.*

SEIGNIORIZE, *v. t.* *see'nyorize.* To lord it over. [*Little used.*] *Halifax.*

SEIGNIORY, *n.* *see'nyory.* [Fr. *seigneurie.*]

1. A lordship; a manor. *Davies. Encyc.*

2. The power or authority of a lord; dominion.

> O'Neal never had any *seignory* over that country, but what he got by encroachment upon the English. *Spenser.*

SEIN, *n.* [Sax. *segne;* Fr. *seine;* Arm. *seigne;* L. *sagena;* Gr. σαγηνη.]

A large net for catching fish. The *seins* used for taking shad in the Connecticut, sometimes sweep nearly the whole breadth of the river.

SE'INER, *n.* A fisher with a sein or net. [*Not much used.*] *Carew.*

SE'ITY, *n.* [L. *se,* one's self.] Something peculiar to a man's self. [*Not well authorized.*] *Tatler.*

SE'IZABLE, *a.* That may be seized; liable to be taken.

SEIZE, *v. t.* [Fr. *saisir;* Arm. *sesiza* or *sesya;* probably allied to *assess,* and to *sit, set.* The sense is to fall on, to throw one's self on, which is nearly the primary sense of *set.* It must be noticed that this word, in writers on law, is usually written *seise;* as also in composition, *disseise, disseisin, redisseise.* But except in law, it is usually or always written *seize.* It is desirable that the orthography should be uniform.]

1. To fall or rush upon suddenly and lay hold on; or to gripe or grasp suddenly. The tiger rushes from the thicket and *seizes* his prey. A dog *seizes* an animal by the throat. The hawk *seizes* a chicken with his claws. The officer *seizes* a thief.

2. To take possession by force, with or without right.

> At last they *seize*
> The scepter, and regard not David's son. *Milton.*

3. To invade suddenly; to take hold of; to come upon suddenly; as, a fever *seizes* the patient.

> And hope and doubt alternate *seize* her soul. *Pope.*

4. To take possession by virtue of a warrant or legal authority. The sherif *seized* the debtor's goods; the whole estate was *seized* and confiscated. We say, to *arrest* a person, to *seize* goods.

5. To fasten; to fix. In *seaman's language,* to fasten two ropes or different parts of one rope together with a cord. *Mar. Dict.*

To be seized of, to have possession; as a griffin *seized of* his prey. A B was *seized* and possessed *of* the manor of Dale. *Spenser.*

To seize on or *upon,* is to fall on and grasp; to take hold on; to take possession. Matt. xxi.

SE'IZED, *pp.* Suddenly caught or grasped; taken by force; invaded suddenly; taken possession of; fastened with a cord; having possession.

SE'IZER, *n.* One that seizes.

SE'IZIN, *n.* [Fr. *saisine.*] In *law,* possession. Seizin is of two sorts, seizin in *deed* or *fact,* and seizin in *law.* Seizin in *fact* or *deed,* is actual or corporal possession; seizin in *law,* is when something is done which the law accounts possession or seizin, as enrollment, or when lands descend to an heir, but he has not yet entered on them. In this case, the law considers the heir as *seized* of the estate, and the person who wrongfully enters on the land is accounted a *disseizor.* *Cowel. Encyc.*

2. The act of taking possession. [*Not used except in law.*]

3. The thing possessed; possession. *Hale.*

Livery of seizin. [See *Livery.*]

Primer seizin. [See *Primer.*]

SE'IZING, *ppr.* Falling on and grasping suddenly; laying hold on suddenly; taking possession by force, or taking by warrant; fastening.

SE'IZING, *n.* The act of taking or grasping suddenly.

2. In *seamen's language,* the operation of fastening together ropes with a cord; also, the cord or cords used for such fastening. *Mar. Dict.*

SE'IZOR, *n.* One who seizes. *Wheaton.*

SE'IZURE, *n.* The act of seizing; the act of laying hold on suddenly; as the *seizure* of a thief.

2. The act of taking possession by force; as the *seizure* of lands or goods: the *seizure* of a town by an enemy; the *seizure* of a throne by an usurper.

3. The act of taking by warrant; as the *seizure* of contraband goods.

4. The thing taken or seized. *Milton.*

5. Gripe; grasp; possession.

> And give me *seizure* of the mighty wealth. *Dryden.*

6. Catch; a catching.

> Let there be no sudden *seizure* of a lapsed syllable, to play upon it. *Watts.*

SE'JANT, *a.* In *heraldry,* sitting, like a cat with the fore feet straight; applied to a lion or other beast. *Encyc.*

SEJU'GOUS, *a.* [L. *sejugis; sex,* six, and *jugum,* yoke.]

In *botany,* a sejugous leaf is a pinnate leaf having six pairs of leaflets. *Martyn.*

SEJUNC'TION, *n.* [L. *sejunctio; se,* from, and *jungo,* to join.]

The act of disjoining; a disuniting; separation. [*Little used.*] *Pearson.*

SEJUNĠ'IBLE, *a.* [supra.] That may be disjoined. [*Little used.*] *Pearson.*

SEKE, for *sick,* obsolete. [See *Sick.*] *Chaucer.*

SEL'COUTH, *a.* [Sax. *sel, seld,* rare, and *couth,* known.]

Rarely known; unusual; uncommon. *Obs.* *Spenser.*

SEL'DOM, *adv.* [Sax. *selden, seldon;* D. *zelden;* G. *selten;* Dan. *selsom, seldsom;* Sw. *sållan, sållsam.* In Danish, *selskab,* [*sel* and *shape,*] is a company, fellowship, or club. *Sel* probably signifies separate, distinct, coinciding with L. *solus.*] Rarely; not often; not frequently.

> Wisdom and youth are *seldom* joined in one. *Hooker.*

SEL'DOM, *a.* Rare; unfrequent. [*Little used.*] *Milton.*

SEL'DOMNESS, *n.* Rareness; uncommonness; infrequency. *Hooker.*

SELD'SHOWN, *a.* [Sax. *seld* and *shown.*] Rarely shown or exhibited. [*Not in use.*] *Shak.*

SELECT', *v. t.* [L. *selectus,* from *seligo; se,* from, and *lego,* to pick, cull or gather.]

To choose and take from a number; to take by preference from among others; to pick out; to cull; as, to *select* the best authors for perusal; to *select* the most interesting and virtuous men for associates.

SELECT', *a.* Nicely chosen; taken from a number by preference; choice: whence, preferable; more valuable or excellent than others; as a body of *select* troops; a *select* company or society; a library consisting of *select* authors.

SELECT'ED, *pp.* Chosen and taken by preference from among a number; picked; culled.

SELECT'EDLY, *adv.* With care in selection. *Haywood.*

SELECT'ING, *ppr.* Choosing and taking from a number; picking out; culling.

SELEC'TION, *n.* [L. *selectio.*] The act of choosing and taking from among a number; a taking from a number by preference.

2. A number of things selected or taken from others by preference. I have a small but valuable *selection* of books.

SELECT'IVE, *a.* Selecting; tending to select. [*Unusual.*] *Fleming.*

SELECT'MAN, *n.* [*select* and *man.*] In *New England,* a town officer chosen annually to manage the concerns of the town, provide for the poor, &c. Their number is usually from three to seven in each town, and these constitute a kind of executive authority.

SELECT'NESS, *n.* The state of being select or well chosen.

SELEC'TOR, *n.* [L.] One that selects or chooses from among a number.

SELE'NIATE, *n.* A compound of selenic acid with a base.

SELEN'IC, *a.* Pertaining to selenium, or extracted from it; as *selenic* acid.

SEL'ENITE, *n.* [Gr. σεληνιτης, from σεληνη, the moon; so called on account of its reflecting the moon's light with brilliancy.]

Foliated or crystalized sulphate of lime. Selenite is a subspecies of sulphate of lime, of two varieties, massive and acicular. *Cleaveland. Kirwan. Nicholson.*

SELENIT'IC, SELENIT'ICAL, *a.* Pertaining to selenite; resembling it, or partaking of its nature and properties.

SELE'NIUM, *n.* [supra.] A new elementary body or substance, extracted from the pyrite of Fahlun in Sweden. It is of a gray dark brown color, with a brilliant metallic luster, and slightly translucent. It is doubted whether it ought to be classed with the metals. *Phillips. Ure.*

SELENIU'RET, SELENU'RET, *n.* A newly discovered mineral, of a shining lead gray color, with a granular texture. It is composed chiefly of selenium, silver and copper. *Cleaveland. Phillips.*

SELENOGRAPH'IC, SELENOGRAPH'ICAL, *a.* [infra.] Belonging to selenography.

SELENOG'RAPHY, *n.* [Gr. σεληνη, the moon, and γραφω, to describe.]

A description of the moon and its phenomena; a branch of cosmography. *Encyc.*

SELF, *a.* or *pron.* plu. *selves*; used chiefly in composition. [Sax. *self, sylf*; Goth. *silba*; Sw. *sielf*; Dan. *selv*; G. *selbst*; D. *zelf.* I know not the primary sense of this word; most probably it is to set or unite, or to separate from others. See *Selvedge.*]

1. In old authors, this word sometimes signifies particular, very, or same. "And on tham *sylfan* geare;" in that same year, that very year. *Sax. Chron.* A. D. 1052, 1061.

> Shoot another arrow that *self* way. *Shak.*
> On these *self* hills. *Raleigh.*
> At that *self* moment enters Palamon. *Dryden.*

In this sense, *self* is an adjective, and is now obsolete, except when followed by *same*; as on the *self-same* day; the *self-same* hour; the *self-same* thing; which is tautology. Matt. viii.

2. In present usage, *self* is united to certain personal pronouns and pronominal adjectives, to express emphasis or distinction; also when the pronoun is used reciprocally. Thus for emphasis, I *myself* will write; I will examine for *myself.* Thou *thyself* shalt go; thou shalt see for *thyself.* You *yourself* shall write; you shall see for *yourself.* He *himself* shall write; he shall examine for *himself.* She *herself* shall write; she shall examine for *herself.* The child *itself* shall be carried; it shall be present *itself.*

Reciprocally, I abhor *myself*; thou enrichest *thyself*; he loves *himself*; she admires *herself*; it pleases *itself*; we value *ourselves*; ye hurry *yourselves*; they see *themselves.* I did not hurt him, he hurt *himself*; he did not hurt me, I hurt *myself.*

Except when added to pronouns used reciprocally, *self* serves to give emphasis to the pronoun, or to render the distinction expressed by it more emphatical. "*I myself* will decide," not only expresses my determination to decide, but the determination that no other shall decide.

Himself, herself, themselves, are used in the nominative case, as well as in the objective.

> Jesus *himself* baptized not, but his disciples. John iv. See Matt. xxiii. 4.

3. *Self* is sometimes used as a noun, noting the individual subject to his own contemplation or action, or noting identity of person. Consciousness makes every one to be what he calls *self.*

> A man's *self* may be the worst fellow to converse with in the world. *Pope.*

4. It also signifies personal interest, or love of private interest; selfishness.

> The fondness we have for *self*—furnishes another long rank of prejudices. *Watts.*

Self is much used in composition.

SELF-ABA'SED, *a.* [*self* and *abase.*] Humbled by conscious guilt or shame.

SELF-ABA'SEMENT, *n.* Humiliation or abasement proceeding from consciousness of inferiority, guilt or shame. *Milner.*

SELF-ABA'SING, *a.* Humbling by the consciousness of guilt or by shame.

SELF-ABU'SE, *n.* [*self* and *abuse.*] The abuse of one's own person or powers. *Shak.*

SELF-ACCU'SING, *a.* [*self* and *accuse.*] Accusing one's self; as a *self-accusing* look. *Sidney.*

SELF-ACTIV'ITY, *n.* [*self* and *activity.*] Self-motion, or the power of moving one's self without foreign aid. *Bentley.*

SELF-ADMIRA'TION, *n.* Admiration of one's self. *Scott.*

SELF-ADMI'RING, *a.* Admiring one's self. *Scott.*

SELF-AFFA'IRS, *n. plu.* [*self* and *affair.*] One's own private business. *Shak.*

SELF-AFFRIGHTED, *a.* [*self* and *affright.*] Frightened at one's self. *Shak.*

SELF-APPLAUSE, *n. self-applauz'.* Applause of one's self.

SELF-APPRÖVING, *a.* That approves of one's own conduct. *Pope.*

SELF-ASSU'MED, *a.* Assumed by one's own act or without authority. *Mitford.*

SELF-BAN'ISHED, *a.* [*self* and *banish.*] Exiled voluntarily.

SELF-BEGOT'TEN, *a.* [*self* and *beget.*] Begotten by one's own powers.

SELF'-BORN, *a.* [*self* and *born.*] Born or produced by one's self.

SELF-CEN'TERED, *a.* [*self* and *center.*] Centered in itself.

> The earth *self-center'd* and unmov'd. *Dryden.*

SELF-CHAR'ITY, *n.* [*self* and *charity.*] Love of one's self. *Shak.*

SELF-COMMU'NICATIVE, *a.* [*self* and *communicative.*]

Imparted or communicated by its own powers. *Norris.*

SELF-CONCE'IT, *n.* [*self* and *conceit.*] A high opinion of one's self; vanity.

SELF-CONCE'ITED, *a.* Vain; having a high or overweening opinion of one's own person or merits. *L'Estrange.*

SELF-CONCE'ITEDNESS, *n.* Vanity; an overweening opinion of one's own person or accomplishments. *Locke.*

SELF-CON'FIDENCE, *n.* [*self* and *confidence.*]

Confidence in one's own judgment or ability; reliance on one's own opinion or powers, without other aid.

SELF-CON'FIDENT, *a.* Confident of one's own strength or powers; relying on the correctness of one's own judgment, or the competence of one's own powers, without other aid.

SELF-CONFI'DING, *a.* Confiding in one's own judgment or powers, without the aid of others. *Pope.*

SELF-CON'SCIOUS, *a.* [*self* and *conscious.*] Conscious in one's self. *Dryden.*

SELF-CON'SCIOUSNESS, *n.* Consciousness within one's self. *Locke.*

SELF-CONSID'ERING, *a.* [*self* and *consider.*]

Considering in one's own mind; deliberating. *Pope.*

SELF-CONSU'MING, *a.* [*self* and *consume.*] That consumes itself. *Pope.*

SELF-CONTRADIC'TION, *n.* [*self* and *contradiction.*]

The act of contradicting itself; repugnancy in terms. To be and not to be at the same time, is a *self-contradiction*; a proposition consisting of two members, one of which contradicts the other.

SELF-CONTRADICT'ORY, *a.* Contradicting itself. *Spectator.*

SELF-CONVICT'ED, *a.* [*self* and *convict.*] Convicted by one's own consciousness, knowledge or avowal.

SELF-CONVIC'TION, *n.* Conviction proceeding from one's own consciousness, knowledge or confession. *Swift.*

SELF-CREA'TED, *a.* Created by one's self; not formed or constituted by another. *Milner.*

SELF-DECE'IT, *n.* [*self* and *deceit.*] Deception respecting one's self, or that originates from one's own mistake; self-deception. *Spectator.*

SELF-DECE'IVED, *a.* [*self* and *deceive.*] Deceived or misled respecting one's self by one's own mistake or error.

SELF-DECE'IVING, *a.* Deceiving one's self.

SELF-DECEP'TION, *n.* [supra.] Deception concerning one's self, proceeding from one's own mistake.

SELF-DEFENSE, *n. self-defens'.* [*self* and *defense.*]

The act of defending one's own person, property or reputation. A man may be justifiable in killing another in *self-defense.*

SELF-DELU'SION, *n.* [*self* and *delusion.*] The delusion of one's self, or respecting one's self. *South.*

SELF-DENI'AL, *n.* [*self* and *denial.*] The denial of one's self; the forbearing to gratify one's own appetites or desires. *South.*

SELF-DENY'ING, *a.* Denying one's self; a forbearing to indulge one's own appetites or desires.

SELF-DEPEND'ENT, SELF-DEPEND'ING, *a.* Depending on one's self. *Scott.*

SELF-DESTRUC'TION, *n.* [*self* and *destruction.*]

The destruction of one's self; voluntary destruction.

SELF-DESTRUC'TIVE, *a.* Tending to the destruction of one's self.

SELF-DETERMINA'TION, *n.* [*self* and *determination.*]

Determination by one's own mind; or determination by its own powers, without extraneous impulse or influence.

SELF-DETERM'INING, *a.* Determining by or of itself; determining or deciding without extraneous power or influence; as the *self-determining* power of the will.

SELF-DEVO'TED, *a.* [*self* and *devote.*] Devoted in person, or voluntarily devoted in person.

SELF-DEVO'TEMENT, *n.* The devoting of one's person and services voluntarily to any difficult or hazardous employment. *Memoirs of Buchanan.*

SELF-DEVOUR'ING, *a.* [*self* and *devour.*] Devouring one's self or itself. *Denham.*

SELF-DIFFU'SIVE, *a.* [*self* and *diffusive.*] Having power to diffuse itself; that diffuses itself. *Norris.*

SELF-ENJOY'MENT, *n.* [*self* and *enjoyment.*] Internal satisfaction or pleasure.

SELF-ESTEE'M, *n.* [*self* and *esteem.*] The esteem or good opinion of one's self. *Milton.*

SELF-ESTIMA'TION, *n.* The esteem or good opinion of one's self. *Milner.*

SELF-EV'IDENCE, *n.* [*self* and *evidence.*] Evidence or certainty resulting from a proposition without proof; evidence that ideas offer to the mind upon bare statement. *Locke.*

SELF-EV'IDENT, *a.* Evident without proof or reasoning; that produces certainty or clear conviction upon a bare presentation to the mind; as a *self-evident* proposition or truth. That two and three make five, is *self-evident.*

SELF-EV'IDENTLY, *adv.* By means of self-evidence.

SELF-EXALTA'TION, *n.* The exaltation of one's self. *Scott.*

SELF-EXALT'ING, *a.* Exalting one's self.

SELF-EXAMINA'TION, *n.* [*self* and *examination.*]

An examination or scrutiny into one's own state, conduct and motives, particularly in regard to religious affections and duties. *South.*

SELF-EXCU'SING, *a.* Excusing one's self. *Scott.*

SELF-EXIST'ENCE, *n.* [*self* and *existence.*]

Inherent existence; the existence possessed by virtue of a being's own nature, and independent of any other being or cause; an attribute peculiar to God. *Blackmore.*

SELF-EXIST'ENT, *a.* Existing by its own nature or essence, independent of any other cause. God is the only *self-existent* being.

SELF-FLAT'TERING, *a.* [*self* and *flatter.*] Flattering one's self.

SELF-FLAT'TERY, *n.* Flattery of one's self.

SELF-GLO'RIOUS, *a.* [*self* and *glorious.*] Springing from vain glory or vanity; vain; boastful. *Dryden.*

SELF-H'ARMING, *a.* [*self* and *harm.*] Injuring or hurting one's self or itself. *Sharp.*

SELF'-HEAL, *n.* [*self* and *heal.*] A plant of the genus Sanicula, and another of the genus Prunella. *Fam. of Plants.*

SELF-HE'ALING, *a.* Having the power or property of healing itself. The *self-healing* power of living animals and vegetables is a property as wonderful as it is indicative of divine goodness.

SELF-HOM'ICIDE, *n.* [*self* and *homicide.*] The killing of one's self. *Hakewill.*

SELF-I'DOLIZED, *a.* Idolized by one's self. *Cowper.*

SELF-IMP'ARTING, *a.* [*self* and *impart.*] Imparting by its own powers and will. *Norris.*

SELF-IMPOS'TURE, *n.* [*self* and *imposture.*]

Imposture practiced on one's self. *South.*

SELF-IN'TEREST, *n.* [*self* and *interest.*] Private interest; the interest or advantage of one's self.

SELF-IN'TERESTED, *a.* Having self-interest; particularly concerned for one's self.

SELF-JUS'TIFIER, *n.* One who excuses or justifies himself. *J. M. Mason.*

SELF-KIN'DLED, *a.* [*self* and *kindle.*] Kindled of itself, or without extraneous aid or power. *Dryden.*

SELF-KNŎWING, *a.* [*self* and *know.*] Knowing of itself, or without communication from another.

SELF-KNOWL'EDGE, *n.* The knowledge of one's own real character, abilities, worth or demerit.

SELF-LŎVE, *n.* [*self* and *love.*] The love of one's own person or happiness.

> *Self-love,* the spring of motion, acts the soul. *Pope.*

SELF-LŎV'ING, *a.* Loving one's self. *Walton.*

SELF'-METAL, *n.* [*self* and *metal.*] The same metal.

SELF-MO'TION, *n.* [*self* and *motion.*] Motion given by inherent powers, without external impulse; spontaneous motion.

> Matter is not endued with *self-motion.* *Cheyne.*

SELF-MÖVED, *a.* [*self* and *move.*] Moved by inherent power without the aid of external impulse. *Pope.*

SELF-MÖVING, *a.* Moving or exciting to action by inherent power, without the impulse of another body or extraneous influence. *Pope.*

SELF-MUR'DER, *n.* [*self* and *murder.*] The murder of one's self; suicide.

SELF-MUR'DERER, *n.* One who voluntarily destroys his own life.

SELF-NEGLECT'ING, *n.* [*self* and *neglect.*] A neglecting of one's self.

> Self-love is not so great a sin as *self-neglecting.* *Shak.*

SELF-OPIN'ION, *n.* [*self* and *opinion.*] One's own opinion. *Collier. Prior.*

SELF-OPIN'IONED, *a.* Valuing one's own opinion highly.

SELF-PARTIAL'ITY, *n.* [*self* and *partiality.*]

That partiality by which a man overrates his own worth when compared with others. *Kames.*

SELF-PLE'ASING, *a.* [*self* and *please.*] Pleasing one's self; gratifying one's own wishes. *Bacon.*

SELF-PRAISE, *n.* [*self* and *praise.*] The praise of one's self; self-applause. *Broome.*

SELF-PREF'ERENCE, *n.* [*self* and *preference.*] The preference of one's self to others.

SELF-PRESERVA'TION, *n.* [*self* and *preservation.*]

The preservation of one's self from destruction or injury. *Milton.*

SELF-REPEL'LENCY, *n.* [*self* and *repellency.*]

The inherent power of repulsion in a body. *Black.*

SELF-REPEL'LING, *a.* [*self* and *repel.*] Repelling by its own inherent power.

SELF-REPRÖVED, *a.* [*self* and *reprove.*] Reproved by consciousness or one's own sense of guilt.

SELF-REPRÖVING, *a.* Reproving by consciousness.

SELF-REPRÖVING, *n.* The act of reproving by a conscious sense of guilt. *Shak.*

SELF-RESTRA'INED, *a.* [*self* and *restrain.*]

Restrained by itself, or by one's own power or will; not controlled by external force or authority. *Dryden.*

SELF-RESTRA'INING, *a.* Restraining or controlling itself.

SELF'-SAME, *a.* [*self* and *same.*] Numerically the same; the very same; identical. *Scripture.*

SELF'-SEEKING, *a.* [*self* and *seek.*] Seeking one's own interest or happiness; selfish. *Arbuthnot.*

SELF-SLAUGHTER, *n.* *self-slau'ter.* [*self* and *slaughter.*]

The slaughter of one's self. *Shak.*

SELF-SUBDU'ED, *a.* [*self* and *subdue.*] Subdued by one's own power or means. *Shak.*

SELF-SUBVERS'IVE, *a.* Overturning or subverting itself. *J. P. Smith.*

SELF-SUFFI''CIENCY, *n.* [*self* and *sufficiency.*]

An overweening opinion of one's own strength or worth; excessive confidence in one's own competence or sufficiency. *Dryden.*

SELF-SUFFI''CIENT, *a.* Having full confidence in one's own strength, abilities or endowments; whence, haughty; overbearing. *Watts.*

SELF-TORMENT'ER, *n.* One who torments himself.

SELF-TORMENT'ING, *a.* [*self* and *torment.*]

Tormenting one's self; as *self-tormenting* sin. *Crashaw.*

SELF-VAL'UING, *a.* Esteeming one's self. *Parnell.*

SELF-WILL', *n.* [*self* and *will.*] One's own will; obstinacy.

SELF-WILL'ED, *a.* Governed by one's own will; not yielding to the will or wishes of others; not accommodating or compliant; obstinate.

SELF-WRONG', *n.* [*self* and *wrong.*] Wrong done by a person to himself. *Shak.*

SELF'ISH, *a.* Regarding one's own interest chiefly or solely; influenced in actions by a view to private advantage. *Spectator.*

SELF'ISHLY, *adv.* In a selfish manner; with regard to private interest only or chiefly. *Pope.*

SELF'ISHNESS, *n.* The exclusive regard of a person to his own interest or happiness; or that supreme self-love or self-preference, which leads a person in his actions to direct his purposes to the advancement of his own interest, power or happiness, without regarding the interest of others. Selfishness, in its worst or unqualified sense, is the very essence of human depravity, and stands in direct opposition to *benevolence*, which is the essence of the divine character. As God is *love*, so man, in his natural state, is *selfishness.*

SELF'NESS, *n.* Self-love; selfishness. [*Not in use.*] *Sidney.*

SELL, for *self*; and *sells* for *selves.* [Scot.] *B. Jonson.*

SELL, *n.* [Fr. *selle*; L. *sella.*] A saddle, and a throne. *Obs.* *Spenser.*

SELL, *v. t.* pret. and pp. *sold.* [Sax. *selan*, *sellan*, *sylan* or *syllan*, to give, grant, yield, assign or *sell*; *syllan to bote*, to give in compensation, to *give to boot*; Sw. *sälia*; Ice. *selia*; Dan. *sælger*; Basque, *saldu.* The primary sense is to deliver, send or transfer, or to put off. The sense of *sell*, as we now understand the word, is wholly derivative; as we see by the Saxon phrases, *syllan to agenne*, to give for one's own; *syllan to gyfe*, to bestow for a gift, to bestow or confer gratis.]

1. To transfer property or the exclusive right of possession to another for an equivalent in money. It is correlative to *buy*, as one party *buys* what the other *sells.* It is distinguished from *exchange* or *barter*, in which one commodity is given for another; whereas in *selling* the consideration is money, or its representative in current notes. To this distinction there may be exceptions. "Esau *sold* his birthright to Jacob for a mess of pottage." But this is unusual. "Let us *sell* Joseph to the Ishmaelites—And they *sold* him for twenty pieces of silver." Gen. xxxvii.

Among the Hebrews, parents had power to *sell* their children.

2. To betray; to deliver or surrender for money or a reward; as, to *sell* one's country.

3. To yield or give for a consideration. The troops fought like lions, and *sold* their lives dearly; that is, they yielded their lives, but first destroyed many, which made it a dear purchase for their enemies.

4. In *Scripture*, to give up to be harassed and made slaves.

He *sold* them into the hands of their enemies. Judg. ii.

5. To part with; to renounce or forsake.

Buy the truth and *sell* it not. Prov. xxiii.

To sell one's self to do evil, to give up one's self to be the slave of sin, and to work wickedness without restraint. 1 Kings xxi. 2 Kings vii.

SELL, *v. i.* To have commerce; to practice selling. *Shak.*

2. To be sold. Corn *sells* at a good price.

SEL'LANDER, *n.* A dry scab in a horse's hough or pastern. *Ainsworth.*

SELL'ER, *n.* The person that sells; a vender.

SELL'ING, *ppr.* Transferring the property of a thing for a price or equivalent in money.

2. Betraying for money.

SELV'EDGE, *n.* [D. *zelf-kant*, self-border; G. *sahl-leiste*, hall-list. The first syllable appears to be *self*, and the last is *edge.*] The edge of cloth, where it is closed by complicating the threads; a woven border, or border of close work. Ex. xxvii.

SELV'EDGED, *a.* Having a selvedge.

SELVES, *plu.* of *self.*

SEM'BLABLE, *a.* [Fr.] Like; similar; resembling. [*Not in use.*] *Shak.*

SEM'BLABLY, *adv.* In like manner. [*Not in use.*] *Shak.*

SEM'BLANCE, *n.* [Fr. *id.*; It. *sembianza*; Sp. *semeja* and *semejanza*; from the root of *similar.*]

1. Likeness; resemblance; actual similitude; as the *semblance* of worth; *semblance* of virtue.

The *semblances* and imitations of shells. *Woodward.*

2. Appearance; show; figure; form.

Their *semblance* kind, and mild their gestures were. *Fairfax.*

SEM'BLANT, *n.* Show; figure; resemblance. [*Not in use.*] *Spenser.*

SEM'BLANT, *a.* Like; resembling. [*Not in use.*] *Prior.*

SEM'BLATIVE, *a.* Resembling; fit; suitable; according to.

And all is *semblative* a woman's part. *Shak.* [*Not in use.*]

SEM'BLE, *v. t.* [Fr. *sembler.*] To imitate; to represent or to make similar.

Where *sembling* art may carve the fair effect. [*Not in use.*] *Prior.*

SEM'I, L. *semi*, Gr. ημι, in composition, signifies half.

SEMI-ACID'IFIED, *a.* or *pp.* Half acidified. [See *Acidify.*]

SEMI-AMPLEX'ICAUL, *a.* [L. *semi*, *amplexus*, or *amplector*, to embrace, and *caulis*, stem.]

In *botany*, embracing the stem half way, as a leaf. *Martyn.*

SEMI-AN'NUAL, *a.* [*semi* and *annual.*] Half yearly.

SEMI-AN'NUALLY, *adv.* Every half year.

SEMI-AN'NULAR, *a.* [L. *semi* and *annulus*, a ring.]

Having the figure of a half circle; that is, half round. *Grew.*

SEMI-AP'ERTURE, *n.* [*semi* and *aperture.*] The half of an aperture.

SEMI-A'RIAN, *n.* [See *Arian.*] In *ecclesiastical history*, the Semi-arians were a branch of the Arians, who in appearance condemned the errors of Arius, but acquiesced in some of his principles, disguising them under more moderate terms. They did not acknowledge the Son to be consubstantial with the Father, that is, of the same substance, but admitted him to be of a like substance with the Father, not by nature, but by a peculiar privilege. *Encyc.*

SEMI-A'RIAN, *a.* Pertaining to semi-arianism.

SEMI-A'RIANISM, *n.* The doctrines or tenets of the Semi-arians. The *semi-arianism* of modern times consists in maintaining the Son to have been from all eternity begotten by the will of the Father. *Encyc.*

SEMI-BARBA'RIAN, *a.* [*semi* and *barbarian.*] Half savage; partially civilized. *Milford.*

SEM'IBREVE, *n.* [*semi* and *breve*; formerly written *semibref.*]

In *music*, a note of half the duration or time of the breve. It is now the measure note by which all others are regulated. It contains the time of two minims, four crotchets, eight quavers, sixteen semiquavers and thirty two demisemiquavers.

SEMI-CAL'CINED, *a.* [*semi* and *calcine.*] Half calcined; as *semi-calcined* iron. *Kirwan.*

SEMI-CAS'TRATE, *v. t.* To deprive of one testicle.

SEMI-CASTRA'TION, *n.* Half castration; deprivation of one testicle. *Brown.*

SEM'ICIRCLE, *n.* [*semi* and *circle.*] The half of a circle; the part of a circle comprehended between its diameter and half of its circumference. *Encyc.*

2. Any body in the form of a half circle.

SEM'ICIRCLED, SEMICIR'CULAR, *a.* Having the form of a half circle. [*Semicircular* is generally used.] *Addison.*

SEM'ICOLON, *n.* [*semi* and *colon.*] In *grammar* and *punctuation*, the point [;] the mark of a pause to be observed in reading or speaking, of less duration than the colon, double the duration of the comma, or half the duration of the period. It is used to distinguish the conjunct members of a sentence. *Encyc.*

SEMI-COLUM'NAR, *a.* [*semi* and *columnar.*]

Like a half column; flat on one side and round on the other; a term of botany, applied to a stem, leaf or petiole. *Martyn.*

SEMI-COM'PACT, *a.* [*semi* and *compact.*] Half compact; imperfectly indurated. *Kirwan.*

SEMI-CRUSTA'CEOUS, *a.* [*semi* and *crustaceous.*] Half crustaceous. *Nat. Hist.*

SEMI-CYLIN'DRIC, SEMI-CYLIN'DRICAL, *a.* [*semi* and *cylindric.*] Half cylindrical. *Lee.*

SEMI-DEIS'TICAL, *a.* Half deistical; bordering on deism. *S. Miller.*

SEMI-DIAM'ETER, *n.* [*semi* and *diameter.*]

Half the diameter; a right line or the length of a right line drawn from the center of a circle or sphere to its circumference or periphery; a radius. *Encyc.*

SEMI-DIAPA'SON, *n.* [*semi* and *diapason.*] In *music*, an imperfect octave, or an octave diminished by a lesser semitone. *Encyc.*

SEMI-DIAPEN'TE, *n.* An imperfect fifth; a hemi-diapente. *Busby.*

SEMI-DIAPHANE'ITY, *n.* [See *Semidiaphanous.*]

Half or imperfect transparency. [*Little used.*] *Boyle.*

[Instead of this, *translucency* is now used.]

SEMI-DIAPH'ANOUS, *a.* [*semi* and *diaphanous.*] Half or imperfectly transparent. *Woodward.*

[Instead of this, *translucent* is now used.]

SEMI-DIATES'SARON, *n.* [*semi* and *diatessaron.*]

In *music*, an imperfect or defective fourth.

SEM'I-DITONE, *n.* [*semi* and It. *ditono.*] In *music*, a lesser third, having its terms as 6 to 5; a hemi-ditone. *Encyc.*

SEM'I-DOUBLE, *n.* [*semi* and *double.*] In *the Romish breviary*, an office or feast celebrated with less solemnity than the double ones, but with more than the single ones. *Bailey.*

SEM'IFLORET, *n.* [*semi* and *floret.*] A half floret, which is tubulous at the beginning, like a floret, and afterwards expanded in the form of a tongue. *Bailey.*

SEMIFLOS'CULOUS, *a.* [*semi* and L. *flosculus*, a little flower. *Semifloscular* is also used, but is less analogical.]

Composed of semiflorets; ligulate; as a *semiflosculous* flower. *Martyn.*

SEMI-FLU'ID, *a.* [*semi* and *fluid.*] Imperfectly fluid. *Arbuthnot.*

SEM'I-FORMED, *a.* [*semi* and *formed.*] Half formed; imperfectly formed; as *semiformed* crystals. *Edwards, W. Indies.*

SEMI-IN'DURATED, *a.* [*semi* and *indurated.*] Imperfectly indurated or hardened.

SEMI-LAPID'IFIED, *a.* [*semi* and *lapidified.*] Imperfectly changed into stone. *Kirwan.*

SEMI-LENTIC'ULAR, *a.* [*semi* and *lenticular.*]

Half lenticular or convex; imperfectly resembling a lens. *Kirwan.*

SEMILU'NAR, **SEMILU'NARY**, *a.* [Fr. *semilunaire*; L. *semi* and *luna*, moon.] Resembling in form a half moon. *Grew.*

SEM'I-METAL, *n.* [*semi* and *metal.*] An imperfect metal, or rather a metal that is not malleable, as bismuth, arsenic, nickel, cobalt, zink, antimony, manganese, tungsten, molybden, and uranite. The name however is usually given to the regulus of these substances. *Nicholson.*

SEMI-METAL'LIC, *a.* Pertaining to a semi-metal, or partaking of its nature and qualities. *Kirwan.*

SEM'INAL, *a.* [Fr. from L. *seminalis*, from *semen*, seed; from the root of *sow.*]

1. Pertaining to seed, or to the elements of production.

2. Contained in seed; radical; rudimental; original; as *seminal* principles of generation; *seminal* virtue. *Glanville. Swift.*

Seminal leaf, the same as seed-leaf.

SEM'INAL, *n.* Seminal state. *Brown.*

SEMINAL'ITY, *n.* The nature of seed; or the power of being produced. *Brown.*

SEM'INARIST, *n.* [from *seminary.*] A Romish priest educated in a seminary. *Sheldon.*

SEM'INARY, *n.* [Fr. *seminaire*; L. *seminarium*, from *semen*, seed; *semino*, to sow.]

1. A seed-plat; ground where seed is sown for producing plants for transplantation; a nursery; as, to transplant trees from a *seminary.* *Mortimer.*

[In this sense, the word is not used in America; being superseded by *nursery.*]

2. The place or original stock whence any thing is brought.

This stratum, being the *seminary* or promptuary, furnishing matter for the formation of animal and vegetable bodies— *Woodward.*

[*Not in use.*]

3. Seminal state. [*Not in use.*] *Brown.*

4. Source of propagation. *Harvey.*

5. A place of education; any school, academy, college or university, in which young persons are instructed in the several branches of learning which may qualify them for their future employments. [*This is the only signification of the word in the United States, at least as far as my knowledge extends.*]

6. A Romish priest educated in a seminary; a seminarist. *B. Jonson.*

SEM'INARY, *a.* Seminal; belonging to seed. *Smith.*

SEM'INATE, *v. t.* [L. *semino.*] To sow; to spread; to propagate. *Waterhouse.*

SEMINA'TION, *n.* [L. *seminatio.*] The act of sowing. *Wotton.*

2. In *botany*, the natural dispersion of seeds. *Martyn.*

SEM'INED, *a.* Thick covered, as with seeds. *Obs.* *B. Jonson.*

SEMINIF'EROUS, *a.* [L. *semen*, seed, and *fero*, to produce.]

Seed-bearing; producing seed. *Darwin.*

SEMINIF'IC, **SEMINIF'ICAL**, *a.* [L. *semen*, seed, and *facio*, to make.]

Forming or producing seed. *Brown.*

SEMINIFICA'TION, *n.* Propagation from the seed or seminal parts. *Hale.*

SEMI-OPA'KE, **SEMI-OPA'COUS**, *a.* [L. *semi* and *opacus.*] Half transparent only. *Boyle.*

SEM'I-OPAL, *n.* A variety of opal. *Jameson.*

SEMI-ORBIC'ULAR, *a.* [*semi* and *orbicular.*]

Having the shape of a half orb or sphere. *Martyn.*

SEMI-OR'DINATE, *n.* [*semi* and *ordinate.*] In *conic sections*, a line drawn at right angles to and bisected by the axis, and reaching from one side of the section to the other; the half of which is properly the semi-ordinate, but is now called the ordinate.

SEMI-OS'SEOUS, *a.* [*semi* and *osseous.*] Half as hard as bone. *Med. and Phys. Journal.*

SEMI-O'VATE, *a.* [*semi* and *ovate.*] Half egg-shaped. *Lee.*

SEMI-OX'YGENATED, *a.* Half saturated with oxygen. *Kirwan.*

SEMI-PAL'MATE, **SEMI-PAL'MATED**, *a.* [*semi* and *palmate.*] Half palmated or webbed. *Nat. Hist.*

SEM'IPED, *n.* [*semi* and L. *pes*, a foot.] A half foot in poetry.

SEMIPE'DAL, *a.* Containing a half foot.

SEMI-PELA'GIAN, *n.* In *ecclesiastical history*, the Semi-pelagians are persons who retain some tincture of the doctrines of Pelagius. See *Pelagianism.* They hold that God has not by predestination dispensed his grace to one more than to another; that Christ died for all men; that the grace purchased by Christ and necessary to salvation, is offered to all men; that man, before he receives grace, is capable of faith and holy desires; and that man being born free, is capable of accepting grace, or of resisting its influences. *Encyc.*

SEMI-PELA'GIAN, *a.* Pertaining to the Semi-pelagians, or their tenets.

SEMI-PELA'GIANISM, *n.* The doctrines or tenets of the Semi-pelagians, supra.

SEMI-PELLU'CID, *a.* [*semi* and *pellucid.*] Half clear, or imperfectly transparent; as a *semi-pellucid* gem. *Woodward.*

SEMI-PELLUCID'ITY, *n.* The quality or state of being imperfectly transparent.

SEMI-PERSPIC'UOUS, *a.* [*semi* and *perspicuous.*]

Half transparent; imperfectly clear. *Grew.*

SEMI-PHLOGIS'TICATED, *a.* [*semi* and *phlogisticated.*] Partially impregnated with phlogiston.

SEMI-PRIMIG'ENOUS, *a.* [*semi* and *primigenous.*]

In *geology*, of a middle nature between substances of primary and secondary formation. *Kirwan.*

SEM'I-PROOF, *n.* [*semi* and *proof.*] Half proof; evidence from the testimony of a single witness. [*Little used.*] *Bailey.*

SEMI-PRO'TOLITE, *n.* [*semi* and Gr. πρωτος, first, and λιθος, stone.]

A species of fossil of a middle nature between substances of primary and those of secondary formation. *Kirwan.*

SEMI-QUAD'RATE, **SEMI-QUAR'TILE**, *n.* [L. *semi* and *quadratus*, or *quartus*, fourth.]

An aspect of the planets, when distant from each other the half of a quadrant, or forty five degrees, one sign and a half. *Bailey.*

SEM'IQUAVER, *n.* [*semi* and *quaver.*] In *music*, a note of half the duration of the quaver; the sixteenth of the semibreve.

SEM'IQUAVER, *v. t.* To sound or sing in semiquavers. *Cowper.*

SEMI-QUIN'TILE, *n.* [L. *semi* and *quintilis.*]

An aspect of the planets, when distant from each other half of the quintile, or thirty six degrees. *Bailey.*

SEMI-SAV'AGE, *a.* [*semi* and *savage.*] Half savage; half barbarian.

SEMI-SAV'AGE, *n.* One who is half savage or imperfectly civilized. *J. Barlow.*

SEMI-SEX'TILE, *n.* [*semi* and *sextile.*] An aspect of the planets, when they are distant from each other the twelfth part of a circle, or thirty degrees. *Bailey.*

SEMI-SPHER'IC, **SEMI-SPHER'ICAL**, *a.* [*semi* and *spherical.*] Having the figure of a half sphere. *Kirwan.*

SEMI-SPHEROID'AL, *a.* [*semi* and *spheroidal.*] Formed like a half spheroid.

SEMITER'TIAN, *a.* [*semi* and *tertian.*] Compounded of a tertian and quotidian ague.

SEMITER'TIAN, *n.* An intermittent compounded of a tertian and a quotidian. *Bailey.*

SEM'ITONE, *n.* [*semi* and *tone.*] In *music*, half a tone; an interval of sound, as between *mi* and *fa* in the diatonic scale, which is only half the distance of the interval between *ut* and *re*, or *sol* and *la.* It is the smallest interval admitted in modern music. *Encyc. Busby.*

SEMITON'IC, *a.* Pertaining to a semitone; consisting of a semitone.

SEMI-TRAN'SEPT, *n.* [*semi* and *transept*; L. *trans* and *septum.*] The half of a transept or cross aisle.

SEMI-TRANSPA'RENT, *a.* [*semi* and *transparent.*] Half or imperfectly transparent.

SEMI-TRANSPA'RENCY, *n.* Imperfect transparency; partial opakeness.

SEMI-VIT'REOUS, *a.* Partially vitreous. *Bigelow.*

SEMI-VITRIFICA'TION, *n.* [*semi* and *vitrification.*] The state of being imperfectly vitrified.

2. A substance imperfectly vitrified.

SEMI-VIT'RIFIED, *a.* [See *Vitrify.*] Half or imperfectly vitrified; partially converted into glass.

SEM'I-VOCAL, *a.* [*semi* and *vocal.*] Pertaining to a semi-vowel; half vocal; imperfectly sounding.

SEM'I-VOWEL, *n.* [*semi* and *vowel.*] In *grammar*, a half vowel, or an articulation which is accompanied with an imperfect sound. Thus *el, em, en*, though uttered with close organs, do not wholly interrupt the sound; and they are called *semi-vowels.*

SEMPERVI'RENT, *a.* [L. *semper*, always, and *virens*, flourishing.]
Always fresh; evergreen. *Lee.*

SEM'PERVIVE, *n.* [L. *semper*, always, and *vivus*, alive.] A plant. *Bacon.*

SEMPITERN'AL, *a.* [Fr. *sempiternel*; L. *sempiternus*; *semper*, always, and *eternus*, eternal.]

1. Eternal in futurity; everlasting; endless; having beginning, but no end.

2. Eternal; everlasting. *Blackmore.*

SEMPITERN'ITY, *n.* [L. *sempiternitas.*] Future duration without end. *Hale.*

SEM'STER, *n.* A seamster; a man who uses a needle. [*Not in use.*]

SEN, *adv.* This word is used by some of our common people for *since.* It seems to be a contraction of *since*, or it is the Sw. *sen*, Dan. *seen*, slow, late.

SEN'ARY, *a.* [L. *seni*, *senarius.*] Of six; belonging to six; containing six.

SEN'ATE, *n.* [Fr. *senat*; It. *senato*; Sp. *senado*; L. *senatus*, from *senex*, old, Ir. *sean*, W. *hen*; Ar. سَنَّ sanna, or سَنَة sanah, to be advanced in years. Under the former verb is the Arabic word signifying a tooth, showing that this is only a dialectical variation of the Heb. שנן. The primary sense is to extend, to advance or to wear. A senate was originally a council of elders.]

1. An assembly or council of senators; a body of the principal inhabitants of a city or state, invested with a share in the government. The *senate* of ancient Rome was one of the most illustrious bodies of men that ever bore this name. Some of the Swiss cantons have a *senate*, either legislative or executive.

2. In *the United States*, senate denotes the higher branch or house of a legislature. Such is the *senate* of the United States, or upper house of the congress; and in most of the states, the higher and least numerous branch of the legislature, is called the *senate.* In the U. States, the *senate* is an elective body.

3. In a looser sense, any legislative or deliberative body of men; as the eloquence of the *senate.*

SEN'ATE-HOUSE, *n.* A house in which a senate meets, or a place of public council. *Shak.*

SEN'ATOR, *n.* A member of a senate. In Rome one of the qualifications of a *senator* was the possession of property to the amount of 80,000 sesterces, about £7000 sterling, or thirty thousand dollars. In Scotland, the lords of session are called *senators* of the college of justice.

2. A counselor; a judge or magistrate. Ps. cv.

SENATO'RIAL, *a.* Pertaining to a senate; becoming a senator; as *senatorial* robes; *senatorial* eloquence.

2. Entitled to elect a senator; as a *senatorial* district. *U. States.*

SENATO'RIALLY, *adv.* In the manner of a senate; with dignity or solemnity.

SEN'ATORSHIP, *n.* The office or dignity of a senator. *Carew.*

SEND, *v. t.* pret. and pp. *sent.* [Sax. *sendan*; Goth. *sandyan*; D. *zenden*; G. *senden*; Sw. *sända*; Dan. *sender.*]

1. In *a general sense*, to throw, cast or thrust; to impel or drive by force to a distance, either with the hand or with an instrument or by other means. We *send* a ball with the hand or with a bat; a bow *sends* an arrow; a cannon *sends* a shot; a trumpet *sends* the voice much farther than the unassisted organs of speech.

2. To cause to be conveyed or transmitted; as, to *send* letters or dispatches from one country to another.

3. To cause to go or pass from place to place; as, to *send* a messenger from London to Madrid.

4. To commission, authorize or direct to go and act.

> I have not *sent* these prophets, yet they ran. Jer. xxiii.

5. To cause to come or fall; to bestow.

> He *sendeth* rain on the just and on the unjust. Matt. v.

6. To cause to come or fall; to inflict.

> The Lord shall *send* upon thee cursing, vexation and rebuke. Deut. xxviii.
>
> If I *send* pestilence among my people. 2 Chron. vii.

7. To propagate; to diffuse.

> Cherubic songs by night from neighb'ring hills
> Aerial music *send.* *Milton.*

To send away, to dismiss; to cause to depart.

To send forth or *out*, to produce; to put or bring forth; as, a tree *sends forth* branches.

2. To emit; as, flowers *send forth* their fragrance. James iii.

SEND, *v. i.* To dispatch an agent or messenger for some purpose.

> See ye how this son of a murderer hath *sent* to take away my head? 2 Kings vi.

So we say, we *sent* to invite guests; we *sent* to inquire into the facts.

To send for, to request or require by message to come or be brought; as, to *send for* a physician; to *send for* a coach. But these expressions are elliptical.

SEN'DAL, *n.* [Sp. *cendal.*] A light thin stuff of silk or thread. [*Not in use.*] *Chaucer.*

SEND'ER, *n.* One that sends. *Shak.*

SEN'EGA, SEN'EKA, *n.* A plant called rattlesnake root, of the genus Polygala.

SENES'CENCE, *n.* [L. *senesco*, from *senex*, old. See *Senate.*]
The state of growing old; decay by time. *Woodward.*

SEN'ESCHAL, *n.* [Fr. *sénéchal*; It. *siniscalco*; Sp. *senescal*; G. *seneschall.* The origin and signification of the first part of the word are not ascertained. The latter part is the Teutonic *schalk* or *scealc*, a servant, as in *marshal.*]
A steward; an officer in the houses of princes and dignitaries, who has the superintendance of feasts and domestic ceremonies. In some instances, the seneschal is an officer who has the dispensing of justice, as the high seneschal of England, &c. *Encyc.*

SEN'GREEN, *n.* A plant, the houseleek, of the genus Sempervivum. *Fam. of Plants.*

SE'NILE, *a.* [L. *senilis.*] Pertaining to old age; proceeding from age. *Boyle.*

SENIL'ITY, *n.* Old age. [*Not much used.*] *Boswell.*

SENIOR, *a.* see'nyor. [L. *senior*, comp. of *senex*, old. See *Senate.*]
Elder or older; but as an adjective, it usually signifies older in office; as the *senior* pastor of a church, where there are colleagues; a *senior* counselor. In such use, *senior* has no reference to age, for a *senior* counselor may be, and often is the younger man.

SENIOR, *n.* see'nyor. A person who is older than another; one more advanced in life.

2. One that is older in office, or one whose first entrance upon an office was anterior to that of another. Thus a senator or counselor of sixty years of age, often has a *senior* who is not fifty years of age.

3. An aged person; one of the oldest inhabitants.

> A *senior* of the place replies. *Dryden.*

SENIOR'ITY, *n.* Eldership; superior age; priority of birth. He is the elder brother, and entitled to the place by *seniority.*

2. Priority in office; as the *seniority* of a pastor or counselor.

SEN'NA, *n.* [Pers. Ar. سَنَا sana. Qu. from Ch. Syr. סנן, to strain, purge, purify. The common pronunciation, *seena*, is incorrect.]
The leaf of the *cassia senna*, a native of the east, used as a cathartic.

SENNIGHT, *n.* sen'nit. [contracted from *sevennight*, as *fortnight* from *fourteennight.*]
The space of seven nights and days; a week. The court will be held this day *sennight*, that is, a week from this day; or the court will be held next Tuesday *sennight*, a week from next Tuesday.

SENOC'ULAR, *a.* [L. *seni*, six, and *oculus*, the eye.] Having six eyes.

> Most animals are binocular, spiders octonocular, and some *senocular.* *Derham.*

SENS'ATED, *a.* [See *Sense.*] Perceived by the senses. [*Not used.*] *Hooke.*

SENSA'TION, *n.* [Fr.; It. *sensazione*; Sp. *sensacion*; from L. *sensus*, *sentio*, to perceive. See *Sense.*]
The perception of external objects by means of the senses. *Encyc.*
Sensation is an exertion or change of the central parts of the sensorium, or of the whole of it, beginning at some of those extreme parts of it which reside in the muscles or organs of sense. The secretion of tears in grief is caused by the *sensation* of pain. Efforts of the will are frequently accom-

panied by painful or pleasurable *sensations.* *Darwin.*

SENSE, *n. sens.* [Fr. *sens;* It. *senso;* Sp. *sentido;* from L. *sensus,* from *sentio,* to feel or perceive; W. *syniaw,* id.; *syn,* sense, feeling, perception; G. *sinn,* sense, mind, intention; D. *zin;* Sw. *sinne;* Dan. *sind, sands.*]

1. The faculty of the soul by which it perceives external objects by means of impressions made on certain organs of the body. *Encyc.*

Sense is a branch of perception. The five *senses* of animals are *sight, hearing, touch, smell* and *taste.*

2. Sensation; perception by the senses. *Bacon.*

3. Perception by the intellect; apprehension; discernment.

This Basilius, having the quick *sense* of a lover— *Sidney.*

4. Sensibility; quickness or acuteness of perception. *Shak.*

5. Understanding; soundness of faculties; strength of natural reason.

Oppress nature sleeps;
This rest might yet have balm'd thy broken *senses.* *Shak.*

6. Reason; reasonable or rational meaning.

He raves; his words are loose
As heaps of sand, and scattering wide from *sense.* *Dryden.*

7. Opinion; notion; judgment.

I speak my private but impartial *sense*
With freedom. *Roscommon.*

8. Consciousness; conviction; as a due *sense* of our weakness or sinfulness.

9. Moral perception.

Some are so hardened in wickedness, as to have no *sense* of the most friendly offices. *L'Estrange.*

10. Meaning; import; signification; as the true *sense* of words or phrases. In interpretation, we are to examine whether words are to be understood in a literal or figurative *sense.* So we speak of a legal *sense,* a grammatical *sense,* an historical *sense, &c.*

Common sense, that power of the mind which, by a kind of instinct, or a short process of reasoning, perceives truth, the relation of things, cause and effect, &c. and hence enables the possessor to discern what is right, useful, expedient or proper, and adopt the best means to accomplish his purpose. This power seems to be the gift of nature, improved by experience and observation.

Moral sense, a determination of the mind to be pleased with the contemplation of those affections, actions or characters of rational agents, which are called good or virtuous. *Encyc.*

SENS'ED, *pp.* Perceived by the senses. [*Not in use.*] *Glanville.*

SENSEFUL, *a. sens'ful.* Reasonable; judicious. [*Not in use.*] *Norris.*

SENSELESS, *a. sens'less.* Wanting the faculty of perception. The body when dead is *senseless;* but a limb or other part of the body may be *senseless,* when the rest of the body enjoys its usual sensibility.

2. Unfeeling; wanting sympathy.

The *senseless* grave feels not your pious sorrows. *Rowe.*

3. Unreasonable; foolish; stupid.

They would repent this their *senseless* perverseness, when it would be too late. *Clarendon.*

4. Unreasonable; stupid; acting without sense or judgment.

They were a *senseless* stupid race. *Swift.*

5. Contrary to reason or sound judgment; as, to destroy by a *senseless* fondness the happiness of children.

6. Wanting knowledge; unconscious; with *of;* as libertines, *senseless of* any charm in love. *Southern.*

7. Wanting sensibility or quick perception. *Peacham.*

SENSELESSLY, *adv. sens'lessly.* In a senseless manner; stupidly; unreasonably; as a man *senselessly* arrogant. *Locke.*

SENSELESSNESS, *n. sens'lessness.* Unreasonableness; folly; stupidity; absurdity. *Grew.*

SENSIBIL'ITY, *n.* [Fr. *sensibilité;* from *sensible.*]

1. Susceptibility of impressions; the capacity of feeling or perceiving the impressions of external objects; *applied to animal bodies;* as when we say, a frozen limb has lost its *sensibility.*

2. Acuteness of sensation; *applied to the body.*

3. Capacity or acuteness of perception; that quality of the soul which renders it susceptible of impressions; delicacy of feeling; as *sensibility* to pleasure or pain; *sensibility* to shame or praise; exquisite *sensibility.*

4. Actual feeling.

This adds greatly to my *sensibility.* *Burke.*

[This word is often used in this manner for *sensation.*]

5. It is sometimes used in the plural.

His *sensibilities* seem rather to have been those of patriotism, than of wounded pride. *Marshall.*

Sensibilities unfriendly to happiness, may be acquired. *Encyc*

6. Nice perception, so to speak, of a balance; that quality of a balance which renders it movable with the smallest weight, or the quality or state of any instrument that renders it easily affected; as the *sensibility* of a balance or of a thermometer. *Lavoisier.*

SENS'IBLE, *a.* [Fr. Sp. *id.;* It. *sensibile.*]

1. Having the capacity of receiving impressions from external objects; capable of perceiving by the instrumentality of the proper organs. We say, the body or the flesh is *sensible,* when it feels the impulse of an external body. It may be more or less *sensible.* *Darwin.*

2. Perceptible by the senses. The light of the moon furnishes no *sensible* heat.

Air is *sensible* to the touch by its motion. *Arbuthnot.*

3. Perceptible or perceived by the mind.

The disgrace was more *sensible* than the pain. *Temple.*

4. Perceiving or having perception, either by the mind or the senses.

A man cannot think at any time, waking or sleeping, without being *sensible* of it. *Locke.*

5. Having moral perception; capable of being affected by moral good or evil.

If thou wert *sensible* of courtesy,
I should not make so great a show of zeal. *Shak.*

6. Having acute intellectual feeling; being easily or strongly affected; as, to be *sensible* of wrong. *Dryden.*

7. Perceiving so clearly as to be convinced; satisfied; persuaded. *Boswell.*

They are now *sensible* it would have been better to comply, than to refuse. *Addison.*

8. Intelligent; discerning; as a *sensible* man.

9. Moved by a very small weight or impulse; as, a *sensible* balance is necessary to ascertain exact weight. *Lavoisier.*

10. Affected by a slight degree of heat or cold; as a *sensible* thermometer. *Thomson.*

11. Containing good sense or sound reason.

He addressed Claudius in the following *sensible* and noble speech. *Henry.*

Sensible note, in music, that which constitutes a third major above the dominant, and a semitone beneath the tonic. *Encyc.*

SENS'IBLE, *n.* Sensation; also, whatever may be perceived. [*Little used.*]

SENS'IBLENESS, *n.* Possibility of being perceived by the senses; as the *sensibleness* of odor or sound.

2. Actual perception by the mind or body; as the *sensibleness* of an impression on the organs. [But qu.]

3. Sensibility; quickness or acuteness of perception; as the *sensibleness* of the eye. *Sharp.*

4. Susceptibility; capacity of being strongly affected, or actual feeling; consciousness; as the *sensibleness* of the soul and sorrow for sin. *Hammond.*

5. Intelligence; reasonableness; good sense.

6. Susceptibility of slight impressions. [See *Sensible,* No. 9, 10.]

SENS'IBLY, *adv.* In a manner to be perceived by the senses; perceptibly to the senses; as pain *sensibly* increased; motion *sensibly* accelerated.

2. With perception, either of mind or body. He feels his loss very *sensibly.*

3. Externally; by affecting the senses. *Hooker.*

4. With quick intellectual perception.

5. With intelligence or good sense; judiciously. The man converses very *sensibly* on all common topics.

SENS'ITIVE, *a.* [It. Sp. *sensitivo;* Fr. *sensitif;* L. *sensitivus,* from *sensus, sentio.*]

1. Having sense or feeling, or having the capacity of perceiving impressions from external objects; as *sensitive* soul; *sensitive* appetite; *sensitive* faculty. *Ray. Dryden.*

2. That affects the senses; as *sensitive* objects. *Hammond.*

3. Pertaining to the senses, or to sensation; depending on sensation; as *sensitive* motions; *sensitive* muscular motions excited by irritation. *Darwin.*

SENS'ITIVELY, *adv.* In a sensitive manner. *Hammond.*

SENS'ITIVE-PLANT, *n.* A plant of the genus Mimosa [mimic,] so called from the sensibility of its leaves and footstalks, which shrink, contract and fall on being slightly touched. *Encyc.*

SENSO'RIAL, *a.* Pertaining to the sensory or sensorium; as *sensorial* faculties; *sensorial* motions or powers. *Darwin.*

SENSO'RIUM, } *n.* [from L. *sensus, sentio,*]
SENS'ORY, } The seat of sense; the brain and nerves. Darwin uses sensorium

to express not only the medullary part of the brain, spinal marrow, nerves, organs of sense and of the muscles, but also that living principle or spirit of animation which resides throughout the body, without being cognizable to our senses, except by its effects. The changes which occasionally take place in the sensorium, as during exertions of volition, or the sensations of pleasure and pain, he terms *sensorial motions.*

2. Organ of sense; as double *sensories*, two eyes, two ears, &c. *Bentley.*

SENSUAL, *a.* [It. *sensuale;* Sp. *sensual;* Fr. *sensuel;* from L. *sensus.*]

1. Pertaining to the senses, as distinct from the mind or soul.

Far as creation's ample range extends,
The scale of *sensual*, mental pow'rs ascends. *Pope.*

2. Consisting in sense, or depending on it; as *sensual* appetites, hunger, lust, &c.
3. Affecting the senses, or derived from them; as *sensual* pleasure or gratification. Hence,
4. In *theology*, carnal; pertaining to the flesh or body, in opposition to the spirit; not spiritual or holy; evil. James iii. Jude 19.
5. Devoted to the gratification of sense; given to the indulgence of the appetites; lewd; luxurious.

No small part of virtue consists in abstaining from that in which *sensual* men place their felicity. *Atterbury.*

SENSU'ALIST, *n.* A person given to the indulgence of the appetites or senses; one who places his chief happiness in carnal pleasures. *South.*

SENSUAL'ITY, *n.* [It. *sensualità;* Sp. *sensualidad;* Fr. *sensualité.*]

Devotedness to the gratification of the bodily appetites; free indulgence in carnal or sensual pleasures.

Those pamper'd animals
That rage in savage *sensuality.* *Shak.*

They avoid dress, lest they should have affections tainted by any *sensuality.* *Addison.*

SENS'UALIZE, *v. t.* To make sensual; to subject to the love of sensual pleasure; to debase by carnal gratifications; as *sensualized* by pleasure. *Pope.*

By the neglect of prayer, the thoughts are *sensualized.* *T. H. Skinner.*

SENS'UALLY, *adv.* In a sensual manner.

SENS'UOUS, *a.* [from *sense.*] Tender; pathetic. [*Not in use.*] *Milton.*

SENT, *pret.* and *pp.* of *send.*

SEN'TENCE, *n.* [Fr.; It. *sentenza;* Sp. *sentencia;* from L. *sententia*, from *sentio*, to think.]

1. In *law*, a judgment pronounced by a court or judge upon a criminal; a judicial decision publicly and officially declared in a criminal prosecution. In *technical language*, sentence is used only for the declaration of judgment against one convicted of a crime. In civil cases, the decision of a court is called a judgment. In criminal cases, *sentence* is a judgment pronounced; doom.
2. In *language not technical*, a determination or decision given, particularly a decision that condemns, or an unfavorable determination.

Let him set out some of Luther's works, that by them we may pass *sentence* upon his doctrines. *Atterbury.*

3. An opinion; judgment concerning a controverted point. Acts xv.
4. A maxim; an axiom; a short saying containing moral instruction. *Broome.*
5. Vindication of one's innocence. Ps. xvii.
6. In *grammar*, a period; a number of words containing complete sense or a sentiment, and followed by a full pause. Sentences are simple or compound. A simple sentence consists of one subject and one finite verb; as, "the Lord reigns." A compound sentence contains two or more subjects and finite verbs, as in this verse,

He fills, he bounds, connects and equals all. *Pope.*

A dark sentence, a saying not easily explained. Dan. viii.

SEN'TENCE, *v. t.* To pass or pronounce the judgment of a court on; to doom; as, to *sentence* a convict to death, to transportation, or to imprisonment.

2. To condemn; to doom to punishment.

Nature herself is *sentenc'd* in your doom. *Dryden.*

SENTEN'TIAL, *a.* Comprising sentences. *Newcome.*

2. Pertaining to a sentence or full period; as a *sentential* pause. *Sheridan.*

SENTEN'TIOUS, *a.* [Fr. *sententieux;* It. *sentenzioso.*]

1. Abounding with sentences, axioms and maxims; short and energetic; as a *sententious* style or discourse; *sententious* truth. *Waller.*

How he apes his sire,
Ambitiously *sententious.* *Addison.*

2. Comprising sentences; as *sententious* marks. *Grew.*

[This should be *sentential.*]

SENTEN'TIOUSLY, *adv.* In short expressive periods; with striking brevity.

Nausicaa delivers her judgment *sententiously*, to give it more weight. *Broome.*

SENTEN'TIOUSNESS, *n.* Pithiness of sentences; brevity with strength.

The Medea I esteem for its gravity and *sententiousness.* *Dryden.*

Sentery, and *sentry*, are corrupted from *sentinel.*

SENTIENT, *a. sen'shent.* [L. *sentiens*, *sentio.*]

That perceives; having the faculty of perception. Man is a *sentient* being; he possesses a *sentient* principle.

SEN'TIENT, *n.* A being or person that has the faculty of perception.

2. He that perceives. *Glanville.*

SEN'TIMENT, *n.* [Fr. *id.;* It. *sentimento;* Sp. *sentimiento;* from L. *sentio*, to feel, perceive or think.]

1. *Properly*, a thought prompted by passion or feeling. *Kames.*
2. In *a popular sense*, thought; opinion; notion; judgment; the decision of the mind formed by deliberation or reasoning. Thus in deliberative bodies, every man has the privilege of delivering his *sentiments* upon questions, motions and bills.
3. The sense, thought or opinion contained in words, but considered as distinct from them. We may like the *sentiment*, when we dislike the language.
4. Sensibility; feeling. *Sheridan.*

SENTIMENT'AL, *a.* Abounding with sentiment, or just opinions or reflections; as a *sentimental* discourse.

2. Expressing quick intellectual feeling.
3. Affecting sensibility; *in a contemptuous sense.* *Sheridan.*

SENTIMENT'ALIST, *n.* One that affects sentiment, fine feeling or exquisite sensibility.

SENTIMENTAL'ITY, *n.* Affectation of fine feeling or exquisite sensibility. *Warton.*

SENT'INEL, *n.* [Fr. *sentinelle;* It. Port. *sentinella;* Sp. *centinela;* from L. *sentio*, to perceive.]

In *military affairs*, a soldier set to watch or guard an army, camp or other place from surprise, to observe the approach of danger and give notice of it. In popular use, the word is contracted into *sentry.*

SEN'TRY, *n.* [See *Sentinel.*]

2. Guard; watch; the duty of a sentinel.

O'er my slumbers *sentry* keep. *Brown.*

SEN'TRY-BOX, *n.* A box to cover a sentinel at his post, and shelter him from the weather.

SE'PAL, *n.* [from L. *sepio.*] In *botany*, the small leaf or part of a calyx. *Necker. Decandolle.*

SEPARABIL'ITY, *n.* [from *separable.*] The quality of being separable, or of admitting separation or disunion.

Separability is the greatest argument of real distinction. *Glanville.*

SEP'ARABLE, *a.* [Fr. from L. *separabilis.* See *Separate.*]

That may be separated, disjoined, disunited or rent; as the *separable* parts of plants; qualities not *separable* from the substance in which they exist.

SEP'ARABLENESS, *n.* The quality of being capable of separation or disunion.

Trials permit me not to doubt of the *separableness* of a yellow tincture from gold. *Boyle.*

SEP'ARATE, *v. t.* [L. *separo;* Fr. *separer;* It. *separare;* Sp. *separar;* Russ. *razberayu.* The Latin word is compounded of *se*, a prefix, and *paro*, evidently coinciding with the oriental ברא or ברר, the sense of which is to throw or drive off. Class Br. No. 7. 8. 9. 10. See *Pare* and *Parry.*]

1. To disunite; to divide; to sever; to part, in almost any manner, either things naturally or casually joined. The parts of a solid substance may be *separated* by breaking, cutting or splitting, or by fusion, decomposition or natural dissolution. A compound body may be *separated* into its constituent parts. Friends may be *separated* by necessity, and must be *separated* by death. The prism *separates* the several kinds of colored rays. A riddle *separates* the chaff from the grain.
2. To set apart from a number for a particular service.

Separate me Barnabas and Saul. Acts xiii.

3. To disconnect; as, to *separate* man and wife by divorce.
4. To make a space between. The Atlantic *separates* Europe from America. A narrow strait *separates* Europe from Africa.

To separate one's self, to withdraw; to depart.

Separate thyself, I pray thee, from me. Gen. xiii.

SEP'ARATE, *v. i.* To part; to be disunited; to be disconnected; to withdraw from each other. The parties *separated*, and each retired.

2. To cleave; to open; as, the parts of a substance *separate* by drying or freezing.

SEP'ARATE, *a.* [L. *separatus.*] Divided from the rest; being parted from another; disjoined; disconnected; *used of things that have been united or connected.* Gen. xlix. 2 Cor. vi.

2. Unconnected; not united; distinct; *used of things that have not been connected.*

Christ was holy, harmless, undefiled, and *separate* from sinners. Heb. vii.

3. Disunited from the body; as a *separate* spirit; the *separate* state of souls. *Locke.*

SEP'ARATED, *pp.* Divided; parted; disunited; disconnected.

SEP'ARATELY, *adv.* In a separate or unconnected state; apart; distinctly; singly. The opinions of the council were *separately* taken.

SEP'ARATENESS, *n.* The state of being separate.

SEP'ARATING, *ppr.* Dividing; disjoining; putting or driving asunder; disconnecting; decomposing.

SEPARA'TION, *n.* [Fr. from L. *separatio*; It. *separazione*; Sp. *separacion.*]

1. The act of separating, severing or disconnecting; disjunction; as the *separation* of the soul from the body.

2. The state of being separate; disunion; disconnection.

All the days of his *separation* he is holy to the Lord. Num. vi.

3. The operation of disuniting or decomposing substances; chemical analysis. *Bacon.*

4. Divorce; disunion of married persons. *Shak.*

SEP'ARATIST, *n.* [Fr. *séparatiste.*] One that withdraws from a church, or rather from an established church, to which he has belonged; a dissenter; a seceder; a schismatic; a sectary. *Bacon.*

SEP'ARATOR, *n.* One that divides or disjoins; a divider.

SEP'ARATORY, *a.* That separates; as *separatory* ducts. [*Little used.*] *Cheyne.*

SEP'ARATORY, *n.* A chimical vessel for separating liquors; and a surgical instrument for separating the pericranium from the cranium. *Parr.*

SEPAWN', **SEPON'**, *n.* A species of food consisting of meal of maiz boiled in water. It is in New York and Pennsylvania what hasty-pudding is in New England.

SEP'IMENT, *n.* [L. *sepimentum*, from *sepio*, to inclose.]

A hedge; a fence; something that separates or defends.

SEPO'SE, *v. t.* *sepo'ze.* [L. *sepono, sepositus.*] To set apart. [*Not in use.*] *Donne.*

SEPOSI''TION, *n.* The act of setting apart; segregation. [*Not in use.*] *Taylor.*

SE'POY, *n.* A native of India, employed as a soldier in the service of European powers.

SEPS, *n.* [L. from Gr. σηπω. Cuvier.] A species of venomous eft or lizard. *Dict. Nat. Hist.*

A genus of lizards, the efts, closely resembling the serpents, from which they scarcely differ, except in their short and often indistinct feet and the marks of an external auditory orifice. *Ed. Encyc.*

SEPT, *n.* [Qu. *sapia*, in the L. *prosapia*; or Heb. שבט. See Class Sb. No. 23.]

A clan, race or family, proceeding from a common progenitor; used of the races or families in Ireland. *Spenser. Davies.*

SEPTAN'GULAR, *a.* [L. *septem*, seven, and *angulus*, angle.] Having seven angles or sides.

SEPTA'RIA, *n.* [L. *septa*, partitions.] A name given to nodules or spheroidal masses of calcarious marl, whose interior presents numerous fissures or seams of some crystalized substance, which divide the mass. *Cleaveland.*

SEPTEM'BER, *n.* [L. from *septem*, seven; Fr. *septembre*; It. *settembre*; Sp. *septiembre.*]

The seventh month from March, which was formerly the first month of the year. September is now the ninth month of the year.

SEPTEM'PARTITE, *a.* Divided into seven parts. *Journ. of Science.*

SEP'TENARY, *a.* [Fr. *septénaire*; It. *settenario*; Sp. *septenario*; L. *septenarius*, from *septem*, seven.]

Consisting of seven; as a *septenary* number. *Watts.*

SEP'TENARY, *n.* The number seven. *Burnet.*

SEPTEN'NIAL, *a.* [L. *septennis*; *septem*, seven, and *annus*, year.]

1. Lasting or continuing seven years; as *septennial* parliaments.

2. Happening or returning once in every seven years; as *septennial* elections in England.

SEPTEN'TRION, *n.* [Fr. from L. *septentrio.*] The north or northern regions. *Shak.*

SEPTEN'TRION, **SEPTEN'TRIONAL**, *a.* [L. *septentrionalis.*] Northern; pertaining to the north.

—From cold *septentrion* blasts. *Milton.*

SEPTENTRIONAL'ITY, *n.* Northerliness. [*A bad word.*]

SEPTEN'TRIONALLY, *adv.* Northerly; towards the north. [*A bad word.*] *Brown.*

SEPTEN'TRIONATE, *v. i.* To tend northerly. *Brown.*

[This word *septentrion* and its derivatives are hardly anglicized; they are harsh, unnecessary and little used, and may well be suffered to pass into disuse.]

SEPT'FOIL, *n.* [L. *septem* and *folium*; seven leafed.] A plant of the genus Tormentilla.

SEP'TIC, **SEP'TICAL**, *a.* [Gr. σηπτικος, from σηπω, to putrefy.] Having power to promote putrefaction. Many experiments were made by Sir John Pringle to ascertain the *septic* and *antiseptic* virtues of natural bodies *Encyc.*

2. Proceeding from or generated by putrefaction; as *septic* acid. *S. L. Mitchill.*

SEP'TIC, *n.* A substance that promotes the putrefaction of bodies. *Encyc.*

SEPTIC'ITY, *n.* Tendency to putrefaction. *Fourcroy.*

SEPTILAT'ERAL, *a.* [L. *septem*, seven, and *latus*, side.] Having seven sides; as a *septilateral* figure. *Brown.*

SEPTIN'SULAR, *a.* [L. *septem*, seven, and *insula*, isle.]

Consisting of seven isles; as the *septinsular* republic of the Ionian isles. *Quart. Rev.*

SEPTUAG'ENARY, *a.* [Fr. *septuagénaire*; L. *septuagenarius*, from *septuaginta*, seventy.] Consisting of seventy. *Brown.*

SEPTUAG'ENARY, *n.* A person seventy years of age.

SEPTUAGES'IMA, *n.* [L. *septuagesimus*, seventieth.]

The third Sunday before Lent, or before Quadragesima Sunday, supposed to be so called because it is about seventy days before Easter. *Encyc.*

SEPTUAGES'IMAL, *a.* [supra.] Consisting of seventy.

Our abridged and *septuagesimal* age. *Brown.*

SEP'TUAGINT, *n.* [L. *septuaginta*, seventy; *septem*, seven, and some word signifying ten.]

A Greek version of the Old Testament, so called because it was the work of *seventy*, or rather of seventy two interpreters. This translation from the Hebrew is supposed to have been made in the reign and by the order of Ptolemy Philadelphus, king of Egypt, about two hundred and seventy or eighty years before the birth of Christ. *Encyc.*

SEP'TUAGINT, *a.* Pertaining to the Septuagint; contained in the Greek copy of the Old Testament.

The *Septuagint* chronology makes fifteen hundred years more from the creation to Abraham, than the present Hebrew copies of the Bible. *Encyc.*

SEP'TUARY, *n.* [L. *septem*, seven.] Something composed of seven; a week. [*Little used.*] *Ash. Cole.*

SEP'TUPLE, *a.* [Low L. *septuplex*; *septem*, seven, and *plico*, to fold.] Seven fold; seven times as much.

SEP'ULCHER, *n.* [Fr. *sepulchre*; Sp. Port. *sepulcro*; It. *sepolcro*; from L. *sepulchrum*, from *sepelio*, to bury, which seems to be formed with a prefix on the Goth. *filhan*, to bury.]

A grave; a tomb; the place in which the dead body of a human being is interred, or a place destined for that purpose. Among the Jews, *sepulchers* were often excavations in rocks. Is. xxii. Matt. xxvii.

SEP'ULCHER, *v. t.* To bury; to inter; to entomb; as obscurely *sepulchered.* *Prior.*

SEPUL'CHRAL, *a.* [L. *sepulchralis*, from *sepulchrum.*]

Pertaining to burial, to the grave, or to monuments erected to the memory of the dead; as a *sepulchral* stone; a *sepulchral* statue; a *sepulchral* inscription. *Milton.*

SEP'ULTURE, *n.* [Fr. from L. *sepultura*, from *sepelio.*]

Burial; interment; the act of depositing the dead body of a human being in the grave.

Where we may royal *sepulture* prepare. *Dryden.*

SEQUA'CIOUS, *a.* [L. *sequax*, from *sequor*, to follow. See *Seek.*] Following; attendant.

Trees uprooted left their place,
Sequacious of the lyre. *Dryden.*

The fond *sequacious* herd. *Thomson.*

2. Ductile; pliant.

The forge was easy, and the matter ductile and *sequacious.* [*Little used.*] *Ray.*

SEQUA'CIOUSNESS, *n.* State of being sequacious; disposition to follow. *Taylor.*

SEQUAC'ITY, *n.* [supra.] A following, or disposition to follow.

2. Ductility; pliableness. [*Little used.*] *Bacon.*

SE'QUEL, *n.* [Fr. *séquelle;* L. It. Sp. *sequela;* from L. *sequor*, to follow.]

1. That which follows; a succeeding part; as the *sequel* of a man's adventures or history.

2. Consequence; event. Let the sun or moon cease, fail or swerve, and the *sequel* would be ruin. *Hooker.*

3. Consequence inferred; consequentialness. [*Little used.*] *Whitgifte.*

SE'QUENCE, *n.* [Fr. from L. *sequens, sequor;* It. *seguenza.*]

1. A following, or that which follows; a consequent. *Brown.*

2. Order of succession.

How art thou a king
But by fair *sequence* and succession? *Shak.*

3. Series; arrangement; method. *Bacon.*

4. In *music*, a regular alternate succession of similar chords. *Busby.*

SE'QUENT, *a.* [supra.] Following; succeeding. *Shak.*

2. Consequential. [*Little used.*]

SE'QUENT, *n.* A follower. [*Not in use.*] *Shak.*

SEQUES'TER, *v. t.* [Fr. *séquestrer;* It. *sequestrare;* Sp. *sequestrar;* Low L. *sequestro*, to sever or separate, to put into the hands of an indifferent person, as a deposit; *sequester*, belonging to mediation or umpirage, and as a noun, an umpire, referee, mediator. This word is probably a compound of *se* and the root of *quæstus, quæsitus*, sought. See *Question.*]

1. To separate from the owner for a time; to seize or take possession of some property which belongs to another, and hold it till the profits have paid the demand for which it is taken.

Formerly the goods of a defendant in chancery, were, in the last resort, *sequestered* and detained to enforce the decrees of the court. And now the profits of a benefice are *sequestered* to pay the debts of ecclesiastics. *Blackstone.*

2. To take from parties in controversy and put into the possession of an indifferent person. *Encyc.*

3. To put aside; to remove; to separate from other things.

I had wholly *sequestered* my civil affairs. *Bacon.*

4. To *sequester one's self*, to separate one's self from society; to withdraw or retire; to seclude one's self for the sake of privacy or solitude; as, to *sequester one's self* from action. *Hooker.*

5. To cause to retire or withdraw into obscurity.

It was his taylor and his cook, his fine fashions and his French ragouts which *sequestered* him. *South.*

SEQUES'TER, *v. i.* To decline, as a widow, any concern with the estate of a husband.

SEQUES'TERED, *pp.* Seized and detained for a time, to satisfy a demand; separated; also, being in retirement; secluded; private; as a *sequestered* situation.

SEQUES'TRABLE, *a.* That may be sequestered or separated; subject or liable to sequestration.

SEQUES'TRATE, *v. t.* To sequester. [It is less used than *sequester*, but exactly synonymous.]

SEQUESTRA'TION, *n.* The act of taking a thing from parties contending for it, and entrusting it to an indifferent person. *Encyc.*

2. In *the civil law*, the act of the ordinary, disposing of the goods and chattels of one deceased, whose estate no one will meddle with. *Encyc.*

3. The act of taking property from the owner for a time, till the rents, issues and profits satisfy a demand.

4. The act of seizing the estate of a delinquent for the use of the state.

5. Separation; retirement; seclusion from society. *South.*

6. State of being separated or set aside. *Shak.*

7. Disunion; disjunction. [*Not in use.*] *Boyle.*

SEQUESTRA'TOR, *n.* One that sequesters property, or takes the possession of it for a time, to satisfy a demand out of its rents or profits. *Taylor.*

2. One to whom the keeping of sequestered property is committed. *Bailey.*

SE'QUIN, *n.* A gold coin of Venice and Turkey, of different value in different places. At Venice, its value is about 9s. 2d. sterling, or $2,04. In other parts of Italy, it is stated to be of 9s. value, or $2. It is sometimes written *chequin* and *zechin.* [See *Zechin.*]

SERAGLIO, *n.* *seral'yo.* [Fr. *sérail;* Sp. *serrallo;* It. *serraglio*, from *serrare*, to shut or make fast, Fr. *serrer;* perhaps from יצר or צרר. Castle deduces the word from the Persian سراي sarai, serai, a great house, a palace. The Portuguese write the word *cerralho*, and Fr. *serrer*, to lock, they write *cerrar*, as do the Spaniards.]

The palace of the Grand Seignior or Turkish sultan, or the palace of a prince. The seraglio of the sultan is a long range of buildings inhabited by the Grand Seignior and all the officers and dependents of his court; and in it is transacted all the business of government. In this also are confined the females of the harem. *Eton.*

SER'APH, *n.* plu. *seraphs;* but sometimes the Hebrew plural, *seraphim*, is used. [from Heb. שרף, to burn.] An angel of the highest order.

As full, as perfect in vile man that mourns,
As the rapt *seraph* that adores and burns. *Pope.*

SERAPH'IC, SERAPH'ICAL, *a.* Pertaining to a seraph; angelic; sublime; as *seraphic* purity; *seraphic* fervor.

2. Pure; refined from sensuality. *Swift.*

3. Burning or inflamed with love or zeal. Thus St. Bonaventure was called the *seraphic* doctor. *Encyc.*

SER'APHIM, *n.* [the Hebrew plural of *seraph.*]

Angels of the highest order in the celestial hierarchy. *Com. Prayer.*

[It is sometimes improperly written *seraphims.*]

SERAS'KIER, *n.* A Turkish general or commander of land forces.

SERASS', *n.* A fowl of the East Indies, of the crane kind. *Dict. Nat. Hist.*

SERE, *a.* Dry; withered; usually written *sear*, which see.

SERE, *n.* [Qu. Fr. *serrer*, to lock or make fast.] A claw or talon. [*Not in use.*] *Chapman.*

SERENA'DE, *n.* [Fr. from It. Sp. *serenata*, from L. *serenus*, clear, serene.]

1. Properly, music performed in a clear night; hence, an entertainment of music given in the night by a lover to his mistress under her window. It consists generally of instrumental music, but that of the voice is sometimes added. The songs composed for these occasions are also called *serenades.* *Encyc.*

2. Music performed in the streets during the stillness of the night; as a midnight *serenade.* *Addison.*

SERENA'DE, *v. t.* To entertain with nocturnal music. *Spectator.*

SERENA'DE, *v. i.* To perform nocturnal music. *Tatler.*

SERENA GUTTA. [See *Gutta Serena.*]

SERENA'TA, *n.* A vocal piece of music on an amorous subject. *Busby.*

SERE'NE, *a.* [Fr. *serein;* It. Sp. *sereno;* L. *serenus;* Russ. *ozariayu.* Heb. Ch. Syr. Ar. זהר to shine. Class Sr. No. 2. 23. 47.]

1. Clear or fair, and calm; as a *serene* sky; *serene* air. *Serene* imports great purity.

2. Bright.

The moon, *serene* in glory, mounts the sky. *Pope.*

3. Calm; unruffled; undisturbed; as a *serene* aspect; a *serene* soul. *Milton.*

4. A title given to several princes and magistrates in Europe; as *serene* highness; most *serene.*

SERE'NE, *n.* A cold damp evening. [*Not in use.*] *B. Jonson.*

SERE'NE, *v. t.* To make clear and calm; to quiet.

2. To clear; to brighten. *Philips.*

SERE'NELY, *adv.* Calmly; quietly.

The setting sun now shone *serenely* bright. *Pope.*

2. With unruffled temper; coolly. *Prior.*

SERE'NENESS, *n.* The state of being serene; serenity.

SEREN'ITUDE, *n.* Calmness. [*Not in use.*] *Wotton.*

SEREN'ITY, *n.* [Fr. *serenité;* L. *serenitas.*]

1. Clearness and calmness; as the *serenity* of the air or sky.

2. Calmness; quietness; stillness; peace.

A general peace and *serenity* newly succeeded general trouble. *Temple.*

3. Calmness of mind; evenness of temper; undisturbed state; coolness.

I cannot see how any men should transgress those moral rules with confidence and *serenity.* *Locke.*

4. A title of respect. *Milton.*

SERF, *n.* [Fr. *serf*; L. *servus*. See *Serve*.] A servant or slave employed in husbandry, and in some countries, attached to the soil and transferred with it. The *serfs* in Poland are slaves. *Coxe.*

SERĠE, *n.* [Fr. *serge*; Sp. *xerga*, coarse freeze, and jargon; It. *sargia*, a coverlet; D. *sergie*.]

A woolen quilted stuff manufactured in a loom with four treddles, after the manner of ratteens. *Encyc.*

SERĠEANT, *n.* *s'arjent.* [Fr. *sergent*; It. *sergente*; Sp. Port. *sargento*; from L. *serviens*, serving, for so was this word written in Latin. But Castle deduces the word from the Persian سرجنك sarchank or sarjank, a prefect, a subaltern military officer. See Cast. Col. 336. If this is correct, two different words are blended.]

1. Formerly, an officer in England, nearly answering to the more modern bailif of the hundred; also, an officer whose duty was to attend on the king, and on the lord high steward in court, to arrest traitors and other offenders. This officer is now called *serjeant at arms*, or *mace*. There are at present other officers of an inferior kind, who attend mayors and magistrates to execute their orders.

2. In *military affairs*, a non-commissioned officer in a company of infantry or troop of dragoons, armed with a halbert, whose duty is to see discipline observed, to order and form the ranks, &c.

3. In *England*, a lawyer of the highest rank, and answering to the doctor of the civil law. *Blackstone.*

4. A title sometimes given to the king's servants; as *sergeant surgeon*, servant surgeon. *Johnson.*

SERĠEANTRY, *n.* *s'arjentry.* In England, sergeantry is of two kinds; *grand sergeantry*, and *petit sergeantry*. *Grand sergeantry*, is a particular kind of knight service, a tenure by which the tenant was bound to do some special honorary service to the king in person, as to carry his banner, his sword or the like, or to be his butler, his champion or other officer at his coronation, to lead his host, to be his marshal, to blow a horn when an enemy approaches, &c. *Cowel. Blackstone.*

Petit sergeantry, was a tenure by which the tenant was bound to render to the king annually some small implement of war, as a bow, a pair of spurs, a sword, a lance, or the like. *Littleton.*

SERĠEANTSHIP, *n.* *s'argentship.* The office of a sergeant.

SERĠE-MAKER, *n.* A manufacturer of serges.

SERI''CEOUS, *a.* [L. *sericus*, from *sericum*, silk.]

Pertaining to silk; consisting of silk; silky. In *botany*, covered with very soft hairs pressed close to the surface; as a *sericeous* leaf. *Martyn.*

SE'RIES, *n.* [L. This word belongs probably to the Shemitic שר, שור, ישר, the primary sense of which is to stretch or strain.]

1. A continued succession of things in the same order, and bearing the same relation to each other; as a *series* of kings; a *series* of successors.

2. Sequence; order; course; succession of things; as a *series* of calamitous events.

3. In *natural history*, an order or subdivision of some class of natural bodies. *Encyc.*

4. In *arithmetic* and *algebra*, a number of terms in succession, increasing or diminishing in a certain ratio; as arithmetical *series* and geometrical *series*. [See *Progression*.]

SER'IN, *n.* A song bird of Italy and Germany.

SE'RIOUS, *a.* [Fr. *serieux*; Sp. *serio*; It. *serio, serioso*; L. *serius*.]

1. Grave in manner or disposition; solemn; not light, gay or volatile; as a *serious* man; a *serious* habit or disposition.

2. Really intending what is said; being in earnest; not jesting or making a false pretense. Are you *serious*, or in jest?

3. Important; weighty; not trifling.

> The holy Scriptures bring to our ears the most *serious* things in the world. *Young.*

4. Particularly attentive to religious concerns or one's own religious state.

SE'RIOUSLY, *adv.* Gravely; solemnly; in earnest; without levity. One of the first duties of a rational being is to inquire *seriously* why he was created, and what he is to do to answer the purpose of his creation.

SE'RIOUSNESS, *n.* Gravity of manner or of mind; solemnity. He spoke with great *seriousness*, or with an air of *seriousness*.

2. Earnest attention, particularly to religious concerns.

> That spirit of religion and *seriousness* vanished all at once. *Atterbury.*

SERMOCINA'TION, *n.* Speech-making. [*Not used.*] *Peacham.*

SERMOCINA'TOR, *n.* One that makes sermons or speeches. [*Not in use.*]

SER'MON, *n.* [Fr. from L. *sermo*, from the root of *sero*, the primary sense of which is to *throw* or *thrust*. See *Assert, Insert*.]

1. A discourse delivered in public by a licensed clergyman for the purpose of religious instruction, and usually grounded on some text or passage of Scripture. Sermons are extemporary addresses, or written discourses.

> His preaching much, but more his practice wrought,
> A living *sermon* of the truths he taught. *Dryden.*

2. A printed discourse.

SER'MON, *v. t.* To discourse as in a sermon. [*Little used.*]

2. To tutor; to lesson; to teach. [*Little used.*] *Shak.*

SER'MON, *v. i.* To compose or deliver a sermon. [*Little used.*] *Milton.*

SER'MONING, *n.* Discourse; instruction; advice. [*Not in use.*] *Chaucer.*

SER'MONIZE, *v. i.* To preach. *Bp. Nicholson.*

2. To inculcate rigid rules. *Chesterfield.*

3. To make sermons; to compose or write a sermon or sermons. [*This is the sense in which this verb is generally used in the U. States.*]

SER'MONIZER, *n.* One that composes sermons.

SER'MONIZING, *ppr.* Preaching; inculcating rigid precepts; composing sermons.

SER'MOUNTAIN, *n.* A plant of the genus Laserpitium; laserwort; seseli. *Lee. Johnson.*

SEROON', *n.* [Sp. *seron*, a frail or basket.]

1. A seroon of almonds is the quantity of two hundred pounds; of anise seed, from three to four hundred weight; of Castile soap, from two hundred and a half to three hundred and three quarters. *Encyc.*

2. A bale or package.

SEROS'ITY, *n.* [Fr. *serosité*. See *Serum*.] In *medicine*, the watery part of the blood. *Encyc.*

SER'OTINE, *n.* A species of bat.

SE'ROUS, *a.* [Fr. *séreux*. See *Serum*.]

1. Thin; watery; like whey; used of that part of the blood which separates in coagulation from the grumous or red part.

2. Pertaining to serum. *Arbuthnot.*

SER'PENT, *n.* [L. *serpens*, creeping; *serpo*, to creep. Qu. Gr. ερπω; or from a root in *Sr*. In Welsh, *sarf*, a serpent, seems to be from *sâr*. The Sanscrit has the word *sarpa*, serpent.]

1. An animal of the order *Serpentes*, [creepers, crawlers,] of the class Amphibia. Serpents are amphibious animals, breathing through the mouth by means of lungs only; having tapering bodies, without a distinct neck; the jaws not articulated, but dilatable, and without feet, fins or ears. Serpents move along the earth by a winding motion, and with the head elevated. Some species of them are viviparous, or rather ovi-viviparous; others are oviparous; and several species are venomous. *Encyc.*

2. In *astronomy*, a constellation in the northern hemisphere, containing, according to the British catalogue, sixty four stars.

3. An instrument of music, serving as a base to the cornet or small shawm, to sustain a chorus of singers in a large edifice. It is so called from its folds or wreaths. *Encyc.*

4. Figuratively, a subtil or malicious person.

5. In *mythology*, a symbol of the sun.

Serpent stones or *snake stones*, are fossil shells of different sizes, found in strata of stones and clays. *Encyc.*

SERPENT-CUCUMBER, *n.* A plant of the genus Trichosanthes.

SER'PENT-EATER, *n.* A fowl of Africa that devours serpents.

SER'PENT-FISH, *n.* A fish of the genus Tænia, resembling a snake, but of a red color. *Dict. Nat. Hist.*

[Qu. *Cepola tænia* or *rubescens*, Linne, the band-fish, Fr. *ruban*.]

SER'PENT'S-TONGUE, *n.* A plant of the genus Ophioglossum.

SERPENTA'RIA, *n.* A plant, called also snake root; a species of Aristolochia. *Encyc.*

SERPENTA'RIUS, *n.* A constellation in the northern hemisphere, containing seventy four stars.

SER'PENTINE, *a.* [L. *serpentinus*, from *serpens*.]

1. Resembling a serpent; usually, winding or turning one way and the other, like a

moving serpent; anfractuous; as a *serpentine* road or course.

2. Spiral; twisted; as a *serpentine* worm of a still.

3. Like a serpent; having the color or properties of a serpent.

Serpentine tongue, in the manege. A horse is said to have a serpentine tongue, when he is constantly moving it, and sometimes passing it over the bit. *Encyc.*

Serpentine verse, a verse which begins and ends with the same word.

SER'PENTINE, SER'PENTINE-STONE, *n.* A species of talck or magnesian stone, usually of an obscure green color, with shades and spots resembling a serpent's skin. *Dict. Nat. Hist.*

Serpentine is often nearly allied to the harder varieties of steatite and potstone. It presents two varieties, precious serpentine, and common serpentine. *Cleaveland.*

SER'PENTIZE, *v. t.* To wind; to turn or bend, first in one direction and then in the opposite; to meander.

> The road *serpentized* through a tall shrubbery. *Barrow, Trav. in Africa.*

SER'PET, *n.* A basket. [*Not in use.*] *Ainsworth.*

SERPIG'INOUS, *a.* [from L. *serpigo*, from *serpo*, to creep.] Affected with serpigo.

SERPI'GO, *n.* [L. from *serpo*, to creep.] A kind of herpes or tetter; called in popular language, a ringworm. *Encyc.*

SER'PULITE, *n.* Petrified shells or fossil remains of the genus Serpula. *Jameson.*

SERR, *v. t.* [Fr. *serrer;* Sp. Port. *cerrar.*] To crowd, press or drive together. [*Not in use.*] *Bacon.*

SER'RATE, SER'RATED, *a.* [L. *serratus*, from *serro*, to saw; *serra*, a saw.] Jagged; notched; indented on the edge, like a saw. In *botany*, having sharp notches about the edge, pointing towards the extremity; as a *serrate* leaf.

When a serrate leaf has small serratures upon the large ones, it is said to be *doubly serrate*, as in the elm. We say also, a *serrate* calyx, corol or stipule.

A *serrate-ciliate* leaf, is one having fine hairs, like the eye lashes, on the serratures.

A *serrature-toothed* leaf, has the serratures toothed.

A *serrulate* leaf, is one finely serrate, with very small notches or teeth. *Martyn.*

SERRA'TION, *n.* Formation in the shape of a saw.

SER'RATURE, *n.* An indenting or indenture in the edge of any thing, like those of a saw. *Martyn.*

SER'ROUS, *a.* Like the teeth of a saw; irregular. [*Little used.*] *Brown.*

SER'RULATE, *a.* Finely serrate; having very minute teeth or notches. *Martyn.*

SER'RY, *v. t.* [Fr. *serrer.*] To crowd; to press together. [*Not used.*] *Milton.*

SE'RUM, *n.* [L.] The thin transparent part of the blood.

2. The thin part of milk; whey.

SER'VAL, *n.* An animal of the feline genus, resembling the lynx in form and size, and the panther in spots; a native of Malabar. *Dict. Nat. Hist.*

SERV'ANT, *n.* [Fr. from L. *servans*, from *servo*, to keep or hold; properly one that waits, that is, stops, holds, attends, or one that is bound.]

1. A person, male or female, that attends another for the purpose of performing menial offices for him, or who is employed by another for such offices or for other labor, and is subject to his command. The word is correlative to *master.* *Servant* differs from *slave*, as the servant's subjection to a master is voluntary, the slave's is not. Every slave is a servant, but every servant is not a slave.

Servants are of various kinds; as *household* or *domestic servants*, menial servants; *laborers*, who are hired by the day, week or other term, and do not reside with their employers, or if they board in the same house, are employed abroad and not in domestic services; *apprentices*, who are bound for a term of years to serve a master, for the purpose of learning his trade or occupation.

In *a legal sense*, stewards, factors, bailiffs and other agents, are *servants* for the time they are employed in such character, as they act in subordination to others.

2. One in a state of subjection.

3. In *Scripture*, a slave; a bondman; one purchased for money, and who was compelled to serve till the year of jubilee; also, one purchased for a term of years. Ex. xxi.

4. The subject of a king; as the *servants* of David or of Saul.

> The Syrians became *servants* to David. 2 Sam. viii.

5. A person who voluntarily serves another or acts as his minister; as Joshua was the *servant* of Moses, and the apostles the *servants* of Christ. So Christ himself is called a *servant*, Is. xlii. Moses is called the *servant* of the Lord. Deut. xxxiv.

6. A person employed or used as an instrument in accomplishing God's purposes of mercy or wrath. So Nebuchadnezzar is called the *servant* of God. Jer. xxv.

7. One who yields obedience to another. The saints are called the *servants* of God, or of righteousness; and the wicked are called the *servants* of sin. Rom. vi.

8. That which yields obedience, or acts in subordination as an instrument. Ps. cxix.

9. One that makes painful sacrifices in compliance with the weakness or wants of others. I Cor. ix.

10. A person of base condition or ignoble spirit. Eccles. x.

11. A word of civility. I am, sir, your humble or obedient *servant.*

> Our betters tell us they are our humble *servants*, but understand us to be their slaves. *Swift.*

Servant of servants, one debased to the lowest condition of servitude. Gen. ix.

SERV'ANT, *v. t.* To subject. [*Not in use.*] *Shak.*

SERVE, *v. t.* *serv.* [Fr. *servir;* It. *servire;* Sp. *servir;* from L. *servio.* This verb is supposed to be from the noun *servus*, a servant or slave, and this from *servo*, to keep. If *servus* originally was a slave, he was probably so named from being *preserved* and taken prisoner in war, or more probably from being bound, and perhaps from the Shemitic צור, צרר, to bind. But the sense of *servant* is generally a waiter, one who attends or waits, and from the sense of stopping, holding, remaining.]

1. To work for; to bestow the labor of body and mind in the employment of another.

> Jacob loved Rachel and said, I will *serve* thee seven years for Rachel thy younger daughter. Gen. xxix.
>
> No man can *serve* two masters. Matt. vi.

2. To act as the minister of; to perform official duties to; as, a minister *serves* his prince.

> Had I served God as diligently as I have *served* the king, he would not have given me over in my gray hairs. *Cardinal Woolsey.*

3. To attend at command; to wait on.

> A goddess among gods, ador'd and *serv'd*
> By angels numberless, thy daily train. *Milton.*

4. To obey servilely or meanly. Be not to wealth a *servant.* *Denham.*

5. To supply with food; as, to be *served* in plate. *Dryden.*

6. To be subservient or subordinate to.

> Bodies bright and greater should not *serve*
> The less not bright. *Milton.*

7. To perform the duties required in; as, the curate *served* two churches.

8. To obey; to perform duties in the employment of; as, to *serve* the king or the country in the army or navy.

9. To be sufficient to, or to promote; as, to *serve* one's turn, end or purpose. *Locke.*

10. To help by good offices; as, to *serve* one's country. *Tate.*

11. To comply with; to submit to.

> They think herein we *serve* the time, because thereby we either hold or seek preferment. *Hooker.*

12. To be sufficient for; to satisfy; to content.

> One half pint bottle *serves* them both to dine,
> And is at once their vinegar and wine. *Pope.*

13. To be in the place of any thing to one. A sofa *serves* the Turks for a seat and a couch.

14. To treat; to requite; as, he *served* me ungratefully; he *served* me very ill. We say also, he *served* me a trick, that is, he deceived me, or practiced an artifice upon me.

15. In *Scripture* and *theology*, to obey and worship; to act in conformity to the law of a superior, and treat him with due reverence.

> Fear the Lord, and *serve* him in sincerity and truth. As for me and my house, we will *serve* the Lord. Josh. xxiv.

16. In *a bad sense*, to obey; to yield compliance or act according to.

> *Serving* divers lusts and pleasures. Tit. iii.

17. To worship; to render homage to; as, to *serve* idols or false gods. Ezek. xx.

18. To be a slave to; to be in bondage to. Gen. xv.

19. To *serve one's self of*, to use; to make use of; *a Gallicism*, [*se servir de.*]

> I will *serve myself of* this concession. *Chillingworth.*

20. To use; to manage; to apply. The guns were well *served.*

21. In *seamen's language*, to wind something round a rope to prevent friction.

To serve up, to prepare and present in a dish; as, to *serve up* a sirloin of beef in plate; figuratively, to prepare.

To serve in, as used by Shakspeare, for *to bring in*, as meat by an attendant, I have never known to be used in America.

To serve out, to distribute in portions; as, to *serve out* provisions to soldiers.

To serve a writ, to read it to the defendant; or to leave an attested copy at his usual place of abode.

To serve an attachment, or *writ of attachment*, to levy it on the person or goods by seizure; or to seize.

To serve an execution, to levy it on lands, goods or person by seizure or taking possession.

To serve a warrant, to read it, and to seize the person against whom it is issued.

In general, to *serve a process*, is to read it so as to give due notice to the party concerned, or to leave an attested copy with him or his attorney, or at his usual place of abode.

To serve an office, to discharge a public duty. [This phrase, I believe, is not used in America. We say, a man *serves in* an office, that is, serves the public in an office.]

SERVE, *v. i. serv.* To be a servant or slave.

> The Lord shall give thee rest from thy sorrow, and from thy fear, and from the hard bondage wherein thou wast made to *serve*. Is. xiv.

2. To be employed in labor or other business for another. Gen. xxix.
3. To be in subjection. Is. xliii.
4. To wait; to attend; to perform domestic offices to another. Luke x.
5. To perform duties, as in the army, navy or in any office. An officer *serves* five years in India, or under a particular commander. The late secretary of the colony, and afterwards state, of Connecticut, was annually appointed, and *served* in the office sixty years.
6. To answer; to accomplish the end.

> She feared that all would not *serve*. *Sidney.*

7. To be sufficient for a purpose.

> This little brand will *serve* to light your fire. *Dryden.*

8. To suit; to be convenient. Take this, and use it as occasion *serves*.
9. To conduce; to be of use.

> Our victory only *served* to lead us on to further visionary prospects. *Swift.*

10. To officiate or minister; to do the honors of; as, to *serve* at a public dinner.

SERV'ED, *pp.* Attended; waited on; worshiped; levied.

SERV'ICE, *n.* [Fr.; It. *servizio*; Sp. *servicio*; from L. *servitium.*]

1. In *a general sense*, labor of body or of body and mind, performed at the command of a superior, or in pursuance of duty, or for the benefit of another. Service is *voluntary* or *involuntary*. *Voluntary* service is that of hired servants, or of contract, or of persons who spontaneously perform something for another's benefit. *Involuntary* service is that of slaves, who work by compulsion.
2. The business of a servant; menial office. *Shak.*
3. Attendance of a servant. *Shak.*
4. Place of a servant; actual employment of a servant; as, to be out of *service*. *Shak.*
5. Any thing done by way of duty to a superior.

> This poem was the last piece of *service* I did for my master king Charles. *Dryden.*

6. Attendance on a superior.

> Madam, I entreat true peace of you,
> Which I will purchase with my duteous *service*. *Shak.*

7. Profession of respect uttered or sent.

> Pray do my *service* to his majesty. *Shak.*

8. Actual duty; that which is required to be done in an office; as, to perform the *services* of a clerk, a sherif or judge.
9. That which God requires of man; worship; obedience.

> God requires no man's *service* upon hard and unreasonable terms. *Tillotson.*

10. Employment; business; office; as, to qualify a man for public *service*.
11. Use; purpose. The guns are not fit for public *service*.
12. Military duty by land or sea; as military or naval *service*.
13. A military achievment. *Shak.*
14. Useful office; advantage conferred; that which promotes interest or happiness. Medicine often does no *service* to the sick; calumny is sometimes of *service* to an author.
15. Favor.

> To thee a woman's *services* are due. *Shak.*

16. The duty which a tenant owes to his lord for his fee. Personal *service* consists in homage and fealty, &c.
17. Public worship, or office of devotion. Divine *service* was interrupted.
18. A musical church composition consisting of choruses, trios, duets, solos, &c.
19. The official duties of a minister of the gospel, as in church, at a funeral, marriage, &c.
20. Course; order of dishes at table.

> There was no extraordinary *service* seen on the board. *Hakewill.*

21. In *seaman's language*, the materials used for serving a rope, as spun yarn, small lines, &c.
22. A tree and its fruit, of the genus Sorbus. The *wild service* is of the genus Cratægus.

Service of a writ, process, &c. the reading of it to the person to whom notice is intended to be given, or the leaving of an attested copy with the person or his attorney, or at his usual place of abode.

Service of an attachment, the seizing of the person or goods according to the direction.

The service of an execution, the levying of it upon the goods, estate or person of the defendant.

SERV'ICEABLE, *a.* That does service; that promotes happiness, interest, advantage or any good; useful; beneficial; advantageous. Rulers may be very *serviceable* to religion by their example. The attentions of my friends were very *serviceable* to me when abroad. Rain and manure are *serviceable* to land.

2. Active; diligent; officious.

> I know thee well, a *serviceable* villain.
> [*Unusual.*] *Shak.*

SERV'ICEABLENESS, *n.* Usefulness in promoting good of any kind; beneficialness.

> All action being for some end, its aptness to be commanded or forbidden must be founded upon its *serviceablenes* or disserviceableness to some end. *Norris.*

2. Officiousness; readiness to do service. *Sidney.*

SERV'IENT, *a.* [L. *serviens.*] Subordinate. [*Not in use.*] *Dyer.*

SERV'ILE, *a.* [Fr. from L. *servilis*, from *servio*, to serve.]

1. Such as pertains to a servant or slave; slavish; mean; such as proceeds from dependence; as *servile* fear; *servile* obedience.
2. Held in subjection; dependent.

> Ev'n fortune rules no more a *servile* land. *Pope.*

3. Cringing; fawning; meanly submissive; as *servile* flattery.

> She must bend the *servile* knee. *Thomson.*

SERV'ILELY, *adv.* Meanly; slavishly; with base submission or obsequiousness.

2. With base deference to another; as, to copy *servilely*; to adopt opinions *servilely*.

SERV'ILENESS, } *n.* Slavery; the condi-
SERVIL'ITY, } tion of a slave or bondman.

> To be a queen in bondage, is more vile
> Than is a slave in base *servility*. *Shak.*

2. Mean submission; baseness; slavishness.
3. Mean obsequiousness; slavish deference; as the common *servility* to custom; to copy manners or opinions with *servility*.

SERV'ING, *ppr.* Working for; acting in subordination to; yielding obedience to; worshiping; also, performing duties; as *serving* in the army.

SERV'ING-MAID, *n.* A female servant; a menial.

SERV'ING-MAN, *n.* A male servant; a menial.

SERV'ITOR, *n.* [It. *servitore*; Sp. *servidor*; Fr. *serviteur*; from L. *servio*, to serve.]

1. A servant; an attendant. *Hooker.*
2. One that acts under another; a follower or adherent. *Davies.*
3. One that professes duty and obedience. *Shak.*
4. In *the university of Oxford*, a student who attends on another for his maintenance and learning; such as is called in Cambridge, a sizer. *Encyc.*

SERV'ITORSHIP, *n.* The office of a servitor. *Boswell.*

SERV'ITUDE, *n.* [Fr. from L. *servitudo* or *servitus*; It. *servitù*. See *Serve.*]

1. The condition of a slave; the state of involuntary subjection to a master; slavery; bondage. Such is the state of the slaves in America. A large portion of the human race are in *servitude*.
2. The state of a servant. [*Less common and less proper.*]
3. The condition of a conquered country.
4. A state of slavish dependence. Some persons may be in love with splendid *servitude*. *South.*
5. Servants, collectively. [*Not in use.*] *Shak.*

SES'AME, } *n.* [Fr. *sesame*; It. *sesamo*; L.
SES'AMUM, } *sesama*; Gr. σησαμη, σησαμον.]

Oily grain; a genus of annual herbaceous plants, from the seeds of which an oil is expressed. One species of it is cultivated in Carolina, and the blacks use the seeds for food. It is called there *bene*. *Encyc. Belve.*

SES'BAN, *n.* A plant; a species of Æschynomene or Bastard sensitive plant. *Encyc.*

SES'ELI, *n.* [L. Gr. *seselis.*] A genus of plants; meadow saxifrage; hartwort. *Encyc.*

SESQUIAL'TER, } *a.* [L. from *sesqui*, the whole and
SESQUIAL'TERAL, } half as much more, and *alter*, other.]

1. In *geometry*, designating a ratio where one quantity or number contains another once, and half as much more; as 9 contains 6 and its half. *Bentley.*

2. A *sesquialteral floret*, is when a large fertile floret is accompanied with a small abortive one. *Martyn.*

SESQUIDU'PLICATE, *a.* [L. *sesqui*, supra, and *duplicatus*, double.]
Designating the ratio of two and a half to one, or where the greater term contains the lesser twice and a half, as that of 50 to 20.

SESQUIP'EDAL, } *a.* [L. *sesqui*, one and a half, and
SESQUIPEDA'LIAN, } *pedalis*, from *pes*, a foot.]
Containing a foot and a half; as a *sesquipedalian* pigmy. *Arbuthnot.*
Addison uses *sesquipedal* as a noun.

SESQUIP'LICATE, *a.* [L. *sesqui*, one and a half, and *plicatus*, *plico*, to fold.]
Designating the ratio of one and a half to one; as the *sesquiplicate* proportion of the periodical times of the planets. *Cheyne.*

SESQUITER'TIAN, } *a.* [L. *sesqui*, one and a half, and
SESQUITER'TIONAL, } *tertius*, third.]
Designating the ratio of one and one third. *Johnson.*

SES'QUITONE, *n.* In *music*, a minor third, or interval of three semitones. *Busby.*

SESS, *n.* [L. *sessio.*] A tax. [*Little used or not at all.* See *Assessment.*]

SES'SILE, *a.* [L. *sessilis.* See *Set.*] In *botany*, sitting on the stem. A *sessile* leaf issues directly from the stem or branch, without a petiole or footstalk. A *sessile* flower has no peduncle. *Sessile* pappus or down has no stipe, but is placed immediately on the seed. *Martyn.*

SES'SION, *n.* [Fr. from L. *sessio*, from *sedeo.* See *Set.*]

1. A sitting or being placed; as the ascension of Christ, and his *session* at the right hand of God. *Hooker.*

2. The actual sitting of a court, council, legislature, &c.; or the actual assembly of the members of these or any similar body for the transaction of business. Thus we say, the court is now in *session*, meaning that the members are assembled for business.

3. The time, space or term during which a court, council, legislature and the like, meet daily for business; or the space of time between the first meeting and the prorogation or adjournment. Thus a *session* of parliament is opened with a speech from the throne, and closed by prorogation. The *session* of a judicial court is called a term. Thus a court may have two *sessions* or four *sessions* annually. The supreme court of the United States has one annual *session*. The legislatures of most of the states have one annual *session* only; some have more. The congress of the United States has one only.

4. *Sessions*, in some of the states, is particularly used for a court of justices, held for granting licenses to innkeepers or taverners, for laying out new highways or altering old ones and the like.

Quarter sessions, in England, is a court held once in every quarter, by two justices of the peace, one of whom is of the quorum, for the trial of small felonies and misdemeanors.

Sessions of the peace, a court consisting of justices of the peace, held in each county for inquiring into trespasses, larcenies, forestalling, &c. and in general, for the conservation of the peace. *Laws of New York.*

SESS'-POOL, *n.* [*sess* and *pool.*] A cavity sunk in the earth to receive and retain the sediment of water conveyed in drains. *Sess-pools* should be placed at proper distances in all drains, and particularly should one be placed at the entrance. *Encyc.*

SES'TERCE, *n.* [Fr. from L. *sestertius.*] A Roman coin or denomination of money, in value the fourth part of a denarius, and originally containing two asses and a half, about two pence sterling or four cents. The sestertium, that is, *sestertium pondus*, was two pounds and a half, or two hundred and fifty denarii; about seven pounds sterling, or thirty one dollars. One qualification of a Roman knight was the possession of estate of the value of four hundred thousand sesterces; that of a senator was double this sum.

Authors mention also a copper *sesterce*, of the value of one third of a penny sterling.

Sesterce was also used by the ancients for a thing containing two wholes and a half; the *as* being taken for the integer. *Encyc.*

SET, *v. t.* pret. pp. *set.* [Sax. *sætan, setan, settan*, to set or place, to *seat* or fix, to appease, to calm, L. *sedo;* to compose, as a book, to dispose or put in order, to establish, found or institute, to possess, to cease; G. *setzen*, to set, to risk or lay, as a wager, to plant, to appoint, to leap or make an onset; D. *zetten;* Sw. *sätta;* Dan. *setter;* W. *sodi*, to fix, to constitute; *gosodi*, to set, to lay, to put, to establish, to ordain; *gosod*, a setting or placing, a *site*, a statute, an onset or assault; L. *sedo, sedeo* and *sido*, coinciding with *sit*, but all of one family. From the Norman orthography of this word, we have *assess, assise.* See *Assess.* Heb. Ch. יסד and שות to set, to place; Syr. ܣܐܡ to found, to establish. Class Sd. No. 31. 56. The primary sense is to throw, to drive, or intransitively, to rush.]

1. To put or place; to fix or cause to rest in a standing posture. We *set* a house on a wall of stone; we *set* a book on a shelf. In this use, *set* differs from *lay;* we *set* a thing on its end or basis; we *lay* it on its side.

2. To put or place in its proper or natural posture. We *set* a chest or trunk on its bottom, not on its end; we *set* a bedstead or a table on its feet or legs.

3. To put, place or fix in any situation. God *set* the sun, moon and stars in the firmament.

I do *set* my bow in the cloud. Gen. ix.

4. To put into any condition or state.

The Lord thy God will *set* thee on high. Deut. xxviii.

I am come to *set* a man at variance against his father. Matt. x.

So we say, to *set in order*, to *set at ease*, to *set to work*, or *at work.*

5. To put; to fix; to attach to.

The Lord *set* a mark upon Cain. Gen. iv.

So we say, to *set* a label on a vial or a bale.

6. To fix; to render motionless; as, the eyes are *set;* the jaws are *set.*

7. To put or fix, as a price. We *set* a price on a house, farm or horse.

8. To fix; to state by some rule.

The gentleman spoke with a *set* gesture and countenance. *Carew.*

The town of Berne has handsome fountains planted at *set* distances from one end of the street to the other. *Addison.*

9. To regulate or adjust; as, to *set* a timepiece by the sun.

He *sets* his judgment by his passion. *Prior.*

10. To fit to music; to adapt with notes; as, to *set* the words of a psalm to music.

Set thy own songs, and sing them to thy lute. *Dryden.*

11. To pitch; to begin to sing in public.

He *set* the hundredth psalm. *Spectator.*

12. To plant, as a shrub, tree or vegetable. *Prior.*

13. To variegate, intersperse or adorn with something fixed; to stud; as, to *set* any thing with diamonds or pearls.

High on their heads, with jewels richly *set*,
Each lady wore a radiant coronet. *Dryden.*

14. To return to its proper place or state; to replace; to reduce from a dislocated or fractured state; as, to *set* a bone or a leg.

15. To fix; to place; as the heart or affections.

Set your affections on things above. Col. iii.
—Minds altogether *set* on trade and profit. *Addison.*

16. To fix firmly; to predetermine.

The heart of the sons of men is fully *set* in them to do evil. Eccles. viii.

Hence we say, a thing is done of *set* purpose; a man is *set*, that is, firm or obstinate in his opinion or way.

17. To fix by appointment; to appoint; to assign; as, to *set* a time for meeting; to *set* an hour or a day. *Bacon. South.*

18. To place or station; to appoint to a particular duty.

Am I a sea or a whale, that thou *settest* a watch over me? Job vii.

19. To stake at play. [*Little used.*] *Prior.*

20. To offer a wager at dice to another. [*Little used.*] *Shak.*

21. To fix in metal.

And him too rich a jewel to be *set*
In vulgar metal for a vulgar use. *Dryden.*

22. To fix; to cause to stop; to obstruct; as, to *set* a coach in the mire. The wagon or the team was *set* at the hill. In some of the states, *stall* is used in a like sense.

23. To embarrass; to perplex.

They are hard *set* to represent the bill as a grievance. *Addison.*

24. To put in good order; to fix for use; to bring to a fine edge; as, to *set* a razor.

25. To loose and extend; to spread; as, to *set* the sails of a ship.

26. To point out without noise or disturbance; as, a dog *sets* birds. *Johnson.*
27. To oppose.
Will you *set* your wit to a fool's? *Shak.*
28. To prepare with runnet for cheese; as, to *set* milk.
29. To dim; to darken or extinguish.
Ahijah could not see; for his eyes were *set* by reason of his age. 1 Kings xiv.

To set by the compass, among seamen, to observe the bearing or situation of a distant object by the compass.

To set about, to begin, as an action or enterprise; to apply to. He has planned his enterprise, and will soon *set about* it.

To set one's self against, to place in a state of enmity or opposition.
The king of Babylon *set himself against* Jerusalem this same day. Ezek. xxiv.

To set against, to oppose; to set in comparison, or to oppose as an equivalent in exchange; as, to *set* one thing *against* another; or to *set off* one thing *against* another.

To set apart, to separate to a particular use; to separate from the rest.
2. To neglect for a time. [*Not in use.*] *Knolles.*

To set aside, to omit for the present; to lay out of the question.
Setting aside all other considerations, I will endeavor to know the truth and yield to that. *Tillotson.*
2. To reject.
I embrace that of the deluge, and *set aside* all the rest. *Woodward.*
3. To annul; to vacate. The court *set aside* the verdict, or the judgment.

To set abroach, to spread. *Shak.*

To set a-going, to cause to begin to move.

To set by, to set apart or on one side; to reject. [In this sense, *by* is emphatical.] *Bacon.*
2. To esteem; to regard; to value. [In this sense, *set* is pronounced with more emphasis than *by*.]

To set down, to place upon the ground or floor.
2. To enter in writing; to register.
Some rules were to be *set down* for the government of the army. *Clarendon.*
3. To explain or relate in writing.
4. To fix on a resolve. [*Little used.*] *Knolles.*
5. To fix; to establish; to ordain.
This law we may name eternal, being that order which God hath *set down* with himself, for himself to do all things by. *Hooker.*

To set forth, to manifest; to offer or present to view. Rom. iii.
2. To publish; to promulgate; to make appear. *Waller.*
3. To send out; to prepare and send.
The Venetian admiral had a fleet of sixty galleys, *set forth* by the Venetians. *Obs.* *Knolles.*
4. To display; to exhibit; to present to view; to show. *Dryden. Milton.*

To set forward, to advance; to move on; also, to promote. *Hooker.*

To set in, to put in the way to begin.
If you please to assist and *set* me *in*, I will recollect myself. *Collier.*

To set off, to adorn; to decorate; to embellish.
They *set off* the worst faces with the best airs. *Addison.*
2. To give a pompous or flattering description of; to eulogize; to recommend; as, to *set off* a character.
3. To place against as an equivalent; as, to *set off* one man's services against another's.
4. To separate or assign for a particular purpose; as, to *set off* a portion of an estate.

To set on or *upon*, to incite; to instigate; to animate to action.
Thou, traitor, hast *set on* thy wife to this. *Shak.*
2. To assault or attack; seldom used transitively, but the passive form is often used.
Alphonsus—was *set upon* by a Turkish pirate and taken. *Knolles.*
3. To employ, as in a task.
Set on thy wife to observe. *Shak.*
4. To fix the attention; to determine to any thing with settled purpose.
It becomes a true lover to have your heart more *set upon* her good than your own. *Sidney.*

To set out, to assign; to allot; as, to *set out* the share of each proprietor or heir of an estate; to *set out* the widow's thirds.
2. To publish. [*Not elegant nor common.*] *Swift.*
3. To mark by boundaries or distinctions of space.
—Determinate portions of those infinite abysses of space and duration, *set out*, or supposed to be distinguished from all the rest by known boundaries. *Locke.*
4. To adorn; to embellish.
An ugly woman in a rich habit, *set out* with jewels, nothing can become. *Dryden.*
5. To raise, equip and send forth; to furnish.
The Venetians pretend they could *set out*, in case of great necessity, thirty men of war. [*Not elegant and little used.*] *Addison.*
6. To show; to display; to recommend; to set off.
I could *set out* that best side of Luther. *Atterbury.*
7. To show; to prove.
Those very reasons *set out* how hainous his sin was. [*Little used and not elegant.*] *Atterbury.*
8. In law, to recite; to state at large. *Judge Sedgwick.*

To set up, to erect; as, to *set up* a building; to *set up* a post, a wall, a pillar.
2. To begin a new institution; to institute; to establish; to found; as, to *set up* a manufactory; to *set up* a school.
3. To enable to commence a new business; as, to *set up* a son in trade.
4. To raise; to exalt; to put in power; as, to *set up* the throne of David over Israel. 2 Sam. iii.
5. To place in view; as, to *set up* a mark.
6. To raise; to utter loudly; as, to *set up* the voice.
I'll *set up* such a note as she shall hear. *Dryden.*
7. To advance; to propose as truth or for reception; as, to *set up* a new opinion or doctrine. *Burnet.*
8. To raise from depression or to a sufficient fortune. This good fortune quite *set* him *up*.
9. In *seaman's language*, to extend, as the shrouds, stays, &c.

To set at naught, to undervalue; to contemn; to despise.
Ye have *set at naught* all my counsel Prov. i.

To set in order, to adjust or arrange; to reduce to method.
The rest will I *set in order* when I come. 1 Cor. xi.

To set eyes on, to see; to behold; or to fix the eyes in looking on; to fasten the eyes on.

To set the teeth on edge, to affect the teeth with a painful sensation.

To set over, to appoint or constitute as supervisor, inspector, ruler or commander.
2. To assign; to transfer; to convey.

To set right, to correct; to put in order.

To set at ease, to quiet; to tranquilize; as, to *set* the heart *at ease*.

To set free, to release from confinement, imprisonment or bondage; to liberate; to emancipate.

To set at work, to cause to enter on work or action; or to direct how to enter on work. *Locke.*

To set on fire, to communicate fire to; to inflame; and figuratively, to enkindle the passions; to make to rage; to irritate; to fill with disorder. James iii.

To set before, to offer; to propose; to present to view. Deut. xi. xxx.

To set a trap, snare or *gin*, to place in a situation to catch prey; to spread; figuratively, to lay a plan to deceive and draw into the power of another.

SET, *v. i.* To decline; to go down; to pass below the horizon; as, the sun *sets;* the stars *set*.
2. To be fixed hard; to be close or firm. *Bacon.*
3. To fit music to words. *Shak.*
4. To congeal or concrete.
That fluid substance in a few minutes begins to *set*. *Boyle.*
5. To begin a journey. The king is *set* from London. [This is obsolete. We now say, to *set out*.]
6. To plant; as, "to sow dry, and to *set* wet." *Old Proverb.*
7. To flow; to have a certain direction in motion; as, the tide *sets* to the east or north; the current *sets* westward.
8. To catch birds with a dog that sets them, that is, one that lies down and points them out, and with a large net. *Boyle.*

To set one's self about, to begin; to enter upon; to take the first steps.

To set one's self, to apply one's self.

To set about, to fall on; to begin; to take the first steps in a business or enterprise. *Atterbury.*

To set in, to begin. Winter in New England, usually *sets in* in December.
2. To become settled in a particular state.
When the weather was *set in* to be very bad. *Addison.*

To set forward, to move or march; to begin to march; to advance.
The sons of Aaron and the sons of Merari *set forward*. Num. x.

To set on, or *upon*, to begin a journey or an enterprise.
He that would seriously *set upon* the search of truth— *Locke.*
2. To assault; to make an attack. *Shak.*

To set out, to begin a journey or course; as, to *set out* for London or from London; to *set out* in business; to *set out* in life or the world.
2. To have a beginning. *Brown.*

To set to, to apply one's self to. *Gov. of the Tongue.*

To set up, to begin business or a scheme of life; as, to *set up* in trade; to *set up* for one's self.

2. To profess openly; to make pretensions. He *sets up* for a man of wit; he *sets up* to teach morality. *Dryden.*

SET, *pp.* Placed; put; located; fixed; adjusted; composed; studded or adorned; reduced, as a dislocated or broken bone.

2. *a.* Regular; uniform; formal; as a *set* speech or phrase; a *set* discourse; a *set* battle.

3. Fixed in opinion; determined; firm; obstinate; as a man *set* in his opinions or way.

4. Established; prescribed; as *set* forms of prayer.

SET, *n.* A number or collection of things of the same kind and of similar form, which are ordinarily used together; as a *set* of chairs; a *set* of tea cups; a *set* of China or other ware.

2. A number of things fitted to be used together, though different in form; as a *set* of dining tables.

A *set* implies more than two, which are called a *pair*.

3. A number of persons customarily or officially associated, as a *set* of men, a *set* of officers; or a number of persons having a similitude of character, or of things which have some resemblance or relation to each other. Hence our common phrase, a *set* of opinions.

This falls into different divisions or *sets* of nations connected under particular religions, &c. *Ward's Law of Nations.*

4. A number of particular things that are united in the formation of a whole; as a *set* of features. *Addison.*

5. A young plant for growth; as *sets* of white thorn or other shrub. *Encyc.*

6. The descent of the sun or other luminary below the horizon; as the *set* of the sun. *Atterbury.*

7. A wager at dice.

That was but civil war, an equal *set*. *Dryden.*

8. A game.

We will, in France, play a *set*
Shall strike his father's crown into the hazard. *Shak.*

SETA'CEOUS, *a.* [L. *seta*, a bristle.] Bristly; set with strong hairs; consisting of strong hairs; as a stiff *setaceous* tail. *Derham.*

2. In *botany*, bristle-shaped; having the thickness and length of a bristle; as a *setaceous* leaf or leaflet. *Martyn.*

Setaceous worm, a name given to a water worm that resembles a horse hair, vulgarly supposed to be an animated hair. But this is a mistake. *Encyc.*

SET-FOIL. [See *Sept-foil.*]

SE'TIFORM, *a.* [L. *seta*, a bristle, and *form.*]

Having the form of a bristle. *Journ. of Science.*

SET'-OFF, *n.* [*set* and *off.*] The act of admitting one claim to counterbalance another. In a *set-off*, the defendant acknowledges the justice of the plaintif's demand, but *sets* up a demand of his own to counterbalance it in whole or in part.

The right of pleading a *set-off* depends on statute. *Blackstone.*

NOTE.—In New England, *offset* is sometimes used for *set-off*. But *offset* has a different sense, and it is desirable that the practice should be uniform, wherever the English language is spoken.

SE'TON, *n.* [Fr. from L. *seta*, a bristle.] In *surgery*, a few horse hairs or small threads, or a twist of silk, drawn through the skin by a large needle, by which a small opening is made and continued for the discharge of humors. *Encyc. Quincy.*

SE'TOUS, *a.* [It. *setoso*; L. *setosus*, from *seta*, a bristle.]

In *botany*, bristly; having the surface set with bristles; as a *setous* leaf or receptacle. *Martyn.*

SETTEE', *n.* [from *set.*] A long seat with a back to it.

2. A vessel with one deck and a very long sharp prow, carrying two or three masts with lateen sails; used in the Mediterranean. *Mar. Dict. Encyc.*

SET'TER, *n.* One that sets; as a *setter on*, or inciter; a *setter up*; a *setter forth*, &c.

2. A dog that beats the field and starts birds for sportsmen.

3. A man that performs the office of a setting dog, or finds persons to be plundered. *South.*

4. One that adapts words to music in composition.

5. Whatever sets off, adorns or recommends. [*Not used.*] *Whitlock.*

SET'TER-WÖRT, *n.* A plant, a species of Helleborus. *Fam. of Plants.*

SET'TING, *ppr.* Placing; putting; fixing; studding; appointing; sinking below the horizon, &c.

SET'TING, *n.* The act of putting, placing, fixing or establishing.

2. The act of sinking below the horizon. The setting of stars is of three kinds, *cosmical*, *acronical*, and *heliacal.* [See these words.]

3. The act or manner of taking birds by a setting dog.

4. Inclosure; as *settings* of stones. Ex. xxviii.

5. The direction of a current at sea.

SET'TING-DOG, *n.* A setter; a dog trained to find and start birds for sportsmen.

SET'TLE, *n.* [Sax. *sell*, *settl*; G. *sessel*; D. *zetel*; L. *sedile.* See *Set.*]

A seat or bench; something to sit on. *Dryden.*

SET'TLE, *v. t.* [from *set.*] To place in a permanent condition after wandering or fluctuation.

I will *settle* you after your old estates. Ezek. xxxvi.

2. To fix; to establish; to make permanent in any place.

I will *settle* him in my house and in my kingdom forever. 1 Chron. xvii.

3. To establish in business or way of life; as, to *settle* a son in trade.

4. To marry; as, to *settle* a daughter.

5. To establish; to confirm.

Her will alone could *settle* or revoke. *Prior.*

6. To determine what is uncertain; to establish; to free from doubt; as, to *settle* questions or points of law. The supreme court have *settled* the question.

7. To fix; to establish; to make certain or permanent; as, to *settle* the succession to a throne in a particular family. So we speak of *settled* habits and *settled* opinions.

8. To fix or establish; not to suffer to doubt or waver.

It will *settle* the wavering and confirm the doubtful. *Swift.*

9. To make close or compact.

Cover ant-hills up that the rain may *settle* the turf before the spring. *Mortimer.*

10. To cause to subside after being heaved and loosened by frost; or to dry and harden after rain. Thus clear weather *settles* the roads.

11. To fix or establish by gift, grant or any legal act; as, to *settle* a pension on an officer, or an annuity on a child.

12. To fix firmly. *Settle* your mind on valuable objects.

13. To cause to sink or subside, as extraneous matter in liquors. In fining wine, we add something to *settle* the lees.

14. To compose; to tranquilize what is disturbed; as, to *settle* the thoughts or mind when agitated.

15. To establish in the pastoral office; to ordain over a church and society, or parish; as, to *settle* a minister. *U. States. Boswell.*

16. To plant with inhabitants; to colonize. The French first *settled* Canada; the Puritans *settled* New England. Plymouth was *settled* in 1620. Hartford was *settled* in 1636. Wethersfield was the first *settled* town in Connecticut.

17. To adjust; to close by amicable agreement or otherwise; as, to *settle* a controversy or dispute by agreement, treaty or by force.

18. To adjust; to liquidate; to balance, or to pay; as, to *settle* accounts.

To settle the land, among seamen, to cause it to sink or appear lower by receding from it.

SET'TLE, *v. i.* To fall to the bottom of liquor; to subside; to sink and rest on the bottom; as, lees or dregs *settle.* Slimy particles in water *settle* and form mud at the bottom of rivers.

This word is used of the extraneous matter of liquors, when it subsides spontaneously. But in chemical operations, when substances mixed or in solution are decomposed, and one component part subsides, it is said to be *precipitated.* But it may also be said to *settle.*

2. To lose motion or fermentation; to deposit, as feces.

A government on such occasions, is always thick before it *settles.* *Addison.*

3. To fix one's habitation or residence. Belgians had *settled* on the southern coast of Britain, before the Romans invaded the isle.

4. To marry and establish a domestic state. Where subsistence is easily obtained, children *settle* at an early period of life.

5. To become fixed after change or fluctuation; as, the wind came about and *settled* in the west. *Bacon.*

6. To become stationary; to quit a rambling or irregular course for a permanent or methodical one.

7. To become fixed or permanent; to take a lasting form or state; as a *settled* conviction.

Chyle—runs through the intermediate colors till it *settles* in an intense red. *Arbuthnot.*

8. To rest; to repose.

When time hath worn out their natural vanity, and taught them discretion, their fondness *settles* on its proper object. *Spectator.*

9. To become calm; to cease from agitation.

Till the fury of his highness *settle*,
Come not before him. *Shak.*

10. To make a jointure for a wife.

He sighs with most success that *settles* well. *Garth.*

11. To sink by its weight; and in loose bodies, to become more compact. We say, a wall *settles;* a house *settles* upon its foundation; a mass of sand *settles* and becomes more firm.

12. To sink after being heaved, and to dry; as, roads *settle* in spring after frost and rain.

13. To be ordained or installed over a parish, church or congregation. A B was invited to *settle* in the first society in New Haven. N D *settled* in the ministry when very young.

14. To adjust differences or accounts; to come to an agreement. He has *settled* with his creditors.

15. To make a jointure for a wife. *Garth.*

SET'TLED, *pp.* Placed; established; fixed; determined; composed; adjusted.

SET'TLEDNESS, *n.* The state of being settled; confirmed state. [*Little used.*] *K. Charles.*

SET'TLEMENT, *n.* The act of settling, or state of being settled.

2. The falling of the foul or foreign matter of liquors to the bottom; subsidence.

3. The matter that subsides; lees; dregs. [Not used. For this we use *settlings.*] *Mortimer.*

4. The act of giving possession by legal sanction.

My flocks, my fields, my woods, my pastures take,
With *settlement* as good as law can make. *Dryden.*

5. A jointure granted to a wife, or the act of granting it. We say, the wife has a competent *settlement* for her maintenance; or she has provision made for her by the *settlement* of a jointure.

6. The act of taking a domestic state; the act of marrying and going to housekeeping.

7. A becoming stationary, or taking a permanent residence after a roving course of life. *L'Estrange.*

8. The act of planting or establishing, as a colony; also, the place, or the colony established; as the British *settlements* in America or India.

9. Adjustment; liquidation; the ascertainment of just claims, or payment of the balance of an account.

10. Adjustment of differences; pacification; reconciliation; as the *settlement* of disputes or controversies.

11. The ordaining or installment of a clergyman over a parish or congregation.

12. A sum of money or other property granted to a minister on his ordination, exclusive of his salary.

13. Legal residence or establishment of a person in a particular parish or town, which entitles him to maintenance if a pauper, and subjects the parish or town to his support. In England, the poor are supported by the parish where they have a *settlement.* In New England, they are supported by the town. In England, the statutes 12 Richard II. and 19 Henry VII. seem to be the first rudiments of parish *settlements.* By statute 13 and 14 Ch. II. a legal *settlement* is declared to be gained by birth, by inhabitancy, by apprenticeship, or by service for forty days. But the gaining of a *settlement* by so short a residence produced great evils, which were remedied by statute 1 James II. *Blackstone.*

14. *Act of settlement*, in British history, the statute of 12 and 13 William III. by which the crown was limited to his present majesty's house, or the house of Orange. *Blackstone.*

SET'TLING, *ppr.* Placing; fixing; establishing; regulating; adjusting; planting or colonizing; subsiding; composing; ordaining or installing; becoming the pastor of a parish or church.

SET'TLING, *n.* The act of making a settlement; a planting or colonizing.

2. The act of subsiding, as lees.

3. The adjustment of differences.

4. *Settlings*, plu. lees; dregs; sediment.

SET'WALL, *n.* [*set* and *wall.*] A plant. The *garden setwall* is a species of Valeriana.

SEVEN, *a.* *sev'n.* [Sax. *seofa, seofan*; Goth. *sibun*; D. *zeeven*; G. *sieben*; Sw. *siu*; Dan. *syv*; L. *septem*, whence Fr. *sept*, It. *sette*, Sp. *siete*, [or the two latter are the W. *saith*, Arm. *saith* or *seiz*;] Sans. *sapta*; Pers. هفت hafat; Zend, *hapte*; Pehlavi, *haft*; Gr. επτα; Ar. سبع; Heb. Ch. Syr. Eth. שבע. In Ch. and Syr. סבע signifies to fill, to satisfy; in Ar. seven, and to make the number seven. In Heb. and Ch. שבע is seven; Ar. شبع to fill. With this orthography coincides the spelling of the Teutonic and Gothic words, whose elements are *Sb*, or their cognates. But the Latin and Sanscrit have a third radical letter, as has the Persic, viz. *t*, and these coincide with the Ar. سبت sabata, to observe the sabbath, to rest, Heb. Ch. Syr. שבת.

It is obvious then that *seven* had its origin in these verbs, and if the Persic and Greek words are from the same source, which is very probable, we have satisfactory evidence that the sibilant letter *s* has been changed into an aspirate. And this confirms my opinion that a similar change has taken place in the Gr. αλς, salt, W. *halen*, and in many other words.]

Four and three; one more than six or less than eight. *Seven* days constitute a week. We read in Scripture of *seven* years of plenty, and *seven* years of famine, *seven* trumpets, *seven* seals, *seven* vials, &c.

SEV'ENFOLD, *a.* [*seven* and *fold.*] Repeated seven times; doubled seven times; increased to seven times the size or amount; as the *sevenfold* shield of Ajax; *sevenfold* rage. *Milton.*

SEV'ENFOLD, *adv.* Seven times as much or often.

Whoever slayeth Cain, vengeance shall be taken on him *sevenfold*. Gen. iv.

SEV'ENNIGHT, *n.* [*seven* and *night.*] A week; the period of seven days and nights; or the time from one day of the week to the next day of the same denomination preceding or following. Our ancestors numbered the diurnal revolutions of the earth by *nights*, as they reckoned the annual revolutions by *winters.* *Sevennight* is now contracted into *sennight*, which see.

SEV'ENSCORE, *n.* [*seven* and *score*, twenty notches or marks.] Seven times twenty, that is, a hundred and forty.

The old countess of Desmond, who lived *sevenscore* years, dentized twice or thrice. *Bacon.*

SEV'ENTEEN, *a.* [Sax. *seofontyne*; seven—ten.] Seven and ten.

SEV'ENTEENTH, *a.* [from *seventeen.* The Saxon *seofon-teotha* or *seofon-teogetha* is differently formed.] The ordinal of seventeen; the seventh after the tenth.

On the *seventeenth* day of the second month—all the fountains of the great deep were broken up. Gen. vii.

SEV'ENTH, *a.* [Sax. *seofetha.*] The ordinal of seven; the first after the sixth.

On the *seventh* day God ended his work which he had made, and he rested on the *seventh* day from all his work which he had made. Gen. ii.

2. Containing or being one part in seven; as the *seventh* part.

SEV'ENTH, *n.* The seventh part; one part in seven.

2. In *music*, a dissonant interval or heptachord. An interval consisting of four tones and two major semitones, is called a *seventh* minor. An interval composed of five tones and a major semitone, is called a *seventh* major. *Encyc. Busby.*

SEV'ENTHLY, *adv.* In the seventh place. *Bacon.*

SEV'ENTIETH, *a.* [from *seventy.*] The ordinal of seventy; as a man in the *seventieth* year of his age. The *seventieth* year begins immediately after the close of the sixty ninth.

SEV'ENTY, *a.* [D. *zeventig*; Sax. *seofa*, seven, and *tig*, ten; Goth. *tig*, Gr. δεκα, ten; but the Saxon writers prefixed *hund*, as *hund-seofontig*. See Lye ad voc. and Sax. Chron. A. D. 1083.] Seven times ten.

That he would accomplish *seventy* years in the desolations of Jerusalem. Dan. ix.

SEV'ENTY, *n.* The Septuagint or seventy translators of the Old Testament into the Greek language.

SEV'ER, *v. t.* [Fr. *sevrer*; It. *sevrare.* There may be a doubt whether *sever* is derived from the Latin *separo.* The French has both *sevrer*, as well as *separer*; and the Italian, *sevrare*, *scevrare* and *sceverare*, as well as *separare*. The It. *scevrare* coincides well in orthography with Eng. *shiver*, and this with Heb. שבר, Ch. Syr. Ar.

תבר to break. The latter are the same word with different prefixes. See Class Br. No. 26. 27.]

1. To part or divide by violence; to separate by cutting or rending; as, to *sever* the body or the arm at a single stroke.

2. To part from the rest by violence; as, to *sever* the head from the body.

3. To separate; to disjoin, as distinct things, but united; as the dearest friends *severed* by cruel necessity.

4. To separate and put in different orders or places.

The angels shall come forth and *sever* the wicked from among the just. Matt. xiii.

5. To disjoin; to disunite; in a general sense, but usually implying violence.

6. To keep distinct or apart. Ex. viii.

7. In *law*, to disunite; to disconnect; to part possession; as, to *sever* an estate in joint-tenancy. *Blackstone.*

SEV'ER, *v. i.* To make a separation or distinction; to distinguish.

The Lord will *sever* between the cattle of Israel and the cattle of Egypt. Ex. ix.

2. To suffer disjunction; to be parted or rent asunder. *Shak.*

SEV'ERAL, *a.* [from *sever.*] Separate; distinct; not common to two or more; as a *several* fishery; a *several* estate. A *several* fishery is one held by the owner of the soil, or by title derived from the owner. A *several* estate is one held by a tenant in his own right, or a distinct estate unconnected with any other person. *Blackstone.*

2. Separate; different; distinct.

Divers sorts of beasts came from *several* parts to drink. *Bacon.*

Four *several* armies to the field are led. *Dryden.*

3. Divers; consisting of a number; more than two, but not very many. *Several* persons were present when the event took place.

4. Separate; single; particular.

Each *several* ship a victory did gain. *Dryden.*

5. Distinct; appropriate.

Each might his *several* province well command,
Would all but stoop to what they understand. *Pope.*

A *joint* and *several* note or bond, is one executed by two or more persons, each of whom is bound to pay the whole, in case the others prove to be insolvent.

SEV'ERAL, *n.* Each particular, or a small number, singly taken.

Several of them neither rose from any conspicuous family, nor left any behind them. *Addison.*

There was not time enough to hear
The *severals*— *Shak.*

[*This latter use, in the plural, is now infrequent or obsolete.*]

2. An inclosed or separate place; inclosed ground; as, they had their *several* for the heathen, their *several* for their own people; put a beast into a *several.* [*These applications are nearly or wholly obsolete.*] *Hooker. Bacon.*

In several, in a state of separation.

Where pastures *in several* be. [*Little used.*] *Tusser.*

SEVERAL'ITY, *n.* Each particular singly taken; distinction. [*Not in use.*] *Bp. Hall.*

SEV'ERALIZE, *v. t.* To distinguish. [*Not in use.*] *Bp. Hall.*

SEV'ERALLY, *adv.* Separately; distinctly; apart from others. Call the men *severally* by name.

I could not keep my eye steady on them *severally* so as to number them. *Newton.*

To be *jointly* and *severally* bound in a contract, is for each obligor to be liable to pay the whole demand, in case the other or others are not able.

SEV'ERALTY, *n.* A state of separation from the rest, or from all others. An estate in *severalty*, is that which the tenant holds in his own right, without being joined in interest with any other person. It is distinguished from joint-tenancy, coparcenary and common. *Blackstone.*

SEV'ERANCE, *n.* Separation; the act of dividing or disuniting. The *severance* of a jointure is made by destroying the unity of interest. Thus when there are two joint-tenants for life, and the inheritance is purchased by or descends upon either, it is a *severance.*

So also when two persons are joined in a writ, and one is nonsuited; in this case *severance* is permitted, and the other plaintif may proceed in the suit. So also in assize, when two or more disseizees appear upon the writ, and not the other, *severance* is permitted. *Blackstone. Encyc.*

SEVE'RE, *a.* [Fr. from L. *severus;* It. Sp. *severo.*]

1. Rigid; harsh; not mild or indulgent; as *severe* words; *severe* treatment; *severe* wrath. *Milton. Pope.*

2. Sharp; hard; rigorous.

Let your zeal—be more *severe* against thyself than against others. *Taylor.*

3. Very strict; or sometimes perhaps, unreasonably strict or exact; giving no indulgence to faults or errors; as *severe* government; *severe* criticism.

4. Rigorous, perhaps cruel; as *severe* punishment; *severe* justice.

5. Grave; sober; sedate to an extreme; opposed to *cheerful, gay, light, lively.*

Your looks must alter, as your subject does,
From kind to fierce, from wanton to *severe.* *Waller.*

6. Rigidly exact; strictly methodical; not lax or airy. I will not venture on so nice a subject with my *severe* style.

7. Sharp; afflictive; distressing; violent; as *severe* pain, anguish, torture, &c.

8. Sharp; biting; extreme; as *severe* cold.

9. Close; concise; not luxuriant.

The Latin, a most *severe* and compendious language— *Dryden.*

10. Exact; critical; nice; as a *severe* test.

SEVE'RELY, *adv.* Harshly; sharply; as, to chide one *severely.*

2. Strictly; rigorously; as, to judge one *severely.*

To be or fondly or *severely* kind. *Savage.*

3. With extreme rigor; as, to punish *severely.*

4. Painfully; afflictively; greatly; as, to be *severely* afflicted with the gout.

5. Fiercely; ferociously.

More formidable Hydra stands within,
Whose jaws with iron teeth *severely* grin. *Dryden.*

SEV'ERITE, *n.* A mineral found near St. Sever, in France, occurring in small masses, white without luster, a little harder than lithomarge. *Phillips.*

SEVER'ITY, *n.* [L. *severitas.*] Harshness; rigor; austerity; want of mildness or indulgence; as the *severity* of a reprimand or reproof.

2. Rigor; extreme strictness; as *severity* of discipline or government.

3. Excessive rigor; extreme degree or amount. *Severity* of penalties or punishments often defeats the object by exciting pity.

4. Extremity; quality or power of distressing; as the *severity* of pain or anguish.

5. Extreme degree; as the *severity* of cold or heat.

6. Extreme coldness or inclemency; as the *severity* of the winter.

7. Harshness; cruel treatment; sharpness of punishment; as *severity* practiced on prisoners of war.

8. Exactness; rigor; niceness; as the *severity* of a test.

9. Strictness; rigid accuracy.

Confining myself to the *severity* of truth. *Dryden.*

SEVRU'GA, *n.* A fish, the *accipenser stellatus.* *Tooke. Pallas.*

SEW, to follow. [*Not used.* See *Sue.*] *Spenser.*

SEW, *v. t.* pronounced *so*, and better written *soe.* [Sax. *siwian, suwian;* Goth. *siuyan;* Sw. *sy;* Dan. *syer;* L. *suo.* This is probably a contracted word, and if its elements are *Sb* or *Sf*, it coincides with the Eth. ሸፈየ shafai, to sew; and the Ar. has إشفي an awl. See Class Sb. No. 85. 100. The Hindoo has *siwawa*, and the Gipsey *siwena.* But the elements are not obvious.]

To unite or fasten together with a needle and thread.

They *sewed* fig leaves together, and made themselves aprons. Gen. iii.

To sew up, to inclose by sewing; to inclose in any thing sewed.

Thou *sewest up* mine iniquity. Job xiv.

Sew me up the skirts of the gown. *Shak.*

SEW, *v. i.* To practice sewing; to join things with stitches.

SEW, *v. t.* [L. *sicco*, to dry.] To drain a pond for taking the fish. *Obs.*

SEW'ED, *pp.* United by stitches.

SEW'EL, *n.* Among *huntsmen*, something hung up to prevent deer from entering a place.

SEW'ER, *n.* [G. *anzucht;* perhaps from the root of *suck*, or L. *sicco.*]

A drain or passage to convey off water under ground; a subterraneous canal, particularly in cities; corruptly pronounced *shore* or *soer.*

SEW'ER, *n.* [D. *schaffer*, from *schaffen*, to provide, to dish up; G. *schaffner;* Dan. *skaffer;* Sw. *skaffare.* See *Shape.*]

An officer who serves up a feast and arranges the dishes. *Obs.* *Milton.*

SEW'ER, *n.* One who sews, or uses the needle.

SEW'ING, *ppr.* Joining with the needle or with stitches.

SEW'STER, *n.* A woman that sews or spins. *Obs.* *B. Jonson.*

SEX, *n.* [Fr. *sexe;* Sp. *sexo;* It. *sesso;* L. *sexus;* qu. G. *sieke*, she, female; from L. *seco*, to divide.]

1. The distinction between male and female; or that property or character by which an animal is male or female. The male sex is usually characterized by muscular strength, boldness and firmness. The female sex is characterized by softness, sensibility and modesty.

In *botany*, the property of plants which corresponds to *sex* in animals. The Linnean system of botany is formed on the doctrine of *sexes* in plants. *Milne.*

2. By way of emphasis, womankind; females.

Unhappy *sex!* whose beauty is your snare. *Dryden.*

The *sex*, whose presence civilizes ours. *Cowper.*

SEXAĠENA'RIAN, *n.* [infra.] A person who has arrived at the age of sixty years. *Cowper.*

SEX'AĠENARY, *a.* [Fr. *sexagénaire;* L. *sexagenarius*, from *sex*, six, and a word signifying ten, seen in *viginti; bis-genti.*]

Designating the number sixty; as a noun, a person sixty years of age; also, something composed of sixty.

SEXAĠES'IMA, *n.* [L. *sexagesimus*, sixtieth.]

The second Sunday before Lent, the next to Shrove-Sunday, so called as being about the 60th day before Easter.

SEXAĠES'IMAL, *a.* Sixtieth; pertaining to the number sixty. *Sexagenary* or *sexagesimal* arithmetic, is a method of computation by sixties, as that which is used in dividing minutes into seconds.

Sexagesimals, or *sexagesimal fractions*, are those whose denominators proceed in the ratio of sixty; as $\frac{1}{60}$, $\frac{1}{3600}$, $\frac{1}{216000}$. The denominator is sixty, or its multiple. These fractions are called also astronomical fractions, because formerly there were no others used in astronomical calculations. *Encyc.*

SEXAN'GLED, } *a.* [L. *sex*, six, and *an-*
SEXAN'GULAR, } *gulus*, angle.] Having six angles; hexagonal. *Dryden.*

SEXAN'GULARLY, *adv.* With six angles; hexagonally.

SEXDEC'IMAL, *a.* [L. *sex*, six, and *decem*, ten.]

In *crystalography*, when a prism or the middle part of a crystal has six faces and two summits, and taken together, ten faces, or the reverse.

SEXDUODEC'IMAL, *a.* [L. *sex*, six, and *duodecim*, twelve.]

In *crystalography*, designating a crystal when the prism or middle part has six faces and two summits, having together twelve faces.

SEXEN'NIAL, *a.* [L. *sex*, six, and *annus*, year.]

Lasting six years, or happening once in six years.

SEXEN'NIALLY, *adv.* Once in six years.

SEX'FID, *a.* [L. *sex*, six, and *findo*, to divide.]

In *botany*, six-cleft; as a *sexfid* calyx or nectary *Martyn.*

SEXLOC'ULAR, *a.* [L. *sex*, six, and *loculus*, a cell.] In *botany*, six-celled; having six cells for seeds; as a *sexlocular* pericarp.

SEX'TAIN, *n.* [L. *sextans*, a sixth, from *sex*, six.] A stanza of six lines.

SEX'TANT, *n.* [L. *sextans*, a sixth. The Romans divided the as into 12 ounces; a sixth, or two ounces, was the *sextans.*]

1. In *mathematics*, the sixth part of a circle. Hence,

2. An instrument formed like a quadrant, excepting that its limb comprehends only 60 degrees, or the sixth part of a circle. *Encyc.*

3. In *astronomy*, a constellation of the southern hemisphere which, according to the British catalogue, contains 41 stars. *Encyc.*

SEX'TARY, *n.* [L. *sextarius.*] A measure of a pint and a half.

SEX'TARY, } *n.* The same as *sacristan.*
SEX'TRY, } [*Not used.*] *Dict.*

SEX'TILE, *n.* [L. *sextilis*, from *sex*, six.] Denoting the aspect or position of two planets, when distant from each other 60 degrees or two signs. This position is marked thus *. *Encyc.*

SEX'TON, *n.* [contracted from *sacristan*, which see.]

An under officer of the church, whose business is to take care of the vessels, vestments, &c. belonging to the church, to attend on the officiating clergyman and perform other duties pertaining to the church, to dig graves, &c. *Encyc.*

SEX'TONSHIP, *n.* The office of a sexton. *Swift.*

SEX'TUPLE, *a.* [Low L. *sextuplus; sex*, six, and *duplus*, double.]

1. Sixfold; six times as much. *Brown.*

2. In *music*, denoting a mixed sort of triple, beaten in double time, or a measure of two times composed of six equal notes, three for each time. *Busby. Encyc.*

SEX'UAL, *a.* [from *sex.*] Pertaining to sex or the sexes; distinguishing the sex; denoting what is peculiar to the distinction and office of male and female; as *sexual* characteristics; *sexual* intercourse, connection or commerce.

2. *Sexual system*, in botany, the system which ascribes to vegetables the distinction of sexes, supposes that plants are male and female, each sex furnished with appropriate organs or parts; the male producing a pollen or dust which fecundates the stigma of the pistil or female organ, and is necessary to render it prolific. It is found however that most plants are hermaphrodite, the male and female organs being contained in the same flower. This doctrine was taught to a certain extent, by Theophrastus, Dioscorides and Pliny among the ancients, but has been more fully illustrated by Cæsalpinus, Grew, Camerarius, Linne and many others among the moderns. *Milne. Encyc.*

SEX'UALIST, *n.* One who believes and maintains the doctrine of sexes in plants; or one who classifies plants by the differences of the sexes and parts of fructification. *Milne. Encyc.*

SEXUAL'ITY, *n.* The state of being distinguished by sex.

SHAB, *v. i.* To play mean tricks. In some parts of New England, it signifies to reject or dismiss; as, a woman *shabs* her suitor. It is however very vulgar and nearly obsolete.

SHAB'BILY, *adv.* [from *shabby.*] Raggedly; with rent or ragged clothes; as, to be clothed *shabbily.*

2. Meanly; in a despicable manner.

SHAB'BINESS, *n.* Raggedness; as the *shabbiness* of a garment.

2. Meanness; paltriness.

SHAB'BY, *a.* [D. *schabbig;* G. *schäbig*, from *schaben*, to rub, to *shave*, to scratch; *schabe*, a moth, a shaving tool, a *scab.* This is a different orthography of *scabby.*]

1. Ragged; torn, or worn to rags; as a *shabby* coat: *shabby* clothes.

2. Clothed with ragged garments.

The dean was so *shabby*— *Swift.*

3. Mean; paltry; despicable; as a *shabby* fellow; *shabby* treatment. *Clarendon.*

[For the idea expressed by *shabby*, there is not a better word in the language.]

SHACK, *n.* In *ancient customs of England*, a liberty of winter pasturage. In Norfolk and Suffolk, the lord of a manor has *shack*, that is, liberty of feeding his sheep at pleasure on his tenants' lands during the six winter months. In Norfolk, shack extends to the common for hogs, in all men's grounds, from harvest to seed-time; whence to go *a-shack*, is to feed at large. *Cowel. Encyc.*

In New England, *shack* is used in a somewhat similar sense for mast or the food of swine, and for feeding at large or in the forest, [for we have no manors,] and I have heard a shiftless fellow, a vagabond, called a *shack.*

SHACK, *v. i.* To shed, as corn at harvest. [*Local.*] *Grose.*

2. To feed in stubble, or upon the waste corn of the field. [*Local.*] *Pegge.*

SHACK'LE, *n.* Stubble.

[In Scotish, *shag* is the refuse of barley, or that which is not well filled, and is given to horses. The word *shack* then is probably from a root which signifies to break, to reject, or to waste, or it may be allied to *shag* and *shake.*]

SHACK'LE, *v. t.* [Sax. *sceacul;* D. *schakel*, a link or mesh; Sax. *sceac-line*, a rope to fasten the foot of a sail. Qu. the root שך. Class Sg. No. 74. But we find the word perhaps in the Ar. شِكَالٌ, from شَكَلَ shakala, to tie the feet of a beast or bird.]

1. To chain; to fetter; to tie or confine the limbs so as to prevent free motion.

So the stretch'd cord the *shackled* dancer tries,
As prone to fall as impotent to rise. *Smith.*

2. To bind or confine so as to obstruct or embarrass action.

You must not *shackle* him with rules about indifferent matters. *Locke.*

SHACK'LE, } *n.* [generally used in the
SHACK'LES, } plural.] Fetters, gyves, handcuffs, cords or something else that confines the limbs so as to restrain the use of them, or prevent free motion. *Dryden.*

2. That which obstructs or embarrasses free action.

His very will seems to be in bonds and *shackles.* *South.*

SHACK'LED, *pp.* Tied; confined; embarrassed.

SHACK'LING, *ppr.* Fettering; binding; confining.

SHAD, *n.* It has no plural termination. *Shad* is singular or plural. [G. *schade.* In W. *ysgadan*, Ir. *sgadan*, is a herring.]
A fish, a species of Clupea. *Shad* enter the rivers in England and America in the spring in immense numbers.

SHAD'DOCK, *n.* A variety of the orange *(Citrus aurantium ;)* pampelmoe. [Fr. *pamplemousse.*] *Lee.*
A large species of orange, *(Citrus decumana.)* *Ed. Encyc.*

SHADE, *n.* [Sax. *scad, scead, sced*, shade; *sceadan*, to separate, divide or shade; G. *schatten*, shadow, and to shade; D. *schaduw, schaduwen*; Dan. *skatterer*, to shade a picture; W. *ysgawd*, a shade; *ysgodi*, to shade or shelter; *cysgodi*, id.; Corn. *skod* or *skez*; Ir. *sgath*, and *sgatham*, to cut off, to shade. The Gr. σκια is probably the same word contracted, and perhaps σκοτος, darkness. In the sense of cutting off or separating, this word coincides exactly, as it does in elements, with the G. *scheiden*, L. *scindo*, for *scido*, which is formed on *cædo*, to strike off. Hence Sax. *gescead*, distinction, L. *scutum*, a shield, Sp. *escudo*; that which cuts off or intercepts. Owen deduces the Welsh word from *cawd*, something that incloses; but probably the sense is that which cuts off or defends.]

1. Literally, the interception, cutting off or interruption of the rays of light; hence, the obscurity which is caused by such interception. *Shade* differs from *shadow*, as it implies no particular form or definite limit; whereas a *shadow* represents in form the object which intercepts the light. Hence when we say, let us resort to the *shade* of a tree, we have no reference to its form; but when we speak of measuring a pyramid or other object by its *shadow*, we have reference to its extent.
2. Darkness; obscurity; as the *shades* of night. The *shade* of the earth constitutes the darkness of night.
3. An obscure place, properly in a grove or close wood, which precludes the sun's rays; and hence, a secluded retreat.
   Let us seek out some desolate *shade*, and there
   Weep our sad bosoms empty. *Shak.*
4. A screen; something that intercepts light or heat.
5. Protection; shelter. [See *Shadow.*]
6. In *painting*, the dark part of a picture. *Dryden.*
7. Degree or gradation of light.
   White, red, yellow, blue, with their several degrees, or *shades* and mixtures, as green, come only in by the eyes. *Locke.*
8. A shadow. [See *Shadow.*]
   Envy will merit, as its *shade*, pursue. *Pope.*
   [This is allowable in poetry.]
9. The soul, after its separation from the body; so called because the ancients supposed it to be perceptible to the sight, not to the touch; a spirit; a ghost; as the *shades* of departed heroes.
   Swift as thought, the flitting *shade*— *Dryden.*

SHADE, *v. t.* [Sax. *sceadan, gesceadan*, to separate, to divide, to *shade.*]

1. To shelter or screen from light by intercepting its rays; and when applied to the rays of the sun, it signifies to shelter from light and heat; as, a large tree *shades* the plants under its branches; *shaded* vegetables rarely come to perfection.
   I went to crop the sylvan scenes,
   And *shade* our altars with their leafy greens. *Dryden.*
2. To overspread with darkness or obscurity; to obscure.
   Thou *shad'st*
   The full blaze of thy beams. *Milton.*
3. To shelter; to hide.
   Ere in our own house I do *shade* my head. *Shak.*
4. To cover from injury; to protect; to screen. *Milton.*
5. To paint in obscure colors; to darken.
6. To mark with gradations of color; as the *shading* pencil. *Milton.*
7. To darken; to obscure.

SHA'DED, *pp.* Defended from the rays of the sun; darkened.

SHA'DER, *n.* He or that which shades.

SHA'DINESS, *n.* [from *shady.*] The state of being shady; umbrageousness; as the *shadiness* of the forest.

SHA'DING, *ppr.* Sheltering from the sun's rays.

SHAD'OW, *n.* [Sax. *scadu, sceadu.* See *Shade.*]

1. Shade within defined limits; obscurity or deprivation of light, apparent on a plane and representing the form of the body which intercepts the rays of light; as the *shadow* of a man, of a tree or a tower. The *shadow* of the earth in an eclipse of the moon is proof of its sphericity.
2. Darkness; shade; obscurity.
   Night's sable *shadows* from the ocean rise. *Denham.*
3. Shelter made by any thing that intercepts the light, heat or influence of the air.
   In secret *shadow* from the sunny ray,
   On a sweet bed of lilies softly laid. *Spenser.*
4. Obscure place; secluded retreat.
   To secret *shadows* I retire. [*Obs.*] *Dryden.*
5. Dark part of a picture. *Obs.* *Peacham.*
   [In the two last senses, *shade* is now used.]
6. A spirit; a ghost. *Obs.*
   [In this sense, *shade* is now used.]
7. In *painting*, the representation of a real shadow.
8. An imperfect and faint representation; opposed to *substance.*
   The law having a *shadow* of good things to come. Heb. x.
9. Inseparable companion.
   Sin and her *shadow*, death. *Milton.*
10. Type; mystical representation.
    Types and *shadows* of that destin'd seed. *Milton.*
11. Protection; shelter; favor. Lam. iv. Ps. xci.
12. Slight or faint appearance. James i.

Shadow of death, terrible darkness, trouble or death. Job iii.

SHAD'OW, *v. t.* To overspread with obscurity.
   The warlike elf much wonder'd at this tree
   So fair and great, that *shadow'd* all the ground. *Spenser.*
   [*Shade* is more generally used.]
2. To cloud; to darken.
   The *shadow'd* livery of the burning sun. *Shak.*
3. To make cool; to refresh by shade; or to shade.
   Flowery fields and *shadowed* waters. *Sidney.*
4. To conceal; to hide; to screen.
   Let every soldier hew him down a bough,
   And bear't before him; thereby shall we *shadow*
   The number of our host. [*Unusual.*] *Shak.*
5. To protect; to screen from danger; to shroud.
   Shadowing their right under your wings of war. *Shak.*
6. To mark with slight gradations of color or light. [In this sense, *shade* is chiefly used.] *Locke.*
7. To paint in obscure colors; as void spaces deeply *shadowed.* *Dryden.*
8. To represent faintly or imperfectly.
   Augustus is *shadowed* in the person of Æneas. *Dryden.*
9. To represent typically. The healing power of the brazen serpent *shadoweth* the efficacy of Christ's righteousness.
   [The two last senses are in use. In place of the others, *shade* is now more generally used.]

SHAD'OWED, *pp.* Represented imperfectly or typically.

SHAD'OW-GRASS, *n.* A kind of grass so called. [*Gramen sylvaticum.*] *Johnson.*

SHAD'OWING, *ppr.* Representing by faint or imperfect resemblance.

SHAD'OWING, *n.* Shade or gradation of light and color. [This should be *shading.*]

SHAD'OWY, *a.* [Sax. *sceadwig.*] Full of shade; dark; gloomy.
   This *shadowy* desert, unfrequented woods. *Shak.*
2. Not brightly luminous; faintly light.
   More pleasant light
   Shadowy sets off the face of things. *Milton.*
3. Faintly representative; typical; as *shadowy* expiations. *Milton.*
4. Unsubstantial; unreal.
   Milton has brought into his poems two actors of a *shadowy* and fictitious nature, in the persons of Sin and Death. *Addison.*
5. Dark; obscure; opake.
   By command ere yet dim night
   Her *shadowy* cloud withdraws. *Milton.*

SHA'DY, *a.* [from *shade.*] Abounding with shade or shades; overspread with shade.
   And Amaryllis fills the *shady* groves. *Dryden.*
2. Sheltered from the glare of light or sultry heat.
   Cast it also that you may have rooms *shady* for summer and warm for winter. *Bacon.*

SHAF'FLE, *v. i.* [See *Shuffle.*] To hobble or limp. [*Not in use.*]

SHAF'FLER, *n.* A hobbler; one that limps. [*Not in use.*]

SHAFT, *n.* [Sax. *sceaft*; D. G. *schaft*; Sw. Dan. *skaft*; L. *scapus*; from the root of *shape*, from setting, or shooting, extending.]

1. An arrow; a missile weapon; as the archer and the *shaft.* *More.*
   So lofty was the pile, a Parthian bow
   With vigor drawn must send the *shaft* below. *Dryden.*

2. In *mining*, a pit or long narrow opening or entrance into a mine. [This may possibly be a different word, as in German it is written *schacht*, Dan. *skægte*.]
3. In *architecture*, the shaft of a column is the body of it, between the base and the capital.
4. Any thing straight; as the *shaft* of a steeple, and many other things. *Peacham.*
5. The stem or stock of a fether or quill.
6. The pole of a carriage, sometimes called *tongue* or *neap*. The thills of a chaise or gig are also called *shafts*.
7. The handle of a weapon.
Shaft, or *white-shaft*, a species of Trochilus or humming bird, having a bill twenty lines in length, and two long white fethers in the middle of its tail. *Encyc.*

SH'AFTED, *a.* Having a handle; a term in heraldry, applied to a spear-head.

SH'AFTMENT, *n.* [Sax. *scæftmund.*] A span, a measure of about six inches. [*Not in use.*] *Ray.*

SHAG, *n.* [Sax. *sceacga*, hair, shag; Dan. *skiæg*; Sw. *skägg*, the beard, a brush, &c. In Eth. ሠቀ shaky, a hair cloth.]
1. Coarse hair or nap, or rough woolly hair.
   True Witney broadcloth, with its shag unshorn. *Gay.*
2. A kind of cloth having a long coarse nap.
3. In *ornithology*, an aquatic fowl, the *Pelecanus graculus*; in the north of England called the *crave*. *Encyc. Ed. Encyc.*

SHAG, *a.* Hairy; shaggy. *Shak.*

SHAG, *v. t.* To make rough or hairy.
   Shag the green zone that bounds the boreal skies. *J. Barlow.*
2. To make rough or shaggy; to deform. *Thomson.*

SHAG'GED, } *a.* Rough with long hair or
SHAG'GY, } wool.
   About his shoulders hangs the *shaggy* skin. *Dryden.*
2. Rough; rugged; as the *shaggy* tops of hills. *Milton.*
   And throw the *shaggy* spoils about your shoulders. *Addison.*

SHAG'GEDNESS, } *n.* The state of being
SHAG'GINESS, } shaggy; roughness with long loose hair or wool.

SHAGREE'N, *n.* [Pers. سغري sagri, the skin of a horse or an ass, &c. dressed.]
A kind of grained lether prepared of the skin of a fish, a species of Squalus. To prepare it, the skin is stretched and covered with mustard seed, which is bruised upon it. The skin is then exposed to the weather for some days, and afterwards tanned. *Encyc.*

SHAGREE'N, *a.* Made of the lether called shagreen.

SHAGREEN, for *chagrin.* [See *Chagrin.*]

SHAH, *n.* A Persian word signifying king. *Eton.*

SHAIK, } *n.* Among the Arabians and
SCHEICH, } Moors, an old man, and hence a chief, a lord, a man of eminence. *Encyc.*

SHAIL, *v. t.* To walk sidewise. [*Low and not in use.*] *L'Estrange.*
[This word is probably the G. *schielen*, Dan. *skieler*, to squint.]

SHAKE, *v. t.* pret. *shook*; pp. *shaken.* [Sax. *sceacan*, to shake, also to flee, to depart, to withdraw; Sw. *skaka*; D. *schokken*, to shake, to jolt, to heap; *schok*, a shock, jolt or bounce; W. *ysgegiaw*, to shake by seizing one by the throat; *cegiaw*, to choke, from *cêg*, a choking, the mouth, an entrance. If the Welsh gives the true origin of this word, it is remarkably expressive, and characteristic of rough manners. I am not confident that the Welsh and Saxon are from a common stock.]
1. To cause to move with quick vibrations; to move rapidly one way and the other; to agitate; as, the wind *shakes* a tree; an earthquake *shakes* the hills or the earth.
   I *shook* my lap, and said, so God *shake* out every man from his house— Neh. v.
   He *shook* the sacred honors of his head. *Dryden.*
   —As a fig tree casteth her untimely fruit, when it is *shaken* of a mighty wind. Rev. vi.
2. To make to totter or tremble.
   The rapid wheels *shake* heav'n's basis. *Milton.*
3. To cause to shiver; as, an ague *shakes* the whole frame.
4. To throw down by a violent motion.
   Macbeth is ripe for *shaking*. *Shak.*
   [But see *shake off*, which is generally used.]
5. To throw away; to drive off.
   'Tis our first intent
   To *shake* all cares and business from our age.
   [See *Shake off.*] *Shak.*
6. To move from firmness; to weaken the stability of; to endanger; to threaten to overthrow. Nothing should *shake* our belief in the being and perfections of God, and in our own accountableness.
7. To cause to waver or doubt; to impair the resolution of; to depress the courage of.
   That ye be not soon *shaken* in mind. 2 Thess. ii.
8. To trill; as, to *shake* a note in music.
To shake hands, sometimes, to unite with; to agree or contract with; more generally, to take leave of, from the practice of shaking hands at meeting and parting. *Shak. K. Charles.*
To shake off, to drive off; to throw off or down by violence; as, to *shake off* the dust of the feet; also, to rid one's self; to free from; to divest of; as, to *shake off* disease or grief; to *shake off* troublesome dependents. *Addison.*

SHAKE, *v. i.* To be agitated with a waving or vibratory motion; as, a tree *shakes* with the wind; the house *shakes* in a tempest.
   The foundations of the earth do *shake*. Is. xxiv.
2. To tremble; to shiver; to quake; as, a man *shakes* in an ague; or he *shakes* with cold, or with terror.
3. To totter.
   Under his burning wheels
   The steadfast empyrean *shook* throughout,
   All but the throne itself of God. *Milton.*

SHAKE, *n.* Concussion; a vacillating or wavering motion; a rapid motion one way and the other; agitation.
   The great soldier's honor was composed of thicker stuff which could endure a *shake*. *Herbert.*
2. A trembling or shivering; agitation.
3. A motion of hands clasped.
   Our salutations were very hearty on both sides, consisting of many kind *shakes* of the hand. *Addison.*
4. In *music*, a trill; a rapid reiteration of two notes comprehending an interval not greater than one whole tone, nor less than a semitone. *Busby.*

SHAKEN, *pp.* sha'kn. Impelled with a vacillating motion; agitated.
2. *a.* Cracked or split; as *shaken* timber.
   Nor is the wood *shaken* nor twisted, as those about Capetown. *Barrow.*
   [Our mechanics usually pronounce this *shaky*, forming the word from *shake*, like *pithy*, from pith.]

SHA'KER, *n.* A person or thing that shakes or agitates; as the *shaker* of the earth. *Pope.*
2. In the United States, *Shakers* is the name given to a very singular sect of Christians, so called from the agitations or movements which characterize their worship.

SHA'KING, *ppr.* Impelling to a wavering motion; causing to vacillate or waver; agitating.
2. Trembling; shivering; quaking.

SHA'KING, *n.* The act of shaking or agitating; brandishing. Job xli.
2. Concussion. *Harmar.*
3. A trembling or shivering. *Waller.*

SHA'KY, *a.* Cracked, as timber. *Chambers.*

SHAL, } *v. i.* *verb auxiliary.* pret. *should.*
SHALL, } [Sax. *scealan*, *scylan*, to be obliged. It coincides in signification nearly with *ought*, it is a duty, it is necessary; D. *zal*, *zul*; G. *soll*; Sw. *skola*, pret. *skulle*; Dan. *skal*, *skulle*, *skulde*. The German and Dutch have lost the palatal letter of the verb; but it appears in the derivative G. *schuld*, guilt, fault, culpability, debt; D. *schuld*, id.; Sw. *skuld*, Dan. *skyld*, debt, fault, guilt; *skylder*, to owe; Sax. *scyld*, debt, offense, L. *scelus*. The literal sense is to hold or be held, hence to owe, and hence the sense of guilt, a being held, bound or liable to justice and punishment. In the Teutonic dialects, *schulden*, *skyld*, are used in the Lord's prayer, as "forgive us our debts," but neither *debt* nor *trespass* expresses the exact idea, which includes sin or crime, and liability to punishment. The word seems to be allied in origin to *skill*, L. *calleo*, to be able, to know. See *Skill*. *Shall* is defective, having no infinitive, imperative or participle. It ought to be written *shal*, as the original has one *l* only, and it has one only in *shalt* and *should*.]
1. *Shall* is primarily in the present tense, and in our mother tongue was followed by a verb in the infinitive, like other verbs. "Ic *sceal* fram the *beon* gefullod." I *have need* to be baptized of thee. Matt. iii. "Ic nu *sceal singan* sar-cwidas." I must now sing mournful songs. *Boethius.*
   We still use *shall* and *should* before another verb in the infinitive, without the sign *to*; but the signification of *shall* is considerably deflected from its primitive sense. It is now treated as a mere auxiliary to other verbs, serving to form some of the tenses. In the present tense, *shall*, before a verb in the infinitive, forms the future tense; but its force and effect are different with the different persons or personal

pronouns. Thus in the first person, *shall* simply foretells or declares what will take place; as, I or we *shall* ride to town on Monday. This declaration simply informs another of a fact that is to take place. The sense of *shall* here is changed from an expression of need or duty, to that of previous statement or information, grounded on intention or resolution. When uttered with emphasis, "I *shall* go," it expresses firm determination, but not a promise.

2. In the second and third persons, *shall* implies a promise, command or determination. "You *shall* receive your wages," "he *shall* receive his wages," imply that you or he *ought* to receive them; but usage gives to these phrases the force of a *promise* in the person uttering them.

When *shall* is uttered with emphasis in such phrases, it expresses determination in the speaker, and implies an authority to enforce the act. "Do you refuse to go? Does he refuse to go? But you or he *shall* go."

3. *Shall I go, shall he go*, interrogatively, asks for permission or direction. But *shall you go*, asks for information of another's intention.

4. But after another verb, *shall*, in the third person, simply foretells. He says that he *shall* leave town to-morrow. So also in the second person; you say that you *shall* ride to-morrow.

5. After *if*, and some verbs which express condition or supposition, *shall*, in all the persons, simply foretells; as,

If { I *shall* say, or we *shall* say,
Thou *shalt* say, ye or you *shall* say,
He *shall* say, they *shall* say.

6. *Should*, in the first person, implies a conditional event. "I *should* have written a letter yesterday, had I not been interrupted." Or it expresses obligation, and that in all the persons.

I *should*, { have paid the bill on de-
Thou *shouldst*, { mand; it was my duty,
He *should*, { your duty, his duty to
You *should*, } pay the bill on demand,
but it was not paid.

7. *Should*, though properly the past tense of *shall*, is often used to express a contingent future event; as, if it *should* rain to-morrow; if you *should* go to London next week; if he *should* arrive within a month. In like manner after *though, grant, admit, allow*.

SHALE, *v. t.* To peel. [*Not in use.* See *Shell.*]

SHALE, *n.* [G. *schale*; a different orthography of *shell*, but not in use. See *Shell.*]

1. A shell or husk. *Shak.*

2. In *natural history*, a species of shist or shistous clay; slate clay; generally of a bluish or yellowish gray color, more rarely of a dark blackish or reddish gray, or grayish black, or greenish color. Its fracture is slaty, and in water it molders into powder. It is often found in strata in coal mines, and commonly bears vegetable impressions. It is generally the forerunner of coal. *Kirwan.*

Bituminous shale is a subvariety of argillaceous slate, is impregnated with bitumen, and burns with flame. *Cleaveland.*

SHALLOON′, *n.* [said to be from *Chalons*, in France; Sp. *chaleon*; Fr. *ras de Chalons.*] A slight woolen stuff. *Swift.*

SHAL′LOP, *n.* [Fr. *chaloupe*; Sp. Port. *chalupa*; G. *schaluppe.* This word is changed into *sloop*; but the two words have now different significations.]

1. A sort of large boat with two masts, and usually rigged like a schooner. *Mar. Dict.*

2. A small light vessel with a small mainmast and fore-mast, with lug-sails. *Encyc.*

SHAL′LOW, *a.* [from *shoal*, Sax. *sceol*, a crowd, or rather *scylf*, a shelf.]

1. Not deep; having little depth; shoal; as *shallow* water; a *shallow* stream; a *shallow* brook. *Dryden.*

2. Not deep; not entering far into the earth; as a *shallow* furrow; a *shallow* trench. *Dryden.*

3. Not intellectually deep; not profound; not penetrating deeply into abstruse subjects; superficial; as a *shallow* mind or understanding; *shallow* skill.

> Deep vers'd in books, and *shallow* in himself. *Milton.*

4. Slight; not deep; as a *shallow* sound. *Bacon.*

SHAL′LOW, *n.* A shoal; a shelf; a flat; a sand-bank; any place where the water is not deep.

> A swift stream is not heard in the channel, but upon *shallows* of gravel. *Bacon.*
>
> Dash'd on the *shallows* of the moving sand. *Dryden.*

SHAL′LOW, *v. t.* To make shallow. [*Little used.*] *Herbert.*

SHAL′LOW-BRAINED, *a.* Weak in intellect; foolish; empty headed. *South.*

SHAL′LOWLY, *adv.* With little depth. *Carew.*

2. Superficially; simply; without depth of thought or judgment; not wisely. *Shak.*

SHAL′LOWNESS, *n.* Want of depth; small depth; as the *shallowness* of water, of a river, of a stream.

2. Superficialness of intellect; want of power to enter deeply into subjects; emptiness; silliness.

SHALM, } *n.* [G. *schalmeie*, from *schallen*,
SHAWM, } to sound. A kind of musical pipe. [*Not used.*] *Knolles.*

SHALO′TE, *n.* The French *echalote* anglicized. [See *Eschalot.*]

SHAL′STONE, *n.* A mineral found only in the Bannet of Temeswar, of a grayish, yellowish or reddish white; tafelspath.

SHALT, the second person singular of *shall*; as, thou *shalt* not steal.

SHAM, *n.* [W. *siom*, vacuity, void, balk, disappointment.]

That which deceives expectation; any trick, fraud or device that deludes and disappoints; delusion; imposture. [*Not an elegant word.*]

> Believe who will the solemn *sham*, not I. *Addison.*

SHAM, *a.* False; counterfeit; pretended; as a *sham* fight.

SHAM, *v. t.* [W. *siomi*, to balk or disappoint.]

To deceive expectation; to trick; to cheat; to delude with false pretenses.

> They find themselves fooled and *shammed* into conviction. [*Not elegant.*] *L'Estrange.*

2. To obtrude by fraud or imposition. *L'Estrange.*

SHAM, *v. i.* To make mocks. *Prior.*

SHAM′AN, *n.* In Russia, a wizard or conjurer, who by enchantment pretends to cure diseases, ward off misfortunes and foretell events. *Encyc.*

SHAM′BLES, *n.* [Sax. *scamel*, L. *scamnum*, a bench, It. *scanno*, Sp. *escaño*; from L. *scando.*]

1. The place where butcher's meat is sold; a flesh-market. 1 Cor. x.

2. In *mining*, a nich or shelf left at suitable distances to receive the ore which is thrown from one to another, and thus raised to the top.

SHAM′BLING, *a.* [from *scamble*, *scambling.*]

Moving with an awkward, irregular, clumsy pace; as a *shambling* trot; *shambling* legs. *Smith.*

SHAM′BLING, *n.* An awkward, clumsy, irregular pace or gait.

SHAME, *n.* [Sax. *scama*, *sceam*, *sceom*; G. *scham*; D. *schaamen*; Sw. Dan. *skam.* Qu. Ar. حَشَمَ chashama, with a prefix, to cause shame, to blush, to reverence. Class Sm. No. 48.]

1. A painful sensation excited by a consciousness of guilt, or of having done something which injures reputation; or by the exposure of that which nature or modesty prompts us to conceal. *Shame* is particularly excited by the disclosure of actions which, in the view of men, are mean and degrading. Hence it is often or always manifested by a downcast look or by blushes, called *confusion of face.*

> Hide, for *shame*,
> Romans, your grandsires' images,
> That blush at their degenerate progeny. *Dryden.*
>
> *Shame* prevails when reason is defeated. *Rambler.*

2. The cause or reason of shame; that which brings reproach, and degrades a person in the estimation of others. Thus an idol is called a *shame.* Hos. ix.

> Guides, who are the *shame* of religion. *South.*

3. Reproach; ignominy; derision; contempt.

> Ye have borne the *shame* of the heathen. Ezek. xxxvi.

4. The parts which modesty requires to be covered.

5. Dishonor; disgrace. Prov. ix.

SHAME, *v. t.* To make ashamed; to excite a consciousness of guilt or of doing something derogatory to reputation; to cause to blush.

> Who *shames* a scribbler, breaks a cobweb through. *Pope.*
>
> I write not these things to *shame* you. 1 Cor. iv.

2. To disgrace.

> And with foul cowardice his carcass *shame.* *Spenser.*

3. To mock at.

> Ye have *shamed* the counsel of the poor. Ps. xiv.

SHAME, *v. i.* To be ashamed.

To its trunk authors give such a magnitude, as I *shame* to repeat. *Raleigh.*

[This verb, I believe, is no longer used intransitively.]

SHA'MED, *pp.* Made ashamed.

SHA'MEFACED, *a.* [Lye supposes this to be a corruption of Sax. *scam-fæst*, shamefast, held or restrained by shame.]

Bashful; easily confused or put out of countenance. A man may be *shamefaced* to excess.

Conscience is a blushing *shamefaced* spirit. *Shak.*

Your *shamefac'd* virtue shunn'd the people's praise. *Dryden.*

SHA'MEFACEDLY, *adv.* Bashfully; with excessive modesty. *Woolton.*

SHA'MEFACEDNESS, *n.* Bashfulness; excess of modesty. *Dryden.*

SHA'MEFUL, *a.* [*shame* and *full.*] That brings shame or disgrace; scandalous; disgraceful; injurious to reputation. It expresses less than *infamous* and *ignominious.*

His naval preparations were not more surprising than his quick and *shameful* retreat. *Arbuthnot.*

2. Indecent; raising shame in others.

Phœbus flying so most *shameful* sight. *Spenser.*

SHA'MEFULLY, *adv.* Disgracefully; in a manner to bring reproach. He *shamefully* deserted his friend.

2. With indignity or indecency; in a manner that may cause shame.

How *shamefully* that maid he did torment. *Spenser.*

SHA'MEFULNESS, *n.* Disgracefulness. *Johnson.*

SHA'MELESS, *a.* [*shame* and *less.*] Destitute of shame; wanting modesty; impudent; brazen-faced; immodest; audacious; insensible to disgrace.

Such *shameless* bards we have. *Pope.*

2. Done without shame; indicating want of shame; as a *shameless* denial of truth.

SHA'MELESSLY, *adv.* Without shame; impudently; as a man *shamelessly* wicked. *Hale.*

SHA'MELESSNESS, *n.* Destitution of shame; want of sensibility to disgrace or dishonor; impudence.

He that blushes not at his crime, but adds *shamelessness* to shame, has nothing left to restore him to virtue. *Taylor.*

SHA'MER, *n.* One who makes ashamed; that which confounds.

SHA'MING, *ppr.* Making ashamed; causing to blush; confounding.

SHAM'MER, *n.* [from *sham.*] One that shams; an impostor. [*Low.*]

SHAMOIS, } *n.* [Fr. *chamois*; It. *camozza*;
SHAM'MY, } Sp. *gamuza*; Port. *gamo*; from Sp. *gama*, a doe, or its root; W. *gavyr*, a goat; Corn. Ir. *gavar.*]

1. A species of wild goat, (*Capra rupicapra*, goat of the rocks,) inhabiting the mountains of Savoy, Piedmont, and the Pyrenees. *Encyc.*

The shamois is now considered as a species of antelope, (*Antelope rupicapra.*) *Ed. Encyc.*

2. A kind of lether prepared from the skin of the wild goat. It is dressed in oil or tanned, and much esteemed for its softness, pliancy and the quality of bearing soap without damage. A great part of the lether which bears this name is counterfeit, being made of the skin of the common goat, the kid, or even of sheep. *Encyc.*

SHAM'ROCK, *n.* The Irish name for three-leafed grass. *Spenser.*

SHANK, *n.* [Sax. *scanc*, *sceanc*; G. D. *schenkel*; Sw. *skank.*]

1. The whole joint from the knee to the ankle. In a horse, the part of the fore leg between the knee and the footlock.

2. The tibia or large bone of the leg; as crooked *shanks.*

3. The long part of an instrument; as the *shank* of a key. *Moxon.*

The beam or shaft of an anchor. *Mar. Dict.*

4. A plant. [*bryonia.*] *Johnson.*

SHANK'ED, *a.* Having a shank.

SHANK'ER, *n.* [from Fr. *chancre.*] A malignant ulcer, usually occasioned by some venereal complaint. *Encyc.*

SHANK-PAINTER, *n.* With *seamen*, a short rope and chain which sustains the shank and flukes of an anchor against the ship's side, as the stopper fastens the ring and stock to the cat-head. *Mar. Dict.*

SHAN'SCRIT, *n.* The Sanscrit, or ancient language of Hindoostan. [See *Sanscrit.*]

SHANTY, for *janty*, gay; showy. [*Not in use or local.*]

SHAPE, *v. t.* pret. *shaped*; pp. *shaped* or *shapen.* [Sax. *sceapian*, *sceppan*, *scipan* or *scyppan*, to form, to create; Sw. *skapa*; Dan. *skaber*; G. *schaffen*, to create, to make or get, to procure, furnish or supply; D. *scheppen*, *schaffen*; Sans. *shafana.* The Sw. has *skaffa*, to provide, and the Dan. *skaffer.*]

1. To form or create.

I was *shapen* in iniquity. Ps. li.

2. To mold or make into a particular form; to give form or figure to; as, to *shape* a garment.

Grace *shap'd* her limbs, and beauty deck'd her face. *Prior.*

3. To mold; to cast; to regulate; to adjust; to adapt to a purpose. He *shapes* his plans or designs to the temper of the times.

4. To direct; as, to *shape* a course. *Denham.*

5. To image; to conceive.

Oft my jealousy
Shapes faults that are not. *Shak.*

SHAPE, *v. i.* To square; to suit; to be adjusted. *Shak.*

SHAPE, *n.* Form or figure as constituted by lines and angles; as the *shape* of a horse or a tree; the *shape* of the head, hand or foot.

2. External appearance.

He beat me grievously in the *shape* of a woman. *Shak.*

3. The form of the trunk of the human body; as a clumsy *shape*; an elegant *shape.*

4. A being as endowed with form.

Before the gates there sat,
On either side, a formidable *shape.* *Milton.*

5. Idea; pattern. *Milton.*

6. Form. This application comes before the legislature in the *shape* of a memorial.

7. Manner.

SHA'PED, } *pp.* Formed; molded; cast;
SHA'PEN, } conceived.

SHA'PELESS, *a.* Destitute of regular form; wanting symmetry of dimensions; as deformed and *shapeless.* *Shak.*

The *shapeless* rock or hanging precipice. *Pope.*

SHA'PELESSNESS, *n.* Destitution of regular form.

SHA'PELINESS, *n.* [from *shapely.*] Beauty or proportion of form. [*Little used.*]

SHA'PELY, *a.* [from *shape.*] Well formed; having a regular shape; symmetrical. *Warton.*

SHA'PESMITH, *n.* [*shape* and *smith.*] One that undertakes to improve the form of the body. [*In burlesque.*] *Garth.*

SHA'PING, *ppr.* Forming; molding; casting; conceiving; giving form.

SH'ARD, *n.* [Sax. *sceard*, from *scearan*, to *shear*, to separate.]

1. A piece or fragment of an earthern vessel or of any brittle substance. *Obs.* *Shak.*

2. The shell of an egg or of a snail. *Gower.*

3. A plant. [*chard.*] *Dryden.*

4. A frith or strait; as a perilous *shard.* *Spenser.*

5. A gap.

6. A fish.

SH'ARDBORN, *a.* [*shard* and *born.*] Born or produced among fragments, or in crevices; as the *shardborn* beetle. *Shak.*

Johnson suggests that *shard* may perhaps signify the sheath of the wings of insects. In this case, the word should be written *shardborne*, and defined, borne in the air by sheathed wings. Such is Todd's explanation of the word in Shakspeare. The word *shard* may perhaps be used for the crustaceous wing of an insect, but I know not that such a sense is legitimate. [See *Sharded.*]

SH'ARDED, *a.* Having wings sheathed with a hard case; as the *sharded* beetle. *Todd*, from *Gower.*

Inhabiting shards. *Johnson*, from *Shak.*

SHARE, *n.* [Sax. *scear*, *sceara*, from *scearan*, to shear; W. *ysgar*, which is a compound.]

1. A part; a portion; a quantity; as a small *share* of prudence or good sense.

2. A part or portion of a thing owned by a number in common; that part of an undivided interest which belongs to each proprietor; as a ship owned in ten *shares*; a Tontine building owned in a hundred *shares.*

3. The part of a thing allotted or distributed to each individual of a number; dividend; separate portion. Each heir has received his *share* of the estate.

4. A part belonging to one; portion possessed.

Nor I without my *share* of fame. *Dryden.*

5. A part contributed. He bears his *share* of the burden.

6. The broad iron or blade of a plow which cuts the ground; or furrow-slice. *Mortimer.*

To go shares, to partake; to be equally concerned. *L'Estrange.*

SHARE, *v. t.* [Sax. *scearan*, *scyran*; but we have *shear* directly from this verb, and *share* seems to be from the noun; W. *ysgariaw.*]

1. To divide; to part among two or more.

Suppose I *share* my fortune equally between my children and a stranger. *Swift.*

And *share* his burden where he *shares* his heart. *Dryden.*

2. To partake or enjoy with others; to seize and possess jointly or in common.

Great Jove with Cesar *shares* his sov'reign sway. *Milton.*
While avarice and rapine *share* the land. *Milton.*

3. To cut; to shear. [*Not now in use.*]

And the *shar'd* visage hangs on equal sides. *Dryden.*

SHARE, *v. i.* To have part.

A right of inheritance gave every one a title to *share* in the goods of his father. *Locke.*

SHA'RE-BONE, *n.* The ossa pubis. *Derham.*

SHA'RED, *pp.* Held or enjoyed with another or others; divided; distributed in shares.

SHA'REHOLDER, *n.* [*share* and *holder.*] One that holds or owns a share in a joint fund or property.

One of the proprietors of the mine, who was a principal *shareholder* in the company, died. *Med. Repos.*

SHA'RER, *n.* A partaker; one that participates any thing with another; one who enjoys or suffers in common with another or others; as a *sharer* in another's good fortune; a *sharer* in the toils of war; a *sharer* in a lady's affections.

SHA'RING, *ppr.* Partaking; having a part with another; enjoying or suffering with others.

SHA'RING, *n.* Participation.

SH'ARK, *n.* [L. *carcharias*; Gr. *χαρχαριας*, from *χαρχαρος*, sharp; Corn. *skarkias.*]

1. A voracious fish of the genus Squalus, of several species. The body is oblong, tapering and rough, and some species have several rows of serrated teeth. The largest grow to the length of thirty feet.

2. A greedy artful fellow; one who fills his pockets by sly tricks. [*Low.*] *South.*

3. Trick; fraud; petty rapine; as, to live upon the *shark.* [*Little used.*] *South.*

4. In *New England*, one that lives by shifts, contrivance or stratagem.

SH'ARK, *v. t.* To pick up hastily, slily or in small quantities. [*Low.*] *Shak.*

SH'ARK, *v. i.* To play the petty thief; or rather to live by shifts and petty stratagems. [In New England, the common pronunciation is *shurk*, but the word rarely implies fraud.]

2. To cheat; to trick. [*Low.*] *Ainsworth.*

3. To fawn upon for a dinner; to beg. *Johnson.*

To shark out, to slip out or escape by low artifices. [*Vulgar.*]

SH'ARKER, *n.* One that lives by sharking; an artful fellow. *Wotton.*

SH'ARKING, *ppr.* Picking up in haste; living by petty rapine, or by shifts and devices.

SH'ARKING, *n.* Petty rapine; trick. *Westfield.*

2. The seeking of a livelihood by shifts and devices.

SH'ARP, *a.* [Sax. *scearp*; D. *scherp*; G. *scharf*; Dan. Sw. *skarp*; Turk. *scerp*: probably from the root of *shear*, *shire*, *short*; the radical letters being *Cr* or *Gr.*]

1. Having a very thin edge or fine point; keen; acute; not blunt. Thus we say, a *sharp* knife, or a *sharp* needle. A *sharp* edge easily severs a substance; a *sharp* point is easily made to penetrate it.

2. Terminating in a point or edge; not obtuse; as, a hill terminates in a *sharp* peak, or a *sharp* ridge.

3. Forming an acute or too small angle at the ridge; as a *sharp* roof.

4. Acute of mind; quick to discern or distinguish; penetrating; ready at invention; witty; ingenious.

Nothing makes men *sharper* than want. *Addison.*

Many other things belong to the material world, wherein the *sharpest* philosophers have not yet obtained clear ideas. *Watts.*

5. Being of quick or nice perception; applied to the senses or organs of perception; as a *sharp* eye; *sharp* sight.

To *sharp* ey'd reason this would seem untrue. *Dryden.*

6. Affecting the organs of taste like fine points; sour; acid; as *sharp* vinegar; *sharp* tasted citrons. *Dryden.*

7. Affecting the organs of hearing like sharp points; piercing; penetrating; shrill; as a *sharp* sound or voice; a *sharp* note or tone; opposed to a *flat* note or sound.

8. Severe; harsh; biting; sarcastic; as *sharp* words; *sharp* rebuke.

—Be thy words severe,
Sharp as he merits; but the sword forbear. *Dryden.*

9. Severely rigid; quick or severe in punishing; cruel.

To that place the *sharp* Athenian law
Cannot pursue us. *Shak.*

10. Eager for food; keen; as a *sharp* appetite.

11. Eager in pursuit; keen in quest.

My fauchion now is *sharp* and passing empty. *Shak*

12. Fierce; ardent; fiery; violent; as a *sharp* contest.

A *sharp* assault already is begun. *Dryden*

13. Keen; severe; pungent; as *sharp* pain.

14. Very painful or distressing; as *sharp* tribulation; a *sharp* fit of the gout.

15. Very attentive or vigilant.

Sharp at her utmost ken she cast her eyes. *Dryden.*

16. Making nice calculations of profit; or close and exact in making bargains or demanding dues. *Swift.*

17. Biting; pinching; piercing; as *sharp* air; *sharp* wind or weather. *Ray.*

18. Subtil; nice; witty; acute; *used of things*; as a *sharp* discourse.

19. Among *workmen*, hard; as *sharp* sand. *Moxon.*

20. Emaciated; lean; thin; as a *sharp* visage. *Milton.*

To brace sharp, in seamanship, to turn the yards to the most oblique position possible, that the ship may lay well up to the wind. *Mar. Dict.*

SH'ARP, *n.* In *music*, an acute sound. *Shak.*

2. A note artificially raised a semitone; or,

3. The character which directs the note to be thus elevated; opposed to a *flat*, which depresses a note a semitone. *Encyc.*

4. A pointed weapon. [*Not in use.*] *Collier.*

SH'ARP, *v. t.* To make keen or acute. *B. Jonson.*

2. To render quick. *Spenser.*

3. To mark with a sharp, in musical composition; or to raise a note a semitone.

SH'ARP, *v. i.* To play tricks in bargaining; to act the sharper. *L'Estrange.*

SH'ARP-EDG'ED, *a.* Having a fine keen edge.

SHARPEN, *v. t.* *shàrpn.* [G. *schärfen*; D. *scherpen*; Sw. *skàrpa.*]

1. To make sharp; to give a keen edge or fine point to a thing; to edge; to point; as, to *sharpen* a knife, an ax or the teeth of a saw; to *sharpen* a sword.

All the Israelites went down to the Philistines to *sharpen* every man his share and his coulter, and his ax and his mattock. 1 Sam. xiii.

2. To make more eager or active; as, to *sharpen* the edge of industry. *Hooker.*

3. To make more pungent and painful. The abuse of wealth and greatness may hereafter *sharpen* the sting of conscience.

4. To make more quick, acute or ingenious. The wit or the intellect is *sharpened* by study.

5. To render perception more quick or acute.

Th' air *sharpen'd* his visual ray
To objects distant far. *Milton.*

6. To render more keen; to make more eager for food or for any gratification; as, to *sharpen* the appetite; to *sharpen* a desire. *Shak. Tillotson.*

7. To make biting, sarcastic or severe.

Sharpen each word. *Smith.*

8. To render less flat, or more shrill or piercing.

Inclosures not only preserve sound, but increase and *sharpen* it. *Bacon.*

9. To make more tart or acid; to make sour; as, the rays of the sun *sharpen* vinegar.

10. To make more distressing; as, to *sharpen* grief or other evil.

11. In *music*, to raise a sound by means of a sharp. *Prof. Fisher.*

SH'ARPEN, *v. i.* To grow or become sharp. *Shak.*

SH'ARPER, *n.* A shrewd man in making bargains; a tricking fellow; a cheat in bargaining or gaming.

Sharpers, as pikes, prey upon their own kind. *L'Estrange.*

SH'ARPLY, *adv.* With a keen edge or a fine point.

2. Severely; rigorously; roughly. Tit. i.

They are to be more *sharply* chastised and reformed than the rude Irish. *Spenser.*

3. Keenly; acutely; vigorously; as the mind and memory *sharply* exercised. *B. Jonson.*

4. Violently; vehemently.

At the arrival of the English embassadors, the soldiers were *sharply* assailed with wants. *Hayward.*

5. With keen perception; exactly; minutely.

You contract your eye, when you would see *sharply.* *Bacon.*

6. Acutely; wittily; with nice discernment.

SH'ARPNESS, *n.* Keenness of an edge or point; as the *sharpness* of a razor or a dart.

2. Not obtuseness. *Wotton.*

3. Pungency; acidity; as the *sharpness* of vinegar. *Watts.*

4. Pungency of pain; keenness; severity of pain or affliction; as the *sharpness* of pain, grief or anguish.

5. Painfulness; afflictiveness; as the *sharpness* of death or calamity.

And the best quarrels in the heat are curst
By those that feel their *sharpness*. *Shak.*

6. Severity of language; pungency; satirical sarcasm; as the *sharpness* of satire or rebuke.

Some did all folly with just *sharpness* blame. *Dryden.*

7. Acuteness of intellect; the power of nice discernment; quickness of understanding; ingenuity; as *sharpness* of wit or understanding. *Dryden. Addison.*

8. Quickness of sense or perception; as the *sharpness* of sight.

9. Keenness; severity; as the *sharpness* of the air or weather.

SH'ARP-SET, *a.* [*sharp* and *set.*] Eager in appetite; affected by keen hunger; ravenous; as an eagle or a lion *sharp-set*. *Brown.*

2. Eager in desire of gratification.

The town is *sharp-set* on new plays. *Pope.*

SH'ARP-SHOOTER, *n.* [*sharp* and *shoot.*] One skilled in shooting at an object with exactness; one skilled in the use of the rifle.

SH'ARP-SIGHTED, *a.* [*sharp* and *sight.*]

1. Having quick or acute sight; as a *sharp-sighted* eagle or hawk.

2. Having quick discernment or acute understanding; as a *sharp-sighted* opponent; *sharp-sighted* judgment.

SH'ARP-VISAGED, *a.* [*sharp* and *visage.*] Having a sharp or thin face. *Hale.*

SH'ARP-WITTED, *a.* Having an acute or nicely discerning mind. *Wotton.*

SHAS'TER, *n.* Among the Hindoos, a sacred book containing the dogmas of the religion of the Bramins and the ceremonies of their worship, and serving as a commentary on the Vedam. It consists of three parts; the first containing the moral law of the Hindoos; the second the rites and ceremonies of their religion; the third the distribution of the people into tribes or classes, with the duties pertaining to each. *Encyc.*

SHAT'TER, *v. t.* [D. *schateren*, to crack, to make a great noise. This word seems to be allied to *scatter* and to *scath*, waste. The sense is to force or drive apart.]

1. To break at once into many pieces; to dash, burst, rend or part by violence into fragments; as, explosion *shatters* a rock or a bomb; lightning *shatters* the sturdy oak; steam *shatters* a boiler; a monarchy is *shattered* by revolt. *Locke.*

2. To rend; to crack; to split; to rive into splinters.

3. To dissipate; to make incapable of close and continued application; as a man of *shattered* humor. *Norris.*

4. To disorder; to derange; to render delirious; as, to *shatter* the brain. The man seems to be *shattered* in his intellect.

SHAT'TER, *v. i.* To be broken into fragments; to fall or crumble to pieces by any force applied.

Some *shatter* and fly in many places. *Bacon.*

SHAT'TER-BRAINED, } *a.* [*shatter* and
SHAT'TER-PATED, } *brain* or *pate.*]

1. Disordered or wandering in intellect.

2. Heedless; wild; not consistent. *Goodman.*

SHAT'TERED, *pp.* Broken or dashed to pieces; rent; disordered.

SHAT'TERING, *ppr.* Dashing or breaking to pieces; rending; disordering.

SHAT'TERS, *n.* [I believe used only in the plural.]

The fragments of any thing forcibly rent or broken; used chiefly or solely in the phrases, to *break* or *rend into shatters*. *Swift.*

SHAT'TERY, *a.* Brittle; easily falling into many pieces; not compact; loose of texture; as *shattery* spar. *Woodward.*

SHAVE, *v. t.* pret. *shaved*; pp. *shaved* or *shaven*. [Sax. *sceafan*, *scafan*; D. *schaaven*; G. *schaben*; Dan. *skaver*; Sw. *skafva.*]

1. To cut or pare off something from the surface of a body by a razor or other edged instrument, by rubbing, scraping or drawing the instrument along the surface; as, to *shave* the chin and cheeks; to *shave* the head of its hair.

He shall *shave* his head in the day of his cleansing. Num. vi.

2. To *shave off*, to cut off.

Neither shall they *shave off* the corner of their beard. Lev. xxi.

3. To pare close.

The bending sythe
Shaves all the surface of the waving green. *Gay.*

4. To cut off thin slices; or to cut in thin slices. *Bacon.*

5. To skim along the surface or near it; to sweep along.

He *shaves* with level wing the deep. *Milton.*

6. To strip; to oppress by extortion; to fleece.

7. To make smooth by paring or cutting off slices; as, to *shave* hoops or staves.

To shave a note, to purchase it at a great discount, a discount much beyond the legal rate of interest. [*A low phrase.*]

SHAVE, *n.* [Sw. *skaf*; G. *schabe*; Sax. *scafa*, *sceafa*; D. *schaaf*, a plane.]

An instrument with a long blade and a handle at each end for shaving hoops, &c.; called also a *drawing knife*.

SHA'VED, *pp.* Pared; made smooth with a razor or other cutting instrument; fleeced.

SHA'VE-GRASS, *n.* A plant of the genus Equisetum.

SHA'VELING, *n.* A man shaved; a friar or religious; *in contempt*. *Spenser.*

SHA'VER, *n.* One that shaves or whose occupation is to shave.

2. One that is close in bargains or a sharp dealer.

This Lewis is a cunning *shaver*. *Swift.*

3. One that fleeces; a pillager; a plunderer.

By these *shavers* the Turks were stripped of all they had. *Knolles.*

SHA'VER, *n.* [Gipsey, *tschabe* or *tschawo*, a boy; *schawo* or *tschawo*, a son; Ar. شاب a youth, from شب shabba, to grow up, to excite.]

A boy or young man. This word is still in common use in New England. It must be numbered among our original words.

SHA'VING, *ppr.* Paring the surface with a razor or other sharp instrument; making smooth by paring; fleecing.

SHA'VING, *n.* The act of paring the surface.

2. A thin slice pared off with a shave, a knife, a plane or other cutting instrument. *Mortimer.*

SHAW, *n.* [Sax. *scua*, *scuwa*; Sw. *skugga*; Dan. *skove*, a thicket, and *skygge*, a shade.]

A thicket; a small wood. [*Local in England. In America not used.*]

SHAW'-FOWL, *n.* [*shaw* and *fowl.*] The representation or image of a fowl made by fowlers to shoot at. *Johnson.*

SHAWL, *n.* A cloth of wool, cotton, silk or hair, used by females as a loose covering for the neck and shoulders. Shawls are of various sizes from that of a handkerchief to that of a counterpane. Shawls were originally manufactured in the heart of India from the fine silky wool of the Thibet sheep, and the best shawls now come from Cashmere; but they are also manufactured in Europe. The largest kinds are used in train-dresses and for long scarfs. *Encyc.*

SHAWM, *n.* [G. *schalmeie*, from *schallen*, to sound.]

A hautboy or cornet; written also *shalm*, but not in use. *Com. Prayer.*

SHE, pronoun personal of the feminine gender. [Sax. *seo*; Goth. *si*; D. *zy*; G. *sie*. The Danes and Swedes use for *he* and *she*, the word from which the English has *hen*; Dan. *han*, he, the male; *hun*, she, the female; *hane*, a cock; Sw. *han*, he; *hanne*, a cock; *hon*, *hennes*, *henne*, she. This is the root of *Henry*. *She* is perhaps the Heb. אשה a woman or wife. In the Saxon, *seo* is used as an adjective, and may be rendered *the* or *a*. It is also used as a relative, answering to *who*, L. *quæ*. It is also used for *he* and *that*. In English, *she* has no variation, and is used only in the nominative case. In the oblique cases, we use *hers* and *her*, a distinct word.]

1. A pronoun which is the substitute for the name of a female, and of the feminine gender; the word which refers to a female mentioned in the preceding or following part of a sentence or discourse.

Then Sarah denied, saying, I laughed not; for *she* was afraid. Gen. xviii.

2. *She* is sometimes used as a noun for *woman* or *female*, and in the plural; but in contempt or in ludicrous language.

Lady, you are the cruell'st *she* alive. *Shak.*

The *shes* of Italy shall not betray
My interest. *Shak.*

3. *She* is used also in composition for female, representing sex; as a *she*-bear; a *she*-cat.

SHE'ADING, *n.* [G. *scheiden*, Sax. *sceadan*, to divide.]

In the isle of Man, a riding, tithing or division, in which there is a coroner or chief constable. The isle is divided into six *sheadings*. *Encyc.*

SHEAF, *n.* plu. *sheaves*. [Sax. *sceaf*; D. *schoof*. It appears to be connected with the D. *schuiven*, *schoof*, to *shove*, Sax. *scufan*. The sense then is a mass or collection driven or pressed together. But the Welsh has *ysgub*, a *sheaf* and a besom, whence *ysgubaw*, to sweep, L. *scopa*, *scopo*, and said to be from *cub*, what is put together, a *cube*. If these are of one family, as I suspect, the root is in Class *Gb*, and the sense to collect or press together.]

1. A quantity of the stalks of wheat, rye,

oats or barley bound together; a bundle of stalks or straw.

—The reaper fills his greedy hands,
And binds the golden *sheaves* in brittle bands. *Dryden.*

2. Any bundle or collection; as a *sheaf* of arrows. *Dryden.*

SHEAF, *v. t.* To collect and bind; to make sheaves. *Shak.*

SHEAL, to *shell*, not used. *Shak.*

SHEAR, *v. t.* pret. *sheared*; pp. *sheared* or *shorn*. The old pret. *shore* is entirely obsolete. [Sax. *scearan, scyran, sciran*, to shear, to divide, whence *share* and *shire*; G. *scheren*, to shear or shave, and to vex, to rail, to *jeer*; *schier dich weg*, get you gone; *schier dich aus dem wege*, move out of the way; D. *scheeren*, to shave, shear, banter, stretch, warp; *de gek scheeren*, to play the fool; *zig weg scheeren*, to *sheer off*; Dan. *skierer*, to cut, carve, saw, hew; *skierts*, a jest, jeer, banter; *skiertser*, to sport, mock, jeer; Sw. *skiăra*, to reap, to mow, to cut off, to cleanse, to rinse; Sans. *schaura* or *chaura*, to shave; W. *ysgar*, a part, a *share*; *ysgariaw*, to separate. The Greek has ξυραω, to shave, and κειρω, to shave, shear, cut off or lay waste. The primary sense is to separate or force off in general; but a prominent signification is to separate by rubbing, as in *scouring*, or as in *shaving*, cutting close to the surface. Hence the sense of *jeering*, as we say, to give one the *rub*. See *Scour* and Class Gr. No. 5. and 8.]

1. To cut or clip something from the surface with an instrument of two blades; to separate any thing from the surface by shears, scissors or a like instrument; as, to *shear* sheep; to *shear* cloth. It is appropriately used for the cutting of wool from sheep or their skins, and for clipping the nap from cloth, but may be applied to other things; as, a horse *shears* the ground in feeding much closer than an ox.

2. To separate by shears; as, to *shear* a fleece.

3. To reap. [*Not in use.*] *Scotish.* *Gower.*

SHEAR, *v. i.* To deviate. [See *Sheer.*]

SHE'ARBILL, *n.* [*shear* and *bill.*] A fowl, the black skimmer or cut-water. (*Rhyncops nigra.*) *Encyc.*

SHEARD, *n.* A shard. [See *Shard.*]

SHE'ARED, *pp.* Clipped; deprived of wool, hair or nap.

SHE'ARER, *n.* One that shears; as a *shearer* of sheep. *Milton.*

SHEARMAN, *n.* *sher'man.* One whose occupation is to shear cloth.

SHEARS, *n. plu.* [from the verb.] An instrument consisting of two blades with a bevel edge, movable on a pin, used for cutting cloth and other substances by interception between the two blades. Shears differ from scissors chiefly in being larger.

Fate urg'd the *shears* and cut the sylph in twain. *Pope.*

2. Something in the form of the blades of shears.

3. Wings. [*Not in use.*] *Spenser.*

4. An engine for raising heavy weights. [See *Sheers.*]

5. The denomination of the age of sheep from the cutting of the teeth; as sheep of one *shear*, two *shear*, &c. [*Local.*] *Mortimer.*

SHE'AR-WATER, *n.* A fowl. [*Larus niger.*] *Ainsworth.*

A species of petrel, (*Procellaria puffinus*, Linn.) found on the coasts of Great Britain and Ireland. *Encyc.*

The cut-water, (*Rhyncops nigra.*) *Bartram.*

SHEAT. [See *Sheet.*]

SHE'AT-FISH, *n.* [G. *scheide*, Cuvier.] A fish, a species of Silurus, having a long slimy body destitute of scales, and the back dusky, like that of the eel. *Dict. Nat. Hist.*

SHEATH, *n.* [Sax. *sceath, scæthe*; G. *scheide*; D. *scheede*; from separating, G. *scheiden*, D. *scheien*, Sax. *sceadan.* See *Shade.*]

1. A case for the reception of a sword or other long and slender instrument; a scabbard. A *sheath* is that which separates, and hence a defense.

2. In *botany*, a membrane investing a stem or branch, as in grasses. *Martyn.*

3. Any thin covering for defense; the wing-case of an insect.

SHEATH, SHEATHE, *v. t.* To put into a case or scabbard; as, to *sheathe* a sword or dagger.

2. To inclose or cover with a sheath or case.

The leopard—keeps the claws of his fore feet turned up from the ground, and *sheathed* in the skin of his toes. *Grew.*

'Tis in my breast she *sheathes* her dagger now. *Dryden.*

3. To cover or line; as, to *sheathe* the bowels with demulcent or mucilaginous substances.

4. To obtund or blunt, as acrimonious or sharp particles. *Arbuthnot.*

5. To fit with a sheath. *Shak.*

6. To case or cover with boards or with sheets of copper; as, to *sheathe* a ship to preserve it from the worms.

To sheathe the sword, a figurative phrase, to put an end to war or enmity; to make peace. It corresponds to the Indian phrase, *to bury the hatchet.*

SHE'ATHED, *pp.* Put in a sheath; inclosed or covered with a case; covered; lined; invested with a membrane.

2. *a.* In *botany*, vaginate; invested by a sheath or cylindrical membranaceous tube, which is the base of the leaf, as the stalk or culm in grasses. *Martyn.*

SHE'ATHING, *ppr.* Putting in a sheath; inclosing in a case; covering; lining; investing with a membrane.

SHE'ATHING, *n.* The casing or covering of a ship's bottom and sides; or the materials for such covering.

SHE'ATHLESS, *a.* Without a sheath or case for covering; unsheathed. *Percy's Masque.*

SHE'ATH-WINGED, *a.* [*sheath* and *wing.*] Having cases for covering the wings; as a *sheath-winged* insect. *Brown.*

SHE'ATHY, *a.* Forming a sheath or case. *Brown.*

SHEAVE, *n.* [In D. *schyf* is a slice, a truckle, a quoit, a fillet, a draughtsman, a pane. In G. *scheibe* is a mark, a pane, a wheel, the knee-pan, a slice.]

In *seamen's language*, a wheel on which the rope works in a block. It is made of hard wood or of metal. When made of wood, it is sometimes *bushed*, that is, has a piece of perforated brass let into its center, the better to sustain the friction of the pin. *Mar. Dict.*

SHEAVE, *v. t.* To bring together; to collect. [*Not in use.*] *Ashmole.*

SHE'AVED, *a.* Made of straw. [*Not in use.*] *Shak.*

SHE'AVE-HOLE, *n.* A channel cut in a mast, yard or other timber, in which to fix a sheave. *Mar. Dict.*

SHECK'LATON, *n.* [Fr. *ciclaton.* Chalmers.]

A kind of gilt lether. [*Not in use.*] *Spenser.*

SHED, *v. t.* pret. and pp. *shed*, [Sax. *scedan*, to pour out. If *s* is a prefix, this word coincides in elements with D. *gieten*, to pour, to cast, G. *giessen*, Eng. *gush.* It coincides also in elements with *shoot.* See the Noun.]

1. To pour out; to effuse; to spill; to suffer to flow out; as, to *shed* tears; to *shed* blood. The *sun* sheds light on the earth; the stars *shed* a more feeble light.

This is my blood of the New Testament, which is *shed* for many for the remission of sins. Matt. xxvi.

2. To let fall; to cast; as, the trees *shed* their leaves in autumn; fowls *shed* their fethers; and serpents *shed* their skin.

3. To scatter; to emit; to throw off; to diffuse; as, flowers *shed* their sweets or fragrance.

SHED, *v. i.* To let fall its parts.

White oats are apt to *shed* most as they lie, and black as they stand. *Mortimer.*

SHED, *n.* [Sax. *sced*, a shade; Sw. *skydd*, a defense; *skydda*, to protect, to defend or shelter; Dan. *skytter*, id.; *skytter*, a shooter; *skyts*, a defense; *skyt*, a gun; *skyder*, to shoot; G. *schützen*, to defend; *schütze*, a shooter; D. *schutten*, to defend, to parry or stop; *schutter*, a *shooter.* It appears that *shed*, the noun and verb, and *shoot*, are from one source, and *shade*, *scud*, *scath*, and several other words, when traced, all terminate in the same radical sense, to thrust, rush or drive.]

1. A slight building; a covering of timber and boards, &c. for shelter against rain and the inclemencies of weather; a poor house or hovel; as a horse-*shed.*

The first Aletes born in lowly *shed.* *Fairfax.*

Sheds of reeds which summer's heat repel. *Sandys.*

2. In composition, effusion; as in blood-*shed.* [See the Verb.]

SHED, *v. t.* To keep off; to prevent from entering; as a hut, umbrella or garment that *sheds* rain.

SHED'DER, *n.* One that sheds or causes to flow out; as a *shedder* of blood.

SHED'DING, *ppr.* Effusing; causing to flow out; letting fall; casting; throwing off; sending out; diffusing; keeping off.

SHEEN, SHEE'NY, *a.* [Sax. *scene*, *scen*, bright. This is the old orthography of *shine*, which see.] Bright; glittering; showy.

Up rose each warrior bold and brave,
Glist'ring in filed steel and armor *sheen.* *Fairfax.*

[*This word is used only in poetry.*]

SHEEN, *n.* Brightness; splendor. *Milton.*

SHEEP, *n. sing.* and *plu.* [Sax. *sceap, scep;* G. *schaf;* D. *schaap;* Bohemian, *skope*, a wether.]

1. An animal of the genus Ovis, which is among the most useful species that the Creator has bestowed on man, as its wool constitutes a principal material of warm clothing, and its flesh is a great article of food. The sheep is remarkable for its harmless temper and its timidity. The varieties are numerous.
2. In contempt, a silly fellow. *Ainsworth.*
3. Figuratively, God's people are called *sheep*, as being under the government and protection of Christ, the great Shepherd. John x.

SHEE'P-BITE, *v. t.* [*sheep* and *bite.*] To practice petty thefts. [*Not in use.*] *Shak.*

SHEE'P-BITER, *n.* One who practices petty thefts. [*Not in use.*] *Shak.*

SHEE'P-COT, *n.* [*sheep* and *cot.*] A small inclosure for sheep; a pen. *Milton.*

SHEE'PFOLD, *n.* [*sheep* and *fold.*] A place where sheep are collected or confined. *Prior.*

SHEE'PHOOK, *n.* [*sheep* and *hook.*] A hook fastened to a pole, by which shepherds lay hold on the legs of their sheep. *Bacon. Dryden.*

SHEE'PISH, *a.* Like a sheep; bashful; timorous to excess , over-modest; meanly diffident. *Locke.*

2. Pertaining to sheep.

SHEE'PISHLY, *adv.* Bashfully; with mean timidity or diffidence.

SHEE'PISHNESS, *n.* Bashfulness; excessive modesty or diffidence; mean timorousness. *Herbert.*

SHEE'P-M'ARKET, *n.* A place where sheep are sold.

SHEE'P-M'ASTER, *n.* [*sheep* and *master.*] A feeder of sheep; one that has the care of sheep.

SHEE'P'S-EYE, *n.* [*sheep* and *eye.*] A modest diffident look, such as lovers cast at their mistresses. *Dryden.*

SHEE'P-SHANK, *n.* [*sheep* and *shank.*] Among *seamen*, a knot in a rope made to shorten it, as on a runner or tie. *Mar. Dict.*

SHEE'P'S-HEAD, *n.* [*sheep* and *head.*] A fish caught on the shores of Connecticut and of Long Island, so called from the resemblance of its head to that of a sheep. It is esteemed delicious food.

SHEE'P-SHEARER, *n.* [*sheep* and *shear.*] One that shears or cuts off the wool from sheep. Gen. xxxviii.

SHEE'P-SHEARING, *n.* The act of shearing sheep.

2. The time of shearing sheep; also, a feast made on that occasion. *South.*

SHEE'P-SKIN, *n.* The skin of a sheep; or lether prepared from it.

SHEE'P-STEALER, *n.* [*sheep* and *steal.*] One that steals sheep.

SHEE'P-STEALING, *n.* The act of stealing sheep.

SHEE'P-WALK, *n.* [*sheep* and *walk.*] Pasture for sheep; a place where sheep feed. *Milton.*

SHEER, *a.* [Sax. *scir, scyr;* G. *schier;* Dan. *skier:* Sans. *charu, tscharu;* from the root of *shear*, to separate; whence *sheer* is clear, pure. It might be deduced from the Shemitic זהר to be clear; Eth. ጸረየ to be clean or pure. But the Danish and Saxon orthography coincides with that of *shear.*]

1. Pure; clear; separate from any thing foreign; unmingled; as *sheer* ale. But this application is unusual. *Shak.*

   We say, *sheer* argument, *sheer* wit, *sheer* falsehood, &c.
2. Clear; thin; as *sheer* muslin.

SHEER, *adv.* Clean; quite; at once. *Obs. Milton.*

SHEER, *v. t.* To shear. [*Not in use.*] *Dryden.*

SHEER, *v. i.* [See *Shear*, the sense of which is to separate.]

1. In *seamen's language*, to decline or deviate from the line of the proper course, as a ship when not steered with steadiness. *Mar. Dict.*
2. To slip or move aside.

To sheer off, to turn or move aside to a distance.

To sheer up, to turn and approach to a place or ship.

SHEER, *n.* The longitudinal curve or bend of a ship's deck or sides.

2. The position in which a ship is sometimes kept at single anchor, to keep her clear of it.

   To *break sheer*, to deviate from that position and risk fouling the anchor. *Mar. Dict.*

SHEER-HULK, *n.* An old ship of war, fitted with sheers or apparatus to fix or take out the masts of other ships. *Mar. Dict.*

SHEE'RLY, *adv.* At once; quite; absolutely. *Obs. Beaum.*

SHEERS, *n. plu.* An engine consisting of two or more pieces of timber or poles, fastened together near the top; used for raising heavy weights, particularly for hoisting the lower masts of ships. *Mar. Dict.*

SHEET, *n.* [Sax. *sceat, sceta, scyta;* L. *scheda;* Gr. *σχεδη.* The Saxon *sceat* signifies a garment, a cloth, towel or napkin; *sceta* is rendered a *sheet*, and the Greek and Latin words signify a table or plate for writing on; from the root of Sax. *sceadan*, to separate, L. *scindo*, Gr. *σχιζω.*]

1. A broad piece of cloth used as a part of bed-furniture.
2. A broad piece of paper as it comes from the manufacturer. *Sheets* of paper are of different sizes, as royal, demi, foolscap, pot and post-paper.
3. A piece of paper printed, folded and bound, or formed into a book in blank, and making four, eight, sixteen or twenty four pages, &c.
4. Any thing expanded; as a *sheet* of water or of fire; a *sheet* of copper, lead or iron.
5. *Sheets*, plu. a book or pamphlet. The following *sheets* contain a full answer to my opponent.
6. A sail.

SHEET, *n.* [Fr. *ecoute;* Sp. Port. *escota;* It. *scotte.* This word seems to be connected with *scot* or *shot;* Sp. *escotar*, to *cut* out clothes, to pay one's *scot* or share of taxes, and in nautical language, to free a ship of water by pumping. The word is probably from that root, or from *shoot.*]

In *nautical language*, a rope fastened to one or both the lower corners of a sail to extend and retain it in a particular situation. When a ship sails with a side-wind, the lower corners of the main and fore-sails are fastened with a tack and a *sheet.* *Mar. Dict.*

SHEET, *v. t.* To furnish with sheets. [*Little used.*]

2. To fold in a sheet. [*Little used.*] *Shak.*
3. To cover as with a sheet; to cover with something broad and thin.

   When snow the pasture *sheets.* *Shak.*

To sheet home, is to haul home a sheet, or extend the sail till the clew is close to the sheet-block.

SHEET-ANCHOR, *n.* The largest anchor of a ship, which in stress of weather is sometimes the seaman's last refuge to prevent the ship from going ashore. Hence,

2. The chief support; the last refuge for safety.

SHEET-COPPER, *n.* Copper in broad thin plates.

SHEE'TING, *n.* Cloth for sheets.

SHEET-IRON, *n.* Iron in sheets or broad thin plates.

SHEET-LEAD, *n.* Lead in sheets.

SHEIK, *n.* In Egypt, a person who has the care of a mosk; a kind of priest. *Encyc.*

SHEK'EL, *n.* [Heb. שקל to weigh; Ch. Syr. Ar. Eth. id.; Eth. to append or suspend; Low L. *siclus;* Fr. *sicle.* From this root we have *shilling.* Payments were originally made by weight, as they still are in some countries. See *Pound.*]

An ancient weight and coin among the Jews and other nations of the same stock. Dr. Arbuthnot makes the weight to have been equal to 9 pennyweights, $2\frac{4}{7}$ grains, Troy weight, and the value 2s. $3\frac{3}{8}$d. sterling, or about half a dollar. Others make its value 2s. 6d. sterling. The golden shekel was worth £1. 16. 6. sterling, about $8, 12. *Encyc.*

SHELD'AFLE, } *n.* A chaffinch.
SHELD'APLE, } *Johnson. Todd.*

This word is also written *shell-apple.* *Ed. Encyc.*

SHEL'DRAKE, *n.* An aquatic fowl of the duck kind, the *Anas tadorna.* It has a greenish black head, and its body is variegated with white. *Encyc.*

SHEL'DUCK, *n.* A species of wild duck. *Mortimer.*

SHELF, *n.* plu. *shelves.* [Sax. *scylf*, whence *scylfan*, to shelve; Fr. *ecueil*, a sand bank.]

1. A platform of boards or planks, elevated above the floor, and fixed or set on a frame or contiguous to a wall, for holding vessels, utensils, books and the like.
2. A sand bank in the sea, or a rock or ledge of rocks, rendering the water shallow and dangerous to ships.
3. In *mining*, fast ground; that part of the internal structure of the earth which lies in an even regular form. *Encyc.*

SHELF'Y, *a.* Full of shelves; abounding with sand banks or rocks lying near the surface of the water and rendering navigation dangerous; as a *shelfy* coast. *Dryden.*

2. Hard; firm. [See *Shelf*, No. 3.] [*Not in use.*] *Carew.*

SHELL, *n.* [Sax. *scyl, scyll, scell*, a shell, and *sceale*, a scale; D. *schil, schaal;* G.

schale; Dan. Sw. *skal*; Fr. *ecaille.* The word primarily signifies that which is peeled or separated, as rind or the outer coat of plants, or their fruit; and as *shells* were used for dishes, the word came to signify a dish. See *Scale.*]

1. The hard or stony covering of certain fruits and of certain animals; as the *shell* of a nut; the *shell* of an oyster or lobster. The *shells* of animals are crustaceous or testaceous; crustaceous, as that of the lobster, and testaceous, as that of the oyster and clam.
2. The outer coat of an egg.
3. The outer part of a house unfinished. We say of a building that wants the interior timbers or finishing, that it is a mere *shell.*
4. An instrument of music, like *testudo* in Latin; the first lyre being made, it is said, by drawing strings over a tortoise shell. *Dryden.*
5. Outer or superficial part; as the *shell* of religion. *Ayliffe.*
6. A bomb.

Fossil shells, shells dug from the earth.

SHELL, *v. t.* To strip or break off the shell; or to take out of the shell; as, to *shell* nuts or almonds.

2. To separate from the ear; as, to *shell* maiz.

SHELL, *v. i.* To fall off, as a shell, crust or exterior coat.

2. To cast the shell or exterior covering. Nuts *shell* in falling.
3. To be disengaged from the husk; as, wheat or rye *shells* in reaping.

SHELL'ED, *pp.* Deprived of the shell; also, separated from the ear; as *shelled* corn or maiz.

SHELL'-FISH, *n.* An aquatic animal whose external covering consists of a shell, crustaceous or testaceous; as lobsters, crabs, oysters, clams, &c.

SHELL'ING, *ppr.* Taking off the shell; casting the external hard covering; separating from the husk and falling.

2. Separating from the ear, as maiz.

SHELL'-MEAT, *n.* Food consisting of shell fish. *Fuller.*

SHELL'-WŎRK, *n.* Work composed of shells, or adorned with them. *Cotgrave.*

SHELL'Y, *a.* Abounding with shells; as the *shelly* shore. *Prior.*

2. Consisting of shells. Lobsters disengage themselves from their *shelly* prisons.

SHEL'TER, *n.* [Sw. *skyla*, to cover; Dan. *skiul*, a shed or cover, a *shelter*; *skiuler*, to hide, conceal, cloke; L. *celo.*]

1. That which covers or defends from injury or annoyance. A house is a *shelter* from rain and other inclemencies of the weather; the foliage of a tree is a *shelter* from the rays of the sun.

> The healing plant shall aid,
> From storms a *shelter*, and from heat a shade. *Pope.*

2. The state of being covered and protected; protection; security.

> Who into *shelter* takes their tender bloom. *Young.*

3. He that defends or guards from danger; a protector. Ps. lxi.

SHEL'TER, *v. t.* To cover from violence, injury, annoyance or attack; as a valley *sheltered* from the north wind by a mountain.

> Those ruins *shelter'd* once his sacred head. *Dryden.*

> We besought the deep to *shelter* us. *Milton.*

2. To defend; to protect from danger; to secure or render safe; to harbor.

> What endless honor shall you gain,
> To save and *shelter* Troy's unhappy train? *Dryden.*

3. To betake to cover or a safe place.

> They *sheltered* themselves under a rock. *Abbot.*

4. To cover from notice; to disguise for protection.

> In vain I strove to check my growing flame,
> Or *shelter* passion under friendship's name. *Prior.*

SHEL'TER, *v. i.* To take shelter.

> There the Indian herdsman shunning heat,
> *Shelters* in cool. *Milton.*

SHEL'TERED, *pp.* Covered from injury or annoyance; defended; protected.

SHEL'TERING, *ppr.* Covering from injury or annoyance; protecting.

SHEL'TERLESS, *a.* Destitute of shelter or protection; without home or refuge.

> Now sad and *shelterless* perhaps she lies. *Rowe.*

SHEL'TERY, *a.* Affording shelter. [*Little used.*] *White.*

SHEL'TIE, *n.* A small but strong horse in Scotland; so called from Shetland, where it is produced. *Encyc.*

SHELVE, *v. t. shelv.* To place on a shelf or on shelves. [*Not in use.*] *Chaucer.*

SHELVE, *v. i. shelv.* [Sax. *scylfan*, to reel.] To incline; to be sloping.

SHELV'ING, *ppr.* or *a.* Inclining; sloping; having declivity.

> With rocks and *shelving* arches vaulted round. *Addison.*

SHELV'Y, *a.* Full of rocks or sand banks; shallow; as a *shelvy* shore. [See *Shelfy.*] *Shak.*

SHEMIT'IC, *a.* Pertaining to Shem, the son of Noah. The *Shemitic* languages are the Chaldee, Syriac, Arabic, Hebrew, Samaritan, Ethiopic and Old Phenician.

SHEND, *v. t.* pret. and pp. *shent.* [Sax. *scendan*; D. *schenden*, to violate, spoil, slander, revile; G. *schänden*, to mar, spoil, disfigure, violate, abuse, debauch. This is from the root of *scandal.*]

1. To injure, mar or spoil. *Obs.*

> That much I fear my body will be *shent.* *Dryden.*

2. To blame, reproach, revile, degrade, disgrace.

> The famous name of knighthood foully *shend.*
> *Obs.* *Spenser.*

3. To overpower or surpass. *Obs.*

> She pass'd the rest as Cynthia doth *shend*
> The lesser stars. *Spenser.*

SHENT, *pp.* Injured. Obsolete unless in poetry.

SHEP'HERD, *n.* [Sax. *sceap-heard* or *hyrd*; *sheep* and *herd.*]

1. A man employed in tending, feeding and guarding sheep in the pasture. *Milton.*
2. A swain; a rural lover. *Raleigh.*
3. The pastor of a parish, church or congregation; a minister of the gospel who superintends a church or parish, and gives instruction in spiritual things. God and Christ are in Scripture denominated *Shepherds*, as they lead, protect and govern their people, and provide for their welfare. Ps. xxiii. lxxx. John x.

SHEP'HERDESS, *n.* A woman that tends sheep; hence, a rural lass.

> She put herself into the garb of a *shepherdess.* *Sidney.*

SHEP'HERDISH, *a.* Resembling a shepherd; suiting a shepherd; pastoral; rustic. *Sidney.*

SHEP'HERDLY, *a.* Pastoral; rustic. *Taylor.*

SHEPHERD'S NEEDLE, *n.* A plant of the genus Scandix; Venus's comb.

SHEPHERD'S POUCH, } *n.* A plant of
SHEPHERD'S PURSE, } the genus Thlaspi.

SHEPHERD'S ROD, *n.* A plant of the genus Dipsacus; teasel.

SHEPHERD'S STAFF, *n.* A plant of the genus Dipsacus.

SHER'BET, *n.* [Pers. شربت. This word, as well as *sirup* and *shrub*, and L. *sorbeo*, is from the Ar. شرب sharaba, to drink, to imbibe.]

A drink composed of water, lemon juice and sugar, sometimes with perfumed cakes dissolved in it, with an infusion of some drops of rose water. Another kind is made with violets, honey, juice of raisins, &c. *Encyc.*

SHERD, *n.* A fragment; usually written *shard*, which see.

SHER'IF, *n.* [Sax. *scir-gerefa*; *scyre*, *scire*, a shire or division, and *gerefa*, a *reeve*, a count, prefect, bailif, provost or steward; G. *graf*, D. *graaf.* *Sherif* is the true orthography.]

An officer in each county, to whom is entrusted the execution of the laws. In England, sherifs are appointed by the king. In the United States, sherifs are elected by the legislature or by the citizens, or appointed and commissioned by the executive of the state. The office of sherif in England is judicial and ministerial. In the United States it is mostly or wholly ministerial. The sherif, by himself or his deputies, executes civil and criminal process throughout the county, has charge of the jail and prisoners, attends courts and keeps the peace.

SHER'IFALTY, }
SHER'IFDŎM, } *n.* The office or jurisdiction of sherif. [I believe none of these words is now in use.
SHER'IFSHIP, }
SHER'IFWICK, }
See *Shrievalty.*]

SHER'RIFFE, *n.* The title of a descendant of Mohammed by Hassan Ibn Ali. *Encyc.*

SHER'RY, *n.* [sometimes written *sherris.*] A species of wine; so called from Xeres in Spain, where it is made.

Shew, *Shewed*, *Shewn.* [See *Show*, *Showed*, *Shown.*]

SHEW-BREAD. [See *Show-bread.*]

SHEW'ER, *n.* One that shows. [See *Shower.*]

SHEWING. [See *Showing.*]

SHIB'BOLETH, *n.* [Heb. an ear of corn, or a stream of water.]

1. A word which was made the criterion by which to distinguish the Ephraimites from the Gileadites. The Ephraimites not be-

ing able to pronounce the letter ש *sh*, pronounced the word *sibboleth*. See Judges xii. Hence,

2. The criterion of a party; or that which distinguishes one party from another; and usually, some peculiarity in things of little importance. *South.*

SHIDE, *n.* [Sax. *sceadan*, to divide.] A piece split off; a cleft; a piece; a billet of wood; a splinter.

[*Not used in New England, and local in England.*]

SHIELD, *n.* [Sax. *scyld*; Sw. *sköld*; Dan. *skiold*, *skildt*; D. G. *schild*. This word is from covering, defending, Sw. *skyla*, to cover; or from separating, Sax. *scylan*, Dan. *skiller*, to separate. Protection is deduced from either, and indeed both may be radically one. See *Shelter*. The L. *scutum* coincides in elements with the Sax. *sceadan*, to separate, and *clypeus* with the Gr. *καλυπτω*, to cover.]

1. A broad piece of defensive armor; a buckler; used in war for the protection of the body. The shields of the ancients were of different shapes and sizes, triangular, square, oval, &c. made of lether or wood covered with lether, and borne on the left arm. This species of armor was a good defense against arrows, darts, spears, &c. but would be no protection against bullets.

2. Defense; shelter; protection; or the person that defends or protects; as a chief, the ornament and *shield* of the nation.

Fear not, Abram; I am thy *shield*, and thy exceeding great reward. Gen. xv.

3. In *heraldry*, the escutcheon or field on which are placed the bearings in coats of arms.

SHIELD, *v. t.* To cover, as with a shield; to cover from danger; to defend; to protect; to secure from assault or injury.

To see the son the vanquish'd father *shield*. *Dryden.*

Hear one that comes to *shield* his injur'd honor. *Smith.*

2. To ward off; to defend against; as clothes to *shield* one from cold.

SHIE'LDED, *pp.* Covered, as with a shield; defended; protected.

SHIE'LDING, *ppr.* Covering, as with a shield; defending from attack or injury; protected.

SHIFT, *v. i.* [Sax. *scyftan*, to order or appoint, to divide or distribute, also to verge or decline, also to drive; D. *schiften*, to divide, distinguish, part, turn, discuss; Dan. *skifte*, a parting, sharing, division, lot, share; *skifter*, to part, share, divide; Sw. *skifta*, to shift, to distribute. This verb is apparently from the same root as *shiver*; Dan. *skifer sig*, to shiver; Sw. *skifta om*, to change. The primary sense is to move, to depart; hence to separate. We observe by the Swedish, that *skifta om*, [*om*, about or round,] was originally the true phrase, to move about or round; and we still say, to *shift about*.]

1. To move; to change place or position. Vegetables are not able to *shift* and seek nutriment. *Woodward.*

2. To change its direction; to vary; as, the wind *shifted* from south to west.

3. To change; to give place to other things. *Locke.*

4. To change clothes, particularly the under garment or chemise. *Young.*

5. To resort to expedients for a livelihood, or for accomplishing a purpose; to move from one thing to another, and seize one expedient when another fails.

Men in distress will look to themselves, and leave their companions to *shift* as well as they can. *L'Estrange.*

6. To practice indirect methods. *Raleigh.*

7. To seek methods of safety.

Nature teaches every creature how to *shift* for itself in cases of danger. *L'Estrange.*

8. To change place; as, a cargo *shifts* from one side to the other.

SHIFT, *v. t.* To change; to alter; as, to *shift* the scenes.

2. To transfer from one place or position to another; as, *shift* the helm; *shift* the sails.

3. To put out of the way by some expedient.

I *shifted* him away. *Shak.*

4. To change, as clothes; as, to *shift* a coat.

5. To dress in fresh clothes. Let him have time to *shift* himself.

To shift about, to turn quite round, to a contrary side or opposite point.

To shift off, to delay; to defer; as, to *shift off* the duties of religion. *Rogers.*

2. To put away; to disengage or disencumber one's self, as of a burden or inconvenience.

SHIFT, *n.* A change; a turning from one thing to another; hence, an expedient tried in difficulty; one thing tried when another fails.

I'll find a thousand *shifts* to get away. *Shak.*

2. In *a bad sense*, mean refuge; last resource.

For little souls on little *shifts* rely. *Dryden.*

3. Fraud; artifice; expedient to effect a bad purpose; or an evasion; a trick to escape detection or evil. *Hooker. South.*

4. A woman's under garment; a chemise.

SHIFT'ED, *pp.* Changed from one place or position to another.

SHIFT'ER, *n.* One that shifts; the person that plays tricks or practices artifice.

2. In *ships*, a person employed to assist the ship's cook in washing, steeping and shifting the salt provisions.

SHIFT'ING, *ppr.* Changing place or position; resorting from one expedient to another.

SHIFT'INGLY, *adv.* By shifts and changes; deceitfully.

SHIFT'LESS, *a.* Destitute of expedients, or not resorting to successful expedients; wanting means to act or live; as a *shiftless* fellow.

SHILF, *n.* [G. *schilf*, sedge.] Straw. *Tooke.*

SHILL, to *shell*, not in use.

SHILL, *v. t.* To put under cover; to sheal. [*Not in use or local.*]

SHIL'LING, *n.* [Sax. *scill*, *scilling*; G. *schilling*; D. *schelling*; Sw. Dan. *skilling*; Fr. *escalin*; It. *scellino*; Sp. *chelin*; Port. *xelim*; from the oriental שקל shakal, to weigh. See *Shekel*.]

An English silver coin equal to twelve pence, or the twentieth part of a pound. The English shilling, or shilling sterling, is equivalent nearly to 22 cents, 22 hundredths, money of the United States. Our ancestors introduced the name with the coin into this country, but by depreciation the value of the shilling sunk in New England and Virginia one fourth, or to a fraction less than 17 cents, in New York to 12½ cents, in Pennsylvania, New Jersey and Maryland to about 11 cents.

This denomination of money still subsists in the United States, although there is no coin of that value current, except the Spanish coin of 12½ cents, which is a shilling in the money of the state of New York. Since the adoption of the present coins of the United States, eagles, dollars, cents, &c. the use of *shilling* is continued only by habit.

SHILLY-SHALLY, *n.* [Russ. *shalyu*, to be foolish, to play the fool, to play wanton tricks.] Foolish trifling; irresolution. [*Vulgar.*]

[This word has probably been written *shill-I-shall-I*, from an ignorance of its origin.]

SHI'LY. [See *Shyly*.]

SHIM'MER, *v. i.* [Sax. *scymrian*; G. *schimmern*; D. *schemeren*; Dan. *skimter*.] To gleam; to glisten. [*Not in use.*] *Chaucer.*

SHIN, *n.* [Sax. *scina*, *scyne*, shin, and *scinban*, shin-bone; G. *schiene*, *schiene-bien*; D. *scheen*, *scheen-been*; Sw. *sken-ben*.]

The fore part of the leg, particularly of the human leg; the fore part of the crural bone, called *tibia*. This bone being covered only with skin, may be named from that circumstance; *skin-bone*; or it may be formed from the root of *chine*, edge.

SHINE, *v. i.* pret. *shined* or *shone*; pp. *shined* or *shone*. [Sax. *scinan*; D. *schuynen*; G. *scheinen*; Sw. *skina*. If *s* is a prefix, this word accords with the root of of L. *canus*, *caneo*; W. *càn*, white, bright. See *Cant*.]

1. To emit rays of light; to give light; to beam with steady radiance; to exhibit brightness or splendor; as, the sun *shines* by day; the moon *shines* by night. *Shining* differs from *sparkling*, *glistening*, *glittering*, as it usually implies a steady radiation or emission of light, whereas the latter words usually imply irregular or interrupted radiation. This distinction is not always observed, and we may say, the fixed stars *shine*, as well as that they *sparkle*. But we never say, the sun or the moon *sparkles*.

2. To be bright; to be lively and animated; to be brilliant.

Let thine eyes *shine* forth in their full luster. *Denham.*

3. To be unclouded; as, the moon *shines*. *Bacon.*

4. To be glossy or bright, as silk.

Fish with their fins and *shining* scales. *Milton.*

5. To be gay or splendid.

So proud she *shined* in her princely state. *Spenser.*

6. To be beautiful.

Once brightest *shin'd* this child of heat and air. *Pope.*

7. To be eminent, conspicuous or distinguished; as, to *shine* in courts. Phil. ii.

Few are qualified to *shine* in company. *Swift.*

8. To give light, real or figurative.

The light of righteousness hath not *shined* to us. *Wisdom.*

9. To manifest glorious excellencies. Ps. lxxx.
10. To be clearly published. Is. ix.
11. To be conspicuously displayed; to be manifest.

Let your light so *shine* before men— Matt. v.

To cause the face to shine, to be propitious. Num. vi. Ps. lxvii.

SHINE, *n.* Fair weather.

Be it fair or foul, rain or *shine*. *Dryden.*

2. Brightness; splendor; luster; gloss.

The glittering *shine* of gold. *Decay of Piety.*

Fair op'ning to some court's propitious *shine*. [*Not elegant.*] *Pope.*

SHI'NESS. [See *Shyness.*]

SHIN'GLE, *n.* [G. *schindel*; Gr. σχινδαλμος; L. *scindula*, from *scindo*, to divide, G. *scheiden.*]

1. A thin board sawed or rived for covering buildings. Shingles are of different lengths, with one end made much thinner than the other for lapping. They are used for covering roofs and sometimes the body of the building.
2. Round gravel, or a collection of roundish stones.

The plain of La Crau in France, is composed of *shingle*. *Pinkerton.*

3. *Shingles*, plu. [L. *cingulum*,] a kind of tetter or herpes which spreads around the body like a girdle; an eruptive disease. *Arbuthnot.*

SHIN'GLE, *v. t.* To cover with shingles; as, to *shingle* a roof.

SHIN'GLED, *pp.* Covered with shingles.

SHIN'GLING, *ppr.* Covering with shingles.

SHI'NING, *ppr.* Emitting light; beaming; gleaming.

2. *a.* Bright; splendid; radiant.
3. Illustrious; distinguished; conspicuous; as a *shining* example of charity.

SHI'NING, *n.* Effusion or clearness of light; brightness. 2 Sam. xxiii.

SHI'NY, *a.* Bright; luminous; clear; unclouded.

Like distant thunder on a *shiny* day. *Dryden.*

SHIP, as a termination, denotes state or office; as in *lordship*. *Steward.*

SHIP. [See *Shape.*]

SHIP, *n.* [Sax. *scip*, *scyp*; D. *schip*; G. *schiff*; Sw. *skepp*; Dan. *skib*; L. *scapha*; from the root of *shape*; Sax. *sceapian*, *scippan*, *scyppan*, to create, form or build.]

In *a general sense*, a vessel or building of a peculiar structure, adapted to navigation, or floating on water by means of sails. In *an appropriate sense*, a building of a structure or form fitted for navigation, furnished with a bowsprit and three masts, a main-mast, a fore-mast and a mizen-mast, each of which is composed of a lower-mast, a top-mast and top-gallant-mast, and square rigged. Ships are of various sizes and fitted for various uses; most of them however fall under the denomination of *ships of war* and *merchants' ships*.

SHIP, *v. t.* [Sax. *scipian.*] To put on board of a ship or vessel of any kind; as, to *ship* goods at Liverpool for New York.

2. To transport in a ship; to convey by water.

The sun no sooner shall the mountains touch,
But we will *ship* him hence. *Shak.*

3. To receive into a ship or vessel; as, to *ship* a sea. *Mar. Dict.*

To ship the oars, to place them in the row-locks. *Mar. Dict.*

To ship off, to send away by water; as, to *ship off* convicts.

SHIP'-BUILDER, SHIP'-BILDER, *n.* [*ship* and *builder.*] A man whose occupation is to construct ships and other vessels; a naval architect; a shipwright.

SHIP'-BUILDING, SHIP'-BILDING, *n.* [*ship* and *build.*] Naval architecture; the art of constructing vessels for navigation, particularly ships and other vessels of a large kind, bearing masts; in distinction from *boat-building*.

SHIP'BOARD, *adv.* [*ship* and *board.*] To go *on shipboard* or *a shipboard* is to go aboard; to enter a ship; to embark; literally, to *go over the side.* It is a peculiar phrase, and not much used. Seamen say, to go *aboard* or *on board.*

To be on ship board, to be in a ship; but seamen generally say, *aboard* or *on board.*

2. *n.* The plank of a ship. Ezek. xxvii. [*Not now used.*]

SHIP'-BOY, *n.* [*ship* and *boy.*] A boy that serves on board of a ship.

SHIP-CARPENTER, *n.* A shipwright; a carpenter that works at ship-building.

SHIP-CH'ANDLER, *n.* [*ship* and *chandler*, G. *handler*, a trader or dealer.]

One who deals in cordage, canvas and other furniture of ships.

SHIP'-HOLDER, *n.* [*ship* and *hold.*] The owner of a ship or of shipping.

SHIP'LESS, *a.* Destitute of ships. *Gray.*

SHIP'MAN, *n.* [*ship* and *man.*] A seaman or sailor. *Obs.* 1 Kings ix. Acts xxviii.

SHIP'M'ASTER, *n.* [*ship* and *master.*] The captain, master or commander of a ship. Jonah i.

SHIP'MENT, *n.* The act of putting any thing on board of a ship or other vessel; embarkation; as, he was engaged in the *shipment* of coal for London.

2. The goods or things shipped, or put on board of a ship or other vessel. We say, the merchants have made large *shipments* to the United States.

The question is whether the share of M in the *shipment*, is exempted from condemnation by reason of his neutral domicil. *J. Story.*

SHIP'-MONEY, *n.* [*ship* and *money.*] In *English history*, an imposition formerly charged on the ports, towns, cities, boroughs and counties of England, for providing and furnishing certain ships for the king's service. This imposition being laid by the king's writ under the great seal, without the consent of parliament, was held to be contrary to the laws and statutes of the realm, and abolished by Stat. 17 Car. 11. *Encyc.*

SHIP'PED, *pp.* Put on board of a ship or vessel; received on board.

SHIP'PEN, *n.* [Sax. *scipen.*] A stable; a cow house. [*Not in use.*] *Chaucer.*

SHIP'PING, *ppr.* Putting on board of a ship or vessel; receiving on board.

2. *a.* Relating to ships; as *shipping* concerns. *Kent.*

SHIP'PING, *n.* Ships in general; ships or vessels of any kind for navigation. The *shipping* of the English nation exceeds that of any other. The tunnage of the *shipping* belonging to the United States is second only to that of Great Britain.

To take shipping, to embark; to enter on board a ship or vessel for conveyance or passage. John vi.

SHIP'-SHAPE, *adv.* In a seamanlike manner. *Mar. Dict.*

SHIP'WRECK, *n.* [*ship* and *wreck.*] The destruction of a ship or other vessel by being cast ashore or broken to pieces by beating against rocks and the like. *Mar. Dict.*

2. The parts of a shattered ship. [*Unusual.*] *Dryden.*
3. Destruction.

To make shipwreck concerning faith, is to apostatize from the love, profession and practice of divine truth which had been embraced. 1 Tim. i.

SHIP'WRECK, *v. t.* To destroy by running ashore or on rocks or sand banks. How many vessels are annually *shipwrecked* on the Bahama rocks!

2. To suffer the perils of being cast away; to be cast ashore with the loss of the ship. The *shipwrecked* mariners were saved. *Addison. Shak.*

SHIP'WRECKED, *pp.* Cast ashore; dashed upon the rocks or banks; destroyed.

SHIP'WRIGHT, *n.* [*ship* and *wright.* See *Work.*]

One whose occupation is to construct ships; a builder of ships or other vessels. *Swift.*

SHIRE, *n.* [Sax. *scir*, *scire*, *scyre*, a division, from *sciran*, to divide. See *Share* and *Shear.* It is pronounced in compound words, *shir*, as in *Hampshire*, *Berkshire.*]

In England, a division of territory, otherwise called a county. The *shire* was originally a division of the kingdom under the jurisdiction of an earl or count, whose authority was entrusted to the *sherif*, [shire-reeve.] On this officer the government ultimately devolved. In the United States, the corresponding division of a state is called a *county*, but we retain *shire* in the compound *half-shire*; as when the county court is held in two towns in the same county alternately, we call one of the divisions a *half-shire*.

In some states, *shire* is used as the constituent part of the name of a county, as *Berkshire*, *Hampshire*, in Massachusetts. These being the names established by law, we say, the *county of Berkshire*, and we cannot with propriety say, the *county of Berks*, for there is no county in Massachusetts thus named.

SHI'RE-MOTE, *n.* [Sax. *scyr-gemote*, shire-meeting.]

Anciently in England, the county court; sherif's turn or court. *Cowel. Blackstone.*

SHIRK, a different spelling of *shark*, which see.

SHIRL, a different spelling of *shorl.* [See *Shorl.*]

SHIR'LEY, *n.* A bird, by some called the greater bullfinch; having the upper part of the body of a dark brown, and the throat and breast red. *Dict.*

SHIRT, *n.* *shurt.* [Dan. *skiorte*, Sw. *skiorta*, a shirt; Dan. *skiort*, a petticoat; Ice. *scyrta.* This word seems to be named from its *shortness* or cutting off, and might have signified originally a somewhat different garment *shortened;* Sax. *scyrt,* short, L. *curtus.*]

A loose garment of linen, cotton or other material, worn by men and boys next the body.

It is folly for a nation to export beef and linen, while a great part of the people are obliged to subsist on potatoes, and have no *shirts* to wear. *A. M.*

SHIRT, *v. t. shurt.* To cover or clothe, as with a shirt. *Dryden.*

2. To change the shirt and put on a clean one.

SHIRTLESS, *a. shurt'less.* Wanting a shirt. *Pope.*

SHIST, SHIST'US, *n.* A species of argillaceous earth or slate; clay slate.

SHIST'IC, SHIST'OUS, *a.* Pertaining to shist, or partaking of its properties.

SHIT'TAH, SHIT'TIM, *n.* In *Scripture,* a sort of precious wood of which the tables, altars and boards of the tabernacle were made among the Jews. The wood is said to be hard, tough and smooth, and very beautiful. *Calmet.*

SHIT'TLE, *a.* [See *Shoot.*] Wavering; unsettled. [*Not used or local.*]

SHITTLE-COCK. [See *Shuttle-cock.*]

SHIT'TLENESS, *n.* Unsettledness; inconstancy. [*Not in use or local.*]

SHIVE, *n. shiv.* [D. *schyf;* G. *scheibe.* If *s* is a prefix, this word agrees radically with *chip.*]

1. A slice; a thin cut; as a *shive* of bread. [*Not in use.*] *Shak.*

2. A thin flexible piece cut off. [*Not in use.*] *Boyle.*

3. A little piece or fragment; as the *shives* of flax made by breaking.

SHIV'ER, *n.* [G. *schiefer,* a splinter, slate; *schiefern,* to shiver, to scale; Dan. *skive,* Sw. *skifva,* a slice; Dan. *skifer, skiver,* a slate; *skifer sig,* to shiver, peel or split, Sw. *skifva sig.*]

1. In *mineralogy,* a species of blue slate; shist; shale.

2. In *seamen's language,* a little wheel; a sheave.

SHIV'ER, *v. t.* [supra. Qu. Heb. שבר to break in pieces. Class Br. No. 26.]

To break into many small pieces or splinters; to shatter; to dash to pieces by a blow.

The ground with *shiver'd* armor strown. *Milton.*

SHIV'ER, *v. i.* To fall at once into many small pieces or parts.

The natural world, should gravity once cease, would instantly *shiver* into millions of atoms. *Woodward.*

2. To quake; to tremble; to shudder; to shake, as with cold, ague, fear or horror.

The man that *shiver'd* on the brink of sin. *Dryden.*

Prometheus is laid
On icy Caucasus to *shiver.* *Swift.*

3. To be affected with a thrilling sensation, like that of chilliness.

Any very harsh noise will set the teeth on edge, and make all the body *shiver.* *Bacon.*

SHIV'ER, *n.* A small piece or fragment into which a thing breaks by any sudden violence.

He would pound thee into *shivers* with his fist, as a sailor breaks a biscuit. *Shak.*

2. A slice; a sliver. *Chaucer.*

SHIV'ERED, *pp.* Broken or dashed into small pieces.

SHIV'ERING, *ppr.* Breaking or dashing into small pieces.

2. Quaking; trembling; shaking, as with cold or fear.

SHIV'ERING, *n.* The act of breaking or dashing to pieces; division; severance.

2. A trembling; a shaking with cold or fear.

SHIV'ER-SPAR, *n.* [G. *schiefer-spath.*] A carbonate of lime, so called from its slaty structure; called also slate-spar. *Phillips.*

SHIV'ERY, *a.* Easily falling into many pieces; not firmly cohering; incompact; as *shivery* stone.

SHOAD, *n.* Among *miners,* a train of metallic stones which serves to direct them in the discovery of mines. *Encyc.*

SHOAD-STONE, *n.* A small stone, smooth, of a dark liver color with a shade of purple. Shoad-stones are loose masses found at the entrance of mines, sometimes running in a straight line from the surface to a vein of ore. They appear to be broken from the strata or larger masses; they usually contain mundic, or marcasitic matter, and a portion of the ore of the mine. *Encyc.*

SHOAL, *n.* [Sax. *sceol,* a crowd. It should rather be written *shole.*]

1. A great multitude assembled; a crowd; a throng; as *shoals* of people. Immense *shoals* of herring appear on the coast in the spring.

The vices of a prince draw *shoals* of followers. *Decay of Piety.*

2. A place where the water of a river, lake or sea is shallow or of little depth; a sand bank or bar; a shallow. The entrance of rivers is often rendered difficult or dangerous by *shoals.*

SHOAL, *v. i.* To crowd; to throng; to assemble in a multitude. The fishes *shoaled* about the place. *Chapman.*

2. To become more shallow. The water *shoals* as we approach the town.

SHOAL, *a.* Shallow; of little depth; as *shoal* water.

SHOALINESS, *n.* [from *shoaly.*] Shallowness; little depth of water.

2. The state of abounding with shoals.

SHOALY, *a.* Full of shoals or shallow places.

The tossing vessel sail'd on *shoaly* ground. *Dryden.*

SHOCK, *n.* [D. *schok,* a bounce, jolt or leap; Fr. *choc,* a striking or dashing against. See *Shake.*]

1. A violent collision of bodies, or the concussion which it occasions; a violent striking or dashing against.

The strong unshaken mounds resist the *shocks*
Of tides and seas. *Blackmore.*

2. Violent onset; conflict of contending armies or foes.

He stood the *shock* of a whole host of foes. *Addison.*

3. External violence; as the *shocks* of fortune. *Addison.*

4. Offense; impression of disgust.

Fewer *shocks* a statesman gives his friend. *Young.*

5. In *electricity,* the effect on the animal system of a discharge of the fluid from a charged body.

6. A pile of sheaves of wheat, rye, &c.

And cause it on *shocks* to be by and by set. *Tusser.*

Behind the master walks, builds up the *shocks.* *Thomson.*

7. In *New England,* the number of sixteen sheaves of wheat, rye, &c. [This is the sense in which this word is generally used with us.]

8. A dog with long rough hair or shag. [from *shag.*]

SHOCK, *v. t.* [D. *schokken;* Fr. *choquer.*]

1. To shake by the sudden collision of a body.

2. To meet force with force; to encounter. *Shak.*

3. To strike, as with horror or disgust; to cause to recoil, as from something odious or horrible; to offend extremely; to disgust. I was *shocked* at the sight of so much misery. Avoid every thing that can *shock* the feelings of delicacy.

Advise him not to *shock* a father's will. *Dryden.*

SHOCK, *v. i.* To collect sheaves into a pile; to pile sheaves. *Tusser.*

SHOCK'ED, *pp.* Struck, as with horror; offended; disgusted.

2. Piled, as sheaves.

SHOCK'ING, *ppr.* Shaking with sudden violence.

2. Meeting in onset or violent encounter.

And now with shouts the *shocking* armies clos'd. *Pope*

3. *a.* Striking, as with horror; causing to recoil with horror or disgust; extremely offensive or disgusting.

The French humor—is very *shocking* to the Italians. *Addison.*

SHOCK'INGLY, *adv.* In a manner to strike with horror or disgust. *Chesterfield.*

SHOD, for shoed, pret. and pp. of *shoe.*

SHÖE, *n.* plu. *shöes.* [Sax. *sceo, sceog;* G. *schuh;* D. *schoen;* Sw. *sko;* Dan. *skoe,* a shoe; *skoer,* to bind with iron, to shoe. It is uncertain to what this word was originally applied, whether to a band of iron, or to something worn on the human foot. It is a contracted word. In G. *handschuh,* hand-shoe, is a glove. The sense is probably a cover, or that which is put on.]

1. A covering for the foot, usually of lether, composed of a thick species for the sole, and a thinner kind for the vamp and quarters. Shoes for ladies often have some species of cloth for the vamp and quarters.

2. A plate or rim of iron nailed to the hoof of a horse to defend it from injury; also, a plate of iron for an ox's hoof, one for each division of the hoof. Oxen are shod in New England, sometimes to defend the hoof from injury in stony places, more generally to enable them to walk on ice, in which case the shoes are armed with sharp points. This is called *calking.*

3. The plate of iron which is nailed to the bottom of the runner of a sleigh, or any vehicle that slides on the snow in winter.

4. A piece of timber fastened with pins to the bottom of the runners of a sled, to prevent them from wearing.

5. Something in form of a shoe.

6. A cover for defense.

Shoe of an anchor, a small block of wood, convex on the back, with a hole to receive the point of the anchor fluke; used to prevent the anchor from tearing the planks of the ship's bow, when raised or lowered. *Mar. Dict.*

SHŌE, *v. t.* pret. and pp. *shod.* To furnish with shoes; to put shoes on; as, to *shoe* a horse or an ox; to *shoe* a sled or sleigh.

2. To cover at the bottom. *Drayton.*

To shoe an anchor, to cover the flukes with a broad triangular piece of plank whose area is larger than that of the fluke. This is intended to give the anchor a stronger hold in soft grounds. *Mar. Dict.*

SHŌEBLACK, *n.* [*shoe* and *black.*] A person that cleans shoes.

SHŌEBOY, *n.* [*shoe* and *boy.*] A boy that cleans shoes.

SHŌEBUCKLE, *n.* [*shoe* and *buckle.*] A buckle for fastening a shoe to the foot.

SHŌEING, *ppr.* Putting on shoes.

SHŌEING-HORN, *n.* [*shoe* and *horn.*] A horn used to facilitate the entrance of the foot into a narrow shoe.

2. Any thing by which a transaction is facilitated; any thing used as a medium; in contempt. *Spectator.*

[*I have never heard this word in America.*]

SHŌE-LEATHER, **SHŌE-LETHER**, *n.* [*shoe* and *lether.*] Lether for shoes.

SHŌELESS, *a.* Destitute of shoes.

Caltrops very much incommoded the *shoeless* Moors. *Dr. Addison.*

SHŌEMAKER, *n.* [*shoe* and *maker.*] One whose occupation or trade is to make shoes and boots.

SHŌER, *n.* One that fits shoes to the feet; one that furnishes or puts on shoes; as a farrier.

SHŌESTRING, *n.* [*shoe* and *string.*] A string used to fasten a shoe to the foot.

SHŌETȲE, *n.* [*shoe* and *tye.*] A ribin used for fastening a shoe to the foot. *Hudibras.*

SHOG, for *shock*, a violent concussion. [*Not in use.*] *Dryden.*

SHOG, *v. t.* To shake; to agitate. [*Not in use.*] *Carew.*

SHOG, *v. i.* To move off; to be gone; to jog. [*Not in use.* See *Jog.*] *Hall.*

SHOG'GING, *n.* Concussion. [*Not in use.*] *Harmar.*

SHOG'GLE, *v. t.* To shake; to joggle. [*Not in use.* See *Joggle.*] *Pegge.*

SHOLE, *n.* [Sax. *sceol*, a crowd.] A throng; a crowd; a great multitude assembled. [This is the better orthography. See *Shoal.*]

SHONE, *pp.* of *shine.*

SHOOK, *pp.* of *shake.*

SHOON, *old plu.* of *shoe.* *Obs.*

SHOOT, *v. t.* pret. and pp. *shot.* The old participle *shotten*, is obsolete. [Sax. *sceotan, scytan*, to shoot, to dart, to rush, to lay out or bestow, to transfer, to point with the finger, whence to lead or direct; G. *schossen*, to shoot, and to pay scot, also *schiessen*, to shoot, to dart; D. *schieten*; Sw. *skiuta*; Dan. *skyder*; Ir. *sceithim*, to vomit; *sciot*, an arrow or dart; It. *scattare*, to shoot an arrow; L. *scateo*, to shoot out water; W. *ysguthaw, ysgudaw*, to scud; *ysgwdu*, to thrust; *ysgythu*, to spout. It is formed with a prefix on *Gd.*]

1. To let fly and drive with force; as, to *shoot* an arrow.

2. To discharge and cause to be driven with violence; as, to *shoot* a ball.

3. To send off with force; to dart.

And from about her *shot* darts of desire. *Milton.*

4. To let off; used of the instrument.

The two ends of a bow *shot* off, fly from one another. *Boyle.*

5. To strike with any thing shot; as, to *shoot* one with an arrow or a bullet.

6. To send out; to push forth; as, a plant *shoots* a branch.

7. To push out; to emit; to dart; to thrust forth.

Beware the secret snake that *shoots* a sting. *Dryden.*

8. To push forward; to drive; to propel; as, to *shoot* a bolt.

9. To push out; to thrust forward.

They *shoot* out the lip. Ps. xxii.

The phrase, to *shoot out the lip*, signifies to treat with derision or contempt.

10. To pass through with swiftness; as, to *shoot* the Stygian flood. *Dryden.*

11. To fit to each other by planing; *a workman's term.*

Two pieces of wood that are *shot*, that is, planed or pared with a chisel. *Moxon*

12. To kill by a ball, arrow or other thing shot; as, to *shoot* a duck.

SHOOT, *v. i.* To perform the act of discharging, sending with force, or driving any thing by means of an engine or instrument; as, to *shoot* at a target or mark.

When you *shoot*, and shut one eye. *Prior.*

The archers have sorely grieved him, and *shot* at him. Gen. xlix.

2. To germinate; to bud; to sprout; to send forth branches.

Onions, as they hang, will *shoot* forth. *Bacon.*

But the wild olive *shoots* and shades the ungrateful plain. *Dryden.*

Delightful task,
To teach the young idea how to *shoot*. *Thomson.*

3. To form by shooting, or by an arrangement of particles into spiculæ. Metals *shoot* into crystals. Every salt *shoots* into crystals of a determinate form.

4. To be emitted, sent forth or driven along.

There *shot* a streaming lamp along the sky. *Dryden.*

5. To protuberate; to be pushed out; to jut; to project. The land *shoots* into a promontory.

6. To pass, as an arrow or pointed instrument; to penetrate.

Thy words *shoot* through my heart. *Addison.*

7. To grow rapidly; to become by rapid growth. The boy soon *shoots* up to a man.

He'll soon *shoot* up a hero. *Dryden.*

8. To move with velocity; as a *shooting* star.

9. To feel a quick darting pain. My temples *shoot.*

To shoot ahead, to outstrip in running, flying or sailing.

SHOOT, *n.* The act of propelling or driving any thing with violence; the discharge of a fire-arm or bow; as a good *shoot.*

The Turkish bow giveth a very forcible *shoot.* *Bacon.*

2. The act of striking or endeavoring to strike with a missive weapon. *Shak.*

3. A young branch.

Prune off superfluous branches and *shoots* of this second spring. *Evelyn.*

4. A young swine. [In New England pronounced *shote.*]

SHOOT'ER, *n.* One that shoots; an archer; a gunner. *Herbert.*

SHOOT'ING, *ppr.* Discharging, as firearms; driving or sending with violence; pushing out; protuberating; germinating; branching; glancing, as pain.

SHOOT'ING, *n.* The act of discharging fire-arms, or of sending an arrow with force; a firing.

2. Sensation of a quick glancing pain.

3. In *sportsmanship*, the act or practice of killing game with guns or fire-arms.

SHOP, *n.* [Norm. *schope*; Sax. *sceoppa*, a depository, from *sceapian*, to form or shape; Sw. *skåp*, a repository; Dan. *skab*, a cupboard or chest of drawers. Qu. Fr. *echoppe.*]

1. A building in which goods, wares, drugs, &c. are sold by retail.

2. A building in which mechanics work, and where they keep their manufactures for sale.

Keep your *shop*, and your *shop* will keep you. *Franklin.*

SHOP, *v. i.* To visit shops for purchasing goods; used chiefly in the participle; as, the lady is *shopping.*

SHOP'BOARD, *n.* [*shop* and *board.*] A bench on which work is performed; as a doctor or divine taken from the *shopboard.* *South.*

SHOP'BOOK, *n.* [*shop* and *book.*] A book in which a tradesman keeps his accounts. *Locke.*

SHOP'KEEPER, *n.* [*shop* and *keep.*] A trader who sells goods in a shop or by retail; in distinction from a merchant, or one who sells by wholesale. *Addison.*

SHOP'LIFTER, *n.* [*shop* and *lift.* See *Lift.*]

One who steals any thing in a shop, or takes goods privately from a shop; one who under pretense of buying goods, takes occasion to steal. *Encyc.*

SHOP'LIFTING, *n.* Larceny committed in a shop; the stealing of any thing from a shop.

SHOP'LIKE, *a.* Low; vulgar. *B. Jonson.*

SHOP'MAN, *n.* [*shop* and *man.*] A petty trader. *Dryden.*

2. One who serves in a shop. *Johnson.*

SHOP'PING, *ppr.* Visiting shops for the purchase of goods.

SHORE, the *old pret.* of *shear.* *Obs.*

SHORE, *n.* [Sax. *score.*] The coast or land adjacent to the ocean or sea, or to a large lake or river. This word is applied primarily to the land contiguous to water; but it extends also to the ground near the border of the sea or of a lake, which is covered with water. We also use the word to express the land near the border of the sea or of a great lake, to an indefinite extent; as when we say, a town stands on the *shore.* We do not apply the word to the land contiguous to a small stream. This we call a bank.

SHORE, *n.* [The popular but corrupt pronunciation of *sewer*; a pronunciation that should be carefully avoided.]

SHORE, *n.* [Sp. Port. *escora*; D. *schoor.*] A prop; a buttress; something that supports a building or other thing. *Watts.*

SHORE, *v. t.* To prop; to support by a post or buttress; usually with *up*; as, to *shore up* a building.

2. To set on shore. [*Not in use.*] *Shak.*

SHO'RED, *pp.* Propped; supported by a prop.

SHO'RELESS, *a.* Having no shore or coast; of indefinite or unlimited extent; as a *shoreless* ocean. *Boyle.*

SHO'RELING, } *n.* In *England*, the skin
SHOR'LING, } of a living sheep shorn, as distinct from the *morling*, or skin taken from a dead sheep. Hence in some parts of England, a *shorling* is a sheep shorn, and *morling* is one that dies. *Encyc.*

SHORL, *n.* [Sw. *skörl*, from *skör*, brittle; Dan. *skiör.*]

A mineral, usually of a black color, found in masses of an indeterminate form, or crystalized in three or nine sided prisms, which when entire are terminated by three sided summits. The surface of the crystals is longitudinally streaked. The amorphous sort presents thin straight distinct columnar concretions, sometimes parallel, sometimes diverging or stelliform. This is called also tourmalin. *Haüy. Werner. Kirwan.*

The shorl of the mineralogists of the last century comprehended a variety of substances which later observations have separated into several species. The green shorl is the epidote, or the vesuvian, or the actinolite. The violet shorl and the lenticular shorl are the axinite. The black volcanic shorl is the augite. The white Vesuvian shorl is the sommite. The white grenatiform is the leucite. The white prismatic is the pycnite, a species of the topaz, and another is a variety of feldspar. Of the blue shorl, one variety is the oxyd of titanium, another the sappare, and another the phosphate of iron. The shorl cruciform is the granatite. The octahedral shorl is the octahedrite or anatase. The red shorl of Hungary and the purple of Madagascar, are varieties of the oxyd of titanium. The spathic shorl is the spodumene. The black shorl and the electric shorl only remain, and to this species the name tourmalin was given by that celebrated mineralogist, the Abbe Haüy. *Gibbs, Journ. of Science.*

Blue shorl is a variety of Hauyne. Red and titanitic shorl is rutile. *Ure.*

SHORLA'CEOUS, *a.* Like shorl; partaking of the nature and characters of shorl. *Kirwan.*

SHORL'ITE, *n.* A mineral of a greenish white color, sometimes yellowish; mostly found in irregular oblong masses or columns, inserted in a mixture of quartz and mica or granite. *Klaproth. Kirwan.*

Shorlite or shorlous topaz, the pycnite of Werner, is of a straw yellow color. *Ure.*

SHORN, *pp.* of *shear.* Cut off; as a lock of wool *shorn.*

2. Having the hair or wool cut off or sheared; as a *shorn* lamb.

3. Deprived; as a prince *shorn* of his honors.

SHORT, *a.* [Sax. *sceort*, *scyrt*; G. *kurz*; D. Sw. Dan. *kort*; Fr. *court*; It. *corto*; L. *curtus*; Ir. *gear*; Russ. *kortayu*, to shorten. It is from cutting off or separating. Qu. Dan. *skiör*, Sw. *skör*, brittle.]

1. Not long; not having great length or extension; as a *short* distance; a *short* ferry; a *short* flight; a *short* piece of timber.

The bed is *shorter* than that a man can stretch himself on it. Is. xxviii.

2. Not extended in time; not of long duration.

The triumphing of the wicked is *short.* Job xx. 1 Thess. ii.

3. Not of usual or sufficient length, reach or extent.

Weak though I am of limb, and *short* of sight. *Pope.*

4. Not of long duration; repeated at small intervals of time; as *short* breath. *Dryden. Sidney.*

5. Not of adequate extent or quantity; not reaching the point demanded, desired or expected; as a quantity *short* of our expectations.

Not therefore am I *short*
Of knowing what I ought. *Milton.*

6. Deficient; defective; imperfect. This account is *short* of the truth.

7. Not adequate; insufficient; scanty; as, provisions are *short*; a *short* allowance of water for the voyage.

8. Not sufficiently supplied; scantily furnished.

The English were inferior in number, and grew *short* in their provisions. *Hayward.*

9. Not far distant in time; future.

He commanded those who were appointed to attend him, to be ready by a *short* day. *Clarendon.*

We now say, at *short* notice. In mercantile language, a note or bill is made payable at *short* sight, that is, in a little time after being presented to the payor.

10. Not fetching a compass; as in the phrase, to *turn short.*

11. Not going to the point intended; as, to stop *short.*

12. Defective in quantity; as sheep *short* of their wool. *Dryden.*

13. Narrow; limited; not extended; not large or comprehensive.

Their own *short* understandings reach
No farther than the present. *Rowe.*

14. Brittle; friable; breaking all at once without splinters or shatters; as marl so *short* that it cannot be wrought into a ball. *Mortimer.*

15. Not bending.

The lance broke *short.* *Dryden.*

16. Abrupt; brief; pointed; petulant; severe. I asked him a question, to which he gave a *short* answer.

To be short, to be scantily supplied; as, to *be short* of bread or water.

To come short, to fail; not to do what is demanded or expected, or what is necessary for the purpose; *applied to persons.* We all *come short* of perfect obedience to God's will.

2. Not to reach or obtain. Rom. iii.

3. To fail; to be insufficient. Provisions *come short.*

To cut short, to abridge; to contract; to make too small or defective; also, to destroy or consume. 2 Kings x.

To fall short, to fail; to be inadequate or scanty; as, provisions *fall short*; money *falls short.*

2. To fail; not to do or accomplish; as, to *fall short* in duty.

3. To be less. The measure *falls short* of the estimate.

To stop short, to stop at once; also, to stop without reaching the point intended.

To turn short, to turn on the spot occupied; to turn without making a compass.

For *turning short* he struck with all his might. *Dryden.*

To be taken short, to be seized with urgent necessity. *Swift.*

In short, in few words; briefly; to sum up or close in a few words.

SHORT, *n.* A summary account; as the *short* of the matter.

The *short* and long in our play is preferred. *Shak.*

SHORT, *adv.* Not long; as *short*-enduring joy; a *short*-breathed man. *Dryden. Arbuthnot.*

In connection with verbs, *short* is a modifying word, or used adverbially; as, to *come short*, &c.

SHORT, *v. t.* To shorten.

2. *v. i.* To fail; to decrease. [*Not in use.*]

SHORT'-BREATHED, *a.* Having short breath or quick respiration.

SHORT'-DATED, *a.* [*short* and *date.*] Having little time to run. *Sandys.*

SHORTEN, *v. t.* *short'n.* [Sax. *scyrtan.*] To make short in measure, extent or time; as, to *shorten* distance; to *shorten* a road; to *shorten* days of calamity. Matt. xxiv.

2. To abridge; to lessen; as, to *shorten* labor or work.

3. To curtail; as, to *shorten* the hair by clipping.

4. To contract; to lessen; to diminish in extent or amount; as, to *shorten* sail; to *shorten* an allowance of provisions.

5. To confine; to restrain.

Here where the subject is so fruitful, I am *shortened* by my chain. *Dryden.*

6. To lop; to deprive.

The youth—*shortened* of his ears. *Dryden.*

SHORTEN, *v. i.* *short'n.* To become short or shorter. The day *shortens* in northern latitudes from June to December.

2. To contract; as, a cord *shortens* by being wet; a metallic rod *shortens* by cold.

SHORT'ENED, *pp.* Made shorter; abridged; contracted.

SHORT'ENING, *ppr.* Making shorter; contracting.

SHORT'ENING, *n.* Something used in cookery to make paste short or friable, as butter or lard.

SHORT'-HAND, *n.* [*short* and *hand.*] Short writing; a compendious method of writing by substituting characters, abbreviations or symbols for words; otherwise called *stenography.* *Locke.*

SHORT'-JOINTED, *a.* [*short* and *joint.*] A horse is said to be *short-jointed*, when the pastern is too short. *Encyc.*

SHORT'-LIVED, *a.* [*short* and *live.*] Not living or lasting long; being of short continuance; as a *short-lived* race of beings; *short-lived* pleasure; *short-lived* passion. *Dryden. Addison.*

SHORT'LY, *adv.* Quickly; soon; in a little time.

The armies came *shortly* in view of each other. *Clarendon.*

2. In few words; briefly; as, to express ideas more *shortly* in verse than in prose. *Pope.*

SHORT'NER, *n.* He or that which shortens. *Swift.*

SHORT'NESS, *n.* The quality of being short in space or time; little length or little duration; as the *shortness* of a journey or of distance; the *shortness* of the days in winter; the *shortness* of life.

2. Fewness of words; brevity; conciseness; as the *shortness* of an essay. The prayers of the church, by reason of their *shortness*, are easy for the memory.

3. Want of reach or the power of retention; as the *shortness* of the memory. *Bacon.*

4. Deficiency; imperfection; limited extent; as the *shortness* of our reason. *Glanville.*

SHORT'-RIB, *n.* [*short* and *rib.*] One of the lower ribs; a rib shorter than the others, below the sternum; a false rib. *Wiseman.*

SHORTS, *n. plu.* The bran and coarse part of meal. [*Local.*]

SHORT-SIGHT, *n.* Short-sightedness; myopy; vision accurate only when the object is near. *Good.*

SHORT-SIGHTED, *a.* [*short* and *sight.*]

1. Not able to see far; having limited vision; *in a literal sense.*

2. Not able to look far into futurity; not able to understand things deep or remote; of limited intellect.

SHORT-SIGHTEDNESS, *n.* A defect in vision, consisting in the inability to see things at a distance, or at the distance to which the sight ordinarily extends. *Short-sightedness* is owing to the too great convexity of the crystaline humor of the eye, by which the rays of light are brought to a focus too soon, that is, before they reach the retina.

2. Defective or limited intellectual sight; inability to see far into futurity or into things deep or abstruse. *Addison.*

SHORT-WAISTED, *a.* [*short* and *waist.*] Having a short waist or body. *Dryden.*

SHORT-WIND'ED, *a.* [*short* and *wind.*] Affected with shortness of breath; having a quick respiration; as asthmatic persons. *May.*

SHORT'-WINGED, *a.* [*short* and *wing.*] Having short wings; as a *short-winged* hawk. *Dryden.*

SHORT-WIT'TED, *a.* Having little wit; not wise; of scanty intellect or judgment. *Hales.*

SHO'RY, *a.* [from *shore.*] Lying near the shore or coast. [*Little used.*] *Burnet.*

SHOT, *pret.* and *pp.* of *shoot.*

SHOT, *n.* [Sax. *scyt;* D. *schoot, schot.* See *Shoot* and *Scot.*]

1. The act of shooting; discharge of a missile weapon.

He caused twenty *shot* of his greatest cannon to be made at the king's army. *Clarendon.*

[*Note.* The plural *shots*, may be used, but *shot* is generally used in both numbers.]

2. A missile weapon, particularly a ball or bullet. *Shot* is properly whatever is discharged from fire-arms or cannon by the force of gunpowder. Shot used in war is of various kinds; as *round shot* or *balls;* those for cannon made of iron, those for muskets and pistols, of lead. Secondly, *double headed shot* or *bar shot*, consisting of a bar with a round head at each end. Thirdly, *chain-shot*, consisting of two balls chained together. Fourthly, *grape-shot*, consisting of a number of balls bound together with a cord in canvas on an iron bottom. Fifthly, *case shot* or *canister shot*, consisting of a great number of small bullets in a cylindrical tin box. Sixthly, *langrel* or *langrage*, which consists of pieces of iron of any kind or shape. *Small shot*, denotes musket balls. *Mar. Dict.*

3. Small globular masses of lead, used for killing fowls and other small animals. These are not called balls or bullets.

4. The flight of a missile weapon, or the distance which it passes from the engine; as a cannon *shot;* a musket *shot;* a pistol *shot;* a bow *shot.*

5. A reckoning; charge or proportional share of expense. [See *Scot.*]

Shot of a cable, in seaman's language, the splicing of two cables together; or the whole length of two cables thus united. A ship will ride easier in deep water with one *shot of cable* thus lengthened, than with three short cables. *Encyc.*

SHOTE, *n.* [Sax. *sceota; from shooting*, darting.]

1. A fish resembling the trout. *Carew.*

2. A young hog. [See *Shoot.*]

SHOT'-FREE, *a.* [*shot* and *free.*] Free from charge; exempted from any share of expense; scot-free.

2. Not to be injured by shot. [*Not used.*] *Feltham.*

3. Unpunished. [*Not used.*]

SHOTTEN, *a.* shot'n. [from *shoot.*] Having ejected the spawn; as a *shotten* herring. *Shak.*

2. Shooting into angles.

3. Shot out of its socket; dislocated; as a bone.

SHOUGH, *n.* shok. A kind of shaggy dog. [*Not in use.* See *Shock.*]

SHOULD. shood. The preterit of *shall*, but now used as an auxiliary verb, either in the past time or conditional present. "He *should* have paid the debt at the time the note became due." *Should* here denotes past time. "I *should* ride to town this day if the weather would permit." Here *should* expresses present or future time conditionally. In the second and third persons, it denotes obligation or duty, as in the first example above.

1. *I should go.* When *should* in this person is uttered without emphasis, it declares simply that an event would take place, on some condition or under other circumstances.

But when expressed with emphasis, *should* in this person denotes obligation, duty or determination.

2. *Thou shouldst* } *go.* *You should* } Without emphasis, *should*, in the second person, is nearly equivalent to *ought;* you ought to go, it is your duty, you are bound to go. [See *Shall.*]

With emphasis, *should* expresses determination in the speaker conditionally to compel the person to act. "If I had the care of you, you *should* go, whether willing or not."

3. *He should go.* *Should*, in the third person, has the same force as in the second.

4. If *I should*, if *you should*, if *he should*, &c. denote a future contingent event.

5. After *should*, the principal verb is sometimes omitted, without obscuring the sense.

So subjects love just kings, or so they *should.* *Dryden.*

That is, so they *should love* them.

6. *Should be*, ought to be; a proverbial phrase, conveying some censure, contempt or irony. Things are not as they *should be.*

The boys think their mother no better than she *should be.* *Addison.*

7. "We think it strange that stones *should* fall from the aerial regions." In this use, *should* implies that stones do fall. In all similar phrases, *should* implies the actual existence of the fact, without a condition or supp sition.

SHOULDER, *n.* [Sax. *sculdre, sculdor, sculder;* G. *schulter;* D. *schouder;* Sw. *skuldra;* Dan. *skulder.*]

1. The joint by which the arm of a human being or the fore leg of a quadruped is connected with the body; or in man, the projection formed by the bones called *scapulæ* or shoulder blades, which extend from the basis of the neck in a horizontal direction.

2. The upper joint of the fore leg of an animal cut for the market; as a *shoulder* of mutton.

3. *Shoulders*, in the plural, the upper part of the back.

Adown her *shoulders* fell her length of hair. *Dryden.*

4. *Figuratively*, support; sustaining power; or that which elevates and sustains.

For on thy *shoulders* do I build my seat. *Shak.*

5. Among artificers, something like the human shoulder; a horizontal or rectangular projection from the body of a thing. *Moxon.*

SHOULDER, *v. t.* To push or thrust with the shoulder; to push with violence.

Around her numberless the rabble flow'd,
Should'ring each other, crowding for a view. *Rowe.*

As they the earth would *shoulder* from her seat. *Spenser.*

2. To take upon the shoulder; as, to *shoulder* a basket.

SHOULDER-BELT, *n.* [*shoulder* and *belt.*] A belt that passes across the shoulder. *Dryden.*

SHOULDER-BLADE, *n.* [*shoulder* and *blade.*] The bone of the shoulder, or blade bone, broad and triangular, covering the hind part of the ribs; called by anatomists *scapula* and *omoplata.* *Encyc.*

SHOULDER-CLAPPER, *n.* [*shoulder* and *clap.*] One that claps another on the shoulder, or that uses great familiarity. [*Not in use.*] *Shak.*

SHOULDER-KNOT, *n.* [*shoulder* and *knot.*] An ornamental knot of ribin or lace worn on the shoulder; an epaulet.

SHOULDER-SHOTTEN, *a.* [*shoulder* and *shot.*]
Strained in the shoulder, as a horse. *Shak.*

SHOULDER-SLIP, *n.* [*shoulder* and *slip.*] Dislocation of the shoulder or of the humerus. *Swift.*

SHOUT, *v. i.* [This word coincides with *shoot*, W. *ysgythu*, to jet, to spout.]
To utter a sudden and loud outcry, usually in joy, triumph or exultation, or to animate soldiers in an onset.

It is not the voice of them that *shout* for mastery. Ex. xxxii.

When ye hear the sound of the trumpet, all the people shall *shout* with a great shout. Josh. vi.

SHOUT, *n.* A loud burst of voice or voices; a vehement and sudden outcry, particularly of a multitude of men, expressing joy, triumph, exultation or animated courage. It is sometimes intended in derision. Josh. vi. Ezra iii.

The Rhodians seeing the enemy turn their backs, gave a great *shout* in derision. *Knolles.*

SHOUT, *v. t.* To treat with shouts or clamor. *Hall.*

SHOUT'ER, *n.* One that shouts. *Dryden.*

SHOUT'ING, *ppr.* Uttering a sudden and loud outcry in joy or exultation.

SHOUT'ING, *n.* The act of shouting; a loud outcry expressive of joy or animation. 2 Sam. vi.

SHŎVE, *v. t.* [Sax. *scufan*, to push or thrust; *scyfan*, to suggest, to hint; D. *schuiven*; G. *schieben*, *schuppen*; Sw. *skuffa*; Dan. *skuffer*. The more correct orthography would be *shuv.*]

1. To push; to propel; to drive along by the direct application of strength without a sudden impulse; particularly, to push a body by sliding or causing it to move along the surface of another body, either by the hand or by an instrument: as, to *shove* a bottle along a table; to *shove* a table along the floor; to *shove* a boat on the water.

And *shove* away the worthy bidden guest. *Milton.*

Shoving back this earth on which I sit. *Dryden.*

2. To push; to press against.

He used to *shove* and elbow his fellow servants to get near his mistress. *Arbuthnot.*

To shove away, to push to a distance; to thrust off.

To shove by, to push away; to delay, or to reject; as, to *shove by* the hearing of a cause; or to *shove by* justice. [*Not elegant.*] *Shak.*

To shove off, to thrust or push away.

To shove down, to overthrow by pushing. *Arbuthnot.*

SHŎVE, *v. i.* To push or drive forward; to urge a course. *Swift.*

2. To push off; to move in a boat or with a pole; as, he *shoved* from shore. *Garth.*

To shove off, to move from shore by pushing with poles or oars.

SHŎVE, *n.* The act of pushing or pressing against by strength, without a sudden impulse. *Swift.*

SHŎVED, *pp.* Pushed; propelled.

SHŎVEL, *n. shuv'l.* [Sax. *scofl*; G. *schaufel*; D. *schoffel*, *schop*; Dan. *skuffe*, a scoop or *shovel*; from *shoving.*]
An instrument consisting of a broad scoop or hollow blade with a handle; used for throwing earth or other loose substances.

SHŎVEL, *v. t.* To take up and throw with a shovel; as, to *shovel* earth into a heap or into a cart, or out of a pit.

2. To gather in great quantities. *Derham.*

SHŎVEL-BOARD, *n.* A board on which they play by sliding metal pieces at a mark. *Dryden.*

SHŎVELED, *pp.* Thrown with a shovel.

SHŎVELER, *n.* [from *shovel.*] A fowl of the genus Anas or duck kind. *Bacon.*

SHŎVELING, *ppr.* Throwing with a shovel.

SHŌW, *v. t.* pret. *showed*; pp. *shown* or *showed*. It is sometimes written *shew*, *shewed*, *shewn*. [Sax. *sceawian*; D. *schouwen*; G. *schauen*; Dan. *skuer*. This word in most of the Teutonic dialects, signifies merely to look, see, view, behold. In Saxon it signifies to show, look, view, explore, regard. This is doubtless a contracted word. If the radical letter lost was a labial, *show* coincides with the Gr. σκοπεω, σκεπτομαι. If a dental has been lost, this word accords with the Sw. *skåda*, to view or behold.]

1. To exhibit or present to the view of others.

Go thy way, *show* thyself to the priest. Matt. viii.

2. To afford to the eye or to notice; to contain in a visible form.

Nor want we skill or art, from whence to raise
Magnificence; and what can heaven *show* more? *Milton.*

3. To make or enable to see. *Milton.*

4. To make or enable to perceive. *Milton.*

5. To make to know; to cause to understand; to make known to; to teach or inform. Job x.

Know, I am sent
To *show* thee what shall come in future days. *Milton.*

6. To prove; to manifest.

I'll *show* my duty by my timely care. *Dryden.*

7. To inform; to teach; with *of*.

The time cometh when I shall no more speak to you in proverbs, but I shall *show* you plainly *of* the Father. John xvi.

8. To point out, as a guide.

Thou shalt *show* them the way in which they must walk. Ex. xviii.

9. To bestow; to confer; to afford; as, to *show* favor or mercy on any person. Ps. cxii. iv.

10. To prove by evidence, testimony or authentic registers or documents.

They could not *show* their father's house. Ezra ii.

11. To disclose; to make known.

I durst not *show* you mine opinion. Job xxxii.

12. To discover; to explain; as, to *show* a dream or interpretation. Dan. ii.

To show forth, to manifest; to publish; to proclaim. 1 Pet. ii.

SHŌW, *v. i.* To appear; to look; to be in appearance.

Just such she *shows* before a rising storm. *Dryden.*

2. To have appearance; to become or suit well or ill.

My lord of York, it better *show'd* with you. *Obs.* *Shak.*

SHŌW, *n.* Superficial appearance; not reality.

Mild heav'n
Disapproves that care, though wise in *show*. *Milton.*

2. A spectacle; something offered to view for money. *Addison.*

3. Ostentatious display or parade.

I envy none their pageantry and *show*. *Young.*

4. Appearance as an object of notice.

The city itself makes the noblest *show* of any in the world. *Addison.*

5. Public appearance, in distinction from concealment; as an open *show*.

6. Semblance; likeness.

In *show* plebeian angel militant. *Milton.*

7. Speciousness; plausibility.

But a short exile must for *show* precede. *Dryden.*

8. External appearance.

And forc'd, at least in *show*, to prize it more. *Dryden.*

9. Exhibition to view; as a *show* of cattle, or cattle-show. *Agricult. Societies.*

10. Pomp; magnificent spectacle.

As for triumphs, masks, feasts, and such *shows*— *Bacon.*

11. A phantom; as a fairy *show*. *Dryden.*

12. Representative action; as a dumb *show*. *Addison.*

13. External appearance; hypocritical pretense.

Who devour widows' houses, and for a *show* make long prayers. Luke xx.

SHŌW-BREAD, } *n.* [*show* and *bread.*]
SHEW'-BREAD, } Among the Jews, bread of exhibition; the loaves of bread which the priest of the week placed before the Lord, on the golden table in the sanctuary. They were shaped like a brick, were ten palms long and five broad, weighing about eight pounds each. They were made of fine flour unleavened, and changed every sabbath. The loaves were twelve in number, and represented the twelve tribes of Israel. They were to be eaten by the priest only. *Encyc.*

SHŌWER, *n.* One who shows or exhibits.

SHOW'ER, *n.* [Sax. *scur*; G. *schauer*, a shower, horror; *schauern*, to shower, to shiver, shudder, quake. Qu. Heb. Ch. Ar. שער to be rough, to shudder.]

1. A fall of rain or hail, of short duration. It may be applied to a like fall of snow, but this seldom occurs. It is applied to a fall of rain or hail of short continuance, of more or less violence, but never to a storm of long continuance.

2. A fall of things from the air in thick succession; as a *shower* of darts or arrows; a *shower* of stones. *Pope.*

3. A copious supply bestowed; liberal distribution; as a great *shower* of gifts. *Shak.*

SHOW'ER, *v. t.* To water with a shower; to wet copiously with rain; as, to *shower* the earth. *Milton.*

2. To bestow liberally; to distribute or scatter in abundance.

Cesar's favor,
That *show'rs* down greatness on his friends. *Addison.*

3. To wet with falling water, as in the shower-bath.

SHOW'ER, *v. i.* To rain in showers.

SHOW'ERED, *pp.* Wet with a shower;

watered abundantly; bestowed or distributed liberally.

SHOW'ERLESS, *a.* Without showers. *Armstrong.*

SHOW'ERY, *a.* Raining in showers; abounding with frequent falls of rain.

SHOWILY, *adv.* In a showy manner; pompously; with parade.

SHOWINESS, *n.* State of being showy; pompousness; great parade.

SHOWISH, *a.* Splendid; gaudy. [*Little used.*] *Swift.*

2. Ostentatious.

SHOWN, *pp.* of *show.* Exhibited; manifested; proved.

SHOWY, *a.* Splendid; gay; gaudy; making a great show; fine. *Addison.*

2. Ostentatious.

SHRAG, *v. t.* To lop. [*Not in use.*]

SHRAG, *n.* A twig of a tree cut off. [*Not in use.*]

SHRAG'GER, *n.* One that lops; one that trims trees. [*Not in use.*]

SHRANK, *pret.* of *shrink*, nearly obsolete.

SHRAP, **SHRAPE**, *n.* A place baited with chaff to invite birds. [*Not in use.*]

SHRED, *v. t.* pret. and pp. *shred.* [Sax. *screadan*, to cut off; Sw. *skräddare*, a tailor.]

To cut into small pieces, particularly narrow and long pieces, as of cloth or lether. It differs from *mince*, which signifies to chop into pieces fine and short.

SHRED, *n.* A long narrow piece cut off; as *shreds* of cloth. *Bacon.*

2. A fragment; a piece; as *shreds* of wit. *Swift.*

SHRED'DING, *ppr.* Cutting into shreds.

SHRED'DING, *n.* That which is cut off; a piece. *Hooker.*

SHREW, *n.* [I know not the original sense of this word. If it signifies a brawler, it may be from D. *schreeuwen*, to brawl, G. *schreien*, Dan. *skriger*. But *beshrew*, in Chaucer, is interpreted to *curse.*]

1. A peevish, brawling, turbulent, vexatious woman. It appears originally to have been applied to males as well as females; but is now restricted to the latter.

> The man had got a *shrew* for his wife, and there could be no quiet in the house with her. *L'Estrange.*

2. A shrew-mouse.

SHREW, *v. t.* To beshrew; to curse. *Obs.* *Chaucer.*

SHREWD, *a.* Having the qualities of a shrew; vexatious; troublesome; mischievous. *Obs.* *Shak.*

2. Sly; cunning; arch; subtil; artful; astute; as a *shrewd* man.

3. Sagacious; of nice discernment; as a *shrewd* observer of men.

4. Proceeding from cunning or sagacity, or containing it; as a *shrewd* saying; a *shrewd* conjecture.

5. Painful; vexatious; troublesome.

> Every of this number
> That have endur'd *shrewd* nights and days with us. *Obs.* *Shak.*

> No enemy is so despicable but he may do one a *shrewd* turn. *Obs.* *L'Estrange.*

SHREWD'LY, *adv.* Mischievously; destructively.

> This practice hath most *shrewdly* past upon thee. *Obs.* *Shak.*

2. Vexatiously; *used of slight mischief.*

> The obstinate and schismatical are like to think themselves *shrewdly* hurt by being cut from that body they chose not to be of. *Obs.* *South.*

> Yet seem'd she not to winch, though *shrewdly* pain'd. *Obs.* *Dryden.*

3. Archly; sagaciously; with good guess; as, I *shrewdly* suspect; he *shrewdly* observed. *Locke.*

SHREWD'NESS, *n.* Sly cunning; archness.

> The neighbors round admire his *shrewdness.* *Swift.*

2. Sagaciousness; sagacity; the quality of nice discernment.

3. Mischievousness; vexatiousness. [*Not in use.*] *Chaucer.*

SHREW'ISH, *a.* Having the qualities of a shrew; froward; peevish; petulantly clamorous.

> My wife is *shrewish* when I keep not hours. *Shak.*

SHREW'ISHLY, *adv.* Peevishly; clamorously; turbulently.

> He speaks very *shrewishly.* *Shak.*

SHREW'ISHNESS, *n.* The qualities of a shrew; frowardness; petulance; turbulent clamorousness.

> I have no gift in *shrewishness.* *Shak.*

SHREW'-MOUSE, *n.* [Sax. *screawa.*] A small animal resembling a mouse, but belonging to the genus Sorex; an animal that burrows in the ground, feeding on corn, insects, &c. It is a harmless animal.

SHRIEK, *v. i.* [Dan. *skriger*; Sw. *skrika*; G. *schreien*; D. *schreijen*; the two latter contracted; W. *ysgreçian*, from *creç*, a scream or shriek, also rough, rugged, Eng. to *creak*, whence *screech*, and vulgarly *screak*; hence W. *ysgreç*, a jay, from its scream; *creg*, hoarse, *crygi*, hoarseness, roughness, from the root of *rugged*, and L. *ruga*, wrinkled, *rugo*, to bray; all from straining, and hence breaking, bursting, cracking; allied to *crack* and *crackle*, It. *scricchiolare.*]

To utter a sharp shrill cry; to scream; as in a sudden fright, in horror or anguish.

> At this she *shriek'd* aloud. *Dryden.*
> It was the owl that *shriek'd.* *Shak.*

SHRIEK, *n.* A sharp shrill outcry or scream, such as is produced by sudden terror or extreme anguish.

> *Shrieks*, clamors, murmurs fill the frighted town. *Dryden.*

SHRIE'KING, *ppr.* Crying out with a shrill voice.

SHRIE'VAL, *a.* Pertaining to a sherif. [*Not in use.*]

SHRIE'VALTY, *n.* [from *sherif.*] Sherifalty; the office of a sherif.

> It was ordained by 28 Ed. 1. that the people shall have election of sherif in every shire, where the *shrievalty* is not of inheritance. *Blackstone.*

SHRIEVE, *n.* Sherif. [*Not in use.*]

SHRIFT, *n.* [Sax. *scrift.*] Confession made to a priest. *Obs.* *Shak.*

SHRIGHT, for *shrieked.* *Chaucer.*

SHRIGHT, *n.* A shriek. [*Not in use.*] *Spenser.*

SHRIKE, *n.* [See *Shriek.*] The butcher-bird; a genus of birds called Lanius, of several species.

SHRILL, *a.* [W. *grill*, a sharp noise; Arm. *scrilh*, a cricket, L. *gryllus*, Fr. *grillon*, Sp. It. *grillo*; It. *strillare*, to scream.]

1. Sharp; acute; piercing; as sound; as a *shrill* voice; *shrill* echoes. *Shak.*

2. Uttering an acute sound; as the cock's *shrill* sounding throat; a *shrill* trumpet.

[Note. A *shrill* sound may be tremulous or trilling; but this circumstance is not essential to it, although it seems to be from the root of *trill.*]

SHRILL, *v. i.* To utter an acute piercing sound.

> Break we our pipes that *shrill'd* as loud as lark. *Spenser.*

SHRILL, *v. t.* To cause to make a shrill sound. *Spenser.*

SHRILL'NESS, *n.* Acuteness of sound; sharpness or fineness of voice. *Smith.*

SHRIL'LY, *adv.* Acutely, as sound; with a sharp sound or voice. *More.*

SHRIMP, *v. t.* [D. *krimpen*; Dan. *skrumper*, to crumple, to shrink; G. *schrumpfen*; W. *crom*, *crwm*, bending or shrinking in.]

To contract. [*Not in use.*] *Echard.*

SHRIMP, *n.* [supra.] A crustaceous animal of the genus Cancer. It has long slender feelers, claws with a single, hooked fang, and three pair of legs. It is esteemed delicious food.

2. A little wrinkled man; a dwarf; in contempt. *Shak.*

SHRINE, *n.* [Sax. *scrin*; G. *schrein*; Sw. *skrin*; L. *scrinium*; It. *scrigno*; Fr. *ecrin.* See *Skreen.*]

A case or box; particularly applied to a case in which sacred things are deposited. Hence we hear much of *shrines* for relics.

> Come, offer at my *shrine*, and I will help thee. *Shak.*

SHRINK, *v. i.* pret. and pp. *shrunk.* The old pret. *shrank* and pp. *shrunken* are nearly obsolete. [Sax. *scrincan.* If *n* is not radical, the root is *rig* or *ryg.*]

1. To contract spontaneously; to draw or be drawn into less length, breadth or compass by an inherent power; as, woolen cloth *shrinks* in hot water; a flaxen or hempen line *shrinks* in a humid atmosphere. Many substances *shrink* by drying.

2. To shrivel; to become wrinkled by contraction; as the skin.

3. To withdraw or retire, as from danger; to decline action from fear. A brave man never *shrinks* from danger; a good man does not *shrink* from duty.

4. To recoil, as in fear, horror or distress. My mind *shrinks* from the recital of our woes.

> What happier natures *shrink* at with affright,
> The hard inhabitant contends is right. *Pope.*

5. To express fear, horror or pain by shrugging or contracting the body. *Shak.*

SHRINK, *v. t.* To cause to contract; as, to *shrink* flannel by immersing it in boiling water.

> O mighty Cesar, dost thou lie so low!
> Are all thy conquests, glories, triumphs, spoils,
> *Shrunk* to this little measure! *Shak.*

SHRINK, *n.* Contraction; a spontaneous drawing into less compass; corrugation. *Woodward.*

2. Contraction; a withdrawing from fear or horror. *Daniel.*

SHRINK'AGE, *n.* A shrinking or contraction into a less compass. Make an allowance for the *shrinkage* of grain in drying.

SHRINK'ER, *n.* One that shrinks; one that withdraws from danger.

SHRINK'ING, *ppr.* Contracting; drawing together; withdrawing from danger; declining to act from fear; causing to contract.

SHRIV'ALTY. [See *Shrievalty.*]

SHRIVE, *v. t.* [Sax. *scrifan*, to take a confession. But the sense seems to be to enjoin or impose penance, or simply to enjoin.]

To hear or receive the confession of; to administer confession; as a priest.

He *shrives* this woman. *Obs.* *Shak.*

SHRIVEL, *v. i.* *shriv'l.* [from the root of *rivel*, Sax. *gerifled.*]

To contract; to draw or be drawn into wrinkles; to shrink and form corrugations; as, a leaf *shrivels* in the hot sun; the skin *shrivels* with age.

SHRIV'EL, *v. t.* To contract into wrinkles; to cause to shrink into corrugations. A scorching sun *shrivels* the blades of corn.

And *shrivel'd* herbs on withering stems decay. *Dryden.*

SHRIV'ELED, *pp.* Contracted into wrinkles.

SHRIV'ELING, *ppr.* Contracting into wrinkles.

SHRI'VER, *n.* [from *shrive.*] A confessor. *Obs.* *Shak.*

SHRI'VING, *n.* Shrift; confession taken. *Obs.* *Spenser.*

SHROUD, *n.* [Sax. *scrud*, clothing.]

1. A shelter; a cover; that which covers, conceals or protects.

Swaddled, as new born, in sable *shrouds.* *Sandys.*

2. The dress of the dead; a winding sheet. *Young.*

3. *Shroud* or *shrouds* of a ship, a range of large ropes extending from the head of a mast to the right and left sides of the ship, to support the mast; as the main *shrouds*; fore *shrouds*; mizen *shrouds.* There are also futtock *shrouds*, bowsprit *shrouds*, &c. *Mar. Dict.*

4. A branch of a tree. [*Not proper.*] *Warton.*

SHROUD, *v. t.* To cover; to shelter from danger or annoyance.

Under your beams I will me safely *shroud.* *Spenser.*

One of these trees with all its young ones, may *shroud* four hundred horsemen. *Raleigh.*

2. To dress for the grave; to cover; as a dead body.

The ancient Egyptian mummies were *shrouded* in several folds of linen besmeared with gums. *Bacon.*

3. To cover; to conceal; to hide; as, to be *shrouded* in darkness.

—Some tempest rise,
And blow out all the stars that light the skies,
To *shroud* my shame. *Dryden.*

4. To defend; to protect by hiding.

So Venus from prevailing Greeks did *shroud*
The hope of Rome, and sav'd him in a cloud. *Waller.*

5. To overwhelm; as, to be *shrouded* in despair.

6. To lop the branches of a tree. [*Unusual or improper.*] *Chambers.*

SHROUD, *v. i.* To take shelter or harbor.

If your stray attendants be yet lodg'd
Or *shroud* within these limits— *Milton.*

SHROUD'ED, *pp.* Dressed; covered; concealed; sheltered; overwhelmed.

SHROUD'ING, *ppr.* Dressing; covering; concealing; sheltering; overwhelming.

SHROUD'Y, *a.* Affording shelter. *Milton.*

SHROVE, *v. i.* To join in the festivities of Shrove-tide. [*Obs.*] *Beaum.*

SHRO'VE-TIDE, SHROVE-TUESDAY, *n.* [from *shrove*, pret. of *shrive*, to take a confession. See *Tide* and *Tuesday.*]

Confession-time; confession-Tuesday; the Tuesday after Quinquagesima Sunday, or the day immediately preceding the first of Lent, or Ash Wednesday; on which day, all the people of England when of the Catholic religion, were obliged to confess their sins one by one to their parish priests; after which they dined on pancakes or fritters. The latter practice still continues. The bell rung on this day is called pancake-bell. *Encyc.*

SHRO'VING, *n.* The festivity of Shrove-tide.

SHRUB, *n.* [Sax. *scrob*, G. *schroff*, rugged; Ir. *sgrabach*, rough. See *Scrub.*]

A low dwarf tree; a woody plant of a size less than a tree; or more strictly, a plant with several permanent woody stems, dividing from the bottom, more slender and lower than in trees. *Encyc.* *Martyn.*

Gooseberries and currants are *shrubs*; oaks and cherries are trees. *Locke.*

SHRUB, *n.* [Ar. شرب drink, and from the same source, *sirup.* The Arabic verb signifies to drink, to imbibe, whence L. *sorbeo.* See *Sherbet* and *Absorb.*]

A liquor composed of acid and sugar, with spirit to preserve it; usually the acid of lemons.

SHRUB, *v. t.* To clear of shrubs. *Anderson.*

SHRUB'BERY, *n.* Shrubs in general.

2. A plantation of shrubs.

SHRUB'BY, *a.* Full of shrubs; as a *shrubby* plain.

2. Resembling a shrub; as plants *shrubby* and curled. *Mortimer.*

3. Consisting of shrubs or brush; as *shrubby* browze. *Philips.*

4. A *shrubby* plant is perennial, with several woody stems. *Martyn.*

SHRUFF, *n.* [G. *schroff*, rugged.] Dross; recrement of metals. [*Not in use.*] *Dict.*

SHRUG, *v. t.* [This word is probably formed from the root of G. *rücken*, the back, D. *rug*, Sax. *hric* or *hryg*, the back, a *ridge*, W. *crug*, a heap, *crwg*, a crook, L. *ruga*, a wrinkle, Eng. *rough.*]

To draw up; to contract; as, to *shrug* the shoulders. The word seems to be limited in its use to the shoulders, and to denote a particular motion which raises the shoulders and rounds the back.

SHRUG, *v. i.* To raise or draw up the shoulders, as in expressing horror or dissatisfaction.

They grin, they *shrug*,
They bow, they snarl, they scratch, they hug. *Swift.*

SHRUG, *n.* A drawing up of the shoulders; a motion usually expressing dislike.

The Spaniards talk in dialogues
Of heads and shoulders, nods and *shrugs.* *Hudibras.*

SHRUG'GING, *ppr.* Drawing up, as the shoulders.

SHRUNK, *pret.* and *pp.* of *shrink.*

SHRUNK'EN, *pp.* of *shrink.* [*Nearly obsolete.*]

SHUD'DER, *v. i.* [G. *schaudern*, *schütteln*; D. *schudden.* This word contains the same elements as the L. *quatio.*]

To quake; to tremble or shake with fear, horror or aversion; to shiver.

I love—alas! I *shudder* at the name. *Smith.*

SHUD'DER, *n.* A tremor; a shaking with fear or horror. *Shak.*

SHUD'DERING, *ppr.* Trembling or shaking with fear or horror; quaking.

SHUF'FLE, *v. t.* [D. *schoffelen*, to shove, to shovel, to shuffle; *dim.* of *shove.* See *Shove* and *Scuffle.*]

1. Properly, to shove one way and the other; to push from one to another; as, to *shuffle* money from hand to hand. *Locke.*

2. To mix by pushing or shoving; to confuse; to throw into disorder; especially, to change the relative positions of cards in the pack.

A man may *shuffle* cards or rattle dice from noon to midnight, without tracing a new idea in his mind. *Rambler.*

3. To remove or introduce by artificial confusion.

It was contrived by your enemies, and *shuffled* into the papers that were seized. *Dryden.*

To shuffle off, to push off; to rid one's self of. When you lay blame to a child, he will attempt to *shuffle* it *off.*

To shuffle up, to throw together in haste; to make up or form in confusion or with fraudulent disorder; as, he *shuffled up* a peace. *Howell.*

SHUF'FLE, *v. i.* To change the relative position of cards in a pack by little shoves; as, to *shuffle* and cut.

2. To change the position; to shift ground; to prevaricate; to evade fair questions; to practice shifts to elude detection.

Hiding my honor in my necessity, I am fain to *shuffle.* *Shak.*

3. To struggle; to shift.

Your life, good master,
Must *shuffle* for itself. *Shak.*

4. To move with an irregular gait; as a *shuffling* nag.

5. To shove the feet; to scrape the floor in dancing. [*Vulgar.*] *Shak.*

SHUF'FLE, *n.* A shoving, pushing or jostling; the act of mixing and throwing into confusion by change of places.

The unguided agitation and rude *shuffles* of matter. *Bentley.*

2. An evasion; a trick; an artifice. *L'Estrange.*

SHUF'FLE-BOARD, the old spelling of *shovel-board.*

SHUF'FLE-CAP, *n.* A play performed by shaking money in a hat or cap. *Arbuthnot.*

SHUF'FLED, *pp.* Moved by little shoves; mixed.

SHUF'FLER, *n.* One that shuffles or prevaricates; one that plays tricks; one that shuffles cards.

SHUF'FLING, *ppr.* Moving by little shoves one way and the other; changing the places of cards; prevaricating; evading; playing tricks.

2. *a.* Evasive; as a *shuffling* excuse.

SHUF'FLING, *n.* The act of throwing into confusion, or of changing the relative position of things by shoving or motion.
2. Trick; artifice; evasion.
3. An irregular gait.
SHUF'FLINGLY, *adv.* With shuffling; with an irregular gait or pace. *Dryden.*
SHUN, *v. t.* [Sax. *scunian, ascunian*; allied perhaps to D. *schuinen*, to slope.]
1. To avoid; to keep clear of; not to fall on or come in contact with; as, to *shun* rocks and shoals in navigation. In *shunning* Scylla, take care to avoid Charybdis.
2. To avoid; not to mix or associate with; as, to *shun* evil company.
3. To avoid; not to practice; as, to *shun* vice.
4. To avoid; to escape; as, to *shun* a blow.
5. To avoid; to decline; to neglect.

I have not *shunned* to declare the whole counsel of God. Acts xx.

SHUN'LESS, *a.* Not to be avoided; inevitable; unavoidable; as *shunless* destiny. [*Little used.*] *Shak.*
SHUN'NED, *pp.* Avoided.
SHUN'NING, *ppr.* Avoiding; keeping clear from; declining.
SHURK. [See *Shark.*]
SHUT, *v. t.* pret. and pp. *shut.* [Sax. *scittan, scyttan*, to bolt or make fast, to shut in. This seems to be derived from or connected with *scyttel*, a bolt or bar, a *scuttle, scytta*, a *shooter*, an archer, *scytan, sceotan, scotian*, to shoot, D. *schutten*, to stop, defend, parry, pound, confine, which seems to be allied to *schutter*, a shooter. So in G. *schützen*, to defend, and *schütze*, a shooter; Dan. *skytter*, to defend; *skytte*, a shooter; Sw. *skydda*, to defend; *skytt*, a marksman. The sense of these words is expressed by *shoot*, and this is the primary sense of a bolt that fastens, from thrusting, driving.]
1. To close so as to hinder ingress or egress; as, to *shut* a door or gate; to *shut* the eyes or the mouth.
2. To prohibit; to bar; to forbid entrance into; as, to *shut* the ports of a kingdom by a blockade.

Shall that be *shut* to man, which to the beast Is open? *Milton.*

3. To preclude; to exclude.

But *shut* from every shore. *Dryden.*

4. To close, as the fingers; to contract; as, to *shut* the hand.
To shut in, to inclose; to confine.

And the Lord *shut* him *in.* Gen. vii.

2. Spoken of points of land, when by the progress of a ship, one point is brought to cover or intercept the view of another. It is then said, we *shut in* such a point, we *shut in* the land; or one point *shuts in* another.
To shut out, to preclude from entering; to deny admission to; to exclude; as, to *shut out* rain by a tight roof. An interesting subject occupying the mind, *shuts out* all other thoughts.
To shut up, to close; to make fast the entrances into; as, to *shut up* a house.
2. To obstruct.

Dangerous rocks *shut up* the passage. *Raleigh.*

3. To confine; to imprison; to lock or fasten in; as, to *shut up* a prisoner.
4. To confine by legal or moral restraint.

Before faith came, we were kept under the law, *shut up* to the faith, which should afterwards be revealed. Gal. iii.

5. To end; to terminate; to conclude.

When the scene of life is *shut up*, the slave will be above his master, if he has acted better. *Collier.*

SHUT, *v. i.* To close itself; to be closed. The door *shuts* of itself; it *shuts* hard. Certain flowers *shut* at night and open in the day.
SHUT, *pp.* Closed; having the entrance barred.
2. *a.* Rid; clear; free. *L'Estrange.*
SHUT, *n.* Close; the act of closing; as the *shut* of a door; the *shut* of evening. [*Little used.*] *Dryden.*
2. A small door or cover. But *shutter* is more generally used.
SHUT'TER, *n.* A person that shuts or closes.
2. A door; a cover; something that closes a passage; as the *shutters* of a window.
SHUT'TING, *ppr.* Closing; prohibiting entrance; confining.
SHUT'TLE, *n.* [from the root of *shoot*; Ice. *skutul.*]
An instrument used by weavers for shooting the thread of the woof in weaving from one side of the cloth to the other, between the threads of the warp.
SHUT'TLE-COCK, *n.* [*shuttle* and *cock* or *cork.*]
A cork stuck with fethers, used to be struck by a battledore in play; also, the play.
SHY, *a.* [G. *scheu*, shy; *scheuchen*, to scare, and *scheuen*, to shun; D. *schuw*, shy; *schuwen*, to shun; Sw. *skygg*, shy, and *sky*, to shun; Dan. *sky*, shy, and *skyer*, to shun, to eschew. In Sp. *esquivo* is *shy*, and *esquivar*, to shun; It. *schifo*, shy, and *schifare*, to shun. The two last mentioned languages have a labial for the last radical, but possibly the words may be of the same family. The G. *scheuchen*, to scare, is our *shoo*, a word used for scaring away fowls.]
1. Fearful of near approach; keeping at a distance through caution or timidity; shunning approach; as a *shy* bird.

She is represented in a *shy* retiring posture. *Addison.*

2. Reserved; not familiar; coy; avoiding freedom of intercourse.

What makes you so *shy*, my good friend? *Arbuthnot.*

3. Cautious; wary; careful to avoid committing one's self or adopting measures.

I am very *shy* of using corrosive liquors in the preparation of medicines. *Boyle.*

4. Suspicious; jealous.

Princes are by wisdom of state somewhat *shy* of their successors. *Wotton.*

SHY'LY, *adv.* In a shy or timid manner; not familiarly; with reserve.
SHY'NESS, *n.* Fear of near approach or of familiarity; reserve; coyness.
SIALOGOGUE, *n.* *sial'ogog.* [Gr. σιαλον, saliva, and αγωγος, leading.]
A medicine that promotes the salivary discharge. *Encyc.*
SIB, a relation, in Saxon, but not in use in English.
SIBE'RIAN, *a.* [Russ. *siver*, north. *Siberia* is formed by annexing the Greek *ia*, country, from the Celtic, to *siver*, north.]
Pertaining to Siberia, a name given to a great and indefinite extent of territory in the north of Asia; as a *Siberian* winter.
SIB'ERITE, *n.* Red tourmalin. *Ure.*
SIB'ILANT, *a.* [L. *sibilo*, to hiss, Fr. *siffler*; Russ. *soplyu, sopyu*, id.]
Hissing; making a hissing sound. *S* and *z* are called *sibilant* letters.
SIB'ILANT, *n.* A letter that is uttered with a hissing of the voice; as *s* and *z.*
SIBILA'TION, *n.* A hissing sound. *Bacon.*
SIB'YL, *n.* [from the L.] In *pagan antiquity*, the Sibyls were certain women said to be endowed with a prophetic spirit. Their number is variously stated; but the opinion of Varro, who states them to have been ten, is generally adopted. They resided in various parts of Persia, Greece and Italy. It is pretended that they wrote certain prophecies on leaves in verse, which are called Sibylline verses, or Sibylline oracles. *Lempriere.*
SIB'YLLINE, *a.* Pertaining to the Sibyls; uttered, written or composed by Sibyls.
SIC'AMORE, *n.* More usually written *sycamore*, which see.
SIC'CATE, *v. t.* To dry. [*Not in use.*]
SICCA'TION, *n.* The act or process of drying. [*Not in use.*]
SIC'CATIVE, *a.* [from L. *sicco*, to dry, Fr. *secher*, It. *seccare*, Sp. *secar*, W. *syçu.*] Drying; causing to dry. *Encyc.*
SIC'CATIVE, *n.* That which promotes the process of drying.
SIC'CITY, *n.* [L. *siccitas.*] Dryness; aridity; destitution of moisture; as the *siccity* of the flesh or of the air. *Brown.*
SICE, *n. size.* [Fr. *six.*] The number six at dice.
SICH, for *such.* [See *Such.*] *Chaucer.*
SICK, *a.* [Sax. *seoc*; D. *ziek*; Sw. *siuk*; Ice. *syke.* Qu. Gr. σικχος, squeamish, lothing.]
1. Affected with nausea; inclined to vomit; as *sick* at the stomach. [*This is probably the primary sense of the word.*] Hence,
2. Disgusted; having a strong dislike to; with *of*; as, to be *sick of* flattery; to be *sick of* a country life.

He was not so *sick of* his master as *of* his work. *L'Estrange.*

3. Affected with disease of any kind; not in health; followed by *of*; as to be *sick of* a fever.
4. Corrupted. [*Not in use nor proper.*] *Shak.*
5. *The sick*, the person or persons affected with disease. *The sick* are healed.
SICK, *v. t.* To make sick. [*Not in use.* See *Sicken.*]
SICK'-BIRTH, *n.* In a ship of war, an apartment for the sick.
SICKEN, *v. t.* *sik'n.* To make sick; to disease.

Raise this to strength, and *sicken* that to death. *Prior.*

2. To make squeamish. It *sickens* the stomach.
3. To disgust. It *sickens* one to hear the fawning sycophant.
4. To impair. [*Not in use.*] *Shak.*
SICK'EN, *v. i.* To become sick; to fall into disease.

The judges that sat upon the jail, and those that attended, *sickened* upon it and died. *Bacon.*

2. To be satiated; to be filled to disgust. *Shak.*

3. To become disgusting or tedious.

The toiling pleasure *sickens* into pain. *Goldsmith.*

4. To be disgusted; to be filled with aversion or abhorrence. He *sickened* at the sight of so much human misery.

5. To become weak; to decay; to languish. Plants often *sicken* and die.

All pleasures *sicken*, and all glories sink. *Pope.*

SICK'ER, *a.* [L. *securus*; Dan. *sikker*; G. *sicher*; D. *zeker.*] Sure; certain; firm. *Obs.* *Spenser.*

SICK'ER, *adv.* Surely; certainly. *Obs.* *Spenser.*

SICK'ERLY, *adv.* Surely. *Obs.*

SICK'ERNESS, *n.* Security. *Obs.* *Spenser.*

SICK'ISH, *a.* [from *sick.*] Somewhat sick or diseased. *Hakewill.*

2. Exciting disgust; nauseating; as a *sickish* taste.

SICK'ISHNESS, *n.* The quality of exciting disgust.

SICKLE, *n.* sik'l. [Sax. *sicel, sicol*; G. *sichel*; D. *zikkel*; Gr. ζαιχλη, ζαγχλον; L. *sicula*, from the root of *seco*, to cut.]

A reaping hook; a hooked instrument with teeth; used for cutting grain.

Thou shalt not move a *sickle* to thy neighbor's standing corn. Deut. xxiii.

SICK'LED, *a.* Furnished with a sickle. *Thomson.*

SICK'LEMAN, } *n.* One that uses a sickle; a reaper. [*Not used in N. England.*] *Shak.*
SICK'LER, }

SICK'LE-WÖRT, *n.* A plant of the genus Coronilla.

SICK'LINESS, *n.* [from *sickly.*] The state of being sickly; the state of being habitually diseased; *applied to persons.*

2. The state of producing sickness extensively; as the *sickliness* of a season.

3. The disposition to generate disease extensively; as the *sickliness* of a climate.

SICK'-LIST, *n.* A list containing the names of the sick.

SICK'LY, *a.* Not healthy; somewhat affected with disease; or habitually indisposed; as a *sickly* person, or a *sickly* constitution; a *sickly* plant.

2. Producing disease extensively; marked with sickness; as a *sickly* time; a *sickly* autumn.

3. Tending to produce disease; as a *sickly* climate.

4. Faint; weak; languid.

The moon grows *sickly* at the sight of day. *Dryden.*

SICK'LY, *v. t.* To make diseased. [*Not in use.*] *Shak.*

SICK'NESS, *n.* [G. *sucht.*] Nausea; squeamishness; as *sickness* of the stomach.

2. State of being diseased.

I do lament the *sickness* of the king. *Shak.*

3. Disease; malady; a morbid state of the body of an animal or plant, in which the organs do not perfectly perform their natural functions.

Trust not too much your now resistless charms;
Those age or *sickness* soon or late disarms. *Pope.*

Himself took our infirmities, and bore our *sicknesses.* Matt. viii.

SIDE, *n.* [Sax. *sid, side, sida*, a side, also wide, like L. *latus*; D. *zyde*, side, flank, page; *zid*, far; G. *seite*; Sw. *sida*; Dan. *side*, a side; *sid* or *siid*, long, trailing; *sidst*, last; Scot. *side*, long. These words indicate the radical sense to be to extend, dilate or draw out.]

1. The broad and long part or surface of a thing, as distinguished from the *end*, which is of less extent and may be a point; as the *side* of a plank; the *side* of a chest; the *side* of a house or of a ship. One *side* of a lens may be concave, the other convex.

Side is distinguished from *edge*; as the *side* of a knife or sword.

2. Margin; edge; verge; border; the exterior line of any thing, considered in length; as the *side* of a tract of land or a field, as distinct from the *end*. Hence we say, the *side* of a river; the *side* of a road; the east and west *side* of the American continent.

3. The part of an animal between the back and the face and belly; the part on which the ribs are situated; as the right *side*; the left *side*. This in quadrupeds is usually the broadest part.

4. The part between the top and bottom; the slope, declivity or ascent, as of a hill or mountain; as the *side* of mount Etna.

5. One part of a thing, or its superficies; as the *side* of a ball or sphere.

6. Any part considered in respect to its direction or point of compass; as to whichever *side* we direct our view. We see difficulties on every *side*.

7. Party; faction; sect; any man or body of men considered as in opposition to another. One man enlists on the *side* of the tories; another on the *side* of the whigs. Some persons change *sides* for the sake of popularity and office, and sink themselves in public estimation.

And sets the passions on the *side* of truth. *Pope.*

8. Interest; favor.

The Lord is on my *side*. Ps. cxviii.

9. Any part being in opposition or contradistinction to another; *used of persons or propositions.* In that battle, the slaughter was great on both *sides*. Passion invites on one *side*; reason restrains on the other.

Open justice bends on neither *side*. *Dryden.*

10. Branch of a family; separate line of descent; as, by the father's *side* he is descended from a noble family; by the mother's *side* his birth is respectable.

11. Quarter; region; part; as from one *side* of heaven to the other.

To take sides, to embrace the opinions or attach one's self to the interest of a party when in opposition to another.

To choose sides, to select parties for competition in exercises of any kind.

SIDE, *a.* Lateral; as a *side* post; but perhaps it would be better to consider the word as compound.

2. Being on the side, or toward the side; oblique; indirect.

The law hath no *side* respect to their persons. *Hooker.*

One mighty squadron with a *side* wind sped. *Dryden.*

So we say, a *side* view, a *side* blow. *Bentley. Pope.*

3. Long; large; extensive. *Obs.* *Shak.*

SIDE, *v. i.* To lean on one side. [*Little used.*] *Bacon.*

2. To embrace the opinions of one party or engage in its interest, when opposed to another party; as, to *side* with the ministerial party.

All *side* in parties and begin th' attack. *Pope.*

SIDE, *v. t.* To stand at the side of. [*Not in use.*] *Spenser.*

2. To suit; to pair. [*Not in use.*] *Clarendon.*

SI'DEBOARD, *n.* [*side* and *board.*] A piece of furniture or cabinet work consisting of a table or box with drawers or cells, placed at the side of a room or in a recess, and used to hold dining utensils, &c.

SI'DE-BOX, *n.* [*side* and *box.*] A box or inclosed seat on the side of a theater, distinct from the seats in the pit.

SI'DE-FLY, *n.* An insect. *Derham.*

SI'DELING, *adv.* [from *sidle*; D. *zydelings.*]

1. Sidewise; with the side foremost; as, to go *sideling* through a crowd. It may be used as a participle; as, I saw him *sideling* through the crowd.

2. Sloping.

SI'DELONG, *a.* [*side* and *long.*] Lateral; oblique; not directly in front; as a *sidelong* glance. *Dryden.*

SI'DELONG, *adv.* Laterally; obliquely; in the direction of the side. *Milton.*

2. On the side; as, to lay a thing *sidelong*. *Evelyn.*

SI'DER, *n.* One that takes a side or joins a party.

2. Cider. [*Not in use.*]

SID'ERAL, } *a.* [L. *sideralis*, from *sidus*, a star.] Pertaining to a star or stars; astral; as *sideral* light.
SIDE'REAL, }

2. Containing stars; starry; as *sidereal* regions.

Sidereal year, in astronomy, the period in which the fixed stars apparently complete a revolution and come to the same point in the heavens.

SID'ERATED, *a.* [L. *sideratus.*] Blasted; planet-struck. *Brown.*

SIDERA'TION, *n.* [L. *sideratio*; *sidero*, to blast, from *sidus*, a star.]

A blasting or blast in plants; a sudden deprivation of sense; an apoplexy; a slight erysipelas. [*Not much used.*] *Ray. Coxe.*

A sphacelus, or a species of erysipelas, vulgarly called a *blast*. *Parr.*

SID'ERITE, *n.* [L. *sideritis*; Gr. *id.* from σιδηρος, iron.]

1. The loadstone; also, iron-wort, a genus of plants; also, the common ground pine (*Teucrium chamæpitys*, Linne.) *Coxe. Encyc. Parr.*

2. In *mineralogy*, a phosphate of iron. *Lavoisier. Fourcroy.*

SIDEROCAL'CITE, *n.* Brown spar. *Ure.*

SIDEROCLEP'TE, *n.* A mineral of a yellowish green color, soft and translucid, occurring in reniform or botryoidal masses. *Saussure.*

SIDEROGRAPH'IC, SIDEROGRAPH'ICAL, *a.* [See *Siderography.*] Pertaining to siderography, or performed by engraved plates of steel; as *siderographic* art; *siderographic* impressions.

SIDEROG'RAPHIST, *n.* One who engraves steel plates, or performs work by means of such plates.

SIDEROG'RAPHY, *n.* [Gr. σιδηρος, steel or iron, and γραφω, to engrave.]
The art or practice of engraving on steel, by means of which, impressions may be transferred from a steel plate to a steel cylinder in a rolling press of a particular construction. *Perkins.*

SI'DE-SADDLE, *n.* [*side* and *saddle.*] A saddle for a woman's seat on horseback.

SIDE-SADDLE FLOWER, *n.* A species of Sarracenia.

SI'DESMAN, *n.* [*side* and *man.*] An assistant to the church warden.
2. A party man. *Milton.*

SI'DETAKING, *n.* A taking sides, or engaging in a party. *Hall.*

SI'DEWAYS, SI'DEWISE, *adv.* [*side* and *way*; but *sidewise* is the proper combination.]
1. Towards one side; inclining; as, to hold the head *sidewise.*
2. Laterally; on one side; as the refraction of light *sidewise.* *Newton.*

SI'DING, *ppr.* Joining one side or party.

SI'DING, *n.* The attaching of one's self to a party.

SI'DLE, *v. i.* To go or move side foremost; as, to *sidle* through a crowd.
2. To lie on the side. *Swift.*

SIEGE, *n.* [Fr. *siége*, a seat, a siege, the *see* of a bishop; Norm. *sage*, a seat; It. *seggia, seggio*; Arm. *sich, sicha, sichenn.* The radical sense is to set, to fall or to throw down; Sax. *sigan*, to fall, set or rush down. These words seem to be connected with *sink*, and with the root of *seal*, L. *sigillum.*]
1. The setting of an army around or before a fortified place for the purpose of compelling the garrison to surrender; or the surrounding or investing of a place by an army, and approaching it by passages and advanced works, which cover the besiegers from the enemy's fire. A *siege* differs from a *blockade*, as in a siege the investing army approaches the fortified place to attack and reduce it by force; but in a blockade, the army secures all the avenues to the place to intercept all supplies, and waits till famine compels the garrison to surrender.
2. Any continued endeavor to gain possession.

> Love stood the *siege*, and would not yield his breast. *Dryden.*

3. Seat; throne. *Obs.* *Spenser.*
4. Rank; place; class. *Obs.* *Shak.*
5. Stool. [*Not in use.*] *Brown.*

SIEGE, *v. t.* To besiege. [*Not in use.*] *Spenser.*

SI'ENITE, *n.* A compound granular rock composed of quartz, hornblend and feldspar, of a grayish color; so called, because there are many ancient monuments consisting of this rock, brought from Syene, in Upper Egypt. *Lunier.*

SIEUR, *n.* [Fr.] A title of respect used by the French.

SIEVE, *n. siv.* [Sax. *sife, syfe*; G. *sieb*; D. *zeef, zift*; the *sifter.* See *Sift.*]
An utensil for separating flour from bran, or the fine part of any pulverized or fine substance from the coarse, by the hand; as a fine *sieve*; a coarse *sieve.* It consists of a hoop with a hair bottom, and performs in the family the service of a bolter in a mill.

SIFT, *v. t.* [Sax. *siftan*; G. *sieben*; D. *ziften.*]
1. To separate by a sieve, as the fine part of a substance from the coarse; as, to *sift* meal; to *sift* powder; to *sift* sand or lime.
2. To separate; to part. *Dryden.*
3. To examine minutely or critically; to scrutinize. Let the principles of the party be thoroughly *sifted.*

> We have *sifted* your objections. *Hooker.*

SIFT'ED, *pp.* Separated by a sieve; purified from the coarser parts; critically examined.

SIFT'ER, *n.* One that sifts; that which sifts; a sieve.

SIFT'ING, *ppr.* Separating the finer from the coarser part by a sieve; critically examining.

SIG, a Saxon word signifying victory, is used in names, as in *Sigbert*, bright victory. It answers to the Greek νιϰ in *Nicander*, and the L. *vic*, in *Victorinus.*

SIGH, *v. i.* [Sax. *sican*, to sigh; D. *zugt*, a sigh; *zugten*, to sigh; Dan. *sukker*; Sw. *sucka*; allied perhaps to *suck*, a drawing in of the breath.]
To inhale a larger quantity of air than usual and immediately expel it; to suffer a single deep respiration.

> He *sighed* deeply in his spirit. Mark viii.

SIGH, *v. t.* To lament; to mourn.

> Ages to come and men unborn
> Shall bless her name and *sigh* her fate. *Prior.*

2. To express by sighs.

> The gentle swain—*sighs* back her grief. *Hoole.*

SIGH, *n.* A single deep respiration; a long breath; the inhaling of a larger quantity of air than usual, and the sudden emission of it. This is an effort of nature to dilate the lungs and give vigor to the circulation of the blood, when the action of the heart and arteries is languid from grief, depression of spirits, weakness or want of exercise. Hence *sighs* are indications of grief or debility.

SIGHER, *n.* One that sighs.

SIGHING, *ppr.* Suffering a deep respiration; taking a long breath.

SIGHING, *n.* The act of suffering a deep respiration, or taking a long breath.

SIGHT, *n.* [Sax. *gesiht*, with a prefix; D. *gezigt*; G. *sicht*; Dan. *sigt*; Sw. *sickt*; from the root of *see.*]
1. The act of seeing; perception of objects by the eye; view; as, to gain *sight* of land; to have a *sight* of a landscape; to lose *sight* of a ship at sea.

> A cloud received him out of their *sight.* Acts i.

2. The faculty of vision, or of perceiving objects by the instrumentality of the eyes. It has been doubted whether moles have *sight.* Milton lost his *sight.* The *sight* usually fails at or before fifty years of age.

> O loss of *sight*, of thee I most complain. *Milton.*

3. Open view; the state of admitting unobstructed vision; a being within the limits of vision. The harbor is in *sight* of the town. The shore of Long Island is in *sight* of New Haven. The White mountain is in plain *sight* at Portland, in Maine; a mountain is or is not within *sight*; an engagement at sea is within *sight* of land.
4. Notice from seeing; knowledge; as a letter intended for the *sight* of one person only.
5. Eye; the instrument of seeing.

> From the depth of hell they lift their *sight.* *Dryden.*

6. An aperture through which objects are to be seen; or something to direct the vision; as the *sight* of a quadrant; the *sight* of a fowling piece or a rifle.
7. That which is beheld; a spectacle; a show; particularly, something novel and remarkable; something wonderful.

> They never saw a *sight* so fair. *Spenser.*
>
> Moses said, I will now turn aside and see this great *sight*, why the bush is not burned. Ex. iii.
>
> Fearful *sights* and great signs shall there be from heaven. Luke xxi.

To take sight, to take aim; to look for the purpose of directing a piece of artillery, &c.

SIGHTED, *a.* In *composition only*, having sight, or seeing in a particular manner; as *long-sighted*, seeing at a great distance; *short-sighted*, able to see only at a small distance; *quick-sighted*, readily seeing, discerning or understanding; *sharp-sighted*, having a keen eye or acute discernment.

SIGHTFULNESS, *n.* Clearness of sight. [*Not in use.*] *Sidney.*

SIGHTLESS, *a.* Wanting sight; blind.

> Of all who blindly creep, or *sightless* soar. *Pope.*

2. Offensive or unpleasing to the eye; as *sightless* stains. [*Not well authorized.*] *Shak.*

SIGHTLINESS, *n.* Comely; having an appearance pleasing to the sight.

SIGHTLY, *a.* Pleasing to the eye; striking to the view.

> Many brave *sightly* horses— *L'Estrange.*
>
> We have thirty members, the most *sightly* of all her majesty's subjects. *Addison.*

2. Open to the view; that may be seen from a distance. We say, a house stands in a *sightly* place.

SIGHTSMAN, *n.* Among *musicians*, one who reads music readily at first sight. *Busby.*

SIG'IL, *n.* [L. *sigillum.*] A seal; signature. *Dryden.*

SIGMOID'AL, *a.* [Gr. σιγμα and ειδος.] Curved like the Greek ς sigma. *Smith. Bigelow.*

The *sigmoid flexure*, in anatomy, is the last curve of the colon, before it terminates in the rectum. *Parr.*

SIGN, *n. sine.* [Fr. *signe*; It. *segno*; Sp. *seña*; L. *signum*; Sax. *segen*; Arm. *sygn, syn*; Ir. *sighin*; G. *zeichen*; Sans. *zaga.* From the last three words it appears that *n* is not radical; the elements being *Sg.* If so, and the G. *zeichen* is of this family, then we learn that *sign* is only a dialectical orthography of *token*, for *zeichen* is the D. *teeken*, Dan. *tegn*, Sw. *tecken*, coinciding perhaps with Gr. δεικνυμι.]

1. A token; something by which another thing is shown or represented; any visible thing, any motion, appearance or event which indicates the existence or approach of something else. Thus we speak of *signs* of fair weather or of a storm, and of external marks which are *signs* of a good constitution.

2. A motion, action, nod or gesture indicating a wish or command.

They made *signs* to his father, how he would have him called. Luke i.

3. A wonder; a miracle; a prodigy; a remarkable transaction, event or phenomenon.

Through mighty *signs* and wonders. Rom. xv. Luke xxi.

4. Some visible transaction, event or appearance intended as proof or evidence of something else; hence, proof; evidence by sight.

Show me a *sign* that thou talkest with me. Judges vi.

5. Something hung or set near a house or over a door, to give notice of the tenant's occupation, or what is made or sold within; as a trader's *sign;* a tailor's *sign;* the *sign* of the eagle.

6. A memorial or monument; something to preserve the memory of a thing.

What time the fire devoured two hundred and fifty men, and they became a *sign*. Num. xxvi.

7. Visible mark or representation; as an outward *sign* of an inward and spiritual grace.

8. A mark of distinction.

9. Typical representation.

The holy symbols or *signs* are not barely significative. *Brerewood.*

10. In *astronomy*, the twelfth part of the ecliptic. The signs are reckoned from the point of intersection of the ecliptic and equator at the vernal equinox, and are named respectively, Aries, Taurus, Gemini, Cancer, Leo, Virgo, Libra, Scorpio, Sagittarius, Capricornus, Aquarius, Pisces. These names are borrowed from the constellations of the zodiac of the same denomination, which were respectively comprehended within the foregoing equal divisions of the ecliptic, at the time when those divisions were first made; but on account of the precession of the equinoxes, the positions of these constellations in the heavens no longer correspond with the divisions of the ecliptic of the same name, but are considerably in advance of them. Thus the constellation Aries, is now in that part of the ecliptic called Taurus.

11. In *algebra*, a character indicating the relation of quantities, or an operation performed by them; as the sign + plus prefixed to a quantity, indicates that the quantity is to be added; the sign — minus, denotes that the quantity to which it is prefixed is to be subtracted. The former is prefixed to quantities called *affirmative* or *positive;* the latter to quantities called *negative*.

12. The subscription of one's name; signature; as a *sign* manual.

13. Among *physicians*, an appearance or symptom in the human body, which indicates its condition as to health or disease.

14. In *music*, any character, as a flat, sharp, dot, &c.

SIGN, *v. t. sine.* To mark with characters or one's name. To *sign a paper, note, deed, &c.* is to write one's name at the foot, or underneath the declaration, promise, covenant, grant, &c., by which the person makes it his own act. To *sign one's name*, is to write or subscribe it on the paper. Signing does not now include sealing.

2. To signify; to represent typically. [*Not in use.*] *Taylor.*

3. To mark.

SIGN, *v. i.* To be a sign or omen. [*Not in use.*] *Shak.*

SIG'NAL, *n.* [Fr. *signal;* Sp. *señal;* from L. *signum.*]

A sign that gives or is intended to give notice; or the notice given. Signals are used to communicate notice, information, orders and the like, to persons at a distance, and by any persons and for any purpose. A signal may be a motion of the hand, the raising of a flag, the firing of a gun, or any thing which, being understood by persons at a distance, may communicate notice.

Signals are particularly useful in the navigation of fleets and in naval engagements. There are *day-signals*, which are usually made by the sails, by flags and pendants, or guns; *night-signals*, which are lanterns disposed in certain figures, or false fires, rockets, or the firing of guns; *fog-signals*, which are made by sounds, as firing of guns, beating of drums, ringing of bells, &c. There are signals of evolution, addressed to a whole fleet, to a division or to a squadron; signals of movements to particular ships; and signals of service, general or particular. Signals used in an army are mostly made by a particular beat of the drum, or by the bugle. *Mar. Dict. Encyc.*

SIG'NAL, *a.* Eminent; remarkable; memorable; distinguished from what is ordinary; as a *signal* exploit; a *signal* service; a *signal* act of benevolence. It is generally but not always used in a good sense.

SIGNAL'ITY, *n.* Quality of being signal or remarkable. [*Not in use.*] *Brown.*

SIG'NALIZE, *v. t.* [from *signal.*] To make remarkable or eminent; to render distinguished from what is common. The soldier who *signalizes* himself in battle, merits his country's gratitude. Men may *signalize* themselves, their valor or their talents.

SIG'NALIZED, *pp.* Made eminent.

SIG'NALIZING, *ppr.* Making remarkable.

SIG'NALLY, *adv.* Eminently; remarkably; memorably; in a distinguished manner.

SIGNA'TION, *n.* Sign given; act of betokening. [*Not in use.*]

SIG'NATORY, *a.* Relating to a seal; used in sealing. *Dict.*

SIG'NATURE, *n.* [Fr. from L. *signo*, to sign.]

1. A sign, stamp or mark impressed.

The brain being well furnished with various traces, *signatures* and images— *Watts.*

The natural and indelible *signature* of God, stamped on the human soul. *Bentley.*

2. In *old medical writers*, an external mark or character on a plant, which was supposed to indicate its suitableness to cure particular diseases, or diseases of particular parts. Thus plants with yellow flowers were supposed to be adapted to the cure of the jaundice, &c.

Some plants bear a very evident *signature* of their nature and use. *More.*

3. A mark for proof, or proof from marks.

4. Sign manual; the name of a person written or subscribed by himself.

5. Among *printers*, a letter or figure at the bottom of the first page of a sheet or half sheet, by which the sheets are distinguished and their order designated, as a direction to the binder. Every successive sheet has a different letter or figure, and if the sheets are more numerous than the letters of the alphabet, then a small letter is added to the capital one; thus A a, B b. In large volumes, the signatures are sometimes composed of letters and figures; thus 5 A, 5 B. But some printers now use figures only for signatures.

6. In *physiognomy*, an external mark or feature by which some persons pretend to discover the nature and qualities of a thing, particularly the temper and genius of persons.

SIG'NATURE, *v. t.* To mark; to distinguish. [*Not in use.*] *Cheyne.*

SIG'NATURIST, *n.* One who holds to the doctrine of signatures impressed upon objects, indicative of character or qualities. [*Little used.*] *Brown.*

SIGNER, *n.* One that signs or subscribes his name; as a memorial with a hundred *signers*.

SIG'NET, *n.* A seal; particularly in Great Britain, the seal used by the king in sealing his private letters, and grants that pass by bill under his majesty's hand.

SIGNIF'ICANCE, } *n.* [from L. *significans*.
SIGNIF'ICANCY, } See *Signify*.]

1. Meaning; import; that which is intended to be expressed; as the *significance* of a nod, or of a motion of the hand, or of a word or expression. *Stillingfleet.*

2. Force; energy; power of impressing the mind; as a duty enjoined with particular *significance*. *Atterbury.*

3. Importance; moment; weight; consequence.

Many a circumstance of less *significancy* has been construed into an overt act of high treason. *Addison.*

SIGNIF'ICANT, *a.* [L. *significans*.] Expressive of something beyond the external mark.

2. Bearing a meaning; expressing or containing signification or sense; as a *significant* word or sound; a *significant* look.

3. Betokening something; standing as a sign of something.

It was well said of Plotinus, that the stars were *significant*, but not efficient. *Raleigh.*

4. Expressive or representative of some fact or event. The passover among the Jews was *significant* of the escape of the Israelites from the destruction which fell

on the Egyptians. The bread and wine in the sacrament are *significant* of the body and blood of Christ.

5. Important; momentous. [*Not in use.*]

SIGNIF'ICANTLY, *adv.* With meaning.

2. With force of expression. *South.*

SIGNIFICA'TION, *n.* [Fr. from L. *significatio.* See *Signify.*]

1. The act of making known, or of communicating ideas to another by signs or by words, by any thing that is understood, particularly by words.

All speaking, or *signification* of one's mind, implies an act or address of one man to another. *South.*

2. Meaning; that which is understood to be intended by a sign, character, mark or word; that idea or sense of a sign, mark, word or expression which the person using it intends to convey, or that which men in general who use it, understand it to convey. The *signification* of words was originally arbitrary, and is dependent on usage. But when custom has annexed a certain sense to a letter or sound, or to a combination of letters or sounds, this sense is always to be considered the *signification* which the person using the word intends to communicate.

So by custom, certain signs or gestures have a determinate *signification.* Such is the fact also with figures, algebraic characters, &c.

SIGNIF'ICATIVE, *a.* [Fr. *significatif.*]

1. Betokening or representing by an external sign; as the *significative* symbols of the eucharist. *Brerewood.*

2. Having signification or meaning; expressive of a certain idea or thing.

Neither in the degrees of kindred were they destitute of *significative* words. *Camden.*

SIGNIF'ICATIVELY, *adv.* So as to represent or express by an external sign. *Usher.*

SIGNIFICA'TOR, *n.* That which signifies. *Burton.*

SIGNIF'ICATORY, *n.* That which betokens, signifies or represents. *Taylor.*

SIG'NIFY, *v. t.* [Fr. *signifier;* L. *significo; signum*, a sign, and *facio*, to make.]

1. To make known something, either by signs or words; to express or communicate to another any idea, thought, wish, purpose or command, either by words, by a nod, wink, gesture, signal or other sign. A man *signifies* his mind by his voice or by written characters; he may *signify* his mind by a nod or other motion, provided the person to whom he directs it, understands what is intended by it. A general or an admiral *signifies* his commands by signals to officers at a distance.

2. To mean; to have or contain a certain sense. The word sabbath *signifies* rest. *Less*, in composition, as in *faithless, signifies* destitution or want. The prefix *re*, in *recommend*, seldom *signifies* any thing.

3. To import; to weigh; to have consequence; *used in particular phrases;* as, it *signifies* much or little; it *signifies* nothing. What does it *signify?* What *signify* the splendors of a court? Confession of sin without reformation of life, can *signify* nothing in the view of God.

4. To make known; to declare.

The government should *signify* to the protestants of Ireland, that want of silver is not to be remedied. *Swift.*

SIG'NIFY, *v. i.* To express meaning with force. [*Little used.*] *Swift.*

SIGNIOR, *n.* *see'nyur.* A title of respect among the Italians. [See *Seignor.*]

SIGNIORIZE, *v. i.* *see'nyurize.* To exercise dominion; or to have dominion. [*Little used.*]

SIGNIORY, *n.* *see'nyury.* A different, but less common spelling of *seigniory*, which see. It signifies lordship, dominion, and in Shakspeare, *seniority.*

SIGN-POST, *n.* [*sign* and *post.*] A post on which a sign hangs, or on which papers are placed to give public notice of any thing. By the laws of some of the New England states, a *sign-post* is to be erected near the center of each town.

SIK, **SIKE**, } *a.* Such. *Obs.* *Spenser.*

SIK'ER, *a.* or *adv.* Sure; surely. *Obs.* [See *Sicker.*]

SIK'ERNESS, *n.* Sureness; safety. *Obs.* *Chaucer.*

SI'LENCE, *n.* [Fr. from L. *silentium*, from *sileo*, to be still; It. *silenzio;* Sp. *silencio.* The sense is to stop or hold; but this may proceed from setting, throwing down. See *Sill.*]

1. In *a general sense*, stillness, or entire absence of sound or noise; as the *silence* of midnight.

2. In *animals*, the state of holding the peace; forbearance of speech in man, or of noise in other animals.

I was dumb with *silence;* I held my peace, even from good. Ps. xxxix.

3. Habitual taciturnity; opposed to *loquacity.* *Shak.*

4. Secrecy. These things were transacted in *silence.*

5. Stillness; calmness; quiet; cessation of rage, agitation or tumult; as the elements reduced to *silence.*

6. Absence of mention; oblivion.

Eternal *silence* be their doom. *Milton.*
And what most merits fame, in *silence* hid. *Milton.*

7. *Silence*, is used elliptically for *let there be silence*, an injunction to keep silence.

SI'LENCE, *v. t.* To oblige to hold the peace; to restrain from noise or speaking.

2. To still; to quiet; to restrain; to appease.

This would *silence* all further opposition. *Clarendon.*

These would have *silenced* their scruples. *Rogers.*

3. To stop; as, to *silence* complaints or clamor.

4. To still; to cause to cease firing; as, to *silence* guns or a battery.

5. To restrain from preaching by revoking a license to preach; as, to *silence* a minister of the gospel. *U. States.*

The Rev. Thomas Hooker, of Chelmsford in Essex, was *silenced* for non-conformity. *B. Trumbull.*

6. To put an end to; to cause to cease.

The question between agriculture and commerce has received a decision which has *silenced* the rivalships between them. *Hamilton.*

SI'LENT, *a.* Not speaking; mute. Ps. xxii.

2. Habitually taciturn; speaking little; not inclined to much talking; not loquacious.

Ulysses, he adds, was the most eloquent and the most *silent* of men. *Broome.*

3. Still; having no noise; as the *silent* watches of the night; the *silent* groves; all was *silent.*

4. Not operative; wanting efficacy. *Raleigh.*

5. Not mentioning; not proclaiming.

This new created world, of which in hell
Fame is not *silent.* *Milton.*

6. Calm; as, the winds were *silent.* *Parnell.*

7. Not acting; not transacting business in person; as a *silent* partner in a commercial house.

8. Not pronounced; having no sound; as, *e* is *silent* in *fable.*

SILEN'TIARY, *n.* One appointed to keep silence and order in court; one sworn not to divulge secrets of state. *Barrow.*

SI'LENTLY, *adv.* Without speech or words.

Each *silently*
Demands thy grace, and seems to watch thy eye. *Dryden.*

2. Without noise; as, to march *silently.*

3. Without mention. He mentioned other difficulties, but this he *silently* passed over. *Locke.*

SI'LENTNESS, *n.* State of being silent; stillness; silence. *Ash.*

SILESIA, *n.* *sile'zha.* A duchy or country now chiefly belonging to Prussia; hence, a species of linen cloth so called; thin coarse linen.

SILESIAN, *a.* *sile'zhan.* Pertaining to Silesia; made in Silesia; as *Silesian* linen.

SI'LEX, **SIL'ICA**, } *n.* One of the supposed primitive earths, usually found in the state of stone. When pure, it is perfectly white or colorless. The purer sorts are mountain crystal and quartz. Recent experiments prove this to be a compound substance, the base of which is a metal called silicium. Silica then is an oxyd of silicium. *Ure.*

SIL'ICE, **SIL'ICULE**, **SIL'ICLE**, } *n.* [L. *silicula*, a little husk.] In *botany*, a little pod or bivalvular pericarp, with seeds attached to both sutures. *Martyn.*

SILICICALCA'RIOUS, *a.* [*silex* and *calcarious.*] Consisting of silex and calcarious matter.

SILICICAL'CE, *n.* [L. *silex* or *silica* and *calx.*]

A mineral of the silicious kind, occurring in amorphous masses; its color is gray or brown. *Cleaveland.*

SILICIF'EROUS, *a.* [L. *silex* and *fero*, to produce.] Producing silex; or united with a portion of silex.

SIL'ICIFY, *v. t.* [L. *silex*, flint, and *facio*, to make.] To convert into silex.

The specimens—found near Philadelphia, are completely *silicified.* *Say.*

SIL'ICIFY, *v. i.* To become silex.

SILICIMU'RITE, *n.* [*silex* and *muria*, brine.] An earth composed of silex and magnesia.

SILI''CIOUS, *a.* Pertaining to silex, or partaking of its nature and qualities.

SILIC'ITED, *a.* Impregnated with silex. *Kirwan, Geol.*

SILIC'IUM, *n.* The undecomposed and perhaps undecomposable base of silex or silica.

SILIC'ULOUS, *a.* Having silicles or little pods, or pertaining to them.

SIL'ING-DISH, *n.* [Dan. *siler*, to strain.] A colander. [*Not in use.*] *Barret.*

SIL'IQUA, *n.* [L.] With *gold finers*, a carat, six of which make a scruple. *Johnson.*

SIL'IQUA, **SIL'IQUE**, *n.* [L. *siliqua.*] A pod; an oblong, membranaceous, bivalvular pericarp, having the seeds fixed to both sutures. *Martyn.*

SIL'IQUOSE, **SIL'IQUOUS**, *n.* [L. *siliquosus.*] Having that species of pericarp called *silique*; as *siliquous* plants. *Martyn.*

SILK, *n.* [Sax. *seolc*; Sw. *silke*; Dan. *id.*; Russ. *schilk*; Ar. Pers. سلك silk; properly any thread, from Ar. سلك salaka, to send or thrust in, to insert, to pass or go.]

1. The fine soft thread produced by the insect called *silk-worm* or *bombyx*. That which we ordinarily call *silk*, is a thread composed of several finer threads which the worm draws from its bowels, like the web of a spider, and with which the silk-worm envelopes itself, forming what is called a *cocoon*. *Encyc.*
2. Cloth made of silk. In this sense, the word has a plural, *silks*, denoting different sorts and varieties, as black *silk*, white *silk*, colored *silks*.
3. The filiform style of the female flower of maiz, which resembles real silk in fineness and softness.

Virginia silk, a plant of the genus Periploca, which climbs and winds about other plants, trees, &c.

SILK, *a.* Pertaining to silk; consisting of silk.

SILK COTTON-TREE, *n.* A tree of the genus Bombax, growing to an immense size; a native of both the Indies. *Encyc.*

SILKEN, *a.* *silk'n.* [Sax. *seolcen.*] Made of silk; as *silken* cloth; a *silken* vail.

2. Like silk; soft to the touch. *Dryden.*
3. Soft; delicate; tender; smooth; as mild and *silken* language.
4. Dressed in silk; as a *silken* wanton. *Shak.*

SILKEN, *v. t.* *silk'n.* To render soft or smooth. *Dyer.*

SILK'INESS, *n.* [from *silky.*] The qualities of silk; softness and smoothness to the feel.

2. Softness; effeminacy; pusillanimity. [*Little used.*] *B. Jonson.*

SILK'MAN, *n.* [*silk* and *man.*] A dealer in silks. *Shak.*

SILK'-MERCER, *n.* [*silk* and *mercer.*] A dealer in silks.

SILK'-WEAVER, *n.* [*silk* and *weaver.*] One whose occupation is to weave silk stuffs. *Watts.*

SILK'-WÖRM, *n.* [*silk* and *worm.*] The worm which produces silk, of the genus Phalæna. Silk-worms are said to have been first introduced into the Roman empire from China, in the reign of Justinian.

SILK'Y, *a.* Made of silk; consisting of silk.

2. Like silk; soft and smooth to the touch.
3. Pliant; yielding. *Shak.*

SILL, *n.* [Sax. *syl*, *syle*, *syll*; Fr. *seuil*; G. *schwelle*; W. *sail*, *syl* or *seiler*, foundation; *seiliaw*, to found; L. *solum*; allied to *solid*. The primary sense is probably to lay, set or throw down.]

1. Properly, the basis or foundation of a thing; appropriately, a piece of timber on which a building rests; the lowest timber of any structure; as the *sills* of a house, of a bridge, of a loom and the like.
2. The timber or stone at the foot of a door; the threshhold.
3. The timber or stone on which a window frame stands; or the lowest piece in a window frame.
4. The shaft or thill of a carriage. [*Local.*] *Grose.*

SIL'LABUB, *n.* A liquor made by mixing wine or cider with milk, and thus forming a soft curd. *King.*

SIL'LILY, *adv.* [from *silly.*] In a silly manner; foolishly; without the exercise of good sense or judgment. *Dryden.*

SIL'LIMANITE, *n.* A mineral found at Saybrook in Connecticut, so named in honor of Prof. Silliman of Yale College. It occurs in long, slender, rhombic prisms, engaged in gneiss. Its color is dark gray and hair brown; luster shining upon the external planes, but brilliant and pseudo-metallic upon those produced by cleavage in a direction parallel with the longer diagonal of the prism. Hardness about the same with quartz. Specific gravity, 3.410.

SIL'LINESS, *n.* Weakness of understanding; want of sound sense or judgment; simplicity; harmless folly. *L'Estrange.*

SIL'LY, *a.* [I have not found this word in any other language; but the Sax. *asealcan* signifies to be dull, inert, lazy. This corresponds with the Ar. كسل *kasela*, to be stupid, Heb. כסל. This may be radically the same word, with a prefix. Class Sl. No. 26.]

1. Weak in intellect; foolish; witless; destitute of ordinary strength of mind; simple; as a *silly* man; a *silly* child
2. Proceeding from want of understanding or common judgment; characterized by weakness or folly; unwise; as *silly* thoughts; *silly* actions; a *silly* scheme; writings stupid or *silly*. *Watts.*
3. Weak; helpless.

> After long storms—
> With which my *silly* bark was toss'd. *Obs.* *Spenser.*

SIL'LYHOW, *n.* The membrane that covers the head of the fetus. [*I believe not used.*] *Brown.*

SILT, *n.* [Sw. *sylta*, to pickle.] Saltness, or salt marsh or mud. [*Not in use in America.*] *Hale.*

SILU'RE, **SILU'RUS**, *n.* The sheat-fish; also, a name of the sturgeon. *Dict. Nat. Hist.*

SIL'VAN, *a.* [L. *silva*, a wood or grove. It is also written *sylvan.*]

1. Pertaining to a wood or grove; inhabiting woods.
2. Woody; abounding with woods.

> Betwixt two rows of rocks, a *silvan* scene. *Dryden.*

SIL'VAN, *n.* Another name of *tellurium*. *Werner.*

SIL'VER, *n.* [Sax. *seolfer*, *siluer*; Goth. *silubr*; G. *silber*; D. *zilver*; Sw. *silfver*; Dan. *sölv*; Lapponic, *sellowpe*. Qu. Russ. *serebro*; *r* for *l*.]

1. A metal of a white color and lively brilliancy. It has neither taste nor smell; its specific gravity is 10.552, according to Bergman, but according to Kirwan it is less. A cubic foot weighs about 660 lbs. Its ductility is little inferior to that of gold. It is harder and more elastic than tin or gold, but less so than copper, platina or iron. It is found native in thin plates or leaves, or in fine threads, or it is found mineralized by various substances. Great quantities of this metal are furnished by the mines of South America, and it is found in small quantities in Norway, Germany, Spain, the United States, &c. *Kirwan.* *Encyc.*
2. Money; coin made of silver.
3. Any thing of soft splendor.

> Pallas—piteous of her plaintive cries,
> In slumber clos'd her *silver*-streaming eyes. *Pope.*

SIL'VER, *a.* Made of silver; as a *silver* cup.

2. White like silver; as *silver* hair. *Shak.*

> Others on *silver* lakes and rivers bath'd
> Their downy breast. *Milton.*

3. White, or pale; of a pale luster; as the *silver* moon.
4. Soft; as a *silver* voice or sound. [Italian, *suono argentino.*] *Spenser.* *Shak.*

SIL'VER, *v. t.* To cover superficially with a coat of silver; as, to *silver* a pin or a dial-plate.

2. To foliate; to cover with tinfoil amalgamated with quicksilver; as, to *silver* glass.
3. To adorn with mild luster; to make smooth and bright.

> And smiling calmness *silver'd* o'er the deep. *Pope.*

4. To make hoary.

> His head was *silver'd* o'er with age. *Gay.*

SIL'VER-BEATER, *n.* [*silver* and *beater.*] One that foliates silver, or forms it into a leaf.

SIL'VER-BUSH, *n.* A plant, a species of Anthyllis.

SIL'VERED, *pp.* Covered with a thin coat of silver; rendered smooth and lustrous; made white or hoary.

SIL'VER-FIR, *n.* A species of fir. *Berkeley.*

SIL'VER-FISH, *n.* A fish of the size of a small carp, having a white color, striped with silvery lines.

SIL'VERING, *ppr.* Covering the surface with a thin coat of silver; foliating; rendering mildly lustrous; rendering white.

SIL'VERING, *n.* The art, operation or practice of covering the surface of any thing with silver; as the *silvering* of copper or brass. *Encyc.*

SIL'VERLING, *n.* A silver coin. Is. vii.

SIL'VERLY, *adv.* With the appearance of silver. *Shak.*

SIL'VERSMITH, *n.* [*silver* and *smith.*] One whose occupation is to work in silver, or in manufactures of which the precious metals form a part.

SIL'VER-THISTLE, *n.* [*silver* and *thistle.*] A plant.

SIL'VER-TREE, *n.* A plant of the genus Protea.

SIL'VER-WEED, *n.* A plant of the genus Potentilla.

SIL'VERY, *a.* [from *silver.*] Like silver; having the appearance of silver; white; of a mild luster.

> Of all the enamel'd race whose *silvery* wing
> Waves to the tepid zephyrs of the spring. *Pope.*

2. Besprinkled or covered with silver.

SIM'AGRE, *n.* [Fr. *simagrée.*] Grimace. [*Not in use.*] *Dryden.*

SIM'AR, **SIMA'RE**, *n.* [Fr. *simarre.*] A woman's robe. [*Not in use.*] *Dryden.*

SIM'ILAR, *a.* [Fr. *similaire*; It. *simile*; Sp. *similar*; L. *similis*; W. *heval, hevalyz*; from *mal*, like, Gr. ὁμαλος. The Welsh *mal* signifies small, light, ground, bruised, smooth, allied to *mill*, W. *malu*, to grind. But I am not confident that these words are of one family.]

Like; resembling; having a like form or appearance. *Similar* may signify exactly alike, or having a general likeness, a likeness in the principal points. Things perfectly *similar* in their nature, must be of the same essence, or homogeneous; but we generally understand *similar* to denote a likeness that is not perfect. Many of the statutes of Connecticut are *similar* to the statutes of Massachusetts on the same subjects. The manners of the several states of New England are *similar*, the people being derived from common ancestors.

SIMILAR'ITY, *n.* Likeness; resemblance; as a *similarity* of features. There is a great *similarity* in the features of the Laplanders and Samoiedes, but little *similarity* between the features of Europeans and the woolly haired Africans.

SIM'ILARLY, *adv.* In like manner; with resemblance. *Reid.*

SIMILE, *n. sim'ily.* [L.] In *rhetoric*, similitude; a comparison of two things which, however different in other respects, have some strong point or points of resemblance; by which comparison, the character or qualities of a thing are illustrated or presented in an impressive light. Thus, the eloquence of Demosthenes was like a rapid torrent; that of Cicero, like a large stream that glides smoothly along with majestic tranquility.

SIMIL'ITUDE, *n.* [Fr. from L. *similitudo.*]

1. Likeness; resemblance; likeness in nature, qualities or appearance; as *similitude* of substance. *Bacon.*

> Let us make man in our image, man
> In our *similitude*— *Milton.*
> Fate some future bard shall join
> In sad *similitude* of griefs to mine. *Pope.*

2. Comparison; simile. [See *Simile.*]

> Tasso, in his *similitudes*, never departed from the woods. *Dryden.*

SIMILITU'DINARY, *a.* Denoting resemblance or comparison. *Coke.*

SIM'ILOR, *n.* A name given to an alloy of red copper and zink, made in the best proportions to imitate silver and gold. *Encyc.*

SIMITAR. [See *Cimeter.*]

SIM'MER, *v. i.* [Qu. Gr. ζυμη, ζυμοω, to ferment.]

To boil gently, or with a gentle hissing. *Simmering* is incipient ebullition, when little bubbles are formed on the edge of the liquor, next to the vessel. These are occasioned by the escape of heat and vapor.

SIM'MERING, *ppr.* Boiling gently.

SIM'NEL, *n.* [Dan. *simle*; Sw. *simla*; G. *semmel.*] A kind of sweet cake; a bun.

SIMO'NIAC, *n.* [Fr. *simoniaque.* See *Simony.*]

One who buys or sells preferment in the church. *Ayliffe.*

SIMONI'ACAL, *a.* Guilty of simony. *Spectator.*

2. Consisting in simony, or the crime of buying or selling ecclesiastical preferment; as a *simoniacal* presentation.

SIMONI'ACALLY, *adv.* With the guilt or offense of simony.

SIMO'NIOUS, *a.* Partaking of simony; given to simony. *Milton.*

SIM'ONY, *n.* [from *Simon* Magus, who wished to purchase the power of conferring the Holy Spirit. Acts viii.]

The crime of buying or selling ecclesiastical preferment; or the corrupt presentation of any one to an ecclesiastical benefice for money or reward. By Stat. 31 Elizabeth, c. vi. severe penalties are enacted against this crime.

SIMOOM', *n.* A hot suffocating wind, that blows occasionally in Africa and Arabia, generated by the extreme heat of the parched deserts or sandy plains. Its approach is indicated by a redness in the air, and its fatal effects are to be avoided by falling on the face and holding the breath. *Encyc.*

SI'MOUS, *a.* [L. *simo*, one with a flat nose, Gr. σιμος.]

1. Having a very flat or snub nose, with the end turned up.

2. Concave; as the *simous* part of the liver. *Brown.*

SIM'PER, *v. i.* To smile in a silly manner. *Shak.*

SIM'PER, *n.* A smile with an air of silliness. *Addison.*

SIM'PERING, *ppr.* Smiling foolishly.

SIM'PERING, *n.* The act of smiling with an air of silliness.

SIM'PERINGLY, *adv.* With a silly smile.

SIM'PLE, *a.* [Fr. from L. *simplex*; *sine*, without, and *plex, plica*, doubling, fold; It. *semplice.*]

1. Single; consisting of one thing; uncompounded; unmingled; uncombined with any thing else; as a *simple* substance; a *simple* idea; a *simple* sound. *Watts.*

2. Plain; artless; not given to design, stratagem or duplicity; undesigning; sincere; harmless.

> A *simple* husbandman in garments gray. *Hubberd.*

3. Artless; unaffected; unconstrained; inartificial; plain.

> In *simple* manners all the secret lies. *Young.*

4. Unadorned; plain; as a *simple* style or narration; a *simple* dress.

5. Not complex or complicated; as a machine of *simple* construction.

6. Weak in intellect; not wise or sagacious; silly.

> The *simple* believeth every word; but the prudent looketh well to his going. Prov. xiv.

7. In *botany*, undivided, as a root, stem or spike; only one on a petiole, as a *simple* leaf; only one on a peduncle, as a *simple* flower; having only one set of rays, as an umbel; having only one row of leaflets, as a *simple* calyx; not plumose or fethered, as a pappus. *Martyn.*

A simple body, in chimistry, is one that has not been decomposed, or separated into two or more bodies.

SIM'PLE, *n.* Something not mixed or compounded. In the *materia medica*, the general denomination of an herb or plant, as each vegetable is supposed to possess its particular virtue, and therefore to constitute a simple remedy. *Encyc. Dryden.*

SIM'PLE, *v. i.* To gather simples or plants.

> As *simpling* on the flowery hills he stray'd. *Garth.*

SIMPLE-MINDED, *a.* Artless; undesigning; unsuspecting. *Blackstone.*

SIM'PLENESS, *n.* The state or quality of being simple, single or uncompounded; as the *simpleness* of the elements. *Digby.*

2. Artlessness; simplicity.

3. Weakness of intellect.

SIM'PLER, *n.* One that collects simples; an herbalist; a simplist.

SIMPLESS, for *simplicity* or *silliness*, is not in use. *Spenser.*

SIM'PLETON, *n.* A silly person; a person of weak intellect; a trifler; a foolish person. *Pope.*

SIMPLI''CIAN, *n.* An artless, unskilled or undesigning person. [*Not in use.*] *Arnway.*

SIMPLIC'ITY, *n.* [L. *simplicitas*; Fr. *simplicité*; It. *simplicità*; Sp. *simplicidad.*]

1. Singleness; the state of being unmixed or uncompounded; as the *simplicity* of metals or of earths.

2. The state of being not complex, or of consisting of few parts; as the *simplicity* of a machine.

3. Artlessness of mind; freedom from a propensity to cunning or stratagem; freedom from duplicity; sincerity.

> Marquis Dorset, a man for his harmless *simplicity* neither misliked nor much regarded. *Hayward.*

4. Plainness; freedom from artificial ornament; as the *simplicity* of a dress, of style, of language, &c. *Simplicity* in writing is the first of excellences.

5. Plainness; freedom from subtilty or abstruseness; as the *simplicity* of scriptural doctrines or truth.

6. Weakness of intellect; silliness. *Hooker.*

Godly simplicity, in Scripture, is a fair open profession and practice of evangelical truth, with a single view to obedience and to the glory of God.

SIMPLIFICA'TION, *n.* [See *Simplify.*] The act of making simple; the act of reducing to simplicity, or to a state not complex. *Ch. Obs.*

SIM'PLIFIED, *pp.* Made simple or not complex.

SIM'PLIFY, *v. t.* [L. *simplex*, simple, and *facio*, to make; Fr. *simplifier.*]

To make simple; to reduce what is complex to greater simplicity; to make plain or easy.

> The collection of duties is drawn to a point, and so far *simplified*. *Hamilton.*
>
> It is important in scientific pursuits, to be cautious in *simplifying* our deductions *Nicholson.*
>
> This is the true way to *simplify* the study of science. *Lavoisier, Trans.*

SIM'PLIFYING, *ppr.* Making simple; rendering less complex.

SIM'PLIST, *n.* One skilled in simples or medical plants. *Brown.*

SIMPLOCE. [See *Symploce.*]

SIM'PLY, *adv.* Without art; without subtilty; artlessly; plainly.

> Subverting worldly strong and worldly wise
> By *simply* meek. *Milton.*

2. Of itself; without addition; alone.

> They make that good or evil, which otherwise of itself were not *simply* the one nor the other. *Hooker.*

3. Merely; solely.

> *Simply* the thing I am
> Shall make me live. *Shak.*

4. Weakly; foolishly.

SIM'ULACHER, *n.* [L. *simulacrum.*] An image. [*Not in use.*] *Elyot.*

SIM'ULAR, *n.* [See *Simulate.*] One who simulates or counterfeits something. [*Not in use.*] *Shak.*

SIM'ULATE, *v. t.* [L. *simulo*, from *similis*, like.]

To feign; to counterfeit; to assume the mere appearance of something, without the reality. The wicked often *simulate* the virtuous and good.

SIM'ULATE, *a.* [L. *simulatus.*] Feigned; pretended. *Bale.*

SIM'ULATED, *pp.* or *a.* Feigned; pretended; assumed artificially. *Chesterfield.*

SIM'ULATING, *ppr.* Feigning; pretending; assuming the appearance of what is not real.

SIMULA'TION, *n.* [Fr. from L. *simulatio.*] The act of feigning to be that which is not; the assumption of a deceitful appearance or character. *Simulation* differs from *dissimulation.* The former denotes the assuming of a false character; the latter denotes the concealment of the true character. Both are comprehended in the word *hypocrisy.*

SIMULTA'NEOUS, *a.* [Fr. *simultanée*; Sp. *simultaneo*; from L. *simul*, at the same time.]

Existing or happening at the same time; as *simultaneous* events. The exchange of ratifications may be *simultaneous.*

SIMULTA'NEOUSLY, *adv.* At the same time.

SIMULTA'NEOUSNESS, *n.* The state or quality of being or happening at the same time; as the *simultaneousness* of transactions in two different places.

SIM'ULTY, *n.* [L. *simultas.*] Private grudge or quarrel. [*Not in use.*] *B. Jonson.*

SIN, *n.* [Sax. *sin* or *syn*; G. *sünde*; D. *zonde*; Sw. Dan. *synd*; Lapponic, Finnish, *sindia*; allied perhaps to Ir. *sainim*, to alter, to vary, to *sunder.* The primary sense is probably to depart, to wander.]

1. The voluntary departure of a moral agent from a known rule of rectitude or duty, prescribed by God; any voluntary transgression of the divine law, or violation of a divine command; a wicked act; iniquity. Sin is either a positive act in which a known divine law is violated, or it is the voluntary neglect to obey a positive divine command, or a rule of duty clearly implied in such command. Sin comprehends not actions only, but neglect of known duty, all evil thoughts, purposes, words and desires, whatever is contrary to God's commands or law. 1 John iii. Matt. xv. James iv.

> Sinners neither enjoy the pleasures of *sin*, nor the peace of piety. *Rob. Hall.*

Among divines, sin is *original* or *actual. Actual* sin, above defined, is the act of a moral agent in violating a known rule of duty. *Original* sin, as generally understood, is native depravity of heart; that want of conformity of heart to the divine will, that corruption of nature or deterioration of the moral character of man, which is supposed to be the effect of Adam's apostasy; and which manifests itself in moral agents by positive acts of disobedience to the divine will, or by the voluntary neglect to comply with the express commands of God, which require that we should love God with all the heart and soul and strength and mind, and our neighbor as ourselves. This native depravity or alienation of affections from God and his law, is supposed to be what the apostle calls the *carnal mind* or *mindedness*, which is enmity against God, and is therefore denominated *sin* or *sinfulness.*

Unpardonable sin, or blasphemy against the Holy Spirit, is supposed to be a malicious and obstinate rejection of Christ and the gospel plan of salvation, or a contemptuous resistance made to the influences and convictions of the Holy Spirit. Matt. xii.

2. A sin-offering; an offering made to atone for sin.

> He hath made him to be *sin* for us, who knew no sin. 2 Cor. v.

3. A man enormously wicked. [*Not in use.*] *Shak.*

Sin differs from *crime*, not in nature, but in application. That which is a *crime* against society, is *sin* against God.

SIN, *v. i.* [Sax. *singian*, *syngian.*] To depart voluntarily from the path of duty prescribed by God to man; to violate the divine law in any particular, by actual transgression or by the neglect or non-observance of its injunctions; to violate any known rule of duty.

> All have *sinned* and come short of the glory of God. Rom. iii.

It is followed by *against.*

> *Against* thee, thee only, have I *sinned.* Ps. li.

2. To offend against right, against men or society; to trespass.

> I am a man
> More *sinn'd* against than *sinning.* *Shak.*

> And who but wishes to invert the laws
> Of order, *sins* against th' eternal cause. *Pope.*

SIN, for *since*, [Scot. *syne*,] obsolete or vulgar.

SIN'APISM, *n.* [L. *sinapis*, *sinape*, mustard, G. *senf*, Sax. *senep.*]

In *pharmacy*, a cataplasm composed of mustard seed pulverized, with some other ingredients, and used as an external application. It is a powerful stimulant. *Encyc.*

SINCE, *prep.* or *adv.* [Sw. *sedan*; Dan. *siden*; D. *sint*; supposed to be contracted from Sax. *siththan*, which is from *sithian*, to pass, to go; and *siththan* may be the participle, and denote past, gone, and hence after, afterward. *Sith* in Saxon, has a like sense. Our early writers used *sith*, *sithen*, *sithence*; the latter is evidently a corruption of *siththan.* It may be doubted whether Sw. *sen*, Dan. *seen*, slow, late, is a contraction of this word; more probably it is not.]

1. After; from the time that. The proper signification of *since* is *after*, and its appropriate sense includes the whole period between an event and the present time. I have not seen my brother *since* January.

> The Lord hath blessed thee, *since* my coming. Gen. xxx.

> —Holy prophets, who have been *since* the world began. Luke i. John ix.

Since then denotes, during the whole time after an event; or at any particular time during that period.

2. Ago; past; before this. "About two years *since*, an event happened," that is, two years having *passed.*

3. Because that; this being the fact that.

> *Since* truth and constancy are vain,
> *Since* neither love nor sense of pain
> Nor force of reason can persuade,
> Then let example be obey'd. *Granville.*

Since, when it precedes a noun, is called a preposition, but when it precedes a sentence it is called an adverb. The truth is, the character of the word is the same in both cases. It is probably an obsolete participle, and according to the usual classification of words, may be properly ranked with the prepositions. In strictness, the last clause of the passage above cited is the case absolute. "The Lord hath blessed thee, *since my coming*," that is, my arrival being *past.* So, *since the world began*, is strictly *past* the world began, the beginning of the world being *past.* In the first case, *since*, considered as a preposition, has *coming*, a noun, for its object, and in the latter case, the clause of a sentence. So we say, *against* your arrival, or *against* you come.

SINCE'RE, *a.* [Fr. from L. *sincerus*, which is said to be composed of *sine*, without, and *cera*, wax; as if applied originally to pure honey.]

1. Pure; unmixed.

> As new-born babes, desire the *sincere* milk of the word. 1 Pet. ii.

> A joy which never was *sincere* till now. *Dryden.*

> There is no *sincere* acid in any animal juice. *Arbuthnot.*

> I would have all gallicisms avoided, that our tongue may be *sincere.* *Felton.*

[This sense is for the most part obsolete. We use the phrases, *sincere* joy, *sincere* pleasure; but we mean by them, *unfeigned*, *real* joy or pleasure.]

2. Unhurt; uninjured.

> Th' inviolable body stood *sincere.* *Obs.* *Dryden.*

3. Being in reality what it appears to be; not feigned; not simulated; not assumed or said for the sake of appearance; real; not hypocritical or pretended. *This is the present use of the word.* Let your intentions be pure and your declarations *sincere.* Let love and friendship be *sincere.* No prayer can avail with a heart-searching God, unless it is *sincere.*

SINCE'RELY, *adv.* Honestly; with real purity of heart; without simulation or disguise; unfeignedly; as, to speak one's mind *sincerely*; to love virtue *incerely.*

SINCE'RENESS, *n.* Sincerity.

SINCER'ITY, *n.* [Fr. *sincerité*; L. *sinceritas.*]

1. Honesty of mind or intention; freedom from simulation or hypocrisy. We may question a man's prudence, when we cannot question his *sincerity.*
2. Freedom from hypocrisy, disguise or false pretense; as the *sincerity* of a declaration or of love.

SIN'CIPUT, *n.* [L.] The fore part of the head from the forehead to the coronal suture. *Encyc.*

SIN'DON, *n.* [L. fine linen.] A wrapper. [*Not in use.*] *Bacon.*

SINE, *n.* [L. *sinus.*] In *geometry*, the right sine of an arch or arc, is a line drawn from one end of that arch, perpendicular to the radius drawn through the other end, and is always equal to half the chord of double the arch. *Harris.*

SI'NECURE, *n.* [L. *sine*, without, and *cura*, cure, care.]

An office which has revenue without employment; in church affairs, a benefice without cure of souls. [*This is the original and proper sense of the word.*]

Sine die, [L. without day.] An adjournment *sine die* is an adjournment without fixing the time of resuming business. When a defendant is suffered to go *sine die*, he is dismissed the court.

SIN'EPITE, *n.* [L. *sinape*, mustard.] Something resembling mustard seed. *De Costa.*

SIN'EW, *n.* [Sax. *sinu, sinw, sinwe*; G. *sehne*; D. *zenuw*; Sw. *sena*; Dan. *sene* or *seene.* The primary sense is stretched, strained, whence the sense of srong; G. *sehnen*, to long; Ir. *sinnim*, to strain.]

1. In *anatomy*, a tendon; that which unites a muscle to a bone.
2. In *the plural*, strength; or rather that which supplies strength. Money is the *sinews* of war. *Dryden.*
3. Muscle; nerve. *Davies.*

SIN'EW, *v. t.* To knit as by sinews. *Shak.*

SIN'EWED, *a.* Furnished with sinews; as a strong-*sinewed* youth.

2. Strong; firm; vigorous.

> When he sees
> Ourselves well *sinewed* to our defense. *Shak.*

SIN'EWLESS, *a.* Having no strength or vigor.

SIN'EW-SHRUNK, *a.* Gaunt-bellied; having the sinews under the belly shrunk by excess of fatigue, as a horse. *Far. Dict.*

SIN'EWY, *a.* Consisting of a sinew or nerve.

> The *sinewy* thread my brain lets fall. *Donne.*

2. Nervous; strong; well braced with sinews; vigorous; firm; as the *sinewy* Ajax. *Shak.*

> The northern people are large, fair complexioned, strong, *sinewy* and courageous. *Hale.*

SIN'FUL, *a.* [from *sin.*] Tainted with sin; wicked; iniquitous; criminal; unholy; as *sinful* men.

> Ah, *sinful* nation, a people laden with iniquity! Is. i.

2. Containing sin, or consisting in sin; contrary to the laws of God; as *sinful* actions; *sinful* thoughts; *sinful* words.

SIN'FULLY, *adv.* In a manner which the laws of God do not permit; wickedly; iniquitously; criminally.

SIN'FULNESS, *n.* The quality of being sinful or contrary to the divine will; wickedness; iniquity; criminality; as the *sinfulness* of an action; the *sinfulness* of thoughts or purposes.

2. Wickedness; corruption; depravity; as the *sinfulness* of men or of the human race.

SING, *v. i.* pret. *sung, sang*; pp. *sung.* [Sax. *singan, syngan*; Goth. *siggwan*; G. *singen*; D. *zingen*; Sw. *siunga*; Dan. *synger.* It would seem from the Gothic that *n* is casual, and the elements *Sg.* If so, it coincides with *say* and *seek*, all signifying to strain, urge, press or drive.]

1. To utter sounds with various inflections or melodious modulations of voice, as fancy may dictate, or according to the notes of a song or tune.

> The noise of them that *sing* do I hear. Ex. xxxii.

2. To utter sweet or melodious sounds, as birds. It is remarkable that the female of no species of birds ever *sings.*

> And *singing* birds in silver cages hung. *Dryden.*

3. To make a small shrill sound; as, the air *sings* in passing through a crevice.

> O'er his head the flying spear
> *Sung* innocent, and spent its force in air. *Pope.*

4. To tell or relate something in numbers or verse.

> *Sing*
> Of human hope by cross event destroy'd. *Prior.*

SING, *v. t.* To utter with musical modulations of voice.

> And they *sing* the song of Moses, the servant of God, and the song of the Lamb. Rev. xv.

2. To celebrate in song; to give praises to in verse.

> The last, the happiest British king,
> Whom thou shalt paint or I shall *sing.* *Addison.*

3. To relate or rehearse in numbers, verse or poetry.

> Arms and the man I *sing.* *Dryden.*

> While stretch'd at ease you *sing* your happy loves. *Dryden.*

SINGE, *v. t.* *sinj.* [Sax. *sængan*; G. *sengen*; D. *zengen.*]

To burn slightly or superficially; to burn the surface of a thing, as the nap of cloth, or the hair of the skin; as, to *singe* off the beard. *Shak.*

> Thus riding on his curls, he seem'd to pass
> A rolling fire along, and *singe* the grass. *Dryden.*

SINGE, *n.* A burning of the surface; a slight burn.

SING'ED, *pp.* Burnt superficially.

SING'EING, *ppr.* Burning the surface.

SING'ER, *n.* [from *sing.*] One that sings.

2. One versed in music, or one whose occupation is to sing; as a chorus of *singers.* *Dryden.*
3. A bird that sings. *Bacon.*

SING'ING, *ppr.* Uttering melodious or musical notes; making a shrill sound; celebrating in song; reciting in verse.

SING'ING, *n.* The act of uttering sounds with musical inflections; musical articulation; the utterance of melodious notes. Cant. ii.

SING'ING-BOOK, *n.* A music book, *as it ought to be called*: a book containing tunes.

SING'INGLY, *adv.* With sounds like singing; with a kind of tune. *North.*

SING'ING-MAN, *n.* [*singing* and *man.*] A man who sings, or is employed to sing; as in cathedrals.

SING'ING-M'ASTER, *n.* A music master; one that teaches vocal music. *Addison.*

SING'ING-WOMAN, *n.* A woman employed to sing.

SIN'GLE, *a.* [L. *singulus*; probably from a root that signifies to *separate.*]

1. Separate; one; only; individual; consisting of one only; as a *single* star; a *single* city; a *single* act.
2. Particular; individual.

> No *single* man is born with a right of controlling the opinions of all the rest. *Pope.*

3. Uncompounded.

> Simple ideas are opposed to complex, and *single* to compound. *Watts.*

4. Alone; having no companion or assistant.

> Who *single* hast maintain'd
> Against revolted multitudes the cause of truth. *Milton.*

5. Unmarried; as a *single* man; a *single* woman.
6. Not double; not complicated; as a *single* thread; a *single* strand of a rope.
7. Performed with one person or antagonist on a side, or with one person only opposed to another; as a *single* fight; a *single* combat.
8. Pure; simple; incorrupt; unbiased; having clear vision of divine truth. Matt. vi.
9. Small; weak; silly. *Obs.* *Beaum. Shak.*
10. In *botany*, a single flower is when there is only one on a stem, and in common usage, one not double. *Martyn.*

SIN'GLE, *v. t.* To select, as an individual person or thing from among a number; to choose one from others.

> —A dog who can *single* out his master in the dark. *Bacon.*

2. To sequester; to withdraw; to retire; as an agent *singling* itself from comforts. [*Not used.*] *Hooker.*
3. To take alone; as men commendable when *singled* from society. [*Not in use.*] *Hooker.*
4. To separate. *Sidney.*

SIN'GLED, *pp.* Selected from among a number.

SIN'GLENESS, *n.* The state of being one only or separate from all others; the opposite of doubleness, complication or multiplicity.

2. Simplicity; sincerity; purity of mind or purpose; freedom from duplicity; as *singleness* of belief; *singleness* of heart. *Hooker. Law.*

SIN'GLY, *adv.* Individually; particularly; as, to make men *singly* and personally good. *Tillotson.*

2. Only; by himself.

> Look thee, 'tis so, thou *singly* honest man. *Shak.*

3. Without partners, companions or associates; as, to attack another *singly.*

> At ombre *singly* to decide their doom. *Dryden.*

4. Honestly; sincerely.

SIN'GULAR, *a.* [Fr. *singulier;* L. *singularis*, from *singulus*, single.]

1. Single; not complex or compound.

That idea which represents one determinate thing, is called a *singular* idea, whether simple, complex or compound. *Watts.*

2. In *grammar*, expressing one person or thing; as the *singular* number. The *singular* number stands opposed to *dual* and *plural.*

3. Particular; existing by itself; unexampled; as a *singular* phenomenon. Your case is hard, but not *singular.*

4. Remarkable; eminent; unusual; rare; as a man of *singular* gravity, or *singular* attainments.

5. Not common; odd; implying something censurable or not approved.

His zeal
None seconded, as *singular* and rash. *Milton.*

6. Being alone; that of which there is but one.

These busts of the emperors and empresses are scarce, and some of them almost *singular* in their kind. *Addison.*

SIN'GULAR, *n.* A particular instance. [*Unusual.*] *More.*

SINGULAR'ITY, *n.* [Fr. *singularité.*] Peculiarity; some character or quality of a thing by which it is distinguished from all, or from most others.

Pliny addeth this *singularity* to that soil, that the second year the very falling of the seeds yieldeth corn. *Raleigh.*

2. An uncommon character or form; something curious or remarkable.

I took notice of this little figure for the *singularity* of the instrument. *Addison.*

3. Particular privilege, prerogative or distinction.

No bishop of Rome ever took upon him this name of *singularity*, (universal bishop.) *Hooker.*

Catholicism—must be understood in opposition to the legal *singularity* of the Jewish nation. *Pearson.*

4. Character or trait of character different from that of others; peculiarity. The *singularity* of living according to the strict precepts of the gospel is highly to be commended.

5. Oddity.

6. Celibacy. [*Not in use.*] *J. Taylor.*

SIN'GULARIZE, *v. t.* To make single. [*Not in use.*]

SIN'GULARLY, *adv.* Peculiarly; in a manner or degree not common to others. It is no disgrace to be *singularly* good.

2. Oddly; strangely.

3. So as to express one or the singular number. *Morton.*

SIN'GULT, *n.* [L. *singultus.*] A sigh. [*Not in use.*]

SIN'ICAL, *a.* [from *sine.*] Pertaining to a sine.

SIN'ISTER, *a.* [L. Probably the primary sense is weak, defective.]

1. Left; on the left hand, or the side of the left hand; opposed to *dexter* or *right;* as the *sinister* cheek; or the *sinister* side of an escutcheon.

2. Evil; bad; corrupt; perverse; dishonest; as *sinister* means; *sinister* purpose.

He scorns to undermine another's interest by any *sinister* or inferior arts. *South.*

3. Unlucky; inauspicious. *B. Jonson.*

Sinister aspect, in astrology, an appearance of two planets happening according to the succession of the signs; as Saturn in Aries, and Mars in the same degree of Gemini. *Encyc.*

SIN'ISTER-HANDED, *a.* Left-handed. [*Not in use.*]

SIN'ISTERLY, *adv.* Absurdly; perversely; unfairly. *A. Wood.*

SINISTROR'SAL, *a.* [*sinister* and Gr. ορσω, to rise.] Rising from left to right, as a spiral line or helix. *Henry.*

SIN'ISTROUS, *a.* Being on the left side; inclined to the left. *Brown.*

2. Wrong; absurd; perverse.

A knave or fool can do no harm, even by the most *sinistrous* and absurd choice. *Bentley.*

SIN'ISTROUSLY, *adv.* Perversely; wrongly.

2. With a tendency to use the left as the stronger hand.

SINK, *v. i.* pret. *sunk;* pp. *id.* The old pret. *sank* is nearly obsolete. [Sax. *sencan, sincan;* Goth. *sigcwan;* G. *sinken;* D. *zinken;* Sw. *siunka;* Dan. *synker;* coinciding with *siege.* Class Sg.]

1. To fall by the force of greater gravity, in a medium or substance of less specific gravity; to subside; opposed to *swim* or *float.* Some species of wood or timber will *sink* in water. Oil will not *sink* in water and many other liquids, for it is specifically lighter.

I *sink* in deep mire. Ps. lxix.

2. To fall gradually.

He *sunk* down in his chariot. 2 Kings ix.

3. To enter or penetrate into any body.

The stone *sunk* into his forehead. 1 Sam. xvii.

4. To fall; to become lower; to subside or settle to a level.

The Alps and Pyrenees *sink* before him. *Addison.*

5. To be overwhelmed or depressed.

Our country *sinks* beneath the yoke. *Shak.*

6. To enter deeply; to be impressed.

Let these sayings *sink* down into your ears. Luke ix.

7. To become deep; to retire or fall within the surface of any thing; as, the eyes *sink* into the head.

8. To fall; to decline; to decay; to decrease. A free state gradually *sinks* into ruin. It is the duty of government to revive a *sinking* commerce.

Let not the fire *sink* or slacken. *Mortimer.*

9. To fall into rest or indolence; as, to *sink* away in pleasing dreams. *Addison.*

10. To be lower; to fall; as, the price of land will *sink* in time of peace.

SINK, *v. t.* To put under water; to immerse in a fluid; as, to *sink* a ship.

2. To make by digging or delving; as, to *sink* a pit or a well.

3. To depress; to degrade. His vices *sink* him in infamy, or in public estimation.

4. To plunge into destruction.

If I have a conscience, let it *sink* me. *Shak.*

5. To cause to fall or to be plunged. *Woodward.*

6. To bring low; to reduce in quantity.

You *sunk* the river with repeated draughts. *Addison.*

7. To depress; to overbear; to crush. This would *sink* the spirit of a hero.

8. To diminish; to lower or lessen; to degrade.

I mean not that we should *sink* our figure out of covetousness. *Rogers.*

9. To cause to decline or fail.

Thy cruel and unnat'ral lust of power
Has *sunk* thy father more than all his years. *Rowe.*

10. To suppress; to conceal; to intervert.

If sent with ready money to buy any thing, and you happen to be out of pocket, *sink* the money, and take up the goods on account. [*Unusual.*] *Swift.*

11. To depress; to lower in value or amount. Great importations may *sink* the price of goods.

12. To reduce; to pay; to diminish or annihilate by payment; as, to *sink* the national debt.

13. To waste; to dissipate; as, to *sink* an estate.

SINK, *n.* [Sax. *sinc.*] A drain to carry off filthy water; a jakes. *Shak. Hayward.*

2. A kind of bason of stone or wood to receive filthy water.

SINK'ING, *ppr.* Falling; subsiding; depressing; declining.

Sinking fund, in *finance*, a fund created for *sinking* or paying a public debt, or purchasing the stock for the government.

SIN'LESS, *a.* [from *sin.*] Free from sin; pure; perfect. Christ yielded a *sinless* obedience.

2. Free from sin; innocent; as a *sinless* soul. *Dryden.*

SIN'LESSNESS, *n.* Freedom from sin and guilt. *Boyle.*

SIN'NER, *n.* One that has voluntarily violated the divine law; a moral agent who has voluntarily disobeyed any divine precept, or neglected any known duty.

2. It is used in contradistinction to *saint*, to denote an unregenerate person; one who has not received the pardon of his sins.

3. An offender; a criminal. *Dryden.*

SIN'NER, *v. i.* To act as a sinner; *in ludicrous language.*

Whether the charmer *sinner* it or saint it. *Pope.*

SIN'-OFFERING, *n.* [*sin* and *offering.*] A sacrifice for sin; something offered as an expiation for sin. Ex. xxix.

SIN'OPER, } **SIN'OPLE,** } *n.* [L. *sinopis;* Gr. σινωπις.] Red ferruginous quartz, of a blood or brownish red color, sometimes with a tinge of yellow. It occurs in small but very perfect crystals, and in masses that resemble some varieties of jasper. *Cleaveland.*

SIN'TER, *n.* In *mineralogy*, calcarious sinter is a variety of carbonate of lime, composed of a series of successive layers, concentric, plane or undulated, and nearly or quite parallel. It appears under various forms. *Cleaveland.*

Silicious sinter is white or grayish, light, brittle, porous, and of a fibrous texture. Opaline silicious sinter somewhat resembles opal. It is whitish, with brownish, blackish or bluish spots, and its fragments present dendritic appearances. *Phillips.*

Pearl sinter or fiorite occurs in stalactitic, cylindrical, botryoidal, and globular masses, white or grayish. *Id.*

SIN'UATE, *v. t.* [L. *sinuo.*] To wind; to turn; to bend in and out. *Woodward.*

SIN'UATE, *a.* In *botany*, a *sinuate* leaf is one that has large curved breaks in the margin, resembling bays, as in the oak. *Martyn.*

SINUA'TION, *n.* A winding or bending in and out. *Hale.*

SINUOS'ITY, *n.* [L. *sinuosus*, *sinus.*] The quality of bending or curving in and out; or a series of bends and turns in arches or other irregular figures.

SIN'UOUS, *a.* [Fr. *sinueux*, from L. *sinus.*] Winding; crooked; bending in and out; as a *sinuous* pipe.

Streaking the ground with *sinuous* trace. *Milton.*

SI'NUS, *n.* [L. a bay.] A bay of the sea; a recess in the shore, or an opening into the land. *Burnet.*

2. In *anatomy*, a cavity in a bone or other part, wider at the bottom than at the entrance. *Encyc.*

3. In *surgery*, a little cavity or sack in which pus is collected; an abscess with only a small orifice. *Encyc. Parr.*

4. An opening; a hollow.

SIP, *v. t.* [Sax. *sipan*, to sip, to drink in, to macerate; D. *sippen*; Dan. *söber*; Sw. *supa*; Ir. *subham*; W. *sipiaw*, to draw the lips; *sipian*, to *sip*; Fr. *soupe*, *souper*; Eng. *sop*, *sup*, *supper*. See Class Sb. No. 79.]

1. To take a fluid into the mouth in small quantities by the lips; as, to *sip* wine; to *sip* tea or coffee. *Pope.*

2. To drink or imbibe in small quantities.

Every herb that *sips* the dew. *Milton.*

3. To draw into the mouth; to extract; as, a bee *sips* nectar from the flowers.

4. To drink out of.

They skim the floods, and *sip* the purple flow'rs. *Dryden.*

SIP, *v. i.* To drink a small quantity; to take a fluid with the lips. *Dryden.*

SIP, *n.* The taking of a liquor with the lips; or a small draught taken with the lips.

One *sip* of this
Will bathe the drooping spirits in delight,
Beyond the bliss of dreams. *Milton.*

SIPE, *v. i.* To ooze; to issue slowly; as a fluid. [*Local.*] *Grose.*

SIPH'ILIS, *n.* [Gr. σιφλος, deformed.] The venereal disease.

SIPHILIT'IC, *a.* Pertaining to the venereal disease, or partaking of its nature.

SI'PHON, *n.* [L. *sipho*, *sipo*; Gr. σιφων; It. *sifone*; Fr. *siphon*; Sp. *sifon*. Qu. from the root of *sip.*]

1. A bent pipe or tube whose legs are of unequal length, used for drawing liquor out of a vessel by causing it to rise over the rim or top. For this purpose, the shorter leg is inserted in the liquor, and the air is exhausted by being drawn through the longer leg. The liquor then rises by the weight of the atmosphere to supply the vacuum, till it reaches the top of the vessel, and then descends in the longer leg of the siphon.

2. The pipe by which the chambers of a shell communicate. *Ed. Encyc.*

SIPHUN'CULATED, *a.* [L. *siphunculus*, a little siphon.] Having a little siphon or spout, as a valve. *Say.*

SIP'PED, *pp.* Drawn in with the lips; imbibed in small quantities.

SIP'PER, *n.* One that sips.

SIP'PET, *n.* A small sop. [*Not in use.*] *Milton.*

SI QUIS. [L. if any one.] These words give name to a notification by a candidate for orders of his intention to inquire whether any impediment may be alledged against him.

SIR, *n. sur.* [Fr. *sire*, and *sieur*, in *monsieur*; Norm. *sire*, lord; Corn. *sira*, father; Heb. שור shur, to sing, to look, observe, watch, also to rule. The primary sense is to stretch, strain, hold, &c. whence the sense of a ruler or chief.]

1. A word of respect used in addresses to men, as *madam* is in addresses to women. It signifies properly *lord*, corresponding to *dominus* in Latin, *don* in Spanish, and *herr* in German. It is used in the singular or plural.

Speak on, *sir*. *Shak.*
But *sirs*, be sudden in the execution. *Shak.*

2. The title of a knight or baronet; as *Sir* Horace Vere. *Bacon.*

3. It is used by Shakspeare for *man.*

In the election of a *sir* so rare. [*Not in use.*]

4. In American colleges, the title of a master of arts.

5. It is prefixed to *loin*, in *sirloin*; as a *sirloin* of beef. This practice is said to have originated in the knighting of a loin of beef by one of the English kings in a fit of good humor. *Addison.*

6. Formerly the title of a priest. *Spenser.*

SIRE, *n.* [supra.] A father; *used in poetry.*

And raise his issue like a loving *sire*. *Shak.*

2. The male parent of a beast; particularly used of horses; as, the horse had a good *sire*, but a bad dam. *Johnson.*

3. It is used in composition; as in *grandsire*, for grandfather; great *grandsire*, great grandfather.

SIRE, *v. t.* To beget; to procreate; *used of beasts.* *Shak.*

SI'RED, *pp.* Begotten.

SIR'EN, *n.* [L.; Fr. *sirène*; It. *sirena*; from Heb. שור shur, to sing.]

1. A mermaid. In *ancient mythology*, a goddess who enticed men into her power by the charms of music, and devoured them. Hence in modern use, an enticing woman; a female rendered dangerous by her enticements.

Sing, *siren*, to thyself, and I will dote. *Shak.*

2. A species of lizard in Carolina, constituting a peculiar genus, destitute of posterior extremities and pelvis. *Cuvier.*

SIR'EN, *a.* Pertaining to a siren, or to the dangerous enticements of music; bewitching; fascinating; as a *siren* song.

SIRI'ASIS, *n.* [Gr. σιριασις. See *Sirius.*] An inflammation of the brain, proceeding from the excessive heat of the sun; phrensy almost peculiar to children. *Johnson. Coxe.*

SIR'IUS, *n.* [L. from the Gr. σειρ, the sun.] The large and bright star called the dog-star, in the mouth of the constellation Canis major.

SIR'LOIN, *n.* A particular piece of beef so called. [See *Sir.*]

SIRNAME, is more correctly written *surname.*

SIRO, *n.* A mite. *Encyc.*

SIROC'CO, *n.* [It. *id.*; Sp. *siroco* or *xaloque.*]

A pernicious wind that blows from the south east in Italy, called the Syrian wind. It is said to resemble the steam from the mouth of an oven.

SIR'RAH, *n.* A word of reproach and contempt; used in addressing vile characters.

Go, *sirrah*, to my cell. *Shak.*

[I know not whence we have this word. The common derivation of it from *sir*, *ha*, is ridiculous.]

SIRT, *n. sert.* [L. *syrtis.*] A quicksand. [*Not in use.*]

SIRUP, *n. sur'up.* [oriental. See *Sherbet* and *Absorb.*]

The sweet juice of vegetables or fruits, or other juice sweetened; or sugar boiled with vegetable infusions. *Coxe.*

SIR'UPED, *a.* Moistened or tinged with sirup or sweet juice. *Drayton.*

SIR'UPY, *a.* Like sirup, or partaking of its qualities. *Mortimer.*

SISE, for *assize.* [*Not used.*]

SIS'KIN, *n.* A bird, the green finch; another name of the aberdavine. *Johnson. Dict. Nat. Hist.*

The siskin or aberdavine is the *Fringilla spinus*; the green finch, the *Fr. chloris*, a different species. *Ed. Encyc.*

SISS, *v. i.* [D. *sissen*; Dan. *suuser*; G. *sausen*; Sw. *susa*, to buzz, rush, hiss, whistle.]

To hiss; *a legitimate word in universal popular use in New England.*

SIS'TER, *n.* [Sax. *sweoster*; D. *zuster*; G. *schwester*; Sw. *syster*; Dan. *söster*; Russ. *sestra*; Pol. *siostra*; Dalmatian, *szesztre.*]

1. A female born of the same parents; correlative to *brother.*

2. A woman of the same faith; a female fellow christian.

If a brother or *sister* be naked and destitute of daily food— James ii.

3. A female of the same kind. *Shak.*

4. One of the same kind, or of the same condition; as *sister*-fruits. *Pope.*

5. A female of the same society; as the nuns of a convent.

SIS'TER, *v. t.* To resemble closely. [*Little used.*] *Shak.*

SIS'TER, *v. i.* To be akin; to be near to. [*Little used.*] *Shak.*

SIS'TERHOOD, *n.* [*sister* and *hood.*] Sisters collectively, or a society of sisters; or a society of females united in one faith or order. *Addison.*

2. The office or duty of a sister. [*Little used.*]

SISTER-IN-LAW, *n.* A husband's or wife's sister. *Ruth.*

SIS'TERLY, *a.* Like a sister; becoming a sister; affectionate; as *sisterly* kindness.

SIT, *v. i.* pret. *sat*; old pp. *sitten.* [Goth. *sitan*; Sax. *sitan* or *sittan*; D. *zitten*; G. *sitzen*; Sw. *sitta*; Dan. *sidder*; L. *sedeo*; It. *sedere*; Fr. *seoir*, whence *asseoir*, to set or place, to lay, to assess, from the participle of which we have *assise*, *assize*, a sitting, a session, whence *size*, by contraction; W. *seza*, to sit habitually; *sezu*, to seat; *gorsez*, a supreme seat; *gorsezu*, to preside; Arm. *aseza*, *diaseza*, *sizhea*, to sit; Ir. *suidhim*, *eisidhim*, and *seisim*; Corn. *seadha*, to *sit*. It coincides with the Ch. Heb. יסד and Heb. שית to set, place or found, and perhaps with the Ar. سد sadda, to stop, close or make firm. See Class Sd. No. 31. 56. See *Set*. The Sp. *sitiar*, to besiege, is the same word differently applied.]

1. To rest upon the buttocks, as animals; as, to *sit* on a sofa or on the ground.
2. To perch; to rest on the feet; as fowls.
3. To occupy a seat or place in an official capacity.

   The scribes and the Pharisees *sit* in Moses' seat. Matt. xxiii.

4. To be in a state of rest or idleness.

   Shall your brethren go to war, and shall ye *sit* here? Num. xxxii.

5. To rest, lie or bear on, as a weight or burden; as, grief *sits* heavy on his heart.
6. To settle; to rest; to abide.

   Pale horror *sat* on each Arcadian face. *Dryden.*

7. To incubate; to cover and warm eggs for hatching; as a fowl.

   As the partridge *sitteth* on eggs and hatcheth them not— Jer. xvii.

8. To be adjusted; to be, with respect to fitness or unfitness; as, a coat *sits* well or ill.

   This new and gorgeous garment, majesty,
   Sits not so easy on me as you think. *Shak.*

9. To be placed in order to be painted; as, to *sit* for one's picture.
10. To be in any situation or condition.

    Suppose all the church lands to be thrown up to the laity; would the tenants *sit* easier in their rents than now? *Swift.*

11. To hold a session; to be officially engaged in public business; as judges, legislators or officers of any kind. The house of commons sometimes *sits* till late at night. The judges or the courts *sit* in Westminster hall. The commissioners *sit* every day.
12. To exercise authority; as, to *sit* in judgment. One council *sits* upon life and death.
13. To be in any assembly or council as a member; to have a seat. 1 Macc.
14. To be in a local position. The wind *sits* fair. [*Unusual.*]

To sit at meat, to be at table for eating.

To sit down, to place one's self on a chair or other seat; as, to *sit down* at a meal.

2. To begin a siege. The enemy *sat down* before the town.
3. To settle; to fix a permanent abode. *Spenser.*
4. To rest; to cease as satisfied.

   Here we cannot *sit down*, but still proceed in our search. *Rogers.*

To sit out, to be without engagement or employment. [*Little used.*] *Saunderson.*

To sit up, to rise or be raised from a recumbent posture.

   He that was dead *sat up*, and began to speak. Luke vii.

2. Not to go to bed; as, to *sit up* late at night; also, to watch; as, to *sit up* with a sick person.

SIT, *v. t.* To keep the seat upon. He *sits* a horse well. [*This phrase is elliptical.*]

2. To *sit me* down, to *sit him* down, to *sit them* down, equivalent to I *seated myself*, &c. are familiar phrases used by good writers, though deviations from strict propriety.

   They *sat them* down to weep. *Milton.*

3. "The court *was sat*," an expression of Addison, is a gross impropriety.

SITE, *n.* [L. *situs*, Eng. *seat*; from the root of L. *sedeo*, to *sit*. The Roman pronunciation was *seetus*.]

1. Situation; local position; as the *site* of a city or of a house.
2. A seat or ground-plot; as a mill-*site*. But we usually say, mill-*seat*, by which we understand the place where a mill stands, or a place convenient for a mill.
3. The posture of a thing with respect to itself.

   The semblance of a lover fix'd
   In melancholy *site*. *Thomson.*

   [*This is improper.*]

SI'TED, *a.* Placed; situated. [*Not in use.*] *Spenser.*

SIT'FAST, *n.* A hard knob growing on a horse's back under the saddle. *Far. Dict.*

SITH, *adv.* [Sax. *sith*, *siththan.*] Since; in later times. *Obs.* *Spenser.*

SITHE, *n.* Time. *Obs.* *Spenser.*

SITHE. [See *Sythe.*]

SITH'ENCE, / **SITH'ES,** } *adv.* [Sax. *siththan.*] Since; in later times. *Obs.* *Spenser.*

SIT'TER, *n.* [from *sit.*] One that sits. The Turks are great *sitters*. *Bacon.*

2. A bird that sits or incubates. *Mortimer.*

SIT'TING, *ppr.* Resting on the buttocks, or on the feet, as fowls; incubating; brooding; being in the actual exercise of authority, or being assembled for that purpose.

2. *a.* In *botany*, sessile.

SIT'TING, *n.* The posture of being on a seat.

2. The act of placing one's self on a seat; as a *sitting* down.
3. The act or time of resting in a posture for a painter to take the likeness. For a portrait, six or seven *sittings* may be required.
4. A session; the actual presence or meeting of any body of men in their seats, clothed with authority to transact business; as a *sitting* of the judges of the king's bench; a *sitting* of the house of commons; during the *sitting* of the supreme court.
5. An uninterrupted application to business or study for a time; course of study unintermitted.

   For the understanding of any one of Paul's epistles, I read it through at one *sitting*. *Locke.*

6. A time for which one sits, as at play, at work or on a visit. *Dryden.*
7. Incubation; a resting on eggs for hatching; as fowls.

   The male bird amuses the female with his songs, during the whole time of her *sitting*. *Addison.*

SIT'UATE, *a.* [Fr. *situer*; It. *situare*, *situato*; Sp. *situar*; from L. *situs*, *sedeo.*]

1. Placed, with respect to any other object; as a town *situate* on a hill or on the sea shore.
2. Placed; consisting.

   Pleasure *situate* in hill and dale. *Milton.*

[*Note.* In the United States, this word is less used than *situated*, but both are well authorized.]

SIT'UATED, *a.* [See *Situate.*] Seated, placed or standing with respect to any other object; as a city *situated* on a declivity, or in front of a lake; a town well *situated* for trade or manufactures; an observatory well *situated* for observation of the stars. New York is *situated* in the forty first degree of N. latitude.

2. Placed or being in any state or condition with regard to men or things. Observe how the executor is *situated* with respect to the heirs.

SITUA'TION, *n.* [Fr.; It. *situazione.*] Position; seat; location in respect to something else. The *situation* of London is more favorable for foreign commerce than that of Paris. The *situation* of a stranger among people of habits differing from his own, cannot be pleasant.

2. State; condition. He enjoys a *situation* of ease and tranquility.
3. Circumstances; temporary state; *used of persons in a dramatic scene.* *Johnson.*
4. Place; office. He has a *situation* in the war department, or under government.

SIV'AN, *n.* The third month of the Jewish ecclesiastical year, answering to part of our May and part of June.

SIX, *a.* [Fr. *six*; L. *sex*; It. *sei*; Sp. *seis*; D. *zes*; G. *sechs*; Dan. Sw. *sex*; Sax. *six*; Gr. ἕξ. Qu. Sans. *shashta*, Heb. שש shish.] Twice three; one more than five.

SIX, *n.* The number of six or twice three.

To be at six and seven, or as more generally used, *at sixes and sevens*, is to be in disorder. *Bacon.* *Swift.* *Shak.*

SIX'FOLD, *a.* [*six* and *fold*; Sax. *six* and *feald.*] Six times repeated; six double; six times as much.

SIX'PENCE, *n.* [*six* and *pence.*] An English silver coin of the value of six pennies; half a shilling.

2. The value of six pennies or half a shilling.

SIX'-PENNY, *a.* Worth sixpence; as a *six-penny* loaf.

SIX'-PETALED, *a.* In *botany*, having six distinct petals or flower leaves. *Martyn.*

SIX'SCORE, *a.* [*six* and *score.*] Six times twenty; one hundred and twenty. *Sandys.*

SIX'TEEN, *a.* [Sax. *sixtene*, *sixtyne.*] Six and ten; noting the sum of six and ten.

SIX'TEENTH, *a.* [Sax. *sixteotha.*] The sixth after the tenth; the ordinal of sixteen.

SIXTH, *a.* [Sax. *sixta.*] The first after the fifth; the ordinal of six.

SIXTH, *n.* The sixth part.

2. In *music*, a hexachord, an interval of two kinds; the minor sixth, consisting of three tones and two semitones major, and the major sixth, composed of four tones and a major semitone. *Rousseau.*

SIXTH'LY, *adv.* In the sixth place. *Bacon.*

SIX'TIETH, *a.* [Sax. *sixteogotha.*] The ordinal of sixty.

SIX'TY, *a.* [Sax. *sixtig.*] Ten times six.

SIX'TY, *n.* The number of six times ten.

SI′ZABLE, *a.* [from *size.*] Of considerable bulk. *Hurd.*

2. Being of reasonable or suitable size; as *sizable* timber.

SIZE, *n.* [either contracted from *assize*, or from the L. *scissus.* I take it to be from the former, and from the sense of setting, as we apply the word to the *assize* of bread.]

1. Bulk; bigness; magnitude; extent of superficies. Size particularly expresses thickness; as the *size* of a tree or of a mast; the *size* of a ship or of a rock. A man may be tall, with little *size* of body.

2. A settled quantity or allowance. [contracted from *assize.*]

3. Figurative bulk; condition as to rank and character; as men of less *size* and quality. [*Not much used.*] *L'Estrange.*

SIZE, *n.* [W. *syth*, stiff, rigid, and *size*; Sp. *sisa*; from the root of *assize*, that which sets or fixes.]

1. A glutinous substance prepared from different materials; used in manufactures.

2. An instrument consistiug of thin leaves fastened together at one end by a rivet; used for ascertaining the size of pearls. *Encyc.*

SIZE, *v. t.* To adjust or arrange according to size or bulk. *Hudibras.*

2. To settle; to fix the standard of; as, to *size* weights and measures. [*Now little used.*]

3. To cover with size; to prepare with size.

4. To swell; to increase the bulk of. *Beaum. and Fletcher.*

5. Among Cornish miners, to separate the finer from the coarser parts of a metal by sifting them through a wire sieve. *Encyc.*

SI′ZED, *pp.* Adjusted according to size; prepared with size.

2. *a.* Having a particular magnitude.

And as my love is siz'd my fear is so. *Shak.*

[*Note.*—This word is used in compounds; as large-*sized*, common-*sized*, middle-*sized*, &c.]

SIZ′EL, *n.* In *coining*, the residue of bars of silver, after pieces are cut out for coins.

SI′ZER, *n.* In *the university of Cambridge*, a student of the rank next below that of a pensioner.

SI′ZINESS, *n.* [from *sizy.*] Glutinousness; viscousness; the quality of size; as the *siziness* of blood.

SI′ZY, *a.* [from *size.*] Glutinous; thick and viscous; ropy; having the adhesiveness of size; as *sizy* blood. *Arbuthnot.*

SKAD′DLE, *n.* [Sax. *scath, sceath.*] Hurt; damage. [*Not in use.*]

SKAD′DLE, *a.* Hurtful; mischievous. [*Not in use.*] *Ray.*

SKAD′DONS, *n.* The embryos of bees. [*Not in use.*] *Bailey.*

SKAIN, *n.* [Fr. *escaigne.*] A knot of thread, yarn or silk, or a number of knots collected.

SKA′INSMATE, *n.* A messmate; a companion. [*Not in use.*] *Shak.*

SKALD, *n.* [Qu. Sw. *scalla*, to sing.] An ancient Scandinavian poet or bard.

SKATE, *n.* [D. *schaats*; probably from the root of *shoot*; It. *scatto*, a slip or slide.]

A sort of shoe furnished with a smooth iron for sliding on ice.

SKATE, *v. i.* To slide or move on skates.

SKATE, *n.* [Sax. *sceadda*; L. *squatus, squatina*; W. *câth vor*, or *morgath*, that is, *sea-cat.* This shows that *skate* is formed on *cat.* The primary sense of *cat*, I do not know; but in W. *câth eithen*, is a hare; that is, *furze* or *gorse cat.*]

A fish of the ray kind, (*Raia Batis;*) called the variegated ray-fish. It is a flat fish, the largest and thinnest of the genus, some of them weighing nearly two hundred pounds. *Dict. Nat. Hist.*

SKA′TER, *n.* One who skates on ice. *Johnson.*

SKEAN, *n.* [Sax. *sægen.*] A short sword, or a knife. [*Not in use.*] *Bacon. Spenser.*

SKEED. [See *Skid.*]

SKEEL, *n.* [G. *schale*, Eng. *shell.*] A shallow wooden vessel for holding milk or cream. [*Local.*] *Grose.*

SKEET, *n.* A long scoop used to wet the sides of ships or the sails. *Mar. Dict.*

SKEG, *n.* A sort of wild plum. *Johnson.*

SKEG′GER, *n.* A little salmon. *Walton.*

SKEL′ETON, *n.* [Fr. *squelette*; It. *scheletro*; Sp. *esqueleto*; Gr. σκελετος, dry, from σκελλω, to dry, that is, to contract; allied perhaps to L. *calleo, callus.*]

1. The bones of an animal body, separated from the flesh and retained in their natural position or connections. When the bones are connected by the natural ligaments, it is called a *natural* skeleton; when by wires, or any foreign substance, an *artificial* skeleton. *Encyc. Wistar.*

2. The compages, general structure or frame of any thing; the principal parts that support the rest, but without the appendages.

3. A very thin or lean person.

SKEL′LUM, *n.* [G. *schelm.*] A scoundrel. [*Not in use.*]

SKEP, *n.* A sort of basket, narrow at the bottom and wide at the top. [*Not used in America.*] *Tusser.*

2. In *Scotland*, the repository in which bees lay their honey. *Johnson.*

SKEPTIC. [See *Sceptic.*]

SKETCH, *n.* [D. *schets*; G. *skizze*; Fr. *esquisse*; Sp. *esquicio*; It. *schizzo*, a sketch, a squirting, a spurt, a gushing, a leap, hop or frisking; *schizzare*, to squirt, to spin, stream or spout. We see the primary sense of the verb is to throw, the sense of *shoot*, It. *scattare*, L. *scateo.*]

An outline or general delineation of any thing; a first rough or incomplete draught of a plan or any design; as the *sketch* of a building; the *sketch* of an essay.

SKETCH, *v. t.* To draw the outline or general figure of a thing; to make a rough draught. *Watts.*

2. To plan by giving the principal points or ideas. *Dryden.*

SKETCH′ED, *pp.* Having the outline drawn.

SKETCH′ING, *ppr.* Drawing the outline.

SKEW, *adv.* [G. *schief*; Dan. *skiæv.*] Awry; obliquely. [See *Askew.*]

SKEW, *v. t.* [Dan. *skiæver*, to twist or distort.]

1. To look obliquely upon; to notice slightly. [*Not in use.*] *Beaum.*

2. To shape or form in an oblique way. [*Not in use.*]

SKEW, *v. i.* To walk obliquely. [*Local.*]

SKEW′ER, *n.* A pin of wood or iron for fastening meat to a spit, or for keeping it in form while roasting. *Dryden.*

SKEW′ER, *v. t.* To fasten with skewers.

SKID, *n.* A curving timber to preserve a ship's side from injury by heavy bodies hoisted or lowered against it; a slider. *Mar. Dict.*

2. A chain used for fastening the wheel of a wagon, to prevent its turning when descending a steep hill. *Encyc.*

SKIFF, *n.* [Fr. *esquif*; It. *schifo*; Sp. *esquifo*; L. *scapha*; G. *schiff*; from the same root as *ship.*]

A small light boat resembling a yawl. *Mar. Dict.*

SKIFF, *v. t.* To pass over in a light boat.

SKILL, *n.* [Sax. *scylan*, to separate, to distinguish; Ice. Sw. *skilia*, Dan. *skiller*, to divide, sever, part; whence *shield*, that which separates, and hence that which protects or defends; D. *scheelen*, to differ; *schillen*, to peel or pare. *Scale* is from the root of these words, as in *shell*, Sax. *scyl*, *sceal.* In Heb. סכל is foolish, perverse, and as a verb, to pervert, to be foolish or perverse; in Ch. to understand or consider, to look, to regard, to cause to know, whence knowledge, knowing, wise, wisdom, understanding; Rab. to be ignorant or foolish; Syr. to be foolish, to wander in mind, also to cause to understand, to know, to perceive, to discern, also to err, to do wrong, to sin, to fail in duty; whence foolish, folly, ignorance, error, sin, and understanding: Sam. to be wont or accustomed, to look or behold. The same verb with ש, Heb. שכל signifies to understand, to be wise, whence wisdom, understanding, also to waste, to scatter or destroy, to bereave, also to prosper; Ch. to understand; שכלל to complete, to perfect; כלל with a prefix. This signifies also to found, to lay a foundation; Syr. to found, also to finish, complete, adorn, from the same root; Ar. شَكَلَ shakala, to bind or tie, whence Eng. *shackles*; also to be dark, obscure, intricate, difficult, to form, to make like, to be of a beautiful form, to know, to be ignorant, to agree, suit or become. These verbs appear to be formed on the root כל, כול to hold or restrain, which coincides in signification with the Ch. Eth. כהל to be able, L. *calleo*, that is, to strain, stretch, reach, and with כלל to perfect, that is, to make sound, or to reach the utmost limit. The sense of folly, error, sin, perverseness, is from wandering, deviation, Gr. σκολιος; the sense of *skill* and understanding is from separation, discernment, or from taking, holding or reaching to, for strength and knowledge are allied, and often from tension. The sense of ignorance and error is from wandering or deviation, or perhaps it proceeds from a negative sense given to the primary verb by the prefix, like *ex* in Latin, and *s* in Italian. The Arabic sense of binding and shackles is from straining. The Eng. *shall* and *should* belong to this family.]

1. The familiar knowledge of any art or science, united with readiness and dexterity in execution or performance, or in the application of the art or science to practical purposes. Thus we speak of the *skill* of a mathematician, of a surveyor, of a physician or surgeon, of a mechanic or seaman. So we speak of *skill* in management or negotiation. *Dryden. Swift.*

2. Any particular art. [*Not in use.*] *Hooker.*

SKILL, *v. t.* To know; to understand. *Obs.*

SKILL, *v. i.* To be knowing in; to be dextrous in performance. *Obs. Spenser.*

2. To differ; to make difference; to matter or be of interest. *Obs. Hooker. Bacon.*

[*This is the Teutonic and Gothic sense of the word.*]

SKILL'ED, *a.* Having familiar knowledge united with readiness and dexterity in the application of it; familiarly acquainted with; followed by *in*; as a professor *skilled in* logic or geometry; one *skilled in* the art of engraving.

SKIL'LESS, *a.* Wanting skill; artless. [*Not in use.*] *Shak.*

SKIL'LET, *n.* [Qu. Fr. *ecuelle, ecuellette.*] A small vessel of iron, copper or other metal, with a long handle; used for heating and boiling water and other culinary purposes.

SKILL'FUL, *a.* Knowing; well versed in any art; hence, dextrous; able in management; able to perform nicely any manual operation in the arts or professions; as a *skillful* mechanic; a *skillful* operator in surgery.

2. Well versed in practice; as a *skillful* physician.

It is followed by *at* or *in*; as *skillful at* the organ; *skillful in* drawing.

SKILL'FULLY, *adv.* With skill; with nice art; dextrously; as a machine *skillfully* made; a ship *skillfully* managed.

SKILL'FULNESS, *n.* The quality of possessing skill; dextrousness; ability to perform well in any art or business, or to manage affairs with judgment and exactness, or according to good taste or just rules; knowledge and ability derived from experience.

SKIL'LING, *n.* An isle or bay of a barn; also. a slight addition to a cottage. [*Local.*]

SKILT, *n.* [See *Skill.*] Difference. *Obs. Cleaveland.*

SKIM, *n.* [a different orthography of *scum*; Fr. *ecume*; It. *schiuma*; G. *schaum*; D. *schuim*; Dan. Sw. *skum*; Ir. *sgeimhim*, to skim.] Scum; the thick matter that forms on the surface of a liquor. [*Little used.*]

SKIM, *v. t.* To take off the thick gross matter which separates from any liquid substance and collects on the surface; as, to *skim* milk by taking off the cream.

2. To take off by skimming; as, to *skim* cream. *Dryden.*

3. To pass near the surface; to brush the surface slightly.

The swallow *skims* the river's wat'ry face. *Dryden.*

SKIM, *v. i.* To pass lightly; to glide along in an even smooth course, or without flapping; as, an eagle or hawk *skims* along the etherial regions.

2. To glide along near the surface; to pass lightly. *Pope.*

3. To hasten over superficially or with slight attention.

They *skim* over a science in a superficial survey. *Watts.*

SKIMBLE-SCAMBLE, *a.* [a duplication of *scamble.*] Wandering; disorderly. [*A low unauthorized word.*] *Shak.*

SKIM'-COULTER, *n.* A coulter for paring off the surface of land.

SKIM'MED, *pp.* Taken from the surface; having the thick matter taken from the surface; brushed along.

SKIM'MER, *n.* An utensil in the form of a scoop; used for skimming liquors.

2. One that skims over a subject. [*Little used.*]

3. A sea fowl, the cut-water, (*Rhyncops nigra.*)

SKIM'-MILK, *n.* Milk from which the cream has been taken.

SKIM'MINGS, *n. plu.* Matter skimmed from the surface of liquors. *Edwards, W. Indies.*

SKIN, *n.* [Sax. *scin*; Sw. *skinn*; Dan. *skind*, a skin; G. *schinden*, to flay; Ir. *scann*, a membrane; W. *ysgin*, a robe made of skin, a pelisse, said to be from *cin*, a spread or covering. But in Welsh, *cèn* is a skin, peel or rind. This may signify a covering, or a peel, from stripping.]

1. The natural covering of animal bodies, consisting of the cuticle or scarf-skin, the rete mucosum, and the cutis or hide. The cuticle is very thin and insensible; the cutis is thicker and very sensible. *Harvey.*

2. A hide; a pelt; the skin of an animal separated from the body, whether green, dry or tanned.

3. The body; the person; *in ludicrous language.* *L'Estrange.*

4. The bark or husk of a plant; the exterior coat of fruits and plants.

SKIN, *v. t.* To strip off the skin or hide; to flay; to peel. *Ellis.*

2. To cover with skin. *Dryden.*

3. To cover superficially. *Addison.*

SKIN, *v. i.* To be covered with skin; as, a wound *skins* over.

SKIN'DEEP, *a.* Superficial; not deep; slight. *Feltham.*

SKIN'FLINT, *n.* [*skin* and *flint.*] A very niggardly person.

SKINK, *n.* [Sax. *scenc.*] Drink; pottage. *Obs. Bacon.*

2. [L. *scincus.*] A small lizard of Egypt; also, the common name of a genus of lizards, with a long body entirely covered with rounded imbricate scales, all natives of warm climates. *Ed. Encyc.*

SKINK, *v. i.* [Sax. *scencan*; G. D. *schenken*; Dan. *skienker*; Sw. *skånka*; Ice. *skenkia*, to bestow, to make a present.] To serve drink. *Obs.*

SKINK'ER, *n.* One that serves liquors. *Obs. Shak.*

SKIN'LESS, *a.* [from *skin.*] Having a thin skin; as *skinless* fruit.

SKIN'NED, *pp.* Stripped of the skin; flayed.

2. Covered with skin.

SKIN'NER, *n.* One that skins.

2. One that deals in skins, pelts or hides.

SKIN'NINESS, *n.* The quality of being skinny.

SKIN'NY, *a.* Consisting of skin, or of skin only; wanting flesh. *Ray. Addison.*

SKIP, *v. i.* [Dan. *kipper*, to leap; Ice. *skopa.*] To leap; to bound; to spring; as a goat or lamb.

The lamb thy riot dooms to bleed to-day,
Had he thy reason, would he *skip* and play? *Pope.*

To skip over, to pass without notice; to omit. *Bacon.*

SKIP, *v. t.* To pass over or by; to omit; to miss.

They who have a mind to see the issue, may *skip* these two chapters. *Burnet.*

SKIP, *n.* A leap; a bound; a spring. *Sidney.*

SKIP'-JACK, *n.* An upstart. *L'Estrange.*

SKIP'-KENNEL, *n.* A lackey; a footboy.

SKIP'PER, *n.* [Dan. *skipper*; D. *schipper.* See *Ship.*] The master of a small trading vessel.

2. [from *skip.*] A dancer.

3. A youngling; a young thoughtless person. *Shak.*

4. The hornfish, so called.

5. The cheese maggot.

SKIP'PET, *n.* [See *Ship* and *Skiff.*] A small boat. [*Not in use.*] *Spenser.*

SKIP'PING, *ppr.* Leaping; bounding.

Skipping notes, in music, are notes that are not in regular course, but separate.

SKIP'PINGLY, *adv.* By leaps.

SKIRMISH, *n. skur'mish.* [Fr. *escarmouche*; It. *scaramuccia*; Sp. *escaramuza*; Port. *escaramuça*; G. *scharmützel*; D. *schermutseling*; Sw. *skårmytsel*; Dan. *skiermydsel*; W. *ysgarm*, outcry; *ysgarmu*, to shout; *ysgarmes*, a shouting, a skirmish; from *garm*, a shout. The primary sense is to throw or drive. In some of the languages, *skirmish* appears to be connected with a word signifying *defense*; but defense is from driving, repelling.]

1. A slight fight in war; a light combat by armies at a great distance from each other, or between detachments and small parties.

2. A contest; a contention.

They never meet but there's a *skirmish* of wit. *Shak.*

SKIRM'ISH, *v. i.* To fight slightly or in small parties.

SKIRM'ISHER, *n.* One that skirmishes.

SKIRM'ISHING, *ppr.* Fighting slightly or in detached parties.

SKIRM'ISHING, *n.* The act of fighting in a loose or slight encounter.

SKIRR, *v. t.* To scour; to ramble over in order to clear. [*Not in use.*] *Shak.*

SKIRR, *v. i.* To scour; to scud; to run hastily. [*Not in use.*] *Shak.*

SKIR'RET, *n.* A plant of the genus Sium. *Lee. Mortimer.*

SKIR'RUS. [See *Scirrhus.*]

SKIRT, *n. skurt.* [Sw. *skiorta*, a shift or close garment; Dan. *skiort*, a petticoat; *skiorte*, a *shirt*, a shift. These words seem to be from the root of *short*, from cutting off.]

1. The lower and loose part of a coat or other garment; the part below the waist; as the *skirt* of a coat or mantle. 1 Sam. xv.

2. The edge of any part of dress. *Addison.*
3. Border ; edge ; margin ; extreme part ; as the *skirt* of a forest ; the *skirt* of a town. *Dryden.*
4. A woman's garment like a petticoat.
5. The diaphragm or midriff in animals.
To spread the skirt over, in Scripture, to take under one's care and protection. Ruth iii.

SKIRT, *v. t.* To border ; to form the border or edge ; or to run along the edge ; as a plain *skirted* by rows of trees ; a circuit *skirted* round with wood. *Addison.*

SKIRT, *v. i.* To be on the border ; to live near the extremity.

Savages—who *skirt* along our western frontiers. *S. S. Smith.*

SKIRT'ED, *pp.* Bordered.

SKIRT'ING, *ppr.* Bordering ; forming a border.

SKIT, *n.* A wanton girl ; a reflection ; a jeer or jibe ; a whim. *Obs.*

SKIT, *v. t.* [Sax. *scitan* ; primarily to throw, to *shoot.*] To cast reflections. [*Local.*] *Grose.*

SKIT'TISH, *a.* [Qu. Fr. *ecouteux.* See *Scud.*]
1. Shy ; easily frightened ; shunning familiarity ; timorous ; as a restif *skittish* jade. *L'Estrange.*
2. Wanton ; volatile ; hasty. *Shak.*
3. Changeable ; fickle ; as *skittish* fortune. *Shak.*

SKIT'TISHLY, *adv.* Shyly ; wantonly ; changeably.

SKIT'TISHNESS, *n.* Shyness ; aptness to fear approach ; timidity.
2. Fickleness ; wantonness.

SKIT'TLES, *n.* Nine pins. *Warton.*

SKOL'EZITE, *n.* A mineral allied to Thomsonite, occurring crystalized and massive, colorless and nearly transparent. When a small portion of it is placed in the exterior flame of the blowpipe, it twists like a worm, [σχωληξ,] becomes opake, and is converted into a blebby colorless glass. *Phillips.*

SKONCE. [See *Sconce.*]

SKOR'ADITE, *n.* [Gr. σχοροδων, garlic ; from its smell under the blowpipe.]
A mineral of a greenish color of different shades, or brown and nearly black, resembling the martial arseniate of copper. It occurs massive, but generally crystalized in rectangular prisms. *Ure. Phillips.*

SKREEN. [See *Screen.*]

SKRINĠE, properly *scringe* ; a vulgar corruption of *cringe.*

SKUE. [See *Skew.*]

SKUG, *v. t.* To hide. [*Local.*]

SKULK, *v. i.* To lurk ; to withdraw into a corner or into a close place for concealment. [See *Sculk.*]

SKULL, *n.* [Sw. *skalle*, skull ; *skal*, a shell ; Dan. *skal*, a shell, the skull, and *skoll*, the skull ; D. *scheel* ; G. *hirn-schale*, brainshell ; Sp. *cholla.* See *Shell.*]
1. The bone that forms the exterior of the head, and incloses the brain ; the brainpan. It is composed of several parts united at the sutures.
2. A person.

Skulls that cannot teach and will not learn. *Cowper.*

3. Skull, for *shoal* or *school*, of fish. [*Not used.*]

SKULL'-ĊAP, *n.* A head piece.
2. A plant of the genus Scutellaria. *Encyc.*

SKUNK, *n.* In America, the popular name of a fetid animal of the weasel kind ; the Viverra Mephitis of Linne.

SKUNK'ĊABBAĠE, } *n.* A plant vulgarly
SKUNK'WEED, } so called, the *Tetodes fœtidus*, so named from its smell. *Bigelow.*

SKUTE, *n.* A boat. [See *Scow.*]

SKȲ, *n.* [Sw. *sky*, Dan. *skye*, a cloud ; Dan. *sky-himmel*, the vault of heaven.]
1. The aerial region which surrounds the earth ; the apparent arch or vault of heaven, which in a clear day is of a blue color. *Milton.*
2. The heavens. *Dryden.*
3. The weather ; the climate. *Johnson.*
4. A cloud ; a shadow. *Obs.* *Gower.*

SKY'-ĈŎLOR, *n.* The color of the sky ; a particular species of blue color ; azure. *Boyle.*

SKY'-ĈŎLORED, *a.* Like the sky in color ; blue ; azure. *Addison.*

SKY'-DȲED, *a.* Colored like the sky. *Pope.*

SKY'EY, *a.* Like the sky ; etherial. *Shak.*

SKY'ISH, *a.* Like the sky, or approaching the sky.

The *skyish* head
Of blue Olympus. [*A bad word.*] *Shak.*

SKY'-L'ARK, *n.* A lark that mounts and sings as it flies. (*Alauda arvensis.*) *Spectator.*

SKY'-LIGHT, *n.* A window placed in the top of a house or ceiling of a room for the admission of light. *Pope.*

SKY'-ROCKET, *n.* A rocket that ascends high and burns as it flies ; a species of fire works. *Addison.*

SLAB, *a.* Thick ; viscous. [*Not used.*] *Shak.*

SLAB, *n.* [W. *llab*, *yslab*, a thin strip.] A plane or table of stone ; as a marble *slab.*
2. An outside piece taken from timber in sawing it into boards, planks, &c.
3. A puddle. [See *Slop.*] *Evelyn.*
Slabs of tin, the lesser masses which the workers cast the metal into. These are run into molds of stone.

SLAB'BER, *v. i.* [D. *slabben* ; G. *schlabben*, *schlabern.*]
To let the saliva or other liquid fall from the mouth carelessly ; to drivel. It is also written *slaver.*

SLAB'BER, *v. t.* To sup up hastily, as liquid food. *Barret.*
2. To wet and foul by liquids suffered to fall carelessly from the mouth.
3. To shed ; to spill.

SLAB'BERER, *n.* One that slabbers ; an idiot.

SLAB'BERING, *ppr.* Driveling.

SLAB'BY, *a.* Thick ; viscous. [*Not much used.*] *Wiseman.*
2. Wet. [See *Sloppy.*]

SLAB'-LINE, *n.* A line or small rope by which seamen truss up the main-sail or fore-sail. *Mar. Dict.*

SLACK, *a.* [Sax. *slæc* ; Sw. *slak* ; W. *llac*, *yslac.* See the Verb.]
1. Not tense ; not hard drawn ; not firmly extended ; as a *slack* rope ; *slack* rigging ; *slack* shrouds.
2. Weak ; remiss ; not holding fast ; as a *slack* hand.
3. Remiss ; backward ; not using due diligence ; not earnest or eager ; as *slack* in duty or service ; *slack* in business.
4. Not violent ; not rapid ; slow ; as a *slack* pace. *Dryden.*
Slack in stays, in seamen's language, slow in going about ; as a ship. *Mar. Dict.*
Slack water, in seamen's language, the time when the tide runs slowly, or the water is at rest ; or the interval between the flux and reflux of the tide. *Mar. Dict.*

SLACK, *adv.* Partially ; insufficiently ; not intensely ; as *slack* dried hops ; bread *slack* baked. *Mortimer.*

SLACK, *n.* The part of a rope that hangs loose, having no stress upon it. *Mar. Dict.*

SLACK, } *v. i.* [Sax. *slacian* ; D.
SLACK'EN, } *slaaken* ; Sw. *slakna* ; W. *yslacâu* and *yslaciaw*, to slacken, to loosen, from *llac*, *llag*, slack, loose, lax, *sluggish.*]
1. To become less tense, firm or rigid ; to decrease in tension ; as, a wet cord *slackens* in dry weather.
2. To be remiss or backward ; to neglect. Deut. xxiii.
3. To lose cohesion or the quality of adhesion ; as, lime *slacks* and crumbles into powder. *Moxon.*
4. To abate ; to become less violent.

Whence these raging fires
Will *slacken*, if his breath stir not their flames. *Milton.*

5. To lose rapidity ; to become more slow ; as, a current of water *slackens* ; the tide *slackens.* *Mar. Dict.*
6. To languish ; to fail ; to flag. *Ainsworth.*

SLACK, } *v. t.* To lessen tension ; to
SLACK'EN, } make less tense or tight ; as, to *slacken* a rope or a bandage.
2. To relax ; to remit ; as, to *slacken* exertion or labor.
3. To mitigate ; to diminish in severity ; as, to *slacken* pain.
4. To become more slow ; to lessen rapidity ; as, to *slacken* one's pace.
5. To abate ; to lower ; as, to *slacken* the heat of a fire.
6. To relieve ; to unbend ; to remit ; as, to *slacken* cares. *Denham.*
7. To withhold ; to use less liberally. *Shak.*
8. To deprive of cohesion ; as, to *slack* lime. *Mortimer.*
9. To repress ; to check.

I should be griev'd, young prince, to think my presence
Unbent your thoughts and *slacken'd* 'em to arms. *Addison.*

10. To neglect.

Slack not the good presage. *Dryden.*

11. To repress, or make less quick or active. *Addison.*

SLACK, *n.* Small coal ; coal broken into small parts. *Eng.*

SLACK, *n.* A valley or small shallow dell. [*Local.*] *Grose.*

SLACK'EN, *n.* Among miners, a spungy semi-vitrified substance which they mix with the ores of metals to prevent their fusion. *Encyc.*

SLACK'LY, *adv.* Not tightly; loosely.
2. Negligently; remissly.

SLACK'NESS, *n.* Looseness; the state opposite to tension; not tightness or rigidness; as the *slackness* of a cord or rope.
2. Remissness; negligence; inattention; as the *slackness* of men in business or duty; *slackness* in the performance of engagements. *Hooker.*
3. Slowness; tardiness; want of tendency; as the *slackness* of flesh to heal. *Sharp.*
4. Weakness; not intenseness. *Brerewood.*

SLADE, *n.* [Sax. *slæd.*] A little dell or valley; also, a flat piece of low moist ground. [*Local.*] *Drayton.*

SLAG, *n.* [Dan. *slagg.*] The dross or recrement of a metal; or vitrified cinders. *Boyle. Kirwan.*

SLAIE, *n. sla.* [Sax. *slæ.*] A weaver's reed.

SLAIN, *pp.* of *slay;* so written for *slayen.* Killed.

SLAKE, *v. t.* [Sw. *slăcka,* Ice. *slæcka,* to quench. It seems to be allied to *lay.*] To quench; to extinguish; as, to *slake* thirst.

And *slake* the heav'nly fire. *Spenser.*

SLAKE, *v. i.* To go out; to become extinct. *Brown.*
2 To grow less tense. [a mistake for *slack.*]

SLAM, *v. t.* [Ice. *lema,* to strike, Old Eng. *lam;* Sax. *hlemman,* to sound.]
1. To strike with force and noise; to shut with violence; as, to *slam* a door.
2. To beat; to cuff. [*Local.*] *Grose.*
3. To strike down; to slaughter. [*Local.*]
4. To win all the tricks in a hand; as we say, to take all at a stroke or dash.

SLAM, *n.* A violent driving and dashing against; a violent shutting of a door.
2. Defeat at cards, or the winning of all the tricks.
3. The refuse of alum-works; used in Yorkshire as a manure, with sea weed and lime. [*Local.*]

SLAM'KIN, SLAM'MERKIN, *n.* [G. *schlampe.*] A slut; a slatternly woman. [*Not used or local.*]

SLA'NDER, *n.* [Norm. *esclaunder;* Fr. *esclandre;* Russ. *klenu, klianu,* to slander; Sw. *klandra,* to accuse or blame.]
1. A false tale or report maliciously uttered, and tending to injure the reputation of another by lessening him in the esteem of his fellow citizens, by exposing him to impeachment and punishment, or by impairing his means of living; defamation. *Blackstone.*

Slander, that worst of poisons, ever finds
An easy entrance to ignoble minds. *Hervey.*

2. Disgrace; reproach; disreputation; ill name. *Shak.*

SLA'NDER, *v. t.* To defame; to injure by maliciously uttering a false report respecting one; to tarnish or impair the reputation of one by false tales, maliciously told or propagated.

SLA'NDERED, *pp.* Defamed; injured in good name by false and malicious reports.

SLA'NDERER, *n.* A defamer; one who injures another by maliciously reporting something to his prejudice.

SLA'NDERING, *ppr.* Defaming.

SLA'NDEROUS, *a.* That utters defamatory words or tales; as a *slanderous* tongue. *Pope.*
2. Containing slander or defamation; calumnious; as *slanderous* words, speeches or reports, false and maliciously uttered.
3. Scandalous; reproachful.

SL'ANDEROUSLY, *adv.* With slander; calumniously; with false and malicious reproach.

SL'ANDEROUSNESS, *n.* The state or quality of being slanderous or defamatory.

SLANG, *old pret.* of *sling.* We now use *slung.*

SLANG, *n.* Low vulgar unmeaning language. [*Low.*]

SLANK, *n.* A plant. [*alga marina.*] *Ainsworth.*

SL'ANT, SL'ANTING, *a.* [Sw. *slinta, slant,* to slip; perhaps allied to W. *ysglent,* a slide; and if *Ln* are the radical letters, this coincides with *lean, incline.*]
Sloping; oblique; inclined from a direct line, whether horizontal or perpendicular; as a *slanting* ray of light; a *slanting* floor.

SL'ANT, *v. t.* To turn from a direct line; to give an oblique or sloping direction to. *Fuller.*

SL'ANT, *n.* An oblique reflection or gibe; a sarcastic remark. [*In vulgar use.*]
2. A copper coin of Sweden, of which 196 pass for one rix-dollar.

SL'ANTINGLY, *adv.* With a slope or inclination; also, with an oblique hint or remark.

SL'ANTLY, SL'ANTWISE, *adv.* Obliquely; in an inclined direction. *Tusser.*

SLAP, *n.* [G. *schlappe,* a slap; *schlappen,* to lap; W. *yslapiaw,* to slap, from *yslab,* that is lengthened, from *llab,* a stroke or slap; *llabiaw,* to slap, to strap. The D. has *flap* and *klap;* It. *schiaffo,* for *schlaffo;* L. *alapa* and *schloppus;* Ch. Syr. צלף. Class Lb. No. 36.]
A blow given with the open hand, or with something broad.

SLAP, *v. t.* To strike with the open hand, or with something broad.

SLAP, *adv.* With a sudden and violent blow. *Arbuthnot.*

SLAP'DASH, *adv.* [*slap* and *dash.*] All at once. [*Low.*]

SLAPE, *a.* Slippery; smooth. [*Local.*] *Grose.*

SLAP'PER, SLAP'PING, *a.* Very large. [*Vulgar.*]

SLASH, *v. t.* [Ice. *slasa,* to strike, to *lash;* W. *llâth.* Qu.]
1. To cut by striking violently and at random; to cut in long cuts.
2. To lash.

SLASH, *v. i.* To strike violently and at random with a sword, hanger or other edged instrument; to lay about one with blows.

Hewing and *slashing* at their idle shades. *Spenser.*

SLASH, *n.* A long cut; a cut made at random. *Clarendon.*

SLASH'ED, *pp.* Cut at random.

SLASH'ING, *ppr.* Striking violently and cutting at random.

SLAT, *n.* [This is doubtless the *sloat* of the English dictionaries. See *Sloat.*]
A narrow piece of board or timber used to fasten together larger pieces; as the *slats* of a cart or a chair.

SLATCH, *n.* In *seamen's language,* the period of a transitory breeze. *Mar. Dict.*
2. An interval of fair weather. *Bailey.*
3. Slack. [See *Slack.*]

SLATE, *n.* [Fr. *eclater,* to split, Sw. *slita;* Ir. *sglata,* a tile. Class Ld.]
1. An argillaceous stone which readily splits into plates; argillite; argillaceous shist.
2. A piece of smooth argillaceous stone, used for covering buildings.
3. A piece of smooth stone of the above species, used for writing on.

SLATE, *v. t.* To cover with slate or plates of stone; as, to *slate* a roof. [It does not signify to *tile.*]

SLATE, SLETE, *v. t.* To set a dog loose at any thing. [*Local.*] *Ray.*

SLA'TE-AX, *n.* A mattock with an ax-end; used in slating. *Encyc.*

SLA'TED, *pp.* Covered with slate.

SLA'TER, *n.* One that lays slates, or whose occupation is to slate buildings.

SLA'TING, *ppr.* Covering with slates.

SLAT'TER, *v. i.* [G. *schlottern,* to hang loosely; *schlotterig,* negligent. See *Slut.*]
1. To be careless of dress and dirty. *Ray.*
2. To be careless, negligent or awkward; to spill carelessly.

SLAT'TERN, *n.* A woman who is negligent of her dress, or who suffers her clothes and furniture to be in disorder; one who is not neat and nice.

SLAT'TERN, *v. t.* To *slattern away,* to consume carelessly or wastefully; to waste. [*Unusual.*] *Chesterfield.*

SLAT'TERNLY, *adv.* Negligently; awkwardly. *Chesterfield.*

SLA'TY, *a.* [from *slate.*] Resembling slate; having the nature or properties of slate; as a *slaty* color or texture; a *slaty* feel.

SLAUGHTER, *n. slaw'ter.* [Sax. *slæge;* D. *slagting;* G. *schlachten,* to kill; Ir. *slaighe; slaighim,* to slay. See *Slay.*]
1. In *a general sense,* a killing. *Applied to men,* slaughter usually denotes great destruction of life by violent means; as the *slaughter* of men in battle.
2. *Applied to beasts,* butchery; a killing of oxen or other beasts for market.

SLAUGHTER, *v. t. slaw'ter.* To kill; to slay; to make great destruction of life; as, to *slaughter* men in battle.
2. To butcher; to kill for the market; as beasts.

SLAUGHTERED, *pp. slaw'tered.* Slain; butchered.

SLAUGHTER-HOUSE, *n. slaw'ter-house.* A house where beasts are butchered for the market.

SLAUGHTERING, *ppr. slaw'tering.* Killing; destroying human life; butchering.

SLAUGHTER-MAN, *n. slaw'ter-man.* One employed in killing. *Shak.*

SLAUGHTEROUS, *a. slaw'terous.* Destructive; murderous. *Shak.*

SLAVE, *n.* [D. *slaaf;* G. *sclave;* Dan. *slave, sclave;* Sw. *slaf;* Fr. *esclave;* Arm. *sclaff;* It. *schiavo;* Sp. *esclavo;* Port. *escravo;* Ir. *sclabhadh.* This word is commonly deduced from *Sclavi, Sclavonians,* the name of a people who were made slaves by the Venetians. But this is not certain.]
1. A person who is wholly subject to the will of another; one who has no will of his own, but whose person and services are wholly under the control of another. In the early state of the world, and to this day among some barbarous nations, pris-

oners of war are considered and treated as *slaves*. The *slaves* of modern times are more generally purchased, like horses and oxen.
2. One who has lost the power of resistance; or one who surrenders himself to any power whatever; as a *slave* to passion, to lust, to ambition. *Waller.*
3. A mean person; one in the lowest state of life.
4. A drudge; one who labors like a slave.
SLAVE, *v. i.* To drudge; to toil; to labor as a slave.
SLA'VEBORN, *a.* Born in slavery.
SLA'VELIKE, *a.* Like or becoming a slave.
SLAV'ER, *n.* [the same as *slabber.*] Saliva driveling from the mouth. *Pope.*
SLAV'ER, *v. i.* To suffer the spittle to issue from the mouth.
2. To be besmeared with saliva. *Shak.*
SLAV'ER, *v. t.* To smear with saliva issuing from the mouth; to defile with drivel.
SLAV'ERED, *pp.* Defiled with drivel.
SLAV'ERER, *n.* A driveler; an idiot.
SLAV'ERING, *ppr.* Letting fall saliva.
SLA'VERY, *n.* [See *Slave.*] Bondage; the state of entire subjection of one person to the will of another.

Slavery is the obligation to labor for the benefit of the master, without the contract or consent of the servant. *Paley.*

Slavery may proceed from crimes, from captivity or from debt. Slavery is also *voluntary* or *involuntary*; *voluntary*, when a person sells or yields his own person to the absolute command of another; *involuntary*, when he is placed under the absolute power of another without his own consent. Slavery no longer exists in Great Britain, nor in the northern states of America.

2. The offices of a slave; drudgery.
SLA'VE-TRADE, *n.* [*slave* and *trade.*] The barbarous and wicked business of purchasing men and women, transporting them to a distant country and selling them for slaves.
SLA'VISH, *a.* Pertaining to slaves; servile; mean; base; such as becomes a slave; as a *slavish* dependence on the great.
2. Servile; laborious; consisting in drudgery; as a *slavish* life.
SLA'VISHLY, *adv.* Servilely; meanly; basely.
2. In the manner of a slave or drudge.
SLA'VISHNESS, *n.* The state or quality of being slavish; servility; meanness.
SLAVON'IC, *a.* Pertaining to the Slavons or ancient inhabitants of Russia.
SLAVON'IC, *n.* The Slavonic language.
SLAY, *v. t.* pret. *slew*; pp. *slain.* [Sax. *slægan, slagan*; Goth. *slahan*; G. *schlagen*; D. *slaaen*; Sw. *slå*; Dan. *slaaer*, to strike, to kill. The proper sense is to *strike*, and as beating was an early mode of killing, this word, like *smile*, came to signify to *kill*. It seems to be formed on the root of *lay*; as we say, to *lay on.*]
1. To kill; to put to death by a weapon or by violence. We say, he *slew* a man with a sword, with a stone, or with a club, or with other arms; but we never say, the sherif *slays* a malefactor with a halter, or a man is *slain* on the gallows or by poison. So that *slay* retains something of its primitive sense of *striking* or *beating*. It is particularly applied to killing in battle, but is properly applied also to the killing of an individual man or beast.
2. To destroy.
SLA'YER, *n.* One that slays; a killer; a murderer; an assassin; a destroyer of life.
SLA'YING, *ppr.* Killing; destroying life.
SLEAVE, *n.* [Ice. *slefa.*] The knotted or entangled part of silk or thread; silk or thread untwisted. *Drayton.*
SLEAVE, *v. t.* To separate threads; or to divide a collection of threads; to sley; *a word used by weavers.*
SLE'AVED, *a.* Raw; not spun or wrought. *Holinshed.*
SLE'AZY, } *a.* [probably from the root of SLEE'ZY, } *loose*; Sax. *lysan, alysan*, to loose.]
Thin; flimsy; wanting firmness of texture or substance; as *sleezy* silk or muslin.
SLED, *n.* [D. *sleede*; G. *schlitten*; Sw. *slåde*; Dan. *slæde*; W. *ysled*; probably from *sliding* or drawing.]
A carriage or vehicle moved on runners, much used in America for conveying heavy weights in winter, as timber, wood, stone and the like.
SLED, *v. t.* To convey or transport on a sled; as, to *sled* wood or timber.
SLED'DED, *pp.* Conveyed on a sled.
2. Mounted on a sled. *Shak.*
SLED'DING, *ppr.* Conveying on a sled.
SLED'DING, *n.* The act of transporting on a sled.
2. The means of conveying on sleds; snow sufficient for the running of sleds. Thus we say in America, when there is snow sufficient to run a sled, it is good *sledding*; the *sledding* is good. Sometimes in New England, there is little or no good *sledding* during the winter.
SLEDGE, *n.* [Sax. *slecge, slege*; D. *sley*; Dan. *slegge*; Sw. *slägga*; from the root of *slay*, to strike.]
1. A large heavy hammer; used chiefly by ironsmiths.
2. In England, a sled; a vehicle moved on runners or on low wheels. In this sense, the word is not used in America; but the same word is used in a somewhat different sense, and written *sleigh.*
SLEEK, *a.* [D. *lekken*, to leak, to smooth or sleek; *gelekt*, made smooth; G. *schlicht*; allied to *lick*, or G. *gleich*, even, equal, *like.* See *Like.*]
1. Smooth; having an even smooth surface; whence, glossy; as *sleek* hair.

So *sleek* her skin, so faultless was her make— *Dryden.*

2. Not rough or harsh.

Those rugged names to our like mouths grow *sleek*— *Milton.*

SLEEK, *n.* That which makes smooth; varnish. [*Little used.*]
SLEEK, *v. t.* To make even and smooth; as, to *sleek* the hair. *B. Jonson.*
2. To render smooth, soft and glossy.

Gentle, my lord, *sleek* o'er your rugged looks. *Shak.*

SLEEK, *adv.* With ease and dexterity; with exactness. [*Vulgar.*]
SLEE'KLY, *adv.* Smoothly; nicely.
SLEE'KNESS, *n.* Smoothness of surface. *Feltham.*
SLEE'KSTONE, *n.* A smoothing stone. *Peacham.*
SLEE'KY, *a.* Of a sleek or smooth appearance. [*Not in use.*] *Thomson.*
SLEEP, *v. i.* pret. and pp. *slept.* [Sax. *slepan, slæpan*; Goth. *slepan*; G. *schlafen*; D. *slaapen.* This word seems to be allied to words which signify to rest or to relax; G. *schlaff.*]
1. To take rest by a suspension of the voluntary exercise of the powers of the body and mind. The proper time to *sleep* is during the darkness of night.
2. To rest; to be unemployed; to be inactive or motionless; as, the sword *sleeps* in its sheath.
3. To rest; to lie or be still; not to be noticed or agitated. The question *sleeps* for the present.
4. To live thoughtlessly.

We *sleep* over our happiness— *Atterbury.*

5. To be dead; to rest in the grave for a time. 1 Thess. iv.
6. To be careless, inattentive or unconcerned; not to be vigilant. *Shak.*
SLEEP, *n.* That state of an animal in which the voluntary exertion of his mental and corporeal powers is suspended, and he rests unconscious of what passes around him, and not affected by the ordinary impressions of external objects. Sleep is generally attended with a relaxation of the muscles, but the involuntary motions, as respiration and the circulation of the blood, are continued. The mind is often very active in sleep; but its powers not being under the control of reason, its exercises are very irregular. Sleep is the natural rest or repose intended by the Creator to restore the powers of the body and mind, when exhausted or fatigued.
Sleep of plants, a state of plants at night, when their leaves droop or are folded. *Linne.*
SLEE'PER, *n.* A person that sleeps; also, a drone or lazy person. *Grew.*
2. That which lies dormant, as a law not executed. [*Not in use.*] *Bacon.*
3. An animal that lies dormant in winter, as the bear, the marmot, &c. *Encyc.*
4. In *building*, the oblique rafter that lies in a gutter. *Encyc.*
5. In *New England*, a floor timber.
6. In *ship-building*, a thick piece of timber placed longitudinally in a ship's hold, opposite the several scarfs of the timbers, for strengthening the bows and stern-frame, particularly in the Greenland ships; or a piece of long compass-timber fayed and bolted diagonally upon the transoms. *Mar. Dict. Encyc.*
7. In *the glass trade*, a large iron bar crossing the smaller ones, hindering the passage of coals, but leaving room for the ashes. *Encyc.*
8. A platform.
9. A fish. [*exocœtus.*] *Ainsworth.*
SLEE'PFUL, *a.* Strongly inclined to sleep. [*Little used.*]
SLEE'PFULNESS, *n.* Strong inclination to sleep. [*Little used.*]
SLEE'PILY, *adv.* Drowsily; with desire to sleep.
2. Dully; in a lazy manner; heavily. *Raleigh.*

3. Stupidly. *Atterbury.*

SLEE'PINESS, *n.* Drowsiness; inclination to sleep. *Arbuthnot.*

SLEE'PING, *ppr.* Resting; reposing in sleep.

SLEE'PING, *n.* The state of resting in sleep.

2. The state of being at rest, or not stirred or agitated. *Shak.*

SLEE'PLESS, *a.* Having no sleep; without sleep; wakeful.

2. Having no rest; perpetually agitated; as Biscay's *sleepless* bay. *Byron.*

SLEE'PLESSNESS, *n.* Want or destitution of sleep.

SLEE'PY, *a.* Drowsy; inclined to sleep.

2. Not awake.

She wak'd her *sleepy* crew. *Dryden.*

3. Tending to induce sleep; soporiferous; somniferous; as a *sleepy* drink or potion. *Milton. Shak.*

4. Dull; lazy; heavy; sluggish. *Shak.*

SLEET, *n.* [Dan. *slud*, loose weather, rain and snow together; Ice. *sletta.*]

1. A fall of hail or snow and rain together, usually in fine particles. *Dryden.*

2. In *gunnery*, the part of a mortar passing from the chamber to the trunnions for strengthening that part. *Encyc.*

SLEET, *v. i.* To snow or hail with a mixture of rain.

SLEE'TY, *a.* Bringing sleet. *Warton.*

2. Consisting of sleet.

SLEEVE, *n.* [Sax. *slef, slyf;* W. *llawes;* said to be from *llaw*, the hand.]

1. The part of a garment that is fitted to cover the arm; as the *sleeve* of a coat or gown.

2. The raveled *sleeve* of care, in Shakspeare. [See *Sleave.*]

To laugh in the sleeve, to laugh privately or unperceived; that is perhaps, originally, by hiding the face under the sleeve or arm. *Arbuthnot.*

To hang on the sleeve, to be or make dependent on others. *Ainsworth.*

SLEEVE, *v. t.* To furnish with sleeves; to put in sleeves.

SLEE'VE-BUTTON, *n.* A button to fasten the sleeve or wristband.

SLEE'VED, *a.* Having sleeves.

SLEE'VELESS, *a.* Having no sleeves; as a *sleeveless* coat. *Sandys.*

2. Wanting a cover, pretext or palliation; unreasonable; as a *sleeveless* tale of transubstantiation; a *sleeveless* errand. [*Little used.*] *Hall. Spectator.*

SLEID, *v. t.* To sley or prepare for use in the weaver's sley or slaie.

SLEIGH, *n. sla.* [probably allied to *sleek.*] A vehicle moved on runners, and greatly used in America for transporting persons or goods on snow or ice. [This word the English write and pronounce *sledge*, and apply it to what we call a *sled.*]

SLEIGHT, *n. slite.* [G. *schlich*, trick, cunning; *schlicht*, plain, sleek; Sw. *slög*, dextrous; D. *sluik*, underhand; *sluiken*, to smuggle; Ir. *slightheach*, sly.]

1. An artful trick; sly artifice; a trick or feat so dextrously performed that the manner of performance escapes observation; as *sleight* of hand, Fr. *legerdemain.* Not improbably *sleight* and Fr. *leger*, light, may have a common origin.

2. Dextrous practice; dexterity.

SLEIGHTFUL, } *a.* Artful; cunningly dex-
SLEIGHTY, } trous.

SLEN'DER, *a.* [Old D. *slinder.* This word is probably formed on the root of *lean*, Teutonic *klein.*]

1. Thin; small in circumference compared with the length; not thick; as a *slender* stem or stalk of a plant.

2. Small in the waist; not thick or gross. A *slender* waist is considered as a beauty.

3. Not strong; small; slight.

Mighty hearts are held in *slender* chains. *Pope.*

4. Weak; feeble; as *slender* hope; *slender* probabilities; a *slender* constitution.

5. Small; inconsiderable; as a man of *slender* parts.

6. Small; inadequate; as *slender* means of support; a *slender* pittance. *Shak.*

7. Not amply supplied.

The good Ostorius often deign'd
To grace my *slender* table *Philips.*

8. Spare; abstemious; as a *slender* diet. *Arbuthnot.*

SLEN'DERLY, *adv.* Without bulk.

2. Slightly; meanly; as a debt to be *slenderly* regarded. *Hayward.*

3. Insufficiently; as a table *slenderly* supplied.

SLEN'DERNESS, *n.* Thinness; smallness of diameter in proportion to the length; as the *slenderness* of a hair. *Newton.*

2. Want of bulk or strength; as the *slenderness* of a cord or chain.

3. Weakness; slightness; as the *slenderness* of a reason. *Whitgifte.*

4. Weakness; feebleness; as the *slenderness* of a constitution.

5. Want of plenty; as the *slenderness* of a supply.

6. Spareness; as *slenderness* of diet.

SLENT, *v. i.* To make an oblique remark. [*Not used.* See *Slant.*]

SLEPT, *pret.* and *pp.* of *sleep.*

SLEW, *pret.* of *slay.*

SLEY, *n.* [Sax. *slæ.*] A weaver's reed. [See *Sleave* and *Sleid.*]

SLEY, *v. t.* To separate; to part threads and arrange them in a reed; as weavers.

SLICE, *v. t.* [G. *schleissen*, to *slit;* Sax. *slitan.*]

1. To cut into thin pieces, or to cut off a thin broad piece. *Sandys.*

2. To cut into parts. *Cleaveland.*

3. To cut; to divide. *Burnet.*

SLICE, *n.* A thin broad piece cut off; as a *slice* of bacon; a *slice* of cheese; a *slice* of bread.

2. A broad piece; as a *slice* of plaster. *Pope.*

3. A peel; a spatula; an instrument consisting of a broad plate with a handle, used by apothecaries for spreading plasters, &c.

4. In *ship-building*, a tapering piece of plank to be driven between the timbers before planking. *Encyc.*

SLI'CED, *pp.* Cut into broad thin pieces.

SLICH, *n.* The ore of a metal when pounded and prepared for working. *Encyc.*

SLI'CING, *ppr.* Cutting into broad thin pieces.

SLICK, the popular pronunciation of *sleek*, and so written by some authors.

SLICK'ENSIDES, *n.* A name which workmen give to a variety of galena in Derbyshire. *Ure.*

SLID, *pret.* of *slide.*

SLID, } *pp.* of *slide.*
SLID'DEN, }

SLID'DER, *v. i.* [Sax. *sliderian, slidrian.* See *Slide.*]

To slide with interruption. [*Not in use.*] *Dryden.*

SLID'DER, } *a.* [See *Slide.*] Slippery.
SLID'DERLY, } [*Not in use.*] *Chaucer.*

SLIDE, *v. i.* pret. *slid;* pp. *slid, slidden.* [Sax. *slidan;* probably *glide*, with a different prefix; G. *gleiten.*]

1. To move along the surface of any body by slipping, or without bounding or rolling; to slip; to glide; as, a sled *slides* on snow or ice; a snow-slip *slides* down the mountain's side.

2. To move along the surface without stepping; as, a man *slides* on ice.

3. To pass inadvertently.

Make a door and a bar for thy mouth; beware thou *slide* not by it. *Ecclus.*

4. To pass smoothly along without jerks or agitation; as, a ship or boat *slides* through the water.

5. To pass in silent unobserved progression.

Ages shall *slide* away without perceiving. *Dryden.*

6. To pass silently and gradually from one state to another; as, to *slide* insensibly into vicious practices, or into the customs of others.

7. To pass without difficulty or obstruction.

Parts answ'ring parts shall *slide* into a whole. *Pope.*

8. To practice sliding or moving on ice.

They bathe in summer, and in winter *slide.* *Waller.*

9. To slip; to fall.

10. To pass with an easy, smooth, uninterrupted course or flow.

SLIDE, *v. t.* To slip; to pass or put in imperceptibly; as, to *slide* in a word to vary the sense of a question. *Watts.*

2. To thrust along; or to thrust by slipping; as, to *slide* along a piece of timber.

SLIDE, *n.* A smooth and easy passage; also, a slider. *Bacon.*

2. Flow; even course. *Bacon.*

SLI'DER, *n.* One that slides.

2. The part of an instrument or machine that slides.

SLI'DING, *ppr.* Moving along the surface by slipping; gliding; passing smoothly, easily or imperceptibly.

SLI'DING, *n.* Lapse; falling; used in *backsliding.*

SLIDING-RULE, *n.* A mathematical instrument used to determine measure or quantity without compasses, by sliding the parts one by another.

SLIGHT, *a.* [D. *slegt;* G. *schlecht*, plain, simple, mean; D. *slegten*, to level; G. *schlecken*, to lick. It seems that *slight* belongs to the family of *sleek*, smooth. Qu. Dan. *slet*, by contraction.]

1. Weak; inconsiderable; not forcible; as a *slight* impulse; a *slight* effort.

2. Not deep; as a *slight* impression.

3. Not violent; as a *slight* disease, illness or indisposition.

4. Trifling; of no great importance.

Slight is the subject, but not so the praise. *Pope.*

5. Not strong; not cogent.

Some firmly embrace doctrines upon *slight* grounds. *Locke.*

6. Negligent; not vehement; not done with effort.

The shaking of the head is a gesture of *slight* refusal. *Bacon.*

7. Not firm or strong; thin; of loose texture; as *slight* silk.

8. Foolish; silly; weak in intellect. *Hudibras.*

SLIGHT, *n.* Neglect; disregard; a moderate degree of contempt manifested negatively by neglect. It expresses less than contempt, disdain and scorn.

2. Artifice; dexterity. [See *Sleight.*]

SLIGHT, *v. t.* To neglect; to disregard from the consideration that a thing is of little value and unworthy of notice; as, to *slight* the divine commands, or the offers of mercy. *Milton. Locke.*

2. To overthrow; to demolish. [*Not used.*] *Clarendon.*

"The rogues *slighted* me into the river," in Shakspeare, is not used. [D. *slegten.*]

To slight over, to run over in haste; to perform superficially; to treat carelessly; as, to *slight over* a theme. *Dryden.*

SLIGHTED, *pp.* Neglected.

SLIGHTEN, *v. t.* To slight or disregard. [*Not in use.*] *Spenser.*

SLIGHTER, *n.* One who neglects.

SLIGHTING, *ppr.* Neglecting; disregarding.

SLIGHTINGLY, *adv.* With neglect; without respect. *Boyle.*

SLIGHTLY, *adv.* Weakly; superficially; with inconsiderable force or effect; in a small degree; as a man *slightly* wounded; an audience *slightly* affected with preaching.

2. Negligently; without regard; with moderate contempt. *Hooker. Shak.*

SLIGHTNESS, *n.* Weakness; want of force or strength; superficialness; as the *slightness* of a wound or an impression.

2. Negligence; want of attention; want of vehemence.

How does it reproach the *slightness* of our sleepy heartless addresses! *Decay of Piety.*

SLIGHTY, *a.* Superficial; slight.

2. Trifling; inconsiderable. *Echard.*

SLI'LY, *adv.* [from *sly.*] With artful or dextrous secrecy.

Satan *slily* robs us of our grand treasure. *Decay of Piety.*

SLIM, *a.* [Ice.] Slender; of small diameter or thickness in proportion to the highth; as a *slim* person; a *slim* tree.

2. Weak; slight; unsubstantial.

3. Worthless.

SLIME, *n.* [Sax. *slim*; Sw. *slem*; D. *slym*; Dan. *sliim*; L. *limus.*]

Soft moist earth having an adhesive quality; viscous mud.

They had brick for stone, and *slime* had they for mortar. Gen. xi.

SLI'ME-PIT, *n.* A pit of slime or adhesive mire.

SLI'MINESS, *n.* The quality of slime; viscosity. *Floyer.*

SLI'MY, *a.* Abounding with slime; consisting of slime.

2. Overspread with slime; as a *slimy* eel.

3. Viscous; glutinous; as a *slimy* soil.

SLI'NESS, *n.* [from *sly.*] Dextrous artifice to conceal any thing; artful secrecy. *Addison.*

SLING, *n.* [D. *slinger.*] An instrument for throwing stones, consisting of a strap and two strings; the stone being lodged in the strap, is thrown by loosing one of the strings. With a *sling* and a stone David killed Goliath.

2. A throw; a stroke. *Milton.*

3. A kind of hanging bandage put round the neck, in which a wounded limb is sustained.

4. A rope by which a cask or bale is suspended and swung in or out of a ship.

5. A drink composed of equal parts of rum or spirit and water sweetened. *Rush.*

SLING, *v. t.* pret. and pp. *slung.* [Sax. *slingan*; D. *slingeren*; Sw. *slinka*, to dangle; Dan. *slingrer*, to reel. The primary sense seems to be to swing.] To throw with a sling.

2. To throw; to hurl. *Addison.*

3. To hang so as to swing; as, to *sling* a pack.

4. To move or swing by a rope which suspends the thing.

SLING'ER, *n.* One who slings or uses the sling.

SLING'ING, *ppr.* Throwing with a sling; hanging so as to swing; moving by a sling.

SLINK, *v. i.* pret. and pp. *slunk.* [Sax. *slincan*; G. *schleichen.*]

1. To sneak; to creep away meanly; to steal away.

He would pinch the children in the dark, and then *slink* into a corner. *Arbuthnot.*

2. To miscarry, as a beast.

SLINK, *v. t.* To cast prematurely; to miscarry of; as the female of a beast.

SLINK, *n.* Produced prematurely, as the young of a beast.

SLIP, *v. i.* [Sax. *slepan*; D. *sleppen*; Sw. *slippa*; Dan. *sliipper*; G. *schlüpfen*; W. *yslib*, smooth, glib, from *llib*; L. *labor*, to slide.]

1. To slide; to glide; to move along the surface of a thing without bounding, rolling or stepping.

2. To slide; not to tread firmly. Walk carefully, lest your foot should *slip.*

3. To move or fly out of place; usually with *out*; as, a bone may *slip out* of its place. *Wiseman.*

4. To sneak; to slink; to depart or withdraw secretly; with *away.*

Thus one tradesman *slips away*
To give his partner fairer play. *Prior.*

5. To err; to fall into error or fault.

One *slippeth* in his speech, but not from his heart. *Ecclus.*

6. To glide; to pass unexpectedly or imperceptibly.

And thrice the flitting shadow *slipp'd* away. *Dryden.*

7. To enter by oversight. An error may *slip* into a copy, notwithstanding all possible care.

8. To escape insensibly; to be lost.

Use the most proper methods to retain the ideas you have acquired, for the mind is ready to let many of them *slip.* *Watts.*

SLIP, *v. t.* To convey secretly.

He tried to *slip* a powder into her drink. *Arbuthnot.*

2. To omit; to lose by negligence. Let us not *slip* the occasion.

And *slip* no advantage
That may secure you. *B. Jonson.*

3. To part twigs from the branches or stem of a tree.

The branches also may be *slipped* and planted. *Mortimer.*

4. To escape from; to leave slily.

Lucentio *slipp'd* me like his greyhound. *Shak.*

From is here understood.

5. To let loose; as, to *slip* the hounds. *Dryden.*

6. To throw off; to disengage one's self from; as, a horse *slips* his bridle.

7. To pass over or omit negligently; as, to *slip* over the main points of a subject.

8. To tear off; as, to *slip* off a twig.

9. To suffer abortion; to miscarry; as a beast.

To slip a cable, to veer out and let go the end. *Mar. Dict.*

To slip on, to put on in haste or loosely; as, to *slip on* a gown or coat.

SLIP, *n.* A sliding; act of slipping.

2. An unintentional error or fault. *Dryden.*

3. A twig separated from the main stock; as the *slip* of a vine.

4. A leash or string by which a dog is held; so called from its being so made as to slip or become loose by relaxation of the hand. *Shak.*

5. An escape; a secret or unexpected desertion.

6. A long narrow piece; as a *slip* of paper. *Addison.*

7. A counterfeit piece of money, being brass covered with silver. [*Not in use.*] *Shak.*

8. Matter found in troughs of grindstones after the grinding of edge-tools. [*Local.*] *Petty.*

9. A particular quantity of yarn. [*Local.*] *Barret.*

10. An opening between wharves or in a dock. [*N. York.*]

11. A place having a gradual descent on the bank of a river or harbor, convenient for ship-building. *Mar. Dict.*

12. A long seat or narrow pew in churches. [*U. States.*]

SLIP'-BOARD, *n.* A board sliding in grooves. *Swift.*

SLIP'-KNOT, *n.* A bow-knot; a knot which will not bear a strain, or which is easily untied. *Johnson. Mar. Dict.*

SLIP'PER, *n.* [Sax.] A kind of shoe consisting of a sole and vamp without quarters, which may be slipped on with ease and worn in undress; a slip-shoe. *Pope.*

2. A kind of apron for children, to be slipped over their other clothes to keep them clean.

3. A plant. [L. *crepis.*]

4. A kind of iron slide or lock for the use of a heavy wagon.

SLIP'PER, *a.* [Sax. *slipur.*] Slippery. [*Not in use.*] *Spenser.*

SLIP'PERED, *a.* Wearing slippers. *Warton.*

SLIP'PERILY, *adv.* [from *slippery.*] In a slippery manner.

SLIP'PERINESS, *n.* The state or quality of being slippery; lubricity; smoothness; glibness; as the *slipperiness* of ice or snow; the *slipperiness* of the tongue.

2. Uncertainty; want of firm footing. *Johnson.*

3. Lubricity of character.

SLIP'PERY, *a.* Smooth; glib; having the quality opposite to adhesiveness; as, oily substances render things *slippery*.

2. Not affording firm footing or confidence; as a *slippery* promise. *Tusser.*

The *slipp'ry* tops of human state. *Cowley.*

3. Not easily held; liable or apt to slip away.

The *slipp'ry* god will try to loose his hold. *Dryden.*

4. Not standing firm; as *slippery* standers. *Shak.*

5. Unstable; changeable; mutable; uncertain; as the *slippery* state of kings. *Denham.*

6. Not certain in its effect; as a *slippery* trick.

7. Lubricous; wanton; unchaste. *Shak.*

SLIP'PY, *a.* Slippery. [Not in use, though regular Sax. *slipeg*.]

SLIP'SHOD, *a.* [*slip* and *shod*.] Wearing shoes like slippers, without pulling up the quarters. *Swift.*

SLIP'STRING, *n.* [*slip* and *string*.] One that has shaken off restraint; a prodigal; called also *slipthrift*, but I believe seldom or never used. *Cotgrave.*

SLIT, *v. t.* pret. *slit*; pp. *slit* or *slitted*. [Sax. *slitan*; Sw. *slita*; G. *schleissen*; D. *slyten*; Dan. *slider*. The two latter signify to wear out or waste. The German has the signification of splitting and of wearing out.]

1. To cut lengthwise; to cut into long pieces or strips; as, to *slit* iron bars into nail rods.

2. To cut or make a long fissure; as, to *slit* the ear or tongue, or the nose. *Temple. Newton.*

3. To cut in general. *Milton.*

4. To rend; to split.

SLIT, *n.* A long cut; or a narrow opening; as a *slit* in the ear.

2. A cleft or crack in the breast of cattle. *Encyc.*

SLIT'TER, *n.* One that slits.

SLIT'TING, *ppr.* Cutting lengthwise.

SLIT'TING-MILL, *n.* A mill where iron bars are slit into nail rods. &c.

SLIVE, *v. i.* To sneak. [*Local.*] *Grose.*

SLIV'ER, *v. t.* [Sax. *slifan*; W. *ysleiviaw*, from *yslaiv*, a slash or slice, from *glaiv*, a sword or cimeter; *llaiv*, shears or a shave; but all probably from the sense of cutting or separating. Class Lb.]

To cut or divide into long thin pieces, or into very small pieces; to cut or rend lengthwise; as, to *sliver* wood.

SLIV'ER, *n.* A long piece cut or rent off, or a piece cut or rent lengthwise. In Scotland, it is said to signify a slice; as a *sliver* of beef.

SLOAT, *n.* [from the root of Dan. *slutter*, to fasten, D. *sluiten*, Sw. *sluta*, G. *schliessen*; from the root of L. *claudo*.]

A narrow piece of timber which holds together larger pieces; as the *sloats* of a cart. [In New England, this is called a *slat*, as the *slats* of a chair, cart, &c.]

SLOB'BER, and its derivatives, are a different orthography of *slabber*, the original pronunciation of which was probably *slobber*. [See *Slabber* and *Slaver*.]

SLOCK, to quench, is a different orthography of *slake*, but not used.

SLOE, *n.* [Sax. *slag*, *sla*; G. *schlehe*; D. *slee*, in *sleepruim*, and *slee* signifies sour; *slee-boom*, the sloe-tree; Dan. *slaae*, *slaaen*, or *slaaen-torne*.]

A small wild plum, the fruit of the black thorn. [*Prunus spinosa.*] *Mortimer.*

SLOOM, *n.* Slumber. [*Not in use or local.*]

SLOOM'Y, *a.* Sluggish; slow. [*Not in use or local.*] *Skinner.*

SLOOP, *n.* [D. *sloep*, *sloepschip*; G. *schaluppe*; Dan. *sluppe*; Fr. *chaloupe*. It is written also *shallop*.]

A vessel with one mast, the main-sail of which is attached to a gaff above, to a boom below, and to the mast on its foremost edge. It differs from a cutter by having a fixed steeving bowsprit, and a jib-stay. Sloops are of various sizes, from the size of a boat to that of more than 100 tons burthen. *Mar. Dict.*

Sloop of war, a vessel of war rigged either as a ship, brig or schooner, and usually carrying from 10 to 18 guns. *Mar. Dict.*

SLOP, *v. t.* [probably allied to *lap*.] To drink greedily and grossly. [*Little used.*]

SLOP, *n.* [probably allied to *slabber*.] Water carelessly thrown about on a table or floor; a puddle; a soiled spot.

2. Mean liquor; mean liquid food.

SLOP, *n.* [Qu. D. *sluif*, a case or cover, or *slof*, an old slipper, or Sax. *slopen*, lax, loose; *toslupan*, to loosen.]

Trowsers; a loose lower garment; drawers; hence, ready made clothes. *Shak.*

SLOP'SELLER, *n.* One who sells ready made clothes.

SLOP'SHOP, *n.* A shop where ready made clothes are sold.

SLOPE, *a.* [This word contains the elements of L. *labor*, *lapsus*, and Eng. *slip*; also of L. *levo*, Eng. *lift*. I know not whether it originally signified ascending or descending, probably the latter.]

Inclined or inclining from a horizontal direction; forming an angle with the plane of the horizon; as *slope* hills. [*Little used.*] *Milton.*

SLOPE, *n.* An oblique direction; a line or direction inclining from a horizontal line; properly, a direction downwards.

2. An oblique direction in general; a direction forming an angle with a perpendicular or other right line.

3. A declivity; any ground whose surface forms an angle with the plane of the horizon; also, an acclivity, as every declivity must be also an acclivity.

SLOPE, *v. t.* To form with a slope; to form to declivity or obliquity; to direct obliquely; to incline; as, to *slope* the ground in a garden; to *slope* a piece of cloth in cutting a garment.

SLOPE, *v. i.* To take an oblique direction; to be declivous or inclined.

SLO'PENESS, *n.* Declivity; obliquity. [*Not much used.*] *Wotton.*

SLO'PEWISE, *adv.* Obliquely. *Carew.*

SLO'PING, *ppr.* Taking an inclined direction.

2. *a.* Oblique; declivous; inclining or inclined from a horizontal or other right line.

SLO'PINGLY, *adv.* Obliquely; with a slope.

SLOP'PINESS, *n.* [from *sloppy*.] Wetness of the earth; muddiness.

SLOP'PY, *a.* [from *slop*.] Wet, as the ground; muddy; plashy.

SLOT, *v. t.* [D. *sluiten*, to shut; G. *schliessen*; Dan. *slutter*; Sw. *sluta*; from the root of L. *claudo*.]

To shut with violence; to slam, that is, to drive. [*Not in use or local.*] *Ray.*

SLOT, *n.* A broad flat wooden bar.

SLOT, *n.* [The Saxon has *slœtinge*, tracks.] The track of a deer. *Drayton.*

SLOTH, *n.* [Sax. *slœwth*, from *slaw*, slow. See *Slow*.]

1. Slowness; tardiness.

I abhor
This dilatory *sloth* and tricks of Rome. *Shak.*

2. Disinclination to action or labor; sluggishness; laziness; idleness.

They change their course to pleasure, ease and *sloth*. *Milton.*

Sloth, like rust, consumes faster than labor wears. *Franklin.*

3. An animal, so called from the remarkable slowness of his motions. There are two species of this animal; the ai or three toed sloth, and the unau or two toed sloth; both found in South America. It is said that its greatest speed seldom exceeds three yards an hour. It feeds on vegetables and ruminates. *Dict. Nat. Hist.*

SLOTH, *v. i.* To be idle. [*Not in use.*] *Gower.*

SLOTH'FUL, *a.* Inactive; sluggish; lazy; indolent; idle.

He that is *slothful* in his work, is brother to him that is a great waster. Prov. xviii.

SLOTH'FULLY, *adv.* Lazily; sluggishly; idly.

SLOTH'FULNESS, *n.* The indulgence of sloth; inactivity; the habit of idleness; laziness.

Slothfulness casteth into a deep sleep. Prov. xix.

SLOT'TERY, *a.* [G. *schlotterig*, negligent; *schlottern*, to hang loosely, to wabble. See *Slut*.]

1. Squalid; dirty; sluttish; untrimmed. [*Not in use.*] *Chaucer.*

2. Foul; wet. [*Not in use.*] *Pryce.*

SLOUCH, *n.* [This word probably belongs to the root of *lag*, *slug*.]

1. A hanging down; a depression of the head or of some other part of the body; an ungainly, clownish gait. *Swift.*

2. An awkward, heavy, clownish fellow. *Gay.*

SLOUCH, *v. i.* To hang down; to have a downcast clownish look, gait or manner. *Chesterfield.*

SLOUCH, *v. t.* To depress; to cause to hang down; as, to *slouch* the hat.

SLOUCH'ING, *ppr.* Causing to hang down.

2. *a.* Hanging down; walking heavily and awkwardly.

SLOUGH, *n. slou.* [Sax. *slog*; W. *yslwç*, a gutter or slough, from *llwç*, a lake.]

1. A place of deep mud or mire; a hole full of mire. *Milton.*

2. [pron. *sluff*.] The skin or cast skin of a serpent. [Its use for the skin in general, in Shakspeare, is not authorized.]

3. [pron. *sluff*.] The part that separates from a foul sore. *Wiseman.*

The dead part which separates from the living in mortification. *Cooper.*

SLOUGH, *v. i. sluff.* To separate from the sound flesh; to come off; as the matter formed over a sore; *a term in surgery.*

To slough off, to separate from the living parts, as the dead part in mortification.

SLOUGHY, *a. slou'y.* Full of sloughs; miry. *Swift.*

SLŎVEN, *n.* [D. *slof,* careless; *sloffen,* to neglect; W. *yslabi,* from *yslab,* extended; Ir. *slapaire.*]

A man careless of his dress, or negligent of cleanliness; a man habitually negligent of neatness and order. *Pope.*

SLŎVENLINESS, *n.* [from *sloven.*] Negligence of dress; habitual want of cleanliness. *Wotton.*

2. Neglect of order and neatness. *Hall.*

SLŎVENLY, *a.* Negligent of dress or neatness; as a *slovenly* man.

2. Loose; disorderly; not neat; as a *slovenly* dress.

SLŎVENLY, *adv.* In a careless, inelegant manner.

SLŎVENRY, *n.* Negligence of order or neatness; dirtiness. [*Not in use.*] *Shak.*

SLŌW, *a.* [Sax. *slaw,* for *slag;* Dan. *slöv,* dull, blunt; contracted from the root of *slack, sluggard, lag.*]

1. Moving a small distance in a long time; not swift; not quick in motion; not rapid; as a *slow* stream; a *slow* motion.

2. Late; not happening in a short time.

> These changes in the heavens though *slow,* produc'd
> Like change on sea and land, sidereal blast. *Milton.*

3. Not ready; not prompt or quick; as *slow* of speech, and *slow* of tongue. Ex. iv.

4. Dull; inactive; tardy.

> The Trojans are not *slow*
> To guard their shore from an expected foe. *Dryden.*

5. Not hasty; not precipitate; acting with deliberation.

> The Lord is merciful, *slow* to anger. *Com. Prayer.*

> He that is *slow* to wrath is of great understanding. Prov. xiv.

6. Dull; heavy in wit. *Pope.*

7. Behind in time; indicating a time later than the true time; as, the clock or watch is *slow.*

8. Not advancing, growing or improving rapidly; as the *slow* growth of arts and sciences.

SLŌW, is used in composition to modify other words; as a *slow-paced* horse.

SLŌW, as a verb, to delay, is not in use. *Shak.*

SLŌW, *n.* [Sax. *sliw.*] A moth. [*Not in use.*] *Chaucer.*

SLŌW'BACK, *n.* A lubber; an idle fellow; a loiterer.

SLŌWLY, *adv.* With moderate motion; not rapidly; not with velocity or celerity; as, to walk *slowly.*

2. Not soon; not early; not in a little time; not with hasty advance; as a country that rises *slowly* into importance.

3. Not hastily; not rashly; not with precipitation; as, he determines *slowly.*

4. Not promptly; not readily; as, he learns *slowly.*

5. Tardily; with slow progress. The building proceeds *slowly.*

SLŌWNESS, *n.* Moderate motion; want of speed or velocity.

> Swiftness and *slowness* are relative ideas. *Watts.*

2. Tardy advance; moderate progression; as the *slowness* of an operation; *slowness* of growth or improvement.

3. Dullness to admit conviction or affection; as *slowness* of heart. *Bentley.*

4. Want of readiness or promptness; dullness of intellect.

5. Deliberation; coolness; caution in deciding.

6. Dilatoriness; tardiness.

SLŌW-WŎRM, } *n.* An insect found on the
SLŌE-WŎRM, } leaves of the sloe-tree, which often changes its skin and assumes different colors. It changes into a four winged fly. *Dict. Nat. Hist.*

SLŌW-WŎRM, *n.* [Sax. *slaw-wyrm.*] A kind of viper, the blind worm, scarcely venomous. *Johnson.*

SLUB'BER, *v. t.* To do lazily, imperfectly or coarsely; to daub; to stain; to cover carelessly. [*Little used and vulgar.*]

SLUB'BERINGLY, *adv.* In a slovenly manner. [*Not used and vulgar.*] *Drayton.*

SLUDĠE, *n.* [D. *slyk,* Sax. *slog,* a slough.] Mud; mire; soft mud. *Mortimer.*

SLUDS, *n.* Among *miners,* half roasted ore.

SLŪE, *v. t.* In *seamen's language,* to turn any thing conical or cylindrical, &c. about its axis without removing it; to turn. *Mar. Dict.*

SLUG, *n.* [allied to *slack, sluggard;* W. *llag;* D. *slak, slek,* a snail.]

1. A drone; a slow, heavy, lazy fellow. *Shak.*

2. A hinderance; obstruction. *Bacon.*

3. A kind of snail, very destructive to plants, of the genus Limax. It is without a shell.

4. [Qu. Sax. *sloca,* a mouthful; D. *slok,* a swallow; or Sax. *slecg,* a sledge.] A cylindrical or oval piece of metal, used for the charge of a gun. *Pope.*

SLUG, *v. i.* To move slowly; to lie idle. *Obs.* *Spenser.*

SLUG, *v. t.* To make sluggish. *Obs.* *Milton.*

SLUG'ABED, *n.* One who indulges in lying abed. [*Not used.*] *Shak.*

SLUG'GARD, *n.* [from *slug* and *ard,* slow kind.]

A person habitually lazy, idle and inactive; a drone. *Dryden.*

SLUG'GARD, *a.* Sluggish; lazy. *Dryden.*

SLUG'GARDIZE, *v. t.* To make lazy. [*Little used.*] *Shak.*

SLUG'GISH, *a.* Habitually idle and lazy; slothful; dull; inactive; as a *sluggish* man.

2. Slow; having little motion; as a *sluggish* river or stream.

3. Inert; inactive; having no power to move itself.

> Matter is *sluggish* and inactive. *Woodward.*

SLUG'GISHLY, *adv.* Lazily; slothfully; drowsily; idly; slowly. *Milton.*

SLUG'GISHNESS, *n.* Natural or habitual indolence or laziness; sloth; dullness; *applied to persons.*

2. Inertness; want of power to move; *applied to inanimate matter.*

3. Slowness; as the *sluggishness* of a stream.

SLUG'GY, *a.* Sluggish. [*Not in use.*] *Chaucer.*

SLŪICE, } *n.* [D. *sluis,* a sluice, a lock; G.
SLUSE, } *schleuse,* a flood-gate, and *schloss,* a lock, from *schliessen,* to shut; Sw. *sluss;* Dan. *sluse;* Fr. *ecluse;* It. *chiusa,* an inclosure. The Dutch *sluiten,* Dan. *slutter,* to shut, are the G. *schliessen;* all formed on the elements *Ld, Ls,* the root of Eng. *lid,* L. *claudo, clausi, clausus;* Low L. *exclusa.* The most correct orthography is *sluse.*]

1. The stream of water issuing through a flood-gate; or the gate itself. If the word had its origin in *shutting,* it denoted the frame of boards or planks which closes the opening of a mill dam; but I believe it is applied to the stream, the gate and channel. It is a common saying, that a rapid stream runs like a *sluse.*

2. An opening; a source of supply; that through which any thing flows.

> Each *sluice* of affluent fortune open'd soon. *Harte.*

SLŪICE, } *v. t.* To emit by flood-gates.
SLUSE, } [*Little used.*] *Milton.*

SLŪICY, } *a.* Falling in streams as from a
SLU'SY, } sluice.

> And oft whole sheets descend of *sluicy* rain. *Dryden.*

SLUM'BER, *v. i.* [Sax. *slumerian;* D. *sluimeren;* G. *schlummern;* Dan. *slummer, slumrer;* Sw. *slumra.*]

1. To sleep lightly; to doze.

> He that keepeth Israel shall neither *slumber* nor sleep. Ps. cxxi.

2. To sleep. *Slumber* is used as synonymous with *sleep,* particularly in the poetic and eloquent style. *Milton.*

3. To be in a state of negligence, sloth, supineness or inactivity.

> Why *slumbers* Pope? *Young.*

SLUM'BER, *v. t.* To lay to sleep.

2. To stun; to stupefy. [*Little used and hardly legitimate.*] *Spenser.* *Wotton.*

SLUM'BER, *n.* Light sleep; sleep not deep or sound.

> From carelessness it shall settle into *slumber,* and from *slumber* it shall settle into a deep and long sleep. *South.*

2. Sleep; repose.

> Rest to my soul, and *slumber* to my eyes. *Dryden.*

SLUM'BERER, *n.* One that slumbers.

SLUM'BERING, *ppr.* Dozing; sleeping.

SLUM'BEROUS, } *a.* Inviting or causing
SLUM'BERY, } sleep; soporiferous.

> While pensive in the *slumberous* shade— *Pope.*

2. Sleepy; not waking. *Shak.*

SLUMP, *v. i.* [G. *schlump,* Dan. Sw. *slump,* a hap or chance, accident, that is, a fall.]

To fall or sink suddenly into water or mud, when walking on a hard surface, as on ice or frozen ground, not strong enough to bear the person. [*This legitimate word is in common and respectable use in New England, and its signification is so appropriate that no other word will supply its place.*]

SLUNG, *pret.* and *pp.* of *sling.*

SLUNK, *pret.* and *pp.* of *slink.*

SLUR, *v. t.* [D. *slordig*, sluttish.] To soil; to sully; to contaminate; to disgrace.

2. To pass lightly; to conceal.

With periods, points and tropes he *slurs* his crimes. *Dryden.*

3. To cheat; to trick. [*Unusual.*] *Prior.*

4. In *music*, to sing or perform in a smooth gliding style. *Busby.*

SLUR, *n.* Properly, a black mark; hence, slight reproach or disgrace. Every violation of moral duty should be a *slur* to the reputation.

2. In *music*, a mark connecting notes that are to be sung to the same syllable, or made in one continued breath of a wind instrument, or with one stroke of a stringed instrument.

SLUSE, a more correct orthography of *sluice*.

SLUSH, *n.* Soft mud, or a soft mixture of filthy substances. [This may be the Eng. *slutch.*]

SLUT, *n.* [D. *slet*, a slut, a rag; G. *schlotterig*, negligent, slovenly; *schlottern*, to hang loosely, to wabble or waddle.]

1. A woman who is negligent of cleanliness, and who suffers her person, clothes, furniture, &c., to be dirty or in disorder. *Shak. King.*

2. A name of slight contempt for a woman. *L'Estrange.*

SLUT'TERY, *n.* The qualities of a slut; more generally, the practice of a slut; neglect of cleanliness and order; dirtiness of clothes, rooms, furniture or provisions. *Drayton.*

SLUT'TISH, *a.* Not neat or cleanly; dirty; careless of dress and neatness; disorderly; as a *sluttish* woman.

2. Disorderly; dirty; as a *sluttish* dress.

3. Meretricious. [*Little used.*] *Holiday.*

SLUT'TISHLY, *adv.* In a sluttish manner; negligently; dirtily.

SLUT'TISHNESS, *n.* The qualities or practice of a slut; negligence of dress; dirtiness of dress, furniture and in domestic affairs generally. *Sidney. Ray.*

SLȲ, *a.* [G. *schlau*; Dan. *slue*. Qu. D. *sluik*, underhand, privately; *sluiken*, to smuggle; which seem to be allied to *sleek* and *sleight.*]

1. Artfully dextrous in performing things secretly, and escaping observation or detection; usually implying some degree of meanness; artfully cunning; *applied to persons*; as a *sly* man or boy.

2. Done with artful and dextrous secrecy; as a *sly* trick.

3. Marked with artful secrecy; as *sly* circumspection. *Milton.*

4. Secret; concealed.

Envy works in a *sly* imperceptible manner. *Watts.*

SLY'-BOOTS, *n.* A sly, cunning or waggish person. [*Low.*]

SLYLY, SLYNESS. [See *Slily*, *Sliness.*]

SMACK, *v. i.* [W. *ysmac*, a stroke; Sax. *smæccan*, to taste; D. *smaaken*; G. *schmecken*; Sw. *smaka*; Dan. *smager*; D. *smak*, a cast or throw. The primary sense is to throw, to strike, whence to touch or taste; Gr. μαχη, a battle; as *battle* from *beat.*]

1. To kiss with a close compression of the lips, so as to make a sound when they separate; to kiss with violence. *Pope.*

2. To make a noise by the separation of the lips after tasting any thing. *Gay.*

3. To have a taste; to be tinctured with any particular taste.

4. To have a tincture or quality infused.

All sects, all ages *smack* of this vice. *Shak.*

SMACK, *v. t.* To kiss with a sharp noise. *Donne.*

2. To make a sharp noise with the lips.

3. To make a sharp noise by striking; to crack; as, to *smack* a whip.

SMACK, *n.* A loud kiss. *Shak.*

2. A quick sharp noise, as of the lips or of a whip.

3. Taste; savor; tincture. *Spenser. Carew.*

4. Pleasing taste. *Tusser.*

5. A quick smart blow.

6. A small quantity; a taste. *Dryden.*

7. [D. *smakschip*. Lye supposes it to be the Sax. *snacca*, from *snaca*, snake, and so named from its form. Qu.] A small vessel, commonly rigged as a cutter, used in the coasting and fishing trade. *Mar. Dict.*

SMALL, *a.* [Sax. *smæl*, *smal*, thin, slender, little; G. *schmal*, D. *smal*, narrow; Dan. *smal*, narrow, strait; *smaler*, to narrow, to diminish; Sw. *smal*; Russ. *malo*, small, little, few; *malyu* and *umaliayu*, to diminish; Slav. to abase; W. *mal*, small, trivial, light, vain, like, similar; *malu*, to grind, and *malau*, to make similar; Gr. ὁμαλος. See *Mill*, *Mold*, *Meal.*]

1. Slender; thin; fine; of little diameter; hence in general, little in size or quantity; not great; as a *small* house; a *small* horse; a *small* farm; a *small* body; *small* particles.

2. Minute; slender; fine; as a *small* voice.

3. Little in degree; as *small* improvement; *small* acquirements; the trouble is *small*.

There arose no *small* stir about that way. Acts ix.

4. Being of little moment, weight or importance; as, it is a *small* matter or thing; a *small* subject.

5. Of little genius or ability; petty; as a *small* poet or musician.

6. Short; containing little; as a *small* essay.

7. Little in amount; as a *small* sum; a *small* price.

8. Containing little of the principal quality, or little strength; weak; as *small* beer.

9. Gentle; soft; not loud. 1 Kings xix.

10. Mean; base; unworthy. [*Colloquial.*]

SMALL, *n.* The small or slender part of a thing; as the *small* of the leg or of the back. *Sidney.*

SMALL, *v. t.* To make little or less. [*Not in use.*]

SMALL'AGE, *n.* A plant of the genus Apium, water parsley. *Lee.*

SMALL-BEER, *n.* [*small* and *beer.*] A species of weak beer.

SMALL-COAL, *n.* [*small* and *coal.*] Little wood coals used to light fires. *Gay.*

SMALL-CRAFT, *n.* [*small* and *craft.*] A vessel, or vessels in general, of a small size, or below the size of ships and brigs intended for foreign trade.

SMALL'ISH, *a.* Somewhat small. *Chaucer.*

SMALL'NESS, *n.* Littleness of size or extent; littleness of quantity; as the *smallness* of a fly or of a horse; the *smallness* of a hill.

2. Littleness in degree; as the *smallness* of trouble or pain.

3. Littleness in force or strength; weakness; as *smallness* of mind or intellectual powers.

4. Fineness; softness; melodiousness; as the *smallness* of a female voice.

5. Littleness in amount or value; as the *smallness* of the sum.

6. Littleness of importance; inconsiderableness; as the *smallness* of an affair.

SMALL-POX', *n.* [*small* and *pox*, *pocks.*] A very contagious disease, characterized by an eruption of pustules on the skin; the variolous disease.

SMALLY, *adv.* *small'-ly.* In a little quantity or degree; with minuteness. [*Little used.*] *Ascham.*

SMALT, *n.* [D. *smelten*, Dan. *smelter*, to melt; G. *schmelz*, from *schmelzen*, to melt, to smelt; Sw. *smält*, id.; a word formed on *melt.*]

A beautiful blue glass of cobalt; flint and potash fused together.

SMAR'AGD, *n.* [Gr. σμαραγδος.] The emerald.

SMARAG'DINE, *a.* [L. *smaragdinus*, from the Greek.]

Pertaining to emerald; consisting of emerald, or resembling it; of an emerald green.

SMARAG'DITE, *n.* A mineral; called also green diallage. *Ure.*

SMAR'IS, *n.* A fish of a dark green color. *Dict. Nat. Hist.*

SM'ART, *n.* [D. *smert*; G. *schmerz*; Dan. *smerte*. This word is probably formed on the root of L. *amarus*, bitter, that is, sharp, like Fr. *piquant*. See the root מרר, Ar. مر. Class Mr. No. 7.]

1. Quick, pungent, lively pain; a pricking local pain, as the pain from puncture by nettles; as the *smart* of bodily punishment.

2. Severe pungent pain of mind; pungent grief; as the *smart* of affliction.

SM'ART, *v. i.* [Sax. *smeortan*; D. *smerten*; G. *schmerzen*; Dan. *smerter.*]

1. To feel a lively pungent pain, particularly a pungent local pain from some piercing or irritating application. Thus Cayenne pepper applied to the tongue makes it *smart*.

2. To feel a pungent pain of mind; to feel sharp pain; as, to *smart* under sufferings.

3. To be punished; to bear penalties or the evil consequences of any thing.

He that is surety for a stranger shall *smart* for it. Prov. xi.

SM'ART, *a.* Pungent; pricking; causing a keen local pain; as a *smart* lash or stroke; a *smart* quality or taste. *Shak. Granville.*

2. Keen; severe; poignant; as *smart* pain or sufferings.

3. Quick; vigorous; sharp; severe; as a *smart* skirmish.

4. Brisk; fresh; as a *smart* breeze.

5. Acute and pertinent; witty; as a *smart* reply; a *smart* saying.

6. Brisk; vivacious; as a *smart* rhetorician.

Who, for the poor renown of being *smart*,
Would leave a sting within a brother's heart? *Young.*

SM'ART, *n.* A cant word for a fellow that affects briskness and vivacity.

SM'ARTEN, *v. t.* To make smart. [*Not in use.*]

SM'ARTLE, *v. i.* To waste away. [*Not in use.*] *Ray.*

SM'ARTLY, *adv.* With keen pain; as, to ake *smartly.*

2. Briskly; sharply; wittily.

3. Vigorously; actively. *Clarendon.*

SM'ARTNESS, *n.* The quality of being smart or pungent; poignancy; as the *smartness* of pain.

2. Quickness; vigor; as the *smartness* of a blow. *Boyle.*

3. Liveliness; briskness; vivacity; wittiness; as the *smartness* of a reply or of a phrase. *Swift.*

SM'ART-WEED, *n.* A name given to the arsmart or *persicaria.*

SMASH, *v. t.* [probably *mash*, with a prefix.] To break in pieces by violence; to dash to pieces; to crush.

Here every thing is broken and *smashed* to pieces. [*Vulgar.*] *Burke.*

SMATCH, *n.* [corrupted from *smack.*]

1. Taste; tincture. [*Not in use or vulgar.*]

2. A bird.

SMAT'TER, *v. i.* [Qu. Dan. *smatter*, to smack, to make a noise in chewing; Sw. *smattra*, to crackle; Ice. *smædr.* It contains the elements of *mutter.*]

1. To talk superficially or ignorantly.

Of state affairs you cannot *smatter.* *Swift.*

2. To have a slight taste, or a slight superficial knowledge.

SMAT'TER, *n.* Slight superficial knowledge. *Temple.*

SMAT'TERER, *n.* One who has only a slight superficial knowledge. *Swift.*

SMAT'TERING, *n.* A slight superficial knowledge. [*This is the word commonly used.*]

SMEAR, *v. t.* [Sax. *smerian, smirian*; D. *smeeren*; G. *schmieren*; Dan. *smörer*; Sw. *smörja*; Ir. *smearam*; Russ. *marayu*; D. *smeer*, G. *schmier*, grease, tallow; Ir. *smear*, id.; Sw. Dan. *smör*, butter. Qu. its alliance with *marrow, marl, mire*, from its softness. See Class Mr. No. 10. 21.]

1. To overspread with any thing unctuous, viscous or adhesive; to besmear; to daub; as, to *smear* any thing with oil, butter, pitch, &c. *Milton. Dryden.*

2. To soil; to contaminate; to pollute; as *smeared* with infamy. *Shak.*

SMEAR, *n.* A fat oily substance; ointment. [*Little used.*]

SME'ARED, *pp.* Overspread with soft or oily matter; soiled.

SME'ARING, *ppr.* Overspreading with any thing soft and oleaginous; soiling.

SME'ARY, *a.* That smears or soils; adhesive. [*Little used.*] *Rowe.*

SMEATH, *n.* A sea fowl.

SMEC'TITE, *n.* [Gr. σμηχτις, deterging.] An argillaceous earth; so called from its property of taking grease out of cloth, &c. *Pinkerton.*

SMEETH, *v. t.* To smoke. [*Not in use.*]

SMEGMAT'IC, *a.* [Gr. σμηγμα, soap.] Being of the nature of soap; soapy; cleansing; detersive.

SMELL, *v. t.* pret. and pp. *smelled, smelt.* [I have not found this word in any other language.] To perceive by the nose, or by the olfactory nerves; to have a sensation excited in certain organs of the nose by particular qualities of a body, which are transmitted in fine particles, often from a distance; as, to *smell* a rose; to *smell* perfumes.

To smell out, is a low phrase signifying to find out by sagacity. *L'Estrange.*

To smell a rat, is a low phrase signifying to suspect strongly.

SMELL, *v. i.* To affect the olfactory nerves; to have an odor or particular scent; followed by *of*; as, to *smell of* smoke; to *smell of* musk.

2. To have a particular tincture or smack of any quality; as, a report *smells* of calumny. [*Not elegant.*] *Shak.*

3. To practice smelling. Ex. xxx.

4. To exercise sagacity. *Shak.*

SMELL, *n.* The sense or faculty by which certain qualities of bodies are perceived through the instrumentality of the olfactory nerves; or the faculty of perceiving by the organs of the nose; one of the five senses. In some species of beasts, the *smell* is remarkably acute, particularly in the canine species.

2. Scent; odor; the quality of bodies which affects the olfactory organs; as the *smell* of mint; the *smell* of geranium.

The sweetest *smell* in the air is that of the white double violet. *Bacon.*

SMELL'ED, SMELT, } *pret.* and *pp.* of *smell.*

SMELL'ER, *n.* One that smells.

SMELL'FEAST, *n.* [*smell* and *feast.*] One that is apt to find and frequent good tables; an epicure; a parasite. *L'Estrange.*

SMELT. [See *Smelled.*]

SMELT, *n.* [Sax.] A small fish that is very delicate food. But in Europe, a fish of the truttaceous kind, so named from its peculiar smell. *Dict. Nat. Hist.*

SMELT, *v. t.* [D. *smelten*; G. *schmelzen*; Dan. *smelter*; Sw. *smälta*, to melt. This is *melt*, with *s* prefixed.] To melt, as ore, for the purpose of separating the metal from extraneous substances.

SMELT'ED, *pp.* Melted for the extraction of the metal.

SMELT'ER, *n.* One that melts ore.

SMELT'ERY, *n.* A house or place for smelting ores.

SMELT'ING, *ppr.* Melting, as ore.

SMELT'ING, *n.* The operation of melting ores for the purpose of extracting the metal.

SMERK, *v. i.* [Sax. *smercian.*] To smile affectedly or wantonly. *Swift.*

2. To look affectedly soft or kind; as a *smerking* countenance; a *smerking* grace. *Young.*

SMERK, *n.* An affected smile.

SMERK, *a.* Nice; smart; janty.

So *smerk*, so smooth he prick'd his ears. *Spenser.*

SMER'LIN, *n.* A fish. *Ainsworth.*

SMEW, *n.* An aquatic fowl, the *Mergus albellus.* *Ed. Encyc.*

SMICK'ER, *v. i.* [Sw. *smickra*, to flatter, Dan. *smigrer.*] To smerk; to look amorously or wantonly. *Kersey.*

SMICK'ERING, *ppr.* Smerking; smiling affectedly.

SMICK'ERING, *n.* An affected smile or amorous look.

SMICK'ET, *n.* Dim. of *smock.* [*Not used.*]

SMID'DY, *n.* [Sax. *smiththa.*] A smithery or smith's workshop. [*Not in use.*]

SMIGHT, for *smite*, in Spenser, is a mistake.

SMILE, *v. i.* [Sw. *smila*; Dan. *smiler.*]

1. To contract the features of the face in such a manner as to express pleasure, moderate joy, or love and kindness; the contrary to *frown.*

The *smiling* infant in his hand shall take
The crested basilisk and speckled snake. *Pope.*

She *smil'd* to see the doughty hero slain. *Pope.*

2. To express slight contempt by a smiling look, implying sarcasm or pity; to sneer.

'Twas what I said to Craggs and Child,
Who prais'd my modesty, and *smil'd.* *Pope.*

3. To look gay and joyous; or to have an appearance to excite joy; as *smiling* spring; *smiling* plenty.

The desert *smil'd*,
And paradise was open'd in the wild. *Pope.*

4. To be propitious or favorable; to favor; to countenance. May heaven *smile* on our labors.

SMILE, *v. t.* To awe with a contemptuous smile. *Young.*

SMILE, *n.* A peculiar contraction of the features of the face, which naturally expresses pleasure, moderate joy, approbation or kindness; opposed to *frown.*

Sweet intercourse of looks and *smiles.* *Milton.*

2. Gay or joyous appearance; as the *smiles* of spring.

3. Favor; countenance; propitiousness; as the *smiles* of providence.

A smile of contempt, a look resembling that of pleasure, but usually or often it can be distinguished by an accompanying archness, or some glance intended to be understood.

SMI'LER, *n.* One who smiles.

SMI'LING, *ppr.* Having a smile on the countenance; looking joyous or gay; looking propitious.

SMI'LINGLY, *adv.* With a look of pleasure.

SMILT, for *smelt.* [*Not in use.*]

SMIRCH, *v. t. smerch.* [from *murk, murky.*] To cloud; to dusk; to soil; as, to *smirch* the face. [*Low.*] *Shak.*

SMIRK, *v. i. smerk.* To look affectedly soft or kind. [See *Smerk.*] *Young.*

SMIT, sometimes used for *smitten.* [See *Smite.*]

SMITE, *v. t.* pret. *smote*; pp. *smitten, smit.* [Sax. *smitan*, to strike; *smitan ofer* or *on*, to put or place, that is, to throw; D. *smyten*, to smite, to cast or throw; G. *schmeissen*, to smite, to fling, to kick, to cast or throw, to fall down, that is, to throw one's self down; Sw. *smida*, to hammer or forge; Dan. *smider*, to forge, to strike, to coin, to invent, devise, counterfeit; D. *smeeden*, to forge; G. *schmieden*, to coin, forge, invent, fabricate. The latter verb seems to be formed on the noun *schmied*, a smith, or *schmiede*, a forge, which is from the root of *smite.* This verb is the L. *mitto*, Fr. *mettre*, with *s* prefixed. Class Md, or Ms. It is no longer in common use, though not entirely obsolete.]

1. To strike; to throw, drive or force against, as the fist or hand, a stone or a

weapon; to reach with a blow or a weapon; as, to *smite* one with the fist; to *smite* with a rod or with a stone.

Whoever shall *smite* thee on the right cheek, turn to him the other also. Matt. v.

2. To kill; to destroy the life of by beating or by weapons of any kind; as, to *smite* one with the sword, or with an arrow or other engine. David *smote* Goliath with a sling and a stone. The Philistines were often *smitten* with great slaughter. [This word, like *slay*, usually or always carries with it something of its original signification, that of *beating*, *striking*, the primitive mode of killing. We never apply it to the destruction of life by poison, by accident or by legal execution.]

3. To blast; to destroy life; as by a stroke or by something sent.

The flax and the barley were *smitten*. Ex. ix.

4. To afflict; to chasten; to punish.

Let us not mistake God's goodness, nor imagine, because he *smites* us, that we are forsaken by him. *Wake.*

5. To strike or affect with passion.

See what the charms that *smite* the simple heart. *Pope.*

Smit with the love of sister arts we came. *Pope.*

To smite with the tongue, to reproach or upbraid. Jer. xviii.

SMITE, *v. i.* To strike; to collide.

The heart melteth and the knees *smite* together. Nah. ii.

SMITE, *n.* A blow. [*Local.*]

SMI'TER, *n.* One who smites or strikes.

I gave my back to the *smiters*. Is. l.

SMITH, *n.* [Sax. *smith*; Dan. Sw. *smed*; D. *smit*; G. *schmied*; from *smiting*.]

1. Literally, the striker, the beater; hence, one who forges with the hammer; one who works in metals; as an iron-*smith*; gold-*smith*; silver-*smith*, &c.

Nor yet the *smith* hath learn'd to form a sword. *Tate.*

2. He that makes or effects any thing. *Dryden.*

Hence the name *Smith*, which, from the number of workmen employed in working metals in early ages, is supposed to be more common than any other.

SMITH, *v. t.* [Sax. *smithian*, to fabricate by hammering.]

To beat into shape; to forge. [*Not in use.*] *Chaucer.*

SMITH'CRAFT, *n.* [*smith* and *craft*.] The art or occupation of a smith. [*Little used.*] *Raleigh.*

SMITH'ERY, *n.* The workshop of a smith.

2. Work done by a smith. *Burke.*

SMITH'ING, *n.* The act or art of working a mass of iron into the intended shape. *Moxon.*

SMITH'Y, *n.* [Sax. *smiththa.*] The shop of a smith. [*I believe never used.*]

SMITT, *n.* The finest of the clayey ore made up into balls, used for marking sheep. *Woodward.*

SMITTEN, *pp.* of *smite*. *smit'n.* Struck; killed.

2. Affected with some passion; excited by beauty or something impressive.

SMIT'TLE, *v. t.* [from *smite.*] To infect. [*Local.*] *Grose.*

SMOCK, *n.* [Sax. *smoc.*] A shift; a chemise; a woman's under garment.

2. In *composition*, it is used for female, or what relates to women; as *smock*-treason. *B. Jonson.*

SMOCK'-FACED, *a.* [*smock* and *face.*] Pale faced; maidenly; having a feminine countenance or complexion. *Fenton.*

SMOCK'-FROCK, *n.* [*smock* and *frock.*] A gaberdine. *Todd.*

SMOCK'LESS, *a.* Wanting a smock. *Chaucer.*

SMOKE, *n.* [Sax. *smoca*, *smec*, *smic*; G. *schmauch*; D. *smook*; W. *ysmwg*, from *mwg*, smoke; Ir. *much*; allied to *muggy*, and I think it allied to the Gr. σμυχω, to consume slowly, to waste.]

1. The exhalation, visible vapor or substance that escapes or is expelled in combustion from the substance burning. It is particularly applied to the volatile matter expelled from vegetable matter, or wood coal, peat, &c. The matter expelled from metallic substances is more generally called *fume*, *fumes*.

2. Vapor; watery exhalations.

SMOKE, *v. i.* [Sax. *smocian*, *smecan*, *smican*; Dan. *smöger*; D. *smooken*; G. *schmauchen.*]

1. To emit smoke; to throw off volatile matter in the form of vapor or exhalation. Wood and other fuel *smokes* when burning; and *smokes* most when there is the least flame.

2. To burn; to be kindled; to rage; in Scripture.

The anger of the Lord and his jealousy shall *smoke* against that man— Deut. xxix.

3. To raise a dust or smoke by rapid motion.

Proud of his steeds, he *smokes* along the field. *Dryden.*

4. To smell or hunt out; to suspect.

I began to *smoke* that they were a parcel of mummers. [*Little used.*] *Addison.*

5. To use tobacco in a pipe or cigar, by kindling the tobacco, drawing the smoke into the mouth and puffing it out.

6. To suffer; to be punished.

Some of you shall *smoke* for it in Rome. *Shak.*

SMOKE, *v. t.* To apply smoke to; to hang in smoke; to scent, medicate or dry by smoke; as, to *smoke* infected clothing; to *smoke* beef or hams for preservation.

2. To smell out; to find out.

He was first *smoked* by the old lord Lafeer. [*Now little used.*] *Shak.*

3. To sneer at; to ridicule to the face. *Congreve.*

SMO'KED, *pp.* Cured, cleansed or dried in smoke.

SMO'KEDRY, *v. t.* To dry by smoke. *Mortimer.*

SMO'KE-JACK, *n.* An engine for turning a spit by means of a fly or wheel turned by the current of ascending air in a chimney.

SMO'KELESS, *a.* Having no smoke; as *smokeless* towers. *Pope.*

SMO'KER, *n.* One that dries by smoke.

2. One that uses tobacco by burning it in a pipe or in the form of a cigar.

SMO'KING, *ppr.* Emitting smoke, as fuel, &c.

2. Applying smoke for cleansing, drying, &c.

3. Using tobacco in a pipe or cigar.

SMO'KING, *n.* The act of emitting smoke.

2. The act of applying smoke to.

3. The act or practice of using tobacco by burning it in a pipe or cigar.

SMO'KY, *a.* Emitting smoke; fumid; as *smoky* fires. *Dryden.*

2. Having the appearance or nature of smoke; as a *smoky* fog. *Harvey.*

3. Filled with smoke, or with a vapor resembling it; thick. New England in autumn frequently has a *smoky* atmosphere.

4. Subject to be filled with smoke from the chimneys or fire-places; as a *smoky* house.

5. Tarnished with smoke; noisome with smoke; as *smoky* rafters; *smoky* cells. *Milton. Denham.*

SMOLDERING, the more correct orthography of *smouldering*, which see.

SMOOR, **SMORE**, *v. t.* [Sax. *smoran.*] To suffocate or smother. [*Not in use.*] *More.*

SMOOTH, *a.* [Sax. *smethe*, *smoeth*; W. *esmwyth*, from *mwyth*; allied to L. *mitis*, Ir. *myth*, *maoth*, soft, tender.]

1. Having an even surface, or a surface so even that no roughness or points are perceptible to the touch; not rough; as *smooth* glass; *smooth* porcelain.

The outlines must be *smooth*, imperceptible to the touch. *Dryden.*

2. Evenly spread; glossy; as a *smooth* haired horse. *Pope.*

3. Gently flowing; moving equably; not ruffled or undulating; as a *smooth* stream; *smooth* Adonis. *Milton.*

4. That is uttered without stops, obstruction or hesitation; voluble; even; not harsh; as *smooth* verse; *smooth* eloquence.

When sage Minerva rose,
From her sweet lips *smooth* elocution flows. *Gay.*

5. Bland; mild; soothing; flattering.

This *smooth* discourse and mild behavior oft
Conceal a traitor— *Addison.*

6. In *botany*, glabrous; having a slippery surface void of roughness.

SMOOTH, *n.* That which is smooth; the smooth part of any thing; as the *smooth* of the neck. Gen. xxvii.

SMOOTH, *v. t.* [Sax. *smethian.*] To make smooth; to make even on the surface by any means; as, to *smooth* a board with a plane; to *smooth* cloth with an iron.

—And *smooth'd* the ruffled sea. *Dryden.*

2. To free from obstruction; to make easy.

Thou, Abelard, the last sad office pay,
And *smooth* my passage to the realms of day. *Pope.*

3. To free from harshness; to make flowing.

In their motions harmony divine
So *smooths* her charming tones. *Milton.*

5. To palliate; to soften; as, to *smooth* a fault. *Shak.*

6. To calm; to mollify; to allay.

Each perturbation *smooth'd* with outward calm. *Milton.*

7. To ease.

The difficulty *smoothed*. *Dryden.*

8. To flatter; to soften with blandishments.

Because I cannot flatter and look fair,
Smile in men's faces, *smooth*, deceive and coy. *Shak.*

SMOOTH'ED, *pp.* Made smooth.

SMOOTHEN, for *smooth*, is used by mechanics; though not, I believe, in the U. States.

SMOOTH'-FACED, *a.* Having a mild, soft look; as *smooth-faced* wooers. *Shak.*

SMOOTH'LY, *adv.* Evenly; not roughly or harshly.
2. With even flow or motion; as, to flow or glide *smoothly.*
3. Without obstruction or difficulty; readily; easily. *Hooker.*
4. With soft, bland, insinuating language.

SMOOTH'NESS, *n.* Evenness of surface; freedom from roughness or asperity; as the *smoothness* of a floor or wall; *smoothness* of the skin; *smoothness* of the water.
2. Softness or mildness to the palate; as the *smoothness* of wine.
3. Softness and sweetness of numbers; easy flow of words.

Virgil, though smooth where *smoothness* is required, is far from affecting it. *Dryden.*

4. Mildness or gentleness of speech; blandness of address. *Shak.*

SMOTE, *pret.* of *smite.*

SMŎTHER, *v. t.* [allied perhaps to Ir. *smuid*, smoke; Sax. *methgian*, to smoke.]
1. To suffocate or extinguish life by causing smoke or dust to enter the lungs; to stifle.
2. To suffocate or extinguish by closely covering, and by the exclusion of air; as, to *smother* a child in bed.
3. To suppress; to stifle; as, to *smother* the light of the understanding. *Hooker.*

SMŎTHER, *v. i.* To be suffocated.
2. To be suppressed or concealed.
3. To smoke without vent. *Bacon.*

SMŎTHER, *n.* Smoke; thick dust. *Shak. Dryden.*
2. A state of suppression. [*Not in use.*] *Bacon.*

SMOUCH, *v. t.* To salute. [*Not in use.*] *Stubbes.*

SMOULDERING, } *a.* [a word formed
SMOULDRY, } from *mold*, *molder*, and therefore it ought to be written *smoldering*. Perhaps we have the word directly from the Dan. *smuler*, *smuller*, Sw. *smola*, *smula*, to crumble or fall to dust; Dan. *smull*, dust; which is from the same root as *mold*, *meal*, &c.]
Burning and smoking without vent. *Dryden.*

SMUG, *a.* [Dan. *smuk*, neat, fine; G. *smuck*; Sax. *smicere.*]
Nice; neat; affectedly nice in dress. [*Not in use or local.*] *Preston.*

SMUG, *v. t.* To make spruce; to dress with affected neatness. [*Not in use.*] *Chaucer.*

SMUG'GLE, *v. t.* [Sw. *smyga*; D. *smokkelen*, which seems to be allied to *smuig*, under hand; *smuigen*, to eat in secret; G. *schmuggeln*; Dan. *smug*, clandestinely. We probably have the root *mug*, in *hugger mugger.*]
1. To import or export secretly goods which are forbidden by the government to be imported or exported; or secretly to import or export dutiable goods without paying the duties imposed by law; to run.
2. To convey clandestinely.

SMUG'GLED, *pp.* Imported or exported clandestinely and contrary to law.

SMUG'GLER, *n.* One that imports or exports goods privately and contrary to law, either contraband goods or dutiable goods, without paying the customs.
2. A vessel employed in running goods.

SMUG'GLING, *ppr.* Importing or exporting goods contrary to law.

SMUG'GLING, *n.* The offense of importing or exporting prohibited goods, or other goods without paying the customs. *Blackstone.*

SMUG'LY, *adv.* Neatly; sprucely. [*Not in use.*] *Gay.*

SMUG'NESS, *n.* Neatness; spruceness without elegance. [*Not in use.*] *Sherwood.*

SMUT, *n.* [Dan. *smuds*; Sax. *smitta*; D. *smet*, a spot or stain; Sw. *smitta*, to taint; D. *smoddig*, dirty; *smodderen*, to *smut*; G. *schmutz.*]
1. A spot made with soot or coal; or the foul matter itself.
2. A foul black substance which forms on corn. Sometimes the whole ear is blasted and converted into *smut.* This is often the fact with maiz. *Smut* lessens the value of wheat.
3. Obscene language.

SMUT, *v. t.* To stain or mark with smut; to blacken with coal, soot or other dirty substance. *Addison.*
2. To taint with mildew. *Bacon.*
3. To blacken; to tarnish.

SMUT, *v. i.* To gather smut; to be converted into smut.

SMUTCH, *v. t.* [from *smoke*; Dan. *smöger.* Qu.]
To blacken with smoke, soot or coal. *B. Jonson.*

[*Note.* We have a common word in New England, pronounced *smooch*, which I take to be *smutch.* It signifies to foul or blacken with something produced by combustion or other like substance.]

SMUT'TILY, *adv.* Blackly; smokily; foully.
2. With obscene language.

SMUT'TINESS, *n.* Soil from smoke, soot, coal or smut.
2. Obsceneness of language.

SMUT'TY, *a.* Soiled with smut, coal, soot or the like.
2. Tainted with mildew; as *smutty* corn.
3. Obscene; not modest or pure; as *smutty* language.

SNACK, *n.* [Qu. from the root of *snatch.*]
1. A share. It is now chiefly or wholly used in the phrase, to *go snacks* with one, that is, to have a share. *Pope.*
2. A slight hasty repast.

SNACK'ET, } *n.* The hasp of a casement.
SNECK'ET, } [*Local.*] *Sherwood.*

SNAC'OT, *n.* A fish. [L. *acus.*] *Ainsworth.*

SNAF'FLE, *n.* [D. *sneb*, *snavel*, bill, beak, snout; G. Dan. Sw. *snabel*; from the root of *nib*, *neb.*]
A bridle consisting of a slender bit-mouth, without branches. *Encyc.*

SNAF'FLE, *v. t.* To bridle; to hold or manage with a bridle.

SNAG, *n.* A short branch, or a sharp or rough branch; a shoot; a knot.

The coat of arms
Now on a naked *snag* in triumph borne. *Dryden.*

2. A tooth, in contempt; or a tooth projecting beyond the rest. *Prior.*

SNAG'GED, } *a.* Full of snags; full of short
SNAG'GY, } rough branches or sharp points; abounding with knots; as a *snaggy* tree; a *snaggy* stick; a *snaggy* oak. *Spenser. More.*

SNAIL, *n.* [Sax. *snægel*, *snegel*; Sw. *snigel*; Dan. *snegel*; G. *schnecke*; dim. from the root of *snake*, *sneak.*]
1. A slimy slow creeping animal, of the genus Helix, and order of Mollusca. The eyes of this insect are in the horns, one at the end of each, which it can retract at pleasure. *Encyc.*
2. A drone; a slow moving person. *Shak.*

SNAIL-CLAVER, } *n.* A plant of the ge-
SNAIL-TREFOIL, } nus Medicago.

SNA'IL-FLOWER, *n.* A plant of the genus Phaseolus.

SNA'IL-LIKE, *a.* Resembling a snail; moving very slowly.

SNA'IL-LIKE, *adv.* In the manner of a snail; slowly.

SNAKE, *n.* [Sax. *snaca*; Dan. *snog*; G. *schnake*; [Sans. *naga.* Qu.] In G. *schnecke*, Dan. *snekke*, is a snail, from the root of Dan. *sniger*, Ir. *snaighim*, Sax. *snican*, to creep, to *sneak.*]
A serpent of the oviparous kind, distinguished from a viper, says Johnson. But in America, the common and general name of serpents, and so the word is used by the poets. *Dryden. Shak.*

SNAKE, *v. t.* In *seamen's language*, to wind a small rope round a large one spirally, the small ropes lying in the spaces between the strands of the large one. This is called also *worming.*

SNA'KEROOT, *n.* [*snake* and *root.*] A plant, a species of birth-wort, growing in North America; the *Aristolochia serpentaria.* *Johnson. Lee.*

SNA'KE'S-HEAD *Iris*, *n.* A plant with a lily shaped flower, of one leaf, shaped like an iris; the hermodactyl, or *Iris tuberosa.* *Miller. Lee.*

SNA'KEWEED, *n.* [*snake* and *weed.*] A plant, bistort, of the genus Polygonum.

SNA'KEWOOD, *n.* [*snake* and *wood.*] The smaller branches of a tree, growing in the isle of Timor and other parts of the east, having a bitter taste, and supposed to be a certain remedy for the bite of the hooded serpent. *Hill.*
It is the wood of the *Strychnos colubrina.* *Parr.*

SNA'KING, *ppr.* Winding small ropes spirally round a large one.

SNA'KY, *a.* Pertaining to a snake or to snakes; resembling a snake; serpentine; winding.
2. Sly; cunning; insinuating; deceitful.

So to the coast of Jordan he directs
His easy steps, girded with *snaky* wiles. *Milton.*

3. Having serpents; as a *snaky* rod or wand. *Dryden.*

That *snaky* headed gorgon shield. *Milton.*

SNAP, *v. t.* [D. *snappen*, *snaauwen*; G. *schnappen*, to snap, to snatch, to gasp or catch for breath; Dan. *snapper*; Sw. *snappa*; from the root of *knap* and D. *knippen.*]
1. To break at once; to break short; as substances that are brittle.

Breaks the doors open, *snaps* the locks. *Prior.*

2. To strike with a sharp sound. *Pope.*
3. To bite or seize suddenly with the teeth. *Addison. Gay.*

4. To break upon suddenly with sharp angry words.
5. To crack; as, to *snap* a whip.
To snap off, to break suddenly.
2. To bite off suddenly. *Wiseman.*
To snap one up, to snap one up short, to treat with sharp words.
SNAP, *v. i.* To break short; to part asunder suddenly; as, a mast or spar *snaps*; a needle *snaps*.

If steel is too hard, that is, too brittle, with the least bending it will *snap*. *Moxon.*

2. To make an effort to bite; to aim to seize with the teeth; as, a dog *snaps* at a passenger; a fish *snaps* at the bait.
3. To utter sharp, harsh, angry words.
SNAP, *n.* A sudden breaking or rupture of any substance.
2. A sudden eager bite; a sudden seizing or effort to seize with the teeth.
3. A crack of a whip.
4. A greedy fellow. *L'Estrange.*
5. A catch; a theft. *Johnson.*
SNAP'-DRAGON, *n.* A plant, calf's snout, of the genus Antirrhinum, and another of the genus Ruellia, and one of the genus Barleria.
2. A play in which raisins are snatched from burning brandy and put into the mouth. *Tatler.*
3. The thing eaten at snap-dragon. *Swift.*
SNAP'PED, *pp.* Broken abruptly; seized or bitten suddenly; cracked, as a whip.
SNAP'PER, *n.* One that snaps. *Shak.*
SNAP'PISH, *a.* Eager to bite; apt to snap; as a *snappish* cur.
2. Peevish; sharp in reply; apt to speak angrily or tartly.
SNAP'PISHLY, *adv.* Peevishly; angrily; tartly.
SNAP'PISHNESS, *n.* The quality of being snappish; peevishness; tartness.
SNAP'SACK, *n.* A knapsack. [*Vulgar.*]
SN'AR, *v. i.* To snarl. [*Not in use.*] *Spenser.*
SNARE, *n.* [Dan. *snare*; Sw. *snara*; Dan. *snore*, a string or cord, D. *snor*; Sw. *snôre*, a line; *snôra*, to lace.]
1. An instrument for catching animals, particularly fowls, by the leg. It consists of a cord or string with slip-knots, in which the leg is entangled. A *snare* is not a net.
2. Any thing by which one is entangled and brought into trouble. 1 Cor. vii.

A fool's lips are the *snare* of his soul. Prov. xviii.

SNARE, *v. t.* [Dan. *snarer.*] To catch with a snare; to ensnare; to entangle; to bring into unexpected evil, perplexity or danger.

The wicked is *snared* in the work of his own hands. Ps. ix.

SNA'RED, *pp.* Entangled; unexpectedly involved in difficulty.
SNA'RER, *n.* One who lays snares or entangles.
SNA'RING, *ppr.* Entangling; ensnaring.
SN'ARL, *v. i.* [G. *schnarren*, to snarl, to speak in the throat; D. *snar*, snappish. This word seems to be allied to *gnarl*, and to proceed from some root signifying to twist, bind or fasten, or to involve, entangle, and thus to be allied to *snare.*]
1. To growl, as an angry or surly dog; to gnarl; to utter grumbling sounds; but it expresses more violence than *grumble.*

That I should *snarl* and bite and play the dog. *Shak.*

2. To speak roughly; to talk in rude murmuring terms.

It is malicious and unmanly to *snarl* at the little lapses of a pen, from which Virgil himself stands not exempted. *Dryden.*

SN'ARL, *v. t.* To entangle; to complicate; to involve in knots; as, to *snarl* the hair; to *snarl* a skain of thread. [*This word is in universal popular use in New England.*]
2. To embarrass.
SN'ARL, *n.* Entanglement; a knot or complication of hair, thread, &c., which it is difficult to disentangle.
SN'ARLER, *n.* One who snarls; a surly growling animal; a grumbling quarrelsome fellow. *Swift.*
SN'ARLING, *ppr* Growling; grumbling angrily.
2. Entangling.
SNA'RY, *a.* [from *snare.*] Entangling; insidious.

Spiders in the vault their *snary* webs have spread. *Dryden.*

SNAST, *n.* [G. *schnautze*, a snout.] The snuff of a candle. [*Not in use.*] *Bacon.*
SNATCH, *v. t.* pret. and pp. *snatched* or *snacht.* [D. *snakken*, to gasp, to catch for breath.]
1. To seize hastily or abruptly.

When half our knowledge we must *snatch*, not take. *Pope.*

2. To seize without permission or ceremony; as, to *snatch* a kiss.
3. To seize and transport away; as, *snatch* me to heaven. *Thomson.*
SNATCH, *v. i.* To catch at; to attempt to seize suddenly.

Nay, the ladies too will be *snatching*. *Shak.*

He shall *snatch* on the right hand, and be hungry. Is. ix.

SNATCH, *n.* A hasty catch or seizing.
2. A catching at or attempt to seize suddenly.
3. A short fit of vigorous action; as a *snatch* at weeding after a shower. *Tusser.*
4. A broken or interrupted action; a short fit or turn.

They move by fits and *snatches*. *Wilkins.*
We have often little *snatches* of sunshine. *Spectator.*

5. A shuffling answer. [*Little used.*] *Shak.*
SNATCH'-BLOCK, *n.* A particular kind of block used in ships, having an opening in one side to receive the bight of a rope. *Mar. Dict.*
SNATCH'ED, *pp.* Seized suddenly and violently.
SNATCH'ER, *n.* One that snatches or takes abruptly. *Shak.*
SNATCH'ING, *ppr.* Seizing hastily or abruptly; catching at.
SNATCH'INGLY, *adv.* By snatching; hastily; abruptly.
SN'ATH, *n.* [Sax. *snæd*; Eng. *snathe*, *sneath.*]
The handle of a sythe. *New England.*
SNATHE, *v. t.* [Sax. *snidan*, *snithan.*] To lop; to prune. [*Not in use.*]
SNAT'TOCK, *n.* [supra.] A chip; a slice. [*Not in use or local.*] *Gayton.*
SNEAK, *v. i.* [Sax. *snican*; Dan. *sniger*, to creep, to move softly. See *Snake.*]
1. To creep or steal away privately; to withdraw meanly, as a person afraid or ashamed to be seen; as, to *sneak* away from company; to *sneak* into a corner or behind a screen.

You skulk'd behind the fence, and *sneak'd* away. *Dryden.*

2. To behave with meanness and servility; to crouch; to truckle.

Will *sneaks* a scriv'ner, an exceeding knave. *Pope.*

SNEAK, *v. t.* To hide. [*Not in use.*] *Wake.*
SNEAK, *n.* A mean fellow.
SNE'AKER, *n.* A small vessel of drink. [*Local.*] *Spectator.*
SNE'AKING, *ppr.* Creeping away slily; stealing away.
2. *a.* Mean; servile; crouching. *Rowe.*
3. Meanly parsimonious; covetous; niggardly.
SNE'AKINGLY, *adv.* In a sneaking manner; meanly. *Herbert.*
SNE'AKINGNESS, *n.* Meanness; niggardliness. *Boyle.*
SNE'AKUP, *n.* A sneaking, cowardly, insidious fellow. [*Not used.*] *Shak.*
SNEAP, *v. t.* [Dan. *snibbe*, reproach, reprimand; *snip*, the end or point of a thing; D. *snip*, a *snipe*, from its bill; *snippen*, to *snip* or *nip*; G. *schneppe*, a peak; from the root of *neb*, *nib*, *nip*, with the sense of shooting out, thrusting like a sharp point.]
1. To check; to reprove abruptly; to reprimand. *Obs.* *Chaucer.*
2. To nip. *Obs.* *Shak.*
SNEB, *v. t.* To check; to reprimand. [The same as *sneap.*] *Spenser.*
SNEEK, *n.* The latch of a door. [*Not in use or local.*]
SNEED, SNEAD, } *n.* A snath. [See *Snath.*]
SNEER, *v. i.* [from the root of L. *naris*, nose; to turn up the nose.]
1. To show contempt by turning up the nose, or by a particular cast of countenance; "naso suspendere adunco."
2. To insinuate contempt by covert expression.

I could be content to be a little *sneered* at. *Pope.*

3. To utter with grimace. *Congreve.*
4. To show mirth awkwardly. *Tatler.*
SNEER, *n.* A look of contempt, or a turning up of the nose to manifest contempt; a look of disdain, derision or ridicule. *Pope.*
2. An expression of ludicrous scorn. *Watts.*
SNEE'RER, *n.* One that sneers.
SNEE'RFUL, *a.* Given to sneering. [*Not in use.*] *Shenstone.*
SNEE'RING, *ppr.* Manifesting contempt or scorn by turning up the nose, or by some grimace or significant look.
SNEE'RINGLY, *adv.* With a look of contempt or scorn.
SNEEZE, *v. i.* [Sax. *niesan*; D. *niezen*; G. *niesen*; Sw. *nysa*; from the root of *nose*, G. *nase*, Dan. *næse*, D. *neus*, L. *nasus*; the primary sense of which is to project.]
To emit air through the nose audibly and violently, by a kind of involuntary convulsive force, occasioned by irritation of the inner membrane of the nose. Thus snuff or any thing that tickles the nose, makes one *sneeze*. *Swift.*

SNEEZE, *n.* A sudden and violent ejection of air through the nose with an audible sound. *Milton.*

SNEE'ZE-WŎRT, *n.* A plant, a species of Achillea, and another of Xeranthemum.

SNEE'ZING, *ppr.* Emitting air from the nose audibly.

SNEE'ZING, *n.* The act of ejecting air violently and audibly through the nose; sternutation.

SNELL, *a.* [Sax. *snel.*] Active; brisk; nimble. [*Not in use.*]

SNET, *n.* The fat of a deer. [*Local among sportsmen.*]

SNEW, *old pret.* of *snow.* *Obs.* *Chaucer.*

SNIB, to nip or reprimand, is only a different spelling of *sneb, sneap. Hubberd's Tale.*

SNICK, *n.* A small cut or mark; a latch. [*Not in use.*]

Snick and snee, a combat with knives. [*Not in use.*]

[*Snee* is a Dutch contraction of *snyden*, to cut.]

SNICK'ER, } *v. i.* [Sw. *niugg*, close. This
SNIG'GER, } can have no connection with *sneer.* The elements and the sense are different.]

To laugh slily; or to laugh in one's sleeve. [*It is a word in common use in New England, not easily defined. It signifies to laugh with small audible catches of voice, as when persons attempt to suppress loud laughter.*]

SNIFF, *v. i.* To draw air audibly up the nose. [See *Snuff.*] *Swift.*

SNIFF, *v. t.* To draw in with the breath. [*Not in use.*] *Todd.*

SNIFF, *n.* Perception by the nose. [*Not in use.*] *Warton.*

SNIFT, *v. i.* To snort. [*Not in use.*]

SNIG, *n.* [See *Snake.*] A kind of eel. [*Local.*] *Grose.*

SNIG'GLE, *v. i.* [supra.] To fish for eels, by thrusting the bait into their holes. [*Local.*] *Walton.*

SNIG'GLE, *v. t.* To snare; to catch. *Beaum.*

SNIP, *v. t.* [D. *snippen*, to nip; *knippen*, to clip. See *Sneap.*]

To clip; to cut off the nip or neb, or to cut off at once with shears or scissors.

SNIP, *n.* A clip; a single cut with shears or scissors. *Shak. Wiseman.*

2. A small shred. *Wiseman.*

3. Share; a snack. [*A low word.*] *L'Estrange.*

SNIPE, *n.* [D. *snip*; G. *schnepfe*; from *neb*, *nib*; so named from its bill.]

1. A bird that frequents the banks of rivers and the borders of fens, distinguished by the length of its bill; the *scolopax gallinago.*

2. A fool; a blockhead. *Shak.*

SNIP'PER, *n.* One that snips or clips.

SNIP'PET, *n.* A small part or share. [*Not in use.*] *Hudibras.*

Snipsnap, a cant word, formed by repeating *snap*, and signifying a tart dialogue with quick replies. *Pope.*

SNITE, *n.* [Sax.] A snipe. [*Not in use.*] *Carew.*

SNITE, *v. t.* [Sax. *snytan.*] To blow the nose. [*Not in use.*] In Scotland, *snite* the candle, snuff it. *Grew.*

SNIVEL, *n.* *sniv'l.* [Sax. *snofel, snyfling.* Qu. *neb, nib, snuff.*]

Snot; mucus running from the nose.

SNIV'EL, *v. i.* To run at the nose.

2. To cry as children, with snuffing or sniveling.

SNIV'ELER, *n.* One that cries with sniveling.

2. One that weeps for slight causes, or manifests weakness by weeping.

SNIV'ELY, *a.* Running at the nose; pitiful; whining.

SNOD, *n.* [Sax.] A fillet. [*Not in use or local.*]

SNOD, *a.* Trimmed; smooth. [*Local.*]

SNOOK, *v. i.* [Sw. *snoka.* Qu. *nook.*] To lurk; to lie in ambush. [*Not in use.*] *Scott.*

SNORE, *v. i.* [Sax. *snora*, a snoring; D. *snorken*; G. *schnarchen*; Sw. *snarka*; from the root of L. *naris*, the nose or nostrils.]

To breathe with a rough hoarse noise in sleep. *Roscommon.*

SNORE, *n.* A breathing with a harsh noise in sleep.

SNO'RER, *n.* One that snores.

SNO'RING, *ppr.* Respiring with a harsh noise.

SNORT, *v. i.* [G. *schnarchen.* See *Snore.*]

1. To force the air with violence through the nose, so as to make a noise, as high spirited horses in prancing and play.

2. To snore. [*Not common.*]

SNORT, *v. t.* To turn up in anger, scorn or derision, as the nose. [*Unusual.*] *Chaucer.*

SNORT'ER, *n.* One that snorts; a snorer.

SNORT'ING, *ppr.* Forcing the air violently through the nose.

SNORT'ING, *n.* The act of forcing the air through the nose with violence and noise. Jer. viii.

2. Act of snoring. [*Unusual.*]

SNOT, *n.* [Sax. *snote*; D. *snot*; Dan. *id.*] Mucus discharged from the nose. *Swift.*

SNOT, *v. t.* [Sax. *snytan.*] To blow the nose. *Sherwood.*

SNOT'TER, *v. i.* To snivel; to sob. [*Local.*] *Grose.*

SNOT'TY, *a.* Foul with snot.

2. Mean; dirty.

SNOUT, *n.* [W. *ysnid*; D. *snuit*; G. *schnautze*, snout; *schnäutzen*, to snuff, to blow the nose, Sax. *snytan*; Sw. *snyte*, Dan. *snude*, snout; *snyder*, to snuff.]

1. The long projecting nose of a beast, as that of swine.

2. The nose of a man; in contempt. *Hudibras.*

3. The nozzle or end of a hollow pipe.

SNOUT, *v. t.* To furnish with a nozzle or point. *Camden.*

SNOUT'ED, *a.* Having a snout. *Heylin.*

SNOUT'Y, *a.* Resembling a beast's snout. *Otway.*

SNOW, *n.* [a contracted word; Sax. *snaw*; Goth. *snaiws*; D. *sneeuw*; G. *schnee*; Dan. *snee*; Sw. *sne*; Sclav. *sneg*; Bohem. *snik*; Ir. *sneacht*; Fr. *neige*; L. *nix*, *nivis*; It. Port. *neve*; Sp. *nieve.* The Latin *nivis*, is contracted from *nigis*, like Eng. *bow*, from Sax. *bugan.* The prefix *s* is common in the other languages.]

1. Frozen vapor; watery particles congealed into white crystals in the air, and falling to the earth. When there is no wind, these crystals fall in flakes or unbroken collections, sometimes extremely beautiful.

2. A vessel equipped with two masts, resembling the main and fore-masts of a ship, and a third small mast just abaft the main-mast, carrying a try-sail. *Mar. Dict.*

SNOW, *v. i.* [Sax. *snawan.*] To fall in snow; as, it *snows*; it *snowed* yesterday.

SNOW, *v. t.* To scatter like snow. *Donne.*

SNOWBALL, *n.* [*snow* and *ball.*] A round mass of snow, pressed or rolled together. *Locke. Dryden.*

SNOWBALL TREE, *n.* A flowering shrub of the genus Viburnum; gelder rose.

SNOW-BIRD, *n.* A small bird which appears in the time of snow, of the genus Emberiza; called also *snow-bunting.*

In the U. States, the *snow-bird* is the *Fringilla nivalis.* *Wilson.*

SNOWBROTH, *n.* [*snow* and *broth.*] Snow and water mixed; very cold liquor. *Shak.*

SNOW-CROWNED, *a.* [*snow* and *crown.*] Crowned or having the top covered with snow. *Drayton.*

SNOWDEEP, *n.* [*snow* and *deep.*] A plant.

SNOW-DRIFT, *n.* [*snow* and *drift.*] A bank of snow driven together by the wind.

SNOW-DROP, *n.* [*snow* and *drop.*] A plant bearing a white flower, cultivated in gardens for its beauty; the *Galanthus nivalis.*

SNOWLESS, *a.* Destitute of snow. *Tooke.*

SNOWLIKE, *a.* Resembling snow.

SNOW-SHOE, *n.* [*snow* and *shoe.*] A shoe or racket worn by men traveling on snow, to prevent their feet from sinking into the snow.

SNOW-SLIP, *n.* [*snow* and *slip.*] A large mass of snow which slips down the side of a mountain, and sometimes buries houses. *Goldsmith.*

SNOW-WHITE, *a.* [*snow* and *white.*] White as snow; very white.

SNOWY, *a.* White like snow. *Shak.*

2. Abounding with snow; covered with snow.

The *snowy* top of cold Olympus. *Milton.*

3. White; pure; unblemished. *Hall.*

SNUB, *n.* [D. *sneb*; a different orthography of *snip, sneap, neb, nib, nip.*]

A knot or protuberance in wood; a snag. [*Not in use.*] *Spenser.*

SNUB, *v. t.* [supra.] To nip; to clip or break off the end. Hence,

2. To check; to reprimand; to check, stop or rebuke with a tart sarcastic reply or remark. [This is the same word radically as *sneap*, *sneb*, and is the word chiefly used.]

SNUB, *v. i.* [G. *schnauben*, to snub, to snort, to pant for, to puff.] To sob with convulsions. [*Not used.*]

SNUB'-NOSE, *n.* A short or flat nose.

SNUB'-NOSED, *a.* Having a short flat nose.

SNUDGE, *v. i.* [Dan. *sniger.* See *Snug.*] To lie close; to snug. [*Not in use or vulgar.*] *Herbert.*

SNUDGE, *n.* A miser, or a sneaking fellow. [*Not in use.*]

SNUFF, *n.* [D. *snuf*, whence *snuffen*, to snuff, to scent; G. *schnuppe*; allied to *snub, neb, nib.*]

1. The burning part of a candle wick, or that which has been charred by the flame, whether burning or not. *Addison.*

2. A candle almost burnt out. *Shak.*

3. Pulverized tobacco, taken or prepared to be taken into the nose.

4. Resentment; huff, expressed by a snuffing of the nose. *Bacon.*

SNUFF, *v. t.* [D. *snuffen*; G. *schnupfen*, to take snuff; *schnuppen*, to snuff a candle.]

1. To draw in with the breath; to inhale; as, to *snuff* the wind. *Dryden.*

2. To scent; to smell; to perceive by the nose. *Dryden.*

3. To crop the snuff, as of a candle; to take off the end of the snuff. *Swift.*

SNUFF, *v. i.* To snort; to inhale air with violence or with noise; as dogs and horses. *Dryden.*

2. To turn up the nose and inhale air in contempt. Mal. ii.

3. To take offense.

SNUFF'BOX, *n.* A box for carrying snuff about the person.

SNUFF'ER, *n.* One that snuffs.

SNUFF'ERS, *n. plu.* An instrument for cropping the snuff of a candle.

SNUF'FLE, *v. i.* [D. *snuffelen*; G. *nüffeln* and *schnuffeln*; Dan. *snövler*, to *snuffle*, to give a crabbed answer, to *snub*.]

To speak through the nose; to breathe hard through the nose, or through the nose when obstructed.

> Some senseless Phillis, in a broken note,
> *Snuffling* at nose— *Dryden.*

SNUF'FLER, *n.* One that snuffles or speaks through the nose when obstructed.

SNUF'FLES, *n.* Obstruction of the nose by mucus.

SNUF'FLING, *n.* A speaking through the nose. *Swift.*

SNUFF'TAKER, *n.* One that takes snuff, or inhales it into the nose.

SNUFF'Y, *a.* Soiled with snuff.

SNUG, *v. i.* [Dan. *sniger*, to sneak; Sax. *snican*, to creep; probably allied to *nigh*, close, Sw. *niugg*. See *Snake*.]

To lie close; as, a child *snugs* to its mother or nurse. *Sidney.*

SNUG, *a.* [Sw. *snygg*, neat.] Lying close; closely pressed; as, an infant lies *snug*.

2. Close; concealed; not exposed to notice.

> At Will's
> Lie *snug* and hear what critics say. *Swift.*

3. Being in good order; all convenient; neat; as a *snug* little farm.

4. Close; neat; convenient; as a *snug* house.

5. Slily or insidiously close.

> When you lay *snug*, to snap young Damon's goat. *Dryden.*

SNUG'GLE, *v. i.* [from *snug*.] To move one way and the other to get a close place; to lie close for convenience or warmth.

SNUG'LY, *adv.* Closely; safely.

SNUG'NESS, *n.* Closeness; the state of being neat or convenient. *Hayley's Cowper.*

SO, *adv.* [Goth. Sax. *swa*; G. *so*; D. *zo*; Dan. *saa*; Sw. *så*; perhaps L. *sic*, contracted, or Heb. שוה to compose, to set. In Ir. *so* is this or that. It is the same in Scots. It is from some root signifying to *set*, to *still*, and this sense is retained in the use of the word by milkmaids, who say to cows, *so, so*, that is, stand still, remain as you are; and in this use, the word may be the original verb.]

1. In like manner, answering to *as*, and noting comparison or resemblance; *as* with the people, *so* with the priest.

2. In such a degree; to that degree.

> Why is his chariot *so* long in coming? Judges v.

3. In such a manner; sometimes repeated, *so* and *so*; as certain colors, mingled *so* and *so*. *Suckling.*

4. It is followed by *as*.

> There is something equivalent in France and Scotland; *so as* it is a hard calumny upon our soil to affirm that so excellent a fruit will not grow here. *Temple.*

But in like phrases, we now use *that*; "*so that* it is a hard calumny;" and this may be considered as the established usage.

5. In the same manner.

> Use your tutor with great respect, and cause all your family to do *so* too. *Locke.*

6. Thus; in this manner; as New York *so* called from the duke of York. I know not why it is, but *so* it is.

> It concerns every man, with the greatest seriousness, to inquire whether these things are *so* or not. *Tillotson.*

7. Therefore; thus; for this reason; in consequence of this or that.

> It leaves instruction, and *so* instructors, to the sobriety of the settled articles of the church. *Holyday.*

> God makes him in his own image an intellectual creature, and *so* capable of dominion. *Locke.*

> This statute made the clipping of coin high treason, which it was not at common law; *so* that this was an enlarging statute. *Blackstone.*

8. On these terms, noting a conditional petition.

> Here then exchange we mutually forgiveness;
> *So* may the guilt of all my broken vows,
> My perjuries to thee be all forgotten. *Rowe.*

So here might be expressed by *thus*, that is, in this manner, by this mutual forgiveness.

9. Provided that; on condition that, [L. *modo*.]

> *So* the doctrine be but wholesome and edifying—though there should be a want of exactness in the manner of speaking and reasoning, it may be overlooked. *Atterbury.*

> I care not who furnishes the means, *so* they are furnished. *Anon.*

10. In like manner, noting the concession of one proposition or fact and the assumption of another; answering to *as*.

> *As* a war should be undertaken upon a just motive, *so* a prince ought to consider the condition he is in when he enters on it. *Swift.*

11. *So* often expresses the sense of a word or sentence going before. In this case it prevents a repetition, and may be considered as a substitute for the word or phrase. "France is highly cultivated, but England is more *so*," that is, *more highly cultivated*. *Arthur Young.*

> To make men *happy*, and to keep them *so*. *Creech.*

12. Thus; thus it is; this is the state.

> How sorrow shakes him!
> *So* now the tempest tears him up by th' roots. *Dryden.*

13. Well; the fact being such. And *so* the work is done, is it?

14. It is sometimes used to express a certain degree, implying comparison, and yet without the corresponding word *as*, to render the degree definite.

> An astringent is not quite *so* proper, where relaxing the urinary passages is necessary. *Arbuthnot.*

That is, not perfectly proper, or not so proper as something else not specified.

15. It is sometimes equivalent to *be it so, let it be so, let it be as it is*, or *in that manner*.

> There is Percy; if your father will do me any honor, *so*; if not, let him kill the next Percy himself. *Shak.*

16. It expresses a wish, desire or petition.

> Ready are the appellant and defendant—
> *So* please your highness to behold the fight. *Shak.*

17. *So much as*, however much. Instead of *so*, we now generally use *as*; *as much as*, that much; whatever the quantity may be.

18. *So so*, or *so* repeated, used as a kind of exclamation; equivalent to well, well; or it is so, the thing is done.

> *So, so*, it works; now, mistress, sit you fast. *Dryden.*

19. *So so*, much as it was; indifferently; not well nor much amiss.

> His leg is but *so so*. *Shak.*

20. *So then*, thus then it is; therefore; the consequence is.

> *So then* the Volscians stand; but as at first
> Ready, when time shall prompt them, to make road
> Upon's again. *Shak.*

SŌAK, *v. t.* [Sax. *socian*; W. *swgiaw*, to soak, and *sugaw*, to suck. To *soak* is to *suck in*; D. *zuigen*, G. *saugen*, Ar. سقى sakai, to imbibe, that is, to draw; Ir. *sughthach*, soaking; perhaps hence Sw. *sackta*, D. *zagt*, soft. Class Sg. No. 36. Heb. Ch. Syr. שקה. No. 82.]

1. To steep; to cause or suffer to lie in a fluid till the substance has imbibed what it can contain; to macerate in water or other fluid; as, to *soak* cloth; to *soak* bread.

2. To drench; to wet thoroughly. The earth is *soaked* with heavy rains.

> Their land shall be *soaked* with blood. Is. xxxiv.

3. To draw in by the pores; as the skin. *Dryden.*

4. To drain. [*Not authorized.*]

SŌAK, *v. i.* To lie steeped in water or other fluid. Let the cloth lie and *soak*.

2. To enter into pores or interstices. Water *soaks* into the earth or other porous matter.

3. To drink intemperately or gluttonously; to drench; as a *soaking* club. [*Low.*] *Locke.*

SŌAKED, *pp.* Steeped or macerated in a fluid; drenched.

SŌAKER, *n.* One that soaks or macerates in a liquid.

2. A hard drinker. [*Low.*]

SŌAKING, *ppr.* Steeping; macerating; drenching; imbibing.

2. *a.* That wets thoroughly; as a *soaking* rain.

SOAL, of a shoe. [See *Sole*.]

SŌAP, *n.* [Sax. *sape*; D. *zeep*; G. *seife*; Sw. *såpa*; Dan. *sæbe*; Fr. *savon*; It. *sapone*; Sp. *xabon*; L. *sapo*; Gr. σαπων; Arm. *savann*; W. *sebon*; Hindoo, *saboon*, *savin*; Gipsey, *sapuna*; Pers. صابون sabun; Ar. صابون sabunon. Class Sb. No. 29.]

A compound of oil and alkali, or oil and earth, and metallic oxyds; usually, a compound of oil and vegetable alkali or lye; used in washing and cleansing, in medicine, &c.

SŌAP, *v. t.* [Sax. *sapan*; D. *zeepen*; G. *seifen*.] To rub or wash over with soap.

SŌAPBERRY TREE, *n.* A tree of the genus Sapindus.

SŌAP-BOILER, *n.* [*soap* and *boiler*.] One whose occupation is to make soap.

SŌAPSTONE, *n.* Steatite; a mineral or species of magnesian earth, usually white or yellow; the lapis ollaris.

SŌAP-SUDS, *n.* Suds; water well impregnated with soap.

SŌAPWÖRT, *n.* A plant of the genus Saponaria.

SŌAPY, *a.* Resembling soap; having the qualities of soap; soft and smooth.

2. Smeared with soap.

SŌAR, *v. i.* [Fr. *essorer*, to soar; *essor*, flight; It. *sorare*; Eth. ሠረረ sarar, to fly, to be lofty. Lud. Col. 109. Class Sr. No. 20.]

1. To fly aloft; to mount upon the wing; as an eagle. Hence,
2. To rise high; to mount; to tower in thought or imagination; to be sublime; as the poet or orator.
3. To rise high in ambition or heroism.

> Valor *soars* above
> What the world calls misfortune. *Addison.*

4. In general, to rise aloft; to be lofty.

SŌAR, *n.* A towering flight. *Milton.*

SŌARING, *ppr.* Mounting on the wing; rising aloft; towering in thought or mind.

SŌARING, *n.* The act of mounting on the wing, or of towering in thought or mind; intellectual flight.

SOB, *v. i.* [Sax. *seobgend*, complaining. Qu.]

To sigh with a sudden heaving of the breast, or a kind of convulsive motion; to sigh with deep sorrow or with tears.

> She sigh'd, she *sobb'd*, and furious with despair,
> She rent her garments, and she tore her hair. *Dryden.*

SOB, *n.* A convulsive sigh or catching of the breath in sorrow; a convulsive act of respiration obstructed by sorrow. *Johnson.*

> Break, heart, or choke with *sobs* my hated breath. *Dryden.*

SOB, *v. t.* To soak. [*Not in use.*] *Mortimer.*

SOB'BING, *ppr.* Sighing with a heaving of the breast.

SO'BER, *a.* [Fr. *sobre*; It. *sobrio*; L. *sobrius*; D. *sober*, poor, mean, spare, sober; Sax. *sifer*, sober, pure, chaste. See *Soft*.]

1. Temperate in the use of spirituous liquors; habitually temperate; as a *sober* man.

> Live a *sober*, righteous and godly life. *Com. Prayer.*

2. Not intoxicated or overpowered by spirituous liquors; not drunken. The sot may at times be *sober*.
3. Not mad or insane; not wild, visionary or heated with passion; having the regular exercise of cool dispassionate reason.

> There was not a *sober* person to be had; all was tempestuous and blustering. *Dryden.*
> No *sober* man would put himself in danger, for the applause of escaping without breaking his neck. *Dryden.*

4. Regular; calm; not under the influence of passion; as *sober* judgment; a man in his *sober* senses.
5. Serious; solemn; grave; as the *sober* livery of autumn.

> What parts gay France from *sober* Spain? *Prior.*
> See her *sober* over a sampler, or gay over a jointed baby. *Pope.*

SO'BER, *v. t.* To make sober; to cure of intoxication.

> There shallow draughts intoxicate the brain,
> And drinking largely *sobers* us again. *Pope.*

SO'BERED, *pp.* Made sober.

SO'BERLY, *adv.* Without intemperance.

2. Without enthusiasm.
3. Without intemperate passion; coolly; calmly; moderately. *Bacon. Locke.*
4. Gravely; seriously.

SO'BERMINDED, *a.* Having a disposition or temper habitually sober, calm and temperate.

SŌBERMINDEDNESS, *n.* Calmness; freedom from inordinate passions; habitual sobriety. *Porteus.*

SO'BERNESS, *n.* Freedom from intoxication; temperance.

2. Gravity; seriousness.
3. Freedom from heat and passion; calmness; coolness.

> The *soberness* of Virgil might have shown him the difference. *Dryden.*

SOBRI'ETY, *n.* [Fr. *sobrieté*; L. *sobrietas*, from *sobrius*.]

1. Habitual soberness or temperance in the use of spirituous liquors; as when we say, a man of *sobriety*. *Hooker. Taylor.*
2. Freedom from intoxication.

> Public *sobriety* is a relative duty. *Blackstone.*

3. Habitual freedom from enthusiasm, inordinate passion or overheated imagination; calmness; coolness; as the *sobriety* of riper years; the *sobriety* of age. *Dryden.*
4. Seriousness; gravity without sadness or melancholy.

> Mirth makes them not mad,
> Nor *sobriety* sad. *Denham.*

SOC, *n.* [Sax. *soc*, from *socan*, *secan*, to *seek*, to follow, L. *sequor*.]

1. Properly, the sequela, secta or suit, or the body of suitors; hence, the power or privilege of holding a court in a district, as in a manor; jurisdiction of causes, and the limits of that jurisdiction. *English Law. Wilkins. Lye.*
2. Liberty or privilege of tenants excused from customary burdens. *Cowel.*
3. An exclusive privilege claimed by millers of grinding all the corn used within the manor or township in which the mill stands. *Grose.*

SOC'AGE, *n.* [from *soc*, supra, a privilege.] In *English law*, a tenure of lands and tenements by a certain or determinate service; a tenure distinct from chivalry or knight's service, in which the render was uncertain. The service must be certain, in order to be denominated *socage*; as to hold by fealty and twenty shillings rent. *Blackstone.*

Socage is of two kinds; *free socage*, where the services are not only certain, but honorable, and *villein socage*, where the services, though certain, are of a baser nature. *Ib.*

SOC'AGER, *n.* A tenant by socage; a socman.

SŌCIABIL'ITY, *n.* [Fr. *sociabilité*.] Sociableness; disposition to associate and converse with others; or the practice of familiar converse.

SO'CIABLE, *a.* [Fr. *sociable*; L. *sociabilis*, from *socius*, a companion, probably from *sequor*, to follow. See *Seek*.]

1. That may be conjoined; fit to be united in one body or company; as *sociable* parts united in one body. *Hooker.*
2. Ready or disposed to unite in a general interest.

> To make man mild, and *sociable* to man. *Addison.*

3. Ready and inclined to join in company or society; or frequently meeting for conversation; as *sociable* neighbors.
4. Inclined to converse when in company; disposed to freedom in conversation; opposed to *reserved* and *taciturn*.
5. Free in conversation; conversing much or familiarly. The guests were very *sociable*.

SO'CIABLENESS, *n.* Disposition to associate; inclination to company and converse; or actual frequent union in society or free converse. This word may signify either the disposition to associate, or the disposition to enter into familiar conversation, or the actual practice of associating and conversing.

SO'CIABLY, *adv.* In a sociable manner; with free intercourse; conversibly; familiarly; as a companion.

SO'CIAL, *a.* [L. *socialis*, from *socius*, companion.]

1. Pertaining to society; relating to men living in society, or to the public as an aggregate body; as *social* interests or concerns; *social* pleasures; *social* benefits; *social* happiness; *social* duties.

> True self-love and *social* are the same. *Pope.*

2. Ready or disposed to mix in friendly converse; companionable.

> Withers, adieu! yet not with thee remove
> Thy martial spirit or thy *social* love. *Pope.*

3. Consisting in union or mutual converse. *Milton.*
4. Disposed to unite in society. Man is a *social* being.

SOCIAL'ITY, *n.* Socialness; the quality of being social. *Sterne.*

SO'CIALLY, *adv.* In a social manner or way.

SO'CIALNESS, *n.* The quality of being social.

SOCI'ETY, *n.* [Fr. *societé*; Sp. *sociedad*; It. *società*; L. *societas*, from *socius*, a companion. See *Sociable*.]

1. The union of a number of rational beings; or a number of persons united, either for a temporary or permanent purpose. Thus

the inhabitants of a state or of a city constitute a *society*, having common interests; and hence it is called a *community*. In a more enlarged sense, the whole race or family of man is a *society*, and called *human society*.

The true and natural foundations of *society*, are the wants and fears of individuals. *Blackstone*.

2. Any number of persons associated for a particular purpose, whether incorporated by law, or only united by articles of agreement; a fraternity. Thus we have bible *societies*, missionary *societies*, and charitable *societies* for various objects; *societies* of mechanics, and learned *societies; societies* for encouraging arts, &c.
3. Company; a temporary association of persons for profit or pleasure. In this sense, *company* is more generally used.
4. Company; fellowship. We frequent the *society* of those we love and esteem.
5. Partnership; fellowship; union on equal terms.

Among unequals what *society* can sort? *Milton*.

Heav'n's greatness no *society* can bear. *Dryden*.

6. Persons living in the same neighborhood, who frequently meet in company and have fellowship. Literary *society* renders a place interesting and agreeable.
7. In *Connecticut*, a number of families united and incorporated for the purpose of supporting public worship, is called an *ecclesiastical society*. This is a parish, except that it has not territorial limits. In Massachusetts, such an incorporated society is usually called a *parish*, though consisting of persons only, without regard to territory.

SOCIN'IAN, *a*. [from *Socinus*, a native of Sienna, in Tuscany, the founder of the sect of Socinians in the 16th century.]
Pertaining to Socinus, or his religious creed.

SOCIN'IAN, *n*. One of the followers of Socinus. *Encyc*.

SOCIN'IANISM, *n*. The tenets or doctrines of Socinus, who held Christ to be a mere man inspired, denied his divinity and atonement, and the doctrine of original depravity. *Encyc*.

SOCK, *n*. [Sax. *socc*; L. *soccus*; Sw. *socka*; G. *socke*; D. *zok*; Dan. *sok*; Fr. *socque*; It. *socco*; Sp. *zoco, zueco*, a wooden shoe, a plinth, whence *zocalo*, Fr. *socle*.]

1. The shoe of the ancient actors of comedy. Hence the word is used for comedy, and opposed to *buskin* or tragedy.

Great Fletcher never treads in buskin here,
Nor greater Jonson dares in *socks* appear. *Dryden*.

2. A garment for the foot, like the foot of a stocking.
3. A plowshare. *Ed. Encyc*.

SOCK'ET, *n*. [Ir. *soicead*.] The little hollow tube or place in which a candle is fixed in the candlestick.

And in the *sockets* oily bubbles dance. *Dryden*.

2. Any hollow thing or place which receives and holds something else; as the *sockets* of the teeth or of the eyes.

His eyeballs in their hollow *sockets* sink. *Dryden*.

Gomphosis is the connection of a tooth to its *socket*. *Wiseman*.

SOCK'ET-CHISEL, *n*. A chisel made with a socket; a stronger sort of chisel. *Moxon*.

SOCK'LESS, *a*. Destitute of socks or shoes. *Beaum*.

SO'CLE, *n*. [See *Sock*.] In *architecture*, a flat square member under the basis of pedestals of vases and statues, serving as a foot or stand.

SOC'MAN, *n*. [See *Socage*.] One who holds lands or tenements by socage. *Cowel*.

SOC'MANRY, *n*. Tenure by socage. [*Not in use*.] *Cowel*.

SOC'OME, *n*. A custom of tenants to grind corn at the lord's mill. [*Not used*.] *Cowel*.

SOC'OTORINE, SOC'OTRINE, *a*. *Socotorine* or *socotrine aloes*, a fine kind of aloes from Socotra, an isle in the Indian ocean. *Encyc*.

SOCRAT'IC, SOCRAT'ICAL, *a*. Pertaining to Socrates, the Grecian sage, or to his language or manner of teaching and philosophizing. The *Socratic* method of reasoning and instruction was by interrogatories.

SOCRAT'ICALLY, *adv*. In the Socratic method. *Goodman*.

SOC'RATISM, *n*. The doctrines or philosophy of Socrates.

SOC'RATIST, *n*. A disciple of Socrates. *Martin*.

SOD, *n*. [D. *zoode*; G. *sode*. I suspect the radical sense is *set*, fixed; W. *sodi*, to set.]
Turf; sward; that stratum of earth on the surface which is filled with the roots of grass, or any portion of that surface. It differs from *clod*, which may be a compact mass of earth without roots; but *sod* is formed by earth held together by roots.

SOD, *a*. Made or consisting of sod.

SOD, *v. t*. To cover with sod; to turf.

SOD, *pret*. of *seethe*; also the passive participle. [See *Sodden*.]

SO'DA, *n*. [G. *soda*; D. *souda*; It. *soda*; Sp. *soda* or *sosa*, glasswort, barilla.]
Mineral fixed alkali; natron; so called because it forms the basis of marine salt. It is found native in Egypt; but it is generally obtained from the salsola kali. Soda is an oxyd, or the protoxyd of sodium, a metal. *Davy*.

SO'DALITE, *n*. A mineral; so called from the large portion of mineral alkali which enters into its composition. It is of a bluish green color, and found crystalized or in masses. *Dict*.

SODAL'ITY, *n*. [L. *sodalitas*, from *sodalis*, a companion.] A fellowship or fraternity. *Stillingfleet*.

SO'DA-WATER, *n*. A very weak solution of soda in water supersaturated with carbonic acid, and constituting a favorite beverage.

SOD'DEN, *pp*. of *seethe*. Boiled; seethed.

SOD'DY, *a*. [from *sod*.] Turfy; consisting of sod; covered with sod.

SOD'ER, *v. t*. [W. *sawd*, juncture; *sawdriaw*, to join, to soder; Fr. *souder*; Arm. *souda* or *soudta*; It. *sodare*, to make firm. It has been taken for granted that this is a contracted word, from L. *solido*, and hence written *solder*. The fact may be doubted; but if true, the settled pronunciation seems to render it expedient to let the contracted orthography remain undisturbed.]
To unite and make solid, as metallic substances; to join separate things or parts of the same thing by a metallic substance in a state of fusion, which hardens in cooling, and renders the joint solid.

SOD'ER, *n*. Metallic cement; a metal or metallic composition used in uniting other metallic substances.

SO'DIUM, *n*. The metallic base of soda. It is soft, sectile, white and opake, and very malleable. It is lighter than water. *Davy*.

SOD'OMITE, *n*. An inhabitant of Sodom.
2. One guilty of sodomy.

SOD'OMY, *n*. A crime against nature.

SOE, *n*. [Scot. *sae*; perhaps *sea*.] A large wooden vessel for holding water; a cowl. [*Local*.] *More*.

Soever, so and ever, found in compounds, as in *whosoever, whatsoever, wheresoever*. See these words. It is sometimes used separate from the pronoun; as, in what things *soever* you undertake, use diligence and fidelity.

SO'FA, *n*. [probably an oriental word. Qu. Sw. *sǒfva*, to lull to sleep.]
An elegant long seat, usually with a stuffed bottom. Sofas are variously made. In the United States, the frame is of mahogany, and the bottom formed of stuffed cloth, with a covering of silk, chintz, calico or hair-cloth. The sofa of the orientals is a kind of alcove raised half a foot above the floor, where visitors of distinction are received. It is also a seat by the side of the room covered with a carpet.

SOF'FIT, *n*. [It. *soffitta*.] In *architecture*, any timber ceiling formed of cross beams, the compartments of which are enriched with sculpture, painting or gilding.
2. The under side or face of an architrave, enriched with compartments of roses. *Encyc*.

SOFT, *a*. [Sax. *softe, softa*. The D. has *zagt*, Sw. *sackta*, D. *sagte*, and the G. *sanft*, in a like sense, but whether allied to *soft*, may be questioned.]

1. Easily yielding to pressure; the contrary of *hard*; as a *soft* bed; a *soft* peach; *soft* earth.
2. Not hard; easily separated by an edged instrument; as *soft* wood. The chestnut is a *soft* wood, but more durable than hickory, which is a very hard wood. So we say, a *soft* stone, when it breaks or is hewed with ease.
3. Easily worked; malleable; as *soft* iron.
4. Not rough, rugged or harsh; smooth to the touch; delicate; as *soft* silk; *soft* raiment; a *soft* skin.
5. Delicate; feminine; as the *softer* sex.
6. Easily yielding to persuasion or motives flexible; susceptible of influence or passion. In both these senses, *soft* is applied to females, and sometimes to males; as a divine of a *soft* and servile temper. *K. Charles*.

One king is too *soft* and easy. *L'Estrange*.

7. Tender; timorous.

However *soft* within themselves they are,
To you they will be valiant by despair. *Dryden*.

8. Mild; gentle; kind; not severe or unfeeling; as a person of a *soft* nature.
9. Civil; complaisant; courteous; as a per-

son of *soft* manners. He has a *soft* way of asking favors.

10. Placid; still; easy.

On her *soft* axle while she paces even,
She bears thee *soft* with the smooth air along. *Milton.*

11. Effeminate; viciously nice.

An idle *soft* course of life is the source of criminal pleasures. *Broome.*

12. Delicate; elegantly tender.

Her form more *soft* and feminine. *Milton.*

13. Weak; impressible.

The deceiver soon found this *soft* place of Adam's. [*Not elegant.*] *Glanville.*

14. Gentle; smooth or melodious to the ear; not loud, rough or harsh; as a *soft* voice or note; a *soft* sound; *soft* accents; *soft* whispers. *Dryden. Pope.*

15. Smooth; flowing; not rough or vehement.

The solemn nightingale tun'd her *soft* lays. *Milton.*

Soft were my numbers, who could take offense? *Pope.*

16. Easy; quiet; undisturbed; as *soft* slumbers.

17. Mild to the eye; not strong or glaring; as *soft* colors; the *soft* coloring of a picture.

The sun shining on the upper part of the clouds, made the *softest* lights imaginable. *Brown.*

18. Mild; warm; pleasant to the feelings; as *soft* air.

19. Not tinged with an acid; not hard; not astringent; as, *soft* water is the best for washing.

20. Mild; gentle; not rough, rude or irritating.

A *soft* answer turneth away wrath. Prov. xv.

SOFT, *adv.* Softly; gently; quietly.

SOFT, *exclam.* for *be soft*, hold; stop; not so fast.

But, *soft*, my muse, the world is wide. *Suckling.*

SOFTEN, *v. t.* *sof'n.* To make soft or more soft; to make less hard.

Their arrow's point they *soften* in the flame. *Gay.*

2. To mollify; to make less fierce or intractable; to make more susceptible of humane or fine feelings; as, to *soften* a hard heart; to *soften* savage natures. The heart is *softened* by pity.

Diffidence conciliates the proud, and *softens* the severe. *Rambler.*

3. To make less harsh or severe; as, to *soften* an expression.

4. To palliate; to represent as less enormous; as, to *soften* a fault.

5. To make easy; to compose; to mitigate; to alleviate.

Music can *soften* pain to ease. *Pope.*

6. To make calm and placid.

Bid her be all that cheers or *softens* life. *Pope.*

7. To make less harsh, less rude, less offensive or violent.

But sweetly temper'd awe, and *soften'd* all he spoke. *Dryden.*

8. To make less glaring; as, to *soften* the coloring of a picture.

9. To make tender; to make effeminate; to enervate; as troops *softened* by luxury.

10. To make less harsh or grating; as, to *soften* the voice.

SOFTEN, *v. i.* *sof'n.* To become less hard; to become more pliable and yielding to pressure; as, iron or wax *softens* in heat; fruits *soften* as they ripen.

2. To become less rude, harsh or cruel; as, savage natures *soften* by civilization.

3. To become less obstinate or obdurate; to become more susceptible of humane feelings and tenderness; to relent. The heart *softens* at the sight of woe.

4. To become more mild; as, the air *softens.*

5. To become less harsh, severe or rigorous.

SOFT'ENED, *pp.* Made less hard or less harsh; made less obdurate or cruel, or less glaring.

SOFT'ENING, *ppr.* Making more soft; making less rough or cruel, &c.

SOFT'ENING, *n.* The act of making less hard, less cruel or obdurate, less violent, less glaring, &c.

SOFT'-HE'ARTED, *a.* Having tenderness of heart; susceptible of pity or other kindly affection; gentle; meek.

SOFT'LING, *n.* An effeminate person; one viciously nice. [*Little used.*] *Woolton.*

SOFT'LY, *adv.* Without hardness.

2. Not with force or violence; gently; as, he *softly* pressed my hand.

3. Not loudly; without noise; as, speak *softly*; walk *softly.*

In this dark silence *softly* leave the town. *Dryden.*

4. Gently; placidly.

She *softly* lays him on a flowery bed. *Dryden.*

5. Mildly; tenderly.

The king must die;
Though pity *softly* pleads within my soul— *Dryden.*

SOFT'NER, *n.* He or that which softens.

2. One that palliates. *Swift.*

SOFT'NESS, *n.* The quality of bodies which renders them capable of yielding to pressure, or of easily receiving impressions from other bodies; opposed to *hardness.*

2. Susceptibility of feeling or passion; as the *softness* of the heart or of our natures.

3. Mildness; kindness; as *softness* of words or expressions. *Watts.*

4. Mildness; civility; gentleness; as *softness* of manners. *Dryden.*

5. Effeminacy; vicious delicacy.

He was not delighted with the *softness* of the court. *Clarendon.*

6. Timorousness; pusillanimity; excessive susceptibility of fear or alarm.

This virtue could not proceed out of fear or *softness.* *Bacon.*

7. Smoothness to the ear; as the *softness* of sounds, which is distinct from *exility* or *fineness.* *Bacon.*

8. Facility; gentleness; candor; easiness to be affected; as *softness* of spirit. *Hooker.*

9. Gentleness, as contrary to *vehemence.*

With strength and *softness*, energy and ease— *Harte.*

10. Mildness of temper; meekness.

For contemplation he and valor form'd,
For *softness* she, and sweet attractive grace. *Milton.*

11. Weakness; simplicity.

12. Mild temperature; as the *softness* of a climate. *Milford.*

SOG'GY, *a.* [allied probably to *soak*, which see; W. *soeg*, and *soegi*, to steep.]

1. Wet; filled with water; soft with moisture; as *soggy* land. Timber that has imbibed water is said to be *soggy.*

2. Steaming with damp. *B. Jonson.*

SOHO, *exclam.* A word used in calling from a distant place; a sportman's halloo. *Shak.*

SOIL, *v. t.* [Sax. *selan*, *sylian*; Dan. *söler*; Sw. *söla*; Fr. *salir*, *souiller*; Arm. *salicza*; Ir. *salaighim.* Class Sl. No. 35. Syr.]

1. To make dirty on the surface; to foul; to dirt; to stain; to defile; to tarnish; to sully; as, to *soil* a garment with dust.

Our wonted ornaments now *soil'd* and stain'd. *Milton.*

2. To cover or tinge with any thing extraneous; as, to *soil* the earth with blood. *Tate.*

3. To dung; to manure. *South.*

To soil a horse, is to purge him by giving him fresh grass. *Johnson.*

To soil cattle, in husbandry, is to feed them with grass daily mowed for them, instead of pasturing them.

SOIL, *n.* [G. *süle.* See the Verb.] Dirt; any foul matter upon another substance; foulness; spot.

2. Stain; tarnish.

A lady's honor—will not bear a *soil.* *Dryden.*

3. The upper stratum of the earth; the mold, or that compound substance which furnishes nutriment to plants, or which is particularly adapted to support and nourish them. [L. *solum*, W. *swl.*]

4. Land; country. We love our native *soil.*

5. Dung; compost.

Improve land by dung and other sort of *soils.* *Mortimer.*

To take soil, to run into the water, as a deer when pursued. *B. Jonson.*

SOIL'ED, *pp.* Fouled; stained; tarnished; manured; fed with grass.

SOIL'INESS, *n.* Stain; foulness. [*Little used.*] *Bacon.*

SOIL'ING, *ppr.* Defiling; fouling; tarnishing; feeding with fresh grass; manuring.

SOIL'ING, *n.* The act or practice of feeding cattle or horses with fresh grass, instead of pasturing them.

SOIL'LESS, *a.* Destitute of soil. *Bigsby.*

SOIL'URE, *n.* [Fr. *souillure.*] Stain; pollution. [*Not in use.*] *Shak.*

SOJOURN, *v. i.* *so'jurn.* [Fr. *sejourner*; It. *soggiornare*, which seems to be formed from the noun *soggiorno*; *sub* and *giorno*, a day.]

To dwell for a time; to dwell or live in a place as a temporary resident, or as a stranger, not considering the place as his permanent habitation. So Abram *sojourned* in Egypt. Gen. xii.

The soldiers assembled at New Castle, and there *sojourned* three days. *Hayward.*

SO'JOURN, *n.* A temporary residence, as that of a traveler in a foreign land. *Milton.*

SO'JOURNER, *n.* A temporary resident; a stranger or traveler who dwells in a place for a time.

We are strangers before thee and *sojourners*, as all our fathers were. 1 Chron. xxix.

SO'JOURNING, *ppr.* Dwelling for a time.

SO'JOURNING, *n.* The act of dwelling in a place for a time; also, the time of abode. Ex. xii.

SO'JOURNMENT, *n.* Temporary residence, as that of a stranger or traveler. *Walsh.*

SOL, *n.* [Norm. *soulze, soulds, souz*, from L. *solidus.*]
1. In France, a small copper coin; a penny; usually *sou* or *sous.* *Encyc.*
2. A copper coin and money of account in Switzerland.

SOL, *n.* [It.] The name of a note in music.

SOL'ACE, *v. t.* [It. *sollazzare*, from L. *solatium; solor*, to comfort, assuage, relieve. See *Console.*]
1. To cheer in grief or under calamity; to comfort; to relieve in affliction; to console; *applied to persons*; as, to *solace* one's self with the hope of future reward.
2. To allay; to assuage; as, to *solace* grief.

SOL'ACE, *v. i.* To take comfort; to be cheered or relieved in grief. *Obs.* *Shak.*

SOL'ACE, *n.* [It. *sollazzo*; L. *solatium.*] Comfort in grief; alleviation of grief or anxiety; also, that which relieves in distress; recreation.

The proper *solaces* of age are not music and compliments, but wisdom and devotion. *Rambler.*

SOL'ACED, *pp.* Comforted; cheered in affliction.

SOL'ACING, *ppr.* Relieving grief; cheering in affliction.

SOLA'CIOUS, *a.* Affording comfort or amusement. [*Not in use.*]

SOLAND'ER, *n.* [Fr. *soulandres.*] A disease in horses. *Dict.*

SOLAN-GOOSE, *n.* The gannet, (*Pelecanus bassanus,*) an aquatic fowl found on the coasts of Great Britain and Ireland. It is nearly of the size of the domestic goose. *Encyc.*

SOLA'NO, *n.* A hot S.E. wind in Spain which produces inflammatory effects on men.

SO'LAR, *a.* [Fr. *solaire*; L. *solaris*, from *sol*, the sun, W. *sûl*, Fr. *soleil*, It. *sole*, Sp. *sol.*]
1. Pertaining to the sun, as the *solar* system; or proceeding from it, as *solar* light; *solar* rays; *solar* influence.
2. Belonging to the sun; as *solar* herbs. [*Not used.*]
3. In *astrology*, born under the predominant influence of the sun; as a *solar* people. *Obs.* *Dryden.*
4. Measured by the progress of the sun, or by its revolution; as the *solar* year.

Solar flowers, are those which open and shut daily, at certain determinate hours. *Linne.*

Solar spots, dark spots that appear on the sun's disk, usually visible only by the telescope, but sometimes so large as to be seen by the naked eye. They adhere to the body of the sun; indicate its revolutions on its axis; are very changeable in their figure and dimensions; and vary in size from mere points to spaces 50.000 miles in diameter.

SÔLD, *pret.* and *pp.* of *sell.*

SÔLD, *n.* [from the root of *soldier*; Norm. *soude.*] Salary; military pay. [*Not in use.*] *Spenser.*

SOL'DAN, for *sultan*, not in use. *Milton.*

SOL'DANEL, *n.* [L. *soldanella.*] A plant.

SOL'DER, *v. t.* [from L. *solido, solidus.*] To unite by a metallic cement. [See *Soder.*]

SOL'DER, *n.* A metallic cement. [See *Soder.*]

SÔLDIER, *n.* *sōljur.* [Fr. *soldat*; Norm. *soudeyer, soudiers*; It. *soldato*; Sp. *soldado*; from L. *solidus*, a piece of money, the pay of a soldier; Norm. *soud*, contracted from *sould*, pay, wages; *soudoyer*, to keep in pay; Sw. *besolda*, to count out money to, to pay; Dan. *besolder*, to give a salary or wages.]
1. A man engaged in military service; one whose occupation is military; a man enlisted for service in an army; a private, or one in the ranks.

There ought to be some time for sober reflection between the life of a *soldier* and his death. *Rambler.*

2. A man enrolled for service, when on duty or embodied for military discipline; a private; as a militia *soldier.*
3. *Emphatically*, a brave warrior; a man of military experience and skill, or a man of distinguished valor. In this sense, an officer of any grade may be denominated a *soldier.* *Shak.*

SÔLDIERESS, *n.* A female soldier. [*Not in use.*] *Beaum.*

SÔLDIERLIKE, } *a.* Like or becoming a
SÔLDIERLY, } real soldier; brave; martial; heroic; honorable.

SÔLDIERSHIP, *n.* Military qualities; military character or state; martial skill; behavior becoming a soldier. *Shak.*

SÔLDIERY, *n.* Soldiers collectively; the body of military men.

I charge not the *soldiery* with ignorance and contempt of learning, without exception. *Swift.*

2. Soldiership; military service. *Obs.* *Sidney.*

SOLE, *n.* [Sax. *sol*; D. *zool*; G. *sohle*; Dan. *sole*; Fr. *id.*; It. *suolo*, soil and sole; Sp. *suela*, the sole of the foot, and *suolo*, soil; L. *solea, solum*; that which sets or is set or laid. The radical sense coincides with that of *sill.*]
1. The bottom of the foot; and by a figure, the foot itself. *Shak. Spenser.*
2. The bottom of a shoe; or the piece of lether which constitutes the bottom.

The caliga was a military shoe with a very thick *sole*, tied above the instep. *Arbuthnot.*

3. The part of any thing that forms the bottom, and on which it stands upon the ground.

Elm is proper for mills, *soles* of wheels, and pipes. *Mortimer.*

4. A marine fish of the genus Pleuronectes, so called probably because it keeps on or near the bottom of the sea. These fish abound on the British coast, and hence the name of *sole bank*, to the southward of Ireland. This fish sometimes grows to the weight of six or seven pounds. *Dict. Nat. Hist.*
5. In *ship-building*, a sort of lining, used to prevent the wearing of any thing.
6. A sort of horn under a horse's hoof. *Encyc.*

SOLE, *v. t.* To furnish with a sole; as, to *sole* a shoe.

SOLE, *a.* [L. *solus*; Fr. *seul*; It. Sp. *solo*; probably from separating; Ar. زال. Class Sl. No. 3.]
1. Single; being or acting without another; individual; only. God is the *sole* creator and sovereign of the world.
2. In *law*, single; unmarried; as a *femme sole.*

SOL'ECISM, *n.* [Gr. σολοικισμος, said to be derived from *Soli*, a people of Attica, who being transplanted to Cilicia, lost the purity of their language.]
1. Impropriety in language, or a gross deviation from the rules of syntax; incongruity of words; want of correspondence or consistency.

A barbarism may be in one word; a *solecism* must be of more. *Johnson, from Cicero.*

2. Any unfitness, absurdity or impropriety. *B. Jonson.*

Cesar, by dismissing his guards and retaining his power, committed a dangerous *solecism* in politics. *Middleton.*

SOL'ECIST, *n.* [Gr. σολοικιςος.] One who is guilty of impropriety in language. *Blackwall.*

SOLECIST'IC, } *a.* Incorrect; incon-
SOLECIST'ICAL, } gruous. *Johnson.*

SOLECIST'ICALLY, *adv.* In a solecistic manner. *Blackwall.*

SOL'ECIZE, *v. i.* [Gr. σολοικιζω.] To commit solecism. *More.*

SO'LELY, *adv.* Singly; alone; only; without another; as, to rest a cause *solely* on one argument; to rely *solely* on one's own strength.

SOLEMN, *a.* *sol'em.* [Fr. *solennel*; It. *solenne*; Sp. *solemne*; L. *solennis*, from *soleo*, to be accustomed, to use, that is, to hold on or continue, as we have *wont*, from G. *wohnen*, to dwell.]
1. Anniversary; observed once a year with religious ceremonies.

The worship of this image was advanced, and a *solemn* supplication observed every year. *Stillingfleet.*

[I doubt the correctness of this definition of Johnson; or whether *solemn*, in our language, ever includes the sense of *anniversary.* In the passage cited, the sense of *anniversary* is expressed by *every year*, and if it is included in *solemn* also, the sentence is tautological. I should say then, that *solemn* in this passage of Stillingfleet, has the sense given in the second definition below.]

2. Religiously grave; marked with pomp and sanctity; attended with religious rites.

His holy rites and *solemn* feasts profan'd. *Milton.*

3. Religiously serious; piously grave; devout; marked by reverence to God; as *solemn* prayer; the *solemn* duties of the sanctuary.
4. Affecting with seriousness; impressing or adapted to impress seriousness, gravity or reverence; sober; serious.

There reign'd a *solemn* silence over all. *Spenser.*

To 'swage with *solemn* touches troubled thoughts. *Milton.*

5. Grave; serious; or affectedly grave; as a *solemn* face.
6. Sacred; enjoined by religion; or attended with a serious appeal to God; as a *solemn* oath.
7. Marked with solemnities; as a *solemn* day.

SOL'EMNESS, *n.* The state or quality of being solemn; reverential manner; gravity; as the *solemness* of public worship.
2. Solemnity; gravity of manner. *Wotton.*

SOLEM'NITY, *n.* [Fr. *solemnité.*] A rite or ceremony annually performed with religious reverence.

Great was the cause: our old *solemnities*
From no blind zeal or fond tradition rise,
But sav'd from death, our Argives yearly pay
These grateful honors to the god of day. *Pope.*

[*Solemnities* seems here to include the sense of *anniversary.* See the fourth line. But in modern usage, that sense is rarely or never attached to the word.]
2. A religious ceremony; a ritual performance attended with religious reverence; as the *solemnity* of a funeral or of a sacrament.
3. A ceremony adapted to impress awe; as the *solemnities* of the last day.
4. Manner of acting awfully serious.

With horrible *solemnity* he caused every thing to be prepared for his triumph of victory. *Sidney.*

5. Gravity; steady seriousness; as the *solemnity* of the Spanish language. *Spectator.*
6. Affected gravity.

Solemnity's a cover for a sot. *Young.*

SOLEMNIZA'TION, *n.* The act of solemnizing; celebration; as the *solemnization* of a marriage. *Bacon.*

SOL'EMNIZE, *v. t.* [Fr. *solenniser*; It. *solennizzare.*]
1. To dignify or honor by ceremonies; to celebrate; as, to *solemnize* the birth of Christ. *Boyle.*

Their choice nobility and flow'r
Met from all parts to *solemnize* this feast. *Milton.*

2. To perform with ritual ceremonies and respect, or according to legal forms; as, to *solemnize* a marriage. *Z. Swift.*
3. To perform religiously once a year. Qu. *Hooker.*
4. To make grave, serious and reverential; as, to *solemnize* the mind for the duties of the sanctuary. [*This use of the word is well authorized in the United States.*]

SOL'EMNLY, *adv.* With gravity and religious reverence. Let us *solemnly* address the throne of grace.
2. With official formalities and by due authority. This question of law has been *solemnly* decided in the highest court.
3. With formal state. *Shak.*
4. With formal gravity and stateliness, or with affected gravity.

—There in deaf murmurs *solemnly* are wise. *Dryden.*

5. With religious seriousness; as, I *solemnly* declare myself innocent.

I do *solemnly* assure the reader— *Swift.*

SO'LENESS, *n.* [from *sole.*] Singleness; a state of being unconnected with others. *Dering.*

SO'LENITE, *n.* Petrified solen, a genus of shells.

SOL-FA, *v. i.* To pronounce the notes of the gammut, ascending or descending, *ut, re, mi, fa, sol, la,* and *e converso.*

SOLIC'IT, *v. t.* [L. *solicito*; Fr. *solliciter*; It. *sollecitare.* I know not whether this word is simple or compound; probably the latter. Qu. L. *lacio.*]
1. To ask with some degree of earnestness; to make petition to; to apply to for obtaining something. This word implies earnestness in seeking, but I think less earnestness than *beg, implore, entreat,* and *importune,* and more than *ask* or *request*; as when we say, a man *solicits* the minister for an office; he *solicits* his father for a favor.

Did I *solicit* thee
From darkness to promote me? *Milton.*

2. To ask for with some degree of earnestness; to seek by petition; as, to *solicit* an office; to *solicit* a favor.
3. To awake or excite to action; to summon; to invite.

That fruit *solicited* her longing eye. *Milton.*

Sounds and some tangible qualities *solicit* their proper senses, and force an entrance to the mind. *Locke.*

4. To attempt; to try to obtain.

I view my crime, but kindle at the view,
Repeat old pleasures and *solicit* new. *Pope.*

5. To disturb; to disquiet; a Latinism rarely used.

But anxious fears *solicit* my weak breast. *Dryden.*

SOLICITA'TION, *n.* Earnest request; a seeking to obtain something from another with some degree of zeal and earnestness; sometimes perhaps, importunity. He obtained a grant by repeated *solicitations.*
2. Excitement; invitation; as the *solicitation* of the senses. *Locke.*

SOLIC'ITED, *pp.* Earnestly requested.

SOLIC'ITING, *ppr.* Requesting with earnestness; asking for; attempting to obtain.

SOLIC'ITOR, *n.* [Fr. *solliciteur.*] One who asks with earnestness; one that asks for another. *Shak.*
2. An attorney, advocate or counselor at law who is authorized to practice in the English court of chancery. In America, an advocate or counselor at law, who, like the attorney general or state's attorney, prosecutes actions for the state.

SOLIC'ITOR-ĠENERAL, *n.* A lawyer in Great Britain, who is employed as counsel for the queen.

SOLIC'ITOUS, *a.* [L. *solicitus.*] Careful; anxious; very desirous, as to obtain something. Men are often more *solicitous* to obtain the favor of their king or of the people, than of their Maker.
2. Careful; anxious; concerned; as respecting an unknown but interesting event; followed usually by *about* or *for.* We say, a man is *solicitous about* the fate of his petition, or *about* the result of the negotiation. He is *solicitous for* the safety of his ship.
3. Anxious; concerned; followed by *for,* as when something is to be obtained. Be not *solicitous for* the future.

SOLIC'ITOUSLY, *adv.* Anxiously; with care and concern. Errors in religion or in science are to be *solicitously* avoided. A wise prince *solicitously* promotes the prosperity of his subjects.

SOLIC'ITRESS, *n.* A female who solicits or petitions.

SOLIC'ITUDE, *n.* [L. *solicitudo.*] Carefulness; concern; anxiety; uneasiness of mind occasioned by the fear of evil or the desire of good. A man feels *solicitude* when his friend is sick. We feel *solicitude* for the success of an enterprise. With what *solicitude* should men seek to secure future happiness.

SOL'ID, *a.* [L. *solidus*; Fr. *solide*; It. Sp. *solido*; from the sense of *setting* or *pressure,* and hence allied to L. *solum,* Eng. *sill.*]
1. Hard; firm; compact; having its constituent particles so close or dense as to resist the impression or penetration of other bodies. Hence solid bodies are not penetrable, nor are the parts movable and easily displaced like those of fluids. *Solid* is opposed to *fluid* and *liquid.*
2. Not hollow; full of matter; as a *solid* globe or cone, as distinguished from a *hollow* one.
3. Having all the geometrical dimensions; cubic; as, a *solid* foot contains 1728 *solid* inches. *Arbuthnot.*

[In this sense, *cubic* is now generally used.]
4. Firm; compact; strong; as a *solid* pier; a *solid* pile; a *solid* wall. *Addison.*
5. Sound; not weakly; as a *solid* constitution of body. [*Sound* is more generally used.] *Watts.*
6. Real; sound; valid; true; just; not empty or fallacious. Wise men seek *solid* reasons for their opinions.
7. Grave; profound; not light, trifling or superficial.

These wanting wit, affect gravity, and go by the name of *solid* men. *Dryden.*

8. In *botany,* of a fleshy, uniform, undivided substance, as a bulb or root; not spungy or hollow within, as a stem. *Martyn.*

A *solid foot,* contains 1728 solid inches, weighing 1000 ounces of rain water.

Solid angle, an angle formed by three or more plain angles meeting in a point.

Solid square, in military language, is a square body of troops; a body in which the ranks and files are equal.

SOL'ID, *n.* A firm compact body. In anatomy and medical science, the bones, flesh and vessels of animal bodies are called *solids,* in distinction from the blood, chyle and other fluids.

SOL'IDATE, *v. t.* [L. *solido.*] To make solid or firm. [*Little used.*] *Cowley.*

SOLIDIFICA'TION, *n.* The act of making solid.

SOLID'IFIED, *pp.* Made solid.

SOLID'IFȲ, *v. t.* [L. *solidus,* solid, and *facio,* to make.]
To make solid or compact. *Kirwan.*

SOLID'IFȲING, *ppr.* Making solid.

SOLID'ITY, *n.* [Fr. *solidité*; L. *soliditas.*]
1. Firmness; hardness; density; compactness; that quality of bodies which resists impression and penetration; opposed to *fluidity.*

That which hinders the approach of two bodies moving one towards another, I call *solidity.* *Locke.*

2. Fullness of matter; opposed to *hollowness.*
3. Moral firmness; soundness; strength; validity; truth; certainty; as opposed to *weakness* or *fallaciousnes*; as the *solidity*

of arguments or reasoning; the *solidity* of principles, truths or opinions. *Addison. Prior.*

4. In *geometry*, the solid contents of a body.

SOL'IDLY, *adv.* Firmly; densely; compactly; as the parts of a pier *solidly* united.

2. Firmly; truly; on firm grounds.

A complete brave man ought to know *solidly* the main end of his being in the world. *Digby.*

SOL'IDNESS, *n.* The quality of being firm, dense or compact; firmness; compactness; solidity; as of material bodies.

2. Soundness; strength; truth; validity; as of arguments, reasons, principles, &c.

SOLIDUN'GULOUS, *a.* [L. *solidus*, solid, and *ungula*, hoof.]

Having hoofs that are whole or not cloven. A horse is a *solidungulous* animal. *Brown. Barrow.*

SOLIFID'IAN, *n.* [L. *solus*, alone, and *fides*, faith.]

One who maintains that faith alone, without works, is necessary to justification. *Hammond.*

SOLIFID'IAN, *a.* Holding the tenets of Solifidians. *Feltham.*

SOLIFID'IANISM, *n.* The tenets of Solifidians.

SOLIL'OQUIZE, *v. i.* To utter a soliloquy.

SOLIL'OQUY, *n.* [Fr. *soliloque*; It. Sp. *soliloquio*; L. *solus*, alone, and *loquor*, to speak.]

1. A talking to one's self; a talking or discourse of a person alone, or not addressed to another person, even when others are present.

Lovers are always allowed the comfort of *soliloquy*. *Spectator.*

2. A written composition, reciting what it is supposed a person speaks to himself.

The whole poem is a *soliloquy*. *Prior.*

SOL'IPED, *n.* [L. *solus*, alone, or *solidus*, and *pes*, foot. But the word is ill formed.]

An animal whose foot is not cloven. *Brown.*

The *solipeds* constitute an order of quadrupeds with undivided hoofs, corresponding to the Linnean genus Equus. *Ed. Encyc.*

SOLITA'IR, *n.* [Fr. *solitaire*, from L. *solitarius*. See *Solitary*.]

1. A person who lives in solitude; a recluse; a hermit. *Pope.*

2. An ornament for the neck. *Shenstone.*

SOLITA'RIAN, *n.* A hermit. *Twisden.*

SOL'ITARILY, *adv.* [from *solitary*.] In solitude; alone; without company.

Feed thy people with thy rod, the flock of thy heritage, that dwell *solitarily* in the wood. Mic. xvi.

SOL'ITARINESS, *n.* The state of being alone; forbearance of company; retirement, or habitual retirement.

At home, in wholesome *solitariness*. *Donne.*

2. Solitude; loneliness; destitution of company or of animated beings; *applied to place*; as the *solitariness* of the country or of a wood.

SOL'ITARY, *a.* [Fr. *solitaire*; L. *solitarius*, from *solus*, alone.]

1. Living alone; not having company. Some of the more ferocious animals are *solitary*, seldom or never being found in flocks or herds. Thus the lion is called a *solitary* animal.

Those rare and *solitary*, these in flocks. *Milton.*

2. Retired; remote from society; not having company, or not much frequented; as a *solitary* residence or place.

3. Lonely; destitute of company; as a *solitary* life.

4. Gloomy; still; dismal.

Let that night be *solitary*, let no joyful voice come therein. Job iii.

5. Single; as a *solitary* instance of vengeance; a *solitary* example.

6. In *botany*, separate; one only in a place; as a *solitary* stipule.

A *solitary flower* is when there is only one to each peduncle; a *solitary seed*, when there is only one in a pericarp. *Martyn.*

SOL'ITARY, *n.* One that lives alone or in solitude; a hermit; a recluse. *Pope.*

SOL'ITUDE, *n.* [Fr. from L. *solitudo*; from *solus*, alone.]

1. Loneliness; a state of being alone; a lonely life.

Whoever is delighted with *solitude*, is either a wild beast or a god. *Bacon.*

2. Loneliness; remoteness from society; destitution of company; *applied to place*; as the *solitude* of a wood or a valley; the *solitude* of the country.

The *solitude* of his little parish is become matter of great comfort to him. *Law.*

3. A lonely place; a desert.

In these deep *solitudes* and awful cells,
Where heavenly-pensive contemplation dwells. *Pope.*

SOLIV'AGANT, *a.* [L. *solivagus*; *solus*, alone, and *vagor*, to wander.] Wandering alone. *Granger.*

SOL'LAR, *n.* [Low L. *solarium*.] A garret or upper room. [*Not in use.*] *Tusser.*

SOLMIZA'TION, *n.* [from *sol*, *mi*, musical notes.]

A solfaing; a repetition or recital of the notes of the gammut. *Burney.*

SO'LO, *n.* [It. from L. *solus*, alone.] A tune, air or strain to be played by a single instrument, or sung by a single voice.

SOLOMON'S LEAF, *n.* A plant.

SOLOMON'S SEAL, *n.* A plant of the genus Convallaria, and another of the genus Uvularia. *Fam. of Plants.*

SOL'STICE, *n.* [Fr. from L. *solstitium*; *sol*, the sun, and *sto*, to stand; It. *solstizio*; Sp. *solsticio*.]

In *astronomy*, the point in the ecliptic at which the sun stops or ceases to recede from the equator, either north in summer, or south in winter; a tropic or tropical point. There are two solstices; the summer solstice, the first degree of Cancer, which the sun enters on the 21st of June, and the winter solstice, the first degree of Capricorn, which the sun enters on the 21st of December.

SOLSTI''TIAL, *a.* Pertaining to a solstice; as a *solstitial* point. *Brown.*

2. Happening at a solstice; usually with us, at the summer solstice or midsummer; as *solstitial* heat. *Milton.*

SOLUBIL'ITY, *n.* [from *soluble*.] The quality of a body which renders it susceptible of solution; susceptibility of being dissolved in a fluid. The *solubility* of resins is chiefly confined to spirits or alcohol.

SOL'UBLE, *a.* [L. *solubilis*, from *solvo*, to melt.]

Susceptible of being dissolved in a fluid; capable of solution. Sugar is *soluble* in water; salt is *soluble* only to a certain extent, that is, till the water is saturated.

SOLU'TE, *a.* [L. *solutus*, *solvo*.] In *a general sense*, loose; free; as a *solute* interpretation. [*Not in use.*] *Bacon.*

2. In *botany*, loose; not adhering; opposed to *adnate*; as a *solute* stipule. *Martyn.*

SOLU'TE, *v. t.* To dissolve. [*Not in use.*] *Bacon.*

SOLU'TION, *n.* [Fr.; It. *soluzione*; Sp. *solucion*; from L. *solutio*, from *solvo*, to loosen, melt, dissolve. See *Solve*.]

1. The act of separating the parts of any body; disruption; breach.

In all bodies there is an appetite of union and evitation of *solution* of continuity. *Bacon.*

2. The operation or process of dissolving or melting in a fluid; as the *solution* of sugar or salt.

[*Note.*—This word is not used in chimistry or mineralogy for the dissolution or melting of bodies by the heat of fire.]

The term *solution* is applied to a very extensive class of phenomena. When a solid disappears in a liquid, if the compound exhibits perfect transparency, we have an example of *solution*. The word is applied both to the *act* of combination and to the *result* of the process. Thus common salt disappears in water, that is, its solution takes place, and the liquid obtained is called a *solution of salt in water*. Solution is the result of attraction or affinity between the fluid and the solid. This affinity continues to operate to a certain point, where it is overbalanced by the cohesion of the solid; it then ceases, the fluid is said to be *saturated*, the point where the operation ceases is called *saturation*, and the fluid is called a *saturated solution*. *Webster's Manual.*

Solution is a true chimical union. *Mixture* is a mere mechanical union of bodies.

3. Resolution; explanation; the act of explaining or removing difficulty or doubt; as the *solution* of a difficult question in morality; the *solution* of a doubt in casuistry.

4. Release; deliverance; discharge. *Barrow.*

5. In *algebra* and *geometry*, the answering of a question, or the resolving of a problem proposed.

Solution of continuity, the separation of connection or connected substances or parts; applied, in surgery, to a fracture, laceration, &c

SOL'UTIVE, *a.* Tending to dissolve; loosening; laxative. *Encyc.*

SOLVABIL'ITY, *n.* Ability to pay all just debts. *Encyc.*

SOLV'ABLE, *a.* That may be solved, resolved or explained.

2. That can be paid. *Tooke.*

SOLVE, *v. t. solv.* [L. *solvo*; Fr. *soudre*; It. *solvere*. Class Sl. Several roots give the sense.]

1. Properly, to loosen or separate the parts of any thing; hence, to explain; to resolve; to eclaircise; to unfold; to clear up; as what is obscure or difficult to be understood; as, to *solve* questions; to *solve* difficulties or a problem.

When God shall *solve* the dark decrees of fate. *Tickel.*

2. To remove; to dissipate; as, to *solve* doubts.

SOLV'ED, *pp.* Explained; removed.

SOLV'ENCY, *n.* [L. *solvens.*] Ability to pay all debts or just claims; as, the *solvency* of a merchant is undoubted. The credit of a nation's notes depends on a favorable opinion of its *solvency*.

SOLVEND', *n.* A substance to be dissolved. *Kirwan.*

SOLV'ENT, *a.* Having the power of dissolving; as a *solvent* body. *Boyle.*

2. Able to pay all just debts. The merchant is *solvent*.

3. Sufficient to pay all just debts. The estate is *solvent*.

SOLV'ENT, *n.* A fluid that dissolves any substance, is called the *solvent*.

SOLV'IBLE, *a.* Solvable, which see.

SOMAT'IC, SOMAT'ICAL, *a.* [Gr. σωματικος, from σωμα, body.] Corporeal; pertaining to a body. [*Not in use.*] *Scott.*

SO'MATIST, *n.* [supra.] One who admits the existence of corporeal or material beings only; one who denies the existence of spiritual substances. *Glanville.*

SOMATOL'OGY, *n.* [Gr. σωμα, body, and λογος, discourse.]
The doctrine of bodies or material substances.

SOMBER, SOMBRE, *a.* [Fr. *sombre*, from Sp. *sombra*, a shade.] Dull; dusky; cloudy; gloomy.

SOMBROUS, *a.* Gloomy. *Stephens.*

SOME, *a. sum.* [Sax. *sum, sume*; D. *sommige*; Sw. *somlige*; Sw. Dan. *som*, who.]

1. Noting a certain quantity of a thing, but indeterminate; a portion greater or less. Give me *some* bread; drink *some* wine; bring *some* water.

2. Noting a number of persons or things, greater or less, but indeterminate.

Some theoretical writers alledge that there was a time when there was no such thing as society. *Blackstone.*

3. Noting a person or thing, but not known, or not specific and definite. *Some* person, I know not who, gave me the information. Enter the city, and *some* man will direct you to the house.

Most gentlemen of property, at *some* period or other of their lives, are ambitious of representing their county in parliament. *Blackstone.*

4. It sometimes precedes a word of number or quantity, with the sense of *about* or *near*, noting want of certainty as to the specific number or amount, but something near it; as a village of *some* eighty houses; *some* two or three persons; *some* seventy miles distant; an object at *some* good distance. *Bacon.*

5. *Some* is often opposed to *others*. *Some* men believe one thing, and *others* another.

6. *Some* is often used without a noun, and then like other adjectives, is a substitute for a noun. We consumed *some* of our provisions, and the rest was given to the poor.

Some to the shores do fly,
Some to the woods. *Daniel.*
Your edicts *some* reclaim from sins,
But most your life and blest example wins. *Dryden.*

7. *Some* is used as a termination of certain adjectives, as in *handsome, mettlesome, blithesome, fullsome, lonesome, gladsome, gamesome*. In these words, *some* has primarily the sense of little, or a certain degree; a little *blithe* or *glad*. But in usage, it rather indicates a considerable degree of the thing or quantity; as *mettlesome*, full of mettle or spirit; *gladsome*, very glad or joyous.

SOMEBODY, *n.* [*some* and *body.*] A person unknown or uncertain; a person indeterminate.

Jesus said, *somebody* hath touched me. Luke viii.

We must draw in *somebody* that may stand
'Twixt us and danger. *Denham.*

2. A person of consideration.

Before these days rose up Theudas, boasting himself to be *somebody*. Acts v.

SOMEDEAL, *adv.* [*some* and *deal.*] In some degree. *Obs.* *Spenser.*

SOM'ERSAULT, SOM'ERSET, *n.* [Sp. *sobresalir*, to exceed in highth, to leap over; *sobresaltar*, to surprise; It. *soprassalire*, to attack unexpectedly; *soprassalto*, an overleap; L. *super* and *salio*, to leap.]
A leap by which a person jumps from a highth, turns over his head and falls upon his feet. *Donne.*

SOMEHOW, *adv.* [*some* and *how.*] One way or other; in some way not yet known. The thing must have happened *somehow* or other.

SOMETHING, *n.* [*some* and *thing.*] An indeterminate or unknown event. *Something* must have happened to prevent the arrival of our friends at the time fixed. I shall call at two o'clock, unless *something* should prevent. [See *Thing.*]

2. A substance or material thing, unknown, indeterminate or not specified. A machine stops because *something* obstructs its motion. There must be *something* to support a wall or an arch.

3. A part; a portion more or less.

Something yet of doubt remains. *Milton.*
Still from his little he could *something* spare,
To feed the hungry and to clothe the bare. *Harte.*

Something of it arises from our infant state. *Watts.*

4. A little; an indefinite quantity or degree. The man asked me a dollar, but I gave him *something* more.

5. Distance not great.

It must be done to-night, and *something* from the palace. *Shak.*

6. *Something* is used adverbially for in some degree; as, he was *something* discouraged; but the use is not elegant. *Temple.*

SOMETIME, *adv.* [*some* and *time.*] Once; formerly.

—That fair and warlike form,
In which the majesty of buried Denmark
Did *sometime* march. *Shak.*

2. At one time or other hereafter.

[*Sometime* is really a compound noun, and *at* is understood before it; *at some time.*]

SOMETIMES, *adv.* [*some* and *times.*] At times; at intervals; not always; now and then. We are *sometimes* indisposed, *sometimes* occupied, *sometimes* at leisure; that is, *at some times*.

It is good that we be *sometimes* contradicted. *Taylor.*

2. At one time; opposed to *another time*.

SOMEWHAT, *n.* [*some* and *what.*] Something, though uncertain what. *Atterbury.*

2. More or less; a certain quantity or degree, indeterminate.

These salts have *somewhat* of a nitrous taste. *Grew.*

3. A part, greater or less.

Somewhat of his good sense will suffer in this transfusion, and much of the beauty of his thoughts will be lost. *Dryden.*

SOMEWHAT, *adv.* In some degree or quantity. This is *somewhat* more or less than was expected; he is *somewhat* aged; he is *somewhat* disappointed; *somewhat* disturbed.

SOMEWHERE, *adv.* [*some* and *where.*] In some place, unknown or not specified; in one place or another. He lives *somewhere* in obscurity. Dryden *somewhere* says, peace to the manes of the dead.

SOMEWHILE, *adv.* [*some* and *while.*] Once; for a time. *Obs.* *Spenser.*

SOMEWHITHER, *adv.* To some indeterminate place. *Johnson.*

SOM'MITE, *n.* Nepheline; a mineral which occurs in small crystals and crystaline grains in the lava of mount Somma on Vesuvius. *Haüy.*

SOMNAMBULA'TION, *n.* [L. *somnus*, sleep, and *ambulo*, to walk.]
The act of walking in sleep. *Beddoes.*

SOMNAM'BULISM, *n.* [supra.] The act or practice of walking in sleep. *Beddoes. Darwin.*

SOMNAM'BULIST, *n.* A person who walks in his sleep. *Beddoes. Porteus.*

SOMNER, for *summoner*. [*Not in use.*]

SOMNIF'EROUS, *a.* [L. *somnifer*; *somnus*, sleep, and *fero*, to bring; Fr. *somnifere*; It. Sp. *somnifero.*]
Causing or inducing sleep; soporiferous; narcotic; as a *somniferous* potion. *Walton.*

SOMNIF'IC, *a.* [L. *somnus*, sleep, and *facio*, to make.] Causing sleep; tending to induce sleep.

SOM'NOLENCE, SOM'NOLENCY, *n.* [Low L. *somnolentia*; from *somnus*, sleep.]
Sleepiness; drowsiness; inclination to sleep. *Gower.*

SOM'NOLENT, *a.* Sleepy; drowsy; inclined to sleep. *Bullokar.*

SON, *n.* [Sax. *sunu*; Goth. *sunus*; G. *sohn*; D. *zoon*; Sw. *son*; Dan. *sön*; Sans. *sunu*; Russ. *syn* or *sin.*]

1. A male child; the male issue of a parent, father or mother. Jacob had twelve *sons*. Ishmael was the *son* of Hagar by Abraham.

2. A male descendant, however distant; hence in the plural, *sons* signifies descendants in general, a sense much used in the Scriptures. The whole human race are styled *sons of Adam*.

3. The compellation of an old man to a young one, or of a confessor to his penitent; a term of affection. Eli called Samuel his *son*.

Be plain, good *son*, and homely in thy drift. *Shak.*

4. A native or inhabitant of a country; as the *sons* of Britain. Let our country never be ashamed of her *sons*.

5. The produce of any thing.

Earth's tall *sons*, the cedar, oak and pine. *Blackmore.*

[*Note.* The primary sense of child is produce, issue; a shoot.]

6. One adopted into a family.

Moses was the *son* of Pharaoh's daughter. Ex. ii.

7. One who is converted by another's instrumentality, is called his *son;* also, one educated by another; as the *sons* of the prophets.

8. Christ is called the *Son* of God, as being conceived by the power of the Holy Spirit, or in consequence of his relation to the Father.

9. *Son* of pride, *sons* of light, *son* of Belial. These are Hebraisms, which denote that persons possess the qualities of pride, of light, or of Belial, as children inherit the qualities of their ancestors.

SON'ATA, *n.* [It. See *Sound.*] A tune intended for an instrument only, as *cantata* is for the voice.

SONG, *n.* [Sax. *song;* D. *zang;* G. *sang, gesang;* Sw. *siöng;* Dan. *sang.* See *Sing.*]

1. In *general*, that which is sung or uttered with musical modulations of the voice, whether of the human voice or that of a bird.

2. A little poem to be sung, or uttered with musical modulations; a ballad. The *songs* of a country are characteristic of its manners. Every country has its love *songs*, its war *songs*, and its patriotic *songs*.

3. A hymn; a sacred poem or hymn to be sung either in joy or thanksgiving, as that sung by Moses and the Israelites after escaping the dangers of the Arabian gulf and of Pharaoh; or of lamentation, as that of David over the death of Saul and Jonathan. *Songs* of joy are represented as constituting a part of heavenly felicity.

4. A lay; a strain; a poem.

The bard that first adorn'd our native tongue,
Tun'd to his British lyre this ancient *song*. *Dryden.*

5. Poetry; poesy; verse.

This subject for heroic *song*
Pleas'd me. *Milton.*

6. Notes of birds. [See Def. 1.]

7. A mere trifle.

The soldier's pay is a *song*. *Silliman.*

Old song, a trifle.

I do not intend to be thus put off with an *old song*. *More.*

SONG'ISH, *a.* Consisting of songs. [*Low and not in use.*] *Dryden.*

SONG'STER, *n.* [*song* and Sax. *steora*, one that steers.]

1. One that sings; one skilled in singing; not often applied to human beings, or only in slight contempt. *Howell.*

2. A bird that sings: as the little *songster* in his cage. [*In this use, the word is elegant.*]

SONG'STRESS, *n.* A female singer. *Thomson.*

SŎN-IN-LAW, *n.* A man married to one's daughter.

SON'NET, *n.* [Fr. from It. *sonetta;* Sp. *soneta.* See *Sound.*]

1. A short poem of fourteen lines, two stanzas of four verses each and two of three each, the rhymes being adjusted by a particular rule. *Milton. Johnson. Busby.*

2. A short poem.

I have a *sonnet* that will serve the turn. *Shak.*

SON'NET, *v. i.* To compose sonnets. *Bp. Hall.*

SONNETEE'R, *n.* [Fr. *sonnetier.*] A composer of sonnets or small poems; a small poet; usually in contempt. *Pope.*

SONOM'ETER, *n.* [L. *sonus*, sound, and Gr. μετρεω, to measure.]

An instrument for measuring sounds or the intervals of sounds. *Ed. Encyc.*

SONORIF'EROUS, *a.* [L. *sonus*, sound, and *fero*, to bring.]

That gives sound; sounding; as the *sonoriferous* particles of bodies. *Derham.*

SONORIF'IC, *a.* [L. *sonus*, sound, and *facio*, to make.]

Producing sound; as the *sonorific* quality of a body. *Watts.*

SONO'ROUS, *a.* [L. *sonorus*, from *sonus*, sound.]

1. Giving sound when struck. Metals are *sonorous* bodies.

2. Loud sounding; giving a clear or loud sound; as a *sonorous* voice.

3. Yielding sound; as, the vowels are *sonorous*. *Dryden.*

4. High sounding; magnificent of sound.

The Italian opera, amidst all the meanness and familiarity of the thoughts, has something beautiful and *sonorous* in the expression. *Addison.*

SONO'ROUSLY, *adv.* With sound; with a high sound.

SONO'ROUSNESS, *n.* The quality of yielding sound when struck, or coming in collision with another body; as the *sonorousness* of metals.

2. Having or giving a loud or clear sound; as the *sonorousness* of a voice or an instrument.

3. Magnificence of sound. *Johnson.*

SŎNSHIP, *n.* [from *son.*] The state of being a son, or of having the relation of a son.

2. Filiation; the character of a son. *Johnson.*

SỌỌN, *adv.* [Sax. *sona;* Goth. *suns.*] In a short time; shortly after any time specified or supposed; as *soon* after sunrise; *soon* after dinner; I shall *soon* return; we shall *soon* have clear weather.

2. Early; without the usual delay; before any time supposed.

How is it that ye have come so *soon* to-day? Ex. ii.

3. Readily; willingly. But in this sense it accompanies *would*, or some other word expressing *will.*

I *would* as *soon* see a river winding among woods or in meadows, as when it is tossed up in so many whimsical figures at Versailles. *Addison.*

As soon as, so soon as, immediately at or after another event. *As soon as* the mail arrives, I will inform you.

As soon as Moses came nigh to the camp, he saw the calf and the dancing. Ex. xxxii.

SỌỌN, *a.* Speedy; quick. [*Not in use.*]

SỌỌNLY, *adv.* Quickly; speedily. [*Not in use.*]

SOOSHONG', **SÖUCHONG'**, } *n.* A kind of black tea.

SOO'SOO, *n.* Among the Bengalese, the name of a cetaceous fish, the Delphinus Gangeticus. *Asiat. Res.*

SỌỌT, *n.* [Sax. Sw. *sot;* Dan. *sod, sood;* Ir. *suth;* W. *swta*, soot, that which is volatile or sudden. But qu. for the word is from the Ar. سَادَ to be black.]

A black substance formed by combustion, or disengaged from fuel in the process of combustion, rising in fine particles and adhering to the sides of the chimney or pipe conveying the smoke. *Soot* consists of oil, carbon and other substances. The *soot* of burnt pine forms lampblack.

SỌỌT, *v. t.* To cover or foul with soot.

SỌỌT'ED, *pp.* Covered or soiled with soot. *Mortimer.*

SOOT'ERKIN, *n.* A kind of false birth fabled to be produced by the Dutch women from sitting over their stoves. *Swift.*

SOOTH, *n.* [Sax. *soth;* Ir. *seadh.*] Truth; reality. *Obs.* *Shak.*

2. Prognostication. *Obs.* *Spenser.*

3. Sweetness; kindness. *Obs.* *Shak.*

SOOTH, *a.* Pleasing; delightful. *Obs.* *Milton.*

2. True; faithful. *Obs.* *Shak.*

SOOTHE, *v. t.* [Sax. *gesothian*, to flatter. There seems to be a connection between this verb and the preceding *sooth.* The sense of *setting*, allaying or softening, would give that of *truth*, and of *sweet*, that is, smooth.]

1. To flatter; to please with blandishments or soft words.

Can I *soothe* tyranny? *Dryden.*

I've tried the force of every reason on him,
Sooth'd and caress'd, been angry, *sooth'd* again— *Addison.*

2. To soften; to assuage; to mollify; to calm; as, to *soothe* one in pain or passion; or to *soothe* pain. It is applied both to persons and things.

3. To gratify; to please.

Sooth'd with his future fame. *Dryden.*

SOOTH'ED, *pp.* Flattered; softened; calmed; pleased.

SOOTH'ER, *n.* A flatterer; he or that which softens or assuages.

SOOTH'ING, *ppr.* Flattering; softening; assuaging.

SOOTH'INGLY, *adv.* With flattery or soft words.

SOOTH'LY, *adv.* In truth; really. *Obs.* *Hales.*

SOOTH'SAY, *v. i.* [*sooth* and *say.*] To foretell; to predict. Acts xvi. [*Little used.*]

SOOTH'SAYER, *n.* A foreteller; a prognosticator; one who undertakes to foretell future events without inspiration.

SOOTH'SAYING, *n.* The foretelling of future events by persons without divine aid or authority, and thus distinguished from *prophecy.*

2. A true saying; truth. *Obs.* *Chaucer.*

SỌỌT'INESS, *n.* [from *sooty.*] The quality of being sooty or foul with soot; fuliginousness.

SỌỌT'ISH, *a.* Partaking of soot; like soot. *Brown.*

SỌỌT'Y, *a.* [Sax. *sotig.*] Producing soot; as *sooty* coal. *Milton.*

2. Consisting of soot; fuliginons; as *sooty* matter. *Wilkins.*

3. Foul with soot.
4. Black like soot; dusky; dark; as the *sooty* flag of Acheron. *Milton.*

SOOT'Y, *v. t.* To black or foul with soot. [*Not authorized.*] *Chapman.*

SOP, *n.* [D. Sax. *sop*; G. *suppe*, soup; Dan. *suppe*; Sw. *soppa*; Sp. *sopa*; It. *zuppa*; Fr. *soupe*. See Class Sb. No. 2. 30. &c. Qu. *soap.*]

1. Any thing steeped or dipped and softened in liquor, but chiefly something thus dipped in broth or liquid food, and intended to be eaten.

Sops in wine, quantity for quantity, inebriate more than wine itself. *Bacon.*

2. Any thing given to pacify; so called from the sop given to Cerberus, in mythology. Hence the phrase, to give a *sop* to Cerberus.

Sop-in-wine, a kind of pink. *Spenser.*

SOP, *v. t.* To steep or dip in liquor.

SOPE. [See *Soap.*]

SOPH, *n.* [L. *sophista.*] In colleges and universities, a student in his second year; a sophomore.

SO'PHI, *n.* A title of the king of Persia. *Shak.*

SOPH'ICAL, *a.* [Gr. σοφος, wise; σοφια, wisdom.]

Teaching wisdom. [*Not in use.*] *Harris.*

SOPH'ISM, *n.* [Fr. *sophisme*; L. *sophisma*; Gr. σοφισμα.]

A specious but fallacious argument; a subtilty in reasoning; an argument that is not supported by sound reasoning, or in which the inference is not justly deduced from the premises.

When a false argument puts on the appearance of a true one, then it is properly called a *sophism* or fallacy. *Watts.*

SOPH'IST, *n.* [L. *sophista*; Fr. *sophiste*; It. *sofista.*]

1. A professor of philosophy; as the *sophists* of Greece. *Temple.*
2. A captious or fallacious reasoner.

SOPH'ISTER, *n.* [supra.] A disputant fallaciously subtil; an artful but insidious logician; as an atheistical *sophister.*

Not all the subtil objections of *sophisters* and rabbies against the gospel, so much prejudiced the reception of it, as the reproach of those crimes with which they aspersed the assemblies of Christians. *Rogers.*

2. A professor of philosophy; a sophist. *Obs.* *Hooker.*

SOPH'ISTER, *v. t.* To maintain by a fallacious argument. [*Not in use.*] *Cobham.*

SOPHIST'IC, SOPHIST'ICAL, *a.* [Fr. *sophistique*; It. *sofistico.*] Fallaciously subtil; not sound; as *sophistical* reasoning or argument.

SOPHIST'ICALLY, *adv.* With fallacious subtilty. *Swift.*

SOPHIST'ICATE, *v. t.* [Fr. *sophistiquer*; Sp. *sofisticar.*]

1. To adulterate; to corrupt by something spurious or foreign; to pervert; as, to *sophisticate* nature, philosophy or the understanding. *Hooker. South.*
2. To adulterate; to render spurious; as merchandise; as, to *sophisticate* wares or liquors.

They purchase but *sophisticated* ware. *Dryden.*

SOPHIST'ICATE, *a.* Adulterated; not pure; not genuine.

So truth, when only one supplied the state,
Grew scarce and dear, and yet *sophisticate.* *Dryden.*

SOPHISTICA'TION, *n.* The act of adulterating; a counterfeiting or debasing the purity of something by a foreign admixture; adulteration. *Boyle. Quincy.*

SOPHIST'ICATOR, *n.* One that adulterates; one who injures the purity and genuineness of any thing by foreign admixture. *Whitaker.*

SOPH'ISTRY, *n.* Fallacious reasoning; reasoning sound in appearance only.

These men have obscured and confounded the nature of things by their false principles and wretched *sophistry.* *South.*

2. Exercise in logic. *Felton.*

SOPH'OMORE, *n.* [See *Soph.*] A student in a college or university, in his second year.

SO'PITE, *v. t.* To lay asleep. [*Not in use.*] *Cheyne.*

SOPI''TION, *n.* [L. *sopio*, to lay asleep.] Sleep. [*Not in use.*] *Brown.*

SOP'ORATE, *v. t.* [L. *soporo.*] To lay asleep. [*Not in use.*]

SOPORIF'EROUS, *a.* [L. *soporifer*; *sopor*, sleep, and *fero*, to bring; from *sopio*, to lull to sleep; Sans. *swapa*, sleep. *Sopio* agrees in elements with *sober.*]

Causing sleep, or tending to produce it; narcotic; opiate; anodyne; somniferous. The poppy possesses *soporiferous* qualities.

SOPORIF'EROUSNESS, *n.* The quality of causing sleep.

SOPORIF'IC, *a.* [L. *sopor*, sleep, and *facio*, to make.]

Causing sleep; tending to cause sleep; narcotic; as the *soporific* virtues of opium. *Locke.*

SOPORIF'IC, *n.* A medicine, drug, plant or other thing that has the quality of inducing sleep.

SO'POROUS, *a.* [L. *soporus*, from *sopor*, sleep.]

Causing sleep; sleepy. *Greenhill.*

SOP'PED, *pp.* [from *sop.*] Dipped in liquid food.

SOP'PER, *n.* [from *sop.*] One that sops or dips in liquor something to be eaten. *Johnson.*

SORB, *n.* [Fr. *sorbe*; It. *sorba, sorbo*; L. *sorbum, sorbus.*] The service tree or its fruit.

SOR'BATE, *n.* A compound of sorbic acid with a base. *Ure.*

SORB'ENT. [See *Absorbent.*]

SORB'IC, *a.* Pertaining to the sorbus or service tree; as *sorbic* acid.

SORB'ILE, *a.* [L. *sorbeo.*] That may be drank or sipped. [*Not in use.*]

SORBI''TION, *n.* [L. *sorbitio.*] The act of drinking or sipping. [*Not in use.*]

SORBON'ICAL, *a.* Belonging to a sorbonist. *Bale.*

SOR'BONIST, *n.* A doctor of the Sorbonne in the university of Paris. Sorbonne is the place of meeting, and hence is used for the whole faculty of theology.

SOR'CERER, *n.* [Fr. *sorcier*; Arm. *sorca*; supposed to be from L. *sors*, lot. But see Class Sr. No. 24. Eth.] A conjurer; an enchanter; a magician.

The Egyptian *sorcerers* contended with Moses. *Watts.*

SOR'CERESS, *n.* A female magician or enchantress. *Milton. Shak.*

SOR'CEROUS, *a.* Containing enchantments. *Chapman.*

SOR'CERY, *n.* Magic; enchantment; witchcraft; divination by the assistance or supposed assistance of evil spirits, or the power of commanding evil spirits. *Encyc.*

Adder's wisdom I have learn'd,
To fence my ears against thy *sorceries.* *Milton.*

SÖRD, for *sward*, is now vulgar. [See *Sward.*]

SORD'AWALITE, *n.* A mineral so named from Sordawald, in Wibourg. It is nearly black, rarely gray or green. *Phillips.*

SOR'DES, *n.* [L.] Foul matter; excretions; dregs; filthy, useless or rejected matter of any kind. *Coxe. Woodward.*

SOR'DET, SOR'DINE, *n.* [Fr. *sourdine*; It. *sordina*; from Fr. *sourd*, L. *surdus*, deaf.]

A little pipe in the mouth of a trumpet to make it sound lower or shriller. *Bailey.*

SOR'DID, *a.* [Fr. *sordide*; It. *sordido*; L. *sordidus*, from *sordes*, filth.] Filthy; foul; dirty; gross.

There Charon stands
A *sordid* god. *Dryden.*

[*This literal sense is nearly obsolete.*]

2. Vile; base; mean; as vulgar, *sordid* mortals. *Cowley.*
3. Meanly avaricious; covetous; niggardly.

He may be old
And yet not *sordid*, who refuses gold. *Denham.*

SOR'DIDLY, *adv.* Meanly; basely; covetously.

SOR'DIDNESS, *n.* Filthiness; dirtiness. *Ray.*

2. Meanness; baseness; as the execrable *sordidness* of the delights of Tiberius. *Cowley.*
3. Niggardliness.

SORE, *n.* [Dan. *saar*, a sore, a wound or an ulcer; D. *zweer*; G. *geschwür*; Sw. *sår*. See the next word.]

1. A place in an animal body where the skin and flesh are ruptured or bruised, so as to be pained with the slightest pressure.
2. An ulcer; a boil.
3. In Scripture, grief; affliction. 2 Chron. vi.

SORE, *a.* [Sax. *sar*, pain, also grievous, painful: D. *zeer*; G. *sehr*; also Sax. *swær*, *swar* or *swer*, heavy, grievous; Dan. *svær*; G. *schwer*; D. *zwaar*. This seems to be radically the same word as the former. See *Sorrow.*]

1. Tender and susceptible of pain from pressure; as, a boil, ulcer or abscess is very *sore*; a wounded place is *sore*; inflammation renders a part *sore.*
2. Tender, as the mind; easily pained, grieved or vexed; very susceptible of irritation from any thing that crosses the inclination.

Malice and hatred are very fretting, and apt to make our minds *sore* and uneasy. *Tillotson.*

3. Affected with inflammation; as *sore* eyes.
4. Violent with pain; severe; afflictive; distressing; as a *sore* disease; *sore* evil or calamity; a *sore* night. *Com. Prayer. Shak.*

5. Severe; violent; as a *sore* conflict.
6. Criminal; evil. *Obs.* *Shak.*
SORE, *adv.* With painful violence; intensely; severely; grievously.
Thy hand presseth me *sore.* *Com. Prayer.*
2. Greatly; violently; deeply. He was *sorely* afflicted at the loss of his son.
Sore sigh'd the knight, who this long sermon heard. *Dryden.*
SORE, *v. t.* To wound; to make sore. *Obs.* *Spenser.*
SORE, *n.* [Fr. *sor-falcon.* *Todd.*] A hawk of the first year. *Spenser.*
2. [Fr. *saur.*] A buck of the fourth year. *Shak.*
SOREHON, } *n.* [Irish and Scottish.] A
SORN, } kind of servile tenure which subjected the tenant to maintain his chieftain gratuitously, whenever he wished to indulge himself in a debauch. So that when a person obtrudes himself on another for bed and board, he is said to *sorn*, or be a *sorner.* *Spenser.* *Macbean.*
SOR'EL, *n.* [*dim.* of *sore.*] A buck of the third year. *Shak.*
SO'RELY, *adv.* [from *sore.*] With violent pain and distress; grievously; greatly; as, to be *sorely* pained or afflicted.
2. Greatly; violently; severely; as, to be *sorely* pressed with want; to be *sorely* wounded.
SO'RENESS, *n.* [from *sore.*] The tenderness of any part of an animal body, which renders it extremely susceptible of pain from pressure; as the *soreness* of a boil, an abscess or wound.
2. Figuratively, tenderness of mind, or susceptibility of mental pain.
SOR'GO, *n.* A plant of the genus Holcus.
SORI'TES, *n.* [L. from Gr. σωρειτης, a heap.]
In *logic*, an argument where one proposition is accumulated on another. Thus,
All men of revenge have their souls often uneasy.
Uneasy souls are a plague to themselves.
Now to be one's own plague is folly in the extreme. *Watts.*
SOROR'ICIDE, *n.* [L. *soror*, sister, and *cædo*, to strike, to kill.]
The murder or murderer of a sister. [Little used, and obviously because the crime is very infrequent.]
SOR'RAĠE, *n.* The blades of green wheat or barley. [*Not used.*] *Dict.*
SOR'RANCE, *n.* In *farriery*, any disease or sore in horses.
SOR'REL, *a.* [Fr. *saure*, yellowish brown; *saurer*, to dry in the smoke; It. *sauro.*] Of a reddish color; as a *sorrel* horse.
SOR'REL, *n.* A reddish color; a faint red.
SOR'REL, *n.* [Sax. *sur*, sour; Dan. *syre*, sorrel; W. *suran.*]
A plant of the genus Rumex, so named from its acid taste. The *wood sorrel* is of the genus Oxalis. The *Indian red* and *Indian white sorrels* are of the genus Hibiscus.
SOR'REL-TREE, *n.* A species of Andromeda.
SOR'RILY, *adv.* [from *sorry.*] Meanly; despicably; pitiably; in a wretched manner.
Thy pipe, O Pan, shall help, though I sing *sorrily.* *Sidney.*

SOR'RINESS, *n.* Meanness; poorness; despicableness.
SOR'RŌW, *n.* [Sax. *sorg;* Goth. *saurga;* Sw. Dan. *sorg*, care, solicitude, sorrow; D. *zorg;* G. *sorge*, care, concern, uneasiness; from the same root as *sore*, heavy.]
The uneasiness or pain of mind which is produced by the loss of any good, real or supposed, or by disappointment in the expectation of good; grief; regret. The loss of a friend we love occasions *sorrow;* the loss of property, of health or any source of happiness, causes *sorrow.* We feel *sorrow* for ourselves in misfortunes; we feel *sorrow* for the calamities of our friends and our country.
A world of woe and *sorrow.* *Milton.*
The safe and general antidote against *sorrow* is employment. *Rambler.*
SOR'RŌW, *v. i.* [Sax. *sarian*, *sargian*, *sorgian*, Goth. *saurgan*, to be anxious, to sorrow.]
To feel pain of mind in consequence of the actual loss of good, or of frustrated hopes of good, or of expected loss of happiness; to grieve; to be sad.
I rejoice not that ye were made sorry, but that ye *sorrowed* to repentance. 1 Cor. vii.
I desire no man to *sorrow* for me. *Hayward.*
Sorrowing most of all for the words which he spoke, that they should see his face no more. Acts xx.
SOR'RŌWED, *pp.* Accompanied with sorrow. [*Not in use.*] *Shak.*
SOR'RŌWFUL, *a.* Sad; grieving for the loss of some good, or on account of some expected evil.
2. Deeply serious; depressed; dejected. 1 Sam. i.
3. Producing sorrow; exciting grief; mournful; as a *sorrowful* accident.
4. Expressing grief; accompanied with grief; as *sorrowful* meat. Job vi.
SOR'RŌWFULLY, *adv.* In a sorrowful manner; in a manner to produce grief.
SOR'RŌWFULNESS, *n.* State of being sorrowful; grief.
SOR'RŌWING, *ppr.* Feeling sorrow, grief or regret.
SOR'RŌWING, *n.* Expression of sorrow. *Browne.*
SOR'RŌWLESS, *a.* Free from sorrow.
SOR'RY, *a.* [Sax. *sarig*, *sari*, from *sar*, sore.]
1. Grieved for the loss of some good; pained for some evil that has happened to one's self or friends or country. It does not ordinarily imply severe grief, but rather slight or transient regret. It may be however, and often is used to express deep grief. We are *sorry* to lose the company of those we love; we are *sorry* to lose friends or property; we are *sorry* for the misfortunes of our friends or of our country.
And the king was *sorry.* Matt. xiv.
2. Melancholy; dismal. *Spenser.*
3. Poor; mean; vile; worthless; as a *sorry* slave; a *sorry* excuse. *L'Estrange.* *Dryden.*
Coarse complexions,
And cheeks of *sorry* grain— *Milton.*
SORT, *n.* [Fr. *sorte;* It. *sorta;* Sp. *suerte;* Port. *sorte;* G. *id.;* D. *soort;* Sw. Dan. *sort;* L. *sors*, lot, chance, state, way, *sort.* This word is from the root of Fr. *sortir*, It. *sortire*, L. *sortior;* the radical sense of which is to start or shoot, to throw or to fall, to come suddenly. Hence *sors* is lot, chance, that which comes or falls. The sense of *sort* is probably derivative, signifying that which is thrown out, separated or selected.]
1. A kind or species; any number or collection of individual persons or things characterized by the same or like qualities; as a *sort* of men; a *sort* of horses; a *sort* of trees; a *sort* of poems or writings. *Sort* is not a technical word, and therefore is used with less precision or more latitude than *genus* or *species* in the sciences.
2. Manner; form of being or acting.
Flowers, in such *sort* worn, can neither be smelt nor seen well by those that wear them. *Hooker.*
To Adam in what *sort* shall I appear? *Milton.*
3. Class or order; as men of the wiser *sort*, or the better *sort;* all *sorts* of people. [See Def. 1.]
4. Rank; condition above the vulgar. [*Not in use.*] *Shak.*
5. A company or knot of people. [*Not in use.*] *Shak.* *Waller.*
6. Degree of any quality.
I shall not be wholly without praise, if in some *sort* I have copied his style. *Dryden.*
7. Lot. *Obs.* *Shak.*
8. A pair; a set; a suit.
SORT, *v. t.* To separate, as things having like qualities from other things, and place them in distinct classes or divisions; as, to *sort* cloths according to their colors; to *sort* wool or thread according to its fineness.
Shell fish have been, by some of the ancients, compared and *sorted* with insects. *Bacon.*
Rays which differ in refrangibility, may be parted and *sorted* from one another. *Newton.*
2. To reduce to order from a state of confusion. [See supra.]
3. To conjoin; to put together in distribution.
The swain perceiving by her words ill *sorted*,
That she was wholly from herself transported-- *Brown.*
4. To cull; to choose from a number; to select.
That he may sort her out a worthy spouse. *Chapman.*
SORT, *v. i.* To be joined with others of the same species.
Nor do metals only *sort* with metals in the earth, and minerals with minerals. *Woodward.*
2. To consort; to associate.
The illiberality of parents towards children, makes them base and *sort* with any company. *Bacon.*
3. To suit; to fit.
They are happy whose natures *sort* with their vocations. *Bacon.*
4. To terminate; to issue; to have success. [Fr. *sortir.*] [*Not in use.*] *Bacon.*
5. To fall out. [*Not in use.*] *Shak.*
SORT'ABLE, *a.* That may be sorted.
2. Suitable; befitting. *Bacon.*
SORT'ABLY, *adv.* Suitably; fitly.
SORT'AL, *a.* Pertaining to or designating a sort. [*Not in use.*] *Locke.*
SORT'ANCE, *n.* Suitableness; agreement. [*Not in use.*] *Shak.*

SORT'ILEGE, *n.* [Fr. from L. *sortilegium ; sors*, lot, and *lego*, to select.]
The act or practice of drawing lots. [*Sortilegy* is not used.] *J. M. Mason.*

SORTILE'GIOUS, *a.* Pertaining to sortilege. *Daubuz.*

SORTI''TION, *n.* [L. *sortitio.*] Selection or appointment by lot. *Bp. Hall.*

SORT'MENT, *n.* The act of sorting; distribution into classes or kinds.
2. A parcel sorted. [This word is superseded by *assortment*, which see.]

SO'RY, *n.* A fossil substance, firm, but of a spungy, cavernous structure, rugged on the surface, and containing blue vitriol; a sulphate of iron. *Dict.*

SOSS, *v. i.* [This word is probably connected with the Armoric *souez*, surprise, the primary sense of which is to fall. See *Souse.*]
To fall at once into a chair or seat; to sit lazily. [*Not in use.*] *Swift.*

SOSS, *n.* A lazy fellow. [Not in use; but some of the common people in New England call a lazy sluttish woman, a *sozzle.*]

SOT, *n.* [Fr. *sot ;* Arm. *sodt;* Sp. *zote, zota ;* Port. *zote ;* D. *zot.* The sense is stupid; Ch. שט. Class Sd. No. 61.]
1. A stupid person; a blockhead; a dull fellow; a dolt. *Shak. South.*
2. A person stupefied by excessive drinking; an habitual drunkard.

> What can ennoble *sots ?* *Pope.*

SOT, *v. t.* To stupefy; to infatuate; to besot.

> I hate to see a brave bold fellow *sotted.* *Dryden.*

[*Not much used.*] [See *Besot.*]

SOT, *v. i.* To tipple to stupidity. [*Little used.*]

SOT'TISH, *a.* Dull; stupid; senseless; doltish; very foolish.

> How ignorant are *sottish* pretenders to astrology! *Swift.*

2. Dull with intemperance.

SOT'TISHLY, *adv.* Stupidly; senselessly; without reason. *Bentley.*

SOT'TISHNESS, *n.* Dullness in the exercise of reason; stupidity.

> Few consider into what a degree of *sottishness* and confirmed ignorance men may sin themselves. *South.*

2. Stupidity from intoxication. *South.*

SÔU, *n.* plu. *sous.* [Fr. *sou, sol.*] A French money of account, and a copper coin, in value the 20th part of a livre or of a franc.

SOUGH, *n. suf.* [Qu. the root of *suck*, to draw.]
A subterraneous drain; a sewer. [*Not in use or local.*] *Ray.*

SOUGHT, *pret.* and *pp.* of *seek.* pron. *sawt.*

> I am found of them who *sought* me not. Is. lxv.

SÔUL, *n.* [Sax. *sawel, sawl* or *saul ; G. seele ;* D. *ziel ;* Dan. *siel ;* Sw. *siäl.*]
1. The spiritual, rational and immortal substance in man, which distinguishes him from brutes; that part of man which enables him to think and reason, and which renders him a subject of moral government. The immortality of the *soul* is a fundamental article of the christian system.

> Such is the nature of the human *soul* that it must have a God, an object of supreme affection. *Edwards.*

2. The understanding; the intellectual principle.

> The eyes of our *souls* then only begin to see, when our bodily eyes are closing. *Law.*

3. Vital principle.

> Thou sun, of this great world both eye and *soul.* *Milton.*

4. Spirit; essence; chief part; as charity, the *soul* of all the virtues.

> Emotion is the *soul* of eloquence. *E. Porter.*

6. Life; animating principle or part; as, an able commander is the *soul* of an army.
7. Internal power.

> There is some *soul* of goodness in things evil. *Shak.*

8. A human being; a person. There was not a *soul* present. In Paris there are more than seven hundred thousand *souls.* London, Westminster, Southwark and the suburbs, are said to contain twelve hundred thousand *souls.*
9. Animal life.

> To deliver their *soul* from death, and to keep them alive in famine. Ps. xxxiii. vii.

10. Active power.

> And heaven would fly before the driving *soul.* *Dryden.*

11. Spirit; courage; fire; grandeur of mind.

> That he wants caution he must needs confess,
> But not a *soul* to give our arms success. *Young.*

12. Generosity; nobleness of mind; *a colloquial use.*
13. An intelligent being.

> Every *soul* in heav'n shall bend the knee. *Milton.*

14. Heart; affection.

> The *soul* of Jonathan was knit with the *soul* of David. 1 Sam. xviii.

15. In *Scripture*, appetite; as the full *soul ;* the hungry *soul.* Prov. xxvii. Job xxxiii.
16. A familiar compellation of a person, but often expressing some qualities of the mind; as alas, poor *soul ;* he was a good *soul.*

SÔUL, *v. t.* To endue with a soul. [*Not used.*] *Chaucer.*

SOUL, SOWL, *v. i.* [Sax. *sufl, sufel*, broth, pottage.] To afford suitable sustenance. [*Not in use.*] *Warner.*

SÔUL-BELL, *n.* The passing bell. *Hall.*

SÔUL-DESTROY'ING, *a.* Pernicious to the soul. Procrastination of repentance and faith is a *soul-destroying* evil.

SÔUL-DISE'ASED, *a.* Diseased in soul or mind. [*Not used.*] *Spenser.*

SÔULED, *a.* Furnished with a soul or mind; as Grecian chiefs largely *souled.* [*Little used.*] *Dryden.*

SÔUL'LESS, *a.* Without a soul, or without greatness or nobleness of mind; mean; spiritless.

> Slave, *soulless* villain. *Shak.*

SÔUL-SCOT, SÔUL-SHOT, *n.* [*soul* and *scot.*] A funeral duty, or money paid by the Romanists in former times for a requiem for the soul. *Ayliffe.*

SÔUL-SELLING, *a.* [*soul* and *sell.*] Selling persons; dealing in the purchase and sale of human beings. *J. Barlow.*

SÔUL-SICK, *a.* [*soul* and *sick.*] Diseased in mind or soul; morally diseased. *Hall.*

SOUND, *a.* [Sax. *sund ;* D. *gezond ;* G. *gesund;* Dan. Sw. *sund ;* Basque, *sendoa ;* L. *sanus ;* Fr. *sain ;* Sp. It. *sano ;* Ch. Syr. חסן. Class Sn. No. 18. 24. 35. It is from driving, or straining, stretching.]
1. Entire; unbroken; not shaky, split or defective; as *sound* timber.
2. Undecayed; whole; perfect, or not defective; as *sound* fruit; a *sound* apple or melon.
3. Unbroken; not bruised or defective; not lacerated or decayed; as a *sound* limb.
4. Not carious; not decaying; as a *sound* tooth.
5. Not broken or decayed; not defective; as a *sound* ship.
6. Whole; entire; unhurt; unmutilated; as a *sound* body.
7. Healthy; not diseased; not being in a morbid state; having all the organs complete and in perfect action; as a *sound* body; *sound* health; a *sound* constitution; a *sound* man; a *sound* horse.
8. Founded in truth; firm; strong; valid; solid; that cannot be overthrown or refuted; as *sound* reasoning; a *sound* argument; a *sound* objection; *sound* doctrine; *sound* principles.
9. Right; correct; well founded; free from error; orthodox. 2 Tim. i.

> Let my heart be *sound* in thy statutes. Ps. cxix.

10. Heavy; laid on with force; as *sound* strokes; a *sound* beating.
11. Founded in right and law; legal; valid; not defective; that cannot be overthrown; as a *sound* title to land; *sound* justice.
12. Fast; profound; unbroken; undisturbed; as *sound* sleep.
13. Perfect, as intellect; not broken or defective; not enfeebled by age or accident; not wild or wandering; not deranged; as a *sound* mind; a *sound* understanding or reason.

SOUND, *adv.* Soundly; heartily.

> So *sound* he slept that nought might him awake. *Spenser.*

SOUND, *n.* The air bladder of a fish.

SOUND, *n.* [Sax. *sund*, a narrow sea or strait, a swimming; Sw. Dan. *sund ;* Pers. شنا shana, a swimming, L. *natatio.* Qu. can this name be given to a narrow sea because wild beasts were accustomed to pass it by swimming, like *Bosporus ;* or is the word from the root of *sound*, whole, denoting a stretch, or narrowness, from stretching, like *straight ?*]
A narrow passage of water, or a strait between the main land and an isle; or a strait connecting two seas, or connecting a sea or lake with the ocean; as the *sound* which connects the Baltic with the ocean, between Denmark and Sweden; the *sound* that separates Long Island from the main land of New York and Connecticut.

SOUND, *n.* [Fr. *sonde ;* Sp. *sonda.* See the following verb.]
An instrument which surgeons introduce into the bladder, in order to discover whether there is a stone in that viscus or not. *Cooper. Sharp.*

SOUND, *v. t.* [Sp. *sondar* or *sondear ;* Fr. *sonder.* This word is probably connected with the L. *sonus*, Eng. *sound*, the primary sense of which is to stretch or reach.]
1. To try, as the depth of water and the quality of the ground, by sinking a plum-

met or lead, attached to a line on which are marked the number of fathoms. The lower end of the lead is covered with tallow, by means of which some portion of the earth, sand, gravel, shells, &c. of the bottom, adhere to it and are drawn up. By these means, and the depth of water and the nature of the bottom, which are carefully marked on good charts, seamen may know how far a ship is from land in the night or in thick weather, and in many cases when the land is too remote to be visible.

2. To introduce a sound into the bladder of a patient, in order to ascertain whether a stone is there or not.

When a patient is to be *sounded*— *Cooper.*

3. To try; to examine; to discover or endeavor to discover that which lies concealed in another's breast; to search out the intention, opinion, will or desires.

I was in jest,
And by that offer meant to *sound* your breast. *Dryden.*

I've *sounded* my Numidians man by man. *Addison.*

SOUND, *v. i.* To use the line and lead in searching the depth of water.

The shipmen *sounded*, and found it twenty fathoms. Acts xxvii.

SOUND, *n.* The cuttle fish. *Ainsworth.*

SOUND, *n.* [Sax. *son*; W. *swn*; Ir. *soin*; Fr. *son*; It. *suono*; Sp. *son*; L. *sonus*, from *sono*, to sound, sing, rattle, beat, &c. This may be a dialectical variation of L. *tonus*, *tono*, which seems to be allied to Gr. *τεινω*, to stretch or strain, L. *teneo*.]

1. Noise; report; the object of hearing; that which strikes the ear; or more philosophically, an impression or the effect of an impression made on the organs of hearing by an impulse or vibration of the air, caused by a collision of bodies or by other means; as the *sound* of a trumpet or drum; the *sound* of the human voice; a horrid *sound*; a charming *sound*; a sharp *sound*; a high *sound*.

2. A vibration of air caused by a collision of bodies or other means, sufficient to affect the auditory nerves when perfect. Some persons are so entirely deaf that they cannot hear the loudest *sounds*. *Audible sounds* are such as are perceptible by the organs of hearing. *Sounds* not audible to men, may be audible to animals of more sensible organs.

3. Noise without signification; empty noise; noise and nothing else.

It is the sense and not the *sound*, that must be the principle. *Locke.*

SOUND, *v. i.* To make a noise; to utter a voice; to make an impulse of the air that shall strike the organs of hearing with a particular effect. We say, an instrument *sounds* well or ill; it *sounds* shrill; the voice *sounds* harsh.

And first taught speaking trumpets how to *sound*. *Dryden.*

2. To exhibit by sound or likeness of sound. This relation *sounds* rather like a fiction than a truth.

3. To be conveyed in sound; to be spread or published.

From you *sounded* out the word of the Lord. 1 Thess. i.

To sound in damages, in law, is when there is no specific value of property in demand to serve as a rule of damages, as in actions of tort or trespass, as distinguished from actions of debt, &c. *Ellsworth.*

SOUND, *v. t.* To cause to make a noise; as, to *sound* a trumpet or a horn.

2. To utter audibly; as, to *sound* a note with the voice.

3. To play on; as, to *sound* an instrument.

4. To order or direct by a sound; to give a signal for, by a certain sound; as, to *sound* a retreat.

5. To celebrate or honor by sounds; to cause to be reported; as, to *sound* one's praise.

6. To spread by sound or report; to publish or proclaim; as, to *sound* the praises or fame of a great man or a great exploit. We sometimes say, to *sound abroad*.

SOUND'-BOARD, SOUND'ING-BOARD, } *n.* A board which propagates the sound in an organ.

To many a row of pipes the *sound-board* breathes. *Milton.*

SOUND'ED, *pp.* Caused to make a noise; uttered audibly.

2. Explored; examined.

SOUND'ING, *ppr.* Causing to sound; uttering audibly.

2. Trying the depth of water by the plummet; examining the intention or will.

3. *a.* Sonorous; making a noise.

4. Having a magnificent sound; as words more *sounding* or significant. *Dryden.*

SOUND'ING, *n.* The act of uttering noise; the act of endeavoring to discover the opinion or desires; the act of throwing the lead.

2. In *surgery*, the operation of introducing the sound into the bladder; called *searching* for the stone. *Cooper.*

SOUND'ING-BOARD, *n.* A board or structure with a flat surface, suspended over a pulpit to prevent the sound of the preacher's voice from ascending, and thus propagating it farther in a horizontal direction. [*Used in American churches.*]

SOUND'ING-ROD, *n.* A rod or piece of iron used to ascertain the depth of water in a ship's hold. It is let down in a groove by a pump. *Mar. Dict.*

SOUND'INGS, *n.* Any place or part of the ocean, where a deep sounding line will reach the bottom; also, the kind of ground or bottom where the lead reaches.

SOUND'LESS, *a.* That cannot be fathomed; having no sound.

SOUND'LY, *adv.* [from *sound*, entire.]

1. Healthily; heartily.

2. Severely; lustily; with heavy blows; smartly; as, to beat one *soundly*.

3. Truly; without fallacy or error; as, to judge or reason *soundly*.

4. Firmly; as a doctrine *soundly* settled. *Bacon.*

5. Fast; closely; so as not to be easily awakened; as, to sleep *soundly*. *Locke.*

SOUND'NESS, *n.* Wholeness; entireness; an unbroken, unimpaired or undecayed state; as the *soundness* of timber, of fruit, of the teeth, of a limb, &c. [See *Sound.*]

2. An unimpaired state of an animal or vegetable body; a state in which the organs are entire and regularly perform their functions. We say, the *soundness* of the body, the *soundness* of the constitution, the *soundness* of health.

3. Firmness; strength; solidity; truth; as *soundness* of reasoning or argument, of doctrine or principles.

4. Truth; rectitude; firmness; freedom from error or fallacy; orthodoxy; as *soundness* of faith.

SÖUP, *n.* [Fr. *soupe*; It. *zuppa*, sop; Sp. *sopa*, sop or soup; G. *suppe*; D. *soep*; Ice. *saup*. See *Sup* and *Sop.*] Broth; a decoction of flesh for food.

SÖUP, *v. t.* To sup; to breathe out. [*Not in use.*] *Wickliffe.*

SÖUP, *v. t.* To sweep. [*Not in use.*] [See *Sweep* and *Swoop.*] *Hall.*

SOUR, *a.* [Sax. *sur*, *surig*; G. *sauer*; D. *zuur*; Sw. *sur*; Dan. *suur*; W. *sûr*; Arm. *sur*; Fr. *sur*, *sure*; Heb. סור to depart, to decline, to turn, as liquors, to become sour. See Class Sr. No. 16. and No. 11.]

1. Acid; having a pungent taste; sharp to the taste; tart; as, vinegar is *sour*; *sour* cider; *sour* beer.

2. Acid and austere or astringent; as, sunripe fruits are often *sour*.

3. Harsh of temper; crabbed; peevish; austere; morose; as a man of a *sour* temper.

4. Afflictive; as *sour* adversities. [*Not in use.*] *Shak.*

5. Expressing discontent or peevishness. He never uttered a *sour* word.

The lord treasurer often looked on me with a *sour* countenance. *Swift.*

6. Harsh to the feelings; cold and damp; as *sour* weather.

7. Rancid; musty.

8. Turned, as milk; coagulated.

SOUR, *n.* An acid substance. *Spenser.*

SOUR, *v. t.* To make acid; to cause to have a sharp taste.

So the sun's heat, with different pow'rs,
Ripens the grape, the liquor *sours*. *Swift.*

2. To make harsh, cold or unkindly.

Tufts of grass *sour* land. *Mortimer.*

3. To make harsh in temper; to make cross, crabbed, peevish or discontented. Misfortunes often *sour* the temper.

Pride had not *sour'd*, nor wrath debas'd my heart. *Harte.*

4. To make uneasy or less agreeable.

Hail, great king!
To *sour* your happiness I must report
The queen is dead. *Shak.*

5. In *rural economy*, to macerate, as lime, and render fit for plaster or mortar. *Encyc.*

SOUR, *v. i.* To become acid; to acquire the quality of tartness or pungency to the taste. Cider *sours* rapidly in the rays of the sun. When food *sours* in the stomach, it is evidence of imperfect digestion.

2. To become peevish or crabbed.

They hinder the hatred of vice from *souring* into severity. *Addison.*

SÖURCE, *n.* [Fr. *source*; Arm. *sourcenn*; either from *sourdre* or *sortir*, or the L. *surgo*. The Italian *sorgente* is from *surgo.*]

1. Properly, the spring or fountain from which a stream of water proceeds, or any collection of water within the earth or upon its surface, in which a stream originates. This is called also the *head* of the stream. We call the water of a spring, where it issues from the earth, the *source* of the stream or rivulet proceeding from it. We say also that springs have their

sources in subterranean ponds, lakes or collections of water. We say also that a large river has its *source* in a lake. For example, the St. Lawrence has its *source* in the great lakes of America.

2. First cause; original; that which gives rise to any thing. Thus ambition, the love of power and of fame, have been the *sources* of half the calamities of nations. Intemperance is the *source* of innumerable evils to individuals.

3. The first producer; he or that which originates; as Greece the *source* of arts. *Waller.*

SOURDET, *n.* [Fr. *sourdine*, from *sourd*, deaf.] The little pipe of a trumpet.

SOUR'-DOCK, *n.* Sorrel, so called.

SOUR'ED, *pp.* Made sour; made peevish.

SOUR'-GOURD, *n.* A plant of the genus Adansonia.

SOUR'ING, *ppr.* Making acid; becoming sour; making peevish.

SOUR'ING, *n.* That which makes acid.

SOUR'ISH, *a.* Somewhat sour; moderately acid; as *sourish* fruit; a *sourish* taste.

SOUR'LY, *adv.* With acidity.

2. With peevishness; with acrimony.

The stern Athenian prince
Then *sourly* smil'd. *Dryden.*

3. Discontentedly. *Brown.*

SOUR'NESS, *n.* Acidity; sharpness to the taste; tartness; as the *sourness* of vinegar or of fruit.

Sourness being one of those simple ideas which one cannot describe. *Arbuthnot.*

2. Asperity; harshness of temper.

Take care that no *sourness* and moroseness mingle with our seriousness of mind. *Nelson.*

SOUR'-SOP, *n.* A plant, the *annona muricata*. *Lee.*

The custard apple. *Miller.*

SÖUS, *n. plu.* of *sou* or *sol.* [See *Sou.*]

SOUSE, *n.* [Ir. *sousgeach*, watery.] Pickle made with salt.

2. Something kept or steeped in pickle.

3. The ears, feet, &c. of swine. [*America.*]

SOUSE, *v. t.* To steep in pickle.

But *souse* the cabbage with a bounteous heart. *Pope.*

2. To plunge into water.

They *soused* me into the Thames, with as little remorse as they drown blind puppies. *Shak.*

SOUSE, *v. i.* [See *Soss.* This word is probably the same as the preceding, to plunge, to dip; I believe from the Armoric.]

To fall suddenly on; to rush with speed; as a hawk on its prey.

Jove's bird will *souse* upon the tim'rous hare. *Dryden.*

SOUSE, *v. t.* To strike with sudden violence. *Shak.*

SOUSE, *adv.* With sudden violence. [*This word is low and vulgar.*]

SÖUTER, *n.* [Sax. *sutere*; L. *sutor.*] A shoemaker; a cobler. [*Not in use.*] *Chaucer.*

SÖUTERLY, *adv.* Like a cobler. [*Not in use.*]

SÖUTERRAIN, *n.* [Fr.; that is, *sub-terrain*, under ground.] A grotto or cavern under ground. [*Not English.*] *Arbuthnot.*

SOUTH, *n.* [Sax. *suth*; G. *sud*; D. *zuid*; Dan. *sud*; Sw. *söder*; Fr. *sud*; Arm. *su.*]

1. The north and south are opposite points in the horizon; each ninety degrees or the quarter of a great circle distant from the east and west. A man standing with his face towards the east or rising sun, has the *south* on his right hand. The meridian of every place is a great circle passing through the north and south points. Strictly, *south* is the horizontal point in the meridian of a place, on the right hand of a person standing with his face towards the east. But the word is applied to any point in the meridian, between the horizon and the zenith.

2. In a less exact sense, any point or place on the earth or in the heavens, which is near the meridian towards the right hand as one faces the east.

3. A southern region, country or place; as the queen of the *south*, in Scripture. So in Europe, the people of Spain and Italy are spoken of as living in the *south*. In the United States, we speak of the states of the *south*, and of the north.

4. The wind that blows from the south. [*Not used.*] *Shak.*

SOUTH, *a.* In *any place north of the tropic of Cancer*, pertaining to or lying in the meridian towards the sun; as a *south* wind.

2. Being in a southern direction; as the *south* sea.

SOUTH, *adv.* Towards the south. A ship sails *south*; the wind blows *south*.

SOUTHE'AST, *n.* The point of the compass equally distant from the south and east. *Bacon.*

SOUTHE'AST, *a.* In the direction of southeast, or coming from the southeast; as a *southeast* wind.

SOUTHE'ASTERN, *a.* Towards the southeast.

SOUTHERLY, *a.* *suth'erly.* Lying at the south, or in a direction nearly south; as a *southerly* point.

2. Coming from the south or a point nearly south; as a *southerly* wind.

SOUTHERN, *a.* *suth'ern.* [Sax. *suth* and *ern*, place.]

1. Belonging to the south; meridional; as the *southern* hemisphere.

2. Lying towards the south; as a *southern* country or climate.

3. Coming from the south; as a *southern* breeze.

SOUTHERNLY, *adv.* *suth'ernly.* Towards the south. *Hakewill.*

SOUTHERNMOST, *a.* *suth'ernmost.* Furthest towards the south.

SOUTHERNWOOD, *n.* *suth'ernwood.* A plant agreeing in most parts with the wormwood. *Miller.*

The southernwood is the *Artemisia abrotanum*, a different species from the wormwood.

SOUTH'ING, *a.* Going towards the south; as the *southing* sun. *Dryden.*

SOUTH'ING, *n.* Tendency or motion to the south. *Dryden.*

2. The *southing* of the moon, the time at which the moon passes the meridian. *Mar. Dict.*

3. Course or distance south; as a ship's *southing*.

SOUTH'MOST, *a.* Furthest towards the south. *Milton.*

SOUTHSAY, **SOUTHSAYER.** } [See *Soothsay.*]

SOUTHWARD, *adv.* *suth'ard.* Towards the south; as, to go *southward*. *Locke.*

SOUTHWARD, *n.* *suth'ard.* The southern regions or countries. *Raleigh.*

SOUTHWEST', *n.* [*south* and *west.*] The point of the compass equally distant from the south and west. *Bacon.*

SOUTHWEST', *a.* Lying in the direction of the southwest; as a *southwest* country.

2. Coming from the southwest; as a *southwest* wind.

SOUTHWEST'ERLY, *a.* In the direction of southwest, or nearly so.

2. Coming from the southwest, or a point near it; as a *southwesterly* wind.

SOUTHWEST'ERN, *a.* In the direction of southwest, or nearly so; as, to sail a *southwestern* course.

SÖUVENANCE, *n.* [Fr.] Remembrance. [*Not English, nor is it used.*] *Spenser.*

SÖUVENIR, *n.* [Fr.] A remembrancer.

SÖVEREIGN, *a.* *suv'eran.* [We retain this barbarous orthography from the Norman *souvereign*. The true spelling would be *suveran*, from the L. *supernus*, *superus*; Fr. *souverain*; It. *sovrano*; Sp. Port. *soberano.*]

1. Supreme in power; possessing supreme dominion; as a *sovereign* prince. God is the *sovereign* ruler of the universe.

2. Supreme; superior to all others; chief. God is the *sovereign* good of all who love and obey him.

3. Supremely efficacious; superior to all others; predominant; effectual; as a *sovereign* remedy.

4. Supreme; pertaining to the first magistrate of a nation; as *sovereign* authority.

SÖVEREIGN, *n.* *suv'eran.* A supreme lord or ruler; one who possesses the highest authority without control. Some earthly princes, kings and emperors are *sovereigns* in their dominions.

2. A supreme magistrate; a king.

3. A gold coin of England, value 20s. or $4.44.

SÖVEREIGNIZE, *v. i.* *suv'eranize.* To exercise supreme authority. [*Not in use.*] *Herbert.*

SÖVEREIGNLY, *adv.* *suv'eranly.* Supremely; in the highest degree.

He was *sovereignly* lovely in himself. [*Little used.*] *Boyle.*

SÖVEREIGNTY, *n.* *suv'eranty.* Supreme power; supremacy; the possession of the highest power, or of uncontrollable power. Absolute *sovereignty* belongs to God only.

SOW, *n.* [Sax. *suga*; Sw. *sugga*; D. *zeug*; G. *sau.*]

1. The female of the hog kind or of swine.

2. An oblong piece of lead. *Ainsworth.*

3. An insect; a milleped. *Ainsworth.*

SOW'-BREAD, *n.* A plant of the genus Cyclamen.

SOW'-BUG, *n.* An insect; a milleped.

SOW'-THISTLE, *n.* A plant of the genus Sonchus. The *downy sow-thistle* is of the genus Andryala.

SÖW, *v. t.* pret. *sowed*; pp. *sowed* or *sown.* [Sax. *sawan*; G. *säen*; D. *zaajen*; Sw. *så*; Dan. *saaer*; Russ. *siyu*; perhaps L. *sevi.* This word is probably contracted.]

1. To scatter on ground, for the purpose of growth and the production of a crop; as, to *sow* good seed; to *sow* a bushel of wheat or rye to the acre; to *sow* oats,

clover or barley; to *sow* seed in drills, or to *sow* it broad cast. Oats and flax should be *sown* early in the spring.

2. To scatter seed over for growth; as, to *sow* ground or land; to *sow* ten or a hundred acres in a year.

3. To spread or to originate; to propagate; as, to *sow* discord.

Born to afflict my Marcia's family,
And *sow* dissension in the hearts of brothers. *Addison.*

4. To supply or stock with seed.

The intellectual faculty is a goodly field, and it is the worst husbandry in the world to *sow* it with trifles. *Hale.*

5. To scatter over; to besprinkle.

He *sow'd* with stars the heaven. *Milton.*
Morn now *sow'd* the earth with orient pearl. *Milton.*

SOW, *v. i.* To scatter seed for growth and the production of a crop. In New England, farmers begin to *sow* in April.

They that *sow* in tears, shall reap in joy. Ps. cxxvi.

SOW, for *sew*, is not in use. [See *Sew*.]

SOWCE, for *souse*. [See *Souse*.]

SOWED, *pp.* Scattered on ground, as seed; sprinkled with seed, as ground. We say, seed is *sowed*; or land is *sowed*.

SOWER, *n.* He that scatters seed for propagation.

Behold, a *sower* went forth to sow. Matt. xiii.

2. One who scatters or spreads; as a *sower* of words. *Hakewill.*

3. A breeder; a promoter; as a *sower* of suits. *Bacon.*

SOWING, *ppr.* Scattering, as seed; sprinkling with seed, as ground; stocking with seed.

SOWING, *n.* The act of scattering seed for propagation.

SOW'INS, *n.* Flummery made of oatmeal somewhat soured. *Mortimer. Swift.* [*Not used, I believe, in America.*]

SOWL, *v. t* To pull by the ears. *Shak.* [*Not used in America.*]

SOWN, *pp.* Scattered, as seed; sprinkled with seed, as ground.

SOY, *n.* A kind of sauce, used in Japan.

SOZ'ZLE, *n.* [See *Soss.*] A sluttish woman, or one that spills water and other liquids carelessly. [*New England.*]

SPAAD, *n.* A kind of mineral; spar. [Sp. *espato.*] *Woodward.*

SPACE. *n.* [Fr. *espace*; Sp. *espacio*; It. *spazio*. L. *spatium*, space; *spatior*, to wander. This word is probably formed on the root of *pateo*. Class Bd.]

1. Room; extension. Space in the abstract, is mere extension.

Pure *space* is capable neither of resistance nor motion. *Locke.*

2. Any quantity of extension. In relation to bodies, *space* is the interval between any two or more objects; as the *space* between two stars or two hills. The quantity of *space* or extent between bodies, constitutes their distance from each other.

3. The distance or interval between lines; as in books. The *spaces* in music are named as well as the lines.

4. Quantity of time; also, the interval between two points of time.

Nine times the *space* that measures day and night— *Milton.*

God may defer his judgments for a time, and give a people a longer *space* for repentance. *Tillotson.*

5. A short time; a while.

To stay your deadly strife a *space*. *Spenser.*

[*This sense is nearly obsolete.*]

SPACE, *v. i.* To rove. [*Not in use.*] *Spenser.*

SPACE, *v. t.* Among *printers*, to make spaces or wider intervals between lines.

SPA'CEFUL, *a.* Wide; extensive. [*Not used.*] *Sandys.*

SPA'CIOUS, *a.* [Fr. *spacieux*; Sp. *spatioso*; It. *spazioso*; L. *spatiosus*.]

1. Wide; roomy; having large or ample room; not narrow; as a *spacious* church; a *spacious* hall or drawing room.

2. Extensive; vast in extent; as the *spacious* earth; the *spacious* ocean.

SPA'CIOUSLY, *adv.* Widely; extensively.

SPA'CIOUSNESS, *n.* Wideness; largeness of extent; roominess; as the *spaciousness* of the rooms in a building.

2. Extensiveness; vastness of extent; as the *spaciousness* of the ocean.

SPAD'DLE, *n.* [*dim.* of *spade.*] A little spade. *Mortimer.*

SPADE, *n.* [Sax. *spad*, *spada*; G. *spaten*; D. *spaade*; Dan. Sw. *spade*; probably from breadth, extension, coinciding with L. *spatula*, from the root of *pateo*.]

1. An instrument for digging, consisting of a broad palm with a handle.

2. A suit of cards.

3. A deer three years old; written also *spaid*.

4. A gelded beast. [L. *spado.*]

SPADE, *v. t.* To dig with a spade; or to pare off the sward of land with a spade.

SPA'DE-BONE, *n.* [*spade* and *bone.*] The shoulder blade. [*I believe little used.*]

SPA'DEFUL. *n.* [*spade* and *full.*] As much as a spade will hold.

SPADI''CEOUS, *a.* [L. *spadiceus*, from *spadix*, a light red color.]

1. Of a light red color, usually denominated *bay*. *Brown.*

2. In *botany*, a *spadiceous flower*, is a sort of aggregate flower, having a receptacle common to many florets, within a spathe, as in palms, dracontium, arum, &c. *Martyn.*

SPADILLE, *n.* *spadil'*. [Fr.] The ace of spades at omber.

SPA'DIX, *n.* [L.] In *botany*, the receptacle in palms and some other plants, proceeding from a spathe. *Martyn.*

SPA'DO, *n.* [L.] A gelding. *Brown.*

SPAGYR'IC, *a.* [L. *spagyricus*.] Chimical. [*Not in use.*]

SPAGYR'IC, *n.* A chimist. [*Not in use.*] *Hall.*

SPAG'YRIST, *n.* A chimist. [*Not in use.*] *Boyle.*

SPA'HEE, } *n.* [Turk. *sipahi*; Pers. *sipahee*.
SPA'HI, } See *Seapoy.*] One of the Turkish cavalry.

SPAKE, *pret.* of *speak*; nearly obsolete. We now use *spoke*.

SPALL, *n.* [Fr. *epaule*; It. *spalla.*] The shoulder. [*Not English.*] *Fairfax.*

2. A chip. [*Not in use.*]

SPALT, } *n.* A whitish scaly mineral, used
SPELT, } to promote the fusion of metals. *Bailey. Ash.*

SPALT, *a.* [Dan. *spalt*, a split; G. *spalten*, to split.] Cracked, as timber. [*N. Eng.*]

SPAN, *n.* [Sax. D. *span*; G. *spanne*; Dan. *spand*, a span in measure; Sw. *span*, a span in measure, and a set of coach horses, G. *gespann*; verbs, Sax. *spannan*, to span, to unite; *gespanian*, to join; D. G. *spannen*; Dan. *spander*, to strain, stretch, bend, yoke. This word is formed on the root of *bend*, L. *pando*. The primary sense is to strain, stretch, extend, hence to join a team, Dan. *forspand*, D. *gespan*.]

1. The space from the end of the thumb to the end of the little finger when extended; nine inches; the eighth of a fathom. *Holder.*

2. A short space of time.

Life's but a *span*; I'll every inch enjoy. *Farquhar.*

3. A *span of horses*, consists of two of nearly the same color, and otherwise nearly alike, which are usually harnessed side by side. The word signifies properly the same as *yoke*, when applied to horned cattle, from buckling or fastening together. But in America, *span* always implies resemblance in color at least; it being an object of ambition with gentlemen and with teamsters to unite two horses abreast that are alike.

4. In *seamen's language*, a small line or cord, the middle of which is attached to a stay.

SPAN, *v. t.* To measure by the hand with the fingers extended, or with the fingers encompassing the object; as, to *span* a space or distance; to *span* a cylinder.

2. To measure.

This soul doth *span* the world. *Herbert.*

SPAN, *v. i.* To agree in color, or in color and size; as, the horses *span* well. [*New England.*]

SPAN, *pret.* of *spin*. *Obs.* We now use *spun*.

SPAN'CEL, *n.* A rope to tie a cow's hind legs. [*Local.*] *Grose.*

SPAN'CEL, *v. t.* To tie the legs of a horse or cow with a rope. [*Local.*] *Malone.*

SPAN'COUNTER, } *n.* A play at which
SPAN'FARTHING, } money is thrown within a span or circuit marked. *Swift.*

SPAN'DREL, *n.* The space between the curve of an arch and the right lines inclosing it.

SPANE, *v. t.* [D. *speenen.*] To wean. [*Not in use.*]

SPANG, *n.* [D. *spange*, a spangle; Gr. φεγγω.]

A spangle or shining ornament; a thin piece of metal or other shining material. [*Not in use.*] *Bacon.*

SPAN'GLE, *n.* [supra.] A small plate or boss of shining metal; something brilliant used as an ornament.

2. Any little thing sparkling and brilliant, like pieces of metal; as crystals of ice.

For the rich *spangles* that adorn the sky. *Waller.*

SPAN'GLE, *v. t.* To set or sprinkle with spangles; to adorn with small distinct brilliant bodies; as a *spangled* breastplate. *Donne.*

What stars do *spangle* heaven with such beauty— *Shak.*

SPAN'GLED, *pp.* Set with spangles.

SPAN'GLING, *ppr.* Adorning with spangles.

SPAN'IEL, *n.* [Fr. *epagneul*; said to be from *Hispaniola*, now *Hayti*.]

1. A dog used in sports of the field, remarkable for his sagacity and obedience. *Dryden.*
2. A mean, cringing, fawning person. *Shak.*

SPAN'IEL, *a.* Like a spaniel; mean; fawning. *Shak.*

SPAN'IEL, *v. i.* To fawn; to cringe; to be obsequious.

SPAN'IEL, *v. t.* To follow like a spaniel.

SPAN'ISH, *a.* Pertaining to Spain.

SPAN'ISH, *n.* The language of Spain.

SPANISH-BROOM, *n.* A plant of the genus Spartium.

SPANISH-BROWN, *n.* A species of earth used in paints.

SPANISH-FLY, *n.* A fly or insect, the *cantharis*, used in vesicatories, or compositions for raising blisters.

SPANISH-NUT, *n.* A plant. *Miller.*

SPANISH-WHITE, *n.* A white earth from Spain, used in paints.

SPANK, *v. t.* [W. *pange*, a blow; allied perhaps to the vulgar *bang*, and found in the Persic.]

To strike with the open hand; to slap. [*A word common in New England.*]

SPANK'ER, *n.* A small coin. *Derham.*

2. In *seamen's language*, a ship's driver; a large sail occasionally set upon the mizen-yard or gaff, the foot being extended by a boom. *Mar. Dict.*
3. One that takes long strides in walking; also, a stout person.

SPANK'ING, *ppr.* Striking with the open hand.

2. *a.* Large; stout. [*Vulgar.*]

SPAN'-LONG, *a.* Of the length of a span. *B. Jonson.*

SPAN'NED, *pp.* Measured with the hand.

SPAN'NER, *n.* One that spans.

2. The lock of a fusee or carbine; or the fusee itself. *Bailey. Bowering.*
3. A wrench or nut screw-driver.

SPAN'-NEW, *a.* [G. *spannen*; allied perhaps to *spangle*.] Quite new; probably *bright-new*.

SPAN'NING, *ppr.* Measuring with the hand; encompassing with the fingers.

SP'AR, *n.* [D. *spar*, a rafter, a shingle; G. *sparren*, a spar, a rafter; Dan. *spar*, a spar, a small beam, the *bar* of a gate; Sw. *sparre*, a rafter; Fr. *barre*; It. *sbarra*, a *bar*; Sp. *esparr*, a fossil; *espar*, a drug. If this word is connected with *spare*, the primary sense is probably *thin*. The sense of *bar* and *spar*, is however more generally derived from thrusting, shooting in length; so *spear* likewise. See *Bar*.]

1. A stone that breaks into a regular shape; marcasite. This name is popularly given to any crystalized mineral of a shining luster. It is the G. *spath*.
2. A round piece of timber. This name is usually given to the round pieces of timber used for the yards and top-masts of ships.
3. The bar of a gate. *Obs.* *Chaucer.*

SP'AR, *v. t.* [Sax. *sparran*; G. *sperren*; from *spar*.]

To bar; to shut close or fasten with a bar. *Obs.* *Chaucer.*

SP'AR, *v. i.* [Sax. *spirian*, to argue or dispute, to *aspire*; Russ. *sporyu*, to dispute, to contend; Ir. *sparnam*. The Saxon word signifies to dispute, also to investigate, to inquire or explore, to follow after. This is another form of the L. *spiro*, Gr. *σπαιρω*, *σπειρω*. The primary sense is to urge, drive, throw, propel.]

1. To dispute; to quarrel in words; to wrangle. [*This is the sense of the word in America.*]
2. To fight with prelusive strokes. *Johnson.*

SP'ARABLE, *n.* [Ir. *sparra*.] Small nails. [*Not in use.*]

SP'ARADRAP, *n.* In pharmacy, a cerecloth. *Wiseman.*

SPARAGE, } [*Vulgar.*] [See *Asparagus*.]
SPARAGUS. }

SPARE, *v. t.* [Sax. *sparian*; D. *spaaren*; G. *sparen*; Dan. *sparer*; Sw. *spara*; Fr. *epargner*. It seems to be from the same root as L. *parco*; It. *sparagnare*.]

1. To use frugally; not to be profuse; not to waste.

   Thou thy Father's thunder did'st not *spare*. *Milton.*

2. To save or withhold from any particular use or occupation. He has no bread to *spare*, that is, to withhold from his necessary uses.

   All the time he could *spare* from the necessary cares of his weighty charge, he bestowed on prayer and serving of God. *Knolles.*

3. To part with without much inconvenience; to do without.

   I could have better *spar'd* a better man. *Shak.*

   Nor can we *spare* you long— *Dryden.*

4. To omit; to forbear. We might have *spared* this toil and expense.

   Be pleas'd your politics to *spare*. *Dryden.*

5. To use tenderly; to treat with pity and forbearance; to forbear to afflict, punish or destroy.

   Spare us, good Lord. *Com. Prayer.*

   Dim sadness did not *spare*
   Celestial visages. *Milton.*

   But man alone can whom he conquers *spare*. *Waller.*

6. Not to take when in one's power; to forbear to destroy; as, to *spare* the life of a prisoner.
7. To grant; to allow; to indulge.

   Where angry Jove did never *spare*
   One breath of kind and temp'rate air. *Roscommon.*

8. To forbear to inflict or impose.

   Spare my sight the pain
   Of seeing what a world of tears it cost you. *Dryden.*

SPARE, *v. i.* To live frugally; to be parsimonious.

   Who at some times spend, at others *spare*,
   Divided between carelessness and care. *Pope.*

2. To forbear; to be scrupulous.

   To pluck and eat my fill I *spar'd* not. *Milton.*

3. To be frugal; not to be profuse.
4. To use mercy or forbearance; to forgive; to be tender.

   The king—was *sparing* and compassionate towards his subjects. *Bacon.*

SPARE, *a.* [Sax. *spær*.] Scanty; parsimonious; not abundant; as a *spare* diet.

   He was *spare* but discreet of speech. *Carew.*

[We more generally use, in the latter application, *sparing*; as, he was *sparing* of words.]

2. That can be dispensed with; not wanted; superfluous. I have no *spare* time on my hands.

   If that no *spare* clothes he had to give. *Spenser.*

3. Lean; wanting flesh; meager; thin.

   O give me your *spare* men, and spare me the great ones. *Shak.*

4. Slow. [*Not in use or local.*] *Grose.*

SPARE, *n.* Parsimony; frugal use. [*Not in use.*] *Bacon.*

SPA'RED, *pp.* Dispensed with; saved; forborne.

SPA'RELY, *adv.* Sparingly. *Milton.*

SPA'RENESS, *n.* State of being lean or thin; leanness. *Hammond.*

SPA'RER, *n.* One that avoids unnecessary expense. *Wotton.*

SPA'RERIB, *n.* [*spare* and *rib*.] The piece of a hog taken from the side, consisting of the ribs with little flesh on them.

SPARGEFAC'TION, *n.* [L. *spargo*, to sprinkle.]

The act of sprinkling. [*Not used.*] *Dict.*

SPA'RING, *ppr.* Using frugally; forbearing; omitting to punish or destroy.

2. *a.* Scarce; little.

   Of this there is with you *sparing* memory, or none. *Bacon.*

3. Scanty; not plentiful; not abundant; as a *sparing* diet.
4. Saving; parsimonious.

   Virgil being so very *sparing* of his words, and leaving so much to be imagined by the reader, can never be translated as he ought in any modern tongue. *Dryden.*

SPA'RINGLY, *adv.* Not abundantly. *Shak.*

2. Frugally; parsimoniously; not lavishly.

   High titles of honor were in the king's minority *sparingly* granted, because dignity then waited on desert. *Hayward.*

   Commend but *sparingly* whom thou dost love. *Denham.*

3. Abstinently; moderately.

   Christians are obliged to taste even the innocent pleasures of life but *sparingly*. *Atterbury.*

4. Seldom; not frequently.

   The morality of a grave sentence, affected by Lucan, is more *sparingly* used by Virgil. *Dryden.*

5. Cautiously; tenderly. *Bacon.*

SPA'RINGNESS, *n.* Parsimony; want of liberality.

2. Caution. *Barrow.*

SP'ARK, *n.* [Sax. *spearc*; D. *spartelen*, to flutter, to sparkle; Dan. *sparker*, to wince or kick. The sense is that which shoots, darts off or scatters; probably allied to L. *spargo* and Russ. *sverkayu*.]

1. A small particle of fire or ignited substance, which is emitted from bodies in combustion, and which either ascends with the smoke, or is darted in another direction. *Pope.*
2. A small shining body or transient light.

   We have here and there a little clear light, and some *sparks* of bright knowledge. *Locke.*

3. A small portion of any thing active. If any *spark* of life is yet remaining.
4. A very small portion. If you have a *spark* of generosity.
5. A brisk, showy, gay man.

   The finest *sparks* and cleanest beaux. *Prior.*

6. A lover.

SP'ARK, *v. i.* To emit particles of fire; to sparkle. [*Not in use.*] *Spenser.*

SP'ARKFUL, *a.* Lively; brisk; gay. *Camden.*

SP'ARKISH, *a.* Airy; gay. *Walsh.*

2. Showy; well dressed; fine. *L'Estrange.*

SP'ARKLE, *n.* A spark. *Dryden.*

2. A luminous particle.

SP'ARKLE, *v. i.* [D. *spartelen.*] To emit sparks; to send off small ignited particles; as burning fuel, &c.

2. To glitter; to glisten; as, a brilliant *sparkles*; *sparkling* colors. *Locke.*

3. To twinkle; to glitter; as *sparkling* stars.

4. To glisten; to exhibit an appearance of animation; as, the eyes *sparkle* with joy. *Milton.*

5. To emit little bubbles, as spiritous liquors; as *sparkling* wine.

SP'ARKLE, *v. t.* To throw about; to scatter. [*Not in use.*] *Sackville.*

SP'ARKLER, *n.* He or that which sparkles; one whose eyes sparkle. *Addison.*

SP'ARKLET, *n.* A small spark. *Cotton.*

SP'ARKLINESS, *n.* Vivacity. [*Not in use.*] *Aubrey.*

SP'ARKLING, *ppr.* or *a.* Emitting sparks; glittering; lively; as *sparkling* wine; *sparkling* eyes.

SP'ARKLINGLY, *adv.* With twinkling or vivid brilliancy.

SP'ARKLINGNESS, *n.* Vivid and twinkling luster.

SP'ARLING, *n.* A smelt. *Cotgrave.*

SPAR'ROW, *n.* [Sax. *speara*; Goth. *sparwa*; G. Dan. *sperling*; Sw. *sparf*; probably allied to *spear* or *spare*, and so named from its smallness.]

A small bird of the genus Fringilla and order of Passers. These birds are frequently seen about houses.

SPAR'ROW-GRASS, a corruption of *asparagus.*

SPAR'ROW-HAWK, } *n.* [Sax. *spearhafoc*; spear-hawk.] A small species of short winged hawk.
SPAR'HAWK,

SP'ARRY, *a.* [from *spar.*] Resembling spar, or consisting of spar; having a confused crystaline structure; spathose.

SPARSE, *a.* spȧrs. [L. *sparsus*, scattered, from *spargo.*]

1. Thinly scattered; set or planted here and there; as a *sparse* population.

2. In *botany*, not opposite, nor alternate, nor in any apparent regular order; applied to branches, leaves, peduncles, &c. *Martyn.*

SPARSE, *v. t.* spȧrs. To disperse. [*Not in use.*] *Spenser.*

SP'ARSED, *a.* Scattered. *Lee.*

SP'ARSEDLY, *adv.* In a scattered manner. *Evelyn.*

SP'ARTAN, *a.* Pertaining to ancient Sparta; hence, hardy; undaunted; as *Spartan* souls; *Spartan* bravery.

SPASM, *n.* [L. *spasmus*; Gr. σπασμα, from σπαω, to draw.]

An involuntary contraction of muscles or muscular fibers in animal bodies; irregular motion of the muscles or muscular fibers; convulsion; cramp. *Coxe.*

SPASMOD'IC, *a.* [Fr. *spasmodique*; It. *spasmodico.*]

Consisting in spasm; as a *spasmodic* affection.

SPASMOD'IC, *n.* A medicine good for removing spasm; but I believe the word generally employed is *anti-spasmodic.*

SPAT, *pret.* of *spit*, but nearly obsolete.

SPAT, *n.* [from the root of *spit*; that which is ejected.]

1. The young of shell fish. *Woodward.*

2. A petty combat; a little quarrel or dissension. [*A vulgar use of the word in New England.*]

SPATHA'CEOUS, *a.* Having a calyx like a sheath.

SPATHE, *n.* [L. *spatha.*] In *botany*, the calyx of a spadix opening or bursting longitudinally, in form of a sheath. It is also applied to the calyx of some flowers which have no spadix, as of narcissus, crocus, iris, &c. *Martyn.*

SPATH'IC, *a.* [G. *spath.*] Foliated or lamellar. *Spathic* iron is a mineral of a foliated structure, and a yellowish or brownish color. *Silliman.*

SPATH'IFORM, *a.* [*spath* and *form.*] Resembling spar in form.

The ocherous, *spathiform* and mineralized forms of uranite— *Lavoisier.*

SPATH'OUS, *a.* Having a calyx like a sheath.

SPATH'ULATE. [See *Spatulate.*]

SPA'TIATE, *v. i.* [L. *spatior.*] To rove; to ramble. [*Not in use.*] *Bacon.*

SPAT'TER, *v. t.* [This root is a derivative of the family of *spit*, or L. *pateo*. See *Sputter.*]

1. To scatter a liquid substance on; to sprinkle with water or any fluid, or with any moist and dirty matter; as, to *spatter* a coat; to *spatter* the floor; to *spatter* the boots with mud. [This word, I believe, is applied always to fluid or moist substances. We say, to *spatter* with water, mud, blood or gravy; but never to *spatter* with dust or meal.]

2. Figuratively, to asperse; to defame. [In this sense, *asperse* is generally used.]

3. To throw out any thing offensive; as, to *spatter* foul speeches. [*Not in use.*] *Shak.*

4. To scatter about; as, to *spatter* water here and there.

SPAT'TER, *v. i.* To throw out of the mouth in a scattered manner; to *sputter.* [See *Sputter.*] *Milton.*

SPAT'TERDASHES, *n. plu.* [*spatter* and *dash.*]

Coverings for the legs to keep them clean from water and mud. [Since boots are generally worn, these things and their name are little used.]

SPAT'TERED, *pp.* Sprinkled or fouled by some liquid or dirty substance.

2. Aspersed.

SPAT'TERING, *ppr.* Sprinkling with moist or foul matter.

2. Aspersing.

SPAT'TLE, *n.* Spittle. [*Not in use.*] *Bale.*

SPAT'TLING-POPPY, *n.* [L. *papaver spumeum.*]

A plant; white behen; a species of Campion.

SPAT'ULA, } *n.* [L. *spathula*, *spatha*, a slice; W. *yspodol*; from the root of L. *pateo*; so named from its breadth, or from its use in spreading s.
SPAT'TLE,

A slice; an apothecaries' instrument for spreading plasters, &c. *Quincy.*

SPAT'ULATE, *a.* [from L. *spathula.*] In *botany*, a spatulate leaf is one shaped like a spatula or battledore, being roundish with a long, narrow, linear base; as in *cistus incanus.* *Martyn.*

SPAV'IN, *n.* [It. *spavenio*, *spavano*, spavin, a cramp; Fr. *eparvin*; Sp. *esparavan*; Port. *esparavam.*]

A tumor or excrescence that forms on the inside of a horse's hough, not far from the elbow; at first like gristle, but afterwards hard and bony. *Far. Dict.*

SPAV'INED, *a.* Affected with spavin. *Goldsmith.*

SPAW, } *n.* A mineral water from a place of this name in Germany. The name may perhaps be applied to other similar waters.
SPA,

2. A spring of mineral water.

SPAWL, *v. i.* [G. *speichel*, spawl; *speien*, to spawl, to spew. *Spew* is a contracted word.]

To throw saliva from the mouth in a scattering form; to disperse spittle in a careless dirty manner.

Why must he sputter, *spawl* and slaver it? *Swift.*

SPAWL, *n.* Saliva or spittle thrown out carelessly. *Dryden.*

SPAWL'ING, *ppr.* Throwing spittle carelessly from the mouth.

SPAWL'ING, *n.* Saliva thrown out carelessly.

SPAWN, *n.* It has no plural. [If this word is not contracted, it belongs to the root of L. *pano*, Sp. *poner*, Fr. *pondre*, to lay eggs. If contracted, it probably belongs to the root of *spew* or *spawl.* The radical sense is that which is ejected or thrown out.]

1. The eggs of fish or frogs, when ejected. *Ray.*

2. Any product or offspring; *an expression of contempt.* *Roscommon.*

3. Offsets; shoots; suckers of plants. [*Not used in America.*]

SPAWN, *v. t.* To produce or deposit, as fishes do their eggs.

2. To bring forth; to generate; *in contempt.* *Swift.*

SPAWN, *v. i.* To deposit eggs, as fish or frogs.

2. To issue, as offspring; *in contempt.* *Locke.*

SPAWN'ED, *pp.* Produced or deposited, as the eggs of fish or frogs.

SPAWN'ER, *n.* The female fish.

The *spawner* and the melter of the barbel cover their spawn with sand. *Walton.*

SPAY, *v. t.* [W. *yspazu*, to exhaust; *dyspazu*, to geld; Arm. *spaza* or *spahein*, to geld; L. *spado*, a gelding; Gr. σπαω, to draw out.]

To castrate the female of a beast by cutting and by taking out the uterus; as, to *spay* a sow. *Mortimer.*

SPA'YED, *pp.* Castrated, as a female beast.

SPA'YING, *ppr.* Castrating, as a female beast.

SPEAK, *v. i.* pret. *spoke*, [*spake*, nearly obs.;] pp. *spoke*, *spoken*. [Sax. *spæcan*, *specan*; It. *spiccar le parole*, to speak distinctly; *spiccare*, to shine, that is, to shoot or thrust forth; Eth. ሰበከ sabak, to preach, to teach, to proclaim. The Sw. has *spå*, Dan. *spaer*, to foretell. It is easy to see that the root of this word is allied to that of *beak*, *peak*, *pick*.]

1. To utter words or articulate sounds, as human beings; to express thoughts by words. Children learn to *speak* at an early age. The organs may be so obstructed that a man may not be able to *speak*.

Speak, Lord, for thy servant heareth. 1 Sam. iii.

2. To utter a speech, discourse or harangue; to utter thoughts in a public assembly. A man may be well informed on a subject, and yet too diffident to *speak* in public.

Many of the nobility made themselves popular by *speaking* in parliament against those things which were most grateful to his majesty. *Clarendon.*

3. To talk; to express opinions; to dispute.

An honest man, sir, is able to *speak* for himself, when the knave is not. *Shak.*

4. To discourse; to make mention of.

Lucan *speaks* of a part of Cesar's army that came to him from the Leman lake. *Addison.*

The Scripture *speaks* only of those to whom it speaks. *Hammond.*

5. To give sound.

Make all your trumpets *speak*. *Shak.*

To speak with, to converse with. Let me *speak with* my son.

SPEAK, *v. t.* To utter with the mouth; to pronounce; to utter articulately; as human beings.

They sat down with him on the ground seven days and seven nights, and none *spoke* a word to him. Job ii.

Speak the word, and my son shall be healed. Matt. viii.

2. To declare; to proclaim; to celebrate.

It is my father's music
To *speak* your deeds. *Shak.*

3. To talk or converse in; to utter or pronounce, as in conversation. A man may know how to read and to understand a language which he cannot *speak*.

4. To address; to accost.

He will smile upon thee, put thee in hope, and *speak* thee fair. *Ecclus.*

5. To exhibit; to make known.

Let heav'n's wide circuit *speak*
The Maker's high magnificence. *Milton.*

6. To express silently or by signs. The lady's looks or eyes *speak* the meaning or wishes of her heart.

7. To communicate; as, to *speak* peace to the soul.

To speak a ship, to hail and speak to her captain or commander.

[*Note.* We say, to *speak* a word or syllable, to *speak* a sentence, an oration, piece, composition, or a dialogue, to *speak* a man's praise, &c.; but we never say, to *speak* an argument, a sermon or a story.]

SPE'AKABLE, *a.* That can be spoken.

2. Having the power of speech. *Milton.*

SPE'AKER, *n.* One that speaks, in whatever manner.

2. One that proclaims or celebrates.

—No other *speaker* of my living actions. *Shak.*

3. One that utters or pronounces a discourse; usually, one that utters a speech in public. We say, a man is a good *speaker*, or a bad *speaker*.

4. The person who presides in a deliberative assembly, preserving order and regulating the debates; as the *speaker* of the house of commons; the *speaker* of a house of representatives.

SPE'AKING, *ppr.* Uttering words; discoursing; talking.

SPE'AKING, *n.* The act of uttering words; discourse.

2. In *colleges*, public declamation.

SPE'AKING-TRUMPET, *n.* A trumpet by which the sound of the human voice may be propagated to a great distance.

SPEAR, *n.* [Sax. *speare*, *spere*; D. G. *speer*; Dan. *spær*; W. *yspar*, from *pâr*, a spear. So W. *ber* is a spear, and a spit, that which shoots to a point. Class Br.]

1. A long pointed weapon, used in war and hunting by thrusting or throwing; a lance. *Milton. Pope.*

2. A sharp pointed instrument with barbs; used for stabbing fish and other animals. *Carew.*

3. A shoot, as of grass; usually *spire*.

SPEAR, *v. t.* To pierce with a spear; to kill with a spear; as, to *spear* a fish.

SPEAR, *v. i.* To shoot into a long stem. [See *Spire*.] *Mortimer.*

SPE'ARED, *pp.* Pierced or killed with a spear.

SPE'AR-FOOT, *n.* [*spear* and *foot*.] The far foot behind; used of a horse. *Encyc.*

SPE'AR-GRASS, *n.* [*spear* and *grass*.] A long stiff grass. *Shak.*

2. In New England, this name is given to a species of Poa.

SPE'ARING, *ppr.* Piercing or killing with a spear.

2. Shooting into a long stem.

SPE'ARMAN, *n.* [*spear* and *man*.] One who is armed with a spear. Ps. lxviii.

SPE'ARMINT, *n.* [*spear* and *mint*.] A plant of the genus Mentha; a species of mint.

SPE'AR-THISTLE, *n.* A plant, a troublesome weed.

SPE'AR-WÕRT, *n.* A plant; the popular name of the *Ranunculus flammula*.

SPECHT, } *n.* A woodpecker. [*Not in use*
SPEIGHT, } *or local.*] *Sherwood.*

SPE''CIAL, *a.* [Fr.; It. *speziale*; Sp. *especial*; from L. *specialis*, from *species*, form, figure, sort, from *specio*, to see. Hence *species* primarily is appearance, that which is presented to the eye. This word and *especial* are the same.]

1. Designating a species or sort.

A *special* idea is called by the schools a species. *Watts.*

2. Particular; peculiar; noting something more than ordinary. She smiles with a *special* grace.

Our Savior is represented every where in Scripture as the *special* patron of the poor and afflicted. *Atterbury.*

3. Appropriate; designed for a particular purpose. A private grant is made by a *special* act of parliament or of congress.

4. Extraordinary; uncommon. Our charities should be universal, but chiefly exercised on *special* opportunities. *Sprat.*

5. Chief in excellence.

The king hath drawn
The *special* head of all the land together. *Shak.*

Special administration, in *law*, is one in which the power of an administrator is limited to the administration of certain specific effects, and not the effects in general of the deceased. *Blackstone.*

Special bail, consists of actual sureties recognized to answer for the appearance of a person in court; as distinguished from *common bail*, which is nominal. *Blackstone.*

Special bailif, is a bailif appointed by the sherif for making arrests and serving processes.

Special contract. [See *Specialty*.]

Special demurrer, is one in which the cause of demurrer is particularly stated.

Special imparlance, is one in which there is a saving of all exceptions to the writ or count, or of all exceptions whatsoever. *Blackstone.*

Special jury, is one which is called upon motion of either party, when the cause is supposed to require it. *Blackstone.*

Special matter in evidence, the particular facts in the case on which the defendant relies.

Special plea, in bar, is a plea which sets forth the particular facts or reasons why the plaintif's demand should be barred, as a release, accord, &c. *Blackstone.*

Special property, a qualified or limited property, as the property which a man acquires in wild animals by reclaiming them.

Special session of a court, an extraordinary session; a session beyond the regular stated sessions; or in corporations and counties in England, a petty session held by a few justices for dispatching small business. *Blackstone.*

Special statute, is a private act of the legislature, such as respects a private person or individual.

Special tail, is where a gift is restrained to certain heirs of the donee's body, and does not descend to the heirs in general. *Blackstone.*

Special verdict, is a verdict in which the jury find the facts and state them as proved, but leave the law arising from the facts to be determined by the court. Another method of finding a special verdict, is when the jury find a verdict generally for the plaintif, but subject to the opinion of the court on a special case stated by the counsel on both sides, with regard to a matter of law. *Blackstone.*

Special warrant, a warrant to take a person and bring him before a particular justice who granted the warrant.

SPE''CIAL, *n.* A particular. [*Not used.*] *Hammond.*

SPE''CIALIZE, *v. t.* To mention specially. [*Not in use.*] *Sheldon.*

SPE''CIALLY, *adv.* Particularly; in a manner beyond what is common, or out of the ordinary course. Every signal deliverance from danger ought to be *specially* noticed as a divine interposition.

2. For a particular purpose. A meeting of the legislature is *specially* summoned.

3. Chiefly; specially.

SPE''CIALTY, *n.* Particularity.

Specialty of rule hath been neglected. *Shak.*

2. A particular or peculiar case.

NOTE. *This word is now little used in the senses above. Its common acceptation is,*

3. A special contract; an obligation or bond; the evidence of a debt by deed or instru-

ment under seal. Such a debt is called a debt by *specialty*, in distinction from *simple contract*. *Blackstone.*

SPECIE, *n.* *spe'shy.* Coin; copper, silver or gold coined and used as a circulating medium of commerce. [See *Special.*]

SPECIES, *n.* *spe'shiz.* [L. from *specio*, to see. See *Special.*]

1. In *zoology*, a collection of organized beings derived from one common parentage by natural generation, characterized by one peculiar form, liable to vary from the influence of circumstances only within certain narrow limits. These accidental and limited variations are *varieties*. Different races from the same parents are called *varieties*.

2. In *botany*, all the plants which spring from the same seed, or which resemble each other in certain characters or invariable forms.

> There are as many *species* as there are different invariable forms or structures of vegetables. *Martyn.*

3. In *logic*, a special idea, corresponding to the specific distinctions of things in nature. *Watts.*

4. Sort; kind; *in a loose sense*; as a *species* of low cunning in the world; a *species* of generosity; a *species* of cloth.

5. Appearance to the senses; visible or sensible representation.

> An apparent diversity between the *species* visible and audible, is that the visible doth not mingle in the medium, but the audible doth. *Bacon*

> The *species* of letters illuminated with indigo and violet. [*Little used.*] *Newton.*

6. Representation to the mind.

> Wit—the faculty of imagination in the writer, which searches over all the memory for the *species* or ideas of those things which it designs to represent. [*Little used.*] *Dryden.*

7. Show; visible exhibition.

> Shows and *species* serve best with the common people. [*Not in use.*] *Bacon.*

8. Coin, or coined silver and gold, used as a circulating medium; as the current *species* of Europe. *Arbuthnot.*

In modern practice, this word is contracted into *specie.* What quantity of *specie* has the bank in its vault? What is the amount of all the current *specie* in the country? What is the value in *specie*, of a bill of exchange? We receive payment for goods in *specie*, not in bank notes.

9. In *pharmacy*, a simple; a component part of a compound medicine. *Johnson. Quincy.*

10. The old pharmaceutical term for powders. *Parr.*

SPECIF'IC, SPECIF'ICAL, *a.* [Fr. *specifique*; It. *specifico.*] That makes a thing of the species of which it is; designating the peculiar property or properties of a thing, which constitute its species, and distinguish it from other things. Thus we say, the *specific* form of an animal or a plant; the *specific* form of a cube or square; the *specific* qualities of a plant or a drug; the *specific* difference between an acid and an alkali; the *specific* distinction between virtue and vice.

> *Specific* difference is that primary attribute which distinguishes each species from one another. *Watts.*

2. In *medicine*, appropriate for the cure of a particular disease; that certainly cures or is less fallible than others; as a *specific* remedy for the gout. The Saratoga waters are found to be a *specific* remedy, or nearly so, for the cure of bilious complaints, so called.

Specific character, in *botany*, a circumstance or circumstances distinguishing one species from every other species of the same genus. *Martyn.*

Specific gravity, in *philosophy*, the weight that belongs to an equal bulk of each body. [See *Gravity.*]

Specific name, in *botany*, is the trivial name, as distinguished from the *generic name.* *Martyn.*

Specific name is now used for the name which, appended to the name of the genus, constitutes the distinctive name of the species; but it was originally applied by Linne to the essential character of the species, or the *essential difference.* The present specific names he at first called the *trivial names.* *Smith.*

SPECIF'IC, *n.* In *medicine*, a remedy that certainly cures a particular disease. *Coxe.*

SPECIF'ICALLY, *adv.* In such a manner as to constitute a species; according to the nature of the species. A body is *specifically* lighter than another, when it has less weight in the same bulk than the other.

> Human reason—differs *specifically* from the fantastick reason of brutes. *Grew.*
>
> —Those several virtues that are *specifically* requisite to a due performance of duty. *South.*

SPECIF'ICATE, *v. t.* [L. *species*, form, and *facio*, to make.]

To show, mark or designate the species, or the distinguishing particulars of a thing; to specify.

SPECIFICA'TION, *n.* The act of determining by a mark or limit; notation of limits.

> This *specification* or limitation of the question hinders the disputers from wandering away from the precise point of inquiry. *Watts.*

2. The act of specifying; designation of particulars; particular mention; as the *specification* of a charge against a military or naval officer.

3. Article or thing specified.

SPEC'IFIED, *pp.* Particularized; specially named.

SPEC'IFY, *v. t.* [Fr. *specifier*; It. *specificare.*]

To mention or name, as a particular thing; to designate in words, so as to distinguish a thing from every other; as, to *specify* the uses of a plant; to *specify* the articles one wants to purchase.

> He has there given us an exact geography of Greece, where the countries and the uses of their soils are *specified.* *Pope.*

SPEC'IFYING, *ppr.* Naming or designating particularly.

SPEC'IMEN, *n.* [L. from *species*, with the termination *men*, which corresponds in sense to the English *hood* or *ness.*]

A sample; a part or small portion of any thing, intended to exhibit the kind and quality of the whole, or of something not exhibited; as a *specimen* of a man's handwriting; a *specimen* of painting or composition; a *specimen* of one's art or skill.

SPE'CIOUS, *a.* [Fr. *specieux*; It. *specioso*; Sp. *especioso*; L. *speciosus.*]

1. Showy; pleasing to the view.

> The rest, far greater part,
> Will deem in outward rites and *specious* forms
> Religion satisfied. *Milton.*

2. Apparently right; superficially fair, just or correct; plausible; appearing well at first view; as *specious* reasoning; a *specious* argument; a *specious* objection; *specious* deeds. Temptation is of greater danger, because it is covered with the *specious* names of good nature, good manners, nobleness of mind, &c.

SPE'CIOUSLY, *adv.* With a fair appearance; with show of right; as, to reason *speciously.*

SPECK, *n.* [Sax. *specca*; D. *spikkel.* In Sp. *peca* is a freckle or spot raised in the skin by the sun. This word may be formed from *peck*, for *peckled* has been used for *speckled*, spotted as though pecked. Qu. Ar. بقع bakaa, to be spotted. Class Bg. No. 31.]

1. A spot; a stain; a small place in any thing that is discolored by foreign matter, or is of a color different from that of the main substance; as a *speck* on paper or cloth.

2. A very small thing.

SPECK, *v. t.* To spot; to stain in spots or drops.

SPECK'LE, *n.* A little spot in any thing, of a different substance or color from that of the thing itself.

SPECK'LE, *v. t.* To mark with small spots of a different color; used chiefly in the participle passive, which see.

SPECK'LED, *pp.* or *a.* Marked with specks; variegated with spots of a different color from the ground or surface of the object; as the *speckled* breast of a bird; a *speckled* serpent.

Speckled bird, a denomination given to a person of doubtful character or principles.

SPECK'LEDNESS, *n.* The state of being speckled. *Ash.*

SPECK'LING, *ppr.* Marking with small spots.

SPEC'TACLE, *n.* [Fr. from L. *spectaculum*, from *specto*, to behold; *specio*, to see; It. *spettacolo.*]

1. A show; something exhibited to view; usually, something presented to view as extraordinary, or something that is beheld as unusual and worthy of special notice. Thus we call things exhibited for amusement, public *spectacles*, as the combats of gladiators in ancient Rome.

> We are made a *spectacle* to the world, and to angels, and to men. 1 Cor. iv.

2. Any thing seen; a sight. A drunkard is a shocking *spectacle.*

3. *Spectacles*, in the plural, glasses to assist the sight.

4. Figuratively, something that aids the intellectual sight.

> Shakspeare—needed not the *spectacles* of books to read nature. *Dryden.*

SPEC'TACLED, *a.* Furnished with spectacles. *Shak.*

SPECTAC'ULAR, *a.* Pertaining to shows. *Hickes.*

SPE€TA'TION, *n.* [L. *spectatio.*] Regard; respect. [*Little used.*] *Harvey.*

SPE€TA'TOR, *n.* [L. whence Fr. *spectateur*; It. *spettatore.*]

1. One that looks on; one that sees or beholds; a beholder; as the *spectators* of a show.

2. One personally present. The *spectators* were numerous.

SPE€TATO'RIAL, *a.* Pertaining to the Spectator. *Addison.*

SPE€TA'TORSHIP, *n.* The act of beholding. *Shak.*

2. The office or quality of a spectator. *Addison.*

SPE€TA'TRESS, **SPE€TA'TRIX**, *n.* [L. *spectatrix.*] A female beholder or looker on. *Rowe.*

SPE€'TER, *n.* [Fr. *spectre*; from L. *spectrum*, from *specto*, to behold.]

1. An apparition; the appearance of a person who is dead; a ghost.

> The ghosts of traitors from the bridge descend,
> With bold fanatic *specters* to rejoice. *Dryden.*

2. Something made preternaturally visible.

3. In *conchology*, a species of voluta, marked with reddish broad bands. *Cyc.*

SPE€'TRUM, *n.* [L.] A visible form; an image of something seen, continuing after the eyes are closed, covered or turned away. This is called an *ocular spectrum*. *Darwin.*

SPE€'ULAR, *a.* [L. *specularis*, from *speculum*, a mirror, from *specio*, to see.]

1. Having the qualities of a mirror or looking glass; having a smooth reflecting surface; as a *specular* metal; a *specular* surface. *Newton.*

2. Assisting sight. [*Improper and not used.*] *Philips.*

3. Affording view. *Milton.*

SPE€'ULATE, *v. i.* [L. *speculor*, to view, to contemplate, from *specio*, to see; Fr. *speculer*; It. *speculare.*]

1. To meditate; to contemplate; to consider a subject by turning it in the mind and viewing it in its different aspects and relations; as, to *speculate* on political events; to *speculate* on the probable results of a discovery. *Addison.*

2. In *commerce*, to purchase land, goods, stock or other things, with the expectation of an advance in price, and of selling the articles with a profit by means of such advance; as, to *speculate* in coffee, or in sugar, or in six per cent stock, or in bank stock.

SPE€'ULATE, *v. t.* To consider attentively; as, to *speculate* the nature of a thing. [*Not in use.*] *Brown.*

SPE€ULA'TION, *n.* Examination by the eye; view. [*Little used.*]

2. Mental view of any thing in its various aspects and relations; contemplation; intellectual examination. The events of the day afford matter of serious *speculation* to the friends of christianity.

> Thenceforth to *speculations* high or deep
> I turn'd my thoughts— *Milton.*

3. Train of thoughts formed by meditation.

> From him Socrates derived the principles of morality and most part of his natural *speculations*. *Temple.*

4. Mental scheme; theory; views of a subject not verified by fact or practice. This globe, which was formerly round only in *speculation*, has been circumnavigated. The application of steam to navigation is no longer a matter of mere *speculation*.

> *Speculations* which originate in guilt, must end in ruin. *R. Hall.*

5. Power of sight.

> Thou hast no *speculation* in those eyes.
> [*Not in use.*] *Shak.*

6. In *commerce*, the act or practice of buying land or goods, &c. in expectation of a rise of price and of selling them at an advance, as distinguished from a regular trade, in which the profit expected is the difference between the retail and wholesale prices, or the difference of price in the place where the goods are purchased, and the place to which they are to be carried for market. In England, France and America, public stock is the subject of continual *speculation*. In the United States, a few men have been enriched, but many have been ruined by *speculation*.

SPE€'ULATIST, *n.* One who speculates or forms theories; a speculator. *Milner.*

SPE€'ULATIVE, *a.* [Fr. *speculatif*; It. *speculativo.*]

1. Given to speculation; contemplative; *applied to persons.*

> The mind of man being by nature *speculative*— *Hooker.*

2. Formed by speculation; theoretical; ideal; not verified by fact, experiment or practice; as a scheme merely *speculative*.

3. Pertaining to view; also, prying. *Bacon.*

SPE€'ULATIVELY, *adv.* In contemplation; with meditation.

2. Ideally; theoretically; in theory only, not in practice. Propositions seem often to be *speculatively* true, which experience does not verify.

SPE€'ULATIVENESS, *n.* The state of being speculative, or of consisting in speculation only.

SPE€'ULATOR, *n.* One who speculates or forms theories. *More.*

2. An observer; a contemplator. *Brown.*

3. A spy; a watcher. *Broome.*

4. In *commerce*, one who buys goods, land or other thing, with the expectation of a rise of price, and of deriving profit from such advance.

SPE€'ULATORY, *a.* Exercising speculation. *Johnson.*

2. Intended or adapted for viewing or espying. *Warton.*

SPE€'ULUM, *n.* [L.; G. D. *spiegel*; Sw. *spegel*; Dan. *spejl.*] A mirror or looking glass.

2. A glass that reflects the images of objects.

3. A metallic reflector used in catadioptric telescopes.

4. In *surgery*, an instrument for dilating and keeping open certain parts of the body. *Coxe.*

SPED, *pret.* and *pp.* of *speed.*

SPEECH, *n.* [Sax. *spæc.* See *Speak.*] The faculty of uttering articulate sounds or words, as in human beings; the faculty of expressing thoughts by words or articulate sounds. *Speech* was given to man by his Creator for the noblest purposes.

2. Language; words as expressing ideas.

> The acts of God to human ears
> Cannot without process of *speech* be told. *Milton.*

3. A particular language, as distinct from others. Ps. xix.

4. That which is spoken; words uttered in connection and expressing thoughts. You smile at my *speech*.

5. Talk; mention; common saying.

> The duke did of me demand,
> What was the *speech* among the Londoners
> Concerning the French journey. *Shak.*

6. Formal discourse in public; oration; harangue. The member has made his first *speech* in the legislature.

7. Any declaration of thoughts.

> I, with leave of *speech* implor'd, repli'd. *Milton.*

SPEECH, *v. i.* To make a speech; to harangue. [*Little used.*]

SPEE'CHLESS, *a.* Destitute or deprived of the faculty of speech. More generally,

2. Mute; silent; not speaking for a time.

> *Speechless* with wonder, and half dead with fear. *Addison.*

SPEE'CHLESSNESS, *n.* The state of being speechless; muteness. *Bacon.*

SPEE'CH-MAKER, *n.* One who makes speeches; one who speaks much in a public assembly.

SPEED, *v. i.* pret. and pp. *sped*, *speeded.* [Sax. *spedian*, *spædan*; D. *spoeden*; G. *spediren*, to send; Gr. σπευδω. The L. *expedio* may be from the same root, which signifies to drive, to hurry, of the family of L. *peto.* Class Bd.]

1. To make haste; to move with celerity. *Shak.*

2. To have success; to prosper; to succeed; that is, to advance in one's enterprise.

> He that's once deni'd will hardly *speed*. *Shak.*

> Those that profaned and abused the second temple, *sped* no better. *South.*

3. To have any condition good or ill; to fare.

> Ships heretofore in seas like fishes *sped*,
> The mightiest still upon the smallest fed. *Waller.*

SPEED, *v. t.* To dispatch; to send away in haste.

> He *sped* him thence home to his habitation. *Fairfax.*

2. To hasten; to hurry; to put in quick motion.

> —But *sped* his steps along the hoarse resounding shore. *Dryden.*

3. To hasten to a conclusion; to execute; to dispatch; as, to *speed* judicial acts. *Ayliffe.*

4. To assist; to help forward; to hasten.

> —With rising gales that *sped* their happy flight. *Dryden.*

5. To prosper; to cause to succeed. May heaven *speed* this undertaking.

6. To furnish in haste.

7. To dispatch; to kill; to ruin; to destroy.

> With a *speeding* thrust his heart he found. *Dryden.*

> A dire dilemma! either way I'm *sped*;
> If foes, they write, if friends they read me dead. *Pope.*

NOTE.—In the phrase, "God speed," there is probably a gross mistake in considering it as equivalent to "may God give you success." The true phrase is probably "*good speed*; *good*, in Saxon, being written *god.* I bid you or wish you *good speed*, that is, good success.

SPEED, *n.* Swiftness; quickness; celerity; *applied to animals.* We say, a man or a horse runs or travels with *speed*; a fowl flies with *speed*. We speak of the *speed* of a fish in the water, but we do not speak of the *speed* of a river, or of wind, or of a falling body. I think however I have seen the word applied to the lapse of time and the motion of lightning, but in poetry only.

2. Haste; dispatch; as, to perform a journey with *speed*; to execute an order with *speed*.

3. Rapid pace; as a horse of *speed*. We say also, high *speed*, full *speed*.

4. Success; prosperity in an undertaking; favorable issue; that is, advance to the desired end.

O Lord God of my master Abraham, I pray thee, send me good *speed* this day. Gen. xxiv.

This use is retained in the proverb, "to make more haste than good *speed*," and in the Scriptural phrase, "to bid one good *speed*," [not *God speed*, as erroneously written.]

SPEE'DILY, *adv.* Quickly; with haste; in a short time.

Send *speedily* to Bertram. *Dryden.*

SPEE'DINESS, *n.* The quality of being speedy; quickness; celerity; haste; dispatch.

SPEE'DWELL, *n.* A plant of the genus Veronica.

SPEE'DY, *a.* Quick; swift; nimble; hasty; rapid in motion; as a *speedy* flight; on *speedy* foot. *Shak.*

2. Quick in performance; not dilatory or slow; as a *speedy* dispatch of business.

SPEET, *v. t.* [D. *speeten*; from the root of *spit*.] To stab. [*Not in use.*]

SPEIGHT, *n.* A woodpecker. [*Not in use or local.*]

SPELK, *n.* [Sax. *spelc.*] A splinter; a small stick or rod used in thatching. [*Local.*] *Grose.*

SPELL, *n.* [Sax. *spel* or *spell*, a story, narration, fable, speech, saying, fame, report, sudden rumor, a magic charm or song. Hence *gospel*, Sax. *god-spell*. In G. *spiel* is play, sport; *spielen*, to play D. *speelen*, Sw. *spela*, Dan. *spiller*. But this is a different application of the same action. The verb primarily signifies to throw or drive, and is probably formed on the root of L. *pello*, Gr. *βαλλω*. See *Peal* and *Appeal*, and Class Bl. No. 1. Eth. In some of the applications of *spell*, we observe the sense of *turn*. We observe the same in *throw, warp, cant*, &c.]

1. A story; a tale. *Obs.* *Chaucer.*

2. A charm consisting of some words of occult power.

Start not; her actions shall be holy;
You hear my *spell* is lawful. *Shak.*
Begin, begin; the mystic *spell* prepare. *Milton.*

3. A turn of work; relief; turn of duty. Take a *spell* at the pump. *Seamen.*

Their toil is so extreme, that they cannot endure it above four hours in a day, but are succeeded by *spells*. *Carew.*

4. In *New England*, a short time; a little time. [*Not elegant.*]

5. A turn of gratuitous labor, sometimes accompanied with presents. People give their neighbors a *spell*. *N. England.*

SPELL, *v. t.* pret. and pp. *spelled* or *spelt*. [Sax. *spellian, spelligan*, to tell, to narrate, to discourse, which gives our sense of *spell* in reading letters; *spelian, speligan*, to take another's turn in labor; D. *spellen*, to spell, as words; Fr. *epeler.*]

1. To tell or name the letters of a word, with a proper division of syllables, for the purpose of learning the pronunciation. In this manner children learn to read by first *spelling* the words.

2. To write or print with the proper letters; to form words by correct orthography.

The word *satire* ought to be *spelled* with *i*, and not with *y*. *Dryden.*

3. To take another's place or turn temporarily in any labor or service. [*This is a popular use of the word in New England.*]

4. To charm; as *spelled* with words of power. *Dryden.*

5. To read; to discover by characters or marks; with *out*; as, to *spell out* the sense of an author. *Milton.*

We are not left to *spell out* a God in the works of creation. *South.*

6. To tell; to relate; to teach. [*Not in use.*] *Warton.*

SPELL, *v. i.* To form words with the proper letters, either in reading or writing. He knows not how to *spell*. Our orthography is so irregular that most persons never learn to *spell*.

2. To read. *Milton.*

SPELL'ED, **SPELT**, } *pret.* and *pp.* of *spell*.

SPELL'ER, *n.* One that spells; one skilled in spelling.

SPELL'ING, *ppr.* Naming the letters of a word, or writing them; forming words with their proper letters.

2. Taking another's turn.

SPELL'ING, *n.* The act of naming the letters of a word, or the act of writing or printing words with their proper letters.

2. Orthography; the manner of forming words with letters. Bad *spelling* is disreputable to a gentleman.

SPELL'ING-BOOK, *n.* A book for teaching children to spell and read.

SPELT, *n.* [Sax. D. *spelte*; G. *spelz*; It. *spelda, spelta.*] A species of grain of the genus Triticum; called also German wheat. *Encyc.*

SPELT, *v. t.* [G. *spalten*; Dan. *spilder.*] To split. [*Not in use.*] *Mortimer.*

SPEL'TER, *n.* [G. D. *spiauter.*] Common zink, which contains a portion of lead, copper, iron, a little arsenic, manganese and plumbago. *Webster's Manual.*

SPENCE, *n. spens.* [Old Fr. *dispense.*] A buttery; a larder; a place where provisions are kept. *Obs.* *Chaucer.*

SPEN'CER, *n.* One who has the care of the spence or buttery. *Obs.*

2. A kind of short coat.

SPEND, *v. t.* pret. and pp. *spent*. [Sax. *spendan*; Sw. *spendera*; Dan. *spanderer*; It. *spendere*; L. *expendo*, from the participle of which is Fr. *depenser*; from the root of L. *pando, pendeo*, the primary sense of which is to strain, to open or spread; allied to *span, pane*, &c. and probably to Gr. *σπενδω*, to pour out.]

1. To lay out; to dispose of; to part with; as, to *spend* money for clothing.

Why do ye *spend* money for that which is not bread? Is. lv.

2. To consume; to waste; to squander; as to *spend* an estate in gaming or other vices.

3. To consume; to exhaust. The provisions were *spent*, and the troops were in want.

4. To bestow for any purpose; often with *on* or *upon*. It is folly to *spend* words in debate *on* trifles.

5. To effuse. [*Little used.*] *Shak.*

6. To pass, as time; to suffer to pass away.

They *spend* their days in wealth, and in a moment go down to the grave. Job xiii.

7. To lay out; to exert or to waste; as, to *spend* one's strength.

8. To exhaust of force; to waste; to wear away; as, a ball had *spent* its force. The violence of the waves was *spent*.

Heaps of *spent* arrows fall and strew the ground. *Dryden.*

9. To exhaust of strength; to harass; to fatigue.

Their bodies *spent* with long labor and thirst— *Knolles.*

SPEND, *v. i.* To make expense; to make disposition of money. He *spends* like a prudent man.

2. To be lost or wasted; to vanish; to be dissipated.

The sound *spendeth* and is dissipated in the open air. *Bacon.*

3. To prove in the use.

—Butter *spent* as if it came from the richer soil. *Temple.*

4. To be consumed. Candles *spend* fast in a current of air. Our provisions *spend* rapidly.

5. To be employed to any use.

The vines they use for wine are so often cut, that their sap *spendeth* into the grapes. [*Unusual.*] *Bacon.*

SPEND'ER, *n.* One that spends; also, a prodigal; a lavisher. *Taylor. Bacon.*

SPEND'ING, *ppr.* Laying out; consuming; wasting; exhausting.

SPEND'ING, *n.* The act of laying out, expending, consuming or wasting. *Whillock.*

SPEND'THRIFT, *n.* [*spend* and *thrift.*] One who spends money profusely or improvidently; a prodigal; one who lavishes his estate. *Dryden. Swift.*

SPE'RABLE, *a.* [L. *sperabilis*, from *spero*, to hope.] That may be hoped. [*Not in use.*] *Bacon.*

SPERM, *n.* [Fr. *sperme*; L. *sperma*; Gr. *σπερμα.*]

1. Animal seed; that by which the species is propagated. *Bacon. Ray.*

2. The head matter of a certain species of whale, called *cachalot*. It is called by the French *blanc de baleine*, the *white of whales*. It is found also in other parts of the body; but it is improperly named, not being a spermatic substance. Of this matter are made candles of a beautiful white color.

3. Spawn of fishes or frogs.

SPERMACE'TI, *n.* [L. *sperma*, sperm, and *cetus*, a whale. It is pronounced as it is written.] The same as *sperm*.

SPERMAT'IC, *a.* Consisting of seed; seminal. *More.*

2. Pertaining to the semen, or conveying it; as *spermatic* vessels. *Ray. Coxe.*

SPERM'ATIZE, *v. i.* To yield seed. [*Not in use.*] *Brown.*

SPERMAT'OCELE, *n.* [Gr. σπερμα, seed, and κηλη, tumor.]
A swelling of the spermatic vessels, or vessels of the testicles. *Coxe.*

SPERSE, *v. t.* To disperse. [*Not in use.*] *Spenser.*

SPET, *v. t.* To spit; to throw out. [*Not used.*]

SPET, *n.* Spittle, or a flow. [*Not in use.*]

SPEW, *v. t.* [Sax. *spiwan*; D. *spuwen*, *spuigen*; G. *speien*, contracted from *speichen*; Sw. *spy*; Dan. *spyer*; L. *spuo.*]
1. To vomit; to puke; to eject from the stomach.
2. To eject; to cast forth.
3. To cast out with abhorrence. Lev. xviii.

SPEW, *v. i.* To vomit; to discharge the contents of the stomach. *B. Jonson.*

SPEW'ED, *pp.* Vomited; ejected.

SPEW'ER, *n.* One who spews.

SPEW'ING, *ppr.* Vomiting; ejecting from the stomach.

SPEW'ING, *n.* The act of vomiting.

SPEW'Y, *a.* Wet; foggy. [*Local.*] *Mortimer.*

SPHAC'ELATE, *v. i.* [See *Sphacelus.*]
1. To mortify; to become gangrenous; as flesh.
2. To decay or become carious, as a bone.

SPHAC'ELATE, *v. t.* To affect with gangrene. *Sharp.*

SPHACELA'TION, *n.* The process of becoming or making gangrenous; mortification. *Med. Repos.*

SPHAC'ELUS, *n.* [Gr. σφακελος, from σφαζω, to kill.]
1. In *medicine* and *surgery*, gangrene; mortification of the flesh of a living animal.
2. Caries or decay of a bone. *Coxe.*

SPHAG'NOUS, *a.* [*sphagnum*, bog-moss. *Linne.*] Pertaining to bog-moss; mossy. *Bigelow.*

SPHENE, *n.* [Gr. σφην, a wedge.] A mineral composed of nearly equal parts of oxyd of titanium, silex and lime. Its colors are commonly grayish, yellowish, reddish and blackish brown, and various shades of green. It is found amorphous and in crystals. *Phillips. Encyc.*

SPHENOID, } **SPHENOID'AL**, } *a.* [Gr. σφην, a wedge, and ειδος, form.] Resembling a wedge.

The *sphenoid bone*, is the pterygoid bone of the basis of the skull. *Coxe.*

SPHERE, *n.* [Fr. from L. *sphæra*, Gr. σφαιρα, whence It. *sfera*, Sp. *esfera*, G. *sphäre.*]
1. In *geometry*, a solid body contained under a single surface, which in every part is equally distant from a point called its center. The earth is not an exact *sphere.* The sun appears to be a *sphere.*
2. An orb or globe of the mundane system.

> First the sun, a mighty *sphere*, he fram'd. *Milton.*

> Then mortal ears
> Had heard the music of the *spheres.* *Dryden.*

3. An orbicular body, or a circular figure representing the earth or apparent heavens. *Dryden.*
4. Circuit of motion; revolution; orbit; as the diurnal *sphere.* *Milton.*
5. The concave or vast orbicular expanse in which the heavenly orbs appear.
6. Circuit of action, knowledge or influence; compass; province; employment. Every man has his particular *sphere* of action, in which it should be his ambition to excel. Events of this kind have repeatedly fallen within the *sphere* of my knowledge. This man treats of matters not within his *sphere.*
6. Rank; order of society. Persons moving in a higher *sphere* claim more deference.

Sphere of activity of a body, the whole space or extent reached by the effluvia emitted from it. *Encyc.*

A right sphere, that aspect of the heavens in which the circles of daily motion of the heavenly bodies, are perpendicular to the horizon. A spectator at the equator views a *right sphere.*

A parallel sphere, that in which the circles of daily motion are parallel to the horizon. A spectator at either of the poles, would view a *parallel sphere.*

An oblique sphere, that in which the circles of daily motion are oblique to the horizon, as is the case to a spectator at any point between the equator and either pole.

Armillary sphere, an artificial representation of the circles of the sphere, by means of brass rings.

SPHERE, *v. t.* To place in a sphere.

> The glorious planet Sol
> In noble eminence enthron'd, and *spher'd*
> Amidst the rest. [*Unusual.*] *Shak.*

2. To form into roundness; as light *sphered* in a radiant cloud. *Milton.*

SPHER'IC, } **SPHER'ICAL**, } *a.* [It. *sferico*; Fr. *spherique*; L. *sphæricus.*]
1. Globular; orbicular; having a surface in every part equally distant from the center; as a *spherical* body. Drops of water take a *spherical* form.
2. Planetary; relating to the orbs of the planets.

> We make guilty of our disasters the sun, the moon and the stars, as if we were villains by *spherical* predominance. *Shak.*

Spherical geometry, that branch of geometry which treats of spherical magnitudes.

Spherical triangle, a triangle formed by the mutual intersection of three great circles of the sphere.

Spherical trigonometry, that branch of trigonometry which teaches to compute the sides and angles of spherical triangles.

SPHER'ICALLY, *adv.* In the form of a sphere.

SPHER'ICALNESS, } **SPHERIC'ITY**, } *n.* The state or quality of being orbicular or spherical; roundness; as the *sphericity* of a drop of water.

SPHER'ICS, *n.* The doctrine of the sphere.

SPHEROID', *n.* [*sphere* and Gr. ειδος, form.]
A body or figure approaching to a sphere, but not perfectly spherical. A spheroid is oblate or prolate. The earth is found to be an *oblate spheroid*, that is, flatted at the poles, whereas some astronomers formerly supposed it to be *prolate* or oblong.

SPHEROID'AL, } **SPHEROID'IC**, } **SPHEROID'ICAL**, } *a.* Having the form of a spheroid. *Cheyne.*
2. In *crystalography*, bounded by several convex faces.

SPHEROID'ITY, *n.* The state or quality of being spheroidal.

SPHEROSID'ERITE, *n.* A substance found in the basaltic compact lava of Steinheim; called also glass lava or hyatite.

SPHER'ULE, *n.* [L. *sphærula.*] A little sphere or spherical body. Mercury or quicksilver when poured upon a plane, divides itself into a great number of minute *spherules.*

SPHER'ULITE, *n.* A variety of obsidian or pearl-stone, found in rounded grains. *Dict. Nat. Hist.*

SPHE'RY, *a.* Belonging to the sphere. *Milton.*
2. Round; spherical. *Shak.*

SPHINC'TER, *n.* [from Gr. σφιγγω, to constrain, to draw close.]
In *anatomy*, a muscle that contracts or shuts; as the *sphincter* labiorum; *sphincter* vesicæ. *Coxe.*

SPHINX, *n.* [Gr. σφιγξ; L. *sphinx.*] A famous monster in Egypt, having the body of a lion and the face of a young woman. *Peacham.*
2. In *entomology*, the hawk-moth, a genus of insects.

SPHRAG'ID, *n.* A species of ocherous clay which falls to pieces in water with the emission of many bubbles; called also earth of Lemnos.

SPIAL, *n.* A spy; a scout. [*Not in use.*] *Bacon.*

SPI'CATE, *a.* [L. *spicatus*, from *spica*, a spike.] Having a spike or ear. *Lee.*

SPICE, *n.* [Fr. *epice*; It. *spezie*; Sp. *especia.*]
1. A vegetable production, fragrant or aromatic to the smell and pungent to the taste; used in sauces and in cookery.
2. A small quantity; something that enriches or alters the quality of a thing in a small degree, as spice alters the taste of a thing.
3. A sample. [Fr. *espece.*]

SPICE, *v. t.* To season with spice; to mix aromatic substances with; as, to *spice* wine.
2. To tincture; as the *spiced* Indian air. *Shak.*
3. To render nice; to season with scruples. *Chaucer.*

SPI'CED, *pp.* Seasoned with spice.

SPI'CER, *n.* One that seasons with spice.
2. One that deals in spice. *Camden.*

SPI'CERY, *n.* [Fr. *epiceries.*] Spices in general; fragrant and aromatic vegetable substances used in seasoning.
2. A repository of spices. *Addison.*

Spick and span, bright; shining; as a garment *spick and span* new, or *span*-new. *Spick* is from the root of the It. *spicco*, brightness; *spiccare*, to shine; *spiccar le parole*, to *speak* distinctly; *spicciare*, to rush out, the radical sense of which is to shoot or dart. *Span* is probably from the root of *spangle*, Gr. φεγγω, G. *spiegel*, a mirror.

SPICK'NEL, } **SPIG'NEL**, } *n.* The herb maldmony or bear wort, *(Dict.)* the *Athamanta Meum (Parr.) Æthusa Meum (Lee.)*

SPICOS'ITY, *n.* [L. *spica.*] The state of having or being full of ears, like corn. [*Not in use.*] *Dict.*

SPIC'ULAR, *a.* [L. *spiculum*, a dart.] Resembling a dart; having sharp points.

SPIC'ULATE, *v. t.* [L. *spiculo*, to sharpen, from *spiculum*, a dart, from *spica*, or its root. See *Spike.*] To sharpen to a point. *Mason.*

SPI'CY, *a.* [from *spice.*] Producing spice; abounding with spices; as the *spicy* shore of Arabia. *Milton.*
2. Having the qualities of spice; fragrant; aromatic; as *spicy* plants.

Led by new stars and borne by *spicy* gales. *Pope.*

SPI'DER, *n.* [I know not from what source this word is derived.]
The common name of the insects of the genus Aranea, remarkable for spinning webs for taking their prey and forming a convenient habitation, and for the deposit of their food.

The *spider's* touch, how exquisitely fine! *Pope.*

SPI'DER-CATCHER, *n.* A bird so called.

SPI'DERLIKE, *a.* Resembling a spider. *Shak.*

SPI'DERWÖRT, *n.* A plant of the genus Anthericum.

SPIG'NEL. [See *Spicknel.*]

SPIG'OT, *n.* [W. *yspigawd*, from *yspig*, Eng. *spike*; from *pig*, Eng. *pike*; Dan. *spiger*, a nail. See *Spike* and *Pike.*]
A pin or peg used to stop a faucet, or to stop a small hole in a cask of liquor. *Swift.*

SPIKE, *n.* [W. *yspig*, supra; D. *spyk*, *spyker*; G. *speiche*; Dan. *spiger*, Sw. *spik*, a nail; L. *spica*, an ear of corn. It signifies a shoot or point. Class Bg. See *Pike.*]
1. A large nail; always in America applied to a nail or pin of metal. A similar thing made of wood is called a peg or pin. In England, it is sometimes used for a sharp point of wood.
2. An ear of corn or grain. It is applied to the heads of wheat, rye and barley; and is particularly applicable to the ears of maiz.
3. A shoot. *Addison.*
4. [L. *spica.*] In *botany*, a species of inflorescence, in which sessile flowers are alternate on a common simple peduncle, as in wheat and rye, lavender, &c. *Martyn.*

SPIKE, *n.* A smaller species of lavender. *Hill.*

SPIKE, *v. t.* To fasten with spikes or long and large nails; as, to *spike* down the planks of a floor or bridge.
2. To set with spikes.

A youth leaping over the *spiked* pales—was caught by the spikes. [*Unusual.*] *Wiseman.*

3. To stop the vent with spikes; as, to *spike* cannon.

SPI'KED, *pp.* Furnished with spikes, as corn; fastened with spikes; stopped with spikes.

SPIKE-LAVENDER, *n.* The *Lavandula spica.* *Ed. Encyc.*

SPI'KELET, *n.* In *botany*, a small spike of a large one; or a subdivision of a spike. *Barton.*

SPIKENARD, *n. spik'nard.* [L. *spica nardi.*]
1. A plant of the genus Nardus.
2. The oil or balsam procured from the spikenard.

SPI'KING, *ppr.* Fastening with spikes; stopping with large nails.

SPI'KY, *a.* Having a sharp point. *Dyer.*

SPILE, *n.* [D. *spil*, a pivot, a spindle; G. *spille*; Ir. *spile*; W. *ebill*; from the root of L. *pilus*, *pilum*, &c.]
1. A small peg or wooden pin, used to stop a hole.
2. A stake driven into the ground to protect a bank, &c.

SPILL, *n.* [a different orthography of *spile*, supra.]
1. A small peg or pin for stopping a cask; as a vent hole stopped with a *spill.* *Mortimer.*
2. A little bar or pin of iron. *Carew.*
3. A little sum of money. [*Not in use.*] *Ayliffe.*

SPILL, *v. t.* pret. *spilled* or *spilt*; pp. *id.* [Sax. *spillan*; D. G. *spillen*; Sw. *spilla*; Dan. *spilder.*]
1. To suffer to fall or run out of a vessel; to lose or suffer to be scattered; applied only to fluids and to substances whose particles are small and loose. Thus we *spill* water from a pail; we *spill* spirit or oil from a bottle; we *spill* quicksilver or powders from a vessel or a paper; we *spill* sand or flour.
2. To suffer to be shed; as, a man *spills* his own blood.
3. To cause to flow out or lose; to shed; as, a man *spills* another's blood. [This is applied to cases of murder or other homicide, but not to venesection. In the latter case we say, to *let* or *take* blood.]

And to revenge his blood so justly *spilt*— *Dryden.*

4. To mischief; to destroy; as, to *spill* the mind or soul; to *spill* glory; to *spill* forms, &c. [*This application is obsolete and now improper.*]
5. To throw away. *Tickel.*
6. In *seamen's language*, to discharge the wind out of the cavity or belly of a sail. *Mar. Dict.*

SPILL, *v. i.* To waste; to be prodigal. [*Not in use.*]
2. To be shed; to be suffered to fall, be lost or wasted.

He was so topfull of himself, that he let it *spill* on all the company. *Watts.*

SPILL'ED, *pp.* Suffered to fall, as liquids; shed.

SPILL'ER, *n.* One that spills or sheds.
2. A kind of fishing line. *Carew.*

SPILL'ING, *ppr.* Suffering to fall or run out, as liquids; shedding.

Spilling-lines, in a ship, are ropes for furling more conveniently the square sails. *Mar. Dict.*

SPILT, *pret.* and *pp.* of *spill.*

SPILTH, *n.* [from *spill.*] Any thing spilt. [*Not in use.*] *Shak.*

SPIN, *v. t.* pret. and pp. *spun.* *Span* is not used. [Sax. Goth. *spinnan*; D. G. *spinnen*; Dan. *spinder*; Sw. *spinna.* If the sense is to draw out or extend, this coincides in origin with *span.*]
1. To draw out and twist into threads, either by the hand or machinery; as, to *spin* wool, cotton or flax; to *spin* goats' hair.

All the yarn which Penelope *spun* in Ulysses' absence did but fill Ithaca with moths. *Shak.*

2. To draw out tediously; to form by a slow process or by degrees; with *out*; as, to *spin out* large volumes on a subject.
3. To extend to a great length; as, to *spin out* a subject.
4. To draw out; to protract; to spend by delays; as, to *spin out* the day in idleness.

By one delay after another, they *spin out* their whole lives. *L'Estrange.*

5. To whirl with a thread; to turn or cause to whirl; as, to *spin* a top.
6. To draw out from the stomach in a filament; as, a spider *spins* a web.

To spin hay, in military language, is to twist it into ropes for convenient carriage on an expedition.

SPIN, *v. i.* To practice spinning; to work at drawing and twisting threads; as, the woman knows how to *spin.*

They neither know to *spin*, nor care to toil. *Prior.*

2. To perform the act of drawing and twisting threads; as, a machine or jenny *spins* with great exactness.
3. To move round rapidly; to whirl; as a top or a spindle.
4. To stream or issue in a thread or small current; as, blood *spins* from a vein. *Drayton.*

SPIN'ACH, } *n.* [L. *spinacia*; It. *spinace*;
SPIN'AGE, } Sp. *espinaca*; Fr. *epinards*; D. *spinagie*; G. *spinat*; Pers. *spanach.*]
A plant of the genus Spinacia.

SPI'NAL, *a.* [See *Spine.*] Pertaining to the spine or back bone of an animal; as the *spinal* marrow; *spinal* muscles; *spinal* arteries. *Arbuthnot. Encyc.*

SPIN'DLE, *n.* [from *spin*; Sax. Dan. *spindel.*]
1. The pin used in spinning wheels for twisting the thread, and on which the thread when twisted, is wound. *Bacon.*
2. A slender pointed rod or pin on which any thing turns; as the *spindle* of a vane.
3. The fusee of a watch.
4. A long slender stalk. *Mortimer.*
5. The lower end of a capstan, shod with iron; the pivot. *Mar. Dict.*

SPIN'DLE, *v. i.* To shoot or grow in a long slender stalk or body. *Bacon. Mortimer.*

SPIN'DLE-LEGS, } *n.* A tall slender
SPIN'DLE-SHANKS, } person; *in contempt.*

SPIN'DLE-SHANKED, *a.* Having long slender legs.

SPIN'DLE-SHAPED, *a.* Having the shape of a spindle; fusiform. *Martyn.*

SPIN'DLE-TREE, *n.* A plant, prick-wood, of the genus Euonymus.

SPINE, *n.* [L. It. *spina*; Fr. *epine*; Sp. *espinazo*; W. *yspin*, from *pin.*]
1. The back bone of an animal. *Coxe.*
2. The shin of the leg. *Coxe.*
3. A thorn; a sharp process from the woody part of a plant. It differs from a prickle, which proceeds from the bark. A spine sometimes terminates a branch or a leaf, and sometimes is axillary, growing at the angle formed by the branch or leaf with the stem. The wild apple and pear are armed with thorns; the rose, bramble, gooseberry, &c. are armed with prickles. *Martyn.*

SPI'NEL, } *n.* [It. *spinella.*] The spinelle
SPINELLE, } ruby, says Haüy, is the true ruby, a gem of a red color, blended with

tints of blue or yellow. It is in grains more or less crystalized. *Haüy. Phillips.*

A subspecies of octahedral corundum. *Jameson.*

SPINELLANE, *n.* A mineral occuring in small crystaline masses and in minute crystals. It has been found only near the lake of Laach. *Phillips.*

SPINES'CENT, *a.* [from *spine.*] Becoming hard and thorny. *Martyn.*

SPIN'ET, *n.* [It. *spinetta;* Fr. *epinette;* Sp. *espineta.*]

An instrument of music resembling a harpsichord, but smaller; a virginal; a clavichord.

SPIN'ET, *n.* [L. *spinetum.*] A small wood or place where briars and thorns grow. [*Not in use.*] *B. Jonson.*

SPINIF'EROUS, *a.* [L. *spina*, spine, and *fero*, to bear.] Producing spines; bearing thorns.

SPINK, *n.* A bird; a finch. *Harte.*

SPIN'NER, *n.* One that spins; one skilled in spinning.

2. A spider. *Shak.*

SPIN'NING, *ppr.* Drawing out and twisting into threads; drawing out; delaying.

SPIN'NING, *n.* The act, practice or art of drawing out and twisting into threads, as wool, flax and cotton.

2. The act or practice of forming webs, as spiders.

SPIN'NING-JENNY, *n.* An engine or complicated machine for spinning wool or cotton, in the manufacture of cloth.

SPIN'NING-WHEEL, *n.* A wheel for spinning wool, cotton or flax into threads. *Gay.*

SPIN'OLET, *n.* A small bird of the lark kind. *Dict. Nat. Hist.*

SPINOS'ITY, *n.* The state of being spiny or thorny; crabbedness. *Glanville.*

SPI'NOUS, *a.* [L. *spinosus*, from *spina.*] Full of spines; armed with thorns; thorny. *Martyn.*

SPI'NOZISM, *n.* The doctrines or principles of Spinoza, a native of Amsterdam, consisting in atheism and pantheism, or naturalism and hulotheism, which allows of no God but nature or the universe.

SPIN'STER, *n.* [*spin* and *ster.*] A woman who spins, or whose occupation is to spin. Hence,

2. In *law*, the common title by which a woman without rank or distinction is designated.

If a gentlewoman is termed a *spinster*, she may abate the writ. *Coke.*

SPIN'STRY, *n.* The business of spinning. *Milton.*

SPIN'THERE, *n.* A mineral of a greenish gray color. *Ure.*

SPI'NY, *a.* [from *spine.*] Full of spines; thorny; as a *spiny* tree.

2. Perplexed; difficult; troublesome. *Digby.*

SPIR'ACLE, *n.* [L. *spiraculum*, from *spiro*, to breathe.]

1. A small aperture in animal and vegetable bodies, by which air or other fluid is exhaled or inhaled; a small hole, orifice or vent; a pore; a minute passage; as the *spiracles* of the human skin.

2. Any small aperture, hole or vent. *Woodward.*

SPI'RAL, *a.* [It. *spirale;* Fr. *spiral;* from L. *spira*, a spire.]

Winding round a cylinder or other round body, or in a circular form, and at the same time rising or advancing forward; winding like a screw. The magnificent column in the Place Vendome, at Paris, is divided by a *spiral* line into compartments. It is formed with *spiral* compartments, on which are engraved figures emblematical of the victories of the French armies. A whirlwind is so named from the *spiral* motion of the air. Water in a tunnel descends in a *spiral* form.

SPI'RALLY, *adv.* In a spiral form or direction; in the manner of a screw. *Ray.*

SPIRA'TION, *n.* [L. *spiratio.*] A breathing. [*Not used.*] *Barrow.*

SPIRE, *n.* [L. *spira;* Gr. σπειρα; Sp. *espira;* from the root of L. *spiro*, to breathe. The primary sense of the root is to throw, to drive, to send, but it implies a winding motion, like *throw*, *warp*, and many others.]

1. A winding line like the threads of a screw; any thing wreathed or contorted; a curl; a twist; a wreath.

His neck erect amidst his circling *spires.* *Milton.*

A dragon's fiery form belied the god;
Sublime on radiant *spires* he rode. *Dryden.*

2. A body that shoots up to a point; a tapering body; a round pyramid or pyramidical body; a steeple.

With glist'ring *spires* and pinnacles adorn'd. *Milton.*

3. A stalk or blade of grass or other plant. How humble ought man to be, who cannot make a single *spire* of grass.

4. The top or uppermost point of a thing. *Shak.*

SPIRE, *v. i.* To shoot; to shoot up pyramidically. *Mortimer.*

2. To breathe. [*Not in use.*]

3. To sprout, as grain in malting.

SPI'RED, *a.* Having a spire. *Mason.*

SPIR'IT, *n.* [Fr. *esprit;* It. *spirito;* Sp. *espiritu;* L. *spiritus*, from *spiro*, to breathe, to blow. The primary sense is to rush or drive.]

1. Primarily, wind; air in motion; hence, breath.

All bodies have *spirits* and pneumatical parts within them. *Bacon.*

[*This sense is now unusual.*]

2. Animal excitement, or the effect of it; life; ardor; fire; courage; elevation or vehemence of mind. The troops attacked the enemy with great *spirit.* The young man has the *spirit* of youth. He speaks or acts with *spirit.* *Spirits*, in the plural, is used in nearly a like sense. The troops began to recover their *spirits.* *Swift.*

3. Vigor of intellect; genius.

His wit, his beauty and his *spirit.* *Butler.*

The noblest *spirit* or genius cannot deserve enough of mankind to pretend to the esteem of heroic virtue. *Temple.*

4. Temper; disposition of mind, habitual or temporary; as a man of a generous *spirit*, or of a revengeful *spirit;* the ornament of a meek and quiet *spirit.*

Let us go to the house of God in the *spirit* of prayer. *Bickersteth.*

5. The soul of man; the intelligent, immaterial and immortal part of human beings. [See *Soul.*]

The *spirit* shall return to God that gave it. Eccles. xii.

6. An immaterial intelligent substance.

Spirit is a substance in which thinking, knowing, doubting, and a power of moving do subsist. *Locke.*

Hence,

7. An immaterial intelligent being.

By which he went and preached to the *spirits* in prison. 1 Pet. iii.

God is a *spirit.* John iv.

8. Turn of mind; temper; occasional state of the mind.

A perfect judge will read each work of wit,
With the same *spirit* that its author writ. *Pope.*

9. Powers of mind distinct from the body.

In *spirit* perhaps he also saw
Rich Mexico, the seat of Montezume. *Milton.*

10. Sentiment; perception.

Your *spirit* is too true, your fears too certain. *Shak.*

11. Eager desire; disposition of mind excited and directed to a particular object.

God has made a *spirit* of building succeed a *spirit* of pulling down. *South.*

12. A person of activity; a man of life, vigor or enterprise.

The watery kingdom is no bar
To stop the foreign *spirits*, but they come. *Shak.*

13. Persons distinguished by qualities of the mind.

Such *spirits* as he desired to please, such would I choose for my judges. *Dryden.*

14. Excitement of mind; animation; cheerfulness; usually in the plural. We found our friend in very good *spirits.* He has a great flow of *spirits.*

—To sing thy praise, would heaven my breath prolong,
Infusing *spirits* worthy such a song. *Dryden.*

15. Life or strength of resemblance; essential qualities; as, to set off the face in its true *spirit.* The copy has not the *spirit* of the original. *Wotton.*

16. Something eminently pure and refined.

Nor doth the eye itself,
That most pure *spirit* of sense, behold itself. *Shak.*

17. That which hath power or energy; the quality of any substance which manifests life, activity, or the power of strongly affecting other bodies; as the *spirit* of wine or of any liquor.

18. A strong, pungent or stimulating liquor, usually obtained by distillation, as rum, brandy, gin, whiskey. In America, *spirit*, used without other words explanatory of its meaning, signifies the liquor distilled from cane-juice, or rum. We say, new *spirit*, or old *spirit*, Jamaica *spirit*, &c.

19. An apparition; a ghost.

20. The renewed nature of man. Matt. xxvi. Gal. v.

21. The influences of the Holy Spirit. Matt. xxii.

Holy Spirit, the third person in the Trinity.

SPIR'IT, *v. t.* To animate; to actuate; as a spirit.

So talk'd the *spirited* sly snake. *Milton.*
[*Little used.*]

2. To animate with vigor; to excite; to encourage; as, civil dissensions *spirit* the ambition of private men. *Swift.*

It is sometimes followed by *up*; as, to *spirit up*. *Middleton.*

3. To kidnap. *Blackstone.*

To spirit away, to entice or seduce.

SPIR'ITALLY, *adv.* By means of the breath. [*Not in use.*] *Holder.*

SPIR'ITED, *pp.* Animated; encouraged; incited.

2. *a.* Animated; full of life; lively; full of spirit or fire; as a *spirited* address or oration; a *spirited* answer. It is used in composition, noting the state of the mind; as in high-*spirited*, low-*spirited*, mean-*spirited*.

SPIR'ITEDLY, *adv.* In a lively manner; with spirit; with strength; with animation.

SPIR'ITEDNESS, *n.* Life; animation.

2. Disposition or make of mind; used in compounds; as high-*spiritedness*, low-*spiritedness*, mean-*spiritedness*, narrow-*spiritedness*.

SPIR'ITFUL, *a.* Lively; full of spirit. [*Not used.*] *Ash.*

SPIR'ITFULLY, *adv.* In a lively manner. [*Not used.*]

SPIR'ITFULNESS, *n.* Liveliness; sprightliness. [*Not used.*] *Harvey.*

SPIR'ITLESS, *a.* Destitute of spirits; wanting animation; wanting cheerfulness; dejected; depressed.

2. Destitute of vigor; wanting life, courage or fire; as a *spiritless* slave.

A man so faint, so *spiritless*,
So dull, so dead in look— *Shak.*

3. Having no breath; extinct; dead. *Greenhill.*

SPIR'ITLESSLY, *adv.* Without spirit; without exertion. *More.*

SPIR'ITLESSNESS, *n.* Dullness; want of life or vigor.

SPIR'ITOUS, *a.* Like spirit; refined; defecated; pure.

More refin'd, more *spiritous* and pure. *Milton.*

2. Fine; ardent; active. *Smith.*

SPIR'ITOUSNESS, *n.* A refined state; fineness and activity of parts; as the thinness and *spiritousness* of liquor. *Boyle.*

SPIR'ITUAL, *a.* [Fr. *spirituel*; It. *spirituale*; L. *spiritualis.*]

1. Consisting of spirit; not material; incorporeal; as a *spiritual* substance or being. The soul of man is *spiritual*.

2. Mental; intellectual; as *spiritual* armor. *Milton.*

3. Not gross; refined from external things; not sensual; relative to mind only; as a *spiritual* and refined religion. *Calamy.*

4. Not lay or temporal; relating to sacred things; ecclesiastical; as the *spiritual* functions of the clergy; the lords *spiritual* and temporal; a *spiritual* corporation.

5. Pertaining to spirit or to the affections; pure; holy.

God's law is *spiritual*; it is a transcript of the divine nature, and extends its authority to the acts of the soul of man. *Brown.*

6. Pertaining to the renewed nature of man; as *spiritual* life.

7. Not fleshly; not material; as *spiritual* sacrifices. 1 Pet. ii.

8. Pertaining to divine things; as *spiritual* songs. Eph. v.

Spiritual court, an ecclesiastical court; a court held by a bishop or other ecclesiastic.

SPIRITUAL'ITY, *n.* Essence distinct from matter; immateriality.

If this light be not spiritual, it approacheth nearest to *spirituality*. *Raleigh.*

2. Intellectual nature; as the *spirituality* of the soul. *South.*

3. Spiritual nature; the quality which respects the spirit or affections of the heart only, and the essence of true religion; as the *spirituality* of God's law.

4. Spiritual exercises and holy affections.

Much of our *spirituality* and comfort in public worship depend on the state of mind in which we come. *Bickersteth.*

5. That which belongs to the church, or to a person as an ecclesiastic, or to religion; as distinct from temporalities.

During the vacancy of a see, the archbishop is guardian of the *spiritualities* thereof. *Blackstone.*

6. An ecclesiastical body. [*Not in use.*] *Shak.*

SPIRITUALIZA'TION, *n.* The act of spiritualizing. In chimistry, the operation of extracting spirit from natural bodies. *Encyc.*

SPIR'ITUALIZE, *v. t.* [Fr. *spiritualiser*, to extract spirit from mixed bodies.]

1. To refine the intellect; to purify from the feculences of the world; as, to *spiritualize* the soul. *Hammond.*

2. In chimistry, to extract spirit from natural bodies.

3. To convert to a spiritual meaning.

SPIR'ITUALLY, *adv.* Without corporeal grossness or sensuality; in a manner conformed to the spirit of true religion; with purity of spirit or heart.

Spiritually minded, under the influence of the Holy Spirit or of holy principles; having the affections refined and elevated above sensual objects, and placed on God and his law. Rom. viii.

Spiritually discerned, known, not by carnal reason, but by the peculiar illumination of the Holy Spirit. 1 Cor. ii.

SPIR'ITUOUS, *a.* [Fr. *spiritueux.*] Containing spirit; consisting of refined spirit; ardent; as *spirituous* liquors. [This might well be written *spiritous.*]

2. Having the quality of spirit; fine; pure; active; as the *spirituous* part of a plant. *Arbuthnot.*

3. Lively; gay; vivid; airy. [*Not in use.*] *Wotton.*

SPIR'ITUOUSNESS, *n.* The quality of being spirituous; ardor; heat; stimulating quality; as the *spirituousness* of liquors.

2. Life; tenuity; activity.

SPIRT. [See *Spurt*, the more correct orthography.]

SPI'RY, *a.* [from *spire.*] Of a spiral form; wreathed; curled; as the *spiry* volumes of a serpent. *Dryden.*

2. Having the form of a pyramid; pyramidical; as *spiry* turrets. *Pope.*

SPISS, *a.* [L. *spissus.*] Thick; close; dense. [*Not in use.*]

SPISS'ITUDE, *n.* [supra.] Thickness of soft substances; the denseness or compactness which belongs to substances not perfectly liquid nor perfectly solid; as the *spissitude* of coagulated blood or of any coagulum.

SPIT, *n.* [Sax. *spitu*; D. *spit*; G. *spiess*; Sw. *spett*; Dan. *spid*; It. *spiedo*; Ice. *spiet*, a spear. It belongs to Class Bd, and is from thrusting, shooting.]

1. An iron prong or bar pointed, on which meat is roasted.

2. Such a depth of earth as is pierced by the spade at once. [D. *spit*, a spade.] *Mortimer.*

3. A small point of land running into the sea, or a long narrow shoal extending from the shore into the sea; as a *spit* of sand.

SPIT, *v. t.* [from the noun.] To thrust a spit through; to put upon a spit; as, to *spit* a loin of veal.

2. To thrust through; to pierce. *Dryden.*

SPIT, *v. t.* pret. and pp. *spit*. *Spat* is obsolete. [Sax. *spittan*; Sw. *spotta*; Dan. *spytter*; G. *spützen*. The sense is to throw or drive. Class Bd.]

1. To eject from the mouth; to thrust out, as saliva or other matter from the mouth.

2. To eject or throw out with violence.

SPIT, *v. i.* To throw out saliva from the mouth. It is a dirty trick to *spit* on the floor or carpet.

SPIT, *n.* [Dan. *spyt.*] What is ejected from the mouth; saliva.

SPIT'AL, } *n.* corrupted from *hospital*.
SPIT'TEL, } "Rob not the *spital*," or charitable foundation. *Johnson.*
[*Vulgar and not in use.*]

SPITCH'COCK, *v. t.* To split an eel lengthwise and broil it. *King.*

SPITCH'COCK, *n.* An eel split and broiled. *Decker.*

SPITE, *n.* [D. *spyt*, spite, vexation; Ir. *spid*. The Fr. has *depit*, Norm. *despite*. The It. *dispetto*, and Sp. *despecho*, seem to be from the L. *despectus*; but *spite* seems to be from a different root.]

Hatred; rancor; malice; malignity; malevolence. *Johnson.*

Spite, however, is not always synonymous with these words. It often denotes a less deliberate and fixed hatred than malice and malignity, and is often a sudden fit of ill will excited by temporary vexation. It is the effect of extreme irritation, and is accompanied with a desire of revenge, or at least a desire to vex the object of ill will.

Be gone, ye critics, and restrain your *spite*;
Codrus writes on, and will for ever write. *Pope.*

In spite of, in opposition to all efforts; in defiance or contempt of. Sometimes *spite of* is used without *in*, but not elegantly. It is often used without expressing any malignity of meaning.

—Whom God made use of to speak a word in season, and saved me *in spite of* the world, the devil and myself. *South.*

In spite of all applications, the patient grew worse every day. *Arbuthnot.*

To owe one a spite, to entertain a temporary hatred for something.

SPITE, *v. t.* To be angry or vexed at.

2. To mischief; to vex; to treat maliciously; to thwart. *Shak.*

3. To fill with spite or vexation; to offend; to vex.

Darius, *spited* at the Magi, endeavored to abolish not only their learning but their language. [*Not used.*] *Temple.*

SPI'TED, *pp.* Hated; vexed.

SPI'TEFUL, *a.* Filled with spite; having a desire to vex, annoy or injure; malignant; malicious.

—A wayward son,
Spiteful and wrathful. *Shak.*

SPI'TEFULLY, *adv.* With a desire to vex, annoy or injure; malignantly; maliciously. *Swift.*

SPI'TEFULNESS, *n.* The desire to vex, annoy or mischief, proceeding from irritation; malice; malignity.

It looks more like *spitefulness* and ill nature, than a diligent search after truth. *Keil.*

SPIT'TED, *pp.* [from *spit.*] Put upon a spit.
2. Shot out into length. *Bacon.*

SPIT'TER, *n.* One that puts meat on a spit.
2. One who ejects saliva from his mouth.
3. A young deer whose horns begin to shoot or become sharp; a brocket or pricket. *Encyc.*

SPIT'TING, *ppr.* Putting on a spit.
2. Ejecting saliva from the mouth.

SPIT'TLE, *n.* [from *spit.*] Saliva; the thick moist matter which is secreted by the salivary glands and ejected from the mouth.
2. A small sort of spade. [*spaddle.*]

SPIT'TLE. [See *Spital.*]

SPIT'TLE, *v. t.* To dig or stir with a small spade. [*Local.*]

SPIT'VENOM, *n.* [*spit* and *venom.*] Poison ejected from the mouth. *Hooker.*

SPLANCHNOL'OGY, *n.* [Gr. σπλαγχνα, bowels, and λογος, discourse.]
1. The doctrine of the viscera; or a treatise or description of the viscera. *Hooper.*
2. The doctrine of diseases of the internal parts of the body. *Coxe.*

SPLASH, *v. t.* [formed on *plash.*] To spatter with water, or with water and mud.

SPLASH, *v. i.* To strike and dash about water.

SPLASH, *n.* Water or water and dirt thrown upon any thing, or thrown from a puddle and the like.

SPLASH'Y, *a.* Full of dirty water; wet; wet and muddy.

SPLAY, *v. t.* [See *Display.*] To dislocate or break a horse's shoulder bone. *Johnson.*
2. To spread. [*Little used.*] *Mease.*

SPLAY, for *display.* [*Not in use.*]

SPLAY, *a.* Displayed; spread; turned outward. *Sidney.*

SPLA'YFOOT, SPLA'YFOOTED, } *a.* Having the foot turned outward; having a wide foot. *Pope.*

SPLA'YMOUTH, *n.* A wide mouth; a mouth stretched by design.

SPLEEN, *n.* [L. *splen*; Gr. σπλην.] The milt; a soft part of the viscera of animals, whose use is not well understood. The ancients supposed this to be the seat of melancholy, anger or vexation. Hence,
2. Anger; latent spite; ill humor. Thus we say, to vent one's *spleen.*

In noble minds some dregs remain,
Not yet purged off, of *spleen* and sour disdain. *Pope.*

3. A fit of anger. *Shak.*
4. A fit; a sudden motion. [*Not used.*] *Shak.*
5. Melancholy; hypochondriacal affections.

—Bodies chang'd to recent forms by *spleen.* *Pope.*

6. Immoderate merriment. [*Not in use.*] *Shak.*

SPLEE'NED, *a.* Deprived of the spleen. *Arbuthnot.*

SPLEE'NFUL, *a.* Angry; peevish; fretful.

Myself have calm'd their *spleenful* mutiny. *Shak.*

2. Melancholy; hypochondriacal. *Pope.*

SPLEE'NLESS, *a.* Kind; gentle; mild. *Obs.* *Chapman.*

SPLEE'NWÖRT, *n.* [L. *splenium.*] A plant of the genus Asplenium; miltwaste.

SPLEE'NY, *a.* Angry; peevish; fretful.

A *spleeny* Lutheran, and not wholesome to
Our cause. *Shak.*

2. Melancholy; affected with nervous complaints.

SPLEN'DENT, *a.* [L. *splendens, splendeo,* to shine.]
1. Shining; glossy; beaming with light; as *splendent* planets; *splendent* metals. *Newton.*
2. Very conspicuous; illustrious. *Wotton.*

SPLEN'DID, *a.* [L. *splendidus,* from *splendeo,* to shine; Fr. *splendide*; It. *splendido*; W. *ysplan,* from *plan,* clear. See *Plain.*]
1. Properly, shining; very bright; as a *splendid* sun. Hence,
2. Showy; magnificent; sumptuous; pompous; as a *splendid* palace; a *splendid* procession; a *splendid* equipage; a *splendid* feast or entertainment.
3. Illustrious; heroic; brilliant; as a *splendid* victory.
4. Illustrious; famous; celebrated; as a *splendid* reputaion.

SPLEN'DIDLY, *adv.* With great brightness or brilliant light.
2. Magnificently; sumptuously; richly; as a house *splendidly* furnished.
3. With great pomp or show. The king was *splendidly* attended.

SPLEN'DOR, *n.* [L. from the Celtic; W. *ysplander,* from *pleiniaw, dyspleiniaw,* to cast rays, from *plan,* a ray, a cion or shoot, a *plane*; whence *plant.* See *Plant* and *Planet.*]
1. Great brightness; brilliant luster; as the *splendor* of the sun.
2. Great show of richness and elegance; magnificence; as the *splendor* of equipage or of royal robes.
3. Pomp; parade; as the *splendor* of a procession or of ceremonies.
4. Brilliance; eminence; as the *splendor* of a victory.

SPLEN'DROUS, *a.* Having splendor. [*Not in use.*] *Drayton.*

SPLEN'ETIC, *a.* [L. *spleneticus.*] Affected with spleen; peevish; fretful.

You humor me when I am sick;
Why not when I am *splenetic?* *Pope.*

SPLEN'ETIC, *n.* A person affected with spleen. *Tatler.*

SPLEN'IC, *a.* [Fr. *splenique.*] Belonging to the spleen; as the *splenic* vein. *Ray.*

SPLEN'ISH, *a.* Affected with spleen; peevish; fretful. *Drayton.*

SPLEN'ITIVE, *a.* Hot; fiery; passionate; irritable. [*Not in use.*]

I am not *splenitive* and rash. *Shak.*

SPLENT, *n.* A callous substance or insensible swelling on the shank-bone of a horse. *Far. Dict.*
2. A splint. [See *Splint.*]

SPLICE, SPLISE, } *v. t.* [Sw. *splissa*; D. *splissen*; G. *spleissen*; Dan. *splidser,* from *splider, splitter,* to *split,* to divide. It should be written *splise.*]
To separate the strands of the two ends of a rope, and unite them by a particular manner of interweaving them; or to unite the end of a rope to any part of another by a like interweaving of the strands. There are different modes of splicing, as the short splice, long splice, eye splice, &c. *Mar. Dict.*

SPLICE, *n.* The union of ropes by interweaving the strands. *Mar. Dict.*

SPLINT, SPLINT'ER, } *n.* [D. *splinter*; G. *splint* or *splitter*; Dan. *splindt.* Qu. is *n* radical?]
1. A piece of wood split off; a thin piece (in proportion to its thickness,) of wood or other solid substance, rent from the main body; as *splinters* of a ship's side or mast, rent off by a shot.
2. In *surgery,* a thin piece of wood or other substance, used to hold or confine a broken bone when set.
3. A piece of bone rent off in a fracture.

SPLINT, SPLINT'ER, } *v. t.* To split or rend into long thin pieces; to shiver; as, the lightning *splinters* a tree.
2. To confine with splinters, as a broken limb.

SPLINT'ER, *v. i.* To be split or rent into long pieces.

SPLINT'ERED, *pp.* Split into splinters; secured by splints.

SPLINT'ERY, *a.* Consisting of splinters, or resembling splinters; as the *splintery* fracture of a mineral, which discovers scales arising from splits or fissures, parallel to the line of fracture. *Kirwan. Fourcroy.*

SPLIT, *v. t.* pret. and pp. *split.* [D. *splitten*; Dan. *splitter*; G. *splittern* or *spleissen*; Eth. ፈለጠ falt, to separate, to divide, the same verb which, in other Shemitic languages, Heb. Ch. Syr. פלט, signifies to escape. See *Spalt.*]
1. To divide longitudinally or lengthwise; to separate a thing from end to end by force; to rive; to cleave; as, to *split* a piece of timber; to *split* a board. It differs from *crack.* To *crack* is to open or partially separate; to *split* is to separate entirely.
2. To rend; to tear asunder by violence; to burst; as, to *split* a rock or a sail.

Cold winter *splits* the rocks in twain. *Dryden.*

3. To divide; to part; as, to *split* a hair. The phrases to *split* the heart, to *split* a ray of light, are now inelegant and obsolete, especially the former. The phrase, to *split* the earth, is not strictly correct.
4. To dash and break on a rock; as, a ship stranded and *split.* *Mar. Dict.*
5. To divide; to break into discord; as a people *split* into parties.
6. To strain and pain with laughter; as, to *split* the sides.

SPLIT, *v. i.* To burst; to part asunder; to suffer disruption; as, vessels *split* by the freezing of water in them. Glass vessels often *split* when heated too suddenly.

2. To burst with laughter.

Each had a gravity would make you *split*. *Pope.*

3. To be broken; to be dashed to pieces. We were driven upon a rock, and the ship immediately *split*. *Swift.*

To split on a rock, to fail; to err fatally; to have the hopes and designs frustrated. *Spectator.*

SPLIT'TER, *n.* One who splits. *Swift.*

SPLIT'TING, *ppr.* Bursting; riving; rending.

SPLUT'TER, *n.* A bustle; a stir. [*A low word and little used.*]

SPLUT'TER, *v. i.* To speak hastily and confusedly. [*Low.*] *Carlton.*

SPOD'UMENE, *n.* [Gr. σποδοω, to reduce to ashes.]

A mineral, called by Haüy *triphane*. It occurs in laminated masses, easily divisible into prisms with rhomboidal bases; the lateral faces smooth, shining and pearly; the cross fracture uneven and splintery. Before the blowpipe it exfoliates into little yellowish or grayish scales; whence its name. *Cleaveland.*

SPOIL, *v. t.* [Fr. *spolier*; It. *spogliare*; L. *spolio*; W. *yspeiliaw*. The sense is probably to pull asunder, to tear, to strip; coinciding with L. *vello*, or with *peel*, or with both. See Class Bl. No. 7. 8. 15. 32.]

1. To plunder; to strip by violence; to rob; with *of*; as, to *spoil* one *of* his goods or possessions.

My sons their old unhappy sire despise,
Spoil'd of his kingdom, and depriv'd of eyes. *Pope.*

2. To seize by violence; to take by force; as, to *spoil* one's goods.

This mount
With all his verdure *spoil'd*— *Milton.*

3. [Sax. *spillan.*] To corrupt; to cause to decay and perish. Heat and moisture will soon *spoil* vegetable and animal substances.

4. To corrupt; to vitiate; to mar.

Spiritual pride *spoils* many graces. *Taylor.*

5. To ruin; to destroy. Our crops are sometimes *spoiled* by insects.

6. To render useless by injury; as, to *spoil* paper by wetting it.

7. To injure fatally; as, to *spoil* the eyes by reading.

SPOIL, *v. i.* To practice plunder or robbery.

—Outlaws which, lurking in woods, used to break forth to rob and *spoil*. *Spenser.*

2. To decay; to lose the valuable qualities; to be corrupted; as, fruit will soon *spoil* in warm weather. Grain will *spoil*, if gathered when wet or moist.

SPOIL, *n.* [L. *spolium.*] That which is taken from others by violence; particularly in war, the plunder taken from an enemy; pillage; booty.

2. That which is gained by strength or effort.

Each science and each art his *spoil*. *Bentley.*

3. That which is taken from another without license.

Gentle gales
Fanning their odoriferous wings, dispense
Native perfumes, and whisper whence they stole
Their balmy *spoils*. *Milton.*

4. The act or practice of plundering; robbery; waste.

The man that hath not music in himself,
Nor is not mov'd with concord of sweet sounds,
Is fit for treason, stratagems and *spoils*. *Shak.*

5. Corruption; cause of corruption.

Villainous company hath been the *spoil* of me. *Shak.*

6. The slough or cast skin of a serpent or other animal. *Bacon.*

SPOIL'ED, *pp.* Plundered; pillaged; corrupted; rendered useless.

SPOIL'ER, *n.* A plunderer; a pillager; a robber.

2. One that corrupts, mars or renders useless.

SPOIL'FUL, *a.* Wasteful; rapacious. [*Little used.*] *Spenser.*

SPOIL'ING, *ppr.* Plundering; pillaging; corrupting; rendering useless.

2. Wasting; decaying.

SPOIL'ING, *n.* Plunder; waste.

SPOKE, *pret.* of *speak.*

SPOKE, *n.* [Sax. *spaca*; D. *spaak*; G. *speiche*. This word, whose radical sense is to shoot or thrust, coincides with *spike*, *spigot*, *pike*, and G. *speien*, contracted from *speichen*, to *spew.*]

1. The radius or ray of a wheel; one of the small bars which are inserted in the hub or nave, and which serve to support the rim or felly. *Swift.*

2. The spar or round of a ladder. [*Not in use in the U. States.*]

SPŌKEN, *pp.* of *speak.* pron. *spo'kn.*

SPO'KE-SHAVE, *n.* A kind of plane to smooth the shells of blocks.

SPO'KESMAN, *n.* [*speak*, *spoke*, and *man.*] One who speaks for another.

He shall be thy *spokesman* to the people. Ex. iv.

SPO'LIATE, *v. t.* [L. *spolio.*] To plunder; to pillage. *Dict.*

SPO'LIATE, *v. i.* To practice plunder; to commit robbery. In time of war, rapacious men are let loose to *spoliate* on commerce.

SPOLIA'TION, *n.* The act of plundering, particularly of plundering an enemy in time of war.

2. The act or practice of plundering neutrals at sea under authority.

3. In *ecclesiastical affairs*, the act of an incumbent in taking the fruits of his benefice without right, but under a pretended title. *Blackstone.*

SPONDA'IC, } SPONDA'ICAL, } *a.* [See *Spondee.*] Pertaining to a spondee; denoting two long feet in poetry.

SPON'DEE, *n.* [Fr. *spondée*; It. *spondeo*; L. *spondæus.*]

A poetic foot of two long syllables. *Broome.*

SPON'DYL, } SPON'DYLE, } *n.* [L. *spondylus*; Gr. σπονδυλος; It. *spondulo.*] A joint of the back bone; a verteber or vertebra. *Coxe.*

SPŎNGE. [See *Spunge.*]

SPŎNK, *n.* [a word probably formed on *punk.*] Touchwood. In Scotland, a match; something dipped in sulphur for readily taking fire. [See *Spunk.*]

SPONS'AL, *a.* [L. *sponsalis*, from *spondeo*, to betroth.] Relating to marriage or to a spouse.

SPON'SION, *n.* [L. *sponsio*, from *spondeo*, to engage.] The act of becoming surety for another.

SPONS'OR, *n.* [L. supra.] A surety; one who binds himself to answer for another, and is responsible for his default. In the church, the *sponsors* in baptism are sureties for the education of the child baptized. *Ayliffe.*

SPONTANE'ITY, *n.* [Fr. *spontaneité*; It. *spontaneità*; L. *sponte*, of free will.]

Voluntariness; the quality of being of free will or accord. *Dryden.*

SPONTA'NEOUS, *a.* [L. *spontaneus*, from *sponte*, of free will.]

1. Voluntary; acting by its own impulse or will without the incitement of any thing external; acting of its own accord; as *spontaneous* motion. *Milton.*

2. Produced without being planted, or without human labor; as a *spontaneous* growth of wood.

Spontaneous combustion, a taking fire of itself. Thus oiled canvas, oiled wool, and many other combustible substances, when suffered to remain for some time in a confined state, suddenly take fire, or undergo *spontaneous combustion.*

SPONTA'NEOUSLY, *adv.* Voluntarily; of his own will or accord; *used of animals*; as, he acts *spontaneously.*

2. By its own force or energy; without the impulse of a foreign cause; *used of things.*

Whey turns *spontaneously* acid. *Arbuthnot.*

SPONTA'NEOUSNESS, *n.* Voluntariness; freedom of will; accord unconstrained; *applied to animals.*

2. Freedom of acting without a foreign cause; *applied to things.*

SPONTOON', *n.* [Fr. Sp. *esponton*; It. *spontaneo.*]

A kind of half pike; a military weapon borne by officers of infantry.

SPOOL, *n.* [G. *spule*; D. *spoel*; Dan. Sw. *spole.*]

A piece of cane or reed, or a hollow cylinder of wood with a ridge at each end; used by weavers to wind their yarn upon in order to slaie it and wind it on the beam. The spool is larger than the quill, on which yarn is wound for the shuttle. But in manufactories, the word may be differently applied.

SPOOL, *v. t.* To wind on spools.

SPOOM, *v. i.* To be driven swiftly; probably a mistake for *spoon.* [See *Spoon*, the verb.]

SPOON, *n.* [Ir. *sponog.*] A small domestic utensil, with a bowl or concave part and a handle, for dipping liquids; as a tea *spoon*; a table *spoon.*

2. An instrument consisting of a bowl or hollow iron and a long handle, used for taking earth out of holes dug for setting posts.

SPOON, *v. i.* To put before the wind in a gale. [*I believe not now used.*]

SPOON'-BILL, *n.* [*spoon* and *bill.*] A fowl of the grallic order, and genus Platatea, so named from the shape of its bill, which is somewhat like a spoon or spatula. Its plumage is white and beautiful.

SPOON'-DRIFT, *n.* In *seamen's language*, a showery sprinkling of sea water, swept from the surface in a tempest. *Mar. Dict.*

SPOON'FUL, *n.* [*spoon* and *full.*] As much as a spoon contains or is able to contain; as a tea *spoonful*; a table *spoonful*.

2. A small quantity of a liquid. *Arbuthnot.*

SPOON'-MEAT, *n.* [*spoon* and *meat.*] Food that is or must be taken with a spoon; liquid food.

Diet most upon *spoon-meats*. *Harvey.*

SPOON'-WORT, *n.* A plant of the genus Cochlearia; scurvy grass.

SPORAD'IC, SPORAD'ICAL, *a.* [Fr. *sporadique*; Gr. σποραδικος, separate, scattered; whence certain isles of Greece were called *Sporades*.]

Separate; single; scattered; used only in reference to diseases. A *sporadic* disease, is one which occurs in particular persons and places, in distinction from an epidemic, which affects persons generally or in great numbers.

Sporadic diseases are opposed to epidemics, as accidental, scattered complaints, neither general nor contagious. *Parr.*

SPORT, *n.* [D. *boert*, jest; *boerten*, to jest; *boertig*, merry, facetious, jocular.]

1. That which diverts and makes merry; play; game; diversion; also, mirth. The word signifies both the cause and the effect; that which produces mirth, and the mirth or merriment produced.

Her *sports* were such as carried riches of knowledge upon the stream of delight. *Sidney.*

Here the word denotes the *cause* of amusement.

They called for Samson out of the prison-house; and he made them *sport*. Judges xvi.

Here sport is the *effect*.

2. Mock; mockery; contemptuous mirth.

Then make *sport* at me, then let me be your jest. *Shak.*

They made a *sport* of his prophets. *Esdras.*

3. That with which one plays, or which is driven about.

To flitting leaves, the *sport* of every wind. *Dryden.*

Never does man appear to greater disadvantage than when he is the *sport* of his own ungoverned passions. *J. Clarke.*

4. Play; idle jingle.

An author who should introduce such a *sport* of words upon our stage, would meet with small applause. *Broome.*

5. Diversion of the field, as fowling, hunting, fishing. *Clarendon.*

In sport. To do a thing *in sport*, is to do it in jest, for play or diversion.

So is the man that deceiveth his neighbor, and saith, am not I *in sport?* Prov. xxvi.

SPORT, *v. t.* To divert; to make merry; *used with the reciprocal pronoun.*

Against whom do ye *sport yourselves?* Is. lvii.

2. To represent by any kind of play.

Now *sporting* on thy lyre the love of youth. *Dryden.*

SPORT, *v. i.* To play; to frolick; to wanton.

See the brisk lambs that *sport* along the mead. *Anon.*

2. To trifle. The man that laughs at religion *sports* with his own salvation.

SPORTER, *n.* One who sports.

SPORTFUL, *a.* Merry; frolicksome; full of jesting; indulging in mirth or play; as a *sportful* companion.

Down he alights among the *sportful* herd. *Milton.*

2. Ludicrous; done in jest or for mere play.

These are no *sportful* productions of the soil. *Bentley.*

SPORTFULLY, *adv.* In mirth; in jest; for the sake of diversion; playfully.

SPORTFULNESS, *n.* Play; merriment; frolick; a playful disposition; playfulness; as the *sportfulness* of kids and lambs.

SPORTIVE, *a.* Gay; merry; wanton; frolicksome.

Is it I
That drive thee from the *sportive* court? *Shak.*

2. Inclined to mirth; playful; as a *sportive* humor.

SPORTIVENESS, *n.* Playfulness; mirth; merriment. *Walton.*

2. Disposition to mirth.

SPORTLESS, *a.* Without sport or mirth; joyless.

SPORTSMAN, *n.* [*sport* and *man.*] One who pursues the sports of the field; one who hunts, fishes and fowls.

2. One skilled in the sports of the field. *Addison.*

SPORT'ULARY, *a.* [from L. *sporta*, a basket, an alms-basket.]

Subsisting on alms or charitable contributions. [*Little used.*] *Hall.*

SPORT'ULE, *n.* [L. *sportula*, a little basket.]

An alms; a dole; a charitable gift or contribution. [*Not in use.*] *Ayliffe.*

SPOT, *n.* [D. *spat*, a spot, spavin, a pop-gun; *spatten*, to *spot*, to *spatter*; Dan. *spette*, a spot, and *spet*, a pecker; *svart spet*, a woodpecker. We see this word is of the family of *spatter*, and that the radical sense is to throw or thrust. A *spot* is made by spattering or sprinkling.]

1. A mark on a substance made by foreign matter; a speck; a blot; a place discolored. The least *spot* is visible on white paper.

2. A stain on character or reputation; something that soils purity; disgrace; reproach; fault; blemish.

Yet Chloe sure was form'd without a *spot*. *Pope.*

See 1 Pet. i. 17. Eph. v. 27.

3. A small extent of space; a place; any particular place.

The *spot* to which I point is paradise. *Milton.*

Fix'd to one *spot*. *Otway.*

So we say, a *spot* of ground, a *spot* of grass or flowers; meaning a place of small extent.

4. A place of a different color from the ground; as the *spots* of a leopard.

5. A variety of the common domestic pigeon, so called from a spot on its head just above its beak.

6. A dark place on the disk or face of the sun or of a planet.

7. A lucid place in the heavens.

Upon the spot, immediately; before moving; without changing place. [So the French say, *sur le champ.*]

It was determined *upon the spot*. *Swift.*

SPOT, *v. t.* To make a visible mark with some foreign matter; to discolor; to stain; as, to *spot* a garment; to *spot* paper.

2. To patch by way of ornament. *Addison.*

3. To stain; to blemish; to taint; to disgrace; to tarnish; as reputation.

My virgin life no *spotted* thoughts shall stain. *Sidney.*

To spot timber, is to cut or chip it, in preparation for hewing.

SPOT'LESS, *a.* Free from spots, foul matter or discoloration.

2. Free from reproach or impurity; pure; untainted; innocent; as a *spotless* mind; *spotless* behavior.

A *spotless* virgin and a faultless wife. *Waller.*

SPOT'LESSNESS, *n.* Freedom from spot or stain; freedom from reproach. *Donne.*

SPOT'TED, *pp.* Marked with spots or places of a different color from the ground; as a *spotted* beast or garment.

SPOT'TEDNESS, *n.* The state or quality of being spotted.

SPOT'TER, *n.* One that makes spots.

SPOT'TINESS, *n.* The state or quality of being spotty.

SPOT'TING, *ppr.* Marking with spots; staining.

SPOT'TY, *a.* Full of spots; marked with discolored places.

SPOUS'AGE, *n.* [See *Spouse.*] The act of espousing. [*Not used.*]

SPOUS'AL, *a.* [from *spouse.*] Pertaining to marriage; nuptial; matrimonial; conjugal; connubial; bridal; as *spousal* rites; *spousal* ornaments. *Pope.*

SPOUS'AL, *n.* [Fr. *epousailles*; Sp. *esponsales*; L. *sponsalia*. See *Spouse.*]

Marriage; nuptials. It is now generally used in the plural; as the *spousals* of Hippolita. *Dryden.*

SPOUSE, *n.* spouz. [Fr. *epouse*; Sp. *esposo*, *esposa*; It. *sposo*, *sposa*; L. *sponsus*, *sponsa*, from *spondeo*, to engage; Ir. *posam*, id. It appears that *n* in *spondeo*, is not radical, or that it has been lost in other languages. The sense of the root is to *put* together, to bind. In Sp. *esposas* signifies manacles.]

One engaged or joined in wedlock; a married person, husband or wife. We say of a man, that he is the *spouse* of such a woman; or of a woman, she is the *spouse* of such a man. *Dryden.*

SPOUSE, *v. t.* spouz. To wed; to espouse. [*Little used.* See *Espouse.*] *Chaucer.*

SPOUS'ED, *pp.* Wedded; joined in marriage; married; but seldom used. The word used in lieu of it is *espoused*. *Milton.*

SPOUSELESS, *a.* spouz'less. Destitute of a husband or of a wife; as a *spouseless* king or queen. *Pope.*

SPOUT, *n.* [D. *spuit*, a spout; *spuiten*, to spout. In G. *spützen* is to *spit*, and *spotten* is to mock, banter, sport. These are of one family; *spout* retaining nearly the primary and literal meaning. Class Bd. See *Bud* and *Pout.*]

1. A pipe, or a projecting mouth of a vessel, useful in directing the stream of a liquid poured out; as the *spout* of a pitcher, of a tea pot or water pot.

2. A pipe conducting water from another pipe, or from a trough on a house.

3. A violent discharge of water raised in a column at sea, like a whirlwind, or by a whirlwind. [See *Water-spout.*]

SPOUT, *v. t.* To throw out, as iquids through a narrow orifice or pipe; as, an elephant *spouts* water from his trunk.

Next on his belly floats the mighty whale—
He *spouts* the tide. *Creech.*

2. To throw out words with affected gravity; to mouth. *Beaum.*

SPOUT, *v. i.* To issue with violence, as a liquid through a narrow orifice or from a spout; as, water *spouts* from a cask or a spring; blood *spouts* from a vein.

All the glittering hill
Is bright with *spouting* rills. *Thomson.*

SPOUT'ED, *pp.* Thrown in a stream from a pipe or narrow orifice.

SPOUT'ING, *ppr.* Throwing in a stream from a pipe or narrow opening; pouring out words violently or affectedly.

SPOUT'ING, *n.* The act of throwing out, as a liquid from a narrow opening; a violent or affected speech; a harangue.

SPRAG, *a.* Vigorous; sprightly. [*Local.*]

[*Note.* In America, this word is, in popular language, pronounced *spry*, which is a contraction of *sprigh*, in *sprightly*.]

SPRAG, *n.* A young salmon. [*Local.*] *Grose.*

SPRAIN, *v. t.* [probably Sw. *sprănga*, to break or loosen; Dan. *sprenger*, to *spring*, to burst or crack; or from the same root.]

To overstrain the ligaments of a joint; to stretch the ligaments so as to injure them, but without luxation or dislocation. *Gay. Encyc.*

SPRAIN, *n.* An excessive strain of the ligaments of a joint without dislocation. *Temple.*

SPRA'INED, *pp.* Injured by excessive straining.

SPRA'INING, *ppr.* Injuring by excessive extension.

SPRAINTS, *n.* The dung of an otter. *Dict.*

SPRANG, *pret.* of *spring*; but *sprung* is more generally used.

SPRAT, *n.* [D. *sprot*; G. *sprotte*; Ir. *sproth.*]

A small fish of the species Clupea.

SPRAWL, *v. i.* [The origin and affinities of this word are uncertain. It may be a contracted word.]

1. To spread and stretch the body carelessly in a horizontal position; to lie with the limbs stretched out or struggling. We say, a person lies *sprawling*; or he *sprawls* on the bed or on the ground. *Hudibras.*

2. To move, when lying down, with awkward extension and motions of the limbs; to scrabble or scramble in creeping.

The birds were not fledged; but in *sprawling* and struggling to get clear of the flame, down they tumbled. *L'Estrange.*

3. To widen or open irregularly, as a body of horse.

SPRAWL'ING, *ppr.* Lying with the limbs awkwardly stretched; creeping with awkward motions; struggling with contorsion of the limbs.

2. Widening or opening irregularly, as cavalry.

SPRAY, *n.* [probably allied to *sprig*. The radical sense is a shoot. Class Rg.]

1. A small shoot or branch; or the extremity of a branch. Hence in England, spray-faggots are bundles of small branches, used as fuel. *Encyc.*

2. Among *seamen*, the water that is driven from the top of a wave in a storm, which spreads and flies in small particles. It differs from *spoon-drift*; as *spray* is only occasional, whereas *spoon-drift* flies continually along the surface of the sea.

SPREAD, SPRED, *v. t.* pret. and pp. *spread* or *spred*. [Sax. *sprædan*, *spredan*; Dan. *spreder*; Sw. *sprida*; D. *spreiden*; G. *spreiten*. This is probably formed on the root of *broad*, G. *breit*; *breiten*, to spread. The more correct orthography is *spred.*]

1. To extend in length and breadth, or in breadth only; to stretch or expand to a broader surface; as, to *spread* a carpet or a table cloth; to *spread* a sheet on the ground.

2. To extend; to form into a plate; as, to *spread* silver. Jer. x.

3. To set; to place; to pitch; as, to *spread* a tent. Gen. xxxiii.

4. To cover by extending something; to reach every part.

And an unusual paleness *spreads* her face. *Granville.*

5. To extend; to shoot to a greater length in every direction, so as to fill or cover a wider space.

The stately trees fast *spread* their branches. *Milton.*

6. To divulge; to propagate; to publish; as news or fame; to cause to be more extensively known; as, to *spread* a report.

In this use, the word is often accompanied with *abroad.*

They, when they had departed, *spread abroad* his fame in all that country. Matt. ix.

7. To propagate; to cause to affect greater numbers; as, to *spread* a disease.

8. To emit; to diffuse; as emanations or effluvia; as, odoriferous plants *spread* their fragrance.

9. To disperse; to scatter over a larger surface; as, to *spread* manure; to *spread* plaster or lime on the ground.

10. To prepare; to set and furnish with provisions; as, to *spread* a table. God *spread* a table for the Israelites in the wilderness.

11. To open; to unfold; to unfurl; to stretch; as, to *spread* the sails of a ship.

SPREAD, SPRED, *v. i.* To extend itself in length and breadth, in all directions, or in breadth only; to be extended or stretched. The larger elms *spread* over a space of forty or fifty yards in diameter; or the shade of the larger elms *spreads* over that space. The larger lakes in America *spread* over more than fifteen hundred square miles.

Plants, if they *spread* much, are seldom tall. *Bacon.*

2. To be extended by drawing or beating; as, a metal *spreads* with difficulty.

3. To be propagated or made known more extensively. Ill reports sometimes *spread* with wonderful rapidity.

4. To be propagated from one to another; as, a disease *spreads* into all parts of a city. The yellow fever of American cities has not been found to *spread* in the country.

SPREAD, SPRED, *n.* Extent; compass.

I have a fine *spread* of improvable land. *Addison.*

2. Expansion of parts.

No flower has that *spread* of the woodbind. *Bacon.*

SPREADER, SPRED'DER, *n.* One that spreads, extends, expands or propagates; as a *spreader* of disease. *Hooker.*

2. One that divulges; one that causes to be more generally known; a publisher; as a *spreader* of news or reports. *Swift.*

SPREADING, SPRED'DING, *ppr.* Extending; expanding; propagating; divulging; dispersing; diffusing.

2. *a.* Extending or extended over a large space; wide; as the *spreading* oak.

Gov. Winthrop and his associates at Charlestown had for a church a large *spreading* tree. *B. Trumbull.*

SPREADING, SPRED'DING, *n.* The act of extending, dispersing or propagating.

SPRENT, *pp.* Sprinkled. *Obs.* [See *Sprinkle.*] *Spenser.*

SPRIG, *n.* [W. *ysbrig*; *ys*, a prefix, and *brig*, top, summit; that is, a shoot, or shooting to a point. Class Brg.]

1. A small shoot or twig of a tree or other plant; a spray; as a *sprig* of laurel or of parsley.

2. A brad, or nail without a head. [*Local.*]

3. The representation of a small branch in embroidery.

4. A small eye-bolt ragged at the point. *Encyc.*

SPRIG, *v. t.* To mark or adorn with the representation of small branches; to work with sprigs; as, to *sprig* muslin.

SPRIG-CRYSTAL, *n.* Crystal found in the form of a hexangular column, adhering to the stone, and terminating at the other end in a point. *Woodward.*

SPRIG'GED, *pp.* Wrought with representations of small twigs.

SPRIG'GING, *ppr.* Working with sprigs.

SPRIG'GY, *a.* Full of sprigs or small branches.

SPRIGHT, SPRITE, *n.* [G. *spriet*, spirit. It should be written *sprite.*]

1. A spirit; a shade; a soul; an incorporeal agent.

Forth he call'd, out of deep darkness dread,
Legions of *sprights*. *Spenser.*
And gaping graves receiv'd the guilty *spright*. *Dryden.*

2. A walking spirit; an apparition. *Locke.*

3. Power which gives cheerfulness or courage.

Hold thou my heart, establish thou my
sprights. [*Not in use.*] *Sidney.*

4. An arrow. [*Not in use.*] *Bacon.*

SPRIGHT, *v. t.* To haunt, as a spright. [*Not used.*] *Shak.*

SPRIGHTFUL, *a.* [This word seems to be formed on the root of *sprag*, a local word, pronounced in America, *spry*. It belongs to the family of *spring* and *sprig.*]

Lively; brisk; nimble; vigorous; gay.

Spoke like a *sprightful* noble gentleman. *Shak.*

Steeds *sprightful* as the light. *Cowley.*

[This word is little used in America. We use *sprightly* in the same sense.]

SPRIGHTFULLY, *adv.* Briskly; vigorously. *Shak.*

SPRIGHTFULNESS, *n.* Briskness; liveliness; vivacity. *Hammond.*

SPRIGHTLESS, *a.* Destitute of life; dull; sluggish; as virtue's *sprightless* cold. *Cowley.*

SPRIGHTLINESS, *n.* [from *sprightly.*] Liveliness; life; briskness; vigor; activity; gayety; vivacity.

In dreams, with what *sprightliness* and alacrity does the soul exert herself. *Addison.*

SPRIGHTLY, *a.* Lively; brisk; animated; vigorous; airy; gay; as a *sprightly* youth; a *sprightly* air; a *sprightly* dance.

The *sprightly* Sylvia trips along the green. *Pope.*

And *sprightly* wit and love inspires. *Dryden.*

SPRING, *v. i.* pret. *sprung*, [*sprang*, not wholly obsolete;] pp. *sprung*. [Sax. *springan*; D. G. *springen*; Dan. *springer*; Sw. *springa*; from the root *Brg*, or *Rg*; *n* probably being casual. The primary sense is to leap, to shoot.]

1. To vegetate and rise out of the ground; to begin to appear; as vegetables.

To satisfy the desolate ground, and cause the bud of the tender herb to *spring forth.* Job xxxviii.

In this sense, *spring* is often or usually followed by *up*, *forth* or *out.*

2. To begin to grow.

The teeth of the young not *sprung*— *Ray.*

3. To proceed, as from the seed or cause.

Much more good of sin shall *spring.* *Milton.*

4. To arise; to appear; to begin to appear or exist.

When the day began to *spring*, they let her go. Judges xxi.

Do not blast my *springing* hopes. *Rowe.*

5. To break forth; to issue into sight or notice.

O *spring* to light; auspicious babe, be born. *Pope.*

6. To issue or proceed, as from ancestors or from a country. Aaron and Moses *sprung* from Levi.

7. To proceed, as from a cause, reason, principle or other original. The noblest title *springs* from virtue.

They found new hope to *spring*
Out of despair. *Milton.*

8. To grow; to thrive.

What makes all this but Jupiter the king,
At whose command we perish and we *spring.* *Dryden.*

9. To proceed or issue, as from a fountain or source. Water *springs* from reservoirs in the earth. Rivers *spring* from lakes or ponds.

10. To leap; to bound; to jump.

The mountain stag that *springs*
From highth to highth, and bounds along the plains— *Philips.*

11. To fly back; to start; as, a bow when bent, *springs* back by its elastic power.

12. To start or rise suddenly from a covert.

Watchful as fowlers when their game will *spring.* *Otway.*

13. To shoot; to issue with speed and violence.

And sudden light
Spring through the vaulted roof— *Dryden.*

14. To bend or wind from a straight direction or plane surface. Our mechanics say, a piece of timber or a plank *springs* in seasoning.

To spring at, to leap towards; to attempt to reach by a leap.

To spring in, to rush in; to enter with a leap or in haste.

To spring forth, to leap out; to rush out.

To spring on or *upon*, to leap on; to rush on with haste or violence; to assault.

SPRING, *v. t.* To start or rouse, as game; to cause to rise from the earth or from a covert; as, to *spring* a pheasant.

2. To produce quickly or unexpectedly.

The nurse, surpris'd with fright,
Starts up and leaves her bed, and *springs* a light. *Dryden.*

[*I have never heard such an expression.*]

3. To start; to contrive or to produce or propose on a sudden; to produce unexpectedly.

The friends to the cause *sprang* a new project. *Swift.*

[In lieu of *spring*, the people in the U. States generally use *start*; to *start* a new project.]

4. To cause to explode; as, to *spring* a mine. *Addison.*

5. To burst; to cause to open; as, to *spring* a leak. When it is said, a vessel has *sprung a leak*, the meaning is, the leak has then commenced.

6. To crack; as, to *spring* a mast or a yard.

7. To cause to close suddenly, as the parts of a trap; as, to *spring* a trap.

To spring a butt, in seamen's language, to loosen the end of a plank in a ship's bottom.

To spring the luff, when a vessel yields to the helm, and sails nearer to the wind than before. *Mar. Dict.*

To spring a fence, for *to leap a fence*, is not a phrase used in this country. *Thomson.*

To spring an arch, to set off, begin or commence an arch from an abutment or pier.

SPRING, *n.* A leap; a bound; a jump; as of an animal.

The pris'ner with a *spring* from prison broke. *Dryden.*

2. A flying back; the resilience of a body recovering its former state by its elasticity; as the *spring* of a bow.

3. Elastic power or force. The soul or the mind requires relaxation, that it may recover its natural *spring.*

Heav'ns! what a *spring* was in his arm. *Dryden.*

4. An elastic body; a body which, when bent or forced from its natural state, has the power of recovering it; as the *spring* of a watch or clock.

5. Any active power; that by which action or motion is produced or propagated.

—Like nature letting down the *springs* of life. *Dryden.*

Our author shuns by vulgar *springs* to move
The hero's glory— *Pope.*

6. A fountain of water; an issue of water from the earth, or the bason of water at the place of its issue. *Springs* are temporary or perennial. From *springs* proceed rivulets, and rivulets united form rivers. Lakes and ponds are usually fed by *springs.*

7. The place where water usually issues from the earth, though no water is there. Thus we say, a *spring* is dry.

8. A source; that from which supplies are drawn. The real christian has in his own breast a perpetual and inexhaustible *spring* of joy.

The sacred *spring* whence right and honor stream. *Davies.*

9. Rise; original; as the *spring* of the day. 1 Sam. ix.

10. Cause; original. The *springs* of great events are often concealed from common observation.

11. The season of the year when plants begin to vegetate and rise; the vernal season. This season comprehends the months of March, April and May, in the middle latitudes north of the equator.

12. In *seamen's language*, a crack in a mast or yard, running obliquely or transversely. [In the sense of *leak*, I believe it is not used.]

13. A rope passed out of a ship's stern and attached to a cable proceeding from her bow, when she is at anchor. It is intended to bring her broadside to bear upon some object. A spring is also a rope extending diagonally from the stern of one ship to the head of another, to make one ship sheer off to a greater distance. *Mar. Dict.*

14. A plant; a shoot; a young tree. [*Not in use.*] *Spenser.*

15. A youth. [*Not in use.*] *Spenser.*

16. A hand; a shoulder of pork. [*Not in use.*] *Beaum.*

SPRING'AL, *n.* A youth. [*Not in use.*] *Spenser.*

SPRING'-BOK, *n.* [D. *spring* and *bok*, a buck or he-goat.] An African animal of the antelope kind. *Barrow.*

SPRINGE, *n. sprinj.* [from *spring.*] A gin; a noose; which being fastened to an elastic body, is drawn close with a sudden spring, by which means it catches a bird.

SPRINGE, *v. t.* To catch in a springe; to ensnare. *Beaum.*

SPRING'ER, *n.* One who springs; one that rouses game.

2. A name given to the grampus.

3. In *architecture*, the rib of a groin or concentrated vault.

SPRING'-HALT, *n.* [*spring* and *halt.*] A kind of lameness in which a horse twitches up his legs. *Shak.*

SPRING'-HEAD, *n.* A fountain or source. [*Useless.*] *Herbert.*

SPRING'INESS, *n.* [from *springy.*] Elasticity; also, the power of springing.

2. The state of abounding with springs; wetness; spunginess; as of land.

SPRING'ING, *ppr.* Arising; shooting up; leaping; proceeding; rousing.

Springing use, in law, a contingent use; a use which may arise upon a contingency. *Blackstone.*

SPRING'ING, *n.* The act or process of leaping, arising, issuing or proceeding.

2. Growth; increase. Ps. lxv.

3. In *building*, the side of an arch contiguous to the part on which it rests.

SPRIN'GLE, *n.* A springe; a noose. [*Not in use.*] *Carew.*

SPRING'-TIDE, *n.* [*spring* and *tide.*] The tide which happens at or soon after the new and full moon, which rises higher than common tides. *Mar. Dict. Dryden.*

SPRING'-WHEAT, *n.* [*spring* and *wheat.*] A species of wheat to be sown in the spring; so called in distinction from *winter* wheat.

SPRING'Y, *a.* [from *spring.*] Elastic; possessing the power of recovering itself when bent or twisted.

2. Having great elastic power. *Arbuthnot.*
3. Having the power to leap; able to leap far.
4. Abounding with springs or fountains; wet; spungy; as *springy* land.

SPRINK'LE, *v. t.* [Sax. *sprengan*; D. *sprenkelen, sprengen*; G. *sprengen*; Dan. *sprinkler*; Ir. *spreighim*. The L. *spargo* may be the same word with the letters transposed, *n* being casual. Class Brg.]
1. To scatter; to disperse; as a liquid or a dry substance composed of fine separable particles; as, Moses *sprinkled* handfuls of ashes towards heaven. Ex. ix.
2. To scatter on; to disperse on in small drops or particles; to besprinkle; as, to *sprinkle* the earth with water; to *sprinkle* a floor with sand; to *sprinkle* paper with iron filings.
3. To wash; to cleanse; to purify.

Having our hearts *sprinkled* from an evil conscience. Heb. x.

SPRINK'LE, *v. i.* To perform the act of scattering a liquid or any fine substance, so that it may fall in small particles.

The priest shall *sprinkle* of the oil with his fingers. Lev. xiv.

Baptism may well enough be performed by *sprinkling* or effusion of water. *Ayliffe.*

2. To rain moderately; as, it *sprinkles*.

SPRINK'LE, *n.* A small quantity scattered; also, an utensil for sprinkling. *Spenser.*

SPRINK'LED, *pp.* Dispersed in small particles, as a liquid or as dust.
2. Having a liquid or a fine substance scattered over.

SPRINK'LER, *n.* One that sprinkles.

SPRINK'LING, *ppr.* Dispersing, as a liquid or as dust.
2. Scattering on, in fine drops or particles.

SPRINK'LING, *n.* The act of scattering in small drops or parcels. *Hall.*
2. A small quantity falling in distinct drops or parts, or coming moderately; as a *sprinkling* of rain or snow.

SPRIT, *v. t.* [Sax. *sprytlan*, to sprout; D. *spruiten*; G. *spriessen*; Dan. *spruder*, *sproyter*, to spurt; Sw. *spritta*, to start. It is of the same family as *sprout*. Class Brd.]
To throw out with force from a narrow orifice; to eject; to spirt. [*Not in use.* See *Spurt.*]

SPRIT, *v. i.* To sprout; to bud; to germinate; as barley steeped for malt. *Mortimer.*

SPRIT, *n.* A shoot; a sprout. *Mortimer.*
2. [D. *spriet.*] A small boom, pole or spar which crosses the sail of a boat diagonally from the mast to the upper aftmost corner, which it is used to extend and elevate. *Mar. Dict.*

SPRITE, *n.* [If from G. *spriet*, this is the most correct orthography. The Welsh has *ysbrid*, a spirit.] A spirit.

SPRI'TEFUL. [See *Sprightful.*]

SPRI'TEFULLY. [See *Sprightfully.*]

SPRI'TELINESS. [See *Sprightliness.*]

SPRI'TELY. [See *Sprightly.*]

SPRIT'-SAIL, *n.* [*sprit* and *sail.*] The sail extended by a sprit.
2. A sail attached to a yard which hangs under the bowsprit. *Mar. Dict.*

SPROD, *n.* A salmon in its second year. *Chambers.*

SPRONG, *old pret.* of *spring*. [Dutch.] [*Not in use.*]

SPROUT, *v. i.* [D. *spruiten*; G. *sprossen*; Sax. *spryttan*; Sp. *brotar*, the same word without *s*. See *Sprit.*]
1. To shoot, as the seed of a plant; to germinate; to push out new shoots. A grain that *sprouts* in ordinary temperature in ten days, may by an augmentation of heat be made to *sprout* in forty eight hours. The stumps of trees often *sprout*, and produce a new forest. Potatoes will *sprout* and produce a crop, although pared and deprived of all their buds or eyes.
2. To shoot into ramifications.

Vitriol is apt to *sprout* with moisture. *Bacon.*

3. To grow, like shoots of plants.

And on the ashes *sprouting* plumes appear. *Tickel.*

SPROUT, *n.* The shoot of a plant; a shoot from the seed, or from the stump or from the root of a plant or tree. The *sprouts* of the cane, in Jamaica are called *ratoons*. *Edwards, W. Ind.*
2. A shoot from the end of a branch. The young shoots of shrubs are called *sprouts*, and in the forest often furnish browse for cattle.

SPROUTS, *n. plu.* Young coleworts. *Johnson.*

SPRUCE, *a.* Nice; trim; neat without elegance or dignity; formerly applied to things with a serious meaning; now applied to persons only.

He is so *spruce*, that he never can be genteel. *Tatler.*

SPRUCE, *v. t.* To trim; to dress with great neatness.

SPRUCE, *v. i.* To dress one's self with affected neatness.

SPRUCE, *n.* The fir-tree; a name given to a species of evergreen, the *Pinus nigra*, which is used in families to give flavor to beer. It is used by way of decoction, or in the essence.

SPRUCE-BEER, *n.* A kind of beer which is tinctured with spruce, either by means of the essence or by decoction.

SPRU'CELY, *adv.* With extreme or affected neatness.

SPRU'CENESS, *n.* Neatness without taste or elegance; trimness; fineness; quaintness.

SPRUE, *n.* A matter formed in the mouth in certain diseases.
2. In *Scotland*, that which is thrown off in casting metals; scoria.

SPRUG, *v. t.* To make smart. [*Not in use.*]

SPRUNG, *pret.* and *pp.* of *spring*. The man *sprung* over the ditch; the mast is *sprung*; a hero *sprung* from a race of kings.

SPRUNT, *v. i.* To spring up; to germinate; to spring forward. [*Not in use.*]

SPRUNT, *n.* Any thing short and not easily bent. [*Not in use.*]
2. A leap; a spring. [*Not in use.*]
3. A steep ascent in a road. [*Local.*]

SPRUNT, *a.* Active; vigorous; strong; becoming strong. [*Not in use.*]

SPRUNT'LY, *adv.* Vigorously; youthfully; like a young man. [*Not in use.*] *B. Jonson.*

SPRY, *a.* Having great power of leaping or running; nimble; active; vigorous. [This word is in common use in New England, and is doubtless a contraction of *sprig*. See *Sprightly.*]

SPUD, *n.* [Dan. *spyd*, a spear; Ice. *spioot*. It coincides with *spit.*] A short knife. [*Little used.*]
2. Any short thing; in contempt. *Swift.*
3. A tool of the fork kind, used by farmers.

SPUD, *v. t.* To dig or loosen the earth with a spud. [*Local.*]

SPUME, *n.* [L. It. *spuma*; Sp. *espuma.*] Froth; foam; scum; frothy matter raised on liquors or fluid substances by boiling, effervescence or agitation.

SPUME, *v. i.* To froth; to foam.

SPUMES'CENCE, *n.* Frothiness; the state of foaming. *Kirwan.*

SPU'MOUS, } *a.* [L. *spumeus.*] Consisting of froth or scum; foamy.
SPU'MY, }

The *spumy* waves proclaim the wat'ry war. *Dryden.*

The *spumous* and florid state of the blood. *Arbuthnot.*

SPUN, *pret.* and *pp.* of *spin*.

SPUNGE, *n.* [L. *spongia*; Gr. σπογγια; Fr. *eponge*; It. *spugna*; Sp. *esponja*; Sax. *spongea*; D. *spons.*]
1. A porous marine substance, found adhering to rocks, shells, &c. under water, and on rocks about the shore at low water. It is generally supposed to be of animal origin, and it consists of a fibrous reticulated substance, covered by a soft gelatinous matter, but in which no polypes have hitherto been observed. It is so porous as to imbibe a great quantity of water, and is used for various purposes in the arts and in surgery. *Encyc. Cuvier.*
2. In *gunnery*, an instrument for cleaning cannon after a discharge. It consists of a cylinder of wood, covered with lamb skin. For small guns, it is commonly fixed to one end of the handle of the rammer.
3. In *the manege*, the extremity or point of a horse-shoe, answering to the heel.

Pyrotechnical spunge, is made of mushrooms or fungi, growing on old oaks, ash, fir, &c. which are boiled in water, dried and beaten, then put in a strong lye prepared with saltpeter, and again dried in an oven. This makes the black match or tinder brought from Germany. *Encyc.*

SPUNGE, *v. t.* To wipe with a wet spunge; as, to *spunge* a slate.
2. To wipe out with a spunge, as letters or writing.
3. To cleanse with a spunge; as, to *spunge* a cannon.
4. To wipe out completely; to extinguish or destroy.

SPUNGE, *v. i.* To suck in or imbibe, as a spunge.
2. To gain by mean arts, by intrusion or hanging on; as an idler who *spunges* on his neighbor.

SPUNG'ED, *pp.* Wiped with a spunge; wiped out; extinguished.

SPUNG'ER, *n.* One who uses a spunge; a hanger on.

SPUNG'IFORM, *a.* [*spunge* and *form.*] Resembling a spunge; soft and porous; porous.

SPUNG'INESS, *n.* The quality or state of being spungy, or porous like spunge. *Harvey.*

SPUNǴ'ING-HOUSE, *n.* A bailif's house to put debtors in.

SPUNǴ'IOUS, *a.* Full of small cavities, like a spunge; as *spungious* bones. *Cheyne.*

SPUNǴ'Y, *a.* Soft and full of cavities; of an open, loose, pliable texture; as a *spungy* excrescence; *spungy* earth; *spungy* cake; the *spungy* substance of the lungs.

2. Full of small cavities; as *spungy* bones.

3. Wet; drenched; soaked and soft, like spunge.

4. Having the quality of imbibing fluids.

SPUN'-HAY, *n.* Hay twisted into ropes for convenient carriage on a military expedition.

SPUNK, *n.* [probably from *punk.*] Touchwood; wood that readily takes fire. Hence,

2. Vulgarly, an inflammable temper; spirit; as a man of *spunk.* Ill natured observations touched his *spunk.* [*Low.*]

SPUN'-Y'ARN, *n.* Among *seamen*, a line or cord formed of two or three rope yarns twisted.

SPUR, *n.* [Sax. *spur;* D. *spoor;* G. *sporn;* Dan. *spore;* Ir. *spor;* W. *yspardun;* Fr. *eperon;* It. *sprone;* coinciding in elements with *spear.* Class Br.]

1. An instrument having a rowel or little wheel with sharp points, worn on horsemen's heels, to prick the horses for hastening their pace.

> Girt with rusty sword and *spur.* *Hudibras.*

Hence, to *set spurs* to a horse, is to prick him and put him upon a run.

2. Incitement; instigation. The love of glory is the *spur* to heroic deeds.

3. The largest or principal root of a tree; hence perhaps, the short wooden buttress of a post; [that is, in both cases, a shoot.]

4. The hard pointed projection on a cock's leg, which serves as an instrument of defense and annoyance. *Ray.*

5. Something that projects; a snag. *Shak.*

6. In *America*, a mountain that shoots from any other mountain or range of mountains, and extends to some distance in a lateral direction, or at right angles.

7. That which excites. We say, upon the *spur* of the occasion; that is, the circumstances or emergency which calls for immediate action.

8. A sea swallow. *Ray.*

9. The hinder part of the nectary in certain flowers, shaped like a cock's spur. *Martyn.*

10. A morbid shoot or excrescence in grain, particularly in rye. [Fr. *ergot.*]

11. In *old fortifications*, a wall that crosses a part of the rampart and joins to the town wall.

SPUR, *v. t.* [Ir. *sporam.*] To prick with spurs; to incite to a more hasty pace; as, to *spur* a horse.

2. To incite; to instigate; to urge or encourage to action, or to a more vigorous pursuit of an object. Some men are *spurred* to action by the love of glory, others by the love of power. Let affection *spur* us to social and domestic duties. *Locke.*

3. To impel; to drive.

> Love will not be *spurr'd* to what it lothes. *Shak.*

4. To put spurs on.

Spurs of the beams, in a ship, are curving timbers, serving as half beams to support the deck, where whole beams cannot be used.

SPUR, *v. i.* To travel with great expedition.

> The Parthians shall be there,
> And *spurring* from the fight, confess their fear. [*Unusual.*] *Dryden.*

2. To press forward.

> Some bold men—by *spurring* on, refine themselves. *Grew.*

SPUR'GALL, *v. t.* [*spur* and *gall.*] To gall or wound with a spur. *Shak.*

SPUR'GALL, *n.* A place galled or excoriated by much using of the spur.

SPUR'GALLED, *pp.* Galled or hurt by a spur; as a *spurgalled* hackney. *Pope.*

SPURǴE, *n.* [Fr. *epurge;* It. *spurgo*, a purge; from L. *purgo, expurgo.*] A plant of the genus Euphorbia.

SPURǴE-FLAX, *n.* A plant. [L. *thymelæa.*]

SPURǴE-LAUREL, *n.* The *Daphne laureola*, a shrub, a native of Europe.

SPURǴE-OLIVE, *n.* Mezereon, a shrub of the genus Daphne.

SPURǴE-WŎRT, *n.* A plant. [L. *xiphion.*]

SPURǴ'ING, for *purging*, not in use. *B. Jonson.*

SPU'RIOUS, *a.* [L. *spurius.*] Not genuine; not proceeding from the true source, or from the source pretended; counterfeit; false; adulterate. *Spurious* writings are such as are not composed by the authors to whom they are ascribed. *Spurious* drugs are common. The reformed churches reject *spurious* ceremonies and traditions.

2. Not legitimate; bastard; as *spurious* issue. By the laws of England, one begotten and born out of lawful matrimony, is a *spurious* child.

Spurious disease, a disease not of the genuine type, but bearing a resemblance in its symptoms.

SPU'RIOUSLY, *adv.* Counterfeitly; falsely.

SPU'RIOUSNESS, *n.* The state or quality of being counterfeit, false or not genuine; as the *spuriousness* of drugs, of coin or of writings.

2. Illegitimacy; the state of being bastard, or not of legitimate birth; as the *spuriousness* of issue.

SPUR'LING, *n.* A small sea fish.

SPUR'LING-LINE, *n.* Among *seamen*, the line which forms the communication between the wheel and the tell-tale.

SPURN, *v. t.* [Sax. *spurnan;* Ir. *sporam;* L. *sperno, aspernor;* from the root of *spur*, or from kicking.]

1. To kick; to drive back or away, as with the foot. *Shak.*

2. To reject with disdain; to scorn to receive or accept. What multitudes of rational beings *spurn* the offers of eternal happiness!

3. To treat with contempt. *Locke.*

SPURN, *v. i.* To manifest disdain in rejecting any thing; as, to *spurn* at the gracious offers of pardon.

2. To make contemptuous opposition; to manifest disdain in resistance.

> Nay more, to *spurn* at your most royal image. *Shak.*

3. To kick or toss up the heels.

> The drunken chairman in the kennel *spurns.* *Gay.*

SPURN, *n.* Disdainful rejection; contemptuous treatment.

> The insolence of office, and the *spurns*
> That patient merit of the unworthy takes. *Shak.*

SPURN'ED, *pp.* Rejected with disdain; treated with contempt.

SPURN'ER, *n.* One who spurns.

SPURN'EY, *n.* A plant. *Dict.*

SPURN'ING, *ppr.* Rejecting with contempt.

SPURN'-WATER, *n.* In *ships*, a channel at the end of a deck to restrain the water.

SPURRE, *n.* A name of the sea swallow.

SPUR'RED, *pp.* Furnished with spurs.

2. *a.* Wearing spurs, or having shoots like spurs.

SPUR'RER, *n.* One who uses spurs.

SPUR'RIER, *n.* One whose occupation is to make spurs.

SPUR-ROY'AL, *n.* A gold coin, first made in the reign of Edward IV. In the reign of James I. its value was fifteen shillings. Sometimes written *spur-rial* or *ryal.* *Beaum.*

SPUR'RY, *n.* A plant of the genus Spergula.

SPURT, *v. t.* [Sw. *spruta;* Dan. *sprуder* and *sproyter*, to spout, to squirt, to syringe. The English word has suffered a transposition of letters. It is from the root of *sprout*, which see.]

To throw out, as a liquid in a stream; to drive or force out with violence, as a liquid from a pipe or small orifice; as, to *spurt* water from the mouth, or other liquid from a tube.

SPURT, *v. i.* To gush or issue out in a stream, as liquor from a cask; to rush from a confined place in a small stream.

> Then the small jet, which hasty hands unlock,
> *Spurts* in the gard'ner's eyes who turns the cock. *Pope.*

SPURT, *n.* A sudden or violent ejection or gushing of a liquid substance from a tube, orifice or other confined place; a jet.

2. A sudden or short occasion or exigency; sudden effort. [*Vulgar.*]

SPURT'LE, *v. t.* [from *spurt.*] To shoot in a scattering manner. [*Little used.*] *Drayton.*

SPUR'WAY, *n.* [*spur* and *way.*] A horse path; a narrow way; a bridle road; a way for a single beast. [*Not used in the U. States.*]

SPUTA'TION, *n.* [L. *sputo*, to spit.] The act of spitting. [*Not used.*] *Harvey.*

SPU'TATIVE, *a.* [supra.] Spitting much; inclined to spit. [*Not used.*] *Wotton.*

SPUT'TER, *v. i.* [D. *spuiten*, to spout; Sw. *spotta;* L. *sputo*, to spit. It belongs to the root of *spout* and *spit;* of the latter it seems to be a diminutive.]

1. To spit, or to emit saliva from the mouth in small or scattered portions, as in rapid speaking.

2. To throw out moisture in small detached parts; as green wood *sputtering* in the flame. *Dryden.*

3. To fly off in small particles with some crackling or noise.

> When sparkling lamps their *sputtering* lights advance. *Dryden.*

4. To utter words hastily and indistinctly; literally, to *spout small;* to speak so rapidly as to emit saliva.

They could neither of them speak their rage, and so they fell a *sputtering* at one another, like two roasting apples. *Congreve.*

SPUT'TER, *v. t.* To throw out with haste and noise; to utter with indistinctness.

In the midst of caresses—to *sputter* out the basest accusations. *Swift.*

SPUT'TER, *n.* Moist matter thrown out in small particles.

SPUT'TERED, *pp.* Thrown out in small portions, as liquids; uttered with haste and indistinctness, as words.

SPUT'TERER, *n.* One that sputters.

SPUT'TERING, *ppr.* Emitting in small particles; uttering rapidly and indistinctly; speaking hastily; spouting.

SPȲ, *n.* [It. *spia*; Fr. *espion*; Sp. *espia*; D. *spiede*; G. *späher*; Dan. *spejder*; W. *yspeiaw*, to espy, to explore; *yspeithiaw*, to look about; *yspaith*, that is open, visible; *paith*, an opening, a prospect, a glance. Class Bd; unless the word is a contraction, and of Class Sg.]

1. A person sent into an enemy's camp to inspect their works, ascertain their strength and their intentions, to watch their movements, and secretly communicate intelligence to the proper officer. By the laws of war among all civilized nations, a *spy* is subjected to capital punishment.
2. A person deputed to watch the conduct of others. *Dryden.*
3. One who watches the conduct of others.

These wretched *spies* of wit. *Dryden.*

SPȲ, *v. t.* To see; to gain sight of; to discover at a distance, or in a state of concealment. It is the same as *espy*; as, to *spy* land from the mast head of a ship.

As tiger *spied* two gentle fawns. *Milton.*

One in reading skipped over all sentences where he *spied* a note of admiration. *Swift.*

2. To discover by close search or examination; as, a lawyer in examining the pleadings in a case, *spies* a defect.
3. To explore; to view, inspect and examine secretly; as a country; usually with *out.*

Moses sent to *spy out* Jaazer, and they took the villages thereof. Num. xxi.

SPȲ, *v. i.* To search narrowly; to scrutinize.

It is my nature's plague
To *spy* into abuse. *Shak.*

SPȲ'-BOAT, *n.* [*spy* and *boat.*] A boat sent to make discoveries and bring intelligence. *Arbuthnot.*

SPȲ'-GLASS, *n.* The popular name of a small telescope, useful in viewing distant objects.

SQUAB, *a.* [In G. *quappe* is a quab, an eelpout; *quabbelig*, plump, sleek; *quabbeln*, to be plump or sleek, and to vibrate, Eng. to *wabble*; Dan. *quabbe*, an eelpout; *quopped.* fat, plump, jolly, our vulgar *whopping*; *quopper*, to shake.]

1. Fat; thick; plump; bulky.

Nor the *squab* daughter, nor the wife were nice. *Betterton.*

2. Unfledged; unfethered; as a *squab* pigeon. *King.*

SQUAB, *n.* A young pigeon or dove. [This word is in common or general use in America, and almost the only sense in which it is used is the one here given. It is sometimes used in the sense of fat, plump.]

2. A kind of sofa or couch; a stuffed cushion. [*Not used in America.*]

SQUAB, *adv.* Striking at once; with a heavy fall; plump.

The eagle dropped the tortoise *squab* upon a rock. [*Low and not used.*] *L'Estrange.*

[The vulgar word *awhap* or *whop*, is used in a like sense in America. It is found in Chaucer.]

SQUAB, *v. i.* To fall plump; to strike at one dash, or with a heavy stroke. [*Not used.*]

SQUAB'BISH, } *a.* Thick; fat; heavy.
SQUAB'BY, } *Harvey.*

SQUAB'BLE, *v. i.* [I know not the origin of this word, but it seems to be from the root of *wabble*; G. *quabbeln*, to vibrate, to quake, to be sleek. See *Squab.*]

1. To contend for superiority; to scuffle; to struggle; as, two persons *squabble* in sport. *Shak.*
2. To contend; to wrangle; to quarrel. *Glanville.*
3. To debate peevishly; to dispute. If there must be disputes, it is less criminal to *squabble* than to murder.

[*Squabble* is not an elegant word in any of its uses. In some of them it is low.]

SQUAB'BLE, *n.* A scuffle; a wrangle; a brawl; a petty quarrel. *Arbuthnot.*

SQUAB'BLER, *n.* A contentious person; a brawler.

SQUAB'BLING, *ppr.* Scuffling; contending; wrangling.

SQUAB'-PIE, *n.* [*squab* and *pie.*] A pie made of squabs or young pigeons.

SQUAD, *n.* [Fr. *escouade.*] A company of armed men; a party learning military exercise; any small party.

SQUAD'RON, *n.* [Fr. *escadron*; It. *squadra*, a squadron, a square; Sp. *esquadron*; from L. *quadratus*, square; *quadro*, to square; allied to *quatuor*, four.]

1. In *its primary sense*, a square or square form; and hence, a square body of troops; a body drawn up in a square. So Milton has used the word.

Those half rounding guards
Just met, and closing stood in *squadron* join'd.

[This sense is probably obsolete, unless in poetry.]

2. A body of troops, infantry or cavalry, indefinite in number.
3. A division of a fleet; a detachment of ships of war, employed on a particular expedition; or one third part of a naval armament. *Mar. Dict.*

SQUAD'RONED, *a.* Formed into squadrons or squares. *Milton.*

SQUAL'ID, *a.* [L. *squalidus*, from *squaleo*, to be foul. Qu. W. *qual*, vile.] Foul; filthy; extremely dirty.

Uncomb'd his locks, and *squalid* his attire. *Dryden.*

SQUAL'IDNESS, *n.* Foulness; filthiness.

SQUALL, *v. i.* [Sw. *sqvåla*; Dan. *squaldrer*, to prate. These words are probably of one family; but *squall*, like *squeal*, is probably from the root of Sax. *gyllan*, to creak, or Heb. קול, D. *gillen*, to *yell*; or is formed from *wail.*]

To cry out; to scream or cry violently; as a woman frightened, or a child in anger or distress; as, the infant *squalled.* *Arbuthnot and Pope.*

SQUALL, *n.* A loud scream; a harsh cry. *Pope.*

2. [Sw. *sqval.*] A sudden gust of violent wind. *Mar. Dict.*

SQUALL'ER, *n.* A screamer; one that cries loud.

SQUALL'ING, *ppr.* Crying out harshly; screaming.

SQUALL'Y, *a.* Abounding with squalls; disturbed often with sudden and violent gusts of wind; as *squally* weather.

2. In *agriculture*, broken into detached pieces; interrupted by unproductive spots. [*Local.*]

SQUA'LOR, *n.* [L.] Foulness; filthiness; coarseness. *Burton.*

SQUAM'IFORM, *a.* [L. *squama*, a scale, and *form.*] Having the form or shape of scales.

SQUAMIG'EROUS, *a.* [L. *squamiger*; *squama*, a scale, and *gero*, to bear.] Bearing or having scales.

SQUA'MOUS, *a.* [L. *squamosus.*] Scaly; covered with scales; as the *squamous* cones of the pine. *Woodward.*

SQUAN'DER, *v. t.* [G. *verschwenden*, probably from *wenden*, to turn.]

1. To spend lavishly or profusely; to spend prodigally; to dissipate; to waste without economy or judgment; as, to *squander* an estate.

They often *squander'd*, but they never gave. *Savage.*

The crime of *squandering* health is equal to the folly. *Rambler.*

2. To scatter; to disperse.

Our *squander'd* troops he rallies. *Dryden.*

[*In this application not now used.*]

SQUAN'DERED, *pp.* Spent lavishly and without necessity or use; wasted; dissipated, as property.

SQUAN'DERER, *n.* One who spends his money prodigally, without necessity or use; a spendthrift; a prodigal; a waster; a lavisher. *Locke.*

SQUAN'DERING, *ppr.* Spending lavishly; wasting.

SQUARE, *a.* [W. *cwâr*; Fr. *carré*, *quarré*; perhaps Gr. αρω, contracted from χαρω. This is probably not a contraction of L. *quadratus.*]

1. Having four equal sides and four right angles; as a *square* room; a *square* figure.
2. Forming a right angle; as an instrument for striking lines *square.* *Moxon.*
3. Parallel; exactly suitable; true.

She's a most triumphant lady, if report be *square* to her. [*Unusual.*] *Shak.*

4. Having a straight front, or a frame formed with straight lines; not curving; as a man of a *square* frame; a *square* built man.
5. That does equal justice; exact; fair; honest; as *square* dealing.
6. Even; leaving no balance. Let us make or leave the accounts *square.*

Three square, five square, having three or five equal sides, &c.; an abusive use of *square.*

Square root, in geometry and arithmetic. The square root of a quantity or number is that which, multiplied by itself, produces the square. Thus 7 is the square root of 49, for 7×7=49.

In *seamen's language*, the yards are square, when they are arranged at right angles with the mast or the keel. The yards and sails are said also to be square, when they are of greater extent than usual. *Mar. Dict.*

SQUARE, *n.* A figure having four equal sides and four right angles.

2. An area of four sides, with houses on each side.

The statue of Alexander VII. stands in the large *square* of the town. *Addison.*

3. The content of the side of a figure squared.

4. An instrument among mechanics by which they form right angles, or otherwise measure angles.

5. In *geometry* and *arithmetic*, a square or square number is the product of a number multiplied by itself. Thus 64 is the square of 8, for $8\times8=64$.

6. Rule; regularity; exact proportion; justness of workmanship and conduct.

They of Galatia much more out of *square*. *Hooker.*

I have not kept my *square*. *Shak.*

[*Not in use.*]

7. A square body of troops; a squadron; as the brave *squares* of war. [*Not in use.*] *Shak.*

8. A quaternion; four. [*Not in use.*] *Shak.*

9. Level; equality.

We live not on the *square* with such as these. *Dryden.*

10. In *astrology*, quartile; the position of planets distant ninety degrees from each other. *Obs.* *Milton.*

11. Rule; conformity; accord. I shall break no *squares* with another for a trifle.

Squares go. Let us see how the *squares go*, that is, how the game proceeds; a phrase taken from the game of chess, the chess board being formed with squares. *L'Estrange.*

SQUARE, *v. t.* [Fr. *equarrir* and *carrer.*]

1. To form with four equal sides and four right angles.

2. To reduce to a square; to form to right angles; as, to *square* mason's work.

3. To reduce to any given measure or standard. *Shak.*

4. To adjust; to regulate; to mold; to shape; as, to *square* our actions by the opinions of others; to *square* our lives by the precepts of the gospel.

5. To accommodate; to fit; as, *square* my trial to my strength. *Milton.*

6. To respect in quartile. *Creech.*

7. To make even, so as to leave no difference or balance; as, to *square* accounts; *a popular phrase.*

8. In *arithmetic*, to multiply a number by itself; as, to *square* the number.

9. In *seamen's language*, to *square the yards*, is to place them at right angles with the mast or keel.

SQUARE, *v. i.* To suit; to fit; to quadrate; to accord or agree. His opinions do not *square* with the doctrines of philosophers.

2. To quarrel; to go to opposite sides.

Are you such fools
To *square* for this? *Shak.*

[*Not in use.*]

SQUA'RENESS, *n.* The state of being square; as an instrument to try the *squareness* of work. *Moxon.*

SQUA'RE-RIGGED, *a.* In *seamen's language*, a vessel is square-rigged when her principal sails are extended by yards suspended by the middle, and not by stays, gaffs, booms and lateen yards. Thus a ship and a brig are *square-rigged* vessels. *Mar. Dict.*

SQUA'RE-SAIL, *n.* In *seamen's language*, a sail extended to a yard suspended by the middle. *Mar. Dict.*

SQUA'RISH, *a.* Nearly square. *Pennant.*

SQUAR'ROUS, *a.* [Qu. Gr. εσχαρα, scurf.] In *botany*, scurfy or ragged, or full of scales; rough; jagged. A *squarrous* calyx consists of scales very widely divaricating; a *squarrous leaf* is divided into shreds or jags, raised above the plane of the leaf, and not parallel to it. *Martyn.*

SQUASH, *v. t.* [from the root of *quash*, L. *quasso*, Fr. *casser.*]

To crush; to beat or press into pulp or a flat mass.

SQUASH, *n.* Something soft and easily crushed. *Shak.*

2. [Qu. Gr. σικυος.] A plant of the genus Cucurbita, and its fruit; a culinary vegetable.

3. Something unripe or soft; *in contempt.*

This *squash*, this gentleman. *Shak.*

4. A sudden fall of a heavy soft body. *Arbuthnot.*

5. A shock of soft bodies.

My fall was stopp'd by a terrible *squash*.

[*Vulgar.*] *Swift.*

SQUAT, *v. i.* [W. *yswatiaw*, from *yswad*, a falling or throw; It. *quatto*, squat, close; *quattare*, to squat, to cower, to lurk. It may perhaps be allied to It. *guatare*, to watch, Fr. *guetter*, to *wait*, to watch.]

1. To sit down upon the hams or heels; as a human being.

2. To sit close to the ground; to cower; as an animal.

3. In *Massachusetts* and *some other states of America*, to settle on another's land without pretense of title; a practice very common in the wilderness.

SQUAT, *v. t.* To bruise or make flat by a fall. [*Not in use.*] *Barret.*

SQUAT, *a.* Sitting on the hams or heels; sitting close to the ground; cowering.

Him there they found,
Squat like a toad, close at the ear of Eve. *Milton.*

2. Short and thick, like the figure of an animal squatting.

The head of the squill insect is broad and *squat*. *Grew.*

SQUAT, *n.* The posture of one that sits on his hams, or close to the ground. *Dryden.*

2. A sudden or crushing fall. [*Not in use.*] *Herbert.*

3. A sort of mineral. *Woodward.*

SQUATT, *n.* Among miners, a bed of ore extending but a little distance.

SQUAT'TER, *n.* One that squats or sits close.

2. In *the U. States*, one that settles on new land without a title.

SQUEAK, *v. i.* [Sw. *sqvåka*, to cry like a frog; G. *quieken*; W. *gwiçian*, to squeak. This word probably belongs to the family of *quack*. Class Gk.]

1. To utter a sharp shrill cry, usually of short duration; to cry with an acute tone, as an animal; or to make a sharp noise, as a pipe or quill, a wheel, a door and the like. Wheels *squeak* only when the axle-tree is dry.

Who can endure to hear one of the rough old Romans, *squeaking* through the mouth of an eunuch? *Addison.*

Zoilus calls the companions of Ulysses, the *squeaking* pigs of Homer. *Pope.*

2. To break silence or secrecy for fear or pain; to speak. *Dryden.*

SQUEAK, *n.* A sharp shrill sound suddenly uttered, either of the human voice or of any animal or instrument, such as a child utters in acute pain, or as pigs utter, or as is made by carriage wheels when dry, or by a pipe or reed.

SQUE'AKER, *n.* One that utters a sharp shrill sound.

SQUE'AKING, *ppr.* Crying with a sharp voice; making a sharp sound; as a *squeaking* wheel.

SQUEAL, *v. i.* [This is only a different orthography of *squall*; Ir. *sgal*, a squealing. See *Squall.*]

To cry with a sharp shrill voice. It is used of animals only, and chiefly of swine. It agrees in sense with *squeak*, except that *squeal* denotes a more continued cry than *squeak*, and the latter is not limited to animals. We say, a *squealing* hog or pig, a *squealing* child; but more generally a *squalling* child.

SQUE'ALING, *ppr.* Uttering a sharp shrill sound or voice; as a *squealing* pig.

SQUE'AMISH, *a.* [probably from the root of *wamble.*]

Literally, having a stomach that is easily turned, or that readily nauseates any thing; hence, nice to excess in taste; fastidious; easily disgusted; apt to be offended at trifling improprieties; scrupulous.

Quoth he, that honor's very *squeamish*
That takes a basting for a blemish. *Hudibras.*

His muse is rustic, and perhaps too plain
The men of *squeamish* taste to entertain. *Southern.*

SQUE'AMISHLY, *adv.* In a fastidious manner; with too much niceness.

SQUE'AMISHNESS, *n.* Excessive niceness; vicious delicacy of taste; fastidiousness; excessive scrupulousness.

The thorough-paced politician must presently laugh at the *squeamishness* of his conscience. *South.*

SQUE'ASINESS, *n.* Nausea. [*Not used.*] [See *Queasiness.*]

SQUE'ASY, *a.* Queasy; nice; squeamish; scrupulous. [*Not used.*] [See *Queasy.*]

SQUEEZE, *v. t.* [Arm. *quasqu*, *goasca*; W. *gwasgu.*]

1. To press between two bodies; to press closely; as, to *squeeze* an orange with the fingers or with an instrument; to *squeeze* the hand in friendship.

2. To oppress with hardships, burdens and taxes; to harass; to crush.

In a civil war, people must expect to be *squeezed* with the burden. *L'Estrange.*

3. To hug; to embrace closely.

4. To force between close bodies; to compel or cause to pass; as, to *squeeze* water through felt.

To squeeze out, to force out by pressure, as a liquid.

SQUEEZE, *v. i.* To press; to urge one's way; to pass by pressing; as, to *squeeze* hard to get through a crowd.

2. To crowd.

To squeeze through, to pass through by pressing and urging forward.

SQUEEZE, *n.* Pressure; compression between bodies. *Phillips.*

2. A close hug or embrace.

SQUEE'ZED, *pp.* Pressed between bodies; compressed; oppressed.

SQUEE'ZING, *ppr.* Pressing; compressing; crowding; oppressing.

SQUEE'ZING, *n.* The act of pressing; compression; oppression.

2. That which is forced out by pressure; dregs.

> The dregs and *squeezings* of the brain. *Pope.*

SQUELCH, } *v. t.* To crush. [*A low word*
SQUELSH, } *and not used.*]

SQUELCH, *n.* A heavy fall. [*Low and not used.*] *Hudibras.*

SQUIB, *n.* [This word probably belongs to the family of *whip*; denoting that which is thrown.]

1. A little pipe or hollow cylinder of paper, filled with powder or combustible matter and sent into the air, burning and bursting with a crack; a cracker.

> Lampoons, like *squibs*, may make a present blaze. *Waller.*

> The making and selling of *squibs* is punishable. *Blackstone.*

2. A sarcastic speech or little censorious writing published; a petty lampoon.

3. A pretty fellow. [*Not in use.*]

> The *squibs*, in the common phrase, are called libellers. *Tatler.*

SQUIB, *v. i.* To throw squibs; to utter sarcastic or severe reflections; to contend in petty dispute; as, two members of a society *squib* a little in debate. [*Colloquial.*]

SQUIB'BING, *ppr.* Throwing squibs or severe reflections.

SQUIB'BING, *n.* The act of throwing squibs or severe reflections.

SQUILL, *n.* [Fr. *squille*, L. *squilla*, a squill, a lobster or prawn; It. *squilla*, a squill, a sea-onion, a little bell; *squillare*, to ring; Sp. *esquila*, a small bell, a shrimp.]

1. A plant of the genus Scilla. It has a large acrid bulbous root like an onion, which is used in medicine.

2. A fish, or rather a crustaceous animal, of the genus Cancer. *Encyc.*

3. An insect, called squill insect from its resemblance to the fish, having a long body covered with a crust, the head broad and squat. *Grew.*

SQUIN'ANCY, *n.* [It. *squinanzia*; Fr. *squinancie.*] The quinsy, which see. [*Squinancy* is not used.]

SQUINT, *a.* [D. *schuin*, sloping, oblique; *schuinte*, a slope; W. *ysgeiniaw*, to spread, to sprinkle, to squint, from *ysgain*, to spread, to sprinkle. We see the sense is to deviate from a direct line, to wander or shoot off.]

1. Looking obliquely; having the optic axes directed to different objects.

2. Looking with suspicion. *Spenser.*

SQUINT, *v. i.* To see obliquely.

> Some can *squint* when they will. *Bacon.*

2. To have the axes of the eyes directed to different objects.

3. To slope; to deviate from a true line; to run obliquely. *Kirwan.*

SQUINT, *v. t.* To turn the eye to an oblique position; to look indirectly; as, to *squint* an eye. *Bacon.*

2. To form the eye to oblique vision.

> He gives the web and the pin, *squints* the eye, and makes the hare-lip. *Shak.*

SQUINT'-EYED, *a.* Having eyes that squint; having oblique vision. *Knolles.*

2. Oblique; indirect; malignant; as *squint-eyed* praise. *Denham.*

3. Looking obliquely or by side glances; as *squint-eyed* jealousy or envy.

SQUINTIFE'GO, *n.* Squinting. [*A cant word and not to be used.*] *Dryden.*

SQUINT'ING, *ppr.* Seeing or looking obliquely; looking by side glances.

SQUINT'ING, *n.* The act or habit of looking obliquely.

SQUINT'INGLY, *adv.* With an oblique look; by side glances.

SQUIN'Y, *v. i.* To look squint. [*A cant word not to be used.*] *Shak.*

SQUIR, *v. t. squur.* To throw; to thrust; to drive. *Obs.* *Tatler.*

SQUIRE, *n.* [a popular contraction of *esquire.* See *Esquire.*]

1. In *Great Britain*, the title of a gentleman next in rank to a knight. *Shak.*

2. In *Great Britain*, an attendant on a noble warrior. *Dryden. Pope.*

3. An attendant at court. *Shak.*

4. In *the United States*, the title of magistrates and lawyers. In New-England, it is particularly given to justices of the peace and judges.

5. The title customarily given to gentlemen.

SQUIRE, *v. t.* To attend as a squire. *Chaucer.*

2. In *colloquial language*, to attend as a beau or gallant for aid and protection; as, to *squire* a lady to the gardens.

SQUI'REHOOD, } *n.* The rank and state of
SQUI'RESHIP, } a squire. *Shelton.*

SQUI'RELY, *a.* Becoming a squire. *Shelton.*

SQUIR'REL, *n. squur'rel.* [Fr. *ecureuil*; L. *sciurus*; Gr. σκιουρος, said to be a compound of σκια, shade, and ουρα, tail.]

A small quadruped of the genus Sciurus, order of Glires, and class Mammalia. The squirrel has two cutting teeth in each jaw, four toes on the fore feet, and five on the hind feet. Several species are enumerated. Among these are the gray, the red, and the black squirrel. These animals are remarkably nimble, running up trees and leaping from branch to branch with surprising agility. They subsist on nuts, of which they lay up a store for winter, some of them in hollow trees, others in the earth. Their flesh is delicate food.

SQUIRREL HUNT, *n.* In *America*, the hunting and shooting of squirrels by a company of men.

SQUIRT, *v. t. squurt.* [from some root in Class *Gr* or *Wr*, signifying to throw or drive.]

To eject or drive out of a narrow pipe or orifice, in a stream; as, to *squirt* water.

SQUIRT, *v. i.* To throw out words; to let fly. [*Not in use.*] *L'Estrange.*

SQUIRT, *n.* An instrument with which a liquid is ejected in a stream with force.

2. A small quick stream.

SQUIRT'ER, *n.* One that squirts.

[*This word in all its forms, is vulgar.*]

Squirting cucumber, a sort of wild cucumber, so called from the sudden bursting of its capsules when ripe; the *Momordica elaterium.*

STAB, *v. t.* [This word contains the elements, and is probably from the primary sense, of the L. *stabilis*, *stabilio*, *stipo*, D. *stippen*, to point or prick, Eng. *stiff*, and a multitude of others in many languages. The radical sense is to thrust; but I know not to what oriental roots they are allied, unless to the Heb. יצב, Ar. وَصَبَ watsaba. Class Sb. No. 35. 37. or Class Db. No. 46. 53. 44.]

1. To pierce with a pointed weapon; as, to be *stabbed* by a dagger or a spear; to *stab* fish or eels.

2. To wound mischievously or mortally; to kill by the thrust of a pointed instrument. *Philips.*

3. To injure secretly or by malicious falsehood or slander; as, to *stab* reputation.

STAB, *v. i.* To give a wound with a pointed weapon.

> None shall dare
> With shorten'd sword to *stab* in closer war. *Dryden.*

2. To give a mortal wound.

> He speaks poniards, and every word *stabs.* *Shak.*

To stab at, to offer a stab; to thrust a pointed weapon at.

STAB, *n.* The thrust of a pointed weapon.

2. A wound with a sharp pointed weapon; as, to fall by the *stab* of an assassin.

3. An injury given in the dark; a sly mischief; as a *stab* given to character.

STAB'BED, *pp.* Pierced with a pointed weapon; killed with a spear or other pointed instrument.

STAB'BER, *n.* One that stabs; a privy murderer.

STAB'BING, *ppr.* Piercing with a pointed weapon; killing with a pointed instrument by piercing the body.

STAB'BING, *n.* The act of piercing with a pointed weapon; the act of wounding or killing with a pointed instrument.

> This statute was made on account of the frequent quarrels and *stabbings* with short daggers. *Blackstone.*

STABIL'IMENT, *n.* [L. *stabilimentum*, from *stabilio*, to make firm. See *Stab.*]

Act of making firm; firm support.

> They serve for *stabiliment*, propagation and shade. *Derham.*

STABIL'ITATE, *v. t.* To make stable; to establish. [*Not used.*] *More.*

STABIL'ITY, *n.* [L. *stabilitas*, from *stabilis.* See *Stab.*]

1. Steadiness; stableness; firmness; strength to stand without being moved or overthrown; as the *stability* of a throne; the *stability* of a constitution of government.

2. Steadiness or firmness of character; firmness of resolution or purpose; the qualities opposite to *fickleness*, *irresolution* or *inconstancy.* We say, a man of little *stability*, or of unusual *stability.*

3. Fixedness; as opposed to *fluidity.* [*I believe not now used.*]

> Since fluidness and *stability* are contrary qualities— *Boyle.*

STA'BLE, *a.* [L. *stabilis*; Fr. *stable*; It. *stabile*. The primary sense is set, fixed. See *Stab.*]

1. Fixed; firmly established; not to be easily moved, shaken or overthrown; as a *stable* government.
2. Steady in purpose; constant; firm in resolution; not easily diverted from a purpose; not fickle or wavering; as a *stable* man; a *stable* character.
3. Fixed; steady; firm; not easily surrendered or abandoned; as a man of *stable* principles.
4. Durable; not subject to be overthrown or changed.

In this region of chance and vanity, where nothing is *stable*— *Rogers.*

STA'BLE, *v. t.* To fix; to establish. [*Not used.*]

STA'BLE, *n.* [L. *stabulum*, that is, a stand, a fixed place, like *stall*. See the latter. These words do not primarily imply a *covering* for horses or cattle.]

A house or shed for beasts to lodge and feed in. In large towns, a stable is usually a building for horses only, or horses and cows, and often connected with a coach house. In the country towns in the northern states of America, a stable is usually an apartment in a barn in which hay and grain are deposited.

STA'BLE, *v. t.* To put or keep in a stable. Our farmers generally *stable* not only horses, but oxen and cows in winter, and sometimes young cattle.

STA'BLE, *v. i.* To dwell or lodge in a stable; to dwell in an inclosed place; to kennel. *Milton.*

STA'BLE-BOY, } *n.* A boy or a man who
STA'BLE-MAN, } attends at a stable. *Swift.*

STA'BLED, *pp.* Put or kept in a stable.

STA'BLENESS, *n.* Fixedness; firmness of position or establishment; strength to stand; stability; as the *stableness* of a throne or of a system of laws.

2. Steadiness; constancy; firmness of purpose; stability; as *stableness* of character, of mind, of principles or opinions.

STA'BLESTAND, *n.* [*stable* and *stand.*] In *law*, when man is found at his standing in the forest with a cross bow bent, ready to shoot at a deer, or with a long bow; or standing close by a tree with grayhounds in a leash ready to slip. This is one of the four presumptions that a man intends stealing the king's deer. *English Law.*

STA'BLING, *ppr.* Putting or keeping in a stable.

STA'BLING, *n.* The act or practice of keeping cattle in a stable.

2. A house, shed or room for keeping horses and cattle.

STAB'LISH, *v. t.* [L. *stabilio*; Fr. *etablir*; It. *stabilire*; Sp. *establecer*. See *Stab.*]

To fix; to settle in a state for permanence; to make firm. [In lieu of this, *establish* is now always used.]

STA'BLY, *adv.* Firmly; fixedly; steadily; as a government *stably* settled.

STACK, *n.* [W. *ystac*, a stack; *ystaca*, a standard, from *tâg*, a state of being stuffed; Dan. *stak*, a pile of hay; Sw. *stack*; Ir. *stacadh*. It signifies that which is set, and coincides with Sax. *stac*, D. *staak*, a stake. *Stock*, *stag*, *stage*, are of the same family, or at least have the same radical sense.]

1. A large conical pile of hay, grain or straw, sometimes covered with thatch. In *America*, the *stack* differs from the *cock* only in size, both being conical. A *long* pile of hay or grain is called a *rick*. In *England*, this distinction is not always observed. This word in Great Britain is sometimes applied to a pile of wood containing 108 cubic feet, and also to a pile of poles; but I believe never in America.

Against every pillar was a *stack* of billets above a man's highth. *Bacon.*

2. A number of funnels or chimneys standing together. We say, a *stack* of chimneys; which is correct, as a *chimney* is a passage. But we also call the whole stack a chimney. Thus we say, the *chimney* rises ten feet above the roof.

STACK, *v. t.* To lay in a conical or other pile; to make into a large pile; as, to *stack* hay or grain.

2. In *England*, to pile wood, poles, &c.

STACK'ED, *pp.* Piled in a large conical heap.

STACK'ING, *ppr.* Laying in a large conical heap.

STACK'ING-BAND, } *n.* A band or rope
STACK'ING-BELT, } used in binding thatch or straw upon a stack.

STACK'ING-STAGE, *n.* A stage used in building stacks.

STACK'-Y'ARD, *n.* A yard or inclosure for stacks of hay or grain.

STAC'TE, *n.* [L. *stacte*; Gr. ςακτη.] A fatty resinous liquid matter, of the nature of liquid myrrh, very odoriferous and highly valued. But it is said we have none but what is adulterated, and what is so called is liquid storax. *Cyc.*

STAD'DLE, *n.* [D. *stutzel*, from *stut*, a prop; *stutten*, to prop; Eng. *stud*; G. *stütze*. It belongs to the root of *stead*, *steady.*]

1. Any thing which serves for support; a staff; a crutch; the frame or support of a stack of hay or grain. *England.*

[*In this sense not used in New England.*]

2. In *New England*, a small tree of any kind, particularly a forest tree. In America, trees are called *staddles* from three or four years old till they are six or eight inches in diameter or more, but in this respect the word is indefinite. This is also the sense in which it is used by Bacon and Tusser.

STAD'DLE, *v. t.* To leave staddles when a wood is cut. *Tusser.*

STAD'DLE-ROOF, *n.* The roof or covering of a stack.

STA'DIUM, *n.* [L.; Gr. ςαδιον.] A Greek measure of 125 geometrical paces; a furlong.

2. The course or career of a race.

STADT'HOLDER, *n.* [D. *stadt*, a city, and *houder*, holder.]

Formerly, the chief magistrate of the United Provinces of Holland; or the governor or lieutenant governor of a province.

STADT'HOLDERATE, *n.* The office of a stadtholder.

ST'AFF, *n.* plu. *staves*. [Sax. *stæf*, a stick or club, a pole, a crook, a prop or support, a letter, an epistle; *stæfn*, *stefn*, the voice; D. *staf*, a staff, scepter or crook; *staaf*, a bar; G. *stab*, a staff, a bar, a rod; Dan. *stab*, *stav*, id.; *stavn*, *stævn*, the prow of a ship, that is, a projection, that which shoots out; Fr. *douve*. The primary sense is to thrust, to shoot. See *Stab.*]

1. A stick carried in the hand for support or defense by a person walking; hence, a support; that which props or upholds. Bread is proverbially called the *staff* of life.

The boy was the very *staff* of my age. *Shak.*

Thy rod and thy *staff*, they comfort me. *Ps.* xxiii.

2. A stick or club used as a weapon.

With forks and *staves* the felon they pursue. *Dryden.*

3. A long piece of wood; a stick; the long handle of an instrument; a pole or stick, used for many purposes.
4. The five lines and the spaces on which music is written.
5. An ensign of authority; a badge of office; as a constable's *staff*. *Shak. Hayward.*
6. The round of a ladder. *Brown.*
7. A pole erected in a ship to hoist and display a flag; called a flag-*staff*. There is also a jack-*staff*, and an ensign-*staff*.
8. [Fr. *estafette*, a courier or express; Dan. *staffette*; It. *staffetta*, an express; *staffiere*, a groom or servant; *staffa*, a stirrup; Sp. *estafeta*, a courier, a general post-office; *estafero*, a foot-boy, a stable-boy, an errand-boy; Port. *estafeta*, an express. This word seems to be formed from It. *staffa*, a stirrup, whence *staffiere*, a stirrup-holder or groom, whence a servant or horseman sent express.] In *military affairs*, an establishment of officers in various departments, attached to an army, or to the commander of an army. The staff includes officers not of the line, as adjutants, quarter-masters, chaplain, surgeon, &c. The staff is the medium of communication from the commander in chief to every department of an army.
9. [Ice. *stef.*] A stanza; a series of verses so disposed that when it is concluded, the same order begins again.

Cowley found out that no kind of *staff* is proper for a heroic poem, as being all too lyrical. *Dryden.*

10. *Stave* and *staves*, plu. of *staff*. [See *Stave.*]

ST'AFFISH, *a.* Stiff; harsh. [*Not in use.*] *Ascham.*

ST'AFF-TREE, *n.* A sort of evergreen privet. *Johnson.*

It is of the genus Celastrus. *Cyc.*

STAG, *n.* [This word belongs to the root of *stick*, *stage*, *stock*. The primary sense is to thrust, hence to fix, to stay, &c.]

1. The male red deer; the male of the hind. *Shak.*
2. A colt or filly; also, a romping girl. [*Local.*] *Grose.*
3. In *New England*, the male of the common ox castrated.

STAG'-BEETLE, *n.* The *Lucanus cervus*, a species of insect. *Encyc.*

STAĠE, *n.* [Fr. *etage*, a story, a degree; Arm. *estaich*; Sax. *stigan*, to go, to ascend; Dan. *stiger*, to step up, to ascend; Sw. *stiga*, to step; *steg*, a step; *stege*, a ladder; D. *stygen*, to mount, G. *steigen.*] Properly, one step or degree of elevation, and what the French call *etage*, we call a *story*. Hence,

1. A floor or platform of any kind elevated above the ground or common surface, as for an exhibition of something to public view; as a *stage* for a mountebank; a *stage* for speakers in public; a *stage* for mechanics. Seamen use floating *stages*, and *stages* suspended by the side of a ship, for calking and repairing.
2. The floor on which theatrical performances are exhibited, as distinct from the *pit*, &c. Hence,
3. The theater; the place of scenic entertainments.

Knights, squires and steeds must enter on the *stage*. *Pope.*

4. Theatrical representations. It is contended that the *stage* is a school of morality. Let it be inquired, where is the person whom the *stage* has reformed?
5. A place where any thing is publicly exhibited.

When we are born, we cry that we are come
To this great *stage* of fools. *Shak.*

6. Place of action or performance; as the *stage* of life.
7. A place of rest on a journey, or where a relay of horses is taken. When we arrive at the next *stage*, we will take some refreshment. Hence,
8. The distance between two places of rest on a road; as a *stage* of fifteen miles.
9. A single step; degree of advance; degree of progression, either in increase or decrease, in rising or falling, or in any change of state; as the several *stages* of a war; the *stages* of civilization or improvement; *stages* of growth in an animal or plant; *stages* of a disease, of decline or recovery; the several *stages* of human life.
10. [instead of *stage-coach*, or *stage-wagon*.] A coach or other carriage running regularly from one place to another for the conveyance of passengers.

I went in the six-penny *stage*. *Swift.*
A parcel sent by the *stage*. *Cowper.*
American usage.

STAĠE, *v. t.* To exhibit publicly. [*Not in use.*] *Shak.*

STA'ĠE-ĊOACH, *n.* [*stage* and *coach*.] A coach that runs by stages; or a coach that runs regularly every day or on stated days, for the conveyance of passengers. *Addison.*

STA'ĠELY, *a.* Pertaining to a stage; becoming the theater. [*Little used.*] *Taylor.*

STA'ĠE-PLAY, *n.* [*stage* and *play*.] Theatrical entertainment. *Dryden.*

STA'ĠE-PLAYER, *n.* An actor on the stage; one whose occupation is to represent characters on the stage. Garrick was a celebrated *stage-player.*

STA'ĠER, *n.* A player. [*Little used.*]
2. One that has long acted on the stage of life; a practitioner; a person of cunning; as an old cunning *stager*; an experienced *stager*; a *stager* of the wiser sort. *Dryden.*

[*I do not recollect to have ever heard this word used in America.*]

STA'ĠERY, *n.* Exhibition on the stage. [*Not in use.*] *Milton.*

STAG-EVIL, *n.* A disease in horses. *Dict.*

STAG'GARD, *n.* [from *stag*.] A stag of four years of age. *Ainsworth.*

STAG'GER, *v. i.* [D. *staggeren*. Kiliaan.]
1. To reel; to vacillate; to move to one side and the other in standing or walking; not to stand or walk with steadiness. *Boyle.*

Deep was the wound; he *stagger'd* with the blow. *Dryden.*

2. To fail; to cease to stand firm; to begin to give way.

The enemy *staggers*. *Addison.*

3. To hesitate; to begin to doubt and waver in purpose; to become less confident or determined. *Shak.*

Abraham *staggered* not at the promise of God through unbelief. Rom. iv.

STAG'GER, *v. t.* To cause to reel. *Shak.*
2. To cause to doubt and waver; to make to hesitate; to make less steady or confident; to shock.

Whoever will read the story of this war, will find himself much *staggered*. *Howell.*

When a prince fails in honor and justice, it is enough to *stagger* his people in their allegiance. *L'Estrange.*

STAG'GERED, *pp.* Made to reel; made to doubt and waver.

STAG'GERING, *ppr.* Causing to reel, to waver or to doubt.

STAG'GERING, *n.* The act of reeling. *Arbuthnot.*
2. The cause of staggering.

STAG'GERINGLY, *adv.* In a reeling manner.
2. With hesitation or doubt.

STAG'GERS, *n. plu.* A disease of horses and cattle, attended with reeling or giddiness; also, a disease of sheep, which inclines them to turn about suddenly. *Cyc.*
2. Madness; wild irregular conduct. [*Not in use.*] *Shak.*

STAG'GER-WŎRT, *n.* A plant, ragwort.

STAG'NANCY, *n.* [See *Stagnant*.] The state of being without motion, flow or circulation, as in a fluid.

STAG'NANT, *a.* [L. *stagnans*, from *stagno*, to be without a flowing motion, It. *stagnare*. Qu. W. *tagu*, to stop.]
1. Not flowing; not running in a current or stream; as a *stagnant* lake or pond; *stagnant* blood in the veins.
2. Motionless; still; not agitated; as water quiet and *stagnant*. *Woodward.*

The gloomy slumber of the *stagnant* soul. *Johnson.*

3. Not active; dull; not brisk; as, business is *stagnant*.

STAG'NATE, *v. i.* [L. *stagno*, *stagnum*; It. *stagnare*.]
1. To cease to flow; to be motionless; as, blood *stagnates* in the veins of an animal; air *stagnates* in a close room.
2. To cease to move; not to be agitated. Water that *stagnates* in a pond or reservoir, soon becomes foul.
3. To cease to be brisk or active; to become dull; as, commerce *stagnates*; business *stagnates*.

STAGNA'TION, *n.* The cessation of flowing or circulation of a fluid; or the state of being without flow or circulation; the state of being motionless; as the *stagnation* of the blood; the *stagnation* of water or air; the *stagnation* of vapors. *Addison.*
2. The cessation of action or of brisk action; the state of being dull; as the *stagnation* of business.

STAG'-WŎRM, *n.* An insect that is troublesome to deer.

STAĠ'YRITE, *n.* An appellation given to Aristotle from the place of his birth.

STAID, *pret.* and *pp.* of *stay*; so written for *stayed*.
2. *a.* [from *stay*, to stop.] Sober; grave; steady; composed; regular; not wild, volatile, flighty or fanciful; as *staid* wisdom.

To ride out with *staid* guides. *Milton.*

STA'IDNESS, *n.* Sobriety; gravity; steadiness; regularity; the opposite of *wildness*.

If he sometimes appears too gay, yet a secret gracefulness of youth accompanies his writings, though the *staidness* and sobriety of age be wanting. *Dryden.*

STAIN, *v. t.* [W. *ystaeniaw*, to spread over, to stain; *ystaenu*, to cover with tin; *ystaen*, that is spread out, or that is sprinkled, a *stain*, *tin*, L. *stannum*; *taen*, a spread, a sprinkle, a layer; *taenu*, to spread, expand, sprinkle, or be scattered. This coincides in elements with Gr. τειѡ. The French *teindre*, Sp. *teñir*, It. *tingere*, Port. *tingir*, to stain, are from the L. *tingo*, Gr. τεγγѡ, Sax. *deagan*, Eng. *dye*; a word formed by different elements. *Stain* seems to be from the Welsh, and if *taen* is not a contracted word, it has no connection with the Fr. *teindre*.]
1. To discolor by the application of foreign matter; to make foul; to spot; as, to *stain* the hand with dye; to *stain* clothes with vegetable juice; to *stain* paper; armor *stained* with blood.
2. To dye; to tinge with a different color; as, to *stain* cloth.
3. To impress with figures, in colors different from the ground; as, to *stain* paper for hangings.
4. To blot; to soil; to spot with guilt or infamy; to tarnish; to bring reproach on; as, to *stain* the character.

Of honor void, of innocence, of faith, of purity,
Our wonted ornaments now soil'd and *stain'd*— *Milton.*

STAIN, *n.* A spot; discoloration from foreign matter; as a *stain* on a garment or cloth.
2. A natural spot of a color different from the ground.

Swift trouts, diversified with crimson *stains*. *Pope.*

3. Taint of guilt; tarnish; disgrace; reproach; as the *stain* of sin.

Nor death itself can wholly wash their *stains*. *Dryden.*

Our opinion is, I hope, without any blemish or *stain* of heresy. *Hooker.*

4. Cause of reproach; shame.

Hereby I will lead her that is the praise and yet the *stain* of all womankind. *Sidney.*

STA'INED, *pp.* Discolored; spotted; dyed; blotted; tarnished.

STA'INER, *n.* One who stains, blots or tarnishes.
2. A dyer.

STA'INING, *ppr.* Discoloring; spotting; tarnishing; dyeing.

STA'INLESS, *a.* Free from stains or spots. *Sidney.*

2. Free from the reproach of guilt; free from sin. *Shak.*

STAIR, *n.* [D. *steiger;* Sax. *stæger;* from Sax. *stigan*, D. G. *steigen*, Goth. *steigan*, to step, to go; Dan. *stiger*, to rise, to step up; Sw. *steg*, a step; Ir. *staighre*. See *Stage.*]

1. A step; a stone or a frame of boards or planks by which a person rises one step. A stair, to make the ascent easy, should not exceed six or seven inches in elevation. When the riser is eight, nine or ten inches in breadth, the ascent by stairs is laborious.

2. *Stairs*, in the plural, a series of steps by which persons ascend to a higher room in a building. [*Stair*, in this sense, is not in use.]

Flight of stairs, may signify the stairs which make the whole ascent of a story; or in winding stairs, the phrase may signify the stairs from the floor to a turn, or from one turn to another.

STA'IRCASE, *n.* [*stair* and *case.*] The part of a building which contains the stairs. Staircases are straight or winding. The straight are called fliers, or direct fliers. Winding stairs, called spiral or cockle, are square, circular or elliptical.

To make a complete *staircase*, is a curious piece of architecture. *Wotton.*

STAKE, *n.* [Sax. *stac;* D. *staak;* Sw. *stake;* Ir. *stac;* It. *steccone*, a stake; *stecca*, a stick; *steccare*, to fence with stakes; Sp. *estaca*, a *stake*, a *stick*. This coincides with *stick*, noun and verb, with *stock*, *stage*, &c. The primary sense is to shoot, to thrust, hence to *set* or fix.]

1. A small piece of wood or timber, sharpened at one end and set in the ground, or prepared for setting, as a support to something. Thus *stakes* are used to support vines, to support fences, hedges and the like. A *stake* is not to be confounded with a *post*, which is a larger piece of timber.

2. A piece of long rough wood.

A sharpen'd *stake* strong Dryas found. *Dryden.*

3. A palisade, or something resembling it. *Milton.*

4. The piece of timber to which a martyr is fastened when he is to be burnt. Hence, to *perish at the stake*, is to die a martyr, or to die in torment. Hence,

5. Figuratively, martyrdom. The *stake* was prepared for those who were convicted of heresy.

6. That which is pledged or wagered; that which is *set*, *thrown down* or *laid*, to abide the issue of a contest, to be gained by victory or lost by defeat.

7. The state of being laid or pledged as a wager. His honor is at *stake*.

8. A small anvil to straighten cold work, or to cut and punch upon. *Moxon.*

STAKE, *v. t.* To fasten, support or defend with stakes; as, to *stake* vines or plants.

2. To mark the limits by stakes; with *out;* as, to *stake out* land; to *stake out* a new road, or the ground for a canal.

3. To wager; to pledge; to put at hazard upon the issue of competition, or upon a future contingency.

I'll *stake* yon lamb that near the fountain plays. *Pope.*

4. To point or sharpen stakes. [*Not used in America.*]

5. To pierce with a stake. *Spectator.*

STA'KED, *pp.* Fastened or supported by stakes; set or marked with stakes; wagered; put at hazard.

STAKE-HEAD, *n.* In *rope-making*, a stake with wooden pins in the upper side to keep the strands apart.

STA'KING, *ppr.* Supporting with stakes; marking with stakes; wagering; putting at hazard.

2. Sharpening; pointing.

STALAC'TIC, } *a.* [from *stalactite.*] Per-
STALAC'TICAL, } taining to stalactite; resembling an icicle. *Kirwan.*

STALAC'TIFORM, } *a.* Like stalactite;
STALACTIT'IFORM, } resembling an icicle. *Phillips.*

STALAC'TITE, *n.* [Gr. σαλακτος, σαλακτις, from σαλαζω, to drop, from σαλαω, L. *stillo.*]

A subvariety of carbonate of lime, usually in a conical or cylindrical form, pendent from the roofs and sides of caverns like an icicle; produced by the filtration of water containing calcarious particles, through fissures and pores of rocks. *Encyc. Cleaveland.*

STALACTIT'IC, *a.* In the form of stalactite, or pendent substances like icicles. *Kirwan.*

STALAG'MITE, *n.* [L. *stalagmium*, a drop; Gr. σαλαγμος, supra.]

A deposit of earthy or calcarious matter, formed by drops on the floors of caverns. *Encyc. Woodward.*

STALAGMIT'IC, *a.* Having the form of stalagmite.

STALAGMIT'ICALLY, *adv.* In the form or manner of stalagmite. *Buckland.*

STAL'DER, *n.* A wooden frame to set casks on. [*Not used in the U. States.*]

STALE, *a.* [I do not find this word in the other Teutonic dialects. It is probably from the root of *still*, G. *stellen*, to set, and equivalent to *stagnant.*]

1. Vapid or tasteless from age; having lost its life, spirit and flavor from being long kept; as *stale* beer.

2. Having lost the life or graces of youth; worn out; decayed; as a *stale* virgin. *Spectator.*

3. Worn out by use; trite; common; having lost its novelty and power of pleasing; as a *stale* remark.

STALE, *n.* [probably that which is set; G. *stellen*. See *Stall.*]

1. Something set or offered to view as an allurement to draw others to any place or purpose; a decoy; a stool-fowl.

Still as he went, he crafty *stales* did lay. *Spenser.*

A pretense of kindness is the universal *stale* to all base projects. *Gov. of the Tongue.*

[*In this sense obsolete.*]

2. A prostitute. *Obs.* *Shak.*

3. Old vapid beer. *Obs.*

4. A long handle; as the *stale* of a rake. [Sax. *stel*, *stele;* D. *steel;* G. *stiel.*] *Mortimer.*

5. A word applied to the king in chess when *stalled* or set; that is, when so situated that he cannot be moved without going into check, by which the game is ended. *Bacon.*

STALE, *v. t.* To make vapid or useless; to destroy the life, beauty or use of; to wear out.

Age cannot wither her, nor custom *stale*
Her infinite variety. *Shak.*

STALE, *v. i.* [G. *stallen;* Dan. *staller;* Sw. *stalla.*]

To make water; to discharge urine; as horses and cattle.

STALE, *n.* Urine; *used of horses and cattle.*

STA'LELY, *adv.* Of old; of a long time. *Obs.* *B. Jonson.*

STA'LENESS, *n.* The state of being stale; vapidness; the state of having lost the life or flavor; oldness; as the *staleness* of beer or other liquors; the *staleness* of provisions. *Bacon. Addison.*

2. The state of being worn out; triteness; commonness; as the *staleness* of an observation.

STALK, *n. stauk.* [Sw. *stielk;* D. *steel;* G. *stiel*, a handle, and a stalk or stem; Sax. *stælg*, a column; Gr. σελεχος; from the root of *stall* and G. *stellen*, to set.]

1. The stem, culm or main body of an herbaceous plant. Thus we speak of a *stalk* of wheat, rye or oats, the *stalks* of maiz or hemp. The *stalk* of herbaceous plants, answers to the *stem* of shrubs and trees, and denotes that which is set, the fixed part of a plant, its support; or it is a shoot.

2. The pedicle of a flower, or the peduncle that supports the fructification of a plant.

3. The stem of a quill. *Grew.*

STALK, *v. i.* [Sax. *stælcan.*] To walk with high and proud steps; usually implying the affectation of dignity, and hence the word usually expresses dislike. The poets however use the word to express dignity of step.

With manly mein he *stalk'd* along the ground. *Dryden.*

Then *stalking* through the deep
He fords the ocean. *Addison.*

2. It is used with some insinuation of contempt or abhorrence. *Johnson.*

Bertran
Stalks close behind her, like a witch's fiend,
Pressing to be employ'd. *Dryden.*
'Tis not to *stalk* about and draw fresh air
From time to time. *Addison.*

3. To walk behind a stalking horse or behind a cover.

The king crept under the shoulder of his led horse, and said, I must *stalk*. *Bacon.*

STALK, *n.* A high, proud, stately step or walk. *Spenser.*

STALK'ED, *a.* Having a stalk.

STALK'ER, *n.* One who walks with a proud step; also, a kind of fishing net.

STALK'ING, *ppr.* Walking with proud or lofty steps.

STALK'ING-HORSE, *n.* A horse, real or factitious, behind which a fowler conceals himself from the sight of the game which he is aiming to kill; hence, a mask; a pretense.

Hypocrisy is the devil's *stalking-horse*, under an affectation of simplicity and religion. *L'Estrange.*

STALK'Y, *a.* Hard as a stalk; resembling a stalk. *Mortimer.*

STALL, *n.* [Sax. *stæl*, *stal*, *stall*, a place, a seat or station, a stable, state, condition;

D. *stal*; G. *stall*, a stable, a stye; Dan. *stald*; Sw. *stall*; Fr. *stalle*; It. *stalla*; W. *ystal*; from the root of G. *stellen*, to set, that is, to throw down, to thrust down; Sans. *stala*, a place. See *Still*.]

1. Primarily, a stand; a station; a fixed spot; hence, the stand or place where a horse or an ox is kept and fed; the division of a stable, or the apartment for one horse or ox. The stable contains eight or ten *stalls*.
2. A stable; a place for cattle.

At last he found a *stall* where oxen stood. *Dryden.*

3. In 1 Kings iv. 26. stall is used for *horse*. "Solomon had forty thousand *stalls* of horses for his chariots." In 2 Chron. ix. 25, stall means *stable*. "Solomon had four thousand *stalls* for horses and chariots." These passages are reconciled by the definition given above; Solomon had four thousand stables, each containing ten stalls; forty thousand stalls.
4. A bench, form or frame of shelves in the open air, where any thing is exposed to sale. It is curious to observe the *stalls* of books in the boulevards and other public places in Paris.
5. A small house or shed in which an occupation is carried on; as a butcher's *stall*. *Spenser.*
6. The seat of a dignified clergyman in the choir.

The dignified clergy, out of humility, have called their thrones by the name of *stalls*. [probably a mistake of the reason.] *Warburton.*

STALL, *v. t.* To put into a stable; or to keep in a stable; as, to *stall* an ox.

Where king Latinus then his oxen *stall'd*. *Dryden.*

2. To install; to place in an office with the customary formalities. [For this, *install* is now used.]
3. To set; to fix; to plunge into mire so as not to be able to proceed; as, to *stall* horses or a carriage.

[This phrase I have heard in Virginia. In New England, *set* is used in a like sense.]

STALL, *v. i.* To dwell; to inhabit.

We could not *stall* together in the world. [*Not in use.*] *Shak.*

2. To kennel.
3. To be set, as in mire.
4. To be tired of eating, as cattle.

STALL'AGE, *n.* The right of erecting stalls in fairs; or rent paid for a stall.

2. In *old books*, laystall; dung; compost.

STALLA'TION, *n.* Installation. [*Not used.*] *Cavendish.*

STALL'-FED, *pp.* Fed on dry fodder, or fattened in a stall or stable. [See *Stall-feed.*]

STALL'-FEED, *v. t.* [*stall* and *feed.*] To feed and fatten in a stable or on dry fodder; as, to *stall-feed* an ox. [This word is used in America to distinguish this mode of feeding from *grass-feeding.*]

STALL'-FEEDING, *ppr.* Feeding and fattening in the stable.

STALLION, *n.* *stal'yun.* [G. *hengst*; Dan. *staldhingst*; Fr. *etalon*; It. *stallone*; from *stall*, or its root, as we now use *stud horse*, from the root of *stud*, *stead*; W. *ystal*, a stall, stock, produce; *ystálu*, to form a stock; *ystalwyn*, a stallion.]

A stone horse; a seed horse; or any male horse not castrated, whether kept for mares or not. According to the Welsh, the word signifies a stock horse, a horse intended for raising stock.

STALL-WORN, in Shakspeare, Johnson thinks a mistake for *stall-worth*, stout.

His *stall-worn* steed the champion stout bestrode. [*The word is not in use.*] *Shak.*

STAM'EN, *n.* plu. *stamens* or *stamina*. [L. This word belongs to the root of *sto*, *stabilis*, or of *stage*.]

1. In *a general sense*, usually in the plural, the fixed, firm part of a body, which supports it or gives it its strength and solidity. Thus we say, the bones are the *stamina* of animal bodies; the ligneous parts of trees are the *stamina* which constitute their strength. Hence,
2. Whatever constitutes the principal strength or support of any thing; as the *stamina* of a constitution or of life; the *stamina* of a state.
3. In *botany*, an organ of flowers for the preparation of the pollen or fecundating dust. It consists of the filament and the anther. It is considered as the male organ of fructification. *Martyn.*

STAM'ENED, *a.* Furnished with stamens.

STAM'IN, *n.* A slight woolen stuff. *Chaucer.*

STAM'INAL, *a.* Pertaining to stamens or stamina; consisting in stamens or stamina. *Med. Repos.*

STAM'INATE, *a.* Consisting of stamens.

STAM'INATE, *v. t.* To endue with stamina.

STAMIN'EOUS, *a.* [L. *stamineus.*] Consisting of stamens or filaments. *Stamineous* flowers have no corol; they want the colored leaves called petals, and consist only of the style and stamina. Linne calls them *apetalous*; others imperfect or incomplete. *Martyn.*

2. Pertaining to the stamen, or attached to it; as a *stamineous* nectary. *Lee.*

STAMINIF'EROUS, *a.* [L. *stamen* and *fero*, to bear.]

A *staminiferous* flower is one which has stamens without a pistil. A *staminiferous* nectary is one that has stamens growing on it. *Martyn.*

STAM'MEL, *n.* A species of red color. *B. Jonson.*

2. A kind of woolen cloth. [See *Stamin.*] *Com. on Chaucer.*

STAM'MER, *v. i.* [Sax. *stamer*, one who stammers; Goth. *stamms*, stammering; Sw. *stamma*; G. *stammeln*; D. *stameren*; Dan. *stammer*; from the root *stam* or *stem*. The primary sense is to stop, to set, to fix. So *stutter* is from the root of *stead*, *stud.*]

Literally, to stop in uttering syllables or words; to stutter; to hesitate or falter in speaking; and hence, to speak with stops and difficulty. Demosthenes is said to have *stammered* in speaking, and to have overcome the difficulty by persevering efforts.

STAM'MER, *v. t.* To utter or pronounce with hesitation or imperfectly. *Beaum.*

STAM'MERER, *n.* One that stutters or hesitates in speaking.

STAM'MERING, *ppr.* Stopping or hesitating in the uttering of syllables and words; stuttering.

2. *a.* Apt to stammer.

STAM'MERING, *n.* The act of stopping or hesitating in speaking; impediment in speech.

STAM'MERINGLY, *adv.* With stops or hesitation in speaking.

STAMP, *v. t.* [D. *stampen*; G. *stampfen*; Dan. *stamper*; Sw. *stampa*; Fr. *estamper*; It. *stampare*; Sp. *estampar*. I know not which is the radical letter, *m* or *p*.]

In *a general sense*, to strike; to beat; to press. Hence,

1. To strike or beat forcibly with the bottom of the foot, or by thrusting the foot downwards; as, to *stamp* the ground.

He frets, he fumes, he stares, he *stamps* the ground. *Dryden.*

[In this sense, the popular pronunciation is *stomp*, with *a* broad.]

2. To impress with some mark or figure; as, to *stamp* a plate with arms or initials.
3. To impress; to imprint; to fix deeply; as, to *stamp* virtuous principles on the heart. [See *Enstamp.*]
4. To fix a mark by impressing it; as a notion of the Deity *stamped* on the mind.

God has *stamped* no original characters on our minds, wherein we may read his being. *Locke.*

5. To make by impressing a mark; as, to *stamp* pieces of silver.
6. To coin; to mint; to form. *Shak.*

STAMP, *v. i.* To strike the foot forcibly downwards.

But starts, exclaims, and *stamps*, and raves, and dies. *Dennis.*

STAMP, *n.* Any instrument for making impressions on other bodies.

'Tis gold so pure,
It cannot bear the *stamp* without alloy. *Dryden.*

2. A mark imprinted; an impression.

That sacred name gives ornament and grace,
And, like his *stamp*, makes basest metals pass. *Dryden.*

3. That which is marked; a thing stamped.

Hanging a golden *stamp* about their necks. *Shak.*

4. A picture cut in wood or metal, or made by impression; a cut; a plate.

At Venice they put out very curious *stamps* of the several edifices which are most famous for their beauty and magnificence. *Addison.*

5. A mark set upon things chargeable with duty to government, as evidence that the duty is paid. We see such *stamps* on English newspapers.
6. A character of reputation, good or bad, fixed on any thing. These persons have the *stamp* of impiety. The Scriptures bear the *stamp* of a divine origin.
7. Authority; current value derived from suffrage or attestation.

Of the same *stamp* is that which is obtruded on us, that an adamant suspends the attraction of the loadstone. *Brown.*

8. Make; cast; form; character; as a man of the same *stamp*, or of a different *stamp*. *Addison.*
9. In *metallurgy*, a kind of pestle raised by a water wheel, for beating ores to pow-

der; any thing like a pestle used for pounding or beating.

STAMP'-DUTY, *n.* [*stamp* and *duty.*] A duty or tax imposed on paper and parchment, the evidence of the payment of which is a stamp.

STAMP'ED, *pp.* Impressed with a mark or figure; coined; imprinted; deeply fixed.

STAMP'ER, *n.* An instrument for pounding or stamping.

STAMP'ING, *ppr.* Impressing with a mark or figure; coining; imprinting.

STAMP'ING-MILL, *n.* An engine used in tin works for breaking or bruising ore.

STAN, as a termination, is said to have expressed the superlative degree; as in *Athelstan*, most noble; *Dunstan*, the highest. But qu. *Stan*, in Saxon, is *stone.*

STANCH, *v. t.* [Fr. *etancher*; Arm. *stançoa*; Sp. Port. *estancar*, to stop, to stanch, to be over tired; It. *stancare*, to weary; Sp. Port. *estancia*, a stay or dwelling for a time, an abode, and a *stanza*; Sp. *estanco*, a stop; hence Fr. *etang*, a pond, and Eng. *tank.*]

In *a general sense*, to stop; to set or fix; but applied only to the blood; to stop the flowing of blood. Cold applications to the neck will often *stanch* the bleeding of the nose. *Bacon.*

STANCH, *v. i.* To stop, as blood; to cease to flow.

Immediately the issue of her blood *stanched.* Luke viii.

STANCH, *a.* [This is the same word as the foregoing, the primary sense of which is to *set*; hence the sense of firmness.]

1. Sound; firm; strong and tight; as a *stanch* ship.
2. Firm in principle; steady; constant and zealous; hearty; as a *stanch* churchman; a *stanch* republican; a *stanch* friend or adherent.

In politics I hear you're *stanch.* *Prior.*

3. Strong; not to be broken. *Shak.*
4. Firm; close.

This is to be kept *stanch.* *Locke.*

A *stanch* hound, is one that follows the scent closely without error or remissness.

STANCH'ED, *pp.* Stopped or restrained from flowing.

STANCH'ER, *n.* He or that which stops the flowing of blood.

STANCH'ING, *ppr.* Stopping the flowing of blood.

STANCH'ION, *n.* [Fr. *etançon*; Arm. *stançonnu* and *stanconni*, to prop. See *Stanch.*]

A prop or support; a piece of timber in the form of a stake or post, used for a support. In *ship-building*, stanchions of wood or iron are of different forms, and are used to support the deck, the quarter rails, the nettings, awnings and the like. *Mar. Dict.*

STANCH'LESS, *a.* That cannot be stanched or stopped. *Shak.*

STANCH'NESS, *n.* Soundness; firmness in principle; closeness of adherence.

STAND, *v. i.* pret. and pp. *stood.* [Sax. Goth. *standan.* This verb, if from the root of G. *stehen*, D. *staaen*, Dan. *staaer*, Sw. *stå*, Sans. *sta*, L. *sto*, is a derivative from the noun, which is formed from the participle of the original verb. In this case, the noun should properly precede the verb. It may be here remarked that if *stan* is the radical word, *stand* and L. *sto* cannot be from the same stock. But *stand* in the pret. is *stood*, and *sto* forms *steti.* This induces a suspicion that *stan* is not the root of *stand*, but that *n* is casual. I am inclined however to believe these words to be from different roots. The Russ. *stoyu*, to stand, is the L. *sto*, but it signifies also to be, to exist, being the substantive verb. So in It. *stare*, Sp. Port. *estar.*]

1. To be upon the feet, as an animal; not to sit, kneel or lie.

The absolution to be pronounced by the priest alone, *standing.* *Com. Prayer.*

And the king turned his face about and blessed all the congregation of Israel, and all the congregation of Israel *stood.* 1 Kings viii.

2. To be erect, supported by the roots, as a tree or other plant. Notwithstanding the violence of the wind, the tree yet *stands.*
3. To be on its foundation; not to be overthrown or demolished; as, an old castle is yet *standing.*
4. To be placed or situated; to have a certain position or location. Paris *stands* on the Seine. London *stands* on the Thames.
5. To remain upright, in a moral sense; not to fall.

To *stand* or fall,
Free in thy own arbitrement it lies. *Milton.*

6. To become erect.

Mute and amaz'd, my hair with horror *stood.* *Dryden.*

7. To stop; to halt; not to proceed.

I charge thee, *stand*,
And tell thy name. *Dryden.*

8. To stop; to be at a stationary point.

Say, at what part of nature will they *stand?* *Pope.*

9. To be in a state of fixedness; hence, to continue; to endure. Our constitution has *stood* nearly forty years. It is hoped it will *stand* for ages.

Commonwealths by virtue ever *stood.* *Dryden.*

10. To be fixed or steady; not to vacillate. His mind *stands* unmoved.
11. To be in or to maintain a posture of resistance or defense. Approach with charged bayonets; the enemy will not *stand.*

The king granted the Jews to *stand* for their life. Esth. viii.

12. To be placed with regard to order or rank. Note the letter that *stands* first in order. Gen. Washington *stood* highest in public estimation. Christian charity *stands* first in the rank of gracious affections.
13. To be in any particular state; to *be*, emphatically expressed, that is, to be fixed or set; *the primary sense of the substantive verb.* How does the value of wheat *stand?* God *stands* in no need of our services, but we always *stand* in need of his aid and his mercy.

Accomplish what your signs foreshow;
I *stand* resign'd. *Dryden.*

14. To continue unchanged or valid; not to fail or become void.

No conditions of our peace can *stand.* *Shak.*

My mercy will I keep for him, and my covenant shall *stand* fast with him. Ps. lxxxix.

15. To consist; to have its being and essence.

Sacrifices—which *stood* only in meats and drinks. Heb. ix.

16. To have a place.

This excellent man, who *stood* not on the advantage-ground before, provoked men of all qualities. *Clarendon.*

17. To be in any state. Let us see how our matters *stand.*

As things now *stand* with us— *Calamy.*

18. To be in a particular respect or relation; as, to *stand* godfather to one. We ought to act according to the relation we *stand* in towards each other.
19. To be, with regard to state of mind.

Stand in awe, and sin not. Ps. iv.

20. To succeed; to maintain one's ground; not to fail; to be acquitted; to be safe.

Readers by whose judgment I would *stand* or fall— *Spectator.*

21. To hold a course at sea; as, to *stand* from the shore; to *stand* for the harbor.

From the same parts of heav'n his navy *stands.* *Dryden.*

22. To have a direction.

The wand did not really *stand* to the metal, when placed under it. *Boyle.*

23. To offer one's self as a candidate.

He *stood* to be elected one of the proctors of the university. *Saunderson.*

24. To place one's self; to be placed.

I *stood* between the Lord and you at that time— Deut. v.

25. To stagnate; not to flow.

—Or the black water of Pomptina *stands.* *Dryden.*

26. To be satisfied or convinced.

Though Page be a secure fool, and *stand* so firmly on his wife's frailty— *Shak.*

27. To make delay. I cannot *stand* to examine every particular.
28. To persist; to persevere.

Never *stand* in a lie when thou art accused. *Taylor.*

29. To adhere; to abide.

Despair would *stand* to the sword. *Daniel.*

30. To be permanent; to endure; not to vanish or fade; as, the color will *stand.*

To stand by, to be near; to be a spectator; to be present. I *stood by* when the operation was performed. This phrase generally implies that the person is inactive, or takes no part in what is done. In seamen's language, to *stand by* is to attend and be ready. *Stand by* the haliards.

2. To be aside; to be placed aside with disregard.

In the mean time, we let the commands *stand by* neglected. *Decay of Piety.*

3. To maintain; to defend; to support; not to desert. I will *stand by* my friend to the last. Let us *stand by* our country. "To *stand by* the Arundelian marbles," in Pope, is to defend or support their genuineness.
4. To rest on for support; to be supported.

This reply *standeth by* conjecture. *Whitgifte.*

To stand for, to offer one's self as a candidate.

How many *stand for* consulships?—Three. *Shak.*

2. To side with; to support; to maintain, or to profess or attempt to maintain. We all *stand for* freedom, *for* our rights or claims.
3. To be in the place of; to be the substitute or representative of. A cipher at the left hand of a figure *stands for* nothing.

I will not trouble myself, whether these names *stand for* the same thing, or really include one another. *Locke.*

4. In *seamen's language*, to direct the course towards.

To stand from, to direct the course from.

To stand one in, to cost. The coat *stands him in* twenty dollars.

To stand in, or *stand in for*, in seamen's language, is to direct a course towards land or a harbor.

To stand off, to keep at a distance. *Dryden.*

2. Not to comply. *Shak.*

3. To keep at a distance in friendship or social intercourse; to forbear intimacy.

We *stand off* from an acquaintance with God. *Atterbury.*

4. To appear prominent; to have relief.

Picture is best when it *standeth off*, as if it were carved. *Wotton.*

To stand off, or *off from*, in seamen's language, is to direct the course from land. To *stand off and on*, is to sail towards land and then from it.

To stand out, to project; to be prominent.

Their eyes *stand out* with fatness. Ps. lxxiii.

2. To persist in opposition or resistance; not to yield or comply; not to give way or recede.

His spirit is come in,
That so *stood out* against the holy church. *Shak.*

3. With seamen, to direct the course from land or a harbor.

To stand to, to ply; to urge efforts; to persevere.

Stand to your tackles, mates, and stretch your oars. *Dryden.*

2. To remain fixed in a purpose or opinion.

I still *stand to* it, that this is his sense. *Stillingfleet.*

3. To abide by; to adhere; as to a contract, assertion, promise, &c.; as, to *stand to* an award; to *stand to* one's word.

4. Not to yield; not to fly; to maintain the ground.

Their lives and fortunes were put in safety, whether they *stood to* it or ran away. *Bacon.*

To stand to sea, to direct the course from land.

To stand under, to undergo; to sustain. *Shak.*

To stand up, to rise from sitting; to be on the feet.

2. To arise in order to gain notice.

Against whom when the accusers *stood up*, they brought no accusation of such things as I supposed. Acts xxv.

3. To make a party.

When we *stood up* about the corn— *Shak.*

To stand up for, to defend; to justify; to support, or attempt to support; as, to *stand up for* the administration.

To stand upon, to concern; to interest. Does it not *stand upon* them to examine the grounds of their opinion? This phrase is, I believe, obsolete; but we say, it *stands us in hand*, that is, it is our concern, it is for our interest.

2. To value; to pride.

We highly esteem and *stand* much *upon* our birth. *Ray.*

3. To insist; as, to *stand upon* security. *Shak.*

To stand with, to be consistent. The faithful servants of God will receive what they pray for, so far as *stands with* his purposes and glory.

It *stands with* reason that they should be rewarded liberally. *Davies.*

To stand together, is used, but the last two phrases are not in very general use, and are perhaps growing obsolete.

To stand against, to oppose; to resist.

To stand fast, to be fixed; to be unshaken or immovable.

To stand in hand, to be important to one's interest; to be necessary or advantageous. It *stands* us *in hand* to be on good terms with our neighbors.

STAND, *v. t.* To endure; to sustain; to bear. I cannot *stand* the cold or the heat.

2. To endure; to resist without yielding or receding.

So had I *stood* the shock of angry fate. *Smith.*

He *stood* the furious foe. *Pope.*

3. To await; to suffer; to abide by.

Bid him disband the legions—
And *stand* the judgment of a Roman senate. *Addison.*

To stand one's ground, to keep the ground or station one has taken; to maintain one's position; in a literal or figurative sense; as, an army *stands its ground*, when it is not compelled to retreat. A man *stands his ground* in an argument, when he is able to maintain it, or is not refuted.

To stand it, to bear; to be able to endure; or to maintain one's ground or state; *a popular phrase.*

To stand trial, is to sustain the trial or examination of a cause; not to give up without trial.

STAND, *n.* [Sans. *stana*, a place, a mansion, state, &c.]

1. A stop; a halt; as, to make a *stand;* to come to a *stand*, either in walking or in any progressive business.

The horse made a *stand*, when he charged them and routed them. *Clarendon.*

2. A station; a place or post where one stands; or a place convenient for persons to remain for any purpose. The sellers of fruit have their several *stands* in the market.

I took my *stand* upon an eminence. *Spectator.*

3. Rank; post; station.

Father, since your fortune did attain
So high a *stand*, I mean not to descend. *Daniel.*

[In lieu of this, *standing* is now used. He is a man of high *standing* in his own country.]

4. The act of opposing.

We have come off
Like Romans; neither foolish in our *stands*,
Nor cowardly in retire. *Shak.*

5. The highest point; or the ultimate point of progression, where a stop is made, and regressive motion commences. The population of the world will not come to a *stand*, while the means of subsistence can be obtained. The prosperity of the Roman empire came to a *stand* in the reign of Augustus; after which it declined.

Vice is at *stand*, and at the highest flow. *Dryden.*

6. A young tree, usually reserved when the other trees are cut. [*English.*]

7. A small table; as a candle-*stand;* or any frame on which vessels and utensils may be laid.

8. In *commerce*, a weight of from two hundred and a half to three hundred of pitch. *Encyc.*

9. Something on which a thing rests or is laid; as a hay-*stand.*

Stand of arms, in military affairs, a musket with its usual appendages, as a bayonet, cartridge box, &c. *Marshall.*

To be at a stand, to stop on account of some doubt or difficulty; hence, to be perplexed; to be embarrassed; to hesitate what to determine, or what to do.

STAND'ARD, *n.* [It. *stendardo;* Fr. *etendard;* Sp. *estandarte;* D. *standaard;* G. *standarte; stand* and *ard*, sort, kind.]

1. An ensign of war; a staff with a flag or colors. The troops repair to their *standard.* The royal *standard* of Great Britain is a flag, in which the imperial ensigns of England, Scotland and Ireland are quartered with the armorial bearings of Hanover.

His armies, in the following day,
On those fair plains their *standards* proud display. *Fairfax.*

2. That which is established by sovereign power as a rule or measure by which others are to be adjusted. Thus the Winchester bushel is the *standard* of measures in Great Britain, and is adopted in the U. States as their *standard.* So of weights and of long measure.

3. That which is established as a rule or model, by the authority of public opinion, or by respectable opinions, or by custom or general consent; as writings which are admitted to be the *standard* of style and taste. Homer's Iliad is the *standard* of heroic poetry. Demosthenes and Cicero are the *standards* of oratory. Of modern eloquence, we have an excellent *standard* in the speeches of lord Chatham. Addison's writings furnish a good *standard* of pure, chaste and elegant English style. It is not an easy thing to erect a *standard* of taste.

4. In *coinage*, the proportion of weight of fine metal and alloy established by authority. The coins of England and of the United States are of nearly the same *standard.*

By the present *standard* of the coinage, sixty two shillings is coined out of one pound weight of silver. *Arbuthnot.*

5. A standing tree or stem; a tree not supported or attached to a wall.

Plant fruit of all sorts and *standard*, mural, or shrubs which lose their leaf. *Evelyn.*

6. In *ship-building*, an inverted knee placed upon the deck instead of beneath it, with its vertical branch turned upward from that which lies horizontally. *Mar. Dict.*

7. In *botany*, the upper petal or banner of a papilionaceous corol. *Martyn.*

STAND'ARD-BEARER, *n.* [*standard* and *bear.*]

An officer of an army, company or troop, that bears a standard; an ensign of infantry or a cornet of horse.

STAND-CROP, *n.* A plant. *Ainsworth.*

STAND'EL, *n.* A tree of long standing. [*Not used.*] *Howell.*

STAND'ER, *n.* One who stands.

2. A tree that has stood long. [*Not used.*] *Ascham.*

STAND'ER-BY, *n.* One that stands near; one that is present; a mere spectator. [We now more generally use *by-stander.*] *Hooker. Addison.*

STAND'ER-GRASS, *n.* A plant. [L. *statyrion.*] *Ainsworth.*

STAND'ING, *ppr.* Being on the feet; being erect. [See *Stand.*]

2. Moving in a certain direction to or from an object.

3. *a.* Settled; established, either by law or by custom, &c.; continually existing; permanent; not temporary; as a *standing* army. Money is the *standing* measure of the value of all other commodities. Legislative bodies have certain *standing* rules of proceeding. Courts of law are or ought to be governed by *standing* rules. There are *standing* rules of pleading. The gospel furnishes us with *standing* rules of morality. The Jews by their dispersion and their present condition, are a *standing* evidence of the truth of revelation and of the prediction of Moses. Many fashionable vices and follies ought to be the *standing* objects of ridicule.

4. Lasting; not transitory; not liable to fade or vanish; as a *standing* color.

5. Stagnant; not flowing; as *standing* water.

6. Fixed; not movable; as a *standing* bed; distinguished from a *truckle* bed. *Shak.*

7. Remaining erect; not cut down; as *standing* corn.

Standing rigging, of a ship. This consists of the cordage or ropes which sustain the masts and remain fixed in their position. Such are the shrouds and stays.

STAND'ING, *n.* Continuance; duration or existence; as a custom of long *standing.*

2. Possession of an office, character or place; as a patron or officer of long *standing.*

3. Station; place to stand in.

I will provide you with a good *standing* to see his entry. *Bacon.*

4. Power to stand.

I sink in deep mire, where there is no *standing.* Ps. lxix.

5. Rank; condition in society; as a man of good *standing* or of high *standing* among his friends.

STAND'ISH, *n.* [*stand* and *dish.*] A case for pen and ink.

I bequeath to Dean Swift my large silver *standish.* *Swift.*

STANE, *n.* [Sax. *stan.*] A stone. [*Local.*] [See *Stone.*]

STANG, *n.* [Sax. *stæng*, *steng*, a pole or stick; Dan. *stang;* G. *stange;* Sw. *stång;* It. *stanga*, a bar; W. *ystang*, a pole or perch; allied to *sting* and *stanchion;* from shooting.]

1. A pole, rod or perch; a measure of land. [*Not in use.*] *Swift.*

2. A long bar; a pole; a shaft.

To ride the stang, is to be carried on a pole on men's shoulders, in derision. [*Local.*] *Todd.*

STANG, *v. i.* To shoot with pain. [*Local.*] *Grose.*

STANK, *a.* Weak; worn out. [*Not in use.*] *Spenser.*

STANK, *v. i.* To sigh. [*Not used.*]

STANK, *old pret.* of *stink.* *Stunk* is now used.

STANK, *n.* [W. *ystanc.* See *Stanch.*] A dam or mound to stop water. [*Local.*]

STAN'NARY, *a.* [from L. *stannum*, tin, Ir. *stan;* W. *ystaen.* See *Tin.*]

Relating to the tin works; as *stannary* courts. *Blackstone.*

STAN'NARY, *n.* A tin mine. *Hall.*

STAN'NEL, } *n.* The kestrel, a species of
STAN'YEL, } hawk; called also *stonegall* and *wind-hover.* *Ed. Encyc.*

STAN'NIC, *a.* Pertaining to tin; procured from tin; as the *stannic* acid. *Lavoisier.*

STAN'ZA, *n.* [It. *stanza*, an abode or lodging, a stanza, that is, a stop; Sp. Port. *estancia*, from *estancar*, to stop; Fr. *stance.* See *Stanch.*]

In *poetry*, a number of lines or verses connected with each other, and ending in a full point or pause; a part of a poem containing every variation of measure in that poem. A stanza may contain verses of a different length or number of syllables, and a different number of verses; or it may consist of verses of equal length. Stanzas are said to have been first introduced from the Italian into French poetry about the year 1580, and thence they were introduced into England. The versions of the Psalms present examples of various kinds of *stanzas.*

Horace confines himself to one sort of verse or *stanza* in every ode. *Dryden.*

STAP'AZIN, *n.* A bird, a species of warbler.

STA'PLE, *n.* [Sax. *stapel*, *stapul*, a stake; D. *stapel*, a pile, stocks, staple; *stapelen*, to pile; G. *stapel*, a stake, a pile or heap, a staple, stocks, a mart; Sw. *stapel;* Dan. *stabel*, a staple; *stabler*, to pile; *stabbe*, a block or log; *stab*, a *staff.* We see this word is from the root of *staff.* The primary sense of the root is to set, to fix. *Staple* is that which is fixed, or a fixed place, or it is a pile or store.]

1. A settled mart or market; an emporium. In England, formerly, the king's *staple* was established in certain ports or towns, and certain goods could not be exported, without being first brought to these ports to be rated and charged with the duty payable to the king or public. The principal commodities on which customs were levied, were *wool*, *skins* and *lether*, and these were originally the *staple* commodities. Hence the words *staple commodities*, came in time to signify the principal commodities produced by a country for exportation or use. Thus cotton is the *staple commodity* of South Carolina, Georgia and other southern states of America. Wheat is the *staple* of Pennsylvania and New York.

2. A city or town where merchants agree to carry certain commodities.

3. The thread or pile of wool, cotton or flax. Thus we say, this is wool of a coarse *staple*, or fine *staple.* In America, cotton is of a short *staple*, long *staple*, fine *staple*, &c. The cotton of short *staple* is raised on the upland; the sea-island cotton is of a fine long *staple.*

4. [W. *ystwfwl.*] A loop of iron, or a bar or wire bent and formed with two points to be driven into wood, to hold a hook, pin, &c. *Pope.*

Staple of land, the particular nature and quality of land.

STA'PLE, *a.* Settled; established in commerce; as a *staple* trade.

2. According to the laws of commerce; marketable; fit to be sold. [*Not much used.*] *Swift.*

3. Chief; principal; regularly produced or made for market; as *staple* commodities. [*This is now the most general acceptation of the word.*]

STA'PLER, *n.* A dealer; as a wool *stapler.*

ST'AR, *n.* [Sax. *steorra;* Dan. Sw. *stierna;* G. *stern;* D. *star;* Arm. Corn. *steren;* Basque, *zarra;* Gr. ἀστηρ; Sans. *tara;* Bengal. *stara;* Pehlavi, *setaram;* Pers. *setareh* or *stara.*]

1. An apparently small luminous body in the heavens, that appears in the night, or when its light is not obscured by clouds or lost in the brighter effulgence of the sun. *Stars* are fixed or planetary. The fixed stars are known by their perpetual twinkling, and by their being always in the same position in relation to each other. The planets do not twinkle, and they revolve about the sun. The stars are worlds, and their immense numbers exhibit the astonishing extent of creation and of divine power.

2. The pole-star. [*A particular application, not in use.*] *Shak.*

3. In *astrology*, a configuration of the planets, supposed to influence fortune. Hence the expression, "You may thank your *stars* for such and such an event."

A pair of *star*-cross'd lovers. *Shak.*

4. The figure of a star; a radiated mark in writing or printing; an asterisk; thus *; used as a reference to a note in the margin, or to fill a blank in writing or printing where letters are omitted.

5. In *Scripture*, Christ is called the *bright and morning star*, the star that ushers in the light of an eternal day to his people. Rev. xxii.

Ministers are also called *stars in Christ's right hand*, as, being supported and directed by Christ, they convey light and knowledge to the followers of Christ. Rev. i.

The twelve stars which form the crown of the church, are the twelve apostles. Rev. xii.

6. The figure of a star; a badge of rank; as *stars* and garters.

The *pole-star*, a bright star in the tail of Ursa minor, so called from its being very near the north pole.

Star of Bethlehem, a flower and plant of the genus Ornithogalum. There is also the star of Alexandria, and of Naples, and of Constantinople, of the same genus. *Cyc. Lee.*

ST'AR, *v. t.* To set or adorn with stars or bright radiating bodies; to bespangle; as a robe *starred* with gems.

ST'AR-APPLE, *n.* A globular or olive-shaped fleshy fruit, inclosing a stone of the same shape. It grows in the warm climates of America, and is eaten by way of dessert. It is of the genus Chrysophyllum. *Miller. Cyc.*

ST'AR-FISH, *n.* [*star* and *fish.*] The sea star or asterias, a genus of marine animals or zoophytes, so named because their body is divided into rays, generally five in number, in the center of which and below is the mouth, which is the only orifice of the alimentary canal. They are covered with a coriaceous skin, armed with points or spines and pierced with numerous small holes, arranged in regular series, through which pass membranaceous *tentacula* or feelers, terminated each by a little disk or cup, by means of which they execute their progressive motions. *Cuvier.*

ST'AR-FLOWER, *n.* A plant, a species of Ornithogalum. *Cyc.*

A plant of the genus Stellaria. *Lee.*

ST'ARGAZER, *n.* [*star* and *gazer.*] One who gazes at the stars; a term of contempt for an astrologer, sometimes used ludicrously for an astronomer.

ST'ARGAZING, *n.* The act or practice of observing the stars with attention; astrology. *Swift.*

ST'AR-GRASS, *n.* [*star* and *grass.*] Starry duck meat, a plant of the genus Callitriche. *Lee.*

ST'AR-HAWK, *n.* A species of hawk so called. *Ainsworth.*

ST'AR-HYACINTH, *n.* A plant of the genus Scilla.

ST'AR-JELLY, *n.* A plant, the Tremella, one of the Fungi; also, star-shoot, a gelatinous substance.

ST'ARLESS, *a.* Having no stars visible or no starlight; as a *starless* night. *Milton. Dryden.*

ST'ARLIGHT, *n.* [*star* and *light.*] The light proceeding from the stars.

> Nor walk by moon
> Or glittering *starlight*, without thee is sweet. *Milton.*

ST'ARLIGHT, *a.* Lighted by the stars, or by the stars only; as a *starlight* evening. *Dryden.*

ST'ARLIKE, *a.* [*star* and *like.*] Resembling a star; stellated; radiated like a star; as *starlike* flowers. *Mortimer.*

2\. Bright; illustrious.

> The having turned many to righteousness shall confer a *starlike* and immortal brightness. *Boyle.*

ST'ARLING, *n.* [Sax. *stær*; Sw. *stare.*]

1\. A bird, the stare, of the genus Sturnus.

2\. A defense to the piers of bridges.

STA'ROST, *n.* In *Poland*, a feudatory; one who holds a fief.

STA'ROSTY, *n.* A fief; an estate held by feudal service.

ST'AR-PAVED, *a.* [*star* and *paved.*] Studded with stars.

> The road of heaven *star-paved.* *Milton.*

ST'AR-PROOF, *a.* [*star* and *proof.* Impervious to the light of the stars; as a *star-proof* elm. *Milton.*

ST'AR-READ, *n.* [*star* and *read.*] Doctrine of the stars; astronomy. [*Not in use.*] *Spenser.*

ST'ARRED, *pp.* or *a.* [from *star.*] Adorned or studded with stars; as the *starred* queen of Ethiopia. *Milton.*

2\. Influenced in fortune by the stars.

> My third comfort,
> *Starr'd* most unluckily— *Shak.*

ST'ARRING, *ppr.* or *a.* Adorning with stars.

2\. Shining; bright; sparkling; as *starring* comets. [*Not in use.*]

ST'ARRY, *a.* [from *star.*] Abounding with stars; adorned with stars.

> Above the clouds, above the *starry* sky. *Pope.*

2\. Consisting of stars; stellar; stellary; proceeding from the stars; as *starry* light; *starry* flame. *Spenser. Dryden.*

3\. Shining like stars; resembling stars; as *starry* eyes. *Shak.*

ST'AR-SHOOT, *n.* [*star* and *shoot.*] That which is emitted from a star.

> I have seen a good quantity of that jelly, by the vulgar called a *star-shoot*, as if it remained upon the extinction of a falling star. *Bacon.*

[The writer once saw the same kind of substance from a brilliant meteor, at Amherst in Massachusetts. See Journ. of Science for a description of it by Rufus Graves, Esq.]

ST'AR-STONE, *n.* Asteria, a kind of extraneous fossil, consisting of regular joints, each of which is of a radiated figure. *Encyc.*

ST'AR-THISTLE, *n.* A plant of the genus Centaurea.

ST'AR-WORT, *n.* A plant of the genus Aster, and another of the genus Iridax. The *yellow star-wort* is of the genus Inula or elecampane.

ST'ARBOARD, *n.* [Sax. *steor-board*; G. *steuerbort*, as if from *steuer*, the rudder or helm; D. *stuur-bord*, as if from *stuur*, helm; Sw. Dan. *styr-bord.* But in Fr. *stribord*, Sp. *estribor*, Arm. *strybourz* or *stribourh*, are said to be contracted from *dexter-bord*, right-side. I know not from what particular construction of a vessel the helm should give name to the right hand side, unless from the tiller's being held by the right hand, or at the right side of the steersman.]

The right hand side of a ship or boat, when a spectator stands with his face towards the head, stem or prow.

ST'ARBOARD, *a.* Pertaining to the right hand side of a ship; being or lying on the right side; as the *starboard* shrouds; *starboard* quarter; *starboard* tack. In seamanship, *starboard*, uttered by the master of a ship, is an order to the helmsman to put the helm to the starboard side. *Mar. Dict.*

ST'ARCH, *n.* [Sax. *stearc*, rigid, stiff; G. *stärke*, strength, starch; *stark*, strong; D. *sterk*, Dan. *stærk*, Sw. *stark*, strong. See *Stare* and *Steer.*]

A substance used to stiffen linen and other cloth. It is the fecula of flour, or a substance that subsides from water mixed with wheat flour. It is sometimes made from potatoes. *Starch* forms the greatest portion of farinaceous substances, particularly of wheat flour, and it is the chief aliment of bread.

ST'ARCH, *a.* Stiff; precise; rigid. *Killingbeck.*

ST'ARCH, *v. t.* To stiffen with starch. *Gay.*

ST'AR-CHAMBER, *n.* Formerly, a court of criminal jurisdiction in England. This court was abolished by Stat. 16 Charles I. See Blackstone, B. iv. ch. xix.

ST'ARCHED, *pp.* Stiffened with starch.

2\. *a.* Stiff; precise; formal. *Swift.*

ST'ARCHEDNESS, *n.* Stiffness in manners; formality. *Addison.*

ST'ARCHER, *n.* One who starches, or whose occupation is to starch. *Johnson.*

ST'ARCHING, *ppr.* Stiffening with starch.

ST'ARCHLY, *adv.* With stiffness of manner; formally.

ST'ARCHNESS, *n.* Stiffness of manner; preciseness.

ST'ARCHY, *a.* Stiff; precise.

STARE, *n.* [Sax. *stær*; G. *stahr*; Sw. *stare.*] A bird, the starling.

STARE, *v. i.* [Sax. *starian*; Dan. *stirrer*; Sw. *stirra*; G. *starren*; D. *staaren.* In Sw. *stirra ut fingren*, is to spread one's fingers. The sense then is to open or extend, and it seems to be closely allied to G. *starr*, stiff, and to *starch*, *stern*, which imply straining, tension.]

1\. To gaze; to look with fixed eyes wide open; to fasten an earnest look on some object. *Staring* is produced by wonder, surprise, stupidity, horror, fright and sometimes by eagerness to hear or learn something, sometimes by impudence. We say, he *stared* with astonishment.

> Look not big, nor *stare*, nor fret. *Shak.*

2\. To stand out; to be prominent.

> Take off all the *staring* straws and jaggs in the hive. [*Not used.*] *Mortimer.*

To stare in the face, to be before the eyes or undeniably evident.

> The law *stares* them in the face, while they are breaking it. *Locke.*

STARE, *n.* A fixed look with eyes wide open. *Dryden.*

STA'RER, *n.* One who stares or gazes.

STA'RING, *ppr.* Gazing; looking with fixed eyes.

ST'ARK, *a.* [Sax. *sterc*, *stearc*; D. *sterk*; G. *stark*, stiff, strong; formed on the root of the G. *starr*, stiff, rigid, Eng. *steer*; from *straining*, *stretching.* See *Starch* and *Steer.*]

1\. Stiff; strong; rugged.

> Many a nobleman lies *stark* and stiff,
> Under the hoofs of vaunting enemies. *Shak.*
> The north is not so *stark* and cold. *Obs.* *B. Jonson.*

2\. Deep; full; profound; absolute.

> Consider the *stark* security
> The commonwealth is in now. *Obs.* *B. Jonson.*

3\. Mere; gross; absolute.

> He pronounces the citation *stark* nonsense. *Collier.*

ST'ARK, *adv.* Wholly; entirely; absolutely; as *stark* mad; *stark* blind; *stark* naked. These are the principal applications of this word now in use. The word is in popular use, but not an elegant word in any of its applications.

ST'ARKLY, *adv.* Stiffly; strongly. *Obs.* *Shak.*

ST'ART, *v. i.* [D. *storten*, to pour, to spill, to fall, to rush, to tumble; Sw. *störta*, to roll upon the head, to pitch headlong. In Sax. *steort* is a tail, that is, a shoot or projection; hence the promontory so called in Devonshire. The word seems to be a derivative from the root of *star*, *steer.* The primary sense is to shoot, to dart suddenly, or to spring.]

1\. To move suddenly, as if by a twitch; as, to *start* in sleep or by a sudden spasm.

2\. To move suddenly, as by an involuntary shrinking from sudden fear or alarm.

> I *start* as from some dreadful dream. *Dryden.*

3. To move with sudden quickness, as with a spring or leap.

A spirit fit to *start* into an empire,
And look the world to law. *Dryden.*

4. To shrink; to wince.

But if he *start*,
It is the flesh of a corrupted heart. *Shak.*

5. To move suddenly aside; to deviate; generally with *from, out of*, or *aside*.

Th' old drudging sun from his long beaten way
Shall at thy voice *start* and misguide the day. *Cowley.*

Keep your soul to the work when ready to *start aside*. *Watts.*

6. To set out; to commence a race, as from a barrier or goal. The horses *started* at the word, go.

At once they *start*, advancing in a line. *Dryden.*

7. To set out; to commence a journey or enterprise. The public coaches *start* at six o'clock.

When two *start* into the world together— *Collier.*

To start up, to rise suddenly, as from a seat or couch; or to come suddenly into notice or importance.

ST'ART, *v. t.* To alarm; to disturb suddenly; to startle; to rouse.

Upon malicious bravery dost thou come,
To *start* my quiet? *Shak.*

2. To rouse suddenly from concealment; to cause to flee or fly; as, to *start* a hare or a woodcock; to *start* game. *Pope.*

3. To bring into motion; to produce suddenly to view or notice.

Brutus will *start* a spirit as soon as Cesar. *Shak.*

The present occasion has *started* the dispute among us. *Lesley.*

So we say, to *start* a question, to *start* an objection; that is, to suggest or propose anew.

4. To invent or discover; to bring within pursuit.

Sensual men agree in the pursuit of every pleasure they can *start*. *Temple.*

5. To move suddenly from its place; to dislocate; as, to *start* a bone.

One *started* the end of the clavicle from the sternum. *Wiseman.*

6. To empty, as liquor from a cask; to pour out; as, to *start* wine into another cask. *Mar. Dict.*

ST'ART, *n.* A sudden motion of the body, produced by spasm; a sudden twitch or spasmodic affection; as a *start* in sleep.

2. A sudden motion from alarm.

The fright awaken'd Arcite with a *start*. *Dryden.*

3. A sudden rousing to action; a spring; excitement.

Now fear I this will give it *start* again. *Shak.*

4. Sally; sudden motion or effusion; a bursting forth; as *starts* of fancy.

To check the *starts* and sallies of the soul. *Addison.*

5. Sudden fit; sudden motion followed by intermission.

For she did speak in *starts* distractedly. *Shak.*

Nature does nothing by *starts* and leaps, or in a hurry. *L'Estrange.*

6. A quick spring; a darting; a shoot; a push; as, to give a *start*.

Both cause the string to give a quicker *start*. *Bacon.*

7. First motion from a place; act of setting out.

The *start* of first performance is all. *Bacon.*

You stand like grayhounds in the slips,
Straining upon the *start*. *Shak.*

To get the start, to begin before another; to gain the advantage in a similar undertaking.

Get the start of the majestic world. *Shak.*

She might have forsaken him, if he had not *got the start* of her. *Dryden.*

ST'ART, *n.* A projection; a push; a horn; a tail. In the latter sense it occurs in the name of the bird *red-start*. Hence *the Start*, in Devonshire.

ST'ARTED, *pp.* Suddenly roused or alarmed; poured out, as a liquid; discovered; proposed; produced to view.

ST'ARTER, *n.* One that starts; one that shrinks from his purpose. *Hudibras.*

2. One that suddenly moves or suggests a question or an objection.

3. A dog that rouses game. *Delany.*

ST'ARTFUL, *a.* Apt to start; skittish.

ST'ARTFULNESS, *n.* Aptness to start.

ST'ARTING, *ppr.* Moving suddenly; shrinking; rousing; commencing, as a jonrney, &c.

ST'ARTING, *n.* The act of moving suddenly.

ST'ARTING-HOLE, *n.* A loophole; evasion. *Martin.*

ST'ARTINGLY, *adv.* By sudden fits or starts. *Shak.*

ST'ARTING-POST, *n.* [*start* and *post*.] A post, stake, barrier or place from which competitors in a race start or begin the race.

ST'ARTISH, *a.* Apt to start; skittish; shy.

ST'ARTLE, *v. i.* [*dim.* of *start*.] To shrink; to move suddenly or be excited on feeling a sudden alarm.

Why shrinks the soul
Back on herself, and *startles* at destruction? *Addison.*

ST'ARTLE, *v. t.* To impress with fear; to excite by sudden alarm, surprise or apprehension; to shock; to alarm; to fright. We were *startled* at the cry of distress. Any great and unexpected event is apt to *startle* us.

The supposition that angels assume bodies, need not *startle* us. *Locke.*

2. To deter; to cause to deviate. [*Little used.*] *Clarendon.*

ST'ARTLE, *n.* A sudden motion or shock occasioned by an unexpected alarm, surprise or apprehension of danger; sudden impression of terror.

After having recovered from my first *startle*, I was well pleased with the accident. *Spectator.*

ST'ARTLED, *pp.* Suddenly moved or shocked by an impression of fear or surprise.

ST'ARTLING, *ppr.* Suddenly impressing with fear or surprise.

ST'ARTUP, *n.* [*start* and *up*.] One that comes suddenly into notice. [Not used. We use *upstart*.] *Shak.*

2. A kind of high shoe. *Hall.*

ST'ARTUP, *a.* Suddenly coming into notice. [*Not used.*] *Warburton.*

ST'ARVE, *v. i.* [Sax. *stearfian*, to perish with hunger or cold; G. *sterben*, to die, either by disease or hunger, or by a wound; D. *sterven*, to die. Qu. is this from the root of Dan. *tarv*, Sw. *tarf*, necessity, want?]

1. To perish; to be destroyed. [*In this general sense, obsolete.*] *Fairfax.*

2. To perish or die with cold; as, to *starve* with cold. [*This sense is retained in England, but not in the U. States.*]

3. To perish with hunger. [*This sense is retained in England and the U. States.*]

4. To suffer extreme hunger or want; to be very indigent.

Sometimes virtue *starves*, while vice is fed. *Pope.*

ST'ARVE, *v. t.* To kill with hunger. Maliciously to *starve* a man is, in law, murder.

2. To distress or subdue by famine; as, to *starve* a garrison into a surrender.

3. To destroy by want; as, to *starve* plants by the want of nutriment.

4. To kill with cold. [*Not in use in the U. States.*]

From beds of raging fire to *starve* in ice
Their soft etherial warmth— *Milton.*

5. To deprive of force or vigor.

The powers of their minds are *starved* by disuse. [*Unusual.*] *Locke.*

ST'ARVED, *pp.* Killed with hunger; subdued by hunger; rendered poor by want.

2. Killed by cold. [*Not in use in the United States.*]

STARVELING, *a.* *st'arvling.* Hungry; lean; pining with want. *Phillips.*

STARVELING, *n.* *st'arvling.* An animal or plant that is made thin, lean and weak through want of nutriment.

And thy poor *starveling* bountifully fed. *Donne.*

ST'ARVING, *ppr.* Perishing with hunger; killing with hunger; rendering lean and poor by want of nourishment.

2. Perishing with cold; killing with cold. [*English.*]

STA'TARY, *a.* [from *state*.] Fixed; settled. [*Not in use.*] *Brown.*

STATE, *n.* [L. *status*, from *sto*, to stand, to be fixed; It. *stato*; Sp. *estado*; Fr. *etát*. Hence G. *stät*, fixed; *statt*, place, abode, stead; *staat*, state; *stadt*, a town or city; D. *staat*, condition, state; *stad*, a city, Dan. Sw. *stad*; Sans. *stidaha*, to stand; Pers. *istaden*, id. *State* is fixedness or standing.]

1. Condition; the circumstances of a being or thing at any given time. These circumstances may be internal, constitutional or peculiar to the being, or they may have relation to other beings. We say, the body is in a sound *state*, or it is in a weak *state*; or it has just recovered from a feeble *state*. The *state* of his health is good. The *state* of his mind is favorable for study. So we say, the *state* of public affairs calls for the exercise of talents and wisdom. In regard to foreign nations, our affairs are in a good *state*. So we say, single *state*, and married *state*.

Declare the past and present *state* of things. *Dryden.*

2. Modification of any thing.

Keep the *state* of the question in your eye. *Boyle.*

3. Crisis; stationary point; highth; point from which the next movement is regression.

Tumors have their several degrees and times, as beginning, augment, *state* and declination. [*Not in use.*] *Wiseman.*

4. Estate; possession. *Obs.* [See *Estate.*] *Daniel.*

5. A political body, or body politic; the whole body of people united under one government, whatever may be the form of the government.

Municipal law is a rule of conduct prescribed by the supreme power in a *state*. *Blackstone.*

More usually the word signifies a political body governed by representatives; a commonwealth; as the *States* of Greece; the *States* of America.

In this sense, *state* has sometimes more immediate reference to the government, sometimes to the people or community. Thus when we say, the *state* has made provision for the paupers, the word has reference to the government or legislature; but when we say, the *state* is taxed to support paupers, the word refers to the whole people or community.

6. A body of men united by profession, or constituting a community of a particular character; as the civil and ecclesiastical *states* in Great Britain. But these are sometimes distinguished by the terms *church* and *state*. In this case, *state* signifies the civil community or government only.

7. Rank; condition; quality; as the *state* of honor. *Shak.*

8. Pomp; appearance of greatness.

In *state* the monarchs march'd. *Dryden.*

Where least of *state*, there most of love is shown. *Dryden.*

9. Dignity; grandeur.

She instructed him how he should keep *state*, yet with a modest sense of his misfortunes. *Bacon.*

10. A seat of dignity.

This chair shall be my *state*. *Shak.*

11. A canopy; a covering of dignity.

His high throne, under *state*
Of richest texture spread— *Milton.*
[*Unusual.*]

12. A person of high rank. [*Not in use.*] *Latimer.*

13. The principal persons in a government.

The bold design
Pleas'd highly those infernal *states*. *Milton.*

14. The bodies that constitute the legislature of a country; as the *states* general.

15. Joined with another word, it denotes public, or what belongs to the community or body politic; as *state* affairs; *state* policy.

STATE, *v. t.* To set; to settle. [See *Stated.*]

2. To express the particulars of any thing in writing; to set down in detail or in gross; as, to *state* an account; to *state* debt and credit; to *state* the amount due.

3. To express the particulars of any thing verbally; to represent fully in words; to narrate; to recite. The witnesses *stated* all the circumstances of the transaction. They are enjoined to *state* all the particulars. It is the business of the advocate to *state* the whole case. Let the question be fairly *stated.*

STA'TED, *pp.* Expressed or represented; told; recited.

2. *a.* Settled; established; regular; occurring at regular times; not occasional; as *stated* hours of business.

3. Fixed; established; as a *stated* salary.

STA'TEDLY, *adv.* Regularly; at certain times; not occasionally. It is one of the distinguishing marks of a good man, that he *statedly* attends public worship.

STA'TELESS, *a.* Without pomp. *J. Barlow.*

STA'TELINESS, *n.* [from *stately.*] Grandeur; loftiness of mien or manner; majestic appearance; dignity.

For *stateliness* and majesty, what is comparable to a horse? *More.*

2. Appearance of pride; affected dignity. *Beaum.*

STA'TELY, *a.* Lofty; dignified; majestic; as *stately* manners; a *stately* gait.

2. Magnificent; grand; as a *stately* edifice; a *stately* dome; a *stately* pyramid.

3. Elevated in sentiment. *Dryden.*

STA'TELY, *adv.* Majestically; loftily. *Milton.*

STA'TEMENT, *n.* The act of stating, reciting or presenting verbally or on paper.

2. A series of facts or particulars expressed on paper; as a written *statement.*

3. A series of facts verbally recited; recital of the circumstances of a transaction; as a verbal *statement.*

STA'TE-MÖNGER, *n.* [*state* and *monger.*] One versed in politics, or one that dabbles in state affairs.

STA'TER, *n.* Another name of the daric, an ancient silver coin weighing about four Attic drachmas, about three shillings sterling, or 61 cents.

STA'TE-ROOM, *n.* [*state* and *room.*] A magnificent room in a palace or great house. *Johnson.*

2. An apartment for lodging in a ship's cabin.

STATES, *n. plu.* Nobility. *Shak.*

STA'TESMAN, *n.* [*state* and *man.*] A man versed in the arts of government; usually, one eminent for political abilities; a politician.

2. A small landholder. *English.*

3. One employed in public affairs. *Pope. Swift.*

STA'TESMANSHIP, *n.* The qualifications or employments of a statesman. *Churchill.*

STA'TESWÖMAN, *n.* A woman who meddles in public affairs; *in contempt.* *Addison.*

STAT'IC, } *a.* [See *Statics.*] Relating
STAT'ICAL, } to the science of weighing bodies; as a *static* balance or engine. *Arbuthnot.*

STAT'ICS, *n.* [Fr. *statique;* It. *statica;* L. *statice;* Gr. ϛατικη.]

1. That branch of mechanics which treats of bodies *at rest.* Dynamics treats of bodies *in motion.*

2. In *medicine,* a kind of epileptics, or persons seized with epilepsies. *Cyc.*

STA'TION, *n.* [Fr. from L. *statio,* from *sto, status;* It. *stazione;* Sp. *estacion.*]

1. The act of standing.

Their manner was to stand at prayer—on which their meetings for that purpose received the name of *stations.* *Obs.* *Hooker.*

2. A state of rest.

All progression is performed by drawing on or impelling forward what was before in *station* or at quiet. [*Rare.*] *Brown.*

3. The spot or place where one stands, particularly where a person habitually stands, or is appointed to remain for a time; as the *station* of a sentinel. Each detachment of troops had its *station.*

4. Post assigned; office; the part or department of public duty which a person is appointed to perform. The chief magistrate occupies the first political *station* in a nation. Other officers fill subordinate *stations.* The office of bishop is an ecclesiastical *station* of great importance. It is the duty of the executive to fill all civil and military *stations* with men of worth.

5. Situation; position.

The fig and date, why love they to remain
In middle *station?* *Prior.*

6. Employment; occupation; business.

By spending the sabbath in retirement and religious exercises, we gain new strength and resolution to perform God's will in our several *stations* the week following. *Nelson.*

7. Character; state.

The greater part have kept their *station.* *Milton.*

8. Rank; condition of life. He can be contented with a humble *station.*

9. In *church history,* the fast of the fourth and sixth days of the week, Wednesday and Friday, in memory of the council which condemned Christ, and of his passion.

10. In *the church of Rome,* a church where indulgences are to be had on certain days. *Encyc.*

STA'TION, *v. t.* To place; to set; or to appoint to the occupation of a post, place or office; as, to *station* troops on the right or left of an army; to *station* a sentinel on a rampart; to *station* ships on the coast of Africa or in the West Indies; to *station* a man at the head of the department of finance.

STA'TIONAL, *a.* Pertaining to a station. *Encyc.*

STA'TIONARY, *a.* Fixed; not moving, progressive or regressive; not appearing to move. The sun becomes *stationary* in Cancer, in its advance into the northern signs. The court in England which was formerly itinerary, is now *stationary.*

2. Not advancing, in a moral sense; not improving; not growing wiser, greater or better; not becoming greater or more excellent. *S. S. Smith.*

3. Respecting place.

The same harmony and *stationary* constitution— *Brown.*

Stationary fever, a fever depending on peculiar seasons. *Coxe.*

STA'TION-BILL, *n.* In *seamen's language,* a list containing the appointed posts of the ship's company, when navigating the ship. *Mar. Dict.*

STA'TIONER, *n.* [from *station,* a state.] A bookseller; one who sells books, paper, quills, inkstands, pencils and other furniture for writing. The business of the bookseller and stationer is usually carried on by the same person.

STA'TIONERY, *n.* The articles usually sold by stationers, as paper, ink, quills, &c.

STA'TIONERY, *a.* Belonging to a stationer.

STA'TIST, *n.* [from *state.*] A statesman; a politician; one skilled in government.

> *Statists* indeed,
> And lovers of their country. [*Not now used.*] *Milton.*

STATIST'IC, STATIST'ICAL, *a.* [from *state* or *statist.*] Pertaining to the state of society, the condition of the people, their economy, their property and resources.

STATIST'ICS, *n.* A collection of facts respecting the state of society, the condition of the people in a nation or country, their health, longevity, domestic economy, arts, property and political strength, the state of the country, &c. *Sinclair. Tooke.*

STAT'UARY, *n.* [It. *statuaria*; Sp. *estatuaria*; from L. *statuarius*, from *statua*, a statue; *statuo*, to set.]

1. The art of carving images as representatives of real persons or things; a branch of sculpture. *Temple.*

[*In this sense the word has no plural.*]

2. [It. *statuario*; Sp. *estatuario.*] One that professes or practices the art of carving images or making statues.

> On other occasions the *statuaries* took their subjects from the poets. *Addison.*

STAT'UE, *n.* [L. *statua*; *statuo*, to set; that which is set or fixed.]

An image; a solid substance formed by carving into the likeness of a whole living being; as a *statue* of Hercules or of a lion.

STAT'UE, *v. t.* To place, as a statue; to form a statue of. *Shak.*

STATU'MINATE, *v. t.* [L. *statumino.*] To prop or support. [*Not in use.*] *B. Jonson.*

STAT'URE, *n.* [L. It. *statura*; Sp. *estatura*; Fr. *stature*; from L. *statuo*, to set.]

The natural highth of an animal body. It is more generally used of the human body.

> Foreign men of mighty *stature* came. *Dryden.*

STAT'URED, *a.* Arrived at full stature. [*Little used.*] *Hall.*

STAT'UTABLE, *a.* [from *statute.*] Made or introduced by statute; proceeding from an act of the legislature; as a *statutable* provision or remedy.

2. Made or being in conformity to statute; as *statutable* measures. *Addison.*

STAT'UTABLY, *adv.* In a manner agreeable to statute.

STAT'UTE, *n.* [Fr. *statut*; It. *statuto*; Sp. *estatuto*; L. *statutum*; from *statuo*, to set.]

1. An act of the legislature of a state that extends its binding force to all the citizens or subjects of that state, as distinguished from an act which extends only to an individual or company; an act of the legislature commanding or prohibiting something; a positive law. *Statutes* are distinguished from *common law.* The latter owes its binding force to the principles of justice, to long use and the consent of a nation. The former owe their binding force to a positive command or declaration of the supreme power.

Statute is commonly applied to the acts of a legislative body consisting of representatives. In monarchies, the laws of the sovereign are called *edicts, decrees, ordinances, rescripts,* &c.

2. A special act of the supreme power, of a private nature, or intended to operate only on an individual or company.

3. The act of a corporation or of its founder, intended as a permanent rule or law; as the *statutes* of a university.

STAT'UTE-MERCHANT, *n.* In *English law*, a bond of record pursuant to the Stat. 13 Edw. 1. acknowledged before one of the clerks of the statutes-merchant and the mayor or chief warden of London, or before certain persons appointed for the purpose; on which, if not paid at the day, an execution may be awarded against the body, lands and goods of the obligor. *Blackstone.*

STAT'UTE-STAPLE, *n.* A bond of record acknowledged before the mayor of the staple, by virtue of which the creditor may forthwith have execution against the body, lands and goods of the debtor, on non-payment. *Blackstone.*

STAT'UTORY, *a.* Enacted by statute; depending on statute for its authority; as a *statutory* provision or remedy.

STAU'ROLITE, STAU'ROTIDE, *n.* [Gr. σαυρος, a cross, and λιθος, stone.] The granatit of Werner or grenatite of Jameson; a mineral crystalized in prisms, either single or intersecting each other at right angles. Its color is white or gray, reddish or brown. It is often opake, sometimes translucent. Its form and infusibility distinguish it from the garnet. It is called by the French, *harmotome.* *Dict. Cleaveland.*

STAVE, *n.* [from *staff*; Fr. *douve, douvain.* It has the first sound of *a*, as in *save.*]

1. A thin narrow piece of timber, of which casks are made. *Staves* make a considerable article of export from New England to the West Indies.

2. A staff; a metrical portion; a part of a psalm appointed to be sung in churches.

3. In *music*, the five horizontal and parallel lines on which the notes of tunes are written or printed; the *staff*, as it is now more generally written.

To stave and tail, to part dogs by interposing a staff and by pulling the tail.

STAVE, *v. t.* pret. *stove* or *staved*; pp. *id.*

1. To break a hole in; to break; to burst; primarily, to thrust through with a staff; as, to *stave* a cask. *Mar. Dict.*

2. To push as with a staff; with *off.*

> The condition of a servant *staves* him *off* to a distance. *South.*

3. To delay; as, to *stave* off the execution of a project.

4. To pour out; to suffer to be lost by breaking the cask.

> All the wine in the city has been *staved.* *Sandys.*

5. To furnish with staves or rundles. [*Not in use.*] *Knolles.*

STAVE, *v. i.* To fight with staves. [*Not in use.*] *Hudibras.*

ST'AVES, *plu.* of *staff*, when applied to a stick, is pronounced with *a* as in *ask*, the Italian sound.

STAW, *v. i.* To be fixed or set. [*Not in use or local.*]

STAY, *v. i.* pret. *staid*, for *stayed.* [Ir. *stadam*; Sp. *estay*, a stay of a ship; *estada*, stay, a remaining; *estiar*, to stop; Port. *estada*, abode; *estaes*, stays of a ship; *estear*, to stay, to prop; W. *ystad*, state; *ystadu*, to stay or remain; Fr. *etai, etayer*; D. *stut, stutten.* This word seems to be connected with *state*, and if so, is a derivative from the root of L. *sto*, to stand. But from the orthography of this word in the Irish, Spanish and Portuguese, and of *steti*, the preterit of *sto*, in Latin, I am led to believe the elementary word was *stad* or *stat.* The sense is to set, stop or hold. It is to be observed further that *stay* may be easily deduced from the G. D. *stag*, a stay; *stag-segel*, stay-sail; W. *tagu*, to stop.]

1. To remain; to continue in a place; to abide for any indefinite time. Do you *stay* here, while I go to the next house. *Stay* here a week. We *staid* at the Hotel Montmorenci.

> *Stay*, I command you; *stay* and hear me first. *Dryden.*

2. To continue in a state.

> The flames augment, and *stay*
> At their full highth, then languish to decay. *Dryden.*

3. To wait; to attend; to forbear to act.

> I *stay* for Turnus. *Dryden.*
> Would ye *stay* for them from having husbands? Ruth i.

4. To stop; to stand still.

> She would command the hasty sun to *stay.* *Spenser.*

5. To dwell.

> I must *stay* a little on one action. *Dryden.*

6. To rest; to rely; to confide in; to trust.

> Because ye despise this word, and trust in oppression, and *stay* thereon— Is. xxx.

STAY, *v. t.* pret. and pp. *staid*, for *stayed.*

1. To stop; to hold from proceeding; to withhold; to restrain.

> All that may *stay* the mind from thinking that true which they heartily wish were false. *Hooker.*
> To *stay* these sudden gusts of passion. *Rowe.*

2. To delay; to obstruct; to hinder from proceeding.

> Your ships are *staid* at Venice. *Shak.*
> I was willing to *stay* my reader on an argument that appeared to me to be new. *Locke.*

3. To keep from departure; as, you might have *staid* me here. *Dryden.*

4. To stop from motion or falling; to prop; to hold up; to support.

> Aaron and Hur *stayed* up his hands. Ex. xvii.
> Sallows and reeds for vineyards useful found
> To *stay* thy vines. *Dryden.*

5. To support from sinking; to sustain with strength; as, to take a luncheon to *stay* the stomach.

STAY, *n.* Continuance in a place; abode for a time indefinite; as, you make a short *stay* in this city.

> Embrace the hero, and his *stay* implore. *Waller.*

2. Stand; stop; cessation of motion or progression.

> Affairs of state seem'd rather to stand at a *stay.* *Hayward.*

[But in this sense, we now use *stand*; to be at a *stand.*]

3. Stop; obstruction; hinderance from progress.

Griev'd with each step, tormented with each *stay*. *Fairfax.*

4. Restraint of passion; moderation; caution; steadiness; sobriety.

With prudent *stay*, he long deferr'd
The rough contention. *Obs.* *Philips.*

5. A fixed state.

Alas, what *stay* is there in human state! *Dryden.*

6. Prop; support.

Trees serve as so many *stays* for their vines. *Addison.*

My only strength and *stay!* *Milton.*

The Lord is my *stay*. Ps. xviii.

The stay and the staff, the means of supporting and preserving life. Is. iii.

7. Steadiness of conduct. *Todd.*

8. In *the rigging of a ship*, a large strong rope employed to support the mast, by being extended from its upper end to the stem of the ship. The *fore-stay* reaches from the foremast head towards the bowsprit end; the *main-stay* extends to the ship's stem; the *mizen-stay* is stretched to a collar on the main-mast, above the quarter deck, &c. *Mar. Dict.*

Stays, in seamanship, implies the operation of going about or changing the course of a ship, with a shifting of the sails. To *be in stays*, is to lie with the head to the wind, and the sails so arranged as to check her progress.

To miss stays, to fail in the attempt to go about. *Mar. Dict.*

STA'YED, *pp.* Staid; fixed; settled; sober. It is now written *staid*, which see.

STA'YEDLY, *adv.* Composedly; gravely; moderately; prudently; soberly. [*Little used.*]

STA'YEDNESS, *n.* Moderation; gravity; sobriety; prudence. [See *Staidness.*]

2. Solidity; weight. [*Little used.*] *Camden.*

STA'YER, *n.* One that stops or restrains; one who upholds or supports; that which props.

STA'YLACE, *n.* A lace for fastening the boddice in female dress. *Swift.*

STA'YLESS, *a.* Without stop or delay. [*Little used.*]

STA'YMAKER, *n.* One whose occupation is to make stays. *Spenser.*

STAYS, *n. plu.* A boddice; a kind of waistcoat stiffened with whalebone or other thing, worn by females. *Gay.*

2. *Stays*, of a ship. [See *Stay.*]

3. Station; fixed anchorage. *Sidney.*

4. Any support; that which keeps another extended.

Weavers, stretch your *stays* upon the weft. *Dryden.*

STA'Y-SAIL, *n.* [*stay* and *sail.*] Any sail extended on a stay. *Mar. Dict.*

STA'Y-TACKLE, *n.* [*stay* and *tackle.*] A large tackle attached to the main-stay by means of a pendant, and used to hoist heavy bodies, as boats, butts of water and the like. *Mar. Dict.*

STEAD, STED, } *n.* [Goth. *stads;* Sax. Dan. *sted;* G. *statt;* D. *stede.* See *Stay.*]

1. Place; *in general.*

Fly this fearful *stead.* *Spenser.*

[*In this sense not used.*]

2. Place or room which another had or might have, noting substitution, replacing or filling the place of another; as, David died and Solomon reigned in his *sted.*

God hath appointed me another seed in *stead* of Abel, whom Cain slew. Gen. iv.

3. The frame on which a bed is laid.

Sallow the feet, the borders and the *sted.* *Dryden.*

[But we never use this word by itself in this sense. We always use *bedstead.*]

To stand in sted, to be of use or great advantage.

The smallest act of charity shall *stand* us *in great stead.* *Atterbury.*

STEAD, STED, in names of places distant from a river or the sea, signifies *place*, as above; but in names of places situated on a river or harbor, it is from Sax. *stathe*, border, bank, shore. Both words perhaps are from one root.

STEAD, *v. t. sted.* To help; to support; to assist; as, it nothing *steads* us. *Obs.* *Shak.*

2. To fill the place of another. *Obs.* *Shak.*

STEAD'FAST, STED'FAST, } *a.* [*stead* and *fast.*] Fast fixed; firm; firmly fixed or established; as the *stedfast* globe of earth. *Spenser.*

2. Constant; firm; resolute; not fickle or wavering.

Abide *stedfast* to thy neighbor in the time of his trouble. *Ecclus.*

Him resist, *stedfast* in the faith. 1 Pet. v.

3. Steady; as *stedfast* sight. *Dryden.*

STEAD'FASTLY, STED'FASTLY, } *adv.* Firmly; with constancy or steadiness of mind.

Steadfastly believe that whatever God has revealed is infallibly true. *Wake.*

STEAD'FASTNESS, STED'FASTNESS, } *n.* Firmness of standing; fixedness in place.

2. Firmness of mind or purpose; fixedness in principle; constancy; resolution; as the *stedfastness* of faith. He adhered to his opinions with *stedfastness.*

STEAD'ILY, STED'DILY, } *adv.* With firmness of standing or position; without tottering, shaking or leaning. He kept his arm *steddily* directed to the object.

2. Without wavering, inconstancy or irregularity; without deviating. He *steddily* pursues his studies.

STEAD'INESS, STED'DINESS, } *n.* Firmness of standing or position; a state of being not tottering or easily moved or shaken. A man stands with *steddiness;* he walks with *steddiness.*

2. Firmness of mind or purpose; constancy; resolution. We say, a man has *steddiness* of mind, *steddiness* in opinion, *steddiness* in the pursuit of objects.

3. Consistent uniform conduct.

Steddiness is a point of prudence as well as of courage. *L'Estrange.*

STEAD'Y, STED'DY, } *a.* [Sax. *stedig.*] Firm in standing or position; fixed; not tottering or shaking; *applicable to any object.*

2. Constant in mind, purpose or pursuit; not fickle, changeable or wavering; not easily moved or persuaded to alter a purpose; as a man *steddy* in his principles, *steddy* in his purpose, *steddy* in the pursuit of an object, *steddy* in his application to business.

3. Regular; constant; undeviating; uniform; as the *steddy* course of the sun. Steer the ship a *steddy* course. A large river runs with a *steddy* stream.

4. Regular; not fluctuating; as a *steddy* breeze of wind.

STEAD'Y, STED'DY, } *v. t.* To hold or keep from shaking, reeling or falling; to support; to make or keep firm. *Steddy* my hand.

STEAK, *n.* [Dan. *steeg, steg*, a piece of roast meat; *steger*, to roast or dress by the fire, to broil, to fry; Sw. *stek*, a steak; *steka*, to roast or broil; G. *stück*, a piece.]

A slice of beef or pork broiled, or cut for broiling. [As far as my observation extends, this word is never applied to any species of meat, except to beef and pork, nor to these dressed in any way except by broiling. Possibly it may be used of a piece fried.]

STEAL, *v. t.* pret. *stole;* pp. *stolen, stole.* [Sax. *stælan, stelan;* G. *stehlen;* D. *steelen;* Dan. *stieler;* Sw. *stiäla;* Ir. *tiallam;* probably from the root of L. *tollo*, to take, to lift.]

1. To take and carry away feloniously, as the personal goods of another. To constitute stealing or theft, the taking must be felonious, that is, with an intent to take what belongs to another, and without his consent. *Blackstone.*

Let him that *stole, steal* no more. Eph. iv.

2. To withdraw or convey without notice or clandestinely.

They could insinuate and *steal* themselves under the same by submission. *Spenser.*

3. To gain or win by address or gradual and imperceptible means.

Variety of objects has a tendency to *steal* away the mind from its steady pursuit of any subject. *Watts.*

So Absalom *stole* the hearts of the men of Israel. 2 Sam. xv.

STEAL, *v. i.* To withdraw or pass privily; to slip along or away unperceived.

Fixed of mind to fly all company, one night she *stole* away. *Sidney.*

From whom you now must *steal* and take no leave. *Shak.*

A soft and solemn breathing sound
Rose like a steam of rich distill'd perfumes,
And *stole* upon the air. *Milton.*

2. To practice theft; to take feloniously. He *steals* for a livelihood.

Thou shalt not *steal.* Ex. xx.

STE'ALER, *n.* One that steals; a thief.

STE'ALING, *ppr.* Taking the goods of another feloniously; withdrawing imperceptibly; gaining gradually.

STE'ALINGLY, *adv.* Slily; privately, or by an invisible motion. [*Little used.*] *Sidney.*

STEALTH, *n. stelth.* The act of stealing; theft.

The owner proveth the *stealth* to have been committed on him by such an outlaw. *Spenser.*

2. The thing stolen; as cabins that are dens to cover *stealth.* [*Not in use.*] *Raleigh.*

3. Secret act; clandestine practice; means unperceived employed to gain an object; way or manner not perceived; *used in a good or bad sense.*

Do good by *stealth*, and blush to find it fame. *Pope.*

The monarch blinded with desire of wealth,
With steel invades the brother's life by *stealth.* *Dryden.*

STEALTHY, *a.* *stelth'y.* Done by stealth; clandestine; unperceived.

Now wither'd murder with his *stealthy* pace
Moves like a ghost. *Shak.*

STEAM, *n.* [Sax. *steam*, *stem*; D. *stoom.*] The vapor of water; or the elastic, aeriform fluid generated by heating water to the boiling point. When produced under the common atmospheric pressure, its elasticity is equivalent to the pressure of the atmosphere, and it is called *low steam*; but when heated in a confined state, its elastic force is rapidly augmented, and it is then called *high steam.* On the application of cold, steam instantly returns to the state of water, and thus forms a sudden vacuum. From this property, and from the facility with which an elastic force is generated by means of steam, this constitutes a mechanical agent at once the most powerful and the most manageable, as is seen in the vast and multiplied uses of the steam engine.

Steam is invisible, and is to be distinguished from the cloud or mist which it forms in the air, that being water in a minute state of division, resulting from the condensation of steam. *D. Olmsted.*

2. In *popular use*, the mist formed by condensed vapor.

STEAM, *v. i.* To rise or pass off in vapor by means of heat; to fume.

Let the crude humors dance
In heated brass, *steaming* with fire intense. *Philips.*

2. To send off visible vapor.

Ye mists that rise from *steaming* lake. *Milton.*

3. To pass off in visible vapor.

The dissolved amber—*steamed* away into the air. *Boyle.*

STEAM, *v. t.* To exhale; to evaporate. [*Not much used.*] *Spenser.*

2. To expose to steam; to apply steam to for softening, dressing or preparing; as, to *steam* cloth; to *steam* potatoes instead of boiling them; to *steam* food for cattle.

STE'AM-BOAT, } *n.* A vessel propelled
STE'AM-VESSEL, } through the water by steam.

STE'AM-BOILER, *n.* A boiler for steaming food for cattle. *Encyc.*

STE'AMED, *pp.* Exposed to steam; cooked or dressed by steam.

STE'AM-ENGINE, *n.* An engine worked by steam.

STE'AMING, *ppr.* Exposing to steam; cooking or dressing by steam; preparing for cattle by steam, as roots.

STEAN, for *stone.* [*Not in use.*]

STE'ARIN, *n.* One of the proximate elements of animal fat, as lard, tallow, &c. The various kinds of animal fat consist of two substances, *stearin* and *elain*; of which the former is solid, and the latter liquid. *D. Olmsted.*

STE'ATITE, *n.* [Gr. στεαρ, στεατος, fat.] Soapstone; so called from its smooth or unctuous feel; a subspecies of rhomboidal mica. It is of two kinds, the common, and the pagodite or lard-stone. It is sometimes confounded with talck, to which it is allied. It is a compact stone, white, green of all shades, gray, brown or marbled, and sometimes herborized by black dendrites. It is found in metalliferous veins, with the ores of copper, lead, zink, silver and tin. *New Dict. of Nat. Hist. Ure.*

STEATIT'IC, *a.* Pertaining to soapstone; of the nature of steatite, or resembling it.

STE'ATOCELE, *n.* [Gr. στεαρ, fat, and κηλη, a tumor.] A swelling of the scrotum, containing fat. *Cyc.*

STEATO'MA, *n.* [Gr.] A species of tumor containing matter like suet. *Coxe.*

STED, STEDFAST. [See *Stead.*]

STEED, *n.* [Sax. *stede.* Qu. *stud*, a stone-horse.] A horse, or a horse for state or war. [This word is not much used in common discourse. It is used in poetry and descriptive prose, and is elegant.]

Stout are our men, and warlike are our *steeds.* *Waller.*

STEEL, *n.* [Sax. *style*; D. *staal*; G. *stahl*; Dan. *staal*; Sw. *stål*; probably from setting, fixing, hardness; G. *stellen.*]

1. Iron combined with a small portion of carbon; iron refined and hardened, used in making instruments, and particularly useful as the material of edged tools. It is called in chimistry, carburet of iron; but this is more usually the denomination of plumbago.

2. *Figuratively*, weapons; particularly, offensive weapons, swords, spears and the like.

Brave Macbeth with his brandish'd *steel.* *Shak.*

—While doubting thus he stood,
Receiv'd the *steel* bath'd in his brother's blood. *Dryden.*

3. Medicines composed of steel, as steel filings.

After relaxing, *steel* strengthens the solids. *Arbuthnot.*

4. Extreme hardness; as heads or hearts of *steel.*

STEEL, *a.* Made of steel; as a *steel* plate or buckle.

STEEL, *v. t.* To overlay, point or edge with steel; as, to *steel* the point of a sword; to *steel* a razor; to *steel* an ax.

2. To make hard or extremely hard.

O God of battles, *steel* my soldiers' hearts. *Shak.*

Lies well *steel'd* with weighty arguments. *Shak.*

3. To make hard; to make insensible or obdurate; as, to *steel* the heart against pity; to *steel* the mind or heart against reproof or admonition.

STEE'LED, *pp.* Pointed or edged with steel; hardened; made insensible.

STEE'LINESS, *n.* [from *steely.*] Great hardness.

STEE'LING, *ppr.* Pointing or edging with steel; hardening; making insensible or unfeeling. *Ch. Relig. Appeal.*

STEE'LY, *a.* Made of steel; consisting of steel.

Broach'd with the *steely* point of Clifford's lance. *Shak.*

Around his shop the *steely* sparkles flew. *Gay.*

2. Hard; firm.

That she would unarm her noble heart of that *steely* resistance against the sweet blows of love. *Sidney.*

STEE'LYARD, *n.* [*steel* and *yard.*] The Roman balance; an instrument for weighing bodies, consisting of a rod or bar marked with notches, designating the number of pounds and ounces, and a weight which is movable along this bar, and which is made to balance the weight of the body by being removed at a proper distance from the fulcrum. The principle of the steelyard is that of the lever; where an equilibrium is produced, when the products of the weights on opposite sides into their respective distances from the fulcrum, are equal to one another. Hence a less weight is made to indicate a greater, by being removed to a greater distance from the fulcrum.

STEEN, } *n.* A vessel of clay or stone. [*Not*
STEAN, } *in use.*]

STEE'NKIRK, *n.* A cant term for a neckcloth. [*Not now in use.*]

STEEP, *a.* [Sax. *steap*; allied to *stoop* and *dip.*] Making a large angle with the plane of the horizon; ascending or descending with great inclination; precipitous; as a *steep* hill or mountain; a *steep* roof; a *steep* ascent; a *steep* declivity.

STEEP, *n.* A precipitous place, hill, mountain, rock or ascent; any elevated object which slopes with a large angle to the plane of the horizon; a precipice.

We had on each side rocks and mountains broken into a thousand irregular *steeps* and precipices. *Addison.*

STEEP, *v. t.* [probably formed on the root of *dip.*] To soak in a liquid; to macerate; to imbue; to keep any thing in a liquid till it has thoroughly imbibed it, or till the liquor has extracted the essential qualities of the substance. Thus cloth is *steeped* in lye or other liquid in bleaching or dyeing. But plants and drugs are *steeped* in water, wine and the like, for the purpose of tincturing the liquid with their qualities.

STEEP, *n.* A liquid for steeping grain or seeds; also, a runnet bag. [*Local.*]

STEE'PED, *pp.* Soaked; macerated; imbued.

STEE'PER, *n.* A vessel, vat or cistern in which things are steeped. *Edwards' W. Indies.*

STEE'PING, *ppr.* Soaking; macerating.

STEE'PLE, *n.* [Sax. *stepel*, *stypel.*] A turret of a church, ending in a point; a spire. It differs from a tower, which usually ends in a square form, though the name is sometimes given to a tower. The bell of a church is usually hung in the steeple.

They, far from *steeples* and their sacred sound— *Dryden.*

STEE'PLED, *a.* Furnished with a steeple; adorned with steeples or towers. *Fairfax.*

STEE'PLE-HOUSE, *n.* A church. [*Not in use.*]

STEE'PLY, *adv.* With steepness; with precipitous declivity.

STEE'PNESS, *n.* The state of being steep; precipitous declivity; as the *steepness* of a hill, a bank or a roof. *Bacon.*

STEE'PY, *a.* Having a steep or precipitou declivity; as *steepy* crags; *a poetical word.*

No more, my goats, shall I behold you climb
The *steepy* cliffs. *Dryden.*

STEER, *n.* [Sax. *steor*, *styre*; D. *stier.*] A young male of the ox kind or common ox. It is rendered in Dutch, a bull; but in the United States, this name is generally given to a castrated male of the ox kind, from two to four years old.

With solemn pomp then sacrific'd a *steer.* *Dryden.*

STEER, *v. t.* [Sax. *steoran*, to steer, to correct or chide, to discipline; G. *steuern*, to hinder, restrain, repress, to curb, to steer, to pilot, to aid, help, support. The verb is connected with or derived from *steuer*, a rudder, a helm, aid, help, subsidy, impost, tax, contribution. D. *stieren*, to steer, to send, and *stuur*, a helm; *stuuren*, to steer, to send; Dan. *styrer*, to govern, direct, manage, steer, restrain, moderate, curb, stem, hinder; *styre*, a helm, rudder or tiller; *styr*, moderation, a tax or assessment; Sw. *styra*, to steer, to restrain; *styre*, a rudder or helm; Arm. *stur*, id.; Ir. *stiuram*. We see the radical sense is to *strain*, variously applied, and this coincides with the root of *starch* and *stark*; stiffness being from stretching.]

1. To direct; to govern; particularly, to direct and govern the course of a ship by the movements of the helm. Hence,
2. To direct; to guide; to show the way or course to.

That with a staff his feeble steps did *steer*. *Spenser.*

STEER, *v. i.* To direct and govern a ship or other vessel in its course. Formerly seamen *steered* by the stars; they now *steer* by the compass.

A ship—where the wind
Veers oft, as oft so *steers* and shifts her sail. *Milton.*

2. To be directed and governed; as, a ship *steers* with ease.
3. To conduct one's self; to take or pursue a course or way.

STEER, *n.* A rudder or helm. [*Not in use.*]

STEE'RAĠE, *n.* The act or practice of directing and governing in a course; as the *steerage* of a ship. *Addison.*

[*In this sense, I believe the word is now little used.*]

2. In *seamen's language*, the effort of a helm, or its effect on the ship. *Mar. Dict.*
3. In *a ship*, an apartment forward of the great cabin, from which it is separated by a bulk-head or partition, or an apartment in the fore part of a ship for passengers. In ships of war it serves as a hall or antichamber to the great cabin. *Mar. Dict.*
4. The part of a ship where the tiller traverses. *Encyc.*
5. Direction; regulation.

He that hath the *steerage* of my course.
[*Little used.*] *Shak.*

6. Regulation or management.

You raise the honor of the peerage,
Proud to attend you at the *steerage*. *Swift.*

7. That by which a course is directed.

Here he hung on high
The *steerage* of his wings— *Dryden.*

[*Steerage*, in the general sense of direction or management, is in popular use, but by no means an elegant word. It is said, a young man when he sets out in life, makes bad *steerage*; but no good writer would introduce the word into elegant writing.]

STEE'RAĠE-WAY, *n.* In *seamen's language*, that degree of progressive movement of a ship, which renders her governable by the helm.

STEE'RED, *pp.* Directed and governed in a course; guided; conducted.

STEE'RER, *n.* One that steers; a pilot. [*Little used.*]

STEE'RING, *ppr.* Directing and governing in a course, as a ship; guiding; conducting.

STEE'RING, *n.* The act or art of directing and governing a ship or other vessel in her course; the act of guiding or managing.

STEE'RING-WHEEL, *n.* The wheel by which the rudder of a ship is turned and the ship steered.

STEE'RLESS, *a.* Having no steer or rudder. [*Not in use.*] *Gower.*

STEE'RSMAN, *n.* [*steer* and *man.*] One that steers; the helmsman of a ship. *Mar. Dict.*

STEE'RSMATE, *n.* [*steer* and *mate.*] One who steers; a pilot. [*Not in use.*] *Milton.*

STEE'VING, *n.* In *seamen's language*, the angle of elevation which a ship's bowsprit makes with the horizon. *Mar. Dict.*

STEG, *n.* [Ice. *stegge.*] A gander. [*Local.*]

STEGANOG'RAPHIST, *n.* [Gr. στεγανος, secret, and γραφω, to write.]
One who practices the art of writing in cipher. *Bailey.*

STEGANOG'RAPHY, *n.* [supra.] The art of writing in ciphers or characters which are not intelligible, except to the persons who correspond with each other. *Bailey.*

STEGNOT'IC, *a.* [Gr. στεγνωτικος.] Tending to bind or render costive. *Bailey.*

STEGNOT'IC, *n.* A medicine proper to stop the orifices of the vessels or emunctories of the body, when relaxed or lacerated. *Cyc.*

STE'INHEILITE, *n.* A mineral, a variety of iolite. *Cleaveland.*

STELE, *n.* A stale or handle; a stalk. *Obs.*

STEL'ECHITE, *n.* A fine kind of storax, in larger pieces than the calamite. *Cyc.*

STEL'LAR, **STEL'LARY**, } *a.* [It. *stellare*; L. *stellaris*, from *stella*, a star.]

1. Pertaining to stars; astral; as *stellar* virtue; *stellar* figure. *Milton. Glanville.*
2. Starry; full of stars; set with stars; as *stellary* regions.

STEL'LATE, **STEL'LATED**, } *a.* [L. *stellatus.*] Resembling a star; radiated.

2. In *botany*, stellate or verticillate leaves are when more leaves than two surround the stem in a whorl, or when they radiate like the spokes of a wheel, or like a star. A *stellate* bristle is when a little star of smaller hairs is affixed to the end; applied also to the stigma. A *stellate* flower is a radiate flower. *Martyn.*

STELLA'TION, *n.* [L. *stella*, a star.] Radiation of light. [*Not in use.*]

STEL'LED, *a.* Starry. [*Not in use.*] *Shak.*

STELLIF'EROUS, *a.* [L. *stella*, a star, and *fero*, to produce.]
Having or abounding with stars.

STEL'LIFORM, *a.* [L. *stella*, star, and *form.*] Like a star; radiated.

STEL'LIFY, *v. t.* To turn into a star. [*Not in use.*] *Chaucer.*

STEL'LION, *n.* [L. *stellio.*] A newt. *Ainsworth.*

STEL'LIONATE, *n.* [Fr. *stellionat*, a cheating: Low L. *stellionatus.*]
In *law*, the crime of selling a thing deceitfully for what it is not, as to sell that for for one's own which belongs to another. [*Not in use.*] *Bacon.*

STEL'LITE, *n.* [L. *stella*, a star.] A name given by some writers to a white stone found on Mount Libanus, containing the lineaments of the star-fish. *Cyc.*

STEL'OCHITE, *n.* A name given to the osteocolla.

STELOG'RAPHY, *n.* [Gr. στηλογραφια; στηλος, a pillar, and γραφω, to write.]
The art of writing or inscribing characters on pillars. *Stackhouse.*

STEM, *n.* [Sax. *stemn*; G. *stamm*, stock, stem, race; D. Sw. *stam*; Dan. *stamme*; Sans. *stamma*. The Latin has *stemma*, in the sense of the stock of a family or race. The primary sense is to set, to fix.]

1. The principal body of a tree, shrub or plant of any kind; the main stock; the firm part which supports the branches.

After they are shot up thirty feet in length, they spread a very large top, having no bough or twig on the *stem*. *Raleigh.*

The low'ring spring with lavish rain,
Beats down the slender *stem* and bearded grain. *Dryden.*

2. The peduncle of the fructification, or the pedicle of a flower; that which supports the flower or the fruit of a plant.
3. The stock of a family; a race or generation of progenitors; as a noble *stem*. *Milton.*

Learn well their lineage and their ancient *stem*. *Tickel.*

4. Progeny, branch of a family.

This is a *stem*
Of that victorious stock. *Shak.*

5. In *a ship*, a circular piece of timber, to which the two sides of a ship are united at the fore end. The lower end of it is scarfed to the keel, and the bowsprit rests upon its upper end. [D. *steven.*] *Mar. Dict.*

From stem to stern, is from one end of the ship to the other, or through the whole length.

STEM, *v. t.* To oppose or resist, as a current; or to make progress against a current. We say, the ship was not able with all her sails to *stem* the tide.

They *stem* the flood with their erected breasts. *Denham.*

2. To stop; to check; as a stream or moving force.

At length Erasmus, that great injur'd name,
Stemm'd the wild torrent of a barb'rous age,
And drove those holy Vandals off the stage. *Pope.*

STEM'-CL'ASPING, *a.* Embracing the stem with its base; amplexicaul; as a leaf or petiole. *Martyn.*

STEM'-LEAF, *n.* A leaf inserted into the stem. *Martyn.*

STEM'LESS, *a.* Having no stem.

STEM'MED, *pp.* Opposed, as a current; stopped.

STEM'MING, *ppr.* Opposing, as a stream; stopping.

STEM'PLE, *n.* In *mining*, a cross bar of wood in a shaft. *Encyc.*

STENCH, *n.* [Sax. *stenc*, *stencg*. See *Stink.*] An ill smell; offensive odor. *Bacon.*

STENCH, *v. t.* To cause to emit a hateful smell. [*Not in use.*] *Mortimer.*

2. To stanch; to stop. [*Not in use.*] *Harvey.*

STENCH'Y, *a.* Having an offensive smell. [*Not in use.*] *Dyer.*

STEN'CIL, *n.* A piece of thin lether or oil cloth, used in painting paper hangings.

STEN'CIL, *v. t.* To paint or color in figures with stencils. *Encyc.*

STENOG'RAPHER, *n.* [Gr. ϛενος, close, narrow, and γραφω, to write.]

One who is skilled in the art of short hand writing.

STENOGRAPH'IC, STENOGRAPH'ICAL, *a.* [supra.] Pertaining to the art of writing in short hand; expressing in characters or short hand.

STENOG'RAPHY, *n.* [supra.] The art of writing in short hand by using abbreviations or characters for whole words. *Encyc.*

STENT, for *stint.* [See *Stint.*]

STENTO'RIAN, *a.* [from *Stentor.*] Extremely loud; as a *stentorian* voice.

2. Able to utter a very loud sound; as *stentorian* lungs.

STENTOROPHON'IC, *a.* [from *Stentor*, a herald in Homer, whose voice was as loud as that of fifty other men, and Gr. φωνη, voice.] Speaking or sounding very loud.

Of this *stentorophonic* horn of Alexander there is a figure preserved in the Vatican. *Derham.*

STEP, *v. i.* [Sax. *stæppan, steppan*; D. *stappen*; Gr. ϛειβω. Qu. Russ. *stopa*, the foot. The sense is to set, as the foot, or more probably to open or part, to stretch or extend.]

1. To move the foot; to advance or recede by a movement of the foot or feet; as, to *step* forward, or to *step* backward.

2. To go; to walk a little distance; as, to *step* to one of the neighbors.

3. To walk gravely, slowly or resolutely.

Home the swain retreats,
His flock before him *stepping* to the fold. *Thomson.*

To step forth, to move or come forth. *Cowley.*

To step aside, to walk to a little distance; to retire from company.

To step in or *into*, to walk or advance into a place or state; or to advance suddenly in. John v.

2. To enter for a short time. I just *stepped into* the house for a moment.

3. To obtain possession without trouble; to enter upon suddenly; as, to *step into* an estate.

To step back, to move mentally; to carry the mind back.

They are *stepping* almost three thousand years *back* into the remotest antiquity. *Pope.*

STEP, *v. t.* To set, as the foot.

2. To fix the foot of a mast in the keel; to erect. *Mar. Dict.*

STEP, *n.* [Sax. *stæp*; D. *stap*; G. *stufe*; W. *tap*, a ledge; *tapiaw*, to form a step or ledge.]

1. A pace; an advance or movement made by one removal of the foot.

2. One remove in ascending or descending; a stair.

The breadth of every single *step* or stair should be never less than one foot. *Wotton.*

3. The space passed by the foot in walking or running. The *step* of one foot is generally five feet; it may be more or less.

4. A small space or distance. Let us go to the gardens; it is but a *step*.

5. The distance between the feet in walking or running.

6. Gradation; degree. We advance in improvement *step* by *step*, or by *steps*.

7. Progression; act of advancing.

To derive two or three general principles of motion from phenomena, and afterwards tell us how the properties and actions of all corporeal things follow from those manifest principles, would be a great *step* in philosophy. *Newton.*

8. Footstep; print or impression of the foot; track. *Dryden.*

9. Gait; manner of walking. The approach of a man is often known by his *step*.

10. Proceeding; measure; action.

The reputation of a man depends on the first *steps* he makes in the world. *Pope.*

11. The round of a ladder.

12. *Steps* in the plural, walk; passage.

Conduct my *steps* to find the fatal tree
In this deep forest. *Dryden.*

13. Pieces of timber in which the foot of a mast is fixed.

STEP, STEPP, *n.* In Russ, an uncultivated desert of large extent. *Tooke.*

[This sense of the Russian word is naturally deducible from Sax. *stepan*, to deprive, infra.]

STEP, Sax. *steop*, from *stepan*, to deprive, is prefixed to certain words to express a relation by marriage.

STEP'-BROTHER, *n.* A brother-in-law, or by marriage.

STEP'-CHILD, *n.* [*step* and *child.*] A son-in-law or daughter-in-law, [a child deprived of its parent.]

STEP'-DAME, *n.* A mother by marriage, [the mother of an orphan or one deprived.]

STEP'-DAUGHTER, *n.* A daughter by marriage, [an orphan daughter.]

STEP'-FATHER, *n.* A father-in-law; a father by marriage only; [the father of an orphan.]

STEP'-MOTHER, *n.* A mother by marriage only; a mother-in-law; [the mother of an orphan.]

STEP'-SISTER, *n.* A sister-in-law, or by marriage, [an orphan sister.]

STEP'-SON, *n.* A son-in-law, [an orphan son.]

[In the foregoing explication of *step*, I have followed Lye. The D. and G. write *stief*, and the Swedes *styf*, before the name; a word which does not appear to be connected with any verb signifying to *bereave*, and the word is not without some difficulties. I have given the explanation which appears to be most probably correct. If the radical sense of *step*, a pace, is to part or open, the word coincides with Sax. *stepan*, to deprive, and in the compounds above, *step* may imply removal or distance.]

STEP'PED, *pp.* Set; placed; erected; fixed in the keel, as a mast.

STEP'PING, *ppr.* Moving, or advancing by a movement of the foot or feet; placing; fixing or erecting, as a mast.

STEP'PING, *n.* The act of walking or running by steps.

STEP'PING-STONE, *n.* A stone to raise the feet above the dirt and mud in walking. *Swift.*

STEP'-STONE, *n.* A stone laid before a door as a stair to rise on in entering the house.

STER, in composition, is from the Sax. *stera*, a director. See *Steer.* It seems primarily to have signified chief, principal or director, as in the L. *minister*, chief servant; but in other words, as in *spinster*, we do not recognize the sense of *chief*, but merely that of a person who carries on the business of spinning.

STERCORA'CEOUS, *a.* [L. *stercoreus*, *stercorosus*, from *stercus*, dung.]

Pertaining to dung, or partaking of its nature. *Arbuthnot.*

STERCORA'RIAN, STER'CORANIST, *n.* [L. *stercus*, dung.] One in the Romish church who held that the host is liable to digestion. *Encyc.*

STER'CORARY, *n.* A place properly secured from the weather for containing dung.

STERCORA'TION, *n.* [L. *stercoratio.*] The act of manuring with dung. *Bacon. Ray.*

STERE, *n.* In *the new French system of measures*, the unit for solid measure, equal to a cubic meter. *Lunier.*

STEREOGRAPH'IC, STEREOGRAPH'ICAL, *a.* [from *stereography.*] Made or done according to the rules of stereography; delineated on a plane; as a *stereographic* chart of the earth.

STEREOGRAPH'ICALLY, *adv.* By delineation on a plane.

STEREOG'RAPHY, *n.* [Gr. ϛερεος, firm, and γραφω, to write.]

The act or art of delineating the forms of solid bodies on a plane; a branch of solid geometry which shows the construction of all solids which are regularly defined. *Encyc.*

STEREOMET'RICAL, *a.* [See *Stereometry.*]

Pertaining to or performed by stereometry.

STEREOM'ETRY, *n.* [Gr. ϛερεος, firm, fixed, and μετρεω, to measure.]

The art of measuring solid bodies, and finding their solid content. *Harris.*

STEREOTOM'ICAL, *a.* Pertaining to or performed by stereotomy.

STEREOT'OMY, *n.* [Gr. ϛερεος, fixed, and τεμνω, to cut.]

The science or art of cutting solids into certain figures or sections, as arches, &c. *Encyc.*

STER'EOTYPE, *n.* [Gr. ϛερεος, fixed, and τυπος, type, form.]

1. Literally, a fixed metal type; hence, a plate of fixed or solid metallic types for printing books. Thus we say, a book is printed *on stereotype*, or *in stereotype*. In the latter use, the word seems rather to signify the workmanship or manner of printing, than the plate.

2. The art of making plates of fixed metallic types, or of executing work on such plates.

STER'EOTYPE, *a.* Pertaining to fixed metallic types.

2. Done on fixed metallic types, or plates of fixed types; as *stereotype* work; *stereotype* printing; a *stereotype* copy of the Bible.

STER'EOTYPE, *v. t.* To make fixed metallic types or plates of type metal, corresponding with the words and letters of a book; to compose a book in fixed types;

as, to *stereotype* the New Testament; certain societies have *stereotyped* the Bible.

STER'EOTYPER, *n.* One who makes stereotype.

STER'EOTYPING, *ppr.* Making stereotype plates for any work; or impressing copies on stereotype plates.

STEREOTYPOG'RAPHER, *n.* A stereotype printer.

STEREOTYPOG'RAPHY, *n.* The art or practice of printing on stereotype. *Entick.*

STER'IL, } *a.* [L. *sterilis*; It. Fr. *sterile*; Sp. *esteril.*] Barren; unfruitful; not fertile; producing little or no crop; as *sterile* land; a *sterile* desert; a *sterile* year. *Bacon.*
STER'ILE, }

2. Barren; producing no young. *More.*

3. Barren of ideas; destitute of sentiment; as a *sterile* production or author.

Sterile flower, in botany, is a term given by Tournefort to the male flower, or that which bears only stamens. *Martyn.*

STERIL'ITY, *n.* [L. *sterilitas*; Fr. *sterilité*; It. *sterilità.*]

1. Barrenness; unproductiveness; unfruitfulness; the quality or state of producing little or nothing; as the *sterility* of land or soil. *Bacon.*

2. Barrenness; unfruitfulness; the state of not producing young; as of animals.

3. Barrenness of ideas or sentiments, as in writings.

4. Want of fertility or the power of producing sentiment; as the *sterility* of an author or of his mind.

STER'ILIZE, *v. t.* To make barren; to impoverish, as land; to exhaust of fertility; as, to *sterilize* soil or land. [*Little used.*] *Woodward.*

2. To deprive of fecundity, or the power of producing young. [*Little used.*]

STER'LET, *n.* A fish of the Caspian and of the rivers in Russia, the *Acipenser ruthenus* of Linne, highly esteemed for its flavor, and from whose roe is made the finest caviare. *Tooke. Coxe.*

STER'LING, *a.* [probably from *Easterling.*]

1. An epithet by which English money of account is distinguished; as a pound *sterling*; a shilling *sterling*; a penny *sterling*. It is not now applied to the coins of England; but *sterling* cost, *sterling* value are used.

2. Genuine; pure; of excellent quality; as a work of *sterling* merit; a man of *sterling* wit or good sense.

STER'LING, *n.* English money.

> And Roman wealth in English *sterling* view. *Arbuthnot.*

In this use, *sterling* may signify English coins.

2. Standard; rate. [*Little used in either sense.*]

STERN, *a.* [Sax. *styrn*, stern; G. *starr*, staring; *störrig*, stubborn. See *Stare*, *Starch*, *Stark*, with which this word is probably connected.]

1. Severe; austere; fixed with an aspect of severity and authority; as a *stern* look; a *stern* countenance; a *stern* frown.

> I would outstare the *sternest* eyes that look. *Shak.*

2. Severe of manner; rigid; harsh; cruel.

> *Stern* as tutors, and as uncles hard. *Dryden.*

> Ambition should be made of *sterner* stuff. *Shak.*

3. Hard; afflictive.

> If wolves had at thy gate howl'd that *stern* time. *Shak.*

4. Rigidly stedfast; immovable.

> *Stern* virtue is the growth of few soils. *Hamilton.*

STERN, *n.* [Sax. *steor* and *ern*, place; the *steer-place*, that is, helm-place.]

1. The hind part of a ship or other vessel, or of a boat; the part opposite to the stem or prow. This part of a ship is terminated by the tafferel above, and by the counters below. *Mar. Dict.*

2. Post of management; direction.

> And sit at chiefest *stern* of public weal. *Shak.*

[Not in use. We now say, to *sit at the helm.*]

3. The hinder part of any thing. [*Not elegant.*] *Spenser.*

By the stern, is a phrase which denotes that a ship is more deeply laden abaft than forward.

STERN'AGE, *n.* Steerage or stern. [*Not in use.*] *Shak.*

STERN'-BOARD, *n.* [*stern* and *board.*] In *seaman's language*, a loss of way in making a tack. To *make a stern-board*, is when by a current or other cause, a vessel has fallen back from the point she had gained in the last tack. *Mar. Dict.*

STERN'-CHASE, *n.* [*stern* and *chase.*] A cannon placed in a ship's stern, pointing backward and intended to annoy a ship that is in pursuit of her. *Mar. Dict.*

STERN'ED, *a.* In compounds, having a stern of a particular shape; as square-*sterned*; pink-*sterned*, &c.

STERN'ER, *n.* [Sax. *steoran*, to steer.] A director. [*Not in use.*] *Clarke.*

STERN'-FAST, *n.* [*stern* and *fast.*] A rope used to confine the stern of a ship or other vessel.

STERN'-FRAME, *n.* [*stern* and *frame.*] The several pieces of timber which form the stern of a ship. *Mar. Dict.*

STERN'LY, *adv.* [See *Stern.*] In a stern manner; with an austere or stern countenance; with an air of authority.

> *Sternly* he pronounc'd
> The rigid interdiction. *Milton.*

STERN'NESS, *n.* Severity of look; a look of austerity, rigor or severe authority; as the *sternness* of one's presence. *Shak.*

2. Severity or harshness of manner; rigor.

> I have *sternness* in my soul enough
> To hear of soldier's work. *Dryden.*

STERN'MOST, *a.* [*stern* and *most.*] Farthest in the rear; farthest astern; as the *sternmost* ship in a convoy. *Mar. Dict.*

STERN'ON, *n.* [Gr.] The breast bone. But *sternum* is chiefly or wholly used.

STERN'-PORT, *n.* [*stern* and *port.*] A port or opening in the stern of a ship. *Mar. Dict.*

STERN'-POST, *n.* [*stern* and *post.*] A straight piece of timber, erected on the extremity of the keel to support the rudder and terminate the ship behind. *Mar. Dict.*

STERN'-SHEETS, *n.* [*stern* and *sheet.*] That part of a boat which is between the stern and the aftmost seat of the rowers; usually furnished with seats for passengers. *Mar. Dict.*

STERN'UM, *n.* [Gr. ϛερνον; from fixing, setting. See *Starch*, *Stark.*] The breast bone; the bone which forms the front of the human chest from the neck to the stomach.

STERNUTA'TION, *n.* [L. *sternutatio.*] The act of sneezing. *Quincy.*

STERNU'TATIVE, *a.* [L. *sternuo*, to sneeze.] Having the quality of provoking to sneeze.

STERNU'TATORY, *a.* [Fr. *sternutatoire*, from L. *sternuo*, to sneeze.] Having the quality of exciting to sneeze.

STERNU'TATORY, *n.* A substance that provokes sneezing.

STERN'-WAY, *n.* [*stern* and *way.*] The movement of a ship backwards, or with her stern foremost. *Mar. Dict.*

STERQUIL'INOUS, *a.* [L. *sterquilinium*, a dunghill.] Pertaining to a dunghill; mean; dirty; paltry. *Howell.*

STERVEN, to *starve*, not in use. *Spenser.*

STETH'ESCOPE, *n.* [Gr. στηθος, the breast, and σκοπεω, to view.] A tubular instrument for distinguishing diseases of the stomach by sounds. *Scudamore.*

STEVE, *v. t.* [from the root of *stow.*] To stow, as cotton or wool in a ship's hold. [*Local.*]

STE'VEDORE, *n.* One whose occupation is to stow goods, packages, &c. in a ship's hold. *N. York.*

STEV'EN, *n.* [Sax. *stefnian*, to call.] An outcry; a loud call; a clamor. [*Not in use.*] *Spenser.*

STEW, *v. t.* [Fr. *etuver*, to stew; *etuve*, a stove; It. *stufare*, to stew; *stufa*, a stove; *stufo*, weary, surfeited; Sp. *estufa*, a stove; *estofa*, stuff quilted; *estofar*, to quilt and to stew; D. *stoof*, a stove; *stooven*, to stew; Dan. *stue*, a room, [See *Stow*,] and *stueovn*, a stove; Sw. *stufva*, to stew and to stow.]

1. To seethe or gently boil; to boil slowly in a moderate manner, or with a simmering heat; as, to *stew* meat; to *stew* apples; to *stew* prunes. *Shak.*

2. To boil in heat.

STEW, *v. i.* To be seethed in a slow gentle manner, or in heat and moisture.

STEW, *n.* A hot house; a bagnio.

> The Lydians were inhibited by Cyrus to use any armor, and give themselves to baths and *stews.* *Abbot.*

2. A brothel; a house of prostitution; but generally or always used in the plural, *stews.* *Bacon. South.*

3. A prostitute. [*Not in use.*]

4. [See *Stow.*] A store pond; a small pond where fish are kept for the table. [*Not used.*]

5. Meat stewed; as a *stew* of pigeons.

6. Confusion, as when the air is full of dust. [D. *stuiven*, to raise a dust; allied to *stew*, and proving that the primary sense of *stew* is to drive or agitate, to stir or excite.] [*Not in use or local.*] *Grose.*

STEW'ARD, *n.* [Sax. *stiward. Ward* is a keeper; but the meaning of the first syllable is not evident. It is probably a contraction of G. *stube*, a room, Eng. *stow*,

Sax. *stow*, place, or *sted*, place, or of Dan. *stöb*, a cup. The *steward* was then originally a chamberlain or a butler.]

1. A man employed in great families to manage the domestic concerns, superintend the other servants, collect the rents or income, keep the accounts, &c. See Gen. xv. 2.—xliii. 19.
2. An officer of state; as lord high *steward*; *steward* of the household, &c. *England.*
3. In *colleges*, an officer who provides food for the students and superintends the concerns of the kitchen.
4. In *a ship of war*, an officer who is appointed by the purser to distribute provisions to the officers and crew. In other ships, a man who superintends the provisions and liquors, and supplies the table.
5. In *Scripture* and *theology*, a minister of Christ, whose duty is to dispense the provisions of the gospel, to preach its doctrines and administer its ordinances.

It is required in *stewards*, that a man be found faithful. 1 Cor. iv.

STEW'ARD, *v. t.* To manage as a steward. [*Not in use.*] *Fuller.*

STEW'ARDLY, *adv.* With the care of a steward. [*Little used.*] *Tooker.*

STEW'ARDSHIP, *n.* The office of a steward. *Calamy.*

STEW'ARTRY, *n.* An overseer or superintendant.

The *stewartry* of provisions. *Tooke.*

STEW'ED, *pp.* Gently boiled; boiled in heat.

STEW'ING, *ppr.* Boiling in a moderate heat.

STEW'ING, *n.* The act of seething slowly.

STEW'ISH, *a.* Suiting a brothel. *Hall.*

STEW'-PAN, *n.* A pan in which things are stewed.

STIB'IAL, *a.* [L. *stibium*, antimony.] Like or having the qualities of antimony; antimonial.

STIBIA'RIAN, *n.* [from L. *stibium.*] A violent man. [*An improper word and not in use.*] *White.*

STIB'IATED, *a.* Impregnated with antimony.

STIB'IUM, *n.* [L.] Antimony.

STIC'ADOS, *n.* A plant. *Ainsworth.*

STICH, *n.* [Gr. ςιχος.] In *poetry*, a verse, of whatever measure or number of feet.

Stich is used in numbering the books of Scripture.

2. In *rural affairs*, an order or rank of trees. [In New England, as much land as lies between double furrows, is called a *stitch*, or a land.]

STICHOM'ETRY, *n.* [Gr. ςιχος, a verse, and μετρον, measure.]

A catalogue of the books of Scripture, with the number of verses which each book contains.

STICH'-WŎRT, **STITCH-WŎRT**, *n.* A plant of the genus Stellaria.

STICK, *n.* [Sax. *sticca*; G. *stecken*; D. *stok*; Dan. *stikke*; Sw. *stake*, *sticka*; It. *stecca.* This word is connected with the verb to *stick*, with *stock*, *stack*, and other words having the like elements. The primary sense of the root is to thrust, to shoot, and to set; Fr. *tige*, a stalk.]

1. The small shoot or branch of a tree or shrub, cut off; a rod; also, a staff; as, to strike one with a *stick.*
2. Any stem of a tree, of any size, cut for fuel or timber. It is applied in America to any long and slender piece of timber, round or square, from the smallest size to the largest, used in the frames of buildings; as a *stick* of timber for a post, a beam or a rafter.
3. Many instruments, long and slender, are called *sticks*; as the composing *stick* of printers.
4. A thrust with a pointed instrument that penetrates a body; a stab.

Stick of eels, the number of twenty five eels. A bind contains ten *sticks.* *Encyc.*

STICK, *v. t.* pret. and pp. *stuck.* [Sax. *stican*, *stician*; G. *stechen*, to sting or prick, and *stecken*, to stick, to adhere; D. *stecken*, to prick or stab; *stikken*, to stitch; Dan. *stikker*, to sting, to prick; Sw. *sticka*; Gr. ςιζω, ςιγμα; W. *ystigaw*; Ir. *steacham.* If formed on the elements *Dg*, *Tg*, this family of words coincides in elements with *tack*, *attack*, *attach.*]

1. To pierce; to stab; to cause to enter, as a pointed instrument; hence, to kill by piercing; as, to *stick* a beast in slaughter. [*A common use of the word.*]
2. To thrust in; to fasten or cause to remain by piercing; as, to *stick* a pin on the sleeve.

The points of spears are *stuck* within the shield. *Dryden.*

3. To fasten; to attach by causing to adhere to the surface; as, to *stick* on a patch or plaster; to *stick* on a thing with paste or glue.
4. To set; to fix in; as, to *stick* card teeth.
5. To set with something pointed; as, to *stick* cards.
6. To fix on a pointed instrument; as, to *stick* an apple on a fork.

STICK, *v. i.* To adhere; to hold to by cleaving to the surface, as by tenacity or attraction; as, glue *sticks* to the fingers; paste *sticks* to the wall, and causes paper to *stick.*

I will cause the fish of thy rivers to *stick* to thy scales. Ezek. xxix.

2. To be united; to be inseparable; to cling fast to, as something reproachful.

If on your fame our sex a blot has thrown,
'Twill ever *stick*, through malice of your own. *Young.*

3. To rest with the memory; to abide. *Bacon.*
4. To stop; to be impeded by adhesion or obstruction; as, the carriage *sticks* in the mire.
5. To stop; to be arrested in a course.

My faltering tongue
Sticks at the sound. *Smith.*

6. To stop; to hesitate. He *sticks* at no difficulty; he *sticks* at the commission of no crime; he *sticks* at nothing.
7. To adhere; to remain; to resist efforts to remove.

I had most need of blessing, and amen
Stuck in my throat. *Shak.*

8. To cause difficulties or scruples; to cause to hesitate.

This is the difficulty that *sticks* with the most reasonable— *Swift.*

9. To be stopped or hindered from proceeding; as, a bill passed the senate, but *stuck* in the house of representatives.

They never doubted the commons; but heard all *stuck* in the lord's house. *Clarendon.*

10. To be embarrassed or puzzled.

They will *stick* long at part of a demonstration, for want of perceiving the connection between two ideas. *Locke.*

11. To adhere closely in friendship and affection.

There is a friend that *sticketh* closer than a brother. Prov. xviii.

To stick to, to adhere closely; to be constant; to be firm; to be persevering; as, to *stick to* a party or cause.

The advantage will be on our side, if we *stick to* its essentials. *Addison.*

To stick by, to adhere closely; to be constant; to be firm in supporting.

We are your only friends; *stick by* us, and we will *stick by* you. *Davenant.*

2. To be troublesome by adhering.

I am satisfied to trifle away my time, rather than let it *stick by* me. *Pope.*

To stick upon, to dwell upon; not to forsake.

If the matter be knotty, the mind must stop and buckle to it, and *stick upon* it with labor and thought. [*Not elegant.*] *Locke.*

To stick out, to project; to be prominent.

His bones that were not seen, *stick out.* Job xxxiii.

STICK'INESS, *n.* [from *stick.*] The quality of a thing which makes it adhere to a plane surface; adhesiveness; viscousness; glutinousness; tenacity; as the *stickiness* of glue or paste.

STICK'LE, *v. i.* [from the practice of prize-fighters, who placed seconds with staves or sticks to interpose occasionally. *Johnson.*]

1. To take part with one side or other.

Fortune, as she wont, turn'd fickle,
And for the foe began to *stickle.* *Hudibras.*

2. To contend; to contest; to altercate. Let the parties *stickle* each for his favorite doctrine.
3. To trim; to play fast and loose; to pass from one side to the other. *Dryden.*

STICK'LE, *v. t.* To arbitrate. [*Not in use.*] *Drayton.*

STICK'LE-BACK, *n.* A small fish of the genus Gasterosteus, of several species. The common species seldom grows to the length of two inches.

Encyc. Dict. Nat. Hist.

STICK'LER, *n.* A sidesman to fencers; a second to a duelist; one who stands to judge a combat.

Basilius the judge, appointed *sticklers* and trumpets whom the others should obey. *Sidney.*

2. An obstinate contender about any thing; as a *stickler* for the church or for liberty.

The tory or high church clergy were the greatest *sticklers* against the exorbitant proceedings of king James. *Swift.*

3. Formerly, an officer who cut wood for the priory of Ederose, within the king's parks of Clarendon. *Cowel.*

STICK'LING, *ppr.* Trimming; contending obstinately or eagerly.

STICK'Y, *a.* Having the quality of adhering to a surface; adhesive; gluey; viscous; viscid; glutinous; tenacious. Gums and resins are *sticky* substances.

STID'DY, *n.* [Ice. *stedia.*] An anvil; also, a smith's shop. [*Not in use or local.*]

STIFF, *a.* [Sax. *stif*; G. *steif*; D. Sw. *styf*; Dan. *stiv*; allied to L. *stipo*, *stabilis*, Eng. *staple*, Gr. ςιφρος, ςιβεω, ςειβω.]

1. Not easily bent; not flexible or pliant; not flaccid; rigid; *applicable to any sub-*

stance; as *stiff* wood; *stiff* paper; cloth *stiff* with starch; a limb *stiff* with frost.

They, rising on *stiff* pinions, tower
The mid aerial sky. *Milton.*

2. Not liquid or fluid; thick and tenacious; inspissated; not soft nor hard. Thus melted metals grow *stiff* as they cool; they are *stiff* before they are hard. The paste is too *stiff*, or not *stiff* enough.

3. Strong; violent; impetuous in motion; as in seamen's language, a *stiff* gale or breeze.

4. Hardy; stubborn; not easily subdued.

How *stiff* is my vile sense! *Shak.*

5. Obstinate; pertinacious; firm in perseverance or resistance.

It is a shame to stand *stiff* in a foolish argument. *Taylor.*

A war ensues; the Cretans own their cause,
Stiff to defend their hospitable laws. *Dryden.*

6. Harsh; formal; constrained; not natural and easy; as a *stiff* formal style.

7. Formal in manner; constrained; affected; starched; not easy or natural; as *stiff* behavior.

The French are open, familiar and talkative; the Italians *stiff*, ceremonious and reserved. *Addison.*

8. Strongly maintained, or asserted with good evidence.

This is *stiff* news. *Shak.*

9. In *seamen's language*, a *stiff* vessel is one that will bear sufficient sail without danger of oversetting.

STIFFEN, *v. t.* *stif'n.* [Sax. *stifian;* Sw. *styfna;* D. *styven;* G. *steifen;* Dan. *stivner*, to stiffen, to starch.]

1. To make stiff; to make less pliant or flexible; as, to *stiffen* cloth with starch.

He *stiffened* his neck and hardened his heart from turning to the Lord God of Israel. 2 Chron. xxxvi.

Stiffen the sinews; summon up the blood. *Shak.*

2. To make torpid; as *stiffening* grief. *Dryden.*

3. To inspissate; to make more thick or viscous; as, to *stiffen* paste.

STIFFEN, *v. i.* *stif'n.* To become stiff; to become more rigid or less flexible.

—Like bristles rose my *stiff'ning* hair. *Dryden.*

2. To become more thick, or less soft; to be inspissated; to approach to hardness; as, melted substances *stiffen* as they cool.

The tender soil then *stiff'ning* by degrees— *Dryden.*

3. To become less susceptible of impression; to become less tender or yielding; to grow more obstinate.

Some souls, we see,
Grow hard and *stiffen* with adversity. *Dryden.*

STIFF'ENING, *ppr.* Making or becoming less pliable, or more thick, or more obstinate.

STIFF'ENING, *n.* Something that is used to make a substance more stiff or less soft.

STIFF'-HE'ARTED, *a.* [*stiff* and *heart.*] Obstinate; stubborn; contumacious.

They are impudent children and *stiff-hearted.* Ezek. ii.

STIFF'LY, *adv.* Firmly; strongly; as the boughs of a tree *stiffly* upheld. *Bacon.*

2. Rigidly; obstinately; with stubbornness. The doctrine of the infallibility of the church of Rome is *stiffly* maintained by its adherents.

STIFF'-NECKED, *a.* [*stiff* and *neck.*] Stubborn; inflexibly obstinate; contumacious; as a *stiff-necked* people; *stiff-necked* pride. *Denham.*

STIFF'NESS, *n.* Rigidness; want of pliableness or flexibility; the firm texture or state of a substance which renders it difficult to bend it; as the *stiffness* of iron or wood; the *stiffness* of a frozen limb. *Bacon.*

2. Thickness; spissitude; a state between softness and hardness; as the *stiffness* of sirup, paste, size or starch.

3. Torpidness; inaptitude to motion.

An icy *stiffness*
Benumbs my blood. *Denham.*

4. Tension; as the *stiffness* of a cord. *Dryden.*

5. Obstinacy; stubbornness; contumaciousness.

The vices of old age have the *stiffness* of it too. *South.*

Stiffness of mind is not from adherence to truth, but submission to prejudice. *Locke.*

6. Formality of manner; constraint; affected precision.

All this religion sat easily upon him, without *stiffness* and constraint. *Atterbury.*

7. Rigorousness; harshness.

But speak no word to her of these sad plights,
Which her too constant *stiffness* doth constrain. *Spenser.*

8. Affected or constrained manner of expression or writing; want of natural simplicity and ease; as *stiffness* of style.

STI'FLE, *v. t.* [The French *etouffer*, to stifle, is nearly allied to *etoffe*, Eng. *stuff*, L. *stupa*. But *stifle* seems to be more nearly allied to L. *stipo* and Eng. *stiff* and *stop;* all however of one family. Qu. Gr. τυφω.]

1. To suffocate; to stop the breath or action of the lungs by crowding something into the windpipe, or by infusing a substance into the lungs, or by other means; to choke; as, to *stifle* one with smoke or dust.

2. To stop; as, to *stifle* the breath; to *stifle* respiration.

3. To oppress; to stop the breath temporarily; as, to *stifle* one with kisses; to be *stifled* in a close room or with bad air.

4. To extinguish; to deaden; to quench; as, to *stifle* flame; to *stifle* a fire by smoke or by ashes.

5. To suppress; to hinder from transpiring or spreading; as, to *stifle* a report.

6. To extinguish; to check or restrain and destroy; to suppress; as, to *stifle* a civil war in its birth. *Addison.*

7. To suppress or repress; to conceal; to withhold from escaping or manifestation; as, to *stifle* passion; to *stifle* grief; to *stifle* resentment.

8. To suppress; to destroy; as, to *stifle* convictions.

STI'FLE, *n.* The joint of a horse next to the buttock, and corresponding to the knee in man; called also the *stifle joint.*

2. A disease in the knee-pan of a horse or other animal. *Cyc.*

STIG'MA, *n.* [L. from Gr. ςιγμα, from ςιζω, to prick or *stick.*]

1. A brand; a mark made with a burning iron.

2. Any mark of infamy; any reproachful conduct which stains the purity or darkens the luster of reputation.

3. In *botany*, the top of the pistil, which is moist and pubescent to detain and burst the pollen or prolific powder. *Martyn.*

STIG'MATA, *n. plu.* The apertures in the bodies of insects, communicating with the tracheæ or air-vessels. *Encyc.*

STIGMAT'IC, } *a.* Marked with a stig-
STIGMAT'ICAL, } ma, or with something reproachful to character. *Shak.*

2. Impressing with infamy or reproach.

STIGMAT'IC, *n.* A notorious profligate, or criminal who has been branded. [*Little used.*]

2. One who bears about him the marks of infamy or punishment. [*Little used.*] *Bullokar.*

3. One on whom nature has set a mark of deformity. [*Little used.*] *Steevens.*

STIGMAT'ICALLY, *adv.* With a mark of infamy or deformity.

STIG'MATIZE, *v. t.* [Fr. *stigmatiser.*] To mark with a brand; *in a literal sense;* as, the ancients *stigmatized* their slaves and soldiers.

2. To set a mark of disgrace on; to disgrace with some note of reproach or infamy.

To find virtue extolled and vice *stigmatized*— *Addison.*

Sour enthusiasts affect to *stigmatize* the finest and most elegant authors, ancient and modern, as dangerous to religion. *Addison.*

STIG'MATIZED, *pp.* Marked with disgrace.

STIG'MATIZING, *ppr.* Branding with infamy.

STI'LAR, *a.* [from *stile.*] Pertaining to the stile of a dial.

Draw a line for the *stilar* line. *Moxon.*

STIL'BITE, *n.* [Gr. ςιλβω, to shine.] A mineral of a shining pearly luster, of a white color, or white shaded with gray, yellow or red. It has been associated with zeolite, and called foliated zeolite, and radiated zeolite. Werner and the French mineralogists divide zeolite into two kinds, mesotype and stilbite; the latter is distinguished by its lamellar structure. *Werner. Jameson. Cleaveland.*

STILE, *n.* [This is another spelling of *style.* See *Style* and *Still.*]

A pin set on the face of a dial to form a shadow.

Erect the *stile* perpendicularly over the substilar line, so as to make an angle with the dialplane equal to the elevation of the pole of your place. *Moxon.*

STILE, *n.* [Sax. *stigel*, a step, ladder, from *stigan*, to step, to walk, to ascend; G. *stegel.* See *Stair.*]

A step or set of steps for ascending and descending, in passing a fence or wall. *Swift.*

STILET'TO, *n.* [It. dim. from *stilo;* Fr. *stylet.* See *Style.*] A small dagger with a round pointed blade.

STILL, *v. t.* [Sax. *stillan;* G. D. *stillen;* Dan. *stiller;* Sw. *stilla*, to *still*, to quiet or appease, that is, to set, to repress; coinciding with G. *stellen*, to put, set, place, Gr. ςελλω, to send, and with *style, stool, stall.*]

1. To stop, as motion or agitation; to check or restrain; to make quiet; as, to *still* the raging sea.
2. To stop, as noise; to silence.

With his name the mothers *still* their babes. *Shak.*

3. To appease; to calm; to quiet; as tumult, agitation or excitement; as, to *still* the passions.

STILL, *a.* Silent; uttering no sound; *applicable to animals or to things.* The company or the man is *still;* the air is *still;* the sea is *still.*

2. Quiet; calm; not disturbed by noise; as a *still* evening.
3. Motionless; as, to stand *still;* to lie or sit *still.*
4. Quiet; calm; not agitated; as a *still* atmosphere.

STILL, *n.* Calm; silence; freedom from noise; as the *still* of midnight. [*A poetic word.*] *Shak.*

STILL, *adv.* To this time; till now.

It hath been anciently reported, and is *still* received. *Bacon.*

[*Still* here denotes this time; set or fixed.]

2. Nevertheless; notwithstanding.

The desire of fame betrays an ambitious man into indecencies that lessen his reputation; he is *still* afraid lest any of his actions should be thrown away in private. *Addison.*

[*Still* here signifies *set, given,* and refers to the whole of the first clause of the sentence. The desire of fame betrays an ambitious man into indecencies that lessen his reputation; *that fact being given* or *set,* or *notwithstanding,* he is afraid, &c.]

3. It precedes or accompanies words denoting increase of degree.

The moral perfections of the Deity, the more attentively we consider them, the more perfectly *still* shall we know them. *Atterbury.*

[*This is not correct.*]

4. Always; ever; continually.

Trade begets trade, and people go much where many people have already gone; so men run *still* to a crowd in the streets, though only to see. *Temple.*

The fewer *still* you name, you wound the more. *Pope.*

5. After that; after what is stated.

In the primitive church, such as by fear were compelled to sacrifice to strange gods, after repented, and kept *still* the office of preaching the gospel. *Whitgifte.*

6. In continuation.

And, like the watchful minutes to the hour,
Still and anon cheer'd up the heavy time. *Shak.*

STILL, *n.* [L. *stillo,* to drop. See *Distill.*] A vessel, boiler or copper used in the distillation of liquors; as vapor ascending out of the *still.* *Newton.*

The word is used in a more general sense for the vessel and apparatus. A still house is also called a still.

STILL, *v. t.* [L. *stillo.*] To expel spirit from liquor by heat and condense it in a refrigeratory; to distill. [See *Distill.*]

STILL, *v. i.* To drop. [*Not in use.* See *Distill.*]

STILLATI''TIOUS, *a.* [L. *stillatitius.*] Falling in drops; drawn by a still.

STILL'ATORY, *n.* An alembic; a vessel for distillation. [*Little used or not at all.*] *Bacon.*

2. A laboratory; a place or room in which distillation is performed. [*Little used.*] *Wotton. More.*

STILL'-BORN, *a.* [*still* and *born.*] Dead at the birth; as a *still-born* child.

2. Abortive; as a *still-born* poem. *Swift.*

STILL'-BURN, *v. t.* [*still* and *burn.*] To burn in the process of distillation; as, to *still-burn* brandy. *Smollett.*

STILL'ED, *pp.* [See *Still,* the verb.] Calmed; appeased; quieted; silenced.

STILL'ER, *n.* One who stills or quiets.

STIL'LICIDE, *n.* [L. *stillicidium; stilla,* a drop, and *cado,* to fall.] A continual falling or succession of drops. [*Not much used.*] *Bacon.*

STILLICID'IOUS, *a.* Falling in drops. *Brown.*

STILL'ING, *ppr.* Calming; silencing; quieting.

STILL'ING, *n.* The act of calming, silencing or quieting.

2. A stand for casks. [*Not used in America.*]

STILL'-LIFE, *n.* [*still* and *life.*] Things that have only vegetable life. *Mason.*

2. Dead animals, or paintings representing the dead. *Gray.*

STILL'NESS, *n.* Freedom from noise or motion; calmness; quiet; silence; as the *stillness* of the night, the air or the sea.

2. Freedom from agitation or excitement; as the *stillness* of the passions.
3. Habitual silence; taciturnity.

The gravity and *stillness* of your youth,
The world hath noted. *Shak.*

STILL'-STAND, *n.* Absence of motion. [*Little used.*]

STIL'LY, *adv.* Silently; without noise.

2. Calmly; quietly; without tumult.

STILPNOSID'ERITE, *n.* [Gr. στιλπνος, shining, and *siderite.*] A mineral of a brownish black color, massive, in curving concretions, splendent and resinous.

STILT, *n.* [G. *stelze;* D. *stelt, stelten;* Dan. *stylter.*] A stilt is a piece of wood with a shoulder, to support the foot in walking. Boys sometimes use *stilts* for raising their feet above the mud in walking, but they are rarely seen.

Men must not walk upon *stilts.* *L'Estrange.*

STILT, *v. t.* To raise on stilts; to elevate. *Young.*

2. To raise by unnatural means.

STIM'ULANT, *a.* [L. *stimulans.*] Increasing or exciting action, particularly the action of the organs of an animal body; stimulating.

STIM'ULANT, *n.* A medicine that excites and increases the action of the moving fibers or organs of an animal body.

STIM'ULATE, *v. t.* [L. *stimulo,* to prick, to goad, to excite; *stimulus,* a goad.] Literally, to prick or goad. Hence,

1. To excite, rouse or animate to action or more vigorous exertion by some pungent motive or by persuasion; as, to *stimulate* one by the hope of reward, or by the prospect of glory.
2. In *medicine,* to excite or increase the action of the moving fibers or organs of an animal body; as, to *stimulate* a torpid limb; or to *stimulate* the stomach and bowels.

STIM'ULATED, *pp.* Goaded; roused or excited to action or more vigorous exertion.

STIM'ULATING, *ppr.* Goading; exciting to action or more vigorous exertion.

STIMULA'TION, *n.* The act of goading or exciting.

2. Excitement; the increased action of the moving fibers or organs in animal bodies.

STIM'ULATIVE, *a.* Having the quality of exciting action in the animal system.

STIM'ULATIVE, *n.* That which stimulates; that which rouses into more vigorous action; that which excites.

STIM'ULATOR, *n.* One that stimulates.

STIM'ULUS, *n.* [L. This word may be formed on the root of *stem,* a shoot.] Literally, a goad; hence, something that rouses from languor; that which excites or increases action in the animal system, as a *stimulus* in medicine; or that which rouses the mind or spirits; as, the hope of gain is a powerful *stimulus* to labor and action.

STING, *v. t.* pret. and pp. *stung.* *Stang* is obsolete. [Goth. *stigcwan;* Sax. *stingan, styngan,* to rush or thrust, hence to sting; G. *stechen,* to stick, to sting; *stachel,* a prick, goad, sting; D. *stecken, steckel;* Dan. *stikker,* to stick, to sting; *sting,* a thrust, a stitch, a sting; Sw. *sticka.* The Dutch has *steng,* a pole or perch; Sw. *stång,* id.; and *stånga,* to push with the horns, to gore. We see that *sting,* is *stick* altered in orthography and pronunciation.]

1. To pierce with the sharp pointed instrument with which certain animals are furnished, such as bees, wasps, scorpions and the like. Bees will seldom *sting* persons, unless they are first provoked.
2. To pain acutely; as, the conscience is *stung* with remorse.

Slander *stings* the brave. *Pope.*

STING, *n.* [Sax. *sting, stincg;* Ice. *staung,* a spear; W. *ystang;* D. *steng,* a pole or perch, Sw. *stång;* It. *stanga,* a bar. These words are all of one family.]

1. A sharp pointed weapon or instrument which certain animals are armed by nature for their defense, and which they thrust from the hinder part of the body to pierce any animal that annoys or provokes them. In most instances, this instrument is a tube, through which a poisonous matter is discharged, which inflames the flesh, and in some instances proves fatal to life.
2. The thrust of a sting into the flesh. The *sting* of most insects produces acute pain.
3. Any thing that gives acute pain. Thus we speak of the *stings* of remorse; the *stings* of reproach.
4. The point in the last verse; as the *sting* of an epigram. *Dryden.*
5. That which gives the principal pain, or constitutes the principal terror.

The *sting* of death is sin. 1 Cor. xv.

STING'ER, *n.* That which stings, vexes or gives acute pain.

STIN'GILY, *adv.* [from *stingy.*] With mean covetousness; in a niggardly manner.

STIN'GINESS, *n.* [from *stingy.*] Extreme avarice; mean covetousness; niggardliness.

STING'LESS, *a.* [from *sting.*] Having no sting.

STIN'GO, *n.* [from the sharpness of the taste.] Old beer. [*A cant word.*] *Addison.*

STIN'GY, *a.* [from straitness; W. *ystang*, something strait; *ystangu*, to straiten, to limit.]

1. Extremely close and covetous; meanly avaricious; niggardly; narrow hearted; as a *stingy* churl. [*A word in popular use, but low and not admissible into elegant writing.*]

STINK, *v. i.* pret. *stank* or *stunk.* [Sax. *stincan*; G. D. *stinken*; Dan. *stinker*; Sw. *stinka.*]

To emit a strong offensive smell. *Locke.*

STINK, *n.* A strong offensive smell. *Dryden.*

STINK'ARD, *n.* A mean paltry fellow.

STINK'ER, *n.* Something intended to offend by the smell. *Harvey.*

STINK'ING, *ppr.* Emitting a strong offensive smell.

STINK'INGLY, *adv.* With an offensive smell. *Shak.*

STINK'POT, *n.* An artificial composition offensive to the smell. *Harvey.*

STINK'STONE, *n.* Swinestone, a variety of compact lucullite; a subspecies of limestone. *Ure.*

STINT, *v. t.* [Sax. *stintan*, to *stint* or *stunt*; Ice. *stunta*; Gr. ςενος, narrow.]

1. To restrain within certain limits; to bound; to confine; to limit; as, to *stint* the body in growth; to *stint* the mind in knowledge; to *stint* a person in his meals.

Nature wisely *stints* our appetite. *Dryden.*

2. To assign a certain task in labor, which being performed, the person is excused from further labor for the day, or for a certain time; *a common popular use of the word in America.*

STINT, *n.* A small bird, the *Tringa cinctus.*

STINT, *n.* Limit; bound; restraint. *Dryden.*

2. Quantity assigned; proportion allotted. The workmen have their *stint.*

Our *stint* of woe
Is common. *Shak.*

STINT'ANCE, *n.* Restraint; stoppage. [*Not used or local.*]

STINT'ED, *pp.* Restrained to a certain limit or quantity; limited.

STINT'ER, *n.* He or that which stints.

STINT'ING, *ppr.* Restraining within certain limits; assigning a certain quantity to; limiting.

STIPE, *n.* [L. *stipes*; Gr. ςυπος, a stake.] In *botany*, the base of a frond; or a species of stem passing into leaves, or not distinct from the leaf. The stem of a fungus is also called *stipe.* The word is also used for the filament or slender stalk which supports the pappus or down, and connects it with the seed. *Martyn.*

STIP'EL, *n.* [See *Stipula.*] In *botany*, a little appendix situated at the base of the folioles. *Decandolle.*

STI'PEND, *n.* [L. *stipendium*; *stips*, a piece of money, and *pendo*, to pay.]

Settled pay or compensation for services, whether daily or monthly wages; or an annual salary.

STI'PEND, *v. t.* To pay by settled wages. *Shelton.*

STIPEND'IARY, *a.* [L. *stipendiarius.*] Receiving wages or salary; performing services for a stated price or compensation.

His great *stipendiary* prelates came with troops of evil appointed horsemen not half full. *Knolles.*

STIPEND'IARY, *n.* [supra.] One who performs services for a settled compensation, either by the day, month or year.

If thou art become
A tyrant's vile *stipendiary*— *Glover.*

STIP'ITATE, *a.* [See *Stipe.*] In *botany*, supported by a stipe; elevated on a stipe; as pappus or down. *Martyn.*

STIP'PLE, *v. t.* To engrave by means of dots, in distinction from engraving in lines. *Todd.*

STIP'PLED, *pp.* Engraved with dots.

STIP'PLING, *ppr.* Engraving with dots.

STIP'PLING, *n.* A mode of engraving on copper by means of dots. *Cyc.*

STIP'TIC. [See *Styptic.*]

STIP'ULA, } *n.* [L. *stipula*, a straw or stub-
STIP'ULE, } ble.]

In *botany*, a scale at the base of nascent petioles or peduncles. Stipules are in pairs or solitary; they are lateral, extrafoliaceous, intrafoliaceous, &c. *Martyn.*

A leafy appendage to the proper leaves or to their footstalks; commonly situated at the base of the latter, in pairs. *Smith.*

STIPULA'CEOUS, } *a.* [from L. *stipula*,
STIP'ULAR, } *stipularis.* See *Stipula.*]

1. Formed of stipules or scales; as a *stipular* bud.

2. Growing on stipules, or close to them; as *stipular* glands. *Martyn. Lee.*

STIP'ULATE, *v. i.* [L. *stipulor*, from *stipes*, or from the primary sense of the root, as in *stipo*, to crowd; whence the sense of agreement, binding, making fast.]

1. To make an agreement or covenant with any person or company to do or forbear any thing; to contract; to settle terms; as, certain princes *stipulated* to assist each other in resisting the armies of France. Great Britain and the United States *stipulate* to oppose and restrain the African slave trade. A has *stipulated* to build a bridge within a given time. B has *stipulated* not to annoy or interdict our trade.

2. To bargain. A has *stipulated* to deliver me his horse for fifty guineas.

STIP'ULATE, *a.* [from *stipula.*] Having stipules on it; as a *stipulate* stalk.

STIP'ULATED, *pp.* Agreed; contracted; covenanted. It was *stipulated* that Great Britain should retain Gibraltar.

STIP'ULATING, *ppr.* Agreeing; contracting; bargaining.

STIPULA'TION, *n.* [Fr. from L. *stipulatio.*]

1. The act of agreeing and covenanting; a contracting or bargaining.

2. An agreement or covenant made by one person with another for the performance or forbearance of some act; a contract or bargain; as the *stipulations* of the allied powers to furnish each his contingent of troops.

3. In *botany*, the situation and structure of the stipules. *Martyn.*

STIP'ULATOR, *n.* One who stipulates, contracts or covenants.

STIP'ULE. [See *Stipula.*]

STIR, *v. t.* *stur.* [Sax. *stirian*, *styrian*; D. *stooren*; G. *stören*, to stir, to disturb; W. *ystwriaw.* This word gives *storm*; Ice. *stir*, war.]

1. To move; to change place in any manner.

My foot I had never yet in five days been able to *stir.* *Temple.*

2. To agitate; to bring into debate.

Stir not questions of jurisdiction. *Bacon.*

3. To incite to action; to instigate; to prompt.

An Até *stirring* him to blood and strife. *Shak.*

4. To excite; to raise; to put into motion.

And for her sake some mutiny will *stir.* *Dryden.*

To stir up, to incite; to animate; to instigate by inflaming passions; as, to *stir up* a nation to rebellion.

The words of Judas were good and able to *stir* them *up* to valor. 2 Macc.

2. To excite; to put into action; to begin; as, to *stir up* a mutiny or insurrection; to *stir up* strife.

3. To quicken; to enliven; to make more lively or vigorous; as, to *stir up* the mind.

4. To disturb; as, to *stir up* the sediment of liquor.

STIR, *v. i.* *stur.* To move one's self. He is not able to *stir.*

2. To go or be carried in any manner. He is not able to *stir* from home, or to *stir* abroad.

3. To be in motion; not to be still. He is continually *stirring.*

4. To become the object of notice or conversation.

They fancy they have a right to talk freely upon every thing that *stirs* or appears. *Watts.*

5. To rise in the morning. [*Colloquial.*] *Shak.*

STIR, *n.* [W. *ystwr.*] Agitation; tumult; bustle; noise or various movements.

Why all these words, this clamor and this *stir?* *Denham.*

Consider, after so much *stir* about the genus and species, how few words have yet settled definitions. *Locke.*

2. Public disturbance or commotion; tumultuous disorder; seditious uproar.

Being advertised of some *stir* raised by his unnatural sons in England, he departed from Ireland without a blow. *Davies.*

3. Agitation of thoughts; conflicting passions. *Shak.*

STIR'IATED, *a.* [L. *stiria*, an icicle.] Adorned with pendants like icicles.

STIR'IOUS, *a.* [supra.] Resembling icicles. [*Not much used.*] *Brown.*

STIRK, *n.* *sturk.* A young ox or heifer. [*Local.*]

STIRP, *n.* *sturp.* [L. *stirps.*] Stock; race; family. [*Not English.*] *Bacon.*

STIR'RED, *pp.* Moved; agitated; put in action.

STIR'RER, *n.* One who is in motion.

2. One who puts in motion.

3. A riser in the morning. *Shak.*

4. An inciter or exciter; an instigator.

5. A *stirrer up*, an exciter; an instigator.

STIR'RING, *ppr.* Moving; agitating; putting in motion.

STIR'RING, *n.* [supra.] The act of moving or putting in motion.

STIRRUP, *n.* *stur'up.* [Sax. *stige-rapa,* step-rope; *stigan,* to step or ascend, and *rap,* rope; G. *steig-bügel,* step-bow or mounting-bow; D. *styg-beugel;* Sw. *stegbögel;* Dan. *stigböjle.* The first stirrups appear to have been ropes.]

A kind of ring or bending piece of metal, horizontal on one side for receiving the foot of the rider, and attached to a strap which is fastened to the saddle; used to assist persons in mounting a horse, and to enable them to sit steadily in riding, as well as to relieve them by supporting a part of the weight of the body.

STIR'RUP-LETHER, *n.* A strap that supports a stirrup.

STITCH, *v. t.* [G. *sticken;* D. *stikken;* Dan. *stikker;* Sw. *sticka.* This is another form of *stick.*]

1. To sew in a particular manner; to sew slightly or loosely; as, to *stitch* a collar or a wristband; to *stitch* the leaves of a book and form a pamphlet.

2. To form land into ridges. [*N. England.*]

To stitch up, to mend or unite with a needle and thread; as, to *stitch up* a rent; to *stitch up* an artery. *Wiseman.*

STITCH, *v. i.* To practice stitching.

STITCH, *n.* A single pass of a needle in sewing.

2. A single turn of the thread round a needle in knitting; a link of yarn; as, to let down a *stitch;* to take up a *stitch.*

3. A land; the space between two double furrows in plowed ground.

4. A local spasmodic pain; an acute lancing pain, like the piercing of a needle; as a *stitch* in the side.

STITCH'ED, *pp.* Sewed slightly.

STITCH'EL, *n.* A kind of hairy wool. [*Local.*]

STITCH'ER, *n.* One that stitches.

STITCH'ERY, *n.* Needlework; *in contempt.* *Shak.*

STITCH'FALLEN, *a.* Fallen, as a stitch in knitting. [*Not in use.*] *Dryden.*

STITCH'ING, *ppr.* Sewing in a particular manner; uniting with a needle and thread.

STITCH'ING, *n.* The act of stitching.

2. Work done by sewing in a particular manner.

3. The forming of land into ridges or divisions.

STITCH'-WÖRT, *n.* A plant, camomile. [L. *anthemis.*] *Ainsworth.*

A plant of the genus Stellaria. *Lee.*

STITH, *a.* [Sax.] Strong; rigid. [*Not in use.*]

STITH'Y, *n.* [supra. Ice. *stedia.*] An anvil. [*Local.*] *Shak.*

2. A disease in oxen.

STIVE, *v. t.* [See *Stuff* and *Stew.*] To stuff up close. [*Not in use.*] *Sandys.*

2. To make hot, sultry and close. [*Not in use.*] *Wotton.*

STI'VER, *n.* [Sw. *stifver;* D. *stuiver.*] A Dutch coin of about the value of a halfpenny sterling, or the cent of the United States. It is also a money of account in Holland and Flanders. *Encyc.*

STÖAK, *v. t.* To stop; to choke; *in seamen's language.*

STOAT, *n.* An animal of the weasel kind; the ermine. This animal is called *stoat* when of a reddish color, and *ermine* when white, as in winter. *Ed. Encyc.*

STO'€AH, *n.* [Ir. and Erse.] An attendant; a wallet boy. [*Not English nor used.*] *Spenser.*

STO€€A'DE, } *n.* STO€€A'DO, } [It. *stoccato,* a thrust, from *stocco,* a stock or race, a rapier or long sword; Sp. *estocada;* Fr. *estocade.* This gives the sense of thrust. But we give the word another signification, from *stock,* a post or fixed piece of timber. The It. *stocco* and Eng. *stock* are the same word.]

1. A stab; a thrust with a rapier. *Shak.*

2. A fence or barrier made with stakes or posts planted in the earth; a slight fortification. [See *Stockade.*]

STO€HAS'TI€, *a.* [Gr. ςοχαςικος.] Conjectural; able to conjecture. [*Not in use.*] *Brown.*

STOCK, *n.* [Sax. *stoc,* a place, the stem of a tree; G. *stock,* a stem, a staff, a *stick,* a block; D. Dan. *stok,* id.; Sw. *stock;* Fr. *estoc;* It. *stocco.* This word coincides with *stake, stick, stack;* that which is set or fixed.]

1. The stem or main body of a tree or other plant; the fixed, strong, firm part; the origin and support of the branches. Job xiv.

2. The stem in which a graft is inserted, and which is its support.

The cion overruleth the *stock* quite. *Bacon.*

3. A post; something fixed, solid and senseless.

When all our fathers worship'd *stocks* and stones. *Milton.*

4. A person very stupid, dull and senseless.

Let's be no stoics, nor no *stocks.* *Shak.*

5. The handle of any thing.

6. The wood in which the barrel of a musket or other fire-arm is fixed.

7. A thrust with a rapier. [*Not in use.*]

8. A cravat or band for the neck.

9. A cover for the leg. *Obs.* [Now *stocking.*]

10. The original progenitor; also, the race or line of a family; the progenitors of a family and their direct descendants; lineage; family. From what *stock* did he spring?

Thy mother was no goddess, nor thy *stock*
From Dardanus— *Denham.*

Men and brethren, children of the *stock* of Abraham— Acts xiii.

11. A fund; capital; the money or goods employed in trade, manufactures, insurance, banking, &c.; as the *stock* of a banking company; the *stock* employed in the manufacture of cotton, in making insurance and the like. *Stock* may be individual or joint.

12. Money lent to government, or property in a public debt; a share or shares of a national or other public debt, or in a company debt. The United States borrow of the bank or of individuals, and sell *stock* bearing an interest of five, six or seven per cent. British *stocks* are the objects of perpetual speculation.

13. Supply provided; store. Every one may be charitable out of his own *stock.* So we say, a *stock* of honor, a *stock* of fame.

Add to that *stock* which justly we bestow. *Dryden.*

14. In *agriculture,* the domestic animals or beasts belonging to the owner of a farm; as a *stock* of cattle or of sheep. It is also used for the crop or other property belonging to the farm. *Encyc.*

15. Living beasts shipped to a foreign country; as, a brig sailed yesterday with *stock* on deck. The cattle are called also *live stock.* *America.*

16. In *the West Indies,* the slaves of a plantation.

17. *Stocks,* plu. a machine consisting of two pieces of timber, in which the legs of criminals are confined by way of punishment.

18. The frame or timbers on which a ship rests while building.

19. The *stock* of an anchor is the piece of timber into which the shank is inserted. *Mar. Dict.*

20. In *book-keeping,* the owner or owners of the books. *Encyc.*

STOCK, *v. t.* To store; to supply; to fill; as, to *stock* the mind with ideas. Asia and Europe are well *stocked* with inhabitants.

2. To lay up in store; as, he *stocks* what he cannot use. *Johnson.*

3. To put in the stocks. [*Little used.*] *Shak.*

4. To pack; to put into a pack; as, to *stock* cards.

5. To supply with domestic animals; as, to *stock* a farm.

6. To supply with seed; as, to *stock* land with clover or herdsgrass. *American farmers.*

7. To suffer cows to retain their milk for 24 hours or more, previous to sale.

To stock up, to extirpate; to dig up. *Edwards, W. Indies.*

STOCKA'DE, *n.* [See *Stoccade.*] In *fortification,* a sharpened post or stake set in the earth.

2. A line of posts or stakes set in the earth as a fence or barrier.

STOCKA'DE, *v. t.* To surround or fortify with sharpened posts fixed in the ground.

STOCKA'DED, *pp.* Fortified with stockades.

STOCKA'DING, *ppr.* Fortifying with sharpened posts or stakes.

STOCK' BROKER, *n.* [*stock* and *broker.*] A broker who deals in the purchase and sale of stocks or shares in the public funds.

STOCK'-DÖVE, *n.* [*stock* and *dove.*] The ring-dove. *Dryden.*

The *stock dove* is the wild pigeon of Europe, *(Columba œnas,)* long considered as the *stock* of the domestic pigeon, but now regarded as a distinct species. The ring-dove is the *Columba palumbus.* *Ed. Encyc.*

STOCK'-FISH, *n.* [*stock* and *fish.*] Cod dried hard and without salt.

STOCK-ĠIL'LYFLOWER, *n.* A plant, a species of Cheiranthus; sometimes written *stock July flower.* *Encyc.* *Fam. of Plants.*

STOCK'ING, *n.* [from *stock;* Ir. *stoca;* supposed by Johnson to be a corruption of *stocken,* plural of *stock.* But qu.]

A garment made to cover the leg.

STOCK'ING, *v. t.* To dress in stockings. *Dryden.*

STOCK'ISH, *a.* Hard; stupid; blockish. [*Little used.*] *Shak.*

STOCK'-JOBBER, *n.* [*stock* and *job.*] One who speculates in the public funds for gain; one whose occupation is to buy and sell stocks.

STOCK'-JOBBING, *n.* The act or art of dealing in the public funds. *Encyc.*

STOCK'-LOCK, *n.* [*stock* and *lock.*] A lock fixed in wood. *Moxon.*

STOCKS. [See under *Stock.*]

STOCK'-STILL, *a.* [*stock* and *still.*] Still as a fixed post; perfectly still.

Our preachers stand *stock-still* in the pulpit. *Anon.*

STOCK'Y, *a.* [from *stock.*] Thick and firm; stout. A *stocky* person is one rather thick than tall or corpulent; one whose bones are covered well with flesh, but without a prominent belly.

STO'IC, *n.* [Gr. στωικος, from στοα, a porch in Athens where the philosopher Zeno taught.]

A disciple of the philosopher Zeno, who founded a sect. He taught that men should be free from passion, unmoved by joy or grief, and submit without complaint to the unavoidable necessity by which all things are governed. *Enfield.*

STO'IC, STO'ICAL, } *a.* Pertaining to the Stoics or to their doctrines.

2. Not affected by passion; unfeeling; manifesting indifference to pleasure or pain.

STO'ICALLY, *adv.* In the manner of the Stoics; without apparent feeling or sensibility; with indifference to pleasure or pain. *Chesterfield.*

STO'ICALNESS, *n.* The state of being stoical; indifference to pleasure or pain.

STO'ICISM, *n.* The opinions and maxims of the Stoics.

2. A real or pretended indifference to pleasure or pain; insensibility.

STOKE, Sax. *stocce, stoc,* place, is the same word as *stock,* differently applied. It is found in many English names of towns.

STOKE, STO'KER, } *n.* One who looks after the fire in a brew-house. [*Local or technical.*] *Green.*

STOLE, *pret.* of *steal.*

STOLE, *n.* [L. It. *stola;* Sp. *estola.*] A long vest or robe; a garment worn by the priests of some denominations when they officiate. It is a broad strip of cloth reaching from the neck to the feet. *Encyc.*

2. [L. *stolo.*] A sucker; a shoot from the root of a plant, by which some plants may be propagated; written also *stool.*

STOLEN, *pp.* *sto'ln.* The passive participle of *steal.*

Stolen waters are sweet. Prov. ix.

STOL'ID, *a.* [L. *stolidus;* from the root of *still, stall,* to set.]

Dull; foolish; stupid. [*Not used.*]

STOLID'ITY, *n.* [supra.] Dullness of intellect; stupidity. [*Little used.*] *Bentley.*

STOLONIF'EROUS, *a.* [L. *stolo,* a sucker, and *fero,* to produce.]

Producing suckers; putting forth suckers; as a *stoloniferous* stem. *Martyn.*

STŎM'ACH, *n.* [L. *stomachus;* Sp. *estomago;* It. *stomacho;* Fr. *estomac.*]

1. In *animal bodies,* a membranous receptacle, the organ of digestion, in which food is prepared for entering into the several parts of the body for its nourishment.

2. Appetite; the desire of food caused by hunger; as a good *stomach* for roast beef. [*A popular use of the word.*]

3. Inclination; liking. *Bacon.*

He which hath no *stomach* to this fight,
Let him depart— *Shak.*

4. Anger; violence of temper.

Stern was his look, and full of *stomach* vain. *Spenser.*

5. Sullenness; resentment; willful obstinacy; stubbornness.

This sort of crying proceeding from pride, obstinacy and *stomach,* the will, where the fault lies, must be bent. *Locke.*

6. Pride; haughtiness.

He was a man
Of an unbounded *stomach,* ever ranking
Himself with princes. *Shak.*

[*Note.* This word in all the foregoing senses, except the first, is nearly obsolete or inelegant.]

STŎM'ACH, *v. t.* [L. *stomachor.*] To resent; to remember with anger.

The lion began to show his teeth, and to *stomach* the affront. *L'Estrange.*

This sense is not used in America, as far as my observation extends. In America, at least in New England, the sense is,

2. To brook; to bear without open resentment or without opposition. [*Not elegant.*]

STŎM'ACH, *v. i.* To be angry. [*Not in use.*] *Hooker.*

STŎM'ACHED, *a.* Filled with resentment. *Shak.*

STŎM'ACHER, *n.* An ornament or support to the breast, worn by females. Is. iii. *Shak.*

STŎM'ACHFUL, *a.* Willfully obstinate; stubborn; perverse; as a *stomachful* boy. *L'Estrange.*

STŎM'ACHFULNESS, *n.* Stubbornness; sullenness; perverse obstinacy.

STOMACH'IC, STOMACH'ICAL, } *a.* Pertaining to the stomach; as *stomachic* vessels. *Harvey.*

2. Strengthening to the stomach; exciting the action of the stomach. *Coxe.*

STOMACH'IC, *n.* A medicine that excites the action and strengthens the tone of the stomach.

STŎM'ACHING, *n.* Resentment. [*Not in use.*]

STŎM'ACHLESS, *a.* Being without appetite. *Hall.*

STŎM'ACHOUS, *a.* Stout; sullen; obstinate. [*Not in use.*] *Spenser.*

STOMP, for *stamp,* which see.

STOND, *n.* [for *stand.*] A stop; a post; a station. *Obs.* [See *Stand.*]

STONE, *n.* [Sax. *stan;* Goth. *staina;* G. *stein;* D. Dan. *steen;* Sw. *sten;* Dalmatian, *sztina;* Croatian, *stine.* This word may be a derivative from the root of *stand,* or it may belong to some root in Class Dn. The primary sense is to set, to fix; Gr. ςενος.]

1. A concretion of some species of earth, as lime, silex, clay and the like, usually in combination with some species of air or gas, with sulphur or with a metallic substance; a hard compact body, of any form and size. In popular language, very large masses of concretions are called *rocks;* and very small concretions are universally called gravel or sand, or grains of sand. Stones are of various degrees of hardness and weight; they are brittle and fusible, but not malleable, ductile, or soluble in water. Stones are of great and extensive use in the construction of buildings of all kinds, for walls, fences, piers, abutments, arches, monuments, sculpture and the like.

When we speak of the substance generally, we use *stone* in the singular; as a house or wall of *stone.* But when we speak of particular separate masses, we say, *a stone,* or *the stones.*

2. A gem; a precious stone.

Inestimable *stones,* unvalu'd jewels. *Shak.*

3. Any thing made of stone; a mirror. *Shak.*

4. A calculous concretion in the kidneys or bladder; the disease arising from a calculus.

5. A testicle.

6. The nut of a drupe or stone fruit; or the hard covering inclosing the kernel, and itself inclosed by the pulpy pericarp. *Martyn.*

7. In *Great Britain,* the weight of fourteen pounds. [8, 12, 14 or 16.]

[*Not used in the United States, except in reference to the riders of horses in races.*]

8. A monument erected to preserve the memory of the dead.

Should some relentless eye
Glance on the *stone* where our cold relics lie— *Pope.*

9. It is used to express torpidness and insensibility; as a heart of *stone.*

I have not yet forgot myself to *stone.* *Pope.*

10. *Stone* is prefixed to some words to qualify their signification. Thus *stone-dead,* is perfectly dead, as lifeless as a stone; *stone-still,* still as a stone, perfectly still; *stone-blind,* blind as a stone, perfectly blind.

To leave no stone unturned, a proverbial expression which signifies to do every thing that can be done; to use all practicable means to effect an object.

Meteoric stones, stones which fall from the atmosphere, as after the displosion of a meteor.

Philosopher's stone, a pretended substance that was formerly supposed to have the property of turning any other substance into gold.

STONE, *a.* Made of stone, or like stone; as a *stone* jug.

STONE, *v. t.* [Sax. *stænan.*] To pelt, beat or kill with stones.

And they *stoned* Stephen calling on God and saying, Lord Jesus, receive my spirit. Acts vii.

2. To harden.

O perjur'd woman, thou dost *stone* my heart. [*Little used.*] *Shak.*

3. To free from stones; as, to *stone* raisins.

4. To wall or face with stones; to line or fortify with stones; as, to *stone* a well; to *stone* a cellar.

STO'NE-BLIND, *a.* [*stone* and *blind.*] Blind as a stone; perfectly blind.

STO'NE-BŌW, *n.* [*stone* and *bow.*] A cross bow for shooting stones.

STO'NE-BREAK, *n.* [*stone* and *break;* L. *saxifraga.*] A plant. *Ainsworth.*

STO'NE-CHAT, STO'NE-CHATTER, } *n.* [*stone* and *chatter.*] A bird, the *Motacilla rubicola.* Linn. *Ainsworth. Ed. Encyc.*

STO'NE-CRAY, *n.* A distemper in hawks.

STO'NE-CROP, *n.* [Sax. *stan-crop.*] A sort of tree. *Mortimer.*

A plant of the genus Sedum; wall-pepper. The stone-crop tree or shrubby glass-wort is of the genus Chenopodium. *Lee.*

STO'NECUTTER, *n.* [*stone* and *cut.*] One whose occupation is to hew stones. *Swift.*

STO'NECUTTING, *n.* The business of hewing stones for walls, steps, cornices, monuments, &c.

STO'NED, *pp.* Pelted or killed with stones; freed from stones; walled with stones.

STO'NE-DEAD, *a.* [*stone* and *dead.*] As lifeless as a stone.

STO'NE-FERN, *n.* [*stone* and *fern.*] A plant. *Ainsworth.*

STO'NE-FLY, *n.* [*stone* and *fly.*] An insect. *Ainsworth.*

STO'NE-FRUIT, *n.* [*stone* and *fruit.*] Fruit whose seeds are covered with a hard shell enveloped in the pulp, as peaches, cherries, plums, &c.; a drupe. *Boyle.*

STO'NE-HAWK, *n.* [*stone* and *hawk.*] A kind of hawk. *Ainsworth.*

STO'NE-HEARTED, STO'NY-HEARTED, *a.* [*stone* and *heart.*] Hard hearted; cruel; pitiless; unfeeling. *Shak.*

STO'NE-HORSE, *n.* [*stone* and *horse.*] A horse not castrated. *Mortimer.*

STO'NE-HOUSE, *n.* [*stone* and *house.*] A house built of stone.

STO'NE-PARSLEY, *n.* A plant of the genus Bubon. *Fam. of Plants.*

STO'NE-PIT, *n.* [*stone* and *pit.*] A pit or quarry where stones are dug. *Woodward.*

STO'NE-PITCH, *n.* [*stone* and *pitch.*] Hard inspissated pitch. *Bacon.*

STO'NE-PLOVER, *n.* [*stone* and *plover.*] A bird. *Ainsworth.*

STO'NER, *n.* One who beats or kills with stones; one who walls with stones.

STO'NE'S-CAST, STO'NE'S-THROW, *n.* [*stone* and *cast* or *throw.*] The distance which a stone may be thrown by the hand.

STO'NE'S-MICKLE, *n.* A bird. *Ainsworth.*

STO'NE-SQUARER, *n.* [*stone* and *square.*] One who forms stones into squares. 1 Kings v.

STO'NE-STILL, *a.* [*stone* and *still.*] Still as a stone; perfectly still or motionless.

STO'NE-WALL, *n.* [*stone* and *wall.*] A wall built of stones.

STO'NE-WARE, *n.* [*stone* and *ware.*] A species of potter's ware of a coarse kind, glazed and baked.

STO'NE-WORK, *n.* [*stone* and *work.*] Work or wall consisting of stone; mason's work of stone. *Mortimer.*

STO'NINESS, *n.* [from *stony.*] The quality of abounding with stones; as, the *stoniness* of ground renders it difficult to till.

2. Hardness of heart. *Hammond.*

STO'NY, *a.* [D. *steenig*; G. *steinig*; Sw. *steneg.*]

1. Made of stone; as a *stony* tower. *Shak.*

2. Consisting of stone; as a *stony* cave. *Milton.*

3. Full of stones; abounding with stones; as *stony* ground.

4. Petrifying; as the *stony* dart of senseless cold. *Spenser.*

5. Hard; cruel; unrelenting; pitiless; as a *stony* heart. *Milton.*

6. Insensible; obdurate; perverse; morally hard.

STOOD, *pret.* of *stand.*

STOOK, *n.* [W. *ystwc*, a shock of grain.] A small collection of sheaves set up in the field. [*Local.*]

STOOK, *v. t.* To set up sheaves of grain in stooks. [*Local.*]

STOOL, *n.* [Sax. *stol*, Goth. *stols*, a seat, a throne; G. *stuhl*, a stool, a stock, a pew, a chair, the see of a bishop; D. Dan. *stoel*, id.; Sw. *stol*; W. *ystal.* This coincides with *stall* and *still.* A *stool* is that which is set, or a seat; Russ. *prestol*, a throne.]

1. A seat without a back; a little form consisting of a board with three or four legs, intended as a seat for one person. *Watts.*

2. The seat used in evacuating the contents of the bowels; hence, an evacuation; a discharge from the bowels.

3. [L. *stolo.*] A sucker; a shoot from the bottom of the stem or the root of a plant. *Edwards, W. Ind.*

Stool of repentance, in Scotland, an elevated seat in the church, on which persons sit as a punishment for fornication and adultery. *Johnson.*

STOOL, *v. i.* In *agriculture*, to ramify; to tiller, as grain; to shoot out suckers.

STOOL'-BALL, *n.* [*stool* and *ball.*] A play in which balls are driven from stool to stool. *Prior.*

STOOM, *v. t.* To put bags of herbs or other ingredients into wine, to prevent fermentation. [*Local.*] *Chambers.*

STOOP, *v. i.* [Sax. *stupian*; D. *stuipen.*]

1. To bend the body downward and forward; as, to *stoop* to pick up a book.

2. To bend or lean forward; to incline forward in standing or walking. We often see men *stoop* in standing or walking, either from habit or from age.

3. To yield; to submit; to bend by compulsion; as, Carthage at length *stooped* to Rome. *Dryden.*

4. To descend from rank or dignity; to condescend. In modern days, attention to agriculture is not called *stooping* in men of property.

> Where men of great wealth *stoop* to husbandry, it multiplieth riches exceedingly. *Bacon.*

5. To yield; to be inferior.

> These are arts, my prince,
> In which our Zama does not *stoop* to Rome. *Addison.*

6. To come down on prey, as a hawk.

> The bird of Jove stoop'd from his airy tour,
> Two birds of gayest plume before him drove. *Milton.*

7. To alight from the wing.

> And *stoop* with closing pinions from above. *Dryden.*

8. To sink to a lower place.

> Cowering low
> With blandishments, each bird *stoop'd* on his wing. *Milton.*

STOOP, *v. t.* To cause to incline downward; to sink; as, to *stoop* a cask of liquor.

2. To cause to submit. [*Little used.*]

STOOP, *n.* The act of bending the body forward; inclination forward.

2. Descent from dignity or superiority; condescension.

> Can any loyal subject see
> With patience such a *stoop* from sovereignty? *Dryden.*

3. Fall of a bird on his prey.

4. In *America*, a kind of shed, generally open, but attached to a house; also, an open place for seats at a door.

STOOP, *n.* [Sax. *stoppa*; D. *stoop*, a measure of about two quarts; Sw. *stop*, a measure of about three pints.]

1. A vessel of liquor; as a *stoop* of wine or ale. *Denham. King.*

2. A post fixed in the earth. [*Local.*]

STOOP'ED, *pp.* Caused to lean.

STOOP'ER, *n.* One that bends the body forward. *Sherwood.*

STOOP'ING, *ppr.* Bending the body forward; yielding; submitting; condescending; inclining.

STOOP'INGLY, *adv.* With a bending of the body forward.

STOOR, *v. i.* To rise in clouds, as dust or smoke; from the Welsh *ystwr*, a stir. [*Local.*]

STOOT'ER, *n.* A small silver coin in Holland, value 2½ stivers. *Encyc.*

STOP, *v. t.* [D. *stoppen*; G. *stopfen*, to stop, to check, to pose, to fill, to cram, to *stuff*, to quilt, to darn, to mend; Dan. *stopper*, to stop, to puzzle, to darn, to cram, to *stuff*; Sw. *stoppa*, to stop, to *stuff*; It. *stoppare*, to stop with tow; *stoppa*, tow, L. *stupa*; Sp. *estopa*, tow; *estofa*, quilted stuff; *estofar*, to quilt, to *stew* meat with wine, spice or vinegar; Port. *estofa*, stuff; *estofar*, to quilt, to stuff; Fr. *etoupe*, tow; *etouper*, to stop with tow; *etouffer*, to choke, to *stifle*, [See *Stifle*;] L. *stupa*, tow; *stipo*, to stuff, to crowd, and *stupeo*, to be stupefied, whence *stupid*, *stupor*, [that is, to *stop*, or a *stop*;] Ir. *stopam*, to stop, to shut. The primary sense is either to cease to move, or to *stuff*, to press, to thrust in, to *cram*; probably the latter.]

1. To close, as an aperture, by filling or by obstructing; as, to *stop* a vent; to *stop* the ears; to *stop* wells of water. 2 Kings iii.

2. To obstruct; to render impassable; as, to *stop* a way, road or passage.

3. To hinder; to impede; to arrest progress; as, to *stop* a passenger in the road; to *stop* the course of a stream.

4. To restrain; to hinder; to suspend; as, to *stop* the execution of a decree.

5. To repress; to suppress; to restrain; as, to *stop* the progress of vice.

6. To hinder; to check; as, to *stop* the approaches of old age or infirmity.

7. To hinder from action or practice.

> Whose disposition, all the world well knows,
> Will not be rubb'd nor *stopp'd*. *Shak.*

8. To put an end to any motion or action; to intercept; as, to *stop* the breath; to *stop* proceedings.

9. To regulate the sounds of musical strings; as, to *stop* a string. *Bacon.*

10. In *seamanship*, to make fast.

11. To point; as a written composition. [*Not in use.*]

STOP, *v. i.* To cease to go forward.

> Some strange commotion
> Is in his brain; he bites his lip, and starts;
> *Stops* on a sudden, looks upon the ground— *Shak.*

2. To cease from any motion or course of

action. When you are accustomed to a course of vice, it is very difficult to *stop*.

The best time to *stop* is at the beginning. *Lesley.*

STOP, *n.* Cessation of progressive motion; as, to make a *stop*. *L'Estrange.*

2. Hinderance of progress; obstruction; act of stopping.

Occult qualities put a *stop* to the improvement of natural philosophy— *Newton.*

3. Repression; hinderance of operation or action.

It is a great step towards the mastery of our desires, to give this *stop* to them. *Locke.*

4. Interruption.

These *stops* of thine fright me the more. *Shak.*

5. Prohibition of sale; as the *stop* of wine and salt. *Temple.*

6. That which obstructs; obstacle; impediment.

A fatal *stop* travers'd their headlong course. *Daniel.*

So melancholy a prospect should inspire us with zeal to oppose some *stop* to the rising torrent. *Rogers.*

7. The instrument by which the sounds of wind music are regulated; as the *stops* of a flute or an organ.

8. Regulation of musical chords by the fingers.

In the *stops* of lutes, the higher they go, the less distance is between the frets. *Bacon.*

9. The act of applying the stops in music.

Th' organ-sound a time survives the *stop*. *Daniel.*

10. A point or mark in writing, intended to distinguish the sentences, parts of a sentence or clauses, and to show the proper pauses in reading. The stops generally used, are the comma, semi-colon, colon and period. To these may be added the marks of interrogation and exclamation.

STOP'-COCK, *n.* [*stop* and *cock.*] A pipe for letting out a fluid, stopped by a turning cock. *Grew.*

STOP'-GAP, *n.* [*stop* and *gap.*] A temporary expedient. [*Not used.*]

STOP'LESS, *a.* Not to be stopped. [*Not in use.*] *Davenant.*

STOP'PAGE, *n.* The act of stopping or arresting progress or motion; or the state of being stopped; as the *stoppage* of the circulation of the blood; the *stoppage* of commerce.

STOP'PED, *pp.* Closed; obstructed; hindered from proceeding; impeded; intercepted.

STOP'PER, *n.* One who stops, closes, shuts or hinders; that which stops or obstructs; that which closes or fills a vent or hole in a vessel.

2. In *seamen's language*, a short piece of rope used for making something fast, as the anchor or cables. Stoppers are also used to prevent the running rigging from coming up, whilst the men are belaying it.

STOP'PER, *v. t.* To close with a stopper.

STOP'PERED, *pp.* Closed with a stopper; as a *stoppered* retort. *Henry.*

STOP'PING, *ppr.* Closing; shutting; obstructing; hindering from proceeding; ceasing to go or move; putting an end to; regulating the sounds of.

STOP'PLE, *n.* [Sw. *stopp.*] That which stops or closes the mouth of a vessel; as a glass *stopple;* a cork *stopple.*

STO'RAGE, *n.* [from *store.*] The act of depositing in a store or warehouse for safe keeping; or the safe keeping of goods in a warehouse.

2. The price charged or paid for keeping goods in a store.

STO'RAX, *n.* [L. *styrax.*] A plant or tree; also, a resinous and odoriferous drug brought from Turkey, but generally adulterated. It imparts to water a yellow color, and has been deemed a resolvent. *Cyc.*

Storax is a solid balsam, either in red tears, or in large cakes, brittle, but soft to the touch, and of a reddish brown color. It is obtained from the *Styrax officinalis,* a tree which grows in the Levant. *Liquid storax,* or *styrax,* is a liquid or semifluid balsam, said to be obtained from the *Liquidamber styraciflua,* a tree which grows in Virginia. It is greenish, of an aromatic taste, and agreeable smell. *Thomson.*

STORE, *n.* [W. *ystor,* that forms a bulk, a store; Sax. Dan. *stor;* Sw. id. great, ample, spacious, main; Ir. *stor, storas;* Heb. Ch. Eth. Ar. אצר atsar. Class Sr. No. 39.]

1. A large number; as a *store* of years. *Obs.* *Dryden.*

2. A large quantity; great plenty; abundance; as a *store* of wheat or provisions. *Bacon.*

3. A stock provided; a large quantity for supply; ample abundance. The troops have great *stores* of provisions and ammunition. The ships have *stores* for a long voyage. [This the present usual acceptation of the word, and in this sense the plural, *stores,* is commonly used. When applied to a single article of supply, it is still sometimes used in the singular; as a good *store* of wine or of bread.]

4. Quantity accumulated; fund; abundance; as *stores* of knowledge.

5. A storehouse; a magazine; a warehouse. Nothing can be more convenient than the *stores* on Central wharf in Boston. *Milton.*

6. In *the United States,* shops for the sale of goods of any kind, by wholesale or retail, are often called *stores.*

In store, in a state of accumulation, *in a literal sense;* hence, in a state of preparation for supply; in a state of readiness. Happiness is laid up *in store* for the righteous; misery is *in store* for the wicked.

STORE, *a.* Hoarded; laid up; as *store* treasure. [*Not in use.*]

STORE, *v. t.* To furnish; to supply; to replenish.

Wise Plato said the world with men was *stor'd.* *Denham.*

Her mind with thousand virtues *stor'd.* *Prior.*

2. To stock against a future time; as a garrison well *stored* with provisions.

One having *stored* a pond of four acres with carp, tench and other fish— *Hale.*

3. To reposit in a store or warehouse for preservation; to warehouse; as, to *store* goods. *Bacon.*

STO'RED, *pp.* Furnished; supplied.

2. Laid up in store; warehoused.

STO'RE-HOUSE, *n.* [*store* and *house.*] A building for keeping grain or goods of any kind; a magazine; a repository; a warehouse.

Joseph opened all the *store-houses* and sold to the Egyptians. Gen. xli.

2. A repository.

The Scripture of God is a *store-house* abounding with inestimable treasures of wisdom and knowledge. *Hooker.*

3. A great mass reposited. [*Not in use.*] *Spenser.*

STO'RE-KEEPER, *n.* [*store* and *keeper.*] A man who has the care of a store.

STO'RER, *n.* One who lays up or forms a store.

STO'RIAL, *a.* [from *story.*] Historical. [*Not in use.*] *Chaucer.*

STO'RIED, *a.* [from *story.*] Furnished with stories; adorned with historical paintings.

Some greedy minion or imperious wife,
The trophied arches, *storied* halls, invade. *Pope.*

2. Related in story; told or recited in history.

STO'RIER, *n.* A relater of stories; a historian. [*Not in use.*]

STO'RIFY, *v. t.* To form or tell stories. [*Not in use.*] *Ch. Relig. Appeal.*

STORK, *n.* [Sax. *storc;* Dan. Sw. *stork.*] A large fowl of the genus Ardea or Heron kind.

STORK'S-BILL, *n.* A plant of the genus Geranium.

STORM, *n.* [Sax. D. Dan. Sw. *storm;* G. *sturm;* W. *ystorm;* D. *stooren,* to disturb; W. *ystwriaw,* Eng. to *stir.* In Italian, *stormo* is a fight, combat, a band or troop; *stormire,* to make a noise; *stormeggiare,* to throng together, to ring the alarm bell. The Italian seems to be from L. *turma.* The primary sense of storm is a rushing, raging or violent agitation.]

1. A violent wind; a tempest. Thus a *storm of wind,* is correct language, as the proper sense of the word is rushing, violence. It has primarily no reference to a fall of rain or snow. But as a violent wind is often attended with rain or snow, the word *storm* has come to be used, most improperly, for a fall of rain or snow without wind.

O beat those *storms,* and roll the seas in vain. *Pope.*

2. A violent assault on a fortified place; a furious attempt of troops to enter and take a fortified place by scaling the walls, forcing the gates and the like. *Dryden.*

3. Violent civil or political commotion; sedition; insurrection; also, clamor; tumult; disturbance of the public peace.

I will stir up in England some black *storms.* *Shak.*

Her sister
Began to scold and raise up such a *storm*— *Shak.*

4. Affliction; calamity; distress; adversity.

A brave man struggling in the *storms* of fate. *Pope.*

5. Violence; vehemence; tumultuous force. *Hooker.*

STORM, *v. t.* To assault; to attack and attempt to take by scaling the walls, forcing gates or breaches and the like; as, to *storm* a fortified town.

STORM, *v. i.* To raise a tempest. *Spenser.*

2. To blow with violence; *impersonally;* as, *it storms.*

3. To rage; to be in a violent agitation of passion; to fume. The master *storms.*

STORM'-BEAT, *a.* [*storm* and *beat.*] Beaten or impaired by storms. *Spenser.*

STORM'ED, *pp.* Assaulted by violence.

STORM'INESS, *n.* Tempestuousness; the state of being agitated by violent winds.

STORM'ING, *ppr.* Attacking with violent force; raging.

STORM'Y, *a.* Tempestuous; agitated with furious winds; boisterous; as a *stormy* season; a *stormy* day or week.

2. Proceeding from violent agitation or fury; as a *stormy* sound; *stormy* shocks. *Addison.*

3. Violent; passionate. [*Unusual.*]

STO'RY, *n.* [Sax. *stær, ster;* It. *storia;* L. *historia;* Gr. ιϛορια.]

1. A verbal narration or recital of a series of facts or incidents. We observe in children a strong passion for hearing *stories.*

2. A written narrative of a series of facts or events. There is probably on record no *story* more interesting than that of Joseph in Genesis.

3. History; a written narrative or account of past transactions, whether relating to nations or individuals.

The four great monarchies make the subject of ancient *story.* *Temple.*

4. Petty tale; relation of a single incident or of trifling incidents. *Addison.*

5. A trifling tale; a fiction; a fable; as the *story* of a fairy. In popular usage, *story* is sometimes a softer term for a lie.

6. A loft; a floor; or a set of rooms on the same floor or level. A story comprehends the distance from one floor to another; as a *story* of nine or ten feet elevation. Hence each floor terminating the space is called a *story;* as a house of one *story,* of two *stories,* of five *stories.* The farm houses in New England have usually two *stories;* the houses in Paris have usually five *stories;* a few have more; those in London four. But in the United States the floor next the ground is the first *story;* in France and England, the first floor or *story,* is the second from the ground.

STO'RY, *v. t.* To tell in historical relation; to narrate.

How worthy he is, I will leave to appear hereafter, rather than *story* him in his own hearing. *Shak.*

It is *storied* of the brazen colossus in Rhodes, that it was seventy cubits high. *Wilkins.*

[*This verb is chiefly used in the passive participle.*]

2. To range one under another. [*Little used.*] *Bentley.*

STO'RY-TELLER, *n.* [*story* and *tell.*] One who tells stories; a narrator of a series of incidents; as an amusing *story-teller.*

2. A historian; *in contempt.* *Swift.*

3. One who tells fictitious stories.

STOT, *n.* [Sax. *stotte,* a poor horse.] A horse. [*Not in use.*] *Chaucer.*

2. A young bullock or steer. [*Not in use or local.*]

STOTE. [See *Stoat.*]

STOUND, *v. i.* [Ice. *stunde.*] To be in pain or sorrow. [*Not in use.*]

2. Stunned. [*Not in use.* See *Astound.*]

STOUND, *n.* Sorrow; grief. [*Not in use.*] *Spenser.*

2. A shooting pain. [*Not in use.*] *Ib.*

3. Noise. [*Not in use.*] *Ib.*

4. Astonishment; amazement. [*Not in use.*] *Gay.*

5. Hour; time; season. [Dan. *stund.*] [*Not in use.*] *Ib.*

6. A vessel to put small beer in. [*Local.*]

STOUR, *n.* [Sax. *styrian,* to stir.] A battle or tumult. *Obs.* *Spenser.*

Stour, signifies a river, as in *Sturbridge.*

STOUT, *a.* [D. *stout,* bold, stout; *stooten,* to push; Dan. *stöder,* to push; *studser,* to strut. The primary sense is to shoot forward or to swell.]

1. Strong; lusty.

A *stouter* champion never handled sword. *Shak.*

2. Bold; intrepid; valiant; brave.

He lost the character of a bold, *stout,* magnanimous man. *Clarendon.*

3. Large; bulky. [*A popular use of the word.*]

4. Proud; resolute; obstinate.

The lords all stand to clear their cause,
Most resolutely *stout.* *Daniel.*

5. Strong; firm; as a *stout* vessel. *Dryden.*

STOUT, *n.* A cant name for strong beer. *Swift.*

STOUT'LY, *adv.* Lustily; boldly; obstinately. He *stoutly* defended himself.

STOUT'NESS, *n.* Strength; bulk.

2. Boldness; fortitude. *Ascham.*

3. Obstinacy; stubbornness. *Shak.*

STOVE, *n.* [Sax. *stofa;* Sw. *stufva;* D. *stoof;* It. *stufa;* Sp. *estufa,* a warm close room, a bath, a room where pitch and tar are heated; *estofar,* to stew meat, and to quilt; Fr. *etuve;* G. *badstube,* a bagnio or hot house; *stube,* a room; *stuben-ofen,* a stove; Dan. *stover,* to stew; *stue,* a room; *stue-ovn,* a stove. This primarily is merely a room, a place. See *Stow.*]

1. A hot house; a house or room artificially warmed. *Bacon.* *Woodward.*

2. A small box with an iron pan, used for holding coals to warm the feet. It is a bad practice for young persons to accustom themselves to sit with a warm *stove* under the feet.

3. An iron box, cylinder or fire-place, in which fire is made to warm an apartment. Stoves for this purpose are of various forms.

4. An iron box, with various apartments in it for cooking; a culinary utensil of various forms.

STOVE, *v. t.* To keep warm in a house or room by artificial heat; as, to *stove* orange trees and myrtles. *Bacon.*

STOVE, *pret.* of *stave.*

STŎV'ER, *n.* [a contraction of *estover.*] Fodder for cattle; primarily, fodder from threshed grain; but in New England, any kind of fodder from the barn or stack.

STOW, *v. t.* [Sax. *stow,* a place, a fixed place or mansion; G. *stauen,* D. *stuwen,* Dan. *stuver,* to stow, to place; Sp. Port. *estivar,* id., coinciding with L. *stipo,* to crowd, to *stuff;* Sp. *estiva,* a rammer; L. *stiva,* the handle of a plow. The sense is to set or throw down, from the more general sense of throwing, driving.]

1. To place; to put in a suitable place or position; as, to *stow* bags, bales or casks in a ship's hold; to *stow* hay in a mow; to *stow* sheaves. The word has reference to the placing of many things, or of one thing among many, or of a mass of things.

2. To lay up; to reposit.

Stow in names, signifies place, as in *Barstow.*

STŌWAĠE, *n.* The act or operation of placing in a suitable position; or the suitable disposition of several things together. The *stowage* of a ship's cargo to advantage requires no little skill. It is of great consequence to make good *stowage.* [*This is the principal use of the word.*]

2. Room for the reception of things to be reposited.

In every vessel there is *stowage* for immense treasures. *Addison.*

3. The state of being laid up. I am curious to have the plate and jewels in safe *stowage.*

4. Money paid for stowing goods. [*Little used.*]

STŌWED, *pp.* Placed in due position or order; reposited.

STŌWING, *ppr.* Placing in due position; disposing in good order.

STRA'BISM, *n.* [L. *strabismus,* from *straba, strabo,* a squint-eyed person.] A squinting; the act or habit of looking asquint.

STRAD'DLE, *v. i.* [from the root of *stride;* Sax. *stredan,* to scatter.] To part the legs wide; to stand or walk with the legs far apart.

STRAD'DLE, *v. t.* To place one leg on one side and the other on the other of any thing; as, to *straddle* a fence or a horse.

STRAD'DLING, *ppr.* Standing or walking with the legs far apart; placing one leg on one side and the other on the other.

STRAGGLE, *v. i. strag'l.* [This word seems to be formed on the root of *stray.* In Sax. *stræçan* is to strew, to spread; D. *strekken,* to stretch; G. *streichen,* to pass, to migrate; W. *treiglaw,* to turn, revolve, wander.]

1. To wander from the direct course or way; to rove. When troops are on the march, let not the men *straggle.*

2. To wander at large without any certain direction or object; to ramble.

The wolf spied a *straggling* kid. *L'Estrange.*

3. To exuberate; to shoot too far in growth. Prune the *straggling* branches of the hedge. *Mortimer.*

4. To be dispersed; to be apart from any main body.

They came between Scylla and Charybdis and the *straggling* rocks. *Raleigh.*

STRAG'GLER, *n.* A wanderer; a rover; one that departs from the direct or proper course; one that rambles without any settled direction. *Swift.*

2. A vagabond; a wandering shiftless fellow.

3. Something that shoots beyond the rest or too far.

4. Something that stands by itself.

STRAG'GLING, *ppr.* Wandering; roving; rambling; being in a separate position.

STR'AHLSTEIN, *n.* [G. *strahl,* a beam or gleam, and *stein,* stone.] Another name of actinolite. *Ure.*

STRAIGHT, *a. strait.* [L. *strictus,* from *stringo;* Sax. *strac;* formed from the root of *reach, stretch, right,* L. *rectus,* G.

recht, Fr. *etroit*, It. *stretto*, in which the palatal letter is lost; but the Spanish retains it in *estrecho, estrechar*. It is lost in the Port. *estreito*. It is customary to write *straight*, for direct or right, and *strait*, for narrow, but this is a practice wholly arbitrary, both being the same word. *Strait* we use in the sense in which it is used in the south of Europe. Both senses proceed from *stretching, straining*.]

1. Right, in a mathematical sense; direct; passing from one point to another by the nearest course; not deviating or crooked; as a *straight* line; a *straight* course; a *straight* piece of timber.
2. Narrow; close; tight; as a *straight* garment. [See *Strait*, as it is generally written.]
3. Upright; according with justice and rectitude; not deviating from truth or fairness.

STRAIGHT, *adv.* Immediately; directly; in the shortest time.

> I know thy generous temper well;
> Fling but th' appearance of dishonor on it,
> It *straight* takes fire, and mounts into a blaze. *Addison.*

STRA'IGHTEN, *v. t. stra'itn.* To make straight; to reduce from a crooked to a straight form. *Hooker.*
2. To make narrow, tense or close; to tighten.
3. To reduce to difficulties or distress.

STRA'IGHTENED, *pp.* Made straight; made narrow.

STRA'IGHTENER, *n.* He or that which straightens.

STRA'IGHTENING, *ppr.* Making straight or narrow.

STRA'IGHTLY, *adv.* In a right line; not crookedly.
2. Tightly; closely.

STRA'IGHTNESS, *n.* The quality or state of being straight; rectitude. *Bacon.*
2. Narrowness; tension; tightness.

STRA'IGHTWAY, *adv.* [*straight* and *way.*] Immediately; without loss of time; without delay.

> He took the damsel by the hand, and said to her, Talitha cumi— And *straightway* the damsel arose. Mark v.

[*Straightways* is obsolete.]

STRAIKS, *n.* Strong plates of iron on the circumference of a cannon wheel over the joints of the fellies.

STRAIN, *v. t.* [Fr. *etreindre*; It. *strignere*; Sp. *estreñir*; L. *stringo*. This word retains its original signification, to stretch. *Strain* is the L. *stringo*, as *straight* is *strictus*, in different dialects.]

1. To stretch; to draw with force; to extend with great effort; as, to *strain* a rope; to *strain* the shrouds of a ship; to *strain* the chords of an instrument.
2. To cause to draw with force, or with excess of exertion; to injure by pressing with too much effort. He *strained* his horses or his oxen by overloading them.
3. To stretch violently or by violent exertion; as, to *strain* the arm or the muscles.
4. To put to the utmost strength. Men in desperate cases will *strain* themselves for relief.
5. To press or cause to pass through some porous substance; to purify or separate from extraneous matter by filtration; to filter; as, to *strain* milk. Water may be *strained* through sand. *Bacon. Arbuthnot.*
6. To sprain; to injure by drawing or stretching.

> Prudes decay'd about-may tack,
> *Strain* their necks with looking back. *Swift.*

7. To make tighter; to cause to bind closer.

> To *strain* his fetters with a stricter care. *Dryden.*

8. To force; to constrain; to make uneasy or unnatural.

> His mirth is forced and *strained*. *Denham.*

STRAIN, *v. i.* To make violent efforts.

> To build his fortune I will *strain* a little. *Shak.*
>
> *Straining* with too weak a wing. *Pope.*

2. To be filtered. Water *straining* through sand becomes pure.

STRAIN, *n.* A violent effort; a stretching or exertion of the limbs or muscles, or of any thing else.
2. An injury by excessive exertion, drawing or stretching. *Grew.*
3. Style; continued manner of speaking or writing; as the genius and *strain* of the book of Proverbs. *Tillotson.*

> So we say, poetic *strains*, lofty *strains*.

4. Song; note; sound; or a particular part of a tune.

> Then heavenly harps a lower *strain* began. *Dryden.*

5. Turn; tendency; inborn disposition.

> Because heretics have a *strain* of madness, he applied her with some corporal chastisements. *Hayward.*

6. Manner of speech or action.

> Such take too high a *strain* at first. *Bacon.*

7. Race; generation; descent.

> He is of a noble *strain*. [*Not in use.*] *Shak.*

8. Hereditary disposition.

> Intemperance and lust breed diseases, which propagated, spoil the *strain* of a nation. [*Not in use.*] *Tillotson.*

9. Rank; character. [*Not in use.*] *Dryden.*

STRA'INABLE, *a.* Capable of being strained. [*Not in use.*] *Bacon.*

STRA'INED, *pp.* Stretched; violently exerted; filtered.

STRA'INER, *n.* That through which any liquid passes for purification; an instrument for filtration.

> The lacteals of animal bodies are the *strainers* to separate the pure emulsion from its feces. *Arbuthnot.*

[*This doctrine is now questioned.*]

STRA'INING, *ppr.* Stretching; exerting with violence; making great efforts; filtering.

STRA'INING, *n.* The act of stretching; the act of filtering; filtration.

STRAINT, *n.* A violent stretching or tension. [*Not in use.*] *Spenser.*

STRAIT, *a.* [See *Straight.*] Narrow; close; not broad.

> *Strait* is the gate, and narrow is the way that leadeth to life, and few there be that find it. Matt. vii.

2. Close; intimate; as a *strait* degree of favor. *Sidney.*
3. Strict; rigorous.

> He now, forsooth, takes on him to reform
> Some certain edicts, and some *strait* decrees. *Shak.*

4. Difficult; distressful.
5. Straight; not crooked.

STRAIT, *n.* [See *Straight.*] A narrow pass or passage, either in a mountain or in the ocean, between continents or other portions of land; as the *straits* of Gibraltar; the *straits* of Magellan; the *straits* of Dover. [*In this sense, the plural is more generally used than the singular, and often without any apparent reason or propriety.*]
2. Distress; difficulty; distressing necessity; formerly written *streight.* [*Used either in the singular or plural.*]

> Let no man who owns a providence, become desperate under any calamity or *strait* whatsoever. *South.*
>
> Ulysses made use of the pretense of natural infirmity to conceal the *straits* he was in at that time in his thoughts. *Broome.*

STRAIT, *v. t.* To put to difficulties. [*Not in use.*] *Shak.*

STRA'ITEN, *v. t. stra'itn.* To make narrow.

> In narrow circuit, *straiten'd* by a foe. *Milton.*

2. To contract; to confine; as, to *straiten* the British commerce. *Addison.*
3. To make tense or tight; as, to *straiten* a cord. *Dunciad.*
4. To distress; to perplex; to press with poverty or other necessity; as, a man *straitened* in his circumstances.
5. To press by want of sufficient room.

> Waters when *straitened*, as at the falls of bridges, give a roaring noise. *Bacon.*

STRA'IT-HANDED, *a.* [*strait* and *hand.*] Parsimonious; sparing; niggardly. [*Not much used.*]

STRAIT-HAND'EDNESS, *n.* Niggardliness; parsimony. *Hall.*

STRA'IT-LACED, *a.* [*strait* and *lace.*]
1. Griped with stays.

> We have few well-shaped that are *strait-laced.* *Locke.*

2. Stiff; constrained. Hence,
3. Rigid in opinion; strict.

STRA'ITLY, *adv.* Narrowly; closely.
2. Strictly; rigorously. [For this, *strictly* is now used.]
3. Closely; intimately.

STRA'ITNESS, *n.* Narrowness; as the *straitness* of a place; *straitness* of mind; *straitness* of circumstances. *Bacon.*
2. Strictness; rigor; as the *straitness* of a man's proceedings. *Shak.*
3. Distress; difficulty; pressure from necessity of any kind, particularly from poverty.
4. Want; scarcity; or rather narrowness; as the *straitness* of the conveniences of life. *Locke.*

STRA'IT-WAISTCOAT, } *n.* An apparatus to confine the limbs of a distracted person.
STRA'IT-JACKET, }

STRAKE, *pret.* of *strike. Obs.* [See *Strike.*]

STRAKE, *n.* [Sp. *traca.*] A streak. [Not used unless in reference to the range of planks in a ship's side. See *Streak.*]
2. A narrow board. [*Not used.*]
3. The iron band of a wheel. [In the United States, this is called a *band*, or the *tire* of a wheel.]

STRAM, *v. i.* [Dan. *strammer*, to stretch, to spread.] To spread out the limbs; to sprawl. [*Local and vulgar.*]

STRAM'ASH, *v. t.* [It. *stramazzare.*] To strike, beat or bang; to break; to destroy. [*Local and vulgar.*] *Grose.*

STRAMIN'EOUS, *a.* [L. *stramineus*, from *stramen*, straw.]

1. Strawy; consisting of straw. *Robinson.*
2. Chaffy; like straw; light. *Burton.*

STRAND, *n.* [Sax. G. D. Dan. Sw. *strand.*]
1. The shore or beach of the sea or ocean, or of a large lake, and perhaps of a navigable river. It is never used of the bank of a small river or pond. The Dutch on the Hudson apply it to a landing place; as the *strand* at Kingston.
2. One of the twists or parts of which a rope is composed. [Russ. *struna*, a cord or string.] *Mar. Dict.*

STRAND, *v. t.* To drive or run aground on the sea shore, as a ship.
2. To break one of the strands of a rope. *Mar. Dict.*

STRAND, *v. i.* To drift or be driven on shore; to run aground; as, a ship *strands* at high water.

STRAND'ED, *pp.* Run ashore.
2. Having a strand broken.

STRAND'ING, *ppr.* Running ashore; breaking a strand.

STRANĠE, *a.* [Fr. *etrange*; It. *strano*, strange, foreign, pale, wan, rude, unpolite; *stranare*, to alienate, to remove, to abuse; *straniare*, to separate; Sp. *extraño*, foreign, extraneous, rare, wild; L. *extraneus*; W. *estronaiz*, strange; *estrawn*, a stranger. The primary sense of the root *tran*, is to depart, to proceed; W. *trawn*, over; *traw*, an advance or distance.]
1. Foreign; belonging to another country.

I do not contemn the knowledge of *strange* and divers tongues. [*This sense is nearly obsolete.*] *Ascham.*

2. Not domestic; belonging to others.

So she impatient her own faults to see,
Turns from herself, and in *strange* things delights. [*Nearly obsolete.*] *Davies.*

3. New; not before known, heard or seen. The former custom was familiar; the latter was new and *strange* to them. Hence,
4. Wonderful; causing surprise; exciting curiosity. It is *strange* that men will not receive improvement, when it is shown to be improvement.

Sated at length, ere long I might perceive
Strange alteration in me. *Milton.*

5. Odd; unusual; irregular; not according to the common way.

He's *strange* and peevish. *Shak.*

6. Remote. [*Little used.*] *Shak.*
7. Uncommon; unusual.

This made David to admire the law of God at that *strange* rate. *Tillotson.*

8. Unacquainted.

They were now at a gage, looking *strange* at one another. *Bacon.*

9. *Strange* is sometimes uttered by way of exclamation.

Strange! what extremes should thus preserve the snow,
High on the Alps, or in deep caves below. *Waller.*

This is an elliptical expression for *it is strange.*

STRANĠE, *v. t.* To alienate; to estrange. [*Not in use.*]

STRANĠE, *v. i.* To wonder; to be astonished. [*Not in use.*] *Glanville.*
2. To be estranged or alienated. [*Not in use.*]

STRANĠELY, *adv.* With some relation to foreigners. *Obs.* *Shak.*
2. Wonderfully; in a manner or degree to excite surprise or wonder.

How *strangely* active are the arts of peace. *Dryden.*

It would *strangely* delight you to see with what spirit he converses. *Law.*

STRANĠENESS, *n.* Foreignness; the state of belonging to another country.

If I will obey the gospel, no distance of place, no *strangeness* of country can make any man a stranger to me. *Sprat.*

2. Distance in behavior; reserve; coldness; forbidding manner.

Will you not observe
The *strangeness* of his alter'd countenance? *Shak.*

3. Remoteness from common manners or notions; uncouthness.

Men worthier than himself
Here tend the savage *strangeness* he puts on. *Shak.*

4. Alienation of mind; estrangement; mutual dislike.

This might seem a means to continue a *strangeness* between the two nations. *Bacon.*
[*This sense is obsolete or little used.*]

5. Wonderfulness; the power of exciting surprise and wonder; uncommonness that raises wonder by novelty.

This raised greater tumults in the hearts of men than the *strangeness* and seeming unreasonableness of all the former articles. *South.*

STRANĠER, *n.* [Fr. *etranger.*] A foreigner; one who belongs to another country. Paris and London are visited by *strangers* from all the countries of Europe.
2. One of another town, city, state or province in the same country. The Commencements in American colleges are frequented by multitudes of *strangers* from the neighboring towns and states.
3. One unknown. The gentleman is a *stranger* to me.
4. One unacquainted.

My child is yet a *stranger* to the world. *Shak.*

I was no *stranger* to the original. *Dryden.*

5. A guest; a visitor. *Milton.*
6. One not admitted to any communication or fellowship.

Melons on beds of ice are taught to bear,
And *strangers* to the sun yet ripen here. *Granville.*

7. In *law*, one not privy or party to an act.

STRANĠER, *v. t.* To estrange; to alienate. [*Not in use.*] *Shak.*

STRAN'GLE, *v. t.* [Fr. *etrangler*; It. *strangolare*; L. *strangulo.*]
1. To choke; to suffocate; to destroy life by stopping respiration.

Our Saxon ancestors compelled the adulteress to *strangle* herself. *Ayliffe.*

2. To suppress; to hinder from birth or appearance. *Shak.*

STRAN'GLED, *pp.* Choked; suffocated; suppressed.

STRAN'GLER, *n.* One who strangles.

STRAN'GLES, *n.* Swellings in a horse's throat.

STRAN'GLING, *ppr.* Choking; suffocating; suppressing.

STRAN'GLING, *n.* The act of destroying life by stopping respiration.

STRAN'GULATED, *a.* Compressed. A hernia or rupture is said to be *strangulated*, when it is so compressed as to cause dangerous symptoms. *Cyc.*

STRANGULA'TION, *n.* [Fr. from L. *strangulatio.*]
1. The act of strangling; the act of destroying life by stopping respiration; suffocation. *Wiseman.*
2. That kind of suffocation which is common to women in hysterics; also, the straitening or compression of the intestines in hernia. *Cyc.*

STRAN'GURY, *n.* [L. *stranguria*; Gr. ϛραγγουρια; ϛραγξ, a drop, and ουρον, urine.] Literally, a discharge of urine by drops; a difficulty of discharging urine, attended with pain.

STRAP, *n.* [D. *strop*, a rope or halter; Dan. Sw. *strop*; Sax. *stropp*; L. *strupus*. *Strap* and *strop* appear to be from *stripping*, and perhaps *stripe* also; all having resemblance to a *strip* of bark peeled from a tree.]
1. A long narrow slip of cloth or lether, of various forms and for various uses; as the *strap* of a shoe or boot; *straps* for fastening trunks or other baggage, for stretching limbs in surgery, &c.
2. In *botany*, the flat part of the corollet in ligulate florets; also, an appendage to the leaf in some grasses. *Martyn.*

STRAP, *v. t.* To beat or chastise with a strap.
2. To fasten or bind with a strap.
3. To rub on a strap for sharpening, as a razor.

STRAPPA'DO, *n.* [It. *strappata*, a pull, strappado; *strappare*, to pull.] A military punishment formerly practiced. It consisted in drawing an offender to the top of a beam and letting him fall, by which means a limb was sometimes dislocated. *Shak.*

STRAPPA'DO, *v. t.* To torture. *Milton.*

STRAP'PING, *ppr.* Drawing on a strap, as a razor.
2. Binding with a strap.
3. *a.* Tall; lusty; as a *strapping* fellow.

STRAP'-SHAPED, *a.* In *botany*, ligulate.

STRA'TA, *n. plu.* [See *Stratum.*] Beds; layers; as *strata* of sand, clay or coal.

STRAT'AĠEM, *n.* [L. *stratagema*; Fr. *stratageme*; It. *stratagemma*; Gr. ϛρατηγημα, from ϛρατηγεω, to lead an army.]
1. An artifice, particularly in war; a plan or scheme for deceiving an enemy. *Shak.*
2. Any artifice; a trick by which some advantage is intended to be obtained.

Those oft are *stratagems* which errors seem. *Pope.*

STRA'TEĠE, } *n.* [Gr. ϛρατηγος.] An Athe-
STRAT'EGUS, } nian general officer. *Mitford.*

STRATH, *n.* [W. *ystrad.*] A vale, bottom or low ground between hills. [*Not in use.*]

STRATIFICA'TION, *n.* [from *stratify.*] The process by which substances in the earth have been formed into strata or layers.
2. The state of being formed into layers in the earth.
3. The act of laying in strata.

STRA'TIFIED, *pp.* Formed into a layer, as a terrene substance.

STRA'TIFȲ, *v. t.* [Fr. *stratifier*, from L. *stratum.*]
1. To form into a layer, as substances in the earth. Thus clay, sand and other species of earth are often found *stratified*.
2. To lay in strata.

STRA'TIFȲING, *ppr.* Arranging in a layer, as terrene substances.

STRATOC'RACY, *n.* [Gr. ςρατος, an army, and κρατεω, to hold.]
A military government; government by military chiefs and an army. *Guthrie.*

STRATOG'RAPHY, *n.* [Gr. ςρατος, an army, and γραφω, to describe.]
Description of armies, or what belongs to an army. [*Not in use.*]

STRA'TUM, *n.* plu. *stratums* or *strata.* The latter is most common. [L. from *sterno*, to spread or lay; Sax. *streone.*]
1. In *geology* and *mineralogy*, a layer; any species of earth, sand, coal and the like, arranged in a flat form, distinct from the adjacent matter. The thicker strata are called *beds;* and these beds are sometimes stratified.
2. A bed or layer artificially made.

STRAUGHT, *pp.* for *stretched. Obs.* *Chaucer.*

STRAW, *n.* [Sax. *streow*, straw, and a stratum or bed; G. *stroh;* D. *stroo;* Dan. *straae;* Sw. *strå;* L. *stramentum*, from *sterno, stravi, stratum.* See *Strew.*]
1. The stalk or stem of certain species of grain, pulse, &c. chiefly of wheat, rye, oats, barley, buckwheat and peas. When used of single stalks, it admits of a plural, *straws. Straws* may show which way the wind blows. We say of grain while growing, the *straw* is large, or it is rusty.
2. A mass of the stalks of certain species of grain when cut, and after being thrashed; as a bundle or a load of *straw.* In this sense, the word admits not the plural number.
3. Any thing proverbially worthless. I care not a *straw* for the play. I will not abate a *straw.* *Hudibras.*

STRAW, *v. t.* To spread or scatter. [See *Strew* and *Strow.*]

STRAW'BERRY, *n.* [*straw* and *berry;* Sax. *straw-berie.*]
A plant and its fruit, of the genus Fragaria. Strawberries are of various kinds, all delicious fruit.

STRAW'BERRY-TREE, *n.* An evergreen tree of the genus Arbutus; the fruit is of a fleshy substance, like a strawberry. *Lee. Miller.*

STRAW'-BUILT, *a.* [*straw* and *built.*]
Constructed of straw; as the suburbs of a *straw-built* citadel. *Milton.*

STRAW'-COLOR, *n.* The color of dry straw; a beautiful yellowish color.

STRAW'-COLORED, *a.* Of a light yellow, the color of dry straw.

STRAW'-CUTTER, *n.* An instrument to cut straw for fodder.

STRAW'-DRAIN, *n.* A drain filled with straw.

STRAW'-STUFFED, *a.* Stuffed with straw. *Hall.*

STRAW'-WORM, *n.* [*straw* and *worm.*] A worm bred in straw.

STRAW'Y, *a.* Made of straw; consisting of straw. *Boyle.*
2. Like straw; light.

STRAY, *v. i.* [The elements of this word are not certainly known. If they are *Strg*, the word coincides with Sax. *stregan, stregan*, to scatter, to spread, the L. *stravi*, Eng. to *strow, strew* or *straw*, also with G. *streichen*, to wander, to strike; both probably from the root of *reach, stretch.* Possibly *stray* is from the It. *straviare*, from L. *extra* and *via.* I am inclined however to refer it to a Teutonic origin. See *Straggle.*]
1. To wander, as from a direct course; to deviate or go out of the way. We say, to *stray* from the path or road into the forest or wood.
2. To wander from company, or from the proper limits; as, a sheep *strays* from the flock; a horse *strays* from an inclosure.
3. To rove; to wander from the path of duty or rectitude; to err; to deviate.

> We have erred and *strayed*— *Com. Prayer.*

4. To wander; to rove at large; to play free and unconfined.

> Lo, the glad gales o'er all her beauties *stray*,
> Breathe on her lips and in her bosom play. *Pope.*

5. To wander; to run a serpentine course.

> Where Thames among the wanton valley *strays.* *Denham.*

STRAY, *v. t.* To mislead. [*Not in use.*] *Shak.*

STRAY, *n.* Any domestic animal that has left an inclosure or its proper place and company, and wanders at large or is lost. The laws provide that *strays* shall be taken up, impounded and advertised.

> Seeing him wander about, I took him up for a *stray.* *Dryden.*

2. The act of wandering. [*Little used.*] *Shak.*

STRA'YER, *n.* A wanderer. [*Little used.*]

STRA'YING, *ppr.* Wandering; roving; departing from the direct course, from the proper inclosure, or from the path of duty.

STREAK, *n.* [Sax. *strica*, a line, direction, course; *strican*, to go; *stric*, a stroke, a plague, and *strec*, a stretch; G. *streich*, a stroke or stripe, and *strich*, id.; D. *streek*, a course; Dan. *streg*, a stroke or line; *strikke*, a cord; *strög*, a stroke, a tract, a row; Sw. *stråk;* Ir. *strioc.* These have all the same elements, and the L. *stria* is probably a contraction of the same word; Sp. *traca*, without a prefix.]
1. A line or long mark, of a different color from the ground; a stripe.

> What mean those color'd *streaks* in heaven? *Milton.*

2. In *a ship*, a uniform range of planks on the side or bottom; sometimes pronounced *strake.* *Mar. Dict.*

STREAK, *v. t.* To form streaks or stripes in; to stripe; to variegate with lines of a different color or of different colors.

> A mule admirably *streaked* and dappled with white and black— *Sandys.*

> Now *streak'd* and glowing with the morning red. *Prior.*

2. To stretch. [*Not elegant.*] *Chapman.*

STREAK, *v. i.* To run swiftly. [*Vulgar in New England.*]

STRE'AKED, *pp.* Marked or variegated with stripes of a different color.

STRE'AKING, *ppr.* Making streaks in.

STRE'AKY, *a.* Having stripes; striped; variegated with lines of a different color.

STREAM, *n.* [Sax. *stream;* G. *strom;* D. *stroom;* Dan. *ström;* Sw. *ström;* W. *ystrym;* Ir. *sreamh* or *sreav.* If *m* is radical, this word belongs to Class Rm.]
1. A current of water or other fluid; a liquid substance flowing in a line or course, either on the earth, as a river or brook, or from a vessel or other reservoir or fountain. Hence,
2. A river, brook or rivulet.
3. A current of water in the ocean; as the gulf *stream.*
4. A current of melted metal or other substance; as a *stream* of lead or iron flowing from a furnace; a *stream* of lava from a volcano.
5. Any thing issuing from a source and moving with a continued succession of parts; as a *stream* of words; a *stream* of sand.

> A *stream* of beneficence. *Atterbury.*

6. A continued current or course; as a *stream* of weather. [*Not used.*] *Raleigh.*

> The *stream* of his life. *Shak.*

7. A current of air or gas, or of light.
8. Current; drift; as of opinions or manners. It is difficult to oppose the *stream* of public opinion.
9. Water.

STREAM, *v. i.* To flow; to move or run in a continuous current. Blood *streams* from a vein.

> Beneath the banks where rivers *stream.* *Milton.*

2. To emit; to pour out in abundance. His eyes *streamed* with tears.
3. To issue with continuance, not by fits.

> From op'ning skies my *streaming* glories shine. *Pope.*

4. To issue or shoot in streaks; as light *streaming* from the east.
5. To extend; to stretch in a long line; as a flag *streaming* in the wind.

STREAM, *v. t.* To mark with colors or embroidery in long tracts.

> The herald's mantle is *streamed* with gold. *Bacon.*

STRE'AMER, *n.* An ensign or flag; a pennon extended or flowing in the wind; *a poetic use of the word.*

> Brave Rupert from afar appears,
> Whose waving *streamers* the glad general knows. *Dryden.*

STRE'AMING, *ppr.* Flowing; running in a current.
2. Emitting; pouring out in abundance; as *streaming* eyes.
3. Flowing; floating loosely; as a flag.

STRE'AMLET, *n.* A small stream; a rivulet; a rill. *Thomson.*

STRE'AM-TIN, *n.* Particles or masses of tin found beneath the surface of alluvial ground. *Encyc.*

STRE'AMY, *a.* Abounding with running water.

> Arcadia,
> However *streamy* now, adust and dry,
> Denied the goddess water. *Prior.*

2. Flowing with a current or streak.

> His nodding helm emits a *streamy* ray. *Pope.*

STREEK, *v. t.* [Sax. *streccan*, to stretch.]
To lay out, as a dead body. [*Not in use.*] *Brand.*

STREET, *n.* [Sax. *stræte, strete;* G. *strasse;* D. *straat;* Sw. *stråt;* Dan. *stræde;* Ir. *sraid;* W. *ystryd;* It. *strada;* Sp. *estrada;* L. *stratum*, from *stratus*, strewed or spread. See *Strew.*]
1. Properly, a paved way or road; but in usage, any way or road in a city, chiefly a main way, in distinction from a lane or alley.
2. Among the people of New England, any public highway.

3. *Streets*, plural, any public way, road or place.

That there be no complaining in our *streets*. Ps. cxliv.

STREE'T-WALKER, *n.* [*street* and *walk.*] A common prostitute that offers herself to sale in the streets.

STREE'T-WARD, *n.* [*street* and *ward.*] Formerly, an officer who had the care of the streets. *Cowel.*

STREIGHT, *n.* A narrow. *Obs.* [See *Strait.*]

STREIGHT, *adv.* Strictly. *Obs.* [See *Strait.*]

STRENE, *n.* Race; offspring. *Obs.* *Chaucer.*

STRENGTH, *n.* [Sax. *strength*, from *streng*, strong. See *Strong.*]

1. That property or quality of an animal body by which it is enabled to move itself or other bodies. We say, a sick man has not *strength* to walk, or to raise his head or his arm. We say, a man has *strength* to lift a weight, or to draw it. This quality is called also *power* and *force.* But *force* is also used to denote the effect of strength exerted, or the quantity of motion. *Strength* in this sense, is positive, or the power of producing positive motion or action, and is opposed to *weakness.*

2. Firmness; solidity or toughness; the quality of bodies by which they sustain the application of force without breaking or yielding. Thus we speak of the *strength* of a bone, the *strength* of a beam, the *strength* of a wall, the *strength* of a rope. In this sense, *strength* is a passive quality, and is opposed to *weakness* or *frangibility.*

3. Power or vigor of any kind.

This act
Shall crush the *strength* of Satan. *Milton.*
Strength there must be either of love or war. *Holyday.*

4. Power of resisting attacks; fastness; as the *strength* of a castle or fort.

5. Support; that which supports; that which supplies strength; security.

God is our refuge and *strength.* Ps. xlvi.

6. Power of mind; intellectual force; the power of any faculty; as *strength* of memory; *strength* of reason; *strength* of judgment.

7. Spirit; animation.

Methinks I feel new *strength* within me rise. *Milton.*

8. Force of writing; vigour; nervous diction. The strength of words, of style, of expression and the like, consists in the full and forcible exhibition of ideas, by which a sensible or deep impression is made on the mind of a hearer or reader. It is distinguished from *softness* or *sweetness.* *Strength* of language enforces an argument, produces conviction, or excites wonder or other strong emotion; *softness* and *sweetness* give pleasure.

And praise the easy vigor of a line,
Where Denham's *strength* and Waller's sweetness join. *Pope.*

9. Vividness; as *strength* of colors or coloring.

10. Spirit; the quality of any liquor which has the power of affecting the taste, or of producing sensible effects on other bodies; as the *strength* of wine or spirit; the *strength* of an acid.

11. The virtue or spirit of any vegetable, or of its juices or qualities.

12. Legal or moral force; validity; the quality of binding, uniting or securing; as the *strength* of social or legal obligations; the *strength* of law; the *strength* of public opinion or custom.

13. Vigor; natural force; as the *strength* of natural affection.

14. That which supports; confidence.

The allies, after a successful summer, are too apt upon the *strength* of it to neglect preparation for the ensuing campaign. *Addison.*

15. Amount of force, military or naval; an army or navy; number of troops or ships well appointed. What is the *strength* of the enemy by land, or by sea?

16. Soundness; force; the quality that convinces, persuades or commands assent; as the *strength* of an argument or of reasoning; the *strength* of evidence.

17. Vehemence; force proceeding from motion and proportioned to it; as the *strength* of wind or a current of water.

18. Degree of brightness or vividness; as the *strength* of light.

19. Fortification; fortress; as an inaccessible *strength.* [*Not in use.*] *Milton.*

20. Support; maintenance of power.

What they boded would be a mischief to us, you are providing shall be one of our principal *strengths.* [*Not used.*] *Sprat.*

STRENGTH, *v. t.* To strengthen. [*Not in use.*]

STRENGTHEN, *v. t.* *strength'n.* To make strong or stronger; to add strength to, either physical, legal or moral; as, to *strengthen* a limb; to *strengthen* an obligation.

2. To confirm; to establish; as, to *strengthen* authority.

3. To animate; to encourage; to fix in resolution.

Charge Joshua, and encourage him, and *strengthen* him. Deut. iii.

4. To cause to increase in power or security.

Let noble Warwick, Cobham and the rest,
With powerful policy *strengthen* themselves. *Shak.*

STRENGTH'EN, *v. i.* To grow strong or stronger.

The disease that shall destroy at length,
Grows with his growth, and *strengthens* with his strength. *Pope.*

STRENGTH'ENED, *pp.* Made strong or stronger; confirmed.

STRENGTH'ENER, *n.* That which increases strength, physical or moral.

2. In *medicine*, something which, taken into the system, increases the action and energy of the vital powers.

STRENGTH'ENING, *ppr.* Increasing strength, physical or moral; confirming; animating.

STRENGTH'LESS, *a.* Wanting strength; destitute of power.

2. Wanting spirit. [*Little used.*] *Boyle.*

STREN'UOUS, *a.* [L. *strenuus;* It. *strenuo;* W. *tren*, force, also impetuous. The sense is pressing, straining or rushing forward.]

1. Eagerly pressing or urgent; zealous; ardent; as a *strenuous* advocate for national rights; a *strenuous* opposer of African slavery.

2. Bold and active; valiant, intrepid and ardent; as a *strenuous* defender of his country.

STREN'UOUSLY, *adv.* With eager and pressing zeal; ardently.

2. Boldly; vigorously; actively.

STREN'UOUSNESS, *n.* Eagerness; earnestness; active zeal; ardor in pursuit of an object, or in opposition to a measure.

STREP'ENT, *a.* [L. *strepens, strepo.*] Noisy; loud. [*Little used.*] *Shenstone.*

STREP'EROUS, *a.* [L. *strepo.*] Loud; boisterous. [*Little used.*]

STRESS, *n.* [W. *trais*, force, violence, oppression; *treissaw*, to force or drive; Ir. *treise*, force; Arm. *treçzen*, a twist; *trozeza, trouezal*, to *truss*, Fr. *trousser.* Hence *distress, trestle*, &c.]

1. Force; urgency; pressure; importance; that which bears with most weight; as the *stress* of a legal question. Consider how much *stress* is laid on the exercise of charity in the New Testament.

This, on which the great *stress* of the business depends— *Locke.*

2. Force or violence; as *stress* of weather.

3. Force; violence; strain.

Though the faculties of the mind are improved by exercise, yet they must not be put to a *stress* beyond their strength. *Locke.*

STRESS, *v. t.* To press; to urge; to distress; to put to difficulties. [*Little used.*] *Spenser.*

STRETCH, *v. t.* [Sax. *streccan;* D. *strekken;* G. *strecken;* Dan. *strekker;* Sw. *sträcka;* probably formed on the root of *reach, right*, L. *rego*, &c.]

1. To draw out to greater length; to extend in a line; as, to *stretch* a cord or a rope.

2. To extend in breadth; as, to *stretch* cloth.

3. To spread; to expand; as, to *stretch* the wings.

4. To reach; to extend.

Stretch thine hand to the poor. *Ecclus.*

5. To spread; to display; as, to *stretch* forth the heavens. *Tillotson.*

6. To draw or pull out in length; to strain; as, to *stretch* a tendon or muscle.

7. To make tense; to strain.

So the *stretch'd* cord the shackled dancer tries. *Smith.*

8. To extend mentally; as, to *stretch* the mind or thoughts.

9. To exaggerate; to extend too far; as, to *stretch* the truth; to *stretch* one's credit.

STRETCH, *v. i.* To be extended; to be drawn out in length or in breadth, or both. A wet hempen cord or cloth contracts; in drying, it *stretches.*

2. To be extended; to spread; as, a lake *stretches* over a hundred miles of earth. Lake Erie *stretches* from Niagara nearly to Huron. Hence,

3. To *stretch to*, is to reach.

4. To be extended or to bear extension without breaking, as elastic substances.

The inner membrane—because it would *stretch* and yield, remained unbroken. *Boyle.*

5. To sally beyond the truth; to exaggerate. A man who is apt to *stretch*, has less credit than others.

6. In *navigation*, to sail; to direct a course. It is often understood to signify to sail under a great spread of canvas close hauled. In this it differs from *stand*, which implies no press of sail. We were *standing* to the

east, when we saw a ship *stretching* to the southward.

7. To make violent efforts in running.

STRETCH, *n.* Extension in length or in breadth; reach; as a great *stretch* of wings. *Ray.*

2. Effort; struggle; strain.

Those put lawful authority upon the *stretch* to the abuse of power, under color of prerogative. *L'Estrange.*

3. Force of body; straining.

By *stretch* of arms the distant shore to gain. *Dryden.*

4. Utmost extent of meaning.

Quotations, in their utmost *stretch*, can signify no more than that Luther lay under severe agonies of mind. *Atterbury.*

5. Utmost reach of power.

This is the utmost *stretch* that nature can. *Granville.*

6. In *sailing*, a tack; the reach or extent of progress on one tack. *Mar. Dict.*

7. Course; direction; as the *stretch* of seams of coal. *Kirwan.*

STRETCH'ED, *pp.* Drawn out in length; extended; exerted to the utmost.

STRETCH'ER, *n.* He or that which stretches.

2. A term in bricklaying. *Moxon.*

3. A piece of timber in building.

4. A narrow piece of plank placed across a boat for the rowers to set their feet against. *Mar. Dict.*

STRETCH'ING, *ppr.* Drawing out in length; extending; spreading; exerting force.

STREW, *v. t.* [Goth. *strawan*; Sax. *streawian*, *streowian*; G. *streuen*; D. *strooijen*; Dan. *ströer*; Sw. *strö*; contracted from *stregan*, which is retained in the Saxon. The Latin has *sterno*, *stravi*; the latter is our *strew*, *straw*. This verb is written *straw*, *strew*, or *strow*; *straw* is nearly obsolete, and *strow* is obsolescent. *Strew* is generally used.]

1. To scatter; to spread by scattering; always applied to dry substances separable into parts or particles; as, to *strew* seed in beds; to *strew* sand on or over a floor; to *strew* flowers over a grave.

2. To spread by being scattered over.

The snow which does the top of Pindus *strew*. *Spenser.*

Is thine alone the seed that *strews* the plain? *Pope.*

3. To scatter loosely.

And *strew'd* his mangled limbs about the field. *Dryden.*

STREW'ED, *pp.* Scattered; spread by scattering; as sand *strewed* on paper.

2. Covered or sprinkled with something scattered; as a floor *strewed* with sand.

STREW'ING, *ppr.* Scattering; spreading over.

STREW'ING, *n.* The act of scattering or spreading over.

2. Any thing fit to be strewed. *Shak.*

STREW'MENT, *n.* Any thing scattered in decoration. [*Not used.*] *Shak.*

STRI'Æ, *n. plu.* [L. See *Streak.*] In *natural history*, small channels in the shells of cockles and in other substances.

STRI'ATE, } *a.* Formed with small channels; channeled.
STRI'ATED, }

2. In *botany*, streaked; marked or scored with superficial or very slender lines; marked with fine parallel lines. *Martyn. Smith.*

Striated fracture, in mineralogy, consists of long narrow separable parts laid on or beside each other. *Kirwan.*

STRI'ATURE, *n.* Disposition of striæ. *Woodward.*

STRICK, *n.* [Gr. στριξ, L. *strix*, a screech-owl.]

A bird of ill omen. [*Not in use.*] *Spenser.*

STRICK'EN, *pp.* of *strike.* Struck; smitten; as the *stricken* deer. [See *Strike.*] *Spenser.*

2. Advanced; worn; far gone.

Abraham was old and well *stricken* in age. Gen xxiv. *Obs.*

STRICK'LE, *n.* [from *strike.*] A strike; an instrument to strike grain to a level with the measure. [In the United States the word *strike* is used.]

2. An instrument for whetting sythes.

STRICT, *a.* [L. *strictus*, from *stringo*; Sax. *stræc.* See *Strain.*]

1. Strained; drawn close; tight; as a *strict* embrace; a *strict* ligature. *Arbuthnot. Dryden.*

2. Tense; not relaxed; as a *strict* or lax fiber. *Arbuthnot.*

3. Exact; accurate; rigorously nice; as, to keep *strict* watch. Observe the *strictest* rules of virtue and decorum.

4. Severe; rigorous; governed or governing by exact rules; observing exact rules; as, the father is very *strict* in observing the sabbath. The master is very *strict* with his apprentices.

5. Rigorous; not mild or indulgent; as *strict* laws.

6. Confined; limited; not with latitude; as, to understand words in a *strict* sense.

STRICT'LY, *adv.* Closely; tightly.

2. Exactly; with nice accuracy; as, patriotism *strictly* so called, is a noble virtue.

3. Positively. He commanded his son *strictly* to proceed no further.

4. Rigorously; severely; without remission or indulgence.

Examine thyself *strictly* whether thou didst not best at first. *Bacon.*

STRICT'NESS, *n.* Closeness; tightness; opposed to *laxity*.

2. Exactness in the observance of rules, laws, rites and the like; rigorous accuracy; nice regularity or precision.

I could not grant too much or distrust too little to men that pretended singular piety and religious *strictness*. *K. Charles.*

3. Rigor; severity.

These commissioners proceeded with such *strictness* and severity as did much obscure the king's mercy. *Bacon.*

STRIC'TURE, *n.* [L. *strictura.* See *Strike* and *Stroke*, which unite with L. *stringo.*]

1. A stroke; a glance; a touch. *Hale.*

2. A touch of criticism; critical remark; censure.

I have given myself the liberty of these *strictures* by way of reflection on every passage. *Hammond.*

3. A drawing; a spasmodic or other morbid contraction of any passage of the body. *Arbuthnot.*

STRIDE, *n.* [Sax. *stræde*, a step; *gestridan*, to stride; *bestridan*, to bestride; probably formed on the root of L. *gradior*, Shemitic רדה, in Syr. to go, Ch. to spread, Sax. *stredan*, id.]

A long step.

Her voice theatrically loud,
And masculine her *stride*. *Swift.*

STRIDE, *v. i.* pret. *strid*, *strode*; pp. *strid*, *stridden.*

1. To walk with long steps.

Mars in the middle of the shining shield
Is grav'd, and *strides* along the field. *Dryden.*

2. To straddle.

STRIDE, *v. t.* To pass over at a step.

See him *stride*
Valleys wide. *Arbuthnot.*

STRI'DING, *ppr.* Walking with long steps; passing over at a step.

STRI'DOR, *n.* [L.] A harsh creaking noise, or a crack. *Dryden.*

STRID'ULOUS, *a.* [L. *stridulus.*] Making a small harsh sound or a creaking. *Brown.*

STRIFE, *n.* [Norm. *estrif.* See *Strive.*] Exertion or contention for superiority; contest of emulation, either by intellectual or physical efforts. *Strife* may be carried on between students or between mechanics.

Thus Gods contended, noble *strife*,
Who most should ease the wants of life. *Congreve.*

2. Contention in anger or enmity; contest; struggle for victory; quarrel or war.

I and my people were at great *strife* with the children of Ammon. Judges xii.

These vows thus granted, rais'd a *strife* above
Betwixt the god of war and queen of love. *Dryden.*

3. Opposition; contrariety; contrast.

Artificial *strife*
Lives in these touches livelier than life. *Shak.*

4. The agitation produced by different qualities; as the *strife* of acid and alkali. [*Little used.*] *Johnson.*

STRI'FEFUL, *a.* Contentious; discordant.

The ape was *strifeful* and ambitious,
And the fox guileful and most covetous. *Spenser.*

STRIG'MENT, *n.* [L. *strigmentum*, from *stringo.*]

Scraping; that which is scraped off. [*Not in use.*] *Brown.*

STRI'GOUS, *a.* [L. *strigosus*, from *strigo.*] In *botany*, a *strigous* leaf is one set with stiff lanceolate bristles. *Martyn.*

STRIKE, *v. t.* pret. *struck*; pp. *struck* and *stricken*; but *struck* is in the most common use. *Strook* is wholly obsolete. [Sax. *astrican*, to strike; D. *stryken*, to strike, and to *stroke*, to smooth, to anoint or rub over, to slide; G. *streichen*, to pass, move or ramble, to depart, to touch, to *stroke*, to glide or glance over, to lower or *strike*, as sails, to curry, [L. *stringo*, *strigil*,] to sweep together, to spread, as a plaster, to play on a violin, to card, as wool, to *strike* or whip, as with a rod; *streich*, *strich*, a stroke, stripe or lash, Eng. *streak*; Dan. *streg*, a stroke; *stryger*, to rub, to *stroke*, to *strike*, to trim, to iron or smooth, to *strike*, as sails, to whip, to play on a violin, to glide along, to plane; Sw. *stryka*, id. We see that *strike*, *stroke* and *streak*, and the L. *stringo*, whence *strain*, *strict*, *stricture*, &c., are all radically one word. *Strong* is of the same family. Hence we see the sense is to rub, to scrape; but it includes often the sense of thrusting. It is to touch or graze with a sweeping or stroke. Hence our sense of *striking* a measure of grain, and *strike, strickle,* and a *stroke* of the pencil in painting. Hence the use of *stricken,* applied to age, worn with age, as in the L. *strigo,* the same word differently applied. Hence also we see the propriety of the use of *stricture,* applied to criticism. It seems to be formed on the root of *rake* and *stretch.*]

1. To touch or hit with some force, either with the hand or an instrument; to give a blow to, either with the open hand, the fist, a stick, club or whip, or with a pointed instrument, or with a ball or an arrow discharged. An arrow *struck* the shield; a ball *strikes* a ship between wind and water.

He at Philippi kept
His sword e'en like a dancer, while I *struck*
The lean and wrinkled Cassius. *Shak.*

2. To dash; to throw with a quick motion.

They shall take of the blood, and *strike* it on the two side-posts. Ex. xii.

3. To stamp; to impress; to coin; as, to *strike* coin at the mint; to *strike* dollars or sovereigns; also, to print; as, to *strike* five hundred copies of a book.

4. To thrust in; to cause to enter or penetrate; as, a tree *strikes* its root deep.

5. To punish; to afflict; as *smite* is also used.

To punish the just is not good, nor to *strike* princes for equity. Prov. xvii.

6. To cause to sound; to notify by sound; as, the clock *strikes* twelve; the drums *strike* up a march. *Shak. Knolles.*

7. In *seamanship,* to lower; to let down; as, to *strike* sail; to *strike* a flag or ensign; to *strike* a yard or a top-mast in a gale; [that is, to run or slip down.] *Mar. Dict.*

8. To impress strongly; to affect sensibly with strong emotion; as, to *strike* the mind with surprise; to *strike* with wonder, alarm, dread or horror.

Nice works of art *strike* and surprise us most upon the first view. *Atterbury.*

They please as beauties, here as wonders *strike.* *Pope.*

9. To make and ratify; as, to *strike* a bargain, L. *fœdus ferire.* This expression probably arose from the practice of the parties striking a victim when they concluded a bargain.

10. To produce by a sudden action.

Waving wide her myrtle wand,
She *strikes* an universal peace through sea and land. *Milton.*

11. To affect in some particular manner by a sudden impression or impulse; as, the plan proposed *strikes* me favorably; to *strike* one dead; to *strike* one blind; to *strike* one dumb. *Shak. Dryden.*

12. To level a measure of grain, salt or the like, by scraping off with a straight instrument what is above the level of the top.

13. To lade into a cooler. *Edwards, W. Indies.*

14. To be advanced or worn with age; *used in the participle;* as, he was *stricken* in years or age; well *struck* in years. *Shak.*

15. To run on; to ground; as a ship.

To strike up, to cause to sound; to begin to beat.

Strike up the drums. *Shak.*

2. To begin to sing or play; as, to *strike up* a tune.

To strike off, to erase from an account; to deduct; as, to *strike off* the interest of a debt.

2. To impress; to print; as, to *strike off* a thousand copies of a book.

3. To separate by a blow or any sudden action; as, to *strike off* a man's head with a cimiter; to *strike off* what is superfluous or corrupt.

To strike out, to produce by collision; to force out; as, to *strike out* sparks with steel.

2. To blot out; to efface; to erase.

To methodize is as necessary as to *strike out.* *Pope.*

3. To form something new by a quick effort; to devise; to invent; to contrive; as, to *strike out* a new plan of finance.

STRIKE, *v. i.* To make a quick blow or thrust.

It pleas'd the king
To *strike* at me upon his misconstruction. *Shak.*

2. To hit; to collide; to dash against; to clash; as, a hammer *strikes* against the bell of a clock.

3. To sound by percussion; to be struck. The clock *strikes.*

4. To make an attack.

A puny subject *strikes*
At thy great glory. *Shak.*

5. To hit; to touch; to act on by appulse.

Hinder light from *striking* on it, and its colors vanish. *Locke.*

6. To sound with blows.

Whilst any trump did sound, or drum *struck* up. *Shak.*

7. To run upon; to be stranded. The ship *struck* at twelve, and remained fast.

8. To pass with a quick or strong effect; to dart; to penetrate.

Now and then a beam of wit or passion *strikes* through the obscurity of the poem. *Dryden.*

9. To lower a flag or colors in token of respect, or to signify a surrender of the ship to an enemy.

10. To break forth; as, to *strike* into reputation. [*Not in use.*]

To strike in, to enter suddenly; also, to recede from the surface, as an eruption; to disappear.

To strike in with, to conform to; to suit itself to; to join with at once. *South.*

To strike out, to wander; to make a sudden excursion; as, to *strike out* into an irregular course of life. *Collier.*

To *strike,* among workmen in manufactories, in England, is to quit work in a body or by combination, in order to compel their employers to raise their wages.

STRIKE, *n.* An instrument with a straight edge for leveling a measure of grain, salt and the like, for scraping off what is above the level of the top. *America.*

2. A bushel; four pecks. [*Local.*] *Tusser.*

3. A measure of four bushels or half a quarter. [*Local.*] *Encyc.*

Strike of flax, a handful that may be hackled at once. [*Local.*]

STRI'KE-BLOCK, *n.* [*strike* and *block.*] A plane shorter than a jointer, used for shooting a short joint. *Moxon.*

STRI'KER, *n.* One that strikes, or that which strikes.

2. In *Scripture,* a quarrelsome man. Tit. i.

STRI'KING, *ppr.* Hitting with a blow; impressing; imprinting; punishing; lowering, as sails or a mast, &c.

2. *a.* Affecting with strong emotions; surprising; forcible; impressive; as a *striking* representation or image.

3. Strong; exact; adapted to make impression; as a *striking* resemblance of features.

STRI'KINGLY, *adv.* In such a manner as to affect or surprise; forcibly; strongly; impressively.

STRI'KINGNESS, *n.* The quality of affecting or surprising.

STRING, *n.* [Sax. *string;* D. Dan. *streng;* G. *strang;* also Dan. *strikke;* G. *strick;* connected with *strong,* L. *stringo,* from drawing, stretching; Ir. *srang,* a string; *sreangaim,* to draw.]

1. A small rope, line or cord, or a slender strip of lether or other like substance, used for fastening or tying things.

2. A ribin.

Round Ormond's knee thou ty'st the mystic *string.* *Prior.*

3. A thread on which any thing is filed; and hence, a line of things; as a *string* of shells or beads. *Addison.*

4. The chord of a musical instrument, as of a harpsichord, harp or violin; as an instrument of ten *strings.* *Scripture.*

5. A fiber, as of a plant.

Duck weed putteth forth a little *string* into the water, from the bottom. *Bacon.*

6. A nerve or tendon of an animal body.

The *string* of his tongue was loosed. Mark vii.

[*This is not a technical word.*]

7. The line or cord of a bow.

He twangs the quiv'ring *string.* *Pope.*

8. A series of things connected or following in succession; any concatenation of things; as a *string* of arguments; a *string* of propositions.

9. In *ship-building,* the highest range of planks in a ship's ceiling, or that between the gunwale and the upper edge of the upper deck ports. *Mar. Dict.*

10. The tough substance that unites the two parts of the pericarp of leguminous plants; as the *strings* of beans.

To have two strings to the bow, to have two expedients for executing a project or gaining a purpose; to have a double advantage, or to have two views. [*In the latter sense, unusual.*]

STRING, *v. t.* pret. and pp. *strung.* To furnish with strings.

Has not wise nature *strung* the legs and feet? *Gay.*

2. To put in tune a stringed instrument.

For here the muse so oft her harp has *strung*— *Addison.*

3. To file; to put on a line; as, to *string* beads or pearls. *Spectator.*

4. To make tense; to strengthen.

Toil *strung* the nerves, and purified the blood. *Dryden.*

5. To deprive of strings; as, to *string* beans.

STRING'ED, *a.* Having strings; as a *stringed* instrument.

2. Produced by strings; as *stringed* noise. *Milton.*

STRIN'GENT, for *astringent,* binding, is not in use. *Thomson.*

STRING'HALT, *n.* [*string* and *halt.*] A sudden twitching of the hinder leg of a horse, or an involuntary or convulsive motion of the muscles that extend or bend the hough. *Far. Dict.*

[This word in some of the United States, is corrupted into *springhalt.*]

STRING'ING, *ppr.* Furnishing with strings; putting in tune; filing; making tense; depriving of strings.

STRING'LESS, *a.* Having no strings.

His tongue is now a *stringless* instrument. *Shak.*

STRING'Y, *a.* Consisting of strings or small threads; fibrous; filamentous; as a *stringy* root. *Grew.*

2. Ropy; viscid; gluey; that may be drawn into a thread.

STRIP, *v. t.* [G. *streifen*, to strip, to flay, to stripe or streak, to graze upon, to swerve, ramble or stroll; D. *streepen*, to stripe, to reprimand; Dan. *striber*, to stripe or streak, and *stripper*, to *strip*, to skin or flay, to ramble; Sax. *bestrypan.* Some of the senses of these verbs seems to be derived from the noun *stripe*, which is probably from *stripping.* Regularly, this verb should be referred to the root of *rip*, L. *rapio.*]

1. To pull or tear off, as a covering; as, to *strip* the skin from a beast; to *strip* the bark from a tree; to *strip* the clothes from a man's back.

2. To deprive of a covering; to skin; to peel; as, to *strip* a beast of his skin; to *strip* a tree of its bark; to *strip* a man of his clothes.

3. To deprive; to bereave; to make destitute; as, to *strip* a man of his possessions.

4. To divest; as, to *strip* one of his rights and privileges. Let us *strip* this subject of all its adventitious glare.

5. To rob; to plunder; as, robbers *strip* a house.

6. To bereave; to deprive; to impoverish; as a man *stripped* of his fortune.

7. To deprive; to make bare by cutting, grazing or other means; as, cattle *strip* the ground of its herbage.

8. To pull off husks; to husk; as, to *strip* maiz, or the ears of maiz. *America.*

9. To press out the last milk at a milking.

10. To unrig; as, to *strip* a ship. *Locke.*

11. To pare off the surface of land in strips, and turn over the strips upon the adjoining surface.

To strip off, to pull or take off; as, to *strip off* a covering; to *strip off* a mask or disguise.

2. To cast off. [*Not in use.*] *Shak.*

3. To separate from something connected. [*Not in use.*]

[We may observe the primary sense of this word is to peel or skin, hence to pull off in a long narrow piece; hence *stripe.*]

STRIP, *n.* [G. *streif*, a stripe, a streak; D. *streep*, a stroke, a line, a stripe; Dan. *stribe.*]

1. A narrow piece, comparatively long; as a *strip* of cloth.

2. Waste, *in a legal sense;* destruction of fences, buildings, timber, &c. [Norm. *estrippe.*] *Massachusetts.*

STRIPE, *n.* [See *Strip.* It is probable that this word is taken from stripping.]

1. A line or long narrow division of any thing, of a different color from the ground; as a *stripe* of red on a green ground; hence, any linear variation of color. *Bacon.*

2. A strip or long narrow piece attached to something of a different color; as a long *stripe* sewed upon a garment.

3. The weal or long narrow mark discolored by a lash or rod.

4. A stroke made with a lash, whip, rod, strap or scourge.

Forty *stripes* may he give him, and not exceed. Deut. xxv.

[A blow with a club is not a *stripe.*]

5. Affliction; punishment; sufferings.

By his *stripes* are we healed. Is. liii.

STRIPE, *v. t.* To make stripes; to form with lines of different colors; to variegate with stripes.

2. To strike; to lash. [*Little used.*]

STRI'PED, *pp.* Formed with lines of different colors.

2. *a.* Having stripes of different colors.

STRI'PING, *ppr.* Forming with stripes.

STRIP'LING, *n.* [from *strip*, *stripe*; primarily a tall slender youth, one that shoots up suddenly.]

A youth in the state of adolescence, or just passing from boyhood to manhood; a lad.

And the king said, inquire thou whose son the *stripling* is. 1 Sam. xviii.

STRIP'PED, *pp.* Pulled or torn off; peeled; skinned; deprived; divested; made naked; impoverished; husked, as maiz.

STRIP'PER, *n.* One that strips.

STRIP'PING, *ppr.* Pulling off; peeling; skinning; flaying; depriving; divesting; husking.

STRIP'PINGS, *n.* The last milk drawn from a cow at a milking. *Grose. New England.*

STRIVE, *v. i.* pret. *strove;* pp. *striven.* [G. *streben;* D. *streeven;* Sw. *sträfva;* Dan. *stræber;* formed perhaps on the Heb. רוב. This word coincides in elements with *drive*, and the primary sense is nearly the same. See *Rival.*]

1. To make efforts; to use exertions; to endeavor with earnestness; to labor hard; *applicable to exertions of body or mind.* A workman *strives* to perform his task before another; a student *strives* to excel his fellows in improvement.

Was it for this that his ambition *strove*
To equal Cesar first, and after Jove? *Cowley.*

Strive with me in your prayers to God for me. Rom. xv.

Strive to enter in at the strait gate. Luke xiii.

2. To contend; to contest; to struggle in opposition to another; to be in contention or dispute; followed by *against* or *with* before the person or thing opposed; as, *strive against* temptation; *strive* for the truth.

My spirit shall not always *strive with* man. Gen. vi.

3. To oppose by contrariety of qualities.

Now private pity *strove* with public hate,
Reason with rage, and eloquence with fate. *Derham.*

4. To vie; to be comparable to; to emulate; to contend in excellence.

Not that sweet grove
Of Daphne by Orontes, and the inspir'd
Castalian spring, might with this paradise
Of Eden *strive.* *Milton.*

STRI'VER, *n.* One that strives or contends; one who makes efforts of body or mind.

STRI'VING, *ppr.* Making efforts; exerting the powers of body or mind with earnestness; contending.

STRI'VING, *n.* The act of making efforts; contest; contention.

Avoid foolish questions and genealogies and contentions, and *strivings* about the law. Tit. iii.

STRI'VINGLY, *adv.* With earnest efforts; with struggles.

STROB'IL, *n.* [L. *strobilus.*] In *botany*, a pericarp formed from an ament by the hardening of the scales. It is made up of scales that are imbricate, from an ament contracted or squeezed together in this state of maturity, as the cone of the pine. *Martyn.*

STROB'ILIFORM, *a.* [L. *strobilus* and *form*, supra.] Shaped like a strobil, as a spike.

STRO'ĈAL, STRO'KAL, *n.* An instrument used by glass-makers to empty the metal from one pot to another. *Encyc.*

STROKE, STROOK, for *struck. Obs.*

STROKE, *n.* [from *strike.*] A blow; the striking of one body against another; *applicable to a club or to any heavy body, or to a rod, whip or lash.* A piece of timber falling may kill a man by its *stroke;* a man when whipped, can hardly fail to flinch or wince at every *stroke.*

Th' oars were silver,
Which to the time of flutes kept *stroke*— *Shak.*

2. A hostile blow or attack.

He entered and won the whole kingdom of Naples without striking a *stroke.* *Bacon.*

3. A sudden attack of disease or affliction; calamity.

At this one *stroke* the man look'd dead in law. *Harte.*

4. Fatal attack; as the *stroke* of death.

5. The sound of the clock.

What is 't o'clock?
Upon the *stroke* of four. *Shak.*

6. The touch of a pencil.

Oh, lasting as those colors may they shine,
Free as thy *stroke*, yet faultless as thy line. *Pope.*

Some parts of my work have been brightened by the *strokes* of your lordship's pencil. *Middleton.*

7. A touch; a masterly effort; as the boldest *strokes* of poetry. *Dryden.*

He will give one of the finishing *strokes* to it. *Addison.*

8. An effort suddenly or unexpectedly produced.

9. Power; efficacy.

He has a great *stroke* with the reader, when he condemns any of my poems, to make the world have a better opinion of them. *Dryden.*

[*I believe this sense is obsolete.*]

9. Series of operations; as, to carry on a great *stroke* in business. [*A common use of the word.*]

10. A dash in writing or printing; a line; a touch of the pen; as a hair *stroke.*

11. In *seamen's language*, the sweep of an oar; as, to row with a long *stroke.*

STROKE, *v. t.* [Sax. *stracan;* Sw. *stryka;* Russ. *strogayu*, *strugayu*, to plane. See *Strike* and *Strict.*]

1. To rub gently with the hand by way of expressing kindness or tenderness; to soothe.

He dried the falling drops, and yet more kind,
He strok'd her cheeks— *Dryden.*

2. To rub gently in one direction. *Gay.*
3. To make smooth.

STRO'KED, *pp.* Rubbed gently with the hand.

STRO'KER, *n.* One who strokes; one who pretends to cure by stroking.

STRO'KESMAN, *n.* In *rowing*, the man who rows the aftmost oar, and whose stroke is to be followed by the rest. *Mar. Dict.*

STRO'KING, *ppr.* Rubbing gently with the hand.

STROLL, *v. i.* [formed probably on *troll*, *roll.*]
To rove; to wander on foot; to ramble idly or leisurely.

These mothers *stroll* to beg sustenance for their helpless infants. *Swift.*

STRŌLL, *n.* A wandering on foot; a walking idly and leisurely.

STRŌLLER, *n.* One who strolls; a vagabond; a vagrant. *Swift.*

STRŌLLING, *ppr.* Roving idly; rambling on foot.

STROM'BITE, *n.* A petrified shell of the genus Strombus. *Jameson.*

STROND, *n.* The beach. [*Not much used.* See *Strand.*]

STRONG, *a.* [Sax. *strong*, *strang* or *streng*; from the latter is formed *strength*; G. *strenge*; D. Dan. *streng*; Sw. *sträng*, strict, severe, rigid. As *n* is casual in this word, the original orthography was *strag*, *streg*, or *strog*, coinciding with L. *strictus*, *stringo*. The sense of the radical word is to stretch, strain, draw, and probably from the root of *stretch* and *reach*. We observe in all the kindred dialects on the continent, the sense of the word is somewhat different from that of the English. The Russ. *strogei*, strict, rigid, severe, retains the original orthography without *n.*]

1. Having physical active power, or great physical power; having the power of exerting great bodily force; vigorous. A patient is recovering from sickness, but is not yet *strong* enough to walk. A *strong* man will lift twice his own weight.

That our oxen may be *strong* to labor. Ps. cxliv.

Orses the *strong* to greater strength must yield. *Dryden.*

2. Having physical passive power; having ability to bear or endure; firm; solid; as a constitution *strong* enough to bear the fatigues of a campaign.
3. Well fortified; able to sustain attacks; not easily subdued or taken; as a *strong* fortress or town.
4. Having great military or naval force; powerful; as a *strong* army or fleet; a *strong* nation; a nation *strong* at sea.
5. Having great wealth, means or resources; as a *strong* house or company of merchants.
6. Moving with rapidity; violent; forcible; impetuous; as a *strong* current of water or wind; the wind was *strong* from the northeast; we had a *strong* tide against us.
7. Hale; sound; robust; as a *strong* constitution.
8. Powerful; forcible; cogent; adapted to make a deep or effectual impression on the mind or imagination; as a *strong* argument; *strong* reasons; *strong* evidence; a *strong* example or instance. He used *strong* language.
9. Ardent; eager; zealous; earnestly engaged; as a *strong* partisan; a *strong* whig or tory.

Her mother, ever *strong* against that match— *Shak.*

10. Having virtues of great efficacy; or having a particular quality in a great degree; as a *strong* powder or tincture; a *strong* decoction; *strong* tea; *strong* coffee.
11. Full of spirit; intoxicating; as *strong* liquors.
12. Affecting the sight forcibly; as *strong* colors.
13. Affecting the taste forcibly; as the *strong* flavor of onions.
14. Affecting the smell powerfully; as a *strong* scent.
15. Not of easy digestion; solid; as *strong* meat. Heb. v.
16. Well established; firm; not easily overthrown or altered; as a custom grown *strong* by time.
17. Violent; vehement; earnest.

Who in the days of his flesh, when he offered up prayers with *strong* crying and tears— Heb. v.

18. Able; furnished with abilities.

I was *stronger* in prophecy than in criticism. *Dryden.*

19. Having great force of mind, of intellect or of any faculty; as a man of *strong* powers of mind; a man of a *strong* mind or intellect; a man of *strong* memory, judgment or imagination.
20. Having great force; comprising much in few words.

Like her sweet voice is thy harmonious song,
As high, as sweet, as easy and as *strong*. *Smith.*

21. Bright; glaring; vivid; as a *strong* light.
22. Powerful to the extent of force named; as an army ten thousand *strong*.

STRON'GER, *a. comp.* of *strong.* Having more strength.

STRON'GEST, *a. superl.* of *strong.* Having most strength.

STRONG'-FISTED, *a.* [*strong* and *fist.*] Having a strong hand; muscular. *Arbuthnot.*

STRONG-HAND, *n.* [*strong* and *hand.*] Violence; force; power.

It was their meaning to take what they needed by *strong-hand.* *Raleigh.*

[*Not properly a compound word.*]

STRONG-HOLD, *n.* [*strong* and *hold.*] A fastness; a fort; a fortified place; a place of security.

STRONG'LY, *adv.* With strength; with great force or power; forcibly; *a word of extensive application.*

2. Firmly; in a manner to resist attack; as a town *strongly* fortified.
3. Vehemently; forcibly; eagerly. The evils of this measure were *strongly* represented to the government.

STRONG'-SET, *a.* [*strong* and *set.*] Firmly set or compacted. *Swift.*

STRONG-WATER, *n.* [*strong* and *water.*] Distilled or ardent spirit. [*Not in use.*] *Bacon.*

STRON'TIAN, *n.* [from *Strontian*, in Argyleshire, where it was first found.]
An earth which, when pure and dry, is perfectly white, and resembles baryte in many of its properties. It is a compound of oxygen and a base to which is given the name *strontium*, in the proportion of 16 per cent. of the former, to 84 per cent. of the latter. *Davy.*

STRON'TIAN, STRONTIT'IC, *a.* Pertaining to strontian.

STRON'TIANITE, *n.* Carbonate of strontian, a mineral that occurs massive, fibrous, stellated, and crystalized in the form of a hexahedral prism, modified on the edges, or terminated by a pyramid. *Phillips.*

Prismatic baryte, a species of heavy spar. *Ure.*

STRON'TIUM, *n.* The base of strontian. *Davy.*

STROOK, for *struck.* [*Not in use.*]

STROP, *n.* A strap. [See *Strap.*] This orthography is particularly used for a strip of lether used for sharpening razors and giving them a fine smooth edge; a razor-strop. But *strap* is preferable.

2. [Sp. *estrovo.*] A piece of rope spliced into a circular wreath, and put round a block for hanging it. *Mar. Dict.*

STRO'PHE, STRO'PHY, *n.* [Fr. *strophe*; It. *strofa*, *strofe*; Gr. στροφη, a turn, from στρεφω, to turn.]
In *Greek poetry*, a stanza; the first member of a poem. This is succeeded by a similar stanza called *antistrophy.*

STROUT, *v. i.* [for *strut.*] To swell; to puff out. [*Not in use.*] *Bacon.*

STROVE, *pret.* of *strive.*

STRŌW, is only a different orthography of *strew.* [See *Strew.*]

STRŌWL, for *stroll*, is not in use. [See *Stroll.*]

STROY, for *destroy*, is not in use. [See *Destroy.*]

STRUCK, *pret.* and *pp.* of *strike.* [See *Strike.*]

STRUCK'EN, the *old pp.* of *strike*, is obsolete.

STRUC'TURE, *n.* [Fr. from L. *structura*, from *struo*, [for *strugo*,] to set or lay; It. *struttura.*]

1. Act of building; practice of erecting buildings.

His son builds on and never is content,
Till the last farthing is in *structure* spent.
[*Rarely used.*] *Dryden.*

2. Manner of building; form; make; construction; as the want of insight into the *structure* and constitution of the terraqueous globe. *Woodward.*
3. Manner of organization of animals and vegetables, &c.
4. A building of any kind, but chiefly a building of some size or of magnificence; an edifice. The iron bridge over the Seine in Paris, is a beautiful *structure.*

There stands a *structure* of majestic frame. *Pope.*

5. In *mineralogy*, the particular arrangement of the integrant particles or molecules of a mineral. *Brongniart.*

STRUDE, } *n.* A stock of breeding mares.
STRODE, } *Bailey.*

STRUG'GLE, *v. i.* [This word may be formed on the root of *stretch, right,* &c. which signifies to strain; or more directly on the same elements in L. *rugo,* to wrinkle, and Eng. *wriggle.* In W. *ystreiglaw* is to turn.]

1. Properly, to strive, or to make efforts with a twisting or with contortions of the body. Hence,

2. To use great efforts; to labor hard; to strive; to contend; as, to *struggle* to save life; to *struggle* with the waves; to *struggle* against the stream; to *struggle* with adversity.

3. To labor in pain or anguish; to be in agony; to labor in any kind of difficulty or distress.

'Tis wisdom to beware,
And better shun the bait than *struggle* in the snare. *Dryden.*

STRUG'GLE, *n.* Great labor; forcible effort to obtain an object, or to avoid an evil; properly, a violent effort with contortions of the body.

2. Contest; contention; strife.

An honest man might look upon the *struggle* with indifference. *Addison.*

3. Agony; contortions of extreme distress.

STRUG'GLER, *n.* One who struggles, strives or contends.

STRUG'GLING, *ppr.* Making great efforts; using violent exertions; affected with contortions.

STRUG'GLING, *n.* The act of striving; vehement or earnest effort.

STRU'MA, *n.* [L.] A glandular swelling; scrofula; the king's evil; a wen. *Wiseman. Coxe.*

STRU'MOUS, *a.* Having swellings in the glands; scrofulous. *Wiseman.*

STRUM'PET, *n.* [Ir. *stribrid, striopach.*] A prostitute.

STRUM'PET, *a.* Like a strumpet; false; inconstant. *Shak.*

STRUM'PET, *v. t.* To debauch. *Shak.*

STRUNG, *pret.* of *string.*

STRUT, *v. i.* [G. *strotzen;* Dan. *strutter.*]

1. To walk with a lofty proud gait and erect head; to walk with affected dignity.

Does he not hold up his head and *strut* in his gait? *Shak.*

2. To swell; to protuberate.

The bellying canvas *strutted* with the gale.
[*Not used.*] *Dryden.*

STRUT, *n.* A lofty proud step or walk with the head erect; affectation of dignity in walking.

STRU'THIOUS, *a.* [L. *struthio.*] Pertaining to or like the ostrich.

STRUT'TER, *n.* One who struts. *Swift.*

STRUT'TING, *ppr.* Walking with a lofty gait and erect head.

STRUT'TING, *n.* The act of walking with a proud gait.

STRUT'TINGLY, *adv.* With a proud lofty step: boastingly.

STRYCH'NIA, *n.* An alkaline substance obtained from the fruit of the *Strychnos nux vomica,* and *Strychnos ignatia.* It is a white substance, crystalized in very small four sided prisms, and intolerably bitter. It acts upon the stomach with violent energy, inducing locked jaw and destroying life. *Ure.*

STUB, *n.* [Sax. *steb;* Dan. *stub;* Sw. *stubbe,* a stock or stem; L. *stipes;* from setting, fixing. See *Stop.*]

1. The stump of a tree; that part of the stem of a tree which remains fixed in the earth when the tree is cut down. [*Stub,* in the United States, I believe is never used for the *stump* of an herbaceous plant.]

2. A log; a block. [*Not in use.*] *Milton.*

STUB, *v. t.* To grub up by the roots; to extirpate; as, to *stub* up edible roots. *Grew.*

2. To strike the toes against a stump, stone or other fixed object. *New England.*

STUB'BED, *a.* Short and thick like something truncated; blunt; obtuse. [Sw. *stubbig.*]

2. Hardy; not nice or delicate. *Berkeley.*

STUB'BEDNESS, *n.* Bluntness; obtuseness.

STUB'BLE, *n.* [D. G. *stoppel;* Sw. *stubb;* L. *stipula.* It is a diminutive of *stub.*]

The stumps of wheat, rye, barley, oats or buckwheat, left in the ground; the part of the stalk left by the sythe or sickle.

After the first crop is off, they plow in the *stubble.* *Mortimer.*

STUB'BLE-GOOSE, *n.* [*stubble* and *goose.*] A goose fed among stubble. *Chaucer.*

STUB'BLE-RAKE, *n.* A rake with long teeth for raking together stubble.

STUB'BORN, *a.* [This word is doubtless formed on the root of *stub* or *stiff,* and denotes fixed, firm. But the origin of the latter syllable is not obvious.]

1. Unreasonably obstinate; inflexibly fixed in opinion; not to be moved or persuaded by reasons; inflexible; as a *stubborn* son; a *stubborn* mind or soul.

The queen is obstinate—
Stubborn to justice. *Shak.*

2. Persevering; persisting; steady; constant; as *stubborn* attention. *Locke.*

3. Stiff; not flexible; as a *stubborn* bow. *Chapman.*

Take a plant of *stubborn* oak. *Dryden.*

4. Hardy; firm; enduring without complaint; as *stubborn* Stoics. *Swift.*

5. Harsh; rough; rugged. [*Little used.*]

6. Refractory; not easily melted or worked; as a *stubborn* ore or metal.

7. Refractory; obstinately resisting command, the goad or the whip; as a *stubborn* ass or horse.

STUB'BORNLY, *adv.* Obstinately; inflexibly; contumaciously.

STUB'BORNNESS, *n.* Perverse and unreasonable obstinacy; inflexibility; contumacy.

Stubbornness and obstinate disobedience must be mastered with blows. *Locke.*

2. Stiffness; want of pliancy.

3. Refractoriness, as of ores.

STUB'BY, *a.* [from *stub.*] Abounding with stubs.

2. Short and thick; short and strong; as *stubby* bristles. *Grew.*

STUB'-NAIL, *n.* [*stub* and *nail.*] A nail broken off; a short thick nail.

STUC'CO, *n.* [It. *id.;* Fr. *stuc;* Sp. *estuco;* allied probably to *stick, stuck.*]

1. A fine plaster composed of lime, sand, whiting and pounded marble; used for covering walls, &c.

2. Work made of stucco.

STUC'CO, *v. t.* To plaster; to overlay with fine plaster.

STUC'COED, *pp.* Overlaid with stucco.

STUC'COING, *ppr.* Plastering with stucco.

STUCK, *pret.* and *pp.* of *stick.*

Stuck o'er with titles, and hung round with strings. *Pope.*

STUCK, *n.* A thrust. [*Not in use.*] *Shak.*

STUCK'LE, *n.* [from *stook.*] A number of sheaves set together in the field. [*Scotish. Not in use in the U. States.*]

STUD, *n.* [Sax. *stod, studu;* Ice. *stod;* D. *stut;* Sw. *stöd;* G. *stütze,* a stay or prop; *stützen,* to butt at, to gore; Dan. *stöder,* to push, to thrust, G. *stossen.* The sense of the root is to set, to thrust. It coincides with *stead,* place, Ir. *stadam,* to stay or stand, *stid,* a prop.]

1. In *building,* a small piece of timber or joist inserted in the sills and beams, between the posts, to support the beams or other main timbers. The boards on the outside and the laths on the inside of a building, are also nailed to the *studs.*

2. A nail with a large head, inserted in work chiefly for ornament; an ornamental knob.

A belt of straw, and ivy buds,
With coral clasps and amber *studs.* *Raleigh.*
Crystal and myrrhine cups, emboss'd with gems
And *studs* of pearl. *Milton.*

3. A collection of breeding horses and mares; or the place where they are kept.

In the *studs* of Ireland, where care is taken, we see horses bred of excellent shape, vigor and fire. *Temple.*

4. A button for a shirt sleeve.

STUD, *v. t.* To adorn with shining studs or knobs.

Their horses shall be trapp'd,
Their harness *studded* all with gold and pearl. *Shak.*

2. To set with detached ornaments or prominent objects.

STUD'DED, *pp.* Adorned with studs.

2. Set with detached ornaments.

The sloping sides and summits of our hills, and the extensive plains that stretch before our view, are *studded* with substantial, neat and commodious dwellings of freemen. *Bp. Hobart.*

STUD'DING, *ppr.* Setting or adorning with studs or shining knobs.

STUD'DING-SAIL, *n.* In *navigation,* a sail that is set beyond the skirts of the principal sails. The studding-sails are set only when the wind is light. They appear like wings upon the yard-arms. *Mar. Dict.*

STU'DENT, *n.* [L. *studens, studeo.* See *Study.*]

1. A person engaged in study; one who is devoted to learning, either in a seminary or in private; a scholar; as the *students* of an academy, of a college or university; a medical *student;* a law *student.*

2. A man devoted to books; a bookish man; as a hard *student;* a close *student.*

Keep a gamester from dice, and a good *student* from his books. *Shak.*

3. One who studies or examines; as a *student* of nature's works.

STUD'-HORSE, *n.* [Sax. *stod-hors;* Low L. *stotarius;* Chaucer, *stot.*]

A breeding horse; a horse kept for propagating his kind.

STUD'IED, *pp.* [from *study.*] Read; closely examined; read with diligence and attention; well considered. The book has been *studied.* The subject has been well *studied.*

2. *a.* Learned; well versed in any branch of learning; qualified by study; as a man well *studied* in geometry, or in law or medical science. *Bacon.*

3. Having a particular inclination. [*Not in use.*] *Shak.*

STUD'IER, *n.* [from *study.*] One who studies; a student.

Lipsius was a great *studier* in the stoical philosophy. *Tillotson.*

STU'DIOUS, *a.* [Fr. *studieux*; L. *studiosus.*]

1. Given to books or to learning; devoted to the acquisition of knowledge from books; as a *studious* scholar.

2. Contemplative; given to thought, or to the examination of subjects by contemplation.

3. Diligent; eager to discover something, or to effect some object; as, be *studious* to please; *studious* to find new friends and allies. *Tickel.*

4. Attentive to; careful; with *of.*

Divines must become *studious of* pious and venerable antiquity. *White.*

5. Planned with study; deliberate.

For the frigid villany of *studious* lewdness, for the calm malignity of labored impiety, what apology can be invented? *Rambler.*

6. Favorable to study; suitable for thought and contemplation; as the *studious* shade. *Thomson.*

Let my due feet never fail,
To walk the *studious* cloister pale. *Milton.*

[*The latter signification is forced and not much used.*]

STU'DIOUSLY, *adv.* With study; with close attention to books.

2. With diligent contemplation. *Dryden.*

3. Diligently; with zeal and earnestness. *Atterbury.*

4. Carefully; attentively.

STU'DIOUSNESS, *n.* The habit or practice of study; addictedness to books. Men of sprightly imagination are not generally the most remarkable for *studiousness.*

STUD'Y, *n.* [Fr. *etude*; L. *studium*, from *studeo*, to study, that is, to *set* the thoughts or mind. See *Assiduous. Studeo* is connected with the English *stud, stead.*]

1. Literally, a setting of the mind or thoughts upon a subject; hence, application of mind to books, to arts or science, or to any subject, for the purpose of learning what is not before known.

Hammond generally spent thirteen hours of the day in *study.* *Fell.*

Study gives strength to the mind; conversation, grace. *Temple.*

2. Attention; meditation; contrivance.

Just men they seem'd, and all their *study* bent
To worship God aright and know his works. *Milton.*

3. Any particular branch of learning that is studied. Let your *studies* be directed by some learned and judicious friend.

4. Subject of attention.

The Holy Scriptures, especially the New Testament, are her daily *study.* *Law.*

5. A building or an apartment devoted to study or to literary employment. *Clarendon. Dryden.*

6. Deep cogitation; perplexity. [*Little used.*] *Bacon.*

STUD'Y, *v. i.* [L. *studeo.*] To fix the mind closely upon a subject; to muse; to dwell upon in thought.

I found a moral first, and then *studied* for a fable. *Swift.*

2. To apply the mind to books. He *studies* eight hours in the day.

3. To endeavor diligently.

That ye *study* to be quiet and do your own business. 1 Thess. iv.

STUD'Y, *v. t.* To apply the mind to; to read and examine for the purpose of learning and understanding; as, to *study* law or theology; to *study* languages.

2. To consider attentively; to examine closely. *Study* the works of nature.

Study thyself; what rank or what degree
Thy wise Creator has ordain'd for thee. *Dryden.*

3. To form or arrange by previous thought; to con over; or to commit to memory; as, to *study* a speech.

STUFF, *n.* [D. *stof, stoffe*; G. *stoff*; Dan. *stöv*; Sw. *stoft*; Goth. *stubyus*; It. *stoffa*; Sp. *estofa*, quilted stuff; *estofar*, to quilt, to *stew.* See *Stove* and *Stew.*]

1. A mass of matter, indefinitely; or a collection of substances; as a heap of dust, of chips or of dross.

2. The matter of which any thing is formed; materials. The carpenter and joiner speak of the *stuff* with which they build; mechanics pride themselves on having their wares made of good *stuff.*

Time is the *stuff* which life is made of. *Franklin.*

Degrading prose explains his meaning ill,
And shows the *stuff*, and not the workman's skill. *Roscommon.*

Cesar hath wept;
Ambition should be made of sterner *stuff.* *Shak.*

3. Furniture; goods; domestic vessels in general.

He took away locks, and gave away the king's *stuff.* [*Nearly obsolete.*] *Hayward.*

4. That which fills any thing.

Cleanse the stuff'd bosom of that perilous *stuff*
That weighs upon the heart. *Shak.*

5. Essence; elemental part; as the *stuff* of the conscience.

6. A medicine. [*Vulgar.*] *Shak.*

7. Cloth; fabrics of the loom; as silk *stuffs*; woolen *stuffs.* In this sense the word has a plural. Stuff comprehends all cloths, but it signifies particularly woolen cloth of slight texture for linings. *Encyc.*

8. Matter or thing; particularly, that which is trifling or worthless; *a very extensive use of the word.* Flattery is fulsome *stuff*; poor poetry is miserable *stuff.*

Anger would indite
Such woful *stuff* as I or Shadwell write. *Dryden.*

9. Among *seamen*, a melted mass of turpentine, tallow, &c. with which the masts, sides and bottom of a ship are smeared. *Mar. Dict.*

STUFF, *v. t.* To fill; as, to *stuff* a bed-tick.

2. To fill very full; to crowd.

This crook drew hazel boughs adown,
And *stuff'd* her apron wide with nuts so brown. *Gay.*

3. To thrust in; to crowd; to press.

Put roses into a glass with a narrow mouth, *stuffing* them close together. *Bacon.*

4. To fill by being put into any thing.

With inward arms the dire machine they load,
And iron bowels *stuff* the dark abode. *Dryden.*

5. To swell or cause to bulge out by putting something in.

Stuff me out with straw. *Shak.*

6. To fill with something improper.

For thee I dim these eyes, and *stuff* this head
With all such reading as was never read. *Pope.*

7. To obstruct, as any of the organs.

I'm *stuff'd*, cousin; I cannot smell. *Shak.*

8. To fill meat with seasoning; as, to *stuff* a leg of veal.

9. To fill the skin of a dead animal for presenting and preserving his form; as, to *stuff* a bird or a lion's skin.

10. To form by filling.

An eastern king put a judge to death for an iniquitous sentence, and ordered his hide to be *stuffed* into a cushion, and placed upon the tribunal. *Swift.*

STUFF, *v. i.* To feed gluttonously.

Taught harmless man to cram and *stuff.* *Swift.*

STUFF'ED, *pp.* Filled; crowded; crammed.

STUFF'ING, *ppr.* Filling; crowding.

STUFF'ING, *n.* That which is used for filling any thing; as the *stuffing* of a saddle or cushion.

2. Seasoning for meat; that which is put into meat to give it a higher relish.

STUKE, for *stucco*, not in use.

STULM, *n.* A shaft to draw water out of a mine. *Bailey.*

STULP, *n.* A post. [*Local.*]

STUL'TIFY, *v. t.* [L. *stultus*, foolish, and *facio*, to make.]

1. To make foolish; to make one a fool. *Burke.*

2. In *law*, to alledge or prove to be insane, for avoiding some act. *Blackstone.*

STULTIL'OQUENCE, *n.* [L. *stultus*, foolish, and *loquentia*, a talking.] Foolish talk; a babbling. *Dict.*

STULTIL'OQUY, *n.* [L. *stultiloquium*, supra.] Foolish talk; silly discourse; babbling. *Taylor.*

STUM, *n.* [D. *stom, stum*, dumb; G. *stumm*, Dan. Sw. *stum*, dumb, mute.]

1. Must; wine unfermented. *Addison.*

2. New wine used to raise fermentation in dead or vapid wines. *B. Jonson.*

3. Wine revived by a new fermentation. *Hudibras.*

STUM, *v. t.* To renew wine by mixing must with it, and raising a new fermentation.

We *stum* our wines to renew their spirits. *Floyer.*

2. To fume a cask of liquor with burning brimstone. [*Local.*]

STUM'BLE, *v. i.* [Ice. *stumra.* This word is probably from a root that signifies to stop or to strike, and may be allied to *stammer.*]

1. To trip in walking or moving in any way upon the legs; to strike the foot so as to fall, or to endanger a fall; *applied to any animal.* A man may *stumble*, as well as a horse.

The way of the wicked is as darkness; they know not at what they *stumble*. Prov. iv.

2. To err; to slide into a crime or an error.

He that loveth his brother, abideth in the light, and there is none occasion of *stumbling* in him. 1 John ii.

3. To strike upon without design; to fall on; to light on by chance. Men often *stumble* upon valuable discoveries.

Ovid *stumbled* by some inadvertence upon Livia in a bath. *Dryden.*

STUM'BLE, *v. t.* To obstruct in progress; to cause to trip or stop.

2. To confound; to puzzle; to put to a nonplus; to perplex.

One thing more *stumbles* me in the very foundation of this hypothesis. *Locke.*

STUM'BLE, *n.* A trip in walking or running.

2. A blunder; a failure.

One *stumble* is enough to deface the character of an honorable life. *L'Estrange.*

STUM'BLED, *pp.* Obstructed; puzzled.

STUM'BLER, *n.* One that stumbles or makes a blunder. *Herbert.*

STUM'BLING, *ppr.* Tripping; erring; puzzling.

STUM'BLING-BLOCK, } *n.* [*stumble* and **STUM'BLING-STONE**, } *block* or *stone.*]

Any cause of stumbling; that which causes to err.

We preach Christ crucified, to the Jews a *stumbling-block*, and to the Greeks foolishness. 1 Cor. i.

This *stumbling-stone* we hope to take away. *Burnet.*

STUMP, *n.* [Sw. Dan. *stump;* Dan. *stumper*, Sw. *stympa*, to mutilate; D. *stomp*, a stump, and blunt; G. *stumpf.*]

1. The stub of a tree; the part of a tree remaining in the earth after the tree is cut down, or the part of any plant left in the earth by the sythe or sickle.

2. The part of a limb or other body remaining after a part is amputated or destroyed; as the *stump* of a leg, of a finger or a tooth. *Dryden. Swift.*

STUMP, *v. t.* To strike any thing fixed and hard with the toe. [*Vulgar.*]

2. To challenge. [*Vulgar.*]

STUMP'Y, *a.* Full of stumps.

2. Hard; strong. [*Little used.*] *Mortimer.*

3. Short; stubby. [*Little used.*]

STUN, *v. t.* [Sax. *stunian;* Fr. *etonner.* The primary sense is to strike or to stop, to blunt, to stupefy.]

1. To make senseless or dizzy with a blow on the head; as, to be *stunned* by a fall, or by a falling timber.

One hung a pole-ax at his saddle bow,
And one a heavy mace to *stun* the foe. *Dryden.*

2. To overpower the sense of hearing; to blunt or stupefy the organs of hearing. To prevent being *stunned*, cannoneers sometimes fill their ears with wool.

3. To confound or make dizzy by loud and mingled sound.

—An universal hubbub wild
Of *stunning* sounds and voices all confus'd. *Milton.*

STUNG, *pret.* and *pp.* of *sting.*

STUNK, *pret.* of *stink.*

STUN'NED, *pp.* Having the sense of hearing overpowered; confounded with noise.

STUN'NING, *ppr.* Overpowering the organs of hearing; confounding with noise.

STUNT, *v. t.* [Ice. *stunta;* Sax. *stintan*, to stint; *stunt*, foolish, stupid. See *Stint.*]

To hinder from growth; *applied to animals and plants;* as, to *stunt* a child; to *stunt* a plant. *Arbuthnot. Pope. Swift.*

STUNT'ED, *pp.* Hindered from growth or increase.

STUNT'EDNESS, *n.* The state of being stunted. *Cheyne.*

STUNT'ING, *ppr.* Hindering from growth or increase.

STUPE, *n.* [L. *stupa*, tow; probably allied to *stuff.*]

Cloth or flax dipped in warm medicaments and applied to a hurt or sore; fomentation; sweating bath. *Wiseman. Coxe.*

STUPE, *v. t.* To foment. *Wiseman.*

STUPE, *n.* A stupid person. [*Not in use.*]

STUPEFAC'TION, *n.* [L. *stupefacio; stupeo*, whence *stupidus*, and *facio.* See *Stop.*]

1. The act of rendering stupid.

2. A stupid or senseless state; insensibility; dullness; torpor; stupidity.

Resistance of the dictates of conscience brings a hardness and *stupefaction* upon it. *South.*

STUPEFAC'TIVE, *a.* Causing insensibility; deadening or blunting the sense of feeling or understanding; narcotic.

Opium hath a *stupefactive* part. *Bacon.*

STU'PEFIER, *n.* [from *stupefy.*] That which causes dullness or stupidity.

STU'PEFY, *v. t.* [Fr. *stupefier;* L. *stupefacio.*]

1. To make stupid; to make dull; to blunt the faculty of perception or understanding; to deprive of sensibility. It is a great sin to attempt to *stupefy* the conscience.

The fumes of passion intoxicate his discerning faculties, as the fumes of drink *stupefy* the brain. *South.*

2. To deprive of material motion.

It is not malleable nor fluent, but *stupefied.* [*Not in use.*] *Bacon.*

STU'PEFYING, *ppr.* Rendering extremely dull or insensible; as the *stupefying* virtues of opium.

[It would be convenient to write *stupifaction, stupifactive*, and place these words after *stupidly.*]

STUPEN'DOUS, *a.* [Low L. *stupendus*, from *stupeo*, to astonish.]

Literally, striking dumb by its magnitude; hence, astonishing; wonderful; amazing; particularly, of astonishing magnitude or elevation; as a *stupendous* pile; a *stupendous* edifice; a *stupendous* mountain; a *stupendous* bridge. *Milton. Dryden.*

STUPEN'DOUSLY, *adv.* In a manner to excite astonishment.

STUPEN'DOUSNESS, *n.* The quality or state of being stupendous or astonishing.

STU'PID, *a.* [Fr. *stupide;* L. *stupidus*, from *stupeo*, to be stupefied, properly to *stop.* See *Stop.*]

1. Very dull; insensible; senseless; wanting in understanding; heavy; sluggish.

O that men should be so *stupid* grown,
As to forsake the living God. *Milton.*
With wild surprise,
A moment *stupid*, motionless he stood. *Thomson.*

2. Dull; heavy; formed without skill or genius.

Observe what loads of *stupid* rhymes
Oppress us in corrupted times. *Swift.*

STUPID'ITY, *n.* [Fr. *stupidité;* L. *stupiditas.*]

Extreme dullness of perception or understanding; insensibility; sluggishness. *Dryden.*

STU'PIDLY, *adv.* With extreme dullness; with suspension or inactivity of understanding; sottishly; absurdly; without the exercise of reason or judgment. *Milton. Dryden.*

STU'PIDNESS, *n.* Stupidity.

STU'POR, *n.* [L.] Great diminution or suspension of sensibility; suppression of sense; numbness; as the *stupor* of a limb. *Arbuthnot.*

2. Intellectual insensibility; moral stupidity; heedlessness or inattention to one's interests.

STU'PRATE, *v. t.* [L. *stupro.*] To ravish; to debauch.

STUPRA'TION, *n.* Rape; violation of chastity by force.

STUR'DILY, *adv.* [from *sturdy.*] Hardily; stoutly; lustily.

STUR'DINESS, *n.* [from *sturdy.*] Stoutness; hardiness; as the *sturdiness* of a school boy. *Locke.*

2. Brutal strength.

STUR'DY, *a.* [G. *störrig*, connected with *storren*, a stub.]

1. Hardy; stout; foolishly obstinate; implying coarseness or rudeness.

This must be done, and I would fain see
Mortal so *sturdy* as to gainsay. *Hudibras.*

A *sturdy* hardened sinner advances to the utmost pitch of impiety with less reluctance than he took the first step. *Atterbury.*

2. Strong; forcible; lusty; as a *sturdy* lout. *Sidney.*

3. Violent; laid on with strength; as *sturdy* strokes. *Spenser.*

4. Stiff; stout; strong; as a *sturdy* oak.

He was not of a delicate contexture, his limbs rather *sturdy* than dainty. *Wotton.*

STUR'DY, *n.* A disease in sheep, marked by dullness and stupor. *Cyc.*

STUR'GEON, *n.* [Fr. *esturgeon;* Sp. *esturion;* It. *storione;* Low L. *sturio;* D. *steur;* G. *stör;* Sw. *stör;* the *stirrer*, one that turns up the mud; G. *stören.*]

A large fish of the genus Acipenser, caught in large rivers. Its flesh is valued for food. *Goldsmith.*

STURK, *n.* [Sax. *styrc.*] A young ox or heifer. [*Scot.*]

STUT'TER, *v. i.* [D. *stotteren;* G. *stottern;* that is, to stop. *Stut* is not used.]

To stammer; to hesitate in uttering words. *Bacon.*

STUT'TERER, *n.* A stammerer.

STUT'TERING, *ppr.* Stammering; speaking with hesitation.

STUT'TERINGLY, *adv.* With stammering.

STȲ, *n.* [Sax. *stige.*] A pen or inclosure for swine.

2. A place of bestial debauchery.

To roll with pleasure in a sensual *sty.* *Milton.*

3. An inflamed tumor on the edge of the eyelid.

STȲ, *v. t.* To shut up in a sty. *Shak.*

STȲ, *v. i.* [Sax. *stigan;* Goth. *steigan.*] To soar; to ascend. [*Not in use.*] [See *Stirrup.*] *Spenser.*

STYCA, *n.* A Saxon copper coin of the lowest value. *Leake.*

STYǴIAN, *a.* [L. *Stygius*, *Styx.*] Pertaining to Styx, fabled by the ancients to be a river of hell over which the shades of the dead passed, or the region of the dead; hence, hellish; infernal.

> At that so sudden blaze, the *Stygian* throng
> Bent their aspect. *Milton.*

STYLE, *n.* [L. *stylus*; D. G. *styl*; It. *stile*; Sp. *estilo*; Fr. *style* or *stile*; Gr. στυλος, a column, a pen or bodkin; from the root of the Teutonic *stellen*, to set or place.]

1. Manner of writing with regard to language, or the choice and arrangement of words; as a harsh *style*; a dry *style*; a tumid or bombastic *style*; a loose *style*; a terse *style*; a laconic or verbose *style*; a flowing *style*; a lofty *style*; an elegant *style*; an epistolary *style*. The character of *style* depends chiefly on a happy selection and arrangement of words.

> Proper words in proper places, make the true definition of *style*. *Swift.*

> Let some lord but own the happy lines,
> How the wit brightens and the *style* refines! *Pope.*

2. Manner of speaking appropriate to particular characters; or in general, the character of the language used.

> No *style* is held for base, where love well named is. *Sidney.*

> According to the usual *style* of dedications. *Middleton.*

So we say, a person addresses another in a *style* of haughtiness, in a *style* of rebuke.

3. Mode of painting; any manner of painting which is characteristic or peculiar.

> The ornamental *style* also possesses its own peculiar merit. *Reynolds.*

4. A particular character of music; as a grave *style*.

5. Title; appellation; as the *style* of majesty.

> Propitious hear our pray'r,
> Whether the *style* of Titan please thee more— *Pope.*

6. Course of writing. [*Not in use.*] *Dryden.*

7. *Style of court*, is properly the practice observed by any court in its way of proceeding. *Ayliffe.*

8. In *popular use*, manner; form; as, the entertainment was prepared in excellent *style.*

9. A pointed instrument formerly used in writing on tables of wax; an instrument of surgery.

10. Something with a sharp point; a graver; the pin of a dial; written also *stile*.

11. In *botany*, the middle portion of the pistil, connecting the stigma with the germ; sometimes called the *shaft*. The *styles* of plants are capillary, filiform, cylindric, subulate, or clavate. *Martyn.*

12. In *chronology*, a mode of reckoning time, with regard to the Julian and Gregorian calendar. Style is *Old* or *New*. The *Old* Style follows the Julian manner of computing the months and days, or the calendar as established by Julius Cesar, in which the year consists of 365 days and 6 hours. This is something more than 11 minutes too much, and in the course of time, between Cesar and pope Gregory XIII. this surplus amounted to 11 days. Gregory reformed the calendar by retrenching 11 days; this reformation was adopted by act of parliament in Great Britain in 1751, by which act eleven days in September, 1752, were retrenched, and the 3d day was reckoned the 14th. This mode of reckoning is called *New* Style.

STYLE, *v. t.* To call; to name; to denominate; to give a title to in addressing. The emperor of Russia is *styled* autocrat; the king of Great Britain is *styled* defender of the faith.

STY'LED, *pp.* Named; denominated; called.

STY'LET, *n.* [from *style.*] A small poniard or dagger. *Encyc.*

STY'LIFORM, *a.* [*style* and *form.*] Like a style, pin or pen.

STY'LING, *ppr.* Calling; denominating.

STY'LITE, *n.* [Gr. στυλος, a column.] In *ecclesiastical history*, the Stylites were a sect of solitaries, who stood motionless on columns or pillars for the exercise of their patience.

STYLOBA'TION, *n.* The pedestal of a column.

STY'LOID, *a.* [L. *stylus* and Gr. ειδος.] Having some resemblance to a style or pen; as the *styloid* process of the temporal bone. *Encyc.*

STYP'TIC, STYP'TICAL, } *a.* [Fr. *styptique*; L. *stypticus*; Gr. στυπτικος; from the root of L. *stipo*, Eng. *stop.*]
That stops bleeding; having the quality of restraining hemorrhage.

STYP'TIC, *n.* A medicine which has the quality of stopping hemorrhage or discharges of blood. Styptics have the quality of astringents, but the word *styptic* is used in a sense different from that of *astringent*, and much more limited. *Styptics* are usually external applications for restraining discharges of blood; *astringents* are usually internal applications for stopping bleeding, or for strengthening the solids. Astringent is the general term; styptic a subdivision of it.

STYPTIC'ITY, *n.* The quality of stanching blood, or stopping hemorrhage.

STYTH'Y, *v. t.* To forge on an anvil. [See *Stithy.*]

SUABIL'ITY, *n.* Liability to be sued; the state of being subject by law to civil process. [*Not much used.*]

SU'ABLE, *a.* [from *sue.*] That may be sued; subject by law to be called to answer in court.

SUADE, for *persuade*, is not in use.

SUAGE, for *assuage*, is not in use.

SU'ANT, *a.* [Fr. *suivant*, from *suivre*, to follow.]
Even; uniform; spread equally over the surface. [*New England, but local.*]

SUA'SIBLE, *a.* [L. *suadeo.*] That may be persuaded or easily persuaded.

SUA'SION, *n.* *sua'zhun.* The act of persuading. [See *Persuade.*]

SUA'SIVE, *a.* [L. *suadeo.*] Having power to persuade. *South.*

SUA'SORY, *a.* [L. *suasorius.*] Tending to persuade; having the quality of convincing and drawing by argument or reason. *Hopkins.*

SUAV'ITY, *n.* [L. *suavitas*; Fr. *suavité*; It. *soavità*; Sp. *suavidad*; from L. *suavis*, sweet.]

1. Sweetness, in a literal sense. [*Not in use.*] *Brown.*

2. Sweetness, in a figurative sense; that which is to the mind what sweetness is to the tongue; agreeableness; softness; pleasantness; as *suavity* of manners; *suavity* of language, conversation or address.

SUB, a Latin preposition, denoting *under* or *below*, used in English as a prefix, to express a subordinate degree. Before *f* and *p* it is changed into those letters, as in *suffer* and *suppose*; and before *m*, into that letter, as in *summon.*

SUBAC'ID, *a.* [*sub* and *acid.*] Moderately acid or sour; as a *subacid* juice. *Arbuthnot.*

SUBAC'ID, *n.* A substance moderately acid.

SUBAC'RID, *a.* [*sub* and *acrid.*] Moderately sharp, pungent or acrid. *Floyer.*

SUBACT', *v. t.* [L. *subactus*, *subago*; *sub* and *ago.*]
To reduce; to subdue. [*Not in use.*] *Bacon.*

SUBAC'TION, *n.* The act of reducing to any state, as of mixing two bodies completely, or of beating them to a powder. *Bacon.*

SUBAĠITA'TION, *n.* [L. *subagitatio.*] Carnal knowledge. *Ch. Relig. Appeal.*

SU'BAH, *n.* In India, a province or viceroyship.

SU'BAHDAR, *n.* In India, a viceroy, or the governor of a province; also, a native of India, who ranks as captain in the European companies.

SU'BAHSHIP, *n.* The jurisdiction of a subahdar.

SUBAL'TERN, *a.* [Fr. *subalterne*; L. *sub* and *alternus.*]
Inferior; subordinate; that in different respects is both superior and inferior; as a *subaltern* officer. It is used chiefly of military officers.

SUBAL'TERN, *n.* A subordinate officer in an army or military body. It is applied to officers below the rank of captain.

SUBALTERN'ATE, *a.* [supra.] Successive; succeeding by turns. *Hooker.*

SUBALTERNA'TION, *n.* State of inferiority or subjection.

2. Act of succeeding by course.

SUBAQUAT'IC, SUBA'QUEOUS, } *a.* [L. *sub* and *aqua*, water.] Being under water, or beneath the surface of water. *Darwin.*

SUBAS'TRAL, *a.* [*sub* and *astral.*] Beneath the stars or heavens; terrestrial. *Warburton.*

SUBASTRIN'GENT, *a.* Astringent in a small degree.

SUBAX'ILLARY, *a.* [L. *sub* and *axilla*, the arm-pit.]
Placed under the axil or angle formed by the branch of a plant with the stem, or by a leaf with the branch. *Darwin.*

SUB-BE'ADLE, *n.* [*sub* and *beadle.*] An inferior or under beadle.

SUB-BRIGADIE'R, *n.* An officer in the horse guards, who ranks as cornet. *Encyc.*

SUBCARBURETED, *a.* Carbureted in an inferior degree; or consisting of one prime of carbon and two of hydrogen. *Ure.*

SUB-CELES'TIAL, *a.* [*sub* and *celestial.*] Being beneath the heavens; as *sub-celestial* glories. *Glanville.*

SUB-CEN'TRAL, *a.* Being under the center. *Say.*

SUB-CH'ANTER, *n.* [*sub* and *chanter.*] An under chanter; a deputy of the precentor of a cathedral. *Johnson.*

SUBCLA'VIAN, *a.* [L. *sub* and *clavis*, a key.]

Situated under the clavicle or collar bone; as the *subclavian* arteries.

SUB-COMMIT'TEE, *n.* [*sub* and *committee.*]

An under committee; a part or division of a committee.

SUB-CONSTELLA'TION, *n.* A subordinate constellation. *Brown.*

SUB-CONTRACT'ED, *a.* [*sub* and *contracted.*]

Contracted after a former contract. *Shak.*

SUB-CON'TRARY, *a.* [*sub* and *contrary.*] Contrary in an inferior degree. In *geometry*, when two similar triangles are so placed as to have a common angle at their vertex, and yet their bases not parallel. *Cyc.*

SUBCORD'ATE, *a.* [L. *sub* and *cor*, the heart.] In shape somewhat like a heart. *Martyn.*

SUBCOS'TAL, *a.* [L. *sub* and *costa*, a rib.]

The *subcostal* muscles are the internal intercostal muscles. *Winslow. Cyc.*

SUBCUTA'NEOUS, *a.* [*sub* and *cutaneous*; L. *cutis*, skin.] Situated under the skin.

SUBCUTIC'ULAR, *a.* [L. *sub* and *cuticula*, cuticle.]

Being under the cuticle or scarf-skin. *Darwin.*

SUBDE'ACON, *n.* [*sub* and *deacon.*] An under deacon; a deacon's servant, in the Romish church. *Ayliffe.*

SUBDE'ACONRY, } *n.* The order and office of subdeacon in the catholic church.
SUBDE'ACONSHIP, }

SUBDE'AN, *n.* [*sub* and *dean.*] An under dean; a dean's substitute or vicegerent. *Ayliffe.*

SUBDE'ANERY, *n.* The office and rank of subdean.

SUBDEC'UPLE, *a.* [L. *sub* and *decuplus.*] Containing one part of ten. *Johnson.*

SUBDENT'ED, *a.* [*sub* and *dent.*] Indented beneath. *Encyc.*

SUBDEPOS'IT, *n.* That which is deposited beneath something else. *Schoolcraft.*

SUBDERISO'RIOUS, *a.* [L. *sub* and *derisor.*] Ridiculing with moderation or delicacy. [*Not in use.*] *More.*

SUBDITI''TIOUS, *a.* [L. *subdititius*, from *subdo*, to substitute.]

Put secretly in the place of something else. [*Little used.*]

SUBDIVERS'IFY, *v. t.* [*sub* and *diversify.*] To diversify again what is already diversified. [*Little used.*] *Hale.*

SUBDIVI'DE, *v. t.* [*sub* and *divide.*] To divide a part of a thing into more parts; to part into smaller divisions.

> In the rise of eight in tones, are two half tones; so as if you divide the tones equally, the eight is but seven whole and equal notes; and if you *subdivide* that into half notes, as in the stops of a lute, it makes the number thirteen. *Bacon.*

> The progenies of Cham and Japhet swarmed into colonies, and those colonies were *subdivided* into many others— *Dryden.*

SUBDIVI'DE, *v. i.* To be subdivided.

SUBDIVI'DED, *pp.* Divided again or into smaller parts.

SUBDIVI'DING, *ppr.* Dividing into smaller parts that which is already divided.

SUBDIVI''SION, *n.* The act of subdividing or separating a part into smaller parts. *Watts.*

2. The part of a thing made by subdividing; the part of a larger part.

> In the decimal table, the *subdivisions* of the cubit, as span, palm, and digit, are deduced from the shorter cubit. *Arbuthnot.*

SUB'DOLOUS, *a.* [L. *subdolus*; *sub* and *dolus*, deceit.]

Sly; crafty; cunning; artful; deceitful. [*Little used.*]

SUBDOM'INANT, *n.* In music, the fourth note above the tonic, being under the dominant.

SUBDU'ABLE, *a.* That may be subdued. *Ward.*

SUBDU'AL, *n.* [from *subdue.*] The act of subduing. *Warburton.*

SUBDU'CE, } *v. t.* [L. *subduco*; *sub* and *duco*, to draw.] To withdraw; to take away.
SUBDUCT', }

> Or from my side *subducting*, took perhaps More than enough. *Milton.*

2. To subtract by arithmetical operation.

> If out of that infinite multitude of antecedent generations we should *subduct* ten— *Hale.*

SUBDUC'TION, *n.* The act of taking away or withdrawing. *Hale.*

2. Arithmetical subtraction. *Hale.*

SUBDUE, *v. t.* *subdu'.* [This is a compound word, and the latter component part is contracted from some word in Class *Db* or *Dg.*]

1. To conquer by force or the exertion of superior power, and bring into permanent subjection; to reduce under dominion. Thus Cesar *subdued* the Gauls; Augustus *subdued* Egypt; the English *subdued* Canada. Subduing implies *conquest* or *vanquishing*, but it implies also more permanence of subjection to the conquering power, than either of these words.

> I will *subdue* all thine enemies. 1 Chron. xvii.

2. To oppress; to crush; to sink; to overpower so as to disable from further resistance.

> Nothing could have *subdu'd* nature
> To such a lowness, but his unkind daughters. *Shak.*

> If aught were worthy to *subdue*
> The soul of man. *Milton.*

3. To tame; to break by conquering a refractory temper or evil passions; to render submissive; as, to *subdue* a stubborn child.
4. To conquer; to reduce to mildness; as, to *subdue* the temper or passions.
5. To overcome by persuasion or other mild means; as, to *subdue* opposition by argument or intreaties.
6. To overcome; to conquer; to captivate; as by charms.
7. To soften; to melt; to reduce to tenderness; as, to *subdue* ferocity by tears.
8. To overcome; to overpower and destroy the force of; as, medicines *subdue* a fever.
9. To make mellow; to break; as land; also, to destroy, as weeds.

SUBDU'ED, *pp.* Conquered and reduced to subjection; oppressed; crushed; tamed; softened.

SUBDUEMENT, *n.* Conquest. [*Not used.*] *Shak.*

SUBDU'ER, *n.* One who conquers and brings into subjection; a tamer. *Spenser.*

2. That which subdues or destroys the force of. *Arbuthnot.*

SUBDU'ING, *ppr.* Vanquishing and reducing to subjection; crushing; destroying the power of resistance; softening.

SUB'DUPLE, *a.* [L. *sub* and *duplus*, double.] Containing one part of two. *Wilkins.*

SUBDU'PLICATE, *a.* [*sub* and *duplicate.*] Having the ratio of the square roots. *Cyc.*

SUBE'QUAL, *a.* [*sub* and *equal.*] Nearly equal. *Martyn.*

SU'BERATE, *n.* [L. *suber*, cork.] A salt formed by the suberic acid in combination with a base. *Chimistry.*

SU'BERIC, *a.* Pertaining to cork, or extracted from it; as *suberic* acid. *Chimistry.*

SUB'EROSE, *a.* [L. *sub* and *erosus*, gnawed.]

In *botany*, having the appearance of being gnawed; appearing as if a little eaten or gnawed. *Martyn.*

SU'BEROUS, *a.* [from L. *suber*, cork.] Corky; soft and elastic.

SUBFUSC', *a.* [L. *subfuscus*; *sub* and *fuscus.*]

Duskish; moderately dark; brownish; tawny. *Tatler.*

SUBGLOB'ULAR, *a.* Having a form approaching to globular. *Say.*

SUBHASTA'TION, *n.* [L. *sub hasta*, under the spear.]

A public sale or auction, so called from the Roman practice. *Burnet.*

SUBHYDROSULPH'URET, *n.* A compound of sulphureted hydrogen with a base, in a less proportion than in hydrosulphuret.

SUBINDICA'TION, *n.* [L. *sub* and *indico.*] The act of indicating by signs. *Barrow.*

SUBINFEUDA'TION, *n.* [*sub* and *infeudation.* See *Feud.*]

1. In *law*, the act of enfeoffing by a tenant or feoffee, who holds lands of the crown; the act of a greater baron, who grants land or a smaller manor to an inferior person. By 34 Edward III. all *subinfeudations* previous to the reign of king Edward I., were confirmed. *Blackstone.*
2. Under tenancy.

> The widow is immediate tenant to the heir, by a kind of *subinfeudation* or under tenancy. *Blackstone.*

SUBINGRES'SION, *n.* [L. *sub* and *ingressus.*]

Secret entrance. [*Not in use.*] *Boyle.*

SUBITA'NEOUS, *a.* [L. *subitaneus.*] Sudden; hasty.

SUB'ITANY, *a.* Sudden. [*Not in use.*]

SUBJA'CENT, *a.* [L. *subjacens*; *sub* and *jaceo*, to lie.] Lying under or below.

2. Being in a lower situation, though not directly beneath. A man placed on a hill, surveys the *subjacent* plain.

SUB'JECT, *a.* [L. *subjectus*, from *subjicio*; *sub* and *jacio*, to throw, that is, to drive or force; It. *suggetto*; Sp. *sujeto.*]

1. Placed or situate under.

—The eastern tower
Whose height commands, as *subject*, all the vale,
To see the fight. *Shak.*

2. Being under the power and dominion of another; as, Jamaica is *subject* to Great Britain.

Esau was never *subject* to Jacob. *Locke.*

3. Exposed; liable from extraneous causes; as a country *subject* to extreme heat or cold.

4. Liable from inherent causes; prone; disposed.

All human things are *subject* to decay. *Dryden.*

5. Being that on which any thing operates, whether intellectual or material; as the *subject*-matter of a discourse. *Dryden.*

6. Obedient. Tit. iii. Col. ii.

SUB'JE€T, *n.* [L. *subjectus; Fr. sujet;* It. *suggetto.*]

1. One that owes allegiance to a sovereign and is governed by his laws. The natives of Great Britain are *subjects* of the British government. The natives of the United States, and naturalized foreigners, are *subjects* of the federal government. Men in free governments, are *subjects* as well as citizens; as citizens, they enjoy rights and franchises; as *subjects,* they are bound to obey the laws.

The *subject* must obey his prince, because God commands it, and human laws require it. *Swift.*

2. That on which any mental operation is performed; that which is treated or handled; as a *subject* of discussion before the legislature; a *subject* of negotiation.

This *subject* for heroic song pleas'd me. *Milton.*

The *subject* of a proposition is that concerning which any thing is affirmed or denied. *Watts.*

3. That on which any physical operation is performed; as a *subject* for dissection or amputation.

4. That in which any thing inheres or exists.

Anger is certainly a kind of baseness, as it appears well in the weakness of those *subjects* in whom it reigns. *Bacon.*

5. The person who is treated of; the hero of a piece.

Authors of biography are apt to be prejudiced in favor of their *subject.* *Middleton.*

6. In *grammar,* the nominative case to a verb passive.

SUBJE€T', *v. t.* To bring under the power or dominion of. Alexander *subjected* a great part of the civilized world to his dominion.

Firmness of mind that *subjects* every gratification of sense to the rule of right reason— *Middleton.*

2. To put under or within the power of.

In one short view *subjected* to our eye,
Gods, emperors, heroes, sages, beauties lie. *Pope.*

3. To enslave; to make obnoxious.

He is the most *subjected,* the most enslaved, who is so in his understanding. *Locke.*

4. To expose; to make liable. Credulity *subjects* a person to impositions.

5. To submit; to make accountable.

God is not bound to *subject* his ways of operation to the scrutiny of our thoughts— *Locke.*

6. To make subservient.

—*Subjected* to his service angel wings. *Milton.*

7. To cause to undergo; as, to *subject* a substance to a white heat; to *subject* it to a rigid test.

SUBJE€T'ED, *pp.* Reduced to the dominion of another; enslaved; exposed; submitted; made to undergo.

SUBJE€T'ING, *ppr.* Reducing to submission; enslaving; exposing; submitting; causing to undergo.

SUBJE€'TION, *n.* The act of subduing; the act of vanquishing and bringing under the dominion of another.

The conquest of the kingdom and the *subjection* of the rebels— *Hale.*

2. The state of being under the power, control and government of another. The safety of life, liberty and property depends on our *subjection* to the laws. The isles of the West Indies are held in *subjection* to the powers of Europe. Our appetites and passions should be in *subjection* to our reason, and our will should be in entire *subjection* to the laws of God.

SUBJE€T'IVE, *a.* Relating to the subject, as opposed to the *object.*

Certainty—is distinguished into objective and *subjective;* objective, is when the proposition is certainly true of itself; and *subjective,* is when we are certain of the truth of it. *Watts.*

SUBJE€T'IVELY, *adv.* In relation to the subject. *Pearson.*

SUBJOIN', *v. t.* [*sub* and *join;* L. *subjungo.*] To add at the end; to add after something else has been said or written; as, to *subjoin* an argument or reason. [*It is never used in a literal physical sense, to express the joining of material things.*]

SUBJOIN'ED, *pp.* Added after something else said or written.

SUBJOIN'ING, *ppr.* Adding after something else said or written.

SUB'JUGATE, *v. t.* [Fr. *subjuguer;* L. *subjugo; sub* and *jugo,* to yoke. See *Yoke.*]
To subdue and bring under the yoke of power or dominion; to conquer by force and compel to submit to the government or absolute control of another.

He *subjugated* a king, and called him his vassal. *Baker.*

[*Subjugate* differs from *subject* only in implying a reduction to a more tyrannical or arbitrary sway; but they are often used as synonymous.]

SUB'JUGATED, *pp.* Reduced to the absolute control of another.

SUB'JUGATING, *ppr.* Conquering and bringing under the absolute power of another.

SUBJUGA'TION, *n.* The act of subduing and bringing under the power or absolute control of another.

SUBJUN€'TION, *n.* The act of subjoining, or state of being subjoined. *Clarke.*

SUBJUN€'TIVE, *a.* [L. *subjunctivus;* Fr. *subjonctif;* It. *soggiunto.* See *Subjoin.*]

1. Subjoined or added to something before said or written.

2. In *grammar,* designating a form of verbs which follow other verbs or words expressing condition, hypothesis or contingency; as, "veni *ut* me *videas,*" I came that you may see me; "*Si fecerint* æquum," if they should do what is just.

3. *Subjunctive* is often used as a noun, denoting the subjunctive mode.

SUB'LANATE, *a.* [L. *sub* and *lana,* wool.] In *botany,* somewhat woolly.

SUBLAPSA'RIAN, } *a.* [L. *sub* and *lapsus,*
SUBLAPS'ARY, } fall.] Done after the apostasy of Adam. [See the Noun.]

SUBLAPSA'RIAN, *n.* One who maintains the sublapsarian doctrine, that the sin of Adam's apostasy being imputed to all his posterity, God in compassion decreed to send his Son to rescue a great number from their lost state, and to accept of his obedience and death on their account. The decree of reprobation, according to the *sublapsarians,* is nothing but a preterition or non-election of persons, whom God left as he found, involved in the guilt of Adam's transgression without any personal sin, when he withdrew some others as guilty as they. *Hammond.*

Sublapsarian is opposed to *supralapsarian.*

SUBLA'TION, *n.* [L. *sublatio.*] The act of taking or carrying away. *Bp. Hall.*

SUBLET', *v. t.* [*sub* and *let.*] To underlet; to lease, as a lessee to another person. [*Unusual.*] *Smollett.*

SUBLEVA'TION, *n.* [L. *sublevo.*] The act of raising on high.

SUBLIEUTEN'ANT, *n.* An officer in the royal regiment of artillery and fusileers, in which are no ensigns, and who is the same as second lieutenant. *Eng.*

SUBLIGA'TION, *n.* [L. *subligo; sub* and *ligo,* to bind.]
The act of binding underneath.

SUBLI'MABLE, *a.* [from *sublime.*] That may be sublimated; capable of being raised by heat into vapor, and again condensed by cold.

SUBLI'MABLENESS, *n.* The quality of being sublimable.

SUB'LIMATE, *v. t.* [from *sublime.*] To bring a solid substance, as camphor or sulphur, into the state of vapor by heat, which on cooling, returns again to the solid state. [See *Sublimation.*]

2. To refine and exalt; to highthen; to elevate.

And as his actions rose, so raise they still their vein,
In words whose weight best suits a *sublimated* strain. *Dryden.*

SUB'LIMATE, *n.* The product of a sublimation. *Corrosive sublimate* is the muriate of mercury when it has undergone sublimation. It is one of the most virulent of the mineral poisons.

Blue sublimate, is a preparation of mercury with flower of brimstone and sal ammoniac; *used in painting.*

SUB'LIMATE, *a.* Brought into a state of vapor by heat and again condensed, as solid substances.

SUB'LIMATED, *pp.* Brought into a state of vapor by heat, as a solid substance; refined.

SUB'LIMATING, *ppr.* Converting into the state of vapor by heat, and condensing; as solid substances.

SUBLIMA'TION, *n.* The operation of bringing a solid substance into the state of vapor by heat, and condensing it again into a solid by cold. Sublimation bears the same relation to a solid, that distillation does to a liquid. Both processes purify the substances to which they are severally applied, by separating them from the fixed and grosser matters with which they are connected.

2. Exaltation; elevation; act of highthening or improving.

Religion, the perfection, refinement and *sublimation* of morality. *South.*

SUBLI'ME, *a.* [L. *sublimis;* Fr. It. Sp. *sublime.*]

1. High in place; exalted aloft.

Sublime on these a tow'r of steel is rear'd. *Dryden.*

2. High in excellence; exalted by nature; elevated.

Can it be that souls *sublime*
Return to visit our terrestrial clime? *Dryden.*

3. High in style or sentiment; lofty; grand.

Easy in style thy work, in sense *sublime.* *Prior.*

4. Elevated by joy; as *sublime* with expectation. *Milton.*

5. Lofty of mein; elevated in manner.

His fair large front and eye *sublime* declar'd
Absolute rule. *Milton.*

SUBLI'ME, *n.* A grand or lofty style; a style that expresses lofty conceptions.

The *sublime* rises from the nobleness of thoughts, the magnificence of words, or the harmonious and lively turn of the phrase— *Addison.*

SUBLI'ME, *v. t.* To sublimate, which see.

2. To raise on high. *Denham.*

3. To exalt; to highten; to improve.

The sun—
Which not alone the southern wit *sublimes,*
But ripens spirits in cold northern climes. *Pope.*

SUBLI'ME, *v. i.* To be brought or changed into a state of vapor by heat, and then condensed by cold, as a solid substance.

Particles of antimony which will not *sublime* alone. *Newton.*

SUBLI'MED, *pp.* Brought into a state of vapor by heat, and when cooled, changed to a solid state.

SUBLI'MELY, *adv.* With elevated conceptions; loftily; as, to express one's self *sublimely.*

In English lays, and all *sublimely* great,
Thy Homer charms with all his ancient heat. *Parnell.*

SUBLI'MENESS, *n.* Loftiness of style or sentiment; sublimity.

SUBLI'MING, *ppr.* Sublimating; exalting.

SUBLIM'ITY, *n.* [Fr. *sublimité;* L. *sublimitas.*]

1. Elevation of place; lofty highth.

2. Highth in excellence; loftiness of nature or character; moral grandeur; as God's incomprehensible *sublimity.* *Raleigh.*

The *sublimity* of the character of Christ owes nothing to his historians. *Buckminster.*

3. In *oratory* and *composition,* lofty conceptions, or such conceptions expressed in corresponding language; loftiness of sentiment or style.

Milton's distinguishing excellence lies in the *sublimity* of his thoughts. *Addison.*

SUBLIN'GUAL, *a.* [L. *sub* and *lingua,* the tongue.]

Situated under the tongue; as the *sublingual* glands. *Coxe.*

SUBLU'NAR, } *a.* [Fr. *sublunaire;* L. *sub*
SUB'LUNARY, } and *luna,* the moon.]

Literally, beneath the moon; but *sublunary,* which is the word chiefly used, denotes merely terrestrial, earthly, pertaining to this world.

All things *sublunary* are subject to change. *Dryden.*

SUBLUXA'TION, *n.* [*sub* and *luxation.*]

In *surgery,* a violent sprain; also, an incomplete dislocation.

SUBMARINE, *a.* [L. *sub* and *marinus,* from *mare,* the sea.]

Being, acting or growing under water in the sea; as *submarine* navigators; *submarine* plants.

SUBMAX'ILLARY, *a.* [L. *sub* and *maxilla,* the jaw-bone.]

Situated under the jaw. *Med. Repos.*

The *submaxillary glands* are two salivary glands, situated, one on either side, immediately within the angle of the lower jaw. *Wistar.*

SUBME'DIANT, *n.* In *music,* the sixth note, or middle note between the octave and subdominant. *Busby.*

SUBMERGE, *v. t. submerj'.* [L. *submergo; sub* and *mergo,* to plunge.]

1. To put under water; to plunge.

2. To cover or overflow with water; to drown.

So half my Egypt was *submerg'd.* *Shak.*

SUBMERGE, *v. i. submerj'.* To plunge under water, as swallows.

SUBMERG'ED, *pp.* Put under water; overflowed.

SUBMERG'ING, *ppr.* Putting under water; overflowing.

SUBMERSE, } *a. submers'.* [L. *submer-*
SUBMERS'ED, } *sus.*] Being or growing under water, as the leaves of aquatic plants.

SUBMER'SION, *n.* [Fr. from L. *submersus.*]

1. The act of putting under water or causing to be overflowed; as the *submersion* of an isle or tract of land. *Hale.*

2. The act of plunging under water; the act of drowning.

SUBMIN'ISTER, } *v. t.* [L. *subministro;*
SUBMIN'ISTRATE, } *sub* and *ministro.*]

To supply; to afford. [*Not in use.*] *Hale.*

SUBMIN'ISTER, *v. i.* To subserve; to be useful to.

Our passions—*subminister* to the best and worst of purposes. *L'Estrange.*

[*Not in use.*] [See *Minister* and *Administer.*]

SUBMIN'ISTRANT, *a.* Subservient; serving in subordination. [*Not in use.*] *Bacon.*

SUBMINISTRA'TION, *n.* The act of furnishing or supplying. [*Not in use.*] *Wotton.*

SUBMISS', *a.* [L. *submissus, submitto.*] Submissive; humble; obsequious. [*Rarely used, and in poetry only.*] *Milton.*

SUBMIS'SION, *n.* [L. *submissio,* from *submitto;* Fr. *soumission;* It. *sommessione.*]

1. The act of submitting; the act of yielding to power or authority; surrender of the person and power to the control or government of another.

Submission, dauphin! 'tis a mere French word;
We English warriors wot not what it means. *Shak.*

2. Acknowledgment of inferiority or dependence; humble or suppliant behavior.

In all *submission* and humility,
York doth present himself unto your highness. *Shak.*

3. Acknowledgment of a fault; confession of error.

Be not as extreme in *submission,* as in offense. *Shak.*

4. Obedience; compliance with the commands or laws of a superior. *Submission* of children to their parents is an indispensable duty.

5. Resignation; a yielding of one's will to the will or appointment of a superior without murmuring. Entire and cheerful *submission* to the will of God is a christian duty of prime excellence.

SUBMISS'IVE, *a.* Yielding to the will or power of another; obedient.

2. Humble; acknowledging one's inferiority; testifying one's submission.

Her at his feet *submissive* in distress,
He thus with peaceful words uprais'd. *Milton.*

SUBMISS'IVELY, *adv.* With submission; with acknowledgment of inferiority; humbly.

The goddess,
Soft in her tone, *submissively* replies. *Dryden.*

SUBMISS'IVENESS, *n.* A submissive temper or disposition.

2. Humbleness; acknowledgment of inferiority.

3. Confession of fault.

Frailty gets pardon by *submissiveness.* *Herbert.*

SUBMISS'LY, *adv.* Humbly; with submission. [*Little used.*] *Taylor.*

SUBMISS'NESS, *n.* Humbleness; obedience. [*Little used.*] *Burton.*

SUBMIT', *v. t.* [L. *submitto; sub,* under, and *mitto,* to send; Fr. *soumettre;* It. *sommettere;* Sp. *someter.*]

1. To let down; to cause to sink or lower.

Sometimes the hill *submits* itself a while. *Dryden.*

[*This use of the word is nearly or wholly obsolete.*]

2. To yield, resign or surrender to the power, will or authority of another; *with the reciprocal pronoun.*

Return to thy mistress, and *submit thyself* under her hand. Gen. xvi.

Wives, *submit yourselves* to your own husbands. Eph. v.

Submit yourselves to every ordinance of man. 1 Pet. ii.

3. To refer; to leave or commit to the discretion or judgment of another; as, to *submit* a controversy to arbitrators; to *submit* a question to the court.

SUBMIT', *v. i.* To surrender; to yield one's person to the power of another; to give up resistance. The enemy *submitted.*

The revolted provinces presently *submitted.* *Middleton.*

2. To yield one's opinion to the opinion or authority of another. On hearing the opinion of the court, the counsel *submitted* without further argument.

3. To be subject; to acquiesce in the authority of another.

To thy husband's will
Thine shall *submit*— *Milton.*

4. To be submissive; to yield without murmuring.

Our religion requires us—to *submit* to pain, disgrace and even death. *Rogers.*

SUBMIT'TED, *pp.* Surrendered; resigned; yielded; referred.

SUBMIT'TER, *n.* One who submits.

SUBMIT'TING, *ppr.* Surrendering; resigning; yielding; referring to another for decision.

SUBMUL'TIPLE, *n.* [See *Multiply.*] A number or quantity which is contained in another a certain number of times, or is an aliquot part of it. Thus 7 is the *submultiple* of 56, being contained in it eight times. The word is used as an adjective also; as a *submultiple* number; *submultiple* ratio. *Cyc.*

SUBNAS'CENT, *a.* [L. *sub* and *nascor.*] Growing underneath.

SUBNECT', *v. t.* [L. *subnecto.*] To tie, buckle or fasten beneath. [*Not in use.*] *Pope.*

SUBNOR'MAL, *n.* [L. *sub* and *norma*, a rule.]
A subperpendicular, or a line under the perpendicular to a curve.

SUBNU'DE, *a.* [L. *sub* and *nudus*, naked.] In *botany*, almost naked or bare of leaves. *Lee.*

SUBOBSCU'RELY, *adv.* Somewhat obscurely or darkly. *Donne.*

SUBOCCIP'ITAL, *a.* Being under the occiput; as the *suboccipital* nerves. *Parr.*

SUBOC'TAVE, } *a.* [L. *sub* and *octavus* or
SUBOC'TUPLE, } *octuple.*] Containing one part of eight. *Wilkins. Arbuthnot.*

SUBOC'ULAR, *a.* [L. *sub* and *oculus.*] Being under the eye. *Barrow.*

SUBORBIC'ULAR, } *a.* [L. *sub* and *orbic-*
SUBORBIC'ULATE, } *ulatus.*] Almost orbiculate or orbicular; nearly circular. *Martyn. Say.*

SUBOR'DINACY, *n.* [See *Subordinate.*]
1. The state of being subordinate or subject to control; as, to bring the imagination to act in *subordinacy* to reason. *Spectator.*
2. Series of subordination. [*Little used.*] *Temple.*

SUBOR'DINANCY, *n.* [Not in use. See *Subordinacy.*]

SUBOR'DINATE, *a.* [L. *sub* and *ordinatus*, from *ordo*, order.]
1. Inferior in order, in nature, in dignity, in power, importance, &c.; as *subordinate* officers.

It was *subordinate*, not enslaved, to the understanding. *South.*

2. Descending in a regular series.

The several kinds and *subordinate* species of each, are easily distinguished. *Woodward*

SUBOR'DINATE, *v. t.* To place in an order or rank below something else; to make or consider as of less value or importance; as, to *subordinate* one creature to another; to *subordinate* temporal to spiritual things.
2. To make subject; as, to *subordinate* the passions to reason. *Scott.*

SUBOR'DINATED, *pp.* Placed in an inferior rank; considered as of inferior importance; subjected.

SUBOR'DINATELY, *adv.* In a lower rank or of inferior importance.
2. In a series regularly descending. *Decay of Piety*

SUBORDINA'TION, *n.* [Fr. See *Subordinate.*]
1. The state of being inferior to another; inferiority of rank or dignity.
2. A series regularly descending.

Natural creatures having a local *subordination*— *Holiday.*

3. Place of rank among inferiors.

—Persons, who in their several *subordinations* would be obliged to follow the example of their superiors. *Swift.*

4. Subjection; state of being under control or government.

The most glorious military achievments would be a calamity and a curse, if purchased at the expense of habits of *subordination* and love of order. *J. Evarts.*

SUBORN', *v. t.* [Fr. *suborner*; It. *subornare*; Sp. *subornar*; L. *suborno*; *sub* and *orno*. The sense of *orno*, in this word, and the primary sense, is to *put on*, to furnish. Hence *suborno*, to furnish privately, that is, to bribe.]
1. In *law*, to procure a person to take such a false oath as constitutes perjury. *Blackstone.*
2. To procure privately or by collusion.

Or else thou art *suborn'd* against his honor. *Shak.*

3. To procure by indirect means.

Those who by despair *suborn* their death. *Dryden.*

SUBORNA'TION, *n.* [Fr.] In *law*, the crime of procuring a person to take such a false oath as constitutes perjury. *Blackstone.*
2. The crime of procuring one to do a criminal or bad action. *Shak. Swift.*

SUBORN'ED, *pp.* Procured to take a false oath, or to do a bad action.

SUBORN'ER, *n.* One who procures another to take a false oath, or to do a bad action.

SUBORN'ING, *ppr.* Procuring one to take a false oath, or to do a criminal action.

SUBO'VATE, *a.* [L. *sub* and *ovatus*, from *ovum*, an egg.]
Almost ovate; nearly in the form of an egg. *Martyn.*

SUBPE'NA, *n.* [L. *sub* and *pœna*, pain, penalty.]
A writ commanding the attendance in court of the person on whom it is served; as witnesses, &c.

SUBPE'NA, *v. t.* To serve with a writ of subpena; to command attendance in court by a legal writ.

SUBPERPENDIC'ULAR, *n.* [*sub* and *perpendicular.*]
A subnormal, which see.

SUBPET'IOLATE, *a.* [*sub* and *petiole.*] In *botany*, having a very short petiole. *Martyn.*

SUBPRI'OR, *n.* [*sub* and *prior.*] The vicegerent of a prior; a claustral officer who assists the prior. *South. Cyc.*

SUBPUR'CHASER, *n.* A purchaser who buys of a purchaser.

SUBQUAD'RATE. *a.* Nearly square. *Say.*

SUBQUAD'RUPLE, *a.* [*sub* and *quadruple.*] Containing one part of four; as *subquadruple* proportion. *Wilkins.*

SUBQUIN'QUEFID, *a.* [*sub* and *quinquefid.*] Almost quinquefid. *Lee.*

SUBQUIN'TUPLE, *a.* [*sub* and *quintuple.*] Containing one part of five; as *subquintuple* proportion. *Wilkins.*

SUBRA'MOUS, *a.* [L. *sub* and *ramosus*, full of branches.]
In *botany*, having few branches. *Lee.*

SUBREC'TOR, *n.* [*sub* and *rector.*] A rector's deputy or substitute. *Walton.*

SUBREP'TION, *n.* [L. *subreptio*, from *subrepo*, to creep under.]
The act of obtaining a favor by surprise or unfair representation, that is, by suppression or fraudulent concealment of facts. *Dict.*

SUBREPTI''TIOUS, *a.* [L. *surreptitius*, supra.]
Falsely crept in; fraudulently obtained. [See *Surreptitious.*]

SUB'ROGATE, *v. t.* [L. *subrogo.*] To put in the place of another. [*Not in use.* See *Surrogate.*]

SUBROGA'TION, *n.* In *the civil law*, the substituting of one person in the place of another and giving him his rights. *Encyc.*

SUBROTUND', *a.* [L. *sub* and *rotundus*, round.] Almost round. *Lee.*

SUBSALI'NE, *a.* Moderately saline or salt. *Encyc.*

SUB'SALT, *n.* A salt with less acid than is sufficient to neutralize its radicals; or a salt having an excess of the base. *Dict.*

SUBSCAP'ULAR, *a.* [L. *sub* and *scapula.*] The *subscapular* artery is the large branch of the axillary artery, which rises near the lowest margin of the scapula. *Cyc.*

SUBSCRI'BE, *v. t.* [L. *subscribo*; *sub* and *scribo*, to write; Fr. *souscrire*; It. *soscrivere*; Sp. *subscribir.*] Literally, to write underneath. Hence,
1. To sign with one's own hand; to give consent to something written, or to bind one's self by writing one's name beneath; as, parties *subscribe* a covenant or contract; a man *subscribes* a bond or articles of agreement.
2. To attest by writing one's name beneath; as, officers *subscribe* their official acts; and secretaries and clerks *subscribe* copies of records.
3. To promise to give by writing one's name; as, each man *subscribed* ten dollars or ten shillings.
4. To submit. [*Not in use.*] *Shak.*

SUBSCRI'BE, *v. i.* To promise to give a certain sum by setting one's name to a paper. The paper was offered and many *subscribed.*
2. To assent; as, I could not *subscribe* to his opinion.

SUBSCRI'BED, *pp.* Having a name or names written underneath. The petition is *subscribed* by two thousand persons.
2. Promised by writing the name and sum. A large sum is *subscribed.*

SUBSCRI'BER, *n.* One who subscribes; one who contributes to an undertaking by subscribing.
2. One who enters his name for a paper, book, map and the like.

SUBSCRI'BING, *ppr.* Writing one's name underneath; assenting to or attesting by writing the name beneath; entering one's name as a purchaser.

SUBSCRIP'TION, *n.* [L. *subscriptio.*] Any thing, particularly a paper, with names subscribed.
2. The act of subscribing or writing one's name underneath; name subscribed; signature.

3. Consent or attestation given by underwriting the name.
4. The act of contributing to any undertaking.
5. Sum subscribed; amount of sums subscribed. We speak of an individual *subscription*, or of the whole *subscription* to a fund.
6. Submission; obedience. [*Not in use.*]

SUBSEC'TION, *n.* [L. *sub* and *sectio.*] The part or division of a section; a subdivision; the section of a section. *Dict.*

SUBSEC'UTIVE, *a.* [L. *subsequor, subsecutus.*]
Following in a train or succession. [*Little used.*]

SUBSEM'ITONE, *n.* In *music*, the sharp seventh or sensible of any key.

SUBSEP'TUPLE, *a.* [L. *sub* and *septuplus.*] Containing one of seven parts. *Wilkins.*

SUB'SEQUENCE, *n.* [L. *subsequor, subsequens: sub* and *sequor*, to follow.]
A following; a state of coming after something. *Grew.*

SUB'SEQUENT, *a.* [Fr. from L. *subsequens*, supra.]
1. Following in time; coming or being after something else at any time, indefinitely; as *subsequent* events; *subsequent* ages or years; a period long *subsequent* to the foundation of Rome.
2. Following in the order of place or succession; succeeding; as a *subsequent* clause in a treaty. What is obscure in a passage may be illustrated by *subsequent* words.

SUB'SEQUENTLY, *adv.* At a later time; in time after something else. Nothing was done at the first meeting; what was *subsequently* transacted, I do not know.
2. After something else in order. These difficulties will be *subsequently* explained.

SUBSERVE, *v. t.* *subserv.'* [L. *subservio; sub* and *servio*, to serve.]
To serve in subordination; to serve instrumentally. In most engines, we make the laws of matter *subserve* the purposes of art.

> Not made to rule,
> But to *subserve* where wisdom bears command. *Milton.*

SUBSERV'IENCE, } *n.* Instrumental use;
SUBSERV'IENCY, } use or operation that promotes some purpose.

> —The body, wherein appears much fitness, use and *subserviency* to infinite functions. *Bentley.*

> There is a regular subordination and *subserviency* among all the parts to beneficial ends. *Cheyne.*

SUBSERV'IENT, *a.* [L. *subserviens.*] Useful as an instrument to promote a purpose; serving to promote some end.

> Hammond had an incredible dexterity, scarcely ever reading any thing which he did not make *subservient* in one kind or other. *Fell.*

2. Subordinate; acting as a subordinate instrument. These are the creatures of God, subordinate to him, and *subservient* to his will.

> These ranks of creatures are *subservient* one to another. *Ray.*

SUBSERV'IENTLY, *adv.* In a subservient manner.

SUBSES'SILE, *a.* [L. *sub* and *sessilis.*] In *botany*, almost sessile; having very short footstalks. *Martyn. Lee.*

SUBSEX'TUPLE, *a.* [L. *sub* and *sextuplus.*] Containing one part in six. *Wilkins.*

SUBSI'DE, *v. i.* [L. *subsido; sub* and *sido*, to settle. See *Set.*]
1. To sink or fall to the bottom; to settle; as lees.
2. To fall into a state of quiet; to cease to rage; to be calmed; to become tranquil. Let the passions *subside.* The tumults of war will *subside.* Christ commanded, and the storm *subsided.*
3. To tend downwards; to sink; as a *subsiding* hill. The land *subsides* into a plain.
4. To abate; to be reduced.

> In cases of danger, pride and envy naturally *subside.* *Middleton.*

SUBSI'DENCE, } *n.* The act or process of
SUBSI'DENCY, } sinking or falling, as the lees of liquors.
2. The act of sinking or gradually descending, as ground. *Burnet.*

SUBSID'IARY, *a.* [Fr. *subsidiaire;* L. *subsidiarius.* See *Subsidy.*]
1. Aiding; assistant; furnishing help. *Subsidiary* troops are troops of one nation hired by another for military service.
2. Furnishing additional supplies; as a *subsidiary* stream.

SUBSID'IARY, *n.* An assistant; an auxiliary; he or that which contributes aid or additional supplies. *Stephens.*

SUB'SIDIZE, *v. t.* [from *subsidy.*] To furnish with a subsidy; to purchase the assistance of another by the payment of a subsidy to him. Great Britain *subsidized* some of the German powers in the late war with France.

SUB'SIDIZED, *pp.* Engaged as an auxiliary by means of a subsidy.

SUB'SIDIZING, *ppr.* Purchasing the assistance of by subsidies.

SUB'SIDY, *n.* [Fr. *subside;* L. *subsidium*, from *subsido*, literally to be or sit under or by.]
1. Aid in money; supply given; a tax; something furnished for aid, as by the people to their prince; as the *subsidies* granted formerly to the kings of England.

> *Subsidies* were a tax, not immediately on property, but on persons in respect of their reputed estates, after the nominal rate of 4s. the pound for lands, and 2s. 8d. for goods. *Blackstone.*

2. A sum of money paid by one prince or nation to another, to purchase the service of auxiliary troops, or the aid of such foreign prince in a war against an enemy. Thus Great Britain paid *subsidies* to Austria and Prussia, to engage them to resist the progress of the French.

SUBSIGN, *v. t.* *subsi'ne.* [L. *subsigno; sub* and *signo*, to sign.]
To sign under; to write beneath. [*Little used.*] *Camden.*

SUBSIGNA'TION, *n.* The act of writing the name under something for attestation. [*Little used.*]

SUBSIST', *v. i.* [Fr. *subsister;* It. *sussistere;* Sp. *subsistir;* L. *subsisto; sub* and *sisto*, to stand, to be fixed.]
1. To be; to have existence; *applicable to matter or spirit.*
2. To continue; to retain the present state.

> Firm we *subsist*, but possible to swerve. *Milton.*

3. To live; to be maintained with food and clothing. How many of the human race *subsist* on the labors of others! How many armies have *subsisted* on plunder!
4. To inhere; to have existence by means of something else; as qualities that *subsist* in substances.

SUBSIST', *v. t.* To feed; to maintain; to support with provisions. The king *subsisted* his troops on provisions plundered from the enemy.

SUBSIST'ENCE, } *n.* [Fr. *subsistence;* It.
SUBSIST'ENCY, } *sussistenza.*] Real being; as a chain of differing *subsistencies.* *Glanville.*

> Not only the things had *subsistence*, but the very images were of some creatures existing. *Stillingfleet.*

2. Competent provisions; means of supporting life.

> His viceroy could only propose to himself a comfortable *subsistence* out of the plunder of his province. *Addison.*

3. That which supplies the means of living; as money, pay or wages.
4. Inherence in something else; as the *subsistence* of qualities in bodies.

SUBSIST'ENT, *a.* [L. *subsistens.*] Having real being; as a *subsistent* spirit. *Brown.*
2. Inherent; as qualities *subsistent* in matter. *Bentley.*

SUB'SOIL, *n.* [*sub* and *soil.*] The bed or stratum of earth which lies between the surface soil and the base on which they rest. *Cyc.*

SUBSPE'CIES, *n.* [*sub* and *species.*] A subordinate species; a division of a species. *Thomson.*

SUB'STANCE, *n.* [Fr.; It. *sustanza;* Sp. *substancia;* L. *substantia, substo; sub* and *sto*, to stand.]
1. In *a general sense*, being; something existing by itself; that which really is or exists; *equally applicable to matter or spirit.* Thus the soul of man is called an immaterial *substance*, a cogitative *substance*, a *substance* endued with thought. We say, a stone is a hard *substance;* tallow is a soft *substance.*
2. That which supports accidents.

> That which subsists by itself is called *substance;* that which subsists in and by another, is called a mode or manner of being. *Watts.*

3. The essential part; the main or material part. In this epitome, we have the *substance* of the whole book.

> This edition is the same in *substance* with the Latin. *Burnet.*

4. Something real, not imaginary; something solid, not empty.

> Heroic virtue did his actions guide,
> And he the *substance*, not th' appearance chose. *Dryden.*

5. Body; corporeal nature or matter.

> The qualities of plants are more various than those of animal *substances.* *Arbuthnot.*

6. Goods; estate; means of living. Job's *substance* was seven thousand sheep, three thousand camels, &c. Job i.

> We are—exhausting our *substance*, but not for our own interest. *Swift.*

SUBSTAN'TIAL, *a.* Belonging to substance; real; actually existing.

> If this atheist would have his chance to be a real and *substantial* agent, he is more stupid than the vulgar. *Bentley.*

2. Real; solid; true; not seeming or imaginary.

If happiness be a *substantial* good. *Denham.*

The *substantial* ornaments of virtue. *L'Estrange.*

3. Corporeal; material.

The rainbow appears like a *substantial* arch in the sky. *Watts.*

4. Having substance; strong; stout; solid; as *substantial* cloth; a *substantial* fence or gate.

5. Possessed of goods or estate; responsible; moderately wealthy; as a *substantial* freeholder or farmer; a *substantial* citizen. *Addison.*

SUBSTANTIAL'ITY, *n.* The state of real existence.

2. Corporeity; materiality.

The soul is a stranger to such gross *substantiality.* *Glanville.*

SUBSTAN'TIALLY, *adv.* In the manner of a substance; with reality of existence.

In him his Father shone, *substantially* express'd. *Milton.*

2. Strongly; solidly. *Clarendon.*

3. Truly; solidly; really.

The laws of this religion would make men, if they would truly observe them, *substantially* religious towards God, chaste and temperate. *Tillotson.*

4. In substance; in the main; essentially. This answer is *substantially* the same as that before given.

5. With competent goods or estate.

SUBSTAN'TIALNESS, *n.* The state of being substantial.

2. Firmness; strength; power of holding or lasting; as the *substantialness* of a wall or column. *Wotton.*

SUBSTAN'TIALS, *n. plu.* Essential parts. *Ayliffe.*

SUBSTAN'TIATE, *v. t.* To make to exist. *Ayliffe.*

2. To establish by proof or competent evidence; to verify; to make good; as, to *substantiate* a charge or allegation; to *substantiate* a declaration.

Canning. Adams. Dexter. Ch. Obs.

SUB'STANTIVE, *a.* Betokening existence; as the *substantive* verb. *Arbuthnot.*

2. Solid; depending on itself. [*Not in use.*] *Bacon.*

SUB'STANTIVE, *n.* In *grammar*, a noun or name; the part of speech which expresses something that exists, either material or immaterial. Thus man, horse, city, goodness, excellence, are *substantives.* [Better called *name*, L. *nomen*, or even *noun*, a corruption of *nomen.*]

SUB'STANTIVELY, *adv.* In substance; essentially.

2. In *grammar*, as a name or noun. An adjective or pronoun may be used *substantively.*

SUB'STILE, *n.* [*sub* and *stile.*] The line of a dial on which the stile is erected. *Encyc.*

SUB'STITUTE, *v. t.* [Fr. *substituer*; It. *sustituire*; Sp. *substituir*; L. *substituo*; *sub* and *statuo*, to set.] To put in the place of another.

Some few verses are inserted or *substituted* in the room of others. *Congreve.*

SUB'STITUTE, *n.* One person put in the place of another to answer the same purpose. A person may be a *substitute* with full powers to act for another in an office. Representatives in legislation are the *substitutes* of their constituents. The orthodox creed of christians is that Christ died as the *substitute* of sinners.

2. One thing put in the place of another. If you have not one medicine, use another as its *substitute.*

SUBSTITU'TION, *n.* The act of putting one person or thing in the place of another to supply its place; as the *substitution* of an agent, attorney or representative to act for one in his absence; the *substitution* of bank notes for gold and silver, as a circulating medium.

2. In *grammar*, syllepsis, or the use of one word for another.

SUBSTRACT', *v. t.* [L. *subtraho*, *subtractum.*] To subtract.

NOTE.—*Substract* was formerly used in analogy with *abstract.* But in modern usage, it is written according to the Latin, *subtract.* See this word and its derivatives.

SUBSTRAC'TION, *n.* In *law*, the withdrawing or withholding of some right. Thus the *substraction* of conjugal rights, is when either the husband or wife withdraws from the other and lives separate. The *substraction* of a legacy, is the withholding or detaining of it from the legatee by the executor. In like manner, the withholding of any service, rent, duty or custom, is a *substraction*, for which the law gives a remedy. *Blackstone.*

SUBSTRA'TUM, *n.* [L. *substratus*, spread under; *sub* and *sterno.*]

1. That which is laid or spread under; a layer of earth lying under another. In *agriculture*, the subsoil. *Cyc.*

2. In *metaphysics*, the matter or substance supposed to furnish the basis in which the perceptible qualities inhere.

SUBSTRUC'TION, *n.* [L. *substructio.*] Under building. *Wotton.*

SUBSTRUC'TURE, *n.* [L. *sub* and *structure.*] An under structure; a foundation.

SUBSTY'LAR, *a.* In *dialing*, the *substylar* line, is a right line on which the gnomon or style is erected at right angles with the plane. *Dict.*

SUB'STYLE, *n.* [*sub* and *style.*] In *dialing*, the line on which the gnomon stands.

SUBSULPH'ATE, *n.* A sulphate with an excess of the base. *Thomson.*

SUBSULT'IVE, } *a.* [from L. *subsultus*, a
SUBSULT'ORY, } leap, from *subsulto*; *sub* and *salio.*]

Bounding; leaping; moving by sudden leaps or starts, or by twitches.

SUBSULT'ORILY, *adv.* In a bounding manner; by leaps, starts or twitches. *Bacon.*

SUBSULT'US, *n.* [L.] In *medicine*, a twitching or convulsive motion; as *subsultus* tendinum. *Coxe.*

SUBSU'ME, *v. t.* [L. *sub* and *sumo.*] To assume as a position by consequence. [*Not used.*] *Hammond.*

SUBTAN'GENT, *n.* In *geometry*, the part of the axis contained between the ordinate and tangent drawn to the same point in a curve.

SUBTEND', *v. t.* [L. *sub* and *tendo*, to stretch.]

To extend under; as the line of a triangle which *subtends* the right angle; to *subtend* the chord of an arch. A line from the eye to a planet, *subtends* an angle of 40 degrees with the horizon.

SUBTEND'ED, *pp.* Extended under.

SUBTEND'ING, *ppr.* Extending under.

SUBTENSE, *n.* *subtens'.* [L. *sub* and *tensus.*] The chord of an arch or arc.

SUBTEP'ID, *a.* [L. *sub* and *tepidus*, warm.] Moderately warm.

SUB'TER, a Latin preposition, signifies *under.*

SUBTER'FLUENT, } *a.* [L. *subterfluens*,
SUBTER'FLUOUS, } *subterfluo.*] Running under or beneath.

SUB'TERFUGE, *n.* [Fr. from L. *subter* and *fugio*, to flee.]

Literally, that to which a person resorts for escape or concealment; hence, a shift; an evasion; an artifice employed to escape censure or the force of an argument, or to justify opinions or conduct.

Affect not little shifts and *subterfuges*, to avoid the force of an argument. *Watts.*

SUBTERRA'NE, *n.* [infra.] A cave or room under ground. *Bryant.*

SUBTERRA'NEAN, } *a.* [L. *subter*, under, and *terra*,
SUBTERRA'NEOUS, } earth; Fr. *souterrain*; It. *sotterraneo.*]

Being or lying under the surface of the earth; situated within the earth or under ground; as *subterranean* springs; a *subterraneous* passage.

[*Subterraneal* and *Subterrany*, are not in use.]

SUBTERRA'NITY, *n.* A place under ground. [*Not in use.*] *Brown.*

SUB'TERRANY, *n.* What lies under ground. [*Not in use.*] *Bacon.*

SUB'TIL, *a.* [Fr. *subtil*; L. *subtilis*; It. *sottile.* This word is often written *subtle*, but less properly.]

1. Thin; not dense or gross; as *subtil* air; *subtil* vapor; a *subtil* medium.

2. Nice; fine; delicate.

I do distinguish plain
Each *subtil* line of her immortal face. *Davies.*

3. Acute; piercing; as *subtil* pain. *Prior.*

4. Sly; artful; cunning; crafty; insinuating; as a *subtil* person; a *subtil* adversary.

5. Planned by art; deceitful; as a *subtil* scheme.

6. Deceitful; treacherous. *Shak.*

7. Refined; fine; acute; as a *subtil* argument.

SUBTIL'IATE, *v. t.* To make thin. [*Not in use.*] *Harvey.*

SUBTILIA'TION, *n.* The act of making thin or rare. [*Not in use.*] *Boyle.*

SUBTIL'ITY, *n.* Fineness. *Smellie.*

SUBTILIZA'TION, *n.* [from *subtilize.*]

1. The act of making subtil, fine or thin. In the laboratory, the operation of making so volatile as to rise in steam or vapor. *Cheyne.*

2. Refinement; extreme acuteness.

SUB'TILIZE, *v. t.* [Fr. *subtiliser*, from L. *subtilis.*]

1. To make thin or fine; to make less gross or coarse. *Cheyne.*

2. To refine; to spin into niceties; as, to *subtilize* arguments.

SUB'TILIZE, *v. i.* To refine in argument; to make very nice distinctions.

In whatever manner the papist might *subtilize*— *Milner.*

SUB'TILLY, *adv.* Thinly; not densely.

2. Finely; not grossly or thickly.

The opakest bodies, if *subtilly* divided—become perfectly transparent. *Newton.*

3. Artfully; cunningly; craftily; as a scheme *subtilly* contrived.

SUB'TILNESS, *n.* Thinness; rareness; as the *subtilness* of air.

2. Fineness; acuteness; as the *subtilness* of an argument.

3. Cunning; artfulness; as the *subtilness* of a foe.

SUB'TILTY, *n.* [Fr. *subtilité*; L. *subtilitas.*]

1. Thinness; fineness; exility; *in a physical sense*; as the *subtilty* of air or light; the *subtilty* of sounds. *Bacon. Grew.*

2. Refinement; extreme acuteness.

Intelligible discourses are spoiled by too much *subtilty* in nice divisions. *Locke.*

3. Slyness in design; cunning; artifice; usually but less properly written *subtlety.*

SUB'TLE, *a.* [See *Subtil.*] Sly in design; artful; cunning; insinuating; *applied to persons*; as a *subtle* foe.

2. Cunningly devised; as a *subtle* stratagem.

SUB'TLY, *adv.* Slyly; artfully; cunningly.

Thou seest how *subtly* to detain thee I devise. *Milton.*

2. Nicely; delicately.

In the nice bee, what sense so *subtly* true. *Pope.*

SUBTRACT', *v. t.* [L. *subtraho, subtractus*; *sub* and *traho*, to draw.]

To withdraw or take a part from the rest; to deduct. *Subtract* 5 from 9, and the remainder is 4.

SUBTRACT'ED, *pp.* Withdrawn from the rest; deducted.

SUBTRACT'ER, *n.* He that subtracts.

2. The number to be taken from a larger number. [*Not used.*] [See *Subtrahend.*]

SUBTRACT'ING, *ppr.* Withdrawing from the rest; deducting.

SUBTRAC'TION, *n.* [L. *subtractio.*] The act or operation of taking a part from the rest.

2. In *arithmetic*, the taking of a lesser number from a greater of the same kind or denomination; an operation by which is found the difference between two sums.

SUBTRACT'IVE, *a.* Tending or having power to subtract.

SUBTRAHEND', *n.* In *arithmetic*, the sum or number to be subtracted or taken from another.

SUBTRI'FID, *a.* Slightly trifid. *Martyn.*

SUBTRIP'LE, *a.* [*sub* and *triple.*] Containing a third or one part of three. *Wilkins.*

SUBTRIP'LICATE, *a.* In the ratio of the cubes.

SUBTU'TOR, *n.* [*sub* and *tutor.*] An under tutor. *Burnet.*

SUB'ULATE, *a.* [L. *subula*, an awl.] In *botany*, shaped like an awl; awl-shaped.

A *subulate* leaf, is linear at the bottom, but gradually tapering towards the end. *Martyn.*

SUB'URB, SUB'URBS, *n.* [L. *suburbium*; *sub* and *urbs*, a city.]

1. A building without the walls of a city, but near them; or more generally, the parts that lie without the walls, but in the vicinity of a city. The word may signify buildings, streets or territory. We say, a house stands in the *suburbs*; a garden is situated in the *suburbs* of London or Paris.

2. The confines; the out part.

The *suburb* of their straw-built citadel. *Milton.*

SUBURB'AN, *a.* [L. *suburbanus.* See *Suburbs.*] Inhabiting or being in the suburbs of a city.

SUB'URBED, *a.* Bordering on a suburb; having a suburb on its out part. *Carew.*

SUBURBICA'RIAN, SUBURB'ICARY, *a.* [Low L. *suburbicarius.*] Being in the suburbs; an epithet applied to the provinces of Italy which composed the ancient diocese of Rome. *Barrow.*

SUBVARI'ETY, *n.* [*sub* and *variety.*] A subordinate variety, or division of a variety. *Mineralogy.*

SUBVENTA'NEOUS, *a.* [L. *subventaneus*; *sub* and *ventus.*] Addle; windy. [*A bad word and not in use.*] *Brown.*

SUBVEN'TION, *n.* [L. *subvenio.*] The act of coming under.

2. The act of coming to relief; support; aid. [*Little used.*] *Spenser.*

SUBVERSE, *v. t.* *subvers'.* To subvert. [*Not in use.*] *Spenser.*

SUBVER'SION, *n.* [Fr. from L. *subversio.* See *Subvert.*]

Entire overthrow; an overthrow of the foundation; utter ruin; as the *subversion* of a government or state; the *subversion* of despotic power; the *subversion* of the constitution or laws; the *subversion* of an empire.

SUBVERS'IVE, *a.* Tending to subvert; having a tendency to overthrow and ruin. Every immorality is *subversive* of private happiness. Public corruption of morals is *subversive* of public happiness.

SUBVERT', *v. t.* [L. *subverto*; *sub* and *verto*, to turn; Fr. Sp. *subvertir*; It. *sovvertere.*]

1. To overthrow from the foundation; to overturn; to ruin utterly. The northern nations of Europe *subverted* the Roman empire. He is the worst enemy of man, who endeavors to *subvert* the christian religion. The elevation of corrupt men to office will slowly, but surely, *subvert* a republican government.

This would *subvert* the principles of all knowledge. *Locke.*

2. To corrupt; to confound; to pervert the mind, and turn it from the truth. 2 Tim. ii.

SUBVERT'ED, *pp.* Overthrown; overturned; entirely destroyed.

SUBVERT'ER, *n.* One who subverts; an overthrower.

SUBVERT'ING, *ppr.* Overthrowing; entirely destroying.

SUBWORK'ER, *n.* [*sub* and *worker.*] A subordinate worker or helper. *South.*

SUCCEDA'NEOUS, *a.* [L. *succedaneus*; *sub* and *cedo.*]

Supplying the place of something else: being or employed as a substitute. *Boyle.*

SUCCEDA'NEUM, *n.* [supra.] That which is used for something else; a substitute. *Warburton.*

SUCCE'DE, SUCCEE'D, *v. t.* The first is the more analogical spelling, as in *concede, recede.* [Fr. *succeder*; It. *succedere*; Sp. *suceder*; L. *succedo*; *sub* and *cedo*, to give way, to pass.]

1. To follow in order; to take the place which another has left; as, the king's eldest son *succeeds* his father on the throne. John Adams *succeeded* Gen. Washington in the presidency of the United States. Lewis XVIII. of France has lately deceased, and is *succeeded* by his brother Charles X.

2. To follow; to come after; to be subsequent or consequent.

Those destructive effects *succeeded* the curse. *Brown.*

3. To prosper; to make successful.

Succeed my wish, and second my design. *Dryden.*

SUCCEE'D, *v. i.* To follow in order.

Not another comfort like to this,
Succeeds in unknown fate. *Shak.*

2. To come in the place of one that has died or quitted the place, or of that which has preceded. Day *succeeds* to night, and night to day.

Enjoy till I return
Short pleasures; for long woes are to *succeed.* *Milton.*

Revenge *succeeds* to love, and rage to grief. *Dryden.*

3. To obtain the object desired; to accomplish what is attempted or intended; to have a prosperous termination. The enemy attempted to take the fort by storm, but did not *succeed.* The assault was violent, but the attempt did not *succeed.*

It is almost impossible for poets to *succeed* without ambition. *Dryden.*

4. To terminate with advantage; to have a good effect.

Spenser endeavored imitation in the Shepherd's Kalendar; but neither will it *succeed* in English. *Dryden.*

5. To go under cover.

Or will you to the cooler cave *succeed?* [*Not much used.*] *Dryden.*

SUCCEE'DED, *pp.* Followed in order; prospered; attended with success.

SUCCEE'DER, *n.* One that follows or comes in the place of another; a successor. [*But the latter word is generally used.*]

SUCCEE'DING, *ppr.* Following in order; subsequent; coming after; as in all *succeeding* ages. He attended to the business in every *succeeding* stage of its progress.

2. Taking the place of another who has quitted the place, or is dead; as a son *succeeding* his father; an officer *succeeding* his predecessor.

3. Giving success; prospering.

SUCCEE'DING, *n.* The act or state of prospering or having success. There is a good prospect of his *succeeding.*

SUCCESS', *n.* [Fr. *succès*; L. *successus*, from *succedo.*]

1. The favorable or prosperous termination of any thing attempted; a termination which answers the purpose intended; *properly in a good sense, but often in a bad sense.*

Or teach with more *success* her son,
The vices of the time to shun. *Waller.*

Every reasonable man cannot but wish me *success* in this attempt. *Tillotson.*

Be not discouraged in a laudable undertaking at the ill *success* of the first attempt. *Anon.*

Military *successes*, above all others, elevate the minds of a people. *Atterbury.*

2. Succession. [*Not in use.*] *Spenser.*

[Note. *Success* without an epithet, generally means a prosperous issue.]

SUCCESS'FUL, *a.* Terminating in accomplishing what is wished or intended; having the desired effect; hence, *in a good sense*, prosperous; fortunate; happy; as a *successful* application of medicine; a *successful* experiment in chimistry or in agriculture; a *successful* enterprise.

2. In *a bad sense;* as a *successful* attempt to subvert the constitution.

SUCCESS'FULLY, *adv.* With a favorable termination of what is attempted; prosperously; favorably.

A reformation *successfully* carried on— *Swift.*

SUCCESS'FULNESS, *n.* Prosperous conclusion; favorable event; success. *Hammond.*

SUCCES'SION, *n.* [Fr. from L. *successio.*]

1. A following of things in order; consecution; series of things following one another, either in time or place. Thus we speak of a *succession* of events in chronology, a *succession* of kings or bishops, and a *succession* of words or sentences.

2. The act of succeeding or coming in the place of another; as, this happened after the *succession* of that prince to the throne. So we speak of the *succession* of heirs to the estates of their ancestors, or collateral *succession.*

3. Lineage; an order or series of descendants.

A long *succession* must ensue. *Milton.*

4. The power or right of coming to the inheritance of ancestors. He holds the property by the title of *succession.*

What people is so void of common sense,
To vote *succession* from a native prince? *Dryden.*

Succession of crops, in agriculture, is more generally called *rotation.*

SUCCESS'IVE, *a.* [Fr. *successif;* It. *successivo.*]

1. Following in order or uninterrupted course, as a series of persons or things, and either in time or place; as the *successive* revolutions of years or ages; the *successive* kings of Egypt. The author holds this strain of declamation through seven *successive* pages or chapters.

Send the *successive* ills through ages down. *Prior.*

2. Inherited by succession; as a *successive* title; a *successive* empire. [*Little used.*] *Shak. Raleigh.*

SUCCESS'IVELY, *adv.* In a series or order, one following another. He left three sons, who all reigned *successively.*

The whiteness at length changed *successively* into blue, indigo and violet. *Newton.*

SUCCESS'IVENESS, *n.* The state of being successive. *Hale.*

SUCCESS'LESS, *a.* Having no success; unprosperous; unfortunate; failing to accomplish what was intended.

Successless all her soft caresses prove. *Pope.*

Best temper'd steel *successless* prov'd in field. *Phillips.*

SUCCESS'LESSNESS, *n.* Unprosperous conclusion. *Boyle.*

SUCCESS'OR, *n.* [L.] One that succeeds or follows; one that takes the place which another has left, and sustains the like part or character; correlative to *predecessor;* as the *successor* of a deceased king; the *successor* of a president or governor; a man's son and *successor.*

A gift to a corporation, either of lands or of chattels, without naming their *successors*, vests an absolute property in them so long as the corporation subsists. *Blackstone.*

SUCCID'UOUS, *a.* [L. *succiduus; sub* and *cado.*] Ready to fall; falling. [*Little used.*]

SUCCIF'EROUS, *a.* [L. *succus*, juice, and *fero*, to bear.] Producing or conveying sap.

SUC'CINATE, *n.* [from L. *succinum*, amber.] A salt formed by the succinic acid and a base.

SUC'CINATED, *a.* Impregnated with the acid of amber.

SUCCINCT', *a.* [L. *succinctus; sub* and *cingo*, to surround.]

1. Tucked up; girded up; drawn up to permit the legs to be free.

His habit fit for speed *succinct.* *Milton.*

[*Little used.*]

2. Compressed into a narrow compass; short; brief; concise; as a *succinct* account of the proceedings of the council.

Let all your precepts be *succinct* and clear. *Roscommon.*

SUCCINCT'LY, *adv.* Briefly; concisely. The facts were *succinctly* stated.

SUCCINCT'NESS, *n.* Brevity; conciseness; as the *succinctness* of a narration.

SUCCIN'IC, *a.* Pertaining to amber; drawn from amber; as the *succinic* acid.

SUC'CINITE, *n.* [L. *succinum*, amber.] A mineral of an amber color, considered as a variety of garnet. It frequently occurs in globular or granular masses, about the size of a pea. *Cleaveland.*

SUC'CINOUS, *a.* Pertaining to amber.

SUC'COR, *v. t.* [Fr. *secourir;* It. *soccorrere;* Sp. *socorrer;* L. *succurro; sub* and *curro*, to run.]

Literally, to run to, or run to support; hence, to help or relieve when in difficulty, want or distress; to assist and deliver from suffering; as, to *succor* a besieged city; to *succor* prisoners.

He is able to *succor* them that are tempted. Heb. ii.

SUC'COR, *n.* Aid; help; assistance; particularly, assistance that relieves and delivers from difficulty, want or distress.

My father
Flying for *succor* to his servant Banister— *Shak.*

2. The person or thing that brings relief. The city when pressed received *succors* from an unexpected quarter.

The mighty *succor* which made glad the foe. *Dryden.*

SUC'CORED, *pp.* Assisted; relieved.

SUC'CORER, *n.* He that affords relief; a helper; a deliverer.

SUC'CORLESS, *a.* Destitute of help or relief. *Thomson.*

SUC'CORY, *n.* Wild endive, a plant of the genus Cichorium.

SUC'COTASH, *n.* In *America*, a mixture of green maiz and beans boiled. The dish, as well as the name, is borrowed from the native Indians.

SUC'CUBA, SUC'CUBUS, *n.* [L. *sub* and *cubo.*] A pretended kind of demon. *Mir. for Mag.*

SUC'CULENCE, SUC'CULENCY, *n.* [See *Succulent.*] Juiciness; as the *succulence* of a peach.

SUC'CULENT, *a.* [Fr.; L. *succulentus*, from *succus*, juice.]

Full of juice; juicy. *Succulent* plants are such as have a juicy and soft stem, as distinguished from such as are ligneous, hard and dry. Thus the grasses are *succulent* herbs, as are peas, beans and the like.

SUCCUMB', *v. i.* [L. *succumbo; sub* and *cumbo, cubo*, to lie down.]

1. To yield; to submit; as, to *succumb* to a foreign power.

2. To yield; to sink unresistingly; as, to *sn*c*cumb* under calamities.

SUCCUMB'ING, *ppr.* Yielding; submitting; sinking.

SUCCUSSA'TION, *n.* [L. *succusso*, to shake.] A trot or trotting. *Brown.*

2. A shaking; succussion.

SUCCUS'SION, *n.* [L. *succussio*, from *succusso*, to shake; *sub* and *quasso.*]

1. The act of shaking; a shake.

2. In *medicine*, a shaking of the nervous parts by powerful stimulants. *Coxe.*

SUCH, *a.* [It is possible that this word may be a contraction of Sax. *swelc, swylc*, G. *solch*, D. *zolk.* More probably it is the Russ. *sitze, sitzev*, our vulgar *sichy.*]

1. Of that kind; of the like kind. We never saw *such* a day; we have never had *such* a time as the present.

It has *as* before the thing to which it relates. Give your children *such* precepts *as* tend to make them wiser and better.

It is to be noted that the definitive adjective *a*, never precedes *such*, but is placed between it and the noun to which it refers; as *such a* man; *such an* honor.

2. The same that. This was the state of the kingdom at *such* time as the enemy landed.

3. The same as what has been mentioned.

That thou art happy, owe to God;
That thou continu'st *such*, owe to thyself. *Milton.*

4. Referring to what has been specified. I have commanded my servant to be at *such* a place.

5. *Such and such*, is used in reference to a person or place of a certain kind.

The sovereign authority may enact a law, commanding *such and such* an action. *South.*

SUCK, *v. t.* [Sax. *sucan, succan;* G. *saugen;* D. *zuigen;* Sw. *suga;* Dan. *suer*, contracted; Ir. *sagham;* W. *sugaw;* L. *sugo;* Fr. *sucer;* It. *succiare, succhiare;* Sp. Port. *sacar*, to draw out.]

1. To draw with the mouth; to draw out, as a liquid from a cask, or milk from the breast; to draw into the mouth. To *suck* is to exhaust the air of the mouth or of a tube; the fluid then rushes into the mouth or tube by means of the pressure of the surrounding air.

2. To draw milk from with the mouth; as, the young of an animal *sucks* the mother or dam, or the breast.

3. To draw into the mouth; to imbibe; as, to *suck* in air; to *suck* the juice of plants.

4. To draw or drain.

Old ocean *suck'd* through the porous globe. *Thomson.*

5. To draw in, as a whirlpool; to absorb. *Dryden.*

6. To inhale.

To suck in, to draw into the mouth; to imbibe; to absorb.

To suck out, to draw out with the mouth; to empty by suction.

To suck up, to draw into the mouth.

SUCK, *v. i.* To draw by exhausting the air, as with the mouth, or with a tube.

2. To draw the breast; as, a child, or the young of any animal, is first nourished by *sucking.*

3. To draw in; to imbibe. *Bacon.*

SUCK, *n.* The act of drawing with the mouth. *Boyle.*

2. Milk drawn from the breast by the mouth. *Shak.*

SUCK'ED, *pp.* Drawn with the mouth, or with an instrument that exhausts the air; imbibed; absorbed.

SUCK'ER, *n.* He or that which draws with the mouth.

2. The embolus or piston of a pump. *Boyle.*

3. A pipe through which any thing is drawn. *Philips.*

4. The shoot of a plant from the roots or lower part of the stem; so called perhaps from its drawing its nourishment from the root or stem.

5. A fish, called also remora; also, a name of the Cyclopterus or lump-fish. *Dict. Nat. Hist.*

6. The name of a common river fish in New England.

SUCK'ER, *v. t.* To strip off shoots; to deprive of suckers; as, to *sucker* maiz.

SUCK'ET, *n.* A sweetmeat for the mouth. *Cleaveland.*

SUCK'ING, *ppr.* Drawing with the mouth or with an instrument; imbibing; absorbing.

SUCK'ING-BOTTLE, *n.* A bottle to be filled with milk for infants to suck instead of the pap. *Locke.*

SUCK'LE, *n.* A teat. [*Not in use.*]

SUCK'LE, *v. t.* To give suck to: to nurse at the breast. Romulus and Remus are fabled to have been *suckled* by a wolf.

SUCK'LED, *pp.* Nursed at the breast.

SUCK'LING, *ppr.* Nursing at the breast.

SUCK'LING, *n.* A young child or animal nursed at the breast. Ps. viii.

2. A sort of white clover. *Cyc.*

SUC'TION, *n.* [Fr.] The act of sucking or drawing into the mouth, as fluids. *Boyle. Arbuthnot.*

2. The act of drawing, as fluids into a pipe or other thing.

SU'DAK, *n.* A fish, a species of Perca. *Tooke.*

SU'DARY, *n.* [L. *sudarium,* from *sudo,* to sweat.]

A napkin or handkerchief. [*Not in use.*] *Wickliffe.*

SUDA'TION, *n.* [L. *sudatio.*] A sweating.

SU'DATORY, *n.* [L. *sudatorium,* from *sudo,* to sweat.]

A hot house; a sweating bath. *Herbert.*

SU'DATORY, *a.* Sweating.

SUD'DEN, *a.* [Sax. *soden;* Fr. *soudain;* Norm. *soubdain;* L. *subitaneus.*]

1. Happening without previous notice; coming unexpectedly, or without the common preparatives.

> And *sudden* fear troubleth thee. Job xxii.
>
> For when they shall say, peace and safety, then *sudden* destruction cometh upon them. 1 Thess. v.

2. Hasty; violent; rash; precipitate; passionate. [*Not in use.*] *Shak.*

SUD'DEN, *n.* An unexpected occurrence; surprise. [*Not in use.*]

On a sudden, sooner than was expected; without the usual preparatives.

> How art thou lost, how *on a sudden* lost! *Milton.*

[*Of a sudden,* is not usual, and is less elegant.]

SUD'DENLY, *adv.* In an unexpected manner; unexpectedly; hastily; without preparation.

> Therefore his calamity shall come *suddenly.* Prov. vi.

2. Without premeditation.

SUD'DENNESS, *n.* State of being sudden; a coming or happening without previous notice. The *suddenness* of the event precluded preparation.

SUDORIF'IC, *a.* [Fr. *sudorifique;* L. *sudor,* sweat, and *facio,* to make.]

Causing sweat; exciting perspiration; as *sudorific* herbs. *Bacon.*

SUDORIF'IC, *n.* A medicine that produces sweat or sensible perspiration. *Coxe.*

SU'DOROUS, *a.* [L. *sudor,* sweat.] Consisting of sweat. *Brown.*

SUDS, *n. sing.* [Qu. W. *suz,* moisture, or its connection with *seethe, sodden.*] Water impregnated with soap.

To be in the suds, to be in turmoil or difficulty; *a familiar phrase.*

SUE, *v. t. su.* [Fr. *suivre,* to follow, L. *sequor.* See *Seek* and *Essay.*]

1. To seek justice or right from one by legal process; to institute process in law against one; to prosecute in a civil action for the recovery of a real or supposed right; as, to *sue* one for debt; to *sue* one for damages in trespass. Matt. v.

2. To gain by legal process.

3. To clean the beak, as a hawk; *a term of falconry.*

To sue out, to petition for and take out; or to apply for and obtain; as, to *sue out* a writ in chancery; to *sue out* a pardon for a criminal.

SUE, *v. i.* To prosecute; to make legal claim; to seek for in law; as, to *sue* for damages.

2. To seek by request; to apply for; to petition; to entreat.

> By adverse destiny constrain'd to *sue*
> For counsel and redress, he *sues* to you. *Pope.*

3. To make interest for; to demand.

> Cesar came to Rome to *sue* for the double honor of a triumph and the consulship. *Middleton.*

SU'ED, *pp.* Prosecuted; sought in law.

SU'ET, *n.* [W. *swyv* and *swyved,* a surface, coating, *suet,* yest, &c.]

The fat of an animal, particularly that about the kidneys; lard. *Wiseman.*

SU'ETY, *a.* Consisting of suet, or resembling it; as a *suety* substance. *Sharp.*

SUF'FER, *v. t.* [L. *suffero; sub,* under, and *fero,* to bear; as we say, to *undergo;* Fr. *souffrir;* It. *sofferire;* Sp. *sufrir.* See *Bear.*]

1. To feel or bear what is painful, disagreeable or distressing, either to the body or mind; to undergo. We *suffer* pain of body; we *suffer* grief of mind. The criminal *suffers* punishment; the sinner *suffers* the pangs of conscience in this life, and is condemned to *suffer* the wrath of an offended God. We often *suffer* wrong; we *suffer* abuse; we *suffer* injustice.

2. To endure; to support; to sustain; not to sink under.

> Our spirit and strength entire,
> Strongly to *suffer* and support our pains. *Milton.*

3. To allow; to permit; not to forbid or hinder. Will you *suffer* yourself to be insulted?

> I *suffer* them to enter and possess. *Milton.*
>
> Thou shalt in any wise rebuke thy neighbor, and not *suffer* sin upon him. Lev. xix.

4. To undergo; to be affected by. Substances *suffer* an entire change by the action of fire, or by entering into new combinations.

5. To sustain; to be affected by; as, to *suffer* loss or damage.

SUF'FER, *v. i.* To feel or undergo pain of body or mind; to bear what is inconvenient. We *suffer* with pain, sickness or sorrow. We *suffer* with anxiety. We *suffer* by evils past and by anticipating others to come. We *suffer* from fear and from disappointed hopes.

2. To undergo, as punishment.

> The father was first condemned to *suffer* on a day appointed, and the son afterwards, the day following. *Clarendon.*

3. To be injured; to sustain loss or damage. A building *suffers* for want of seasonable repairs. It is just that we should *suffer* for neglect of duty.

> Public business *suffers* by private infirmities. *Temple.*

SUF'FERABLE, *a.* That may be tolerated or permitted; allowable.

2. That may be endured or borne. *Wotton.*

SUF'FERABLY, *adv.* Tolerably; so as to be endured. *Addison.*

SUF'FERANCE, *n.* The bearing of pain; endurance; pain endured; misery.

> He must not only die,
> But thy unkindness shall the death draw out
> To ling'ring *sufferance.* *Shak.*

2. Patience; moderation; a bearing with patience.

> But hasty heat temp'ring with *sufferance* wise. *Spenser.*

3. Toleration; permission; allowance; negative consent by not forbidding or hindering.

> In process of time, sometimes by *sufferance,* sometimes by special leave and favor, they erected to themselves oratories. *Hooker.*
>
> In their beginning, they are weak and wan,
> But soon through *sufferance* grow to fearful end. *Spenser.*

An estate at sufferance, in law, is where a person comes into possession of land by lawful title, but keeps it after the title ceases, without positive leave of the owner. *Blackstone.*

SUF'FERED, *pp.* Borne; undergone; permitted; allowed.

SUF'FERER, *n.* One who endures or undergoes pain, either of body or mind; one who sustains inconvenience or loss; as *sufferers* by poverty or sickness. Men are *sufferers* by fire or losses at sea; they are *sufferers* by the ravages of an enemy; still more are they *sufferers* by their own vices and follies.

2. One that permits or allows.

SUF'FERING, *ppr.* Bearing; undergoing pain, inconvenience or damage; permitting; allowing.

SUF'FERING, *n.* The bearing of pain, inconvenience or loss; pain endured; distress, loss or injury incurred; as *suffer-*

ings by pain or sorrow; *sufferings* by want or by wrongs.

SUFFICE, *v. i.* *suffi'ze.* [Fr. *suffire*; L. *sufficio*; *sub* and *facio*.]

To be enough or sufficient; to be equal to the end proposed.

> To recount Almighty works
> What words or tongue of seraph can *suffice?* *Milton.*

SUFFICE, *v. t.* *suffi'ze.* To satisfy; to content; to be equal to the wants or demands of.

> Let it *suffice* thee; speak no more to me of this matter. Deut. iii.
> Lord, show us the Father, and it *sufficeth* us. John xiv. Ruth ii.

2. To afford; to supply.

> The pow'r appeas'd, with wind *suffic'd* the sail. [*Not in use.*] *Dryden.*

SUFFICED, *pp.* *suffi'zed.* Satisfied; adequately supplied.

SUFFI''CIENCY, *n.* The state of being adequate to the end proposed.

> His *sufficiency* is such, that he bestows and possesses, his plenty being unexhausted. *Boyle.*

2. Qualification for any purpose.

> I am not so confident of my own *sufficiency* as not willingly to admit the counsel of others. *K. Charles.*

3. Competence; adequate substance or means.

> An elegant *sufficiency*, content. *Thomson.*

4. Supply equal to wants; ample stock or fund. *Watts.*

5. Ability; adequate power.

> Our *sufficiency* is of God. 2 Cor. iii.

6. Conceit; self-confidence. [See *Self-sufficiency*.]

SUFFI''CIENT, *a.* [L. *sufficiens*.] Enough; equal to the end proposed; adequate to wants; competent; as provision *sufficient* for the family; water *sufficient* for the voyage; an army *sufficient* to defend the country.

> My grace is *sufficient* for thee. 2 Cor. xii.

2. Qualified; competent; possessing adequate talents or accomplishments; as a man *sufficient* for an office. *Shak.*

3. Fit; able; of competent power or ability.

> Who is *sufficient* for these things? 2 Cor. ii.

SUFFI''CIENTLY, *adv.* To a sufficient degree; enough; to a degree that answers the purpose, or gives content; as, we are *sufficiently* supplied with food and clothing; a man *sufficiently* qualified for the discharge of his official duties.

SUFFICING, *ppr.* *suffi'zing.* Supplying what is needed; satisfying.

SUFFI'SANCE, *n.* [Fr.] Sufficiency; plenty. [*Not in use.*] *Spenser.*

SUF'FIX, *n.* [L. *suffixus*, *suffigo*; *sub* and *figo*, to fix.]

A letter or syllable added or annexed to the end of a word. *Parkhurst. M. Stuart.*

SUFFIX', *v. t.* To add or annex a letter or syllable to a word.

SUFFIX'ED, *pp.* Added to the end of a word.

SUFFIX'ING, *ppr.* Adding to the end of a word.

SUFFLAM'INATE, *v. t.* [L. *sufflamen*, a stop.]

To stop; to impede. [*Not in use.*] *Barrow.*

SUFFLA'TE, *v. t.* [L. *sufflo*; *sub* and *flo*, to blow.]

To blow up; to inflate. [*Little used.*] *Bailey.*

SUFFLA'TION, *n.* [L. *sufflatio*.] The act of blowing up or inflating. *Coles.*

SUF'FOCATE, *v. t.* [Fr. *suffoquer*; It. *suffogare*; Sp. *sufocar*; L. *suffoco*; *sub* and *focus*, or its root.]

1. To choke or kill by stopping respiration. Respiration may be stopped by the interception of air, as in hanging and strangling, or by the introduction of smoke, dust or mephitic air into the lungs. Men may be *suffocated* by the halter; or men may be *suffocated* in smoke or in carbonic acid gas, as in mines and wells.

> And let not hemp his windpipe *suffocate.* *Shak.*

2. To stifle; to destroy; to extinguish; as, to *suffocate* fire or live coals.

> A swelling discontent is apt to *suffocate* and strangle without passage. *Collier.*

SUF'FOCATE, *a.* Suffocated. *Shak.*

SUF'FOCATED, *pp.* Choked; stifled.

SUF'FOCATING, *ppr.* Choking; stifling.

SUF'FOCATINGLY, *adv.* So as to suffocate; as *suffocatingly* hot.

SUFFOCA'TION, *n.* The act of choking or stifling; a stopping of respiration, either by intercepting the passage of air to and from the lungs, or by inhaling smoke, dust or air that is not respirable.

2. The act of stifling, destroying or extinguishing.

SUF'FOCATIVE, *a.* Tending or able to choke or stifle; as *suffocative* catarrhs. *Arbuthnot.*

SUFFOS'SION, *n.* [L. *suffossio*; *sub* and *fodio*, to dig.]

A digging under; an undermining. *Bp. Hall.*

SUF'FRAGAN, *a.* [Fr. *suffragant*; It. *suffraganeo*; L. *suffragans*, assisting; *suffragor*, to vote for, to favor.] Assisting; as a *suffragan* bishop.

SUF'FRAGAN, *n.* A bishop, considered as an assistant to his metropolitan; or rather, an assistant bishop. By 26 Hen. VIII. *suffragans* are to be denominated from some principal place in the diocese of the prelate whom they are to assist. *Bp. Barlow.*

SUF'FRAGANT, *n.* An assistant; a favorer; one who concurs with. *Obs.* *Taylor.*

SUF'FRAGATE, *v. t.* [L. *suffragor*.] To vote with. [*Not in use.*] *Hale.*

SUF'FRAGATOR, *n.* [L.] One who assists or favors by his vote. *Bp. of Chester.*

SUF'FRAGE, *n.* [L. *suffragium*; Fr. *suffrage*; Sax. *frægnan*, to ask, G. *fragen*.]

1. A vote; a voice given in deciding a controverted question, or in the choice of a man for an office or trust. Nothing can be more grateful to a good man than to be elevated to office by the unbiased *suffrages* of free enlightened citizens.

> Lactantius and St. Austin confirm by their *suffrages* the observation made by heathen writers. *Atterbury.*

2. United voice of persons in public prayer.

3. Aid; assistance; *a Latinism.* [*Not in use.*]

SUFFRAG'INOUS, *a.* [L. *suffrago*, the pastern or hough.]

Pertaining to the knee joint of a beast. *Brown.*

SUFFRU''TICOUS, *a.* [L. *sub* and *fruticosus*; *frutex*, a shrub.]

In *botany*, under-shrubby, or part shrubby; permanent or woody at the base, but the yearly branches decaying; as sage, thyme, hyssop, &c. *Martyn. Cyc.*

SUFFU'MIGATE, *v. t.* [L. *suffumigo*.] To apply fumes or smoke to the internal parts of the body, as in medicine.

SUFFUMIGA'TION, *n.* Fumigation; the operation of smoking any thing, or rather of applying fumes to the internal parts of the body.

2. A term applied to all medicines that are received into the body in the form of fumes. *Cyc.*

SUFFU'MIGE, *n.* A medical fume. *Harvey.*

SUFFU'SE, *v. t.* *suffu'ze.* [L. *suffusus*, *suffundo*; *sub* and *fundo*, to pour.]

To overspread, as with a fluid or tincture; as eyes *suffused* with tears; cheeks *suffused* with blushes.

> When purple light shall next *suffuse* the skies. *Pope.*

SUFFU'SED, *pp.* Overspread, as with a fluid or with color.

SUFFU'SION, *n.* [Fr. from L. *suffusio*.]

1. The act or operation of overspreading, as with a fluid or with a color.

2. The state of being suffused or spread over.

> To those that have the jaundice or like *suffusion* of eyes, objects appear of that color. *Ray.*

3. That which is suffused or spread over.

SUG, *n.* [L. *sugo*, to suck.] A kind of worm. *Walton.*

SUGAR, *n.* SHUG'AR. [Fr. *sucre*; Arm. *sucr*; Sp. *azucar*; It. *zucchero*; G. *zucker*; D. *suiker*; Dan. *sokker*, *sukker*; Sw. *socker*; W. *sugyr*; Ir. *siacra*; L. *saccharum*; Gr. σακχαρον; Pers. Ar. سُكَّر sukkar; Sans. *scharkara*; Slavonic, *zakar*. It is also in the Syr. and Eth.]

1. A well known substance manufactured chiefly from the sugar cane, *arundo saccharifera*; but in the United States, great quantities of this article are made from the sugar maple; and in France, a few years since, it was extensively manufactured from the beet. The saccharine liquor is concentrated by boiling, which expels the water; lime is added to neutralize the acid that is usually present; the grosser impurities rise to the surface, and are separated in the form of scum; and finally as the liquor cools, the sugar separates from the melasses in grains. The sirup or melasses is drained off, leaving the sugar in the state known in commerce by the name of *raw* or *muscovado* sugar. This is farther purified by means of clay, or more extensively by bullocks' blood, which forming a coagulum, envelops the impurities. Thus clarified, it takes the names of *lump*, *loaf*, *refined*, &c. according to the different degrees of purification. Sugar is a proximate element of the vegetable kingdom, and is found in most ripe fruits, and many farinaceous roots. By fermentation, sugar is converted into alcohol, and hence forms the basis of those substances which are used for making intoxicating

liquors, as melasses, grapes, apples, malt, &c.

The *ultimate* elements of sugar are oxygen, carbon and hydrogen. Of all vegetable principles, it is considered by Dr. Rush as the most wholesome and nutritious.

2. A chimical term: as the *sugar* of lead.

SUGAR, *v. t.* SHUG'AR. To impregnate, season, cover, sprinkle or mix with sugar. *Crashaw.*

2. To sweeten.

But flattery still in *sugar'd* words betrays. *Denham.*

Sugar of lead, acetate of lead.

SUGAR-CANDY, *n.* [*sugar* and *candy.*] Sugar clarified and concreted or crystalized, in which state it becomes transparent.

SUG'AR-CANE, *n.* [*sugar* and *cane.*] The cane or plant from whose juice sugar is obtained.

SUG'AR-HOUSE, *n.* A building in which sugar is refined.

SUG'AR-LOAF, *n.* A conical mass of refined sugar.

SUG'AR-MILL, *n.* A machine for pressing out the juice of the sugar cane.

SUG'AR-MITE, *n.* [*sugar* and *mite.*] A winged insect; lepisma.

The *lepisma saccharina*, is an apterous or wingless insect, covered with silvery scales. *Ed. Encyc.*

SUG'AR-PLUM, *n.* [*sugar* and *plum.*] A species of sweetmeat in small balls.

SUG'ARY, *a.* Tinctured or sweetened with sugar; sweet; tasting like sugar.

2. Fond of sugar, or of sweet things. *Todd.*

3. Containing sugar. *Ash.*

4. Like sugar. *Ash.*

SUGES'CENT, *a.* [L. *sugens*, sucking.] Relating to sucking. *Paley.*

SUG'GEST, *v. t.* [L. *suggero, suggestus*; *sub* and *gero*; It. *suggerire*; Fr. *suggerer.*]

1. To hint; to intimate or mention in the first instance; as, to *suggest* a new mode of cultivation; to *suggest* a different scheme or measure; to *suggest* a new idea.

2. To offer to the mind or thoughts.

Some ideas are *suggested* to the mind by all the ways of sensation and reflection. *Locke.*

3. To seduce; to draw to ill by insinuation.

Knowing that tender youth is soon *suggested.* [*Not in use.*] *Shak.*

4. To inform secretly.

We must *suggest* the people. *Shak.* [*Not in use.*]

SUGGEST'ED, *pp.* Hinted; intimated.

SUGGEST'ER, *n.* One that suggests.

SUGGES'TION, *n.* [Fr.; from *suggest.*] A hint; a first intimation, proposal or mention. The measure was adopted at the *suggestion* of an eminent philosopher.

2. Presentation of an idea to the mind; as the *suggestions* of fancy or imagination; the *suggestions* of conscience.

3. Insinuation; secret notification or incitement. *Shak.*

4. In *law*, information without oath.

SUGGEST'IVE, *a.* Containing a hint or intimation.

SUG'GIL, *v. t.* [L. *suggillo.*] To defame. [*Not in use.*] *Parker.*

SUG'GILATE, *v. t.* [L. *suggillo.*] To beat black and blue. [*Not in use.*] *Wiseman.*

SUGGILA'TION, *n.* A black and blue mark; a blow; a bruise. [*Not in use.*]

SUICI'DAL, *a.* Partaking of the crime of suicide.

SU'ICIDE, *n.* [Fr. from L. *suicidium*; *se* and *cædo*, to slay.]

1. Self-murder; the act of designedly destroying one's own life. To constitute suicide, the person must be of years of discretion and of sound mind. *Blackstone.*

2. One guilty of self-murder; a felo de se.

SUICISM, for *suicide*, is not in use.

SUIL'LAGE, *n.* [Fr. *souillage.*] Drain of filth. *Obs.* *Wotton.*

SU'ING, *ppr.* of *sue.* Prosecuting.

SU'ING, *n.* [Fr. *suer*, to sweat, L. *sudo.*] The process of soaking through any thing. [*Not in use.*] *Bacon.*

SUIT, *n.* [Norm. *suit* or *suyt*; Fr. *suite*, from *suivre*, to follow, from L. *sequor.* See *Seek.* In Law Latin, *secta* is from the same source.]

Literally, a following; and so used in the old English statutes.

1. Consecution; succession; series; regular order; as the same kind and *suit* of weather. [*Not now so applied.*] *Bacon.*

2. A set; a number of things used together, and in a degree necessary to be united, in order to answer the purpose; as a *suit* of curtains; a *suit* of armor; sometimes with less dependence of the particular parts on each other, but still united in use; as a *suit* of clothes; a *suit* of apartments.

3. A set of the same kind or stamp; as a *suit* of cards.

4. Retinue; a company or number of attendants or followers; attendance; train; as a nobleman and his *suit.* [This is sometimes pronounced as a French word, *sweet*; but in all its senses, this is the same word, and the affectation of making it French in one use and English in another, is improper, not to say ridiculous.]

5. A petition; a seeking for something by petition or application.

Many shall make *suit* to thee. Job xi.

6. Solicitation of a woman in marriage; courtship. *Shak.*

7. In *law*, an action or process for the recovery of a right or claim; legal application to a court for justice; prosecution of right before any tribunal; as a civil *suit*; a criminal *suit*; a *suit* in chancery.

In England, the several *suits* or remedial instruments of justice, are distinguished into three kinds, actions personal, real, and mixed. *Blackstone.*

8. Pursuit; prosecution; chase. *Spenser. Cyc.*

Suit and service, in feudal law, the duty of feudatories to attend the courts of their lords or superiors in time of peace, and in war, to follow them and perform military service. *Blackstone.*

To bring suit, a phrase in law, denoting literally to bring *secta*, followers or witnesses to prove the plaintif's demand. The phrase is antiquated, or rather it has changed its signification; for to *bring a suit*, now is to institute an action.

Out of suits, having no correspondence. *Shak.*

Suit-covenant, in law, is a covenant to sue at a certain court. *Bailey.*

Suit-court, in law, the court in which tenants owe attendance to their lord. *Bailey.*

SUIT, *v. t.* To fit; to adapt; to make proper. *Suit* the action to the word. *Suit* the gestures to the passion to be expressed. *Suit* the style to the subject.

2. To become; to be fitted to.

Ill *suits* his cloth the praise of railing well. *Dryden.*

Raise her notes to that sublime degree,
Which *suits* a song of piety and thee. *Prior.*

2. To dress; to clothe.

Such a Sebastian was my brother too,
So went he *suited* to his watery tomb. *Shak.*

4. To please; to make content. He is well *suited* with his place.

SUIT, *v. i.* To agree; to accord; as, to *suit with*; to *suit to.* Pity *suits with* a noble nature. *Dryden.*

Give me not an office
That *suits with* me so ill— *Addison.*

The place itself was *suiting to* his care. *Dryden.*

[The use of *with*, after *suit*, is now most frequent.]

SUITABLE, *a.* Fitting; according with; agreeable to; proper; becoming; as ornaments *suitable* to one's character and station; language *suitable* to the subject.

2. Adequate. We cannot make *suitable* returns for divine mercies.

SUITABLENESS, *n.* Fitness; propriety; agreeableness; a state of being adapted or accommodated. Consider the laws, and their *suitableness* to our moral state.

SUITABLY, *adv.* Fitly; agreeably; with propriety. Let words be *suitably* applied.

SUITED, *pp.* Fitted; adapted; pleased.

SUITING, *ppr.* Fitting; according with; becoming; pleasing.

SUITOR, *n.* One that sues or prosecutes a demand of right in law, as a plaintif, petitioner or appellant.

2. One who attends a court, whether plaintif, defendant, petitioner, appellant, witness, juror and the like. These, in legal phraseology, are all included in the word *suitors.*

3. A petitioner; an applicant.

She hath been a *suitor* to me for her brother. *Shak.*

4. One who solicits a woman in marriage; a wooer; a lover.

SUITRESS, *n.* A female supplicant. *Rowe.*

SUL'CATE, SUL'CATED, } *a.* [L. *sulcus*, a furrow.] In *botany*, furrowed; grooved; scored with deep broad channels longitudinally; as a *sulcated* stem. *Martyn.*

SUL'KINESS, *n.* [from *sulky.*] Sullenness; sourness; moroseness.

SUL'KY, *a.* [Sax. *solcen*, sluggish.] Sullen; sour; heavy; obstinate; morose.

While these animals remain in their inclosures, they are *sulky.* *As. Res.*

SUL'KY, *n.* A carriage for a single person.

SUL'LAGE, *n.* [See *Sulliage.*] A drain of filth, or filth collected from the street or highway. *Cyc.*

SUL'LEN, *a.* [perhaps set, fixed, and allied to *silent*, *sill*, &c.]

1. Gloomily angry and silent; cross; sour; affected with ill humor.

> And *sullen* I forsook th' imperfect feast. *Prior.*

2. Mischievous; malignant.

> Such *sullen* planets at my birth did shine. *Dryden.*

3. Obstinate; intractable.

> Things are as *sullen* as we are. *Tillotson.*

4. Gloomy; dark; dismal.

> Why are thine eyes fix'd to the *sullen* earth? *Shak.*

> Night with her *sullen* wings. *Milton.*
> No cheerful breeze this *sullen* region knows. *Pope.*

5. Heavy; dull; sorrowful.

> Be thou the trumpet of our wrath,
> And *sullen* presage of your own decay. *Shak.*

SUL'LENLY, *adv.* Gloomily; malignantly; intractably; with moroseness. *Dryden.*

SUL'LENNESS, *n.* Ill nature with silence; silent moroseness; gloominess; malignity; intractableness. *Milton. Temple.*

SUL'LENS, *n. plu.* A morose temper; gloominess. [*Not in use.*] *Shak.*

SUL'LIAGE, *n.* [Fr. *souillage.*] Foulness; filth. [*Not in use.*]

SUL'LIED, *pp.* Soiled; tarnished; stained.

SUL'LY, *v. t.* [Fr. *souiller;* from the root of *soil,* G. *süle.*]

1. To soil; to dirt; to spot; to tarnish.

> And statues *sullied* yet with sacrilegious smoke. *Roscommon.*

2. To tarnish; to darken.

> Let there be no spots to *sully* the brightness of this solemnity. *Atterbury.*

3. To stain; to tarnish; as the purity of reputation; as virtues *sullied* by slanders; character *sullied* by infamous vices.

SUL'LY, *v. i.* To be soiled or tarnished.

> Silvering will *sully* and canker more than gilding. *Bacon.*

SUL'LY, *n.* Soil; tarnish; spot.

> A noble and triumphant merit breaks through little spots and *sullies* on his reputation. *Spectator.*

SUL'LYING, *ppr.* Soiling; tarnishing; staining.

SUL'PHATE, *n.* [from *sulphur.*] A neutral salt formed by sulphuric acid in combination with any base; as *sulphate* of lime. *Lavoisier.*

SULPHAT'IC, *a.* Pertaining to sulphate.

SUL'PHITE, *n.* [from *sulphur.*] A salt or definite compound formed by a combination of sulphurous acid with a base. *Lavoisier.*

SUL'PHUR, *n.* [L. whence Fr. *soufre;* It. *zolfo;* Sp. *azufre;* Port. *enxofre;* D. *solfer.*]

A simple combustible mineral substance, of a yellow color, brittle, insoluble in water, but fusible by heat. It is called also *brimstone,* that is, *burn-stone,* from its great combustibility. It burns with a blue flame and a peculiar suffocating odor. Sulphur native or prismatic is of two kinds, common and volcanic. *Nicholson. Ure.*

SUL'PHURATE, *a.* [L. *sulphuratus.*] Belonging to sulphur; of the color of sulphur. [*Little used.*] *More.*

SUL'PHURATE, *v. t.* To combine with sulphur.

SUL'PHURATED, *pp.* Combined or impregnated with sulphur; as *sulphurated* hydrogen gas. *Lavoisier.*

SULPHURA'TION, *n.* Act of addressing or anointing with sulphur. *Bentley.*

SUL'PHURE, SUL'PHURET, *n.* A combination of sulphur with a metallic, earthy or alkaline base; as a *sulphuret* of potash. *Lavoisier. Hooper.*

SULPHU'REOUS, *a.* Consisting of sulphur; having the qualities of sulphur or brimstone; impregnated with sulphur.

> Her snakes untied, *sulphureous* waters drink. *Pope.*

SULPHU'REOUSLY, *adv.* In a sulphureous manner.

SULPHU'REOUSNESS, *n.* The state of being sulphureous.

SUL'PHURETED, *a.* Applied to gaseous bodies holding sulphur in solution; as *sulphureted* hydrogen.

SUL'PHURIC, *a.* Pertaining to sulphur; more strictly, designating an acid formed by sulphur saturated with oxygen; as *sulphuric* acid, formerly called vitriolic acid, or oil of vitrol. *Chimistry.*

SUL'PHUROUS, *a.* Like sulphur; containing sulphur; also, designating an acid formed by sulphur subsaturated with oxygen. This is called *sulphurous acid.*

SUL'PHUR-WORT, *n.* A plant, hog's fennel, of the genus Peucedanum.

SUL'PHURY, *a.* Partaking of sulphur; having the qualities of sulphur.

SUL'TAN, *n.* [Qu. Ch. Syr. Heb. שלט to rule.]

An appellation given to the emperor of the Turks, denoting ruler or commander.

SULTA'NA, SUL'TANESS, *n.* The queen of a sultan; the empress of the Turks. *Cleaveland.*

SUL'TAN-FLOWER, *n.* A plant, a species of Centaurea.

SUL'TANRY, *n.* An eastern empire; the dominions of a sultan. *Bacon.*

SUL'TRINESS, *n.* [from *sultry.*] The state of being sultry; heat with a moist or close air.

SUL'TRY, *a.* [G. *schwül,* sultry; Sax. *swolath, swole,* heat, G. *schwüle.* See *Swelter.*]

1. Very hot, burning and oppressive; as Libya's *sultry* deserts. *Addison.*
2. Very hot and moist, or hot, close, stagnant and unelastic; as air or the atmosphere. A *sultry* air is usually enfeebling and oppressive to the human body.

> Such as born beneath the burning sky
> And *sultry* sun, betwixt the tropics lie. *Dryden.*

SUM, *n.* [Fr. *somme;* G. *summe;* D. *som;* Dan. *sum;* Sw. L. *summa,* a sum; Sax. *somed,* L. *simul,* together; Sax. *somnian,* to assemble. These words may be from the root of Ch. סום, Syr. ܣܘܡ, Heb. שום to set or place.]

1. The aggregate of two or more numbers, magnitudes, quantities or particulars; the amount or whole of any number of individuals or particulars added. The *sum* of 5 and 7 is 12.

> How precious are thy thoughts to me, O God! how great is the *sum* of them! Ps. cxxxix.

> Take the *sum* of all the congregation. Num. i.

[*Sum* is now applied more generally to numbers, and *number* to persons.]

2. A quantity of money or currency; any amount indefinitely. I sent him a *sum* of money, a small *sum,* or a large *sum.* I received a large *sum* in bank notes.
3. Compendium; abridgment; the amount; the substance. This is the *sum* of all the evidence in the case. This is the *sum* and substance of all his objections. The *sum* of all I have said is this.

The phrase, *in sum,* is obsolete or nearly so.

> *In sum,* the gospel considered as a law, prescribes every virtue to our conduct, and forbids every sin. *Rogers.*

4. Highth; completion.

> Thus have I told thee all my state, and brought
> My story to the *sum* of earthly bliss. *Milton.*

SUM, *v. t.* To add particulars into one whole; to collect two or more particular numbers into one number; to cast up; usually followed by *up,* but it is superfluous. Custom enables a man to *sum up* a long column of figures with surprising facility and correctness.

> The hour doth rather *sum up* the moments, than divide the day. *Bacon.*

2. To bring or collect into a small compass; to comprise in a few words; to condense. He *summed* up his arguments at the close of his speech, with great force and effect.

> "Go to the ant, thou sluggard," in few words, *sums* up the moral of this fable. *L'Estrange.*

3. In *falconry,* to have fethers full grown.

> With prosperous wing full *summ'd.* *Milton.*
> [*Unusual.*]

SUMAC, SUMACH, *n.* *shu'mak.* [Fr. *sumach;* G. *id.;* D. *sumak;* Ar. Pers. سُمَّاق.]

A plant or shrub of the genus Rhus, of many species, some of which are used in tanning and dyeing, and in medicine.

SUM'LESS, *a.* Not to be computed; of which the amount cannot be ascertained.

> The *sumless* treasure of exhausted mines. *Pope.*

SUM'MARILY, *adv.* [from *summary.*] In a summary manner; briefly; concisely; in a narrow compass or in few words. The Lord's prayer teaches us *summarily* the things we are to ask for.

2. In a short way or method.

> When the parties proceed *summarily,* and they choose the ordinary way of proceeding, the cause is made plenary. *Ayliffe.*

SUM'MARY, *a.* [Fr. *sommaire;* from *sum,* or L. *summa.*]

Reduced into a narrow compass, or into few words; short; brief; concise; compendious; as a *summary* statement of arguments or objections; a *summary* proceeding or process.

SUM'MARY, *n.* An abridged account; an abstract, abridgment or compendium, containing the sum or substance of a fuller account; as the comprehensive *summary* of our duty to God in the first table of the law.

SUM'MED, *pp.* [from *sum.*] Collected into a total amount; fully grown, as fethers.

SUM'MER, *n.* One who casts up an account. *Sherwood.*

SUM'MER, *n.* [Sax. *sumer, sumor;* G. Dan. *sommer;* D. *zomer;* Sw. *sommar;* Ir. *samh,* the sun, and summer, and *samhradh,* summer.]

With us, the season of the year comprehended in the months June, July and August; during which time, the sun being north of the equator, shines more directly upon this part of the earth, which, together with the increased length of the days, renders this the hottest period of the year. In latitudes south of the equator, just the opposite takes place, or it is summer there when it is winter here.

The entire year is also sometimes divided into summer and winter, the former signifying the warmer and the latter the colder part of the year.

SUM'MER, *v. i.* To pass the summer or warm season.

The fowls shall *summer* upon them. Is. xviii.

SUM'MER, *v. t.* To keep warm. [*Little used.*] *Shak.*

SUM'MER, *n.* [Fr. *sommier*, a hair quilt, the sound-board of an organ, the winter and head of a printer's press, a large beam and a sumpter horse; W. *sumer*, that which supports or keeps together, a summer. From the latter explanation, we may infer that *summer* is from the root of *sum*.]

1. A large stone, the first that is laid over columns and pilasters, beginning to make a cross vault; or a stone laid over a column, and hollowed to receive the first haunce of a platband. *Cyc.*

2. A large timber supported on two stone piers or posts, serving as a lintel to a door or window, &c. *Cyc.*

3. A large timber or beam laid as a central floor timber, inserted into the girders, and receiving the ends of the joists and supporting them. This timber is seen in old buildings in America and in France. In America, it is wholly laid aside. It is called in England *summer-tree*.

SUM'MER-COLT, *n.* The undulating state of the air near the surface of the ground when heated. [*Not used in America.*]

SUMMER-CYPRESS, *n.* A plant, a species of Chenopodium.

SUMMER-FAL'LOW, *n.* [See *Fallow.*] Naked fallow; land lying bare of crops in summer.

SUMMER-FAL'LOW, *v. t.* To plow and work repeatedly in summer, to prepare for wheat or other crop.

SUM'MER-HOUSE, *n.* A house or apartment in a garden to be used in summer. *Pope. Watts.*

2. A house for summer's residence.

SUM'MERSET, *n.* [corruption of Fr. *soubresaut.*]

A high leap in which the heels are thrown over the head. *Hudibras. Walton.*

SUM'MER-WHEAT, *n.* Spring wheat.

SUM'MING, *ppr.* of *sum.* Adding together.

SUM'MIST, *n.* One that forms an abridgment. [*Little used.*] *Dering.*

SUM'MIT, *n.* [L. *summitas*, from *summus*, highest.]

1. The top; the highest point; as the *summit* of a mountain.

2. The highest point or degree; utmost elevation. The general arrived to the *summit* of human fame.

SUM'MON, *v. t.* [L. *submoneo*; *sub* and *moneo*; Fr. *sommer.* See *Admonish.*]

1. To call, cite or notify by authority to appear at a place specified, or to attend in person to some public duty, or both; as, to *summon* a jury; to *summon* witnesses.

The parliament is *summoned* by the king's writ or letter. *Blackstone.*

Nor trumpets *summon* him to war. *Dryden.*

2. To give notice to a person to appear in court and defend.

3. To call or command.

Love, duty, safety *summon* us away. *Pope.*

4. To call up; to excite into action or exertion; with *up.* *Summon up* all your strength or courage.

Stiffen the sinews, *summon up* the blood. *Shak.*

SUM'MONED, *pp.* Admonished or warned by authority to appear or attend to something; called or cited by authority.

SUM'MONER, *n.* One who summons or cites by authority. In England, the sheriff's messenger, employed to warn persons to appear in court.

SUM'MONING, *ppr.* Citing by authority to appear or attend to something.

SUM'MONS, *n.* with a plural termination, but used in the singular number; as a *summons is* prepared. [L. *submoneas.*] A call by authority or the command of a superior to appear at a place named, or to attend to some public duty.

This *summons* he resolved not to disobey. *Fell.*

He sent to summon the seditious and to offer pardon; but neither *summons* nor pardon was regarded. *Hayward.*

2. In *law*, a warning or citation to appear in court; or a written notification signed by the proper officer, to be served on a person, warning him to appear in court at a day specified, to answer to the demand of the plaintif.

SUMOOM', *n.* A pestilential wind of Persia. [See *Simoom.*]

SUMP, *n.* In *metallurgy*, a round pit of stone, lined with clay, for receiving the metal on its first fusion.

2. A pond of water reserved for salt-works.

3. In *mining*, a pit sunk below the bottom of the mine.

SUMP'TER, *n.* [Fr. *sommier*; It. *somaro.*]

A horse that carries clothes or furniture; a baggage-horse; usually called a pack-horse. *Shak.*

SUMP'TION, *n.* [L. *sumo, sumptus.*] A taking. [*Not in use.*] *Taylor.*

SUMP'TUARY, *a.* [L. *sumptuarius*, from *sumptus*, expense; Fr. *somptuaire.*]

Relating to expense. *Sumptuary* laws or regulations are such as restrain or limit the expenses of citizens in apparel, food, furniture, &c. *Sumptuary* laws are abridgments of liberty, and of very difficult execution. They can be justified only on the ground of extreme necessity.

SUMPTUOS'ITY, *n.* [from *sumptuous.*] Expensiveness; costliness. [*Not in use.*] *Raleigh.*

SUMP'TUOUS, *a.* [L. *sumptuosus*; It. *suntuoso*; from *sumptus*, cost, expense.]

Costly; expensive; hence, splendid; magnificent; as a *sumptuous* house or table; *sumptuous* apparel.

We are too magnificent and *sumptuous* in our tables and attendance. *Atterbury.*

SUMP'TUOUSLY, *adv.* Expensively; splendidly; with great magnificence. *Bacon. Swift.*

SUMP'TUOUSNESS, *n.* Costliness; expensiveness.

I will not fall out with those who can reconcile *sumptuousness* and charity. *Boyle.*

2. Splendor; magnificence.

SUN, *n.* [Sax. *sunna*; Goth. *sunno*; G. *sonne*; D. *zon.* The Danish has *Söndag*, Sunday, Slav. *Sonze.* Qu. W. *tan*, Ir. *teine*, fire, and *shan*, in *Bethshan.*]

1. The splendid orb or luminary which, being in or near the center of our system of worlds, gives light and heat to all the planets. The light of the sun constitutes the day, and the darkness which proceeds from its absence, or the shade of the earth, constitutes the night. Ps. cxxxvi.

2. In *popular usage*, a sunny place; a place where the beams of the sun fall; as, to stand in the *sun*, that is, to stand where the direct rays of the sun fall.

3. Any thing eminently splendid or luminous; that which is the chief source of light or honor. The natives of America complain that the *sun* of their glory is set.

I will never consent to put out the *sun* of sovereignty to posterity. *K. Charles.*

4. In *Scripture*, Christ is called the *sun* of righteousness, as the source of light, animation and comfort to his disciples.

5. The luminary or orb which constitutes the center of any system of worlds. The fixed stars are supposed to be *suns* in their respective systems.

Under the sun, in the world; on earth; a proverbial expression.

There is no new thing *under the sun.* Eccles. i.

SUN, *v. t.* To expose to the sun's rays; to warm or dry in the light of the sun; to insolate; as, to *sun* cloth; to *sun* grain.

—Then to *sun* thyself in open air. *Dryden.*

SUN'BEAM, *n.* [*sun* and *beam.*] A ray of the sun. Truth written with a *sunbeam*, is truth made obviously plain.

Gliding through the even on a *sunbeam.* *Milton.*

SUN'-BEAT, *a.* [*sun* and *beat.*] Struck by the sun's rays; shone brightly on. *Dryden.*

SUN'-BRIGHT, *a.* [*sun* and *bright.*] Bright as the sun; like the sun in brightness; as a *sun-bright* shield; a *sun-bright* chariot. *Spenser. Milton.*

How and which way I may bestow myself
To be regarded in her *sun-bright* eye. *Shak.*

SUN'-BURNING, *n.* [*sun* and *burning.*] The burning or tan occasioned by the rays of the sun on the skin. *Boyle.*

SUN'BURNT, *a.* [*sun* and *burnt.*] Discolored by the heat or rays of the sun; tanned; darkened in hue; as a *sunburnt* skin.

Sunburnt and swarthy though she be. *Dryden.*

2. Scorched by the sun's rays; as a *sunburnt* soil. *Blackmore.*

SUN'CLAD, *a.* [*sun* and *clad.*] Clad in radiance or brightness.

SUN'DAY, *n.* [Sax. *sunna-dæg*; G. *sonntag*; D. *zondag*; Dan. *söndag*; Sw. *söndag*; so called because this day was anciently dedicated to the sun, or to its worship.]

The christian sabbath; the first day of the week, a day consecrated to rest from secular employments, and to religious worship. It is called also the Lord's day. Many pious persons however discard the use of *Sunday*, and call the day the *sabbath.*

SUN'DER, *v. t.* [Sax. *sundrian, syndrian;* G. *sondern;* Dan. *sönder*, torn in pieces; Sw. *söndra*, to divide.]

1. To part; to separate; to divide; to disunite in almost any manner, either by rending, cutting or breaking; as, to *sunder* a rope or cord; to *sunder* a limb or joint; to *sunder* friends, or the ties of friendship. The executioner *sunders* the head from the body at a stroke. A mountain may be *sundered* by an earthquake.

Bring me lightning, give me thunder;
—Jove may kill, but ne'er shall *sunder*. *Granville.*

2. To expose to the sun. [*Provincial in England.*]

SUN'DER, *n.* *In sunder*, in two.

He cutteth the spear *in sunder*. Ps. xlvi.

SUN'DERED, *pp.* Separated; divided; parted.

SUN'DERING, *ppr.* Parting; separating.

SUN'-DEW, *n.* [*sun* and *dew.*] A plant of the genus Drosera. *Lee.*

SUN'-DIAL, *n.* [*sun* and *dial.*] An instrument to show the time of day, by means of the shadow of a gnomon or style on a plate. *Locke.*

SUN'-DRIED, *a.* [*sun* and *dry.*] Dried in the rays of the sun.

SUN'DRY, *a.* [Sax. *sunder*, separate.] Several; divers; more than one or two. [This word, like *several*, is indefinite; but it usually signifies a small number, sometimes many.]

I have composed *sundry* collects. *Saunderson.*

Sundry foes the rural realm surround. *Dryden.*

SUN'FISH, *n.* [*sun* and *fish.*] A name of the diodon, a genus of fishes of a very singular form, appearing like the fore part of the body of a very deep fish amputated in the middle. *Dict. Nat. Hist.*

The sunfish is the *Tetraodon mola* of Linne. *Cyc.*

2. The basking shark. *Cyc.*

SUN'FLOWER, *n.* [*sun* and *flower.*] A plant of the genus Helianthus; so called from the form and color of its flower, or from its habit of turning to the sun. The *bastard sunflower* is of the genus Helenium; the *dwarf sunflower* is of the genus Rudbeckia, and another of the genus Tetragonotheca; the *little sunflower* is of the genus Cistus. *Fam. of Plants.*

SUNG, *pret.* and *pp.* of *sing.*

While to his harp divine Amphion *sung*. *Pope.*

SUNK, *pret.* and *pp.* of *sink.*

Or toss'd by hope, or *sunk* by care. *Prior.*

SUN'LESS, *a.* [*sun* and *less.*] Destitute of the sun or its rays; shaded. *Thomson.*

SUN'LIKE, *a.* [*sun* and *like.*] Resembling the sun. *Cheyne.*

SUN'NY, *a.* [from *sun.*] Like the sun; bright. *Spenser.*

2. Proceeding from the sun; as *sunny* beams. *Spenser.*

3. Exposed to the rays of the sun; warmed by the direct rays of the sun; as the *sunny* side of a hill or building.

Her blooming mountains and her *sunny* shores. *Addison.*

4. Colored by the sun.

Her *sunny* locks
Hang on her temples like a golden fleece. *Shak.*

SUN'PROOF, *a.* [*sun* and *proof.*] Impervious to the rays of the sun. *Peele.*

SUN'RISE, SUN'RISING, *n.* [*sun* and *rise.*] The first appearance of the sun above the horizon in the morning; or more generally, the time of such appearance, whether in fair or cloudy weather. *Raleigh.*

2. The east.

SUN'SET, SUN'SETTING, *n.* [*sun* and *set.*] The descent of the sun below the horizon; or the time when the sun sets; evening. *Raleigh. Dryden.*

SUN'SHINE, *n.* [*sun* and *shine.*] The light of the sun, or the place where it shines; the direct rays of the sun, or the place where they fall.

But all *sunshine*, as when his beams at noon
Culminate from th' equator. *Milton.*

2. A place warmed and illuminated; warmth; illumination.

The man that sits within a monarch's heart,
And ripens in the *sunshine* of his favor. *Shak.*

SUN'SHINE, SUN'SHINY, *a.* Bright with the rays of the sun; clear, warm or pleasant; as a *sunshiny* day; *sunshiny* weather. *Boyle.*

2. Bright like the sun.

—Flashing beams of that *sunshiny* shield. *Spenser.*

SUP, *v. t.* [Sax. *supan;* D. *zuipen;* Fr. *souper*. See *Soup* and *Sip.*]

To take into the mouth with the lips, as a liquid; to take or drink by a little at a time; to sip.

There I'll *sup*
Balm and nectar in my cup. *Crashaw.*

SUP, *v. i.* To eat the evening meal.

When they had *supped*, they brought Tobias in. *Tobit.*

SUP, *v. t.* To treat with supper.

Sup them well. [*Not in use.*] *Shak.*

SUP, *n.* A small mouthful, as of liquor or broth; a little taken with the lips; a sip.

Tom Thumb got a little *sup*. *Drayton.*

SUPER, a Latin preposition, Gr. ὑπερ, signifies *above, over, excess*. It is much used in composition.

SU'PERABLE, *a.* [L. *superabilis*, from *supero*, to overcome.]

That may be overcome or conquered. These are *superable* difficulties.

SU'PERABLENESS, *n.* The quality of being conquerable or surmountable.

SU'PERABLY, *adv.* So as may be overcome.

SUPERABOUND', *v. i.* [*super* and *abound.*]

To be very abundant or exuberant; to be more than sufficient. The country *superabounds* with corn.

SUPERABOUND'ING, *ppr.* Abounding beyond want or necessity; abundant to excess or a great degree.

SUPERABUND'ANCE, *n.* More than enough; excessive abundance: as a *superabundance* of the productions of the earth. *Woodward.*

SUPERABUND'ANT, *a.* Abounding to excess; being more than is sufficient; as *superabundant* zeal. *Swift.*

SUPERABUND'ANTLY, *adv.* More than sufficiently. *Cheyne.*

SUPERACID'ULATED, *a.* [*super* and *acidulated.*] Acidulated to excess.

SUPERADD', *v. t.* [*super* and *add.*] To add over and above; to add to what has been added.

2. To add or annex something extrinsic.

The strength of a living creature, in those external motions, is something distinct from and *superadded* to its natural gravity. *Wilkins.*

SUPERADD'ED, *pp.* Added over and above.

SUPERADD'ING, *ppr.* Adding over and above; adding something extrinsic.

SUPERADDI''TION, *n.* [*super* and *addition.*]

1. The act of adding to something, or of adding something extraneous. *More.*

2. That which is added.

This *superaddition* is nothing but fat. *Arbuthnot.*

SUPERADVE'NIENT, *a.* [L. *superadveniens.*]

1. Coming upon; coming to the increase or assistance of something.

When a man has done bravely by the *superadvenient* assistance of his God— *More.*

2. Coming unexpectedly. [*This word is little used.*]

SUPERANGEL'IC, *a.* [*super* and *angelic.*] Superior in nature or rank to the angels. One class of Unitarians believe Christ to be a *superangelic* being.

SUPERAN'NUATE, *v. t.* [L. *super* and *annus*, a year.]

To impair or disqualify by old age and infirmity; as a *superannuated* magistrate. *Swift.*

SUPERAN'NUATE, *v. i.* To last beyond the year. [*Not in use.*] *Bacon.*

SUPERAN'NUATED, *pp.* Impaired or disqualified by old age.

SUPERANNUA'TION, *n.* The state of being too old for office or business, or of being disqualified by old age.

SUPERB', *a.* [Fr. *superbe;* L. *superbus*, proud, from *super.*]

1. Grand; magnificent; as a *superb* edifice; a *superb* colonnade.

2. Rich; elegant; as *superb* furniture or decorations.

3. Showy; pompous; as a *superb* exhibition.

4. Rich; splendid; as a *superb* entertainment.

5. August; stately.

SUPERB'LY, *adv.* In a magnificent or splendid manner; richly; elegantly.

SUPERC'ARGO, *n.* [*super* and *cargo.*] An officer or person in a merchant's ship, whose business is to manage the sales and superintend all the commercial concerns of the voyage.

SUPERCELES'TIAL, *a.* [*super* and *celestial.*]

Situated above the firmament or great vault of heaven.

Trans. Pausanias. Raleigh. Woodward.

SUPERCIL'IARY, *a.* [L. *super* and *cilium*, the eyebrow.] Situated or being above the eyebrow. *As. Res.*

The *superciliary arch*, is the bony superior arch of the orbit. *Cyc.*

SUPERCIL'IOUS, *a.* [L. *superciliosus.* See above.]

1. Lofty with pride; haughty; dictatorial; overbearing; as a *supercilious* officer.

2. Manifesting haughtiness, or proceeding from it; overbearing; as a *supercilious* air; *supercilious* behavior.

SUPERCIL'IOUSLY, *adv.* Haughtily; dogmatically; with an air of contempt. *Clarendon.*

SUPERCIL'IOUSNESS, *n.* Haughtiness; an overbearing temper or manner.

SUPERCONCEP'TION, *n.* [*super* and *conception.*] A conception after a former conception. *Brown.*

SUPERCON'SEQUENCE, *n.* [*super* and *consequence.*] Remote consequence. [*Not used.*] *Brown.*

SUPERCRES'CENCE, *n.* [L. *super* and *crescens.*]
That which grows upon another growing thing. *Brown.*

SUPERCRES'CENT, *a.* [supra.] Growing on some other growing thing. *Johnson.*

SUPEREM'INENCE, SUPEREM'INENCY, *n.* [L. *super* and *emineo.*] Eminence superior to what is common; distinguished eminence; as the *supereminence* of Cicero as an orator; the *supereminence* of Dr. Johnson as a writer, or of lord Chatham as a statesman.

SUPEREM'INENT, *a.* Eminent in a superior degree; surpassing others in excellence; as a *supereminent* divine; the *supereminent* glory of Christ.

SUPEREM'INENTLY, *adv.* In a superior degree of excellence; with unusual distinction.

SUPERER'OGANT, *a.* Supererogatory, which see. *Stackhouse.*

SUPERER'OGATE, *v. i.* [L. *super* and *erogatio, erogo.*]
To do more than duty requires. Aristotle's followers have *supererogated* in observance. [*Little used.*] *Glanville.*

SUPEREROGA'TION, *n.* [supra.] Performance of more than duty requires.

> There is no such thing as works of *supererogation.* *Tillotson.*

SUPEREROG'ATIVE, *a.* Supererogatory. [*Not much used.*] *Stafford.*

SUPEREROG'ATORY, *a.* Performed to an extent not enjoined or not required by duty; as *supererogatory* services. *Howell.*

SUPERESSEN'TIAL, *a.* [*super* and *essential.*]
Essential above others, or above the constitution of a thing. *Pausanias, Trans.*

SUPEREXALT', *v. t.* [*super* and *exalt.*] To exalt to a superior degree. *Barrow.*

SUPEREXALTA'TION, *n.* [*super* and *exaltation.*] Elevation above the common degree. *Holiday.*

SUPEREX'CELLENCE, *n.* [*super* and *excellence.*] Superior excellence.

SUPEREX'CELLENT, *a.* Excellent in an uncommon degree; very excellent. *Decay of Piety.*

SUPEREXCRES'CENCE, *n.* [*super* and *excrescence.*] Something superfluously growing. *Wiseman.*

SUPERFECUND'ITY, *n.* [*super* and *fecundity.*] Superabundant fecundity or multiplication of the species. *Paley.*

SUPERFE'TATE, *v. i.* [L. *super* and *fœtus.*] To conceive after a prior conception.

> The female is said to *superfetate.* *Grew.*

SUPERFETA'TION, *n.* A second conception after a prior one, and before the birth of the first, by which two fetuses are growing at once in the same matrix. *Howell.*

SU'PERFETE, *v. i.* To superfetate. [*Little used.*] *Howell.*

SU'PERFETE, *v. t.* To conceive after a former conception. [*Little used.*] *Howell.*

SU'PERFICE, *n.* Superficies; surface. [*Little used.*] [See *Superficies.*]

SUPERFI''CIAL, *a.* [It. *superficiale*; Sp. *superficial*; Fr. *superficiel*; from *superficies.*]
1. Being on the surface; not penetrating the substance of a thing; as a *superficial* color; a *superficial* covering.
2. Composing the surface or exterior part; as, soil constitutes the *superficial* part of the earth.
3. Shallow; contrived to cover something.

> This *superficial* tale
> Is but a preface to her worthy praise. *Shak.*

4. Shallow; not deep or profound; reaching or comprehending only what is obvious or apparent; as a *superficial* scholar; *superficial* knowledge. *Dryden.*

SUPERFICIAL'ITY, *n.* The quality of being superficial. [*Not much used.*] *Brown.*

SUPERFI''CIALLY, *adv.* On the surface only; as a substance *superficially* tinged with a color.
2. On the surface or exterior part only; without penetrating the substance or essence; as, to survey things *superficially.* *Milton.*
3. Without going deep or searching things to the bottom; slightly. He reasons *superficially.*

> I have laid down *superficially* my present thoughts. *Dryden.*

SUPERFI''CIALNESS, *n.* Shallowness; position on the surface.
2. Slight knowledge; shallowness of observation or learning; show without substance.

SUPERFI''CIES, *n.* [L. from *super*, upon, and *facies*, face.]
The surface; the exterior part of a thing. A superficies consists of length and breadth; as the *superficies* of a plate or of a sphere. Superficies is rectilinear, curvilinear, plane, convex or concave.

SU'PERFINE, *a.* [*super* and *fine.*] Very fine or most fine; surpassing others in fineness; as *superfine* cloth. The word is chiefly used of cloth, but sometimes of liquors: as *superfine* wine or cider; and of other things, as *superfine* wire; *superfine* flour.

SUPER'FLUENCE, *n.* [L. *super* and *fluo*, to flow.] Superfluity; more than is necessary. [*Little used.*] *Hammond.*

SUPERFLU'ITANCE, *n.* [L. *super* and *fluito*, to float.]
The act of floating above or on the surface. [*Little used.*] *Brown.*

SUPERFLU'ITANT, *a.* Floating above or on the surface. [*Little used.*] *Brown.*

SUPERFLU'ITY, *n.* [Fr. *superfluité*; It. *superfluità*; L. *superfluitas*; *super* and *fluo*, to flow.]
1. Superabundance; a greater quantity than is wanted; as a *superfluity* of water or provisions.
2. Something that is beyond what is wanted; something rendered unnecessary by its abundance. Among the *superfluities* of life we seldom number the abundance of money.

SUPER'FLUOUS, *a.* [L. *superfluus*, overflowing; *super* and *fluo*, to flow.]
1. More than is wanted; rendered unnecessary by superabundance; as a *superfluous* supply of corn.
2. More than sufficient; unnecessary; useless; as a composition abounding with *superfluous* words. *Superfluous* epithets rather enfeeble than strengthen description. If what has been said will not convince, it would be *superfluous* to say more.

Superfluous interval, in music, is one that exceeds a true diatonic interval by a semitone minor. *Cyc.*

Superfluous polygamy, (*Polygamia superflua,*) a kind of inflorescence or compound flower, in which the florets of the disk are hermaphrodite and fertile, and those of the ray, though female or pistiliferous only, are also fertile; designating the second order of the class *Syngenesia* of Linne. *Martyn.*

Superfluous sound or *tone*, is one which contains a semitone minor more than a tone. *Cyc.*

SUPER'FLUOUSLY, *adv.* With excess; in a degree beyond what is necessary.

SUPER'FLUOUSNESS, *n.* The state of being superfluous or beyond what is wanted.

SU'PERFLUX, *n.* [L. *super* and *fluxus.*] That which is more than is wanted. [*Little used.*] *Shak.*

SUPERFOLIA'TION, *n.* [*super* and *foliation.*] Excess of foliation. [*Not used.*] *Brown.*

SUPERHU'MAN, *a.* [*super* and *human.*] Above or beyond what is human; divine.

SUPERIMPOSE, *v. t.* *superimpo'ze.* [*super* and *impose.*]
To lay or impose on something else; as a stratum of earth *superimposed* on a different stratum. *Kirwan.*

SUPERIMPO'SED, *pp.* Laid or imposed on something. *Humboldt.*

SUPERIMPO'SING, *ppr.* Laying on something else.

SUPERIMPOSI''TION, *n.* The act of laying or the state of being placed on something else. *Kirwan.*

SUPERIMPREGNA'TION, *n.* [*super* and *impregnation.*]
The act of impregnating upon a prior impregnation; impregnation when previously impregnated. *Coxe.*

SUPERINCUM'BENT, *a.* [*super* and *incumbent.*] Lying or resting on something else.

SUPERINDU'CE, *v. t.* [*super* and *induce.*] To bring in or upon as an addition to something; as, to *superinduce* a virtue or quality upon a person not before possessing it.

> Long custom of sinning *superinduces* upon the soul new and absurd desires. *South.*

SUPERINDU'CED, *pp.* Induced or brought upon something.

SUPERINDU'CING, *ppr.* Inducing on something else.

SUPERINDUC'TION, *n.* The act of superinducing.

> The *superinduction* of ill habits quickly defaces the first rude draught of virtue. *South.*

SUPERINJEC'TION, *n.* [*super* and *injection.*]
An injection succeeding another. *Dict.*

SUPERINSPECT′, *v. t.* [*super* and *inspect.*] To oversee; to superintend by inspection. [*Little used.*]

SUPERINSTITU′TION, *n.* [*super* and *institution.*]

One institution upon another; as when A is instituted and admitted to a benefice upon a title, and B is instituted and admitted upon the presentation of another. *Bailey.*

SUPERINTELLEC′TUAL, *a.* [*super* and *intellectual.*]

Being above intellect. *Pausanias, Trans.*

SUPERINTEND′, *v. t.* [*super* and *intend.*] To have or exercise the charge and oversight of; to oversee with the power of direction; to take care of with authority; as, an officer *superintends* the building of a ship or the construction of a fort. God exercises a *superintending* care over all his creatures.

SUPERINTEND′ED, *pp.* Overseen; taken care of.

SUPERINTEND′ENCE, SUPERINTEND′ENCY, *n.* The act of superintending; care and oversight for the purpose of direction, and with authority to direct.

SUPERINTEND′ENT, *n.* One who has the oversight and charge of something, with the power of direction; as the *superintendent* of an alms-house or work-house; the *superintendent* of public works; the *superintendent* of customs or finance.

2. An ecclesiastical superior in some reformed churches.

SUPERINTEND′ING, *ppr.* Overseeing with the authority to direct what shall be done and how it shall be done.

SUPE′RIOR, *a.* [Sp. L. from *super*, above; Fr. *superieur*; It. *superiore.*]

1. Higher; upper; more elevated in place; as the *superior* limb of the sun; the *superior* part of an image. *Newton.*

2. Higher in rank or office; more exalted in dignity; as a *superior* officer; a *superior* degree of nobility.

3. Higher or greater in excellence; surpassing others in the greatness, goodness or value of any quality; as a man of *superior* merit, of *superior* bravery, of *superior* talents or understanding, of *superior* accomplishments.

4. Being beyond the power or influence of; too great or firm to be subdued or affected by; as a man *superior* to revenge.

> There is not on earth a spectacle more worthy than a great man *superior* to his sufferings. *Spectator.*

5. In *botany*, a *superior flower* has the receptacle of the flower above the germ; a *superior germ* is included within the corol. *Martyn.*

SUPE′RIOR, *n.* One who is more advanced in age. Old persons or elders are the *superiors* of the young.

2. One who is more elevated in rank or office.

3. One who surpasses others in dignity, excellence or qualities of any kind. As a writer of pure English, Addison has no *superior.*

4. The chief of a monastery, convent or abbey.

SUPERIOR′ITY, *n.* Pre-eminence; the quality of being more advanced or higher, greater or more excellent than another in any respect; as *superiority* of age, of rank or dignity, of attainments or excellence. The *superiority* of others in fortune and rank, is more readily acknowledged than *superiority* of understanding.

SUPERLA′TION, *n.* [L. *superlatio.*] Exaltation of any thing beyond truth or propriety. [*I believe not used.*] *B. Jonson.*

SUPER′LATIVE, *a.* [Fr. *superlatif*; L. *superlativus*; *super* and *latio, latus, fero.*]

1. Highest in degree; most eminent; surpassing all other; as a man of *superlative* wisdom or prudence, of *superlative* worth; a woman of *superlative* beauty.

2. Supreme; as the *superlative* glory of the divine character.

3. In *grammar*, expressing the highest or utmost degree; as the *superlative* degree of comparison.

SUPER′LATIVE, *n.* In *grammar*, the superlative degree of adjectives, which is formed by the termination *est*, as *meanest highest, bravest*; or by the use of *most*, as *most* high, *most* brave; or by *least*, as *least* amiable.

SUPER′LATIVELY, *adv.* In a manner expressing the utmost degree.

> I shall not speak *superlatively* of them. *Bacon.*

2. In the highest or utmost degree. Tiberius was *superlatively* wicked; Clodius was *superlatively* profligate.

SUPER′LATIVENESS, *n.* The state of being in the highest degree.

SUPERLU′NAR, SUPERLU′NARY, *a.* [L. *super* and *luna*, the moon.]

Being above the moon; not sublunary or of this world.

> The head that turns at *superlunar* things. *Pope.*

SUPERMUN′DANE, *a.* [*super* and *mundane.*] Being above the world. *Paus. Trans.*

SUPERN′AL, *a.* [L. *supernus, super.*] Being in a higher place or region; locally higher; as the *supernal* orbs; *supernal* regions. *Raleigh.*

2. Relating to things above; celestial; heavenly; as *supernal* grace.

> Not by the sufferings of *supernal* pow'r. *Milton.*

SUPERNA′TANT, *a.* [L. *supernatans, supernato*; *super* and *nato*, to swim.]

Swimming above; floating on the surface; as oil *supernatant* on water. *Boyle.*

SUPERNATA′TION, *n.* The act of floating on the surface of a fluid. *Bacon.*

SUPERNAT′URAL, *a.* [*super* and *natural.*] Being beyond or exceeding the powers or laws of nature; miraculous. A *supernatural* event is one which is not produced according to the ordinary or established laws of natural things. Thus if iron has more specific gravity than water, it will sink in that fluid; and the floating of iron on water must be a *supernatural* event. Now no human being can alter a law of nature; the floating of iron on water therefore must be caused by divine power specially exerted to suspend, in this instance, a law of nature. Hence *supernatural* events or miracles can be produced only by the immediate agency of divine power.

SUPERNAT′URALLY, *adv.* In a manner exceeding the established course or laws of nature. The prophets must have been *supernaturally* taught or enlightened, for their predictions were beyond human foreknowledge.

SUPERNAT′URALNESS, *n.* The state or quality of being beyond the power or ordinary laws of nature.

SUPERNU′MERARY, *a.* [Fr. *supernumeraire*; L. *super* and *numerus*, number.]

1. Exceeding the number stated or prescribed; as a *supernumerary* officer in a regiment; a *supernumerary* canon in the church.

2. Exceeding a necessary, a usual or a round number; as *supernumerary* addresses; *supernumerary* expense. *Addison. Fell.*

SUPERNU′MERARY, *n.* A person or thing beyond the number stated, or beyond what is necessary or usual. On the reduction of the regiments, several *supernumeraries* were to be provided for.

SUPERPARTIC′ULAR, *a.* [*super* and *particular.*]

Noting a ratio when the excess of the greater term is a unit; as the ratio of 1 to 2, or of 3 to 4. *Encyc.*

SUPERP′ARTIENT, *a.* [L. *super* and *partio.*]

Noting a ratio when the excess of the greater term is more than a unit; as that of 3 to 5, or of 7 to 10. *Encyc.*

SU′PERPLANT, *n.* [*super* and *plant.*] A plant growing on another plant; as the misletoe. [*Not used.*] [We now use *parasite.*] *Bacon.*

SUPERPLUS′AGE, *n.* [L. *super* and *plus.*] That which is more than enough; excess. [We now use *surplusage*, which see.] *Fell.*

SUPERPON′DERATE, *v. t.* [L. *super* and *pondero.*]

To weigh over and above. [*Not used.*] *Dict.*

SUPERPOSE, *v. t.* *superpo′ze.* [*super* and Fr. *poser*, to lay.]

To lay upon, as one kind of rock on another.

SUPERPO′SED, *pp.* Laid or being upon something. *Humboldt.*

SUPERPO′SING, *ppr.* Placing upon something.

SUPERPOSI″TION, *n.* [*super* and *position.*]

1. A placing above; a lying or being situated above or upon something; as the *superposition* of rocks. *Humboldt.*

2. That which is situated above or upon something else.

SU′PERPRAISE, *v. t.* *su′perpraze.* To praise to excess. *Shak.*

SUPERPROPORTION, *n.* [*super* and *proportion.*] Overplus of proportion. *Digby.*

SUPERPURGA′TION, *n.* [*super* and *purgation.*] More purgation than is sufficient. *Wiseman.*

SUPERREFLEC′TION, *n.* [*super* and *reflection.*]

The reflection of an image reflected. *Bacon.*

SUPERREWARD′, *v. t.* To reward to excess. *Bacon.*

SUPERROY′AL, *a.* [*super* and *royal.*] Larger than royal; denoting the largest species of printing paper.

SUPERSA′LIENCY, *n.* [L. *super* and *salio*, to leap.]

The act of leaping on any thing. [*Little used.*] *Brown.*

SUPERSA'LIENT, *a.* Leaping upon.

SU'PERSALT, *n.* In chimistry, a salt with an excess of acid, as supertartrate of potash. *Cyc.*

SUPERSAT'URATE, *v. t.* [L. *super* and *saturo.*] To saturate to excess. *Chimistry.*

SUPERSAT'URATED, *pp.* Saturated to excess.

SUPERSAT'URATING, *ppr.* Saturating or filling to excess.

SUPERSATURA'TION, *n.* The operation of saturating to excess; or the state of being thus saturated. *Fourcroy.*

SUPERSCRI'BE, *v. t.* [L. *super* and *scribo*, to write.]

To write or engrave on the top, outside or surface; or to write the name or address of one on the outside or cover; as, to *superscribe* a letter.

SUPERSCRI'BED, *pp.* Inscribed on the outside.

SUPERSCRI'BING, *ppr.* Inscribing, writing or engraving on the outside, or on the top.

SUPERSCRIP'TION, *n.* The act of superscribing.

2. That which is written or engraved on the outside, or above something else. *Waller.*

The *superscription* of his accusation was written over, THE KING OF THE JEWS. Mark xv. Luke xxiii.

3. An impression of letters on coins. Matt. xxii.

SUPERSEC'ULAR, *a.* [*super* and *secular.*] Being above the world or secular things.

SUPERSE'DE, *v. t.* [L. *supersedeo; super* and *sedeo*, to sit.]

1. Literally, to set above; hence, to make void, inefficacious or useless by superior power, or by coming in the place of; to set aside; to render unnecessary; to suspend. The use of artillery in making breaches in walls, has *superseded* the use of the battering ram. The effect of passion is to *supersede* the workings of reason. *South.*

Nothing is supposed that can *supersede* the known laws of natural motion. *Bentley.*

2. To come or be placed in the room of; hence, to displace or render unnecessary; as, an officer is *superseded* by the appointment of another person.

SUPERSE'DEAS, *n.* In *law*, a writ of *supersedeas*, is a writ or command to suspend the powers of an officer in certain cases, or to stay proceedings. This writ does not destroy the power of an officer, for it may be revived by another writ called a *procedendo.* *Blackstone.*

SUPERSE'DED, *pp.* Made void; rendered unnecessary or inefficacious; displaced; suspended.

SUPERSE'DING, *ppr.* Coming in the place of; setting aside; rendering useless; displacing; suspending.

SUPERSE'DURE, *n.* The act of superseding; as the *supersedure* of trial by jury. [*New.*] *Hamilton, Fed.*

SUPERSERV'ICEABLE, *a.* [*super* and *serviceable.*]

Over officious; doing more than is required or desired. [*Not in use.*] *Shak.*

SUPERSTI''TION, *n.* [Fr. from L. *superstitio, superslo; super* and *sto*, to stand.]

1. Excessive exactness or rigor in religious opinions or practice; extreme and unnecessary scruples in the observance of religious rites not commanded, or of points of minor importance; excess or extravagance in religion; the doing of things not required by God, or abstaining from things not forbidden; or the belief of what is absurd, or belief without evidence. *Brown.*

Superstition has reference to God, to religion, or to beings superior to man. *Encyc.*

2. False religion; false worship.

3. Rite or practice proceeding from excess of scruples in religion. In this sense, it admits of a plural.

They the truth
With *superstitions* and traditions taint. *Milton.*

4. Excessive nicety; scrupulous exactness.

5. Belief in the direct agency of superior powers in certain extraordinary or singular events, or in omens and prognostics.

SUPERSTI''TIONIST, *n.* One addicted to superstition. *More.*

SUPERSTI''TIOUS, *a.* [Fr. *superstitieux;* L. *superstitiosus.*]

1. Over scrupulous and rigid in religious observances; addicted to superstition; full of idle fancies and scruples in regard to religion; as *superstitious* people.

2. Proceeding from superstition; manifesting superstition; as *superstitious* rites; *superstitious* observances.

3. Over exact; scrupulous beyond need.

Superstitious use, in law, the use of land for a religious purpose, or by a religious corporation.

SUPERSTI''TIOUSLY, *adv.* In a superstitious manner; with excessive regard to uncommanded rites or unessential opinions and forms in religion. *Bacon.*

2. With too much care; with excessive exactness or scruple.

3. With extreme credulity in regard to the agency of superior beings in extraordinary events.

SUPERSTI''TIOUSNESS, *n.* Superstition.

SUPERSTRA'IN, *v. t.* [*super* and *strain.*] To overstrain or stretch. [*Little used.*] *Bacon.*

SUPERSTRA'TUM, *n.* [*super* and *stratum.*] A stratum or layer above another, or resting on something else. *Asiat. Res.*

SUPERSTRUCT', *v. t.* [L. *superstruo; super* and *struo*, to lay.] To build upon; to erect.

This is the only proper basis on which to *superstruct* first innocence and then virtue.
[*Little used.*] *Decay of Piety.*

SUPERSTRUC'TION, *n.* An edifice erected on something.

My own profession hath taught me not to erect new *superstructions* on an old ruin. *Denham.*

SUPERSTRUCT'IVE, *a.* Built or erected on something else. *Hammond.*

SUPERSTRUCT'URE, *n.* Any structure or edifice built on something else; particularly, the building raised on a foundation. This word is used to distinguish what is erected on a wall or foundation from the foundation itself.

2. Any thing erected on a foundation or basis. In education, we begin with teaching languages as the foundation, and proceed to erect on that foundation the *superstructure* of science.

SUPERSUBSTAN'TIAL, *a.* [*super* and *substantial.*]

More than substantial; being more than substance. *Cyc.*

SUPERSUL'PHATE, *n.* Sulphate with an excess of acid.

SUPERSUL'PHURETED, *a.* Combined with an excess of sulphur. *Aikin.*

SUPERTERRE'NE, *a.* [*super* and *terrene.*] Being above ground, or above the earth. *Hill.*

SUPERTERRES'TRIAL, *a.* Being above the earth, or above what belongs to the earth. *Buckminster.*

SUPERTON'IC, *n.* In *music*, the note next above the key-note. *Busby.*

SUPERTRAG'ICAL, *a.* Tragical to excess. *Warton.*

SUPERVACA'NEOUS, *a.* [L. *supervacaneus; super* and *vaco*, to make void.]

Superfluous; unnecessary; needless; serving no purpose. *Howell.*

SUPERVACA'NEOUSLY, *adv.* Needlessly.

SUPERVACA'NEOUSNESS, *n.* Needlessness. *Bailey.*

SUPERVE'NE, *v. i.* [L. *supervenio; super* and *venio.*]

1. To come upon as something extraneous.

Such a mutual gravitation can never *supervene* to matter, unless impressed by divine power. *Bentley.*

2. To come upon; to happen to.

SUPERVE'NIENT, *a.* Coming upon as something additional or extraneous.

That branch of belief was in him *supervenient* to christian practice. *Hammond.*

Divorces can be granted, *a mensa et toro*, only for *supervenient* causes. *Z. Swift.*

SUPERVEN'TION, *n.* The act of supervening.

SUPERVI'SAL, } *n.* { *supervi'zal,*
SUPERVI''SION, } *n.* { *supervizh'on.*

[from *supervise.*] The act of overseeing; inspection; superintendence. *Tooke. Walsh.*

SUPERVI'SE, *n.* *supervi'ze.* Inspection. [*Not used.*] *Shak.*

SUPERVI'SE, *v. t.* [L. *super* and *visus, video*, to see.]

To oversee; to superintend; to inspect; as, to *supervise* the press for correction.

SUPERVI'SED, *pp.* Inspected.

SUPERVI'SING, *ppr.* Overseeing; inspecting; superintending.

SUPERVI'SOR, *n.* An overseer; an inspector; a superintendent; as the *supervisor* of a pamphlet. *Dryden.*

SUPERVI'VE, *v. t.* [L. *super* and *vivo*, to live.]

To live beyond; to outlive. The soul will *supervive* all the revolutions of nature. [*Little used.*] [See *Survive.*]

SUPINA'TION, *n.* [L. *supino.*] The act of lying or state of being laid with the face upward.

2. The act of turning the palm of the hand upwards. *Lawrence's Lect.*

SUPINA'TOR, *n.* In *anatomy*, a muscle that turns the palm of the hand upward.

SUPI'NE, *a.* [L. *supinus.*] Lying on the back, or with the face upward; opposed to *prone.*

2. Leaning backward; or inclining with exposure to the sun.

If the vine
On rising ground be plac'd on hills *supine*— *Dryden.*

3. Negligent; heedless; indolent; thoughtless; inattentive.

He became pusillanimous and *supine*, and openly exposed to any temptation. *Woodward.*

These men suffer by their *supine* credulity. *K. Charles.*

SU'PINE, *n.* [L. *supinum.*] In *grammar*, a word formed from a verb, or a modification of a verb.

SUPI'NELY, *adv.* With the face upward.

2. Carelessly; indolently; drowsily; in a heedless, thoughtless state.

Who on beds of sin *supinely* lie. *Sandys.*

SUPI'NENESS, *n.* A lying with the face upward.

2. Indolence; drowsiness; heedlessness. Many of the evils of life are owing to our own *supineness.*

SUPINITY, for *supineness*, is not used.

SUP'PAGE, *n.* [from *sup.*] What may be supped; pottage. [*Not in use.*] *Hooker.*

SUPPALPA'TION, *n.* [L. *suppalpor; sub* and *palpor*, to stroke.]
The act of enticing by soft words. [*Not used.*] *Hall.*

SUPPARASITA'TION, *n.* [L. *supparasitor; sub* and *parasite.*]
The act of flattering merely to gain favor. [*Not in use.*] *Hall.*

SUPPEDA'NEOUS, *a.* [L. *sub* and *pes*, the foot.]
Being under the feet. *Brown.*

SUPPED'ITATE, *v. t.* [L. *suppedito.*] To supply. [*Not used.*] *Hammond.*

SUPPEDITA'TION, *n.* [L. *suppeditatio.*] Supply; aid afforded. [*Little used.*] *Bacon.*

SUP'PER, *n.* [Fr. *souper.* See *Sup.*] The evening meal. People who dine late, eat no *supper*. The dinner of fashionable people would be the *supper* of rustics.

SUP'PERLESS, *a.* Wanting supper: being without supper; as, to go *supperless* to bed. *Spectator.*

SUPPLANT', *v. t.* [Fr. *supplanter; L. supplanto; sub* and *planta*, the bottom of the foot.] To trip up the heels.

Supplanted down he fell. *Milton.*

2. To remove or displace by stratagem; or to displace and take the place of; as, a rival *supplants* another in the affections of his mistress, or in the favor of his prince.

Suspecting that the courtier had *supplanted* the friend. *Fell.*

3. To overthrow; to undermine.

SUPPLANTA'TION, *n.* The act of supplanting.

SUPPLANT'ED, *pp.* Tripped up; displaced.

SUPPLANT'ER, *n.* One that supplants.

SUPPLANT'ING, *ppr.* Tripping up the heels; displacing by artifice.

SUP'PLE, *a.* [Fr. *souple;* Arm. *soublat, soublein*, to bend.]

1. Pliant; flexible; easily bent; as *supple* joints; *supple* fingers. *Bacon. Temple.*

2. Yielding; compliant; not obstinate.

If punishment—makes not the will *supple*, it hardens the offender. *Locke.*

3. Bending to the humor of others; flattering; fawning. *Addison.*

4. That makes pliant; as *supple* government. *Shak.*

SUP'PLE, *v. t.* To make soft and pliant; to render flexible; as, to *supple* lether.

2. To make compliant.

A mother persisting till she had *suppled* the will of her daughter. *Locke.*

SUP'PLE, *v. i.* To become soft and pliant; as stones *suppled* into softness. *Dryden.*

SUP'PLED, *pp.* Made soft and pliant; made compliant.

SUP'PLEMENT, *n.* [Fr. from L. *supplementum, suppleo; sub* and *pleo*, to fill.]

1. Literally, a supply; hence, an addition to any thing by which its defects are supplied, and it is made more full and complete. The word is particularly used of an addition to a book or paper.

2. Store; supply. [*Not in use.*] *Chapman.*

3. In *trigonometry*, the quantity by which an arc or an angle falls short of 180 degrees or a semicircle.

SUPPLEMENT'AL, } *a.* Additional; added to supply
SUPPLEMENT'ARY, } what is wanted; as a *supplemental* law or bill.

SUP'PLENESS, *n.* [from *supple.*] Pliancy; pliableness; flexibility; the quality of being easily bent; as the *suppleness* of the joints.

2. Readiness of compliance; the quality of easily yielding; facility; as the *suppleness* of the will. *Locke.*

SUP'PLETORY, *a.* [from L. *suppleo*, to supply.]
Supplying deficiencies; as a *suppletory* oath. *Blackstone.*

SUP'PLETORY, *n.* That which is to supply what is wanted. *Hammond.*

SUPPLI'AL, *n.* The act of supplying. [*Not used.*] *Warburton.*

SUPPLI'ANCE, *n.* Continuance. [*Not in use.*] *Shak.*

SUP'PLIANT, *a.* [Fr. from *supplier*, to entreat, contracted from L. *supplico*, to *supplicate; sub* and *plico*, to fold. See *Comply* and *Apply.*]

1. Entreating; beseeching; supplicating; asking earnestly and submissively.

The rich grow *suppliant*, and the poor grow proud. *Dryden.*

2. Manifesting entreaty; expressive of humble supplication.

To bow and sue for grace with *suppliant* knee. *Milton.*

SUP'PLIANT, *n.* A humble petitioner; one who entreats submissively.

Spare this life, and hear thy *suppliant's* pray'r. *Dryden.*

SUP'PLIANTLY, *adv.* In a suppliant or submissive manner.

SUP'PLICANT, *a.* [L. *supplicans.*] Entreating; asking submissively. *Bp. Bull.*

SUP'PLICANT, *n.* One that entreats; a petitioner who asks earnestly and submissively.

The wise *supplicant*—left the event to God. *Rogers.*

SUP'PLICATE, *v. t.* [L. *supplico; sub* and *plico.* See *Suppliant.*]

1. To entreat for; to seek by earnest prayer; as, to *supplicate* blessings on christian efforts to spread the gospel.

2. To address in prayer; as, to *supplicate* the throne of grace.

SUP'PLICATE, *v. i.* To entreat; to beseech; to implore; to petition with earnestness and submission.

A man cannot brook to *supplicate* or beg. *Bacon.*

SUPPLICA'TION, *n.* [Fr. from L. *supplicatio.*]

1. Entreaty; humble and earnest prayer in worship. In all our *supplications* to the Father of mercies, let us remember a world lying in ignorance and wickedness.

2. Petition; earnest request.

3. In *Roman antiquity*, a religious solemnity observed in consequence of some military success. It consisted in sacrifices, feasting, offering thanks, and praying for a continuance of success. *Encyc.*

SUP'PLICATORY, *a.* Containing supplication; humble; submissive. *Johnson.*

SUPPLI'ED, *pp.* [from *supply.*] Fully furnished; having a sufficiency.

SUPPLI'ER, *n.* He that supplies.

SUPPLY', *v. t.* [L. *suppleo; sub* and *pleo*, disused, to fill; Fr. *suppleer;* Sp. *suplir;* It. *supplire.*]

1. To fill up, as any deficiency happens; to furnish what is wanted; to afford or furnish a sufficiency; as, to *supply* the poor with bread and clothing; to *supply* the daily wants of nature; to *supply* the navy with masts and spars; to *supply* the treasury with money. The city is well *supplied* with water.

I wanted nothing fortune could *supply.* *Dryden.*

2. To serve instead of.

Burning ships the banish'd sun *supply.* *Waller.*

3. To give; to bring or furnish.

Nearer care *supplies*
Sighs to my breast, and sorrow to my eyes. *Prior.*

4. To fill vacant room.

The sun was set, and Vesper to *supply*
His absent beams, had lighted up the sky. *Dryden.*

5. To fill; as, to *supply* a vacancy.

6. In *general*, to furnish; to give or afford what is wanted.

Modern infidelity *supplies* no such motives. *Rob. Hall.*

SUPPLY', *n.* Sufficiency for wants given or furnished. The poor have a daily *supply* of food; the army has ample *supplies* of provisions and munitions of war. Customs, taxes and excise constitute the *supplies* of revenue.

SUPPLY'ING, *ppr.* Yielding or furnishing what is wanted; affording a sufficiency.

SUPPLY'MENT, *n.* A furnishing. [*Not in use.*] *Shak.*

SUPPORT, *v. t.* [Fr. *supporter;* It. *sopportare;* L. *supporto; sub* and *porto*, to carry.]

1. To bear; to sustain; to uphold; as, a prop or pillar *supports* a structure; an abutment *supports* an arch; the stem of a tree *supports* the branches. Every edifice must have a foundation to *support* it; a rope or cord *supports* a weight.

2. To endure without being overcome; as, to *support* pain, distress or misfortunes.

This fierce demeanor and his insolence,
The patience of a God could not *support*. *Dryden.*

3. To bear; to endure; as, to *support* fatigues or hardships; to *support* violent exertions. The eye will not *support* the light of the sun's disk.
4. To sustain; to keep from fainting or sinking; as, to *support* the courage or spirits.
5. To sustain; to act or represent well; as, to *support* the character of king Lear; to *support* the part assigned.
6. To bear; to supply funds for or the means of continuing; as, to *support* the annual expenses of government.
7. To sustain; to carry on; as, to *support* a war or a contest; to *support* an argument or debate.
8. To maintain with provisions and the necessary means of living; as, to *support* a family; to *support* a son in college; to *support* the ministers of the gospel.
9. To maintain; to sustain; to keep from failing; as, to *support* life; to *support* the strength by nourishment.
10. To sustain without change or dissolution; as, clay *supports* an intense heat.
11. To bear; to keep from sinking; as, water *supports* ships and other bodies; air *supports* a balloon.
12. To bear without being exhausted; to be able to pay; as, to *support* taxes or contributions.
13. To sustain; to maintain; as, to *support* a good character.
14. To maintain; to verify; to make good; to substantiate. The testimony is not sufficient to *support* the charges; the evidence will not *support* the statements or allegations; the impeachment is well *supported* by evidence.
15. To uphold by aid or countenance; as, to *support* a friend or a party.
16. To vindicate; to maintain; to defend successfully; as, to be able to *support* one's own cause.

SUPPORT, *n.* The act or operation of upholding or sustaining.
2. That which upholds, sustains or keeps from falling, as a prop, a pillar, a foundation of any kind.
3. That which maintains life; as, food is the *support* of life, of the body, of strength. Oxygen or vital air has been supposed to be the *support* of respiration and of heat in the blood.
4. Maintenance; subsistence; as an income sufficient for the *support* of a family; or revenue for the *support* of the army and navy.
5. Maintenance; an upholding; continuance in any state, or preservation from falling, sinking or failing; as taxes necessary for the *support* of public credit; a revenue for the *support* of government.
6. In *general*, the maintenance or sustaining of any thing without suffering it to fail, decline or languish; as the *support* of health, spirits, strength or courage; the *support* of reputation, credit, &c.
7. That which upholds or relieves; aid; help; succor; assistance.

SUPPORTABLE, *a.* [Fr.] That may be upheld or sustained.
2. That may be borne or endured; as, the pain is *supportable*, or not *supportable*. Patience renders evils *supportable*.
3. Tolerable; that may be borne without resistance or punishment; as, such insults are not *supportable*.
4. That can be maintained; as, the cause or opinion is *supportable*.

SUPPORTABLENESS, *n.* The state of being tolerable. *Hammond.*

SUPPORTANCE, *n.* Maintenance; support. [*Not in use.*]

SUPPORTA'TION, *n.* Maintenance; support. [*Not in use.*]

SUPPORTED, *pp.* Borne; endured; upheld; maintained; subsisted; sustained; carried on.

SUPPORTER, *n.* One that supports or maintains.
2. That which supports or upholds; a prop, a pillar, &c.

The sockets and *supporters* of flowers are figured. *Bacon.*

3. A sustainer; a comforter.

The saints have a companion and *supporter* in all their miseries. *South.*

4. A maintainer; a defender.

Worthy *supporters* of such a reigning impiety. *South.*

5. One who maintains or helps to carry on; as the *supporters* of a war.
6. An advocate; a defender; a vindicator; as the *supporters* of religion, morality, justice, &c.
7. An adherent; one who takes part; as the *supporter* of a party or faction.
8. In *ship-building*, a knee placed under the cat-head.
9. *Supporters*, in heraldry, are figures of beasts that appear to support the arms. *Johnson.*

SUPPORTFUL, *a.* Abounding with support. [*Not used.*]

SUPPORTING, *ppr.* Bearing; enduring; upholding; sustaining; maintaining; subsisting; vindicating.

SUPPORTLESS, *a.* Having no support. *Battle of Frogs and Mice.*

SUPPORTMENT, *n.* Support. [*Not in use.*] *Wotton.*

SUPPO'SABLE, *a.* [from *suppose.*] That may be supposed; that may be imagined to exist. That is not a *supposable* case.

SUPPO'SAL, *n.* [from *suppose.*] Position without proof; the imagining of something to exist; supposition.

Interest, with a Jew, never proceeds but upon *supposal* at least, of a firm and sufficient bottom. *Obs.* *South.*

SUPPOSE, *v. t.* suppo'ze. [Fr. *supposer*; L. *suppositus, suppono*; It. *supporre*; Sp. *suponer*; *sub* and *pono*, to *put.*]
1. To lay down or state as a proposition or fact that may exist or be true, though not known or believed to be true or to exist; or to imagine or admit to exist, for the sake of argument or illustration. Let us *suppose* the earth to be the center of the system, what would be the consequence?

When we have as great assurance that a thing is, as we could possibly, *supposing* it were, we ought not to doubt of its existence. *Tillotson.*

2. To imagine; to believe; to receive as true.

Let not my lord *suppose* that they have slain all the young men, the king's sons; for Amnon only is dead. 2 Sam. xiii.

3. To imagine; to think.

I *suppose*,
If our proposals once again were heard— *Milton.*

4. To require to exist or be true. The existence of things *supposes* the existence of a cause of the things.

One falsehood *supposes* another, and renders all you say suspected. *Female Quixote.*

5. To put one thing by fraud in the place of another. [*Not in use.*]

SUPPO'SE, *n.* Supposition; position without proof.

—Fit to be trusted on a bare *suppose*
That he is honest. [*Not in use.*] *Dryden.*

SUPPO'SED, *pp.* Laid down or imagined as true; imagined; believed; received as true.

SUPPO'SER, *n.* One who supposes. *Shak.*

SUPPO'SING, *ppr.* Laying down or imagining to exist or be true; stating as a case that may be; imagining; receiving as true.

SUPPOSI''TION, *n.* The act of laying down, imagining or admitting as true or existing, what is known not to be true, or what is not proved.
2. The position of something known not to be true or not proved; hypothesis.

This is only an infallibility upon *supposition* that if a thing be true, it is impossible to be false. *Tillotson.*

3. Imagination; belief without full evidence.

SUPPOSITI''TIOUS, *a.* [L. *supposititius*, from *suppositus, suppono.*]
Put by trick in the place or character belonging to another; not genuine; as a *supposititious* child; a *supposititious* writing. *Addison.*

SUPPOSITI''TIOUSNESS, *n.* The state of being supposititious.

SUPPOS'ITIVE, *a.* Supposed; including or implying supposition. *Chillingworth.*

SUPPOS'ITIVE, *n.* [supra.] A word denoting or implying supposition. *Harris.*

SUPPOS'ITIVELY, *adv.* With, by or upon supposition. *Hammond.*

SUPPOS'ITORY, *n.* [Fr. *suppositoire.*] In *medicine*, a long cylindrical body introduced into the rectum to procure stools when clysters cannot be administered. *Parr.*

SUPPRESS', *v. t.* [L. *suppressus, supprimo*; *sub* and *premo*, to press.]
1. To overpower and crush; to subdue; to destroy; as, to *suppress* a rebellion; to *suppress* a mutiny or riot; to *suppress* opposition.

Every rebellion when it is *suppressed*, makes the subject weaker, and the government stronger. *Davies.*

2. To keep in; to restrain from utterance or vent; as, to *suppress* the voice; to *suppress* sighs.
3. To retain without disclosure; to conceal; not to tell or reveal; as, to *suppress* evidence.

She *suppresses* the name, and this keeps him in a pleasing suspense. *Broome.*

4. To retain without communication or making public; as, to *suppress* a letter; to *suppress* a manuscript.

5. To stifle; to stop; to hinder from circulation; as, to *suppress* a report.
6. To stop; to restrain; to obstruct from discharges; as, to *suppress* a diarrhea, a hemorrhage and the like.

SUPPRESS'ED, *pp.* Crushed; destroyed; retained; concealed; stopped; obstructed.

SUPPRESS'ING, *ppr.* Subduing; destroying; retaining closely; concealing; hindering from disclosure or publication; obstructing.

SUPPRES'SION, *n.* [Fr. from L. *suppressio.*]
1. The act of suppressing, crushing or destroying; as the *suppression* of a riot, insurrection or tumult.
2. The act of retaining from utterance, vent or disclosure; concealment; as the *suppression* of truth, of reports, of evidence and the like.
3. The retaining of any thing from public notice; as the *suppression* of a letter or any writing.
4. The stoppage, obstruction or morbid retention of discharges; as the *suppression* of urine, of diarrhea or other discharge.
5. In *grammar* or *composition*, omission; as the *suppression* of a word.

SUPPRESS'IVE, *a.* Tending to suppress; subduing; concealing. *Seward.*

SUPPRESS'OR, *n.* One that suppresses; one that subdues; one that prevents utterance, disclosure or communication.

SUP'PURATE, *v. i.* [L. *suppuro*; *sub* and *pus, puris*; Fr. *suppurer*; It. *suppurare.*] To generate pus; as, a boil or abscess *suppurates.*

SUP'PURATE, *v. t.* To cause to suppurate. [*In this sense, unusual.*] *Arbuthnot.*

SUP'PURATING, *ppr.* Generating pus.

SUPPURA'TION, *n.* [Fr. from L. *suppuratio.*]
1. The process of generating purulent matter, or of forming pus, as in a wound or abscess; one of the natural terminations of healthy inflammation. *Cyc. Cooper. Wiseman.*
2. The matter generated by suppuration.

SUP'PURATIVE, *a.* [Fr. *suppuratif.*] Tending to suppurate; promoting suppuration.

SUP'PURATIVE, *n.* A medicine that promotes suppuration.

SUPPUTA'TION, *n.* [L. *supputatio*, *supputo*; *sub* and *puto*, to think.] Reckoning; account; computation. *Holder.*

SUPPU'TE, *v. t.* [L. *supputo*, supra.] To reckon; to compute. [*Not in use.*]

SUPRA, a Latin preposition, signifying *above, over* or *beyond.*

SUPRA-AX'ILLARY, *a.* [*supra* and *axil.*] In *botany*, growing above the axil; inserted above the axil; as a peduncle. [See *Suprafoliaceous.*] *Lee.*

SUPRACIL'IARY, *a.* [L. *supra* and *cilium*, eyebrow.] Situated above the eyebrow. *Ure.*

SUPRA-DECOM'POUND, *a.* [*supra* and *decompound.*] More than decompound; thrice compound. A *supra-decompound leaf*, is when a petiole divided several times, connects many leaflets; each part forming a decompound leaf. *Martyn.*

SUPRAFOLIA'CEOUS, *a.* [L. *supra* and *folium*, a leaf.] In *botany*, inserted into the stem above the leaf or petiole, or axil, as a peduncle or flower. *Martyn.*

SUPRALAPSA'RIAN, } *a.* [L. *supra* and
SUPRALAP'SARY, } *lapsus*, fall.]
Antecedent to the apostasy of Adam.

SUPRALAPSA'RIAN, *n.* One who maintains that God, antecedent to the fall of man or any knowledge of it, decreed the apostasy and all its consequences, determining to save some and condemn others, and that in all he does he considers his own glory only. *Encyc.*

SUPRAMUN'DANE, *a.* [L. *supra* and *mundus*, the world.] Being or situated above the world or above our system.

SUPRA-ORB'ITAL, *a.* [*supra* and *orbit.*] Being above the orbit of the eye.

SUPRARE'NAL, *a.* [L. *supra* and *ren, renes*, the kidneys.] Situated above the kidneys.

SUPRASCAP'ULARY, *a.* [L. *supra* and *scapula.*] Being above the scapula.

SUPRAVUL'GAR, *a.* [*supra* and *vulgar.*] Being above the vulgar or common people. *Collier.*

SUPREM'ACY, *n.* [See *Supreme.*] State of being supreme or in the highest station of power; highest authority or power; as the *supremacy* of the king of Great Britain; or the *supremacy* of parliament.

> The usurped power of the pope being destroyed, the crown was restored to its *supremacy* over spiritual men and causes. *Blackstone.*

Oath of supremacy, in Great Britain, an oath which acknowledges the supremacy of the king in spiritual affairs, and renounces or abjures the pretended supremacy of the pope.

SUPRE'ME, *a.* [L. *supremus*, from *supra*; Fr. *suprême.*]
1. Highest in authority; holding the highest place in government or power. In the United States, the congress is *supreme* in regulating commerce and in making war and peace. The parliament of Great Britain is *supreme* in legislation; but the king is *supreme* in the administration of the government. In the universe, God only is the *supreme* ruler and judge. His commands are *supreme*, and binding on all his creatures.
2. Highest, greatest or most excellent; as *supreme* love; *supreme* glory; *supreme* degree.
3. It is sometimes used in a bad sense; as *supreme* folly or baseness, folly or baseness carried to the utmost extent. [*A bad use of the word.*]

SUPRE'MELY, *adv.* With the highest authority. He rules *supremely.*
2. In the highest degree; to the utmost extent; as *supremely* blest. *Pope.*

SUR, a prefix, from the French, contracted from L. *super, supra*, signifies *over, above, beyond, upon.*

SURADDI''TION, *n.* [Fr. *sur*, on or upon, and *addition.*] Something added to the name. [*Not used.*] *Shak.*

SU'RAL, *a.* [L. *sura.*] Being in or pertaining to the calf of the leg; as the *sural* artery. *Wiseman.*

SU'RANCE, for *assurance*, not used. *Shak.*

SUR'BASE, *n.* [*sur* and *base.*] A border or molding above the base. *Pennant.*

SUR'BASED, *a.* Having a surbase, or molding above the base.

SURBA'TE, *v. t.* [It. *sobattere*; either L. *sub* and *battere*, or *solea*, sole, and *battere*, to beat the sole or hoof.]
1. To bruise or batter the feet by travel.

> Chalky land *surbates* and spoils oxen's feet. *Mortimer.*

2. To harass; to fatigue. *Clarendon.*

SURBA'TED, *pp.* Bruised in the feet; harassed; fatigued.

SURBA'TING, *ppr.* Bruising the feet of; fatiguing.

Surbeat or *surbet*, for *surbate*, not in use.

SURBED', *v. t.* [*sur* and *bed.*] To set edgewise, as a stone; that is, in a position different from that which it had in the quarry. *Plot.*

SURCE'ASE, *v. i.* [Fr. *sur* and *cesser*, to cease.]
1. To cease; to stop; to be at an end. *Donne.*
2. To leave off; to practice no longer; to refrain finally.

> So pray'd he, whilst an angel's voice from high,
> Bade him *surcease* to importune the sky. *Harte.*

[This word is entirely useless, being precisely synonymous with *cease*, and it is nearly obsolete.]

SURCE'ASE, *v. t.* To stop; to cause to cease. *Obs.*

SURCE'ASE, *n.* Cessation; stop. *Obs.*

SURCH'ARGE, *v. t.* [Fr. *surcharger*; *sur* and *charge.*]
1. To overload; to overburden; as, to *surcharge* a beast or a ship; to *surcharge* a cannon.

> Your head reclin'd, as hiding grief from view,
> Droops like a rose *surcharg'd* with morning dew. *Dryden.*

2. In *law*, to overstock; to put more cattle into a common than the person has a right to do, or more than the herbage will sustain. *Blackstone.*

SURCH'ARGE, *n.* An excessive load or burden; a load greater than can be well borne. *Bacon.*

SURCH'ARGED, *pp.* Overloaded; overstocked.

SURCH'ARGER, *n.* One that overloads or overstocks.

SURCH'ARGING, *ppr.* Overloading; burdening to excess; overstocking with cattle or beasts.

SUR'CINGLE, *n.* [Fr. *sur*, upon, and L. *cingulum*, a belt.]
1. A belt, band or girth which passes over a saddle, or over any thing laid on a horse's back, to bind it fast.
2. The girdle of a cassoc. *Marvel.*

SUR'CINGLED, *a.* Girt; bound with a surcingle. *Hall.*

SUR'CLE, *n.* [L. *surculus.*] A little shoot; a twig; a sucker.

SUR'COAT, *n.* [Fr. *sur* and Eng. *coat.*] A short coat worn over the other clothes. *Camden.*

SUR'CREW, *n.* [*sur* and *crew.*] Additional crew or collection. [*Not in use.*] *Wotton.*

SUR'CULATE, *v. t.* [L. *surculo.*] To prune. [*Not in use.*]

SURCULA'TION, *n.* The act of pruning. [*Not in use.*] *Brown.*

SURD, *a.* [L. *surdus*, deaf.] Deaf; not having the sense of hearing. [*Not used.*]

2. Unheard. [*Not used.*]

3. Designating a quantity whose root cannot be exactly expressed in numbers.

SURD, *n.* In *algebra*, a quantity whose root cannot be exactly expressed in numbers. Thus 2 is a surd number, because there is no number which multiplied into itself, will exactly produce 2.

SURD'ITY, *n.* Deafness. [*Not used.*]

SURE, *a. shure.* [Fr. *sûr, seur*; Arm. *sur*; Norm. *seor, seur.* In G. *zwar* signifies indeed, to be sure, it is true; which leads me to suspect *sure* to be contracted from the root of *sever*, in L. *assevero*, and to be connected with *swear*, and perhaps with L. *verus*; *s* being the remains of a prefix.]

1. Certain; unfailing; infallible.

The testimony of the Lord is *sure*. Ps. xix.

We have also a more *sure* word of prophecy. 2 Pet. i.

2. Certainly knowing, or having full confidence.

We are *sure* that the judgment of God is according to truth— Rom. ii.

Now we are *sure* that thou knowest all things. John xvi.

3. Certain; safe; firm; permanent.

Thy kingdom shall be *sure* to thee. Dan. iv.

4. Firm; stable; steady; not liable to failure, loss or change; as a *sure* covenant. 2 Sam. xxiii. Neh. ix. Is. xxviii.

The Lord will make my lord a *sure* house. 1 Sam. xxv.

So we say, to stand *sure*, to be *sure* of foot.

5. Certain of obtaining or of retaining; as, to be *sure* of game; to be *sure* of success; to be *sure* of life or health.

6. Strong; secure; not liable to be broken or disturbed.

Go your way, make it as *sure* as ye can. Math. xxvii.

7. Certain; not liable to failure. The income is *sure*.

To be sure, or *be sure*, certainly. Shall you go? *be sure* I shall.

To make sure, to make certain; to secure so that there can be no failure of the purpose or object.

Make sure of Cato. *Addison.*

A peace cannot fail, provided we *make sure* of Spain. *Temple.*

Give all diligence to *make* your calling and election *sure*. 2 Pet. i.

SURE, *adv.* Certainly; without doubt; doubtless.

Sure the queen would wish him still unknown. *Smith.*

[But in this sense, *surely* is more generally used.]

SUREFOOT'ED, *a.* [*sure* and *foot.*] Not liable to stumble or fall; as a *surefooted* horse.

SU'RELY, *adv.* Certainly; infallibly; undoubtedly.

In the day thou eatest thereof, thou shalt *surely* die. Gen. ii.

He that created something out of nothing, *surely* can raise great things out of small. *South.*

2. Firmly; without danger of falling.

He that walketh uprightly, walketh *surely*. Prov. x.

SU'RENESS, *n.* Certainty.

For more *sureness* he repeats it. [*Little used.*] *Woodward.*

SU'RETISHIP, *n.* [from *surety.*] The state of being surety; the obligation of a person to answer for another, and make good any debt or loss which may occur from another's delinquency.

He that hateth *suretiship* is sure. Prov. xi.

SU'RETY, *n.* [Fr. *sureté.*] Certainty; indubitableness.

Know of a *surety*, that thy seed shall be a stranger in a land that is not theirs— Gen. xv.

2. Security; safety.

Yet for the more *surety* they looked round about. *Sidney.*

3. Foundation of stability; support.

We our state
Hold, as you yours, while our obedience holds;
On other *surety* none. *Milton.*

4. Evidence; ratification; confirmation.

She call'd the saints to *surety*,
That she would never put it from her finger,
Unless she gave it to yourself. *Shak.*

5. Security against loss or damage; security for payment.

There remains unpaid
A hundred thousand more, in *surety* of the which
One part of Aquitain is bound to us. *Shak.*

6. In *law*, one that is bound with and for another; one who enters into a bond or recognizance to answer for another's appearance in court, or for his payment of a debt or for the performance of some act, and who, in case of the principal debtor's failure, is compellable to pay the debt or damages; a bondsman; a bail.

He that is *surety* for a stranger, shall smart for it. Prov. xi.

Thy servant became *surety* for the lad to my father. Gen. xliv.

7. In *Scripture*, Christ is called "the *surety* of a better testament." Heb. vii. 22. He undertook to make atonement for the sins of men, and thus prepare the way to deliver them from the punishment to which they had rendered themselves liable.

8. A hostage.

SURF, *n.* The swell of the sea which breaks upon the shore, or upon sand banks or rocks. *Mar. Dict.*

2. In *agriculture*, the bottom or conduit of a drain. [*Local.*]

SUR'FACE, *n.* [F. *sur*, upon, and *face.*] The exterior part of any thing that has length and breadth; one of the limits that terminates a solid; the superficies; outside; as the *surface* of the earth; the *surface* of the sea; the *surface* of a diamond; the *surface* of the body; the *surface* of a cylinder; an even or an uneven *surface*; a smooth or rough *surface*; a spherical *surface*. *Newton. Pope.*

SURFEIT, *v. t. sur'fit.* [Fr. *sur*, over, and *faire, fait*, to do, L. *facio.*]

1. To feed with meat or drink, so as to oppress the stomach and derange the functions of the system; to overfeed and produce sickness or uneasiness.

2. To cloy; to fill to satiety and disgust. He *surfeits* us with his eulogies.

SUR'FEIT, *v. i.* To be fed till the system is oppressed and sickness or uneasiness ensues.

They are as sick that *surfeit* with too much, as they that starve with nothing. *Shak.*

SUR'FEIT, *n.* Fullness and oppression of the system, occasioned by excessive eating and drinking. He has not recovered from a *surfeit*.

2. Excess in eating and drinking.

Now comes the sick hour that his *surfeit* made. *Shak.*

SUR'FEITED, *pp.* Surcharged and oppressed with eating and drinking to excess; cloyed.

SUR'FEITER, *n.* One who riots; a glutton. *Shak.*

SUR'FEITING, *ppr.* Oppressing the system by excessive eating and drinking; cloying; loading or filling to disgust.

SUR'FEITING, *n.* The act of feeding to excess; gluttony. Luke xxi.

SUR'FEIT-WATER, *n.* [*surfeit* and *water.*] Water for the cure of surfeits. *Locke.*

SURĠE, *n.* [L. *surgo*, to rise; Sans. *surgo*, highth.]

1. A large wave or billow; a great rolling swell of water. [*It is not applied to small waves, and is chiefly used in poetry and eloquence.*]

He flies aloft, and with impetuous roar,
Pursues the foaming *surges* to the shore. *Dryden.*

2. In *ship-building*, the tapered part in front of the whelps, between the chocks of a capstan, on which the messenger may surge. *Cyc.*

SURĠE, *v. t.* To let go a portion of a rope suddenly. *Surge* the messenger. *Mar. Dict.*

SURĠE, *v. i.* To swell; to rise high and roll; as waves.

The *surging* waters like a mountain rise. *Spenser.*

2. To slip back; as, the cable *surges*.

SURĠELESS, *a. surj'less.* Free from surges; smooth; calm.

SUR'ĠEON, *n. sur'jen.* [contracted from *chirurgeon.*]

One whose profession or occupation is to cure diseases or injuries of the body by manual operation. In a more general sense, one whose occupation is to cure external diseases, whether by manual operation, or by medicines externally or internally.

SUR'ĠERY, *n.* Properly, the act of healing by manual operation; or that branch of medical science which treats of manual operations for the healing of diseases or injuries of the body. In a more general sense, the act of healing external diseases by manual operation or by medicines; or that branch of medical science which has for its principal object the cure of external injuries. *Cooper.*

SUR'ĠICAL, *a.* Pertaining to surgeons or surgery; done by means of surgery.

SUR'ĠING, *ppr.* Swelling and rolling, as billows.

Surging waves against a solid rock. *Milton.*

SUR'ĠY, *a.* Rising in surges or billows; full of surges; as the *surgy* main. *Pope.*

SU'RICATE, *n.* An animal like the ichneumon; the four toed weasel. *Dict.*

SUR'LILY, *adv.* [from *surly.*] In a surly, morose manner.

SUR'LINESS, *n.* Gloomy moroseness; crabbed ill nature; as the *surliness* of a dog.

SUR'LING, *n.* A sour morose fellow. [*Not in use.*] *Camden.*

SUR'LY, *a.* [W. *swr*, surly, snarling; *swri*, surliness, sullenness. Qu. its alliance with *sour.*]

1. Gloomily morose; crabbed; snarling; sternly sour; rough; cross and rude; as a *surly* groom; a *surly* dog.

That *surly* spirit, melancholy. *Shak.*

2. Rough; dark; tempestuous.

Now soften'd into joy the *surly* storm. *Thomson.*

SURMI'SAL, *n.* Surmise. [*Not in use.*]

SURMISE, *v. t.* *surmi'ze.* [Norm. *surmys*, alledged; *surmitter*, to surmise, to accuse, to suggest; Fr. *sur* and *mettre*, to put.]

To suspect; to imagine without certain knowledge; to entertain thoughts that something does or will exist, but upon slight evidence.

It wafted nearer yet, and then she knew
That what before she but *surmis'd*, was true. *Dryden.*

This change was not wrought by altering the form or position of the earth, as was *surmised* by a very learned man, but by dissolving it. *Woodward.*

SURMI'SE, *n.* Suspicion; the thought or imagination that something may be, of which however there is no certain or strong evidence; as the *surmises* of jealousy or of envy.

We double honor gain
From his *surmise* prov'd false. *Milton.*

No man ought to be charged with principles he disowns, unless his practices contradict his professions; not upon small *surmises.* *Swift.*

SURMI'SED, *pp.* Suspected; imagined upon slight evidence.

SURMI'SER, *n.* One who surmises.

SURMI'SING, *ppr.* Suspecting; imagining upon slight evidence.

SURMI'SING, *n.* The act of suspecting; surmise; as evil *surmisings.* 1 Tim. vi.

SURMOUNT', *v. t.* [Fr. *surmonter; sur* and *monter*, to ascend.]

1. To rise above.

The mountains of Olympus, Atho and Atlas, *surmount* all winds and clouds. *Raleigh.*

2. To conquer; to overcome; as, to *surmount* difficulties or obstacles.

3. To surpass; to exceed.

What *surmounts* the reach
Of human sense— *Milton.*

SURMOUNT'ABLE, *a.* That may be overcome; superable.

SURMOUNT'ED, *pp.* Overcome; conquered; surpassed.

SURMOUNT'ER, *n.* One that surmounts.

SURMOUNT'ING, *ppr.* Rising above; overcoming; surpassing.

SURMUL'LET, *n.* A fish of the genus Mullus, *(M. barbatus,)* remarkable for the brilliancy of its colors, and for the changes which they undergo as the fish expires. The name is also applied to other species of the genus. *Ed. Encyc.*

SUR'MULOT, *n.* A name given by Buffon to the brown or Norway rat. *Ed. Encyc.*

SUR'NAME, *n.* [Fr. *surnom;* It. *soprannome;* Sp. *sobrenombre;* L. *super* and *nomen.*]

1. An additional name; a name or appellation added to the baptismal or christian name, and which becomes a family name. Surnames, with us, originally designated occupation, estate, place of residence, or some particular thing or event that related to the person. Thus William *Rufus* or *red;* Edmund *Ironsides;* Robert *Smith*, or the *smith;* William *Turner.*

2. An appellation added to the original name.

My *surname* Coriolanus. *Shak.*

SURNA'ME, *v. t.* [Fr. *surnommer.*] To name or call by an appellation added to the original name.

Another shall subscribe with his hand unto the Lord, and *surname* himself by the name of Israel. Is. xliv.

And Simon he *surnamed* Peter. Mark iii.

SURNA'MED, *pp.* Called by a name added to the christian or original name.

SURNA'MING, *ppr.* Naming by an appellation added to the original name.

SUROX'YD, *n.* [*sur* and *oxyd.*] That which contains an addition of oxyd. [*Little used.*]

SUROX'YDATE, *v. t.* To form a suroxyd. [*Little used.*]

SURP'ASS, *v. t.* [Fr. *surpasser; sur* and *passer*, to pass beyond.]

To exceed; to excel; to go beyond in any thing good or bad. Homer *surpasses* modern poets in sublimity. Pope *surpasses* most other poets in smoothness of versification. Achilles *surpassed* the other Greeks in strength and courage. Clodius *surpassed* all men in the profligacy of his life. Perhaps no man ever *surpassed* Washington in genuine patriotism and integrity of life.

SURP'ASSABLE, *a.* That may be exceeded. *Dict.*

SURP'ASSED, *pp.* Exceeded; excelled.

SURP'ASSING, *ppr.* Exceeding; going beyond.

2. *a.* Excellent in an eminent degree; exceeding others.

O thou, that with *surpassing* glory crown'd— *Milton.*

SURP'ASSINGLY, *adv.* In a very excellent manner; or in a degree surpassing others.

SURPLICE, *n.* *sur'plis.* [Fr. *surplis;* Sp. *sobrepelliz;* L. *super pellicium*, above the robe of fur.]

A white garment worn by clergymen of some denominations over their other dress, in their ministrations. It is particularly the habit of the clergy of the church of England.

SUR'PLICED, *a.* Wearing a surplice. *Mallet.*

SUR'PLICE-FEES, *n.* [*surplice* and *fees.*] Fees paid to the clergy for occasional duties. *Warton.*

SUR'PLUS, *n.* [Fr. *sur* and *plus*, L. *id.*, more.]

1. Overplus; that which remains when use is satisfied; excess beyond what is prescribed or wanted. In the United States, the *surplus* of wheat and rye not required for consumption or exportation, is distilled.

2. In *law*, the residuum of an estate, after the debts and legacies are paid.

SURPLUS'AGE, *n.* Surplus; as *surplusage* of grain or goods beyond what is wanted.

2. In *law*, something in the pleadings or proceedings not necessary or relevant to the case, and which may be rejected.

3. In *accounts*, a greater disbursement than the charge of the accountant amounteth to. *Rees.*

SURPRISAL, *n.* *surpri'zal.* [See *Surprise.*] The act of surprising or coming upon suddenly and unexpectedly; or the state of being taken unawares.

SURPRISE, *v. t.* *surpri'ze.* [Fr. from *surprendre; sur* and *prendre*, to take; It. *sorpresa, sorprendere;* Sp. *sorpresa, sorprehender;* L. *super, supra*, and *prendo*, to take.]

1. To come or fall upon suddenly and unexpectedly; to take unawares.

The castle of Macduff I will *surprise.* *Shak.*

Who can speak
The mingled passions that *surpris'd* his heart. *Thomson.*

2. To strike with wonder or astonishment by something sudden, unexpected or remarkable, either in conduct, words or story, or by the appearance of something unusual. Thus we are *surprised* at desperate acts of heroism, or at the narration of wonderful events, or at the sight of things of uncommon magnitude or curious structure.

3. To confuse; to throw the mind into disorder by something suddenly presented to the view or to the mind.

Up he starts, discover'd and *surpris'd.* *Milton.*

SURPRI'SE, *n.* The act of coming upon unawares, or of taking suddenly and without preparation. The fort was taken by *surprise.*

2. The state of being taken unexpectedly.

3. An emotion excited by something happening suddenly and unexpectedly, as something novel told or presented to view. Nothing could exceed his *surprise* at the narration of these adventures. It expresses less than *wonder* and *astonishment.*

4. A dish with nothing in it. [*Not in use.*] *King.*

SURPRI'SED, *pp.* Come upon or taken unawares; struck with something novel or unexpected.

SURPRI'SING, *ppr.* Falling on or taking suddenly or unawares; striking with something novel; taking by a sudden or unexpected attack.

2. *a.* Exciting surprise; extraordinary; of a nature to excite wonder and astonishment; as *surprising* bravery; *surprising* patience; a *surprising* escape from danger.

SURPRI'SINGLY, *adv.* In a manner or degree that excites surprise. He exerted himself *surprisingly* to save the life of his companion.

SUR'QUEDRY, *n.* [*sur* and Norm. F. *cuider*, to think. Qu. Sp. *cuidar*, to heed. See *Heed.*] Overweening pride; arrogance. [*Not in use.*] *Spenser.*

SURREBUT', *v. i.* [*sur* and *rebut.*] In *legal pleadings*, to reply, as a plaintif, to a defendant's rebutter.

SURREBUT'TER, *n.* The plaintif's reply in pleading to a defendant's rebutter. *Blackstone.*

SURREJOIN', *v. i.* [*sur* and *rejoin.*] In *legal pleadings*, to reply, as a plaintif to a defendant's rejoinder.

SURREJOIN'DER, *n.* The answer of a plaintif to a defendant's rejoinder.

SURREN'DER, *v. t.* [Fr. *sur*, L. *sursum*, and *rendre*, to render.]

1. To yield to the power of another; to give or deliver up possession upon compulsion or demand; as, to *surrender* one's person to an enemy, or to commissioners of bankrupt; to *surrender* a fort or a ship. [To *surrender up* is not elegant.]
2. To yield; to give up; to resign in favor of another; as, to *surrender* a right or privilege; to *surrender* a place or an office.
3. To give up; to resign; as, to *surrender* the breath.
4. In *law*, to yield an estate, as a tenant, into the hands of the lord for such purposes as are expressed in the act. *Blackstone.*
5. To yield to any influence, passion or power; as, to *surrender* one's self to grief, to despair, to indolence or to sleep.

SURREN'DER, *v. i.* To yield; to give up one's self into the power of another. The enemy seeing no way of escape, *surrendered* at the first summons.

SURREN'DER, *n.* The act of yielding or resigning one's person or the possession of something, into the power of another; as the *surrender* of a castle to an enemy; the *surrender* of a right or of claims.

2. A yielding or giving up.
3. In *law*, the yielding of an estate by a tenant to the lord, for such purposes as are expressed by the tenant in the act. *Blackstone.*

SURREN'DERED, *pp.* Yielded or delivered to the power of another; given up; resigned.

SURRENDEREE', *n.* In *law*, a person to whom the lord grants surrendered land; the *cestuy que use.*

SURREN'DERING, *ppr.* Yielding or giving up to the power of another; resigning.

SURREN'DEROR, *n.* The tenant who surrenders an estate into the hands of his lord.

> Till the admittance of *cestuy que use*, the lord takes notice of the *surrenderor* as his tenant. *Blackstone.*

SURREN'DRY, *n.* A surrender. [*Surrender* is the most elegant and best authorized.]

SURREP'TION, *n.* [L. *surreptus*, *surrepo*; *sub* and *repo*, to creep.]

A coming unperceived; a stealing upon insensibly. [*Little used.*]

SURREPTI''TIOUS, *a.* [L. *surreptitius*, supra.]

Done by stealth or without proper authority; made or introduced fraudulently; as a *surreptitious* passage in a manuscript.

> A correct copy of the Dunciad, the many *surreptitious* ones have rendered necessary. *Letter to Publisher of Dunciad.*

SURREPTI''TIOUSLY, *adv.* By stealth; without authority; fraudulently.

SUR'ROGATE, *n.* [L. *surrogatus*, *surrogo*, *subrogo*; *sub* and *rogo*, to propose. *Rogo*, to ask or propose, signifies primarily to reach, put or thrust forward; and *subrogo* is to put or set in the place of another.]

In *a general sense*, a deputy; a delegate; a substitute; particularly, the deputy of an ecclesiastical judge, most commonly of a bishop or his chancellor. In some of the United States, the judge of probate, of wills and testaments.

SUR'ROGATE, *v. t.* To put in the place of another. [*Little used.*]

SURROGA'TION, *n.* The act of substituting one person in the place of another. [*Little used.*]

SURROUND', *v. t.* [*sur* and *round*, Fr. *rond.*]

1. To encompass; to environ; to inclose on all sides; as, to *surround* a city. They *surrounded* a body of the enemy.
2. To lie or be on all sides of; as, a wall or ditch *surrounds* the city.

SURROUND'ED, *pp.* Encompassed; inclosed; beset.

SURROUND'ING, *ppr.* Encompassing; inclosing; lying on all sides of.

SURSOL'ID, *n.* [*sur* and *solid*, or *surdesolid.*]

In *mathematics*, the fifth power of a number; or the product of the fourth multiplication of a number considered as the root. Thus $3\times3=9$, the square of 3, and $9\times3=27$, the third power or cube, and $27\times3=81$, the fourth power, and $81\times3=243$, which is the *sursolid* of 3.

SURSOL'ID, *a.* Denoting the fifth power.

Sursolid problem, is that which cannot be resolved but by curves of a higher kind than the conic sections. *Rees.*

SURTÖUT, *n.* [Fr. *sur-tout*, over all.] A man's coat to be worn over his other garments.

SUR'TURBRAND, *n.* Fibrous brown coal or bituminous wood; so called in Iceland. *Ure.*

SURVE'NE, *v. t.* [Fr. *survenir*; *sur* and *venir*, to come.]

To supervene; to come as an addition; as a suppuration that *survenes* lethargies. [*Little used.*] *Harvey.*

SURVEY, *v. t.* [Norm. *surveer*, *surveoir*; *sur* and Fr. *voir*, to see or look, contracted from L. *video*, *videre.*]

1. To inspect or take a view of; to view with attention, as from a high place; as, to stand on a hill, and *survey* the surrounding country. It denotes more particular and deliberate attention than *look* or *see.*
2. To view with a scrutinizing eye; to examine.

> With such alter'd looks,
> All pale and speechless, he *survey'd* me round. *Dryden.*

3. To examine with reference to condition, situation and value; as, to *survey* a building to determine its value and exposure to loss by fire.
4. To measure, as land; or to ascertain the contents of land by lines and angles.
5. To examine or ascertain the position and distances of objects on the shore of the sea, the depth of water, nature of the bottom, and whatever may be necessary to facilitate the navigation of the waters and render the entrance into harbors, sounds and rivers easy and safe. Thus officers are employed to *survey* the coast and make charts of the same.
6. To examine and ascertain, as the boundaries and royalties of a manor, the tenure of the tenants, and the rent and value of the same.
7. To examine and ascertain, as the state of agriculture.

SUR'VEY, *n.* [formerly accented on the last syllable.]

1. An attentive view; a look or looking with care. He took a *survey* of the whole landscape.

> Under his proud *survey* the city lies. *Denham.*

2. A particular view; an examination of all the parts or particulars of a thing, with a design to ascertain the condition, quantity or quality; as a *survey* of the stores, provisions or munitions of a ship. So also a *survey* of roads and bridges is made by proper officers; a *survey* of buildings is intended to ascertain their condition, value and exposure to fire. A *survey* of land includes mensuration and the ascertainment of quantity. A *survey* of a harbor, sound or coast comprehends an examination of the distance and bearing of points of land, isles, shoals, depth of water, course of channels, &c. A *survey* of agriculture includes a view of the state of property, buildings, fences, modes of cultivation, crops, gardens, orchards, woods, livestock, &c. And in general, *survey* denotes a particular view and examination of any thing.
3. In *the United States*, a district for the collection of the customs, under the inspection and authority of a particular officer.

Trigonometrical survey, the measurement of an arc of the meridian by means of a series of triangles.

SURVEYED, *pp.* Viewed with attention; examined; measured.

SURVEYING, *ppr.* Viewing with attention; examining particularly; measuring.

SURVEYING, *n.* That branch of mathematics which teaches the art of measuring land.

SURVEYOR, *n.* An overseer; one placed to superintend others. *Shak.*

2. One that views and examines for the purpose of ascertaining the condition, quantity or quality of any thing; as a *surveyor* of land; a *surveyor* of highways; *surveyors* of ordnance. In the customs, a gauger; an officer who ascertains the contents of casks, and the quantity of liquors subject to duty; also in the United States, an officer who ascertains the weight and quantity of goods subject to duty.

SURVEYOR-GENERAL, *n.* A principal surveyor; as the *surveyor-general* of the king's manors, or of woods and parks in England. In the United States, the chief surveyor of lands; as the *surveyor-general* of the United States, or of a particular state.

SURVEYORSHIP, *n.* The office of a surveyor.

SURVIEW', *v. t.* To survey. [*Not in use.*] *Spenser.*

SUR'VIEW, *n.* Survey. [*Not in use.*]

SURVI'SE, *v. t.* [Fr. *sur* and *viser.*] To look over. [*Not in use.*] *B. Jonson.*

SURVI'VAL, *n.* [See *Survive.*] A living beyond the life of another person, thing or event; an outliving.

SURVI'VANCE, *n.* Survivorship. [*Little used.*] *Hume.*

SURVI'VE, *v. t.* [Fr. *survivre; sur* and *vivre*, to live; It. *sopravvivere*; Sp. *sobrevivir*; L. *supervivo.*]

1. To outlive; to live beyond the life of another; as, the wife *survives* her husband; or a husband *survives* his wife.

2. To outlive any thing else; to live beyond any event. Who would wish to *survive* the ruin of his country? Many men *survive* their usefulness or the regular exercise of their reason.

SURVI'VE, *v. i.* To remain alive.

> Try pleasure,
> Which when no other enemy *survives*,
> Still conquers all the conquerors. *Denham.*

SURVI'VENCY, *n.* A surviving; survivorship.

SURVI'VER, *n.* One that outlives another. [See *Survivor.*]

SURVI'VING, *ppr.* Outliving; living beyond the life of another, or beyond the time of some event.

2. *a.* Remaining alive; yet living; as *surviving* friends or relatives.

SURVI'VOR, *n.* One who outlives another.

2. In *law*, the longer liver of two joint tenants, or of any two persons who have a joint interest in any thing. *Blackstone.*

SURVI'VORSHIP, *n.* The state of outliving another.

2. In *law*, the right of a joint tenant or other person who has a joint interest in an estate, to take the whole estate upon the death of the other. When there are more than two joint tenants, the whole estate remains to the last survivor by right of *survivorship.* *Blackstone.*

SUSCEPTIBIL'ITY, *n.* [from *susceptible.*] The quality of admitting or receiving either something additional, or some change, affection or passion; as the *susceptibility* of color in a body; *susceptibility* of culture or refinement; *susceptibility* of love or desire, or of impressions.

SUSCEP'TIBLE, *a.* [Fr. from L. *suscipio*, to take; *sub* and *capio.*]

1. Capable of admitting any thing additional, or any change, affection or influence; as a body *susceptible* of color or of alteration; a body *susceptible* of pain; a heart *susceptible* of love or of impression.

2. Tender; capable of impression; impressible. The minds of children are more *susceptible* than those of persons more advanced in life.

3. Having nice sensibility; as a man of a *susceptible* heart.

SUSCEP'TIBLENESS, *n.* Susceptibility, which see.

SUSCEP'TION, *n.* The act of taking. [*But little used.*] *Ayliffe.*

SUSCEP'TIVE, *a.* Capable of admitting; readily admitting. Our natures are *susceptive* of errors. *Watts.*

SUSCEPTIV'ITY, *n.* Capacity of admitting. [*Little used.*] *Wollaston.*

SUSCEP'TOR, *n.* [L.] One who undertakes; a godfather.

SUSCIP'IENCY, *n.* Reception; admission.

SUSCIP'IENT, *a.* Receiving; admitting.

SUSCIP'IENT, *n.* One who takes or admits; one that receives. *Bp. Taylor.*

SUS'CITATE, *v. t.* [Fr. *susciter;* L. *suscito; sub* and *cito.*] To rouse; to excite; to call into life and action. *Brown.*

SUSCITA'TION, *n.* The act of raising or exciting. *Pearson.*

SUS'LIK, *n.* A spotted animal of the rat kind. A quadruped of the genus Arctomys, of a yellowish brown color, with small white spots; the earless marmot. *Ed. Encyc.*

SUSPECT', *v. t.* [L. *suspectus, suspicio; sub* and *specio*, to see or view.]

1. To mistrust; to imagine or have a slight opinion that something exists, but without proof and often upon weak evidence or no evidence at all. We *suspect* not only from fear, jealousy or apprehension of evil, but in modern usage, we *suspect* things which give us no apprehension.

> Nothing makes a man *suspect* much, more than to know little. *Bacon.*
> From her hand I could *suspect* no ill. *Milton.*

2. To imagine to be guilty, but upon slight evidence or without proof. When a theft is committed, we are apt to *suspect* a person who is known to have been guilty of stealing; but we often *suspect* a person who is innocent of the crime.

3. To hold to be uncertain; to doubt; to mistrust; as, to *suspect* the truth of a story.

4. To hold to be doubtful. The veracity of a historian, and the impartiality of a judge, should not be *suspected.*

5. To conjecture. *Philosophy of Rhetoric.*

SUSPECT', *v. i.* To imagine guilt.

> If I *suspect* without cause, why then let me be your jest. *Shak.*

SUSPECT', *a.* Doubtful. [*Not much used.*] *Glanville.*

SUSPECT', *n.* Suspicion. [*Obs.*] *Bacon. Shak.*

SUSPECT'ABLE, *a.* That may be suspected.]*Little used.*]

SUSPECT'ED, *pp.* Imagined without proof; mistrusted.

SUSPECT'EDLY, *adv.* So as to excite suspicion; so as to be suspected.

SUSPECT'EDNESS, *n.* State of being suspected or doubted. *Robinson.*

SUSPECT'ER, *n.* One who suspects.

SUSPECT'FUL, *a.* Apt to suspect or mistrust. *Bailey.*

SUSPECT'ING, *ppr.* Imagining without evidence; mistrusting upon slight grounds.

SUSPECT'LESS, *a.* Not suspecting; having no suspicion. *Herbert.*

2. Not suspected; not mistrusted. *Beaum.*

SUSPEND', *v. t.* [Fr. *suspendre;* It. *sospendere;* Sp. *suspender;* L. *suspendo; sub* and *pendo*, to hang.]

1. To hang; to attach to something above; as, to *suspend* a ball by a thread; to *suspend* the body by a cord or by hooks; a needle *suspended* by a loadstone.

2. To make to depend on. God hath *suspended* the promise of eternal life on the condition of faith and obedience.

3. To interrupt; to intermit; to cause to cease for a time.

> The guard nor fights nor flies; their fate so near
> At once *suspends* their courage and their fear. *Denham.*

4. To stay; to delay; to hinder from proceeding for a time.

> *Suspend* your indignation against my brother. *Shak.*
> I *suspend* their doom. *Milton.*

5. To hold in a state undetermined; as, to *suspend* one's choice or opinion. *Locke.*

6. To debar from any privilege, from the execution of an office, or from the enjoyment of income.

> Good men should not be *suspended* from the exercise of their ministry and deprived of their livelihood, for ceremonies which are acknowledged indifferent. *Sanderson.*

7. To cause to cease for a time from operation or effect; as, to *suspend* the habeas corpus act.

SUSPEND'ED, *pp.* Hung up; made to depend on; caused to cease for a time; delayed; held undetermined; prevented from executing an office or enjoying a right.

SUSPEND'ER, *n.* One that suspends.

2. *Suspenders*, plu. straps worn for holding up pantaloons, &c.; braces.

SUSPEND'ING, *ppr.* Hanging up; making to depend on; intermitting; causing to cease for a time; holding undetermined; debarring from action or right.

SUSPENSE, *n. suspens'.* [L. *suspensus.*] A state of uncertainty; indetermination; indecision. A man's mind is in *suspense*, when it is balancing the weight of different arguments or considerations, or when it is uncertain respecting facts unknown, or events not in his own power.

> Ten days the prophet in *suspense* remain'd. *Denham.*

2. Stop; cessation for a time.

> A cool *suspense* from pleasure or from pain. *Pope.*

3. In *law*, suspension; a temporary cessation of a man's right; as when the rent or other profits of land cease by unity of possession of land and rent.

SUSPENSE, *a. suspens'.* Held from proceeding. [*Little used.*] *Milton.*

SUSPENSIBIL'ITY, *n.* The capacity of being suspended or sustained from sinking: as the *suspensibility* of indurated clay in water. *Kirwan.*

SUSPENS'IBLE, *a.* Capable of being suspended or held from sinking.

SUSPEN'SION, *n.* [Fr. from L. *suspensio.* See *Suspend.*]

1. The act of hanging up, or of causing to hang by being attached to something above.

2. The act of making to depend on any thing for existence or taking place; as the *suspension* of payment on the performance of a condition.

3. The act of delaying; delay; as the *suspension* of a criminal's execution; called a respite or reprieve.

4. Act of withholding or balancing the judgment; forbearance of determination; as the *suspension* of opinion, of judgment, of decision or determination. *Suspension* of judgment often proceeds from doubt or ignorance of facts.

5. Temporary cessation; interruption; in-

termission; as the *suspension* of labor or of study; the *suspension* of pain.
6. Temporary privation of powers, authority or rights; usually intended as a censure or punishment; as the *suspension* of an ecclesiastic or minister for some fault. This may be merely a *suspension* of his office, or it may be both of his office and his income. A military or naval officer's *suspension* takes place when he is arrested.
7. Prevention or interruption of operation; as the *suspension* of the habeas corpus act.
8. In *rhetoric*, a keeping of the hearer in doubt and in attentive expectation of what is to follow, or what is to be the inference or conclusion from the arguments or observations.
9. In *Scot's law*, a stay or postponement of execution of a sentence condemnatory, by means of letters of suspension granted on application to the lord ordinary. *Cyc.*
10. In *mechanics*, points of suspension, in a balance, are the points in the axis or beam where the weights are applied, or from which they are suspended. *Cyc.*
11. In *music*, every sound of a chord to a given base, which is continued to another base, is a *suspension*. *Cyc.*
Suspension of arms, in war, a short truce or cessation of operations agreed on by the commanders of the contending parties, as for burying the dead, making proposals for surrender or for peace, &c. *Cyc.*

SUSPENS'IVE, *a.* Doubtful. *Beaum.*

SUSPENS'OR, *n.* In *anatomy*, a bandage to suspend the scrotum.

SUSPENS'ORY, *a.* That suspends; suspending; as a *suspensory* muscle.

SUSPENS'ORY, *n.* That which suspends or holds up; a truss.

SUS'PICABLE, *a.* [L. *suspicor.*] That may be suspected; liable to suspicion. [*Not in use.*] *More.*

SUSPI''CION, *n.* [Fr. from L. *suspicio.* See *Suspect.*]
The act of suspecting; the imagination of the existence of something without proof, or upon very slight evidence, or upon no evidence at all. *Suspicion* often proceeds from the apprehension of evil; it is the offspring or companion of jealousy.

> *Suspicions* among thoughts, are like bats among birds; they ever fly by twilight. *Bacon.*

SUSPI''CIOUS, *a.* [L. *suspiciosus.*] Inclined to suspect; apt to imagine without proof.

> Nature itself, after it has done an injury, will ever be *suspicious*, and no man can love the person he suspects. *South.*

2. Indicating suspicion or fear.

> We have a *suspicious*, fearful, constrained countenance. *Swift.*

3. Liable to suspicion; adapted to raise suspicion; giving reason to imagine ill; as an author of *suspicious* innovations. *Hooker.*

> I spy a black *suspicious* threat'ning cloud. *Shak.*

4. Entertaining suspicion; given to suspicion.

> Many mischievous insects are daily at work to make men of merit *suspicious* of each other. *Pope.*

SUSPI''CIOUSLY, *adv.* With suspicion.
2. So as to excite suspicion. *Sidney.*

SUSPI''CIOUSNESS, *n.* The quality of being liable to suspicion, or liable to be suspected; as the *suspiciousness* of a man's appearance, of his weapons or of his actions.
2. The quality or state of being apt to suspect; as the *suspiciousness* of a man's temper or mind.

SUSPI'RAL, *n.* [L. *suspiro*, to breathe; *sub* and *spiro.*]
1. A breathing hole; a vent or ventiduct. *Rees.*
2. A spring of water passing under ground towards a cistern or conduit. [*Local.*] *Rees.*

SUSPIRA'TION, *n.* [L. *suspiratio, suspiro*, to sigh; *sub* and *spiro*, to breathe.]
The act of sighing or fetching a long and deep breath; a sigh. *More.*

SUSPI'RE, *v. i.* [supra.] To sigh; to fetch a long deep breath; to breathe. [*Little used.*] *Shak.*

SUSPI'RED, *pp.* or *a.* Wished for; desired. [*Not in use.*]

SUSTA'IN, *v. t.* [L. *sustineo; sub* and *teneo*, to hold under; Fr. *soutenir;* It. *sostenere;* Sp. *sostener, sustentar.*]
1. To bear; to uphold; to support; as, a foundation *sustains* the superstructure; pillars *sustain* an edifice; a beast *sustains* a load.
2. To hold; to keep from falling; as, a rope *sustains* a weight.
3. To support; to keep from sinking in despondence. The hope of a better life *sustains* the afflicted amidst all their sorrows.
4. To maintain; to keep alive; to support; to subsist; as provisions to *sustain* a family or an army.
5. To support in any condition by aid; to assist or relieve.

> His sons, who seek the tyrant to *sustain*. *Dryden.*

6. To bear; to endure without failing or yielding. The mind stands collected and *sustains* the shock.

> Shall Turnus then such endless toil *sustain?* *Dryden.*

7. To suffer; to bear; to undergo.

> You shall *sustain* more new disgraces. *Shak.*

8. To maintain; to support; not to dismiss or abate. Notwithstanding the plea in bar or in abatement, the court *sustained* the action or suit.
9. To maintain as a sufficient ground. The testimony or the evidence is not sufficient to *sustain* the action, the accusation, the charges, or the impeachment.
10. In *music*, to continue, as the sound of notes through their whole length. *Busby.*

SUSTA'IN, *n.* That which upholds. [*Not in use.*] *Milton.*

SUSTA'INABLE, *a.* That may be sustained or maintained. The action is not *sustainable.*

SUSTA'INED, *pp.* Borne; upheld; maintained; supported; subsisted; suffered.

SUSTA'INER, *n.* He or that which sustains, upholds or suffers.

SUSTA'INING, *ppr.* Bearing; upholding; maintaining; suffering; subsisting.

SUSTAL'TIC, *a.* [Gr. συςαλτικος.] Mournful; affecting; an epithet given to a species of music by the Greeks. *Busby.*

SUS'TENANCE, *n.* [Norm. Fr.; from *sustain.*]
1. Support; maintenance; subsistence; as the *sustenance* of the body; the *sustenance* of life.
2. That which supports life; food; victuals; provisions. This city has ample *sustenance.*

SUSTEN'TACLE, *n.* [L. *sustentaculum.*] Support. [*Not in use.*] *More.*

SUSTENTA'TION, *n.* [Fr. from L. *sustentatio, sustento.*]
1. Support; preservation from falling. *Boyle.*
2. Use of food. *Brown.*
3. Maintenance; support of life. *Bacon.*

SUSURRA'TION, *n.* [L. *susurratio; susurro*, to whisper.] A whispering; a soft murmur.

SU'TILE, *a.* [L. *sutilis*, from *suo*, to sew.] Done by stitching. [*Not in use.*] *Boswell.*

SUT'LER, *n.* [D. *zoetelaar*, as if from *zoet*, sweet. But in German, *sudelkoch* is a paltry victualer, as if from *sudeln*, to soil; *sudler*, a dirty fellow. In Danish, *sudelkock* is a pastry cook, from the same root; *sudler*, to soil. The Danish may be the original signification.]
A person who follows an army and sells to the troops provisions and liquors.

SUT'LING, *a.* Belonging to sutlers; engaged in the occupation of a sutler. *Tatler.*

SUTTEE', *n.* In the Sanscrit, or sacred language of the Hindoos, a female deity.
2. A widow who immolates herself on the funeral pile of her husband.
3. The sacrifice of burning a widow on the the funeral pile of her husband.

SUT'TLE, *a.* *Suttle weight*, in commerce, is when tret is allowed; neat weight. *Dict.*

SU'TURE, *n.* [L. *sutura*, from *suo*, to sew.]
1. Literally, a sewing; hence, the uniting of the parts of a wound by stitching. *Coxe.*
2. The seam or joint which unites the bones of the skull; or the peculiar articulation or connection of those bones; as the coronal *suture;* the sagittal *suture.*

SUV'ERAN, *a.* [Fr. *souverain;* Sp. Port. *soberano;* It. *sovrano;* from L. *supernus, superus, super.* The barbarous Norman word *souvereign*, seems to be formed of L. *super* and *regnum;* a strange blunder.]
1. Supreme in power; possessing supreme dominion; as a *suveran* prince. The Creator is the *suveran* ruler of the universe.
2. Supreme; chief; superior to all others.
3. Supremely efficacious; superior to all others; as a *suveran* remedy.
4. Supreme; pertaining to the first magistrate of a nation; as *suveran* authority.

SUV'ERAN, *n.* A supreme lord or ruler; one who possesses the highest authority without control. Some kings are *suverans* in their dominions; the authority of others is limited. The Creator is the *suveran* of all that he has made.
2. A supreme magistrate, lord or king.

> O let my *suv'ran* turn away his face. *Shak.*

SUV'ERANLY, *adv.* Supremely; in the highest degree. *Obs.* *Boyle.*

SUV'ERANTY, *n.* Supreme power; supremacy; the possession of uncontrollable power. Absolute *suveranty* belongs only to God.

SWAB, *n.* [Sax. *swebban*, to sweep; formed perhaps on the root of *wipe*, as G. *schweben*, to wave or soar, is on that of *wave*, and D. *zweepen*, on that of *whip*.]

A mop for cleaning floors; on board of ships, a large mop or bunch of old rope yarn, used to clean the deck and cabin.

SWAB, *v. t.* [supra.] To clean with a mop; to wipe when wet or after washing; as, to *swab* the deck of a ship.

SWAB'BER, *n.* [D. *zwabber.*] One that uses a swab to clean a floor or deck; on board of ships of war, an inferior officer, whose business is to see that the ship is kept clean.

SWAD, *n.* A pod, as of beans or peas. [*Local.*]

2. A short fat person. *Obs.* *B. Jonson.*

3. In *New England*, a lump, mass or bunch; also, a crowd. [*Vulgar.*]

SWAD'DLE, *v. t.* [Sax. *swathe*, *swethel*, a border, fringe or band; *beswethan*, to swathe; D. *zwaad*, G. *schwaden*, a *swath.*]

1. To swathe; to bind, as with a bandage; to bind tight with clothes; used generally of infants; as, to *swaddle* a child.

They *swaddled* me in my night-gown. *Addison.*

2. To beat; to cudgel. [*Low and not in use.*] *Hudibras.*

SWAD'DLE, *n.* Clothes bound tight around the body.

They put me in bed in all my *swaddles*. *Addison.*

SWAD'DLED, *pp.* Swathed; bound in tight clothes.

SWAD'DLING, *ppr.* Swathing; binding in tight clothes.

SWAD'DLING-BAND, } *n.* A band or
SWAD'DLING-CLOTH, } cloth wrapped round an infant. Luke ii.

SWAG, *v. i.* [Qu. Sax. *sigan*, to fall; Ice. *sweigia*; Sw. *svag*, Dan. *id.* feeble; Dan. *svækker*, to weaken. See *Weak.*]

To sink down by its weight; to lean. *Grew.*

SWAG'-BELLIED, *a.* Having a prominent overhanging belly. *Shak.*

SWAGE, *v. t.* [probably allied to *swag* and *weak*; from falling or throwing down.]

To ease; to soften; to mitigate.

Apt words have power to *swage*
The tumors of a troubled mind. *Milton.*

[See *Assuage*, which is the word now used.]

SWAG'GER, *v. i.* [Sax. *swegan*, to sound or rattle.]

To bluster; to bully; to boast or brag noisily; to be tumultuously proud.

What a pleasure it is to *swagger* at the bar. *Arbuthnot.*

To be great is not to *swagger* at our footmen. *Collier.*

SWAG'GERER, *n.* A blusterer; a bully; a boastful noisy fellow. *Shak.*

SWAG'GERING, *ppr.* Blustering; boasting noisily.

SWAG'GING, *ppr.* Sinking or inclining.

SWAG'GY, *a.* [from *swag.*] Sinking, hanging or leaning by its weight. *Brown.*

SWAIN, *n.* [Sax. *swein*, *swan*, a boy, a youth, a servant, a herdsman; Sw. *sven*, a boy; Dan. *svend*; Ice. *svein.*]

1. A young man. *Spenser.*

2. A country servant employed in husbandry. *Shak.*

3. A pastoral youth. [*It is used chiefly in this sense, and in poetry.*]

Blest *swains!* whose nymphs in every grace excel. *Pope.*

SWA'INISH, *a.* Rustic. *Milton.*

SWA'INMOTE, } [*swain* and *mote*, meet-
SWE'INMOTE, } *n.* ing.] In *England*, a
SWAN'IMOTE, } court held before the verderors of the forest as judges, by the steward of the court, thrice every year; the swains or freeholders within the forest composing the jury. Its principal jurisdiction is to inquire into the oppressions and grievances committed by the officers of the forest. It receives and tries also presentments certified from the court of attachments against offenses in vert and venison. This court is incident to a forest, as a court of piepoudre is to a fair. *Blackstone.*

SWALE, *n.* [probably from *vale.*] A local word in New England, signifying an interval or vale; a tract of low land.

2. In *England*, a shade. *Cyc.*

SWALE, *v. i.* To waste. [See *Sweal.*]

SWALE, *v. t.* To dress a hog for bacon, by singeing or burning off his hair. [*Local.*] *Cyc.*

SWAL'LET, *n.* [See *Well.*] Among *the tin miners*, water breaking in upon the miners at their work. *Bailey.*

SWAL'LOW, *n.* [Sax. *swalewe*; D. *zwaluw*; G. *schwalbe*; Dan. *svale*; Sw. *svala.*]

A bird of the genus Hirundo, of many species, among which are the chimney swallow and the martin.

SWAL'LOW-FISH, *n.* A sea fish of the genus Trigla, called in Cornwall, *tub-fish*; remarkable for the size of its gill-fins. It is called also the *sapphirine gurnard.* *Cyc.*

SWAL'LOW-FLY, *n.* The name of the chelidonius, a fly remarkable for its swift and long flight. *Cyc.*

SWAL'LOW'S-TAIL, *n.* In *joinery* and *carpentry*, the same as *dove-tail.*

SWAL'LOW-STONE, *n.* *Chelidonius lapis*, a stone which Pliny and other authors affirm to be found in the stomachs of young swallows. *Cyc.*

SWAL'LOW-TAIL, *n.* A plant, a species of willow. *Bacon.*

SWAL'LOW-WORT, *n.* A plant of the genus Asclepias; *hirundinaria.* It grows in the southern part of Europe, and is said to have been successfully used as a medicine, chiefly in dropsical cases. *Cyc.*

The *African swallow-wort* is of the genus Stapelia. *Lee.*

SWAL'LOW, *v. t.* [Sax. *swelgan*, *swilgan*, to swallow, to swill; D. *zwelgen*; Sw. *svälja*, to swallow; *svalg*, the throat; Dan. *svælger.* Qu. the Fr. *avaler*, with a prefix, and the root of *fall.*]

1. To take into the stomach; to receive through the gullet or œsophagus into the stomach; as, to *swallow* food or drink. Food should be well chewed before it is *swallowed.*

2. To absorb; to draw and sink into an abyss or gulf; to ingulf; usually followed by *up.* The Malstrom off the coast of Norway, it is said, will *swallow up* a ship.

In bogs *swallow'd up* and lost. *Milton.*

The earth opened and *swallowed* them *up.* Num. xvi.

3. To receive or embrace, as opinions or belief, without examination or scruple; to receive implicitly. *Locke.*

4. To engross; to appropriate.

Homer—has *swallowed up* the honor of those who succeeded him. *Pope.*

5. To occupy; to employ.

The necessary provision of life *swallows* the greatest part of their time. *Locke.*

6. To seize and waste.

Corruption *swallow'd* what the liberal hand
Of bounty scatter'd. *Thomson.*

7. To engross; to engage completely.

The priest and the prophet have erred through strong drink; they are *swallowed up* of wine. Is. xxviii.

8. To exhaust; to consume. His expenses *swallow up* all his income.

SWAL'LOW, *n.* The gullet or œsophagus; the throat.

2. Voracity. *South.*

3. As much as is swallowed at once.

SWAL'LOWED, *pp.* Taken into the stomach; absorbed; received without scruple; engrossed; wasted; exhausted.

SWAL'LOWER, *n.* One who swallows; also, a glutton. *Tatler.*

SWAL'LOWING, *ppr.* Taking into the stomach; absorbing; ingulfing; receiving implicitly; engrossing; wasting; exhausting.

SWAL'LOWING, *n.* The act of taking into the stomach or of absorbing; the act of receiving implicitly; the act of engrossing.

SWAM, *pret.* of *swim.*

SWAMP, *n.* [Sax. *swam*, a fungus or mushroom; Goth. *swamms*, a spunge, G. *schwamm*, D. *zwam*, Dan. *svamp*; Sw. *id.* a spunge, a fungus.]

Spungy land; low ground filled with water; soft wet ground. In *New England*, I believe this word is never applied to marsh, or the boggy land made by the overflowing of salt water, but always to low soft ground in the interior country; wet and spungy land, but not usually covered with water. This is the true meaning of the word. *Swamps* are often mowed. In *England*, the word is explained in books by boggy land, morassy or marshy ground.

SWAMP, *v. t.* To plunge, whelm or sink in a swamp; to plunge into difficulties inextricable.

SWAMP'Y, *a.* Consisting of swamp; like a swamp; low, wet and spungy; as *swampy* land.

SWAMP-ORE, *n.* In *mineralogy*, an ore of iron found in swamps and morasses; called also bog-ore, or indurated bog iron ore. Its color is a dark yellowish brown or gray; its fracture is earthy, and it contains so much phosphoric acid as to injure its tenacity. *Cyc.*

SWAN, *n.* [Sax. *swan*; D. *zwaan*; G. *schwan*; Dan. *svane*; Sw. *svan.* Qu. *wan*, white, with a prefix.]

A large aquatic fowl of the genus Anas, of two varieties, the wild and the tame. The plumage is of a pure white color, and its long arching neck gives it a noble appearance. *Cyc.*

SWANG, *n.* A piece of low land or green sward, liable to be covered with water. [*Local in England.*]

SWANSDOWN, *n.* A fine soft thick woolen cloth.

SWAN'SKIN, *n.* [*swan* and *skin.*] A species of flannel of a soft texture, thick and warm.

SWAP, *adv.* [Qu. *sweep.*] Hastily; at a snatch. [*A low word and local.*]

SWAP, *v. t.* To exchange; to barter; to swop. [See *Swop.*] [*This word is not elegant, but common in colloquial language in America.*]

SWAPE, *n.* [Qu. *sweep.*] A pole supported by a fulcrum on which it turns, used for raising water from a well, for churning, &c. [This Bailey spells *swipe*, and in N. England it is pronounced *sweep*, as in *well-sweep.*]

SWARD, *n.* [Sax. *sweard*; Dan. *svær*; D. *zwoord*; G. *schwarte*, rind, skin; W. *gweryd*, an excretion, sward, moss.]

1. The skin of bacon. [*Local.*]
2. The grassy surface of land; turf; that part of the soil which is filled with the roots of grass, forming a kind of mat. When covered with green grass, it is called *green sward.*

SWARD, *v. t.* To produce sward; to cover with sward. *Mortimer.*

SWARD'-CUTTER, *n.* An instrument for cutting sward across the ridges.

SWARD'Y, *a.* Covered with sward or grass; as *swardy* land.

SWARE, *old pret.* of *swear.* We now use *swore.*

SWARE, } *n.* A copper coin and money
SCHWARE, } of account in Bremen, value one fifth of a groat, and 72 groats make a thaler, [dollar.]

SWARM, *n.* *sworm.* [Sax. *swearm*; G. *schwarm*; D. *zwerm*; Dan. *sverm*; Sw. *svårm.* This seems to be formed on the root of *warm.* The Sp. *hervir*, to boil, to swarm, is the L. *ferveo*, and boiling is very expressive of the motions of a swarm of bees. See the Verb.]

1. In *a general sense*, a large number or body of small animals or insects, particularly when in motion; but *appropriately*, a great number of honey bees which emigrate from a hive at once, and seek new lodgings under the direction of a queen; or a like body of bees united and settled permanently in a hive. The bees that leave a hive in spring, are the young bees produced in the year preceding. Ex. viii. Judges xiv.
2. A swarm or multitude; particularly, a multitude of people in motion. *Swarms* of northern nations overran the south of Europe in the fifth century.

Note.—The application of this word to inanimate things, as swarms of *advantages*, by Shakspeare, and swarms of *themes*, by Young, is not legitimate, for the essence of the word is motion.

SWARM, *v. i.* *sworm.* [Sax. *swearmian*; D. *zwermen*; G. *schwärmen*; Dan. *svermer*; Sw. *svårma*, to swarm, to rove, to wander, to swerve.]

1. To collect and depart from a hive by flight in a body, as bees. Bees *swarm* in warm, clear days in summer.
2. To appear or collect in a crowd; to run; to throng together; to congregate in a multitude.

In crowds around the *swarming* people join. *Dryden.*

3. To be crowded; to be thronged with a multitude of animals in motion. The forests in America often *swarm* with wild pigeons. The northern seas in spring *swarm* with herrings.

Every place *swarms* with soldiers. *Spenser.*

[Such phrases as "life *swarms* with ills," "those days *swarmed* with fables," are not legitimate, or wholly obsolete. *Brown. Young.*]

4. To breed multitudes. *Milton.*
5. To climb, as a tree, by embracing it with the arms and legs, and scrambling.

At the top was placed a piece of money, as a prize for those who could *swarm* up and seize it. *Coxe's Russ.*

Note.—This, by the common people in New England, is pronounced *squirm* or *squurm*, and it is evidently formed on *worm*, indicating that *worm* and *warm*, on which *swarm* and *squirm* are formed, are radically the same word. The primary sense is to bend, wind, twist, as a worm, or a swarm of bees. It may be formed on the root of *veer, vary.*

SWARM, *v. t.* To crowd or throng. [*Not in use.*]

SWART, } *a.* *swort.* [Sax. *swart*, *sweart*;
SWARTH, } *sworth.* Sw. *svart*; Dan. *sværte*; G. *schwarz*; D. *zwart.*]

1. Being of a dark hue; moderately black; tawny.

A nation strange with visage *swart.* *Spenser.*

[I believe *swart* and *swarth* are never used in the United States, certainly not in New England. *Swarthy* is a common word.]

2. Gloomy; malignant. [*Not in use.*] *Milton.*

SWART, *v. t.* To make tawny. *Brown.*

SWARTH, } *n.* An apparition. [*Not us-*
SWAIRTH, } *ed in New England.*]

SWARTH'ILY, *adv.* [from *swarthy.*] Duskily; with a tawny hue.

SWARTH'INESS, *n.* Tawniness; a dusky or dark complexion.

SWARTH'Y, *a.* [See *Swart.*] Being of a dark hue or dusky complexion; tawny. In warm climates, the complexion of men is universally *swarthy* or black. The Moors, Spaniards and Italians are more *swarthy* than the French, Germans and English.

Their *swarthy* hosts would darken all our plains. *Addison.*

2. Black; as the *swarthy* African.

SWART'INESS, *n.* A tawny color. *Sherwood.*

SWART'ISH, *a.* Somewhat dark or tawny.

SWART'Y, *a.* Swarthy; tawny. *Burton.*

SWARVE, *v. i.* To swerve. [*Not in use.*] *Spenser.*

SWASH, *n.* An oval figure, whose moldings are oblique to the axis of the work. *Moxon.*

[*A cant word.* Johnson.]

SWASH, *n.* A blustering noise; a vaporing. [*Not in use or vulgar.*]

2. Impulse of water flowing with violence. In the southern states of America, *swash* or *swosh* is a name given to a narrow sound or channel of water lying within a sand bank, or between that and the shore. Many such are found on the shores of the Carolinas.

SWASH, *v. i.* [D. *zwetsen*, to boast.] To bluster; to make a great noise; to vapor or brag. [*Not in use.*] *Shak.*

SWASH, } *a.* Soft, like fruit too ripe.
SWASH'Y, } [*Local.*] *Pegge.*

SWASH'-BUCKLER, *n.* A sword-player; a bully or braggadocio. [*Not in use.*] *Milton.*

SWASH'ER, *n.* One who makes a blustering show of valor or force of arms. [*Not in use.*] *Shak.*

SWAT, } *v. i.* To sweat. *Obs.*
SWATE, } *Chaucer.*

SWATCH, *n.* A swath. [*Not in use.*] *Tusser.*

SWATH, *n.* *swoth.* [Sax. *swathe*, a track, a border or fringe, a band; D. *zwaad*; G. *schwaden.*]

1. A line of grass or grain cut and thrown together by the sythe in mowing or cradling.
2. The whole breadth or sweep of a sythe in mowing or cradling; as a wide *swath.* *Farmers.*
2. A band or fillet. They wrapped me in a hundred yards of *swath.* *Guardian.*

SWATHE, *v. t.* To bind with a band, bandage or rollers; as, to *swathe* a child.

2. To bind or wrap.

Their children are never *swathed* or bound about with any thing when first born. *Abbot.*

SWAY, *v. t.* [D. *zwaaijen*, to turn, to wield, to swing, to sway. This word is probably formed on the root of *weigh, wave*, Sax. *wæg, weg*, and *swag*, and probably *swing* is written for *swig*, and is of the same family; Ice. *sweigia*; Sw. *sviga.*]

1. To move or wave; to wield with the hand; as, to *sway* the scepter.
2. To bias; to cause to lean or incline to one side. Let not temporal advantages *sway* you from the line of duty. The king was *swayed* by his council from the course he intended to pursue.

As bowls run true by being made
On purpose false, and to be *sway'd.*
Hudibras.

3. To rule; to govern; to influence or direct by power and authority, or by moral force.

This was the race
To *sway* the world, and land and sea subdue.
Dryden.

She could not *sway* her house. *Shak.*

Take heed lest passion *sway*
Thy judgment to do aught which else free will
Would not admit. *Milton.*

SWAY, *v. i.* To be drawn to one side by weight; to lean. A wall *sways* to the west.

The balance *sways* on our part. *Bacon.*

[This sense seems to indicate that this word and *swag*, are radically one.]

2. To have weight or influence.

The example of sundry churches—doth *sway* much. *Hooker.*

3. To bear rule; to govern.

Had'st thou *sway'd* as kings should do— *Shak.*

4. In *seamen's language*, to hoist; particularly applied to the lower yards and to the topmast yards, &c.

SWAY, *n.* The swing or sweep of a weapon.

To strike with huge two-handed *sway.* *Milton*

2. Any thing moving with bulk and power.

Are not you mov'd when all the *sway* of earth
Shakes like a thing unfirm? *Shak.*

3. Preponderation; turn or cast of balance.

—Expert
When to advance, or stand, or turn the *sway* of battle. *Milton.*

4. Power exerted in governing; rule; dominion; control.

When vice prevails and impious men bear *sway*,
The post of honor is a private station. *Addison.*

5. Influence; weight or authority that inclines to one side; as the *sway* of desires. All the world is subject to the *sway* of fashion.

SWA'YED, *pp.* Wielded; inclined to one side; ruled; governed; influenced; biased.

SWA'YING, *ppr.* Wielding; causing to lean; biasing; ruling.

SWA'YING, *n.* *Swaying of the back*, among beasts, is a kind of lumbago, caused by a fall or by being overloaded. *Cyc.*

SWEAL, *v. i.* [Sax. *swelan*; sometimes written *swale*. In America, it is pronounced as written, *sweal* or *sweel*.]

1. To melt and run down, as the tallow of a candle; to waste away without feeding the flame.
2. To blaze away.

SWE'ALING, *ppr.* Melting and wasting away.

SWEAR, *v. i.* pret. *swore*, [formerly *sware*;] pp. *sworn*. [Sax. *swerian*, *swerigan*; Goth. *swaran*; D. *zweeren*; G. *schwören*; Sw. *svåria*, to swear, and *svara*, to answer; Dan. *sværger*, to swear, and *svarer*, to answer. The latter seems to be from *svarrer*, to turn, Eng. *veer*. *Swear* seems to be allied to *aver* and the L. *assevero*, and to belong to the root *Wr*.]

1. To affirm or utter a solemn declaration, with an appeal to God for the truth of what is affirmed.

Ye shall not *swear* by my name falsely. Lev. xix.

But I say unto you, *swear* not at all. Matt. v.

2. To promise upon oath.

Jacob said, *swear* to me this day; and he *swore* to him. Gen. xxv.

3. To give evidence on oath; as, to *swear* to the truth of a statement. He *swore* that the prisoner was not present at the riot.
4. To be profane; to practice profaneness. Certain classes of men are accustomed to *swear*. For men to *swear* is sinful, disreputable and odious; but for females or ladies to *swear*, appears more abominable and scandalous.

SWEAR, *v. t.* To utter or affirm with a solemn appeal to God for the truth of the declaration; as, to *swear* on oath. [This seems to have been the primitive use of *swear*; that is, to affirm.]

2. To put to an oath; to cause to take an oath; as, to *swear* witnesses in court; to *swear* a jury; the witness has been *sworn*; the judges are *sworn* into office.
3. To declare or charge upon oath; as, to *swear* treason against a man.
4. To obtest by an oath.

Now by Apollo, king, thou *swear'st* thy gods in vain. *Shak.*

To swear the peace against one, to make oath that one is under the actual fear of death or bodily harm from the person; in which case the person must find sureties of the peace.

SWEARER, *n.* One who swears; one who calls God to witness for the truth of his declaration.

2. A profane person.

Then the liars and *swearers* are fools. *Shak.*

SWEARING, *ppr.* Affirming upon oath; uttering a declaration, with an appeal to God for the truth of it.

2. Putting upon oath; causing to swear.

SWEARING, *n.* The act or practice of affirming on oath. *Swearing* in court is lawful.

2. Profaneness. All *swearing* not required by some law, or in conformity with law, is criminal. False *swearing* or perjury is a crime of a deep dye.

SWEAT, *n. swet.* [Sax. *swat*; D. *zweet*; G. *schweiss*; Dan. *sveed*; Sw. *svett*; L. *sudor*.]

1. The fluid or sensible moisture which issues out of the pores of the skin of an animal.

In the *sweat* of thy face shalt thou eat bread. Gen. iii.

2. Labor; toil; drudgery. *Milton.*
3. Moisture evacuated from any substance; as the *sweat* of hay or grain in a mow or stack.

SWEAT, *v. i. swet.* pret. and pp. *sweat* or *sweated*. *Swot* is obsolete. [Sax. *swætan*; Sw. *svetta*; Dan. *sveeder*; D. *zweeten*; G. *schwitzen*; L. *sudo*; Fr. *suer*.]

1. To emit sensible moisture through the pores of the skin; to perspire. Horses *sweat*; oxen *sweat* little or not at all.]
2. To toil; to labor; to drudge.

He'd have the poets *sweat*. *Waller.*

3. To emit moisture, as green plants in a heap.

SWEAT, *v. t. swet.* To emit or suffer to flow from the pores; to exsude.

For him the rich Arabia *sweats* her gums. *Dryden.*

2. To cause to emit moisture from the pores of the skin. His physicians attempted to *sweat* him by the most powerful sudorifics. They *sweat* him profusely.

SWEAT'ER, *n.* One that causes to sweat.

SWEAT'INESS, *n.* The state of being sweaty or moist with sweat.

SWEAT'ING, *ppr.* Emitting moisture from the pores of the skin; throwing out moisture; exsuding.

2. Causing to emit moisture upon the skin.

SWEAT'ING-BATH, *n.* A sudatory; a bath for exciting sensible perspiration or sweat; a hypocaust or stove. *Cyc.*

SWEAT'ING-HOUSE, *n.* A house for sweating persons in sickness. *Cyc.*

SWEAT'ING-IRON, *n.* A kind of knife or a piece of a sythe, used to scrape off sweat from horses. *Cyc.*

SWEAT'ING-ROOM, *n.* A room for sweating persons.

2. In *rural economy*, a room for sweating cheese and carrying off the superfluous juices. *Cyc.*

SWEAT'ING-SICKNESS, *n.* A febril epidemic disease which prevailed in some countries of Europe, but particularly in England, in the 15th and 16th centuries. Its first appearance was in the army of the earl of Richmond, afterward Henry VII. on his landing at Milford haven, in 1485. The invasion of the disease was sudden, and usually marked by a local affection producing the sensation of intense heat, afterwards diffusing itself over the whole body, and immediately followed by profuse sweating, which continued through the whole course of the disease or till death, which often happened in a few hours. *Cyc.*

SWEAT'Y, *a.* Moist with sweat; as a *sweaty* skin; a *sweaty* garment.

2. Consisting of sweat.

No noisy whiffs or *sweaty* streams. *Swift.*

3. Laborious; toilsome; as the *sweaty* forge. *Prior.*

SWEDE, *n.* A native of Sweden.

2. A Swedish turnep.

SWE'DISH, *a.* Pertaining to Sweden.

SWE'DISH-TURNEP, *n.* The ruta baga, a hard sort of turnep, of two kinds, the white and the yellow. The latter is most valued. *Cyc.*

SWEEP, *v. t.* pret. and pp. *swept*. [Sax. *swapan*, *sweopan*. It seems to be allied to *swab*, and may be formed on the root of *wipe*.]

1. To brush or rub over with a brush, broom or besom, for removing loose dirt; to clean by brushing; as, to *sweep* a chimney or a floor. When we say, to *sweep* a room, we mean, to *sweep* the floor of the room; and to *sweep* the house, is to *sweep* the floors of the house.
2. To carry with a long swinging or dragging motion; to carry with pomp.

And like a peacock, *sweep* along his tail. *Shak.*

3. To drive or carry along or off by a long brushing stroke or force, or by flowing on the earth. Thus the wind *sweeps* the snow from the tops of the hills; a river *sweeps* away a dam, timber or rubbish; a flood *sweeps* away a bridge or a house. Hence,
4. To drive, destroy or carry off many at a stroke, or with celerity and violence; as, a pestilence *sweeps* off multitudes in a few days. The conflagration *swept* away whole streets of houses.

I have already *swept* the stakes. *Dryden.*

5. To rub over.

Their long descending train,
With rubies edg'd and sapphires, *swept* the plain. *Dryden.*

6. To strike with a long stroke.

Wake into voice each silent string,
And *sweep* the sounding lyre. *Pope.*

7. To draw or drag over; as, to *sweep* the bottom of a river with a net, or with the bight of a rope, to hook an anchor. *Mar. Dict.*

SWEEP, *v. i.* To pass with swiftness and violence, as something broad or brushing the surface of any thing; as a *sweeping* rain; a *sweeping* flood. A fowl that flies near the surface of land or water, is said to *sweep* along near the surface.

2. To pass over or brush along with celerity and force; as, the wind *sweeps* along the plain.
3. To pass with pomp; as, a person *sweeps* along with a trail.

She *sweeps* it through the court with troops of ladies. *Shak.*

3. To move with a long reach; as a *sweeping* stroke. *Dryden.*

SWEEP, *n.* The act of sweeping.

2. The compass of a stroke; as a long *sweep.*

3. The compass of any turning body or motion; as the *sweep* of a door.

4. The compass of any thing flowing or brushing; as, the flood carried away every thing within its *sweep.*

5. Violent and general destruction; as the *sweep* of an epidemic disease. *Graunt.*

6. Direction of any motion not rectilinear; as the *sweep* of a compass.

7. The mold of a ship when she begins to compass in, at the rung heads; also, any part of a ship shaped by the segment of a circle; as a floor-*sweep*; a back-*sweep*, &c.

8. Among *refiners of metals*, the almond-furnace.

9. Among *seamen*, a large oar, used to assist the rudder in turning a ship in a calm, or to increase her velocity in a chase, &c.

Sweep of the tiller, a circular frame on which the tiller traverses in large ships.

SWEE'PER, *n.* One that sweeps.

SWEE'PING, *ppr.* Brushing over; rubbing with a broom or besom; cleaning with a broom or besom; brushing along; passing over; dragging over.

SWEE'PINGS, *n. plu.* Things collected by sweeping; rubbish. The *sweepings* of streets are often used as manure.

SWEE'P-NET, *n.* [*sweep* and *net.*] A large net for drawing over a large compass.

SWEE'PSTAKE, *n.* [*sweep* and *stake.*] A man that wins all; usually *sweepstakes.* *Shak.*

SWEE'PY, *a.* Passing with speed and violence over a great compass at once.

The branches bend before their *sweepy* sway. *Dryden.*

2. Strutting.

3. Wavy.

SWEET, *a.* [Sax. *swete*; D. *zoet*; G. *süss*; Sw. *söt*; Dan. *söd*; Sans. *swad.* Qu. L. *suavis.*]

1. Agreeable or grateful to the taste; as, sugar or honey is *sweet.*

2. Pleasing to the smell; fragrant; as a *sweet* rose; *sweet* odor; *sweet* incense. Ex. xxvi.

3. Pleasing to the ear; soft; melodious; harmonious; as the *sweet* notes of a flute or an organ; *sweet* music; a *sweet* voice.

4. Pleasing to the eye; beautiful; as a *sweet* face; a *sweet* color or complexion; a *sweet* form. *Shak.*

5. Fresh; not salt; as *sweet* water. *Bacon.*

6. Not sour; as *sweet* fruits; *sweet* oranges.

7. Mild; soft; gentle.

Canst thou bind the *sweet* influences of Pleiades? Job xxxviii.

8. Mild; soft; kind; obliging; as *sweet* manners.

9. Grateful; pleasing.

Sweet interchange of hill and valley. *Milton.*

10. Making soft or excellent music; as a *sweet* singer.

11. Not stale; as *sweet* butter. The bread is *sweet.*

12. Not turned; not sour; as *sweet* milk.

13. Not putrescent or putrid; as, the meat is *sweet.*

SWEET, *n.* Something pleasing or grateful to the mind; as the *sweets* of domestic life.

A little bitter mingled in our cup, leaves no relish of the *sweet.* *Locke.*

2. A sweet substance; particularly, any vegetable juice which is added to wines to improve them. *Encyc.*

3. A perfume. *Prior. Dryden.*

4. A word of endearment.

5. Cane juice, melasses, or other sweet vegetable substance. *Edwards, W. Indies.*

SWEE'T-APPLE, *n.* [*sweet* and *apple.*] The *Annona squamosa.* *Lee.*

SWEE'T-BREAD, *n.* [*sweet* and *bread.*] The pancreas of a calf.

SWEE'T-BRIAR, *n.* [*sweet* and *briar.*] A shrubby plant of the genus Rosa, cultivated for its fragrant smell.

SWEE'T-BROOM, *n.* [*sweet* and *broom.*] A plant. *Ainsworth.*

SWEET-CIC'ELY, *n.* A plant of the genus Scandix.

SWEET-CIS'TUS, *n.* A shrub, the gum-cistus. *Mason.*

SWEET-CORN, *n.* A variety of the maiz, of a sweet taste.

SWEET-FLAG, *n.* A plant of the genus Acorus.

SWEET-GUM, *n.* A tree of the genus Liquidambar.

SWEET-JOHN'S, *n.* A plant, a species of Dianthus.

SWEET-MAUD'LIN, *n.* A species of Achillea.

SWEET-M'ARJORAM, *n.* A very fragrant plant, of the genus Origanum.

SWEET-PEA, *n.* A pea cultivated for ornament, of the genus Lathyrus. *Cyc.*

SWEET-ROOT, *n.* The liquorice, or Glycyrrhiza.

SWEET-RUSH, *n.* Another name of the sweet-flag, a species of Acorus.

SWEE'T-SOP, *n.* A name of the *Annona squamosa.* *Lee.*

SWEET-SUL'TAN, *n.* A plant, a species of Centaurea.

SWEET-WEED, *n.* A plant of the genus Capraria, and another of the genus Scoparia.

SWEET-WIL'LIAM, *n.* The name of several species of pink, of the genus Dianthus. *Cyc.*

The *Dianthus barbatus*, a species of pink of many varieties. *Encyc. Lee.*

SWEET-WIL'LOW, *n.* A plant, the *Myrica gale*, or Dutch myrtle. *Lee.*

SWEET-WOOD, *n.* A plant, a species of Laurus. *Lee.*

SWEETEN, *v. t.* *swee'tn.* To make sweet; as, to *sweeten* tea or coffee.

2. To make pleasing or grateful to the mind; as, to *sweeten* life; to *sweeten* friendship.

3. To make mild or kind; as, to *sweeten* the temper.

4. To make less painful; as, to *sweeten* the cares of life.

5. To increase agreeable qualities; as, to *sweeten* the joys or pleasures of life.

6. To soften; to make delicate.

Corregio has made his name immortal by the strength he has given to his figures, and by *sweetening* his lights and shades. *Dryden.*

7. To make pure and salubrious by destroying noxious matter; as, to *sweeten* rooms or apartments that have been infected; to *sweeten* the air.

8. To make warm and fertile; as, to dry and *sweeten* soils.

9. To restore to purity; as, to *sweeten* water, butter or meat.

SWEETEN, *v. i.* *swee'tn.* To become sweet. *Bacon.*

SWEE'TENED, *pp.* Made sweet, mild or grateful.

SWEE'TENER, *n.* He or that which sweetens; he that palliates; that which moderates acrimony.

SWEE'TENING, *ppr.* Making sweet or grateful.

SWEE'T-HE'ART, *n.* A lover or mistress. *Shak.*

SWEE'TING, *n.* A sweet apple. *Ascham.*

2. A word of endearment. *Shak.*

SWEE'TISH, *a.* Somewhat sweet or grateful to the taste. *Encyc.*

SWEE'TISHNESS, *n.* The quality of being sweetish. *Berkley.*

SWEE'TLY, *adv.* In a sweet manner; gratefully; agreeably.

He *sweetly* temper'd awe. *Dryden.*
No poet ever *sweetly* sung,
Unless he was, like Phœbus, young. *Swift.*

SWEE'TMEAT, *n.* [*sweet* and *meat.*] Fruit preserved with sugar; as peaches, pears, melons, nuts, orange peel, and the like.

SWEE'TNESS, *n.* The quality of being sweet, in any of its senses; as gratefulness to the taste; or to the smell, fragrance; agreeableness to the ear, melody; as *sweetness* of the voice; *sweetness* of elocution. *Middleton.*

2. Agreeableness of manners; softness; mildness; obliging civility; as *sweetness* of behavior.

3. Softness; mildness; amiableness; as *sweetness* of temper.

SWEE'T-SCENTED, *a.* [*sweet* and *scent.*] Having a sweet smell; fragrant.

SWEE'T-SMELLING, *a.* [*sweet* and *smell.*] Having a sweet smell; fragrant.

SWELL, *v. i.* pret. *swelled*; pp. *swelled.* *Swollen* is nearly obsolete. [Sax. *swellan*; D. *zwellen*; G. *schwellen*; Dan. *svæller*; Sw. *svälla.* Qu. is it not from the verb to *well*, or its root?]

1. To grow larger; to dilate or extend the exterior surface or dimensions by matter added to the interior part, or by expansion of the inclosed substance. Thus the legs *swell* in dropsy; a bruised part *swells*; a tumor *swells*; a bladder *swells* by inflation.

2. To increase in size or extent by any addition; as, a river *swells* and overflows its banks.

3. To rise or be driven into waves or billows. In a tempest, the ocean *swells* into waves mountain high.

4. To be puffed up or bloated; as, to *swell* with pride.

5. To be bloated with anger; to be exasperated. He *swells* with rage.

6. To be inflated; to belly; as *swelling* sails.

7. To be turgid or bombastic; as *swelling* words; a *swelling* style. *Roscommon.*

8. To protuberate; to bulge out; as, a cask *swells* in the middle.

9. To be elated; to rise into arrogance.

Your equal mind yet *swells* not into state. *Dryden.*

10. To grow more violent; as, a moderate passion may *swell* to fury.

11. To grow upon the view; to become larger.

—And monarchs to behold the *swelling* scene. *Shak.*

12. To become larger in amount. Many little debts added, *swell* to a great amount.

13. To become louder; as, a sound gradually *swells* as it approaches.

14. To strut; to look big.

—*Swelling* like a turkey cock. *Shak.*

15. To rise in altitude; as, land *swells* into hills.

SWELL, *v. t.* To increase the size, bulk or dimensions of; to cause to rise, dilate or increase. Rains and dissolving snow *swell* the rivers in spring, and cause floods. Jordan is *swelled* by the snows of mount Libanus.

2. To aggravate; to highten.

It is low ebb with the accuser, when such peccadillos are put to *swell* the charge. *Atterbury.*

3. To raise to arrogance; as, to be *swelled* with pride or haughtiness.

4. To enlarge. These sums *swell* the amount of taxes to a fearful size. These victories served to *swell* the fame of the commander.

5. In *music*, to augment, as the sound of a note.

SWELL, *n.* Extension of bulk. *Shak.*

2. Increase, as of sound; as the *swell* of a note.

3. A gradual ascent or elevation of land; as an extensive plain abounding with little *swells.*

4. A wave or billow; more generally, a succession of large waves; as, a heavy *swell* sets into the harbor. *Swell* is also used to denote the waves or fluctuation of the sea after a storm, and the waves that roll in and break upon the shore.

5. In *an organ*, a certain number of pipes inclosed in a box, which being uncovered, produce a *swell* of sound. *Busby.*

SWELL'ED, *pp.* Enlarged in bulk; inflated; tumefied.

SWELL'ING, *ppr.* Growing or enlarging in its dimensions; growing tumid; inflating; growing or making louder.

SWELL'ING, *n.* A tumor, or any morbid enlargement of the natural size; as a *swelling* on the hand or leg.

2. Protuberance; prominence.

The superficies of such plates are not even, but have many cavities and *swellings.* *Newton.*

3. A rising or enlargement by passion; as the *swellings* of anger, grief or pride. *Tatler.*

SWELT, for *swelled*, is not in use. *Spenser.*

SWELT, *v. i.* [Sax. *sweltan;* Goth. *swiltan; ga-swiltan*, to perish, to die; properly to fail, to swoon. Qu. is not this formed on the root of *wilt?*]

To faint; to swoon. *Obs.* *Chaucer.*

SWELT, *v. t.* To overpower, as with heat; to cause to faint. *Obs.* [We now use *swelter.*] *Hall.*

SWELT'ER, *v. i.* [from *swelt.*] To be overcome and faint with heat; to be ready to perish with heat.

SWELT'ER, *v. t.* To oppress with heat. *Bentley.*

SWELT'ERED, *pp.* Oppressed with heat.

SWELT'ERING, *ppr.* Fainting or languishing with heat; oppressing with heat.

SWELT'RY, *a.* Suffocating with heat; oppressive with heat; sultry. [See *Sultry*, which is probably a contraction of *sweltry.*]

SWEPT, *pret.* and *pp.* of *sweep.*

SWERD, for *sward*, is not in use.

SWERVE, *v. i. swerv.* [D. *zwerven*, to swerve, to rove. In sense it coincides with the verb to *swarm*, and in German it is rendered *schwärmen.* It seems to be formed on *warp*, and all may spring from the root of *veer.* See *Vary.*]

1. To wander; to rove. *Sidney.*

The *swerving* vines on the tall elms prevail. *Dryden.*

2. To wander from any line prescribed, or from a rule of duty; to depart from what is established by law, duty or custom; to deviate.

I *swerve* not from thy commandments. *Com. Prayer.*

They *swerve* from the strict letter of the law. *Clarendon.*

Many who, through the contagion of evil example, *swerve* exceedingly from the rules of their holy religion— *Atterbury.*

3. To bend; to incline. *Milton.*

4. To climb or move forward by winding or turning.

The tree was high,
Yet nimbly up from bough to bough I *swerv'd.* *Dryden.*

[This use of the word coincides with that of *swarm*, which see.]

SWERV'ING, *ppr.* Roving; wandering; deviating from any rule or standard; inclining; climbing or moving by winding and turning.

SWERV'ING, *n.* The act of wandering; deviation from any rule, law, duty or standard.

SWIFT, *a.* [Sax. *swift*, from *swifan*, to turn, to rove, to wander, to whirl round; D. *zweeven*, to rove, to hover, to fluctuate; Dan. *svæver;* Sw. *svåfva;* G. *schweben*, to wave, soar or hover. The latter appear to be formed on the root of *wave.* See *Swivel* and *Waft.*]

1. Moving a great distance or over a large space in a short time; moving with celerity or velocity; fleet; rapid; quick; speedy. We say, *swift* winds, a *swift* stream, *swift* lightnings, *swift* motion, *swift* as thought, a fowl *swift* of wing, a man *swift* of foot. *Swift* is applicable to any kind of motion.

2. Ready; prompt.

Let every man be *swift* to hear, slow to speak, slow to wrath. James i.

3. Speedy; that comes without delay.

There shall be false teachers among you, who shall privily bring in damnable heresies, even denying the Lord that bought them, and bring upon themselves *swift* destruction. 2 Pet. ii.

SWIFT, *n.* The current of a stream. [*Little used.*] *Walton.*

2. In *domestic affairs*, a reel or turning instrument for winding yarn. [*This is a sense directly from the Saxon verb.*]

3. A bird, a species of swallow, so called from the rapidity of its flight. *Derham.*

4. The common newt or eft, a species of lizard. *Cyc.*

SWIFT'ER, *n.* In *a ship*, a rope used to confine the bars of the capstan in their sockets, while men are turning it; also, a rope used to encircle a boat longitudinally, to strengthen and defend her sides from the impulse of other boats. Swifters also are two shrouds fixed on the starboard and larboard sides of the lower masts, above all the other shrouds, to give the masts additional security.

SWIFT'ER, *v. t.* To stretch, as shrouds by tackles.

SWIFT'LY, *adv.* Fleetly; rapidly; with celerity; with quick motion or velocity.

Pleas'd with the passage, we slide *swiftly* on. *Dryden.*

SWIFT'NESS, *n.* Speed; rapid motion; quickness; celerity; velocity; rapidity. *Swiftness* is a word of general import, applicable to every kind of motion, and to every thing that moves; as the *swiftness* of a bird; the *swiftness* of a stream; *swiftness* of descent in a falling body; *swiftness* of thought, &c.

SWIG, *v. t.* or *i.* [Ice. *swiga.* Qu. *suck.*] To drink by large draughts; to suck greedily.

SWIG, *n.* A large draught. [*Vulgar.*]

2. In *seamen's language*, a pulley with ropes which are not parallel.

SWIG, *v. t.* [Sax. *swigan*, to stupefy.] To castrate, as a ram, by binding the testicles tight with a string. [*Local.*] *Cyc.*

SWILL, *v. t.* [Sax. *swelgan, swylgan*, to swallow.]

1. To drink grossly or greedily; as, to *swill* down great quantities of liquors. *Arbuthnot.*

2. To wash; to drench. *Shak.*

3. To inebriate; to swell with fullness.

I should be loth
To meet the rudeness and *swill'd* insolence
Of such late wassailers. *Milton.*

SWILL, *n.* Large draughts of liquor; or drink taken in excessive quantities.

2. The wash or mixture of liquid substances, given to swine; called in some places *swillings.*

SWILL'ED, *pp.* Swallowed grossly in large quantities.

SWILL'ER, *n.* One who drinks voraciously.

SWILL'ING, *ppr.* Swallowing excessive quantities of liquors.

SWILL'INGS, *n.* Swill.

SWIM, *v. i.* pret. *swam;* pp. *swum.* [Sax. *swimman;* D. *zwemmen*, to swim; *zwymen*, to swoon; G. *schwemmen, schwimmen;* Dan. *svimler, svömmer;* Sw. *svima*, to swoon.]

1. To float; to be supported on water or other fluid; not to sink. Most species of wood will *swim* in water. Any substance will *swim*, whose specific gravity is less than that of the fluid in which it is immersed.

2. To move progressively in water by means of the motion of the hands and feet, or of fins. In Paris, boys are taught to *swim* by instructors appointed for that purpose. Is. xxv.

Leap in with me into this angry flood,
And *swim* to yonder point. *Shak.*

3. To float; to be borne along by a current. In all states there are men who will *swim* with the tide of popular opinion.

4. To glide along with a smooth motion, or with a waving motion.

She with pretty and with *swimming* gait. *Shak.*

A hov'ring mist came *swimming* o'er his sight. *Dryden.*

5. To be dizzy or vertiginous; to have a waving motion of the head or a sensation of that kind, or a reeling of the body. The head *swims* when we walk on high.

6. To be floated; to be overflowed or drenched; as, the earth *swims* in rain. *Spectator.*

Sudden the ditches swell, the meadows *swim.* *Thomson.*

All the night I make my bed to *swim;* I water my couch with my tears. Ps. vi.

7. To overflow; to abound; to have abundance.

They now *swim* in joy. *Milton.*

SWIM, *v. t.* To pass or move on; as, to *swim* a stream. Deer are known to *swim* rivers and sounds.

Sometimes he thought to *swim* the stormy main. *Dryden.*

2. To immerse in water that the lighter parts may swim; as, to *swim* wheat for seed. *Encyc.*

SWIMM, *n.* The bladder of fishes, by which they are said to be supported in water. *Grew.*

SWIM'MER, *n.* One that swims.

2. A protuberance on the leg of a horse. *Far. Dict.*

SWIM'MING, *ppr.* Floating on a fluid; moving on a fluid; having a waving or reeling motion; overflowing; abounding.

SWIM'MING, *n.* The act or art of moving on the water by means of the limbs; a floating.

2. Dizziness.

SWIM'MINGLY, *adv.* Smoothly; without obstruction; with great success. [*Not elegant.*]

SWIN'DLE, *v. t.* [D. *zwendelen.*] To cheat and defraud grossly, or with deliberate artifice; as, to *swindle* a man out of his property.

SWIN'DLED, *pp.* Grossly cheated and defrauded.

SWIN'DLER, *n.* [G. *schwindler.*] A cheat; a rogue; one who defrauds grossly, or one who makes a practice of defrauding others by imposition or deliberate artifice.

SWINE, *n. sing.* and *plu.* [Sax. *swin;* Sw. Dan. *svin;* D. *zwyn;* G. *schwein.* It is found in the Fr. *marsouin,* a porpess; L. *mare,* the sea, and *swine;* the sea hog; Port. *suino,* pertaining to swine; Polish, *svinia;* Bohemian, *swine;* Corn. *swynia.*]

A hog; a quadruped of the genus Sus, which furnishes man with a large portion of his most nourishing food. The fat or lard of this animal enters into various dishes in cookery. The swine is a heavy, stupid animal, and delights to wallow in the mire.

SWI'NE-BREAD, *n.* A kind of plant, truffle. *Bailey.*

SWI'NE-CASE, SWI'NE-COAT, SWI'NE-CRUE, } *n.* A hog sty; a pen for swine. [*Local.*]

SWI'NE-GRASS, *n.* A plant. [L. *centinodia,* knot grass. *Ainsworth.*]

SWI'NEHERD, *n.* [*swine* and *herd.*] A keeper of swine. *Tusser.*

SWI'NE-OAT, *n.* [*swine* and *oat.*] A kind of oats, cultivated for the use of pigs, as in Cornwall; the *Avena nuda* of botanists. *Cyc.*

SWI'NE-PIPE, *n.* [*swine* and *pipe.*] A bird, the red-wing. [*Local.*] *Cyc.*

SWI'NE-POCKS, SWI'NE-POX, } *n.* The chicken-pocks. [*Local.*]

A variety of the chicken-pocks, with acuminated vesicles containing a watery fluid; the water pox. *Good.*

SWI'NE'S CRESS, *n.* A species of cress, of the genus Cochlearia.

SWI'NE-STONE, *n.* [*swine* and *stone.*] A name given to those kinds of limestone which, when rubbed, emit a fetid odor, resembling that of naphtha combined with sulphureted hydrogen. *Cyc.*

SWI'NE-STY, *n.* A sty or pen for swine.

SWI'NE-THISTLE, *n.* A plant, the sow thistle. *Cyc.*

SWING, *v. i.* pret. and pp. *swung.* [G. *schwingen,* to swing, to brandish, to beat with a swingle staff; D. *zwingelen,* to beat; Sw. *svinga;* Dan. *svinger,* to swing, to brandish, to soar. It seems that this is the Sax. *swingan,* to beat, strike, flagellate, whence to *swingle* flax. *Swing* seems to be formed on the root of *wag.*]

1. To move to and fro, as a body suspended in the air; to wave; to vibrate.

I tried if a pendulum would *swing* faster, or continue *swinging* longer in our receiver, if exhausted. *Boyle.*

2. To practice swinging; as, a man *swings* for health or pleasure.

3. To move or float; also, to turn round an anchor; as, a ship *swings* with the tide. *Mar. Dict.*

SWING, *v. t.* To make to play loosely; to cause to wave or vibrate; as a body suspended in the air.

2. To whirl round in the air.

—*Swing* thee in air, then dash thee down. *Milton.*

3. To wave; to move to and fro; as, a man *swings* his arms when he walks.

He *swings* his tail, and swiftly turns him round. *Dryden.*

4. To brandish; to flourish.

SWING, *n.* A waving or vibratory motion; oscillation; as the *swing* of a pendulum.

2. Motion from one side to the other. A haughty man struts or walks with a *swing.*

3. A line, cord or other thing suspended and hanging loose; also, an apparatus suspended for persons to swing in.

4. Influence or power of a body put in motion.

The ram that batters down the wall,
For the great *swing* and rudeness of his poise— *Shak.*

5. Free course; unrestrained liberty or license.

Take thy *swing.* *Dryden.*

To prevent any thing which may prove an obstacle to the full *swing* of his genius. *Burke.*

6. The sweep or compass of a moving body.

7. Unrestrained tendency; as the prevailing *swing* of corrupt nature; the *swing* of propensities. *South. Glanville.*

SWING'-BRIDGE, *n.* [*swing* and *bridge.*] A bridge that may be moved by swinging; used on canals.

SWINGE, *v. t.* *swinj.* [Sax. *swingan,* supra.]

1. To beat soundly; to whip; to bastinade; to chastise; to punish.

You *swing'd* me for my love. *Shak.*
—And *swinges* his own vices in his son. *Dryden.*

2. To move as a lash. [*Not in use.*] *Milton.*

[*This verb is obsolescent and vulgar.*]

SWINGE, *n.* *swinj.* A sway; a swing; the sweep of any thing in motion. [*Not in use.*] *Waller.*

SWINGE-BUCKLER, *n.* *swinj'-buckler.* A bully; one who pretends to feats of arms. [*Not in use.*] *Shak.*

SWING'ER, *n.* One who swings; one who hurls.

SWING'ING, *ppr.* of *swing.* Waving; vibrating; brandishing.

SWING'ING, *n.* The act of swinging; an exercise for health or pleasure.

SWING'ING, *ppr.* of *swinge.* Beating soundly.

2. *a.* Huge; very large. [*Vulgar.*]

SWING'INGLY, *adv.* Vastly; hugely. [*Vulgar.*]

SWIN'GLE, *v. i.* [from *swing.*] To dangle; to wave hanging.

2. To swing for pleasure. [*Not in use.*]

SWIN'GLE, *v. t.* [Sax. *swingan,* to beat. See *Swing.*]

To beat; to clean flax by beating it with a wooden instrument resembling a large knife, and called in New England a *swingling knife.* Flax is first broke and then *swingled.*

SWIN'GLE, *n.* In wire-works, a wooden spoke fixed to the barrel that draws the wire; also, a crank. *Cyc.*

SWIN'GLED, *pp.* Beat and cleaned by a swingling knife.

SWIN'GLE-TREE, *n.* A whiffle-tree or whipple-tree.

SWIN'GLING, *ppr.* Beating and cleaning, as flax.

SWIN'GLING-KNIFE, SWIN'GLE, } *n.* A wooden instrument like a large knife, about two feet long, with one thin edge, used for cleaning flax of the shives.

SWIN'GLING-TOW, *n.* The coarse part of flax, separated from the finer by swingling and hatcheling.

SWING'-TREE, *n.* [*swing* and *tree.*] The bar of a carriage to which the traces are fastened. In America, it is often or generally called the *whiffle-tree,* or *whipple-tree.*

SWING'-WHEEL, *n.* [*swing* and *wheel.*] In a time piece, the wheel which drives the pendulum. In a watch, or balance-clock, it is called the crown-wheel. *Cyc.*

SWI'NISH, *a.* [from *swine.*] Befitting swine; like swine; gross; hoggish; brutal; as a *swinish* drunkard or sot; *swinish* gluttony.

SWINK, *v. i.* [Sax. *swincan.*] To labor; to toil; to drudge. *Obs.* *Spenser.*

SWINK, *v. t.* To overlabor. *Obs.* *Milton.*

SWINK, *n.* Labor; toil; drudgery. *Obs.* *Spenser.*

SWINK'ER, *n.* A laborer; a plowman. *Obs.* *Chaucer.*

SWIPE, *n.* A swape or sweep, which see.

SWIP'PER, *a.* [Sax. *swipan,* to move quick.] Nimble; quick. [*Not in use.*]

SWISS, *n.* A native of Switzerland or Swisserland.

2. The language of Swisserland.

SWITCH, *n.* [Sw. *svege.*] A small flexible twig or rod.

On the medal, Mauritania leads a horse by a thread with one hand, and in the other holds a *switch.* *Addison.*

SWITCH, *v. t.* To strike with a small twig or rod; to beat; to lash. *Chapman.*

SWITCH, *v. i.* To walk with a jerk. [*Obsolete or local.*]

SWIVEL, *n. swiv'l.* [from Sax. *swifan*, to turn or whirl round; or from the root of *whiffle*, which see. In D. *weifelen* is to palter, to waver, to whiffle.]

1. A ring which turns upon a staple; or a strong link of iron used in mooring ships, and which permits the bridles to be turned round; any ring or staple that turns. *Mar. Dict.*

2. A small cannon or piece of artillery, carrying a shot of half a pound, fixed on a socket on the top of a ship's side, stern or bow, or in her tops, in such a manner as to be turned in any direction. *Mar. Dict.*

SWIVEL, *v. i. swiv'l.* To turn on a staple, pin or pivot.

SWIV'EL-HOOK, *n.* A hook that turns in the end of an iron block strap, for the ready taking the turns out of a tackle. *Cyc.*

SWOB, *n.* A mop. [See *Swab.*]

SWOB, *v. t.* To clean or wipe with a swob. [See *Swab.*]

SWOB'BER, *n.* One who swabs or cleans with a mop. [See *Swabber.*]

2. *Swobbers*, four privileged cards, only used incidentally in betting at the game of whist. *Swift.*

SWOLLEN, } *pp.* of *swell*; irregular and ob-
SWOLN, } solescent. The regular participle, *swelled*, is to be preferred.

SWOM, *old pret.* of *swim*, is obsolete. We now use *swum* and *swam.*

SWOON, *v. i.* [Sax. *aswunan.* Qu. *wane, vain, vanish.*]

To faint; to sink into a fainting fit, in which there is a suspension of the apparent vital functions and mental powers.

The most in years *swoon'd* first away for pain. *Dryden.*

He seemed ready to *swoon* away in the surprise of joy. *Tatler.*

SWOON, *n.* A fainting fit; lipothymy; syncope. *Coxe.*

SWOON'ING, *ppr.* Fainting away.

SWOON'ING, *n.* The act of fainting; syncope. *Hall.*

SWOOP, *v. t.* [This is probably from *sweep*, or the same root.]

1. To fall on at once and seize; to catch while on the wing; as, a hawk *swoops* a chicken; a kite *swoops* up a mouse.

2. To seize; to catch up; to take with a sweep. *Glanville.*

3. To pass with violence. [*Not in use.*] *Drayton.*

SWOOP, *v. i.* To pass with pomp. *Drayton.*

SWOOP, *n.* A falling on and seizing, as of a rapacious fowl on his prey.

The eagle fell—and carried away a whole litter of cubs at a *swoop.* *L'Estrange.*

SWOP, *v. t.* To exchange; to barter; to give one commodity for another. [See *Swap.* This is a common word, but not in elegant use.]

SWŌRD, *n.* [Sax. *sword, sweord*; G. *schwert*; D. *zwaard*; Dan. *sværd*; Sw. *svård.*]

1. An offensive weapon worn at the side, and used by hand either for thrusting or cutting.

2. Figuratively, destruction by war.

I will bring a *sword* upon you. Lev. xxvi. Is. li.

3. Vengeance or justice.

She quits the balance, and resigns the *sword.* *Dryden.*

4. Emblem of authority and power.

The ruler—beareth not the *sword* in vain. Rom. xiii.

5. War; dissension.

I came not to send peace, but a *sword.* Matt. x.

6. Emblem of triumph and protection.

The Lord—the *sword* of thy excellence. Deut. xxxiii.

SWŌRD-BEĀRER, *n.* [*sword* and *bear.*] An officer in the city of London, who carries a sword as an emblem of justice before the lord mayor when he goes abroad.

SWŌRD-BELT, *n.* [*sword* and *belt.*] A belt by which a sword is suspended and borne by the side.

SWŌRD-BLADE, *n.* [*sword* and *blade.*] The blade or cutting part of a sword.

SWŌRDED, *a.* Girded with a sword. *Milton.*

SWŌRDER, *n.* A soldier; a cut-throat. [*Not in use.*] *Shak.*

SWŌRD-FIGHT, *n.* [*sword* and *fight.*] Fencing; a combat or trial of skill with swords.

SWŌRD-FISH, *n.* [*sword* and *fish.*] A genus of fishes called in ichthyology, xiphias; so named from the nose, snout or upper jaw, which is shaped like a sword. *Cyc.*

SWŌRD-GRASS, *n.* [*sword* and *grass.*] A kind of sedge, glader; the sweet rush, a species of Acorus. *Ainsworth. Cyc.*

SWŌRD-KNOT, *n.* [*sword* and *knot.*] A ribin tied to the hilt of a sword. *Pope.*

SWŌRD-LAW, *n.* [*sword* and *law.*] Violence; government by force. *Milton.*

SWŌRD-MAN, *n.* [*sword* and *man.*] A soldier; a fighting man. *Shak.*

SWŌRD-PLAYER, *n.* [*sword* and *player.*] A fencer; a gladiator; one who exhibits his skill in the use of the sword. *Hakewill.*

SWŌRD-SHAPED, *a.* [*sword* and *shape.*] Ensiform; shaped like a sword; as a *sword-shaped* leaf. *Martyn.*

SWORE, *pret.* of *swear.*

SWORN, *pp.* of *swear.* The officers of government are *sworn* to a faithful discharge of their duty.

Sworn friends, is a phrase equivalent to determined, close or firm friends.

I am *sworn* brother, sweet,
To grim necessity. *Shak.*

Sworn enemies, are determined or irreconcilable enemies.

SWOUND, *v. i.* To swoon. [*Not in use.*] *Shak.*

SWUM, *pret.* and *pp.* of *swim.*

SWUNG, *pret.* and *pp.* of *swing.*

SYB, } *a.* [Sax.] Related by blood. *Obs.*
SIB, }

SYBARIT'IC, } *a.* [from *Sybaritæ*, in-
SYBARIT'ICAL, } habitants of Sybaris, in Italy, who were proverbially voluptuous.]

Luxurious; wanton. *Bp. Hall.*

SYCAMINE. [See *Sycamore.*]

SYC'AMORE, *n.* [Gr. συκαμινος, συκομορος, from συκος, a fig, and μορος.]

A species of fig-tree. The name is also given to the *Acer majus*, [*A. pseudo-platanus*,] a species of maple. *Cyc. Lee.*

This name is also given to the plane tree or button-wood, of the genus Platanus. *Pursh.*

SYC'AMORE-MOTH, *n.* A large and beautiful moth or night butterfly; so called because its caterpillar feeds on the leaves of the sycamore. *Cyc.*

SYC'ITE, *n.* [Gr. συκος, fig.] Fig-stone; a name which some authors give to nodules of flint or pebbles which resemble a fig. *Cyc.*

SYC'OPHANCY, *n.* [infra.] Originally, information of the clandestine exportation of figs; hence, mean talebearing; obsequious flattery; servility.

SYC'OPHANT, *n.* [Gr. συκοφαντη; συκος, a fig, and φαινω, to discover.]

Originally, an informer against those who stole figs, or exported them contrary to law, &c. Hence in time it came to signify a talebearer or informer, in general; hence, a parasite; a mean flatterer; especially a flatterer of princes and great men; hence, a deceiver; an impostor. Its most general use is in the sense of an obsequious flatterer or parasite. *Encyc. Potter's Antiq.*

SYC'OPHANT, } *v. t.* To play the syc-
SYC'OPHANTIZE, } ophant; to flatter meanly and officiously; to inform or tell tales for gaining favor.

SYCOPHANT'IC, *a.* Talebearing; more generally, obsequiously flattering; parasitic; courting favor by mean adulation.

2. *Sycophantic plants*, or *parasites*, are such as adhere to other plants, and depend on them for support.

SYC'OPHANTRY, *n.* Mean and officious talebearing or adulation. *Barrow.*

SYDNE'AN, } *a.* Denoting a species of
SYDNE'IAN, } white earth brought from Sidney cove in South Wales. *Kirwan.*

SYENITE. [See *Sienite.*]

SYKE, *n.* A small brook or rill in low ground. [*Local.*]

SYLLAB'IC, } *a.* [from *syllable.*] Per-
SYLLAB'ICAL, } taining to a syllable or syllables; as *syllabic* accent.

2. Consisting of a syllable or syllables; as a *syllabic* augment.

SYLLAB'ICALLY, *adv.* In a syllabic manner.

SYLLABICA'TION, *n.* The act of forming syllables; the act or method of dividing words into syllables. *Ash.*

SYL'LABLE, *n.* [L. *syllaba*; Gr. συλλαβη, from συλλαμβανω, to comprehend; συν and λαμβανω, to take.]

1. A letter, or a combination of letters, uttered together, or at a single effort or impulse of the voice. A vowel may form a syllable by itself, as *a*, the definitive, or in *amen*; *e* in *even*; *o* in *over*, and the like. A syllable may also be formed of a vowel and one consonant, as in *go, do, in, at*; or a syllable may be formed by a vowel with two articulations, one preceding, the other following it, as in *can, but, tun*; or a

syllable may consist of a combination of consonants, with one vowel or diphthong, as *strong, short, camp, voice.*

A syllable sometimes forms a word, and is then significant, as in *go, run, write, sun, moon.* In other cases, a syllable is merely part of a word, and by itself is not significant. Thus *ac*, in *active*, has no signification.

At least one vowel or open sound is essential to the formation of a syllable; hence in every word there must be as many syllables as there are single vowels, or single vowels and diphthongs. A word is called according to the number of syllables it contains, viz.

Monosyllable, a word of one syllable.
Dissyllable, a word of two syllables.
Trisyllable, a word of three syllables.
Polysyllable, a word of many syllables.

2. A small part of a sentence or discourse; something very concise. This account contains not a *syllable* of truth.

Before a *syllable* of the law of God was written. *Hooker.*

SYL'LABLE, *v. t.* To utter; to articulate. [*Not used.*] *Milton.*

SYL'LABUB, *n.* A compound drink made of wine and milk; a different orthography of *sillabub.*

SYL'LABUS, *n.* [L. from the same source as *syllable.*]
An abstract; a compendium containing the heads of a discourse.

SYLLEP'SIS, *n.* [Gr. συλληψις. See *Syllable.*]
1. In *grammar*, a figure by which we conceive the sense of words otherwise than the words import, and construe them according to the intention of the author; otherwise called *substitution.*
2. The agreement of a verb or adjective, not with the word next to it, but with the most worthy in the sentence; as, *rex* et regina *beati.*

SYL'LOGISM, *n.* [L. *syllogismus*; Gr. συλλογισμος; συν, with, and λεγω, to speak; λογιζομαι, to think.]
A form of reasoning or argument, consisting of three propositions, of which the two first are called the *premises*, and the last the *conclusion.* In this argument, the conclusion necessarily follows from the premises; so that if the two first propositions are true, the conclusion must be true, and the argument amounts to demonstration. Thus,

A plant has not the power of locomotion;
An oak is a plant;
Therefore an oak has not the power of locomotion.

These propositions are denominated the major, the minor, and the conclusion.

SYLLOGIS'TIC, SYLLOGIS'TICAL, *a.* Pertaining to a syllogism; consisting of a syllogism, or of the form of reasoning by syllogisms; as *syllogistic* arguments or reasoning.

SYLLOGIS'TICALLY, *adv.* In the form of a syllogism; by means of syllogisms; as, to reason or prove *syllogistically.*

SYLLOGIZA'TION, *n.* A reasoning by syllogisms. *Harris.*

SYL'LOGIZE, *v. i.* To reason by syllogisms.

Men have endeavored to teach boys to *syllogize*, or to frame arguments and refute them, without real knowledge. *Watts.*

SYL'LOGIZER, *n.* One who reasons by syllogisms.

SYL'LOGIZING, *ppr.* Reasoning by syllogisms.

SYLPH, *n.* [Fr. *sylphide*; Gr. σιλφη, a moth, a beetle.]
An imaginary being inhabiting the air. *Temple. Pope.*

SYL'VA, *n.* [L. a wood or forest.] In *poetry*, a poetical piece composed in a start or kind of transport.
2. A collection of poetical pieces of various kinds. *Cyc.*

SYLVAN. [See *Silvan.*]

SYL'VAN, *n.* A fabled deity of the wood; a satyr; a faun; sometimes perhaps, a rustic.

Her private orchards, wall'd on ev'ry side,
To lawless *sylvans* all access deni'd. *Pope.*

SYL'VANITE, *n.* Native tellurium, a metallic substance recently discovered. *Dict. Ure.*

SYMBAL. [See *Cymbal.*]

SYM'BOL, *n.* [L. *symbolum*; Gr. συμβολον; συν, with, and βαλλω, to throw; συμβαλλω, to compare.]
1. The sign or representation of any moral thing by the images or properties of natural things. Thus the lion is the *symbol* of courage; the lamb is the *symbol* of meekness or patience. Symbols are of various kinds, as types, enigmas, parables, fables, allegories, emblems, hieroglyphics, &c. *Encyc.*
2. An emblem or representation of something else. Thus in the eucharist, the bread and wine are called *symbols* of the body and blood of Christ.
3. A letter or character which is significant. The Chinese letters are most of them *symbols.* The *symbols* in algebra are arbitrary.
4. In medals, a certain mark or figure representing a being or thing, as a trident is the *symbol* of Neptune, the peacock of Juno, &c.
5. Among christians, an abstract or compendium; the creed, or a summary of the articles of religion. *Baker.*
6. Lot; sentence of adjudication. [*Not in use.*] *Taylor.*

SYMBOL'IC, SYMBOL'ICAL, *a.* Representative; exhibiting or expressing by resemblance or signs; as, the figure of an eye is *symbolical* of sight and knowledge. The ancients had their *symbolical* mysteries.

The sacrament is a representation of Christ's death, by such *symbolical* actions as he appointed. *Taylor.*

Symbolical philosophy, is the philosophy expressed by hieroglyphics.

SYMBOL'ICALLY, *adv.* By representation or resemblance of properties; by signs; typically. Courage is *symbolically* represented by a lion.

SYM'BOLISM, *n.* Among chimists, consent of parts. *Encyc.*

SYMBOLIZA'TION, *n.* [See *Symbolize.*]
The act of symbolizing; resemblance in properties. *Brown.*

SYM'BOLIZE, *v. i.* [Fr. *symboliser.*] To have a resemblance of qualities or properties.

The pleasing of color *symbolizeth* with the pleasing of a single tone to the ear; but the pleasing of order doth *symbolize* with harmony. *Bacon.*

They both *symbolize* in this, that they love to look upon themselves through multiplying glasses. *Howell.*

SYM'BOLIZE, *v. t.* To make to agree in properties.
2. To make representative of something.

Some *symbolize* the same from the mystery of its colors. *Brown.*

SYM'BOLIZING, *ppr.* Representing by some properties in common; making to agree or resemble in properties.

SYM'METRAL, *a.* [from *symmetry.*] Commensurable. *More.*

SYMME'TRIAN, SYM'METRIST, *n.* [from *symmetry.*] One eminently studious of proportion or symmetry of parts. *Sidney. Wotton.*

SYMMET'RICAL, *a.* [from *symmetry.*] Proportional in its parts; having its parts in due proportion, as to dimensions; as a *symmetrical* body or building.

SYMMET'RICALLY, *adv.* With due proportion of parts.

SYM'METRIZE, *v. t.* To make proportional in its parts; to reduce to symmetry. *Burke.*

SYM'METRY, *n.* [Gr. συμμετρια; συν, with, together, and μετρον, measure; μετρεω, to measure; Fr. *symetrie*; It. Sp. *simetria.*]
A due proportion of the several parts of a body to each other; adaptation of the dimensions of the several parts of a thing to each other; or the union and conformity of the members of a work to the whole. Symmetry arises from the proportion which the Greeks call analogy, which is the relation of conformity of all the parts to a certain measure; as the *symmetry* of a building or an animal body. *Cyc.*
Uniform symmetry, in architecture, is where the same ordonnance reigns throughout the whole.
Respective symmetry, is where only the opposite sides are equal to each other. *Cyc.*

SYMPATHET'IC, SYMPATHET'ICAL, *a.* [Fr. *sympathique.* See *Sympathy.*]
1. Pertaining to sympathy.
2. Having common feeling with another; susceptible of being affected by feelings like those of another, or of feelings in consequence of what another feels; as a *sympathetic* heart.
3. Among *physicians*, produced by sympathy. A *sympathetic* disease is one which is produced by sympathy, or by a remote cause, as when a fever follows a local injury. In this case, the word is opposed to *idiopathetic*, which denotes a disease produced by a proximate cause, or an original disease. Thus an epilepsy is *sympathetic*, when it is produced by some other disease. *Cyc.*
4. Among *chimists* and *alchimists*, an epithet applied to a kind of powder, possessed of the wonderful property that if spread on a cloth dipped in the blood of a wound, the wound will be healed, though the patient is at a distance. This opinion is discarded as charlatanry.

This epithet is given also to a species of ink or liquor, with which a person may write letters which are not visible till something else is applied.

5. In *anatomy*, sympathetic is applied to two nerves, from the opinion that their communications are the cause of sympathies. One of these is the great intercostal nerve; the other is the facial nerve. *Cyc.*

SYMPATHET'ICALLY, *adv.* With sympathy or common feeling; in consequence of sympathy; by communication from something else.

SYM'PATHIZE, *v. i.* [Fr. *sympathiser.* See *Sympathy.*]

1. To have a common feeling, as of bodily pleasure or pain.

> The mind will *sympathize* so much with the anguish and debility of the body, that it will be too distracted to fix itself in meditation. *Buckminster.*

2. To feel in consequence of what another feels; to be affected by feelings similar to those of another, in consequence of knowing the person to be thus affected. We *sympathize* with our friends in distress; we feel some pain when we see them pained, or when we are informed of their distresses, even at a distance.

[It is generally and properly used of suffering or pain, and not of pleasure or joy. It may be sometimes used with greater latitude.]

3. To agree; to fit. [*Not in use.*] *Dryden.*

SYM'PATHY, *n.* [Gr. συμπαθεια, συμπαθεω; συν, with, and παθος, passion.]

1. Fellow feeling; the quality of being affected by the affection of another, with feelings correspondent in kind, if not in degree. We feel *sympathy* for another when we see him in distress, or when we are informed of his distresses. This *sympathy* is a correspondent feeling of pain or regret.

> *Sympathy* is produced through the medium of organic impression. *Chipman.*
>
> I value myself upon *sympathy;* I hate and despise myself for envy. *Kames.*

2. An agreement of affections or inclinations, or a conformity of natural temperament, which makes two persons pleased with each other. *Encyc.*

> To such associations may be attributed most of the *sympathies* and antipathies of our nature. *Anon.*

3. In *medicine*, a correspondence of various parts of the body in similar sensations or affections; or an affection of the whole body or some part of it, in consequence of an injury or disease of another part, or of a local affection. Thus a contusion on the head will produce nausea and vomiting. This is said to be by *sympathy*, or consent of parts. *Cyc.*

4. In *natural history*, a propension of inanimate things to unite, or to act on each other. Thus we say, there is a *sympathy* between the lodestone and iron. *Cyc.*

SYMPHO'NIOUS, *a.* [from *symphony.*] Agreeing in sound; accordant; harmonious.

> —Sounds
> *Symphonious* of ten thousand harps. *Milton.*

SYM'PHONY, *n.* [L. *symphonia;* Fr. *symphonie;* Gr. συμφωνια; συν, with, and φωνη, voice.]

1. A consonance or harmony of sounds, agreeable to the ear, whether the sounds are vocal or instrumental, or both.

> The trumpets sound,
> And warlike *symphony* is heard around. *Dryden.*

2. A musical instrument, mentioned by French writers.

3. A full concert.

4. An overture or other composition for instruments.

SYM'PHYSIS, *n.* [Gr. συμφυσις; συν, together, and φυω, to grow.]

1. In *anatomy*, the union of bones by cartilage; a connection of bones without a movable joint. *Coxe. Cyc.*

2. In *surgery*, a coalescence of a natural passage; also, the first intention of cure in a wound. *Coxe.*

SYMPOSIAC, *a.* *sympo'ziac.* [Gr. συμποσια, a drinking together; συν, together, and πινω, to drink.]

Pertaining to compotations and merry-making; happening where company is drinking together; as *symposiac* meetings. *Brown.*

> *Symposiac* disputations. *Arbuthnot.*

[*Not much used.*]

SYMPO'SIAC, *n.* A conference or conversation of philosophers at a banquet. *Plutarch.*

SYMPOSIUM, *n.* *sympo'zium.* [supra.] A drinking together; a merry feast. *Warton.*

SYMP'TOM, *n.* [Fr. *symptome;* Gr. συμπτωμα, a falling or accident, from συν, with, and πιπτω, to fall.]

1. Properly, something that happens in concurrence with another thing, as an attendant. Hence in *medicine*, any affection which accompanies disease; a perceptible change in the body or its functions, which indicates disease. The causes of disease often lie beyond our sight, but we learn the nature of them by the *symptoms.* Particular *symptoms* which more uniformly accompany a morbid state of the body, and are characteristic of it, are called *pathognomonic* or *diagnostic symptoms.*

2. A sign or token; that which indicates the existence of something else; as, open murmurs of the people are a *symptom* of disaffection to law or government.

SYMPTOMAT'IC, SYMPTOMAT'ICAL, *a.* Pertaining to symptoms; happening in concurrence with something; indicating the existence of something else.

2. In *medicine*, a *symptomatic* disease is one which proceeds from some prior disorder in some part of the body. Thus a *symptomatic* fever may proceed from local pain or local inflammation. It is opposed to *idiopathic.* *Encyc. Coxe.*

3. According to symptoms; as a *symptomatical* classification of diseases.

SYMPTOMAT'ICALLY, *adv.* By means of symptoms; in the nature of symptoms. *Wiseman.*

SYMPTOMATOL'OGY, *n.* [Gr. συμπτωμα and λογος, discourse.]

The doctrine of symptoms; that part of the science of medicine which treats of the symptoms of diseases. *Coxe.*

SYNAGOG'ICAL, *a.* [from *synagogue.*] Pertaining to a synagogue. *Dict.*

SYNAGOGUE, *n.* *syn'agog.* [Fr. from Gr. συναγωγη; συν, together, and αγω, to drive; properly an assembly.]

1. A congregation or assembly of Jews, met for the purpose of worship or the performance of religious rites.

2. The house appropriated to the religious worship of the Jews.

3. The court of the seventy elders among the Jews, called the great synagogue. *Cyc.*

SYN'AGRIS, *n.* A fish caught in the Archipelago, resembling the dentex. It has a sharp back, and is reckoned a species of Sparus. *Cyc.*

SYNALE'PHA, *n.* [Gr. συναλοιφη.] In *grammar*, a contraction of syllables by suppressing some vowel or diphthong at the end of a word, before another vowel or diphthong; as *ill' ego* for *ille ego.*

SYN'ARCHY, *n.* [Gr. συναρχια.] Joint rule or sovereignty. *Stackhouse.*

SYNAR'ESIS, SYNAR'ESY, *n.* [Gr. συναιρεσις.] Contraction; the shortening of a word by the omission of a letter, as *ne'er* for *never.* *Addison.*

SYNARTHRO'SIS, *n.* [Gr. συν, with, and αρθροω, to articulate.]

Union of bones without motion; close union; as in sutures, symphysis and the like. *Coxe.*

SYNAX'IS, *n.* [Gr. from συναγω, to congregate; συν and αγω.]

A congregation; also, a term formerly used for the Lord's supper. *Saxon Laws.*

SYNCHONDRO'SIS, *n.* [Gr. συν and χονδρος, cartilage.]

The connection of bones by means of cartilage or gristle. *Wiseman.*

SYN'CHRONAL, *a.* [Gr. συν, with, and χρονος, time.]

Happening at the same time; simultaneous.

SYN'CHRONAL, *n.* [supra.] That which happens at the same time with something else, or pertains to the same time. *More.*

SYNCHRON'ICAL, *a.* [See *Synchronism.*] Happening at the same time; simultaneous. *Boyle.*

SYN'CHRONISM, *n.* [Gr. συν, with, and χρονος, time.]

Concurrence of two or more events in time; simultaneousness. *Hale.*

SYN'CHRONIZE, *v. i.* [supra.] To agree in time; to be simultaneous. *Robinson.*

SYN'CHRONOUS, *a.* Happening at the same time; simultaneous. *Arbuthnot.*

SYN'CHRONOUSLY, *adv.* [supra.] At the same time.

SYN'COPATE, *v. t.* [See *Syncope.*] To contract, as a word, by taking one or more letters or syllables from the middle.

2. In *music*, to prolong a note begun on the unaccented part of a bar, to the accented part of the next bar; or to connect the last note of a bar with the first of the following; or to end a note in one part, in the middle of a note of another part.

SYN'COPATED, *pp.* Contracted by the loss of a letter from the middle of the word.

2. Inverted, as the measure in music.

SYNCOPA'TION, *n.* The contraction of a word by taking a letter, letters or a syllable from the middle.

2. In *music*, an interruption of the regular measure; an inversion of the order of notes; a prolonging of a note begun on the unaccented part of a bar, to the accented part of the next bar; also, a driving note, when a shorter note at the beginning of a measure is followed by two or more longer notes before another short note occurs, equal to that which occasioned the driving, to make the number even. *Encyc.*

SYN'COPE, SYN'COPY, *n.* [Gr. συγκοπη, from συγκοπτω; συν and κοπτω, to cut off.]
1. In *music*, the same as *syncopation;* the division of a note introduced when two or more notes of one part answer to a single note of another.
2. In *grammar*, an elision or retrenchment of one or more letters or a syllable from the middle of a word.
3. In *medicine*, a fainting or swooning; a diminution or interruption of the motion of the heart, and of respiration, accompanied with a suspension of the action of the brain and a temporary loss of sensation, volition and other faculties. *Cyc.*

SYN'COPIST, *n.* One who contracts words.

SYN'COPIZE, *v. t.* To contract by the omission of a letter or syllable.

SYN'DIC, *n.* [L. *syndicus;* Gr. συνδικος; συν, with, and δικη, justice.]
An officer of government, invested with different powers in different countries; a kind of magistrate entrusted with the affairs of a city or community. In Geneva, the *syndic* is the chief magistrate. Almost all the companies in Paris, the university, &c., have their *syndics.* The university of Cambridge has its *syndics.*

SYN'DICATE, *n.* In some countries on the European continent, a council; a branch of government. *Burnet.*

SYN'DICATE, *v. t.* To judge, or to censure.

SYN'DROME, SYN'DROMY, *n.* [Gr. συνδρομη, a running together.]
1. Concurrence. *Glanville.*
2. In *medicine*, the concourse or combination of symptoms in a disease. *Cyc.*

SYNEC'DOCHE, SYNEC'DOCHY, *n.* [Gr. συνεκδοχη; συν and εκδεχομαι, to take.]
In *rhetoric*, a figure or trope by which the whole of a thing is put for a part, or a part for the whole; as the genus for the species, or the species for the genus, &c. *Cyc.*

SYNECDOCH'ICAL, *a.* Expressed by synecdoche; implying a synecdoche. *Boyle.*

SYN'GENESE, *n.* [Gr. συν, with, and γενεσις, generation, origin.]
In *botany*, a plant whose stamens are united in a cylindrical form by the anthers.

SYNGENE'SIAN, *a.* Pertaining to the class syngenesia.

SYNNEURO'SIS, *n.* [Gr. συν and νευρον, a nerve.]
In *anatomy*, the connection of parts by means of ligaments, as in the movable joints. *Coxe. Parr.*

SYN'OD, *n.* [Gr. συνοδος, a convention; συν and οδος, way.]
1. In *church history*, a council or meeting of ecclesiastics to consult on matters of religion. Synods are of four kinds, 1. *General* or *ecumenical*, which are composed of bishops from different nations. 2. *National*, in which the bishops of one nation only meet, to determine points of doctrine or discipline. 3. *Provincial*, in which the bishops of one province only meet. This is called a convocation. 4. *Diocesan.*
In Scotland, a synod is composed of several adjoining presbyteries. The members are the ministers, and a ruling elder from each parish. A synod in the United States is constituted in like manner as in Scotland.
2. A meeting, convention or council; as a *synod* of gods.

> Let us call to *synod* all the blest. *Milton.*

3. In *astronomy*, a conjunction of two or more planets or stars in the same optical place of the heavens. *Encyc.*

SYN'ODAL, *n.* Anciently, a pecuniary rent, paid to the bishop or archdeacon at the time of his Easter visitation, by every parish priest; a procuration. *Encyc.*

> *Synodals* are due of common right to the bishop only. *Gibson.*

2. Constitutions made in provincial or diocesan synods, are sometimes called *synodals.* *Encyc.*

SYN'ODAL, SYNOD'IC, SYNOD'ICAL, *a.* Pertaining to a synod; transacted in a synod; as *synodical* proceedings or forms; a *synodical* epistle. *Stillingfleet.*

Synodical month, in astronomy, is the period from one conjunction of the moon with the sun to another. This is called also a lunation, because in the course of it the moon exhibits all its phases. This month consists of 29 days, 12 hours, 44 minutes, 3 seconds and 11 thirds. *Kepler. Encyc.*

SYNOD'ICALLY, *adv.* By the authority of a synod. *Sanderson.*

SYNOM'OSY, *n.* [Gr. συνωμοσια; συν, with, and ομνυμι, to swear.]
Sworn brotherhood; a society in ancient Greece nearly resembling a modern political club. *Mitford.*

SYN'ONYM, *n.* [Gr. συνωνυμος; συν, with, and ονομα, name.]
A name, noun or other word having the same signification as another, is its *synonym.* Two words containing the same idea are *synonyms.*

> He has extricated the *synonyms* of former authors. *Coxe's Russ.*

SYNON'YMA, *n. plu.* Words having the same signification. But *synonyms* is a regular English word.

SYNON'YMAL, *a.* Synonymous. [*Not in use.*]

SYNON'YMIST, *n.* Among *botanists*, a person who collects the different names or synonyms of plants, and reduces them to one another. *Cyc.*

SYNON'YMIZE, *v. t.* To express the same meaning in different words. *Camden.*

SYNON'YMOUS, *a.* Expressing the same thing; conveying the same idea. We rarely find two words precisely *synonymous. Wave* and *billow* are sometimes *synonymous*, but not always. When we speak of the large rolling swell of the sea, we may call it a *wave* or a *billow;* but when we speak of the small swell of a pond, we may call it a *wave*, but we may not call it a *billow.*

SYNON'YMOUSLY, *adv.* In a synonymous manner; in the same sense; with the same meaning. Two words may be used *synonymously* in some cases and not in others.

SYNON'YMY, *n.* The quality of expressing the same meaning by different words.
2. In *rhetoric*, a figure by which synonymous words are used to amplify a discourse.

SYNOP'SIS, *n.* [Gr. συνοψις; συν, with, and οψις, view.]
A general view, or a collection of things or parts so arranged as to exhibit the whole or the principal parts in a general view.

SYNOP'TIC, SYNOP'TICAL, *a.* Affording a general view of the whole, or of the principal parts of a thing; as a *synoptic* table. *Buckland.*

SYNOP'TICALLY, *adv.* In such a manner as to present a general view in a short compass.

SYNO'VIA, SYN'OVY, *n.* In *anatomy*, the fluid secreted into the cavities of joints, for the purpose of lubricating them. *Cyc.*

SYNO'VIAL, *a.* [supra.] Pertaining to synovia; secreting a lubricating fluid; as the *synovial* membrane; *synovial* gland. *Cyc.*

SYNTAC'TIC, SYNTAC'TICAL, *a.* [See *Syntax.*] Pertaining to syntax, or the construction of sentences.
2. According to the rules of syntax or construction. *Encyc.*

SYNTAC'TICALLY, *adv.* In conformity to syntax.

SYN'TAX, *n.* [L. *syntaxis;* Gr. συνταξις; συν, together, and τασσω, to put.]
1. In *grammar*, the construction of sentences; the due arrangement of words in sentences, according to established usage. Syntax includes concord and regimen, or the agreement and government of words. Words, in every language, have certain connections and relations, as verbs and adjectives with nouns, which relations must be observed in the formation of sentences. A gross violation of the rules of syntax is a *solecism.*
2. Connected system or order; union of things. [*Not in use.*] *Glanville.*

SYN'THESIS, *n.* [Gr. συνθεσις; συν, and τιθημι, to put or set.]
1. Composition, or the putting of two or more things together, as in compound medicines. *Cyc.*
2. In *logic*, composition, or that process of reasoning in which we advance by a regular chain from principles before established or assumed, and propositions already proved, till we arrive at the conclusion. *Synthesis* is the opposite of *analysis* or *resolution.* *Encyc.*
3. In *surgery*, the operation by which divided parts are reunited. *Cyc.*
4. In *chimistry*, the uniting of elements into a compound; the opposite of *analysis*, which is the separation of a compound into its constituent parts. That water is composed of oxygen and hydrogen, is proved both by analysis and *synthesis.*

SYNTHET'IC, SYNTHET'ICAL, *a.* Pertaining to synthesis; consisting in synthesis or composition; as the *synthetic* method of reasoning, as opposed to the *analytical.*

SYNTHET'ICALLY, *adv.* By synthesis; by composition.

SYN'THETIZE, *v. t.* To unite in regular structure. [*Not much used.*]

SYNTON'IC, *a.* [Gr. συν, with, and τονος, tone.] In *music*, sharp; intense. *Rousseau.*

SYPH'ILIS. [See *Siphilis.*]

SY'PHON, *n.* [Gr. σιφων.] A tube or pipe. More correctly *siphon*, which see.

SYR'IAC, *n.* The language of Syria, especially the ancient language of that country.

SYR'IAC, *a.* [from *Syria.*] Pertaining to Syria, or its language; as the *Syriac* version of the Pentateuch; *Syriac* Bible.

SYR'IACISM, *n.* A Syrian idiom. *Milton.*

SYR'IAN, *a.* Pertaining to Syria.

SYR'IANISM, *n.* A Syrian idiom, or a peculiarity in the Syrian language. *Paley.*

SYR'IASM, *n.* The same as *syrianism.* *Warburton. Stuart.*

SYRIN'GA, *n.* [Gr. συριγξ, συριγγος, a pipe.] A genus of plants, the lilac.

SYRINGE, *n. syr'inj.* [supra.] An instrument for injecting liquids into animal bodies, into wounds, &c.; or an instrument in the form of a pump, serving to imbibe any fluid, and then to expel it with force.

SYR'INGE, *v. t.* To inject by means of a pipe or syringe; to wash and cleanse by injections from a syringe.

SYRINGOT'OMY, *n.* [Gr. συριγξ, a pipe, and τεμνω, to cut.]
The operation of cutting for the fistula. *Cyc.*

SYR'TIS, *n.* [L.] A quicksand. [*Not English.*] *Milton.*

SYRUP. [See *Sirup.*]

SYS'TASIS, *n.* [Gr. συςασις.] The consistence of a thing; constitution. [*Little used.*] *Burke.*

SYS'TEM, *n.* [Fr. *systéme*; L. *systema*; Gr. συςημα; συν and ιςημι, to set.]
1. An assemblage of things adjusted into a regular whole; or a whole plan or scheme consisting of many parts connected in such a manner as to create a chain of mutual dependencies; or a regular union of principles or parts forming one entire thing. Thus we say, a *system* of logic, a *system* of philosophy, a *system* of government, a *system* of principles, the solar *system*, the Copernican *system*, a *system* of divinity, a *system* of law, a *system* of morality, a *system* of husbandry, a *system* of botany or of chimistry.
2. Regular method or order.
3. In *music*, an interval compounded or supposed to be compounded of several lesser intervals, as the fifth octave, &c. the elements of which are called *diastems.* *Busby.*

SYSTEMAT'IC, SYSTEMAT'ICAL, *a.* Pertaining to system; consisting in system; methodical; formed with regular connection and adaptation or subordination of parts to each other, and to the design of the whole; as a *systematic* arrangement of plants or animals; a *systematic* course of study.
2. Proceeding according to system or regular method; as a *systematic* writer.

SYSTEMAT'ICALLY, *adv.* In the form of a system; methodically. *Boyle.*

SYS'TEMATIST, *n.* One who forms a system, or reduces to system.

SYSTEMIZA'TION, *n.* [from *systemize.*] The act or operation of systemizing; the reduction of things to system or regular method.

SYS'TEMIZE, *v. t.* To reduce to system or regular method; as, to *systemize* the principles of moral philosophy; to *systemize* plants or fossils.

SYS'TEMIZED, *pp.* Reduced to system or method.

SYS'TEMIZER, *n.* One who reduces things to system.

SYS'TEMIZING, *ppr.* Reducing to system or due method.

SYS'TEM-MAKER, *n.* One who forms a system.

SYS'TEM-MONGER, *n.* One given to the forming of systems. *Chesterfield.*

SYS'TOLE, SYS'TOLY, *n.* [Gr. συςολη, from συςελλω, to contract; συν and ςελλω, to send.]
1. In *grammar*, the shortening of a long syllable.
2. In *anatomy*, the contraction of the heart for expelling the blood and carrying on the circulation. [See *Diastole.*]

SYS'TYLE, *n.* [Gr. συν, with or together, and ςυλος, a column.]
In *architecture*, the manner of placing columns, where the place between the two shafts consists of two diameters or four modules. *Encyc.*

SYTHE, *n.* [Sax. *sithe*; D. *seissen*; Ch. חצר, Syr. ܚܨܕ, Ar. حصد hatzada, to reap; deriv. Ar. a sickle; Sam. ࠇࠑࠃ to reap; Eth. ዐጸደ atzad, to reap, and deriv. a sickle; Heb. Ch. מעצר from the same root, an ax. These verbs seem to be the same, with different prefixes, and from this evidently is derived *sythe*, which is written incorrectly *scythe.*]
1. An instrument for mowing grass, or cutting other grain or vegetables. It consists of a long curving blade with a sharp edge, made fast to a handle, which in New England is called a *snath*, and which is bent into a convenient form for swinging the blade to advantage. The blade is hung to the snath at an acute angle.
In *mythology*, Saturn or Time is represented with a sythe, the emblem of destruction.
2. The curved sharp blade used anciently in war chariots.

SYTHE, *v. t.* To mow. [*Not in use.*] *Shak.*

SY'THED, *a.* Armed with sythes, as a chariot.

SY'THEMAN, *n.* One who uses a sythe; a mower.

SYZ'YGY, *n.* [Gr. συζυγια; συν and ζυγοω, to join.]
The conjunction or opposition of a planet with the sun, or of any two of the heavenly bodies. On the phenomena and circumstances of the *syzygies*, depends a great part of the lunar theory. *Encyc.*

T.

T is the twentieth letter of the English Alphabet, and a close consonant. It represents a close joining of the end of the tongue to the root of the upper teeth, as may be perceived by the syllables *at, et, ot, ut*, in attempting to pronounce which, the voice is completely intercepted. It is therefore numbered among the mutes, or close articulations, and it differs from *d* chiefly in its closeness; for in pronouncing *ad, ed*, we perceive the voice is not so suddenly and entirely intercepted, as in pronouncing *at* and *et.* *T* by itself has one sound only, as in *take, turn, bat, bolt, smite, bitter.* So we are accustomed to speak; but in reality, *t* can be hardly said to have any sound at all. Its use, like that of all mute articulations, is to modify the manner of uttering the vocal sound which precedes or follows it.

When *t* is followed by *h*, as in *think* and *that*, the combination really forms a distinct sound for which we have no single character. This combination has two sounds in English; aspirated, as in *think*, and vocal, as in *that.*

The letters *ti*, before a vowel, and unaccented, usually pass into the sound of *sh*, as in *nation, motion, partial, substantiate*; which are pronounced *nashon, moshon, parshal, substanshate.* In this case, *t* loses entirely its proper sound or use, and being blended with the subsequent letter, a new sound results from the combination, which is in fact a simple sound. In a few words, the combination *ti* has the sound of the English *ch*, as in *Christian, mixtion, question.*

T is convertible with *d.* Thus the Germans write *tag*, where we write *day*, and *gut*, for *good.* It is also convertible with *s* and *z*, for the Germans write *wasser*, for *water*, and *zahm*, for *tame.*

T. as an abbreviation, stands for *theologia*; as, S. T. D. *sanctæ theologiæ doctor*, doctor of divinity. In ancient monuments and writings, T. is an abbreviature, which stands for *Titus, Titius* or *Tullius.*

As a numeral, T, among the Latins, stood for 160, and with a dash over the top, T, for 160,000. *Encyc.*

In *music*, T. is the initial of tenor, vocal and instrumental; of *tacet*, for silence, as *adagio tacet*, when a person is to rest during the whole movement. In concertos and symphonies, it is the initial of *tutti*, the whole band, after a solo. It sometimes stands for *tr.* or *trillo*, a shake.

TAB'ARD, *n.* [W. *tabar*, from *tâb*, a spread or surface; It. *tabarra.*]

A short gown; a herald's coat. [*Not used in the U. States.*]

TAB'ARDER, *n.* One who wears a tabard.

TABASHEER, *n.* A Persian word signifying a concretion found in the joints of the bamboo, said by Dr. Russel to be the juice of the plant thickened and hardened; by others, to be pure silex. It is highly valued in the E. Indies as a medicine, for the cure of bilious vomitings, bloody flux, piles, &c. *Encyc. Thomson.*

TAB'BIED, *pp.* Watered; made wavy.

TAB'BY, *a.* [See the Noun.] Brinded; brindled; diversified in color; as a *tabby* cat. *Addison.*

TAB'BY, *n.* [Fr. *tabis*; It. Sp. Port. *tabi*; Dan. *tabin*; D. *tabbyn*; G. *tobin*; Arm. *taftas*, taffeta. Qu. Fr. *taveler*, to spot.]

1. A kind of waved silk, usually watered. It is manufactured like taffeta, but is thicker and stronger. The watering is given to it by the calender. *Cyc.*

2. A mixture of stone or shells and mortar, which becomes hard as a rock; used in Morocco.

TAB'BY, *v. t.* To water or cause to look wavy; as, to *tabby* silk, mohair, ribin, &c. This is done by a calender without water. *Cyc.*

TAB'BYING, *n.* The passing of stuffs under a calender to give them a wavy appearance.

TABEFAC'TION, *n.* [L. *tabeo*, to waste, and *facio*, to make. See *Tabefy.*]

A wasting away; a gradual losing of flesh by disease.

TAB'EFY, *v. i.* [Heb. Ch. דאב to pine; or Ar. ذَبَّ tabba, to be weakened, to perish. Class Db.] To consume; to waste gradually; to lose flesh. [*Little used.*] *Harvey.*

TABERD. [See *Tabard.*]

TAB'ERNACLE, *n.* [L. *tabernaculum*, a tent, from *taberna*, a shop or shed, from *tabula*, a board; or rather from its root. See *Table.*]

1. A tent. Num. xxiv. Matt. xvii.

2. A temporary habitation. *Milton.*

3. Among *the Jews*, a movable building, so contrived as to be taken to pieces with ease and reconstructed, for the convenience of being carried during the wanderings of the Israelites in the wilderness. It was of a rectangular figure, thirty cubits long, ten broad, and ten high. The interior was divided into two rooms by a vail or curtain, and it was covered with four different spreads or carpets. *Cruden.*

It is also applied to the temple. Ps. xv.

4. A place of worship; a sacred place. *Addison.*

5. Our natural body. 2 Cor. v. 2 Pet. i.

6. God's gracious presence, or the tokens of it. Rev. xxi.

7. An ornamented chest placed on Roman catholic altars as a receptacle of the ciborium and pyxis.

TAB'ERNACLE, *v. i.* To dwell; to reside for a time; to be housed; as we say, Christ *tabernacled* in the flesh.

TABERNAC'ULAR, *a.* Latticed. *Warton.*

TAB'ID, *a.* [Fr. *tabide*; L. *tabidus*, from *tabeo*, to waste.] Wasted by disease; consumptive.

> In *tabid* persons, milk is the best restorative. *Arbuthnot.*

TAB'IDNESS, *n.* State of being wasted by disease; consumptiveness.

TAB'LATURE, *n.* [from *table.*] Painting on walls and ceilings; a single piece comprehended in one view, and formed according to one design. *Johnson. Lord Shaftsbury.*

2. In *music*, the expression of sounds or notes of composition by letters of the alphabet or ciphers, or other characters not used in modern music. In a stricter sense, the manner of writing a piece for the lute, theorbo, guitar, base viol, or the like; which is done by writing on several parallel lines, (each of which represents a string of the instrument,) certain letters of the alphabet, referring to the frets on the neck of the instrument, each letter directing how some note is to be sounded. *Cyc.*

3. In *anatomy*, a division or parting of the skull into two tables. *Cyc.*

TA'BLE, *n.* [Fr. from L. *tabula*; It. *tavola*; Sp. *tabla*; W. *tavell*, a flat mass, a tablet, a slice, a spread; *tâb*, *tâv*, a spread, an extended surface; *tavlu*, to throw, to project; *tavu*, to spread or overspread; Sax. *tæfl*, a die, a table-man; D. *tafel*, a board, a table, whence in ships, *tafferel*; G. Sw. *tafel*, a board or table; Russ. *id.*; Fr. *tableau*, a picture.]

1. A flat surface of some extent, or a thing that has a flat surface; as a *table* of marble.

2. An article of furniture, consisting usually of a frame with a surface of boards or of marble, supported by legs, and used for a great variety of purposes, as for holding dishes of meat, for writing on, &c.

> The nymph the *table* spread. *Pope.*

3. Fare or entertainment of provisions; as, he keeps a good *table.*

4. The persons sitting at table or partaking of entertainment.

> I drink to th' general joy of the whole *table.* *Shak.*

5. A tablet; a surface on which any thing is written or engraved. The ten commandments were written on two *tables* of stone. Ex. xxxii.

> Written—not on *tables* of stone, but on fleshly *tables* of the heart. 2 Cor. iii.

6. A picture, or something that exhibits a view of any thing on a flat surface.

> Saint Anthony has a *table* that hangs up to him from a poor peasant. *Addison.*

7. Among *Christians*, the table, or Lord's table, is the sacrament, or holy communion of the Lord's supper.

8. The altar of burnt-offering. Mal. i.

9. In *architecture*, a smooth, simple member or ornament of various forms, most usually in that of a long square.

10. In *perspective*, a plain surface, supposed to be transparent and perpendicular to the horizon. It is called also *perspective plane.* *Cyc.*

11. In *anatomy*, a division of the cranium or skull. The cranium is composed of two tables or lamins, with a cellular structure between them, called the *meditallium* or *diploë.* *Cyc. Wistar.*

12. In *the glass manufacture*, a circular sheet of finished glass, usually about four feet in diameter, each weighing from ten to eleven pounds. Twelve of these are called a side or crate of glass.

13. In *literature*, an index; a collection of heads or principal matters contained in a book, with references to the pages where each may be found; as a *table* of contents. *Watts.*

14. A synopsis; many particulars brought into one view. *B. Jonson.*

15. The palm of the hand.

> Mistress of a fairer *table*
> Hath not history nor fable. *B. Jonson.*

16. Draughts; small pieces of wood shifted on squares.

> We are in the world like men playing at *tables.* *Taylor.*

17. In *mathematics*, tables are systems of numbers calculated to be ready for expediting operations; as a *table* of logarithms; a multiplication *table.*

18. *Astronomical tables*, are computations of the motions, places and other phenomena of the planets, both primary and secondary. *Cyc.*

19. In *chimistry*, a list or catalogue of substances or their properties; as a *table* of known acids; a *table* of acidifiable bases; a *table* of binary combinations; a *table* of specific gravities. *Lavoisier.*

20. In *general*, any series of numbers formed on mathematical or other correct principles.

21. A division of the ten commandments; as the first and second *tables.* The first table comprehends our more immediate duties to God; the second table our more immediate duties to each other.

22. Among *jewelers*, a table diamond or other precious stone, is one whose upper surface is quite flat, and the sides only cut in angles. *Cyc.*

23. A list or catalogue; as a *table* of stars.

Raised table, in *sculpture*, an embossment in a frontispiece for an inscription or other ornament, supposed to be the abacus of Vitruvius. *Cyc.*

Round table. Knights of the round table, are a military order instituted by Arthur, the first king of the Britons, A. D. 516.

Twelve tables, the laws of the Romans, so called probably, because engraved on so many tables.

To turn the tables, to change the condition or fortune of contending parties; a metaphorical expression taken from the vicissitudes of fortune in gaming. *Dryden.*

To serve tables, to provide for the poor; or to distribute provisions for their wants. Acts vi.

TA'BLE, *v. i.* To board; to diet or live at the table of another. Nebuchadnezzar *tabled* with the beasts. *South.*

TA'BLE, *v. t.* To form into a table or catalogue; as, to *table* fines. In England, the chirographer *tables* the fines of every county, and fixes a copy in some open place of the court. *Cyc.*

2. To board; to supply with food.

3. To let one piece of timber into another by alternate scores or projections from the middle. *Cyc.*

TA'BLE-BED, *n.* [*table* and *bed.*] A bed in the form of a table.

TA'BLE-BEER, *n.* [*table* and *beer.*] Beer for the table, or for common use; small beer.

TA'BLE-BOOK, *n.* [*table* and *book.*] A book on which any thing is engraved or written without ink.

Put into your *table-book* whatever you judge worthy. *Dryden.*

TA'BLE-CLOTH, *n.* [*table* and *cloth.*] A cloth for covering a table, particularly for spreading on a table before the dishes are set for meals.

TA'BLED, *pp.* Formed into a table.

TA'BLE-LAND, *n.* [*table* and *land.*] Elevated flat land.

TA'BLE-MAN, *n.* [*table* and *man.*] A man at draughts; a piece of wood. *Bacon.*

TA'BLER, *n.* One who boards. *Ainsworth.*

TA'BLES, *n. plu.* A board used for backgammon.

TAB'LET, *n.* A small table or flat surface.

2. Something flat on which to write, paint, draw or engrave.

Through all Greece the young gentlemen learned to design on *tablets* of boxen wood. *Dryden.*

The pillar'd marble, and the *tablet* brass. *Prior.*

3. A medicine in a square form. *Tablets* of arsenic were formerly worn as a preservative against the plague. *Bacon.*

A solid kind of electuary or confection, made of dry ingredients, usually with sugar, and formed into little flat squares; called also *lozenge* and *troche.* *Cyc.*

TA'BLE-TALK, *n.* [*table* and *talk.*] Conversation at table or at meals.

He improves by the *table-talk.* *Guardian.*

TA'BLING, *ppr.* Boarding; forming into a table; letting one timber into another by scores.

TA'BLING, *n.* A forming into tables; a setting down in order.

2. The letting of one timber into another by alternate scores or projections, as in shipbuilding. *Cyc.*

3. In *sail-making*, a broad hem made on the skirts of sails by turning over the edge of the canvas, and sewing it down. *Cyc.*

TABOO', *n.* In *the isles of the Pacific*, a word denoting prohibition or religious interdict, which is of great force among the inhabitants.

TABOO', *v. t.* To forbid, or to forbid the use of; to interdict approach or use; as, to *taboo* the ground set apart as a sanctuary for criminals. *Tabooed* ground is held sacred and inviolable.

TA'BOR, *n.* [W. *tabwrz*; Ir. *tabar*; Old Fr. *tabour.* This in some languages, is written *tambour*, and *timbrel.* The *atabal* of the Spaniards is probably of the same family. It is probably named from striking, beating; Eng. *tap*, Gr. τυπτω, Syr. ܛܒܠ Ar. طبج. Class Db. No. 28.]

A small drum used as an accompaniment to a pipe or fife. *Cyc.*

TA'BOR, *v. i.* To strike lightly and frequently.

Her maids shall lead her as with the voice of doves, *taboring* upon their breasts. Nah. ii.

2. To play on a tabor or little drum.

TA'BORER, *n.* One who beats the tabor. *Shak.*

TAB'ORET, *n.* [from *tabor.*] A small tabor. *Spectator.*

TAB'ORIN, **TABORI'NE**, } *n.* [Fr. *tabourin*; from *tabor.*] A tabor; a small drum. *Shak.*

TAB'RERE, *n.* A taborer. *Obs.* *Spenser.*

TAB'RET, *n.* [See *Tabor.*] A tabor. 1 Sam. xviii.

TAB'ULAR, *a.* [L. *tabularis*, from *tabula*, table.]

1. In the form of a table; having a flat or square surface.

2. Having the form of lamina or plates.

3. Set down in tables; as a *tabular* list of substances.

4. Set in squares. *Johnson.*

Tabular crystal, one in which the prism is very short. *Phillips.*

Tabular spar, in mineralogy, a species of limestone, generally of a grayish white color. It occurs either massive or crystalized, in rectangular four sided tables. *Haüy.*

Tabular spar is the schaalstein of Werner, and the prismatic augite of Jameson.

TAB'ULATE, *v. t.* To reduce to tables or synopses.

2. To shape with a flat surface. *Johnson.*

TAB'ULATED, *pp.* Having a flat or square flat surface; as a *tabulated* diamond. *Grew.*

TACAMAHAC'A, **TACAMAHAC'**, } *n.* A tree of a sweet fragrance, planted in gardens as an ornament. It is of the genus Populus, [*P. balsamifera.*]

2. A resin brought from America in large oblong masses wrapped in flag leaves, of a light brown color, and an aromatic smell between that of lavender and musk. It is obtained from the Fagara octandra, and it is said also, from the Populus balsamifera. *Thomson.*

TA'CE, from L. *taceo*, a term used in Italian music, directing to be silent.

TA'CET, in *music*, is used when a vocal or instrumental part is to be silent during a whole movement. *Cyc.*

TACH, **TACHE**, } *n.* [See *Tack.*] Something used for taking hold or holding; a catch; a loop; a button. It is found in Scripture, but I believe is not now used in discourse or writing. Ex. xxvi.

TACHYG'RAPHY, *n.* [Gr. ταχυς, quick, and γραφω, to write.]

The art or practice of quick writing. [We now use *stenography*, and *short hand writing.*]

TAC'IT, *a.* [Fr. *tacite*; L. *tacitus*, from *taceo*, to be silent, that is, to stop, or to close. See *Tack.*]

Silent; implied, but not expressed. *Tacit* consent is consent by silence, or not interposing an objection. So we say, a *tacit* agreement or covenant of men to live under a particular government, when no objection or opposition is made; a *tacit* surrender of a part of our natural rights; a *tacit* reproach, &c.

TAC'ITLY, *adv.* Silently; by implication; without words; as, he *tacitly* assented.

TAC'ITURN, *a.* [L. *taciturnus.*] Habitually silent; not free to converse; not apt to talk or speak. *Smollett.*

TACITURN'ITY, *n.* [Fr. *taciturnité*, from L. *taciturnitas*, from *taceo*, to be silent.] Habitual silence or reserve in speaking.

Too great loquacity, and too great *taciturnity* by fits. *Arbuthnot.*

TACK, *v. t.* [Gr. τασσω, to set, place, ordain, the root of which was ταγω, as appears from its derivatives, ταγεις, ταγμα. Hence Fr. *attacher*, It. *attaccare*, Sp. *atacar*, W. *tagu*, to stop, Sp. *taco*, a stopper. See *Attach.* The primary sense is probably to thrust or send.]

1. To fasten; to attach. In the solemn or grave style, this word now appears ludicrous; as, to get a commendam *tacked* to their sees. *Swift.*

—And *tack* the center to the sphere. *Herbert.*

2. To unite by stitching together; as, to *tack* together the sheets of a book; to *tack* one piece of cloth to another. [*In the familiar style, this word is in good use.*]

3. To fasten slightly by nails; as, to *tack* on a board or shingle.

TACK, **TACHE**, } *n.* [Fr. *tache.*] A spot. [*Not used.*]

TACK, *n.* [Ir. *taca*; Arm. *tach.*] A small nail.

2. A rope used to confine the foremost lower corners of the courses and stay-sails, when the wind crosses the ship's course obliquely; also, a rope employed to pull the lower corner of a studding sail to the boom. Hence,

3. The part of a sail to which the tack is usually fastened; the foremost lower corner of the courses. Hence,

4. The course of a ship in regard to the position of her sails; as the starboard *tack*, or larboard *tack*; the former when she is close-hauled with the wind on her starboard, the latter when close hauled with the wind on her larboard. *Mar. Dict.*

To hold tack, to last or hold out. *Tusser.*

Tack of a flag, a line spliced into the eye at the bottom of the tabling, for securing the flag to the halliards.

TACK, *v. i.* To change the course of a ship by shifting the tacks and position of the sails from one side to the other. *Mar. Dict.*

TACK, *n.* In rural economy, a shelf on which cheese is dried. [*Local.*]

Tack of land, the term of a lease. [*Local.*]

TACK'ER, *n.* One who tacks or makes an addition.

TACK'ET, *n.* A small nail. *Barret.*

TACK'ING, *ppr.* Changing a ship's course.

TACK'LE, *n.* [D. *takel*, a pulley and tackle; *takelen*, to rig; G. *takel*, *takeln*; Sw. *tackel*, *tackla*; Dan. *takkel*, *takler*; W. *taclu*, to put in order, to dress, deck, set right; *taclau*, tackling, accouterments; *tacyl*, a tool. This seems to belong to the family of *tack*, Gr. τασσω. The primary sense is to put on, or to set or to put in order.]

1. A machine for raising or lowering heavy weights, consisting of a rope and blocks, called a pulley. *Mar. Dict.*

2. Instruments of action; weapons.

She to her *tackle* fell. *Hudibras.*

3. An arrow. *Chaucer.*

4. The rigging and apparatus of a ship.

Tackle-fall, the rope, or rather the end of the rope of a pulley, which falls and by which it is pulled.

Ground-tackle, anchors, cables, &c.

Gun-tackle, the instruments for hauling cannon in or out.

Tack-tackle, a small tackle to pull down the tacks of the principal sails. *Mar. Dict.*

TACK'LE, *v. t.* To harness; as, to *tackle* a horse into a gig, sleigh, coach or wagon. [*A legitimate and common use of the word in America.*]

2. To seize; to lay hold of; as, a wrestler *tackles* his antagonist; a dog *tackles* the game. This is a common popular use of the word in New England, though not elegant. But it retains the primitive idea, to put on, to fall or throw on. [See *Attack.*]

3. To supply with tackle. *Beaum.*

TACK'LED, *pp.* Harnessed; seized.

2. Made of ropes tacked together.

My man shall
Bring thee cords, made like a *tackled* stair. *Shak.*

TACK'LING, *ppr.* Harnessing; putting on harness; seizing; falling on.

TACK'LING, *n.* Furniture of the masts and yards of a ship, as cordage, sails, &c.

2. Instruments of action; as fishing *tackling.* *Walton.*

3. Harness; the instruments of drawing a carriage.

TACKS'MAN, *n.* One who holds a tack or lease of land from another; a tenant or lessee. [*Local.*]

TACT, *n.* [L. *tactus*, from *tango*, [for *tago*,] to touch; Fr. *tact*; It. *tatto*; Sp. *tacto.*]

1. Touch; feeling: formerly, the stroke in beating time in music. [Dan. *tagt.*]

2. Peculiar skill or faculty; nice perception or discernment. *Am. Review.*

TAC'TIC, TAC'TICAL, *a.* [See *Tactics.*] Pertaining to the art of military and naval dispositions for battle, evolutions, &c.

TACTI''CIAN, *n.* [See *Tactics.*] One versed in tactics.

TAC'TICS, *n.* [Gr. τακτικος, from τασσω, ταττω, to set, to appoint; ταξις, order; Fr. *tactique.* See *Tack.*]

1. The science and art of disposing military and naval forces in order for battle and performing military and naval evolutions. In the most extensive sense, tactics, *la grande tactique* of the French, comprehends every thing that relates to the order, formation and disposition of armies, their encampments, &c.

2. The art of inventing and making machines for throwing darts, arrows, stones and other missile weapons. *Cyc.*

TAC'TILE, TAC'TIL, *a.* [Fr. *tactile*, from L. *tactilis*, from *tango*, to touch.]

Tangible; susceptible of touch; that may be felt; as *tactile* sweets; *tactile* qualities. *Hale.*

TACTIL'ITY, *n.* Tangibleness; perceptibility of touch.

TAC'TION, *n.* [Fr. from L. *tactio*, *tango*, to touch.] The act of touching; touch.

TADOR'NA, *n.* [Sp. *tadorno.*] A name of the shel-drake, vulpanser, or borough-duck. *Cyc.*

TAD'POLE, *n.* [Sax. *tade*, toad, with *pola*, coinciding with L. *pullus*, young.]

A frog in its first state from the spawn; a porwiggle.

TAF'ELSPATH, *n.* A lamellar mineral of a yellowish grey or rose white, forming masses of prisms interlaced in the gang, chiefly lime and silex. *Cyc.*

TAF'FEREL, *n.* [D. *taffereel*, from *tafel*, table.]

The upper part of a ship's stern, which is flat like a table on the top, and sometimes ornamented with carved work. *Mar. Dict. Cyc.*

TAF'FETA, *n.* [Fr. *tafetas*, *taffetas*; Sp. *tafetan*; It. *taffetta*; D. *taf*; G. *taffet.*]

A fine smooth stuff of silk, having usually a remarkable gloss. *Taffetas* are of all colors. *Cyc.*

TAG, *n.* [Sw. *tagg*, a point or prickle; Ice. *tag*; Dan. *tagger*, *takker.* The primary sense is probably a shoot, coinciding with the first syllable of L. *digitus*, [See *Toe*;] or the sense is from putting on, as in *tackle.* In Goth. *taga* is hair, the hair of the head, that which is shot out, or that which is thick. The latter sense would show its alliance to the W. *tagu*, to choke.]

1. A metallic point put to the end of a string.

2. Something mean and paltry; as *tag*-rag people. [*Vulgar.*] *Shak.*

3. A young sheep. [*Local.*]

TAG, *v. t.* To fit with a point; as, to *tag* lace.

2. To fit one thing to another; to append to.

His courteous host
Tags every sentence with some fawning word. *Dryden.*

3. To join or fasten. *Swift.*

TAG, *n.* A play in which the person gains who tags, that is, touches another. This was a common sport among boys in Connecticut formerly, and it may be still. The word is inserted here for the sake of the evidence it affords of the affinity of languages, and of the original orthography of the Latin *tango*, to touch, which was *tago.* This vulgar *tag* is the same word; the primitive word retained by the common people. It is used also as a verb, to *tag.* [See *Touch.*]

TAG-SORE, *n.* A disease in sheep. *Cyc.*

TAG-TAIL, *n.* [*tag* and *tail.*] A worm which has its tail of another color. *Walton.*

TAIL, *n.* [Sax. *tægl*; Ice. *tagl*; dim. of *tag*, a shoot, or from Goth. *taga*, hair.]

1. The part of an animal which terminates its body behind. In many quadrupeds, the tail is a shoot or projection covered with hair. In fowls, the tail consists of fethers, or is covered with them, which serve to assist in the direction of their flight. In fishes the tail is formed usually by a gradual sloping of the body, ending in a fin. The tail of a fish may assist the animal in steering, but its principal use is to propel the fish forward. It is the instrument of swimming.

2. The lower part, noting inferiority.

The Lord will make thee the head, and not the *tail.* Deut. xxviii.

3. Any thing hanging long; a catkin. *Harvey.*

4. The hinder part of any thing. *Butler.*

5. In *anatomy*, that tendon of a muscle which is fixed to the movable part. *Cyc.*

6. In *botany*, the *tail of a seed*, is a downy or fethery appendage to certain seeds, formed of the permanent elongated style. *Cyc.*

7. *Horse's tail*, among *the Tartars* and *Chinese*, is an ensign or flag; among *the Turks*, a standard borne before the grand visier, bashaws and the sangiacs. For this purpose, it is fitted to a half-pike with a gold button, and is called *toug.* There are bashaws of one, two and three *tails.* *Cyc.*

8. In *heraldry*, the tail of a hart.

9. In *music*, the part of a note running upwards or downwards.

10. The extremity or last end; as the *tail* of a storm.

Tail of a comet, a luminous train which extends from the nucleus in a direction opposite to the sun.

To turn tail, is to run away; to flee.

Tail of a lock, on a canal, the lower end, or entrance into the lower pond.

Tail-piece, of a violin, is a piece of ebony attached to the end of the instrument, to which the strings are fastened. *Cyc.*

TAIL, *n.* [Fr. *tailler*, Sp. *tallar*, It. *tagliare*, Port. *talhar*, Ir. *tallam*, to cut off; W. *toli*, to curtail, to separate, to *deal* out, from *tawl*, a sending or throwing, a cast or throw, a separation, diminution, interruption. This is from the same root as *deal.* Class Dl. No. 15. See *Deal.*]

In *law*, an estate in tail is a limited fee; an estate limited to certain heirs, and from which the other heirs are precluded. Estates tail are *general* or *special*; *general*, where lands and tenements are given to one, and to the heirs of his body begotten; *special*, where the gift is restrained to certain heirs of the donee's body, as to his heirs by a particular woman named. [See *Entail.*] *Blackstone.*

TAIL, *v. t.* To pull by the tail. *Hudibras.*

TA'ILAGE, TAL'LIAGE, *n.* [Fr. *tailler*, to cut off.] Literally, a share; hence, a tax or toll. *Obs.* *Blackstone.*

TA'ILED, *a.* Having a tail. *Grew.*

TA'ILINGS, *n. plu.* [from *tail.*] The lighter parts of grain blown to one end of the heap in winnowing. [*Local.*] *Cyc.*

TA'ILOR, *n.* [Fr. *tailleur*, from *tailler*, to cut, It. *tagliare*, Ir. *tallam.*]

One whose occupation is to cut out and make men's garments.

TA'ILOR, *v. i.* To practice making men's clothes. *Green.*

TA'ILORESS, *n.* A female who makes garments for men.

TA'ILORING, *n.* The business of a tailor.

TAINT, *v. t.* [Fr. *teindre*, to dye or stain; L. *tingo*; Gr. τεγγω, to dye, literally to dip, primarily to thrust, the sense of L. *tango*; and *n* not being radical, the real word is *tego* or *tago*, coinciding with Eng. *duck*; hence its sense in *extinguo.* See *Dye*, *Attaint* and *Tinge.*]

1. To imbue or impregnate, as with some extraneous matter which alters the sensible qualities of the substance.

The spaniel struck
Stiff by the *tainted* gale— *Thomson.*

2. *More generally*, to impregnate with something odious, noxious or poisonous; as, putrid substances *taint* the air.

3. To infect; to poison. The breath of consumptive lungs is said to *taint* sound lungs. *Harvey.*

4. To corrupt, as by incipient putrefaction; as *tainted* meat.

5. To stain; to sully; to tarnish.

We come not by the way of accusation
To *taint* that honor every good tongue blesses. *Shak.*

6. To corrupt, as blood; to attaint. [*Not in use.*] [See *Attaint.*]

TAINT, *v. i.* To be infected or corrupted; to be touched with something corrupting.

I cannot *taint* with fear. *Shak.*

2. To be affected with incipient putrefaction. Meat soon *taints* in warm weather.

TAINT, *n.* Tincture; stain.

2. Infection; corruption; depravation. Keep children from the *taint* of low and vicious company.

3. A stain; a spot; a blemish on reputation. *Shak.*

4. An insect; a kind of spider. *Brown.*

TA'INTED, *pp.* Impregnated with something noxious, disagreeable to the senses or poisonous; infected; corrupted; stained.

TA'INTFREE, *a.* [*taint* and *free.*] Free from taint or guilt. *Heath.*

TA'INTING, *ppr.* Impregnating with something foul or poisonous; infecting; corrupting; staining.

TA'INTLESS, *a.* Free from taint or infection; pure. *Swift.*

TA'INTURE, *n.* [L. *tinctura.*] Taint; tinge; defilement; stain; spot. [*Not much used.*] *Shak.*

TAJACU, TAJASSU, } *n.* The peccary or Mexican hog.

TAKE, *v. t.* pret. *took;* pp. *taken.* [Sax. *tæcan*, to *take*, and to *teach;* also *thicgan*, to take, as food; Sw. *taga;* Dan. *tager;* Ice. *taka;* Gr. *δεχομαι;* L. *doceo.* This word seems to be allied to *think*, for we say, I *think* a thing to be so, or I *take* it to be so. It seems also to be allied to Sax. *teogan*, to draw, to *tug*, L. *duco;* for we say, to *take* a likeness, and to *draw* a likeness. We use *taking* also for engaging, attracting. We say, a child *takes* to his mother or nurse, and a man *takes* to drink; which seem to include *attaching* and holding. We observe that *take* and *teach* are radically the same word.]

1. In *a general sense*, to get hold or gain possession of a thing in almost any manner, either by receiving it when offered, or by using exertion to obtain it. *Take* differs from *seize*, as it does not always imply haste, force or violence. It more generally denotes to gain or receive into possession in a peaceable manner, either passively or by active exertions. Thus,

2. To receive what is offered.

Then I *took* the cup at the Lord's hand. Jer. xxv.

3. To lay hold of; to get into one's power for keeping.

No man shall *take* the nether or the upper millstone to pledge. Deut. xxiv.

4. To receive with a certain affection of mind. He *takes* it in good part; or he *takes* it very ill.

5. To catch by surprise or artifice; to circumvent.

Men in their loose unguarded hours they *take*,
Not that themselves are wise, but others weak. *Pope.*

6. To seize; to make prisoner. The troops entered, slew and *took* three hundred janizaries. *Knolles.*

This man was *taken* of the Jews. Acts xxiii.

7. To captivate with pleasure; to engage the affections; to delight.

Neither let her *take* thee with her eyelids. Prov. vi.

Cleombrotus was so *taken* with this prospect, that he had no patience. *Wake.*

8. To get into one's power by engines or nets; to entrap; to ensnare; as, to *take* foxes with traps; to *take* fishes with nets, or with hook and line.

9. To understand in a particular sense; to receive as meaning. I *take* your meaning.

You *take* me right. *Bacon.*

Charity, *taken* in its largest extent, is nothing else but the sincere love to God and our neighbor. *Wake.*

10. To exact and receive.

Take no usury of him or increase. Lev. xxv.

11. To employ; to occupy. The prudent man always *takes* time for deliberation, before he passes judgment.

12. To agree to; to close in with; to comply with.

I *take* thee at thy word. *Rowe.*

13. To form and adopt; as, to *take* a resolution. *Clarendon.*

14. To catch; to embrace; to seize; as, to *take* one by the hand; to *take* in the arms.

15. To admit; to receive as an impression; to suffer; as, to *take* a form or shape.

Yet thy moist clay is pliant to command;
Now *take* the mold— *Dryden.*

16. To obtain by active exertion; as, to *take* revenge or satisfaction for an injury.

17. To receive; to receive into the mind.

They *took* knowledge of them that they had been with Jesus. Acts iv.

It appeared in his face that he *took* great contentment in this our question. *Bacon.*

18. To swallow, as meat or drink; as, to *take* food; to *take* a glass of wine.

19. To swallow, as medicine; as, to *take* pills; to *take* stimulants.

20. To choose; to elect. *Take* which you please. But the sense of *choosing*, in this phrase, is derived from the connection of *take* with *please.* So we say, *take* your choice.

21. To copy.

Beauty alone could beauty *take* so right. *Dryden.*

22. To fasten on; to seize. The frost has *taken* the corn; the worms have *taken* the vines.

Wheresoever he *taketh* him, he teareth him, and he foameth— Mark ix.

23. To accept; not to refuse. He offered me a fee, but I would not *take* it.

Ye shall *take* no satisfaction for the life of a murderer. Num. xxxv.

24. To adopt.

I will *take* you to me for a people. Ex. vi.

25. To admit.

Let not a widow be *taken* into the number under threescore. 1 Tim. v.

26. To receive, as any temper or disposition of mind; as, to *take* shame to one's self; to *take* delight; to *take* pride or pleasure.

27. To endure; to bear without resentment; or to submit to without attempting to obtain satisfaction. He will *take* an affront from no man. Cannot you *take* a jest?

28. To draw; to deduce.

The firm belief of a future judgment is the most forcible motive to a good life, because *taken* from this consideration of the most lasting happiness and misery. *Tillotson.*

29. To assume; as, I *take* the liberty to say. *Locke.*

30. To allow; to admit; to receive as true, or not disputed; as, to *take* a thing for granted.

31. To suppose; to receive in thought; to entertain in opinion; to understand. This I *take* to be the man's motive.

He *took* that for virtue and affection which was nothing but vice in disguise. *South.*

You'd doubt his sex, and *take* him for a girl. *Tate.*

32. To seize; to invade; as, to be *taken* with a fever.

33. To have recourse to; as, the sparrow *takes* a bush; the cat *takes* a tree. [In this sense, we usually say, the bird *takes to* a bush, the squirrel *takes to* a tree.]

34. To receive into the mind.

Those do best, who *take* material hints to be judged by history. *Locke.*

35. To hire; to rent; to obtain possession on lease; as, to *take* a house or farm for a year.

36. To admit in copulation.

37. To draw; to copy; to paint a likeness; as a likeness *taken* by Reynolds.

38. To conquer and cause to surrender; to gain possession of by force or capitulation; as, to *take* an army, a city or a ship.

39. To be discovered or detected. He was *taken* in the very act.

40. To require or be necessary. It *takes* so much cloth to make a coat.

To take away, to deprive of; to bereave; as a bill for *taking away* the votes of bishops.

By your own law I *take* your life *away.* *Dryden.*

2. To remove; as, to *take away* the consciousness of pleasure. *Locke.*

To take care, to be careful; to be solicitous for.

Doth God *take care* for oxen? 1 Cor. ix.

2. To be cautious or vigilant. *Take care* not to expose your health.

To take care of, to superintend or oversee; to have the charge of keeping or securing.

To take a course, to resort to; to have recourse to measures.

The violence of storming is the *course* which God is forced to *take* for the destroying of sinners. *Hammond.*

To take one's own course, to act one's pleasure; to pursue the measures of one's own choice.

To take down, to reduce; to bring lower; to depress; as, to *take down* pride, or the proud.

2. To swallow; as, to *take down* a potion.

3. To pull down; to pull to pieces; as, to *take down* a house or a scaffold.

4. To write; as, to *take down* a man's words at the time he utters them.

To take from, to deprive of.

I will smite thee, and *take* thine head *from* thee. 1 Sam. xvii.

2. To deduct; to subtract; as, to *take* one number *from* another.
3. To detract; to derogate. *Dryden.*
To take heed, to be careful or cautious.
Take heed what doom against yourself you give. *Dryden.*
To take heed to, to attend to with care. *Take heed to* thy ways.
To take hold, to seize; to fix on.
To take in, to inclose; to fence. *Mortimer.*
2. To encompass or embrace; to comprise; to comprehend.
3. To draw into a smaller compass; to contract; to brail or furl; as, to *take in* sail.
4. To cheat; to circumvent; to gull. [*Not elegant.*]
5. To admit; to receive; as, a vessel will *take in* more water. The landlord said he could *take in* no more lodgers.
6. To win by conquest. [*Not in use.*] *Felton.*
7. To receive into the mind or understanding.
Some bright genius can *take in* a long train of propositions. *Watts.*
To take in hand, to undertake; to attempt to execute any thing. Luke i.
To take notice, to observe; or to observe with particular attention.
2. To show by some act that observation is made; to make remark upon. He heard what was said, but *took* no *notice* of it.
To take oath, to swear with solemnity, or in a judicial manner.
To take off, to remove, in various ways; to remove from the top of any thing; as, to *take off* a load; to *take off* one's hat, &c.
2. To cut off; as, to *take off* the head or a limb.
3. To destroy; as, to *take off* life.
4. To remove; to invalidate; as, to *take off* the force of an argument.
5. To withdraw; to call or draw away.
Keep foreign ideas from *taking off* the mind from its present pursuit. *Locke.*
6. To swallow; as, to *take off* a glass of wine.
7. To purchase; to take from in trade.
The Spaniards having no commodities that we will *take off*— *Locke.*
8. To copy.
Take off all their models in wood. *Addison.*
9. To imitate; to mimic.
10. To find place for; as more scholars than preferments can *take off*.
To take off from, to lessen; to remove in part. This *takes off from* the deformity of vice.
To take order with, to check. [*Not much used.*] *Bacon.*
To take out, to remove from within a place; to separate; to deduct.
2. To draw out; to remove; to clear or cleanse from; as, to *take out* a stain or spot from cloth; to *take out* an unpleasant taste from wine.
To take part, to share. *Take part* in our rejoicing.
To take part with, to unite with; to join with.
To take place, to happen; to come, or come to pass.
2. To have effect; to prevail.
Where arms *take place*, all other pleas are vain. *Dryden.*
To take effect, to have the intended effect; to be efficacious.
To take root, to live and grow; as a plant.
2. To be established; as principles.
To take up, to lift; to raise.
2. To buy or borrow; as, to *take up* goods to a large amount; to *take up* money at the bank.
3. To begin; as, to *take up* a lamentation. Ezek. xix.
4. In *surgery*, to fasten with a ligature.
5. To engross; to employ; to engage the attention; as, to *take up* the time.
6. To have final recourse to.
Arnobius asserts that men of the finest parts *took up* their rest in the christian religion. *Addison.*
7. To seize; to catch; to arrest; as, to *take up* a thief; to *take up* vagabonds.
8. To admit.
The ancients *took up* experiments upon credit. *Bacon.*
9. To answer by reproof; to reprimand.
One of his relations *took* him *up* roundly. *L'Estrange.*
10. To begin where another left off.
Soon as the evening shades prevail,
The moon *takes up* the wondrous tale. *Addison.*
11. To occupy; to fill; as, to *take up* a great deal of room.
12. To assume; to carry on or manage for another; as, to *take up* the quarrels of our neighbors.
13. To comprise; to include.
The noble poem of Palemon and Arcite—*takes up* seven years. *Dryden.*
14. To adopt; to assume; as, to *take up* current opinions.
They *take up* our old trade of conquering. *Dryden.*
15. To collect; to exact a tax. *Knolles.*
16. To pay and receive; as, to *take up* a note at the bank. *Johnson's Reports.*
To take up arms, } to begin war; to begin
To take arms, } resistance by force.
To take upon, to assume; to undertake. He *takes upon* himself to assert that the fact is capable of proof.
2. To appropriate to; to admit to be imputed to; as, to *take upon* one's self a punishment.
To take side, to join one of two differing parties; to take an interest in one party.
To take to heart, to be sensibly affected by; to feel any thing sensibly.
To take advantage of, to catch by surprise; or to make use of a favorable state of things to the prejudice of another.
To take the advantage of, to use any advantage offered.
To take air, to be divulged or made public; to be disclosed; as a secret.
To take the air, to expose one's self to the open air.
To take a course, to begin a certain direction or way of proceeding.
To take leave, to bid adieu or farewell.
To take breath, to rest; to be recruited or refreshed.
To take aim, to direct the eye or a weapon to a particular object.
To take along, to carry, lead or convey.
To take a way, to begin a particular course or direction.
TAKE, *v. i.* To move or direct the course; to resort to, or to attach one's self; to betake one's self. The fox being hard pressed *took* to the hedge. My friend has left his music and *taken* to books.
The defluxion *taking* to his breast, wasted his lungs. *Bacon.*
2. To please; to gain reception. The play will not *take*, unless it is set off with proper scenes.
Each wit may praise it for his own dear sake,
And hint he writ it, if the thing should *take*. *Addison.*
3. To have the intended or natural effect.
In impressions from mind to mind, the impression *taketh*. *Bacon.*
4. To catch; to fix, or be fixed. He was inoculated, but the infection did not *take*.
When flame *taketh* and openeth, it giveth a noise. *Bacon.*
To take after, to learn to follow; to copy; to imitate; as, he *takes after* a good pattern.
2. To resemble; as, the son *takes after* his father.
To take in with, to resort to. *Bacon.*
To take for, to mistake; to suppose or think one thing to be another.
The lord of the land *took* us *for* spies. Gen. xlii.
To take on, to be violently affected; as, the child *takes on* at a great rate.
2. To claim, as a character.
I *take* not *on* me here as a physician. *Shak.*
To take to, to apply to; to be fond of; to become attached to; as, to *take to* books; to *take to* evil practices.
2. To resort to; to betake to.
Men of learning who *take to* business, discharge it generally with greater honesty than men of the world. *Addison.*
To take up, to stop.
Sinners at last *take up* and settle in a contempt of all religion. [*Not in use.*] *Tillotson.*
2. To reform. [*Not in use.*] *Locke.*
To take up with, to be contented to receive; to receive without opposition; as, to *take up with* plain fare.
In affairs which may have an extensive influence on our future happiness, we should not *take up with* probabilities. *Watts.*
2. To lodge; to dwell. [*Not in use.*] *South.*
To take with, to please. The proposal *takes* well *with* him.
TAKEN, *ta'kn. pp.* of *take.* Received; caught; apprehended; captivated, &c.
TA'KER, *n.* One that takes or receives; one who catches or apprehends.
2. One that subdues and causes to surrender; as the *taker* of captives or of a city.
TA'KING, *ppr.* Receiving; catching; getting possession; apprehending.
2. *a.* Alluring; attracting.
TA'KING, *n.* The act of gaining possession; a seizing; seizure; apprehension.
2. Agitation; distress of mind.
What a *taking* was he in, when your husband asked what was in the basket? *Shak.*
TA'KINGNESS, *n.* The quality of pleasing. *Taylor.*
TALAPOIN', *n.* In Siam, a priest, or one devoted to religion; also, a species of monkey.
TAL'BOT, *n.* A sort of dog, noted for his quick scent and eager pursuit of game. [The figure of a dog is said to be borne in the arms of the Talbot family.] *Cyc. Johnson.*

TALCK, } *n.* [G. *talk*, isinglass; *talg*, tallow; Sw. *talk*, *talg*, id.; Dan. *tælg*, *talg*, tallow, and *talk*, *talgsteen*, tallow-stone; D. *talk*, tallow; Port. Sp. *talco*. This word, if written *talck*, would admit of a regular adjective, *talcky*.]
TALC, }

A species of magnesian earth, consisting of broad flat smooth lamins or plates, unctuous to the touch, of a shining luster, translucent, and often transparent. By the action of fire, the lamins open a little, the fragment swells, and the extremities are with difficulty fused into a white enamel. When rubbed with resin, talck acquires positive electricity. Its prevailing colors are white, apple-green and yellow. *Cyc. Kirwan.*

Of this mineral, Jameson's sixth subspecies of rhomboidal mica, there are two kinds, common and indurated. *Ure.*

TALCK'ITE, *n.* A species of talck of a loose form.

TALCK'OUS, *a.* Talcky. [But *talcous* or *talckous* is ill formed.]

TALCK'Y, *a.* Like talck; consisting of talck; as a *talcky* feel; a *talcky* substance.

2. Containing talck.

TALE, *n.* [See *Tell.*] A story; a narrative; the rehearsal of a series of events or adventures, commonly some trifling incidents; or a fictitious narrative; as the *tale* of a tub; Marmontel's *tales*; idle *tales*. Luke xxiv.

We spend our years as a *tale* that is told. Ps. xc.

2. Oral relation. *Shak.*

3. Reckoning; account set down. Ex. v.

In packing, they keep a just *tale* of the number. *Carew.*

4. Number reckoned.

—The ignorant who measure by *tale*, not by weight. *Hooker.*

5. A telling; information; disclosure of any thing secret.

Birds—are aptest by their voice to tell *tales* what they find. *Bacon.*

In thee are men that carry *tales* to shed blood. Ezek. xxii.

6. In *law*, a count or declaration. [*Tale*, in this sense, is obsolete.]

7. In *commerce*, a weight for gold and silver in China and other parts of the E. Indies; also, a money of account. In China, each tale is 10 maces=100 candareens=1000 cash. *Cyc.*

TALE, *v. i.* To tell stories. *Obs.* *Gower.*

TA'LEBEARER, *n.* [*tale* and *bear.*] A person who officiously tells tales; one who impertinently communicates intelligence or anecdotes, and makes mischief in society by his officiousness.

Where there is no *talebearer*, the strife ceaseth. Prov. xxvi.

TA'LEBEARING, *a.* Officiously communicating information.

TA'LEBEARING, *n.* The act of informing officiously; communication of secrets maliciously.

TA'LEFUL, *a.* Abounding with stories. *Thomson.*

TAL'ENT, *n.* [L. *talentum*; Gr. ταλαντον, from ταλαω, to bear, allied to L. *tollo*. The word is said to have originally signified a balance or scales.]

1. Among the ancients, a weight, and a coin. The true value of the talent cannot well be ascertained, but it is known that it was different among different nations. The Attic talent, the weight, contained 60 Attic minæ, or 6000 Attic drachmæ, equal to 56 pounds, eleven ounces, English troy weight. The mina being reckoned equal to £3 4*s.* 7*d.* sterling, or fourteen dollars and a third nearly, the talent was of the value of £193 15*s.* sterling, about $861 dollars. Other computations make it £225 sterling.

The Romans had the great talent and the little talent; the great talent is computed to be equal to £99 6*s.* 8*d.* sterling, and the little talent to £75 sterling.

2. *Talent*, among the Hebrews, was also a gold coin, the same with a shekel of gold; called also stater, and weighing only four drachmas.

But the Hebrew talent of silver, called *cicar*, was equivalent to three thousand shekels, or one hundred and thirteen pounds, ten ounces and a fraction, troy weight. *Arbuthnot.*

3. Faculty; natural gift or endowment; a metaphorical application of the word, said to be borrowed from the Scriptural parable of the talents. Matt. xxv.

He is chiefly to be considered in his three different *talents*, as a critic, a satirist, and a writer of odes. *Dryden.*

'Tis not my *talent* to conceal my thoughts. *Addison.*

4. Eminent abilities; superior genius; as, he is a man of *talents*.

[*Talent*, in the singular, is sometimes used in a like sense.]

5. Particular faculty; skill. He has a *talent* at drawing.

6. [Sp. *talante*, manner of performing any thing, will, disposition.] Quality; disposition. *Swift.*

TAL'ENTED, *a.* Furnished with talents; possessing skill or talents. *Ch. Spectator.*

TA'LES, *n.* [L. *talis*, plu. *tales.*] In law, *tales de circumstantibus*, spectators in court, from whom the sherif is to select men to supply any defect of jurors who are impanneled, but who may not appear, or may be challenged.

TA'LETELLER, *n.* One who tells tales or stories. *Guardian.*

Talionis, lex talionis, [L.] in *law*, the law of retaliation. [See *Retaliate.*]

TAL'ISMAN, *n.* [said to be Arabic or Persian.]

1. A magical figure cut or engraved under certain superstitious observances of the configuration of the heavens, to which wonderful effects are ascribed; or it is the seal, figure, character or image of a heavenly sign, constellation or planet, engraven on a sympathetic stone, or on a metal corresponding to the star, in order to receive its influence. The talismans of the Samothracians were pieces of iron, formed into images and set in rings, &c. They were held to be preservatives against all kinds of evils. *Cyc.*

Talismans are of three kinds, *astronomical, magical* and *mixed.* Hence,

2. Something that produces extraordinary effects; as a *talisman* to destroy diseases. *Swift.*

TALISMAN'IC, *a.* Magical; having the properties of a talisman or preservative against evils by secret influence. *Addison.*

TALK, *v. i.* *tauk.* [Dan. *tolker*, Sw. *tolka*, to interpret, translate, explain; D. *tolken*, id.; Russ. *tolkuyu*, id. This is probably the same word differently applied. The word is formed from *tell.* See *Tell*, for the Danish and Swedish.]

1. To converse familiarly; to speak, as in familiar discourse, when two or more persons interchange thoughts.

I will buy with you, sell with you, *talk* with you; but I will not eat with you. *Shak.*

In Æsop's time
When all things *talk'd*, and *talk'd* in rhyme. *B. Trumbull.*

I will come down and *talk* with thee. Num. xi.

Did not our heart burn within us, while he *talked* with us by the way? Luke xxiv.

2. To prate; to speak impertinently. *Milton.*

3. *To talk of*, to relate; to tell; to give account. Authors *talk of* the wonderful remains of Palmyra.

The natural histories of Switzerland *talk* much *of* the fall of these rocks, and the great damage done. *Addison.*

So shall I *talk of* thy wondrous works. Ps. cxix.

4. To speak; to reason; to confer.

Let me *talk* with thee of thy judgments. Jer. xii.

To talk to, in *familiar language*, to advise or exhort; or to reprove gently. I will *talk to* my son respecting his conduct.

TALK, *n.* *tauk.* Familiar converse; mutual discourse; that which is uttered by one person in familiar conversation, or the mutual converse of two or more.

Should a man full of *talk* be justified? Job xi.
In various *talk* th' instructive hours they past. *Pope.*

2. Report; rumor.

I hear a *talk* up and down of raising money. *Locke.*

3. Subject of discourse. This noble achievment is the *talk* of the whole town.

4. Among *the Indians of North America*, a public conference, as respecting peace or war, negotiation and the like; or an official verbal communication made from them to another nation or its agents, or made to them by the same.

TALK, a mineral. [See *Talck.*]

TALKATIVE, *a.* *tauk'ativ.* Given to much talking; full of prate; loquacious; garrulous. One of the faults of old age is to be *talkative.*

TALKATIVENESS, *n.* *tauk'ativness.* Loquacity; garrulity; the practice or habit of speaking much in conversation. *Swift.*

TALKER, *n.* *tauk'er.* One who talks; also, a loquacious person, male or female; a prattler. *Shak.*

2. A boaster. *Taylor.*

TALKING, *ppr.* *tauk'ing.* Conversing; speaking in familiar conversation. Matt. xvii.

2. *a.* Given to talking; loquacious; as *talking age.* *Goldsmith.*

TALKING, *n.* *tauk'ing.* The act of conversing familiarly; as foolish *talking.* Eph. v.

TALL, *a.* [W. *tal*; *talâu*, to grow *tall*. The primary sense is to stretch or extend; W. *tellu*, to stretch; Sp. *talla*, raised work, also stature; *talle*, shape, size; *tallo*, a shoot or sprout; *talludo*, tall, slender; *talon*, the heel, that is, a shoot; Port. *talo*, a stalk; *taludo*, stalky; Ar. طال taula, to be long, to spread, to be extended, to defer or delay, that is, to draw out in time, Eng. *dally*, Class Dl. No. 20.; allied probably to L. *tollo*, Gr. τελλω. In Sw. *tall* is a pine-tree.]

1. High in stature; long and comparatively slender; applied to a person, or to a standing tree, mast or pole. *Tall* always refers to something erect, and of which the diameter is small in proportion to the highth. We say, a *tall* man or woman, a *tall* boy for his age; a *tall* tree, a *tall* pole, a *tall* mast; but we never say, a *tall* house or a *tall* mountain. The application of the word to a palace or its shadow, in Waller, is now improper.

Dark shadows cast, and as his palace *tall*. *Waller.*

2. Sturdy; lusty; bold. [*Unusual.*] *Shak.*

TAL'LAĠE, TAL'LIAĠE, *n.* [Fr. *tailler*, to cut of. See *Tail.*]

Anciently, a certain rate or tax paid by barons, knights and inferior tenants, towards the public expenses. When it was paid out of knight's fees, it was called *scutage*; when by cities and burghs, *talliage*; when upon lands not held by military tenure, *hidage*. *Blackstone.*

TAL'LAĠE, *v. t.* To lay an impost. *Bp. Ellis.*

TALL'NESS, *n.* Highth of stature. [See *Tall.*]

TAL'LŌW, *n.* [Dan. *tælg*; D. *talk*; G. Sw. *talg*; Eth. ጠለለ to be fat; Ar. طلّ talla, to be moist. Class Dl. No. 21.]

A sort of animal fat, particularly that which is obtained from animals of the sheep and ox kinds. We speak of the *tallow* of an ox or cow, or of sheep. This substance grows chiefly about the kidneys and on the intestines. The fat of swine we never call *tallow*, but *lard* or *suet*. I see in English books, mention is made of the tallow of hogs, [See *Cyclopedia*, article *Tallow*;] but in America I never heard the word thus applied. It may be applied to the fat of goats and deer. The fat of bears we call bear's grease. Tallow is applied to various uses, but chiefly to the manufacture of candles.

TAL'LŌW, *v. t.* To grease or smear with tallow.

2. To fatten; to cause to have a large quantity of tallow; as, to *tallow* sheep. *Farmers.*

TAL'LŌW-CANDLE, *n.* A candle made of tallow.

TAL'LŌW-CH'ANDLER, *n.* [*chandler* is generally supposed to be from the Fr. *chandelier*, and the word to signify *tallow-candler*, a maker of candles; for in Fr. *chandelier* is a tallow-chandler. See *Corn-chandler.*]

One whose occupation is to make, or to make and sell tallow candles.

TAL'LŌWED, *pp.* Greased or smeared with tallow.

2. Made fat; filled with tallow.

TAL'LŌWER, *n.* An animal disposed to form tallow internally. *Cyc.*

TAL'LŌW-FACED, *a.* Having a sickly complexion; pale. *Burton.*

TAL'LŌWING, *ppr.* Greasing with tallow.

2. Causing to gather tallow; *a term in agriculture.*

TAL'LŌWING, *n.* The act, practice or art of causing animals to gather tallow; or the property in animals of forming tallow internally; *a term in agriculture.* *Cyc.*

TAL'LŌWISH, *a.* Having the properties or nature of tallow.

TAL'LŌWY, *a.* Greasy; having the qualities of tallow.

TAL'LY, *n.* [Fr. *tailler*, Port. *talhar*, Sp. *tallar*, to cut. See *Tail.*]

1. A piece of wood on which notches or scores are cut, as the marks of number. In purchasing and selling, it is customary for traders to have two sticks, or one stick cleft into two parts, and to mark with a score or notch on each, the number or quantity of goods delivered; the seller keeping one stick, and the purchaser the other. Before the use of writing, this or something like it was the only method of keeping accounts, and *tallies* are received as evidence in courts of justice. In the English exchequer are *tallies* of loans, one part being kept in the exchequer, the other being given to the creditor in lieu of an obligation for money lent to government. *Cyc.*

2. One thing made to suit another.

They were framed the *tallies* for each other. *Dryden.*

TAL'LY, *v. t.* To score with correspondent notches; to fit; to suit; to make to correspond.

They are not so well *tallied* to the present juncture. *Pope.*

2. In *seamanship*, to pull aft the sheets or lower corners of the main and fore-sail.

TAL'LY, *v. i.* To be fitted; to suit; to correspond.

I found pieces of tiles that exactly *tallied* with the channel. *Addison.*

TALL'Y, *adv.* Stoutly; with spirit. *Obs.* *Beaum.*

TAL'LYING, *ppr.* Fitting to each other; making to correspond.

2. Agreeing; corresponding.

3. Hauling aft the corners of the main and fore-sail. *Mar. Dict.*

TAL'LYMAN, *n.* [*tally* and *man.*] One who sells for weekly payment. *Dict.*

2. One who keeps the tally, or marks the sticks.

TAL'MUD, *n.* [Ch. from למד lamad, to teach.]

The body of the Hebrew laws, traditions and explanations; or the book that contains them. The Talmud contains the laws, and a compilation of expositions of duties imposed on the people, either in Scripture, by tradition, or by authority of their doctors, or by custom. It consists of two parts, the *Mischna*, and the *Gemara*; the former being the *written* law, the latter a collection of traditions and comments of Jewish doctors. *Encyc.*

TAL'MUDIC, TALMU'DICAL, *a.* Pertaining to the Talmud; contained in the Talmud; as *Talmudic* fables. *Enfield.*

TAL'MUDIST, *n.* One versed in the Talmud.

TALMUDIST'IC, *a.* Pertaining to the Talmud; resembling the Talmud.

TAL'ON, *n.* [Fr. Sp. *talon*, the heel, that is, a shoot or protuberance. See *Tall.*]

1. The claw of a fowl. *Bacon.*

2. In *architecture*, a kind of molding, concave at the bottom, and convex at the top. When the concave part is at the top, it is called an inverted talon. It is usually called by workmen an ogee, or O G, and by authors an upright or inverted cymatium. *Cyc.*

TA'LUS, *n.* [L. *talus*, the ankle.] In *anatomy*, the astragalus, or that bone of the foot which is articulated to the leg.

2. In *architecture*, a slope; the inclination of any work.

3. In *fortification*, the slope of a work, as a bastion, rampart or parapet. *Cyc.*

TA'MABLE, *a.* [from *tame.*] That may be tamed; capable of being reclaimed from wildness or savage ferociousness; that may be subdued.

TA'MABLENESS, *n.* The quality of being tamable.

TAM'ARIN, *n.* A small monkey of South America, with large ears; the great eared monkey, *(Simia midas.)* *Cyc.*

TAM'ARIND, *n.* [Sp. *tamarindo*; Port. plu. *tamarindos*; It. *tamarino*, *tamarindi*; Fr. *tamarin*; said to be a compound of תמר the palm tree, and *indus* or *ind*, the root of *India.*]

A tree, a native of the East Indies, and of Arabia and Egypt. It is cultivated in both the Indies for the sake of its shade and for its cooling, grateful acid fruit, the pulp of which, mixed with boiled sugar, is imported into northern countries. The stem of the tree is lofty, large, and crowned with wide spreading branches; the flowers are in simple clusters, terminating the short lateral branches. *Cyc.*

TAM'ARINDS, *n. plu.* The preserved seed-pods of the tamarind, which abound with an acid pulp. *Cyc.*

TAM'ARISK, *n.* A tree or shrub of the genus Tamarix, of several species. *Cyc.*

TAM'BAC, *n.* A mixture of gold and copper, which the people value more highly than gold itself. *Cyc.*

TAM'BOR, *n.* [Sp. Port. *tambor*, a drum; It. *tamburo*. The *m* is probably casual. See *Tabor.*]

1. A small drum, used by the Biscayans as an accompaniment to the flageolet. *Cyc.*

2. In *architecture*, a term applied to the Corinthian and Composite capitals, which bear some resemblance to a drum. It is also called the vase, and campana, or the bell.

3. A little box of timber work covered with a ceiling, within the porches of certain churches.

4. A round course of stones, several of which form the shaft of a pillar, not so high as a diameter.

5. In *the arts*, a species of embroidery, wrought on a kind of cushion or spherical body, which is properly the *tambor*,

and so named from its resemblance to a drum.

TAM'BOR, *v. t.* To embroider with a tambor.

TAM'BORIN, *n.* [Fr. *tambourin*, from *tambour*, tabor; Sp. *tamboril*. See *Tabor*.]

1. A small drum.

2. A lively French dance, formerly in vogue in operas. *Cyc.*

TAME, *a.* [Sax. Dan. D. *tam*; Sw. *tam*, *tamd*; G. *zahm*. See the Verb.]

1. That has lost its native wildness and shyness; mild; accustomed to man; domestic; as a *tame* deer; a *tame* bird.

2. Crushed; subdued; depressed; spiritless.

And you, *tame* slaves of the laborious plow. *Roscommon.*

3. Spiritless; unanimated; as a *tame* poem. [*Not elegant nor in use.*]

TAME, *v. t.* [Sax. *tamian*, *getemian*; Goth. *ga-tamyan*; Dan. *tæmmer*; Sw. *tämia*; D. *tammen*; G. *zahmen*; L. *domo*; Gr. δαμαω; Fr. *dompter*; Sp. Port. *domar*; It. *domare*; Ch. Heb. דום to be silent, dumb; or Ar. كظم to restrain, to stop, shut, silence, subdue, tame. See Class Dm. No. 3. 25. and No. 23. 24.]

1. To reclaim; to reduce from a wild to a domestic state; to make gentle and familiar; as, to *tame* a wild beast.

2. To civilize; as, to *tame* the ferocious inhabitants of the forest.

3. To subdue; to conquer; to depress; as, to *tame* the pride or passions of youth.

4. To subdue; to repress; as wildness or licentiousness.

The tongue can no man *tame*. James iii.

TA'MED, *pp.* Reclaimed from wildness; domesticated; made gentle; subdued.

TA'MELESS, *a.* Wild; untamed; untamable. [*Not much used.*] *Hall.*

TA'MELY, *adv.* With unresisting submission; meanly; servilely; without manifesting spirit; as, to submit *tamely* to oppression; to bear reproach *tamely*.

TA'MENESS, *n.* The quality of being tame or gentle; a state of domestication.

2. Unresisting submission; meanness in bearing insults or injuries; want of spirit. *Rogers.*

TA'MER, *n.* One that tames or subdues; one that reclaims from wildness. *Pope.*

TA'MING, *ppr.* Reclaiming from a wild state; civilizing; subduing.

TAM'INY, } *n.* A woolen stuff. *Johnson.*
TAM'MY, }

TAM'KIN, *n.* A stopper. [See *Tampion*.]

TAM'PER, *v. i.* To meddle; to be busy; to try little experiments; as, to *tamper* with a disease.

2. To meddle; to have to do with without fitness or necessity.

'Tis dangerous *tamp'ring* with a muse. *Roscommon.*

3. To deal; to practice secretly.

Others *tamper'd*
For Fleetwood, Desborough and Lambert. *Hudibras.*

TAM'PERING, *ppr.* Meddling; dealing; practicing secretly.

TAM'PERING, *n.* The act of meddling or practicing secretly.

TAMP'ING, *n.* [allied probably to *tame*, *dam*, *stem*, *stamp*, &c.] The matter that is driven into the hole bored into any thing for blasting. The powder being first put into the hole, and a tube for a conductor of the fire, the hole is rammed to fullness with brick-dust or other matter. This is called *tamping*.

TAM'PION, } *n.* [Fr. *tampon*; Arm. *tapon*.] The stopper of a cannon or other piece of ordnance, consisting of a cylinder of wood. *Mar. Dict.*
TOM'PION, }

TAM'POE, *n.* A fruit of the East Indies, somewhat resembling an apple. It is eaten by the natives, and called sometimes mangoustan, though a different fruit and less agreeable to the taste. *Cyc.*

TAM'TAM, *n.* A large flat drum used by the Hindoos.

TAN, *v. t.* [Fr. *tanner*, to tan; *tanne*, a little black spot on the face; It. *tane*, tawny color. Gregoire, in his Armoric dictionary, suggests that this may be from *tan* or *dan*, which in Leon signifies an oak. But this is very doubtful. In Ir. *tionus* signifies a *tan-house*, and *tionsonaim* is to drop or distill. *Spotting* is often from sprinkling, and *dyeing* from dipping. In Gaelic, *dean* is color. It seems to be allied to *tawny*, and perhaps to *dun*.]

1. In *the arts*, to convert animal skins into lether by steeping them in an infusion of oak or some other bark, by which they are impregnated with tannin, an astringent substance which exists in several species of bark, and thus rendered firm, durable, and in some degree, impervious to water.

2. To make brown; to imbrown by exposure to the rays of the sun; as, to *tan* the skin.

His face all *tann'd* with scorching sunny rays. *Spenser.*

TAN, *n.* The bark of the oak, &c. bruised and broken by a mill for tanning hides. It bears this name before and after it has been used. Tan, after being used in tanning, is used in gardening for making hotbeds; and it is also made into cakes and used as fuel.

TAN'-BED, *n.* [*tan* and *bed*.] In *gardening*, a bed made of tan; a bark bed.

TAN'-PIT, *n.* [*tan* and *pit*.] A bark pit; a vat in which hides are laid in tan.

TAN'-SPUD, *n.* [*tan* and *spud*.] An instrument for peeling the bark from oak and other trees. [*Local.*]

TAN'-STOVE, *n.* [*tan* and *stove*.] A hot house with a bark bed.

TAN'-VAT, *n.* [*tan* and *vat*.] A vat in which hides are steeped in liquor with tan.

TANG, *n.* [Gr. ταγγη, rancor; ταγγος, rancid; It *tanfo*.]

1. A strong taste; particularly, a taste of something extraneous to the thing itself; as, wine or cider has a *tang* of the cask. *Locke.*

2. Relish; taste. [*Not elegant.*]

3. Something that leaves a sting or pain behind.

She had a tongue with a *tang*. *Shak.*

4. Sound; tone. [*Not in use.*] *Holder.*

TANG, *v. i.* To ring with. [*Not in use.*] *Shak.*

[This may be allied to *ding*, *dong*.]

TAN'GENT, *n.* [Fr. *tangente*; L. *tangens*, touching. See *Touch*.] In *geometry*, a right line which touches a curve, but which when produced, does not cut it. In *trigonometry*, the tangent of an arc, is a right line touching the arc at one extremity, and terminated by a secant passing through the other extremity.

TANGIBIL'ITY, *n.* [from *tangible*.] The quality of being perceptible to the touch or sense of feeling.

TAN'GIBLE, *a.* [from L. *tango*, to touch.]

1. Perceptible by the touch; tactile.

2. That may be possessed or realized.

TAN'GLE, *v. t.* [This word, if *n* is casual, seems to be allied to the W. *tagu*, to choke, Goth. *taga*, hair; from crowding together. In Ar. دجا signifies to involve.]

1. To implicate; to unite or knit together confusedly; to interweave or interlock, as threads, so as to make it difficult to ravel the knot.

2. To ensnare; to entrap; as, to be *tangled* in the folds of dire necessity. *Milton.*

Tangled in amorous nets. *Milton.*

3. To embroil; to embarrass.

When my simple weakness strays,
Tangled in forbidden ways. *Crashaw.*

[*Entangle*, the compound, is the more elegant word.]

TAN'GLE, *v. i.* To be entangled or united confusedly.

TAN'GLE, *n.* A knot of threads or other things united confusedly, or so interwoven as not to be easily disengaged; as hair or yarn in *tangles*. *Milton.*

2. A kind of sea weed.

TAN'IST, *n.* [Gaelic, *tanaiste*, a lord, the governor of a country; in Ireland, the heir apparent of a prince; probably from *tan*, a region or territory, or from the Gr. δυναςης, a lord, which is from δυναμαι, to be powerful or able, the root of the Gaelic *duine*, a man. But both may be of one family, the root *tan*, *ten*, Gr. τεινω, L. *teneo*, W. *tannu*, to stretch, strain or hold.]

Among the descendants of the Celts in Ireland, a lord, or the proprietor of a tract of land; a governor or captain. This office or rank was elective, and often obtained by purchase or bribery. *Davies.*

TAN'ISTRY, *n.* [Gaelic, *tanaisteachd*.] In Ireland, a tenure of lands by which the proprietor had only a life estate, and to this he was admitted by election. The primitive intention seems to have been that the inheritance should descend to the oldest or most worthy of the blood and name of the deceased. This was in reality giving it to the strongest, and the practice often occasioned bloody wars in families. *Davies. Cyc.*

TANK, *n.* [Fr. *etang*, a pond; Sp. *estanque*; Port. *tanque*; Sans. *tanghi*; Japan, *tange*. This seems to be from the root of *stanch*, to stop, to hold.]

A large bason or cistern; a reservoir of water. *Dryden.*

TANK'ARD, *n.* [Ir. *tancaird*; Gaelic, *tancard*; *tank* and *ard*.] A large vessel for liquors, or a drinking vessel, with a cover.

Marius was the first who drank out of a silver *tankard*, after the manner of Bacchus. *Arbuthnot.*

TANK'ARD-TURNEP, *n.* A sort of turnep that stands high above the ground. *Cyc.*

TAN'LING, *n.* One tanned or scorched by the heat of the sun.

TAN'NED, *pp.* [from *tan.*] Converted into lether. [See *Tan.*]

2. Darkened by the rays of the sun.

TAN'NER, *n.* One whose occupation is to tan hides, or convert them into lether by the use of tan.

TAN'NERY, *n.* The house and apparatus for tanning.

TAN'NIERS, *n.* A variety of the *arum esculentum*, an esculent root. *Mease.*

TAN'NIN, *n.* The chimical name of that astringent substance contained in vegetables, particularly in the bark of the oak and chesnut, and in gall-nuts; the substance used to change raw hides into lether.

TAN'NING, *ppr.* Converting raw hides into lether.

TAN'NING, *n.* The practice, operation and art of converting the raw hides of animals into lether by the use of tan.

TAN'REC, *n.* A quadruped of the Indies, larger than a rat. Qu.

TAN'SY, *n.* *s* as *z.* [Fr. *tanaisie*; It. Sp. *tanaceto*; L. *tanacetum.* Qu. Gr. *αθανασια*, immortality. This is doubtful and rather improbable.]

A plant of the genus Tanacetum, of many species. It is extremely bitter to the taste, and used for medicinal and culinary purposes. *Cyc.*

TANT, *n.* A small spider with two eyes and eight long legs, and of an elegant scarlet color. *Cyc.*

TAN'TALISM, *n.* [See *Tantalize.*] The punishment of Tantalus; a teasing or tormenting by the hope or near approach of good which is not attainable.

Is not such a provision like *tantalism* to this people? *J. Quincy.*

TAN'TALITE, *n.* The ore of tantalum or columbium, a newly discovered metal. It is of an iron black color, sometimes with a tinge of blue. It is imbedded in angular pieces, from the size of a pea to that of a hazel-nut. *Cyc.*

TANTALIZA'TION, *n.* The act of tantalizing.

TAN'TALIZE, *v. t.* [from *Tantalus*, in fable, who was condemned for his crimes to perpetual hunger and thirst, with food and water near him which he could not reach.]

To tease or torment by presenting some good to the view and exciting desire, but continually frustrating the expectations by keeping that good out of reach; to tease; to torment.

Thy vain desires, at strife
Within themselves, have *tantaliz'd* thy life. *Dryden.*

TAN'TALIZED, *pp.* Teased or tormented by the disappointment of the hope of good.

TAN'TALIZER, *n.* One that tantalizes.

TAN'TALIZING, *ppr.* Teasing or tormenting by presenting to the view some unattainable good.

TAN'TALUM, *n.* Columbium, the metal obtained from tantalite, newly discovered. *Thomson. Cyc.*

TANT'AMOUNT, *a.* [L. *tantus*, so much, and *amount.*]

Equal; equivalent in value or signification; as a sum *tantamount* to all our expenses. Silence is sometimes *tantamount* to consent.

TAN'TIVY, *adv.* [said to be from the note of a hunting horn; L. *tanta vi.*] To ride *tantivy*, is to ride with great speed. *Johnson.*

TANT'LING, *n.* [See *Tantalize.*] One seized with the hope of pleasure unattainable. *Shak.*

TAP, *v. t.* [Fr. *taper*; Arm. *tapa*, *tapein*; Dan. *tapper*, to throb; Gr. *τυπτω*, *τυπος*. See Class Db. No. 28.]

To strike with something small, or to strike a very gentle blow; to touch gently; as, to *tap* one with the hand; to *tap* one on the shoulder with a cane.

TAP, *v. i.* To strike a gentle blow. He *tapped* at the door.

TAP, *v. t.* [Sax. *tæppan*; Sw. *tappa*; Dan. *tapper*; D. *tappen*; G. *zapfen.*]

1. To pierce or broach a cask, and insert a tap.

2. To open a cask and draw liquor. *Addison.*

3. To pierce for letting out a fluid; as, to *tap* a tumor; to *tap* a dropsical person. *Sharp.*

4. To box, or bore into; as, to *tap* a maple tree to obtain the sap for making sugar. *Mease.*

TAP, *n.* A gentle blow; a slight blow with a small thing.

She gives her right hand woman a *tap* on the shoulder. *Addison.*

2. A spile or pipe for drawing liquor from a cask. [But in Sp. *tapar* is to stop, and a *tap* may be a stopper. In this case, the verb to *tap*, should follow the noun.]

TAPE, *n.* [Sax. *tæppe.*] A narrow fillet or band; a narrow piece of woven work, used for strings and the like; as curtains tied with *tape.* *Pope.*

TA'PER, *n.* [Sax. *taper*, *tapur.* Qu. It. *doppiere*, a torch, W. *tampyr.*]

A small wax candle; a small lighted wax candle, or a small light.

Get me a *taper* in my study, Lucius. *Shak.*

TA'PER, *a.* [supposed to be from the form of a taper.]

Regularly narrowed towards the point; becoming small towards one end; conical; pyramidical; as *taper* fingers. *Dryden.*

TA'PER, *v. i.* To diminish or become gradually smaller towards one end; as, a sugar loaf *tapers* towards a point.

TA'PER, *v. t.* To make gradually smaller in diameter.

TA'PERING, *ppr.* Making gradually smaller.

2. *a.* Becoming regularly smaller in diameter towards one end; gradually diminishing towards a point.

TA'PERNESS, *n.* The state of being taper.

TAP'ESTRY, *n.* [Fr. *tapis*, a carpet; *tapisserie*, hangings, tapestry; L. *tapes*, tapestry; Fr. *se tapir*, to crouch, to lie flat; Sp. *tapiz*, tapestry, and a grass-plot; It. *tappelo*, a carpet; *tappezzeria*, tapestry; Arm. *tapiçz*, a carpet; *tapiçziry*, tapestry. Qu. from weaving or spreading.]

A kind of woven hangings of wool and silk, often enriched with gold and silver, representing figures of men, animals, landscapes, &c. *Cyc.*

TA'PET, *n.* [supra.] Worked or figured stuff. *Spenser.*

TAPETI, *n.* An American animal of the hare kind. *Dict. Nat. Hist.*

TA'PE-WŎRM, *n.* [*tape* and *worm.*] A worm bred in the human intestines or bowels. The body is jointed, and each joint has its mouth.

TAP'-HOUSE, *n.* [*tap* and *house.*] A house where liquors are retailed.

TA'PIR, *n.* A quadruped of S. America, about 6 feet long and 3½ high, resembling a hog in shape, with a short movable proboscis. It frequents the water, like the hippopotamus. *Ed. Encyc.*

TA'PIS, *n.* [Fr.] Tapestry. Upon the *tapis*, under consideration, or on the table.

TAP'PED, *pp.* Broached; opened.

TAP'PING, *ppr.* Broaching; opening for the discharge of a fluid.

TAP'-ROOT, *n.* [*tap* and *root.*] The main root of a plant, which penetrates the earth directly downwards to a considerable depth. *Cyc. Mortimer.*

TAP'STER, *n.* One whose business is to draw ale or other liquor. *Swift.*

T'AR, *n.* [Sax. *tare*, *tyr*, *tyrwa*; D. *teer*; G. *theer*; Sw. *tiara*; Dan. *tiere*; Gaelic, *tearr.* In D. *teeren* signifies to smear with tar or pitch, and to pine, waste, consume, digest, prey, subsist, feast, and *teer* is tender, as well as tar. The D. *teeren*, is the G. *zehren*, Dan. *tærer*, Sw. *tåra*, to fret, gnaw, consume; Eng. *tare*, in commerce. *Tar* then is from flowing, or from wasting, perhaps in combustion.]

1. A thick resinous substance of a dark brown or black color, obtained from pine and fir trees, by burning the wood with a close smothering heat. *Encyc. Cyc.*

Tar inspissated is called pitch, and is much used in ships and cordage. *Cyc.*

2. A sailor; so called from his tarred clothes.

T'AR, *v. t.* To smear with tar; as, to *tar* ropes.

2. [Sax. *tiran*, *tyrian.*] To tease; to provoke. [*Not in use.*] *Shak.*

TARA'BE, *n.* A large parrot with a red head. *Cyc.*

TARAN'TULA, *n.* [It. *tarantella.*] A species of spider, the *Aranea tarantula*, so called, it is said, from Tarentum in Apulia, where this animal is mostly found; a venomous insect, whose bite gives name to a new disease, called *tarantismus.* This is said to be cured by music.

TARAN'TULATE, *v. t.* To excite or govern emotions by music.

TAR'AQUIRA, *n.* A species of American lizard. *Cyc.*

TARDA'TION, *n.* [L. *tardo.* See *Tardy.*] The act of retarding or delaying. [*Not used.* We use for this, *retardation.*]

T'ARDIGRADE, T'ARDIGRADOUS, } *a.* [L. *tardigradus*; *tardus*, slow, and *gradus*, step.]

Slow-paced; moving or stepping slowly. *Brown.*

T'ARDIGRADE, *n.* The tardigrades are a genus of edentate quadrupeds, including the genus Bradypus or sloth.

T'ARDILY, *adv.* [from *tardy.*] Slowly; with slow pace or motion. *Shak.*

T'ARDINESS, *n.* [from *tardy.*] Slowness, or the slowness of motion or pace.
2. Unwillingness; reluctance manifested by slowness.
3. Lateness; as the *tardiness* of witnesses or jurors in attendance; the *tardiness* of students in attending prayers or recitation.

T'ARDITY, *n.* [L. *tarditas.*] Slowness; tardiness. [*Not used.*]

T'ARDY, *a.* [Fr. *tardif;* Sp. It. *tardo*, from L. *tardus;* from W. *tariaw*, to strike against, to stop, to stay, to *tarry*, whence *target; tar*, a shock; *taran*, that gives a shock, a clap of thunder; *taranu*, to thunder. We see the word is a derivative from a root signifying to strike, to clash, to dash against, hence to retard or stop.]
1. Slow; with a slow pace or motion.

And check the *tardy* flight of time. *Sandys.*

2. Late; dilatory; not being in season.

The *tardy* plants in our cold orchards plac'd. *Waller.*

You may freely censure him for being *tardy* in his payments. *Arbuthnot.*

3. Slow; implying reluctance.

Tardy to vengeance, and with mercy brave. *Prior.*

4. Unwary. [*Not in use.*] *Hudibras.*
5. Criminal. [*Not in use.*] *Collier.*

T'ARDY, *v. i.* [Fr. *tarder.*] To delay. [*Not in use.*]

T'ARDY-GAITED, *a.* [*tardy* and *gait.*] Slow-paced; having a slow step or pace.

The mellow horn
Chides the *tardy-gaited* morn. *Clifton.*

TARE, *n.* [I know not the origin of this word. See the next word.]
1. A weed that grows among corn. *Locke.*

Declare to us the parable of the *tares* of the field. Matt. xiii.

2. In *agriculture*, a plant of the vetch kind, of which there are two sorts, the purple flowered spring or summer tare, and the purple-flowered wild or winter tare. It is much cultivated in England for fodder. *Cyc.*

TARE, *n.* [Fr. *id.;* It. Sp. *tara;* D. *tarra;* It. *tarare*, to abate; Dan. *tærer*, to waste, Sw. *tåra*, D. *teeren*, G. *zehren.*]
In *commerce*, deficiency in the weight or quantity of goods by reason of the weight of the cask, bag or other thing containing the commodity, and which is weighed with it; hence, the allowance or abatement of a certain weight or quantity from the weight or quantity of a commodity sold in a cask, chest, bag or the like, which the seller makes to the buyer on account of the weight of such cask, chest or bag; or the abatement may be on the price of the commodity sold. When the tare is deducted, the remainder is called the *net* or *neat* weight.

TARE, *v. t.* To ascertain or mark the amount of tare. *Laws of Penn.*

TARE, *old pret.* of *tear.* We now use *tore.*

TA'RED, *pp.* Having the tare ascertained and marked.

T'ARGE, for *target*, is obsolete. *Spenser.*

T'ARGET, *n.* [Sax. *targ, targa;* Fr. *targe;* It. *targa;* W. *targed*, from *taraw*, to strike, whence *tariad*, a striking against or collision, a stopping, a staying, a *tarrying; tariaw*, to strike against, to stop, to *tarry.* We see that *target* is that which stops; hence a defense; and from the root of *tarry* and *tardy.*]
1. A shield or buckler of a small kind, used as a defensive weapon in war.
2. A mark for the artillery to fire at in their practice.

T'ARGETED, *a.* Furnished or armed with a target. *Gauden.*

T'ARGETEE'R, *n.* One armed with a target. *Chapman.*

T'ARGUM, *n.* [Ch. תרגום targum, interpretation.]
A translation or paraphrase of the sacred Scriptures in the Chaldee language or dialect. Of these the *Targum* of Jonathan, and that of Onkelos, are held in most esteem by the Jews.

T'ARGUMIST, *n.* The writer of a Targum. *Parkhurst.*

TAR'IF, *n.* [Fr. *tarif;* It. *tariffa;* Sp. *tarifa*, a book of prices or rates.]
1. Properly, a list or table of goods with the duties or customs to be paid for the same, either on importation or exportation, whether such duties are imposed by the government of a country, or agreed on by the princes or governments of two countries holding commerce with each other.
2. A list or table of duties or customs to be paid on goods imported or exported.

TAR'IF, *v. t.* To make a list of duties on goods.

TAR'IN, *n.* A bird of the genus Fringilla, kept in cages for its beauty and fine notes; the citrinella. *Cyc.*

TA'RING, *ppr.* Ascertaining or marking the amount of tare.

T'ARN, *n.* [Ice. *tiorn.*] A bog; a marsh; a fen.

T'ARNISH, *v. t.* [Fr. *ternir, ternissant.*]
1. To sully; to soil by an alteration induced by the air, or by dust and the like; to diminish or destroy luster; as, to *tarnish* a metal; to *tarnish* gilding; to *tarnish* the brightness or beauty of color.
2. To diminish or destroy the purity of; as, to *tarnish* reputation or honor.

T'ARNISH, *v. i.* To lose luster; to become dull; as, polished substances or gilding will *tarnish* in the course of time. Metals *tarnish* by oxydation.

T'ARNISHED, *pp.* Sullied; having lost its brightness by oxydation, or by some alteration induced by exposure to air, dust and the like.

Gold and silver, when *tarnished*, resume their brightness by setting them over certain lyes. Copper and pewter, &c. *tarnished*, recover their luster with tripoli and potashes. *Cyc.*

T'ARNISHING, *ppr.* Sullying; losing brightness.

TARPAU'LIN, *n.* [from *tar.*] A piece of canvas well daubed with tar, and used to cover the hatchways of a ship to prevent rain or water from entering the hold.
2. A sailor; *in contempt.* *Dennis.*

TAR'RACE, TAR'RASS, TER'RASS, TRASS, *n.* A volcanic earth, resembling puzzolana, used as a cement; or a coarse sort of plaster or mortar, durable in water, and used to line cisterns and other reservoirs of water. The Dutch tarrass is made of a soft rock stone found near Collen, on the lower part of the Rhine. It is burnt like lime, and reduced to powder in mills. It is of a grayish color. *Cyc.*

TAR'RAGON, *n.* A plant of the genus Artemisia, *(A. dracunculus,)* celebrated for perfuming vinegar in France. *Ed. Encyc. Mease.*

T'ARRED, *pp.* Smeared with tar.

TAR'RIANCE, *n.* [from *tarry.*] A tarrying; delay; lateness. [*Not in use.*]

TAR'RIER, *n.* A dog. [See *Terrier.*]
2. [from *tarry.*] One who tarries or delays.

T'ARRING, *ppr.* Smearing with tar. *Shak.*

TAR'ROCK, *n.* A sea fowl of the genus Larus or gull kind, the *L. tridactylus.* It is of the size of the common pigeon, and is remarkable for having no hind toe, but in lieu of it a small protuberance. *Cyc.*

TAR'RY, *v. i.* [W. *tariaw*, to strike against any thing, to stop, to stay, to tarry; Ir. Gaelic, *tairisim.* It is of the same family as *tardy* and *target.* The primary sense is to thrust or drive, hence to strike against, to stop; W. *tarw*, L. *taurus*, a bull, is from the same root.]
1. To stay; to abide; to continue; to lodge.

Tarry all night and wash your feet. Gen. xix.

2. To stay behind. Ex. xii.
3. To stay in expectation; to wait.

Tarry ye here for us, till we come again to you. Ex. xxiv.

4. To delay; to put off going or coming; to defer.

Come down to me, *tarry* not. Gen. xlv.

5. To remain; to stay.

He that telleth lies, shall not *tarry* in my sight. Ps. ci.

TAR'RY, *v. t.* To wait for.

I cannot *tarry* dinner. [*Not in use.*] *Shak.*

T'ARRY, *a.* [from *tar.*] Consisting of tar, or like tar. *More.*

TAR'RYING, *ppr.* Staying; delaying.

TAR'RYING, *n.* Delay. Ps. xl.
[*This word is in respectable use.*]

T'ARSEL, *n.* A kind of hawk. *Shak.*

T'ARSUS, *n.* [Gr. ταρσος; Fr. *tarse.*] That part of the foot to which the leg is articulated, the front of which is called the *instep.* *Cyc.*

T'ART, *a.* [Sax. *teart;* D. *taartig.* See the next word.]
1. Acid; sharp to the taste; acidulous; as a *tart* apple.
2. Sharp; keen; severe; as a *tart* reply; *tart* language; a *tart* rebuke.

T'ART, *n.* [D. *taart;* Sw. *tart;* Fr. *tarte;* It. *torta;* G. *torte;* Sp. *tarta.* The Italian and German orthography seem to connect this word with *torto*, L. *tortus*, twisted; and this may be the primary sense of *tart*, acid, sharp, and hence this noun, something acid or made of acid fruit. But qu.]
A species of pie or pastry, consisting of fruit baked on paste.

T'ARTAN, *n.* [Sp. It. *tartana.*] A small coasting vessel with one mast and a bowsprit, and the principal sail, which is very large, extended by a lateen-yard. *Mar. Dict.*

T'ARTAR, *n.* [Fr. *tartre;* Sp. *tartaro;* from *tart*, acid.]
1. An acid concrete salt, formed from wines completely fermented, and adhering to the sides of the casks in the form of a hard

crust. It is white or red, the white being most esteemed. In its crude state, it is much used as a flux in the assaying of ores. *Nicholson. Cyc.*

Tartar is a supertartrate of potash; that is, a compound of tartaric acid and potash, having the acid in excess. *D. Olmsted.*

2. A person of a keen irritable temper.

3. A native of Tartary; a corruption of *Tatar.*

T'ARTAR, *n.* [L. *Tartarus.*] Hell. [*Not in use.*] *Shak.*

TARTA'REAN, TARTA'REOUS, *a.* Hellish; pertaining to Tartarus. *Milton.*

TARTA'REOUS, *a.* Consisting of tartar; resembling tartar, or partaking of its properties. *Grew.*

TARTAR'IC, TARTA'REAN, *a.* Pertaining to Tartary, in Asia.

Tartaric acid, the acid of tartar.

T'ARTARIN, *n.* [from *tartar.*] Fixed vegetable alkali or potash.

T'ARTARINATED, *a.* Combined with tartarin.

T'ARTARIZE, *v. t.* To impregnate with tartar; to refine by means of the salt of tartar. *Cyc.*

T'ARTARIZED, *pp.* Impregnated with tartar; refined by tartar.

T'ARTARIZING, *ppr.* Impregnating with tartar; refining by means of the salt of tartar.

T'ARTAROUS, *a.* Containing tartar; consisting of tartar, or partaking of its qualities.

T'ARTARUM, *n.* A preparation of tartar, called petrified tartar. *Cyc.*

T'ARTISH, *a.* [from *tart.*] Somewhat tart.

T'ARTLY, *adv.* Sharply; with acidity.

2. Sharply; with poignancy; severely; as, to reply or rebuke *tartly.*

3. With sourness of aspect. *Shak.*

T'ARTNESS, *n.* Acidity; sharpness to the taste; as the *tartness* of wine or fruit.

2. Sharpness of language or manner; poignancy; keenness; severity; as the *tartness* of rebuke.

T'ARTRATE, T'ARTRITE, *n.* [from *tartar.*] A salt formed by the combination of tartarous or tartaric acid with a base; as *tartrite* of potash; *tartrite* of soda. *Cyc.*

T'ARTUFFISH, *a.* [Fr. *tartuffe*, a hypocrite.]

Precise; formal. [*Not in use.*] *Sterne.*

T'AR-WATER, *n.* [*tar* and *water.*] A cold infusion of tar, used as a medicine. *Cyc.*

T'ASK, *n.* [Fr. *tache*; W. *tasg*, a bond, a pledge, that which is settled or agreed to be done, a job, a *task*; Gaelic, Ir. *tasg*, task, and *tasgaire*, a slave; It. *tassa.* The sense is that which is *set* or fixed, from throwing or putting on.]

1. Business imposed by another, often a definite quantity or amount of labor. Each man has his *task.* When he has performed his *task*, his time is his own. Ex. v.

2. Business; employment.

His mental powers were equal to greater *tasks.* *Atterbury.*

3. Burdensome employment.

To take to task, to reprove; to reprimand; as, to *take* one *to task* for idleness. *Addison.*

T'ASK, *v. t.* [W. *tasgu*, to bind, to rate, to task, to spring, start, leap back, to urge.]

1. To impose a task; to assign to one a definite amount of business or labor.

2. To burden with some employment; to require to perform.

There *task* thy maids, and exercise the loom. *Dryden.*

T'ASKED, *pp.* Required to perform something.

T'ASKER, *n.* One that imposes a task.

T'ASKING, *ppr.* Imposing a task on; requiring to perform.

T'ASKMASTER, *n.* [*task* and *master.*] One who imposes a task, or burdens with labor. Sinful propensities and appetites are men's most unrelenting *taskmasters.* They condemn us to unceasing drudgery, and reward us with pain, remorse and poverty. Next to our sinful propensities, fashion is the most oppressive *taskmaster.*

2. One whose office is to assign tasks to others. Ex. i. iii.

TAS'SEL, *n.* [W. *tasel*, a sash, a bandage, a fringe, a tassel; *tasiaw*, to tie; *tas*, that binds or hems in; It. *tassello*, the collar of a cloke.]

1. A sort of pendant ornament, attached to the corners of cushions, to curtains and the like, ending in loose threads.

2. A small ribin of silk sowed to a book, to be put between the leaves. *Cyc.*

3. In *building*, tassels are the pieces of boards that lie under the mantle-tree.

4. A burr. [See *Teasel.*]

5. A male hawk; properly *terzol*, It. *terzuolo.*

TAS'SELED, *a.* Furnished or adorned with tassels; as the *tasseled* horn. *Milton.*

TAS'SES, *n. plu.* Armor for the thighs; appendages to the ancient corslet, consisting of skirts of iron that covered the thighs. They were fastened to the cuirass with hooks.

TASTABLE, *a.* [from *taste.*] That may be tasted; savory; relishing.

TĀSTE, *v. t.* [Fr. *tâter*, to feel; It. *tastare*; Norm. *taster*, to touch, to try; G. D. *tasten*; Dan. *tasser.* The Dutch has *toetsen*, to touch, to try, to *test*; Dan. *taster and*, to attack or assault. This shows that the primary sense is to thrust or drive; allied perhaps to *dash*; hence to strike, to touch, to bring one thing in contact with another.]

1. To perceive by means of the tongue; to have a certain sensation in consequence of something applied to the tongue, the organ of taste; as, to *taste* bread; to *taste* wine; to *taste* a sweet or an acid.

2. To try the relish of by the perception of the organs of taste.

3. To try by eating a little; or to eat a little.

Because I *tasted* a little of this honey. 1 Sam. xiv.

4. To essay first. *Dryden.*

5. To have pleasure from. *Carew.*

6. To experience; to feel; to undergo.

That he by the grace of God should *taste* death for every man. Heb. ii.

7. To relish intellectually; to enjoy.

Thou, Adam, wilt *taste* no pleasure. *Milton.*

8. To experience by shedding, as blood.

When Commodus had once *tasted* human blood, he became incapable of pity or remorse. *Gibbon.*

TĀSTE, *v. i.* To try by the mouth; to eat or drink; or to eat or drink a little only; as, to *taste* of each kind of wine.

2. To have a smack; to excite a particular sensation, by which the quality or flavor is distinguished; as, butter *tastes* of garlic; apples boiled in a brass-kettle, sometimes *taste* of brass.

3. To distinguish intellectually.

Scholars, when good sense describing,
Call it *tasting* and imbibing. *Swift.*

4. To try the relish of any thing. *Taste* of the fruits; *taste* for yourself.

5. To be tinctured; to have a particular quality or character.

Ev'ry idle, nice and wanton reason
Shall, to the king, *taste* of this action. *Shak.*

6. To experience; to have perception of.

The valiant never *taste* of death but once. *Shak.*

7. To take to be enjoyed.

Of nature's bounty men forbore to *taste.* *Waller.*

8. To enjoy sparingly.

For age but *tastes* of pleasures, youth devours. *Dryden.*

9. To have the experience or enjoyment of.

They who have *tasted* of the heavenly gift, and the good word of God. Heb. vi.

TĀSTE, *n.* The act of tasting; gustation. *Milton.*

2. A particular sensation excited in an animal by the application of a substance to the tongue, the proper organ; as the *taste* of an orange or an apple; a bitter *taste*; an acid *taste*; a sweet *taste.*

3. The sense by which we perceive the relish of a thing. This sense appears to reside in the tongue or its papillæ. Men have a great variety of *tastes.* In the influenza of 1790, the *taste*, for some days, was entirely extinguished.

4. Intellectual relish; as, he had no *taste* of true glory. *Addison.*

I have no *taste*
Of popular applause. *Dryden.*

[*Note.* In this use, the word is now followed by *for.* "He had no *taste for* glory." When followed by *of*, the sense is ambiguous, or rather it denotes experience, trial.]

5. Judgment; discernment; nice perception, or the power of perceiving and relishing excellence in human performances; the faculty of discerning beauty, order, congruity, proportion, symmetry, or whatever constitutes excellence, particularly in the fine arts and belles lettres. *Taste* is not wholly the gift of nature, nor wholly the effect of art. It depends much on culture. We say, a good *taste*, or a fine *taste.* *Gerard.*

6. Style; manner, with respect to what is pleasing; as a poem or music composed in good *taste.* *Cyc.*

7. Essay; trial; experiment. [*Not in use.*] *Shak.*

8. A small portion given as a specimen.

9. A bit; a little piece tasted or eaten.

TĀSTED, *pp.* Perceived by the organs of taste; experienced.

TĀSTEFUL, *a.* Having a high relish; savory; as *tasteful* herbs. *Pope.*

2. Having good taste.

TĀSTEFULLY, *adv.* With good taste.

TĀSTELESS, *a.* Having no taste; insipid; as *tasteless* fruit.

2. Having no power of giving pleasure; as *tasteless* amusements.
3. Having no power to perceive taste. [*Not used.*]
4. Having no intellectual gust. [*Little used.*]

TĀSTELESSNESS, *n.* Want of taste or relish; insipidness; as the *tastelessness* of fruit.
2. Want of perception of taste. [*Not in use.*]
3. Want of intellectual relish. [*Not in use.*]

TĀSTER, *n.* One who tastes.
2. One who first tastes food or liquor.

Thy tutor be thy *taster*, e'er thou eat. *Dryden.*

3. A dram cup. *Ainsworth.*

TĀSTILY, *adv.* With good taste.

TĀSTING, *ppr.* Perceiving by the tongue.
2. Trying; experiencing; enjoying or suffering.

TĀSTING, *n.* The act of perceiving by the tongue.
2. The sense by which we perceive or distinguish savors; or the perception of external objects through the instrumentality of the tongue or organs of taste.

TĀSTY, *a.* Having a good taste, or nice perception of excellence; *applied to persons;* as a *tasty* lady.
2. Being in conformity to the principles of good taste; elegant; as *tasty* furniture; a *tasty* dress.

TAT'TER, *v. t.* [Qu. Sax. *totæran;* compounded of *tæran*, to *tear*, and the prefix *to.*]
To rend or tear into rags. [*Not used except in the participle.*]

TAT'TER, *n.* A rag, or a part torn and hanging to the thing; chiefly used in the plural, *tatters.*

TATTERDEMA'LION, *n.* A ragged fellow. *L'Estrange.*

TAT'TERED, *pp.* or *a.* Rent; torn; hanging in rags; as a *tattered* garment.

Where wav'd the *tatter'd* ensigns of Rag-fair. *Pope.*

TAT'TLE, *v. i.* [D. *tateren;* It. *tattamellare.*]
1. To prate; to talk idly; to use many words with little meaning.

Excuse it by the *tattling* quality of age, which is always narrative. *Dryden.*

2. To tell tales; to communicate secrets; as a *tattling* girl.

TAT'TLE, *n.* Prate; idle talk or chat; trifling talk.

They told the *tattle* of the day. *Swift.*

TAT'TLER, *n.* One who tattles; an idle talker; one that tells tales.

TAT'TLING, *ppr.* Talking idly; telling tales.
2. *a.* Given to idle talk; apt to tell tales.

TATTOO', *n.* [If this word was originally *taptoo* or *tapto*, it is from the Fr. *tapoter*, to beat; *tapotez tous*, beat, all of you; from *taper*, Gr. τυπτω, Eng. *tap.*]
A beat of drum at night, giving notice to soldiers to retreat, or to repair to their quarters in garrison, or to their tents in camp. *Cyc.*

TATTOO', *v. t.* [In the South Sea isles.] To prick the skin, and stain the punctured spots with a black substance, forming lines and figures upon the body. In some isles, the inhabitants *tattoo* the face, in others only the body. The same practice exists among other rude nations. *Barrow. Makenzie.*

TATTOO', *n.* Figures on the body made by punctures and stains in lines and figures.

TATTOO'ED, *pp.* Marked by stained lines and figures on the body.

TATTOO'ING, *ppr.* Marking with various figures by stained lines.

TAU, *n.* The toad fish of Carolina, a species of Gadus, *(G. tau.)* *Cyc.*
2. A species of beetle; also, a species of moth, *(Phalena;)* also, a kind of fly, [*Musca.)* *Cyc.*

TAUGHT, *a.* taut. [from the root of *tight.*] Stretched; not slack. *Mar. Dict.*

TAUGHT, *pret.* and *pp.* of *teach.* pron. *taut.* [L. *doctus.*]
Experience *taught* him wisdom. He has been *taught* in the school of experience.

T'AUNT, *v. t.* [Qu. Fr. *tancer*, to rebuke or chide; W. *tantiaw*, to stretch; or Pers. تَوانِيدن to pierce with words.]
1. To reproach with severe or insulting words; to revile; to upbraid.

When I had at my pleasure *taunted* her— *Shak.*

2. To exprobrate; to censure.

Rail thou in Fulvia's phrase, and *taunt* my faults. *Shak.*

T'AUNT, *n.* Upbraiding words; bitter or sarcastic reproach; insulting invective.

With scoffs and scorns, and contumelious *taunts.* *Shak.*

With sacrilegious *taunt* and impious jest. *Prior.*

T'AUNTED, *pp.* Upbraided with sarcastic or severe words.

T'AUNTER, *n.* One who taunts, reproaches or upbraids with sarcastic or censorious reflections.

T'AUNTING, *ppr.* Treating with severe reflections; upbraiding.

T'AUNTINGLY, *adv.* With bitter and sarcastic words; insultingly; scoffingly.

TAUR'ICORNOUS, *a.* [L. *taurus*, a bull, and *cornu*, horn.]
Having horns like a bull. *Brown.*

TAUR'IFORM, *a.* [L. *taurus*, a bull, and *form.*]
Having the form of a bull. *Faber.*

TAUR'US, *n.* [L.; W. *tarw.*] The bull; one of the twelve signs of the zodiac, and the second in order, or that next to Aries. This constellation, according to the British catalogue, contains 141 stars. *Cyc.*

TAUTOLOG'IC, } *a.* [See *Tautology.*]
TAUTOLOG'ICAL, } Repeating the same thing; having the same signification; as a *tautological* expression or phrase.

Tautological echo, an echo that repeats the same sound or syllable many times.

TAUTOL'OGIST, *n.* One who uses different words or phrases in succession to express the same sense.

TAUTOL'OGIZE, *v. i.* To repeat the same thing in different words.

TAUTOL'OGY, *n.* [Gr. ταυτολογια; ταυτος, the same, and λογος, word or expression.]
A repetition of the same meaning in different words; needless repetition of a thing in different words or phrases; or a representation of any thing as the cause, condition or consequence of itself, as in the following lines. *Cyc.*

The dawn is overcast, the morning low'rs,
And heavily in clouds brings on the day. *Addison.*

TAV'ERN, *n.* [Fr. *taverne;* W. *tavarn;* L. *taberna; tab*, the root of *table*, a board, and Sax. *ærn*, place.]
A house licensed to sell liquors in small quantities, to be drank on the spot. In some of the United States, *tavern* is synonymous with *inn* or *hotel*, and denotes a house for the entertainment of travelers, as well as for the sale of liquors, licensed for that purpose.

TAV'ERNER, } *n.* One who keeps
TAV'ERN-KEEPER, } a tavern. In the United States, one who is licensed to sell liquors to be drank in his house, and to entertain travelers and lodgers, together with the horses or oxen composing their teams. *Taverners* are by law to be provided with suitable beds for their guests, and with fodder for horses and cattle. *Laws of Conn.*

TAV'ERN-H'AUNTER, *n.* [*tavern* and *haunt.*]
One who frequents taverns; one who spends his time and substance in tippling in taverns.

TAV'ERNING, *n.* A feasting at taverns. *Hall.*

TAV'ERN-MAN, *n.* [*tavern* and *man.*] The keeper of a tavern. [*Not in use.*]
2. A tippler.

TAW, *v. t.* [Sax. *tawian;* D. *touwen.* In Sax. *teagan* has the like signification. In Persic, تَاوِيدن is to scrape and curry hides.]
To dress white lether or alum lether; to dress and prepare skins in white, as the skins of sheep, lambs, goats and kids, for gloves and the like. *Cyc.*

TAW, *n.* A marble to be played with. *Swift.*

TAW'DRILY, *adv.* In a tawdry manner.

TAW'DRINESS, *n.* [from *tawdry.*] Tinsel in dress; excessive finery; ostentatious finery without elegance.

A clumsy person makes his ungracefulness more ungraceful by *tawdriness* of dress. *Richardson.*

TAW'DRY, *a.* Very fine and showy in colors without taste or elegance; having an excess of showy ornaments without grace; as a *tawdry* dress; *tawdry* fethers; *tawdry* colors.

He rails from morning to night at essenced fops and *tawdry* courtiers. *Spectator.*

TAW'DRY, *n.* A slight ornament. *Drayton.*

TAW'ED, *pp.* Dressed and made white, as lether.

TAW'ER, *n.* A dresser of white lether.

TAW'ING, *ppr.* Dressing, as white lether.

TAW'ING, *n.* The art and operation of preparing skins and forming them into white lether.

TAW'NY, *a.* [Fr. *tanné*, from *tanner*, to tan.]
Of a yellowish dark color, like things tanned, or persons who are sun-burnt; as a *tawny*

Moor or Spaniard; the *tawny* sons of Numidia; the *tawny* lion. *Addison. Milton.*

TAX, *n.* [Fr. *taxe;* Sp. *tasa;* It. *tassa;* from L. *taxo,* to tax. If from the Gr. ταξις, τασσω, the root was *tago,* the sense of which was to set, to thrust on. But this is doubtful. It may be allied to *task.*]

1. A rate or sum of money assessed on the person or property of a citizen by government, for the use of the nation or state. *Taxes,* in free governments, are usually laid upon the property of citizens according to their income, or the value of their estates. *Tax* is a term of general import, including almost every species of imposition on persons or property for supplying the public treasury, as tolls, tribute, subsidy, excise, impost, or customs. But more generally, *tax* is limited to the sum laid upon polls, lands, houses, horses, cattle, professions and occupations. So we speak of a land *tax,* a window *tax,* a *tax* on carriages, &c. Taxes are *annual* or *perpetual.*

2. A sum imposed on the persons and property of citizens to defray the expenses of a corporation, society, parish or company; as a city *tax,* a county *tax,* a parish *tax,* and the like. So a private association may lay a *tax* on its members for the use of the association.

3. That which is imposed; a burden. The attention that he gives to public business is a heavy *tax* on his time.

4. Charge; censure. *Clarendon.*

5. Task.

TAX, *v. t.* [L. *taxo;* Fr. *taxer;* It. *tassare.*]

1. To lay, impose or assess upon citizens a certain sum of money or amount of property, to be paid to the public treasury, or to the treasury of a corporation or company, to defray the expenses of the government or corporation, &c.

We are more heavily *taxed* by our idleness, pride and folly, than we are *taxed* by government. *Franklin.*

2. To load with a burden or burdens.

The narrator—never *taxes* our faith beyond the obvious bounds of probability. *J. Sparks.*

3. To assess, fix or determine judicially, as the amount of cost on actions in court; as, the court *taxes* bills of cost.

4. To charge; to censure; to accuse; usually followed by *with;* as, to *tax* a man *with* pride. He was *taxed with* presumption.

Men's virtues I have commended as freely as I have *taxed* their crimes. *Dryden.*

[To *tax of* a crime, is not in use, nor to *tax for.* Both are now improper.]

TAX'ABLE, *a.* That may be taxed; liable by law to the assessment of taxes; as *taxable* estate. By the laws of some states, polls are not *taxable* after the age of seventy.

2. That may be legally charged by a court against the plaintif or defendant in a suit; as *taxable* costs.

TAXA'TION, *n.* [Fr. from L. *taxatio.*] A taxing; the act of laying a tax, or of imposing taxes on the subjects of a state by government, or on the members of a corporation or company by the proper authority. *Taxation* is probably the most difficult subject of legislation.

2. Tax; sum imposed. [*Little used.*]

He daily such *taxations* did exact— *Daniel.*

3. Charge; accusation. [*Little used.*] *Shak.*

4. The act of taxing or assessing a bill of cost.

TAX'ED, *pp.* Rated; assessed; accused.

TAX'ER, *n.* One who taxes.

2. In Cambridge, two officers chosen yearly to see the true guage of weights and measures observed. *Cyc.*

TAX'IARCH, *n.* [Gr. ταξιαρχης; ταξις, order, and αρχος, chief.]

An Athenian military officer commanding a taxis or battalion. *Mitford.*

TAX'IDERMY, *n.* [Gr. ταξις, order, and δερμα, skin.]

The art of preparing and preserving specimens of animals.

TAX'ING, *ppr.* Imposing a tax; assessing, as a bill of cost; accusing.

TAX'ING, *n.* The act of laying a tax; taxation. Luke ii.

TAXON'OMY, *n.* [Gr. ταξις, order, and νομος, law.]

Classification; a term used by a French author to denote the classification of plants. *Decandolle, Theor. Elem. de la Botanique.*

TEA, *n.* [Chinese, *tcha* or *tha.* Grosier. Russ. *tshai;* Sp. *te;* It. *tè;* Fr. *thé.*]

1. The leaves of the tea-tree as dried and imported. There are several kinds of tea, as imperial tea, hyson and young hyson, called green teas; souchong and bohea, called black teas, &c.

2. A decoction or infusion of tea leaves in boiling water. *Tea* is a refreshing beverage.

3. Any infusion or decoction of vegetables; as sage *tea;* camomile *tea,* &c.

TE'A-BOARD, *n.* [*tea* and *board.*] A board to put tea furniture on.

TE'A-CANISTER, *n.* [*tea* and *canister.*] A canister or box in which tea is kept.

TE'A-CUP, *n.* [*tea* and *cup.*] A small cup in which tea is drank.

TE'A-DRINKER, *n.* [*tea* and *drinker.*] One who drinks much tea.

TE'A-PLANT, *n.* The tea-tree.

TE'A-POT, *n.* [*tea* and *pot.*] A vessel with a spout, in which tea is made, and from which it is poured into tea-cups.

TE'A-SAUCER, *n.* [*tea* and *saucer.*] A small saucer in which a tea-cup is set.

TE'A-SPOON, *n.* [*tea* and *spoon.*] A small spoon used in drinking tea and coffee.

TE'A-TABLE, *n.* [*tea* and *table.*] A table on which tea furniture is set, or at which tea is drank.

TE'A-TREE, *n.* [*tea* and *tree.*] The tree or plant that produces the leaves which are imported and called *tea.* The generic name given to it by Linne, is *thea.* It is a native of China, Japan and Tonquin, but has recently been introduced into S. America. *Encyc.*

TEACH, *v. t.* pret. and pp. *taught.* [Sax. *tæcan,* to *teach,* and to *take;* L. *doceo;* Ir. *deachtaim,* to teach, to dictate; Gaelic, *deachdam,* which seems to be the L. *dico, dicto,* and both these and the Gr. δειχω, to show, may be of one family; all implying sending, passing, communicating, or rather leading, drawing.]

1. To instruct; to inform; to communicate to another the knowledge of that of which he was before ignorant.

He will *teach* us of his ways, and we will walk in his paths. Is. ii.

Lord, *teach* us to pray, as John also *taught* his disciples. Luke xi.

2. To deliver any doctrine, art, principles or words for instruction. One sect of ancient philosophers *taught* the doctrines of stoicism, another those of epicureanism.

In vain they worship me, *teaching* for doctrines the commandments of men. Matt. xv.

3. To tell; to give intelligence. *Tusser.*

4. To instruct, or to practice the business of an instructor; to use or follow the employment of a preceptor; as, a man *teaches* school for a livelihood.

5. To show; to exhibit so as to impress on the mind.

If some men *teach* wicked things, it must be that others may practice them. *South.*

6. To accustom; to make familiar.

They have *taught* their tongue to speak lies. Jer. ix.

7. To inform or admonish; to give previous notice to.

For he *taught* his disciples, and said—Mark ix.

8. To suggest to the mind.

For the Holy Spirit shall *teach* you in that same hour what ye ought to say. Luke xii.

9. To signify or give notice.

He *teacheth* with his fingers. Prov. vi.

10. To counsel and direct. Hab. ii.

TEACH, *v. i.* To practice giving instruction; to perform the business of a preceptor.

The heads thereof judge for reward, and the priests thereof *teach* for hire. Mic. iii.

TEACH, *n.* [Ir. Gaelic, *teagham,* to heat.] In sugar works, the last boiler. *Edwards, W. Ind.*

TE'ACHABLE, *a.* That may be taught; apt to learn; also, readily receiving instruction; docile.

We ought to bring our minds free, unbiased and *teachable,* to learn our religion from the word of God. *Watts.*

TE'ACHABLENESS, *n.* The quality of being capable of receiving instruction; more generally, a willingness or readiness to be informed and instructed; docility; aptness to learn.

TE'ACHER, *n.* One who teaches or instructs.

2. An instructor; a preceptor; a tutor; one whose business or occupation is to instruct others.

3. One who instructs others in religion; a preacher; a minister of the gospel.

The *teachers* in all the churches assembled themselves. *Raleigh.*

4. One who preaches without regular ordination. *Swift.*

TE'ACHING, *ppr.* Instructing; informing.

TE'ACHING, *n.* The act or business of instructing.

2. Instruction.

TEAD, } *n.* [L. *tæda.*] A torch; a flambeau.
TEDE, } [*Not in use.*] *Spenser.*

TEAGUE, *n. teeg.* An Irishman; *in contempt.* *Johnson.*

TEAK, } *n.* A tree of the East Indies, which
TEEK, } furnishes an abundance of ship timber. The generic name given to it by Linne, is Tectona. *Cyc.*

TEAL, *n.* [D. *taling.*] An aquatic fowl of the genus Anas, the smallest of the duck kind. *Cyc.*

TEAM, *n.* [Sax. *team*, offspring, progeny, race of descendants, hence a suit or long series; *tyman*, to *teem*, to bear, to bring forth, also to call, to summon. The primary sense is to shoot out or extend.]

1. Two or more horses, oxen or other beasts harnessed together to the same vehicle for drawing, as to a coach, chariot, wagon, cart, sled, sleigh and the like. It has been a great question whether *teams* of horses or oxen are most advantageously employed in agriculture. In land free from stones and stumps and of easy tillage, it is generally agreed that horses are preferable for *teams*.

2. Any number passing in a line; a long line.

> Like a long *team* of snowy swans on high. *Dryden.*

[*This is the primary sense, but is rarely used.*]

TE'AMSTER, *n.* [*team* and *ster.*] One who drives a team.

TE'AM-WŎRK, *n.* [*team* and *work.*] Work done by a team, as distinguished from personal labor. *New England.*

TEAR, *n.* [Gaelic, *dear*, *deur*; Goth. *tagr*, contracted in Sax. *tear*; G. *zähre*; Sw. *tår*; Dan. *taare*; W. *daigyr*; Gr. δακρυ; from flowing or pouring forth; Ar. تاق tauka, to burst forth, as tears, or ودق wadaka, to drop or distil. See Class Dg. No. 16. 24. and 48. 63.]

1. Tears are the limpid fluid secreted by the lacrymal gland, and appearing in the eyes, or flowing from them. A *tear*, in the singular, is a drop or a small quantity of that fluid. Tears are excited by passions, particularly by grief. This fluid is also called forth by any injury done to the eye. It serves to moisten the cornea and preserve its transparency, and to remove any dust or fine substance that enters the eye and gives pain.

2. Something in the form of a transparent drop of fluid matter.

TEAR, *v. t.* pret. *tore*; pp. *torn*; old pret. *tare*, obs. [Sax. *tæran*, to tear; *tiran*, *tyran*, *tyrian*, *tyrigan*, to fret, gnaw, provoke; Russ. *deru*, to tear. In Sw. *tära* is to fret, consume, waste; Dan. *tærer*, id.; D. *teeren*, G. *zehren*, id. These are probably the same word varied in signification, and they coincide with L. *tero*, Gr. τειρω. In W. *tori*, Arm. *torri*, Corn. *terhi*, is to break; Ch. Syr. תרע, to tear, to rend. Class Dr. No. 42. 51.]

1. To separate by violence or pulling; to rend; to lacerate; as, to *tear* cloth; to *tear* a garment; to *tear* the skin or flesh. We use *tear* and *rip* in different senses. To *tear* is to rend or separate the *texture* of cloth; to *rip* is to open a *seam*, to separate parts sewed together.

2. To wound; to lacerate.

> The women beat their breasts, their cheeks they *tear*. *Shak.*

3. To rend; to break; to form fissures by any violence; as, torrents *tear* the ground. *Dryden.*

4. To divide by violent measures; to shatter; to rend; as a state or government *torn* by factions. *Locke.*

5. To pull with violence; as, to *tear* the hair. *Dryden.*

6. To remove by violence; to break up.

> Or on rough seas from their foundation *torn*. *Dryden.*

7. To make a violent rent.

> In the midst, a *tearing* groan did break
> The name of Antony. *Shak.*

To tear from, to separate and take away by force; as an isle *torn from* its possessor.

> The hand of fate
> Has *torn* thee *from* me. *Addison.*

To tear off, to pull off by violence; to strip.

To tear out, to pull or draw out by violence; as, to *tear out* the eyes.

To tear up, to rip up; to remove from a fixed state by violence; as, to *tear up* a floor; to *tear up* the foundations of government or order.

TEAR, *v. i.* To rave; to rage; to rant; to move and act with turbulent violence; as a mad bull. *L'Estrange.*

TEAR, *n.* A rent; a fissure. [*Little used.*]

TEARER, *n.* One who tears or rends any thing.

2. One that rages or raves with violence.

TE'AR-FALLING, *a.* [*tear* and *fall.*] Shedding tears; tender; as *tear-falling* pity. *Shak.*

TE'ARFUL, *a.* [*tear* and *full.*] Abounding with tears; weeping; shedding tears; as *tearful* eyes. *Shak.*

TEARING, *ppr.* [from *tear*, to rend.] Rending; pulling apart; lacerating; violent; raging.

TE'ARLESS, *a.* Shedding no tears; without tears; unfeeling. *Sandys.*

TEASE, *v. t.* *s* as *z*. [Sax. *tæsan*, to pull or tear.]

1. To comb or card, as wool or flax.

2. To scratch, as cloth in dressing, for the purpose of raising a nap.

3. To vex with importunity or impertinence; to harass, annoy, disturb or irritate by petty requests, or by jests and raillery. Parents are often *teased* by their children into unreasonable compliances.

> My friends *tease* me about him, because he has no estate. *Spectator.*

TE'ASED, *pp.* Carded.

2. Vexed; irritated or annoyed.

TE'ASEL, *n.* *tee'zl.* [Sax. *tæsl.*] A plant of the genus Dipsacus, one kind of which bears a large burr which is used for raising a nap on woolen cloth. Hence,

2. The burr of the plant.

TE'ASELER, *n.* One who uses the teasel for raising a nap on cloth. *Kelham.*

TE'ASER, *n.* One that teases or vexes.

TE'ASING, *ppr.* Combing; carding; scratching for the purpose of raising a nap; vexing with importunity.

TEAT, } *n.*
TIT, } [Sax. *tit*, *titt*, as it is usually pronounced to this day; G. *zitze*; D. *tet*; W. *têth*; Corn. *titi*; Ir. *did*; Basque, *titia*; Gaelic, *did*; Fr. *teton*, breast, It. *tetta*; Port. Sp. *teta*; Gr. τιτθος. It coincides with *tooth*, *teeth* in elements, and radical sense, which is a shoot.]

The projecting part of the female breast; the dug of a beast; the pap of a woman; the nipple. It consists of an elastic erectile substance, embracing the lactiferous ducts, which terminate on its surface, and thus serves to convey milk to the young of animals.

TEATHE, *n.* The soil or fertility left on lands by feeding them. [*Local.*]

TEATHE, *v. t.* To feed and enrich by live stock. [*Local.*]

TECH'ILY, *adv.* [from *techy*, so written for *touchy.*] Peevishly; fretfully; frowardly.

TECH'INESS, *n.* Peevishness; fretfulness. *Bp. Hall.*

TECH'NIC, } *a.*
TECH'NICAL, } [L. *technicus*; Gr. τεχνικος, from τεχνη, art, artifice, from τευχω, to fabricate, make or prepare. This word and τασσω have the same elements.]

1. Pertaining to art or the arts. A *technical* word is a word that belongs properly or exclusively to an art; as the verb to *smelt*, belongs to metallurgy. So we say, *technical* phrases, *technical* language. Every artificer has his *technical* terms.

2. Belonging to a particular profession; as, the words of an indictment must be *technical*. *Blackstone, Index.*

> It is of the utmost importance clearly to understand the *technical* terms used by the eastern theologians. *Prof. Lee.*

TECH'NICALLY, *adv.* In a technical manner; according to the signification of terms of art or the professions.

TECH'NICALNESS, } *n.*
TECHNICAL'ITY, } The quality or state of being technical or peculiar to the arts. *Forster.*

TECH'NICS, *n.* The doctrine of arts in general; such branches of learning as respect the arts.

TECHNOLOG'ICAL, *a.* [See *Technology.*]

1. Pertaining to technology. *Beddoes. Tooke.*

2. Pertaining to the arts; as *technological* institutes. *Journ. of Science.*

TECHNOL'OGIST, *n.* One who discourses or treats of arts, or of the terms of art.

TECHNOL'OGY, *n.* [Gr. τεχνη, art, and λογος, word or discourse.]

1. A description of arts; or a treatise on the arts.

2. An explanation of the terms of the arts. *Crabbe.*

TECH'Y, *a.* [so written for *touchy.*] Peevish; fretful; irritable. [More correctly *touchy.*] *Shak.*

TECTON'IC, *a.* [Gr. τεκτονικος, from τευχω, to fabricate.]

Pertaining to building. *Bailey.*

TED, *v. t.* [W. *têd* and *têz*, [*teth*,] a spread; *tedu*, to distend.]

Among *farmers*, to spread; to turn new mowed grass from the swath, and scatter it for drying. [*Local.*] *Mortimer. Milton.*

TED'DED, *pp.* Spread from the swath; as *tedded* grass. *Milton.*

TED'DER, *n.* [W. *tid*, a chain; Ir. *tead*, *teidin*; Gaelic, *tead*, *teidin*, *teud*, a chain, cord or rope; Sw. *tiuder*; probably from extending. See *Ted.*]

1. A rope or chain by which an animal is tied that he may feed on the ground to the extent of the rope and no further. Hence the popular saying, a person has gone to the length of his *tedder*.

2. That by which one is restrained. *Child.*

TED'DER, *v. t.* To tie with a tedder; to permit to feed to the length of a rope or chain.

2. To restrain to certain limits.

Te deum, a hymn to be sung in churches or on occasions of joy; so called from the first words.

> *Te deum* was sung at St. Paul's after the victory. *Bacon.*

TE'DIOUS, *a.* [Sp. It. *tedioso*, from *tedio*, L. *tædium;* probably connected with W. *ted*, tedder, from the sense of drawing out.]

1. Wearisome; tiresome from continuance, prolixity, or slowness which causes prolixity. We say, a man is *tedious* in relating a story; a minister is *tedious* in his sermon. We say also, a discourse is *tedious*, when it wearies by its length or dullness.
2. Slow; as a *tedious* course. *Harte.*

TE'DIOUSLY, *adv.* In such a manner as to weary.

TE'DIOUSNESS, *n.* Wearisomeness by length of continuance or by prolixity; as the *tediousness* of an oration or argument.

2. Prolixity; length. *Shak.*
3. Tiresomeness; quality of wearying; as the *tediousness* of delay.
4. Slowness that wearies.

TE'DIUM, *n.* [L. *tædium.*] Irksomeness; wearisomeness. *Cowper.*

TEEM, *v. i.* [Sax. *tyman*, to bring forth, to bear; *team*, offspring; also *tyman, teamian*, to call, to summon; D. *teemen*, to whine, to cant, that is, to throw.]

1. To bring forth, as young.

> If she must *teem*,
> Create her child of spleen— *Shak.*

2. To be pregnant; to conceive; to engender young.

> *Teeming* buds and cheerful greens appear. *Dryden.*

2. To be full; to be charged; as a breeding animal; to be prolific. Every head *teems* with politics. *Addison.*
4. To bring forth; to produce, particularly in abundance. The earth *teems* with fruits; the sea *teems* with fishes.

TEEM, *v. t.* To produce; to bring forth.

> What's the newest grief?
> Each minute *teems* a new one. *Shak.*

[*This transitive sense is not common.*]

2. To pour. [*Not in use.*] *Swift.*

TEE'MER, *n.* One that brings forth young.

TEE'MFUL, *a.* Pregnant; prolific.

2. Brimful. *Ainsworth.*

TEE'MING, *ppr.* Producing young.

TEE'MLESS, *a.* Not fruitful or prolific; barren; as the *teemless* earth. *Dryden.*

TEEN, *n.* [infra.] Grief; sorrow. [*Not in use.*] *Spenser.*

TEEN, *v. t.* [Sax. *teonan, tynan*, to irritate.] To excite; to provoke. [*Not in use.*]

TEENS, *n.* [from *teen*, ten.] The years of one's age reckoned by the termination *teen*. These years begin with *thirteen*, and end with *nineteen*. Miss is in her *teens.*

TEETH, *plu.* of *tooth*, which see.

In the teeth, directly; in direct opposition; in front.

> Nor strive with all the tempest *in my teeth.* *Pope.*

TEETH, *v. i.* [from the noun.] To breed teeth.

TEE'THING, *ppr.* Breeding teeth; undergoing dentition.

TEE'THING, *n.* The operation or process of the first growth of teeth, or the process by which they make their way through the gums, called *dentition.*

TEG'ULAR, *a.* [L. *tegula*, a tile, from *tego*, to cover or make close.]

Pertaining to a tile; resembling a tile; consisting of tiles.

TEG'ULARLY, *adv.* In the manner of tiles on a roof. *Kirwan.*

TEG'UMENT, *n.* [L. *tegumentum*, from *tego*, to cover.]

A cover or covering; seldom used except in reference to the covering of a living body. [See *Integument.*]

TEH-HEE, a sound made in laughing.

TEH-HEE, *v. i.* To laugh. [*A cant word.*]

TEIL, TEIL-TREE, } *n.* [L. *tilia;* Ir. *teile.*] The lime tree, otherwise called the linden.

TEINT, *n.* [Fr. *teint*, from *teindre*, L. *tingo*, to dye.] Color; tinge. [See *Tint.*]

TEL'ARY, *a.* [L. *tela*, a web.] Pertaining to a web.

2. Spinning webs; as a *telary* spider. [*Little used.*] *Brown.*

TEL'EGRAPH, *n.* [Gr. τηλε, at a distance, and γραφω, to write.]

A machine for communicating intelligence from a distance by various signals or movements previously agreed on; which signals represent letters, words or ideas which can be transmitted from one station to another, as far as the signals can be seen. This machine was invented by the French about the year 1793 or 1794, and is now adopted by other nations. *Cyc.*

TELEGRAPH'I€, *a.* Pertaining to the telegraph; made by a telegraph; as *telegraphic* movements or signals; *telegraphic* art.

2. Communicated by a telegraph; as *telegraphic* intelligence.

TELEOL'OGY, *n.* [Gr. τελος, end, and λογος, discourse.]

The science of the final causes of things.

TEL'ESCOPE, *n.* [Fr. from Gr. τελος, end, or τηλε, at a distance, probably the latter, and σκοπεω, to see; It. Sp. *telescopio.*]

An optical instrument employed in viewing distant objects, as the heavenly bodies. It assists the eye chiefly in two ways; first, by enlarging the visual angle under which a distant object is seen, and thus magnifying that object; and secondly, by collecting and conveying to the eye a larger beam of light than would enter the naked organ, and thus rendering objects distinct and visible which would otherwise be indistinct or invisible. Its essential parts are the *object glass*, which collects the beam of light and forms an image of the object, and the *eye glass*, which is a microscope by which the image is magnified. *D. Olmsted.*

TEL'ESCOPE-SHELL, *n.* In *conchology*, a species of turbo with plane, striated and numerous spires. *Cyc.*

TELES€OP'I€, TELES€OP'I€AL, } *a.* Pertaining to a telescope; performed by a telescope; as a *telescopic* view.

2. Seen or discoverable only by a telescope; as *telescopic* stars.

TELE'SIA, *n.* Sapphire. *Ure.*

TEL'ESM, *n.* [Ar.] A kind of amulet or magical charm. *Gregory.*

TELESMAT'I€, TELESMAT'I€AL, } *a.* Pertaining to telesms; magical. *Gregory.*

TELES'TI€, *n.* [Gr. τελος, end, and ςιχος, a verse.]

A poem in which the final letters of the lines make a name.

Paus. Trans. B. Jonson.

TELL, *v. t.* pret. and pp. *told.* [Sax. *tellan;* G. *zahlen;* D. *tellen*, to count, number or tell; Dan. *tæler*, to count; *taler*, to talk, speak, reason; Sw. *tala*, to speak, to talk; *tal*, talk, discourse, speech, number; Dan. *tale*, Ice. *tala*, id. The primary sense is to throw or drive, L. *telum*, Ar. دل dalla. Class Dl. No. 6. So L. *appello* and *peal*, L. *pello*, Gr. βαλλω.]

1. To utter; to express in words; to communicate to others.

> I will not eat till I have *told* my errand. Gen. xxiv.

2. To relate; to narrate; to rehearse particulars; as, to *tell* a story. Gen. xxxvii.

> And not a man appears to *tell* their fate. *Pope.*

3. To teach; to inform; to make known; to show by words. *Tell* us the way.

> Why didst thou not *tell* me that she was thy wife? Gen. xii.

4. To discover; to disclose; to betray.

> They will *tell* it to the inhabitants of this land. Num. xiv.

5. To count; to number.

> Look now towards heaven, and *tell* the stars. Gen. xv.

6. To relate in confession; to confess or acknowledge.

> *Tell* me now what thou hast done. Josh. vii.

7. To publish.

> *Tell* it not in Gath. 2 Sam. i.

8. To unfold; to interpret; to explain. Ezek. xxiv.
9. To make excuses.

> Tush, never *tell* me. [*Not elegant.*] *Shak.*

10. To make known.

> Our feelings *tell* us how long they ought to have submitted. *Junius.*

11. To discover; to find; to discern. The colors are so blended that I cannot *tell* where one ends and the other begins.

Tell, though equivalent in some respects to *speak* and *say*, has not always the same application. We say, to *tell* this, that or what, to *tell* a story, to *tell* a word, to *tell* truth or falsehood, to *tell* a number, to *tell* the reasons, to *tell* something or nothing; but we never say, to *tell* a speech, discourse or oration, or to *tell* an argument or a lesson. It is much used in commands. *Tell* me the whole story; *tell* me all you know, or all that was said. *Tell* has frequently the sense of *narrate;* which *speak* and *say* have not.

TELL, *v. i.* To give an account; to make report.

> —That I may publish with the voice of thanksgiving, and *tell* of all thy wondrous works. Ps. xxvi.

To tell of, *To tell on*, } to inform. You must not disobey; I will *tell of* you if you do. This is a common popular use of the word. To *tell on*, is quite vulgar as well as improper.

TELL'ER, *n.* One that tells, relates or communicates the knowledge of something.

2. One who numbers.
3. In *the exchequer of England*, there are four officers called *tellers*, whose business is to receive all moneys due to the crown, and throw down a bill through a pipe into the tally-court, where it is received by the auditor's clerks, who write the words of the bill on a tally, and deliver it to be entered by the clerk of the pell. The tally is then split by the two deputy chamberlains, who have their seals, and while the senior deputy reads the one part, the junior examines the other with the other two clerks. [This word is supposed to be from *tally*, being in ancient records written *tallier.*] *Cyc.*
4. An officer of a bank, who receives and pays money on checks.

TEL'LINITE, *n.* [from *tellina*, a genus of testaceous animals.]
Petrified or fossil shells of the genus Tellina. *Kirwan.*

TELL'-TALE, *a.* Telling tales; babbling. *Shak.*

TELL'-TALE, *n.* [*tell* and *tale.*] One who officiously communicates information of the private concerns of individuals; one who tells that which prudence should suppress, and which if told, often does mischief among neighbors. *Milton. Shak.*
2. A movable piece of ivory or lead on a chamber organ, that gives notice when the wind is exhausted. *Busby.*
3. In *seamanship*, a small piece of wood, traversing in a groove across the front of the poop deck, and which, by communicating with a small barrel on the axis of the steering wheel, indicates the situation of the helm. *Mar. Dict.*

TEL'LURATE, *n.* A compound of tellurium and a base.

TEL'LURETED, *a.* Tellureted hydrogen is hydrogen combined with tellurium in a gaseous form. *Ure.*

TELLU'RIUM, *n.* A metal recently discovered by Klaproth, combined with gold and silver in the ores, and received from the bannat of Temeswar. The ores are denominated *native*, *graphic*, *yellow*, and *black*. The native tellurium is of a color between tin and silver, and sometimes inclines to a steel gray. The graphic tellurium is steel gray; but sometimes white, yellow or lead gray. These ores are found massive or crystalized. *Cyc.*

TEM'ACHIS, *n.* [Gr. τεμαχος, a piece.] A genus of fossils of the class of gypsums, softer than others, and of a bright glittering hue. *Cyc.*

TEMERA'RIOUS, *a.* [Fr. *temeraire;* L. *temerarius;* from the root of *time*, *tempest*, which see. The sense is rushing or advancing forward.]
1. Rash; headstrong; unreasonably adventurous; despising danger; as *temerarious* folly. *L'Estrange.*
2. Careless; heedless; done at random; as the *temerarious* dash of an unguided pen. [*This word is not much used.*] *Ray.*

TEMERA'RIOUSLY, *adv.* Rashly; with excess of boldness. *Swift.*

TEMER'ITY, *n.* [L. *temeritas;* properly a rushing forward.]
1. Rashness; unreasonable contempt of danger; as the *temerity* of a commander in war.
2. Extreme boldness.
> The figures are bold even to *temerity*. *Cowley.*

TEM'IN, *n.* A money of account in Algiers, equivalent to 2 carubes, or 29 aspers, about 34 cents, or 17*d.* sterling. *Cyc.*

TEM'PER, *v. t.* [L. *tempero*, to mix or moderate; It. *temperare;* Sp. *templar*, to temper, to soften or moderate, to anneal, as glass, to tune an instrument, to trim sails to the wind; Fr. *temperer*, to temper, allay or abate; W. *tymperu*, to temper, to mollify; *tym*, space; *tymp*, enlargement, birth, season. The latter unites this word with *time*, the primary sense of which is to fall, to rush, and to *temper* may be primarily to restrain, to lay or allay, to cause to subside.]
1. To mix so that one part qualifies the other; to bring to a moderate state; as, to *temper* justice with mercy. *Milton.*
2. To compound; to form by mixture; to qualify, as by an ingredient; or in general, to mix, unite or combine two or more things so as to reduce the excess of the qualities of either, and bring the whole to the desired consistence or state.
> Thou shalt make it a perfume, a confection after the art of the apothecary, *tempered* together, pure and holy. Ex. xxx.

3. To unite in due proportion; to render symmetrical; to adjust, as parts to each other.
> God hath *tempered* the body together. 1 Cor. xii.

4. To accommodate; to modify.
> Thy sustenance serving to the appetite of the eater, *tempered* itself to every man's liking. *Wisdom.*

5. To soften; to mollify; to assuage; to soothe; to calm; to reduce any violence or excess.
> Solon—labored to *temper* the warlike courages of the Athenians with sweet delights of learning. *Spenser.*

> Woman! nature made thee
> To *temper* man; we had been brutes without you. *Otway.*

6. To form to a proper degree of hardness; as, to *temper* iron or steel.
> The *temper'd* metals clash, and yield a silver sound. *Dryden.*

7. To govern; *a Latinism.* [*Not in use.*] *Spenser.*
8. In *music*, to modify or amend a false or imperfect concord by transferring to it a part of the beauty of a perfect one, that is, by dividing the tones. *Cyc.*

TEM'PER, *n.* Due mixture of different qualities; or the state of any compound substance which results from the mixture of various ingredients; as the *temper* of mortar.
2. Constitution of body. [In this sense we more generally use *temperament.*]
3. Disposition of mind; the constitution of the mind, particularly with regard to the passions and affections; as a calm *temper;* a hasty *temper;* a fretful *temper*. This is applicable to beasts as well as to man.
> Remember with what mild
> And gracious *temper* he both heard and judg'd. *Milton.*

4. Calmness of mind; moderation.
> Restore yourselves unto your *tempers*, fathers. *B. Jonson.*

> To fall with dignity, with *temper* rise. *Pope.*

5. Heat of mind or passion; irritation. The boy showed a great deal of *temper* when I reproved him.

So we say, a man of violent *temper*, when we speak of his irritability. [*This use of the word is common, though a deviation from its original and genuine meaning.*]
6. The state of a metal, particularly as to its hardness; as the *temper* of iron or steel. *Sharp.*
7. Middle course; mean or medium. *Swift.*
8. In *sugar works*, white lime or other substance stirred into a clarifier filled with cane-juice, to neutralize the superabundant acid. *Edwards, W. Indies.*

TEM'PERAMENT, *n.* [Fr. from L. *temperamentum.*]
1. Constitution; state with respect to the predominance of any quality; as the *temperament* of the body.
> Bodies are denominated hot and cold, in proportion to the present *temperament* of that part of our body to which they are applied. *Locke.*

2. Medium; due mixture of different qualities.
> The common law—has reduced the kingdom to its just state and *temperament*. *Hale.*

3. In *music*, temperament is an operation which, by means of a slight alteration in the intervals, causes the difference between two contiguous sounds to disappear, and makes each of them appear identical with the other. *Rousseau.*

Temperament is the accommodation or adjustment of the imperfect sounds, by transferring a part of their defects to the more perfect ones, to remedy in part the false intervals of instruments of fixed sounds, as the organ, harpsichord, forte piano, &c. *Busby.*
> The harshness of a given concord increases with the *temperament*. *Prof. Fisher.*

TEMPERAMENT'AL, *a.* Constitutional. [*Not much used.*] *Brown.*

TEM'PERANCE, *n.* [Fr. from L. *temperantia*, from *tempero.*]
1. Moderation; particularly, habitual moderation in regard to the indulgence of the natural appetites and passions; restrained or moderate indulgence; as *temperance* in eating and drinking; *temperance* in the indulgence of joy or mirth. *Temperance* in eating and drinking is opposed to *gluttony* and *drunkenness*, and in other indulgences, to *excess*.
2. Patience; calmness; sedateness; moderation of passion.
> He calm'd his wrath with goodly *temperance*. [*Unusual.*] *Spenser.*

TEM'PERATE, *a.* [L. *temperatus.*] Moderate; not excessive; as *temperate* heat; a *temperate* climate; *temperate* air. *Bacon.*
2. Moderate in the indulgence of the appetites and passions; as *temperate* in eating and drinking; *temperate* in pleasures; *temperate* in speech.
> Be sober and *temperate*, and you will be healthy. *Franklin.*

3. Cool; calm; not marked with passion; not violent; as a *temperate* discourse or address; *temperate* language.
4. Proceeding from temperance; as *temperate* sleep. *Pope.*
5. Free from ardent passion.
> She is not hot, but *temperate* as the morn. *Shak.*

Temperate zone, the space on the earth between the tropics and the polar circles, where the heat is less than in the tropics, and the cold less than in the polar circles.

TEM'PERATELY, *adv.* Moderately; without excess or extravagance.

2. Calmly; without violence of passion; as, to reprove one *temperately.*

3. With moderate force.

> Winds that *temperately* blow. *Addison.*

TEM'PERATENESS, *n.* Moderation; freedom from excess; as the *temperateness* of the weather or of a climate.

2. Calmness; coolness of mind. *Daniel.*

TEM'PERATIVE, *a.* Having the power or quality of tempering.

TEM'PERATURE, *n.* [Fr. from L. *temperatura.*]

1. In *physics*, the state of a body with regard to heat or cold, as indicated by the thermometer; or the degree of free caloric which a body possesses, when compared with other bodies. When a body applied to another, either excites the sensation of heat, or expands that body, we say it is of a *higher temperature*; that is, it possesses more free caloric. When it excites the sensation of cold, or contracts another body, it is said to be of a *lower temperature.* Thus we speak of the *temperature* of air, of water, of a climate, &c.; two countries of the same *temperature.*

2. Constitution; state; degree of any quality.

> Memory depends upon the consistence and *temperature* of the brain. *Watts.*

3. Moderation; freedom from immoderate passions.

> In that proud port, which her so goodly graceth,
> Most goodly *temperature* you may descry.
> [*Not in use.*] *Spenser.*

TEM'PERED, *pp.* Duly mixed or modified; reduced to a proper state; softened; allayed; hardened.

2. Adjusted by musical temperament.

3. *a.* Disposed; as a well *tempered*, good *tempered*, or bad *tempered* man.

TEM'PERING, *ppr.* Mixing and qualifying; qualifying by mixture; softening; mollifying; reducing to a state of moderation; hardening.

TEM'PEST, *n.* [Fr. *tempête*; L. *tempestas*; Sp. *tempestad*; It. *tempesta*; from L. *tempus*, time, season. The primary sense of *tempus*, time, is a falling, or that which falls, comes or happens, from some verb which signifies to fall or come suddenly, or rather to drive, to rush. *Time* is properly a coming, a season, that which presents itself, or is present. The sense of *tempest*, is from the sense of rushing or driving. See *Temerity* and *Temerarious.*]

1. An extensive current of wind, rushing with great velocity and violence; a storm of extreme violence. We usually apply the word to a steady wind of long continuance; but we say also of a tornado, it blew a *tempest.* The currents of wind are named, according to their respective degrees of force or rapidity, a *breeze*, a *gale*, a *storm*, a *tempest*; but *gale* is also used as synonymous with *storm*, and *storm* with *tempest.* *Gust* is usually applied to a sudden blast of short duration. A tempest may or may not be attended with rain, snow or hail.

> We, caught in a fiery *tempest*, shall be hurl'd
> Each on his rock transfix'd— *Milton.*

2. A violent tumult or commotion; as a popular or political *tempest*; the *tempest* of war.

3. Perturbation; violent agitation; as a *tempest* of the passions.

TEM'PEST, *v. t.* To disturb as by a tempest. [*Little used.*] *Milton.*

TEM'PEST-BEATEN, *a.* [*tempest* and *beat.*] Beaten or shattered with storms. *Dryden.*

TEMPESTIV'ITY, *n.* [L. *tempestivus.*] Seasonableness. [*Not in use.*] *Brown.*

TEM'PEST-TOST, *a.* [*tempest* and *tost.*] Tossed or driven about by tempests. *Shak.*

TEMPEST'UOUS, *a.* [Sp. *tempestuoso*; It. *tempestoso*; Fr. *tempêtueux.*]

1. Very stormy; turbulent; rough with wind; as *tempestuous* weather; a *tempestuous* night.

2. Blowing with violence; as a *tempestuous* wind.

TEMPEST'UOUSLY, *adv.* With great violence of wind or great commotion; turbulently. *Milton.*

TEMPEST'UOUSNESS, *n.* Storminess; the state of being tempestuous or disturbed by violent winds; as the *tempestuousness* of the winter or of weather.

TEM'PLAR, *n.* [from the *Temple*, a house near the Thames, which originally belonged to the knights Templars. The latter took their denomination from an apartment of the palace of Baldwin II. in Jerusalem, near the temple.]

1. A student of the law. *Pope.*

2. *Templars, knights of the Temple*, a religious military order, first established at Jerusalem in favor of pilgrims traveling to the Holy Land. The order originated with some persons who, in 1118, devoted themselves to the service of God, promising to live in perpetual chastity, obedience and poverty, after the manner of canons. In 1228, this order was confirmed in the council of Troyes, and subjected to a rule of discipline. It flourished, became immensely rich, and its members became so insolent and vicious, that the order was suppressed by the council of Vienne, in 1312. *Cyc.*

TEM'PLE, *n.* [Fr.; L. *templum*; It. *tempio*; Sp. *templo*; W. *temyl*, temple, that is extended, a seat; *temlu*, to form a seat, expanse or temple; Gaelic, *teampul.*]

1. A public edifice erected in honor of some deity. Among pagans, a building erected to some pretended deity, and in which the people assembled to worship. Originally, temples were open places, as the Stonehenge in England. In Rome, some of the temples were open, and called *sacella*; others were roofed, and called *ædes.* The most celebrated of the ancient pagan temples were that of Belus in Babylon, that of Vulcan at Memphis, that of Jupiter at Thebes, that of Diana at Ephesus, that of Apollo in Miletus, that of Jupiter Olympius in Athens, and that of Apollo at Delphi. The most celebrated and magnificent temple erected to the true God, was that built by Solomon in Jerusalem.

In *Scripture*, the tabernacle is sometimes called by this name. 1 Sam. i.—iii.

2. A church; an edifice erected among christians as a place of public worship.

> Can he whose life is a perpetual insult to the authority of God, enter with any pleasure a *temple* consecrated to devotion and sanctified by prayer? *Buckminster.*

3. A place in which the divine presence specially resides; the church as a collective body. Eph. ii.

4. In *England*, the *Temples* are two inns of court, thus called because anciently the dwellings of the knights Templars. They are called the Inner and the Middle Temple.

TEM'PLE, *n.* [L. *tempus*, *tempora.* The primary sense of the root of this word is to fall. See *Time.*]

1. Literally, the fall of the head; the part where the head slopes from the top.

2. In *anatomy*, the anterior and lateral part of the head, where the skull is covered by the temporal muscles. *Cyc.*

TEM'PLE, *v. t.* To build a temple for; to appropriate a temple to. [*Little used.*] *Feltham.*

TEM'PLET, *n.* A piece of timber in a building; as a *templet* under a girder. *Moxon.*

TEM'PORAL, *a.* [Fr. *temporel*; from L. *temporalis*, from *tempus*, time.]

1. Pertaining to this life or this world or the body only; secular; as *temporal* concerns; *temporal* affairs. In this sense, it is opposed to *spiritual.* Let not *temporal* affairs or employments divert the mind from spiritual concerns, which are far more important.

In this sense also it is opposed to *ecclesiastical*; as *temporal* power, that is, secular, civil or political power; *temporal* courts, those which take cognizance of civil suits. *Temporal* jurisdiction is that which regards civil and political affairs.

2. Measured or limited by time, or by this life or this state of things; having limited existence; opposed to *eternal.*

> The things which are seen are *temporal*, but the things which are not seen are eternal. 2 Cor. iv.

3. In *grammar*, relating to a tense; as a *temporal* augment.

4. [Fr. *temporal.*] Pertaining to the temple or temples of the head; as the *temporal* bone; a *temporal* artery or vein; *temporal* muscle.

TEMPORAL'ITIES, } *n.* Secular possessions; revenues
TEM'PORALS, }
of an ecclesiastic proceeding from lands, tenements, or lay-fees, tithes and the like. It is opposed to *spiritualities.* *Bacon.*

TEM'PORALLY, *adv.* With respect to time or this life only. *South.*

TEM'PORALNESS, *n.* Worldliness. [*Not used.*]

TEM'PORALTY, *n.* The laity; secular people. [*Little used.*]

2. Secular possessions. [See *Temporalities.*]

TEMPORA'NEOUS, *a.* Temporary. [*Little used.*]

TEM'PORARILY, *adv.* For a time only; not perpetually.

TEM'PORARINESS, *n.* [from *temporary.*] The state of being temporary; opposed to *perpetuity.*

TEM'PORARY, *a.* [L. *temporarius.*] Lasting for a time only; existing or continuing for a limited time; as, the patient has obtained *temporary* relief. There is a *temporary* cessation of hostilities. There is a *temporary* supply of provisions. In times of great danger, Rome appointed a *temporary* dictator.

TEMPORIZA'TION, *n.* The act of temporizing.

TEM'PORIZE, *v. i.* [Fr. *temporiser;* from L. *tempus*, time.]

1. To comply with the time or occasion; to humor or yield to the current of opinion or to circumstances; *a conduct that often indicates obsequiousness.*

> They might their grievance inwardly complain,
> But outwardly they needs must *temporize.* *Daniel.*

2. To delay; to procrastinate.

> Well, you will *temporize* with the hours. [*Little used.*] *Shak.*

3. To comply. [*Not in use.*] *Shak.*

TEM'PORIZER, *n.* One who yields to the time, or complies with the prevailing opinions, fashions or occasions; a trimmer. *Shak.*

TEM'PORIZING, *ppr.* Complying with the time, or with the prevailing humors and opinions of men; time-serving.

TEMPT, *v. t.* [Arm. *tempti;* L. *tento;* Fr. *tenter;* It. *tentare;* Sp. *tentar.* It is from the root of L. *teneo*, Gr. τεινω, and the primary sense is to strain, urge, press.]

1. To incite or solicit to an evil act; to entice to something wrong by presenting arguments that are plausible or convincing, or by the offer of some pleasure or apparent advantage as the inducement.

> My lady Gray *tempts* him to this harsh extremity. *Shak.*
>
> Every man is *tempted*, when he is drawn away by his own lust and enticed. James i.

2. To provoke; to incite.

> *Tempt* not the brave and needy to despair. *Dryden.*

3. To solicit; to draw; *without the notion of evil.*

> Still his strength conceal'd,
> Which *tempted* our attempt, and wrought our fall. *Milton.*

4. To try; to venture on; to attempt.

> E'er leave be giv'n to *tempt* the nether skies. *Dryden.*

5. In *Scripture*, to try; to prove; to put to trial for proof.

> God did *tempt* Abraham. Gen. xxii.
>
> Ye shall not *tempt* the Lord your God. Deut. vi.

TEMPT'ABLE, *a.* Liable to be tempted. *Swift.*

TEMPTA'TION, *n.* The act of tempting; enticement to evil by arguments, by flattery, or by the offer of some real or apparent good.

> When the devil had ended all the *temptation*, he departed from him for a season. Luke iv.

2. Solicitation of the passions; enticements to evil proceeding from the prospect of pleasure or advantage.

3. The state of being tempted or enticed to evil. When by human weakness you are led into *temptation*, resort to prayer for relief.

4. Trial.

> Lead us not into *temptation.* *Lord's Prayer.*

5. That which is presented to the mind as an inducement to evil.

> Dare to be great without a guilty crown,
> View it, and lay the bright *temptation* down. *Dryden.*

6. In *colloquial language*, an allurement to any thing indifferent, or even good.

TEMPT'ED, *pp.* Enticed to evil; provoked; tried.

TEMPT'ER, *n.* One that solicits or entices to evil.

> Those who are bent to do wickedly, will never want *tempters* to urge them on. *Tillotson.*

2. The great adversary of man; the devil. Matt. iv.

TEMPT'ING, *ppr.* Enticing to evil; trying.

2. *a.* Adapted to entice or allure; attractive; as *tempting* pleasures.

TEMPT'INGLY, *adv.* In a manner to entice to evil; so as to allure.

TEMPT'RESS, *n.* A female who entices.

TEMSEBREAD, TEM'SED-BREAD, *n.* [Fr. *tamiser*, It. *tamisare, tamigiare*, to sift; Fr. *tamis*, It. *tamiso, tamigio*, a sieve.]

Bread made of flour better sifted than common flour. [*I know not where this word is used.*] *Johnson.*

TEM'ULENCE, TEM'ULENCY, *n.* [L. *temulentia.*] Intoxication; inebriation; drunkenness. [*Not used.*]

TEM'ULENT, *a.* [L. *temulentus.*] Intoxicated. [*Not in use.*]

TEM'ULENTIVE, *a.* Drunken; in a state of inebriation. [*Not in use.*]

TEN, *a.* [Sax. *tyn;* D. *tien;* G. *zehn;* Dan. *tie;* Sw. *tio.* I suppose this word to be contracted from the Gothic *tiguns*, ten, from *tig*, ten. If so, this is the Greek δεκα, L. *decem*, W. *deg*, Gaelic, *deich*, Fr. *dix*, It. *dieci*, Sp. *diez.*]

1. Twice five; nine and one.

> With twice *ten* sail I cross'd the Phrygian sea. *Dryden.*

2. It is a kind of proverbial number.

> There's a proud modesty in merit,
> Averse to begging, and resolv'd to pay
> *Ten* times the gift it asks. *Dryden.*

The meaning in this use is, a great deal more, indefinitely.

TEN'ABLE, *a.* [Fr. from L. *teneo*, to hold. See *Tenant.*]

That may be held, maintained or defended against an assailant, or against attempts to take it; as a *tenable* fortress. The works were not deemed *tenable.* The ground taken in the argument is not *tenable.*

TENA'CIOUS, *a.* [L. *tenax*, from *teneo*, to hold; Fr. *tenace.*]

1. Holding fast, or inclined to hold fast; inclined to retain what is in possession; as men *tenacious* of their just rights. Men are usually *tenacious* of their opinions, as well as of their property. *Locke. Arbuthnot.*

2. Retentive; apt to retain long what is committed to it; as a *tenacious* memory. *Locke.*

3. Adhesive; apt to adhere to another substance; as oily, glutinous or viscous matter. Few substances are so *tenacious* as tar.

4. Niggardly; close fisted. *Ainsworth.*

TENA'CIOUSLY, *adv.* With a disposition to hold fast what is possessed.

2. Adhesively.

3. Obstinately; with firm adherence.

TENA'CIOUSNESS, *n.* The quality of holding fast; unwillingness to quit, resign or let go; as a man's *tenaciousness* of his rights or opinions.

2. Adhesiveness; stickiness; as the *tenaciousness* of clay or glue.

3. Retentiveness; as the *tenaciousness* of memory.

TENAC'ITY, *n.* [Fr. *tenacité;* L. *tenacitas*, from *teneo*, to hold.]

1. Adhesiveness; that quality of bodies which makes them stick or adhere to others; glutinousness; stickiness; as the *tenacity* of oils, of glue, of tar, of starch and the like.

2. That quality of bodies which keeps them from parting, without considerable force; cohesiveness; the effect of attraction; opposed to *brittleness* or *fragility.* *Cyc.*

TEN'ACY, *n.* Tenaciousness. [*Not in use.*] *Barrow.*

TENA'IL, *n.* [Fr. *tenaille*, from *tenir*, L. *teneo*, to hold.]

In *fortification*, an outwork consisting of two parallel sides with a front, in which is a re-entering angle. It is simple or double. *Cyc.*

TEN'AILLON, *n.* In *fortification*, tenaillons are works constructed on each side of the ravelins, like the lunets, but differing in this, that one of the faces of the tenaillon is in the direction of the ravelin, whereas that of the lunet is perpendicular to it. *Cyc.*

TEN'ANCY, *n.* [Sp. *tenencia;* Fr. *tenant*, L. *tenens.*]

In *law*, a holding or possession of lands or tenements; tenure; as *tenancy* in fee simple; *tenancy* in tail; *tenancy* by the curtesy; *tenancy* at will. *Tenancy* in common happens where there is a unity of possession merely. *Blackstone.*

TEN'ANT, *n.* [Fr. *tenant*, from *tenir*, to hold, L. *teneo;* Gr. τεινω, to strain, stretch, extend; W. *tannu*, to stretch; *tynu*, to pull; *tyn*, a stretch; *ten*, drawn; It. *tenere*, Sp. *tener*, to hold.]

1. A person holding land or other real estate under another, either by grant, lease or at will; one who has the occupation or temporary possession of lands or tenements whose title is in another; as a *tenant* in tail; *tenant* in common; *tenant* by the curtesy; *tenant* in parcenary; *tenant* for life; *tenant* at will; *tenant* in dower.

2. One who has possession of any place; a dweller.

> The happy *tenant* of your shade. *Cowley.*

Tenant in capite, or *tenant in chief*, by the laws of England, is one who holds immediately of the king. According to the feudal system, all lands in England are considered as held immediately or mediately of the king, who is stiled lord paramount. Such tenants however are considered as having the fee of the lands and permanent possession. *Blackstone.*

TEN'ANT, *v. t.* To hold or possess as a tenant.

> Sir Roger's estate is *tenanted* by persons who have served him or his ancestors. *Addison.*

TEN'ANTABLE, *a.* Fit to be rented; in a state of repair suitable for a tenant.

TEN'ANTED, *pp.* Held by a tenant.

TEN'ANTING, *ppr.* Holding as a tenant.

TEN'ANTLESS, *a.* Having no tenant; unoccupied; as a *tenantless* mansion. *Thodey.*

TEN'ANTRY, *n.* The body of tenants; as the *tenantry* of a manor or a kingdom. *Paley.*

2. Tenancy. [*Not in use.*] *Ridley.*

TENCH, *n.* [Fr. *tenche*; Sp. *tenca*; L. *tinca.*] A fish of the genus Cyprinus, found in ponds and rivers.

TEND, *v. t.* [contracted from *attend*, L. *attendo*; *ad* and *tendo*, to stretch, W. *tannu.* Attention denotes a straining of the mind.]

1. To watch; to guard; to accompany as an assistant or protector.

And flaming ministers to watch and *tend*
Their earthly charge— *Milton.*

There is a pleasure in that simplicity, in beholding princes *tending* their flocks. *Pope.*

2. To hold and take care of; as, to *tend* a child.

3. To be attentive to.

Unsuck'd of lamb or kid that *tend* their play. *Milton.*

TEND, *v. i.* [L. *tendo*; Fr. *tendre*; It. *tendere*; formed on L. *teneo*, Gr. τεινω.]

1. To move in a certain direction.

Having overheard two gentlemen *tending* towards that sight— *Wotton.*

Here Dardanus was born, and hither *tends.* *Dryden.*

2. To be directed to any end or purpose; to aim at; to have or give a leaning.

The laws of our religion *tend* to the universal happiness of mankind. *Tillotson.*

3. To contribute. Our petitions, if granted, might *tend* to our destruction. *Hammond.*

4. [for *attend.*] To attend; to wait as attendants or servants.

He *tends* upon my father. *Shak.*
[*Colloquial.*]

5. To attend as something inseparable. [*Not in use.*] *Shak.*

6. To wait; to expect. [*Not in use.*] *Shak.*

7. To swing round an anchor, as a ship. *Mar. Dict.*

TEND'ANCE, *n.* Attendance; state of expectation.

2. Persons attending. *Shak.*

3. Act of waiting; attendance. *Shak.*

4. Care; act of tending. *Milton.*

[This word is entirely obsolete in all its senses. We now use *attendance.*]

TEND'ED, *pp.* Attended; taken care of; nursed; as an infant, or a sick person.

TEND'ENCY, *n.* [from *tend*; L. *tendens*, tending.]

Drift; direction or course towards any place, object, effect or result. Read such books only as have a good moral *tendency.* Mild language has a *tendency* to allay irritation.

Writings of this kind, if conducted with candor, have a more particular *tendency* to the good of their country. *Addison.*

TEND'ER, *n.* [from *tend.*] One that attends or takes care of; a nurse.

2. A small vessel employed to attend a larger one for supplying her with provisions and other stores, or to convey intelligence and the like. *Mar. Dict.*

3. [Fr. *tendre*, to reach.] In *law*, an offer, either of money to pay a debt, or of service to be performed, in order to save a penalty or forfeiture which would be incurred by non-payment or non-performance; as the *tender* of rent due, or of the amount of a note or bond with interest. To constitute a legal tender, such money must be offered as the law prescribes; the offer of bank notes is not a legal tender. So also the tender must be at the time and place where the rent or debt ought to be paid, and it must be to the full amount due.

There is also a *tender* of issue in pleadings, a *tender* of an oath, &c.

4. Any offer for acceptance. The gentleman made me a *tender* of his services.

5. The thing offered. This money is not a legal *tender.*

6. Regard; kind concern. [*Not in use.*] *Shak.*

TEND'ER, *v. t.* [Fr. *tendre*, to reach or stretch out; L. *tendo.*]

1. To offer in words; or to exhibit or present for acceptance.

All conditions, all minds *tender* down
Their service to lord Timon. *Shak.*

2. To hold; to esteem.

Tender yourself more dearly. *Shak.*
[*Not in use.*]

3. To offer in payment or satisfaction of a demand, for saving a penalty or forfeiture; as, to *tender* the amount of rent or debt.

TEN'DER, *a.* [Fr. *tendre*; It. *tenero*; Port. *tênro*; Ir. Gaelic, *tin*; W. *tyner*; L. *tener*; allied probably to *thin*, L. *tenuis*, W. *tenau*; Ar. ودن wadana, to be soft or thin. Class Dn. No 12. and see No. 25.]

1. Soft; easily impressed, broken, bruised or injured; not firm or hard; as *tender* plants; *tender* flesh; *tender* grapes. Deut. xxxii. Cant. ii.

2. Very sensible to impression and pain; easily pained.

Our bodies are not naturally more *tender* than our faces. *L'Estrange.*

3. Delicate; effeminate; not hardy or able to endure hardship.

The *tender* and delicate woman among you. Deut. xxviii.

4. Weak; feeble; as *tender* age. Gen. xxxiii.

5. Young and carefully educated. Prov. iv.

6. Susceptible of the softer passions, as love, compassion, kindness; compassionate; pitiful; easily affected by the distresses of another, or anxious for another's good; as the *tender* kindness of the church; a *tender* heart.

7. Compassionate; easily excited to pity, forgiveness or favor.

The Lord is pitiful, and of *tender* mercy. James v. Luke i.

8. Exciting kind concern.

I love Valentine;
His life's as *tender* to me as his soul. *Shak.*

9. Expressive of the softer passions; as a *tender* strain.

10. Careful to save inviolate, or not to injure; with *of.* Be *tender of* your neighbor's reputation.

The civil authority should be *tender of* the honor of God and religion. *Tillotson.*

11. Gentle; mild; unwilling to pain.

You that are so *tender* o'er his follies,
Will never do him good. *Shak.*

12. Apt to give pain; as, that is a *tender* subject; things that are *tender* and unpleasing. *Bacon.*

13. Adapted to excite feeling or sympathy; pathetic; as *tender* expressions; *tender* expostulations.

TEND'ERED, *pp.* Offered for acceptance.

TEN'DER-HE'ARTED, *a.* [*tender* and *heart.*]

1. Having great sensibility; susceptible of impressions or influence.

—When Rehoboam was young and *tender-hearted*, and could not withstand them. 2 Chron. xiii.

2. Very susceptible of the softer passions of love, pity or kindness.

Be ye kind one to another, and *tender-hearted.* Eph. iv.

TENDER-HE'ARTEDNESS, *n.* Susceptibility of the softer passions.

TEND'ERING, *ppr.* Offering for acceptance.

TEN'DERLING, *n.* A fondling; one made tender by too much kindness.

2. The first horns of a deer.

TEN'DERLOIN, *n.* A tender part of flesh in the hind quarter of beef.

TEN'DERLY, *adv.* With tenderness; mildly; gently; softly; in a manner not to injure or give pain.

Brutus *tenderly* reproves. *Pope.*

2. Kindly; with pity or affection.

TEN'DERNESS, *n.* The state of being tender or easily broken, bruised or injured; softness; brittleness; as the *tenderness* of a thread; the *tenderness* of flesh.

2. The state of being easily hurt; soreness; as the *tenderness* of flesh when bruised or inflamed.

3. Susceptibility of the softer passions; sensibility.

Well we know your *tenderness* of heart. *Shak.*

4. Kind attention; anxiety for the good of another, or to save him from pain. *Bacon.*

5. Scrupulousness; caution; extreme care or concern not to give or to commit offense; as *tenderness* of conscience. *South.*

6. Cautious care to preserve or not to injure; as a *tenderness* of reputation. *Gov. of the Tongue.*

7. Softness of expression; pathos.

TEND'ING, *ppr.* Having a certain direction; taking care of.

TEND'ING, *n.* In seaman's language, a swinging round or movement of a ship upon her anchor.

TEN'DINOUS, *a.* [Fr. *tendineux*; It. *tendinoso*; from L. *tendines*, tendons, from *tendo*, to stretch.]

1. Pertaining to a tendon; partaking of the nature of tendons.

2. Full of tendons; sinewy; as nervous and *tendinous* parts. *Wiseman.*

TEND'MENT, *n.* Attendance; care. *Obs.* *Hall.*

TEN'DON, *n.* [L. *tendo*; Gr. τενων; from τεινω, L. *teneo*, *tendo.*]

In *anatomy*, a hard insensible cord or bundle of fibers, by which a muscle is attached to a bone.

TEN'DRAC, *n.* An animal of the hedgehog kind, found in the E. Indies. *Dict. Nat. Hist.*

TEN'DRIL, *n.* [Fr. *tendron*, from *tenir*, to hold.]
A clasp or clasper of a vine or other climbing or creeping plant; a filiform spiral shoot, that winds round another body. *Tendrils* or claspers are given to plants that have weak stalks. *Ray.*
They are also given to creeping vines which require support on the earth.
TEN'DRIL, *a.* Clasping; climbing; as a tendril. *Dyer.*
TEN'EBROUS, TENE'BRIOUS, *a.* [L. *tenebrosus*, from *tenebræ*, darkness.] Dark; gloomy. *Young.*
TENE'BROUSNESS, TENEBROS'ITY, *n.* Darkness; gloom.
TEN'EMENT, *n.* [Fr.; Low L. *tenementum*, from *teneo*, to hold.]
1. In *common acceptation*, a house; a building for a habitation; or an apartment in a building, used by one family.
2. A house or lands depending on a manor; or a fee farm depending on a superior. *Cyc.*
3. In *law*, any species of permanent property that may be held, as land, houses, rents, commons, an office, an advowson, a franchise, a right of common, a peerage, &c. These are called free or frank tenements.
The thing held is a *tenement*, and the possessor of it a *tenant*, and the manner of possession is called *tenure*. *Blackstone.*
TENEMENT'AL, *a.* Pertaining to tenanted lands; that is or may be held by tenants.
Tenemental lands they distributed among their tenants. *Blackstone.*
TENEMENT'ARY, *a.* That is or may be leased; held by tenants. *Spelman.*
TENER'ITY, *n.* Tenderness. [*Not in use.*]
TENES'MUS, *n.* [L. literally a straining or stretching.]
A painful, ineffectual and repeated effort, or a continual and urgent desire to go to stool. *Coxe. Cyc.*
TEN'ET, *n.* [L. *tenet*, he holds.] Any opinion, principle, dogma or doctrine which a person believes or maintains as true; as the *tenets* of Plato or of Cicero. The *tenets* of christians are adopted from the Scriptures; but different interpretations give rise to a great diversity of *tenets*.
TEN'FOLD, *a.* [*ten* and *fold.*] Ten times more.
Fire kindled into *tenfold* rage. *Milton.*
TEN'NANTITE, *n.* [from *Tennant.*] A subspecies of gray copper; a mineral of a lead color, or iron black, massive or crystalized, found in Cornwall, England. *Ure.*
TEN'NIS, *n.* [If this word is from L. *teneo*, Fr. *tenir*, it must be from the sense of holding on, continuing to keep in motion.]
A play in which a ball is driven continually or kept in motion by rackets.
TEN'NIS, *v. t.* To drive a ball. *Spenser.*
TEN'ON, *n.* [Fr. from *tenir*, L. *teneo*, to hold.]
In *building* and *cabinet work*, the end of a piece of timber, which is fitted to a mortise for insertion, or inserted, for fastening two pieces of timber together. The form of a tenon is various, as square, dovetailed, &c.
TEN'OR, *n.* [L. *tenor*, from *teneo*, to hold; that is, a holding on in a continued course; Fr. *teneur*; It. *tenore*; Sp. *tenor.*]
1. Continued run or currency; whole course or strain. We understand a speaker's intention or views from the *tenor* of his conversation, that is, from the general course of his ideas, or general purport of his speech.
Does not the whole *tenor* of the divine law positively require humility and meekness to all men? *Sprat.*
2. Stamp; character. The conversation was of the same *tenor* as that of the preceding day.
This success would look like chance, if it were not perpetual and always of the same *tenor*. *Dryden.*
3. Sense contained; purport; substance; general course or drift; as close attention to the *tenor* of the discourse. Warrants are to be executed according to their form and *tenor*. *Locke.*
Bid me tear the bond.
—When it is paid according to the *tenor*. *Shak.*
4. [Fr. *tenor.*] In *music*, the natural pitch of a man's voice in singing; hence, the part of a tune adapted to a man's voice, the second of the four parts, reckoning from the base; and originally the air, to which the other parts were auxiliary.
5. The persons who sing the tenor, or the instrument that plays it.
TENSE, *a. tens.* [L. *tensus*, from *tendo*, to stretch.]
Stretched; strained to stiffness; rigid; not lax; as a *tense* fiber.
For the free passage of the sound into the ear, it is requisite that the tympanum be *tense*. *Holder.*
TENSE, *n. tens.* [corrupted from Fr. *temps*, L. *tempus.*]
In *grammar*, time, or a particular form of a verb, or a combination of words, used to express the time of action, or of that which is affirmed; or tense is an inflection of verbs by which they are made to signify or distinguish the time of actions or events.
The primary simple tenses are three; those which express time *past, present*, and *future*; but these admit of modifications, which differ in different languages. The English language is rich in *tenses*, beyond any other language in Europe.
TENSENESS, *n. tens'ness.* The state of being tense or stretched to stiffness; stiffness; opposed to *laxness*; as the *tenseness* of a string or fiber; *tenseness* of the skin. *Sharp.*
TENS'IBLE, *a.* Capable of being extended. *Bacon.*
TENS'ILE, *a.* Capable of extension. *Bacon.*
TEN'SION, *n.* [Fr. from L. *tensio*, *tendo.*]
1. The act of stretching or straining; as the *tension* of the muscles.
2. The state of being stretched or strained to stiffness; or the state of being bent or strained; as, different degrees of *tension* in chords give different sounds; the greater the *tension*, the more acute the sound.
3. Distension.
TENS'IVE, *a.* Giving the sensation of tension, stiffness or contraction; as a *tensive* pain. *Floyer.*
TENS'OR, *n.* In *anatomy*, a muscle that extends or stretches a part.
TENSURE, the same as *tension*, and not used. *Bacon.*
TENT, *n.* [W. *tent*, from *ten*, *tyn*, stretched; Fr. *tente*; Sp. *tienda*; L. *tentorium*, from *tendo*, to stretch.]
1. A pavilion or portable lodge consisting of canvas or other coarse cloth, stretched and sustained by poles; used for sheltering persons from the weather, particularly soldiers in camp. The wandering Arabs and Tartars lodge in *tents*. The Israelites lodged in *tents* forty years, while they were in the desert.
2. In *surgery*, a roll of lint or linen, used to dilate an opening in the flesh, or to prevent the healing of an opening from which matter or other fluid is discharged. *Cyc.*
TENT, *n.* [Sp. *tinto*, deep colored, from L. *tinctus.*]
A kind of wine of a deep red color, chiefly from Galicia or Malaga in Spain.
TENT, *v. i.* To lodge as in a tent; to tabernacle. *Shak.*
TENT, *v. t.* To probe; to search as with a tent; as, to *tent* a wound.
I'll *tent* him to the quick. *Shak.*
2. To keep open with a tent. *Wiseman.*
TEN'TACLE, *n.* [Tech. L. *tentacula.*] A filiform process or organ, simple or branched, on the bodies of various animals of the Linnean class Vermes, and of Cuvier's Mollusca, Annelides, Echinodermata, Actinia, Medusæ, Polypi, &c. either an organ of feeling, prehension or motion, sometimes round the mouth, sometimes on other parts of the body.
TENT'AGE, *n.* An encampment. [*Unusual.*] *Drayton.*
TENTA'TION, *n.* [Fr. from L. *tentatio*; *tento*, to try.] Trial; temptation. [*Little used.*] *Brown.*
TENT'ATIVE, *a.* [Fr.] Trying; essaying.
TENT'ATIVE, *n.* An essay; trial. *Berkeley.*
TENT'ED, *a.* Covered or furnished with tents; as soldiers.
2. Covered with tents; as a *tented* field.
TENT'ER, *n.* [L. *tendo*, *tentus*, to stretch.] A hook for stretching cloth on a frame.
To be on the tenters, to be on the stretch; to be in distress, uneasiness or suspense. *Hudibras.*
TENT'ER, *v. t.* To hang or stretch on tenters. *Bacon.*
TENT'ER, *v. i.* To admit extension.
Woolen cloths will *tenter*. *Bacon.*
TENT'ERED, *pp.* Stretched or hung on tenters.
TENT'ER-GROUND, *n.* Ground on which tenters are erected.
TEN'TERING, *ppr.* Stretching or hanging on tenters.
TENTH, *a.* [from *ten.*] The ordinal of ten; the first after the ninth.
TENTH, *n.* The tenth part.
2. Tithe; the tenth part of annual produce or increase. The *tenth* of income is payable to the clergy in England, as it was to the priests among the Israelites.
3. In *music*, the octave of the third; an interval comprehending nine conjoint degrees, or ten sounds, diatonically divided. *Busby.*
TENTH'LY, *adv.* In the tenth place.
TENTIG'INOUS, *a.* [L. *tentigo*, a stretching.] Stiff; stretched. [*Not in use.*] *Dict.*

TENT'ORY, *n.* [L. *tentorium.*] The awning of a tent. *Evelyn.*

TENT'WÖRT, *n.* [*tent* and *wort.*] A plant of the genus Asplenium.

TENUIFO'LIOUS, *a.* [L. *tenuis* and *folium.*] Having thin or narrow leaves.

TENU'ITY, *n.* [Fr. *tenuité*; L. *tenuitas*, from *tenuis*, thin. See *Thin.*]

1. Thinness; smallness in diameter; exility; thinness, applied to a broad substance, and slenderness, applied to one that is long; as the *tenuity* of paper or of a leaf; the *tenuity* of a hair or filament.

2. Rarity; rareness; thinness; as of a fluid; as the *tenuity* of the air in the higher regions of the atmosphere; the *tenuity* of the blood. *Bacon.*

3. Poverty. [*Not in use.*] *K. Charles.*

TEN'UOUS, *a.* [L. *tenuis.*] Thin; small; minute. *Brown.*

2. Rare.

TEN'URE, *n.* [Fr. from *tenir*, L. *teneo*, to hold.]

1. A holding. In *English law*, the manner of holding lands and tenements of a superior. All the species of ancient tenures may be reduced to four, three of which subsist to this day. 1. Tenure by knight service, which was the most honorable. This is now abolished. 2. Tenure in free socage, or by a certain and determinate service, which is either free and honorable, or villein and base. 3. Tenure by copy of court roll, or copyhold tenure. 4. Tenure in ancient demain. There was also tenure in frankalmoign, or free alms. The tenure in free and common socage has absorbed most of the others. *Blackstone.*

In the United States, almost all lands are held in fee simple; not of a superior, but the whole right and title to the property being vested in the owner.

Tenure in general, then, is the particular manner of holding real estate, as by exclusive title or ownership, by fee simple, by fee tail, by curtesy, in dower, by copyhold, by lease, at will, &c.

2. The consideration, condition or service which the occupier of land gives to his lord or superior for the use of his land.

3. Manner of holding in general. In absolute governments, men hold their rights by a precarious *tenure.*

TEPEFAC'TION, *n.* [L. *tepefacio*; *tepidus*, warm, and *facio*, to make.]

The act or operation of warming, making tepid or moderately warm.

TEP'EFȲ, *v. t.* [L. *tepefacio.*] To make moderately warm. *Goldsmith.*

TEP'EFȲ, *v. i.* To become moderately warm.

TEP'ID, *a.* [L. *tepidus*, from *tepeo*, to be warm; Russ. *toplyu.*]

Moderately warm; lukewarm; as a *tepid* bath; *tepid* rays; *tepid* vapors.

Tepid mineral waters, are such as have less sensible cold than common water. *Cyc.*

TEP'IDNESS, *n.* Moderate warmth; lukewarmness. *Rambler.*

TE'POR, *n.* [L.] Gentle heat; moderate warmth. *Arbuthnot.*

TER'APHIM, *n.* [Heb.] Household deities or images.

TERATOL'OGY, *n.* [Gr. τερας, a prodigy, and λογος, discourse.]

Bombast in language; affectation of sublimity. [*Not used.*] *Bailey.*

TERCE, *n. ters.* [Sp. *tercia*; Fr. *tiers*, *tierce*, a third.]

A cask whose contents are 42 gallons, the third of a pipe or butt.

TER'CEL, *n.* The male of the common falcon (*Falco peregrinus.*) *Ed. Encyc.*

TERCE-MAJOR, *n.* A sequence of the three best cards.

TER'EBINTH, *n.* [Fr. *terebinthe*; Gr. τερεβινθος.] The turpentine tree. *Spenser.*

TEREBIN'THINATE, *a.* Terebinthine; impregnated with the qualities of turpentine. *Ramsay.*

TEREBIN'THINE, *a.* [L. *terebinthinus*, from *terebinthina*, turpentine.]

Pertaining to turpentine; consisting of turpentine, or partaking of its qualities.

TER'EBRATE, *v. t.* [L. *terebro*, *tero.*] To bore; to perforate with a gimlet. [*Little used.*] *Derham.*

TEREBRA'TION, *n.* The act of boring. [*Little used.*] *Bacon.*

TEREBRAT'ULITE, *n.* Fossil terebratula, a kind of shell.

TERE'DO, *n.* [L. from *tero*, to wear.] A worm that bores and penetrates the bottom of ships; or rather a genus of worms, so called.

TER'EK, *n.* A water fowl with long legs.

TER'ET, } *a.* [L. *teres.*] Round and tapering; columnar; as the stem of a plant. *Martyn.*
TERE'TE, }

TERĠEM'INAL, } *a.* [L. *tergeminus.*] Thrice double; as a *tergeminate* leaf. *Martyn.*
TERĠEM'INATE, }

TERĠEM'INOUS, *a.* [supra.] Threefold.

TERĠIF'ETOUS, *a.* *Tergifetous plants*, are such as bear their seeds on the back of their leaves, as ferns. *Cyc.*

TER'ĠIVERSATE, *v. i.* [L. *tergum*, the back, and *verto*, to turn.] To shift; to practice evasion. [*Little used.*] *Bailey.*

TERĠIVERSA'TION, *n.* A shifting; shift; subterfuge; evasion.

Writing is to be preferred before verbal conferences, as being more free from passion and *tergiversation.* *Bramhall.*

2. Change; fickleness of conduct.

The colonel, after all his *tergiversation*, lost his life in the king's service. *Clarendon.*

TERM, *n.* [Gr. τερμα; Fr. *terme*; It. *termine*; Sp. *termino*; L. *terminus*, a limit or boundary; W. *terv*, *tervyn*, from *terv*, extreme.]

1. A limit; a bound or boundary; the extremity of any thing; that which limits its extent.

Corruption is a reciprocal to generation, and they two are as nature's two *terms* or boundaries. *Bacon.*

2. The time for which any thing lasts; any limited time; as the *term* of five years; the *term* of life.

3. In *geometry*, a point or line that limits. A line is the *term* of a superficies, and a superficies is the *term* of a solid.

4. In *law*, the limitation of an estate; or rather the whole time or duration of an estate; as a lease for the *term* of life, for the *term* of three lives, for the *term* of twenty one years.

5. In *law*, the time in which a court is held or open for the trial of causes. In England, there are four terms in the year; Hilary term, from January 23d to February 12th; Easter term, from Wednesday, fortnight after Easter, to the Monday next after Ascension day; Trinity term, from Friday next after Trinity Sunday to the Wednesday, fortnight after; and Michaelmas term, from November 6th to the 28th. These terms are observed by the courts of king's bench, the common pleas and exchequer, but not by the parliament, the chancery or by inferior courts. The rest of the year is called vacation. In the United States, the terms to be observed by the tribunals of justice, are prescribed by the statutes of congress and of the several states.

6. In *universities* and *colleges*, the time during which instruction is regularly given to students, who are obliged by the statutes and laws of the institution to attend to the recitations, lectures and other exercises.

7. In *grammar*, a word or expression; that which fixes or determines ideas.

In painting, the greatest beauties cannot be always expressed for want of *terms.* *Dryden.*

8. In *the arts*, a word or expression that denotes something peculiar to an art; as a technical *term.*

9. In *logic*, a syllogism consists of three terms, the major, the minor, and the middle. The predicate of the conclusion is called the major term, because it is the most general, and the subject of the conclusion is called the minor term, because it is less general. These are called the extremes; and the third term, introduced as a common measure between them, is called the mean or middle term. Thus in the following syllogism.

Every vegetable is combustible;
Every tree is a vegetable;
Therefore every tree is combustible.

Combustible is the predicate of the conclusion, or the major term; *every tree* is the minor term; *vegetable* is the middle term. *Hedge's Logic.*

10. In *architecture*, a kind of statues or columns adorned on the top with the figure of a head, either of a man, woman or satyr. Terms are sometimes used as consoles, and sustain entablatures; and sometimes as statues to adorn gardens. *Cyc.*

11. Among *the ancients*, terms, *termini miliares*, were the heads of certain divinities placed on square land-marks of stone, to mark the several stadia on roads. These were dedicated to Mercury, who was supposed to preside over highways. *Cyc.*

12. In *algebra*, a member of a compound quantity; as *a*, in a+b; or *ab*, in ab+cd. *Day.*

13. Among *physicians*, the monthly courses of females are called *terms.* *Bailey.*

14. In *contracts*, *terms*, in the plural, are conditions; propositions stated or promises made, which when assented to or accepted by another, settle the contract and bind the parties. A engages to build a house for B for a specific sum of money, in a given time; these are his *terms.* When B promises to give to A that sum for building the house, he has agreed to the *terms*; the contract is completed and binding upon both parties.

Terms of proportion, in mathematics, are such numbers, letters or quantities as are compared one with another.

To make terms, to come to an agreement.

To come to terms, to agree; to come to an agreement.

To bring to terms, to reduce to submission or to conditions.

TERM, *v. t.* To name; to call; to denominate.

Men *term* what is beyond the limits of the universe, imaginary space. *Locke.*

TER'MAGANCY, *n.* [from *termagant.*] Turbulence; tumultuousness; as a violent *termagancy* of temper. *Baker.*

TER'MAGANT, *a.* [In Sax. *tir* or *tyr* is a deity, Mars or Mercury, and a prince or lord. As a prefix, it augments the sense of words, and is equivalent to *chief* or *very great.* The Sax. *magan*, Eng. *may*, is a verb denoting to be able, to prevail; from the sense of straining, striving or driving. Qu. the root of *stir.*]

Tumultuous; turbulent; boisterous or furious; quarrelsome; scolding.

The eldest was a *termagant*, imperious, prodigal, profligate wench. *Arbuthnot.*

TER'MAGANT, *n.* A boisterous, brawling, turbulent woman. It seems in Shakspeare to have been used of men. In ancient farces and puppet-shows, *termagant* was a vociferous, tumultuous deity.

She threw his periwig into the fire. Well, said he, thou art a brave *termagant*. *Tatler.*

The sprites of fiery *termagants* in flame— *Pope.*

TERM'ED, *pp.* Called; denominated.

TERM'ER, *n.* One who travels to attend a court term. *Spenser.*

TERM'ER, } **TERM'OR**, } *n.* One who has an estate for a term of years or life. *Blackstone.*

TERM'-FEE, *n.* Among lawyers, a fee or certain sum charged to a suitor for each term his cause is in court.

TERM'INABLE, *a.* [from *term.*] That may be bounded; limitable. *Dict.*

TERM'INAL, *a.* [from L. *terminus.*] In *botany*, growing at the end of a branch or stem; terminating; as a *terminal* scape, flower or spike. *Martyn.*

2. Forming the extremity; as a *terminal* edge.

TERM'INATE, *v. t.* [Fr. *terminer;* L. *termino;* Sp. *terminar;* It. *terminare;* from L. *terminus*, W. *tervyn.*]

1. To bound; to limit; to set the extreme point or side of a thing; as, to *terminate* a surface by a line.

2. To end; to put an end to; as, to *terminate* a controversy.

TERM'INATE, *v. i.* To be limited; to end; to come to the furthest point in space; as, a line *terminates* at the equator; the torrid zone *terminates* at the tropics.

2. To end; to close; to come to a limit in time. The session of congress, every second year, must *terminate* on the third of March.

The wisdom of this world, its designs and efficacy, *terminate* on this side heaven. *South.*

TERM'INATED, *pp.* Limited; bounded; ended.

TERM'INATING, *ppr.* Limiting; ending; concluding.

TERMINA'TION, *n.* The act of limiting or setting bounds; the act of ending or concluding.

2. Bound; limit in space or extent; as the *termination* of a line.

3. End in time or existence; as the *termination* of the year or of life; the *termination* of happiness.

4. In *grammar*, the end or ending of a word; the syllable or letter that ends a word. Words have different *terminations* to express number, time and sex.

5. End; conclusion; result.

6. Last purpose. *White.*

7. Word; term. [*Not in use.*] *Shak.*

TERMINA'TIONAL, *a.* Forming the end or concluding syllable. *Walker.*

TERM'INATIVE, *a.* Directing termination. *Bp. Rust.*

TERM'INATIVELY, *adv.* Absolutely; so as not to respect any thing else. *Taylor.*

TERM'INATOR, *n.* In *astronomy*, a name sometimes given to the circle of illumination, from its property of terminating the boundaries of light and darkness. *Cyc.*

TERM'INER, *n.* A determining; as in *oyer* and *terminer.*

TERM'ING, *ppr.* Calling; denominating.

TERM'INIST, *n.* In *ecclesiastical history*, a sect of christians who maintain that God has fixed a certain term for the probation of particular persons, during which time they have the offer of grace, but after which God no longer wills their salvation. *Cyc.*

TERMINOL'OGY, *n.* [L. *terminus*, or Gr. τερμα, and λογος.] The doctrine of terms; a treatise on terms.

2. In *natural history*, that branch of the science which explains all the terms used in the description of natural objects. *Ed. Encyc.*

TERMIN'THUS, *n.* [Gr. τερμινθος, a pine nut.]

In *surgery*, a large painful tumor on the skin, thought to resemble a pine nut. *Cyc.*

TERM'LESS, *a.* Unlimited; boundless; as *termless* joys. *Raleigh.*

TERM'LY, *a.* Occurring every term; as a *termly* fee. *Bacon.*

TERM'LY, *adv.* Term by term; every term; as a fee *termly* given. *Bacon.*

TERN, *n.* [L. *sterna.*] A common name of certain aquatic fowls of the genus Sterna; as the great tern or sea swallow, *(S. hirundo,)* the black tern, the lesser tern, or hooded tern, and the foolish tern, or noddy, *(S. stolida.)* The brown tern, or brown gull, *(S. obscura,)* is considered as the young of the pewit gull or sea-crow, before molting. *Ed. Encyc.*

TERN, *a.* [L. *ternus.*] Threefold; consisting of three.

Tern leaves, in threes, or three by three; expressing the number of leaves in each whorl or set.

Tern peduncles, three growing together from the same axil.

Tern flowers, growing three and three together. *Martyn.*

TERN'ARY, *a.* [L. *ternarius*, of three.] Proceeding by threes; consisting of three.

The *ternary* number, in antiquity, was esteemed a symbol of perfection and held in great veneration. *Cyc.*

TERN'ARY, } **TERN'ION**, } *n.* [L. *ternarius, ternio.*] The number three. *Holder.*

TERN'ATE, *a.* [L. *ternus, terni.*] In *botany*, a *ternate* leaf, is one that has three leaflets on a petiole, as in trefoil, strawberry, bramble, &c. There are leaves also *biternate* and *triternate*, having three ternate or three biternate leaflets. *Martyn.*

These leaves must not be confounded with *folia terna*, which are leaves that grow three together in a whorl, on a stem or branch. *Cyc.*

Ternate bat, a species of bat of a large kind, found in the isle Ternate, and other East India isles. [See *Vampyre.*]

Terra Japonica, catechu, so called.

Terra Lemnia, a species of red bolar earth.

Terra ponderosa, baryte; heavy spar.

Terra Sienna, a brown bole or ocher from Sienna in Italy.

TER'RACE, *n.* [Fr. *terrasse;* It. *terrazzo;* Sp. *terrado;* from L. *terra*, the earth.]

1. In *gardening*, a raised bank of earth with sloping sides, laid with turf, and graveled on the top for a walk. *Cyc.*

2. A balcony or open gallery. *Johnson.*

3. The flat roof of a house. All the buildings of the oriental nations are covered with *terraces*, where people walk or sleep.

TER'RACE, *v. t.* To form into a terrace.

2. To open to the air and light. *Wotton.*

TER'RACED, *pp.* Formed into a terrace; having a terrace. *Thomson.*

TER'RAÇING, *ppr.* Forming into a terrace; opening to the air.

TER'RAPIN, *n.* A name given to a species of tide-water tortoise.

TERRA'QUEOUS, *a.* [L. *terra*, earth, and *aqua*, water; W. *tir*, Sans. *dara*, earth.]

Consisting of land and water, as the globe or earth. This epithet is given to the earth in regard to the surface, of which more than three fifths consist of water, and the remainder of earth or solid materials.

TER'RAR, *n.* A register of lands. [*Not in use.*] *Cowel.*

TERRE-BLUE, *n.* [Fr. *terre*, earth, and *blue.*]

A kind of earth. *Woodward.*

TERRE-MOTE, *n.* [L. *terra*, earth, and *motus*, motion.]

An earthquake. [*Not in use.*] *Gower.*

TERRE-PLEIN, } **TERRE-PLAIN**, } *n.* [Fr. *terre*, earth, and *plein*, full.] In *fortification*, the top, platform or horizontal surface of a rampart, on which the cannon are placed.

TERRE-TEN'ANT, } **TER-TEN'ANT**, } *n.* [Fr. *terre-tenant.*] One who has the actual possession of land; the occupant.

TERRE-VERTE, *n.* [Fr. *terre*, earth, and *verd, verte*, green.]

A species of green earth, used by painters. It is an indurated clay, found in the earth in large flat masses, imbedded in strata of other species of earth. It is of a fine regular structure, and of a smooth glossy surface. It is found in Cyprus, France and Italy. *Cyc.*

TER'REL, *n.* [from *terra.*] Little earth, a magnet of a just spherical figure, and so placed that its poles, equator, &c. correspond exactly to those of the world.

TERRE'NE, *a.* [L. *terrenus*, from *terra*, W. *tir*, earth.]

1. Pertaining to the earth; earthy; as *terrene* substance.
2. Earthly; terrestrial.
God set before him a mortal and immortal life, a nature celestial and *terrene*. *Raleigh.*

TER'REOUS, *a.* [L. *terreus*, from *terra*, earth.]
Earthy; consisting of earth; as *terreous* substances; *terreous* particles. *Brown.*

TERRES'TRIAL, *a.* [L. *terrestris*, from *terra*, the earth.]
1. Pertaining to the earth; existing on the earth; as *terrestrial* animals; bodies *terrestrial.* 1 Cor. xv.
2. Consisting of earth; as the *terrestrial* globe.
3. Pertaining to the world, or to the present state; sublunary. Death puts an end to all *terrestrial* scenes.

TERRES'TRIALLY, *adv.* After an earthly manner. *More.*

TERRES'TRIOUS, *a.* Earthy. [*Little used.*]
2. Pertaining to the earth; being or living on the earth; terrestrial. *Brown.*

TER'RIBLE, *a.* [Fr. from L. *terribilis*, from *terreo*, to frighten.]
1. Frightful; adapted to excite terror; dreadful; formidable.
Prudent in peace, and *terrible* in war. *Prior.*
The form of the image was *terrible.* Dan. ii.
2. Adapted to impress dread, terror or solemn awe and reverence.
The Lord thy God is among you, a mighty God and *terrible.* Deut. vii.
Let them praise thy great and *terrible* name, for it is holy. Ps. xcix.
He hath done for thee these great and *terrible* things, which thine eyes have seen. Deut. x.
3. *adv.* Severely; very; so as to give pain; as *terrible* cold; *a colloquial phrase.*

TER'RIBLENESS, *n.* Dreadfulness; formidableness; the quality or state of being terrible; as the *terribleness* of a sight.

TER'RIBLY, *adv.* Dreadfully; in a manner to excite terror or fright.
When he ariseth to shake *terribly* the earth. Is. ii.
2. Violently; very greatly.
The poor man squalled *terribly.* *Swift.*

TER'RIER, *n.* [Fr. from *terra*, earth.] A dog or little hound, that creeps into the ground after animals that burrow. *Dryden.*
2. A lodge or hole where certain animals, as foxes, rabbits, badgers and the like, secure themselves. *Cyc.*
3. *Originally*, a collection of acknowledgments of the vassals or tenants of a lordship, containing the rents and services they owed to the lord, &c.; at present, a book or roll in which the lands of private persons or corporations are described by their site, boundaries, number of acres, &c. *Cyc.*
4. A wimble, auger or borer. [L. *tero.*] *Ainsworth.*

TERRIF'IC, *a.* [L. *terrificus*, from *terreo*, *terror*, and *facio.*]
Dreadful; causing terror; adapted to excite great fear or dread; as a *terrific* form; *terrific* sight.

TER'RIFIED, *pp.* Frightened; affrighted.

TER'RIFY, *v. t.* [L. *terror* and *facio*, to make.]
To frighten; to alarm or shock with fear.
They were *terrified* and affrighted. Luke xxiv.
When ye shall hear of wars and commotions, be not *terrified.* Luke xxi. Job vii.

TER'RIFYING, *ppr.* Frightening; affrighting.

TERRIG'ENOUS, *a.* [L. *terrigena*, one born of the earth; *terra* and *gigno.*] Earth-born; produced by the earth.

TERRITO'RIAL, *a.* [from *territory.*] Pertaining to territory or land; as *territorial* limits; *territorial* jurisdiction. *Tooke.*
2. Limited to a certain district. Rights may be personal or *territorial.*

TERRITO'RIALLY, *adv.* In regard to territory; by means of territory. *E. Everett.*

TER'RITORY, *n.* [Fr. *territoire*; It. Sp. *territorio*; L. *territorium*, from *terra*, earth.]
1. The extent or compass of land within the bounds or belonging to the jurisdiction of any state, city or other body.
Linger not in my *territories.* *Shak.*
They erected a house within their own *territory.* *Hayward.*
Arts and sciences took their rise and flourished only in those small *territories* where the people were free. *Swift.*
2. A tract of land belonging to and under the dominion of a prince or state, lying at a distance from the parent country or from the seat of government; as the *territories* of the East India Company; the *territories* of the United States; the *territory* of Mishigan; Northwest *territory.* These districts of country, when received into the union and acknowledged to be states, lose the appellation of *territory.* *Constitution of the U. States.*

TER'ROR, *n.* [L. *terror*, from *terreo*, to frighten; Fr. *terreur*; It. *terrore.*]
1. Extreme fear; violent dread; fright; fear that agitates the body and mind.
The sword without, and *terror* within. Deut. xxxii.
The *terrors* of God do set themselves in array against me. Job vi.
Amaze and *terror* seiz'd the rebel host. *Milton.*
2. That which may excite dread; the cause of extreme fear.
Rulers are not a *terror* to good works, but to the evil. Rom. xiii.
Those enormous *terrors* of the Nile. *Prior.*
3. In *Scripture*, the sudden judgments of God are called *terrors.* Ps. lxxiii.
4. The threatenings of wicked men, or evil apprehended from them. 1 Pet. iii.
5. Awful majesty, calculated to impress fear. 2 Cor. v.
6. Death is emphatically styled the *king of terrors.*

TERSE, *a. ters.* [L. *tersus*, from *tergo*, to wipe.]
Cleanly written; neat; elegant without pompousness; as *terse* language; a *terse* style.
Diffus'd, yet *terse*, poetical, though plain. *Harte.*

TERSELY, *adv. ters'ly.* Neatly.

TERSENESS, *n. ters'ness.* Neatness of style; smoothness of language. *Warton.*

TER-TEN'ANT, *n.* [Fr. *terre* and *tenant.*] The occupant of land.

TER'TIALS, *n.* In *ornithology*, fethers near the junction of the wing with the body.

TER'TIAN, *a.* [L. *tertianus*, from *tertius*, third.]
Occurring every other day; as a *tertian* fever.

TER'TIAN, *n.* A disease or fever whose paroxysms return every other day; an intermittent occurring after intervals of about forty eight hours. *Cyc.* *Coxe.*
2. A measure of 84 gallons, the third part of a tun. *Obs.*

TER'TIARY, *a.* Third; of the third formation. *Tertiary* mountains are such as result from the ruins of other mountains promiscuously heaped together. *Kirwan.*
Tertiary formation, in *geology*, a series of horizontal strata, more recent than chalk beds, consisting chiefly of sand and clay, and frequently embracing vast quantities of organic remains of the larger animals. It comprehends the *alluvial* formation, which embraces those deposits only which have resulted from causes still in operation; and the *diluvial* formation, which is constituted of such deposits as are supposed to have been produced by the deluge. *D. Olmsted.*

TER'TIATE, *v. t.* [L. *tertius*, third; *tertio*, to do every third day.]
1. To do any thing the third time. *Johnson.*
2. To examine the thickness of the metal at the muzzle of a gun; or in general, to examine the thickness to ascertain the strength of ordnance.

TES'SELATE, *v. t.* [L. *tessela*, a little square stone.]
To form into squares or checkers; to lay with checkered work.

TES'SELATED, *pp.* Checkered; formed in little squares or mosaic work; as a *tesselated* pavement.
2. In *botany*, spotted or checkered like a chess board; as a *tesselated* leaf. *Martyn.*

TESSELA'TION, *n.* Mosaic work, or the operation of making it. *Forsyth, Italy.*

TESSERA'IC, *a.* [L. *tessera*, a square thing.]
Diversified by squares; tesselated. *Atkyns.*

TEST, *n.* [L. *testa*, an earthen pot; It. *testa* or *testo*; Fr. *têt.*]
1. In *metallurgy*, a large cupel, or a vessel in the nature of a cupel, formed of wood ashes and finely powdered brick dust, in which metals are melted for trial and refinement. *Cyc.*
2. Trial; examination by the cupel; hence, any critical trial and examination.
Thy virtue, prince, has stood the *test* of fortune
Like purest gold— *Addison.*
3. Means of trial.
Each *test* and every light her muse will bear. *Dryden.*
4. That with which any thing is compared for proof of its genuineness; a standard.
—Life, force and beauty must to all impart,
At once the source, the end and *test* of art. *Pope.*
5. Discriminative characteristic; standard.
Our *test* excludes your tribe from benefit. *Dryden.*
6. Judgment; distinction.
Who would excel, when few can make a *test*
Betwixt indifferent writing and the best? *Dryden.*
7. In *chimistry*, a substance employed to detect any unknown constituent of a compound, by causing it to exhibit some

known property. Thus ammonia is a *test* of copper, because it strikes a blue color with that metal, by which a minute quantity of it can be discovered when in combination with other substances. *D. Olmsted.*

TEST, *n.* [L. *testis*, a witness, properly one that affirms.]

In *England*, an oath and declaration against transubstantiation, which all officers, civil and military, are obliged to take within six months after their admission. They were formerly obliged also to receive the sacrament, according to the usage of the church of England. These requisitions are made by Stat. 25 Charles II. which is called the *test act*. The test of 7 Jac. 1. was removed in 1753. *Blackstone.*

TEST, *v. t.* To compare with a standard; to try; to prove the truth or genuineness of any thing by experiment or by some fixed principle or standard; as, to *test* the soundness of a principle; to *test* the validity of an argument.

The true way of *testing* its character, is to suppose it [the system] will be persevered in. *Edin. Review.*

Experience is the surest standard by which to *test* the real tendency of the existing constitution. *Washington's Address.*

To *test* this position— *Hamilton, Rep.*

In order to *test* the correctness of this system— *Adams' Lect.*

This expedient has been already *tested*. *Walsh, Rev.*

2. To attest and date; as a writing *tested* on such a day.

3. In *metallurgy*, to refine gold or silver by means of lead, in a test, by the destruction, vitrification or scorification of all extraneous matter.

TEST'ABLE, *a.* [L. *testor*. See *Testament.*]

That may be devised or given by will. *Blackstone.*

TESTACEOG'RAPHY, *n.* [See *Testaceology.*]

TESTACEOL'OĠY, TESTAL'OĠY, } *n.* [L. *testacea*, or *testa*, and Gr. λογος.]

The science of testaceous vermes, or of those soft and simple animals which have a testaceous covering; a branch of vermeology. [Words thus formed of two languages are rather anomalous, and the first for its length is very objectionable.]

TESTA'CEOUS, *a.* [L. *testaceus*, from *testa*, a shell. The primary sense of *testa, testis, testor*, &c. is to thrust or drive; hence the sense of hardness, compactness, in *testa* and *testis*; and hence the sense of *attest, contest, detest, testator, testament*, all implying a sending, driving, &c.]

Pertaining to shells; consisting of a hard shell, or having a hard continuous shell. *Testaceous animals* are such as have a strong thick entire shell, as oysters and clams; and are thus distinguished from *crustaceous animals*, whose shells are more thin and soft, and consist of several pieces jointed, as lobsters. *Cyc.*

Testaceous medicines, are all preparations of shells and like substances, as the powders of crabs' claws, pearl, &c. *Encyc.*

TEST'AMENT, *n.* [Fr. from L. *testamentum*, from *testor*, to make a will.]

1. A solemn authentic instrument in writing, by which a person declares his will as to the disposal of his estate and effects after his death. This is otherwise called a *will*. A testament, to be valid, must be made when the testator is of sound mind, and it must be subscribed, witnessed and published in such manner as the law prescribes.

A man in certain cases may make a valid will by words only, and such will is called *nuncupative*. *Blackstone.*

2. The name of each general division of the canonical books of the sacred Scriptures; as the Old *Testament*; the New *Testament*. The name is equivalent to *covenant*, and in our use of it, we apply it to the books which contain the old and new dispensations; that of Moses, and that of Jesus Christ.

TESTAMENT'ARY, *a.* Pertaining to a will or to wills; as *testamentary* causes in law.

2. Bequeathed by will; given by testament; as *testamentary* charities. *Atterbury.*

3. Done by testament or will.

Testamentary guardian of a minor, is one appointed by the deed or will of a father, until the child becomes of age.

TESTAMENTA'TION, *n.* The act or power of giving by will. [*Little used.*] *Burke.*

TEST'ATE, *a.* [L. *testatus.*] Having made and left a will; as, a person is said to die *testate.*

TESTA'TION, *n.* [L. *testatio*. A witnessing or witness. *Bp. Hall.*

TESTA'TOR, *n.* [L.] A man who makes and leaves a will or testament at death.

TESTA'TRIX, *n.* A woman who makes and leaves a will at death.

TEST'ED, *pp.* Tried or approved by a test. *Shak. Parkhurst.*

TEST'ER, *n.* [Fr. *tête*, head.] The top covering of a bed, consisting of some species of cloth, supported by the bedstead.

TEST'ER, TEST'ON, } *n.* A French coin, of the value of about six pence sterling.

TEST'ICLE, *n.* [L. *testiculus*; literally a hard mass, like *testa*, a shell.]

The testicles are male organs of generation, consisting of glandular substances, whose office is to secrete the fecundating fluid. *Cyc.*

TESTIC'ULATE, *a.* In *botany*, shaped like a testicle. *Lee.*

TESTIFICA'TION, *n.* [L. *testificatio*. See *Testify.*]

The act of testifying or giving testimony or evidence; as a direct *testification* of our homage to God. *South.*

TESTIFICA'TOR, *n.* One who gives witness or evidence.

TEST'IFIED, *pp.* [from *testify.*] Given in evidence; witnessed; published; made known.

TEST'IFIER, *n.* [from *testify.*] One who testifies; one who gives testimony or bears witness to prove any thing.

TEST'IFȲ, *v. i.* [L. *testificor*; *testis* and *facio*; It. *testificare*; Sp. *testificar.*]

1. To make a solemn declaration, verbal or written, to establish some fact; to give testimony for the purpose of communicating to others a knowledge of something not known to them.

Jesus needed not that any should *testify* of man, for he knew what was in man. John ii.

2. In *judicial proceedings*, to make a solemn declaration under oath, for the purpose of establishing or making proof of some fact to a court; to give testimony in a cause depending before a tribunal.

One witness shall not *testify* against any person to cause him to die. Num. xxxv.

3. To declare a charge against one.

O Israel, I will *testify* against thee. Ps. l.

4. To protest; to declare against.

I *testified* against them in the day wherein they sold victuals. Neh. xiii.

TEST'IFȲ, *v. t.* To affirm or declare solemnly for the purpose of establishing a fact.

We speak that we do know, and *testify* that we have seen. John iii.

2. In *law*, to affirm or declare under oath before a tribunal, for the purpose of proving some fact.

3. To bear witness to; to support the truth of by testimony.

To *testify* the gospel of the grace of God. Acts xx.

4. To publish and declare freely.

Testifying both to the Jews, and also to the Greeks, repentance towards God and faith towards our Lord Jesus Christ. Acts xx.

TEST'IFȲING, *ppr.* Affirming solemnly or under oath, for the purpose of establishing a fact; giving testimony; bearing witness; declaring.

TEST'ILY, *adv.* [from *testy.*] Fretfully; peevishly; with petulance.

TESTIMO'NIAL, *n.* [Fr. from L. *testimonium.*]

A writing or certificate in favor of one's character or good conduct. *Testimonials* are required on many occasions. A person must have *testimonials* of his learning and good conduct, before he can obtain license to preach. *Testimonials* are to be signed by persons of known respectability of character.

TEST'IMONY, *n.* [L. *testimonium.*] A solemn declaration or affirmation made for the purpose of establishing or proving some fact. Such affirmation in judicial proceedings, may be verbal or written, but must be under oath. *Testimony* differs from *evidence*; *testimony* is the declaration of a witness, and *evidence* is the effect of that declaration on the mind, or the degree of light which it affords.

2. Affirmation; declaration. These doctrines are supported by the uniform *testimony* of the fathers. The belief of past facts must depend on the evidence of human *testimony*, or the *testimony* of historians.

3. Open attestation; profession.

Thou for the *testimony* of truth hast borne Universal reproach. *Milton.*

4. Witness; evidence; proof of some fact.

Shake off the dust under your feet, for a *testimony* against them. Mark vi.

5. In *Scripture*, the two tables of the law.

Thou shalt put into the ark the *testimony* which I shall give thee. Ex. xxv.

6. The book of the law.

He brought forth the king's son—and gave him the *testimony*. 2 Kings xi.

7. The gospel, which testifies of Christ and declares the will of God. 1 Cor. ii. 2 Tim. i.

8. The ark. Ex. xvi.

9. The word of God; the Scriptures.

The *testimony* of the Lord is sure, making wise the simple. Ps. xix.

10. The laws or precepts of God. "I love thy *testimonies*." "I have kept thy *testimonies*." *Psalms.*

11. That which is equivalent to a declaration; manifestation.

Sacrifices were appointed by God for a *testimony* of his hatred of sin. *Clarke.*

12. Evidence suggested to the mind; as the *testimony* of conscience. 2 Cor. i.

13. Attestation; confirmation.

TEST'IMONY, *v. t.* To witness. [*Not in use.*] *Shak.*

TEST'INESS, *n.* [from *testy.*] Fretfulness; peevishness; petulance.

Testiness is a disposition or aptness to be angry. *Locke.*

TEST'ING, *ppr.* [from *test.*] Trying for proof; proving by a standard or by experiment.

A plan for *testing* alkalies— *Ure.*

TEST'ING, *n.* The act of trying for proof.

2. In *metallurgy*, the operation of refining large quantities of gold or silver by means of lead, in the vessel called a *test.* In this process, the extraneous matter is vitrified, scorified or destroyed, and the metal left pure. This operation is performed in the manner of cupellation. *Cyc.*

TESTOON', *n.* A silver coin in Italy and Portugal. In Florence, the testoon is worth two lire or three paoli, about seventeen pence sterling, or thirty two cents. At Lisbon, the testoon, as a money of account, is valued at 100 rees, about seven pence sterling, or twelve and a half cents.

TEST'-PAPER, *n.* A paper impregnated with a chimical re-agent, as litmus, &c. *Parke.*

TESTU'DINAL, *a.* Pertaining to the tortoise, or resembling it. *Fleming.*

TESTU'DINATED, *a.* [L. *testudo*, a tortoise.] Roofed; arched.

TESTUDIN'EOUS, *a.* Resembling the shell of a tortoise.

TESTU'DO, *n.* [L.] A tortoise. Among the Romans, a cover or skreen which a body of troops formed with their shields or targets, by holding them over their heads when standing close to each other. This cover resembled the back of a tortoise, and served to shelter the men from darts, stones and other missiles. A similar defense was sometimes formed of boards and moved on wheels.

2. In *medicine*, a broad soft tumor between the skull and the skin, called also *talpa* or mole, as resembling the subterraneous windings of the tortoise or mole. *Cyc.*

TEST'Y, *a.* [from Fr. *teste, tête*, the head, or from the same root.]

Fretful; peevish; petulant; easily irritated. Pyrrhus cured his *testy* courtiers with a kick.

Must I stand and crouch under your *testy* humor? *Shak.*

TET'ANUS, *n.* [Gr. τετανος, stretched.] A spasmodic contraction of the muscles of voluntary motion, particularly of those which shut the lower jaw; the locked jaw. *Cyc.*

TETAUG', *n.* The name of a fish on the coast of New England; called also black fish.

TETCH'INESS, } See *Techiness*, *Techy*.
TETCH'Y. } [corrupted from *touchy*, *touchiness.*] [*Not in use.*]

TETE, *n.* [Fr. head.] False hair; a kind of wig or cap of false hair.

Tete-a-tete, [Fr.] head to head; cheek by jowl; in private.

TETH'ER, *n.* [See *Tedder.*] A rope or chain by which a beast is confined for feeding within certain limits.

TETH'ER, *v. t.* To confine, as a beast, with a rope or chain for feeding within certain limits. [It would be well to write this word uniformly *tedder.*]

TET'RACHORD, *n.* [Gr. τετταρα, four, and χορδη, a chord.]

In *ancient music*, a diatessaron; a series of four sounds, of which the extremes, or first and last, constituted a fourth. These extremes were immutable; the two middle sounds were changeable. *Cyc.*

TET'RAD, *n.* [Gr. τετρας, the number four.] The number four; a collection of four things.

TETRADAC'TYLOUS, *a.* [Gr. τετρα and δακτυλος.] Having four toes.

TETRADIAP'ASON, *n.* [Gr. τετρα, four, and *diapason.*]

Quadruple diapason or octave; a musical chord, otherwise called a quadruple eighth or twenty ninth. *Cyc.*

TETRADRACH'MA, *n.* [Gr. τετρα and δραχμη.]

In *ancient coinage*, a silver coin worth four drachmas, 3*s.* sterling, or 66⅔ cents; the drachma being estimated at 9*d.* sterling, or 16⅔ cents.

TETRADYNAM'IAN, *n.* [Gr. τετρα and δυναμις, power, strength.]

In *botany*, a plant having six stamens, four of which are longer than the others.

TETRADYNAM'IAN, *a.* Having six stamens, four of which are uniformly longer than the others.

TET'RAGON, *n.* [Gr. τετραγωνος; τετρα, for τεσσαρες, four, and γωνια, an angle.]

1. In *geometry*, a figure having four angles; a quadrangle; as a square, a rhombus, &c.

2. In *astrology*, an aspect of two planets with regard to the earth, when they are distant from each other ninety degrees, or the fourth of a circle.

TETRAG'ONAL, *a.* Pertaining to a tetragon; having four angles or sides. Thus a square, a parallelogram, a rhombus, and a trapezium, are *tetragonal* figures.

2. In *botany*, having four prominent longitudinal angles, as a stem. *Martyn.*

TET'RAGONISM, *n.* The quadrature of the circle. *Cyc.*

TET'RAGYN, *n.* [Gr. τετρα, four, and γυνη, a female.] In *botany*, a plant having four pistils.

TETRAGYN'IAN, *a.* Having four pistils.

TETRAHE'DRAL, *a.* [See *Tetrahedron.*]

1. Having four equal triangles. *Bailey.*

2. In *botany*, having four sides, as a pod or silique. *Martyn.*

TETRAHE'DRON, *n.* [Gr. τετρα, four, and εδρα, side.]

In *geometry*, a figure comprehended under four equilateral and equal triangles; or one of the five regular Platonic bodies of that figure. *Cyc.*

TETRAHEXAHE'DRAL, *a.* [Gr. τετρα, four, and *hexahedral.*]

In *crystalography*, exhibiting four ranges of faces, one above another, each range containing six faces.

TETRAM'ETER, *n.* [Gr. τετρα, four, and μετρον, measure.]

In *ancient poetry*, an iambic verse consisting of four feet, found in the comic poets. *Cyc.*

A verse consisting of four measures or eight feet. *Ash.*

TETRAN'DER, *n.* [Gr. τετρα, four, and ανηρ, a male.] In *botany*, a plant having four stamens.

TETRAN'DRIAN, *a.* Having four stamens.

TETRAPET'ALOUS, *a.* [Gr. τετρα, four, and πεταλον, leaf.]

In *botany*, containing four distinct petals or flower leaves; as a *tetrapetalous* corol. *Martyn.*

TETRAPH'YLLOUS, *a.* [Gr. τετρα, four, and φυλλον, leaf.]

In *botany*, having four leaves; consisting of four distinct leaves or leaflets; as a *tetraphyllous* calyx. *Martyn.*

TET'RAPTOTE, *n.* [Gr. τετρα, four, and πτωσις, case.]

In *grammar*, a noun that has four cases only; as L. *astus*, &c.

TE'TRARCH, *n.* [Gr. τετραρχης; τετρα, four, and αρχη, rule.]

A Roman governor of the fourth part of a province; a subordinate prince. In time, this word came to denote any petty king or sovereign.

TETR'ARCHATE, *n.* The fourth part of a province under a Roman tetrarch; or the office or jurisdiction of a tetrarch.

TETR'ARCHICAL, *a.* Pertaining to a tetrarchy. *Herbert.*

TET'RARCHY, *n.* The same as *tetrarchate.*

TETRASPERM'OUS, *a.* [Gr. τετρα, four, and σπερμα, seed.] In *botany*, containing four seeds. *Martyn.*

A *tetraspermous plant*, is one which produces four seeds in each flower, as the rough-leaved or verticillate plants. *Martyn.*

TETRAS'TICH, *n.* [Gr. τετραϛιχος; τετρα, four, and ϛιχος, verse.]

A stanza, epigram or poem consisting of four verses. *Pope.*

TET'RASTYLE, *n.* [Gr. τετρα, four, and ϛυλος, column.]

In *ancient architecture*, a building with four columns in front. *Cyc.*

TETRASYLLAB'IC, } *a.* Consisting of
TETRASYLLAB'ICAL, } four syllables. *Cyc.*

TETRASYL'LABLE, *n.* [Gr. τετρα, four, and συλλαβη, syllable.] A word consisting of four syllables.

TET'RIC, }
TET'RICAL, } *a.* [L. *tetricus.*] Froward; perverse; harsh; sour;
TET'RICOUS, } rugged. [*Not in use.*] *Knolles.*

TETRIC'ITY, *n.* Crabbedness; perverseness. [*Not in use.*]

TET'TER, *n.* [Sax. *teter, tetr*; allied perhaps to L. *titillo.*]

1. In *medicine*, a common name of several cutaneous diseases, consisting of an eruption of vesicles or pustules, in distinct or confluent clusters, spreading over the body in various directions and hardening into scabs or crusts. It includes the shingles,

ring-worm, milky scale *(crusta lactea,)* scald head, &c. *Good.*

2. In *farriery*, a cutaneous disease of animals, of the ring-worm kind, which spreads on the body in different directions, and occasions a troublesome itching. *Cyc.*

TET'TER, *v. t.* To affect with the disease called *tetters.*

TET'TISH, *a.* [Qu. Fr. *tête*, head.] Captious; testy. [*Not in use.*]

TEUTON'IC, *a.* Pertaining to the Teutons, a people of Germany, or to their language; as a noun, the language of the Teutons, the parent of the German Dutch, and Anglo Saxon or native English.

Teutonic order, a military religious order of knights, established toward the close of the twelfth century, in imitation of the Templars and Hospitallers. It was composed chiefly of Teutons or Germans, who marched to the Holy Land in the crusades, and was established in that country for charitable purposes. It increased in numbers and strength till it became master of all Prussia, Livonia and Pomerania. *Cyc.*

TEW, *v. t.* To work; to soften. [*Not in use.*] [See *Taw.*]

2. To work; to pull or tease; *among seamen.*

TEW, *n.* [probably *tow.*] Materials for any thing. [*Not in use.*] *Skinner.*

2. An iron chain. [*Not in use.*] *Ainsworth.*

TEW'EL, *n.* [Fr. *tuyau.*] An iron pipe in a forge to receive the pipe of a bellows. *Moxon.*

TEW'TAW, *v. t.* To beat; to break. [*Not in use.*] [See *Tew.*] *Mortimer.*

TEXT, *n.* [Fr. *texte*; L. *textus*, woven; It. *testo.* See *Texture.*]

1. A discourse or composition on which a note or commentary is written. Thus we speak of the *text* or original of the Scripture, in relation to the comments upon it. Infinite pains have been taken to ascertain and establish the genuine original *text.*

2. A verse or passage of Scripture which a preacher selects as the subject of a discourse.

> How oft, when Paul has serv'd us with a *text*,
> Has Epictetus, Plato, Tully preach'd. *Cowper.*

3. Any particular passage of Scripture, used as authority in argument for proof of a doctrine. In modern sermons, *texts* of Scripture are not as frequently cited as they were formerly.

4. In *ancient law authors*, the four Gospels, by way of eminence. *Cyc.*

TEXT, *v. t.* To write, as a text. [*Not much used.*] *Beaum.*

TEXT'-BOOK, *n.* In *universities* and *colleges*, a classic author written with wide spaces between the lines, to give room for the observations or interpretation dictated by the master or regent. *Cyc.*

2. A book containing the leading principles or most important points of a science or branch of learning, arranged in order for the use of students.

TEXT-HAND, *n.* A large hand in writing; so called because it was the practice to write the text of a book in a large hand, and the notes in a smaller hand.

TEXT'ILE, *a.* [L. *textilis.*] Woven, or capable of being woven.

TEXT'ILE, *n.* That which is or may be woven. *Bacon. Wilkins.*

TEXT'-MAN, *n.* A man ready in the quotation of texts. *Saunderson.*

TEXTO'RIAL, *a.* [L. *textor.*] Pertaining to weaving.

TEXT'RINE, *a.* Pertaining to weaving; as the *textrine* art. *Derham.*

TEXT'UAL, *a.* Contained in the text. *Milton.*

2. Serving for texts. *Bp. Hall.*

TEXT'UALIST, } *n.* [Fr. *textuaire*, from
TEXT'UARY, } *texte.*] One who is well versed in the Scriptures, and can readily quote texts.

2. One who adheres to the text.

TEXT'UARY, *a.* Textual; contained in the text. *Brown.*

2. Serving as a text; authoritative. *Glanville.*

TEXT'UIST, *n.* One ready in the quotation of texts.

TEX'TURE, *n.* [L. *textura*, *textus*, from *texo*, to weave.]

1. The act of weaving.

2. A web; that which is woven.

> Others, far in the grassy dale,
> Their humble *texture* weave. *Thomson.*

3. The disposition or connection of threads, filaments or other slender bodies interwoven; as the *texture* of cloth or of a spider's web.

4. The disposition of the several parts of any body in connection with each other; or the manner in which the constituent parts are united; as the *texture* of earthy substances or fossils; the *texture* of a plant; the *texture* of paper, of a hat or skin; a loose *texture*; or a close compact *texture.*

5. In anatomy. [See *Tissue.*]

THACK, for *thatch*, is local. [See *Thatch.*]

THAL'LITE, *n.* [Gr. θαλλος, a green twig.] In *mineralogy*, a substance variously denominated by different authors. It is the epidote of Haüy, the delphinite of Saussure, and the pistacite of Werner. It occurs both crystalized and in masses. *Cyc.*

THAM'MUZ, *n.* The tenth month of the Jewish civil year, containing 29 days, and answering to a part of June and a part of July.

2. The name of a deity among the Phenicians.

THAN, *adv.* [Sax. *thanne*; Goth. *than*; D. *dan.* This word signifies also *then*, both in English and Dutch. The Germans express the sense by *als*, as.]

This word is placed after some comparative adjective or adverb, to express comparison between what precedes and what follows. Thus Elijah said, I am not better *than* my fathers. Wisdom is better *than* strength. Israel loved Joseph more *than* all his children. All nations are counted less *than* nothing. I who am less *than* the least of all saints. The last error shall be worse *than* the first. He that denies the faith is worse *than* an infidel.

After *more*, or an equivalent termination, the following word implies *less*, or *worse*; after *less*, or an equivalent termination, it implies *more* or *better.*

THANE, *n.* [Sax. *thegn*, *thægn*, a minister or servant; *thegnian*, *thenian*, to serve; D. G. *dienen*, to serve; Sw. *tiena*, to serve; *tienare*, a servant; Dan. *tiener*, to serve; *tiener*, a servant. If *g* is radical, this word belongs to Class Dg; if not, to Class Dn. No. 10.]

The thanes in England were formerly persons of some dignity; of these there were two orders, the king's thanes, who attended the Saxon and Danish kings in their courts, and held lands immediately of them; and the ordinary thanes, who were lords of manors, and who had a particular jurisdiction within their limits. After the conquest, this title was disused, and *baron* took its place.

THA'NE-LANDS, *n.* Lands granted to thanes.

THA'NESHIP, *n.* The state or dignity of a thane; or his seignory.

THANK, *v. t.* [Sax. *thancian*; G. D. *danken*; Ice. *thacka*: Sw. *tacka*; Dan. *takker.* We see by the Gothic dialects that *n* is not radical. To ascertain the primary sense, let us attend to its compounds; G. *abdanken*, [which in English would be *off-thank*,] to dismiss, discharge, discard, send away, put off, to disband or break, as an officer; *verdanken*, to owe or be indebted; D. *afdanken*, to cashier or discharge. These senses imply a sending. Hence *thank* is probably from the sense of giving, that is, a render or return.]

1. To express gratitude for a favor; to make acknowledgments to one for kindness bestowed.

> We are bound to *thank* God always for you. 2 Thess. i.
>
> Joab bowed himself and *thanked* the king. 2 Sam. xiv.

2. It is used ironically.

> Weigh the danger with the doubtful bliss,
> And *thank* yourself, if aught should fall amiss. *Dryden.*

THANK, } *n. generally in the plural.* [Sax.
THANKS, } *thanc*; Gaelic, *tainc.*] Expression of gratitude; an acknowledgment made to express a sense of favor or kindness received. Gratitude is the feeling or sentiment excited by kindness; *thanks* are the expression of that sentiment. Luke vi.

> *Thanks* be to God, who giveth us the victory. 1 Cor. xv.
>
> *Thanks* be to God for his unspeakable gift. 2 Cor. ix.
>
> He took bread and gave *thanks* to God. Acts xxvii.

THANK'ED, *pp.* Having received expressions of gratitude.

THANK'FUL, *a.* [Sax. *thancfull*; Gaelic, *taincal.*]

Grateful; impressed with a sense of kindness received, and ready to acknowledge it. The Lord's supper is to be celebrated with a *thankful* remembrance of his sufferings and death.

> Be *thankful* to him, and bless his name. Ps. c.

THANK'FULLY, *adv.* With a grateful sense of favor or kindness received.

> If you have liv'd, take *thankfully* the past. *Dryden.*

THANK'FULNESS, *n.* Expression of gratitude; acknowledgment of a favor.

2. Gratitude; a lively sense of good received.

The celebration of these holy mysteries being ended, retire with all *thankfulness* of heart for having been admitted to that heavenly feast. *Taylor.*

THANK'ING, *ppr.* Expressing gratitude for good received.

THANK'LESS, *a.* Unthankful; ungrateful; not acknowledging favors.

That she may feel
How sharper than a serpent's tooth it is
To have a *thankless* child. *Shak.*

2. Not deserving thanks, or not likely to gain thanks; as a *thankless* office. *Wotton.*

THANK'LESSNESS, *n.* Ingratitude; failure to acknowledge a kindness. *Donne.*

THANK'-OFFERING, *n.* [*thank* and *offering.*]

An offering made in acknowledgment of mercy. *Watts.*

THANKSGIVE, *v. t.* thanksgiv'. [*thanks* and *give.*]

To celebrate or distinguish by solemn rites. [*Not in use.*] *Mede.*

THANKSGIV'ER, *n.* One who gives thanks or acknowledges a kindness. *Barrow.*

THANKSGIV'ING, *ppr.* Rendering thanks for good received.

THANKSGIV'ING, *n.* The act of rendering thanks or expressing gratitude for favors or mercies.

Every creature of God is good, and nothing to be refused, if received with *thanksgiving.* 1 Tim. iv.

2. A public celebration of divine goodness; also, a day set apart for religious services, specially to acknowledge the goodness of God, either in any remarkable deliverance from calamities or danger, or in the ordinary dispensation of his bounties. The practice of appointing an annual *thanksgiving* originated in New England.

THANK'-WORTHY, *a.* [*thank* and *worthy.*]

Deserving thanks; meritorious. 1 Pet. ii.

TH'ARM, *n.* [Sax. *thearm*; G. D. *darm.*] Intestines twisted into a cord. [*Local.*]

THAT, *an adjective, pronoun* or *substitute.* [Sax. *thæt, that*; Goth. *thata*; D. *dat*; G. *das*; Dan. *det*; Sw. *det.* Qu. Gr. ταυτος. This word is called in Saxon and German, an article, for it sometimes signifies *the.* It is called also in Saxon a pronoun, equivalent to *id, istud,* in Latin. In Swedish and Danish it is called a pronoun of the neuter gender. But these distinctions are groundless and of no use. It is probably from the sense of setting.]

1. *That* is a word used as a definitive adjective, pointing to a certain person or thing before mentioned, or supposed to be understood. "Here is *that* book we have been seeking this hour." "Here goes *that* man we were talking of."

It shall be more tolerable for Sodom and Gomorrah in the day of judgment, than for *that* city. Matt. x.

2. *That* is used definitively, to designate a specific thing or person emphatically.

The woman was made whole from *that* hour. Matt. ix.

In these cases, *that* is an adjective. In the two first examples, *the* may be substituted for it. "Here is *the* book we have been seeking." "Here goes *the* man we were talking of." But in other cases, *the* cannot supply its place, and *that* may be considered as more emphatically definitive than *the.*

3. *That* is used as the representative of a noun, either a person or a thing. In this use, it is often a pronoun and a relative. When it refers to persons, it is equivalent to *who,* and when it refers to a thing, it is equivalent to *which.* In this use, it represents either the singular number or the plural.

He *that* reproveth a scorner, getteth to himself shame. Prov. ix.

They *that* hate me without a cause, are more than the hairs of my head. Ps. lxiii.

A judgment *that* is equal and impartial, must incline to the greater probabilities. *Wilkins.*

They shall gather out of his kingdom all things *that* offend. Matt. xiii.

4. *That* is also the representative of a sentence or part of a sentence, and often of a series of sentences. In this case, *that* is not strictly a pronoun, a word standing for a noun; but is, so to speak, a *pro-sentence,* the substitute for a sentence, to save the repetition of it.

And when Moses heard *that,* he was content. Lev. x.

That here stands for the whole of what Aaron had said, or the whole of the preceding verse.

I will know your business, *that* I will. *Shak.*

Ye defraud, and *that* your brethren. 1 Cor. vi.

That sometimes in this use, precedes the sentence or clause to which it refers.

That be far from thee, to do after this manner, *to slay the righteous with the wicked.* Gen. xviii.

That here represents the clause in italics.

5. *That* sometimes is the substitute for an adjective. You alledge that the man is *innocent*; *that* he is not.

6. *That,* in the following use, has been called a conjunction. "I heard *that* the Greeks had defeated the Turks." But in this case, *that* has the same character as in No. 4. It is the representative of the part of the sentence which follows, as may be seen by inverting the order of the clauses. "The Greeks had defeated the Turks; I heard *that.*" "It is not *that* I love you less." *That* here refers to the latter clause of the sentence, as a kind of demonstrative.

7. *That* was formerly used for *that which,* like *what.*

We speak *that* we do know, and testify *that* we have seen. John iii.

[This use is no longer held legitimate.]

8. *That* is used in opposition to *this,* or by way of distinction.

If the Lord will, we shall live, and do this or *that.* James iv.

9. When *this* and *that* refer to foregoing words, *this,* like the Latin *hic,* and French *ceci,* refers to the latter, and *that* to the former. It is the same with *these* and *those.*

Self-love and *reason* to one end aspire,
Pain their aversion, pleasure their desire,
But greedy *that,* its object would devour,
This taste the honey, and not wound the flow'r. *Pope.*

10. *That* sometimes introduces an explanation of something going before. "Religion consists in living up to those principles; *that* is, in acting in conformity to them." Here *that* refers to the whole first clause of the sentence.

11. "Things are preached, not in *that* they are taught, but in *that* they are published." Here *that* refers to the words which follow it.

So when *that* begins a sentence. "*That* we may fully understand the subject, let us consider the following propositions." *That* denotes purpose, or rather introduces the clause expressing purpose, as will appear by restoring the sentence to its natural order. "Let us consider the following propositions, *that,* [for the purpose expressed in the following clause,] we may fully understand the subject." "Attend *that* you may receive instruction." Here also *that* expresses purpose elliptically; "attend for the purpose *that,* you may receive instruction;" *that* referring to the last member.

In that, a phrase denoting consequence, cause or reason; *that* referring to the following sentence.

THATCH, *n.* [Sax. *thac,* connected with *theccan, thecan,* to cover, L. *tego,* Eng. *deck*; G. *dach,* a roof; D. *dak*; Sw. *tak*; Dan. *tag, tække*; Gaelic, *tughe, tuighe.* The primary sense is to put on, to spread over or make close.]

Straw or other substance used to cover the roofs of buildings, or stacks of hay or grain, for securing them from rain, &c.

THATCH, *v. t.* To cover with straw, reeds or some similar substance; as, to *thatch* a house or a stable, or a stack of grain.

THATCH'ED, *pp.* Covered with straw or thatch.

THATCH'ER, *n.* One whose occupation is to thatch houses.

THATCH'ING, *ppr.* Covering with straw or thatch.

THATCH'ING, *n.* The act or art of covering buildings with thatch, so as to keep out water.

THAUMATUR'GIC, THAUMATUR'GICAL, } *a.* [See *Thaumaturgy.*] Exciting wonder. *Burton.*

THAU'MATURGY, *n.* [Gr. θαυμα, a wonder, and εργον, work.]

The act of performing something wonderful. *Warton.*

THAW, *v. i.* [Sax. *thawan*; G. *thauen*; D. *dooyen*; Dan. *töer*; Sw. *töa*; Gr. τηκω. Class Dg.]

1. To melt, dissolve or become fluid, as ice or snow. [It is remarkable that this word is used only of things that congeal by frost. We never say, to *thaw* metal of any kind.]

2. To become so warm as to melt ice and snow; *used of weather.*

THAW, *v. t.* To melt; to dissolve; as ice, snow, hail or frozen earth.

THAW, *n.* The melting of ice or snow; the resolution of ice into the state of a fluid; liquefaction by heat, of any thing congealed by frost.

THAW'ED, *pp.* Melted, as ice or snow.

THAW'ING, *ppr.* Dissolving; resolving into a fluid; liquefying; as any thing frozen.

THE, *an adjective*, or *definitive adjective*. [Sax. *the*; D. *de*. Qu. Ch. דא.]

1. This adjective is used as a definitive, that is, before nouns which are specific or understood; or it is used to limit their signification to a specific thing or things, or to describe them; as *the* laws of the twelve tables. *The* independent tribunals of justice in our country, are *the* security of private rights, and *the* best bulwark against arbitrary power. *The* sun is *the* source of light and heat.

   This he calls *the* preaching of the cross. *Simeon.*

2. *The* is also used rhetorically before a noun in the singular number, to denote a species by way of distinction; a single thing representing the whole. *The* fig tree putteth forth her green figs; *the* almond tree shall flourish; *the* grasshopper shall be a burden.

3. In *poetry*, *the* sometimes loses the final vowel before another vowel.

   Th' adorning thee with so much art,
   Is but a barb'rous skill. *Cowley.*

4. *The* is used before adjectives in the comparative and superlative degree. *The longer* we continue in sin, *the more difficult* it is to reform. *The most strenuous* exertions will be used to emancipate Greece. *The most* we can do is to submit; *the best* we can do; *the worst* that can happen.

THE'ARCHY, *n.* [Gr. θεος, God, and αρχη, rule.]

Government by God; more commonly called *theocracy*. *Ch. Relig. Appeal.*

THE'ATER, **THE'ATRE**, *n.* [Fr. *theatre*; L. *theatrum*; Gr. θεατρον, from θεαομαι, to see.]

1. Among *the ancients*, an edifice in which spectacles or shows were exhibited for the amusement of spectators.
2. In *modern times*, a house for the exhibition of dramatic performances, as tragedies, comedies and farces; a play-house; comprehending the stage, the pit, the boxes, galleries and orchester.
3. Among *the Italians*, an assemblage of buildings, which by a happy disposition and elevation, represents an agreeable scene to the eye. *Cyc.*
4. A place rising by steps or gradations like the seats of a theater.

   Shade above shade, a woody *theater*
   Of stateliest view— *Milton.*

5. A place of action or exhibition; as the *theater* of the world.
6. A building for the exhibition of *scholastic* exercises, as at Oxford, or for other exhibitions.

Anatomical theater, a hall with several rows of seats, disposed in the manner of an amphitheater, and a table turning on a pivot in the middle, for anatomical demonstrations. *Cyc.*

THE'ATINS, *n.* An order of regular priests in Naples, who have no property, nor do they beg, but wait for what providence sends them. They have their name from the chief of the order.

THE'ATRAL, *a.* Belonging to a theater. [*Not in use.*]

THEAT'RIC, **THEAT'RICAL**, *a.* Pertaining to a theater or to scenic representations; resembling the manner of dramatic performers; as *theatrical* dress; *theatrical* performances; *theatrical* gestures.

THEAT'RICALLY, *adv.* In the manner of actors on the stage; in a manner suiting the stage.

THEAVE, **THAVE**, *n.* An ewe of the first year. [*Local.*]

THEE, *pron.* obj. case of *thou*. [contracted from Sax. *thec*; Cimb. *thig*; Francic, *thec*; Goth. *thuk*. See *Thou.*]

THEE, *v. i.* [Goth. *thihan*; Sax. *thean.*] To thrive; to prosper. *Obs.* *Chaucer.*

THEFT, *n.* [Sax. *thyfthe*. See *Thief.*] The act of stealing. In *law*, the private, unlawful, felonious taking of another person's goods or movables, with an intent to steal them. To constitute *theft*, the taking must be in private or without the owner's knowledge, and it must be unlawful or felonious, that is, it must be with a design to deprive the owner of his property privately and against his will. Theft differs from *robbery*, as the latter is a violent taking from the person, and of course not private.

2. The thing stolen. Ex. xxii.

THEFT'-BOTE, *n.* [*theft* and Sax. *bote*, compensation.]

In *law*, the receiving of a man's goods again from a thief; or a compensation for them, by way of composition, and to prevent the prosecution of the thief. This in England subjects a person to a heavy fine, as by this means the punishment of the criminal is prevented.

THEIR, *a. pronom.* [Sax. *hiora*; Ice. *theirra.*]

1. *Their* has the sense of a pronominal adjective, denoting *of them*, or the possession of two or more; as *their* voices; *their* garments; *their* houses; *their* land; *their* country.
2. *Theirs* is used as a substitute for the adjective and the noun to which it refers, and in this case, it may be the nominative to a verb. "Our land is the most extensive, but *theirs* is the best cultivated." Here *theirs* stands as the representative of *their land*, and is the nominative to *is*.

   Nothing but the name of zeal appears
   'Twixt our best actions and the worst of *theirs*. *Denham.*

   In this use, *theirs* is not in the possessive case, for then there would be a double possessive.

THE'ISM, *n.* [from Gr. θεος, God.] The belief or acknowledgment of the existence of a God, as opposed to *atheism*. *Theism* differs from *deism*, for although deism implies a belief in the existence of a God, yet it signifies in modern usage a denial of revelation, which *theism* does not.

THE'IST, *n.* One who believes in the existence of a God.

THEIS'TIC, **THEIS'TICAL**, *a.* Pertaining to theism, or to a theist; according to the doctrine of theists.

THEM, *pron.* the objective case of *they*, and of both genders. [In our mother tongue, *them* is an adjective, answering to *the*, in the dative and ablative cases of both numbers. The common people continue to use it in the plural number as an adjective, for they say, bring *them* horses, or *them* horses are to be led to water.]

Go ye to *them* that sell, and buy for yourselves. Matt. xxv.

Then shall the king say to *them* on his right hand, come, ye blessed of my Father— Matt. xxv.

THEME, *n.* [L. *thema*; Gr. θεμα, from τιθημι, to set or place.]

1. A subject or topic on which a person writes or speaks. The preacher takes a text for the *theme* of his discourse.

   When a soldier was the *theme*, my name
   Was not far off. *Shak.*

2. A short dissertation composed by a student. *Milton.*
3. In *grammar*, a radical verb, or the verb in its primary absolute sense, not modified by inflections; as the infinitive mode in English. But a large portion of the words called *themes* in Greek, are not the radical words, but are themselves derivative forms of the verb. The fact is the same in other languages.
4. In *music*, a series of notes selected as the text or subject of a new composition.

THEMSELVES, a compound of *them* and *selves*, and added to *they* by way of emphasis or pointed distinction. Thus we say, *they themselves* have done the mischief; they cannot blame others. In this case, *themselves* is in the nominative case, and may be considered as an emphatical pronoun.

In some cases, *themselves* is used without *they*, and stands as the only nominative to the following verb. *Themselves* have done the mischief.

This word is used also in the objective case after a verb or preposition. Things in *themselves* innocent, may under certain circumstances cease to be so.

They open to *themselves* at length the way. *Milton.*

THEN, *adv.* [Goth. Sax. *thanne*; G. *dann*; D. *dan*. See *Thence.*]

1. At that time, referring to a time specified, either past or future.

   And the Canaanite was *then* in the land. Gen. xii.

   That is, when Abram migrated and came into Canaan.

   Now I know in part, but *then* shall I know even as I am known. 1 Cor. xii.

2. Afterward; soon afterward or immediately.

   First be reconciled to thy brother, and *then* come and offer thy gift. Matt. v.

3. In that case; in consequence. Gal. iii. Job iii.

   If all this be so, *then* man has a natural freedom. *Locke.*

4. Therefore; for this reason.

   Now *then* be all thy weighty cares away. *Dryden.*

5. At another time; as *now* and *then*, at one time and another. *Milton.*
6. That time.

   Till *then* who knew
   The force of those dire arms? *Milton.*

THENCE, *adv.* *thens.* [Sax. *thanan*, *thanon*; G. *dannen*; from *than*, *dann*, then, supra. *Then* signifies properly place, or set time, from *setting*, and *thence* is derived from it. So the Germans say, *von dannen*, from *thence*.]

1. From that place.

   When you depart *thence*, shake off the dust of your feet. Mark vi.

It is more usual, though not necessary, to use *from* before *thence.*

Then will I send and fetch thee *from thence.* Gen. xxvii.

2. From that time.

There shall be no more *thence* an infant of days. Is. lxv.

3. For that reason.

Not to sit idle with so great a gift
Useless, and *thence* ridiculous, about him. *Milton.*

THENCEFORTH, *adv. thens'forth.* [*thence* and *forth.*] From that time.

If the salt hath lost its savor, it is *thenceforth* good for nothing. Matt. v.

This is also preceded by *from,* though not from any necessity.

And *from thenceforth* Pilate sought to release him. John xix.

THENCEFOR'WARD, *adv.* [*thence* and *forward.*] From that time onward. *Kettlewell.*

THENCEFROM', *adv.* [*thence* and *from.*] From that place. [*Not in use.*] *Smith.*

THEOC'RACY, *n.* [Fr. *theocracie;* It. *teocrazia;* Sp. *teocracia;* Gr. θεος, God, and κρατος, power; κρατεω, to hold.]

Government of a state by the immediate direction of God; or the state thus governed. Of this species the Israelites furnish an illustrious example. The *theocracy* lasted till the time of Saul.

THEOCRAT'IC, THEOCRAT'ICAL, *a.* Pertaining to a theocracy; administered by the immediate direction of God; as the *theocratical* state of the Israelites. The government of the Israelites was *theocratic.*

THE'ODICY, *n.* [Gr. θεος, and L. *dico,* to speak.]

The science of God; metaphysical theology. *Leibnitz. Encyc.*

THEOD'OLITE, *n.* [Qu. Gr. θεω, to run, and δολιχος, long.]

An instrument for taking the hights and distances of objects, or for measuring horizontal and vertical angles in land-surveying. *Johnson. Cyc.*

THEOG'ONY, *n.* [Fr. *theogonie;* Gr. θεογονια; θεος, God, and γονη, or γινομαι, to be born.]

In *mythology,* the generation of the gods; or that branch of heathen theology which taught the genealogy of their deities. Hesiod composed a poem concerning that theogony, or the creation of the world and the descent of the gods.

THEOL'OGASTER, *n.* A kind of quack in divinity; as a quack in medicine is called *medicaster.* *Burton.*

THEOLO'GIAN, *n.* [See *Theology.*] A divine; a person well versed in theology, or a professor of divinity. *Milton.*

THEOLOG'IC, THEOLOG'ICAL, *a.* [See *Theology.*] Pertaining to divinity, or the science of God and of divine things; as a *theological* treatise; *theological* criticism. *Swift. Cyc.*

THEOLOG'ICALLY, *adv.* According to the principles of theology.

THEOL'OGIST, *n.* A divine; one studious in the science of divinity, or one well versed in that science.

THEOL'OGIZE, *v. t.* To render theological. *Glanville.*

2. *v. i.* To frame a system of theology. [*Little used.*]

THEOL'OGIZER, *n.* A divine, or a professor of theology. [*Unusual.*] *Boyle.*

THE'OLOGUE, for *theologist,* is not in use.

THEOL'OGY, *n.* [Fr. *theologie;* It. Sp. *teologia;* Gr. θεολογια; θεος, God, and λογος, discourse.]

Divinity; the science of God and divine things; or the science which teaches the existence, character and attributes of God, his laws and government, the doctrines we are to believe, and the duties we are to practice. Theology consists of two branches, *natural* and *revealed. Natural theology* is the knowledge we have of God from his works, by the light of nature and reason. *Revealed theology* is that which is to be learned only from revelation.

Moral theology, teaches us the divine laws relating to our manners and actions, that is, our moral duties.

Speculative theology, teaches or explains the doctrines of religion, as objects of faith.

Scholastic theology, is that which proceeds by reasoning, or which derives the knowledge of several divine things from certain established principles of faith. *Tillotson. Cyc.*

THEOM'ACHIST, *n.* [Gr. θεος, God, and μαχη, combat.] One who fights against the gods. *Bailey.*

THEOM'ACHY, *n.* [supra.] A fighting against the gods, as the battle of the giants with the gods.

2. Opposition to the divine will.

THEOP'ATHY, *n.* [Gr. θεος, God, and παθος, passion.]

Religious suffering; suffering for the purpose of subduing sinful propensities. *Quart. Review.*

THEOR'BO, *n.* [It. *tiorba;* Fr. *tuorbe* or *teorbe.*]

A musical instrument made like a large lute, except that it has two necks or juga, the second and longer of which sustains the four last rows of chords, which are to give the deepest sounds. The theorbo has eight base or thick strings twice as long as those of the lute, which excess of length renders the sound exceedingly soft, and continues it a great length of time. *Cyc.*

THE'OREM, *n.* [Fr. *theoreme;* Sp. It. *teorema;* Gr. θεωρημα, from θεωρεω, to see.]

1. In *mathematics,* a proposition which terminates in theory, and which considers the properties of things already made or done; or it is a speculative proposition deduced from several definitions compared together.

A theorem is a proposition to be proved by a chain of reasoning. A theorem is something to be *proved;* a problem is something to be *done.* *Day.*

2. In *algebra* or *analysis,* it is sometimes nsed to denote a rule, particularly when that rule is expressed by symbols. *Cyc.*

A universal theorem, extends to any quantity without restriction.

A particular theorem, extends only to a particular quantity.

A negative theorem, expresses the impossibility of any assertion.

A local theorem, is that which relates to a surface.

A solid theorem, is that which considers a space terminated by a solid, that is, by any of the three conic sections.

THEOREMAT'IC, THEOREMAT'ICAL, THEOREM'IC, *a.* Pertaining to a theorem; comprised in a theorem; consisting of theorems; as *theoremic* truth. *Grew.*

THEORET'IC, THEORET'ICAL, *a.* [Gr. θεωρητικος. See *Theory.*]

Pertaining to theory; depending on theory or speculation; speculative; terminating in theory or speculation; not practical; as *theoretical* learning; *theoretic* sciences. The sciences are divided into *theoretical,* as theology, philosophy and the like, and *practical,* as medicine and law.

THEORET'ICALLY, *adv.* In or by theory; in speculation; speculatively; not practically. Some things appear to be *theoretically* true, which are found to be practically false.

THE'ORIC, *n.* Speculation. *Shak.*

THEOR'IC, for *theoretic,* is not now used. [See *Theoretic.*]

Theoric revenue, in ancient Athens, was the revenue of the state appropriated to the support of theatrical exhibitions. *Milford.*

THE'ORIST, *n.* One who forms theories; one given to theory and speculation.

The greatest *theorists* have given the preference to such a government as that of this kingdom. *Addison.*

THE'ORIZE, *v. i.* To form a theory or theories; to speculate; as, to *theorize* on the existence of phlogiston.

THE'ORY, *n.* [Fr. *theorie;* It. *teoria;* L. *theoria;* Gr. θεωρια, from θεωρεω, to see or contemplate.]

1. Speculation; a doctrine or scheme of things, which terminates in speculation or contemplation, without a view to practice. It is here taken in an unfavorable sense, as implying something visionary.

2. An exposition of the general principles of any science; as the *theory* of music.

3. The science distinguished from the art; as the *theory* and practice of medicine.

4. The philosophical explanation of phenomena, either physical or moral; as Lavoisier's *theory* of combustion; Smith's *theory* of moral sentiments.

Theory is distinguished from *hypothesis* thus; a theory is founded on inferences drawn from principles which have been established on independent evidence; a hypothesis is a proposition assumed to account for certain phenomena, and has no other evidence of its truth, than that it affords a satisfactory explanation of those phenomena. *D. Olmsted.*

THEOSOPH'IC, THEOSOPH'ICAL, *a.* Pertaining to theosophism or to theosophists; divinely wise.

THEOS'OPHISM, *n.* [Gr. θεος, God, and σοφισμα, comment; σοφος, wise.]

Pretension to divine illumination; enthusiasm.

THEOS'OPHIST, *n.* One who pretends to divine illumination; one who pretends to derive his knowledge from divine revelation. *Enfield.*

THEOS'OPHY, *n.* Divine wisdom; godliness. *Ed. Encyc.*

2. Knowledge of God. *Good.*

THERAPEU'TIC, *a.* [Gr. θεραπευτικος, from θεραπευω, to nurse, serve or cure.]

Curative; that pertains to the healing art; that is concerned in discovering and applying remedies for diseases.

Medicine is justly distributed into prophylactic, or the art of preserving health, and *therapeutic*, or the art of restoring it. *Watts.*

THERAPEU'TICS, *n.* That part of medicine which respects the discovery and application of remedies for diseases. Therapeutics teaches the use of diet and of medicines. *Cyc.*

2. A religious sect described by Philo. They were devotees to religion.

THERE, *adv.* [Sax. *thær*; Goth. *thar*; D. *daar*; Sw. *där*; Dan. *der.* This word was formerly used as a pronoun, as well as an adverb of place. Thus in Saxon, *thærto* was *to him, to her*, or *to it.*]

1. In that place.

The Lord God planted a garden eastward in Eden, and *there* he put the man whom he had formed. Gen. ii.

2. It is sometimes opposed to *here*; *there* denoting the place most distant.

Darkness *there* might well seem twilight *here.* *Milton.*

3. *Here* and *there*, in one place and another; as *here* a little and *there* a little.

4. It is sometimes used by way of exclamation, calling the attention to something distant; as *there, there*; see *there*; look *there.*

5. *There* is used to begin sentences, or before a verb; sometimes pertinently, and sometimes without signification; but its use is so firmly established that it cannot be dispensed with.

Wherever *there* is sense or perception, there some idea is actually produced. *Locke.*

There have been that have delivered themselves from their ills by their good fortune or virtue. *Suckling.*

And *there* came a voice from heaven, saying, thou art my beloved Son. Mark i.

6. In composition, *there* has the sense of a pronoun, as in Saxon; as *thereby*, which signifies *by that.*

THEREABOUT', **THEREABOUTS'**, *adv.* [*there* and *about.* The latter is less proper, but most commonly used.]

1. Near that place. *Shak.*

2. Nearly; near that number, degree or quantity; as ten men or *thereabouts.*

3. Concerning that. [*Not much used.*] Luke xxiv.

THERE'AFTER, *adv.* [*there* and *after.* Sax. *thær-æfter*, after that.]

1. According to that; accordingly.

When you can draw the head indifferently well, proportion the body *thereafter.* *Peacham.*

2. After that. *Spenser.*

THEREAT', *adv.* [*there* and *at.*] At that place.

Wide is the gate, and broad is the way, that leadeth to destruction, and many there are who go in *thereat.* Matt. vii.

2. At that; at that thing or event; on that account.

Every error is a stain to the beauty of nature; for which cause it blusheth *thereat.* *Hooker.*

THEREBY', *adv.* [*there* and *by.*] By that; by that means; in consequence of that.

Acquaint now thyself with him, and be at peace; *thereby* good shall come to thee. Job xxii.

THEREFOR', *adv.* [*there* and *for.*] For that or this, or it.

THEREFORE, *adv. ther'fore.* [*there* and *for.*]

1. For that; for that or this reason, referring to something previously stated.

I have married a wife, and *therefore* I cannot come. Luke xiv.

2. Consequently.

He blushes; *therefore* he is guilty. *Spectator.*

3. In return or recompense for this or that.

What shall we have *therefore?* Matt. xix.

THEREFROM', *adv.* [*there* and *from.*] From this or that.

—Turn not aside *therefrom* to the right hand or to the left. Josh. xxiii.

THEREIN', *adv.* [*there* and *in.*] In that or this place, time or thing.

Bring forth abundantly in the earth and multiply *therein.* Gen. ix.

Ye shall keep the sabbath—whosoever doeth any work *therein*—that soul shall be cut off. Ex. xxxi.

Therein our letters do not well agree. *Shak.*

THEREINTO', *adv.* [*there* and *into.*] Into that. *Bacon.*

THEREOF', *adv.* [*there* and *of.*] Of that or this.

In the day thou eatest *thereof*, thou shalt surely die. Gen. ii.

THEREON', *adv.* [*there* and *on.*] On that or this.

Then the king said, hang him *thereon.* Esth. vii.

THEREOUT', *adv.* [*there* and *out.*] Out of that or this. Lev. ii.

THERETO', **THEREUNTO'**, *adv.* [*there* and *to* or *unto.*] To that or this.

Add the fifth part *thereto.* Lev. v.

THEREUN'DER, *adv.* [*there* and *under.*] Under that or this. *Raleigh.*

THEREUPON', *adv.* [*there* and *upon.*] Upon that or this.

The remnant of the house of Judah, they shall feed *thereupon.* Zeph. ii.

2. In consequence of that.

He hopes to find you forward,
And *thereupon* he sends you this good news. *Shak.*

3. Immediately.

THEREWHI'LE, *adv.* [*there* and *while.*] At the same time. *Obs.* *Wickliffe.*

THEREWITH', *adv.* [*there* and *with.*] With that or this.

I have learned in whatever state I am, *therewith* to be content. Phil. iv.

THEREWITHAL', *adv.* [*there* and *withal.*]

1. Over and above.

2. At the same time.

3. With that. [*This word is obsolete.*]

[The foregoing compounds of *there* with the prepositions, are for the most part deemed inelegant and obsolete. Some of them however are in good use, and particularly in the law style.]

THERF-BREAD, *n. therf'bred.* [Sax. *thærf*, *theorf*, unfermented.] Unleavened bread. [*Not in use.*] *Wickliffe.*

THE'RIAC, *n.* [L. *theriaca*, Gr. θηριακη, treacle.]

A name given by the ancients to various compositions esteemed efficacious against the effects of poison, but afterwards restrained chiefly to what has been called *Theriaca Andromachi*, or *Venice-treacle*, which is a compound of sixty four drugs, prepared, pulverized, and reduced by means of honey to an electuary. *Cyc.*

THE'RIAC, **THERI'ACAL**, *a.* Pertaining to theriac; medicinal. *Bacon.*

THER'MAL, *a.* [L. *thermæ*, warm baths; Gr. θερμαι, from θερω, to warm.] Pertaining to heat; warm.

Thermal waters, are warm or tepid mineral waters, whose heat varies from 92° to 112°. *Parr.*

THER'MOLAMP, *n.* [Gr. θερμος, warm, from θερμη, heat, and *lamp.*]

An instrument for furnishing light by means of inflammable gas. *Med. Repos.*

THERMOM'ETER, *n.* [Gr. θερμος, warm, from θερμη, heat, and μετρον, measure.]

An instrument for measuring heat; founded on the property which heat possesses of expanding all bodies, the rate or quantity of expansion being supposed proportional to the degree of heat applied, and hence indicating that degree. The thermometer indicates only the *sensible* heat of bodies, and gives us no information respecting the quantity of latent heat, or of combined heat, which those bodies may contain. *D. Olmsted.*

THERMOMET'RICAL, *a.* Pertaining to a thermometer; as the *thermometrical* scale or tube.

2. Made by a thermometer; as *thermometrical* observations.

THERMOMET'RICALLY, *adv.* By means of a thermometer.

THER'MOSCOPE, *n.* [Gr. θερμη, heat, and σκοπεω, to see.]

An instrument showing the temperature of the air, or the degree of heat and cold. *Arbuthnot.*

THESE, *pron.* plu. of *this.* pronounced *theez*, and used as an adjective or substitute. *These* is opposed to *those*, as *this* is to *that*, and when two persons or things or collections of things are named, *these* refers to the things or persons which are nearest in place or order, or which are last mentioned.

Some place the bliss in action, some in ease;
Those call it pleasure, and contentment *these.* *Pope.*

Here *these* is a substitute for *these persons*, and for the persons last mentioned, who place their bliss in ease.

THE'SIS, *n.* [L. *thesis*; Gr. θεσις, a position, from τιθημι, to set.]

1. A position or proposition which a person advances and offers to maintain, or which is actually maintained by argument; a theme; a subject.

2. In *logic*, every proposition may be divided into *thesis* and *hypothesis.* Thesis contains the thing affirmed or denied, and hypothesis the conditions of the affirmation or negation. *Cyc.*

THET'ICAL, *a.* [from Gr. θετικος. See *Thesis.*] Laid down. *More.*

THEUR'GIC, **THEUR'GICAL**, *a.* [from *theurgy.*] Pertaining to the power of performing supernatural things.

Theurgic hymns, songs of incantation.

THE'URGIST, *n.* One who pretends to or is addicted to theurgy. *Hallywell.*

THE'URGY, *n.* [Gr. θεουργια; θεος, God, and εργον, work.]

The art of doing things which it is the peculiar province of God to do; or the power or act of performing supernatural things by invoking the names of God or of subordinate agents; magic. This has been divided by some writers into three parts; *theurgy*, or the operation by divine or celestial means; *natural magic*, performed by the powers of nature; and *necromancy*, which proceeds by invoking demons. *Cyc.*

THEW, *n.* [Sax. *theaw*; Gr. ἔθος.] Manner; custom; habit; form of behavior. [*Not in use.*] *Spenser.*

2. Brawn. [*Not in use.*] *Shak.*

THEW'ED, *a.* Accustomed; educated. [*Not in use.*] *Spenser.*

THEY, *pron. plu.*; objective case, *them.* [Sax. *thæge*; Goth. *thai, thaim.*]

1. The men, the women, the animals, the things. It is never used adjectively, but always as a pronoun referring to persons, or as a substitute referring to things.

They and their fathers have transgressed against me. Ezek. ii.

They of Italy salute you. Heb. xiii.

Blessed are *they* who hunger and thirst after righteousness. Matt. v.

2. It is used indefinitely, as our ancestors used *man*, and as the French use *on*. *They* say, [*on dit*,] that is, it is said by persons, indefinitely.

THI'BLE, *n.* A slice; a skimmer; a spatula. [*Not in use or local.*] *Ainsworth.*

THICK, *a.* [Sax. *thic, thicca*; G. *dick, dicht*; D. *dik, digt*; Sw. *tiock*; Dan. *tyk* and *digt*, thick, tight; Gael. Ir. *tiugh*; W. *tew*, contracted. See Class Dg. No 3. 8. 10. 22. 36. 57. The sense is probably taken from driving, forcing together or pressing.]

1. Dense; not thin; as *thick* vapors; a *thick* fog.

2. Inspissated; as, the paint is too *thick*.

3. Turbid; muddy; feculent; not clear; as, the water of a river is *thick* after a rain.

4. Noting the diameter of a body; as a piece of timber seven inches *thick*.

My little finger shall be *thicker* than my father's loins. 1 Kings xii.

5. Having more depth or extent from one surface to its opposite than usual; as a *thick* plank; *thick* cloth; *thick* paper.

6. Close; crowded with trees or other objects; as a *thick* forest or wood; *thick* grass; *thick* corn.

The people were gathered *thick* together. *Locke.*

7. Frequent; following each other in quick succession. The shot flew *thick* as hail.

Favors came *thick* upon him. *Wotton.*

Not *thicker* billows beat the Libyan main. *Dryden.*

8. Set with things close to each other; not easily pervious.

Black was the forest, *thick* with beech it stood. *Dryden.*

9. Not having due distinction of syllables or good articulation; as a *thick* utterance. He speaks too *thick*.

10. Dull; somewhat deaf; as *thick* of hearing.

THICK, *n.* The thickest part, or the time when any thing is thickest.

In the *thick* of the dust and smoke he presently entered his men. *Knolles.*

2. A thicket. [*Not in use.*] *Drayton.*

Thick and *thin*, whatever is in the way.

Through *thick* and *thin* she follow'd him. *Hudibras.*

THICK, *adv.* Frequently; fast.

I hear the trampling of *thick* beating feet. *Dryden.*

2. Closely; as a plat of ground *thick* sown. *Norris.*

3. To a great depth, or to a thicker depth than usual; as a bed covered *thick* with tan; land covered *thick* with manure.

Thick and threefold, in quick succession, or in great numbers. [*Not in use.*] *L'Estrange.*

THICK, *v. i.* To become thick or dense. [*Not used.*] *Spenser.*

THICKEN, *v. t.* *thik'n.* [Sax. *thiccian.*] To make thick or dense.

2. To make close; to fill up interstices; as, to *thicken* cloth.

3. To make concrete; to inspissate; as, to *thicken* paint, mortar or a liquid.

4. To strengthen; to confirm.

And this may help to *thicken* other proofs. [*Not used.*] *Shak.*

5. To make frequent, or more frequent; as, to *thicken* blows.

6. To make close, or more close; to make more numerous; as, to *thicken* the ranks.

THICKEN, *v. i.* *thik'n.* To become thick or more thick; to become dense; as, the fog *thickens*.

2. To become dark or obscure.

Thy luster *thickens*
When he shines by. *Shak.*

3. To concrete; to be consolidated; as, the juices of plants *thicken* into wood.

4. To be inspissated; as, vegetable juices *thicken*, as the more volatile parts are evaporated.

5. To become close, or more close or numerous.

The press of people *thickens* to the court. *Dryden.*

6. To become quick and animated.

The combat *thickens*. *Addison.*

7. To become more numerous; to press; to be crowded. Proofs of the fact *thicken* upon us at every step.

THICK'ENED, *pp.* Made dense, or more dense; made more close or compact; made more frequent; inspissated.

THICK'ENING, *ppr.* Making dense or more dense, more close, or more frequent; inspissating.

THICK'ENING, *n.* Something put into a liquid or mass to make it more thick.

THICK'ET, *n.* A wood or collection of trees or shrubs closely set; as a ram caught in a *thicket*. Gen. xxii.

THICK'HEADED, *a.* Having a thick skull; dull; stupid.

THICK'ISH, *a.* Somewhat thick.

THICK'LY, *adv.* Deeply; to a great depth. *Boyle.*

2. Closely; compactly.

3. In quick succession.

THICK'NESS, *n.* The state of being thick; denseness; density; as the *thickness* of fog, vapor or clouds.

2. The state of being concrete or inspissated; consistence; spissitude; as the *thickness* of paint or mortar; the *thickness* of honey; the *thickness* of the blood.

3. The extent of a body from side to side, or from surface to surface; as the *thickness* of a tree; the *thickness* of a board; the *thickness* of the hand; the *thickness* of a layer of earth.

4. Closeness of the parts; the state of being crowded or near; as the *thickness* of trees in a forest; the *thickness* of a wood.

5. The state of being close, dense or impervious; as the *thickness* of shades. *Addison.*

6. Dullness of the sense of hearing; want of quickness or acuteness; as *thickness* of hearing. *Swift.*

THICK'SET, *a.* [*thick* and *set.*] Close planted; as a *thickset* wood. *Dryden.*

2. Having a short thick body.

THICK'SKULL, *n.* [*thick* and *skull.*] Dullness; or a dull person; a blockhead. *Entick.*

THICK'SKULLED, *a.* Dull; heavy; stupid; slow to learn.

THICK'SKIN, *n.* [*thick* and *skin.*] A coarse gross person; a blockhead. *Entick.*

THICK'SPRUNG, *a.* [*thick* and *sprung.*] Sprung up close together. *Entick. Shak.*

THIEF, *n.* plu. *thieves.* [Sax. *theof*; Sw. *tiuf*; D. *dief*; G. *dieb*; Goth. *thiubs*; Dan. *tyv.*] A person guilty of theft.

1. One who secretly, unlawfully and feloniously takes the goods or personal property of another. The *thief* takes the property of another privately; the robber by open force. *Blackstone.*

2. One who takes the property of another wrongfully, either secretly or by violence. Job xxx.

A certain man went down from Jerusalem to Jericho, and fell among *thieves*, who stripped him of his raiment. Luke x.

3. One who seduces by false doctrine. John x.

4. One who makes it his business to cheat and defraud; as a den of *thieves*. Matt. xxi.

5. An excrescence in the snuff of a candle. *May.*

THIE'F-CATCHER, *n.* [*thief* and *catch.*] One who catches thieves, or whose business is to detect thieves and bring them to justice.

THIE'F-LEADER, *n.* [*thief* and *lead.*] One who leads or takes a thief. [*Not much used.*]

THIE'F-TAKER, *n.* [*thief* and *taker.*] One whose business is to find and take thieves and bring them to justice.

THIEVE, *v. i.* [from *thief.*] To steal; to practice theft.

THIE'VERY, *n.* The practice of stealing; theft. [See *Theft.*]

Among the Spartans, *thievery* was a practice morally good and honest. *South.*

2. That which is stolen. *Shak.*

THIE'VISH, *a.* Given to stealing; addicted to the practice of theft; as a *thievish* boy.

Or with a base and boist'rous sword enforce
A *thievish* living on the common road. *Shak.*

2. Secret; sly; acting by stealth; as *thievish* minutes. *Shak.*

3. Partaking of the nature of theft; as a *thievish* practice.

THIE'VISHLY, *adv.* In a thievish manner; by theft.

THIE'VISHNESS, *n.* The disposition to steal.

2. The practice or habit of stealing.

THIGH, *n.* [Sax. *thegh, theo* or *theoh*; D. *dye*; G. *dick-bein*, thick-bone. The German explains the word; *thigh* is *thick.*]

That part of men, quadrupeds and fowls, which is between the leg and the trunk.

As the word signifies, it is the *thick* part of the lower limbs.

THILK, *pron.* [Sax. *thilc.*] The same. *Obs.* *Spenser.*

THILL, *n.* [Sax. *thil* or *thill.*] The shaft of a cart, gig or other carriage. The thills are the two pieces of timber extending from the body of the carriage on each side of the last horse, by which the carriage is supported in a horizontal position.

THILL'ER, } *n.* The horse which
THILL'-HORSE, } goes between the thills or shafts, and supports them. In a team, the last horse. *Cyc.* *Shak.*

THIM'BLE, *n.* [I know not the origin or primary sense of this word. Possibly it may be from *thumb.* In Gaelic, *temeheal* is a cover.]

1. A kind of cap or cover for the finger, usually made of metal, used by tailors and seamstresses for driving the needle through cloth.
2. In *sea language*, an iron ring with a hollow or groove round its whole circumference, to receive the rope which is spliced about it. *Mar. Dict.*

THIME. [See *Thyme.*]

THIN, *a.* [Sax. *thinn*, *thynn*; G. *dünn*; D. *dun*; Sw. *tunn*; Dan. *tynd*; W. *tenau*, *teneu*; L. *tenuis*; Gaelic, *tanadh*; Russ. *tonkei.* Qu. Gr. *ςενος*, narrow. It appears to be connected with W. *ten*, *tan*, stretched, extended, Gr. *τεινω.* Qu. Ar. ودن. In sense it is allied to Syr. Heb. Ch. Eth. קטן, but I know not whether the first consonant of this word is a prefix. See Class Dn. No. 12. 25.]

1. Having little thickness or extent from one surface to the opposite; as a *thin* plate of metal; *thin* paper; a *thin* board; a *thin* covering.
2. Rare; not dense; applied to fluids or to soft mixtures; as *thin* blood; *thin* milk; *thin* air.

   In the day, when the air is more *thin.* *Bacon.*

3. Not close; not crowded; not filling the space; not having the individuals that compose the thing in a close or compact state; as, the trees of a forest are *thin;* the corn or grass is *thin.* A *thin* audience in church is not uncommon. Important legislative business should not be transacted in a *thin* house.
4. Not full or well grown.

   Seven *thin* ears. Gen. xli.

5. Slim; small; slender; lean. A person becomes *thin* by disease. Some animals are naturally *thin.*
6. Exile; small; fine; not full.

   Thin hollow sounds, and lamentable screams. *Dryden.*

7. Not thick or close; of a loose texture; not impervious to the sight; as a *thin* vail.
8. Not crowded or well stocked; not abounding.

   Ferrara is very large, but extremely *thin* of people. *Addison.*

9. Slight; not sufficient for a covering; as a *thin* disguise.

THIN, *adv.* Not thickly or closely; in a scattered state; as seed sown *thin.*

Spain is *thin* sown of people. *Bacon.*

THIN, *v. t.* [Sax. *thinnian*; Russ. *tonyu*; L. *tenuo.* See *Attenuate.*]

1. To make thin; to make rare or less thick; to attenuate; as, to *thin* the blood.
2. To make less close, crowded or numerous; as, to *thin* the ranks of an enemy; to *thin* the trees or shrubs of a thicket.
3. To attenuate; to rarefy; to make less dense; as, to *thin* the air; to *thin* the vapors.

THINE, *pronominal adj.* [Goth. *theins*, *theina;* Sax. *thin;* G. *dein;* Fr. *tien;* probably contracted from *thigen.* See *Thou.*]

Thy; belonging to thee; relating to thee; being the property of thee. It was formerly used for *thy*, before a vowel.

Then thou mightest eat grapes thy fill, at *thine* own pleasure. Deut. xxxii.

But in common usage, *thy* is now used before a vowel in all cases.

The principal use of *thine* now is when a verb is interposed between this word and the noun to which it refers. I will not take any thing that is *thine.* *Thine* is the kingdom, and the power, and the glory.

In the following passage, *thine* is used as a substitute for *thy righteousness.*

I will make mention of *thy righteousness*, even of *thine* only. Ps. lxxi.

In some cases, it is preceded by the sign of the possessive case, like nouns, and is then also to be considered as a substitute.

If any *of thine* be driven out to the utmost parts of heaven— Deut. xxx.

It is to be observed that *thine*, like *thou*, is used only in the solemn style. In familiar and common language, *your* and *yours* are always used in the singular number as well as the plural.

THING, *n.* [Sax. *thing*, a thing, a cause; *for his thingon*, for his cause or sake; also, *thing* and *gething*, a meeting, council or convention; *thingan*, *thingian*, to hold a meeting, to plead, to supplicate; *thingere*, an intercessor; *thingung*, intercession; G. *ding*, a thing, a court; *dingen*, to go to law, to hire or haggle; *Dingstag*, Tuesday, [*thing's day;*] *beding*, condition, clause; *bedingen*, to agree, to bargain or contract, to cheapen; D. *ding*, thing, business; *dingen*, to plead, to attempt, to cheapen; *dingbank*, the bar; *dingdagen*, session-days; *dinger*, *dingster*, a pleader; *dingtaal*, plea; *Dingsdag*, Tuesday; *beding*, condition, agreement; *bedingen*, to condition; Sw. *ting*, thing, cause, also a court, assizes; *tinga*, to hire, bargain or agree; Dan. *ting*, a thing, affair, business, case, a court of justice; *tinger*, to strike up a bargain, to haggle; *tingbog*, records of a court, [*thing-book;*] *tingdag*, the court day, the assizes; *tinghold*, jurisdiction; *tingmænd*, jurors, jury, [*thing-men;*] *tingsag*, a cause or suit at law, [*thing-sake.*] The primary sense of *thing* is that which comes, falls or happens, like *event*, from L. *evenio.* The primary sense of the root, which is *tig* or *thig*, is to press, urge, drive or strain, and hence its application to courts, or suits at law; a seeking of right. We observe that *Dingsdag*, *Dingdag*, in some of the dialects signifies *Tuesday*, and this from the circumstance that that day of the week was, as it still is in some states, the day of opening courts; that is, *litigation day*, or *suitors' day*, a day of striving for justice; or perhaps *combat-day*, the day of trial by battle. This leads to the unfolding of another fact. Among our ancestors, *Tig* or *Tiig*, was the name of the deity of combat and war, the Teutonic Mars; that is, strife, combat deified. This word was contracted into *tiw* or *tu*, and hence *Tiwes-dæg* or *Tues-dæg*, Tuesday, the day consecrated to *Tiig*, the god of war. But it seems this is merely the day of commencing court and trial; *litigation day.* This *Tiig*, the god of war, is *strife*, and this leads us to the root of *thing*, which is to drive, urge, strive. So *res*, in Latin, is connected with *reus*, accused. For words of like signification, see *Sake* and *Cause.*]

1. An event or action; that which happens or falls out, or that which is done, told or proposed. This is the general signification of the word in the Scriptures; as after these *things*, that is, events.

   And the *thing* was very grievous in Abraham's sight, because of his son. Gen. xxi.

   Then Laban and Bethuel answered and said, the *thing* proceedeth from the Lord. Gen. xxiv.

   And Jacob said, all these *things* are against me. Gen. xlii.

   I will tell you by what authority I do these *things.* Matt. xxi.

   These *things* said Esaias when he saw his glory. John xii.

   In learning French, choose such books as will teach you *things* as well as language. *Jay to Littlepage.*

2. Any substance; that which is created; any particular article or commodity.

   He sent after this manner; ten asses laden with the good *things* of Egypt— Gen. xlii.

   They took the *things* which Micah had made. Judges xviii.

3. An animal; as every living *thing;* every creeping *thing.* Gen. i.

   [*This application of the word is improper, but common in popular and vulgar language.*]

4. A portion or part; something.

   Wicked men who understand any *thing* of wisdom— *Tillotson.*

5. In contempt.

   I have a *thing* in prose. *Swift.*

6. Used of persons in contempt.

   See, sons, what *things* you are. *Shak.*
   The poor *thing* sigh'd. *Addison.*
   I'll be this abject *thing* no more. *Granville.*

7. Used in a sense of honor.

   —— I see thee here,
   Thou noble *thing!* *Shak.*

THINK, *v. i.* pret. and pp. *thought*, pron. *thaut.* [Sax. *thincan*, *thencan*; Goth. *thagkyan*; Sw. *tycka* and *tænka*; Dan. *tykker* and *tænker;* D. *denken*, to think, and *gedagt*, thought; G. *denken*, to think, and *gedächtniss*, remembrance; *gedanke*, thought; *nachdenken*, to ponder or meditate; Gr. *δοκεω*; Syr. Ch. דוק; allied to L. *duco.* We observe *n* is casual, and omitted in the participle *thought.* The sense seems to be to set in the mind, or to draw out, as in meditation. Class Dg. No. 9.]

1. To have the mind occupied on some subject; to have ideas, or to revolve ideas in the mind.

   —For that I am
   I know, because I *think.* *Dryden.*

These are not matters to be slightly *thought* on. *Tillotson.*

2. To judge; to conclude; to hold as a settled opinion. I *think* it will rain to-morrow. I *think* it not best to proceed on our journey.

Let them marry to whom they *think* best. Num. xxxvi.

3. To intend.

Thou *thought'st* to help me. *Shak.*

I *thought* to promote thee to great honor. Num. xxiv.

4. To imagine; to suppose; to fancy.

Edmund, I *think*, is gone
In pity of his misery, to dispatch
His 'nighted life. *Shak.*

Let him that *thinketh* he standeth, take heed lest he fall. 1 Cor. x.

5. To muse; to meditate.

While Peter *thought* on the vision—Acts x.

Think much, speak little. *Dryden.*

6. To reflect; to recollect or call to mind.

And when Peter *thought* thereon, he wept. Mark xiv.

7. To consider; to deliberate. *Think* how this thing could happen.

He *thought* within himself, saying, what shall I do? Luke xii.

8. To presume.

Think not to say within yourselves, we have Abraham to our father— Matt. iii.

9. To believe; to esteem.

To think on or *upon*, to muse on; to meditate on.

If there be any virtue, and if there be any praise, *think on* these things. Phil. iv.

2. To light on by meditation. He has just *thought on* an expedient that will answer the purpose.

3. To remember with favor.

Think upon me, my God, for good. Neh. v.

To think of, to have ideas come into the mind. He *thought of* what you told him. I would have sent the books, but I did not *think of* it.

To think well of, to hold in esteem; to esteem.

THINK, *v. t.* To conceive; to imagine.

Charity—*thinketh* no evil. 1 Cor. xiii.

2. To believe; to consider; to esteem.

Nor *think* superfluous others' aid. *Milton.*

3. To seem or appear, as in the phrases, *me thinketh* or *methinks*, and *methought.* These are genuine Saxon phrases, equivalent to *it seems to me, it seemed to me.* In these expressions, *me* is actually in the dative case; almost the only instance remaining in the language. Sax. "genoh *thuht*," satis visum est, it appeared enough or sufficient; "*me thincth*," mihi videtur, it seems to me; I perceive.

To think much, to grudge.

He *thought* not *much* to clothe his enemies. *Milton.*

To think much of, to hold in high esteem.

To think scorn, to disdain. Esth. iii.

THINK'ER, *n.* One who thinks; but chiefly, one who thinks in a particular manner; as a close *thinker*; a deep *thinker*; a coherent *thinker.* *Locke. Swift.*

THINK'ING, *ppr.* Having ideas; supposing; judging; imagining; intending; meditating.

2. *a.* Having the faculty of thought; cogitative: capable of a regular train of ideas. Man is a *thinking* being.

THINK'ING, *n.* Imagination; cogitation; judgment.

I heard a bird so sing,
Whose music, to my *thinking*, pleas'd the king. *Shak.*

THIN'LY, *adv.* [from *thin.*] In a loose scattered manner; not thickly; as ground *thinly* planted with trees; a country *thinly* inhabited.

THIN'NESS, *n.* The state of being thin; smallness of extent from one side or surface to the opposite; as the *thinness* of ice; the *thinness* of a plate; the *thinness* of the skin.

2. Tenuity; rareness; as the *thinness* of air or other fluid.

3. A state approaching to fluidity, or even fluidity; opposed to *spissitude*; as the *thinness* of honey, of white wash or of paint.

4. Exility; as the *thinness* of a point.

5. Rareness; a scattered state; paucity; as the *thinness* of trees in a forest; the *thinness* of inhabitants.

THIRD, *a. thurd.* [Sax. *thridda;* Goth. *thridya*; G. *dritte*; D. *derde*; Sw. Dan. *tredie*; Fr. *tiers*; L. *tertius*; Gr. *τριτος*; W. *trydy.*]

The first after the second; the ordinal of three. The *third* hour in the day among the ancients, was nine o'clock in the morning.

Third estate, in the British nation, is the commons; or in the legislature, the house of commons.

Third order, among the Catholics, is a sort of religious order that observes the same rule and the same manner of life in proportion as some other two orders previously instituted; as the *third order* of Franciscans, instituted by St. Francis in 1221. *Cyc.*

Third point or *tierce point*, in architecture, the point of section in the vertex of an equilateral triangle. *Cyc.*

Third rate, in navies. A third rate ship carries from 64 to 80 guns.

Third sound, in music. See the noun *Third.*

THIRD, *n. thurd.* The third part of any thing. A man takes land and tills it for one *third* of the produce; the owner taking two *thirds.*

2. The sixtieth part of a second of time.

3. In *music*, an interval containing three diatonic sounds; the major composed of two tones, called by the Greeks ditone, and the minor called hemiditone, consisting of a tone and a half. *Rousseau. Busby.*

THIRDBŎROUGH, *n. thurd'burro.* [*third* and *borough.*] An under constable. *Johnson.*

THIRD'INGS, *n.* The third year of the corn or grain growing on the ground at the tenant's death, due to the lord for a heriot, within the manor of Turfat in Herefordshire. *Cyc.*

THIRD'LY, *adv.* In the third place. *Bacon.*

THIRDS, *n. plu.* The third part of the estate of a deceased husband, which by law the widow is entitled to enjoy during her life. *N. England.*

THIRL, *v.t. thurl.* [Sax. *thirlian.*] To bore; to perforate. It is now written *drill* and *thrill.* [See these words, and see *Nostril.*]

THIRLAGE, *n. thurl'age.* In *English customs*, the right which the owner of a mill possesses by contract or law, to compel the tenants of a certain district to bring all their grain to his mill for grinding. *Cyc.*

THIRST, *n. thurst.* [Sax. *thurst, thyrst*; G. *durst*; D. *dorst*; Sw. *törst*; Dan. *törst*, from *tör*, dry; *törrer*, to dry, D. *dorren*, L. *torreo*, Sw. *torka.*]

1. A painful sensation of the throat or fauces, occasioned by the want of drink.

Wherefore is it that thou hast brought us out of Egypt, to kill us and our children and our cattle with *thirst?* Ex. xvii.

2. A vehement desire of drink. Ps. civ.

3. A want and eager desire after any thing.

Thirst of worldly good. *Fairfax.*

Thirst of knowledge. *Milton.*

Thirst of praise. *Granville.*

Thirst after happiness. *Cheyne.*

But *for* is now more generally used after *thirst*; as a *thirst for* worldly honors; a *thirst for* praise.

4. Dryness; drouth.

The rapid current, through veins
Of porous earth with kindly *thirst* updrawn,
Rose a fresh fountain— *Milton.*

THIRST, *v. i. thurst.* [Sax. *thyrstan*; D. *dorsten*; G. *dursten*; Sw. *törsta*; Dan. *törster.*]

1. To experience a painful sensation of the throat or fauces for want of drink.

The people *thirsted* there for water. Ex. xvii.

2. To have a vehement desire for any thing.

My soul *thirsteth* for the living God. Ps. xlii.

THIRST, *v. t.* To want to drink; as, to *thirst* blood. [*Not English.*] *Prior.*

THIRST'INESS, *n.* [from *thirsty.*] The state of being thirsty; thirst. *Wotton.*

THIRST'ING, *ppr.* Feeling pain for want of drink; having eager desire.

THIRST'Y, *a.* [from *thirst.*] Feeling a painful sensation of the throat or fauces for want of drink.

Give me a little water, for I am *thirsty.* Judges iv.

I was *thirsty*, and ye gave me no drink. Matt. xxv.

2. Very dry; having no moisture; parched.

The *thirsty* land shall become springs of water. Is. xxxv.

3. Having a vehement desire of any thing; as in blood-*thirsty.* Is. xliv. lxv.

THIRTEEN, *a. thur'teen.* [Sax. *threottyne*; *three* and *ten*; Sw. *tretton*; G. *dreyzehn*; D. *dertien.*] Ten and three; as *thirteen* times.

THIRTEENTH, *a. thur'teenth.* [supra.] The third after the tenth; the ordinal of thirteen; as the *thirteenth* day of the month.

THIRTEENTH, *n. thur'teenth.* In *music*, an interval forming the octave of the sixth, or sixth of the octave. *Busby.*

THIRTIETH, *a. thur'tieth.* [from *thirty*; Sax. *thrittigotha.*]

The tenth threefold; the ordinal of thirty; as the *thirtieth* day of the month.

THIRTY, *a. thur'ty.* [Sax. *thrittig*; G. *dreissig*; D. *dertig.*]

Thrice ten; ten three times repeated; or twenty and ten. The month of June consists of *thirty* days. Joseph was *thirty* years old when he stood before Pharaoh.

THIS, *definitive adjective* or *substitute.* plur. *these.* [Sax. *this*; Dan. plu. *disse*; Sw. *dessa, desse*; G. *das, dessen*; D. *deeze, dit.*]

1. *This* is a definitive, or definitive adjective, denoting something that is present or near in place or time, or something just mentioned. Is *this* your younger brother? What trespass is *this* which ye have committed?

Who did sin, *this* man or his parents, that he was born blind? John ix.

When they heard *this*, they were pricked to the heart. Acts ii.

In the latter passage, *this* is a substitute for what had preceded, viz. the discourse of Peter just delivered. In like manner, *this* often represents a word, a sentence or clause, or a series of sentences or events.

In some cases, it refers to what is future, or to be immediately related.

But know *this*, that if the good man of the house had known in what watch the thief would come, he would have watched, and would not have suffered his house to be broken up. Matt. xxiv.

Here *this* refers to the whole subsequent member of the sentence.

2. *By this*, is used elliptically for *by this time;* as, *by this* the mail has arrived.

3. *This* is used with words denoting time past; as, I have taken no snuff for *this* month; and often with plural words. I have not wept *this* forty years.

In this case, *this*, in the singular, refers to the whole term of time, or period; *this period* of forty years. *Dryden.*

4. *This* is opposed to *that.*

This way and *that* the wav'ring sails they bend. *Pope.*

A body of *this* or *that* denomination is produced. *Boyle.*

This and *that*, in this use, denote difference indefinitely.

5. When *this* and *that* refer to different things before expressed, *this* refers to the thing last mentioned, and *that* to the thing first mentioned. [See *These.*]

Their judgment in *this* we may not, and in in *that* we need not, follow. *Hooker.*

6. It is sometimes opposed to *other.*

Consider the arguments which the author had to write *this*, or to design the *other*, before you arraign him. *Dryden.*

THISTLE, *n. this'l.* [Sax. *thistel;* G. D. *distel;* Sw. *tistel.*]

The common name of numerous prickly plants of the class *Syngenesia*, and several genera; as the common corn thistle, or Canada thistle, of the genus Serratula or Cnicus; the spear thistle of the genus Cnicus; the milk thistle of the genus Carduus; the blessed thistle of the genus Centaurea; the globe thistle of the genus Echinops; the cotton thistle of the genus Onopordon; and the sow thistle of the genus Sonchus. The name is also given to other prickly plants not of the class *Syngenesia;* as the fuller's thistle or teasel of the genus Dipsacus, and the melon thistle and torch thistle of the genus Cactus. *Lee. Bigelow.*

One species of thistle, *(Cnicus arvensis,)* grows in fields among grain, and is extremely troublesome to farmers. It is called in America the Canada thistle, as it first appeared in Canada, where it was probably introduced from France, as it abounds in Normandy, and also in England. A larger species in America *(Cnicus lanceolatus,)* is indigenous, but it spreads slowly and gives no trouble.

Thorns also and *thistles* shall it bring forth to thee. Gen. iii.

THISTLY, *a. this'ly.* Overgrown with thistles; as *thistly* ground.

THITH'ER, *adv.* [Sax. *thider, thyder.*] To that place; opposed to *hither.*

This city is near, O let me escape *thither.* Gen. xix.

Where I am, *thither* ye cannot come. John vii.

2. To that end or point.

Hither and thither, to this place and to that; one way and another.

THITH'ERWARD, *adv.* [*thither* and *ward.*] Toward that place.

They shall ask the way to Zion, with their faces *thitherward.* Jer. l.

THO, a contraction of *though.* [See *Though.*]

2. *Tho*, for Sax. *thonne*, then. [*Not in use.*] *Spenser.*

THOLE, *n.* [Sax. *thol;* Ir. Gaelic, *dula*, a pin or peg.]

1. A pin inserted into the gunwale of a boat, to keep the oar in the row-lock, when used in rowing. *Mar. Dict.*

2. The pin or handle of a sythe-snath.

THOLE, *v. t.* [Sax. *tholian;* Goth. *thulan;* G. D. *dulden;* Sw. *tåla;* L. *tollo, tolero.*]

To bear; to endure; to undergo. *Obs.* *Gower.*

THOLE, *v. i.* [supra.] To wait. [*Local.*]

THOLE, *n.* [L. *tholus.*] The roof of a temple. [*Not used or local.*]

THO'MAISM, } *n.* The doctrine of St.
THO'MISM, } Thomas Aquinas with respect to predestination and grace.

THO'MIST, *n.* A follower of Thomas Aquinas, in opposition to the Scotists.

THOM'SONITE, *n.* [from *Thomson.*] A mineral of the zeolite family, occurring generally in masses of a radiated structure.

THONG, *n.* [Sax. *thwang.*] A strap of lether, used for fastening any thing.

And nails for loosen'd spears, and *thongs* for shields provide. *Dryden.*

THORAC'IC, *a.* [L. *thorax*, the breast.] Pertaining to the breast; as the *thoracic* arteries. *Coxe.*

The *thoracic duct*, is the trunk of the absorbent vessels. It runs up along the spine from the receptacle of the chyle to the left subclavian vein, in which it terminates. *Cyc. Parr.*

THORAC'ICS, *n. plu.* In *ichthyology*, an order of bony fishes, respiring by means of gills only, the character of which is that the bronchia are ossiculated, and the ventral fins are placed underneath the thorax, or beneath the pectoral fins. *Linne. Cyc.*

THO'RAL, *a.* [L. *thorus*, or rather *torus.*] Pertaining to a bed. *Ayliffe.*

THO'RAX, *n.* [L.] In *anatomy*, that part of the human skeleton which consists of the bones of the chest; also, the cavity of the chest. *Cyc.*

THORI'NA, *n.* A newly discovered earth, resembling zirconia, found in gadolinite by Berzelius. *Ure.*

THORN, *n.* [Sax. *thorn;* G. *dorn;* D. *doorn;* Dan. *torne;* Slav. *tern;* Goth. *thaurnus;* W. *draen.* Qu. is not the latter contracted from the Gaelic *dreaghum?*]

1. A tree or shrub armed with spines or sharp ligneous shoots; as the black *thorn;* white *thorn*, &c. The word is sometimes applied to a bush with prickles; as a rose on a *thorn.*

2. A sharp ligneous or woody shoot from the stem of a tree or shrub; a sharp process from the woody part of a plant; a spine. *Thorn* differs from *prickle;* the latter being applied to the sharp points issuing from the bark of a plant and not attached to the wood, as in the rose and bramble. But in common usage, thorn is applied to the prickle of the rose, and in fact the two words are used promiscuously.

3. Any thing troublesome. St. Paul had a *thorn* in the flesh. 2 Cor. xii. Num. xxxiii.

4. In *Scripture*, great difficulties and impediments.

I will hedge up thy way with *thorns.* Hos. ii.

5. Worldly cares; things which prevent the growth of good principles. Matt. xiii.

THORN'-APPLE, *n.* [*thorn* and *apple.*] A plant of the genus Datura; a popular name of the *Datura Stramonium*, or apple of Peru. *Bigelow.*

THORN'-BACK, *n.* [*thorn* and *back.*] A fish of the ray kind, which has prickles on its back. *Cyc.*

THORN'-BUSH, *n.* A shrub that produces thorns.

THORN'-BUT, *n.* A fish, a but or turbot. *Ainsworth.*

THORN'-HEDGE, *n.* [*thorn* and *hedge.*] A hedge or fence consisting of thorn.

THORN'LESS, *a.* Destitute of thorns; as a *thornless* shrub or tree. *Muhlenberg.*

THORN'Y, *a.* Full of thorns or spines; rough with thorns; as a *thorny* wood; a *thorny* tree; a *thorny* diadem or crown. *Dryden. Raleigh.*

2. Troublesome; vexatious; harassing; perplexing; as *thorny* care; the *thorny* path of vice.

3. Sharp; pricking; vexatious; as *thorny* points. *Shak.*

THORN'Y REST-HARROW, *n.* A plant. *Cyc.*

THORN'Y-TREFOIL, *n.* A plant of the genus Fagonia. *Lee.*

THŎROUGH, *a. thur'ro.* [Sax. *thurh;* G. *durch;* D. *door.* In these languages, the word is a preposition; but as a preposition we write it *through.* See this word. It is evidently from the root of *door*, which signifies a passage, and the radix of the word signifies to pass.]

1. Literally, passing through or to the end; hence, complete; perfect; as a *thorough* reformation; *thorough* work; a *thorough* translator; a *thorough* poet. *Dryden.*

2. Passing through; as *thorough* lights in a house. *Bacon.*

THŎROUGH, *prep. thur'ro.* From side to side, or from end to end.

2. By means of. [*Not now used.*] [See *Through.*]

THŎROUGH, *n. thur'ro.* An inter-furrow between two ridges. *Cyc.*

THŎROUGH-BASE, *n. thur'ro-base.* [*thorough* and *base.*]

In *music*, an accompaniment to a continued base by figures. *Cyc.*

THŎROUGH-BRED, *a. thur'ro-bred.* [*thorough* and *bred.*] Completely taught or accomplished.

THŎROUGH-FARE, *n. thur'ro-fare.* [*thorough* and *fare.*]

1. A passage through; a passage from one street or opening to another; an unobstructed way.

2. Power of passing. *Milton.*

THŎROUGHLY, *adv. thur'roly.* Fully; entirely; completely; as a room *thoroughly* swept; a business *thoroughly* performed. Let the matter be *thoroughly* sifted. Let every part of the work be *thoroughly* finished.

THŎROUGH-PACED, *a. thur'ro-paced.* [*thorough* and *paced.*]

Perfect in what is undertaken; complete; going all lengths; as a *thorough-paced* tory or whig. *Swift.*

THŎROUGH-SPED, *a. thur'ro-sped.* [*thorough* and *sped.*]

Fully accomplished; thorough-paced. *Swift.*

THŎROUGH-STITCH, *adv. thur'ro-stitch.* [*thorough* and *stitch.*]

Fully; completely; going the whole length of any business. [*Not elegant.*] *L'Estrange.*

THŎROUGH-WAX, *n. thur'ro-wax.* [*thorough* and *wax.*] A plant of the genus Bupleurum. *Lee.*

THŎROUGH-WŎRT, *n. thur'ro-wort.* The popular name of a plant, the *Eupatorium perfoliatum*, a native of N. America. It is valued in medicine.

THORP, Sax. *thorpe*; D. *dorp*; G. *dorf*; Sw. Dan. *torp*; W. *trev*; Gaelic, Ir. *treabh*; L. *tribus.* The word in Welsh signifies a dwelling place, a homestead, a hamlet, a town. When applied to a single house, it answers to the Sax. *ham*, a house, whence *hamlet* and *home.* In the Teutonic dialects, it denotes a village. The primary sense is probably a house, a habitation, from fixedness; hence a hamlet, a village, a tribe; as in rude ages the dwelling of the head of a family was soon surrounded by the houses of his children and descendants. In our language, it occurs now only in names of places and persons.

THOS, *n.* An animal of the wolf kind, but larger than the common wolf. It is common in Surinam. It preys on poultry and water fowls. *Cyc.*

THOSE, *pron. s* as *z.* plu. of *that*; as *those* men; *those* temples. When *those* and *these* are used in reference to two things or collections of things, *those* refers to the first mentioned, as *these* does to the last mentioned. [See *These*, and the example there given.]

THOU, *pron.* in the obj. *thee.* [Sax. *thu*; G. Sw. Dan. *du*; L. Fr. It. Sp. Port. *tu*; Sans. *tuam.* The nominative case is probably contracted, for in the oblique cases it is in Sw. and Dan. *dig*, in Goth. *thuk*, Sax. *thec.* So in Hindoo, *tu* in the nominative, makes in the dative, *tuko*; Gipsey, *tu*, *tuke.* In Russ. the verb is *tukayu*, to thou.]

The second personal pronoun, in the singular number; the pronoun which is used in addressing persons in the solemn style.

> Art *thou* he that should come? Matt. xi.
>
> I will fear no evil, for *thou* art with me. Ps. xxiii.

Thou is used only in the solemn style, unless in very familiar language, and by the Quakers.

THOU, *v. t.* To treat with familiarity.

> If thou *thouest* him some thrice, it shall not be amiss. *Shak.*

THOU, *v. i.* To use thou and thee in discourse.

THOUGH, *v. i. tho.* [Sax. *theah*; Goth. *thauh*; G. *doch*; Sw. *dock*; D. Dan. *dog.* This is the imperative of a verb; Ir. *daighim*, to give, D. *dokken.*]

1. Grant; admit; allow. "If thy brother be waxen poor—thou shalt relieve him; yea, *though* he be a stranger." *Grant* or *admit* the fact that he is a stranger, yet thou shalt relieve him. Lev. xxv.

> *Though* he slay me, yet will I trust in him. Job xiii.

That is, *grant* or *admit* that he shall slay me, yet will I trust in him.

> *Though* hand join in hand, the wicked shall not be unpunished. Prov. xi.

That is, *admit* the fact that the wicked unite their strength, yet this will not save them from punishment.

> Not that I so affirm, *though* so it seem. *Milton.*

That is, *grant* that it seems so, yet I do not so affirm.

2. Used with *as.*

> In the vine were three branches, and it was *as though* it budded. Gen. xl.

So we use *as if*; it was *as if* it budded; and *if* is *gif*, give. The appearance was like the real fact, *if* admitted or true.

3. It is used in familiar language, at the end of a sentence.

> A good cause would do well *though.* *Dryden.*

This is generally or always elliptical, referring to some expression preceding or understood.

4. It is compounded with *all*, in *although*, which see.

THOUGHT, *pret.* and *pp.* of *think*; pronounced *thaut.*

THOUGHT, *n. thaut.* [primarily the passive participle of *think*, supra; Sax. *theaht.*]

1. Properly, that which the mind thinks. Thought is either the act or operation of the mind, when attending to a particular subject or thing, or it is the idea consequent on that operation. We say, a man's *thoughts* are employed on government, on religion, on trade or arts, or his *thoughts* are employed on his dress or his means of living. By this we mean that the mind is directed to that particular subject or object; that is, according to the literal import of the verb *think*, the mind, the intellectual part of man, is *set* upon such an object, it holds it in view or contemplation, or it extends to it, it stretches to it.

> *Thought* cannot be superadded to matter, so as in any sense to render it true that matter can become cogitative. *Dwight.*

2. Idea; conception. I wish to convey my *thoughts* to another person. I employ words that express my *thoughts*, so that he may have the same ideas; in this case, our *thoughts* will be alike.

3. Fancy; conceit; something framed by the imagination.

> *Thoughts* come crowding in so fast upon me, that my only difficulty is to choose or reject. *Dryden.*

4. Reflection; particular consideration.

> Why do you keep alone?
> Using those *thoughts* which should have died
> With them they think on. *Shak.*

5. Opinion; judgment.

> Thus Bethel spoke, who always speaks his *thoughts.* *Pope.*

6. Meditation; serious consideration.

> Pride, of all others the most dangerous fault,
> Proceeds from want of sense or want of *thought.* *Roscommon.*

7. Design; purpose.

> All their *thoughts* are against me for evil. Ps. lvi. xxxiii. Jer. xxix.

8. Silent contemplation. *Shak.*

9. Solicitude; care; concern.

> Hawis was put in trouble, and died with *thought* and anguish before his business came to an end. *Bacon.*

10. Inward reasoning; the workings of conscience.

> Their *thoughts* the meanwhile accusing or else excusing one another. Rom. ii.

11. A small degree or quantity; as a *thought* longer; a *thought* better. [*Not in use.*] *Hooker. Sidney.*

To take thought, to be solicitous or anxious. Matt. vi.

THOUGHT'FUL, *a.* Full of thought; contemplative; employed in meditation; as a man of *thoughtful* mind.

2. Attentive; careful; having the mind directed to an object; as *thoughtful* of gain. *Philips.*

3. Promoting serious thought; favorable to musing or meditation.

> War, horrid war, your *thoughtful* walks invades. *Pope.*

4. Anxious; solicitous.

> Around her crowd distrust and doubt and fear,
> And *thoughtful* foresight, and tormenting care. *Prior.*

THOUGHT'FULLY, *adv.* With thought or consideration; with solicitude.

THOUGHT'FULNESS, *n.* Deep meditation. *Blackmore.*

2. Serious attention to spiritual concerns.

3. Anxiety; solicitude.

THOUGHT'LESS, *a.* Heedless; careless; negligent.

> *Thoughtless* of the future. *Rogers.*

2. Gay; dissipated.

3. Stupid; dull.

> *Thoughtless* as monarch oaks that shade the plain. *Dryden.*

THOUGHT'LESSLY, *adv.* Without thought; carelessly; stupidly. *Garth.*

THOUGHT'LESSNESS, *n.* Want of thought; heedlessness; carelessness; inattention.

THOUGHT'SICK, *a.* [*thought* and *sick.*] Uneasy with reflection. *Shak.*

THOU'SAND, *a. s* as *z.* [Sax. *thusend*; Goth. *thusund*; G. *tausend*; D. *duizend*; Sw. *tusend*; Dan. *tusind.*]

1. Denoting the number of ten hundred.

2. Proverbially, denoting a great number indefinitely. It is a *thousand* chances to one that you succeed.

THOU'SAND, *n.* The number of ten hundred.

> A *thousand* shall fall at thy side, and ten *thousand* at thy right hand. Ps. xci.

Thousand is sometimes used plurally without the plural termination, as in the passage above, ten *thousand*; but it often takes the plural termination. In former times, how many *thousands* perished by famine!

THOU'SANDTH, *a.* The ordinal of thousand; as the *thousandth* part of a thing; also proverbially, very numerous.

THOU'SANDTH, *n.* The thousandth part of any thing; as two *thousandths* of a tax.

THOWL. [See *Thole.*]

THRACK, *v. t.* To load or burden. [*Not in use.*] *South.*

THRALL, *n.* [Sax. *thrall*, a slave or servant; Dan. *træl*; Sw. *träl*; Ice. *troel*; Ir. *trail*; Gaelic, *traill.*]

1. A slave.

2. Slavery. *Obs.*

THRALL, *v. t.* To enslave. *Obs.* [*Enthrall* is in use.]

THRALL'DOM, *n.* [Dan. *trældom.*] Slavery; bondage; a state of servitude. The Greeks lived in *thralldom* under the Turks, nearly four hundred years.

He shall rule, and she in *thralldom* live.
[*This word is in good use.*] *Dryden.*

THRAP'PLE, *n.* The windpipe of an animal. [*Not an English word.*] *Scott.*

THRASH, *v. t.* [Sax. *tharscan* or *therscan*; G. *dreschen*; D. *dorschen*; Sw. *tröska*; Ice. *therskia.* It is written *thrash* or *thresh.* The common pronunciation is *thrash.*]

1. To beat out grain from the husk or pericarp with a flail; as, to *thrash* wheat, rye or oats.

2. To beat corn off from the cob or spike; as, to *thrash* maiz.

3. To beat soundly with a stick or whip; to drub. *Shak.*

THRASH, *v. i.* To practice thrashing; to perform the business of thrashing; as a man who *thrashes* well.

2. To labor; to drudge.

I rather would be Mevius, *thrash* for rhymes,
Like his, the scorn and scandal of the times— *Dryden.*

THRASH'ED, *pp.* Beaten out of the husk or off the ear.

2. Freed from the grain by beating.

THRASH'ER, *n.* One who thrashes grain.

THRASH'ING, *ppr.* Beating out of the husk or off the ear; beating soundly with a stick or whip.

THRASH'ING, *n.* The act of beating out grain with a flail; a sound drubbing.

THRASH'ING-FLOOR, *n.* [*thrash* and *floor.*]

A floor or area on which grain is beaten out. *Dryden.*

THRASON'ICAL, *a.* [from *Thraso*, a boaster in old comedy.]

1. Boasting; given to bragging.

2. Boastful; implying ostentatious display. *Shak.*

THRAVE, *n.* [Sax. *draf*, a drove.] A drove; a herd. [*Not in use.*]

THRAVE, *n.* [W. *dreva*, twenty four; *drev*, a bundle or tie.]

The number of two dozen. [*Not in use.*]

THREAD, } *n.* [Sax. *thred*, *thræd*; D. *draad*;
THRED, } Sw. *tråd*; Dan. *traad*; probably from drawing.]

1. A very small twist of flax, wool, cotton, silk or other fibrous substance, drawn out to considerable length.

2. The filament of a flower. *Botany.*

3. The filament of any fibrous substance, as of bark.

4. A fine filament or line of gold or silver.

5. *Air-threads*, the fine white filaments which are seen floating in the air in summer, the production of spiders.

6. Something continued in a long course or tenor; as the *thread* of a discourse. *Burnet.*

7. The prominent spiral part of a screw.

THREAD, } *v. t.* To pass a thread through
THRED, } the eye; as, to *thread* a needle.

2. To pass or pierce through, as a narrow way or channel.

They would not *thread* the gates. *Shak.*
Heavy trading ships—*threading* the Bosporus. *Mitford.*

THREAD'BARE, } *a.* [*thread* and *bare.*]
THRED'BARE, } Worn to the naked thread; having the nap worn off; as a *threadbare* coat; *threadbare* clothes. *Spenser. Dryden.*

2. Worn out; trite; hackneyed; used till it has lost its novelty or interest; as a *threadbare* subject; state topics and *threadbare* quotations. *Swift.*

THREAD'BARENESS, } *n.* The state of
THRED'BARENESS, } being threadbare or trite.

THREAD'EN, } *a.* Made of thread; as
THRED'EN, } *threaden* sails. [*Little used.*] *Shak.*

THREAD'-SHAPED, } *a.* In *botany*, fili-
THRED'-SHAPED, } form.

THREAD'Y, } *a.* Like thread or filaments;
THRED'Y, } slender. *Granger.*

2. Containing thread. *Dyer.*

THREAP, *v. t.* [Sax. *threapian*, or rather *threagan.*]

To chide, contend or argue. [*Local.*] *Ainsworth.*

THREAT, *n. thret.* [Sax. *threat.* See the Verb.]

A menace; denunciation of ill; declaration of an intention or determination to inflict punishment, loss or pain on another.

There is no terror, Cassius, in your *threats.* *Shak.*

THREAT, *v. t. thret.* To threaten, which see. *Threat* is used only in poetry. *Dryden.*

THREATEN, *v. t. thret'n.* [Sax. *threatian*, from *threat.* But *threat* appears to be contracted from *threagan*, which is written also *threawian*; D. *dreigen*; G. *drohen*; Dan. *tretter*, to chide, to scold, dispute, wrangle.]

1. To declare the purpose of inflicting punishment, pain or other evil on another, for some sin or offense; to menace. God *threatens* the finally impenitent with everlasting banishment from his presence.

2. To menace; to terrify or attempt to terrify by menaces; as for extorting money. To send *threatening* letters is a punishable offense.

3. To charge or enjoin with menace, or with implied rebuke; or to charge strictly.

Let us straitly *threaten* them, that they speak henceforth to no man in his name. Acts iv.

4. To menace by action; to present the appearance of coming evil; as, rolling billows *threaten* to overwhelm us.

5. To exhibit the appearance of something evil or unpleasant approaching; as, the clouds *threaten* us with rain or a storm.

THREATENED, *pp. thret'nd.* Menaced with evil.

THREATENER, *n. thret'ner.* One that threatens. *Milton.*

THREATENING, *ppr. thret'ning.* Menacing; denouncing evil.

2. *a.* Indicating a threat or menace; as a *threatening* look.

3. Indicating something impending; as, the weather is *threatening*; the clouds have a *threatening* aspect.

THREATENING, *n. thret'ning.* The act of menacing; a menace; a denunciation of evil, or declaration of a purpose to inflict evil on a person or country, usually for sins and offenses. The prophets are filled with God's *threatenings* against the rebellious Jews. Acts iv.

THREATENINGLY, *adv. thret'ningly.* With a threat or menace; in a threatening manner. *Shak.*

THREATFUL, *a. thret'ful.* Full of threats; having a menacing appearance; minacious. *Spenser.*

THREE, *a.* [Sax. *threo*, *thri*, *thry* and *thrig*; Sw. Dan. *tre*; G. *drei*; D. *drie*; Fr. *trois*; It. *tre*; Sp. L. *tres*; Gael. W. *tri*; Gipsey, *tre*; Gr. τρεις; Sans. *treja*, *tri.* I know not the last radical, nor the primary sense of *three.* Owen in his Welsh Dictionary, suggests that it signifies *fixed*, *firm.* But see *Extricate* and *Trick.* It is probably contracted from *thrig.*]

1. Two and one.

I offer thee *three* things. 2 Sam. xxiv.

2. It is often used like other adjectives, without the noun to which it refers.

Abishai—attained not to the first *three.* 2 Sam. xxiii.

3. Proverbially, a small number.

Away, thou *three*-inched fool. *Shak.*
[*I believe obsolete.*]

THREE-CAP'SULED, *a.* Tricapsular.

THREE-CEL'LED, *a.* Trilocular.

THREE-CLEFT', *a.* Trifid.

THREE'-CORNERED, *a.* [*three* and *corner.*]

1. Having three corners or angles; as a *three-cornered* hat.

2. In *botany*, having three sides, or three prominent longitudinal angles, as a stem. *Martyn.*

THREE'-FLOWERED, *a.* [*three* and *flower.*]

Bearing three flowers together. *Martyn.*

THREE'FOLD, *a.* [*three* and *fold.*] Three-double; consisting of three; or thrice repeated, as *threefold* justice. *Raleigh.*

A *threefold* cord is not quickly broken. Eccles. iv.

THREE'-GRAINED, *a.* Tricoccous.

THREE'-LEAVED, *a.* [*three* and *leaf.*] Consisting of three distinct leaflets; as a *three-leaved* calyx. *Martyn.*

THREE'-LOBED, *a.* [*three* and *lobe.*] A *three-lobed leaf*, is one that is divided to the middle into three parts, standing wide from each other and having convex margins. *Martyn.*

THREE'-NERVED, *a.* [*three* and *nerve.*] A *three-nerved leaf*, has three distinct vessels or nerves running longitudinally without branching. *Martyn.*

THREE'-PARTED, *a.* [*three* and *parted.*] Tripartite. A *three-parted leaf*, is divided into three parts down to the base, but not entirely separate. *Martyn.*

THREE'-PENCE, *n. thrip'ence.* [*three* and *pence.*]

A small silver coin of three times the value of a penny. *Shak.*

THREE'-PENNY, *a.* *thrip'enny.* Worth three pence only; mean.

THREE'-PETALED, *a.* [*three* and *petal.*] Tripetalous; consisting of three distinct petals; as a corol. *Botany.*

THREE'-PILE, *n.* [*three* and *pile.*] An old name for good velvet. *Shak.*

THREE'-PILED, *a.* Set with a thick pile. *Obs.* *Shak.*

THREE'-POINTED, *a.* Tricuspidate.

THREE'SCORE, *a.* [*three* and *score.*] Thrice twenty; sixty; as *threescore* years.

THREE'-SEEDED, *a.* [*three* and *seed.*] Containing three seeds; as a *three-seeded* capsule. *Botany.*

THREE'-SIDED, *a.* [*three* and *side.*] Having three plane sides; as a *three-sided* stem, leaf, petiole, peduncle, scape, or pericarp. *Martyn.*

THREE'-VALVED, *a.* [*three* and *valve.*] Trivalvular; consisting of three valves; opening with three valves; as a *three-valved* pericarp. *Lee. Martyn.*

THRENE, *n.* [Gr. θρηνος.] Lamentation. [*Not used.*] *Shak.*

THREN'ODY, *n.* [Gr. θρηνος, lamentation, and ωδη, ode.]
A song of lamentation. *Herbert.*

THRESH, *v. t.* To thrash. [See *Thrash.*] The latter is the popular pronunciation, but the word is written *thrash* or *thresh*, indifferently. [See the derivation and definitions under *Thrash.*]

THRESH'ER, *n.* The sea fox. *Cyc.*

THRESH'HŎLD, *n.* [Sax. *therscwald*; G. *thürschwelle*; Sw. *trŏskel*; Ice. *throsulldur.* The Saxon and Swedish words seem by their orthography to be connected with *thrash*, *thresh*, and the last syllable to be *wald*, wood; but the German word is obviously compounded of *thür*, door, and *schwelle*, sill; door-sill.]

1. The door-sill; the plank, stone or piece of timber which lies at the bottom or under a door, particularly of a dwelling house, church, temple or the like; hence, entrance; gate; door.

2. Entrance; the place or point of entering or beginning. He is now at the *threshhold* of his argument.

> Many men that stumble at the *threshhold.* *Shak.*

THREW, *pret.* of *throw.*

THRICE, *adv.* [from *three*; perhaps *three*, and L. *vice*; or a change of Fr. *tiers.*]

1. Three times.

> Before the cock crow, thou shalt deny me *thrice.* Matt. xxvi.

2. Sometimes used by way of amplification; very.

> *Thrice* noble Lord, let me entreat of you
> To pardon me. *Shak.*

THRID, *v. t.* [W. *treiziaw*, to penetrate; *treidiaw*, to course, to range.]
To slide through a narrow passage; to slip, shoot or run through, as a needle, bodkin, or the like.

> Some *thrid* the mazy ringlets of her hair. *Pope.*

THRID'DED, *pp.* Slid through.

THRID'DING, *ppr.* Sliding through; causing to pass through.

THRIFT, *n.* [from *thrive.*] Frugality; good husbandry; economical management in regard to property.

> The rest—willing to fall to *thrift*, prove very good husbands. *Spenser.*

2. Prosperity; success and advance in the acquisition of property; increase of worldly goods; gain.

> I have a mind presages me such *thrift.* *Shak.*

3. Vigorous growth, as of a plant.

4. In *botany*, a plant of the genus Statice.

THRIFT'ILY, *adv.* Frugally; with parsimony.

2. With increase of worldly goods.

THRIFT'INESS, *n.* Frugality; good husbandry; as *thriftiness* to save; *thriftiness* in preserving one's own. *Wotton. Spenser.*

2. Prosperity in business; increase of property.

THRIFT'LESS, *a.* Having no frugality or good management; profuse; extravagant; not thriving. *Shak.*

THRIFT'Y, *a.* Frugal; sparing; using economy and good management of property.

> I am glad he has so much youth and vigor left, of which he has not been *thrifty.* *Swift.*

2. *More generally*, thriving by industry and frugality; prosperous in the acquisition of worldly goods; increasing in wealth; as a *thrifty* farmer or mechanic.

3. Thriving; growing rapidly or vigorously; as a plant.

4. Well husbanded.

> I have five hundred crowns,
> The *thrifty* hire I sav'd under your father. *Shak.*

THRILL, *n.* [See the Verb.] A drill.

2. A warbling. [See *Trill.*]

3. A breathing place or hole. *Herbert.*

THRILL, *v. t.* [Sax. *thyrlian*, *thirlian*; D. *drillen*, to *drill*, to bore; *trillen*, to shiver, pant, quaver; G. *drillen*, to drill; *triller*, a shake; *trillern*, to *trill*; Dan. *driller*, to bore, to drill; *trilder*, Sw. *trilla*, to roll; Dan. *trille*, a trill; W. *troliaw*, to troll or roll; all probably of one family, from the root of *roll.* See *Drill.*]

1. To bore; to drill; to perforate by turning a gimblet or other similar instrument. [But in the literal sense, *drill* is now chiefly or wholly used. Spenser used it literally in the clause, "with *thrilling* point of iron brand."]

2. To pierce; to penetrate; as something sharp.

> The cruel word her tender heart so *thrill'd*,
> That sudden cold did run through every vein. *Spenser.*

> A servant that he bred, *thrill'd* with remorse. *Shak.*

THRILL, *v. i.* To pierce; to penetrate; as something sharp; particularly, to cause a tingling sensation that runs through the system with a slight shivering; as, a sharp sound *thrills* through the whole frame. *Addison.*

> A faint cold fear *thrills* through my veins. *Shak.*

2. To feel a sharp shivering sensation running through the body.

> To seek sweet safety out
> In vaults and prisons; and to *thrill* and shake— *Shak.*

THRILL'ED, *pp.* Penetrated; pierced.

THRILL'ING, *ppr.* Perforating; drilling.

2. Piercing; penetrating; having the quality of penetrating; passing with a tingling, shivering sensation.

3. Feeling a tingling, shivering sensation running through the system.

THRING, *v. t.* To press, crowd or throng. [*Not used.*] *Chaucer.*

THRIS'SA, *n.* A fish of the herring kind.

THRIVE, *v. i.* pret. *thrived*; pp. *thrived*, *thriven.* [Dan. *trives*, to thrive, to increase; Sw. *trifvas.* It may belong to the family of *trip*, to hasten, or to that of *drive.*]

1. To prosper by industry, economy and good management of property; to increase in goods and estate. A farmer *thrives* by good husbandry. When the body of laboring men *thrive*, we pronounce the state prosperous.

> Diligence and humility is the way to *thrive* in the riches of the understanding, as well as in gold. *Watts.*

2. To prosper in any business; to have increase or success.

> O son, why sit we here, each other viewing
> Idly, while Satan our great author *thrives*? *Milton.*

> They by vices *thrive.* *Sandys.*

3. To grow; to increase in bulk or stature; to flourish. Young cattle *thrive* in rich pastures; and trees *thrive* in a good soil.

4. To grow; to advance; to increase or advance in any thing valuable.

THRI'VER, *n.* One that prospers in the acquisition of property.

THRI'VING, *ppr.* Prospering in worldly goods.

2. *a.* Being prosperous or successful; advancing in wealth; increasing; growing; as a *thriving* mechanic; a *thriving* trader.

THRI'VINGLY, *adv.* In a prosperous way.

THRI'VINGNESS, } *n.* Prosperity; growth;
THRI'VING, } increase. *Decay of Piety.*

THRO, a contraction of *through*, not now used.

THROAT, *n.* [Sax. *throta*, *throte*; D. *strote*; Russ. *grud.*]

1. The anterior part of the neck of an animal, in which are the gullet and windpipe, or the passages for the food and breath.

In *medicine*, the fauces; all that hollow or cavity which may be seen when the mouth is wide open. *Cyc.*

2. In *seamen's language*, that end of a gaff which is next the mast. *Mar. Dict.*

3. In *ship-building*, the inside of the knee-timber at the middle or turns of the arms; also, the inner part of the arms of an anchor where they join the shank; and the middle part of a floor-timber. *Cyc.*

Throat-brails, brails attached to the gaff, close to the mast.

Throat-halliards, are those that raise the throat of the gaff. *Mar. Dict.*

THRŎAT, *v. t.* To mow beans in a direction against their bending. [*Local.*] *Cyc.*

THROAT-PIPE, *n.* [*throat* and *pipe.*] The windpipe or weasand.

THRŎAT-WŎRT, *n.* [*throat* and *wort.*] A plant of the genus Campanula, a perennial weed common in pasture-ground; also, a plant of the genus Trachelium. *Cyc. Lee.*

THRŌATY, *a.* Guttural. *Howell.*

THROB, *v. i.* [perhaps allied to *drive* and to *drub;* at least its elements and signification coincide; Gr. θορυβεω.]

To beat, as the heart or pulse, with more than usual force or rapidity; to beat in consequence of agitation; to palpitate. The heart *throbs* with joy, desire or fear; the violent action of the heart is perceived by a *throbbing* pulse.

My heart *throbs* to know one thing. *Shak.*

We apply the word also to the breast.

Here may his head live on my *throbbing* breast. *Shak.*

THROB, *n.* A beat or strong pulsation; a violent beating of the heart and arteries; a palpitation.

Thou talk'st like one who never felt
Th' impatient *throbs* and longings of a soul
That pants and reaches after distant good. *Addison.*

THROB'BING, *ppr.* Beating with unusual force, as the heart and pulse; palpitating.

THROB'BING, *n.* The act of beating with unusual force, as the heart and pulse; palpitation.

THROD'DEN, *v. i.* To grow; to thrive. [*Not in use or local.*] *Grose.*

THRŌE, *n.* [Sax. *throwian,* to suffer, to agonize; but this is the same word as *throw,* and the sense is to strain, as in twisting, to struggle.]

Extreme pain; violent pang; anguish; agony. It is particularly applied to the anguish of travail in child-birth.

My *throes* came thicker, and my cries increas'd. *Dryden.*

THRŌE, *v. i.* To agonize; to struggle in extreme pain.

THRŌE, *v. t.* To put in agony. *Shak.*

THRONE, *n.* [L. *thronus;* Gr. θρονος; Fr. *trone.*]

1. A royal seat; a chair of state. The throne is sometimes an elegant chair richly ornamented with sculpture and gilding, raised a step above the floor, and covered with a canopy.
2. The seat of a bishop. *Ayliffe.*
3. In *Scripture,* sovereign power and dignity.

Only in the *throne* will I be greater than thou. Gen. xli.

Thy *throne,* O God, is forever. Ps. xlv.

4. Angels. Col. i.
5. The place where God peculiarly manifests his power and glory.

The heaven is my *throne,* and the earth my footstool. Is. lxvi.

THRONE, *v. t.* To place on a royal seat; to enthrone.

2. To place in an elevated position; to give an elevated place to; to exalt.

True image of the Father, whether thron'd
In the bosom of bliss and light of light. *Milton.*

THRO'NED, *pp.* Placed on a royal seat, or on an elevated seat; exalted.

THRONG, *n.* [Sax. *thrang;* Ir. *drong;* G. D. *drang.* See the Verb.]

1. A crowd; a multitude of persons or of living beings pressing or pressed into a close body or assemblage; as a *throng* of people at a play-house.
2. A great multitude; as the heavenly *throng.*

THRONG, *v. i.* [Sax. *thringan;* D. *dringen;* G. *drängen;* Dan. *trænger;* Sw. *trånga.* If *n* is not radical, this word coincides with Sw. *tryka,* Dan. *trykker,* to press, to print. Class Rg.]

To crowd together; to press into a close body, as a multitude of persons; to come in multitudes.

I have seen
The dumb men *throng* to see him. *Shak.*

THRONG, *v. t.* To crowd or press, as persons; to oppress or annoy with a crowd of living beings.

Much people followed him, and *thronged* him. Mark v.

THRONG'ED, *pp.* Crowded or pressed by a multitude of persons.

THRONG'ING, *ppr.* Crowding together; pressing with a multitude of persons.

THRONG'ING, *n.* The act of crowding together.

THRONG'LY, *adv.* In crowds. [*Not in use.*] *More.*

THROP'PLE, *n.* The windpipe of a horse. [*Local.*] *Cyc.*

THROSTLE, *n. thros'l.* [Sax. *throstle;* G. *drossel.*]

A bird of the genus Turdus, the song-thrush.

THROS'TLING, *n.* A disease of cattle of the ox kind, occasioned by a swelling under their throats, which unless checked, will choke them. *Cyc.*

THROT'TLE, *n.* [from *throat.*] The windpipe or larynx. *Brown.*

THROT'TLE, *v. i.* To choke; to suffocate; or to obstruct so as to endanger suffocation. *Milton. Dryden.*

2. To breathe hard, as when nearly suffocated.

THROT'TLE, *v. t.* To utter with breaks and interruptions, as a person half suffocated.

Throttle their practic'd accents in their fears. *Shak.*

THROUGH, *prep. thru.* [Sax. *thurh;* D. *door;* G. *durch;* W. *trwy* or *trw,* whence *trwyaw,* to pervade; Ir. *treoghdham,* Gaelic, *treaghaim,* to pierce or bore.]

1. From end to end, or from side to side; from one surface or limit to the opposite; as, to bore *through* a piece of timber, or *through* a board; a ball passes *through* the side of a ship.
2. Noting passage; as, to pass *through* a gate or avenue.

Through the gates of iv'ry he dismiss'd
His valiant offspring. *Dryden.*

3. By transmission, noting the means of conveyance.

Through these hands this science has passed with great applause. *Temple.*

Material things are presented only *through* their senses. *Cheyne.*

4. By means of; by the agency of; noting instrumentality. This signification is a derivative of the last.

Through the scent of water it will bud. Job xiv.

Some *through* ambition, or *through* thirst of gold,
Have slain their brothers, and their country sold. *Dryden.*

Sanctify them *through* thy truth. John xvii.

The gift of God is eternal life *through* Jesus Christ our Lord. Rom. vi.

5. Over the whole surface or extent; as, to ride *through* the country.

Their tongue walketh *through* the earth. Ps. lxxiii.

6. Noting passage among or in the midst of; as, to move *through* water, as a fish; to run *through* a thicket, as a deer.

THROUGH, *adv. thru.* From one end or side to the other; as, to pierce a thing *through.*

2. From beginning to end; as, to read a letter *through.*
3. To the end; to the ultimate purpose; as, to carry a project *through.*

To carry through, to complete; to accomplish.

To go through, to prosecute a scheme to the end.

2. To undergo; to sustain; as, to *go through* hardships.

THROUGH-BRED, should be *thorough-bred.*

THROUGH-LIGHTED, should be *thorough-lighted.* [*Not used.*]

THROUGHLY, *adv. thru'ly.* Completely; fully; wholly. *Bacon.*

2. Without reserve; sincerely. *Tillotson.*

[For this, *thoroughly* is now used.]

THROUGHOUT, *prep. thruout'.* [*through* and *out.*]

Quite through; in every part; from one extremity to the other. This is the practice *throughout* Ireland. A general opinion prevails *throughout* England. *Throughout* the whole course of his life, he avoided every species of vice.

THROUGHOUT, *adv. thruout'.* In every part. The cloth was of a piece *throughout.*

THROUGH-PACED. [*Not used.*] [See *Thorough-paced.*] *More.*

THRŌVE, *old pret.* of *thrive.*

THRŌW, *v. t.* pret. *threw;* pp. *thrown.* [Sax. *thrawan;* perhaps D. *draaijen,* to turn, wind, twist, whirl; G. *drehen;* W. *troi.* The Saxon word signifies to twist, to turn, to curl, to throw, and to revolve. It is contracted, and probably coincides in elements with Gr. τρεχω, to run, for this was applied primarily to wheels, as we see by its derivatives, τροχος, a wheel, τροχιλος, a top, L. *trochilus.*]

1. Properly, to hurl; to whirl; to fling or cast in a winding direction.
2. To fling or cast in any manner; to propel; to send; to drive to a distance from the hand or from an engine. Thus we *throw* stones or dust with the hand; a cannon *throws* a ball; a bomb *throws* a shell. The Roman balistæ *threw* various weapons. A fire engine *throws* water to extinguish flames.
3. To wind; as, to *throw* silk.
4. To turn; as, to *throw* balls in a lathe. [*Not in general use.*]
5. To venture at dice.

Set less than thou *throwest.* *Shak.*

6. To cast; to divest or strip one's self of; to put off; as, a serpent *throws* his skin. *Shak.*
7. To cast; to send.

I have *thrown*
A brave defiance in king Henry's teeth. *Shak.*

8. To put on; to spread carelessly.

O'er his fair limbs a flow'ry vest he *threw.* *Pope.*

9. To overturn; to prostrate in wrestling; as, a man *throws* his antagonist.

10. To cast; to drive by violence; as a vessel or sailors *thrown* upon a rock.

To throw away, to lose by neglect or folly; to spend in vain; as, to *throw away* time; to *throw away* money.

2. To bestow without a compensation.

3. To reject; as, to *throw away* a good book, or a good offer. *Taylor.*

To throw by, to lay aside or neglect as useless; as, to *throw by* a garment.

To throw down, to subvert; to overthrow; to destroy; as, to *throw down* a fence or wall.

2. To bring down from a high station; to depress. *Spectator.*

To throw in, to inject.

2. To put in; to deposit with others; also, to give up or relinquish.

To throw off, to expel; to clear from; as, to *throw off* a disease.

2. To reject; to discard; as, to *throw off* all sense of shame; to *throw off* a dependent.

To throw on, to cast on; to load.

To throw out, to cast out; to reject or discard; to expel. *Swift.*

2. To utter carelessly; to speak; as, to *throw out* insinuations or observations.

3. To exert; to bring forth into act.

She *throws out* thrilling shrieks. *Spenser.*

4. To distance; to leave behind. *Addison.*

5. To exclude; to reject. The bill was *thrown out* on the second reading.

To throw up, to resign; as, to *throw up* a commission.

2. To resign angrily.

Bad games are *thrown up* too soon. *Hudibras.*

3. To discharge from the stomach. *Arbuthnot.*

To throw one's self down, to lie down.

To throw one's self on, to resign one's self to the favor, clemency or sustaining power of another; to repose. *Taylor.*

THROW, *v. i.* To perform the act of throwing.

2. To cast dice.

To throw about, to cast about; to try expedients. [*Not much used.*] *Spenser.*

THROW, *n.* The act of hurling or flinging; a cast; a driving or propelling from the hand or from an engine.

He heav'd a stone, and rising to the *throw*,
He sent it in a whirlwind at the foe. *Addison.*

2. A cast of dice; and the manner in which dice fall when cast; as a good *throw*. None but a fool hazards all upon one *throw*.

3. The distance which a missile is or may be thrown; as a stone's *throw*.

4. A stroke; a blow.

Nor shield defend the thunder of his *throws*. *Spenser.*

5. Effort; violent sally.

Your youth admires
The *throws* and swellings of a Roman soul. *Addison.*

6. The agony of travail. [See *Throe.*]

7. A turner's lathe. [*Local.*]

THROWER, *n.* One that throws; one that twists or winds silk; a throwster.

THROWN, *pp.* of *throw.* Cast; hurled; wound or twisted.

THROWSTER, *n.* One that twists or winds silk.

THRUM, *n.* [Ice. *thraum*; G. *trumm*; D. *drom*, the end of a thing; Gr. *θρυμμα*, a fragment; *θρυπτω*, to break.] The ends of weaver's threads.

2. Any coarse yarn. *Bacon.*

3. *Thrums*, among *gardeners*, the thread-like internal bushy parts of flowers; the stamens.

THRUM, *v. i.* [D. *trom*, a drum.] To play coarsely on an instrument with the fingers. *Dryden.*

THRUM, *v. t.* To weave; to knot; to twist; to fringe. *Cavendish.*

2. Among *seamen*, to insert short pieces of rope-yarn or spun yarn in a sail or mat. *Dict.*

THRUSH, *n.* [Sax. *drisc*; G. *drossel*; W. *tresglen*; Sw. *trast.*]

1. A bird, a species of Turdus, the largest of the genus; the *Turdus viscivorus* or missel-bird. *Cyc. Ed. Encyc.*

2. [Qu. *thrust.*] An affection of the inflammatory and suppurating kind, in the feet of the horse and some other animals. In the horse it is in the frog. *Cyc.*

3. In *medicine*, (L. *apthæ*,) ulcers in the mouth and fauces. *Coxe. Arbuthnot.*

THRUST, *v. t.* pret. and pp. *thrust.* [L. *trudo, trusum, trusito*; Ch. טרד; Ar. طرد tarada. Class Rd. No. 63.]

1. To push or drive with force; as, to *thrust* any thing with the hand or foot, or with an instrument.

Neither shall one *thrust* another. Joel ii. John xx.

2. To drive; to force; to impel.

To thrust away or *from*, to push away; to reject. Acts vii.

To thrust in, to push or drive in.

Thrust in thy sickle and reap. Rev. xiv.

To thrust on, to impel; to urge. *Shak.*

To thrust off, to push away.

To thrust through, to pierce; to stab. Num. xxv. 2 Sam. xviii.

To thrust out, to drive out or away; to expel. Ex. xii.

To thrust one's self, to obtrude; to intrude; to enter where one is not invited or not welcome. *Locke.*

To thrust together, to compress.

THRUST, *v. i.* To make a push; to attack with a pointed weapon; as, a fencer *thrusts* at his antagonist.

2. To enter by pushing; to squeeze in.

And *thrust* between my father and the god. *Dryden.*

3. To intrude. *Rowe.*

4. To push forward; to come with force; to press on.

Young, old, *thrust* there
In mighty concourse. *Chapman.*

THRUST, *n.* A violent push or driving, as with a pointed weapon, or with the hand or foot, or with any instrument; a word much used in fencing.

Polites Pyrrhus with his lance pursues,
And often reaches, and his *thrusts* renews. *Dryden.*

2. Attack; assault.

There is one *thrust* at your pure, pretended mechanism. *More.*

[Note. *Push* and *shove* do not exactly express the sense of *thrust*. The two former imply the application of force by one body already in contact with the body to be impelled. *Thrust* on the contrary, often implies the impulse or application of force by a moving body, a body in motion before it reaches the body to be impelled. This distinction does not extend to every case.]

THRUST'ER, *n.* One who thrusts or stabs.

THRUST'ING, *ppr.* Pushing with force; driving; impelling; pressing.

THRUST'ING, *n.* The act of pushing with force.

2. In dairies, the act of squeezing curd with the hand, to expel the whey. [*Local.*] *Cyc.*

THRUST'INGS, *n.* In *cheese-making*, the white whey, or that which is last pressed out of the curd by the hand, and of which butter is sometimes made. *Cyc.*

[*The application of this word to cheese-making, is, I believe, entirely unknown in New England.*]

THRUST'ING-SCREW, *n.* A screw for pressing curd in cheese-making. [*Local.*]

THRUS'TLE, *n.* The thrush. [See *Throstle.*]

THRȲ-FAL'LOW, *v. t.* [*thrice* and *fallow.*] To give the third plowing in summer. *Tusser.*

THU'LITE, *n.* A rare mineral of a peach blossom color, found in Norway. *Ure.*

THUMB, THUM, *n.* [Sax. *thuma*; G. *daumen*; D. *duim*; Dan. *tomme*; Sw. *tumme.*]

The short thick finger of the human hand, or the corresponding member of other animals. [The common orthography is corrupt. The real word is *thum.*]

THUMB, THUM, *v. t.* To handle awkwardly; to play with the fingers; as, to *thum* over a tune.

2. To soil with the fingers.

THUMB, THUM, *v. i.* To play on with the fingers.

THUMB'-BAND, THUM'-BAND, *n.* [*thum* and *band.*] A twist of any thing as thick as the thum. *Mortimer.*

THUMB'ED, THUM'MED, *a.* Having thumbs.

THUM'ERSTONE, *n.* A mineral so called from *Thum*, in Saxony, where it was found. It is called also *axinite*, from the resemblance of its flat sharp edges to that of an ax. It is either massive or crystalized; its crystals are in the form of a compressed oblique rhomboidal prism. It is of the silicious kind, and of a brown gray or violet color. *Cyc.*

THUM'MIM, *n. plu.* A Hebrew word denoting perfections. The *Urim* and *Thummim* were worn in the breastplate of the high priest, but what they were, has never been satisfactorily ascertained.

THUMP, *n.* [It. *thombo.*] A heavy blow given with any thing that is thick, as with a club or the fist, or with a heavy hammer, or with the britch of a gun.

The watchman gave so great a *thump* at my door, that I awaked at the knock. *Tatler.*

THUMP, *v. t.* To strike or beat with something thick or heavy. *Shak.*

THUMP, *v. i.* To strike or fall on with a heavy blow.

A watchman at night *thumps* with his pole. *Swift.*

THUMP'ER, *n.* The person or thing that thumps.

THUMP'ING, *ppr.* Striking or beating with something thick or blunt.

2. *a.* Heavy.

3. Vulgarly, stout; fat; large.

THUM'-RING, *n.* A ring worn on the thum. *Shak.*

THUM'-STALL, *n.* [*thum* and *stall.*] A kind of thimble or ferule of iron, horn or lether, with the edges turned up to receive the thread in making sails. It is worn on the thum to tighten the stitches. *Cyc.*

THUN'DER, *n.* [Sax. *thunder, thunor*; G. *donner*; D. *donder*; Sw. *dunder*; Dan. *dundren*; L. *tonitru*, from *tono*, to sound; Fr. *tonnerre*; It. *tuono*; Pers. تُنْدُر thondor.]

1. The sound which follows an explosion of electricity or lightning; the report of a discharge of electrical fluid, that is, of its passage from one cloud to another, or from a cloud to the earth, or from the earth to a cloud. When this explosion is near to a person, the thunder is a rattling or clattering sound, and when distant, the sound is heavy and rumbling. The fact is in some degree the same with the report of a cannon. This sharpness or acuteness of the sound when near, and the rumbling murmur when distant, are the principal distinctions in thunder. [Thunder is not *lightning*, but the effect of it. See Johnson's Dictionary, under *thunder.*]

There were *thunders* and lightnings. Ex. xix.

2. Thunder is used for *lightning*, or for a *thunderbolt*, either originally through ignorance, or by way of metaphor, or because the lightning and thunder are closely united.

The revenging gods
'Gainst parricides all the *thunder* bend. *Shak.*

3. Any loud noise; as the *thunder* of cannon.

Sons of *thunder*. Mark iii.

4. Denunciation published; as the *thunders* of the Vatican.

THUN'DER, *v. i.* To sound, rattle or roar, as an explosion of electricity.

Canst thou *thunder* with a voice like him? Job xl.

2. To make a loud noise, particularly a heavy sound of some continuance.

His dreadful voice no more
Would *thunder* in my ears. *Milton.*

3. To rattle, or give a heavy rattling sound.

And roll the *thund'ring* chariot o'er the ground. *J. Trumbull.*

THUN'DER, *v. t.* To emit with noise and terror.

Oracles severe
Were daily *thunder'd* in our gen'ral's ear. *Dryden.*

2. To publish any denunciation or threat.

An archdeacon, as being a prelate, may *thunder* out an ecclesiastical censure. *Ayliffe.*

THUN'DERBOLT, *n.* [*thunder* and *bolt.*]

1. A shaft of lightning; a brilliant stream of the electrical fluid, passing from one part of the heavens to another, and particularly from the clouds to the earth. Ps. lxxviii.

2. Figuratively, a daring or irresistible hero; as the Scipios, those *thunderbolts* of war. *Dryden.*

3. Fulmination; ecclesiastical denunciation.

He severely threatens such with the *thunderbolt* of excommunication. *Hakewill.*

4. In *mineralogy*, thunder-stone. *Spectator.*

THUN'DER-CLAP, *n.* [*thunder* and *clap.*] A burst of thunder; sudden report of an explosion of electricity.

When suddenly the *thunder-clap* was heard. *Dryden.*

THUN'DER-CLOUD, *n.* [*thunder* and *cloud.*] A cloud that produces lightning and thunder.

THUN'DERER, *n.* He that thunders. *Waller. Dryden.*

THUN'DER-HOUSE, *n.* An instrument for illustrating the manner in which buildings receive damage by lightning. *Cyc.*

THUN'DERING, *ppr.* Making the noise of an electrical explosion; uttering a loud sound; fulminating denunciations.

THUN'DERING, *n.* The report of an electrical explosion; thunder.

Entreat the Lord that there be no more mighty *thunderings* and hail. Ex. ix.

THUN'DEROUS, *a.* Producing thunder.

How he before the *thunderous* throne doth lie. [*Little used.*] *Milton.*

THUN'DER-SHOWER, *n.* [*thunder* and *shower.*] A shower accompanied with thunder.

THUN'DER-STONE, *n.* A stone, otherwise called *brontia.* *Cyc.*

THUN'DER-STORM, *n.* [*thunder* and *storm.*]

A storm accompanied with lightning and thunder. Thunder clouds are often driven by violent winds. In America, the violence of the wind at the commencement, is sometimes equal to that of a hurricane, and at this time the explosions of electricity are the most terrible. This violence of the wind seldom continues longer than a few minutes, and after this subsides, the rain continues, but the peals of thunder are less frequent. These violent showers sometimes continue for hours; more generally, they are of shorter duration.

THUN'DER-STRIKE, *v. t.* [*thunder* and *strike.*]

1. To strike, blast or injure by lightning. [*Little used in its literal sense.*] *Sidney.*

2. To astonish or strike dumb, as with something terrible. [*Little used except in the participle.*]

THUN'DER-STRUCK, *pp.* or *a.* Astonished; amazed; struck dumb by something surprising or terrible suddenly presented to the mind or view. [*This is a word in common use.*]

THU'RIBLE, *n.* [L. *thuribulum*, from *thus, thuris*, frankincense.]

A censer; a pan for incense. [*Not in use.*] *Cowel.*

THURIF'EROUS, *a.* [L. *thurifer*; *thus* and *fero*, to bear.] Producing or bearing frankincense.

THURIFICA'TION, *n.* [L. *thus, thuris*, and *facio*, to make.]

The act of fuming with incense; or the act of burning incense. *Stillingfleet.*

THURS'DAY, *n.* [Dan. *Torsdag*, that is, *Thor's day*, the day consecrated to *Thor*, the god of thunder, answering to the Jove of the Greeks and Romans, L. *dies Jovis*; It. *Giovedi*; Sp. *Jueves*; Fr. *Jeudi*. So in G. *donnerstag*, D. *donderdag*, thunder-day. This *Thor* is from the root of W. *taran*, thunder; *taraw*, to strike, hit or produce a shock; Gaelic, Ir. *toirn*, a great noise; *toirneas*, thunder. The root of the word signifies to drive, to rush, to strike. In Sw. *thordon* is thunder.] The fifth day of the week.

THUS, *adv.* [Sax. *thus*; D. *dus.*] In this or that manner; on this wise; as, *thus* saith the Lord; the Pharisee prayed *thus.*

Thus did Noah, according to all that God commanded him. Gen. vi.

2. To this degree or extent; as *thus* wise; *thus* peaceable. *Holyday.*

Thus far extend, *thus* far thy bounds— *Milton.*

3. In the phrase, *thus much*, it seems to be an adjective, equivalent to *this much.*

THWACK, *v. t.* [Qu. Sax. *thaccian*, to feel or stroke lightly. It does not well accord with this verb. The word *twit* is the Sax. *æthwitan*, or *othwitan*, a compound of *æth* or *oth*, to or at, and *witan*. In like manner, *thwack* may be formed from our vulgar *whack*, which is precisely the Eth. ወቀዐ wakea, Ar. وَقَعَ wakaa, to strike.]

To strike with something flat or heavy; to bang; to beat or thrash. *Arbuthnot.*

THWACK, *n.* A heavy blow with something flat or heavy. *Addison.*

THWACK'ING, *ppr.* Striking with a heavy blow.

THWAITE, *n.* A fish, a variety of the shad. *Cyc.*

2. A plain parcel of ground, cleared of wood and stumps, inclosed and converted to tillage. [*Local.*]

THWART, *a.* thwort. [D. *dwars*; Dan. *tver, tvert, tvers*; Sw. *tvärs, tvart*; probably a compound of Sax. *æth, oth*, to, and the root of *veer*, L. *verto, versus.*]

Transverse; being across something else.

Mov'd contrary with *thwart* obliquities. *Milton.*

THWART, *v. t.* thwort. To cross; to be, lie or come across the direction of something.

Swift as a shooting star
In autumn *thwarts* the night. *Milton.*

2. To cross, as a purpose; to oppose; to contravene; hence, to frustrate or defeat. We say, to *thwart* a purpose, design or inclination; or to *thwart* a person.

If crooked fortune had not *thwarted* me. *Shak.*

The proposals of the one never *thwarted* the inclinations of the other. *South.*

THWART, *v. i.* To be in opposition.

—A proposition that shall *thwart* at all with these internal oracles. [*Unusual and improper.*] *Locke.*

THWART, *n.* The seat or bench of a boat on which the rowers sit. *Mar. Dict.*

THWART'ED, *pp.* Crossed; opposed; frustrated.

THWART'ER, *n.* A disease in sheep, indicated by shaking, trembling or convulsive motions. *Cyc.*

THWART'ING, *ppr.* Crossing; contravening; defeating.

THWART'ING, *n.* The act of crossing or frustrating.

THWART'INGLY, *adv.* In a cross direction; in opposition.

THWART'NESS, *n.* Untowardness; perverseness. *Hall.*

THWART'SHIPS, *adv.* Across the ship. *Mar. Dict.*

THWITE, *v. t.* [Sax. *thwitan.*] To cut or clip with a knife. [*Local.*] *Chaucer.*

THWIT'TLE, *v. t.* To whittle. [See *Whittle.*] *Chaucer.*

THȲ, *a.* [contracted from *thine*, or from some other derivative of *thou*. It is probable that the pronoun was originally *thig*, *thug* or *thuk*, and the adjective *thigen*. See *Thou.*]

Thy is the adjective of *thou*, or a pronominal adjective, signifying of thee, or belonging to thee, like *tuus* in Latin. It is used in the solemn and grave style.

These are *thy* works, parent of good. *Milton.*

Thyine wood, a precious wood, mentioned Rev. xviii.

THY'ITE, *n.* The name of a species of indurated clay, of the morochthus kind, of a smooth regular texture, very heavy, of a shining surface, and of a pale green color. *Cyc.*

THYME, *n.* usually pronounced improperly, *time*. [Fr. *thym*; L. *thymus*; Gr. *θυμος*.]

A plant of the genus Thymus. The garden thyme is a warm pungent aromatic, much used to give a relish to seasonings and soups.

Thymus. [Gr. *θυμος*.] In *anatomy*, a glandular body, divided into lobes, situated behind the sternum in the duplicature of the mediastinum. It is largest in the fetus, diminishes after birth, and in adults often entirely disappears. It has no excretory duct, and its use is unknown. In calves it is called *sweatbread.* *Hooper. Wistar. Parr.*

THY'MY, *a.* Abounding with thyme; fragrant.

THY'ROID, *a.* [Gr. *θυρεος*, a shield, and *ειδος*, form.]

Resembling a shield; applied to one of the cartilages of the larynx, so called from its figure, to a gland situated near that cartilage, and to the arteries and veins of the gland. *Cyc.*

The *thyroid cartilage* constitutes the anterior, superior, and largest part of the larynx. *Hooper.*

The *thyroid gland* is situated on the sides and front of the lower part of the larynx, and the upper part of the trachea. It is copiously supplied with blood, but is not known to furnish any secretion. It is the seat of the bronchocele or goiter. *Hooper. Parr.*

THYRSE, *n.* [L. *thyrsus*; Gr. *θυρσος*.] In *botany*, a species of inflorescence; a panicle contracted into an ovate form, or a dense or close panicle, more or less of an ovate figure, as in the lilac. *Martyn. Smith.*

THȲSELF', *pron.* [*thy* and *self*.] A pronoun used after *thou*, to express distinction with emphasis. "*Thou thyself* shalt go;" that is, thou shalt go and no other. It is sometimes used without *thou*, and in the nominative as well as objective case.

These goods *thyself* can on *thyself* bestow. *Dryden.*

TI'AR, } *n.* [Fr. *tiare*; L. Sp. It. *tiara*;
TIA'RA, } Gr. *τιαρα*; Sax. *tyr*. See Syr. ܟܕܪ chadar, Class Dr. No. 15, and Heb. עטר atar, No. 34. From the former probably the Latins had their *cidaris*, and *tiara* from the latter; the same word with different prefixes.]

1. An ornament or article of dress with which the ancient Persians covered their heads; a kind of turban. As different authors describe it, it must have been of different forms. The kings of Persia alone had a right to wear it straight or erect; the lords and priests wore it depressed, or turned down on the fore side. Xenophon says the tiara was encompassed with the diadem, at least in ceremonials. *Cyc.*

2. An ornament worn by the Jewish high priest. Ex. xxviii.

3. The pope's triple crown. The tiara and keys are the badges of the papal dignity; the tiara of his civil rank, and the keys of his jurisdiction. It was formerly a round high cap. It was afterward encompassed with a crown, then with a second and a third. *Cyc.*

TIB'IAL, *a.* [L. *tibia*, a flute, and the large bone of the leg.]

1. Pertaining to the large bone of the leg; as the *tibial* artery; *tibial* nerve. *Med. Repos.*

2. Pertaining to a pipe or flute.

TIB'URO, *n.* A fish of the shark kind.

TICE, for *entice.* [*Not in use.*] *Beaum.*

TICK, *n.* [In Gaelic, *doigh* is trust. But I suspect *tick* to signify a cut, a notch, W. *twc*, from the manner of keeping accounts among unlettered men. See *Dock* and *Ticket.*]

Credit; trust; as, to buy upon *tick*. *Locke.*

TICK, *n.* [Fr. *tique*; G. *zecke*; It. *zecca.*] A little animal of a livid color and globose-ovate form, that infests sheep, dogs, goats, cows, &c., a species of Acarus. *Cyc.*

TICK, *n.* [D. *teek*, *tyk*; probably from covering, L. *tego*, Eng. to *deck*; Russ. *tik*, tent-cloth.]

The cover or case of a bed, which contains the fethers, wool or other material.

TICK, *v. i.* [from *tick*, credit.] To run upon score.

2. To trust. *Arbuthnot.*

TICK, *v. i.* [D. *tikken*. It coincides in elements with L. *tango*, *tago.*]

To beat; to pat; or to make a small noise by beating or otherwise; as a watch.

TICK-BEAN, *n.* A small bean employed in feeding horses and other animals. *Cyc.*

TICK'EN, *n.* Cloth for bed-ticks or cases for beds.

TICK'ET, *n.* [Fr. *etiquette*; W. *tocyn*, a short piece or slip, a ticket, from *tociaw*, to curtail, to clip, to *dock*. We have *dock* and *docket* from the same root. It denotes a piece or slip of paper.]

1. A piece of paper or a card, which gives the holder a right of admission to some place; as a *ticket* for the play-house or for other exhibition.

2. A piece of paper or writing, acknowledging some debt, or a certificate that something is due to the holder. *Spenser.*

3. A piece of paper bearing some number in a lottery, which entitles the owner to receive such prize as may be drawn against that number. When it draws no prize, it is said to draw a blank, and the holder has nothing to receive.

TICK'ET, *v. t.* To distinguish by a ticket. *Bentley.*

TICK'LE, *v. t.* [*dim.* of *touch*; perhaps directly from *tick*, to pat, or it is the L. *titillo*, corrupted.]

1. To touch lightly and cause a peculiar thrilling sensation, which cannot be described. A slight sensation of this kind may give pleasure, but when violent it is insufferable.

2. To please by slight gratification. A glass of wine may *tickle* the palate.

Such a nature
Tickled with good success. *Shak.*

TICK'LE, *v. i.* To feel titillation.

He with secret joy therefore
Did *tickle* inwardly in every vein. *Spenser.*

TICK'LE, *a.* Tottering; wavering, or liable to waver and fall at the slightest touch; unstable; easily overthrown.

Thy head stands so *tickle* on thy shoulders, that a milkmaid, if in love, may sigh it off. *Shak.*

The state of Normandy
Stands on a *tickle* point. *Shak.*

[This word is wholly obsolete, at least in N. England. *Ticklish* is the word used.]

TICK'LENESS, *n.* Unsteadiness. [*Not in use.*] *Chaucer.*

TICK'LER, *n.* One that tickles or pleases.

TICK'LING, *ppr.* Affecting with titillation.

TICK'LING, *n.* The act of affecting with titillation.

TICK'LISH, *a.* Sensible to slight touches; easily tickled. The bottom of the foot is very *ticklish*, as are the sides. The palm of the hand, hardened by use, is not *ticklish.*

2. Tottering; standing so as to be liable to totter and fall at the slightest touch; unfixed; easily moved or affected.

Ireland was a *ticklish* and unsettled state. *Bacon.*

3. Difficult; nice; critical; as, these are *ticklish* times. *Swift.*

TICK'LISHNESS, *n.* The state or quality of being *ticklish* or very sensible.

2. The state of being tottering or liable to fall.

3. Criticalness of condition or state.

TICK-SEED, *n.* A plant of the genus Coreopsis, and another of the genus Corispernum. *Lee.*

TICK'TACK, *n.* A game at tables. *Bailey.*

TID, *a.* [Sax. *tydder.*] Tender; soft; nice.

TID'BIT, *n.* [*tid* and *bit*.] A delicate or tender piece.

TID'DLE, } *v. t.* To use with tenderness;
TID'DER, } to fondle.

TIDE, *n.* [Sax. *tidan*, to happen; *tid*, time, season, opportunity, an hour; G. *zeit*; D. *tyd*; Sw. Dan. *tid*. This word is from a root that signifies to come, to happen, or to fall or rush, as in *betide*; corresponding in sense with time, season, hour, opportunity. *Tid*, time, is the fall, the occasion, the event. Its original meaning is entirely obsolete, except in composition, as in *Shrovetide*, *Whitsuntide.*]

1. Time; season.

Which, at the appointed *tide*,
Each one did make his bride. *Spenser.*

[*This sense is obsolete.*]

2. The flow of the water in the ocean and seas, twice in a little more than twenty four hours; the *flux* and *reflux*, or ebb and flow. We commonly distinguish the flow or rising of the water by the name of *flood-tide*, and the reflux by that of *ebb-tide*. There is much less *tide* or rise of water in the main ocean, at a distance from land,

than there is at the shore, and in sounds and bays.

2. Stream; course; current; as the *tide* of the times.

> Time's ungentle *tide*. *Byron.*

3. Favorable course.

> There is a *tide* in the affairs of men,
> Which taken at the flood, leads on to fortune. *Shak.*

4. Violent confluence. [*Not in use.*] *Bacon.*

5. Among *miners*, the period of twelve hours. *Cyc.*

6. Current; flow of blood.

> And life's red *tide* runs ebbing from the wound. *Battle of Frogs and Mice.*

TIDE, *v. t.* To drive with the stream. *Dryden.*

TIDE, *v. i.* To work in or out of a river or harbor by favor of the tide, and anchor when it becomes adverse. *Mar. Dict.*

TI'DE-GATE, *n.* A gate through which water passes into a basin when the tide flows, and which is shut to retain the water from flowing back at the ebb.

2. Among *seamen*, a place where the tide runs with great velocity. *Mar. Dict.*

TI'DE-MILL, *n.* [*tide* and *mill.*] A mill that is moved by tide water; also, a mill for clearing lands from tide water.

TI'DES-MAN, *n.* An officer who remains on board of a merchant's ship till the goods are landed, to prevent the evasion of the duties.

TI'DE-WAITER, *n.* [*tide* and *waiter.*] An officer who watches the landing of goods, to secure the payment of duties.

TI'DE-WAY, *n.* [*tide* and *way.*] The channel in which the tide sets. *Mar. Dict.*

TI'DILY, *adv.* [from *tidy.*] Neatly; with neat simplicity; as a female *tidily* dressed.

TI'DINESS, *n.* Neatness without richness or elegance; neat simplicity; as the *tidiness* of dress.

2. Neatness; as the *tidiness* of rooms.

TI'DINGS, *n. plu.* [Sw. *tidning*; Dan. *tidende*, news. It is the participle of Sax. *tidan*, to happen, or some other verb connected with *tide*, and denotes coming, or that which arrives.]

News; advice; information; intelligence; account of what has taken place, and was not before known.

> I shall make my master glad with these *tidings*. *Shak.*
>
> Behold I bring you good *tidings* of great joy, which shall be to all people. Luke ii.

TI'DY, *a.* [from *tide*, time, season; Dan. Sw. *tidig*, seasonable.]

1. In *its primary sense*, seasonable; favorable; being in proper time; as weather fair and *tidy*. *Tusser.*

2. Neat; dressed with neat simplicity; as a *tidy* lass; the children are *tidy;* their dress is *tidy;* that is primarily, proper for the time or occasion.

3. Neat; being in good order. The apartments are well furnished and *tidy*.

TĪE, TȲE, } *v. t.* [Sax. *tian*, for *tigan*, to bind; *tig, tige*, a tie, a purse. The primary sense is to strain, and hence its alliance to *tug*, to draw, Sw. *tiga*, L. *taceo*, to be silent. The Gr. δεω may be the same word. On account of the participle *tying*, it might be well to write the verb *tye*.]

1. To bind; to fasten with a band or cord and knot.

> My son, keep thy father's commandments—bind them continually upon thine heart, and *tie* them about thy neck. Prov. vi.

2. To fold and make fast; as, to *tie* a knot.

3. To knit; to complicate.

> We do not *tie* this knot with an intention to puzzle the argument. *Burnet.*

4. To fasten; to hold; to unite so as not to be easily parted.

> In bond of virtuous love together *tied*. *Fairfax.*

5. To oblige; to constrain; to restrain; to confine. People in their jealousy, may *tie* the hands of their ministers and public agents, so as to prevent them from doing good.

> Not *tied* to rules of policy, you find
> Revenge less sweet than a forgiving mind. *Dryden.*

6. In *music*, to unite notes by a cross line, or by a curve line drawn over them.

To tie up, to confine; to restrain; to hinder from motion or action; as, to *tie up* the tongue; to *tie up* the hands. *Addison.*

To tie down, to fasten so as to prevent from rising.

2. To restrain; to confine; to hinder from action.

TIE, *n.* A knot; fastening.

2. Bond; obligation, moral or legal; as the sacred *ties* of friendship or of duty; the *ties* of allegiance.

3. A knot of hair. *Young.*

TĪED, TȲED, } *pp.* Bound; fastened with a knot; confined; restrained; united, as notes.

TIĒR, *n.* [Heb. טור tur. Class Dr. No. 24. See *Tire.*]

A row; a rank; particularly when two or more rows are placed one above another; as a *tier* of seats in a church or theater. Thus in ships of war, the range of guns on one deck and one side of a ship, is called a *tier*. Those on the lower deck are called the lower *tier*, and those above, the middle or upper *tiers*. Ships with three *tiers* of guns are three deckers.

The *tiers* of a cable are the ranges of fakes or windings of a cable, laid one within another when coiled.

Tier, in organs, is a rank or range of pipes in the front of the instrument, or in the interior, when the compound stops have several ranks of pipes. *Cyc.*

TIERCE, *n.* *ters.* [Fr. from *tiers*, third.] A cask whose content is one third of a pipe, that is, forty gallons; or it may be the measure.

2. In *Ireland*, a weight by which provisions are sold. The *tierce* of beef for the navy, is 304*lb.* and for India, 336*lb.*

3. In *music*, a third.

4. In *gaming*, a sequence of three cards of the same color.

5. A thrust in fencing.

TIERCEL, TIERCELET, } *n.* In *falconry*, a name given to the male hawk, as being a third part less than the female. *Cyc.*

TIERCET, *n. ter'cet.* [from *tierce.*] In *poetry*, a triplet; three lines, or three lines rhyming.

TIFF, *n.* [Qu. *tipple, tope.*] Liquor; or rather a small draught of liquor. [*Vulgar.*] *Philips.*

2. A pet or fit of peevishness. *Johnson.*

[*I know not where this word is used in the latter sense.*]

TIFF, *v. i.* To be in a pet. [*Low.*] *Johnson.*

TIFF, *v. t.* To dress. [*Not in use.*]

TIF'FANY, *n.* [According to the Italian and Spanish Dictionaries, this word is to be referred to *taffeta.*] A species of gauze or very thin silk.

Tiffe-de-mer, a species of sea plant, so called by Count Marsigli, from its resemblance to the heads of the *Typha palustris*, or cat's tail. It has a smooth surface and a velvety look. It grows to two feet in highth, and is elegantly branched. It grows on rocks and stones, and when first taken out of the sea, is full of a yellow viscous water, but when this is pressed out and the substance is dried, it becomes of a dusky brown color. *Cyc.*

TIG, *n.* A play. [See *Tag.*]

TĬĠE, *n.* [Fr. a stalk.] The shaft of a column from the astragal to the capital. *Bailey.*

TI'GER, *n.* [Fr. *tigre*; It. *tigro*; L. *tigris*; said to be from גיר, gir, a dart; whence תגיר tiger.]

A fierce and rapacious animal of the genus Felis, *(F. tigris;)* one of the largest and most terrible of the genus, inhabiting Africa and Asia. The American tiger is the *Felis onça*. There is also the tiger cat or *Felis capensis*.

TI'GER-FOOTED, *a.* Hastening to devour; furious. *Entick.*

TI'GERISH, *a.* Like a tiger.

TI'GER'S-FOOT, *n.* A plant of the genus Ipomœa. *Lee.*

TI'GER-SHELL, *n.* [*tiger* and *shell.*] A name given to the red voluta, with large white spots. In the Linnean system, the *tiger-shell* is a species of Cypræa. *Cyc.*

TIGH, *n.* In *Kent*, a close or inclosure.

TIGHT, *a.* [G. *dicht;* D. Sw. Dan. *digt;* allied to *thick* and *tie*, and to Sw. *tiga*, to be silent, L. *taceo;* that is, close, closely compressed; Russ. *tugei*, stiff. See *Tack.*]

1. Close; compact; not loose or open; having the joints so close that no fluid can enter or escape; not leaky; as a *tight* ship, or a *tight* cask.

2. Close; not admitting much air; as a *tight* room.

3. Sitting close to the body; as a *tight* coat or other garment.

4. Close; not having holes or crevices; not loose; applied to many vessels, &c.

5. Close; hard; as a *tight* bargain. [*In common use in America.*]

6. Close; parsimonious; saving; as a man *tight* in his dealings. [*In common use in America.*]

7. Closely dressed; not ragged.

> I'll spin and card, and keep our children *tight*. *Gay.*

8. Hardy; adroit. *Shak.*

[*Note.* This is the *taugt* or *taught* of seamen, applied to a rope stretched. The primary sense is strained.]

TĪGHTEN, *v. t. ti'tn.* To draw tighter; to straiten; to make more close in any manner.

TĪGHTER, *n.* A ribin or string used to draw clothes closer. [*Not used.*]

2. More tight.

TIGHTLY, *adv.* Closely; compactly.

2. Neatly; adroitly.

TIGHTNESS, *n.* Closeness of joints; compactness; straitness.

2. Neatness, as in dress.

3. Parsimoniousness; closeness in dealing.

TI'GRESS, *n.* [from *tiger.*] The female of the tiger.

TIKE, *n.* A tick. [See *Tick.*]

TIKE, *n.* [Celtic, *tiak, tiac,* a plowman; Arm. *tiec,* a housekeeper.]

1. A countryman or clown.

2. A dog. *Shak.*

TILE, *n.* [Sax. *tigel;* D. *tegel* or *tichgel;* G. *ziegel;* Dan. Sw. *tegel;* L. *tegula;* It. *tegola;* Sp. *teja,* contracted. This word is undoubtedly from the root of L. *tego,* to cover, Eng. to *deck.*]

1. A plate or piece of baked clay, used for covering the roofs of buildings.

The pins for fastening *tiles* are made of oak or fir. *Moxon.*

2. In *metallurgy,* a small flat piece of dried earth, used to cover vessels in which metals are fused.

3. A piece of baked clay used in drains.

TILE, *v. t.* To cover with tiles; as, to *tile* a house.

2. To cover, as tiles.

The muscle, sinew and vein,
Which *tile* this house, will come again. *Donne.*

TILE-EARTH, *n.* A species of strong clayey earth; stiff and stubborn land. [*Local.*] *Cyc.*

TI'LED, *pp.* Covered with tiles.

TILE-ORE, *n.* A subspecies of octahedral red copper ore. *Ure.*

TI'LER, *n.* A man whose occupation is to cover buildings with tiles. *Bacon.*

TI'LING, *ppr.* Covering with tiles.

TI'LING, *n.* A roof covered with tiles. Luke v.

2. Tiles in general.

TILL, *n.* A vetch; a tare. [*Local.*]

TILL, } *n.* A money box in a shop; a
TILL'ER, } drawer.

TILL, *prep.* or *adv.* [Sax. *til, tille;* Sw. Dan. *til;* Sax. *atillan,* to reach or come to. This word in Sw. and Dan. as in Scottish, signifies *to* or *at,* and is the principal word used where we use *to.* The primary sense of the verb is expressed in the Saxon.]

1. To the time or time of. I did not see the man *till* the last time he came; I waited for him *till* four o'clock; I will wait *till* next week.

Till now, to the present time. I never heard of the fact *till now.*

Till then, to that time. I never heard of the fact *till then.*

2. It is used before verbs and sentences in a like sense, denoting to the time specified in the sentence or clause following. I will wait *till* you arrive.

He said to them, occupy *till* I come. Luke xix.

Certain Jews—bound themselves under a curse, saying that they would neither eat nor drink *till* they had killed Paul. Acts xxiii.

Meditate so long *till* you make some act of prayer to God. *Taylor.*

[*Note.*—In this use, *till* is not a conjunction; it does not connect sentences like *and,* or like *or.* It neither denotes union nor separation, nor an alternative. It has always the same office, except that it precedes a single word or a single sentence; the time to which it refers being in one case expressed by a single word, as *now,* or *then,* or *time,* with *this,* or *that,* &c. and in the other by a verb with its adjuncts; as, occupy *till I come.* In the latter use, *till* is a preposition preceding a sentence, like *against,* in the phrase, *against* I come.]

TILL, *v. t.* [Sax. *tilian, tiligan,* to work, to *toil,* to cultivate, to prepare; W. *telu,* to strain. In G. *bestellen,* from *stellen,* to set, to put in order, has the sense of *tilling,* cultivating. These words are doubtless of one family.]

1. To labor; to cultivate; to plow and prepare for seed, and to dress crops. This word includes not only plowing but harrowing, and whatever is done to prepare ground for a crop, and to keep it free from weeds.

The Lord God sent him forth from the garden of Eden to *till* the ground from whence he was taken. Gen. iii.

2. In *the most general sense,* to till may include every species of husbandry, and this may be its sense in Scripture.

TILL'ABLE, *a.* Capable of being tilled; arable; fit for the plow. *Carew.*

TILL'AGE, *n.* The operation, practice or art of preparing land for seed, and keeping the ground free from weeds which might impede the growth of crops. Tillage includes manuring, plowing, harrowing and rolling land, or whatever is done to bring it to a proper state to receive the seed, and the operations of plowing, harrowing and hoeing the ground, to destroy weeds and loosen the soil after it is planted; culture; a principal branch of agriculture. *Tillage* of the earth is the principal as it was the first occupation of man, and no employment is more honorable.

TILL'ED, *pp.* Cultivated; prepared for seed and kept clean.

TILL'ER, *n.* One who tills; a husbandman; a cultivator; a plowman.

2. The bar or lever employed to turn the rudder of a ship.

3. A small drawer; a till.

4. Among *farmers,* the shoot of a plant, springing from the root or bottom of the original stalk; also, the sprout or young tree that springs from the root or stump.

5. A young timber tree. [*Local.*]

TILL'ER, *v. i.* To put forth new shoots from the root, or round the bottom of the original stalk; as we say, wheat or rye *tillers;* it spreads by *tillering.* The common orthography is *tiller.* Sir Joseph Banks writes it *tillow.*

TILL'ERING, *ppr.* Sending out new shoots round the bottom of the original stem.

TILLERING, *n.* The act of sending forth young shoots from the root or around the bottom of the original stalk.

TILL'ER-ROPE, *n.* The rope which forms a communication between the fore end of the tiller and the wheel. *Mar. Dict.*

TILL'ING, *ppr.* Cultivating.

TILL'ING, *n.* The operation of cultivating land; culture.

TILL'MAN, *n.* A man who tills the earth; a husbandman. *Obs.* *Tusser.*

TILL'Y-FALLY, } *adv.* or *a.* A word for-
TILL'Y-VALLY, } merly used when any thing said was rejected as trifling or impertinent. *Obs.*

TILT, *n.* [Sax. *teld;* Dan. *telt;* Ice. *tiald;* W. *telu,* to stretch over.]

1. A tent; a covering over head. *Denham.*

2. The cloth covering of a cart or wagon.

3. The cover of a boat; a small canopy or awning of canvas or other cloth, extended over the stern sheets of a boat. *Mar. Dict.*

TILT, *v. t.* To cover with a cloth or awning. *Philips.*

TILT, *n.* [See the Verb.] A thrust; as a *tilt* with a lance. *Addison.*

2. Formerly, a military exercise on horseback, in which the combatants attacked each other with lances; as *tilts* and tournaments.

3. A large hammer; a tilt-hammer; used in iron manufactures.

4. Inclination forward; as the *tilt* of a cask; or a cask is *a-tilt.*

TILT, *v. t.* [Sax. *tealtian,* to lean, to incline, to nod; Dan. *tylder,* to pour out, to decant. In D. *tillen* signifies to lift, L. *tollo.* This is probably a derivative verb.]

1. To incline; to raise one end, as of a cask, for discharging liquor; as, to *tilt* a barrel.

2. To point or thrust, as a lance.

Sons against fathers *tilt* the fatal lance. *Philips.*

3. To hammer or forge with a tilt-hammer or tilt; as, to *tilt* steel to render it more ductile. *Cyc.*

4. To cover with a tilt.

TILT, *v. i.* To run or ride and thrust with a lance; to practice the military game or exercise of thrusting at each other on horseback. *Milton.*

2. To fight with rapiers.

Swords out and *tilting* one at other's breast. *Shak.*

3. To rush, as in combat. *Collier.*

4. To play unsteadily; to ride, float and toss.

The fleet swift *tilting* o'er the surges flew. *Pope.*

5. To lean; to fall, as on one side.

The trunk of the body is kept from *tilting* forward by the muscles of the back. *Grew.*

TILT'-BOAT, *n.* A boat covered with canvas or other cloth.

TILT'ED, *pp.* Inclined; made to stoop; covered with cloth or awning.

2. Hammered; prepared by beating; as steel.

TILT'ER, *n.* One who tilts; one who uses the exercise of pushing a lance on horseback; one who fights.

Let me alone to match your *tilter.* *Granville.*

2. One who hammers with a tilt.

TILTH, *n.* [Sax. *tilth;* from *till.*] That which is tilled; tillage ground. [*Not in use.*]

2. The state of being tilled or prepared for a crop. We say, land is in good *tilth,* when it is manured, plowed, broken and mellowed for receiving the seed. We say also, ground is in bad *tilth.* When we say, land is *in tilth,* we mean in good condition for the seed; *not in tilth,* in a bad condition.

TILT'-HAMMER, *n.* [*tilt* and *hammer.*] A heavy hammer used in iron works, which is lifted by a wheel.

TILT'ING, *ppr.* Inclining; causing to stoop or lean; using the game of thrusting with the lance on horseback; also, hammering with a tilt-hammer.

TIM'BAL, *n.* A kettle drum.

TIM'BER, *n.* [Sax. *timber*, wood, a tree, structure; *timbrian*, to build, to edify, in a moral sense; Goth. *timbryan*, to construct; Sw. *timmer*, wood fit for building; *timra*, to build, to frame; Dan. *tömmer*, timber; *tömrer*, to build; D. *timmer*, an apartment; *timber*, a crest; *timmeren*, to build; *timmerhout*, timber; G. *zimmer*, an apartment; *zimmern*, to square, fit, fabricate; *zimmerholz*, timber. If *m* is radical, which is probable, this word coincides with Gr. δεμω, L. *domus*, a house, and Gr. δεμας, the body. The primary sense is probably to set, lay or found.]

1. That sort of wood which is proper for buildings or for tools, utensils, furniture, carriages, fences, ships and the like. We apply the word to standing trees which are suitable for the uses above mentioned, as a forest contains excellent *timber*; or to the beams, rafters, scantling, boards, planks, &c. hewed or sawed from such trees. Of all the species of trees useful as *timber*, in our climate, the white oak and the white pine hold the first place in importance.
2. The body or stem of a tree. *Shak.*
3. The materials; *in irony.*

Such dispositions—are the fittest *timber* to make politics of. *Bacon.*

4. A single piece or squared stick of wood for building, or already framed.

Many of the *timbers* were decayed. *Coxe's Switzerland.*

5. In *ships*, a timber is a rib or curving piece of wood, branching outward from the keel in a vertical direction. One *timber* is composed of several pieces united in one frame. *Mar. Dict*

TIM'BER, *v. t.* To furnish with timber. [See *Timbered.*]

TIM'BER, *v. i.* To light on a tree. [*Not in use.*] *L'Estrange.*

2. In *falconry*, to make a nest. *Cyc.*

Timber or *timmer of furs*, as of martens, ermines, sables and the like, denotes forty skins; of other skins, one hundred and twenty. *Laws of Ed. Confessor.*

Timbers of ermine, in *heraldry*, denote the ranks or rows of ermine in noblemen's coats.

TIM'BERED, *pp.* or *a.* Furnished with timber; as a well *timbered* house. In the United States, we say, land is well *timbered*, when it is covered with good timber trees.

2. Built; formed; contrived. [*Little used.*] *Wotton.*

TIM'BER-HEAD, *n.* [*timber* and *head.*] In *ships*, the top end of a timber, rising above the gunwale, and serving for belaying ropes, &c.; otherwise called *kevel-head.* *Mar. Dict.*

TIM'BERING, *ppr.* Furnishing with timber.

TIM'BER-SOW, *n.* A worm in wood. *Bacon.*

TIM'BER-TREE, *n.* [*timber* and *tree.*] A tree suitable for timber.

TIM'BER-WŎRK, *n.* [*timber* and *work.*] Work formed of wood.

TIM'BER-Y'ARD, *n.* [*timber* and *yard.*] A yard or place where timber is deposited.

TIM'BRE, *n.* [D. *timber.*] A crest on a coat of arms. It ought to be written *timber.*

TIM'BREL, *n.* [Sp. *tamboril*, a tabor or drum; It. *tamburo*; Fr. *tambourin*, *tambour*; Ir. *tiompan*; L. *tympanum*; Gr. τυμπανον. This is probably the same as *tabor*, or from the same root; *m* being casual. It is from beating; Gr. τυπτω.]

An instrument of music; a kind of drum, tabor or tabret, which has been in use from the highest antiquity.

And Miriam took a *timbrel* in her hand—and all the women went out after her with *timbrels* and with dances. Ex. xv.

TIM'BRELED, *a.* Sung to the sound of the timbrel. *Milton.*

TIME, *n.* [Sax. *tim*, *tima*, time in general; Dan. *time*, Sw. *timme*, an hour; L. *tempus*; It. Port. *tempo*; Sp. *tiempo*; Fr. *temps*, time in general; all from the root of the Sw. *tima*, to happen, to come, to befall; but the root in some of its applications, must have signified to rush with violence. Hence the sense of *temples*, L. *tempora*, the falls of the head, also *tempest*, &c. See *Tempest.* *Time* is primarily equivalent to *season*; to the Gr. ωρα in its original sense, *opportunity*, *occasion*, a fall, an event, that which comes.]

1. A particular portion or part of duration, whether past, present or future. The *time* was; the *time* has been; the *time* is; the *time* will be.

Lost *time* is never found again. *Franklin.*

God, who at sundry times, and in divers manners, spoke in *time* past to the fathers by the prophets. Heb. i.

2. A proper time; a season.

There is a *time* to every purpose. Eccles. iii.

The *time* of figs was not yet. Mark xi.

3. Duration.

The equal and uniform flux of *time* does not affect our senses. *Cyc.*

Time is *absolute* or *relative*; *absolute* time is considered without any relation to bodies or their motions. *Relative* time is the sensible measure of any portion of duration, by means of motion. Thus the diurnal revolution of the sun measures a space of time or duration. Hence,

4. A space or measured portion of duration. We were in Paris two months, and all that *time* enjoyed good health.
5. Life or duration, in reference to occupation. One man spends his *time* in idleness; another devotes all his *time* to useful purposes.

Believe me, your *time* is not your own; it belongs to God, to religion, to mankind. *Buckminster.*

6. Age; a part of duration distinct from other parts; as ancient *times*; modern *times*. The Spanish armada was defeated in the *time* of Queen Elizabeth.
7. Hour of travail.

She was within one month of her *time*. *Clarendon.*

8. Repetition; repeated performance, or mention with reference to repetition. The physician visits his patient three *times* in a day.
9. Repetition; doubling; addition of a number to itself; as, to double cloth four *times*; four *times* four amount to sixteen.
10. Measure of sounds in music; as common *time*, and treble *time*. In concerts, it is all important that the performers keep *time*, or exact *time*.
11. The state of things at a particular period; as when we say, good *times*, or bad *times*, hard *times*, dull *times* for trade, &c. In this sense, the plural is generally used.
12. In *grammar*, tense.

In time, in good season; sufficiently early. He arrived *in time* to see the exhibition.

2. A considerable space of duration; process or continuation of duration. You must wait patiently; you will *in time* recover your health and strength.

At times, at distinct intervals of duration. *At times* he reads; *at* other *times*, he rides.

The spirit began to move him *at times*. Judges xiii.

Time enough, in season; early enough.

Stanley at Bosworth-field, came *time enough* to save his life. *Bacon.*

To lose time, to delay.

2. To go too slow; as, a watch or clock *loses time.*

Apparent time, in *astronomy*, true solar time, regulated by the apparent motions of the sun.

Mean time, equated time, a mean or average of apparent time.

Siderial time, is that which is shown by the diurnal revolutions of the stars.

TIME, *v. t.* To adapt to the time or occasion; to bring, begin or perform at the proper season or time; as, the measure is well *timed*, or ill *timed.* No small part of political wisdom consists in knowing how to *time* propositions and measures.

Mercy is good, but kings mistake its *timing*. *Dryden.*

2. To regulate as to time; as, he *timed* the stroke. *Addison.*
3. To measure; as in music or harmony. *Shak.*

TI'MED, *pp.* Adapted to the season or occasion.

TI'MEFUL, *a.* Seasonable; timely; sufficiently early. [*Not much used.*] *Raleigh.*

TI'MEIST, *n.* In *music*, a performer who keeps good time. *Busby.*

TI'ME-KEEPER, *n.* [*time* and *keeper.*] A clock, watch or other chronometer.

TI'MELESS, *a.* Unseasonable; done at an improper time.

Nor fits it to prolong the heav'nly feast
Timeless— [*Not used.*] *Pope.*

2. Untimely; immature; done or suffered before the proper time; as a *timeless* grave. [*Not used.*] *Shak.*

TI'MELESSLY, *adv.* Unseasonably. *Milton.*

TI'MELINESS, *n.* [from *timely.*] Seasonableness; a being in good time.

TI'MELY, *a.* Seasonable; being in good time; sufficiently early. The defendant had *timely* notice of this motion. *Timely* care will often prevent great evils.

2. Keeping time or measure. [*Not used.*] *Spenser.*

TI'MELY, *adv.* Early; soon; in good season.

Timely advis'd, the coming evil shun. *Prior.*

TI'ME-PIECE, *n.* [*time* and *piece.*] A clock, watch or other instrument to measure or show the progress of time; a chronometer.

TI'ME-PLEASER, *n.* *s* as *z.* [*time* and *please.*]

One who complies with the prevailing opinions, whatever they may be. *Shak.*

TI'ME-SERVER, *n.* [*time* and *serve.*] One who adapts his opinions and manners to the times; one who obsequiously complies with the ruling power. *Hall.*

TI'ME-SERVING, *a.* Obsequiously complying with the humors of men in power.

TI'ME-SERVING, *n.* An obsequious compliance with the humors of men in power, which implies a surrender of one's independence, and sometimes of one's integrity.

TI'ME-WORN, *a.* Impaired by time. *Irving.*

TIM'ID, *a.* [Fr. *timide*; L. *timidus*, from *timeo*, to fear; Gaelic, *tim*, *time*, fear; Sp. *temblar*, to shake with fear; *temer*, to fear. The sense is probably to shake, or to fail, fall, recede or shrink.]

Fearful; wanting courage to meet danger; timorous; not bold.

Poor is the triumph o'er the *timid* hare. *Thomson.*

TIMID'ITY, *n.* [Fr. *timidité*; L. *timiditas.*] Fearfulness; want of courage or boldness to face danger; timorousness; habitual cowardice. *Timidity* in one person may be a good trait of character, while in another it is a deep reproach.

TIM'IDLY, *adv.* In a timid manner; weakly; without courage.

TIM'IDNESS, *n.* Timidity.

TIMOC'RACY, *n.* [Gr. τιμη, honor, worth, and κρατεω, to hold.]

Government by men of property, who are possessed of a certain income. *Gillies' Aristotle.*

TIMONEE'R, *n.* [Fr. *timon*; L. *temo.*] A helmsman. *Mar. Dict.*

TIM'OROUS, *a.* [It. *timoroso*; from L. *timor.* See *Timid.*]

1. Fearful of danger; timid; destitute of courage; as a *timorous* female.

2. Indicating fear; full of scruples; as *timorous* doubts; *timorous* beliefs. *Brown. Prior.*

TIM'OROUSLY, *adv.* Fearfully; timidly; without boldness; with much fear.

Let dastard souls be *timorously* wise. *Philips.*

TIM'OROUSNESS, *n.* Fearfulness; timidity; want of courage. *Swift.*

TIMOUS, *a.* [from *time.*] Early; timely. [*Not in use.*] *Bacon.*

TIMOUSLY, *adv.* In good season. [*Not in use.*] *Ch. Relig. Appeal.*

TIN, *n.* [Sax. D. *tin*; G. *zinn*; Sw. *tenn*; Dan. *tin*, pewter, and *tinblik*, tin, that is, *tin-plate*; Ir. *stan*; W. *ystaen*, that is spread or is sprinkled over, a stain, and tin; Corn. *staen*; Arm. *stean*; Fr. *etain*; L. *stannum*; Sp. *estaño*; Port. *estanho*; It. *stagno.* The latter signifies tin, pewter, and a pond, L. *stagnum.*]

1. A white metal, with a slight tinge of yellow. It is soft, non-elastic, very malleable, and when a bar of it is bent near the ear, distinguished by a crackling sound called the *cry* of tin. It is used for culinary vessels, being for this purpose usually combined with lead, forming *pewter*; and alloyed with small proportions of antimony, copper and bismuth, is formed into various wares resembling silver, under the names of *block-tin*, *brittania*, &c. Equal parts of tin and lead compose *soder.* Tin united with copper in different proportions, forms *bronze*, *bell-metal*, and *speculum-metal.* *D. Olmsted.*

2. Thin plates of iron covered with tin.

TIN, *v. t.* To cover with tin, or overlay with tinfoil.

TINCT, *v. t.* [L. *tingo*, *tinctus.*] To stain or color; to imbue. *Obs.*

TINCT, *n.* Stain; color. [Obsolete. We now use *tinge* and *tincture.*]

TINC'TURE, *n.* [L. *tinctura*; Fr. *teinture.* See *Tinge.*]

1. The finer and more volatile parts of a substance, separated by a menstruum; or an extract of a part of the substance of a body, communicated to the menstruum. Hence,

2. In *medicine*, a spiritous solution of such of the proximate principles of vegetables and animals as are soluble in pure alcohol or proof-spirit; wine or spirits containing medicinal substances in solution. *Cyc. Coxe.*

3. A tinge or shade of color; as a *tincture* of red.

4. Slight taste superadded to any substance; as a *tincture* of orange-peel.

5. Slight quality added to any thing; as a *tincture* of French manners.

All manners take a *tincture* from our own. *Pope.*

TINC'TURE, *v. t.* To tinge; to communicate a slight foreign color to; to impregnate with some extraneous matter.

A little black paint will *tincture* and spoil twenty gay colors. *Watts.*

2. To imbue the mind; to communicate a portion of any thing foreign; as a mind *tinctured* with scepticism.

TINC'TURED, *pp.* Tinged; slightly impregnated with something foreign.

TINC'TURING, *ppr.* Tinging; imbuing; impregnating with a foreign substance.

TIND, *v. t.* [Sax. *tendan*, *tynan*, to kindle; Goth. *tandyan*; Sw. *tända*; Dan. *tænder*; Eng. *tine*; *tinder*, G. *zunder*; probably allied to Ir. Gaelic, *teine*, fire, W. Corn. Arm. *tan*; and perhaps our word *sun* is of the same family.] To kindle. *Obs.* But hence,

TIND'ER, *n.* [Sax. *tyndre.*] Something very inflammable used for kindling fire from a spark; as scorched linen. *Swift.*

TIND'ER-BOX, *n.* [*tinder* and *box.*] A box in which tinder is kept. *Atterbury.*

TIND'ERLIKE, *a.* [*tinder* and *like.*] Like tinder; very inflammable. *Shak.*

TINE, *v. t.* [Sax. *tynan.*] To kindle; to set on fire. *Obs.* [See *Tind.*] *Spenser.*

TINE, *v. t.* [Sax. *tynan*; L. *teneo.*] To shut or inclose; to fill. [*Not in use or local.*]

TINE, *n.* [Sax. *tindes*; Ice. *tindr*; probably the L. *dens*, G. *zahn*, W. *dant*, a tooth; at any rate, it is a shoot.]

1. The tooth or spike of a fork; a prong; also, the tooth of a harrow or drag.

2. Trouble; distress. [*Not in use.*] *Spenser.*

TINE, *v. i.* [Sax. *tynan*; from *teine*, *tan*, fire, supra.]

To rage; to smart; to fight. *Obs.* *Spenser.*

TI'NEMAN, *n.* Anciently an officer of the forest in England, who had the nocturnal care of vert and venison. *Cyc.*

TI'NET, *n.* [*tine*, to shut, supra.] In *old writers*, brushwood and thorns for making and repairing hedges. *Cyc.*

TINFOIL, *n.* [*tin* and L. *folium*, a leaf.] Tin reduced to a thin leaf.

TING, *n.* A sharp sound. [*Not in use.* Children use *ding*, *dong.* See *Tingle.*]

TING, *v. i.* To sound or ring. [*Not in use.*]

TINGE, *v. t.* [L. *tingo*; Gr. τεγγω; Sax. *deagan*; Eng. to *dye*; G. *tunken*, to dip; Fr. *teindre*, to stain. See *Dye.* Ar. طاح to perish, to *die*, to *tinge.* Class Dg. No. 40. See also No. 8. and 19. Tinging is from dipping. The primary sense of the verb is to plunge, or to throw down, to thrust, and intransitively to fall; hence we see the words to *die*, that is, to fall or perish, and to *dye*, or color, may be from one root.]

To imbue or impregnate with something foreign; to communicate the qualities of one substance, in some degree, to another, either by mixture, or by adding them to the surface; as, to *tinge* a blue color with red; an infusion *tinged* with a yellow color by saffron; to *tinge* a decoction with a *bitter* taste. The jaundice *tinges* the eyes with yellow.

The virtues of sir Roger, as well as his imperfections, are *tinged* with extravagance. *Addison.*

TINGE, *n.* Color; dye; taste; or rather a slight degree of some color, taste, or something foreign, infused into another substance or mixture, or added to it; tincture; as a red color that has a *tinge* of blue; a dish of food that has a *tinge* of orange peel in its taste.

TING'ED, *pp.* Imbued or impregnated with a small portion of something foreign.

TING'ENT, *a.* Having the power to tinge.

As for the white part, it appeared much less enriched with the *tingent* property. *Boyle.*

[*Little used.*]

TING'ING, *ppr.* Imbuing or impregnating with something foreign.

TIN'-GLASS, *n.* Bismuth, which see.

TIN'GLE, *v. i.* [W. *tincial*, *tincian* or *tinciaw*, to tink, to tinkle or tingle, to ring, to draw or drain the last drop. Qu. D. *tintelen*, Fr. *tinter*, L. *tinnio.*]

1. To feel a kind of thrilling sound.

At which both the ears of every one that heareth it shall *tingle.* 1 Sam. iii.

2. To feel a sharp thrilling pain.

The pale boy senator yet *tingling* stands. *Pope.*

3. To have a thrilling sensation, or a sharp slight penetrating sensation.

They suck pollution through their *tingling* veins. *Tickel.*

TING'LING, *ppr.* Having a thrilling sensation.

TING'LING, *n.* A thrilling sensation.

TINK, *v. i.* [W. *tinciaw*, supra.] To make a sharp shrill noise; to tinkle. [*The latter is generally used.*]

TINK'AL, *n.* Borax in its crude state or unrefined. It consists of small crystals of a yellowish color, and is unctuous to the feel. *Dict.*

TINK'ER, *n.* [W. *tincerz*, the ringer, from *tinciaw*, to ring.] A mender of brass kettles, pans and the like.

TINK'ERLY, *adv.* In the manner of a tinker. *Hackengill.*

TINK'LE, *v. i.* [W. *tincial*, supra, under *tingle.*]

1. To make small quick sharp sounds, as by striking on metal; to clink.

—And have not charity, I am become as sounding brass, or a *tinkling* cymbal. 1 Cor. xiii. Is. iii.

The sprightly horse
Moves to the music of his *tinkling* bells. *Dodsley.*

The moment the money *tinkles* in the chest, the soul mounts out of purgatory. *Tetzel in Milner.*

2. To hear a small sharp sound.

And his ears *tinkled*, and his color fled. *Dryden.*

TINK'LE, *v. t.* To cause to clink or make sharp quick sounds.

TINK'LING, *ppr.* Making a small quick sharp noise.

TINK'LING, *n.* A small quick sharp sound.

Making a *tinkling* with their feet. Is. iii.

TIN'MAN, *n.* [*tin* and *man.*] A manufacturer of tin vessels; a dealer in tin ware. *Prior.*

TIN'-MINE, *n.* [*tin* and *mine.*] A mine where tin is obtained.

TIN'NED, *pp.* Covered with tin.

TIN'NER, *n.* [from *tin.*] One who works in the tin mines. *Bacon.*

TIN'NING, *ppr.* [from *tin.*] Covering with tin or tinfoil.

TIN'NING, *n.* The act, art or practice of covering or lining any thing with melted tin or with tinfoil, as kitchen utensils, locks, bits, &c.

TIN'NY, *a.* Abounding with tin. *Drayton.*

TIN'PENNY, *n.* [*tin* and *penny.*] A customary duty in England, formerly paid to tithingmen. *Bailey.*

TIN'SEL, *n.* [Fr. *etincelle*, a spark.] Something very shining and gaudy; something superficially shining and showy, or having a false luster, and more gay than valuable.

Who can discern the *tinsel* from the gold? *Dryden.*

If the man will too curiously examine the superficial *tinsel* good, he undeceives himself to his cost. *Norris.*

2. A kind of shining cloth. *Fairfax.*

3. A kind of lace.

TIN'SEL, *a.* Gaudy; showy to excess; specious; superficial.

TIN'SEL, *v. t.* To adorn with something glittering and showy without much value; to make gaudy.

She, *tinsel'd* o'er in robes of varying hues— *Pope.*

TIN'SELED, *pp.* Decorated with gaudy ornaments.

TIN'SELING, *ppr.* Adorning with tinsel or superficial luster.

TINT, *n.* [It. *tinta*; Fr. *teint*; from L. *tinctus*, *tingo*. See *Tinge.*]

A dye; a color, or rather a slight coloring or tincture distinct from the ground or principal color; as red with a blue *tint*, or *tint* of blue. In painting, *tints* are the colors considered as more or less bright, deep or thin, by the due use and intermixture of which a picture receives its shades, softness and variety.

Or blend in beauteous *tint* the color'd mass. *Pope.*

Their vigor sickens, and their *tints* decline. *Harte.*

TINT, *v. t.* To tinge; to give a slight coloring to. *Seward.*

TIN'-WÖRM, *n.* [*tin* and *worm.*] An insect. *Bailey.*

TIN'Y, *a.* [from the root of *thin*, which see.] Very small; little; puny. [*A word used by children, and in burlesque.*]

When that I was a little *tiny* boy. *Shak.*

TIP, *n.* [D. *tip*, a different orthography of *top*; G. *zipfel*; that is, a shoot or extension to a point. Qu. Eth. ጥቤ thybe, the nipple.]

1. The end; the point or extremity of any thing small; as the *tip* of the finger; the *tip* of a spear; the *tip* of the tongue; the *tip* of the ear. *Addison. Pope.*

2. One part of the play at nine-pins. *Dryden.*

3. In *botany*, an anther. *Withering.*

TIP, *v. t.* To form a point with something; to cover the tip, top or end; as, to *tip* any thing with gold or silver.

With truncheon *tipp'd* with iron head. *Hudibras.*

Tipp'd with jet,
Fair ermines spotless as the snows they press. *Thomson.*

2. [for *tap.*] To strike slightly, or with the end of any thing small; to tap.

A third rogue *tips* me by the elbow. *Swift.*

3. To lower one end, or throw upon the end; as, to *tip* a cart for discharging a load. [*N. England.*]

To tip the wink, to direct a wink, or to wink to another for notice. *Pope.*

TIP, *v. i.* In the phrase, to *tip off*, that is, to fall headlong; hence, to die.

TIP'PED, } **TIPT**, } *pp.* Having the end covered.

TIP'PET, *n.* [Sax. *tæppet.* It seems to be formed from *tæppe*, tape.]

A narrow garment or covering for the neck, worn by females. It is now made of fur, though formerly of some kind of cloth. *Bacon.*

TIP'PING, *ppr.* Covering the end or tip.

TIP'PLE, *v. i.* [Qu. D. *zuipen*; Fr. *toper.* This word and *tope* are probably of one family, and I suspect them to be from the root of *dip.* See *Drink.*]

To drink spiritous or strong liquors habitually; to indulge in the frequent and improper use of spiritous liquors. When a man begins to *tipple*, let his creditors secure their debts.

TIP'PLE, *v. t.* To drink, as strong liquors, in luxury or excess.

—Himself for saving charges
A peel'd, slic'd onion eats, and *tipples* verjuice. *Dryden.*

TIP'PLE, *n.* Drink; liquor taken in tippling. *L'Estrange.*

TIP'PLED, *pp.* Drank in excess.

2. *a.* Intoxicated; inebriated. *Dryden.*

TIP'PLER, *n.* One who habitually indulges in the excessive use of spiritous liquors; a drunkard; a sot. It however signifies often a person who habitually drinks strong liquors, without absolute drunkenness.

TIP'PLING, *ppr.* Indulging in the habitual use of strong or spiritous liquors.

TIP'PLING, *n.* The habitual practice of drinking strong or spiritous liquors; a drinking to excess.

TIP'PLING-HOUSE, *n.* [*tipple* and *house.*] A house in which liquors are sold in drams or small quantities, and where men are accustomed to spend their time and money in excessive drinking.

TIP'-STAFF, *n.* [*tip* and *staff.*] An officer who bears a staff tipped with metal; a constable.

2. A staff tipped with metal. *Bacon.*

TIP'SY, *a.* [from *tipple.*] Fuddled; overpowered with strong drink; intoxicated.

TIP'TOE, *n.* [*tip* and *toe.*] The end of the toe.

Upon his *tiptoes* stalketh stately by. *Spenser.*

To be or *to stand a tiptoe*, to be awake or alive to any thing; to be roused; as, to *be a tiptoe* with expectation.

TIP'TOP, *n.* The highest or utmost degree.

TIRA'DE, *n.* [It. *tirata*; Fr. *tirade*, a train or series, from *tirer*, to draw.]

1. Formerly in French music, the filling of an interval by the intermediate diatonic notes. *Cyc.*

2. In *modern usage*, a strain or flight; a series of violent declamation.

Here he delivers a violent *tirade* against all persons who profess to know any thing about angels. *Quart. Review.*

TIRE, *n.* [Heb. טור tur, a row or series. See Class Dr. No. 24. 34. 35. 38. and No. 15.]

1. A tier; a row or rank. This is the same word as *tier*, differently written. [See *Tier* and *Tour.*]

2. A head dress; something that encompasses the head. [See *Tiara.*] Ezek. xxiv. Is. iii.

On her head she wore a *tire* of gold. *Spenser.*

3. Furniture; apparatus; as the *tire* of war. *Philips.*

4. Attire. [See *Attire.*]

5. A band or hoop of iron, used to bind the fellies of wheels, to secure them from wearing and breaking; as cart-*tire*; wagon-*tire*. This tire however is generally formed of different pieces, and is not one entire hoop.

TIRE, *v. t.* To adorn; to attire; to dress; as the head. *Obs.* [See *Attire.*] 2 Kings ix.

TIRE, *v. t.* [Sax. *teorian*, *ateorian*, *geteorian*, to fail. In D. *teeren* signifies to *tar*, to pine, to waste or consume, to digest; Gr. τειρω; L. *tero.* In Ir. and Gaelic, *tor*, *toras*, *tuirse*, is weariness; *tuirsighim*, to weary, to *tire.*]

1. To weary; to fatigue; to exhaust the strength by toil or labor; as, to *tire* a horse or an ox. A long day's work in summer will *tire* the laborer.

Tir'd with toil, all hopes of safety past. *Dryden.*

2. To weary; to fatigue; to exhaust the power of attending, or to exhaust patience with dullness or tediousness. A dull advocate may *tire* the court and jury, and injure his cause.

To tire out, to weary or fatigue to excess; to harass. *Tickel.*

TIRE, *v. i.* To become weary; to be fatigued; to have the strength fail; to have the patience exhausted. A feeble body soon *tires* with hard labor.

TI'RED, *pp.* Wearied; fatigued.

TI'REDNESS, *n.* The state of being wearied; weariness. *Hakewill.*

TI'RESÖME, *a.* Wearisome; fatiguing; exhausting the strength; as a *tiresome* day's work; a *tiresome* journey.

2. Tedious; exhausting the patience; as a *tiresome* discourse. The debates in congress are said to be sometimes very *tiresome.*

TI'RESÖMENESS, *n.* The act or quality of tiring or exhausting strength or patience; wearisomeness; tediousness; as the *tiresomeness* of work or of a dull speaker.

TI'REWÖMAN, *n.* [*tire* and *woman.*] A woman whose occupation is to make head dresses. *Locke.*

TI'RING, *ppr.* Wearying; fatiguing; exhausting strength or patience.

TI'RING-HOUSE, TI'RING-ROOM, *n.* The room or place where players dress for the stage. *Shak.*

TIR'WIT, *n.* A bird. [L. *vanellus.*] *Ainsworth.*

N. B. The lapwing is called teewit in Scotland, (*Ed. Encyc.*) and the lapwing is the vanellus.

'TIS, a contraction of *it is.*

TIS'IC, TIS'ICAL, *a.* *s* as z. [for *phthisic, phthisical.*] Consumptive.

TIS'IC, *n.* *s* as z. [supra.] Consumption; morbid waste.

TIS'RI, *n.* The first Hebrew month of the civil year, and the seventh of the ecclesiastical; answering to a part of our September and a part of October.

TISSUE, *n. tish'u.* [Fr. *tissu,* woven; *tisser,* to lay the ground-work of lace, to weave.]

1. Cloth interwoven with gold or silver, or with figured colors.

> A robe of *tissue,* stiff with golden wire. *Dryden.*

2. In *anatomy,* texture or organization of parts. The peculiar intimate structure of a part is called its *tissue.* A part of a fibrous structure is called a *fibrous tissue.* The organs of the body are made up of simpler elements, some generally diffused through the body, and others peculiar to particular organs. These simpler structures are called the *tissues* of the body; as the cellular *tissue;* the mucous *tissue,* &c. The *cellular tissue* is the cellular membrane. *Bichat. Cyc.*

3. A connected series; as, the whole story is a *tissue* of forgeries or of falsehood.

TIS'SUE, *v. t.* To form tissue; to interweave; to variegate.

> The chariot was covered with cloth of gold *tissued* upon blue. *Bacon.*

TIS'SUED, *pp.* Interwoven; formed with variegated work.

TIS'SUING, *ppr.* Interweaving; forming with variegated work.

TIT, *n.* A small horse, *in contempt;* a woman, *in contempt;* a small bird; a titmouse or tomtit.

TI'TAN, TITA'NIUM, *n.* In *mineralogy,* a metal of modern discovery, and of a dark copper color, first found in Cornwall in England. It occurs in different states of oxydation or intermixture, in various parts of the world. It exists in three different states of oxydation; the first is blue or purple, the second red, and the third white. The ores of this metal are called menachanite, from Menachan in Cornwall, where it was originally found; iserine, from the river Iser, in Silesia; nigrine, from its black color; sphene, rutile, and octahedrite.

TITA'NIAN, TITANIT'IC, *a.* Pertaining to titanium.

TITANIF'EROUS, *a.* [*titan* or *titanium,* and L. *fero.*] Producing titanium; as *titaniferous* pyrites. *Cleaveland.*

TI'TANITE, *n.* An ore or oxyd of titanium, commonly of a reddish brown color, when it is opake; it occurs also in prismatic crystals terminated by pyramids of a blood red color, and is then translucent or transparent. *Phillips.*

TIT'BIT, *n.* A tender piece. [See *Tidbit.*]

TI'THABLE, *a.* Subject to the payment of tithes. *Swift.*

TITHE, *n.* [Sax. *teotha,* probably contracted from *teogetha,* as the verb is *teighthian,* to decimate. See *Ten.*]

The tenth part of any thing; but appropriately, the tenth part of the increase annually arising from the profits of land and stock, allotted to the clergy for their support. Tithes are *personal, predial,* or *mixed; personal,* when accruing from labor, art, trade and navigation; *predial,* when issuing from the earth, as hay, wood and fruit; and *mixed,* when accruing from beasts, which are fed from the ground. *Blackstone.*

TITHE, *v. t.* To levy a tenth part on; to tax to the amount of a tenth.

> When thou hast made an end of *tithing* all the tithes of thine increase. Deut. xxvi.
>
> Ye *tithe* mint and rue. Luke xi.

TITHE, *v. i.* To pay tithes. *Tusser.*

TI'THED, *pp.* Taxed a tenth.

TI'THE-FREE, *a.* Exempt from the payment of tithes.

TI'THE-PAYING, *a.* Paying tithes; subjected to pay tithes. *Franklin.*

TI'THER, *n.* One who collects tithes.

TI'THING, *ppr.* Levying a tax on, to the amount of a tenth.

TI'THING, *n.* A decennary; a number or company of ten householders, who dwelling near each other, were sureties or free-pledges to the king for the good behavior of each other. The institution of tithings in England is ascribed to Alfred. *Blackstone.*

TI'THINGMAN, *n.* [*tithing* and *man.*]

1. The chief man of a tithing; a headborough; one elected to preside over the tithing. *Blackstone.*

2. A peace officer; an under constable.

3. In *New England,* a parish officer annually elected to preserve good order in the church during divine service, and to make complaint of any disorderly conduct.

TITH'YMAL, *n.* [Fr. *lithymale;* Gr. τιθυμαλος, from τιτθος, the breast.]

A plant, milk thistle, of the genus Euphorbia.

TIT'ILLATE, *v. i.* [L. *titillo.*] To tickle.

> The pungent grains of *titillating* dust. *Pope.*

TIT'ILLATING, *ppr.* Tickling.

TITILLA'TION, *n.* [Fr. from L. *titillatio.*]

1. The act of tickling; or the state of being tickled. *Bacon. Arbuthnot.*

2. Any slight pleasure.

> The products of those *titillations* that reach no higher than the senses. *Glanville.*

TIT'L'ARK, *n.* [*tit* and *lark.*] A small bird, a species of Alauda or lark.

TI'TLE, *n.* [L. *titulus;* It. *titolo.* This may belong to the family of Gr. τιθημι, to set or put; Sax. *tithian,* to give.]

1. An inscription put over any thing as a name by which it is known.

2. The inscription in the beginning of a book, containing the subject of the work, and sometimes the author's name.

3. In *the civil* and *canon laws,* a chapter or division of a book.

4. An appellation of dignity, distinction or pre-eminence given to persons; as duke, marquis and the like. *Cyc.*

5. A name; an appellation.

> Ill worthy I such *title* should belong
> To me transgressor. *Milton.*

6. Right; or that which constitutes a just cause of exclusive possession; that which is the foundation of ownership; as a good *title* to an estate; or an imperfect *title.* The lowest degree of *title* is naked possession, then comes the right of possession, and lastly the right of property, all which united complete the title. *Blackstone.*

But *possession* is not essential to a complete title. A title to personal property may be acquired by occupancy. A *claim* is not a *title.*

7. The instrument which is evidence of a right.

8. In *the canon law,* that by which a beneficiary holds a benefice. This is true and valid, or colorable. A *valid* title gives a right to the benefice. A *colorable* title appears to be valid, but is not. *Cyc.*

9. In *ancient church records,* a church to which a priest was ordained, and where he was to reside. *Cowel.*

TI'TLE, *v. t.* To name; to call; to entitle. *Milton.*

TI'TLED, *pp.* Called; named.

2. *a.* Having a title.

TI'TLELESS, *a.* Not having a title or name. [*Not in use.*] *Shak.*

TI'TLE-PAGE, *n.* [*title* and *page.*] The page of a book which contains its title.

TI'TLING, *ppr.* Calling; denominating; entitling.

TIT'MOUSE, *n.* [*tit,* small, and *mouse.*] A small bird of the genus Parus. *Dryden.*

TIT'TER, *v. i.* To laugh with the tongue striking against the root of the upper teeth; to laugh with restraint. *Pope.*

TIT'TER, *n.* A restrained laugh.

2. A weed.

TIT'TLE, *n.* [from *tit,* small.] A small particle; a minute part; a jot; an iota.

TIT'TLE-TATTLE, *n.* [*tattle,* doubled.]

1. Idle trifling talk; empty prattle. *Prior.*

2. An idle trifling talker. [*Less proper.*]

TIT'TLE-TATTLE, *v. i.* To talk idly; to prate. *Sidney.*

TITUBA'TION, *n.* [L. *titubo,* to stumble.] The act of stumbling.

TIT'ULAR, *a.* [Fr. *titulaire;* from L. *titulus.*]

1. Existing in title or name only; nominal; having or conferring the title only; as a *titular* king or prince.

2. Having the title to an office or dignity without discharging the duties of it.

> Both Valerius and Austin were *titular* bishops. *Ayliffe.*

TIT'ULAR, } *n.* A person invested with
TIT'ULARY, } a title, in virtue of which he holds an office or benefice, whether he performs the duties of it or not. *Cyc.*

TITULAR'ITY, *n.* The state of being titular. *Brown.*

TIT'ULARLY, *adv.* Nominally; by title only.

TIT'ULARY, *a.* Consisting in a title. *Bacon.*

2. Pertaining to a title. *Bacon.*

TIV'ER, *n.* A kind of ocher which is used in marking sheep in some parts of England. [*Local.*] *Cyc.*

TIV'ER, *v. t.* To mark sheep with tiver, in different ways and for different purposes. [*Local.*]

TIV'ERING, *ppr.* Marking with tiver. [*Local.*]

TIV'ERING, *n.* The act or practice of marking with tiver. [*Local.*] *Cyc.*

TIV'Y, *adv.* [See *Tantivy.*] With great speed; a huntsman's word or sound. *Dryden.*

TO, *prep.* [Sax. *to;* D. *te* or *toe;* G. *zu;* Ir. Gaelic, *do;* Corn. *tho.* This is probably a contracted word, but from what verb it is not easy to ascertain. The sense is obvious; it denotes passing, moving towards. The pronunciation is *to* or *too*, and this depends much on its application or its emphasis.]

1. Noting motion towards a place; opposed to *from*, or placed after another word expressing motion *towards.* He is going *to* church.
2. Noting motion towards a state or condition. He is going *to* a trade; he is rising *to* wealth and honor.
3. Noting accord or adaptation; as an occupation suited *to* his taste; she has a husband *to* her mind.
4. Noting address or compellation, or the direction of a discourse. These remarks were addressed *to* a large audience.

> *To* you, my noble lord of Westmoreland;
> I pledge your grace. *Shak.*

5. Noting attention or application.

> Go, buckle *to* the law. *Dryden.*
> Meditate upon these things; give yourself wholly *to* them. 1 Tim. iv.

6. Noting addition.

> Add *to* your faith, virtue. 2 Pet. i.
> Wisdom he has, and *to* his wisdom, courage. *Denham.*

7. Noting opposition. They engaged hand *to* hand.
8. Noting amount, rising to. They met us, *to* the number of three hundred.
9. Noting proportion; as, three is *to* nine as nine is *to* twenty seven. It is ten *to* one that you will offend by your officiousness.
10. Noting possession or appropriation. We have a good seat; let us keep it *to* ourselves.
11. Noting perception; as a substance sweet *to* the taste; an event painful *to* the mind.
12. Noting the subject of an affirmation.

> I have a king's oath *to* the contrary. *Shak.*

13. In comparison of.

> All that they did was piety *to* this. *B. Jonson.*

14. As far as.

> Few of the Esquimaux can count *to* ten. *Quart. Rev.*

15. Noting intention.

> —Marks and points out each man of us *to* slaughter. *B. Jonson.*

[In this sense, *for* is now used.]

16. After an adjective, noting the object; as deaf *to* the cries of distress; alive *to* the sufferings of the poor. He was attentive *to* the company, or *to* the discourse.
17. Noting obligation; as duty *to* God and *to* our parents.
18. Noting enmity; as a dislike *to* spirituous liquors.
19. Towards; as, she stretched her arms *to* heaven. *Dryden.*
20. Noting effect or end. The prince was flattered *to* his ruin. He engaged in a war *to* his cost. Violent factions exist *to* the prejudice of the state.

> Numbers were crowded *to* death. *Clarendon.*

21. *To*, as a sign of the infinitive, precedes the radical verb. Sometimes it is used instead of the ancient form, *for to*, noting purpose. David in his life time intended *to* build a temple. The legislature assembles annually *to* make and amend laws. The court will sit in February *to* try some important causes.
22. It precedes the radical verb after adjectives, noting the object; as ready *to* go; prompt *to* obey; quick *to* hear, but slow *to* censure.
23. It precedes the radical verb, noting the object.

> The delay of our hopes teaches us *to* mortify our desires. *Smallridge.*

24. It precedes the radical verb, noting consequence.

> I have done my utmost to lead my life so pleasantly as *to* forget my misfortunes. *Pope.*

25. It notes extent, degree or end. He languishes *to* death, even *to* death. The water rises *to* the highth of twenty feet. The line extends from one end *to* the other.
26. After the substantive verb, and with the radical verb, it denotes futurity. The construction, we *are to* meet at ten o'clock, every man at death *is to* receive the reward of his deeds, is a particular form of expressing future time.
27. After *have*, it denotes duty or necessity. I *have* a debt *to* pay on Saturday.
28. *To-day, to-night, to-morrow*, are peculiar phrases derived from our ancestors. *To* in the two first, has the sense or force of *this; this day, this night.* In the last, it is equivalent to *in* or *on; in* or *on* the morrow. The words may be considered as compounds, *to-day, to-night, to-morrow*, and usually as adverbs. But sometimes they are used as nouns; as, *to-day* is ours. *Cowley.*

To and fro, backward and forward. In this phrase, *to* is adverbial.

To the face, in presence of; not in the absence of.

> I withstood him *face to face.* Gal. ii.
> *To-morrow, to-morrow*, and *to-morrow*,
> Creeps in this petty pace from day to day. *Shak.*

[NOTE.—In the foregoing explanation of *to*, it is to be considered that the definition given is not always the sense of *to* by itself, but the sense rather of the word preceding it, or connected with it, or of *to* in connection with other words. In general, *to* is used in the sense of moving towards a place, or towards an object, or it expresses direction *towards* a place, end, object or purpose.]

To is often used adverbially to modify the sense of verbs; as, to *come to;* to *heave to.* The sense of such phrases is explained under the verbs respectively.

In popular phrases like the following, "I will not come; you shall *to*, or *too*, a genuine Saxon phrase, *to* denotes moreover, besides, L. *insuper.*

TOAD, *n.* [Sax. *tade, tadige.*] A paddoc, an animal of the genus Rana, the *Rana Bufo* of Linne; a small clumsy animal, the body warty, thick and disgusting to the sight, but perfectly harmless, and indeed it is said to be useful in gardens by feeding on noxious worms.

TOAD-EATER, *n.* A vulgar name given to a fawning, obsequious parasite; a mean sycophant.

TOAD-FISH, *n.* [*toad* and *fish.*] A fish of the genus Lophius, the fishing frog. *Cyc.*

TOAD-FLAX, *n.* [*toad* and *flax.*] A plant of the genus Antirrhinum; snap-dragon; calves' snout.

TOADISH, *a.* Like a toad. [*Not used.*] *Stafford.*

TOAD-STONE, *n.* [*toad* and *stone.*] In *mineralogy*, a sort of trap rock, of a brownish gray color. The toad-stone of Derbyshire is generally a dark brown basaltic amygdaloid, composed of basalt and green earth, and containing oblong cavities filled with calcarious spar. *Cyc.*

TOAD-STOOL, *n.* [*toad* and *stool.*] A sort of fungous plant that grows in moist and rich grounds like a mushroom.

TOAST, *v. t.* [Sp. Port. *tostar*, to *toast* or roast. Qu. are these from the L. *tostus?*]

1. To dry and scorch by the heat of a fire; as, to *toast* bread or cheese. [*It is chiefly limited in its application to these two articles.*]
2. To warm thoroughly; as, to *toast* the feet. [*Not much used.*]
3. To name when a health is drank; to drink to the health in honor of; as, to *toast* a lady. Addison writes "to *toast* the health;" a form of expression I believe not now used.

TOAST, *n.* Bread dried and scorched by the fire; or such bread dipped in melted butter, or in some liquor. Dry toast is bread scorched, or it is scorched bread with butter spread upon it. Soft toast is made by immersing toasted bread in melted butter, and called dipped toast.

2. A female whose health is drank in honor or respect.

> The wise man's passion, and the vain man's *toast.* *Pope.*

3. He or that which is named in honor in drinking.

TOASTED, *pp.* Scorched by heat; named in drinking the health.

TOASTER, *n.* One who toasts.

2. An instrument for toasting bread or cheese.

TO'ASTING, *ppr.* Scorching by fire; drinking to the honor of.

TOBAC'CO, *n.* [so named from *Tabaco*, a province of Yucatan, in Spanish America, where it was first found by the Spaniards.]

A plant, a native of America, of the genus Nicotiana, much used for smoking and chewing and in snuff. As a medicine, it is narcotic. Tobacco has a strong disagreeable smell, and an acrid taste. When first used it sometimes occasions vomiting; but the practice of using it in any form, soon conquers distaste, and forms a relish for it that is strong and almost unconquerable.

TOBAC'CONIST, *n.* A dealer in tobacco; also, a manufacturer of tobacco.

TOBAC'CO-PIPE, *n.* [*tobacco* and *pipe.*] A pipe used for smoking tobacco, often made of clay and baked, sometimes of other material.

TOBAC'CO-PIPE CLAY, *n.* A species of clay; called also cimolite.

TOBACCO-PIPE FISH, *n.* A name of the *Syngnathus Acus* of Linne; called also needle-fish. *Cyc.*

TOCK'AY, *n.* A species of spotted lizard in India. *Cyc.*

TOC'SIN, *n.* [Fr.; Armoric, *tocq*, a stroke, from the root of *touch*, and *sonn* or *seing*, sound.]
An alarm bell, or the ringing of a bell for the purpose of alarm.

TOD, *n.* [In Gaelic, *tod* is a clod, a mass.]
1. A bush; a thick shrub. *Obs.* *Spenser.*
2. A quantity of wool of twenty eight pounds, or two stone.
3. A fox. *B. Jonson.*

TOD, *v. t.* To weigh; to produce a tod. [*Not in use.*] *Shak.*

TO-DAY, *n.* [*to* and *day.*] The present day.

TOD'DY, *n.* A juice drawn from various kinds of the palm in the E. Indies; or a liquor prepared from it.
2. A mixture of spirit and water sweetened. *Toddy* differs from *grog* in having a greater proportion of spirit, and in being sweetened.

TO'DY, *n.* A genus of insectivorous birds, of the order of Picæ; natives of warm climates. *Cyc.* *Ed. Encyc.*

TOE, *n.* [Sax. *ta*; G. *zehe*; Sw. *tå*; Dan. *taae*; Fr. *doigt du pied*; L. *digitus*. *Toe* is contracted from *tog*, the primary word on which L. *digitus* is formed, coinciding with *dug*, and signifying a shoot. Class Dg.]
1. One of the small members which form the extremity of the foot, corresponding to a finger on the hand. The toes in their form and structure resemble the fingers, but are shorter.
2. The fore part of the hoof of a horse. and of other hoofed animals.
3. The member of a beast's foot corresponding to the toe in man.

TOFO'RE, *prep.* or *adv.* [Sax. *toforan*; *to* and *fore.*]
Before; formerly. *Obs.* *Shak.*

TOFT, *n.* [probably from the root of *tuft.*]
1. A grove of trees. *Cyc.*
2. [Dan. *tofte* or *tomt.*] In *law books*, a place where a messuage has stood, but is decayed. *Cowel.* *Cyc.*

TO'GATED, } *a.* [L. *toga*, a gown; *togatus*,
TO'GED, } gowned.] Gowned; dressed in a gown; wearing a gown; as *toged* consuls. *Shak.*

TOGETH'ER, *adv.* [Sax. *togæthre*; *to* and *gather.*]
1. In company. We walked *together* to the wood.
2. In or into union.

> The king joined humanity and policy *together.* *Bacon.*

3. In the same place; as, to live *together* in one house.
4. In the same time; as, to live *together* in the same age.
5. In concert; as, the allies made war upon France *together.*
6. Into junction or a state of union; as, to sew, knit, pin or fasten two things *together*; to mix things *together.*

Together with, in union with; in company or mixture with.

> Take the bad *together with* the good. *Dryden.*

TOG'GEL, *n.* A small wooden pin tapering towards both ends. *Mar. Dict.*

TOIL, *v. i.* [Sax. *teolan*, *tiolan*, to strive, strain, urge, to prepare, to heal, to *toil*, and *tilian*, *tiligan*, to prepare or provide, to *till*, to *toil*, to study or be solicitous; Russ. *dialayu*. The primary sense is expressed in the Saxon, to strain, to urge. Class Dl.]
To labor; to work; to exert strength with pain and fatigue of body or mind, particularly of the body, with efforts of some continuance or duration.

> Master, we have *toiled* all night and caught nothing. Luke v.

TOIL, *v. t.* To *toil out*, to labor; to work out.

> *Toil'd out* my uncouth passage— *Milton.*

2. To weary; to overlabor; as *toil'd* with works of war. [*Not in use nor proper.*] *Shak.*

TOIL, *n.* Labor with pain and fatigue; labor that oppresses the body or mind. *Toil* may be the labor of the field or the workshop, or of the camp. What *toils* men endure for the acquisition of wealth, power and honor! Gen. v.

TOIL, *n.* [Fr. *toiles*, snare, trap; Ir. *dul*, a snare or gin; L. *tela*, a web; from spreading, extending or laying.]
A net or snare; any thread, web or string spread for taking prey.

> A fly falls into the *toils* of a spider. *L'Estrange.*

TOIL'ER, *n.* One who toils, or labors with pain.

TOIL'ET, *n.* [Fr. *toilette*, from *toile*, cloth.]
1. A covering or cloth of linen, silk or tapestry, spread over a table in a chamber or dressing room. Hence,
2. A dressing table. *Pope.*

TOIL'ING, *ppr.* Laboring with pain.

TOIL'SOME, *a.* Laborious; wearisome; attended with fatigue and pain; as *toilsome* work; a *toilsome* task.

> What can be *toilsome* in these pleasant walks? *Milton.*

2. Producing toil; as a *toilsome* day or journey.

TOIL'SOMENESS, *n.* Laboriousness; wearisomeness.

TOISE, *n. tois.* [Fr.] A fathom or long measure in France, containing six feet; but the French foot is longer than the English, 76 being equal to 81 English feet.

TOKA'Y, *n.* A kind of wine produced at Tokay in Hungary, made of white grapes. It is distinguished from other wines by its aromatic taste. It is not good till it is about three years old, and it continues to improve as long as it is kept.

TOKEN, *n. to'kn.* [Sax. *tacn*, *tacen*; Goth. *taikns*; D. *teeken*; Dan. *tegn*; Sw. *teckn*; G. *zeichen*. This may be the same word as the L. *signum*, dialectically varied, or from the same radix; Gr. δεικνυμι.]
1. A sign; something intended to represent or indicate another thing or an event. Thus the rainbow is a *token* of God's covenant established with Noah. The blood of the paschal lamb, sprinkled on the doors of the Hebrews, was a *token* to the destroying angel of God's will that he should pass by those houses. Gen. ix. Ex. xii.

> Show me a *token* for good. Ps. lxxxvi.

2. A mark. In pestilential diseases, tokens are livid spots upon the body, which indicate the approach of death. *Cyc.*
3. A memorial of friendship; something by which the friendship of another person is to be kept in mind. *Shak.*
4. In *coinage*, tokens were coins struck in the reign of Elizabeth in the cities of Bristol, Oxford and Worcester, and also by private persons, which were put into circulation, and upon being returned, the issuer gave the value of them in current money. *Cyc.*
5. In *printing*, ten quires of paper; an extra quire is usually added to every other token, when counted out for the press.

TO'KEN, *v. t.* To make known. [*Not in use.*] *Shak.*

TO'KENED, *a.* Being marked with spots. *Shak.*

TOL, *v. t.* [L. *tollo.*] To take away; a law term. *Cyc.*

TO'LA, *n.* In India, a weight for gold and silver, but different in different places.

TOLD, *pret.* and *pp.* of *tell.*

> Who *told* thee that thou wast naked? Gen. iii.
>
> Thou hast mocked me, and *told* me lies. Judges xvi.
>
> —Sheep and oxen that could not be *told.* 1 Kings viii.

TOL-BOOTH. [See *Toll-booth.*]

TOLE, *v. t.* [I know not from what source we have this word; but it coincides with the Ar. دَلَّ dalla, to draw. The Ethiopic has ተለወ talwa, to follow, and አተለወ to cause to follow. It is a legitimate word and in good use.]
To draw or cause to follow by presenting something pleasing or desirable to view; to allure by some bait. Thus our farmers *tole* sheep and make them follow, by holding to them a measure of corn or some portion of fodder. In New England, it is applied only to the alluring of beasts. Locke has applied it to men.

TO'LED, *pp.* Drawn; allured; induced to follow.

TOL'ERABLE, *a.* [Fr. from L. *tolerabilis*. See *Tolerate.*]
1. That may be borne or endured; supportable, either physically or mentally. The cold in Canada is severe, but *tolerable*. The insults and indignities of our enemies are not *tolerable.*

> It shall be more *tolerable* for the land of Sodom and Gomorrah in the day of judgment, than for that city. Matt. x.

2. Moderately good or agreeable; not contemptible; not very excellent or pleasing, but such as can be borne or received without disgust, resentment or opposition; as a *tolerable* translation; a *tolerable* entertainment; a *tolerable* administration. *Swift.*

TOL'ERABLENESS, *n.* The state of being tolerable.

TOL'ERABLY, *adv.* Supportably; in a manner to be endured.

2. Moderately well; passably; not perfectly; as a constitution *tolerably* firm. The advocate speaks *tolerably* well.

TOL'ERANCE, *n.* [L. *tolerantia*, from *tolero*, to bear.]

The power or capacity of enduring; or the act of enduring.

> Diogenes one frosty morning came to the market place shaking, to show his *tolerance*. *Bacon.*

[Little used. But *intolerance* is in common use.]

TOL'ERANT, *a.* Enduring; indulgent; favoring toleration.

TOL'ERATE, *v. t.* [Fr. *tolerer*; L. *tolero*, from *tollo*, to lift; Ch. טול to lift or raise. Class Dl. No. 3, and see No. 6. 7. 18. 20. 28. 32.]

To suffer to be or to be done without prohibition or hinderance; to allow or permit negatively, by not preventing; not to restrain; as, to *tolerate* opinions or practices. The protestant religion is *tolerated* in France, and the Roman Catholic in Great Britain.

> Crying should not be *tolerated* in children. *Locke.*

> The law of love *tolerates* no vice, and patronizes every virtue. *G. Spring.*

TOL'ERATED, *pp.* Suffered; allowed; not prohibited or restrained.

TOL'ERATING, *ppr.* Enduring; suffering to be or to be done; allowing; not restraining.

TOLERA'TION, *n.* [L. *toleratio.*] The act of tolerating; the allowance of that which is not wholly approved; appropriately, the allowance of religious opinions and modes of worship in a state, when contrary to or different from those of the established church or belief. *Toleration* implies a right in the sovereign to control men in their opinions and worship, or it implies the actual exercise of power in such control. Where no power exists or none is assumed to establish a creed and a mode of worship, there can be no *toleration*, in the strict sense of the word, for one religious denomination has as good a right as another to the free enjoyment of its creed and worship.

TŌLL, *n.* [Sax. *toll*; D. *tol*; Sw. *tull*; Dan. *told*; G. *zoll*; W. *toll*, a fraction, a toll; *toli* and *toliaw*, to curtail, to diminish, to take away, to spare or save, to *deal* out, from *tawl*, a throw, a casting off, a separation, a cutting off; *tolli*, from *toll*, to subtract, to take *toll*; Gr. τελος, toll, custom, and end, exit, from cutting off; Fr. *tailler*, to cut off, [See *Tail*;] Ir. *deilim*, to separate; *dail*, a share, Eng. *dole*; *diolam*, to sell, to exchange, to pay *toll*. This is from the root of *deal*. See *Deal*, Sax. *bedælan*. Class Dl. No. 12.]

1. A tax paid for some liberty or privilege, particularly for the privilege of passing over a bridge or on a highway, or for that of vending goods in a fair, market or the like.

2 A liberty to buy and sell within the bounds of a manor. *Cyc.*

3. A portion of grain taken by a miller as a compensation for grinding.

TŌLL, *v. i.* To pay toll or tallage. *Shak.*

2. To take toll, as by a miller. *Tusser.*

TŌLL, *v. i.* [W. *tol*, *tolo*, a loud sound, a din; Pers. تَالِيدَن talidan, to sound, to ring. We see that W. *tawl*, supra, is a throw or cast, a driving, and this is the radical sense of *sound.*]

To sound or ring, as a bell, with strokes uniformly repeated at intervals, as at funerals, or in calling assemblies, or to announce the death of a person.

> Now sink in sorrows with a *tolling* bell. *Pope.*

TŌLL, *v. t.* [supra.] To cause a bell to sound with strokes slowly and uniformly repeated, as for summoning public bodies or religious congregations to their meetings, or for announcing the death of a person, or to give solemnity to a funeral. *Tolling* is a different thing from *ringing*.

TŌLL, *v. t.* [L. *tollo.*] To take away; to vacate; to annul; a law term.

2. To draw. [See *Tole.*] *Bacon.*

TŌLL, *n.* A particular sounding of a bell.

TŌLL-BĀR, *n.* [*toll* and *bar.*] A bar or beam used for stopping boats on a canal at the toll-house.

TŌLL-BOOTH, *n.* [*toll* and *booth.*] A place where goods are weighed to ascertain the duties or toll.

2. A prison. *Ainsworth.*

TŌLL-BOOTH, *v. t.* To imprison in a tollbooth. *Corbet.*

TŌLL-BRIDGE, *n.* A bridge where toll is paid for passing it.

TŌLL-GATE, *n.* A gate where toll is taken.

TŌLL-GATHERER, *n.* The man who takes toll.

TŌLL-HOUSE, *n.* A house or shed placed by a road near a toll-gate, or at the end of a toll-bridge, or by a canal, where the man who takes the toll remains.

TŌLLING, *ppr.* Causing to sound in a slow grave manner.

2. Taking away; removing.

3. Sounding, as a bell.

TOLU BALSAM, *n.* Balsam of Tolu, a balsam produced from a tree growing in Tolu, in S. America. *Cyc.*

TOLUTA'TION, *n.* [L. *toluto.*] A pacing or ambling. [*Not used.*] *Brown. Hudibras.*

TOM'AHAWK, *n.* An Indian hatchet.

TOM'AHAWK, *v. t.* To cut or kill with a hatchet called a tomahawk.

TOMA'TO, *n.* A plant, and its fruit, a species of Solanum. It is called sometimes the *love-apple.*

TŌMB, *n. toom.* [Fr. *tombe, tombeau*; W. *tom, tomen, twm, twmp*, a mound, a heap; Ir. *tuoma*; Sp. *tumba*; L. *tumulus*, a heap or hillock; *tumeo*, to swell; Gr. τυμβος. Class Dm. This name was given to a place for the dead by men who raised a heap of earth over the dead.]

1. A grave; a pit in which the dead body of a human being is deposited.

> As one dead in the bottom of a *tomb.* *Shak.*

2. A house or vault formed wholly or partly in the earth, with walls and a roof for the reception of the dead.

3. A monument erected to preserve the memory of the dead.

TŌMB, *v. t.* To bury; to inter. [See *Entomb.*]

TOM'BAC, *n.* A white alloy of copper; a metallic composition made by mixing and fusing together a large quantity of zink with a smaller quantity of copper, with arsenic.

TŌMBLESS, *a.* Destitute of a tomb or sepulchral monument.

TOM'BOY, *n.* [*Tom, Thomas*, and *boy.*] A rude boisterous boy; also in sarcasm, a romping girl. [*Vulgar.*]

TŌMBSTONE, *n.* [*tomb* and *stone.*] A stone erected over a grave, to preserve the memory of the deceased; a monument.

TOME, *n.* [Fr. from Gr. τομος, a piece or section, from τεμνω, to cut off.]

A book; as many writings as are bound in a volume, forming the part of a larger work. It may be applied to a single volume.

TOMENT'OUS, *a.* [L. *tomentum*, down.] In *botany*, downy; nappy; cottony; or flocky; covered with hairs so close as scarcely to be discernible, or with a whitish down, like wool; as a *tomentous* stem or leaf. *Martyn. Lee.*

TO-MOR'ROW, *n.* [*to* and *morrow.*] The day after the present.

> One to-day is worth two *to-morrows.* *Franklin.*

TOM'PION, *n.* [Fr. *tampon*, a stopple.] The stopper of a cannon. [See *Tampion.*]

TOM'TIT, *n.* A little bird, the titmouse.

TON, the termination of names of places, is *town.*

TON, *n.* [Fr.] The prevailing fashion.

TŌN, *n.* [Sax. *tunna*; Fr. *tonne*; Sp. *tonel*, a cask, a tun or butt.]

The weight of twenty hundred gross. [See *Tun.*] This is false orthography. The word is from the Saxon *tunna*, a cask, and the sense of weight is taken from that of a cask or butt.

TONE, *n.* [Fr. *ton*; Sp. *tono*; It. *tuono*; Sw. G. *ton*; D. *toon*; Dan. *tone*; L. *tonus*; Gr. τονος, sound; L. *tono*, Gr. τονοω, to sound, from the root of τεινω, to strain or stretch. The L. *sonus* is probably the same word in a different dialect.]

1. Sound, or a modification of sound; any impulse or vibration of the air which is perceptible by the ear; as a low *tone*, high *tone*, or loud *tone*; a grave *tone*; an acute *tone*; a sweet *tone*; a harsh *tone*.

2. Accent; or rather, a particular inflection of the voice, adapted to express emotion or passion; *a rhetorical sense of the word.* *E. Porter.*

> Eager his *tone*, and ardent were his eyes. *Dryden.*

3. A whining sound; a whine; a kind of mournful strain of voice; as, children often read with a *tone.*

4. An affected sound in speaking.

5. In *music*, an interval of sound; as, the difference between the diapente and diatessaron, is a *tone*. Of tones there are two kinds, major and minor. The tone major is in the ratio of 8 to 9, which results from the difference between the fourth and fifth. The tone minor is as 9 to 10, resulting from the difference between the minor third and the fourth. *Cyc.*
6. The tone of an instrument, is its peculiar sound with regard to softness, evenness and the like. *Cyc.*
7. In *medicine*, that state of organization in a body, in which the animal functions are healthy and performed with due vigor. *Tone*, in its primary signification, is *tension*, and tension is the primary signification of strength. Hence its application to the natural healthy state of animal organs. Tone therefore in medicine, is the strength and activity of the organs, from which proceed healthy functions. So we say, the body is in a *sound* state, the health is *sound* or *firm*.

TONE, *v. t.* To utter with an affected tone.
2. To tune. [See *Tune*.]

TO'NED, *a.* Having a tone; used in composition; as high-*toned;* sweet-*toned.*

TO'NELESS, *a.* Having no tone; unmusical. *Entick.*

TO'NE-SYLLABLE, *a.* An accented syllable. *M. Stuart.*

TONG, *n.* [See *Tongs.*] The catch of a buckle. [*Not used.*] [See *Tongue.*] *Spenser.*

TONGS, *n. plu.* [Sax. Dan. D. *tang*; G. *zange*; Sw. *tång*; Ice. *taung*; Gaelic, *teangas.* This seems by its orthography to be the same word as *tongue, tongues,* and to signify projections, shoots.]
An instrument of metal, consisting of two parts or long shafts joined at one end; used for handling things, particularly fire or heated metals. We say, a *pair of tongs,* a smith's *tongs.*

TŎNGUE, TUNG, *n.* [Sax. *tung, tunga*; Goth. *tuggo*; Sw. *tunga*; Dan. *tunge*; D. *tong*; G. *zunge*; Ir. and Gaelic, *teanga*; Ant. L. *tingua.* We see by the Gothic, that *n* is not radical; the word belongs to Class *Dg.* It signifies a shoot or extension, like L. *digitus* and *dug.* Our common orthography is incorrect; the true spelling is *tung.*]
1. In man, the instrument of taste, and the chief instrument of speech; and in other animals, the instrument of taste. It is also an instrument of deglutition. In some animals, the tongue is used for drawing the food into the mouth, as in animals of the bovine genus, &c. Other animals lap their drink, as dogs.

The tongue is covered with membranes, and the outer one is full of papillæ of a pyramidical figure, under which lies a thin, soft, reticular coat perforated with innumerable holes, and always lined with a thick and white or yellowish mucus. *Cyc.*

2. Speech; discourse; sometimes, fluency of speech.

> Much *tongue* and much judgment seldom go together. *L'Estrange.*

3. The power of articulate utterance; speech.

> Parrots imitating human *tongue.* *Dryden.*

4. Speech, as well or ill used; mode of speaking.

> Keep a good *tongue* in thy head. *Shak.*
> The *tongue* of the wise is health. Prov. xii.

5. A language; the whole sum of words used by a particular nation. The English *tongue*, within two hundred years, will probably be spoken by two or three hundred millions of people in North America.
6. Speech; words or declarations only; opposed to *thoughts* or *actions.*

> Let us not love in word, neither in *tongue*, but in deed and in truth. 1 John iii.

7. A nation, as distinguished by their language.

> I will gather all nations and *tongues.* Is. lxvi.

8. A point; a projection; as the *tongue* of a buckle or of a balance.
9. A point or long narrow strip of land, projecting from the main into a sea or a lake.
10. The taper part of any thing; in the rigging of a ship, a short piece of rope spliced into the upper part of standing backstays, &c. to the size of the mast-head.

To hold the tongue, to be silent. *Addison.*

TŎNGUE, TUNG, *v. t.* To chide; to scold.

> How might she *tongue* me. *Shak.*

TŎNGUE, TUNG, *v. i.* To talk; to prate. *Shak.*

TŎNGUED, TUNG'ED, *a.* Having a tongue.

> *Tongued* like the night-crow. *Donne.*

TŎNGUE-GR'AFTING, TUNG'-GR'AFTING, *n.* A mode of grafting by inserting the end of a cion in a particular manner.

TŎNGUELESS, TUNG'LESS, *a.* Having no tongue.
2. Speechless; as a *tongueless* block. *Shak.*
3. Unnamed; not spoken of.

> One good deed dying *tongueless.* *Shak.*

[*Not used.*]

TŎNGUE-PAD, TUNG'-PAD, *n.* A great talker. [*Not in use.*] *Tatler.*

TŎNGUE-SHAPED, TUNG'-SHAPED, *a.* In *botany*, a *tongue-shaped leaf*, is linear and fleshy, blunt at the end, convex underneath, and having usually a cartilaginous border. *Martyn.*

TŎNGUE-TIE, TUNG'-TIE, *v. t.* [*tongue* and *tie.*] To deprive of speech or the power of speech, or of distinct articulation. *Goodman.*

TŎNGUE-TIED, TUNG'-TIED, *a.* Destitute of the power of distinct articulation; having an impediment in the speech. *Holder.*
2. Unable to speak freely, from whatever cause.

> Love and *tongue-tied* simplicity. *Shak.*

TON'IC, *a.* [from Gr. τονος, L. *tonus.* See *Tone.*]
1. Literally, increasing tension; hence, increasing strength, as *tonic* power.
2. In *medicine*, increasing strength, or the tone of the animal system; obviating the effects of debility, and restoring healthy functions.
3. Relating to tones or sounds.
4. Extended. [*Not in use.*] *Brown.*

Tonic spasm, in *medicine*, a rigid contraction of the muscles without relaxation, as in tetanus, &c. *Hooper.*

TON'IC, *n.* A medicine that increases the tone of the muscular fiber, and gives vigor and action to the system.
A medicine which increases the tone or strength of the body. *Parr.*
2. In *music*, the key-note or principal sound which generates all the rest. [Fr. *tonique.*] *Cyc.*
3. In *music*, a certain degree of tension, or the sound produced by a vocal string in a given degree of tension.

TO-NIGHT, *n.* [*to* and *night.*] The present night, or the night after the present day.

TŎN'NAGE, *n.* [from *ton*, a corrupt orthography. See *Tun.*]
1. The weight of goods carried in a boat or ship.
2. The cubical content or burthen of a ship in tuns; or the amount of weight which she may carry.
3. A duty or impost on ships, estimated per tun; or a duty, toll or rate payable on goods per tun, transported on canals.

TON'SIL, *n.* [L. *tonsillæ.* This word seems to be formed from *tonsus, tondeo*, to clip.]
In *anatomy*, a glandular body at the passage from the mouth to the pharynx. The *tonsils* are called also from their shape, *amygdalæ*, and in popular language, *almonds.* The tonsils have several excretory ducts opening into the mouth. *Cyc. Hooper.*

TON'SIL, *a.* That may be clipped. *Mason.*

TON'SURE, *n.* [Fr. from L. *tonsura*, from *tonsus*, shaved; *tondeo*, to clip or shave.]
1. The act of clipping the hair, or of shaving the head; or the state of being shorn. *Addison.*
2. In *the Romish church*, tonsure is the first ceremony used for devoting a person to the service of God and the church; the first degree of the clericate, given by a bishop, who cuts off a part of his hair with prayers and benedictions. Hence *tonsure* is used to denote entrance or admission into holy orders. *Cyc.*
3. In *the Romish church*, the corona or crown which priests wear as a mark of their order and of their rank in the church. *Cyc.*

TONTĬNE, *n.* [Fr. *tontine*; said to be from its inventor, *Tonti*, an Italian.]
An annuity on survivorship; or a loan raised on life-annuities, with the benefit of survivorship. Thus an annuity is shared among a number, on the principle that the share of each, at his death, is enjoyed by the survivors, until at last the whole goes to the last survivor, or to the last two or three, according to the terms on which the money is advanced.

TO'NY, *n.* A simpleton. [*Ludicrous.*] *Dryden.*

TOO, *adv.* [Sax. *to.*]
1. Over; more than enough; noting excess; as, a thing is *too* long, *too* short, or *too* wide; *too* high; *too* many; *too* much.

> His will *too* strong to bend, *too* proud to learn. *Cowley.*

2. Likewise; also; in addition.

> A courtier and a patriot *too.* *Pope.*
> Let those eyes that view
> The daring crime, behold the vengeance *too.* *Pope.*

3. *Too, too*, repeated, denotes excess emphatically; but this repetition is not in respectable use.

TOOK, *pret.* of *take.*

Enoch was not, for God *took* him. Gen. v.

TOOL, *n.* [Sax. *tol.* Qu. Fr. *outil.* In old Law Latin, we find *attile, attilia*, stores, tools, implements. Qu. *artillery*, by corruption.]

1. An instrument of manual operation, particularly such as are used by farmers and mechanics; as the *tools* of a joiner, cabinet-maker, smith or shoemaker.
2. A person used as an instrument by another person; *a word of reproach.* Men of intrigue always have their *tools*, by whose agency they accomplish their purposes.

TOOL, *v. t.* To shape with a tool. *Entick.*

TOOM, *a.* Empty. [*Not in use.*] *Wickliffe.*

TOOT, *v. i.* [Sax. *totian*, to shoot, to project; D. *toeten*, to blow the horn; *toet-horn*, a bugle horn; G. *düten;* Sw. *tiuta.* This word corresponds in elements with Gr. τιθημι and W. *dodi*, to put, set, lay, give; L. *do, dedi.* The Saxon expresses the primary sense.]

1. To stand out or be prominent. [*Not in use.*] *Howell.*
2. To make a particular noise with the tongue articulating with the root of the upper teeth, at the beginning and end of the sound; also, to sound a horn in a particular manner.

This writer should wear a *tooting* horn. *Howell.*

3. To peep; to look narrowly. [*Not in use, and probably a mistaken interpretation.*] *Spenser.*

TOOT, *v. t.* To sound; as, to *toot* the horn.

TOOT'ER, *n.* One who plays upon a pipe or horn. *B. Jonson.*

TOOTH, *n.* plu. *teeth.* [Sax. *toth*, plu. *teth.* It corresponds with W. *did* and *têth*, a *teat*, Gaelic, *did, dead*, and with *toot*, supra; signifying a shoot. If *n* is not radical in the L. *dens*, Gr. οδους, οδοντος, this is the same word.]

1. A bony substance growing out of the jaws of animals, and serving as the instrument of mastication. The *teeth* are also very useful in assisting persons in the utterance of words, and when well formed and sound, they are ornamental. The teeth of animals differ in shape, being destined for different offices. The front teeth in men and quadrupeds are called *incisors*, or *incisive* or *cutting teeth;* next to these are the pointed teeth, called *canine* or *dog teeth;* and on the sides of the jaws are the *molar teeth* or *grinders.*
2. Taste; palate.

These are not dishes for thy dainty *tooth.* *Dryden.*

3. A tine; a prong; something pointed and resembling an animal tooth; as the *tooth* of a rake, a comb, a card, a harrow, a saw, or of a wheel. The teeth of a wheel are sometimes called *cogs*, and are destined to catch corresponding parts of other wheels.

Tooth and nail, [by biting and scratching,] with one's utmost power; by all possible means. *L'Estrange.*

To the teeth, in open opposition; directly to one's face.

That I shall live, and tell him *to his teeth.* *Shak.*

To cast in the teeth, to retort reproachfully; to insult to the face. *Hooker.*

In spite of the teeth, in defiance of opposition; in opposition to every effort. *Shak.*

To show the teeth, to threaten.

When the law *shows her teeth*, but dares not bite. *Young.*

TOOTH, *v. t.* To furnish with teeth; as, to *tooth* a rake.

2. To indent; to cut into teeth; to jag; as, to *tooth* a saw.
3. To lock into each other. *Moxon.*

TOOTH'ACHE, *n.* [*tooth* and *ache.*] Pain in the teeth.

TOOTHACHE-TREE, *n.* A shrub of the genus Zanthoxylum. *Lee.*

TOOTH'-DRAWER, *n.* [*tooth* and *draw.*] One whose business is to extract teeth with instruments. *Wiseman.*

TOOTH'-DRAWING, *n.* The act of extracting a tooth; the practice of extracting teeth.

TOOTH'ED, *pp.* or *a.* Having teeth or jags. In *botany*, dentate; having projecting points, remote from each other, about the edge. *Martyn. Smith.*

TOOTH'-EDGE, *n.* [*tooth* and *edge.*] The sensation excited by grating sounds, and by the touch of certain substances. *Darwin.*

TOOTH'FUL, *a.* Palatable. [*Not in use.*]

TOOTH'LESS, *a.* Having no teeth. *Dryden.*

TOOTH'LETTED, *a.* In *botany*, denticulate; having very small teeth or notches; as a leaf. *Martyn.*

TOOK'PICK, } *n.* [*tooth* and *pick.*] An instrument for
TOOTH'PICKER, } cleaning the teeth of substances lodged between them. *Shak.*

TOOTH'SOME, *a.* Palatable; grateful to the taste. *Carew.*

TOOTH'SOMENESS, *n.* Pleasantness to the taste.

TOOTH'WORT, *n.* A plant whose roots resemble human teeth, such as the *Lathræa squamaria*, various species of Dentaria, the *Ophrys corallorrhiza*, &c. This name is also given to the lead-wort, of the genus Plumbago, from its toothed corol. *Cyc.*

TOOTH'Y, *a.* Toothed; having teeth. *Croxall.*

TOOT'ING, *ppr.* Sounding in a particular manner.

TOP, *n.* [Sax. D. Dan. *top;* Sw. *topp;* W. *tob* or *top; topiaw*, to top, to form a crest.]

1. The highest part of any thing; the upper end, edge or extremity; as the *top* of a tree; the *top* of a spire; the *top* of a house; the *top* of a mountain.
2. Surface; upper side; as the *top* of the ground.
3. The highest place; as the *top* of preferment. *Locke. Swift.*
4. The highest person; the chief. *Shak.*
5. The utmost degree.

The *top* of my ambition is to contribute to that work. *Pope.*
If you attain the *top* of your desires in fame— *Pope.*

6. The highest rank. Each boy strives to be at the *top* of his class, or at the *top* of the school.
7. The crown or upper surface of the head. *Shak.*
8. The hair on the crown of the head; the forelock. *Shak.*
9. The head of a plant. *Watts.*
10. [G. *topf.*] An inverted conoid which children play with by whirling it on its point, continuing the motion with a whip. *Shak.*
11. In *ship-building*, a sort of platform, surrounding the head of the lower mast and projecting on all sides. It serves to extend the shrouds, by which means they more effectually support the mast; and in ships of war, the top furnishes a convenient stand for swivels and small arms to annoy the enemy. *Cyc.*

TOP'-ARMOR, *n.* In *ships*, a railing on the top, supported by stanchions and equipped with netting.

TOP'-BLOCK, *n.* In *ships*, a block hung to an eye-bolt in the cap, used in swaying and lowering the top-mast.

TOP'-CHAIN, *n.* In *ships*, a chain to sling the lower yards in time of action, to prevent their falling when the ropes by which they are hung, are shot away.

TOP'-CLOTH, *n.* In *ships*, a piece of canvas used to cover the hammocks which are lashed to the top in action.

TOP'-DRAINING, *n.* The act or practice of draining the surface of land.

TOP'-DRESSING, *n.* A dressing of manure laid on the surface of land. *Cyc.*

TOP'FULL, *a.* [*top* and *full.*] Full to the brim. *Watts.*

TOP-GAL'LANT, *a.* [See *Top-sail.*]

2. Highest; elevated; splendid; as a *top-gallant* spark. *L'Estrange.*

TOP-HEAVY, *a. top'-hevy.* [*top* and *heavy.*] Having the top or upper part too heavy for the lower. *Wotton.*

TOP'-KNOT, *n.* [*top* and *knot.*] A knot worn by females on the top of the head.

TOP'LESS, *a.* Having no top; as a *topless* highth. *Chapman.*

TOP'MAN, *n.* [*top* and *man.*] The man who stands above in sawing.

2. In *ships*, a man standing in the top.

TOP'-MAST, *n.* In *ships*, the second mast, or that which is next above the lower mast. Above that is the top-gallant-mast.

TOP'-MOST, *a.* [*top* and *most.*] Highest; uppermost; as the *topmost* cliff; the *topmost* branch of a tree. *Dryden. Addison.*

TOP'-PROUD, *a.* [*top* and *proud.*] Proud to the highest degree. *Shak.*

TOP'-ROPE, *n.* A rope to sway up a top-mast, &c.

TOP'-SAIL, *n.* A sail extended across the top-mast, above which is the top-gallant-sail.

TOP'-SHAPED, *a.* In *botany*, turbinate.

TOP'-SOILING, *n.* The act or art of taking off the top-soil of land, before a canal is begun.

TOP'-STONE, *n.* A stone that is placed on the top, or which forms the top.

TOP'-TACKLE, *n.* A large tackle hooked to the lower end of the top-mast top-rope and to the deck. *Mar. Dict.*

TOP, *v. i.* To rise aloft; to be eminent; as lofty ridges and *topping* mountains. *Derham.*

2. To predominate; as *topping* passions; *topping* uneasiness.

3. To excel; to rise above others.

But write thy best and *top*— *Dryden.*

TOP, *v. t.* To cover on the top; to tip; to cap.

—A mount
Of alabaster, *topp'd* with golden spires. *Milton.*

Mountains *topp'd* with snow. *Waller.*

2. To rise above.

A gourd—climbing by the boughs twined about them, till it *topped* and covered the tree. *L'Estrange.*

Topping all others in boasting. *Shak.*

3. To outgo; to surpass.

4. To crop; to take off the top or upper part.

Top your rose trees a little with your knife near a leaf-bud. *Evelyn.*

So in America we say, to *top* corn, that is maiz, by cutting off the stalk just above the ear.

5. To rise to the top of; as, he *topped* the hill. *Denham.*

6. To perform eminently. [*Not in use.*]

TO'PAN, *n.* A name of the horned Indian raven, or rhinoceros bird. *Cyc.*

TO'PARCH, *n.* [Gr. τοπος, place, and αρχος, a chief.] The principal man in a place or country.

TO'PARCHY, *n.* A little state, consisting of a few cities or towns; a petty country governed by a toparch. Judea was formerly divided into ten *toparchies.*

TO'PAZ, *n.* [Gr. τοπαζιον.] A mineral, said to be so called from Topazos, a small isle in the Arabic gulf, where the Romans obtained a stone which they called by this name, but which is the chrysolite of the moderns. The topaz is of a yellowish color. It sometimes occurs in masses, but more generally crystalized in rectangular octahedrons. Topaz is valued as a gem or precious stone, and is used in jewelry. It consists of silex, fluoric acid and alumin, in the following proportions; alumin 57 parts, silex 34, and fluoric acid 7 or 8. *Dict. Nat. Hist.*

Of topaz there are three subspecies, common topaz, shorlite and physalite. *Jameson.*

TOPAZ'OLITE, *n.* A variety of precious garnet, of a topaz yellow color, or an olive green. *Ure. Cleaveland.*

TOPE, *n.* A fish of the shark kind, the *squalus galeus* of Linne. *Cyc.*

TOPE, *v. i.* [Fr. *toper.* Qu. *dip.*] To drink hard; to drink strong or spiritous liquors to excess.

If you *tope* in form, and treat— *Dryden.*

TO'PER, *n.* One who drinks to excess; a drunkard; a sot.

TOP'ET, *n.* A small bird, the crested titmouse.

N. B. The crested titmouse of Latham, *Parus bicolor*, is the toupet titmouse of Pennant. *Ed. Encyc.*

TOPH, **TOPH'IN**, } *n.* [from the Latin.] A kind of sandstone.

TOPHA'CEOUS, *a.* Gritty; sandy; rough; stony. *Arbuthnot.*

TO'PHET, *n.* [Heb תפה tophet, a drum.] Hell; so called from a place east of Jerusalem where children were burnt to Moloch, and where drums were used to drown their cries.

TO'PHI, *n.* Ducksten; a stone formed by earthy depositions; called also tufa or trass.

TOP'IARY, *a.* [L. *topiarius*, ornamented.] Shaped by clipping or cutting. *Butler.*

TOP'IC, *n.* [Gr. τοπος, place; L. *topicus, topica*; Sans. *topu.*]

1. Any subject of discourse or argument. The Scriptures furnish an unlimited number of *topics* for the preacher, and *topics* infinitely interesting.

2. In *rhetoric*, a probable argument drawn from the several circumstances and places of a fact. Aristotle wrote a book of *topics.* Cicero defines *topics* to be the art of finding arguments. *Cyc.*

3. Principle of persuasion.

Contumacious persons whom no *topics* can work upon. *Wilkins.*

4. In *medicine*, an external remedy; a remedy to be applied outwardly to a particular part of the body, as a plaster, a poultice, a blister and the like. *Cyc.*

TOP'IC, **TOP'ICAL**, } *a.* [supra.] Pertaining to a place; limited; local; as a *topical* remedy.

2. Pertaining to a topic or subject of discourse, or to a general head.

TOP'ICALLY, *adv.* Locally; with limitation to a part.

2. With application to a particular part; as a remedy *topically* applied.

TOPOG'RAPHER, *n.* [See *Topography.*] One who describes a particular place, town, city or tract of land.

TOPOGRAPH'IC, **TOPOGRAPH'ICAL**, } *a.* Pertaining to topography; descriptive of a place.

TOPOGRAPH'ICALLY, *adv.* In the manner of topography.

TOPOG'RAPHY, *n.* [Gr. τοπος, place, and γραφη, description.] The description of a particular place, city, town, manor, parish or tract of land. It is of more limited application than *chorography.*

TOP'PED, **TOPT**, } *pp.* or *a.* Covered on the top; capped; surpassed; cropped; having the top cut off.

TOP'PING, *ppr.* Covering the top; capping; surpassing; cropping; lopping.

2. *a.* Fine; gallant. *Johnson.*

[*But Johnson's definition is probably incorrect.*]

3. Proud; assuming superiority. [*This is the sense in which the common people of N. England use the word, and I believe the true sense, but it is not elegant.*]

TOP'PING, *n.* In *seamen's language*, the act of pulling one extremity of a yard higher than the other. *Mar. Dict.*

TOP'PING-LIFT, *n.* A large strong tackle employed to suspend or top the outer end of a gaff, or of the boom of a main-sail, in a brig or schooner. *Mar. Dict.*

TOP'PINGLY, *adv.* Proudly; with airs of disdain. [*Not an elegant word, nor much used.*]

TOP'PLE, *v. i.* [from *top.*] To fall forward; to pitch or tumble down.

Though castles *topple* on their warders' heads. *Shak.*

[*This word is used chiefly of children when beginning to walk.*]

TOP'PLING, *ppr.* Falling forward.

TOPSY-TUR'VY, *adv.* In an inverted posture; with the top or head downwards; as, to turn a carriage *topsy-turvy.* *South.*

TOQUET, *n.* *toka'.* [Fr. a cap.] A kind of bonnet or head dress for women.

TOR, *n.* [Sax. *tor*; L. *turris.*] A tower; a turret; also, a high pointed hill; *used in names.*

TORCH, *n.* [It. *torcia*; Sp. *antorcha*; Fr. *torche*; D. *toorts*; probably a twist; It. *torciare*, to twist, Sp. *torcêr*, W. *torçi*, L. *torqueo, tortus.*]

A light or luminary formed of some combustible substance, as of resinous wood or of candles.

They light the nuptial *torch.* *Milton.*

TORCH'-BEARER, *n.* [*torch* and *bear.*] One whose office is to carry a torch. *Sidney.*

TORCH'ER, *n.* One that gives light. [*Not used.*] *Shak.*

TORCH'-LIGHT, *n.* [*torch* and *light.*] The light of a torch or of torches.

2. A light kindled to supply the want of the sun. *Bacon.*

TORCH'-THISTLE, *n.* A plant of the genus Cactus. *Lee.*

The common name of a subdivision of the genus Cactus, called also *cereus*, from *cera*, wax, from the resemblance of the stems to a wax candle. *Torch-thistle* is from the prickly stems, used by the Indians for torches. *Cyc.*

TORCH'-WORT, *n.* A plant. *More.*

TORE, *pret.* of *tear.* He *tore* his robe.

TORE, *n.* [perhaps from *tear*; W. *tori*, to break.]

The dead grass that remains on mowing land in winter and spring. [*Used in New England.*] *Mortimer.*

TORE, *n.* [L. *torus.*] In *architecture*, a large round molding on the base of a column. It is distinguished from the astragal by its size. The bases of the Tuscan and Doric columns have only one tore, which is between the plinth and listel. In the Attic base there are two. *Cyc.*

TOREUMATOG'RAPHY, *n.* [Gr. τορευμα, sculpture, and γραφη, description.]

A description of ancient sculptures and basso-relievos. *Cyc.*

TOR'MENT, *n.* [Fr. *tourment*; L. *tormentum*; It. Sp. *tormento*; probably from the root of L. *torqueo, torno*, Eng. *tour*; that is, from twisting, straining.]

1. Extreme pain; anguish; the utmost degree of misery, either of body or mind.

The more I see
Pleasure about me, so much I feel
Torment within me. *Milton.*

Lest they also come into this place of *torment.* Luke xvi. Rev. ix. xiv.

2. That which gives pain, vexation or misery.

They brought to him all sick people that were taken with divers diseases and *torments.* Matt. iv.

3. An engine for casting stones. *Elyot.*

TORMENT', *v. t.* To put to extreme pain or anguish; to inflict excruciating pain and misery, either of body or mind.

Art thou come hither to *torment* us before the time? Matt. viii.

He shall be *tormented* with fire and brimstone. Rev. xiv.

2. To pain; to distress.

Lord, my servant lieth at home sick of the palsy, grievously *tormented*. Matt. viii.

3. To tease; to vex; to harass; as, to be *tormented* with importunities, or with petty annoyances.

4. To put into great agitation.

They soaring on main wing
Tormented all the air. [*Unusual.*] *Milton.*

TORMENT'ED, *pp.* Pained to extremity; teased; harassed.

TORMENT'IL, *n.* [Fr. *tormentille;* It. *tormentilla.*]
A genus of plants, the septfoil. The root is used in medicines as a powerful astringent, and for alleviating gripes or *tormina*, whence its name. *Cyc.*

TORMENT'ING, *ppr.* Paining to an extreme degree; inflicting severe distress and anguish; teasing; vexing.

TORMENT'ING, *n.* In *agriculture*, an imperfect sort of horse-hoeing. *Cyc.*

TORMENT'OR, *n.* He or that which torments; one who inflicts penal anguish or tortures. *Milton. Dryden.*

2. In *agriculture*, an instrument for reducing a stiff soil. *Cyc.*

TORN, *pp.* of *tear.*

Neither shall ye eat any flesh that is *torn* by the beasts in the field. Ex. xxii.

TORNA'DO, *n.* [from the root of *turn;* that is, a whirling wind. The Sp. Port. *tornada* is a return.]
A violent gust of wind, or a tempest, distinguished by a whirling motion. Tornadoes of this kind happen after extreme heat, and sometimes in the United States, rend up fences and trees, and in a few instances have overthrown houses and torn them to pieces. Tornadoes are usually accompanied with severe thunder, lightning and torrents of rain; but they are of short duration, and narrow in breadth.

TO'ROUS, *a.* [L. *torosus.*] In *botany*, protuberant; swelling in knobs, like the veins and muscles; as a *torous* pericarp. *Martyn.*

TORPE'DO, *n.* [L. from *torpeo*, to be numb.]
The cramp fish or electric ray, *Raia torpedo.* This fish is usually taken in forty fathoms water, on the coast of France and England, and in the Mediterranean. A touch of this fish occasions a numbness in the limb, accompanied with an indescribable and painful sensation, and is really an electric shock. When dead, the fish loses its power of producing this sensation. *Cyc.*

TOR'PENT, *a.* [L. *torpens, torpeo.*] Benumbed; torpid; having no motion or activity; incapable of motion.

A frail and *torpent* memory. *Evelyn.*

TOR'PENT, *n.* In *medicine*, that which diminishes the exertion of the irritative motions. *Darwin.*

TORPES'CENCE, *n.* A state of insensibility; torpidness; numbness; stupidity.

TORPES'CENT, *a.* [L. *torpescens.*] Becoming torpid or numb. *Shenstone.*

TOR'PID, *a.* [L. *torpidus, torpeo;* perhaps W. *torp*, a lump.]

1. Having lost motion or the power of exertion and feeling; numb; as a *torpid* limb.

Without heat all things would be *torpid*. *Ray.*

2. Dull; stupid; sluggish; inactive. The mind as well as the body becomes *torpid* by indolence. Impenitent sinners remain in a state of *torpid* security. *Barrington.*

TORPID'ITY, *n.* Torpidness.

TOR'PIDNESS, } *n.* The state of being torpid; numbness. Torpidness may amount to total insensibility or loss of sensation.
TOR'PITUDE, }

2. Dullness; inactivity; sluggishness; stupidity.

TOR'POR, *n.* [L.] Numbness; inactivity; loss of motion, or of the power of motion. Torpor may amount to a total loss of sensation, or complete insensibility. It may however be applied to the state of a living body which has not lost all power of feeling and motion.

2. Dullness; laziness; sluggishness; stupidity.

TORPORIF'IC, *a.* [L. *torpor* and *facio.*] Tending to produce torpor.

TORREFAC'TION, *n.* [Fr. from L. *torrefacio; torridus* and *facio.*]

1. The operation of drying by a fire.

2. In *metallurgy*, the operation of roasting ores.

3. In *pharmacy*, the drying or roasting of drugs on a metalline plate, placed over or before coals of fire, till they become friable to the fingers, or till some other desired effect is produced. *Cyc.*

TOR'REFIED, *pp.* Dried; roasted; scorched. *Torrefied earth*, in agriculture, is that which has undergone the action of fire. *Cyc.*

TOR'REFY, *v. t.* [L. *torrefacio;* L. *torridus, torreo*, and *facio;* Fr. *torrefier.*]

1. To dry by a fire. *Brown.*

2. In *metallurgy*, to roast or scorch, as metallic ores.

3. In *pharmacy*, to dry or parch, as drugs, on a metalline plate till they are friable, or are reduced to any state desired.

TOR'REFYING, *ppr.* Drying by a fire; roasting; parching.

TOR'RENT, *n.* [L. *torrens.* This is the participle of *torreo*, to parch. But the sense of the word *torrent*, allies it to the W. *tori*, to break, and the Eng. *tear.* They are all of one family, denoting violent action.]

1. A violent rushing stream of water or other fluid; a stream suddenly raised and running rapidly, as down a precipice; as a *torrent* of lava.

2. A violent or rapid stream; a strong current; as a *torrent* of vices and follies; a *torrent* of corruption.

Erasmus, that great injur'd name,
Stemm'd the wild *torrent* of a barb'rous age. *Pope*

TOR'RENT, *a.* Rolling or rushing in a rapid stream; as waves of *torrent* fire.

TORRICEL'LIAN, *a.* Pertaining to Torricelli, an Italian philosopher and mathematician, who discovered the true principle on which the barometer is constructed.

Torricellian tube, is a glass tube thirty or more inches in length, open at one end, and hermetically sealed at the other.

Torricellian vacuum, a vacuum produced by filling a tube with mercury, and allowing it to descend till it is counterbalanced by the weight of an equal column of the atmosphere, as in the barometer.

TOR'RID, *a.* [L. *torridus*, from *torreo*, to roast.]

1. Parched; dried with h at; as a *torrid* plain or desert.

2. Violently hot; burning or parching; as a *torrid* heat. *Milton.*

Torrid zone, in geography, that space or broad belt of the earth included between the tropics, over which the sun is vertical at some period every year, and where the heat is always great.

TOR'RIDNESS, *n.* The state of being very hot or parched.

TORSE, *n.* [Fr. *torse;* L. *tortus.*] In *heraldry*, a wreath.

TOR'SEL, *n.* [supra.] Any thing in a twisted form; as *torsels* for mantle-trees. *Moxon.*

TOR'SION, *n.* [L. *torsio*, from *torqueo*, to twist.] The act of turning or twisting.

Torsion balance, an instrument for estimating very minute forces by the motion of an index attached to the ends of two fine wires, which twist around each other. *D. Olmsted.*

TOR'SO, *n.* [It.] The trunk of a statue, mutilated of head and limbs; as the *torso* of Hercules.

TOR'STEN, *n.* An iron ore of a bright bluish black, &c.

TORT, *n.* [Fr. from L. *tortus*, twisted, from *torqueo.* The primary sense is to turn or strain, hence to twist.]

1. In *law*, any wrong or injury. *Torts* are injuries done to the person or property of another, as trespass, assault and battery, defamation and the like. *Blackstone.*

2. Mischief; calamity. [*Except in the legal sense above explained, it is obsolete.*] *Spenser.*

TORT'ILE, } *a.* [L. *tortilis.*] Twisted; wreathed; coiled. In botany, coiled like a rope; as a *tortile* awn. *Martyn.*
TORT'IL, }

TOR'TION, *n.* [L. *tortus.*] Torment; pain. [*Not in use.*] *Bacon.*

TOR'TIOUS, *a.* [from *tort.*] Injurious; done by wrong.

2. In *law*, implying tort, or injury for which the law gives damages.

TORT'IVE, *a.* [L. *tortus.*] Twisted; wreathed. *Shak.*

TORTOISE, *n. tor'tis.* [from L. *tortus*, twisted.]

1. An animal of the genus Testudo, covered with a shell or crust.

2. In *the military art*, a defense used by the ancients, formed by the troops arranging themselves in close order and placing their bucklers over their heads, making a cover resembling a tortoise-shell.

TOR'TOISE-SHELL, *n.* [*tortoise* and *shell.*] The shell or rather scales of the tortoise, used in inlaying and in various manufactures. *Cyc.*

TORTUOS'ITY, *n.* [from *tortuous.*] The state of being twisted or wreathed; wreath; flexure. *Brown.*

TORT'UOUS, *a.* [L. *tortuosus;* Fr. *tortueux.*]

1. Twisted; wreathed; winding; as a *tortuous* train; a *tortuous* leaf or corol, in botany. *Milton. Martyn.*

2. Tortious. [*Not used.*] [See *Tortious.*] *Spenser.*

TORT'UOUSNESS, *n.* The state of being twisted.

TORT'URE, *n.* [Fr. *torture;* It. Sp. *tortura;* from L. *tortus, torqueo*, to twist, W. *torçi;* probably from the root of *turn.* See *Tour.*]

1. Extreme pain; anguish of body or mind; pang; agony; torment.

Ghastly spasm or racking *torture*. *Milton.*

2. Severe pain inflicted judicially, either as a punishment for a crime, or for the purpose of extorting a confession from an accused person. Torture may be and is inflicted in a variety of ways, as by water or fire, or by the boot or thumbkin. But the most usual mode is by the rack or wheel. *Paley. Cyc.*

TORT'URE, *v. t.* To pain to extremity; to torment.

2. To punish with torture; to put to the rack; as, to *torture* an accused person.

3. To vex; to harass. *Addison.*

4. To keep on the stretch, as a bow. [*Not in use.*] *Bacon.*

TORT'URED, *pp.* Tormented; stretched on the wheel; harassed.

TORT'URER, *n.* One who tortures; a tormenter. *Bacon.*

TORT'URING, *ppr.* Tormenting; stretching on the rack; vexing.

TORT'URINGLY, *adv.* So as to torture or torment. *Beaum.*

TORT'UROUS, *a.* Tormenting. [*Not in use.*] *More.*

TOR'ULOSE, *a.* In *botany*, swelling a little. *Martyn.*

TO'RUS, *n.* A molding. [See *Tore.*]

TORV'ITY, *n.* [L. *torvitas*; from twisting, supra.] Sourness or severity of countenance.

TORV'OUS, *a.* [L. *torvus*, from the root of *torqueo*, to twist.]

Sour of aspect; stern; of a severe countenance. *Derham.*

TO'RY, *n.* [said to be an Irish word, denoting a robber; perhaps from *tor*, a bush, as the Irish banditti lived in the mountains or among trees.]

The name given to an adherent to the ancient constitution of England and to the apostolical hierarchy. The tories form a party which are charged with supporting more arbitrary principles in government than the whigs, their opponents.

In America, during the revolution, those who opposed the war, and favored the claims of Great Britain, were called *tories.*

TO'RYISM, *n.* The principles of the tories.

TOSE, *v. t. s* as *z.* To tease wool. [*Not in use or local.*]

TOSS, *v. t.* pret. and pp. *tossed* or *tost.* [W. *tosiaw*, to toss, to jerk.]

1. To throw with the hand; particularly, to throw with the palm of the hand upward, or to throw upward; as, to *toss* a ball.

2. To throw with violence. *Shak.*

3. To lift or throw up with a sudden or violent motion; as, to *toss* the head; or to *toss* up the head.

He *toss'd* his arm aloft. *Addison.*

4. To cause to rise and fall; as, to be *tossed* on the waves.

We, being exceedingly *tossed* with a tempest— Acts xxvii.

5. To move one way and the other. Prov. xxi.

6. To agitate; to make restless.

Calm region once,
And full of peace, now *tost* and turbulent. *Milton.*

7. To keep in play; to tumble over; as, to spend four years in *tossing* the rules of grammar. *Ascham.*

TOSS, *v. i.* To fling; to roll and tumble; to writhe; to be in violent commotion.

To *toss* and fling, and to be restless, only frets and enrages our pain. *Tillotson.*

2. To be tossed. *Shak.*

To toss up, is to throw a coin into the air and wager on what side it will fall. *Brampston.*

TOSS, *n.* A throwing upward or with a jerk; the act of tossing; as the *toss* of a ball.

2. A throwing up of the head; a particular manner of raising the head with a jerk. It is much applied to horses, and may be applied to an affected manner of raising the head in men.

TOSS'ED, *pp.* Thrown upward suddenly or with a jerk; made to rise and fall suddenly.

TOSS'EL. [See *Tassel.*]

TOSS'ER, *n.* One who tosses.

TOSS'ING, *ppr.* Throwing upward with a jerk; raising suddenly; as the head.

TOSS'ING, *n.* The act of throwing upward; a rising and falling suddenly; a rolling and tumbling.

Dire was the *tossing*, deep the groans. *Milton.*

TOSS'-POT, *n.* [*toss* and *pot.*] A toper; one habitually given to strong drink.

TOST, *pret.* and *pp.* of *toss.*

In a troubled sea of passion *tost.* *Milton.*

TO'TAL, *a.* [Fr.; L. *totalis, totus*; W. *twt.*]

1. Whole; full; complete; as *total* darkness; a *total* departure from the evidence; a *total* loss; the *total* sum or amount.

2. Whole; not divided.

—Myself the *total* crime. *Milton.*

TO'TAL, *n.* The whole; the whole sum or amount. These sums added, make the grand *total* of five millions.

TOTAL'ITY, *n.* [Fr. *totalité.*] The whole sum; whole quantity or amount.

TO'TALLY, *adv.* Wholly; entirely; fully; completely; as, to be *totally* exhausted; all hope *totally* failed; he was *totally* absorbed in thought.

TO'TALNESS, *n.* Entireness.

TOTE, *v. t.* To carry or convey. [*A word used in slaveholding countries; said to have been introduced by the blacks.*]

TOT'TER, *v. i.* [This may be allied to *titter.*]

1. To shake so as to threaten a fall; to vacillate; as, an old man *totters* with age; a child *totters* when he begins to walk.

2. To shake; to reel; to lean.

As a bowing wall shall ye be, and as a *tottering* fence. Ps. lxii.

Troy nods from high, and *totters* to her fall. *Dryden.*

TOT'TERING, *ppr.* Shaking, as threatening a fall; vacillating; reeling; inclining.

TOT'TERY, *a.* Shaking; trembling or vacillating as if about to fall; unsteady. [*Not in use.*] [Spenser wrote *tottle*, as the common people of New England still pronounce it.]

TOU'CAN, *n.* A fowl of the genus Ramphastos; also, a constellation of nine small stars. *Cyc.*

TOUCH, *v. t. tuch.* [Fr. *toucher*; Arm. *touicha, touchan* or *touchein*; Goth. *tekan, attekan*; G. *ticken*; D. *tekken*; Sp. Port. *tocar*; It. *toccare*; Gr. *θιγω*; L. *tango*, originally *tago*, [our vulgar *tag*;] pret. *tetigi*, pp. *tactus.* The sense is to thrust or strike. Class Dg. It appears by the laws of Numa Pompilius, that in his days this word was written without *n.* "Pellex aram Junonis ne *tagito.*"]

1. To come in contact with; to hit or strike against.

He *touched* the hollow of his thigh. Gen. xxxii. Matt. ix.

Esther drew near, and *touched* the top of the scepter. Esth. v.

2. To perceive by the sense of feeling.

Nothing but body can be *touch'd* or *touch.* *Creech.*

3. To come to; to reach; to attain to.

The god vindictive doom'd them never more,
Ah men unbless'd! to *touch* that natal shore. *Pope.*

4. To try, as gold with a stone.

Wherein I mean to *touch* your love indeed— *Shak.*

5. To relate to; to concern.

The quarrel *toucheth* none but thee alone. *Shak.*

[*This sense is now nearly obsolete.*]

6. To handle slightly. *Brown.*

7. To meddle with. I have not *touched* the books.

8. To affect.

What of sweet
Hath *touch'd* my sense, flat seems to this. *Milton.*

9. To move; to soften; to melt.

The tender sire was *touch'd* with what he said. *Addison.*

10. To mark or delineate slightly.

The lines, though *touch'd* but faintly— *Pope.*

11. To infect; as men *touched* with pestilent diseases. [*Little used.*] *Bacon.*

12. To make an impression on.

Its face must be—so hard that the file will not *touch* it. *Moxon.*

13. To strike, as an instrument of music; to play on.

They *touch'd* their golden harps. *Milton.*

14. To influence by impulse; to impel forcibly.

No decree of mine,
To *touch* with lightest moment of impulse
His free will. *Milton.*

15. To treat slightly. In his discourse, he barely *touched* upon the subject deemed the most interesting.

16. To afflict or distress. Gen. xxvi.

To touch up, to repair; or to improve by slight touches or emendations. *Addison.*

To touch the wind, in seamen's language, is to keep the ship as near the wind as possible.

TOUCH, *v. i. tuch.* To be in contact with; to be in a state of junction, so that no space is between. Two spheres *touch* only at points. *Johnson.*

2. To fasten on; to take effect on.

Strong waters will *touch* upon gold, that will not *touch* silver. *Bacon.*

3. To treat of slightly in discourse. *Addison.*

To touch at, to come or go to, without stay. The ship *touched at* Lisbon.

The next day we *touched at* Sidon. Acts xxvii.

To touch on or *upon*, to mention slightly.

If the antiquaries have *touched upon* it, they have immediately quitted it. *Addison.*

2. In the sense of *touch at.* [*Little used.*]

TOUCH, *n. tuch.* Contact; the hitting of two bodies; the junction of two bodies at the surface, so that there is no space between them. The mimosa shrinks at the slightest *touch.*

2. The sense of feeling; one of the five senses. We say, a thing is cold or warm to the *touch*; silk is soft to the *touch*,

The spider's *touch* how exquisitely fine! *Pope.*

3. The act of touching. The *touch* of cold water made him shrink.

4. The state of being touched.

—That never *touch* was welcome to thy hand
Unless I touch'd. *Shak.*

5. Examination by a stone. *Shak.*

6. Test; that by which any thing is examined.

Equity, the true *touch* of all laws. *Carew.*

7. Proof; tried qualities.

My friends of noble *touch.* *Shak.*

8. Single act of a pencil on a picture.

Never give the least *touch* with your pencil, till you have well examined your design. *Dryden.*

9. Feature; lineament.

Of many faces, eyes and hearts,
To have the *touches* dearest priz'd. *Shak.*

10. Act of the hand on a musical instrument.

Soft stillness and the night
Become the *touches* of sweet harmony. *Shak.*

11. Power of exciting the affections.

Not alone
The death of Fulvia, with more urgent *touches,*
Do strongly speak t' us. *Shak.*

12. Something of passion or affection.

He both makes intercession to God for sinners, and exercises dominion over all men, with a true, natural and sensible *touch* of mercy. *Hooker.*

13. Particular application of any thing to a person.

Speech of *touch* towards others should be sparingly used. *Obs.* *Bacon.*

14. A stroke; as a *touch* of raillery; a satiric *touch.* *Addison.*

15. Animadversion; censure; reproof.

I never bore any *touch* of conscience with greater regret. *K. Charles.*

16. Exact performance of agreement.

I keep *touch* with my promise. *Obs.* *More.*

17. A small quantity intermixed.

Madam, I have a *touch* of your condition. *Shak.*

18. A hint; suggestion; slight notice.

A small *touch* will put him in mind of them. *Bacon.*

19. A cant word for a slight essay.

Print my preface in such form as, in the bookseller's phrase, will make a sixpenny *touch.* [*Not in use.*] *Swift.*

20. In *music,* the resistance of the keys of an instrument to the fingers; as a heavy *touch,* or light *touch.*

21. In *music,* an organ is said to have a good *touch* or stop, when the keys close well.

22. In *ship-building,* touch is the broadest part of a plank worked top and butt; or the middle of a plank worked anchor-stock fashion; also, the angles of the stern timbers at the counters. *Cyc.*

TOUCHABLE, *a. tuch'able.* That may be touched; tangible.

TOUCH-HOLE, *n. tuch'-hole.* [*touch* and *hole.*]

The vent of a cannon or other species of fire-arms, by which fire is communicated to the powder of the charge. It is now called the vent.

TOUCHINESS, *n. tuch'iness.* [from *touchy.*] Peevishness; irritability; irascibility. *King Charles.*

TOUCHING, *ppr. tuch'ing.* Coming in contact with; hitting; striking; affecting.

2. Concerning; relating to; with respect to.

Now as *touching* things offered to idols— 1 Cor. viii.

3. *a.* Affecting; moving; pathetic.

TOUCHING, *n. tuch'ing.* Touch; the sense of feeling.

TOUCHINGLY, *adv. tuch'ingly.* In a manner to move the passions; feelingly. *Garth.*

TOUCH-ME-NOT, *n.* A plant of the genus Impatiens, and another of the genus Momordica.

TOUCH-NEEDLE, *n. tuch'-needle.* [*touch* and *needle.*]

Touch-needles are small bars of gold, silver and copper, each pure and in all proportions, prepared for trying gold and silver by the touchstone, by comparison with the mark they leave upon it. *Cyc.*

TOUCHSTONE, *n. tuch'stone.* [*touch* and *stone.*]

1. A stone by which metals are examined; a black, smooth, glossy stone. The touchstone of the ancients was called *lapis Lydius,* from Lydia in Asia Minor, where it was found.

2. Any test or criterion by which the qualities of a thing are tried; as money, the *touchstone* of common honesty. *L'Estrange.*

Irish touchstone, is the basalt, the stone which composes the Giant's causey. This is said also to be an excellent touchstone.

TOUCH-WOOD, *n. tuch'-wood.* [*touch* and *wood.*]

Decayed wood, used like a match for taking fire from a spark. *Howell.*

TOUCHY, *a. tuch'y.* [vulgarly *techy.*] Peevish; irritable; irascible; apt to take fire. [*Not elegant.*] *Arbuthnot.*

TOUGH, *a. tuf.* [Sax. *toh*; D. *taai*; G. *zähe.* Qu. *tight, thick.*]

1. Having the quality of flexibility without brittleness; yielding to force without breaking. The ligaments of animals and of India rubber are remarkably *tough. Tough* timber, like young ash, is the most proper for the shafts and springs of a carriage.

2. Firm; strong; not easily broken; able to endure hardship; as an animal of a *tough* frame. *Dryden.*

3. Not easily separated; viscous; clammy; tenacious; ropy; as *tough* phlegm.

4. Stiff; not flexible.

TOUGHEN, *v. i. tuf'n.* To grow tough. *Mortimer.*

TOUGHEN, *v. t. tuf'n.* To make tough.

TOUGHLY, *adv. tuf'ly.* In a tough manner.

TOUGHNESS, *n. tuf'ness.* The quality of a substance which renders it in some degree flexible, without brittleness or liability to fracture; flexibility with a firm adhesion of parts; as the *toughness* of steel. *Dryden.*

2. Viscosity; tenacity; clamminess; glutinousness; as the *toughness* of mucus.

3. Firmness; strength of constitution or texture. *Shak.*

TOUPE'E, } **TOUPET,** } *n.* [Fr. *toupet,* from *touffe,* a *tuft,* or its root.] A little tuft; a curl or artificial lock of hair.

TÖUR, *n.* [Fr. *tour,* a turn; D. *toer*; Heb. תור, Ar. تار taura, to go round. Class Dr. No. 38.]

1. Literally, a going round; hence, a journey in a circuit; as the *tour* of Europe; the *tour* of France or England.

2. A turn; a revolution; as the *tours* of the heavenly bodies. [*Not now in use.*]

3. A turn; as a *tour* of duty; a military use of the word.

4. A tress or circular border of hair on the head, worn sometimes by both sexes. *Cyc.*

5. A tower. [*Not in use.*]

TÖURIST, *n.* One who makes a tour, or performs a journey in a circuit.

TÖURMALIN, } **TUR'MALIN,** } *n.* [probably a corruption of *tournamal,* a name given to this stone in Ceylon.]

In *mineralogy,* a silicious stone, sometimes used as a gem by jewelers, remarkable for exhibiting electricity by heat or friction. It occurs in long prisms deeply striated. Its fracture is conchoidal, and its internal luster vitreous. *Cyc.*

Turmalin is considered as a variety of shorl. *Cleaveland.*

TÖURN, *n.* The sherif's turn or court; also, a spinning wheel. [*Not American.*]

TOURNAMENT, *n. turn'ament.* [from Fr. *tourner,* to turn.]

A martial sport or exercise formerly performed by cavaliers to show their address and bravery. These exercises were performed on horseback, and were accompanied with tilting, or attacks with blunted lances and swords. *Bacon.*

TOURNEQUET, *n. turn'eket.* [Fr.] A surgical instrument or bandage which is straitened or relaxed with a screw, and used to check hemorrhages. *Cyc.*

TOURNEY, *n. turn'ey.* A tournament, supra.

TOURNEY, *v. i. turn'ey.* To tilt; to perform tournaments. *Spenser.*

TOUSE, *v. t. touz.* [G. *zausen,* to pull.] To pull; to haul; to tear. [Hence *Towser.*]

As a bear whom angry curs have *tous'd.* *Spenser.*

TOUS'EL, *v. t. s* as *z.* The same as *touse*; to put into disorder; to tumble; to tangle. [*Used by the common people of New England.*]

TÖW, *v. t.* [Sax. *teogan, teon*; Fr. *touer*; G. *ziehen,* to pull; *zug,* a pulling, a *tug*; L. *duco.* See Class Dg. No. 62. 64.]

To drag, as a boat or ship, through the water by means of a rope. *Towing* is performed by another boat or ship, or by men on shore, or by horses. Boats on canals are usually *towed* by horses.

TÖW, *n.* [Sax. *tow*; Fr. *etoupe*; L. *stupa*; It. *stoppa*; Sp. *estopa.* It coincides with *stuff.*]

The coarse and broken part of flax or hemp, separated from the finer part by the hatchel or swingle.

TÖWAGE, *n.* [from *tow,* the verb.] The act of towing.

2. The price paid for towing. *Walsh.*

TO'WARD, } **TO'WARDS,** } *prep.* [Sax. *toward*; *to* and *ward, weard*; L. *versus, verto.*]

1. In the direction to.

He set his face *toward* the wilderness. Num. xxiv.

2. With direction to, in a moral sense; with respect to; regarding.

His eye shall be evil *toward* his brother. Deut. xxviii.

Herein do I exercise myself to have always a conscience void of offense *toward* God and *toward* men. Acts xxiv.

Hearing of thy love and faith which thou hast *toward* the Lord Jesus Christ, and *toward* all saints. Philemon 5.

3. With ideal tendency to.

This was the first alarm England received *towards* any trouble. *Clarendon.*

4. Nearly.

I am *towards* nine years older since I left you. *Swift.*

TO'WARD, TO'WARDS, } *adv.* Near; at hand; in a state of preparation.

TO'WARD, *a.* Ready to do or learn; not froward; apt; as a *toward* youth.

TO'WARDLINESS, *n.* [from *towardly.*] Readiness to do or learn; aptness; docility

The beauty and *towardliness* of these children moved her brethren to envy. *Raleigh.*

TO'WARDLY, *a.* Ready to do or learn; apt; docile; tractable; compliant with duty. *Bacon.*

TO'WARDNESS, *n.* Docility; towardliness. *South.*

TOW'EL, *n.* [Fr. *touaille;* Gaelic, *tubailt;* It. *tovaglia;* Port. *toalha;* Arm. *touailhon;* Sp. *toballa, tobaja, toaja,* or *toalla.* In Italian the word signifies a table cloth.]
A cloth used for wiping the hands and for other things.

TOW'ER, *n.* [Sax. *tor, tirre;* Ir. *tor;* Fr. Arm. *tour;* Sp. It. Port. *torre;* W. *twr,* a heap or pile; Corn. *id.;* G. *thurm;* D. *torm;* L. *turris;* Gr. τυρσις; Heb. טורה. Class Dr. No. 24.]

1. A building, either round or square, raised to a considerable elevation and consisting of several stories. When towers are erected with other buildings, as they usually are, they rise above the main edifice. They are generally flat on the top, and thus differ from steeples or spires. Before the invention of guns, places were fortified with *towers,* and attacked with movable *towers* mounted on wheels, which placed the besiegers on a level with the walls. *Cyc.*
2. A citadel; a fortress. Ps. lxi.
3. A high head dress. *Hudibras.*
4. High flight; elevation. *Johnson.*

Tower bastion, in fortification, a small tower in the form of a bastion, with rooms or cells underneath for men and guns. *Cyc.*

Tower of London, a citadel containing an arsenal. It is also a palace where the kings of England have sometimes lodged. *Cyc.*

TOW'ER, *v. i.* To rise and fly high; to soar; to be lofty.

Sublime thoughts, which *tower* above the clouds. *Locke.*

TOW'ERED, *a.* Adorned or defended by towers. *Milton.*

TOW'ERING, *ppr.* Rising aloft; mounting high; soaring.

2. *a.* Very high; elevated; as a *towering* highth.

TOW'ER-MUSTARD, *n.* [*tower* and *mustard.*] A plant of the genus Turritis. *Lee.*

TOW'ERY, *a.* Having towers; adorned or defended by towers; as *towery* cities. *Pope.*

TŌWING, *ppr.* Drawing on water, as a boat.

TŌWING-PATH, *n.* A path used by men or horses that tow boats.

To wit, to know; namely.

TŌW-LINE, *n.* [*tow* and *line.*] A small hawser, used to tow a ship, &c.

TOWN, *n.* [Sax. *tun;* W. *din, dinas,* a fortified hill, a fort; Gaelic, *dun;* Sax. *dun, dune,* a hill, whence *downs.* The Sax. *tun* signifies an inclosure, a garden, a village, a town, and *tynan* is to shut, to make fast; G. *zaun,* a hedge; D. *tun,* a garden. If the original word signified a hill, the sense is a mass or collection. But probably the original word signified fortified, and the rude fortifications of uncivilized men were formed with hedges and stakes; hence also a garden. See *Garden* and *Tun.*]

1. Originally, a walled or fortified place; a collection of houses inclosed with walls, hedges or pickets for safety. Rahab's house was on the *town* wall. Josh. ii.

A *town* that hath gates and bars. 1 Sam. xxiii.

2. Any collection of houses, larger than a village. In this use the word is very indefinite, and a *town* may consist of twenty houses, or of twenty thousand.
3. In *England,* any number of houses to which belongs a regular market, and which is not a city or the see of a bishop. *Johnson.*

A town, in modern times, is generally without walls, which is the circumstance that usually distinguishes it from a city. *Cyc.*

In *the United States,* the circumstance that distinguishes a town from a city, is generally that a city is incorporated with special privileges, and a town is not. But a city is often called a *town.*

4. The inhabitants of a town. The *town* voted to send two representatives to the legislature, or they voted to lay a tax for repairing the highways. *New England. Chapman.*
5. In *popular usage,* in America, a township; the whole territory within certain limits.
6. In *England,* the court end of London. *Pope.*
7. The inhabitants of the metropolis. *Pope.*
8. The metropolis. The gentleman lives in *town* in winter; in summer he lives in the country. The same form of expression is used in regard to other populous towns.

TOWN'-CLERK, *n.* [*town* and *clerk.*] An officer who keeps the records of a town, and enters all its official proceedings.

TOWN-CRI'ER, *n.* [*town* and *cry.*] A public crier; one who makes proclamation. *Shak.*

TOWN'-HOUSE, *n.* [*town* and *house.*] The house where the public business of the town is transacted by the inhabitants in legal meeting. *New England.*

2. A house in town; in opposition to a house in the country.

TOWN'ISH, *a.* Pertaining to the inhabitants of a town; like the town.

TOWN'LESS, *a.* Having no town. *Howell.*

TOWN'SHIP, *n.* The district or territory of a town. In *New England,* the states are divided into townships of five, six, seven, or perhaps ten miles square, and the inhabitants of such townships are invested with certain powers for regulating their own affairs, such as repairing roads, providing for the poor, &c.

TOWNS'MAN, *n.* [*town* and *man.*] An inhabitant of a place; or one of the same town with another.

2. A selectman; an officer of the town in New England, who assists in managing the affairs of the town. [See *Selectmen.*]

TOWN'-TALK, *n.* [*town* and *talk.*] The common talk of a place, or the subject of common conversation.

TŌW-ROPE, *n.* [*tow* and *rope.*] Any rope used in towing ships or boats. *Mar. Dict.*

TOWS'ER, *n.* [from *touse.*] The name of a dog.

TOX'ICAL, *a.* [L. *toxicum.*] Poisonous. [*Little used.*]

TOXICOL'OGY, *n.* [Gr. τοξικον, poison, and λογος, discourse.]
A discourse on poisons; or the doctrine of poisons. *Orfila. Coxe.*

TOY, *n.* [Qu. D. *tooi,* tire, ornament.]

1. A plaything for children; a bawble.
2. A trifle; a thing for amusement, but of no real value.
3. An article of trade of little value.

They exchange gold and pearl for *toys.* *Abbot.*

4. Matter of no importance.

Nor light and idle *toys* my lines may vainly swell. *Drayton.*

5. Folly; trifling practice; silly opinion.
6. Amorous dalliance; play; sport. *Milton.*
7. An old story; a silly tale. *Shak.*
8. Slight representation; as the *toy* of novelty. *Hooker.*
9. Wild fancy; odd conceit. *Shak.*

TOY, *v. i.* [Dan. *töver,* Sw. *töfva,* to stay, to tarry, to dally. This seems to be the true origin of *toy,* supra.] To dally amorously; to trifle; to play.

TOY, *v. t.* To treat foolishly. [*Not used.*] *Dering.*

TOY'ER, *n.* One who toys; one who is full of trifling tricks.

TOY'FUL, *a.* Full of trifling play. *Donne.*

TOY'ING, *ppr.* Dallying; trifling.

TOY'ISH, *a.* Trifling; wanton. *Crowley.*

TOY'ISHNESS, *n.* Disposition to dalliance or trifling.

TOY'MAN, *n.* [*toy* and *man.*] One that deals in toys.

TOY'SHOP, *n.* [*toy* and *shop.*] A shop where toys are sold.

TŌZE, *v. t.* To pull by violence. [See *Touse.*]

TRACE, *n.* [Fr. *id.;* It. *traccia;* Sp. *traza;* L. *tractus, tracto.* See *Track,* and the verb *Trace.*]

1. A mark left by any thing passing; a footstep; a track; a vestige; as the *trace* of a carriage or sled; the *trace* of a man or of a deer.
2. Remains; a mark, impression or visible appearance of any thing left when the thing itself no longer exists. We are told that there are no *traces* of ancient Babylon now to be seen.

The shady empire shall retain no *trace*
Of war or blood, but in the sylvan chase. *Pope.*

TRACE, *n.* [Fr. *tirasse;* or W. *tres.* See *Trestle.*]

Traces, in a harness, are the straps, chains or ropes by which a carriage or sleigh is drawn by horses. [Locally these are called *tugs;* Sax. *teogan*, to draw.]

TRACE, *v. t.* [Fr. *tracer;* It. *tracciare;* Sp. *trazare;* L. *tracto*, from *traho*, Eng. to *draw*, to *drag.*]

1. To mark out; to draw or delineate with marks; as, to *trace* a figure with a pencil; to *trace* the outline of any thing.

2. To follow by some mark that has been left by something which has preceded; to follow by footsteps or tracks.

You may *trace* the deluge quite round the globe. *Burnet.*

I feel thy power to *trace* the ways
Of highest agents. *Milton.*

3. To follow with exactness.

That servile path thou nobly do'st decline,
Of *tracing* word by word, and line by line. *Denham.*

4. To walk over.

We do *trace* this alley up and down. *Shak.*

TRA'CEABLE, *a.* That may be traced. *Drummond.*

TRA'CED, *pp.* Marked out; delineated; followed.

TRA'CER, *n.* One that traces or follows by marks.

TRA'CERY, *n.* Ornamental stone work. *Warton.*

TRA'CHEA, *n.* [Low L. from Gr. τραχυς, rough.] In *anatomy*, the windpipe.

TRA'CHEAL, *a.* Pertaining to the trachea or windpipe; as the *tracheal* artery. *Coxe.*

TRA'CHEOCELE, *n.* [*trachea* and κηλη, a tumor.]

An enlargement of the thyroid gland; bronchocele or goiter. *Cyc.*

TRACHEOT'OMY, *n.* [*trachea* and τεμνω, to cut.]

In *surgery*, the operation of making an opening into the windpipe. *Cyc.*

TRA'CHYTE, *n.* [Gr. τραχυς, rough.] A species of volcanic rock, composed of crystals of glassy feldspar, sometimes with crystals of hornblend, mica, iron pyrite, &c. *Daubeny. Journ. of Science.*

TRACHYT'IC, *a.* Pertaining to trachyte, or consisting of it.

TRA'CING, *ppr.* [from *trace.*] Marking out; drawing in lines; following by marks or footsteps.

Tracing lines, in a ship, are lines passing through a block or thimble, and used to hoist a thing higher.

TRA'CING, *n.* Course; regular track or path. *Davies.*

TRACK, *n.* [It. *traccia;* Sp. *traza;* Fr. *trace.* See *Trace.* *Track* is properly a mark made by drawing, not by stepping; the latter is a derivative sense.]

1. A mark left by something that has passed along; as the *track* of a ship, a wake; the *track* of a meteor; the *track* of a sled or sleigh.

2. A mark or impression left by the foot, either of man or beast. Savages are said to be wonderfully sagacious in finding the *tracks* of men in the forest.

3. A road; a beaten path.

Behold Torquatus the same *track* pursue. *Dryden.*

4. Course; way; as the *track* of a comet.

TRACK, *v. t.* To follow when guided by a trace, or by the footsteps, or marks of the feet; as, to *track* a deer in the snow.

2. To tow; to draw a boat on the water in a canal.

TRACK'ED, *pp.* Followed by the footsteps.

TRACK'ING, *ppr.* Following by the impression of the feet; drawing a boat; towing.

TRACK'LESS, *a.* Having no track; marked by no footsteps; untrodden; as a *trackless* desert.

TRACK'-ROAD, *n.* [*track* and *road.*] A towing-path. *Cyc.*

TRACK'-SCOUT, *n.* [*track* and D. *schuit*, boat.]

A boat or vessel employed on the canals in Holland, usually drawn by a horse. *Cyc.*

TRACT, *n.* [L. *tractus;* It. *tratto;* Fr. *trait;* from L. *traho*, Fr. *traire*, to draw.]

1. Something drawn out or extended.

2. A region, or quantity of land or water, of indefinite extent. We may apply *tract* to the sandy and barren desert of Syria and Arabia, or to the narrow vales of Italy and Sardinia. We say, a rich *tract* of land in Connecticut or Ohio, a stony *tract*, or a mountainous *tract.* We apply *tract* to a single farm, or to a township or state.

3. A treatise; a written discourse or dissertation of indefinite length, but generally not of great extent.

4. In *hunting*, the trace or footing of a wild beast. *Cyc.*

5. Treatment; exposition. [*Not in use.*] *Shak.*

6. Track. [*Not in use.*]

7. Continuity or extension of any thing; as a *tract* of speech. [*Not much used.*]

8. Continued or protracted duration; length; extent; as a long *tract* of time. *Milton.*

TRACT, *v. t.* To trace out; to draw out. [*Not in use.*]

TRACTABIL'ITY, *n.* [from *tractable.*] The quality or state of being tractable or docile; docility; tractableness. *Beddoes.*

TRACT'ABLE, *a.* [L. *tractabilis*, from *tracto*, to handle or lead; Fr. *traitable;* It. *trattabile.*]

1. That may be easily led, taught or managed; docile; manageable; governable; as *tractable* children; a *tractable* learner. *Locke.*

2. Palpable; such as may be handled; as *tractable* measures. *Holder.*

TRACT'ABLENESS, *n.* The state or quality of being tractable or manageable; docility; as the *tractableness* of children. *Locke.*

TRACT'ABLY, *adv.* In a tractable manner; with ready compliance.

TRACT'ATE, *n.* [L. *tractatus.*] A treatise; a tract. [*Not now in use.*] *Brown. Hale.*

TRACTA'TION, *n.* [L. *tractatio.*] Treatment or handling of a subject; discussion. *Bp. Hall.*

TRACTA'TRIX, *n.* In *geometry*, a curve line.

TRACT'ILE, *a.* [L. *tractus.*] Capable of being drawn out in length; ductile.

Bodies are *tractile* or intractile. *Bacon.*

TRACTIL'ITY, *n.* The quality of being tractile; ductility. *Derham.*

TRAC'TION, *n.* [L. *tractus, traho.*] The act of drawing, or state of being drawn; as the *traction* of a muscle. *Holder.*

2. Attraction; a drawing towards. *Cyc.*

TRACT'OR, *n.* That which draws, or is used for drawing. *Journ. of Science.*

TRADE, *n.* [Sp. Port. *trato; tratar*, to handle, to trade; It. *tratta, trattare;* from L. *tracto*, to handle, use, *treat.* The Fr. *traite, traiter*, are the same words.]

1. The act or business of exchanging commodities by barter; or the business of buying and selling for money; commerce; traffick; barter. Trade comprehends every species of exchange or dealing, either in the produce of land, in manufactures, in bills or money. It is however chiefly used to denote the barter or purchase and sale of goods, wares and merchandise, either by wholesale or retail. Trade is either *foreign*, or *domestic* or *inland.* *Foreign* trade consists in the exportation and importation of goods, or the exchange of the commodities of different countries. *Domestic* or *home* trade is the exchange or buying and selling of goods within a country. Trade is also by the wholesale, that is, by the package or in large quantities, or it is by retail, or in small parcels. The *carrying* trade is that of transporting commodities from one country to another by water.

2. The business which a person has learned and which he carries on for procuring subsistence or for profit; occupation; particularly, mechanical employment; distinguished from the liberal arts and learned professions, and from agriculture. Thus we speak of the *trade* of a smith, of a carpenter or mason. But we never say, the *trade* of a farmer or of a lawyer or physician.

3. Business pursued; occupation; *in contempt;* as, piracy is their *trade.*

Hunting their sport, and plund'ring was their *trade.* *Dryden.*

4. Instruments of any occupation.

The shepherd bears
His house and household goods, his *trade* of war. *Dryden.*

5. Employment not manual; habitual exercise. *Bacon.*

6. Custom; habit; standing practice.

Thy sin's not accidental, but a *trade.* *Shak.*

7. Men engaged in the same occupation. Thus booksellers speak of the customs of the *trade.*

TRADE, *v. i.* To barter, or to buy and sell; to deal in the exchange, purchase or sale of goods, wares and merchandise, or any thing else; to traffick; to carry on commerce as a business. Thus American merchants *trade* with the English at London and at Liverpool; they *trade* with the French at Havre and Bordeaux, and they *trade* with Canada. The country shopkeepers *trade* with London merchants. Our banks are permitted to *trade* in bills of exchange.

2. To buy and sell or exchange property, in a single instance. Thus we say, a man treats with another for his farm, but cannot *trade* with him. A *traded* with B for a horse or a number of sheep.

3. To act merely for money.

How did you dare
To *trade* and traffick with Macbeth? *Shak.*

4. To have a trade wind.

They on the *trading* flood ply tow'rd the pole. [*Unusual.*] *Milton.*

TRADE, *v. t.* To sell or exchange in commerce.

They *traded* the persons of men. Ezek. xxvii.

[*This, I apprehend, must be a mistake; at least it is not to be vindicated as a legitimate use of the verb.*]

TRA'DED, *a.* Versed; practiced. [*Not in use.*] *Shak.*

TRA'DEFUL, *a.* Commercial; busy in traffick. *Spenser.*

TRA'DER, *n.* One engaged in trade or commerce; a dealer in buying and selling or barter; as a *trader* to the East Indies; a *trader* to Canada; a country *trader.*

TRA'DESFOLK, *n.* People employed in trade. [*Not in use.*] *Swift.*

TRA'DESMAN, *n.* [*trade* and *man.*] A shopkeeper. A merchant is called a *trader*, but not a *tradesman.* *Johnson.*

[In America, a shopkeeper is usually called a *retailer.*]

TRA'DE-WIND, *n.* [*trade* and *wind.*] A wind that favors trade. A trade wind is a wind that blows constantly in the same direction, or a wind that blows for a number of months in one direction, and then changing, blows as long in the opposite direction. These winds in the East Indies are called *monsoons*, which are periodical. On the Atlantic, within the tropics, the trade winds blow constantly from the eastward to the westward.

TRA'DING, *ppr.* Trafficking; exchanging commodities by barter, or buying and selling them.

2. *a.* Carrying on commerce; as a *trading* company.

TRA'DING, *n.* The act or business of carrying on commerce.

TRADI''TION, *n.* [Fr. from L. *traditio*, from *trado*, to deliver.]

1. Delivery; the act of delivering into the hands of another.

A deed takes effect only from the *tradition* or delivery. *Blackstone.*

The sale of a movable is completed by simple *tradition.* *Cyc.*

2. The delivery of opinions, doctrines, practices, rites and customs from father to son, or from ancestors to posterity; the transmission of any opinions or practice from forefathers to descendants by oral communication, without written memorials. Thus children derive their vernacular language chiefly from *tradition.* Most of our early notions are received by *tradition* from our parents.

3. That which is handed down from age to age by oral communication. The Jews pay great regard to *tradition* in matters of religion, as do the Romanists. Protestants reject the authority of *tradition* in sacred things, and rely only on the written word. *Traditions* may be good or bad, true or false.

Stand fast, and hold the *traditions* which ye have been taught, whether by word or our epistle. 2 Thess. ii.

Why do ye also transgress the commandment of God by your *traditions?* Matt. xv.

TRADI''TIONAL, TRADI''TIONARY, *a.* Delivered orally from father to son; communicated from ancestors to descendants by word only; transmitted from age to age without writing; as *traditional* opinions; *traditional* evidence; the *traditional* expositions of the Scriptures.

The reveries of the Talmud, a collection of Jewish *traditionary* interpolations, are unrivaled in the regions of absurdity. *Buckminster.*

2. Observant of tradition. [*Not used.*]

TRADI''TIONALLY, *adv.* By transmission from father to son, or from age to age; as an opinion or doctrine *traditionally* derived from the apostles, is of no authority.

TRADI''TIONARY, *n.* Among the Jews, one who acknowledges the authority of traditions, and explains the Scriptures by them. The word is used in opposition to Cairite, one who denies the authority of traditions.

TRADI''TIONER, TRADI''TIONIST, *n.* One who adheres to tradition. *Gregory.*

TRAD'ITIVE, *a.* [Fr. from L. *trado.*] Transmitted or transmissible from father to son, or from age to age, by oral communication.

Suppose we on things *traditive* divide. *Dryden.*

TRAD'ITOR, *n.* [L.] A deliverer; a name of infamy given to christians who delivered the Scriptures or the goods of the church to their persecutors, to save their lives. *Milner.*

TRADU'CE, *v. t.* [L. *traduco; trans*, over, and *duco*, to lead; Fr. *traduire;* It. *tradurre.*]

1. To represent as blamable; to condemn.

The best stratagem that Satan hath, is by *traducing* the form and manner of the devout prayers of God's church. *Hooker.*

2. To calumniate; to vilify; to defame; willfully to misrepresent.

As long as men are malicious and designing, they will be *traducing.* *Gov. of the Tongue.*

He had the baseness to *traduce* me in libel. *Dryden.*

3. To propagate; to continue by deriving one from another.

From these only the race of perfect animals was propagated and *traduced* over the earth. [*Not in use.*] *Hale.*

TRADU'CED, *pp.* Misrepresented; calumniated.

TRADU'CEMENT, *n.* Misrepresentation; ill founded censure; defamation; calumny. [*Little used.*] *Shak.*

TRADU'CENT, *a.* Slandering; slanderous. *Entick.*

TRADU'CER, *n.* One that traduces; a slanderer; a calumniator.

TRADU'CIBLE, *a.* That may be orally derived or propagated. [*Little used.*] *Hale.*

TRADU'CING, *ppr.* Slandering; defaming; calumniating.

TRADU'CINGLY, *adv.* Slanderously; by way of defamation.

TRADUC'TION, *n.* [L. *traductio.*] Derivation from one of the same kind; propagation.

If by *traduction* came thy mind,
Our wonder is the less to find
A soul so charming from a stock so good. *Dryden.*

2. Tradition; transmission from one to another; as traditional communication and *traduction* of truth. [*Little used.*] *Hale.*

3. Conveyance; transportation; act of transferring; as the *traduction* of animals from Europe to America by shipping. *Hale.*

4. Transition. *Bacon.*

TRADUC'TIVE, *a.* Derivable; that may be deduced. *Warburton.*

TRAF'FICK, *n.* [Fr. *trafic;* It. *traffico;* Sp. *trafago;* a compound of L. *trans*, Celtic *tra*, and *facio*, or some other verb of the like elements.]

1. Trade; commerce, either by barter or by buying and selling. This word, like *trade*, comprehends every species of dealing in the exchange or passing of goods or merchandise from hand to hand for an equivalent, unless the business of retailing may be excepted. It signifies appropriately foreign trade, but is not limited to that.

My father,
A merchant of great *traffick* through the world. *Shak.*

2. Commodities for market. *Gay.*

TRAF'FICK, *v. i.* [Fr. *trafiquer;* It. *trafficare;* Sp. *traficar* or *trafagar.*]

1. To trade; to pass goods and commodities from one person to another for an equivalent in goods or money; to barter; to buy and sell wares; to carry on commerce. The English and Americans *traffick* with all the world. Gen. xlii.

2. To trade meanly or mercenarily. *Shak.*

TRAF'FICK, *v. t.* To exchange in traffick.

TRAF'FICKABLE, *a.* Marketable. [*Not in use.*] *Bp. Hall.*

TRAF'FICKER, *n.* One who carries on commerce; a trader; a merchant. Is. viii. *Shak.*

TRAF'FICKING, *ppr.* Trading; bartering; buying and selling goods, wares and commodities.

TRAG'ACANTH, *n.* [L. *tragacanthum;* Gr. τραγακανθα; τραγος, a goat, and ακανθα, thorn.]

1. Goat's thorn; a plant of the genus Astragalus, of several species, growing in Syria, Candia, &c. almost all of which were included by Linne in the tragacanthas, and all of which produce the gum tragacanth.

2. A gum obtained from the goat's thorn. It comes in small contorted pieces resembling worms. It is of different colors; that which is white, clear, smooth and vermicular, is the best. It is somewhat soft to the touch, but only imperfectly soluble. It is softening, and used in coughs and catarrhs. *Nicholson. Cyc.*

TRAGE'DIAN, *n.* [L. *tragœdus.* See *Tragedy.*] A writer of tragedy. *Stillingfleet.*

2. *More generally*, an actor of tragedy. *Dryden.*

TRAG'EDY, *n.* [Fr. *tragedie;* It. Sp. *tragedia;* Gr. τραγῳδια; said to be composed of τραγος, a goat, and ῳδη, a song, because originally it consisted in a hymn sung in honor of Bacchus by a chorus of music, with dances and the sacrifice of a goat.]

1. A dramatic poem representing some signal action performed by illustrious persons, and generally having a fatal issue. Æschylus is called the father of *tragedy.*

All our *tragedies* are of kings and princes. *Taylor.*

2. A fatal and mournful event; any event in which human lives are lost by human violence, more particularly by unauthorized violence.

TRAǴIC, } *a.* [L. *tragicus*; Fr. *tragique*;
TRAǴICAL, } It. *tragico.*]
1. Pertaining to tragedy; of the nature or character of tragedy; as a *tragic* poem; a *tragic* play or representation. *Shak.*
2. Fatal to life; mournful; sorrowful; calamitous; as the *tragic* scenes of Hayti the *tragic* horrors of Scio and Missilonghi; the *tragical* fate of the Greeks.
3. Mournful; expressive of tragedy, the loss of life, or of sorrow.

I now must change those notes to *tragic*. *Milton*

TRAǴICALLY, *adv.* In a tragical manner: with fatal issue; mournfully; sorrowfully. The play ends *tragically.*

TRAǴICALNESS, *n.* Fatality; mournfulness; sadness.

We moralize the fable in the *tragicalness* of the event. *Decay of Piety*

TRAǴI-COMEDY, *n.* [Fr. *tragi-comedie*; *tragedy* and *comedy.*]
A kind of dramatic piece representing some action passed among eminent persons, the event of which is not unhappy, in which serious and comic scenes are blended; a species of composition not now used, or held in little estimation. *Cyc.*

TRAǴI-COMIC, } *a.* Pertaining to
TRAǴI-COMICAL, } tragi-comedy; partaking of a mixture of grave and comic scenes.

TRAǴI-COMICALLY, *adv.* In a tragi-comical manner.

TRAIL, *v. t.* [W. *rhel*, a flagging, a trailing; *rhelyw*, a trail; Sp. *traillar*, to level the ground; *trailla*, a leash, packthread, an instrument for leveling the ground; W. *trail*, a drawing over, a trail, a turn, as if from *traigyl*, a turn or revolution; *treilliaw*, to turn, to roll, to traverse, to dredge; Gaelic, *triallam*, to go, to walk, [qu. *travel*;] Port. *tralho*, a fishing net, as if from drawing, L. *traho*; D. *treillen*, to draw, to tow; Norm. *trailler*, to search for. The Welsh seems to accord with *troll*; the others appear to be formed on *drag*, L. *traho.* Qu.]
1. To hunt by the track. [See the Norman, supra.]
2. To draw along the ground. *Trail* your pikes.

And hung his head, and *trail'd* his legs along. *Dryden.*

They shall not *trail* me through the streets
Like a wild beast. *Milton.*

That long behind he *trails* his pompous robe. *Pope.*

3. To lower; as, to *trail* arms.
4. In *America*, to tread down grass by walking through; to lay flat; as, to *trail* grass.

TRAIL, *v. i.* To be drawn out in length.

When his brother saw the red blood *trail.* *Spenser.*

TRAIL, *n.* Track followed by the hunter; scent left on the ground by the animal pursued.

How cheerfully on the false *trail* they cry. *Shak.*

2. Any thing drawn to length; as the *trail* of a meteor; a *trail* of smoke. *Dryden.*

When lightning shoots in glitt'ring *trails* along. *Rowe.*

3. Any thing drawn behind in long undulations; a train.

And drew behind a radiant *trail* of hair. *Pope.*

4. The entrails of a fowl; applied sometimes to those of sheep. *Smollet.*

Trail-boards, in ship-building, a term for the carved work between the cheeks of the head, at the heel of the figure. *Cyc.*

TRAILED, *pp.* Hunted by the tracks; laid flat; drawn along on the ground; brought to a lower position; as *trailed* arms.

TRA'ILING, *ppr.* Hunting by the track; drawing on the ground; treading down; laying flat; bringing to a lower position; drawing out in length.

Since the flames pursu'd the *trailing* smoke— *Dryden.*

Swift men of foot whose broad-set backs their *trailing* hair did hide. *Chapman.*

TRAIN, *v. t.* [Fr. *trainer*; It. *trainare*, *tranare*, to draw or drag; Sp. *traina*, a train of gunpowder. Qu. *drain*, or is it a contracted word, from L. *traho*, to *draw?*]
1. To draw along.

In hollow cube he *train'd*
His devilish enginery. *Milton.*

2. To draw; to entice; to allure.

If but twelve French
Were there in arms, they would be as a call
To *train* ten thousand English to their side. *Shak.*

3. To draw by artifice or stratagem.

O *train* me not, sweet mermaid, with thy note. *Shak.*

4. To draw from act to act by persuasion or promise.

We did *train* him on. *Shak.*

5. To exercise; to discipline; to teach and form by practice; as, to *train* the militia to the manual exercise; to *train* soldiers to the use of arms and to tactics. Abram armed his *trained* servants. Gen. xiv.

The warrior horse here bred he's taught to *train.* *Dryden.*

6. To break, tame and accustom to draw; as oxen.
7. In *gardening*, to lead or direct and form to a wall or espalier; to form to a proper shape by growth, lopping or pruning; as, to *train* young trees.
8. In *mining*, to trace a lode or any mineral appearance to its head.

To train or *train up*, to educate; to teach; to form by instruction or practice; to bring up.

Train up a child in the way he should go, and when he is old he will not depart from it. Prov. xxii.

The first christians were, by great hardships, *trained up* for glory. *Tillotson.*

TRAIN, *n.* Artifice; stratagem of enticement.

Now to my charms,
And to my wily *trains.* *Milton.*

2. Something drawn along behind, the end of a gown, &c.; as the *train* of a gown or robe.
3. The tail of a fowl.

The *train* steers their flight, and turns their bodies, like the rudder of a ship. *Ray.*

4. A retinue; a number of followers or attendants.

My *train* are men of choice and rarest parts. *Shak.*

The king's daughter with a lovely *train.* *Addison.*

5. A series; a consecution or succession of connected things.

Rivers now stream and draw their humid *train.* *Milton.*

Other truths require a *train* of ideas placed in order. *Locke.*

—The *train* of ills our love would draw behind it. *Addison.*

6. Process; regular method; course. Things are now in a *train* for settlement.

If things were once in this *train*—our duty would take root in our nature. *Swift.*

7. A company in order; a procession.

Fairest of stars, last in the *train* of night. *Milton.*

8. The number of beats which a watch makes in any certain time. *Cyc.*
9. A line of gunpowder, laid to lead fire to a charge, or to a quantity intended for execution.

Train of artillery, any number of cannon and mortars accompanying an army.

TRA'INABLE, *a.* That may be trained. [*Little used.*]

TRA'IN-BAND, *n.* [*train* and *band.*] A band or company of militia. *Train-bands*, in the plural, militia; so called because trained to military exercises.

TRA'IN-BEARER, *n.* [*train* and *bearer.*] One who holds up a train.

TRA'INED, *pp.* Drawn; allured; educated; formed by instruction.

TRA'INING, *ppr.* Drawing; alluring; educating; teaching and forming by practice.

TRA'INING, *n.* The act or process of drawing or educating; education. In *gardening*, the operation or art of forming young trees to a wall or espalier, or of causing them to grow in a shape suitable for that end. *Cyc.*

TRA'IN-OIL, *n.* [*train* and *oil.*] The oil procured from the blubber or fat of whales by boiling. *Cyc.*

TRA'IN-ROAD, *n.* [*train* and *road.*] In *mines*, a slight rail-way for small wagons. *Cyc.*

TRA'INY, *a.* Belonging to train-oil. [*Not in use.*] *Gay.*

TRAIPSE, *v. i.* To walk sluttishly or carelessly. [*A low word.*]

TRAIT, *n.* [Fr. *trait*, from *traire*, to draw; L. *tractus.* See *Tract* and *Treat.*]
1. A stroke; a touch.

By this single *trait*, Homer makes an essential difference between the Iliad and Odyssey. *Broome.*

2. A line; a feature; as a *trait* of character.

TRA'ITOR, *n.* [Fr. *traître*; Arm. *treitre*, *treytor*; Sp. *traidor*; from L. *traditor*; *trado*, to deliver.]
1. One who violates his allegiance and betrays his country; one guilty of treason; one who, in breach of trust, delivers his country to its enemy, or any fort or place entrusted to his defense, or who surrenders an army or body of troops to the enemy, unless when vanquished; or one who takes arms and levies war against his country; or one who aids an enemy in conquering his country. [See *Treason.*]
2. One who betrays his trust.

TRA'ITORLY, *a.* Treacherous. [*Not in use.*]

TRA'ITOROUS, *a.* Guilty of treason; treacherous; perfidious; faithless; as a *traitorous* officer or subject.
2. Consisting in treason; partaking of treason: implying breach of allegiance; as a *traitorous* scheme or conspiracy.

TRA'ITOROUSLY, *adv.* In violation of allegiance and trust; treacherously; perfidiously.

They had *traitorously* endeavored to subvert the fundamental laws. *Clarendon.*

TRA'ITOROUSNESS, *n.* Treachery; the quality of being treasonable. *Scott.*

TRA'ITRESS, *n.* A female who betrays her country or her trust. *Dryden.*

TRAJECT', *v. t.* [L. *trajectus, trajicio; trans* and *jacio*, to throw.]

To throw or cast through; as, to *traject* the sun's light through three or more cross prisms. *Newton.*

TRAJ'ECT, *n.* A ferry; a passage, or place for passing water with boats. *Shak.*

TRAJECT'ING, *ppr.* Casting through.

TRAJEC'TION, *n.* The act of casting or darting through. *Boyle.*

2. Transportation.

3. Emission. *Brown.*

TRAJECT'ORY, *n.* The orbit of a comet; the path described by a comet in its motion, which Dr. Halley supposes to be elliptical. *Cyc.*

TRALA'TION, *n.* [from L. *translatio.*] A change in the use of a word, or the use of a word in a less proper, but more significant sense. *Bp. Hall.*

TRALATI''TIOUS, *a.* [L. *translatus, transfero.*] Metaphorical; not literal.

TRALATI''TIOUSLY, *adv.* Metaphorically; not in a literal sense. *Holder.*

TRALIN'EATE, *v. t.* [L. *trans* and *linea*, line.] To deviate from any direction. [*Not in use.*] *Dryden.*

TRALU'CENT, *a.* [L. *tralucens; trans* and *luceo.*] Transparent; clear. *Davies.*

TRAM'MEL, *n.* [Fr. *tramail*, a drag-net; *tra* and *mail.* In Sp. *traba* is a fetter, Fr. *entraves.* This seems to be a different word.]

1. A kind of long net for catching birds or fishes.

The *trammel* differs not much from the shape of the bunt. *Carew.*

2. A kind of shackles used for regulating the motions of a horse, and making him amble.

3. An iron hook, of various forms and sizes, used for hanging kettles and other vessels over the fire.

4. *Trammels*, in mechanics, a joiner's instrument for drawing ovals upon boards. One part consists of a cross with two grooves at right angles; the other is a beam carrying two pins which slide in those grooves, and also the describing pencil. *Cyc.*

TRAM'MEL, *v. t.* [Sp. *trabar*, to join, to seize, to shackle. Qu.]

1. To catch; to intercept. *Shak.*

2. To confine; to hamper; to shackle.

TRAM'MELED, *pp.* Caught; confined; shackled.

2. In *the manege*, a horse is said to be trammeled, when he has blazes or white marks on the fore and hind foot of one side. *Cyc.*

TRAM'MELING, *ppr.* Catching; confining; shackling.

TRAMON'TANE, *n.* One living beyond the mountain; a stranger.

TRAMON'TANE, *a.* [It. *tramontana; tra*, L. *trans*, beyond, and *mons*, mountain.]

Lying or being beyond the mountain; foreign; barbarous. The Italian painters apply this epithet to all such as live north of the Alps, as in Germany and France; and a north wind is called a *tramontane* wind. The French lawyers call certain Italian canonists *tramontane* or *ultramontane* doctors; considering them as favoring too much the court of Rome. *Cyc.*

TRAMP, *v. t.* [Sw. *trampa.*] To tread.

TRAMP, *v. i.* To travel; to wander or stroll.

TRAMP'ER, *n.* A stroller; a vagrant or vagabond.

TRAM'PLE, *v. t.* [Gr. *trampeln, trampen;* Dan. *tramper;* Sw. *trampa.* If *m* is casual, as I suppose, these words are the D. *trappen*, to tread; *trap*, a step.]

1. To tread under foot; especially, to tread upon with pride, contempt, triumph or scorn.

Neither cast ye your pearls before swine, lest they *trample* them under their feet. Matt. vii.

2. To tread down; to prostrate by treading; as, to *trample* grass.

3. To treat with pride, contempt and insult.

TRAM'PLE, *v. i.* To tread in contempt.

Diogenes *trampled* on Plato's pride with greater of his own. *Gov. of the Tongue.*

2. To tread with force and rapidity. *Dryden.*

TRAM'PLE, *n.* The act of treading under foot with contempt. *Milton.*

TRAM'PLED, *pp.* Trod on; trodden under foot.

TRAM'PLER, *n.* One that tramples; one that treads down.

TRAM'PLING, *ppr.* Treading under foot; prostrating by treading; treading with contempt and insult.

TRANA'TION, *n.* [L. *trano.*] The act of passing over by swimming. [*Not in use.*]

TR'ANCE, *n.* tr'ans. [Fr. *transe;* supposed to be from the L. *transitus*, a passing over; *transeo*, to pass over; *trans* and *eo.* The L. *trans* seems to be the W. *tra*, It. *tra* and *tras*, Sp. *tras*, and Fr. *tres*, very; so that it may be inferred that *n* is not radical.]

An ecstasy; a state in which the soul seems to have passed out of the body into celestial regions, or to be rapt into visions.

My soul was ravish'd quite as in a *trance.* *Spenser.*

While they made ready, he fell into a *trance*, and saw heaven opened. Acts x.

TR'ANCED, *a.* Lying in a trance or ecstasy.

And there I left him *tranc'd.* *Shak.*

TRAN'GRAM, *n.* An odd thing intricately contrived. [*It is said to be a cant word, and is not used.*] *Arbuthnot.*

Trannel, used by Moxon, is a mistake for *tree-nail*, pronounced by ship-builders, *trunnel.*

TRAN'QUIL, *a.* [Fr. *tranquille;* L. *tranquillus.*]

Quiet; calm; undisturbed; peaceful; not agitated. The atmosphere is *tranquil.* The state is *tranquil.* A *tranquil* retirement is desirable; but a *tranquil* mind is essential to happiness.

TRAN'QUILIZE, *v. t.* To quiet; to allay when agitated; to compose; to make calm and peaceful; as, to *tranquilize* a state disturbed by factions or civil commotions; to *tranquilize* the mind.

Religion haunts the imagination of the sinner, instead of *tranquilizing* his heart. *Rob. Hall.*

TRAN'QUILIZED, *pp.* Quieted; calmed; composed.

TRAN'QUILIZING, *ppr.* Quieting; composing.

TRANQUIL'LITY, *n.* [L. *tranquillitas.*] Quietness; a calm state; freedom from disturbance or agitation. We speak of the *tranquillity* of public affairs, of the state, of the world, the *tranquillity* of a retired life, the *tranquillity* of mind proceeding from conscious rectitude.

TRAN'QUILLY, *adv.* Quietly; peacefully.

TRAN'QUILNESS, *n.* Quietness; peacefulness.

TRANSACT', *v. t.* [L. *transactus, transigo; trans* and *ago;* to act or drive through.]

To do; to perform; to manage; as, to *transact* commercial business. We *transact* business in person or by an agent.

TRANSACT'ED, *pp.* Done; performed; managed.

TRANSACT'ING, *ppr.* Managing; performing.

TRANSAC'TION, *n.* The doing or performing of any business; management of any affair.

2. That which is done; an affair. We are not to expect in history a minute detail of every *transaction.*

3. In *the civil law*, an adjustment of a dispute between parties by mutual agreement.

TRANSACT'OR, *n.* One who performs or conducts any business. *Derham.*

TRANSAL'PINE, *a.* [L. *trans*, beyond, and *Alpine*, of the Alps.]

Lying or being beyond the Alps in regard to Rome, that is, on the north or west of the Alps; as *Transalpine* Gaul; opposed to *Cisalpine.*

TRANSAN'IMATE, *v. t.* [*trans* and *animate.*]

To animate by the conveyance of a soul to another body. *King.*

TRANSANIMA'TION, *n.* [L. *trans* and *anima.*]

Conveyance of the soul from one body to another; transmigration. [*The latter is the word generally used.*] *Brown.*

TRANSATLAN'TIC, *a.* [L. *trans*, beyond, and *Atlantic.*]

Lying or being beyond the Atlantic. When used by a person in Europe or Africa, *transatlantic* signifies being in America; when by a person in America, it denotes being or lying in Europe or Africa. We apply it chiefly to something in Europe.

TRANSCEND', *v. t.* [L. *transcendo; trans* and *scando*, to climb.]

1. To rise above; to surmount; as lights in the heavens *transcending* the region of the clouds.

2. To pass over; to go beyond.

It is a dangerous opinion to such hopes as shall *transcend* their limits. *Bacon.*

3. To surpass; to outgo; to excel; to exceed.

How much her worth *transcended* all her kind. *Dryden.*

TRANSCEND', *v. i.* To climb. [*Not in use.*] *Brown.*

TRANSCEND'ED, *pp.* Overpassed; surpassed; exceeded.

TRANSCEND'ENCE, TRANSCEND'ENCY, *n.* Superior excellence; supereminence.

2. Elevation above truth; exaggeration. *Bacon.*

TRANSCEND'ENT, *a.* [L. *transcendens.*] Very excellent; superior or supreme in excellence; surpassing others; as *transcendent* worth; *transcendent* valor.

Cloth'd with *transcendent* brightness. *Milton.*

TRANSCENDENT'AL, *a.* Supereminent; surpassing others; as *transcendental* being or qualities. *Grew.*

Transcendental quantities, among geometricians, are indeterminate ones, or such as cannot be expressed or fixed to any constant equation.

Transcendental curve, is such as cannot be defined by any algebraic equation, or of which, when it is expressed by an equation, one of the terms is a variable quantity. *Cyc.*

TRANSCEND'ENTLY, *adv.* Very excellently; supereminently; by way of eminence.

The law of christianity is eminently and *transcendently* called the word of truth. *South.*

TRANS'COLATE, *v. t.* [L. *trans* and *colo*, to strain.]

To strain; to cause to pass through a sieve or colander. *Harvey.*

TRANSCRI'BE, *v. t.* [L. *transcribo; trans*, over, and *scribo*, to write.]

To copy; to write over again or in the same words; to write a copy of any thing; as, to *transcribe* Livy or Tacitus; to *transcribe* a letter.

TRANSCRI'BED, *pp.* Copied.

TRANSCRI'BER, *n.* A copier; one who writes from a copy. *Addison.*

TRANSCRI'BING, *ppr.* Writing from a copy; writing a copy.

TRAN'SCRIPT, *n.* [L. *transcriptum.*] A copy; a writing made from and according to an original; a writing or composition consisting of the same words with the original.

The decalogue of Moses was but a *transcript*, not an original. *South.*

2. A copy of any kind.

The Roman learning was a *transcript* of the Grecian. *Glanville.*

TRANSCRIP'TION, *n.* [Fr.] The act of copying. Corruptions creep into books by repeated *transcriptions.*

TRANSCRIPT'IVELY, *adv.* In manner of a copy. *Brown.*

TRANSCUR', *v.i.* [L. *transcurro; trans* and *curro*, to run.]

To run or rove to and fro. [*Little used.*] *Bacon.*

TRANSCUR'SION, *n.* [supra.] A rambling or ramble; a passage beyond certain limits; extraordinary deviation; as the *transcursion* of a comet. *More.*

I am to make often *transcursions* into the neighboring forests as I pass along. *Howell.*

[NOTE. *Excursion* has in a great measure superseded this word.]

TRANSDUC'TION, *n.* [L. *trans* and *duco.*] The act of conveying over. *Entick.*

TRANSE, *n.* Ecstasy. [See *Trance.*]

TRANSELEMENTA'TION, *n.* [*trans* and *element.*]

The change of the elements of one body into those of another, as of the bread and wine into the actual body and blood of Christ; transubstantiation. *Burnet.*

TRAN'SEPT, *n.* [L. *trans* and *septum.*] In *ancient churches*, the aisle extending across the nave and main aisles. *Cyc.*

TRANSFER', *v. t.* [L. *transfero; trans* and *fero*, to carry.]

1. To convey from one place or person to another; to transport or remove to another place or person; as, to *transfer* the laws of one country to another. The seat of government was *transferred* from New York to Albany. We say, a war is *transferred* from France to Germany. Pain or the seat of disease in the body, is often *transferred* from one part to another.

2. To make over; to pass; to convey, as a right, from one person to another; to sell; to give. The title to land is *transferred* by deed. The property of a bill of exchange may be *transferred* by indorsement. Stocks are *transferred* by assignment, or entering the same under the name of the purchaser in the proper books.

TRANS'FER, *n.* The removal or conveyance of a thing from one place or person to another.

2. The conveyance of right, title or property, either real or personal, from one person to another, either by sale, by gift or otherwise.

TRANSFER'ABLE, *a.* That may be transferred or conveyed from one place or person to another.

2. Negotiable, as a note, bill of exchange or other evidence of property, that may be conveyed from one person to another by indorsement or other writing. The stocks of the public and of companies are *transferable.*

TRANSFER'RED, *pp.* Conveyed from one to another.

TRANSFERREE', *n.* The person to whom a transfer is made. *Hamilton.*

TRANSFER'RER, *n.* One who makes a transfer or conveyance.

TRANSFER'RING, *ppr.* Removing from one place or person to another; conveying to another, as a right.

TRANSFIGURA'TION, *n.* [Fr. See *Transfigure.*]

1. A change of form; particularly, the supernatural change in the personal appearance of our Savior on the mount. See Matt. xvii.

2. A feast held by the Romish church on the 6th of August, in commemoration of the miraculous change above mentioned. *Cyc.*

TRANSFIG'URE, *v. t.* [L. *trans* and *figura; Fr. transfigurer.*]

To transform; to change the outward form or appearance.

—And was *transfigured* before them. Matt. xvii.

TRANSFIG'URED, *pp.* Changed in form.

TRANSFIG'URING, *ppr.* Transforming; changing the external form.

TRANSFIX', *v. t.* [L. *transfixus, transfigo; trans* and *figo.*]

To pierce through, as with a pointed weapon; as, to *transfix* one with a dart or spear. *Dryden.*

TRANSFIX'ED, *pp.* Pierced through.

TRANSFIX'ING, *ppr.* Piercing through with a pointed weapon.

TRANSFORM', *v. t.* [Fr. *transformer;* L. *trans* and *forma.*]

1. To change the form of; to change the shape or appearance; to metamorphose; as a caterpillar *transformed* into a butterfly.

2. To change one substance into another; to transmute. The alchimists sought to *transform* lead into gold.

3. In *theology*, to change the natural disposition and temper of man from a state of enmity to God and his law, into the image of God, or into a disposition and temper conformed to the will of God.

Be ye *transformed* by the renewing of your mind. Rom. xii.

4. To change the elements, bread and wine, into the flesh and blood of Christ. *Romish Church.*

5. Among *the mystics*, to change the contemplative soul into a divine substance, by which it is lost or swallowed up in the divine nature.

6. In *algebra*, to change an equation into another of a different form, but of eqnal value.

TRANSFORM', *v. i.* To be changed in form; to be metamorphosed.

His hair *transforms* to down. *Addison.*

TRANSFORMA'TION, *n.* The act or operation of changing the form or external appearance.

2. Metamorphosis; change of form in insects; as from a caterpillar to a butterfly.

3. Transmutation; the change of one metal into another, as of copper or tin into gold.

4. The change of the soul into a divine substance, as among the mystics.

5. Transubstantiation.

6. In *theology*, a change of heart in man, by which his disposition and temper are conformed to the divine image; a change from enmity to holiness and love.

7. In *algebra*, the change of an equation into one of a different form, but of equal value. *Cyc.*

TRANSFORM'ED, *pp.* Changed in form or external appearance; metamorphosed; transmuted; renewed.

TRANSFORM'ING, *ppr.* Changing the form or external appearance; metamorphosing; transmuting; renewing.

2. *a.* Effecting or able to effect a change of form or state; as the *transforming* power of true religion.

TRANSFREIGHT, *v. i. transfra'te.* To pass over the sea. [*Not in use.*] *Waterland.*

TRANSFRETA'TION, *n.* [L. *trans* and *fretum*, a strait.]

The passing over a strait or narrow sea. [*Little used.*] *Davies.*

TRANSFUSE, *v. t. transfu'ze.* [L. *transfusus, transfundo; trans* and *fundo.*]

1. To pour, as liquor, out of one vessel into another.

2. To transfer, as blood, from one animal to another.

3. To cause to pass from one to another; to cause to be instilled or imbibed; as, to *transfuse* a spirit of patriotism from one to another; to *transfuse* a love of letters.

TRANSFU'SED, *pp.* Poured from one vessel into another.

TRANSFU'SIBLE, *a.* That may be transfused, &c. *Boyle.*

TRANSFU'SING, *ppr.* Pouring out of one vessel into another; transferring.

TRANSFUSION, *n. transfu'zhon.* The act of pouring, as liquor, out of one vessel into another. In chimistry and pharmacy, *transfusions* of liquors are frequent. *Cyc.*

2. The act or operation of transferring the blood of one animal into the vascular system of another by means of a tube. *Cyc.*

TRANSGRESS', *v. t.* [Fr. *transgresser*; L. *transgressus, transgredior*; *trans* and *gradior*, to pass.]

1. To pass over or beyond any limit; to surpass. *Dryden.*

2. In *a moral sense*, to overpass any rule prescribed as the limit of duty; to break or violate a law, civil or moral. To *transgress* a divine law, is sin. Legislators should not *transgress* laws of their own making.

TRANSGRESS', *v. i.* To offend by violating a law; to sin. 1 Chron. ii.

TRANSGRESS'ED, *pp.* Overpassed; violated.

TRANSGRESS'ING, *ppr.* Passing beyond; surpassing; violating; sinning.

TRANSGRES'SION, *n.* [Fr.] The act of passing over or beyond any law or rule of moral duty; the violation of a law or known principle of rectitude; breach of command.

He mourned because of the *transgression* of them that had been carried away. Ezra x.

Forgive thy people all their *transgressions.* 1 Kings viii.

2. Fault; offense; crime. *Shak.*

TRANSGRES'SIONAL, *a.* That violates a law or rule of duty.

TRANSGRESS'IVE, *a.* Faulty; culpable; apt to transgress. *Brown.*

TRANSGRESS'OR, *n.* One who breaks a law or violates a command; one who violates any known rule or principle of rectitude; a sinner.

The way of *transgressors* is hard. Prov. xiii.

TRANSHA'PE, *v. t.* [*trans* and *shape.*] To transform. [*Not in use.*] *Shak.*

TRANSHIP', *v. t.* [*trans* and *ship.*] To convey from one ship to another; *a commercial word.*

TRANSHIP'MENT, *n.* The act of transferring, as goods, from one ship to another.

TRANSHIP'PED, *pp.* Carried from one ship to another.

TRANSHIP'PING, *ppr.* Carrying from one ship to another.

TRANSIENT, *a. tran'shent.* [L. *transiens, transeo*; *trans* and *eo.*]

1. Passing; not stationary; hence, of short duration; not permanent; not lasting or durable. How *transient* are the pleasures of this life!

—Measur'd this *transient* world. *Milton.*

2. Hasty; momentary; imperfect; as a *transient* view of a landscape.

Transient person, a person that is passing or traveling through a place; one without a settled habitation.

TRAN'SIENTLY, *adv.* [supra.] In passage; for a short time; not with continuance.

I touch here but *transiently*—on some few of those many rules of imitating nature, which Aristotle drew from Homer. *Dryden.*

TRAN'SIENTNESS, *n.* [supra.] Shortness of continuance; speedy passage.

TRANSIL'IENCE, TRANSIL'IENCY, *n.* [L. *transiliens, transilio*; *trans* and *salio.*]

A leap from thing to thing. [*Not much used.*] *Glanville.*

TRANS'IT, *n.* [L. *transitus*, from *transeo.*]

1. A passing; a passing over or through; conveyance; as the *transit* of goods through a country.

2. In *astronomy*, the passing of one heavenly body over the disk of another and larger. I witnessed the *transit* of Venus over the sun's disk, June 3, 1769. When a smaller body passes behind a larger, it is said to suffer an *occultation.*

3. The passage of one heavenly body over the meridian of another.

TRANS'IT, *v. t.* To pass over the disk of a heavenly body. *Cyc.*

TRANS'IT-DUTY, *n.* A duty paid on goods that pass through a country.

TRANSI''TION, *n. transizh'on.* [L. *transitio.*] Passage from one place or state to another; change; as the *transition* of the weather from hot to cold. Sudden *transitions* are sometimes attended with evil effects.

The spots are of the same color throughout, there being an immediate *transition* from white to black. *Woodward.*

2. In *rhetoric*, a passing from one subject to another. This should be done by means of some connection in the parts of the discourse, so as to appear natural and easy.

He with *transition* sweet new speech resumes. *Milton.*

3. In *music*, a change of key from major to minor, or the contrary; or in short, a change from any one genus or key to another; also, the softening of a disjunct interval by the introduction of intermediate sounds. *Cyc. Busby.*

Transition rocks, in geology, rocks supposed to have been formed when the world was passing from an uninhabitable to a habitable state. These rocks contain few organic remains, and when they occur with others, lie immediately over those which contain none, and which are considered as primitive. *Werner. Cyc.*

TRANS'ITIVE, *a.* Having the power of passing. *Bacon.*

2. In *grammar*, a transitive verb is one which is or may be followed by an object; a verb expressing an action which passes from the agent to an object, from the subject which *does*, to the object on which it *is done.* Thus, "Cicero *wrote* letters to Atticus." In this sentence, the act of writing, performed by Cicero, the agent, terminates on letters, the object. All verbs not passive, may be arranged in two classes, *transitive* and *intransitive.* In English, this division is correct and complete.

TRANS'ITORILY, *adv.* [See *Transitory.*] With short continuance.

TRANS'ITORINESS, *n.* A passing with short continuance; speedy departure or evanescence. Who is not convinced of the *transitoriness* of all sublunary happiness?

TRANS'ITORY, *a.* [L. *transitorius.*] Passing without continuance; continuing a short time; fleeting; speedily vanishing.

O Lord, comfort and succor all them who, in this *transitory* life, are in trouble. *Com. Prayer.*

2. In *law*, a transitory action, is one which may be brought in any county, as actions for debt, detinue, slander and the like. It is opposed to *local.* *Blackstone.*

TRANSLA'TABLE, *a.* [from *translate.*] Capable of being translated or rendered into another language.

TRANSLA'TE, *v. t.* [L. *translatus*, from *transfero*; *trans*, over, and *fero*, to bear; Sp. *trasladar*; It. *traslatare.*]

1. To bear, carry or remove from one place to another. It is applied to the removal of a bishop from one see to another.

The bishop of Rochester, when the king would have *translated* him to a better bishoprick, refused. *Camden.*

2. To remove or convey to heaven, as a human being, without death.

By faith Enoch was *translated*, that he should not see death. Heb. xvi.

3. To transfer; to convey from one to another. 2 Sam. iii.

4. To cause to remove from one part of the body to another; as, to *translate* a disease.

5. To change.

Happy is your grace,
That can *translate* the stubbornness of fortune
Into so quiet and so sweet a style. *Shak.*

6. To interpret; to render into another language; to express the sense of one language in the words of another. The Old Testament was *translated* into the Greek language more than two hundred years before Christ. The Scriptures are now *translated* into most of the languages of Europe and Asia.

7. To explain.

TRANSLA'TED, *pp.* Conveyed from one place to another; removed to heaven without dying; rendered into another language.

TRANSLA'TING, *ppr.* Conveying or removing from one place to another; conveying to heaven without dying; interpreting in another language.

TRANSLA'TION, *n.* [Fr. from L. *translatio.*]

1. The act of removing or conveying from one place to another; removal; as the *translation* of a disease from the foot to the breast.

2. The removal of a bishop from one see to another.

3. The removal of a person to heaven without subjecting him to death.

4. The act of turning into another language; interpretation; as the *translation* of Virgil or Homer.

5. That which is produced by turning into another language; a version. We have a good *translation* of the Scriptures.

TRANSLA'TIVE, *a.* Taken from others.

TRANSLA'TOR, *n.* One who renders into another language; one who expresses the sense of words in one language by equivalent words in another.

TRANS'LATORY, *a.* Transferring; serving to translate. *Arbuthnot.*

TRANSLA'TRESS, *n.* A female translator.

TRANSLOCA'TION, *n.* [L. *trans* and *locatio, loco.*]

Removal of things reciprocally to each others' places; or rather substitution of one thing for another.

There happened certain *translocations* of animal and vegetable substances at the deluge. *Woodward.*

TRANSLU'CENCY, *n.* [L. *translucens*; *trans*, through, and *luceo*, to shine.]

1. The property of admitting rays of light to pass through, but not so as to render objects distinguishable. *Mineralogy.*

2. Transparency.

TRANSLU'CENT, *a.* In *mineralogy*, transmitting rays of light, but not so as to render objects distinctly visible. *Cleaveland.*

2. Transparent; clear.

Replenish'd from the cool *translucent* springs. *Pope.*

TRANSLU'CID, *a.* [L. *translucidus*, supra.]

Transparent; clear. [See *Translucent.*] *Bacon.*

TRANSMARI'NE, *a.* [L. *transmarinus*; *trans* and *marinus*; *mare*, sea.] Lying or being beyond the sea. *Howell.*

TRANSMEW', *v. t.* [Fr. *transmuer*; L. *transmuto.*]

To transmute; to transform; to metamorphose. [*Not in use.*] *Spenser.*

TRANS'MIGRANT, *a.* [See *Transmigrate.*] Migrating; passing into another country or state for residence, or into another form or body.

TRANS'MIGRANT, *n.* One who migrates or leaves his own country and passes into another for settlement. *Bacon.*

2. One who passes into another state or body.

TRANS'MIGRATE, *v. i.* [L. *transmigro*; *trans* and *migro*, to migrate.]

1. To migrate; to pass from one country or jurisdiction to another for the purpose of residing in it; as men or families. *Brown.*

2. To pass from one body into another.

Their souls may *transmigrate* into each other. *Howell.*

TRANS'MIGRATING, *ppr.* Passing from one country, state or body into another.

TRANSMIGRA'TION, *n.* The passing of men from one country to another for the purpose of residence, particularly of a whole people.

2. The passing of a thing into another state, as of one substance into another. *Hooker.*

3. The passing of the soul into another body, according to the opinion of Pythagoras.

TRANS'MIGRATOR, *n.* One who transmigrates. *Ellis.*

TRANSMI'GRATORY, *a.* Passing from one place, body or state to another. *Faber.*

TRANSMISSIBIL'ITY, *n.* [from *transmissible.*] The quality of being transmissible.

TRANSMIS'SIBLE, *a.* [See *Transmit.*]

1. That may be transmitted or passed from one to another. *Blackstone. Burke.*

2. That may be transmitted through a transparent body.

TRANSMIS'SION, *n.* [Fr. from L. *transmissio.*]

1. The act of sending from one place or person to another; as the *transmission* of letters, writings, papers, news and the like, from one country to another; or the *transmission* of rights, titles or privileges from father to son, and from one generation to another. *Newton. Bacon.*

2. The passing of a substance through any body, as of light through glass.

TRANSMIS'SIVE, *a.* Transmitted; derived from one to another.

Itself a sun, it with *transmissive* light
Enlivens worlds denied to human sight. *Prior.*

TRANSMIT', *v. t.* [L. *transmitto*; *trans* and *mitto*, to send.]

1. To send from one person or place to another; as, to *transmit* a letter or a memorial; to *transmit* dispatches; to *transmit* money or bills of exchange from one city or country to another. Light is *transmitted* from the sun to the earth; sound is *transmitted* by means of vibrations of the air. Our civil and religious privileges have been *transmitted* to us from our ancestors; and it is our duty to *transmit* them to our children.

2. To suffer to pass through; as, glass *transmits* light; metals *transmit* electricity.

TRANSMIT'TAL, *n.* Transmission. *Swift.*

TRANSMIT'TED, *pp.* Sent from one person or place to another; caused or suffered to pass through.

TRANSMIT'TER, *n.* One who transmits.

TRANSMIT'TIBLE, *a.* That may be transmitted.

TRANSMIT'TING, *ppr.* Sending from one person or place to another; suffering to pass through.

TRANSMUTABIL'ITY, *n.* [See *Transmute.*]

Susceptibility of change into another nature or substance.

TRANSMU'TABLE, *a.* [from *transmute.*] Capable of being changed into a different substance, or into something of a different form or nature.

The fluids and solids of an animal body are *transmutable* into one another. *Arbuthnot.*

TRANSMU'TABLY, *adv.* With capacity of being changed into another substance or nature.

TRANSMUTA'TION, *n.* [L. *transmutatio.*]

1. The change of any thing into another substance, or into something of a different nature. For a long time, the *transmutation* of base metals into gold was deemed practicable, but nature proved refractory, and the alchimists were frustrated.

2. In *chimistry*, the transmutation of one substance into another is very easy and common, as of water into gas or vapor, and of gases into water.

3. In *geometry*, the change or reduction of one figure or body into another of the same area or solidity, but of a different form; as of a triangle into a square. *Cyc.*

4. The change of colors, as in the case of a decoction of the nephritic wood. *Cyc.*

5. In *the vegetable economy*, the change of a plant into another form; as of wheat into chess, according to the popular opinion. [See *Chess.*]

TRANSMU'TE, *v. t.* [L. *transmuto*; *trans* and *muto*, to change.]

To change from one nature or substance into another. Water may be *transmuted* into ice, and ice into water; the juices of plants are *transmuted* into solid substances; but human skill has not been able to *transmute* lead or copper into gold.

A holy conscience sublimates every thing; it *transmutes* the common affairs of life into acts of solemn worship to God. *J. M. Mason.*

The caresses of parents and the blandishments of friends, *transmute* us into idols. *Buckminster.*

TRANSMU'TED, *pp.* Changed into another substance or nature.

TRANSMU'TER, *n.* One that transmutes.

TRANSMU'TING, *ppr.* Changing or transforming into another nature or substance.

TRAN'SOM, *n.* [L. *transenna*, from *trans*, over, across.]

1. A beam or timber extended across the stern-post of a ship, to strengthen the aftpart and give it due form. *Mar. Dict.*

2. In *architecture*, the piece that is framed across a double light window; or a lintel over a door; the vane of a cross-staff. *Cyc. Johnson.*

TRANS'PADANE, *a.* [L. *trans* and *Padus*, the river Po.] Being beyond the river Po. *Stephens.*

TRANSPA'RENCY, *n.* [See *Transparent.*] That state or property of a body by which it suffers rays of light to pass through it, so that objects can be distinctly seen through it; diaphaneity. This is a property of glass, water and air, which when clear, admit the free passage of light. Transparency is opposed to *opakeness.*

TRANSPA'RENT, *a.* [Fr. *id.*; L. *trans* and *pareo*, to appear.]

1. Having the property of transmitting rays of light so that bodies can be distinctly seen through; pervious to light; diaphanous; pellucid; as *transparent* glass; a *transparent* diamond; opposed to *opake.*

2. Admitting the passage of light; open; porous; as a *transparent* vail. *Dryden.*

TRANSPA'RENTLY, *adv.* Clearly; so as to be seen through.

TRANSPA'RENTNESS, *n.* The quality of being transparent; transparency.

TRANSP'ASS, *v. t.* [*trans* and *pass.*] To pass over. [*Not in use.*] *Gregory.*

TRANSP'ASS, *v. i.* To pass by or away. [*Not in use.*] *Daniel.*

TRANSPIC'UOUS, *a.* [L. *trans* and *specio*, to see.] Transparent; pervious to the sight.

The wide *transpicuous* air. *Milton.*

TRANSPIERCE, *v. t.* *transpers'.* [Fr. *transpercer.*]

To pierce through; to penetrate; to permeate; to pass through.

His forceful spear the sides *transpierc'd.* *Dryden.*

TRANSPIERCED, *pp.* *transpers'ed.* Pierced through; penetrated.

TRANSPIERCING, *ppr.* *transpers'ing.* Penetrating; passing through.

TRANSPI'RABLE, *a.* [Fr.; from *transpire.*] Capable of being emitted through pores.

TRANSPIRA'TION, *n.* [Fr.; from *transpire.*]

The act or process of passing off through the pores of the skin; cutaneous exhalation; as the *transpiration* of obstructed fluids. *Sharp.*

TRANSPI'RE, *v. t.* [Fr. *transpirer*; L. *transpiro*; *trans* and *spiro.*]

To emit through the pores of the skin; to to send off in vapor.

TRANSPI'RE, *v. i.* To be emitted through the pores of the skin; to exhale; to pass off in insensible perspiration; as, fluids *transpire* from the human body.

2. To escape from secrecy; to become public. The proceedings of the council have not yet *transpired.*

3. To happen or come to pass.

TRANSPI'RING, *ppr.* Exhaling; passing off in insensible perspiration; becoming public.

TRANSPLA'CE, *v. t.* [*trans* and *place.*] To remove; to put in a new place.

It was *transplaced* from the left side of the Vatican to a more eminent place. [*Little used.*] *Wilkins.*

TRANSPLANT', *v. t.* [Fr. *transplanter; trans* and *plant,* L. *planto.*]

1. To remove and plant in another place; as, to *transplant* trees.

2. To remove and settle or establish for residence in another place; as, to *transplant* inhabitants. Salmaneser *transplanted* the Cuthites to Samaria.

3. To remove. *Clarendon. Milton.*

TRANSPLANTA'TION, *n.* The act of transplanting; the removal of a plant or of a settled inhabitant to a different place for growth or residence.

2. Removal; conveyance from one to another. Formerly men believed in the *transplantation* of diseases. *Baker. Cyc.*

TRANSPLANT'ED, *pp.* Removed and planted or settled in another place.

TRANSPLANT'ER, *n.* One who transplants.

2. A machine for transplanting trees.

TRANSPLANT'ING, *ppr.* Removing and planting or settling in another place.

TRANSPLEND'ENCY, *n.* [L. *trans* and *splendens.* See *Splendor.*] Supereminent splendor. *More.*

TRANSPLEND'ENT, *a.* Resplendent in the highest degree.

TRANSPLEND'ENTLY, *adv.* With eminent splendor. *More.*

TRANSPŌRT, *v. t.* [L. *transporto; trans* and *porto,* to carry.]

1. To carry or convey from one place to another, either by means of beasts or vehicles on land, or by ships in water, or by balloons in air; as, to *transport* the baggage of an army; to *transport* goods from one country to another; to *transport* troops over a river.

2. To carry into banishment, as a criminal. Criminals are *transported* as a punishment for their crimes, which often amounts to banishment.

3. To hurry or carry away by violence of passion.

They laugh as if *transported* with some fit
Of passion. *Milton.*

4. To ravish with pleasure; to bear away the soul in ecstasy; as, to be *transported* with joy. *Milton.*

5. To remove from one place to another, as a ship by means of hawsers and anchors. *Mar. Dict.*

TRANS'PŌRT, *n.* Transportation; carriage; conveyance.

The Romans stipulated with the Carthaginians to furnish them with ships for *transport* and war. *Arbuthnot.*

2. A ship or vessel employed for carrying soldiers, warlike stores or provisions from one place to another, or to convey convicts to the place of their destination.

3. Rapture; ecstasy. The news of victory was received with *transports* of joy.

4. A convict transported or sentenced to exile.

TRANSPŌRTABLE, *a.* That may be transported. *Beddoes.*

TRANSPŌRTANCE, *n.* Conveyance. [*Not in use.*] *Shak.*

TRANSPORTA'TION, *n.* The act of carrying or conveying from one place to another, either on beasts or in vehicles, by land or water, or in air. Goods in Asia are *transported* on camels; in Europe and America, either on beasts or on carriages or sleds. But *transportation* by water is the great means of commercial intercourse.

2. Banishment for felony.

3. Transmission; conveyance. *Dryden.*

4. Transport; ecstasy. [*Little used.*] *South.*

5. Removal from one country to another; as the *transportation* of plants.

TRANSPŌRTED, *pp.* Carried; conveyed; removed; ravished with delight.

TRANSPŌRTEDLY, *adv.* In a state of rapture.

TRANSPŌRTEDNESS, *n.* A state of rapture. *Bp. Hall.*

TRANSPŌRTER, *n.* One who transports or removes.

TRANSPŌRTING, *ppr.* Conveying or carrying from one place to another; removing; banishing for a crime.

2. *a.* Ravishing with delight; bearing away the soul in pleasure; extatic; as *transporting* joy.

TRANSPŌRTMENT, *n.* Transportation. [*Little used.*] *Hall.*

TRANSPŌSAL, *n.* *transpo'zal.* [from *transpose.*]

The act of changing the places of things, and putting each in the place which was before occupied by the other.

TRANSPOSE, *v. t.* *transpo'ze.* [Fr. *transposer; trans* and *poser,* to put.]

1. To change the place or order of things by putting each in the place of the other; as, to *transpose* letters, words or propositions. *Locke.*

2. To put out of place. *Shak.*

3. In *algebra,* to bring any term of an equation over to the other side. Thus if $a+b=c$, and we make $a=c-b$, then b is said to be *transposed.*

4. In *grammar,* to change the natural order of words.

5. In *music,* to change the key.

TRANSPO'SED, *pp.* Being changed in place and one put in the place of the other.

TRANSPO'SING, *ppr.* Changing the place of things and putting each in the place of the other.

2. Bringing any term of an equation over to the other side.

3. Changing the natural order of words.

TRANSPOSI''TION, *n.* [Fr. from L. *transpositio.*]

1. A changing of the places of things and putting each in the place before occupied by the other; as the *transposition* of words in a sentence.

2. The state of being reciprocally changed in place. *Woodward.*

3. In *algebra,* the bringing of any term of an equation to the other side.

4. In *grammar,* a change of the natural order of words in a sentence. The Latin and Greek languages admit *transposition* without inconvenience, to a much greater extent than the English.

5. In *music,* a change in the composition, either in the transcript or the performance, by which the whole is removed into another key. *Busby.*

TRANSPOSI''TIONAL, *a.* Pertaining to transposition. *Pegge.*

TRANSPOS'ITIVE, *a.* Made by transposing; consisting in transposition.

TRANSUBSTAN'TIATE, *v. t.* [Fr. *transubstantier; trans* and *substance.*]

To change to another substance; as, to *transubstantiate* the sacramental elements, bread and wine, into the flesh and blood of Christ, according to the popish doctrine.

TRANSUBSTANTIA'TION, *n.* Change of substance. In *the Romish theology,* the supposed conversion of the bread and wine in the eucharist, into the body and blood of Christ. *Cyc.*

TRANSUBSTAN'TIATOR, *n.* One who maintains the popish doctrine of transubstantiation. *Barrow.*

TRANSUDA'TION, *n.* [from *transude.*]

The act or process of passing off through the pores of a substance; as sweat or other fluid. *Boyle.*

TRANSU'DATORY, *a.* Passing by transudation.

TRANSU'DE, *v. i.* [L. *trans* and *sudo,* to sweat.]

To pass through the pores or interstices of texture, as perspirable matter or other fluid; as, liquor may *transude* through lether, or through wood.

TRANSU'DING, *ppr.* Passing through the pores of a substance, as sweat or other fluid.

TRANSU'ME, *v. t.* [L. *transumo; trans* and *sumo,* to take.] To take from one to another. [*Little used.*]

TRANSUMPT', *n.* A copy or exemplification of a record. [*Not in use.*] *Herbert.*

TRANSUMP'TION, *n.* The act of taking from one place to another. [*Little used.*] *South.*

TRANSVEC'TION, *n.* [L. *transvectio.*] The act of conveying or carrying over.

TRANSVERS'AL, *a.* [Fr. from L. *trans* and *versus.*]

Running or lying across; as a *transversal* line. *Hale.*

TRANSVERS'ALLY, *adv.* In a direction crosswise. *Wilkins.*

TRANSVERSE, *a.* *transvers'.* [L. *transversus; trans* and *versus, verto.*]

1. Lying or being across or in a cross direction; as a *transverse* diameter or axis. *Transverse* lines are the diagonals of a square or parallelogram. Lines which intersect perpendiculars, are also called *transverse.*

2. In *botany,* a *transverse* partition, in a pericarp, is at right angles with the valves, as in a silique. *Martyn.*

TR'ANSVERSE, *n.* The longer axis of an ellipse.

TRANSVERSE, *v. t. transvers'.* To overturn. [*Little used.*]

TRANSVERSELY, *adv. transvers'ly.* In a cross direction; as, to cut a thing *transversely.*

At Stonehenge, the stones lie *transversely* upon each other. *Stillingfleet.*

TRAN'TERS, *n. plu.* Men who carry fish from the sea coast to sell in the inland countries. [*Not American.*] *Bailey.*

TRAP, *n.* [Sax. *trapp, trepp;* Fr. *trape;* It. *trapola;* Sp. *trampa.*]

1. An engine that shuts suddenly or with a spring, used for taking game; as a *trap* for foxes. A trap is a very different thing from a *snare;* though the latter word may be used in a figurative sense for a trap.
2. An engine for catching men. [*Not used in the U. States.*]
3. An ambush; a stratagem; any device by which men or other animals may be caught unawares.

Let their table be made a snare and a *trap.* Rom. xi.

4. A play in which a ball is driven with a stick.

TRAP, *n.* [Sw. *trappa*, Dan. *trappe*, a stair or stairs.]

In *mineralogy*, a name given to rocks characterized by a columnar form, or whose strata or beds have the form of steps or a series of stairs. Kirwan gives this name to two families of basalt. It is now employed to designate a rock or aggregate in which hornblend predominates, but it conveys no definite idea of any one species; and under this term are comprehended hornblend, hornblend slate, greenstone, greenstone slate, amygdaloid, basalt, wacky, clinkstone porphyry, and perhaps hypersthene rock, augite rock, and some varieties of sienite. *Cleaveland.*

TRAP, *v. t.* To catch in a trap; as, to *trap* foxes or beaver.

2. To ensnare; to take by stratagem.

I *trapp'd* the foe. *Dryden.*

3. To adorn; to dress with ornaments. [See *Trappings.*] [*The verb is little used.*] *Spenser.*

TRAP, *v. i.* To set traps for game; as, to *trap* for beaver.

TRAPAN', *v. t.* [Sax. *treppan;* from *trap.*] To ensnare; to catch by stratagem. *South.*

TRAPAN', *n.* A snare; a stratagem.

TRAPAN'NER, *n.* One who ensnares.

TRAPAN'NING, *ppr.* Ensnaring.

TRAP'-DOOR, *n.* [*trap* and *door.*] A door in a floor, which shuts close like a valve. *Ray.*

TRAPE, *v. i.* To traipse; to walk carelessly and sluttishly. [*Not much used.*]

TRAPES, *n.* A slattern; an idle sluttish woman.

TRAPE'ZIAN, *a.* [See *Trapezium.*] In *crystalography*, having the lateral planes composed of trapeziums situated in two ranges, between two bases.

TRAPE'ZIFORM, *a.* Having the form of a trapezium.

TRAPEZIHE'DRON, *n.* [L. *trapezium* and Gr. εδρα, side.]

A solid bounded by twenty four equal and similar trapeziums. *Cleaveland.*

TRAPE'ZIUM, *n.* plu. *trapezia* or *trapeziums.* [L. from Gr. τραπεζιον, a little table.]

1. In *geometry*, a plane figure contained under four unequal right lines, none of them parallel. *Cyc.*
2. In *anatomy*, a bone of the carpus.

TRAPEZOID', *n.* [L. *trapezium* and Gr. ειδος.]

An irregular solid figure having four sides, no two of which are parallel to each other; also, a plane four sided figure having two of the opposite sides parallel to each other. *Cyc. Olmsted.*

TRAPEZOID'AL, *a.* Having the form of a trapezoid.

2. Having the surface composed of twenty four trapeziums, all equal and similar. *Cleaveland.*

TRAP'PINGS, *n. plu.* [from *trap.* The primary sense is that which is set, spread or put on.]

1. Ornaments of horse furniture.

Caparisons and steeds,
Bases and tinsel *trappings*— *Milton.*

2. Ornaments; dress; external and superficial decorations.

These but the *trappings* and the suits of woe. *Shak.*

Trappings of life, for ornament, not use. *Dryden.*

Affectation is part of the *trappings* of folly. *Rambler.*

TRAP'POUS, *a.* [from *trap*, in geology. It ought to be *trappy.*]

Pertaining to trap; resembling trap, or partaking of its form or qualities. *Kirwan.*

TRAP'-STICK, *n.* A stick with which boys drive a wooden ball; hence, a slender leg. *Addison.*

TRAP'-TUFF, *n.* Masses of basalt, amygdaloid, hornblend, sandstones, &c., cemented. *Ure.*

TRASH, *n.* [In G. *drüse* is a gland; *drusen*, dregs. In Sw. *trasa* is a rag. The word may be allied to *thrash.*]

1. Any waste or worthless matter.

Who steals my money, steals *trash.* *Shak.*

2. Loppings of trees; bruised canes, &c. In the West Indies, the decayed leaves and stems of canes are called *field-trash;* the bruised or macerated rind of canes is called *cane-trash;* and both are called *trash.* *Edwards, W. Indies.*
3. Fruit or other matter improper for food, but eaten by children, &c. It is used particularly of unripe fruits.
4. A worthless person. [*Not proper.*] *Shak.*
5. A piece of lether or other thing fastened to a dog's neck to retard his speed.

TRASH, *v. t.* To lop; to crop. *Warburton.*

2. To strip of leaves; as, to *trash* ratoons. *Edwards, W. Indies.*
3. To crush; to humble; as, to *trash* the Jews. *Hammond.*
4. To clog; to encumber; to hinder. *Shak.*

TRASH, *v. i.* To follow with violence and trampling. *Todd.*

TRASH'Y, *a.* Waste; rejected; worthless; useless. *Dryden.*

TRASS, *n.* Pumiceous conglomerate, a volcanic production; a gray or yellowish porous substance.

TRAU'LISM, *n.* A stammering. [*Not in use.*]

TRAUMAT'IC, *a.* [Gr. τραυμα, a wound.]

1. Pertaining to or applied to wounds. *Coxe.*
2. Vulnerary; adapted to the cure of wounds. *Wiseman.*

TRAUMAT'IC, *n.* A medicine useful in the cure of wounds.

TRAV'AIL, *v. i.* [Fr. *travailler;* W. *travaelu*, to toil; a compound of W. *tra*, that is, *tras*, L. *trans*, over, beyond, and *mael*, work, Eng. *moil;* It. *travagliare;* Sp. *trabajar.*]

1. To labor with pain; to toil.
2. To suffer the pangs of childbirth; to be in labor. Gen. xxxv.

TRAV'AIL, *v. t.* To harass; to tire; as troubles sufficient to *travail* the realm. [*Not in use.*] *Hayward.*

TRAV'AIL, *n.* Labor with pain; severe toil.

As every thing of price, so doth this require *travail.* *Obs.* *Hooker.*

2. Labor in childbirth; as a severe *travail;* an easy *travail.*

TRAV'AILING, *ppr.* Laboring with toil; laboring in childbirth. Is. xlii.

TRAVE, **TRAV'IS**, } *n.* [Sp. *traba;* Fr. *entraves.* See *Trammel.*]

1. A wooden frame to confine a horse while the smith is setting his shoes. This is not used for horses in America, but a similar frame is used for confining oxen for shoeing.
2. Beam; a lay of joists; a traverse. *Wood.*

TRAV'EL, *v. i.* [a different orthography and application of *travail.*]

1. To walk; to go or march on foot; as, to *travel* from London to Dover, or from New York to Philadelphia. So we say, a man ordinarily *travels* three miles an hour. [This is the proper sense of the word, which implies *toil.*]
2. To journey; to ride to a distant place in the same country; as, a man *travels* for his health; he is *traveling* to Virginia. A man *traveled* from London to Edinburgh in five days.
3. To go to a distant country, or to visit foreign states or kingdoms, either by sea or land. It is customary for men of rank and property to *travel* for improvement. Englishmen *travel* to France and Italy. Some men *travel* for pleasure or curiosity; others *travel* to extend their knowledge of natural history.
4. To pass; to go; to move. News *travels* with rapidity.

Time *travels* in divers paces with divers persons. *Shak.*

5. To labor. [See *Travail.*]
6. To move, walk or pass, as a beast, a horse, ox or camel. A horse *travels* fifty miles in a day; a camel, twenty.

TRAVEL, *v. t.* To pass; to journey over; as, to *travel* the whole kingdom of England.

I *travel* this profound. *Milton.*

2. To force to journey.

The corporations—shall not be *traveled* forth from their franchises. [*Not used.*] *Spenser.*

TRAV'EL, *n.* A passing on foot; a walking.

2. Journey; a passing or riding from place to place.

His *travels* ended at his country seat. *Dryden.*

3. *Travel* or *travels*, a journeying to a dis-

tant country or countries. The gentleman has just returned from his *travels*.

4. The distance which a man rides in the performance of his official duties; or the fee paid for passing that distance; as the *travel* of the sherif is twenty miles; or that of a representative is seventy miles. His *travel* is a dollar for every twenty miles. *U. States.*

5. *Travels*, in the plural, an account of occurrences and observations made during a journey; as a book of *travels*; the title of a book that relates occurrences in traveling; as *travels* in Italy.

6. Labor; toil; labor in childbirth. [See *Travail.*]

TRAV'ELED, *pp.* Gained or made by travel; as *traveled* observations. [*Unusual.*] *Quart. Rev.*

2. *a.* Having made journeys. *Wotton.*

TRAV'ELER, *n.* One who travels in any way. Job xxxi.

2. One who visits foreign countries.

3. In *ships*, an iron thimble or thimbles with a rope spliced round them, forming a kind of tail or a species of grommet. *Mar. Dict.*

TRAV'ELING, *ppr.* Walking; going; making a journey. Matt. xxv.

2. *a.* Incurred by travel; as *traveling* expenses.

3. Paid for travel; as *traveling* fees.

TRAV'EL-TAINTED, *a.* [*travel* and *tainted.*]

Harassed; fatigued with travel. [*Not in use.*] *Shak.*

TRAV'ERS, *adv.* [Fr. See *Traverse.*] Across; athwart. [*Not used.*] *Shak.*

TRAV'ERSABLE, *a.* [See *Traverse*, in law.] That may be traversed or denied; as a *traversable* allegation.

TRAV'ERSE, *adv.* [Fr. *a travers.*] Athwart; crosswise.

The ridges of the field lay *traverse*. *Hayward.*

TRAV'ERSE, *prep.* [supra.] Through crosswise.

He *traverse*
The whole battalion views their order due.
[*Little used.*] *Milton.*

TRAV'ERSE, *a.* [Fr. *traverse; tra, tras*, and L. *versus; transversus.*]

Lying across; being in a direction across something else; as paths cut with *traverse* trenches. *Hayward.*

Oak—may be trusted in *traverse* work for summers. *Wotton.*

TRAV'ERSE, *n.* [supra.] Any thing laid or built across.

There is a *traverse* placed in the loft where she sitteth. *Bacon.*

2. Something that thwarts, crosses or obstructs; a cross accident. He is satisfied he should have succeeded, had it not been for unlucky *traverses* not in his power.

3. In *fortification*, a trench with a little parapet for protecting men on the flank; also, a wall raised across a work. *Cyc.*

4. In *navigation*, traverse-sailing is the mode of computing the place of a ship by reducing several short courses made by sudden shifts or turns, to one longer course. *D. Olmsted.*

5. In *law*, a denial of what the opposite party has advanced in any stage of the pleadings. When the *traverse* or denial comes from the defendant, the issue is tendered in this manner, "and of this he puts himself on the country." When the *traverse* lies on the plaintif, he prays "this may be inquired of by the country." *Blackstone.*

The technical words introducing a traverse are *absque hoc*, without this; that is, without this which follows.

6. A turning; a trick.

TRAV'ERSE, *v. t.* To cross; to lay in a cross direction.

The parts should be often *traversed* or crossed by the flowing of the folds. *Dryden.*

2. To cross by way of opposition; to thwart; to obstruct.

Frog thought to *traverse* this new project. *Arbuthnot.*

3. To wander over; to cross in traveling; as, to *traverse* the habitable globe.

What seas you *travers'd*, and what fields you fought. *Pope.*

4. To pass over and view; to survey carefully.

My purpose is to *traverse* the nature, principles and properties of this detestable vice, ingratitude. *South.*

5. To turn and point in any direction; as, to *traverse* a cannon. *Cyc.*

6. To plane in a direction across the grain of the wood; as, to *traverse* a board. *Cyc.*

7. In *law pleadings*, to deny what the opposite party has alleged. When the plaintif or defendant advances new matter, he avers it to be true, and *traverses* what the other party has affirmed. So to *traverse* an indictment or an office, is to deny it.

To traverse a yard, in sailing, is to brace it aft.

TRAV'ERSE, *v. i.* In *fencing*, to use the posture or motions of opposition or counteraction.

To see thee fight, to see thee *traverse*— *Shak.*

2. To turn, as on a pivot; to move round; to swivel. The needle of a compass *traverses*; if it does not *traverse* well, it is an unsafe guide.

3. In *the manege*, to cut the tread crosswise, as a horse that throws his croup to one side and his head to the other. *Cyc.*

TRAV'ERSE-BOARD, *n.* [*traverse* and *board.*]

In *a ship*, a small board to be hung in the steerage, and bored full of holes upon lines, showing the points of compass upon it. By moving a peg on this, the steersman keeps an account of the number of glasses a ship is steered on any point. *Cyc. Mar. Dict.*

TRAV'ERSE-TABLE, *n.* [*traverse* and *table.*]

In *navigation*, a table of difference of latitude and departure.

TRAV'ERSING, *ppr.* Crossing; passing over; thwarting; turning; denying.

TRAV'ESTIED, *pp.* Disguised by dress; turned into ridicule.

TRAV'ESTIN, *n.* [It. *travestino.*] A kind of white spongy stone found in Italy. *Ed. Encyc.*

TRAV'ESTY, *a.* [infra.] Having an unusual dress; disguised by dress so as to be ridiculous. It is applied to a book or composition translated in a manner to make it burlesk.

TRAV'ESTY, *n.* A parody; a burlesk translation of a work. *Travesty* may be intended to ridicule absurdity, or to convert a grave performance into a humorous one.

TRAV'ESTY, *v. t.* [Fr. *travestir*; It. *travestire; tra, tras*, over, and Fr. *vestir, vêtir*, to clothe.]

To translate into such language as to render ridiculous or ludicrous.

G. Battista Lalli *travestied* Virgil, or turned him into Italian burlesk verse. *Cyc. Good's Sacred Idyls.*

TRAY, *n.* [Sw. *tråg*, Sax. *trog*, Dan. *trug*, a *trough.* It is the same word as *trough*, differently written; L. *trua.*]

A small trough or wooden vessel, sometimes scooped out of a piece of timber and made hollow, used for making bread in, chopping meat and other domestic purposes.

TRA'Y-TRIP, *n.* A kind of play. *Shak.*

TRE'ACHER, } **TRE'ACHETOUR**, } *n.* [Fr. *tricheur.*] A traitor. *Obs.* **TRE'ACHOUR**, } *Spenser.*

TREACHEROUS, *a.* *trech'erous.* [See *Treachery.*]

Violating allegiance or faith pledged; faithless; traitorous to the state or sovereign; perfidious in private life; betraying a trust. A man may be *treacherous* to his country, or *treacherous* to his friend, by violating his engagements or his faith pledged.

TREACHEROUSLY, *adv. trech'erously.* By violating allegiance or faith pledged; by betraying a trust; faithlessly; perfidiously; as, to surrender a fort to an enemy *treacherously*; to disclose a secret *treacherously.*

You *treacherously* practic'd to undo me. *Otway.*

TREACHEROUSNESS, *n. trech'erousness.* Breach of allegiance or of faith; faithlessness; perfidiousness.

TREACHERY, *n. trech'ery.* [Fr. *tricherie*, a cheating; *tricher*, to cheat. This word is of the family of *trick, intrigue, intricate.*]

Violation of allegiance or of faith and confidence. The man who betrays his country in any manner, violates his allegiance, and is guilty of *treachery.* This is treason. The man who violates his faith pledged to his friend, or betrays a trust in which a promise of fidelity is implied, is guilty of *treachery.* The disclosure of a secret committed to one in confidence, is *treachery.* This is perfidy.

TRE'ACLE, *n.* [Fr. *theriaque*; It. *teriaca*; Sp. *triaca*; L. *theriaca*; Gr. θηριακη, from θηρ, a wild beast; θηριακα φαρμακα.]

1. The spume of sugar in sugar refineries. Treacle is obtained in refining sugar; melasses is the drainings of crude sugar. Treacle however is often used for melasses.

2. A saccharine fluid, consisting of the inspissated juices or decoctions of certain vegetables, as the sap of the birch, sycamore, &c. *Cyc.*

3. A medicinal compound of various ingredients. [See *Theriaca.*]

TRE'ACLE-MUSTARD, *n.* A plant of the genus Thlaspi, whose seeds are used in the theriaca; Mithridate mustard. *Cyc.*

TRE'ACLE-WATER, *n.* A compound cordial, distilled with a spiritous menstruum from any cordial and sudorific drugs and herbs, with a mixture of Venice treacle. *Cyc.*

TREAD, *v. i. tred.* pret. *trod;* pp. *trod, trodden.* [Sax. *trædan, tredan;* Goth. *trudan;* D. *tred*, a step; *treeden*, to tread; G. *treten;* Dan. *træder;* Sw. *tråda;* Gaelic, *troidh*, the foot; W. *troed*, the foot; *troediaw*, to use the foot, to tread. It coincides in elements with L. *trudo.*]

1. To set the foot.

Where'er you *tread*, the blushing flow'rs shall rise. *Pope.*

Fools rush in where angels fear to *tread*. *Burke.*

2. To walk or go.

Every place whereon the soles of your feet shall *tread*, shall be yours. Deut. xi.

3. To walk with form or state.

Ye that stately *tread*, or lowly creep. *Milton.*

4. To copulate, as fowls. *Shak.*

To tread or *tread on*, to trample; to set the foot on in contempt.

Thou shalt *tread upon* their high places. Deut. xxxiii.

TREAD, *v. t. tred.* To step or walk on.

Forbid to *tread* the promis'd land he saw. *Prior.*

2. To press under the feet.
3. To beat or press with the feet; as, to *tread* a path; to *tread* land when too light; a well *trodden* path.
4. To walk in a formal or stately manner.

He thought she *trod* the ground with greater grace. *Dryden.*

5. To crush under the foot; to trample in contempt or hatred, or to subdue. Ps. xliv. lx.
6. To compress, as a fowl.

To tread the stage, to act as a stage-player; to perform a part in a drama.

To tread or *tread out*, to press out with the feet; to press out wine or wheat; as, to *tread out* grain with cattle or horses.

They *tread* their wine presses and suffer thirst. Job xxiv.

TREAD, *n. tred.* A step or stepping; pressure with the foot; as a nimble *tread;* cautious *tread;* doubtful *tread.* *Milton. Dryden.*

2. Way; track; path. [*Little used.*] *Shak.*
3. Compression of the male fowl.
4. Manner of stepping; as, a horse has a good *tread.*

TREADER, *n. tred'er.* One who treads. Is. xvi.

TREADING, *ppr. tred'ing.* Stepping; pressing with the foot; walking on.

TREADLE, } *n.* The part of a loom or
TRED'DLE, } other machine which is moved by the *tread* or foot.

2. The albuminous cords which unite the yelk of the egg to the white.

TREAGUE, *n. treeg.* [Goth. *triggwa;* It. *tregua;* Ice. *trigd*, a truce, a league.]

A truce. *Obs.* *Spenser.*

TREASON, *n. tree'zn.* [Fr. *trahison;* Norm. *trahir*, to draw in, to betray, to commit treason, Fr. *trahir*, L. *traho.* See *Draw* and *Drag.*]

Treason is the highest crime of a civil nature of which a man can be guilty. Its signification is different in different countries. In general, it is the offense of attempting to overthrow the government of the state to which the offender owes allegiance, or of betraying the state into the hands of a foreign power. In monarchies, the killing of the king, or an attempt to take his life, is treason. In England, to imagine or compass the death of the king, or of the prince, or of the queen consort, or of the heir apparent of the crown, is high treason; as are many other offenses created by statute.

In the United States, treason is confined to the actual levying of war against the United States, or in adhering to their enemies, giving them aid and comfort. *Constitution of U. States.*

Treason in Great Britain, is of two kinds, *high treason* and *petit treason.* *High treason* is a crime that immediately affects the king or state; such as the offenses just enumerated. *Petit treason* involves a breach of fidelity, but affects individuals. Thus for a wife to kill her husband, a servant his master or lord, or an ecclesiastic his lord or ordinary, is *petit treason.* But in the United States this crime is unknown; the killing in the latter cases being murder only.

TREASONABLE, *a. tree'znable.* Pertaining to treason; consisting of treason; involving the crime of treason, or partaking of its guilt.

Most men's heads had been intoxicated with imaginations of plots and *treasonable* practices. *Clarendon.*

TREASONOUS, for *treasonable*, is not in use.

TREASURE, *n. trezh'ur.* [Fr. *tresor;* Sp. It. *tesauro;* L. *thesaurus;* Gr. θησαυρος.]

1. Wealth accumulated; particularly, a stock or store of money in reserve. Henry VII. was frugal and penurious, and collected a great *treasure* of gold and silver.
2. A great quantity of any thing collected for future use.

We have *treasures* in the field, of wheat and of barley, and of oil and of honey. Jer. xli.

3. Something very much valued. Ps. cxxxv.

Ye shall be a peculiar *treasure* to me. Ex. xix.

4. Great abundance.

In whom are hid all the *treasures* of wisdom and knowledge. Col. ii.

TREASURE, *v. t. trezh'ur.* To hoard; to collect and reposit, either money or other things, for future use; to lay up; as, to *treasure* gold and silver; usually with *up.* Sinners are said to *treasure up* wrath against the day of wrath. Rom. ii.

TREASURE-CITY, *n. trezh'ur-city.* A city for stores and magazines. Ex. i.

TREASURED, *pp. trezh'ured.* Hoarded; laid up for future use.

TREASURE-HOUSE, *n. trezh'ur-house.* A house or building where treasures and stores are kept. *Taylor.*

TREASURER, *n. trezh'urer.* One who has the care of a treasure or treasury; an officer who receives the public money arising from taxes and duties or other sources of revenue, takes charge of the same, and disburses it upon orders drawn by the proper authority. Incorporated companies and private societies have also their *treasurers.*

In England, the lord high treasurer is the principal officer of the crown, under whose charge is all the national revenue.

The treasurer of the household, in the absence of the lord-steward, has power with the controller and other officers of the Green-cloth, and the steward of the Marshalsea, to hear and determine treasons, felonies and other crimes committed within the king's palace. There is also the treasurer of the navy, and the treasurers of the county. *Cyc.*

TREASURERSHIP, *n. trezh'urership.* The office of treasurer.

TREASURESS, *n. trezh'uress.* A female who has charge of a treasure. *Dering.*

TREASURE-TROVE, *n. trezh'ur-trove.* [*treasure* and Fr. *trouvé*, found.]

Any money, bullion and the like, found in the earth, the owner of which is not known. *Eng. Law.*

TREASURY, *n. trezh'ury.* A place or building in which stores of wealth are reposited; particularly, a place where the public revenues are deposited and kept, and where money is disbursed to defray the expenses of government.

2. A building appropriated for keeping public money. John viii.
3. The officer or officers of the treasury department.
4. A repository of abundance. Ps. cxxxv.

TREAT, *v. t.* [Fr. *traiter;* It. *trattare;* Sp. *tratar;* L. *tracto;* Sax. *trahtian.*]

1. To handle; to manage; to use. Subjects are usually faithful or treacherous, according as they are well or ill *treated.* To *treat* prisoners ill, is the characteristic of barbarians. Let the wife of your bosom be kindly *treated.*
2. To discourse on. This author *treats* various subjects of morality.
3. To handle in a particular manner, in writing or speaking; as, to *treat* a subject diffusely.
4. To entertain without expense to the guest.
5. To negotiate; to settle; as, to *treat* a peace. [*Not in use.*] *Dryden.*
6. To manage in the application of remedies; as, to *treat* a disease or a patient.

TREAT, *v. i.* To discourse; to handle in writing or speaking; to make discussions. Cicero *treats* of the nature of the gods; he *treats* of old age and of duties.

2. To come to terms of accommodation.

Inform us, will the emp'ror *treat?* *Swift.*

3. To make gratuitous entertainment. It is sometimes the custom of military officers to *treat* when first elected.

To treat with, to negotiate; to make and receive proposals for adjusting differences. Envoys were appointed to *treat with* France, but without success.

TREAT, *n.* An entertainment given; as a parting *treat.* *Dryden.*

2. Something given for entertainment; as a rich *treat.*
3. *Emphatically*, a rich entertainment.

TRE'ATABLE, *a.* Moderate; not violent.

The heats or the colds of seasons are less *treatable* than with us. [*Not in use.*] *Temple.*

TRE'ATABLY, *adv.* Moderately. [*Not in use.*] *Hooker.*

TRE'ATED, *pp.* Handled; managed; used; discoursed on; entertained.

TRE'ATER, *n.* One that treats; one that handles or discourses on; one that entertains.

TRE'ATING, *ppr.* Handling; managing; using; discoursing on; entertaining.

TRE'ATISE, *n.* [L. *tractatus.*] A tract; a written composition on a particular subject, in which the principles of it are discussed or explained. A treatise is of an indefinite length; but it implies more form and method than an essay, and less fullness or copiousness than a system. *Cyc.*

TRE'ATISER, *n.* One who writes a treatise. [*Not used.*] *Featley.*

TRE'ATMENT, *n.* [Fr. *traitement.*] Management; manipulation; manner of mixing or combining, of decomposing and the like; as the *treatment* of substances in chimical experiments.

2. Usage; manner of using; good or bad behavior towards.

Accept such *treatment* as a swain affords. *Pope.*

3. Manner of applying remedies to cure; mode or course pursued to check and destroy; as the *treatment* of a disease.

4. Manner of applying remedies to; as the *treatment* of a patient.

TRE'ATY, *n.* [Fr. *traité*; It. *trattato.*] Negotiation; act of treating for the adjustment of differences, or for forming an agreement; as, a *treaty* is on the carpet.

He cast by *treaty* and by trains
Her to persuade. *Spenser.*

2. An agreement, league or contract between two or more nations or sovereigns, formally signed by commissioners properly authorized, and solemnly ratified by the several sovereigns or the supreme power of each state. Treaties are of various kinds, as *treaties* for regulating commercial intercourse, *treaties* of alliance, offensive and defensive, *treaties* for hiring troops, *treaties* of peace, &c.

3. Intreaty. [*Not in use.*] *Shak.*

TRE'ATY-MAKING, *a.* The treaty-making power is lodged in the executive government. In monarchies, it is vested in the king or emperor; in the United States of America, it is vested in the president, by and with the consent of the senate.

TREBLE, *a.* *trib'l.* [Fr. *triple*; L. *triplex*, *triplus*; *tres*, three, and *plexus*, fold. This should be written *trible.*]

1. Threefold; triple; as a lofty tower with *treble* walls. *Dryden.*

2. In *music*, acute; sharp; as a *treble* sound. *Bacon.*

3. That plays the highest part or most acute sounds; that plays the treble; as a *treble* violin. *Cyc.*

TREBLE, *n.* *trib'l.* In *music*, the part of a symphony whose sounds are highest or most acute. This is divided into first or highest treble, and second or base treble. *Cyc.*

TREBLE, *v. t.* *trib'l.* [L. *triplico*; Fr. *tripler.*]

To make thrice as much; to make threefold. Compound interest soon *trebles* a debt.

TREBLE, *v. i.* *trib'l.* To become threefold. A debt at compound interest soon *trebles* in amount.

TREBLENESS, *n.* *trib'lness.* The state of being treble; as the *trebleness* of tones. *Bacon.*

TREBLY, *adv.* *trib'ly.* In a threefold number or quantity; as a good deed *trebly* recompensed.

TREE, *n.* [Sax. *treo*, *treow*; Dan. *træ*; Sw. *trå*, wood, and *träd*, a tree; Gr. δρυς; Slav. *drevo*. Qu. W. *dar*, an oak; Sans. *taru*, a tree. It is not easy to ascertain the real original orthography; most probably it was as in the Swedish or Greek.]

1. The general name of the largest of the vegetable kind, consisting of a firm woody stem springing from woody roots, and spreading above into branches which terminate in leaves. A tree differs from a shrub principally in size, many species of trees growing to the highth of fifty or sixty feet, and some species to seventy or eighty, and a few, particularly the pine, to a much greater highth.

Trees are of various kinds; as *nuciferous*, or nut-bearing trees; *bacciferous*, or berry-bearing; *coniferous*, or cone-bearing, &c. Some are forest-trees, and useful for timber or fuel; others are fruit-trees, and cultivated in gardens and orchards; others are used chiefly for shade and ornament.

2. Something resembling a tree, consisting of a stem or stalk and branches; as a genealogical *tree*.

3. In *ship-building*, pieces of timber are called *chess-trees*, *cross-trees*, *roof-trees*, *tressel-trees*, *&c.*

4. In *Scripture*, a cross.

—Jesus, whom they slew and hanged on a *tree*. Acts x.

5. Wood. *Obs.* *Wickliffe.*

TREE'-FROG, *n.* [*tree* and *frog.*] A species of frog, the *Rana arborea*, found on trees and shrubs; called by the older writers, *Ranunculus viridis*. *Cyc.*

TREE-GERMANDER, *n.* A plant of the genus Teucrium. *Cyc.*

TREE'-LOUSE, *n.* [*tree* and *louse.*] An insect of the genus Aphis.

TREE'-MOSS, *n.* A species of lichen. *Cyc.*

TREEN, *a.* Wooden; made of wood. *Obs.* *Camden.*

TREEN, *n.* The old plural of *tree*. *Obs.* *B. Jonson.*

TREE'-NAIL, *n.* [*tree* and *nail*; commonly pronounced *trunnel.*]

A long wooden pin, used in fastening the planks of a ship to the timbers. *Mar. Dict.*

TREE-OF-LIFE, *n.* An evergreen tree of the genus Thuja.

TREE'-TOAD, *n.* [*tree* and *toad.*] A small species of toad in N. America, found on trees. This animal croaks chiefly in the evening and after a rain.

TRE'FOIL, *n.* [Fr. *trèfle*; L. *trifolium*; *tres*, three, and *folium*, leaf.]

The common name for many plants of the genus Trifolium; also, in *agriculture*, a name of the *medicago tupulina*, a plant resembling clover, with yellow flowers, much cultivated for hay and fodder. *Cyc.*

TREILLAGE, *n.* *trel'lage.* [Fr. from *treillis*, trellis.]

In *gardening*, a sort of rail-work, consisting of light posts and rails for supporting espaliers, and sometimes for wall trees. *Cyc.*

TREL'LIS, *n.* [Fr. *treillis*, grated work.] In *gardening*, a structure or frame of cross-barred work, or lattice work, used like the treillage for supporting plants.

TREL'LISED, *a.* Having a trellis or trellises. *Herbert.*

TREM'BLE, *v. i.* [Fr. *trembler*; L. *tremo*; Gr. τρεμω; It. *tremare*; Sp. *tremer.*]

1. To shake involuntarily, as with fear, cold or weakness; to quake; to quiver; to shiver; to shudder.

Frighted Turnus *trembled* as he spoke. *Dryden.*

2. To shake; to quiver; to totter.

Sinai's gray top shall *tremble*. *Milton.*

3. To quaver; to shake, as sound; as when we say, the voice *trembles*.

TREM'BLEMENT, *n.* In *French music*, a trill or shake.

TREM'BLER, *n.* One that trembles.

TREM'BLING, *ppr.* Shaking, as with fear, cold or weakness; quaking; shivering.

TREM'BLINGLY, *adv.* So as to shake; with shivering or quaking.

Tremblingly she stood. *Shak.*

TREM'BLING-POPLAR, *n.* The aspen-tree, so called.

TREMEN'DOUS, *a.* [L. *tremendus*, from *tremo*, to tremble.]

1. Such as may excite fear or terror; terrible; dreadful. Hence,

2. Violent; such as may astonish by its force and violence; as a *tremendous* wind; a *tremendous* shower; a *tremendous* shock or fall; a *tremendous* noise.

TREMEN'DOUSLY, *adv.* In a manner to terrify or astonish; with great violence.

TREMEN'DOUSNESS, *n.* The state or quality of being tremendous, terrible or violent.

TREM'OLITE, *n.* A mineral, so called from Tremola, a valley in the Alps, where it was discovered. It is classed by Haüy with hornblend or amphibole, and called amphibole grammatite. It is of three kinds, asbestous, common, and glassy tremolite; all of a fibrous or radiated structure, and of a pearly color. *Kirwan. Cyc.*

Tremolite is a subspecies of straight edged augite. *Ure.*

TRE'MOR, *n.* [L. from *tremo.*] An involuntary trembling; a shivering or shaking; a quivering or vibratory motion; as the *tremor* of a person who is weak, infirm or old.

He fell into a universal *tremor*. *Harvey.*

TREM'ULOUS, *a.* [L. *tremulus*, from *tremo*, to tremble.]

1. Trembling; affected with fear or timidity; as a *trembling* christian. *Decay of Piety.*

2. Shaking; shivering; quivering; as a *tremulous* limb; a *tremulous* motion of the hand or the lips; the *tremulous* leaf of the poplar. *Holder. Thomson.*

TREM'ULOUSLY, *adv.* With quivering or trepidation.

TREM'ULOUSNESS, *n.* The state of trembling or quivering; as the *tremulousness* of an aspen leaf.

TREN, *n.* A fish spear. *Ainsworth.*

TRENCH, *v. t.* [Fr. *trancher*, to cut; It. *trincea*, a trench; *trinciare*, to cut; Sp. *trincar*, *trinchear*; Arm. *troucha*; W. *tryçu.*]

1. To cut or dig, as a ditch, a channel for water, or a long hollow in the earth. We *trench* land for draining. [*This is the appropriate sense of the word.*]

2. To fortify by cutting a ditch and raising a rampart or breast-work of earth thrown

out of the ditch. [In this sense, *entrench* is more generally used.]
3. To furrow; to form with deep furrows by plowing.
4. To cut a long gash. [*Not in use.*] *Shak.*

TRENCH, *v. i.* To encroach. [See *Entrench.*]

TRENCH, *n.* A long narrow cut in the earth; a ditch; as a *trench* for draining land.
2. In *fortification*, a deep ditch cut for defense, or to interrupt the approach of an enemy. The wall or breast-work formed by the earth thrown out of the ditch, is also called a *trench*, as also any raised work formed with bavins, gabions, woolpacks or other solid materials. Hence the phrases, to *mount the trenches*, to *guard the trenches*, to *clear the trenches*, &c.
To open the trenches, to begin to dig, or to form the lines of approach.

TRENCH'ANT, *a.* [Fr. *tranchant.*] Cutting; sharp. [*Little used.*] *Spenser.*

TRENCH'ED, *pp.* Cut into long hollows or ditches; furrowed deep.

TRENCH'ER, *n.* [Fr. *tranchoir.*] A wooden plate. *Trenchers* were in use among the common people of New England till the revolution.
2. The table. *Shak.*
3. Food; pleasures of the table.

It would be no ordinary declension that would bring some men to place their *summum bonum* upon their *trenchers*. *South.*

TRENCH'ER-FLY, *n.* [*trencher* and *fly.*] One that haunts the tables of others; a parasite. *L'Estrange.*

TRENCH'ER-FRIEND, *n.* [*trencher* and *friend.*]
One who frequents the tables of others; a spunger.

TRENCH'ER-MAN, *n.* [*trencher* and *man.*]
1. A feeder; a great eater. *Shak.*
2. A cook. *Obs.*

TRENCH'ER-MATE, *n.* [*trencher* and *mate.*]
A table companion; a parasite. *Hooker.*

TRENCH'ING, *ppr.* Cutting into trenches; digging; ditching.

TRENCH'-PLOW, *n.* [*trench* and *plow.*] A kind of plow for opening land to a greater depth than that of common furrows. *Cyc.*

TRENCH'-PLOW, *v. t.* [*trench* and *plow.*] To plow with deep furrows.

TRENCH'-PLOWING, *n.* The practice or operation of plowing with deep furrows, for the purpose of loosening the land to a greater depth than usual. *Cyc.*

TREND, *v. i.* [This word seems to be allied to *trundle*, or to *run.*]
To run; to stretch; to tend; to have a particular direction; as, the shore of the sea *trends* to the southwest.

TREND, *n.* That part of the stock of an anchor from which the size is taken. *Cyc.*

TREND, *v. t.* In rural economy, to free wool from its filth. [*Local.*] *Cyc.*

TREND'ER, *n.* One whose business is to free wool from its filth. [*Local.*] *Cyc.*

TREND'ING, *ppr.* Running; tending.
2. Cleaning wool. [*Local.*]

TREND'ING, *n.* The operation of freeing wool from filth of various kinds. *Cyc.*

TREN'DLE, *n.* [Sax.; probably connected with *trundle;* Sw. *trind*, round; that is, *round*, with a prefix.]
Any thing round used in turning or rolling; a little wheel.

TREN'TAL, TREN'TALS, *n.* [Fr. *trente*, thirty; contracted from L. *triginta*, It. *trenta.*]
An office for the dead in the Romish service, consisting of thirty masses rehearsed for thirty days successively after the party's death. *Cyc.*

TREPAN', *n.* [Fr. *trepan;* It. *trapano;* Gr. τρυπανον, from τρυπαω, to bore; τρυπα, a hole; τρυω. Qu. L. *tero*, *terebra*, on the root *Rp.*]
In *surgery*, a circular saw for perforating the skull. It resembles a wimble. *Cyc.*

TREPAN', *v. t.* To perforate the skull and take out a piece; a surgical operation for relieving the brain from pressure or irritation. *Cyc.*
Trepan, a snare, and *trepan*, to ensnare, are from *trap*, and written *trapan*, which see.

TREPAN'NED, *pp.* Having the skull perforated.

TREPAN'NER, *n.* One who trepans.

TREPAN'NING, *ppr.* Perforating the skull with a trepan.

TREPAN'NING, *n.* The operation of making an opening in the skull, for relieving the brain from compression or irritation. *Cyc.*

TREPH'INE, *n.* [See *Trepan.*] An instrument for trepanning, more modern than the trepan. It is a circular or cylindrical saw, with a handle like that of a gimblet, and a little sharp perforator, called the center-pin. *Cyc.*

TREPH'INE, *v. t.* To perforate with a trephine; to trepan. *Cyc.*

TREP'ID, *a.* [L. *trepidus.*] Trembling; quaking. [*Not used.*]

TREPIDA'TION, *n.* [L. *trepidatio*, from *trepido*, to tremble; Russ. *trepeg*, a trembling; *trepeschu*, to tremble.]
1. An involuntary trembling; a quaking or quivering, particularly from fear or terror; hence, a state of terror. The men were in great *trepidation*.
2. A trembling of the limbs, as in paralytic affections.
3. In *the old astronomy*, a libration of the eighth sphere, or a motion which the Ptolemaic system ascribes to the firmament, to account for the changes and motion of the axis of the world. *Cyc.*
4. Hurry; confused haste.

TRES'PASS, *v. i.* [Norm. *trespasser;* *tres*, L. *trans*, beyond, and *passer*, to pass.]
1. Literally, to pass beyond; hence primarily, to pass over the boundary line of another's land; to enter unlawfully upon the land of another. A man may *trespass* by walking over the ground of another, and the law gives a remedy for damages sustained.
2. To commit any offense or to do any act that injures or annoys another; to violate any rule of rectitude to the injury of another.

If any man shall *trespass* against his neighbor, and an oath be laid upon him— 1 Kings viii. See Luke xvii. 3. and 4.

3. In *a moral sense*, to transgress voluntarily any divine law or command; to violate any known rule of duty.

In the time of his disease did he *trespass* yet more. 2 Chron. xxviii.

We have *trespassed* against our God. Ezra x.

4. To intrude; to go too far; to put to inconvenience by demand or importunity; as, to *trespass* upon the time or patience of another.

TRES'PASS, *n.* In *law*, violation of another's rights, not amounting to treason, felony, or misprision of either. Thus to enter another's close, is a *trespass;* to attack his person is a *trespass.* When violence accompanies the act, it is called a trespass *vi et armis.*
2. Any injury or offense done to another.

If ye forgive not men their *trespasses*, neither will your Father forgive your *trespasses.* Matt. vi.

3. Any voluntary transgression of the moral law; any violation of a known rule of duty; sin. Col. ii.

You hath he quickened, who were dead in *trespasses* and sins. Eph. ii.

TRES'PASSER, *n.* One who commits a trespass; one who enters upon another's land or violates his rights.
2. A transgressor of the moral law; an offender; a sinner.

TRES'PASSING, *ppr.* Entering another man's inclosure; injuring or annoying another; violating the divine law or moral duty.

TRESS, *n.* [Fr. Dan. *tresse;* Sw. *tress*, a lock or weft of hair; Dan. *tresser*, Sw. *tressa*, Russ. *tresuyu*, to weave, braid or twist. The Sp. has *trenza*, and the Port. *trança*, a tress. The French may possibly be from the It. *treccia*, but probably it is from the north of Europe.] A knot or curl of hair; a ringlet.

Fair *tresses* man's imperial race ensnare. *Pope.*

TRESS'ED, *a.* Having tresses.
2. Curled; formed into ringlets. *Spenser.*

TRESS'URE, *n.* In *heraldry*, a kind of border. *Warton.*

TRES'TLE, *n.* *tres'l.* [Fr. *tréteau*, for *tresteau;* W. *três*, a trace, a chain, a stretch, labor; *tresiaw*, to labor, that is, to strain; *trestyl*, a strainer, a trestle. This root occurs in *stress* and *distress.*]
1. The frame of a table. [Qu. D. *driestal*, a three-legged stool.]
2. A movable form for supporting any thing.
3. In *bridges*, a frame consisting of two posts with a head or cross beam and braces, on which rest the string-pieces. [This is the use of the word in New England. It is vulgarly pronounced *trussel* or *trussl.*]
Trestle-trees, in a ship, are two strong bars of timber, fixed horizontally on the opposite sides of the lower mast-head, to support the frame of the top and the topmast. *Mar. Dict.*

TRET, *n.* [probably from L. *tritus*, *tero*, to wear.]
In *commerce*, an allowance to purchasers, for waste or refuse matter, of four per cent. on the weight of commodities. It is said this allowance is nearly discontinued. *Cyc.*

TRETH'INGS, *n.* [W. *trêth*, a tax; *trethu*, to tax.]

Taxes; imposts. [*I know not where used. It is unknown, I believe, in the United States.*]

TREV'ET, *n.* [*three-feet, tripod; Fr. trepied.*] A stool or other thing that is supported by three legs.

TREY, *n.* [L. *tres*, Eng. *three*, Fr. *trois.*] A three at cards; a card of three spots. *Shak.*

TRI, a prefix in words of Greek and Latin origin, signifies *three*, from Gr. τρεις.

TRI'ABLE, *a.* [from *try.*] That may be tried; that may be subjected to trial or test. *Boyle.*

2. That may undergo a judicial examination; that may properly come under the cognizance of a court. A cause may be *triable* before one court, which is not *triable* in another. In England, testamentary causes are *triable* in the ecclesiastical courts.

TRIACONTAHE'DRAL, *a.* [Gr. τριακοντα, thirty, and εδρα, side.]

Having thirty sides. In *mineralogy*, bounded by thirty rhombs. *Cleaveland.*

TRI'ACONTER, *n.* [Gr. τριακοντηρης.] In ancient Greece, a vessel of thirty oars. *Milford.*

TRI'AD, *n.* [L. *trias*, from *tres*, three.] The union of three; three united. In *music*, the common chord or harmony, consisting of the third, fifth and eighth. *Busby.*

TRI'AL, *n.* [from *try.*] Any effort or exertion of strength for the purpose of ascertaining its effect, or what can be done. A man tries to lift a stone, and on *trial* finds he is not able. A team attempts to draw a load, and after unsuccessful *trial*, the attempt is relinquished.

2. Examination by a test; experiment; as in chimistry and metallurgy.

3. Experiment; act of examining by experience. In gardening and agriculture, we learn by *trial* what land will produce; and often, repeated *trials* are necessary.

4. Experience; suffering that puts strength, patience or faith to the test; afflictions or temptations that exercise and prove the graces or virtues of men.

> Others had *trial* of cruel mockings and scourgings. Heb. xi.

5. In *law*, the examination of a cause in controversy between parties, before a proper tribunal. Trials are *civil* or *criminal.* Trial in civil causes, may be by record or inspection; it may be by witnesses and jury, or by the court. By the laws of England and of the United States, trial by jury, in criminal cases, is held sacred. No criminal can be legally deprived of that privilege.

6. Temptation; test of virtue.

> Every station is exposed to some *trials*. *Rogers.*

7. State of being tried. *Shak.*

TRIAL'ITY, *n.* [from *three.*] Three united; state of being three. [*Little used.*] *Wharton.*

TRIAN'DER, *n.* [Gr. τρεις, three, and ανηρ, a male.] A plant having three stamens.

TRIAN'DRIAN, *a.* Having three stamens.

TRI'ANGLE, *n.* [Fr. from L. *triangulum; tres, tria*, three, and *angulus*, a corner.]

In *geometry*, a figure bounded by three lines, and containing three angles. The three angles of a triangle are equal to two right angles, or the number of degrees in a semicircle.

If the three lines or sides of a triangle are all right, it is a *plane* or *rectilinear* triangle.

If all the three sides are equal, it is an *equilateral* triangle.

If two of the sides only are equal, it is an *isosceles* or *equicrural* triangle.

If all the three sides are unequal, it is a *scalene* or *scalenous* triangle.

If one of the angles is a right angle, the triangle is *rectangular.*

If one of the angles is obtuse, the triangle is called *obtusangular* or *amblygonous.*

If all the angles are acute, the triangle is *acutangular* or *oxygonous.*

If the three lines of a triangle are all curves, the triangle is said to be *curvilinear.*

If some of the sides are right and others curve, the triangle is said to be *mixtilinear.*

If the sides are all arcs of great circles of the sphere, the triangle is said to be *spherical.* *Cyc.*

TRIAN'GLED, *a.* Having three angles.

TRIAN'GULAR, *a.* Having three angles.

In *botany*, a *triangular stem* has three prominent longitudinal angles; a *triangular leaf* has three prominent angles, without any reference to their measurement or direction. *Martyn. Smith.*

TRIAN'GULARLY, *adv.* After the form of a triangle. *Harris.*

TRIA'RIAN, *a.* [L. *triarii.*] Occupying the third post or place. *Cowley.*

TRIBE, *n.* [W. *trev;* Gael. *treabh;* Sax. *thorpe*, D. *dorp*, G. *dorf*, Sw. Dan. *torp*, a hamlet or village; L. *tribus.* We have *tribe* from the last. In Welsh, the word signifies a dwelling place, homestead, hamlet or town, as does the Sax. *thorpe.* The Sax. *træf* is a tent; Russ. *derevni*, an estate, a hamlet. From the sense of house, the word came to signify a family, a race of descendants from one progenitor, who originally settled round him and formed a village.]

1. A family, race or series of generations, descending from the same progenitor and kept distinct, as in the case of the twelve tribes of Israel, descended from the twelve sons of Jacob.

2. A division, class or distinct portion of people, from whatever cause that distinction may have originated. The city of Athens was divided into ten *tribes.* Rome was originally divided into three *tribes;* afterward the people were distributed into thirty *tribes*, and afterwards into thirty five. *Rom. Hist.*

3. A number of things having certain characters or resemblances in common; as a *tribe* of plants; a *tribe* of animals.

Linneus distributed the vegetable kingdom into three tribes, viz. *monocotyledonous, dicotyledonous*, and *acotyledonous* plants, and these he subdivided into *gentes* or nations. *Martyn.*

By recent naturalists, *tribe* has been used for a division of animals or vegetables, intermediate between order and genus. Cuvier divides his orders into *families*, and his families into *tribes*, including under the latter one or more *genera.* Leach, in his arrangement of insects, makes his tribes, on the contrary, the primary subdivisions of his orders, and his families subordinate to them, and immediately including the genera. *Cuvier. Ed. Encyc.*

Tribes of plants, in *gardening*, are such as are related to each other by some natural affinity or resemblance; as by their duration, the *annual, biennial*, and *perennial* tribes; by their roots, as the *bulbous, tuberous*, and *fibrous-rooted* tribes; by the loss or retention of their leaves, as the *deciduous* and *ever-green* tribes; by their fruits and seeds, as the *leguminous, bacciferous, coniferous, nuciferous* and *pomiferous* tribes, &c. *Cyc.*

4. A division; a number considered collectively.

5. A nation of savages; a body of rude people united under one leader or government; as the *tribes* of the six nations; the Seneca *tribe* in America.

6. A number of persons of any character or profession; *in contempt;* as the scribbling *tribe.* *Roscommon.*

TRIBE, *v. t.* To distribute into tribes or classes. [*Not much used.*] *Bp. Nicholson.*

TRIB'LET, / TRIB'OULET, *n.* A goldsmith's tool for making rings. *Ainsworth.*

TRIBOM'ETER, *n.* [Gr. τριβω, to rub or wear, and μετρον, measure.]

An instrument to ascertain the degree of friction. *Cyc. Entick.*

TRI'BRACH, *n.* [Gr. τρεις, three, and βραχυς, short.]

In *ancient prosody*, a poetic foot of three short syllables, as *mĕlĭŭs.*

TRIBRAC'TEATE, *a.* Having three bracts about the flower. *Decandolle.*

TRIBULA'TION, *n.* [Fr. from L. *tribulo*, to thrash, to beat.]

Severe affliction; distresses of life; vexations. In *Scripture*, it often denotes the troubles and distresses which proceed from persecution.

> When *tribulation* or persecution ariseth because of the word, he is offended. Matt. xiii.
>
> In the world ye shall have *tribulation.* John xvi.

TRIBU'NAL, *n.* [L. *tribunal*, from *tribunus*, a tribune, who administered justice.]

1. Properly, the seat of a judge; the bench on which a judge and his associates sit for administering justice.

2. More generally, a court of justice; as, the house of lords in England is the highest *tribunal* in the kingdom.

3. [Fr. *tribunel.*] In *France*, a gallery or eminence in a church or other place, in which the musical performers are placed for a concert.

TRIB'UNARY, *a.* [from *tribune.*] Pertaining to tribunes.

TRIB'UNE, *n.* [Fr. *tribun;* L. *tribunus*, from *tribus*, tribe; Sp. It. *tribuno.*]

1. In *ancient Rome*, an officer or magistrate chosen by the people to protect them from the oppression of the patricians or nobles, and to defend their liberties against any attempts that might be made upon them by the senate and consuls. These magistrates were at first two, but their number was increased ultimately to ten. There were also military tribunes, officers of the army, each of whom commanded a divis-

ion or legion. In the year of Rome 731, the senate transferred the authority of the tribunes to Augustus and his successors. There were also other officers called tribunes; as *tribunes* of the treasury, of the horse, of the making of arms, &c. *Cyc.*
2. In *France*, a pulpit or elevated place in the chamber of deputies, where a speaker stands to address the assembly.

TRIB'UNESHIP, *n.* The office of a tribune. *Addison.*

TRIBUNI''CIAN, } *a.* Pertaining to tribunes; as *tribunician* power or authority. *Middleton.*
TRIBUNI''TIAL,
2. Suiting a tribune.

TRIB'UTARY, *a.* [from *tribute.*] Paying tribute to another, either from compulsion, as an acknowledgment of submission, or to secure protection, or for the purpose of purchasing peace. The republic of Ragusa is *tributary* to the grand seignor. Many of the powers of Europe are *tributary* to the Barbary states.
2. Subject; subordinate.
He, to grace his *tributary* gods— *Milton.*
3. Paid in tribute.
No flatt'ry tunes these *tributary* lays. *Concanen.*
4. Yielding supplies of any thing. The Ohio has many large *tributary* streams; and is itself *tributary* to the Mississippi.

TRIB'UTARY, *n.* One that pays tribute or a stated sum to a conquering power, for the purpose of securing peace and protection, or as an acknowledgment of submission, or for the purchase of security. What a reproach to nations that they should be the *tributaries* of Algiers!

TRIB'UTE, *n.* [Fr. *tribut;* L. *tributum,* from *tribuo,* to give, bestow or divide.]
1. An annual or stated sum of money or other valuable thing, paid by one prince or nation to another, either as an acknowledgment of submission, or as the price of peace and protection, or by virtue of some treaty. The Romans made all their conquered countries pay *tribute,* as do the Turks at this day; and in some countries the *tribute* is paid in children. *Cyc.*
2. A personal contribution; as a *tribute* of respect.
3. Something given or contributed.

TRICAP'SULAR, *a.* [L. *tres,* three, and *capsula,* a little chest.]
In *botany,* three-capsuled; having three capsules to each flower. *Martyn.*

TRICE, *v. t.* [W. *treisiaw,* to seize.] In *seamen's language,* to haul and tie up by means of a small rope or line. *Mar. Dict.*

TRICE, *n.* A very short time; an instant; a moment.
If they get never so great spoil at any time, they waste the same in a *trice.* *Spenser.*
A man shall make his fortune in a *trice.* *Young.*

TRICHOT'OMOUS, *a.* [See *Trichotomy.*] Divided into three parts, or divided by threes; as a *trichotomous* stem. *Martyn.*

TRICHOT'OMY, *n.* [Gr. τριχα, three, and τεμνω, to cut or divide.] Division into three parts. *Watts.*

TRICK, *n.* [D. *trek,* a pull or drawing, a *trick; trekken,* to *draw,* to *drag; bedriegen,* to cheat; *driegen,* to tack or baste; G. *triegen,* to deceive; *trug, betrug,* fraud, *trick;* Dan. *trekke,* a trick; *trekker,* to draw, to entice; Fr. *tricher,* to cheat; It. *treccare,* to cheat; *trecca,* a huckster; *treccia,* a lock of hair, from folding, involving, Gr. θριξ; Sp. *trica,* a quibble; L. *tricor,* to play tricks, to trifle, to baffle. We see the same root in the Low L. *intrico,* to fold, and in *intrigue.* *Trick* is from *drawing,* that is, a drawing aside, or a folding, interweaving, implication.]
1. An artifice or stratagem for the purpose of deception; a fraudful contrivance for an evil purpose, or an underhand scheme to impose upon the world; a cheat or cheating. We hear of *tricks* in bargains, and *tricks* of state.
He comes to me for counsel, and I show him a *trick.* *South.*
2. A dextrous artifice.
On one nice *trick* depends the gen'ral fate. *Pope.*
3. Vicious practice; as the *tricks* of youth.
4. The sly artifice or legerdemain of a juggler; as the *tricks* of a merry Andrew.
5. A collection of cards laid together.
6. An unexpected event.
Some *trick* not worth an egg. [*Unusual.*] *Shak.*
7. A particular habit or manner; as, he has a *trick* of drumming with his fingers, or a *trick* of frowning. [*This word is in common use in America, and by no means vulgar.*]

TRICK, *v. t.* To deceive; to impose on; to defraud; to cheat; as, to *trick* another in the sale of a horse.

TRICK, *v. t.* [W. *treciaw,* to furnish or harness, to trick out; *trec,* an implement, harness, gear, from *rhêç,* a breaking forth, properly a throwing or extending. This may be a varied application of the foregoing word.]
To dress; to decorate; to set off; to adorn fantastically.
Trick her off in air. *Pope.*
It is often followed by *up, off,* or *out.*
People are lavish in *tricking up* their children in fine clothes, yet starve their minds. *Locke.*

TRICK, *v. i.* To live by deception and fraud. *Dryden.*

TRICK'ED, *pp.* Cheated; deceived; dressed.

TRICK'ER, } *n.* One who tricks; a deceiver; a cheat.
TRICK'STER,

TRICK'ER, *n.* A trigger. [See *Trigger.*]

TRICK'ERY, *n.* The art of dressing up; artifice; stratagem. *Parr. Burke.*

TRICK'ING, *ppr.* Deceiving; cheating; defrauding.
2. Dressing; decorating.

TRICK'ING, *n.* Dress; ornament. *Shak.*

TRICK'ISH, *a.* Artful in making bargains; given to deception and cheating; knavish. *Pope.*

TRICK'LE, *v. i.* [allied perhaps to Gr. τρεχω, to run, and a diminutive.]
To flow in a small gentle stream; to run down; as, tears *trickle* down the cheek; water *trickles* from the eaves.
Fast beside there *trickled* softly down
A gentle stream. *Spenser.*

TRICK'LING, *ppr.* Flowing down in a small gentle stream.

TRICK'LING, *n.* The act of flowing in a small gentle stream.
He wakened by the *trickling* of his blood. *Wiseman.*

TRICK'MENT, *n.* Decoration. [*Not used.*]

TRICK'SY, *a.* [from *trick.*] Pretty; brisk. [*Not much used.*] *Shak.*

TRICK'-TRACK, *n.* A game at tables.

TRICLIN'IARY, *a.* [L. *tricliniaris,* from *triclinium,* a couch to recline on at dinner.]
Pertaining to a couch for dining, or to the ancient mode of reclining at table.

TRICOC'COUS, *a.* [L. *tres,* three, and *coccus,* a berry.]
A tricoccous or three-grained capsule is one which is swelling out in three protuberances, internally divided into three cells, with one seed in each; as in Euphorbia. *Martyn.*

TRICOR'PORAL, *a.* [L. *tricorpor; tres* and *corpus.*] Having three bodies. *Todd.*

TRICUS'PIDATE, *a.* [L. *tres,* three, and *cuspis,* a point.]
In *botany,* three-pointed; ending in three points; as a *tricuspidate* stamen.

TRIDAC'TYLOUS, *a.* [Gr. τρεις, three, and δακτυλος, a toe.] Having three toes.

TRIDE, *a.* Among hunters, short and ready; fleet; as a *tride* pace. *Bailey. Cyc.*

TRI'DENT, *n.* [Fr. from L. *tridens; tres,* three, and *dens,* tooth.]
In *mythology,* a kind of scepter or spear with three prongs, which the fables of antiquity put into the hands of Neptune, the deity of the ocean.

TRI'DENT, } *a.* Having three teeth or prongs.
TRI'DENTED,

TRIDENT'ATE, *a.* [L. *tres* and *dens,* tooth.] Having three teeth. *Lee.*

TRIDIAPA'SON, *n.* [*tri* and *diapason.*] In *music,* a triple octave or twenty second. *Busby.*

TRI'DING. [See *Trithing.*]

TRIDODECAHE'DRAL, *a.* [Gr. τρεις, three, and *dodecahedral.*]
In *crystalography,* presenting three ranges of faces, one above another, each containing twelve faces.

TRID'UAN, *a.* [L. *triduum; tres* and *dies,* day.]
Lasting three days, or happening every third day. [*Little used.*]

TRIEN'NIAL, *a.* [Fr. *triennal;* L. *triennis, triennium; tres,* three, and *annus,* year.]
1. Continuing three years; as *triennial* parliaments.
2. Happening every three years; as *triennial* elections. *Triennial* elections and parliaments were established in England in 1695; but these were discontinued in 1717, and septennial elections and parliaments were adopted, which still continue.

TRIEN'NIALLY, *adv.* Once in three years.

TRI'ER, *n.* [from *try.*] One who tries; one who makes experiments; one who examines any thing by a test or standard.
2. One who tries judicially; a judge who tries a person or cause; a juryman. [See *Trior.*]
3. A test; that which tries or approves. *Shak.*

TRI'ERARCH, *n.* [Gr. τριηρης, a trireme, and αρχος, a chief.]
In *ancient Greece,* the commander of a trireme; also, a commissioner who was obliged to build ships and furnish them at his own expense. *Mitford.*

TRIETER'ICAL, *a.* [L. *trietericus; tres,* three, and Gr. ετος, year.]

Triennial; kept or occurring once in three years. [*Little used.*] *Gregory.*

TRI'FALLOW, *v. t.* [L. *tres*, three, and *fallow.*]

To plow land the third time before sowing. *Mortimer.*

TRIF'ID, *a.* [L. *trifidus ; tres*, three, and *findo*, to divide.]

In *botany*, divided into three parts by linear sinuses with strait margins; three-cleft. *Martyn.*

TRIFIS'TULARY, *a.* [L. *tres* and *fistula*, a pipe.] Having three pipes. *Brown.*

TRI'FLE, *n.* [It coincides with *trivial*, which see.]

A thing of very little value or importance; *a word applicable to any thing and every thing of this character.*

> With such poor *trifles* playing. *Drayton.*
> Moments make the year, and *trifles*, life. *Young.*
> *Trifles*
> Are to the jealous confirmations strong. *Shak.*

TRI'FLE, *v. i.* To act or talk without seriousness, gravity, weight or dignity; to act or talk with levity.

> They *trifle*, and they beat the air about nothing which toucheth us. *Hooker.*

2. To indulge in light amusements. *Law.*

To trifle with, to mock; to play the fool with; to treat without respect or seriousness.

To trifle with, } to spend in vanity; to waste
To trifle away, } to no good purpose; as, to *trifle with* time, or to *trifle away* time; to *trifle with* advantages.

TRI'FLE, *v. t.* To make of no importance. [*Not in use.*]

TRI'FLER, *n.* One who trifles or acts with levity. *Bacon.*

TRI'FLING, *ppr.* Acting or talking with levity, or without seriousness or being in earnest.

2. *a.* Being of small value or importance; trivial; as a *trifling* debt; a *trifling* affair.

TRI'FLING, *n.* Employment about things of no importance.

TRI'FLINGLY, *adv.* In a trifling manner; with levity; without seriousness or dignity. *Locke.*

TRI'FLINGNESS, *n.* Levity of manners; lightness. *Entick.*

2. Smallness of value; emptiness; vanity.

TRIF'LOROUS, *a.* [L. *tres*, three, and *flos, floris*, flower.]

Three-flowered; bearing three flowers; as a *triflorous* peduncle. *Martyn.*

TRIFO'LIATE, *a.* [L. *tres*, three, and *folium*, leaf.] Having three leaves. *Harte.*

TRIFO'LIOLATE, *a.* Having three folioles. *Decandolle.*

TRI'FOLY, *n.* Sweet trefoil. [See *Trefoil.*] *Mason.*

TRI'FORM, *a.* [L. *triformis ; tres* and *forma.*]

Having a triple form or shape; as the *triform* countenance of the moon. *Milton.*

TRIG, *v. t.* [W. *trigaw*. See *Trigger.*] To fill; to stuff. [*Not in use.*]

2. To stop; as a wheel. *Bailey.*

TRIG, *a.* Full; trim; neat. [*Not in use.*]

TRIG'AMY, *n.* [Gr. τρεις, three, and γαμος, marriage.]

State of being married three times; or the state of having three husbands or three wives at the same time. *Herbert.*

TRIG'GER, *n.* [W. *trigaw*, to stop; Dan. *trekker*, to draw; *trykker*, to press or pinch; or *trygger*, to make sure; *trug*, Sw. *trygg*, safe, secure; *trycka*, to press. This is the Eng. *true*, or from the same root.]

1. A catch to hold the wheel of a carriage on a declivity.

2. The catch of a musket or pistol; the part which being pulled, looses the lock for striking fire.

TRIGIN'TALS, *n.* [L. *triginta.*] Trentals; the number of thirty masses to be said for the dead.

TRIG'LYPH, *n.* [Gr. τρεις, three, and γλυφη, sculpture.]

An ornament in the frieze of the Doric column, repeated at equal intervals. Each triglyph consists of two entire gutters or channels, cut to a right angle, called *glyphs*, and separated by three interstices, called *femora.* *Cyc.*

TRIG'ON, *n.* [Gr. τρεις, three, and γωνια, angle.]

1. A triangle; a term used in astrology; also, trine, an aspect of two planets distant 120 degrees from each other. *Cyc.*

2. A kind of triangular lyre or harp.

TRIG'ONAL, } *a.* Triangular; having
TRIG'ONOUS, } three angles or corners.

2. In *botany*, having three prominent longitudinal angles. *Martyn.*

TRIGONOMET'RICAL, *a.* Pertaining to trigonometry; performed by or according to the rules of trigonometry.

TRIGONOMET'RICALLY, *adv.* According to the rules or principles of trigonometry. *Asiat. Res.*

TRIGONOM'ETRY, *n.* [Gr. τριγωνος, a triangle, and μετρεω, to measure.]

The measuring of triangles; the science of determining the sides and angles of triangles, by means of certain parts which are given. When this science is applied to the solution of plane triangles, it is called *plane* trigonometry; when its application is to spherical triangles, it is called *spherical* trigonometry.

TRI'GYN, *n.* [Gr. τρεις, three, and γυνη, a female.] In *botany*, a plant having three pistils.

TRIGYN'IAN, *a.* Having three pistils.

TRIHE'DRAL, *a.* [See *Trihedron.*] Having three equal sides.

TRIHE'DRON, *n.* [Gr. τρεις, three, and εδρα, side.] A figure having three equal sides.

TRIJU'GOUS, *a.* [L. *tres*, three, and *jugum*, yoke.]

In *botany*, having three pairs. A *trijugous* leaf is a pinnate leaf with three pairs of leaflets. *Martyn.*

TRILAT'ERAL, *a.* [Fr. from L. *tres*, three, and *latus*, side.] Having three sides.

TRILIT'ERAL, *a.* [L. *tres*, three, and *litera*, letter.]

Consisting of three letters; as a *triliteral* root or word.

TRILIT'ERAL, *n.* A word consisting of three letters.

TRILL, *n.* [It. *trillo ;* Dan. *trille ;* G. *triller ;* W. *treilliaw*, to turn, to roll. But the latter may be contracted from *treiglaw*, to turn; *traill, traigyl*, a turn or roll, from the root of *draw, drag.* *Trill* coincides with *thirl* and *drill ;* D. *drillen.* Qu. *reel.*]

A quaver; a shake of the voice in singing, or of the sound of an instrument. [See *Shake.*]

TRILL, *v. t.* [It. *trillare.*] To utter with a quavering or tremulousness of voice; to shake.

> The sober-suited songstress *trills* her lay. *Thomson.*

TRILL, *v. i.* To flow in a small stream, or in drops rapidly succeeding each other; to trickle.

> And now and then an ample tear *trill'd* down
> Her delicate cheek. *Shak.*

2. To shake or quaver; to play in tremulous vibrations of sound.

> To judge of *trilling* notes and tripping feet. *Dryden.*

TRILL'ED, *pp.* Shaken; uttered with rapid vibrations.

TRILL'ING, *ppr.* Uttering with a quavering or shake.

TRILLION, *n.* *tril'yun.* [a word formed arbitrarily of *three*, or Gr. τριτος, and *million.*]

The product of a million multiplied by a million, and that product multiplied by a million; or the product of the square of a million multiplied by a million. Thus 1.000,000 × 1.000,000 = 1.000,000,000,000, and this product multiplied by a million = 1,000,000,000,000,000,000.

TRILO'BATE, *a.* [L. *tres* and *lobus.*] Having three lobes. *Journ. of Science.*

TRILOC'ULAR, *a.* [L. *tres* and *locus*, a cell.]

In *botany*, three-celled; having three cells for seeds; as a *trilocular* capsule.

TRILU'MINAR, } *a.* [L. *tres* and *lumen*,
TRILU'MINOUS, } light.] Having three lights.

TRIM, *a.* [Sax. *trum*, firm, stable, strong, secure; *tryman, getrymian*, to make firm, to strengthen, to prepare, to order or dispose, to exhort, persuade or animate. The primary sense is to set, to strain, or to make straight.]

Firm; compact; tight; snug; being in good order. We say of a ship, she is *trim*, or *trim-built ;* every thing about the man is *trim.* We say of a person, he is *trim*, when his body is well shaped and firm; and we say, his dress is *trim*, when it sits closely to his body and appears tight and snug; and of posture we say, a man or a soldier is *trim*, when he stands erect. It is particularly applicable to soldiers, and in Saxon, *truma* is a troop or body of soldiers.

TRIM, *v. t.* [Sax. *trumian, trymian*, to make firm or strong, to strengthen, to prepare, to put in order.]

1. In *a general sense*, to make right, that is, to put in due order for any purpose.

> The hermit *trimm'd* his little fire. *Goldsmith.*

2. To dress; to put the body in a proper state.

> I was *trimm'd* in Julia's gown. *Shak.*

3. To decorate; to invest or embellish with extra ornaments; as, to *trim* a gown with lace. *Dryden.*

4. To clip, as the hair of the head; also, to shave; that is, to put in due order.

5. To lop, as superfluous branches; to prune; as, to *trim* trees. *Mortimer.*
6. To supply with oil; as, to *trim* a lamp.
7. To make neat; to adjust.

> I found her *trimming* up the diadem
> On her dead mistress— *Shak.*

8. In *carpentry*, to dress, as timber; to make smooth.
9. To adjust the cargo of a ship, or the weight of persons or goods in a boat, so equally on each side of the center and at each end, that she shall sit well on the water and sail well. Thus we say, to *trim* a ship or a boat.
10. To rebuke; to reprove sharply; *a popular use of the word.*
11. To arrange in due order for sailing; as, to *trim* the sails.

To trim in, in *carpentry*, to fit, as a piece of timber into other work. *Moxon.*

To trim up, to dress; to put in order.

TRIM, *v. i.* To balance; to fluctuate between parties, so as to appear to favor each. *South.*

TRIM, *n.* Dress; gear; ornaments. *Dryden.*

2. The state of a ship or her cargo, ballast, masts, &c., by which she is well prepared for sailing.

Trim of the masts, is their position in regard to the ship and to each other, as near or distant, far forward or much aft, erect or raking. *Mar. Dict.*

Trim of sails, is that position and arrangement which is best adapted to impel the ship forward. *Mar. Dict.*

TRIM'ETER, *n.* A poetical division of verse, consisting of three measures. *Lowth.*

TRIM'ETER, TRIMET'RICAL, *a.* [Gr. τριμετρος, three measures.] Consisting of three poetical measures, forming an iambic of six feet. *Roscommon.*

TRIM'LY, *adv.* Nicely; neatly; in good order. *Spenser.*

TRIM'MED, *pp.* Put in good order; dressed; ornamented; clipped; shaved; balanced; rebuked.

TRIM'MER, *n.* One that trims; a time-server.

2. A piece of timber fitted in.

> All the joists and the *trimmers* for the stair case— *Moxon.*

TRIM'MING, *ppr.* Putting in due order; dressing; decorating; pruning; balancing; fluctuating between parties.

TRIM'MING, *n.* Ornamental appendages to a garment, as lace, ribins and the like.

TRIM'NESS, *n.* Neatness; snugness; the state of being close and in good order.

TRI'NAL, *a.* [L. *trinus*, three.] Threefold. *Milton.*

TRINE, *a.* Threefold; as *trine* dimension, that is, length, breadth and thickness.

TRINE, *n.* [supra.] In *astrology*, the aspect of planets distant from each other 120 degrees, forming the figure of a trigon or triangle. *Cyc. Johnson.*

TRINE, *v. t.* To put in the aspect of a trine. *Dryden.*

TRINERV'ATE, *a.* [L. *tres* and *nervus.*] In *botany*, having three nerves or unbranched vessels meeting behind or beyond the base. *Martyn.*

TRI'NERVE, TRI'NERVED, *a.* In *botany*, a *trinerved* or three-nerved leaf, has three nerves or unbranched vessels meeting in the base of the leaf. *Martyn.*

TRIN'GLE, *n.* [Fr.] In *architecture*, a little square member or ornament, as a listel, reglet, platband and the like, but particularly a little member fixed exactly over every triglyph. *Cyc.*

TRINITA'RIAN, *a.* Pertaining to the Trinity, or to the doctrine of the Trinity.

TRINITA'RIAN, *n.* One who believes the doctrine of the Trinity.

2. One of an order of religious, who made it their business to redeem christians from infidels.

TRIN'ITY, *n.* [L. *trinitas; tres* and *unus, unitas*, one, unity.]

In *theology*, the union of three persons in one Godhead, the Father, the Son, and the Holy Spirit.

> In my whole essay, there is not any thing like an objection against the *Trinity*. *Locke.*

TRINK'ET, *n.* [If *n* is casual, this is from W. *treciaw*, to furnish. See *Trick.*]

1. A small ornament, as a jewel, a ring and the like. *Dryden. Swift.*
2. A thing of little value; tackle; tools. *Tusser. L'Estrange.*

TRINO'MIAL, *a.* [L. *tres* and *nomen.*] In *mathematics*, a *trinomial* root, is a root consisting of three parts, connected by the signs + or —. Thus $x+y+z$, or $a+b-c$.

TRINO'MIAL, *n.* A root of three terms or parts.

TRI'O, *n.* A concert of three parts; three united.

TRIOB'OLAR, *a.* [L. *triobolaris; tres* and *obolus.*]

Of the value of three oboli; mean; worthless. [*Not used.*] *Cheyne.*

TRIOCTAHE'DRAL, *a.* [*tri* and *octahedral.*]

In *crystalography*, presenting three ranges of faces, one above another, each range containing eight faces.

TRIOC'TILE, *n.* [L. *tres*, three, and *octo*, eight.]

In *astrology*, an aspect of two planets with regard to the earth, when they are three octants or eight parts of a circle, that is, 135 degrees, distant from each other. *Cyc.*

TRI'OR, TRI'ER, *n.* [from *try.*] In *law*, a person appointed by the court to examine whether a challenge to a panel of jurors, or to any juror, is just. The *triors* are two indifferent persons. *Cyc.*

TRIP, *v. t.* [G. *trippeln*; D. *trippen*; Sw. *trippa*; Dan. *tripper*; W. *tripiaw*, to trip, to stumble; from *rhip*, a skipping. See טרף and טרב in Castle.]

1. To supplant; to cause to fall by striking the feet suddenly from under the person; usually followed by *up*; as, to *trip up* a man in wrestling; to *trip up* the heels. *Shak.*
2. To supplant; to overthrow by depriving of support. *Bramhall.*
3. To catch; to detect. *Shak.*
4. To loose an anchor from the bottom by its cable or buoy-rope. *Mar. Dict.*

TRIP, *v. i.* To stumble; to strike the foot against something, so as to lose the step and come near to fall; or to stumble and fall.

2. To err; to fail; to mistake; to be deficient.

> Virgil pretends sometimes to *trip*. *Dryden.*

TRIP, *v. i.* [Ar. طرب *tariba*, to move lightly; allied perhaps to Sw. *trappa*, Dan. *trappe*, G. *treppe*, stairs.]

1. To run or step lightly; to walk with a light step.

> She bounded by and *tripp'd* so light
> They had not time to take a steady sight. *Dryden.*

> Thus from the lion *trips* the trembling doe. *Dryden.*

2. To take a voyage or journey.

TRIP, *n.* A stroke or catch by which a wrestler supplants his antagonist.

> And watches with a *trip* his foe to foil. *Dryden.*

2. A stumble by the loss of foot-hold, or a striking of the foot against an object.
3. A failure; a mistake.

> Each seeming *trip*, and each digressive start. *Harte.*

4. A journey; or a voyage.

> I took a *trip* to London on the death of the queen. *Pope.*

5. In *navigation*, a single board in plying to windward. *Cyc.*
6. Among *farmers*, a small flock of sheep, or a small stock of them. [*Local.*] *Cyc.*

TRIP'ARTITE, *a.* [Fr. from L. *tripartitus; tres*, three, and *partitus*, divided; *partior.*]

1. Divided into three parts. In botany, a *tripartite* leaf is one which is divided into three parts down to the base, but not wholly separate. *Martyn.*
2. Having three corresponding parts or copies; as indentures *tripartite.*

TRIPARTI''TION, *n.* A division by three, or the taking of a third part of any number or quantity. *Cyc.*

TRIPE, *n.* [Fr. *id.*; Sp. *tripa*; It. *trippa*; G. *tripp*; Russ. *trebucha*; W. *tripa*, from *rhip*, from *rhib*, a streak or dribblet. In Sp. *tripe*, Dan. *trip*, is shag, plush. This word is probably from tearing, ripping, like *strip.*]

1. Properly, the entrails; but in common usage, the large stomach of ruminating animals, prepared for food.
2. In ludicrous language, the belly. *Johnson.*

TRIP'EDAL, *a.* [L. *tres* and *pes.*] Having three feet.

TRI'PE-MAN, *n.* A man who sells tripe. *Swift.*

TRIPEN'NATE, TRIPIN'NATE, *a.* [L. *tres* and *penna* or *pinna.*] In *botany*, a *tripinnate* leaf is a species of superdecompound leaf, when a petiole has bipinnate leaves ranged on each side of it, as in common fern. *Martyn.*

TRIPER'SONAL, *a.* [L. *tres* and *persona.*] Consisting of three persons. *Milton.*

TRIPET'ALOUS, *a.* [Gr. τρεις, three, and πεταλον, leaf.]

In *botany*, three-petaled; having three petals or flower leaves.

TRI'PHANE, *n.* A mineral, spodumene. *Ure.*

TRIPH'THONG, *n.* [Gr. τρεις, three, and φθογγη, sound.]

A coalition of three vowels in one compound sound, or in one syllable, as in *adieu, eye.*

TRIPHTHON'GAL, *a.* Pertaining to a triphthong; consisting of a triphthong.

TRIPH'YLLOUS, *a.* [Gr. τρεις, three, and φυλλον, leaf.]
In *botany*, three-leaved; having three leaves.

TRIP'LE, *a.* [Fr. from L. *triplex, triplus; tres* and *plico*, to fold.]
1. Threefold; consisting of three united; as a *triple* knot; a *triple* tie.

By thy *triple* shape as thou art seen— *Dryden.*

2. Treble; three times repeated. [See *Treble.*]
Triple time, in music, is that in which each bar is divided into three measures or equal parts, as three minims, three crotchets, three quavers, &c.

TRIP'LE, *v. t.* To treble; to make threefold or thrice as much or as many. [Usually written *treble.*] *Lee.*

TRIP'LET, *n.* [from *triple.*] Three of a kind, or three united.
2. In *poetry*, three verses rhyming together.
3. In *music*, three notes sung or played in the time of two.

TRIP'LICATE, *a.* [L. *triplicatus, triplico; tres* and *plico*, to fold.]
Made thrice as much; threefold.
Triplicate ratio, is the ratio which cubes bear to each other. *Cyc.*

TRIPLICA'TION, *n.* The act of trebling or making threefold, or adding three together. *Glanville.*
2. In *the civil law*, the same as sur-rejoinder in common law.

TRIPLIC'ITY, *n.* [Fr. *triplicité*; from L. *triplex.*]
Trebleness; the state of being threefold. *Watts.*

TRIP'LY-RIBBED, *a.* [*triple* and *rib.*] In *botany*, having a pair of large ribs branching off from the main one above the base, as in the leaves of many species of sunflower. *Smith.*

TRIP'-MADAM, *n.* A plant. *Mortimer.*

TRI'POD, *n.* [L. *tripus, tripodis*; Gr. τριπους; τρεις, three, and πους, foot.]
A bench, stool or seat supported by three legs, on which the priest and sibyls in ancient times were placed to render oracles. *Dryden. Cyc.*

TRIP'OLI, *n.* In *mineralogy*, a mineral originally brought from Tripoli, used in polishing stones and metals. It has a dull argillaceous appearance, but is not compact. It has a fine hard grain, but does not soften by water, or mix with it. It is principally composed of silex. *Cyc.*

TRIP'OLINE, *a.* Pertaining to tripoli.

TRI'POS, *n.* A tripod, which see.

TRIP'PED, *pp.* [from *trip.*] Supplanted.

TRIP'PER, *n.* One who trips or supplants; one that walks nimbly.

TRIP'PING, *ppr.* Supplanting; stumbling; falling; stepping nimbly.
2. *a.* Quick; nimble. *Milton.*

TRIP'PING, *n.* The act of tripping.
2. A light dance. *Milton.*
3. The loosing of an anchor from the ground by its cable or buoy-rope.

TRIP'PINGLY, *adv.* Nimbly; with a light nimble quick step; with agility.

Sing and dance it *trippingly.* *Shak.*

Speak the speech *trippingly* on the tongue. *Shak.*

TRIP'TOTE, *n.* [Gr. τρεις, three, and πτωσις, case.]
In *grammar*, a name having three cases only. *Clarke.*

TRIPU'DIARY, *a.* [L. *tripudium.*] Pertaining to dancing; performed by dancing. *Brown.*

TRIPUDIA'TION, *n.* [L. *tripudio*, to dance.]
Act of dancing. *Johnson.*

TRIPYR'AMID, *n.* [L. *tres* and *pyramis.*] In *mineralogy*, a genus of spars, the body of which is composed of single pyramids, each of three sides, affixed by their base to some solid body. *Cyc.*

TRIQUE'TROUS, *a.* [L. *triquetrus*, from *triquetra*, a triangle.]
Three-sided; having three plane sides. *Encyc.*

TRIRA'DIATED, *a.* [L. *tres* and *radius.*] Having three rays.

TRI'REME, *n.* [L. *triremis; tres* and *remus.*]
A galley or vessel with three benches or ranks of oars on a side. *Mitford.*

TRIRHOMBOID'AL, *a.* [*tri* and *rhomboidal.*] Having the form of three rhombs.

TRISACRAMENTA'RIAN, *n.* [L. *tres*, three, and *sacrament.*]
One of a religious sect who admit of three sacraments and no more. *Cyc.*

TRISAG'ION, *n.* [Gr. τρεις, three, and αγιος, holy.]
A hymn in which the word *holy* is repeated three times. *Bull. Cyc.*

TRISECT', *v. t.* [L. *tres*, three, and *seco*, to cut.]
To cut or divide into three equal parts. *Allen.*

TRISECT'ED, *pp.* Divided into three equal parts.

TRISECT'ING, *ppr.* Dividing into three equal parts.

TRISEC'TION, *n.* [L. *tres* and *sectio*, a cutting.]
The division of a thing into three parts; particularly in geometry, the division of an angle into three equal parts. *Cyc.*

TRISEP'ALOUS, *a.* In *botany*, having three sepals to a calyx. *Decandolle.*

TRIS'PAST, TRISPAS'TON, *n.* [Gr. τρεις and σπαω, to draw.] In *mechanics*, a machine with three pulleys for raising great weights. *Cyc.*

TRISPERM'OUS, *a.* [Gr. τρεις, three, and σπερμα, seed.]
Three-seeded; containing three seeds; as a *trispermous* capsule.

TRIST, TRIST'FUL, *a.* [L. *tristis*, sad.] Sad; sorrowful; gloomy. [*Not used.*] *Shak.*

TRIPERSONAL'ITY, *n.* The state of existing in three persons in one Godhead. *Milton.*

TRISULC', *n.* [L. *trisulcus.*] Something having three points. [*Not in use.*] *Brown.*

TRISYLLAB'IC, TRISYLLAB'ICAL, *a.* [from *trisyllable.*] Pertaining to a trisyllable; consisting of three syllables; as a *trisyllabic* word or root.

TRISYL'LABLE, *n.* [L. *tres*, three, and *syllaba*, syllable.] A word consisting of three syllables.

TRITE, *a.* [L. *tritus*, from *tero*, to wear.]
Worn out; common; used till so common as to have lost its novelty and interest; as a *trite* remark; a *trite* subject. *Swift.*

TRI'TELY, *adv.* In a common manner.

TRI'TENESS, *n.* Commonness; staleness; a state of being worn out; as the *triteness* of an observation or a subject.

TRITERN'ATE, *a.* [L. *tres*, three, and *ternate.*]
Having three biternate leaves, or the divisions of a triple petiole subdivided into threes; a species of superdecompound leaf. *Martyn. Lee.*

TRITHE'ISM, *n.* [Fr. *tritheisme;* Gr. τρεις, three, and θεος, God.]
The opinion or doctrine that there are three Gods in the Godhead.

TRITHE'IST, *n.* One who believes that there are three distinct Gods in the Godhead, that is, three distinct substances, essences or hypostases. *Encyc.*

TRITHEIS'TIC, *a.* Pertaining to tritheism.

TRITHE'ITE, *n.* A tritheist.

TRI'THING, *n.* [from *three.*] One of the divisions of the county of York in England, which is divided into three parts. It is now called *Riding.* *Blackstone.*

TRIT'ICAL, *a.* [from *trite.*] Trite; common. [*Not in use.*]

TRIT'ICALNESS, *n.* Triteness. [*Not used.*] *Warton.*

TRI'TON, *n.* In *mythology*, a fabled sea demi-god, supposed to be the trumpeter of Neptune. He is represented by poets and painters as half man and half fish. *Cyc.*
2. A genus of the molluscal order of worms. *Linne. Cyc.*
3. A bird of the West Indies, famous for its notes. *Ray. Cyc.*

TRI'TONE, *n.* [L. *tres* and *tonus.*] In *music*, a false concord, consisting of three tones, two major and one minor tone, or of two tones and two semitones; a dissonant interval. *Cyc.*

TRITOX'YD, *n.* [Gr. τριτος, third, and *oxyd.*]
In *chimistry*, a substance oxydized in the third degree. *Thomson.*

TRIT'URABLE, *a.* [See *Triturate.*] Capable of being reduced to a fine powder by pounding, rubbing or grinding. *Brown.*

TRIT'URATE, *v. t.* [L. *trituro*, from *tritus*, *tero*, to wear.]
To rub or grind to a very fine powder, and properly to a finer powder than that made by pulverization.

TRIT'URATED, *pp.* Reduced to a very fine powder.

TRIT'URATING, *ppr.* Grinding or reducing to a very fine powder.

TRITURA'TION, *n.* The act of reducing to a fine powder by grinding.

TRI'TURE, *n.* A rubbing or grinding. [*Not used.*] *Cheyne.*

TRITU'RIUM, *n.* A vessel for separating liquors of different densities.

TRI'UMPH, *n.* [Fr. *triomphe;* It. *trionfo;* Sp. *triunfo;* L. *triumphus;* Gr. θριαμβος.]
1. Among *the ancient Romans*, a pompous ceremony performed in honor of a victorious general, who was allowed to enter

the city crowned, originally with laurel, but in later times with gold, bearing a truncheon in one hand and a branch of laurel in the other, riding in a chariot drawn by two white horses, and followed by the kings, princes and generals whom he had vanquished, loaded with chains and insulted by mimics and buffoons. The triumph was of two kinds, the greater and the less. The lesser triumph was granted for a victory over enemies of less considerable power, and was called an *ovation.*

2. State of being victorious.

Hercules from Spain
Arriv'd in *triumph*, from Geryon slain. *Dryden.*

3. Victory; conquest.

The vain coquets the trifling *triumphs* boast. *Logie.*

4. Joy or exultation for success.

Great *triumph* and rejoicing was in heav'n. *Milton.*

5. A card that takes all others; now written *trump*, which see.

TRI'UMPH, *v. i.* To celebrate victory with pomp; to rejoice for victory.

How long shall the wicked *triumph?* Ps. xciv.

2. To obtain victory.

There fix thy faith, and *triumph* o'er the world. *Rowe.*

Attir'd with stars, we shall forever sit
Triumphing over death. *Milton.*

3. To insult upon an advantage gained.

Let not my enemies *triumph* over me. Ps. xxv.

Sorrow on all the pack of you
That *triumph* thus upon my misery. *Shak.*

4. To be prosperous; to flourish.

Where commerce *triumph'd* on the favoring gales. *Trumbull.*

To triumph over, to succeed in overcoming; to surmount; as, to *triumph over* all obstacles.

TRIUMPH'AL, *a.* [Fr. from L. *triumphalis.*] Pertaining to triumph; used in a triumph; as a *triumphal* crown or car; a *triumphal* arch. *Pope. Swift.*

TRIUMPH'AL, *n.* A token of victory. *Milton.*

TRIUMPH'ANT, *a.* [L. *triumphans.*] Celebrating victory; as a *triumphant* chariot. *South.*

2. Rejoicing as for victory.

Successful beyond hope to lead you forth
Triumphant out of this infernal pit. *Milton.*

3. Victorious; graced with conquest.

So shall it be in the church *triumphant.* *Perkins.*

Athena, war's *triumphant* maid— *Pope.*

4. Celebrating victory; expressing joy for success; as a *triumphant* song.

TRIUMPH'ANTLY, *adv.* In a triumphant manner; with the joy and exultation that proceeds from victory or success.

Through armed ranks *triumphantly* she drives. *Granville.*

2. Victoriously; with success.

Triumphantly tread on thy country's ruin. *Shak.*

3. With insolent exultation. *South.*

TRI'UMPHER, *n.* One who triumphs or rejoices for victory; one who vanquishes.

2. One who was honored with a triumph in Rome. *Peacham.*

TRI'UMPHING, *ppr.* Celebrating victory with pomp; vanquishing; rejoicing for victory; insulting on an advantage.

TRI'UMVIR, *n.* [L. *tres*, three, and *vir*, man.] One of three men united in office. The triumvirs, L. *triumviri*, of Rome, were three men who jointly obtained the sovereign power in Rome. The first of these were Cesar, Crassus and Pompey.

TRIUM'VIRATE, *n.* A coalition of three men; particularly, the union of three men who obtained the government of the Roman empire.

2. Government by three men in coalition.

TRI'UNE, *a.* [L. *tres* and *unus.*] Three in one; an epithet applied to God, to express the unity of the Godhead in a trinity of persons. *Cyc.*

TRIU'NITY, *n.* Trinity. [*Not used.*]

TRIV'ANT, *n.* A truant. *Burton.*

TRIVALV'ULAR, *a.* Three-valved; having three valves.

TRIVERB'IAL, *a.* [L. *triverbium.*] Triverbial days, in the Roman calendar, were juridical or court days, days allowed to the pretor for hearing causes; called also *dies fasti.* There were only twenty eight in the year. *Cyc.*

TRIV'ET, *n.* A three legged stool. [See *Trevet.*]

TRIV'IAL, *a.* [Fr. from L. *trivialis*; probably from Gr. τριβω, L. *tero, trivi*, to wear, or from *trivium*, a highway.]

1. Trifling; of little worth or importance; inconsiderable; as a *trivial* subject; a *trivial* affair. *Dryden. Pope.*

2. Worthless; vulgar. *Roscommon.*

Trivial name, in *natural history*, the common name for the species, which added to the generic name forms the complete denomination of the species; the specific name. Thus in *Lathyrus aphaca, Lathyrus* is the generic name, and *aphaca* the trivial or specific name, and the two combined form the complete denomination of the species. Linne at first applied the term *specific name* to the essential character of the species, now called the *specific definition* or *difference*; but it is now applied solely to the trivial name. *Martyn. Cyc.*

TRIVIAL'ITY, *n.* Trivialness. [*Not much used.*]

TRIV'IALLY, *adv.* Commonly; vulgarly.

2. Lightly; inconsiderably; in a trifling degree.

TRIV'IALNESS, *n.* Commonness.

2. Lightness; unimportance.

TROAT, *v. i.* To cry, as a buck in rutting time. *Dict.*

TROAT, *n.* The cry of a buck in rutting time.

TRO'€AR, *n.* [Fr. *un trois quart*, expressive of its triangular point.] A surgical instrument for tapping dropsical persons and the like.

TRO€HA'I€, **TRO€HA'I€AL**, *a.* [See *Trochee.*] In *poetry*, consisting of trochees; as *trochaic* measure or verse.

TRO€HAN'TER, *n.* [Gr. τροχαντηρ.] In *anatomy*, the trochanters are two processes of the thigh bone, called *major* and *minor*, the major on the outside, and the minor on the inside. *Coxe. Cyc.*

TRO'€HE, *n.* [Gr. τροχος, a wheel.] A form of medicine in a cake or tablet, or a stiff paste cut into proper portions and dried. It is made by mixing the medicine with sugar and the mucilage of gum tragacanth, intended to be gradually dissolved in the mouth and slowly swallowed, as a demulcent to sheath the epiglottis, and as a remedy for the bronchocele.

TRO'€HEE, *n.* [L. *trochæus*; Gr. τροχαιος, from τρεχω.] In *verse*, a foot of two syllables, the first long and the second short.

TRO€HIL'I€, *a.* Having power to draw out or turn round.

TRO€HIL'I€S, *n.* [Gr. τροχιλια, from τρεχω; L. *trochilus.*] The science of rotary motion.

TRO'€HILUS, **TRO'€HIL**, *n.* [L. *trochilus*; Gr. τροχιλος, from τρεχω, to run.]

1. An aquatic bird, a swift runner, with long legs, which is said to get its meat out of the crocodile's mouth. *Ainsworth.*

2. A name given to the golden crowned wren. *Cyc.*

3. In *zoology*, the humming bird or honeysucker, a kind of beautiful little birds, natives of America. *Cyc.*

4. In *architecture*, a hollow ring round a column; called also scotia, and by workmen, the casement. *Cyc.*

TRO'€HINGS, *n.* The small branches on the top of a deer's head. *Cyc.*

TRO'€HISCH, *n.* [Gr. τροχισκος.] A kind of tablet or lozenge. *Bacon.*

TRO'€HITE, *n.* [L. *trochus*; Gr. τρεχω, to run.]

1. In *natural history*, a kind of figured fossil stone, resembling parts of plants, called St. Cuthbert's beads. These stones are usually of a brownish color; they break like spar, and are easily dissolved in vinegar. Their figure is generally cylindrical, sometimes a little tapering. Two, three or more of these joined, constitute an *entrochus.* *Cyc.*

2. Fossil remains of the shells called *trochus.*

TRO€H'LEA, *n.* [L. a pulley, from Gr. τρεχω, to run.] A pulley-like cartilage, through which the tendon of the trochleary muscle passes. *Coxe. Parr.*

TRO€H'LEARY, *a.* [from L. *trochlea.*] Pertaining to the trochlea; as the *trochleary* muscle, the superior oblique muscle of the eye; the *trochleary* nerve, the pathetic nerve, which goes to that muscle. *Parr.*

TRO'€HOID, *n.* [Gr. τροχος, L. *trochus*, from τρεχω, to run, and ειδος.] In *geometry*, a curve generated by the motion of a wheel; the cycloid. *Cyc.*

TROD, *pret.* of *tread.*

TROD, **TRODDEN**, *pp.* of *tread.*

Jerusalem shall be *trodden* down by the Gentiles. Luke xxi.

TRODE, *old pret.* of *tread.*

TRODE, *n.* Tread; footing. *Obs.* *Spenser.*

TROG'LODYTE, *n.* [Gr. τρωγλη, a cavern, and δυω, to enter.] The Troglodytes were a people of Ethiopia, represented by the ancients as living in caves, about whom we have many fables. *Cyc.*

TROLL, *v. t.* [G. *trollen*; W. *troliaw*, to troll, to roll; *troelli*, to turn, wheel or whirl; *troell*, a wheel, a reel; *trol*, a roller. It is probably formed on *roll.*]

To move in a circular direction; to roll; to move volubly; to turn; to drive about.

They learn to roll the eye, and *troll* the tongue.

Troll about the bridal bowl. *B. Jonson.*

TROLL, *v. i.* To roll; to run about; as, to *troll* in a coach and six. *Swift.*

2. Among *anglers*, to fish for pikes with a rod whose line runs on a wheel or pulley. *Gay. Cyc.*

TROLLED, *pp.* Rolled; turned about.

TROLLING, *ppr.* Rolling; turning; driving about; fishing with a rod and reel.

TROL′LOP, *n.* [G. *trolle;* from *troll*, strolling.]

A stroller; a loiterer; a woman loosely dressed; a slattern. *Milton.*

TROLLOPEE′, *n.* Formerly, a loose dress for females. *Obs. Goldsmith.*

TROL′MYDAMES, *n.* [Fr. *trou-madame.*] The game of nine-holes. *Shak.*

TROMP, *n.* [See *Trumpet.*] A blowing machine formed of a hollow tree, used in furnaces.

TROMP′IL, *n.* An aperture in a tromp.

TRON′AĢE, *n.* Formerly, a toll or duty paid for weighing wool. *Cyc.*

TRONA′TOR, *n.* An officer in London, whose business was to weigh wool.

TRON′€O, *n.* [L. *truncus.*] A term in Italian music, directing a note or sound to be cut short, or just uttered and then discontinued. *Cyc.*

TRONE, *n.* A provincial word in some parts of England for a small drain. *Cyc.*

TROOP, *n.* [Fr. *troupe;* It. *truppa;* Sp. Port. *tropa;* Dan. D. *trop;* G. *trupp;* Sw. *tropp.* The Gaelic *trapan*, a bunch or cluster, is probably the same word. The sense is a crowd, or a moving crowd.]

1. A collection of people; a company; a number; a multitude. Gen. xlix. 2 Sam. xxiii. Hos. vii.

That which should accompany old age,
As honor, love, obedience, *troops* of friends,
I must not look to have. *Shak.*

2. A body of soldiers. But applied to infantry, it is now used in the plural, *troops*, and this word signifies soldiers in general, whether more or less numerous, including infantry, cavalry and artillery. We apply the word to a company, a regiment or an army. The captain ordered his *troops* to halt; the colonel commanded his *troops* to wheel and take a position on the flank; the general ordered his *troops* to attack; the *troops* of France amounted to 400,000 men.

3. *Troop*, in the singular, a small body or company of cavalry, light horse or dragoons, commanded by a captain.

4. A company of stage-players. *Coxe's Russ.*

TROOP, *v. i.* To collect in numbers.

Armies at the call of trumpet,
Troop to their standard. *Milton.*

2. To march in a body.

I do not, as an enemy to peace,
Troop in the throngs of military men. *Shak.*

3. To march in haste or in company. *Shak. Chapman.*

TROOP′ER, *n.* A private or soldier in a body of cavalry; a horse soldier.

TROOP′ING, *ppr.* Moving together in a crowd; marching in a body.

TROPE, *n.* [L. *tropus;* Gr. τροπος, from τρεπω, to turn; W. *trova*, a turn, a *tropic; trovâu*, to turn.]

In *rhetoric*, a word or expression used in a different sense from that which it properly signifies; or a word changed from its original signification to another, for the sake of giving life or emphasis to an idea, as when we call a stupid fellow an ass, or a shrewd man a fox.

Tropes are chiefly of four kinds, metaphor, metonymy, synecdoche, and irony. Some authors make figure the genus, of which trope is a species; others make them different things, defining trope to be a change of sense, and figure to be any ornament, except what becomes so by such change.

TRO′PHIED, *a.* [from *trophy.*] Adorned with trophies.

—The *trophied* arches, storied halls invade. *Pope.*

TRO′PHY, *n.* [L. *tropæum;* Gr. τροπαιον; Fr. *trophée;* Sp. It. *trofeo.*]

1. Among *the ancients*, a pile of arms taken from a vanquished enemy, raised on the field of battle by the conquerors; also, the representation of such a pile in marble, on medals and the like; or according to others, trophies were trees planted in conspicuous places of the conquered provinces, and hung with the spoils of the enemy, in memory of the victory. Hence,

2. Any thing taken and preserved as a memorial of victory, as arms, flags, standards and the like, taken from an enemy.

Around the posts hung helmets, darts and spears,
And captive chariots, axes, shields and bars,
And broken beaks of ships, the *trophies* of their wars. *Dryden.*

3. In *architecture*, an ornament representing the stem of a tree, charged or encompassed with arms and military weapons, offensive and defensive. *Cyc.*

4. Something that is evidence of victory; memorial of conquest.

Present every hearer to Christ as a *trophy* of grace.

TRO′PHY-MŎNEY, *n.* A duty paid in England annually by house-keepers, towards providing harness, drums, colors, &c. for the militia. *Cyc.*

TROP′I€, *n.* [Fr. *tropique;* L. *tropicus;* from the Gr. τροπη, a turning; τρεπω, to turn.]

1. In *astronomy*, a circle of the sphere drawn through a solstitial point, parallel to the equator; or the line which bounds the sun's declination from the equator, north or south. This declination is twenty-three degrees and a half nearly. There are two tropics; the tropic of Cancer, on the north of the equator, and the tropic of Capricorn on the south.

2. *Tropics*, in geography, are two lesser circles of the globe, drawn parallel to the equator through the beginning of Cancer and of Capricorn.

TROP′I€AL, *a.* Pertaining to the tropics; being within the tropics; as *tropical* climates; *tropical* latitudes; *tropical* heat; *tropical* winds.

2. Incident to the tropics; as *tropical* diseases.

3. [from *trope.*] Figurative; rhetorically changed from its proper or original sense.

The foundation of all parables is some analogy or similitude between the *tropical* or allusive part of the parable, and the thing intended by it. *South.*

Tropical writing or *hieroglyphic*, is such as represents a thing by qualities which resemble it. *Warburton.*

TROP′I€ALLY, *adv.* In a tropical or figurative manner. *Enfield.*

TROP′I€-BIRD, *n.* An aquatic fowl of the genus Phaeton, with a long slender tail and remarkable powers of flight. *Ed. Encyc.*

TRO′PIST, *n.* [from *trope.*] One who explains the Scriptures by tropes and figures of speech; one who deals in tropes.

TROPOLOĠ′I€AL, *a.* [See *Tropology.*] Varied by tropes; changed from the original import of the words.

TROPOL′OĠY, *n.* [Gr. τροπος, trope, and λογος, discourse.]

A rhetorical mode of speech, including tropes, or change from the original import of the word. *Brown.*

TROSS′ERS, *n.* Trowsers. [*Not used.*] [See *Trowsers.*] *Shak.*

TROT, *v. i.* [Fr. *trotter;* G. *trotten*, to trot, to tread; It. *trottare;* Sp. Port. *trotar;* allied probably to *tread* and to *strut.*]

1. To move faster than in walking, as a horse or other quadruped, by lifting one fore foot and the hind foot of the opposite side at the same time. *Cyc.*

2. To walk or move fast; or to run.

He that rises late must *trot* all day, and will scarcely overtake his business at night. *Franklin.*

TROT, *n.* The pace of a horse or other quadruped, when he lifts one fore foot and the hind foot of the opposite side at the same time. This pace is the same as that of a walk, but more rapid. The trot is often a jolting hard motion, but in some horses, it is as easy as the amble or pace, and has a more stately appearance.

2. An old woman; *in contempt.*

TROTH, *n.* [Sax. *treothe;* the old orthography of *truth.* See *Truth.*]

1. Belief; faith; fidelity; as, to plight one's *troth.* *Obs.* *Shak.*

2. Truth; verity; veracity; as in *troth;* by my *troth.* *Obs.*

TROTH′LESS, *a.* Faithless; treacherous. *Obs.* *Fairfax.*

TROTH′-PLIGHT, *v. t.* To betroth or affiance. *Obs.*

TROTH′-PLIGHT, *a.* Betrothed; espoused; affianced. *Obs.* *Shak.*

TROTH′-PLIGHT, *n.* The act of betrothing or plighting faith.

TROT′TER, *n.* A beast that trots, or that usually trots.

2. A sheep's foot.

TROT′TING, *ppr.* Moving with a trot; walking fast, or running.

TROUBLE, *v. t.* *trub′l.* [Fr. *troubler;* It. *turbare;* Sp. Port. *turbar;* L. *turbo;* Gaelic, *treabhlaim*, which seems to be connected with *treabham*, to plow, that is, to turn or to stir, W. *torva*, L. *turba*, a crowd, and perhaps *trova*, a turn; Gr. τρεπω. The primary sense is to turn or to stir, to whirl about, as in L. *turbo*, *turbinis*, a whirlwind. Hence the sense of agitation, disturbance.]

1. To agitate; to disturb; to put into confused motion.

God looking forth will *trouble* all his host. *Milton.*

An angel went down at a certain season into the pool, and *troubled* the water. John v.

2. To disturb; to perplex.

Never *trouble* yourself about those faults which age will cure. *Locke.*

3. To afflict; to grieve; to distress.

Those that *trouble* me, rejoice when I am moved. Ps. xiii.

4. To busy; to cause to be much engaged or anxious.

Martha, thou art careful, and *troubled* about many things. Luke x.

5. To tease; to vex; to molest.

The boy so *troubles* me,
'Tis past enduring. *Shak.*

6. To give occasion for labor to. I will not *trouble* you to deliver the letter. I will not *trouble* myself in this affair.

7. To sue for a debt. He wishes not to *trouble* his debtors.

TROUBLE, *n. trub'l.* Disturbance of mind; agitation; commotion of spirits; perplexity; *a word of very extensive application.*

2. Affliction; calamity.

He shall deliver thee in six *troubles.* Job v.
Redeem Israel, O God, out of all his *troubles.* Ps. xxv.

3. Molestation; inconvenience; annoyance.

Lest the fiend some new *trouble* raise. *Milton.*

4. Uneasiness; vexation. *Milton.*

5. That which gives disturbance, annoyance or vexation; that which afflicts.

TROUBLED, *pp. trub'ld.* Disturbed; agitated; afflicted; annoyed; molested.

TROUBLER, *n. trub'ler.* One who disturbs; one who afflicts or molests; a disturber; as a *troubler* of the peace.

The rich *troublers* of the world's repose. *Waller.*

TROUBLESŎME, *a. trub'lsome.* Giving trouble or disturbance; molesting; annoying; vexatious. In warm climates, insects are very *troublesome.*

2. Burdensome; tiresome; wearisome.

My mother will never be *troublesome* to me. *Pope.*

3. Giving inconvenience to. I wish not to be *troublesome* as a guest.

4. Teasing; importunate; as a *troublesome* applicant.

TROUBLESŎMELY, *adv. trub'lsomely.* In a manner or degree to give trouble; vexatiously.

TROUBLESŎMENESS, *n. trub'lsomeness.*
1. Vexatiousness; the quality of giving trouble or of molesting. *Bacon.*

2. Unseasonable intrusion; importunity.

TROUBLE-STATE, *n.* A disturber of the community. [*Not used.*]

TROUBLING, *ppr. trub'ling.* Disturbing; agitating; molesting; annoying; afflicting.

TROUBLING, *n. trub'ling.* The act of disturbing or putting in commotion. John v.

2. The act of afflicting.

TROUBLOUS, *a. trub'lus.* Agitated; tumultuous; full of commotion.

A tall ship toss'd in *troublous* seas. *Spenser.*

2. Full of trouble or disorder; tumultuous; full of affliction.

The street shall be built again, and the wall, even in *troublous* times. Dan. ix.

TROUGH, *n. trauf.* [Sax. D. G. *trog;* Dan. *trug;* It. *truogo.*]

1. A vessel hollow longitudinally, or a large log or piece of timber excavated longitudinally on the upper side; used for various purposes.

2. A tray. [*This is the same word dialectically altered.*]

3. A canoe; the rude boat of uncivilized men. *Abbot.*

4. The channel that conveys water, as in mills.

The *trough* of the sea, the hollow between waves.

TROUL, for *troll.* [See *Troll.*]

TROUNCE, *v. t. trouns.* [Qu. Fr. *tronçon, tronçonner.*]

To punish, or to beat severely. [*A low word.*]

TROUSE, *n. trooz.* [See *Trowsers.*] A kind of trowsers worn by children.

TROUT, *n.* [Sax. *truht;* Fr. *truite;* It. *trota;* D. *truit;* L. *trutta;* Sp. *trucha.* *Trout* is contracted from *trocta.*]

A river fish of the genus Salmo, variegated with spots, and esteemed as most delicate food.

TROUT'-CŎLORED, *a.* White with spots of black, bay or sorrel; as a *trout-colored* horse.

TROUT'-FISHING, *n.* The fishing for trouts.

TROUT'-STREAM, *n.* A stream in which trout breed.

TRO'VER, *n.* [Fr. *trouver,* It. *trovare,* to find; Sw. *träffa,* to hit; Dan. *treffer,* to meet with; *træf,* an accident; D. G. *treffen,* to meet, to hit.] Trover is properly the finding of any thing. Hence,

1. In *law,* the gaining possession of any goods, whether by finding or by other means.

2. An action which a man has against another who has found or obtained possession of any of his goods, and who refuses to deliver them on demand. This is called an action of *trover* and *conversion.* In this case, the trover or finding is an immaterial fact, but the plaintif must prove his own property, and the possession and conversion of the goods by the defendant. *Blackstone.*

TRŌW, *v. i.* [Sax. *treowian, treowan,* to believe, to trust; G. *trauen;* Sw. *tro;* Dan. *troer;* contracted from *trogan,* and coinciding with the root of *truth.* See *True.*]

To believe; to trust; to think or suppose. *Obs.* *Spenser. Hooker.*

TRŌW, is used in the imperative, as a word of inquiry. What means the fool, *trow?*

TROW'EL, *n.* [Fr. *truelle;* L. *trulla;* D. *troffel.* Qu. D. G. *treffen,* to hit, to strike, hence to put on.]

1. A mason's tool, used in spreading and dressing mortar, and breaking bricks to shape them.

2. A gardener's tool, somewhat like a trowel, made of iron and scooped; used in taking up plants and for other purposes. *Cyc.*

TROWS'ERS, *n. plu. s* as *z.* [Gaelic, *triusan;* Fr. *trousse,* a truss, a bundle; W. *trws,* a garment that covers; *trouse,* dress; *trwsa,* a truss, a packet; *trwsiaw,* to dress; Gaelic, *trusam,* to gird or *truss* up.]

A loose garment worn by males, extending from the waist to the knee or to the ankle, and covering the lower limbs.

TROY, } *n.* [said to have been
TROY-WEIGHT, } named from *Troyes,* in France, where it was first adopted in Europe. The troy ounce is supposed to have been brought from Cairo during the crusades. Some persons however say that the original name was *tron.*]

The weight by which gold and silver, jewels, &c. are weighed. In this weight, 20 grains = a scruple, 3 scruples = a dram, 8 drams = an ounce, and 12 ounces = one pound.

TRU'ANT, *a.* [Fr. *truand.*] Idle; wandering from business; loitering; as a *truant* boy.

While *truant* Jove, in infant pride,
Play'd barefoot on Olympus' side. *Trumbull.*

TRU'ANT, *n.* An idler; an idle boy. *Dryden.*

TRU'ANT, *v. i.* To idle away time; to loiter or be absent from employment. *Shak.*

TRU'ANTLY, *adv.* Like a truant; in idleness.

TRU'ANTSHIP, *n.* Idleness; neglect of employment. *Ascham.*

TRUBS, *n.* An herb. *Ainsworth.*

TRUB'TAIL, *n.* A short squat woman. *Obs.* *Ainsworth.*

TRUCE, *n.* [Goth. *triggwa;* It. *tregua;* Norm. *trewe;* Ice. *trigd;* Cimbric, *trugth;* properly a league or pact, from the root of *trick,* to make fast, to fold. See *True.*]

1. In *war,* a suspension of arms by agreement of the commanders; a temporary cessation of hostilities, either for negotiation or other purpose.

2. Intermission of action, pain or contest; temporary cessation; short quiet.

There he may find
Truce to his restless thoughts. *Milton.*

TRU'CE-BREAKER, *n.* [*truce* and *breaker.*] One who violates a truce, covenant or engagement. 2 Tim. iii.

TRUCH'MAN, *n.* An interpreter. [See *Dragoman.*]

TRUCIDA'TION, *n.* [L. *trucido,* to kill.] The act of killing.

TRUCK, *v. i.* [Fr. *troquer;* Sp. Port. *trocar;* allied probably to W. *trwc,* L. *trochus,* a round thing, Eng. *truck;* Gr. τροχος, τρεχω.]

To exchange commodities; to barter. Our traders *truck* with the Indians, giving them whiskey and trinkets for skins. [*Truck* is now vulgar.]

TRUCK, *v. t.* To exchange; to give in exchange; to barter; as, to *truck* knives for gold dust. [*Vulgar.*] *Swift.*

TRUCK, *n.* Permutation; exchange of commodities; barter.

2. A small wooden wheel not bound with iron; a cylinder.

3. A small wheel; hence *trucks,* a low carriage for carrying goods, stone, &c. Indeed this kind of carriage is often called a *truck,* in the singular.

TRUCK'AĠE, *n.* The practice of bartering goods. *Milton.*

TRUCK'ER, *n.* One who trafficks by exchange of goods.

TRUCK'ING, *ppr.* Exchanging goods; bartering.

TRUCK'LE, *n.* A small wheel or caster. *Hudibras.*

TRUCK'LE, *v. i.* [*dim.* of *truck.*] To yield or bend obsequiously to the will of another; to submit; to creep. Small states must *truckle* to large ones.

Religion itself is forced to *truckle* with worldly policy. *Norris.*

TRUCK'LE-BED, *n.* [*truckle* and *bed.*] A bed that runs on wheels and may be pushed under another; a trundle-bed.

TRUCK'LING, *ppr.* Yielding obsequiously to the will of another.

TRU'CULENCE, *n.* [L. *truculentia*, from *trux*, fierce, savage.]

1. Savageness of manners; ferociousness.
2. Terribleness of countenance.

TRU'CULENT, *a.* Fierce; savage; barbarous; as the *truculent* inhabitants of Scythia. *Ray.*

2. Of a ferocious aspect.
3. Cruel; destructive; as a *truculent* plague. *Harvey.*

TRUDGE, *v. i.* To travel on foot. The father rode; the son *trudged* on behind.

2. To travel or march with labor.

—And *trudg'd* to Rome upon my naked feet. *Dryden.*

TRUE, *a.* [Sax. *treow*, *treowe*, faithful, and as a noun, faith, trust; Sw. *tro*; Dan. *troe*; G. *treu*; D. *trouw*, trust, loyalty, fidelity, faith; *trouwen*, to marry; Goth. *triggus*, faithful; *triggwa.* a pact or league, a *truce.* This is the real orthography, coinciding with Sw. *trygg*, Dan. *tryg*, safe, secure, and W. *trigiaw*, to stay, to tarry, to dwell, that is, to stop, to set. The primary sense of the root is to make close and fast, to set, or to stretch, strain, and thus make straight and close.]

1. Conformable to fact; being in accordance with the actual state of things; as a *true* relation or narration; a *true* history. A declaration is *true*, when it states the facts. In this sense, *true* is opposed to *false*.
2. Genuine; pure; real; not counterfeit, adulterated or false; as *true* balsam; the *true* bark; *true* love of country; a *true* christian.

—The *true* light which lighteth every man that cometh into the world. John i.

3. Faithful; steady in adhering to friends, to promises, to a prince or to the state; loyal; not false, fickle or perfidious; as a *true* friend; a *true* lover; a man *true* to his king, *true* to his country, *true* to his word; a husband *true* to his wife; a wife *true* to her husband; a servant *true* to his master; an officer *true* to his charge.
4. Free from falsehood; as a *true* witness.
5. Honest; not fraudulent; as good men and *true*.

If king Edward be as *true* and just— *Shak.*

6. Exact; right to precision; conformable to a rule or pattern; as a *true* copy; a *true* likeness of the original.
7. Straight; right; as a *true* line; the *true* course of a ship.
8. Not false or pretended; real; as, Christ was the *true* Messiah.
9. Rightful; as, George IV. is the *true* king of England.

TRUEBORN, *a.* [*true* and *born.*] Of genuine birth; having a right by birth to any title; as a *trueborn* Englishman. *Shak.*

TRUEBRED, *a.* [*true* and *bred.*] Of a genuine or right breed; as a *truebred* beast. *Dryden.*

2. Being of genuine breeding or education; as a *truebred* gentleman.

TRUEHE'ARTED, *a.* [*true* and *heart.*] Being of a faithful heart; honest; sincere; not faithless or deceitful; as a *truehearted* friend.

TRUEHE'ARTEDNESS, *n.* Fidelity; loyalty; sincerity.

TRUELOVE, *n.* [*true* and *love.*] One really beloved.

2. A plant, the herb Paris.

TRUELOVE-KNOT, *n.* [Qu. is not this from the Dan. *trolover*, to betroth, to promise in marriage; *troe*, true, and *lover*, to promise; the knot of faithful promise or engagement.]

A knot composed of lines united with many involutions; the emblem of interwoven affection or engagements.

TRUENESS, *n.* Faithfulness; sincerity.

2. Reality; genuineness.
3. Exactness; as the *trueness* of a line.

TRUEPENNY, *n.* [*true* and *penny.*] A familiar phrase for an honest fellow. *Bacon.*

TRUF'FLE, *n.* [Fr. *truffe*; Sp. *trufa*, deceit, imposition, and *truffles*; and if this vegetable is named from its growth under ground, it accords with It. *truffare*, to deceive.]

A subterraneous vegetable production, or a kind of mushroom, of a fleshy fungous structure and roundish figure; an esculent substance, much esteemed. It is of the genus Tuber. *Cyc.*

TRUF'FLE-WORM, *n.* A worm found in truffles, the larva of a fly. *Cyc.*

TRUG, *n.* A hod. This is our *trough* and *tray*; the original pronunciation being retained in some parts of England. The word was also used formerly for a measure of wheat, as much, I suppose as was carried in a trough; three *trugs* making two bushels.

TRU'ISM, *n.* [from *true.*] An undoubted or self-evident truth.

Trifling *truisms* clothed in great swelling words of vanity— *J. P. Smith.*

TRULL, *n.* [W. *troliaw*, to troll or roll, whence *stroll*; or *truliaw*, to drill. Qu. Gr. ματρυλλη.] A low vagrant strumpet.

TRULLIZA'TION, *n.* [L. *trullisso.*] The laying of strata of plaster with a trowel.

TRU'LY, *adv.* [from *true.*] In fact; in deed; in reality.

2. According to truth; in agreement with fact; as, to see things *truly*; the facts are *truly* represented.
3. Sincerely; honestly; really; faithfully; as, to be *truly* attached to a lover. The citizens are *truly* loyal to their prince or their country.
4. Exactly; justly; as, to estimate *truly* the weight of evidence.

TRUMP, *n.* [It. *tromba*; Gaelic, *trompa.* See *Trumpet.*]

1. A trumpet; a wind instrument of music; a poetical word used for *trumpet.* It is seldom used in prose, in common discourse; but is used in Scripture, where it seems peculiarly appropriate to the grandeur of the subject.

At the last *trump*; for the trumpet shall sound, and the dead shall be raised. 1 Cor. xv. 1 Thess. iv.

2. [contracted from *triumph*, It. *trionfo*, Fr. *triomphe.*] A winning card; one of the suit of cards which takes any of the other suits.
3. An old game with cards.

To put to the trumps, / *To put on the trumps*, } to reduce to the last expedient, or to the utmost exertion of power.

TRUMP, *v. t.* To take with a trump card.

2. To obtrude; also, to deceive. [Fr. *tromper.*] [*Not in use.*]

To trump up, to devise; to seek and collect from every quarter.

TRUMP, *v. i.* To blow a trumpet. *Wickliffe.*

TRUMP'ERY, *n.* [Fr. *tromperie.*] Falsehood; empty talk. *Raleigh.*

2. Useless matter; things worn out and cast side.

[*This is the sense of the word in New England.*]

TRUMP'ET, *n.* [It. *tromba*, *trombetta*; Sp. *trompa*, *trompeta*; Fr. *trompette*; Gaelic, *trompa*, *trompaid*; G. *trompete*; D. Sw. *trompet*; Dan. *trompette*; Arm. *trompett.* The radical letters and the origin are not ascertained.]

1. A wind instrument of music, used chiefly in war and military exercises. It is very useful also at sea, in speaking with ships. There is a speaking trumpet, and a hearing trumpet. They both consist of long tubular bodies, nearly in the form of a parabolic conoid, with wide mouths.

The *trumpet's* loud clangor
Excites us to arms. *Dryden.*

2. In the military style, a trumpeter.

He wisely desired that a *trumpet* might be first sent for a pass. *Clarendon.*

3. One who praises or propagates praise, or is the instrument of propagating it. A great politician was pleased to be the *trumpet* of his praises.

TRUMP'ET, *v. t.* To publish by sound of trumpet; also, to proclaim; as, to *trumpet* good tidings.

They did nothing but publish and *trumpet* all the reproaches they could devise against the Irish. *Bacon.*

TRUMP'ETED, *pp.* Sounded abroad; proclaimed.

TRUMP'ETER, *n.* One who sounds a trumpet. *Dryden.*

2. One who proclaims, publishes or denounces.

These men are good *trumpeters.* *Bacon.*

3. A bird, a variety of the domestic pigeon. Also, a bird of South America, the *agami*, of the genus Psophia, about the size of the domestic fowl; so called from its uttering a hollow noise, like that of a trumpet. *Cyc. Ed. Encyc.*

TRUMP'ET-FISH, *n.* A fish of the genus Centriscus, *(C. scolopax;)* called also the bellows fish. *Cyc.*

TRUMP'ET-FLOWER, *n.* A flower of the genus Bignonia, and another of the genus Lonicera. *Cyc.*

TRUMPET HONEYSUCKLE, *n.* A plant of the genus Lonicera.

TRUMP'ETING, *ppr.* Blowing the trumpet; proclaiming.

TRUMP'ET-SHELL, *n.* The name of a genus of univalvular shells, of the form of a trumpet, (*Buccinum*, Linne.) *Cyc.*

TRUMP'ET-TONGUED, *a.* Having a tongue vociferous as a trumpet. *Shak.*

TRUMP'LIKE, *a.* Resembling a trumpet. *Chapman.*

TRUNC'ATE, *v. t.* [L. *trunco*, to cut off, W. *tryçu*, Arm. *troucha*; coinciding with Fr. *trancher*.] To cut off; to lop; to maim.

TRUNC'ATE, *a.* In *botany*, appearing as if cut off at the tip; ending in a tranverse line; as a *truncate* leaf. *Martyn.*

TRUNC'ATED, *pp.* Cut off; cut short; maimed. A *truncated* cone is one whose vertex is cut off by a plane parallel to its base.

2. Appearing as if cut off; plane; having no edge; as a mineral substance. *Phillips.*

TRUNC'ATING, *ppr.* Cutting off.

TRUNCA'TION, *n.* The act of lopping or cutting off.

TRUN'CHEON, *n.* [Fr. *tronçon*, from *tronc*, trunk, L. *truncus*.]

A short staff; a club; a cudgel; a battoon; used by kings and great officers as a mark of command.

> The marshal's *truncheon* nor the judge's robe. *Shak.*

TRUN'CHEON, *v. t.* To beat with a truncheon; to cudgel. *Shak.*

TRUNCHEONEE'R, *n.* A person armed with a truncheon.

TRUN'DLE, *v. i.* [Sax. *trændle*, *trendle*, any round body; Dan. Sw. *trind*, round; W. *trôn*, a circle, a round, a throne; *trôni*, to rim; from the root of *rundle*, *round*.]

1. To roll, as on little wheels; as, a bed *trundles* under another.

2. To roll; as a bowl.

TRUN'DLE, *v. t.* To roll, as a thing on little wheels; as, to *trundle* a bed or a gun-carriage.

TRUN'DLE, *n.* A round body; a little wheel, or a kind of low cart with small wooden wheels.

TRUN'DLE-BED, *n.* A bed that is moved on trundles or little wheels; called also *truckle-bed*.

TRUN'DLE-TAIL, *n.* A round tail; a dog so called from his tail. *Shak.*

TRUNK, *n.* [Fr. *tronc*; It. *troncone*; Sp. *tronco*; L. *truncus*, from *trunco*, to cut off. The primitive Celtic word of this family is in Fr. *trancher*, It. *trinciare*, Sp. *trincar*, *trinchar*. The *n* is not radical, for in Arm. the word is *troucha*, W. *tryçu*.]

1. The stem or body of a tree, severed from its roots. This is the proper sense of the word. But surprising as it may seem, it is used most improperly to signify the stem of a standing tree or vegetable, in general. *Milton. Dryden.*

2. The body of an animal without the limbs. *Shak.*

3. The main body of any thing; as the *trunk* of a vein or of an artery, as distinct from the branches.

4. The snout or proboscis of an elephant; the limb or instrument with which he feeds himself.

5. A slender, oblong, hollow body, joined to the fore part of the head of many insects, by means of which they suck the blood of animals or the juices of vegetables.

6. In *architecture*, the fust or shaft of a column.

7. A long tube through which pellets of clay are blown. *Ray.*

8. A box or chest covered with skin.

Fire-trunks, in fire ships, wooden funnels fixed under the shrouds to convey or lead the flames to the masts and rigging.

TRUNK, *v. t.* To lop off; to curtail; to truncate. [*Not in use.*] *Spenser.*

TRUNK'ED, *pp.* Cut off; curtailed. *Obs.*

2. Having a trunk. *Howell.*

TRUNK'-HOSE, *n.* [*trunk* and *hose*.] Large breeches formerly worn. *Prior.*

TRUN'NION, *n.* [Fr. *trognon*.] The trunnions of a piece of ordnance, are two knobs which project from the opposite sides of a piece, whether gun, mortar or howitzer, and serve to support it on the cheeks of the carriage. *Mar. Dict.*

TRUN'NION-PLATE, *n.* The trunnion plates are two plates in traveling carriages, mortars and howitzers, which cover the upper parts of the side-pieces, and go under the trunnions. *Cyc.*

TRUN'NION-RING, *n.* A ring on a cannon next before the trunnions.

TRU'SION, *n.* *tru'zhon*. [L. *trudo*.] The act of pushing or thrusting. *Bentley.*

TRUSS, *n.* [Fr. *trousse*; Dan. *trosse*, a cord or rope; Sw. *tross*; W. *trwsa*, a truss, a packet. See *Trowsers*.]

1. In *a general sense*, a bundle; as a *truss* of hay or straw. A *truss* of hay in England is half a hundred. A *truss* of straw is of different weights in different places.

2. In *surgery*, a bandage or apparatus used in cases of ruptures, to keep up the reduced parts and hinder further protrusion, and for other purposes. *Cyc.*

3. Among *botanists*, a truss or bunch is a tuft of flowers formed at the top of the main stalk or stem of certain plants. *Cyc.*

4. In *navigation*, a machine to pull a lower yard close to its mast and retain it firmly in that position. *Cyc.*

5. [See *Trous*.]

TRUSS, *v. t.* To bind or pack close. *Shak.*

2. To skewer; to make fast.

To truss up, to strain; to make close or tight.

TRUSS'ED, *pp.* Packed or bound closely.

TRUSS'ING, *ppr.* Packing or binding closely.

TRUST, *n.* [Dan. *tröst*, consolation; *tröster*, to comfort, that is, to strengthen; *miströster*, to distrust, to discourage; Sw. *tröst*, confidence, trust, consolation; *tröst a*, to console; *misströsta*, to distrust, to despair. The Saxon has *trywsian*, to trust, to obligate. Qu. Gr. θαρσω.]

1. Confidence; a reliance or resting of the mind on the integrity, veracity, justice, friendship or other sound principle of another person.

> He that putteth his *trust* in the Lord shall be safe. Prov. xxix.

2. He or that which is the ground of confidence.

> O Lord God, thou art my *trust* from my youth. Ps. lxxi.

3. Charge received in confidence.

> Reward them well, if they observe their *trust*. *Denham.*

4. That which is committed to one's care. Never violate a sacred *trust*.

5. Confident opinion of any event.

> His *trust* was with th' Eternal to be deem'd
> Equal in strength. *Milton.*

6. Credit given without examination; as, to take opinions on *trust*.

7. Credit on promise of payment, actual or implied; as, to take or purchase goods on *trust*.

8. Something committed to a person's care for use or management, and for which an account must be rendered. Every man's talents and advantages are a *trust* committed to him by his Maker, and for the use or employment of which he is accountable.

9. Confidence; special reliance on supposed honesty.

10. State of him to whom something is entrusted.

> I serve him truly, that will put me in *trust*. *Shak.*

11. Care; management. 1 Tim. vi.

12. In *law*, an estate, devised or granted in confidence that the devisee or grantee shall convey it, or dispose of the profits, at the will of another; an estate held for the use of another. *Blackstone.*

TRUST, *v. t.* To place confidence in; to rely on. We cannot *trust* those who have deceived us.

> He that *trusts* every one without reserve, will at last be deceived. *Rambler.*

2. To believe; to credit.

> *Trust* me, you look well. *Shak.*

3. To commit to the care of, in confidence. *Trust* your Maker with yourself and all your concerns.

4. To venture confidently.

> Fool'd by thee, to *trust* thee from my side. *Milton.*

5. To give credit to; to sell to upon credit, or in confidence of future payment. The merchants and manufacturers *trust* their customers annually with goods to the value of millions.

> It is happier to be sometimes cheated, than not to *trust*. *Rambler.*

TRUST, *v. i.* To be confident of something present or future.

> I *trust* to come to you, and speak face to face. 2 John 12.
>
> We *trust* we have a good conscience. Heb. xiii.

2. To be credulous; to be won to confidence.

> Well, you may fear too far—
> Safer than *trust* too far. *Shak.*

To trust in, to confide in; to place confidence in; to rely on; *a use frequent in the Scriptures*.

> *Trust in* the Lord, and do good. Ps. xxxvii.
>
> They shall be greatly ashamed that *trust in* graven images. Is. xlii.

To trust to, to depend on; to have confidence in; to rely on.

> The men of Israel—*trusted to* the liers in wait. Judges xx.

TRUST'ED, *pp.* Confided in; relied on; depended on; *applied to persons*.

2. Sold on credit; as goods or property.

3. Delivered in confidence to the care of another; as letters or goods *trusted* to a carrier or bailee.

TRUSTEE', *n.* A person to whom any thing or business is committed, in confidence that he will discharge his duty. The *trustee* of an estate is one to whom it is devised or granted in trust, or for the use of another.

2. A person to whom is confided the management of an institution; as the *trustees* of a college or of an academy.

TRUST'ER, *n.* One who trusts or gives credit.

TRUST'ILY, *adv.* [from *trusty.*] Faithfully; honestly; with fidelity.

TRUST'INESS, *n.* [from *trusty.*] That quality of a person by which he deserves the confidence of others; fidelity; faithfulness; honesty; as the *trustiness* of a servant.

TRUST'ING, *ppr.* Confiding in; giving credit; relying on.

TRUST'INGLY, *adv.* With trust or implicit confidence.

TRUST'LESS, *a.* Not worthy of trust; unfaithful. *Spenser.*

TRUST'Y, *a.* That may be safely trusted; that justly deserves confidence; fit to be confided in; as a *trusty* servant. *Addison.*

2. That will not fail; strong; firm; as a *trusty* sword. *Spenser.*

TRUTH, *n.* [Sax. *treowth*, truth, and troth; G. *treue*, D. *getrouwheid*, fidelity, from *trouw*, trust, faith, fidelity, whence *trouwen*, to marry.]

1. Conformity to fact or reality; exact accordance with that which is, or has been, or shall be. The *truth* of history constitutes its whole value. We rely on the *truth* of the scriptural prophecies.

My mouth shall speak *truth*. Prov. viii.

Sanctify them through thy *truth;* thy word is *truth*. John xvii.

2. True state of facts or things. The duty of a court of justice is to discover the *truth*. Witnesses are sworn to declare the *truth*, the whole *truth*, and nothing but the *truth*.

3. Conformity of words to thoughts, which is called *moral truth*.

Shall *truth* fail to keep her word? *Milton.*

4. Veracity; purity from falsehood; practice of speaking truth; habitual disposition to speak truth; as when we say, a man is a man of *truth*.

5. Correct opinion. *Harte.*

6. Fidelity; constancy.

The thoughts of past pleasure and *truth*,
The best of all blessings below. *Song.*

7. Honesty; virtue.

It must appear
That malice bears down *truth*. *Shak.*

8. Exactness; conformity to rule.

Plows, to go true, depend much on the *truth* of the iron work. [*Not in use.*] *Mortimer.*

9. Real fact or just principle; real state of things. There are innumerable *truths* with which we are not acquainted.

10. Sincerity.

God is a spirit, and they that worship him must worship in spirit and in *truth*. John iv.

11. The *truth* of God, is his veracity and faithfulness. Ps. lxxi.

Or his revealed will.

I have walked in thy *truth*. Ps. xxvi.

12. Jesus Christ is called *the truth*. John xiv.

13. It is sometimes used by way of concession.

She said, *truth*, Lord; yet the dogs eat of the crums— Matt. xv.

That is, it is a truth; what you have said, I admit to be true.

In truth, in reality; in fact.

Of a truth, in reality; certainly.

To do truth, is to practice what God commands. John iii.

TRUTHFUL, *a.* Full of truth. *Barrington.*

TRUTHLESS, *a.* Wanting truth; wanting reality.

2. Faithless. *Fuller.*

TRUTINA'TION, *n.* [L. *trutina*, a balance; *trutinor*, to weigh.] The act of weighing. [*Not used.*] *Brown.*

TRUTTA'CEOUS, *a.* [from L. *trutta*, trout.] Pertaining to the trout; as fish of the *truttaceous* genus. *Dict. Nat. Hist.*

TRY, *v. i.* [This word is from the root of Dan. *trekker*, to draw, or *trykker*, Sw. *trycka*, to press, to urge; *trachta*, to seek or strive to obtain; D. *tragten*, to endeavor; Dan. *tragter*, id. The primary sense of all these words is to strain, to use effort, to stretch forward.]

To exert strength; to endeavor; to make an effort; to attempt. *Try* to learn; *try* to lift a weight. The horses *tried* to draw the load. [*These phrases give the true sense.*]

TRY, *v. t.* To examine; to make experiment on; to prove by experiment.

Come, *try* upon yourselves what you have seen me. *Shak.*

2. To experience; to have knowledge by experience of.

Or *try* the Libyan heat, or Scythian cold. *Dryden.*

3. To prove by a test; as, to *try* weights and measures by a standard; to *try* one's opinions by the divine oracles.

4. To act upon as a test.

The fire sev'n times *tried* this. *Shak.*

5. To examine judicially by witnesses and the principles of law; as causes *tried* in court.

6. To essay; to attempt.

Let us *try* advent'rous work. *Milton.*

7. To purify; to refine; as silver seven times *tried*.

8. To search carefully into. Ps. xi.

9. To use as means; as, to *try* remedies for a disease.

10. To strain; as, to *try* the eyes; *the literal sense of the word.*

To try tallow, &c. is to melt and separate it from the membranes.

To try out, to pursue efforts till a decision is obtained.

TRY'ING, *ppr.* Exerting strength; attempting.

2. Examining by searching or comparison with a test; proving; using; straining, &c.

3. *a.* Adapted to try, or put to severe trial.

TRY'-SAIL, *n.* A sail used by a ship in a storm; literally the *strain-sail.*

TUB, *n.* [D. *tobbe;* G. *zuber;* Gaelic, *tubag.*]

1. An open wooden vessel formed with staves, heading and hoops; used for various domestic purposes, as for washing, for making cheese, &c.

2. A state of salivation; so called because the patient was formerly sweated in a tub. [*Not in use.*] *Shak.*

3. A certain quantity; as a *tub* of tea, which is 60 pounds; a *tub* of camphor, from 56 to 80 pounds; a *tub* of vermilion, from 3 to 4 hundred pounds. [*Local.*] *Cyc.*

4. A wooden vessel in which vegetables are planted, for the sake of being movable and set in a house in cold weather.

TUB, *v. t.* To plant or set in a tub.

TUB'BER, *n.* In Cornwall, a mining instrument, called in other places a beele. The man who uses this tool is called *tubber-man* or *beel-man*. *Cyc.*

TUB'BING, *ppr.* Setting in a tub.

TUBE, *n.* [Fr. *tube;* L. *tubus.*] A pipe; a siphon; a canal or conduit; a hollow cylinder, either of wood, metal or glass, used for the conveyance of fluids, and for various other purposes.

2. A vessel of animal bodies or plants, which conveys a fluid or other substance.

3. In *botany*, the narrow hollow part of a monopetalous corol, by which it is fixed to the receptacle. *Martyn.*

4. In *artillery*, an instrument of tin, used in quick firing. *Cyc.*

TUBE, *v. t.* To furnish with a tube; as, to *tube* a well. *Journ. of Science.*

TU'BER, *n.* In *botany*, a knob in roots, solid, with the component particles all similar. *Martyn.*

TU'BERCLE, *n.* [Fr. *tubercule*, from L. *tuberculum*, from *tuber*, a bunch.]

1. A pimple; a small push, swelling or tumor on animal bodies.

2. A little knob, like a pimple, on plants; a little knob or rough point on the leaves of some lichens, supposed to be the fructification. *Martyn.*

TUBER'CULAR, } *a.* Full of knobs or
TUBER'CULOUS, } pimples. *Fourcroy.*

2. Affected with tubercles. *Journ. of Science.*

TUBER'CULATE, *a.* Having small knobs or pimples, as a plant. *Lee.*

TU'BEROSE, *n.* [L. *tuberosa.*] A plant with a tuberous root and a liliaceous flower, the *Polianthus tuberosa;* formerly called the tuberous hyacinth. *Cyc.*

TU'BEROUS, *a.* [from L. *tuber*, a bunch.] Knobbed. In *botany*, consisting of roundish fleshy bodies, or tubers, connected into a bunch by intervening threads; as the roots of artichokes and potatoes. *Martyn.*

TUB'-FISH, *n.* [*tub* and *fish.*] A species of Trigla, sometimes called the flying-fish. *Cyc.*

TU'BIPORE, *n.* [*tube* and *pore.*] A genus of zoophytes or corals. *Cyc.*

TU'BIPORITE, *n.* Fossil tubipores.

TUB'-MAN, *n.* In the exchequer, a barrister so called. *Eng.*

TU'BULAR, *a.* [from L. *tubus.*] Having the form of a tube or pipe; consisting of a pipe; fistular; as a *tubular* snout; a *tubular* calyx. *Martyn.*

TU'BULE, *n.* [L. *tubulus.*] A small pipe or fistular body. *Woodward.*

TU'BULIFORM, *a.* Having the form of a tube. *Kirwan.*

TU'BULOUS, *a.* Longitudinally hollow.

2. Containing tubes; composed wholly of tubulous florets; as a *tubulous* compound flower.

3. In *botany*, having a bell-shaped border, with five reflex segments, rising from a tube; as a *tubulous* floret. *Martyn.*

TUCH, *n.* A kind of marble. *Herbert.*

TUCK, *n.* [Gaelic, *tuca*; W. *twca*; from the sense of cutting or thrusting, and the root of *dock*. The It. has *stocco*, and the Fr. *estoc*.]

1. A long narrow sword.
2. A kind of net. *Carew.*
3. [from the verb following.] In *a ship*, the part where the ends of the bottom planks are collected under the stern. *Cyc.*
4. A fold; a pull; a lugging. [See *Tug*.]

TUCK, *v. t.* [In G. *zucken* signifies to stir, to stoop, to shrug. In some parts of England, this verb signifies to full, as cloth; Ir. *tucalam*.]

1. To thrust or press in or together; to fold under; to press into a narrower compass; as, to *tuck* up a bed; to *tuck* up a garment; to *tuck* in the skirt of any thing. *Addison.*
2. To inclose by tucking close around; as, to *tuck* a child into a bed. *Locke.*
3. To full, as cloth. [*Local.*]

TUCK, *v. i.* To contract; to draw together. [*Not in use.*] *Sharp.*

TUCK'ER, *n.* A small piece of linen for shading the breast of women. *Addison.*

2. A fuller, whence the name. [*Local.*]

TUCK'ET, *n.* [It. *tocato*, a touch.] A flourish in music; a voluntary; a prelude.

2. [It. *tocchetto.*] A steak; a collop.

TUCK'ETSONANCE, *n.* The sound of the tucket, an ancient instrument of music. *Shak.*

TUCK'ING, *ppr.* Pressing under or together; folding.

TUESDAY, *n.* *s* as *z*. [Sw. *Tisdag*; Dan. *Tirsdag*; D. *Dingsdag*; G. *Dingstag*; Sax. *Tiwæsdæg* or *Tuesdæg*, from *Tig*, *Tiig*, or *Tuisco*, the Mars of our ancestors, the deity that presided over combats, strife and litigation. Hence *Tuesday* is court day, assize day; the day for combat or commencing litigation. See *Thing*.] The third day of the week.

TU'FA, } *n.* [It. *tufo*, porous ground; Fr.
TUF, } *tuf*, soft gravel-stone or sandstone; G. *tof*.]

A stone or porous substance formed by depositions from springs or rivulets, containing much earthy matter in solution. Tufa is also formed by the concretion of loose volcanic dust or cinders, cemented by water, or by the consolidation of mud thrown out of volcanoes. The disintegration and subsequent consolidation of basaltic rocks, forms a kind of tufa, called by the German geologists, *trap-tuff*. *Cyc.*

TUFA'CEOUS, *a.* Pertaining to tufa; consisting of tufa, or resembling it.

TUFFOON', *n.* [a corruption of *typhon*.] A violent tempest or tornado with thunder and lightning, frequent in the Chinese sea and the gulf of Tonquin.

TUFT, *n.* [W. *twf*; Fr. *touffe*, *toupet*; Sw. *tofs*; Sp. *tupe*, a tuft; *tupir*, to press together; *tupa*, satiety.]

1. A collection of small things in a knot or bunch; as a *tuft* of flowers; a *tuft* of fethers; a *tuft* of grass or hair. A *tuft* of fethers forms the crest of a bird. *Dryden. Addison.*
2. A cluster; a clump; as a *tuft* of trees; a *tuft* of olives. *Shak.*
3. In *botany*, a head of flowers, each elevated on a partial stalk, and all forming together a dense roundish mass. The word is sometimes applied to other collections, as little bundles of leaves, hairs and the like. *Cyc.*

TUFT, *v. t.* To separate into tufts.

2. To adorn with tufts or with a tuft. *Thomson.*

TUF-TAF'FETA, *n.* A villous kind of silk. [*Not in use.*]

TUFT'ED, *pp.* or *a.* Adorned with a tuft, as the *tufted* duck; growing in a tuft or clusters, as a *tufted* grove. *Milton. Pope.*

TUFT'Y, *a.* Abounding with tufts; growing in clusters; bushy. *Thomson.*

TUG, *v. t.* [Sax. *teogan*, *teon*; G. *ziehen*, to draw; *zug*, a *tug*; Fr. *touer*; L. *duco*. See *Tow*, to drag.]

1. To pull or draw with great effort; to drag along with continued exertion; to haul along.

> There sweat, there strain, *tug* the laborious oar. *Roscommon.*

2. To pull; to pluck.

> —To ease the pain
> His *tugg'd* ears suffer'd with a strain. *Hudibras.*

TUG, *v. i.* To pull with great effort; as, to *tug* at the oar; to *tug* against the stream.

2. To labor; to strive; to struggle.

> They long wrestled and strenuously *tugged* for their liberty. [*This is not elegant.*] *Howe.*

TUG, *n.* [G. *zug*.] A pull with the utmost effort.

> At the *tug* he falls—
> Vast ruins come along— *Dryden.*

2. A sort of carriage, used in some parts of England for conveying bavins or faggots and other things. *Cyc.*
3. In *some parts of New England*, the traces of a harness are called *tugs*.

TUG'GER, *n.* One who tugs, or pulls with great effort.

TUG'GING, *ppr.* Pulling or dragging with great exertion; hauling.

TUG'GINGLY, *adv.* With laborious pulling. *Bailey.*

TUI''TION, *n.* [L. *tuitio*, from *tueor*, to see, behold, protect, &c. This verb is probably contracted from *tugo*, Ir. *tuighim*. If so, it coincides with the Dan. *tugt*, education, *tugter*, to chastise, D. *tugt*, G. *zucht*. In this case, it coincides nearly with L. *duco*, to lead.]

1. Guardianship; superintending care over a young person; the particular watch and care of a tutor or guardian over his pupil or ward.
2. *More especially*, instruction; the act or business of teaching the various branches of learning. We place our children under the preceptors of academies for *tuition*. [*This is now the common acceptation of the word.*]
3. The money paid for instruction. In our colleges, the *tuition* is from thirty to forty dollars a year.

TULIP, *n.* [Fr. *tulipe*; L. *tulipa*; It. *tulipano*; Sp. *tulipan*; D. *tulp*; G. *tulpe*; Sw. *tulpan*; Dan. *tulipan*.]

A plant and a flower of the genus Tulipa, of a great variety of colors, and much cultivated for its beauty.

TU'LIP-TREE, *n.* An American tree bearing flowers resembling the tulip, of the genus Liriodendron. Also, a tree of the genus Magnolia. *Lee.*

TUM'BLE, *v. i.* [Sax. *tumbian*, to tumble, to dance; Sw. *tumla*, to fall, to tumble; Dan. *tumler*, to shake, toss, reel, tumble; Fr. *tomber*; Sp. *tumbar*, to *tumble*, roll, keel, as a ship, to throw down; *tumba*, a *tomb*, a vault, a *tumble* or fall; L. *tumulus*, *tumultus*, *tumeo*; It. *tomare*, to fall; *tombolare*, to tumble; W. *twmp*, a hillock. The sense of *tumble* is derivative, probably from that of roundness, and this from swelling or turning.]

1. To roll; to roll about by turning one way and the other; as, a person in pain *tumbles* and tosses. *Shak.*
2. To fall; to come down suddenly and violently; as, to *tumble* from a scaffold.
3. To roll down. The stone of Sisyphus is said to have *tumbled* to the bottom, as soon as it was carried up the hill. *Addison.*
4. To play mountebank tricks. *Rowe.*

TUM'BLE, *v. t.* To turn over; to turn or throw about for examination or searching; sometimes with *over*; as, to *tumble over* books or papers; to *tumble over* clothes. [To *tumble over in thought*, is not elegant.]

2. To disturb; to rumple; as, to *tumble* a bed.

To tumble out, to throw or roll out; as, to *tumble out* casks from a store.

To tumble down, to throw down carelessly. *Locke.*

TUM'BLE, *n.* A fall. *L'Estrange.*

TUM'BLED, *pp.* Rolled; disturbed; rumpled; thrown down.

TUM'BLER, *n.* One who tumbles; one who plays the tricks of a mountebank. *Pope.*

2. A large drinking glass.
3. A variety of the domestic pigeon, so called from his practice of tumbling or turning over in flight. It is a short-bodied pigeon, of a plain color, black, blue or white. *Cyc.*
4. A sort of dog, so called from his practice of tumbling before he attacks his prey. *Swan.*

TUM'BLING, *ppr.* Rolling about; falling; disturbing; rumpling.

Tumbling-home, in *a ship*, is the inclination of the top-sides from a perpendicular, towards the center of the ship; or the part of a ship which falls inward above the extreme breadth. *Cyc. Mar. Dict.*

TUM'BLING-BAY, *n.* In a canal, an overfall or weir. *Cyc.*

TUM'BREL, *n.* [Fr. *tombereau*, from *tomber*. See *Tumble*.]

1. A ducking stool for the punishment of scolds.
2. A dung-cart. *Tusser. Tatler.*
3. A cart or carriage with two wheels, which accompanies troops or artillery, for conveying the tools of pioneers, cartridges and the like.

TUM'BRIL, *n.* A contrivance of the basket kind, or a kind of cage of osiers, willows, &c. for keeping hay and other food for sheep. *Cyc.*

TUMEFAC'TION, *n.* [L. *tumefacio*, to make tumid. See *Tumid*.]

The act or process of swelling or rising into a tumor; a tumor; a swelling.

TU'MEFIED, *pp.* [from *tumefy.*] Swelled; enlarged; as a *tumefied* joint. *Wiseman.*

TU'MEFȲ, *v. t.* [L. *tumefacio; tumidus, tumeo,* and *facio.*] To swell, or cause to swell.

TU'MEFȲ, *v. i.* To swell; to rise in a tumor.

TU'MEFȲING, *ppr.* Swelling; rising in a tumor.

TU'MID, *a.* [L. *tumidus,* from *tumeo,* to swell.]

1. Being swelled, enlarged or distended; as a *tumid* leg; *tumid* flesh.

2. Protuberant; rising above the level.

So high as heav'd the *tumid* hills. *Milton.*

3. Swelling in sound or sense; pompous; puffy; bombastic; falsely sublime; as a *tumid* expression; a *tumid* style. *Boyle.*

TU'MIDLY, *adv.* In a swelling form.

TU'MIDNESS, *n.* A swelling or swelled state.

TU'MITE, *n.* A mineral. [See *Thummerstone.*]

TU'MOR, *n.* [L. from *tumeo,* to swell.] In *surgery,* a swelling; a morbid enlargement of any part of the body; *a word of very comprehensive signification.*

The morbid enlargement of a particular part, without being caused by inflammation. *Parr.*

Any swelling which arises from the growth of distinct superfluous parts or substances, which did not make any part of the original structure of the body, or from a morbid increase in the bulk of other parts, which naturally and always existed in the human frame. *Cyc.*

The term *tumor* is limited by Abernethy to such swellings as arise from new productions, and includes only the *sarcomatous* and *encysted* tumors. *Parr.*

An *encysted tumor* is one which is formed in a membrane called a *cyst,* connected with the surrounding parts by the neighboring cellular substance. There are also fatty tumors, called *lipomatous* or *adipose, (adipose sarcoma,)* formed by an accumulation of fat in a limited extent of the cellular substance. *Cyc.*

2. Affected pomp; bombast in language; swelling words or expressions; false magnificence or sublimity. [*Little used.*] *Wotton.*

TU'MORED, *n.* Distended; swelled. *Junius.*

TU'MOROUS, *a.* Swelling; protuberant. *Wotton.*

2. Vainly pompous; bombastic; as language or style. [*Little used.*] *B. Jonson.*

TUMP, *n.* [infra.] A little hillock.

TUMP, *v. t.* [W. *twmp,* a round mass, a hillock; L. *tumulus.* See *Tomb.*]

In *gardening,* to form a mass of earth or a hillock round a plant; as, to *tump* teasel. [This English phrase is not used in America, but it answers nearly to our *hilling.* See *Hill.*]

TUMP'ED, *pp.* Surrounded with a hillock of earth.

TUMP'ING, *ppr.* Raising a mass of earth round a plant.

TU'MULAR, *a.* [L. *tumulus,* a heap.] Consisting in a heap; formed or being in a heap or hillock. *Pinkerton.*

TU'MULATE, *v. i.* To swell. [*Not in use.*]

TUMULOS'ITY, *n.* [infra.] Hilliness. *Bailey.*

TU'MULOUS, *a.* [L. *tumulosus.*] Full of hills. *Bailey.*

TU'MULT, *n.* [L. *tumultus,* a derivative from *tumeo,* to swell.]

1. The commotion, disturbance or agitation of a multitude, usually accompanied with great noise, uproar and confusion of voices.

What meaneth the noise of this *tumult?* 1 Sam. iv.

Till in loud *tumult* all the Greeks arose. *Pope.*

2. Violent commotion or agitation with confusion of sounds; as the *tumult* of the elements. *Spectator.*

3. Agitation; high excitement; irregular or confused motion; as the *tumult* of the spirits or passions.

4. Bustle; stir.

TU'MULT, *v. i.* To make a tumult; to be in great commotion. *Milton.*

TUMULT'UARILY, *adv.* [from *tumultuary.*] In a tumultuary or disorderly manner.

TUMULT'UARINESS, *n.* Disorderly or tumultuous conduct; turbulence; disposition to tumult. *K. Charles.*

TUMULT'UARY, *a.* [Fr. *tumultuaire;* from L. *tumultus.*]

1. Disorderly; promiscuous; confused; as a *tumultuary* conflict. *K. Charles.*

2. Restless; agitated; unquiet.

Men who live without religion, live always in a *tumultuary* and restless state. *Atterbury.*

TUMULT'UATE, *v. i.* [L. *tumultuo.*] To make a tumult. [*Not used.*] *South.*

TUMULTUA'TION, *n.* Commotion; irregular or disorderly movement; as the *tumultuation* of the parts of a fluid. *Boyle.*

TUMULT'UOUS, *a.* [Fr. *tumultueux.*] Conducted with tumult; disorderly; as a *tumultuous* conflict; a *tumultuous* retreat.

2. Greatly agitated; irregular; noisy; confused; as a *tumultuous* assembly or meeting.

3. Agitated; disturbed; as a *tumultuous* breast.

4. Turbulent; violent; as a *tumultuous* speech.

5. Full of tumult and disorder; as a *tumultuous* state or city. *Sidney.*

TUMULT'UOUSLY, *adv.* In a disorderly manner; by a disorderly multitude.

TUMULT'UOUSNESS, *n.* The state of being tumultuous; disorder; commotion.

TUN, *n.* [Sax. Sw. *tunna,* a cask; Fr. *tonne, tonneau;* Ir. *tonna;* Arm. *tonnell;* Sp. Port. *tonel, tonelada;* G. *tonne;* D. *ton;* W. *tynell,* a barrel or tun. This word seems to be from the root of L. *teneo,* to hold, Gr. τεινω, to stretch, W. *tyn,* stretched, strained, tight, *tynâu,* to strain, to tighten; and this seems also to be the Sax. *tun,* a *town,* for this word signifies also a garden, evidently from enclosing, and a class, from collecting or holding.]

1. In *a general sense,* a large cask; an oblong vessel bulging in the middle, like a pipe or puncheon, and girt with hoops.

2. A certain measure for liquids, as for wine, oil, &c.

3. A quantity of wine, consisting of two pipes or four hogsheads, or 252 gallons. In different countries, the tun differs in quantity.

4. In *commerce,* the weight of twenty hundreds gross, each hundred consisting of 112*lb.*=2240*lb.* But by a law of Connecticut, passed June 1827, gross weight is abolished, and a tun is the weight of 2000*lb.* It is also a practice in N. York to sell by 2000*lb.* to the tun.

5. A certain weight by which the burden of a ship is estimated; as a ship of three hundred *tuns,* that is, a ship that will carry three hundred times two thousand weight. Forty two cubic feet are allowed to a *tun.*

6. A certain quantity of timber, consisting of forty solid feet if round, or fifty four feet if square. *Cyc.*

7. Proverbially, a large quantity. *Shak.*

8. In *burlesque,* a drunkard. *Dryden.*

9. At the end of names, *tun, ton,* or *don,* signifies *town,* village, or hill.

TUN, *v. t.* To put into casks. *Bacon. Boyle.*

TU'NABLE, *a.* [from *tune.*] Harmonious; musical.

And *tunable* as sylvan pipe or song. *Milton.*

2. That may be put in tune.

TU'NABLENESS, *n.* Harmony; melodiousness.

TU'NABLY, *adv.* Harmoniously; musically.

TUN'-BELLIED, *a.* [*tun* and *belly.*] Having a large protuberant belly. *Entick.*

TUN'-DISH, *n.* [*tun* and *dish.*] A tunnel.

TUNE, *n.* [Fr. *ton;* It. *tuono;* D. *toon;* W. *ton;* Ir. *tona;* L. *tonus.* It is a different spelling of *tone,* which see.]

1. A series of musical notes in some particular measure, and consisting of a single series, for one voice or instrument, the effect of which is melody; or a union of two or more series or parts to be sung or played in concert, the effect of which is harmony. Thus we say, a merry *tune,* a lively *tune,* a grave *tune,* a psalm *tune,* a martial *tune.*

2. Sound; note. *Shak.*

3. Harmony; order; concert of parts.

A continual parliament I thought would but keep the commonweal in *tune.* *K. Charles.*

4. The state of giving the proper sounds; as when we say, a harpsichord is in *tune;* that is, when the several chords are of that tension, that each gives its proper sound, and the sounds of all are at due intervals, both of tones and semitones.

5. Proper state for use or application; right disposition; fit temper or humor. The mind is not in *tune* for mirth.

A child will learn three times as fast when he is in *tune,* as he will when he is dragged to his task. *Locke.*

TUNE, *v. t.* To put into a state adapted to produce the proper sounds; as, to *tune* a forte-piano; to *tune* a violin.

Tune your harps. *Dryden.*

2. To sing with melody or harmony.

Fountains, and ye that warble as ye flow
Melodious murmurs, warbling *tune* his praise. *Milton.*

So we say of birds, they *tune* their notes or lays.

3. To put into a state proper for any purpose, or adapted to produce a particular effect. [*Little used.*] *Shak.*

TUNE, *v. i.* To form one sound to another.
While *tuning* to the waters' fall
The small birds sang to her. *Drayton.*
2. To utter inarticulate harmony with the voice.

TU'NED, *pp.* Uttered melodiously or harmoniously; put in order to produce the proper sounds.

TU'NEFUL, *a.* Harmonious; melodious; musical; as *tuneful* notes; *tuneful* birds. *Milton. Dryden.*

TU'NELESS, *a.* Unmusical; unharmonious.
2. Not employed in making music; as a *tuneless* harp.

TU'NER, *n.* One who tunes. *Shak.*
2. One whose occupation is to tune musical instruments.

TUNG, *n.* A name given by the Indians to a small insect, called by the Spaniards *pique*, which inserts its eggs within the human skin; an insect very troublesome in the East and West Indies. *Cyc.*

TUNG, *n.* [Sax. *tung, tunga*; Goth. *tugga*; Sw. *tunga*; Dan. *tunge*; D. *tong*; G. *zunge*. The common orthography, *tongue*, is incorrect.]
In man, the instrument of taste, and the chief instrument of speech. [See *Tongue*.]

TUNG'STATE, *n.* A salt formed of tungstenic acid and a base.

TUNG'STEN, *n.* [Sw. Dan. *tung*, heavy, and *sten*, stone.]
In *mineralogy*, a mineral of a yellowish or grayish white color, of a lamellar structure, and infusible by the blowpipe. It occurs massive or crystalized, usually in octahedral crystals. This is an ore. The same name is given to the metal obtained from this ore. This metal is procured in small panes as fine as sand, of a strong metallic luster, an iron gray color, and slightly agglutinated. It is one of the hardest of the metals, and very brittle. *Fourcroy. Cyc.*

TUNGSTEN'IC, *a.* Pertaining to or procured from tungsten.

TU'NIC, *n.* [Fr. *tunique*; L. *tunica*. See *Town* and *Tun*.]
1. A kind of waistcoat or under garment worn by men in ancient Rome and the east. In the later ages of the republic, the tunic was a long garment with sleeves. *Cyc.*
2. Among the religious, a woolen shirt or under garment. *Cyc.*
3. In *anatomy*, a membrane that covers or composes some part or organ; as the *tunics* or coats of the eye; the *tunics* of the stomach, or the membranous and muscular layers which compose it. *Cyc.*
4. A natural covering; an integument; as the *tunic* of a seed.
The *tunic* of the seed, is the *arillus*, a covering attached to the base only of the seed, near the *hilum* or scar, and enveloping the rest of the seed more or less completely and closely. *Cyc.*

TU'NICATED, *a.* In *botany*, covered with a tunic or membranes; coated; as a stem.
A *tunicated bulb*, is one composed of numerous concentric coats, as an onion. *Martyn.*

TU'NICLE, *n.* [from *tunic*.] A natural covering; an integument. *Ray. Bentley.*

TU'NING, *ppr.* Uttering harmoniously or melodiously; putting in due order for making the proper sounds.

TU'NING-FORK, *n.* A steel instrument consisting of two prongs and a handle; used for tuning instruments. *Busby.*

TU'NING-HAMMER, *n.* An instrument for tuning instruments of music. *Busby.*

TUNK'ER, *n.* [G. *tunken*, to dip.] The tunkers are a religious sect in Pennsylvania, of German origin, resembling English baptists.

TUN'NAGE, *n.* [from *tun*.] The amount of tuns that a ship will carry; the content or burthen of a ship. A ship pays duty according to her *tunnage*.
2. The duty charged on ships according to their burthen, or the number of tuns at which they are rated. *U. States' Laws.*
3. A duty laid on liquors according to their measure. *Cyc.*
4. A duty paid to mariners by merchants for unloading their ships, after a rate by the tun. *Cyc.*
5. The whole amount of shipping, estimated by the tuns.

TUN'NEL, *n.* [Fr. *tonnelle*.] A vessel with a broad mouth at one end, and a pipe or tube at the other, for conveying liquor into casks.
2. The opening of a chimney for the passage of smoke; called generally a *funnel*.
3. A large subterraneous arch through a hill for a canal and the passage of boats. Smaller drains or culverts are also called *tunnels*. *Cyc.*

TUN'NEL, *v. t.* To form like a tunnel; as, to *tunnel* fibrous plants into nests. *Derham.*
2. To catch in a net called a tunnel-net.
3. To form with net-work. *Derham.*

TUN'NEL-KILN, *n.* A lime-kiln in which coal is burnt, as distinguised from a *flame-kiln*, in which wood or peat is used. *Cyc.*

TUN'NEL-NET, *n.* A net with a wide mouth at one end and narrow at the other. *Cyc.*

TUN'NEL-PIT, *n.* A shaft sunk from the top of the ground to the level of an intended tunnel, for drawing up the earth and stones.

TUN'NING, *ppr.* Putting into casks.

TUN'NY, *n.* [It. *tonno*; Fr. *thon*; G. *thunfisch*; L. *thynnus*.]
A fish of the genus Scomber, the Spanish mackerel. The largest weigh upwards of four hundred pounds. *Cyc.*

TUP, *n.* A ram. [*Local.*]

TUP, *v. t.* [Gr. τυπτω.] To butt, as a ram. [*Local.*]
2. To cover, as a ram. [*Local.*]

TU'PELO, *n.* A tree of the genus Nyssa. *Drayton. Mease.*

TUP'-MAN, *n.* A man who deals in tups. [*Local.*]

TUR'BAN, *n.* [Ar.] A head dress worn by the orientals, consisting of a cap, and a sash of fine linen or taffeta artfully wound round it in plaits. The cap is red or green, roundish on the top, and quilted with cotton. The sash of the Turks is white linen; that of the Persians is red woolen. *Cyc.*
2. In *conchology*, the whole set of whirls of a shell. *Cyc.*

TUR'BANED, *a.* Wearing a turban; as a *turbaned* Turk. *Shak.*

TUR'BAN-SHELL, *n.* In *natural history*, a genus of shells, or rather of sea urchins, *(echinodermata,)* of a hemispheric or spheroidal shape, the *Cidaris* of Klein.

TUR'BAN-TOP, *n.* A plant of the genus Helvella; a kind of fungus or mushroom. *Cyc.*

TUR'BARY, *n.* [from *turf*; Latinized, *turbaria*.]
1. In *law*, a right of digging turf on another man's land. *Common of turbary*, is the liberty which a tenant enjoys of digging turf on the lord's waste.
2. The place where turf is dug. *Cowel.*

TUR'BID, *a.* [L. *turbidus*, from *turbo*, to disturb, that is, to stir, to turn.]
Properly, having the lees disturbed; but in a more general sense, muddy; foul with extraneous matter; thick, not clear; *used of liquids of any kind*; as *turbid* water; *turbid* wine. Streams running on clay generally appear to be *turbid*. This is often the case with the river Seine.

TUR'BIDLY, *adv.* Proudly; haughtily; *a Latinism.* [*Not in use.*] *Young.*

TUR'BIDNESS, *n.* Muddiness; foulness.

TURBIL'LION, *n.* [Fr. *tourbillon*.] A whirl; a vortex. *Spectator.*

TUR'BINATE, **TUR'BINATED**, } *a.* [L. *turbinatus*, formed like a top, from *turbo*, *turben*, a top.]
1. In *conchology*, spiral, or wreathed conically from a larger base to a kind of apex; as *turbinated* shells. *Cyc.*
2. In *botany*, shaped like a top or cone inverted; narrow at the base, and broad at the apex; as a *turbinated* germ, nectary or pericarp. *Lee.*
3. Whirling. [*Little used.*]

TURBINA'TION, *n.* The act of spinning or whirling, as a top.

TUR'BINITE, **TUR'BITE**, } *n.* A petrified shell of the turbo kind. *Cyc. Kirwan.*

TUR'BIT, *n.* A variety of the domestic pigeon, remarkable for its short beak; called by the Dutch *kort-bek*, short beak. *Cyc. Ed. Encyc.*
2. The turbot. *Cyc.*

TUR'BITH, **TUR'PETH**, } *n.* A root brought from the East Indies, particularly from Cambaya, Surat and Goa, or from Ceylon. It is the cortical part of the root of a species of Convolvulus. That sold in the shops is a longish root, of the thickness of the finger, resinous, heavy, and of a brownish hue without, but whitish within. It is cathartic. *Cyc.*
Turbith or *turpeth mineral*, is the yellow precipitate of mercury, called sometimes yellow subsulphate of mercury, or subdeutosulphate. *Ure.*

TUR'BOT, *n.* [Fr.] A fish of the genus Pleuronectes, [fishes which swim on the side.] It grows to the weight of twenty or thirty pounds, and is much esteemed by epicures.

TUR'BULENCE, **TUR'BULENCY**, } *n.* [See *Turbulent*.] A disturbed state; tumult; confusion; as the *turbulence* of the times; *turbulence* in political affairs. *Milton.*
2. Disorder or tumult of the passions; as *turbulence* of mind. *Dryden.*

3. Agitation; tumultuousness; as *turbulence* of blood. *Swift.*

4. Disposition to resist authority; insubordination; as the *turbulence* of subjects.

TUR'BULENT, *a.* [L. *turbulentus*, from *turbo*, to disturb.]

1. Disturbed; agitated; tumultuous; being in violent commotion; as the *turbulent* ocean.

> Calm region once,
> And full of peace, now tost and *turbulent*. *Milton.*

> The *turbulent* mirth of wine. *Dryden.*

2. Restless; unquiet; refractory; disposed to insubordination and disorder; as *turbulent* spirits.

3. Producing commotion.

> Whose heads that *turbulent* liquor fills with fumes. *Milton.*

TUR'BULENTLY, *adv.* Tumultuously; with violent agitation; with refractoriness.

TUR'CISM, *n.* The religion of the Turks.

TURF, *n.* [Sax. *tyrf*; D. *turf*; G. Sw. *torf*; Fr. *tourbe*; Ir. *tarp*, a clod. The word seems to signify a collection, a mass, or perhaps an excrescence.]

1. That upper stratum of earth and vegetable mold, which is filled with the roots of grass and other small plants, so as to adhere and form a kind of mat. This is otherwise called *sward* and *sod*.

2. Peat; a peculiar kind of blackish, fibrous, vegetable, earthy substance, used as fuel. [Dryden and Addison wrote *turfs*, in the plural. But when turf or peat is cut into small pieces, the practice now is to call them *turves*.]

3. Race-ground; or horse-racing.

> The honors of the *turf* are all our own. *Cowper.*

TURF, *v. t.* To cover with turf or sod; as, to *turf* a bank or the border of a terrace.

TURF'-COVERED, *a.* Covered with turf. *Tooke.*

TURF'-DRAIN, *n.* A drain filled with turf or peat. *Cyc.*

TURF'ED, *pp.* Covered with turf or green sod.

TURF'-HEDGE, *n.* A hedge or fence formed with turf and plants of different kinds. *Cyc.*

TURF'-HOUSE, *n.* A house or shed formed of turf, common in the northern parts of Europe. *Cyc. Tooke.*

TURF'INESS, *n.* [from *turfy*.] The state of abounding with turf, or of having the consistence or qualities of turf.

TURF'ING, *ppr.* Covering with turf.

TURF'ING, *n.* The operation of laying down turf, or covering with turf.

TURF'ING-IRON, *n.* An implement for paring off turf. *Cyc.*

TURF'ING-SPADE, *n.* An instrument for under-cutting turf, when marked out by the plow. *Cyc.*

TURF'-MOSS, *n.* A tract of turfy, mossy, or boggy land. *Cyc.*

TURF'-SPADE, *n.* A spade for cutting and digging turf, longer and narrower than the common spade. *Cyc.*

TURF'Y, *a.* Abounding with turf.

2. Having the qualities of turf.

TUR'GENT, *a.* [L. *turgens*, from *turgeo*, to swell.] Swelling; tumid; rising into a tumor or puffy state; as when the humors are *turgent*. *Gov. of the Tongue.*

TURGES'CENCE, TURGES'CENCY, *n.* [L. *turgescens.*] The act of swelling.

2. The state of being swelled. *Brown.*

3. Empty pompousness; inflation; bombast.

TUR'GID, *a.* [L. *turgidus*, from *turgeo*, to swell.]

1. Swelled; bloated; distended beyond its natural state by some internal agent or expansive force.

> A bladder held by the fire grew *turgid*. *Boyle.*

More generally, the word is applied to an enlarged part of the body; as a *turgid* limb.

2. Tumid; pompous; inflated; bombastic; as a *turgid* style; a *turgid* manner of talking. *Watts.*

TURGID'ITY, *n.* State of being swelled; tumidness.

TUR'GIDLY, *adv.* With swelling or empty pomp.

TUR'GIDNESS, *n.* A swelling or swelled state of a thing; distention beyond its natural state by some internal force or agent, as in a limb.

2. Pompousness; inflated manner of writing or speaking; bombast; as the *turgidness* of language or style.

TURIONIF'EROUS, *a.* [L. *turio*, a shoot, and *fero*, to bear.] Producing shoots. *Barton.*

TUR'KEY, TUR'KY, *n.* [As this fowl was not brought from Turkey, it would be more correct to write the name *turky*.]

A large fowl, the Meleagris gallopavo, a distinct genus. It is a native of America, and its flesh furnishes most delicious food. Wild turkies abound in the forests of America, and domestic turkies are bred in other countries, as well as in America.

TUR'KEY-STONE, *n.* Another name of the oil-stone, from Turkey.

TURK'OIS, *n.* [Fr. *turquoise*; from *Turkey*.]

A mineral, called also calaite, brought from the east; of a beautiful light green color, occurring in thin layers, or in rounded masses, or in reniform masses, with a botryoidal surface. It is susceptible of a high polish, and is used in jewelry. It is usually written in the French manner.

TURK'S-CAP, *n.* A plant of the genus Lilium.

TURK'S-HEAD, *n.* A plant of the genus Cactus.

TURK'S-TURBAN, *n.* A plant of the genus Ranunculus.

TURM, *n.* [L. *turma.*] A troop. [*Not English.*] *Milton.*

TUR'MALIN, *n.* An electric stone. [See *Tourmalin.*]

TUR'MERIC, *n.* [It. *turtumaglio.* Thomson says, Sans. Pers. *zur*, yellow, and *mirich*, pepper.]

Indian saffron; a medicinal root brought from the East Indies, the root of the *Curcuma longa.* It is externally grayish, but internally of a deep lively yellow or saffron color. It has a slight aromatic smell, and a bitterish, slightly acrid taste. It is used for dyeing, and in some cases, as a medicine. This name is sometimes given to the blood-root of America. *Cyc. Bigelow.*

TURMOIL', *n.* [I know not the origin of this word; but it is probably from the root of the L. *turba, turbo, turma*, or of *turn.*]

Disturbance; tumult; harassing labor; trouble; molestation by tumult.

> There I'll rest, as after much *turmoil*
> A blessed soul doth in Elysium. *Shak.*

TURMOIL', *v. t.* To harass with commotion.

> It is her fatal misfortune—to be miserably tossed and *turmoiled* with these storms of affliction. *Spenser.*

2. To disquiet; to weary. *Milton.*

TURMOIL', *v. i.* To be disquieted; to be in commotion. *Milton.*

TURN, *v. t.* [Sax. *turnan, tyrnan*; L. *torno*; Gr. τορνοω; Fr. *tourner*; Arm. *turnein*; It. *torno*, a wheel, L. *turnus*; *torniare*, to turn; *tornare*, to return; *torneare, tornire*, to turn, to fence round, to tilt; *torniamento*, tournament; Sp. *torno, tornear*; G. *turnier*, a tilt; Sw. *tornera*, to run tilt, Dan. *turnerer*; W. *twrn*, turn, from *tur*, a turning; Gaelic, *turna*, a spinning wheel; *turnoir*, a turner. This is probably a derivative verb from the root of Ar. دَارَ daura, to turn. Class Dr. No. 3, and see No 15. 13. 18. 38.]

1. To cause to move in a circular course; as, to *turn* a wheel; to *turn* a spindle; to *turn* the body.

2. To change or shift sides; to put the upper side downwards, or one side in the place of the other. It is said a hen *turns* her eggs often when sitting.

3. To alter, as a position.

> Expert
> When to advance, or stand, or *turn* the sway of battle. *Milton.*

4. To cause to preponderate; to change the state of a balance; as, to *turn* the scale. *Dryden.*

5. To bring the inside out; as, to *turn* a coat.

6. To alter, as the posture of the body, or direction of the look.

> The monarch *turns* him to his royal guest. *Pope.*

7. To form on a lathe; to make round.

8. To form; to shape; *used in the participle*; as a body finely *turned*.

> His limbs how *turn'd*. *Pope.*

9. To change; to transform; as, to *turn* evil to good; to *turn* goods into money.

> Impatience *turns* an ague into a fever. *Taylor.*

> I pray thee, *turn* the counsel of Ahithophel into foolishness. 2 Sam. xv.

10. To metamorphose; as, to *turn* a worm into a winged insect.

11. To alter or change, as color; as, to *turn* green to blue.

12. To change or alter in any manner; to vary. *Shak.*

13. To translate; as, to *turn* Greek into English.

> —Who *turns* a Persian tale for half a crown. *Pope.*

14. To change, as the manner of writing; as, to *turn* prose into verse.

15. To change, as from one opinion or party to another; as, to *turn* one from a tory

to a whig; to *turn* a Mohammedan or a pagan to a Christian.

16. To change in regard to inclination or temper.

Turn thee to me, and have mercy upon me. Ps. xxv.

17. To change or alter from one purpose or effect to another.

God will make these evils the occasion of greater good, by *turning* them to our advantage. *Tillotson.*

18. To transfer.

Therefore he slew him, and *turned* the kingdom to David. 1 Chron. x.

19. To cause to nauseate or lothe; as, to *turn* the stomach.

20. To make giddy.

Eastern priests in giddy circles run,
And *turn* their heads to imitate the sun. *Pope.*

21. To infatuate; to make mad, wild or enthusiastic; as, to *turn* the brain. *Addison.*

22. To change direction to or from any point; as, to *turn* the eyes to the heavens; to *turn* the eyes from a disgusting spectacle.

23. To direct by a change to a certain purpose or object; to direct, as the inclination, thoughts or mind. I have *turned* my mind to the subject.

My thoughts are *turn'd* on peace. *Addison.*

24. To revolve; to agitate in the mind.

Turn those ideas about in your mind. *Watts.*

25. To bend from a perpendicular direction; as, to *turn* the edge of an instrument.

26. To move from a direct course or strait line; to cause to deviate; as, to *turn* a horse from the road, or a ship from her course.

27. To apply by a change of use.

When the passage is open, land will be *turned* most to cattle. *Temple.*

28. To reverse.

The Lord thy God will *turn* thy captivity, and have compassion upon thee. Deut. xxx.

29. To keep passing and changing in the course of trade; as, to *turn* money or stock two or three times in the year.

30. To adapt the mind; *chiefly in the participle.*

He was perfectly well *turned* for trade. *Addison.*

31. To make acid; to sour; as, to *turn* cider or wine; to *turn* milk.

32. To persuade to renounce an opinion; to dissuade from a purpose, or cause to change sides. You cannot *turn* a firm man.

To turn aside, to avert.

To turn away, to dismiss from service; to discard; as, to *turn away* a servant.

2. To avert; as, to *turn away* wrath or evil.

To turn back, to return; as, to *turn back* goods to the seller. [*Little used.*] *Shak.*

To turn down, to fold or double down.

To turn in, to fold or double; as, to *turn in* the edge of cloth.

To turn off, to dismiss contemptuously; as, to *turn off* a sycophant or parasite.

2. To give over; to resign. We are not so wholly *turned off* from that reversion.

3. To divert; to deflect; as, to *turn off* the thoughts from serious subjects.

To be turned of, to be advanced beyond; as, to *be turned of* sixty six.

To turn out, to drive out; to expel; as, to *turn* a family *out* of doors, or *out* of the house.

2. To put to pasture; as cattle or horses.

To turn over, to change sides; to roll over.

2. To transfer; as, to *turn over* a business to another hand.

3. To open and examine one leaf after another; as, to *turn over* a concordance. *Swift.*

4. To overset.

To turn to, to have recourse to.

Helvetius' tables may be *turned to* on all occasions. *Locke.*

To turn upon, to retort; to throw back; as, to *turn* the arguments of an opponent *upon* himself. *Atterbury.*

To turn the back, to flee; to retreat. Ex. xxiii.

To turn the back upon, to quit with contempt; to forsake.

To turn the die or *dice,* to change fortune.

TURN, *v. i.* To move round; to have a circular motion; as, a wheel *turns* on its axis; a spindle *turns* on a pivot; a man *turns* on his heel.

2. To be directed.

The understanding *turns* inwards on itself, and reflects on its own operations. *Locke.*

3. To show regard by directing the look towards any thing.

Turn mighty monarch, *turn* this way;
Do not refuse to hear. *Dryden.*

4. To move the body round. He *turned* to me with a smile.

5. To move; to change posture. Let your body be at rest; do not *turn* in the least.

6. To deviate; as, to *turn* from the road or course.

7. To alter; to be changed or transformed; as, wood *turns* to stone; water *turns* to ice; one color *turns* to another.

8. To become by change; as, the fur of certain animals *turns* in winter.

Cygnets from gray *turn* white. *Bacon.*

9. To change sides. A man in a fever *turns* often. *Swift.*

10. To change opinions or parties; as, to *turn* Christian or Mohammedan.

11. To change the mind or conduct.

Turn from thy fierce wrath. Ex. xxxii.

12. To change to acid; as, milk *turns* suddenly during a thunder storm.

13. To be brought eventually; to result or terminate in. This trade has not *turned* to much account or advantage. The application of steam *turns* to good account, both on land and water.

14. To depend on for decision. The question *turns* on a single fact or point.

15. To become giddy.

I'll look no more,
Lest my brain *turn*. *Shak.*

16. To change a course of life; to repent.

Turn ye, *turn* ye from your evil ways, for why will ye die? Ezek. xxxiii.

17. To change the course or direction; as, the tide *turns.*

To turn about, to move the face to another quarter.

To turn away, to deviate.

2. To depart from; to forsake.

To turn in, to bend inwards.

2. To enter for lodgings or entertainment. Gen. xix.

3. To go to bed.

To turn off, to be diverted; to deviate from a course. The road *turns off* to the left.

To turn on or *upon,* to reply or retort.

2. To depend on.

To turn out, to move from its place, as a bone.

2. To bend outwards; to project.

3. To rise from bed; also, to come abroad.

To turn over, to turn from side to side; to roll; to tumble.

2. To change sides or parties.

To turn to, to be directed; as, the needle *turns to* the magnetic pole.

To turn under, to bend or be folded downwards.

To turn up, to bend or be doubled upwards.

TURN, *n.* The act of turning; movement or motion in a circular direction, whether horizontally, vertically or otherwise; a revolution; as the *turn* of a wheel.

2. A winding; a meandering course; a bend or bending; as the *turn* of a river. *Addison.*

3. A walk to and fro.

I will take a *turn* in your garden. *Dryden.*

4. Change; alteration; vicissitude; as the *turns* and varieties of passions. *Hooker.*

Too well the *turns* of mortal chance I know. *Pope.*

5. Successive course.

Nobleness and bounty—which virtues had their *turns* in the king's nature. *Bacon.*

6. Manner of proceeding; change of direction. This affair may take a different *turn* from that which we expect.

7. Chance; hap; opportunity.

Every one has a fair *turn* to be as great as he pleases. *Collier.*

8. Occasion; incidental opportunity.

An old dog falling from his speed, was loaded at every *turn* with blows and reproaches. *L'Estrange.*

9. Time at which, by successive vicissitudes, any thing is to be had or done. They take each other's *turn*.

His *turn* will come to laugh at you again. *Denham.*

10. Action of kindness or malice.

Thanks are half lost when good *turns* are delay'd. *Fairfax.*

Some malicious natures place their delight in doing ill *turns.* *L'Estrange.*

11. Reigning inclination or course. Religion is not to be adapted to the *turn* and fashion of the age.

12. A step off the ladder at the gallows. *Butler.*

13. Convenience; occasion; purpose; exigence; as, this will not serve his *turn*. *Clarendon. Temple.*

14. Form; cast; shape; manner; in a literal or figurative sense; as the *turn* of thought; a man of a sprightly *turn* in conversation.

The *turn* of his thoughts and expression is unharmonious. *Dryden.*

Female virtues are of a domestic *turn*. *Addison.*

The Roman poets, in their description of a beautiful man, often mention the *turn* of his neck and arms. *Addison.*

15. Manner of arranging words in a sentence.

16. Change; new position of things. Some evil happens at every *turn* of affairs.

17. Change of direction; as the *turn* of the tide from flood to ebb.

18. One round of a rope or cord.
19. In *mining*, a pit sunk in some part of a drift. *Cyc.*
20. *Turn* or *tourn*, in law. The sherif's turn is a court of record, held by the sherif twice a year in every hundred within his county. [*England.*]

By turns, one after another; alternately. They assist each other *by turns*.

2. At intervals.

They feel *by turns* the bitter change. *Milton.*

To take turns, to take each other's places alternately.

TURN'-BENCH, *n.* [*turn* and *bench.*] A kind of iron lathe. *Moxon.*

TURN'COAT, *n.* [*turn* and *coat.*] One who forsakes his party or principles. *Shak.*

TURN'ED, *pp.* Moved in a circle; changed.

TUR'NEP, *n.* [a compound of *tur*, round, and Sax. *næpe*, L. *napus*, a turnep.]
A bulbous root or plant of the genus Brassica, of great value for food; an esculent root of several varieties.

TURN'ER, *n.* One whose occupation is to form things with a lathe; one who turns.

TURN'ERITE, *n.* A rare mineral occurring in small crystals of a yellowish brown color, externally brilliant and translucent. *Phillips.*

TURN'ERY, *n.* The art of forming into a cylindrical shape by the lathe.
2. Things made by a turner or in the lathe.

TURN'ING, *ppr.* Moving in a circle; changing; winding.

TURN'ING, *n.* A winding; a bending course; flexure; meander.
2. Deviation from the way or proper course.

TURN'INGNESS, *n.* Quality of turning; tergiversation. [*Not in use.*] *Sidney.*

TURN'PIKE, *n.* [*turn* and *pike.*] Strictly, a frame consisting of two bars crossing each other at right angles, and turning on a post or pin, to hinder the passage of beasts, but admitting a person to pass between the arms.
2. A gate set across a road to stop travelers and carriages till toll is paid for keeping the road in repair.
3. A turnpike road.
4. In *military affairs*, a beam filled with spikes to obstruct passage. *Cyc.*

TURN'PIKE, *v. t.* To form, as a road, in the manner of a turnpike road; to throw the path of a road into a rounded form. *Med. Repos.*

TURN'PIKE-ROAD, *n.* A road on which turnpikes or toll-gates are established by law, and which are made and kept in repair by the toll collected from travelers or passengers who use the road. *Cyc.*

TURN'SERVING, *n.* [*turn* and *serve.*] The act or practice of serving one's turn or promoting private interest. *Bacon.*

TURN'-SICK, *a.* [*turn* and *sick.*] Giddy. *Bacon.*

TURN'SOLE, *n.* [*turn* and L. *sol*, the sun.] A plant of the genus Heliotropium, so named because its flower is supposed to turn towards the sun.

TURN'SPIT, *n.* [*turn* and *spit.*] A person who turns a spit.

His lordship is his majesty's *turnspit*. *Burke.*

2. A variety of the dog, so called from turning the spit.

TURN'STILE, *n.* [*turn* and *stile.*] A turnpike in a foot-path. *Gay.*

TURN'STONE, *n.* [*turn* and *stone.*] A bird, called the sea-dotterel, the *Tringa morinella*, a little larger than an English blackbird. This bird takes its name from its practice of turning up small stones in search of insects. *Cyc.*

TUR'PENTINE, *n.* [L. *terebinthina*; Sp. It. *trementina*; G. *terpentin*. I know not the origin of this word; the first syllable may coincide with the root of *tar*.]
A transparent resinous substance, flowing naturally or by incision from several species of trees, as from the pine, larch, fir, &c. Common turpentine is of about the consistence of honey; but there are several varieties. *Cyc.*

TUR'PENTINE-TREE, *n.* A tree of the genus Pistacia, which produces not only its proper fruit, but a kind of horn which grows on the surface of its leaves. This is found to be an excrescence, the effect of the puncture of an insect, and is produced in the same manner as the galls of other plants. *Cyc.*

TURP'ITUDE, *n.* [Fr. from L. *turpitudo*, from *turpis*, foul, base.]
1. Inherent baseness or vileness of principle in the human heart; extreme depravity.
2. Baseness or vileness of words or actions; shameful wickedness. *South.*

TUR'REL, *n.* A tool used by coopers. *Sherwood.*

TUR'RET, *n.* [L. *turris.*] A little tower; a small eminence or spire attached to a building and rising above it.

And lift her *turrets* nearer to the sky. *Pope.*

2. In *the art of war*, movable turrets, used formerly by the Romans, were buildings of a square form, consisting of ten or even twenty stories, and sometimes one hundred and twenty cubits high, moved on wheels. They were employed in approaches to a fortified place, for carrying soldiers, engines, ladders, casting-bridges and other necessaries. *Cyc.*

TUR'RETED, *a.* Formed like a tower; as a *turreted* lamp. *Bacon.*
2. Furnished with turrets.

TUR'RILITE, *n.* The fossil remains of a spiral multilocular shell. *Ed. Encyc.*

TUR'TLE, *n.* [Sax. *id.*; Fr. *tourterelle*; L. *turtur*; Gaelic, *turtuir*; It. *tortora*, *tortola*, *tortorella*.]
1. A fowl of the genus Columba; called also the *turtle dove*, and *turtle pigeon*. It is a wild species, frequenting the thickest parts of the woods, and its note is plaintive and tender. *Ed. Encyc.*
2. The name sometimes given to the common tortoise.
3. The name given to the large sea-tortoise. *Cyc.*

TUR'TLE-DŎVE, *n.* A species of the genus Columba. [See *Turtle.*]

TUR'TLE-SHELL, *n.* [*turtle* and *shell.*] A shell, a beautiful species of Murex; also, tortoise-shell.

TUS'CAN, *a.* Pertaining to Tuscany in Italy; an epithet given to one of the orders of columns, the most ancient and simple.

TUS'CAN, *n.* An order of columns.

TUSH, an exclamation, indicating check, rebuke or contempt. *Tush, tush*, never tell me such a story as that.

TUSH, *n.* [Sax. *tux.*] A tooth.

TUSK, *n.* [Sax. *tux.*] The long pointed tooth of certain rapacious, carnivorous or fighting animals; as the *tusks* of the boar.

TUSK, *v. i.* To gnash the teeth, as a boar. *Obs.* *B. Jonson.*

TUSK'ED, TUSK'Y, *a.* Furnished with tusks; as the *tusky* boar. *Dryden.*

TUS'SLE, *n.* A struggle; a conflict. [*Vulgar.*] [See *Touse.*]

TUS'SUC, TUS'SOC, *n.* A tuft of grass or twigs. *Obs.* *Grew.*

TUT, an exclamation, used for checking or rebuking.

TUT, *n.* An imperial ensign of a golden globe with a cross on it.

Tut bargain, among *miners*, a bargain by the lump. [Qu. L. *totus.*] *Cyc.*

TU'TELAGE, *n.* [from L. *tutela*, protection, from *tueor*, to defend.]
1. Guardianship; protection; *applied to the person protecting*; as, the king's right of seignory and *tutelage*. *Bacon.*
2. State of being under a guardian.

TU'TELAR, TU'TELARY, *a.* [L. *tutelaris*, supra.] Having the guardianship or charge of protecting a person or a thing; guardian; protecting; as *tutelary* genii; *tutelary* goddesses. *Temple. Dryden.*

TU'TENAG, *n.* The Chinese name of zink. Sometimes the word is used to denote a metallic compound brought from China, called Chinese copper or white copper, consisting of copper, zink and iron. *Cyc. Fourcroy.*

TU'TOR, *n.* [L. from *tueor*, to defend; Fr. *tuteur.*]
1. In *the civil law*, a guardian; one who has the charge of a child or pupil and his estate.
2. One who has the care of instructing another in various branches or in any branch of human learning. Some gentlemen employ a *tutor* to teach in their families, others to attend a son in his travels.
3. In *universities* and *colleges*, an officer or member of some hall, who has the charge of instructing the students in the sciences and other branches of learning.

In *the American colleges*, tutors are graduates selected by the governors or trustees, for the instruction of undergraduates of the three first years. They are usually officers of the institution, who have a share, with the president and professors, in the government of the students.

TU'TOR, *v. t.* To teach; to instruct. *Shak.*
2. To treat with authority or severity. *Addison.*
3. To correct.

TU'TORAGE, *n.* In *the civil law*, guardianship; the charge of a pupil and his estate. In France, *tutorage* does not expire till the pupil is twenty five years of age.
2. The authority or solemnity of a tutor. [*Little used.*]

TU'TORED, *pp.* Instructed; corrected; disciplined.

TU'TORESS, *n.* A female tutor; an instructress; a governess. *More.*

TU'TORING, *ppr.* Teaching; directing; correcting.

TU'TORING, *n.* The act of instructing; education.

TU'TRIX, *n.* A female guardian. *Smollett.*

TUT'SAN, *n.* A plant, park-leaves, of the genus Hypericum. *Lee.*

TUT'TI, *n.* [L. *toti.*] In Italian music, a direction for all to play in full concert.

TUT'TY, *n.* [It. *tuzia ;* Low L. *tutia.*] An argillaceous ore of zink, found in Persia, formed on cylindric molds into tubular pieces, like the bark of a tree. It is said to be made of a glutinous, argillaceous earth, like clay, which is put into pots, moistened and baked. *Cyc.*

TUZ, *n.* [Qu. *touse.*] A lock or tuft of hair. [*Not in use.*] *Dryden.*

TWAIN, *a.* or *n.* [Sax. *twegen ;* Sw. *tvenne ;* Dan. *tvende*, for *tvegende.* Whether *two* is contracted from *tweg*, is not apparent, but we see in the Danish *tvende*, the first syllable of twenty ; *twen-tig*, two tens.] Two.

When old winter splits the rocks in *twain.* *Dryden.*

[*Nearly obsolete in common discourse, but used in poetry and burlesque.*]

TWAIT, *n.* A fish.

2. In old writers, wood grubbed up and converted into arable land. [*Local.*] *Cyc.*

TWANG, *v. i.* [D. *dwang*, Dan. *tvang*, Sw. *tvång*, G. *zwang*, force, compulsion ; G. *zwängen, zwingen*, D. *dwingen*, Sw. *tvinga*, Dan. *tvinger*, to constrain.]

To sound with a quick sharp noise ; to make the sound of a string which is stretched and suddenly pulled ; as the *twanging* bows. *Philips.*

TWANG, *v. t.* To make to sound, as by pulling a tense string and letting it go suddenly. *Shak.*

Sound the tough horn, and *twang* the quivering string. *Pope.*

TWANG, *n.* A sharp quick sound ; as the *twang* of a bowstring ; a *twang* of the nose. *Butler.*

2. An affected modulation of the voice ; a kind of nasal sound.

He has a *twang* in his discourse. *Arbuthnot.*

TWAN'GLE, *v. i.* To twang. *Shak.*

TWANG'ING, *ppr.* Making a sharp sound.

2. *a.* Contemptibly noisy. *Shak.*

TWANK, a corruption of *twang.* *Addison.*

'TWAS, a contraction of *it was.*

TWAT'TLE, *v. i.* [G. *schwatzen*, with a different prefix. See *Twitter.*]

To prate ; to talk much and idly ; to gabble ; to chatter ; as a *twattling* gossip. *L'Estrange.*

TWAT'TLE, *v. t.* To pet ; to make much of. [*Local.*] *Grose.*

TWAT'TLING, *ppr.* or *a.* Prating ; gabbling ; chattering.

TWAT'TLING, *n.* The act of prating ; idle talk.

TWAY, for *twain*, two. [*Not in use.*] *Spenser.*

TWA'Y-BLADE, } *n.* [*tway* and *blade.*] A
TWȲ-BLADE, } plant of the genus Ophris ; a polypetalous flower, consisting of six dissimilar leaves, of which the five upper ones are so disposed as to represent, in some measure, a helmet, the under one being headed and shaped like a man. *Lee. Miller.*

TWEAG, } *v. t.* [Sax. *twiccian*, to twitch ;
TWEAK, } G. *zwicken ;* D. *zwikken.* It is radically the same word as *twitch*, and of the same signification.]

To twitch ; to pinch and pull with a sudden jerk ; as, to *tweag* or *tweak* the nose. *Shak. Swift.*

TWEAG, *n.* Distress ; a pinching condition. [*Not in use.*] *Arbuthnot.*

TWEE'DLE, *v. t.* To handle lightly ; used of awkward fiddling. Qu. *Addison.*

TWEEL, *v. t.* To weave with multiplied leases in the harness, by increasing the number of threads in each split of the reed, and the number of treddles, &c. *Cyc.*

TWEE'ZER-CASE, *n.* A case for carrying tweezers.

TWEE'ZERS, *n.* [This seems to be formed on the root of *vise*, an instrument for pinching.] Nippers ; small pinchers used to pluck out hairs.

TWELFTH, *a.* [Sax. *twelfta ;* Sw. *tolfte ;* Dan. *tolvte ;* D. *twaalfde ;* G. *zwölfte.*]

The second after the tenth ; the ordinal of twelve.

TWELFTH-TIDE, *n.* [*twelfth* and *tide.*] The twelfth day after christmas. *Tusser.*

TWELVE, *a.* *twelv.* [Sax. *twelf ;* D. *twaalf ;* G. *zwölf ;* Sw. *tolf ;* Dan. *tolv.* Qu. *two left* after ten.]

The sum of two and ten ; twice six ; a dozen. *Twelve* men compose a petty jury.

TWELVEMONTH, *n.* *twelv'month.* [*twelve* and *month.*]

A year, which consists of twelve calendar months.

I shall laugh at this a *twelvemonth* hence. *Shak.*

TWELVEPENCE, *n.* *twelv'pence.* [*twelve* and *pence.*] A shilling.

TWELVEPENNY, *a.* *twelv'penny.* Sold for a shilling ; worth a shilling ; as a *twelve-penny* gallery. *Dryden.*

TWELVESCORE, *a.* *twelv'score.* [*twelve* and *score.*] Twelve times twenty ; two hundred and forty. *Dryden.*

TWEN'TIETH, *a.* [Sax. *twentigtha*, *twentogotha.* See *Twenty.*] The ordinal of twenty ; as the *twentieth* year. *Dryden.*

TWEN'TY, *a.* [Sax. *twenti, twentig ;* composed of *twend, twenne, twæn*, two, and Goth. *tig*, ten, Gr. δεκα, L. *decem*, W. *deg.* See *Twain.*]

1. Twice ten ; as *twenty* men ; *twenty* years.

2. Proverbially, an indefinite number.

Maximilian, upon *twenty* respects, could not have been the man. *Bacon.*

TWI'BIL, *n.* [*two* and *bil.*] A kind of mattock, and a halbert.

TWICE, *adv.* [from *two.*] Two times.

He *twice* essay'd to cast his son in gold. *Dryden.*

2. Doubly ; as *twice* the sum. He is *twice* as fortunate as his neighbor.

3. *Twice* is used in composition ; as in *twice-told*, *twice*-born, *twice*-planted, *twice*-conquered.

TWIDLE, for *tweedle.* [See *Tweedle.*]

TWI'FALLOW, *v. t.* [*twi*, two, and *fallow.*] To plow a second time land that is fallowed.

TWI'FALLOWED, *pp.* Plowed twice, as summer fallow.

TWI'FALLOWING, *ppr.* Plowing a second time.

TWI'FALLOWING, *n.* The operation of plowing a second time, as fallow land, in preparing it for seed.

TWI'FOLD, *a.* Twofold. *Obs.* *Spenser.*

TWIG, *n.* [Sax. *twig ;* D. *twyg ;* G. *zweig.* Qu. L. *vigeo*, with a prefix.]

A small shoot or branch of a tree or other plant, of no definite length or size.

The Britons had boats made of willow *twigs*, covered on the outside with hides. *Raleigh.*

TWIG'GEN, *a.* Made of twigs ; wicker. *Grew.*

TWIG'GY, *a.* Full of twigs ; abounding with shoots. *Evelyn.*

TWI'LIGHT, *n.* [Sax. *tweon-leoht*, doubtful light, from *tweon, tweogan*, to doubt, from *twegen*, two.]

1. The faint light which is reflected upon the earth after sunset and before sunrise ; crepuscular light. In latitudes remote from the equator, the *twilight* is of much longer duration than at and near the equator.

2. Dubious or uncertain view ; as the *twilight* of probability. *Locke.*

TWI'LIGHT, *a.* Obscure ; imperfectly illuminated ; shaded.

O'er the *twilight* groves and dusky caves. *Pope.*

2. Seen or done by twilight. *Milton.*

TWILL, *v. t.* To weave in ribs or ridges ; to quill. [See *Quill.*]

TWILT, *n.* A quilt. [*Local.*] *Grose.*

TWIN, *n.* [Sax. *twinan*, to twine ; from *two.*]

1. One of two young produced at a birth by an animal that ordinarily brings but one ; used mostly in the plural, *twins ;* applied to the young of beasts, as well as to human beings.

2. A sign of the zodiac ; Gemini. *Thomson.*

3. One very much resembling another.

TWIN, *a.* Noting one of two born at a birth ; as a *twin* brother or sister.

2. Very much resembling.

3. In *botany*, swelling out into two protuberances, as an anther or germ. *Martyn.*

TWIN, *v. i.* To be born at the same birth. *Shak.*

2. To bring two at once. *Tusser.*

3. To be paired ; to be suited. *Sandys.*

[*This verb is little used.*]

TWIN, *v. t.* To separate into two parts. *Chaucer.*

TWIN'-BORN, *a.* [*twin* and *born.*] Born at the same birth.

TWINE, *v. t.* [Sax. *twinan ;* D. *twynen ;* Sw. *tvinna ;* Dan. *tvinder ;* from *two.*]

1. To twist ; to wind, as one thread or cord around another, or as any flexible substance around another body ; as fine *twined* linen. Ex. xxxix.

2. To unite closely ; to cling to ; to embrace.

3. To gird ; to wrap closely about.

Let wreaths of triumph now my temples *twine.* *Pope.*

TWINE, *v. i.* To unite closely, or by interposition of parts.

Friends now fast sworn, who *twine* in love— *Shak.*

2. To wind ; to bend ; to make turns.

As rivers, though they bend and *twine*— *Swift.*

3. To turn round ; as, her spindles *twine.* *Chapman.*

TWINE, *n.* A strong thread composed of two or three smaller threads or strands twisted together ; used for binding small parcels, and for sewing sails to their bolt-ropes, &c. Twine of a stronger kind is used for nets.

2. A twist; a convolution; as Typhon's snaky *twine*. *Milton.*

3. Embrace; act of winding round. *Philips.*

TWI'NED, *pp.* Twisted; wound round.

TWINĠE, *v. t. twinj.* [Sw. *tvinga*, D. *dwingen*, Dan. *tvinger*, G. *zwingen*, to constrain; but the sense is primarily to *twitch.* See *Twang, Tweak, Twitch.*]

1. To affect with a sharp sudden pain; to torment with pinching or sharp pains.

> The gnat *twinged* the lion till he made him tear himself, and so he mastered him. *L'Estrange.*

2. To pinch; to tweak; to pull with a jerk; as, to *twinge* one by the ears and nose. *Hudibras.*

TWINĠE, *v. i. twinj.* To have a sudden, sharp, local pain, like a twitch; to suffer a keen spasmodic or shooting pain; as, the side *twinges.* [*This is the sense in which this word is generally used within the limits of my acquaintance.*]

TWINĠE, *n. twinj.* A sudden sharp pain; a darting local pain of momentary continuance; as a *twinge* in the arm or side.

2. A sharp rebuke of conscience.

3. A pinch; a tweak; as a *twinge* of the ear. *L'Estrange.*

TWINĠ'ING, *ppr.* Suffering a sharp local pain of short continuance; pinching with a sudden pull.

TWINĠ'ING, *n.* The act of pinching with a sudden twitch; a sudden, sharp, local pain.

TWI'NING, *ppr.* Twisting; winding round; uniting closely to; embracing.

2. In *botany*, ascending spirally around a branch, stem or prop. *Martyn.*

TWINK. [See *Twinkle.*]

TWIN'KLE, *v. i.* [Sax. *twinclian*; most probably formed from *wink*, with the prefix *eth, ed*, or *oth*, like *twit.*]

1. To sparkle; to flash at intervals; to shine with a tremulous intermitted light, or with a broken quivering light. The fixed stars *twinkle*; the planets do not.

> These stars do not *twinkle*, when viewed through telescopes that have large apertures. *Newton.*

2. To open and shut the eye by turns; as the *twinkling* owl. *L'Estrange.*

3. To play irregularly; as, her eyes will *twinkle.* *Donne.*

TWIN'KLE, TWIN'KLING, } *n.* A sparkling; a shining with intermitted light; as the *twinkling* of the stars.

2. A motion of the eye. *Dryden.*

3. A moment; an instant; the time of a wink.

> In a moment, in the *twinkling* of an eye, at the last trump—the dead shall be raised incorruptible. 1 Cor. xv.

TWIN'KLING, *ppr.* Sparkling.

TWIN'LING, *n.* [from *twin.*] A twin lamb. *Tusser.*

TWIN'NED, *a.* [from *twin.*] Produced at one birth, like twins; united. *Milton.*

TWIN'NER, *n.* [from *twin.*] A breeder of twins. *Tusser.*

TWIN'TER, *n.* [*two* and *winter.*] A beast two winters old. [*Local.*] *Grose.*

TWIRE, *v. i.* To take short flights; to flutter; to quiver; to twitter. [*Not in use.*] *Chaucer. Beaum.*

TWIRL, *v. t. twurl.* [D. *dwarlen*; G. *querlen*; formed on *whirl.* The German coincides with our vulgar *quirl.*]

To move or turn round with rapidity; to whirl ronnd.

> See ruddy maids,
> Some taught with dextrous hand to *twirl* the wheel— *Dodsley.*

TWIRL, *v. i.* To revolve with velocity; to be whirled round.

TWIRL, *n.* A rapid circular motion; quick rotation.

2. Twist; convolution. *Woodward.*

TWIRL'ED, *pp.* Whirled round.

TWIRL'ING, *ppr.* Turning with velocity; whirling.

TWIST, *v. t.* [Sax. *getwistan*; D. *twisten*, to dispute, Sw. *tvista*; Dan. *tvister*, to dispute, to litigate; G. *zwist*, a dispute. In all the dialects except ours, this word is used figuratively, but it is remarkably expressive and well applied.]

1. To unite by winding one thread, strand or other flexible substance round another; to form by convolution, or winding separate things round each other; as, to *twist* yarn or thread. So we say, to double and *twist.*

2. To form into a thread from many fine filaments; as, to *twist* wool or cotton.

3. To contort; to writhe; as, to *twist* a thing into a serpentine form. *Pope.*

4. To wreathe; to wind; to encircle.

> —Pillars of smoke *twisted* about with wreaths of flame. *Burnet.*

5. To form; to weave; as, to *twist* a story. *Shak.*

6. To unite by intertexture of parts; as, to *twist* bays with ivy. *Waller.*

7. To unite; to enter by winding; to insinuate; as, avarice *twists* itself into all human concerns.

8. To pervert; as, to *twist* a passage in an author.

9. To turn from a straight line.

TWIST, *v. i.* To be contorted or united by winding round each other. Some strands will *twist* more easily than others.

TWIST, *n.* A cord, thread or any thing flexible, formed by winding strands or separate things round each other.

2. A cord; a string; a single cord.

3. A contortion; a writhe. *Addison.*

4. A little roll of tobacco.

5. Manner of twisting. *Arbuthnot.*

6. A twig. [*Not in use.*]

TWIST'ED, *pp.* Formed by winding threads or strands round each other.

TWIST'ER, *n.* One that twists.

2. The instrument of twisting. *Wallis.*

TWIST'ING, *ppr.* Winding different strands or threads round each other; forming into a thread by twisting.

TWIT, *v. t.* [Sax. *othwitan, edwitan, ætwitan*, to reproach, to upbraid; a compound of *ad, æth*, or *oth*, and *witan.* The latter verb signifies to know, Eng. to *wit*, and also to impute, to ascribe, to prescribe or appoint, also to reproach; and with *ge*, a different prefix, *gewitan*, to depart. The original verb then signifies to set, send or throw. We have in this word decisive evidence that the first letter *t*, is a prefix, the remains of *æth* or *oth*, a word that probably coincides with the L. *ad*, to; and hence we may fairly infer that the other words in which *t* precedes *w*, are also compound. That some of them are so, appears evident from other circumstances.]

To reproach; to upbraid; as for some previous act. He *twitted* his friend of falsehood.

> With this these scoffers *twitted* the christians. *Tillotson.*
>
> Æsop minds men of their errors, without *twitting* them for what is amiss. *L'Estrange.*

TWITCH, *v. t.* [Sax. *twiccian.* See *Twang.*] To pull with a sudden jerk; to pluck with a short, quick, motion; to snatch; as, to *twitch* one by the sleeve; to *twitch* a thing out of another's hand; to *twitch* off clusters of grapes.

TWITCH, *n.* A pull with a jerk; a short, sudden, quick pull; as a *twitch* by the sleeve.

2. A short spasmodic contraction of the fibers or muscles; as a *twitch* in the side; convulsive *twitches.* *Sharp.*

TWITCH'ED, *pp.* Pulled with a jerk.

TWITCH'ER, *n.* One that twitches.

TWITCH'-GRASS, *n.* Couch grass; a species of grass which it is difficult to exterminate. But qu. is not this word a corruption of *quitch-grass, or quich-grass?*

TWITCH'ING, *ppr.* Pulling with a jerk; suffering short spasmodic contractions.

TWIT'TED, *pp.* Upbraided.

TWIT'TER, *v. t.* [D. *kwetteren*; Dan. *quidrer*; Sw. *quittra.*]

1. To make a succession of small, tremulous, intermitted noises; as, the swallow *twitters.* *Dryden.*

2. To make the sound of a half suppressed laugh.

TWIT'TER, *n.* [from *twit.*] One who twits or reproaches.

TWIT'TER, *n.* A small intermitted noise, as in half suppressed laughter; or the sound of a swallow.

TWIT'TERING, *ppr.* Uttering a succession of small interrupted sounds, as in a half suppressed laugh, or as a swallow.

TWIT'TING, *ppr.* Upbraiding; reproaching.

TWIT'TINGLY, *adv.* With upbraiding. *Junius.*

TWIT'TLE-TWATTLE, *n.* Tattle; gabble. [*Vulgar.*] *L'Estrange.*

'TWIXT, a contraction of *betwixt*, used in poetry.

TWŌ, *a.* [Sax. *twa*; Goth. *twa, twai, twos*; D. *twee*; G. *zwei*; Sw. *två*; Ir. Gaelic, *da* or *do*; Russ. *tva, tvoe*; Slav. *dwa*; Sans. *dui, dwaja*; Gipsey, *duj*; Hindoo, Ch. Pers. *du*; L. *duo*; Gr. δυο; It. *due*; Sp. *dos*; Port. *dous*; Fr. *deux.*]

1. One and one. Two similar horses used together, are called a span, or a pair.

2. *Two* is used in composition; as in *two*-legged. Man is a *two*-legged animal.

TWŌ-CAP'SULED, *a.* Bicapsular.

TWŌ-CEL'LED, *a.* Bilocular.

TWŌ-CLEFT, *a.* Bifid.

TWŌEDĠED, *a.* Having two edges, or edges on both sides; as a *two-edged* sword.

TWŌ-FLOWERED, *a.* Bearing two flowers at the end, as a peduncle.

TWŌFŌLD, *a.* [*two* and *fold.*] Two of the same kind, or two different things existing together; as *twofold* nature; a *twofold* sense; a *twofold* argument.
2. Double; as *twofold* strength or desire.
3. In *botany*, two and two together, growing from the same place; as *twofold* leaves. *Martyn.*

TWŌFŌLD, *adv.* Doubly; in a double degree. Matt. xxiii.

TWŌ-FORKED, *a.* Dichotomous.

TWŌ-HANDED, *a.* Having two hands; an epithet used as equivalent to large, stout and strong. *Milton.*

TWŌ-LEAVED, *a.* Diphyllous.

TWŌ-LŌBED, *a.* Bilobate.

TWŌ-P'ARTED, *a.* Bipartite.

TWŌ-PENCE, *n.* A small coin. *Shak.*

TWŌ-PETALED, *a.* Dipetalous.

TWŌ-SEEDED, *a.* In *botany*, dispermous; containing two seeds, as a fruit; having two seeds to a flower, as a plant. *Martyn.*

TWŌ-TIPPED, *a.* Bilabiate.

TWŌ-TŎNGUED, *a.* Double-tongued; deceitful. *Sandys.*

TWŌ-VALVED, *a.* Bivalvular, as a shell, pod, or glume.

TYE, *v. t.* [See *Tie*, the more usual orthography, and *Tying.*]
To bind or fasten.

TȲE, *n.* A knot. [See *Tie.*]
2. A bond; an obligation.

> By the soft *tye* and sacred name of friend. *Pope.*

3. In *ships*, a runner or short thick rope.

TY'ER, *n.* One who ties or unites. *Fletcher.*

TYGER. [See *Tiger.*]

TY'ING, *ppr.* [See *Tie* and *Tye.*] Binding; fastening. [As this participle must be written with *y*, it might be well to write the verb *tye.*]

TYKE, *n.* A dog; or one as contemptible as a dog. *Shak.*

TYM'BAL, *n.* [Fr. *timbale*; It. *taballo*; Sp. *timbal.* *M* is probably not radical. It is from beating, Gr. τυπτω.]
A kind of kettle drum.

> A *tymbal's* sound were better than my voice. *Prior.*

TYM'PAN, *n.* [L. *tympanum.* See *Tymbal.*]
1. A drum; hence, the barrel or hollow part of the ear behind the membrane of the tympanum. *Hooper.*
2. The area of a pediment; also, the part of a pedestal called the trunk or dye. *Cyc.*
3. The pannel of a door.
4. A triangular space or table in the corners or sides of an arch, usually enriched with figures. *Cyc.*
5. Among *printers*, a frame covered with parchment or cloth, on which the blank sheets are put in order to be laid on the form to be impressed.

TYM'PANITES, *n.* In *medicine*, a flatulent distention of the belly; wind dropsy; tympany. *Cyc.*

TYM'PANIZE, *v. i.* To act the part of a drummer.

TYM'PANIZE, *v. t.* To stretch, as a sk n over the head of a drum.

TYM'PANUM, *n.* The drum of the ear. [See *Tympan.*]
2. In *mechanics*, a wheel placed round an axis. *Cyc.*

TYM'PANY, *n.* A flatulent distention of the belly. [See *Tympanites.*]

TYN'Y, *a.* Small. [See *Tiny.*]

TYPE, *n.* [Fr. *type*; L. *typus*; Gr. τυπος, from the root of *tap*, Gr. τυπτω, to beat, strike, impress.]
1. The mark of something; an emblem; that which represents something else.

> Thy emblem, gracious queen, the British rose,
> *Type* of sweet rule and gentle majesty. *Prior.*

2. A sign; a symbol; a figure of something to come; as, Abraham's sacrifice and the paschal lamb, were *types* of Christ. To this word is opposed *antitype.* Christ, in this case, is the *antitype.*
3. A model or form of a letter in metal or other hard material; used in printing.
4. In *medicine*, the form or character of a disease, in regard to the intension and remission of fevers, pulses, &c.; the regular progress of a fever. *Cyc.* *Coxe.*
5. In *natural history*, a general form, such as is common to the species of a genus, or the individuals of a species.
6. A stamp or mark. *Shak.*

TYPE, *v. t.* To prefigure; to represent by a model or symbol beforehand. [*Little used.*] *White.*

TY'PE-METAL, *n.* A compound of lead and antimony, with a small quantity of copper or brass.

TY'PHOID, *a.* [*typhus* and Gr. ειδος, form.] Resembling typhus; weak; low. *Say.*

TY'PHUS, *a.* [from Gr. τυφω, to inflame or heat. Hippocrates gave this name to a fever which produced great heat in the eyes. *Parr.* But the Gr. τυφος is smoke; so Sp. *tufo*, a warm exhalation.]
A typhus disease or fever is accompanied with great debility. The word is sometimes used as a noun.

TYP'IC, } *a.* Emblematic; figurative;
TYP'ICAL, } representing something future by a form, model or resemblance. Abraham's offering of his only son Isaac, was *typical* of the sacrifice of Christ. The brazen serpent was *typical* of the cross.
Typic fever, is one that is regular in its attacks; opposed to *erratic fever.* *Cyc.*

TYP'ICALLY, *adv.* In a typical manner; by way of image, symbol or resemblance.

TYP'ICALNESS, *n.* The state of being typical.

TYP'IFIED, *pp.* Represented by symbol or emblem.

TYP'IFȲ, *v. t.* To represent by an image, form, model or resemblance. The washing of baptism *typifies* the cleansing of the soul from sin by the blood of Christ. Our Savior was *typified* by the goat that was slain. *Brown.*

TYP'IFȲING, *ppr.* Representing by model or emblem.

TYP'OCOSMY, *n.* [Gr. τυπος and κοσμος.] A representation of the world. [*Not much used.*] *Camden.*

TȲPOG'RAPHER, *n.* [See *Typography.*] A printer. *Warton.*

TȲPOGRAPH'IC, } *a.* Pertaining to
TȲPOGRAPH'ICAL, } printing; as the *typographic* art.
2. Emblematic.

TȲPOGRAPH'ICALLY, *adv.* By means of types; after the manner of printers.
2. Emblematically; figuratively.

TȲPOG'RAPHY, *n.* [Gr. τυπος, type, and γραφω, to write.]
1. The art of printing, or the operation of impressing letters and words on forms of types.
2. Emblematical or hieroglyphic representation. *Brown.*

TYP'OLITE, *n.* [Gr. τυπος, form, and λιθος, stone.]
In *natural history*, a stone or fossil which has on it impressions or figures of plants and animals. *Cyc.*

TY'RAN, *n.* A tyrant. [*Not in use.*] *Spenser.*

TYR'ANNESS, *n.* [from *tyrant.*] A female tyrant. *Spenser.* *Akenside.*

TȲRAN'NIC, } *a.* [Fr. *tyrannique*; Gr.
TȲRAN'NICAL, } τυραννικος.] Pertaining to a tyrant; suiting a tyrant; arbitrary; unjustly severe in government; imperious; despotic; cruel; as a *tyrannical* prince; a *tyrannical* master; *tyrannical* government or power.

> Our sects a more *tyrannic* power assume. *Roscommon.*

> Th' oppressor rul'd *tyrannic* where he durst. *Pope.*

TȲRAN'NICALLY, *adv.* With unjust exercise of power; arbitrarily; oppressively.

TȲRAN'NICALNESS, *n.* Tyrannical disposition or practice. *Ch. Relig. Appeal.*

TȲRAN'NICIDE, *n.* [L. *tyrannus*, tyrant, and *cædo*, to kill.]
1. The act of killing a tyrant.
2. One who kills a tyrant. *Hume.*

TYR'ANNING, *ppr.* or *a.* Acting as a tyrant. [*Not used.*] *Spenser.*

TYR'ANNIZE, *v. i.* [Fr. *tyranniser.*] To act the tyrant; to exercise arbitrary power; to rule with unjust and oppressive severity; to exercise power over others not permitted by law or required by justice, or with a severity not necessary to the ends of justice and government. A prince will often *tyrannize* over his subjects; republican legislatures sometimes *tyrannize* over their fellow citizens; masters sometimes *tyrannize* over their servants or apprentices. A husband may not *tyrannize* over his wife and children.

TYR'ANNOUS, *a.* Tyrannical; arbitrary; unjustly severe; despotic. *Sidney.*

TYR'ANNY, *n.* [Fr. *tyrannie*; from *tyran.*]
1. Arbitrary or despotic exercise of power; the exercise of power over subjects and others with a rigor not authorized by law or justice, or not requisite for the purposes of government. Hence tyranny is often synonymous with *cruelty* and *oppression.*
2. Cruel government or discipline; as the *tyranny* of a master.
3. Unresisted and cruel power.
4. Absolute monarchy cruelly administered.
5. Severity; rigor; inclemency.

> The *tyranny* o' th' open night. *Shak.*

TY'RANT, *n.* [L. *tyrannus*; Gr. τυραννος. The Welsh has *teyrn*, a king or sovereign, which Owen says is compounded of *te*, [that spreads,] and *gyrn*, imperious, supreme, from *gyr*, a driving. The Gaelic has *tiarna* and *tighearna*, a lord, prince or ruler, from *tigh*, a house; indicating that the word originally signified the master of a family merely, or the head of a clan. There is some uncertainty as to the real origin of the word. It signified originally merely a chief, king or prince.]

1. A monarch or other ruler or master, who uses power to oppress his subjects; a person who exercises unlawful authority, or lawful authority in an unlawful manner; one who by taxation, injustice or cruel punishment, or the demand of unreasonable services, imposes burdens and hardships on those under his control, which law and humanity do not authorize, or which the purposes of government do not require.

2. A despotic ruler; a cruel master; an oppressor.

> Love, to a yielding heart is a king, to a resisting heart is a *tyrant*. *Sidney.*

TY'RO, *n.* A beginner. [See *Tiro.*]

TȲTHE. [See *Tithe.*]

TȲTHING. [See *Tithing.*]

TZ'AR, *n.* The emperor of Russia.

TZARI'NA, *n.* The empress of Russia.

U.

U is the twenty first letter and the fifth vowel in the English Alphabet. Its true primary sound in Anglo Saxon, was the sound which it still retains in most of the languages of Europe; that of *oo* in *cool*, *tool*, answering to the French *ou*, in *tour*. This sound was changed, probably under the Norman kings, by the attempt made to introduce the Norman French language into common use. However this fact may be, the first, or long and proper sound of *u*, in English, is now not perfectly simple, and it cannot be strictly called a *vowel*. The sound seems to be nearly that of *eu*, shortened and blended. This sound however is not precisely that of *eu* or *yu*, except in a few words, as in *unite*, *union*, *uniform*; the sound does not begin with the distinct sound of *e*, nor end in the distinct sound of *oo*, unless when prolonged. It cannot be well expressed in letters. This sound is heard in the unaffected pronunciation of *annuity*, *numerate*, *brute*, *mute*, *dispute*, *duke*, *true*, *truth*, *rule*, *prudence*, *opportunity*, *infusion*.

Some modern writers make a distinction between the sound of *u*, when it follows *r*, as in *rude*, *truth*, and its sound when it follows other letters, as in *mute*, *duke*; making the former sound equivalent to *oo*; *rood*, *trooth*; and the latter a diphthong equivalent to *eu* or *yu*. This is a mischievous innovation, and not authorized by any general usage either in England or the United States. The difference, very nice indeed, between the sound of *u* in *mute*, and in *rude*, is owing entirely to the articulation which precedes that letter. For example, when a labial precedes *u*, we enter on its sound with the lips closed, and in opening them to the position required for uttering *u*, there is almost necessarily a slight sound of *e* formed before we arrive at the proper sound of *u*. When *r* precedes *u*, the mouth is open before the sound of *u* is commenced. But in both cases, *u* is to be considered as having the same sound.

In some words, as in *bull*, *full*, *pull*, the sound of *u* is that of the Italian *u*, the French *ou*, but shortened. This is a vowel.

U has another short sound, as in *tun*, *run*, *sun*, *turn*, *rub*. This also is a vowel.

U'BEROUS, *a.* [L. *uber.*] Fruitful; copious. [*Little used.*]

U'BERTY, *n.* [L. *ubertas*, from *uber*, fruitful or copious.] Abundance; fruitfulness. [*Little used.*]

UBICA'TION, } *n.* [L. *ubi*, where.] The
UBI'ETY, } state of being in a place; local relation. [*Not much used.*] *Glanville.*

UBIQ'UITARINESS, *n.* Existence every where. [*Little used.*] *Fuller.*

UBIQ'UITARY, *a.* [L. *ubique*, from *ubi*. where.]

Existing every where, or in all places. *Howell.*

UBIQ'UITARY, *n.* [supra.] One that exists every where. *Hall.*

UBIQ'UITY, *n.* [L. *ubique*, every where.] Existence in all places or every where at the same time; omnipresence. The *ubiquity* of God is not disputed by those who admit his existence. *South.*

UD'DER, *n.* [Sax. *uder*; G. *euter*; D. *uyer*; Gr. ουθαρ.]

The breast of a female; but the word is applied chiefly or wholly to the glandular organ of female breasts, in which the milk is secreted and retained for the nourishment of their young, commonly called the *bag*, in cows and other quadrupeds.

UD'DERED, *a.* Furnished with udders. *Gay.*

UG'LILY, *adv.* In an ugly manner; with deformity.

UG'LINESS, *n.* [from *ugly.*] Total want of beauty; deformity of person; as old age and *ugliness*. *Dryden.*

2. Turpitude of mind; moral depravity; lothesomeness.

> Their dull ribaldry must be offensive to any one who does not, for the sake of the sin, pardon the *ugliness* of its circumstances. *South.*

UG'LY, *a.* [W. *hag*, a cut or gash; *hagyr*, ugly, rough. See *Hack.*]

Deformed; offensive to the sight; contrary to beauty; hateful; as an *ugly* person; an *ugly* face.

> O I have pass'd a miserable night,
> So full of *ugly* sights, of ghastly dreams. *Shak.*
> Fellow, begone; I cannot bear thy sight;
> This news hath made thee a most *ugly* man. *Ib.*

UKA'SE, *n.* In Russia, a proclamation or imperial order published.

UL'CER, *n.* [Fr. *ulcere*; It. *ulcera*; L. *ulcus*; Gr. ελκος.]

A sore; a solution of continuity in any of the soft parts of the body, attended with a secretion of pus or some kind of discharge. *Ulcers* on the lungs are seldom healed. *Cooper.*

UL'CERATE, *v. i.* To be formed into an ulcer; to become ulcerous.

UL'CERATE, *v. t.* [Fr. *ulcerer*; L. *ulcero.*] To affect with an ulcer or with ulcers. *Harvey.*

UL'CERATED, *pp.* Affected with ulcers.

UL'CERATING, *ppr.* Turning to an ulcer; generating ulcers.

ULCERA'TION, *n.* [Fr. from L. *ulceratio.*]

1. The process of forming into an ulcer; or the process of becoming ulcerous.

2. An ulcer; a morbid sore that discharges pus or other fluid. *Arbuthnot.*

UL'CERED, *a.* Having become an ulcer. *Temple.*

UL'CEROUS, *a.* Having the nature or character of an ulcer; discharging purulent or other matter. *Harvey.*

2. Affected with an ulcer or with ulcers.

UL'CEROUSNESS, *n.* The state of being ulcerous.

UL'CUSLE, *n.* [L. *ulcusculum*, from *ulcus.*] A little ulcer.

U'LE-TREE, *n.* In *botany*, the Castilla, a genus of trees, whose milky juice yields that kind of elastic gum, called by the Mexicans *ule*. *Cyc.*

ULIG'INOUS, *a.* [L. *uliginosus*, from *uligo*, ooziness.]

Muddy; oozy; slimy. *Woodward.*

UL'LAGE, *n.* In *commerce*, the wantage of casks of liquor, or what a cask wants of being full. *Cyc.*

UL'MIN, *n.* [L. *ulmus*, elm.] A substance obtained from the elm tree, of very singular properties. It resembles gum, but is hard, of a black color, and considerably bitter. In its original state, it is soluble in water, and insoluble in alcohol or ether; but when nitric or oxymuriatic acid is poured into its solution, it changes into a resinous substance no longer soluble in water, but soluble in alcohol. *Cyc.*

A substance originally obtained in the state of an exsudation from the *elm*; but it is found to be a constituent of the bark of almost all trees. *Thomson.*

ULNAGE. [See *Alnage*, *Aunage.*]

UL'NAR, *a.* [L. *ulna.*] Pertaining to the ulna or cubit; as the *ulnar* nerve. *Coxe.*

ULTE'RIOR, *a.* [L. comparative.] Further; as *ulterior* demands; *ulterior* propositions. What *ulterior* measures will be adopted is uncertain. *Smollett.*

2. In *geography*, being or situated beyond or on the further side of any line or boundary; opposed to *citerior*, or hither.

UL'TIMATE, *a.* [L. *ultimus*, furthest.]

1. Furthest; most remote; extreme. We have not yet arrived at the *ultimate* point of progression.

2. Final; being that to which all the rest is directed, as to the main object. The *ultimate* end of our actions should be the glory of God, or the display of his exalted excellence. The *ultimate* end and aim of men is to be happy, and to attain to this end, we must yield that obedience which will honor the law and character of God.

3. Last in a train of consequences; intended in the last resort.

Many actions apt to procure fame, are not conducive to this our *ultimate* happiness. *Addison.*

4. Last; terminating; being at the furthest point. *Darwin.*

5. The last into which a substance can be resolved; constituent. *Darwin.*

UL'TIMATELY, *adv.* Finally; at last; in the end or last consequence. Afflictions often tend to correct immoral habits, and *ultimately* prove blessings.

ULTIMA'TUM, *n.* [L.] In *diplomacy*, the final propositions, conditions or terms offered as the basis of a treaty; the most favorable terms that a negotiator can offer, and the rejection of which usually puts an end to negotiation. It is sometimes used in the plural, *ultimata.*

2. Any final proposition or condition.

ULTIM'ITY, *n.* The last stage or consequence. [*Little used.*] *Bacon.*

ULTRAMARINE, *a.* [L. *ultra*, beyond, and *marinus*, marine.]

Situated or being beyond the sea. *Ainsworth.*

ULTRAMARINE, *n.* [supra.] A beautiful and durable sky-blue; a color formed of the mineral called lapis lazuli, and consisting of little else than oxyd of iron. *Klaproth.*

2. Azure-stone. *Ure.*

Ultramarine ashes, a pigment which is the residuum of lapis lazuli, after the ultramarine has been extracted. Their appearance is that of the ultramarine, a little tinged with red, and diluted with white. *Cyc.*

ULTRAMON'TANE, *a.* [Fr. from L. *ultra* and *montanus*, from *mons*, mountain.]

Being beyond the mountain. Thus France, with regard to Italy, is an *ultramontane* country.

Pouffin is the only *ultramontane* painter whom the Italians seem to envy. *Cyc.*

ULTRAMUN'DANE, *a.* [L. *ultra* and *mundus*, world.]

Being beyond the world, or beyond the limits of our system.

ULTRO'NEOUS, *a.* [L. *ultro*, of one's own accord.] Spontaneous; voluntary. [*Not used.*]

U'LULATE, *v. i.* [L. *ululo*, to howl.] To howl, as a dog or wolf. *Herbert.*

ULULA'TION, *n.* A howling, as of the wolf or dog.

UM'BEL, *n.* [L. *umbella*, a screen or fan.] In *botany*, a particular mode of inflorescence or flowering, which consists of a number of flower-stalks or rays, nearly equal in length, spreading from a common center, their summits forming a level, convex, or even globose surface, more rarely a concave one, as in the carrot. It is simple or compound; in the latter, each peduncle bears another little umbel, umbellet or umbellicle. *Cyc. Martyn.*

Umbel is sometimes called a *rundle*, from its roundness.

UM'BELLAR, *a.* Pertaining to an umbel; having the form of an umbel.

UM'BELLATE, } *a.* Bearing umbels;
UM'BELLATED, } consisting of an umbel; growing on an umbel; as *umbellate* plants or flowers.

UM'BELLET, } *n.* A little or partial um-
UMBEL'LICLE, } bel. *Martyn.*

UMBELLIF'EROUS, *a.* [L. *umbella* and *fero*, to bear.]

Producing the inflorescence called an umbel; bearing umbels; as *umbelliferous* plants.

UM'BER, *n.* In *natural history*, an ore of iron, a fossil of a brown, yellowish, or blackish brown color, so called from Ombria in Italy, where it was first obtained. It is used in painting. A specimen from Cyprus afforded, of a hundred parts, 48 parts of oxyd of iron, 20 of oxyd of manganese, the remainder silex, alumin and water. *Cyc*

UM'BER, *n.* A fowl of Africa, called the African crow.

The *Scopus umbretta*, a fowl of the grallic order, inhabiting Africa. *Cyc.*

UM'BER, *n.* A fish of the truttaceous kind, called the *grayling*, or *thymallus*; a fresh water fish of a fine taste. *Cyc.*

UM'BER, *v. t.* To color with umber; to shade or darken. *Shak.*

UM'BERED, *a.* [L. *umbra*, a shade.] Shaded; clouded. *Shak.*

2. [from *umber.*] Painted with umber.

UMBIL'IC, *n.* [infra.] The navel; the center. *Herbert.*

UMBIL'IC, } *a.* [L. *umbilicus*, the navel.]
UMBIL'ICAL, } Pertaining to the navel; as *umbilical* vessels; *umbilical* region.

Umbilical points, in *mathematics*, the same as *foci.*

Umbilical vessels, in *vegetables*, are the small vessels which pass from the heart of the seed into the side seed-lobes, and are supposed to imbibe the saccharine, farinaceous or oily matter which is to support the new vegetable in its germination and infant growth. *Cyc. Darwin.*

UMBIL'ICATE, } *a.* Navel-shaped;
UMBIL'ICATED, } formed in the middle like a navel; as a flower, fruit, or leaf. *Martyn. Cyc.*

UM'BLES, *n.* [Fr.] The entrails of a deer. *Dict.*

UM'BO, *n.* [L.] The boss or protuberant part of a shield. *Cyc. Swift.*

UMBOLDILITE, *n.* [from *Humboldt.*] A newly discovered Vesuvian mineral, whose primitive form is a right rectangular prism, with a square base, its color brown, inclining to yellowish or greenish yellow. *Journ. of Science.*

UM'BRA, *n.* A fish caught in the Mediterranean, generally about 12 or 14 inches long, but sometimes growing to the weight of 60 pounds. It is called also *chromis* and *corvo.* *Cyc.*

UM'BRAGE, *n.* [Fr. *ombrage*, from *ombre*, L. *umbra*, a shade.]

1. A shade; a skreen of trees; as the *umbrage* of woods. *Milton.*

2. Shadow; shade; slight appearance.

The opinion carries no show of truth nor *umbrage* of reason on its side. *Woodward. Obs.* [See *Shadow.*]

3. Suspicion of injury; offense; resentment. The court of France took *umbrage* at the conduct of Spain.

UMBRA'GEOUS, *a.* [Fr. *ombrageux.*] Shading; forming a shade; as *umbrageous* trees or foliage. *Thomson.*

2. Shady; shaded; as an *umbrageous* grotto or garden.

Umbrageous grots, and caves of cool recess. *Milton.*

3. Obscure. *Wotton.*

UMBRA'GEOUSNESS, *n.* Shadiness; as the *umbrageousness* of a tree. *Raleigh.*

UM'BRATE, *v. t.* [L. *umbro*, to shade.] To shade; to shadow. [*Little used.*]

UM'BRATED, *pp.* Shaded; shadowed. *Ch. Relig. Appeal.*

UMBRAT'IC, } *a.* [L. *umbraticus.*] Shad-
UMBRAT'ICAL, } owy; typical. *Barrow.*

2. Keeping in the shade or at home. *B. Jonson.*

UM'BRATILE, *a.* [L. *umbratilis.*] Being in the shade. *Johnson.*

2. Unreal; unsubstantial. *B. Jonson.*

3. Being in retirement; secluded; as an *umbratile* life. [*Little used.*] *Bacon.*

UMBRA'TIOUS, *a.* [See *Umbrage.*] Suspicious; apt to distrust; captious; disposed to take umbrage. [*Little used*] *Wotton.*

UM'BREL, } *n.* [from L. *umbra*, shade.]
UMBREL'LA, } A shade, skreen or guard, carried in the hand for sheltering the person from the rays of the sun, or from rain or snow. It is formed of silk, cotton or other cloth extended on strips of elastic whalebone, inserted in or fastened to a rod or stick. [See *Parasol.*]

UMBRIE'RE, *n.* The visor of a helmet. *Spenser.*

UMBROS'ITY, *n.* [L. *umbrosus.*] Shadiness. [*Little used.*] *Brown.*

UM'PIRAGE, *n.* [from *umpire.*] The power, right or authority of an umpire to decide. *President's Message, Oct.* 1803.

2. The decision of an umpire.

UM'PIRE, *n.* [Norm. *impere*; L. *imperium*, contracted, as in *empire.*]

1. A third person called in to decide a controversy or question submitted to arbitrators, when the arbitrators do not agree in opinion.

2. A person to whose sole decision a controversy or question between parties is referred. Thus the emperor of Russia was constituted *umpire* between Great Britain and the United States, to decide the controversy respecting the slaves carried from the states by the British troops.

UM'PIRE, *v. t.* To arbitrate; to decide as umpire; to settle, as a dispute. [*Little used.*] *Bacon.*

UN, a prefix or inseparable preposition, Sax. *un* or *on*, usually *un*, G. *un*, D. *on*, Sans.

an, is the same word as the L. *in*. It is a particle of negation, giving to words to which it is prefixed, a negative signification. We use *un* or *in* indifferently for this purpose; and the tendency of modern usage is to prefer the use of *in*, in some words, where *un* was formerly used. *Un* admits of no change of *n* into *l*, *m* or *r*, as *in* does, in *illuminate*, *immense*, *irresolute*. It is prefixed generally to adjectives and participles, and almost at pleasure. In a few instances, it is prefixed to verbs, as in *unbend*, *unbind*, *unharness*. As the compounds formed with *un* are so common and so well known, the composition is not noticed under the several words. For the etymologies, see the simple words.

UNABA'SED, *a.* Not abased; not humbled.

UNABASH'ED, *a.* Not abashed; not confused with shame, or by modesty. *Pope.*

UNABA'TED, *a.* Not abated; not diminished in strength or violence. The fever remains *unabated*.

UNABBRE'VIATED, *a.* Not abbreviated; not shortened.

UNABET'TED, *a.* Not abetted; not aided.

UNABIL'ITY, } *n.* Want of ability. [*Not*
UNA'BLENESS, } *used.* We use *inability*.]

UNABJU'RED, *a.* Not abjured; not renounced on oath.

UNA'BLE, *a.* Not able; not having sufficient strength or means; impotent; weak in power, or poor in substance. A man is *unable* to rise when sick; he is *unable* to labor; he is *unable* to support his family or to purchase a farm; he is *unable* for a particular enterprise.

2. Not having adequate knowledge or skill. A man is *unable* to paint a good likeness; he is *unable* to command a ship or an army.

UNABOL'ISHABLE, *a.* Not abolishable; that may not be abolished, annulled or destroyed. *Milton.*

UNABOL'ISHED, *a.* Not abolished; not repealed or annulled; remaining in force. *Hooker.*

UNABRIDG'ED, *a.* Not abridged; not shortened.

UNAB'ROGATED, *a.* Not abrogated; not annulled.

UNABSOLV'ED, *a.* *s* as *z.* Not absolved; not acquitted or forgiven.

UNABSORB'ABLE, *a.* Not absorbable; not capable of being absorbed. *Davy.*

UNABSORB'ED, *a.* Not absorbed; not imbibed. *Davy.*

UNACCEL'ERATED, *a.* Not accelerated; not hastened.

UNACCENT'ED, *a.* Not accented; having no accent; as an *unaccented* syllable. *Holder.*

UNACCEPT'ABLE, *a.* Not acceptable; not pleasing; not welcome; not such as will be received with pleasure. *Clarendon.*

UNACCEPT'ABLENESS, *n.* The state of not pleasing. *Collier.*

UNACCEPT'ABLY, *adv.* In an unwelcome or unpleasing manner.

UNACCEPT'ED, *a.* Not accepted or received; rejected. *Prior.*

UNACCESS'IBLE, *a.* Inaccessible. [*This latter word is now used.*]

UNACCESS'IBLENESS, *n.* State of not being approachable; inaccessibleness. [*The latter is the word now used.*]

UNACCOM'MODATED, *a.* Not accommodated; not furnished with external conveniences. *Shak.*

2. Not fitted or adapted. *Mitford.*

UNACCOM'MODATING, *a.* Not accommodating; not ready to oblige; uncompliant.

UNACCOMPANIED, *a.* Not attended; having no attendants, companions or followers. *Hayward.*

2. Having no appendages.

UNACCOM'PLISHED, *a.* Not accomplished; not finished; incomplete. *Dryden.*

2. Not refined in manners; not furnished with elegant literature or with polish of manners.

UNACCOM'PLISHMENT, *n.* Want of accomplishment or execution. *Milton.*

UNACCORD'ING, *a.* Not according; not agreeing. *Fearn.*

UNACCOUNTABIL'ITY, *n.* The state or quality of not being accountable; or the state of being unaccountable for. *Swift.*

UNACCOUNT'ABLE, *a.* Not to be accounted for. Such folly is *unaccountable*.

2. Not explicable; not to be solved by reason or the light possessed; not reducible to rule. The union of soul and body is to us *unaccountable*. *Swift.*

3. Not subject to account or control; not subject to answer; not responsible.

UNACCOUNT'ABLENESS, *n.* Strangeness.

2. Irresponsibility.

UNACCOUNT'ABLY, *adv.* In a manner not to be explained; strangely. *Addison.*

UNACCRED'ITED, *a.* Not accredited; not received; not authorized. The minister or the consul remained *unaccredited*.

UNAC'CURATE, *a.* Inaccurate; not correct or exact. [But *inaccurate* is now used.] *Boyle.*

UNAC'CURATENESS, *n.* Want of correctness. [But we now use *inaccurateness*, or *inaccuracy*.]

UNACCU'SED, *a.* *s* as *z.* Not accused; not charged with a crime or fault.

UNACCUS'TOMED, *a.* Not accustomed; not used; not made familiar; not habituated; as a bullock *unaccustomed* to the yoke. Jer. xxxi.

2. New; not usual; not made familiar; as *unaccustomed* air; *unaccustomed* ideas. *Watts.*

UNACHIE'VABLE, *a.* That cannot be done or accomplished. *Farindon.*

UNACHIE'VED, *a.* Not achieved; not accomplished or performed.

UNACKNOWL'EDGED, *a.* Not acknowledged; not recognized; as an *unacknowledged* agent or consul.

2. Not owned; not confessed; not avowed; as an *unacknowledged* crime or fault.

UNACQUA'INTANCE, *n.* Want of acquaintance or familiarity; want of knowledge; followed by *with*; as an utter *unacquaintance with* his design. *South.*

UNACQUA'INTED, *a.* Not well known; unusual.

And th' *unacquainted* light began to fear.
[*Not in use.*] *Spenser.*

2. Not having familiar knowledge; followed by *with*.

My ears are *unacquainted*
With such bold truths. *Denham.*

UNACQUA'INTEDNESS, *n.* Want of acquaintance. *Whiston.*

UNACQUI'RED, *a.* Not acquired; not gained.

UNACQUIT'TED, *a.* Not acquitted; not declared innocent.

UNACT'ED, *a.* Not acted; not performed; not executed. *Shak.*

UNACT'IVE, *a.* Not active; not brisk. [We now use *inactive*.]

2. Having no employment.

3. Not busy; not diligent; idle.

4. Having no action or efficacy. [See *Inactive*.]

UNACT'UATED, *a.* Not actuated; not moved. *Glanville.*

UNADAPT'ED, *a.* Not adapted; not suited. *Mitford.*

UNADDICT'ED, *a.* Not addicted; not given or devoted.

UNADJUDG'ED, *a.* Not adjudged; not judicially decided.

UNADJUST'ED, *a.* Not adjusted; not settled; not regulated; as differences *unadjusted*.

2. Not settled; not liquidated; as *unadjusted* accounts.

UNADMIN'ISTERED, *a.* Not administered.

UNADMI'RED, *a.* Not admired; not regarded with great affection or respect. *Pope.*

UNADMI'RING, *a.* Not admiring.

UNADMON'ISHED, *a.* Not admonished; not cautioned, warned or advised. *Milton.*

UNADOPT'ED, *a.* Not adopted; not received as one's own.

UNADO'RED, *a.* Not adored; not worshiped. *Milton.*

UNADORN'ED, *a.* Not adorned; not decorated; not embellished. *Milton.*

UNADUL'TERATED, *a.* Not adulterated; genuine; pure. *Addison.*

UNADUL'TEROUS, *a.* Not guilty of adultery.

UNADUL'TEROUSLY, *adv.* Without being guilty of adultery.

UNADVENT'UROUS, *a.* Not adventurous; not bold or resolute. *Milton.*

UNADVI'SABLE, *a.* *s* as *z.* Not advisable; not to be recommended; not expedient; not prudent.

UNADVI'SED, *a.* *s* as *z.* Not prudent; not discrete. *Shak.*

2. Done without due consideration; rash; as an *unadvised* measure or proceeding. *Shak.*

UNADVI'SEDLY, *adv.* *s* as *z.* Imprudently; indiscretely; rashly; without due consideration. *Hooker.*

UNADVI'SEDNESS, *n.* *s* as *z.* Imprudence; rashness.

UNA'ERATED, *a.* Not combined with carbonic acid.

UNAF'FABLE, *a.* Not affable; not free to converse; reserved.

UNAFFECT'ED, *a.* Not affected; plain; natural; not labored or artificial; simple; as *unaffected* ease and grace.

2. Real; not hypocritical; sincere; as *unaffected* sorrow. *Dryden.*

3. Not moved; not having the heart or passions touched. Men often remain *unaf-*

fected under all the solemn monitions of Providence.

UNAFFECT'EDLY, *adv.* Really; in sincerity; without disguise; without attempting to produce false appearances. He was *unaffectedly* cheerful. *Locke.*

UNAFFECT'ING, *a.* Not pathetic; not adapted to move the passions.

UNAFFEC'TIONATE, *a.* Not affectionate; wanting affection.

UNAFFIRM'ED, *a.* Not affirmed; not confirmed.

UNAFFLICT'ED, *a.* Not afflicted; free from trouble.

UNAFFRIGHTED, *a.* Not frightened.

UNAG'GRAVATED, *a.* Not aggravated.

UNAG'ITATED, *a.* Not agitated; calm.

UNAGREE'ABLE, *a.* Not consistent; unsuitable. *Milton.*

UNAGREE'ABLENESS, *n.* Unsuitableness; inconsistency with. *Decay of Piety.*

UNA'IDABLE, *a.* Not to be aided or assisted. [*Not used.*]

UNA'IDED, *a.* Not aided; not assisted. *Blackmore.*

UNA'IMING, *a.* Having no particular aim or direction. *Granville.*

UNA'KING, *a.* Not aking; not giving or feeling pain. *Shak.*

UNAL'ARMED, *a.* Not alarmed; not disturbed with fear. *Cowper.*

UNA'LIENABLE, *a.* Not alienable; that cannot be alienated; that may not be transferred; as *unalienable* rights. *Swift.*

UNA'LIENABLY, *adv.* In a manner that admits of no alienation; as property *unalienably* vested.

UNA'LIENATED, *a.* Not alienated; not transferred; not estranged.

UNALLA'YED, *a.* Not allayed; not appeased or quieted.

2. For *unalloyed.* [See *Unalloyed.*]

UNALLE'VIATED, *a.* Not alleviated; not mitigated.

UNALLI'ABLE, *a.* That cannot be allied or connected in amity. *Cheyne.*

UNALLI'ED, *a.* Having no alliance or connection, either by nature, marriage or treaty; as *unallied* families or nations, or substances.

2. Having no powerful relation.

UNALLOW'ED, *a.* Not allowed; not permitted.

UNALLOY'ED, *a.* Not alloyed; not reduced by foreign admixture; as metals *unalloyed.*

I enjoyed *unalloyed* satisfaction in his company. *Mitford.*

UNALLU'RED, *a.* Not allured; not enticed.

UNALLU'RING, *a.* Not alluring; not tempting. *Mitford.*

UN'ALMSED, *a.* unàmzed. Not having received alms. *Pollok.*

UNAL'TERABLE, *a.* Not alterable; unchangeable; immutable. *South.*

UNAL'TERABLENESS, *n.* Unchangeableness; immutability. *Woodward.*

UNAL'TERABLY, *adv.* Unchangeably; immutably.

UNAL'TERED, *a.* Not altered or changed. *Dryden.*

UNAMA'ZED, *a.* Not amazed; free from astonishment. *Milton.*

UNAMBIG'UOUS, *a.* Not ambiguous; not of doubtful meaning; plain; clear; certain. *Chesterfield.*

UNAMBIG'UOUSLY, *adv.* In a clear, explicit manner.

UNAMBIG'UOUSNESS, *n.* Clearness; explicitness.

UNAMBI''TIOUS, *a.* Not ambitious; free from ambition.

2. Not affecting show; not showy or prominent; as *unambitious* ornaments.

UNAMBI''TIOUSNESS, *n.* Freedom from ambition.

UNAMEND'ABLE, *a.* Not capable of emendation. *Pope.*

UNAMEND'ED, *a.* Not amended; not rectified. *Ash.*

UNA'MIABLE, *a.* Not amiable; not conciliating love; not adapted to gain affection. *Spectator.*

UNA'MIABLENESS, *n.* Want of amiableness.

UNAMU'SED, *a.* s as z. Not amused; not entertained.

UNAMU'SING, *a.* s as z. Not amusing; not affording entertainment. *Roscoe. Mitford.*

UNAMU'SIVE, *a.* Not affording amusement.

UNANALOG'ICAL, *a.* Not analogical.

UNANAL'OGOUS, *a.* Not analogous; not agreeable to. *Darwin.*

UNAN'ALYSED, *a.* s as z. Not analysed; not resolved into simple parts. *Boyle.*

UNAN'CHORED, *a.* Not anchored; not moored. *Pope.*

UNANE'LED, *a.* Not having received extreme unction. [See *Anneal.*] *Shak.*

UNAN'GULAR, *a.* Having no angles. *Good.*

UNAN'IMALIZED, *a.* Not formed into animal matter.

UNAN'IMATED, *a.* Not animated; not possessed of life.

2. Not enlivened; not having spirit; dull.

UNAN'IMATING, *a.* Not animating; dull.

UNANIM'ITY, *n.* [Fr. *unanimité*; L. *unus*, one, and *animus*, mind.]

Agreement of a number of persons in opinion or determination; as, there was perfect *unanimity* among the members of the council.

UNAN'IMOUS, *a.* Being of one mind; agreeing in opinion or determination; as, the house of assembly was *unanimous*; the members of the council were *unanimous.*

2. Formed by unanimity; as a *unanimous* vote.

UNAN'IMOUSLY, *adv.* With entire agreement of minds. *Addison.*

UNAN'IMOUSNESS, *n.* The state of being of one mind.

2. Proceeding from unanimity; as the *unanimousness* of a vote.

UNANNE'ALED, *a.* Not annealed; not tempered by heat; suddenly cooled.

UNANNEX'ED, *a.* Not annexed; not joined.

UNANNOY'ED, *a.* Not annoyed or incommoded.

UNANOINT'ED, *a.* Not anointed.

2. Not having received extreme unction. *Shak.*

UN'ANSWERABLE, *a.* Not to be satisfactorily answered; not capable of refutation; as an *unanswerable* argument.

UN'ANSWERABLENESS, *n.* The state of being unanswerable.

UN'ANSWERABLY, *adv.* In a manner not to be answered; beyond refutation. *South.*

UN'ANSWERED, *a.* Not answered; not opposed by a reply. *Milton.*

2. Not refuted. *Hooker.*

3. Not suitably returned. *Dryden.*

UNAPOC'RYPHAL, *a.* Not apocryphal; not of doubtful authority. *Milton.*

UNAPPALL'ED, *a.* Not appalled; not daunted; not impressed with fear.

With eyes erect and visage *unappall'd.* *Smith.*

UNAPPAR'ELED, *a.* Not appareled; not clothed. *Bacon.*

UNAPPA'RENT, *a.* Not apparent; obscure; not visible. *Milton.*

UNAPPE'ALABLE, *a.* Not appealable; admitting no appeal; that cannot be carried to a higher court by appeal; as an *unappealable* cause.

UNAPPE'ASABLE, *a.* s as z. Not to be appeased or pacified; as an *unappeasable* clamor.

2. Not placable; as *unappeasable* wrath.

UNAPPE'ASED, *a.* s as z. Not appeased; not pacified. *Dryden.*

UNAPPLI'ABLE, *a.* Inapplicable. [*Little used.*] *Milton.*

UNAP'PLICABLE, *a.* Inapplicable; that cannot be applied. [We now use *inapplicable.*]

UNAPPLI'ED, *a.* Not applied; not used according to the destination; as *unapplied* funds.

UNAP'POSITE, *a.* s as z. Not apposite; not suitable. *Gerard.*

UNAPPRE'CIATED, *a.* Not duly estimated or valued.

UNAPPREHEND'ED, *a.* Not apprehended; not taken.

2. Not understood. *Hooker.*

UNAPPREHENS'IBLE, *a.* Not capable of being understood. *South.*

UNAPPREHENS'IVE, *a.* Not apprehensive; not fearful or suspecting.

2. Not intelligent; not ready of conception. *South.*

UNAPPRI'SED, *a.* s as z. Not apprised; not previously informed.

UNAPPRŌACHABLE, *a.* That cannot be approached; inaccessible.

UNAPPRŌACHABLENESS, *n.* Inaccessibleness.

UNAPPRŌACHED, *a.* Not approached; not to be approached. *Milton.*

UNAPPRO'PRIATED, *a.* Not appropriated; not applied or directed to be applied to any specific object; as money or funds. *Hamilton.*

2. Not granted or given to any person, company or corporation; as *unappropriated* lands. *B. Trumbull.*

UNAPPRÖVED, *a.* Not approved; not having received approbation. *Milton.*

UNAPT', *a.* Not apt; not ready or propense.

A soldier, *unapt* to weep. *Shak.*

2. Dull; not ready to learn.

3. Unfit; not qualified; not disposed; with

to, before a verb, and *for*, before a noun; as *unapt to* admit a conference with reason. *Hooker.*

Unapt for noble, wise, spiritual employments. *Taylor.*

4. Improper; unsuitable. *Johnson.*

UNAPT'LY, *adv.* Unfitly; improperly. *Grew.*

UNAPT'NESS, *n.* Unfitness; unsuitableness. *Spenser.*

2. Dullness; want of quick apprehension. *Shak.*

3. Unreadiness; disqualification; want of propension. The mind, by excess of exertion, gets an *unaptness* to vigorous attempts. *Locke.*

UN'ARGUED, *a.* Not argued; not debated.

2. Not disputed; not opposed by argument. *Milton.*

3. Not censured; *a Latinism.* [*Not used.*] *B. Jonson.*

UN'ARM, *v. t.* To disarm; to strip of armor or arms. [*Not used.*] [See *Disarm.*] *Shak.*

UN'ARMED, *a.* Not having on arms or armor; not equipped. Man is born *unarmed.* It is mean to attack even an enemy *unarmed.*

2. Not furnished with scales, prickles or other defense; as animals and plants.

UNARRA'IGNED, *a.* Not arraigned; not brought to trial. *Daniel.*

UNARRANGED, *a.* Not arranged; not disposed in order.

UNARRA'YED, *a.* Not arrayed; not dressed. *Dryden.*

2. Not disposed in order.

UNARRI'VED, *a.* Not arrived. [*Ill formed.*] *Young.*

UN'ARTED, *a.* Ignorant of the arts. [*Not in use.*] *Waterhouse.*

UN'ARTFUL, *a.* Not artful; artless; not having cunning. *Dryden.*

2. Wanting skill. [*Little used.*] *Cheyne.*

UN'ARTFULLY, *adv.* Without art; in an unartful manner. *Swift.*

[In lieu of these words, *artless* and *artlessly* are generally used.]

UNARTIC'ULATED, *a.* Not articulated or distinctly pronounced. *Encyc.*

UNARTIFI''CIAL, *a.* Not artificial; not formed by art.

UNARTIFI''CIALLY, *adv.* Not with art; in a manner contrary to art. *Derham.*

UNASCEND'IBLE, *a.* That cannot be ascended. *Marshall.*

UNASCERTA'INABLE, *a.* That cannot be ascertained, or reduced to a certainty; that cannot be certainly known.

The trustees are *unascertainable.* *Wheaton's Rep.*

UNASCERTA'INED, *a.* Not reduced to a certainty; not certainly known. *Hamilton.*

UN'ASKED, *a.* Not asked; unsolicited; as, to bestow favors *unasked;* that was an *unasked* favor.

2. Not sought by entreaty or care.

The bearded corn ensu'd
From earth *unask'd.* *Dryden.*

UNASPECT'IVE, *a.* Not having a view to. *Feltham.*

UNAS'PIRATED, *a.* Having no aspirate. *Farr.*

UNASPI'RING, *a.* Not aspiring; not ambitious. *Rogers.*

UNASSA'ILABLE, *a.* Not assailable; that cannot be assaulted. *Shak.*

UNASSA'ILED, *a.* Not assailed; not attacked by violence.

To keep my life and honor *unassail'd.* *Milton.*

UNASSAULT'ED, *a.* Not assaulted; not attacked.

UNASSA'YED, *a.* Not essayed; not attempted. [We now use *unessayed.*]

2. Not subjected to assay or trial.

UNASSEM'BLED, *a.* Not assembled or congregated.

UNASSERT'ED, *a.* Not asserted; not affirmed; not vindicated.

UNASSESS'ED, *a.* Not assessed; not rated.

UNASSIGNABLE, *a.* Not assignable; that cannot be transferred by assignment or indorsement. *Jones. Wheaton.*

UNASSIGNED, *a.* Not assigned; not declared; not transferred.

UNASSIM'ILATED, *a.* Not assimilated; not made to resemble.

2. In *physiology*, not formed or converted into a like substance; not animalized, as food. *Med. Repos.*

UNASSIST'ED, *a.* Not assisted; not aided or helped; as *unassisted* reason. *Rogers.*

UNASSIST'ING, *a.* Giving no help. *Dryden.*

UNASSO'CIATED, *a.* Not associated; not united with a society.

2. In *Connecticut*, not united with an association; as an *unassociated* church.

UNASSORT'ED, *a.* Not assorted; not distributed into sorts.

UNASSU'MING, *a.* Not assuming; not bold or forward; not making lofty pretensions; not arrogant; modest; as an *unassuming* youth; *unassuming* manners.

UNASSU'RED, *a.* [See *Sure.*] Not assured; not confident; as an *unassured* countenance. *Glanville.*

2. Not to be trusted; as an *unassured* foe. *Spenser.*

3. Not insured against loss; as goods *unassured.*

UNATO'NABLE, *a.* Not to be appeased; not to be reconciled. *Milton.*

UNATO'NED, *a.* Not expiated.

A brother's blood yet *unaton'd.* *Rowe.*

UNATTACH'ED, *a.* Not attached; not arrested. *Junius.*

2. Not closely adhering; having no fixed interest; as *unattached* to any party.

3. Not united by affection.

UNATTACK'ED, *a.* Not attacked; not assaulted.

UNATTA'INABLE, *a.* Not to be gained or obtained; as *unattainable* good.

UNATTA'INABLENESS, *n.* The state of being beyond the reach or power. *Locke.*

UNATTA'INTED, *a.* Not attainted; not corrupted.

UNATTEM'PERED, *a.* Not tempered by mixture.

UNATTEMPT'ED, *a.* Not attempted; not tried; not essayed.

Things *unattempted* yet in prose or rhyme. *Milton.*

UNATTEND'ED, *a.* Not attended; not accompanied; having no retinue or attendance. *Milton.*

2. Forsaken. *Shak.*

3. Not medically attended; not dressed; as *unattended* wounds. *Mitford.*

UNATTEND'ING, *a.* Not attending or listening; not being attentive.

Ill is lost that praise
That is address'd to *unattending* ears. *Milton.*

UNATTEN'TIVE, *a.* Not regarding; inattentive. [*The latter word is now used.*]

UNATTEST'ED, *a.* Not attested; having no attestation. *Barrow.*

UNATTI'RED, *a.* Not attired; not adorned.

UNATTRACT'ED, *a.* Not attracted: not affected by attraction.

UNAUGMENT'ED, *a.* Not augmented or increased; in grammar, having no augment, or additional syllable. *Richardson.*

UNAUTHEN'TIC, *a.* Not authentic; not genuine or true.

UNAUTHEN'TICATED, *a.* Not authenticated; not made certain by authority.

UNAU'THORIZED, *a.* Not authorized; not warranted by proper authority; not duly commissioned.

UNAVA'ILABLE, *a.* Not available; not having sufficient power to produce the intended effect; not effectual; vain; useless. *Hooker.*

UNAVA'ILABLENESS, *n.* Inefficacy; uselessness. *Sandys.*

UNAVA'ILING, *a.* Not having the effect desired; ineffectual; useless; vain; as *unavailing* efforts; *unavailing* prayers.

UNAVENG'ED, *a.* Not avenged; not having obtained satisfaction; as, a person is *unavenged.*

2. Not punished; as, a crime is *unavenged.*

UNAVERT'ED, *a.* Not averted; not turned away.

UNAVOID'ABLE, *a.* That cannot be made null or void. *Blackstone.*

2. Not avoidable; not to be shunned; inevitable; as *unavoidable* evils.

3. Not to be missed in ratiocination. *Locke.*

UNAVOID'ABLENESS, *n.* The state of being unavoidable; inevitableness. *Glanville.*

UNAVOID'ABLY, *adv.* Inevitably; in a manner that prevents failure or escape.

UNAVOID'ED, *a.* Not avoided or shunned.

2. Inevitable. [*Not legitimate.*] *B. Jonson.*

UNAVOW'ED, *a.* Not avowed; not acknowledged; not owned; not confessed.

UNAWA'KED, } *a.* Not awakened; not
UNAWA'KENED, } roused from sleep.

2. Not roused from spiritual slumber or stupidity. *Scott.*

UNAWA'RE, *a.* Without thought, inattentive. *Swift.*

UNAWA'RE, } *adv.* Suddenly; unexpect-
UNAWA'RES, } edly; without previous preparation. The evil came upon us *unawares.*

2. Without premeditated design. He killed the man *unawares.*

At unawares, unexpectedly.

He breaks *at unawares* upon our walks. *Dryden.*

UNAW'ED, *a.* Not awed; not restrained by fear; undaunted. *Dryden.*

UNBACK'ED, *a.* Not having been backed; as an *unbacked* colt.

2. Not tamed; not taught to bear a rider. *Shak.*

3. Unsupported; left without aid. *Daniel.*

UNBA'KED, *a.* Not baked.

UNBAL'ANCED, *a.* Not balanced; not poised; not in equipoise.

Let earth *unbalanc'd* from her orbit fly. *Pope.*

2. Not adjusted; not settled; not brought to an equality of debt and credit; as an *unbalanced* account.

3. Not restrained by equal power; as *unbalanced* parties. *J. Adams.*

UNBAL'LAST, *v. i.* To free from ballast; to discharge the ballast from. *Mar. Dict.*

UNBAL'LASTED, *a.* Freed from ballast.

2. *a.* Not furnished with ballast; not kept steady by ballast or by weight; unsteady; as *unballasted* wits.

"*Unballast* vessel," for *unballasted*, in Addison, is an unauthorized phrase.

UNBAND'ED, *a.* Stripped of a band; having no band. *Shak.*

UNBAN'NERED, *a.* Having no banner. *Pollok.*

UNBAPTI'ZED, *a.* Not baptized. *Hooker.*

UNB'AR, *v. t.* To remove a bar or bars from; to unfasten; to open; as, to *unbar* a gate.

UNB'ARBED, *a.* Not shaven. [*Not in use.*] *Shak.*

UNB'ARKED, *a.* Stripped of its bark. *Bacon.*

[We now use *barked* in the same sense.]

UNB'ARRED, *pp.* Having its bars removed; unfastened.

UNB'ARRING, *ppr.* Removing the bars from; unfastening.

UNBASH'FUL, *a.* Not bashful; bold; impudent. *Shak.*

UNBA'TED, *a.* Not repressed; not blunted. [*Not in use.*]

UNBA'THED, *a.* Not bathed; not wet. *Dryden.*

UNBAT'TERED, *a.* Not battered; not bruised or injured by blows. *Shak.*

UNBA'Y, *v. t.* To open; to free from the restraint of mounds.

I ought to *unbay* the current of my passions. [*Not in use.*] *Norris.*

UNBEARDED, *a. unberd'ed.* Having no beard; beardless.

UNBEARING, *a.* Bearing or producing no fruit. *Dryden.*

UNBE'ATEN, *a.* Not beaten; not treated with blows. *Corbet.*

2. Untrod; not beaten by the feet; as *unbeaten* paths. *Roscommon.*

UNBEAU'TEOUS, } *a.* [See *Beauty.*] Not
UNBEAU'TIFUL, } beautiful; having no beauty. *Hammond.*

UNBECOME, *v. t.* Not to become; not to be suitable to; to misbecome. [*Not used.*] *Sherlock.*

UNBECOMING, *a.* Unsuitable; improper for the person or character; indecent; indecorous.

My grief lets *unbecoming* speeches fall. *Dryden.*

UNBECOMINGLY, *adv.* In an unsuitable manner; indecorously. *Barrow.*

UNBECOMINGNESS, *n.* Unsuitableness to the person, character or circumstances; impropriety; indecorousness. *Locke.*

UNBED', *v. t.* To raise or rouse from bed.

Eels *unbed* themselves and stir at the noise of thunder. *Walton.*

UNBED'DED, *pp.* Raised from bed; disturbed.

UNBED'DING, *ppr.* Raising from bed.

UNBEFIT'TING, *a.* Not befitting; unsuitable; unbecoming. *Swift.*

UNBEFRIENDED, *a. unbefrend'ed.* Not befriended; not supported by friends; having no friendly aid. *Killingbeck.*

UNBEGET', *v. t.* To deprive of existence. *Dryden.*

UNBEGOT', } *a.* Not generated; eter-
UNBEGOT'TEN, } nal. *Stillingfleet.*

2. Not yet generated. *Shak.*

3. Not begotten; not generated. *South.*

UNBEGUI'LE, *v. t.* To undeceive; to free from the influence of deceit.

Then *unbeguile* thyself. *Donne.*

UNBEGUI'LED, *pp.* Undeceived.

UNBEGUN', *a.* Not begun. *Hooker.*

UNBEHELD', *a.* Not beheld; not seen; not visible. *Milton.*

UNBE'ING, *a.* Not existing. [*Not in use.*] *Brown.*

UNBELIE'F, *n.* [Sax. *ungeleafa.*] Incredulity; the withholding of belief; as, *unbelief* is blind. *Milton.*

2. Infidelity; disbelief of divine revelation. *Hooker.*

3. In *the New Testament*, disbelief of the truth of the gospel, rejection of Christ as the Savior of men, and of the doctrines he taught; distrust of God's promises and faithfulness, &c. Matt. xiii. Mark xvi. Heb. iii. Rom. iv.

4. Weak faith. Mark ix.

UNBELIE'VE, *v. t.* To discredit; not to believe or trust. *Wotton.*

2. Not to think real or true. *Dryden.*

UNBELIE'VED, *pp.* Not believed; discredited.

UNBELIE'VER, *n.* An incredulous person; one who does not believe.

2. An infidel; one who discredits revelation, or the mission, character and doctrines of Christ. 2 Cor. vi.

UNBELIE'VING, *a.* Not believing; incredulous.

2. Infidel; discrediting divine revelation, or the mission, character and doctrines of Christ; as the *unbelieving* Jews. Acts xiv. Rev. xxi.

UNBELOVED, *a.* Not loved. *Dryden.*

UNBEMOANED, *a.* Not lamented. *Pollok.*

UNBEND', *v. t.* To free from flexure; to make straight; as, to *unbend* a bow. *Dryden.*

2. To relax; to remit from a strain or from exertion; to set at ease for a time; as, to *unbend* the mind from study or care. *Denham.*

3. To relax effeminately.

You *unbend* your noble strength. *Shak.*

4. In *seamanship*, to take the sails from their yards and stays; also, to cast loose a cable from the anchors; also, to untie one rope from another. *Mar. Dict.*

UNBEND'ING, *ppr.* Relaxing from any strain; remitting; taking from their yards, &c., as sails.

2. *a.* Not suffering flexure.

3. Unyielding; resolute; inflexible; *applied to persons.*

4. Unyielding; inflexible; firm; *applied to things*; as *unbending* truth. *J. M. Mason.*

5. Devoted to relaxation.

I hope it may entertain your lordship at an *unbending* hour. *Rowe.*

UNBEN'EFICED, *a.* Not enjoying or having a benefice. *Dryden.*

UNBENEV'OLENT, *a.* Not benevolent; not kind. *Rogers.*

UNBENIGHTED, *a.* Never visited by darkness. *Milton.*

UNBENIGN, *a.* Not benign; not favorable or propitious; malignant. *Milton.*

UNBENT', *pp.* of *unbend.* Relaxed; remitted; relieved from strain or exertion. *Denham.*

2. In *seamen's language*, taken from the yards; loosed; as, the sails are *unbent*; the cable is *unbent.*

3. Not strained; unstrung; as a bow *unbent.*

4. Not crushed; not subdued; as, the soul is *unbent* by woes.

UNBEQUE'ATHED, *a.* Not bequeathed; not given by legacy.

UNBESEE'MING, *a.* Unbecoming; not befitting; unsuitable.

UNBESOUGHT, *a. unbesaut'.* Not besought; not sought by petition or entreaty. *Milton.*

UNBESPO'KEN, *a.* Not bespoken, or ordered beforehand.

UNBEST'ARRED, *a.* Not adorned or distinguished by stars. *Pollok.*

UNBESTOWED, *a.* Not bestowed; not given; not disposed of.

UNBETRA'YED, *a.* Not betrayed. *Daniel.*

UNBEWA'ILED, *a.* Not bewailed; not lamented. *Shak.*

UNBEWITCH', *v. t.* To free from fascination. *South.*

UNBI'AS, *v. t.* To free from bias or prejudice.

The truest service a private man can do his country, is to *unbias* his mind, as much as possible, between the rival powers. *Swift.*

UNBI'ASED, *pp.* Freed from prejudice or bias.

2. *a.* Free from any undue partiality or prejudice; impartial; as an *unbiased* mind; *unbiased* opinion or decision.

UNBI'ASEDLY, *adv.* Without prejudice; impartially.

UNBI'ASEDNESS, *n.* Freedom from bias or prejudice. *Bp. Hall.*

UNBID', } *a.* Not bid; not command-
UNBID'DEN, } ed. *Milton.*

2. Spontaneous; as, thorns shall the earth produce *unbid.* *Milton.*

3. Uninvited; not requested to attend; as *unbidden* guests. *Shak.*

UNBIG'OTED, *a.* Free from bigotry. *Addison*

UNBIND, *v. t.* To untie; to remove a band from; to unfasten; to loose; to set free from shackles. *Unbind* your fillets; *unbind* the prisoner's arms; *unbind* the load.

UNBISH'OP, *v. t.* To deprive of episcopal orders. *South.*

UNBIT', *a.* Not bitten. *Young.*

UNBIT', *v. t.* In *seamanship*, to remove the turns of a cable from off the bitts. *Mar. Dict.*

2. To unbridle.

UNBIT'TED, *pp.* Removed from the bitts; unbridled.

UNBIT'TING, *ppr.* Unbridling; removing from the bitts.

UNBLA'MABLE, *a.* Not blamable; not culpable; innocent. *Bacon.*

UNBLA'MABLENESS, *n.* State of being chargeable with no blame or fault. *More.*

UNBLA'MABLY, *adv.* In such a manner as to incur no blame. 1 Thess. ii.

UNBLA'MED, *a.* Not blamed; free from censure. *Pope.*

UNBL'ASTED, *a.* Not blasted; not made to wither. *Peacham.*

UNBLEE'DING, *a.* Not bleeding; not suffering loss of blood. *Byron.*

UNBLEM'ISHABLE, *a.* Not capable of being blemished. *Milton.*

UNBLEM'ISHED, *a.* Not blemished; not stained; free from turpitude or reproach; *in a moral sense;* as an *unblemished* reputation or life.

2. Free from deformity.

UNBLENCH'ED, *a.* Not disgraced; not injured by any stain or soil; as *unblenched* majesty. *Milton.*

UNBLENCH'ING, *a.* Not shrinking or flinching; firm.

UNBLEND'ED, *a.* Not blended; not mingled. *Glanville.*

UNBLEST', *a.* Not blest; excluded from benediction. *Bacon.*

2. Wretched; unhappy. *Prior.*

UNBLIGHTED, *a.* Not blighted; not blasted. *Cowper.*

UNBLINDED, *a.* Not blinded.

UNBLOODED, *a.* Not stained with blood. *Shak.*

UNBLOODY, *a.* Not stained with blood.

2. Not shedding blood; not cruel. *Dryden.*

UNBLOS'SOMING, *a.* Not producing blossoms. *Mason.*

UNBLOWN, *a.* Not blown; not having the bud expanded. *Shak.*

2. Not extinguished. *More.*

3. Not inflated with wind. *Sandys.*

UNBLUNT'ED, *a.* Not made obtuse or dull; not blunted. *Cowley.*

UNBLUSH'ING, *a.* Not blushing; destitute of shame; impudent. *Thomson.*

UNBLUSH'INGLY, *adv.* In an impudent manner.

UNBOASTFUL, *a.* Not boasting; unassuming; modest. *Thomson.*

UNBOD'IED, *a.* Having no material body; incorporeal; as *unbodied* spirits. *Watts.*

2. Freed from the body. *Spenser.*

UNBOIL'ED, *a.* Not boiled; as *unboiled* rice. *Bacon.*

UNBOLT, *v. t.* To remove a bolt from; to unfasten; to open; as, to *unbolt* a gate. *Shak.*

UNBOLTED, *a.* Freed from fastening by bolts.

2. Unsifted; not bolted; not having the bran or coarse part separated by a bolter; as *unbolted* meal.

UNBONNETED, *a.* Having no bonnet on. *Shak.*

UNBOOK'ISH, *a.* Not addicted to books or reading.

2. Not cultivated by erudition. *Shak.*

UNBORN', UN'BORN, } *a.* [It is accented either on the first or second syllable.] Not born; not brought into life; future.

> Some *unborn* sorrow, ripe in fortune's womb. *Shak.*

> The woes to come, the children yet *unborn*
> Shall feel this day. *Shak.*

UNBOR'ROWED, *a.* Not borrowed; genuine; original; native; one's own; as *unborrowed* beauties; *unborrowed* gold; *unborrowed* excellence.

UNBOSOM, *v. t.* *s* as *z.* To disclose freely one's secret opinions or feelings. *Milton.*

2. To reveal in confidence.

UNBOSOMED, *pp.* Disclosed, as secrets; revealed in confidence.

UNBOSOMING, *ppr.* Disclosing, as secrets; revealing in confidence.

UNBOT'TOMED, *a.* Having no bottom; bottomless.

> The dark, *unbottom'd,* infinite abyss. *Milton.*

2. Having no solid foundation. *Hammond.*

UNBOUGHT, *a. unbaut'.* Not bought; obtained without money or purchase.

> The *unbought* dainties of the poor. *Dryden.*

2. Not having a purchaser. *Locke.*

UNBOUND', *a.* Not bound; loose; wanting a cover; as *unbound* books.

2. Not bound by obligation or covenant.

3. *pret.* of *unbind.*

UNBOUND'ED, *a.* Having no bound or limit; unlimited in extent; infinite; interminable; as *unbounded* space; *unbounded* power.

2. Having no check or control; unrestrained. The young man has *unbounded* license. His extravagance is *unbounded.*

UNBOUND'EDLY, *adv.* Without bounds or limits.

UNBOUND'EDNESS, *n.* Freedom from bounds or limits. *Cheyne.*

UNBOUN'TEOUS, *a.* Not bounteous; not liberal. *Milton.*

UNBOW', *v. t.* To unbend. *Fuller.*

UNBOW'ED, *a.* Not bent; not arched. *Shak.*

UNBOW'EL, *v. t.* To deprive of the entrails; to exenterate; to eviscerate. *Decay of Piety.*

UNBOW'ELED, *pp.* Eviscerated.

UNBOW'ELING, *ppr.* Taking out the bowels.

UNBRA'CE, *v. t.* To loose; to relax; as, to *unbrace* a drum; to *unbrace* the arms; to *unbrace* the nerves.

UNBRA'ID, *v. t.* To separate the strands of a braid; to disentangle.

UNBRA'IDED, *pp.* Disentangled, as the strands of a braid.

UNBRA'IDING, *ppr.* Separating the strands of a braid.

UNBR'ANCHED, *a.* Not ramified; not shooting into branches.

UNBR'ANCHING, *a.* Not dividing into branches. *Goldsmith.*

UNBREAST, *v. t. unbrest'.* To disclose or lay open. *P. Fletcher.*

UNBRE'ATHED, *a.* Not exercised.

> Our *unbreath'd* memories. *Shak.*

UNBRE'ATHING, *a.* Unanimated; as *unbreathing* stones. *Shak.*

UNBRED', *a.* Not well bred; not polished in manners; ill educated; rude; as *unbred* minds; *unbred* servants. *Locke.*

2. Not taught; as *unbred* to spinning. *Dryden.*

UNBREE'CHED, *a.* Having no breeches. *Shak.*

UNBREW'ED, *a.* Not mixed; pure; genuine. *Young.*

UNBRI'BABLE, *a.* That cannot be bribed. [*Not used.*] *Feltham.*

UNBRI'BED, *a.* Not bribed; not corrupted by money; not unduly influenced by money or gifts. *Dryden.*

UNBRI'DLE, *v. t.* To free from the bridle.

UNBRI'DLED, *pp.* Loosed from the bridle.

2. *a.* Unrestrained; licentious; as *unbridled* lust; *unbridled* boldness; *unbridled* passions.

UNBRO'KE, UNBRO'KEN, } *a.* Not broken; not violated. Preserve your vows *unbroken.*

2. Not weakened; not crushed; not subdued.

> How broad his shoulders spread, by age *unbroke.* *Pope.*

3. Not tamed; not taught; not accustomed to the saddle, harness or yoke; as an *unbroken* horse or ox.

UNBROTHERLY, *a.* Not becoming a brother; not suitable to the character and relation of a brother; unkind. [*Unbrotherlike* is not used.]

UNBRUISED, *a.* *s* as *z.* Not bruised; not crushed or hurt. *Shak.*

UNBUCK'LE, *v. t.* To loose from buckles; to unfasten; as, to *unbuckle* a shoe; to *unbuckle* a girdle; to *unbuckle* a helm. *Shak.*

UNBUCK'LED, *pp.* Loosed from buckles; unfastened.

UNBUCK'LING, *ppr.* Loosing from buckles; unfastening.

UNBUILD, UNBILD', } *v. t.* To demolish what is built; to raze; to destroy. *Milton.*

UNBUILT, UNBILT', } *a.* Not yet built; not erected.

UNBURIED, *a. unber'ried.* Not buried; not interred. *Dryden.*

UNBURN'ED, UNBURNT', } *a.* Not burnt; not consumed by fire.

2. Not injured by fire; not scorched.

3. Not baked, as brick.

UNBURN'ING, *a.* Not consuming away by fire.

UNBUR'THEN, UNBUR'DEN, } *v. t.* To rid of a load; to free from a burden; to ease. *Shak.*

2. To throw off. *Shak.*

3. To relieve the mind or heart by disclosing what lies heavy on it. *Shak.*

UNBUR'THENED, UNBUR'DENED, } *pp.* Freed from a load; thrown off; eased; relieved.

UNBUR'THENING, UNBUR'DENING, } *ppr.* Freeing from a load or burden; relieving from what is a burden.

UNBUSIED, *a. unbiz'zied.* Not busied; not employed; idle. *Bp. Rainbow.*

UNBUT'TON, *v. t.* To loose from being fastened by buttons; to loose buttons. *Shak.*

UNBUT'TONED, *pp.* Loosed from buttons. *Addison.*

UNCA'GE, *v. t.* To loose from a cage.

UNCA'GED, *pp.* Released from a cage or from confinement.

UNCAL'CINED, *a.* Not calcined. *Boyle.*

UN€AL'€ULATED, *a.* Not subjected to calculation. *J. Barlow.*
UN€AL'€ULATING, *a.* Not making calculations.
UN€ALL'ED, *a.* Not called; not summoned; not invited. *Milton.*
Uncalled for, not required; not needed or demanded.
UN€'ALM, *v. t.* To disturb. [*Not in use, and an ill word.*] *Dryden.*
UN€AN'CELED, *a.* Not canceled; not erased; not abrogated or annulled. *Dryden.*
UN€AN'DID, *a.* Not candid; not frank or sincere; not fair or impartial.
UN€ANON'I€AL, *a.* Not agreeable to the canons; not acknowledged as authentic. *Barrow.*
UN€ANON'I€ALNESS, *n* The state of being uncanonical. *Lloyd.*
UN€AN'OPIED, *a.* Not covered by a canopy.
UN€AP', *v. t.* To remove a cap or cover; to open; as, to *uncap* a vein.
UN€A'PABLE, *a.* Incapable. [The latter word has superseded *uncapable.*]
UN€AP'PED, *pp.* Opened.
UN€AP'TIVATED, *a.* Not captivated. *Rambler.*
Uncared for, not regarded; not heeded. *Hooker.*
UN€'ARNATE, *a.* Not fleshly. *Brown.*
UN€'ARPETED, *a.* Not covered with a carpet.
UN€A'SE, *v. t.* To disengage from a covering; to take off or out.
2. To flay; to strip. *L'Estrange.*
UN€A'SED, *pp.* Stripped of a covering or case.
UN€A'SING, *ppr.* Disengaging from a cover.
UN€AS'TRATED, *a.* Not castrated.
UN€AT'E€HISED, *a.* *s* as *z.* Not catechis untaught. *Milton.*
UN€AUGHT, *a.* *uncaut'.* Not yet caught or taken. *Shak.*
UN€AUS'ED, *a.* *s* as *z.* Having no precedent cause; existing without an author.
UN€AU'TIOUS, *a.* Not cautious; not wary; heedless. [*Incautious* is now generally used.] *Dryden.*
UNCE'ASING, *a.* Not ceasing; not intermitting; continual.
UNCE'ASINGLY, *adv.* Without intermission or cessation; continually.
UNCEL'EBRATED, *a.* Not celebrated; not solemnized. *Milton.*
UNCELES'TIAL, *a.* Not heavenly. *Feltham.*
UNCEN'SURABLE, *a.* Not worthy of censure. *Dwight.*
UNCEN'SURED, *a.* Not censured; exempt from blame or reproach.

Whose right it is *uncensur'd* to be dull. *Pope.*

UNCEN'TRICAL, *a.* Not central; distant from the center.
UNCEREMO'NIAL, *a.* Not ceremonial.
UNCEREMO'NIOUS, *a.* Not ceremonious; not formal.
UNCER'TAIN, *a.* Not certain; doubtful; not certainly known. It is *uncertain* who will be the next president.
2. Doubtful; not having certain knowledge.

Man without the protection of a superior Being—is *uncertain* of every thing that he hopes for. *Tillotson.*

3. Not sure in the consequence.

Or whistling slings dismiss'd the *uncertain* stone. *Gay.*

4. Not sure; not exact.

Soon bent his bow, *uncertain* in his aim. *Dryden.*

5. Unsettled; irregular. *Hooker.*
UNCER'TAINLY, *adv.* Not surely; not certainly. *Dryden.*
2. Not confidently.

—Standards that cannot be known at all, or but imperfectly and *uncertainly.* *Locke.*

UNCER'TAINTY, *n.* Doubtfulness; dubiousness. The truth is not ascertained; the latest accounts have not removed the *uncertainty.*
2. Want of certainty; want of precision; as the *uncertainty* of the signification of words.
3. Contingency.

Steadfastly grasping the greatest and most slippery *uncertainties.* *South.*

4. Something unknown.

Our shepherd's case is every man's case that quits a certainty for an *uncertainty.* *L'Estrange.*

UNCES'SANT, *a.* Continual; incessant. [*The latter is the word now used.*]
UNCES'SANTLY, *adv.* Incessantly. *Obs.*
UNCHA'IN, *v. t.* To free from chains or slavery. *Prior.*
UNCHA'INED, *pp.* Disengaged from chains, shackles or slavery.
UNCHA'INING, *ppr.* Freeing from chains, bonds or restraint.
UNCHANĠEABLE, *a.* Not capable of change; immutable; not subject to variation. God is an *unchangeable* being.
UNCHANĠEABLENESS, *n.* The state or quality of being subject to no change; immutability. *Newton.*
UNCHANĠEABLY, *adv.* Without change; immutably.
UNCHANĠED, *a.* Not changed or altered. *Dryden.*
2. Not alterable.
UNCHANĠING, *a.* Not changing; suffering no alteration.
UN€HARA€TERIS'TI€, *a.* Not characteristic; not exhibiting a character. *Gregory.*
UNCH'ARĠE, *v.t.* To retract an accusation. [*Not used.*]
UNCH'ARĠED, *a.* Not charged; not loaded. *Shak.*
UNCHAR'ITABLE, *a.* Not charitable; contrary to charity, or the universal love prescribed by christianity; as *uncharitable* opinions or zeal.
UNCHAR'ITABLENESS, *n.* Want of charity. If we hate our enemies we sin; we are guilty of *uncharitableness.*
UNCHAR'ITABLY, *adv.* In a manner contrary to charity.
UNCH'ARM, *v. t.* To release from some charm, fascination, or secret power. *Beaum.*
UNCH'ARMED, *a.* Not charmed; not fascinated.
UNCH'ARMING, *a.* Not charming; no longer able to charm. *Dryden.*
UNCHA'RY, *a.* Not wary; not frugal. [*Not used.*] *Shak.*
UNCHĀSTE, *a.* Not chaste; not continent; not pure; libidinous; lewd. *Sidney. Milton.*
UNCHĀSTELY, *adv.* Incontinently; lewdly. *Milton.*
UNCHASTI'SABLE, *a.* [See *Chastise.*] That cannot be chastised. *Milton.*
UNCHASTI'SED, *a.* Not chastised; not punished.
2. Not corrected; not restrained.
UNCHAS'TITY, *n.* Incontinence; lewdness; unlawful indulgence of the sexual appetite. *Woodward.*
UNCHECK'ED, *a.* Not checked; not restrained; not hindered. *Milton.*
2. Not contradicted. *Shak.*
UNCHEE'RFỤL, *a.* Not cheerful; sad. *Shak.*
UNCHEE'RFỤLNESS, *n.* Want of cheerfulness; sadness. *Spectator.*
UNCHEE'RY, *a.* Dull; not enlivening. *Sterne.*
UNCHEW'ED, *a.* Not chewed or masticated. *Dryden.*
UNCHILD, *v. t.* To bereave of children. [*Not in use.*] *Shak.*
UN€HRIS'TIAN, *a.* Contrary to the laws of christianity; as an *unchristian* reflection; *unchristian* temper or conduct.
2. Not evangelized; not converted to the christian faith; infidel.
UN€HRIS'TIAN, *v. t.* To deprive of the constituent qualities of christianity. *South.*
UN€HRIS'TIANIZE, *v. t.* To turn from the christian faith; to cause to degenerate from the belief and profession of christianity. *Buchanan.*
UN€HRIS'TIANLY, *a.* Contrary to the laws of christianity; unbecoming christians. *Milton.*
UN€HRIS'TIANLY, *adv.* In a manner contrary to christian principles. *Bedell.*
UN€HRIS'TIANNESS, *n.* Contrariety to christianity. *K. Charles.*
UNCHURCH', *v. t.* To expel from a church; to deprive of the character and rights of a church. *Milner.*
UNCHURCH'ED, *pp.* Expelled from a church.
UNCHURCH'ING, *ppr.* Expelling from a church.
UN'CIAL, *a.* [L. *uncialis.*] Pertaining to letters of a large size, used in ancient manuscripts.
UN'CIAL, *n.* An uncial letter.
UN'CINATE, *a.* [L. *uncinatus*, from *uncus*, a hook.] In *botany*, hooked at the end. *Martyn.*
UNCIR'€UMCISED, *a.* *s* as *z.* Not circumcised. *Scripture.*
UNCIR€UMCI''SION, *n.* Absence or want of circumcision. *Hammond.*
UNCIR€UMS€RI'BED, *a.* Not circumscribed; not bounded; not limited.

Where the prince is *uncircumscribed*, obedience ought to be unlimited. *Addison.*

UNCIR'€UMSPE€T, *a.* Not circumspect; not cautious. *Hayward.*
UNCIR€UMSTAN'TIAL, *a.* Not important. [*Not in use.*] *Brown.*
UNCIV'IL, *a.* Not civil; not complaisant; not courteous in manners; *applied to persons.*
2. Not polite; rude; *applied to manners*; as *uncivil* behavior.

UNCIVILIZA'TION, *n.* A state of savageness; rude state. *Dict.*

UNCIV'ILIZED, *a.* Not reclaimed from savage life; as the *uncivilized* inhabitants of Canada or New Zealand.

2. Coarse; indecent; as the most *uncivilized* words in our language. [*Not in use.*] *Addison.*

UNCIV'ILLY, *adv.* Not complaisantly; not courteously; rudely. *Brown.*

UNCLAD', *a.* Not clad; not clothed.

UNCLA'IMED, *a.* Not claimed; not demanded; not called for; as *unclaimed* dividends of a bank.

UNCLAR'IFIED, *a.* Not purified; not fined; not depurated by a separation of feculent or foreign matter.

UNCL'ASP, *v. t.* To loose a clasp; to open what is fastened with a clasp; as, to *unclasp* a book. *Shak.*

UNCL'ASPING, *ppr.* Loosing a clasp.

UNCLASS'IC, UNCLASS'ICAL, *a.* Not classic; not according to the best models of writing.

2. Not pertaining to the classic writers; as *unclassic* ground.

UN'CLE, *n.* [Fr. *oncle*; contracted from L. *avunculus.*] The brother of one's father or mother.

UNCLE'AN, *a.* Not clean; foul; dirty; filthy.

2. In *the Jewish law*, ceremonially impure, not cleansed by ritual practices. Num. xix. Lev. xi. Rom. xiv.

3. Foul with sin. Matt. x.

That holy place where no *unclean* thing shall enter. *Rogers.*

4. Not in covenant with God. 1 Cor. vii.

5. Lewd; unchaste.

Adultery of the heart, consisting of inordinate and *unclean* affections. *Perkins.*

No *unclean* person—hath any inheritance in the kingdom of Christ and of God. Eph. v.

UNCLE'ANABLE, *a.* That cannot be cleansed. *Swift.*

UNCLEANLINESS, *n.* *unclen'liness.* Want of cleanliness; filthiness. *Clarendon.*

UNCLEANLY, *a.* *unclen'ly.* Foul; filthy; dirty. *Shak.*

2. Indecent; unchaste; obscene.

It is a pity that these harmonious writers have indulged any thing *uncleanly* or impure to defile their paper. *Watts.*

UNCLE'ANNESS, *n.* Foulness; dirtiness; filthiness.

Be not troublesome to thyself or to others by *uncleanness.* *Taylor.*

2. Want of ritual or ceremonial purity. Lev. xv.

3. Moral impurity; defilement by sin; sinfulness.

I will save you from all your *uncleanness.* Ezek. xxxvi.

4. Lewdness; incontinence. Col. iii. 2 Pet. ii.

UNCLEANSED, *a.* *unclenz'ed.* Not cleansed; not purified. *Bacon.*

UNCLENCH', *v. t.* To open the closed hand; as, to *unclench* the fist. *Garth.*

UNCLENCH'ED, *pp.* Opened; unclosed.

UNCLEW', *v. t.* To undo; to unwind, unfold or untie.

UNCLIP'PED, *a.* Not clipped; not cut; not diminished or shortened by clipping; as *unclipped* money; *unclipped* hair.

UNCLOG', *v. t.* To disencumber of difficulties and obstructions; to free from incumbrances, or any thing that retards motion.

UNCLOG'GED, *pp.* or *a.* Disencumbered; set free from obstructions.

UNCLOG'GING, *ppr.* Disencumbering.

UNCLOIS'TER, *v. t.* To release from a cloister or from confinement; to set at liberty. *Norris.*

UNCLOIS'TERED, *pp.* Released from a cloister or from confinement.

UNCLOIS'TERING, *ppr.* Releasing from confinement.

UNCLO'SE, *v. t.* *s* as *z.* To open; to break the seal of; as, to *unclose* a letter. *Pope.*

2. To disclose; to lay open.

UNCLO'SED, *pp.* Opened.

2. *a.* Not separated by inclosures; open. *Clarendon.*

3. Not finished; not concluded. *Madison.*

4. Not closed; not sealed.

UNCLO'SING, *ppr.* Opening; breaking the seal of.

UNCLO'THE, *v. t.* To strip of clothes; to make naked; to divest.

To have a distinct knowledge of things, we must *unclothe* them. *Watts.*

UNCLO'THED, *pp.* Stripped of clothing or covering.

Not for that we would be *unclothed*, but clothed upon. 2 Cor. v.

UNCLO'THEDLY, *adv.* Without clothing. *Bacon.*

UNCLO'THING, *ppr.* Stripping of clothing.

UNCLOUD', *v. t.* To unvail; to clear from obscurity or clouds.

UNCLOUD'ED, *a.* Not cloudy; free from clouds; clear; as an *unclouded* sky.

2. Not darkened; not obscured.

UNCLOUD'EDNESS, *n.* Freedom from clouds; clearness.

2. Freedom from obscurity or gloom. *Boyle.*

UNCLOUD'ING, *ppr.* Clearing from clouds or obscurity.

UNCLOUD'Y, *a.* Not cloudy; clear; free from clouds, obscurity or gloom. *Gay.*

UNCLUTCH', *v. t.* To open something closely shut.

Unclutch his griping hand. *Decay of Piety.*

UNCOAG'ULABLE, *a.* That cannot be coagulated. *Good.*

UNCOAG'ULATED, *a.* Not coagulated or concreted.

UNCŌATED, *a.* Not coated; not covered with a coat.

UNCOCK'ED, *a.* Not cocked, as a gun.

2. Not made into cocks, as hay.

3. Not set up, as the brim of a hat.

UNCOIF', *v. t.* To pull the cap off. *Arbuthnot.*

UNCOIF'ED, *a.* Not wearing a coif. *Young.*

UNCOIL', *v. t.* To unwind or open, as the turns of a rope or other line.

UNCOIL'ED, *pp.* Opened; unwound.

UNCOIN'ED, *a.* Not coined; as *uncoined* silver.

UNCOLLECT'ED, *a.* Not collected; not received; as *uncollected* taxes; debts *uncollected.*

2. Not collected; not recovered from confusion, distraction or wandering; as the mind yet *uncollected.*

UNCOLLECT'IBLE, *a.* Not collectible; that cannot be collected or levied, or paid by the debtor; as *uncollectible* taxes; *uncollectible* debts. *Wolcott.*

UNCŎLORED, *a.* Not colored; not stained or dyed. *Bacon.*

2. Not hightened in description.

UNCŌMBED, *a.* Not combed; not dressed with a comb. *Dryden.*

UNCOMBI'NABLE, *a.* Not capable of being combined. *Davy.*

UNCOMBI'NED, *a.* Not combined; separate; simple.

UNCŎMELINESS, *n.* Want of comeliness; want of beauty or grace; as *uncomeliness* of person, of dress or behavior. *Locke. Wotton.*

UNCŎMELY, *a.* Not comely; wanting grace; as an *uncomely* person; *uncomely* dress; *uncomely* manners.

2. Unseemly; unbecoming; unsuitable.

UNCŎMFORTABLE, *a.* Affording no comfort; gloomy.

Christmas—the most *uncomfortable* time of the year. *Addison.*

2. Giving uneasiness; as an *uncomfortable* seat or condition.

UNCŎMFORTABLENESS, *n.* Want of comfort or cheerfulness. *Taylor.*

2. Uneasiness.

UNCŎMFORTABLY, *adv.* In an uncomfortable manner; without comfort or cheerfulness, in an uneasy state.

UNCOMM'ANDED, *a.* Not commanded; not required by precept, order or law; as *uncommanded* austerities. *South.*

UNCOMMEND'ABLE, *a.* Not commendable; not worthy of commendation; illaudable. *Feltham.*

UNCOMMEND'ED, *a.* Not praised; not commended. *South.*

UNCOMMER'CIAL, *a.* Not commercial; not carrying on commerce.

UNCOMMIS'ERATED, *a.* Not commiserated; not pitied.

UNCOMMIS'SIONED, *a.* Not commissioned; not having a commission. *Tooke.*

UNCOMMIT'TED, *a.* Not committed. *Hammond.*

UNCOM'MON, *a.* Not common; not usual; rare; as an *uncommon* season; an *uncommon* degree of cold or heat; *uncommon* courage.

2. Not frequent; not often seen or known; as an *uncommon* production.

UNCOM'MONLY, *adv.* Rarely; not usually.

2. To an uncommon degree.

UNCOM'MONNESS, *n.* Rareness of occurrence; infrequency. The *uncommonness* of a thing often renders it valuable.

UNCOMMU'NICATED, *a.* Not communicated; not disclosed or delivered to others.

2. Not imparted to or from another; as the *uncommunicated* perfections of God.

UNCOMMU'NICATIVE, *a.* Not communicative; not free to communicate to others; reserved.

UNCOMPACT', *a.* Not compact; not firm; not of close texture; loose. *Addison.*

UNCOMPACT'ED, *a.* Not compact; not firm. *Johnson.*

UNCOMPANIED, *a.* Having no companion. [*Unaccompanied* is mostly used.] *Fairfax.*

UNCOMPAS'SIONATE, *a.* Not compassionate; having no pity. *Shak.*

UNCOMPAS'SIONED, *a.* Not pitied.

UNCOMPEL'LABLE, *a.* Not compellable; that cannot be forced or compelled. *Feltham.*

UNCOMPEL'LED, *a.* Not forced; free from compulsion. *Pope.*

UNCOM'PENSATED, *a.* Not compensated; unrewarded.

UNCOMPLA'INING, *a.* Not complaining; not murmuring; not disposed to murmur.

UNCOM'PLAISANT, *a.* *s* as *z.* Not complaisant; not civil; not courteous. *Locke.*

UNCOM'PLAISANTLY, *adv.* Uncivilly; discourteously.

UNCOMPLE'TE, *a.* Not complete; not finished; not perfect. [But *incomplete* is chiefly used.]

UNCOMPLE'TED, *a.* Not finished; not completed.

UNCOMPLY'ING, *a.* Not complying; not yielding to request or command; unbending.

UNCOMPOUND'ED, *a.* Not compounded; not mixed.

Hardness may be reckoned the property of all *uncompounded* matter. *Newton.*

2. Simple; not intricate. *Hammond.*

UNCOMPOUND'EDNESS, *n.* Freedom from mixture; simplicity of substance. *Hammond.*

UNCOMPREHENS'IVE, *a.* Not comprehensive.

2. Unable to comprehend. *South.*

UNCOMPRESS'ED, *a.* Not compressed; free from compression. *Boyle.*

UNCOM'PROMISING, *a.* *s* as *z.* Not compromising; not agreeing to terms; not complying. *Review.*

UNCONCE'IVABLE, *a.* Not to be conceived or understood; that cannot be comprehended. *Locke.*

[But *inconceivable* is chiefly used.]

UNCONCE'IVABLENESS, *n.* The state or quality of being inconceivable. [*Little used.*] *Locke.*

UNCONCE'IVED, *a.* Not thought; not imagined. *Creech.*

UNCONCERN', *n.* Want of concern; absence of anxiety; freedom from solicitude. *Swift.*

UNCONCERN'ED, *a.* Not concerned; not anxious; feeling no solicitude. He is *unconcerned at* what has happened. He is *unconcerned about* or *for* the future.

Happy mortals, *unconcerned for* more. *Dryden.*

[It has *at* sometimes before a past event, but *about* or *for* is more generally used before a past or future event.]

2. Having no interest in. He is *unconcerned* in the events of the day.

UNCONCERN'EDLY, *adv.* Without interest or affection; without anxiety.

And *unconcern'dly* cast his eyes around. *Dryden.*

UNCONCERN'EDNESS, *n.* Freedom from concern or anxiety. *South.*

UNCONCERN'ING, *a.* Not interesting; not affecting; not belonging to one. [*Not used.*] *Addison.*

UNCONCERN'MENT, *n.* The state of having no share. [*Not used.*] *South.*

UNCONCIL'IATED, *a.* Not reconciled.

UNCONCIL'IATING, *a.* Not conciliating; not adapted or disposed to gain favor, or to reconciliation.

UNCONCLU'DIBLE, *a.* Not determinable. [*Not used.*] *More.*

UNCONCLU'DING, **UNCONCLU'DENT**, } *a.* Not decisive; not inferring a plain or certain conclusion or consequence. [*Little used.*] *Hale. Locke.*

[In the place of these, *inconclusive* is generally used.]

UNCONCLU'DINGNESS, *n.* Quality of being inconclusive. [*Not used.*] *Boyle.*

UNCONCLU'SIVE, *a.* Not decisive. [But *inconclusive* is now used.] *Hammond.*

UNCONCOCT'ED, *a.* Not concocted; not digested. *Brown.*

UNCONDEM'NED, *a.* Not condemned; not judged guilty.

—A man that is a Roman, and *uncondemned.* Acts xxii.

2. Not disapproved; not pronounced criminal; as a practice yet *uncondemned.* *Locke.*

UNCONDENS'ABLE, *a.* That cannot be condensed.

UNCONDENS'ED, *a.* Not condensed.

UNCONDI''TIONAL, *a.* Absolute; unreserved; not limited by any conditions. We are required to make an *unconditional* surrender of ourselves to our Maker. The king demanded *unconditional* submission.

O pass not, Lord, an absolute decree,
Or bind thy sentence *unconditional.* *Dryden.*

UNCONDI''TIONALLY, *adv.* Without conditions; without terms of limitation; without reservation. The troops did not surrender *unconditionally*, but by capitulation.

UNCONFESS'ED, *a.* Not confessed; not acknowledged.

UNCONFI'NABLE, *a.* Unbounded. [*Not used.*] *Shak.*

2. That cannot be confined or restrained. *Thomson.*

UNCONFI'NED, *a.* Not confined; free from restraint; free from control. *Pope.*

2. Having no limits; illimitable; unbounded. *Spectator.*

UNCONFI'NEDLY, *adv.* Without confinement or limitation. *Barrow.*

UNCONFIRM'ED, *a.* Not fortified by resolution; weak; raw; as troops *unconfirmed* by experience.

2. Not confirmed; not strengthened by additional testimony.

His witness *unconfirm'd.* *Milton.*

3. Not confirmed according to the church ritual.

UNCONFORM', *a.* Unlike; dissimilar; not analogous. [*Not in use.*] *Milton.*

UNCONFORM'ABLE, *a.* Not consistent; not agreeable; not conforming.

Moral evil is an action *unconformable* to the rule of our duty. *Watts.*

UNCONFORM'ITY, *n.* Incongruity; inconsistency; want of conformity. *South.*

UNCONFU'SED, *a.* *s* as *z.* Free from confusion or disorder. *Locke.*

2. Not embarrassed.

UNCONFU'SEDLY, *adv.* *s* as *z.* Without confusion or disorder. *Locke.*

UNCONFU'TABLE, *a.* Not confutable; not to be refuted or overthrown; that cannot be disproved or convicted of error; as an *unconfutable* argument. *Sprat.*

UNCONGE'ALABLE, *a.* Not capable of being congealed.

UNCONGE'ALED, *a.* Not frozen; not congealed; not concreted. *Brown.*

UNCONGE'NIAL, *a.* Not congenial.

UNCON'JUGAL, *a.* Not suitable to matrimonial faith; not befitting a wife or husband. *Milton.*

UNCONJUNC'TIVE, *a.* That cannot be joined. [*Little used.*] *Milton.*

UNCONNECT'ED, *a.* Not connected; not united; separate.

2. Not coherent; not joined by proper transitions or dependence of parts; loose; vague; desultory; as an *unconnected* discourse.

UNCONNI'VING, *a.* Not conniving; not overlooking or winking at. *Milton.*

UNCON'QUERABLE, *a.* Not conquerable; invincible; that cannot be vanquished or defeated; that cannot be overcome in contest; as an *unconquerable* foe.

2. That cannot be subdued and brought under control; as *unconquerable* passions or temper.

UNCON'QUERABLY, *adv.* Invincibly; insuperably; as foes *unconquerably* strong. *Pope.*

UNCON'QUERED, *a.* Not vanquished or defeated.

2. Unsubdued; not brought under control.

3. Invincible; insuperable. *Sidney.*

UNCONSCIEN'CIOUS, *a.* Not conscientious; not regulated or limited by conscience. *Kent.*

UNCON'SCIONABLE, *a.* Unreasonable; exceeding the limits of any reasonable claim or expectation; as an *unconscionable* request or demand. *L'Estrange.*

2. Forming unreasonable expectations. You cannot be so *unconscionable* as to expect this sacrifice on my part.

3. Enormous; vast; as *unconscionable* size or strides. [*Not elegant.*]

4. Not guided or influenced by conscience. *South.*

UNCON'SCIONABLENESS, *n.* Unreasonableness of hope or claim.

UNCON'SCIONABLY, *adv.* Unreasonably; in a manner or degree that conscience and reason do not justify. *Hudibras.*

UNCON'SCIOUS, *a.* Not conscious; having no mental perception; as *unconscious* causes. *Blackmore.*

2. Not conscious; not knowing; not perceiving; as *unconscious* of guilt or error.

UNCON'SCIOUSLY, *adv.* Without perception; without knowledge.

UNCON'SCIOUSNESS, *n.* Want of perception; want of knowledge.

UNCON'SECRATE, *v. t.* To render not sacred; to desecrate. [*Not used.*] *South.*

UNCON'SECRATED, *a.* Not consecrated; not set apart for a sacred use by religious ceremonies; not dedicated or devoted; as a temple *unconsecrated*; *unconsecrated* bread.

Unconsented to, not consented to; not yielded; not agreed to. *Wake.*

UNCONSENT'ING, *a.* Not consenting; not yielding consent.

UNCONSID'ERED, *a.* Not considered; not attended to. *Shak.*

UNCONSO'LED, *a.* Not consoled; not comforted.

UNCONSOL'IDATED, *a.* Not consolidated or made solid.

UNCONSO'LING, *a.* Not consoling; affording no comfort. *Buckminster.*

UNCON'SONANT, *a.* Not consonant; not consistent; incongruous; unfit. [*Little used.*] *Hooker.*

UNCONSPI'RINGNESS, *n.* Absence of plot or conspiracy. [*An ill formed word and not used.*] *Boyle.*

UNCON'STANT, *a.* Not constant; not steady or faithful; fickle; changeable. [*Inconstant* is now used.] *Shak.*

UNCONSTITU'TIONAL, *a.* Not agreeable to the constitution; not authorized by the constitution; contrary to the principles of the constitution. It is not *unconstitutional* for the king of Great Britain to declare war without the consent of parliament; but for the president of the United States to declare war, without an act of congress authorizing it, would be *unconstitutional.*

UNCONSTITUTIONAL'ITY, *n.* The quality of being unauthorized by the constitution, or contrary to its provisions or principles. The supreme court has power to decide upon the *unconstitutionality* of a law.

UNCONSTITU'TIONALLY, *adv.* In a manner not warranted by or contrary to the constitution.

UNCONSTRA'INED, *a.* Free from constraint; acting voluntarily; voluntary. *Dryden.*

2. Not proceeding from constraint; as actions.

UNCONSTRA'INEDLY, *adv.* Without force or constraint; freely; spontaneously; voluntarily. *South.*

UNCONSTRA'INT, *n.* Freedom from constraint; ease. *Felton.*

UNCONSULT'ING, *a.* Taking no advice; rash; imprudent. *Sidney.*

UNCONSU'MED, *a.* Not consumed; not wasted, expended or dissipated; not destroyed. *Milton.*

UNCONSUM'MATE, *a.* Not consummated. *Dryden.*

UNCONTEM'NED, *a.* Not despised; not contemned. *Shak.*

Uncontended for, not contended for; not urged for.

UNCONTEND'ING, *a.* Not contending; not contesting; not disputing.

UNCONTENT'ED, *a.* Not contented; not satisfied. *Dryden.*

UNCONTENT'INGNESS, *n.* Want of power to satisfy. [*Not in use.*] *Boyle.*

UNCONTEST'ABLE, *a.* Indisputable; not to be controverted. [*Incontestible* is the word now used.]

UNCONTEST'ED, *a.* Not contested; not disputed.

2. Evident; plain. *Blackmore.*

UNCONTRADICT'ED, *a.* Not contradicted; not denied. *Pearson.*

UNCON'TRITE, *a.* Not contrite; not penitent. *Hammond.*

UNCONTRI'VED, *a.* Not contrived; not formed by design. *Dwight.*

UNCONTRI'VING, *a.* Not contriving; improvident. *Goldsmith.*

UNCONTROLLABLE, *a.* That cannot be controlled; ungovernable; that cannot be restrained; as an *uncontrollable* temper; *uncontrollable* subjects.

2. That cannot be resisted or diverted; as *uncontrollable* events.

3. Indisputable; irrefragable; as an *uncontrollable* maxim; the king's *uncontrollable* title to the English throne.

UNCONTROLLABLY, *adv.* Without power of opposition.

2. In a manner or degree that admits of no restraint or resistance; as a stream *uncontrollably* violent.

UNCONTROLLED, *a.* Not governed; not subjected to a superior power or authority; not restrained.

2. Not resisted; unopposed. *Dryden.*

3. Not convinced; not refuted. [*Unusual.*] *Hayward.*

UNCONTROLLEDLY, *adv.* Without control or restraint; without effectual opposition. *Decay of Piety.*

UNCON'TROVERTED, *a.* Not disputed; not contested; not liable to be called in question. *Glanville.*

UNCONVERS'ABLE, *a.* Not free in conversation; not social; reserved.

2. Not suited to conversation. *Rogers.*

UNCON'VERSANT, *a.* Not conversant; not familiarly acquainted with. *Mitford.*

UNCONVERT'ED, *a.* Not converted; not changed in opinion; not turned from one faith to another.

2. Not persuaded of the truth of the christian religion; as *unconverted* pagans. *Addison. Hooker.*

3. Not renewed; not regenerated; not having the natural enmity of the heart subdued, and a principle of grace implanted. *Baxter.*

4. Not turned or changed from one form to another.

UNCONVERT'IBLE, *a.* That cannot be converted or changed in form. Lead is *unconvertible* into silver.

UNCONVIN'CED, *a.* Not convinced; not persuaded. *Locke.*

UNCORD', *v. t.* To loose from cords; to unfasten or unbind; as, to *uncord* a bed; to *uncord* a package.

UNCORK', *v. t.* To draw the cork from; as, to *uncork* a bottle.

UNCORK'ED, *pp.* Not having the cork drawn.

UNCORK'ING, *ppr.* Drawing the cork from.

UNCOR'ONETED, *a.* Not honored with a coronet or title. *Pollok.*

UNCORP'ULENT, *a.* Not corpulent; not fleshy. *Pollok.*

UNCORRECT'ED, *a.* Not corrected; not revised; not rendered exact; as an *uncorrected* copy of a writing.

2. Not reformed; not amended; as life or manners *uncorrected.*

UNCOR'RIGIBLE, *a.* That cannot be corrected; depraved beyond correction. [For this, *incorrigible* is now used.]

UNCORRUPT', *a.* Not corrupt; not depraved; not perverted; not tainted with wickedness; not influenced by iniquitous interest; as an *uncorrupt* judgment; *uncorrupt* manners. *Hooker.*

UNCORRUPT'ED, *a.* Not corrupted; not vitiated; not depraved; as the dictates of *uncorrupted* reason; *uncorrupted* records. *Dryden. Locke.*

UNCORRUPT'EDNESS, *n.* State of being uncorrupted. *Milton.*

UNCORRUPT'IBLE, *a.* That cannot be corrupted. [But *incorruptible* is the word now used.]

UNCORRUPT'LY, *adv.* With integrity; honestly. *Ch. Relig. Appeal.*

UNCORRUPT'NESS, *n.* Integrity; uprightness. Tit. ii.

UNCOUN'SELABLE, *a.* Not to be advised; not consistent with good advice or prudence. *Clarendon.*

UNCOUNT'ABLE, *a.* That cannot be counted; innumerable. *Raleigh.*

UNCOUNT'ED, *a.* Not counted; not numbered. *Shak.*

UNCOUN'TERFEIT, *a.* Not counterfeit; not spurious; genuine; as *uncounterfeit* zeal. *Sprat.*

UNCOUNTERM'ANDED, *a.* Not countermanded.

UNCOUPLE, *v. t. uncup'pl.* To loose dogs from their couples; to set loose; to disjoin. *Shak. Dryden.*

UNCOUPLED, *pp. uncup'pled.* Disjoined; set free.

UNCOUPLING, *ppr. uncup'pling.* Disuniting; setting free.

UNCOURTEOUS, *a. uncurt'eous.* Uncivil; unpolite; not kind and complaisant. *Sidney.*

UNCOURT'EOUSLY, *adv.* Uncivilly; unpolitely.

UNCOURT'EOUSNESS, *n.* Incivility; disobliging treatment.

UNCOURTLINESS, *n.* Unsuitableness of manners to a court; inelegance; as *uncourtliness* of manners or phrases. *Addison.*

UNCOURTLY, *a.* Inelegant of manners; not becoming a court; not refined; unpolite; as *uncourtly* behavior or language. *Swift.*

2. Not courteous or civil; as an *uncourtly* speech.

3. Not versed in the manners of a court.

UNCÖUTH, *a.* [Sax. *uncuth*, unknown.] Odd; strange; unusual; not rendered pleasing by familiarity; as an *uncouth* phrase or expression; *uncouth* manners; *uncouth* dress.

UNCÖUTHLY, *adv.* Oddly; strangely. *Dryden.*

UNCÖUTHNESS, *n.* Oddness; strangeness; want of agreeableness derived from familiarity; as the *uncouthness* of a word or of dress.

UNCŎVENANTED, *a.* Not promised by covenant; not resting on a covenant or promise. *S. Miller.*

UNCŎVER, *v. t.* To divest of a cover: to remove any covering from; *a word of general use.*

2. To deprive of clothes; to strip; to make naked. *Shak.*

3. To unroof, as a building.

4. To take off the hat or cap; to bare the head.

5. To strip of a vail, or of any thing that conceals; to lay open; to disclose to view.

UN€ÖVERED, *pp.* Divested of a covering or clothing; laid open to view; made bare.

UN€ÖVERING, *ppr.* Divesting of a cover or of clothes; stripping of a vail; laying open to view.

UN€REA'TE, *v. t.* To annihilate; to deprive of existence.

Who can *uncreate* thee, thou shalt know. *Milton.*

UN€REA'TED, *pp.* Reduced to nothing; deprived of existence.

2. *a.* Not yet created; as misery *uncreated.* *Milton.*

3. Not produced by creation. God is an *uncreated* being. *Locke.*

UN€RED'IBLE, *a.* Not to be believed; not entitled to credit. [For this, *incredible* is used.]

UN€RED'ITABLE, *a.* Not in good credit or reputation; not reputable. *Hammond.*

2. Not for the credit or reputation. *Mitford.*

UN€RED'ITABLENESS, *n.* Want of reputation. *Decay of Piety.*

2. The quality of being disreputable.

UN€RED'ITED, *a.* Not believed. *Warner.*

UN€RIT'I€AL, *a.* Not critical.

2. Not according to the just rules of criticism. *M. Stuart.*

UN€ROP'PED, *a.* Not cropped; not gathered. *Milton.*

UN€ROSS'ED, *a.* Not crossed; not canceled. *Shak.*

2. Not thwarted; not opposed.

UN€ROWD'ED, *a.* Not crowded; not compressed; not straitened for want of room.

UN€ROWN', *v. t.* To deprive of a crown; to dethrone.

2. To pull off the crown. *Dryden.*

UN€ROWN'ED, *pp.* Deprived of a crown.

2. *a.* Not crowned; having no crown.

UN€ROWN'ING, *ppr.* Depriving of a crown.

UN€RYS'TALIZABLE, *a.* Not susceptible of crystalization. *Ure.*

UN€RYS'TALIZED, *a.* Not crystalized.

UN€'TION, *n.* [Fr. *onction*; L. *unctio*, from *ungo*, to anoint.]

1. The act of anointing. *Hooker.*

2. Unguent; ointment. [*Unusual.*] *Dryden.*

3. The act of anointing medically; as mercurial *unction.* *Arbuthnot.*

4. Any thing softening or lenitive. *Shak.*

5. That which excites piety and devotion. *Johnson.*

6. Richness of gracious affections.

7. Divine or sanctifying grace. 1 John i.

Extreme unction, the rite of anointing in the last hours; or the application of sacred oil to the parts where the five senses reside. *Cyc.*

UN€TUOS'ITY, *n.* Oiliness; fatness; the quality of being greasy. *Brown.*

UN€'TUOUS, *a.* Fat; oily; greasy. *Milton. Dryden.*

2. Having a resemblance to oil; as the *unctuous* feel of a stone.

UN€'TUOUSNESS, *n.* Fatness; oiliness.

2. The quality of resembling oil.

UN€ULL'ED, *a.* Not gathered.

2. Not separated; not selected.

UN€UL'PABLE, *a.* Not blamable; not faulty. *Hooker.*

UN€ULT', *a.* [*un* and L. *cultus.*] Uncultivated; rude; illiterate. [*Not in use.*] *Ch. Relig. Appeal.*

UN€UL'TIVABLE, *a.* Not capable of being tilled or cultivated.

UN€UL'TIVATED, *a.* Not cultivated; not tilled; not used in tillage; as an *uncultivated* tract of land.

2. Not instructed; not civilized; rude; rough in manners; as an *uncultivated* nation or age. *Locke. Roscommon.*

UN€UM'BERED, *a.* Not burdened; not embarrassed. *Dryden.*

UN€U'RABLE, *a.* Incurable. [*The latter is mostly used.*]

UN€U'RABLY, *adv.* Incurably.

UN€URB'ABLE, *a.* That cannot be curbed or checked. [*Not in use.*] *Shak.*

UN€URB'ED, *a.* Not curbed; not restrained; licentious. *Shak.*

UN€URL', *v. t.* To loose from ringlets.

The lion *uncurls* his angry mane. *Dryden.*

UN€URL', *v. i.* To fall from a curled state, as ringlets; to become straight. *Shak.*

UN€URL'ED, *pp.* Loosed from ringlets.

2. *a.* Not curled; not formed into ringlets.

UN€URL'ING, *ppr.* Loosing from ringlets.

UN€UR'RENT, *a.* Not current; not passing in common payment; as *uncurrent* coin or notes. *Shak.*

UN€URSE, *v. t. uncurs'.* To free from any execration. [*Not used.*] *Shak.*

UN€URS'ED, } *a.* Not cursed; not execra-
UN€URST', } ted. *K. Charles.*

UN€URTA'ILED, *a.* Not curtailed; not shortened.

UN€US'TOMARY, *a.* Not customary; not usual. *Dwight.*

UN€US'TOMED, *a.* Not subjected to customs or duty. *Ash.*

2. That has not paid duty, or been charged with customs. *Smollett.*

UN€UT', *a.* Not cut; as trees *uncut.* *Waller.*

UNDAM', *v. t.* To free from a dam, mound or obstruction. *Dryden.*

UNDAM'AĠED, *a.* Not damaged; not made worse; as *undamaged* goods.

UNDAMP'ED, *a.* Not damped; not depressed.

UNDAN'ĠEROUS, *a.* Not dangerous. *Thomson.*

UND'ARKENED, *a.* Not darkened or obscured.

UN'DATED, *a.* [L. *undatus*; *unda*, a wave.] Waved; rising and falling in waves towards the margin, as a leaf. *Lee.*

UNDA'TED, *a.* Not dated; having no date.

UND'AUNTED, *a.* Not daunted; not subdued or depressed by fear; intrepid. *Dryden.*

UND'AUNTEDLY, *adv.* Boldly; intrepidly. *South.*

UND'AUNTEDNESS, *n.* Boldness; fearless bravery; intrepidity. *Pope.*

UNDAWN'ING, *a.* Not yet dawning; not growing light; not opening with brightness. *Cowper.*

UNDAZ'ZLED, *a.* Not dazzled; not confused by splendor. *Milton. Boyle.*

UNDE'AF, *v. t.* To free from deafness. [*Not in use.*]

UNDEBA'SED, *a.* Not debased; not adulterated. *Shak.*

UNDEBAUCH'ED, *a.* Not debauched; not corrupted; pure. *Dryden.*

UNDE€'AGON, *n.* [L. *undecim*, eleven, and Gr. γωνια, angle.] A figure of eleven angles or sides.

UNDE€A'YED, *a.* Not decayed; not impaired by age or accident; being in full strength. *Dryden.*

UNDE€A'YING, *a.* Not decaying; not suffering diminution or decline.

2. Immortal; as the *undecaying* joys of heaven.

UNDEÇE'IVABLE, *a.* That cannot be deceived; not subject to deception. *Holder.*

UNDEÇE'IVE, *v. t.* To free from deception, cheat, fallacy or mistake, whether caused by others or by ourselves. If we rely on our own works for salvation, the Scriptures may *undeceive* us.

UNDEÇE'IVED, *pp.* Disabused of cheat, deception or fallacy.

2. Not deceived; not misled or imposed on.

UNDEÇE'IVING, *ppr.* Freeing from deception or fallacy.

UNDE'ÇENCY, *n.* Unbecomingness; indecency. [*The latter word is now used.*]

UNDE'ÇENT, *a.* Not decent; indecent. [*The latter is the word used.*]

UNDE'ÇENTLY, *adv.* Indecently. [*The latter is the word used.*]

UNDEÇI'DABLE, *a.* That cannot be decided. *South.*

UNDEÇI'DED, *a.* Not decided; not determined; not settled. *Hooker.*

UNDEÇI'PHERABLE, *a.* That cannot be deciphered.

UNDEÇI'PHERED, *a.* Not deciphered or explained.

UNDEÇI'SIVE, *a.* Not decisive; not conclusive; not determining the controversy or contest. *Granville.*

UNDECK', *v. t.* To divest of ornaments. *Shak.*

UNDECK'ED, *pp.* Deprived of ornaments.

2. *a.* Not decked; not adorned. *Milton.*

UNDE€LA'RED, *a.* Not declared; not avowed.

UNDE€LI'NABLE, *a.* That cannot be declined.

2. Not to be avoided. *Hacket.*

UNDE€LI'NED, *a.* Not deviating; not turned from the right way. *Sandys.*

2. Not varied in termination; as a noun *undeclined.*

UNDE€OMPO'SABLE, *a.* *s* as *z.* Not admitting decomposition; that cannot be decomposed. *Chimistry.*

UNDE€OMPO'SED, *a.* *s* as *z.* Not decomposed; not separated; as constituent particles. *Ib.*

UNDE€OMPOUND'ED, *a.* Not decompounded. *Davy.*

UNDE€'ORATED, *a.* Not adorned; not embellished; plain.

To leave the character of Christ *undecorated*, to make its own impression. *Buckminster.*

UNDED'I€ATED, *a.* Not dedicated; not consecrated.

2. Not inscribed to a patron.

UNDEE'DED, *a.* Not signalized by any great action. *Shak.*

2. Not transferred by deed; as *undeeded* land. [*Local.*]

UNDEFA'ÇEABLE, *a.* That cannot be defaced.

UNDEFA'ÇED, *a.* Not deprived of its form; not disfigured; as an *undefaced* statue.

UNDEFE'ASIBLE, *a.* *s* as *z.* Not defeasible. [But *indefeasible* is chiefly used.]

UNDEFEND'ED, *a.* Not defended; not protected.

2. Not vindicated.

3. Open to assault; being without works of defense.

UNDEFI'ED, *a.* Not set at defiance; not challenged. *Spenser.*

UNDEFI'LED, *a.* Not defiled; not polluted; not vitiated. *Milton.*

UNDEFI'NABLE, *a.* Not definable; not capable of being described or limited; as the *undefinable* bounds of space. *Grew.*

2. That cannot be described by interpretation or definition.

Simple ideas are *undefinable.* *Locke.*

UNDEFI'NABLENESS, *n.* The quality or state of being undefinable. *E. T. Fitch.*

UNDEFI'NED, *a.* Not defined; not described by definition or explanation.

2. Not having its limits described.

UNDEFLOUR'ED, *a.* Not debauched; not vitiated. *Milton.*

UNDEFORM'ED, *a.* Not deformed; not disfigured. *Pope.*

UNDEFRAUD'ED, *a.* Not defrauded.

UNDEFRA'YED, *a.* Not defrayed; not paid.

UNDEGRA'DED, *a.* Not degraded.

UNDE'IFY, *v. t.* To reduce from the state of Deity. *Addison.*

UNDEL'EGATED, *a.* Not delegated; not deputed; not granted; as *undelegated* authority; *undelegated* powers.

UNDELIB'ERATED, *a.* Not carefully considered; as an *undeliberated* measure. [*Not correct.*] *Clarendon.*

UNDELIB'ERATING, *a.* Not deliberating; not hesitating; hasty; prompt.

UNDELIGHTED, *a.* Not delighted; not well pleased. *Milton.*

UNDELIGHTFUL, *a.* Not giving delight or great pleasure. *Clarendon.*

UNDELIV'ERED, *a.* Not delivered; not communicated.

UNDEM'ANDED, *a.* Not demanded; not required.

UNDEMOL'ISHED, *a.* Not demolished; not pulled down. *Swift.*

2. Not destroyed.

UNDEMON'STRABLE, *a.* Not capable of fuller evidence. *Hooker.*

2. Not capable of demonstration.

UNDENI'ABLE, *a.* That cannot be denied; as *undeniable* evidence.

UNDENI'ABLY, *adv.* So plainly as to admit no contradiction or denial. *Dryden.*

UNDEPEND'ING, *a.* Not dependent. *Milton.*

UNDEPLO'RED, *a.* Not lamented. *Dryden.*

UNDEPO'SABLE, *a.* *s* as *z.* That cannot be deposed from office. *Milton.*

UNDEPRA'VED, *a.* Not corrupted; not vitiated.

UNDEP'RECATED, *a.* Not deprecated.

UNDEPRE'CIATED, *a.* Not depreciated; not lowered in value. *Walsh.*

UNDEPRI'VED, *a.* Not deprived; not divested of by authority; not stripped of any possession.

UN'DER, *prep.* [Goth. *undar;* Sax. *under;* D. *onder;* G. *unter;* probably compounded of *on* and *nether;* *on the nether* side.]

1. Beneath; below; so as to have something over or above. He stood *under* a tree; the carriage is *under* cover. We may see things *under* water; we have a cellar *under* the whole house.

2. In a state of pupilage or subjection to; as a youth *under* a tutor; a ward *under* a guardian; colonies *under* the British government.

I also am a man *under* authority, having soldiers *under* me. Matt. viii.

3. In a less degree than. The effect of medicine is sometimes *under* and sometimes above or over its natural strength. *Hooker.*

4. For less than. He would not sell the horse *under* forty pounds.

5. Less than; below. There are parishes in England *under* forty pounds a year.

6. With the pretense of; with the cover or pretext of. He does this *under* the name of love. This argument is not to be evaded *under* some plausible distinction.

7. With less than.

Several young men could never leave the pulpit *under* half a dozen conceits. *Swift.*

8. In a degree, state or rank inferior to.

It was too great an honor for any man *under* a duke. *Addison.*

9. In a state of being loaded; in a state of bearing or being burdened; as, to travel *under* a heavy load; to live *under* extreme oppression.

10. In a state of oppression or subjection to, the state in which a person is considered as bearing or having any thing laid upon him; as, to have fortitude *under* the evils of life; to have patience *under* pain, or *under* misfortunes; to behave like a christian *under* reproaches and injuries.

11. In a state of liability or obligation. No man shall trespass but *under* the pains and penalties of the law. Attend to the conditions *under* which you enter upon your office. We are *under* the necessity of obeying the laws. Nuns are *under* vows of chastity. We all lie *under* the curse of the law, until redeemed by Christ.

12. In the state of bearing and being known by; as men trading *under* the firm of Wright & Co.

13. In the state of; in the enjoyment or possession of. We live *under* the gospel dispensation.

14. During the time of. The American revolution commenced *under* the administration of lord North.

15. Not having reached or arrived to; below. He left three sons *under* age.

16. Represented by; in the form of. Morpheus is represented *under* the figure of a boy asleep. [But *morph,* in Ethiopic, signifies cessation, rest.]

17. In the state of protection or defense. *Under* favor of the prince, our author was promoted. The enemy landed *under* cover of their batteries.

18. As bearing a particular character.

The duke may be mentioned *under* the double capacity of a poet and a divine. *Felton.*

19. Being contained or comprehended in.

Under this head may be mentioned the contests between the popes and the secular princes. *Lesley.*

20. Attested by; signed by. Here is a deed *under* his hand and seal.

He has left us evidence *under* his own hand. *Locke.*

21. In a state of being handled, treated or discussed, or of being the subject of. The bill is now *under* discussion. We shall have the subject *under* consideration next week.

22. In subordination to. *Under* God, this is our only safety.

23. In subjection or bondage to; ruled or influenced by; *in a moral sense;* within the dominion of.

They are all *under* sin. Rom. iii.

Under a signature, bearing, as a name or title.

Under way, in seamen's language, moving; in a condition to make progress.

To keep under, to hold in subjection or control; to restrain.

I *keep under* my body. 1 Cor. ix.

UN'DER, *a.* Lower in degree; subject; subordinate; as an *under* officer; *under* sherif.

Under is much used in composition. For the etymologies, see the principal words.

UNDERAC'TION, *n.* Subordinate action; action not essential to the main story.

The least episodes or *underactions*—are parts necessary to the main design. *Dryden.*

UNDERA'GENT, *n.* A subordinate agent. *South.*

UNDERBEAR, *v. t.* To support; to endure. *Shak.*

2. To line; to guard; as cloth of gold *underborne* with blue tinsel. *Obs.* *Shak.*

UNDERBEARER, *n.* In funerals, one who sustains the corpse.

UNDERBID', *v. t.* To bid or offer less than another; as in auctions, when a contract or service is set up to the lowest bidder.

UN'DERBRED, *a.* Of inferior breeding or manners. *Observer.*

UN'DERBRUSH, *n.* Shrubs and small trees in a wood or forest, growing under large trees.

UNDERBUY, *v. t.* To buy at less than a thing is worth. [*Not used.*] *Beaum.*

UNDERCHAMBERLAIN, *n.* A deputy chamberlain of the exchequer.

UN'DERCLERK, *n.* A clerk subordinate to the principal clerk.

UN'DERCROFT, *n.* A vault under the choir or chancel of a church; also, a vault or secret walk under ground. *Bullokar.*

UNDERCUR'RENT, *n.* A current below the surface of the water. *Mar. Dict.*

UNDERDITCH', *v. t.* To form a deep ditch or trench to drain the surface of land.

UNDERDÖ, *v. i.* To act below one's abilities. *B. Jonson.*

2. To do less than is requisite. *Grew.*

UN'DERDOSE, *n.* A quantity less than a dose.

UNDERDO'SE, *v. i.* To take small doses. *Cheyne.*

UN'DERDRAIN, *n.* A drain or trench below the surface of the ground.

UNDERDRA'IN, *v. t.* To drain by cutting a deep channel below the surface.

UNDERFAC'TION, *n.* A subordinate faction. *Decay of Piety.*

UNDERF'ARMER, *n.* A subordinate farmer.

UNDERFEL'LOW, *n.* A mean sorry wretch. *Sidney.*

UNDERFIL'LING, *n.* The lower part of a building. *Wotton.*

UNDERFONG′, *v. t.* [Sax. *fangan*, to seize.] To take in hand. *Obs.* *Spenser.*

UN′DERFOOT, *adv.* Beneath. *Milton.*

UN′DERFOOT, *a.* Low; base; abject; trodden down. *Milton.*

UNDERFUR′NISH, *v. t.* To supply with less than enough. *Collier.*

UNDERFUR′NISHED, *pp.* Supplied with less than enough.

UNDERFUR′NISHING, *ppr.* Furnishing with less than enough.

UNDERFUR′ROW, *adv.* In agriculture, to *sow underfurrow*, is to plow in seed. This phrase is applied to other operations, in which something is covered by the furrow-slice.

UNDERGIRD′, *v. t.* [See *Gird.*] To bind below; to gird round the bottom. Acts xxvii.

UNDERGO′, *v. t.* To suffer; to endure something burdensome or painful to the body or the mind; as, to *undergo* toil and fatigue; to *undergo* pain; to *undergo* grief or anxiety; to *undergo* the operation of amputation.

2. To pass through. Bread in the stomach *undergoes* the process of digestion; it *undergoes* a material alteration.

3. To sustain without fainting, yielding or sinking. Can you *undergo* the operation, or the fatigue?

4. To be the bearer of; to possess.

> Virtues—
> As infinite as man may *undergo*. *Shak.*

[*Not in use.*]

5. To support; to hazard.

> I have mov'd certain Romans
> To *undergo* with me an enterprise. *Obs.* *Shak.*

6. To be subject to.

> Claudio *undergoes* my challenge. *Obs.* *Shak.*

UNDERGO′ING, *ppr.* Suffering; enduring.

UNDERGONE, *pp.* *undergawn′.* Borne; suffered; sustained; endured. Who can tell how many evils and pains he has *undergone?*

UNDERGRAD′UATE, *n.* A student or member of a university or college, who has not taken his first degree.

UNDERGROUND′, *n.* A place or space beneath the surface of the ground. *Shak.*

UN′DERGROUND, *a.* Being below the surface of the ground; as an *underground* story or apartment.

UNDERGROUND′, *adv.* Beneath the surface of the earth.

UN′DERGROWTH, *n.* That which grows under trees; shrubs or small trees growing among large ones. *Milton.*

UN′DERHAND, *adv.* By secret means; in a clandestine manner. *Hooker.*

2. By fraud; by fraudulent means. *Dryden.*

UN′DERHAND, *a.* Secret; clandestine; usually implying meanness or fraud, or both. He obtained the place by *underhand* practices.

UNDERHAND′ED, *a.* Underhand; clandestine. [*This is the word in more general use in the United States.*]

UNDERI′VED, *a.* Not derived; not borrowed; not received from a foreign source.

UNDERKEE′PER, *n.* A subordinate keeper. *Gray.*

UNDERLA′BORER, *n.* A subordinate workman. *Wilkins.*

UNDERLA′ID, *pp.* or *a.* [from *underlay.*] Having something lying or laid beneath; as sand *underlaid* with clay.

UNDERLA′Y, *v. t.* To lay beneath; to support by something laid under.

UNDERLE′AF, *n.* A sort of apple good for cider. *Cyc.* *Mortimer.*

UNDERLET′, *v. t.* To let below the value. *Smollett.*

2. To let or lease, as a lessee or tenant; to let under a lease.

> It is a matter of much importance—that the tenant should have power to *underlet* his farms. *Cyc.*

UNDERLET′TER, *n.* A tenant who leases.

UNDERLET′TING, *ppr.* Letting or leasing under a lease, or by a lessee.

UNDERLET′TING, *n.* The act or practice of letting lands by lessees or tenants. [This is called also *subletting.*]

UNDERLI′NE, *v. t.* To mark with a line below the words; sometimes called *scoring.*

2. To influence secretly. [*Not used.*] *Wotton.*

UNDERLI′NED, *pp.* Marked with a line underneath.

UN′DERLING, *n.* An inferior person or agent; a mean sorry fellow. *Milton.*

UNDERLI′NING, *ppr.* Marking with a line below.

UN′DERLOCK, *n.* A lock of wool hanging under the belly of a sheep. *Cyc.*

UN′DERMASTER, *n.* A master subordinate to the principal master. *Lowth.*

UN′DERMEAL, *n.* A repast before dinner. *B. Jonson.*

UNDERMI′NE, *v. t.* To sap; to excavate the earth beneath, for the purpose of suffering to fall, or of blowing up; as, to *undermine* a wall.

2. To excavate the earth beneath. Rapid streams often *undermine* their banks and the trees growing upon them.

3. To remove the foundation or support of any thing by clandestine means; as, to *undermine* reputation; to *undermine* the constitution of the state.

> He should be warned who are like to *undermine* him. *Locke.*

UNDERMI′NED, *pp.* Sapped; having the foundation removed.

UNDERMI′NER, *n.* One that saps, or excavates the earth beneath any thing.

2. One that clandestinely removes the foundation or support; one that secretly overthrows; as an *underminer* of the church.

UNDERMI′NING, *ppr.* Sapping; digging away the earth beneath; clandestinely removing the supports of.

UN′DERMOST, *a.* Lowest in place beneath others.

2. Lowest in state or condition.

> The party that is *undermost.* *Addison.*

UN′DERN, *n.* [Sax.] The third hour of the day, or nine o'clock. [*Not in use.*] *Chaucer.*

UNDERNE′ATH, *adv.* [*under* and *neath.* See *Nether.*]

Beneath; below; in a lower place.

> Or sullen Mole that runneth *underneath.* *Milton.*

> The slate did not lie flat upon it, but left a free passage *underneath.* *Addison.*

UNDERNE′ATH, *prep.* Under; beneath.

> *Underneath* this stone doth lie
> As much beauty as could die. *B. Jonson.*

UNDEROF′FICER, *n.* A subordinate officer.

UNDEROG′ATORY, *a.* Not derogatory. *Boyle.*

UN′DERPART, *n.* A subordinate part. *Dryden.*

UNDERPET′TICOAT, *n.* A petticoat worn under a shirt or another petticoat. *Spectator.*

UNDERPIN′, *v. t.* To lay stones under the sills of a building, on which it is to rest.

2. To support by some solid foundation; or to place something underneath for support.

UNDERPIN′NED, *pp.* Supported by stones or a foundation.

UNDERPIN′NING, *ppr.* Placing stones under the sills for support.

UNDERPIN′NING, *n.* The act of laying stones under sills.

2. The stones on which a building immediately rests.

UN′DERPLOT, *n.* A series of events in a play, proceeding collaterally with the main story, and subservient to it. *Dryden.*

2. A clandestine scheme.

UNDERPRA′ISE, *v. t.* *s* as *z.* To praise below desert. *Dryden.*

UNDERPRI′ZE, *v. t.* To value at less than the worth; to undervalue. *Shak.*

UNDERPRI′ZED, *pp.* Undervalued.

UNDERPRI′ZING, *ppr.* Undervaluing.

UNDERPROP′, *v. t.* To support; to uphold.

> And *underprop* the head that bears the crown. *Fenton.*

UNDERPROPORTIONED, *a.* Having too little proportion.

> Scanty and *underproportioned* returns of civility. *Collier.*

UNDERPULL′ER, *n.* An inferior puller. [*Not in use.*] *Collier.*

UNDERRA′TE, *v. t.* To rate too low; to rate below the value; to undervalue. *Buck.*

UN′DERRATE, *n.* A price less than the worth; as, to sell a thing at an *underrate.*

UNDERRUN′, *v. t.* To pass under in a boat. *Mar. Dict.*

To underrun a tackle, to separate its parts and put them in order. *Mar. Dict.*

UNDERSAT′URATED, *a.* Not fully saturated; *a chimical term.*

UNDERSA′Y, *v. t.* To say by way of derogation or contradiction. [*Not in use.*] *Spenser.*

UNDERSEC′RETARY, *n.* A secretary subordinate to the principal secretary. *Bacon.*

UNDERSELL′, *v. t.* To sell the same articles at a lower price than another.

UNDERSELL′ING, *ppr.* Selling at a lower price.

UNDERSERV′ANT, *n.* An inferior servant. *Grew.*

UNDERSET′, *v. t.* To prop; to support. *Bacon.*

UN′DERSET, *n.* A current of water below the surface. *Mar. Dict.*

UNDERSET′TER, *n.* A prop; a pedestal; a support. 1 Kings vii.

UNDERSET′TING, *ppr.* Propping; supporting.

UNDERSET′TING, *n.* The lower part; the pedestal. *Wotton.*

UNDER-SHER′IF, *n.* A sherif's deputy.

UNDERSHER′IFRY, *n.* The office of an under-sherif. [*Not in use.*]

UN'DERSHOT, *a.* Moved by water passing under the wheel; opposed to *overshot;* as an *undershot* mill or mill-wheel.

UN'DERSHRUB, *n.* A low shrub, permanent and woody at the base, but the yearly branches decaying. *Barton. Martyn.*

UN'DERSOIL, *n.* Soil beneath the surface; subsoil. *Asiat. Res.*

UN'DERSONG, *n.* Chorus; burden of a song.

Menalcas shall sustain his *undersong.* *Dryden.*

UNDERSTAND', *v. t.* pret. and pp. *understood.* [*under* and *stand.* The sense is to support or hold in the mind.]

1. To have just and adequate ideas of; to comprehend; to know; as, to *understand* a problem in Euclid; to *understand* a proposition or a declaration.

2. To have the same ideas as the person who speaks, or the ideas which a person intends to communicate. I *understood* the preacher; the court perfectly *understand* the advocate or his argument.

3. To receive or have the ideas expressed or intended to be conveyed in a writing or book; to know the meaning. It is important that we should *understand* the sacred oracles.

4. To know the meaning of signs, or of any thing intended to convey ideas; as, to *understand* a nod, a wink, or a motion.

5. To suppose to mean.

The most learned interpreters *understood* the words of sin, and not of Abel. *Locke.*

6. To know by experience. *Milton.*

7. To know by instinct.

—Amorous intent, well *understood.* *Milton.*

8. To interpret, at least mentally. *Stillingfleet.*

9. To know another's meaning. *Milton.*

10. To hold in opinion with conviction. *Milton.*

11. To mean without expressing.

War then, war,
Open or *understood,* must be resolv'd. *Milton.*

12. To know what is not expressed. *Milton.*

I bring them to receive
From thee their names, and pay thee fealty
With low subjection; *understand* the same
Of fish. *Milton.*

13. To learn; to be informed. I *understand* that congress have passed the bill.

UNDERSTAND', *v. i.* To have the use of the intellectual faculties; to be an intelligent and conscious being.

All my soul be
Imparadis'd in you, in whom alone
I *understand,* and grow, and see. *Donne.*

2. To be informed by another; to learn.

I *understood* of the evil that Eliashib did. Neh. xiii.

UNDERSTAND'ABLE, *a.* That can be understood. [*Not much used.*] *Chillingworth.*

UNDERSTAND'ER, *n.* One who understands or knows by experience. [*Little used.*] *Beaum.*

UNDERSTAND'ING, *ppr.* Comprehending; apprehending the ideas or sense of another, or of a writing; learning or being informed.

2. *a.* Knowing; skillful. He is an *understanding* man.

UNDERSTAND'ING, *n.* The faculty of the human mind by which it apprehends the real state of things presented to it, or by which it receives or comprehends the ideas which others express and intend to communicate. The understanding is called also the *intellectual faculty.* It is the faculty by means of which we obtain a great part of our knowledge. Luke xxiv. Eph. i.

By *understanding* I mean that faculty whereby we are enabled to apprehend the objects of knowledge, generals or particulars, absent or present, and to judge of their truth or falsehood, good or evil. *Watts.*

There is a spirit in man, and the inspiration of the Almighty giveth him *understanding.* Job xxxii.

2. Knowledge; exact comprehension.

Right *understanding* consists in the perception of the visible or probable agreement or disagreement of ideas. *Locke.*

3. Intelligence between two or more persons; agreement of minds; union of sentiments. There is a good *understanding* between the minister and his people.

UNDERSTAND'INGLY, *adv.* Intelligibly; with full knowledge or comprehension of a question or subject; as, to vote upon a question *understandingly;* to act or judge *understandingly.*

The gospel may be neglected, but it cannot be *understandingly* disbelieved. *J. Hawes.*

UNDERSTOOD', *pret.* and *pp.* of *understand.*

UN'DERSTRAPPER, *n.* A petty fellow; an inferior agent. *Swift.*

UNDERSTRA'TUM, *n.* Subsoil; the bed or layer of earth on which the mold or soil rests. *Cyc.*

UNDERSTRO'KE, *v. t.* To underline. *Swift.*

UNDERTA'KABLE, *a.* That may be undertaken. [*Not in use.*] *Chillingworth.*

UNDERTA'KE, *v. t.* pret. *undertook;* pp. *undertaken.* [*under* and *take.*]

1. To engage in; to enter upon; to take in hand; to begin to perform. When I *undertook* this work, I had a very inadequate knowledge of the extent of my labors.

2. To covenant or contract to perform or execute. A man *undertakes* to erect a house, or to make a mile of canal, when he enters into stipulations for that purpose.

3. To attempt; as when a man *undertakes* what he cannot perform.

4. To assume a character. [*Not in use.*] *Shak.*

5. To engage with; to attack.

Your lordship should not *undertake* every companion you offend. [*Not in use.*] *Shak.*

6. To have the charge of.

—Who *undertakes* you to your end. *Shak.* [*Not in use.*]

UNDERTA'KE, *v. i.* To take upon or assume any business or province.

O Lord, I am oppressed; *undertake* for me. Is. xxxviii.

2. To venture; to hazard. They dare not *undertake.*

3. To promise; to be bound.

I dare *undertake* they will not lose their labor. *Woodward.*

To undertake for, to be bound; to become surety for.

UNDERTA'KEN, *pp.* of *undertake.* The work was *undertaken* at his own expense.

UNDERTA'KER, *n.* One who undertakes; one who engages in any project or business. *Clarendon.*

2. One who stipulates or covenants to perform any work for another. *Swift.*

3. One who manages funerals. *Young.*

UNDERTA'KING, *ppr.* Engaging in; taking in hand; beginning to perform; stipulating to execute.

UNDERTA'KING, *n.* Any business, work or project which a person engages in, or attempts to perform; an enterprise. The canal, or the making of the canal, from the Hudson to lake Erie, a distance of almost four hundred miles, was the greatest *undertaking* of the kind in modern times. The attempt to find a navigable passage to the Pacific round North America, is a hazardous *undertaking,* and probably useless to navigation.

UNDERTEN'ANT, *n.* The tenant of a tenant; one who holds lands or tenements of a tenant.

UN'DERTIME, *n.* Undern-tide; the time after dinner, or in the evening. [*Not in use.*] *Spenser.*

UNDERTOOK', *pret.* of *undertake.*

UNDERTREASURER, *n. undertrezh'urer.* A subordinate treasurer.

UNDERVALUA'TION, *n.* The act of valuing below the real worth; rate not equal to the worth.

UNDERVAL'UE, *v. t.* To value, rate or estimate below the real worth.

2. To esteem lightly; to treat as of little worth.

In comparison of the discharge of my duties, I *undervalued* all designs of authority. *Atterbury.*

3. To despise; to hold in mean estimation.

I write not this with the least intention to *undervalue* the other parts of poetry. *Dryden.*

UNDERVAL'UE, *n.* Low rate or price; a price less than the real worth. *Hamilton.*

UNDERVAL'UED, *pp.* Estimated at less than the real worth; slighted; despised.

UNDERVAL'UER, *n.* One who esteems lightly. *Walton.*

UNDERVAL'UING, *ppr.* Estimating at less than the real worth; slighting; despising.

UNDERWENT', *pret.* of *undergo.* He *underwent* severe trials.

UN'DERWOOD, *n.* Small trees that grow among large trees. *Mortimer.*

UN'DERWÖRK, *n.* Subordinate work; petty affairs. *Addison.*

UNDERWÖRK', *v. t.* To destroy by clandestine measures. *Shak.*

2. To work or labor upon less than is sufficient or proper. *Dryden.*

3. To work at a less price than others in the like employment; as, one mason may *underwork* another; a shoemaker cannot *underwork* a joiner.

UN'DERWÖRKER, *n.* One who underworks; or a subordinate workman.

UNDERWÖRK'ING, *ppr.* Destroying clandestinely; working at a less price than others in the like employment.

UNDERWORKMAN, *n.* A subordinate workman.

UNDERWRI'TE, *v. t.* [See *Write.*] To write under something else.

The change I have made, I have here *underwritten.* *Saunderson.*

2. To subscribe. We whose names are *underwritten*, agree to pay the sums expressed against our respective names.

3. To subscribe one's name for insurance; to set one's name to a policy of insurance, for the purpose of becoming answerable for loss or damage, for a certain premium per cent. Individuals *underwrite* policies of insurance, as well as companies.

The broker who procures insurance, ought not, by *underwriting* the policy, to deprive the parties of his unbiased testimony. *Marshall.*

UNDERWRI'TE, *v. i.* To practice insuring.

UN'DERWRITER, *n.* One who insures; an insurer; so called because he underwrites his name to the conditions of the policy.

UNDERWRI'TING, *ppr.* Writing under something.

2. Subscribing a policy; insuring.

UNDERWRI'TING, *n.* The act or practice of insuring ships, goods, houses, &c.

UNDERWRIT'TEN, *pp.* Written under; subscribed.

UNDESCEND'IBLE, *a.* Not descendible; not capable of descending to heirs.

UNDESCRI'BED, *a.* Not described. *Hooker.*

UNDESCRI'ED, *a.* Not descried; not discovered; not seen. *Wollaston.*

UNDESERV'ED, *a. s* as *z.* Not deserved; not merited. *Sidney.*

UNDESERV'EDLY, *adv.* Without desert, either good or evil. *Milton. Dryden.*

UNDESERV'EDNESS, *n.* Want of being worthy. *Newton.*

UNDESERV'ER, *n.* One of no merit. *Shak.*

UNDESERV'ING, *a.* Not deserving; not having merit. God continually supplies the wants of his *undeserving* creatures.

2. Not meriting; with *of*; as a man *undeserving of* happiness, or *of* punishment. [*This is rather harsh and unusual.*] *Sidney. Pope.*

UNDESERV'INGLY, *adv.* Without meriting any particular advantage or harm. *Milton.*

UNDESIGNED, *a.* Not designed; not intended; not proceeding from purpose; as, to do an *undesigned* injury.

UNDESIGNEDLY, *adv.* Without design or intention.

UNDESIGNEDNESS, *n.* Freedom from design or set purpose. *Paley.*

UNDESIGNING, *a.* Not acting with set purpose.

2. Sincere; upright; artless; having no artful or fraudulent purpose. It is base to practice on *undesigning* minds.

UNDESI'RABLE, *a. s* as *z.* Not to be desired; not to be wished; not pleasing. *Milton.*

UNDESI'RED, *a. s* as *z.* Not desired, or not solicited.

UNDESI'RING, *a.* Not desiring; not wishing. *Dryden.*

UNDESPA'IRING, *a.* Not yielding to despair. *Dyer.*

UNDESTROY'ABLE, *a.* Indestructible. [*Not in use.*] *Boyle.*

UNDESTROY'ED, *a.* Not destroyed; not wasted; not ruined. *Locke.*

UNDETECT'ED, *a.* Not detected; not discovered; not laid open. *R. G. Harper.*

UNDETERM'INABLE, *a.* That cannot be determined or decided. *Locke.*

UNDETERM'INATE, *a.* Not determinate; not settled or certain. [But *indeterminate* is now generally used.]

UNDETERM'INATENESS, *n.* Uncertainty; unsettled state.

UNDETERMINA'TION, *n.* Indecision; uncertainty of mind. [See *Indetermination*, which is chiefly used.]

UNDETERM'INED, *a.* Not determined; not settled; not decided. *Locke.*

2. Not limited; not defined; indeterminate. *Hale.*

UNDETER'RED, *a.* Not deterred; not restrained by fear or obstacles. *Mitford.*

UNDETEST'ING, *a.* Not detesting; not abhorring. *Thomson.*

UNDEVEL'OPED, *a.* Not opened or unfolded.

UNDE'VIATING, *a.* Not deviating; not departing from the way, or from a rule, principle or purpose; steady; regular; as an *undeviating* course of virtue. *Panoplist.*

2. Not erring; not wandering; not crooked. *Cowper.*

UNDE'VIATINGLY, *adv.* Without wandering; steadily; regularly.

UNDEVO'TED, *a.* Not devoted. *Clarendon.*

UNDEVOUT', *a.* Not devout; having no devotion.

UNDEX'TROUS, *a.* Not dextrous; clumsy.

UNDIAPH'ANOUS, *a.* Not transparent; not pellucid. *Boyle.*

UNDID', *pret.* of *undo.*

UNDIG'ENOUS, *a.* [L. *unda*, wave, and Gr. *γενος*, kind.] Generated by water. *Kirwan.*

UNDIGEST'ED, *a.* Not digested; not subdued by the stomach; crude. *Arbuthnot.*

UNDIGHT, *v. t.* To put off. *Obs.* *Spenser.*

UNDIG'NIFIED, *a.* Not dignified; common; mean. *Swift.*

UNDIMIN'ISHABLE, *a.* Not capable of diminution. *Scott.*

UNDIMIN'ISHED, *a.* Not diminished; not lessened; unimpaired. *Milton. Dryden.*

UNDIMIN'ISHING, *a.* Not diminishing; not becoming less.

UNDINT'ED, *a.* Not impressed by a blow. *Shak.*

UNDIPLOMAT'IC, *a.* Not according to the rules of diplomatic bodies.

UNDIP'PED, *a.* Not dipped; not plunged. *Dryden.*

UNDIRECT'ED, *a.* Not directed; not guided; left without direction.

2. Not addressed; not superscribed; as a letter.

UNDISAPPOINT'ED, *a.* Not disappointed. *Elphinstone.*

UNDISCERN'ED, *a.* Not discerned; not seen; not observed; not descried; not discovered; as truths *undiscerned.* *Brown.*

UNDISCERN'EDLY, *adv.* In such a manner as not to be discovered or seen. *Boyle.*

UNDISCERN'IBLE, *a.* That cannot be discerned, seen or discovered; invisible; as *undiscernible* objects or distinctions. *Rogers.*

UNDISCERN'IBLENESS, *n.* The state or quality of being undiscernible.

UNDISCERN'IBLY, *adv.* In a way not to be discovered or seen; invisibly; imperceptibly. *South.*

UNDISCERN'ING, *a.* Not discerning; not making just distinctions; wanting judgment or the power of discrimination.

UNDISCERN'ING, *n.* Want of discernment. *Spectator.*

UNDIS'CIPLINED, *a.* Not disciplined; not duly exercised and taught; not subdued to regularity and order; raw; as *undisciplined* troops; *undisciplined* valor. *Madison:*

2. Not instructed; untaught; as *undisciplined* minds.

UNDISCLOSE, *v. t.* *undisclo'ze.* Not to discover. [*A bad word.*] *Daniel.*

UNDISCLO'SED, *a.* Not disclosed; not revealed.

UNDISCOLORED, *a.* Not discolored; not stained.

UNDISCORD'ING, *a.* Not disagreeing; not jarring in music; harmonious; as *undiscording* voices. *Milton.*

UNDISCOVERABLE, *a.* That cannot be discovered or found out; as *undiscoverable* principles.

UNDISCOVERABLY, *adv.* In a manner not to be discovered.

UNDISCOVERED, *a.* Not discovered; not seen; not descried. *Dryden.*

UNDISCRE'TE, *a.* Not discrete; not prudent or wise. [Instead of this, *indiscrete* is used.]

UNDISCRE'TELY, *adv.* Indiscretely. [See *Indiscretely.*]

UNDISCUSS'ED, *a.* Not discussed; not argued or debated. *Du Ponceau.*

UNDISGRA'CED, *a.* Not disgraced or dishonored.

UNDISGUISED, *a.* [See *Guise.*] Not disguised; not covered with a mask, or with a false appearance. *Dryden.*

2. Open; frank; candid; plain; artless. *Rogers.*

UNDISHON'ORED, *a.* [See *Honor.*] Not dishonored; not disgraced. *Shak.*

UNDISMA'YED, *a.* Not dismayed; not disheartened by fear; not discouraged; as troops *undismayed.*

UNDISOBLI'GING, *a.* Inoffensive. [*Little used.*] *Brown.*

UNDISOR'DERED, *a. s* as *z.* Not disordered; not disturbed.

UNDISPENS'ED, *a.* Not dispensed.

2. Not freed from obligation.

UNDISPENS'ING, *a.* Not allowing to be dispensed with. *Milton.*

UNDISPERS'ED, *a.* Not dispersed; not scattered. *Boyle.*

UNDISPLA'YED, *a.* Not displayed; not unfolded.

Undisposed of, not disposed of; not bestowed; not parted with; as employments *undisposed of.* *Swift.*

UNDIS'PUTABLE, *a.* Not disputable. [But the word now used is *indisputable.*]

UNDISPU'TED, *a.* Not disputed; not contested; not called in question; as an *undisputed* title; *undisputed* truth. *Dryden.*

UNDISQUI'ETED, *a.* Not disquieted; not disturbed. *Tooke.*

UNDISSEM'BLED, *a.* Not dissembled; open; undisguised; unfeigned; as *undissembled* friendship or piety. *Warton. Atterbury.*

UNDISSEM'BLING, *a.* Not dissembling; not exhibiting a false appearance; not false. *Thomson.*

UNDIS'SIPATED, *a.* Not dissipated; not scattered. *Boyle.*

UNDISSOLV'ABLE, *a.* [See *Dissolve.*] That cannot be dissolved or melted. *Greenhill.*

2. That may not be loosened or broken; as the *undissolvable* ties of friendship.

UNDISSOLV'ED, *a.* Not dissolved; not melted. *Cowper.*

UNDISSOLV'ING, *a.* Not dissolving; not melting; as the *undissolving* ice of the Alps.

UNDISTEM'PERED, *a.* Not diseased; free from malady.

2. Free from perturbation. *Temple.*

UNDISTEND'ED, *a.* Not distended; not enlarged.

UNDISTILL'ED, *a.* Not distilled.

UNDISTIN'GUISHABLE, *a.* That cannot be distinguished by the eye; not to be distinctly seen. *Shak.*

2. Not to be known or distinguished by the intellect, by any peculiar property. *Locke.*

UNDISTIN'GUISHABLY, *adv.* Without distinction; so as not to be known from each other, or to be separately seen. *Barrow.*

UNDISTIN'GUISHED, *a.* Not distinguished; not so marked as to be distinctly known from each other.

Undistinguish'd seeds of good and ill. *Dryden.*

2. Not separately seen or descried. *Dryden.*

3. Not plainly discerned. *Swift.*

4. Having no intervenient space. *Shak.*

5. Not marked by any particular property. *Denham.*

6. Not treated with any particular respect. *Pope.*

7. Not distinguished by any particular eminence.

UNDISTIN'GUISHING, *a.* Making no difference; not discriminating; as *undistinguishing* favor.

Undistinguishing distribution of good and evil. *Addison.*

UNDISTORT'ED, *a.* Not distorted; not perverted. *More.*

UNDISTRACT'ED, *a.* Not perplexed by contrariety or confusion of thoughts, desires or concerns. *Boyle.*

UNDISTRACT'EDLY, *adv.* Without disturbance from contrariety of thoughts or multiplicity of concerns. *Boyle.*

UNDISTRACT'EDNESS, *n.* Freedom from disturbance or interruption from contrariety or multiplicity of thoughts and concerns. *Boyle.*

UNDISTRIB'UTED, *a.* Not distributed or allotted.

UNDISTURB'ED, *a.* Free from interruption; not molested or hindered; as *undisturbed* with company or noise.

2. Free from perturbation of mind; calm; tranquil; placid; serene; not agitated. To be *undisturbed* by danger, by perplexities, by injuries received, is a most desirable object.

3. Not agitated; not stirred; not moved; as the surface of water *undisturbed*. *Dryden.*

UNDISTURB'EDLY, *adv.* Calmly; peacefully. *Locke.*

UNDISTURB'EDNESS, *n.* Calmness; tranquillity; freedom from molestation or agitation.

UNDIVERS'IFIED, *a.* Not diversified; not varied; uniform. *Roscoe.*

UNDIVERT'ED, *a.* Not diverted; not turned aside.

2. Not amused; not entertained or pleased.

UNDIVI'DABLE, *a.* That cannot be divided; not separable; as an *undividable* scene. *Shak.*

UNDIVI'DED, *a.* Not divided; not separated or disunited; unbroken; whole; as *undivided* attention or affections.

2. In *botany*, not lobed, cleft or branched. *Cyc.*

UNDIVI'DEDLY, *adv.* So as not to be parted. *Feltham.*

UNDIVORCED, *a.* Not divorced; not separated. *Young.*

UNDIVULG'ED, *a.* Not divulged; not revealed or disclosed; secret. *Belknap. Robertson.*

UNDÖ, *v. t.* pret. *undid*; pp. *undone.* To reverse what has been done; to annul; to bring to naught any transaction. We can *undo* many kinds of work; but we cannot *undo* crimes, errors or faults.

To-morrow ere the setting sun,
She'd all *undo* what she had done. *Swift.*

2. To loose; to open; to take to pieces; to unravel; to unfasten; to untie; as, to *undo* a knot. *Waller.*

3. To ruin; to bring to poverty; to impoverish. Many are *undone* by unavoidable losses; but more *undo* themselves by vices and dissipation, or by indolence.

4. To ruin, in a moral sense; to bring to everlasting destruction and misery.

5. To ruin in reputation.

UNDOCK', *v. t.* To take out of dock; as, to *undock* a ship. *Encyc.*

UNDÖER, *n.* One who undoes or brings destruction; one who reverses what has been done; one who ruins the reputation of another.

UNDÖING, *ppr.* Reversing what has been done; ruining.

UNDÖING, *n.* The reversal of what has been done.

2. Ruin; destruction. *Hooker.*

UNDŎNE, *pp.* Reversed; annulled.

2. Ruined; destroyed.

When the legislature is corrupted, the people are *undone.* *J. Adams.*

3. *a.* Not done; not performed; not executed. We are apt to leave *undone* what we ought to do.

UNDOUBTED, *a. undout'ed.* Not doubted; not called in question; indubitable; indisputable; as *undoubted* proof; *undoubted* truth. *Milton.*

UNDOUBTEDLY, *adv. undout'edly.* Without doubt; without question; indubitably. *Tillotson.*

UNDOUBTFUL, *a. undout'ful.* Not doubtful; not ambiguous; plain; evident. *Shak.*

UNDOUBTING, *a. undout'ing.* Not doubting; not hesitating respecting facts; not fluctuating in uncertainty; as an *undoubting* believer; an *undoubting* faith. *Hammond.*

UNDRA'INED, *a.* Not drained; not freed from water.

UNDRAMAT'IC, } *a.* Not dramatic; **UNDRAMAT'ICAL**, } not according to the rules of the drama, or not suited to the drama. *Young.*

UNDRAWN', *a.* Not drawn; not pulled by an external force. *Milton.*

2. Not allured by motives or persuasion.

3. Not taken from the box; as an *undrawn* ticket.

UNDREADED, *a. undred'ed.* Not dreaded; not feared. *Milton.*

UNDRE'AMED, *a.* Not dreamed; not thought of. *Shak.*

UNDRESS', *v. t.* To divest of clothes; to strip. *Addison.*

2. To divest of ornaments, or the attire of ostentation; to disrobe. *Prior.*

UN'DRESS, *n.* A loose negligent dress. *Dryden.*

UNDRESS'ED, *pp.* Divested of dress; disrobed.

2. *a.* Not dressed; not attired.

3. Not prepared; as meat *undressed.*

4. Not pruned; not trimmed; not put in order; as an *undressed* vineyard.

UNDRI'ED, *a.* Not dried; wet; moist; as *undried* cloth.

2. Not dried; green; as *undried* hay; *undried* hops. *Mortimer.*

UNDRIV'EN, *a.* Not driven; not impelled. *Dryden.*

UNDROOP'ING, *a.* Not drooping; not sinking; not despairing. *Thomson.*

UNDROSS'Y, *a.* Free from dross or recrement. *Pope.*

UNDROWN'ED, *a.* Not drowned. *Shak.*

UNDU'BITABLE, *a.* Not to be doubted; unquestionable. [But the word now used is *indubitable.*]

UNDŪE, *a.* Not due; not yet demandable of right; as a debt, note or bond *undue.*

2. Not right; not legal; improper; as an *undue* proceeding.

3. Not agreeable to a rule or standard, or to duty; not proportioned; excessive; as an *undue* regard to the externals of religion; an *undue* attachment to forms; an *undue* rigor in the execution of law.

UNDU'KE, *v. t.* To deprive of dukedom. *Swift.*

UN'DULARY, *a.* [L. *undula*, a little wave.] Playing like waves; waving. *Brown.*

UN'DULATE, } *a.* Wavy; waved ob- **UN'DULATED**, } tusely up and down, near the margin, as a leaf or corol. *Lee. Smith.*

UN'DULATE, *v. t.* [L. *undula*, a little wave; *unda*, a wave; Low L. *undulo.*] To move back and forth, or up and down, as waves; to cause to vibrate.

Breath vocalized, that is, vibrated and *undulated*— *Holder.*

UN'DULATE, *v. i.* To vibrate; to move back and forth; to wave; as *undulating* air. *Pope.*

UN'DULATING, *ppr.* Waving; vibrating.

2. *a.* Wary; rising and falling.

UN'DULATINGLY, *adv.* In the form of waves.

UNDULA'TION, *n.* [from *undulate.*] A waving motion or vibration; as the *undulations* of a fluid, of water or air; the *undulations* of sound. The *undulations* of a fluid are propagated in concentric circles.

2. In *medicine*, a particular uneasy sensation of an undulatory motion in the heart. *Cyc.*

3. In *music*, a rattling or jarring of sounds, as when discordant notes are sounded together. It is called also *beat.* *Cyc.*

4. In *surgery*, a certain motion of the matter of an abscess when pressed, which indicates its maturity or fitness for opening. *Cyc.*

UN'DULATORY, *a.* [from *undulate.*] Moving in the manner of waves; or resembling the motion of waves, which successively rise or swell and fall. We speak of the *undulatory* motion of water, of air or other fluid, and this *undulatory* motion of air is supposed to be the cause of sounds. This is sometimes called *vibratory;* but *undulatory* seems to be most correct.

UNDULL', *v. t.* To remove dullness or obscurity; to clear; to purify. [*Not used.*] *Whitlock.*

UNDU'LY, *adv.* Not according to duty or propriety.

2. Not in proper proportion; excessively. His strength was *unduly* exerted.

UNDU'RABLE, *a.* Not durable; not lasting. [*Not in use.*] *Arnway.*

UNDUST', *v. t.* To free from dust. [*Not in use.*] *Mountague.*

UNDU'TEOUS, *a.* Not performing duty to parents and superiors; not obedient; as an *unduteous* child, apprentice or servant. *Dryden.*

UNDU'TIFUL, *a.* Not obedient; not performing duty; as an *undutiful* son or subject. *Tillotson.*

UNDU'TIFULLY, *adv.* Not according to duty; in a disobedient manner. *Dryden.*

UNDU'TIFULNESS, *n.* Want of respect; violation of duty; disobedience; as the *undutifulness* of children or subjects.

UNDY'ING, *a.* Not dying; not perishing.

2. Not subject to death; immortal; as the *undying* souls of men.

UNEARNED, *a.* *unern'ed.* Not merited by labor or services.

> Hoping heaven will bless
> Thy slighted fruits, and give thee bread *unearn'd.* *Philips.*

UNEARTHED, *a.* *unerth'ed.* Driven from a den, cavern or burrow. *Thomson.*

UNEARTHLY, *a.* *unerth'ly.* Not terrestrial. *Shak.*

UNE'ASILY, *adv.* *s* as *z.* With uneasiness or pain.

> He lives *uneasily* under the burden. *L'Estrange.*

2. With difficulty; not readily. *Boyle.*

UNE'ASINESS, *n.* A moderate degree of pain; restlessness; want of ease; disquiet.

2. Unquietness of mind; moderate anxiety or perturbation; disquietude.

3. That which makes uneasy or gives trouble; ruggedness; as the *uneasiness* of the road. [*Unusual.*] *Burnet.*

UNE'ASY, *a.* *s* as *z.* Feeling some degree of pain; restless; disturbed; unquiet. The patient is *uneasy.*

2. Giving some pain; as an *uneasy* garment.

3. Disturbed in mind; somewhat anxious; unquiet. He is *uneasy* respecting the success of his project.

> The soul, *uneasy* and confin'd from home,
> Rests and expatiates in a life to come. *Pope.*

4. Constraining; cramping; as *uneasy* rules. *Roscommon.*

5. Constrained; stiff; not graceful; not easy; as an *uneasy* deportment. *Locke.*

6. Giving some pain to others; disagreeable; unpleasing.

> A sour, untractable nature makes him *uneasy* to those who approach him. *Spectator.*

7. Difficult.

> Things—so *uneasy* to be satisfactorily understood. [*Not in use.*] *Boyle.*

UNE'ATABLE, *a.* Not eatable; not fit to be eaten. *Miller.*

UNE'ATEN, *a.* Not eaten; not devoured. *Clarendon.*

UNE'ATH, *adv.* [*un* and Sax. *eath*, easy.]

1. Not easily. [*Not in use.*] *Shak.*

2. Beneath; below. [*Not in use.*] [See *Neither* and *Beneath.*] *Spenser.*

UNECLIPS'ED, *a.* Not eclipsed; not obscured.

UNED'IFYING, *a.* Not edifying; not improving to the mind. *Atterbury.*

UNED'UCATED, *a.* Not educated; illiterate.

UNEFFA'CED, *a.* Not effaced; not obliterated. *Cheyne.*

UNEFFECT'UAL, *a.* Ineffectual. [*The latter is the word now used.*]

UNELAS'TIC, *a.* Not elastic; not having the property of recovering its original state, when bent or forced out of its form.

UNELA'TED, *a.* Not elated; not puffed up.

UNEL'BOWED, *a.* Not attended by any at the elbow. *Pope.*

UNELECT'ED, *a.* Not elected; not chosen; not preferred. *Shak.*

UNEL'EGANT, *a.* Not elegant. [*Not used.*] [See *Inelegant.*]

UNEL'IGIBLE, *a.* Not proper to be chosen; ineligible. [*The latter is the word now used.*]

UNEMAN'CIPATED, *n.* Not emancipated or liberated from slavery.

UNEMB'ALMED, *a.* Not embalmed.

UNEMBAR'RASSED, *a.* Not embarrassed; not perplexed in mind; not confused. The speaker appeared *unembarrassed.*

2. Free from pecuniary difficulties or incumbrances. He or his property is *unembarrassed.*

3. Free from perplexing connection; as, the question comes before the court *unembarrassed* with irrelevant matter.

UNEMBIT'TERED, *a.* Not embittered; not aggravated. *Roscoe.*

UNEMBOD'IED, *a.* Free from a corporeal body; as *unembodied* spirits. *Elliott.*

2. Not embodied; not collected into a body; as *unembodied* militia. *Smollett.*

UNEMPHAT'IC, *a.* Having no emphasis.

UNEMPLOY'ED, *a.* Not employed; not occupied; not busy; at leisure; not engaged. *Addison.*

2. Not being in use; as *unemployed* capital or money.

UNEMPOW'ERED, *a.* Not empowered or authorized.

UNEMP'TIABLE, *a.* Not to be emptied; inexhaustible. [*Not in use.*] *Hooker.*

UNEM'ULATING, *a.* Not emulating; not striving to excel. *Ruffhead.*

UNENCH'ANTED, *a.* Not enchanted; that cannot be enchanted. *Milton.*

UNENCUM'BER, *v. t.* To free from incumbrance.

UNENCUM'BERED, *pp.* Disengaged from incumbrance.

2. *a.* Not encumbered; not burdened.

UNENDOW'ED, *a.* Not endowed; not furnished; not invested; as a man *unendowed* with virtues.

2. Not furnished with funds; as an *unendowed* college or hospital.

UNENDU'RING, *a.* Not lasting; of temporary duration. *Dwight.*

UNEN'ERVATED, *a.* Not enervated or weakened. *Beattie.*

UNENGA'GED, *a.* Not engaged; not bound by covenant or promise; free from obligation to a particular person; as, a lady is *unengaged.*

2. Free from attachment that binds; as, her affections are *unengaged.*

3. Unemployed; unoccupied; not busy.

4. Not appropriated; as *unengaged* revenues. [We generally say, *unappropriated* revenue or money.]

UNENGA'GING, *a.* Not adapted to engage or win the attention or affections; not inviting.

UNENJOY'ED, *a.* Not enjoyed; not obtained; not possessed. *Dryden.*

UNENJOY'ING, *a.* Not using; having no fruition. *Creek.*

UNENL'ARGED, *a.* Not enlarged; narrow. *Watts.*

UNENLIGHTENED, *a.* Not enlightened; not illuminated. *Atterbury.*

UNENSLA'VED, *a.* Not enslaved; free. *Addison.*

UNENTAN'GLE, *v. t.* To free from complication or perplexity; to disentangle. *Donne.*

UNENTAN'GLED, *pp.* Disentangled.

2. *a.* Not entangled; not complicated; not perplexed.

UNEN'TERPRISING, *a.* Not enterprising; not adventurous.

UNENTERTA'INING, *a.* Not entertaining or amusing; giving no delight. *Pope.*

UNENTERTA'ININGNESS, *n.* The quality of being unentertaining or dull.

UNENTHRALL'ED, *a.* Not enslaved; not reduced to thralldom.

UNENTÖMBED, *a.* Not buried; not interred. *Dryden.*

UNEN'VIED, *a.* Not envied; exempt from the envy of others.

UNEN'VIOUS, *a.* Not envious; free from envy.

UNEP'ITAPHED, *a.* Having no epitaph. *Pollok.*

UNE'QUABLE, *a.* Different from itself; different at different times; not uniform; diverse; as *unequable* motions; *unequable* months or seasons. *Bentley.*

UNE'QUAL, *a.* [L. *inæqualis.*] Not equal; not even; not of the same size, length,

breadth, quantity, &c.; as men of *unequal* stature; houses of *unequal* dimensions.
2. Not equal in strength, talents, acquirements, &c.; inferior.
3. Not equal in age or station; inferior.
4. Insufficient; inadequate. His strength is *unequal* to the task.
5. Partial; unjust; not furnishing equivalents to the different parties; as an *unequal* peace; an *unequal* bargain.
6. Disproportioned; ill matched.

Against *unequal* arms to fight in pain. *Milton.*

7. Not regular; not uniform; as *unequal* pulsations. *Dryden.*
8. In *botany*, having the parts not corresponding in size, but in proportion only, as a corol; rugged, not even or smooth, as the surface of a leaf or stem. *Martyn. Cyc.*

An *unequal leaf*, is when the two halves, separated by the mid-rib, are unequal in dimensions, and their bases not parallel; called also an *oblique leaf*. *Smith. Cyc.*

UNE'QUALABLE, *a.* Not to be equaled. *Boyle.*

UNE'QUALED, *a.* Not to be equaled; unparalleled; unrivaled; *in a good or bad sense;* as *unequaled* excellence; *unequaled* ingratitude or baseness.

UNE'QUALLY, *adv.* Not equally; in different degrees; in disproportion to each other.
2. Not with like sentiments, temper or religious opinions or habits. 2 Cor. vi.

UNE'QUALNESS, *n.* State of being unequal; inequality. *Temple.*

UNEQ'UITABLE, *a.* Not equitable; not just.
2. Not impartial. [*Inequitable* is generally used.]

UNEQUIV'OCAL, *a.* Not equivocal; not doubtful; clear; evident; as *unequivocal* evidence.
2. Not ambiguous; not of doubtful signification; not admitting different interpretations; as *unequivocal* words or expressions.

UNEQUIV'OCALLY, *adv.* Without doubt; without room to doubt; plainly; with full evidence.

UNER'RABLE, *a.* Incapable of erring; infallible. *Sheldon.*

UNER'RABLENESS, *n.* Incapacity of error. *Decay of Piety.*

UNER'RING, *a.* Committing no mistake; incapable of error; as the *unerring* wisdom of God.
2. Incapable of failure; certain. He takes *unerring* aim.

UNER'RINGLY, *adv.* Without mistake. *Glanville.*

UNESCHEW'ABLE, *a.* Unavoidable. [*Not in use.*] *Carew.*

UNESPI'ED, *a.* Not espied; not discovered; not seen. *Dryden.*

UNESSA'YED, *a.* Not essayed; unattempted. *Milton.*

UNESSEN'TIAL, *a.* Not essential; not absolutely necessary; not of prime importance.
2. Not constituting the essence.
3. Void of real being; as *unessential* night. *Milton.*

UNESSEN'TIAL, *n.* Something not constituting essence, or not of absolute necessity. Forms are among the *unessentials* of religion.

UNESTAB'LISH, *v. t.* To unfix; to deprive of establishment. [*Little used.*] *Milton.*

UNESTAB'LISHED, *a.* Not established; not permanently fixed.

UNEVANGEL'ICAL, *a.* Not orthodox; not according to the gospel. *Milner.*

UNEVEN, *a.* une'vn. Not even; not level; as an *uneven* road or way; *uneven* ground. *Addison.*
2. Not equal; not of equal length.

Hebrew verse consists of *uneven* feet. *Peacham.*

3. Not uniform; as an *uneven* temper.

UNE'VENLY, *adv.* In an uneven manner.

UNE'VENNESS, *n.* Surface not level; inequality of surface; as the *unevenness* of ground or of roads. *Ray.*
2. Turbulence; change; want of uniformity; as the *unevenness* of king Edward's reign. [*Unusual.*] *Hale.*
3. Want of uniformity; as *unevenness* of temper.
4. Want of smoothness.

UNEV'ITABLE, *a.* Not to be escaped; unavoidable. [The word now used is *inevitable.*]

UNEXACT', *a.* Not exact. [See *Inexact*, which is generally used.]

UNEXACT'ED, *a.* Not exacted; not taken by force. *Dryden.*

UNEXAG'GERATED, *a.* Not exaggerated. *Buckminster.*

UNEXAG'GERATING, *a.* Not enlarging in description.

UNEXAM'INABLE, *a.* Not to be examined or inquired into. *Milton.*

UNEXAM'INED, *a.* Not examined; not interrogated strictly; as a *witness.*
2. Not inquired into; not investigated; as a question.
3. Not discussed; not debated.

UNEXAM'PLED, *a.* Having no example or similar case; having no precedent; unprecedented; unparalleled; as the *unexampled* love and sufferings of our Savior.

UNEXCEP'TIONABLE, *a.* Not liable to any exception or objection; unobjectionable; as *unexceptionable* conduct; *unexceptionable* testimony.

UNEXCEP'TIONABLENESS, *n.* State or quality of being unexceptionable. *More.*

UNEXCEP'TIONABLY, *adv.* In a manner liable to no objection; as a point *unexceptionably* proved.

UNEXCI'SED, *a.* *s* as *z.* Not charged with the duty of excise.

UNEXCI'TED, *a.* Not excited; not roused. *Brown.*

UNEXCOG'ITABLE, *a.* Not to be found out. [*Not in use.*] *Raleigh.*

UNEXCOMMU'NICATED, *a.* Not excommunicated. *Scott.*

UNEXCU'SABLE, *a.* *s* as *z.* Not excusable. [We now use *inexcusable.*]

UNEXCU'SABLENESS, *n.* Inexcusableness, which see.

UNEX'ECUTED, *a.* Not performed; not done; as a task, business or project *unexecuted.*
2. Not signed or sealed; not having the proper attestations or forms that give validity; as a contract or deed *unexecuted.*

UNEX'EMPLARY, *a.* Not exemplary; not according to example. *Swift.*

UNEXEM'PLIFIED, *a.* Not exemplified; not illustrated by example. *Boyle.*

UNEXEMPT', *a.* Not exempt; not free by privilege. *Milton.*

UNEX'ERCISED, *a.* *s* as *z.* Not exercised; not practiced; not disciplined; not experienced. *Dryden.*

UNEXERT'ED, *a.* Not called into action; not exerted. *Brown.*

UNEXHAUST'ED, *a.* Not exhausted; not drained to the bottom, or to the last article. *Addison.*
2. Not spent; as *unexhausted* patience or strength.

UNEXIST'ENT, *a.* Not existing. *Brown.*

UNEX'ORCISED, *a.* *s* as *z.* Not exorcised; not cast out by exorcism.

UNEXPAND'ED, *a.* Not expanded; not spread out. *Blackmore.*

UNEXPECTA'TION, *n.* Want of foresight. [*Not in use.*] *Bp. Hall.*

UNEXPECT'ED, *a.* Not expected; not looked for; sudden; not provided against. *Hooker.*

UNEXPECT'EDLY, *adv.* At a time or in a manner not expected or looked for; suddenly.

UNEXPECT'EDNESS, *n.* The quality of being unexpected, or of coming suddenly and by surprise. *Watts.*

UNEXPEC'TORATING, *a.* Not expectorating; not discharging from the throat or lungs.

UNEXPE'DIENT, *a.* Not expedient. [But *inexpedient* is the word now used.]

UNEXPEND'ED, *a.* Not expended; not laid out. There is an *unexpended* balance of the appropriation.

UNEXPENS'IVE, *a.* Not expensive; not costly. *Milton.*

UNEXPE'RIENCED, *a.* Not experienced; not versed; not acquainted by trial or practice. *Dryden.*
2. Untried; *applied to things.* [*Unusual.*] *Cheyne.*

UNEXPERT', *a.* Wanting skill; not ready or dextrous in performance. *Prior.*

UNEXPI'RED, *a.* Not expired; not ended.

UNEXPLA'INABLE, *a.* That cannot be explained. *Med. Repos.*

UNEXPLO'RED, *a.* Not explored; not searched or examined by the eye; unknown.
2. Not examined intellectually.

UNEXPO'SED, *a.* *s* as *z.* Not laid open to view; concealed. *R. G. Harper.*
2. Not laid open to censure.

UNEXPOUND'ED, *a.* Not expounded; not explained.

UNEXPRESS'ED, *a.* Not expressed; not mentioned or named; not exhibited.

UNEXPRESS'IBLE, *a.* That cannot be expressed. [But *inexpressible* is the word now used.]

UNEXPRESS'IVE, *a.* Not having the power of expressing.
2. Inexpressible; unutterable. *Shak.*

UNEXTEND'ED, *a.* Occupying no assignable space; having no dimensions; as a spiritual, an *unextended* substance. *Locke.*

UNEXTINCT', *a.* Not extinct; not being destroyed; not having perished.

UNEXTIN'GUISHABLE, *a.* That cannot be extinguished; unquenchable; as *unextinguishable* fire.
2. That cannot be annihilated or repressed; as an *unextinguishable* thirst for knowledge. [But *inextinguishable* is more generally used.]

UNEXTIN'GUISHABLY, *adv.* In a manner or degree that precludes extinction. *Johnson.*

UNEXTIN'GUISHED, *a.* Not extinguished; not quenched; not entirely repressed. *Dryden.*

UNEX'TIRPATED, *a.* Not extirpated; not rooted out.

UNEXTORT'ED, *a.* Not extorted; not wrested.

UNEXTRACT'ED, *a.* Not extracted or drawn out.

UNFA'DED, *a.* Not faded; not having lost its strength of color.
2. Unwithered; as a plant. *Dryden.*

UNFA'DING, *a.* Not liable to lose strength or freshness of coloring.
2. Not liable to wither; as *unfading* laurels. *Pope.*

UNFA'DINGNESS, *n.* The state or quality of being unfading. *Hall.*

UNFA'ILABLE, *a.* That cannot fail. [*Not in use.*] *Hall.*

UNFA'ILABLENESS, *n.* The quality of being unfailable. [*Not in use.*] *Hall.*

UNFA'ILING, *a.* Not liable to fail; not capable of being exhausted; as an *unfailing* spring; *unfailing* sources of supply.
2. That does not fail; certain; as an *unfailing* promise.

UNFA'ILINGNESS, *n.* The state of being unfailing. *Hall.*

UNFA'INTING, *a.* Not fainting; not sinking; not failing under toil. *Sandys.*

UNFA'IR, *a.* Not honest; not impartial; disingenuous; using trick or artifice; as an *unfair* dealer.
2. Not honest; not just; not equal; as *unfair* practices.
3. Proceeding from trick or dishonesty; as *unfair* advantages.

UNFA'IRLY, *adv.* Not in a just or equitable manner. *Parnell.*

UNFA'IRNESS, *n.* Dishonest or disingenuous conduct or practice; use of trick or artifice; *applied to persons.* He is noted for his *unfairness* in dealing.
2. Injustice; want of equitableness; as the *unfairness* of a proceeding.

UNFA'ITHFUL, *a.* Not observant of promises, vows, allegiance or duty; violating trust or confidence; treacherous; perfidious; as an *unfaithful* subject; an *unfaithful* husband or wife; an *unfaithful* servant; an *unfaithful* bailee or agent.
2. Not performing the proper duty.

> My feet through wine *unfaithful* to their weight— *Pope.*

3. Impious; infidel. *Milton.*
4. Negligent of duty; as an *unfaithful* workman.

UNFA'ITHFULLY, *adv.* In violation of promises, vows or duty; treacherously; perfidiously. *Bacon.*
2. Negligently; imperfectly; as work *unfaithfully* done.

UNFA'ITHFULNESS, *n.* Neglect or violation of vows, promises, allegiance or other duty; breach of confidence or trust reposed; perfidiousness; treachery; as the *unfaithfulness* of a subject to his prince or the state; the *unfaithfulness* of a husband to his wife, or of a wife to her husband; the *unfaithfulness* of an agent, servant or officer.

UNFAL'CATED, *a.* Not curtailed; having no deductions. *Swift.*

UNFALL'EN, *a.* Not fallen. *Young.*

UNFAL'LOWED, *a.* Not fallowed. *Philips.*

UNFAMIL'IAR, *a.* Not accustomed; not common; not rendered agreeable by frequent use. *Warton.*

UNFAMILIAR'ITY, *n.* Want of familiarity. *Johnson.*

UNFASH'IONABLE, *a.* Not fashionable; not according to the prevailing mode; as *unfashionable* dress or language.
2. Not regulating dress or manners according to the reigning custom; as an *unfashionable* man.

UNFASH'IONABLENESS, *n.* Neglect of the prevailing mode; deviation from reigning custom. *Locke.*

UNFASH'IONABLY, *adv.* Not according to the fashion; as, to be *unfashionably* dressed.

UNFASH'IONED, *a.* Not modified by art; amorphous; shapeless; not having a regular form; as a lifeless lump *unfashioned.* *Dryden. Good.*

UNF'AST, *a.* Not safe; not secure.

UNF'ASTEN, *v. t.* To loose; to unfix; to unbind; to untie.

UNF'ASTENED, *pp.* Loosed; untied; unfixed.

UNF'ATHERED, *a.* Fatherless. *Shak.*

UNF'ATHERLY, *a.* Not becoming a father; unkind. *Cowper.*

UNFATH'OMABLE, *a.* That cannot be sounded by a line; as an *unfathomable* lake. *Addison.*
2. So deep or remote that the limit or extent cannot be found. The designs of Providence are often *unfathomable.*

UNFATH'OMABLENESS, *n.* The state of being unfathomable. *Norris.*

UNFATH'OMABLY, *adv.* So as not to be capable of being sounded. *Thomson.*

UNFATH'OMED, *a.* Not sounded; not to be sounded. *Dryden.*

UNFATIGUED, *a.* *unfatee'ged.* Not wearied; not tired. *Philips.*

UNFAULT'Y, *a.* Free from fault; innocent. *Milton.*

UNFA'VORABLE, *a.* Not favorable; not propitious; not disposed or adapted to countenance or support. We found the minister's opinion *unfavorable* to our project. The committee made a report *unfavorable* to the petitioner.
2. Not propitious; not adapted to promote any object; as weather *unfavorable* for harvest.
3. Not kind; not obliging.
4. Discouraging; as *unfavorable* prospects.

UNFA'VORABLENESS, *n.* Unpropitiousness; unkindness; want of disposition to countenance or promote.

UNFA'VORABLY, *adv.* Unpropitiously; unkindly; so as not to countenance, support or promote; in a manner to discourage.

UNFA'VORED, *a.* Not favored; not assisted. *Goldsmith.*

UNFE'ARED, *a.* Not affrighted; not daunted. [*Not in use.*] *B. Jonson.*
2. Not feared; not dreaded. *Milton.*

UNFE'ASIBLE, *a.* *s* as *z.* That cannot be done; impracticable.

UNFEATH'ERED, } *a.* Having no fethers;
UNFETH'ERED, } unfledged; implumous; naked of fethers. *Dryden.*

UNFE'ATURED, *a.* Wanting regular features; deformed.

> Visage rough,
> Deform'd, *unfeatur'd.* *Dryden.*

UNFED', *a.* Not fed; not supplied with food. *Spenser.*

UNFEE'D, *a.* Not feed; not retained by a fee.
2. Unpaid; as an *unfeed* lawyer. *Shak.*

UNFEE'LING, *a.* Insensible; void of sensibility.
2. Cruel; hard.

UNFEE'LINGLY, *adv.* In an unfeeling or cruel manner.

UNFEE'LINGNESS, *n.* Insensibility; hardness of heart; cruelty. *Darwin.*

UNFEIGNED, *a.* Not feigned; not counterfeit; not hypocritical; real; sincere; as *unfeigned* piety to God; *unfeigned* love to man.

UNFEIGNEDLY, *adv.* Without hypocrisy; really; sincerely.

> He pardoneth all them that truly repent, and *unfeignedly* believe his holy gospel. *Com. Prayer.*

UNFELIC'ITATING, *a.* Not producing felicity. [*Unusual.*] *J. Lathrop.*

UNFEL'LOWED, *a.* Not matched.

UNFELT', *a.* Not felt; not perceived. *Dryden.*

UNFENCE, *v. t.* *unfens'.* To strip of fence; to remove a fence from. *South.*

UNFEN'CED, *pp.* Deprived of a fence.
2. *a.* Not fenced; not inclosed; defenseless; as a tract of land *unfenced.*

UNFERMENT'ED, *a.* Not fermented; not having undergone the process of fermentation; as liquor.
2. Not leavened; as bread.

UNFER'TILE, *a.* Not fertile; not rich; not having the qualities necessary to the production of good crops.
2. Barren; unfruitful; bare; waste.
3. Not prolific.

[This word is not obsolete, but *infertile* is much used instead of it.]

UNFET'TER, *v. t.* To loose from fetters; to unchain; to unshackle.
2. To free from restraint; to set at liberty; as, to *unfetter* the mind.

UNFET'TERED, *pp.* Unchained; unshackled; freed from restraint.
2. *a.* Not restrained.

UNFET'TERING, *ppr.* Unchaining; setting free from restraint.

UNFIG'URED, *a.* Representing no animal form. *Wotton.*

UNFIL'IAL, *a.* Unsuitable to a son or child; undutiful; not becoming a child. *Shak.*

UNFILL'ED, *a.* Not filled; not fully supplied. *Taylor.*

UNFIN'ISHED, *a.* Not finished; not complete; not brought to an end; imperfect; wanting the last hand or touch; as an *unfinished* house; an *unfinished* painting. *Dryden.*

UNFI'RED, *a.* Not fired; not inflamed.

UNFIRM', *a.* [See *Firm.*] Not firm; weak; feeble; infirm.

[*Note.* When we speak of the weakness of the human frame, we use *infirm.* When we speak of the weakness of other things, as a bridge, wall and the like, we say, it is *unfirm.*]

2. Not stable; not well fixed.

With feet *unfirm.* *Dryden.*

UNFIRM'NESS, *n.* A weak state; instability.

UNFIT', *a.* Not fit; improper; unsuitable. *Milton.*

2. Unqualified; as a man *unfit* for an office.

UNFIT', *v. t.* To disable; to make unsuitable; to deprive of the strength, skill or proper qualities for any thing. Sickness *unfits* a man for labor.

2. To disqualify; to deprive of the moral or mental qualities necessary for any thing. Sin *unfits* us for the society of holy beings.

UNFIT'LY, *adv.* Not properly; unsuitably.

UNFIT'NESS, *n.* Want of suitable powers or qualifications, physical or moral; as the *unfitness* of a sick man for labor, or of an ignorant man for office; the *unfitness* of sinners for the enjoyments of heaven.

2. Want of propriety or adaptation to character or place; as *unfitness* of behavior or of dress.

UNFIT'TED, *pp.* Rendered unsuitable; disqualified.

UNFIT'TING, *ppr.* Rendering unsuitable; disqualifying.

2. *a.* Improper; unbecoming.

UNFIX', *v. t.* To loosen from any fastening; to detach from any thing that holds; to unsettle; to unhinge; as, to *unfix* the mind or affections.

2. To make fluid; to dissolve.

Nor can the rising sun
Unfix their frosts. *Dryden.*

UNFIX'ED, *pp.* Unsettled; loosened.

2. *a.* Wandering; erratic; inconstant; having no settled habitation.

3. Having no settled view or object of pursuit.

UNFIX'ING, *ppr.* Unsettling; loosening.

UNFLAG'GING, *a.* Not flagging; not drooping; maintaining strength or spirit. *South.*

UNFLAT'TERED, *a.* Not flattered. *Young.*

UNFLAT'TERING, *a.* Not flattering; not gratifying with obsequious behavior; not coloring the truth to please.

2. Not affording a favorable prospect; as, the weather is *unflattering.*

UNFLEDG'ED, *a.* Not yet furnished with fethers; implumous; as an *unfledged* bird.

2. Young; not having attained to full growth. *Shak.*

UNFLESH'ED, *a.* Not fleshed; not seasoned to blood; raw; as an *unfleshed* hound; *unfleshed* valor. *Shak.*

UNFOIL'ED, *a.* Not vanquished; not defeated. *Temple.*

UNFŌLD, *v. t.* To open folds; to expand; to spread out.

2. To open any thing covered or close; to lay open to view or contemplation; to disclose; to reveal; as, to *unfold* one's designs; to *unfold* the principles of a science.

3. To declare; to tell; to disclose.

Unfold the passion of my love. *Shak.*

4. To display; as, to *unfold* the works of creation.

5. To release from a fold or pen; as, to *unfold* sheep. *Shak.*

UNFŌLDED, *pp.* Opened; expanded; revealed; displayed; released from a fold.

UNFŌLDING, *ppr.* Opening; expanding; disclosing; displaying; releasing from a fold.

UNFŌLDING, *n.* The act of expanding, displaying or disclosing; disclosure.

UNFOOL', *v. t.* To restore from folly. [*Not in use.*]

UNFORBEARING, *a.* Not forbearing.

UNFORBID', UNFORBID'DEN, } *a.* Not forbid; not prohibited; *applied to persons.* *Milton.*

2. Allowed; permitted; legal; *applied to things.*

UNFORBID'DENNESS, *n.* The state of being unforbidden. [*Not in use.*] *Boyle.*

UNFORCED, *a.* Not forced; not compelled; not constrained. *Dryden.*

2. Not urged or impelled. *Donne.*

3. Not feigned; not hightened; natural; as *unforced* passions; *unforced* expressions of joy.

4. Not violent; easy; gradual; as an easy and *unforced* ascent. *Denham.*

5. Easy; natural; as an *unforced* posture.

UNFŌRCIBLE, *a.* Wanting force or strength; as an *unforcible* expression. *Hooker.*

UNFŌRDABLE, *a.* Not fordable; that cannot be forded, or passed by wading; as an *unfordable* river. *Whitaker.*

UNFOREBO'DING, *a.* Giving no omens. *Pope.*

UNFOREKNŌWN, *a.* Not previously known or foreseen. *Milton.*

UNFORESEE'ABLE, *a.* That cannot be foreseen. [*A bad word and not in use.*] *South.*

UNFORESEE'N, *a.* Not foreseen; not foreknown. *Dryden.*

UNFO'RESKINNED, *a.* Circumcised. [*Bad.*] *Milton.*

UNFORETŌLD, *a.* Not predicted.

UNFOREWARN'ED, *a.* [See *Warn.*] Not previously warned or admonished.

UNFOR'FEITED, *a.* Not forfeited. *Rogers.*

UNFORGIV'EN, *a.* Not forgiven; not pardoned.

UNFORGIV'ING, *a.* Not forgiving; not disposed to overlook or pardon offenses; implacable. *Dryden.*

UNFORGOT', UNFORGOT'TEN, } *a.* Not forgot; not lost to memory. *Knolles.*

2. Not overlooked; not neglected.

UNFORM', *v. t.* To destroy; to unmake; to decompose or resolve into parts. *Good.*

UNFORM'ED, *a.* Not molded into regular shape; as *unformed* matter. *Spectator.*

UNFORSA'KEN, *a.* Not forsaken; not deserted; not entirely neglected.

UNFOR'TIFIED, *a.* Not fortified; not secured from attack by walls or mounds. *Pope.*

2. Not guarded; not strengthened against temptations or trials; weak; exposed; defenseless; as an *unfortified* mind.

3. Wanting securities or means of defense. *Collier.*

UNFOR'TUNATE, *a.* Not successful; not prosperous; as an *unfortunate* adventure; an *unfortunate* voyage; *unfortunate* attempts; an *unfortunate* man; an *unfortunate* commander; *unfortunate* business.

UNFOR'TUNATELY, *adv.* Without success; unsuccessfully; unhappily. The scheme *unfortunately* miscarried.

UNFOR'TUNATENESS, *n.* Ill luck; ill fortune; failure of success. *Sidney.*

UNFOS'TERED, *a.* Not fostered; not nourished.

2. Not countenanced by favor; not patronized.

UNFOUGHT, *a. unfaut'.* Not fought. *Knolles.*

UNFOUL'ED, *a.* Not fouled; not polluted; not soiled; not corrupted; pure. *Young.*

UNFOUND', *a.* Not found; not met with. *Dryden.*

UNFOUND'ED, *a.* Not founded; not built or established.

2. Having no foundation; vain; idle; as *unfounded* expectations.

UNFRA'MABLE, *a.* Not to be framed or molded. [*Not in use.*] *Hooker.*

UNFRA'MABLENESS, *n.* The quality of not being framable. [*Not in use.*] *Sanderson.*

UNFRA'MED, *a.* Not framed; not fitted for erection; as *unframed* timber.

2. Not formed; not constructed; not fashioned. *Dryden.*

UNFRATERN'AL, *a.* Not brotherly.

UNFREE', *a.* Not free; as *unfree* peasants. *Tooke.*

UNFRE'QUENCY, *n.* The state of being unfrequent. *Cowper.*

UNFRE'QUENT, *a.* Not frequent; not common; not happening often; infrequent. *Brown.*

UNFRE'QUENT, *v. t.* To cease to frequent. [*Not in use.*] *Philips.*

UNFRE'QUENTED, *a.* Rarely visited; seldom resorted to by human beings; as an *unfrequented* place or forest. *Addison.*

UNFRE'QUENTLY, *adv.* Not often; seldom. *Brown.*

UNFRI'ABLE, *a.* Not easily crumbled. *Paley.*

UNFRIENDED, *a. unfrend'ed.* Wanting friends; not countenanced or supported. *Shak.*

UNFRIEND'LINESS, *n.* Want of kindness; disfavor. *Boyle.*

UNFRIEND'LY, *a.* Not friendly; not kind or benevolent; as an *unfriendly* neighbor.

2. Not favorable; not adapted to promote or support any object; as weather *unfriendly* to health.

UNFROCK', *v. t.* To divest. *Hurd.*

UNFRO'ZEN, *a.* Not frozen; not congealed. *Boyle.*

UNFRU'GAL, *a.* Not frugal; not saving or economical.

UNFRUITFUL, *a.* Not producing fruit; barren; as an *unfruitful* tree.

2. Not producing offspring; not prolific; barren; as an *unfruitful* female.

3. Not producing good effects or works; as an *unfruitful* life.

4. Unproductive; not fertile; as an *unfruitful* soil.

UNFRUITFULNESS, *n.* Barrenness; infecundity; unproductiveness; *applied to persons or things.*

UNFRUS'TRABLE, *a.* That cannot be frustrated. *Edwards.*

UNFULFILL'ED, *a.* Not fulfilled; not accomplished; as a prophecy or prediction *unfulfilled.*

UNFU'MED, *a.* Not fumigated.

2. Not exhaling smoke; not burnt. *Milton.*

UNFUND'ED, *a.* Not funded; having no permanent funds for the payment of its interest; as an *unfunded* debt. *Hamilton.*

UNFURL', *v. t.* To loose and unfold; to expand; to open or spread; as, to *unfurl* sails.

UNFURL'ED, *pp.* Unfolded; expanded.

UNFURL'ING, *ppr.* Unfolding; spreading.

UNFUR'NISH, *v. t.* To strip of furniture; to divest; to strip.

2. To leave naked. *Shak.*

UNFUR'NISHED, *a.* Not furnished; not supplied with furniture; as an *unfurnished* room or house.

2. Unsupplied with necessaries or ornaments.

3. Empty; not supplied.

UNFU'SED, *a. s* as *z.* Not fused; not melted.

UNFU'SIBLE, *a. s* as *z.* Infusible. [*The latter word is generally used.*]

UNGA'INABLE, *a.* That cannot be gained. [*Little used.*] *Pierce.*

UNGA'INFUL, *a.* Unprofitable; not producing gain. *Hall.*

UNGA'INLY, *a.* [Sax. *ungægne.*] Not expert or dextrous; clumsy; awkward; uncouth; as an *ungainly* strut in walking. *Swift.*

[I believe *ungain* is not used.]

UNGALL'ED, *a.* Unhurt; not galled. *Shak.*

UNG'ARNISHED, *a.* Not garnished or furnished; unadorned.

UNGAR'RISONED, *a.* Not garrisoned; not furnished with troops for defense.

UNG'ARTERED, *a.* Being without garters. *Shak.*

UNGATH'ERED, *a.* Not gathered; not cropped; not picked. *Dryden.*

UNGE'AR, *v. t.* To unharness; to strip of gear.

UNGE'ARED, *pp.* Unharnessed.

UNGE'ARING, *ppr.* Stripping of harness or gear.

UNĠEN'ERATED, *a.* Having no beginning; unbegotten. *Raleigh.*

UNĠEN'ERATIVE, *a.* Begetting nothing. *Shak.*

UNĠEN'EROUS, *a.* Not of a noble mind; not liberal; *applied to persons;* as an *ungenerous* man or prince.

2. Not noble; not liberal; *applied to things;* as an *ungenerous* act. *Pope.*

3. Dishonorable; ignominious.

> The victor never will impose on Cato
> *Ungen'rous* terms. *Addison.*

UNĠEN'EROUSLY, *adv.* Unkindly; dishonorably.

UNĠE'NIAL, *a.* Not favorable to nature or to natural growth; as *ungenial* air; *ungenial* soils.

> Sullen seas that wash th' *ungenial* pole. *Thomson.*

UNĠENTEE'L, *a.* Not genteel; *used of persons;* not consistent with polite manners or good breeding; *used of manners.*

UNĠENTEE'LLY, *adv.* Uncivilly; not with good manners.

UNĠEN'TLE, *a.* Not gentle; harsh; rude. *Shak.*

UNĠEN'TLEMANLIKE, *a.* Not like a gentleman. *Chesterfield.*

UNĠEN'TLEMANLY, *a.* Not becoming a gentleman.

UNĠEN'TLENESS, *n.* Want of gentleness; harshness; severity; rudeness. *Tusser.*

2. Unkindness; incivility. *Shak.*

UNĠEN'TLY, *adv.* Harshly; with severity; rudely. *Shak.*

UNĠEOMET'RICAL, *a.* Not agreeable to the rules of geometry. *Cheyne.*

UNGIFT'ED, *a.* Not gifted; not endowed with peculiar faculties. *Arbuthnot.*

UNGILD'ED, } *a.* Not gilt; not overlaid
UNGILT', } with gold.

UNGIRD', *v. t.* [See *Gird.*] To loose from a girdle or band; to unbind. Gen. xxiv.

UNGIRD'ED, *pp.* Loosed from a girth or band.

UNGIRD'ING, *ppr.* Loosing from a girdle or band.

UNGIRT', *pp.* Unbound.

2. *a.* Loosely dressed. *Waller.*

UNGIV'ING, *a.* Not bringing gifts. *Dryden.*

UNGLA'ZED, *a.* Not furnished with glass; as, the windows are *unglazed;* the house is yet *unglazed.*

2. Wanting glass windows.

3. Not covered with vitreous matter; as *unglazed* potters' ware.

UNGLO'RIFIED, *a.* Not glorified; not honored with praise or adoration.

UNGLO'RIOUS, *a.* Not glorious; bringing no glory or honor. *J. Lathrop.*

UNGLŎVE, *v. t.* To take off the gloves. [*Not in use.*] *Beaum.*

UNGLŎVED, *a.* Having the hand naked. [*Little used.*] *Bacon.*

UNGLŪE, *v. t.* To separate any thing that is glued or cemented. *Swift.*

UNGLU'ED, *pp.* Loosed from glue or cement.

UNGLU'ING, *ppr.* Separating what is cemented.

UNGOD', *v. t.* To divest of divinity. *Dryden.*

UNGOD'LILY, *adv.* Impiously; wickedly. *Gov. of the Tongue.*

UNGOD'LINESS, *n.* Impiety; wickedness; disregard of God and his commands, and neglect of his worship; or any positive act of disobedience or irreverence.

> The wrath of God is revealed from heaven against all *ungodliness.* Rom. i.

UNGOD'LY, *a.* Wicked; impious; neglecting the fear and worship of God, or violating his commands. 1 Pet. iv.

2. Sinful; contrary to the divine commands; as *ungodly* deeds. Jude iv.

3. Polluted by wickedness; as an *ungodly* day. *Shak.*

UNGO'RED, *a.* Not gored; not wounded with a horn.

2. Not wounded.

UNGORĠ'ED, *a.* Not gorged; not filled; not sated. *Dryden.*

UNGOT', } *a.* Not gained.
UNGOT'TEN, }

2. Not begotten. *Shak.*

UNGŎVERNABLE, *a.* That cannot be governed; that cannot be ruled or restrained.

2. Licentious; wild; unbridled; as *ungovernable* passions. *Atterbury.*

UNGŎVERNABLY, *adv.* So as not to be governed or restrained. *Goldsmith.*

UNGŎVERNED, *a.* Not being governed.

2. Not subjected to laws or principles; not restrained or regulated; unbridled; licentious; as *ungoverned* appetite; *ungoverned* passions.

UNGOWN'ED, *a.* Not having or not wearing a gown. *Pollok.*

UNGRA'CEFUL, *a.* Not graceful; not marked with ease and dignity; wanting beauty and elegance; as *ungraceful* manners. Without politeness, learning is *ungraceful.* *Locke. Addison.*

UNGRA'CEFULLY, *adv.* Awkwardly; inelegantly.

UNGRA'CEFULNESS, *n.* Want of gracefulness; want of ease and dignity; want of elegance; awkwardness; as *ungracefulness* of manners.

UNGRA'CIOUS, *a.* Wicked; odious; hateful. *Shak. Dryden.*

2. Offensive; unpleasing; as *ungracious* manners.

3. Unacceptable; not well received; not favored.

> Any thing of grace towards the Irish rebels was as *ungracious* at Oxford as at London. *Clarendon.*

UNGRA'CIOUSLY, *adv.* With disfavor. The proposal was received *ungraciously.*

2. Not in a pleasing manner.

UNGRAMMAT'ICAL, *a.* Not according to the established and correct rules of grammar.

UNGRAMMAT'ICALLY, *adv.* In a manner contrary to the rules of grammar.

UNGR'ANTED, *a.* Not granted; not bestowed; not transferred by deed or gift; as *ungranted* lands. *U. States. Hamilton.*

2. Not granted; not yielded; not conceded in argument.

UNGRA'TE, *a.* Not agreeable; ungrateful. [*Not in use.*] *Taylor. Swift.*

UNGRA'TEFUL, *a.* Not grateful; not feeling thankful for favors.

2. Not making returns, or making ill returns for kindness. *South.*

3. Making no returns for culture; as an *ungrateful* soil.

4. Unpleasing; unacceptable. Harsh sounds are *ungrateful* to the ear.

UNGRA'TEFULLY, *adv.* With ingratitude. *Wake.*

2. Unpleasingly; unacceptably.

UNGRA'TEFULNESS, *n.* Ingratitude; want of due feelings of kindness for favors received; ill return for good.

2. Disagreeableness; unpleasing quality.

UNGRAT'IFIED, *a.* Not gratified; not compensated.

2. Not pleased.

3. Not indulged; as *ungratified* appetite.

UNGRA'VELY, *adv.* Without gravity or seriousness.

UNGROUND'ED, *a.* Having no foundation or support; as *ungrounded* hopes or confidence.

UNGROUND'EDLY, *adv.* Without ground or support; without reason. *Ray.*

UNGROUND'EDNESS, *n.* Want of foundation or support. *Steele.*

UNGRUDĠ'ING, *a.* Not grudging; freely giving.

UNGRUDG'INGLY, *adv.* Without ill will; heartily; cheerfully; as, to bestow charity *ungrudgingly.*

UNGU'ARDED, *a.* Not guarded; not watched.

2. Not defended; having no guard.

3. Careless; negligent; not attentive to danger; not cautious; as, to be *unguarded* in conversation.

4. Negligently said or done; not done or spoken with caution; as an *unguarded* expression or action.

UNGU'ARDEDLY, *adv.* Without watchful attention to danger; without caution; carelessly; as, to speak or promise *unguardedly.*

UN'GUENT, *n.* [L. *unguentum,* from *ungo,* to anoint.]

Ointment; a soft composition used as a topical remedy, as for sores, burns and the like. An unguent is stiffer than a liniment. but softer than a cerate. *Cyc.*

UNGUENT'OUS, *a.* Like unguent, or partaking of its qualities.

UNGUESS'ED, *a.* [See *Guess.*] Not obtained by guess or conjecture. *Spenser.*

UNGUEST'LIKE, *a.* [See *Guest.*] Not becoming a guest. *Milton.*

UNGUIC'ULAR, *a.* [L. *unguis,* the nail.] In *botany,* of the length of the human nails, or half an inch. *Lee. Martyn.*

UNGUIC'ULATE, UNGUIC'ULATED, *a.* [L. *unguis,* a claw.] Clawed; having claws. *Encyc.*

2. In *botany,* clawed; having a narrow base; as the petal in a polypetalous corol. *Martyn.*

UNGUI'DED, *a.* Not guided; not led or conducted.

2. Not regulated.

UNGUILTY, *a. ungilt'y.* Not guilty; not stained with crime; innocent. *Spenser.*

UN'GUINOUS, *a.* [L. *unguinosus.*] Oily; unctuous; consisting of fat or oil, or resembling it. *Forster, North. Voyages.*

UN'GULA, *n.* [L. a hoof.] In *geometry,* a section or part of a cylinder, cut off by a plane oblique to the base.

UN'GULATE, *a.* Shaped like a hoof.

UNHAB'ITABLE, *a.* [Fr. *inhabitable;* L. *inhabitabilis, inhabito.*]

That cannot be inhabited by human beings; uninhabitable. [*The latter word is generally used.*]

UNHABIT'UATED, *a.* Not habituated; not accustomed. *Tooke.*

UNHACK'ED, *a.* Not hacked; not cut, notched or mangled. *Shak.*

UNHACK'NEYED, *a.* Not hackneyed; not much used or practiced.

UNHA'LE, *a.* Unsound; not entire; not healthy.

UNHAL'LOW, *v. t.* To profane; to desecrate.

The vanity *unhallows* the virtue. *L'Estrange.*

UNHAL'LOWED, *pp.* Profaned; deprived of its sacred character.

2. *a.* Profane; unholy; impure; wicked. *Milton. Dryden.*

In the cause of truth, no *unhallowed* violence—is either necessary or admissible. *E. D. Griffin.*

UNHAND', *v. t.* To loose from the hand; to let go. *Shak.*

UNHAND'ILY, *adv.* Awkwardly; clumsily.

UNHAND'INESS, *n.* Want of dexterity; clumsiness.

UNHAND'LED, *a.* Not handled; not treated; not touched. *Shak.*

UNHAND'SÖME, *a.* Ungraceful; not beautiful.

I cannot admit that there is any thing *unhandsome* or irregular in the globe. *Woodward.*

2. Unfair; illiberal; disingenuous.

3. Uncivil; unpolite.

UNHAND'SÖMELY, *adv.* Inelegantly; ungracefully.

2. Illiberally; unfairly.

3. Uncivilly; unpolitely.

UNHAND'SÖMENESS, *n.* Want of beauty and elegance.

2. Unfairness; disingenuousness.

3. Incivility.

UNHAND'Y, *a.* Not dextrous; not skillful; not ready in the use of the hands; awkward; as a person *unhandy* at his work.

2. Not convenient; as an *unhandy* posture for writing.

UNHANG', *v. t.* To divest or strip of hangings, as a room.

2. To take from the hinges; as, to *unhang* a gate.

UNHANG'ED, UNHUNG', *a.* Not hung upon a gallows; not punished by hanging. *Shak.*

UNHAP', *n.* Ill luck; misfortune. [*Not in use.*] *Sidney.*

UNHAP'PIED, *a.* Made unhappy. [*Not in use.*] *Shak.*

UNHAP'PILY, *adv.* Unfortunately; miserably; calamitously. *Milton.*

UNHAP'PINESS, *n.* Misfortune; ill luck. *Burnet.*

2. Infelicity; misery.

It is our great *unhappiness,* when any calamities fall upon us, that we are uneasy and dissatisfied. *Wake.*

[But it usually expresses less than *misery* or *wretchedness.*]

3. Mischievous prank. [*Not in use.*] *Shak.*

UNHAP'PY, *a.* Unfortunate; unlucky. He has been *unhappy* in his choice of a partner. Affairs have taken an *unhappy* turn.

2. Not happy; in a degree miserable or wretched. She is *unhappy* in her marriage. Children sometimes render their parents *unhappy.*

3. Evil; calamitous; marked by infelicity; as an *unhappy* day.

This *unhappy* morn. *Milton.*

4. Mischievous; irregular. *Shak.*

UNHAR'ASSED, *a.* Not harassed; not vexed or troubled. *Trumbull.*

UNH'ARBOR, *v. t.* To drive from harbor or shelter.

UNH'ARBORED, *a.* Not sheltered, or affording no shelter. *Milton.*

UNH'ARDENED, *a.* Not hardened; not indurated; as metal.

2. Not hardened; not made obdurate; as the heart. *Shak.*

UNH'ARDY, *a.* Not hardy; feeble; not able to endure fatigue.

2. Not having fortitude; not bold; timorous. *Milton.*

UNH'ARMED, *a.* Unhurt; uninjured; unimpaired. *Locke.*

UNH'ARMFUL, *a.* Not doing harm; harmless; innoxious.

Themselves *unharmful,* let them live unharm'd. *Dryden.*

UNHARMO'NIOUS, *a.* Not having symmetry or congruity; disproportionate. *Milton.*

2. Discordant; unmusical; jarring; as sounds. *Swift.*

UNHARMO'NIOUSLY, *adv.* With jarring; discordantly.

UNH'ARNESS, *v. t.* To strip of harness; to loose from harness or gear.

2. To disarm; to divest of armor.

UNHATCH'ED, *a.* Not hatched; not having left the egg.

2. Not matured and brought to light; not disclosed.

UNHAZ'ARDED, *a.* Not hazarded; not put in danger; not exposed to loss; not adventured. *Milton.*

UNHEAD, *v. t. unhed'.* To take out the head of; as, to *unhead* a cask.

UNHEADED, *pp. unhed'ed.* Having the head taken out.

UNHEADING, *ppr. unhed'ing.* Taking out the head of.

UNHEALTHFUL, *a. unhelth'ful.* Not healthful; injurious to health; insalubrious; unwholesome; noxious; as an *unhealthful* climate or air.

2. Abounding with sickness or disease; sickly; as an *unhealthful* season.

UNHEALTHFULNESS, *n. unhelth'fulness.*

1. Unwholesomeness; insalubriousness; noxiousness to health.

2. The state of being sickly; as the *unhealthfulness* of the autumn.

UNHEALTHILY, *adv. unhelth'ily.* In an unwholesome or unsound manner. *Milton.*

UNHEALTHINESS, *n. unhelth'iness.* Want of health; habitual weakness or indisposition; *applied to persons.*

2. Unsoundness; want of vigor; as the *unhealthiness* of trees or other plants.

3. Unfavorableness to health; as the *unhealthiness* of a climate.

UNHEALTHY, *a. unhelth'y.* Wanting health; wanting a sound and vigorous state of body; habitually weak or indisposed; as an *unhealthy* person.

2. Unsound; wanting vigor of growth; as an *unhealthy* plant.

3. Sickly; abounding with disease; as an *unhealthy* season or city.

4. Insalubrious; unwholesome; adapted to generate diseases; as an *unhealthy* climate or country.

5. Morbid; not indicating health.

UNHE'ARD, *a.* Not heard; not perceived by the ear. *Milton.*

2. Not admitted to audience.

What pangs I feel, unpitied and *unheard!* *Dryden.*

3. Not known in fame; not celebrated.

Nor was his name *unheard.* *Milton.*

4. Unheard of; obscure; not known by fame. *Granville.*

Unheard of, new; unprecedented. *Swift.*

UNHE'ART, *v. t.* To discourage; to depress; to dishearten. [*Not in use.*] *Shak.*

UNHE'ATED, *a.* Not heated; not made hot. *Boyle.*

UNHEDǴED, *a.* Not hedged; not surrounded by a hedge.

UNHEE'DED, *a.* Not heeded; disregarded; neglected.

The world's great victor passed *unheeded* by. *Pope.*

UNHEE'DFUL, *a.* Not cautious; inattentive; careless. *Beaum.*

UNHEE'DING, *a.* Not heeding; careless; negligent. *Dryden.*

UNHEE'DY, *a.* Precipitate; sudden. *Spenser.*

UNHE'LE, *v. t.* To uncover. [*Not in use.*] *Spenser.*

UNHELM'ED, *a.* Having no helm. *Pollok.*

UNHELP'ED, *a.* Unassisted; having no aid or auxiliary; unsupported. *Dryden.*

UNHELP'FUL, *a.* Affording no aid. *Shak.*

UNHES'ITATING, *a.* Not hesitating; not remaining in doubt; prompt; ready. *Eclec. Review.*

UNHES'ITATINGLY, *adv.* Without hesitation or doubt.

UNHEWN', *a.* Not hewn; rough. *Dryden.*

UNHI'DEBOUND, *a.* Lax of maw; capacious. [*Not used.*] *Milton.*

UNHIN'DERED, *a.* Not hindered; not opposed; exerting itself freely. *S. Clarke.*

UNHINǴE, *v. t. unhinj'.* To take from the hinges; as, to *unhinge* a door.

2. To displace; to unfix by violence. *Blackmore.*

3. To unfix; to loosen; to render unstable or wavering; as, to *unhinge* the mind; to *unhinge* opinions.

UNHOARD, *v. t.* To steal from a hoard; to scatter.

UNHO'LINESS, *n.* Want of holiness; an unsanctified state of the heart.

2. Impiety; wickedness; profaneness. *Raleigh.*

UNHO'LY, *a.* Not holy; not renewed and sanctified. 2 Tim. iii.

2. Profane; not hallowed; not consecrated; common. Heb. x.

3. Impious; wicked.

4. Not ceremonially purified. Lev. x.

UNHON'EST, *a.* [See *Honest.*] Dishonest; dishonorable. *Obs.* *Ascham.*

UNHON'ORED, *a.* [See *Honor.*] Not honored; not regarded with veneration; not celebrated. *Dryden.*

UNHOOK', *v. t.* To loose from a hook.

UNHOOP', *v. t.* To strip of hoops. *Addison.*

UNHO'PED, *a.* Not hoped for; not so probable as to excite hope.

With *unhop'd* success. *Dryden.*

Unhoped for, unhoped, as above.

UNHO'PEFUL, *a.* Such as leaves no room to hope. *Boyle.*

UNHORN'ED, *a.* Having no horns. *Tooke.*

UNHORSE, *v. t. unhors'.* To throw from a horse; to cause to dismount. *Shak.*

UNHORS'ED, *pp.* Thrown from a horse. *Dryden.*

UNHORS'ING, *ppr.* Throwing from a horse; dismounting.

UNHOS'PITABLE, *a.* Not kind to strangers. [But *inhospitable* is the word now used.]

UNHOS'TILE, *a.* Not belonging to a public enemy. *Philips.*

UNHOUSE, *v. t. unhouz'.* To drive from the house or habitation; to dislodge. *Milton.*

2. To deprive of shelter.

UNHOUS'ED, *pp.* Driven from a house or habitation. *Shak.*

2. *a.* Wanting a house; homeless. *Shak.*

3. Having no settled habitation. *Shak.*

4. Destitute of shelter or cover. Cattle in severe weather should not be left *unhoused.*

UNHOUS'ELED, *a.* *s* as *z.* Not having received the sacrament. *Shak.*

UNHU'MAN, *a.* Inhuman. [But *inhuman* is the word used.]

UNHU'MANIZE, *v. t.* To render inhuman or barbarous. *J. Barlow.*

UNHUM'BLED, *a.* Not humbled; not affected with shame or confusion; not contrite in spirit. *Milton.*

2. In *theology*, not having the will and the natural enmity of the heart to God and his law, subdued.

UNHURT', *a.* Not hurt; not harmed; free from wound or injury. *Dryden.*

UNHURT'FUL, *a.* Not hurtful; harmless; innoxious. *Shak.*

UNHURT'FULLY, *adv.* Without harm; harmlessly. *Pope.*

UNHUS'BANDED, *a.* *s* as *z.* Deprived of support; neglected. *Browne.*

2. Not managed with frugality.

UNHUSK'ED, *a.* Not being stripped of husks.

UNICAP'SULAR, *a.* [L. *unus*, one, and *capsula*, chest.]

Having one capsule to each flower, as a pericarp. *Martyn.*

U'NICORN, *n.* [L. *unicornis; unus*, one, and *cornu*, horn.]

1. An animal with one horn; the monoceros. This name is often applied to the rhinoceros.

2. The *sea unicorn* is a fish of the whale kind, called narwal, remarkable for a horn growing out at his nose. *Cyc.*

3. A fowl. *Grew.*

Fossil unicorn, or *fossil unicorn's horn*, a substance used in medicine, a terrene crustaceous spar. *Cyc.*

UNICORN'OUS, *a.* Having only one horn. *Brown.*

UNIDE'AL, *a.* Not ideal; real. *Johnson.*

UNIF'LOROUS, *a.* [L. *unus*, one, and *flos*, flower.]

Bearing one flower only; as a *uniflorous* peduncle. *Martyn.*

U'NIFORM, *a.* [L. *uniformis; unus*, one, and *forma*, form.]

1. Having always the same form or manner; not variable. Thus we say, the dress of the Asiatics is *uniform*, or has been *uniform* from early ages. So we say, it is the duty of a christian to observe a *uniform* course of piety and religion.

2. Consistent with itself; not different; as, one's opinions on a particular subject have been *uniform.*

3. Of the same form with others; consonant; agreeing with each other; conforming to one rule or mode.

How far churches are bound to be *uniform* in their ceremonies, is doubted. *Hooker.*

4. Having the same degree or state; as *uniform* temperature.

Uniform motion. The motion of a body is *uniform*, when it passes over equal spaces in equal times. *D. Olmsted.*

Uniform matter, is that which is all of the same kind and texture. *Cyc.*

U'NIFORM, *n.* The particular dress of soldiers, by which one regiment or company is distinguished from another, or a soldier from another person. We say, the *uniform* of a company of militia, the *uniform* of the artillery or matross companies, the *uniform* of a regiment, &c. This dress is called a *uniform*, because it is alike among all the soldiers.

UNIFORM'ITY, *n.* Resemblance to itself at all times; even tenor; as the *uniformity* of design in a poem.

2. Consistency; sameness; as the *uniformity* of a man's opinions.

3. Conformity to a pattern or rule; resemblance, consonance or agreement; as the *uniformity* of different churches in ceremonies or rites.

4. Similitude between the parts of a whole; as the *uniformity* of sides in a regular figure. Beauty is said to consist in *uniformity* with variety. *Cyc.*

5. Continued or unvaried sameness or likeness.

Uniformity must tire at last, though it is a *uniformity* of excellence. *Johnson.*

Act of uniformity, in England, the act of parliament by which the form of public prayers, administration of sacraments and other rites, is prescribed to be observed in all the churches. 1 Eliz. and 13 and 14 Car. 11.

U'NIFORMLY, *adv.* With even tenor; without variation; as a temper *uniformly* mild.

2. Without diversity of one from another.

UNIǴEN'ITURE, *n.* [L. *unigenitus; unus* and *genitus.*]

The state of being the only begotten.

UNIǴ'ENOUS, *a.* [L. *unigena.*] Of one kind; of the same genus. *Kirwan.*

UNILA'BIATE, *a.* In *botany*, having one lip only, as a corol. *Martyn.* *Asiat. Res.*

UNILAT'ERAL, *a.* [L. *unus*, one, and *latus*, side.]

1. Being on one side or party only. [*Unusual.*]

2. Having one side.

A *unilateral raceme*, is when the flowers grow only on one side of the common peduncle. *Martyn.*

UNILIT'ERAL, *a.* [L. *unus*, one, and *litera*, letter.] Consisting of one letter only.

UNILLU'MINATED, *a.* Not illuminated; not enlightened; dark.

2. Ignorant.

UNILLUS'TRATED, *a.* Not illustrated; not made plain. *Good.*

UNILOC'ULAR, *a.* [L. *unus*, one, and *loculus*, cell.]

Having one cell only; as a *unilocular* pericarp.

UNIMAǴ'INABLE, *a.* Not to be imagined; not to be conceived. *Tillotson.*

UNIMAǴ'INABLY, *adv.* To a degree not to be imagined. *Boyle.*

UNIMAǴ'INED, *a.* Not imagined; not conceived.

UNIMBU'ED, *a.* Not imbued; not tinctured. *Drake.*

UNIM'ITABLE, *a.* That cannot be imitated. [But the word now used is *inimitable.*]

UNIM'ITATED, *a.* Not imitated. *Johnson.*

UNIMMOR'TAL, *a.* Not immortal; perishable. *Milton.*

UNIMPA'IRABLE, *a.* Not liable to waste or diminution. *Hakewill.*

UNIMPA'IRED, *a.* Not impaired; not diminished; not enfeebled by time or injury; as an *unimpaired* constitution.

UNIMPAS'SIONED, *a.* Not endowed with passions. *Thomson.*

2. Free from passion; calm; not violent; as an *unimpassioned* address.

UNIMPE'ACHABLE, *a.* That cannot be impeached; that cannot be accused; free from stain, guilt or fault; as an *unimpeachable* reputation.

2. That cannot be called in question; as an *unimpeachable* claim or testimony.

UNIMPE'ACHED, *a.* Not impeached; not charged or accused; fair; as an *unimpeached* character.

2. Not called in question; as testimony *unimpeached.*

UNIMPE'DED, *a.* Not impeded; not hindered. *Rawle.*

UNIM'PLICATED, *a.* Not implicated; not involved. *Mitford.*

UNIMPLI'ED, *a.* Not implied; not included by fair inference. *Madison.*

UNIMPLO'RED, *a.* Not implored; not solicited. *Milton.*

UNIMPORT'ANT, *a.* Not important; not of great moment.

2. Not assuming airs of dignity. *Pope.*

UNIMPORTU'NED, *a.* Not importuned; not solicited.

UNIMPO'SING, *a.* *s* as *z.* Not imposing; not commanding respect.

2. Not enjoining as obligatory; voluntary. *Thomson.*

UNIMPREG'NATED, *a.* Not impregnated.

UNIMPRESS'IVE, *a.* Not impressive; not forcible; not adapted to affect or awaken the passions. *Beddoes.*

UNIMPRÖVABLE, *a.* Not capable of improvement, melioration or advancement to a better condition. *Rambler.*

2. Incapable of being cultivated or tilled. *Wolcott.*

UNIMPRÖVABLENESS, *n.* The quality of being not improvable. *Hammond.*

UNIMPRÖVED, *a.* Not improved; not made better or wiser; not advanced in knowledge, manners or excellence. *Rawle. Pope. Glanville.*

2. Not used for a valuable purpose. How many advantages *unimproved* have we to regret!

3. Not used; not employed. *Hamilton. Ramsay.*

4. Not tilled; not cultivated; as *unimproved* land or soil; *unimproved* lots of ground. *Laws of Penn. Franklin. Ramsay.*

5. Uncensured; not disapproved. [This sense, from the L. *improbo*, is entirely obsolete.]

UNIMPRÖVING, *a.* Not improving; not tending to advance or instruct. *Johnson.*

UNIMPU'TABLE, *a.* Not imputable or chargeable to.

UNINCH'ANTED, *a.* Not enchanted; not affected by magic or enchantment; not haunted. [Usually *unenchanted.*]

UNINCRE'ASABLE, *a.* Admitting no increase. [*Not in use.*] *Boyle.*

UNINCUM'BERED, *a.* Not incumbered; not burdened.

2. Free from any temporary estate or interest, or from mortgage, or other charge or debt; as an estate *unincumbered* with dower.

UNINDEBT'ED, *a.* Not indebted.

2. Not borrowed. [*Unusual.*] *Young.*

UNINDIF'FERENT, *a.* Not indifferent; not unbiased; partial; leaning to one party. *Hooker.*

UNINDORS'ED, *a.* Not indorsed; not assigned; as an *unindorsed* note or bill.

UNINDUS'TRIOUS, *a.* Not industrious; not diligent in labor, study or other pursuit. *Decay of Piety.*

UNINFECT'ED, *a.* Not infected; not contaminated or affected by foul infectious air.

2. Not corrupted.

UNINFEC'TIOUS, *a.* Not infectious; not foul; not capable of communicating disease.

UNINFLA'MED, *a.* Not inflamed; not set on fire. *Bacon.*

2. Not highly provoked.

UNINFLAM'MABLE, *a.* Not inflammable; not capable of being set on fire. *Boyle.*

UNIN'FLUENCED, *a.* Not influenced; not persuaded or moved by others, or by foreign considerations; not biased; acting freely.

2. Not proceeding from influence, bias or prejudice; as *uninfluenced* conduct or actions.

UNINFORM'ED, *a.* Not informed; not instructed; untaught. *Milton.*

2. Unanimated; not enlivened. *Spectator.*

UNINFORM'ING, *a.* Not furnishing information; uninstructive. *Mitford.*

UNINGE'NIOUS, *a.* Not ingenious; dull. *Burke.*

UNINGEN'UOUS, *a.* Not ingenuous; not frank or candid; disingenuous. *Decay of Piety.*

UNINHAB'ITABLE, *a.* Not inhabitable; that in which men cannot live; unfit to be the residence of men. *Raleigh.*

UNINHAB'ITABLENESS, *n.* The state of being uninhabitable.

UNINHAB'ITED, *a.* Not inhabited by men; having no inhabitants. *Swift.*

UNINI''TIATED, *a.* Not initiated.

UNIN'JURED, *a.* Not injured; not hurt; suffering no harm. *Milton.*

UNINQUIS'ITIVE, *a.* *s* as *z.* Not inquisitive; not curious to search and inquire. *Warton.*

UNINSCRI'BED, *a.* Not inscribed; having no inscription. *Pope.*

UNINSPI'RED, *a.* Not having received any supernatural instruction or illumination. *Locke.*

UNINSTRUCT'ED, *a.* Not instructed or taught; not educated.

2. Not directed by superior authority; not furnished with instructions.

UNINSTRUCT'IVE, *a.* Not instructive; not conferring improvement. *Addison.*

UNIN'SULATED, *a.* Not insulated; not being separated or detached from every thing else. *Ure.*

UNINSU'RED, *a.* [See *Sure.*] Not insured; not assured against loss.

UNINTEL'LIGENT, *a.* Not having reason or consciousness; not possessing understanding. *Bentley.*

2. Not knowing; not skillful; dull. *Locke.*

UNINTELLIGIBIL'ITY, *n.* The quality of being not intelligible. *Burnet.*

UNINTEL'LIGIBLE, *a.* Not intelligible; that cannot be understood. *Swift.*

UNINTEL'LIGIBLY, *adv.* In a manner not to be understood.

UNINTEND'ED, *a.* Not intended; not designed. *Locke.*

UNINTEN'TIONAL, *a.* Not intentional; not designed; done or happening without design. *Boyle.*

UNINTEN'TIONALLY, *adv.* Without design or purpose.

UNIN'TERESTED, *a.* Not interested; not having any interest or property in; having nothing at stake; as, to be *uninterested* in any business or calamity.

2. Not having the mind or the passions engaged; as, to be *uninterested* in a discourse or narration.

UNIN'TERESTING, *a.* Not capable of exciting an interest, or of engaging the mind or passions; as an *uninteresting* story or poem.

UNINTERMIS'SION, *n.* Defect or failure of intermission. *Parker.*

UNINTERMIT'TED, *a.* Not intermitted; not interrupted; not suspended for a time; continued. *Hale.*

UNINTERMIT'TING, *a.* Not intermitting; not ceasing for a time; continuing.

UNINTERMIT'TINGLY, *adv.* Without cessation; continually. *Mitford.*

UNINTERMIX'ED, *a.* Not intermixed; not mingled.

UNIN'TERPOLATED, *a.* Not interpolated; not inserted at a time subsequent to the original writing.

UNINTERRUPT'ED, *a.* Not interrupted; not broken. *Addison.*

2. Not disturbed by intrusion or avocation.

UNINTERRUPT'EDLY, *adv.* Without interruption; without disturbance.

UNINTRENCH'ED, *a.* Not intrenched; not defended by intrenchments. *Pope.*

UNIN'TRICATED, *a.* Not perplexed; not obscure or intricate. [*Not in use.*] *Hammond.*

UNINTRODU'CED, *a.* Not introduced; not properly conducted; obtrusive. *Young.*

UNINU'RED, *a.* Not inured; not hardened by use or practice. *Philips.*

UNINVENT'ED, *a.* Not invented; not found out. *Milton.*

UNINVEST'ED, *a.* Not invested; not clothed. *Dwight.*

2. Not converted into some species of property less fleeting than money; as money *uninvested.* *Hamilton.*

UNINVES'TIGABLE, *a.* That cannot be investigated or searched out. *Ray.*

UNINVID'IOUS, *a.* Not invidious.

UNINVI'TED, *a.* Not invited; not requested; not solicited. *Philips.*

U'NION, *n.* [Fr. *union;* It. *unione;* L. *unio,* to unite, from *unus,* one.]
1. The act of joining two or more things into one, and thus forming a compound body or a mixture; or the junction or coalition of things thus united. *Union* differs from *connection,* as it implies the bodies to be in contact, without an intervening body; whereas things may be *connected* by the intervention of a third body, as by a cord or chain.

One kingdom, joy and *union* without end. *Milton.*

2. Concord; agreement and conjunction of mind, will, affections or interest. Happy is the family where perfect *union* subsists between all its members.
3. The junction or united existence of spirit and matter; as the *union* of soul and body.
4. Among *painters,* a symmetry and agreement between the several parts of a painting. *Cyc.*
5. In *architecture,* harmony between the colors in the materials of a building. *Cyc.*
6. In *ecclesiastical affairs,* the combining or consolidating of two or more churches into one. This cannot be done without the consent of the bishop, the patron, and the incumbent. Union is by *accession,* when the united benefice becomes an accessory of the principal; by *confusion,* where the two titles are suppressed, and a new one created, including both; and by *equality,* where the two titles subsist, but are equal and independent. *Cyc.*
7. States united. Thus the United States of America are sometimes called *the Union.* *Marshall. Hamilton.*
8. A pearl. [L. *unio.*] [*Not in use.*]

Union, or *Act of union,* the act by which Scotland was united to England, or by which the two kingdoms were incorporated into one, in 1707.

Legislative union, the union of Great Britain and Ireland, in 1800.

Union by the first intention, in *surgery,* the process by which the opposite surfaces of recent wounds grow together and unite without suppuration, when they are kept in contact with each other; the result of a wonderful self-healing power in living bodies. *Cyc.*

UNIP'AROUS, *a.* [L. *unus,* one, and *pario,* to bear.] Producing one at a birth. *Brown.*

UNIRA'DIATED, *a.* Having one ray. *Encyc.*

UNIR'RITATED, *a.* Not irritated; not fretted.
2. Not provoked or angered.

UNIR'RITATING, *a.* Not irritating or fretting.
2. Not provoking.
3. Not exciting. *Beddoes.*

U'NISON, *n.* [L. *unus,* one, and *sonus,* sound.]
1. In *music,* an accordance or coincidence of sounds, proceeding from an equality in the number of vibrations made in a given time by a sonorous body. If two chords of the same matter have equal length, thickness and tension, they are said to be in *unison,* and their sounds will be in *unison.* Sounds of very different qualities and force may be in unison; as the sound of a bell may be in unison with a sound of a flute. Unison then consists in sameness of degree, or similarity in respect to gravity or acuteness, and is applicable to any sound, whether of instruments or of the human organs, &c.
2. A single unvaried note. *Pope.*

In unison, in agreement; in harmony.

U'NISON, *a.* Sounding alone.

Sounds intermix'd with voice,
Choral or *unison.*

UNIS'ONANCE, *n.* Accordance of sounds.

What constitutes *unisonance* is the equality of the number of vibrations of two sonorous bodies, in equal times. *Cyc.*

UNIS'ONANT, *a.* Being in unison; having the same degree of gravity or acuteness.

UNIS'ONOUS, *a.* Being in unison. *Busby.*

U'NIT, *n.* [L. *unus,* one; *unitas,* unity.]
1. One; a word which denotes a single thing or person; the least whole number.

Units are the integral parts of any large number. *Watts.*

2. In *mathematics,* any known determinate quantity, by the constant repetition of which, any other quantity of the same kind is measured. [See *Unity.*] *D. Olmsted.*

UNITA'RIAN, *n.* [L. *unitus, unus.*] One who denies the doctrine of the trinity, and ascribes divinity to God the Father only. The Arian and Socinian are both comprehended in the term *Unitarian.*

UNITA'RIAN, *a.* Pertaining to Unitarians, or to the doctrine of the unity of the Godhead.

UNITA'RIANISM, *n.* The doctrines of Unitarians, who contend for the unity of the Godhead, in opposition to the Trinitarians, and who of course deny the divinity of Christ.

UNI'TE, *v. t.* [L. *unio, unitus;* Fr. Sp. *unir;* It. *unire.*]
1. To put together or join two or more things, which make one compound or mixture. Thus we *unite* the parts of a building to make one structure. The kingdoms of England, Scotland and Ireland *united,* form one empire. So we *unite* spirit and water and other liquors. We *unite* strands to make a rope. The states of North America *united,* form one nation.
2. To join; to connect in a near relation or alliance; as, to *unite* families by marriage; to *unite* nations by treaty.
3. To make to agree or be uniform; as, to *unite* a kingdom in one form of worship; to *unite* men in opinions. *Clarendon.*
4. To cause to adhere; as, to *unite* bricks or stones by cement.
5. To join in interest or fellowship. Gen. xlix.
6. To tie; to splice; as, to *unite* two cords or ropes.
7. To join in affection; to make near; as, to *unite* hearts in love.

To unite the heart, to cause all its powers and affections to join with order and delight in the same objects. Ps. lxxxvi.

UNI'TE, *v. i.* To join in an act; to concur; to act in concert. All parties *united* in petitioning for a repeal of the law.
2. To coalesce; to be cemented or consolidated; to combine; as, bodies *unite* by attraction or affinity.
3. To grow together, as the parts of a wound.

The spur of a young cock grafted into the comb, will *unite* and grow. *Duhamel.*

4. To coalesce, as sounds.
5. To be mixed. Oil and water will not *unite.*

UNI'TED, *pp.* Joined; made to agree; cemented; mixed; attached by growth.

United flowers, are such as have the stamens and pistils in the same flower. *Cyc.*

UNI'TER, *n.* The person or thing that unites.

UNI'TING, *ppr.* Joining; causing to agree; consolidating; coalescing; growing together.

UNI''TION, *n.* Junction; act of uniting. [*Not in use.*] *Wiseman.*

U'NITIVE, *a.* Having the power of uniting. [*Not used.*] *Norris.*

U'NITY, *n.* [L. *unitas.*] The state of being one; oneness. *Unity* may consist of a simple substance or existing being, as the soul; but usually it consists in a close junction of particles or parts, constituting a body detached from other bodies. Unity is a thing undivided itself, but separate from every other thing. *School Philosophy.*
2. Concord; conjunction; as a *unity* of proofs. *Shak.*
3. Agreement; uniformity; as *unity* of doctrine; *unity* of worship in a church. *Hooker.*
4. In *christian theology,* oneness of sentiment, affection or behavior.

How good and how pleasant it is for brethren to dwell together in *unity!* Ps. cxxxiii.

5. In *mathematics,* the abstract expression for any unit whatsoever. The number 1 is *unity,* when it is not applied to any particular object; but a *unit,* when it is so applied. *D. Olmsted.*
6. In *poetry,* the principle by which a uniform tenor of story and propriety of representation is preserved. In the drama, there are three unities; the unity of *action,* that of *time,* and that of *place.* In the epic poem, the great and almost only *unity* is that of action.
7. In *music,* such a combination of parts as to constitute a whole; or a kind of symmetry of style and character. *Rousseau.*
8. In *law,* the properties of a joint estate are derived from its *unity,* which is fourfold; unity of *interest,* unity of *title,* unity of *time,* and unity of *possession;* in other words, joint-tenants have one and the same interest, accruing by one and the same conveyance, commencing at the same time, and held by one and the same undivided possession. *Blackstone.*
9. In *law,* unity of possession, is a joint possession of two rights by several titles, as when a man has a lease of land upon a certain rent, and afterwards buys the fee simple. This is a *unity* of possession, by which the lease is extinguished.

Unity of faith, is an equal belief of the same truths of God, and possession of the grace of faith in like form and degree. *Brown.*

Unity of spirit, is the oneness which subsists between Christ and his saints, by which the same spirit dwells in both, and both have the same disposition and aims; and it is the oneness of christians among themselves, united under the same head, having the same spirit dwelling in them, and possessing the same graces, faith, love, hope, &c. *Brown.*

U'NIVALVE, *a.* [L. *unus*, one, and *valvæ.*] Having one valve only, as a shell or pericarp.

U'NIVALVE, *n.* A shell having one valve only. The *univalves* form one of the three divisions into which shells are usually divided. *Linne.*

UNIVALV'ULAR, *a.* Having one valve only; as a *univalvular* pericarp or shell. *Martyn. Cyc.*

UNIVERS'AL, *a.* [L. *universalis*; *unus* and *versor.*]

1. All; extending to or comprehending the whole number, quantity or space; as *universal* ruin; *universal* good; *universal* benevolence.

The *universal* cause
Acts not by partial, but by general laws. *Pope.*

2. Total; whole.

From harmony, from heav'nly harmony,
This *universal* frame began. *Dryden.*

3. Comprising all the particulars; as *universal* kinds. *Davies.*

4. In *botany*, a *universal umbel*, is a primary or general umbel; the first or largest set of rays in a compound umbel; opposed to *partial*. A *universal involucre* is placed at the foot of a universal umbel. *Martyn.*

Universal instrument, is one which measures all kinds of distances, lengths, &c.; as the pantometer or holometer. *Cyc.*

Universal dial, is a dial by which the hour may be found by the sun in any part of the world, or under any elevation of the pole.

Universal proposition. [See the Noun.] *Cyc.*

UNIVERS'AL, *n.* [See the Adjective.] In *logic*, a universal is *complex* or *incomplex*. A *complex universal*, is either a universal proposition, as "every whole is greater than its parts," or whatever raises a manifold conception in the mind, as the definition of a reasonable animal.

An *incomplex universal*, is what produces one conception only in the mind, and is a simple thing respecting many; as human nature, which relates to every individual in which it is found. *Cyc.*

2. The whole; the general system of the universe. [*Not in use.*]

UNIVERS'ALISM, *n.* In *theology*, the doctrine or belief that all men will be saved or made happy in a future life.

UNIVERS'ALIST, *n.* One who holds the doctrine that all men will be saved.

UNIVERSAL'ITY, *n.* The state of extending to the whole; as the *universality* of a proposition; the *universality* of sin: the *universality* of the deluge. *Woodward.*

UNIVERS'ALLY, *adv.* With extension to the whole; in a manner to comprehend all; without exception. Air is a fluid *universally* diffused. God's laws are *universally* binding on his creatures.

[NOTE.—*Universal* and its derivatives are used in common discourse for *general*. This kind of universality is by the schoolmen called *moral*, as admitting of some exceptions, in distinction from *metaphysical*, which precludes all exceptions.]

UNIVERS'ALNESS, *n.* Universality.

U'NIVERSE, *n.* [Fr. *univers*; L. *universitas.*] The collective name of heaven and earth, and all that belongs to them; the whole system of created things; the το παν of the Greeks, and the *mundus* of the Latins.

UNIVERS'ITY, *n.* An assemblage of colleges established in any place, with professors for instructing students in the sciences and other branches of learning, and where degrees are conferred. A university is properly a universal school, in which are taught all branches of learning, or the four faculties of theology, medicine, law, and the sciences and arts. *Cyc.*

UNIV'OCAL, *a.* [L. *unus*, one, and *vox*, word.]

1. Having one meaning only. A *univocal* word is opposed to an *equivocal*, which has two or more significations. *Watts.*

2. Having unison of sounds; as the octave in music and its replicates. *Rousseau.*

3. Certain; regular; pursuing always one tenor. [*Little used.*] *Brown.*

UNIV'OCALLY, *adv.* In one term; in one sense.

How is sin *univocally* distinguished into venial and mortal, if the venial be not sin? *Hale.*

2. In one tenor. [*Little used.*] *Ray.*

UNIVOCA'TION, *n.* Agreement of name and meaning. *Cyc.*

U'NIVOQUE, U'NIVOKE, } *a.* In *music*, univocal concords are the octave and its recurrences, above or below. *Cyc.*

UNJOINT', *v. t.* To disjoint. *Fuller.*

UNJOINT'ED, *a.* Disjointed; separated. *Milton.*

2. Having no joint or articulation; as an *unjointed* stem. *Botany.*

UNJOY'OUS, *a.* Not joyous; not gay or cheerful. *Thomson.*

UNJUDG'ED, *a.* Not judged; not judicially determined. *Prior.*

UNJUST', *a.* Not just; acting contrary to the standard of right established by the divine law; not equitable; as an *unjust* man.

2. Contrary to justice and right; wrongful; as an *unjust* sentence; an *unjust* demand; an *unjust* accusation.

UNJUST'IFIABLE, *a.* Not justifiable; that cannot be proved to be right; not to be vindicated or defended; as an *unjustifiable* motive or action. *Atterbury.*

UNJUST'IFIABLENESS, *n.* The quality of not being justifiable. *Clarendon.*

UNJUST'IFIABLY, *adv.* In a manner that cannot be justified or vindicated.

UNJUST'IFIED, *a.* Not justified or vindicated.

2. Not pardoned. *J. M. Mason.*

UNJUST'LY, *adv.* In an unjust manner; wrongfully.

UNKED, UNKID, } for *uncouth*, odd; strange. [*Not in use.*]

UNKEM'MED, UNKEMPT', } *a.* Uncombed; unpolished. *Spenser.*
[*Obsolete, except in poetry.*]

UNKEN'NEL, *v. t.* To drive from his hole; as, to *unkennel* a fox. *Shak.*

2. To rouse from secrecy or retreat. *Shak.*

3. To release from a kennel.

UNKEN'NELED, *pp.* Driven or let loose from confinement, as a fox or dog.

UNKENT', *a.* [*un* and *ken*, to know.] Unknown. *Obs.* *Spenser.*

UNKEPT', *a.* Not kept; not retained; not preserved.

2. Not observed; not obeyed; as a command. *Hooker.*

UNKERN'ELED, *a.* Destitute of a kernel. *Pollok.*

UNKIND, *a.* Not kind; not benevolent; not favorable; not obliging. *Shak.*

2. Unnatural. *Spenser.*

UNKINDLY, *a.* Unnatural; contrary to nature; as an *unkindly* crime. *Spenser.*

2. Unfavorable; malignant; as an *unkindly* fog. *Milton.*

UNKINDLY, *adv.* Without kindness; without affection; as, to treat one *unkindly.*

2. In a manner contrary to nature; unnaturally.

All works of nature,
Abortive, monstrous, or *unkindly* mix'd. *Milton.*

UNKINDNESS, *n.* Want of kindness; want of natural affection; want of good will.

2. Disobliging treatment; disfavor.

UNKING', *v. t.* To deprive of royalty. *Shak.*

UNKING'LIKE, UNKING'LY, } *a.* Unbecoming a king; not noble. *Milner. Shak.*

UNKISS'ED, *a.* Not kissed. *Shak.*

UNKLE. [See *Uncle.*]

UNKNIGHTLY, *a.* Unbecoming a knight. *Sidney.*

UNKNIT', *v. t.* To separate threads that are knit; to open; to loose work that is knit or knotted. *Shak.*

2. To open. *Shak.*

UNKNOT', *v. t.* To free from knots; to untie.

UNKNOW, *v. t.* To cease to know. [*Not in use.*]

UNKNOWABLE, *a.* That cannot be known. *Watts.*

UNKNOWING, *a.* Not knowing; ignorant; with *of.*

Unknowing of deceit. *Pope.*

UNKNOWINGLY, *adv.* Ignorantly; without knowledge or design. *Addison.*

UNKNOWN, *a.* Not known. The author of the invention is *unknown.*

2. Greater than is imagined. *Bacon.*

3. Not having had cohabitation. *Shak.*

4. Not having communication. *Addison.*

UNLA'BORED, *a.* Not produced by labor; as *unlabored* harvests. *Dryden.*

2. Not cultivated by labor; not tilled. *Blackmore.*

3. Spontaneous; voluntary; that offers without effort; natural.

And from the theme *unlabor'd* beauties rise. *Tickel.*

4. Easy; natural; not stiff; as an *unlabored* style. *Roscoe.*

UNLABO'RIOUS, *a.* Not laborious; not difficult to be done. *Milton.*

UNLA'CE, *v. t.* To loose from lacing or fastening by a cord or strings passed through loops and holes; as, to *unlace* a helmet or a garment.

2. To loose a woman's dress.

3. To divest of ornaments. *Shak.*

4. In *sea language*, to loose and take off a bonnet from a sail.

UNLA'CED, *pp.* Loosed from lacing; unfastened.

UNLA'CING, *ppr.* Loosing from lacing or fastening.

UNLACK'EYED, *a.* Unattended with a lackey. *Cowper.*

UNLA'DE, *v. t.* To unload; to take out the cargo of; as, to *unlade* a ship.

2. To unload; to remove, as a load or burden. Acts xxi.

UNLA'DEN, *pp.* of *lade.* Unloaded.

UNLA'ID, *a.* Not placed; not fixed. *Hooker.*

2. Not allayed; not pacified; not suppressed. *Milton.*

3. Not laid out, as a corpse. *B. Jonson.*

UNLAMENT'ED, *a.* Not lamented; whose loss is not deplored.

Thus *unlamented* pass the proud away. *Pope.*

UNL'ARDED, *a.* Not intermixed or inserted for improvement. *Chesterfield.*

UNLATCH', *v. i.* To open or loose by lifting the latch.

UNLAU'RELED, *a.* Not crowned with laurel; not honored. *Byron.*

UNLAV'ISH, *a.* Not lavish; not profuse; not wasteful.

UNLAV'ISHED, *a.* Not lavished; not spent wastefully.

UNLAW', *v. t.* To deprive of the authority of law. *Milton.*

UNLAW'FUL, *a.* Not lawful; contrary to law; illegal; not permitted by law. *Dryden.*

Unlawful assembly, in *law*, the meeting of three or more persons to commit an unlawful act.

UNLAW'FULLY, *adv.* In violation of law or right; illegally. *Taylor.*

2. Illegitimately; not in wedlock; as a child *unlawfully* born. *Addison.*

UNLAW'FULNESS, *n.* Illegality; contrariety to law. *South.*

2. Illegitimacy.

UNLEARN', *v. t. unlern'.* To forget or lose what has been learned. It is most important to us all to *unlearn* the errors of our early education.

I had learned nothing right; I had to *unlearn* every thing. *Luther* in *Milner.*

UNLEARN'ED, *pp.* Forgotten.

2. *a.* Not learned; ignorant; illiterate; not instructed. *Dryden.*

3. Not gained by study; not known. *Milton.*

4. Not suitable to a learned man; as *unlearned* verses. *Shak.*

UNLEARN'EDLY, *adv.* Ignorantly. *Brown.*

UNLEARN'EDNESS, *n.* Want of learning; illiterateness. *Sylvester.*

UNLEAVENED, *a. unlev'ened.* Not leavened; not raised by leaven, barm or yeast. Ex. xii.

UNLEC'TURED, *a.* Not taught by lecture. *Young.*

UNLEISURED, *a. unlezh'ured.* Not having leisure. [*Not in use.*] *Milton.*

UNLENT,' *a.* Not lent.

UNLESS', *conj.* [Sax. *onlesan*, to loose or release.]

Except; that is, remove or dismiss the fact or thing stated in the sentence or clause which follows. "We cannot thrive, *unless* we are industrious and frugal." The sense will be more obvious with the clauses of the sentence inverted. *Unless*, [remove this fact, suppose it not to exist,] *we are industrious and frugal*, we cannot thrive. *Unless* then answers for a negation. If we are *not* industrious, we cannot thrive.

UNLES'SONED, *a.* Not taught; not instructed. *Shak.*

UNLET'TERED, *a.* Unlearned; untaught; ignorant. *Dryden.*

UNLET'TEREDNESS, *n.* Want of learning. *Waterhouse.*

UNLEV'ELED, *a.* Not leveled; not laid even. *Tickel.*

UNLIBID'INOUS, *a.* Not libidinous; not lustful. *Milton.*

UNLI'CENSED, *a.* Not licensed; not having permission by authority; as an *unlicensed* innkeeper.

The vending of ardent spirits, in places licensed or *unlicensed*, is a tremendous evil. *L. Beecher.*

UNLICK'ED, *a.* Shapeless; not formed to smoothness; as an *unlicked* bear whelp. *Shak.*

UNLIGHTED, *a.* Not lighted; not illuminated. *Prior.*

2. Not kindled or set on fire.

UNLIGHTSÔME, *a.* Dark; gloomy; wanting light. *Milton.*

UNLI'KE, *a.* Dissimilar; having no resemblance. Never were two men more *unlike.* The cases are entirely *unlike.*

2. Improbable; unlikely. *Bacon.*

UNLI'KELIHOOD, } *n.* Improbability.
UNLI'KELINESS, } *South. Locke.*

UNLI'KELY, *a.* Improbable; such as cannot be reasonably expected; as an *unlikely* event. The thing you mention is very *unlikely.*

2. Not promising success. He employs very *unlikely* means to effect his object.

UNLI'KELY, *adv.* Improbably. *Addison.*

UNLI'KENESS, *n.* Want of resemblance; dissimilitude. *Dryden.*

UNLIM'BER, *a.* Not limber; not flexible; not yielding.

UNLIM'ITABLE, *a.* Admitting no limits; boundless. [We now use *illimitable.*]

UNLIM'ITED, *a.* Not limited; having no bounds; boundless. *Boyle.*

2. Undefined; indefinite; not bounded by proper exceptions; as *unlimited* terms.

3. Unconfined; not restrained.

Ascribe not to God such an *unlimited* exercise of mercy as may destroy his justice. *Rogers.*

Unlimited problem, is one which is capable of infinite solutions. *Cyc.*

UNLIM'ITEDLY, *adv.* Without bounds. *Decay of Piety.*

UNLIM'ITEDNESS, *n.* The state of being boundless, or of being undefined. *Johnson.*

UNLIN'EAL, *a.* Not in a line; not coming in the order of succession. *Shak.*

UNLINK', *v. t.* To separate links; to loose; to unfasten; to untwist. *Shak.*

UNLIQ'UIDATED, *a.* Not liquidated; not settled; not having the exact amount ascertained; as an *unliquidated* debt; *unliquidated* accounts. *Hamilton.*

2. Unpaid; unadjusted. *Wheaton.*

UNLIQ'UIFIED, *a.* Unmelted; not dissolved. *Addison.*

UNLIQ'UORED, *a.* Not moistened; not smeared with liquor; not filled with liquor. *Bp. Hall. Milton.*

UNLIS'TENING, *a.* Not listening; not hearing; not regarding. *Thomson.*

UNLI'VELINESS, *n.* Want of life; dullness. *Milton.*

UNLI'VELY, *a.* Not lively; dull.

UNLÔAD, *v. t.* To take the load from; to discharge of a load or cargo; as, to *unload* a ship; to *unload* a cart.

2. To disburden; as, to *unload* a beast.

3. To disburden; to relieve from any thing onerous or troublesome. *Shak.*

UNLÔADED, *pp.* Freed from a load or cargo; disburdened.

UNLÔADING, *ppr.* Freeing from a load or cargo; disburdening; relieving of a burden.

UNLO'CATED, *a.* Not placed; not fixed in a place.

2. In *America*, unlocated lands are such new or wild lands as have not been surveyed, appropriated or designated by marks, limits or boundaries, to some individual, company or corporation.

UNLOCK', *v. t.* To unfasten what is locked; as, to *unlock* a door or a chest.

2. To open, in general; to lay open.

Unlock your springs, and open all your shades. *Pope.*

UNLOCK'ED, *pp.* Opened.

2. *a.* Not locked; not made fast.

Unlooked for, not expected; not foreseen. *Bacon.*

UNLOOSE, *v. t. unloos'.* To loose. [An ill formed word, as it expresses the same idea as *loose.*]

UNLOOSE, *v. i. unloos'.* To fall in pieces; to lose all connection or union. *Collier.*

UNLÖSABLE, *a. s* as *z.* That cannot be lost. [*Not in use.*] *Boyle.*

UNLÖVED, *a.* Not loved. *Sidney.*

UNLÖVELINESS, *n.* Want of loveliness; unamiableness; want of the qualities which attract love. *Sidney.*

UNLÖVELY, *a.* Not lovely; not amiable; destitute of the qualities which attract love, or possessing qualities that excite dislike.

UNLÖVING, *a.* Not loving; not fond. *Shak.*

UNLUCK'ILY, *adv.* Unfortunately; by ill fortune. *Addison.*

UNLUCK'INESS, *n.* Unfortunateness; ill fortune.

2. Mischievousness. *Addison.*

UNLUCK'Y, *a.* Unfortunate; not successful; as an *unlucky* man.

2. Unfortunate; not resulting in success; as an *unlucky* adventure; an *unlucky* throw of dice; an *unlucky* game.

[This word is usually applied to incidents in which success depends on single events, to games of hazard, &c. rather than to things which depend on a long series of events, or on the ordinary course of providence. Hence we say, a man is *unlucky* in play or in a lottery; but not that a farmer is *unlucky* in his husbandry, or a commander *unlucky* in the result of a campaign.]

3. Unhappy; miserable; subject to frequent misfortunes. *Spenser.*

4. Slightly mischievous; mischievously

waggish; as an *unlucky* boy; an *unlucky* wag.
5. Ill omened; inauspicious.
Haunt me not with that *unlucky* face. *Dryden.*

UNLUS'TROUS, *a.* Wanting luster; not shining. *Shak.*

UNLUST'Y, *a.* Not lusty; not stout; weak.

UNLU'TE, *v. t.* To separate things cemented or luted; to take the lute or clay from.

UNLU'TED, *pp.* Separated, as luted vessels.

UNLU'TING, *ppr.* Separating, as luted vessels.

UNMA'DE, *pp.* Deprived of its form or qualities. *Woodward.*
2. *a.* Not made; not yet formed. *Spenser.*
3. Omitted to be made. *Blackmore.*

UNMAGNET'IC, *a.* Not having magnetic properties. *Cavallo.*

UNMA'IDENLY, *a.* Not becoming a maiden. *Hall.*

UNMA'IMED, *a.* Not maimed; not disabled in any limb; sound; entire. *Pope.*

UNMA'KABLE, *a.* Not possible to be made. [*Little used.*] *Grew.*

UNMA'KE, *v. t.* To destroy the form and qualities which constitute a thing what it is.
God does not make or *unmake* things to try experiments. *Burnet.*
2. To deprive of qualities before possessed.

UNMA'KING, *ppr.* Destroying the peculiar properties of a thing.

UNMALLEABIL'ITY, *n.* The quality or state of being unmalleable.

UNMAL'LEABLE, *a.* Not malleable; not capable of being hammered into a plate, or of being extended by beating.

UNMAN', *v. t.* To deprive of the constitutional qualities of a human being, as reason, &c. *South.*
2. To deprive of men; as, to *unman* a ship.
3. To emasculate; to deprive of virility.
4. To deprive of the courage and fortitude of a man; to break or reduce into irresolution; to dishearten; to deject. *Dryden. Pope.*
5. To dispeople; as towns *unmanned.* *Goldsmith.*

UNMAN'AGEABLE, *a.* Not manageable; not easily restrained, governed or directed; not controllable.
2. Not easily wielded. *Locke.*

UNMAN'AGED, *a.* Not broken by horsemanship. *Taylor.*
2. Not tutored; not educated. *Felton.*

UNMAN'LIKE, } *a.* Not becoming a human being. *Collier.*
UNMAN'LY, }
2. Unsuitable to a man; effeminate.
Unmanly warmth and tenderness of love. *Addison.*
3. Not worthy of a noble mind; ignoble; base; ungenerous; cowardly.

UNMAN'NED, *pp.* Deprived of the qualities of a man.

UNMAN'NERED, *a.* Uncivil; rude. *B. Jonson.*

UNMAN'NERLINESS, *n.* Want of good manners; breach of civility; rudeness of behavior. *Locke.*

UNMAN'NERLY, *a.* Ill bred; not having good manners; rude in behavior; as an *unmannerly* youth.
2. Not according to good manners; as an *unmannerly* jest. *Swift.*

UNMAN'NERLY, *adv.* Uncivilly. *Shak.*

UNMANUFAC'TURED, *a.* Not manufactured; not wrought into the proper form for use.

UNMANU'RED, *a.* Not manured; not enriched by manure.
2. Uncultivated. *Spenser.*

UNM'ARKED, *a.* Not marked; having no mark.
2. Unobserved; not regarded; undistinguished. *Pope.*

UNM'ARRED, *a.* Not marred; not injured; not spoiled; not obstructed.

UNMAR'RIABLE, *a.* Not marriageable. [*Little used.*] *Milton.*

UNMAR'RIED, *a.* Not married; having no husband or no wife. *Bacon.*

UNMAR'RY, *v. t.* To divorce. *Milton.*

UNM'ARSHALED, *a.* Not disposed or arranged in due order.

UNM'ASCULATE, *v. t.* To emasculate. *Fuller.*

UNM'ASCULINE, *a.* Not masculine or manly; feeble; effeminate. *Milton.*

UNM'ASK, *v. t.* To strip of a mask or of any disguise; to lay open what is concealed. *Roscommon.*

UNM'ASK, *v. i.* To put off a mask.

UNM'ASKED, *pp.* Stripped of a mask or disguise.
2. *a.* Open; exposed to view. *Dryden.*

UNM'ASTERABLE, *a.* That cannot be mastered or subdued. [*Not in use.*] *Brown.*

UNM'ASTERED, *a.* Not subdued; not conquered.
2. Not conquerable.
He cannot his *unmaster'd* grief sustain. *Dryden.*

UNMATCH'ABLE, *a.* That cannot be matched; that cannot be equaled; unparalleled. *Hooker.*

UNMATCH'ED, *a.* Matchless; having no match or equal. *Dryden.*

UNME'ANING, *a.* Having no meaning or signification; as *unmeaning* words.
2. Not expressive; not indicating intelligence; as an *unmeaning* face.
There pride sits blazon'd on th' *unmeaning* brow. *Trumbull.*

UNMEANT, *a. unment'.* Not meant; not intended. *Dryden.*

UNMEASURABLE, *a. unmezh'urable.* That cannot be measured; unbounded; boundless. *Swift.*
[For this, *immeasurable* is generally used.]

UNMEAS'URABLY, *adv.* Beyond all measure. *Howell.*

UNMEAS'URED, *a.* Not measured; plentiful beyond measure. *Milton.*
2. Immense; infinite; as *unmeasured* space. *Blackmore.*

UNMECHAN'ICAL, *a.* Not mechanical; not according to the laws or principles of mechanics.

Unmeddled with, not meddled with; not touched; not altered. *Carew.*

UNMED'DLING, *a.* Not meddling; not interfering with the concerns of others; not officious. *Chesterfield.*

UNMED'DLINGNESS, *n.* Forbearance of interposition. [*Not in use.*] *Hall.*

UNMED'ITATED, *a.* Not meditated; not prepared by previous thought. *Milton.*

UNMEE'T, *a.* Not fit; not proper; not worthy or suitable. *Milton. Prior.*

UNMEE'TLY, *adv.* Not fitly; not properly; not suitably. *Spenser.*

UNMEE'TNESS, *n.* Unfitness; unsuitableness. *Milton.*

UNMEL'LOWED, *a.* Not mellowed; not fully matured. *Shak.*

UNMELO'DIOUS, *a.* Not melodious; wanting melody; harsh. *Herbert.*

UNMELT'ED, *a.* Undissolved; not melted. *Waller.*
2. Not softened.

UNMEN'TIONED, *a.* Not mentioned; not named. *Clarendon.*

UNMER'CANTILE, *a.* Not according to the customs and rules of commerce.

UNMER'CHANTABLE, *a.* Not merchantable; not of a quality fit for the market.

UNMER'CIFUL, *a.* Not merciful; cruel; inhuman to such beings as are in one's power; not disposed to spare or forgive. *Rogers.*
2. Unconscionable; exorbitant; as *unmerciful* demands. *Pope.*

UNMER'CIFULLY, *adv.* Without mercy or tenderness; cruelly. *Addison.*

UNMER'CIFULNESS, *n.* Want of mercy; want of tenderness and compassion towards those who are in one's power; cruelty in the exercise of power or punishment. *Taylor.*

UNMER'ITABLE, *a.* Having no merit or desert. [*Not in use.*] *Shak.*

UNMER'ITED, *a.* Not merited; not deserved; obtained without service or equivalent; as *unmerited* promotion.
2. Not deserved; cruel; unjust; as *unmerited* sufferings or injuries.

UNMER'ITEDNESS, *n.* State of being unmerited. *Boyle.*

UNMET', *a.* Not met. *B. Jonson.*

UNMETAL'LIC, *a.* Not metallic; not having the properties of metal; not belonging to metals. *Encyc.*

UNMIGHTY, *a.* Not mighty; not powerful.

UNMILD, *a.* Not mild; harsh; severe; fierce.

UNMILDNESS, *n.* Want of mildness; harshness. *Milton.*

UNMIL'ITARY, *a.* Not according to military rules or customs.

UNMILK'ED, *a.* Not milked. *Pope.*

UNMILL'ED, *a.* Not milled; not indented or grained; as *unmilled* coin.

UNMINDED, *a.* Not minded; not heeded. *Milton.*

UNMINDFUL, *a.* Not mindful; not heedful; not attentive; regardless; as *unmindful* of laws; *unmindful* of health or of duty. *Milton.*

UNMINDFULLY, *adv.* Carelessly; heedlessly.

UNMINDFULNESS, *n.* Heedlessness; inattention; carelessness.

UNMIN'GLE, *v. t.* To separate things mixed. *Bacon.*

UNMIN'GLEABLE, *a.* That cannot be mixed. [*Not in use.*] *Boyle.*

UNMIN'GLED, *a.* Not mingled; not mixed; pure. *Pope.*
2. Pure; not vitiated or alloyed by foreign admixture; as *unmingled* joy.

UNMINISTE'RIAL, *a.* Not ministerial.

UNMI'RY, *a.* Not miry; not muddy; not foul with dirt. *Gay.*

UNMISS'ED, *a.* Not missed; not perceived to be gone or lost. *Gray.*

UNMISTA'KEABLE, *a.* That cannot be mistaken. [*Little used.*] *Cheyne.*

UNMISTA'KEN, *a.* Not mistaken; sure. *Trumbull.*

UNMISTRUST'ING, *a.* Not mistrusting; not suspecting; unsuspicious.

UNMIT'IGABLE, *a.* Not capable of being mitigated, softened or lessened. *Shak.*

UNMIT'IGATED, *a.* Not mitigated; not lessened; not softened in severity or harshness. *Shak.*

UNMIX'ED, **UNMIXT'**, *a.* Not mixed; not mingled; pure; unadulterated; unvitiated by foreign admixture. *Bacon.*

2. Pure; unalloyed; as *unmixed* pleasure.

UNMOANED, *a.* Not lamented. *Shak.*

UNMOD'IFIABLE, *a.* That cannot be modified or altered in form; that cannot be reduced to a more acceptable or desired form.

UNMOD'IFIED, *a.* Not modified; not altered in form; not qualified in meaning.

UNMO'DISH, *a.* Not modish; not according to custom. *Pope.*

UNMOIST', *a.* Not moist; not humid; dry. *Philips.*

UNMOIST'ENED, *a.* Not made moist or humid. *Boyle.*

UNMOLD, *v. t.* To change the form; to reduce from any form.

UNMOLDED, *pp.* Not changed in form.

2. *a.* Not molded; not shaped or formed.

UNMOLEST'ED, *a.* Not molested; not disturbed; free from disturbance. *Pope.*

UNMONEYED, *a.* Not having money. *Shenstone.*

UNMONOP'OLIZE, *v. t.* To recover from being monopolized. [*Not in use.*] *Milton.*

UNMONOP'OLIZED, *a.* Not monopolized.

UNMOOR', *v. t.* In *sea language*, to bring to the state of riding with a single anchor, after having been moored by two or more cables. *Cyc.*

2. To loose from anchorage. *Pope.*

UNMOOR'ED, *pp.* Loosed from anchorage, or brought to ride with a single anchor.

UNMOOR'ING, *ppr.* Loosing from anchorage, or bringing to ride with a single anchor.

UNMOR'ALIZED, *a.* Untutored by morality; not conformed to good morals. *Norris.*

UNMORT'GAGED, *a.* [See *Mortgage.*] Not mortgaged; not pledged. *Addison. Dryden.*

UNMOR'TIFIED, *a.* Not mortified; not shamed.

2. Not subdued by sorrow; as *unmortified* sin.

UNMOUNT'ED, *a.* Not mounted. *Unmounted* dragoons are such as have not horses.

UNMOURNED, *a.* Not lamented. *Rogers.*

UNMÖVABLE, *a.* That cannot be moved or shaken; firm; fixed. *Locke.* [*Immovable* is more generally used.]

UNMOVED, *a.* Not moved; not transferred from one place to another. *Locke.*

2. Not changed in purpose; unshaken; firm. *Milton.*

3. Not affected; not having the passions excited; not touched or impressed. *Pope.*

4. Not altered by passion or emotion. *Dryden.*

UNMÖVING, *a.* Having no motion. *Cheyne.*

2. Not exciting emotion; having no power to affect the passions.

UNMUF'FLE, *v. t.* To take a covering from the face. *Milton.*

2. To remove the muffling of a drum.

UNMUR'MURED, *a.* Not murmured at. *Beaum.*

UNMUR'MURING, *a.* Not murmuring; not complaining; as *unmurmuring* patience.

UNMU'SICAL, *a.* *s* as *z.* Not musical; not harmonious or melodious.

2. Harsh; not pleasing to the ear. *B. Jonson.*

UNMU'TILATED, *a.* Not mutilated; not deprived of a member or part; entire.

UNMUZ'ZLE, *v. t.* To loose from a muzzle. *Shak.*

UNNA'MED, *a.* Not named; not mentioned. *Milton.*

UNNA'TIVE, *a.* Not native; not natural; forced. *Thomson.*

UNNAT'URAL, *a.* Contrary to the laws of nature; contrary to the natural feelings. *L'Estrange.*

2. Acting without the affections of our common nature; as an *unnatural* father or son.

3. Not in conformity to nature; not agreeable to the real state of persons or things; not representing nature; as affected and *unnatural* thoughts; *unnatural* images or descriptions.

UNNAT'URALIZE, *v. t.* To divest of natural feelings. *Hales.*

UNNAT'URALIZED, *pp.* Divested of natural feelings.

2. *a.* Not naturalized; not made a citizen by authority.

UNNAT'URALLY, *adv.* In opposition to natural feelings and sentiments. *Tillotson.*

UNNAT'URALNESS, *n.* Contrariety to nature. *Sidney.*

UNNAV'IGABLE, *a.* Not navigable. [But *innavigable* is more generally used.]

UNNAV'IGATED, *a.* Not navigated; not passed over in ships or other vessels. *Cook's Voyages.*

UNNEC'ESSARILY, *adv.* Without necessity; needlessly. *Hooker.*

UNNEC'ESSARINESS, *n.* The state of being unnecessary; needlessness.

UNNEC'ESSARY, *a.* Not necessary; needless; not required by the circumstances of the case; useless; as *unnecessary* labor or care; *unnecessary* rigor. *Dryden.*

UNNECES'SITATED, *a.* Not required by necessity. *Eton.*

UNNEE'DFUL, *a.* Not needful; not wanted; needless. *Milton.*

UNNEIGHBORLY, *a.* Not suitable to the duties of a neighbor; not becoming persons living near each other; not kind and friendly.

UNNEIGHBORLY, *adv.* In a manner not suitable to a neighbor; in a manner contrary to the kindness and friendship which should subsist among neighbors. *Shak.*

UNNERV'ATE, *a.* Not strong; feeble. [*Not in use.*] *Broome.*

UNNERVE, *v. t.* *unnerv'.* To deprive of nerve, force or strength; to weaken; to enfeeble; as, to *unnerve* the arm. *Addison.*

UNNERV'ED, *pp.* Deprived of strength. *Shak.*

2. *a.* Weak; feeble.

UNNETH, **UNNETHES**, *adv.* Scarcely; hardly. *Obs.* [See *Uneath.*] *Spenser.*

UNNEU'TRAL, *a.* Not neutral; not uninterested.

UNNO'BLE, *a.* Not noble; ignoble; mean. *Shak.*

UNNO'TED, *a.* Not noted; not observed; not heeded; not regarded. *Pope.*

2. Not honored.

UNNO'TICED, *a.* Not observed; not regarded.

2. Not treated with the usual marks of respect; not kindly and hospitably entertained.

UNNUM'BERED, *a.* Not numbered; innumerable; indefinitely numerous. *Prior.*

UNNUR'TURED, *a.* Not nurtured; not educated.

UNOBEYED, *a.* Not obeyed. *Milton.*

UNOBJECT'ED, *a.* Not objected; not charged as a fault or error. *Atterbury.*

UNOBJEC'TIONABLE, *a.* Not liable to objection; that need not be condemned as faulty, false or improper. *Stephens.*

UNOBJEC'TIONABLY, *adv.* In a manner not liable to objection.

UNOBNOX'IOUS, *a.* Not liable; not exposed to harm. *Milton.*

UNOBSCU'RED, *a.* Not obscured; not darkened. *Milton.*

UNOBSE'QUIOUS, *a.* Not obsequious; not servilely submissive.

UNOBSE'QUIOUSLY, *adv.* Not with servile submissiveness.

UNOBSE'QUIOUSNESS, *n.* Want of servile submissiveness or compliance; incompliance.

UNOBSERV'ABLE, *a.* *s* as *z.* That is not observable; not discoverable. *Boyle.*

UNOBSERV'ANCE, *n.* Want of observation; inattention; regardlessness. *Whitlock.*

UNOBSERV'ANT, *a.* Not observant; not attentive; heedless. *Glanville.*

2. Not obsequious.

UNOBSERV'ED, *a.* Not observed; not noticed; not seen; not regarded; not heeded. *Bacon.*

UNOBSERV'ING, *a.* Not observing; inattentive; heedless. *Dryden.*

UNOBSTRUCT'ED, *a.* Not obstructed; not filled with impediments; as an *unobstructed* stream or channel.

2. Not hindered; not stopped. *Blackmore.*

UNOBSTRUCT'IVE, *a.* Not presenting any obstacle. *Blackmore.*

UNOBTA'INABLE, *a.* That cannot be obtained; not within reach or power.

UNOBTA'INED, *a.* Not obtained; not gained; not acquired. *Hooker.*

UNOBTRU'SIVE, *a.* Not obtrusive; not forward; modest. *Young.*

UNOB'VIOUS, *a.* Not obvious; not readily occurring to the view or the understanding. *Boyle.*

UNOC'CUPIED, *a.* Not occupied; not possessed; as *unoccupied* land.

2. Not engaged in business; being at leisure. The man is *unoccupied.*
3. Not employed or taken up; as time *unoccupied.*
UNOFFEND'ED, *a.* Not offended; not having taken offense.
UNOFFEND'ING, *a.* Not offending; not giving offense.
2. Not sinning; free from sin or fault.
3. Harmless; innocent.
UNOFFENS'IVE, *a.* Not offensive; giving no offense; harmless. [For this, *inoffensive* is more generally used.]
UNOF'FERED, *a.* Not offered; not proposed to acceptance. *Clarendon.*
UNOFFI''CIAL, *a.* Not official; not pertaining to office.
2. Not proceeding from the proper officer or from due authority; as *unofficial* news or notice.
UNOFFI''CIALLY, *adv.* Not officially; not in the course of official duty. The man was *unofficially* informed by the sherif or commander.
UNOF'TEN, *adv.* Rarely. [*Not used.*]
UNOIL', *v. t.* To free from oil. *Dryden.*
UNOIL'ED, *pp.* Freed from oil.
2. *a.* Not oiled; free from oil.
UNO'PENED, *a.* Not opened; remaining fast, close, shut or sealed. *Chesterfield.*
UNO'PENING, *a.* Not opening. *Pope.*
UNOP'ERATIVE, *a.* Not operative; producing no effect. [But *inoperative* is generally used.] *South.*
UNOPPO'SED, *a.* *s* as *z.* Not opposed; not resisted; not meeting with any obstruction; as an army or stream *unopposed.* *Dryden.*
UNOPPRESS'ED, *a.* Not oppressed; not unduly burdened.
UNOR'DERLY, *a.* Not orderly; disordered; irregular. [*Disorderly* is more generally used.] *Sanderson.*
UNOR'DINARY, *a.* Not ordinary; not common. [*Not in use.*] *Locke.*
UNOR'GANIZED, *a.* Not organized; not having organic structure or vessels for the preparation, secretion and distribution of nourishment, &c. Metals are *unorganized* bodies. [This word is in use, but *inorganized* is also used.]
UNORIG'INAL, *a.* Not original; derived.
2. Having no birth; ungenerated. *Milton.*
UNORIG'INATED, *a.* Not originated; having no birth or creation.

God is underived, *unoriginated* and self-existent. *Stephens.*

UNORNAMENT'AL, *a.* Not ornamental. *West.*
UNOR'NAMENTED, *a.* Not ornamented; not adorned; plain. *Coventry.*
UNOR'THODOX, *a.* Not orthodox; not holding the genuine doctrines of the Scriptures. *Decay of Piety.*
UNOSTENTA'TIOUS, *a.* Not ostentatious; not boastful; not making show and parade; modest.
2. Not glaring; not showy; as *unostentatious* coloring.
UNOWED, *a.* Not owed; not due.
UNOWNED, *a.* Not owned; having no known owner; not claimed.
2. Not avowed; not acknowledged as one's own; not admitted as done by one's self.

UNOX'YGENATED, UNOX'YGENIZED, } *a.* Not having oxygen in combination.
UNPACIF'IC, *a.* Not pacific; not disposed to peace; not of a peaceable disposition. *Warton.*
UNPAC'IFIED, *a.* Not pacified; not appeased; not calmed. *Browne.*
UNPACK', *v. t.* To open, as things packed; as, to *unpack* goods.
2. To disburden. [*Little used.*] *Shak.*
UNPACK'ED, *pp.* Opened, as goods.
2. *a.* Not packed; not collected by unlawful artifices; as an *unpacked* jury. *Hudibras.*
UNPACK'ING, *ppr.* Opening, as a package.
UNPA'ID, *a.* Not paid; not discharged; as a debt. *Milton.*
2. Not having received his due; as *unpaid* workmen. *Pope.*
Unpaid for, not paid for; taken on credit.
UNPA'INED, *a.* Not pained; suffering no pain. *Milton.*
UNPA'INFUL, *a.* Not painful; giving no pain. *Locke.*
UNPAL'ATABLE, *a.* Not palatable; disgusting to the taste. *Collier.*
2. Not such as to be relished; disagreeable; as an *unpalatable* law. *Dryden.*
UNPALL'ED, *a.* Not deadened.
UNPAN'OPLIED, *a.* Destitute of panoply or complete armor. *Pollok.*
UNPAR'ADISE, *v. t.* To deprive of happiness like that of paradise; to render unhappy. *Young.*
UNPAR'AGONED, *a.* Unequaled; unmatched. *Shak.*
UNPAR'ALLELED, *a.* Having no parallel or equal; unequaled; unmatched. *Addison.*

The *unparalleled* perseverance of the armies of the U. States, under every suffering and discouragement, was little short of a miracle. *Washington.*

UNP'ARDONABLE, *a.* Not to be forgiven; that cannot be pardoned or remitted; as an *unpardonable* sin. *Rogers.*
UNP'ARDONABLY, *adv.* Beyond forgiveness. *Atterbury.*
UNP'ARDONED, *a.* Not pardoned; not forgiven; as *unpardoned* offenses. *Rogers.*
2. Not having received a legal pardon. The convict returned *unpardoned.*
UNP'ARDONING, *a.* Not forgiving; not disposed to pardon. *Dryden.*
UNP'ARLIAMENT'ARINESS, *n.* Contrariety to the rules, usages or constitution of parliament. *Clarendon.*
UNP'ARLIAMENT'ARY, *a.* Contrary to the usages or rules of proceeding in parliament.
2. Contrary to the rules or usages of legislative bodies.
UNP'ARTED, *a.* Not parted; not divided; not separated. *Prior.*
UNP'ARTIAL, *a.* Not partial. [*Not in use.*] [See *Impartial.*]
UNP'ARTIALLY, *adv.* Fairly; impartially. [*Not used.*]
UNP'ASSABLE, *a.* Not admitting persons to pass; impassable; as *unpassable* roads, rivers or mountains. [*Impassable* is more generally used.]

2. Not current; not received in common payments; as *unpassable* notes or coins. [Instead of this, *uncurrent* and *not current* are now used.]
UNPAS'SIONATE, UNPAS'SIONATED, } *a.* Calm; free from passion; impartial. [Instead of these words, *dispassionate* is now used.]
UNPAS'SIONATELY, *adv.* Without passion; calmly. [For this, *dispassionately* is now used.] *K. Charles.*
UNP'ASTORAL, *a.* Not pastoral; not suitable to pastoral manners. *Warton.*
UNPAT'ENTED, *a.* Not granted by patent. *Cranch.*
UNP'ATHED, *a.* Unmarked by passage; not trodden. *Shak.*
2. Not being beaten into a path; as *unpathed* snow.
UNPATHET'IC, *a.* Not pathetic; not adapted to move the passions or excite emotion. *Warton.*
UNPAT'RONIZED, *a.* Not having a patron; not supported by friends. *Johnson.*
UNPAT'TERNED, *a.* Having no equal. *Beaum.*
UNPA'VED, *a.* Not paved; not covered with stone.
UNPAWN'ED, *a.* Not pawned; not pledged. *Pope.*
UNPA'Y, *v. t.* To undo. [*Not in use.*] *Shak.*
2. Not to pay or compensate. [*Not used.*]
UNPE'ACEABLE, *a.* Not peaceable; quarrelsome. *Hammond.*
UNPE'ACEABLENESS, *n.* Unquietness; quarrelsomeness. *Parker.*
UNPE'ACEFUL, *a.* Not pacific or peaceful; unquiet. *Cowley.*
UNPED'IGREED, *a.* Not distinguished by a pedigree. *Pollok.*
UNPEG', *v. t.* To loose from pegs; to open.
2. To pull out the peg from.
UNPELT'ED, *a.* Not pelted; not assailed with stones.
UNPEN', *v. t.* To let out or suffer to escape by breaking a dam or opening a pen.

If a man *unpens* another's water— *Blackstone.*

UNPE'NAL, *a.* Not penal; not subject to a penalty. *Clarendon.*
UNPEN'ETRABLE, *a.* Not to be penetrated. [But *impenetrable* is chiefly used.]
UNPEN'ITENT, *a.* Not penitent. [But *impenitent* is the word now used.]
UNPEN'NED, *pp.* Unfastened; let out.
UNPEN'NING, *ppr.* Suffering to escape; unlocking.
UNPEN'SIONED, *a.* Not pensioned; not rewarded by a pension; as an *unpensioned* soldier.
2. Not kept in pay; not held in dependence by a pension. *Pope.*
UNPEOPLE, *v. t.* To deprive of inhabitants; to depopulate; to dispeople. *Milton. Dryden.*
UNPEOPLED, *pp.* Depopulated; dispeopled.
UNPEOPLING, *ppr.* Depopulating.
UNPERCE'IVABLE, *a.* Not to be perceived; not perceptible.
UNPERCE'IVED, *a.* Not perceived; not heeded; not observed; not noticed. *Milton.*
UNPERCE'IVEDLY, *adv.* So as not to be perceived. *Boyle.*

UNPER'FECT, *a.* Not perfect; not complete. [But the word now used is *imperfect.*]

UNPER'FECTED, *a.* Not perfected; not completed. *Hammond.*

UNPER'FECTNESS, *n.* Want of perfectness; incompleteness. [*Imperfectness* and *imperfection* are now used.]

UNPER'FORATED, *a.* Not perforated; not penetrated by openings.

UNPERFORM'ED, *a.* Not performed; not done; not executed; as, the business remains *unperformed.*

2\. Not fulfilled; as an *unperformed* promise. *Taylor.*

UNPERFORM'ING, *a.* Not performing; not discharging its office. *Dryden.*

UNPER'ISHABLE, *a.* Not perishable; not subject to decay. [The word now used is *imperishable.*]

UNPER'ISHING, *a.* Not perishing; durable.

UNPER'MANENT, *a.* Not permanent; not durable.

UNPER'JURED, *a.* Free from the crime of perjury. *Dryden.*

UNPERPLEX', *v. t.* To free from perplexity. *Donne.*

UNPERPLEX'ED, *a.* Not perplexed; not harassed; not embarrassed.

2\. Free from perplexity or complication; simple.

UNPER'SPIRABLE, *a.* That cannot be perspired, or emitted through the pores of the skin. *Arbuthnot.*

UNPERSUA'DABLE, *a.* That cannot be persuaded, or influenced by motives urged. *Sidney.*

UNPERVERT'ED, *a.* Not perverted; not wrested or turned to a wrong sense or use.

UNPET'RIFIED, *a.* Not petrified; not converted into stone.

UNPHILOSOPH'IC, } *a.* Not according
UNPHILOSOPH'ICAL, } to the rules or principles of sound philosophy; contrary to philosophy or right reason. *Newton.*

UNPHILOSOPH'ICALLY, *adv.* In a manner contrary to the principles of sound philosophy or right reason. *South.*

UNPHILOSOPH'ICALNESS, *n.* Incongruity with philosophy. *Norris.*

UNPHILOS'OPHIZE, *v. t.* To degrade from the character of a philosopher. *Pope.*

UNPHILOS'OPHIZED, *pp.* or *a.* Degraded from the rank of a philosopher.

2\. Not sophisticated or perverted by philosophy; as *unphilosophized* revelation. *Good.*

UNPHYS'ICKED, *a. s* as *z.* Not influenced by medicine; not physicked. [*Not used.*] *Howell.*

UNPIERCED, *a. unpers'ed.* Not pierced; not penetrated. *Gay.*

UNPIL'LARED, *a.* Deprived of pillars; as an *unpillared* temple. *Pope.*

UNPIL'LOWED, *a.* Having no pillow; having the head not supported. *Milton.*

UNPIN', *v. t.* To loose from pins; to unfasten what is held together by pins; as, to *unpin* a frock; to *unpin* the frame of a building.

UNPINK'ED, *a.* Not pinked; not marked or set with eyelet holes. *Shak.*

UNPIT'IED, *a.* Not pitied; not compassionated; not regarded with sympathetic sorrow. *Dryden. Pope.*

UNPIT'IFUL, *a.* Having no pity; not merciful. *Davies.*

2\. Not exciting pity.

UNPIT'IFULLY, *adv.* Unmercifully; without mercy. *Shak.*

UNPIT'YING, *a.* Having no pity; showing no compassion. *Granville.*

UNPLA'CABLE, *a.* Not to be appeased. [*Implacable* is the word now used.]

UNPLA'CED, *a.* Having no office or employment under the government. *Pope.*

UNPLAGUED, *a.* Not plagued; not harassed; not tormented. *Shak.*

UNPLANT'ED, *a.* Not planted; of spontaneous growth. *Waller.*

UNPL'ASTERED, *a.* Not plastered.

UNPLAUS'IBLE, *a. s* as *z.* Not plausible; not having a fair appearance; as arguments not *unplausible.* *Milton.*

UNPLAUS'IBLY, *adv. s* as *z.* Not with a fair appearance. *Swift.*

UNPLAUS'IVE, *a.* Not approving; not applauding.

UNPLE'ADABLE, *a.* That cannot be pleaded. *South.*

UNPLEASANT, *a. unplez'ant.* Not pleasant; not affording pleasure; disagreeable. *Hooker.*

UNPLEASANTLY, *adv. unplez'antly.* In a manner not pleasing; uneasily. *Pope.*

UNPLEASANTNESS, *n. unplez'antness.* Disagreeableness; the state or quality of not giving pleasure. *Hooker.*

UNPLE'ASED, *a. s* as *z.* Not pleased; displeased. *Dryden.*

UNPLE'ASING, *a.* Offensive; disgusting. *Milton. Dryden.*

UNPLE'ASINGLY, *adv.* In a manner to displease.

UNPLE'ASINGNESS, *n.* Want of qualities to please. *Milton.*

UNPLEDG'ED, *a.* Not pledged; not mortgaged.

UNPLI'ABLE, *a.* Not pliable; not easily bent.

UNPLI'ANT, *a.* Not pliant; not easily bent; stiff. *Wotton.*

2\. Not readily yielding the will; not compliant.

UNPLOW'ED, *a.* Not plowed. *Mortimer.*

UNPLU'ME, *v. t.* To strip of plumes or fethers; to degrade. *Glanville.*

UNPLU'MED, *pp.* or *a.* Deprived of plumes; destitute of plumes.

UNPLUN'DERED, *a.* Not plundered or stripped.

UNPOET'IC, } *a.* Not poetical; not hav-
UNPOET'ICAL, } ing the beauties of verse.

2\. Not becoming a poet. *Corbet.*

UNPOET'ICALLY, *adv.* In a manner not comporting with the nature of poetry.

2\. In a manner unbecoming a poet.

UNPOINT'ED, *a.* Having no point or sting. *B. Jonson.*

2\. Not having marks by which to distinguish sentences, members and clauses in writing.

3\. Not having the vowel points or marks; as an *unpointed* manuscript in Hebrew or Arabic. *M. Stuart.*

UNPOIS'ON, *v. t. s* as *z.* To remove or expel poison. *South.*

UNPOIZ'ED, *a.* Not poized; not balanced. *Thomson.*

UNPO'LARIZED, *a.* Not polarized; not having polarity.

UNPOL'ICIED, *a.* Not having civil polity, or a regular form of government.

UNPOL'ISHED, *a.* Not polished; not made smooth or bright by attrition. *Stillingfleet.*

2\. Not refined in manners; uncivilized; rude; plain. *Dryden.*

UNPOLI'TE, *a.* Not refined in manners; not elegant.

2\. Not civil; not courteous; rude. [See *Impolite.*]

UNPOLI'TELY, *adv.* In an uncivil or rude manner.

UNPOLI'TENESS, *n.* Want of refinement in manners; rudeness.

2\. Incivility; want of courtesy.

UNPOLLED, *a.* Not registered as a voter.

2\. Unplundered; not stripped. *Fanshaw.*

UNPOLLU'TED, *a.* Not polluted; not defiled; not corrupted.

UNPOP'ULAR, *a.* Not popular; not having the public favor; as an *unpopular* magistrate.

2\. Not pleasing the people; as an *unpopular* law.

UNPOPULAR'ITY, *n.* The state of not enjoying the public favor, or of not pleasing the people.

UNPORTABLE, *a.* Not to be carried. *Raleigh.*

UNPORTIONED, *a.* Not endowed or furnished with a portion or fortune; as an *unportioned* daughter.

UNPORTUOUS, *a.* Having no ports. *Burke.*

UNPOSSESS'ED, *a.* Not possessed; not held; not occupied. *Milton.*

UNPOSSESS'ING, *a.* Having no possessions. *Shak.*

UNPOS'SIBLE, *a.* Not possible. *Obs.* [The word now used is *impossible.*]

UNPOW'DERED, *a.* Not sprinkled with powder.

UNPRAC'TICABLE, *a.* Not feasible; that cannot be performed. [The word now used is *impracticable.*]

UNPRAC'TICED, *a.* Not having been taught by practice; not skilled; not having experience; raw; unskillful. *Shak.*

2\. Not known; not familiar by use. [*Not used.*] *Prior.*

UNPRA'ISED, *a. s* as *z.* Not praised; not celebrated. *Milton. Dryden.*

UNPRECA'RIOUS, *a.* Not dependent on another; not uncertain. *Blackmore.*

UNPREC'EDENTED, *a.* Having no precedent or example; not preceded by a like case; not having the authority of prior example. *Swift.*

UNPRECI'SE, *a.* Not precise; not exact. *Warton.*

UNPREDES'TINED, *a.* Not previously determined or destined. *Milton.*

UNPREDICT', *v. t.* To retract prediction. *Milton.*

UNPREFER'RED, *a.* Not preferred; not advanced. *Collier.*

UNPREG'NANT, *a.* Not pregnant.

2\. Not prolific: not quick of wit. *Shak.*

UNPREJU'DICATE, *a.* Not prepossessed by settled opinions. [*Little used.*] *Taylor.*

UNPREJ'UDICED, *a.* Not prejudiced; free from undue bias or prepossession; not preoccupied by opinion; impartial; as an *unprejudiced* mind. *Addison.*
2. Not warped by prejudice; as an *unprejudiced* judgment.
UNPRELAT'I€AL, *a.* Unsuitable to a prelate. *Clarendon.*
UNPREMED'ITATED, *a.* Not previously meditated or prepared in the mind.
2. Not previously purposed or intended; not done by design.
UNPREPA'RED, *a.* Not prepared; not ready; not fitted or furnished by previous measures. *Milton.*
2. Not prepared by holiness of life for the event of death and a happy immortality. *Roscommon.*
UNPREPA'REDNESS, *n.* State of being unprepared.
UNPREPOSSESS'ED, *a.* Not prepossessed; not biased by previous opinions; not partial. *South.*
UNPREPOSSESS'ING, *a.* Not having a winning appearance.
UNPRESS'ED, *a.* Not pressed. *Shak. Tickel.*
2. Not enforced. *Clarendon.*
UNPRESUMP'TUOUS, *a.* [See *Presume.*] Not presumptuous; not rash; modest; submissive. *Cowper.*
UNPRETEND'ING, *a.* Not claiming distinction; modest. *Pope.*
UNPREVA'ILING, *a.* Being of no force; vain. *Shak.*
UNPREVENT'ED, *a.* Not prevented; not hindered. *Shak.*
2. Not preceded by any thing. *Obs. Milton.*
UNPRIEST, *v. t.* To deprive of the orders of a priest. *Milton.*
UNPRIESTLY, *a.* Unsuitable to a priest. *Bale.*
UNPRINCE, *v. t. unprins'.* To deprive of principality or sovereignty. *Swift.*
UNPRINCELY, *a. unprins'ly.* Unbecoming a prince; not resembling a prince. *K. Charles.*
UNPRIN'CIPLED, *a.* Not having settled principles; as souls *unprincipled* in virtue. *Milton.*
2. Having no good moral principles; destitute of virtue; not restrained by conscience; profligate.
UNPRINT'ED, *a.* Not printed; as a literary work. *Pope.*
2. Not stamped with figures; white; as *unprinted* cotton.
UNPRIS'ONED, *a. s* as *z.* Set free from confinement. *Donne.*
UNPRI'ZABLE, *a.* Not valued; not of estimation.
UNPRI'ZED, *a.* Not valued. *Shak.*
UNPRO€LA'IMED, *a.* Not proclaimed; not notified by public declaration. *Milton.*
UNPRODU€'TIVE, *a.* Not productive; barren. *Burke.*
2. *More generally,* not producing large crops; not making profitable returns for labor; as *unproductive* land.
3. Not profitable; not producing profit or interest; as capital; as *unproductive* funds or stock.
4. Not efficient; not producing any effect.

UNPRODU€'TIVENESS, *n.* The state of being unproductive; as land, stock, capital, labor, &c.
UNPROFA'NED, *a.* Not profaned; not violated. *Dryden.*
UNPROFES'SIONAL, *a.* Not pertaining to one's profession. *Beddoes.*
2. Not belonging to a profession.
UNPROFI''CIENCY, *n.* Want of proficiency or improvement. *Hall.*
UNPROF'ITABLE, *a.* Bringing no profit; producing no gain beyond the labor, expenses and interest of capital; as *unprofitable* land; *unprofitable* stock; *unprofitable* employment.
2. Producing no improvement or advantage; useless; serving no purpose; as an *unprofitable* life; *unprofitable* study. Job xv.
3. Not useful to others.
4. Misimproving talents; bringing no glory to God; as an *unprofitable* servant. Matt. xxv.
UNPROF'ITABLENESS, *n.* The state of producing no profit or good; uselessness; inutility. *Addison.*
UNPROF'ITABLY, *adv.* Without profit; without clear gain; as capital *unprofitably* employed.
2. Without any good effect or advantage; to no good purpose. *Addison.*
UNPROF'ITED, *a.* Not having profit or gain. *Shak.*
UNPROHIB'ITED, *a.* Not prohibited; not forbid; lawful.
UNPROJE€T'ED, *a.* Not planned; not projected. *South.*
UNPROLIF'I€, *a.* Not prolific; barren; not producing young or fruit. *Hale.*
2. Not producing in abundance.
UNPROM'ISING, *a.* Not promising; not affording a favorable prospect of success, of excellence, of profit, &c.; as an *unpromising* youth; an *unpromising* season.
UNPROMPT'ED, *a.* Not prompted; not dictated.
2. Not excited or instigated.
UNPRONOUNCEABLE, *a. unpronouns'able.* That cannot be pronounced. [*Unusual.*] *Walker.*
UNPRONOUNC'ED, *a.* Not pronounced; not uttered. *Milton.*
UNPROP', *v. t.* To remove a prop from; to deprive of support.
UNPROP'ER, *a.* Not fit or proper. *Obs.* [*Improper* is the word now used.]
UNPROP'ERLY, *adv.* Unfitly. *Obs.* [See *Improperly.*]
UNPROPHET'I€, } *a.* Not foreseeing
UNPROPHET'I€AL, } or not predicting future events.
UNPROPI''TIOUS, *a.* Not propitious; not favorable; not disposed to promote; inauspicious. *Pope.*
UNPROPI''TIOUSLY, *adv.* Unfavorably; unkindly.
UNPROPÖRTIONABLE, *a.* Wanting due proportion.
UNPROPÖRTIONATE, *a.* Wanting proportion; disproportionate; unfit.
UNPROPÖRTIONED, *a.* Not proportioned; not suitable. *Shak.*
UNPROPO'SED, *a. s* as *z.* Not proposed; not offered. *Dryden.*
UNPROP'PED, *a.* Not propped; not supported or upheld. *Milton.*

UNPROS'PEROUS, *a.* Not prosperous; not attended with success; unfortunate. *Pope.*
UNPROS'PEROUSLY, *adv.* Unsuccessfully; unfortunately. *Taylor.*
UNPROS'PEROUSNESS, *n.* Want of success; failure of the desired result. *Hammond.*
UNPROS'TITUTED, *a.* Not prostituted; not debased.
UNPROTE€T'ED, *a.* Not protected; not defended. *Hooker.*
2. Not countenanced; not supported.
UNPROTRA€T'ED, *a.* Not protracted; not drawn out in length.
UNPRÖVED, *a.* Not proved; not known by trial. *Spenser.*
2. Not established as true by argument, demonstration or evidence.
UNPROVI'DE, *v. t.* To unfurnish; to divest or strip of qualifications. *Southern.*
UNPROVI'DED, *pp.* Divested of qualifications.
2. *a.* Not provided; unfurnished; unsupplied. *Dryden.*
UNPROV'IDENT, *a.* Improvident. *Obs.*
UNPROVI''SIONED, *a. s* as *z.* Not furnished with provisions. *Pollok.*
UNPROVO'KED, *a.* Not provoked; not incited; *applied to persons.*
2. Not proceeding from provocation or just cause; as an *unprovoked* attack. *Addison.*
UNPROVO'KING, *a.* Giving no provocation or offense. *Fleetwood.*
UNPRUDEN'TIAL, *a.* Imprudent. [*Not used.*] *Milton.*
UNPRU'NED, *a.* Not pruned; not lopped. *Shak.*
UNPUB'LI€, *a.* Not public; private; not generally seen or known. *Taylor.*
UNPUB'LISHED, *a.* Not made public; secret; private. *Shak.*
2. Not published; as a manuscript or book. *Pope.*
UNPUN€'TUAL, *a.* Not punctual; not exact in time. *Pope.*
UNPUN€TUAL'ITY, *n.* Want of punctuality.
UNPUN€'TUATED, *a.* Not punctuated; not pointed. *Busby.*
UNPUN'ISHED, *a.* Not punished; suffered to pass without punishment or with impunity; as a thief *unpunished;* an *unpunished* crime. *Dryden.*
UNPUN'ISHING, *a.* Not punishing.
UNPUR'CHASED, *a.* Not purchased; not bought. *Denham.*
UNPU'RE, *a.* Not pure; impure. *Obs.* [See *Impure.*]
UNPURG'ED, *a.* Not purged; unpurified. *Milton.*
UNPU'RIFIED, *a.* Not purified; not freed from recrement or foul matter.
2. Not cleansed from sin; unsanctified. *Decay of Piety.*
UNPUR'POSED, *a.* Not intended; not designed. *Shak.*
UNPURS'ED, *a.* Robbed of a purse. *Pollok.*
UNPURSU'ED, *a.* Not pursued; not followed; not prosecuted. *Milton.*
UNPU'TREFIED, *a.* Not putrefied; not corrupted. *Bacon.*
UNQU'AFFED, *a.* Not quaffed; not drank. *Byron.*

UNQUAL'IFIED, *a.* Not qualified; not fit; not having the requisite talents, abilities or accomplishments. *Swift.*
2. Not having taken the requisite oath or oaths.
3. Not modified or restricted by conditions or exceptions; as *unqualified* praise.

UNQUAL'IFY, *v. t.* To divest of qualifications. [But instead of this, *disqualify* is now used.]

UNQUAL'ITIED, *a.* Deprived of the usual faculties. [*Not in use.*] *Shak.*

UNQUAR'RELABLE, *a.* That cannot be impugned. [*Not in use.*] *Brown.*

UNQUEE'N, *v. t.* To divest of the dignity of queen. *Shak.*

UNQUELL'ED, *a.* Not quelled; not subdued. *Thomson.*

UNQUENCH'ABLE, *a.* That cannot be quenched; that will never be extinguished; inextinguishable. Matt. iii. Luke iii.

UNQUENCH'ABLENESS, *n.* The state or quality of being inextinguishable. *Hakewill.*

UNQUENCH'ABLY, *adv.* In a manner or degree so as not to be quenched.

UNQUENCH'ED, *a.* Not extinguished. *Bacon.*

UNQUES'TIONABLE, *a.* Not to be questioned; not to be doubted; indubitable; certain; as *unquestionable* evidence or truth; *unquestionable* courage. *Addison.*

UNQUES'TIONABLY, *adv.* Without doubt; indubitably. *Sprat.*

UNQUES'TIONED, *a.* Not called in question; not doubted.
2. Not interrogated; having no questions asked; not examined. *Dryden.*
3. Indisputable; not to be opposed. *B. Jonson.*

UNQUES'TIONING, *a.* Not calling in question; not doubting; unhesitating. *J. M. Mason.*

UNQUICK', *a.* Not quick; slow.
2. Not alive; motionless. [*Not in use.*] *Daniel.*

UNQUICK'ENED, *a.* Not animated; not matured to vitality; as *unquickened* progeny. *Blackstone.*

UNQUI'ET, *a.* Not quiet; not calm or tranquil; restless; uneasy; as an *unquiet* person; an *unquiet* mind.
2. Agitated; disturbed by continual motion; as the *unquiet* ocean.
3. Unsatisfied; restless. *Pope.*

UNQUI'ET, *v. t.* To disquiet. [*Not in use.*] *Herbert.*

UNQUI'ETLY, *adv.* In an unquiet state; without rest; in an agitated state. *Shak.*

UNQUI'ETNESS, *n.* Want of quiet; want of tranquillity; restlessness; uneasiness. *Taylor. Denham.*
2. Want of peace; as of a nation. *Spenser.*
3. Turbulence; disposition to make trouble or excite disturbance. *Dryden.*

UNQUI'ETUDE, *n.* Uneasiness; restlessness. *Obs.* [For this, *disquietude* and *inquietude* are used.]

UNRACK'ED, *a.* Not racked; not poured from the lees.

UNRA'KED, *a.* Not raked; as land *unraked.*
2. Not raked together; not raked up; as fire. *Shak.*

UNRAN'SACKED, *a.* Not ransacked; not searched.
2. Not pillaged. *Knolles.*

UNRAN'SOMED, *a.* Not ransomed; not liberated from captivity or bondage by payment for liberty. *Pope.*

UNRASH', *a.* Not rash; not presumptuous. *Clarendon.*

UNRAV'EL, *v. t.* To disentangle; to disengage or separate threads that are knit.
2. To free; to clear from complication or difficulty. *Addison.*
3. To separate connected or united parts; to throw into disorder.

Nature all *unravel'd.* *Dryden.*

4. To unfold, as the plot or intrigue of a play. *Pope.*

UNRAV'EL, *v. i.* To be unfolded; to be disentangled.

UNRAV'ELMENT, *n.* The development of the plot in a play. *Mickel.*

UNRA'ZORED, *a.* Unshaven. *Milton.*

UNRE'ACHED, *a.* Not reached; not attained to. *Dryden.*

UNREAD, *a. unred'.* Not read; not recited; not perused. *Hooker. Dryden.*
2. Untaught; not learned in books. *Dryden.*

UNREADINESS, *n. unred'iness.* Want of readiness; want of promptness or dexterity. *Hooker.*
2. Want of preparation. *Taylor.*

UNREADY, *a. unred'y.* Not ready; not prepared; not fit. *Shak.*
2. Not prompt; not quick. *Brown.*
3. Awkward; ungainly. *Bacon.*

UNRE'AL, *a.* Not real; not substantial; having appearance only. *Milton. Shak.*

UNREAL'ITY, *n.* Want of reality or real existence. *Fearn.*

UNRE'APED, *a.* Not reaped; as *unreaped* wheat; an *unreaped* field.

UNRE'ASONABLE, *a.* *s* as *z.* Not agreeable to reason. *Hooker.*
2. Exceeding the bounds of reason; claiming or insisting on more than is fit; as an *unreasonable* demand.
3. Immoderate; exorbitant; as an *unreasonable* love of life or of money.
4. Irrational. [In this sense, see *Irrational.*]

UNRE'ASONABLENESS, *n.* Inconsistency with reason; as the *unreasonableness* of sinners.
2. Exorbitance; excess of demand, claim, passion and the like; as the *unreasonableness* of a proposal.

UNRE'ASONABLY, *adv.* In a manner contrary to reason.
2. Excessively; immoderately; more than enough.

UNRE'ASONED, *a.* Not reasoned. *Burke.*

UNRE'AVE, *v. t.* [See *Reave*, *Unreeve* and *Ravel.*] To unwind; to disentangle; to loose. *Spenser.*
2. Not to rive; not to tear asunder; not to unroof. [*Not in use.*] *Hall.*

UNREBA'TED, *a.* Not blunted. *Hakewill.*

UNREBU'KABLE, *a.* Not deserving rebuke; not obnoxious to censure. 1 Tim. vi.

UNRECE'IVED, *a.* Not received; not taken; as sacraments *unreceived.*
2. Not come into possession; as a letter *unreceived.*
3. Not adopted; not embraced; as opinions *unreceived.*

UNRECK'ONED, *a.* Not reckoned or enumerated. *Bp. Gardiner.*

UNRECLA'IMABLE, *a.* That cannot be reclaimed, reformed or domesticated.

UNRECLA'IMED, *a.* Not reclaimed; not brought to a domestic state; not tamed; as a wild beast *unreclaimed.*
2. Not reformed; not called back from vice to virtue. *Rogers.*

UNREC'OMPENSED, *a.* Not recompensed; not rewarded.

UNRECONCI'LABLE, *a.* That cannot be reconciled; that cannot be made consistent with; as two *unreconcilable* propositions. [In this sense, *irreconcilable* is generally used.]
2. Not reconcilable; not capable of being appeased; implacable. *Shak.*
3. That cannot be persuaded to lay aside enmity or opposition, and to become friendly or favorable; as *unreconcilable* neighbors.

[*Irreconcilable* is generally used.]

UNRECONCI'LED, *a.* Not reconciled; not made consistent.
2. Not appeased; not having become favorable.
3. In *a theological sense*, not having laid aside opposition and enmity to God; not having made peace with God through faith in Christ.

UNRECORD'ED, *a.* Not recorded; not registered; as an *unrecorded* deed or lease.
2. Not kept in remembrance by public monuments.

Not *unrecorded* in the rolls of fame. *Pope.*

UNRECOUNT'ED, *a.* Not recounted; not told; not related or recited. *Shak.*

UNRECÓVERABLE, *a.* That cannot be recovered; past recovery. *Feltham.*
2. That cannot be regained.

UNRECÓVERED, *a.* Not recovered; not recalled into possession; not regained. *Drayton.*
2. Not restored to health.

UNRECRUITABLE, *a.* That cannot be recruited.
2. Incapable of recruiting. [*Bad and not used.*] *Milton.*

UNREC'TIFIED, *a.* Not rectified; not corrected or set right.

UNRECU'RING, *a.* That cannot be cured. [*Not in use.*] *Shak.*

UNREDEE'MABLE, *a.* That cannot be redeemed.

UNREDEE'MED, *a.* Not redeemed; not ransomed.
2. Not paid; not recalled into the treasury or bank by payment of the value in money; as *unredeemed* bills, notes or stock.

UNREDRESS'ED, *a.* Not redressed; not relieved from injustice; *applied to persons.*
2. Not removed; not reformed; as *unredressed* evils.

UNREDU'CED, *a.* Not reduced; not lessened in size, quantity or amount.

UNREDU'CIBLE, *a.* Not capable of reduction. *Ash.*

UNREDU'CIBLENESS, *n.* The quality of not being capable of reduction. *South.*

UNREEVE, *v. t.* *unree'v.* To withdraw or take out a rope from a block, thimble, &c. [See *Unreave.*]

UNREFI'NED, *a.* Not refined; not purified; as *unrefined* sugar.
2. Not refined or polished in manners.

UNREFORM'ABLE, *a.* Not capable of being put into a new form. *Hammond.*
2. That cannot be reformed or amended. *Cowper.*

UNREFORM'ED, *a.* Not reformed; not reclaimed from vice; as an *unreformed* youth.
2. Not amended; not corrected; as *unreformed* manners; *unreformed* vices.
3. Not reduced to truth and regularity; not freed from error; as an *unreformed* calendar. *Holder.*

UNREFRACT'ED, *a.* Not refracted, as rays of light.

UNREFRESH'ED, *a.* Not refreshed; not relieved from fatigue; not cheered.

UNREFRESH'ING, *a.* Not refreshing; not invigorating; not cooling; not relieving from depression or toil. *Beddoes.*

UNREG'ARDED, *a.* Not regarded; not heeded; not noticed; neglected; slighted. *Dryden. Swift.*

UNREG'ARDFUL, *a.* Not giving attention; heedless; negligent.

UNREGEN'ERACY, *n.* State of being unregenerate or unrenewed in heart. *Hammond.*

UNREGEN'ERATE, *a.* Not regenerated; not renewed in heart; remaining at enmity with God. *Stephens.*

UNREG'ISTERED, *a.* Not registered; not recorded. *Shak.*

UNREG'ULATED, *a.* Not regulated; not reduced to order. *Milner.*

UNREINED, *a.* Not restrained by the bridle. *Milton.*

UNREJOIC'ING, *a.* Unjoyous; gloomy; sad. *Thomson.*

UNRELA'TED, *a.* Not related by blood or affinity.
2. Having no connection with.

UNREL'ATIVE, *a.* Not relative; not relating; having no relation to. *Chesterfield.* [*Irrelative* is more generally used.]

UNREL'ATIVELY, *adv.* Without relation to. [*Little used.*] *Bolingbroke.*

UNRELENT'ING, *a.* Not relenting; having no pity; hard; cruel; as an *unrelenting* heart.
2. Not yielding to pity; as *unrelenting* cruelty.
3. Not yielding to circumstances; inflexibly rigid; as an *unrelenting* rule. *Paley.*

UNRELIE'VABLE, *a.* Admitting no relief or succor. *Boyle.*

UNRELIE'VED, *a.* Not relieved; not eased or delivered from pain.
2. Not succored; not delivered from confinement or distress; as a garrison *unrelieved.*
3. Not released from duty; as an *unrelieved* sentinel.

UNREM'ARKABLE, *a.* Not remarkable; not worthy of particular notice.
2. Not capable of being observed. *Digby.*

UNREM'ARKED, *a.* Not remarked; unobserved. *Melmoth.*

UNREME'DIABLE, *a.* That cannot be cured; admitting no remedy. *Sidney.*

UNREM'EDIED, *a.* Not cured; not remedied. *Milton.*

UNREMEM'BERED, *a.* Not remembered; not retained in the mind; not recollected. *Wotton.*

UNREMEM'BERING, *a.* Having no memory or recollection. *Dryden.*

UNREMEM'BRANCE, *n.* Forgetfulness; want of remembrance. [*Not in use.*] *Watts.*

UNREMIT'TED, *a.* Not remitted; not forgiven; as punishment *unremitted.*
2. Not having a temporary relaxation; as pain *unremitted.*
3. Not relaxed; not abated.

UNREMIT'TING, *a.* Not abating; not relaxing for a time; incessant; continued; as *unremitting* exertions.

UNREMIT'TINGLY, *adv.* Without abatement or cessation. *Fleming.*

UNREMÖVABLE, *a.* That cannot be removed; fixed. *Shak.*

UNREMÖVABLENESS, *n.* The state or quality of being fixed and not capable of being removed. *Hall.*

UNREMÖVABLY, *adv.* In a manner that admits of no removal. *Shak.*

UNREMÖVED, *a.* Not removed; not taken away.
2. Not capable of being removed.
Like Atlas *unremov'd.* *Milton.*

UNRENEW'ED, *a.* Not made anew; as, the lease is *unrenewed.*
2. Not regenerated; not born of the Spirit; as a heart *unrenewed.*

UNREPA'ID, *a.* Not repaid; not compensated; not recompensed; as a kindness *unrepaid.* *Johnson.*

UNREPE'ALED, *a.* Not repealed; not revoked or abrogated; remaining in force.

UNREPENT'ANCE, *n.* State of being impenitent. [*Little used.*] *Warton.*

UNREPENT'ANT, } *a.* Not repenting; not
UNREPENT'ING, } penitent; not contrite for sin. *Dryden.*

UNREPENT'ED, *a.* Not repented of. *Hooker.*

UNREPI'NING, *a.* Not repining; not peevishly murmuring or complaining. *Rowe.*

UNREPI'NINGLY, *adv.* Without peevish complaints.

UNREPLEN'ISHED, *a.* Not replenished; not filled; not adequately supplied. *Boyle.*

UNREPO'SED, *a.* *s* as *z.* Not reposed.

UNREPRESENT'ED, *a.* *s* as *z.* Not represented; having no one to act in one's stead.

UNREPRIE'VABLE, *a.* That cannot be reprieved or respited from death.

UNREPRIE'VED, *a.* Not reprieved; not respited.

UNREPROACHED, *a.* Not upbraided; not reproached.

UNREPRÖVABLE, *a.* Not deserving reproof; that cannot be justly censured. Col. i.

UNREPRÖVED, *a.* Not reproved; not censured. *Sandys.*
2. Not liable to reproof or blame. *Milton.*

UNREPUG'NANT, *a.* Not repugnant; not opposite. *Hooker.*

UNREP'UTABLE, *a.* Not reputable. [For this, *disreputable* is generally used.]

UNREQUEST'ED, *a.* Not requested; not asked. *Knolles.*

UNREQUI'TABLE, *a.* Not to be retaliated. *Boyle.*

UNREQUI'TED, *a.* Not requited; not recompensed.

UNRES'CUED, *a.* Not rescued; not delivered. *Pollok.*

UNRESENT'ED, *a.* *s* as *z.* Not resented; not regarded with anger. *Rogers.*

UNRESERVE, *n.* *unrezerv'.* Absence of reserve; frankness; freedom of communication. *Warton.*

UNRESERV'ED, *a.* Not reserved; not retained when a part is granted.
2. Not limited; not withheld in part; full; entire; as *unreserved* obedience to God's commands. *Rogers.*
3. Open; frank; concealing or withholding nothing; free; as an *unreserved* disclosure of facts.

UNRESERV'EDLY, *adv.* Without limitation or reservation. *Boyle.*
2. With open disclosure; frankly; without concealment. *Pope.*

UNRESERV'EDNESS, *n.* Frankness; openness; freedom of communication; unlimitedness. *Boyle. Pope.*

UNRESIST'ED, *a.* [See *Resist.*] Not resisted; not opposed. *Bentley.*
2. Resistless; such as cannot be successfully opposed. *Pope.*

UNRESIST'IBLE, *a.* Irresistible. *Temple.*

UNRESIST'ING, *a.* Not making resistance; yielding to physical force or to persuasion. *Dryden.*
2. Submissive; humble. *Buckminster.*

UNRESIST'INGLY, *adv.* Without resistance. *Randolph.*

UNRESOLV'ABLE, *a.* *s* as *z.* That cannot be solved or resolved. *South.*

UNRESOLV'ED, *a.* *s* as *z.* Not resolved; not determined. *Shak.*
2. Not solved; not cleared. *Locke.*

UNRESOLV'ING, *a.* *s* as *z.* Not resolving; undetermined. *Dryden.*

UNRESPECT'ABLE, *a.* Not respectable. [*Not used.*] *Malone.*

UNRESPECT'ED, *a.* Not respected; not regarded with respect. *Shak.*

UNRESPECT'IVE, *a.* Inattentive; taking little notice. [*Not in use.*] *Shak.*

UNRES'PITED, *a.* Not respited.
2. Admitting no pause or intermission. *Milton.*

UNRESPONS'IBLE, *a.* Not answerable; not liable.
2. Not able to answer; not having the property to respond. [*Irresponsible* is also used in the like sense.]

UNREST', *n.* Unquietness; uneasiness. [*Not in use.*] *Spenser. Wotton.*

UNREST'ING, *a.* Not resting; continually in motion. *Byron.*

UNRESTO'RED, *a.* Not restored; not having recovered health.
2. Not restored to a former place, to favor, or to a former condition.

UNRESTRA'INABLE, *a.* That cannot be restrained. *Darwin.*

UNRESTRA'INED, *a.* Not restrained; not controlled; not confined; not hindered. *Dryden.*
2. Licentious; loose. *Shak.*

3. Not limited; as an *unrestrained* power; *unrestrained* truth.

UNRESTRA'INT, *n.* Freedom from restraint.

UNRESTRICT'ED, *a.* Not restricted; not limited or confined. *Smollett.*

UNRETRACT'ED, *a.* Not retracted; not recalled. *Collier.*

UNREVE'ALED, *a.* Not revealed; not discovered; not disclosed. *Pope.*

UNREVENG'ED, *a.* Not revenged; as an injury *unrevenged.*

2. Not vindicated by just punishment.

Scipio's ghost walks *unreveng'd.* *Addison.*

UNREVENGEFUL, *a.* *unrevenj'ful.* Not disposed to revenge. *Hacket.*

UNREV'ENUED, *a.* Not furnished with a revenue. *Pollok.*

UNREV'EREND, *a.* Not reverend.

2. Disrespectful; irreverent; as an *unreverend* tongue. *Shak.*

UNREV'ERENT, *a.* Irreverent. [*The latter is chiefly used.*]

UNREV'ERENTLY, *adv.* Irreverently, which see.

UNREVERS'ED, *a.* Not reversed; not annulled by a counter decision; as a judgment or decree *unreversed.*

UNREVI'SED, *a.* *s* as z. Not revised; not reviewed; not corrected.

UNREVI'VED, *a.* Not revived; not recalled into life or force.

UNREVO'KED, *a.* Not revoked; not recalled; not annulled. *Milton.*

UNREWARD'ED, *a.* Not rewarded; not compensated. *Pope.*

UNRID'DLE, *v. t.* To solve or explain; as, to *unriddle* an enigma or mystery.

2. To explain.

And where you can't *unriddle*, learn to trust. *Parnell.*

UNRID'DLED, *pp.* Explained; interpreted.

UNRID'DLER, *n.* One who explains an enigma.

UNRID'DLING, *ppr.* Solving; explaining.

UNRIDIC'ULOUS, *a.* Not ridiculous.

UNRI'FLED, *a.* Not rifled; not robbed; not stripped. *Hume.*

UNRIG', *v. t.* To strip of both standing and running rigging. *Mar. Dict.*

UNRIG'GED, *pp.* Stripped of rigging.

UNRIG'GING, *ppr.* Stripping of rigging.

UNRIGHT, *a.* Not right; wrong. *Obs.*

UNRIGHTEOUS, *a.* *unri'chus.* [Sax. *unrihtwis;* that is, not right-wise.]

1. Not righteous; not just; not conformed in heart and life to the divine law; evil; wicked; *used of persons.*

2. Unjust; contrary to law and equity; as an *unrighteous* decree or sentence.

UNRIGHTEOUSLY, *adv.* *unri'chusly.* Unjustly; wickedly; sinfully. *Dryden.*

UNRIGHTEOUSNESS, *n.* *unri'chusness.* Injustice; a violation of the divine law, or of the plain principles of justice and equity; wickedness. *Unrighteousness* may consist of a single unjust act, but more generally, when applied to persons, it denotes an habitual course of wickedness. Rom. i. vi. 2 Cor. vi.

Every transgression of the law is *unrighteousness.* *Hall.*

UNRIGHTFUL, *a.* Not rightful; not just. *Shak.*

UNRING', *v. t.* To deprive of a ring or of rings. *Hudibras.*

UNRI'OTED, *a.* Free from rioting. [*Not used.*] *May.*

UNRIP', *v. t.* To rip. [*This word is not merely useless, but improper.*] *Bacon.*

UNRI'PE, *a.* Not ripe; not mature; not brought to a state of perfection; as *unripe* fruit. *Shak.*

2. Not seasonable; not yet proper.

He fix'd his *unripe* vengeance to defer. *Dryden.*

3. Not prepared; not completed; as an *unripe* scheme.

4. Too early; as the *unripe* death of Dorilaus. [*Unusual.*] *Sidney.*

UNRI'PENED, *a.* Not ripened; not matured. *Addison.*

UNRI'PENESS, *n.* Want of ripeness; immaturity; as the *unripeness* of fruit or of a project.

UNRI'VALED, *a.* Having no rival; having no competitor. *Pope.*

2. Having no equal; peerless.

UNRIV'ET, *v. t.* To loose from rivets; to unfasten. *Hale.*

UNRIV'ETED, *pp.* Loosed from rivets; unfastened.

UNRIV'ETING, *ppr.* Unfastening; loosing from rivets.

UNRO'BE, *v. t.* To strip of a robe; to undress; to disrobe. *Young.*

UNROLL, *v. t.* To open what is rolled or convolved; as, to *unroll* cloth.

2. To display. *Dryden.*

UNROLLED, *pp.* Opened, as a roll; displayed.

UNROLLING, *ppr.* Opening, as a roll; displaying.

UNRO'MANIZED, *a.* Not subjected to Roman arms or customs. *Whitaker.*

UNROMAN'TIC, *a.* Not romantic; not fanciful. *Swift.*

UNROOF', *v. t.* To strip off the roof or covering of a house.

UNROOF'ED, *pp.* Stripped of the roof.

UNROOF'ING, *ppr.* Stripping of the roof.

UNROOST'ED, *a.* Driven from the roost. *Shak.*

UNROOT', *v. t.* To tear up by the roots; to extirpate; to eradicate; as, to *unroot* an oak. *Dryden.*

UNROOT', *v. i.* To be torn up by the roots.

UNROUGH, *a.* *unruff'.* Not rough; unbearded; smooth. *Shak.*

UNROUND'ED, *a.* Not made round. *Donne.*

UNROUT'ED, *a.* Not routed; not thrown into disorder. *Beaum.*

UNROY'AL, *a.* Not royal; unprincely. *Sidney.*

UNRUF'FLE, *v. i.* To cease from being ruffled or agitated; to subside to smoothness. *Addison.*

UNRUF'FLED, *a.* Calm; tranquil; not agitated.

Calm and *unruffled* as a summer's sea. *Addison.*

2. Not disturbed; not agitated; as an *unruffled* temper.

UNRU'LED, *a.* Not ruled; not governed; not directed by superior power or authority. *Spenser.*

UNRU'LINESS, *n.* [from *unruly.*] Disregard of restraint; licentiousness; turbulence; as the *unruliness* of men, or of their passions.

2. The disposition of a beast to break over fences and wander from an inclosure; the practice of breaking or leaping over fences.

UNRU'LY, *a.* Disregarding restraint; licentious; disposed to violate laws; turbulent; ungovernable; as an *unruly* youth.

The tongue can no man tame; it is an *unruly* evil. James iv.

2. Accustomed to break over fences and escape from inclosures; apt to break or leap fences; as an *unruly* ox.

The owner of the *unruly* ox paid a sum of money, as a civil penalty for the ransom of his life. *S. E. Dwight.*

UNRU'MINATED, *a.* Not well chewed; not well digested. *Bolingbroke.*

UNRUM'PLE, *v. t.* To free from rumples; to spread or lay even. *Addison.*

UNSADDEN, *v. t.* *unsad'n.* To relieve from sadness. *Whitlock.*

UNSAD'DLE, *v. t.* To strip of a saddle; to take the saddle from; as, to *unsaddle* a horse.

UNSAD'DLED, *pp.* Divested of the saddle.

2. *a.* Not saddled; not having a saddle on.

UNSA'FE, *a.* Not safe; not free from danger; exposed to harm or destruction. *Milton. Dryden.*

2. Hazardous; as an *unsafe* adventure.

UNSA'FELY, *adv.* Not safely; not without danger; in a state exposed to loss, harm or destruction. *Grew.*

UNSA'FETY, *n.* State of being unsafe; exposure to danger. *Bacon.*

UNSAID, *a.* *unsed'.* Not said; not spoken; not uttered. *Dryden.*

UNSA'INT, *v. t.* To deprive of saintship. *South.*

UNSA'INTED, *pp.* Not sainted.

UNSA'LABLE, *a.* Not salable; not in demand; not meeting a ready sale; as *unsalable* goods.

UNSALT'ED, *a.* Not salted; not pickled; fresh; as *unsalted* meat.

UNSALU'TED, *a.* Not saluted; not greeted.

UNSANC'TIFIED, *a.* Not sanctified; unholy. *Thodey.*

2. Not consecrated.

UNSANC'TIONED, *a.* Not sanctioned; not ratified; not approved; not authorized. *Walsh.*

UNSAN'DALED, *a.* Not wearing sandals.

UNSA'TED, *a.* Not sated; not satisfied or satiated. *Shenstone.*

UNSA'TIABLE, *a.* That cannot be satisfied. [But *insatiable* is generally used.]

UNSA'TIATE, *a.* Not satisfied. *Obs.* *More.*

[*Insatiate* is the word now used.]

UNSATISFAC'TION, *n.* Dissatisfaction. *Brown.*

UNSATISFAC'TORILY, *adv.* So as not to give satisfaction.

UNSATISFAC'TORINESS, *n.* The quality or state of not being satisfactory; failure to give satisfaction. *Boyle.*

UNSATISFAC'TORY, *a.* Not giving satisfaction; not convincing the mind.

2. Not giving content; as an *unsatisfactory* compensation.

UNSAT'ISFIABLE, *a.* That cannot be satisfied. *Taylor.*

UNSAT'ISFIED, *a.* Not satisfied; not having enough; not filled; not gratified to the full; as *unsatisfied* appetites or desires.

2. Not content; not pleased; as, to be *unsatisfied* with the choice of an officer; to be *unsatisfied* with the wages or compensation allowed.

3. Not settled in opinion; not resting in confidence of the truth of any thing; as, to be *unsatisfied* as to the freedom of the will.

4. Not convinced or fully persuaded. The judges appeared to be *unsatisfied* with the evidence.

5. Not fully paid.

An execution returned *unsatisfied*. *Daggett, Wheaton's Rep.*

UNSAT'ISFIEDNESS, *n.* The state of being not satisfied or content.

UNSAT'ISFȲING, *a.* Not affording full gratification of appetite or desire; not giving content; not convincing the mind. *Addison.*

UNSAT'URATED, *a.* Not saturated; not supplied to the full. *Chimistry.*

UNSA'VED, *a.* Not saved; not having eternal life. *Pollok.*

UNSA'VORILY, *adv.* So as to displease or disgust. *Milton.*

UNSA'VORINESS, *n.* A bad taste or smell. *Johnson.*

UNSA'VORY, *a.* Tasteless; having no taste. Job vi.

2. Having a bad taste or smell. *Milton. Brown.*

3. Unpleasing; disgusting. *Hooker. Shak.*

UNSA'Y, *v. t.* pret. and pp. *unsaid.* To recant or recall what has been said; to retract; to deny something declared.

Say and *unsay*, feign, flatter or abjure. *Milton.*

UNSCA'LY, *a.* Not scaly; having no scales. *Gay.*

UNSCAN'NED, *a.* Not measured; not computed. *Shak.*

UNSCA'RED, *a.* Not scared; not frightened away.

UNSC'ARRED, *a.* Not marked with scars or wounds. *Shak.*

UNSCAT'TERED, *a.* Not scattered; not dispersed; not thrown into confusion.

UNSCHOL'ARLY, *a.* Not suitable to a scholar. [*A bad word.*] *Asiat. Res.*

UNSCHOLAS'TIC, *a.* Not bred to literature; as *unscholastic* statesmen. *Locke.*

2. Not scholastic.

UNSCHOOL'ED, *a.* Not taught; not educated; illiterate. *Hooker.*

UNSCIENTIF'IC, *a.* Not scientific; not according to the rules or principles of science.

UNSCIENTIF'ICALLY, *adv.* In a manner contrary to the rules or principles of science.

UNSCIN'TILLATING, *a.* Not sparkling; not emitting sparks. *J. Barlow.*

UNSCORCH'ED, *a.* Not scorched; not affected by fire. *Shak.*

UNSCO'RIFIED, *a.* Not scorified; not converted into dross.

UNSCOUR'ED, *a.* Not scoured; not cleaned by rubbing; as *unscoured* armor. *Shak.*

UNSCRATCH'ED, *a.* Not scratched; not torn. *Shak.*

UNSCREE'NED, *a.* Not screened; not covered; not sheltered; not protected. *Boyle.*

UNSCREW', *v. t.* To draw the screws from; to loose from screws; to unfasten. *Burnet.*

UNSCREW'ED, *pp.* Loosed from screws.

UNSCREW'ING, *ppr.* Drawing the screws from.

UNSCRIP'TURAL, *a.* Not agreeable to the Scriptures; not warranted by the authority of the word of God; as an *unscriptural* doctrine.

UNSCRIP'TURALLY, *adv.* In a manner not according with the Scriptures.

UNSCRU'PULOUS, *a.* Not scrupulous; having no scruples. *Mitford.*

UNSCRU'PULOUSNESSS, *n.* Want of scrupulousness. *Ib.*

UNSCRU'TABLE. [See *Inscrutable.*]

UNSCUTCH'EONED, *a.* Not honored with a coat of arms. *Pollok.*

UNSE'AL, *v. t.* To break or remove the seal of; to open what is sealed; as, to *unseal* a letter.

UNSE'ALED, *pp.* Opened, as something sealed.

2. *a.* Not sealed; having no seal, or the seal broken. *Shak.*

UNSE'ALING, *ppr.* Breaking the seal of; opening.

UNSE'AM, *v. t.* To rip; to cut open. *Shak.*

UNSEARCHABLE, *a. unserch'able.* That cannot be searched or explored; inscrutable; hidden; mysterious.

The counsels of God are to us *unsearchable.* *Rogers.*

UNSEARCHABLENESS, *n. unserch'ableness.* The quality or state of being unsearchable, or beyond the power of man to explore. *Bramhall.*

UNSEARCHABLY, *adv. unserch'ably.* In a manner so as not to be explored.

UNSEARCHED, *a. unserch'ed.* Not searched; not explored; not critically examined.

UNSEASONABLE, *a. unsee'znable.* Not seasonable; not being in the proper season or time. He called at an *unseasonable* hour.

2. Not suited to the time or occasion; unfit; untimely; ill timed; as *unseasonable* advice; an *unseasonable* digression.

3. Late; being beyond the usual time. He came home at an *unseasonable* time of night.

4. Not agreeable to the time of the year; as an *unseasonable* frost. The frosts of 1816, in June, July and August, in New England, were considered *unseasonable*, as they were unusual.

UNSE'ASONABLENESS, *n.* [supra.] The quality or state of being unseasonable, ill timed, or out of the usual time.

UNSE'ASONABLY, *adv.* Not seasonably; not in due time, or not in the usual time; not in the time best adapted to success. *Dryden. Arbuthnot.*

UNSEASONED, *a. unsee'znd.* Not seasoned; not exhausted of the natural juices and hardened for use; as *unseasoned* wood, boards, timber, &c.

2. Not inured; not accustomed; not fitted to endure any thing by use or habit; as, men *unseasoned* to tropical climates are exposed to fevers.

3. Unformed; not qualified by use or experience; as an *unseasoned* courtier. *Shak.*

4. Not salted; not sprinkled, filled or impregnated with any thing to give relish; as *unseasoned* meat.

5. Unseasonable. [*Not in use.*] *Shak.*

UNSE'AT, *v. t.* To throw from the seat. *Cowper.*

UNSE'ATED, *pp.* Thrown from the seat.

2. *a.* Not seated; having no seat or bottom.

3. Not settled with inhabitants; as *unseated* lands. [We usually say, *unsettled.*] *Wolcott.*

UNSE'AWORTHY, *a.* Not fit for a voyage; not able to sustain the violence of the sea; as, the ship is *unseaworthy.*

UNSEC'ONDED, *a.* Not seconded; not supported. The motion was *unseconded;* the attempt was *unseconded.*

2. Not exemplified a second time. [*Not in use.*] *Brown.*

UNSE'CRET, *a.* Not secret; not close; not trusty. *Shak.*

UNSE'CRET, *v. t.* To disclose; to divulge. [*Not used.*] *Bacon.*

UNSEC'ULARIZE, *v. t.* To detach from secular things; to alienate from the world. *Ch. Obs.*

UNSECU'RE, *a.* Not secure; not safe. [But *insecure* is generally used.]

UNSEDU'CED, *a.* Not seduced; not drawn or persuaded to deviate from the path of duty. *Milton.*

UNSEE'DED, *a.* Not seeded; not sown. [*Local.*] *N. England.*

UNSEE'ING, *a.* Wanting the power of vision; not seeing. *Shak.*

UNSEE'M, *v. i.* Not to seem. [*Not in use.*] *Shak.*

UNSEE'MLINESS, *n.* Uncomeliness; indecency; indecorum; impropriety. *Hooker.*

UNSEE'MLY, *a.* Not fit or becoming; uncomely; unbecoming; indecent.

My sons, let your *unseemly* discord cease. *Dryden.*

UNSEE'MLY, *adv.* Indecently; unbecomingly. *Philips.*

UNSEE'N, *a.* Not seen; not discovered. *Milton.*

2. Invisible; not discoverable; as the *unseen* God.

3. Unskilled; inexperienced. [*Not in use.*] *Clarendon.*

UNSE'IZED, *a.* Not seized; not apprehended.

2. Not possessed; not taken into possession. *Dryden.*

UNSEL'DOM, *adv.* Not seldom.

UNSELECT'ED, *a.* Not selected; not separated by choice.

UNSELECT'ING, *a.* Not selecting.

UNSELF'ISH, *a.* Not selfish; not unduly attached to one's own interest. *Spectator.*

UNSENS'IBLE, *a.* Not sensible. [But *insensible* is now used.]

UNSENT', *a.* Not sent; not dispatched; not transmitted.

Unsent for, not called or invited to attend. *Taylor.*

UNSEP'ARABLE, *a.* That cannot be parted. [But *inseparable* is now used.]

UNSEP'ARATED, *a.* Not separated or parted. *Pope.*

UNSEP'ULCHERED, *a.* Having no grave; unburied. *Chapman.*

UNSERV'ED, *a.* Not served.

UNSERV'ICEABLE, *a.* Not serviceable; not bringing advantage, use, profit or convenience; useless; as an *unserviceable* utensil or garment; an *unserviceable* tract of land; *unserviceable* muskets.

UNSERV'ICEABLENESS, *n.* The quality or state of being useless; unfitness for use. *Sanderson.*

UNSERV'ICEABLY, *adv.* Without use; without advantage. *Woodward.*

UNSET', *a.* Not set; not placed. *Hooker.*
2. Not sunk below the horizon.

UNSET'TLE, *v. t.* To unfix; to move or loosen from a fixed state; to unhinge; to make uncertain or fluctuating; as, to *unsettle* doctrines and opinions.
2. To move from a place. *L'Estrange.*
3. To overthrow. *Fleetwood.*

UNSET'TLE, *v. i.* To become unfixed. *Shak.*

UNSET'TLED, *pp.* Unfixed; unhinged; rendered fluctuating.
2. *a.* Not settled; not fixed; not determined; as doctrines, questions, opinions and the like.
3. Not established. *Dryden.*
4. Not regular; unequal; changeable; as an *unsettled* season; *unsettled* weather. *Bentley.*
5. Not having a legal settlement in a town or parish.
6. Having no fixed place of abode. *Hooker.*
7. Not having deposited its fecal matter; turbid; as *unsettled* liquor.
8. Having no inhabitants; not occupied by permanent inhabitants; as *unsettled* lands in America. *Belknap. Hamilton.*

UNSET'TLEDNESS, *n.* The state of being unfixed, unsettled or undetermined.
2. Irresolution; fluctuation of mind or opinions.
3. Uncertainty.
4. Want of fixedness; fluctuation. *South.*

UNSET'TLEMENT, *n.* Unsettled state; irresolution. *Barrow.*

UNSET'TLING, *ppr.* Unfixing; removing from a settled state.

UNSEV'ERED, *a.* Not severed; not parted; not divided. *Shak.*

UNSEX', *v. t.* To deprive of the sex, or to make otherwise than the sex commonly is. *Shak.*

UNSHACK'LE, *v. t.* To unfetter; to loose from bonds; to set free from restraint; as, to *unshackle* the hands; to *unshackle* the mind.

UNSHACK'LED, *pp.* Loosed from shackles or restraint.

UNSHACK'LING, *ppr.* Liberating from bonds or restraint.

UNSHA'DED, *a.* Not shaded; not overspread with shade or darkness. *Boyle.*
2. Not clouded; not having shades in coloring.

UNSHAD'OWED, *a.* Not clouded; not darkened.

UNSHA'KABLE, *a.* That cannot be shaken. [*Not in use.*] *Shak.*

UNSHA'KED, for *unshaken*, not in use. *Shak.*

UNSHA'KEN, *a.* Not shaken; not agitated; not moved; firm; fixed.
2. Not moved in resolution; firm; steady.
3. Not subject to concussion.

UNSHA'MED, *a.* Not shamed; not ashamed; not abashed. *Dryden.*

UNSHA'MEFACED, *a.* Wanting modesty; impudent.

UNSHA'MEFACEDNESS, *n.* Want of modesty; impudence. *Chalmers.*

UNSHA'PE, *v. t.* To throw out of form or into disorder; to confound; to derange. [*Little used.*] *Shak.*

UNSHA'PEN, *a.* Misshapen; deformed; ugly. *Addison.*

UNSHA'RED, *a.* Not shared; not partaken or enjoyed in common; as *unshared* bliss. *Milton.*

UNSHE'ATH, } *v. t.* To draw from the sheath or scabbard.
UNSHE'ATHE, }
Unsheath thy sword. *Shak.*
To unsheath the sword, to make war.

UNSHE'ATHED, *pp.* Drawn from the sheath.

UNSHE'ATHING, *ppr.* Drawing from the scabbard.

UNSHED', *a.* Not shed; not spilt; as blood *unshed.* *Milton.*

UNSHEL'TERED, *a.* Not sheltered; not screened; not defended from danger or annoyance. *Decay of Piety.*

UNSHIE'LDED, *a.* Not defended by a shield; not protected; exposed. *Dryden.*

UNSHIP', *v. t.* To take out of a ship or other water craft; as, to *unship* goods.
2. To remove from the place where it is fixed or fitted; as, to *unship* an oar; to *unship* capstan bars. *Mar. Dict.*

UNSHIP'PED, *pp.* Removed from a ship or from its place.
2. Destitute of a ship.

UNSHOCK'ED, *a.* Not shocked; not disgusted; not astonished. *Tickel.*

UNSHOD', *a.* Not shod; having no shoes. *Clarendon.*

UNSHOOK', *a.* Not shaken; not agitated. *Pope.*

UNSHORN, *a.* Not shorn; not sheared; not clipped; as *unshorn* locks. *Milton.*

UNSHOT', *a.* Not hit by shot. *Waller.*
2. Not shot; not discharged.

UNSHOUT', *v. t.* To retract a shout. [*Not in use.*] *Shak.*

UNSHOW'ERED, *a.* Not watered or sprinkled by showers; as *unshowered* grass. *Milton.*

UNSHRINK'ING, *a.* Not shrinking; not withdrawing from danger or toil; not recoiling; as *unshrinking* firmness.

UNSHRUNK', *a.* Not shrunk; not contracted.

UNSHUN'NABLE, *a.* That cannot be shunned; inevitable. [*Not in use.*] *Shak.*

UNSHUN'NED, *a.* Not shunned; not avoided.

UNSHUT', *a.* Not shut; open; unclosed.

UNSIFT'ED, *a.* Not sifted; not separated by a sieve. *May.*
2. Not critically examined; untried.
Unsight unseen, a vulgar phrase, denoting *unseeing unseen*, or *unseen* repeated; as, to buy a thing *unsight unseen*, that is, without seeing it.

UNSIGHTED, *a.* Not seen; invisible. *Obs.* *Shak.*

UNSIGHTLINESS, *n.* Disagreeableness to the sight; deformity; ugliness. *Wiseman.*

UNSIGHTLY, *a.* Disagreeable to the eye; ugly; deformed. *Milton.*

UNSIG'NALIZED, *a.* Not signalized or distinguished.

UNSIGNIF'ICANT, *a.* Having no meaning. *Obs.* [See *Insignificant.*]

UNSIL'VERED, *a.* Not covered with quicksilver; as an *unsilvered* mirror. *Ure.*

UNSINCE'RE, *a.* Not sincere; hypocritical. [See *Insincere.*]
2. Not genuine; adulterated. *Boyle.*
3. Not sound; not solid.
[Obsolete in the two last significations, and for the first, *insincere* is generally used.]

UNSINCER'ITY, *n.* Insincerity; cheat. [*Not used.*] [See *Insincerity.*]

UNSIN'EW, *v. t.* To deprive of strength. *Dryden.*

UNSIN'EWED, *pp.* or *a.* Deprived of strength or force; weak; nerveless. *Shak.*

UNSIN'EWING, *ppr.* Depriving of strength; enfeebling.

UNSING'ED, *a.* Not singed; not scorched. *Brown.*

UNSIN'GLED, *a.* Not singled; not separated. *Dryden.*

UNSINK'ING, *a.* Not sinking; not failing.

UNSIN'NING, *a.* Committing no sin; impeccable; untainted with sin; as *unsinning* obedience. *Rogers.*

UNSI'ZABLE, *a.* Not being of the proper size, magnitude or bulk. *Smollett.*

UNSI'ZED, *a.* Not sized; as *unsized* paper.

UNSKILL'ED, *a.* Wanting skill; destitute of readiness or dexterity in performance. *Pope.*
2. Destitute of practical knowledge. *Dryden.*

UNSKILL'FUL, *a.* Not skillful; wanting the knowledge and dexterity which are acquired by observation, use and experience; as an *unskillful* surgeon; an *unskillful* mechanic; an *unskillful* logician.

UNSKILL'FULLY, *adv.* Without skill, knowledge or dexterity; clumsily. *Shak.*

UNSKILL'FULNESS, *n.* Want of art or knowledge; want of that readiness in action or execution, which is acquired by use, experience and observation. *Taylor.*

UNSLA'IN, *a.* Not slain; not killed. *Dryden.*

UNSLA'KED, *a.* Not slaked; unquenched; as *unslaked* thirst.

UNSLAK'ED, *a.* Not saturated with water; as *unslaked* lime.

UNSLEE'PING, *a.* Not sleeping; ever wakeful. *Milton.*

UNSLING', *v. t.* In *seamen's language*, to take off the slings of a yard, a cask, &c.

UNSLIP'PING, *a.* Not slipping; not liable to slip. *Shak.*

UNSLOW, *a.* Not slow. [*Not in use.*]

UNSLUM'BERING, *a.* Never sleeping or slumbering; always watching or vigilant. *Thodey.*

UNSMIRCH'ED, *a.* Not stained; not soiled or blacked. *Shak.*

UNSMO'KED, *a.* Not smoked; not dried in smoke.
2. Not used in smoking, as a pipe. *Swift.*

UNSMOOTH', *a.* Not smooth; not even; rough. *Milton.*

UNSO'BER, *a.* Not sober. [*Not used.*]

UNSO'CIABLE, *a.* Not suitable to society; not having the qualities which are proper for society, and which render it agreeable; as an *unsociable* temper.

2. Not apt to converse; not free in conversation; reserved.

UNSO'CIABLY, *adv.* Not kindly.

2. With reserve.

UNSO'CIAL, *a.* Not adapted to society; not beneficial to society. *Shenstone.*

UNSOCK'ET, *v. t.* To loose or take from a socket. *Swift.*

UNSOFT', *a.* Not soft; hard. [*Not used.*] *Chaucer.*

UNSOFT', *adv.* Not with softness. *Obs.* *Spenser.*

UNSOIL'ED, *a.* Not soiled; not stained; unpolluted. *Dryden.*

2. Not disgraced; not tainted; as character.

UNSŌLD, *a.* Not sold; not transferred for a consideration.

UNSŌLDIERED, *a.* Not having the qualities of a soldier. [*Not in use.*] *Beaum.*

UNSŌLDIERLIKE, } *a.* [See *Soldier.*] Un-
UNSŌLDIERLY, } becoming a soldier. *Broome.*

UNSOLIC'ITED, *a.* Not solicited; not requested; unasked. *Halifax.*

2. Not asked for; as an *unsolicited* favor.

UNSOLIC'ITOUS, *a.* Not solicitous; not anxious; not very desirous.

UNSOL'ID, *a.* Not solid; not firm; not substantial; as *unsolid* arguments or reasoning; an *unsolid* foundation.

2. Fluid. *Locke.*

UNSOLV'ABLE, *a.* That cannot be solved; inexplicable. *More.*

UNSOLV'ED, *a.* Not solved; not explained. *Watts.*

UNSO'NABLE, *a.* That cannot be sounded. *Obs.*

UNSOOT, for *unsweet. Obs.* *Spenser.*

UNSOPHIS'TICATED, *a.* Not adulterated by mixture; not counterfeit; pure; as *unsophisticated* drugs; *unsophisticated* arguments. *Locke.*

UNSOR'RŌWED, *a.* Not lamented; not bewailed. *Hooker.*

UNSORT'ED, *a.* Not separated into sorts; not distributed according to kinds or classes; as *unsorted* types; *unsorted* ideas. *Watts.*

UNSOUGHT, *a. unsaut'.* Not sought; not searched for.

2. Had without searching; as *unsought* honor; *unsought* ideas. *Locke.*

UNSŌUL, *v. t.* To deprive of mind or understanding. *Shelton.*

UNSOUND', *a.* Not sound; defective; as *unsound* timber.

2. Infirm; sickly; as *unsound* in health; an *unsound* constitution.

3. Not orthodox; defective; as *unsound* in faith; *unsound* doctrine. *Milner.*

4. Not sound in character; not honest; not faithful; not to be trusted; defective; deceitful. *Shak.*

5. Not true; not solid; not real; not substantial; as *unsound* pleasures; *unsound* delights. *Spenser.*

6. Not close; not compact; as *unsound* cheese. *Mortimer.*

7. Not sincere; not faithful; as *unsound* love. *Gay.*

8. Not solid; not material. *Spenser.*

9. Erroneous; wrong; deceitful; sophistical; as *unsound* arguments.

10. Not strong; as *unsound* ice.

11. Not fast; not calm; as *unsound* sleep.

12. Not well established; defective; questionable; as *unsound* credit. *Hamilton.*

UNSOUND'ED, *a.* Not sounded; not tried with the lead.

UNSOUND'LY, *adv.* Not with soundness; as, he reasons *unsoundly;* he sleeps *unsoundly.*

UNSOUND'NESS, *n.* Defectiveness; as the *unsoundness* of timber.

2. Defectiveness of faith; want of orthodoxy. *Hooker.*

3. Corruptness; want of solidity; as the *unsoundness* of principles. *Hooker.*

4. Defectiveness; as the *unsoundness* of fruit.

5. Infirmity; weakness; as of body; as the *unsoundness* of the body or constitution.

UNSOUR'ED, *a.* Not made sour. *Bacon.*

2. Not made morose or crabbed. *Dryden.*

UNSŌWED, } *a.* Not sown; not sowed
UNSŌWN, } as *unsown* or *unsowed* ground. *Bacon.*

2. Not scattered on land for seed; as seed *unsown.*

3. Not propagated by seed scattered; as *unsown* flowers. *Dryden.*

UNSPA'RED, *a.* Not spared. *Milton.*

UNSPA'RING, *a.* Not parsimonious; liberal; profuse. *Milton.*

2. Not merciful or forgiving. *Milton.*

UNSPA'RINGNESS, *n.* The quality of being liberal or profuse. *Milford.*

UNSPE'AK, *v. t.* To recant; to retract what has been spoken. *Shak.*

UNSPE'AKABLE, *a.* That cannot be uttered; that cannot be expressed; unutterable; as *unspeakable* grief or rage. 2 Cor. xii.

Joy *unspeakable* and full of glory. 1 Pet. i.

UNSPE'AKABLY, *adv.* In a manner or degree that cannot be expressed; inexpressibly; unutterably.

UNSPEC'IFIED, *a.* Not specified; not particularly mentioned. *Brown.*

UNSPE'CIOUS, *a.* Not specious; not plausible. *Asiat. Res.*

UNSPEC'ULATIVE, *a.* Not speculative or theoretical.

UNSPED', *a.* Not performed; not dispatched. *Obs.* *Garth.*

UNSPENT', *a.* Not spent; not used or wasted; as water in a cistern *unspent.*

2. Not exhausted; as strength or force *unspent.*

3. Not having lost its force or impulse; as an *unspent* ball.

UNSPHE'RE, *v. t.* To remove from its orb. *Shak.*

UNSPI'ED, *a.* Not searched; not explored. *Milton.*

2. Not seen; not discovered. *Tickel.*

UNSPILT', *a.* Not spilt; not shed.

2. Not spoiled. [*Not in use.*] *Tusser.*

UNSPIR'IT, *v. t.* To depress in spirits; to dispirit; to dishearten. [Little used. The word used is *dispirit.*]

UNSPIR'ITED, *pp.* Dispirited.

UNSPIR'ITUAL, *a.* Not spiritual; carnal; worldly. *Swift.*

UNSPIR'ITUALIZE, *v. t.* To deprive of spirituality. *South.*

UNSPLIT', *a.* Not split; as, *unsplit* wood will not season.

UNSPOIL'ED, *a.* Not spoiled; not corrupted; not ruined; not rendered useless. *Pope.*

2. Not plundered; not pillaged.

UNSPOT'TED, *a.* Not stained; free from spot.

2. Free from moral stain; untainted with guilt; unblemished; immaculate; as *unspotted* reputation.

UNSPOT'TEDNESS, *n.* State of being free from stain or guilt. *Feltham.*

UNSQUA'RED, *a.* Not made square; as *unsquared* timber.

2. Not regular; not formed. *Shak.*

UNSQUI'RE, *v. t.* To divest of the title or privilege of an esquire. *Swift.*

UNSTA'BLE, *a.* [L. *instabilis.*] Not stable; not fixed.

2. Not steady; inconstant; irresolute; wavering. James i.

UNSTA'BLENESS, *n.* Instability.

UNSTA'ID, *a.* Not steady; mutable; not settled in judgment; volatile; fickle; as *unstaid* youth. *Shak.*

UNSTA'IDNESS, *n.* Unfixed or volatile state or disposition; mutability; fickleness; indiscretion.

2. Uncertain motion; unsteadiness. *Sidney.*

UNSTA'INED, *a.* Not stained; not dyed.

2. Not polluted; not tarnished; not dishonored; as an *unstained* character.

UNST'ANCHED, *a.* Not stanched; not stopped; as blood.

UNSTA'TE, *v. t.* To deprive of dignity. *Shak.*

UNSTAT'UTABLE, *a.* Contrary to statute; not warranted by statute. *Swift.*

UNSTEADFAST, *a. unsted'fast.* Not fixed; not standing or being firm.

2. Not firmly adhering to a purpose.

UNSTEADFASTNESS, *n. unsted'fastness.* Want of steadfastness; instability; inconstancy. *K. James.*

UNSTEADILY, *adv. unsted'ily.* Without steadiness; in a wavering, vacillating manner.

2. Inconstantly; in a fickle manner.

3. Not in the same manner at different times; variously. *Locke.*

UNSTEADINESS, *n. unsted'iness.* Unstableness; inconstancy; want of firmness; irresolution; mutableness of opinion or purpose. *Addison.*

2. Frequent change of place; vacillation.

UNSTEADY, *a. unsted'y.* Not steady; not constant; irresolute. *Denham.*

2. Mutable; variable; changeable; as *unsteady* winds.

3. Not adhering constantly to any fixed plan or business.

UNSTEE'PED, *a.* Not steeped; not soaked. *Bacon.*

UNSTIM'ULATED, *a.* Not stimulated; not excited; as *unstimulated* nature. *L. Beecher.*

UNSTIM'ULATING, *a.* Not exciting motion or action.

UNSTING', *v. t.* To disarm of a sting. *South.*

Elegant dissertations on virtue and vice—will not *unsting* calamity. *J. M. Mason.*

UNSTING'ED, *pp.* Deprived of its sting. *Pollok.*

UNSTINT'ED, *a.* Not stinted; not limited. *Skelton.*

UNSTIRRED, *a. unstur'red.* Not stirred; not agitated. *Boyle.*

UNSTITCH', *v. t.* To open by picking out stitches. *Collier.*

UNSTITCH'ED, *a.* Not stitched.

UNSTOOP'ING, *a.* Not stooping; not bending; not yielding; as *unstooping* firmness. *Shak.*

UNSTOP', *v. t.* To free from a stopple, as a bottle or cask.

2. To free from any obstruction; to open. *Boyle.*

UNSTOP'PED, *pp.* Opened.

2. *a.* Not meeting any resistance. *Dryden.*

UNSTOP'PING, *ppr.* Taking out a stopper; opening; freeing from obstruction.

UNSTO'RED, *a.* Not stored; not laid up in store; not warehoused.

2. Not supplied with stores; as a fort *unstored* with provisions.

UNSTORM'ED, *a.* Not assaulted; not taken by assault. *Addison.*

UNSTRA'INED, *a.* Not strained; as *unstrained* oil.

2. Easy; not forced; natural; as an *unstrained* derivation. *Hakewill.*

UNSTRA'ITENED, *a.* Not straitened; not contracted.

UNSTRA'TIFIED, *a.* Not stratified; not formed or being in strata or layers. *Cleaveland.*

UNSTRENGTH'ENED, *a.* Not strengthened; not supported; not assisted. *Hooker.*

UNSTRING', *v. t.* To relax tension; to loosen; as, to *unstring* the nerves.

2. To deprive of strings; as, to *unstring* a harp.

3. To loose; to untie.

4. To take from a string; as, to *unstring* beads.

UNSTRUCK', *a.* Not struck; not impressed; not affected; as *unstruck* with horror. *Philips.*

UNSTUD'IED, *a.* Not studied; not premeditated. *Dryden.*

2. Not labored; easy; natural; as an *unstudied* style.

UNSTU'DIOUS, *a.* Not studious; not diligent in study. *Dwight.*

UNSTUFF'ED, *a.* Not stuffed; not filled; not crowded. *Shak.*

UNSUBDU'ED, *a.* Not subdued; not brought into subjection; not conquered; as nations or passions *unsubdued.*

UNSUB'JECT, *a.* Not subject; not liable; not obnoxious.

UNSUBJECT'ED, *a.* Not subjected; not subdued.

UNSUBMIS'SIVE, *a.* Not submissive; disobedient.

UNSUBMIT'TING, *a.* Not submitting; not obsequious; not readily yielding. *Thomson.*

UNSUBOR'DINATED, *a.* Not subordinated or reduced to subjection.

UNSUBORN'ED, *a.* Not suborned; not procured by secret collusion. *Ash. Hume.*

UNSUB'SIDIZED, *a.* Not engaged in another's service by receiving subsidies.

UNSUBSTAN'TIAL, *a.* Not substantial; not solid. *Milton.*

2. Not real; not having substance. *Addison.*

UNSUCCEE'DED, *a.* Not succeeded; not followed. *Milton.*

UNSUCCESS'FUL, *a.* Not successful; not producing the desired event; not fortunate. *Addison.*

UNSUCCESS'FULLY, *adv.* Without success; without a favorable issue; unfortunately. *South.*

UNSUCCESS'FULNESS, *n.* Want of success or favorable issue.

UNSUCCESS'IVE, *a.* Not proceeding by a flux of parts or by regular succession. *Hale.*

UNSUCK'ED, *a.* Not having the breasts drawn. *Milton.*

UNSUF'FERABLE, *a.* Not sufferable; not to be endured; intolerable. [But the word now used is *insufferable.*]

UNSUF'FERABLY, *adv.* So as not to be endured. [For this, *insufferably* is chiefly used.]

UNSUF'FERING, *a.* Not suffering; not tolerating. *Young.*

UNSUFFI''CIENCE, *n.* Inability to answer the end proposed. [For this, *insufficiency* is used.]

UNSUFFI''CIENT, *a.* Not sufficient; inadequate. [For this, *insufficient* is now used.]

UNSUGARED, *a.* UNSHOOG'ARED. Not sweetened with sugar. *Bacon.*

UNSUITABLE, *a.* Not suitable; unfit; not adapted; as timber *unsuitable* for a bridge.

2. Unbecoming; improper; as a dress *unsuitable* for a clergyman; *unsuitable* returns for favors.

UNSUITABLENESS, *n.* Unfitness; incongruity; impropriety. *South.*

UNSUITABLY, *adv.* In a manner unbecoming or improper.

2. Incongruously; as a man and wife *unsuitably* matched.

UNSUITED, *a.* Not suited; not fitted; not adapted; not accommodated.

UNSUITING, *a.* Not fitting; not becoming. *Shak.*

UNSUL'LIED, *a.* Not sullied; not stained; not tarnished.

2. Not disgraced; free from imputation of evil.

UNSUNG', *a.* Not sung; not celebrated in verse; not recited in verse. *Addison.*

UNSUN'NED, *a.* Not having been exposed to the sun. *Milton.*

UNSUPER'FLUOUS, *a.* Not more than enough. *Milton.*

UNSUPPLANT'ED, *a.* Not supplanted; not overthrown by secret means or stratagem.

UNSUPPLI'ED, *a.* Not supplied; not furnished with things necessary. *Dryden.*

UNSUPPORTABLE, *a.* That cannot be supported; intolerable. [But *insupportable* is generally used.]

UNSUPPORTABLENESS, *n.* Insupportableness. [*The latter is chiefly used.*]

UNSUPPORTABLY, *adv.* Insupportably. [*The latter is generally used.*]

UNSUPPORTED, *a.* Not supported; not upheld; not sustained. *Milton.*

2. Not countenanced; not assisted. *Brown.*

UNSUPPRESS'ED, *a.* Not suppressed; not subdued; not extinguished.

UNSU'RE, *a.* [See *Sure.*] Not fixed; not certain. *Pope.*

UNSURMOUNT'ABLE, *a.* That cannot be surmounted or overcome; insuperable. *Locke.*

UNSURP'ASSED, *a.* Not surpassed; not exceeded.

UNSUSCEP'TIBLE, *a.* Not susceptible; not capable of admitting or receiving; as a heart *unsusceptible* of impressions; a substance *unsusceptible* of change or of permanent colors.

UNSUSPECT', for *unsuspected*, is not in use.

UNSUSPECT'ED, *a.* Not suspected; not considered as likely to have done an evil act, or to have a disposition to evil. *Swift. Dryden.*

UNSUSPECT'EDLY, *adv.* In a manner to avoid suspicion. *Pope.*

UNSUSPECT'ING, *a.* Not imagining that any ill is designed; free from suspicion. *Pope.*

UNSUSPI''CIOUS, *a.* Having no suspicion; not indulging the imagination of evil in others; as an *unsuspicious* youth.

2. Not to be suspected; as *unsuspicious* testimony. *Mitford.*

UNSUSPI''CIOUSLY, *adv.* Without suspicion.

UNSUSTA'INABLE, *a.* Not sustainable; that cannot be maintained or supported; as *unsustainable* pain; a suit in law *unsustainable.*

UNSUSTA'INED, *a.* Not sustained; not supported; not seconded.

UNSWA'THE, *v. t.* To take a swathe from; to relieve from a bandage. *Addison.*

UNSWA'YABLE, *a.* That cannot be swayed, governed or influenced by another. [*Little used.*] *Shak.*

UNSWA'YED, *a.* Not swayed; not wielded; as a scepter.

2. Not biased; not controlled or influenced.

UNSWEAR, *v. t.* To recant or recall an oath. *Spenser.*

UNSWEAT, *v. t. unswet'.* To ease or cool after exercise or toil. [*A bad word and not used.*] *Milton.*

UNSWEATING, *a. unswet'ing.* Not sweating. *Dryden.*

UNSWEE'T, *a.* Not sweet. [*Little used.*] *Spenser.*

UNSWEPT', *a.* Not cleaned with a broom; not swept; not brushed. *Shak.*

UNSWORN, *a.* Not sworn; not bound by an oath; not having taken an oath; as, the witness is *unsworn.*

UNSYMMET'RICAL, *a.* Wanting symmetry or due proportion of parts.

UNSYSTEMAT'IC, } *a.* Not systematic; not having regular order, distribution or arrangement of parts. *Ames.*
UNSYSTEMAT'ICAL, }

UNSYS'TEMIZED, *a.* Not systemized; not arranged in due order; not formed into system.

UNTACK', *v. t.* To separate what is tacked; to disjoin; to loosen what is fast. *Milton.*

UNTA'INTED, *a.* Not rendered impure by admixture; not impregnated with foul matter; as *untainted* air.

2. Not sullied; not stained; unblemished; as *untainted* virtue or reputation.
3. Not rendered unsavory by putrescence; as *untainted* meat.
4. Not charged with a crime; not accused; as, he lived *untainted*. *Shak.*

UNTA'INTEDLY, *adv.* Without spot; without blemish; without imputation of crime.

UNTA'INTEDNESS, *n.* State or quality of being untainted; purity. *Hall.*

UNTAKEN, *a.* *unta'kn.* Not taken; not seized; not apprehended; as a thief *untaken.*
2. Not reduced; not subdued; as *untaken* Troy. *Pope.*
3. Not swallowed.

Untaken away, not removed. 2 Cor. iii.

Untaken up, not occupied; not filled. *Boyle.*

Untalked of, not talked of; not made the subject of conversation.

UNTA'MABLE, *a.* That cannot be tamed or domesticated; that cannot be reclaimed from a wild state. *Grew.*
2. Not to be subdued or reduced to control.

UNTA'MED, *a.* Not reclaimed from wildness; not domesticated; not made familiar with man; as an *untamed* beast.
2. Not subdued; not brought under control; as a turbulent, *untamed* mind. *Dryden.*
3. Not softened or rendered mild by culture; as an *untamed* people. *Spenser.*

UNTAN'GLE, *v. t.* To disentangle; to loose from tangles or intricacy; as, to *untangle* thread.

Untangle this cruel chain. *Prior.*

UNTAN'GLED, *pp.* Disentangled.

UNTAN'GLING, *ppr.* Disentangling.

UNT'ARNISHED, *a.* Not soiled; not tarnished; not stained; unblemished; as *untarnished* silk; *untarnished* reputation.

UNTÄSTED, *a.* Not tasted; not tried by the taste or tongue.
2. Not enjoyed; as *untasted* pleasures.

UNTÄSTEFUL, *a.* Having no taste; being without taste.

UNTÄSTEFULLY, *adv.* Without taste or gracefulness; in bad taste. *Br. Rev.*

UNTÄSTING, *a.* Not tasting; not perceiving by the taste. *Smith.*

UNTAUGHT, *a.* *untaut'.* Not taught; not instructed; not educated; unlettered; illiterate. *Dryden.*
2. Unskilled; new; not having use or practice.

A tongue *untaught* to plead for favor. *Shak.*

UNTAX'ED, *a.* Not taxed; not charged with taxes.
2. Not accused.

UNTE'ACH, *v. t.* pret. and pp. *untaught.* To cause to forget or lose what has been taught.

Experience will *unteach* us. *Brown.*

UNTE'ACHABLE, *a.* That cannot be taught or instructed; indocile. *Milton.*

UNTE'ACHABLENESS, *n.* The quality of not readily receiving instruction; indocility. *Scott.*

UNTEE'MING, *a.* Not producing young; barren.

UNTEM'PERATE, *a.* Intemperate. [*The latter is now used.*]

UNTEM'PERED, *a.* Not tempered; not duly mixed for use; not durable or strong.

UNTEMPT'ED, *a.* Not tempted; not tried by enticements or persuasions; not invited by any thing alluring.

UNTEN'ABLE, *a.* Not tenable; that cannot be held in possession; as an *untenable* post or fort. *Dryden. Clarendon.*
2. That cannot be maintained or supported; not defensible; as an *untenable* doctrine; *untenable* ground in argument.

UNTEN'ANTABLE, *a.* Not fit for an occupant; not in suitable repair or condition for a tenant.

UNTEN'ANTED, *a.* Not occupied by a tenant; not inhabited. *Temple.*

UNTEND'ED, *a.* Not tended; not having any attendant. *Thomson.*

UNTEN'DER, *a.* Not tender; not soft.
2. Wanting sensibility or affection. *Shak.*

UNTEND'ERED, *a.* Not tendered; not offered; as *untendered* money or tribute. *Shak.*

UNTENT', *v. t.* To bring out of a tent. [*Little used.*] *Shak.*

UNTENT'ED, *a.* Not having a medical tent applied. *Shak.*

UNTER'RIFIED, *a.* Not terrified; not affrighted; not daunted. *Milton.*

UNTEST'ED, *a.* Not tested; not tried by a standard. *Adams' Lect.*

UNTHANK'ED, *a.* Not thanked; not repaid with acknowledgments. *Dryden.*
2. Not received with thankfulness; as an *unthanked* reprieve. [*Unusual.*] *Dryden.*

UNTHANK'FUL, *a.* Not thankful; ungrateful; not making acknowledgments for good received.

For he is kind to the *unthankful* and to the evil. Luke vi.

UNTHANK'FULLY, *adv.* Without thanks; without a grateful acknowledgment of favors. *Boyle.*

UNTHANK'FULNESS, *n.* Neglect or omission of acknowledgment for good received; want of a sense of kindness or benefits; ingratitude.

Immoderate favors breed first *unthankfulness*, and afterwards hate. *Hayward.*

[See Tacitus' Ann. iv. 18.]

UNTHAW'ED, *a.* Not thawed; not melted or dissolved; as ice or snow. *Pope.*

UNTHINK', *v. t.* To dismiss a thought. *Shak.*

UNTHINK'ING, *a.* Not thinking; not heedful; thoughtless; inconsiderate; as *unthinking* youth.
2. Not indicating thought or reflection; as a round *unthinking* face. *Pope.*

UNTHINK'INGNESS, *n.* Want of thought or reflection; habitual thoughtlessness. *Halifax.*

UNTHORN'Y, *a.* Not thorny; free from thorns. *Brown.*

UNTHOUGHTFUL, *a.* *unthaut'ful.* Thoughtless; heedless. *Cowley.*

Unthought of, not thought of; not regarded; not heeded. *Shak.*

UNTHREAD, *v. t.* *unthred'.* To draw or take out a thread from; as, to *unthread* a needle.
2. To loose. *Milton.*

UNTHREAD'ED, *pp.* Deprived of a thread.

UNTHREAD'ING, *ppr.* Depriving of a thread.

UNTHREATENED, *a.* *unthret'ened.* Not threatened; not menaced. *K. Charles.*

UN'THRIFT, *n.* A prodigal; one who wastes his estate by extravagance. *Dryden.*

UNTHRIFT'ILY, *adv.* Without frugality. *Collier.*

UNTHRIFT'INESS, *n.* Waste of property without necessity or use; prodigality; profusion. *Hayward.*

UNTHRIFT'Y, *a.* Prodigal; lavish; profuse; spending property without necessity or use. *Sidney.*
2. Not thriving; not gaining property; as an *unthrifty* farmer.
3. Not gaining flesh; as an *unthrifty* ox.
4. Not vigorous in growth, as a plant.

UNTHRI'VING, *a.* Not thriving; not prospering in temporal affairs; not gaining property.

UNTHRO'NE, *v. t.* To remove from a throne, or from supreme authority; to dethrone.

UNTI'DY, *a.* Not tidy; not seasonable; not ready.
2. Not neatly dressed; not in good order.

UNTI'E, *v. t.* To loosen, as a knot; to disengage the parts that form a knot. *Untie* the knot.
2. To unbind; to free from any fastening; as, to *untie* an iron chain. *Waller.*
3. To loosen from coils or convolution; as snakes *untied.* *Pope.*
4. To loose; to separate something attached; as, to *untie* the tongue.
5. To resolve; to unfold; to clear. *Watts.*

UNTI'ED, *pp.* Loosed, as a knot; unbound; separated; resolved.
2. *a.* Not tied; not bound or gathered in a knot; loose.
3. Not fastened with a knot.
4. Not held by any tie or band.

UNTIL', *prep.* [*un* and *till.* See *Till.*] To; *used of time.*

He and his sons were priests of the tribe of Dan, *until* the day of the captivity. Judges xviii.

2. To; *used of objects.* *Obs.* *Spenser.*
3. Preceding a sentence or clause, to; that is, to the event mentioned, or the time of it; as, *until* this hour; *until* this year.

The scepter shall not depart from Judah—*until* Shiloh come. Gen. xlix.

4. To the point or place of.

In open prospect nothing bounds our eye,
Until the earth seems join'd unto the sky. *Dryden.*

5. To the degree that.

Thou shalt push Syria, *until* they be consumed. 2 Chron. xviii.

[Note. *Until* is always the same part of speech in fact, and has the same signification. The only difference is, that it is followed sometimes by a single word denoting time, and in other cases by a verb denoting an event, or a word denoting place or degree. The sense is in all cases *to;* and *till* may be used as its substitute, and in modern usage it is most common.]

UNTI'LE, *v. t.* To take the tiles from; to uncover by removing tiles. *Swift.*

UNTILL'ED, *a.* Not tilled; not cultivated. *Mortimer.*

UNTIM'BERED, *a.* Not furnished with timber. *Shak.*
2. Not covered with timber trees; as *untimbered* land.

UNTI'MELY, *a.* Happening before the usual time; as *untimely* frost.

2. Happening before the natural time; premature; as *untimely* death; *untimely* fate. *Dryden.*

UNTI'MELY, *adv.* Before the natural time.
—What is *untimely* done. *Shak.*

UNTINC'TURED, *a.* Not tinctured; not tinged. *Goldsmith.*

UNTING'ED, *a.* Not tinged; not stained; not discolored; as water *untinged; untinged* beams of light. *Boyle.*
2. Not infected. *Swift.*

UNTI'RABLE, *a.* That cannot be wearied; indefatigable; unwearied. *Shak.*

UNTI'RED, *a.* Not tired; not exhausted by labor. *Dryden.*

UNTI'RING, *a.* Not becoming tired or exhausted; as *untiring* patience.

UNTI'TLED, *a.* Having no title; as an *untitled* tyrant. *Shak.*

UN'TO, *prep.* a compound of *un,* [on,] and *to;* of no use in the language, as it expresses no more than *to.* I do not find it in our mother tongue, nor is it ever used in popular discourse. It is found in writers of former times, but is entirely obsolete.

UNTOLD, *a.* Not told; not related; not revealed. *Waller. Dryden.*
2. Not numbered; as money *untold.*

UNTOMB, *v. t. untoom'.* To disinter. *Fuller.*

UNTOOTH'SOME, *a.* Not pleasant to the taste.

UNTOUCHED, *a. untuch'ed.* Not touched; not reached; not hit. *Stephens.*
2. Not moved; not affected; as the heart *untouched.*
3. Not meddled with; as books *untouched* for years.

UNTO'WARD, *a.* Froward; perverse; refractory; not easily guided or taught. Acts ii.
2. Awkward; ungraceful; as *untoward* words. *Creech.*
3. Inconvenient; troublesome; unmanageable; as an *untoward* vow. *Hudibras.*

UNTO'WARDLY, *adv.* In a froward or perverse manner; perversely; ungainly. *Tillotson.*

UNTO'WARDLY, *a.* Awkward; perverse; froward. *Locke.*

UNTO'WARDNESS, *n.* Awkwardness; frowardness; perverseness. *Bp. Wilson.*

UNTRA'CEABLE, *a.* That cannot be traced or followed. *South.*

UNTRA'CED, *a.* Not traced; not followed.
2. Not marked by footsteps. *Denham.*
3. Not marked out.

UNTRACK'ED, *a.* Not tracked; not marked by footsteps.
2. Not followed by the tracks.

UNTRACT'ABLE, *a.* [L. *intractabilis.*] Not tractable; not yielding to discipline; stubborn; indocile; ungovernable; as an *untractable* son. *Locke.*
2. Rough; difficult. *Milton.*
3. Not yielding to the heat or to the hammer; as an ore.
[*Intractable* is more generally used.]

UNTRACT'ABLENESS, *n.* Refractoriness; stubbornness; unwillingness to be governed, controlled or managed. *Locke.*

UNTRA'DING, *a.* Not engaged in commerce; as an *untrading* country or city.

UNTRA'INED, *a.* Not trained; not disciplined; not skillful. *Milton.*
2. Not educated; not instructed.
My wit *untrained.* *Shak.*
3. Irregular; ungovernable; as *untrained* hope. *Herbert.*

UNTRAM'MELED, *a.* Not trammeled; not shackled. *Herbert.*

UNTRANSFER'ABLE, *a.* That cannot be transferred or passed from one to another; as power or right *untransferable.*

UNTRANSFER'RED, *a.* Not transferred; not conveyed or assigned to another; as titles or rights *untransferred.*

UNTRANSLA'TABLE, *a.* Not capable of being translated. *Gray.*

UNTRANSLA'TED, *a.* Not translated or rendered into another language.

UNTRANSPA'RENT, *a.* Not transparent; not diaphanous; opake; not permeable by light. *Boyle.*

UN'TRANSPOSED, *a. untranspo'zed.* Not transposed; having the natural order. *Rambler.*

UNTRAV'ELED, *a.* Not traveled; not trodden by passengers; as an *untraveled* forest.
2. Having never seen foreign countries; as an *untraveled* Englishman. *Addison.*

UNTRAV'ERSED, *a.* Not traversed; not passed over.

UNTREAD, *v. t. untred'.* To tread back; to go back in the same steps. *Shak.*

UNTREASURED, *a. untrezh'ured.* Not treasured; not laid up; not reposited. *Shak.*

UNTRE'ATABLE, *a.* Not treatable; not practicable. [*Not used.*] *Decay of Piety.*

UNTREM'BLING, *a.* Not trembling or shaking; firm; steady. *Montgomery.*

UNTRI'ED, *a.* Not tried; not attempted. *Milton.*
2. Not yet experienced; as *untried* sufferings.
3. Not having passed trial; not heard and determined in law. The cause remains *untried.*

UNTRIM'MED, *a.* Not trimmed; not pruned; not dressed; not put in order.

UNTRI'UMPHABLE, *a.* That admits no triumph. [*Barbarous and not used.*] *Hudibras.*

UNTRI'UMPHED, *a.* Not triumphed over.

UNTROD', } *a.* Not having been trod;
UNTROD'DEN, } not passed over; not marked by the feet. *Milton. Addison.*

UNTROLLED, *a.* Not bolled; not rolled along. *Dryden.*

UNTROUBLED, *a. untrub'led.* Not troubled; not disturbed by care, sorrow or business; free from trouble. *Shak.*
2. Not agitated; not ruffled; not confused; free from passion; as an *untroubled* mind. *Milton.*
3. Not agitated; not moved; as an *untroubled* lake.
4. Not disturbed or interrupted in the natural course; as *untroubled* nature. *Spenser.*
5. Not foul; not turbid; clear; as an *untroubled* stream.

UNTROUB'LEDNESS, *n.* State of being free from trouble; unconcern. [*Not used.*] *Hammond.*

UNTRUE, *a.* Not true; false; contrary to the fact. The story is *untrue.*
2. Not faithful to another; not fulfilling the duties of a husband, wife, vassal, &c.; false; disloyal. *Dryden.*
3. Inconstant; as a lover.

UNTRU'LY, *adv.* Not truly; falsely; not according to reality.

UNTRUSS', *v. t.* To untie or unfasten; to loose from a truss; to let out. *Dryden.*

UNTRUSS'ED, *a.* Not trussed; not tied up.

UNTRUST'INESS, *n.* Unfaithfulness in the discharge of a trust.

UNTRUST'Y, *a.* Not trusty; not worthy of confidence; unfaithful.

UNTRUTH, *n.* Contrariety to truth; falsehood.
2. Want of veracity. *Sandys.*
3. Treachery; want of fidelity. *Obs.* *Shak.*
4. False assertion.
No *untruth* can possibly avail the patron and defender long. *Hooker.*

UNTUCK'ERED, *a.* Having no tucker; as an *untuckered* neck. *Addison.*

UNTU'NABLE, *a.* Not harmonious; not musical. *Bacon.*
2. Not capable of making music. *Tatler.*
3. Not capable of being tuned or brought to the proper pitch.

UNTU'NE, *v. t.* To make incapable of harmony.
Untune that string. *Shak.*
2. To disorder.
Untun'd and jarring senses. *Shak.*

UNTURN'ED, *a.* Not turned. He left no stone *unturned.*

UNTU'TORED, *a.* Uninstructed; untaught; as *untutored* infancy. *Prior.*

UNTWI'NE, *v. t.* To untwist. *Waller.*
2. To open; to disentangle. *Bacon.*
3. To separate, as that which winds or clasps. *Ascham.*

UNTWIST', *v. t.* To separate and open, as threads twisted; or to turn back that which is twisted.
2. To open; to disentangle; as intricacy.

UNTY. [See *Untie.*]

UNU'NIFORM, *a.* Not uniform; wanting uniformity. [*Little used.*]

UNUPHELD', *a.* Not upheld; not sustained. *Pollok.*

UNURG'ED, *a.* Not urged; not pressed with solicitation. *Shak.*

UNU'SED, *a. s* as *z.* Not put to use; not employed.
2. That has never been used.
3. Not accustomed; as hands *unused* to labor; hearts *unused* to deceit.

UNU'SEFUL, *a.* Useless; serving no good purpose. *Philips.*

UNU'SUAL, *a. s* as *z.* Not usual; not common; rare; as an *unusual* season; a person of *unusual* graces or erudition.

UNU'SUALLY, *adv. s* as *z.* Not commonly; not frequently; rarely. This summer, 1828, has been *unusually* rainy.

UNU'SUALNESS, *n. s* as *z.* Uncommonness; infrequency; rareness of occurrence. *Broome.*

UNUT'TERABLE, *a.* That cannot be uttered or expressed; ineffable; inexpressible; as *unutterable* anguish; *unutterable* joy.

UNVA'IL, *v. t.* To remove a vail from; to uncover; to disclose to view. She *unvailed* her face.

UNVAL'UABLE, *a.* Being above price; invaluable. [But *invaluable* is the word now used.]

UNVAL'UED, *a.* Not valued; not prized; neglected. *Shak.*

2. Inestimable; not to be valued. *Shak.*
3. Not estimated; not having the value set.

UNVAN'QUISHABLE, *a.* That cannot be conquered. *Bp. King.*

UNVAN'QUISHED, *a.* Not conquered; not overcome. *Milton.*

UNVA'RIABLE, *a.* Not variable; not changeable or alterable. [But *invariable* is the word now used.]

UNVA'RIED, *a.* Not varied; not altered; not diversified.

UNVA'RIEGATED, *a.* Not variegated; not diversified.

UNV'ARNISHED, *a.* Not overlaid with varnish.
2. Not artificially colored or adorned; not artfully embellished; plain.

I will a round *unvarnish'd* tale deliver. *Shak.*

UNVA'RYING, *a.* Not altering; not liable to change; uniform. *Locke.*

UNVEIL. [See *Unvail.*]

UNVEILEDLY, *adv.* Plainly; without disguise. [*Little used.*]

UNVEN'ERABLE, *a.* Not venerable; not worthy of veneration. *Shak.*

UNVEN'TILATED, *a.* Not fanned by the wind; not purified by a free current of air.

UNVERD'ANT, *a.* Not verdant; not green; having no verdure. *Congreve.*

UNVER'ITABLE, *a.* Not true. [*Not in use.*] *Brown.*

UNVERS'ED, *a.* Not skilled; not versed; unacquainted; as *unversed* in spinning. *Blackmore.*

UNVEX'ED, *a.* Not vexed; not troubled; not disturbed or irritated. *Dryden.*

UNVI'OLATED, *a.* Not violated; not injured; as *unviolated* honor.
2. Not broken; not transgressed; as laws *unviolated.*

UNVIR'TUOUS, *a.* Not virtuous; destitute of virtue. *Shak.*

UNVIS'ARD, *v. t.* *s* as z. To unmask. *Milton.*

UNVIS'ITED, *a.* *s* as z. Not visited; not resorted to; not frequented.

UNVI'TAL, *a.* Not vital; not affecting life. *Med. Repos.*

UNVI''TIATED, } *a.* Not vitiated; not
UNVI''CIATED, } corrupted. *B. Jonson.*

UNVIT'RIFIED, *a.* Not vitrified; not converted into glass.

UNVOL'ATILIZED, *a.* Not volatilized. *Aikin.*

UNVO'TE, *v. t.* To contravene by vote a former vote; to annul a former vote. *Burke.*

UNVOW'ELED, *a.* Having no vowels. *Skinner.*

UNVOY'AGEABLE, *a.* Not to be navigated or passed over on a fluid. [*Not used.*] *Milton.*

UNVUL'GAR, *a.* Not common. *B. Jonson.*

UNVUL'NERABLE, *a.* Not vulnerable; that cannot be wounded. [*Invulnerable* is mostly used.]

Unwaited on, not attended.

UNWA'KENED, *a.* Not awakened; not roused from sleep or stupidity.

UNWALL'ED, *a.* Not surrounded, fortified or supported by a wall. *Knolles.*

UNWA'RES, *adv.* Unexpectedly. [For this, *unawares* is used.]

UNWA'RILY, *adv.* Without vigilance and caution; heedlessly. *Digby.*

UNWA'RINESS, *n.* Want of vigilance; want of caution; carelessness; heedlessness. *Spectator.*

UNWAR'LIKE, *a.* [See *War.*] Not fit for war; not used to war; not military. *Waller.*

UNWARM'ED, *a.* [See *Warm.*] Not warmed.
2. Not excited; not animated. *Addison.*

UNWARN'ED, *a.* [See *Warn.*] Not cautioned; not previously admonished of danger. *Locke.*

UNWARP', *v. t.* [See *Warp.*] To reduce back what is warped. *Evelyn.*

UNWARP'ED, *a.* Not warped; not biased; not turned from the true direction; impartial. *Thomson.*

UNWARP'ING, *a.* Not bending; unyielding; not deviating. *Dwight.*

UNWAR'RANTABLE, *a.* Not defensible; not vindicable; not justifiable; illegal; unjust; improper. *South.*

UNWAR'RANTABLY, *adv.* In a manner that cannot be justified. *Wake.*

UNWAR'RANTED, *a.* Not warranted; not authorized.
2. Not ascertained; not assured or certain.
3. Not covenanted to be good, sound, or of a certain quality; as an *unwarranted* horse.

UNWA'RY, *a.* Not vigilant against danger; not cautious; unguarded; precipitate. *Locke. Dryden.*
2. Unexpected. *Obs.*

UNWASH'ED, } *a.* Not washed; not
UNWASH'EN, } cleansed by water. Matt. xv.

UNWASTED, *a.* Not lost by extravagance or negligence; not lavished away; not dissipated.
2. Not consumed by time or violence.
3. Not lost by exhaustion, evaporation or other means.

UNWASTING, *a.* Not growing less; not decaying. *Pope.*

UNWATERED, *a.* [See *Water.*] Not watered; dry. *Pope.*

UNWA'YED, *a.* Not used to travel. [*Bad and not used.*] *Suckling.*

UNWE'AKENED, *a.* Not weakened; not enfeebled. *Boyle.*

UNWEALTHY, *a.* *unwelth'y.* Not wealthy. *Langhorne.*

UNWEAPONED, *a.* *unwep'nd.* Not furnished with weapons or offensive arms. *Raleigh.*

UNWE'ARIABLE, *a.* That cannot be wearied; indefatigable. [*Little used.*] *Hooker.*

UNWE'ARIED, *a.* Not tired; not fatigued. *Dryden.*
2. Indefatigable; continual; that does not tire or sink under fatigue; as *unwearied* perseverance. *Rogers.*

UNWE'ARIEDLY, *adv.* Without tiring or sinking under fatigue.

UNWE'ARIEDNESS, *n.* State of being unwearied. *Baxter.*

UNWE'ARY, *a.* Not weary; not tired.

UNWE'ARY, *v. t.* To refresh after fatigue. *Temple.*

UNWED', *a.* Unmarried. *Shak.*

UNWED'DED, *a.* Unmarried; remaining single.

UNWEDGEABLE, *a.* *unwedj'able.* Not to be split with wedges. [*Barbarous and not used.*] *Shak.*

UNWEE'DED, *a.* Not weeded; not cleared of weeds. *Shak.*

UNWEE'PED. [See *Unwept.*]

UNWEE'TING, *a.* [See *Weet* and *Wit.*] Ignorant; unknowing. *Obs.* *Spenser.*

UNWEE'TINGLY, *adv.* Ignorantly. *Obs.* *Spenser.*

UNWEIGHED, *a.* Not weighed; not having the weight ascertained.

Solomon left all the vessels *unweighed.* 1 Kings vii.

2. Not deliberately considered and examined; as, to leave arguments or testimony *unweighed.*
3. Not considerate; negligent; as words *unweighed.* *Pope.*

UNWEIGHING, *a.* Inconsiderate; thoughtless. *Shak.*

UNWEL'COME, *a.* Not welcome; not grateful; not pleasing; not well received; as *unwelcome* news; an *unwelcome* guest.

UNWELL', *a.* Not well; indisposed; not in good health. [It expresses less than *sick.*]

UNWELL'NESS, *n.* State of being indisposed. [*Not in use.*] *Chesterfield.*

UNWEPT', *a.* Not lamented; not mourned. The profligate lives despised, and dies *unwept.*

UNWET', *a.* Not wet or moist. *Dryden.*

UNWHIP'PED, } *a.* Not whipped; not cor-
UNWHIPT', } rected with the rod. *Pope.*

UNWHO'LE, *a.* [See *Whole.*] Not sound; infirm. [*Not in use.*]

UNWHO'LESOME, *a.* Not wholesome; unfavorable to health; insalubrious; as *unwholesome* air or food. *Bacon.*
2. Pernicious; as *unwholesome* advice.

UNWHO'LESOMENESS, *n.* Insalubrity; state or quality of being injurious or noxious to health; as the *unwholesomeness* of a climate.

UNWIE'LDILY, *adv.* Heavily; with difficulty. *Dryden.*

UNWIE'LDINESS, *n.* Heaviness; difficulty of being moved; as the *unwieldiness* of a corpulent body. *Donne.*

UNWIE'LDY, *a.* That is moved with difficulty; unmanageable; bulky; ponderous; as an *unwieldy* bulk; an *unwieldy* rock.

UNWILL'ED, *a.* Not willed; not produced by the will.

UNWILL'ING, *a.* Not willing; loth; disinclined; reluctant; as an *unwilling* servant.

UNWILL'INGLY, *adv.* Not with good will; not cheerfully; reluctantly.

UNWILL'INGNESS, *n.* Lothness; disinclination; reluctance.

UNWIND, *v. t.* pret. and pp. *unwound.* To wind off; to loose or separate what is wound or convolved; as, to *unwind* thread or a ball.
2. To disentangle. *Hooker.*

UNWIND, *v. i.* To admit evolution. *Mortimer.*

UNWI'PED, *a.* Not cleaned by rubbing. *Shak.*

UNWI'SE, *a.* *s* as z. Not wise; not choosing the best means for the end; defective

in wisdom; as an *unwise* man; *unwise* kings.
2. Not dictated by wisdom; not adapted to the end; as *unwise* measures.
UNWI'SELY, *adv.* Not wisely; not prudently; as *unwisely* rigid; *unwisely* studious.
UNWISH', *v. t.* To wish that which is, not to be. [*Not in use.*] *Shak.*
UNWISH'ED, *a.* Not wished; not sought; not desired. *Pope.*
UNWIST,' *a.* Not known. *Obs. Spenser.*
UNWIT', *v. t.* To deprive of understanding. [*Not in use.*] *Shak.*
UNWITHDRAW'ING, *a.* Not withdrawing; continually liberal. *Milton.*
UNWITH'ERED, *a.* Not withered or faded.
UNWITH'ERING, *a.* Not liable to wither or fade. *Cowper.*
UNWITHSTOOD', *a.* Not opposed. *Philips.*
UNWIT'NESSED, *a.* Not witnessed; not attested by witnesses; wanting testimony.
UNWIT'TILY, *adv.* Without wit. *Cowley.*
UNWIT'TINGLY, *adv.* Without knowledge or consciousness; ignorantly; as, he has *unwittingly* injured himself, or his neighbor.
UNWIT'TY, *a.* Not witty; destitute of wit. *Shenstone.*
UNWI'VED, *a.* Having no wife. [*Not used.*] *Selden.*
UNWŎMAN, *v. t.* To deprive of the qualities of a woman. *Sandys.*
UNWŎMANLY, *a.* Unbecoming a woman.
UNWŎNTED, *a.* Unaccustomed; unused; not made familiar by practice; as a child *unwonted* to strangers; sea calves *unwonted* to fresh water. *May.*
2. Uncommon; unusual; infrequent; rare; as an *unwonted* meteor; *unwonted* changes. *Dryden.*
UNWŎNTEDNESS, *n.* Uncommonness; rareness. *Taylor.*
UNWOO'ED, *a.* Not wooed; not courted. *Shak.*
UNWŎRKING, *a.* Living without labor. *Locke.*
UNWŎRMED, *a.* Not wormed. [*Not used.*] *Beaum.*
UNWŎRN, *a.* Not worn; not impaired. *Young.*
UNWŎRSHIPED, *a.* Not worshiped; not adored. *Milton.*
UNWŎRSHIPING, *a.* Not worshiping; habitually neglecting the worship of God. *J. M. Matthews.*
UNWŎRTHILY, *adv.* [See *Worthy* and *Worth.*]
Not according to desert; without due regard to merit; as, to treat a man *unworthily.*
UNWŎRTHINESS, *n.* Want of worth or merit.
UNWŎRTHY, *a.* Not deserving; followed by *of.* As sinners, we are utterly *unworthy of* the divine favor.
2. Not deserving; wanting merit. Receive your *unworthy* son into favor. One great evil of government is that *unworthy* men are elected or appointed to fill important offices.
3. Unbecoming; vile; base; as *unworthy* usage or treatment. *Dryden.*
4. Not suitable; inadequate. This opinion is *unworthy* of its author.
UNWOUND', *pp.* of *wind.* Wound off; untwisted. *Mortimer.*
UNWOUND'ED, *a.* Not wounded; not hurt; not injured in body; as *unwounded* enemies. *Milton.*
2. Not hurt; not offended; as *unwounded* ears. *Pope.*
UNWRAP', *v. t.* To open what is wrapped or folded.
UNWRE'ATH, *v. t.* To untwist or untwine. *Boyle.*
UNWRIN'KLE, *v. t.* To reduce wrinkles; to smooth. *Anacharsis.*
UNWRI'TING, *a.* Not writing; not assuming the character of an author; as an *unwriting* citizen.
UNWRITTEN, *a. unrit'n.* Not written; not reduced to writing; verbal.
2. Blank; containing no writing. *South.*
Unwritten doctrines, in religion, are such as have been handed down by word of mouth; oral or traditional doctrines.
Unwritten laws, are such as have been delivered down by tradition or in songs. Such were the laws of the early nations of Europe.

The *unwritten laws* of England and of the United States, called *common law,* are such as have not the authority of statutes, not having originated from any legislative act, or originating from some act not now extant. These laws are now contained in the reports of judicial decisions.

UNWROUGHT, *a. unraut'.* Not labored; not manufactured; not reduced to due form. *Dryden.*
UNWRUNG, *a. unrung'.* Not pinched. *Shak.*
UNYIE'LDED, *a.* Not yielded; not conceded; not given up. *Dryden.*
UNYIE'LDING, *a.* Not yielding to force or persuasion; unbending; unpliant; stiff; firm; obstinate. *Med. Repos.*
2. Not giving place. *Thomson.*
UNYO'KE, *v. t.* To loose from a yoke; to free from a yoke.

Unyoke the steers. *Shak.*

2. To part; to disjoin. *Shak.*
UNYO'KED, *pp.* Freed from the yoke.
2. *a.* Not having worn the yoke. *Dryden.*
3. Licentious; unrestrained. *Shak.*
UNYO'KING, *ppr.* Freeing from the yoke.
UNZO'NED, *a.* Not bound with a girdle; as an *unzoned* bosom. *Prior.*
UP, *adv.* [Sax. *up, upp*; G. *auf*; D. Dan. *op*; Sw. *up.*]
1. Aloft; on high.

But *up* or down— *Milton.*

2. Out of bed. He is not *up.* *Shak.*
3. Having risen from a seat.

Sir Roger was *up.* *Addison.*

4. From a state of concealment or discumbiture.
5. In a state of being built.

Up with my tent. *Shak.*

6. Above the horizon. The sun is *up.*
7. To a state of excitement. He was wrought *up* to a rage.
8. To a state of advance or proficiency.

—Till we have wrought ourselves *up* to this degree of christian indifference. *Atterbury.*

9. In a state of elevation or exaltation.

Those that were *up,* kept others low. *Spenser.*

10. In a state of climbing or ascending. We went *up* to the city or town.
11. In a state of insurrection.

The gentle archbishop of York is *up.* *Shak.*
My soul is *up* in arms. *Dryden.*

12. In a state of being increased or raised. The river is *up*; the flood is *up.* *Dryden.*
13. In a state of approaching; as, *up* comes a fox. *L'Estrange.*
14. In order. He drew *up* his regiment.
15. From younger to elder years; as from his youth *up.*
Up and down, from one place to another; here and there.
2. From one state or position to another; backwards and forwards.
Up to, to an equal highth with; as *up to* the chin in water.
2. To a degree or point adequate. Live *up to* the principles professed.
Up with, raise; lift; as, *up with* the fist; *up with* the timber.
Up is much used to modify the actions expressed by verbs. It is very often useful and necessary; very often useless.
To bear up, to sustain.
To go up, to ascend.
To lift up, to raise.
To get up, to rise from bed or a seat.
To bind up, to bind together.
To blow up, to inflate; to distend; to inflame.
To grow up, to grow to maturity.
Up stream, from the mouth towards the head of a stream; against the stream; hence *up* is in a direction towards the head of a stream or river; as *up* the country.
Up sound, in the direction from the sea; opposed to *down sound,* that is, in the direction of the ebb tide.
Up is used elliptically for *get up,* expressing a command or exhortation.

Up, let us be going. Judges xix.

UP, *prep.* From a lower to a higher place. Go *up* the hill. *Bacon.*
UPBEAR, *v. t.* pret. *upbore*; pp. *upborne.* [*up* and *bear.* See *Bear.*]
1. To raise aloft; to lift; to elevate. *Milton.*
2. To sustain aloft; to support in an elevated situation.

Upborne they fly. *Pope.*

3. To support; to sustain. *Spenser.*
UPBIND, *v. t.* To bind up. *Collins.*
UPBLŎW, *v. t.* To blow up. [*Not used.*] *Spenser.*
UPBRA'ID, *v. t.* [Sax. *upgebredan,* to reproach; *gebrædan,* to roast, to dilate or extend, to draw, as a sword; *bredan,* to braid; Dan. *bebrejder,* to upbraid.]
1. To charge with something wrong or disgraceful; to reproach; to cast in the teeth; followed by *with* or *for,* before the thing imputed; as, to *upbraid* a man *for* his folly or his intemperance.

Yet do not
Upbraid us *with* our distress. *Shak.*
He *upbraided* them *with* their unbelief. Matt. xvi.

[The use of *to* and *of,* after *upbraid,* as to *upbraid* a man *of* his gain by iniquity, to *upbraid to* a man his evil practices, has been long discontinued.]

2. To reproach; to chide.

God who giveth to all men liberally, and *upbraideth* not. James i.

3. To reprove with severity.

Then he began to *upbraid* the cities wherein most of his mighty works were done—Matt. xi.

4. To bring reproach on. *Addison.*

How much doth thy kindness *upbraid* my wickedness! *Sidney.*

5. To treat with contempt. *Obs.* *Spenser.*

UPBRA'IDED, *pp.* Charged with something wrong or disgraceful; reproached; reproved.

UPBRA'IDER, *n.* One who upbraids or reproves.

UPBRA'IDING, *ppr.* Accusing; casting in the teeth; reproaching; reproving.

UPBRA'IDING, *n.* A charging with something wrong or disgraceful; the act of reproaching or reproving.

I have too long borne
Your blunt *upbraidings.* *Shak.*

2. The reproaches or accusations of conscience.

UPBRAY, for *upbraid,* to shame, is not in use. *Spenser.*

UPBROUGHT, *a.* *upbraut'.* Brought up; educated. [*Not in use.*] *Spenser.*

UP'CAST, *a.* Cast up; *a term in bowling.*

2. Thrown upwards; as with *upcast* eyes. *Dryden.*

UP'CAST, *n.* In *bowling,* a cast; a throw. *Shak.*

UPDRAW', *v. t.* To draw up. [*Not in use.*] *Milton.*

UPGATH'ER, *v. t.* To contract. [*Not in use.*] *Spenser.*

UPGROW, *v. i.* To grow up. [*Not in use.*] *Milton.*

UP'HAND, *a.* Lifted by the hand. *Moxon.*

UPHE'AVE, *v. t.* To heave or lift up.

UPHELD', *pret.* and *pp.* of *uphold.* Sustained; supported.

UP'HILL, *a.* Difficult, like the act of ascending a hill; as *uphill* labor. *Clarissa.*

UPHOARD, *v. t.* To hoard up. [*Not used.*] *Spenser.* *Shak.*

UPHOLD, *v. t.* pret. and pp. *upheld.* [*Upholden* is obsolete.]

1. To lift on high; to elevate. *Dryden.*

2. To support; to sustain; to keep from falling or slipping.

Honor shall *uphold* the humble in spirit. Prov. xxix.

3. To keep from declension. *Atterbury.*

4. To support in any state. *Raleigh.*

5. To continue; to maintain. *Hooker.*

6. To keep from being lost.

Faulconbridge,
In spite of spite, alone *upholds* the day. *Shak.*

7. To continue without failing. *Holder.*

8. To continue in being. *Hakewill.*

UPHOLDER, *n.* One that upholds; a supporter; a defender; a sustainer. *Swift.* *Hale.*

2. An undertaker; one who provides for funerals. *Gay.*

UPHOLSTERER, *n.* [from *up* and *hold.*] One who furnishes houses with beds, curtains and the like. *Pope.*

UPHOLSTERY, *n.* Furniture supplied by upholsterers.

UP'LAND, *n.* [*up* and *land.*] High land; ground elevated above the meadows and intervals which lie on the banks of rivers, near the sea, or between hills; land which is generally dry. It is opposed to meadow, marsh, swamp, interval, &c. Uplands are particularly valuable as affording pasture for sheep.

UP'LAND, *a.* Higher in situation; being on upland; as *upland* inhabitants.

2. Pertaining to uplands; as *upland* pasturage.

UPLAND'ISH, *a.* Pertaining to uplands; dwelling on high lands or mountains. *Chapman.*

UPLA'Y, *v. t.* To lay up; to hoard. [*Not in use.*] *Donne.*

UPLE'AD, *v. t.* To lead upwards. *Milton.*

UPLED', *pp.* Led upwards.

UPLIFT', *v. t.* To raise aloft; to raise; to elevate; as, to *uplift* the arm. It is chiefly used in the participle; as *uplifted* eyes; *uplifted* arms. *Milton.* *Swift.*

UPLIFT'ED, *pp.* Raised high; lifted; elevated.

UPLOOK', *v. t.* To look up. [*Not in use.*] *Shak.*

UP'MOST, *a.* [*up* and *most.*] Highest; topmost. [Little used. We generally use *uppermost.*] *Dryden.*

UPON', *prep.* [Sax. *ufan, ufon* or *ufe.* This is probably *up* and *on;* the Sax. *ufe* being the G. *auf,* up.] On. *Upon* has the sense of *on,* and might perhaps be wholly dispensed with.

1. Resting or being on the top or surface; as being *upon* a hill, or *upon* a rock; *upon* a field; *upon* a table; *upon* a river; *upon* the altar; *upon* the roof. He has his coat *upon* his back; his hat is *upon* his head.

2. In a state of resting or dependence; as *upon* this condition; he will contract with you *upon* these terms. *Upon* our repentance we hope to be forgiven.

3. Denoting resting, as a burden. Impose *upon* yourself this task.

4. In the direction or part of; as *upon* the right hand.

5. Relating to. They are now engaged *upon* the affairs of the bank.

6. In consideration of; as *upon* the whole matter. *Dryden.*

7. Near to; as a village *upon* the Thames.

8. With, or having received. He came *upon* an hour's warning.

9. On the occasion of; engaged in for the execution of. He sent the officer *upon* a bold enterprise.

10. In; during the time of; as *upon* the seventh day; *upon* the first of January.

11. Noting security; as, to borrow money *upon* lands, or *upon* mortgage.

12. Noting approach or attack.

The Philistines be *upon* thee, Samson. Judges xvi.

13. Noting exposure or incurring some danger or loss. You do this *upon* pain of death, or *upon* the penalties of the law.

14. At the time of; on occasion of. What was their conduct *upon* this event?

15. By inference from, or pursuing a certain supposition. *Upon* his principles, we can have no stable government.

16. Engaged in. What is he *upon*? *Locke.*

17. Having a particular manner. The horse is now *upon* a hard trot. *Dryden.*

18. Resting or standing, as on a condition. He is put *upon* his good behavior.

19. Noting means of subsistence or support. Cattle live *upon* grass.

20. Noting dependence for subsistence; as, paupers come *upon* the parish or town.

To take upon, to assume.

To assume upon, in *law,* to promise; to undertake.

UP'PER, *a.* [*comp.* from *up.*] Higher in place; as the *upper* lip; the *upper* side of a thing. An *upper* story is a higher one; *the upper* story is the highest. So *the upper* deck of a ship.

2. Superior in rank or dignity; as the *upper* house of a legislature.

Upper hand, advantage; superiority.

Upper-works, in a ship, the parts above water when the ship is properly balanced for a voyage; or that part which is above the main wale. *Cyc.*

UP'PERMOST, *a.* [*superl.; upper* and *most.*]

1. Highest in place; as the *uppermost* seats.

2. Highest in power or authority.

Whatever faction happens to be *uppermost*— *Swift.*

3. Predominant; most powerful. *Dryden.*

UPRA'ISE, *v. t.* *s* as *z.* [*up* and *raise.*] To raise; to lift up. *Milton.*

UPRE'AR, *v. t.* [*up* and *rear.*] To rear up; to raise. *Gay.*

UPRIGHT, *a.* *upri'te* or *up'rite.* [*up* and *right.* This word is marked in books with the accent on the first syllable. But it is frequently pronounced with the accent on the second, and the accent on the first syllable of its derivatives is inadmissible.]

1. Erect; perpendicular to the plane of the horizon; as an *upright* tree; an *upright* post. Among *mechanics,* plumb.

2. Erected; pricked up; shooting directly from the body.

All have their ears *upright*— *Spenser.*
With chatt'ring teeth and bristling hair *upright.* *Dryden.*

3. Honest; just; adhering to rectitude in all social intercourse; not deviating from correct moral principles; as an *upright* man. Job i.

4. Conformable to moral rectitude.

Conscience rewards *upright* conduct with pleasure. *J. M. Mason.*

UP'RIGHT, *n.* In *architecture,* a representation or draught of the front of a building; called also an elevation, or orthography. *Cyc.*

2. Something standing erect or perpendicular.

UPRIGHTLY, *adv.* In a direction perpendicular to the plane of the horizon; in an erect position.

2. Honestly; with strict observance of rectitude; as, to live *uprightly.* *Dryden.*

He that walketh *uprightly,* walketh surely. Prov. x.

UPRIGHTNESS, *n.* Perpendicular erection. *Waller.*

2. Honesty; integrity in principle or practice; conformity to rectitude and justice in social dealings.

The truly upright man is inflexible in his *uprightness.* *Atterbury.*

UPRI'SE, *v. i.* *s* as *z.* pret. *uprose;* pp. *uprisen.* To rise from bed or from a seat.

Uprose the virgin with the morning light. *Pope.*

2. To ascend above the horizon.

Uprose the sun. *Cowley.*

3. To ascend, as a hill. *Obs.* *Shak.*

UPRI'SE, *n.* A rising; appearance above the horizon. *Obs.* *Shak.*

UPRI'SING, *ppr.* Rising; ascending.

UPRI'SING, *n.* The act of rising.

Thou knowest my down-sitting and mine *uprising.* Ps. cxxxix.

UP'ROAR, *n.* [D. *oproer;* G. *aufruhr; auf,* up, and *rühren,* to stir, to beat, D. *roeren,* Sw. *röra.* In verse it is sometimes accented on the second syllable.]

Great tumult; violent disturbance and noise; bustle and clamor.

The Jews who believed not—set all the city in an *uproar.* Acts xvii.

Horror thus prevail'd,
And wild uproar. *Philips.*

UPRŌAR, *v. t.* To throw into confusion. [*Not in use.*]

UPROLL, *v. t.* [*up* and *roll.*] To roll up. *Milton.*

UPROOT', *v. t.* [*up* and *root.*] To root up; to tear up by the roots; as, to *uproot* the hills or trees. *Dryden.*

UPROUSE, *v. t. uprouz.* [*up* and *rouse.*] To rouse from sleep; to awake. *Shak.*

UPSET', *v. t.* [*up* and *set.*] To overturn; to overthrow; to overset; as a carriage.

UP'SHOT, *n.* [*up* and *shot.*] Final issue; conclusion; end; as the *upshot* of the matter.

Here is the *upshot* and result of all. *Burnet.*

Upside down, the upper part undermost. As a phrase, this denotes in confusion; in complete disorder. *South.*

UP'SPRING, *n.* [*up* and *spring.*] An upstart. [*Not in use.*] *Shak.*

UPSPRING', *v. i.* To spring up. [*Not in use.*] *Sackville.*

UPSTAND', *v. i.* To be erected. [*Not used.*] *May.*

UPST'ART, *v. i.* [*up* and *start.*] To start or spring up suddenly. *Dryden.*

UP'START, *n.* One that suddenly rises from low life to wealth, power or honor. *Spenser.*

2. Something that springs up suddenly. *Milton. Bacon.*

UP'START, *a.* Suddenly raised. *Shak.*

UPSTA'Y, *v. t.* [*up* and *stay.*] To sustain; to support. *Milton.*

UPSWARM', *v. t.* [See *Swarm.*] To raise in a swarm. [*Not in use.*] *Shak.*

UPTA'KE, *v. t.* [*up* and *take.*] To take into the hand. [*Not in use.*] *Spenser.*

UPTEAR, *v. t.* [*up* and *tear.*] To tear up. *Milton.*

UPTRA'IN, *v. t.* [*up* and *train.*] To train up; to educate. [*Not in use.*] *Spenser.*

UPTURN', *v. t.* [*up* and *turn.*] To turn up; to throw up; as, to *upturn* the ground in plowing. *Milton. Pope.*

UP'WARD, *a.* [*up* and *ward,* Sax. *weard,* L. *versus.*]

Directed to a higher place; as with *upward* eye; with *upward* speed. *Dryden. Prior.*

UP'WARD, *n.* The top. [*Not in use.*] *Shak.*

UP'WARD, **UP'WARDS**, *adv.* Toward a higher place; opposed to *downward.*

Upward I lift my eye. *Watts.*

2. Toward heaven and God.

Looking inward, we are struck dumb; looking *upward,* we speak and prevail. *Hooker.*

3. With respect to the higher part.

Upward man,
Downward fish. *Milton.*

4. More than, indefinitely. *Upwards* of ten years have elapsed; *upwards* of a hundred men were present.

5. Toward the source. Trace the stream *upwards.*

And trace the muses *upwards* to their spring. *Pope.*

UPWHIRL, *v. i. upwhurl'.* [*up* and *whirl.*] To rise upwards in a whirl; to whirl upwards. *Milton.*

UPWHIRL', *v. t.* To raise upwards in a whirling direction.

UPWIND, *v. t.* [*up* and *wind.*] To wind up. *Spenser.*

URAN-GLIM'MER, *n.* An ore of uranium; uran-mica; chalcolite.

U'RANITE, *n.* An ore or phosphate of uranium, called also uran-glimmer, and uran-mica. It is of a lemon yellow gold color, or yellowish brown, sometimes of an apple green or emerald color. It occurs crystalized in rectangular prisms, in imperfect octahedrons, &c. Its structure is lamellar, and it yields to the knife. *Cyc. Phillips.*

Uranite is found in primitive earths, in three states, crystalized, compact, and pulverulent. *Lavoisier. Dict. Nat. Hist.*

URANIT'IC, *a.* Pertaining to uranite, or resembling it.

URA'NIUM, *n.* [Gr. ουρανος, heaven, or a planet so called.]

A metal discovered in 1789 by Klaproth, in the mineral called pechblend. It is occasionally found native in uran-ocher and uran-mica; but more generally it is obtained from pechblend, in which it exists with iron, copper, lead, and sometimes with arsenic, cobalt and zink. *Henry.*

URAN-O'CHER, *n.* Pechblend, an ore of uranium, containing the metal in an oxydized state. It is brown, grayish, black, and brownish black; occurring massive, globular, reniform, disseminated, and pulverulent. *Cyc. Ure. Phillips.*

URANOL'OGY, *n.* [Gr. ουρανος, heaven, and λογος, discourse.]

A discourse or treatise on the heavens. *Mitchill.*

UR'BANE, *a.* [L. *urbanus,* from *urbs,* a city.] Civil; courteous in manners; polite.

URBAN'ITY, *n.* [Fr. *urbanité;* L. *urbanitas,* from *urbs,* a city.]

1. That civility or courtesy of manners which is acquired by associating with well bred people; politeness; polished manners. *Dryden. Brown.*

2. Facetiousness. *L'Estrange.*

UR'BANIZE, *v. t.* To render civil and courteous; to polish. *Howell.*

UR'CEOLATE, *a.* [L. *urceolus, urceus,* a pitcher.]

In *botany,* shaped like a pitcher; swelling out like a pitcher; as a calyx or corol. *Martyn. Lee.*

UR'CHIN, *n.* [Arm. *heureuchin;* L. *erinaceus.*] A name given to the hedgehog.

2. A name of slight anger given to a child; as, the little *urchin* cried.

URE, *n.* Use; practice. [Obsolete, but retained in *inure.*]

U'REA, *n.* A substance obtained from urine. *Ure.*

U'RETER, *n.* [Gr. ουρητηρ, from ουρεω. See *Urine.*]

A tube conveying the urine from the kidney to the bladder. There are two ureters, one on each side. *Coxe. Quincy.*

URE'THRA, *n.* [Gr. ουρηθρα, from ουρεω. See *Urine.*]

The canal by which the urine is conducted from the bladder and discharged. *Coxe.*

URGE, *v. t.* [L. *urgeo.* This belongs probably to the family of Gr. ειργω and L. *arceo.*]

1. To press; to push; to drive; to impel; to apply force to, in almost any manner.

And great Achilles *urge* the Trojan fate. *Dryden.*

2. To press the mind or will; to press by motives, arguments, persuasion or importunity.

My brother
Did *urge* me in his act. *Shak.*

3. To provoke; to exasperate.

Urge not my father's anger. *Shak.*

4. To follow close; to impel.

Heir *urges* heir, like wave impelling wave. *Pope.*

5. To labor vehemently; to press with eagerness.

Through the thick deserts headlong *urg'd* his flight. *Pope.*

6. To press; as, to *urge* an argument; to *urge* a petition; to *urge* the necessity of a case.

7. To importune; to solicit earnestly. He *urged* his son to withdraw.

8. To apply forcibly; as, to *urge* an ore with intense heat.

URGE, *v. i.* To press forward; as, he strives to *urge* upward.

URG'ED, *pp.* Pressed; impelled; importuned.

URG'ENCY, *n.* Pressure; importunity; earnest solicitation; as the *urgency* of a request.

2. Pressure of necessity; as the *urgency* of want or distress; the *urgency* of the occasion.

URG'ENT, *a.* Pressing with importunity. Ex. xii.

2. Pressing with necessity; violent; vehement; as an *urgent* case or occasion.

URG'ENTLY, *adv.* With pressing importunity; violently; vehemently; forcibly.

URG'ER, *n.* One who urges; one who importunes.

URGE-WŎNDER, *n.* A sort of grain. *Mortimer.*

URG'ING, *ppr.* Pressing; driving; impelling.

2. *a.* Pressing with solicitations; importunate.

U'RIC, *a.* In *chimistry,* the uric acid, called also lithic acid, is obtained from urinary calculi.

U'RIM, *n.* [Heb. אורים.] The Urim and Thummim, among the Israelites, signify lights and perfections. These were a kind of ornament belonging to the habit of the high priest, in virtue of which he gave oracular answers to the people; but what they were has not been satisfactorily ascertained. *Cyc.*

U'RINAL, *n.* [Fr. *urinal;* L. *urinalis,* from *urina,* urine.]

1. A bottle in which urine is kept for inspection.
2. A vessel for containing urine.
3. In *chimistry*, an oblong glass vessel, used in making solutions. *Cyc.*

U'RINARY, *a.* [from *urine.*] Pertaining to urine; as the *urinary* bladder; *urinary* calculi; *urinary* abscesses.

U'RINARY, URINA'RIUM, } *n.* In *agriculture*, a reservoir or place for the reception of urine, &c. for manure. *Cyc.*

U'RINATIVE, *a.* Provoking urine. *Bacon.*

URINA'TOR, *n.* [L. from *urino*, to dive.] A diver; one who plunges and sinks in water in search of something, as for pearls. *Ray.*

U'RINE, *n.* [L. *urina*; Gr. ουρον, from ουρεω; G. *harn, harnen.*]
An animal fluid or liquor secreted by the kidneys, whence it is conveyed into the bladder by the ureters, and through the urethra discharged. The urine of beasts is sometimes called *stale.*

U'RINE, *v. i.* [supra.] To discharge urine. *Bacon.*

U'RINOUS, *a.* Pertaining to urine, or partaking of its qualities. *Arbuthnot.*

URN, *n.* [L. *urna.*] A kind of vase of a roundish form, largest in the middle; used as an ornament. *Cyc.*
2. A vessel for water.
3. A vessel in which the ashes of the dead were formerly kept.
4. A Roman measure for liquids, containing about three gallons and a half, wine measure. It was half the amphora, and four times the congius. *Cyc.*

UROS'COPY, *n.* [Gr. ουρον and σκεπτω.] Inspection of urine. *Brown.*

UR'RY, *n.* A sort of blue or black clay, lying near a vein of coal. *Mortimer.*

UR'SA, *n.* [L.] The bear, a constellation, the greater and lesser bear, near the north pole.

UR'SIFORM, *a.* [L. *ursa*, bear, and *form.*] In the shape of a bear.

UR'SINE, *a.* [L. *ursinus.*] Pertaining to or resembling a bear.

UR'SULINE, *a.* Denoting an order of nuns who observe the rule of St. Austin; so called from their institutress, St. Ursula. *Cyc.*

U'RUS, URE, } *n.* [L. *urus.*] The wild bull.

US, *pron.* objective case of *we.*

> Give *us* this day our daily bread. *Lord's Prayer.*

U'SAGE, *n. s* as *z.* [Fr. from *user*, to use. See *Use.*]
1. Treatment; an action or series of actions performed by one person towards another, or which directly affect him; as good *usage*; ill *usage*; hard *usage*. Gentle *usage* will often effect what harsh *usage* will not. The elephant may by governed by mild *usage.*
2. Use, or long continued use; custom; practice. Uninterrupted *usage* for a long time, or immemorial *usage* constitutes prescription. Custom is a local *usage*; prescription is a personal *usage*. In language, *usage* is the foundation of all rules.

> Of things once received and confirmed by use, long *usage* is a law sufficient. *Hooker.*

3. Manners; behavior. *Obs.* *Spenser.*

U'SAGER, *n. s* as *z.* [Fr.] One who has the use of any thing in trust for another. [*Not in use.*] *Daniel.*

U'SANCE, *n. s* as *z.* [Fr.] Use; proper employment. *Spenser.*
2. Usury; interest paid for money. *Shak.*
3. In *commerce*, a determinate time fixed for the payment of bills of exchange, reckoned either from the day of their date, or the day of their acceptance. It is thus called because this time is settled by *usage*, or the custom of places on which the bills are drawn. In France, the usance for bills drawn from Spain and Portugal, is sixty days. At London, the usance for bills drawn from Holland, Germany or France, is one month. The usance is very different in different countries and cities. *Cyc.*

USE, *n.* [L. *usus*; It. *uso*; Fr. *us*, plu.]
1. The act of handling or employing in any manner, and for any purpose, but especially for a profitable purpose; as the *use* of a pen in writing; the *use* of books in study; the *use* of a spade in digging. Use is of two kinds; that which employs a thing, without destroying it or its form, as the *use* of a book or of a farm; or it is the employment of a thing which destroys or wastes it, as the *use* of bread for provision; the *use* of water for turning a mill.
2. Employment; application of any thing to a purpose, good or bad. It is our duty to make a faithful *use* of our opportunities and advantages for improvement.

> Books can never teach the *use* of books. *Bacon.*

3. Usefulness; utility; advantage; production of benefit. The value of a thing is to be estimated by its *use*. His friendship has been of *use* to me.

> 'Tis *use* alone that sanctifies expense. *Pope.*

4. Need of employment, or occasion to employ. I have no further *use* for this book.
5. Power of receiving advantage. [*Unusual.*] *Dryden.*
6. Continued practice or employment.

> Sweetness, truth, and every grace,
> Which time and *use* are wont to teach. *Waller.*

7. Custom; common occurrence.

> O Cesar, these things are beyond all *use.* [*Unusual.*] *Shak.*

8. Interest; the premium paid for the possession and employment of borrowed money. *South.*
9. In *law*, the benefit or profit of lands and tenements. Use imports a trust and confidence reposed in a man for the holding of lands. He to whose *use* or benefit the trust is intended, shall enjoy the profits. An estate is granted and limited to A for the *use* of B.

Statute of Uses, in England, the Stat. 27 Henry VIII. Cap. 10. which transfers uses into possession, or which unites the use and possession.

Cestuy que use, in law, the person who has the use of lands and tenements.

Contingent use, in law. A contingent or springing use, is where the use is suspended on a future event.

Resulting use, is one which, being limited by the deed, expires or cannot vest, and results or returns to him who raised it, after such expiration.

Secondary or *shifting use*, is that which though executed, may change from one to another by circumstances. *Blackstone.*

In use, in employment; as, the book is now *in use.*
2. In customary practice or observance. Such words, rites and ceremonies, have long been *in use.*

USE, *v. t. s* as *z.* [Fr. *user*; It. *usare*; Sp. *usar*; L. *utor, usus*; Gr. εθω.]
1. To employ; to handle, hold, occupy or move for some purpose; as, to *use* a plow; to *use* a chair; to *use* a book; to *use* time. Most men *use* the right hand with more convenience than the left, and hence its name, *right.*
2. To waste, consume or exhaust by employment; as, to *use* flour for food; to *use* beer for drink; to *use* water for irrigation, or for turning the wheel of a mill.
3. To accustom; to habituate; to render familiar by practice; as men *used* to cold and hunger; soldiers *used* to hardships and danger. *Addison. Swift.*
4. To treat; as, to *use* one well or ill; to *use* people with kindness and civility; to *use* a beast with cruelty.

> Cato has *us'd* me ill. *Addison.*

5. To practice customarily.

> *Use* hospitality one to another. 1 Pet. iv.

To use one's self, to behave. *Obs.* *Shak.*

USE, *v. i. s* as *z.* To be accustomed; to practice customarily.

> They *use* to place him that shall be their captain on a stone. *Spenser.*

2. To be wont.

> Fears *use* to be represented in an imaginary fashion. *Bacon.*

3. To frequent; to inhabit.

> Where never foot did *use.* *Spenser.*

U'SED, *pp. s* as *z.* Employed; occupied; treated.

U'SEFUL, *a.* Producing or having power to produce good; beneficial; profitable; helpful towards advancing any purpose; as vessels and instruments *useful* in a family; books *useful* for improvement; *useful* knowledge; *useful* arts.

U'SEFULLY, *adv.* In such a manner as to produce or advance some end; as instruments or time *usefully* employed.

U'SEFULNESS, *n.* Conduciveness to some end, properly to some valuable end; as the *usefulness* of canal navigation; the *usefulness* of machinery in manufactures.

U'SELESS, *a.* Having no use; unserviceable; producing no good end; answering no valuable purpose; not advancing the end proposed; as a *useless* garment; *useless* pity. *Gay.*

U'SELESSLY, *adv.* In a useless manner; without profit or advantage. *Locke.*

U'SELESSNESS, *n.* Unserviceableness; unfitness for any valuable purpose, or for the purpose intended; as the *uselessness* of pleasure.

U'SER, *n. s* as *z.* One who uses, treats or occupies.

USH'ER, *n.* [Fr. *huissier*, a door-keeper, from *huis*, It. *uscio*, a door.]
1. Properly, an officer or servant who has the care of the door of a court, hall, chamber or the like; hence, an officer whose business is to introduce strangers, or to walk before a person of rank. In the king's household there are four gentle-

men-ushers of the privy chamber. There is also an usher of the exchequer, who attends the barons, sherifs, juries, &c. *Cyc. England.*

2. An under-teacher or assistant to the preceptor of a school.

USH'ER, *v. t.* To introduce, as a forerunner or harbinger; to forerun.

The stars that *usher* evening, rose. *Milton.*

The Examiner was *ushered* into the world by a letter, setting forth the great genius of the author. *Addison.*

USH'ERED, *pp.* Introduced.

USH'ERING, *ppr.* Introducing, as a forerunner.

USQUEBAUGH, *n.* [Ir. *uisge*, water, and *bagh*, life.]

A compound distilled spirit. From this word, by corruption, we have *whiskey*.

US'TION, *n.* [Fr. *ustion;* L. *ustio*, from *uro, ustus*, to burn.]

The act of burning; the state of being burnt.

USTO'RIOUS, *a.* [supra.] Having the quality of burning. *Watts.*

USTULA'TION, *n.* [L. *ustulatus.*] The act of burning or searing. *Petty.*

2. In *metallurgy*, ustulation is the operation of expelling one substance from another by heat, as sulphur and arsenic from ores, in a muffle.

3. In *pharmacy*, the roasting or drying of moist substances so as to prepare them for pulverizing; also, the burning of wine. *Cyc.*

U'SUAL, *a. s* as z. [Fr. *usuel;* from *use.*] Customary; common; frequent; such as occurs in ordinary practice, or in the ordinary course of events. Rainy weather is not *usual* in this climate.

Consultation with oracles was formerly a thing very *usual*. *Hooker.*

U'SUALLY, *adv. s* as z. Commonly; customarily; ordinarily. Men *usually* find some excuse for their vices. It is *usually* as cold in North America in the fortieth degree of latitude, as it is in the west of Europe in the fiftieth.

U'SUALNESS, *n. s* as z. Commonness; frequency.

USUCAP'TION, *n.* [L. *usus*, use, and *capio*, to take.]

In *the civil law*, the same as *prescription* in the common law; the acquisition of the title or right to property by the uninterrupted and undisputed possession of it for a certain term prescribed by law.

U'SUFRUCT, *n.* [L. *usus*, use, and *fructus*, fruit.]

The temporary use and enjoyment of lands or tenements; or the right of receiving the fruits and profits of lands or other thing, without having the right to alienate or change the property. *Cyc.*

USUFRUCT'UARY, *n.* A person who has the use and enjoyment of property for a time, without having the title or property. *Johnson.*

U'SURE, *v. i. s* as z. To practice usury. [*Not in use.*] *Shak.*

U'SURER, *n. s* as z. [See *Usury.*] Formerly, a person who lent money and took interest for it.

2. In *present usage*, one who lends money at a rate of interest beyond the rate established by law.

USU'RIOUS, *a. s* as z. Practicing usury; taking exorbitant interest for the use of money; as a *usurious* person.

2. Partaking of usury; containing usury; as a *usurious* contract, which by statute is void.

USU'RIOUSLY, *adv.* In a usurious manner.

USU'RIOUSNESS, *n.* The state or quality of being usurious.

USURP', *v. t. s* as z. [Fr. *usurper;* L. *usurpo.*]

To seize and hold in possession by force or without right; as, to *usurp* a throne; to *usurp* the prerogatives of the crown; to *usurp* power. To *usurp* the right of a patron, is to oust or dispossess him.

Vice sometimes *usurps* the place of virtue. *Denham.*

[*Usurp* is not applied to common dispossession of private property.]

USURPA'TION, *n.* [supra.] The act of seizing or occupying and enjoying the property of another, without right; as the *usurpation* of a throne; the *usurpation* of the supreme power. *Usurpation*, in a peculiar sense, denotes the absolute ouster and dispossession of the patron of a church, by presenting a clerk to a vacant benefice, who is thereupon admitted and instituted. *Cyc.*

USURP'ED, *pp.* Seized or occupied and enjoyed by violence, or without right.

USURP'ER, *n.* One who seizes or occupies the property of another without right; as the *usurper* of a throne, of power, or of the rights of a patron. *Shak. Dryden. Cyc.*

USURP'ING, *ppr.* Seizing or occupying the power or property of another without right.

The worst of tyrants, an *usurping* crowd. *Pope.*

USURP'INGLY, *adv.* By usurpation; without just right or claim. *Shak.*

U'SURY, *n. s* as z. [Fr. *usure;* L. *usura*, from *utor*, to use.]

1. Formerly, interest; or a premium paid or stipulated to be paid for the use of money. [*Usury* formerly denoted any legal interest, but in this sense, the word is no longer in use.]

2. In *present usage*, illegal interest; a premium or compensation paid or stipulated to be paid for the use of money borrowed or retained, beyond the rate of interest established by law.

3. The practice of taking interest. *Obs.* *Bacon.*

UTEN'SIL, *n.* [Fr. *utensile.* This seems to be formed on the participle of the L. *utor.*]

An instrument; that which is used; particularly, an instrument or vessel used in a kitchen, or in domestic and farming business.

U'TERINE, *a.* [Fr. *uterin;* L. *uterinus*, from *uterus.*]

Pertaining to the womb. *Uterine* brother or sister, is one born of the same mother, but by a different father. *Cyc.*

UTERO-GESTA'TION, *n.* Gestation in the womb from conception to birth. *Pritchard.*

U'TERUS, *n.* [L.] The womb.

UTIL'ITY, *n.* [Fr. *utilité;* L. *utilitas*, from *utor*, to use.]

Usefulness; production of good; profitableness to some valuable end; as the *utility* of manures upon land; the *utility* of the sciences; the *utility* of medicines.

U'TILIZE, *v. t.* [It. *utilizzare;* Sp. *utilizar;* from *utile, util*, useful.] To gain; to acquire. [*Rare.*] *Journ. of Science.*

U'TIS, *n.* Bustle; stir. [*Not in use.*] *Shak.*

UT'MOST, *a.* [Sax. *utmæst, utmest; ut*, out, and *mest*, most; that is, to the *outermost* point.]

1. Extreme; being at the furthest point or extremity; as the *utmost* limit of North America; the *utmost* limits of the land; the *utmost* extent of human knowledge.

2. Being in the greatest or highest degree; as the *utmost* assiduity; the *utmost* harmony; the *utmost* misery or happiness; the *utmost* peril. *Shak.*

UT'MOST, *n.* The most that can be; the greatest power, degree or effort. He has done his *utmost.* Try your *utmost.*

I will be free
Even to the *utmost* as I please in words. *Shak.*

UTO'PIAN, *a.* [from More's *Utopia.*] Ideal; chimerical; fanciful; not well founded.

U'TRICLE, *n.* [L. *utriculus*, a little bag or bottle.]

1. A little bag or bladder; a little cell; a reservoir in plants to receive the sap. *Fourcroy. Martyn.*

2. A capsule of one cell, and containing a solitary seed, often very thin and semitransparent, constantly destitute of valves, and falling with the seed. *Gærtner. Cyc. Smith.*

UTRIC'ULAR, *a.* Containing utricles; furnished with glandular vessels like small bags; as plants. *Lee.*

UT'TER, *a.* [Sax.; that is, *outer.*] Situated on the outside or remote from the center. *Milton.*

2. Placed or being beyond any compass; out of any place; as the *utter* deep. *Milton.*

3. Extreme; excessive; utmost; as *utter* darkness.

4. Complete; total; final; as *utter* ruin.

5. Peremptory; absolute; as an *utter* refusal or denial.

6. Perfect; mere; quite; as *utter* strangers.

UT'TER, *v. t.* To speak; to pronounce; to express; as, to *utter* words; to *utter* sounds. *Addison.*

2. To disclose; to discover; to divulge; to publish. He never *utters* a syllable of what I suppose to be intended as a secret.

3. To sell; to vend; as, to *utter* wares. [*This is obsolete, unless in the law style.*]

4. To put or send into circulation; to put off, as currency, or cause to pass in commerce; as, to *utter* coin or notes. A man *utters* a false note, who gives it in payment, knowing it to be false.

UT'TERABLE, *a.* That may be uttered, pronounced or expressed.

UT'TERANCE, *n.* The act of uttering words; pronunciation; manner of speaking; as a good or bad *utterance.*

They began to speak with other tongues, as the spirit gave them *utterance.* Acts ii.

2. Emission from the mouth; vocal expression; as the *utterance* of sounds.
3. [Fr. *outrance.*] Extremity; furthest part. [*Not in use.*] *Shak.*

UT'TERED, *pp.* Spoken; pronounced; disclosed; published; put into circulation.

UT'TERER, *n.* One who utters; one who pronounces.
2. One who divulges or discloses.
3. One who puts into circulation.
4. A seller; a vender.

UT'TERING, *ppr.* Pronouncing; disclosing; putting into circulation; selling.

UT'TERLY, *adv.* To the full extent; fully; perfectly; totally; as *utterly* tired; *utterly* debased; *utterly* lost to all sense of shame; it is *utterly* vain; *utterly* out of my power.

UT'TERMOST, *a.* [*utter* and *most.*] Extreme; being in the furthest, greatest or highest degree; as the *uttermost* extent or end; the *uttermost* distress.

UT'TERMOST, *n.* The greatest. The *uttermost* we can do is to be patient.

To the uttermost, in the most extensive degree; fully. Heb. vii.

U'VEOUS, *a.* [L. *uva,* a grape.] Resembling a grape. *Ray.*

The *uveous* coat of the eye, or *uvea,* is the posterior lamin of the iris; so called by the ancients, because in the animals which they dissected, it resembles an unripe grape. *Parr.*

U'VULA, *n.* [L.] A soft round spungy body, suspended from the palate near the foramina of the nostrils, over the glottis. *Wiseman.*

The small conical body projecting from the middle of the soft palate. *Cyc.*

UXO'RIOUS, *a.* [L. *uxorius,* from *uxor,* wife.]

Submissively fond of a wife. *Bacon.*

UXO'RIOUSLY, *adv.* With fond or servile submission to a wife. *Dryden.*

UXO'RIOUSNESS, *n.* Connubial dotage; foolish fondness for a wife. *More.*

V.

V is the twenty second letter of the English Alphabet, and a labial articulation, formed by the junction of the upper teeth with the lower lip, as in pronouncing *av, ev, ov, vain.* It is not a close articulation, but one that admits of some sound. It is nearly allied to *f,* being formed by the same organs; but *v* is vocal, and *f* is aspirate, and this constitutes the principal difference between them. *V* and *u* were formerly the same letter, derived no doubt from the oriental *vau* or *waw,* but they have now as distinct uses as any two letters in the alphabet, and are therefore to be considered as different letters. *V* has one sound only, as in *very, vote, lavish.*

As a numeral, V stands for 5. With a dash over it, in old books, V̄, it stands for 5000.

V. R. among the Romans, stood for *uti rogas,* as you desire; V. C. for *vir consularis;* V. G. for *verbi gratia;* V. L. for *videlicet.*

In music for instruments, V. stands for *violin;* V. V. for *violins.*

VA'CANCY, *n.* [L. *vacans,* from *vaco,* to be empty; Fr. *vacance;* It. *vacanza;* Sp. *vacancia;* W. *gwag;* Heb. בק to empty. Class Bg. No. 28.]
1. Empty space; vacuity. [In this sense, *vacuity* is now generally used.] *Shak.*
2. Chasm; void space between bodies or objects; as a *vacancy* between two beams or boards in a building; a *vacancy* between two buildings; a *vacancy* between words in a writing. *Watts.*
3. The state of being destitute of an incumbent; want of the regular officer to officiate in a place. Hence also it signifies the office, post or benefice which is destitute of an incumbent; as a *vacancy* in a parish; *vacancies* in the treasury or war office. There is no *vacancy* on the bench of the supreme court.
4. Time of leisure; freedom from employment; intermission of business.

> Those little *vacancies* from toils are sweet. *Dryden.*

5. Listlessness; emptiness of thought. *Wotton.*
6. A place or office not occupied, or destitute of a person to fill it; as a *vacancy* in a school.

VA'CANT, *a.* [Fr.; from L. *vacans.*] Empty; not filled; void of every substance except air, as a *vacant* space between houses; *vacant* room. *Milton.*
2. Empty; exhausted of air; as a *vacant* receiver. *Boyle.*
3. Free; unincumbered; unengaged with business or care.

> Philosophy is the interest of those only who are *vacant* from the affairs of the world. *More.*

4. Not filled or occupied with an incumbent or possessor; as a *vacant* throne; a *vacant* parish.
5. Being unoccupied with business; as *vacant* hours; *vacant* moments. *Addison.*
6. Empty of thought; thoughtless; not occupied with study or reflection; as a *vacant* mind.
7. Indicating want of thought.

> The duke had a pleasant and *vacant* face. *Wotton.*

8. In *law,* abandoned; having no heir; as *vacant* effects or goods.

VA'CATE, *v. t.* To annul; to make void; to make of no authority or validity; as, to *vacate* a commission; to *vacate* a charter.

> The necessity of observing the Jewish sabbath was *vacated* by the apostolical institution of the Lord's day. *Nelson.*

2. To make vacant; to quit possession and leave destitute. It was resolved by parliament that James had *vacated* the throne of England.
3. To defeat; to put an end to.

> He *vacates* my revenge. *Dryden.*
> [*Unusual.*]

VA'CATED, *pp.* Annulled; made void; made vacant.

VA'CATING, *ppr.* Making void; making vacant.

VACA'TION, *n.* [Fr. from L. *vacatio.*] The act of making void, vacant, or of no validity; as the *vacation* of a charter.
2. Intermission of judicial proceedings; the space of time between the end of one term and the beginning of the next; non-term.
3. The intermission of the regular studies and exercises of a college or other seminary, when the students have a recess.
4. Intermission of a stated employment.
5. The time when a see or other spiritual dignity is vacant.

> During the *vacation* of a bishopric, the dean and chapter are guardians of the spiritualities. *Cyc.*

6. Leisure; freedom from trouble or perplexity. [*Now little used.*] *Hammond.*

VAC'CARY, *n.* [L. *vacca,* a cow.] An old word signifying a cow house, dairy house, or a cow pasture. *Bailey. Cyc.*

VAC'ILLANCY, *n.* [L. *vacillans,* from *vacillo,* to waver, Eng. to *waggle,* from the root of *wag,* which see.]

A state of wavering; fluctuation; inconstancy. *More.*

VAC'ILLANT, *a.* [supra.] Wavering; fluctuating; unsteady. *Smellie.*

VAC'ILLATE, *v. i.* [L. *vacillo;* G. *wackeln;* Eng. to *waggle,* a diminutive of *wag.* See *Wag.*]
1. To waver; to move one way and the other; to reel or stagger.
2. To fluctuate in mind or opinion; to waver; to be unsteady or inconstant.

VAC'ILLATING, *ppr.* Wavering; reeling; fluctuating.
2. *a.* Unsteady; inclined to fluctuate.

VACILLA'TION, *n.* [Fr. from L. *vacillatio.*]
1. A wavering; a moving one way and the other; a reeling or staggering.
2. Fluctuation of mind; unsteadiness; change from one object to another. *S. Lee.*

VAC'CINATE, *v. t.* [L. *vacca,* a cow.] To inoculate with the cow-pox, or a virus originally taken from cows, called *vaccine* matter.

VAC'CINATED, *pp.* Inoculated with the cow-pox.

VAC'CINATING, *ppr.* Inoculating with the cow-pox.

VACCINA'TION, *n.* The act, art or practice of inoculating persons with the cow-pox.

VAC'CINE, *a.* [L. *vaccinus,* from *vacca,* a cow.]

Pertaining to cows; originating with or derived from cows; as the *vaccine* disease or cow-pox.

VACUA'TION, *n.* [L. *vacuo.*] The act of emptying. [*Little used.*] [See *Evacuation.*]

VAC'UIST, *n.* [from *vacuum.*] One who holds to the doctrine of a vacuum in nature; opposed to a *plenist.* *Boyle.*

VACU'ITY, *n.* [L. *vacuitas*, from *vacuus.*]
1. Emptiness; a state of being unfilled.
 Hunger is such a state of *vacuity* as to require a fresh supply. *Arbuthnot.*
2. Space unfilled or unoccupied, or occupied with an invisible fluid only.
 A *vacuity* is interspersed among the particles of matter. *Bentley.*
3. Emptiness; void.
 God only can fill every *vacuity* of the soul. *Rogers.*
4. Inanity; emptiness; want of reality. *Granville.*
5. Vacuum, which see.

VAC'UOUS, *a.* Empty; unfilled; void. *Milton.*

VAC'UOUSNESS, *n.* The state of being empty. *Mountague.*

VAC'UUM, *n.* [L.] Space empty or devoid of all matter or body. Whether there is such a thing as an absolute *vacuum* in nature, is a question which has been much controverted. The Peripatetics assert that nature abhors a *vacuum.*
Torricellian vacuum, the vacuum produced by filling a tube with mercury, and allowing it to descend till it is counterbalanced by the weight of the atmosphere, as in the barometer invented by Torricelli.

VADE, *v. i.* [L. *vado.*] To vanish; to pass away. [*Not in use.*] *Wotton.*

VADE-ME'CUM, *n.* [L. go with me.] A book or other thing that a person carries with him as a constant companion; a manual.

VAG'ABOND, *a.* [L. *vagabundus*, from *vagor*, to wander; from the root of *wag.*]
1. Wandering; moving from place to place without any settled habitation; as a *vagabond* exile. *Shak.*
2. Wandering; floating about without any certain direction; driven to and fro.
 Like to a *vagabond* flag upon the stream. *Shak.*

VAG'ABOND, *n.* [supra.] A vagrant; one who wanders from town to town or place to place, having no certain dwelling, or not abiding in it. By the laws of England and of the United States, *vagabonds* are liable to be taken up and punished.

VAG'ABONDRY, *n.* A state of wandering in idleness.

VAGA'RY, *n.* [L. *vagus*, wandering.] A wandering of the thoughts; a wild freak; a whim; a whimsical purpose.
 They chang'd their minds,
 Flew off, and into strange *vagaries* fell.
 Milton.

VA'GIENT, *a.* [L. *vagiens.*] Crying like a child. [*Not in use.*] *More.*

VAG'INAL, *a.* [L. *vagina*, a sheath. See *Wain.*]
Pertaining to a sheath, or resembling a sheath; as a *vaginal* membrane.

VAG'INANT, *a.* [L. *vagina.*] In *botany*, sheathing; as a *vaginant* leaf, one investing the stem or branch by its base, which has the form of a tube. *Martyn.*

VAG'INATED, *a.* In *botany*, sheathed; invested by the tubular base of the leaf; as a stem. *Martyn.*

VAGINOPEN'NOUS, *a.* [L. *vagina* and *penna.*]
Having the wings covered with a hard case or sheath, as insects.

VA'GOUS, *a.* [L. *vagus*; Fr. *vague.*] Wandering; unsettled. [*Little used.*] *Ayliffe.*

VA'GRANCY, *n.* [from *vagrant.*] A state of wandering without a settled home. *Vagrancy* in idle strollers or vagabonds, is punishable by law.

VA'GRANT, *a.* [L. *vagor.*] Wandering from place to place without any settled habitation; as a *vagrant* beggar.
2. Wandering; unsettled; moving without any certain direction.
 That beauteous Emma *vagrant* courses took. *Prior.*

VA'GRANT, *n.* [Norm. *vagarant.*] An idle wanderer; a vagabond; one who strolls from place to place; a sturdy beggar; one who has no settled habitation, or who does not abide in it.
 Vagrants and outlaws shall offend thy view. *Prior.*

VAGUE, *a. vāg.* [Fr. from L. *vagus*, wandering.]
1. Wandering; vagrant; vagabond; as *vague* villains. [*In this literal sense, not used.*] *Hayward.*
2. Unsettled; unfixed; undetermined; indefinite. He appears to have very *vague* ideas of this subject.
3. Proceeding from no known authority; flying; uncertain; as a *vague* report.

VAIL, *n.* [Fr. *voile*; It. *velo*; L. *velum*, from *velo*, to cover, to spread over; Gaelic, *falach*, a vail. It is correctly written *vail*, for *e*, in Latin, is our *a.*]
1. Any kind of cloth which is used for intercepting the view and hiding something; as the *vail* of the temple among the Israelites.
2. A piece of thin cloth or silk stuff, used by females to hide their faces. In some eastern countries, certain classes of females never appear abroad without *vails.*
3. A cover; that which conceals; as the *vail* of oblivion.
4. In *botany*, the membranous covering of the germen in the *Musci* and *Hepaticæ*; the calypter. *Cyc.*
5. *Vails*, money given to servants. [*Not used in America.*] *Dryden.*

VAIL, *v. t.* [L. *velo.*] To cover; to hide from the sight; as, to *vail* the face.

VAIL, *v. t.* [Fr. *avaler.*] To let fall.
 They stiffly refused to *vail* their bonnets.
 [*I believe wholly obsolete.*] *Carew.*
2. To let fall; to lower; as, to *vail* the topsail. *Obs.*
3. To let fall; to sink. *Obs.* *Shak.*

VAIL, *v. i.* To yield or recede; to give place; to show respect by yielding.
 Thy convenience must *vail* to thy neighbor's necessity. *Obs.* *South.*

VA'ILED, *pp.* Covered; concealed.

VA'ILER, *n.* One who yields from respect. *Obs.* *Overbury.*

VA'ILING, *ppr.* Covering; hiding from the sight.

VAIN, *a.* [Fr. *vain*; It. *vano*; L. *vanus*; Gaelic, *fann*, weak; *faon*, void; W. *gwan*; Sans. *vana*; probably allied to Eng. *wan*, *wane*, *want.*]
1. Empty; worthless; having no substance, value or importance. 1 Pet. i.
 To your *vain* answer will you have recourse. *Blackmore.*
 Every man walketh in a *vain* show. Ps. xxxix.
 Why do the people imagine a *vain* thing? Ps. ii.
2. Fruitless; ineffectual. All attempts, all efforts were *vain.*
 Vain is the force of man. *Dryden.*
3. Proud of petty things, or of trifling attainments; elated with a high opinion of one's own accomplishments, or with things more showy than valuable; conceited.
 The minstrels play'd on every side,
 Vain of their art— *Dryden.*
4. Empty; unreal; as a *vain* chimera.
5. Showy; ostentatious.
 Load some *vain* church with old theatric state. *Pope.*
6. Light; inconstant; worthless. Prov. xii.
7. Empty; unsatisfying. The pleasures of life are *vain.*
8. False; deceitful; not genuine; spurious. James i.
9. Not effectual; having no efficacy.
 Bring no more *vain* oblations. Is. i.
In vain, to no purpose; without effect; ineffectual.
 In vain they do worship me. Matt. xv.
To take the name of God in vain, to use the name of God with levity or profaneness.

VAINGLO'RIOUS, *a.* [*vain* and *glorious.*]
1. Vain to excess of one's own achievments; elated beyond due measure; boastful.
 Vainglorious man. *Spenser.*
2. Boastful; proceeding from vanity.
 Arrogant and *vainglorious* expression. *Hale.*

VAINGLO'RIOUSLY, *adv.* With empty pride. *Milton.*

VAINGLO'RY, *n.* [*vain* and *glory.*] Exclusive vanity excited by one's own performances; empty pride; undue elation of mind.
 He hath nothing of *vainglory.* *Bacon.*
 Let nothing be done through strife or *vainglory.* Phil. ii.

VA'INLY, *adv.* Without effect; to no purpose; ineffectually; in vain.
 In weak complaints you *vainly* waste your breath. *Dryden.*
2. Boastingly; with vaunting; proudly; arrogantly.
 Humility teaches us not to think *vainly* nor vauntingly of ourselves. *Delany.*
3. Idly; foolishly.
 Nor *vainly* hope to be invulnerable. *Milton.*

VA'INNESS, *n.* The state of being vain; inefficacy; ineffectualness; as the *vainness* of efforts.
2. Empty pride; vanity.

VAIR, *n.* In *heraldry*, a kind of fur or doubling, consisting of divers little piecees, argent and azure, resembling a bell-glass. *Cyc.* *Chambers.*

VAIR, VA'IRY, } *a.* In *heraldry*, charged with vair; variegated with argent and azure colors, when the term is *vairy proper*; and with other colors, when it is *vair* or *vairy composed.* *Todd.* *Cyc.*

VA'IVODE, *n.* [Sclav.] A prince of the Dacian provinces; sometimes written *waiwode*, for this is the pronunciation.

VAL'ANCE, *n.* [Qu. Fr. *avalant*, falling; Norm. *valaunt*, descending.]
The fringes of drapery hanging round the tester and head of a bed. *Swift.*

VAL'ANCE, *v. t.* To decorate with hanging fringes. *Shak.*

VALE, *n.* [Fr. *val*; It. *valle*; L. *vallis*. Qu. W. *gwael*, low, and Eng. to *fall*, Fr. *avaler*.]
1. A tract of low ground or of land between hills; a valley. [*Vale* is used in poetry, and *valley* in prose and common discourse.]

In those fair *vales*, by nature form'd to please. *Harte.*

2. A little trough or canal; as a pump *vale* to carry off the water from a ship's pump.
3. *Vales*, money given to servants. [*avails.*] [*Not used in America.*]

VALEDIC'TION, *n.* [L. *valedico*; *vale*, farewell, and *dico*, to say.] A farewell; a bidding farewell.

VALEDIC'TORY, *a.* Bidding farewell; as a *valedictory* oration.

VALEDIC'TORY, *n.* An oration or address spoken at commencement, in American colleges, by a member of the class which receive the degree of bachelor of arts, and take their leave of college and of each other.

VAL'ENTINE, *n.* A sweetheart or choice made on Valentine's day. *Wotton.*
2. A letter sent by one young person to another on Valentine's day. *Burton.*

VALE'RIAN, *n.* A plant of the genus Valeriana, of many species.

VAL'ET, *n.* [Fr.; formerly written *vadlet*, *valect*, *vallet*, &c.]
1. A waiting servant; a servant who attends on a gentleman's person.
2. In *the manege*, a kind of goad or stick armed with a point of iron. *Cyc.*

VALETUDINA'RIAN, **VALETU'DINARY**, } *a.* [L. *valetudinarius*, from *valetudo*, from *valeo*, to be well.]
Sickly; weak; infirm; seeking to recover health.

VALETUDINA'RIAN, **VALETU'DINARY**, } *n.* A person of a weak, infirm or sickly constitution; one who is seeking to recover health.

Valetudinarians must live where they can command and scold. *Swift.*

VAL'IANCE, *n.* *val'yance.* Bravery; valor. [*Not in use.*] *Spenser.*

VALIANT, *a.* *val'yant.* [Fr. *vaillant*, from *valoir*, L. *valeo*, to be strong.]
1. Primarily, strong; vigorous in body; as a *valiant* fencer. *Walton.*
2. Brave; courageous; intrepid in danger; heroic; as a *valiant* soldier.

Be thou *valiant* for me, and fight the Lord's battles. 1 Sam. xviii.

3. Performed with valor; bravely conducted; heroic; as a *valiant* action or achievment; a *valiant* combat. *Nelson.*

VAL'IANTLY, *adv.* Stoutly; vigorously; with personal strength.
2. Courageously; bravely; heroically.

VAL'IANTNESS, *n.* Stoutness; strength.
2. *Most generally*, valor; bravery; intrepidity in danger.

Achimetes, having won the top of the walls, by the *valiantness* of the defendants was forced to retire. *Knolles.*

VAL'ID, *a.* [Fr. *valide*; L. *validus*, from *valeo*, to be strong. The primary sense of the root is to strain or stretch.]
1. Having sufficient strength or force; founded in truth; sound; just; good; that can be supported; not weak or defective; as a *valid* reason; a *valid* argument; a *valid* objection.
2. Having legal strength or force; efficacious; executed with the proper formalities; that cannot be rightfully overthrown or set aside; supportable by law or right; as a *valid* deed; a *valid* covenant; a *valid* instrument of any kind; a *valid* claim or title; a *valid* marriage.
3. Strong; powerful; *in a literal sense*; as *valid* arms. [*Not in use.*]

VALID'ITY, *n.* [Fr. *validité*; from *valid.*]
1. Strength or force to convince; justness; soundness; as the *validity* of an argument or proof; the *validity* of an objection.
2. Legal strength or force; that quality of a thing which renders it supportable in law or equity; as the *validity* of a will; the *validity* of a grant; the *validity* of a claim or of a title. Certain forms and solemnities are usually requisite to give *validity* to contracts and conveyances of rights.
3. Value. [*Not in use.*] *Shak.*

VAL'IDLY, *adv.* In a valid manner; in such a manner or degree as to make firm or to convince.

VAL'IDNESS, *n.* Validity, which see.

VALÏSE, *n.* [Fr.] A horseman's case or portmanteau.

VALLAN'CY, *n.* [from *valance.*] A large wig that shades the face. *Dryden.*

VALLA'TION, *n.* [L. *vallatus*, from *vallum*, a wall.] A rampart or entrenchment. *Warton.*

VAL'LEY, *n.* plu. *valleys.* [Fr. *vallée*; L. *vallis.* See *Vale.*]
1. A hollow or low tract of land between hills or mountains.
2. A low extended plain, usually alluvial, penetrated or washed by a river. The *valley* of the Connecticut is remarkable for its fertility and beauty.

Ye mountains, sink; ye *valleys*, rise;
Prepare the Lord his way. *Watts.*

3. In *building*, a gutter over the sleepers in the roof of a building. *Cyc.*

VAL'LUM, *n.* [L.] A trench or wall. *Warton.*

VAL'OR, *n.* [L. *valor*; Fr. *valeur*; from L. *valeo*, to be strong, to be worth.]
Strength of mind in regard to danger; that quality which enables a man to encounter danger with firmness; personal bravery; courage; intrepidity; prowess.

When *valor* preys on reason,
It eats the sword it fights with. *Shak.*
For contemplation he and *valor* form'd. *Milton.*

Ad valorem, in commerce, according to the value; as an *ad valorem* duty.

VAL'OROUS, *a.* Brave; courageous; stout; intrepid; as a *valorous* knight.

VAL'OROUSLY, *adv.* In a brave manner; heroically.

VAL'UABLE, *a.* [Fr. *valable*; from *value.*]
1. Having value or worth; having some good qualities which are useful and esteemed; precious; as a *valuable* horse; *valuable* land; a *valuable* house.
2. Worthy; estimable; deserving esteem; as a *valuable* friend; a *valuable* companion.

VALUA'TION, *n.* [from *value.*] The act of estimating the value or worth; the act of setting a price; as the just *valuation* of civil and religious privileges.
2. Apprizement; as a *valuation* of lands for the purpose of taxation.
3. Value set upon a thing; estimated worth.

So slight a *valuation*. *Shak.*

VALUA'TOR, *n.* One who sets a value; an apprizer.

VALUE, *n.* *val'u.* [Fr. *valoir*, *valu*; from L. *valor*, from *valeo*, to be worth; It. *valore*; Sp. *valor.*]
1. Worth; that property or those properties of a thing which render it useful or estimable; or the degree of that property or of such properties. The *real* value of a thing is its utility, its power or capacity of procuring or producing good. Hence the *real* or *intrinsic* value of iron, is far greater than that of gold. But there is, in many things, an *estimated* value, depending on opinion or fashion, such as the *value* of precious stones. The *value* of land depends on its fertility, or on its vicinity to a market, or on both.
2. Price; the rate of worth set upon a commodity, or the amount for which a thing is sold. We say, the *value* of a thing is what it will bring in market.
3. Worth; *applied to persons.*

Ye are all physicians of no *value*. Job xiii.
Ye are of more *value* than many sparrows. Matt. x.

4. High rate.

Cesar is well acquainted with your virtue,
And therefore sets this *value* on your life. *Addison.*

5. Importance; efficacy in producing effects; as considerations of no *value*.

—Before events shall have decided on the *value* of the measures. *Marshall.*

6. Import; precise signification; as the *value* of a word or phrase. *Mitford.*

VALUE, *v. t.* *val'u.* To estimate the worth of; to rate at a certain price; to apprize; as, to *value* lands or goods.
2. To rate at a high price; to have in high esteem; as a *valued* poem or picture. A man is apt to *value* his own performances at too high a rate; he is even disposed to *value* himself for his humility.
3. To esteem; to hold in respect and estimation; as, to *value* one for his works or virtues.
4. To take account of.

The mind doth *value* every moment. *Bacon.*

5. To reckon or estimate with respect to number or power.

The queen is *valu'd* thirty thousand strong. *Shak.*

6. To consider with respect to importance.

The king must take it ill,
So slightly *valu'd* in his messenger. *Shak.*
Neither of them *valued* their promises according to the rules of honor or integrity. *Clarendon.*

7. To raise to estimation.

Some *value* themselves to their country by jealousies to the crown. [*Not in use.*] *Temple.*

8. To be worth. [*Not in use.*] *Shak.*

VAL'UED, *pp.* Estimated at a certain rate; apprized; esteemed.

VAL'UELESS, *a.* Being of no value; having no worth.

VAL'UER, *n.* One who values; an apprizer; one who holds in esteem.

VAL'UING, *ppr.* Setting a price on; estimating the worth of; esteeming.

VALV'ATE, *a.* [See *Valve.*] Having or resembling a valve.

VALVE, *n. valv.* [L. *valvæ*, folding doors; coinciding with *volvo.*]

1. A folding door.

> Swift through the *valves* the visionary fair
> Repass'd. *Pope.*

2. A lid or cover so formed as to open a communication in one direction, and close it in the other. Thus the valve of a common pump opens upwards to admit the water, and closes downwards to prevent its return.

3. In *anatomy*, a membranous partition within the cavity of a vessel, which opens to allow the passage of a fluid in one direction, and shuts to prevent its regurgitation. *Parr.*

4. In *botany*, the outer coat, shell or covering of a capsule or other pericarp, or rather one of the pieces which compose it; also, one of the leaflets composing the calyx and corol in grasses. *Martyn.*

5. One of the pieces or divisions in bivalve and multivalve shells. *Ed. Encyc.*

VALV'ED, *a.* Having valves; composed of valves.

VALV'LET, VALV'ULE, } *n.* A little valve; one of the pieces which compose the outer covering of a pericarp.

VALV'ULAR, *a.* Containing valves. *Moor. Med. Dict.*

VAMP, *n.* [W. *gwam*, that incloses, or goes partly round.] The upper lether of a shoe.

VAMP, *v. t.* To piece an old thing with a new part; to repair.

> I had never much hopes of your *vamped* play. *Swift.*

VAMP'ED, *pp.* Pieced; repaired.

VAMP'ER, *n.* One who pieces an old thing with something new.

VAMP'ING, *ppr.* Piecing with something new.

VAMP'IRE, *n.* [G. *vampyr.*] In *mythology*, an imaginary demon, which was fabled to suck the blood of persons during the night.

2. In *zoology*, a species of large bat, the *Vespertilio vampyrus* of Linne, called also the ternate bat. It inhabits Guinea, Madagascar, the E. India Isles, New Holland and New Caledonia. These animals fly in flocks, darkening the air by their numbers. It is said that this bat will insinuate his tongue into the vein of an animal imperceptibly, and suck his blood while asleep. This name is also given by Buffon to a species of large bat in South America, the *V. spectrum* of Linne. *Cyc.*

VAN, *n.* [The radical word from which is formed the Fr. *avant, avancer*, Eng. *advance, advantage.* It is from the root of L. *venio*, the primary sense of which is to pass.]

1. The front of an army; or the front line or foremost division of a fleet, either in sailing or in battle.

2. Among *farmers*, a fan for winnowing grain. [This in New England is always pronounced *fan*, which see. But the winnowing machine has nearly superseded the use of it.]

3. In *mining*, the cleansing of ore or tin stuff by means of a shovel. *Cyc.*

4. A wing with which the air is beaten.

> He wheel'd in air, and stretch'd his *vans* in vain. *Dryden.*

VAN, *v. t.* [Fr. *vanner.*] To fan. [*Not in use.*] [See *Fan.*]

VAN-CŌURIERS, *n.* [Fr. *avant-coureurs.*] In *armies*, light armed soldiers sent before armies to beat the road upon the approach of an enemy; precursors. *Cyc.*

VAN'DAL, *n.* [It signifies a wanderer.] A ferocious, cruel person.

VANDAL'IC, *a.* Pertaining to the Vandals; designating the south shore of the Baltic, where once lived the Vandals, a nation of ferocious barbarians; hence, ferocious; rude; barbarous.

VAN'DALISM, *n.* Ferocious cruelty; indiscriminate destruction of lives and property. *Ramsay.*

VANDY'KE, *n.* A small round handkerchief with a collar for the neck, worn by females.

VANE, *n.* [D. *vaan.* The primary sense is extended.]

A plate placed on a spindle, at the top of a spire, for the purpose of showing by its turning and direction, which way the wind blows. In *ships*, a piece of bunting is used for the same purpose.

VAN-FOSS, *n.* A ditch on the outside of the counterscarp. *Cyc.*

VANG, *n.* The vangs of a ship are a sort of braces to steady the mizen-gaff. *Cyc.*

2. The thin membranous part or web of a fether. *Derham.*

VAN'-GU'ARD, *n.* [*van* and *guard.*] The troops who march in front of an army; the first line.

VANIL'LA, *n.* A genus of plants which have an unctuous aromatic taste, and a fragrant smell; natives of South America and the W. Indies. *Cyc.*

VAN'ISH, *v. i.* [L. *vanesco*; Fr. *evanouir*; It. *svanire*; from L. *vanus*, vain, or its root; Eng. to *wane.* The primary sense is to withdraw or depart.]

1. To disappear; to pass from a visible to an invisible state; as, vapor *vanishes* from the sight by being dissipated. Light *vanishes*, when the rays of the illuminating body are intercepted; darkness *vanishes* before the rising sun.

2. To disappear; to pass beyond the limit of vision; as, a ship *vanishes* from the sight of spectators on land.

3. To disappear; to pass away; to be annihilated or lost. How cheering is the well founded hope of enjoying delights which can never *vanish!*

VAN'ISHED, *a.* Having no perceptible existence. *Pope.*

VAN'ISHING, *ppr.* Disappearing; passing from the sight or possession; departing forever.

VAN'ITY, *n.* [Fr. *vanité*; L. *vanitas*, from *vanus*, vain.]

1. Emptiness; want of substance to satisfy desire; uncertainty; inanity.

> *Vanity* of *vanities*, saith the preacher; all is *vanity.* Eccles. i.

2. Fruitless desire or endeavor.

> *Vanity* possesseth many who are desirous to know the certainty of things to come. *Sidney.*

3. Trifling labor that produces no good. *Raleigh.*

4. Emptiness; untruth.

> Here I may well show the *vanity* of what is reported in the story of Walsingham. *Davies.*

5. Empty pleasure; vain pursuit; idle show; unsubstantial enjoyment.

> Sin with *vanity* had fill'd the works of men. *Milton.*

> Think not when woman's transient breath is fled,
> That all her *vanities* at once are dead;
> Succeeding *vanities* she still regards. *Pope.*

6. Ostentation; arrogance. *Raleigh.*

7. Inflation of mind upon slight grounds; empty pride, inspired by an overweening conceit of one's personal attainments or decorations. Fops cannot be cured of their *vanity.*

> *Vanity* is the food of fools. *Swift.*
> No man sympathizes with the sorrows of *vanity.* *Johnson.*

VAN'QUISH, *v. t.* [Fr. *vaincre*; L. *vinco*; It. *vincere*; Sp. *vincer*; probably allied to L. *vincio*, to bind.]

1. To conquer; to overcome; to subdue in battle; as an enemy.

> They *vanquished* the rebels in all encounters. *Clarendon.*

2. To defeat in any contest; to refute in argument. *Atterbury.*

VAN'QUISH, *n.* A disease in sheep, in which they pine away.

VAN'QUISHABLE, *a.* That may be conquered. *Gayton.*

VAN'QUISHED, *pp.* Overcome in battle; subdued; defeated.

VAN'QUISHER, *n.* A conqueror; a victor. *Milton.*

VAN'QUISHING, *ppr.* Conquering; subduing; defeating; refuting.

VAN'SIRE, *n.* In *zoology*, a species of weasel with short ears, found in Madagascar. *Cyc.*

V'ANT, *v. i.* [Fr. *vanter.*] To boast. [This is the more correct orthography. See *Vaunt.*]

V'ANTAĠE, *n.* [Sp. *ventaja*; from the root of L. *venio.* See *Advantage* and *Van.*]

1. Gain; profit. *Obs.*

2. Superiority; state in which one has better means of action or defense than another. [This, I believe, is used only in the compound, *vantage-ground.*]

3. Opportunity; convenience. *Obs.* *Shak.*

V'ANTAĠE, *v. t.* To profit. [*Not in use.*]

V'ANTAĠE-GROUND, *n.* Superiority of state or place; the place or condition which gives one an advantage over another.

VANT'BRASS, *n.* [Fr. *avant-bras.*] Armor for the arm. *Obs.* *Milton.*

VAP'ID, *a.* [L. *vapidus.* The radical verb is not in the Latin, but the sense must be to pass or fly off, to escape; or to strike down, L. *vapulo.* It is probably allied to *vapor.*]

1. Having lost its life and spirit; dead; spiritless; flat; as *vapid* beer; a *vapid* state of the blood.

2. Dull; unanimated.

VAP'IDNESS, *n.* The state of having lost its life or spirit; deadness; flatness; as the *vapidness* of ale or cider.

2. Dullness; want of life or spirit.

VA'POR, *n.* [L. Sp. *vapor;* Fr. *vapeur;* It. *vapore.* It is probably from a verb signifying to depart, to fly off.]

1. In *a general sense*, an invisible elastic fluid, rendered aeriform by heat, and capable of being condensed, or brought back to the liquid or solid state, by cold. The vapor of water is distinguished by the name of *steam*, which see.

2. A visible fluid floating in the atmosphere. All substances which impair the transparency of the atmosphere, as smoke, fog, &c. are in common language called *vapors*, though the term *vapor* is technically applied only to an invisible and condensible substance, as in No. 1.; fog, &c. being vapor condensed, or water in a minute state of division. *Vapor* rising into the higher regions of the atmosphere, and condensed in large volumes, forms *clouds*. *D. Olmsted.*

3. Substances resembling smoke, which sometimes fill the atmosphere, particularly in America during the autumn.

4. Wind; flatulence. *Bacon.*

5. Mental fume; vain imagination, unreal fancy. *Hammond.*

6. *Vapors*, a disease of nervous debility, in which a variety of strange images float in the brain, or appear as if visible. Hence hypochondriacal affections and spleen are called *vapors*.

7. Something unsubstantial, fleeting or transitory.

> For what is your life? It is even a *vapor*, that appeareth for a little time, and then vanisheth away. James iv.

VA'POR, *v. i.* [L. *vaporo.*] To pass off in fumes or a moist floating substance; to steam; to be exhaled; to evaporate. [In this sense, *evaporate* is generally used.]

2. To emit fumes.

> Running water *vapors* not so much as standing water. [*Little used.*] *Bacon.*

3. To bully; to boast or vaunt with a vain ostentatious display of worth; to brag. [*This is the most usual signification of the word.*]

> And what in real value's wanting,
> Supply with *vaporing* and ranting. *Hudibras.*

VA'POR, *v. t.* To emit, cast off or scatter in fumes or stream; as, to *vapor* away a heated fluid.

> Another sighing *vapors* forth his soul. *B. Jonson.*

VAPORABIL'ITY, *n.* The quality of being capable of vaporization. *Dispensatory.*

VAP'ORABLE, *a.* Capable of being converted into vapor by the agency of caloric.

VAP'ORATE, *v. i.* To emit vapor. [See *Evaporate.*]

VAPORA'TION, *n.* [L. *vaporatio.*] The act or process of converting into vapor, or of passing off in vapor.

VA'POR-BATH, *n.* [*vapor* and *bath.*] The application of vapor to the body in a close place.

2. In *chimistry*, an apparatus for heating bodies by the fumes of hot water. *Cyc.*

VA'PORED, *a.* Moist; wet with vapors.

2. Splenetic; peevish. *Green.*

VA'PORER, *n.* A boaster; one who makes a vaunting display of his prowess or worth; a braggart.

VAPORIF'I€, *a.* [L. *vapor* and *facio*, to make.] Forming into vapor; converting into steam, or expelling in a volatile form, as fluids.

VA'PORING, *ppr.* Boasting; vaunting ostentatiously and vainly.

VA'PORINGLY, *adv.* In a boasting manner.

VA'PORISH, *a.* Full of vapors.

2. Hypochondriac; splenetic; affected by hysterics.

VAPORIZA'TION, *n.* The artificial formation of vapor.

VAP'ORIZE, *v. t.* To convert into vapor by the application of heat or artificial means.

VAP'ORIZE, *v. i.* To pass off in vapor.

VAP'ORIZED, *pp.* Expelled in vapor.

VAP'ORIZING, *ppr.* Converting into vapor.

VA'POROUS, *a.* [Fr. *vaporeux.*] Full of vapors or exhalations; as the *vaporous* air of valleys. *Derham.*

2. Vain; unreal; proceeding from the vapors. *Bacon.*

3. Windy; flatulent; as, *vaporous* food is the most easily digested. *Arbuthnot.*

VA'POROUSNESS, *n.* State of being full of vapors.

VA'PORY, *a.* Vaporous; full of vapors. *Thomson.*

2. Hypochondriac; splenetic; peevish. *Thomson.*

VAPULA'TION, *n.* [L. *vapulo.*] The act of beating or whipping. [*Not in use.*]

VARE, *n.* [Sp. *vara.*] A wand or staff of justice. [*Not in use.*] *Howell.*

VAR'E€, *n.* The French name for kelp or incinerated sea weed; wrack. *Ure.*

VA'RI, *n.* In *zoology*, a species of quadruped, the maucauco or *Lemur catta* of Linne, having its tail marked with rings of black and white; a native of Madagascar. The *vari* of Buffon is the black maucauco, *L. macaco* of Linne, with the neck bearded, like a ruff. *Cyc. Ed. Encyc.*

VA'RIABLE, *a.* [Fr. See *Vary.*] That may vary or alter; capable of alteration in any manner; changeable; as *variable* winds or seasons; *variable* colors.

2. Susceptible of change; liable to change; mutable; fickle; unsteady; inconstant; as, the affections of men are *variable;* passions are *variable*.

> His heart I know, how *variable* and vain. *Milton.*

3. In *mathematics*, subject to continual increase or decrease; in opposition to *constant*, retaining the same value.

VA'RIABLE, *n.* In *mathematics*, a quantity which is in a state of continual increase or decrease. The indefinitely small quantity by which a variable is continually increased or diminished, is called its *differential*, and the method of finding these quantities, the *differential calculus*. *Hutton.*

VA'RIABLENESS, *n.* Susceptibility of change; liableness or aptness to alter; changeableness; as the *variableness* of the weather.

2. Inconstancy; fickleness; unsteadiness; levity; as the *variableness* of human passions.

VA'RIABLY, *adv.* Changeably; with alteration; in an inconstant or fickle manner.

VA'RIANCE, *n.* [See *Vary.*] In *law*, an alteration of something formerly laid in a writ; or a difference between a declaration and a writ, or the deed on which it is grounded.

2. Any alteration or change of condition.

3. Difference that produces dispute or controversy; disagreement; dissension; discord. A mere *variance* may become a war. Without a spirit of condescension, there will be an everlasting *variance*.

At variance, in disagreement; in a state of difference or want of agreement.

2. In a state of dissension or controversy; in a state of enmity.

VA'RIATE, *v. t.* To alter; to make different. *King.*

2. To vary. [*A bad word.*]

VARIA'TION, *n.* [Fr. from L. *variatio.* See *Vary.*]

1. Alteration; a partial change in the form, position, state or qualities of the same thing; as a *variation* of color in different lights; a *variation* in the size of a plant from day to day; the unceasing, though slow *variation* of language; a *variation* in a soil from year to year. Our opinions are subject to continual *variations*.

> The essences of things are conceived not capable of such *variation*. *Locke.*

2. Difference; change from one to another.

> In some other places are born more females than males; which, upon this *variation* of proportion, I recommend to the curious. *Graunt.*

3. In *grammar*, change of termination of nouns and adjectives, constituting what is called case, number and gender; as the *variation* of words.

4. Deviation; as a *variation* of a transcript from the original. *Dryden.*

5. In *astronomy*, the variation of the moon is the third inequality in her motion; by which, when out of the quadratures, her true place differs from her place twice equated. *Cyc.*

6. In *geography* and *navigation*, the deviation of the magnetic needle from the true north point; called also *declination*. *Cyc.*

The variation of the needle at New Haven, in 1820, as ascertained from the mean of numerous observations made by Professor Fisher, was $4^{\circ}.\ 25'\frac{42}{100}$ west.

7. In *music*, the different manner of singing or playing the same air or tune, by subdividing the notes into several others of less value, or by adding graces, yet so that the tune itself may be discovered through all its embellishments. *Cyc.*

VAR'I€OCELE, *n.* [L. *varix*, a dilated vein, and Gr. κηλη, a tumor.] In *surgery*, a varicous enlargement of the veins of the spermatic cord; or more generally, a like enlargement of the veins of the scrotum. *Cyc.*

VAR'I€OSE, } *a.* [L. *varicosus*, having en-
VAR'I€OUS, } larged veins.]

1. Preternaturally enlarged, or permanently dilated, as a vein.

2. Swelled; puffy; as an ulcer on the legs of beasts. *Cyc.*

VA'RIED, *pp.* of *vary*. Altered; partially changed; changed.

VA'RIEGATE, *v. t.* [It. *varieggiare;* from L. *vario, varius.* See *Vary.*]

To diversify in external appearance; to mark with different colors; as, to *variegate* a floor with marble of different colors.

The shells are filled with a white spar, which *variegates* and adds to the beauty of the stone. *Woodward.*

Ladies like *variegated* tulips show. *Pope.*

VA'RIEGATED, *pp.* Diversified in colors or external appearance. *Variegated leaves*, in botany, are such as are irregularly marked with white or yellow spots. *Cyc.*

VA'RIEGATING, *ppr.* Diversifying with colors.

VARIEGA'TION, *n.* The act of diversifying, or state of being diversified by different colors; diversity of colors.

VARI'ETY, *n.* [Fr. *varieté*; L. *varietas*, from *vario*, to vary.]

1. Intermixture of different things, or of things different in form; or a succession of different things.

Variety is nothing else but a continued novelty. *South.*

The *variety* of colors depends on the composition of light. *Newton.*

2. One thing of many which constitute variety. In this sense, it has a plural; as the *varieties* of a species.

3. Difference; dissimilitude.

There is a *variety* in the tempers of good men. *Atterbury.*

4. Variation; deviation; change from a former state. [*Little used.*] *Hale.*

5. Many and different kinds. The shopkeeper has a great *variety* of cottons and silks.

He wants to do a *variety* of good things. *Law.*

6. In *natural history*, a difference not permanent or invariable, but occasioned by an accidental change; as a *variety* of any species of plant.

Naturalists formerly erred very much in supposing an accidental *variety* of plants, animals or minerals, to be a distinct species. Ray has established a good test for *varieties* in botany. A plant is distinct, which propagates itself in its own form by its seed; but when the difference disappears in the new plant, it is only a variety. Variety then is a difference between individuals, not permanent nor important enough to constitute a distinct species; such as in size, color, fullness, curling, &c.

7. Different sort; as *varieties* of soil or land.

VA'RIOLITE, *n.* [L. *varius* and Gr. λιθος, stone.]

In *mineralogy*, a kind of porphyritic rock, in which the imbedded substances are imperfectly crystalized, or are rounded, giving the stone a spotted appearance. *Cyc.*

Variolites are fragments of primitive glandular rocks. *Dict. Nat. Hist.*

VA'RIOLOID, *n.* [L. *variolæ* and Gr. ειδος, form.]

The name recently given to a disease resembling the small pox.

VA'RIOLOUS, *a.* [L. *variolæ*, from *vario*, to diversify.] Pertaining to or designating the small pox.

VA'RIOUS, *a.* [L. *varius*. See *Vary*.] Different; several; manifold; as men of *various* names and *various* occupations.

2. Changeable; uncertain; unfixed.

The names of mixed modes—are very *various* and doubtful. *Locke.*

3. Unlike each other; diverse. *Dryden.*

So many and so *various* laws are giv'n. *Milton.*

4. Variegated; diversified. *Milton.*

VA'RIOUSLY, *adv.* In different ways; with change; with diversity; as objects *variously* represented; flowers *variously* colored. The human system is *variously* affected by different medicines.

VA'RIX, *n.* [L.] An uneven swelling of a dilated vein. *Cyc.*

2. In *beasts*, a sort of puffy dilatation or enlargement in some part of a vein, forming a kind of knot. *Cyc.*

V'ARLET, *n.* [Old Fr. See *Valet*.] Anciently, a servant or footman. *Tusser.*

2. A scoundrel; a rascal; as an impudent *varlet*. *Addison.*

V'ARLETRY, *n.* The rabble; the crowd. [*Not in use.*] *Shak.*

V'ARNISH, *n.* [Fr. *vernis*; Sp. *barniz*; Port. *verniz*; It. *vernice*; Low L. *vernix*; G. *firniss*; D. *vernis*.]

1. A thick, viscid, glossy liquid, laid on work by painters and others, to give it a smooth hard surface and a beautiful gloss. Varnishes are made of different materials and for different purposes. Amber varnish is made of amber, lintseed oil, litharge and turpentine. Black varnish, for japanning wood and lether, is made by mixing lampblack with a proper quantity of a strong solution of gum-lac in spirit of wine. *Cyc.*

2. An artificial covering to give a fair appearance to any act or conduct.

V'ARNISH, *v. t.* [Fr. *vernisser*, *vernir*.] To lay varnish on; to cover with a liquid, for giving any thing a glossy surface; as, to *varnish* a sideboard or table.

2. To cover with something that gives a fair external appearance.

Close ambition, *varnish'd* o'er with zeal. *Milton.*

3. To give a fair external appearance in words; to give a fair coloring to; as, to *varnish* errors or deformity.

Cato's voice was ne'er employ'd
To clear the guilty, and to *varnish* crimes. *Addison.*

And bow the knee to pomp that loves to *varnish* guilt. *Byron.*

V'ARNISHED, *pp.* Covered with varnish; made glossy.

2. Rendered fair in external appearance.

V'ARNISHER, *n.* One who varnishes, or whose occupation is to varnish.

2. One who disguises or palliates; one who gives a fair external appearance. *Pope.*

V'ARNISHING, *ppr.* Laying on varnish; giving a fair external appearance.

V'ARNISH-TREE, *n.* The *Rhus vernix*, poison ash, or poison oak. *Lee.*

V'ARVELS, } *n.* [Fr. *vervel.*] Silver rings
VER'VELS, } about the legs of a hawk, on which the owner's name is engraved. *Dict.*

VA'RY, *v. t.* [L. *vario*; Fr. *varier*; Sp. *variar*; It. *variare*; probably allied to Eng. *veer*, Sp. *birar*, L. *verto*, Eth. በረየ bari, whence አስተበረየ to alternate. See Class Br. No. 11. and No. 23.]

1. To alter in form, appearance, substance or position; to make different by a partial change; as, to *vary* a thing in dimensions; to *vary* its properties, proportions or nature; to *vary* the posture or attitude of a thing; to *vary* one's dress.

2. To change to something else.

Gods, that never change their state,
Vary oft their love and hate. *Waller.*

We are to *vary* the customs according to the time and country where the scene of action lies. *Dryden.*

3. To make of different kinds.

God hath *varied* the inclinations of men, according to the variety of actions to be performed. *Browne.*

4. To diversify; to variegate.

God hath here
Varied his bounty so with new delights. *Milton.*

VA'RY, *v. i.* To alter or be altered in any manner; to suffer a partial change. Colors often *vary* when held in different positions. Customs *vary* from one age to another, until they are entirely changed.

2. To be changeable; to alter; as the *varying* hues of the clouds; the *varying* plumage of a dove.

3. To differ or be different; to be unlike. The laws of different countries *vary*. The laws of France *vary* from those of England.

4. To be changed; to become different. The man *varies* in his opinions; his opinions *vary* with the times.

5. To become unlike one's self; to alter.

He *varies* from himself no less. *Pope.*

6. To deviate; to depart; as, to *vary* from the law; to *vary* from the rules of justice or reason. *Locke.*

7. To alter or change in succession.

While fear and anger, with alternate grace,
Pant in her breast, and *vary* in her face. *Addison.*

8. To disagree; to be at variance; as, men *vary* in opinion.

VA'RY, *n.* Alteration; change. [*Not in use.*] *Shak.*

VA'RYING, *ppr.* Altering; changing; deviating.

VAS'CULAR, *a.* [L. *vasculum*, a vessel, from *vas*, id.]

1. Pertaining to the vessels of animal or vegetable bodies; as the *vascular* functions.

2. Full of vessels; consisting of animal or vegetable vessels, as arteries, veins, lacteals and the like; as the *vascular* system. Animal flesh is all *vascular*, none of it parenchymous. *Cyc.*

VASCULAR'ITY, *n.* The state of being vascular. *Med. Repos.*

VASCULIF'EROUS, *a.* [L. *vasculum* and *fero*, to bear.]

Vasculiferous plants are such as have seed vessels divided into cells. *Cyc.*

VASE, *n.* [Fr. from L. *vas*, *vasa*, a vessel; It. *vaso*.]

1. A vessel for domestic use, or for use in temples; as a *vase* for sacrifice, an urn, &c.

2. An ancient vessel dug out of the ground or from rubbish, and kept as a curiosity.

3. In *architecture*, an ornament of sculpture, placed on socles or pedestals, representing the vessels of the ancients, as incense-pots, flower-pots, &c. They usually crown or finish façades or frontispieces. *Cyc.*

4. The body of the Corinthian and Composite capital; called also the tambor or drum.

5. Among *florists*, the calyx of a plant, as of a tulip. *Cyc.*
6. Among *goldsmiths*, the middle of a church candlestick. *Cyc.*
7. A solid piece of ornamental marble. *Johnson.*

VAS'SAL, *n.* [Fr. *vassal*; It. *vassallo*; Sp. *vasallo*; W. *gwâs*, a boy or youth, a page, a servant; *gwasâu*, to serve.]
1. A feudatory; a tenant; one who holds land of a superior, and who vows fidelity and homage to him. A *rear* vassal is one who holds of a lord who is himself a vassal.
2. A subject; a dependant. *Hooker.*
3. A servant. *Shak.*
4. In *common language*, a bondman; a political slave. We will never be the *vassals* of a foreign prince

VAS'SAL, *v. t.* To subject to control; to enslave.

VAS'SALAGE, *n.* [Fr. *vasselage*; Sp. *vasalage.*]
1. The state of being a vassal or feudatory.
2. Political servitude; dependence; subjection; slavery. The Greeks were long held in *vassalage* by the Turks.

VAS'SALED, *pp.* or *a.* Enslaved; subjected to absolute power; as a *vassaled* land. *Trumbull.*

V'AST, *a.* [L. *vastus*; Fr. *vaste*; It. *vasto*. The primary sense of the root must be to part or spread, as this is connected with the verb to *waste*.]
1. Being of great extent; very spacious or large; as the *vast* ocean; a *vast* abyss; the *vast* empire of Russia; the *vast* plains of Syria; the *vast* domains of the Almighty.
2. Huge in bulk and extent; as the *vast* mountains of Asia; the *vast* range of the Andes.
3. Very great in numbers or amount; as a *vast* army; *vast* numbers or multitudes were slain; *vast* sums of money have been expended to gratify pride and ambition.
4. Very great in force; mighty; as *vast* efforts; *vast* labor.
5. Very great in importance; as a subject of *vast* concern.

V'AST, *n.* An empty waste.

> Through the *vast* of heav'n it sounded. *Milton.*
> The watery *vast*. *Pope.*

VASTA'TION, *n.* [L. *vastatio*, from *vasto*, to waste.]
A laying waste; waste; depopulation. [*Devastation* is generally used.]

VASTID'ITY, *n.* Vastness; immensity. [*Not English.*] *Shak.*

V'ASTLY, *adv.* Very greatly; to a great extent or degree; as a space *vastly* extended. Men differ *vastly* in their opinions and manners.

V'ASTNESS, *n.* Great extent; immensity; as the *vastness* of the ocean or of space.
2. Immense bulk and extent; as the *vastness* of a mountain.
3. Immense magnitude or amount; as the *vastness* of an army, or of the sums of money necessary to support it.
4. Immense importance.

V'ASTY, *a.* Being of great extent; very spacious.

> I can call spirits from the *vasty* deep.
> [*Little used.*] *Shak.*

VAT, *n.* [D. *vat*; Sax. *fat*; G. *fass.*] A large vessel or cistern for holding liquors in an immature state; as *vats* for wine.

> Let him produce his *vats* and tubs, in opposition to heaps of arms and standards. *Addison.*

2. A square box or cistern in which hides are laid for steeping in tan.
3. An oil measure in Holland; also, a wine measure.
4. A square hollow place on the back of a calcining furnace, where tin ore is laid to dry. *Cyc.*

VAT'ICAN, *n.* In Rome, the celebrated church of St. Peter; and also, a magnificent palace of the pope; situated at the foot of one of the seven hills on which Rome was built. Hence the phrase, the *thunders of the Vatican*, meaning the anathemas or denunciations of the pope.

VAT'ICIDE, *n.* [L. *vates*, a prophet, and *cædo*, to kill.]
The murderer of a prophet. *Pope.*

VATIC'INAL, *a.* [L. *vaticinor*, to prophesy.] Containing prophecy. *Warton.*

VATIC'INATE, *v. i.* [L. *vaticinor*, from *vates*, a prophet.]
To prophesy; to foretell; to practice prediction. [*Little used.*] *Howell.*

VATICINA'TION, *n.* Prediction; prophecy. *Bentley.*

VAULT, *n.* [Fr. *voûte*; It. *volta*, a vault; *volto*, the face, visage, and a vault, L. *vultus*; a derivative of L. *volvo*, *volutus*; Sp. *voltear*, to turn, to tumble.]
1. A continued arch, or an arched roof. Vaults are of various kinds, circular, elliptical, single, double, cross, diagonal, Gothic, &c. *Cyc.*
2. A cellar.

> To banish rats that haunt our *vault*. *Swift.*

3. A cave or cavern.

> The silent *vaults* of death, unknown to light. *Sandys.*

4. A repository for the dead. *Shak.*
5. In *the manege*, the leap of a horse.

VAULT, *v. t.* To arch; to form with a vault; or to cover with a vault; as, to *vault* a passage to a court.

VAULT, *v. i.* [Sp. *voltear*; It. *voltare*; Fr. *vautrer.*]
1. To leap; to bound; to jump; to spring.

> *Vaulting* ambition, which o'erleaps itself— *Shak.*
> Leaning on his lance, he *vaulted* on a tree. *Dryden.*
> Lucan *vaulted* upon Pegasus with all the heat and intrepidity of youth. *Addison.*

2. To tumble; to exhibit feats of tumbling or leaping.

VAULT'AGE, *n.* Vaulted work; an arched cellar. [*Not in use.*] *Shak.*

VAULT'ED, *pp.* Arched; concave; as a *vaulted* roof.
2. Covered with an arch or vault.
3. *a.* In *botany*, arched like the roof of the mouth, as the upper lip of many ringent flowers. *Martyn.*

VAULT'ER, *n.* One that vaults; a leaper; a tumbler.

VAULT'ING, *ppr.* Arching; covering with an arch.
2. Leaping; tumbling; exhibiting feats of leaping.

VAULT'Y, *a.* Arched; concave. [*Not in use.*] *Shak.*

V'AUNT, *v. i.* [Fr. *vanter*; It. *vantarsi*, from *vanto*, a boasting, from *vano*, vain, L. *vanus*. This ought to be written *vant.*]
To boast; to make a vain display of one's own worth, attainments or decorations; to talk with vain ostentation; to brag.

> Pride—prompts a man to *vaunt* and overvalue what he is. *Gov. of the Tongue.*

V'AUNT, *v. t.* To boast of; to make a vain display of.

> My vanquisher, spoil'd of his *vaunted* spoil. *Milton.*
> Charity *vaunteth* not itself. 1 Cor. xiii.

V'AUNT, *n.* Boast; a vain display of what one is or has, or has done; ostentation from vanity.

> Him I seduc'd
> With other *vaunts* and other promises. *Milton.*

V'AUNT, *n.* [Fr. *avant.*] The first part. [*Not used.*] *Shak.*

VAUNT-COURIER, *n.* [Fr. *avant-coureur.*] A precursor. *Shak.*

V'AUNTED, *pp.* Vainly boasted of or displayed.

V'AUNTER, *n.* A vain conceited boaster; a braggart; a man given to vain ostentation. *Spenser.*

V'AUNTFUL, *a.* Boastful; vainly ostentatious.

V'AUNTING, *ppr.* Vainly boasting; ostentatiously setting forth what one is or has.

V'AUNTINGLY, *adv.* Boastfully; with vain ostentation. *Shak.*

V'AUNT-MURE, *n.* [Fr. *avant-mur.*] A false wall; a work raised in front of the main wall. *Camden.*

VAV'ASOR, *n.* [This word in old books is variously written, *valvasor*, *vavasour*, *valvasour*. It is said to be from *vassal*. But qu.]
Camden holds that the *vavasor* was next below a baron. Du Cange maintains that there were two sorts of vavasors; the greater, who held of the king, such as barons and counts; and the lesser, called *valvasini*, who held of the former. The dignity or rank is no longer in use, and the name is known only in books. *Cyc.*

VAV'ASORY, *n.* The quality or tenure of the fee held by a vavasor. *Cyc.*

VA'WARD, *n.* [*van* and *ward.*] The fore part. *Obs.* *Shak.*

VEAL, *n.* [Fr. *veau*, a calf; probably contracted from L. *vitellus.*]
The flesh of a calf killed for the table.

VEC'TION, *n.* [L. *vectio*, from *veho*, to carry.]
The act of carrying, or state of being carried. [*Not in use.*]

VECTITA'TION, *n.* [L. *vectito.*] A carrying. [*Not in use.*] *Arbuthnot.*

VEC'TOR, *n.* [L. from *veho*, to carry.] In *astronomy*, a line supposed to be drawn from any planet moving round a center or the focus of an ellipsis, to that center or focus.

VEC'TURE, *n.* [L. *vectura*, from *veho*, supra.]
A carrying; carriage; conveyance by carrying. [*Little used.*] *Bacon.*

VEDA, *n. vedaw'.* The name of the collective body of the Hindoo sacred writings. These are divided into four parts or vedas. The word is sometimes written *vedam*. *Sir W. Jones.* *Colebrooke.*

VEDET′, VEDETTE, *n.* [Fr. *vedette;* It. *vedetta,* from *vedere,* L. *video,* to see.] A sentinel on horseback.

VEER, *v. i.* [Fr. *virer;* Sp. *birar;* D. *vieren;* allied probably to L. *vario* and *verto.* See *Ware.*]

To turn; to change direction; as, the wind *veers* to the west or north.

And as he leads, the following navy *veers.* *Dryden.*

And turn your *veering* heart with ev'ry gale. *Roscommon.*

To veer and haul, as wind, to alter its direction.

VEER, *v. t.* To turn; to direct to a different course.

To veer out, to suffer to run or to let out to a greater length; as, to *veer out* a rope.

To veer away, to let out; to slacken and let run; as, to *veer away* the cable. This is called also *paying out* the cable.

To veer and haul, to pull tight and slacken alternately. *Mar. Dict.*

VEE′RABLE, *a.* Changeable; shifting. [*Not in use.*] *Randolph.*

VEE′RED, *pp.* Turned; changed in direction; let out.

VEE′RING, *ppr.* Turning; letting out to a greater length.

VEGETABIL′ITY, *n.* [from *vegetable.*] Vegetable nature; the quality of growth without sensation. *Brown.*

VEG′ETABLE, *n.* [Fr. from *vegeter,* L. *vigeo,* to grow.]

1. A plant; an organized body destitute of sense and voluntary motion, deriving its nourishment through pores or vessels on its outer surface, in most instances adhering to some other body, as the earth, and in general, propagating itself by seeds. Some vegetables have spontaneous motion, as the sunflower. Vegetables alone have the power of deriving nourishment from inorganic matter, or organic matter entirely decomposed.

2. In *a more limited sense,* vegetables are such plants as are used for culinary purposes and cultivated in gardens, or are destined for feeding cattle and sheep. Vegetables for these uses are such as are of a more soft and fleshy substance than trees and shrubs; such as cabbage, cauliflower, turneps, potatoes, peas, beans, &c.

VEG′ETABLE, *a.* Belonging to plants; as a *vegetable* nature; *vegetable* qualities; *vegetable* juices.

2. Consisting of plants; as the *vegetable* kingdom.

3. Having the nature of plants; as a *vegetable* body.

VEG′ETATE, *v. i.* [L. *vegeto;* Fr. *vegeter;* from L. *vigeo,* to flourish.]

To sprout; to germinate; to grow; as plants; to grow and be enlarged by nutriment imbibed from the earth, air or water, by means of roots and leaves. Plants will not *vegetate* without a certain degree of heat; but some plants *vegetate* with less heat than others. Potatoes will *vegetate* after they are pared.

See dying vegetables life sustain,
See life dissolving *vegetate* again. *Pope.*

VEG′ETATING, *ppr.* Germinating; sprouting; growing; as plants.

VEGETA′TION, *n.* [Fr.] The process of growing, as plants, by means of nourishment derived from the earth, or from water and air, and received through roots and leaves. We observe that *vegetation* depends on heat as the moving principle, and on certain substances which constitute the nutriment of plants. Rapid *vegetation* is caused by increased heat and a rich soil.

2. Vegetables or plants in general. In June, *vegetation* in our climate wears a beautiful aspect.

Vegetation of salts, so called, consists in certain concretions formed by salts, after solution in water, when set in the air for evaporation. These concretions appear round the surface of the liquor, affixed to the sides of the vessel.

VEG′ETATIVE, *a.* [Fr. *vegetatif.*] Growing, or having the power of growing, as plants. *Raleigh.*

2. Having the power to produce growth in plants; as the *vegetative* properties of soil. *Broome.*

VEG′ETATIVENESS, *n.* The quality of producing growth.

VEGE′TE, *a.* [L. *vegetus.*] Vigorous; active. [*Little used.*] *Wallis.*

VEG′ETIVE, *a.* [L. *vegeto, vigeo.*] Vegetable; having the nature of plants; as *vegetive* life. [*Little used.*] *Tusser.*

VEG′ETIVE, *n.* A vegetable. [*Not in use.*] *Sandys.*

VEG′ETO-ANIMAL, *a. Vegeto-animal matter,* is a term formerly applied to vegetable gluten, which is found in the seeds of certain plants, in a state of union with farina or starch. It is remarkably elastic, and when dry, semi-transparent. By distillation it affords, like animal substances, alkaline water, concrete volatile alkali, and an empyreumatic oil. *Cyc. Fourcroy.*

VEGE′TOUS, *a.* Vigorous; lively; vegete. [*Not in use.*] *B. Jonson.*

VE′HEMENCE, VE′HEMENCY, *n.* [Fr. *vehemence;* from L. *vehemens,* from *veho,* to carry, that is, to rush or drive.]

1. Violence; great force; properly, force derived from velocity; as the *vehemence* of wind. But it is applied to any kind of forcible action; as, to speak with *vehemence.*

2. Violent ardor; great heat; animated fervor; as the *vehemence* of love or affection; the *vehemence* of anger or other passion.

I tremble at his *vehemence* of temper. *Addison.*

VE′HEMENT, *a.* [Fr. from L. *vehemens.*]

1. Violent; acting with great force; furious; very forcible; as a *vehement* wind; a *vehement* torrent; a *vehement* fire or heat.

2. Very ardent; very eager or urgent; very fervent; as a *vehement* affection or passion; *vehement* desire; vehement eloquence. *Milton.*

VE′HEMENTLY, *adv.* With great force and violence.

2. Urgently; forcibly; with great zeal or pathos. *Tillotson.*

VE′HICLE, *n.* [Fr. *vehicule;* L. *vehiculum,* from *veho,* to carry.]

1. That in which any thing is or may be carried; any kind of carriage moving on land, either on wheels or runners. This word comprehends coaches, chariots, gigs, sulkies, wagons, carts of every kind, sleighs and sleds. These are all *vehicles.* But the word is more generally applied to wheel carriages, and rarely I believe to water craft.

2. That which is used as the instrument of conveyance. Language is the *vehicle* which conveys ideas to others. Letters are *vehicles* of communication.

A simple style forms the best *vehicle* of thought to a popular assembly. *Wirt.*

VE′HICLED, *a.* Conveyed in a vehicle. *Green.*

VEIL, *n.* [L. *velum.*] A cover; a curtain; something to intercept the view and hide an object.

2. A cover; a disguise. [See *Vail.* The latter orthography gives the Latin pronunciation as well as the English, and is to be preferred.]

VEIL, *v. t.* To cover with a veil; to conceal.

2. To invest; to cover.

3. To hide. [See *Vail.*]

VEIN, *n.* [Fr. *veine;* L. *vena,* from the root of *venio,* to come, to pass. The sense is a passage, a conduit.]

1. A vessel in animal bodies, which receives the blood from the extreme arteries, and returns it to the heart. The veins may be arranged in three divisions. 1. Those that commence from the capillaries all over the body, and return the blood to the heart. 2. The pulmonary veins. 3. The veins connected with the vena portarum, in which the blood that has circulated through the organs of digestion, is conveyed to the liver. *Cyc.*

2. In *plants,* a tube or an assemblage of tubes, through which the sap is transmitted along the leaves. The term is more properly applied to the finer and more complex ramifications, which interbranch with each other like net-work; the larger and more direct assemblages of vessels being called *ribs* and *nerves.* Veins are also found in the calyx and corol of flowers. *Cyc.*

The vessels which branch or variously divide over the surface of leaves are called *veins.* *Martyn.*

3. In *geology,* a fissure in rocks or strata, filled with a particular substance. Thus metallic *veins* intersect rocks or strata of other substances. Metalliferous *veins* have been traced in the earth for miles; some in South America are said to have been traced eighty miles. Many species of stones, as granite, porphyry, &c. are often found in *veins.* *Cyc.*

4. A streak or wave of different color, appearing in wood, marble, and other stones; variegation.

5. A cavity or fissure in the earth or in other substance.

6. Tendency or turn of mind; a particular disposition or cast of genius; as a rich *vein* of wit or humor; a satirical *vein.*

Invoke the muses, and improve my *vein.* *Waller.*

7. Current.

He can open a *vein* of true and noble thinking. *Swift.*

8. Humor; particular temper. *Shak.*

9. Strain; quality; as my usual *vein.* *Oldham.*

VEINED, *a.* [from *vein.*] Full of veins; streaked; variegated; as *veined* marble.

2. In *botany,* having vessels branching over the surface, as a leaf.

VEINLESS, *a.* In *botany*, having no veins; as a *veinless* leaf. *Barton.*

VEINY, *a.* Full of veins; as *veiny* marble. *Thomson.*

VELIF'EROUS, *a.* [L. *velum*, a sail, and *fero*, to bear.] Bearing or carrying sails. *Evelyn.*

VELITA'TION, *n.* [L. *velitatio.*] A dispute or contest; a slight skirmish. [*Not in use.*] *Burton.*

VELL, *n.* [Qu. *fell*, a skin.] A rennet bag. [*Local.*]

VELL, *v. t.* [Qu. *fell*, a skin.] To cut off the turf or sward of land. [*Local.*] *Cyc.*

VELLE'ITY, *n.* [Fr. *velleité;* from L. *velle*, to will.]
A term by which the schools express the lowest degree of desire. *Locke.*

VEL'LICATE, *v. t.* [L. *vellico*, from *vello*, to pull. It may be from the root of *pull.*]
To twitch; to stimulate; applied to the muscles and fibers of animals; to cause to twitch convulsively. *Cyc.*

VEL'LICATED, *pp.* Twitched or caused to twitch.

VEL'LICATING, *ppr.* Twitching; convulsing.

VELLICA'TION, *n.* The act of twitching, or of causing to twitch.
2. A twitching or convulsive motion of a muscular fiber.

VEL'LUM, *n.* [Fr. *velin.* It coincides with *fell*, D. *vel*, skin; probably from the root of L. *vello.*]
A finer kind of parchment or skin, rendered clear and white for writing.

VELOC'ITY, *n.* [Fr. *velocité;* L. *velocitas*, from *velox*, swift, allied to *volo*, to fly.]
1. Swiftness; celerity; rapidity; as the *velocity* of wind; the *velocity* of a planet or comet in its orbit or course; the *velocity* of a cannon ball; the *velocity* of light. In these phrases, *velocity* is more generally used than *celerity.* We apply *celerity* to animals; as, a horse or an ostrich runs with *celerity*, and a stream runs with *rapidity* or *velocity:* but bodies moving in the air or in ethereal space, move with greater or less *velocity*, not *celerity.* This usage is arbitrary, and perhaps not universal.
2. In *philosophy*, velocity is that affection of motion by which a body moves over a certain space in a certain time. Velocity is in direct proportion to the space over which a body moves. Velocity is *absolute* or *relative; absolute*, when a body moves over a certain space in a certain time; *relative*, when it has respect to another moving body. *Velocity* is also *uniform* or *equal;* or it is *unequal*, that is, retarded or accelerated.

VEL'URE, *n.* [Fr. *velours.*] Velvet. *Obs.* *Shak.*

VEL'VET, *n.* [It. *velluto;* Sp. *velludo;* Fr. *velours;* L. *vellus*, hair, nap.]
A rich silk stuff, covered on the outside with a close, short, fine, soft shag or nap. The name is given also to cotton stuffs.

VEL'VET, *v. t.* To paint velvet. *Peacham.*

VEL'VET, VEL'VETED, } *a.* Made of velvet; or soft and delicate, like velvet.

VELVETEE'N, *n.* A kind of cloth made in imitation of velvet.

VEL'VETING, *n.* The fine shag of velvet. *Cyc.*

VEL'VETY, *a.* Made of velvet, or like velvet; soft; smooth; delicate. *Med. Repos.*

VE'NAL, *a.* [L. *vena*, a vein.] Pertaining to a vein or to veins; contained in the veins; as *venal* blood. [See *Venous*, which is generally used.]

VE'NAL, *a.* [L. *venalis*, from *veneo*, to be sold.]
1. Mercenary; prostitute; that may be bought or obtained for money or other valuable consideration; as a *venal* muse; *venal* services.
2. That may be sold; set to sale; as, all offices are *venal* in a corrupt government.
3. Purchased; as a *venal* vote. *Junius.*

VENAL'ITY, *n.* Mercenariness; the state of being influenced by money; prostitution of talents, offices or services for money or reward; as the *venality* of a corrupt court.

VEN'ARY, *a.* [L. *venor*, to hunt.] Relating to hunting.

VENAT'IC, VENAT'ICAL, } *a.* [L. *venaticus*, from *venor*, to hunt.] Used in hunting.

VENA'TION, *n.* [L. *venatio*, from *venor*, to hunt.]
1. The act or practice of hunting. *Brown.*
2. The state of being hunted. *Brown.*

VEND, *v. t.* [L. *vendo;* Fr. *vendre;* It. *vendere;* Sp. *vender.*]
To sell; to transfer a thing and the exclusive right of possessing it, to another person for a pecuniary equivalent; as, to *vend* goods; to *vend* meat and vegetables in market. Vending differs from *barter.* We *vend* for money; we *barter* for commodities. *Vend* is applicable only to wares, merchandize, or other small articles, not to lands and tenements. We never say, to *vend* a farm, a lease, or a bond, a right or a horse.

VEND'ED, *pp.* Sold; transferred for money; as goods.

VENDEE', *n.* The person to whom a thing is sold.

VEND'ER, *n.* [Fr. *vendeur.*] A seller; one who transfers the exclusive right of possessing a thing, either his own, or that of another as his agent. Auctioneers are the *venders* of goods for other men.

VENDIBIL'ITY, VEND'IBLENESS, } *n.* The state of being vendible or salable.

VEND'IBLE, *a.* [L. *vendibilis.*] Salable; that may be sold; that can be sold; as *vendible* goods. Vendible differs from *marketable;* the latter signifies *proper* or *fit for market*, according to the laws or customs of a place. *Vendible* has no reference to such legal fitness.

VEND'IBLE, *n.* Something to be sold or offered for sale. *Mitford.*

VEND'IBLY, *adv.* In a salable manner.

VENDITA'TION, *n.* [L. *venditatio.*] A boastful display. [*Not in use.*] *B. Jonson.*

VENDI''TION, *n.* [Fr. from L. *venditio.*] The act of selling; sale.

VEND'OR, *n.* A vender; a seller.

VENDUE, *n.* [Fr. *vendu*, sold.] Auction; a public sale of any thing by outcry, to the highest bidder.

VENDUE-M'ASTER, *n.* One who is authorized to make sale of any property to the highest bidder, by notification and public outcry; an auctioneer.

VENEE'R, *v. t.* [G. *furnieren.* This word seems to be from the root of *furnish*, the primary sense of which is to *put on.*]
To inlay; to lay thin slices or leaves of fine wood of different kinds on a ground of common wood.

VENEE'R, *n.* Thin slices of wood for inlaying.

VENEE'RED, *pp.* Inlaid; ornamented with marquetry.

VENEE'RING, *ppr.* Inlaying; adorning with inlaid work.

VENEE'RING, *n.* The act or art of inlaying, of which there are two kinds; one, which is the most common, consists in making compartments of different woods; the other consists in making representations of flowers, birds and other figures. The first is more properly *veneering;* the last is *marquetry.* *Cyc.*

VEN'EFICE, *n.* [L. *veneficium.*] The practice of poisoning. [*Not in use.*]

VENEFI''CIAL, VENEFI''CIOUS, } *a.* [L. *veneficium.*] Acting by poison; bewitching. [*Little used.*] *Brown.*

VENEFI''CIOUSLY, *adv.* By poison or witchcraft. [*Little used.*] *Brown.*

VEN'EMOUS. [See *Venomous.*]

VEN'ENATE, *v. t.* [L. *veneno; venenum*, poison, W. *gwenwyn;* from raging.]
To poison; to infect with poison. [*Not used.*] *Harvey.*

VENENA'TION, *n.* The act of poisoning.
2. Poison; venom. [*Not used.*] *Brown.*

VENE'NE, VENE'NOSE, } *a.* [Fr. *veneneux.*] Poisonous; venomous. [*Not used.*] *Harvey.*

VENERABIL'ITY, *n.* State or quality of being venerable. [*Not used.*] *More.*

VEN'ERABLE, *a.* [Fr. from L. *venerabilis*, from *veneror*, to honor, to worship.]
1. Worthy of veneration or reverence; deserving of honor and respect; as a *venerable* magistrate; a *venerable* parent.
2. Rendered sacred by religious associations, or being consecrated to God and to his worship; to be regarded with awe and treated with reverence; as the *venerable* walls of a temple or church.

> The places where saints have suffered for the testimony of Christ—rendered *venerable* by their death. *Hooker.*

VEN'ERABLENESS, *n.* The state or quality of being venerable. *South.*

VEN'ERABLY, *adv.* In a manner to excite reverence.

> —An awful pile! stands *venerably* great. *Addison.*

VEN'ERATE, *v. t.* [Fr. *venerer;* L. *veneror.*]
To regard with respect and reverence; to reverence; to revere. We *venerate* an old faithful magistrate; we *venerate* parents and elders; we *venerate* men consecrated to sacred offices. We *venerate* old age or gray hairs. We *venerate*, or ought to *venerate*, the gospel and its precepts.

> And seem'd to *venerate* the sacred shade. *Dryden.*

VEN'ERATED, *pp.* Reverenced; treated with honor and respect.

VEN'ERATING, *ppr.* Regarding with reverence.

VENERA'TION, *n.* [Fr. from L. *veneratio.*]

The highest degree of respect and reverence; respect mingled with some degree of awe; a feeling or sentiment excited by the dignity and superiority of a person, or by the sacredness of his character, and with regard to place, by its consecration to sacred services.

We find a secret awe and *veneration* for one who moves above us in a regular and illustrious course of virtue. *Addison.*

VEN'ERATOR, *n.* One who venerates and reverences.

VENE'REAL, *a.* [L. *venereus*, from *Venus*; W. *Gwener*, from *gwen*, white, fair. See *Venus*.]

1. Pertaining to the pleasures of sexual commerce. A *venereal* person is one addicted to sexual pleasures or venery. *Cyc.*
2. Proceeding from sexual intercourse; as the *venereal* disease; *venereal* virus or poison.
3. Adapted to the cure of the lues venerea; as *venereal* medicines.
4. Adapted to excite venereal desire; aphrodisiac; provocative. *Cyc.*
5. Consisting of copper, called by chimists formerly *Venus*. *Obs.* *Boyle.*

VENE'REAN, *a.* Venereal. [*Not used.*] *Howell.*

VENE'REOUS, *a.* [L. *venereus*.] Lustful; libidinous. *Derham.*

VEN'EROUS, for *venereous*. [*Not used.*]

VEN'ERY, *n.* [from *Venus*.] The pleasures of the bed.

Contentment, without the pleasure of lawful *venery*, is continence; of unlawful, chastity. *Grew.*

VEN'ERY, *n.* [Fr. *venerie*; from L. *venor*, to hunt, that is, to drive or rush.]

The act or exercise of hunting; the sports of the chase.

Beasts of *venery* and fishes. *Brown.*

VENESEC'TION, *n.* [L. *vena*, vein, and *sectio*, a cutting.]

The act or operation of opening a vein for letting blood; blood-letting; phlebotomy. *Cyc.* *Wiseman.*

VEN'EY, *n.* [Fr. *venez*, from *venir*, to come.] A bout; a thrust; a hit; a turn at fencing.

Three *veneys* for a dish of stewed prunes. *Obs.* *Shak.*

VENGE, *v. t.* *venj.* [Fr. *venger*.] To avenge; to punish. [*Not in use.*] [See *Avenge* and *Revenge*.] *Shak.*

VENGEABLE, *a.* *venj'able.* [from *venge*.] Revengeful; as *vengeable* despite. [*Not in use.*] *Spenser.*

VENGEANCE, *n.* *venj'ance.* [Fr. from *venger*, to revenge, L. *vindico*.]

The infliction of pain on another, in return for an injury or offense. Such infliction, when it proceeds from malice or mere resentment, and is not necessary for the purposes of justice, is revenge, and a most hainous crime. When such infliction proceeds from a mere love of justice, and the necessity of punishing offenders for the support of the laws, it is *vengeance*, and is warrantable and just. In this case, vengeance is a just retribution, recompense or punishment. In this latter sense the word is used in Scripture, and frequently applied to the punishments inflicted by God on sinners.

To me belongeth *vengeance* and recompense. Deut. xxxii.

The Lord will take *vengeance* on his adversaries. Nah. i.

With a vengeance, in familiar language, signifies with great violence or vehemence; as, to strike one *with a vengeance*.

Formerly, *what a vengeance*, was a phrase used for *what* emphatical.

But *what a vengeance* makes thee fly? *Hudibras.*

VENGEFUL, *a.* *venj'ful.* Vindictive; retributive; as God's *vengeful* ire. *Milton.*

2. Revengeful.

VENGEMENT, *n.* *venj'ment.* Avengement; penal retribution. [*Avengement* is generally used.]

VENG'ER, *n.* An avenger. [*Not in use.*] *Spenser.*

VE'NIABLE, *a.* [See *Venial*.] Venial; pardonable. [*Not in use.*] *Brown.*

VE'NIABLY, *adv.* Pardonably; excusably. [*Not used.*] *Brown.*

VE'NIAL, *a.* [It. *veniale*; Sp. *venial*; Fr. *veniel*; from L. *venia*, pardon, leave to depart, from the root of *venio*, and signifying literally a going or passing.]

1. That may be forgiven; pardonable; as a *venial* fault or transgression. The reformed churches hold all sins to be *venial*, through the merits of the Redeemer; but the most trifling sins not to be *venial*, except through the righteousness and atonement of Christ.
2. In *familiar language*, excusable; that may be allowed or permitted to pass without censure; as a *venial* slip or fault.
3. Allowed.

Permitting him the while
Venial discourse unblam'd. *Milton.*

VE'NIALNESS, *n.* State of being excusable or pardonable.

Venire facias, or *venire*, in *law*, a writ or precept directed to the sherif, requiring him to summon twelve men, to try an issue between parties. It is also a writ in the nature of a summons to cause the party indicted on a penal statute, to appear.

VENISON, *n.* *ven'izn*, or *ven'zn*. [Fr. *venaison*, from L. *venatio*, a hunting, from *venor*, to hunt.]

The flesh of beasts of game, or of such wild animals as are taken in the chase. It is however, in the United States, applied exclusively to the flesh of the deer or cervine genus of animals.

VEN'OM, *n.* [Fr. *venin*; It. *veneno*; L. *venenum*; W. *gwenwyn*. It appears by the Welsh word and its affinities, that the primary sense is raging, furious, and hence it is to be referred to the root of L. *venor*, to hunt, to drive or chase; *venio*, to come. See *Venus*, &c.]

1. Poison; matter fatal or injurious to life. *Venom* is generally used to express noxious matter that is applied externally, or that is discharged from animals, as that of bites and stings of serpents, scorpions, &c.; and *poison*, to express substances taken into the stomach. *Cyc.*
2. Spite; malice.

VEN'OM, *v. t.* To poison; to infect with venom. [Little used, but *envenom* is in use and elegant. *Venom* may be elegantly used in poetry.]

VEN'OMOUS, *a.* Poisonous; noxious to animal life; as, the bite of a serpent may be *venomous*. The sack at the base of the rattlesnake's teeth, contains *venomous* matter.

2. Noxious; mischievous; malignant; as a *venomous* progeny. *Brown.*
3. Spiteful; as a *venomous* writer.

VEN'OMOUSLY, *adv.* Poisonously; malignantly; spitefully. *Dryden.*

VEN'OMOUSNESS, *n.* Poisonousness; noxiousness to animal life.

2. Malignity; spitefulness.

VE'NOUS, *a.* [L. *venosus*, from *vena*, a vein.]

1. Pertaining to a vein or to veins; contained in veins; as *venous* blood, which is distinguishable from arterial blood by its darker color.
2. In *botany*, veined. A *venous leaf*, has vessels branching, or variously divided, over its surface. *Martyn.*

VENT, *n.* [Fr. *vente*, Sp. *venta*; sale, from *vendre*, Sp. *vender*; from the root of L. *venio*, Eng. *wind*, &c.; properly a passage.]

1. A small aperture; a hole or passage for air or other fluid to escape; as the *vent* of a cask.
2. The opening in a cannon or other piece of artillery, by which fire is communicated to the charge.
3. Passage from secrecy to notice; publication. *Wotton.*
4. The act of opening. *Phillips.*
5. Emission; passage; escape from confinement; as, his smothered passions urge for *vent*.
6. Discharge; utterance; means of discharge.

Had like grief been dew'd in tears,
Without the *vent* of words— *Milton.*

7. Sale; as the *vent* of a thousand copies of a treatise. *Pope.*
8. Opportunity to sell; demand.

There is no *vent* for any commodity except wool. *Temple.*

9. An inn; a baiting place. [*Not in use.*]

To give vent to, to suffer to escape; to let out; to pour forth.

VENT, *v. t.* To let out at a small aperture.

2. To let out; to suffer to escape from confinement; to utter; to pour forth; as, to *vent* passion or complaint.

The queen of heav'n did thus her fury *vent*. *Dryden.*

3. To utter; to report. [*Not in use.*] *Stephens.*
4. To publish.

The sectators did greatly enrich their inventions by *venting* the stolen treasures of divine letters. [*Not used.*] *Raleigh.*

5. To sell.

Therefore did those nations *vent* such spice. [*Not in use.*] *Raleigh.*

[Instead of *vent* in the latter sense, we use *vend*.]

VENT, *v. i.* To snuff. [*Not in use.*] *Spenser.*

VENT'AGE, *n.* A small hole. [*Not in use.*] *Shak.*

VENT'AIL, *n.* [Fr. a folding door.] That part of a helmet made to be lifted up; the part intended for the admission of air, or for breathing.

VENTAN'NA, } *n.* [Sp. *ventana.*] A window. [*Not English.*] *Dryden.*
VENTAN'A, }

VENT'ER, *n.* One who utters, reports or publishes. *Barrow.*

VEN'TER, *n.* [L.] In *anatomy*, the abdomen, or lower belly; formerly applied to any large cavity containing viscera, as the head, thorax and abdomen, called the three *venters.* *Parr.*

2. The womb; and hence, mother. A has a son B by one *venter*, and a daughter C by another *venter;* children by different *venters.* *Law Language.*

3. The belly of a muscle.

VEN'TIDUCT, *n.* [L. *ventus*, wind, and *ductus*, a canal; It. *ventidotti.*]

In *building*, a passage for wind or air; a subterraneous passage or spiracle for ventilating apartments. *Cyc.*

VEN'TILATE, *v. t.* [L. *ventilo*, from *ventus*, wind; Fr. *ventiler.*]

1. To fan with wind; to open and expose to the free passage of air or wind; as, to *ventilate* a room; to *ventilate* a cellar.

2. To cause the air to pass through; as, to *ventilate* a mine.

3. To winnow; to fan; as, to *ventilate* wheat.

4. To examine; to discuss; that is, to agitate; as, to *ventilate* questions of policy. [*Not now in use.*]

VEN'TILATED, *pp.* Exposed to the action of the air; fanned; winnowed; discussed.

VEN'TILATING, *ppr.* Exposing to the action of wind; fanning; discussing.

VENTILA'TION, *n.* [Fr. from L. *ventilatio.*]

1. The act of ventilating; the act or operation of exposing to the free passage of air, or of causing the air to pass through any place, for the purpose of expelling impure air and dissipating any thing noxious.

2. The act of fanning or winnowing, for the purpose of separating chaff and dust.

3. Vent; utterance. [*Not in use.*] *Wotton.*

4. Refrigeration. [*Not in use.*] *Harvey.*

VEN'TILATOR, *n.* An instrument or machine for expelling foul or stagnant air from any close place or apartment, and introducing that which is fresh and pure. Ventilators are of very different constructions and sizes.

VENTOS'ITY, *n.* [Fr. *ventosité;* from L. *ventosus.*] Windiness; flatulence. *Bacon.*

VEN'TRAL, *a.* [from L. *venter*, belly.] Belonging to the belly.

The *ventral fins*, in fishes, are placed between the anus and the throat. *Ed. Encyc.*

VEN'TRICLE, *n.* [L. *ventriculus*, from *venter*, belly.]

In *a general sense*, a small cavity in an animal body. It is applied to the stomach. It is also applied to two cavities of the heart, which propel the blood into the arteries. The word is also applied to cavities in different parts of the brain. *Cyc.*

VEN'TRICOUS, *a.* [L. *ventricosus*, from *venter*, belly.]

In *botany*, bellied; distended; swelling out in the middle; as a *ventricous* perianth. *Martyn.*

VENTRIC'ULOUS, *a.* [supra.] Somewhat distended in the middle.

VENTRIL'OQUISM, } *n.* [L. *venter*, belly, and *loquor*, to speak.]
VENTRIL'OQUY, }

The act, art or practice of speaking in such a manner that the voice appears to come, not from the person, but from some distant place, as from the opposite side of the room, from the cellar, &c.

VENTRIL'OQUIST, *n.* One who speaks in such a manner that his voice appears to come from some distant place.

The ancient *ventriloquists* seemed to speak from their bellies. *Encyc.*

VENTRIL'OQUOUS, *a.* Speaking in such a manner as to make the sound appear to come from a place remote from the speaker.

VEN'TURE, *n.* [Fr. *aventure;* It. Sp. *ventura;* from L. *venio, ventus, venturus*, to come.]

1. A hazard; an undertaking of chance or danger; the risking of something upon an event which cannot be foreseen with tolerable certainty.

I, in this *venture*, double gains pursue. *Dryden.*

2. Chance; hap; contingency; luck; an event that is not or cannot be foreseen. *Bacon.*

3. The thing put to hazard; particularly, something sent to sea in trade.

My *ventures* are not in one bottom trusted. *Shak.*

At a venture, at hazard; without seeing the end or mark; or without foreseeing the issue.

A bargain *at a venture* made. *Hudibras.*

A certain man drew a bow *at a venture.* 1 Kings xxii.

VEN'TURE, *v. i.* To dare; to have courage or presumption to do, undertake or say. A man *ventures* to mount a ladder; he *ventures* into battle; he *ventures* to assert things which he does not know.

2. To run a hazard or risk.

Who freights a ship to *venture* on the seas. *Dryden.*

To venture at, } to dare to engage in; to attempt without any certainty of success. It is rash to *venture upon* such a project.
To venture on or *upon,* }

And when I *venture at* the comic style. *Waller.*

VEN'TURE, *v. t.* To expose to hazard; to risk; as, to *venture* one's person in a balloon.

2. To put or send on a venture or chance; as, to *venture* a horse to the West Indies.

VEN'TURED, *pp.* Put to the hazard; risked.

VEN'TURER, *n.* One who ventures or puts to hazards.

VEN'TURESOME, *a.* Bold; daring; intrepid; as a *venturesome* boy.

VEN'TURESOMELY, *adv.* In a bold, daring manner.

VEN'TURING, *ppr.* Putting to hazard; daring.

VEN'TURING, *n.* The act of putting to risk; a hazarding.

VEN'TUROUS, *a.* Daring; bold; hardy; fearless; intrepid; adventurous; as a *venturous* soldier.

With *vent'rous* arm
He pluck'd, he tasted. *Milton.*

VEN'TUROUSLY, *adv.* Daringly; fearlessly; boldly. *Bacon.*

VEN'TUROUSNESS, *n.* Boldness; hardiness; fearlessness; intrepidity. The event made them repent of their *venturousness.*

VEN'UE, } *n.* [L. *vicinia;* Norm. *visne.*] In *law*, a neighborhood or near place; the place where an action is laid. In certain cases, the court has power to change the *venue.* *Cyc.*
VISNE, }

The twelve men who are to try the cause, must be of the same *venue* where the demand is made. *Blackstone.*

VEN'UE, *n.* A thrust. [See *Veney.*]

VEN'ULITE, *n.* A petrified shell of the genus Venus.

VE'NUS, *n.* [L.; W. *Gwener*, from *gwen*, white, fair, the feminine of *gwyn*, white, fair, that affords happiness; also *gwyn*, rage, violent impulse of the mind, lust, smart; *gwynâu*, to whiten; *gwynt*, wind, L. *ventus; gwynawg*, full of rage; *gwent*, an open country; *gwenu*, to smile; *gwenwyn*, poison, L. *venenum*, Eng. *venom; gwenwynaw*, to poison, to fret or irritate. These affinities lead to the true origin of these words. The primary sense of the root is to shoot or rush, as light or wind. From light is derived the sense of white, fair, Venus, or it is from opening, parting; and from rushing, moving, comes *wind*, and the sense of raging, fury, whence L. *venenum*, poison, that which frets or causes to rage. These words all coincide with L. *venio*, which signifies to rush, to fall, to happen; *venor*, to hunt, &c. The Greeks had the same idea of the goddess of love, viz. that her name signified fairness, whiteness, and hence the fable that she sprung from froth, whence her Greek name Αφροδιτη, from αφρος, froth.]

1. In *mythology*, the goddess of beauty and love; that is, beauty or love deified; just as the Gaelic and Irish *diana*, swiftness, impetuosity, is denominated the goddess of hunting.

2. In *astronomy*, one of the inferior planets, whose orbit is between the earth and Mercury; a star of brilliant splendor.

3. In *the old chimistry*, a name given to copper.

VENUS'S COMB, *n.* A plant of the genus Scandix; shepherd's needle. *Lee.*

VENUS'S LOOKING-GLASS, *n.* A plant of the genus Campanula.

VENUS'S NAVELWORT, *n.* A plant of the genus Cynoglossum.

VENUST', *a.* [L. *venustus.*] Beautiful. [*Not used.*]

VERA'CIOUS, *a.* [L. *verax*, from *verus*, true.]

1. Observant of truth; habitually disposed to speak truth.

2. True. [*Little used.*] *Pinkerton.*

VERAC'ITY, *n.* [It. *veracità;* from L. *verax*, from *verus*, true.]

1. Habitual observance of truth, or habitual truth; as a man of *veracity.* His *veracity* is not called in question. The question of the court is, whether you know the witness to be a man of *veracity.* We rely on history, when we have confidence in the *veracity* and industry of the historian.

"The *veracity* of facts," is not correct language. *Truth* is applicable to men and to facts; *veracity* to men only, or to sentient beings.

2. Invariable expression of truth; as the *veracity* of our senses. *Kames.*

VERAN'DA, *n.* An oriental word denoting a kind of open portico, formed by extending a sloping roof beyond the main building. *Todd.*

VERA'TRIA, *n.* [L. *veratrum*, hellebore.] A newly discovered vegetable alkali, extracted from the white hellebore. *Ure.*

VERB, *n.* [L. *verbum*; Fr. *verbe*; Sp. It. *verbo*; Ir. *fearb*; probably from the root of L. *fero*.]

1. In *grammar*, a part of speech that expresses action, motion, being, suffering, or a request or command to do or forbear any thing. The verb affirms, declares, asks or commands; as, I *write*; he *runs*; the river *flows*; they *sleep*; we *see*; they *are deceived*; *depart*; *go*; *come*; *write*; *does* he *improve*?

When the action expressed by a verb is exerted on an object, or terminates upon it, the act is considered as passing to that object, and the verb is called *transitive*; as, I *read* Livy. When the act expressed by the verb, terminates in the agent or subject, the verb is called *intransitive*; as, I *run*; I *walk*; I *sleep*.

When the agent and object change places, and the agent is considered as the instrument by which the object is affected, the verb is called *passive*; as, Goliath *was slain* by David.

2. A word. *South.*

VERB'AL, *a.* [Fr.; L. *verbalis.*] Spoken; expressed to the ear in words; not written; as a *verbal* message; a *verbal* contract; *verbal* testimony.

2. Oral; uttered by the mouth. *Shak.*

3. Consisting in mere words; as a *verbal* reward.

4. Respecting words only; as a *verbal* dispute.

5. Minutely exact in words, or attending to words only; as a *verbal* critic.

6. Literal; having word answering to word; as a *verbal* translation.

7. In *grammar*, derived from a verb; as a *verbal* noun.

8. Verbose; abounding with words. [*Not in use.*] *Shak.*

VERBAL'ITY, *n.* Mere words; bare literal expressions. *Brown.*

VERB'ALIZE, *v. t.* To convert into a verb.

VERB'ALLY, *adv.* In words spoken; by words uttered; orally. *South.*

2. Word for word; as, to translate *verbally.* *Dryden.*

VERBA'TIM, *adv.* [L.] Word for word; in the same words; as, to tell a story *verbatim* as another has related it.

VERB'ERATE, *v. t.* [L. *verbero.*] To beat; to strike. [*Not in use.*]

VERBERA'TION, *n.* A beating or striking; blows. *Arbuthnot.*

2. The impulse of a body, which causes sound. *Cyc.*

VERB'IAĠE, *n.* [Fr.] Verbosity; use of many words without necessity; superabundance of words.

VERBO'SE, *a.* [L. *verbosus.*] Abounding in words; using or containing more words than are necessary; prolix; tedious by a multiplicity of words; as a *verbose* speaker; a *verbose* argument.

VERBOS'ITY, } *n.* Employment of a
VERBO'SENESS, } superabundance of words; the use of more words than are necessary; as the *verbosity* of a speaker.

2. Superabundance of words; prolixity; as the *verbosity* of a discourse or argument.

VER'DANCY, *n.* [See *Verdant.*] Greenness. *Norris.*

VER'DANT, *a.* [Fr. *verdoyant*; L. *viridans*, from *viridis*, from *vireo*, to be green. The radical sense of the verb is to grow or advance with strength.]

1. Green; fresh; covered with growing plants or grass; as *verdant* fields; a *verdant* lawn.

2. Flourishing.

VER'DERER, } *n.* [Fr. *verdier*, from *verd*,
VER'DEROR, } green; or Low L. *viridarius.*]

An officer in England, who has the charge of the king's forest, to preserve the vert and venison, keep the assizes, view, receive and enroll attachments and presentments of all manner of trespasses. *Blackstone.*

VER'DICT, *n.* [L. *verum dictum*, true declaration.]

1. The answer of a jury given to the court concerning any matter of fact in any cause, civil or criminal, committed to their trial and examination. In criminal causes, the jury decide the law as well as the fact. Verdicts are *general* or *special*; *general*, when they decide in general terms, or in the terms of the general issue, as *no wrong*, *no disseisin*; *special*, when the jury find and state the facts at large, and as to the law, pray the judgment of the court. *Blackstone.*

2. Decision; judgment; opinion pronounced; as, to be condemned by the *verdict* of the public.

> These enormities were condemned by the *verdict* of common humanity. *South.*

VER'DIGRIS, *n.* [Fr. *verd* and *gris*; greengray.]

Rust of copper, or an acetate of copper, formed by the combination of an acid with copper. *Ure.*

VER'DITER, *n.* [*verde-terre*, green earth; *terre-verte.*]

A preparation of copper sometimes used by painters, &c. for a blue, but more generally mixed with a yellow for a green color. It is a factitious substance or blue pigment, obtained by adding chalk or whiting to a solution of copper in nitric acid or aqua fortis. *Encyc. Ure.*

VER'DURE, *n.* [Fr.; from L. *vireo.*] Green; greenness; freshness of vegetation; as the *verdure* of the meadows in June; the *verdure* of spring.

VER'DUROUS, *a.* Covered with green; clothed with the fresh color of vegetables; as *verdurous* pastures. *Philips.*

VER'ECUND, *a.* [L. *verecundus.*] Bashful; modest. [*Not much used.*] *Wotton.*

VERECUND'ITY, *n.* Bashfulness; modesty; blushing. [*Not in much use.*]

VERĠE, *n. verj.* [Fr.; It. *verga*, L. *virga*, a rod, that is, a shoot.]

1. A rod, or something in the form of a rod or staff, carried as an emblem of authority; the mace of a dean. *Swift.*

2. The stick or wand with which persons are admitted tenants, by holding it in the hand, and swearing fealty to the lord. On this account, such tenants are called *tenants by the verge.* *Cyc. England.*

3. In *law*, the compass or extent of the king's court, within which is bounded the jurisdiction of the lord steward of the king's household; so called from the verge or staff which the marshal bears. *Cowel.*

4. The extreme side or end of any thing which has some extent of length; the brink; edge; border; margin. [This seems to be immediately connected with the L. *vergo.*]

5. Among *gardeners*, the edge or outside of a border; also, a slip of grass adjoining to gravel-walks, and dividing them from the borders in the parterre-garden. *Cyc.*

6. A part of a time piece.

VERĠE, *v. i.* [L. *vergo.*] To tend downwards; to bend; to slope; as, a hill *verges* to the north.

2. To tend; to incline; to approach.

> I find myself *verging* to that period of life which is to be labor and sorrow. *Swift.*

VERĠ'ER, *n.* He that carries the mace before the bishop, dean, &c. *Farquhar. Cyc.*

2. An officer who carries a white wand before the justices of either bench in England. *Cyc.*

VERĠ'ING, *ppr.* Bending or inclining; tending.

VER'GOULEUSE, *n.* A species of pear; contracted to *vergaloo.*

VERID'ICAL, *a.* [L. *veridicus*; *verus* and *dico.*] Telling truth. [*Not used.*]

VER'IFIABLE, *a.* [from *verify.*] That may be verified; that may be proved or confirmed by incontestable evidence. *South.*

VERIFICA'TION, *n.* [Fr. See *Verify.*] The act of verifying or proving to be true; the act of confirming or establishing the authenticity of any powers granted, or of any transaction, by legal or competent evidence.

VER'IFIED, *pp.* Proved; confirmed by competent evidence.

VER'IFIER, *n.* One that proves or makes appear to be true.

VER'IFȲ, *v. t.* [Fr. *verifier*; L. *verus*, true, and *facio*, to make; W. *gwir*, pure, true, ether, purity; *gwiraw*, to verify.]

1. To prove to be true; to confirm.

> This is *verified* by a number of examples. *Bacon.*

2. To fulfill, as a promise; to confirm the truth of a prediction; to show to be true. The predictions of this venerable patriot have been *verified.* Gen. xlii. 1 Kings viii.

3. To confirm or establish the authenticity of any thing by examination or competent evidence. The first act of the house of representatives is to *verify* their powers, by exhibiting their credentials to a committee of the house, or other proper authority. *U. States.*

VER'IFȲING, *ppr.* Proving to be true; confirming; establishing as authentic.

VER'ILY, *adv.* [from *very.*] In truth; in fact; certainly.

2. Really; truly; with great confidence. It was *verily* thought the enterprise would succeed.

VERISIM'ILAR, *a.* [L. *verisimilis ; verus*, true, and *similis*, like.] Having the appearance of truth ; probable ; likely. *White.*

VERISIMIL'ITUDE, *n.* [L. *verisimilitudo.*] The appearance of truth ; probability ; likelihood.

Verisimilitude and opinion are an easy purchase ; but true knowledge is dear and difficult. *Glanville.*

VERISIMIL'ITY, for *verisimilitude*, is not in use.

VER'ITABLE, *a.* [Fr.] True ; agreeable to fact. [*Little used.*] *Shak.*

VER'ITABLY, *adv.* In a true manner. [*Not in use.*]

VER'ITY, *n.* [Fr. *verité ;* L. *veritas*, from *verus*, true ; W. *gwirez ;* Sans. *wartha.*]

1. Truth ; consonance of a statement, proposition or other thing to fact. 1 Tim. ii.

It is a proposition of eternal *verity*, that none can govern while he is despised. *South.*

2. A true assertion or tenet.

By this it seems to be a *verity*. *Davies.*

3. Moral truth ; agreement of the words with the thoughts. *Johnson.*

VER'JUICE, *n.* [Fr. *verjus*, that is, *verd jus*, the juice of green fruits.]

A liquor expressed from wild apples, sour grapes, &c. used in sauces, ragouts and the like. It is used also in the purification of wax for candles, in poultices, &c. *Cyc.*

VERMEIL. [See *Vermilion.*]

VERMEOL'OGIST, *n.* [infra.] One who treats of vermes.

VERMEOL'OGY, *n.* [L. *vermes*, worms, and Gr. λογος, discourse.]

A discourse or treatise on vermes, or that part of natural history which treats of vermes. [*Little used.*]

VERMICEL'LI, *n.* [It. *vermicello*, a little worm, L. *vermiculus*, from *vermis*, a worm.]

In *cookery*, little rolls or threads of paste, or a composition of flour, eggs, sugar and saffron ; used in soups and pottages.

VERMIC'ULAR, *a.* [L. *vermiculus*, a little worm, from *vermis*, a worm.]

Pertaining to a worm ; resembling a worm ; particularly, resembling the motion of a worm ; as the *vermicular* motion of the intestines, called also *peristaltic*. *Cyc.*

Vermicular or *vermiculated work*, in sculpture, a sort of ornament consisting of frets or knots, in Mosaic pavements, winding and representing the tracks of worms.

VERMIC'ULATE, *v. t.* [L. *vermiculatus.*] To inlay; to form work by inlaying, resembling the motion or the tracks of worms.

VERMIC'ULATED, *pp.* Formed in the likeness of the motion of a worm.

VERMIC'ULATING, *ppr.* Forming so as to resemble the motion of a worm.

VERMICULA'TION, *n.* The act or operation of moving in the form of a worm ; continuation of motion from one part to another, as in the peristaltic motion of the intestines. *Hale.*

2. The act of forming so as to resemble the motion of a worm.

VERM'ICULE, *n.* [L. *vermiculus.*] A little worm or grub. *Derham.*

VERMIC'ULOUS, *a.* [L. *vermiculosus.*] Full of worms or grubs.

2. Resembling worms.

VERM'IFORM, *a.* [L. *vermis*, a worm, and *forma*, form.]

Having the form or shape of a worm; as the *vermiform* process of the cerebellum.

VERM'IFUGE, *n.* [L. *vermis*, a worm, and *fugo*, to expel.]

A medicine or substance that destroys or expels worms from animal bodies ; an anthelmintic.

VER'MIL, VERMILION, } *n. vermil'yon.* [Fr. *vermeil, vermillon ;* It. *vermiglione ;* from L. *vermiculus, vermes ;* a name sometimes improperly given to the kermes. See *Crimson.*]

1. The cochineal, a small insect found on a particular plant. [*Improper or obsolete.*]

2. Red sulphuret of mercury ; a bright, beautiful red color of two sorts, natural and artificial. The *natural* is found in silver mines, in the form of a ruddy sand, which is to be prepared by purification or washing, and then levigated with water on a stone. The *factitious* or *common* vermilion is made of artificial cinnabar, ground with white wine, and afterwards with the white of an egg.

3. Any beautiful red color. In blushing, the delicate cheek is covered with *vermilion.*

VERMILION, *v.t. vermil'yon.* To dye red ; to cover with a delicate red.

VERMIL'IONED, *pp.* or *a.* Dyed or tinged with a bright red.

VERM'IN, *n. sing.* and *plu. ;* used chiefly in the plural. [Fr. It. *vermine ;* from L. *vermes*, worms.]

1. All sorts of small animals which are destructive to grain or other produce ; all noxious little animals or insects, as squirrels, rats, mice, worms, grubs, flies, &c.

These *vermin* do great injuries in the field. *Mortimer.*

2. Used of noxious human beings in contempt ; as base *vermin.* *Hudibras.*

VERM'INATE, *v. i.* [L. *vermino.*] To breed vermin.

VERMINA'TION, *n.* The breeding of vermin. *Derham.*

2. A griping of the bowels.

VERM'INOUS, *a.* Tending to breed vermin.

The *verminous* disposition of the body. *Harvey.*

VERMIP'AROUS, *a.* [L. *vermes*, worms, and *pario*, to bear.] Producing worms. *Brown.*

VERMIV'OROUS, *a.* [L. *vermes*, worms, and *voro*, to devour.]

Devouring worms ; feeding on worms. *Vermivorous* birds are very useful to the farmer.

VERNAC'ULAR, *a.* [L. *vernaculus*, born in one's house, from *verna*, a servant.]

1. Native ; belonging to the country of one's birth. English is our *vernacular* language. The *vernacular* idiom is seldom perfectly acquired by foreigners.

2. Native ; belonging to the person by birth or nature. *Milner.*

A *vernacular disease*, is one which prevails in a particular country or district; more generally called *endemic.*

VERNAC'ULOUS, *a.* [supra.] Vernacular ; also, scoffing. *Obs.* *Brown. Spenser.*

VER'NAL, *a.* [L. *vernalis*, from *ver*, spring.]

1. Belonging to the spring ; appearing in spring ; as *vernal* bloom.

Vernal flowers are preparatives to autumnal fruits. *Rambler.*

2. Belonging to youth, the spring of life.

Vernal signs, the signs in which the sun appears in the spring.

Vernal equinox, the equinox in spring or March ; opposed to the *autumnal* equinox, in September.

VER'NANT, *a.* [L. *vernans ; verno*, to flourish.] Flourishing, as in spring ; as *vernant* flowers. *Milton.*

VER'NATE, *v. i.* To become young again. [*Not in use.*]

VERNA'TION, *n.* [L. *verno.*] In *botany*, the disposition of the nascent leaves within the bud. It is called also *foliation* or *leafing.* *Martyn.*

VER'NIER, *n.* [from the inventor.] A graduated index which subdivides the smallest divisions on a straight or circular scale. *Cyc.*

VERNIL'ITY, *n.* [L. *vernilis*, from *verna*, a slave.] Servility ; fawning behavior, like that of a slave. [*Not in use.*] *Bailey.*

VERON'ICA, *n.* [*vera-icon*, true image.]

1. A portrait or representation of the face of our Savior on handkerchiefs.

2. In *botany*, a genus of plants, Speedwell.

VER'RUCOUS, *a.* [L. *verruca*, a wart ; *verrucosus*, full of warts.]

Warty ; having little knobs or warts on the surface ; as a *verrucous* capsule. *Martyn.*

VERSABIL'ITY, VERS'ABLENESS, } *n.* [L. *versabilis*, from *versor*, to turn.]

Aptness to be turned round. [*Not used.*] *Dict.*

VERS'ABLE, *a.* [supra.] That may be turned. [*Not used.*]

VERSAL, for *universal.* [*Not used or very vulgar.*]

VERS'ATILE, *a.* [L. *versatilis*, from *versor*, to turn.]

1. That may be turned round ; as a *versatile* boat or spindle. *Harte.*

2. Liable to be turned in opinion ; changeable ; variable ; unsteady ; as a man of *versatile* disposition.

3. Turning with ease from one thing to another ; readily applied to a new task, or to various subjects ; as a man of *versatile* genius.

4. In *botany*, a *versatile anther* is one fixed by the middle on the point of the filament, and so poised as to turn like the needle of a compass ; fixed by its side, but freely movable. *Lee. Martyn.*

VERSATIL'ITY, *n.* The quality of being versatile ; aptness to change ; readiness to be turned ; variableness.

2. The faculty of easily turning one's mind to new tasks or subjects ; as the *versatility* of genius.

VERSE, *n. vers.* [L. *versus ;* Fr. *vers ;* from L. *verto*, to turn.]

1. In *poetry*, a line, consisting of a certain number of long and short syllables, disposed according to the rules of the species of poetry which the author intends to compose. Verses are of various kinds, as *hexameter, pentameter*, and *tetrameter*, &c. according to the number of feet in each. A verse of twelve syllables is called an

Alexandrian or *Alexandrine.* Two or more verses form a stanza or strophe.

2. Poetry; metrical language.

Virtue was taught in *verse.* *Prior.*

Verse embalms virtue. *Donne.*

3. A short division of any composition, particularly of the chapters in the Scriptures. The author of the division of the Old Testament into *verses,* is not ascertained. The New Testament was divided into *verses* by Robert Stephens.

4. A piece of poetry. *Pope.*

5. A portion of an anthem to be performed by a single voice to each part.

6. In a song or ballad, a stanza is called a *verse.*

Blank verse, poetry in which the lines do not end in rhymes.

Heroic verse, usually consists of ten syllables, or in English, of five accented syllables, constituting five feet.

VERSE, *v. t.* To tell in verse; to relate poetically.

Playing on pipes of corn, and *versing* love. *Shak.*

To be versed, [L. *versor,*] to be well skilled; to be acquainted with; as, *to be versed* in history or in geometry.

VERSE-MAN, *n.* [*verse* and *man.*] A writer of verses; *in ludicrous language. Prior.*

VERS'ER, *n.* A maker of verses; a versifier. *B. Jonson.*

VERS'ICLE, *n.* [L. *versiculus.*] A little verse. [*Not used.*]

VERS'ICOLOR, VERS'ICOLORED, *a.* [L. *versicolor.*] Having various colors; changeable in color.

VERSIC'ULAR, *a.* Pertaining to verses; designating distinct divisions of a writing.

VERSIFICA'TION, *n.* [Fr. from *versifier.*] The act, art or practice of composing poetic verse. Versification is the result of art, labor and rule, rather than of invention or the fire of genius. It consists in adjusting the long and short syllables, and forming feet into harmonious measure. *Cyc.*

VERS'IFICATOR, *n.* A versifier. [*Little used.*] [See *Versifier.*]

VERS'IFIED, *pp.* [from *versify.*] Formed into verse.

VERS'IFIER, *n.* One who makes verses. Not every *versifier* is a poet.

2. One who converts into verse; or one who expresses the ideas of another, written in prose; as, Dr. Watts was a *versifier* of the Psalms.

VERS'IFY, *v. i.* To make verses.

I'll *versify* in spite, and do my best. *Dryden.*

VERS'IFY, *v. t.* To relate or describe in verse.

I'll *versify* the truth. *Daniel.*

2. To turn into verse; as, to *versify* the Psalms.

VER'SION, *n.* [Fr. from L. *versio.*] A turning; a change or transformation; as the *version* of air into water. [*Unusual.*] *Bacon.*

2. Change of direction; as the *version* of the beams of light. [*Unusual.*] *Bacon.*

3. The act of translating; the rendering of thoughts or ideas expressed in one language, into words of like signification in another language. How long was Pope engaged in the *version* of Homer?

4. Translation; that which is rendered from another language. We have a good *version* of the Scriptures. There is a good *version* of the Pentateuch in the Samaritan. The Septuagint *version* of the Old Testament was made for the benefit of the Jews in Alexandria.

VERST, *n.* A Russian measure of length, containing 1166⅔ yards, or 3500 feet; about three quarters of an English mile.

VERT, *n.* [Fr. *verd,* green, L. *viridis.*] In *the forest laws,* every thing that grows and bears a green leaf within the forest. To preserve *vert* and venison, is the duty of the verderer. *England.*

2. In *heraldry,* a green color.

VERT'EBER, VERT'EBRA, *n.* [L. *vertebra,* from *verto,* to turn.] A joint of the spine or back-bone of an animal.

VERT'EBRAL, *a.* Pertaining to the joints of the spine or back-bone.

2. Having a back-bone or spinal joints; as *vertebral* animals.

VERT'EBRAL, *n.* An animal of the class which have a back-bone.

VERT'EBRATED, *a.* [L. *vertebratus.*] Having a back-bone, or vertebral column, containing the spinal marrow, as an animal; as man, quadrupeds, fowls, amphibia, and fishes. *Cuvier.*

VERT'EX, *n.* [L. from *verto,* to turn; primarily a round point.]

1. The crown or top of the head. *Coxe.*

2. The top of a hill or other thing; the point of a cone, pyramid, angle or figure; the pole of a glass, in optics. The vertex of a curve, is the point from which the diameter is drawn, or the intersection of the diameter and the curve.

3. In *astronomy,* the zenith; the point of the heavens perpendicularly over the head. *Cyc.*

VERT'ICAL, *a.* [Fr. from L. *vertex.*]

1. Placed or being in the zenith, or perpendicularly over the head. The sun is *vertical* to the inhabitants within the tropics at certain times every year.

2. Being in a position perpendicular to the plane of the horizon.

Vertical leaves, in botany, are such as stand so erect, that neither of the surfaces can be called the upper or under.

Vertical anthers, are such as terminate the filaments, and being inserted by their base, stand no less upright than the filaments themselves. *Cyc.*

Vertical circle, in astronomy, a great circle passing through the zenith and the nadir. The meridian of any place is a *vertical circle.* The vertical circles are called azimuths. *Cyc.*

Vertical line, in conics, is a right line drawn on the vertical plane, and passing through the vertex of the cone. *Cyc.*

Vertical plane, in conics, is a plane passing through the vertex of a cone, and through its axis.

Prime vertical, a great circle of the sphere, perpendicular to the horizon, and passing through the zenith and the east and west points.

VERT'ICALLY, *adv.* In the zenith.

VERT'ICALNESS, *n.* The state of being in the zenith, or perpendicularly over the head. [*Verticality* is not used.]

VERT'ICIL, *n.* [L. *verticillus,* from *vertex,* supra.]

In *botany,* a little whirl; a mode of inflorescence, in which the flowers surround the stem in a kind of ring. *Cyc.*

VERTIC'ILLATE, *a.* [supra.] In *botany,* verticillate flowers are such as grow in a whirl, or round the stem in rings, one above another, at each joint. The term is also applied in this sense to leaves and branches. Verticillate plants are such as bear whirled flowers. *Martyn. Lee.*

VERTIC'ITY, *n.* [from *vertex,* supra.] The power of turning; revolution; rotation. *Locke.*

2. That property of the lodestone by which it turns to some particular point.

The attraction of the magnet was known long before its *verticity.* *Cyc.*

VERTIG'INOUS, *a.* [L. *vertiginosus.*]

1. Turning round; whirling; rotary; as a *vertiginous* motion. *Bentley.*

2. Giddy; affected with vertigo. *Woodward.*

VERTIG'INOUSNESS, *n.* Giddiness; a whirling, or sense of whirling; unsteadiness. *Taylor.*

VERT'IGO, *n.* [L. from *verto,* to turn.] Giddiness; dizziness or swimming of the head; an affection of the head, in which objects appear to move in various directions, though stationary, and the person affected finds it difficult to maintain an erect posture. *Cyc.*

VER'VAIN, *n.* A plant of the genus Verbena, or rather the genus so called.

VERVAIN-MALLOW, *n.* A species of mallow, the *Malva alcea.* *Cyc.*

VER'VELS, *n.* [Fr. *vervelle.*] Labels tied to a hawk. *Ainsworth.*

VER'Y, *a.* [Fr. *vrai;* L. *verus.*] True; real.

Whether thou be my *very* son Esau or not. Gen. xxvii.

He that repeateth a matter, separateth *very* friends. Prov. xvii.

So we say, in *very* deed, in the *very* heavens, this is the *very* man we want. In these phrases, *very* is emphatical; but its signification is *true, real.*

VER'Y, *adv.* As an adverb, or modifier of adjectives and adverbs, *very* denotes in a great degree, an eminent or high degree, but not generally the highest; as a *very* great mountain; a *very* bright sun; a *very* cold day; a *very* pernicious war; a *very* benevolent disposition; the river flows *very* rapidly.

VES'ICANT, *n.* [infra.] A blistering application; an epispastic. *Bigelow.*

VES'ICATE, *v. t.* [L. *vesica,* a little bladder, Gr. φυσχη, from φυσαω, to inflate.]

To blister; to raise little bladders, or separate the cuticle by inflaming the skin. Celsus recommends to *vesicate* the external parts of wounds. *Wiseman.*

VES'ICATED, *pp.* Blistered.

VES'ICATING, *ppr.* Blistering.

VESICA'TION, *n.* The process of raising blisters or little cuticular bladders on the skin.

VES'ICATORY, *n.* [Fr. *vesicatoire.*] A blistering application or plaster; an epispastic. Vesicatories made of cantharides, are more powerful than sinapisms, or preparations of mustard.

VES'ICLE, *n.* [L. *vesicula.* See *Vesicate.*]
1. A little bladder, or a portion of the cuticle separated from the skin and filled with some humor.
2. Any small membranous cavity in animals or vegetables. The lungs consist of *vesicles* admitting air. *Ray. Cyc.*

VESIC'ULAR, } *a.* Pertaining to vesicles;
VESIC'ULOUS, } consisting of vesicles.
2. Hollow; full of interstices. *Cheyne.*
3. Having little bladders or glands on the surface, as the leaf of a plant.

VESIC'ULATE, *a.* Bladdery; full of bladders.

VES'PER, *n.* [L. This word and *Hesperus* are probably of one origin, and both from the root of *west.*]
1. The evening star; Venus; also, the evening.
2. *Vespers,* in the plural, the evening song or evening service in the Romish church.
Sicilian vespers, the era of the general massacre of the French in Sicily, on Easter evening, 1282, at the toll of the bell for vespers.

VES'PERTINE, *a.* [L. *vespertinus.* See *Vesper.*]
Pertaining to the evening; happening or being in the evening.

VES'SEL, *n.* [It. *vasello,* from *vaso,* a vase or vessel; Fr. *vaisseau*; Sp. *vasija*; from L. *vas, vasis.* This word is probably the English *vat,* in a different dialect; G. *fass,* a vat; *gefäss,* a vessel; *fassen,* to hold; allied probably to *fast, fasten.* The Sp. *vasija* is from the Latin; but the Spanish has also *baxel,* a general name of all floating buildings; probably of Celtic origin.]
1. A cask or utensil proper for holding liquors and other things, as a tun, a pipe, a puncheon, a hogshead, a barrel, a firkin, a bottle, a kettle, a cup, a dish, &c.
2. In *anatomy,* any tube or canal, in which the blood and other humors are contained, secreted or circulated, as the arteries, veins, lymphatics, spermatics, &c. *Cyc.*
3. In *the physiology of plants,* a canal or tube of very small bore, in which the sap is contained and conveyed; also, a bag or utricle, filled with pulp, and serving as a reservoir for sap; also, a spiral canal, usually of a larger bore, for receiving and distributing air. *Martyn. Grew.*
4. Any building used in navigation, which carries masts and sails, from the largest ship of war down to a fishing sloop. In general however, *vessel* is used for the smaller ships, brigs, sloops, schooners, luggers, scows, &c. *Mar. Dict.*
5. Something containing. *Milton.*
Vessels of wrath, in *Scripture,* are such persons as are to receive the full effects of God's wrath and indignation, as a punishment for their sins.
Vessels of mercy, are persons who are to receive the effects of God's mercy, or future happiness and glory.
Chosen vessels, ministers of the gospel, as appointed to bear the glad news of salvation to others; called also *earthern vessels,* on account of their weakness and frailty.

VES'SEL, *v. t.* To put into a vessel. [*Not in use.*] *Bacon.*

VES'SETS, *n.* A kind of cloth. Qu.

VES'SICON, } *n.* [L. *vesica.*] A soft swel-
VES'SIGON, } ling on a horse's leg, called a *windgall.* *Cyc.*

VEST, *n.* [Fr. *veste*; It. *vesta*; L. *vestis,* a coat or garment; *vestio,* to cover or clothe, Goth. *vestyan*; W. *gwisg.*]
1. An outer garment.

> Over his lucid arms
> A military *vest* of purple flow'd. *Milton.*

2. In *common speech,* a man's under garment; a short garment covering the body, but without sleeves, worn under the coat; called also *waistcoat.*

VEST, *v. t.* To clothe; to cover, surround or encompass closely.

> With ether *vested* and a purple sky. *Dryden.*

2. To dress; to clothe with a long garment; as the *vested* priest. *Milton.*
To vest with, to clothe; to furnish with; to invest with; as, to *vest* a man *with* authority; to *vest* a court *with* power to try cases of life and death; to *vest* one *with* the right of seizing slave-ships.

> Had I been *vested with* the monarch's pow'r. *Prior.*

To vest in, to put in possession of; to furnish with; to clothe with. The supreme executive power in England is *vested in* the king; in the United States, it is *vested in* the president.
2. To clothe with another form; to convert into another substance or species of property; as, to *vest* money *in* goods; to *vest* money *in* land or houses; to *vest* money *in* bank stock, or *in* six per cent. stock; to *vest* all one's property *in* the public funds.

VEST, *v. i.* To come or descend to; to be fixed; to take effect, as a title or right. Upon the death of the ancestor, the estate, or the right to the estate, *vests* in the heir at law.

VEST'AL, *a.* [L. *vestalis,* from *Vesta,* the goddess of fire, Gr. εϛια.]
1. Pertaining to Vesta, the goddess of fire among the Romans, and a virgin.
2. Pure; chaste. *Shak.*

VEST'AL, *n.* A virgin consecrated to Vesta, and to the service of watching the sacred fire, which was to be perpetually kept burning upon her altar. The *Vestals* were six in number, and they made a vow of perpetual virginity.

VEST'ED, *pp.* Clothed; covered; closely encompassed.
2. *a.* Fixed; not in a state of contingency or suspension; as *vested* rights.
Vested legacy, in law, a legacy the right to which commences *in presenti,* and does not depend on a contingency, as a legacy to one, to be paid when he attains to twenty one years of age. This is a *vested* legacy, and if the legatee dies before the testator, his representative shall receive it. *Blackstone.*
Vested remainder, is where the estate is invariably fixed, to remain to a determinate person, after the particular estate is spent. This is called a remainder executed, by which a present interest passes to the party, though to be enjoyed in future. *Blackstone.*

VES'TIBULE, *n.* [Fr.; L. *vestibulum.*]
1. The porch or entrance into a house, or a large open space before the door, but covered. Vestibules for magnificence are usually between the court and garden.
2. A little antechamber before the entrance of an ordinary apartment.
3. An apartment in large buildings, which presents itself into a hall or suit of rooms or offices. An area in which a magnificent staircase is carried up is sometimes called a *vestibule.*
4. In *anatomy,* a cavity belonging to the labyrinth of the ear. *Cyc.*

VES'TIGE, *n.* [Fr.; L. *vestigium.* This word and *vestibule,* show that some verb signifying to tread, from which they are derived, is lost.]
A track or footstep; the mark of the foot left on the earth; but mostly used for the mark or remains of something else; as the *vestiges* of ancient magnificence in Palmyra; *vestiges* of former population.

VEST'ING, *ppr.* [from *vest.*] Clothing; covering; closely encompassing; descending to and becoming permanent, as a right or title; converting into other species of property, as money.

VEST'ING, *n.* Cloth for vests; vest patterns. *U. States.*

VEST'MENT, *n.* [L. *vestimentum,* from *vestio,* to clothe; Fr. *vêtement.*]
A garment; some part of clothing or dress; especially some part of outer clothing; but it is not restricted to any particular garment.

> The sculptor could not give *vestments* suitable to the quality of the persons represented. *Dryden.*

VEST'RY, *n.* [L. *vestiarium*; Fr. *vestiaire.*]
1. A room appendant to a church, in which the sacerdotal vestments and sacred utensils are kept, and where parochial meetings are held.
2. A parochial assembly, so called because held in the vestry.

> The council are chosen by the *vestry.* *Clarendon.*

VEST'RY-CLERK, *n.* [*vestry* and *clerk.*] An officer chosen by the vestry, who keeps the parish accounts and books. *Cyc.*

VEST'RY-MAN, *n.* [*vestry* and *man.*] In London, *vestry-men* are a select number of principal persons of every parish, who choose parish officers and take care of its concerns. *Cyc.*

VEST'URE, *n.* [Fr. *vêture.* See *Vest.*] A garment; a robe.

> There polish'd chests embroider'd *vesture* grac'd. *Pope.*

2. Dress; garments in general; habit; clothing; vestment; as the *vesture* of priests.
3. Clothing; covering.

> Rocks, precipices and gulfs appareled with a *vesture* of plants. *Bentley.*
> —And gild the humble *vestures* of the plain. *Trumbull.*

4. In *old law books,* the corn with which land was covered; as the *vesture* of an acre.
5. In *old books,* seisin; possession. *Obs.*

VESU'VIAN, *a.* Pertaining to Vesuvius, a volcano near Naples.

VESU'VIAN, *n.* In *mineralogy,* a subspecies of pyramidical garnet, a mineral found in the vicinity of Vesuvius, classed with the family of garnets; called by Haüy idocrase. It is generally crystalized in four sided prisms, the edges of which are truncated, forming prisms of eight, fourteen or sixteen sides. It sometimes occurs massive. It is composed chiefly of silex, lime and alumin, with a portion of oxyd of iron, and oxyd of manganese. *Dict. Ure.*

VETCH, *n.* [Fr. *vesce;* It. *veccia;* L. *vicia;* Sp. *veza;* D. *wik, wikke,* vetch, and a weight; *wikken,* to weigh; G. *wicke,* a vetch; *wickel,* a roller; *wichtig,* weighty; *wickeln,* to wind up. We see *vetch* is from the root of *weigh, wag, wiggle,* and signifies a little roller.]
A plant of the leguminous kind, with papilionaceous flowers, of the genus Vicia. It is a common name of most species of the genus. The name is also applied, with various epithets, to many other leguminous plants of different genera; as the *chichling vetch,* of the genus Lathyrus; the *horseshoe vetch,* of the genus Hippocrepis; the *milk vetch,* of the genus Astragalus, &c. *Lee.*

VETCH'LING, *n.* [from *vetch.*] In *botany,* a name of the *Lathyrus aphaca,* expressive of its diminutive size. The *meadow vetchling* is a wild plant common in meadows, which makes good hay.

VETCH'Y, *a.* Consisting of vetches or of pea straw; as a *vetchy* bed. *Spenser.*
2. Abounding with vetches.

VET'ERAN, *a.* [L. *veteranus,* from *vetero,* to grow old, from *vetus,* old.]
Having been long exercised in any thing; long practiced or experienced; as a *veteran* officer or soldier; *veteran* skill. *Thomson.*

VET'ERAN, *n.* One who has been long exercised in any service or art, particularly in war; one who has grown old in service and has had much experience.

> Ensigns that pierc'd the foe's remotest lines,
> The hardy *veteran* with tears resigns. *Addison.*

VETERINA'RIAN, *n.* [L. *veterinarius.*] One skilled in the diseases of cattle or domestic animals. *Brown.*

VET'ERINARY, *a.* [supra.] Pertaining to the art of healing or treating the diseases of domestic animals, as oxen, horses, sheep, &c. A *veterinary* college was established in England in 1792, at St. Pancras, in the vicinity of London. The improvement of the *veterinary* art is of great importance to the agricultural interest.

VE'TO, *n.* [L. *veto,* I forbid.] A forbidding; prohibition; or the right of forbidding; applied to the right of a king or other magistrate or officer to withhold his assent to the enactment of a law, or the passing of a decree. Thus the king of Great Britain has a *veto* upon every act of parliament; he sometimes prevents the passing of a law by his *veto.*

VEX, *v. t.* [L. *vexo;* Fr. *vexer;* It. *vessare;* Sp. *vexar.*]
1. To irritate; to make angry by little provocations; *a popular use of the word.*
2. To plague; to torment; to harass; to afflict.

> Ten thousand torments *vex* my heart. *Prior.*

3. To disturb; to disquiet; to agitate.

> White curl the waves, and the *vex'd* ocean roars. *Pope.*

4. To trouble; to distress.

> I will also *vex* the hearts of many people. Ezek. xxxii.

5. To persecute. Acts xii.
6. To stretch, as by hooks. [*Not in use.*] *Dryden.*

VEX, *v. i.* To fret; to be teased or irritated. *Chapman.*

VEXA'TION, *n.* [Fr. from L. *vexatio.*] The act of irritating, or of troubling, disquieting and harassing.
2. State of being irritated or disturbed in mind.
3. Disquiet; agitation; great uneasiness.

> Passions too violent—afford us *vexation* and pain. *Temple.*

4. The cause of trouble or disquiet.

> Your children were *vexation* to your youth. *Shak.*

5. Afflictions; great troubles; severe judgments.

> The Lord shall send on thee cursing, *vexation* and rebuke. Deut. xxviii.

6. A harassing by law. *Bacon.*
7. A slight teasing trouble.

VEXA'TIOUS, *a.* Irritating; disturbing or agitating to the mind; causing disquiet; afflictive; as a *vexatious* controversy; a *vexatious* neighbor.
2. Distressing; harassing; as *vexatious* wars. *South.*
3. Full of trouble and disquiet.

> He leads a *vexatious* life. *Digby.*

4. Teasing; slightly troublesome; provoking.
A *vexatious suit,* in law, is one commenced for the purpose of giving trouble, or without cause.

VEXA'TIOUSLY, *adv.* In a manner to give great trouble or disquiet.

VEXA'TIOUSNESS, *n.* The quality of giving great trouble and disquiet, or of teasing and provoking.

VEX'ED, *pp.* Teased; provoked; irritated; troubled; agitated; disquieted; afflicted.

VEX'ER, *n.* One who vexes, irritates or troubles.

VEX'IL, *n.* [L. *vexillum,* a standard.] A flag or standard. In *botany,* the upper petal of a papilionaceous flower. *Martyn.*

VEX'ILLARY, *n.* A standard bearer.

VEX'ILLARY, *a.* Pertaining to an ensign or standard.

VEXILLA'TION, *n.* [L. *vexillatio.*] A company of troops under one ensign.

VEX'ING, *ppr.* Provoking; irritating; afflicting.

VEX'INGLY, *adv.* So as to vex, tease or irritate. *Tatler.*

VI'AL, *n.* [Fr. *viole;* Gr. φιαλη; L. *phiala.*] A phial; a small bottle of thin glass, used particularly by apothecaries and druggists.

> Samuel took a *vial* of oil, and poured it on his head. 1 Sam. x.

Vials of God's wrath, in Scripture, are the execution of his wrath upon the wicked for their sins. Rev. xvi.

VI'AL, *v. t.* To put in a vial. *Milton.*

VI'AND, *n.* [Fr. *viande;* from It. *vivanda;* L. *vivendus, vivo,* to live.] Meat dressed; food.

> *Viands* of various kinds allure the taste. *Pope.*

[*It is used chiefly in the plural.*]

VIAT'IC, *a.* [L. *viaticum,* from *via,* way.] Pertaining to a journey or to traveling.

VIAT'ICUM, *n.* [L. supra.] Provisions for a journey.
2. Among *the ancient Romans,* an allowance to officers who were sent into the provinces to exercise any office or perform any service, also to the officers and soldiers of the army. *Cyc.*
3. In *the Romish church,* the communion or eucharist given to persons in their last moments.

VI'BRANT, } *n.* [L. *vibrans.*] A name given
VIB'RION, } to the ichneumon fly, from the continual vibration of its antennæ. *Cyc.*

VI'BRATE, *v. i.* [L. *vibro;* It. *vibrare.* This word belongs to the root of Eng. *wabble;* W. *gwibiaw,* to wander, to move in a circular or serpentine direction.]
1. To swing; to oscillate; to move one way and the other; to play to and fro; as, the pendulum of a clock *vibrates* more or less rapidly, as it is shorter or longer. The chords of an instrument *vibrate* when touched.
2. To quiver; as, a whisper *vibrates* on the ear. *Pope.*
3. To pass from one state to another; as, a man *vibrates* from one opinion to another.

VI'BRATE, *v. t.* To brandish; to move to and fro; to swing; as, to *vibrate* a sword or staff. The pendulum of a clock *vibrates* seconds.
2. To cause to quiver.

> Breath vocalized, that is, *vibrated* or undulated, may differently affect the lips, and impress a swift tremulous motion. *Holder.*

VI'BRATED, *pp.* Brandished; moved one way and the other.

VIBRATIL'ITY, *n.* Disposition to preternatural vibration or motion. [*Not much used.*] *Rush.*

VI'BRATING, *ppr.* Brandishing; moving to and fro, as a pendulum or musical chord.

VIBRA'TION, *n.* [Fr. from L. *vibro.*] The act of brandishing; the act of moving or state of being moved one way and the other in quick succession.
2. In *mechanics,* a regular reciprocal motion of a body suspended; a motion consisting of continual reciprocations or returns; as of the pendulum of a chronometer. This is frequently called *oscillation.* The number of *vibrations* in a given time depends on the length of the vibrating body; a pendulum three feet long, makes only ten *vibrations* while one of nine inches makes twenty. The *vibrations* of a pendulum are somewhat slower at or near the equator than in remote latitudes. The *vibrations* of a pendulum are isochronal in the same climate. *Cyc.*
3. In *physics,* alternate or reciprocal motion; as the *vibrations* of the nervous fluid, by which sensation has been supposed to be produced, by impressions of external objects propagated thus to the brain. *Cyc.*
4. In *music,* the motion of a chord, or the undulation of any body, by which sound is produced. The acuteness, elevation and gravity of sound, depend on the length of the chord and its tension.

VIBRAT'IUNCLE, *n.* A small vibration. *Chambers. Cyc.*

VI'BRATIVE, *a.* That vibrates. *Newton.*

VI'BRATORY, *a.* Vibrating; consisting in vibration or oscillation; as a *vibratory* motion.

2. Causing to vibrate.

VIC'AR, *n.* [Fr. *vicaire*; It. *vicario*; L. *vicarius*, from *vicis*, a turn, or its root.]

1. In *a general sense*, a person deputed or authorized to perform the functions of another; a substitute in office. The pope pretends to be *vicar* of Jesus Christ on earth. He has under him a grand vicar, who is a cardinal, and whose jurisdiction extends over all priests, regular and secular.

2. In *the canon law*, the priest of a parish, the predial tithes of which are impropriated or appropriated, that is, belong to a chapter or religious house, or to a layman, who receives them, and only allows the vicar the smaller tithes or a salary. *Cyc.*

Apostolical vicars, are those who perform the functions of the pope in churches or provinces committed to their direction. *Cyc.*

VIC'ARAGE, *n.* The benefice of a vicar. A vicarage by endowment, becomes a benefice distinct from the parsonage. *Cyc.*

VICAR-GEN'ERAL, *n.* A title given by Henry VIII. to the earl of Essex, with power to oversee all the clergy, and regulate all church affairs. It is now the title of an office, which, as well as that of official principal, is united in the chancellor of the diocese. The business of the vicar-general is to exercise jurisdiction over matters purely spiritual. *Cyc.*

VICA'RIAL, *a.* [from *vicar.*] Pertaining to a vicar; small; as *vicarial* tithes.

VICA'RIATE, *a.* Having delegated power, as vicar. *Barrow.*

VICA'RIATE, *n.* A delegated office or power. *Lord North.*

VICA'RIOUS, *a.* [L. *vicarius.*] Deputed; delegated; as *vicarious* power or authority.

2. Acting for another; filling the place of another; as a *vicarious* agent or officer.

3. Substituted in the place of another; as a *vicarious* sacrifice. The doctrine of *vicarious* punishment has occasioned much controversy.

VICA'RIOUSLY, *adv.* In the place of another; by substitution. *Burke.*

VIC'ARSHIP, *n.* The office of a vicar; the ministry of a vicar.

VICE, *n.* [Fr. *vice*; It. *vizio*; Sp. *vicio*; L. *vitium*; W. *gwyd.*]

1. Properly, a spot or defect; a fault; a blemish; as the *vices* of a political constitution. *Madison.*

2. In *ethics*, any voluntary action or course of conduct which deviates from the rules of moral rectitude, or from the plain rules of propriety; any moral unfitness of conduct, either from defect of duty, or from the transgression of known principles of rectitude. *Vice* differs from *crime*, in being less enormous. We never call murder or robbery a *vice*; but every act of intemperance, all falsehood, duplicity, deception, lewdness and the like, is a *vice*. The excessive indulgence of passions and appetites which in themselves are innocent, is a *vice*. The smoking of tobacco and the taking of snuff, may in certain cases be innocent and even useful, but these practices may be carried to such an excess as to become *vices*. This word is also used to denote a habit of transgressing; as a life of *vice*. *Vice* is rarely a solitary invader; it usually brings with it a frightful train of followers.

3. Depravity or corruption of manners; as an age of *vice*.

> When *vice* prevails, and impious men bear sway,
> The post of honor is a private station. *Addison.*

4. A fault or bad trick in a horse.

5. The fool or punchinello of old shows.

> His face made of brass, like a *vice* in a game. *Tusser.*

6. An iron press. [This should be written *vise.*]

7. A gripe or grasp. [*Not in use.*] *Shak.*

VICE, *v. t.* To draw by a kind of violence. [*Not in use.*] [See *Vise.*] *Shak.*

VICE, L. *vice*, in the turn or place, is used in composition to denote one *qui vicem gerit*, who acts in the place of another, or is second in authority.

VICE-AD'MIRAL, *n.* In the navy, the second officer in command. His flag is displayed at the fore top-gallant-mast head. *Mar. Dict.*

2. A civil officer in Great Britain, appointed by the lords commissioners of the admiralty, for exercising admiralty jurisdiction within their respective districts.

VICE-AD'MIRALTY, *n.* The office of a vice-admiralty; a vice-admiralty court.

VICE-A'GENT, *n.* [*vice* and *agent.*] One who acts in the place of another. *Hooker.*

VICE-CH'AMBERLAIN, } *n.* An officer in
VICE-CHAMBERLAIN, } court, next in command to the lord chamberlain. *England.*

VICE-CH'ANCELLOR, *n.* An officer in a university in England, a distinguished member, who is annually elected to manage the affairs in the absence of the chancellor. *Cyc.*

VICE-CONSUL, *n.* One who acts in the place of a consul.

VI'CED, *a.* Vitious; corrupt. [*Not in use.*] *Shak.*

VICE-DO'GE, *n.* A counsellor at Venice, who represents the doge when sick or absent. *Cyc.*

VICEGE'RENCY, *n.* [See *Vicegerent.*] The office of a vicegerent; agency under another; deputed power; lieutenancy. *South.*

VICEGE'RENT, *n.* [L. *vicem gerens*, acting in the place of another.] A lieutenant; a vicar; an officer who is deputed by a superior or by proper authority to exercise the powers of another. Kings are sometimes called God's *vicegerents*. It is to be wished they would always deserve the appellation.

VICEGE'RENT, *a.* Having or exercising delegated power; acting by substitution, or in the place of another. *Milton.*

VICE-LEG'ATE, *n.* An officer employed by the pope to perform the office of spiritual and temporal governor in certain cities, when there is no legate or cardinal to command there. *Cyc.*

VIC'ENARY, *a.* [L. *vicenarius.*] Belonging to twenty.

VICE-PRES'IDENT, *n.* *s* as *z*. An officer next in rank below a president. *U. States.*

VI'CEROY, *n.* [Fr. *viceroi.*] The governor of a kingdom or country, who rules in the name of the king with regal authority, as the king's substitute. *Swift.*

VICEROY'ALTY, *n.* The dignity, office or jurisdiction of a viceroy.

VI'CEROYSHIP, *n.* The dignity, office or jurisdiction of a viceroy.

VI'CETY, *n.* Nicety; exactness. [*Not in use; probably a mistake.*] *B. Jonson.*

VI''CIATE, *v. t.* [L. *vitio*. This verb is usually written *vitiate*; but as *vice*, from L. *vitium*, is established, it would be well to write the verb *viciate*, as we write *appreciate* and *depreciate*, from L. *pretium.*]

1. To injure the substance or properties of a thing so as to impair its value, and lessen or destroy its use; to make less pure, or wholly impure; to deprave, in a physical or moral sense; as, to *viciate* the blood; to *viciate* taste or style; to *viciate* morals.

2. To render defective and thus destroy the validity of; to invalidate by defect; as, to *viciate* a deed or bond.

VI''CIATED, *pp.* Depraved; impaired in substance or quality; rendered defective and void.

VI''CIATING, *ppr.* Injuring in substance or properties; rendering defective; making void.

VICIA'TION, *n.* Depravation; corruption.

VIC'INAGE, *n.* [from L. *vicinia*, neighborhood; *vicinus*, near.] Neighborhood; the place or places adjoining or near. A jury must be of the *vicinage*, or body of the county.

In law, *common because of vicinage*, is where the inhabitants of two townships contiguous to each other, have usually intercommoned with one another; the beasts of one straying into the other's fields without molestation from either. *Blackstone.*

VIC'INAL, } *a.* Near; neighboring. [*Lit-*
VIC'INE, } *tle used.*] *Glanville.*

VICIN'ITY, *n.* [L. *vicinitas.*] Nearness in place; as the *vicinity* of two country seats.

2. Neighborhood; as a seat in the *vicinity* of the metropolis.

3. Neighboring country. Vegetables produced in the *vicinity* of the city, are daily brought to market. The *vicinity* is full of gardens.

VICIOS'ITY, *n.* Depravity; corruption of manners. [But *viciousness* is generally used.]

VI''CIOUS, *a.* [Fr. *vicieux*; L. *vitiosus.*]

1. Defective; imperfect; as a system of government *vicious* and unsound. *Harte.*

2. Addicted to vice; corrupt in principles or conduct; depraved; wicked; habitually transgressing the moral law; as a *vicious* race of men; *vicious* parents; *vicious* children.

3. Corrupt; contrary to moral principles or to rectitude; as *vicious* examples; *vicious* conduct.

4. Corrupt, in a physical sense; foul; impure; insalubrious; as *vicious* air.

5. Corrupt; not genuine or pure; as *vicious* language; *vicious* idioms.

6. Unruly; refractory; not well tamed or broken; as a *vicious* horse. *N. Eng.*

VI′′CIOUSLY, *adv.* Corruptly; in a manner contrary to rectitude, moral principles, propriety or purity.

2. Faultily; not correctly. *Burnet.*

VI′′CIOUSNESS, *n.* Addictedness to vice; corruptness of moral principles or practice; habitual violation of the moral law, or of moral duties; depravity in principles or in manners.

What makes a governor justly despised, is *viciousness* and ill morals. *South.*

2. Unruliness; refractoriness; as of a beast. *N. England.*

VICIS′SITUDE, *n.* [L. *vicissitudo;* from *vicis,* a turn.]

1. Regular change or succession of one thing to another; as the *vicissitudes* of day and night, and of winter and summer; the *vicissitudes* of the seasons.

2. Change; revolution; as in human affairs. We are exposed to continual *vicissitudes* of fortune.

VICISSITU′DINARY, *a.* Changing in succession. *Donne.*

VICON′TIEL, *a.* [*vice-comitalia.* See *Viscount.*]

In *old law books,* pertaining to the sherif. *Vicontiel rents,* are certain rents for which the sherif pays a rent to the king.

Vicontiel writs, are such as are triable in the county or sherif court. *Cyc.*

VICON′TIELS, *n.* Things belonging to the sherif; particularly, farms for which the sherif pays rent to the king. *Cyc.*

VI′COUNT, *n.* [*vice-comes.*] In *law books,* the sherif.

2. A degree of nobility next below a count or earl. [See *Viscount.*] *Cyc.*

VIC′TIM, *n.* [L. *victima;* Fr. *victime.*]

1. A living being sacrificed to some deity, or in the performance of a religious rite; usually, some beast slain in sacrifice: but human beings have been slain by some nations, for the purpose of appeasing the wrath or conciliating the favor of some deity.

2. Something destroyed; something sacrificed in the pursuit of an object. How many persons have fallen *victims* to jealousy, to lust, to ambition!

VIC′TIMATE, *v. t.* To sacrifice. [*Not in use.*] *Bullokar.*

VIC′TOR, *n.* [L. from *vinco, victus,* to conquer, or the same root. *N* not being radical, the root is *vico* or *vigo;* Sax. *wig, wigg,* war; *wiga,* a warrior, a hero, a *victor; wigan,* to war, to fight. The primary sense is to urge, drive or strive, hence to subdue.]

1. One who conquers in war; a vanquisher; one who defeats an enemy in battle. *Victor* differs from *conqueror.* We apply *conqueror* to one who subdues countries, kingdoms or nations; as, Alexander was the *conqueror* of Asia or India, or of many nations, or of the world. In such phrases, we cannot substitute *victor.* But we use *victor,* when we speak of one who overcomes a particular enemy, or in a particular battle; as, Cesar was *victor* at Pharsalia. The duke of Wellington was *victor* at Waterloo. *Victor* then is not followed by the possessive case; for we do not say, Alexander was the *victor of* Darius, though we say, he was *victor at* Arbela. *Johnson.*

2. One who vanquishes another in private combat or contest; as a *victor* in the Olympic games.

3. One who wins, or gains the advantage.

In love, the *victors* from the vanquish'd fly;
They fly that wound, and they pursue that die. *Waller.*

4. Master; lord.

These, *victor* of his health, his fortune, friends. [*Not usual nor legitimate.*] *Pope.*

VIC′TORESS, *n.* A female who vanquishes. *Spenser.*

VICTO′RIOUS, *a.* [Fr. *victorieux.*] Having conquered in battle or contest; having overcome an enemy or antagonist; conquering; vanquishing; as a *victorious* general; *victorious* troops; a *victorious* admiral or navy.

2. That produces conquest; as a *victorious* day. *Pope.*

3. Emblematic of conquest; indicating victory; as brows bound with *victorious* wreaths. *Shak.*

VICTO′RIOUSLY, *adv.* With conquest; with defeat of an enemy or antagonist; triumphantly; as, grace will carry us *victoriously* through all difficulties. *Hammond.*

VICTO′RIOUSNESS, *n.* The state of being victorious.

VIC′TORY, *n.* [L. *victoria,* from *vinco, victus,* to conquer; Fr. *victoire.*]

1. Conquest; the defeat of an enemy in battle, or of an antagonist in contest; a gaining of the superiority in war or combat. *Victory* supposes the power of an enemy or an antagonist to prove inferior to that of the victor. *Victory* however depends not always on superior skill or valor; it is often gained by the fault or mistake of the vanquished.

Victory may be honorable to the arms, but shameful to the counsels of a nation. *Bolingbroke.*

2. The advantage or superiority gained over spiritual enemies, over passions and appetites, or over temptations, or in any struggle or competition.

Thanks be to God, who giveth us the *victory,* through our Lord Jesus Christ. 1 Cor. xv.

VIC′TRESS, *n.* A female that conquers. *Shak.*

VICTUAL. [See *Victuals.*]

VICTUAL, *v. t.* *vit'l.* [from *victual,* the noun.]

1. To supply with provisions for subsistence; as, to *victual* an army; to *victual* a garrison.

2. To store with provisions; as, to *victual* a ship.

VICTUALED, *pp.* *vit'ld.* Supplied with provisions.

VICTUALER, *n.* *vit'ler.* One who furnishes provisions.

2. One who keeps a house of entertainment.

3. A provision-ship; a ship employed to carry provisions for other ships, or for supplying troops at a distance.

VICTUALING, *ppr.* *vit'ling.* Supplying with provisions.

VICTUALING-HOUSE, *n.* A house where provision is made for strangers to eat.

VICTUALS, *n.* *vit'lz.* [Fr. *victuailles;* It. *vettovaglia;* Sp. *vitualla;* from L. *victus,* food, from the root of *vivo,* which was *vigo* or *vico,* coinciding with *vigeo;* Basque, *vicia,* life. This word is now never used in the singular.]

Food for human beings, prepared for eating; that which supports human life; provisions; meat; sustenance. We never apply this word to that on which beasts or birds feed, and we apply it chiefly to food for men when cooked or prepared for the table. We do not now give this name to flesh, corn or flour, in a crude state; but we say, the *victuals* are well cooked or dressed, and in great abundance. We say, a man eats his *victuals* with a good relish.

Such phrases as to buy *victuals* for the army or navy, to lay in *victuals* for the winter, &c. are now obsolete. We say, to buy *provisions;* yet we use the verb, to *victual* an army or ship.

VIDEL′ICET, *adv.* [L. for *videre licet.*] To wit; namely. An abbreviation for this word is *viz.*

VID′UAL, *a.* [L. *viduus,* deprived.] Belonging to the state of a widow. [*Not used.*]

VIDU′ITY, *n.* [L. *viduitas.*] Widowhood. [*Not used.*]

VIE, *v. i.* [Sax. *wigan,* to war, to contend, that is, to strain, to urge, to press. See *Victor.*]

To strive for superiority; to contend; to use effort in a race, contest, competition, rivalship or strife. How delightful it is to see children *vie* with each other in diligence and in duties of obedience.

In a trading nation, the younger sons may be placed in a way of life to *vie* with the best of their family. *Addison.*

VIE, *v. t.* To show or practice in competition; as, to *vie* power; to *vie* charities. [*Not legitimate.*]

2. To urge; to press.

She hung about my neck, and kiss and kiss
She *vied* so fast. [*Not in use.*] *Shak.*

VIELLEUR, *n.* A species of fly in Surinam, less than the lantern fly. *Cyc.*

VIEW, *v. t.* *vu.* [Fr. *vue,* from *voir,* to see, contracted from L. *videre,* Russ. *viju.* The primary sense is to reach or extend to.]

1. To survey; to examine with the eye; to look on with attention, or for the purpose of examining; to inspect; to explore. *View* differs from *look, see,* and *behold,* in expressing more particular or continued attention to the thing which is the object of sight. We ascended mount Holyoke, and *viewed* the charming landscape below. We *viewed* with delight the rich valleys of the Connecticut about the town of Northampton.

Go up and *view* the country. Josh. vii.
I *viewed* the walls of Jerusalem. Neh. vii.

2. To see; to perceive by the eye. *Pope.*

3. To survey intellectually; to examine with the mental eye; to consider. *View* the subject in all its aspects.

VIEW, *n.* *vu.* Prospect; sight; reach of the eye.

The walls of Pluto's palace are in *view.* *Dryden.*

2. The whole extent seen. Vast or extensive *views* present themselves to the eye.

3. Sight; power of seeing, or limit of sight. The mountain was not within our *view.*

4. Intellectual or mental sight. These things

give us a just *view* of the designs of providence.

5. Act of seeing. The facts mentioned were verified by actual *view*.

6. Sight; eye.

Objects near our *view* are thought greater than those of larger size, that are more remote. *Locke.*

7. Survey; inspection; examination by the eye. The assessors took a *view* of the premises.

Surveying nature with too nice a *view*. *Dryden.*

8. Intellectual survey; mental examination. On a just *view* of all the arguments in the case, the law appears to be clear.

9. Appearance; show.

Graces—
Which, by the splendor of her *view*
Dazzled, before we never knew. *Waller.*

10. Display; exhibition to the sight or mind.

To give a right *view* of this mistaken part of liberty— *Locke.*

11. Prospect of interest.

No man sets himself about any thing, but upon some *view* or other, which serves him for a reason. *Locke.*

12. Intention; purpose; design. With that *view* he began the expedition. With a *view* to commerce, he passed through Egypt.

13. Opinion; manner of seeing or understanding. These are my *views* of the policy which ought to be pursued.

View of frankpledge, in *law*, a court of record, held in a hundred, lordship or manor, before the steward of the leet. *Blackstone.*

Point of view, the direction in which a thing is seen.

VIEWED, *pp.* *vu'ed.* Surveyed; examined by the eye; inspected; considered.

VIEWER, *n.* *vu'er.* One who views, surveys or examines.

2. In *New England*, a town officer whose duty is to inspect something; as a *viewer* of fences, who inspects them to determine whether they are sufficient in law.

VIEWING, *ppr.* *vu'ing.* Surveying; examining by the eye or by the mind; inspecting; exploring.

VIEWING, *n.* *vu'ing.* The act of beholding or surveying.

VIEWLESS, *a.* *vu'less.* That cannot be seen; not being perceivable by the eye; invisible; as *viewless* winds. *Shak.*

Swift through the valves the visionary fair
Repass'd, and *viewless* mix'd with common air. *Pope.*

VIGESIMA'TION, *n.* [L. *vigesimus*, twentieth.]
The act of putting to death every twentieth man. *Bailey.*

VIG'IL, *n.* [L. *vigilia*; Fr. *vigile*; L. *vigil*, waking, watchful; *vigilo*, to watch. This is formed on the root of Eng. *wake*, Sax. *wæcan*, *wecan*. The primary sense is to stir or excite, to rouse, to agitate.]

1. Watch; devotion performed in the customary hours of rest or sleep.

So they in heav'n their odes and *vigils* tun'd. *Milton.*

2. In *church affairs*, the eve or evening before any feast, the ecclesiastical day beginning at six o'clock in the evening, and continuing till the same hour the following evening; hence, a religious service performed in the evening preceding a holiday. *Cyc.*

3. A fast observed on the day preceding a holiday; a wake. *Cyc.*

4. Watch; forbearance of sleep; as the *vigils* of the card table. *Addison.*

Vigils or *watchings* of flowers, a term used by Linne to express a peculiar faculty belonging to the flowers of certain plants, of opening and closing their petals at certain hours of the day. *Cyc.*

VIG'ILANCE, *n.* [Fr. from L. *vigilans*. See *Vigil*.]

1. Forbearance of sleep; a state of being awake. *Parr.*

2. Watchfulness; circumspection; attention of the mind in discovering and guarding against danger, or providing for safety. *Vigilance* is a virtue of prime importance in a general. The *vigilance* of the dog is no less remarkable than his fidelity.

3. Guard; watch.

In at this gate none pass
The *vigilance* here plac'd. [*Unusual.*] *Milton.*

VIG'ILANCY, for *vigilance*, is not used.

VIG'ILANT, *a.* [Fr. from L. *vigilans.*] Watchful; circumspect; attentive to discover and avoid danger, or to provide for safety.

Take your places and be *vigilant.* *Shak.*
Be sober, be *vigilant.* 1 Pet. v.

VIG'ILANTLY, *adv.* [supra.] Watchfully; with attention to danger and the means of safety; circumspectly.

VIGNETTE, } *n.* [Fr. *vignette*, from *vigne*,
VIGNET', } a vine.] An ornament placed at the beginning of a book, preface or dedication; a head piece. These vignets are of various forms; often they are wreaths of flowers or sprigs.

VIG'OR, *n.* [L. from *vigeo*, to be brisk, to grow, to be strong; allied to *vivo*, *vixi*, to live, and to Sax. *wigan*, to carry on war, and to *wake*.]

1. Active strength or force of body in animals; physical force.

The *vigor* of this arm was never vain. *Dryden.*

2. Strength of mind; intellectual force; energy. We say, a man possesses *vigor* of mind or intellect.

3. Strength or force in vegetable motion; as, a plant grows with *vigor*.

4. Strength; energy; efficacy.

In the fruitful earth
His beams, unactive else, their *vigor* find. *Milton.*

VIG'OR, *v. t.* To invigorate. [*Not in use.*] *Feltham.*

VIG'OROUS, *a.* Full of physical strength or active force; strong; lusty; as a *vigorous* youth; a *vigorous* body.

2. Powerful; strong; made by strength, either of body or mind; as a *vigorous* attack; *vigorous* exertions. The enemy expects a *vigorous* campaign.

The beginnings of confederacies have been *vigorous* and successful. *Davenant.*

VIG'OROUSLY, *adv.* With great physical force or strength; forcibly; with active exertions; as, to prosecute an enterprise *vigorously.*

VIG'OROUSNESS, *n.* The quality of being vigorous or possessed of active strength.

[*Vigor* and all its derivatives imply active strength, or the power of action and exertion, in distinction from passive strength, or strength to endure.]

VILD, } *a.* Vile. [*Not in use.*] *Spenser.*
VI'LED, }

VILE, *a.* [L. *vilis*; Fr. Sp. *vil*; It. *vile*; Gr. φαυλος.]

1. Base; mean; worthless; despicable.

The inhabitants account gold a *vile* thing. *Abbot.*

A man in *vile* raiment. James ii.

Wherefore are we counted as beasts, and reputed as *vile* in your sight? Job xviii.

2. Morally base or impure; sinful; depraved by sin; wicked; hateful in the sight of God and of good men. The sons of Eli made themselves *vile.* 1 Sam. iii.

Behold I am *vile*; what shall I answer? Job xl.

VI'LED, *a.* Abusive; scurrilous; defamatory. [*Not in use.*] *Hayward.*

VI'LELY, *adv.* Basely; meanly; shamefully; as Hector *vilely* dragged about the walls of Troy. *Philips.*

2. In a cowardly manner. 2 Sam. i.

The Volscians *vilely* yielded the town. *Shak.*

VI'LENESS, *n.* Baseness; meanness; despicableness.

His *vileness* us shall never awe. *Drayton.*

2. Moral baseness or depravity; degradation by sin; extreme wickedness; as the *vileness* of mankind. *Prior.*

VIL'IFIED, *pp.* [from *vilify.*] Defamed; traduced; debased.

VIL'IFIER, *n.* One who defames or traduces.

VIL'IFY, *v. t.* [from *vile.*] To make vile; to debase; to degrade.

Their Maker's image
Forsook them, when themselves they *vilified*
To serve ungovern'd appetite. *Milton.*

2. To defame; to traduce; to attempt to degrade by slander.

Many passions dispose us to depress and *vilify* the merit of one rising in the esteem of mankind. *Addison.*

[*This is the most usual sense of the verb.*]

VIL'IFYING, *ppr.* Debasing; defaming.

VIL'IPEND, *v. t.* [L. *vilipendo.*] To despise. [*Not in use.*]

VILIPEND'ENCY, *n.* Disesteem; slight. [*Not in use.*]

VIL'ITY, *n.* Vileness; baseness. [*Not in use.*] *Kennet.*

VILL, *n.* [L. *villa*; Fr. *ville.*] A village; a small collection of houses. *Hale.*

The statute of Exeter, 14 Edward I. mentions *entire-vills*, *demi-vills*, and *hamlets.* *Cyc.*

VIL'LA, *n.* [L. *villa*; Fr. *ville*; Gaelic, *bail.*]
A country seat or a farm, furnished with a mansion and convenient out-houses. *Cyc.*

VIL'LAGE, *n.* [Fr.; from *villa.*] A small assemblage of houses, less than a town or city, and inhabited chiefly by farmers and other laboring people. In England, it is said that a *village* is distinguished from a town by the want of a market. *Cyc.*

In the United States, no such distinction exists, and any small assemblage of houses in the country is called a *village.*

VIL'LAGER, *n.* An inhabitant of a village. *Milton.*

VIL'LAGERY, *n.* A district of villages. *Shak.*

VIL'LAIN, } *n.* [Fr. *vilain;* It. Sp. *villano;*
VIL'LAN, } Norm. *vilaint.* According to the French orthography, this word is formed from *vile;* but the orthography in other languages connects this word with *vill, village,* and this is probably the true origin. It would be well to write *villan.*]

1. In *feudal law,* a villain or villein is one who holds lands by a base or servile tenure, or in *villenage.* Villains were of two sorts; *villains regardant,* that is, annexed to the manor, *adscriptitii glebæ;* or *villains in gross,* that is, annexed to the person of their lord, and transferable from one to another. *Blackstone.*

2. A vile wicked person; a man extremely depraved, and capable or guilty of great crimes. We call by the name of *villain,* the thief, the robber, the burglarian, the murderer, the incendiary, the ravisher, the seducer, the cheat, the swindler, &c.

Calm thinking *villains,* whom no faith could fix. *Pope.*

VIL'LAKIN, *n.* A little village; a word used by Gay.

VIL'LANAGE, *n.* The state of a villain; base servitude.

2. A base tenure of lands; tenure on condition of doing the meanest services for the lord; usually written *villenage.*

3. Baseness; infamy. [See *Villany.*]

VIL'LANIZE, *v. t.* To debase; to degrade; to defame; to revile.

Were virtue by descent, a noble name
Could never *villanize* his father's fame.
[*Little used.*] *Dryden.*

VIL'LANIZED, *pp.* Defamed; debased. [*Little used.*]

VIL'LANIZING, *ppr.* Defaming; debasing. [*Little used.*]

VIL'LANOUS, } *a.* [from *villain.*] Base;
VIL'LAINOUS, } very vile.

2. Wicked; extremely depraved; as a *villanous* person or wretch.

3. Proceeding from extreme depravity; as a *villanous* action.

4. Sorry; vile; mischievous; *in a familiar sense;* as a *villanous* trick of the eye. *Shak.*

Villanous judgment, in old law, a judgment that casts reproach on the guilty person.

VIL'LANOUSLY, *adv.* Basely; with extreme wickedness or depravity.

VIL'LANOUSNESS, *n.* Baseness; extreme depravity.

VIL'LANY, } *n.* Extreme depravity; atro-
VIL'LAINY, } cious wickedness; as the *villany* of the thief or the robber; the *villany* of the seducer.

The commendation is not in his wit, but in his *villany.* *Shak.*

2. A crime; an action of deep depravity. In this sense, the word has a plural.

Such *villanies* roused Horace into wrath. *Dryden.*

VILLAT'IC, *a.* [L. *villaticus.*] Pertaining to a village.

Tame *villatic* fowl. *Milton.*

VIL'LENAGE, *n.* [from *villain.*] A tenure of lands and tenements by base services. *Blackstone.*

VIL'LOUS, *a.* [L. *villosus,* from *villus,* hair, Eng. *wool.*]

1. Abounding with fine hairs or wooly substance; nappy; shaggy; rough; as a *villous* coat.

The *villous coat* of the stomach and intestines is the inner mucous membrane, so called from the innumerable villi or fine fibrils with which its internal surface is covered. *Cyc. Parr.*

2. In *botany,* pubescent; covered with soft hairs.

VIM'INAL, *a.* [L. *viminalis.*] Pertaining to twigs; consisting of twigs; producing twigs.

VIMIN'EOUS, *a.* [L. *vimineus,* from *vimen,* a twig.] Made of twigs or shoots.

In the hive's *vimineous* dome. *Prior.*

VINA'CEOUS, *a.* [L. *vinaceus.*] Belonging to wine or grapes. *White.*

VIN'CIBLE, *a.* [from L. *vinco,* to conquer. See *Victor.*]

Conquerable; that may be overcome or subdued.

He not *vincible* in spirit— *Hayward.*

VIN'CIBLENESS, *n.* The capacity of being conquered; conquerableness. *Dict.*

VINC'TURE, *n.* [L. *vinctura.*] A binding. [*Not in use.*]

VINDE'MIAL, *a.* [L. *vindemialis,* from *vindemia,* vintage; *vinea* and *demo.*] Belonging to a vintage or grape harvest.

VINDE'MIATE, *v. i.* [supra.] To gather the vintage. *Evelyn.*

VINDEMIA'TION, *n.* The operation of gathering grapes. *Bailey.*

VINDICABIL'ITY, *n.* The quality of being vindicable, or capable of support or justification. *Journ. of Science.*

VIN'DICABLE, *a.* [infra.] That may be vindicated, justified or supported. *Dwight.*

VIN'DICATE, *v. t.* [L. *vindico.*] To defend; to justify; to support or maintain as true or correct, against denial, censure or objections.

When the respondent denies any proposition, the opponent must *vindicate* it. *Watts.*

Laugh where we must, be candid where we can;
But *vindicate* the ways of God to man. *Pope.*

2. To assert; to defend with success; to maintain; to prove to be just or valid; as, to *vindicate* a claim or title.

3. To defend with arms, or otherwise; as, to *vindicate* our rights.

4. To avenge; to punish; as a war to *vindicate* or punish infidelity. *Bacon.*

God is more powerful to exact subjection and to *vindicate* rebellion. *Pearson.*

[*This latter use is entirely obsolete.*]

VIN'DICATED, *pp.* Defended; supported; maintained; proved to be just or true.

VIN'DICATING, *ppr.* Defending; supporting against denial, censure, charge or impeachment; proving to be true or just; defending by force.

VINDICA'TION, *n.* [Fr. from L. *vindico.*]

1. The defense of any thing, or a justification against denial or censure, or against objections or accusations; as the *vindication* of opinions or of a creed; the *vindication* of the Scriptures against the objections and cavils of infidels.

2. The act of supporting by proof or legal process; the proving of any thing to be just; as the *vindication* of a title, claim or right.

3. Defense by force or otherwise; as the *vindication* of the rights of man; the *vindication* of our liberties or the rights of conscience.

VIN'DICATIVE, *a.* Tending to vindicate.

2. Revengeful. [This is now generally *vindictive.*]

VIN'DICATOR, *n.* One who vindicates; one who justifies or maintains; one who defends. *Dryden.*

VIN'DICATORY, *a.* Punitory; inflicting punishment; avenging.

The afflictions of Job were not *vindicatory* punishments. *Bramhall.*

2. Tending to vindicate; justificatory.

VINDIC'TIVE, *a.* [Fr. *vindicatif.*] Revengeful; given to revenge.

I am *vindictive* enough to repel force by force. *Dryden.*

VINDIC'TIVELY, *adv.* By way of revenge; revengefully.

VINDIC'TIVENESS, *n.* A revengeful temper.

2. Revengefulness.

VINE, *n.* [L. *vinea;* Fr. *vigne;* from the It. *vigna,* Sp. *viña,* a vineyard; W. *gwinien,* vine, and *gwin,* wine. See *Wine.*]

1. A plant that produces grapes, of the genus Vitis, and of a great number of varieties.

2. The long slender stem of any plant, that trails on the ground, or climbs and supports itself by winding round a fixed object, or by seizing any fixed thing with its tendrils or claspers. Thus we speak of the hop *vine,* the bean *vine,* the *vines* of melons, squashes, pumpkins, and other cucurbitaceous plants.

VI'NED, *a.* Having leaves like those of the vine. *Wotton.*

VI'NE-DRESSER, *n.* [*vine* and *dresser.*] One who dresses, trims, prunes and cultivates vines.

VI'NE-FRETTER, *n.* [*vine* and *fret.*] A small insect that injures vines, the aphis or puceron.

VIN'EGAR, *n.* [Fr. *vin,* wine, and *aigre,* sour.]

1. Vegetable acid; an acid liquor obtained from wine, cider, beer or other liquors, by the second or acetous fermentation. Vinegar may differ indefinitely in the degree of its acidity. When highly concentrated, it is called *radical vinegar.*

2. Any thing really or metaphorically sour. [*Not in use.*] *Shak.*

Vinegar of lead, a liquor formed by digesting ceruse or litharge with a sufficient quantity of vinegar to dissolve it.

VI'NE-GRUB, *n.* [*vine* and *grub.*] A little insect that infests vines; the vine-fretter or puceron. *Cyc.*

VI'NERY, *n.* In *gardening,* an erection for supporting vines and exposing them to artificial heat, consisting of a wall with stoves and flues.

VINEYARD, } *n.* [Sax. *vingeard;* Ir. *fion-*
VIN'YARD, } *ghort.* The correct orthography, from the Saxon, is *vinyard.*]

A plantation of vines producing grapes; properly, an inclosure or yard for grapevines.

VIN'NEWED, *a.* [Sax. *fynig.*] Moldy; musty. [*Not in use.*] *Newton.*

VIN'NEWEDNESS, *n.* Mustiness; moldiness. [*Not in use.*] *Barret.*

VIN'NY, *a.* [supra.] Moldy; musty. [*Not in use.*]

VIN'OLENCY, *n.* [L. *vinolentia*, from *vinum*, wine.] Drunkenness. [*Not used.*]

VIN'OLENT, *a.* Given to wine. [*Not used.*]

VINOS'ITY, *n.* State or quality of being vinous. *Scott.*

VI'NOUS, *a.* [Fr. *vineux*, from L. *vinum*, wine.]
Having the qualities of wine; pertaining to wine; as a *vinous* taste; a *vinous* flavor; *vinous* fermentation.

VINT'AGE, *n.* [Fr. *vendange*, from L. *vindemia.*]
1. The produce of the vine for the season. The *vintage* is abundant.
2. The time of gathering the crop of grapes.
3. The wine produced by the crop of grapes in one season. *Cyc.*

VINT'AGER, *n.* One that gathers the vintage.

VINT'NER, *n.* One who deals in wine; a wine-seller.

VINT'RY, *n.* A place where wine is sold. *Ainsworth.*

VI'NY, *a.* Belonging to vines; producing grapes.
2. Abounding in vines. *P. Fletcher.*

VI'OL, *n.* [Fr. *viole*; It. Sp. *viola*; Ir. *biol.*] A stringed musical instrument, of the same form as the violin, but larger, and having formerly six strings, to be struck with a bow. Viols are of different kinds. The largest of all is the *base viol*, whose tones are deep, soft and agreeable. The violin now takes the place of the old viol.

> Me softer airs befit, and softer strings
> Of lute, or *viol*, still more apt for mournful things. *Milton.*

VI'OLABLE, *a.* [L. *violabilis*. See *Violate.*]
That may be violated, broken or injured.

VIOLA'CEOUS, *a.* [L. *viola*, a violet.] Resembling violets. *Encyc.*

VI'OLATE, *v. t.* [Fr. *violer*; L. *violo*; It. *violare*; Sp. *violar.*]
1. To injure; to hurt; to interrupt; to disturb; as, to *violate* sleep. *Milton.*

> Kindness for man, and pity for his fate,
> May mix with bliss and yet not *violate*. *Dryden.*

2. To break; to infringe; to transgress; as, to *violate* the laws of the state, or the rules of good breeding; to *violate* the divine commands; to *violate* one's vows or promises. Promises and commands may be *violated* negatively, by non-observance.
3. To injure; to do violence to.

> Forbid to *violate* the sacred fruit. *Milton.*

4. To treat with irreverence; to profane; as, to *violate* the sanctity of a holy place.
5. To ravish; to compress by force.

VI'OLATED, *pp.* Injured; broken; transgressed; ravished.

VI'OLATING, *ppr.* Injuring; infringing; ravishing.

VIOLA'TION, *n.* [Fr.] The act of violating or injuring; interruption, as of sleep or peace.
2. Infringement; transgression; non-observance; as the *violation* of law or positive command; a *violation* of covenants, engagements and promises; a *violation* of vows.
3. Act of irreverence; profanation or contemptuous treatment of sacred things; as the *violation* of a church.
4. Ravishment; rape.

VI'OLATOR, *n.* One who violates, injures, interrupts or disturbs; as a *violator* of repose.
2. One who infringes or transgresses; as a *violator* of law.
3. One who profanes or treats with irreverence; as a *violator* of sacred things.
4. A ravisher.

VI'OLENCE, *n.* [L. *violentia.*] Physical force; strength of action or motion; as the *violence* of a storm; the *violence* of a blow or of a conflict.
2. Moral force; vehemence. The critic attacked the work with *violence*.
3. Outrage; unjust force; crimes of all kinds.

> The earth was filled with *violence*. Gen. vi.

4. Eagerness; vehemence.

> You ask with *violence*. *Shak.*

5. Injury; infringement. Offer no *violence* to the laws, or to the rules of civility.
6. Injury; hurt.

> Do *violence* to no man. Luke iii.

7. Ravishment; rape.

To do violence to or *on*, to attack; to murder.

> But, as it seems, *did violence on* herself. *Shak.*

To do violence to, to outrage; to force; to injure. He *does violence to* his own opinions.

VI'OLENCE, *v. t.* To assault; to injure; also, to bring by violence. [*Little used.*] *B. Jonson. Feltham.*

VI'OLENT, *a.* [Fr.; L. *violentus.*] Forcible; moving or acting with physical strength; urged or driven with force; as a *violent* wind; a *violent* stream; a *violent* assault or blow; a *violent* conflict.
2. Vehement; outrageous; as a *violent* attack on the minister.
3. Produced or continued by force; not spontaneous or natural.

> No *violent* state can be perpetual. *Burnet.*

4. Produced by violence; not natural; as a *violent* death.
5. Acting by violence; assailant; not authorized.

> Some *violent* hands were laid on Humphry's life. *Shak.*

6. Fierce; vehement; as a *violent* philippic; a *violent* remonstrance.

> We might be reckoned fierce and *violent*. *Hooker.*

7. Severe; extreme; as *violent* pains.
8. Extorted; not voluntary.

> Vows made in pain, are *violent* and void. *Milton.*

Violent presumption, in law, is presumption that arises from circumstances which necessarily attend such facts. Such circumstances being proved, the mind infers with confidence that the fact has taken place, and this confidence is a *violent presumption*, which amounts to proof.

VI'OLENT, *n.* An assailant. [*Not in use.*]

VI'OLENT, *v. t.* To urge with violence. [*Not used.*] *Fuller.*

VI'OLENTLY, *adv.* With force; forcibly; vehemently; as, the wind blows *violently*.

> Forfeitures must not be exacted *violently*. *Taylor.*

VI'OLET, *n.* [Fr. *violette*; It. *violetto*; L. *viola.*]
A plant and flower of the genus Viola, of many species.

VI'OLIN, *n.* [It. *violino*; Fr. *violon*; from *viol.*]
A musical instrument with four strings, played with a bow; a fiddle; one of the most perfect and most powerful instruments that has been invented. *Cyc.*

VI'OLINIST, *n.* A person skilled in playing on a violin. *Farey.*

VI'OLIST, *n.* A player on the viol. *Todd.*

VIOLONCEL'LO, *n.* [It.] A stringed instrument of music; a base viol of four strings, or a little base violin with long large strings, giving sounds an octave lower than the base violin. *Encyc.*

VIOLO'NO, *n.* A double base, a deep toned instrument. *Busby.*

VI'PER, *n.* [L. *vipera*; Fr. *vipere*; W. *gwiber*, from *gwib*, a quick course, a driving, flying or serpentine motion, a wandering.]
1. A serpent, a species of coluber, whose bite is remarkably venomous.

> A *viper* came out of the heat, and fastened on his hand. Acts xxix.

2. A person or thing mischievous or malignant. *Shak.*

VI'PERINE, *a.* [L. *viperinus.*] Pertaining to a viper or to vipers.

VI'PEROUS, *a.* [L. *vipereus.*] Having the qualities of a viper; malignant; venomous; as a *viperous* tongue. *Shak.*

VIPER'S BUGLOSS, *n.* A plant of the genus Echium.

VIPER'S GRASS, *n.* A plant of the genus Scorzonera.

VIRA'GO, *n.* [L. from *vir*, a man.] A woman of extraordinary stature, strength and courage; a female who has the robust body and masculine mind of a man; a female warrior.

> To arms! to arms! the fierce *virago* cries. *Pope.*

2. In common language, a bold, impudent, turbulent woman; a termagant.

VIRE, *n.* [Sp. *vira.*] An arrow. *Obs. Gower.*

VI'RELAY, *n.* [Fr. *virelai*, from *virer*, to turn.]
A song or little poem among the Provençal poets in France; a roundelay. It sometimes consisted of two rhymes only, and short verses, with stops. *Johnson. Cyc.*

> To which a lady sung a *virelay*. *Dryden.*

VI'RENT, *a.* [L. *virens*, from *vireo*, to flourish or be green.]
Green; verdant; fresh. *Brown.*

VIR'GATE, *a.* nearly *vurgate.* [L. *virga*, a rod.]
In *botany*, having the shape of a rod or wand; as a *virgate* stem.

VIR'GATE, *n.* A yardland. *Warton.*

VIRGE. [See *Verge.*]

VIRGIL'IAN, *a.* Pertaining to Virgil, the Roman poet.
2. Resembling the style of Virgil. *Young.*

VIR'GIN, *n.* nearly *vur'gin.* [It. *virgine*; Sp. *virgen*; Fr. *vierge*; L. *virgo.*]
1. A woman who has had no carnal knowledge of man.
2. A woman not a mother. [*Unusual.*] *Milton.*
3. The sign Virgo. [See *Virgo.*] *Milton.*

VIR'GIN, *a.* Pure; untouched; as *virgin* gold. *Woodward.*
2. Fresh; new; unused; as *virgin* soil. *Belknap.*

3. Becoming a virgin; maidenly; modest; indicating modesty; as a *virgin* blush; *virgin* shame. *Cowley.*
4. Pure; chaste.
VIR'ĠIN, *v. i.* To play the virgin; *a cant word.* *Shak.*
VIR'ĠINAL, *a.* Pertaining to a virgin; maidenly; as *virginal* chastity. *Hammond.*
VIR'ĠINAL, *n.* A keyed instrument of one string, jack and quill to each note, like a spinet, but in shape resembling the forte piano; *out of use.* *Cyc.* *Bacon.*
VIR'ĠINAL, *v. i.* To pat; to strike as on a virginal. [*A cant word.*] *Shak.*
VIRĠIN'ITY, *n.* [L. *virginitas.*] Maidenhood; the state of having had no carnal knowledge of man.
VIR'ĠIN'S BOWER, *n.* A plant of the genus Clematis.
VIR'GO, *n.* [L.] A sign of the zodiac which the sun enters in August; a constellation, containing according to the British catalogue, one hundred and ten stars. *Cyc.*
VIRID'ITY, *n.* [L. *viriditas,* from *vireo,* to be green.]
Greenness; verdure; the color of fresh vegetables. *Evelyn.*
VI'RILE, *a.* [L. *virilis,* from *vir,* a man, Sax. *wer;* Sans. *vira,* strong; from the root of L. *vireo.*]
1. Pertaining to a man, in the eminent sense of the word, [not to *man,* in the sense of the human race;] belonging to the male sex; as *virile* age.
2. Masculine; not *puerile* or *feminine;* as *virile* strength or vigor.
VIRIL'ITY, *n.* [Fr. *virilité;* L. *virilitas.*]
1. Manhood; the state of the male sex, which has arrived to the maturity and strength of a man, and to the power of procreation.
2. The power of procreation.
3. Character of man. [*Unusual.*]
VIR'TU, *n.* [It.] A love of the fine arts; a taste for curiosities. *Chesterfield.*
VIR'TUAL, *a.* [Fr. *virtuel;* from *virtue.* See *Virtue.*]
1. Potential; having the power of acting or of invisible efficacy without the material or sensible part.

> Every kind that lives,
> Fomented by his *virtual* power, and warm'd. *Milton.*

> Neither an actual nor *virtual* intention of the mind, but only that which may be gathered from the outward acts. *Stillingfleet.*

2. Being in essence or effect, not in fact; as the *virtual* presence of a man in his agent or substitute.
VIRTUAL'ITY, *n.* Efficacy. *Brown.*
VIR'TUALLY, *adv.* In efficacy or effect only; by means of some virtue or influence, or the instrumentality of something else. Thus the sun is *virtually* on earth by its light and heat. The citizens of an elective government are *virtually* present in the legislature by their representatives. A man may *virtually* agree to a proposition by silence or withholding objections. *Addison.* *Cyc.*
VIR'TUATE, *v. t.* To make efficacious. [*Not in use.*] *Harvey.*
VIRTUE, *n.* *vur'tu.* [Fr. *vertu;* It. *virtu;* Sp. *vertud;* L. *virtus,* from *vireo,* or its root. See *Worth.* The radical sense is strength, from straining, stretching, extending. This is the primary sense of L. *vir,* a man. Class Br.]
1. Strength; that substance or quality of physical bodies, by which they act and produce effects on other bodies. In this literal and proper sense, we speak of the *virtue* or *virtues* of plants in medicine, and the *virtues* of drugs. In decoctions, the *virtues* of plants are extracted. By long standing in the open air, the *virtues* are lost.
2. Bravery; valor. This was the predominant signification of *virtus* among the Romans.

> Trust to thy single *virtue.* *Shak.*

[*This sense is nearly or quite obsolete.*]
3. Moral goodness; the practice of moral duties and the abstaining from vice, or a conformity of life and conversation to the moral law. In this sense, *virtue* may be, and in many instances must be, distinguished from *religion.* The practice of moral duties merely from motives of convenience, or from compulsion, or from regard to reputation, is *virtue,* as distinct from *religion.* The practice of moral duties from sincere love to God and his laws, is virtue and religion. In this sense it is true,

> That *virtue* only makes our bliss below. *Pope.*

> *Virtue* is nothing but voluntary obedience to truth. *Dwight.*

4. A particular moral excellence; as the *virtue* of temperance, of chastity, of charity.

> Remember all his *virtues.* *Addison.*

5. Acting power; something efficacious.

> Jesus, knowing that *virtue* had gone out of him, turned— Mark iii.

6. Secret agency; efficacy without visible or material action.

> She moves the body which she doth possess,
> Yet no part toucheth, but by *virtue's* touch. *Davies.*

7. Excellence; or that which constitutes value and merit.

> —Terence, who thought the sole grace and *virtue* of their fable, the sticking in of sentences. *B. Jonson.*

8. One of the orders of the celestial hierarchy.

> Thrones, dominations, princedoms, *virtues,* powers. *Milton.*

9. Efficacy; power.

> He used to travel through Greece by *virtue* of this fable, which procured him reception in all the towns. *Addison.*

10. Legal efficacy or power; authority. A man administers the laws by *virtue* of a commission.
In virtue, in consequence; by the efficacy or authority.

> This they shall attain, partly *in virtue* of the promise of God, and partly *in virtue* of piety. *Atterbury.*

VIR'TUELESS, *a.* Destitute of virtue.
2. Destitute of efficacy or operating qualities.

> *Virtueless* she wish'd all herbs and charms. *Fairfax.*

VIRTUO'SO, *n.* [It.] A man skilled in the fine arts, particularly in music; or a man skilled in antiquities, curiosities and the like.

> *Virtuoso* the Italians call a man who loves the noble arts, and is a critic in them. *Dryden.*

VIRTUO'SOSHIP, *n.* The pursuits of a virtuoso. *Hurd.*
VIR'TUOUS, *a.* Morally good; acting in conformity to the moral law; practicing the moral duties, and abstaining from vice; as a *virtuous* man.
2. Being in conformity to the moral or divine law; as a *virtuous* action; a *virtuous* life.

> The mere performance of *virtuous* actions does not denominate an agent virtuous. *Price.*

3. Chaste; *applied to women.*
4. Efficacious by inherent qualities; as *virtuous* herbs; *virtuous* drugs. [*Not in use.*] *Chapman.*
5. Having great or powerful properties; as *virtuous* steel; a *virtuous* staff; a *virtuous* ring. [*Not in use.*] *Milton.* *Spenser.*
6. Having medicinal qualities. [*Not used.*] *Bacon.*
VIR'TUOUSLY, *adv.* In a virtuous manner; in conformity with the moral law or with duty; as a life *virtuously* spent. *Denham.*

> A child *virtuously* educated. *Addison.*

VIR'TUOUSNESS, *n.* The state or character of being virtuous. *Spenser.*
VIR'ULENCE, } *n.* [from *virulent.*] That
VIR'ULENCY, } quality of a thing which renders it extremely active in doing injury; acrimony; malignancy; as the *virulence* of poison.
2. Acrimony of temper; extreme bitterness or malignity; as the *virulence* of enmity or malice; the *virulence* of satire; to attack a man with *virulence.* *Addison.*
VIR'ULENT, *a.* [L. *virulentus,* from *virus,* poison, that is, strength, from the same root as *vir, vireo.* See *Venom.*]
1. Extremely active in doing injury; very poisonous or venomous. No poison is more *virulent* than that of some species of serpents.
2. Very bitter in enmity; malignant; as a *virulent* invective.
VIR'ULENTLY, *adv.* With malignant activity; with bitter spite or severity.
VI'RUS, *n.* [L. See *Virulent.*] Foul or contagious matter of an ulcer, pustule, &c.; poison.
VIS'AGE, *n.* *s* as *z.* [Fr.; from It. *visaggio;* from L. *visus, video.*]
The face; the countenance or look of a person, or of other animal; chiefly applied to human beings; as a wolfish *visage.* *Shak.*

> Love and beauty still that *visage* grace. *Waller.*

> His *visage* was so marred, more than any man. Is. lii.

VIS'AĠED, *a.* Having a visage or countenance. *Milton.*
VIS-A-VIS, *n.* [Fr. opposite, face to face.] A carriage in which two persons sit face to face.
VIS'CERA, *n.* [L.] The bowels or intestines; the contents of the abdomen and thorax.
In its most general sense, the organs contained in any cavity of the body, particularly in the three venters, the head, thorax and abdomen. *Cyc.* *Parr.*
VIS'CERAL, *a.* [L. *viscera.*] Pertaining to the viscera or intestines.
2. Feeling; having sensibility. [*Unusual.*] *Reynolds.*

VIS′CERATE, *v. t.* [supra.] To exenterate; to embowel; to deprive of the entrails or viscera. [*Eviscerate* is generally used.]

VIS′CID, *a.* [L. *viscidus; viscus*, birdlime.] Glutinous; sticky; tenacious; not readily separating; as, turpentine, tar, gums, &c. are more or less *viscid*.

VISCID′ITY, *n.* Glutinousness; tenacity; stickiness.

2. Glutinous concretion. *Floyer.*

VISCOS′ITY, **VIS′COUSNESS**, *n.* Glutinousness; tenacity; viscidity; that quality of soft substances which makes them adhere so as not to be easily parted.

VISCOUNT, *n. vi′count.* [L. *vice-comes*; Fr. *vicomte.*]

1. An officer who formerly supplied the place of the count or earl; the sherif of the county. *England.*

2. A degree or title of nobility next in rank to an earl. *Cowel. England.*

VISCOUNTESS, *n. vi′countess.* The lady of a viscount; a peeress of the fourth order. *Johnson.*

VISCOUNTSHIP, **VISCOUNTY**, *n. vi′countship.* *vi′county.* The quality and office of a viscount. *Williams.*

VIS′COUS, *a.* [Fr. *visqueux*; from L. *viscus*, birdlime.]

Glutinous; clammy; sticky; adhesive; tenacious; as a *viscous* juice.

VISE, *n.* [Fr. *vis*, a screw.] An engine or instrument for griping and holding things, closed by a screw; *used by artificers.*

VISH′NU, *n.* In *the Hindoo mythology*, the name of one of the chief deities of the trimurti or triad. He is the second person of this unity, and a personification of the preserving powers. *Cyc. Encyc.*

VISIBIL′ITY, *n.* s as z. [from *visible*; Fr. *visibilité.*]

1. The state or quality of being perceivable to the eye; as the *visibility* of minute particles, or of distant objects.

2. The state of being discoverable or apparent; conspicuousness; as the perpetual *visibility* of the church. *Stillingfleet.*

VIS′IBLE, *a.* s as z. [Fr. from L. *visibilis.*]

1. Perceivable by the eye; that can be seen; as a *visible* star; the least spot is *visible* on white paper; air agitated by heat becomes *visible*; as the air near a heated stove, or over a dry sandy plain, appears like pellucid waves.

Virtue made *visible* in outward grace. *Young.*

2. Discovered to the eye; as *visible* spirits. *Shak.*

3. Apparent; open; conspicuous. Factions at court became more *visible*. *Clarendon.*

Visible church, in theology, the apparent church of Christ; the whole body of professed believers in Christ, as contradistinguished from the real or *invisible* church, consisting of sanctified persons.

Visible horizon, the line that bounds the sight.

VIS′IBLENESS, *n.* State or quality of being visible; visibility.

VIS′IBLY, *adv.* In a manner perceptible to the eye. The day is *visibly* governed by the sun; the tides are *visibly* governed by the moon.

VI″SION, *n.* s as z. [Fr. from L. *visio*, from *video, visus.*]

1. The act of seeing external objects; actual sight.

Faith here is turned into *vision* there. *Hammond.*

2. The faculty of seeing; sight. *Vision* is far more perfect and acute in some animals than in man.

3. Something imagined to be seen, though not real; a phantom; a specter.

No dreams, but *visions* strange. *Sidney.*

4. In *Scripture*, a revelation from God; an appearance or exhibition of something supernaturally presented to the minds of the prophets, by which they were informed of future events. Such were the *visions* of Isaiah, of Amos, of Ezekiel, &c.

5. Something imaginary; the production of fancy. *Locke.*

6. Any thing which is the object of sight. *Thomson.*

VI″SIONAL, *a.* Pertaining to a vision. *Waterland.*

VI″SIONARY, *a.* [Fr. *visionnaire.*] Affected by phantoms; disposed to receive impressions on the imagination.

Or lull to rest the *visionary* maid. *Pope.*

2. Imaginary; existing in imagination only; not real; having no solid foundation; as a *visionary* prospect; a *visionary* scheme or project.

VI″SIONARY, *n.* One whose imagination is disturbed.

2. One who forms impracticable schemes; one who is confident of success in a project which others perceive to be idle and fanciful. [*Visionist*, in a like sense, is not used.]

VIS′IT, *v. t.* s as z. [L. *visito*; Fr. *visiter*; It. *visitare*; from L. *viso*, to go to see; W. *gwest, gwesta*, to visit, to go about; *gwest*, a going, a visit; *gwes*, that is going or moving. We see the sense is to go, to move to.]

1. To go or come to see; to attend. The physician *visits* his patient and prescribes. One friend *visits* another from respect or affection. Paul and Barnabas *visited* the churches they had planted, to know their state and confirm their faith. Men *visit* England, France or Italy in their travels.

2. To go or come to see for inspection, examination, correction of abuses, &c.; as, a bishop *visits* his diocese; a superintendant *visits* those persons or works which are under his care.

3. To salute with a present.

Samson *visited* his wife with a kid. Judges xv.

4. To go to and to use; as, to *visit* the springs.

To visit in mercy, in *Scriptural language*, to be propitious; to grant requests; to deliver from trouble; to support and comfort. It is thus God *visits* his people. Gen. xxi. Zech. x. Luke xii.

To visit with the rod, to punish. Ps. lxxxix.

To visit in wrath, or *visit iniquity* or *sins upon*, to chastise; to bring judgments on; to afflict. Ex. xx.

To visit the fatherless and widow, or *the sick and imprisoned*, to show them regard and pity, and relieve their wants. Matt xxv. James i.

VIS′IT, *v. i.* To keep up the interchange of civilities and salutations; to practice going to see others. We ought not to *visit* for pleasure or ceremony on the sabbath.

VIS′IT, *n.* The act of going to see another, or of calling at his house; a waiting on; as a *visit* of civility or respect; a *visit* of ceremony; a short *visit*; a long *visit*; a pleasant *visit*.

2. The act of going to see; as a *visit* to Saratoga or to Niagara.

3. A going to see or attending on; as the *visit* of a physician.

4. The act of going to view or inspect; as the *visit* of a trustee or inspector.

VIS′ITABLE, *a.* Liable or subject to be visited. All hospitals built since the reformation are *visitable* by the king or lord chancellor.

VIS′ITANT, *n.* One that goes or comes to see another; one who is a guest in the house of a friend.

When the *visitant* comes again he is no more a stranger. *South.*

VISITA′TION, *n.* [Fr. from L. *visito.*] The act of visiting.

Nothing but peace and gentle *visitation*. *Shak.*

2. Object of visit.

O flowers!
My early *visitation* and my last. *Milton.*
[*Unusual.*]

3. In *law*, the act of a superior or superintending officer, who visits a corporation, college, church or other house, to examine into the manner in which it is conducted, and see that its laws and regulations are duly observed and executed. In England, the *visitation* of the diocese belongs to the bishop; parochial *visitation* belongs peculiarly to the archdeacons. *Cyc.*

4. In *Scripture*, and in *a religious sense*, the sending of afflictions and distresses on men to punish them for their sins, or to prove them. Hence afflictions, calamities and judgments are called *visitations*.

What will ye do in the day of *visitation?* Is. x.

5. Communication of divine love; exhibition of divine goodness and mercy. *Hooker.*

VIS′ITED, *pp.* Waited on; attended; inspected; subjected to sufferings; favored with relief or mercy.

VIS′ITING, *ppr.* Going or coming to see; attending on, as a physician; inspecting officially; afflicting; showing mercy to.

2. *a.* Authorized to visit and inspect; as a *visiting* committee.

VIS′ITING, *n.* The act of going to see or of attending; visitation.

VIS′ITOR, *n.* [Fr. *visiteur.*] One who comes or goes to see another, as in civility or friendship.

2. A superior or person authorized to visit a corporation or any institution, for the purpose of seeing that the laws and regulations are observed, or that the duties and conditions prescribed by the founder or by law, are duly performed and executed.

The king is the *visitor* of all lay corporations. *Blackstone.*

VISITO′RIAL, *a.* [from *visitor*; written improperly *visitatorial.*]

Belonging to a judicial visitor or superintendant.

An archdeacon has *visitorial* power in parishes *Ayliffe.*

VI'SIVE, *a.* [from L. *visus.*] Pertaining to the power of seeing; formed in the act of seeing. [*Not in use.*] *Brown.*

VISNE, *n. veen.* [Norm. from L. *vicinia.*] Neighborhood. [See *Venue.*]

VIS'NOMY, *n.* [a barbarous contraction of *physiognomy.*] Face; countenance. [*Not in use.*] *Spenser.*

VI'SOR, *n. s* as *z.* [Fr. *visiere;* It. *visiera;* from L. *visus, video;* written also *visard, visar, vizard.*]

1. A head piece or mask used to disfigure and disguise.

My weaker government since, makes you pull off the *visor.* *Sidney.*

Swarms of knaves the *visor* quite disgrace. *Young.*

2. A perforated part of a helmet. *Sidney.*

VI'SORED, *a.* Wearing a visor; masked; disguised. *Milton.*

VIS'TA, *n.* [It. sight; from L. *visus, video.*] A view or prospect through an avenue, as between rows of trees; hence, the trees or other things that form the avenue.

The finish'd garden to the view
Its *vistas* opens and its alleys green. *Thomson.*

VIS'UAL, *a. s* as *z.* [Fr. *visuel;* It. *visuale;* from L. *visus.*]

Pertaining to sight; used in sight; serving as the instrument of seeing; as the *visual* nerve. *Bacon. Milton.*

The air,
No where so clear, sharpen'd his *visual* ray. *Milton.*

Visual point, in *perspective*, a point in the horizontal line, in which all the ocular rays unite. *Cyc.*

Visual rays, lines of light, imagined to come from the object to the eye. *Cyc.*

VI'TAL, *a.* [L. *vitalis*, from *vita*, life. This must be a contraction of *victa*, for *vivo* forms *vixi, victus;* Gr. *βιος*, from *βιοω*, contracted.]

1. Pertaining to life, either animal or vegetable; as *vital* energies; *vital* powers.

2. Contributing to life; necessary to life; as *vital* air; *vital* blood.

3. Containing life.

Spirits that live throughout,
Vital in every part— *Milton.*
And *vital* virtue infus'd, and *vital* warmth. *Milton.*

4. Being the seat of life; being that on which life depends.

The dart flew on, and pierc'd a *vital* part. *Pope.*

5. Very necessary; highly important; essential. Religion is a business of *vital* concern. Peace is of *vital* importance to our country.

6. So disposed as to live.

Pythagoras and Hippocrates affirm the birth of the seventh month to be *vital.* *Brown.*

[*Little used.*]

Vital air, pure air or oxygen gas, which is essential to animal life.

VITAL'ITY, *n.* [from *vital.*] Power of subsisting in life; the principle of animation, or of life; as the *vitality* of vegetable seeds or of eggs. *Ray.*

2. The act of living; animation.

VI'TALIZE, *v. t.* To give life. *Trans. Pausanias.*

VI'TALLY, *adv.* In such a manner as to give life.

The organic structure of human bodies, by which they are fitted to live and move, and to be *vitally* informed by the soul, is the workmanship of a most wise and beneficent maker. *Bentley.*

2. Essentially; as *vitally* important.

VI'TALS, *n. plu.* Parts of animal bodies essential to life, such as the viscera. *Prior.*

2. The part essential to life, or to a sound state. Corruption of manners preys upon the *vitals* of a state.

VIT'ELLARY, *n.* [L. *vitellus*, the yelk of an egg.]

The place where the yelk of an egg swims in the white. [*Little used.*] *Brown.*

VI''TIATE, *v. t.* [L. *vitio.* See *Vice* and *Viciate.*]

1. To injure the substance or qualities of a thing, so as to impair or spoil its use and value. Thus we say, luxury *vitiates* the humors of the body; evil examples *vitiate* the morals of youth; language is *vitiated* by foreign idioms.

This undistinguishing complaisance will *vitiate* the taste of readers. *Garth.*

2. To render defective; to destroy; as the validity or binding force of an instrument or transaction. Any undue influence exerted on a jury *vitiates* their verdict. Fraud *vitiates* a contract.

VI''TIATED, *pp.* Depraved; rendered impure; rendered defective and void.

VI''TIATING, *ppr.* Depraving; rendering of no validity.

VITIA'TION, *n.* The act of vitiating; depravation; corruption; as the *vitiation* of the blood. *Harvey.*

2. A rendering invalid; as the *vitiation* of a contract.

VITILIT'IGATE, *v.i.* [L. *vitiosus* and *litigo.*] To contend in law litigiously or cavilously. [*Not in use.*]

VITILITIGA'TION, *n.* Cavilous litigation. [*Not in use.*] *Hudibras.*

Vitious, vitiously, vitiousness. [See *Vicious* and its derivatives.]

VITREO-ELEC'TRIC, *a.* Containing or exhibiting positive electricity, or that which is excited by rubbing glass. *Ure.*

VIT'REOUS, *a.* [L. *vitreus*, from *vitrum*, glass or woad; W. *gwydyr*, glass, a greenish blue color.] Pertaining to glass.

2. Consisting of glass; as a *vitreous* substance.

3. Resembling glass; as the *vitreous* humor of the eye, so called from its resembling melted glass. [See *Humor.*]

VIT'REOUSNESS, *n.* The quality or state of being vitreous; resemblance of glass.

VITRES'CENCE, *n.* [from L. *vitrum*, glass.] Glassiness; or the quality of being capable of conversion into glass; susceptibility of being formed into glass. *Kirwan.*

VITRES'CENT, *a.* Capable of being formed into glass; tending to become glass.

VITRES'CIBLE, *a.* That can be vitrified. *Encyc.*

VITRIFAC'TION, *n.* [See *Vitrify.*] The act, process or operation of converting into glass by heat; as the *vitrifaction* of sand, flint and pebbles with alkaline salts.

VIT'RIFIABLE, *a.* [from *vitrify.*] Capable of being converted into glass by heat and fusion. Flint and alkaline salts are *vitrifiable.*

VIT'RIFICABLE, for *vitrifiable.* [*Not used.*]

VIT'RIFICATE, for *vitrify.* [*Not used.*] *Bacon.*

VITRIFICA'TION, for *vitrifaction.* [See *Vitrifaction*, which is generally used.]

VIT'RIFIED, *pp.* Converted into glass.

VIT'RIFORM, *a.* [L. *vitrum*, glass, and *form.*]

Having the form or resemblance of glass. *Fourcroy.*

VIT'RIFY, *v. t.* [L. *vitrum*, glass, and *facio*, to make.]

To convert into glass by fusion or the action of heat; as, to *vitrify* sand and alkaline salts.

VIT'RIFY, *v. i.* To become glass; to be converted into glass.

Chimists make vessels of animal substances calcined, which will not *vitrify* in the fire. *Arbuthnot.*

VIT'RIOL, *n.* [Fr. *vitriol;* It. *vitriuolo;* Sp. *vitriolo;* from L. *vitrum*, glass; perhaps from its color.]

1. In *mineralogy*, native vitriol is a substance of a grayish or yellowish white color, apple green, or sky blue, and when decomposed, covered with an ochery crust. It occurs in masses, disseminated, stalactical, or capillary. Externally, it is dull and rough; internally, it is more or less shining, with a vitreous silky structure. It is called by manufacturers *copperas*, a name derived from the flower or efflorescence of copper. This substance is seen only in cabinets.

2. In *chimistry*, a combination of the acid of sulphur with any metallic substance; but chiefly *green vitriol*, or sulphate of iron; *blue vitriol*, or sulphate of copper, and *white vitriol*, or sulphate of zink. *Cyc. Fourcroy.*

All metals may be converted into *vitriols*, by dissolving them with acid spirits, and suffering them to stand and crystalize.

VIT'RIOLATE, *v. t.* To convert, as sulphur in any compound, into sulphuric acid, formerly called vitriolic acid. Thus the sulphuret of iron *vitriolated*, becomes sulphate of iron, or green vitriol.

VIT'RIOLATED, *pp.* Converted into sulphuric acid or vitriol.

VIT'RIOLATING, *ppr.* Turning into sulphuric acid or vitriol.

VITRIOLA'TION, *n.* The act or process of converting into sulphuric acid or vitriol.

VITRIOL'IC, *a.* Pertaining to vitriol; having the qualities of vitriol, or obtained from vitriol.

Vitriolic acid, in modern chimistry is denominated *sulphuric acid*, the base of it being sulphur; sulphur completely saturated with oxygen.

VIT'RIOLIZABLE, *a.* Capable of being converted into sulphuric acid.

VITRIOLIZA'TION. [See *Vitriolation.*]

VIT'RIOLIZE. [See *Vitriolate.*]

VIT'RIOLIZED. [See *Vitriolated.*]

VIT'RIOLIZING. [See *Vitriolating.*]

VIT'ULINE, *a.* [L. *vitulinus.*] Belonging to a calf, or to veal.

VITU'PERABLE, *a.* [See *Vituperate.*] Blameworthy; censurable. [*Not used.*]

VITU'PERATE, *v. t.* [L. *vitupero.*] To blame; to censure. [*Little used.*]

VITUPERA'TION, *n.* [L. *vituperatio.*] Blame; censure. [*Little used.*]

VITU'PERATIVE, *a.* Uttering or writing censure; containing censure. *Pope.*

VIVA'CIOUS, *a.* [L. *vivax*, from *vivo*, to live.]

1. Lively; active; sprightly in temper or conduct. *Howell.*

2. Long lived. [*Not in use.*] *Bentley.*

3. Having vigorous powers of life; as *vivacious* plants. *Med. Repos.*

VIVA'CIOUSNESS, *n.* Activity; liveliness; sprightliness of temper or behavior; vivacity. *Dryden.*

2. Power of living; also, long life. [*Not in use.*] *Brown. Boyle.*

VIVAC'ITY, *n.* [Fr. *vivacité*; L. *vivacitas.*]

1. Liveliness; sprightliness of temper or behavior; as a lady of great *vivacity.*

2. Air of life and activity; as *vivacity* of countenance.

3. Life; animation; spirits; as the *vivacity* of a discourse.

4. Power of living. [*Not used.*] *Boyle.*

5. Longevity. [*Not in use.*] *Brown.*

VI'VARY, *n.* [L. *vivarium*, from *vivo*, to live.]

A warren; a place for keeping living animals, as a pond, a park, &c. *Cowel.*

Viva voce, [L.] by word of mouth; as, to vote *viva voce.*

VIVE, *a.* [Fr. *vif*; L. *vivus.*] Lively; forcible. [*Not in use.*] *Bacon.*

VI'VELY, *adv.* In a lively manner. [*Not used.*]

VI'VENCY, *n.* [L. *vivens*, from *vivo.*] Manner of supporting life or vegetation. [*Not in use.*] *Brown.*

VIVES, *n.* A disease of animals, particularly of horses, seated in the glands under the ear, where a tumor is formed which sometimes ends in suppuration. *Cyc.*

VIV'IANITE, *n.* A phosphate of iron, of various shades of blue and green. *Phillips.*

VIV'ID, *a.* [L. *vividus*, from *vivo*, to live.]

1. Lively; sprightly; active.

> Body is a fit workhouse for sprightly *vivid* faculties to exert themselves in. *South.*

2. Lively; sprightly; forming brilliant images, or painting in lively colors; as a *vivid* imagination.

3. Bright; strong; exhibiting the appearance of life or freshness; as the *vivid* colors of the rainbow; the *vivid* green of flourishing vegetables.

> Arts which present, with all the *vivid* charms of painting, the human face and human form divine. *Bp. Hobart.*

VIV'IDLY, *adv.* With life; with strength.

> Sensitive objects affect a man much more *vividly* than those which affect only his mind. *South.*

2. With brightness; in bright colors. *Boyle.*

3. In glowing colors; with animated exhibition to the mind. The orator *vividly* represented the miseries of his client.

VIV'IDNESS, *n.* Life; strength; sprightliness.

2. Strength of coloring; brightness.

VIVIF'IC, } *a.* [L. *vivificus.* See *Vivify.*]
VIVIF'ICAL, } Giving life; reviving; enlivening. *Bailey.*

VIV'IFICATE, *v. t.* [L. *vivifico*; *vivus*, alive, and *facio*, to make.]

1. To give life to; to animate. [See *Vivify.*] *More.*

2. In *chimistry*, to recover from such a change of form as seems to destroy the essential qualities; or to give to natural bodies new luster, force and vigor. *Cyc.*

VIVIFICA'TION, *n.* The act of giving life; revival. *Bacon.*

2. Among *chimists*, the act of giving new luster, force and vigor; as the *vivification* of mercury. *Cyc.*

VIV'IFICATIVE, *a.* Able to animate or give life. *More.*

VIV'IFIED, *pp.* Revived; endued with life.

VIV'IFY, *v. t.* [Fr. *vivifier*; L. *vivifico*; *vivus*, alive, and *facio*, to make.]

To endue with life; to animate; to make to be living.

> Sitting on eggs doth *vivify*, not nourish. *Bacon.*

VIV'IFYING, *ppr.* Enduing with life; communicating life to.

VIVIP'AROUS, *a.* [L. *vivus*, alive, and *pario*, to bear.]

1. Producing young in a living state, as all mammifers; as distinguished from *oviparous*, producing eggs, as fowls. If fowls were *viviparous*, it is difficult to see how the female would fly during pregnancy.

2. In *botany*, producing its offspring alive, either by bulbs instead of seeds, or by the seeds themselves germinating on the plant, instead of falling, as they usually do; as a *viviparous* plant. *Martyn.*

VIX'EN, *n.* [*vixen* is a she fox, or a fox's cub.]

A froward, turbulent, quarrelsome woman. *Shak.*

VIX'ENLY, *a.* Having the qualities of a vixen. *Barrow.*

VIZ. a contraction of *videlicet*; to wit, that is, namely.

VIZ'ARD, *n.* A mask. [See *Visor.*]

VIZ'ARD, *v. t.* To mask.

VIZ'IER, } *n.* [Ar. from وزر wazara, to
VI'ZER, } bear, to sustain, to administer.] The chief minister of the Turkish empire.

VO'CABLE, *n.* [L. *vocabulum*; It. *vocabolo.* See *Voice.*]

A word; a term; a name. *Asiat. Res.*

VOCAB'ULARY, *n.* [Fr. *vocabulaire*, from L. *vocabulum*, a word.]

A list or collection of the words of a language, arranged in alphabetical order and explained; a dictionary or lexicon. We often use *vocabulary* in a sense somewhat different from that of *dictionary*, restricting the signification to the list of words; as when we say, the *vocabulary* of Johnson is more full or extensive than that of Entick. We rarely use the word as synonymous with *dictionary*, but in the other countries the corresponding word is so used, and this may be so used in English.

VO'CAL, *a.* [Fr. from L. *vocalis.* See *Voice.*]

1. Having a voice.

> To hill or valley, fountain or fresh shade,
> Made *vocal* by my song. *Milton.*

2. Uttered or modulated by the voice; as *vocal* melody; *vocal* prayer; *vocal* praise.

Vocal music, music made by the voice, in distinction from instrumental music; hence, music or tunes set to words, to be performed by the human voice.

VO'CAL, *n.* Among the Romanists, a man who has a right to vote in certain elections. *Cyc.*

VOCAL'ITY, *n.* [L. *vocalitas.*] Quality of being utterable by the voice; as the *vocality* of the letters. *Holder.*

VO'CALIZE, *v. t.* To form into voice; to make vocal.

> It is one thing to give impulse to breath alone, and another to *vocalize* that breath. *Holder.*

VO'CALIZED, *pp.* Made vocal; formed into voice.

VO'CALIZING, *ppr.* Forming into voice or sound.

VO'CALLY, *adv.* With voice; with an audible sound.

2. In words; as, to express desires *vocally.* *Hale.*

VOCA'TION, *n.* [Fr. from L. *vocatio*, from *voco*, to call. See *Voice.*]

1. Among *divines*, a calling by the will of God; or the bestowment of God's distinguishing grace upon a person or nation, by which that person or nation is put in the way of salvation; as the *vocation* of the Jews under the old dispensation, and of the Gentiles under the gospel.

2. Summons; call; inducement.

> What can be urged for them who, not having the *vocation* of poverty to scribble, out of mere wantonness make themselves ridiculous! *Dryden.*

3. Designation or destination to a particular state or profession.

> None is to enter the ecclesiastic or monastic state, without a particular *vocation.* *Cyc.*

4. Employment; calling; occupation; trade; a word that includes professions as well as mechanical occupations. Let every divine, every physician, every lawyer, and every mechanic, be faithful and diligent in his *vocation.*

VOC'ATIVE, *a.* [Fr. *vocatif*; L. *vocativus.*] Relating to calling; as the *vocative* case in grammar.

VOC'ATIVE, *n.* In *grammar*, the fifth case or state of nouns in the Latin language; or the case in any language, in which a word is placed when the person is addressed; as *Domine*, O Lord.

VOCIF'ERATE, *v. i.* [L. *vocifero*; *vox* and *fero.*] To cry out with vehemence; to exclaim.

VOCIF'ERATE, *v. t.* To utter with a loud voice.

VOCIF'ERATING, *ppr.* Crying out with vehemence; uttering with a loud voice.

VOCIFERA'TION, *n.* A violent outcry; vehement utterance of the voice. *Arbuthnot.*

VOCIF'EROUS, *a.* Making a loud outcry; clamorous; noisy; as *vociferous* heralds. *Chapman.*

VOGUE, *n.* vōg. [Fr. *vogue*, a rowing; It. *voga*, a rowing, mode, fashion; *vogare*, to row; Sp. *voga*; *vogar*, to row. This word belongs to the family of *Bg*, *Wg.* See *Wag* and *Way.* The sense of *vogue* is way, or the *going* of the world.]

The way or fashion of people at any particular time; temporary mode, custom or practice; popular reception for the time. We say, a particular form of dress is now in *vogue*; an amusing writer is now in *vogue*; such opinions are now in *vogue.*

The phrase, the *vogue of the world*, used by good writers formerly, is nearly or quite obsolete.

Use may revive the obsoletest word,
And banish those that now are most in *vogue*.
Roscommon.

VOICE, *n.* [Fr. *voix*; L. *vox*; It. *voce*; Sp. *voz*; Gaelic, *bagh*, a word; *baigham*, to speak to; Ir. *focal*, a word; Sans. *vach*, to speak, L. *voco*. The sense of the verb is to throw, to drive out sound; and *voice* is that which is driven out.]

1. Sound or audible noise uttered by the mouth, either of human beings or of other animals. We say, the *voice* of a man is loud or clear; the *voice* of a woman is soft or musical; the *voice* of a dog is loud or harsh; the *voice* of a bird is sweet or melodious. The *voice* of human beings is articulate; that of beasts, inarticulate. The *voices* of men are different, and when uttered together, are often dissonant.
2. Any sound made by the breath; as the trumpet's *voice*.
3. A vote; suffrage; opinion or choice expressed. Originally *voice* was the oral utterance of choice, but it now signifies any vote however given.

Some laws ordain, and some attend the choice
Of holy senates, and elect by *voice*. *Dryden.*

I have no words;
My *voice* is in my sword. *Shak.*

4. Language; words; expression.

Let us call on God in the *voice* of his church. *Fell.*

5. In *Scripture*, command; precept.

Ye would not be obedient to the *voice* of the Lord your God. Deut. viii.

6. Sound.

After the fire, a still small *voice*. 1 Kings xix.
Canst thou thunder with a *voice* like him? Job xl.
The floods have lifted up their *voice*. Ps. xciii.

7. Language; tone; mode of expression.

I desire to be present with you now, and to change my *voice*. Gal. iv.

8. In *grammar*, a particular mode of inflecting or conjugating verbs; as the active *voice*; the passive *voice*.

VOICE, *v. t.* To rumor; to report.

It was *voiced* that the king purposed to put to death Edward Plantagenet. [*Little used.*] *Shak.*

2. To fit for producing the proper sounds; to regulate the tone of; as, to *voice* the pipes of an organ. *Ed. Encyc.*
3. To vote.

VOICE, *v. i.* To clamor; to exclaim. *Obs.* *Bacon.*

VOIC'ED, *pp.* Fitted to produce the proper tones.

2. *a.* Furnished with a voice. *Denham.*

VOICELESS, *a.* *vois'less.* Having no voice or vote. *Coke.*

VOID, *a.* [Fr. *vuide*; It. *voto*; L. *viduus*; Sw. *öde*; G. Dan. *öde*, waste, which seems to be the Eng. *wide*; so *waste* and *vast* are from one root. It coincides with Gr. ἰδιος, and the root of L. *divido*, Ar. بدّ badda, to separate. Class Bd. No. 1. See also No. 48.]

1. Empty; vacant; not occupied with any visible matter; as a *void* space or place. 1 Kings xxii.
2. Empty; without inhabitants or furniture. Gen. i.
3. Having no legal or binding force; null; not effectual to bind parties, or to convey or support a right; not sufficient to produce its effect. Thus a deed not duly signed and sealed, is *void*. A fraudulent contract is *void*, or may be rendered *void*.

My word shall not return to me *void*, but it shall accomplish that which I please. Is. lv.
I will make *void* the counsel of Judah and Jerusalem in this place. Jer. xix.

4. Free; clear; as a conscience *void* of offense. Acts xxiv.
5. Destitute; as *void* of learning; *void* of reason or common sense.

He that is *void* of wisdom, despiseth his neighbor. Prov. xi.

6. Unsupplied; vacant; unoccupied; having no incumbent.

Divers offices that had been long *void*. *Camden.*

7. Unsubstantial; vain.

Lifeless idol, *void* and vain. *Pope.*

Void space, in physics, a vacuum.
To make void, to violate; to transgress.

They have *made void* thy law. Ps. cxix.

2. To render useless or of no effect. Rom. iv.

VOID, *n.* An empty space; a vacuum.

Pride, where wit fails, steps in to our defense,
And fills up all the mighty *void* of sense. *Pope.*

Th' illimitable *void*. *Thomson.*

VOID, *v. t.* To quit; to leave.

Bid them come down,
Or *void* the field. *Shak.*

2. To emit; to send out; to evacuate; as, to *void* excrementitious matter; to *void* worms.
3. To vacate; to annul; to nullify; to render of no validity or effect.

It had become a practice—to *void* the security given for money borrowed. *Clarendon.*

4. To make or leave vacant.

VOID, *v. i.* To be emitted or evacuated. *Wiseman.*

VOID'ABLE, *a.* That may be annulled or made void, or that may be adjudged void, invalid or of no force.

—Such administration is not void, but *voidable* by sentence. *Ayliffe.*

2. That may be evacuated.

VOID'ANCE, *n.* The act of emptying.

2. The act of ejecting from a benefice; ejection.
3. Vacancy; want of an incumbent. *Cyc.*
4. Evasion; subterfuge. *Bacon.*

VOID'ED, *pp.* Thrust out; evacuated.

2. *a.* In *heraldry*, having the inner or middle part cut out, as an ordinary. *Cyc.*

VOID'ER, *n.* A basket in which broken meat is carried from the table. *Cleaveland.*

2. One who evacuates.
3. One who nullifies.
4. In *heraldry*, one of the ordinaries, whose figure is much like that of the flanch or flasque.
5. In *agriculture*, a provincial name of a kind of shallow basket of open work. *England.*

VOID'ING, *ppr.* Ejecting; evacuating.

2. Making or declaring void, or of no force.
3. Quitting; leaving.
4. *a.* Receiving what is ejected; as a *voiding* lobby. *Shak.*

VOID'NESS, *n.* Emptiness; vacuity; destitution.

2. Nullity; inefficacy; want of binding force.
3. Want of substantiality. *Hakewill.*

VOI'TURE, *n.* [Fr. *id.*; It. *vettura*, from L. *vectus*, *veho.*] Carriage. [*Not English.*] *Arbuthnot.*

VOLAL'KALI, *n.* Volatile alkali; *by contraction.* *Kirwan, Geol.*

VO'LANT, *a.* [Fr. flying, from *voler*, L. *volo*, to fly.]

1. Flying; passing through the air; as *volant* automata. *Wilkins.*
2. Nimble; active; as *volant* touch. *Milton.*
3. In *heraldry*, represented as flying or having the wings spread.

VOL'ATILE, *a.* [Fr. from L. *volatilis*, from *volo*, to fly.]

1. Flying; passing through the air on wings, or by the buoyant force of the atmosphere.
2. Having the power to fly; as, birds are *volatile* animals. *Ray. Bacon.*
3. Capable of wasting away, or of easily passing into the aeriform state. Thus substances which affect the smell with pungent or fragrant odors, as musk, hartshorn and essential oils, are called *volatile* substances, because they waste away on exposure to the atmosphere. Alcohol and ether are called *volatile* liquids for a similar reason, and because they easily pass into the state of vapor on the application of heat. On the contrary, gold is a *fixed* substance, because it does not suffer waste even when exposed to the heat of a furnace; and oils are called *fixed*, when they do not evaporate on simple exposure to the atmosphere.
4. Lively; gay; full of spirit; airy; hence, fickle; apt to change; as a *volatile* temper. *Watts.*

You are as giddy and *volatile* as ever. *Swift.*

VOL'ATILE, *n.* A winged animal. [*Little used.*] *Brown.*

VOL'ATILENESS, VOLATIL'ITY, } *n.* [Fr. *volatilité.*] Disposition to exhale or evaporate; the quality of being capable of evaporation; that property of a substance which disposes it to rise and float in the air, and thus to be dissipated; as the *volatility* of fluids. Ether is remarkable for its *volatility*. Many or most solid bodies are susceptible of *volatility* by the action of intense heat.

By the spirit of a plant we understand that pure elaborated oil, which by reason of its extreme *volatility*, exhales spontaneously, and in which the odor or smell consists. *Arbuthnot.*

2. Great sprightliness; levity; liveliness; whence, mutability of mind; fickleness; as the *volatility* of youth.

VOLATILIZA'TION, *n.* [from *volatilize.*] The act or process of rendering volatile, or rather of causing to rise and float in the air. *Boyle.*

VOL'ATILIZE, *v. t.* [Fr. *volatiliser.*] To render volatile; to cause to exhale or evaporate; to cause to pass off in vapor or invisible effluvia, and to rise and float in the air.

The water—dissolving the oil, and *volatilizing* it by the action. *Newton.*

VOL'ATILIZED, *pp.* Rendered volatile; caused to rise and float in air.

VOL'ATILIZING, *ppr.* Rendering volatile; causing to rise and float in air.

VOLCAN'IC, *a.* [from *volcano.*] Pertaining to volcanoes; as *volcanic* heat.
2. Produced by a volcano; as *volcanic* tufa.
3. Changed or affected by the heat of a volcano.

VOL'CANIST, *n.* [from *volcano.*] One versed in the history and phenomena of volcanoes.
2. One who believes in the effects of eruptions of fire in the formation of mountains.

VOL'CANITE, *n.* A mineral, otherwise called augite.

VOLCAN'ITY, *n.* The state of being volcanic or of volcanic origin.

VOLCANIZA'TION, *n.* [from *volcanize.*] The process of undergoing volcanic heat and being affected by it.

VOL'CANIZE, *v. t.* To subject to or cause to undergo volcanic heat and to be affected by its action. *Spallanzani.*

VOL'CANIZED, *pp.* Affected by volcanic heat.

VOLCA'NO, *n.* [It. from *Vulcan.*] In *geology*, an opening in the surface of the earth or in a mountain, from which smoke, flames, stones, lava or other substances are ejected. Such are seen in Etna and Vesuvius in Sicily and Italy, and Hecla in Iceland. It is vulgarly called a *burning mountain.* Herschel has discovered a *volcano* in the moon.
2. The mountain that ejects fire, smoke, &c.

VOLE, *n.* [Fr. from *voler*, to fly.] A deal at cards that draws all the tricks. *Swift.*

VO'LERY, *n.* [Fr. *volerie*, from *voler*, to fly.]
1. A flight of birds. *Locke.*
2. A large bird-cage, in which the birds have room to fly. *Cyc.*

VOLITA'TION, *n.* [L. *volito*, dim. of *volo*, to fly.] The act of flying; flight. *Brown.*

VOLI''TION, *n.* [L. *volitio*, from *volo*, to will. See *Will.*]
1. The act of willing; the act of determining choice, or forming a purpose. There is a great difference between actual *volition*, and the approbation of judgment. *South.*

Volition is the actual exercise of the power which the mind has of considering or forbearing to consider an idea. *Locke.*

2. The power of willing or determining.

VOL'ITIVE, *a.* Having the power to will.

They not only perfect the intellectual faculty, but the *volitive.* *Hale.*

VOL'LEY, *n.* plu. *volleys.* [Fr. *volée*, a flight, from *voler*, to fly, L. *volo.*]
1. A flight of shot; the discharge of many small arms at once. *Waller.*
2. A burst or emission of many things at once; as a *volley* of words. *Shak.*

But rattling nonsense in full *volleys* breaks. *Pope.*

VOL'LEY, *v. t.* To discharge with a volley.

VOL'LEY, *v. i.* To throw out or discharge at once. *Shak.*

VOL'LEYED, *a.* [from *volley.*] Disploded; discharged with a sudden burst; as *volleyed* thunder. *Milton. Philips.*

VOLT, *n.* [Fr. *volte*, a ring; It. *volta*, a turn; from L. *volutus, volvo.*]
1. A round or circular tread; a gait of two treads, made by a horse going sideways round a center. *Far. Dict.*
2. In *fencing*, a sudden movement or leap to avoid a thrust.

Volta, in Italian music, signifies that the part is to be repeated one, two or more times.

VOLTA'IC, *a.* Pertaining to Volta, the discoverer of voltaism; as the *voltaic* pile.

Voltaic apparatus, the apparatus used for accumulating galvanic electricity. The agent itself is denominated *galvanism*, after its discoverer Galvani, while the instruments used for exciting and accumulating it, are called *voltaic*, in honor of Volta, who first contrived this kind of apparatus.

Voltaic pile, a column formed by successive pairs of metallic disks, as silver and zink, with moistened cloth between every two contiguous pairs.

Voltaic battery, the larger forms of voltaic apparatus, used for accumulating galvanic electricity.

VOL'TAISM, *n.* [from *Volta*, an Italian.] That branch of electrical science which has its source in the chimical action between metals and different liquids. It is more properly called *galvanism*, from Galvani, who first proved or brought into notice its remarkable influence on animals.

VOLU'BILATE, }
VOL'UBILE, } *a.* In *gardening*, a volubilate stem is one that climbs by winding or twining round another body. *Cyc.*

VOLUBIL'ITY, *n.* [Fr. *volubilité*; L. *volubilitas*, from *volvo*, to roll.]
1. The capacity of being rolled; aptness to roll; as the *volubility* of a bowl. *Watts.*
2. The act of rolling.

By irregular *volubility.* *Hooker.*

3. Ready motion of the tongue in speaking; fluency of speech.

She ran over the catalogue of diversions with such a *volubility* of tongue, as drew a gentle reprimand from her father. *Female Quixote.*

4. Mutability; liableness to revolution; as the *volubility* of human affairs. [*Unusual.*] *L'Estrange.*

VOL'UBLE, *a.* [L. *volubilis.*] Formed so as to roll with ease, or to be easily set in motion; apt to roll; as *voluble* particles of matter. *Boyle.*
2. Rolling; having quick motion.

This less *voluble* earth. *Milton.*

3. Nimble; active; moving with ease and smoothness in uttering words; fluent; as a flippant, *voluble* tongue.
4. Fluent; flowing with ease and smoothness; as a *voluble* speech. *Shak.*
5. Having fluency of speech.

Cassio, a knave very *voluble.* *Shak.*

VOL'UBLY, *adv.* In a rolling or fluent manner. *Hudibras.*

VOL'UME, *n.* [Fr. from L. *volumen*, a roll; *volvo*, to roll. To make *u* long, in this word, is palpably wrong.]
1. Primarily a roll, as the ancients wrote on long strips of bark, parchment or other material, which they formed into rolls or folds. Of such volumes, Ptolemy's library in Alexandria contained 3 or 700,000.
2. A roll or turn; as much as is included in a roll or coil; as the *volume* of a serpent. *Dryden.*
3. Dimensions; compass; space occupied; as the *volume* of an elephant's body; a *volume* of gas. *Darwin. Parke.*
4. A swelling or spherical body.

The undulating billows rolling their silver *volumes.* *Irving.*

5. A book; a collection of sheets of paper, usually printed or written paper, folded and bound, or covered. A book consisting of sheets once folded, is called a folio, or a folio *volume*; of sheets twice folded, a quarto; and thus according to the number of leaves in a sheet, it is called an octavo, or a duodecimo. The Scriptures or sacred writings, bound in a single *volume*, are called the Bible. The number of *volumes* in the Royal Library, in Rue de Richlieu, at Paris, is variously estimated. It is probable it may amount to 400,000.

An odd *volume* of a set of books, bears not the value of its proportion to the set. *Franklin.*

6. In *music*, the compass of a voice from grave to acute; the tone or power of voice. *Busby.*

VOL'UMED, *a.* Having the form of a volume or roll; as *volumed* mist. *Percy's Masque.*

VOLU'MINOUS, *a.* Consisting of many coils or complications.

The serpent roll'd *voluminous* and vast. *Milton.*

2. Consisting of many volumes or books. The collections of Muratori and of the Byzantine history, are very *voluminous.*
3. Having written much, or made many volumes; as a *voluminons* writer.
4. Copious; diffusive. He was too *voluminous* in discourse. [*Not in use.*]

VOLU'MINOUSLY, *adv.* In many volumes; very copiously. *Granville.*

VOLU'MINOUSNESS, *n.* State of being bulky or in many volumes.

VOL'UMIST, *n.* One who writes a volume; an author. [*Not in use.*] *Milton.*

VOL'UNTARILY, *adv.* [from *voluntary.*] Spontaneously; of one's own will; without being moved, influenced or impelled by others.

To be agents *voluntarily* in our own destruction, is against God and nature. *Hooker.*

VOL'UNTARINESS, *n.* The state of being voluntary or optional.

VOL'UNTARY, *a.* [Fr. *volontaire*; L. *voluntarius*, from *voluntas*, will, from *volo.*]
1. Acting by choice or spontaneously; acting without being influenced or impelled by another.
2. Free, or having power to act by choice; not being under restraint; as, man is a *voluntary* agent. *Hooker.*
3. Proceeding from choice or free will.

That sin or guilt pertains exclusively to *voluntary* action, is the true principle of orthodoxy. *N. W. Taylor.*

4. Willing; acting with willingness.

She fell to lust a *voluntary* prey. *Pope.*

5. Done by design; purposed; intended. If a man kills another by lopping a tree, here is no *voluntary* murder.
6. Done freely, or of choice; proceeding from free will. He went into *voluntary* exile. He made a *voluntary* surrender.
7. Acting of his own accord; spontaneous; as the *voluntary* dictates of knowledge.
8. Subject to the will; as the *voluntary* motions of an animal. Thus the motion of a

leg or an arm is *voluntary*, but the motion of the heart is *involuntary*.

A *voluntary escape*, in *law*, is the escape of a prisoner by the express consent of the sherif.

Voluntary jurisdiction, is that which is exercised in doing that which no one opposes; as in granting dispensations, &c.

Voluntary affidavit or *oath*, is one made in an extra-judicial matter.

Voluntary waste, is that which is committed by positive acts.

VOL'UNTARY, *n.* One who engages in any affair of his own free will; a volunteer. [In this sense, *volunteer* is now generally used.]

2. In *music*, a piece played by a musician extemporarily, according to his fancy. In the Philosophical Transactions, we have a method of writing *voluntaries*, as fast as the musician plays the notes. This is by a cylinder turning under the keys of the organ. *Cyc.*

3. A composition for the organ.

VOLUNTEE'R, *n.* [Fr. *volontaire*.] A person who enters into military or other service of his own free will. In military affairs, volunteers enter into service voluntarily, but when in service they are subject to discipline and regulations like other soldiers. They sometimes serve gratuitously, but often receive a compensation.

VOLUNTEE'R, *a.* Entering into service of free will; as *volunteer* companies.

VOLUNTEE'R, *v. t.* To offer or bestow voluntarily, or without solicitation or compulsion; as, to *volunteer* one's services.

VOLUNTEE'R, *v. i.* To enter into any service of one's free will, without solicitation or compulsion. He *volunteered* in that undertaking.

[*These verbs are in respectable use.*]

VOLUP'TUARY, *n.* [L. *voluptuarius*, from *voluptas*, pleasure.]

A man addicted to luxury or the gratification of the appetite, and to other sensual pleasures. *Atterbury.*

VOLUP'TUOUS, *a.* [Fr. *voluptueux*; L. *voluptuosus*.]

Given to the enjoyments of luxury and pleasure; indulging to excess in sensual gratifications.

Soften'd with pleasure and *voluptuous* life. *Milton.*

VOLUP'TUOUSLY, *adv.* Luxuriously; with free indulgence of sensual pleasures; as, to live *voluptuously*.

VOLUP'TUOUSNESS, *n.* Luxuriousness; addictedness to pleasure or sensual gratification.

Where no *voluptuousness*, yet all delight. *Donne.*

VOLUTA'TION, *n.* [L. *volutatio*, from *voluto*, from *volvo*, Eng. to *wallow*.]

A wallowing; a rolling of the body on the earth. [See *Wallow*.]

VOLU'TE, *n.* [Fr. *volute*; It. *voluta*; from L. *volutus*, *volvo*.]

1. In *architecture*, a kind of spiral scroll, used in the Ionic and Composite capitals, of which it is a principal ornament. The number of *volutes* in the Ionic order, is four; in the Composite, eight. There are also eight angular volutes in the Corinthian capital, accompanied with eight smaller ones, called helices. *Cyc.*

2. In *natural history*, a genus of shells. *Say.*

VOLU'TION, *n.* A spiral turn.

VOL'UTITE, *n.* A petrified shell of the genus Voluta. *Jameson.*

VOL'VIC, *a.* Denoting a species of stone or lava.

VOM'IC, *a.* The *vomic* nut, *nux vomica*, is the seed of the *Strychnos nux vomica*, a native of the East Indies. It is a very active poison. *Cyc.*

VOM'ICA, *n.* [L.] An encysted tumor on the lungs. *Arbuthnot.*

VOM'IT, *v. i.* [L. *vomo*; Fr. *vomir*; It. *vomire*; Sans. *vamathu*. Probably the Gr. εμεω is the same word, with the loss of its first letter.]

To eject the contents of the stomach by the mouth. Some persons *vomit* with ease, as do cats and dogs. But horses do not *vomit*. *Cyc.*

VOM'IT, *v. t.* To throw up or eject from the stomach; to discharge from the stomach through the mouth. It is followed often by *up* or *out*, but without necessity and to the injury of the language. In the yellow fever, the patients often *vomit* dark colored matter, like coffee grounds.

The fish *vomited out* Jonah upon the dry land. Jonah ii.

2. To eject with violence from any hollow place. Volcanoes *vomit* flames, ashes, stones and liquid lava.

VOM'IT, *n.* The matter ejected from the stomach. *Sandys.*

2. That which excites the stomach to discharge its contents; an emetic.

Black vomit, the dark colored matter ejected from the stomach in the last stage of the yellow fever or other malignant disease; hence, the yellow fever, vulgarly so called.

VOM'ITED, *pp.* Ejected from the stomach through the mouth, or from any deep place through an opening.

VOM'ITING, *ppr.* Discharging from the stomach through the mouth, or ejecting from any deep place.

VOM'ITING, *n.* The act of ejecting the contents of the stomach through the mouth. *Vomiting* is an inverted action of the stomach. *Cyc.*

2. The act of throwing out substances with violence from a deep hollow, as a volcano, &c.

VOMI''TION, *n.* The act or power of vomiting. *Grew.*

VOM'ITIVE, *a.* [Fr. *vomitif*.] Causing the ejection of matter from the stomach; emetic. *Brown.*

VOM'ITORY, *a.* [L. *vomitorius*.] Procuring vomits; causing to eject from the stomach; emetic. *Brown.*

VOM'ITORY, *n.* An emetic. *Harvey.*

2. A door. *Gibbon.*

VORA'CIOUS, *a.* [Fr. It. *vorace*; L. *vorax*, from *voro*, to devour; Heb. Ch. בער to clear away, to consume; Gr. βορα, food. Class Br. No. 6.]

1. Greedy for eating; ravenous; very hungry; as a *voracious* man or appetite.

2. Rapacious; eager to devour; as *voracious* animals.

3. Ready to swallow up; as a *voracious* gulf or whirlpool.

VORA'CIOUSLY, *adv.* With greedy appetite; ravenously.

VORA'CIOUSNESS, *n.* Greediness of appetite; ravenousness; eagerness to devour; rapaciousness.

VORAC'ITY, *n.* Greediness of appetite; voraciousness.

Creatures by their *voracity* pernicious, have commonly fewer young. *Derham.*

VORAG'INOUS, *a.* [L. *voraginosus*, *vorago*.] Full of gulfs. *Scott.*

VOR'TEX, *n.* plu. *vortices* or *vortexes*. [L. from *verto*, Ant. *vorto*, to turn.]

1. A whirlpool; a whirling or circular motion of water, forming a kind of cavity in the center of the circle, and in some instances, drawing in water or absorbing other things.

2. A whirling of the air; a whirlwind. *Cyc.*

3. In the *Cartesian system*, the circular motion originally impressed on the particles of matter, carrying them around their own axes, and around a common center. By means of these *vortices*, Descartes attempted to account for the formation of the universe.

VOR'TICAL, *a.* Whirling; turning; as a *vortical* motion. *Newton. Bentley.*

VO'TARESS, *n.* A female devoted to any service, worship or state of life.

No rosary this *votaress* needs. *Cleaveland.*

VO'TARIST, *n.* [See *Votary*.] One devoted or given up to any person or thing, to any service, worship or pursuit.

I am no idle *votarist*. *Shak.*

[*Votary is now used.*]

VO'TARY, *a.* [from L. *votus*, from *voveo*. See *Vow*.]

Devoted; promised; consecrated by a vow or promise; consequent on a vow.

Votary resolution is made equipollent to custom. *Bacon.*

VO'TARY, *n.* One devoted, consecrated or engaged by a vow or promise; hence more generally, one devoted, given or addicted to some particular service, worship, study or state of life. Every goddess of antiquity had her *votaries*. Every pursuit or study has now its *votaries*. One is a *votary* to mathematics, another is a *votary* to music, and alas, a great portion of the world are *votaries* of sensual pleasures.

It was the coldness of the *votary*, not the prayer, which was in fault. *Fell.*

VOTE, *n.* [It. Sp. *voto*; L. *votum*, from *voveo*, to vow. *Votum* is properly wish or will.]

1. Suffrage; the expression of a wish, desire, will, preference or choice, in regard to any measure proposed, in which the person voting has an interest in common with others, either in electing a man to office, or in passing laws, rules, regulations and the like. This vote or expression of will may be given by holding up the hand, by rising and standing up, by the voice, *(viva voce,)* by ballot, by a ticket or otherwise. All these modes and others are used. Hence

2. That by which will or preference is expressed in elections, or in deciding propositions; a ballot; a ticket, &c.; as a written *vote*.

3. Expression of will by a majority; legal decision by some expression of the minds of a number; as, the *vote* was unanimous.

4. United voice in public prayer.

VOTE, *v. i.* To express or signify the mind, will or preference, in electing men to office, or in passing laws, regulations and the like, or in deciding on any proposition in which one has an interest with others. In elections, men are bound to *vote* for the best men to fill offices, according to their best knowledge and belief.

To *vote* for a duelist, is to assist in the prostration of justice, and indirectly to encourage the crime. *L. Beecher.*

VOTE, *v. t.* To choose by suffrage; to elect by some expression of will; as, the citizens *voted* their candidate into office with little opposition.

2. To enact or establish by vote or some expression of will. The legislature *voted* the resolution unanimously.

3. To grant by vote or expression of will.

Parliament *voted* them a hundred thousand pounds. *Swift.*

VO'TED, *pp.* Expressed by vote or suffrage; determined.

VO'TER, *n.* One who has a legal right to vote or give his suffrage.

VO'TING, *ppr.* Expressing the mind, will or preference in election, or in determining questions proposed; giving a vote or suffrage; electing, deciding, giving or enacting by vote.

VO'TIVE, *a.* [Fr. *votif;* L. *votivus,* from *votus,* vowed.]

Given by vow; devoted; as *votive* offerings. *Votive* medals, are those on which vows of the people for emperors or empresses are expressed.

Venus, take my *votive* glass. *Prior.*

VOUCH, *v. t.* [Norm. *voucher;* L. *voco.* See *Voice.*]

1. To call to witness; to obtest.

And *vouch* the silent stars and conscious moon. *Dryden.*

2. To declare; to affirm; to attest; to warrant; to maintain by affirmations.

They made him ashamed to *vouch* the truth of the relation, and afterward to credit it. *Atterbury.*

2. To warrant; to confirm; to establish proof.

The consistency of the discourse—*vouches* it to be worthy of the great apostle. *Locke.*

4. In *law,* to call into court to warrant and defend, or to make good a warranty of title.

He *vouches* the tenant in tail, who *vouches* over the common vouchee. *Blackstone.*

VOUCH, *v. i.* To bear witness; to give testimony or full attestation. I cannot *vouch* for the truth of the report.

He declares he will not believe her, till the elector of Hanover shall *vouch* for the truth of what she has so solemnly affirmed. *Swift.*

VOUCH, *n.* Warrant; attestation. *Shak.*

VOUCH'ED, *pp.* Called to witness; affirmed or fully attested; called into court to make good a warranty.

VOUCHEE', *n.* In *law,* the person who is vouched or called into court to support or make good his warranty of title in the process of common recovery. *Blackstone.*

VOUCH'ER, *n.* One who gives witness or full attestation to any thing.

The great writers of that age stand up together as *vouchers* for each other's reputation. *Spectator.*

2. In *law,* the act of calling in a person to make good his warranty of title.

3. A book, paper or document which serves to vouch the truth of accounts, or to confirm and establish facts of any kind. The merchant's books are his *vouchers* for the correctness of his accounts. Notes, bonds, receipts and other writings, are used as *vouchers* in proving facts.

VOUCH'ER, } *n.* In *law,* the tenant in a
VOUCH'OR, } writ of right; one who calls in another to establish his warranty of title. In common recoveries, there may be a single *voucher,* or double *vouchers.* *Blackstone.*

VOUCH'ING, *ppr.* Calling to witness; attesting by affirmation; calling in to maintain warranty of title.

VOUCHSA'FE, *v. t.* [*vouch* and *safe;* to vouch or answer for safety.]

1. To permit to be done without danger.

2. To condescend to grant.

Shall I *vouchsafe* your worship a word or two? *Shak.*

It is not said by the apostle that God *vouchsafed* to the heathen the means of salvation. *South.*

VOUCHSA'FE, *v. i.* To condescend; to deign; to yield.

Vouchsafe, illustrious Ormond, to behold
What pow'r the charms of beauty had of old. *Dryden.*

VOUCHSA'FED, *pp.* Granted in condescension.

VOUCHSA'FEMENT, *n.* Grant in condescension; as, God's greatest communicated *vouchsafements.* *Boyle.*

VOUCHSA'FING, *ppr.* Condescending to grant; deigning.

VOW, *n.* [Fr. *voeu;* It. *voto;* L. *votum,* from *voveo,* to vow; probably a contracted word.]

1. A solemn promise made to God, or by a pagan to his deity. The Roman generals when they went to war, sometimes made a *vow* that they would build a temple to some favorite deity, if he would give them victory. A *vow* is a promise of something to be given or done hereafter.

A person is constituted a religious by taking three *vows,* of chastity, of poverty, and of obedience. Among the Israelites, the *vows* of children were not binding, unless ratified by the express or tacit consent of their father. Num. xxx.

2. A solemn promise; as the *vows* of unchangeable love and fidelity. In a moral and religious sense, *vows* are promises to God, as they appeal to God to witness their sincerity, and the violation of them is a most hainous offense.

VOW, *v. t.* [Fr. *vouer;* L. *voveo.*] To give, consecrate or dedicate to God by a solemn promise. When Jacob went to Mesopotamia, he *vowed* to God a tenth of his substance, and his own future devotion to his service. Gen. xxviii.

When thou *vowest* a vow, defer not to pay it. Eccles. v.

2. To devote. *Spenser.*

VOW, *v. i.* To make vows or solemn promises. He that *vows,* must be careful to perform.

VOW'ED, *pp.* Solemnly promised to God; given or consecrated by solemn promise.

VOW'EL, *n.* [L. *vocalis,* from *voco;* Fr. *voyelle;* It. *vocale.*]

1. In *grammar,* a simple sound; a sound uttered by simply opening the mouth or organs; as the sound of *a, e, o.*

2. The letter or character which represents a simple sound.

VOW'EL, *a.* Pertaining to a vowel; vocal.

VOW'ELED, *a.* Furnished with vowels.

VOW'ER, *n.* One who makes a vow.

VOW'-FELLOW, *n.* [*vow* and *fellow.*] One bound by the same vow. [*Little used.*]

VOW'ING, *ppr.* Making a vow.

VOY'AGE, *n.* [Fr. from *voie,* or the same root, Eng. *way,* Sax. *wæg, weg.* See *Wag* and *Way.*]

1. A passing by sea or water from one place, port or country to another, especially a passing or journey by water to a distant place or country. Captain L. made more than a hundred *voyages* to the West Indies. A *voyage* over lake Superior is like a *voyage* to Bermuda.

2. The practice of traveling. [*Not in use.*] *Bacon.*

VOY'AĠE, *v. i.* To sail or pass by water. *Pope.*

VOY'AĠE, *v. t.* To travel; to pass over.

I with pain
Voyag'd th' unreal, vast, unbounded deep. *Milton.*

VOY'AĠER, *n.* One who sails or passes by sea or water.

A private *voyager* I pass the main. *Pope.*

VULCANIST. [See *Volcanist.*]

VULCANO. [See *Volcano.*[

VUL'GAR, *a.* [Fr. *vulgaire;* It. *vulgare;* L. *vulgaris,* from *vulgus,* the common people, that is, the crowd, Eng. *folk.*]

1. Pertaining to the common unlettered people; as *vulgar* life.

2. Used or practiced by common people; as *vulgar* sports.

3. Vernacular; national.

It might be more useful to the English reader, to write in our *vulgar* language. *Fell.*

4. Common; used by all classes of people; as the *vulgar* version of the Scriptures.

5. Public; as *vulgar* report.

6. Mean; rustic; rude; low; unrefined; as *vulgar* minds; *vulgar* manners.

7. Consisting of common persons.

In reading an account of a battle, we follow the hero with our whole attention, but seldom reflect on the *vulgar* heaps of slaughter. *Rambler.*

Vulgar fractions, in arithmetic, fractions expressed by a numerator and denominator; thus $\frac{2}{5}$.

VUL'GAR, *n.* The common people. [*It has no plural termination, but has often a plural verb.*]

The *vulgar* imagine the pretender to have been a child imposed on the nation. *Swift.*

VUL'GARISM, *n.* Grossness of manners; vulgarity. [*Little used.*]

2. A vulgar phrase or expression. [*This is the usual sense of the word.*]

VULGAR'ITY, *n.* Mean condition in life; the state of the lower classes of society. *Brown.*

2. Grossness or clownishness of manners or language; as *vulgarity* of behavior; *vulgarity* of expression or language. *Dryden.*

VUL'GARIZE, *v. t.* To make vulgar. *Foster.*

VUL'GARLY, *adv.* Commonly; in the ordinary manner among the common people.

Such an one we *vulgarly* call a desperate person. *Hammond.*

2. Meanly; rudely; clownishly.

VUL'GATE, *n.* A very ancient Latin version of the Scriptures, and the only one which the Romish church admits to be authentic. It is so called from its common use in the Latin church. *Cyc.*

VUL'GATE, *a.* Pertaining to the old Latin version of the Scriptures.

VUL'NERABLE, *a.* [Fr. from L. *vulnero*, to wound, from *vulnus*, a wound.]

1. That may be wounded; susceptible of wounds or external injuries; as a *vulnerable* body.

Achilles was *vulnerable* in his heel; and there will never be wanting a Paris to infix the the dart. *Dwight.*

2. Liable to injury; subject to be affected injuriously; as a *vulnerable* reputation.

VUL'NERARY, *a.* [Fr. *vulneraire;* L. *vulnerarius.*] Useful in healing wounds; adapted to the cure of external injuries; as *vulnerary* plants or potions. *Cyc.*

VUL'NERARY, *n.* Any plant, drug or composition, useful in the cure of wounds. Certain unguents, balsams and the like, are used as *vulneraries.*

VUL'NERATE, *v. t.* [L. *vulnero.*] To wound; to hurt. [*Not in use.*] *Glanville.*

VULNERA'TION, *n.* The act of wounding. [*Not in use.*] *Pearson.*

VUL'PINE, *a.* [L. *vulpinus*, from *vulpes*, a fox. *Vulpes* is our English *wolf*, the same word applied to a different animal.] Pertaining to the fox; cunning; crafty; artful.

VUL'PINITE, *n.* [from *Vulpino*, in Italy.] A mineral of a grayish white color, splendent and massive; its fracture foliated. It consists of the sulphate of lime and silica. *Ure.*

VUL'TUR, VUL'TURE, *n.* [L. *vultur.*] A genus of fowls, belonging to the order of Accipiters. The bill is straight, but hooked at the end, and covered at the base by a cere or skin. The head is naked. There are thirteen species, all carnivorous and rapacious. The vultur is one of the largest kinds of fowls, and the condor of South America, one of this family, is the largest species of flying animals that has been discovered. *Cyc.*

VUL'TURINE, *a.* [L. *vulturinus.*] Belonging to the vultur; having the qualities of the vultur; resembling the vultur; rapacious.

W.

W is the twenty third letter of the English Alphabet. It takes its written form and its name from the union of two V's, this being the form of the Roman capital letter which we call U. The name, *double u*, being given to it from its form or composition, and not from its sound, ought not to be retained. Every letter should be named from its sound, especially the vowels. W is properly a vowel, a simple sound, formed by opening the mouth with a close circular configuration of the lips. It is precisely the *ou* of the French, and the *u* of the Spaniards, Italians and Germans. With the other vowels it forms diphthongs, which are of easy pronunciation; as in *well, want, will, dwell;* pronounced *ooell, ooant, ooill, dooell.* In English, it is always followed by another vowel, except when followed by *h*, as is *when;* but this case is an exception only in writing, and not in pronunciation, for *h* precedes *w* in utterance; *when* being pronounced *hooen.* In Welsh, *w*, which is sounded as in English, is used without another vowel, as in *fwl*, a fool; *dwn*, dun; *dwb*, mortar; *gwn*, a gun, and a gown.

It is not improbable that the Romans pronounced *v* as we do *w*, for their *volvo* is our *wallow;* and *volo, velle*, is the English *will*, G. *wollen.* But this is uncertain. The German *v* has the sound of the English *f*, and *w* that of the English *v*.

W, at the end of words, is often silent after *a* and *o*, as in *law, saw, low, sow.* In many words of this kind, *w* represents the Saxon *g;* in other cases, it helps to form a diphthong, as in *now, vow, new, strew.*

WAB'BLE, *v. i.* [W. *gwibiaw*, to wander, to move in a circular form.]

To move from one side to the other; to vacillate; as a turning or whirling body. So it is said a top *wabbles*, when it is in motion, and deviates from a perpendicular direction; a spindle *wabbles*, when it moves one way and the other. [*This word is applied chiefly to bodies when turning with a circular motion, and its place cannot be supplied by any other word in the language. It is neither low nor barbarous.*]

WACK'E, WACK'Y, *n.* A rock nearly allied to basalt, of which it may be regarded as a more soft and earthy variety. Its color is a greenish gray, brown or black. It is opake, yields easily to the knife, and has a greasy feel. Its principal ingredient is silex. Gray wacky is a different species of rock, being a kind of sandstone. *Cyc.*

Wacky is a mineral substance intermediate between clay and basalt. *Ure.*

WAD, *n.* [G. *watte;* Dan. *vat*, a wad; that is, a mass or collection.]

1. A little mass of some soft or flexible material, such as hay, straw, tow, paper, or old rope-yarn, used for stopping the charge of powder in a gun and pressing it close to the shot, or for keeping the powder and shot close.

2. A little mass, tuft or bundle, as of hay or peas.

WAD, WADD, *n.* In *mineralogy*, black wadd is a species of the ore of manganese, of which there are four kinds; fibrous, ochery, pulverulent ochery, and dendritic. In some places, plumbago or black lead is called wad or wadd. *Cyc.*

WAD'DED, *a.* Formed into a wad or mass.

WAD'DING, *n.* [G. *watte.*] A wad, or the materials for wads; any pliable substance of which wads may be made.

2. A kind of soft stuff of loose texture, used for stuffing garments.

WAD'DLE, *v. i.* [This seems to be a diminutive formed on the root of *wade*, L. *vado*, to go; G. *waten*, to wade; *watscheln*, to waddle.]

1. To move one way and the other in walking; to deviate to one side and the other; to vacillate; as, a child *waddles* when he begins to walk; very fat people walk with a kind of *waddling* pace. So we say, a duck or a goose *waddles.*

2. To walk with a waddling motion.

And hardly *waddles* forth to cool— *Swift.*

WAD'DLING, *ppr.* Moving from side to side in walking.

WAD'DLINGLY, *adv.* With a vacillating gait. *Entick.*

WADE, *v. i.* [Sw. *vada;* D. *waaden;* G. *waten;* Dan. *vader;* Fr. *gueer*, for *gueder;* It. *guadare;* Sp. *vadear*, L. *vado*, to go.]

1. To walk through any substance that yields to the feet; as, to *wade* through water; to *wade* through sand or snow. To *wade* over a river, is to walk through on the bottom. Fowls that *wade* have long legs.

2. To move or pass with difficulty or labor; as, judges *wade* through an intricate law case. It is not my purpose to *wade* through these controversies.

The king's admirable conduct has *waded* through all these difficulties. *Davenant.*

—And *wades* through fumes, and gropes his way. *Dryden.*

WADE, *v. t.* To pass by walking on the bottom; as, to *wade* a river. [This is a common expression, but elliptical for to *wade through* a river.]

WA'DING, *ppr.* Walking through a substance that yields to the feet, as through water or sand.

WAD'SETT, *n.* An ancient tenure or lease of land in the Highlands of Scotland, which seems to have been upon a kind of mortgage. [Sax. *wæd, wed*, a pledge.] *Cyc.*

WAD'SETTER, *n.* One who holds by wadsett. *Cyc.*

WA'FER, *n.* [D. *wafel;* G. *waffel;* Dan. *vaffel;* Sw. *våffla;* Russ. *vaphel;* Fr. *gauffre.*]

1. A thin cake or leaf; as a *wafer* of bread given by the Romanists in the eucharist.
2. A thin leaf of paste, or a composition of flour, the white of eggs, isinglass and yeast, spread over with gum-water and dried; used in sealing letters.

WA'FER, *v. t.* To seal or close with a wafer.

W'AFT, *v. t.* [perhaps from *wave*; if so, it belongs to the root of *wag*.]
1. To bear through a fluid or buoyant medium; to convey through water or air; as, a balloon was *wafted* over the channel.

Speed the soft intercourse from soul to soul,
And *waft* a sigh from Indus to the pole. *Pope.*

2. To convey; as ships. *Cyc.*
3. To buoy; to cause to float; to keep from sinking. *Brown.*
4. To beckon; to give notice by something in motion. [*Not in use.*]

[This verb is regular. But *waft* was formerly used by some writers for *wafted.*]

W'AFT, *v. i.* To float; to be moved or to pass in a buoyant medium.

And now the shouts *waft* near the citadel. *Dryden.*

W'AFT, *n.* A floating body; also, a signal displayed from a ship's stern, by hoisting an ensign furled in a roll, to the head of the staff. *Cyc.*

W'AFTAĠE, *n.* Conveyance or transportation through a buoyant medium, as air or water. [*Not in use.*] *Shak.*

W'AFTED, *pp.* Borne or conveyed through air or water.

W'AFTER, *n.* He or that which wafts; a passage boat.
2. The conductor of vessels at sea; *an old word.*

W'AFTING, *ppr.* Carrying through a buoyant medium.

W'AFTURE, *n.* The act of waving. [*Not in use.*] *Shak.*

WAG, *v. t.* [Sax. *wagian* and *wecgan*; G. *bewegen*; D. *beweegen*, to move, to stir; *weegen*, to *weigh*; G. *wägen*, to *weigh*; Sw. *våga*, Dan. *vajer*, to wag, to weigh. This is the radix of the L. *vacillo*, Eng. *fickle*, *wagon*, *wain*, *way*, *wave*, *waggle*, &c.]

To move one way and the other with quick turns; to move a little way, and then turn the other way; as, to *wag* the head.

Every one that passeth thereby shall be astonished, and *wag* his head. Jer. xviii. Matt. xxvii.

[*Wag* expresses particularly the motion of the head and body used in buffoonery, mirth, derision, sport and mockery. It is applied also to birds and beasts; as, to *wag* the tail.]

WAG, *v. i.* To be quick in ludicrous motion; to stir.

'Tis merry in hall, where beards *wag* all. *Shak.*

Tremble and start at *wagging* of a straw. *Shak.*

2. To go; to depart; to pack off.

I will provoke him to't, or let him *wag.* *Shak.*

3. To be moved one way and the other.

The resty sieve *wagg'd* ne'er the more. *Dryden.*

WAG, *n.* [from the verb.] A droll; a man full of low sport and humor; a ludicrous fellow.

We wink at *wags*, when they offend. *Dryden.*

The counsellor never pleaded without a piece of packthread in his hand, which he used to twist about his finger all the while he was speaking; the *wags* used to call it the thread of his discourse. *Addison.*

WAĠE, *v. t.* [G. *wagen*; D. *waagen*; Sw. *våga*, to venture, to dare, to wage; Fr. *gager*, for *guager*, to lay or bet; from the root of *wag*. The sense is to throw, to lay or throw down, as a glove or gauntlet.]
1. To lay; to bet; to throw down, as a pledge; to stake; to put at hazard on the event of a contest. This is the common popular sense of the word in New England; as, to *wage* a dollar; to *wage* a horse.
2. To venture; to hazard.

To wake and *wage* a danger profitless. *Shak.*

3. To make; to begin; to carry on; that is, to go forward or advance to attack, as in invasion or aggression; used in the phrase, to *wage war.* He *waged* war with all his enemies.

He ponder'd, which of all his sons was fit
To reign, and *wage* immortal *war* with wit. *Dryden.*

4. To set to hire.

Thou must *wage*
Thy works for wealth. *Spenser.*
[*Not in use.*]

5. To take to hire; to hire for pay; to employ for wages; as *waged* soldiers. He was well *waged* and rewarded. [Fr.] *Obs.* *Raleigh.*

To wage one's law, to give security to make one's law. The defendant is then to swear that he owes nothing to the plaintif, and eleven neighbors, called compurgators, are to avow upon their oaths, that they believe in their consciences that he has declared the truth. This is called *wager of law.* *Blackstone.*

WA'ĠED, *pp.* Laid; deposited; as a pledge; made or begun, as war.

WA'ĠER, *n.* Something deposited, laid or hazarded on the event of a contest or some unsettled question; a bet.

Besides these plates for horse-races, the *wagers* may be as the persons please. *Temple.*

If any atheist can stake his soul for a *wager* against such an inexhaustible disproportion— *Bentley.*

2. Subject on which bets are laid. *Sidney.*
3. In *law*, an offer to make oath of innocence or non-indebtedness; or the act of making oath, together with the oaths of eleven compurgators, to fortify the defendant's oath.

Wager of battle, is when the tenant in a writ of right, offers to prove his right by the body of his champion, and throwing down his glove as a gage or pledge, thus wages or stipulates battle with the champion of the demandant, who by taking up the glove, accepts the challenge. The champions, armed with batons, enter the list, and taking each other by the hand, each swears to the justice of the cause of the party for whom he appears; they then fight till the stars appear, and if the champion of the tenant can defend himself till that time, his cause prevails. *Blackstone.*

WA'ĠER, *v. t.* To lay; to bet; to hazard on the issue of a contest, or on some question that is to be decided, or on some casualty. *Dryden.*

WA'ĠERED, *pp.* Laid; pledged; as a bet.

WA'ĠERER, *n.* One who wagers or lays a bet.

WA'ĠERING, *ppr.* Laying; betting.

Wagering policy, in commerce, a policy of insurance, insuring a sum of money when no property is at hazard; as a policy to insure money on a ship when no property is on board; that is, insurance, interest or no interest: or a wagering policy may be a policy to insure property which is already insured. Such policies in England, are by Statute 19 Geo. III. made null and void.

WA'ĠES, *n.* plural in termination, but singular in signification. [Fr. *gage, gages.*]
1. Hire; reward; that which is paid or stipulated for services, but chiefly for services by manual labor, or for military and naval services. We speak of servant's *wages*, a laborer's *wages*, or soldier's *wages*; but we never apply the word to the rewards given to men in office, which are called *fees* or *salary*. The word is however sometimes applied to the compensation given to representatives in the legislature. [*U. States.*]

Tell me, what shall thy *wages* be? Gen. xxix.

Be content with your *wages*. Luke iii.

2. Reward; fruit; recompense; that which is given or received in return.

The *wages* of sin is death. Rom. vi.

WAG'GEL, **WAG'EL**, *n.* A name given in Cornwall to the martinazzo, dung-hunter, or dung-bird, a species of Larus or sea-gull, (L. *parasiticus.*) *Cyc. Dict. Nat. Hist. Ed. Encyc.*

WAG'GERY, *n.* [from *wag.*] Mischievous merriment; sportive trick or gayety; sarcasm in good humor; as the *waggery* of a school boy. *Locke.*

WAG'GISH, *a.* Mischievous in sport; roguish in merriment or good humor; frolicksome; as a company of *waggish* boys. *L'Estrange.*
2. Done, made or laid in waggery or for sport; as a *waggish* trick.

WAG'GISHLY, *adv.* In a waggish manner; in sport.

WAG'GISHNESS, *n.* Mischievous sport; wanton merriment. *Bacon.*

WAG'GLE, *v. i.* [D. *waggelen*; G. *wackeln*; L. *vacillo*; dim. of *wag.*]

To waddle; to reel or move from side to side.

Why do you go nodding and *waggling* so? *L'Estrange.*

WAG'GLE, *v. t.* To move one way and the other; as, a bird *waggles* its tail.

WAG'ON, *n.* [D. G. *wagen*; Sw. *vagn*; Sax. *wægn*, *wæn*; W. *gwain*, a wagon, wain or sheath, L. *vagina*, the latter being from *wag*, and signifying a passage; Gaelic, *baighin*, a wagon; Malabar, *uagaham*; Sans. *wahana*. The old orthography, *waggon*, seems to be falling into disuse. See *Wag.*]
1. A vehicle moved on four wheels, and usually drawn by horses; used for the transportation of heavy commodities. In America, light wagons are used for the conveyance of families, and for carrying

light commodities to market, particularly a very light kind drawn by one horse.
2. A chariot. [*Not in use.*] *Spenser.*
WAG'ON, *v. t.* To transport in a wagon. Goods are *wagoned* from London to the interior.
WAG'ON, *v. i.* To practice the transportation of goods in a wagon. The man *wagons* between Philadelphia and Pittsburg.
WAG'ONAGE, *n.* Money paid for carriage in a wagon.
WAG'ONER, *n.* One who conducts a wagon.
2. A constellation, Charles' wain.
WAG'ONING, *ppr.* Transporting in a wagon.
WAG'ONING, *n.* The business of transporting in a wagon.
WAG'TAIL, *n.* [*wag* and *tail.*] A small bird, a species of Motacilla.
WAID, *a.* Crushed. [*Not in use.*] *Shak.*
WAIF, *n.* [Norm. *wef, weif;* from *waive.*] Goods found, of which the owner is not known. These were originally such goods as a thief, when pursued, threw away to prevent being apprehended. They belong to the king, unless the owner makes fresh suit of the felon, takes him and brings him to justice. *Blackstone.*
WAIL, *v. t.* [Ice. *væla;* It. *guaiolare;* Gaelic, *guilam* or *uaill;* W. *gwylaw* and *wylaw;* Arm. *goela,* to howl; Heb. Ar. אכל.]
To lament; to moan; to bewail.

Or if no more her absent lord she *wails*— *Pope.*

WAIL, *v. i.* To weep; to express sorrow audibly.

Therefore I will *wail* and howl. Mic. i.

WAIL, *n.* Loud weeping; violent lamentation.
WA'ILFUL, *a.* Sorrowful; mournful. *Shak.*
WA'ILING, *ppr.* Lamenting with audible cries.
WA'ILING, *n.* Loud cries of sorrow; deep lamentation.

There shall be *wailing* and gnashing of teeth. Matt. xiii.

WA'ILMENT, *n.* Lamentation. *Hacket.*
WAIN, *n.* [Sax. *wæn,* W. *gwain;* contracted. See *Wagon.*]
1. A wagon; a carriage for the transportation of goods on wheels.
2. A constellation, Charles' wain.
WA'INAGE, *n.* A finding of carriages. *Ainsworth.*
WA'IN-BOTE, *n.* Timber for wagons or carts. *Eng. Law.*
WA'IN-HOUSE, *n.* A house or shed for wagons and carts. [*Local.*] *Cyc.*
WA'IN-ROPE, *n.* A rope for binding a load on a wagon; a cart-rope. *Shak.*
WA'INSCOT, *n.* [D. *wagenschot.*] In building, timber-work serving to line the walls of a room, being made in panels.
WA'INSCOT, *v. t.* To line with boards; as, to *wainscot* a hall.

Music sounds better in chambers *wainscoted* than hanged. *Bacon.*

2. To line with different materials.

The other is *wainscoted* with looking-glass. *Addison.*

WA'INSCOTED, *pp.* Lined with boards or panels.
WA'INSCOTING, *ppr.* Lining with boards.
WAIR, *n.* A piece of timber two yards long, and a foot broad. [*I know not where used.*] *Bailey.*
WAIST, *n.* [W. *gwâsg,* pressure, squeeze, the *waist,* the part where the girdle is tied; allied to *squeeze.*]
1. That part of the human body which is immediately below the ribs or thorax; or the small part of the body between the thorax and hips.
2. That part of a ship which is between the quarter deck and forecastle. But in many ships now built, there is no quarter deck, and in such the waist is the middle part of the ship.
WA'ISTBAND, *n.* The band or upper part of breeches, trowsers or pantaloons, which encompasses the waist.
WAISTCLOTHS, *n.* Coverings of canvas or tarpauling for the hammocks, stowed on the gangways, between the quarter deck and forecastle. *Mar. Dict.*
WA'ISTCOAT, *n.* [*waist* and *coat.*] A short coat or garment for men, extending no lower than the hips, and covering the waist; a vest. This under garment is now generally called in America a *vest.*
WA'ISTER, *n.* In *ships,* waisters are men who are stationed in the waist in working the ship. *Mar. Dict.*
WAIT, *v. i.* [Fr. *guetter;* It. *guatare;* W. *gweitiaw,* to wait; *gwaid,* attendance. The sense is to stop, or to continue.]
1. To stay or rest in expectation; to stop or remain stationary, till the arrival of some person or event. Thus we say, I went to the place of meeting, and there *waited* an hour for the moderator or chairman. I will go to the hotel, and there *wait* till you come. We will *wait* for the mail.
2. To stay proceedings, or suspend any business, in expectation of some person, event, or the arrival of some hour. The court was obliged to *wait* for a witness.
3. To rest in expectation and patience.

All the days of my appointed time will I *wait,* till my change come. Job xiv.

4. To stay; not to depart.

Haste, my dear father, 'tis no time to *wait.* *Dryden.*

5. To stay; to continue by reason of hinderance.
6. To lie in ambush, as an enemy.

Such ambush *waited* to intercept thy way. *Milton.*

To wait on or *upon,* to attend, as a servant; to perform menial services for; as, to *wait on* a gentleman; to *wait on* the table.
To wait on, to attend; to go to see; to visit on business or for ceremony. Tell the gentleman I will *wait on* him at ten o'clock.
2. To pay servile or submissive attendance.
3. To follow, as a consequence; as the ruin that *waits on* such a supine temper. [Instead of this, we use *await.*]
4. To look watchfully.

It is a point of cunning to *wait on* him with whom you speak, with your eye. *Bacon.*

[*Unusual.*]
5. To attend to; to perform.

Aaron and his sons shall *wait on* their priest's office. Num. iii. viii. Rom. xii.

6. To be ready to serve; to obey. Ps. xxv. Prov. xx.
To wait at, to attend in service; to perform service at. 1 Cor. ix.
To wait for, to watch, as an enemy. Job xv.
WAIT, *v. t.* To stay for; to rest or remain stationary in expectation of the arrival of.

Aw'd with these words, in camps they still abide,
And *wait* with longing eyes their promis'd guide. *Dryden.*

[Elliptical for *wait for.*]
2. To attend; to accompany with submission or respect.

He chose a thousand horse, the flow'r of all
His warlike troops, to *wait* the funeral. *Dryden.*

[*This use is not justifiable, but by poetical license.*]
3. To attend as a consequence of something.

Such doom *waits* luxury— *Philips.*

[Not in use. In this sense we use *attend* or *attend on.*]
WAIT, *n.* Ambush. As a noun, this word is used only in certain phrases. *To lie in wait,* is to lie in ambush; to be secreted in order to fall by surprise on an enemy; hence figuratively, to lay snares, or to make insidious attempts, or to watch for the purpose of ensnaring. Josh. viii.
In wait, is used in a like sense by Milton.
To lay wait, to set an ambush. Jer. ix.
WA'ITER, *n.* One who waits; an attendant; a servant in attendance.

The *waiters* stand in ranks; the yeoman cry,
Make room, as if a duke were passing by. *Swift.*

2. A server; a vessel on which tea furniture, &c. is carried.
WA'ITING, *ppr.* Staying in expectation.
Waiting on, attending; accompanying; serving.
Waiting for, staying for the arrival of.
Waiting at, staying or attending at in expectation or in service.
In waiting, in attendance.
WA'ITING-MAID, WA'ITING-WÖMAN, } *n.* An upper servant who attends a lady. *Waiting-gentlewoman* is sometimes, though less commonly used.
WAITS, *n.* [Goth. *wahts,* watch.] Itinerant nocturnal musicians. [*Not in use.*] *Beaum.*
2. Nocturnal musicians who attended great men. *Cyc.*
WAIVE, *n.* A woman put out of the protection of the law. *Cyc.*
WA'IWODE, *n.* In the Turkish empire, the governor of a small province or town; a general. *Cyc.*
WAKE, *v. i.* [Goth. *wakan;* Sax. *wæcan;* G. *wachen;* D. *waaken, wekken;* Sw. *våcka, up-våcka;* Dan. *vækker;* L. *vigil, vigilo.* The root *wak* is allied to *wag.* The primary sense is to stir, to rouse, to excite. The transitive verb in Saxon, is written *wæcan, wecan;* but both are from one root.]
1. To be awake; to continue awake; to watch; not to sleep. Ps. cxxvii.

The father *waketh* for the daughter. *Ecclus.*
Though wisdom *wakes,* suspicion sleeps. *Milton.*

I cannot think any time, *waking* or sleeping, without being sensible of it. *Locke.*

2. To be excited or roused from sleep; to awake; to be awakened. He *wakes* at the slightest noise.
3. To cease to sleep; to awake.

4. To be quick; to be alive or active. *Dryden.*

5. To be excited from a torpid state; to be put in motion. The dormant powers of nature *wake* from their frosty slumbers.

Gentle airs to fan the earth now *wak'd.* *Milton.*

WAKE, *v. t.* To rouse from sleep.

The angel that talked with me, came again and *waked* me. Zech. iv.

2. To arouse; to excite; to put in motion or action.

Prepare war, *wake up* the mighty men. Joel iii.

[The use of *up* is common, but not necessary.]

To *wake* the soul by tender strokes of art. *Pope.*

3. To bring to life again, as if from the sleep of death.

To second life
Wak'd in the renovation of the just. *Milton.*

WAKE, *n.* The feast of the dedication of the church, formerly kept by watching all night. *Dryden. King.*

2. Vigils; state of forbearing sleep.

—Their merry *wakes* and pastimes keep. *Milton.*

3. Act of waking. [*Old song.*]

Wake of a ship, the track it leaves in the water, formed by the meeting of the water, which rushes from each side to fill the space which the ship makes in passing through it.

To be in the wake of a ship, is to be in her track, or in a line with her keel.

WA'KEFUL, *a.* Not sleeping; indisposed to sleep.

Dissembling sleep, but *wakeful* with the fright— *Dryden.*

2. Watchful; vigilant.

WA'KEFULLY, *adv.* With watching or sleeplessness.

WA'KEFULNESS, *n.* Indisposition to sleep.

2. Forbearance of sleep; want of sleep. *Bacon.*

WAKEN, *v. i.* *wa'kn.* [This seems to be the Saxon infinitive retained.] To wake; to cease to sleep; to be awakened.

Early Turnus *wak'ning* with the light. *Dryden.*

WAKEN, *v. t.* *wa'kn.* To excite or rouse from sleep.

Go, *waken* Eve. *Milton.*

2. To excite to action or motion.

Then Homer's and Tyrtæus' martial muse
Waken'd the world. *Roscommon.*

3. To excite; to produce; to rouse into action.

They introduce
Their sacred song, and *waken* raptures high. *Milton.*

WA'KENED, *pp.* Roused from sleep; excited into action.

WA'KENER, *n.* One who rouses from sleep. *Feltham.*

WA'KENING, *ppr.* Rousing from sleep or stupidity; calling into action.

WA'KER, *n.* One who watches; one who rouses from sleep. *B. Jonson.*

WA'KE-ROBIN, *n.* A plant of the genus Arum.

WA'KING, *ppr.* Being awake; not sleeping.

2. Rousing from sleep; exciting into motion or action.

WA'KING, *n.* The period of being awake. *Butler.*

2. Watch. *Obs.*

WALE, *n.* [This may be the W. *gwialen*, a rod or twig, or from the same root.]

1. In cloth, a ridge or streak rising above the rest. We say, cloth is wove with a *wale.*

2. A streak or stripe; the mark of a rod or whip on animal flesh.

Wales of a ship, an assemblage of strong planks, extending along a ship's sides throughout the whole length, at different bights, and serving to strengthen the decks and form the curves. They are distinguished into the *main wale* and the *channel wale.* *Mar. Dict.*

WA'LE-KNOT, } *n.* A single wale-knot is
WALL-KNOT, } made by untwisting the ends of a rope, and making a bight with the first strand; then passing the second over the end of the first, and the third over the end of the second, and through the bight of the first. The double is made by passing the ends, singly, close underneath the first wale, and thrusting them upwards through the middle, only the last end comes up under two bights. *Cyc.*

WALK, *v. i.* *wauk.* [Sax. *wealcan*, to roll or revolve; *wealcere*, a fuller, whence the name *Walker;* D. *walken*, to work a hat; G. *walken*, to full, to felt hats; *walker*, a fuller, Sw. *valkare;* Dan. *valker*, to full or mill cloth; *valker*, a fuller; *valke*, a pad or stuffed roll; G. *wallen*, to stir, to be agitated, to rove, to travel, to wander. From the same root are Russ. *valyu*, G. *wälzen*, to roll, and *wälsch*, foreign, Celtic, Welsh, that is, wanderers. The primary sense is simply to move or press, but appropriately to roll, to press by rolling, as in hatting, and this is the origin of *walker*, for the practice of felting hats must have preceded that of fulling cloth in mills. Our ancestors appropriated the verb to moving on the feet, and the word is peculiarly expressive of that rolling or wagging motion which marks the walk of clownish people.]

1. To move slowly on the feet; to step slowly along; to advance by steps moderately repeated; as animals. Walking in men differs from running only in the rapidity and length of the steps; but in quadrupeds, the motion or order of the feet is sometimes changed.

At the end of twelve months, he *walked* in the palace of the kingdom of Babylon. Dan. iv.

When Peter had come down out of the ship, he *walked* on the water, to go to Jesus. Matt. xiv.

2. To move or go on the feet for exercise or amusement. Hundreds of students daily *walk* on Downing terrace in Cambridge.

3. To appear, as a specter.

The spirits of the dead
May *walk* again. *Shak.*

4. To act on any occasion.

Do you think I'd *walk* in any plot?
Obs. *B. Jonson.*

5. To be in motion, as a clamorous tongue.

Her tongue did *walk*
In foul reproach. *Obs.* *Spenser.*

6. To act or move on the feet in sleep.

When was it she last *walk'd?* *Shak.*

[But this is unusual. When we speak of noctambulation, we say, to *walk in sleep.*]

7. To range; to be stirring.

Affairs that *walk*,
As they say spirits do at midnight. *Shak.*

[*Unusual.*]

8. To move off; to depart.

When he comes forth he will make their cows and garrans *walk.* [*Not elegant.*] *Spenser.*

9. In *Scripture*, to live and act or behave; to pursue a particular course of life.

To walk with God, to live in obedience to his commands, and have communion with him. Gen. v.

To walk in darkness, to live in ignorance, error and sin, without comfort. 1 John i.

To walk in the light, to live in the practice of religion, and to enjoy its consolations. 1 John i.

To walk by faith, to live in the firm belief of the gospel and its promises, and to rely on Christ for salvation. 2 Cor. v.

To walk through the fire, to be exercised with severe afflictions. Is. xliii.

To walk after the flesh, to indulge sensual appetites, and to live in sin. Rom. viii.

To walk after the Spirit, to be guided by the counsels and influences of the Spirit and by the word of God, and to live a life of holy deportment. *Ib.*

To walk in the flesh, to live this natural life, which is subject to infirmities and calamities. 2 Cor. x.

To walk in, to enter, as a house. *Walk in*, gentlemen.

WALK, *v. t.* *wauk.* To pass through or upon; as, to *walk* the streets. [This is eliptical for to *walk in* or *through* the street.]

2. To cause to walk or step slowly; to lead, drive or ride with a slow pace. He found the road so bad he was obliged to *walk* his horse. The coachman *walked* his horses from Woodbridge to Princeton.

WALK, *n.* *wauk.* The act of walking; the act of moving on the feet with a slow pace.

2. The act of walking for air or exercise; as a morning *walk;* an evening *walk.* *Pope.*

3. Manner of walking; gait; step. We often know a person in a distant apartment by his *walk.*

4. Length of way or circuit through which one walks; or a place for walking; as a long *walk;* a short *walk.* The gardens of the Tuilerie and of the Luxemburgh are very pleasant *walks.*

5. An avenue set with trees. *Milton.*

6. Way; road; range; place of wandering.

The mountains are his *walks.* *Sandys.*
The starry *walks* above. *Dryden.*

7. Region; space.

He opened a boundless *walk* for his imagination. *Pope.*

8. Course of life or pursuit. This is not within the *walk* of the historian.

9. The slowest pace of a horse, ox or other quadruped.

10. A fish. [A mistake for *whelk.*] *Ainsworth.*

11. In *the West Indies*, a plantation of canes, &c. *Edwards, W. Ind.*

A *sheep walk*, so called, is high and dry land where sheep pasture.

WALKABLE, *a.* *wauk'able.* Fit to be walked on. [*Not much used.*] *Swift.*

WALKER, *n.* *wauk'er.* One who walks.
2. In our mother tongue, a fuller.
3. In *law*, a forest officer appointed to walk over a certain space for inspection; a forester.
4. One who deports himself in a particular manner.
5. A fulling-mill. [*Not in use or local.*]

WALKING, *ppr.* *wauk'ing.* Moving on the the legs with a slow pace; moving; conducting one's self.

WALKING, *n.* *wauk'ing.* The act of moving on the feet with a slow pace.

WALK'ING-STAFF, WALK'ING-STICK, *n.* A staff or stick carried in the hand for support or amusement in walking.

WALK-MILL, *n.* *wauk'-mill.* A fulling-mill. [*Local.*] *Cyc.*

WALL, *n.* [L. *vallum*; Sax. *weal*; D. *wal*; Ir. Gaelic, *balla* and *fal*; Russ. *val*; W. *gwal.* In L. *vallus* is a stake or post, and probably *vallum* was originally a fence of stakes, a palisade or stockade; the first rude fortification of uncivilized men. The primary sense of *vallus* is a shoot, or that which is set, and the latter may be the sense of *wall*, whether it is from *vallus*, or from some other root.]
1. A work or structure of stone, brick or other materials, raised to some highth, and intended for a defense or security. *Walls* of stone, with or without cement, are much used in America for fences on farms; *walls* are laid as the foundations of houses and the security of cellars. *Walls* of stone or brick form the exterior of buildings, and they are often raised round cities and forts as a defense against enemies.
2. *Walls*, in the plural, is used for fortifications in general; works for defense.

> I rush undaunted to defend the *walls.* *Dryden.*

3. A defense; means of security or protection. 1 Sam. xxv.

To take the wall, to take the upper or most honorable place.

> I will *take the wall* of any man or maid of Montague's. *Shak.*

WALL-CREEPER, *n.* A small bird of the genus Certhia; the spider-catcher. *Ed. Encyc.*

WALL'-CRESS, *n.* [*wall* and *cress.*] A plant of the genus Arabis. *Cyc.*
2. A plant of the genus Turritis. *Lee.*

WALL'-EYE, *n.* [*wall* and *eye.*] A disease in the crystaline humor of the eye; the glaucoma.
2. In *horses*, an eye in which the iris is of a very light gray color. *Cyc.*

WALL'-EYED, *a.* Having white eyes. *Johnson.*

WALL'-FLOWER, *n.* [*wall* and *flower.*] A plant of the genus Cheiranthus; a species of stock gillyflower.

WALL'-FRUIT, *n.* [*wall* and *fruit.*] Fruit which, to be ripened, must be planted against a wall.

WALL-LOUSE, *n.* [*wall* and *louse.*] An insect or small bug. [L. *cimex.*] *Ainsworth.*

WALL'-MOSS, *n.* A species of moss growing on walls.

WALL-PEN'NYWORT, *n.* A plant of the genus Cotyledon.

WALL-PEPPER, *n.* A plant of the genus Sedum.

WALL-PIE, *n.* A plant, a species of Asplenium. *Lee.*

WALL'-SIDED, *a.* Having sides nearly perpendicular, as a ship.

WALL'-SPRING, *n.* A spring of water issuing from stratified rocks.

WALL-WORT, *n.* A plant, the dwarf elder or danewort; a species of Sambucus.

WALL, *v. t.* To inclose with a wall; as, to *wall* a city.
2. To defend by walls.

> And terror of his name that *walls* us in
> From danger. *Denham.*

3. To fill up with a wall.

WALL'ED, *pp.* Inclosed or fortified with a wall.

WALL'ER, *n.* One who builds walls in the country. *Cyc.*

WALL'ERITE, *n.* A mineral, or variety of clay, found in small compact masses of the size of a nut, white and opake, or yellowish and translucent. *Cleaveland.*

WAL'LET, *n.* A bag for carrying the necessaries for a journey or march; a knapsack.
2. Any thing protuberant and swagging; as *wallets* of flesh. *Shak.*

WALL'ING, *ppr.* Inclosing or fortifying with a wall.

WALL'ING, *n.* Walls in general; materials for walls.

WAL'LOP, *v. i.* [formed on G. *wallen*, Sax. *wealan*, to boil or bubble; D. *opwallen*; Eng. to *well.* See *Well.*]
To boil with a continued bubbling or heaving and rolling of the liquor, with noise.

WAL'LOPING, *ppr.* Boiling with a heaving and noise.

WAL'LOW, *v. i.* [Sax. *wealwian*; Sw. *välfva*; Goth. *walugan*; G. *walzen.* The latter is the Eng. *welter*, but of the same family; L. *volvo*; Sp. *volver*; Russ. *valyu, baliayu.* This verb seems to be connected with *well, walk, &c.*]
1. To roll one's body on the earth, in mire, or on other substance; to tumble and roll in water. Swine *wallow* in the mire.
2. To move heavily and clumsily.

> Part huge of bulk,
> *Wallowing* unwieldy, enormous in their gait,
> Tempest the ocean. [*Unusual.*] *Milton.*

3. To live in filth or gross vice; as man *wallowing* in his native impurity. *South.*

WAL'LOW, *v. t.* To roll one's body.

> *Wallow* thyself in ashes. Jer. vi.

WAL'LOW, *n.* A kind of rolling walk.

WAL'LOWER, *n.* One that rolls in mire.

WAL'LOWING, *ppr.* Rolling the body on any thing.

WAL'NUT, *n.* [D. *walnoot*; Sax. *walh*, foreign, and *hnuta*, nut. The Germans call it *wälsche nuss*, Welsh nut, that is, foreign or Celtic nut.]
A tree and its fruit, of the genus Juglans. The black walnut, so called, grows in America, and is indigenous in the southern and middle states, as far north as the river Hudson. That is said to be the limit of its indigenous growth, but when transplanted, it grows well in the eastern states.
In America there are several species of hickory nut, called by this name.

WAL'RUS, *n.* [G. *wall*, as in *wallfisch*, a whale, and *ross*, a horse.]
The morse or sea horse, an animal of the northern seas, of the genus Trichechus.

WAL'TRON, *n.* Another name of the walrus. *Woodward.*

WALTZ, *n.* [G. *walzen*, to roll.] A modern dance and tune, the measure of whose music is triple; three quavers in a bar. *Busby.*

WAM'BLE, *v. i.* [D. *wemelen*; Dan *vamler*; Sw. *våmjas.*]
To be disturbed with nausea; as a *wambling* stomach. [*Vulgar.*] *L'Estrange.*

WAM'BLE-CROPPED, *a.* Sick at the stomach. [*Vulgar.*]

WAMPEE', *n.* A plant, a species of Arum.

WAM'PUM, *n.* Shells or strings of shells, used by the American Indians as money or a medium of commerce. These strings of shells when united, form a broad belt, which is worn as an ornament or girdle. It is sometimes called wampumpeague, and wompeague, or wampampeague, of which *wampum* seems to be a contraction. *Winthrop. Gookin.*

WAN, *a.* [Sax. *wan, wann*, deficient; *wanian*, to fail, to *wane*; *wan*, pale, that is, deficient in color; allied probably to *vain.* Qu. W. *gwan*, weak, and *gwyn*, white. The primary sense is to withdraw or depart.] Pale; having a sickly hue; languid of look.

> Sad to view, his visage pale and *wan.* *Spenser.*
>
> Why so pale and *wan*, fond lover? *Suckling.*

WAN, for *won*; *pret.* of *win.* *Obs.*

WAND, *n.* [D. *vaand.*] A small stick; a rod. If a child runs away, a few strokes of a *wand* will bring him back.
2. A staff of authority; as a silver *wand.* *Milton.*
3. A rod used by conjurers or diviners.

> Picus bore a buckler in his hand,
> His other wav'd a long divining *wand.* *Dryden.*

WAN'DER, *v. i.* [Sax. *wandrian*; D. *wandelen*, to walk; G. *wandeln*, to wander, to walk, to change, exchange or transform; Sw. *vånda*, to turn; *vandra*, to wander; Dan. *vandler*, to walk, to wander, to trade; *vandel*, behavior, deportment, conversation; It. *andare*, Sp. Port. *andar*, to go; Sans. *andara*, a wanderer.]
1. To rove; to ramble here and there without any certain course or object in view; as, to *wander* over the fields; to *wander* about the town, or about the country. Men may sometimes *wander* for amusement or exercise. Persons sometimes *wander* because they have no home and are wretched, and sometimes because they have no occupation.

> They *wandered* about in sheep-skins and goat-skins. Heb. xi.
>
> He *wandereth* abroad for bread. Job xv.
>
> He was *wandering* in the field. Gen. xxxvii.

2. To leave home; to depart; to migrate.

> When God caused me to *wander* from my father's house— Gen. xx.

3. To depart from the subject in discussion; as, to *wander* from the point.
4. In *a moral sense*, to stray; to deviate; to depart from duty or rectitude.

> O let me not *wander* from thy commandments. Ps. cxix.

5. To be delirious; not to be under the guidance of reason; as, the mind *wanders*.

WAN'DER, *v. t.* To travel over without a certain course.

Wand'ring many a famous realm. [*Elliptical.*] *Milton.*

WAN'DERER, *n.* A rambler; one that roves; one that deviates from duty.

WAN'DERING, *ppr.* Roving; rambling; deviating from duty.

WAN'DERING, *n.* Peregrination; a traveling without a settled course.

2. Aberration; mistaken way; deviation from rectitude; as a *wandering* from duty.

3. A roving of the mind or thoughts from the point or business in which one ought to be engaged. *Locke.*

4. The roving of the mind in a dream.

5. The roving of the mind in delirium.

6. Uncertainty; want of being fixed. *Locke.*

WAN'DERINGLY, *adv.* In a wandering or unsteady manner. *Taylor.*

WANDEROO', *n.* A baboon of Ceylon and Malabar.

WANE, *v. i.* [Sax. *wanian*, to fail, fall off or decrease.]

1. To be diminished; to decrease; particularly applied to the illuminated part of the moon. We say, the moon *wanes*, that is, the visible or illuminated part decreases.

Waning moons their settled periods keep. *Addison.*

2. To decline; to fail; to sink; as the *waning* age of life.

You saw but sorrow in its *waning* form. *Dryden.*

Land and trade ever will wax and *wane* together. *Child.*

WANE, *v. t.* To cause to decrease. *Obs.* *B. Jonson.*

WANE, *n.* Decrease of the illuminated part of the moon, to the eye of a spectator.

2. Decline; failure; diminution; decrease; declension.

You are cast upon an age in which the church is in its *wane*. *South.*

WANG, *n.* [Sax. *wang, weng, wong.*] The jaw, jaw-bone or cheek bone. [*Little used or vulgar.*]

2. The latchet of a shoe. [Sax. *sceo-thwang*, shoe-thong.] [*Not in use.*]

WANG-TOOTH, *n.* A jaw-tooth. *Cyc.*

WAN'HOPE, *n.* Want of hope. [*Not used.*]

WAN'HORN, *n.* A plant of the genus Kaempferia. *Lee.*

WA'NING, *ppr.* Decreasing; failing; declining.

WAN'LY, *adv.* In a pale manner; palely.

WAN'NED, *a.* Made wan or pale. *Shak.*

WAN'NESS, *n.* Paleness; a sallow, dead, pale color; as the *wanness* of the cheeks after a fever.

WAN'NISH, *a.* Somewhat wan; of a pale hue. *Fairfax.*

WANT, *n. waunt.* [Sax. *wan*, supra; *wanian*, to fail; Goth. *wan*, deficiency, want. This seems to be primarily a participle of *wane.*]

1. Deficiency; defect; the absence of that which is necessary or useful; as a *want* of power or knowledge for any purpose; *want* of food and clothing. The *want* of money is a common *want*. 2 Cor. viii. ix.

From having wishes in consequence of our *wants*, we often feel *wants* in consequence of our wishes. *Rambler.*

2. Need; necessity; the effect of deficiency.

Pride is as loud a beggar as *want*, and more saucy. *Franklin.*

3. Poverty; penury; indigence.

Nothing is so hard for those who abound in riches as to conceive how others can be in *want*. *Swift.*

4. The state of not having. I cannot write a letter at present for *want* of time.

5. That which is not possessed, but is desired or necessary for use or pleasure.

Habitual superfluities become actual *wants*. *Paley.*

6. A mole. *Heylin.*

WANT, *v. t. waunt.* To be destitute; to be deficient in; not to have; *a word of general application*; as, to *want* knowledge; to *want* judgment; to *want* learning; to *want* food and clothing; to *want* money.

2. To be defective or deficient in. Timber may *want* strength or solidity to answer its purpose.

3. To fall short; not to contain or have. The sum *wants* a dollar of the amount of debt.

Nor think, though men were none,
That heaven would *want* spectators, God *want* praise. *Milton.*

4. To be without.

The unhappy never *want* enemies. *Richardson.*

5. To need; to have occasion for, as useful, proper or requisite. Our manners *want* correction. In winter we *want* a fire; in summer we *want* cooling breezes. We all *want* more public spirit and more virtue.

6. To wish for; to desire. Every man *wants* a little pre-eminence over his neighbor. Many *want* that which they cannot obtain, and which if they could obtain, would certainly ruin them.

What *wants* my son? *Addison.*

WANT, *v. i. waunt.* To be deficient; not to be sufficient.

As in bodies, thus in souls, we find
What *wants* in blood and spirits, swell'd with wind. *Pope.*

2. To fail; to be deficient; to be lacking.

No time shall find me *wanting* to my truth. *Dryden.*

3. To be missed; not to be present. The jury was full, *wanting* one.

4. To fall short; to be lacking.

Twelve, *wanting* one, he slew. *Dryden.*

WANT'AGE, *n.* Deficiency; that which is wanting.

WANT'ED, *pp.* Needed; desired.

WANT'ING, *ppr.* Needing; lacking; desiring.

2. *a.* Absent; deficient. One of the twelve is *wanting*. We have the means, but the application is *wanting*.

3. Slack; deficient. I shall not be *wanting* in exertion.

WANT'LESS, *a.* Having no want; abundant; fruitful. *Warner.*

WAN'TON, *a.* [W. *gwantan*, apt to run off, variable, fickle, wanton; *gwantu*, to thrust, to sever; allied probably to *wander.*]

1. Wandering or roving in gayety or sport; sportive; frolicksome; darting aside, or one way and the other. *Wanton* boys kill flies for sport.

Note a wild and *wanton* herd. *Shak.*

2. Moving or flying loosely; playing in the wind.

She
Her unadorned golden tresses wore
Dishevel'd, but in *wanton* ringlets wav'd. *Milton.*

3. Wandering from moral rectitude; licentious; dissolute; indulging in sensuality without restraint; as men grown *wanton* by prosperity. *Roscommon.*

My plenteous joys,
Wanton in fullness— *Shak.*

4. *More appropriately*, deviating from the rules of chastity; lewd; lustful; lascivious; libidinous.

Thou art froward by nature, enemy to peace,
Lascivious, *wanton*. *Shak.*

Ye have lived in pleasure on the earth, and been *wanton*. James v.

5. Disposed to unchastity; indicating wantonness. Is. iii.

6. Loose; unrestrained; running to excess.

How does your tongue grow *wanton* in her praise! *Addison.*

7. Luxuriant; overgrown.

What we by day lop overgrown,
One night or two with *wanton* growth derides,
Tending to wild. *Milton.*

8. Extravagant; as *wanton* dress. *Milton.*

9. Not regular; not turned or formed with regularity.

The quaint mazes in the *wanton* green. *Milton.*

WAN'TON, *n.* A lewd person; a lascivious man or woman. *South. Shak.*

2. A trifler; an insignificant flutterer. *Shak.*

3. A word of slight endearment.

Peace, my *wanton*— [*Little used.*] *B. Jonson.*

WAN'TON, *v. i.* To rove and ramble without restraint, rule or limit; to revel; to play loosely.

Nature here
Wanton'd as in her prime. *Milton.*

Her golden tresses *wanton* in the wind. *Anon.*

2. To ramble in lewdness; to play lasciviously. *Prior.*

3. To move briskly and irregularly.

WAN'TONING, *ppr.* Roving; flying loosely; playing without restraint; indulging in licentiousness.

WAN'TONIZE, *v. i.* To behave wantonly. [*Not in use.*]

WAN'TONLY, *adv.* Loosely; without regularity or restraint; sportively; gayly; playfully; lasciviously.

WAN'TONNESS, *n.* Sportiveness; gayety; frolicksomeness; waggery.

—As sad as night,
Only for *wantonness*. *Shak.*

2. Licentiousness; negligence of restraint.

The tumults threatened to abuse all acts of grace, and turn them into *wantonness*. *K. Charles.*

3. Lasciviousness; lewdness. Rom. xiii. 2 Pet. ii.

WANT'-WIT, *n.* [*want* and *wit.*] One destitute of wit or sense; a fool. [*Not in much use.*] *Shak.*

WAN'TY, *n.* [D. *want*, cordage, tackling. Qu.]

A broad strap of lether, used for binding a load upon the back of a beast. [*Local.*] *Tusser.*

WAP'ACUT, *n.* The spotted owl of Hudson's bay.

WA'PED, *a.* [from the root of L. *vapulo*, to strike, and *awhap*, *whap*, which the common people in N. England use, and pronounce *whop*.]

Dejected; cast down; crushed by misery. [*Not in use.*] *Shak.*

WAP'ENTAKE, **WAP'ENTAC**, *n.* [Sax. *wæpen-tac*; but it is rather Gothic, as this division of a county was peculiar to the northern counties; *wæpen*, a weapon, and *tac*, *tace*, touch; Goth. *tekan*. See *Touch*. This name had its origin in a custom of touching lances or spears when the hundreder or chief entered on his office. "Cum quis accipiebat præfecturam wapentachii, die statuto in loco ubi consueverant congregari, omnes majores natu contra eum conveniebant, et descendente eo de equo suo, omnes assurgebant ei. Ipse vero erecta lancea sua, ab omnibus secundum morem fœdus accipiebat: omnes enim quotquot venissent cum lanceis suis ipsius hastam tangebant, et ita se confirmabant per contactum armorum, pace palam concessa. *Wæpnu* enim arma sonat; *tac*, tactus est—hac de causa totus ille conventus dicitur *wapentac*, eo quod per tactum armorum suorum ad invicem confœderati sunt."
LL. Edward Confessor 33. *Wilkins.*

Lye seems to doubt this explanation of the word *wapentac*, because the word *tac* is not found in the Saxon. He seems not to have considered that the word is known only in the north of England, where the Gothic dialects prevailed; and surely the word must have been understood in the age of Edward the Confessor.]

In some northern counties of England, a division or district, answering to the hundred or cantred in other counties. The name was first given to the meeting, supra. *Selden. Blackstone. Wilkins.*

WAPP, *n.* In *a ship*, the rope with which the shrouds are set taught in wale-knots. *Cyc.*

WAP'PE, *n.* A species of cur, said to be so called from his voice. His only use is to alarm the family by barking when any person approaches the house. *Cyc.*

WAP'PER, *n.* A fish; a name given to the smaller species of the river gudgeon. *Cyc.*

WAR, *n. waur.* [Sax. *wær*; Fr. *guerre*; It. Sp. Port. *guerra*; D. *warren*, to quarrel, wrangle, entangle; Dan. *virrer*; G. *verwirren*, to perplex, embroil, disturb. The primary sense of the root is to strive, struggle, urge, drive, or to turn, to twist.]

1. A contest between nations or states, carried on by force, either for defense, or for revenging insults and redressing wrongs, for the extension of commerce or acquisition of territory, or for obtaining and establishing the superiority and dominion of one over the other. These objects are accomplished by the slaughter or capture of troops, and the capture and destruction of ships, towns and property. Among rude nations, war is often waged and carried on for plunder. As war is the contest of nations or states, it always implies that such contest is authorized by the monarch or the sovereign power of the nation. When war is commenced by attacking a nation in peace, it is called an *offensive* war, and such attack is *aggressive*. When war is undertaken to repel invasion or the attacks of an enemy, it is called *defensive*, and a defensive war is considered as justifiable. Very few of the wars that have desolated nations and deluged the earth with blood, have been justifiable. Happy would it be for mankind, if the prevalence of christian principles might ultimately extinguish the spirit of war, and if the ambition to be great, might yield to the ambition of being good.

Preparation for *war* is sometimes the best security for peace. *Anon.*

2. In *poetical language*, instruments of war.

His complement of stores, and total *war*. *Prior.*

3. *Poetically*, forces; army.

O'er the embattled ranks the waves return,
And overwhelm their *war*. *Milton.*

4. The profession of arms; art of war; as a fierce man of *war*. Is. ii. *Wisdom.*

5. Hostility; state of opposition or contest; act of opposition. *Shak.*

6. Enmity; disposition to contention.

The words of his mouth were smoother than butter, but *war* was in his heart. Ps. lv.

Man of war, in naval affairs, a ship of large size, armed and equipped for attack or defense.

Holy war, a crusade; a war undertaken to deliver the Holy Land, or Judea, from infidels. These *holy wars* were carried on by most unholy means.

WAR, *v. i.* To make war; to invade or attack a nation or state with force of arms; to carry on hostilities; or to be in a state of contest by violence.

He teacheth my hands to *war*. 2 Sam. xxii.

And they *warred* against the Midianites. Num. xxxi.

Why should I *war* without the walls of Troy? *Shak.*

2. To contend; to strive violently; to be in a state of opposition.

Lusts which *war* against the soul. 1 Pet. ii.

WAR, *v. t.* To make war upon; as, to *war* the Scot. [*Not used.*]

2. To carry on a contest.

That thou mightest *war* a good warfare. 1 Tim. i.

WAR'-BEAT, **WAR'-BEATEN**, *a.* [*war* and *beat*.] Worn down in war. *J. Barlow.*

WAR'BLE, *v. t.* [G. *wirbeln*, to turn, whirl, warble; *wirbel*, a whirl, a vortex; *wirbelbein*, a turning bone or joint, L. *vertebra*; Dan. *hvirvler*, Eng. to *whirl*. These words are all of one family; L. *verto*, Eng. *veer*, *vary*, *&c.*]

1. To quaver a sound or the voice; to modulate with turns or variations. Certain birds are remarkable for *warbling* their songs.

2. To cause to quaver.

And touch the *warbled* string. *Milton.*

3. To utter musically; to be modulated.

If she be right invok'd with *warbled* song. *Milton.*

Warbling sweet the nuptial lay. *Trumbull.*

WAR'BLE, *v. i.* To be quavered or modulated.

Such strains ne'er *warble* in the linnet's throat. *Gay.*

2. To be uttered melodiously; as *warbling* lays.

For *warbling* notes from inward cheering flow. *Sidney.*

3. To sing.

Birds on the branches *warbling*. *Milton.*

WAR'BLED, *pp.* Quavered; modulated; uttered musically.

WAR'BLER, *n.* A singer; a songster; *used of birds.*

In lulling strains the fether'd *warblers* woo. *Tickel.*

2. The common name of a genus of small birds *(Sylvia,)* comprising most of the small woodland songsters of Europe and N. America. They feed on insects and are very lively and active. The blue-bird is a species of the genus. *Ed. Encyc. Wilson.*

WAR'BLES, *n.* In *farriery*, small hard tumors on the backs of horses, occasioned by the heat of the saddle in traveling, or by the uneasiness of its situation; also, small tumors produced by the larvas of the gad fly, in the backs of horses, cattle, &c. *Cyc.*

WAR'BLING, *ppr.* Quavering the voice; modulating notes; singing.

2. *a.* Filled with musical notes; as the *warbling* glade. *Trumbull.*

WAR'BLING, *n.* The act of shaking or modulating notes; singing.

WARD, in composition, as in *toward*, *homeward*, is the Sax. *weard*, from the root of L. *verto*, &c. It corresponds to the L. *versus*.

WARD, *v. t. waurd.* [Sax. *weardian*; Sw. *vårda*; Dan. *værger*; probably from Sax. *warian*, *werian*; Goth. *waryan*; D. *weeren*, to defend, guard, prevent; W. *gwaru*, to fend; allied to *wary*, *aware*; Fr. *garder*, for *guarder*, It. *guardare*, Sp. *guardar*. The primary sense is to repel, to keep off; hence to stop; hence to defend by repelling or other means.]

1. To guard; to keep in safety; to watch.

Whose gates he found fast shut, ne living wight
To *ward* the same— *Spenser.*

[In this sense, *ward* is obsolete, as we have adopted the French of the same word, to *guard*. We now never apply *ward* to the thing to be defended, but always to the thing against which it is to be defended. We *ward off* a blow or dagger, and we *guard* a person or place.]

2. To defend; to protect.

Tell him it was a hand that *warded* him
From thousand dangers. *Shak.*

[Obs. See the remark, supra.]

3. To fend off; to repel; to turn aside any thing mischievous that approaches.

Now *wards* a falling blow, now strikes again. *Daniel.*

The pointed jav'lin *warded* off his rage. *Addison.*

It instructs the scholar in the various methods of *warding off* the force of objections. *Watts.*

[This is the present use of *ward*. To *ward off* is now the more general expression, nor can I, with Johnson, think it less elegant.]

WARD, *v. i. waurd.* To be vigilant; to keep guard. *Obs.*

2. To act on the defensive with a weapon.

She drove the stranger to no other shift, than to *ward* and go back. *Sidney.*

And on their *warding* arms light bucklers bear. *Dryden.*

WARD, *n.* Watch; act of guarding.

Still when she slept, he kept both watch and *ward.* *Spenser.*

2. Garrison; troops to defend a fort; as small *wards* left in forts. [*Not in use.*] *Spenser.*
3. Guard made by a weapon in fencing.

For want of other *ward,*
He lifted up his hand his front to guard. *Dryden.*

4. A fortress; a strong hold. *Shak.*
5. One whose business is to guard, watch and defend; as a fire-*ward.*
6. A certain district, division or quarter of a town or city, committed to an alderman. There are twenty six *wards* in London.
7. Custody; confinement under guard. Pharaoh put his butler and baker in *ward.* Gen. xl.
8. A minor or person under the care of a guardian. See Blackstone's chapter on the rights and duties of guardian and *ward.*
9. The state of a child under a guardian.

I must attend his majesty's commands, to whom I am now in *ward.* *Shak.*

10. Guardianship; right over orphans.

It is inconvenient in Ireland, that the *wards* and marriages of gentlemen's children should be in the disposal of any of those lords. *Spenser.*

11. The division of a forest.
12. The division of a hospital.
13. A part of a lock which corresponds to its proper key.

WARD'ED, *pp.* Guarded.

Warded off, prevented from attacking or injuring.

WARD'EN, *n.* A keeper; a guardian.

2. An officer who keeps or guards; a keeper; as the *warden* of the fleet or fleet prison.
3. A large pear.

Warden of the cinque ports, in England, an officer or magistrate who has the jurisdiction of a port or haven. There are five such ports.

Warden of a university, is the master or president.

WARD'ER, *n.* A keeper; a guard.

The *warders* of the gate. *Dryden.*

2. A truncheon by which an officer of arms forbad fight. *Shak.*

Warders of the tower, officers who attend state prisoners.

WARD'MOTE, *n.* [*ward* and Sax. *mote*, meeting.]

In *law*, a court held in each ward in London.

WARD'ROBE, *n.* [*ward* and *robe*; Fr. *garde-robe.*]

1. A room or apartment where clothes or wearing apparel is kept.
2. Wearing apparel in general.

WARD'-ROOM, *n.* [*ward* and *room.*] In *a ship*, a room over the gun-room, where the lieutenants and other principal officers sleep and mess. *Mar. Dict.*

WARD'SHIP, *n.* Guardianship; care and protection of a ward.

2. Right of guardianship.

Wardship is incident to tenure in socage. *Blackstone.*

3. Pupilage; state of being under a guardian. *K. Charles.*

WARD'-STAFF, *n.* A constable's or watchman's staff.

WARE, *pret.* of *wear*, obs. It is now written *wore.*

WARE, *a.* [Sax. *war*; Dan. *vær.* It belongs to the root of *ward.* We never use *ware* by itself. But we use it in *aware, beware*, and in *wary.* It was formerly in use.]

1. Being in expectation of; provided against. 2 Tim. iv.
2. Wary; cautious. *Milton.*

WARE, *v. i.* To take heed of. [We now use *beware* as a single word, though in fact it is not.]

Then *ware* a rising tempest on the main.
Obs. *Dryden.*

WARE, *v. t.* pret. *wore.* [This is evidently from the root of *veer.* See *Veer.*]

To cause a ship to change her course from one board to the other, by turning her stern to the wind; opposed to *tacking*, in which the head is turned to the wind; as, to *ware* ship. We *wore* ship and stood to the southward.

WARE, *n.* plu. *wares.* [Sax. *ware*; D. *waar*; G. *waare*; Sw. *vara*; Dan. *vare.*]

Goods; commodities; merchandise; *usually in the plural*; but we say, China *ware*, earthern-*ware*, potters' *ware.* It was formerly used in the singular, and may be so used still.

Let the dark shop commend the *ware.* *Cleaveland.*

Sea ware, a marine plant, a species of Fucus. *Lee.*

WA'REFUL, *a.* [from *ware*, wary.] Wary; watchful; cautious. [*Not used.*]

WA'REFULNESS, *n.* Wariness; cautiousness. *Obs.*

WA'REHOUSE, *n.* [*ware* and *house.*] A storehouse for goods. *Addison.*

WA'REHOUSE, *v. t.* *s* as *z.* To deposit or secure in a warehouse.

WA'REHOUSED, *pp.* Placed in a store for safe keeping.

WA'REHOUSING, *ppr.* Repositing in a store for safe keeping.

WA'RELESS, *a.* Unwary; incautious. *Obs.* *Spenser.*

2. Suffered unawares. *Obs.*

WA'RELY, *adv.* Cautiously. *Obs.* [See *Warily.*]

WAR'FARE, *n.* [*war* and *fare*, Sax. *faran*, to go.] Military service; military life; war.

The Philistines gathered their armies for *warfare.* 1 Sam. xxviii.

2. Contest; struggle with spiritual enemies.

The weapons of our *warfare* are not carnal. 2 Cor. x.

WAR'FARE, *v. i.* To lead a military life; to carry on continual wars.

In that credulous *warfaring* age. [*Little used.*] *Camden.*

WAR'HABLE, *a.* [*war* and L. *habilis.*] Fit for war. [*Not in use.*] *Spenser.*

WAR'HOOP, *n.* [*war* and *hoop.*] The savage yell of war; a yell uttered on entering into battle.

WA'RILY, *adv.* [from *wary.*] Cautiously; with timorous prudence or wise foresight. Great enterprises are to be conducted *warily.* Change of laws should be *warily* proceeded in. *Hooker.*

WAR'INE, *n.* A species of monkey of S. America. *Dict. Nat. Hist.*

WA'RINESS, *n.* Caution; prudent care to foresee and guard against evil. The road was so slippery, and the danger so great, that we were obliged to proceed with *wariness.*

To determine what are little things in religion, great *wariness* is to be used. *Sprat.*

WARK, *n.* Work; a building. *Spenser.*
[It is obsolete, except in *bulwark.*]

WAR'LIKE, *a.* [*war* and *like.*] Fit for war; disposed for war; as a *warlike* state.

Old Siward with ten thousand *warlike* men. *Shak.*

2. Military; pertaining to war; as *warlike* toil. *Milton.*
3. Having a martial appearance.
4. Having the appearance of war.

WAR'LIKENESS, *n.* A warlike disposition or character. [*Little used.*] *Sandys.*

WAR'LING, *n.* One often quarreled with; a word coined perhaps to rhyme with *darling.* [*Not in use.*] *Camden.*

WAR'LOCK, } *n.* [*wær-loga*, in Saxon, sig-
WAR'LUCK, } nifies perfidious, false to covenants. Qu. Ice. *vard-lookr.*]

A male witch; a wizard. *Dryden.*
[*This word is not in use.*]

WARM, *a.* *waurm.* [Goth. D. G. *warm*; Sax. *wearm*; Sw. Dan. *varm*; Ant. L. *formus.* This word is probably a derivative from the root of L. *ferveo*, whence *fermentum*, Eng. *barm.* See *Swarm.*]

1. Having heat in a moderate degree; not cold; as *warm* blood; *warm* milk. The flesh of living animals is *warm*, if their blood is *warm.* But some animals have not *warm* blood.
2. Subject to heat; having prevalence of heat, or little or no winter; as the *warm* climate of Egypt.
3. Zealous; ardent; as, to be *warm* in the cause of our country or of religion.

Each *warm* wish springs mutual from the heart. *Pope.*

4. Habitually ardent or passionate; keen; irritable; as a *warm* temper.
5. Easily excited or provoked; irritable; as *warm* passions.
6. Violent; furious; as a *warm* contest. We shall have *warm* work to-day.
7. Busy in action; heated in action; ardent. Be *warm* in fight.
8. Fanciful; enthusiastic; as a *warm* head.
9. Vigorous; sprightly.

Now *warm* in youth, now withering in thy bloom,
Lost in a convent's solitary gloom. *Pope.*

WARM, *v. t.* [Sax. *wearmian*; Goth. *warmyan.*]

1. To communicate a moderate degree of heat to; as, a stove *warms* an apartment. The sun in summer *warms* the earth, and gives life to vegetation.
2. To make engaged or earnest; to interest; to engage; to excite ardor or zeal in; as, to *warm* the heart with love or zeal.

I formerly *warmed* my head with reading controversial writings. *Pope.*

WARM, *v. i.* To become moderately heated. The earth soon *warms* in a clear day in summer.

2. To become ardent or animated. The speaker should *warm* as he proceeds in the argument, for as he becomes animated, he excites more interest in his audience.

WARM'ED, *pp.* Moderately heated; made ardent; excited.

WARM'ING, *ppr.* Making moderately hot; making ardent or zealous.

WARM'ING-PAN, *n.* [*warm* and *pan.*] A covered pan with a long handle, for warming a bed with ignited coals.

WARM'ING-STONE, *n.* [*warm* and *stone.*] A stone dug in Cornwall, which retains heat a great while, and has been found to give ease in internal hemorrhoids. *Ray.*

WARM'LY, *adv.* With gentle heat. *Milton.*

2. Eagerly; earnestly; ardently; as, to espouse *warmly* the cause of Bible societies.

WARM'NESS, WARMTH, *n.* Gentle heat; as the *warmth* of the blood.

2. Zeal; ardor; fervor; as the *warmth* of love or of piety.

3. Earnestness; eagerness. The cause of the Greeks has been espoused with *warmth* by all parties in free countries.

4. Excitement; animation; as the *warmth* of passion. The preacher declaimed with great *warmth* against the vices of the age.

5. Fancifulness; enthusiasm; as *warmth* of head. *Temple.*

6. In *painting*, the fiery effect given to a red color by a small addition of yellow. *Cyc.*

WARN, *v. t.* *waurn.* [Sax. *warnian*; Sw. *varna*; G. *warnen*; formed on the root of *ware, wary*, Sax. *warian.* This is our *garnish*, as used in law, Norm. *garnisher*; also *garner*, for *guarner*, to warn, to admonish or give notice.]

1. To give notice of approaching or probable danger or evil, that it may be avoided; to caution against any thing that may prove injurious.

> Juturna *warns* the Daunian chief
> Of Lausus' danger— *Dryden.*

> Being *warned* of God in a dream, that they should not return to Herod, they departed into their own country another way. Matt. ii.

2. To caution against evil practices. 1 Thess. v.

3. To admonish of any duty.

> Cornelius—was *warned* from God by an holy angel to send for thee. Acts x.

4. To inform previously; to give notice to. *Shak.*

> —*Warn'd* of th' ensuing fight. *Dryden.*

5. To notify by authority; to summon; as, to *warn* the citizens to meet on a certain day; to *warn* soldiers to appear on parade.

6. To ward off. [*Not in use.*] *Spenser.*

WARN'ED, *pp.* Cautioned against danger; admonished of approaching evil; notified.

WARN'ER, *n.* An admonisher.

WARN'ING, *ppr.* Cautioning against danger; admonishing; giving notice to; summoning to meet or appear.

WARN'ING, *n.* Caution against danger, or against faults or evil practices which incur danger.

> Could *warning* make the world more just or wise. *Dryden.*

> Hear the word at my mouth, and give them *warning* from me. Ezek. iii.

2. Previous notice; as a short *warning*. He had a month's *warning*. *Dryden.*

WAR'-OFFICE, *n.* An office in which the military affairs of a country are superintended and managed. *U. States.*

WARP, *n.* *waurp.* [Sax. *wearp*; D. *werp*, a cast or throw. See the Verb.]

1. In *manufactures*, the threads which are extended lengthwise in the loom, and crossed by the woof.

2. In *a ship*, a rope employed in drawing, towing or removing a ship or boat; a towing line. *Mar. Dict.*

3. In *agriculture*, a slimy substance deposited on land by marine tides, by which a rich alluvial soil is formed. [*Local.*] *Cyc.*

4. In *cows*, a miscarriage. [See the Verb.] [*Local.*]

WARP, *v. i.* [Sax. *weorpan, wurpan, wyrpan*, to throw, to return; G. *werfen*, to cast or throw, to whelp; D. *werpen*, to throw or fling, to whelp, kitten or litter; Dan. *værper*, to lay eggs; *varper*, to tow; Sw. *vărpa*, to lay eggs; Ir. Gaelic, *fiaram*, to bend, twist, incline.]

1. To turn, twist or be twisted out of a straight direction; as, a board *warps* in seasoning, or in the heat of the sun, by shrinking.

> They clamp one piece of wood to the end of another, to keep it from casting or *warping*. *Moxon.*

2. To turn or incline from a straight, true or proper course; to deviate.

> There's our commission,
> From which we would not have you *warp*. *Shak.*

> Methinks
> My favor here begins to *warp*. *Shak.*

3. To fly with a bending or waving motion; to turn and wave, like a flock of birds or insects. The following use of *warp* is inimitably beautiful.

> As when the potent rod
> Of Amram's son, in Egypt's evil day,
> Wav'd round the coast, up called a pitchy cloud
> Of locusts, *warping* on the eastern wind— *Milton.*

4. To slink; to cast the young prematurely; as cows.

> In an enclosure near a dog-kennel, eight heifers out of twenty *warped.* [*Local.*] *Cyc.*

WARP, *v. t.* To turn or twist out of shape, or out of a straight direction, by contraction. The heat of the sun *warps* boards and timber.

2. To turn aside from the true direction; to cause to bend or incline; to pervert.

> This first avow'd, nor folly *warp'd* my mind. *Dryden.*

> I have no private considerations to *warp* me in this controversy. *Addison.*

> —Zeal, to a degree of warmth able to *warp* the sacred rule of God's word. *Locke.*

3. In *seamen's language*, to tow or move with a line or warp, attached to buoys, to anchors or to other ships, &c. by which means a ship is drawn, usually in a bending course or with various turns.

4. In *rural economy*, to cast the young prematurely. [*Local.*] *Cyc.*

5. In *agriculture*, to inundate, as land, with sea water; or to let in the tide, for the purpose of fertilizing the ground by a deposit of warp or slimy substance. *Warp* here is the *throw*, or that which is cast by the water. [*Local in Lincolnshire and Yorkshire, Eng.*] *Cyc.*

6. In *rope-making*, to run the yarn off the winches into hauls to be tarred.

To warp water, in Shakspeare, is forced and unusual; indeed it is not English.

WARP'ED, *pp.* Twisted by shrinking or seasoning; turned out of the true direction; perverted; moved with a warp; overflowed.

WARP'ING, *ppr.* Turning or twisting; causing to incline; perverting; moving with a warp; enriching by overflowing with tide water.

WARP'ING-BANK, *n.* A bank or mound of earth raised round a field for retaining the water let in from the sea. [*Local.*] *Cyc.*

WARP'ING-CLOUGH, WARP'ING-HATCH, WARP'ING-SLUICE, *n.* A flood gate to let in tide water upon land. [*Local.*]

WARP'ING-CUT, WARP'ING-DRAIN, WARP'ING-GUTTER, *n.* An open passage or channel for discharging the water from lands inundated. [*Local.*] *Cyc.*

WARP'ING-HOOK, *n.* A hook used by rope-makers for hanging the yarn on, when warping into hauls for tarring. *Cyc.*

WARP'ING-POST, *n.* A strong post used in warping rope yarn. *Cyc.*

WAR'PROOF, *n.* [*war* and *proof.*] Valor tried by war.

WAR'RANT, *v. t.* [Gaelic, *barantas*, a warrant or pledge; *baranta*, a *warrantee* or surety; W. *gwarantu*, to warrant or guarantee; *gwarant*, warrant, attestation, authority, security; said to be from *gwar*, smooth, placid, secure; Norm. *garranty*, warranted, proved; *garren*, [*guarren*,] a *warren*; Fr. *garantir*, [*guarantir*,] to warrant; *garenne*, a *warren*; It. *guarentire*. This is from the root of *guard, warren* and *wary*. The primary sense of the root is to stop or hold, or to repel, and thus guard by resisting danger; as we say, to *keep off*. Hence the sense of security. The Welsh sense of smooth, placid, is derivative, either from security, or from repressing. See *Guard* and *Garrison.*]

1. To authorize; to give authority or power to do or forbear any thing, by which the person authorized is secured or saved harmless from any loss or damage by the act. A commission *warrants* an officer to seize an enemy. We are not *warranted* to resist legitimate government, except in extreme cases.

2. To maintain; to support by authority or proof.

> Reason *warrants* it, and we may safely receive it as true.

3. To justify.

> True fortitude is seen in great exploits,
> That justice *warrants*, and that wisdom guides. *Addison.*

4. To secure; to exempt; to privilege.

> I'll *warrant* him from drowning. *Shak.*

> In a place
> Less *warranted* than this, or less secure,
> I cannot be— *Milton.*

5. To declare with assurance.

> My neck is as smooth as silk, I *warrant* ye. *L'Estrange.*

6. In *law*, to secure to a grantee an estate granted; to assure.

7. To secure to a purchaser of goods the title to the same; or to indemnify him against loss.

8. To secure to a purchaser the good quality of the goods sold. [See *Warranty.*]

9. To assure that a thing is what it appears to be, which implies a covenant to make good any defect or loss incurred by it.

WAR'RANT, *n.* An act, instrument or obligation, by which one person authorizes another to do something which he has not otherwise a right to do; an act or instrument investing one with a right or authority, and thus securing him from loss or damage; *a word of general application.*

2. A precept authorizing an officer to seize an offender and bring him to justice. A general *warrant* to seize suspected persons, is illegal.

3. Authority; power that authorizes or justifies any act. Those who preach the gospel have the *warrant* of Scripture. We have the *warrant* of natural right to do what the laws do not forbid; but civility and propriety may sometimes render things improper, which natural right warrants.

4. A commission that gives authority, or that justifies.

5. A voucher; that which attests or proves.

6. Right; legality.

There's *warrant* in that theft
Which steals itself when there's no mercy left. *Obs.* *Shak.*

7. A writing which authorizes a person to receive money or other thing.

Warrant of attorney, that by which a man appoints another to act in his name, and warrants his transaction.

Land warrant, is an instrument or writing issued by the proper officer, authorizing a person to locate or take up a tract of new or uncultivated land. *U. States.*

Search warrant, a precept authorizing a person to enter houses, shops, &c. to search for a criminal, for stolen or smuggled goods.

Warrant officer, an officer holding a warrant from the navy board, such as the master, surgeon, purser, &c. of a ship.

WAR'RANTABLE, *a.* Authorized by commission, precept or right; justifiable; defensible. The seizure of a thief is always *warrantable* by law and justice. Falsehood is never *warrantable.*

His meals are coarse and short, his employment *warrantable.* *South*

WAR'RANTABLENESS, *n.* The quality of being justifiable. *Sidney.*

WAR'RANTABLY, *adv.* In a manner that may be justified; justifiably. *Wake.*

WAR'RANTED, *pp.* Authorized; justified; secured; assured by covenant or by implied obligation.

WARRANTEE', *n.* The person to whom land or other thing is warranted. *Ch. Justice Parsons.*

WAR'RANTER, *n.* One who gives authority or legally empowers.

2. One who assures, or covenants to assure; one who contracts to secure another in a right, or to make good any defect of title or quality; as the *warranter* of a horse.

WAR'RANTING, *ppr.* Authorizing; empowering.

2. Assuring; securing to another a right, or covenanting to make good a defect of title in lands, or of quality in goods.

WAR'RANTISE, *n.* Authority; security. [*Not in use.*] *Shak.*

WAR'RANTOR, *n.* One who warrants.

WAR'RANTY, *n.* In *law*, a promise or covenant by deed, made by the bargainer for himself and his heirs, to warrant or secure the bargainee and his heirs against all men in the enjoyment of an estate or other thing granted. Such warranty passes from the seller to the buyer, from the feoffor to the feoffee, and from the releaser to the releasee. Warranty is *real*, when annexed to lands and tenements granted in fee or for life, &c. and is in deed or in law; and *personal*, when it respects goods sold or their quality.

In common recoveries, a fictitious person is called to warranty. In the sale of goods or personal property, the seller warrants the title; for warranty is express or implied. If a man sells goods which are not his own, or which he has no right to sell, the purchaser may have satisfaction for the injury. And if the seller expressly warrants the goods to be sound and not defective, and they prove to be otherwise, he must indemnify the purchaser; for the law implies a contract in the warranty, to make good any defect. But the warranty must be at the time of sale, and not afterwards. *Blackstone.*

2. Authority; justificatory mandate or precept.

If they disobey any precept, that is no excuse to us, nor gives us any *warranty* to disobey likewise. *Kettlewell.*

[In this sense, *warrant* is now used.]

3. Security.

The stamp was a *warranty* of the public. *Locke.*

WAR'RANTY, *v. t.* To warrant; to guaranty. [*A useless word.*]

WARRA'Y, *v. t.* [Fr. *guerroyer*, from *guerre.*] To make war upon. *Obs.* *Spenser.*

WARRE, *a.* [Sax. *wærra*, for *wærsa.*] Worse. *Obs.* *Spenser.*

WAR'REN, *n.* [from the root of *wear*, an inclosed place; Fr. *garenne*; D. *waarande*; Goth. *waryan*, Sax. *warian*, to defend. See *Guard*, *Warrant* and *Wary.*]

1. A piece of ground appropriated to the breeding and preservation of rabbits.

2. In *law*, a franchise or place privileged by prescription or grant from the king, for keeping beasts and fowls. The *warren* is the next franchise in degree to the park; and a forest, which is the highest in dignity, comprehends a chase, a park and a free warren. *Cyc.*

3. A place for keeping fish in a river. *Cyc.*

WAR'RENER, *n.* The keeper of a warren. *Johnson.*

WAR'RIANGLE, *n.* A hawk. *Ainsworth.*

WAR'RIOR, *n.* [from *war*; Fr. *guerrier*; It. *guerriere*; Sp. *guerrero*, *guerreador.*]

1. In *a general sense*, a soldier; a man engaged in military life.

2. Emphatically, a brave man; a good soldier.

WAR'RIORESS, *n.* A female warrior. *Spenser.*

WART, *n. waurt.* [Sax. *weart*; D. *wrat*; G. *warze*; Sw. *vårta*; L. *verruca*; Fr. *verrue.*]

1. A hard excrescence on the skin of animals, which is covered with the production of the cuticle. In *horses*, warts are spungy excrescences on the hinder pasterns, which suppurate. *Cyc.*

2. A protuberance on trees.

WART'ED, *a.* In *botany*, having little knobs on the surface; verrucose; as a *warted* capsule. *Martyn.*

WART'WÖRT, *n.* A plant of the genus Euphorbia or spurge, which is studded with hard warty knobs; also, a plant of the genus Heliotropium, and another of the genus Lapsana. *Cyc. Lee.*

WART'Y, *a.* Having warts; full of warts; overgrown with warts; as a *warty* leaf. *Lee.*

2. Of the nature of warts.

WAR'-WORN, *a.* [*war* and *worn.*] Worn with military service; as a *war-worn* coat; a *war-worn* soldier.

WA'RY, *a.* [Sax. *wær*; Ice. *var.* See *Ware* and *Warn.*]

Cautious of danger; carefully watching and guarding against deception, artifices and dangers; scrupulous; timorously prudent. Old men are usually more *wary* than the young. It is incumbent on a general in war to be always *wary.*

WAS, *s* as *z*; the past tense of the substantive verb; Sax. Goth. *wesan*; L. *esse*, for *vesse*, to be, to exist, whence Eng. *is*, in the present tense, and *was* in the past; as, I *was*; he *was.*

WASH, *v. t.* [Sax. *wæscan*; G. *waschen*; D. *wasschen.*]

1. To cleanse by ablution, or by rubbing in water; as, to *wash* the hands or the body; to *wash* garments.

2. To wet; to fall on and moisten; as, the rain *washes* the flowers or plants.

3. To overflow. The tides *wash* the meadows.

4. To overflow or dash against; to cover with water; as, the waves *wash* the strand or shore; the sea *washes* the rocks on the shore or beach.

5. To scrub in water; as, to *wash* a deck or a floor.

6. To separate extraneous matter from; as, to *wash* ore; to *wash* grain.

7. In *painting*, to lay a color over any work with a pencil, to give it the proper tints, and make it appear more natural. Thus work is *washed* with a pale red to imitate brick, &c.

8. To rub over with some liquid substance; as, to *wash* trees for removing insects or diseases.

9. To squeeze and cleanse in water; as, to *wash* wool. So sheep are said to be *washed*, when they are immersed in water and their wool squeezed, by which means it is cleansed.

10. To cleanse by a current of water; as, showers *wash* the streets.

11. To overlay with a thin coat of metal; as steel *washed* with silver.

12. To purify from the pollution of sin.

But ye are *washed*, but ye are sanctified. 1 Cor. vi.

To wash a ship, to bring all her guns to one side to make her heel, and then to wash and scrape her side.

WASH, *v. i.* To perform the act of ablution.

Wash in Jordan seven times. 2 Kings v.

[*Elliptical.*]

2. To perform the business of cleansing clothes in water.

She can *wash* and scour. *Shak.*

To wash off, in calico-printing, to soak and

rinse printed calicoes, to dissolve and remove the gum and paste. *Cyc.*

WASH, *n.* Alluvial matter; substances collected and deposited by water; as the *wash* of a river.

2. A bog; a marsh; a fen.

Neptune's salt *wash.* *Shak.*

3. A cosmetic; as a *wash* for the face, to help the complexion.

4. A lotion; a medical liquid preparation for external application.

5. A superficial stain or color. *Collier.*

6. Waste liquor of a kitchen for hogs.

7. The act of washing the clothes of a family; or the whole quantity washed at once. There is a great *wash*, or a small *wash.*

8. With *distillers*, the fermentable liquor made by dissolving the proper subject for fermentation and distillation in common water. In the distillery of malt, the wash is made by mixing the water hot, with the malt ground into meal. *Cyc.*

9. The shallow part of a river, or arm of the sea; as the *washes* in Lincolnshire. *Cyc.*

10. The blade of an oar; the thin part, which enters the water and by whose impulse the boat is moved.

11. The color laid on a picture to vary its tints.

12. A substance laid on boards or other work for beauty or preservation.

13. A thin coat of metal.

14. In *the W. Indies*, a mixture of dunder, melasses, water and scummings, for distillation. *Edwards, W. Ind.*

WASH'-BALL, *n.* [*wash* and *ball.*] A ball of soap, to be used in washing the hands or face.

WASH'-BOARD, *n.* [*wash* and *board.*] A broad thin plank, fixed occasionally on the top of a boat or other small vessels' side, to prevent the sea from breaking over; also, a piece of plank on the sill of a lower deck port for the same purpose. *Mar. Dict.*

2. A board in a room, next to the floor.

WASH'ED, *pp.* Cleansed in water; purified.

2. Overflowed; dashed against with water.

3. Covered over with a thin coat, as of metal.

WASH'ER, *n.* One who washes.

2. An iron ring between the nave of a wheel and the linch-pin.

WASH'ER-WOMAN, *n.* A woman that washes clothes for others or for hire.

WASH'ING, *ppr.* Cleansing with water; purifying; overflowing; overspreading.

WASH'ING, *n.* The act of cleansing with water; ablution. Heb. ix.

2. A wash; or the clothes washed.

WASH'-POT, *n.* A vessel in which any thing is washed. *Cowley.*

WASH'-TUB, *n.* A tub in which clothes are washed.

WASH'Y, *a.* [from *wash.*] Watery; damp; soft; as the *washy* ooze. *Milton.*

2. Weak; not solid. *Wotton.*

3. Weak; not firm or hardy; liable to sweat profusely with labor; as a *washy* horse. [*New England.*]

WASP, *n.* [Sax. *wæsp* or *wæps*; D. *wesp*; G. *wespe*; L. *vespa*; Fr. *guèpe*; Sp. *avispa*; Port. *bespa.*]

In *entomology*, a genus of insects, Vespa, of the order of Hymenopters. The mouth is horny, the jaw compressed, without a proboscis; the feelers four, unequal and filiform; the eyes lunated; the body smooth; the sting concealed, and the upper wings plicated. Wasps construct combs, and rear their young in the cells. The sting is painful. *Cyc.*

WASP'-FLY, *n.* A species of fly resembling a wasp, but having no sting, and but two wings. *Cyc.*

WASP'ISH, *a.* Snappish; petulant; irritable; irascible; quick to resent any trifling affront.

Much do I suffer, much, to keep in peace
This jealous, *waspish*, wrong-head, rhyming race. *Pope.*

WASP'ISHLY, *adv.* Petulantly; in a snappish manner.

WASP'ISHNESS, *n.* Petulance; irascibility; snappishness.

WAS'SAIL, *n.* [Sax. *wæs-hæl*, health-liquor.]

1. A liquor made of apples, sugar and ale, formerly much used by English good-fellows. *Johnson.*

2. A drunken bout. *Shak.*

3. A merry song. *Ainsworth.*

[*This word is unknown in America.*]

WAS'SAIL, *v. i.* To hold a merry drinking meeting.

WAS'SAIL-BOWL, *n.* A bowl for holding wassail.

WAS'SAIL-CUP, *n.* A cup in which wassail was carried to the company. *Cyc.*

WAS'SAILER, *n.* A toper; a drunkard. *Milton.*

WAST, past tense of the substantive verb, in the second person; as, thou *wast.*

WASTE, *v. t.* [Sax. *westan*, *awestan*; G. *verwüsten*; D. *verwoesten*; L. *vasto*; It. *guastare*; Sp. Port. *gastar*, for *guastar*; Fr. *gâter*; Arm. *goasta*. The W. *gwasgaru*, to scatter, seems to be compound. The primary sense is probably to scatter, to spread. Class Bz. No. 2.]

1. To diminish by gradual dissipation or loss. Thus disease *wastes* the patient; sorrows *waste* the strength and spirits.

2. To cause to be lost; to destroy by scattering or by injury. Thus cattle *waste* their fodder when fed in the open field.

3. To expend without necessity or use; to destroy wantonly or luxuriously; to squander; to cause to be lost through wantonness or negligence. Careless people *waste* their fuel, their food or their property. Children *waste* their inheritance.

And *wasted* his substance with riotous living. Luke xv.

4. To destroy in enmity; to desolate; as, to *waste* an enemy's country.

5. To suffer to be lost unnecessarily; or to throw away; as, to *waste* the blood and treasure of a nation.

6. To destroy by violence.

The Tyber
Insults our walls, and *wastes* our fruitful grounds. *Dryden.*

7. To impair strength gradually.

Now *wasting* years my former strength confounds. *Broome.*

8. To lose in idleness or misery; to wear out.

Here condemn'd
To *waste* eternal days in woe and pain. *Milton.*

9. To spend; to consume.

O were I able
To *waste* it all myself, and leave you none. *Milton.*

10. In *law*, to damage, impair or injure, as an estate, voluntarily, or by suffering the buildings, fences, &c. to go to decay. See the Noun.

11. To exhaust; to be consumed by time or mortality.

Till your carcasses be *wasted* in the wilderness. Num. xiv.

12. To scatter and lose for want of use or of occupiers.

Full many a flow'r is born to blush unseen,
And *waste* its sweetness on the desert air. *Gray.*

WASTE, *v. i.* To dwindle; to be diminished; to lose bulk or substance gradually; as, the body *wastes* in sickness.

The barrel of meal shall not *waste.* 1 Kings xvii.

2. To be diminished or lost by slow dissipation, consumption or evaporation; as, water *wastes* by evaporation; fuel *wastes* in combustion.

3. To be consumed by time or mortality.

But man dieth, and *wasteth* away. Job xiv.

WASTE, *a.* Destroyed; ruined.

The Sophi leaves all *waste* in his retreat. *Milton.*

2. Desolate; uncultivated; as a *waste* country; a *waste* howling wilderness. Deut. xxxii.

3. Destitute; stripped; as lands laid *waste.*

4. Superfluous; lost for want of occupiers.

—And strangled with her *waste* fertility. *Milton.*

5. Worthless; that which is rejected, or used only for mean purposes; as *waste* wood.

6. That of which no account is taken, or of which no value is found; as *waste* paper.

7. Uncultivated; untilled; unproductive.

There is yet much *waste* land in England. *Cyc.*

Laid waste, desolated; ruined.

WASTE, *n.* The act of squandering; the dissipation of property through wantonness, ambition, extravagance, luxury or negligence.

For all this *waste* of wealth, and loss of blood. *Milton.*

2. Consumption; loss; useless expense; any loss or destruction which is neither necessary nor promotive of a good end; a loss for which there is no equivalent; as a *waste* of goods or money; a *waste* of time; a *waste* of labor; a *waste* of words.

Little *wastes* in great establishments, constantly occurring, may defeat the energies of a mighty capital. *L. Beecher.*

3. A desolate or uncultivated country. The plains of Arabia are mostly a wide *waste.*

4. Land untilled, though capable of tillage; as the *wastes* in England.

5. Ground, space or place unoccupied; as the etherial *waste.*

In the dead *waste* and middle of the night. *Shak.*

6. Region ruined and deserted.

All the leafy nation sinks at last,
And Vulcan rides in triumph o'er the *waste.* *Dryden.*

7. Mischief; destruction.

He will never, I think, in the way of *waste*, attempt us again. *Shak.*

3. In *law*, spoil, destruction or injury done to houses, woods, fences, lands, &c., by a tenant for life or for years, to the prejudice of the heir, or of him in reversion or remainder. Waste is *voluntary*, as by pulling down buildings; or *permissive*, as by suffering them to fall for want of necessary repairs. Whatever does a lasting damage to the freehold, is a *waste*. *Blackstone.*

WASTED, *pp.* Expended without necessity or use; lost through negligence; squandered.

2. Diminished; dissipated; evaporated; exhausted.

3. Desolated; ruined; destroyed.

WASTEFUL, *a.* Lavish; prodigal; expending property, or that which is valuable, without necessity or use; *applied to persons.*

2. Destructive to property; ruinous; as *wasteful* practices or negligence; *wasteful* expenses.

3. Desolate; unoccupied; untilled; uncultivated.

In wilderness and *wasteful* deserts stray'd. *Spenser.*

WASTEFULLY, *adv.* In a lavish manner; with prodigality; in useless expenses or consumption.

Her lavish hand is *wastefully* profuse. *Dryden.*

WASTEFULNESS, *n.* Lavishness; prodigality; the act or practice of expending what is valuable without necessity or use.

WASTE-GATE, *n.* A gate to let the water of a pond pass off when it is not wanted. *Cyc.*

WAS'TEL, *n.* A particular sort of bread; fine bread or cake. *Lowth. Cyc.*

WASTENESS, *n.* A desolate state; solitude.

That day is a day of wrath, a day of trouble and distress, a day of *wasteness*. Zeph. i.

WASTER, *n.* One who is prodigal; one who squanders property; one who consumes extravagantly or without use.

He also that is slothful in his work, is brother to him who is a great *waster*. Prov. xviii.

Sconces are great *wasters* of candles. *Swift.*

2. A kind of cudgel. *Beaum.*

WASTETHRIFT, *n.* [*waste* and *thrift.*] A spendthrift. *Beaum.*

WASTE-WIER, *n.* An overfall or wier for the superfluous water of a canal. *Cyc.*

WASTING, *ppr.* Lavishing prodigally; expending or consuming without use; diminishing by slow dissipation; desolating; laying waste.

Wasting and relentless war has made ravages, with but few and short intermissions, from the days of the tyrant Nimrod down to the Nimrod of our own age. *J. Lyman.*

2. *a.* Diminishing by dissipation or by great destruction; as a *wasting* disease.

WASTREL, *n.* A state of waste or common. [*Local.*]

WASTREL, WASTOREL, *n.* Waste substances; any thing cast away as bad. [*Local.*] *Cyc.*

WATCH, *n.* [Sax. *wæcca*, from *wæcan*, *wæccan*, to *wake*; Sw. *vacht* or *vakt*, watch, guard; *vachta*, to *watch*; Dan. *vagt*. It is from the same root as *wake*, which see.]

1. Forbearance of sleep.

2. Attendance without sleep.

All the long night their mournful *watch* they keep. *Addison.*

3. Attention; close observation. Keep *watch* of the suspicious man.

4. Guard; vigilance for keeping or protecting against danger.

He kept both *watch* and ward. *Spenser.*

5. A watchman, or watchmen; men set for a guard, either one person or more, set to espy the approach of an enemy or other danger, and to give an alarm or notice of such danger; a sentinel; a guard. He kept a *watch* at the gate. *Bacon.*

Ye have a *watch*; go your way, make it as sure as ye can. Matt. xxvii.

6. The place where a guard is kept.

He upbraids Iago, that he made him
Brave me upon the *watch*. *Shak.*

7. Post or office of a watchman.

As I did stand my *watch* upon the hill— *Shak.*

8. A period of the night, in which one person or one set of persons stand as sentinels; or the time from one relief of sentinels to another. This period among the Israelites, seems to have been originally four hours, but was afterwards three hours, and there were four watches during the night. Hence we read in Scripture of the morning watch, and of the second, third and fourth watch; the evening watch commencing at six o'clock, the second at nine, the third at twelve, and the fourth at three in the morning. Ex. xiv. Matt. xiv. Luke xii.

9. A small time piece or chronometer, to be carried in the pocket or about the person, in which the machinery is moved by a spring.

10. At *sea*, the space of time during which one set or division of the crew remain on deck to perform the necessary duties. This is different in different nations. *Cyc.*

To be on the watch, to be looking steadily for some event.

WATCH, *v. i.* [Sax. *wacian*, *wæcan*; Sw. *våcka*, *upvåcka*; Dan. *vækker*; G. *wachen*; Russ. *vetchayu.*]

1. To be awake; to be or continue without sleep.

I have two nights *watch'd* with you. *Shak.*

2. To be attentive; to look with attention or steadiness. *Watch* and see when the man passes.

3. To look with expectation.

My soul waiteth for the Lord more than they that *watch* for the morning. Ps. cxxx.

4. To keep guard; to act as sentinel; to look for danger.

He gave signal to the minister that *watch'd*. *Milton.*

5. To be attentive; to be vigilant in preparation for an event or trial, the time of whose arrival is uncertain.

Watch therefore; for ye know not what hour your Lord doth come. Matt. xxiv.

6. To be insidiously attentive; as, to *watch* for an opportunity to injure another.

7. To attend on the sick during the night; as, to *watch* with a man in a fever.

To watch over, to be cautiously observant of; to inspect, superintend and guard from error and danger. It is our duty constantly to *watch over* our own conduct and that of our children.

WATCH, *v. t.* To guard; to have in keeping.

Flaming ministers *watch* and tend their charge. *Milton.*

2. To observe in ambush; to lie in wait for.

Saul also sent messengers to David's house to *watch* him, and to slay him. 1 Sam. xix.

3. To tend; to guard.

Paris *watched* the flocks in the groves of Ida. *Broome.*

4. To observe in order to detect or prevent, or for some particular purpose; as, to *watch* a suspected person; to *watch* the progress of a bill in the legislature.

WATCH'ED, *pp.* Guarded; observed with steady vigilance.

WATCH'ER, *n.* One who sits up or continues awake; particularly, one who attends upon the sick during the night.

2. A diligent observer; as an attentive *watcher* of the works of nature. [*Not in use.*] *More.*

WATCH'ET, *a.* [Sax. *wæced*, weak.] Pale or light blue.

Who stares in Germany at *watchet* eyes?
[*Not in use.*] *Dryden.*

WATCH'FUL, *a.* Vigilant; attentive; careful to observe; observant; cautious. It has *of* before the thing to be regulated, as to be *watchful of* one's behavior; and *against*, before the thing to be avoided, as to be *watchful against* the growth of vicious habits. *Locke. Law.*

WATCH'FULLY, *adv.* Vigilantly; heedfully; with careful observation of the approach of evil, or attention to duty. *Boyle.*

WATCH'FULNESS, *n.* Vigilance; heedfulness; heed; suspicious attention; careful and diligent observation for the purpose of preventing or escaping danger, or of avoiding mistakes and misconduct.

2. Wakefulness; indisposition or inability to sleep.

Watchfulness—often precedes too great sleepiness. *Arbuthnot.*

WATCH-GLASS, *n.* [*watch* and *glass.*] In *ships*, a half hour glass, used to measure the time of a watch on deck.

2. A concavo-convex glass for covering the face or dial of a watch.

WATCH'-HOUSE, *n.* [*watch* and *house.*] A house in which a watch or guard is placed. *Gay.*

WATCH'ING, *ppr.* Being awake; guarding; attending the sick; carefully observing.

WATCH'ING, *n.* Wakefulness; inability to sleep. *Wiseman.*

WATCH'-LIGHT, *n.* [*watch* and *light.*] A candle with a rush wick. *Addison.*

WATCH'MAKER, *n.* [*watch* and *maker.*] One whose occupation is to make and repair watches.

WATCH'MAN, *n.* [*watch* and *man.*] A sentinel; a guard. *Swift.*

WATCH'TOWER, *n.* [*watch* and *tower.*] A tower on which a sentinel is placed to watch for enemies or the approach of danger. *Bacon.*

WATCH'WORD, *n.* [*watch* and *word.*] The word given to sentinels, and to such as have occasion to visit the guards, used as a signal by which a friend is known from an enemy, or a person who has a right to pass the watch, from one who has not.

WATER, *n.* *wau'ter.* [Sax. *wæter, wæs*; D. *water*; G. *wasser*; Dan. *vater*; Sw. *vatten*; Goth. *wato*; Russ. *voda*. This may be from the root of *wet*, Gr. ὑετος. In Ar. *wadi* signifies a stream, or the channel where water flows in winter, but which is dry in summer; a thing common on the plains of Syria and Arabia.]

1. A fluid, the most abundant and most necessary for living beings of any in nature, except air. Water when pure, is colorless, destitute of taste and smell, ponderous, transparent, and in a very small degree compressible. It is reposited in the earth in inexhaustible quantities, where it is preserved fresh and cool, and from which it issues in springs, which form streams and rivers. But the great reservoirs of water on the globe are the ocean, seas and lakes, which cover more than three fifths of its surface, and from which it is raised by evaporation, and uniting with the air in the state of vapor, is wafted over the earth, ready to be precipitated in the form of rain, snow or hail.

Water by the abstraction or loss of heat, becomes solid, or in other words, is converted into ice or snow; and by heat it is converted into steam, an elastic vapor, one of the most powerful agents in nature. Modern chimical experiments prove that water is a compound substance, consisting of a combination of oxygen and hydrogen gases, or rather the bases or ponderable matter of those gases; or about two volumes or measures of hydrogen gas and one of oxygen gas. The proportion of the ingredients in weight, is nearly 85 parts of oxygen to 15 of hydrogen. *Lavoisier. Vauquelin. Fourcroy.*

2. The ocean; a sea; a lake; a river; any great collection of water; as in the phrases, to go by *water*, to travel by *water*.

3. Urine; the animal liquor secreted by the kidneys and discharged from the bladder.

4. The color or luster of a diamond or pearl, sometimes perhaps of other precious stones; as a diamond of the first *water*, that is, perfectly pure and transparent. Hence the figurative phrase, a man or a genius of the *first water*, that is, of the first excellence.

5. *Water* is a name given to several liquid substances or humors in animal bodies; as the *water* of the pericardium, of dropsy, &c. *Cyc.*

Mineral waters, are those waters which are so impregnated with foreign ingredients, such as gaseous, sulphureous and saline substances, as to give them medicinal, or at least sensible properties. Most natural waters contain more or less of these foreign substances, but the proportion is generally too minute to affect the senses. *D. Olmsted.*

To hold water, to be sound or tight. [*Obsolete or vulgar.*] *L'Estrange.*

WATER-BEARER, *n.* [*water* and *bearer.*] In *astronomy*, a sign of the zodiac, called also Aquarius, from L. *aqua*, water.

WATER-BELLOWS, *n.* [*water* and *bellows.*] A machine for blowing air into a furnace, by means of a column of water falling through a vertical tube. *Cyc.*

WATER-BORNE, *n.* Borne by the water; floated; having water sufficient to float; as ships *water-borne* by the flowing tide. *Smollett.*

WATER-CAL'AMINT, *n.* [*water* and *calamint.*] A species of mint or Mentha. *Cyc.*

WATER-CARRIAGE, *n.* [*water* and *carriage.*]

1. Transportation or conveyance by water; or the means of transporting by water.

2. A vessel or boat. [*Not in use.*] *Arbuthnot.*

WATER-CART, *n.* [*water* and *cart.*] A cart bearing a large cask of water which is conveyed into a cylinder full of holes, by means of which the water is sprinkled upon the ground.

WATER-CLOCK, *n.* [*water* and *clock.*] The clepsydra; an instrument or machine serving to measure time by the fall of a certain quantity of water. *Encyc.*

WATER-COLOR, *n.* [*water* and *color.*] Water-colors, in painting or limning, are colors diluted and mixed with gum-water. Water-colors are so called in distinction from oil-colors. *Encyc.*

WATER-COURSE, *n.* [*water* and *course.*]

1. A stream of water; a river or brook. Is. xliv.

2. A channel or canal for the conveyance of water, particularly in draining lands.

WATER-CRESS, *n.* [*water* and *cress.*] A small creeping plant or weed growing in watery places. *Cyc.*

A plant, a species of Sisymbrium. *Lee.*

WATER-CROWFOOT, *n.* [*water* and *crowfoot.*] A plant on which cows are said to be fond of feeding. *Cyc.*

WATER-DROP, *n.* [*water* and *drop.*] A drop of water. *Shak.*

WATER-DROPWORT, *n.* A plant of the genus Œnanthe. *Lee.*

WATER-EL'EPHANT, *n.* A name given to the hippopotamus.

WATER-ENGINE, *n.* [*water* and *engine.*] An engine to raise water; or an engine moved by water.

WATERFALL, *n.* [*water* and *fall.*] A fall or perpendicular descent of the water of a river or stream, or a descent nearly perpendicular; a cascade; a cataract. But the word is generally used of the fall of a small river or rivulet. It is particularly used to express a cascade in a garden, or an artificial descent of water, designed as an ornament. *Cyc.*

WATER-FLAG, *n.* [*water* and *flag.*] Water flower de luce, a species of Tris.

WATER-FLOOD, *n.* [*water* and *flood.*] A flood of water; an inundation.

WATER-FLY, *n.* [*water* and *fly.*] An insect that is seen on the water.

WATER-FOWL, *n.* [*water* and *fowl.*] A fowl that frequents the water, or lives about rivers, lakes, or on or near the sea; an aquatic fowl. Of aquatic fowls, some are waders, or furnished with long legs; others are swimmers, and are furnished with webbed feet.

WATER-FOX, *n.* [*water* and *fox.*] A name given to the carp, on account of its cunning. *Walton.*

WATER-FURROW, *n.* [*water* and *furrow.*] In *agriculture*, a deep furrow made for conducting water from the ground and keeping it dry.

WATER-FURROW, *v. t.* To plow or open water furrows.

WATER-GAGE, } *n.* [*water* and *gage.*]
WATER-GUAGE, } An instrument for measuring or ascertaining the depth or qnantity of water.

WATER-GALL, *n.* A cavity made in the earth by a torrent of water.

2. An appearance in the rainbow. *Steevens.*

WATER-GER'MANDER, *n.* A plant of the genus Teucrium. *Cyc.*

WATER-GOD, *n.* [*water* and *god.*] A deity that presides over the water.

WATER-GRUEL, *n.* [*water* and *gruel.*] A liquid food, composed of water and a small portion of meal or other farinaceous substance boiled.

WATER-HAMMER, *n.* A column of water in a vacuum, which not being supported as in the air, falls against the end of the vessel with a peculiar noise. It may be formed by corking a vessel of water while it is boiling. The vapor condensing as it cools, a vacuum is formed.

WATER-HAIR-GRASS, *n.* A species of grass, the *Aira aquatica.* *Cyc.*

WATER-HEMP-AGRIMONY, *n.* A plant of the genus Bidens. *Lee.*

WATER-HEN, *n.* [*water* and *hen.*] A water fowl of the genus Fulica, the gallinula or moorhen; also, a species of Rallus, the soree, inhabiting Virginia and Carolina. *Cyc.*

WATER-HOG, *n.* [*water* and *hog.*] A quadruped of S. America, the *Cavia capybara.* *Linne.*

WATER-LAUREL, *n.* [*water* and *laurel.*] A plant.

WATER-LEAF, *n.* [*water* and *leaf.*] A plant of the genus Hydrophyllum. *Lee.*

WATERLESS, *a.* Destitute of water. *Tooke.*

WATER-LEVEL, *n.* [*water* and *level.*] The level formed by the surface of still water.

WATER-LILY, *n.* [*water* and *lily.*] A plant of the genus Nymphæa. *Lee.*

WATER-LINE, *n.* [*water* and *line.*] A horizontal line supposed to be drawn about a ship's bottom, at the surface of the water. This is higher or lower, according to the depth of water necessary to float her. *Mar. Dict. Cyc.*

WATER-LOGGED, *a.* [*water* and *log.*] Lying like a log on the water. A ship is said to be *water-logged*, when by leaking and receiving a great quantity of water into her hold, she has become so heavy as not to be manageable by the helm, and to be at the mercy of the waves. *Cyc.*

WATERMAN, *n.* [*water* and *man.*] A boatman; a ferryman; a man who manages water-craft. *Gay.*

WATER-MARK, *n.* [*water* and *mark.*] The mark or limit of the rise of a flood. *Dryden.*

WATER-MEL'ON, *n.* [*water* and *melon.*] A plant and its fruit, of the genus Cucurbita, (*C. citrullus.*) This plant requires a warm climate to bring it to perfection. It also requires a dry, sandy, warm soil, and will not grow well in any other. The fruit abounds with a sweetish liquor resembling water in color, and the pulp is remarkably rich and delicious.

WATER-MILL, *n.* [*water* and *mill.*] A mill whose machinery is moved by water, and thus distinguished from a wind-mill.

WATER-MINT. [See *Water-calamint.*]

WATER-NEWT, *n.* [*water* and *newt.*] An animal of the lizard tribe, [*Lacerta aquatica.*]

WATER-OR'DEAL, *n.* [*water* and *ordeal.*] A judicial trial of persons accused of crimes, by means of water; formerly in use among illiterate and superstitious nations.

WATER-OU'ZEL, *n.* [*water* and *ouzel.*] A fowl of the genus Sturnus. *Linne.*

The *water-ouzel* is the *Turdus cinctus* of Latham. *Ed. Encyc.*

WATER-P'ARSNEP, *n.* [*water* and *parsnep.*] A plant of the genus Sium. *Lee.*

WATER-PŌA, *n.* A species of grass, the *Poa aquatica.* *Cyc.*

WATER-POISE, *n.* *s* as *z.* [*water* and *poise.*]

An instrument for examining the purity of water.

WATER-POT, *n.* [*water* and *pot.*] A vessel for holding or conveying water, or for sprinkling water on cloth in bleaching, or on plants, &c.

WATER-PROOF, *a.* [*water* and *proof.*] Impervious to water; so firm and compact as not to admit water; as *water-proof* cloth, lether or felt.

WATER-RAD'ISH, *n.* [*water* and *radish.*] A species of water-cresses. *Johnson.*

Water-cress, a species of Sisymbrium. *Lee.*

WATER-RAIL, *n.* [*water* and *rail.*] A fowl of the genus Rallus.

WATER-RAT, *n.* [*water* and *rat.*] An animal of the genus Mus, which lives in the banks of streams or lakes.

WATER-ROCKET, *n.* [*water* and *rocket.*]
1. A species of water-cresses. *Johnson.*
2. A kind of fire-work to be discharged in the water.

WATER-ROT, *v. t.* [*water* and *rot.*] To rot by steeping in water; as, to *water-rot* hemp or flax.

WATER-ROTTED, *pp.* Rotted by being steeped in water.

WATER-ROTTING, *ppr.* Rotting in water.

WATER-SAIL, *n.* [*water* and *sail.*] A small sail used under a studding sail or driver boom. *Mar. Dict.*

WATER-SAPPHIRE, *n.* [*water* and *sapphire.*] A kind of blue precious stone.

WATER-SHOOT, *n.* [*water* and *shoot.*] A sprig or shoot from the root or stock of a tree. [*Local.*]

WATER-SNAKE, *n.* [*water* and *snake.*] A snake that frequents the water.

WATER-SŌAK, *v. t.* [*water* and *soak.*] To soak or fill the interstices with water.

WATER-SŌAKED, *pp.* Soaked or having its interstices filled with water; as *water-soaked* wood; a *water-soaked* hat.

WATER-SŌLDIER, *n.* A plant of the genus Stratiotes. *Cyc.*

WATER-SPANIEL, *n.* [*water* and *spaniel.*] A dog so called. *Sidney.*

WATER-SPOUT, *n.* [*water* and *spout.*] At sea, a vertical column of water, raised from the surface of the sea and driven furiously by the wind. *Mar. Dict.*

WATER-TABLE, *n.* [*water* and *table.*] In *architecture*, a ledge in the wall of a building, about eighteen or twenty inches from the ground.

WATER-TATH, *n.* In *England*, a species of coarse grass growing in wet grounds, and supposed to be injurious to sheep. *Cyc.*

WATER-THERMOM'ETER, *n.* An instrument for ascertaining the precise degree of cold at which water ceases to be condensed. *Cyc.*

WATER-TIGHT, *a.* [*water* and *tight.*] So tight as not to admit water.

WATER-TRE'FOIL, *n.* A plant. *Mortimer.*

WATER-VIOLET, *n.* [*water* and *violet.*] A plant of the genus Hottonia. *Miller. Lee.*

WATER-WAY, *n.* [*water* and *way.*] In *a ship's deck*, a piece of timber, forming a channel for conducting water to the scuppers.

WATER-WHEEL, *n.* [*water* and *wheel.*]
1. A wheel moved by water.
2. An engine for raising water from a deep well.

WATER-WILLOW, *n.* [*water* and *willow.*] A plant. [L. *lysimachia.*] *Ainsworth.*

WATER-WITH, *n.* [*water* and *with.*] A plant. *Derham.*

WATER-WŎRK, *n.* [*water* and *work.*] Water-works are hydraulic machines or engines, particularly such as form artificial fountains, spouts and the like.

WATER-WŎRT, *n.* A plant of the genus Elatine. *Lee.*

WATER, *v. t.* *wau'ter.* To irrigate; to overflow with water, or to wet with water; as, to *water* land. Showers *water* the earth.
2. To supply with water. The hilly lands of New England are remarkably well *watered* with rivers and rivulets.
3. To supply with water for drink; as, to *water* cattle and horses.
4. To diversify; to wet and calender; to give a wavy appearance to; as, to *water* silk.

WATER, *v. i.* *wau'ter.* To shed water or liquid matter. His eyes began to *water.*
2. To get or take in water. The ship put into port to *water.*

The mouth waters, a phrase denoting that a person has a longing desire.

WATERAGE, *n.* Money paid for transportation by water.

WATERED, *pp.* Overspread or sprinkled with water; made wet; supplied with water; made lustrous by being wet and calendered.

WATERER, *n.* One who waters. *Carew.*

WATERINESS, *n.* [from *watery.*] Moisture; humidity; a state of abounding with water. *Arbuthnot.*

WATERING, *ppr.* Overflowing; sprinkling or wetting with water; supplying with water; giving water for drink; giving a wavy appearance to.

WATERING, *n.* The act of overflowing or sprinkling with water; the act of supplying with water for drink or other purposes; the act of wetting and calendering for giving luster to, as cloth.
2. The place where water is supplied.

WATERING-PLACE, *n.* A place to which people resort for mineral water, or for the use of water in some way or other.

WATERING-TROUGH, *n.* A trough in which cattle and horses drink.

WATERISH, *a.* Resembling water; thin, as a liquor. *Dryden.*
2. Moist; somewhat watery; as *waterish* land. *Hale.*

WATERISHNESS, *n.* Thinness, as of a liquor; resemblance to water.

Waterishness, which is like the serosity of our blood. *Floyer.*

WATERLESS, *a.* Destitute of water. *Mitford.*

WATERY, *a.* Resembling water; thin or transparent, as a liquid; as *watery* humors.

The oily and *watery* parts of the aliment. *Arbuthnot.*

2. Tasteless; insipid; vapid; spiritless; as *watery* turneps. *Philips.*
3. Wet; abounding with water; as *watery* land; *watery* eyes. *Prior.*
4. Pertaining to water; as the *watery* god. *Dryden.*
5. Consisting of water; as a *watery* desert. *Milton.*

WAT'TLE, *n.* [Sax. *watel*, a twig; allied perhaps to *withe*, L. *vitis;* that is, a shoot.]
1. Properly, a twig or flexible rod; and hence, a hurdle.
2. The fleshy excrescence that grows under the throat of a cock or turkey, or a like substance on a fish. *Cyc. Walton.*
3. A rod laid on a roof to support the thatch.

WAT'TLE, *v. t.* To bind with twigs.
2. To twist or interweave twigs one with another; to plat; to form a kind of network with flexible branches; as, to *wattle* a hedge. *Mortimer.*

WAT'TLED, *pp.* Bound or interwoven with twigs.

WAT'TLING, *ppr.* Interweaving with twigs.

WAUL, *v. i.* To cry, as a cat.

WAUL'ING, *ppr.* Crying, as a cat.

WAVE, *n.* [Sax. *weg*, *wæg*, a wave, a way; both the same word, and both coinciding with the root of *wag*, *wagon*, *vacillate*, *weigh*, &c. The sense is a going, a moving, appropriately a moving one way and the other; G. *woge;* Sw. *våg;* Ir. *buaice.*]
1. A moving swell or volume of water; usually, a swell raised and driven by wind. A pebble thrown into still water produces *waves*, which form concentric circles, receding from the point where the pebble fell. But waves are generally raised and driven by wind, and the word comprehends any moving swell on the surface of water, from the smallest ripple to the billows of a tempest.

The *wave* behind impels the *wave* before. *Pope.*

2. Unevenness; inequality of surface. *Newton.*
3. The line or streak of luster on cloth watered and calendered.

WAVE, *v. i.* [Sax. *wafian;* probably a corrupt orthography.]

1. To play loosely; to move like a wave, one way and the other; to float; to undulate.

His purple robes *wav'd* careless to the wind. *Trumbull.*

2. To be moved, as a signal. *B. Jonson.*
3. To fluctuate; to waver; to be in an unsettled state. *Obs.*

WAVE, *v. t.* [See *Waver.*] To raise into inequalities of surface. *Shak.*

2. To move one way and the other; to brandish; as, to *wave* the hand; to *wave* a sword. *Milton. Dryden.*
3. To waft; to remove any thing floating. *Brown.*
4. To beckon; to direct by a waft or waving motion. *Shak.*

WAVE, *v. t.* [Norm. *weyver*, to *wave* or *waive*; *waifnez*, waived; *wefs, weifs*, waifs.]

1. To put off; to cast off; to cast away; to reject; as, to *wave* goods stolen; usually written *waive.*
2. To quit; to depart from.

He resolved not to *wave* his way. *Wotton.*

3. To put off; to put aside for the present, or to omit to pursue; as, to *wave* a motion. He offered to *wave* the subject. [*This is the usual sense.*]

WA'VED, *pp.* Moved one way and the other; brandished.

2. Put off; omitted.
3. *a.* In *heraldry*, indented.
4. Variegated in luster; as *waved* silk.
5. In *botany*, undate; rising and falling in waves on the margin, as a leaf. *Lee.*

WA'VELESS, *a.* Free from waves; undisturbed; unagitated; as the *waveless* sea.

WA'VELLITE, *n.* [from *Wavel*, the discoverer.]

A mineral, a phosphate or sub-phosphate of alumin; commonly found in crystals, which usually adhere and radiate, forming hemispherical or globular concretions, from a very small size to an inch in diameter. The form of the crystal is usually that of a rhombic prism with dihedral terminations. *Phillips.*

WAVE-LOAF, *n.* [*wave* and *loaf.*] A loaf for a wave-offering.

WA'VE-OFFERING, *n.* An offering made with waving towards the four cardinal points. Num. xviii.

WA'VER, *v. i.* [Sax. *wafian*; Dan. *svæver*, from *væver*, to weave, that is, to move one way and the other.]

1. To play or move to and fro; to move one way and the other. *Boyle.*
2. To fluctuate; to be unsettled in opinion; to vacillate; to be undetermined; as, to *waver* in opinion; to *waver* in faith.

Let us hold fast the profession of our faith without *wavering.* Heb. x.

3. To totter; to reel; to be in danger of falling. *Holyday.*

WA'VER, *n.* A name given to a sapling or young timber tree in England. [*Local.*]

WA'VERER, *n.* One who wavers; one who is unsettled in doctrine, faith or opinion.

WA'VERING, *ppr.* or *a.* Fluctuating; being in doubt; undetermined.

WA'VERINGNESS, *n.* State or quality of being wavering. *Mountague.*

WAVE-SUBJECT'ED, *a.* Subject to be overflowed. *Goldsmith.*

WA'VE-WORN, *a.* [*wave* and *worn.*] Worn by the waves.

The shore that o'er his *wave-worn* basis bow'd. *Shak.*

WA'VING, *ppr.* Moving as a wave; playing to and fro; brandishing.

WA'VY, *a.* [from *wave.*] Rising or swelling in waves; full of waves; as the *wavy* sea. *Chapman.*

2. Playing to and fro; undulating.

Let her glad valleys smile with *wavy* corn. *Prior.*

3. Undulating on the border or on the surface; *a botanical use.*

Wawes or *waes*, for *waves.* [*Not in use.*] *Spenser.*

WAX, *n.* [Sax. *wæx, wex*; G. *wachs*; D. *wasch*; Sw. *vax*; Russ. *vaksa*; L. *viscus, viscum.*]

1. A thick, viscid, tenacious substance, collected by bees, or excreted from their bodies, and employed in the construction of their cells; usually called *bees' wax.* Its native color is yellow, but it is bleached for candles, &c.
2. A thick tenacious substance excreted in the ear.
3. A substance secreted by certain plants, forming a silvery powder on the leaves and fruit, as in the wax-palm and wax-myrtle. *Cyc.*
4. A substance found on the hinder legs of bees, which is supposed to be their food.
5. A substance used in sealing letters; called sealing-wax, or Spanish wax. This is a composition of gum-lacca and resin, colored with some pigment. *Cyc.*
6. A thick substance used by shoemakers for rubbing their thread.

WAX, *v. t.* To smear or rub with wax; as, to *wax* a thread or a table.

WAX, *v. i.* pret. *waxed*; pp. *waxed* or *waxen.* [Sax. *weaxan*; G. *wachsen*; Sw. *våxa*; allied probably to L. *augeo, auxi*, Gr. *αεξω* and *αυξω.*]

1. To increase in size; to grow; to become larger; as the *waxing* and the waning moon. *Hakewill.*
2. To pass from one state to another; to become; as, to *wax* strong; to *wax* warm or cold; to *wax* feeble; to *wax* hot; to *wax* old; to *wax* worse and worse. *Scripture.*

WAX'-BILL, *n.* A bird, a species of Loxia.

WAX'-CANDLE, *n.* [*wax* and *candle.*] A candle made of wax.

WAX'-CHANDLER, *n.* [*wax* and *chandler.*] A maker of wax candles.

WAX'ED, *pp.* Smeared or rubbed with wax.

WAX'EN, *a.* Made of wax; as *waxen* cells. *Milton.*

WAX'ING, *ppr.* Growing; increasing; becoming; smearing with wax.

WAX'ING, *n.* In *chimistry*, the preparation of any matter to render it fit for melting; also, the process of stopping out colors in calico-printing. *Cyc.*

WAX-MYRTLE, *n.* The bayberry, or *Myrica cerifera*, a shrub of N. America, the berries of which are covered with a greenish wax, called myrtle wax, or bayberry tallow. *Bigelow.*

WAX-P'ALM, *n.* A species of palm, the *Ceroxylon andicola*, a native of the Andes, the stem of which is covered with a secretion, consisting of two thirds resin and one third wax. *Cyc.*

WAX'-WORK, *n.* Figures formed of wax, in imitation of real beings.

WAX'Y, *a.* Soft like wax; resembling wax; viscid; adhesive.

WAY, *n.* [Sax. *wæg, weg*; G. D. *weg*; Dan. *vej*; Sw. *våg*; L. It. *via*; Fr. *voie*; coinciding in origin with *wag, weigh, wagon, vogue*, &c.]

1. Literally, a passing; hence, a passage; the place of passing; hence, a road of any kind; a highway; a private road; a lane; a street; any place for the passing of men, cattle or other animals; *a word of very comprehensive signification.*
2. Length of space; as a great *way*; a little *way.*
3. Course; direction of motion or travel. What *way* did he take? Which *way* shall I go? Keep in the *way* of truth and knowledge.

Mark what *way* I make. *Shak.*

4. Passage; room for passing. Make *way* for the jury.
5. Course, or regular course.

And let eternal justice take the *way.* *Dryden.*

6. Tendency to any meaning or act.

There is nothing in the words that sounds that *way.* *Atterbury.*

7. Sphere of observation.

The general officers and the public ministers that fell in my *way*— *Temple.*

8. Manner of doing any thing; method; means of doing. Seek the best *way* of learning, and pursue it.

By noble *ways* we conquest will prepare. *Dryden.*

9. Method; scheme of management.

What impious *ways* my wishes took. *Prior.*

10. Manner of thinking or behavior; particular turn of opinion; determination or humor. Let him have his *way*, when that will not injure him, or any other person. But multitudes of children are ruined by being permitted to have their *way.*
11. Manner; mode. In no *way* does this matter belong to me. We admire a person's *way* of expressing his ideas.
12. Method; manner of practice. Find, if you can, the easiest *way* to live.

Having lost the *way* of nobleness. *Sidney.*

13. Method or plan of life and conduct. Instruct your children in the right *way.*

Her *ways* are *ways* of pleasantness, and all her paths are peace. Prov. iii.

All flesh had corrupted his *way.* Gen. vi.

14. Course; process of things, good or bad. Things are in a prosperous *way.*
15. Right method to act or know.

We are quite out of the *way.* *Locke.*

16. General scheme of acting.

Men who go out of the *way* to hint free things, must be guilty of absurdity or rudeness. *Clarissa.*

17. *Ways*, plu. the timbers on which a ship is lanched.

To make way, to give room for passing; or to make a vacancy.

To give way, to recede; to make room; or to yield; to concede the place or opinion to another.

To make one's way, to advance in life by efforts; to advance successfully,

By the way, en passant, as we proceed; a phrase introducing something in discourse, not immediately connected with the subject.

To go one's way, or *to come one's way*, to go or come along. *Shak.*

To go the way of all the earth, to die.

In the way, a phrase noting obstruction. What is there *in the way* of your success?

In *Scripture*, the *ways* of God, are his providential government, or his works. Rom. xi. Job xl.

Way and *ways* are used in certain phrases, in the sense of *wise*. He is no *ways* a match for his antagonist.

'Tis no *way* the interest even of the priesthood. *Pope.*

To be under way, in seamen's language, to be in motion, as when a ship begins to move. So a ship is said to have *head-way*, when she moves forward in her course, and *stern-way*, when she is driven astern. She is said also to *gather way*, or to *lose way*. *Lee-way* is a movement of a ship aside of her course, or to the leeward.

Milky way, in *astronomy*, the galaxy; a broad luminous belt or space in the heavens, supposed to be occasioned by the blended light of an immense number of stars. By means of a telescope of uncommon magnifying powers, Dr. Herschel has been able to ascertain this fact, by distinguishing the stars.

Covert way, in *fortification*, a passage covered from the enemy's fire.

Ways and *means*, in *legislation*, means for raising money; resources for revenue.

Way-going crop, among farmers, is the crop which is taken from the ground the year the tenant leaves the farm. [*England.*] *Cyc.*

WA'Y-BREAD, *n.* A name given to the herb plantain *(plantago.)* [*Local.*] *Cyc.*

WA'YFARER, *n.* [*way* and *fare*, Sax. *faran*, to go.] A traveler; a passenger. *Carew.*

WA'YFARING, *a.* [supra.] Traveling; passing; being on a journey. Judges xix.

WA'YFARING-TREE, *n.* A shrub, a species of Viburnum. *Cyc.*

WAYLA'ID, *pp.* Watched in the way. [See *Waylay.*]

WAYLA'Y, *v. t.* [*way* and *lay.*] To watch insidiously in the way, with a view to seize, rob or slay; to beset in ambush; as, to *waylay* a traveler. *Milton. Dryden.*

[*In this word there is little difference of accent.*]

WAYLA'YER, *n.* One who waits for another in ambush, with a view to seize, rob or slay him.

WA'Y-LEAVE, *n.* A provincial term for the ground purchased for a wagon-way between coal-pits and a river. [*Local.*] *Cyc.*

WA'YLESS, *a.* Having no road or path; pathless; trackless. *Drayton.*

WA'Y-MAKER, *n.* One who makes a way; a precursor. *Bacon.*

WA'Y-M'ARK, *n.* [*way* and *mark.*] A mark to guide in traveling. Jer. xxxi.

WA'YMENT, *v. i.* [Sax. *wa*, woe.] To lament. [*Not in use.*] *Spenser.*

WA'Y-PANE, *n.* A slip left for cartage in watered land. [*Local.*] *Cyc.*

WA'Y-THISTLE, *n.* A troublesome plant or perennial weed. *Cyc.*

WA'YWARD, *a.* [*way* and *ward.*] Froward; peevish; perverse; liking his own way.

Wayward beauty doth not fancy move. *Fairfax.*

WA'Y-WARDEN, *n.* In local usage, the surveyor of a road. *Eng.*

WA'YWARDLY, *adv.* Frowardly; perversely. *Sidney.*

WA'YWARDNESS, *n.* Frowardness; perverseness. *Wotton.*

WA'Y-WISER, *n.* An instrument for measuring the distance which one has traveled on the road; called also perambulator, and podometer, or pedometer. *Cyc.*

WA'YWODE, } *n.* In *the Ottoman empire*,
WA'IWODE, } the governor of a small town or province, which not forming a pashawlic, is the appendage of some great officer; also, a mussulman charged with the collection of taxes, or with the police of a place.

2. In *Poland*, the governor of a province. *Cyc.*

WA'YWODESHIP, *n.* The province or jurisdiction of a waywode. *Eton.*

WE, *pron.* plu. of *I;* or rather a different word, denoting the person speaking and another or others with him. *I* and *John*, the speaker calls *we*, or *I* and *John* and *Thomas;* or *I* and many others. In the objective case, *us.*

We is used to express men in general, including the speaker.

Vice seen too oft, familiar with her face,
We first endure, then pity, then embrace. *Pope.*

WEAK, *a.* [Sax. *waac*, *wace;* G. *weich*, *schwach;* D. *zwak;* Dan. *veeg*, *væg;* Sw. *vek.* The primary sense of the root is to yield, fail, give way, recede, or to be soft.]

1. Having little physical strength; feeble. Children are born *weak;* men are rendered *weak* by disease.

2. Infirm; not healthy; as a *weak* constitution.

3. Not able to bear a great weight; as a *weak* bridge; *weak* timber.

4. Not strong; not compact; easily broken; as a *weak* ship; a *weak* rope.

5. Not able to resist a violent attack; as a *weak* fortress.

6. Soft; pliant; not stiff.

7. Low; small; feeble; as a *weak* voice.

8. Feeble of mind; wanting spirit; wanting vigor of understanding; as a *weak* prince; a *weak* magistrate.

To think every thing disputable, is a proof of a *weak* mind and captious temper. *Beattie.*

9. Not much impregnated with ingredients, or with things that excite action, or with stimulating and nourishing substances; as *weak* broth; *weak* tea; *weak* toddy; a *weak* solution; a *weak* decoction.

10. Not politically powerful; as a *weak* nation or state.

11. Not having force of authority or energy; as a *weak* government.

12. Not having moral force or power to convince; not well supported by truth or reason; as a *weak* argument.

13. Not well supported by argument; as *weak* reasoning.

14. Unfortified; accessible; impressible; as the *weak* side of a person.

15. Not having full conviction or confidence; as *weak* in faith.

16. *Weak* land is land of a light thin soil. [*I believe never used in New England.*] *Cyc.*

WEAK, *v. t.* To make weak. [*Not used.*]

WEAK, *v. i.* To become weak. [*Not used.*] *Chaucer.*

WEAKEN, *v. t.* wee'kn. [Sax. *wacan*, to languish, to vacillate.]

1. To lessen the strength of, or to deprive of strength; to debilitate; to enfeeble; as, to *weaken* the body; to *weaken* the mind; to *weaken* the hands of the magistrate; to *weaken* the force of an objection or an argument.

2. To reduce in strength or spirit; as, to *weaken* tea; to *weaken* any solution or decoction.

WE'AKENED, *pp.* Debilitated; enfeebled; reduced in strength.

WE'AKENER, *n.* He or that which weakens.

WE'AKENING, *ppr.* Debilitating; enfeebling; reducing the strength or vigor of any thing.

WE'AK-HE'ARTED, *a.* Having little courage; dispirited.

WE'AKLING, *n.* A feeble creature. *Shak.*

WE'AKLY, *adv.* Feebly; with little physical strength; faintly; not forcibly; as a fortress *weakly* defended.

2. With want of efficacy.

Was plighted faith so *weakly* seal'd above? *Dryden.*

3. With feebleness of mind or intellect; indiscretely; injuriously.

Beneath pretended justice *weakly* fall. *Dryden.*

4. Timorously; with little courage or fortitude.

WE'AKLY, *a.* Not strong of constitution; infirm; as a *weakly* woman; a man of a *weakly* constitution. *Raleigh.*

WE'AKNESS, *n.* Want of physical strength; want of force or vigor; feebleness; as the *weakness* of a child; the *weakness* of an invalid; the *weakness* of a wall or bridge, or of thread or cordage.

2. Want of sprightliness.

Soft, without *weakness;* without glaring, gay. *Pope.*

3. Want of steadiness.

By such a review, we shall discern and strengthen our *weaknesses.* *Rogers.*

4. Infirmity; unhealthiness; as *weakness* of constitution. *Temple.*

5. Want of moral force or effect upon the mind; as the *weakness* of evidence; the *weakness* of arguments.

6. Want of judgment; feebleness of mind; foolishness.

All wickedness is *weakness.* *Milton.*

7. Defect; failing; fault; *with a plural.*

Many take pleasure in spreading abroad the *weaknesses* of an exalted character. *Spectator.*

WE'AKSIDE, *n.* [*weak* and *side.*] Foible; deficience; failing; infirmity. *Temple.*

WEAL, *n.* [Sax. *wela;* G. *wohl;* Dan. *vel;* from the same root as *well*, Sw. *väl;* L. *valeo*, to be strong, to *avail*, to *prevail.* The primary sense of *weal* is strength, soundness, from the sense of straining, stretching or advancing.]

1. A sound state of a person or thing; a state which is prosperous, or at least not unfortunate, not declining; prosperity; happiness.

As we love the *weal* of our souls and bodies. *Bacon.*

The *weal* or wo in thee is plac'd. *Milton.*

So we say, the public *weal*, the general *weal*, the *weal* of the nation or state. *B. Trumbull.*

2. Republic; state; public interest. [But we now use *commonwealth*, in the sense of *state.*]

WEAL, *n.* The mark of a stripe. [See *Wale.*]

Weald, wald, walt, wold, in Saxon and other Teutonic dialects, signifies a wood or forest. It is found in names, as in *Walt-ham*, wood-house; corruptly pronounced *Waltham.*

WE'ALSMAN, *n.* [*weal* and *man.*] A name given sneeringly to a politician. *Shak.*

WEALTH, *n.* *welth.* [from *weal*; Sax. *welega, welga*, rich.] Prosperity; external happiness. *Obs.*

2. Riches; large possessions of money, goods or land; that abundance of worldly estate which exceeds the estate of the greater part of the community; affluence; opulence.

Each day new *wealth* without their care provides. *Dryden.*

WEALTH'ILY, *adv.* Richly. *Shak.*

WEALTH'INESS, *n.* State of being wealthy; richness.

WEALTH'Y, *a.* Rich; having large possessions in lands, goods, money or securities, or larger than the generality of men; opulent; affluent. As wealth is a comparative thing, a man may be *wealthy* in one place, and not so in another. A man may be deemed *wealthy* in a village, who would not be so considered in London.

WEAN, *v. t.* [Sax. *wenan, gewœnan*, to accustom; from the root of *wone, wont*; *gewunian*, to delay; D. *wenan, afwenan*; G. *entwöhnen*; Sw. *vånja.* See *Wont.*]

1. To accustom and reconcile, as a child or other young animal, to a want or deprivation of the breast.

And the child grew, and was *weaned.* Gen. xxi.

2. To detach or alienate, as the affections, from any object of desire; to reconcile to the want or loss of any thing; as, to *wean* the heart from temporal enjoyments.

WE'ANED, *pp.* Accustomed or reconciled to the want of the breast or other object of desire.

WE'ANEL, **WE'ANLING**, } *n.* A child or other animal newly weaned. *Milton.*

WE'ANING, *ppr.* Accustoming or reconciling, as a young child or other animal, to a want of the breast; reconciling to the want of any object of desire.

WEAPON, *n.* *wep'n.* [Sax. *wæpn, wepn*; D. G. *wapen*; Dan. *vaaben*; Sw. *vapen.* This word seems to be from some root signifying to strike, L. *vapulo*, our vulgar *whap, awhap.*]

1. Any instrument of offense; any thing used or designed to be used in destroying or annoying an enemy. The *weapons* of rude nations are clubs, stones and bows and arrows. Modern *weapons* of war are swords, muskets, pistols, cannon and the like.

2. An instrument for contest, or for combating enemies.

The *weapons* of our warfare are not carnal. 2 Cor. x.

3. An instrument of defense.

4. *Weapons*, in *botany*, arms; thorns, prickles, and stings, with which plants are furnished for defense; enumerated among the *fulcres* by Linne. *Martyn.*

WEAPONED, *a.* *wep'nd.* Armed; furnished with weapons or arms; equipped. *Hayward.*

WEAP'ONLESS, *a.* Unarmed; having no weapon. *Milton.*

WEAP'ON-SALVE, *n.* [*weapon* and *salve.*] A salve which was supposed to cure the wound, by being applied to the weapon that made it. *Obs.* *Boyle.*

WEAR, *v. t.* pret. *wore*; pp. *worn.* [W. *gwariaw*, to spend or consume; Sax. *weran, werian*, to carry, to wear, as arms or clothes.]

1. To waste or impair by rubbing or attrition; to lessen or diminish by time, use or instruments. A current of water often *wears* a channel in limestone.

2. To carry appendant to the body, as clothes or weapons; as, to *wear* a coat or a robe; to *wear* a sword; to wear a *crown.*

On her white breast a sparkling cross she *wore.* *Pope.*

3. To have or exhibit an appearance; to bear; as, she *wears* a smile on her countenance.

4. To affect by degrees.

Trials *wear* us into a liking of what possibly, in the first essay, displeased us. *Locke.*

To wear away, to consume; to impair, diminish or destroy by gradual attrition or decay. *Dryden.*

To wear off, to diminish by attrition or slow decay. *South.*

To wear out, to consume; to render useless by attrition or decay; as, to *wear out* a coat or a book.

2. To consume tediously; as, to *wear out* life in idle projects.

3. To harass; to tire.

He shall *wear out* the saints of the Most High. Dan. vii.

4. To waste the strength of; as an old man *worn out* in the service of his country.

WEAR, *v. i.* To be wasted; to be diminished by attrition, by use, or by time.

Thou wilt surely *wear* away. Ex. xviii.

2. To be tediously spent.

Thus *wore* out night. *Milton.*

3. To be consumed by slow degrees. It is better to *wear* out, than to rust out.

To wear off, to pass away by degrees. The follies of youth *wear off* with age.

WEAR, *n.* The act of wearing; diminution by friction; as the *wear* and tear of a garment.

2. The thing worn.

WEAR, *n.* [Sax. *wær, wer*; from the root of *werian*, to hold, defend, protect; D. *waaren* or *weeren*; often written *wier.* See *Warren* and *Guard.*]

1. A dam in a river to stop and raise the water, for conducting it to a mill, or for taking fish.

2. An instrument or kind of basket work for catching fish.

WEARABLE, *a.* That can be worn. *Swift.*

WEARD, Sax. a warden, in names, denotes watchfulness or care, but it must not be confounded with *ward*, in *toward.*

WEARER, *n.* [from *wear.*] One who wears or carries as appendant to the body; as the *wearer* of a cloke, a sword or a crown.

2. That which wastes or diminishes.

WE'ARINESS, *n.* [from *weary.*] The state of being weary or tired; that lassitude or exhaustion of strength which is induced by labor; fatigue.

With *weariness* and wine oppress'd. *Dryden.*

2. Lassitude; uneasiness proceeding from continued waiting, disappointed expectation or exhausted patience, or from other cause.

WEARING, *ppr.* Bearing on or appendant to the person; diminishing by friction; consuming.

2. *a.* Denoting what is worn; as *wearing* apparel.

WEARING, *n.* Clothes; garments. *Obs.* *Shak.*

WEARISH, *a.* Boggy; watery. [*Not in use.*]

2. Weak; washy. [*Not in use.*] *Carew.*

WE'ARISŎME, *a.* [from *weary.*] Causing weariness; tiresome; tedious; fatiguing; as a *wearisome* march; a *wearisome* day's work.

Wearisome nights are appointed unto me. Job vii.

WE'ARISŎMELY, *adv.* Tediously; so as to cause weariness. *Raleigh.*

WE'ARISŎMENESS, *n.* The quality of exhausting strength or patience; tiresomeness; tediousness; as the *wearisomeness* of toil, or of waiting long in anxious expectation.

WE'ARY, *a.* [Sax. *werig*; allied perhaps to *wear.*]

1. Having the strength much exhausted by toil or violent exertion; tired; fatigued.

[It should be observed however that this word expresses less than *tired*, particularly when applied to a beast; as a *tired* horse. It is followed by *of*, before the cause of fatigue; as, to be *weary of* marching; to be *weary of* reaping; to be *weary of* study.]

2. Having the patience exhausted, or the mind yielding to discouragement. He was *weary* of asking for redress.

3. Causing weariness; tiresome; as a *weary* way; a *weary* life. *Spenser.* *Shak.*

WE'ARY, *v. t.* [from the adjective.] To reduce or exhaust the physical strength of the body; to tire; to fatigue; as, to *weary* one's self with labor or traveling.

The people shall *weary* themselves for very vanity. Hab. ii.

2. To make impatient of continuance.

I stay too long by thee; I *weary* thee. *Shak.*

3. To harass by any thing irksome; as, to be *wearied* of waiting for the arrival of the post.

To weary out, to subdue or exhaust by fatigue.

WE'ASAND, **WE'SAND**, } *n.* *s* as *z.* [Sax. *wasend, wæsend*; perhaps from the root of *wheeze*, and Goth. *ond*, Dan. *aande*, breath.]

The windpipe or trachea; the canal through which air passes to and from the lungs.

WE'ASEL, } *n. s* as z. [Sax. *wesle;* Dan.
WEE'SEL, } *vesel;* G. *wiesel;* D. *weezel.* I know not the meaning of this name. In G. *wiese* is a meadow.]

A small animal of the genus Mustela, which lives under the roots of trees, or in other holes, and feeds on small birds, but particularly on mice. A weasel that frequents barns and corn-houses, frees them from rats and mice, and is sometimes deemed a very useful inmate.

WE'ASEL-COOT, *n.* The red headed smew or *Mergus minutus.* *Cyc.*

WEATHER, *n. weth'er.* [Sax. *weder, wæder* or *wether;* G. *wetter;* D. *weder* or *weer;* Dan. *vejr;* Sw. *våder;* Sans. *widara,* a storm. The primary sense of this word is air, wind or atmosphere; probably the Gr. αιθηρ, whence *ether.*] Properly, the air; hence,

1. The state of the air or atmosphere with respect to heat or cold, wetness or dryness, calm or storm, clearness or cloudiness, and the like; as warm *weather;* cold *weather;* wet *weather;* dry *weather;* calm *weather;* tempestuous *weather;* fair *weather;* cloudy *weather;* hazy *weather,* and the like.
2. Change of the state of the air. *Bacon.*
3. Storm; tempest. *Dryden.*

[*These last significations are not now in use, unless by a poetic license.*]

Stress of weather, violent winds; force of tempests.

WEATHER, *v. t. weth'er.* To air; to expose to the air. [*Rarely used.*] *Spenser. Tusser.*

2. In *seamen's language,* to sail to the windward of something else; as, to *weather* a cape; to *weather* another ship. As this is often difficult, hence,
3. To pass with difficulty. *Hale.*

To weather a point, to gain or accomplish it against opposition. *Addison.*

To weather out, to endure; to hold out to the end; as, to *weather out* a storm. *Addison.*

Weather is used with several words, either as an adjective, or as forming part of a compound word.

WEATH'ER-BEATEN, *a.* [*weather* and *beaten.*]

Beaten or harassed by the weather. *Milton. Dryden.*

WEATH'ER-BIT, *n.* A turn of the cable about the end of the windlass, without the knight-heads. *Cyc.*

WEATH'ER-BOARD, *n.* That side of a ship which is towards the wind; the windward side. So in other words, *weather* signifies towards the wind or windward; as in *weather*-bow, *weather*-braces, *weather*-gage, *weather*-lifts, *weather*-quarter, *weather*-shrouds, *weather*-side, *weather*-shore, &c.

WEATH'ER-BOARDING, *n.* The act of nailing up boards against a wall; or the boards themselves. *Cyc.*

WEATH'ER-BOARDS, *n.* Pieces of plank placed in the ports of a ship, when laid up in ordinary. *Mar. Dict.*

WEATH'ER-CLOTHS, *n.* Long pieces of canvas or tarpauling used to preserve the hammocks from injury by the weather when stowed, or to defend persons from the wind and spray. *Mar. Dict.*

WEATH'ER-COCK, *n.* [*weather* and *cock.*]

1. Something in the shape of a cock placed on the stop of a spire, which by turning, shows the direction of the wind; a vane, or weather-vane.
2. Any thing or person that turns easily and frequently; a fickle, inconstant person. *Dryden.*

WEATH'ER-DRIVEN, *a.* [*weather* and *driven.*]

Driven by winds or storms; forced by stress of weather. *Carew.*

WEATH'ER-FEND, *v. t.* [*weather* and *fend.*] To shelter.

WEATH'ER-GAGE, *n.* [*weather* and *gage.*] Something that shows the weather. Qu. *Hudibras.*

A ship is said to have the *weather-gage* of another, when she is at the windward of her.

WEATH'ER-GLASS, *n.* [*weather* and *glass.*] An instrument to indicate the state of the atmosphere. This word includes the barometer, thermometer, hygrometer, manometer, and anemometer. *Cyc.*

WEATH'ER-HELM, *n.* [*weather* and *helm.*] A ship is said to carry a *weather-helm,* when she is inclined to come too near the wind. *Mar. Dict.*

WEATH'ERMOST, *a.* [*weather* and *most.*] Being farthest to the windward.

WEATH'ER-PROOF, *a.* [*weather* and *proof.*] Proof against rough weather.

WEATH'ER-ROLL, *n.* [*weather* and *roll.*] The roll of a ship to the windward; opposed to *lee-lurch.*

WEATH'ER-SPY, *n.* [*weather* and *spy.*] A star-gazer; one that foretells the weather. [*Little used.*] *Donne.*

WEATH'ER-TIDE, *n.* [*weather* and *tide.*] The tide which sets against the lee side of a ship, impelling her to the windward. *Mar. Dict.*

WEATH'ER-WISE, *a.* [*weather* and *wise.*] Skillful in foreseeing the changes or state of the weather.

WEATH'ER-WISER, *n.* Something that foreshows the weather. [*Not used.*] *Derham.*

WEATH'ERED, *pp.* Passed to the windward; passed with difficulty.

WEATH'ERING, *ppr.* Passing or sailing to the windward; passing with difficulty.

WEAVE, *v. t.* pret. *wove;* pp. *woven, wove.* The regular form, *weaved,* is rarely or never used. [Sax. *wefan;* G. *weben;* D. *weeven;* Sw. *våfva;* Dan. *væver;* Pers. *baftan;* Gr. υφαω.]

1. To unite threads of any kind in such a manner as to form cloth. This is done by crossing the threads by means of a shuttle. The modes of weaving, and the kinds of texture, are various. The threads first laid in length are called the *warp;* those which cross them in the direction of the breadth, are called the *weft* or *woof.*
2. To unite any thing flexible; as, to *weave* twigs.
3. To unite by intermixture or close connection; as a form of religion *woven* into the civil government. *Addison.*
4. To interpose; to insert.

This *weaves* itself perforce into my business. *Shak.*

WEAVE, *v. i.* To practice weaving; to work with a loom.

WE'AVER, *n.* One who weaves; one whose occupation is to weave.

2. The common name of the genus Ploceus, of several species, natives of Africa and the E. Indies; so called because they construct curious and often pensile nests, by interweaving twigs and fibers. *Ed. Encyc.*

WE'AVER-FISH, *n.* A kind of fish, [L. *araneus piscis.*] [See *Weever.*] *Ainsworth.*

WE'AVING, *ppr.* Forming cloth by intertexture of threads.

WE'AVING, *n.* The act or art of forming cloth in a loom, by the union or intertexture of threads.

2. The task or work to be done in making cloth.

WEB, *n.* [Sax. *web;* Sw. *våf.* See *Weave.*]

1. Texture of threads; plexus; any thing woven. Penelope devised a *web* to deceive her wooers. *Spenser.*
2. *Locally,* a piece of linen cloth. *England. Ireland.*
3. A dusky film that forms over the eye and hinders the sight; suffusion. *Shak.*
4. Some part of a sword. Qu. *net-work* of the handle or hilt. *Shak. Fairfax.*
5. In *ship-building,* the thin partition on the inside of the rim, and between the spokes of a sheave. *Cyc.*
6. In *ornithology,* the membrane which unites the toes of many water-fowls.

Spider's web, a plexus of very delicate threads or filaments which a spider spins from its bowels, and which serves as a net to catch flies or other insects for its food.

Web of a coulter, is the thin sharp part.

WEB'BED, *a.* [from *web.*] Having the toes united by a membrane, or web; as the *webbed* feet of aquatic fowls.

WEB'-FOOTED, *a.* [*web* and *foot.*] Having webbed feet; palmiped. A goose, or duck, is a *web-footed* fowl.

WED, *v. t.* [Sax. *weddian,* to covenant, to promise, to marry; Sw. *vädja;* Dan. *vedder,* to wager; W. *gwezu;* L. *vador,* to give bail, or *fœdus,* a league; probably both are of one family.]

1. To marry; to take for husband or for wife.

—Since the day
I saw thee first, and *wedded* thee. *Milton.*

2. To join in marriage.

And Adam, *wedded* to another Eve,
Shall live with her— *Milton.*

3. To unite closely in affection; to attach firmly. We are apt to be *wedded* to our own customs and opinions.

Men are *wedded* to their lusts. *Tillotson.*

4. To unite for ever.

Thou art *wedded* to calamity. *Shak.*

5. To espouse; to take part with.

They *wedded* his cause. *Obs. Clarendon.*

WED, *v. i.* To marry; to contract matrimony.

When shall I *wed?* *Shak.*

WED, *n.* A pledge.

WED'DED, *pp.* Married; closely attached.

WED'DING, *ppr.* Marrying; uniting with in matrimony.

WED'DING, *n.* Marriage; nuptials; nuptial ceremony; nuptial festivities.

Let her beauty be her *wedding* dower. *Shak.*

WED'DING-CLOTHES, *n.* [*wedding* and *clothes.*]
Garments for a bride or a bridegoom, to be worn at marriage.

WED'DING-DAY, *n.* [*wedding* and *day.*] The day of marriage.

WED'DING-FEAST, *n.* [*wedding* and *feast.*]
A feast or entertainment prepared for the guests at a wedding.

WEDǴE, *n.* [Sax. *wecg*, *wæcg*; Dan. *veg*; Sw. *vigg*; D. *wig*. This word signifies a mass, a lump.]
1. A mass of metal; as a *wedge* of gold or silver. Josh. vii.
2. A piece of metal, particularly iron, thick at one end and sloping to a thin edge at the other, used in splitting wood, rocks, &c. This is one of the five mechanical powers. A like piece of wood is by some persons called a wedge, or a glut.
3. Something in the form of a wedge. Sometimes bodies of troops are drawn up in the form of a *wedge*.

WEDǴE, *v. t.* To cleave with a wedge; to rive. [*Little used.*]
2. To drive as a wedge is driven; to crowd or compress closely. We were *wedged* in by the crowd.
3. To force, as a wedge forces its way; as, to *wedge* one's way. *Milton.*
4. To fasten with a wedge or with wedges; as, to *wedge* on a sythe; to *wedge* in a rail or a piece of timber.
5. To fix in the manner of a wedge.

Wedg'd in the rocky shoals, and sticking fast. *Dryden.*

WEDǴ'ED, *pp.* Split with a wedge; fastened with a wedge; closely compressed.

WEDǴE-SHAPED, *a.* [*wedge* and *shape.*] Having the shape of a wedge; cuneiform.
A *wedge-shaped* leaf is broad and abrupt at the summit, and tapering down to the base. *Smith.*

WEDǴ'ING, *ppr.* Cleaving with a wedge; fastening with wedges; compressing closely.

WED'LOCK, *n.* [Qu. *wed* and *lock*, or Sax. *lac*, a gift.] Marriage; matrimony. *Addison.*

WED'LOCK, *v. t.* To marry. [*Little used.*] *Milton.*

WED'LOCKED, *pp.* United in marriage. [*Little used.*] *Milton.*

WEDNESDAY, *n.* wenz'day. [Sax. *Wodensdæg*, Woden's day; Sw. *Odensdag* or *Onsdag*; from *Wodin* or *Odin*, a deity or chief among the northern nations of Europe.]
The fourth day of the week; the next day after Tuesday.

WEE, *a.* [contracted from G. *wenig.*] Small; little. [*Not in use.*]

WEE'CHELM, } *n.* A species of elm.
WITCH'-ELM, } *Bacon.*

WEED, *n.* [Sax. *weod.*] The general name of any plant that is useless or noxious. The word therefore has no definite application to any particular plant or species of plants; but whatever plants grow among corn, grass, or in hedges, and which are either of no use to man or injurious to crops, are denominated *weeds.*
2. Any kind of unprofitable substance among ores in mines, as mundic or marcasite. [*Local.*]

WEED, *n.* [Sax. *wæd*, *wæda*, a vestment, any garment, that which is put on.]
1. Properly, a garment, as in Spenser, but now used only in the plural, *weeds*, for the mourning apparel of a female; as a widow's *weeds.* *Milton.*
2. An upper garment. *Obs.* *Chapman.*

WEED, *v. t.* [Sax. *weodian*; D. *weeden.*]
1. To free from noxious plants; as, to *weed* corn or onions; to *weed* a garden.
2. To take away, as noxious plants; as, to *weed* a writing of invectives.
3. To free from any thing hurtful or offensive; as, to *weed* a kingdom of bad subjects.
4. To root out vice; as, to *weed* the hearts of the young. *Locke. Ascham.*

WEE'DED, *pp.* Freed from weeds or whatever is noxious.

WEE'DER, *n.* One that weeds or frees from any thing noxious.

WEE'D-HOOK, } *n.* [*weed* and *hook.*]
WEE'DING-HOOK, } A hook used for cutting away or extirpating weeds. *Tusser.*

WEE'DING, *ppr.* Freeing from weeds or whatever is noxious to growth.

WEE'DING, *n.* The operation of freeing from noxious weeds, as a crop. *Cyc.*

WEE'DING-CHISEL, *n.* *s* as *z.* A tool with a divided chisel point, for cutting the roots of large weeds within the ground. *Cyc.*

WEE'DING-FORCEPS, } *n.* An instru-
WEE'DING-TONGS, } ment for taking up some sorts of plants in weeding.

WEE'DING-FORK, *n.* A strong three-pronged fork, used in cleaning ground of weeds.

WEE'DING-RHIM, *n.* An implement somewhat like the frame of a wheel-barrow, used for tearing up weeds on summer fallows, &c.; used in Kent, Eng. *Cyc.*

WEE'DLESS, *a.* Free from weeds or noxious matter. *Dryden.*

WEE'DY, *a.* Consisting of weeds; as *weedy* trophies. *Shak.*
2. Abounding with weeds; as *weedy* grounds; a *weedy* garden; *weedy* corn.

WEEK, *n.* [Sax. *weoc*; D. *week*; G. *woche*; Dan. *uge*; Sw. *vecka.*]
1. The space of seven days.

I fast twice in the *week*. Luke xviii.

2. In *Scripture*, a prophetic week, is a week of years, or seven years. Dan. ix.

WEE'K-DAY, *n.* [*week* and *day.*] Any day of the week except the sabbath. *Pope.*

WEE'KLY, *a.* Coming, happening or done once a week; hebdomadary; as a *weekly* payment of bills; a *weekly* gazette; a *weekly* allowance. *Dryden. Swift.*

WEE'KLY, *adv.* Once a week; by hebdomadal periods; as, each performs service *weekly.* *Ayliffe.*

WEEL, *n.* [See *Well.* Sax. *wæl*, from *weallan*, to boil.] A whirlpool. [*Not in use.*]

WEEL, } *n.* A kind of twiggin trap or
WEE'LY, } snare for fish. *Carew.*

WEEN, *v. i.* [Sax. *wenan*, to think, suppose or hope, and to *wean.* The sense is to set, fix or hold in the mind; G. *wähnen*, to imagine; D. *waanen.*]
To think; to imagine; to fancy. *Spenser. Milton.*
[*Obsolete, except in burlesque.*]

WEE'NING, *ppr.* Thinking; imagining. *Obs.*

WEEP, *v. i.* pret. and pp. *wept.* *Weeped*, I believe, is never used. [Sax. *wepan*; evidently the same word as *whoop.* See *Whoop.* The primary sense is to cry out.]
1. To express sorrow, grief or anguish by outcry. This is the original sense. But in present usage, to manifest and express grief by outcry or by shedding tears.

They all *wept* sore, and fell on Paul's neck, and kissed him. Acts xx.

Phocion was rarely seen to *weep* or to laugh. *Mitford.*

2. To shed tears from any passion. Persons sometimes *weep* for joy.
3. To lament; to complain. Num. xi.

WEEP, *v. t.* To lament; to bewail; to bemoan.

We wand'ring go
Through dreary wastes, and *weep* each other's woe. *Pope.*

2. To shed moisture; as, to *weep* tears of joy.

Groves whose rich trees *wept* od'rous gum and balm. *Milton.*

3. To drop; as the *weeping* amber. *Pope.*
4. To abound with wet; as *weeping* grounds. *Mortimer.*

WEE'PER, *n.* One who weeps; one who sheds tears. *Dryden.*
2. A white border on the sleeve of a mourning coat. *Johnson.*
3. A species of monkey, the *Simia Capucina.* *Cyc.*

WEE'PING, *ppr.* Lamenting; shedding tears.

WEE'PING, *n.* Lamentation.

WEE'PING-ROCK, *n.* [*weep* and *rock.*] A porous rock from which water gradually issues.

WEE'PING-SPRING, *n.* A spring that slowly discharges water.

WEEPING-WILLOW, *n.* A species of willow, whose branches grow very long and slender, and hang down nearly in a perpendicular direction.

WEE'RISH, *a.* Insipid; weak; washy; surly. [*Not in use.*] *Ascham.*

WEE'SEL, the more proper spelling of *weasel.*

WEET, *v. i.* pret. *wot.* [Sax. *witan*; D. *weeten*; Sw. *veta*; G. *wissen*; Russ. *vidayu*; allied probably to L. *video*, Gr. *ειδω.*] To know. *Obs.*

WEE'TLESS, *a.* Unknowing. *Obs.*

WEE'VER, *n.* A fish, called also sea-dragon. [L. *araneus.*] *Cyc.*
A fish of the genus Trachinus, the spines of whose dorsal fins are supposed to be poisonous. *Ed. Encyc.*

WEE'VIL, *n.* [Sax. *wefl*; G. *wibel.*] A small insect that does great damage to wheat or other corn, by eating into the grains and devouring the farinaceous part. This insect is of the beetle kind, somewhat larger than a louse. *Cyc.*

WEFT, *old pret.* of *wave.* *Spenser.*

WEFT, *n.* [from *weave.*] The woof of cloth; the threads that cross the warp.
2. A web; a thing woven. *Cyc.*

WEFT, *n.* A thing waved, waived, or cast away. [*Not used.*] [See *Waif.*]

WEFT'AGE, *n.* Texture. [*Not used.*] *Grew.*

WEIGH, *v. t.* *wa.* [Sax. *wæg*, *weg*, a balance; *wægan*, to weigh, to bear, to carry, L. *veho*; D. *weegen*, *wikken*; G. *wägen*; Sw. *våga*; Dan. *vejer*, to weigh; Russ.

vaga, a balance; Amharic, አዋቂ awaki, weight. See *Wag.*]

1. To examine by the balance; to ascertain the weight, that is, the force with which a thing tends to the center of gravity; as, to *weigh* sugar; to *weigh* gold.

2. To be equivalent to in weight; that is, according to the Saxon sense of the verb, to lift to an equipoise a weight on the other side of the fulcrum. Thus when a body balances a weight of twenty eight pounds avoirdupois, it lifts or bears it, and is said to *weigh* so much. It *weighs* a quarter of a hundred.

3. To raise; to lift; as an anchor from the ground, or any other body; as, to *weigh* anchor; to *weigh* an old hulk.

4. To pay, allot or take by weight.

They *weighed* for my price thirty pieces of silver. Zech. xi.

5. To ponder in the mind; to consider or examine for the purpose of forming an opinion or coming to a conclusion; as, to *weigh* the advantages and disadvantages of a scheme.

Regard not who it is which speaketh, but *weigh* only what is spoken. *Hooker.*

6. To compare by the scales.

Here in nice balance truth with gold she *weighs*. *Pope.*

7. To regard; to consider as worthy of notice.

I *weigh* not you. *Shak.*

To weigh down, to overbalance.

2. To oppress with weight; to depress.

WEIGH, *v. i.* To have weight; as, to *weigh* lighter or heavier. *Brown.*

2. To be considered as important; to have weight in the intellectual balance. This argument *weighs* with the considerate part of the community.

3. To bear heavily; to press hard.

—Cleanse the stuff'd bosom of that perilous stuff,
Which *weighs* upon the heart. *Shak.*

To weigh down, to sink by its own weight.

WEIGH, *n.* A certain quantity. A *weigh* of wool, cheese, &c., is 256lb. avoirdupois; a *weigh* of corn is forty bushels; of barley or malt, six quarters. *Encyc. Cyc.*

WEIGHABLE, *a.* That may be weighed.

WEIGHED, *pp.* Examined by the scales; having the weight ascertained.

2. Considered.

3. *a.* Experienced; as a young man not *weighed* in state affairs. [*Not in use.*] *Bacon.*

WEIGHER, *n.* One who weighs.

2. An officer whose duty is to weigh commodities.

WEIGHING, *ppr.* Examining by scales; considering.

WEIGHING, *n.* The act of ascertaining weight.

2. As much as is weighed at once; as a *weighing* of beef.

WEIGHING-CAGE, *n.* A cage in which small living animals may be conveniently weighed. *Cyc.*

WEIGHING-HOUSE, *n.* A building furnished with a dock and other conveniences for weighing commodities and ascertaining the tunnage of boats to be used on a canal. *Cyc.*

WEIGHING-MACHINE, *n.* A machine for weighing heavy bodies, and particularly wheel carriages, at turnpike gates. *Cyc. England.*

2. A machine for weighing cattle.

WEIGHT, *n. wate.* [Sax. *wiht*; Sw. *vigt*. See *Weigh.*]

1. The quantity of a body, ascertained by the balance; in a philosophical sense, that quality of bodies by which they tend towards the center of the earth in a line perpendicular to its surface. In short, weight is gravity, and the weight of a particular body is the amount of its gravity, or of the force with which it tends to the center. The weight of a body is in direct proportion to its quantity of matter. *Newton.*

2. A mass of iron, lead, brass or other metal, to be used for ascertaining the weight of other bodies; as a *weight* of an ounce, a pound, a quarter of a hundred, &c. The *weights* of nations are different, except those of England and the United States, which are the same.

3. A ponderous mass; something heavy.

A man leaps better with *weights* in his hands. *Bacon.*

4. Pressure; burden; as the *weight* of grief; *weight* of care; *weight* of business; *weight* of government.

5. Importance; power; influence; efficacy; consequence; moment; impressiveness; as an argument of great *weight*; a consideration of vast *weight*. The dignity of a man's character adds *weight* to his words.

WEIGHTILY, *adv.* Heavily; ponderously.

2. With force or impressiveness; with moral power.

WEIGHTINESS, *n.* Ponderousness; gravity; heaviness.

2. Solidity; force; impressiveness; power of convincing; as the *weightiness* of an argument. *Locke.*

3. Importance. *Hayward.*

WEIGHTLESS, *a.* Having no weight; light. *Dryden.*

WEIGHTY, *a.* Having great weight; heavy; ponderous; as a *weighty* body.

2. Important; forcible; momentous; adapted to turn the balance in the mind, or to convince; as *weighty* reasons; *weighty* matters; *weighty* considerations or arguments. *Shak.*

3. Rigorous; severe; as our *weightier* judgment. [*Not in use.*] *Shak.*

WEIRD, *a.* Skilled in witchcraft. [*Not in use.*] *Shak.*

WEIVE, for *waive*. [*Not in use.*] *Gower.*

WELAWAY, an exclamation expressive of grief or sorrow, equivalent to *alas*. It is a compound of Sax. *wa*, wo, and *la*, oh. The original is *wa-la*, which is doubtless the origin of our common exclamation, *O la*, and to this, *wa*, wo, is added. The true orthography would be *wa la wa*. But the word is. I believe, wholly obsolete.

WEL'COME, *a.* [Sax. *wil-cuma*; *well* and *come*; that is, your coming is pleasing to me.]

1. Received with gladness; admitted willingly to the house, entertainment and company; as a *welcome* guest.

2. Grateful; pleasing; as a *welcome* present; *welcome* news.

3. Free to have or enjoy gratuitously. You are *welcome* to the use of my library.

To bid welcome, to receive with professions of kindness. *Bacon.*

WEL'COME, is used elliptically for *you are welcome*.

Welcome, great monarch, to your own. *Dryden.*

Welcome to our house, an herb.

WEL'COME, *n.* Salutation of a new comer.

Welcome ever smiles— *Shak.*

2. Kind reception of a guest or new comer. We entered the house and found a ready *welcome*.

Truth finds an entrance and a *welcome* too. *South.*

WEL'COME, *v. t.* [Sax. *wilcumian.*] To salute a new comer with kindness; or to receive and entertain hospitably, gratuitously and cheerfully.

Thus we salute thee with our early song,
And *welcome* thee, and wish thee long. *Milton.*

WEL'COMED, *pp.* Received with gladness and kindness.

WEL'COMELY, *adv.* In a welcome manner. *Brown.*

WEL'COMENESS, *n.* Gratefulness; agreeableness; kind reception. *Boyle.*

WEL'COMER, *n.* One who salutes or receives kindly a new comer. *Shak.*

WEL'COMING, *ppr.* Saluting or receiving with kindness a new comer or guest.

WELD, } *n.* A plant of the genus Reseda,
WOLD, } used by dyers to give a yellow color, and sometimes called *dyers' weed*. It is much cultivated in Kent for the London dyers. *Cyc.*

WELD, *v. t.* To wield. *Obs.* *Spenser.*

WELD, *v. t.* [Sw. *välla*, to weld; G. *wellen*, to join; D. *wellen*, to well, to spring, to soder.]

To unite or hammer into firm union, as two pieces of iron, when heated almost to fusion.

WELD'ED, *pp.* Forged or beat into union in an intense heat.

WELD'ER, *n.* One who welds iron.

2. A manager; an actual occupant. [*Not in use.*] *Swift.*

WELD'ING, *ppr.* Uniting in an intense heat.

WELD'ING-HEAT, *n.* The heat necessary for welding iron bars, which is said to be 60° by Wedgwood's pyrometer, and 8877° by Fahrenheit.

WEL'FARE, *n.* [*well* and *fare*, a good going; G. *wohlfahrt*; D. *welvaart*; Sw. *välfart*; Dan. *velfærd.*]

1. Exemption from misfortune, sickness, calamity or evil; the enjoyment of health and the common blessings of life; prosperity; happiness; *applied to persons*.

2. Exemption from any unusual evil or calamity; the enjoyment of peace and prosperity, or the ordinary blessings of society and civil government; *applied to states*.

WELK, *v. i.* [G. D. *welken*, to wither, to fade, to decay; primarily to shrink or contract, as things in drying, whence the Saxon *weolc*, a whilk or whelk, a shell; from its wrinkles.]

To decline; to fade; to decay; to fall.

When ruddy Phœbus 'gins to *welk* in west. *Obs.* *Spenser.*

WELK, *v. t.* To contract; to shorten.

Now sad winter *welked* hath the day— *Spenser.*

[*This word is obsolete. But its signification has heretofore been misunderstood.*]

WELK'ED, *pp.* or *a.* Contracted into wrinkles or ridges.

—Horns *welk'd* and wav'd like the enridged sea. *Obs.* *Shak.*

WELK'IN, *n.* [Sax, *wolc, wolcen*, a cloud, the air, ether, the vault of heaven; G. *wolke*, a cloud. Qu. Sax. *wealcan*, to roll, to full.]

The visible regions of the air; the vault of heaven. *Chaucer. Milton.*

[*This is obsolete, unless in poetry.*]

Welkin eye, in Shakspeare, is interpreted by Johnson, a blue eye, from *welkin*, the sky; by Todd, a rolling eye, from Sax. *wealcan*, to roll; and by Entick, a languishing eye. See *Welk*. It is obsolete, at least in New England.

WELK'ING, *ppr.* Fading; declining; contracting.

WELL, *n.* [Sax. *well*, a spring or fountain; *wellan*, to *well*, to boil or bubble, to spring, to rise; D. *wel, wellen*, id.; G. *quelle*, a spring; *quellen*, to spring, to issue forth, to gush, to well, to swell; *wallen*, to swell. In G. *welle* is a wave. On this word I suppose *swell* to be formed.]

1. A spring; a fountain; the issuing of water from the earth.

Begin then, sisters of the sacred *well*. *Milton.*

[*In this sense, obsolete.*]

2. A pit or cylindrical hole, sunk perpendicularly into the earth to such a depth as to reach a supply of water, and walled with stone to prevent the earth from caving in.

3. In *ships*, an apartment in the middle of a ship's hold, to inclose the pumps, from the bottom to the lower deck. *Mar. Dict.*

4. In *a fishing vessel*, an apartment in the middle of the hold, made tight at the sides, but having holes perforated in the bottom to let in fresh water for the preservation of fish, while they are transported to market. *Mar. Dict.*

5. In *the military art*, a hole or excavation in the earth, in mining, from which run branches or galleries. *Cyc.*

WELL'-DRAIN, *n.* [*well* and *drain.*] A drain or vent for water, somewhat like a well or pit, serving to discharge the water of wet land. *Cyc.*

WELL'-DRAIN, *v. t.* To drain land by means of wells or pits, which receive the water, and from which it is discharged by machinery. *Cyc.*

WELL'-HOLE, WELL, } *n.* In *architecture*, the hole or space left in a floor for the stairs. *Moxon.*

WELL'-ROOM, *n.* [*well* and *room.*] In a boat, a place in the bottom where the water is collected, and whence it is thrown out with a scoop.

WELL'-SPRING, *n.* [*well* and *spring.*] A source of continual supply. Prov. xvi.

WELL'-WATER, *n.* [*well* and *water.*] The water that flows into a well from subterraneous springs; water drawn from a well.

WELL, *v. i.* [Sax. *wellan.*] To spring; to issue forth, as water from the earth. [*Little used.*] *Spenser. Dryden.*

WELL, *v. t.* To pour forth. *Obs.* *Spenser.*

WELL, *a.* [Sax. *wel* or *well*; G. *wohl*; D. *wel*; Sw. *väl*; Dan. *vel*; W. *gwell*, better; *gwella*, to make better, to mend, to improve; Arm. *guellaat*; L. *valeo*, to be strong; Sans. *bala, bali*, strength. The primary sense of *valeo* is to strain, stretch, whence to advance, to prevail, to gain, according to our vulgar phrase, to *get ahead*, which coincides with *prosper*, Gr. προσφερω. I do not find *well* used in other languages as an adjective, but it is so used in English. See *Weal.*]

1. Being in health; having a sound body, with a regular performance of the natural and proper functions of all the organs; *applied to animals*; as a *well* man; the patient has recovered, and is perfectly *well*.

While you are *well*, you may do much good. *Taylor.*

Is your father *well*? Gen. xliii.

2. Fortunate; convenient; advantageous; happy. It is *well* for us that we are sequestered so far from the rest of the world.

It was *well* with us in Egypt. Num. xi.

3. Being in favor.

He was *well* with Henry the fourth. *Dryden.*

WELL, *adv.* In a proper manner; justly; rightly; not ill or wickedly. James ii.

If thou doest not *well*, sin lieth at the door. Gen. iv.

2. Skillfully; with due art; as, the work is *well* done; he writes *well*; he rides *well*; the plot is *well* laid, and *well* executed.

3. Sufficiently; abundantly.

Lot—beheld all the plain of Jordan, that it was *well* watered every where. Gen. xiii.

4. Very much; to a degree that gives pleasure. I liked the entertainment *well*.

5. Favorably; with praise.

All the world speaks *well* of you. *Pope.*

6. Conveniently; suitably; advantageously. This is all the mind can *well* contain. I cannot *well* attend the meeting.

7. To a sufficient degree; perfectly. I know not *well* how to execute this task.

8. Thoroughly; fully. Let the cloth be *well* cleansed. Let the steel be *well* polished.

She looketh *well* to the ways of her household. Prov. xxxi.

9. Fully; adequately.

We are *well* able to overcome it. Num. xiii.

10. Far; as, to be *well* advanced in life.

As well as, together with; not less than; one as much as the other; as a sickness long *as well as* severe. London is the largest city in Europe, *as well as* the principal banking city.

Well enough, in a moderate degree; so as to give satisfaction, or so as to require no alteration.

Well is him, seems to be elliptical for *well is to him.*

Well is prefixed to many words, expressing what is right, fit, laudable, or not defective; as *well*-affected; *well*-designed; *well*-directed; *well*-ordered; *well*-formed; *well*-meant; *well*-minded; *well*-seasoned; *well*-tasted.

Well is sometimes used elliptically for *it is well*, and as an expression of satisfaction with what has been said or done; and sometimes it is merely expletive. *Well*, the work is done. *Well*, let us go. *Well, well*, be it so.

WELL'ADAY, alas, Johnson supposes to be a corruption of *welaway*, which see. *Shak. Gay.*

WELLBE'ING, *n.* [*well* and *being.*] Welfare; happiness; prosperity; as, virtue is essential to the *wellbeing* of men or of society.

WELL-BELOVED, *a.* Greatly beloved. Mark xii.

WELL'-BORN, *a.* [*well* and *born.*] Born of a noble or respectable family; not of mean birth. *Waller. Dryden.*

WELL'-BRED, *a.* [*well* and *bred.*] Educated to polished manners; polite. *Roscommon.*

WELL-DONE, *exclam.* [*well* and *done.*] A word of praise; bravely; nobly; in a right manner.

WELLFARE, is now written *welfare.*

WELL-FA'VORED, *a.* Handsome; well formed; beautiful; pleasing to the eye. Gen. xxix.

WELL-GROUND'ED, *a.* [*well* and *ground.*] Well founded; having a solid foundation.

WELL'-HEAD, *n.* [*well* and *head.*] A source, spring or fountain. *Obs.* *Spenser.*

WELL-INTEN'TIONED, *a.* Having upright intentions or purpose. *Milner.*

WELL-MAN'NERED, *a.* [*well* and *manner.*] Polite; well-bred; complaisant. *Dryden.*

WELL'-MEANER, *n.* [*well* and *mean.*] One whose intention is good. *Dryden.*

WELL'-MEANING, *a.* Having a good intention. *Killingbeck.*

WELL-MET', *exclam.* A term of salutation denoting joy at meeting.

WELL-MINDED, *a.* [*well* and *mind.*] Well disposed; having a good mind.

WELL-MOR'ALIZED, *a.* Regulated by good morals. *Milner.*

WELL'-NATURED, *a.* [*well* and *natured.*] Good natured; kind. *Dryden.*

WELL'-NIGH, *adv.* [*well* and *nigh.*] Almost; nearly.

WELL'-SPENT, *a.* [*well* and *spent.*] Spent or passed in virtue; as a *well-spent* life; *well-spent* days. *Pope.*

WELL'-SPOKEN, *a.* [*well* and *speak.*]

1. Speaking well; speaking with fitness or grace; or speaking kindly.

2. Spoken with propriety; as *well-spoken* words.

WELL-WILL'ER, *n.* [*well* and *will.*] One who means kindly. *Sidney. Hooker.*

WELL-WISH', *n.* [*well* and *wish.*] A wish of happiness. *Addison.*

WELL-WISH'ER, *n.* [supra.] One who wishes the good of another. *Addison.*

WELSH, *a.* [Sax. *weallisc*, from *wealh*, a foreigner; *weallian*, to wander; G. *wälsch*, foreign, strange, Celtic, *Welsh*; *Walsche sprache*, the Italian language, that is, foreign, or Celtic.] Pertaining to the Welsh nation.

WELSH, *n.* The language of Wales or of the Welsh.

2. The general name of the inhabitants of Wales. The word signifies foreigners or wanderers, and was given to this people by other nations, probably because they came from some distant country. The Welsh call themselves *Cymry*, in the plu-

ral, and a Welshman *Cymro*, and their country *Cymru*, of which the adjective is *Cymreig*, and the name of their language, *Cymraeg*. They are supposed to be the *Cimbri* of Jutland. *Owen.*

WELT, *n.* [W. *gwald*, from *gwal*, a fence, a *wall*; *gwaliaw*, to inclose; *gwaldu*, to hem. See *Wall*.]

A border; a kind of hem or edging, as on a garment or piece of cloth, or on a shoe. *Bacon.*

WELT, *v. t.* To furnish with a welt; to sew on a border.

WEL'TER, *v. i.* [Sax. *wæltan*; Sw. *vältra*; G. *walzen*; Dan. *vælter*; allied probably to *wallow*, L. *voluto*.]

To roll, as the body of an animal; but usually, to roll or wallow in some foul matter; as, to *welter* in blood or in filth. *Dryden.*

WEL'TERING, *ppr.* Rolling; wallowing; as in mire, blood, or other filthy matter.

WEM, *n.* [Sax.] A spot; a scar. *Obs.* *Brerewood.*

WEM, *v. t.* [Sax. *wemman*.] To corrupt. *Obs.*

WEN, *n.* [Sax. *wenn*; D. *wen*; Arm. *guennaen*, a wart.]

An encysted swelling or tumor; also, a fleshy excrescence growing on animals, sometimes to a large size. *Cyc.*

WENCH, *n.* [Sax. *wencle*. Qu. G. *wenig*, little.]

1. A young woman. [*Little used.*] *Sidney. Donne.*

2. A young woman of ill fame. *Prior.*

3. In *America*, a black or colored female servant; a negress.

WENCH, *v. i.* To frequent the company of women of ill fame. *Addison.*

WENCH'ER, *n.* A lewd man. *Grew.*

WENCH'ING, *ppr.* Frequenting women of ill fame.

WEND, *v. i.* [Sax. *wendan*.] To go; to pass to or from. [Obsolete, except in poetry; but its preterit, *went*, is in common use.]

2. To turn round. *Obs.* [*Wend* and *wind* are from the same root.]

WEN'NEL, *n.* A weanel. [See *Weanel*.] *Obs.*

WEN'NISH, WEN'NY, } *a.* [from *wen*.] Having the nature of a wen.

WENT, *pret.* of the obsolete verb *wend*. We now arrange *went* in grammar as the preterit of *go*, but in origin it has no connection with it.

WEPT, *pret.* and *pp.* of *weep*.

When he had come near, he beheld the city and *wept* over it. Luke xix.

WERE, pron. *wer*, which when prolonged, becomes *ware*. This is used as the imperfect tense plural of *be*; we *were*, you *were*, they *were*; and in some other tenses. It is the Danish verb *værer*, to be, to exist, Sw. *vara*, and in origin has no connection with *be*, nor with *was*. It is united with *be*, to supply its want of tenses, as *went* is with *go*.

WERE, *n.* A dam. [See *Wear*.]

WER'EGILD, *n.* [Sax. *wer*, man, and the estimated value of a man, and *gild*, *geld*, money.]

Formerly, the price of a man's head; a compensation paid for a man killed, partly to the king for the loss of a subject, and partly to the lord of the vassal, and partly to the next of kin. It was paid by the murderer. *Blackstone.*

WERNE'RIAN, *a.* Pertaining to Werner, the German mineralogist, who arranged minerals in classes, &c. according to their external characters.

WER'NERITE, *n.* A mineral, regarded by Werner as a subspecies of scapolite; called foliated scapolite. It is named from that distinguished mineralogist, Werner. It is found massive, and crystalized in octahedral prisms with four sided pyramidical terminations, disseminated in rocks of grayish or red feldspar. It is imperfectly lamellar, of a greenish, grayish, or olive green color, with a pearly or resinous luster. It is softer than feldspar, and melts into a white enamel.

WERT, the second person singular of the subjunctive imperfect tense of *be*. [See *Were*.]

Werth, *worth*, in names, signifies a farm, court or village, from Sax. *weorthig*. *Lye, Dict.*

WE'SIL, for *weasand*. [*Not in use.*]

WEST, *n.* [Sax. D. G. *west*; Dan. *vest*; Sw. *vester*; Fr. *ouest*. This word probably signifies decline or fall, or departure; as in L. *occidens*, and in other cases. In elements, it coincides with *waste*.]

1. In strictness, that point of the horizon where the sun sets at the equinox, or any point in a direct line between the spectator or other object, and that point of the horizon; or west is the intersection of the prime vertical with the horizon, on that side where the sun sets. *West* is directly opposite to *east*, and one of the cardinal points. In a less strict sense, west is the region of the hemisphere near the point where the sun sets when in the equator. Thus we say, a star sets in the *west*, a meteor appears in the *west*, a cloud rises in the *west*.

2. A country situated in the region towards the sun-setting, with respect to another. Thus in the United States, the inhabitants of the Atlantic states speak of the inhabitants of Ohio, Kentucky or Missouri, and call them people of the *west*; and formerly, the empire of Rome was called the empire of the *West*, in opposition to the empire of the *East*, the seat of which was Constantinople.

WEST, *a.* Being in a line towards the point where the sun sets when in the equator; or in a looser sense, being in the region near the line of direction towards that point, either on the earth or in the heavens.

This shall be your *west* border. Num. xxxiv.

2. Coming or moving from the west or western region; as a *west* wind.

WEST, *adv.* To the western region; at the westward; more westward; as, Ireland lies *west* of England.

WEST, *v. i.* To pass to the west; to set, as the sun. [*Not in use.*] *Chaucer.*

WEST'ERING, *a.* Passing to the west. [*I believe not now used.*] *Milton.*

WEST'ERLY, *a.* Being towards the west; situated in the western region; as the *westerly* parts of England. *Graunt.*

2. Moving from the westward; as a *westerly* wind.

WEST'ERLY, *adv.* Tending, going or moving towards the west; as a man traveling *westerly*.

WEST'ERN, *a.* [*west* and Sax. *ærn*, place.]

1. Being in the west, or in the region nearly in the direction of west; being in that quarter where the sun sets; as the *western* shore of France; the *western* ocean.

2. Moving in a line to the part where the sun sets; as, the ship makes a *western* course.

WEST'ING, *n.* Space or distance westward; or departure; as the *westing* and southing of a ship.

WEST'WARD, *adv.* [Sax. *westweard*; *west* and *weard*, L. *versus*.]

Towards the west; as, to ride or sail *westward*.

WEST'WARDLY, *adv.* In a direction towards the west; as, to pass *westwardly*.

WET, *a.* [Sax. *wæt*; Sw. *väta*, Dan. *væde*, moisture, Gr. ὑετος; L. *udus*.]

1. Containing water, as *wet* land, or a *wet* cloth; or having water or other liquid upon the surface, as a *wet* table. *Wet* implies more water or liquid than *moist* or *humid*.

2. Rainy; as *wet* weather; a *wet* season.

WET, *n.* Water or wetness; moisture or humidity in considerable degree. Wear thick shoes or pattens to keep your feet from the *wet*.

2. Rainy weather; foggy or misty weather. *Swift.*

WET, *v. t.* pret. and pp. *wet*. But *wetted* is sometimes used. [Sax. *wætan*; Sw. *väta*; Dan. *væder*.]

1. To fill or moisten with water or other liquid; to sprinkle or humectate; to cause to have water or other fluid adherent to the surface; to dip or soak in liquor; as, to *wet* a spunge; to *wet* the hands; to *wet* cloth.

Wet the thirsty earth with falling show'rs. *Milton.*

2. To moisten with drink. *Walton.*

WETH'ER, *n.* [Sax. *wether* or *wedder*. In Dan. *væder* is a ram.] A ram castrated.

WET'NESS, *n.* The state of being wet, either by being soaked or filled with liquor, or by having a liquid adherent to the surface; as the *wetness* of land; the *wetness* of a cloth. It implies more water or liquid than *humidness* or *moisture*.

2. A watery or moist state of the atmosphere; a state of being rainy, foggy or misty; as the *wetness* of weather or the season.

WET'TISH, *a.* Somewhat wet; moist; humid.

WEX, *v. t.* or *i.* To grow; to wax. [*Not to be used.*] [See *Wax*.]

WE'ZAND, for *weasand*. [See the latter.]

[NOTE.—In words beginning with *wh*, the letter *h*, or aspirate, when both letters are pronounced, precedes the sound of *w*. Thus *what*, *when*, are pronounced *hwat*, *hwen*. So they were written by our ancestors, and so they ought to be written still, as they are by the Danes and Swedes.]

WHACK, *v. t.* To strike. This is probably the primary word on which is formed *thwack*. [See *Twit*.] *Whack* is a vulgar word.

WHALE, *n.* [Sax. *hwal*, *hwæl*; G. *wallfisch*, from *wallen*, to stir, agitate or rove; D. *walvisch*; Sw. Dan. *hval*. This fish is named from roundness, or from rolling;

for in Dan. *hvalt* is arched or vaulted; *hvæller*, to arch or vault, D. *welven*.]

The general name of an order of animals inhabiting the ocean, arranged in zoology under the name of *Cete* or *Cetacea*, and belonging to the class *Mammalia* in the Linnean system. The common whale is of the genus Balæna. It is the largest animal of which we have any account, and probably the largest in the world. It is sometimes ninety feet in length in the northern seas, and in the torrid zone much larger. The whale furnishes us with oil, whalebone, &c. [See *Cachalot*.]

WHA'LEBONE, *n.* [*whale* and *bone*.] A firm elastic substance taken from the upper jaw of the whale, used as a stiffening in stays, fans, screens, &c.

WHA'LE-FISHERY, *n.* The fishery or occupation of taking whales.

WHA'LY, *a.* Marked with streaks; properly *wealy*.

WHAME, *n.* A species of fly, tabanus, the burrel fly, that annoys horses.

WHANG, *n.* [Sax. *thwang*.] A lether thong. [*Not in use.*]

WHANG, *v. t.* To beat. [*Not in use or local.*] *Grose.*

WHAP, *n.* A blow. [*Vulgar.*] [See *Awhap*.]

WHAP'PER, *n.* Something uncommonly large of the kind. So *thumper* is connected with *thump*, to strike with a heavy blow. [*Vulgar.*]

WHARF, *n.* *hworf.* [Sax. *hwarf*, *hweorf*; D. *werf*; Dan. *verf*; Russ. *vorph*. In D. *werven* signifies to raise or levy. In the plural, *wharfs* and *wharves* are both used.]

A perpendicular bank or mound of timber or stone and earth, raised on the shore of a harbor, or extending some distance into the water, for the convenience of lading and unlading ships and other vessels. This name is also given to the wider part of a canal, where boats lie while loading and unloading. The two longest *wharfs* in New England are at Boston and at New Haven. The latter is much the longest, extending into the harbor about three quarters of a mile.

WHARF, *v. t.* To guard or secure by a wharf or firm wall of timber or stone; as, the western bank of the Connecticut is *wharfed* at Hartford, to prevent the river from wearing away the land.

WHARF'AGE, *n.* The fee or duty paid for the privilege of using a wharf for loading or unloading goods, timber, wood, &c.

WHARF'ING, *n.* Wharfs in general.

WHARF'INGER, *n.* A man who has the care of a wharf, or the proprietor of a wharf.

WHAT, *pronoun relative* or *substitute.* [Sax. *hwæt*; Goth. *waiht*; D. *wat*; G. *was*; Dan. Sw. *hvad*; Scot. *quhat*; L. *quod*, *quid*. The Sax. *hwæt*, *hwat*, signifies brisk, lively, vigorous; which shows that this pronoun is the same word as *wight*, a living being, from the root of the L. *vivo*, for *vigo*. See *Wight*. The Gothic *h*, represents the Latin *c*, in *victus*.]

1. That which. Say *what* you will, is the same as say *that which* you will.
2. Which part. Consider *what* is due to nature, and *what* to art or labor.
3. *What* is the substitute for a sentence or clause of a sentence. "I tell thee *what*, corporal, I could tear her." Here *what* relates to the last clause, "I could tear her;" this is *what* I tell you.
4. *What* is used as an adjective, of both genders, often in specifying sorts or particulars. See *what* colors this silk exhibits. I know *what* qualities you desire in a friend; that is, I know the *qualities which* you desire.
5. *What* is much used in asking questions. *What* sort of character is this? *What* poem is this? *What* man is this we see coming?
6. *What time*, at the time or on the day when.

   What time the morn mysterious visions brings. *Pope.*

7. To how great a degree.

   What partial judges are our love and hate! *Dryden.*

8. Whatever.

   Whether it was the shortness of his foresight, the strength of his will—or *what* it was— *Bacon.*

9. Some part, or some. "The year before, he had so used the matter, that *what* by force, *what* by policy, he had taken from the christians above thirty castles;" that is, he had taken above thirty castles, a part or some by force, a part or some by policy; or *what* may be interpreted *partly*. *Knolles.*

Sometimes *what* has no verb to govern it, and it must be considered as adverbially used. "*What* with carrying apples and fuel, he finds himself in a hurry;" that is, partly, in part.

10. *What* is sometimes used elliptically for *what is this*, or *how is this?*

    What! could ye not watch with me one hour? Matt. xxvi.

11. *What* is used interrogatively and elliptically, as equivalent to *what will be the consequence? What will follow?* as in the phrase, *what* if I undertake this business myself?

What though, that is, grant this or that; allow it to be so.

What ho, an exclamation of calling.

WHAT, *n.* Fare; things; matter. [*Not in use.*] *Spenser.*

WHATEV'ER, *pron.* [*what* and *ever*.] Being this or that; being of one nature or another; being one thing or another; any thing that may be. *Whatever* is read, let it be read with attention. *Whatever* measure may be adopted, let it be with due caution. *Whatever* you do, let it be done with prudence.

2. All that; the whole that; all particulars that.

   At once came forth *whatever* creeps. *Milton.*

WHATSOEV'ER, a compound of *what*, *so*, and *ever*, has the sense of *whatever*, and is less used than the latter. Indeed it is nearly obsolete. *Whatso*, in a like sense, is entirely obsolete.

WHEAL, *n.* A pustule. [See *Weal*.]

WHEAT, *n.* [Sax. *hwæte*; Goth. *hwit*; Ice. *hveitenu*; G. *weitzen*; Sw. *hvete*; Dan. *hvede*; D. *weit*. Qu. Heb. חטה; Syr. id.]

A plant of the genus Triticum, and the seed of the plant, which furnishes a white flour for bread, and next to rice, is the grain most generally used by the human race. Of this grain the varieties are numerous, as red wheat, white wheat, bald wheat, bearded wheat, winter wheat, summer wheat, &c.

WHE'AT-BIRD, *n.* A bird that feeds on wheat. *Virginia.*

WHE'AT-EAR, *n.* The English name of the *Motacilla œnanthe*; called also *white-tail* and *fallow-finch*. *Cyc.*

WHEATEN, *a.* *hwee'tn.* Made of wheat; as *wheaten* bread. *Arbuthnot. Pope.*

WHE'AT-PLUM, *n.* A sort of plum.

WHEE'DLE, *v. t.* [Qu. Gr. γοητευω, or χωτιλλω.] To flatter; to entice by soft words.

   To learn th' unlucky art of *wheedling* fools. *Dryden.*

WHEE'DLE, *v. i.* To flatter; to coax.

WHEE'DLED, *pp.* Flattered; enticed; coaxed.

WHEE'DLING, *ppr.* Flattering; enticing by soft words.

WHEE'DLING, *n.* The act of flattering or enticing.

WHEEL, *n.* [Sax. *hweol*, *hweohl*, *hweogl*, *hweogul*; D. *wiel*; Sw. *hiul*. This seems to have *Wg* or *Hg* for its elements. See Syr. and Ar. No. 16. 17. Class Cg.]

1. A circular frame of wood, iron or other metal, consisting of a nave or hub, into which are inserted spokes which sustain a rim or felly; the whole turning on an axis. The name is also given to a solid circular or round piece of wood or metal, which revolves on an axis. The wheel and axle constitute one of the mechanical powers.
2. A circular body. *Shak.*
3. A carriage that moves on wheels. *Pope.*
4. An instrument for torturing criminals; as an examination made by the rack and the *wheel*. *Addison.*
5. A machine for spinning thread, of various kinds.
6. Rotation; revolution; turn; as the vicissitude and *wheel* of things. *South.*
7. A turning about; a compass.

   He throws his flight in many an airy *wheel*. *Milton.*

8. In *pottery*, a round board turned by a lathe in a horizontal position, on which the clay is shaped by the hand.

WHEEL-ANIMAL, *n.* A genus of animalcules, with arms for taking their prey, resembling wheels. *Cyc.*

WHEE'L-BARROW, *n.* [*wheel* and *barrow*.] A barrow moved on a single wheel.

WHEE'L-BOAT, *n.* [*wheel* and *boat*.] A boat with wheels, to be used either on water or upon inclined planes or rail-ways.

WHEE'L-CARRIAGE, *n.* [*wheel* and *carriage*.] A carriage moved on wheels.

WHEE'LER, *n.* A maker of wheels. *Obs.*

WHEE'L-FIRE, *n.* [*wheel* and *fire*.] In *chimistry*, a fire which encompasses the crucible without touching it. *Cyc.*

WHEE'L-SHAPED, *a.* [*wheel* and *shape*.] In *botany*, rotate; monopetalous, expanding into a flat border at top, with scarcely any tube; as a *wheel-shaped* corol. *Smith.*

WHEE'L-WRIGHT, *n.* [*wheel* and *wright*.] A man whose occupation is to make wheels and wheel-carriages, as carts and wagons.

WHEEL, *v. t.* To convey on wheels; as, to *wheel* a load of hay or wood.

2. To put into a rotary motion; to cause to turn round. *Milton.*

WHEEL, *v. i.* To turn on an axis. *Bentley.*
2. To turn; to move round; as, a body of troops *wheel* to the right or left.
3. To fetch a compass.

Then *wheeling* down the steep of heav'n he flies. *Pope.*

4. To roll forward.

Thunder
Must *wheel* on th' earth, devouring where it rolls. *Milton.*

WHEE'LED, *pp.* Conveyed on wheels; turned; rolled round.

WHEE'LING, *ppr.* Conveying on wheels or in a wheel-carriage; turning.

WHEE'LING, *n.* The act of conveying on wheels.
2. The act of passing on wheels, or convenience for passing on wheels. We say, it is good *wheeling*, or bad *wheeling*, according to the state of the roads.
3. A turning or circular movement of troops embodied.

WHEE'LY, *a.* Circular; suitable to rotation. *Philips.*

WHEEZE, *v. i.* [Sax. *hweosan*; Arm. *chueza*; Sw. *hes*, hoarse; Dan. *hvæser*; Sw. *hvåsa*, to hiss, to *whiz*; Dan. *hvaes*, a *whistling*. *Wheese*, *whiz*, and probably *whisper*, are of one family, and accord with the root of the L. *fistula.*]
To breathe hard and with an audible sound, as persons affected with asthma. *Dryden. Swift.*

WHEE'ZING, *ppr.* Breathing with difficulty and noise.

WHELK, *n.* A wrinkle; inequality on the surface; protuberance; a pustule. [See *Welk* and *Weal.*]
2. A shell of the genus Buccinum, or trumpet-shell, univalvular, spiral and gibbous, with an oval aperture ending in a short canal or gutter. *Linne. Cyc.*

WHELK'Y, *a.* Protuberant; embossed; rounded. *Spenser.*

WHELM, *v. t.* [Sax. *ahwylfan*; Goth. *hulyan*; Ice. *wilma* or *hwilma.*]
1. To cover with water or other fluid; to cover by immersion in something that envelops on all sides; as, to *whelm* a person or a company in the seas; to *whelm* a caravan in sand or dust.
2. To cover completely; to immerse deeply; to overburden; as, to *whelm* one in sorrows.
3. To throw over so as to cover. [*Not used.*] *Mortimer.*

WHELM'ED, *pp.* Covered, as by being plunged or immersed.

WHELM'ING, *ppr.* Covering, as by immersion.

WHELP, *n.* [Dan. *hvalp*; Sw. *valp*; D. *welp*. This word coincides in elements with *wolf*, L. *vulpes.*]
1. The young of the canine species, and of several other beasts of prey; a puppy; a cub; as a bear robbed of her *whelps*; lion's *whelps.*
2. A son; *in contempt.* *Shak.*
3. A young man; *in contempt.* *Addison.*

WHELP, *v. i.* To bring forth young, as the female of the canine species and some other beasts of prey. *Boyle.*

WHEN, *adv.* [Goth. *hwan*; Sax. *hwænne*; G. *wann*; D. *wanneer*; L. *quando*; Gaelic, *cuinne.*]
1. At the time. We were present *when* Gen. La Fayette embarked at Havre for New York.
2. At what time, interrogatively.

When shall these things be? Matt. xxiv.

3. Which time.

I was adopted heir by his consent;
Since *when*, his oath is broke. *Shak.*

4. After the time that. *When* the act is passed, the public will be satisfied.
5. At what time.

Kings may
Take their advantage, *when* and how they list. *Daniel.*

When as, at the time when; what time. *Obs.*

When as sacred light began to dawn. *Milton.*

WHENCE, *adv.* [Sax. *hwanon.*] From what place.

Whence and what art thou? *Milton.*

2. From what source. *Whence* shall we derive hope? *Whence* comes this honor?

Whence hath this man this wisdom? Matt. xiii.

3. From which premises, principles or facts. These facts or principles are admitted, *whence* it follows, that judgment must be entered for the plaintif.
4. How; by what way or means. Mark xii.
5. In general, from which person, cause, place, principle or circumstance.

From whence may be considered as tautological, *from* being implied in *whence*; but the use is well authorized, and in some cases the use of it seems to give force or beauty to the phrase. We ascended the mountain, *from whence* we took a view of the beautiful plains below.

Of whence, is not now used.

WHENCESOEV'ER, *adv.* [*whence*, *so*, and *ever.*]
From what place soever; from what cause or source soever.

Any idea, *whencesoever* we have it— *Locke.*

WHENCEVER. [See *Whensoever.*]

WHENEV'ER, *adv.* [*when* and *ever.*] At whatever time. *Whenever* you come, you will be kindly received.

WHENSOEV'ER, *adv.* [*when*, *so*, and *ever.*] At what time soever; at whatever time. *Locke.*

WHERE, *adv.* [Sax. *hwær*; Goth. *hwar*; Sw. *hvar*; D. *waar.*]
1. At which place or places.

She visited the place *where* first she was so happy— *Sidney.*
In all places *where* I record my name, I will come to thee and I will bless thee. Ex. xx.

2. At or in what place.

Adam, *where* art thou? Gen. iii.

3. At the place in which.

Where I thought the remnant of my age
Should have been cherish'd by her child-like duty. *Shak.*

4. Whither; to what place, or from what place. *Where* are you going? *Where* are you from? [These uses of *where* are common, and the first cannot be condemned as vulgar.]

Any where, in any place. I sought the man, but could not find him *any where*.

[Note. *Where* seems to have been originally a noun, and was so used by Spenser. "He shall find no *where* safe to him." In this sense, it is obsolete; yet it implies place, its original signification.]

WHEREABOUT', *adv.* [*where* and *about.*]
1. Near what place. *Whereabout* did you meet your friend?
2. Near which place. *Shak.*
3. Concerning which.

The object *whereabout* they are conversant. *Hooker.*

WHEREAS, *adv. s* as *z.* [*where* and *as.*]
1. When in fact or truth, implying opposition to something that precedes.

Are not those found to be the greatest zealots, who are most notoriously ignorant? *whereas* true zeal should always begin with true knowledge. *Sprat.*

2. The thing being so that; considering that things are so; implying an admission of facts, sometimes followed by a different statement, and sometimes by inferences or something consequent, as in the law style, where a preamble introduces a law.

Whereas wars are generally causes of poverty— *Bacon.*

3. Whereat; at which place. *Obs.* *Spenser.*
4. But on the contrary. [See No. 1.] *Woodward.*

WHEREAT', *adv.* [*where* and *at.*] At which.

Whereat he was no less angry and ashamed, than desirous to obey Zelmane. *Sidney.*

2. At what, interrogatively. *Whereat* are you offended?

WHEREBY', *adv.* [*where* and *by.*] By which.

You take my life,
When you do take the means *whereby* I live. *Shak.*

2. By what, interrogatively.

Whereby shall I know this? Luke i.

WHEREFORE, *adv.* [*where* and *for.*] For which reason.

Wherefore by their fruits ye shall know them. Matt. vii.

2. Why; for what reason.

Wherefore didst thou doubt? Matt. xiv.

WHEREIN', *adv.* [*where* and *in.*] In which; in which thing, time, respect, book, &c. This is the thing *wherein* you have erred.
2. In what.

Yet ye say, *wherein* have we wearied him? Mal. ii.

WHEREINTŌ', *adv.* [*where* and *into.*] Into which. *Obs.* *Bacon.*

WHERENESS, *n.* Ubiety; imperfect locality.

A point hath no dimensions, but only a *whereness*, and is next to nothing. *Grew.*
[*This word is not used, nor has it any intelligible signification.*]

WHEREOF', *adv.* [*where* and *of.*] Of which. We are not guilty of the crime *whereof* we are accused.
2. Of what. *Whereof* was this house built? *Obs.*

How this world, when and *whereof* created— *Milton.*

WHEREON', *adv.* [*where* and *on.*] On which; as the ground *whereon* we tread.
2. On what. *Whereon* do we stand? *Obs.*

WHERESO, *adv. Obs.* [See *Wheresoever.*]

WHERESOEV'ER, *adv.* [*where*, *so*, and *ever.*]
In what place soever; in whatever place, or in any place indefinitely. Seize the thief, *wheresoever* he may be found. [*Wherever* is the preferable word.].

WHERETHROUGH, through which, is not in use.

WHERETŌ, *adv.* [*where* and *to.*] To which.

Whereto we have already attained— Phil. iii.

2. To what; to what end. [*Little used.*]

WHEREUNTO′, *adv.* [*where* and *unto.*] The same as *whereto.* [*Little used.*]

WHEREUPON′, *adv.* Upon which.

The townsmen mutinied and sent to Essex, *whereupon* he came thither. *Clarendon.*

WHEREV′ER, *adv.* [*where* and *ever.*] At whatever place.

He cannot but love virtue, *wherever* it is. *Atterbury.*

WHEREWITH′, *adv.* [*where* and *with.*] With which.

The love *wherewith* thou hast loved me. John xvii.

2. With what, interrogatively.

Wherewith shall I save Israel? Judges vi.

WHEREWITHAL′, *adv.* [See *Withal.*] [*where, with,* and *all.*] The same as *wherewith.*

WHER′RET, *v. t.* [G. *wirren.* Qu.] To hurry; to trouble; to tease; to give a box on the ear. [*Low and not used in America.*]

WHER′RET, *n.* A box on the ear. [*Not in use.*] *Beaum.*

WHER′RY, *n.* [a different orthography of *ferry*, formed with a strong breathing; like *whistle*, from the root of L. *fistula.*]

1. A boat used on rivers. The name is given to several kinds of light boats. It is also applied to some decked vessels used in fishing, in different parts of Great Britain and Ireland. *Mar. Dict.*

2. A liquor made from the pulp of crabs after the verjuice is expressed; sometimes called *crab-wherry.* [*Local.*]

WHET, *v. t.* pret. and pp. *whetted* or *whet.* [Sax. *hwettan ;* Sw. *hvässa ;* Dan. *hvas,* sharp; *hvedser,* to whet; D. *wetten*; G. *wetzen.*]

1. To rub for the purpose of sharpening, as an edge tool; to sharpen by attrition; as, to *whet* a sythe or an ax.

2. To provoke; to excite; to stimulate; as, to *whet* the appetite.

3. To provoke; to make angry or acrimonious.

Since Cassius first did *whet* me against Cesar, I have not slept. *Shak.*

To whet on or *whet forward,* to urge on; to instigate. [*Not used nor proper.*] *Shak.*

WHET, *n.* The act of sharpening by friction.

2. Something that provokes or stimulates the appetite; as sips, drams and *whets.* *Spectator.*

WHETH′ER, *pronoun* or *substitute.* [Sax. *hwæther.* This word seems to be connected with *what* and the L. *uter*, the latter not being aspirated. The sense seems to be *what*, or *which of two*, referring either to persons or to sentences.]

1. Which of two.

Whether of them twain did the will of his father? Matt. xxi.

Here *whether* is a substitute for *one of two*, and signifies *which ; which* of the two; but in this sense it is obsolete.

2. Which of two alternatives, expressed by a sentence or the clause of a sentence, and followed by *or.* "Resolve *whether* you will go *or* not;" that is, you will go or not go; resolve *which.*

[Note. In the latter use, which is now most common, *whether* is called an adverb. This is a mistake. It is the same part of speech as in the former example. The only difference is that in the former example it represents or refers to a noun, and in the latter to a sentence or clause.]

WHET′STONE, *n.* [*whet* and *stone.*] A stone used for sharpening edged instruments by friction.

WHET′STONE-SLATE, } *n.* Novaculite
WHET′-SLATE, } or coticular shist, a variety of slate used for sharpening instruments of iron. The light green colored variety from the Levant is the most valuable. It should be kept in a damp place, that it may not become too dry and hard.

WHET′TED, *pp.* Rubbed for sharpening; sharpened; provoked; stimulated.

WHET′TER, *n.* He or that which whets or sharpens.

WHET′TING, *ppr.* Rubbing for the purpose of making sharp; sharpening; provoking; inciting; stimulating.

WHEW′ER, *n.* Another name of the widgeon. [*Local.*]

WHEY, *n.* [Sax. *hwæg ;* D. *wei* or *hui.*] The serum or watery part of milk, separated from the more thick or coagulable part, particularly in the process of making cheese. In this process, the thick part is called *curd*, and the thin part *whey.*

WHEYEY, *a.* Partaking of whey; resembling whey. *Bacon.*

WHEYISH, *a.* Having the qualities of whey. *Philips.*

WHEY-TUB, *n.* A tub in which whey stands for yielding cream, &c. *Cyc.*

WHICH, *pron. relative* or *substitute.* [I have not found this word in any other language, and I think it not probable that it is a contraction of Sax. *hwilc*, G. *welcher*, D. *welk*, &c. If not, it may be from the root of *quick.* See *What* and *Wight.*]

1. A word called a relative or pronoun relative, because it relates to another word or thing, usually to some word that precedes it in the sentence. I call it also a *substitute*, as it supplies the place of a noun, or of an adjective, or of a sentence or clause. 1. "The garden *which* I cultivate," that is, the garden, *which garden* I cultivate. 2. "We are bound to obey all the divine commands, *which* we cannot do without divine aid." Here *which* represents the words, *obey the divine commands.* 3. "You declared him to be innocent, *which* he is not." Here *which* stands for *innocent.*

In the foregoing uses, *which* is not used in the masculine gender, that is, it does not in modern usage represent a person.

2. *Which* is much used in asking questions, for the purpose of obtaining the designation of a particular person or thing by the answer, and in this use, it is of the masculine as well as of the neuter gender. There are two or three things to be done; *which* shall I do first? *Which* man is it?

Which of you convinceth me of sin? John viii.

For *which* of those works do ye stone me? John x.

3. That which. "Take *which* you will," that is, take any one of the whole.

The which, by the which. The use of *the* before *which*, is obsolete.

WHICHEV′ER, } *pron.* Whether one
WHICHSOEV′ER, } or the other. *Whichever* road you take, it will conduct you to town.

WHIFF, *n.* [W. *çwif*, a whiff or puff, a hiss; *çwifiaw*, to whiff, and *çwaf*, a quick gust.]

1. A sudden expulsion of air from the mouth; a puff; as the *whiff* of a smoker.

And seasons his *whiffs* with impertinent jokes. *Pope.*

2. In *ichthyology*, a species of Pleuronectes or flounder. *Ed. Encyc.*

WHIFF, *v. t.* To puff; to throw out in whiffs; to consume in whiffs.

WHIF′FLE, *v. i.* [D. *weifelen*, to waver; *zweeven*, to hover. This accords in sense with G. *zweifeln*, to doubt, which would seem to be from *zwei*, two, or its root. The G. has also *schweifen*, to rove or wander, which seems to be allied to *sweep.* The D. has also *twyffelen*, to doubt, from *twee*, two, or its root; Sw. *tvifla*, Dan. *tvivler*, from the root of *two.* Yet *whiffle* seems to be directly from *whiff.*]

To start, shift and turn; to change from one opinion or course to another; to use evasions; to prevaricate; to be fickle and unsteady.

A person of a *whiffling* and unsteady turn of mind, cannot keep close to a point of controversy. *Watts.*

WHIF′FLE, *v. t.* To disperse with a puff; to scatter. *More.*

WHIF′FLE, *n.* Anciently, a fife or small flute.

WHIF′FLER, *n.* One who whiffles or frequently changes his opinion or course; one who uses shifts and evasions in argument.

2. A harbinger; perhaps one who blows the horn or trumpet. *Shak.*

3. A young man who goes before a company in London on occasions of public solemnity. *Cyc.*

WHIF′FLING, *ppr.* Shifting and turning; prevaricating; shuffling.

WHIF′FLING, *n.* Prevarication.

WHIG, *n.* [Sax. *hwæg.* See *Whey.*] Acidulated whey, sometimes mixed with butter milk and sweet herbs; used as a cooling beverage. [*Local.*]

WHIG, *n.* [origin uncertain.] One of a political party which had its origin in England in the seventeenth century, in the reign of Charles I. or II., when great contests existed respecting the royal prerogatives and the rights of the people. Those who supported the king in his high claims, were called *tories*, and the advocates of popular rights were called *whigs.* During the revolution in the United States, the friends and supporters of the war and the principles of the revolution, were called *whigs*, and those who opposed them, were called *tories* and *royalists.*

Where then, when tories scarce get clear,
Shall *whigs* and congresses appear? *M'Fingal.*

WHIG′GARCHY, *n.* Government by whigs. [*Cant.*] *Swift.*

WHIG′GISH, *a.* Pertaining to whigs; partaking of the principles of whigs. *Swift.*

WHIG′GISM, *n.* The principles of a whig. *Swift.*

WHILE, *n.* [Sax. *hwile ;* Goth. *hweila ;* G. *weil ;* D. *wyl*, time, while; Dan. *hvile*, Sw. *hvila*, repose; W. *çwyl*, a turn, Ir. *foil.* See the Verb.]

Time; space of time, or continued duration. He was some *while* in this country. One *while* we thought him innocent.

Pausing a *while*, thus to herself she mus'd. *Milton.*

Worth while, worth the time which it requires; worth the time and pains; hence, worth the expense. It is not always *worth while* for a man to prosecute for small debts.

WHILE, *adv.* During the time that. *While* I write, you sleep.

2. As long as.

Use your memory, and you will sensibly experience a gradual improvement, *while* you take care not to overload it. *Watts.*

3. At the same time that. *Pope.*

WHILE, *v.t.* [W. *çwylaw*, to turn, to run a course, to bustle; Eth. ወዐለ waala, to pass the time, to spend the day or life, to remain; Amharic, id.; Dan. *hviler*, Sw. *hvila*, to rest or repose; Ir. *foillim*, to stay, to rest, to tarry; G. *weilen*, *verweilen*, to abide, to stay; D. *verwylen*, id. Qu. the identity of these words.]

To while away, as time, in English, is to loiter; or more generally, to cause time to pass away pleasantly, without irksomeness; as, we *while away* time in amusements or diversions.

Let us *while away* this life. *Pope.*

WHILE, *v. i.* To loiter. *Spectator.*

WHILE'RE, *adv.* [*while* and *ere.*] A little while ago. *Obs.*

WHI'LING, *ppr.* Loitering; passing time agreeably, without impatience or tediousness.

WHILK, *n.* A shell. [See *Whelk.*]

WHI'LOM, *adv.* [Sax. *hwilon.*] Formerly; once; of old. *Obs.* *Spenser.*

WHILST, *adv.* The same as *while*, which see. *Whiles* is not used.

WHIM, *n.* [Ice. *hwima*; W. *çwim*, a brisk motion, a turn; *çwimiaw*, to move round briskly; Sp. *quimera*, a whim, a wild fancy, a scuffle.]

1. Properly, a sudden turn or start of the mind; a freak; a fancy; a capricious notion. We say, every man has his *whims*. [See *Freak* and *Caprice.*]

All the superfluous *whims* relate. *Swift.*

2. A low wit; *a cant word.* *Addison.*

WHIM'PER, *v. i.* [G. *wimmern.*] To cry with a low, whining, broken voice; as, a child *whimpers.* *Locke.*

WHIM'PERING, *ppr.* Crying with a low broken voice.

WHIM'PERING, *n.* [supra.] A low muttering cry.

WHIMPLED, a word used by Shakspeare, is perhaps a mistake for *whimpered.* There is no such word in the English.

WHIM'SEY, *n.* *s* as *z.* [from *whim.*] A whim; a freak; a capricious notion; as the *whimseys* of poets.

Men's follies, *whimsies*, and inconstancy. *Swift.*

WHIM'SICAL, *a.* Full of whims; freakish; having odd fancies; capricious.

My neighbors call me *whimsical.* *Addison.*

WHIM'SICALLY, *adv.* [supra.] In a whimsical manner; freakishly.

WHIM'SICALNESS, *n.* [supra.] Freakishness; whimsical disposition; odd temper.

WHIN, *n.* [In W. *çwyn* is a weed; L. *genista spinosa.*] Gorse; furze; a plant of the genus Ulex. *Tusser.* *Lee.*

WHIN'-AX, *n.* [*whin* and *ax.*] An instrument used for extirpating whin from land. *Cyc.*

WHIN'BREL, } *n.* A bird resembling the
WHIM'BREL, } curlew. *Dict. Nat. Hist.*

WHIN'-CHAT, *n.* A bird, a species of warbler, the *Motacilla rubetra*, Linn. *Ed. Encyc.*

WHINE, *v.t.* [Sax. *wanian* and *cwanian*; Goth. *hwainon*; Dan. *hviner*, to whine, and to *whinny*, as a horse; Sw. *hvina*, to squeal or squeak; W. *açwyn*, to complain; L. *hinnio*, and qu. *gannio.*]

To express murmurs by a plaintive cry; to moan with a puerile noise; to murmur meanly.

They came—with a *whining* accent craving liberty. *Sidney.*

Then, if we *whine*, look pale— *Shak.*

WHINE, *n.* A plaintive tone; the nasal puerile tone of mean complaint; mean or affected complaint. *Rowe.*

WHI'NER, *n.* One who whines.

WHI'NING, *ppr.* Expressing murmurs by a mean plaintive tone or cant.

WHIN'NY, *v. i.* [L. *hinnio*; from the root of *whine.*] To utter the sound of a horse; to neigh.

WHIN'OC, *n.* [G. *wenig*, small.] The small pig of a litter. *N. England.*

WHIN'-STONE, *n.* [*whin* and *stone*; Scot. *quhyn-stane.*]

Whin-stone or whin is a provincial name given to basaltic rocks, and applied by miners to any kind of dark colored and hard unstratified rock which resists the point of the pick. Veins of dark basalt or green-stone, are frequently called *whin-dykes.* *Cyc.*

WHIN'-YARD, *n.* A sword; *in contempt.* *Hudibras.*

WHIP, *v. t.* [Sax. *hweopan*, to whip, and to *weep*, that is, to *whoop* or *hoop*; D. *wippen*, to shake, to move or wag, to give the strapado; *zweepen*, to whip; Dan. *vipper*, to swing; W. *çwipiaw*, to move briskly, to *whip*; *çwip*, a quick flirt or turn. The sense is well expressed by the Welsh, and we say, a man *whips* round a corner, when running he suddenly turns. It seems to be allied to *wipe* and *sweep*, and L. *vapulo*, and implies a sweeping throw or thrust.]

1. To strike with a lash or sweeping cord; as, to *whip* a horse.

2. To sew slightly. *Gay.*

3. To drive with lashes; as, to *whip* a top.

4. To punish with the whip; as, to *whip* a vagrant; to *whip* one thirty nine lashes; to *whip* a perverse boy.

Who, for false quantities, was *whipp'd* at school. *Dryden.*

5. To lash with sarcasm.

They would *whip* me with their fine wits. *Shak.*

6. To strike; to thrash; to beat out, as grain, by striking; as, to *whip* wheat. [*Not in use in the U. States.*] *Cyc.*

To whip about or *round*, to wrap; to inwrap; as, to *whip* a line round a rod. *Moxon.*

To whip out, to draw nimbly; to snatch; as, to *whip out* a sword or rapier from its sheath.

To whip from, to take away suddenly.

To whip into, to thrust in with a quick motion. He *whipped* his hand *into* his pocket.

To whip up, to seize or take up with a quick motion. She *whipped up* the child, and ran off. Among seamen, to hoist with a whip or small tackle.

WHIP, *v. i.* To move nimbly; to start suddenly and run; or to turn and run; as, the boy *whipped* away in an instant; he *whipped* round the corner; he *whipped* into the house, and was out of sight in a moment.

WHIP, *n.* [Sax. *hweop.*] An instrument for driving horses or other teams, or for correction, consisting of a lash tied to a handle or rod.

2. In *ships*, a small tackle, used to hoist light bodies. *Mar. Dict.*

Whip and spur, with the utmost haste.

WHIP'-CORD, *n.* [*whip* and *cord.*] Cord of which lashes are made. *Dryden.*

WHIP'-GRAFT, *v. t.* [*whip* and *graft.*] To graft by cutting the cion and stock in a sloping direction, so as to fit each other, and by inserting a tongue on the cion into a slit in the stock.

WHIP'-GRAFTING, *n.* The act or practice of grafting by cutting the cion and stock with a slope, to fit each other, &c. *Encyc.*

WHIP'-HAND, *n.* [*whip* and *hand.*] Advantage over; as, he has the *whip-hand* of her. *Dryden*

WHIP'-LASH, *n.* [*whip* and *lash.*] The lash of a whip. *Tusser.*

WHIP'PED, *pp.* Struck with a whip; punished; enwrapped; sewed slightly.

WHIP'PER, *n.* One who whips; particularly, an officer who inflicts the penalty of legal whipping.

WHIP'PING, *ppr.* Striking with a whip; punishing with a whip; enwrapping.

WHIP'PING, *n.* The act of striking with a whip, or of punishing; the state of being whipped.

WHIP'PING-POST, *n.* [*whipping* and *post.*] A post to which offenders are tied when whipped.

WHIP'PLE-TREE, *n.* [*whip* and *tree*; but qu. is it not *whiffle-tree*?]

The bar to which the traces or tugs of a harness are fastened, and by which a carriage, a plow, a harrow or other implement is drawn.

WHIP'POWIL, *n.* The popular name of an American bird, so called from its note, or the sounds of its voice. [Not *whip-poor-will.*]

WHIP'-SAW, *n.* [*whip* and *saw.*] A saw to be used by two persons.

WHIP'-STAFF, *n.* [*whip* and *staff.*] In *ships*, a bar by which the rudder is turned. In small vessels this is called the *tiller.*

WHIP'STER, *n.* A nimble fellow. *Prior.*

WHIP'-STITCH, *v. t.* [*whip* and *stitch.*] In *agriculture*, to half-plow or to rafter land. This word, I believe, is not used in America. The practice of *whip-stitching* resembles what is called in America *ridging.*

WHIP'-STOCK, *n.* [*whip* and *stock.*] The rod or staff to which the lash of a whip is fastened.

WHIPT, *pp.* of *whip*; sometimes used for *whipped.*

WHIR, *v. i.* *hwur.* To whirl round with noise; to fly with noise.

WHIR, *v. t.* To hurry.

WHIRL, *v. t.* *hwurl.* [Sax. *hwyrfan*; D. *wervelen*; G. *wirbeln*, to whirl, to *warble*; Dan. *hvirveler*, Sw. *hvirfla*, to whirl; Dan. *hvirvelbeen*, whirl-bone, vertebra; *hvirvelsoe*, whirl-sea, a whirlpool; Sw. *hvirfvel*, Ice. *whirla*, a whirl. We see that *whirl* and *warble* are dialectical forms of the same word, and both probably from the root of L. *verto* and Eng. *veer.*]

To turn round rapidly; to turn with velocity.

He *whirls* his sword around without delay. *Dryden.*

WHIRL, *v. i.* To be turned round rapidly; to move round with velocity; as the *whirling* spindles of a cotton machine or wheels of a coach.

The wooden engine flies and *whirls* about. *Dryden.*

2. To move hastily.

—But *whirl'd* away, to shun his hateful sight. *Dryden.*

WHIRL, *n.* [G. *wirbel*; Dan. *hvirvel.*] A turning with rapidity or velocity; rapid rotation or circumvolution; quick gyration; as the *whirl* of a top; the *whirl* of a wheel; the *whirl* of time; the *whirls* of fancy. *Creech. Pope.*

2. Any thing that moves or is turned with velocity, particularly on an axis or pivot.

3. A hook used in twisting.

4. In *botany*, a species of inflorescence, consisting of many subsessile flowers surrounding the stem in a ring. It is also written *whorl* and *wherl.* *Martyn.*

WHIRL'-BAT, *n.* [*whirl* and *bat.*] Any thing moved with a whirl as preparatory for a blow, or to augment the force of it. Poets use it for the ancient cestus.

The *whirl-bat* and the rapid race shall be
Reserv'd for Cesar. *Dryden.*

WHIRL'-BL'AST, *n.* [*whirl* and *blast.*] A whirling blast of wind. *Entick.*

WHIRL'-BONE, *n.* [*whirl* and *bone.*] The patella; the cap of the knee; the knee-pan. *Ainsworth.*

WHIRL'ED, *pp.* Turned round with velocity.

2. In *botany*, growing in whirls; bearing whirls; verticillate.

WHIRL'IGIG, *n.* [*whirl* and *gig.*] A toy which children spin or whirl round. *Johnson.*

2. In *military antiquities*, an instrument for punishing petty offenders, as sutlers, brawling women, &c.; a kind of wooden cage turning on a pivot, in which the offender was whirled round with great velocity. *Cyc.*

WHIRL'ING, *ppr.* Turning or moving round with velocity.

WHIRL'ING-TABLE, *n.* A machine contrived to exhibit and demonstrate the principal laws of gravitation, and of the planetary motions in curvilinear orbits. *Cyc.*

WHIRL-PIT, *n.* A whirlpool. [*Not used.*]

WHIRL'POOL, *n.* [*whirl* and *pool.*] An eddy of water; a vortex or gulf where the water moves round in a circle. In some cases, a whirlpool draws things to its center and absorbs them, as is the case with the Maelstrom off the coast of Norway.

WHIRL'WIND, *n.* [*whirl* and *wind.*] A violent wind moving in a circle, or rather in a spiral form, as if moving round an axis; this axis or the perpendicular column moving horizontally, raising and whirling dust, leaves and the like.

WHIRRAW'. [See *Hoora.*]

WHIR'RING, *n.* The sound of a partridge's or pheasant's wings.

[Note.—*Whir* is used by the common people in New England in an adverbial manner, to express the rapid flight or the sound of any thing thrown. See *Whir.*]

WHISK, *n.* [G. D. *wisch*, a wisp.] A small bunch of grass, straw, hair or the like, used for a brush; hence, a brush or small besom.

2. Part of a woman's dress; a kind of tippet. *Child.*

WHISK, *v. t.* To sweep, brush or wipe with a whisk.

2. To sweep along; to move nimbly over the ground. *Hudibras.*

WHISK, *v. i.* To move nimbly and with velocity. *Purchas.*

WHISK'ER, *n.* [from *whisk.*] Long hair growing on the human cheek. *Pope.*

WHISK'ERED, *a.* Formed into whiskers; furnished with whiskers.

WHISK'ET, *n.* A basket. [*Local.*]

WHISK'ING, *ppr.* Brushing; sweeping along; moving with velocity along the surface.

WHIS'KY, *n.* [Ir. *uisge*, water, whence *usquebaugh*; W. *wysg*, a stream.]

A spirit distilled from grain. In the north of England, the name is given to the spirit drawn from barley. In the United States, whisky is generally distilled from wheat, rye or maiz.

WHIS'PER, *v. i.* [Sax. *hwisprian*; Dan. *hvisker*; Sw. *hviska*, to buzz, to *whisper*; allied to *whistle*, *wheeze*, and L. *fistula.* The word seems by its sound to be an onomatopy, as it expresses a sibilant sound or breathing.]

1. To speak with a low hissing or sibilant voice. It is ill manners to *whisper* in company.

The hollow *whisp'ring* breeze— *Thomson.*

2. To speak with suspicion or timorous caution.

3. To plot secretly; to devise mischief.

All that hate me *whisper* together against me. Ps. xli.

WHIS'PER, *v. t.* To address in a low voice. He *whispers* the man in the ear. [But this is elliptical for *whispers to.*]

2. To utter in a low sibilant voice. He *whispered* a word in my ear.

3. To prompt secretly; as, he came to *whisper* Woolsey. *Shak.*

WHIS'PER, *n.* A low soft sibilant voice; or words uttered with such a voice.

The *whisper* cannot give a tone. *Bacon.*
Soft *whispers* through th' assembly went. *Dryden.*

2. A cautious or timorous speech.

3. A hissing or buzzing sound.

WHIS'PERED, *pp.* Uttered in a low voice; uttered with suspicion or caution.

WHIS'PERER, *n.* One who whispers.

2. A tattler; one who tells secrets; a conveyer of intelligence secretly. *Bacon.*

3. A backbiter; one who slanders secretly. Prov. xvi.

WHIS'PERING, *ppr.* Speaking in a low voice; telling secretly; backbiting.

WHIS'PERING, *n.* The act of speaking with a low voice; the telling of tales, and exciting of suspicions; a backbiting.

WHIS'PERINGLY, *adv.* In a low voice.

WHIST, *a.* [Corn. *huist*, silence.] Silent; mute; still; not speaking; not making a noise.

The winds with wonder *whist*,
Smoothly the waters kiss'd. *Milton.*

[This adjective, like some others, always follows its noun. We never say, *whist* wind; but the wind is *whist.*]

Whist is used for *be silent. Whist, whist*, that is, *be silent* or *still.*

WHIST, *n.* A game at cards, so called because it requires silence or close attention. It is not in America pronounced *whisk.*

WHIS'TLE, *v. i.* *hwis'l.* [Sax. *hwistlan*; Sw. *hvissla*; Dan. *hvidsler*; L. *fistula*, a whistle; allied to *whisper.*]

1. To utter a kind of musical sound, by pressing the breath through a small orifice formed by contracting the lips.

While the plowman near at hand,
Whistles o'er the furrow'd land. *Milton*

2. To make a sound with a small wind instrument.

3. To sound shrill, or like a pipe.

The wild winds *whistle*, and the billows roar. *Pope.*

WHIS'TLE, *v. t.* To form, utter or modulate by whistling; as, to *whistle* a tune or air.

2. To call by a whistle; as, he *whistled* back his dog.

WHIS'TLE, *n.* [Sax. *hwistle*; L. *fistula.*]

1. A small wind instrument. *Bacon.*

2. The sound made by a small wind instrument.

3. Sound made by pressing the breath through a small orifice of the lips.

4. The mouth; the organ of whistling. [*Vulgar.*]

5. A small pipe, used by a boatswain to summon the sailors to their duty; the boatswain's call. *Mar. Dict.*

6. The shrill sound of winds passing among trees or through crevices, &c.

7. A call, such as sportsmen use to their dogs.

WHIS'TLED, *pp.* Sounded with a pipe; uttered in a whistle.

WHIS'TLE-FISH, *n.* A local name of a species of Gadus, with only two fins on the back; the *Mustela fluviatilis.* *Cyc.*

WHIS'TLER, *n.* One who whistles.

WHIS'TLING, *ppr.* Uttering a musical sound through a small orifice of the lips; sounding with a pipe; making a shrill sound, as wind.

WHIS'TLY, *adv.* Silently.

WHIT, *n.* [Sax. *wiht*, a creature, also a thing, something, any thing. This is probably from the root of L. *vivo, victum.*]

A point; a jot; the smallest part or particle imaginable. It is used without a preposition. He is not a *whit* the wiser for experience.

It does not me a *whit* displease. *Cowley.*

The regular construction would be *by* a whit, or *in* a whit. In these phrases, *a whit* may be interpreted by *in the least, in the smallest degree.*

WHITE, *a.* [Sax. *hwit*; Sw. *hvit*; Dan. *hvid*; D. *wit*; G. *weiss.*]

1. Being of the color of pure snow; snowy; not dark; as *white* paper; a *white* skin.
2. Pale; destitute of color in the cheeks, or of the tinge of blood color; as *white* with fear.
3. Having the color of purity; pure; clean; free from spot; as *white* robed innocence.
4. Gray; as *white* hair; a venerable man, *white* with age.
5. Pure; unblemished.

No *whiter* page than Addison's remains. *Pope.*

6. In *a scriptural sense*, purified from sin; sanctified. Ps. li.

WHI'TE-BAIT, *n.* [*white* and *bait.*] A very small delicate fish, of the genus Clupea.

WHI'TE-BEAM, *n.* The white-leaf tree, a species of Cratægus. *Lee.*

WHI'TE-BEAR, *n.* [*white* and *bear.*] The bear that inhabits the polar regions.

WHITE-BRANT, *n.* [*white* and *brant.*] A species of the duck kind, the *Anas hyperborea.* *Cyc.*

WHI'TE-BUG, *n.* [*white* and *bug.*] An insect of the bug kind, which injures vines and some other species of fruit. *Cyc.*

WHITE-CAM'PION, *n.* [*white* and *campion.*]
A pernicious perennial weed, growing in corn land, pastures and hedges. *Cyc.*

WHITE-CAT'ERPILLAR, *n.* An insect of a small size, called sometimes the borer, that injures the gooseberry bush. *Cyc.*

WHITE-CEN'TAURY, *n.* An annual weed in woods and other places. It is said to form the basis of the famous Portland powder for the gout. *Cyc.*

WHITE-CLOVER, *n.* A small species of perennial clover, bearing white flowers. It furnishes excellent food for cattle and horses, as well as for the honey bee.

WHI'TE-CROP, *n.* White crops, in agriculture, are such as lose their green color or become white in ripening, as wheat, rye, barley and oats.

WHITE-D'ARNEL, *n.* A prolific and troublesome weed, growing among corn. *Cyc.*

WHI'TE-EAR, } *n.* A bird, the fallow
WHI'TE-TAIL, } finch.

WHITE-FACE, } *n.* A white mark in the
WHITE-BLAZE, } forehead of a horse, descending almost to the nose. *Cyc.*

WHI'TE-FILM, *n.* A white film growing over the eyes of sheep and causing blindness. *Cyc.*

WHI'TE-FOOT, *n.* A white mark on the foot of a horse, between the fetlock and the coffin. *Cyc.*

WHITE-HONEYSUCKLE, *n.* A name sometimes given to the white clover. *Cyc.*

WHITE-HORSE-FISH, *n.* In *ichthyology*, the *Raia aspera nostras* of Willoughby, and the *Raia fullonica* of Linne. It has a rough spiny back, and on the tail are three rows of strong spines. It grows to the size of the skate. *Cyc.*

WHITE-LAND, *n.* A name which the English give to a tough clayey soil, of a whitish hue when dry, but blackish after rain. *Cyc.*

WHITE-LEAD, *n.* A carbonate of lead, much used in painting. It is prepared by exposing sheets of lead to the fumes of an acid, usually vinegar, and suspending them in the air until the surface becomes incrusted with a white coat, which is the substance in question. *D. Olmsted.*

WHI'TE-LIMED, *a.* Whitewashed, or plastered with lime.

WHITE-LINE, *n.* Among *printers*, a void space, broader than usual, left between lines. *Cyc.*

WHI'TE-LIVERED, *a.* [*white* and *liver.*]
1. Having a pale look; feeble; cowardly.
2. Envious; malicious.

WHITE-MAN'GANESE, *n.* An ore of manganese; carbonated oxydized manganese.

WHI'TE-MEAT, *n.* [*white* and *meat.*] Meats made of milk, butter, cheese, eggs and the like. *Spenser.*

WHITE-POP'LAR, *n.* A tree of the poplar kind, sometimes called the abele tree.

WHITE-POP'PY, *n.* A species of poppy, sometimes cultivated for the opium which is obtained from its juice by evaporation.

WHI'TE-POT, *n.* [*white* and *pot.*] A kind of food made of milk, cream, eggs, sugar, &c. baked in a pot. *King.*

WHITE-PRECIP'ITATE, *n.* Carbonate of mercury.

WHITE-PYR'ITE, } *n.* [*white* and *pyrite*;
WHITE-PYRI'TES, } Fr. *sulfure blanc.*]
An ore of a tin-white color, passing into a brass-yellow and steel-gray, occurring in octahedral crystals, sometimes stalactitical and botryoidal. It contains 46 parts of iron, and 54 of sulphur. *Cyc.*

WHI'TE-RENT, *n.* [*white* and *rent.*] In *Devon* and *Cornwall*, a rent or duty of eight pence, payable yearly by every tinner to the duke of Cornwall, as lord of the soil. *Cyc.*

WHI'TE-SALT, *n.* Salt dried and calcined; decrepitated salt.

WHI'TESTER, *n.* A bleacher. [*Local.*]

WHI'TESTONE, *n.* In *geology*, the *weiss stein* of Werner, and the eurite of some geologists; a species of rocks, composed essentially of feldspar, but containing mica and other minerals. *Cyc.*

WHITE-SWELLING, *n.* [*white* and *swelling.*]
A swelling or chronic enlargement of the joints, circumscribed, without any alteration in the color of the skin, sometimes hard, sometimes yielding to pressure, sometimes indolent, but usually painful. *Cyc.*

WHI'TE-TAIL, *n.* A bird, the wheat-ear, a species of Motacilla.

WHITE-THORN, *n.* A species of thorn, called also haw-thorn, of the genus Cratægus.

WHITE-THROAT, *n.* A small bird that frequents gardens and hedges, the *Motacilla sylvia.* *Linne. Cyc. Ed. Encyc.*

WHITE-VIT'RIOL, *n.* In *mineralogy*, sulphate of zink, a natural salt. *Cyc.*

WHI'TEWASH, *n.* [*white* and *wash.*] A wash or liquid composition for whitening something; a wash for making the skin fair.
2. A composition of lime and water, used for whitening the plaster of walls, &c.

WHI'TEWASH, *v. t.* To cover with a white liquid composition, as with lime and water, &c.
2. To make white; to give a fair external appearance.

WHI'TEWASHED, *pp.* Covered or overspread with a white liquid composition.

WHI'TE-WASHER, *n.* One who whitewashes the walls or plastering of apartments.

WHI'TEWASHING, *ppr.* Overspreading or washing with a white liquid composition.

WHI'TE-WATER, *n.* A disease of sheep, of the dangerous stomachic kind. *Cyc.*

WHI'TE-WAX, *n.* Bleached wax.

WHI'TE-WINE, *n.* Any wine of a clear transparent color, bordering on white, as Madeira, Sherry, Lisbon, &c.; opposed to wine of a deep red color, as Port and Burgundy.

WHI'TEWOOD, *n.* A species of timber tree growing in N. America, the Liriodendron, or tulip tree. *Mease.*
The name of certain species of Bignonia. *Lee.*

WHITE, *n.* One of the natural colors of bodies, but not strictly a color, for it is said to be a composition of all the colors; destitution of all stain or obscurity on the surface; whiteness. We say, bleached cloth is of a good *white*; attired in a robe of *white.*
2. A white spot or thing; the mark at which an arrow is shot. *Dryden.*

White of the eye, that part of the ball of the eye surrounding the iris or colored part. It owes its whiteness to the *tunica albuginea* or *adnata*, a partial covering of the forepart of the eye, formed by the expansion of the tendons of the muscles which move the eye-ball. *Parr.*

White of an egg, the albumen, or pellucid viscous fluid, which surrounds the vitellus or yelk. *Parr.*
An analogous part, in the seeds of plants, is called the *albumen* or *white.* It is a farinaceous fleshy or horny substance, which makes up the chief bulk of some seeds, as in grasses, corn, palms and lilies, never rising out of the ground nor performing the office of leaves, but destined solely to nourish the germinating embryo, till its roots can perform their office. It is the *perispermum* of Jussieu. *Gærtner. Smith.*

Spanish white, a substance used in painting, prepared from chalk, by separating from the latter its silicious impurities.

WHITE, *v. t.* To make white; to whiten; to whitewash; as *whited* sepulchers. Mark ix. Matt. xxiii.

WHI'TED, *pp.* Made white; whitened.

WHI'TELY, *adv.* Coming near to white. [*Not used.*] *Shak.*

WHITEN, *v. t. hwi'tn.* To make white; to bleach; to blanch; as, to *whiten* cloth.

WHI'TEN, *v. i.* To grow white; to turn or become white. The hair *whitens* with age; the sea *whitens* with foam; the trees in spring *whiten* with blossoms.

WHI'TENED, *pp.* Made white; bleached.

WHI'TENER, *n.* One who bleaches or makes white.

WHI'TENESS, *n.* The state of being white; white color, or freedom from any darkness or obscurity on the surface.
2. Paleness; want of a sanguineous tinge in the face. *Shak.*

3. Purity; cleanness; freedom from stain or blemish. *Dryden.*

WHITES, *n.* The fluor albus, a disease of females.

WHITH'ER, *adv.* [Sax. *hwyder.*] To what place, interrogatively. *Whither* goest thou?

Whither away so fast? *Shak.*

2. To what place, absolutely.

I stray'd, I knew not *whither.* *Milton.*

3. To which place, relatively.

Whither when as they came, they fell at words. *Spenser.*

4. To what point or degree.

5. Whithersoever.

WHITHERSOEV'ER, *adv.* [*whither* and *soever.*]

To whatever place. I will go *whithersoever* you lead.

WHI'TING, *n.* [from *white.*] A small sea fish, the *Asellus mollis* or *albus,* a species of Gadus. *Cyc.*

2. The same as Spanish white, which see.

WHI'TISH, *a.* [from *white.*] Somewhat white; white in a moderate degree. *Boyle.*

WHI'TISHNESS, *n.* [supra.] The quality of being somewhat white. *Boyle.*

WHIT'LEATHER, } *n.* [*white* and *leather.*]
WHIT'LETHER, } Lether dressed with alum, remarkable for its toughness. *Chapman.*

In *common use,* the ligaments of animals, when in food.

WHIT'LOW, *n.* [Sax. *hwit,* white, and *low,* a flame. Qu.]

1. In *surgery,* paronychia, a swelling or inflammation about the nails or ends of the fingers, or affecting one or more of the phalanges of the fingers, generally terminating in an abscess. There are four or five varieties of this swelling. 1. The *cutaneous paronychia,* which raises the cuticle, forming a kind of vesicle filled with a limpid serum, or bloody fluid. 2. The *subcutaneous paronychia,* a tumor attended with acute pain. It is seated in the cellular membrane under the skin. 3. The *subungual paronychia,* which occurs under the nail. It commences with inflammatory symptoms, but is less painful than the former. 4. There is also the *paronychia of the periosteum,* and the *paronychia of the tendons* or *theca.* *Cyc.*

2. In *sheep,* the whitlow is a disease of the feet, of an inflammatory kind. It occurs round the hoof, where an acrid matter is collected, which ought to be discharged. *Cyc.*

WHIT'LOW-GRASS, *n.* Mountain knotgrass, a species of Illecebrium, *(I. paronychia.)* *Cyc.*

2. A name given to certain species of Draba. *Cyc.*

The *rue-leaved whitlow-grass* is a species of Saxifraga. *Lee.*

WHIT'SOUR, *n.* A sort of apple.

WHIT'STER, *n.* A whitener; a bleacher. *Obs.* *Shak.*

WHIT'SUL, *n.* A provincial name of milk, sour milk, cheese curds and butter. *Carew.*

WHIT'SUNTIDE, *n.* [*white, Sunday,* and *tide.*]

The feast or season of Pentecost; so called it is said, because, in the primitive church, those who had been newly baptized appeared at church between Easter and Pentecost in white garments. *Johnson. Cyc.*

WHIT'TEN-TREE, *n.* A sort of tree. *Ainsworth.*

WHIT'TLE, *n.* [Sax. *hwitel, hwitle.*] A small pocket knife. [*In this sense, I believe the word is not used in America.*]

2. A white dress for a woman; a double blanket worn by west countrywomen in England, over the shoulders, like a cloke. [*Not used in the U. States.*] *Dict.*

WHIT'TLE, *v. t.* To pare or cut off the surface of a thing with a small knife. Some persons have a habit of *whittling,* and are rarely seen without a penknife in their hands for that purpose. [*This is, I believe, the only use of this word in New England.*]

2. To edge; to sharpen. [*Not in use.*] *Hakewill.*

WHI'TY-BROWN, *a.* Of a color between white and brown. [*Local in England.*] *Pegge.*

WHIZ, *v. t.* [It seems to be allied to *hiss.*] To make a humming or hissing sound, like an arrow or ball flying through the air.

It flew, and *whizzing* cut the liquid way. *Dryden.*

WHIZ, *n.* A hissing sound.

WHIZ'ZING, *ppr.* Making a humming or hissing sound.

WHŎ, *pron. relative.* pron. hoo. [Sax. *hwa;* D. *wie;* L. *qui;* Fr. *que;* It. *chi;* Sp. *quien;* Ir. *cia;* Russ. *koi;* Pers. *ki.* *Who* is undoubtedly a contracted word in English as in Latin. See *What* and *Wight.*]

1. *Who* is a pronoun relative, always referring to persons. It forms *whose* in the genitive or possessive case, answering to the L. *cujus,* and *whom* in the objective or accusative case. *Who, whose* and *whom,* are in both numbers. Thus we say, the man or woman *who* was with us; the men or women *who* were with us; the men or women *whom* we saw.

2. Which of many. Are you satisfied *who* did the mischief?

3. It is much used in asking questions; as, *who* am I? *Who* art thou? *Who* is this? *Who* are these? In this case, the purpose is to obtain the name or designation of the person or character.

4. It has sometimes a disjunctive sense.

There thou tell'st of kings, and *who* aspire;
Who fall, *who* rise, *who* triumph, *who* do moan. *Daniel.*

5. *Whose* is of all genders. *Whose* book is this?

The question *whose* solution I require— *Dryden.*

As who should say, elliptically for *as one who should say.* *Collier.*

WHŎEV'ER, *pron.* [*who* and *ever.*] Any one without exception; any person whatever. The person who trespasses shall be punished, *whoever* he may be.

WHOLE, *a. hole.* [In Sax. *walg, onwalg,* is whole, sound, entire. In D. *heel, geheel,* has a like sense, from the root of *heal;* G. *heil;* Sw. *hel;* Dan. *heel;* W. *oll* or *holl;* Gr. ὁλος; Ir. *uile.* This seems to be connected with *heal, hale.* Of this, the derivative *wholesome,* is evidence. See Class Gl. No. 19. 31. 35.]

1. All; total; containing the total amount or number, or the entire thing; as the *whole* earth; the *whole* world; the *whole* solar system; the *whole* army; the *whole* nation.

2. Complete; entire; not defective or imperfect; as a *whole* orange; the egg is *whole;* the vessel is *whole.*

3. Unimpaired; unbroken; uninjured.

My life is yet *whole* in me. 2 Sam. i.

4. Sound; not hurt or sick.

They that are *whole* need not a physician. Matt. ix.

5. Restored to health and soundness; sound; well.

Thy faith hath made thee *whole.* Mark v.
His hand was restored *whole.* Mark iii.

WHOLE, *n.* The entire thing; the entire or total assemblage of parts. The *whole* of religion is contained in the short precept, "Love God with all your heart, and your neighbor as yourself."

Fear God and keep his commandments, for this is the *whole* duty of man. Eccles. xii.

2. A system; a regular combination of parts. *Pope.*

WHO'LESALE, *n.* [*whole* and *sale.*] Sale of goods by the piece or large quantity; as distinguished from *retail.* Some traders sell either by *wholesale* or retail.

2. The whole mass.

Some from vanity or envy, despise a valuable book, and throw contempt upon it by *wholesale.* *Watts.*

WHO'LESALE, *a.* [supra.] Buying and selling by the piece or quantity; as a *wholesale* merchant or dealer.

2. Pertaining to the trade by the piece or quantity; as the *wholesale* price.

WHO'LESŎME, *a.* [*whole* and *some;* G. *heilsam.*]

1. Tending to promote health; favoring health; salubrious; as *wholesome* air or diet; a *wholesome* climate.

2. Sound; contributing to the health of the mind; favorable to morals, religion or prosperity; as *wholesome* advice; *wholesome* doctrines; *wholesome* truths.

3. Useful; salutary; conducive to public happiness, virtue or peace; as a *wholesome* law.

4. That utters sound words.

A *wholesome* tongue is a tree of life. Prov. xv.

5. Kindly; pleasing; as a *wholesome* answer. *Shak.*

Wholesome ship, a ship that will try, hull and ride well. *Dict.*

WHO'LESŎMELY, *adv.* In a wholesome or salutary manner; salubriously.

WHO'LESŎMENESS, *n.* The quality of contributing to health; salubrity; as the *wholesomeness* of air or diet.

2. Salutariness; conduciveness to the health of the mind or of the body politic; as the *wholesomeness* of doctrines or laws.

WHOLLY, *adv.* Entirely; completely; perfectly.

Nor *wholly* overcome, nor *wholly* yield. *Dryden.*

2. Totally; in all the parts or kinds.

They employed themselves *wholly* in domestic life. *Addison.*

WHŎM, *pron.* hoom. The objective of *who,* coinciding with the L. *quem* and *quam.*

Whom have I in heaven but thee? Ps. lxxiii.

WHŎMSOEV'ER, *pron.* [*whom* and *soever.*] Any person without exception.

With *whomsoever* thou findest thy goods, let him not live. Gen. xxxi.

WHOOBUB, for *hubbub*. [*Not in use.*] *Shak.*

WHOOP, *n. hoop.* [This is the same as *hoop*, but aspirated; Goth. *wopyan*, to whoop, to call: Sax. *hweopan*, to *weep*, and to *whip*. The sense is to drive out the voice.]

1. A shout of pursuit *Addison.*
2. A shout of war; a particular cry of troops when they rush to the attack. The Indians of America are remarkable for their war *whoop*.
3. The bird called *hoopoe* or *upupa*.

WHOOP, *v. i.* To shout with a particular voice. *Shak.*

WHOOP, *v. t.* To insult with shouts. *Dryden.*

WHOOT, *v. i. hoot.* [See *Hoot.*]

WHOP, *n.* [the vulgar pronunciation of *whap*, or *awhap*.]

A sudden fall, or the suddenness of striking in a fall.

WHORE, *n. hore.* [W. *huran*, from *huriaw*, to hire; *hur*, that which is fixed or set, *hire*, wages; Sax. *hor-cwen*, hore-woman; Sw. *hora*, *hor-kåna*; Dan. *hore*, *hore-kone*; G. *hure*; D. *hoer*. The correct orthography is *hore*.]

A harlot; a courtesan; a concubine; a prostitute.

WHORE, *v. i.* [supra.] To have unlawful sexual commerce; to practice lewdness.

WHORE, *v. t.* To corrupt by lewd intercourse. [*Little used.*] *Congreve.*

WHOREDŎM, *n. ho'redom.* Lewdness; fornication; practice of unlawful commerce with the other sex. It is applied to either sex, and to any kind of illicit commerce.

2. In *Scripture*, idolatry; the desertion of the worship of the true God, for the worship of idols. *Prophets.*

WHO'REM'ASTER, *n.* [supra.] One who practices lewdness.

WHO'REMŎNGER, *n.* The same as *whoremaster*.

WHO'RESŎN, *n.* A bastard; *a word used generally in contempt.* *Shak.*

WHO'RISH, *a.* Lewd; unchaste; addicted to unlawful sexual pleasures; incontinent.

WHO'RISHLY, *adv.* In a lewd manner.

WHO'RISHNESS, *n.* The practice of lewdness; the character of a lewd woman. *Hale.*

WHŎRL, } [See *Whirl.*]
WHŎRLE. }

WHŎRT, *n.* The fruit of the whortleberry; or the shrub.

WHŎRTLEBERRY, *n.* [Sax. *heort-berg*, hart-berry. The Germans call it *heidelbeere*, heath-berry.]

A plant or shrub and its fruit, of the genus Vaccinium.

WHŎSE, *hooz.* The possessive or genitive case of *who* or *which*; applied to persons or things. We say, the person *whose* merits are known; the garment *whose* color is admired.

WHŎSESOEV'ER, *pron.* [*whose* and *soever.*] Of any person whatever. John xx.

WHŎ'SO, *pron. hooso.* Any person whatever. *Obs.*

WHŎSOEV'ER, *pron.* [*who*, *so*, and *ever.*] Any one; any person whatever.

Whosoever will, let him take of the water of life freely. Rev. xxii.

WHUR, *v. i.* To pronounce the letter *r* with too much force.

WHUR, *n.* The sound of a body moving through the air with velocity. [See *Whir.*]

WHURT, *n.* A whortleberry or bilberry. [See *Whort.*]

WHȲ, *adv.* [Sax. *hwi*, and *for hwi*, or *for hwig*, for why. *Hwi*, *hwig*, coincides in elements with *which*. So *pourquoi* in French, is the same; *pour* and L. *quid*, *quod*; for what. The original phrase is *for what, for why.*]

1. For what cause or reason, interrogatively.

Turn ye, turn ye, for *why* will ye die? Jer. xxvii.

2. For which reason or cause, relatively.

No ground of enmity,
Why he should mean me ill. *Milton.*

3. For what reason or cause; for which; relatively.

Turn the discourse; I have a reason *why*
I would not have you speak so tenderly. *Dryden.*

4. It is used sometimes emphatically, or rather as an expletive.

If her chill heart I cannot move,
Why, I'll enjoy the very love. *Cowley.*

WI, from the Gothic *weiha*, signifies *holy*. It is found in some names, as in *Wibert*, holy-bright, or bright holy, eminent for sanctity; Dan. *vier*, to consecrate, Sw. *viga*.

WIC, WICK, a termination, denotes jurisdiction, as in *bailiwick*. Its primary sense is a village or mansion, L. *vicus*, Sax. *wic* or *wyc*; hence it occurs in *Berwick*, *Harwich*, *Norwich*, &c. It signifies also a bay or a castle. *Gibson.*

WICK, *n.* [Sax. *weoc*; Sw. *veke*, a wick or match; Ir. *buaic.*]

A number of threads of cotton or some similar substance, loosely twisted into a string, round which wax or tallow is applied by means of melting and running in a mold, and thus forming a candle or torch.

WICK'ED, *a.* [Sw. *vika*, to decline, to err, to deviate, also to fold; Sax. *wican*, to recede, to slide, to fall away; *wicelian*, to *vacillate*, to stumble. It seems to be connected in origin with *wag*, and Sax. *wicca*, witch. The primary sense is to wind and turn, or to depart, to fall away.]

1. Evil in principle or practice; deviating from the divine law; addicted to vice; sinful; immoral. This is a word of comprehensive signification, extending to every thing that is contrary to the moral law, and both to persons and actions. We say, a *wicked* man, a *wicked* deed, *wicked* ways, *wicked* lives, a *wicked* heart, *wicked* designs, *wicked* works.

No man was ever *wicked* without secret discontent. *Rambler.*

2. A word of slight blame; as the *wicked* urchin.
3. Cursed; baneful; pernicious; as *wicked* words, words pernicious in their effects. *Obs.*

[This last signification may throw some light on the word *witch.*]

The wicked, in Scripture, persons who live in sin; transgressors of the divine law; all who are unreconciled to God, unsanctified or impenitent.

WICK'EDLY, *adv.* In a manner or with motives and designs contrary to the divine law; viciously; corruptly; immorally.

All that do *wickedly* shall be stubble. Mal. iv.

I have sinned, and I have done *wickedly*. 2 Sam. xxiv.

WICK'EDNESS, *n.* Departure from the rules of the divine law; evil disposition or practices; immorality; crime; sin; sinfulness; corrupt manners. Wickedness generally signifies evil practices.

What *wickedness* is this that is done among you? Judges xx.

But *wickedness* expresses also the corrupt dispositions of the heart.

Their inward part is very *wickedness*. Ps. v.

In heart ye work *wickedness*. Ps. lviii.

WICK'EN, } *n.* The *Sorbus aucuparia*, mountain ash, or roan-tree. *Lee.*
WICK'EN-TREE, }

WICK'ER, *a.* [Dan. *vien*, probably contracted from *vigen*. The Eng. *twig*, G. *zweig*, D. *twyg*, are probably formed on the simple word *wig*, from the root of L. *vigeo*, to grow. The word signifies a shoot.]

Made of twigs or oziers; as a *wicker* basket; a *wicker* chair. *Spenser. Peacham.*

WICK'ET, *n.* [Fr. *guichet*; W. *gwiced*, a little door, from *gwig*, a narrow place, a corner.]

A small gate.

The *wicket*, often open'd, knew the key. *Dryden.*

WICK'LIFFITE, *n.* A follower of Wickliffe, the English reformer.

WIDE, *a.* [Sax. *wid*, *wide*; D. *wyd*; G. *weit*; Sw. Dan. *vid*; Sans. *vidi*, breadth; Ar. بَدَّ badda, to separate; allied to *void*, *divide*, *widow*, Ir. *feadh*, &c. See Class Bd. No. 1.]

1. Broad; having a great or considerable distance or extent between the sides; opposed to *narrow*; as *wide* cloth; a *wide* table; a *wide* highway; a *wide* bed; a *wide* hall or entry. In this use, *wide* is distinguished from *long*, which refers to the extent or distance between the *ends*.
2. Broad; having a great extent each way; as a *wide* plain; the *wide* ocean.
3. Remote; distant. This position is very *wide* from the truth. *Hammond.*
4. Broad to a certain degree; as three feet *wide*.

WIDE, *adv.* At a distance; far. His fame was spread *wide*.

2. With great extent; used chiefly in composition; as *wide*-skirted meads; *wide*-waving swords; *wide*-wasting pestilence; *wide*-spreading evil.

WI'DELY, *adv.* With great extent each way. The gospel was *widely* disseminated by the apostles.

2. Very much; to a great distance; far. We differ *widely* in opinion.

WI'DEN, *v. t.* To make wide or wider; to extend in breadth; as, to *widen* a field; to *widen* a breach.

[NOTE.—In America, females say, to *widen* a stocking.]

WI'DEN, *v. i.* To grow wide or wider; to enlarge; to extend itself.

And arches *widen*, and long aisles extend. *Pope.*

WI'DENED, *pp.* Made wide or wider; extended in breadth.

WI'DENESS, *n.* Breadth; width; great extent between the sides; as the *wideness* of a room.

2. Large extent in all directions; as the *wideness* of the sea or ocean.

WI'DENING, *ppr.* Extending the distance between the sides; enlarging in all directions.

WID'GEON, *n.* A fowl of the duck kind, or genus Anas, having a black bill, the head and upper part of the neck of a bright bay, the back and sides waved with black and white, and the belly white. *Dict. Nat. Hist.*

WID'OW, *n.* [Sax. *widew;* G. *wittwe;* D. *weduwe;* Dan. *vidue;* L. *vidua;* Fr. *veuve;* It. *vedova;* Sp. *viuda;* Sans. *widhava;* Russ. *vdova;* from the root of *wide, void.* See *Wide.*]

A woman who has lost her husband by death. Luke ii.

Widow's chamber, in London, the apparel and furniture of the bed-chamber of the widow of a freeman, to which she is entitled. *Cyc.*

WID'OW, *v. t.* To bereave of a husband; but rarely used except in the participle. *Dryden.*

2. To endow with a widow's right. [*Unusual.*]

3. To strip of any thing good. *Shak.*

The *widow'd* isle in mourning— *Dryden.*

WID'OW-BENCH, *n.* [*widow* and *bench.*] In *Sussex*, that share which a widow is allowed of her husband's estate, besides her jointure. *Cyc.*

WID'OWED, *pp.* Bereaved of a husband by death.

2. Deprived of some good; stripped.

Trees of their shrivel'd fruits
Are *widow'd.* *Philips.*

WID'OWER, *n.* A man who has lost his wife by death.

WID'OWHOOD, *n.* The state of being a widow.

2. Estate settled on a widow. [*Not in use.*] *Shak.*

WID'OW-HUNTER, *n.* [*widow* and *hunter.*] One who seeks or courts widows for a jointure or fortune. *Addison.*

WID'OWING, *ppr.* Bereaving of a husband; depriving; stripping.

WID'OW-MAKER, *n.* [*widow* and *maker.*] One who makes widows by destroying lives. *Shak.*

WID'OW-WAIL, *n.* In *botany*, a plant of the genus Cneorum. *Lee.*

WIDTH, *n.* [from *wide;* G. *weite;* D. *wydte.*]

Breadth; wideness; the extent of a thing from side to side; as the *width* of cloth; the *width* of a door. *Dryden.*

WIELD, *v. t.* [Sax. *wealdan, waldan;* Goth. *ga-waldan*, to govern; *wald*, power, dominion; Dan. *vælde*, power; *gevalt*, force, authority; Sw. *välde*, power; allied to L. *valeo*, Eng. *well.* The primary sense of power and strength is to stretch or strain. This seems to be the Russ. *vladyu*, to rule, and *wald* or *vlad*, in names, as *Waldemir, Vlademir.*]

1. To use with full command or power, as a thing not too heavy for the holder; to manage; as, to *wield* a sword; to *wield* the scepter.

Part *wield* their arms, part curb the foaming steed. *Milton.*

2. To use or employ with the hand.

Nothing but the influence of a civilized power could induce a savage to *wield* a spade. *S. S. Smith.*

3. To handle; in an ironical sense.

Base Hungarian wight, wilt thou the spigot *wield?* *Shak.*

To wield the scepter, to govern with supreme command.

WIE'LDED, *pp.* Used with command; managed.

WIE'LDING, *ppr.* Using with power; managing.

WIE'LDLESS, *a.* Unmanageable. *Spenser.*

WIE'LDY, *a.* That may be wielded; manageable.

WI'ERY, *a.* [from *wire.*] Made of wire; having the properties of wire. It would be better written *wiry.*

2. [Sax. *wær*, a pool.] Wet; marshy. [*Not in use.*] *Shak.*

WIFE, *n.* plu. *wives.* [Sax. *wif;* D. *wyf;* G. *weib*, a woman.]

1. The lawful consort of a man; a woman who is united to a man in the lawful bonds of wedlock; the correlative of *husband.*

The husband of one *wife.* 1 Tim. iii.

Let every one of you in particular, so love his *wife* even as himself, and let the *wife* see that she reverence her husband. Eph. v.

2. A woman of low employment; as strawberry *wives.* [*Not in use.*] *Shak.*

WIG, in Saxon, signifies war. It is found in some names.

WIG, *n.* [G. *weck*, wig, and *weck-butter*, roll butter. It would seem that the sense is a roll or twist interwoven.]

1. A covering for the head, consisting of hair interwoven or united by a kind of network; formerly much worn by men.

2. A sort of cake. *Obs.* *Ainsworth.*

WIGEON. [See *Widgeon.*]

WIGHT, *n.* [Sax. *wiht*, G. *wicht*, a living being, Goth. *waiht;* L. *victum*, from *vivo*, to live, originally *vigo* or *vico*, and probably allied to *vigeo.* This, in the Celtic form, would be *quic* or *qwig*, Eng. *quick*, alive; and hence L. *qui, quæ, quid, quod*, contracted from *quic, quiced, quoced:* Scot. *quhat.* The letter *h*, in the Gothic and Scotish, representing the *c* of the Latin, proves the word to be thus contracted.]

A being; a person. It is obsolete, except in irony or burlesque. [See *Aught.*]

The *wight* of all the world who lov'd thee best. *Dryden.*

WIGHT, *a.* [Sax. *hwæt.*] Swift; nimble. *Obs.* *Spenser.*

[This seems to be a dialectical form of *quick.*]

WIGHTLY, *adv.* Swiftly; nimbly. *Obs.* *Spenser.*

WIG'WAM, *n.* An Indian cabin or hut, so called in America. It is sometimes written *weekwam.*

WILD, *a.* [Sax. D. G. *wild;* Sw. Dan. *vild;* W. *gwyllt;* connected with Sax. *wealh*, a traveler, foreigner or pilgrim; G. *wälsch*, Celtic, Welsh; *wallen*, to rove, Sw. *villa, förvilla.* The sense is obvious.]

1. Roving; wandering; inhabiting the forest or open field; hence, not tamed or domesticated; as a *wild* boar; a *wild* ox; a *wild* cat; a *wild* bee.

2. Growing without culture; as *wild* parsnep; *wild* cherry; *wild* tansy. *Wild* rice, a palatable and nutritious food, grows spontaneously in the lakes and ponds of the North West territory. *J. Morse.*

3. Desert; not inhabited; as a *wild* forest. *Milton.*

4. Savage; uncivilized; not refined by culture; as the *wild* natives of Africa or America.

5. Turbulent; tempestuous; irregular; as a *wild* tumult.

The *wild* winds howl. *Addison.*

6. Licentious; ungoverned; as *wild* passions.

Valor grown *wild* by pride— *Prior.*

7. Inconstant; mutable; fickle.

In the ruling passion, there alone
The *wild* are constant, and the cunning known. *Pope.*

8. Inordinate; loose.

A fop well dress'd, extravagant and *wild.* *Dryden.*

9. Uncouth; loose.

—What are these,
So wither'd, and so *wild* in their attire? *Shak.*

10. Irregular; disorderly; done without plan or order; as, to make *wild* work. *Milton.*

11. Not well digested; not framed according to the ordinary rules of reason; not being within the limits of probable practicability; imaginary; fanciful; as a *wild* project or scheme; *wild* speculations.

12. Exposed to the wind and sea; as a *wild* roadstead. *Mar. Dict.*

13. Made or found in the forest; as *wild* honey.

Wild is prefixed to the names of many plants, to distinguish them from such of the name as are cultivated in gardens, as *wild* basil, *wild* parsnep, *wild* carrot, *wild* olive, &c.

WILD, *n.* A desert; an uninhabited and uncultivated tract or region; a forest or sandy desert; as the *wilds* of America; the *wilds* of Africa; the sandy *wilds* of Arabia.

Then Libya first, of all her moisture drain'd,
Became a barren waste, a *wild* of sand. *Addison.*

WILDFIRE, *n.* [*wild* and *fire.*] A composition of inflammable materials.

Brimstone, pitch, *wildfire*, burn easily, and are hard to quench. *Bacon.*

2. A disease of sheep, attended with inflammation of the skin; a kind of erysipelas. *Cyc.*

WILD-FOWL, *n.* [*wild* and *fowl.*] Fowls of the forest, or untamed.

WILD-GOOSE, *n.* [*wild* and *goose.*] An aquatic fowl of the genus Anas, the *Anas anser*, a fowl of passage. These geese fly to the south in autumn, and return to the north in the spring. This species is the stock of the common domestic goose. The wild goose of N. America, also migratory, is a distinct species, the *Anas Canadensis.*

Wild-goose chase, the pursuit of something as unlikely to be caught as the wild goose. *Shak.*

WILD-HONEY, *n.* [*wild* and *honey.*] Honey that is found in the forest, in hollow trees or among rocks.

WILD-LAND, *n.* [*wild* and *land.*] Land not cultivated, or in a state that renders it unfit for cultivation.

2. In America, forest; land not settled and cultivated.

WILD-SERVICE, *n.* A plant. *Miller.*

The wilder myrtle-leaved service is a tree of the genus Cratægus, *(C. torminalis.)* *Lee.*

WIL'DER, *v. t.* [Dan. *vilder*, from *vild*, wild.]

To lose or cause to lose the way or track; to puzzle with mazes or difficulties; to bewilder.

Long lost and *wilder'd* in the maze of fate. *Pope.*

WIL'DERED, *pp.* Lost in a pathless tract; puzzled.

WIL'DERING, *ppr.* Puzzling.

WIL'DERNESS, *n.* [from *wild.*] A desert; a tract of land or region uncultivated and uninhabited by human beings, whether a forest or a wide barren plain. In the United States, it is applied only to a forest. In Scripture, it is applied frequently to the deserts of Arabia. The Israelites wandered in the *wilderness* forty years.

2. The ocean.

The wat'ry *wilderness* yields no supply. *Waller.*

3. A state of disorder. [*Not in use.*] *Milton.*

4. A wood in a garden, resembling a forest.

WILDING, *n.* A wild sour apple. *Mortimer.*

WILDLY, *adv.* Without cultivation. *More.*

2. Without tameness.

3. With disorder; with perturbation or distraction; with a fierce or roving look; as, to start *wildly* from one's seat; to stare *wildly.*

4. Without attention; heedlessly. *Shak.*

5. Capriciously; irrationally; extravagantly.

Who is there so *wildly* sceptical as to question whether the sun will rise in the east? *Wilkins.*

6. Irregularly.

She, *wildly* wanton, wears by night away
The sign of all our labors done by day. *Dryden.*

WILDNESS, *n.* Rudeness; rough uncultivated state; as the *wildness* of a forest or heath. *Prior.*

2. Inordinate disposition to rove; irregularity of manners; as the *wildness* of youth. *Shak.*

3. Savageness; brutality. *Sidney.*

4. Savage state; rudeness.

5. Uncultivated state; as the *wildness* of land.

6. A wandering; irregularity.

Delirium is but a short *wildness* of the imagination. *Watts.*

7. Alienation of mind. *Shak.*

8. State of being untamed.

9. The quality of being undisciplined, or not subjected to method or rules.

Is there any danger that this discipline will tame too much the fiery spirit, the enchanting *wildness*, and magnificent irregularity of the orator's genius? *Wirt.*

WILDS, *n.* Among *farmers*, the part of a plow by which it is drawn. [*Local.*]

WILE, *n.* [Sax. *wile*; Ice. *wul*; W. *fel*, fine, subtil.]

A trick or stratagem practiced for ensnaring or deception; a sly, insidious artifice.

That ye may be able to stand against the *wiles* of the devil. Eph. vi.

WILE, *v. t.* To deceive; to beguile. [*Little used.*] *Spenser.*

WI'LILY, *adv.* [from *wily.*] By stratagem; with insidious art. Josh. ix.

WI'LINESS, *n.* [from *wily.*] Cunning; guile.

WILK, } *n.* [G. *welken*, to wither, or
WHILK, } cause to wither.] A species of shell. [See *Welk.*]

WILL, *n.* [Sax. *willa*; Goth. *wilja*; D. *wil* or *wille*; G. *wille*; Sw. *vilje*; Dan. *villie*; W. *gwyll*; Ir. *ail*; Gr. βουλη, counsel; Slav. *volia*. See the Verb.]

1. That faculty of the mind by which we determine either to do or forbear an action; the faculty which is exercised in deciding, among two or more objects, which we shall embrace or pursue. The will is directed or influenced by the judgment. The understanding or reason compares different objects, which operate as motives; the judgment determines which is preferable, and the *will* decides which to pursue. In other words, we *reason* with respect to the value or importance of things; we then *judge* which is to be preferred; and we *will* to take the most valuable. These are but different operations of the mind, soul, or intellectual part of man. Great disputes have existed respecting the freedom of the *will.*

Will is often quite a different thing from *desire.*

A power over a man's subsistence, amounts to a power over his *will.* *Federalist, Hamilton.*

2. Choice; determination. It is my *will* to prosecute the trespasser.

3. Choice; discretion; pleasure.

Go, then, the guilty at thy *will* chastise. *Pope.*

4. Command; direction.

Our prayers should be according to the *will* of God. *Law.*

5. Disposition; inclination; desire. "What is your *will*, Sir?" In this phrase, the word may also signify determination, especially when addressed to a superior.

6. Power; arbitrary disposal.

Deliver me not over to the *will* of my enemies. Ps. xxvii.

7. Divine determination; moral purpose or counsel.

Thy *will* be done. *Lord's Prayer.*

8. Testament; the disposition of a man's estate, to take effect after his death. *Wills* are *written*, or *nuncupative*, that is, *verbal.* *Blackstone.*

Good will, favor; kindness. *Shak.*

2. Right intention. Phil. i.

Ill will, enmity; unfriendliness. It expresses less than *malice.*

To have one's will, to obtain what is desired.

At will. To hold an estate *at the will* of another, is to enjoy the possession at his pleasure, and be liable to be ousted at any time by the lessor or proprietor.

Will with a wisp, Jack with a lantern; ignis fatuus; a luminous appearance sometimes seen in the air over moist ground, supposed to proceed from hydrogen gas.

WILL, *v. t.* [Sax. *willan*; Goth. *wilyan*; D. *willen*; G. *wollen*; Sw. *vilja*; Dan. *ville*; L. *volo, velle*; Gr. βουλομαι; Fr. *vouloir*; It. *volere*. The sense is to set, or to set forward, to stretch forward. The sense is well expressed by the L. *propono.*]

1. To determine; to decide in the mind that something shall be done or forborne; implying power to carry the purpose into effect. In this manner God *wills* whatever comes to pass. So in the style of princes; "we *will* that execution be done."

A man that sits still is said to be at liberty, because he can walk if he *wills* it. *Locke.*

2. To command; to direct.

'Tis yours, O queen! to *will*
The work which duty bids me to fulfill. *Dryden.*

3. To be inclined or resolved to have.

There, there, Hortensio, *will* you any wife? *Shak.*

4. To wish; to desire. What *will* you?

5. To dispose of estate and effects by testament.

6. It is sometimes equivalent to *may be.* Let the circumstances be what they *will*; that is, any circumstances, of whatever nature.

7. *Will* is used as an auxiliary verb, and a sign of the future tense. It has different significations in different persons.

1. *I will* go, is a present promise to go; and with an emphasis on *will*, it expresses determination.

2. *Thou wilt* go, *you will* go, express foretelling; simply stating an event that is to come.

3. *He will* go, is also a foretelling. The use of *will* in the plural, is the same. *We will*, promises; *ye will, they will*, foretell.

WILL'ED, *pp.* Determined; resolved; desired.

2. Disposed of by will or testament.

WILL'ER, *n.* One who wills.

WILL'FUL, *a.* [*will* and *full.*] Governed by the will without yielding to reason; obstinate; stubborn; perverse; inflexible; as a *willful* man.

2. Stubborn; refractory; as a *willful* horse.

WILL'FULLY, *adv.* Obstinately; stubbornly.

2. By design; with set purpose.

If we sin *willfully* after that we have received the knowledge of the truth, there remaineth no more sacrifice for sins. Heb. x.

WILL'FULNESS, *n.* Obstinacy; stubbornness; perverseness.

Sins of presumption are such as proceed from pride, arrogance, *willfulness*, and haughtiness of men's heart. *Perkins.*

WILL'ING, *ppr.* Determining; resolving; desiring.

2. Disposing of by will.

WILL'ING, *a.* [Sw. Dan. *villig.*] Free to do or grant; having the mind inclined; disposed; not averse. Let every man give, who is able and *willing.*

2. Pleased; desirous.

Felix, *willing* to show the Jews a pleasure. Acts xxiv.

3. Ready; prompt.

He stoop'd with weary wings and *willing* feet. *Milton.*

4. Chosen; received of choice or without reluctance; as, to be held in *willing* chains.

5. Spontaneous.

No spouts of blood run *willing* from a tree. *Dryden.*

6. Consenting. *Milton.*

WILL'ING-HE'ARTED, *a.* Well disposed; having a free heart. Ex. xxxv.

WILL'INGLY, *adv.* With free will; without reluctance; cheerfully.

2. By one's own choice.

The condition of that people is not so much to be envied as some would *willingly* represent it. *Addison.*

WILL'INGNESS, *n.* Free choice or consent of the will; freedom from reluctance; readiness of the mind to do or forbear.

Sweet is the love that comes with *willingness.* *Dryden.*

WIL'LOW, *n.* [Sax. *welig*; D. *wilge*; W. *gwial*, twigs; also *helig*, L. *salix.*]

A tree of the genus Salix. There are several species of willow, the white, the black, the purple or red, the sallow, and the broad leaved willow, &c. A species called the *weeping willow*, has long and slender branches which droop and hang downward, the *Salix Babylonica.*

WIL'LOWED, *a.* Abounding with willows. *Collins.*

WIL'LOW-GALL, *n.* A protuberance on the leaves of willows. *Cyc.*

WIL'LOW-HERB, *n.* The purple loosestrife, a plant of the genus Lythrum; also, the yellow loosestrife, of the genus Lysimachia; also, the French willow, of the genus Epilobium. *Lee. Cyc.*

WIL'LOWISH, *a.* Like the color of the willow. *Walton.*

WIL'LOW-TUFTED, *a.* Tufted with willows. *Goldsmith.*

WIL'LOW-WEED, *n.* A name sometimes given to the smartweed or persicaria. *Cyc.*

WIL'LOW-WŎRT, *n.* A plant. *Miller.*

WIL'LOWY, *a.* Abounding with willows. *Gray.*

WILT, *v. i.* [G. D. *welken*, to fade; that is, to shrink or withdraw.]

To begin to wither; to lose freshness and become flaccid, as a plant when exposed to great heat in a dry day, or when first separated from its root.

This is a legitimate word, for which there is no substitute in the language. It is not synonymous with *wither*, as it expresses only the beginning of withering. A *wilted* plant often revives and becomes fresh; not so a *withered* plant.

WILT, *v. t.* To cause to begin to wither; to make flaccid; as a green plant.

2. To cause to languish; to depress or destroy the vigor and energy of.

Despots have *wilted* the human race into sloth and imbecility. *Dwight.*

WILT'ED, *pp.* Having become flaccid and lost its freshness, as a plant.

WILT'ING, *ppr.* Beginning to fade or wither.

WI'LY, *a.* [from *wile.*] Cunning; sly; using craft or stratagem to accomplish a purpose; subtil; as a *wily* adversary.

WIM'BLE, *n.* [W. *guimbill*, a gimlet; *çwimiaw*, to move round briskly. See *Whim.*]

An instrument for boring holes, turned by a handle.

WIM'BLE, *a.* Active; nimble. *Obs.* *Spenser.*

WIM'BREL, *n.* A bird of the curlew kind, a species of Scolopax, [*S. phæopus.*] *Cyc.*

WIM'PLE, *n.* [G. *wimpel*, a pendant; Dan. *vimpel*; W. *gwempyl*, a vail, a wimple; Fr. *guimpe*, a neck handkerchief.] A hood or vail. *Obs.* Is. iii.

WIM'PLE, *v. t.* To draw down, as a vail. *Obs.* *Spenser.*

WIN, *v. t.* pret. and pp. *won.* [Sax. *winnan*, to labor, to toil, to gain by labor, to *win*; D. *winnen*; G. *gewinnen*; Sw. *vinna.*]

1. To gain by success in competition or contest; as, to *win* the prize in a game; to *win* money; to *win* a battle, or to *win* a country. Battles are *won* by superior strength or skill.

—Who thus shall Canaan *win.* *Milton.*

2. To gain by solicitation or courtship.

3. To obtain; to allure to kindness or compliance. Thy virtue *won* me. *Win* your enemy by kindness.

4. To gain by persuasion or influence; as, an orator *wins* his audience by argument. The advocate has *won* the jury.

And Mammon *wins* his way, where seraphs might despair. *Byron.*

WIN, *v. t.* To gain the victory.

Nor is it aught but just
That he, who in debate of truth hath *won*,
Should *win* in arms. *Milton.*

To win upon, to gain favor or influence; as, to *win upon* the heart or affections. *Dryden.*

2. To gain ground.

The rabble will in time *win upon* power. *Shak.*

To win of, to be conqueror. *Shak.*

WINCE, *v. i.* [Fr. *guincher*, to twist; *guingois*, crookedness, W. *gwing*; *gwingaw*, to wriggle, to wince.]

1. To shrink, as from a blow or from pain; to start back.

I will not stir nor *wince.* *Shak.*

2. To kick or flounce when uneasy, or impatient of a rider; as, a horse *winces.* *Hudibras.*

WIN'CER, *n.* One that winces, shrinks or kicks.

WINCH, *n.* [Sax. *wince*; Fr. *guincher*, to twist.]

A windlass; or an instrument with which to turn or strain something forcibly; as a *winch* to strain the cord of a bedstead, or to turn a wheel.

WINCH, *v. i.* To wince; to shrink; to kick with impatience or uneasiness. [This is a more correct orthography than *wince.*]

WINCH'ING, } *ppr.* Flinching; shrinking;
WIN'CING, } kicking.

WIN'COPIPE, *n.* The vulgar name of a little flower, that, when it opens in the morning, bodes a fair day. *Bacon.*

WIND, *n.* [Sax. D. G. *wind*; Sw. Dan. *vind*; W. *gwynt*; L. *ventus*; It. *vento*; Sp. *viento*; Fr. *vent.* This word accords with L. *venio*, *ventum*, and the Teutonic *wendan*, Eng. *went.* The primary sense is to move, flow, rush or drive along.]

1. Air in motion with any degree of velocity, indefinitely; a current of air. When the air moves moderately, we call it a light wind, or a breeze; when with more velocity, we call it a fresh breeze, and when with violence, we call it a gale, storm or tempest. The word *gale* is used by the poets for a moderate breeze, but seamen use it as equivalent to *storm.*

Winds are denominated from the point of compass from which they blow; as a *north* wind; an *east* wind; a *south* wind; a *west* wind; a *southwest* wind, &c.

2. The *four winds*, the cardinal points of the heavens.

Come from the *four winds*, O breath, and breathe upon these slain. Ezek. xxxvii.

This sense of the word seems to have had its origin with the orientals, as it was the practice of the Hebrews to give to each of the four cardinal points the name of *wind.*

3. Direction of the wind from other points of the compass than the cardinal, or any point of compass; as a compass of eight *winds.* *Obs.* *Heylin.*

4. Breath; power of respiration.

If my *wind* were but long enough to say my prayers, I would repent. *Shak.*

5. Air in motion from any force or action; as the *wind* of a cannon ball; the *wind* of a bellows.

6. Breath modulated by the organs or by an instrument.

Their instruments were various in their kind,
Some for the bow, and some for breathing *wind.* *Dryden.*

7. Air impregnated with scent.

A pack of dog-fish had him in the *wind.* *Swift.*

8. Any thing insignificant or light as wind.

Think not with *wind* of airy threats to awe. *Milton.*

9. Flatulence; air generated in the stomach and bowels; as, to be troubled with *wind.*

10. The name given to a disease of sheep, in which the intestines are distended with air, or rather affected with a violent inflammation. It occurs immediately after shearing. *Cyc.*

Down the wind, decaying; declining; in a state of decay; as, he went *down the wind.* [*Not used.*] *L'Estrange.*

To take or *have the wind*, to gain or have the advantage. *Bacon.*

To take wind, or *to get wind*, to be divulged; to become public. The story *got wind*, or *took wind.*

In the wind's eye, in seamen's language, towards the direct point from which the wind blows.

Between wind and water, denoting that part of a ship's side or bottom which is frequently brought above water by the rolling of the ship, or fluctuation of the water's surface.

To carry the wind, in the manege, is when a horse tosses his nose as high as his ears.

Constant or *perennial wind*, a wind that blows constantly from one point of the compass; as the trade wind of the tropics.

Shifting, *variable* or *erratic winds*, are such as are changeable, now blowing from one point and now from another, and then ceasing altogether.

Stated or *periodical wind*, a wind that constantly returns at a certain time, and blows steadily from one point for a certain time. Such are the monsoons in India, and land and sea breezes.

Trade wind, a wind that blows constantly from one point, such as the tropical wind in the Atlantic.

WIND'AGE, *n.* [Sp. *viento*, wind, windage.] The difference between the diameter of a piece and that of a ball or shell. *Cyc.*

WIND'BOUND, *a.* [*wind* and *bound.*] Prevented from sailing by a contrary wind. *Mar. Dict.*

WIND'-DROPSY, *n.* [*wind* and *dropsy.*] A swelling of the belly from wind in the intestines; tympanites. *Coxe.*

WIND'-EGG, *n.* [*wind* and *egg.*] An addle egg.

WIND'ER, *v.t.* To fan; to clean grain with a fan. [*Local.*]

WIND'ER-MEB, *n.* A bird of the genus Larus, or gull-kind. *Cyc.*

WIND'FALL, *n.* [*wind* and *fall.*] Fruit blown off the tree by wind.

2. An unexpected legacy.

WIND'-FALLEN, *a.* Blown down by the wind. *Drayton.*

WIND'-FLOWER, *n.* [*wind* and *flower.*] A plant, the anemone.

WIND'-FURNACE, *n.* [*wind* and *furnace.*] A furnace in which the air is supplied by an artificial current, as from a bellows.

WIND'-GAGE, *n.* [*wind* and *gage.*] An instrument for ascertaining the velocity and force of wind. *Cyc.*

WIND'-GALL, *n.* [*wind* and *gall.*] A soft tumor on the fetlock joints of a horse.

WIND'-GUN, *n.* An air gun; a gun discharged by the force of compressed air.

WIND' HATCH, *n.* [*wind* and *hatch.*] In mining, the opening or place where the ore is taken out of the earth. *Cyc.*

WIND'-HÔVER, *n.* [*wind* and *hover.*] A species of hawk; called also the *stannel*, but more usually the *kestrel.* *Cyc.*

WIND'INESS, *n.* [from *windy.*] The state of being windy or tempestuous; as the *windiness* of the weather or season.

2. Fullness of wind; flatulence. *Harvey.*

3. Tendency to generate wind; as the *windiness* of vegetables.

4. Tumor; puffiness.

The swelling *windiness* of much knowledge. *Brerewood.*

WIND'-INSTRUMENT, *n.* An instrument of music, played by wind, chiefly by the breath; as a flute, a clarinet, &c. *Cyc.*

WIND'LAS, } *n.* [*wind* and *lace.* Qu.] A
WIND'LASS, } machine for raising great weights, consisting of a cylinder or roller of timber, moving on its axis and turned by levers, with a rope or chain attached to the weight.

2. A handle by which any thing is turned. [*Not in use.*] *Shak.*

WIND'LE, *n.* A spindle; a kind of reel.

WIND'-MILL, *n.* [*wind* and *mill.*] A mill turned by the wind. *Mortimer.*

WIND'PIPE, *n.* [*wind* and *pipe.*] The passage for the breath to and from the lungs; the trachea.

WIND'-PUMP, *n.* [*wind* and *pump.*] A pump moved by wind, useful in draining lands. *Cyc.*

WIND'-RODE, *n.* A term used by seamen to signify a ship when riding with wind and tide opposed to each other, driven to the leeward of her anchor.

WIND'RÔW, *n.* [*wind* and *row.*] A row or line of hay, raked together for the purpose of being rolled into cocks or heaps. [*This is the only use of the word in New England.*]

2. The green border of a field, dug up in order to carry the earth on other land to mend it. *Cyc.*

3. A row of peats set up for drying; or a row of pieces of turf, sod or sward, cut in paring and burning. *Cyc.*

WIND'-SAIL, *n.* [*wind* and *sail.*] A wide tube or funnel of canvas, used to convey a stream of air into the lower apartments of a ship. *Mar. Dict.*

WIND'SEED, *n.* A plant of the genus Arctolis. *Lee.*

WIND'-SHOCK, *n.* [*wind* and *shock.*] A sort of bruise or shiver in a tree. *Cyc.*

WIND'-TIGHT, *a.* [*wind* and *tight.*] So tight as to prevent the passing of wind. *Hall.*

WIND'WARD, *n.* [*wind* and *ward.*] The point from which the wind blows; as, to ply to the *windward.*

WIND'WARD, *a.* [*wind* and *ward.*] Being on the side towards the point from which the wind blows; as the *windward* shrouds.

WIND'WARD, *adv.* Towards the wind.

WIND'Y, *a.* Consisting of wind; as a *windy* tempest. *Shak.*

2. Next the wind; as the *windy* side. *Shak.*

3. Tempestuous; boisterous; as *windy* weather.

4. Puffy; flatulent; abounding with wind. *Arbuthnot.*

5. Empty; airy; as *windy* joy. *Milton.*

WIND, *v. t.* pret. and pp. *wound.* [Sax. *windan*; G. D. *winden*; from *wind*, or the same root.]

1. To blow; to sound by blowing or inflation.

Wind the shrill horn. *Pope.*

2. To turn; to move, or cause to turn.

To turn and *wind* a fiery Pegasus. *Shak.*

3. To turn round some fixed object; to bind, or to form into a ball or coil by turning; as, to *wind* thread on a spool; to *wind* thread into a ball; to *wind* a rope into a coil.

4. To introduce by insinuation. The child *winds* himself into my affections.

They have little arts and dexterities to *wind* in such things into discourse. *Gov. of the Tongue.*

5. To change; to vary.

Were our legislature vested in the prince, he might *wind* and turn our constitution at his pleasure. *Addison.*

6. To entwist; to enfold; to encircle. *Shak.*

7. [With *i* short, as in *win.*] To nose; to perceive or to follow by the scent; as, hounds *wind* an animal.

8. To ventilate; to expose to the wind; to winnow.

To wind off, [with *i* long,] to unwind.

To wind out, to extricate. *Clarendon.*

To wind up, to bring to a small compass, as a ball of thread. *Locke.*

2. To bring to a conclusion or settlement; as, to *wind up* one's affairs.

3. To put in a state of renovated or continued motion.

Fate seem'd to *wind* him *up* for fourscore years. *Dryden.*

To wind up a clock, is to wind the cord by which the weights are suspended, round an axis or pin.

To wind up a watch, is to wind the spring round its axis or pin.

4. To raise by degrees.

Thus they *wound up* his temper to a pitch— *Atterbury.*

5. To straiten, as a string; to put in tune.

Wind up the slacken'd strings of thy lute. *Waller.*

6. To put in order for regular action. *Shak.*

WIND, *v. i.* To turn; to change.

So swift your judgments turn and *wind.* *Dryden.*

2. To turn around something; as, vines *wind* around a pole.

3. To have a circular direction; as *winding* stairs.

4. To crook; to bend. The road *winds* in various places.

5. To move round; as, a hare pursued turns and *winds.*

To wind out, to be extricated; to escape.

Long lab'ring underneath, ere they could *wind*
Out of such prison. *Milton.*

WINDER, *n.* One who winds.

WINDING, *ppr.* Turning; binding about; bending.

2. *a.* Bending; twisting from a direct line or an even surface.

WINDING, *n.* A turn or turning; a bend; flexure; meander; as the *windings* of a road or stream.

2. A call by the boatswain's whistle.

WINDING-ENGINE, *n.* An engine employed in mining, to draw up buckets from a deep pit. *Cyc.*

WINDING-SHEET, *n.* [*winding* and *sheet.*] A sheet in which a corpse is wrapped. *Bacon.*

WINDING-TACKLE, *n.* [*winding* and *tackle.*] A tackle consisting of one fixed triple block, and one double or triple movable block. *Dict.*

WIND'ÔW, *n.* [Dan. *vindue*; Sp. *ventana*, from the same root as *venta*, sale, *vent* of goods. The word in Spanish signifies also a nostril, that is, a passage. *Ventaja* is advantage; *ventalla*, a valve, and *ventalle*, a *fan*; *ventear*, to blow. Hence we see that *vent*, L. *vendo*, *wind*, *fan*, and *van*, Fr. *avant*, are all of one family. So is also the L. *fenestra*, Fr. *fenêtre*, D. *venster*, G. *fenster*, Ir. *fineog*. The vulgar pronunciation is *windor*, as if from the Welsh *gwyntdor*, wind-door.]

1. An opening in the wall of a building for the admission of light, and of air when necessary. This opening has a frame on the sides, in which are set movable sashes, containing panes of glass. In the U. States, the sashes are made to rise and fall, for the admission or exclusion of air. In France, *windows* are shut with frames or sashes that open and shut vertically, like the leaves of a folding door.

2. An aperture or opening.

A *window* shalt thou make to the ark. Gen. vi.

3. The frame or other thing that covers the aperture.

Ere I let fall the *windows* of mine eyes. *Shak.*

4. An aperture; or rather the clouds or water-spouts.

The *windows* of heaven were opened. Gen. vii.

5. Lattice or casement; or the network of wire used before the invention of glass. Judges v.

6. Lines crossing each other.

Till he has *windows* on his bread and butter. *King.*

WIND'OW, *v.t.* To furnish with windows. *Wotton. Pope.*

2. To place at a window. [*Unusual.*] *Shak.*
3. To break into openings. [*Unusual.*] *Shak.*

WIND'ŌW-BLIND, *n.* [*window* and *blind.*] A blind to intercept the light of a window. Venetian *window-blinds* are now much used in the United States.

WIND'OW-FRAME, *n.* [*window* and *frame.*] The frame of a window which receives and holds the sashes.

WIND'ŌW-GLASS, *n.* [*window* and *glass.*] Panes of glass for windows.

WIND'ŌW-SASH, *n.* [*window* and *sash.*] The sash or light frame in which panes of glass are set for windows.

WIND'ŌWY, *a.* Having little crossings like the sashes of a window. *Donne.*

WINE, *n.* [Sax. *win*; G. *wein*; D. *wyn*; Sw. Dan. *vin*; W. *gwin*; Russ. *vino*; L. *vinum*; It. Sp. *vino*; Fr. *vin*; Ir. *fion*; Gr. *οινος*; Eolic, *Fοινος*; Eth. ወይን wine; Heb. יין. This oriental word seems to be connected with עין a fountain, and ענה anah, to thrust, to press, or press out.]

1. The fermented juice of grapes; as the *wine* of the Madeira grape; the *wine* of Burgundy or Oporto.
2. The juice of certain fruits, prepared with sugar, spirits, &c.; as currant *wine*; gooseberry *wine*.
3. Intoxication.

> Noah awoke from his *wine*. Gen. ix.

4. Drinking.

> They that tarry long at the *wine*. Prov. xxiii.

Corn and wine, in Scripture, are put for all kinds of necessaries for subsistence. Ps.

Bread and wine, in the Lord's supper, are symbols of the body and blood of Christ.

WI'NE-BIBBER, *n.* One who drinks much wine; a great drinker. Prov. xxiii.

WI'NE-CASK, *n.* [*wine* and *cask.*] A cask in which wine is or has been kept.

WI'NE-FLY, *n.* A small fly found in empty wine casks.

WI'NE-GLASS, *n.* [*wine* and *glass.*] A small glass in which wine is drank.

WI'NELESS, *a.* Destitute of wine; as *wineless* life. *Swift.*

WI'NE-MEASURE, *n.* [See *Measure.*] The measure by which wines and other spirits are sold, smaller than beer measure.

WI'NE-MERCHANT, *n.* A merchant who deals in wines.

WI'NE-PRESS, *n.* [*wine* and *press.*] A place where grapes are pressed.

WING, *n.* [Sax. *gehwing*; Sw. Dan. *vinge*. The word signifies the side, end or extremity.]

1. The limb of a fowl by which it flies. In a few species of fowls, the wings do not enable them to fly; as is the case with the dodo, ostrich, great auk, and penguin; but in the two former, the wings assist the fowls in running.
2. The limb of an insect by which it flies.
3. In *botany*, the side petal of a papilionaceous corol; also, an appendage of seeds, by means of which they are wafted in the air and scattered; also, any membranous or leafy dilatation of a footstalk, or of the angles of a stem, branch or flower stalk, or of a calyx. *Martyn. Cyc.*
4. Flight; passage by the wing; as, to be on the *wing*; to take *wing*.
5. Means of flying; acceleration. Fear adds *wings* to flight.
6. Motive or incitement of flight.

> Then fiery expedition be my *wing*. *Shak.*

7. The flank or extreme body or part of an army. *Dryden.*
8. Any side-piece. *Mortimer.*
9. In *gardening*, a side-shoot. *Cyc.*
10. In *architecture*, a side-building, less than the main edifice.
11. In *fortification*, the longer sides of horn-works, crown-works, &c. *Cyc.*
12. In *a fleet*, the ships on the extremities, when ranged in a line, or when forming the two sides of a triangle.
13. In *a ship*, the wings are those parts of the hold and orlop deck, which are nearest the sides.
14. In *Scripture*, protection; generally in the plural. Ps. lxiii. Ex. xix.

On the wings of the wind, with the utmost velocity. Ps. xviii.

WING, *v. t.* To furnish with wings; to enable to fly or to move with celerity.

> Who heaves old ocean, and who *wings* the storms. *Pope.*

2. To supply with side bodies; as on either side well *winged*. *Shak.*
3. To transport by flight.

> I, an old turtle,
> Will *wing* me to some wither'd bough. *Shak.*
>
> Edge the keen sword, and *wing* th' unerring ball. *Trumbull.*

To wing a flight, to exert the power of flying.

WING'ED, *pp.* Furnished with wings; transported by flying.

2. *a.* Having wings; as a *winged* fowl. Gen. i.
3. Swift; rapid; as with *winged* haste. *Shak.*
4. Wounded; hurt.
5. In *botany*, furnished with longitudinal membranous appendages, as a *winged* stalk or stem; or with downy or hairy appendages, as *winged* seeds. *Cyc.*

Winged petiole, having a thin membrane or border on each side, or dilated on the sides. *Martyn.*

Winged leaf, a pennate leaf; a species of compound leaf, wherein a simple leaf has several leaflets fastened to each side of it. *Martyn.*

6. In *heraldry*, represented with wings, or having wings of a different color from the body.
7. Fanned with wings; swarming with birds. *Milton.*

WINGED-PEA, *n.* A plant. *Miller.*

WING'-FOOTED, *a.* [*wing* and *foot.*] Swift; moving with rapidity; fleet. *Drayton.*

WING'LESS, *a.* Having no wings; not able to ascend or fly.

WING-SHELL, *n.* [*wing* and *shell.*] The shell that covers the wing of insects.

WING'Y, *a.* Having wings; rapid; as *wingy* speed. *Addison.*

WINK, *v. i.* [Sax. *wincian*; D. *wenken*; G. *winken*; Sw. *vinka*; Dan. *vinker*; W. *gwing*, a wink; *gwingaw*, to wriggle, to wink, to wince. *Wink* and *wince* are radically one word.]

1. To shut the eyes; to close the eyelids.

> They are not blind, but they *wink*. *Tillotson.*

2. To close and open the eyelids.
3. To give a hint by a motion of the eyelids.

> *Wink* at the footman to leave him without a plate. *Swift.*

4. To close the eyelids and exclude the light.

> Or *wink* as cowards and afraid. *Prior.*

5. To be dim; as a *winking* light. *Dryden.*

To wink at, to connive at; to seem not to see; to tolerate; to overlook, as something not perfectly agreeable; as, to *wink at* faults. *Roscommon.*

WINK, *n.* The act of closing the eyelids.

I lay awake, and could not sleep a *wink*.

> I could eclipse and cloud them with a *wink*. *Donne.*

2. A hint given by shutting the eye with a significant cast. *Swift.*

WINK'ER, *n.* One who winks. *Pope.*

WINK'ING, *ppr.* Shutting the eyes; shutting and opening the eyelids; hinting by closing the eye; conniving at; overlooking.

WINK'INGLY, *adv.* With the eye almost closed. *Peacham.*

WIN'NER, *n.* [from *win.*] One who gains by success in competition or contest.

WIN'NING, *ppr.* [from *win.*] Gaining by success in competition or contest.

2. *a.* Attracting; adapted to gain favor; charming; as a *winning* address.

WIN'NING, *n.* The sum won or gained by success in competition or contest.

WIN'NŌW, *v. t.* [L. *evanno*, from *vannus*, a fan; D. G. *wannen*; from the root of *fan* and *wind*. The Sax. has *windwian*, to wind.]

1. To separate and drive off the chaff from grain by means of wind. Grain is *winnowed* by a fan, or by a machine, or by pouring it out of a vessel in a current of air.
2. To fan; to beat as with wings. *Milton.*
3. To examine; to sift for the purpose of separating falsehood from truth.

> *Winnow* well this thought. *Dryden.*

4. To separate, as the bad from the good. *Shak.*

WIN'NŌW, *v. i.* To separate chaff from corn.

> *Winnow* not with every wind. *Ecclus.*

WIN'NŌWED, *pp.* Separated from the chaff by wind; sifted; examined.

WIN'NŌWER, *n.* One who winnows.

WIN'NŌWING, *ppr.* Separating from the chaff by wind; examining.

WIN'TER, *n.* [Sax. G. D. Sw. Dan.; from *wind*, or its root; Goth. *wintrus.*]

1. The cold season of the year. Astronomically considered, winter commences in northern latitudes when the sun enters Capricorn, or at the solstice about the 21st of December, and ends at the equinox in March; but in ordinary discourse, the three *winter* months are December, January, and February. Our Saxon ancestors reckoned the years by winters; as ten *winters*; thirty *winters*. In tropical climates, there are two winters annually; but they cannot be said to be cold. In the temperate and frigid climates, there is one winter only in the year.

2. The part of a printing press which sustains the carriage.

WIN'TER, *v. i.* To pass the winter. He *wintered* in Italy. Cattle *winter* well on good fodder.

WIN'TER, *v. t.* To feed or manage during the winter. To *winter* young cattle on straw, is not profitable. Delicate plants must be *wintered* under cover.

WINTER-AP'PLE, *n.* [*winter* and *apple.*] An apple that keeps well in winter.

WINTER-B'ARLEY, *n.* [*winter* and *barley.*] A kind of barley which is sowed in autumn.

WIN'TER-BEATEN, *a.* [*winter* and *beat.*] Harassed by the severe weather of winter. *Spenser.*

WIN'TER-BERRY, *n.* [*winter* and *berry.*] A plant of the genus Prinos. *Lee.*

WIN'TER-BLOOM, *n.* [*winter* and *bloom.*] A plant of the genus Azalea. *Lee.*

WINTER-CHER'RY, *n.* [*winter* and *cherry.*] A plant of the genus Physalis, and its fruit, which is of the size of a cherry. *Lee. Miller.*

WINTER-CITRON, *n.* [*winter* and *citron.*] A sort of pear.

WIN'TER-CRESS, *n.* [*winter* and *cress.*] A plant of the genus Erysimum.

WINTER-CROP', *n.* [*winter* and *crop.*] A crop which will bear the winter, or which may be converted into fodder during the winter. *Cyc.*

WINTER-FAL'LOW, *n.* [*winter* and *fallow.*] Ground that is fallowed in winter.

WINTER-G'ARDEN, *n.* [*winter* and *garden.*] An ornamental garden for winter.

WIN'TER-GREEN, *n.* [*winter* and *green.*] A plant of the genus Pyrola, useful as a vulnerary. *Cyc.*

WIN'TER-KILL, *v. t.* [*winter* and *kill.*] To kill by means of the weather in winter; as, to *winter-kill* wheat or clover. *New-England.*

WIN'TER-KILL, *v. i.* To be killed by the winter. Wheat is liable to *winter-kill* in moist land.

WIN'TER-KILLED, *pp.* Killed by the winter, as grain.

WIN'TER-KILLING, *ppr.* Killing by the weather in winter.

WIN'TER-LODGE, } *n.* [*winter* and *lodge.*] In
WIN'TER-LODGMENT, } *botany*, the hybernacle of a plant, which protects the embryo or future shoot from injuries during the winter. It is either a bud or a bulb. *Encyc.*

WIN'TER-PEAR, *n.* [*winter* and *pear.*] Any pear that keeps well in winter.

WINTER-QUARTERS, *n.* [*winter* and *quarters.*]
The quarters of an army during the winter; a winter residence or station.

WIN'TER-RIG, *v. t.* [*winter* and *rig.*] To fallow or till in winter. [*Local.*]

WINTER-SOL'STICE, *n.* [*winter* and *solstice.*]
The solstice of the winter, which takes place when the sun enters Capricorn, December 21st.

WIN'TERED, *pp.* Kept through the winter.

WIN'TERING, *ppr.* Passing the winter; keeping in winter.

WIN'TERLY, *a.* Such as is suitable to winter. [*Little used.*] *Shak.*

WIN'TERY, *a.* Suitable to winter; brumal; hyemal; cold; stormy. *Dryden.*

WI'NY, *a.* [from *wine.*] Having the taste or qualities of wine. *Bacon.*

WIPE, *v. t.* [Sax. *wipian.*] To rub with something soft for cleaning; to clean by rubbing; as, to *wipe* the hands or face with a towel. Luke vii.

2. To strike off gently.

> Some nat'ral tears they dropp'd, but *wip'd* them soon. *Milton.*

3. To cleanse from evil practices or abuses; to overturn and destroy what is foul and hateful.

> I will *wipe* Jerusalem as a man *wipeth* a dish. 2 Kings xxi.

4. To cheat; to defraud. *Spenser.*

To wipe away, to cleanse by rubbing or tersion; as, to *wipe away* a stain or reproach.

To wipe off, to clear away. *Wipe off* this foul stain; *wipe off* the dust.

To wipe out, to efface; to obliterate. *Wipe out* the blot.

WIPE, *n.* The act of rubbing for the purpose of cleaning.

2. A blow; a stroke.

3. A gibe; a jeer; a severe sarcasm. *Swift.*

4. A bird. [Sw. *vipa*, the lapwing.] *Ainsworth.*

WI'PED, *pp.* Rubbed for cleaning; cleaned by rubbing; cleared away; effaced.

WI'PER, *n.* One who wipes.

2. The instrument used for wiping.

WI'PING, *ppr.* Rubbing with a cloth or other soft thing for cleaning; clearing away; effacing.

WIRE, *n.* [Sw. *vir*; Ice *wijr.*] A thread of metal; any metallic substance drawn to an even thread.

WIRE, *v. t.* To bind with wire; to apply wire to, as in bottling liquors.

WI'REDRAW, *v. t.* [*wire* and *draw.*] To draw a metal into wire, which is done by drawing it through a hole in a plate of steel.

2. To draw into length. *Arbuthnot.*

3. To draw by art or violence.

> My sense has been *wiredrawn* into blasphemy. *Dryden.*

4. To draw or spin out to great length and tenuity; as, to *wiredraw* an argument.

WI'REDRAWER, *n.* One who draws metal into wire. *Locke.*

WI'REDRAWING, *ppr.* Drawing a metal into wire.

2. Drawing to a great length or fineness.

WI'REDRAWN, *pp.* Drawn into wire; drawn out to great length or fineness.

WI'RE-GRATE, *n.* [*wire* and *grate.*] A grate or contrivance of fine wire work to keep insects out of vineries, hot houses, &c. *Cyc.*

WI'RE-HEEL, *n.* [*wire* and *heel.*] A defect and disease in the feet of a horse or other beast. *Cyc.*

WI'RE-WORM, *n.* [*wire* and *worm.*] A mischievous worm that sometimes injures grain.

WI'RY, *a.* Made of wire; like wire.

WIS, *v. t.* pret. *wist.* [G. *wissen*; D. *weeten*; Dan. *vider*; Sw. *veta.* This is the Sax. *witan*, to *wit.*]
To think; to suppose; to imagine. *Obs.* *Spenser.*

WIS'DOM, *n. s* as z. [Sax. *id.*; *wise* and *dom*; G. *weisheit*, [*wisehood*;] D. *wysheid*; Sw. *visdom* and *vishet*; Dan. *visdom* or *viisdom.* See *Wise.* *Wisdom*, it seems, is from the Gothic dialect.]

1. The right use or exercise of knowledge; the choice of laudable ends, and of the best means to accomplish them. This is wisdom in *act*, *effect*, or *practice.* If wisdom is to be considered as a *faculty* of the mind, it is the faculty of discerning or judging what is most just, proper and useful, and if it is to be considered as an *acquirement*, it is the knowledge and use of what is best, most just, most proper, most conducive to prosperity or happiness. Wisdom in the first sense, or *practical wisdom*, is nearly synonymous with *discretion.* It differs somewhat from *prudence*, in this respect; *prudence* is the exercise of sound judgment in avoiding evils; *wisdom* is the exercise of sound judgment either in avoiding evils or attempting good. *Prudence* then is a species, of which *wisdom* is the genus.

> *Wisdom* gained by experience, is of inestimable value. *Scott.*

> It is hoped that our rulers will act with dignity and *wisdom*; that they will yield every thing to reason, and refuse every thing to force. *Ames.*

2. In *Scripture*, human learning; erudition; knowledge of arts and sciences.

> Moses was learned in all the *wisdom* of the Egyptians. Acts vii.

3. Quickness of intellect; readiness of apprehension; dexterity in execution; as the *wisdom* of Bezaleel and Aholiab. Ex. xxxi.

4. Natural instinct and sagacity. Job xxxix.

5. In *Scripture theology*, wisdom is true religion; godliness; piety; the knowledge and fear of God, and sincere and uniform obedience to his commands. This is the *wisdom* which is from above. Ps. xc. Job xxviii.

6. Profitable words or doctrine. Ps. xxxvii.

The wisdom of this world, mere human erudition; or the carnal policy of men, their craft and artifices in promoting their temporal interests; called also *fleshly wisdom.* 1 Cor. ii. 2. Cor. i.

The wisdom of words, artificial or affected eloquence; or learning displayed in teaching. 1 Cor. i. ii.

WISE, *a. s* as z. [Sax. *wis*, *wise*; G. *weise*; D. *wys*; Sw. *vis*; Dan. *viis*; Sax. *wissan*, G. *wissen*, to know; Sans. *vid.* This in Dutch, is *weeten*, to know, which is the Goth. Sax. *witan*, Eng. to *wit.* So that *wise*, *wit*, *weet*, *wot*, are all from one root, or dialectical forms of the same word; Ir. *fois*, *feas*, knowledge; W. *gwys*, *gwyz*, Sans. *widja*, intelligence. In general, the radical sense of *know* is to reach or to hold, from extension, stretching. In this case, it may be to show, to disclose, from a like sense; for in Sw. *visa*, Dan. *viser*, G. *weisen*, D. *wysen*, is to show. In this case, L. *video*, *visum*, which seems to be connected with this word, may coincide in origin with *wide.* *Wistful*, attentive, eager, is from reaching forward.]

1. Properly, having knowledge; hence, having the power of discerning and judging correctly, or of discriminating between what is true and what is false; between what is fit and proper, and what is im-

proper; as a *wise* prince; a *wise* magistrate. Solomon was deemed the *wisest* man. But a man may be *speculatively* and not *practically* wise. Hence,
2. Discrete and judicious in the use or application of knowledge; choosing laudable ends, and the best means to accomplish them. This is to be *practically* wise. Gen. xli.
3. Skillful; dextrous.
They are *wise* to do evil, but to do good they have no knowledge. Jer. iv.
4. Learned; knowing; as the *wise* and the unwise. Rom. i.
5. Skilled in arts, science, philosophy, or in magic and divination. 2 Sam. xiv.
6. Godly; pious. Prov. xiii.
—The holy Scriptures, which are able to make thee *wise* to salvation. 2 Tim. iii.
7. Skilled in hidden arts; *a sense somewhat ironical;* as the *wise* woman of Brainford. *Shak.*
8. Dictated or guided by wisdom; containing wisdom; judicious; well adapted to produce good effects; *applicable to things;* as a *wise* saying; a *wise* scheme or plan; *wise* conduct or management; a *wise* determination.
9. Becoming a wise man; grave; discrete; as *wise* deportment. *Milton.*

WISE, *n. s* as z. [Sax. *wise;* G. *weise;* D. *wys;* Sw. *vis;* Dan. *viis;* Fr. *guise;* It. *guisa;* Arm. *guis.*]
Manner; way of being or acting.
This song she sings in most commanding *wise.* *Sidney.*
In fittest *wise.* *Spenser.*
In the foregoing form, this word is obsolete, The use of it is now very limited. It is common in the following phrases.
1. *In any wise.*
If he that sanctified the field will *in any wise* redeem it— Lev. xxvii.
Fret not thyself *in any wise.* Ps. xxxvii.
2. *On this wise.*
On this wise ye shall bless the children of Israel. Num. vi.
3. *In no wise.*
He shall *in no wise* lose his reward. Matt. x.
It is used in composition, as in *likewise, otherwise, lengthwise,* &c. By mistake, *ways* is often used for it; as *lengthways,* for *lengthwise.*

WI'SEAȻRE, *n.* more correctly *wisesager.* [G. *weissager; weise* and *sager,* a sayer, a predicter or foreteller.]
One who makes pretensions to great wisdom; hence in contempt, a simpleton; a dunce. *Addison.*

WISE-HE'ARTED, *a.* [*wise* and *heart.*] Wise; knowing; skillful. Ex. xxviii.

WI'SELING, *n.* One who pretends to be wise. *Donne.*

WI'SELY, *adv.* Prudently; judiciously; discretely; with wisdom. Prov. xvi. xxi.
2. Craftily; with art or stratagem.
Let us deal *wisely* with them. Ex. i.

WI'SENESS, *n.* Wisdom. *Obs.* *Spenser.*

WISH, *v. i.* [Sax. *wiscan;* Cimbric, *oska.* In all the other Teutonic and Gothic dialects, the corresponding word is written with *n;* D. *wenschen;* G. *wünschen;* Dan. *önsker;* Sw. *önska.* This is probably the same word.]
1. To have a desire, or strong desire, either for what is or is not supposed to be obtainable. It usually expresses less than *long;* but sometimes it denotes to long or wish earnestly. We often *wish* for what is not obtainable.
This is as good an argument as an antiquary could *wish* for. *Arbuthnot.*
They have more than heart could *wish.* Ps. lxxiii.
I *wish* above all things that thou mayest prosper. 3 John 2.
They cast four anchors out of the stern, and *wished* for the day. Acts xxvii.
2. To be disposed or inclined; as, to *wish* well to another's affairs. *Addison.*
3. It sometimes partakes of hope or fear. I *wish* the event may prove fortunate, or less calamitous than we apprehend.

WISH, *v. t.* To desire. I *wish* your prosperity.
Let them be driven backward and put to shame, that *wish* me evil. Ps. xl.
2. To long for; to desire eagerly or ardently. It has this sense when expressed with emphasis.
3. To recommend by wishing.
I would not *wish* them to a fairer death. *Shak.*
4. To imprecate; as, to *wish* curses on an enemy. *Shak.*
5. To ask; to express desire. *Clarendon.*

WISH, *n.* Desire; sometimes, eager desire. Job xxxiii.
2. Desire expressed. *Pope.*
Blister'd be thy tongue
For such a *wish.* *Shak.*
3. Thing desired. He has his *wish.*
The difference between *wish* and *desire* seems to be, that *desire* is directed to what is obtainable, and a *wish* may be directed to what is obtainable or not. *Kames.*

WISH'ED, *pp.* Desired; or ardently desired.

WISH'ER, *n.* One who desires; one who expresses a wish. *Shak.*

WISH'FUL, *a.* Having desire, or ardent desire.
2. Showing desire; as *wishful* eyes.
3. Desirable; exciting wishes. [*Bad.*] *Chapman.*

WISH'FULLY, *adv.* With desire or ardent desire.
2. With the show of desiring.

WISH'ING, *ppr.* Desiring.

WISK'ET, *n.* A basket. *Ainsworth.*

WISP, *n.* [Dan. *visk,* a wisp, a whisk; *visker,* to whisk, to rub or wipe; G. D. *wisch.*]
A small bundle of straw or other like substance; as a *wisp* of straw; a *wisp* of hay; a *wisp* of herbs. *Shak.* *Bacon.*

WIST, *pret.* of *wis.* *Obs.*

WIST'FUL, *a.* [from *wist.* The sense is stretching or reaching towards.] Full of thoughts; earnest; attentive.
Why—dost thou so *wistful* seem? *Gay.*

WIST'FULLY, *adv.* Attentively; earnestly. *Hudibras.*

WIS'TIT, *n.* The striated monkey; a small species of monkey from S. America, with an annulated tail, the *ouistiti* of Buffon. *Cuvier.* *Ed. Encyc.*

WIST'LY, *adv.* Earnestly. *Obs.* *Shak.*

WIT, *v. i.* [Sax. Goth. *witan,* D. *weeten,* G. *wissen,* to know; Sans. *vid.* See *Wise.*]
To know. This verb is used only in the infinitive, *to wit,* namely, that is to say. [L. *videlicet,* i. e. *videre licet.*]

WIT, *n.* [Sax. *wit* or *ge-wit;* G. *witz;* Dan. *vid.* See the Verb and *Wise.*]
1. Primarily, the intellect; the understanding or mental powers.
Will puts in practice what the *wit* deviseth. *Davies.*
For *wit* and power their last endeavors bend
T' outshine each other. *Dryden.*
2. The association of ideas in a manner natural, but unusual and striking, so as to produce surprise joined with pleasure. Wit is defined
What oft was thought, but ne'er so well express'd. *Pope.*
Wit consists in assembling and putting together with quickness, ideas in which can be found resemblance and congruity, by which to make up pleasant pictures and agreeable visions in the fancy. *Locke.*
Wit consists chiefly in joining things by distant and fanciful relations, which surprise us because they are unexpected. *Kames.*
Wit is a propriety of thoughts and words; or in other terms, thoughts and words elegantly adapted to the subject. *Dryden.*
3. The faculty of associating ideas in a new and unexpected manner.
4. A man of genius; as, the age of Addison abounded with *wits.*
A *wit* herself, Amelia weds a *wit.* *Young.*
5. A man of fancy or wit.
Intemperate *wits* will spare neither friend nor foe. *L'Estrange.*
6. Sense; judgment.
He wants not *wit* the danger to decline. *Dryden.*
7. Faculty of the mind. *Shak.*
8. *Wits,* in the plural, soundness of mind; intellect not disordered; sound mind. No man in his *wits* would venture on such an expedition. Have you lost your *wits?* Is he out of his *wits?*
9. Power of invention; contrivance; ingenuity. He was at his *wits'* end. *Hooker.*

WITCH, *n.* [Sax. *wicca.* See *Wicked.*] A woman who by compact with the devil, practices sorcery or enchantment.
2. A woman who is given to unlawful arts.
3. [Sax. *wic.*] A winding sinuous bank. *Obs.* *Spenser.*

WITCH, *v. t.* To bewitch; to fascinate; to enchant.
I'll *witch* sweet ladies with my words and looks. *Shak.*

WITCH'ȻR'AFT, *n.* [*witch* and *craft.*] The practices of witches; sorcery; enchantments; intercourse with the devil. *Bacon.*
2. Power more than natural.
He hath a *witchcraft*
Over the king in's tongue. *Shak.*

WITCH'-ELM, *n.* A kind of elm. *Scott.*

WITCH'ERY, *n.* Sorcery; enchantment. *Milton.*
2. Fascination.

WITCH'-HAZEL, *n.* A species of elm, (*Ulmus montana.*) *Cyc.*
2. The hop-hornbeam, (*Carpinus ostrya.*) *Lee.*
The *Virginian witch-hazel* is the *Hamemelis virginica,* a shrub which flowers in autumn when its leaves are falling. *Lee.* *Bigelow.*

WIT'-ȻRACKER, *n.* [*wit* and *cracker.*] One who breaks jests; a joker. [*Not in use.*] *Shak.*

WIT'-ȻR'AFT, *n.* [*wit* and *craft.*] Contrivance; invention. *Obs.* *Camden.*

WITE, *v. t.* [Sax. *witan;* the root of *twit.*] To reproach; to blame. *Obs.* *Spenser.*

WITE, *n.* Blame; reproach. *Obs.*

WI'TELESS, *a.* Blameless. *Obs.* *Spenser.*

WIT'-FISH, *n.* [white fish; D. *witvisch.*] An East Indian fish of the size of a whiting; also, another East Indian fish, the *Albula Indica* of Ray. *Cyc.*

WITH, *prep.* [Sax. *with*, near or against; Goth. *ga-withan*, to join. The primary sense is to press, or to *meet*, to unite; hence in composition, it denotes opposition, as in *withstand* and *withdraw;* hence *against*, Sax. *wither*, G. *wider.*]

1. By, noting cause, instrument or means. We are distressed *with* pain; we are elevated *with* joy. *With* study men become learned and respectable. Fire is extinguished *with* water.
2. On the side of, noting friendship or favor.
   Fear not, for I am *with* thee. Gen. xxvi.
3. In opposition to; in competition or contest; as, to struggle *with* adversity. The champions fought *with* each other an hour. He will lie *with* any man living.
4. Noting comparison. The fact you mention compares well *with* another I have witnessed.
5. In company. The gentlemen traveled *with* me from Boston to Philadelphia.
6. In the society of. There is no living *with* such neighbors.
7. In connection, or in appendage. He gave me the Bible, and *with* it the warmest expressions of affection.
8. In mutual dealing or intercourse.
   I will buy *with* you, sell *with* you— *Shak.*
9. Noting confidence. I will trust you *with* the secret.
10. In partnership. He shares the profits *with* the other partners. I will share *with* you the pleasures and the pains.
11. Noting connection.
    Nor twist our fortunes *with* your sinking fate. *Dryden.*
12. Immediately after.
    With this he pointed to his face. *Dryden.*
13. Among. I left the assembly *with* the last.
    Tragedy was originally *with* the ancients a piece of religious worship. *Rymer.*
14. Upon.
    Such arguments had invincible force *with* those pagan philosophers. *Addison.*
15. In consent, noting parity of state.
    See! where on earth the flow'ry glories lie,
    With her they flourish'd, and *with* her they die. *Pope.*

With and *by* are closely allied in many of their uses, and it is not easy to lay down a rule by which their uses may be distinguished. It is observed by Johnson that *with* seems rather to denote an instrument, and *by* a cause; as, he killed an enemy *with* a sword, but he died *by* an arrow. But this rule is not always observed.

With, in composition, signifies for the most part opposition, privation; or separation, departure.

WITH, WITHE, *n.* [Sax. *withig;* Sw. *vidja;* L. *vitis, vitex;* probably a shoot.]

1. A willow twig.
2. A band consisting of a twig, or twigs twisted. *K. Charles.*

WITHAL, *adv.* *withaul'.* [*with* and *all.*] With the rest; together with; likewise; at the same time.
   If you choose that, then I am yours *withal.* *Shak.*
   How modest in exception, and *withal*
   How terrible in constant resolution! *Shak.*

2. It is sometimes used for *with.* But the word is not elegant, nor much used.

WITHDRAW', *v. t.* [*with* and *draw.*] To take back; to take from.
   It is impossible that God should *withdraw* his presence from any thing. *Hooker.*
   We say, to *withdraw* capital from a bank or stock in trade, to *withdraw* aid or assistance.

2. To recall; to cause to retire or leave; to call back or away. France has *withdrawn* her troops from Spain.

WITHDRAW', *v. i.* To retire; to retreat; to quit a company or place. We *withdrew* from the company at ten o'clock.
   She from her husband soft *withdrew.* *Milton.*

WITHDRAW'ING, *ppr.* Taking back; recalling; retiring.

WITHDRAW'ING-ROOM, *n.* A room behind another room for retirement; a drawing room. *Mortimer.*

WITHDRAW'MENT, *n.* The act of withdrawing or taking back; a recalling. *Ch. Obs.*
   Their *withdrawment* from the British and Foreign Bible Society, would tend to paralyze their exertions. *Simeon.*

WITHDRAWN', *pp.* of *withdraw.* Recalled; taken back.

WITH'ER, *v. i.* [W. *gwiz*, dried, withered; *gwizoni*, to wither; Sax. *gewitherod*, withered; Ir. *fothadh.*]

1. To fade; to lose its native freshness; to become sapless; to dry.
   It shall *wither* in all the leaves of her spring. Ezek. xvii.
2. To waste; to pine away; as animal bodies; as a *withered* hand. Matt. xii.
3. To lose or want animal moisture.
   Now warm in love, now *with'ring* in the grave. *Dryden.*

WITH'ER, *v. t.* To cause to fade and become dry; as, the sun *withereth* the grass. James i.

2. To cause to shrink, wrinkle and decay, for want of animal moisture.
   Age cannot *wither* her. *Shak.*

WITH'ER-BAND, *n.* [*withers* and *band.*] A piece of iron laid under a saddle near a horse's withers, to strengthen the bow. *Far. Dict.*

WITH'ERED, *pp.* Faded; dried; shrunk.

WITH'EREDNESS, *n.* The state of being withered.

WITH'ERING, *ppr.* Fading; becoming dry.

WITH'ERITE, *n.* In *mineralogy*, a carbonate of baryte, first discovered by Dr. Withering; rhomboidal baryte. It is white, gray, or yellow. *Ure. Cyc.*

WITH'ERNAM, *n.* [Sax. *wither*, against, and *naman*, to take.]

In withernam, in law, a second or reciprocal distress, in lieu of a first distress which has been eloigned; reprisal. *Blackstone.*

WITH'ERS, *n.* [This seems to signify a joining, from the root of *with.*] The juncture of the shoulder bones of a horse, at the bottom of the neck. *Far. Dict.*

WITH'ER-WRUNG, *a.* Injured or hurt in the withers, as a horse. *Cyc.*

WITHHELD', *pret.* and *pp.* of *withhold.*

WITHHOLD, *v. t.* pret. and pp. *withheld.* [*with* and *hold.*]

1. To hold back; to restrain; to keep from action.
   Withhold—your hasty hand. *Spenser.*
   If our passions may be *withheld.* *Kettlewell.*
2. To retain; to keep back; not to grant; as, to *withhold* assent to a proposition. The sun does not *withhold* his light.

WITHHOLDEN, *pp.* The old participle of *withhold;* now obsolete. We use *withheld.*

WITHHOLDER, *n.* One that withholds.

WITHHOLDING, *ppr.* Holding back; restraining; retaining; not granting.

WITHIN', *prep.* [Sax. *withinnan.*] In the inner part; as the space *within* the walls of a house; a man contented and happy *within* himself. *Tillotson.*

2. In the limits or compass of; not beyond; used of place and time. The object is *within* my sight; *within* the knowledge of the present generation; *within* a month or a year.
3. Not reaching to any thing external.
   Were every action concluded *within* itself— *Locke.*
4. In the compass of; not longer ago than.
   Within these five hours Hastings liv'd
   Untainted. *Shak.*
5. Not later than; as, *within* five days from this time, it will be fair weather.
6. In the reach of.
   Both he and she are still *within* my pow'r. *Dryden.*
7. Not exceeding. Keep your expenses *within* your income.
8. In the heart or confidence of. [*Inelegant.*] *South.*
9. In the house; in any inclosure.

WITHIN', *adv.* In the inner part; inwardly; internally.
   The wound festers *within.* *Carew.*

2. In the mind.
   Ills from *within* thy reason must prevent. *Dryden.*

WITHINSI'DE, *adv.* [*within* and *side.*] In the inner parts. [*Bad.*] *Sharp.*

WITHOUT', *prep.* [Sax. *withutan;* *with* and *out.*]

1. Not with; as *without* success.
2. In a state of destitution or absence from.
   There is no living with thee nor *without* thee. *Tatler.*
3. In a state of not having, or of destitution. How many live all their life *without* virtue, and *without* peace of conscience.
4. Beyond; not within.
   Eternity, before the world and after, is *without* our reach. *Burnet.*
5. Supposing the negation or omission of.
   Without the separation of the two monarchies, the most advantageous terms from the French must end in our destruction. *Addison.*
6. Independent of; not by the use of. Men like to live *without* labor.
   Wise men will do it *without* a law. *Bacon.*
7. On the outside of; as *without* the gate; *without* doors.

8. With exemption from. That event cannot happen *without* great damage to our interests.

9. Unless; except.

Without, when it precedes a sentence or member of a sentence, has been called a conjunction. This is a mistake. "You will not enjoy health, *without* you use much exercise." In this sentence, *without* is a preposition still, but followed by a member of a sentence, instead of a single noun. It has no property of a connective or conjunction, and does not fall within the definition. You will not enjoy health, this fact following being removed, or not taking place; *you use exercise*. This use of *without*, is nearly superseded by *unless* and *except*, among good writers and speakers; but is common in popular discourse or parlance.

WITHOUT', *adv.* Not on the inside; not within.

These were from *without* the growing miseries. *Milton.*

2. Out of doors.

3. Externally; not in the mind.

Without were fightings, within were fears. 2 Cor. vii.

WITHOUT'EN, for *withoutan*, the Saxon word, is obsolete. *Spenser.*

WITHSTAND', *v. t.* [*with* and *stand*. See *Stand.*]

To oppose; to resist, either with physical or moral force; as, to *withstand* the attack of troops; to *withstand* eloquence or arguments.

When Peter was come to Antioch, I *withstood* him to his face. Gal. ii.

WITHSTAND'ER, *n.* One that opposes; an opponent; a resisting power. *Raleigh.*

WITHSTAND'ING, *ppr.* Opposing; making resistance.

WITH-VINE, } *n.* A local name for the
WITH-WINE, } couch-grass. *Cyc.*

WITH'WIND, *n.* A plant. [L. *convolvulus.*]

WITH'Y, *n.* [Sax. *withig.*] A large species of willow. *Cyc.*

WITH'Y, *a.* Made of withs; like a with; flexible and tough.

WIT'LESS, *a.* [*wit* and *less.*] Destitute of wit or understanding; inconsiderate; wanting thought; as a *witless* swain; *witless* youth. *Philips.*

2. Indiscrete; not under the guidance of judgment; as *witless* bravery. *Shak.*

WIT'LESSLY, *adv.* Without the exercise of judgment.

WIT'LING, *n.* [*dim.* from *wit.*] A person who has little wit or understanding; a pretender to wit or smartness.

A beau and *witling* perish'd in the throng. *Pope.*

WIT'NESS, *n.* [Sax. *witnesse*, from *witan*, to know.]

1. Testimony; attestation of a fact or event.

If I bear *witness* of myself, my *witness* is not true. John v.

2. That which furnishes evidence or proof.

Laban said, this heap is a *witness* between me and thee this day. Gen. xxxi.

3. A person who knows or sees any thing; one personally present; as, he was *witness*; he was an eye-*witness*. 1 Pet. v.

4. One who sees the execution of an instrument, and subscribes it for the purpose of confirming its authenticity by his testimony.

5. One who gives testimony; as, the *witnesses* in court agreed in all essential facts.

With a witness, effectually; to a great degree; with great force, so as to leave some mark as a testimony behind. He struck *with a witness*. [*Not elegant.*]

WIT'NESS, *v. t.* To see or know by personal presence. I *witnessed* the ceremonies in New York, with which the ratification of the constitution was celebrated, in 1788.

2. To attest; to give testimony to; to testify to something.

Behold, how many things they *witness* against thee. Mark xv.

3. To see the execution of an instrument, and subscribe it for the purpose of establishing its authenticity; as, to *witness* a bond or a deed.

WIT'NESS, *v. i.* To bear testimony.

The men of Belial *witnessed* against him, even against Naboth. 1 Kings xxi.

2. To give evidence.

The shew of their countenance doth *witness* against them. Is. iii.

WIT'NESSED, *pp.* Seen in person; testified; subscribed by persons present; as a deed *witnessed* by two persons.

WIT'NESSING, *ppr.* Seeing in person; bearing testimony; giving evidence.

WIT'-SNAPPER, *n.* [*wit* and *snap.*] One who affects repartee. [*Not in use.*] *Shak.*

WIT'-ST'ARVED, *a.* Barren of wit; destitute of genius. *Examiner.*

WIT'TED, *a.* Having wit or understanding; as a quick *witted* boy.

WIT'TICISM, *n.* [from *wit.*] A sentence or phrase which is affectedly witty; a low kind of wit.

—He is full of conceptions, points of epigram, and *witticisms;* all which are below the dignity of heroic verse. *Addison.*

WIT'TILY, *adv.* [from *wit.*] With wit; with a delicate turn or phrase, or with an ingenious association of ideas. *Sidney.*

2. Ingeniously; cunningly; artfully.

Who his own harm so *wittily* contrives. *Dryden.*

WIT'TINESS, *n.* [from *witty.*] The quality of being witty. *Spenser.*

WIT'TINGLY, *adv.* [See *Wit.*] Knowingly; with knowledge; by design.

He knowingly and *wittingly* brought evil into the world. *More.*

WIT'TOL, *n.* [Sax. from *witan*, to know.] A man who knows his wife's infidelity and submits to it; a tame cuckold. *Shak.*

WIT'TOLLY, *adv.* Like a tame cuckold. *Shak.*

WIT'TY, *a.* [from *wit.*] Possessed of wit; full of wit; as a *witty* poet.

2. Judicious; ingenious; inventive.

3. Sarcastic; full of taunts.

Honeycomb was unmercifully *witty* upon the women. *Spectator.*

WIT'WALL, *n.* A bird, the great spotted woodpecker. *Ainsworth. Cyc.*

WIT'-WŎRM, *n.* [*wit* and *worm.*] One that feeds on wit. [*Not in use.*] *B. Jonson.*

WIVE, *v. i.* [from *wife.*] To marry. [*Not in use.*] *Shak.*

WIVE, *v. t.* To match to a wife. *Shak.*

2. To take for a wife. [*Not in use.*] *Shak.*

WI'VEHOOD, *n.* Behavior becoming a wife. [It should be *wifehood.*] *Obs.* *Spenser.*

WI'VELESS, *a.* Not having a wife. [It should be *wifeless.*]

WI'VELY, *a.* Pertaining to a wife. [It should be *wifely.*] *Sidney.*

WI'VER, } *n.* A kind of heraldric dra-
WIV'ERIN, } gon. *Thynne.*

WIVES, *plu.* of *wife*

WIZ'ARD, *n.* [from *wise.*] A conjurer; an enchanter; a sorcerer. Lev. xx.

The wily *wizard* must be caught. *Dryden.*

WIZ'ARD, *a.* Enchanting; charming. *Collins.*

2. Haunted by wizards. *Milton.*

WIZ'EN, *v. i.* [Sax. *wisnian, weosnian.*] To wither; to dry. [*Local.*]

WO, *n.* [Sax. *wa;* L. *væ;* Gr. *ουαι*; W. *gwae;* G. *weh;* D. *wee;* Sw. *ve.*]

1. Grief; sorrow; misery; a heavy calamity.

One *wo* is past; and behold, there come two *woes* more hereafter. Rev. ix.

They weep each other's *wo.* *Pope.*

2. A curse.

Can there be a *wo* or curse in all the stores of vengeance, equal to the malignity of such a practice? *South.*

3. *Wo* is used in denunciation, and in exclamations of sorrow.

Wo is me; for I am undone. Is. vi.

This is properly the Saxon dative, "*wo* is *to* me."

"*Wo worth* the day." This is also the dative; *wo be to* the day; Sax. *wurthan, weorthan* or *wyrthan*, to be, to become.

Wo is a noun, and if used as an adjective, it is improperly used. "*Wo* to you that are rich." "*Wo* to that man, by whom the offense cometh;" that is, misery, calamity, be or will be to him.

WŌAD, *n.* [Sax. *wad* or *waad;* G. *waid, weid;* D. *weede;* Fr. *guede;* It. *guado.* Qu. *weed.*]

A plant of the genus Isatis, cultivated for the use of dyers. The woad blue is a very deep blue, and is the base of many other colors or shades of color. Woad is first bruised in a mill, and then made into balls. It grows wild in France and along the coasts of the Baltic. The term *woad* is applied to the Reseda, weld or wold, and to the *Genista tinctoria* or dyer's broom. *Cyc.*

WŌAD-MILL, *n.* A mill for bruising and preparing woad.

WO'BEGONE, *a.* [*wo, be*, and *gone.*] Overwhelmed with wo; immersed in grief and sorrow.

So *wobegone* was he with pains of love. *Fairfax.*

WODA'NIUM, *n.* A metal recently discovered in a species of pyrite, found in Hungary, which had been supposed to be an ore of cobalt. It has a bronze yellow color. *Cyc.*

WOESŎME, *a. wo'sum.* Woful. [*Not in use.*] *Langhorne.*

WOFT, for *waft.* [*Not in use.*] *Shak.*

WO'FUL, *a.* Sorrowful; distressed with grief or calamity; afflicted.

How many *woful* widows left to bow
To sad disgrace! *Daniel.*

2. Sorrowful; mournful; full of distress; as *woful* day. Jer. xvii.

3. Bringing calamity, distress or affliction; as a *woful* event; *woful* want.
4. Wretched; paltry.

What *woful* stuff this madrigal would be. *Pope.*

WO'FULLY, *adv.* Sorrowfully; mournfully; in a distressing manner.
2. Wretchedly; extremely; as, he will be *wofully* deceived.

WO'FULNESS, *n.* Misery; calamity.

WOLD, in Saxon, is the same as *wald* and *weald*, a wood, sometimes perhaps a lawn or plain. *Wald* signifies also power, dominion, from *waldan*, to rule. These words occur in names.

WOLF, *n.* WULF. [Sax. *wulf*; G. D. *wolf*; Sw. *ulf*; Dan. *ulv*; Russ. *volk*; L. *vulpes*, a fox, the same word differently applied. The Gr. is αλωπηξ.]
1. An animal of the genus Canis, a beast of prey that kills sheep and other small domestic animals; called sometimes the wild dog. The wolf is crafty, greedy and ravenous.
2. A small white worm or maggot, which infests granaries. *Cyc.*
3. An eating ulcer. *Brown.*

WOLF-DOG, *n.* A dog of a large breed, kept to guard sheep. *Tickel.*
2. A dog supposed to be bred between a dog and a wolf. *Johnson.*

WOLF-FISH, *n.* A fish, the *lupus marinus*, (the *Anarrhichas lupus* of Linne;) a fierce voracious fish of the northern seas. *Cyc.*

WOLF'ISH, *a.* Like a wolf; having the qualities or form of a wolf; as a *wolfish* visage; *wolfish* designs. *Shak.*

WOLF'-NET, *n.* A kind of net used in fishing, which takes great numbers. *Cyc.*

WOL'FRAM, *n.* In *mineralogy*, an ore of tungsten. Its color is generally a brownish or grayish black; when cut with a knife, it gives a reddish brown streak. It occurs massive and crystalized, and in concentric lamellar concretions. *Cyc.*

WOLF'S-BANE, *n.* A poisonous plant of the genus Aconitum; aconite.
2. The winter aconite, or Helleborus hyemalis. *Lee.*

WOLF'S-CLAW, *n.* A plant of the genus Lycopodium. *Lee.*

WOLF'S-MILK, *n.* An herb. *Ainsworth.*

WOLF'S-PEACH, *n.* A plant of the genus Solanum, *(S. lycopersicum.)* *Lee.*

WOL'VERIN, **WOLVERE'NE**, } *n.* The glutton, a carnivorous animal of voracious appetite. *Dict. Nat. Hist.*

The name *wolverene* is applied to an animal of N. America, considered by Linne as a peculiar species, *(Ursus luscus,)* but which has been since regarded as a variety of the glutton, *(U. gulo.)* *Ed. Encyc.*

WOLV'ISH, *a.* More properly *wolfish*, which see.

WÖMAN, *n.* plu. *women.* [a compound of *womb* and *man*. It is the same word as L. *fœmina*; the Latins writing *f* for *w*. The plural as written, seems to be *womb-men.* But we pronounce it *wimen*, and so it ought to be written, for it is from the Saxon *wifman*, wife-man.]
1. The female of the human race, grown to adult years.

And the rib, which the Lord God had taken from the man, made he a *woman.* Gen. ii.

Women are soft, mild, pitiful, and flexible. *Shak.*

We see every day *women* perish with infamy, by having been too willing to set their beauty to show. *Rambler.*

I have observed among all nations that the *women* ornament themselves more than the men; that wherever found, they are the same kind, civil, obliging, humane, tender beings, inclined to be gay and cheerful, timorous and modest. *Ledyard.*

2. A female attendant or servant. *Shak.*

WÖMAN, *v. t.* To make pliant. *Shak.*

WÖMANED, *a.* Accompanied or united with a woman. [*Not used.*] *Shak.*

WÖMAN-HATER, *n.* [*woman* and *hater.*] One who has an aversion to the female sex. *Swift.*

WÖMANHOOD, *n.* [*woman* and *hood.*] The state, character or collective qualities of a woman. *Spenser.*

WÖMANISE, *v. t.* To make effeminate. [*Not used.*]

WÖMANISH, *a.* Suitable to a woman; having the qualities of a woman; feminine; as *womanish* habits; *womanish* tears; a *womanish* voice. *Dryden. Shak.*

WÖMANKIND, *n.* [*woman* and *kind.*] The female sex; the race of females of the human kind. *Addison.*

WÖMANLY, *a.* Becoming a woman; feminine; as *womanly* behavior. *Arbuthnot.*

A blushing *womanly* discovering grace. *Donne.*

WÖMANLY, *adv.* In the manner of a woman.

WÖMB, *n.* woom. [Sax. *wamb*; Goth. *wamba*; Sw. *våmb*; Dan. *vom*; Scot. *wame*; G. *wampe*, belly, a dewlap; D. *wam.*]
1. The uterus or matrix of a female; that part where the young of an animal is conceived and nourished till its birth. *Cyc.*
2. The place where any thing is produced.

The *womb* of earth the genial seed receives. *Dryden.*

3. Any large or deep cavity. *Addison.*

Womb of the morning, in Scripture, the clouds, which distill dew; supposed to be emblematic of the church bringing forth multitudes to Christ. Ps. cx.

WÖMB, *v. t.* To inclose; to breed in secret. [*Not in use.*] *Shak.*

WOM'BAT, *n.* An animal of New Holland, of the opossum family. *Cyc.*

WÖMBY, *a.* woom'y. Capacious. [*Not in use.*] *Shak.*

WOMEN, *n. plu.* of *woman.* pron. *wim'en.* But it is supposed the word we pronounce is from Sax. *wifman*, and therefore should be written *wimen.*

WŎN, *pret.* and *pp.* of *win*; as victories *won.*

WŎN, **WONE**, } *v. i.* [Sax. *wunian*; G. *wohnen*; D. *woonen*, to dwell, to continue; Ir. *fanaim.*]
To dwell; to abide. *Obs.* Its participle is retained in *wont*, that is, *woned.* *Milton.*

WŎN, *n.* A dwelling. *Obs.* *Spenser.*

WŎNDER, *n.* [Sax. G. *wunder*; D. *wonder*; Sw. Dan. *under*; qu. Gr. φαινω, to show; and hence a sight; or from the root of the Sp. *espanto*, a panic.]
1. That emotion which is excited by novelty, or the presentation to the sight or mind, of something new, unusual, strange, great, extraordinary, or not well understood; something that arrests the attention by its novelty, grandeur or inexplicableness. *Wonder* expresses less than *astonishment*, and much less than *amazement.* It differs from *admiration*, in not being necessarily accompanied with love, esteem or approbation, nor directed to persons. But *wonder* sometimes is nearly allied to *astonishment*, and the exact extent of the meaning of such words can hardly be graduated.

They were filled with *wonder* and amazement. Acts iii.

Wonder is the effect of novelty upon ignorance. *Johnson.*

2. Cause of wonder; that which excites surprise; a strange thing; a prodigy.

To try things oft, and never to give over, doth *wonders.* *Bacon.*

I am as a *wonder* to many. Ps. lxxi.

3. Any thing mentioned with surprise.

Babylon, the *wonder* of all tongues. *Milton.*

Wonders of the world. The seven wonders of the world were the Egyptian pyramids, the mausoleum erected by Artemisia, the temple of Diana at Ephesus, the walls and hanging gardens of Babylon, the colossus at Rhodes, the statue of Jupiter Olympius, and the Pharos or watch-tower of Alexandria.
4. A miracle. Ex. iii.

WONDER, *v. i.* [Sax. *wundrian.*] To be affected by surprise or admiration.

I could not sufficiently *wonder* at the intrepidity of these diminutive mortals. *Swift.*

We cease to *wonder* at what we understand. *Johnson.*

WŎNDERER, *n.* One who wonders.

WŎNDERFUL, *a.* Adapted to excite wonder or admiration; exciting surprise; strange; astonishing. Job xlii.

WŎNDERFULLY, *adv.* In a manner to excite wonder or surprise.

I will praise thee, for I am fearfully and *wonderfully* made. Ps. cxxxix.

WŎNDERFULNESS, *n.* The state or quality of being wonderful. *Sidney.*

WŎNDERING, *ppr.* Indulging or feeling wonder. Gen. xxiv. Luke xxiv.

WŎNDERMENT, *n.* Surprise; astonishment; a wonderful appearance. [*Vulgar.*]

WŎNDERSTRUCK, *a.* [*wonder* and *struck.*] Struck with wonder, admiration and surprise. *Dryden.*

WŎNDER-WŎRKING, *a.* Doing wonders or surprising things.

WŎNDROUS, *a.* Admirable; marvelous; such as may excite surprise and astonishment; strange.

That I may publish with the voice of thanksgiving, and tell of all thy *wondrous* works. Ps. xxvi.

WŎNDROUS, *adv.* In a wonderful or surprising degree; as a place *wondrous* deep; you are *wondrous* fair; *wondrous* fond of peace. These phrases of Cowley, Dryden and Pope, are admissible only in the ludicrous and burlesque style.

WŎNDROUSLY, *adv.* In a strange or wonderful manner or degree.

Chloe complains, and *wondrously's* aggriev'd. *Glanville.*

WŎNT, a contraction of *woll not*, that is, *will not.*

WŎNT, *a.* [*wont* is strictly the participle passive of *won*, *wone*; Sax. *wunian*, to dwell, to remain, to endure, to exist, to consist; G. *wohnen*, D. *woonen*. But the D. has *wennen*, Sw. *vänia*, Dan. *vænner*, to accustom; Ir. *fanaim*, to remain. In English, the verb is obsolete; but we retain the participle in use, and form it into a verb. See the Verb.]

Accustomed; habituated; using or doing customarily.

If the ox were *wont* to push with his horn— Ex. xxi.

They were *wont* to speak in old time, saying— 2 Sam. xx. See Matt. xxvii. 15. Luke xxii. 39.

WŎNT, *n.* Custom; habit; use. *Obs.* *Sidney. Hooker.*

WŎNT, *v. i.* To be accustomed or habituated; to be used.

A yearly solemn feast she *wont* to make. *Spenser.*

Wherewith he *wont* to soar so high. *Obs.* *Waller.*

WŎNTED, *pp.* Accustomed; used.

Again his *wonted* weapon prov'd. *Spenser.*

2. Accustomed; made familiar by use.

She was *wonted* to the place, and would not remove. *L'Estrange.*

WŎNTEDNESS, *n.* The state of being accustomed. *King Charles.*

WŎNTLESS, *a.* Unaccustomed; unused. *Obs.* *Spenser.*

WOO, *v. t.* [Sax. *wogan*, whence *awogod*, wooed.]

1. To court; to solicit in love.

My proud rival *wooes*
Another partner to his throne and bed— *Philips.*

Each, like the Grecian artist, *wooes*
The image he himself has wrought. *Prior.*

2. To court solicitously; to invite with importunity.

Thee, chantress, oft the woods among,
I *woo* to hear thy even song. *Milton.*

WOO, *v. i.* To court; to make love. *Dryden.*

WOOD, *a.* [Sax. *wod.*] Mad; furious. *Obs.* *Spenser.*

WOOD, *n.* [Sax. *wuda, wudu*; D. *woud*; W. *gwyz.*]

1. A large and thick collection of trees; a forest.

Light thickens, and the crow
Makes wing to the rooky *wood.* *Shak.*

2. The substance of trees; the hard substance which composes the body of a tree and its branches, and which is covered by the bark.

3. Trees cut or sawed for the fire. *Wood* is yet the principal fuel in the U. States.

4. An idol. Hab. ii.

WOOD, *v. i.* To supply or get supplies of wood.

WOOD-ANEM'ONE, *n.* A plant. [See *Anemone.*]

WOOD'-ASHES, *n.* [*wood* and *ashes.*] The remains of burnt wood or plants. [This word is used in England to distinguish these ashes from the remains of coal. In the U. States, where wood chiefly is burnt, the people usually say simply *ashes*. But as coal becomes more used, the English distinction will be necessary.]

WOOD'-BIND, } *n.* A name given to the
WOOD'-BINE, } honeysuckle, a species of Lonicera. *Lee.*

WOOD'-BOUND, *a.* [*wood* and *bound.*] Encumbered with tall woody hedgerows.

WOOD'-CHAT, *n.* A species of butcher bird.

WOOD'CHUK, *n.* [*wood* and *chuk*, a hog.] [See *Chuk.*]

The popular name in New England of a species of the Marmot tribe of animals, the *Arctomys monax*. It burrows and is dormant in winter.

WOOD'-COAL, *n.* [*wood* and *coal.*] Charcoal.

WOOD'-COCK, *n.* [*wood* and *cock.*] A fowl of the genus Scolopax, inhabiting the northern parts of the European continent in summer, but frequenting England in winter. The woodcock of the U. States is a smaller species. *Cyc.*

WOOD'-COCK SHELL, *n.* A name given by English naturalists to a peculiar kind of the purpura, called by the French *becasse*; of two species, the prickly and the smooth. *Cyc.*

WOOD'-DRINK, *n.* [*wood* and *drink.*] A decoction or infusion of medicinal woods.

WOOD'ED, *a.* Supplied or covered with wood; as land *wooded* and watered. *Arbuthnot.*

WOOD'EN, *a.* [from *wood.*] Made of wood; consisting of wood; as a *wooden* box; a *wooden* leg; a *wooden* horse.

2. Clumsy; awkward.

When a bold man is put out of countenance, he makes a very *wooden* figure on it. *Collier.*

WOOD-ENGRA'VING, *n.* Xylography; the art of engraving on wood, or of cutting figures of natural objects on wood. *Cyc.*

WOOD'-FRETTER, *n.* [*wood* and *fret.*] An insect or worm that eats wood. *Ainsworth.*

WOOD-HOLE, *n.* [*wood* and *hole.*] A place where wood is laid up. *Philips.*

WOOD-HOUSE, *n.* [*wood* and *house.*] A house or shed in which wood is deposited and sheltered from the weather. *U. States.*

WOOD'ING, *ppr.* Getting or supplying with wood. *Washington.*

WOOD'-LAND, *n.* [*wood* and *land.*] Land covered with wood, or land on which trees are suffered to grow, either for fuel or timber. *America.*

2. In *England*, a soil which, from its humidity and color, resembles the soil in woods. *Cyc.*

WOOD'-L'ARK, *n.* [*wood* and *lark.*] A bird, a species of lark.

WOOD'-LAYER, *n.* [*wood* and *layer.*] A young oak or other timber plant, laid down in a hedge among the white thorn or other plants used in hedges. *Cyc.*

WOOD'LESS, *a.* Destitute of wood. *Mitford.*

WOOD'-LOCK, *n.* [*wood* and *lock.*] In *ship-building*, a piece of elm, close fitted and sheathed with copper, in the throating or score of the pintle, to keep the rudder from rising. *Cyc.*

WOOD'-LOUSE, *n.* [*wood* and *louse.*] An insect, the milleped. *Dict. Nat. Hist.*

WOOD'MAN, *n.* [*wood* and *man.*] A forest officer, appointed to take care of the king's wood. *England.*

2. A sportsman; a hunter. *Milton. Pope.*

WOOD'-MEIL, *n.* A coarse hairy stuff made of Iceland wool, used to line the ports of ships of war. *Cyc.*

WOOD'-MITE, *n.* [*wood* and *mite.*] A small insect found in old wood.

WOOD'-MŎNGER, *n.* [*wood* and *monger.*] A wood seller.

WOOD'-MOTE, *n.* [*wood* and *mote.*] In England, the ancient name of the forest court; now the court of attachment. *Cyc.*

WOOD'NESS, *n.* Anger; madness; rage. *Obs.* *Fisher.*

WOOD'-NIGHTSHADE, *n.* A plant.

WOOD'-NOTE, *n.* [*wood* and *note.*] Wild music.

—Or sweetest Shakspeare, fancy's child,
Warble his native *wood-notes* wild. *Milton.*

WOOD'-NYMPH, *n.* [*wood* and *nymph.*] A fabled goddess of the woods; a dryad.

The *wood-nymphs* deck'd with daisies trim. *Milton.*

WOOD-OF'FERING, *n.* Wood burnt on the altar. Neh. x.

WOOD'PECKER, *n.* [*wood* and *peck.*] A bird of the genus Picus, that pecks holes in trees, or that picks insects from the bark.

WOOD'-PIGEON, *n.* [*wood* and *pigeon.*] The ring-dove, (*Columba palumbus.*) *Ed. Encyc.*

WOOD-PU'CERON, *n.* [*wood* and *puceron.*] A small insect of the puceron kind, of a grayish color, having two hollow horns on the hinder part of its body. It resembles the puceron of the alder, but it penetrates into the wood. *Cyc.*

WOOD'REVE, *n.* [*wood* and *reve.*] In England, the steward or overseer of a wood.

WOOD'-ROOF, } *n.* [*wood* and *roof* or *ruff.*]
WOOD'-RUFF, } A plant of the genus Asperula. *Cyc.*

WOOD'-SAGE, *n.* [*wood* and *sage.*] A plant of the genus Teucrium. *Lee.*

WOOD'-SARE, *n.* A kind of froth seen on herbs. *Bacon.*

WOOD-SEERE, *n.* The time when there is no sap in a tree. *Tusser.*

WOOD'-SHOCK, *n.* The fisher or wejack, a quadruped of the weasel kind in North America.

WOOD'-SOOT, *n.* [*wood* and *soot.*] Soot from burnt wood, which has been found useful as a manure. *Cyc.*

WOOD'-SORREL, *n.* [*wood* and *sorrel.*] A plant of the genus Oxalis. *Lee.*

WOOD'-SPITE, *n.* [*wood* and *spite.*] A name given in some parts of England to the green woodpecker.

WOOD'-STONE, *n.* [*wood* and *stone.*] A blackish gray silicious stone, a subspecies of horn-stone. *Ure.*

WOOD'-WARD, *n.* [*wood* and *ward.*] An officer of the forest, whose duty is to guard the woods. *Cyc. England.*

WOOD'-WASH, *n.* A name sometimes applied to dyer's broom. *Cyc.*

WOOD' WAXEN, *n.* A plant of the genus Genista; dyer's broom. *Fam. of Plants. Lee.*

WOOD'-WŎRM, *n.* [*wood* and *worm.*] A worm that is bred in wood. *Johnson.*

WOOD'Y, *a.* [from *wood.*] Abounding with wood; as *woody* land; a *woody* region.

—Secret shades
Of *woody* Ida's inmost grove. *Milton.*

2. Consisting of wood; ligneous; as the *woody* parts of plants.

3. Pertaining to woods; sylvan; as *woody* nymphs. *Spenser.*

WOO'ER, *n.* [from *woo.*] One who courts, or solicits in love. *Bacon.*
WOOF, *n.* [Sax. *weft*, from *wefan*, to weave; Sw. *väf*; Gr. *υφη*.]
1. The threads that cross the warp in weaving; the weft. *Bacon.*
2. Texture; cloth; as a pall of softest *woof.* *Pope.*
WOO'ING, *ppr.* [from *woo.*] Courting; soliciting in love.
WOO'INGLY, *adv.* Enticingly; with persuasiveness; so as to invite to stay. *Shak.*
WOOL, *n.* [Sax. *wul*; G. *wolle*; D. *wol*; Sw. *ull*; Dan. *uld*; Russ. *volna*; Basque, *ulea.* Qu. Gr. *ουλος*, soft; *ιουλος*, down; or L. *vellus*, from *vello*, to pull off.]
1. That soft species of hair which grows on sheep and some other animals, which in fineness sometimes approaches to fur. The word generally signifies the fleecy coat of the sheep, which constitutes a most essential material of clothing in all cold and temperate climates.
2. Short thick hair.
3. In *botany*, a sort of pubescence, or a clothing of dense curling hairs on the surface of certain plants. *Martyn.*
WOOL'-BALL, *n.* A ball or mass of wool found in the stomach of sheep. *Cyc.*
WOOL'-COMBER, *n.* One whose occupation is to comb wool.
WOOLD, *v. t.* [D. *woelen*, *bewoelen*; G. *wühlen.*]
To wind, particularly to wind a rope round a mast or yard, when made of two or more pieces, at the place where they are fished, for confining and supporting them. *Mar. Dict.*
WOOLD'ED, *pp.* Bound fast with ropes; wound round.
WOOLD'ER, *n.* A stick used in woolding. *Mar. Dict.*
WOOLD'ING, *ppr.* Binding fast with ropes; winding round.
WOOLD'ING, *n.* The act of winding, as a rope round a mast.
2. The rope used for binding masts and spars.
WOOL'-DRIVER, *n.* [*wool* and *driver.*] One who buys wool and carries it to market.
WOOL'EN, *a.* Made of wool; consisting of wool; as *woolen* cloth.
2. Pertaining to wool; as *woolen* manufactures.
WOOL'EN, *n.* Cloth made of wool. *Pope.*
WOOL'EN-DRAPER, *n.* One who deals in woolen goods.
WOOL'FEL, *n.* [*wool* and *fel*, L. *pellis.*] A skin with the wool; a skin from which the wool has not been sheared or pulled. *Davies.*
WOOL'INESS, *n.* [from *woolly.*] The state of being woolly.
WOOL'LY, *a.* Consisting of wool; as a *woolly* covering; a *woolly* fleece. *Dryden.*
2. Resembling wool; as *woolly* hair. *Shak.*
3. Clothed with wool; as *woolly* breeders. *Shak.*
4. In *botany*, clothed with a pubescence resembling wool. *Martyn.*
WOOLLY-PASTINUM, *n.* A name given in the East Indies to a species of red orpiment or arsenic. *Cyc.*

WOOL'PACK, *n.* [*wool* and *pack.*] A pack or bag of wool.
2. Any thing bulky without weight. *Cleaveland.*
WOOL'SACK, *n.* [*wool* and *sack.*] A sack or bag of wool.
2. The seat of the lord chancellor and of the judges in the house of lords. *Eng.*
WOOL'-STAPLE, *n.* [*wool* and *staple.*] A city or town where wool used to be brought to the king's staple for sale.
WOOL-STA'PLER, *n.* One who deals in wool.
WOOL'-TRADE, *n.* [*wool* and *trade.*] The trade in wool.
WOOL'WARD, *adv.* In wool. [*Not in use.*]
WOOL'-WINDER, *n.* [*wool* and *wind.*] A person employed to wind or make up wool into bundles to be packed for sale. *Cyc.*
WOOP, *n.* A bird. [L. *rubicilla.*]
WOOS, *n.* A plant; sea weed.
WOOTS, *n.* Indian steel, a metallic substance imported from the East Indies; valued as the material of edge-tools. It has in combination a minute portion of alumin and silica. *Webster's Manual.*
WŎRD, *n.* [Sax. *word* or *wyrd*; G. *wort*; D. *woord*; Dan. Sw. *ord*; Sans. *wartha.* This word is probably the participle of a root in *Br*, and radically the same as L. *verbum*; Ir. *abairim*, to speak. A *word* is that which is uttered or thrown out.]
1. An articulate or vocal sound, or a combination of articulate and vocal sounds, uttered by the human voice, and by custom expressing an idea or ideas; a single component part of human speech or language. Thus *a* in English is a word; but few words consist of one letter only. Most words consist of two or more letters, as *go, do, shall*, called monosyllables, or of two or more syllables, as *honor, goodness, amiable.*
2. The letter or letters, written or printed, which represent a sound or combination of sounds.
3. A short discourse.

Shall I vouchsafe your worship a *word* or two? *Shak.*

4. Talk; discourse.

Why should calamity be full of *words?* *Shak.*

Be thy *words* severe. *Dryden.*

5. Dispute; verbal contention; as, some *words* grew between us.
6. Language; living speech; oral expression. The message was delivered by *word* of mouth.
7. Promise. He gave me his *word* he would pay me.

Obey thy parents; keep thy *word* justly. *Shak.*

8. Signal; order; command.

Give the *word* through. *Shak.*

9. Account; tidings; message. Bring me *word* what is the issue of the contest.
10. Declaration; purpose expressed.

I know you brave, and take you at your *word.* *Dryden.*

11. Declaration; affirmation.

I desire not the reader should take my *word.* *Dryden.*

12. The Scripture; divine revelation, or any part of it. This is called the *word* of God.
13. Christ. John i.
14. A motto; a short sentence; a proverb. *Spenser.*
A good word, commendation; favorable account.

And gave the harmless fellow *a good word.* *Pope.*

In word, in declaration only.

Let us not love *in word* only, neither in tongue; but in deed and in truth. 1 John iii.

WŎRD, *v. i.* To dispute. [*Little used.*] *L'Estrange.*
WŎRD, *v. t.* To express in words. Take care to *word* ideas with propriety.

The apology for the king is the same, but *worded* with greater deference to that great prince. *Addison.*

WŎRD-CATCHER, *n.* One who cavils at words. *Pope.*
WŎRDED, *pp.* Expressed in words.
WŎRDER, *n.* A speaker. [*Not in use.*] *Whitlock.*
WŎRDINESS, *n.* [from *wordy.*] The state or quality of abounding with words. *Ash.*
WŎRDING, *ppr.* Expressing in words.
WŎRDING, *n.* The act of expressing in words.
2. The manner of expressing in words. The *wording* of the ideas is very judicious.
WŎRDISH, *a.* Respecting words. [*Not used.*] *Sidney.*
WŎRDISHNESS, *n.* Manner of wording. [*Not used.*]
WŎRDLESS, *a.* Not using words; not speaking; silent. *Shak.*
WŎRDY, *a.* Using many words; verbose; as a *wordy* speaker; a *wordy* orator. *Spectator.*
2. Containing many words; full of words.

We need not lavish hours in *wordy* periods. *Philips.*

WORE, *pret.* of *wear.* He *wore* gloves.
WORE, *pret.* of *ware.* They *wore* ship.
WŎRK, *v. i.* pret. and pp. *worked* or *wrought.* [Sax. *weorcan*, *wircan*, *wyrcan*; Goth. *waurkyan*; D. *werken*; G. *wirken*; Sw. *virka*, *verka*; Dan. *virker*; Gr. *εργαζομαι.*]
1. In *a general sense*, to move, or to move one way and the other; to perform; as in popular language it is said, a mill or machine *works* well.
2. To labor; to be occupied in performing manual labor, whether severe or moderate. One man *works* better than another; one man *works* hard; another *works* lazily.
3. To be in action or motion; as the *working* of the heart. *Shak.*
4. To act; to carry on operations.

Our better part remains
To *work* in close design. *Milton.*

5. To operate; to carry on business; to be customarily engaged or employed in. Some *work* in the mines, others in the loom, others at the anvil.

They that *work* in fine flax. Is. xix.

6. To ferment; as, unfermented liquors *work* violently in hot weather.
7. To operate; to produce effects by action or influence.

All things *work* together for good to them that love God. Rom. viii.

This so *wrought* upon the child, that afterwards he desired to be taught. *Locke.*

8. To obtain by diligence. [*Little used.*] *Shak.*

9. To act or operate on the stomach and bowels; as a cathartic.

10. To labor; to strain; to move heavily; as, a ship *works* in a tempest.

11. To be tossed or agitated.

Confus'd with *working* sands and rolling waves. *Addison.*

12. To enter by working; as, to *work* into the earth.

To work on, to act on; to influence.

To work up, to make way.

Body shall *up* to spirit *work*. *Milton.*

To work to windward, among seamen, to sail or ply against the wind; to beat. *Mar. Dict.*

WŎRK, *v. t.* To move; to stir and mix; as, to *work* mortar.

2. To form by labor; to mold, shape or manufacture; as, to *work* wood or iron into a form desired, or into an utensil; to *work* cotton or wool into cloth.

3. To bring into any state by action. A foul stream, or new wine or cider, *works* itself clear.

4. To influence by acting upon; to manage; to lead.

And *work* your royal father to his ruin. *Philips.*

5. To make by action, labor or violence. A stream *works* a passage or a new channel.

Sidelong he *works* his way. *Milton.*

6. To produce by action, labor or exertion.

We might *work* any effect—only by the unity of nature. *Bacon.*

Each herb he knew, that *works* or good or ill. *Harte.*

7. To embroider; as, to *work* muslin.

8. To direct the movements of, by adapting the sails to the wind; as, to *work* a ship.

9. To put to labor; to exert.

Work every nerve. *Addison.*

10. To cause to ferment, as liquor.

To work out, to effect by labor and exertion.

Work out your own salvation with fear and trembling. Phil. ii.

2. To erase; to efface. [*Not used.*]

3. To solve, as a problem.

To work up, to raise; to excite; as, to *work up* the passions to rage.

The sun that rolls his chariot o'er their heads,
Works up more fire and color in their cheeks. *Addison.*

2. To expend in any work, as materials. They have *worked up* all the stock.

To work double tides, in the language of seamen, to perform the labor of three days in two; a phrase taken from the practice of working by the night tide as well as by the day.

To work into, to make way, or to insinuate; as, to *work* one's self *into* favor or confidence.

To work a passage, among seamen, to pay for a passage by doing duty on board of the ship.

WŎRK, *n.* [Sax. *weorc*; D. G. *werk*; Dan. Sw. *verk*; Gr. εργον.]

1. Labor; employment; exertion of strength; particularly in man, manual labor.

2. State of labor; as, to be at *work*.

3. Awkward performance. What *work* you make!

4. That which is made or done; as good *work*, or bad *work*. *Milton.*

5. Embroidery; flowers or figures wrought with the needle.

6. Any fabric or manufacture.

7. The matter on which one is at work. In rising she dropped her *work*.

8. Action; deed; feat; achievment; as the *works* of bloody Mars. *Pope.*

9. Operation.

As to the composition or dissolution of mixed bodies, which is the chief *work* of elements— *Digby.*

10. Effect; that which proceeds from agency.

Fancy
Wild *work* produces oft, and most in dreams. *Milton.*

11. Management; treatment. *Shak.*

12. That which is produced by mental labor; a composition; a book; as the *works* of Addison.

13. *Works*, in the plural, walls, trenches and the like, made for fortifications.

14. In *theology*, moral duties or external performances, as distinct from *grace*.

To set to work, } to employ; to engage in
To set on work, } any business. *Hooker.*

WŎRKED, *pp.* Moved; labored; performed; managed; fermented.

WŎRKER, *n.* One that works; one that performs.

WŎRK-FELLŎW, *n.* One engaged in the same work with another. Rom. xvi.

WŎRK-FŌLK, *n.* Persons that labor. *Obs.* *Beaum.*

WŎRKHOUSE, } *n.* A house where
WŎRKING-HOUSE, } any manufacture is carried on.

2. Generally, a house in which idle and vicious persons are confined to labor.

WŎRKING, *ppr.* Moving; operating; laboring; fermenting.

WŎRKING, *n.* Motion; the act of laboring. *Shak.*

2. Fermentation. *Bacon.*

3. Movement; operation; as the *workings* of fancy.

WŎRKING-DAY, *n.* [*work* and *day.*] Any day of the week, except the sabbath.

WŎRKMAN, *n.* [*work* and *man.*] Any man employed in labor, whether in tillage or manufactures.

2. By way of eminence, a skillful artificer or laborer.

WŎRKMANLIKE, *a.* Skillful; well performed.

WŎRKMANLY, *a.* Skillful; well performed.

WŎRKMANLY, *adv.* In a skillful manner; in a manner becoming a workman. *Tusser.*

WŎRKMANSHIP, *n.* Manufacture; something made, particularly by manual labor. Ex. xxxi.

2. That which is effected, made or produced. Eph. ii.

3. The skill of a workman; or the execution or manner of making any thing. The *workmanship* of this cloth is admirable.

4. The art of working. *Woodward.*

WŎRK'MASTER, *n.* [*work* and *master.*] The performer of any work. *Spenser.*

WŎRKSHOP, *n.* [*work* and *shop.*] A shop where any manufacture is carried on.

WŎRK'WŎMAN, *n.* A woman who performs any work; or one skilled in needle work. *Spenser.*

WŎRLD, *n.* [Sax. *weorold*, *woruld*; D. *waereld*; Sw. *verld*. This seems to be a compound word, and probably is named from roundness, the vault; but this is not certain.]

1. The universe; the whole system of created globes or vast bodies of matter.

2. The earth; the terraqueous globe; sometimes called the *lower world*.

3. The heavens; as when we speak of the heavenly *world*, or upper *world*.

4. System of beings; or the orbs which occupy space, and all the beings which inhabit them. Heb. xi.

God—hath in these last days spoken to us by his Son, whom he hath appointed heir of all things; by whom also he made the *worlds*. Heb. i.

There may be other *worlds*, where the inhabitants have never violated their allegiance to their Almighty sovereign. *W. B. Sprague.*

5. Present state of existence; as while we are in the *world*.

Behold, these are the ungodly who prosper in the *world*. Ps. lxxiii.

6. A secular life. By the *world* we sometimes understand the things of this world, its pleasures and interests. A great part of mankind are more anxious to enjoy the *world* than to secure divine favor.

7. Public life, or society; as banished from the *world*. *Shak.*

8. Business or trouble of life.

From this *world*-wearied flesh. *Shak.*

9. A great multitude or quantity; as a *world* of business; a *world* of charms. *Milton.*

10. Mankind; people in general; *in an indefinite sense*. Let the *world* see your fortitude.

Whose disposition, all the *world* well knows— *Shak.*

11. Course of life. He begins the *world* with little property, but with many friends.

12. Universal empire.

This through the east just vengeance hurl'd,
And lost poor Antony the *world*. *Prior.*

13. The customs and manners of men; the practice of life. A knowledge of the *world* is necessary for a man of business; it is essential to politeness.

14. All the world contains.

Had I a thousand *worlds*, I would give them all for one year more to devote to God. *Law.*

15. The principal nations or countries of the earth. Alexander conquered the *world*.

16. The Roman empire. *Scripture.*

17. A large tract of country; a wide compass of things.

I must descry new *worlds*. *Cowley.*

18. The inhabitants of the earth; the whole human race. John iii.

19. The carnal state or corruption of the earth; as the present evil *world*; the course of this *world*. Gal. i. Eph. ii.

20. The ungodly part of the world.

I pray not for the *world*, but for them that thou hast given me. John xvii.

21. Time; as in the phrase, *world* without end.

22. A collection of wonders. [*Not in use.*]

In the world, in possibility. All the precaution *in the world* would not save him.

For all the world, exactly. [*Little used.*] *Sidney.*

2. For any consideration.

WŎRLDLINESS, *n.* [from *world.*] A predominant passion for obtaining the good things of this life; covetousness; addictedness to gain and temporal enjoyments.

WŎRLDLING, *n.* A person whose soul is set upon gaining temporal possessions; one devoted to this world and its enjoyments.

If we consider the expectations of futurity, the *worldling* gives up the argument. *Rogers.*

WŎRLDLY, *a.* Secular; temporal; pertaining to this world or life, in contradistinction to the life to come; as *worldly* pleasures; *worldly* affairs; *worldly* estate; *worldly* honor; *worldly* lusts. Tit. ii.

2. Devoted to this life and its enjoyments; bent on gain; as a *worldly* man; a *worldly* mind.

3. Human; common; belonging to the world; as *worldly* actions; *worldly* maxims.

WŎRLDLY, *adv.* With relation to this life.

Subverting *worldly* strong and *worldly* wise
By simply meek. *Milton.*

WŎRLDLY-MINDED, *a.* Devoted to the acquisition of property and to temporal enjoyments.

WŎRLDLY-MINDEDNESS, *n.* A predominating love and pursuit of this world's goods, to the exclusion of piety and attention to spiritual concerns.

WŎRM, *n.* [Sax. *wyrm*; G. *wurm*; D. *worm*; Dan. *orm*; Sw. *id.* a serpent. This word is probably named from a winding motion, and the root of *swarm.*]

1. In *common usage*, any small creeping animal, or reptile, either entirely without feet, or with very short ones, including a great variety of animals of different classes and orders, viz. certain small serpents, as the blind-worm or slow-worm; the larvas of insects, viz. grubs, caterpillars and maggots, as the wood-worm, canker-worm, silk-worm, (the larva of a moth *(Phalæna,)* which spins the filaments of which silk is made,) the grub that injures corn, grass, &c., the worms that breed in putrid flesh, the bots in the stomach of horses, and many others; certain wingless insects, as the glow-worm; the intestinal worms, or such as breed in the cavities and organs of living animals, as the tape-worm, the round-worm, the fluke, &c.; and numerous animals found in the earth, and in water, particularly in the sea, as the earth-worm or *lumbricus*, the hair-worm or *gordius*, the *teredo*, or worm that bores into the bottom of ships, &c. *Worms*, in the plural, in common usage, is used for intestinal worms, or those which breed in the stomach and bowels, particularly the round and thread worms, *(lumbrici* and *ascarides,)* which are often found there in great numbers; as we say, a child has *worms.*

2. In *zoology*, the term *Vermes* or *worms* has been applied to different divisions of invertebral animals, by different naturalists. Linne's class of *Vermes*, includes the following orders, viz. *Intestina*, including the proper intestinal worms, the earth-worm, the hair-worm, the *teredo*, and some other marine worms; *Mollusca*, including the slug, and numerous soft animals inhabiting the water, particularly the sea; *Testacea*, including all the proper shell-fish; *Zoophyta*, or compound animals, including corals, polypes, and spunges; and *Infusoria*, or simple microscopic animalcules. His character of the class is, —— spiracles obscure, jaws various, organs of sense usually tentacula, no brain, ears nor nostrils, limbs wanting, frequently hermaphrodite. This class includes all the invertebral animals, except the insects and *crustacea*. The term *Vermes* has been since greatly limited, particularly by the French naturalists. Lamarck confined it to the intestinal worms, and some others, whose organization is equally imperfect. The character of his class is, suboviparous, body soft, highly reproductive, undergo no metamorphosis; no eyes, nor articulated limbs, nor radiated disposition of internal organs. *Linne. Cyc.*

3. Remorse; that which incessantly gnaws the conscience; that which torments.

Where their *worm* dieth not. Mark ix.

4. A being debased and despised.

I am a *worm*, and no man. Ps. xxii.

5. A spiral instrument or iron screw, used for drawing wads and cartridges from cannon or small arms.

6. Something spiral, vermiculated, or resembling a worm; as the threads of a screw. *Moxon.*

7. In *chimistry* and *distilleries*, a spiral leaden pipe placed in a tub of water, through which the vapor passes in distillation, and in which it is cooled and condensed. It is called also a *serpentine.*

8. A small worm-like ligament situated beneath a dog's tongue. *Cyc.*

WŎRM, *v. i.* To work slowly, gradually and secretly.

When debates and fretting jealousy
Did *worm* and work within you more and more,
Your color faded. *Herbert.*

WŎRM, *v. t.* To expel or undermine by slow and secret means.

They find themselves *wormed* out of all power. *Swift.*

2. To cut something, called a worm, from under the tongue of a dog. *Cyc.*

3. To draw the wad or cartridge from a gun; to clean by the worm.

4. To wind a rope spirally round a cable, between the strands; or to wind a smaller rope with spun yarn. *Mar. Dict.*

To worm one's self into, to enter gradually by arts and insinuations; as *to worm one's self into* favor.

WŎRM-EATEN, *a.* [*worm* and *eat.*] Gnawed by worms; as *worm-eaten* boards, planks or timber.

2. Old; worthless. *Raleigh.*

WŎRMED, *pp.* Cleared by a worm or screw.

WŎRM-GRASS, *n.* A plant of the genus Spigalia.

WŎRMING, *ppr.* Entering by insinuation; drawing, as a cartridge; clearing, as a gun.

WŎRMLIKE, *a.* Resembling a worm; spiral; vermicular.

WŎRM-POWDER, *n.* A powder used for expelling worms from the stomach and intestines.

WŎRM-SEED, *n.* A seed which has the property of expelling worms from the stomach, bowels and intestines. It is said to be brought from Persia, and to be the produce of a species of Artemisia. *Cyc.*

2. A plant of the genus Chenopodium. *Lee.*

WŎRM-TINCTURE, *n.* A tincture prepared from earth-worms dried, pulverized and mixed with oil of tartar, spirit of wine, saffron and castor. *Cyc.*

WŎRMWOOD, *n.* [Sax. *wermod*; G. *wermuth.*]

A plant, the *artemisia.* It has a bitter nauseous taste; but it is stomachic and corroborant. *Cyc.*

Tree-wormwood, a species of Artemisia, with woody stalks. *Cyc.*

WŎRMWOOD-FLY, *n.* A small black fly, found on the stalks of wormwood. *Cyc.*

WŎRMY, *a.* Containing a worm; abounding with worms.

2. Earthy; groveling.

WŎRN, *pp.* of *wear*; as a garment long *worn.*

Worn out, consumed or rendered useless by wearing.

WOR'NIL, *n.* A maggot that infests the backs of cows. *Derham.*

WOR'RAL, *n.* An animal of the lizard kind, about four feet long and eight inches broad, with a forked tongue. It feeds on flies, and is harmless. It is found in Egypt. *Pococke. Cyc.*

WŎRRIED, *pp.* [from *worry.*] Harassed; fatigued.

WŎRRIER, *n.* [from *worry.*] One that worries or harasses.

WŎRRY, *v. t.* [Sax. *werig*, malign, vexatious; *werigan*, *werian*, to disturb, to tease, to harass, to *weary*; or Dan. *uroe*, trouble, Sw. *oro.* The sense of *tearing* does not properly belong to this word. It may have that sense as secondary.]

1. To tease; to trouble; to harass with importunity, or with care and anxiety. Persons are often *worried* with care and solicitude.

Let them rail
And then *worry* one another at their pleasure. *Rowe.*

Worry him out till he gives his consent. *Swift.*

A church *worried* with reformation. *South.*

2. To fatigue; to harass with labor; *a popular sense of the word.*

3. To harass by pursuit and barking; as, dogs *worry* sheep.

4. To tear; to mangle with the teeth.

5. To vex; to persecute brutally.

WŎRRYING, *ppr.* Teasing; troubling; harassing; fatiguing; tearing.

WŎRSE, *a.* [Sax. *wærse, wyrse*; Dan. *verre*; Sw. *värre.* This adjective has the signification of the comparative degree, and as *bad* has no comparative and superlative, *worse* and *worst* are used in lieu of them, although radically they have no relation to *bad.*]

1. More evil; more bad or ill; more depraved and corrupt; *in a moral sense.*

Evil men and seducers shall wax *worse* and *worse.* 2 Tim. iii.

There are men who seem to believe they are not bad, while another can be found *worse.* *Rambler.*

2. In *a physical sense*, in regard to health, more sick.

She was nothing bettered, but rather grew *worse.* Mark v.

3. More bad; less perfect or good. This carriage is *worse* for wear.

The worse, the loss; the disadvantage.

Judah was put to *the worse* before Israel. 2 Kings xiv.

2. Something less good. Think not *the worse* of him for his enterprise.

WORSE, *adv.* In a manner more evil or bad.

We will deal *worse* with thee than with them. Gen. xix.

WORSE, to put to disadvantage, is not in use. [See *Worst.*] *Milton.*

WORSEN, *v. t.* To worse. [*Not in use.*] *Milton.*

WORSER, is a vulgar word, and not used in good writing or speaking.

WORSHIP, *n.* [Sax. *weorthscype*; *worth* and *ship*; the state of worth or worthiness. See *Worth.*]

1. Excellence of character; dignity; worth; worthiness.

—Elfin born of noble state,
And muckle *worship* in his native land. *Spenser.*

In this sense, the word is nearly or quite obsolete; but hence,

2. A title of honor, used in addresses to certain magistrates and others of respectable character.

My father desires your *worship's* company. *Shak.*

3. A term of ironical respect. *Pope.*

4. *Chiefly* and *eminently*, the act of paying divine honors to the Supreme Being; or the reverence and homage paid to him in religious exercises, consisting in adoration, confession, prayer, thanksgiving and the like.

The *worship* of God is an eminent part of religion. *Tillotson.*
Prayer is a chief part of religious *worship.* *Ibm.*

5. The homage paid to idols or false gods by pagans; as the *worship* of Isis.

6. Honor; respect; civil deference.

Then shalt thou have *worship* in the presence of them that sit at meat with thee. Luke xiv.

7. Idolatry of lovers; obsequious or submissive respect. *Shak.*

WORSHIP, *v. t.* To adore; to pay divine honors to; to reverence with supreme respect and veneration.

Thou shalt *worship* no other God. Ex. xxxiv.
Adore and *worship* God supreme. *Milton.*

2. To respect; to honor; to treat with civil reverence.

Nor *worship'd* with a waxen epitaph. *Shak.*

3. To honor with extravagant love and extreme submission; as a lover.

With bended knees I daily *worship* her. *Carew.*

WORSHIP, *v. i.* To perform acts of adoration.

2. To perform religious service.

Our fathers *worshiped* in this mountain. John iv.

WORSHIPED, *pp.* Adored; treated with divine honors; treated with civil respect.

WORSHIPER, *n.* One who worships; one who pays divine honors to any being; one who adores. *South.*

WORSHIPFUL, *a.* Claiming respect; worthy of honor from its character or dignity.

This is *worshipful* society. *Shak.*

2. A term of respect, sometimes ironically.

WORSHIPFULLY, *adv.* Respectfully. *Shak.*

WORSHIPING, *ppr.* Adoring; paying divine honors to; treating with supreme reverence; treating with extreme submission.

WORST, *a.* [*superl.* of *worse*, which see.]

1. Most bad; most evil; *in a moral sense*; as the *worst* man; the *worst* sinner.

2. Most severe or dangerous; most difficult to heal; as the *worst* disease.

3. Most afflictive, pernicious or calamitous; as the *worst* evil that can befall a state or an individual.

WORST, *n.* The most evil state; *in a moral sense.*

2. The most severe or aggravated state; the highth; as, the disease is at the *worst.*

3. The most calamitous state. Be armed against the *worst.*

WORST, *v. t.* To get the advantage over in contest; to defeat; to overthrow. It is madness to contend, when we are sure to be *worsted.*

WORSTED, *pp.* Defeated; overthrown.

WORSTED, *n.* WUST'ED. [The origin of this word is uncertain. It is usually supposed to take its name from a town in England or in Flanders: but in Norman, *worstetz* is mentioned; as *lit de worstetz*, a bed of *worsted.*]

Yarn spun from combed wool; a particular kind of woolen yarn.

WORST'ED, *a.* Consisting of worsted; made of worsted yarn; as *worsted* stockings.

WORT, *n.* [Sax. *wyrt*; G. *wurz*; Sw. *ort*; Dan. *urt*; Fr. *vert, verd*; from the root of L. *vireo*, to grow; *viridis*, green.]

1. A plant; an herb; now used chiefly or wholly in compounds; as in *mugwort, liverwort, spleenwort.*

2. A plant of the cabbage kind.

3. New beer unfermented, or in the act of fermentation; the sweet infusion of malt. *Bacon. Cyc.*

WORTH, a termination, signifies a farm or court; as in *Wordsworth.*

WORTH, *v. i.* [Sax. *weorthan*, to be.] This verb is now used only in the phrases, wo *worth* the day, wo *worth* the man, &c., in which the verb is in the imperative mode, and the noun in the dative; wo *be to* the day.

WORTH, *n.* [Sax. *weorth, wurth, wyrth*; G. *werth*; D. *waarde*; Sw. *vård*; Dan. *værd*; W. *gwerth*; L. *virtus*, from the root of *vireo.* The primary sense is strength.]

1. Value; that quality of a thing which renders it useful, or which will produce an equivalent good in some other thing. The *worth* of a day's labor may be estimated in money, or in wheat. The *worth* of labor is settled between the hirer and the hired. The *worth* of commodities is usually the price they will bring in market; but *price* is not always *worth.*

2. Value of mental qualities; excellence; virtue; usefulness; as a man or magistrate of great *worth.*

As none but she, who in that court did dwell,
Could know such *worth*, or *worth* describe so well. *Waller.*

All *worth* consists in doing good, and in the disposition by which it is done. *Dwight.*

3. Importance; valuable qualities; *applied to things*; as, these things have since lost their *worth.*

WORTH, *a.* Equal in value to. Silver is scarce *worth* the labor of digging and refining. In one country, a day's labor is *worth* a dollar; in another, the same labor is not *worth* fifty cents. It is *worth* while to consider a subject well before we come to a decision.

If your arguments produce no conviction, they are *worth* nothing to me. *Beattie.*

2. Deserving of; in a good or bad sense, but chiefly in a good sense. The castle is *worth* defending.

To reign is *worth* ambition, though in hell. *Milton.*
This is life indeed, life *worth* preserving. *Addison.*

3. Equal in possessions to; having estate to the value of. Most men are estimated by their neighbors to be *worth* more than they are. A man *worth* a hundred thousand dollars in the United States, is called rich; but not so in London or Paris.

Worthiest of blood, an expression in law, denoting the preference of sons to daughters in the descent of estates.

WORTHILY, *adv.* In a manner suited to; as, to walk *worthily* of our extraction. [*Bad.*] *Ray.*

2. Deservedly; according to merit.

You *worthily* succeed not only to the honors of your ancestors, but also to their virtues. *Dryden.*

3. Justly; not without cause.

I affirm that some may very *worthily* deserve to be hated. *South.*

WORTHINESS, *n.* Desert; merit.

The prayers which our Savior made, were for his own *worthiness* accepted. *Hooker.*

2. Excellence; dignity; virtue.

Who is sure he hath a soul, unless
It see and judge and follow *worthiness?* *Donne.*

3. Worth; quality or state of deserving. *Sidney.*

WORTHLESS, *a.* Having no value; as a *worthless* garment; a *worthless* ship.

2. Having no value of character or no virtue; as a *worthless* man or woman.

3. Having no dignity or excellence; as a *worthless* magistrate.

WORTHLESSNESS, *n.* Want of value; want of useful qualities; as the *worthlessness* of an old garment or of barren land.

2. Want of excellence or dignity; as the *worthlessness* of a person.

WORTHY, *a.* [G. *wurdig*; D. *waardig*; Sw. *vårdig.*]

1. Deserving; such as merits; having worth or excellence; equivalent; with *of*, before the thing deserved. She has married a man *worthy of* her.

Thou art *worthy of* the sway. *Shak.*
I am not *worthy of* the least of all the mercies— Gen. xxxii.

2. Possessing worth or excellence of qualities; virtuous; estimable; as a *worthy* citizen; a *worthy* magistrate.

Happier thou may'st be, *worthier* canst not be. *Milton.*
This *worthy* mind should worthy things embrace. *Davies.*

3. Suitable; having qualities suited to; either in a good or bad sense; equal in value; as flowers *worthy* of paradise.

4. Suitable to any thing bad.

The merciless Macdonald,
Worthy to be a rebel. *Shak.*

5. Deserving of ill; as things *worthy* of stripes. Luke xii.

WOR̃THY, *n.* A man of eminent worth; a man distinguished for useful and estimable qualities; a man of valor; *a word much used in the plural;* as the *worthies* of the church; political *worthies;* military *worthies.* *Holyday. Milton.*

WOR̃THY, *v. t.* To render worthy; to exalt. [*Not in use.*] *Shak.*

WOT, *v. i.* [originally *wat;* the preterite of Sax. *witan*, to know; formerly used also in the present tense.]
To know; to be aware. *Obs.* *Spenser.*

WOULD. WUD. *pret.* of *will*, G. *wollen*, L. *volo.*

Would is used as an auxiliary verb in conditional forms of speech. "I *would* go, *if* I could." This form of expression denotes *will* or *resolution*, under a condition or supposition.

You *would* go, } denote simply an *event*,
He *would* go, } under a condition or supposition.

The condition implied in *would* is not always expressed. "By pleasure and pain, I *would* be understood to mean what delights or molests us—"; that is, *if it should be asked* what I mean by pleasure and pain, I *would* thus explain what I wish to have understood. In this form of expression, which is very common, there seems to be an implied allusion to an inquiry, or to the supposition of something not expressed.

Would has the sense of *wish* or *pray*, particularly in the phrases, "*would* to God," "*would* God we had died in Egypt," "I *would* that ye knew what conflict I have;" that is, I could *wish* such a thing, *if* the wish could avail. Here also there is an implied condition.

Would is used also for *wish to do*, or *to have.* What *wouldst* thou? What *would* he?

WOULD'ING, *n.* Motion of desire. [*Not in use.*] *Hammond.*

WOUND, *n.* [Sax. *wund;* D. *wond;* G. *wunde;* W. *gwanu*, to thrust, to stab.]

1. A breach of the skin and flesh of an animal, or of the bark and wood of a tree, or of the bark and substance of other plants, caused by violence or external force. The self-healing power of living beings, animal or vegetable, by which the parts separated in *wounds*, tend to unite and become sound, is a remarkable proof of divine benevolence and wisdom.
2. Injury; hurt; as a *wound* given to credit or reputation.

WOUND, *v. t.* To hurt by violence; as, to *wound* the head or the arm; to *wound* a tree.

He was *wounded* for our transgressions. Is. liii.

WOUND, *pret.* and *pp.* of *wind.*

WOUND'ED, *pp.* Hurt; injured.

WOUND'ER, *n.* One that wounds.

WOUND'ING, *ppr.* Hurting; injuring.

WOUND'ING, *n.* Hurt; injury. Gen. iv.

WOUND'LESS, *a.* Free from hurt or injury.

WOUND'WOR̃T, *n.* The name of several plants; one, a species of Achillea; another, a species of Stachys; another, a species of Laserpitium; another, a species of Solidago; and another a species of Senecio. *Cyc.*

WOUND'Y, *a.* Excessive. [*Not English.*]

WOVE, *pret.* of *weave*, sometimes the participle.

WOX, WOXEN, for *waxed.* [*Not in use.*]

NOTE. *W* before *r* is always silent.

WRACK, WRECK, } *n.* [See *Wreck.*] A name given to a marine plant which is of great utility as a manure. It is called sometimes *sea-wrack* or *sea-wreck*, and *sea-oak* and *sea-tangle.* It is the *Fucus vesiculosus* of Linne, a plant found on rocks left dry at low water. The stalk runs along the middle of the leaf, and is terminated by watery bladders. *Cyc.*

The *grass wrack* is of the genus Zostera. *Lee.*

Wrack, and *to wrack.* [See *Wreck.*]

WRAIN-BOLT. [See *Wring-bolt.*]

WRAN'GLE, *v. i.* [from the root of *wring*, Sw. *vrånga;* that is, to wring, to twist, to struggle, to contend; or it is from the root of *ring*, to sound.]
To dispute angrily; to quarrel peevishly and noisily; to brawl; to altercate.

For a score of kingdoms you should *wrangle.* *Shak.*

He did not know what it was to *wrangle* on indifferent points. *Addison.*

WRAN'GLE, *v. t.* To involve in contention. [*Little used.*] *Sanderson.*

WRAN'GLE, *n.* An angry dispute; a noisy quarrel. *Swift.*

WRAN'GLER, *n.* An angry disputant; one who disputes with heat or peevishness; as a noisy contentious *wrangler.* *Watts.*

Senior wrangler, in the university of Cambridge, the student who passes the best examination in the senate house. Then follow the second, third, &c. wranglers.

WRAN'GLESOME, *a.* Contentious; quarrelsome. *Moor.*

WRAN'GLING, *ppr.* Disputing or contending angrily.

WRAN'GLING, *n.* The act of disputing angrily.

WRAP, *v. t.* pret. and pp. *wrapped* or *wrapt.*

1. To wind or fold together. John xx.
2. To involve; to cover by winding something round; often with *up;* as, to *wrap up* a child in its blanket; *wrap* the body well with flannel in winter.

I, *wrapt* in mist
Of midnight vapor, glide obscure. *Milton.*

3. To involve; to hide; as truth *wrapt* in tales.
4. To comprise; to contain.

Leontine's young wife, in whom all his happiness was *wrapped* up, died in a few days after the death of her daughter. *Addison.*

5. To involve totally.

Things reflected on in gross and transiently, are thought to be *wrapped* in impenetrable obscurity. *Locke.*

6. To inclose.
7. To snatch up; to transport. This is an error. It ought to be *rapt.* [See *Rap* and *Rapt.*]

WRAP'PED, WRAPT, } *pp.* Wound; folded; inclosed.

WRAP'PER, *n.* One that wraps.

2. That in which any thing is wrapped or inclosed.

WRAP'PING, *ppr.* Winding; folding; involving; inclosing.

2. *a.* Used or designed for wrapping or covering; as *wrapping* paper.

WRAP'-RASCAL, *n.* An upper coat. *Jamieson.*

WRASS, WRASSE, } *n.* A fish, the *Labrus tinca* of Linne, called by authors, *turdus vulgaris*, or *tinca marina*, the *sea-tench*, and sometimes *old-wife.* It resembles the carp in figure, and is covered with large scales. The name is also applied to other species of the genus Labrus. *Cyc. Ed. Encyc.*

WR'ATH, *n.* [Sax. *wrath, wræth;* Sw. D. *vrede;* W. *irad*, of which L. *ira* is a contraction; Ar. أرث to provoke. Class Rd. No. 36.]

1. Violent anger; vehement exasperation; indignation; as the *wrath* of Achilles.

When the *wrath* of king Ahasuerus was appeased— Esth. ii.

O Lord—in *wrath* remember mercy. Hab. iii.

2. The effects of anger. Prov. xxvii.
3. The just punishment of an offense or crime. Rom. xiii.

God's wrath, in Scripture, is his holy and just indignation against sin. Rom. i.

WR'ATHFUL, *a.* Very angry; greatly incensed. The king was very *wrathful.*

2. Springing from wrath, or expressing it; as *wrathful* passions; a *wrathful* countenance.

WR'ATHFULLY, *adv.* With violent anger. *Shak.*

WR'ATHFULNESS, *n.* Vehement anger.

WR'ATHLESS, *a.* Free from anger. *Waller.*

WR'ATHY, *a.* Very angry; *a colloquial word.*

WRAWL, *v. i.* [Sw. *vråla*, to bawl.] To cry, as a cat. [*Not in use.*] *Spenser.*

WREAK, *v. t.* [Sax. *wræcan, wræccan;* D. *wreeken;* G. *rächen;* perhaps allied to *break.* The sense is to drive or throw, to dash with violence. See Ar. حرج. Class Rg. No. 32. and No. 48.]

1. To execute; to inflict; to hurl or drive; as, to *wreak* vengeance on an enemy.

On me let death *wreak* all his rage. *Milton.*

2. To revenge.

Come *wreak* his loss, whom bootless ye complain. *Fairfax.*

Another's wrongs to *wreak* upon thyself. *Spenser.*

[*This latter sense is nearly or quite obsolete.*]

WREAK, for *reck*, to care, is a mistake. *Shak.*

WREAK, *n.* Revenge; vengeance; furious passion. *Obs.* *Shak. Spenser.*

WRE'AKFUL, *a.* Revengeful; angry. *Shak.*

WRE'AKLESS, *a.* Unrevengeful; weak. *Shak.*

WREATH, *n.* [Sax. *wræth, wreoth.* See *Writhe.*]

1. Something twisted or curled; as a *wreath* of flowers. Hence,
2. A garland; a chaplet.

Nor wear his brows victorious *wreaths.*

WREATH, *v. t.* pret. *wreathed;* pp. *wreathed, wreathen.*

1. To twist; to convolve; to wind one about another; as, to *wreath* a garland of flowers.
2. To interweave; to entwine; as chains of *wreathed* work.

3. To encircle, as a garland.

The flow'rs that *wreath* the sparkling bowl. *Prior.*

4. To encircle as with a garland; to dress in a garland.

And with thy winding ivy *wreaths* her lance. *Dryden.*

WREATH, *v.i.* To be interwoven or entwined; as a bower of *wreathing* trees. *Dryden.*

WRE'ATHED, *pp.* Twisted; entwined; interwoven.

WRE'ATHING, *ppr.* Twisting; entwining; encircling.

WRE'ATHY, *a.* Twisted; curled; spiral; as a *wreathy* spire.

WRECK, *n.* [Dan. *vrag*, a *wreck*, *shipwreck*; Sw. *vrak*, refuse; Sax. *wræc*, *wræcca*, an exile, a wretch; D. *wrak*, broken, a wreck. This word signifies properly that which is cast, driven or dashed, or that which is broken.]

1. Destruction; properly, the destruction of a ship or vessel on the shore. Hence,

2. The ruins of a ship stranded; a ship dashed against rocks or land and broken, or otherwise rendered useless by violence and fracture.

3. Dissolution by violence; ruin; destruction.

The *wreck* of matter and the crush of worlds. *Addison.*

4. The remains of any thing ruined; dead weeds and grass.

5. In *metallurgy*, the vessel in which ores are washed the third time.

6. *Wreck*, for *wreak*, is less proper. [See also *Rack.*]

WRECK, *v. t.* [Sw. *vråka*, to throw away.]

1. To strand; to drive against the shore, or dash against rocks, and break or destroy. The ship Diamond of New York, was *wrecked* on a rock in Cardigan Bay, on the coast of Wales.

2. To ruin; as, they *wreck* their own fortunes.

3. *Wreck*, for *wreak*, is improper. *Shak.*

WRECK, *v. i.* To suffer wreck or ruin. *Milton.*

WRECK'ED, *pp.* Dashed against the shore or on rocks; stranded and ruined.

WRECK'FUL, *a.* Causing wreck.

WRECK'ING, *ppr.* Stranding; running on rocks or on shore; ruining.

WREN, *n.* [Sax. *wrenna*; Ir. *drean.*] A small bird of the genus Motacilla.

WRENCH, *v. t.* [G. *verrenken*; D. *verwringen*. See *Wring*. Qu. Ir. *freanc.*]

1. To pull with a twist; to wrest, twist or force by violence; as, to *wrench* a sword from another's hand.

2. To strain; to sprain; to distort.

You *wrenched* your foot against a stone. *Swift.*

WRENCH, *n.* A violent twist, or a pull with twisting.

2. A sprain; an injury by twisting; as in a joint. *Locke.*

3. An instrument for screwing or unscrewing iron work.

4. Means of compulsion. [*Not used.*] *Bacon.*

5. In *the plural*, sleights; subtilties. *Obs.* *Chaucer.*

WREST, *v. t.* [Sax. *wræstan*; G. *reissen*, to wrest, to snatch or pull, to burst, to tear; Dan. *vrister*. Qu. L. *restis*, a rope.]

1. To twist or extort by violence; to pull or force from by violent wringing or twisting; as, to *wrest* an instrument from another's hands.

2. To take or force from by violence. The enemy made a great effort, and *wrested* the victory from our hands.

But fate has *wrested* the confession from me. *Addison.*

3. To distort; to turn from truth or twist from its natural meaning by violence; to pervert.

Wrest once the law to your authority. *Shak.*

Thou shalt not *wrest* the judgment of the poor. Ex. xxiii.

Which they that are unlearned and unstable *wrest*, as they do also the other Scriptures, to their own destruction. 2 Pet. iii.

WREST, *n.* Distortion; violent pulling and twisting; perversion. *Hooker.*

2. Active or moving power. [*Not used.*] *Spenser.*

3. An instrument to tune.

WREST'ED, *pp.* Pulled with twisting; distorted; perverted.

WREST'ER, *n.* One who wrests or perverts.

WREST'ING, *ppr.* Pulling with a twist; distorting; perverting.

WRESTLE, *v. i. res'l.* [Sax. *wræstlian* or *wraxlian*; D. *worstelen*. If *wraxlian* is the true orthography, this word belongs to Class *Rg*; otherwise it is from *wrest.*]

1. To strive with arms extended, as two men, who seize each other by the collar and arms, each endeavoring to throw the other by tripping up his heels and twitching him off his center.

Another, by a fall in *wrestling*, started the end of the clavicle from the sternum. *Wiseman.*

2. To struggle; to strive; to contend.

We *wrestle* not against flesh and blood. Eph. vi.

WRES'TLER, *n.* One who wrestles; or one who is skillful in wrestling.

WRES'TLING, *ppr.* Striving to throw; contending.

WRES'TLING, *n.* Strife; struggle; contention.

WRETCH, *n.* [Sax. *wræcca*, one who is driven, an exile. See *Wreck* and ערך. Class Rg. No. 48.]

1. A miserable person; one sunk in the deepest distress; as a forlorn *wretch.*

2. A worthless mortal; as a contemptible *wretch.*

3. A person sunk in vice; as a profligate *wretch.*

4. It is sometimes used by way of slight or ironical pity or contempt.

Poor *wretch* was never frighted so. *Drayton.*

5. It is sometimes used to express tenderness; as we say, *poor thing.* *Shak.*

WRETCH'ED, *a.* Very miserable; sunk into deep affliction or distress, either from want, anxiety or grief.

The *wretched* find no friends. *Dryden.*

2. Calamitous; very afflicting; as the *wretched* condition of slaves in Algiers.

3. Worthless; paltry; very poor or mean; as a *wretched* poem; a *wretched* cabin.

4. Despicable; hatefully vile and contemptible. He was guilty of *wretched* ingratitude.

WRETCH'EDLY, *adv.* Most miserably; very poorly. The prisoners were *wretchedly* lodged.

2. Unhappily; as two wars *wretchedly* entered upon. *Clarendon.*

3. Meanly; despicably; as a discourse *wretchedly* delivered.

WRETCH'EDNESS, *n.* Extreme misery or unhappiness, either from want or sorrow; as the *wretchedness* of poor mendicants.

We have, with the feeling, lost the very memory of such *wretchedness* as our forefathers endured— *Raleigh.*

The prodigal brought nothing to his father but his rags and *wretchedness.* *Dwight.*

2. Meanness; despicableness; as the *wretchedness* of a performance.

WRETCHLESS, for *reckless*, } are improper.
WRETCHLESSNESS, for *recklessness*, }

WRIG, for *wriggle.* [*Not in use.*]

WRIG'GLE, *v. i.* [W. *rhuglaw*, to move briskly; D. *wriggelen* or *wrikken.*]

To move the body to and fro with short motions.

Both he and his successors would often *wriggle* in their seats, as long as the cushion lasted. *Swift.*

WRIG'GLE, *v. t.* To put into a quick reciprocating motion; to introduce by a shifting motion.

Wriggling his body to recover
His seat, and cast his right leg over. *Hudibras.*

WRIG'GLER, *n.* One who wriggles.

WRIG'GLING, *ppr.* Moving the body one way and the other with quick turns.

WRIGHT, *n.* [Sax. *wryhta*; from the root of *work.*]

An artificer; one whose occupation is some kind of mechanical business; a workman; a manufacturer. This word is now chiefly used in compounds, as in *shipwright*, *wheelwright.*

WRING, *v. t.* pret. and pp. *wringed* and *wrung*. The latter is chiefly used. [Sax. *wringan*; G. *ringen*; D. *wringen*; Dan. *vrænger*; Sw. *vrånga*; Dan. *ringer*. The sense is to strain.]

1. To twist; to turn and strain with violence; as, to *wring* clothes in washing.

2. To squeeze; to press; to force by twisting; as, to *wring* water out of a wet garment.

3. To writhe; as, to *wring* the body in pain.

4. To pinch.

The king began to find where his shoe did *wring* him. *Obs.* *Bacon.*

If he had not been too much grieved and *wrung* by an uneasy and strait fortune— *Obs.* *Clarendon.*

5. To distress; to press with pain.

Didst thou taste but half the griefs,
That *wring* my soul, thou couldst not talk thus coldly. *Addison.*

6. To distort; to pervert.

How dare these men thus *wring* the Scriptures? *Whitgifte.*

7. To persecute with extortion.

These merchant adventurers have been often wronged and *wringed* to the quick. *Hayward.*

8. To bend or strain out of its position, as, to *wring* a mast. *Mar. Dict.*

To wring off, to force off or separate by wringing; as, to *wring off* the head of a fowl.

To wring out, to force out; to squeeze out by twisting; as, to *wring out* dew or water. Judges vi.

2. To free from a liquor by wringing; as, to *wring out* clothes.

To wring from, to force from by violence; to extort; as revenues *wrung from* the poor; to *wring from* one his rights; to *wring* a secret *from* one.

WRING, *v. i.* To writhe; to twist; as with anguish. *Shak.*

WRING, *n.* Action of anguish. *Hall.*

WRING'-BOLT, *n.* [*wring* and *bolt.*] A bolt used by shipwrights, to bend and secure the planks against the timbers till they are fastened by bolts, spikes and tree-nails. *Mar. Dict.*

WRING'ED, *pp.* Twisted; pressed; distressed; extorted.

WRING'ER, *n.* One who wrings; one that forces water out of any thing by wringing.

WRING'ING, *ppr.* Twisting; writhing; extorting.

WRING'-STAVES, *n.* Strong bars of wood used in applying wring-bolts. *Mar. Dict.*

WRINK'LE, *n.* [Sax. *wrincle*; Sw. *rynka*; Dan. *rynke*. This coincides with *ring*, a circle. The Dutch write this word *krinkle*, and *kring* is *ring*. The G. *runzel* is probably of the same family, formed on *Rg*; Ir. *rang*. If *n* is casual, the root coincides with L. *ruga*, a wrinkle, and W. *rhyç*, a furrow.]

1. A small ridge or prominence, or a furrow, formed by the shrinking or contraction of any smooth substance; corrugation; a crease; as *wrinkles* in the face or skin.

2. A fold or rumple in cloth.

3. Roughness; unevenness.

Not the least *wrinkle* to deform the sky. *Dryden.*

WRINK'LE, *v. t.* [Sax. *wrinclian*; Sw. *rynka*; Dan. *rynker*.]

1. To contract into furrows and prominences; to corrugate; as, to *wrinkle* the skin; to *wrinkle* the brow.

Her *wrinkled* form in black and white array'd. *Pope.*

2. To make rough or uneven.

A keen north wind, blowing dry,
Wrinkled the face of deluge, as decay'd. *Milton.*

WRINK'LE, *v. i.* To shrink into furrows and ridges.

WRINK'LED, *pp.* Contracted into ridges and furrows.

WRINK'LING, *ppr.* Shrinking; contracting into furrows and ridges.

WRIST, *n.* [Sax. *wrist*; allied probably to *wrest* and *wrestle*; that is, a twist or junction.]

1. The joint by which the hand is united to the arm.

2. In *the manege*, the *bridle wrist* is that of the cavalier's left hand. *Cyc.*

WRIST'BAND, *n.* [*wrist* and *band.*] That band or part of a shirt sleeve which covers the wrist.

WRIT, *n.* [from *write.*] That which is written. In this sense, *writ* is particularly applied to the Scriptures, or books of the Old and New Testament; as holy *writ*; sacred *writ*.

2. In *law*, a precept issued from the proper authority to the sherif, his deputy or other subordinate officer, commanding him to perform some act, as to summon a defendant into court to answer, and the like.

In England, writs are issued from some court under seal. In some of the United States, writs are issued by any single judge or justice of the peace, in the name and by the authority of the state.

In some of the United States, the writ in a civil suit, contains both the summons and the plaintif's declaration or cause of action set forth at large, and a writ is either a summons or an attachment.

Writs are *original* or *judicial*. An *original* writ, in England, is issued from the high court of chancery. A *judicial* writ is issued by order of a court upon a special occasion, during the pendency of the suit.

Writs are of various kinds; as writs of *assize*; writs of *capias*; writs of *distringas*, &c.

3. A legal instrument. *Shak.*

WRIT, *pret.* of *write*, is not now used. [See *Write* and *Wrote.*]

WRITE, *v. t.* pret. *wrote*; pp. *writ*, *written*. [Sax. *writan*, *awritan*, *gewritan*; Ice. *rita*; Goth. *writs*, a letter. The sense is to scrape, to scratch, to rub; probably from the root of *grate* and L. *rado*.]

1. To form by a pen on paper or other material, or by a graver on wood or stone; as, to *write* the characters called letters; to *write* figures. We *write* characters on paper with pen and ink; we *write* them on stone with a graving tool.

2. To express by forming letters and words on paper or stone; as, to *write* a deed; to *write* a bill of divorcement. The ten commandments were *written* with the finger of God on tables of stone. Ex. xxxi.

3. To engrave. [*See the preceding definition.*]

4. To impress durably. *Write* useful truths on the heart.

5. To compose or produce, as an author.

6. To copy; to transcribe.

7. To communicate by letter.

I chose to *write* the thing I durst not speak
To her I lov'd. *Prior.*

WRITE, *v. i.* To perform the act of forming characters, letters or figures, as representatives of sounds or ideas. Learn to *write* when young.

2. To be employed as a clerk or an amanuensis. A *writes* for B. D *writes* in one of the public offices.

3. To play the author; as, he thinks, he speaks, he *writes*, he sings.

4. To recite or relate in books. Josephus *wrote* of the wars of the Jews.

5. To send letters.

He *wrote* for all the Jews concerning their freedom. *Esdras.*

6. To call one's self; to be entitled; to use the style of.

Those who began to *write* themselves men, but thought it no shame to learn. *Fell.*

7. To compose; to frame or combine ideas and express them in words.

They can *write* up to the dignity and character of their authors. *Felton.*

WRI'TER, *n.* One who writes or has written.

2. An author.

3. A clerk or amanuensis.

Writer of the tallies, an officer of the exchequer of England; a clerk to the auditor of the receipt, who writes upon the tallies the whole of the tellers' bills. *Cyc.*

WRITHE, *v. t.* [Sax. *writhan*; Sw. *vrida*; Dan. *vrider*.]

1. To twist; to distort.

Her mouth she *writh'd*. *Dryden.*

2. To twist with violence; as, to *writhe* the body. *Addison.*

3. To wrest; to distort; to torture; as, to *writhe* words. *Obs.* *Hooker.*

WRITHE, *v. i.* To twist; to be distorted; as, to *writhe* with agony. *Addison.*

WRI'THED, *pp.* Twisted; distorted.

WRI'THING, *ppr.* Twisting; distorting.

WRITH'LE, *v. t.* [from *writhe.*] To wrinkle. [*Not in use.*] *Spenser.*

WRI'TING, *ppr.* Forming, as characters, with a pen, style or graver.

2. *a.* Used or intended for writing; as *writing* paper.

WRI'TING, *n.* The act or art of forming letters and characters, on paper, wood, stone or other material, for the purpose of recording the ideas which characters and words express, or of communicating them to others by visible signs. We hardly know which to admire most, the ingenuity or the utility of the art of *writing*.

2. Any thing written or expressed in letters; hence, any legal instrument, as a deed, a receipt, a bond, an agreement, &c.

3. A book; any written composition; a pamphlet; as the *writings* of Addison.

4. An inscription. John xix.

5. *Writings*, plu. conveyances of lands; deeds; or any official papers.

WRI'TING-MA'STER, *n.* One who teaches the art of penmanship.

WRIT'TEN, *pp.* Expressed in letters.

Written laws, statutes; laws enacted by the supreme power and recorded; as contradistinguished from *unwritten* or *common* law.

WRIZ'ZLED, for *writhled.* [*Not in use.*] *Spenser.*

WRO'KEN, for *wreaked.* [*Not in use.*] *Spenser.*

WRONG, *a.* [Sw. *vrång*; Dan. *vrang*; properly the participle of *wring*, Sw. *vrånga*, Dan. *vrænger*.] Literally wrung, twisted or turned from a straight line or even surface. Hence,

1. Not physically right; not fit or suitable; as the *wrong* side of a garment. You hold the book the *wrong* end uppermost. There may be something *wrong* in the construction of a watch or an edifice.

2. Not morally right; that deviates from the line of rectitude prescribed by God; not just or equitable; not right or proper; not legal; erroneous; as a *wrong* practice; *wrong* ideas; a *wrong* course of life; *wrong* measures; *wrong* inclinations and desires; a *wrong* application of talents; *wrong* judgment. Hab. i.

3. Erroneous; not according to truth; as a *wrong* statement.

WRONG, *n.* Whatever deviates from moral rectitude; any injury done to another; a trespass; a violation of right. Wrongs are *private* or *public*. *Private* wrongs are civil injuries, immediately affecting individuals; *public* wrongs are crimes and misdemeanors which affect the community. *Blackstone.*

Sarai said to Abraham, my *wrong* be on thee. Gen. xvi.

Friend, I do thee no *wrong*. Matt. xx.

The obligation to redress a *wrong*, is at least as binding as that of paying a debt. *E. Everett.*

WRONG, *adv.* Not rightly; amiss; morally ill; erroneously.

Ten censure *wrong* for one that writes amiss. *Pope.*

WRONG, *v. t.* To injure; to treat with injustice; to deprive of some right, or to withhold some act of justice from. We *wrong* a man, when we defraud him, and when we trespass on his property. We *wrong* a man, when we neglect to pay him his due. Philemon 18.

2. To do injustice to by imputation; to impute evil unjustly. If you suppose me capable of a base act, you *wrong* me.

WRONG'-DÖER, *n.* One who injures another, or does wrong.

WRONG'-DÖING, *n.* Evil or wicked act or action.

WRONG'ED, *pp.* Treated unjustly; injured.

WRONG'ER, *n.* One who injures another.

WRONG'FUL, *a.* Injurious; unjust; as a *wrongful* taking of property; *wrongful* dealing.

WRONG'FULLY, *adv.* Unjustly; in a manner contrary to the moral law or to justice; as, to accuse one *wrongfully*; to suffer *wrongfully*.

WRONG'HEAD, WRONGHEAD'ED, *a.* [*wrong* and *head.*] Wrong in opinion or principle; having a perverse understanding; perverse.

WRONGHEAD'EDNESS, *n.* Perverseness; erroneousness.

WRONG'LESSLY, *adv.* Without injury to any one. [*Not used.*] *Sidney.*

WRONG'LY, *adv.* In a wrong manner; unjustly; amiss. He judges *wrongly* of my motives.

WRONG'NESS, *n.* Wrong disposition; error. *Butler.*

WROTE, *pret.* of *write*. He *wrote* a letter yesterday. Herodotus *wrote* his history more than two thousand years ago.

[Note. *Wrote* is not now used as the participle.]

WROTH, *a. rauth.* [Sax. *wræth, wrath.* See *Wrath.*]

Very angry; much exasperated.

Cain was very *wroth*, and his countenance fell. Gen. iv.

I was *wroth* with my people. Is. xlvii.

[*An excellent word and not obsolete.*]

WROUGHT, *pret.* and *pp.* of *work. raut.* [Sax. *worhte*, the pret. and pp. of *wircan, weorcan*, to work.]

1. Worked; formed by work or labor; as *wrought* iron.

2. Effected; performed.

She hath *wrought* a good work upon me. Matt. xxvi.

3. Effected; produced. He *wrought* the public safety. A great change was *wrought* in his mind.

This *wrought* the greatest confusion in the unbelieving Jews. *Addison.*

4. Used in labor.

The elders of that city shall take a heifer that hath not been *wrought* with. Deut. xxi

5. Worked; driven; as infection *wrought* out of the body. [*Not used.*] *Bacon.*

6. Actuated.

Vain Morat, by his own rashness *wrought*— *Dryden.*

7. Worked; used; labored in. The mine is still *wrought*.

8. Formed; fitted.

He that hath *wrought* us for the self-same thing is God. 2 Cor. v.

9. Guided; managed. [*Not used.*] *Milton.*

10. Agitated; disturbed.

My dull brain was *wrought*
With things forgot. *Shak.*

Wrought on or *upon*, influenced; prevailed on. His mind was *wrought upon* by divine grace.

Wrought to or *up to*, excited; inflamed. Their minds were *wrought up to* a violent passion. She was *wrought up to* the tenderest emotions of pity.

WRUNG, *pret.* and *pp.* of *wring*.

WRȲ, *a.* [Goth. *wraicwa*, or Dan. *vrier*, to twist, contracted from *vrider*, Eng. to *writhe.*]

1. Twisted; turned to one side; distorted; as a *wry* neck; a *wry* mouth.

2. Deviating from the right direction; as *wry* words.

3. Wrested; perverted; as, to put a *wry* sense on an author's words. *Atterbury.*

WRȲ, *v. i.* To be writhed or distorted. [*Not used.*]

WRȲ, *v. t.* To distort; to wrest. [*Not used.*]

WRY'NECK, *n.* [*wry* and *neck.*] A twisted or distorted neck; a deformity in which the neck is drawn to one side, and at the same time somewhat forwards. *Cyc.*

2. A disease of the spasmodic kind in sheep, in which the head is drawn to one side. *Cyc.*

3. In *ornithology*, a bird resembling the woodpeckers, the *Yunx torquilla*; so called from the singular manner in which, when surprised, it turns its head over its shoulders. *Ed. Encyc.*

WRY'NECKED, *a.* Having a distorted neck.

WRY'NESS, *n.* The state of being wry or distorted. *Mountague.*

WYCH-ELM, *n.* A variety of the elm, or a peculiar species, (*Ulmus glabra.*) *Cyc.*

X.

X, the twenty fourth letter of the English Alphabet, is borrowed from the Greek. In the middle and at the end of words, it has the sound of *ks*, as in *wax, lax, luxury.* At the beginning of a word, it has precisely the sound of z. It is used as an initial, in a few words borrowed from the Greek.

As a numeral, X stands for ten. It represents one V, which stands for five, placed on the top of another. When laid horizontally, thus ⋈, it stands for a thousand, and with a dash over it, thus X̄, it stands for ten thousand. As an abbreviation, X. stands for *Christ*, as in Xn. *Christian*; Xm. *Christmas.*

XAN'THID, XAN'THIDE, *n.* A compound of xanthogene and a metal. *Henry.*

XAN'THOGENE, *n.* [Gr. ξανθος, yellow, and γενναω, to generate.]

The base of a new acid, produced by the mixture of a solution of pure potassa with bisulphuret of carbon. This acid contains sulphur, carbon, and hydrogen. It is named from the yellow color of its compounds. *Henry. Zeise.*

XEBEC', *n.* A small three masted vessel, used in the Mediterranean sea. With a fair wind, in good weather, it carries two large square sails; when close hauled, it carries large lateen sails. *Mar. Dict.*

XEROCOLLYR'IUM, *n.* [Gr. ξηρος, dry, and κολλυριον.] A dry collyrium or eye-salve. *Coxe.*

XEROMY'RUM, *n.* [Gr. ξηρος, dry, and μυρον, ointment.] A dry ointment. *Coxe.*

XEROPH'AGY, *n.* [Gr. ξηρος, dry, and φαγω, to eat.]

The eating of dry meats, a sort of fast among the primitive christians.

XEROPH'THALMY, *n.* [Gr. ξηρος, dry, and οφθαλμια.]

A dry red soreness or itching of the eyes, without swelling or a discharge of humors.

XIPH'IAS, *n.* [Gr. from ξιφος, a sword.] The sword-fish.

2. A comet shaped like a sword.

XIPH'OID, *a.* [supra.] The *xiphoid* or *ensiform cartilage*, is a small cartilage placed at the bottom of the breast bone. *Cyc. Coxe.*

XYLOG'RAPHY, *n.* [Gr. ξυλον, wood, and γραφω, to engrave.]

Wood-engraving; the act or art of cutting figures in wood, in representation of natural objects.

XYS'TER, *n.* [Gr. ξυσρον, from ξυω, to scrape.]

A surgeon's instrument for scraping bones.

Y.

Y, the twenty fifth letter of the English Alphabet, is taken from the Greek *v*. At the beginning of words, it is called an articulation or consonant, and with some propriety perhaps, as it brings the root of the tongue in close contact with the lower part of the palate, and nearly in the position to which the close *g* brings it. Hence it has happened that in a great number of words, *g* has been changed into *y*, as the Sax. *gear*, into *year*; *geornian*, into *yearn*; *gyllan*, into *yell*; *gealew*, into *yellow*.

In the middle and at the end of words, *y* is precisely the same as *i*. It is sounded as *i* long, when accented, as in *defy*, *rely*; and as *i* short, when unaccented, as in *vanity*, *glory*, *synonymous*. This latter sound is a vowel. At the beginning of words, *y* answers to the German and Dutch *j*.

Y, as a numeral, stands for 150, and with a dash over it, Ȳ, for 150,000.

YACHT, *n.* *yot.* [D. *jagt*; G. *jacht*, from *jagen*. It is properly a boat drawn by horses.]

A vessel of state used to convey princes, embassadors and other great personages from one place to another. The royal yachts are rigged as ketches, except the principal one, which is equipped as a ship. The smaller yachts are rigged as sloops. *Mar. Dict.*

YAGER, *n.* *yaw'ger.* [G. *jäger*, from *jagen*, to chase.] A horseman.

YA'HOO, *n.* A word used by Chesterfield, I suppose for a savage, or a person resembling a savage.

YAK, *n.* A species of ox, with cylindric horns curving outwards, long pendent hair, and villous horselike tail; the grunting ox of Pennant. This ox is found in Thibet. *Cyc.*

YAM, *n.* A large esculent root growing in tropical climates.

YAM'BOO, *n.* A kind of plant producing fruit like a plum.

YAN'KEE, *n.* A corrupt pronunciation of the word *English* by the native Indians of America. *Heckewelder.*

YAN'OLITE, *n.* A mineral, called also axinite or thumerstone, whose crystals resemble an ax. *Ure.*

YAP, to bark, is not a legitimate word.

YAP'ON, *n.* The cassine or South Sea tea.

The Ilex cassine or youpon, is a shrub growing in the S. States, used as a tea and a medicine. *Mease.*

Y'ARD, *n.* [Sax. *geard*, *gerd*, *gyrd*, a rod, that is, a shoot.]

1. A measure of three feet or thirty six inches. It is just seven ninths of the Paris ell.

2. [Sax. *gyrdan*, to inclose; Dan. *gierde*, a hedge, an inclosure; *gierder*, to hedge in, Sw. *gårda*.] An inclosure; usually, a small inclosed place in front of or around a house or barn. The yard in front of a house is called a *court*, and sometimes a *court-yard*. In the United States, a small yard is fenced round a barn for confining cattle, and called *barn-yard* or *cow-yard*.

3. In *ships*, a long slender piece of timber, nearly cylindrical, suspended upon the mast, by which a sail is extended.

Yard of land, in old books, a certain quantity of land, but different in different counties. In some counties it was 15 acres, in others 20 or 24, and even 40.

Dock-yard, a place where ships are laid up.

Prison yard, primarily an inclosure about a prison, or attached to it. Hence *liberty of the yard*, is a liberty granted to persons imprisoned for debt, of walking in the yard, or within any other limits prescribed by law, on his giving bond not to go beyond those limits. *U. States.*

Y'ARD, *v. t.* To confine cattle to the yard; as, to *yard* cows. [*A farmer's word.*]

Y'ARD-ARM, *n.* [*yard* and *arm*.] Either half of a ship's yard, from the center or mast to the end.

Y'ARD-STICK, *n.* [*yard* and *stick*.] A stick three feet in length, used as a measure of cloth, &c.

Y'ARD-WAND, *n.* [*yard* and *wand*.] A measure of a yard; now *yard-stick.*

YARE, *a.* [Sax. *gearw*, prepared; from the root of *gear*. See *Eager*.]

Ready; dextrous; eager. *Obs.* *Shak.*

YA'RELY, *adv.* Readily; dextrously; skillfully. *Obs.* *Shak.*

Y'ARN, *n.* [Sax. *gearn*; G. Ice. Sw. *garn*; D. *garen*.]

1. Spun wool; woolen thread; but it is applied also to other species of thread, as to cotton and linen.

2. In *rope-making*, one of the threads of which a rope is composed. It is spun from hemp.

Y'ARR, *v. i.* [Low L. *hirrio*; Celtic, *gar*, W. *garw*, rough.]

To growl or snarl, as a dog. [*Not in use.*] *Ainsworth.*

YAR'RISH, *a.* Having a rough dry taste. [*Local.*]

YAR'ROW, *n.* [Sax. *gearwe*; Sp. *yaro*.] A plant of the genus Achillea; the milfoil, or plant of a thousand leaves.

YATE, in the north of England, is used for *gate*.

YAW, *n.* The African name of a raspberry. *Cyc.*

YAW, *v. i.* To rise in blisters, breaking in white froth, as cane juice in the sugar works. [Qu. *yew*. See *Yew*.] *West Indies.*

2. In *navigation*, to deviate from the line of her course, as a ship. *Mar. Dict.*

YAWL, *n.* A small ship's boat, usually rowed by four or six oars.

YAWL, *v. i.* To cry out. [See *Yell*.]

YAWN, *v. i.* [Sax. *geonan*, *gynian*; G. *gähnen*; W. *agenu*; Gr. *χαινω*.]

1. To gape; to oscitate; to have the mouth open involuntarily through drowsiness or dullness.

> The lazy, *yawning* drone. *Shak.*
>
> And while above he spends his breath,
> The *yawning* audience nod beneath. *Trumbull.*

2. To open wide; as, wide *yawns* the gulf below.

3. To express desire by yawning; as, to *yawn* for fat livings. *Hooker.*

YAWN, *n.* A gaping; an involuntary opening of the mouth from drowsiness; oscitation.

> One person yawning in company will produce a spontaneous *yawn* in all present. *N. Chipman.*

2. An opening wide. *Addison.*

YAWN'ING, *ppr.* Gaping; opening wide.

2. *a.* Sleepy; drowsy; dull. *Shak.*

YAWN'ING, *n.* The act of gaping or opening wide.

YAWS, *n.* A severe cutaneous disease, which is indigenous in Africa, and from Africa it has been introduced into the W. Indies. It is said to be so named from *yaw*, a raspberry. It is called by nosologists *frambœsia*, from the French *framboise*, a raspberry. It is propagated solely by the infection of the matter of the pustules, applied to a part of the body where the skin is broken. It affects a person but once. *Cyc.*

YCLAD', *pp.* Clad. [This word and the following retain the *y*, which is the remains of the Saxon *ge*, prefixed to verbs. But it is obsolete, except in poetry, and perhaps in burlesque only.]

YCLEP'ED, *pp.* of Sax. *ge-clypian*, *clepan*, to call. [See *Yclad*.] Called; named. It is obsolete, except in burlesque.

YDRAD', *pp.* Dreaded. *Obs.* *Spenser.*

YE, *pron.* [Sax. *ge*.] The nominative plural of the second person, of which *thou* is the singular. But the two words have no radical connection. *Ye* is now used only in the sacred and solemn style. In common discourse and writing, *you* is exclusively used.

> But *ye* are washed, but *ye* are sanctified. 1 Cor. vi.

YEA, *adv.* *yā.* [Sax. *gea*, *geac*; G. D. Dan. *ja*; Sw. *jaka*, to consent. Class Cg. No. 25. 26.]

1. Yes; a word that expresses affirmation or assent. Will you go? *yea.* It sometimes introduces a subject, with the sense of indeed, verily, truly, it is so.

> *Yea*, hath God said, ye shall not eat of every tree in the garden? Gen. iii.
>
> Let your communication be *yea*, *yea*; nay, nay. Matt. v.

2. It sometimes enforces the sense of something preceding; not only so, but more.

> Therein I do rejoice; *yea*, and will rejoice. Phil. i.

3. In Scripture, it is used to denote certainty, consistency, harmony and stability.

All the promises of God in him are *yea*, and in him are amen. 2 Cor. i.

[In this use, the word may be considered a noun.]

Yea is used only in the sacred and solemn style. [See *Yes.*]

YEAD, } **GEAD,** } *v. i.* To go. *Obs.* *Spenser.*

YEAN, *v. i.* [Sax. *eanian.*] To bring forth young, as a goat or sheep; to lamb. [*Obsolete or local.*]

YE'ANED, *pp.* Brought forth.

YE'ANLING, *n.* The young of sheep; a lamb. [*Obsolete or local.*]

YEAR, *n.* [Sax. *gear;* G. *jahr;* D. *jaar;* Sw. *år;* Dan. *aar;* Sans. *jahran;* probably a course or circle; the root *gar, ger,* signifying to run.]

1. The space or period of time in which the sun moves through the twelve signs of the ecliptic, or whole circle, and returns to the same point. This is the solar year, and the year, in the strict and proper sense of the word. It is called also the tropical year. This period comprehends what are called the twelve calendar months, or 365 days, 5 hours, and 49 minutes, within a small fraction. But in popular usage, the year consists of 365 days, and every fourth year of 366; a day being added to February, on account of the 5 hours and 49 minutes.

2. The time in which any planet completes a revolution; as the *year* of Jupiter or of Saturn.

3. The time in which the fixed stars make a revolution, is called the *great year.*

4. *Years,* in the plural, is sometimes equivalent to age or old age: as a man in *years.*

In *popular language,* year is often used for *years.* The horse is ten *year* old.

Sidereal year, the time in which the sun, departing from any fixed star, returns to the same. This is 365 days, 6 hours, 6 minutes, and 11, 5 seconds.

Anomalistical year, the time that elapses from the sun's leaving its apogee, till it returns to it; which is 365 days, 6 hours, 14 minutes.

Civil year, the year which any nation has contrived for the computation of time.

Bissextile or *leap year,* the year consisting of 366 days.

Lunar year, consists of 12 lunar months.

Lunar astronomical year, consists of 12 lunar synodical months, or 354 days, 8 hours, 48 minutes, 36 seconds.

Common lunar year, consists of 12 lunar civil months, or 354 days.

Embolismic or *intercalary year,* consists of 13 lunar civil months, and contains 384 days.

Julian year, established by Julius Cesar, consists of 365 days, 6 hours.

Gregorian year, is the Julian year corrected, and is the year now generally used in Europe. From the difference between this and the Julian year, arises the distinction of Old and New Style.

Sabbatic year, among the Israelites, was every seventh year, when their land was suffered to lie untilled. *Cyc.* *Encyc.*

The *civil* or *legal year,* in England, formerly commenced on the 25th day of March. This practice continued till after the settlement of America, and the first settlers of New England observed it for many years.

YE'AR-BOOK, *n.* [*year* and *book.*] A book containing annual reports of cases adjudged in the courts of England.

YE'ARED, *a.* Containing years. [*Not in use.*] *B. Jonson.*

YE'ARLING, *n.* A young beast one year old, or in the second year of his age.

YE'ARLING, *a.* Being a year old; as a *yearling* heifer.

YE'ARLY, *a.* Annual; happening, accruing or coming every year; as a *yearly* rent or income.

2. Lasting a year; as a *yearly* plant.

3. Comprehending a year; as the *yearly* circuit or revolution of the earth.

YE'ARLY, *adv.* Annually; once a year; as blessings *yearly* bestowed.

YEARN, } **YERN,** } *v. i.* [Sax. *geornian, giernan, gyrnan, earnian,* to desire, to yearn; Sw. *gerna,* willingly, Dan. *gierne,* G. *gern,* D. *gaarne.* The sense is to *strain,* or stretch forward. We have *earnest* from the same root.]

1. To be strained; to be pained or distressed; to suffer.

Falstaff, he is dead,
And we must *yearn* therefore. *Shak.*

2. *Usually,* to long; to feel an earnest desire; that is literally, to have a desire or inclination stretching towards the object or end. 1 Kings iii.

Joseph made haste, for his bowels did *yearn* upon his brother. Gen. xliii.

Your mother's heart *yearns* towards you. *Addison.*

—Anticlus, unable to control,
Spoke loud the language of his *yearning* soul. *Pope.*

YEARN, } **YERN,** } *v. t.* To pain; to grieve; to vex.

She laments for it, that it would
Yearn your heart to see it. *Shak.*

It *yearns* me not if men my garments wear. *Obs.* *Shak.*

YEARN'FUL, } **YERN'FUL,** } *a.* Mournful; distressing. *Obs.*

YEARN'ING, } **YERN'ING,** } *ppr.* Longing; having longing desire.

YEARN'ING, } **YERN'ING,** } *n.* Strong emotions of desire, tenderness or pity.

YEAST, *n.* [Sax. *gist,* yeast, a guest, also a storm; *yst,* a storm; G. *gäscht,* yeast, and *gast,* a guest; *gäschen,* to foam or froth; D. *gist,* yeast; *gisten,* to ferment. This coincides with *gas* and *ghost.* The primary sense of the noun is wind, spirit, flatulence or froth, from rushing; Ch. נפח to inflate. Class Gs. No. 18.]

1. Barm; the foam, froth or flower of beer or other liquor in fermentation; used for raising dough for bread or cakes, and making it light and puffy.

2. Spume or foam of water. [*Not in use.*] *Shak.*

YE'ASTY, *a.* Frothy; foamy; spumy; like yeast.

YELK, *n.* [Sax. *gealew,* yellow; G. *gelb,* yellow. See *Gold* and *Yellow.*]

The yellow part of an egg; the vitellus. It is sometimes written and pronounced *yolk,* but *yelk* is the proper word. *Yolk* is a corruption.

YELL, *v. i.* [Sax. *giellan, gyllan;* D. *gillen;* Sw. *gälla,* to ring. It agrees in elements with *call.*]

To cry out with a hideous noise; to cry or scream as with agony or horror. Savages *yell* most frightfully when they are rushing to the first onset of battle.

Nor the night raven, that still deadly *yells.* *Spenser.*

YELL, *n.* A sharp, loud, hideous outcry.

Their hideous *yells*
Rend the dark welkin. *Phillips.*

YELL'ING, *ppr.* Uttering hideous outcries; shrieking; as *yelling* monsters. *Milton.*

YELL'ING, *n.* The act of screaming hideously.

YEL'LOW, *a.* [Sax. *gealew,* yellow; *gealla,* gall; G. *gelb;* D. *geel;* Dan. *guul;* Sw. *gål, gul.* Hence *gold,* Dan. *guld.* The Fr. *jaune* is the same word, contracted from *jaulne,* as it is written in the Norman; It. *giallo;* Russ. *jelknu,* to become yellow; *jeltnie,* yellow; L. *galbanus.* Qu. *gilvus.* The root is the Celtic *gal, geal,* bright. See *Gold.* Class Gl. No. 7.]

Being of a bright color; of the color of gold. *Newton.*

YEL'LOW, *n.* A bright color, reflecting the most light of any, after white. It is one of the simple or primitive colors.

YEL'LOW-BLOSSOMED, *a.* Furnished or adorned with yellow flowers. *Goldsmith.*

YEL'LOW-BOY, *n.* A gold coin. [*Vulgar.*]

YEL'LOW-EARTH, *n.* A soft yellow mineral found at Wehraw, in Upper Lusatia, united with clay and argillaceous ironstone.

YELLOW-FE'VER, *n.* A malignant disease of warm climates, which often suffuses the skin with a yellowish color.

YEL'LOW-GOLDS, *n.* A flower. *B. Jonson.*

YEL'LOW-HAMMER, *n.* A bird of the genus Emberiza. Its throat and the crown of the head, are yellow. *Cyc.*

YEL'LOWISH, *a.* Somewhat yellow; as, amber is of a *yellowish* color. *Woodward.*

YEL'LOWISHNESS, *n.* The quality of being somewhat yellow. *Boyle.*

YEL'LOWNESS, *n.* The quality of being yellow; as the *yellowness* of an orange.

2. Jealousy. [*Not in use.*] *Shak.*

YEL'LOWS, *n.* A disease of horses, cattle and sheep, in which the eyes are tinged with a yellow color, proceeding often from obstructions in the gall-ducts. It is relieved by purges. *Cyc.*

YELP, *v. i.* [Sax. *gealpan,* to bray; Dan. *gylper,* to croak.]

To bark, as a beagle-hound after his prey, or as other dog.

YELP'ING, *ppr.* Barking in a particular manner.

YEN'ITE, *n.* A mineral found in the isle of Elba, and in other places, of a brown or brownish black color. It is arranged with the chrysolite family, but differs much from other species of it. It resembles hornblend, or rather black epidote. It occurs both crystalized and massive; the form of the crystals being that of a rhomboidal prism. It consists chiefly of silex, lime, and oxyd of manganese. *Cyc.* *Phillips.*

This mineral is called yenite or jenite,

in commemoration of the battle of Jena, and lievrite, from its discoverer. *Cleaveland.*

YEOMAN, *n.* [Sax. *gemæne*, common, Sw. *gemen*, Dan. *gemeen*. See *Common*.]

1. A common man, or one of the plebeians, of the first or most respectable class; a freeholder; a man free born. A yeoman in England is considered as next in order to the gentry. The word is little used in the United States, unless as a title in law-proceedings and instruments, designating occupation, and this only in particular states. But *yeomanry* is much used.

2. An officer in the king's household, of a middle rank between a gentleman and a groom. *Eng.*

3. In *ships*, an inferior officer under the boatswain, gunner or carpenters, charged with the stowage, account and distribution of the stores. *Mar. Dict.*

4. A name or title of certain soldiers; as *yeomen* of the guard.

YEOMANLY, *a.* Pertaining to a yeoman. *B. Jonson.*

YEOMANRY, *n.* The collective body of yeomen or freeholders. Thus the common people in America, are called the *yeomanry*.

YERK, *v. t.* [This seems to be the Heb. Ch. ירק, Eth. ወረቀ waraka, to spit, that is, to thrust out. It is the same as *jerk*. Class Rg. No. 35.]

To throw or thrust with a sudden smart spring; as, horses *yerk* their heels. *Far. Dict.*

YERK, *n.* A sudden or quick thrust or motion.

YERK'ING, *ppr.* Thrusting with a quick spring.

YERN. [See *Yearn*.]

YES, *adv.* [Sax. *gise*.] A word which expresses affirmation or consent; opposed to *no*; as, are you married, madam? *yes.*

It is used like *yea*, to enforce by repetition or addition, something which precedes. You have done all this; *yes*, you have done more.

> *Yes*, you despise the man to books confin'd. *Pope.*

YEST. [See *Yeast*.]

YES'TER, *a.* [G. *gestern*; D. *gisteren*; Sax. *gystern*; L. *hesternus*.]

Last; last past; next before the present; as *yester* sun. *Dryden.*

[NOTE. This is seldom used except in the compounds which follow.]

YES'TERDAY, *n.* [Sax. *gyrstan-dæg*, *gyrsternlic dæg*. See *Yester*.]

1. The day last past; the day next before the present.

> All our *yesterdays* have lighted fools
> The way to dusty death. *Shak.*
>
> We are but of *yesterday*, and know nothing. Job viii.

2. *Yesterday* is used generally without a preposition; as, I went to town *yesterday*. *Yesterday* we received letters from our friends. In this case, a preposition is understood; as *on yesterday*, or *during yesterday*. The word may be considered as adverbially used.

YES'TERNIGHT, *n.* [*yester* and *night*.]

1. The last night.

2. It is used without a preposition. My brother arrived *yesternight*; where *on* or *during* is understood, but it may be considered as adverbially used.

YESTY. [See *Yeasty*.]

YET, *conj.* [Sax. *get*, *gyt*; Gr. ετι; W. *etto*. It seems to be from the root of the verb *get*.]

Nevertheless; notwithstanding; however. I come to you in the spirit of peace; *yet* you will not receive me.

> *Yet* I say unto you, that Solomon in all his glory, was not arrayed like one of these. Matt. vi.

YET, *adv.* Beside; over and above. There is one reason *yet* further to be alledged.

2. Still; the state remaining the same.

> They attest facts they had heard while they were *yet* heathens. *Addison.*

3. At this time; so soon. Is it time to go? Not *yet*.

4. At least; at all.

> A man that would form a comparison between Quintilian's declamations, if *yet* they are Quintilian's— *Baker.*

5. It is prefixed to words denoting extension of time or continuance.

> A little longer; *yet* a little longer. *Dryden.*

6. Still; in a new degree. The crime becomes *yet* blacker by the pretense of piety.

7. Even; after all; a kind of emphatical addition to a negative.

> Men may not too rashly believe the confessions of witches, nor *yet* the evidence against them. *Bacon.*

8. Hitherto. You have *yet* done nothing; you have as *yet* done less than was expected.

Yeven, for *given*, is not in use. *Spenser.*

YEW, *n.* [Sax. *iw*; W. *yw* or *ywen*; G. *eibe* or *eibenbaum*; D. *ibenboom*; Fr. *if*.]

An evergreen tree of the genus Taxus, valued for its wood or timber.

YEW, *v. i.* To rise, as scum on the brine in boiling at the salt works. [See *Yaw*.] *Cyc.*

YEW'EN, *a.* Made of yew. *Hubberd.*

YEX, *n.* [Sax. *geocsa*. See *Hiccough*.] A hiccough. [*Little used.*]

YEX, *v. i.* To hiccough.

YFE'RE, *adv.* Together. [*Not in use.*] *Spenser.*

YIELD, *v. t.* [Sax. *gieldan*, *gildan*, *gyldan*, to render, to pay. But the word seems to be directly from the W. *gildiaw*, to produce, to yield, to concede, to contribute. The sense is obvious.]

1. To produce, as land, stock or funds; to give in return for labor, or as profit. Lands *yield* not more than three per cent. annually; houses *yield* four or five per cent. Maiz on good land, *yields* two or three hundred fold.

2. To produce, in general. Most vegetable juices *yield* a salt.

3. To afford; to exhibit. The flowers in spring *yield* a beautiful sight.

4. To allow; to concede; to admit to be true; as, to *yield* the point in debate. We *yield* that there is a God.

5. To give, as claimed of right; as, to *yield* due honors; to *yield* due praise.

6. To permit; to grant.

> Life is but air,
> That *yields* a passage to the whistling sword. *Dryden.*

7. To emit; to give up. To *yield* the breath, is to expire.

8. To resign; to give up; sometimes with *up* or *over*; as, to *yield up* their own opinions. We *yield* the place to our superiors.

9. To surrender; sometimes with *up*; as, to *yield* a fortress to the enemy; or to *yield up* a fortress.

YIELD, *v. i.* To give up the contest; to submit.

> He saw the fainting Grecians *yield*. *Dryden.*

2. To comply with; as, I *yielded* to his request.

3. To give way; not to oppose. We readily *yield* to the current of opinion; we *yield* to customs and fashions.

4. To give place, as inferior in rank or excellence. They will *yield* to us in nothing.

> Tell me in what more happy fields
> The thistle springs, to which the lily *yields*? *Pope.*

YIELDABLENESS, *n.* Disposition to comply. [*A bad word and not used.*]

YIELDANCE, *n.* Act of producing; concession. [*Not used.*] *Hall.*

YIELDED, *pp.* Produced; afforded; conceded; allowed; resigned; surrendered.

YIELDER, *n.* One who yields.

YIELDING, *ppr.* Producing; affording; conceding; resigning; surrendering; allowing.

2. *a.* Inclined to give way or comply; flexible; accommodating; as a *yielding* temper.

YIELDING, *n.* Act of producing; act of surrendering; submission. *Shak.*

YIELDINGLY, *adv.* With compliance.

YIELDINGNESS, *n.* Disposition to comply; quality of yielding. *Paley.*

YO'JAN, *n.* In the E. Indies, a measure or distance of five miles. *Asiat. Res.*

YOKE, *n.* [Sax. *geoc* or *ioc*; D. *juk*; G. *joch*; Sw. *ok*; Sans. *yuga*; Fr. *joug*; It. *giogo*; Sp. *yugo*; L. *jugum*; Gr. ζευγος; Slav. Russ. *igo*; Ch. Syr. Ar. זוג zug, to join, L. *jungo*, Gr. ζυγοω.]

1. A piece of timber, hollowed or made curving near each end, and fitted with bows for receiving the necks of oxen; by which means two are connected for drawing. From a ring or hook in the bow, a chain extends to the thing to be drawn, or to the yoke of another pair of oxen behind.

2. A mark of servitude; slavery; bondage.

> Our country sinks beneath the *yoke*. *Shak.*

3. A chain; a link; a bond of connection; as the *yoke* of marriage. *Dryden.*

4. A couple; a pair; as a *yoke* of oxen.

5. Service.

> My *yoke* is easy. Matt. xi.

YOKE, *v. t.* To put a yoke on; to join in a yoke; as, to *yoke* oxen, or a pair of oxen.

2. To couple; to join with another.

> Cassius, you are *yoked* with a lamb. *Shak.*

3. To enslave; to bring into bondage. *Shak.*

4. To restrain; to confine. Libertines like not to be *yoked* in marriage.

> The words and promises that *yoke*
> The conqueror, are quickly broke. *Hudibras.*

YO'KED, *pp.* Confined in a yoke; joined; coupled.

YO'KE-ELM, *n.* A tree.

YO'KE-FELLOW, } *n.* [*yoke* and *fellow* or
YO'KE-MATE, } *mate*.] An associate or companion.

2. A mate; a fellow. *Spectator.*

YO'KING, *ppr.* Putting a yoke on; joining; coupling.

YŌLD, for *yielded.* [*Not in use.*] *Spenser.*

YŌLK, *n.* The yelk of an egg. [See *Yelk.*]

2. The unctuous secretion from the skin of sheep, which renders the pile soft and pliable. *Cyc.*

3. The *vitellus*, a part of the seed of plants, so named by Gærtner, from its supposed analogy with the yelk of an egg. It is characterized as very firmly and inseparably connected with the embryo, yet never rising out of the integuments of the seed in germination, but absorbed, like the *albumen*, (see *White* and *Perisperm*,) for the nourishment of the embryo. When the albumen is present, it is always situated between it and the embryo. In the grasses it forms a scale between the embryo and albumen. It is considered by Smith as a subterraneous cotyledon. *Cyc. Smith.*

YON, YOND, YON'DER, } *a.* [Sax. *geond.* This seems to be formed from *gan*, to go, or its root, and signifies properly *gone*; or it is from *geonan*, to open; whence distant. The G. *jener*, and D. *gins*, *ginder*, may be the same word, or from the same root.]

Being at a distance within view.

> *Yonder* men are too many for an embassy. *Bacon.*
>
> Read thy lot in *yon* celestial sign. *Milton.*
>
> *Yon* flowery arbors, *yonder* alleys green. *Milton.*

YON, YOND, YON'DER, } *adv.* At a distance within view. When we use this word, we often point the hand or direct the eye to the place or object.

> First and chiefest, with thee bring
> Him that *yon* soars on golden wing. *Milton.*
>
> *Yonder* are two apple women scolding. *Arbuthnot.*

YOND, *a.* Mad; furious, or alienated in mind; that is, *gone*, wandering, and allied to the preceding. *Obs.* *Spenser.*

YORE, *adv.* [Sax. *geara.* It probably signifies past, gone, from the root of *year.*]

Long. *Obs.* *Spenser.*

Of yore, of old time; long ago; as in times or days *of yore*.

> But Satan now is wiser than *of yore*. *Pope.*

YOU, *pron. yu.* [Sax. *eow*, *iu*, *iuch*; G. *euch*; Arm. *chuy*; D. *gu* or *yu*, thou. *You* has been considered as in the plural only, and is so treated in the Saxon grammar. But from the Belgic dialect, it appears to be in the singular as well as the plural, and our universal popular usage, in applying it to a single person with a verb in the singular number, is correct. *Yourself* is in the singular number.]

1. The pronoun of the second person, in the nominative or objective case. In familiar language, it is applied to an individual, as *thou* is in the solemn style. In the plural, it is used in the solemn style in the objective case.

> In vain *you* tell your parting lover,
> *You* wish fair winds may waft him over. *Prior.*
>
> He that despiseth *you*, despiseth me. Luke x.

2. *You* is used, like *on* in French, for any one. This at a distance looks like a rock; but as *you* approach it, *you* see a little cabin.

YOUNG, *a. yung.* [Sax. *iong*, *geong*; G. *jung*; D. *jong*; Sw. Dan. *ung*; Arm. *yaouncq*; W. *ieuanc*; Sans. *yuwana*; L. *juvenis.* Qu. Ch. Syr. Heb. Sam. ינק to suck. The Welsh makes the word a compound, and the origin is not evident.]

1. Not having been long born; being in the first part of life; not old: *used of animals*; as a *young* child; a *young* man; a *young* fawn.

2. Being in the first part of growth; as a *young* plant; a *young* tree.

3. Ignorant; weak; or rather, having little experience.

> Come, elder brother, thou'rt too *young* in this. *Shak.*

YOUNG, *n.* The offspring of animals, either a single animal, or offspring collectively. The cow will take care of her *young*, as will the hen. Animals make provision for their *young*.

YOUNGER, *a. comp. yun'ger.* Not so old as another. A person of ninety years old is *younger* than one of a hundred, though certainly not a *young* man, nor in the first part of life.

YOUNGEST, *a. superl. yun'gest.* Having the least age. There are three persons living, the *youngest* of whom is ninety years old.

YOUNGISH, *a. yung'ish.* Somewhat young. *Tatler.*

YOUNGLING, *n. yung'ling.* [Sax. *geongling.*]

Any animal in the first part of life. *Dryden.*

YOUNGLY, *adv. yung'ly.* Early in life. *Shak.*

2. Ignorantly; weakly. [*Little used.*]

YOUNGSTER, *n. yung'ster.* A young person; a lad; *a colloquial word.* *Shak.*

YOUNGTH, for *youth*, is not in use. *Spenser.*

YOUNK'ER, *n.* Among seamen, a stripling in the service.

YOUR, *a. pronom.* pron. *yure.* [from *you*; Sax. *eower*; G. *euer.*]

1. Belonging to you; equally applicable to both numbers; as *your* father; *your* heart; *your* prince; *your* subjects.

2. It is used indefinitely.

> *Your* medalist and *your* critic are much nearer related than the world imagine. *Addison.*

3. *Yours* is used as a substitute for a noun in the nominative or objective. This book is *yours*. I have no pen; give me *yours*. My sword and *yours* are kin. *Shak.*

YOURSELF, *pron.* plu. *yourselves.* [*your* and *self.*]

1. A word added to *you*, to express distinction emphatically between you and other persons. This work you must do *yourself*; or you *yourself* must do it; that is, *you* and no other person.

> Sometimes it is used without *you*.
>
> Allow obedience, if *yourselves* are old. *Shak.*

2. It is used as the reciprocal pronoun. You love only *yourself*; you have brought this calamity on *yourselves*; be but *yourselves*.

YOUTH, *n. yuth.* [Sax. *iuguth*, *iugoth*, *iogoth*, *geogath*; G. *jugend*; D. *jougd.*]

1. The part of life that succeeds to childhood. In *a general sense*, youth denotes the whole early part of life, from infancy to manhood; but it is not unusual to divide the stages of life into *infancy*, *childhood*, *youth*, and *manhood*. In this sense the word can have no plural.

> Those who pass their *youth* in vice, are justly condemned to spend their age in folly. *Rambler.*

2. A young man. In this sense it has a plural.

> Seven *youths* from Athens yearly sent— *Dryden.*

3. A young person, male or female.

4. Young persons, collectively.

> It is fit to *youth* to read the best authors first. *B. Jonson.*

YOUTHFUL, *a.* Young; as two *youthful* knights. *Dryden.*

2. Pertaining to the early part of life; as *youthful* days; *youthful* age.

3. Suitable to the first part of life; as *youthful* thoughts; *youthful* sports.

4. Fresh; vigorous; as in youth. *Bentley.*

YOUTHFULLY, *adv.* In a youthful manner.

YOUTHLY, *a.* Young; early in life. *Obs.* *Spenser.*

YOUTHY, *a.* Young. [*Bad and not used.*] *Spectator.*

YPIGHT, *a.* Fixed, that is, pitched. *Obs.* *Spenser.*

YT'TRIA, *n.* [so called from *Ytterby*, a quarry in Sweden.]

One of the earths. It has the appearance of a fine white powder, without taste or smell. It is insoluble in water, and does not affect vegetable blues. It combines with acids and forms salts. Its base is yttrium. *Cyc. Ure. Davy.*

YT'TRIOUS, *a.* Pertaining to yttria; containing yttria; as the *yttrious* oxyd of columbium. *Cleaveland.*

YT'TRIUM, *n.* The base of yttria.

YTTRO-CE'RITE, *n.* A mineral, consisting of the oxyd of cerium, yttria, lime and fluoric acid.

YTTRO-COL'UMBITE, *n.* A mineral containing yttria.

YTTRO-TAN'TALITE, *n.* A mineral found in kidney-form masses; an ore of tantalum.

YUCK, *v. i.* To itch. [*Local.*] *Grose.*

YUFTS, *n.* Russia lether, prepared from ox hides in a peculiar manner. *Tooke.*

YUG, YOG, } *n.* In the mythology of India, an age; one of the ages into which the Hindoos divide the duration or existence of the world.

YU'LAN, *n.* A beautiful flowering tree of China. *Grosier.*

YULE, *n.* [Sax. *iule*, *geohol*, *gehul*, *geol*; Arm. *gouel*, *gouil*, a feast; W. *gwyl*, a holiday.]

The name anciently given to Christmas, or the feast of the nativity of our Savior.

YUX, *n.* A hiccough. [*Not used.*]

YUX, *v. i.* To hiccough. *Obs.*

Z.

Z, the last letter of the English Alphabet, is a sibilant articulation, and is merely a vocal *S.* It bears the same relation to *s,* as *v* does to *f.* With us it has not a compound sound, nor is it a double consonant, as in the Italian and German. It is as simple in its sound as *S.*

As a numeral, Z stands for 2000, and with a dash over it, Z̄, for 2,000,000. It is pronounced zee.

ZA'BAISM. [See *Sabianism.*]

ZA€'€HO, *n.* The lowest part of the pedestal of a column.

ZAF'FER, *n.* The residuum of cobalt, after the sulphur, arsenic and other volatile matters have been expelled by calcination; so that it is a gray or dark gray oxyd of cobalt, mixed with a portion of silex. *Cyc.*

ZA'NY, *n.* [It. *zanni,* a buffoon.] A merry andrew; a buffoon. *Pope.*

ZA'NY, *v. t.* To mimic. *Beaum.*

ZAP'OTE, *n.* In *Mexico,* the generic name of fruits which are roundish and contain a hard stone; the species are various.

ZAR'NICH, *n.* [See *Arsenic.*] The name of a genus of fossils, which are inflammable, of a plain uniform structure, not flexible or elastic, soluble in oil, and burning with a whitish flame and noxious smell like garlic. This substance is supposed to be sulphureted arsenic. Of this genus there are four species; one the real sandarach; another is sold under the name of orpiment. *Cyc.*

ZEA, *n.* The generic name of maiz.

ZEAL, *n.* [Gr. ζηλος; L. *zelus.*] Passionate ardor in the pursuit of any thing. Excessive *zeal* may rise to enthusiasm. In general, *zeal* is an eagerness of desire to accomplish or obtain some object, and it may be manifested either in favor of any person or thing, or in opposition to it, and in a good or bad cause.

Zeal, the blind conductor of the will. *Dryden.*

They have a *zeal* of God, but not according to knowledge. Rom. x.

A *zeal* for liberty is sometimes an eagerness to subvert, with little care what shall be established. *Johnson.*

ZEALOT, *n.* zel'ot. One who engages warmly in any cause, and pursues his object with earnestness and ardor. It is generally used in dispraise, or applied to one whose ardor is intemperate and censurable.

The fury of *zealots* was one cause of the destruction of Jerusalem. *K. Charles.*

ZEALOT'I€AL, *a.* Ardently zealous. [*Little used.*] *Strype.*

ZEALOUS, *a.* zel'us. Warmly engaged or ardent in the pursuit of an object.

Being thus saved himself, he may be *zealous* in the salvation of souls. *Law.*

ZEALOUSLY, *adv.* zel'usly. With passionate ardor; with eagerness.

It is good to be *zealously* affected always in a good thing. Gal. iv.

ZEALOUSNESS, *n.* zel'usness. The quality of being zealous; zeal.

ZE'BRA, *n.* An animal of the genus Equus, beautifully marked with stripes; a native of Africa.

ZE'BU, *n.* A variety of the common ox, with a hump on the shoulders. It is found in the E. Indies and resembles the *bos Indicus,* or Indian ox, but is very small, being sometimes little larger than a dog. *Cyc.*

ZE'€HIN, *n.* A Venetian gold coin; usually written *sequin,* which see. If named from *Zecha,* the place where minted, this is the correct orthography.

ZED'OARY, *n.* A medicinal root, belonging to a plant growing in the East Indies, whose leaves resemble those of ginger, only they are longer and broader. It comes in oblong pieces, about the thickness of the little finger, and two or three inches in length. It is a warm stomachic. *Cyc.*

ZEINE, *n.* A substance of a yellowish color, soft, insipid, and elastic, procured from the seeds of the *Zea Mays* or Indian corn. *Gorham.*

ZEMINDAR, *n.* [from *zem, zemin,* land.] In India, a feudatory or landholder who governs a district of country and collects taxes. *Asiat. Res.*

ZEMINDARY, *n.* The jurisdiction of a zemindar.

ZEND, *n.* A language that formerly prevailed in Persia.

ZEND'AVESTA, *n.* Among the Persees, a sacred book ascribed to Zoroaster, and reverenced as a bible, or sole rule of faith and practice. It is often called *Zend,* by contraction.

ZE'NITH, *n.* [Fr.; It. *zenit;* Sp. *zenit* or *cenit.* I have not found the oriental original.]

That point in the visible celestial hemisphere, which is vertical to the spectator, and from which a direct perpendicular line passing through the spectator, and extended, would proceed to the center of the earth. It is opposed to *nadir.*

ZE'OLITE, *n.* [Gr. ζεω, to boil, to foam, and λιθος, stone.]

A mineral, so named by Cronstedt from its intumescence before the blowpipe. Many substances have been confounded under this name, particularly such as are fusible by the blowpipe without addition, and exhibit a phosphoric brilliancy at the moment of fusion. Haüy makes two species of zeolite, which he calls mesotype and stilbite. Werner makes four subspecies, which he calls mealy zeolite, fibrous zeolite, radiated zeolite, and foliated zeolite. He makes zeolite a generic name, and Jameson, who adopts this theory, arranges in this family prehnite, zeolite, apophyllite, cubicite, called by Haüy analcime, chabasite, cross-stone, laumonite, dipyre, natrolite, and wavellite. *Cyc.*

Zeolite commonly occurs in a four sided prism, terminated by a four sided pyramid; often in small fibrous masses. *Cleaveland.*

ZEOLIT'I€, *a.* Pertaining to zeolite; consisting of zeolite, or resembling it.

ZEOLIT'IFORM, *a.* Having the form of zeolite.

ZEPH'YR, *n.* [L. *zephyrus;* Gr. ζεφυρος.] The west wind; and poetically, any soft, mild, gentle breeze. The poets personify Zephyrus, and make him the most mild and gentle of all the sylvan deities. *Cyc.*

Mild as when *Zephyrus* on Flora breathes. *Milton.*

ZER'DA, *n.* An animal of the canine genus, found in the desert of Zaara, beyond mount Atlas. It is about ten inches in length, with a pointed nose, long whiskers, large black vivid eyes, and remarkably swift of foot. Its color is a yellowish pale brown. *Dict. Nat. Hist.*

ZE'RO, *n.* [It.] Cipher; nothing. The point of a thermometer from which it is graduated. Zero, in the thermometers of Celsius and Reaumur, is at the point at which water congeals. The zero of Fahrenheit's thermometer is fixed at the point at which the mercury stands when immersed in a mixture of snow and common salt. In Wedgewood's pyrometer, the zero corresponds with 1077° on Fahrenheit's scale.

ZEST, *n.* [Pers. زستن zistan, to peel. Class Sd.]

1. A piece of orange or lemon peel, used to give flavor to liquor; or the fine thin oil that spurts out of it when squeezed; also, the woody thick skin quartering the kernel of a walnut. *Cyc.*
2. Relish; something that gives a pleasant taste; or the taste itself.

ZEST, *v. t.* To give a relish or flavor to; to highten taste or relish.

2. To cut the peel of an orange or lemon from top to bottom into thin slips; or to squeeze the peel over the surface of any thing. *Cyc.*

ZE'TA, *n.* A Greek letter.

2. A little closet or chamber, with pipes running along the walls, to convey into it fresh air, or warm vapor from below. *Cyc.*

ZETET'I€, *a.* [Gr. ζητεω, to seek.] That seeks; that proceeds by inquiry. The *zetetic* method in mathematics, is that used in investigation, or the solution of problems. *Cyc.*

ZEUG'MA, *n.* [Gr. ζευγμα, from ζευγνυω, to join. See *Yoke.*]

A figure in grammar by which an adjective or verb which agrees with a nearer word, is by way of supplement, referred to another more remote. Thus in Virgil, "Hic illius *arma,* hic *currus fuit;*" where *fuit,* which agrees directly with *currus*, is referred also to *arma*. *Cyc.*

ZIB'ET, *n.* [See *Civet.*] An animal of the genus Viverra; the ash-gray weasel, striated with black undulations, and an annulated tail. It may be called the Indian civet, as it resembles the African civet. *Cyc.*

ZIG'ZAG, *a.* Having short turns.

ZIG'ZAG, *n.* Something that has short turns or angles.

ZIG'ZAG, *v. t.* To form with short turns.

Ziment water, or *copper water*, is a name given to water found in copper mines; water impregnated with copper.

ZIM'OME, } *n.* [Gr. ζυμη.] One of the con-
ZYM'OME, } stituents of gluten. *Ure.*

ZINK, *n.* [G. Sw. Dan. *zink.* The common orthography, *zinc*, is erroneous.]

A metal of a brilliant white color, with a shade of blue, and appearing as if composed of plates adhering together. It is not brittle, but less malleable than copper, lead or tin. When heated however, it is malleable, and may be drawn into plates. *Cyc.*

ZINKIF'EROUS, *a.* [*zink* and L. *fero.*] Producing zink; as *zinkiferous* ore. *Journ. of Science.*

ZINK'Y, *a.* Pertaining to zink, or having its appearance.

Some effervesce with acids, some not, though soluble therein, as to the *zinky* part. *Kirwan.*

The *zinky* ores are said to be grayer than other ores. *Ibm.*

ZIR'CON, *n.* Called also jargon of Ceylon, a mineral originally found in Ceylon, in the sands of rivers, along with spinel, sapphire, tourmalin, and iron sand. Zircon, hyacinth, and zirconite, are regarded as varieties of the same species. They are essentially composed of the earth zirconia, with silex, and a minute portion of iron. The primitive form of the crystals is an octahedron, composed of two four sided prisms. The common form is a rectangular four sided prism. *Haüy. Brongniart. Cyc.*

ZIRCO'NIA, *n.* A peculiar earth obtained from the gem zircon; a fine white powder. *Cyc.*

ZIR'CONITE, *n.* A variety of the zircon.

ZIRCO'NIUM, *n.* The metallic basis of zirconia.

ZIV'OLO, *n.* A bird resembling the yellow hammer, and by some considered as the same species. *Dict. Nat. Hist.*

ZIZ'EL, *n.* The suslik or earless marmot, a small quadruped found in Poland and the south of Russia. *Cuvier. Cyc.*

ZOC'CO, } [It. *zoccolo*; from L. *soccus*,
ZO'CLE, } *n.* a sock.] A square body
ZOC'COLO, } under the base of a pedestal, &c. serving for the support of a bust, statue or column. *Cyc.*

ZO'DIAC, *n.* [Fr. *zodiaque*; It. Sp. *zodiaco*; L. *zodiacus*; Gr. ζωδιακος, from ζωον, an animal.]

A broad circle in the heavens, containing the twelve signs through which the sun passes in its annual course. The center of this belt is the ecliptic, which is the path of the sun. It intersects the equator at an angle of 23 degrees and a half or rather 29 minutes. This is called its obliquity.

2. A girdle. *Milton.*

ZODI'ACAL, *a.* Pertaining to the zodiac.

Zodiacal light, a luminous track or space in the heavens, resembling that of the milky way, sometimes appearing after sunset and before sunrising.

ZOI'SITE, *n.* [from *Van Zois*, its discoverer.]

A mineral regarded as a variety of epidote. It occurs in deeply striated rhomboidal prisms, much compressed and rounded; its colors gray, yellowish or bluish gray, brown, grayish yellow, or reddish white. *Cleaveland.*

This is called also a subspecies of prismatoidal augite. *Cyc. Thomson.*

ZONE, *n.* [L. *zona*; Gr. ζωνη.] A girdle.

An embroider'd *zone* surrounds her waist. *Dryden.*

2. In *geography*, a division of the earth, with respect to the temperature of different latitudes. The zones are five; the torrid zone, extending from tropic to tropic 46°, 56′, or 23° 28′ on each side of the equator; two temperate or variable zones, situated between the tropics and polar circles; and two frigid zones, situated between the polar circles and the poles.

3. Circuit; circumference. *Milton.*

Ciliary zone, in *anatomy*, the black impression of the ciliary processes on the vitreous humor of the eye. *Cyc.*

ZO'NED, *a.* Wearing a zone. *Pope.*

ZON'NAR, *n.* A belt or girdle, which the Christians and Jews in the Levant are obliged to wear, to distinguish them from the Mohammedans. *Cyc.*

ZOÖG'RAPHER, *n.* [See *Zoography.*] One who describes animals, their forms and habits.

ZOÖGRAPH'ICAL, *a.* Pertaining to the description of animals.

ZOÖG'RAPHY, *n.* [Gr. ζωον, an animal, and γραφω, to describe.]

A description of animals, their forms and habits. [But *zoology* is generally used.]

ZO'OLITE, *n.* [Gr. ζωον, an animal, and λιθος, stone.] An animal substance petrified or fossil. *Morin.*

ZOÖLOG'ICAL, *a.* [from *zoology.*] Pertaining to zoology, or the science of animals.

ZOÖLOG'ICALLY, *adv.* According to the principles of zoology. *Lawrence.*

ZOÖL'OGIST, *n.* [from *zoology.*] One who is well versed in the natural history of animals, or who describes animals.

ZOÖL'OGY, *n.* [Gr. ζωον, an animal, and λογος, discourse.]

A treatise on animals, or the science of animals; that branch of natural history which respects the forms, classification, history and habits of animals, particularly of brutes or irrational animals.

ZOÖN'IC, *a.* [Gr. ζωον, an animal.] Pertaining to animals; as the *zoonic* acid, obtained from animal substances.

ZOÖN'OMY, *n.* [Gr. ζωον, an animal, and νομος, law.]

The laws of animal life, or the science which treats of the phenomena of animal life, their causes and relations. *Darwin.*

ZOOPHITE. [See *Zoophyte.*]

ZOÖPH'ORIC, *a.* [Gr. ζωον, an animal, and φορεω, to bear.]

The zoophoric column is one which supports the figure of an animal.

ZOÖPH'ORUS, *n.* [supra.] In *ancient architecture*, the same with the *frieze* in modern architecture; a part between the architrave and cornice; so called from the figures of animals carved upon it. *Dict.*

ZO'OPHYTE, *n.* [Gr. ζωον, an animal, and φυτον, a plant.]

In *natural history*, a body supposed to partake of the nature both of an animal and a vegetable, such as madrepores, millepores, corallines, &c. *Cyc.*

ZOÖPHYTOLOG'ICAL, *a.* Pertaining to zoophytology.

ZOÖPHYTOL'OGY, *n.* [*zoophyte* and Gr. λογος, discourse.] The natural history of zoophytes. *Ed. Encyc.*

ZOÖT'OMIST, *n.* [See *Zootomy.*] One who dissects the bodies of brute animals; a comparative anatomist.

ZOÖT'OMY, *n.* [Gr. ζωον, an animal, and τεμνω, to cut.]

Anatomy; particularly, the dissecting of bodies of beasts or brute animals; comparative anatomy, or the anatomy of brute animals.

ZOR'IL, *n.* A fetid animal of the weasel kind, found in S. America. [In Sp. *zorro* is a fox, and *zorillo*, the whelp of a fox.] *Cyc.*

ZUF'FOLO, *n.* [It. *zufolo*, from *zufolare*, to hiss or whistle, L. *sufflo.*]

A little flute or flageolet, especially that which is used to teach birds. *Busby.*

ZU'MATE, *n.* [See *Zumic.*] A combination of the zumic acid and a salifiable base. *Ure.*

ZU'MIC, *a.* [Gr. ζυμη, ferment.] The zumic acid is procured from many acescent vegetable substances. *Ure.*

ZUMOLOG'ICAL, *a.* [See *Zumology.*] Pertaining to zumology.

ZUMOL'OGIST, *n.* One who is skilled in the fermentation of liquors.

ZUMOL'OGY, *n.* [Gr. ζυμη, ferment, from ζυμοω, to ferment, and λογος, discourse.]

A treatise on the fermentation of liquors, or the doctrine of fermentation. *Cyc.*

ZUMOSIM'ETER, *n.* [Gr. ζυμωσις, fermentation, and μετρεω, to measure.]

An instrument proposed by Swammerdam for ascertaining the degree of fermentation occasioned by the mixture of different liquids, and the degree of heat which they acquire in fermentation. *Cyc.*

ZUR'LITE, *n.* A newly discovered Vesuvian mineral, whose primitive form is a cube, or according to some authors, a rectangular prism. *Journ. of Science.*

ZYGODAC'TYLOUS, *a.* [Gr. ζευγω, to join, and δακτυλος, a finger.]

Having the toes disposed in pairs; distinguishing an order of fowls which have the feet furnished with two toes before and two behind, as the parrot, woodpecker, &c. *Ed. Encyc.*

ZYGOMAT'IC, *a.* [Gr. ζευγμα, a joining.] Pertaining to a bone of the head, called also *os jugale*, or cheek bone, or to the bony arch under which the temporal muscle passes. The term *zygoma* is applied both to the bone and the arch. *Cyc.*

Zygomatic arch. [See *Zygomatic.*]

Zygomatic bone, the cheek bone.

Zygomatic muscles, two muscles of the face, which rise from the zygomatic bone, and are inserted into the corner of the mouth.

Zygomatic processes, the processes of the temporal and cheek bones, which unite to form the zygomatic arch.

Zygomatic suture, the suture which joins the zygomatic processes of the temporal and cheek bones. *Parr.*

ADDITIONS.

ABANDON.
5. In *commerce*, to relinquish to insurers all claim to a ship or goods insured, as a preliminary towards recovering for a total loss. *Park.*

ABANDONMENT.
2. In *commerce*, the relinquishing to underwriters all the property saved from loss by shipwreck, capture or other peril stated in the policy. This *abandonment* must be made before the insured can demand indemnification for a total loss. *Park.*

ABLE. [Norm. *ablez, hable; habler*, to enable, from L. *habilis.*]

ABSCISSION.
2. In *rhetoric*, a figure of speech, when having begun to say a thing, a speaker stops abruptly, as supposing the matter sufficiently understood. Thus, "He is a man of so much honor and candor, and such generosity—but I need say no more."

AL'GATES, *adv.* [Sax. *algeats; all* and *geat*, a gait, a way.] By all means; on any terms. *Obs.*

ALIENISM, *n. āl'yenizm.* The state of being an alien.

The law was very gentle in the construction of the disability of *alienism*. *Kent.*

ALLO'DIUM. [add to the etymology what follows.]

[In Sw. *odal*, and in Dan. *odel*, signify *allodial;* the word being used as an adjective; Sw. *odalgods*, that is, *odal goods*, signifies allodial lands; and *odaljord*, odal earth, is used as its synonym. *Odalmān*, is one who possesses allodial land; *odalbonde* is a yeoman or freeholder; *odelt* signifies undivided; *o* in Swedish being a prefix, answering to the English *un*, and giving to words a negative signification. If *o* in *odal* is this prefix, and *dal* from the root of *deal*, the word signifies *undivided*. But some obscurity rests on this word.]

AMATO'RIOUS, *a.* Pertaining to love. *Milton.*

AMBIL'EVOUS, *a.* [L. *ambo*, both, and *lævus*, left.] Left handed on both sides. [*Not in use.*] *Brown.*

ANCIENT. We usually apply both *ancient* and *old* to things subject to gradual decay. We say, an *old* man, an *ancient* record; but never the *old* sun, *old* stars, an *old* river or mountain.

ANIMALIZE.
2. To convert into animal matter.

ANSWER.
8. The reply of a legislative body or house to an address or message of the supreme magistrate.

APPROACHING, *ppr.* Drawing nearer; advancing nearer.

APRON.
6. A piece of lether or other thing to be spread before a person riding in a gig, chaise or sulky, to defend him from rain, snow or dust.

ARE, *n.* [L. *area.*] In *France*, a measure, the new square perch, containing a hundred square meters, a little less than two square perches of 22 feet, in the ancient measure. *Lunier.*

ATROCIOUS.
Very grievous; violent; as *atrocious* distempers. *Obs.* *Cheyne.*

AUTOCH'THON, *n.* [Gr. αυτοχθων.] One who rises or grows out of the earth.

BAR'RATROUS, *a.* Tainted with barratry.

BAR'RATROUSLY, *adv.* In a barratrous manner. *Kent.*

BARRELED.
2. In *composition*, having a barrel or tube; as a double-*barreled* gun.

BASIL'ICAL, *a.* *s* as *z*. In the manner of a public edifice or cathedral. *Forsyth.*

BAWL'ER, *n.* One who bawls.

BA'REHEADEDNESS, *n.* State of being bareheaded.

BE'ASTISH, *a.* Like a beast; brutal.

BET'TERING-HOUSE, *n.* A house for the reformation of offenders.

BEWA'ILER, *n.* One who laments.

BLE'AKISH, *a.* Moderately bleak.

BO'NUS, *n.* [L.] A premium given for a charter or other privilege granted to a company.

BOOK'STORE, *n.* A shop where books are sold.

BLEB'BY, *a.* Full of blebs. *Phillips.*

BREAKFAST, *v. t. brek'fast.* To furnish with the first meal in the morning.

BRU'TISM, *n.* The nature or characteristic qualities or actions of a brute; extreme stupidity or beastly vulgarity. *Dwight.*

BURGLA'RIAN, *n.* A person guilty of burglary.

CAPSULE.
2. A small saucer, made of clay for roasting samples of ores, or for melting them.

CEMENTI'TIOUS, *a.* Having the quality of cementing. *Forsyth.*

CEREMO'NIALLY, *adv.* According to rites and ceremonies; as a person *ceremonially* unclean; an act *ceremonially* unlawful. *Milton.*

CHUNK, *n.* A short thick piece of wood. [*Colloquial.*]

CHYLIF'EROUS, *a.* [L. *chylus* and *fero.*] Transmitting chyle. *Cheyne.*

CHYMIFICA'TION, *n.* The process of becoming or of forming chyme.

CHYM'IFIED, *pp.* Formed into chyme. *Good.*

CHYM'IFY, *v. t.* To form into chyme.

CIRCUMSTAN'TIAL, *n.* *Circumstantials*, in the plural, are things incident to the main subject, but of less importance; opposed to *essentials;* as the *circumstantials* of religion. *Addison.*

Close communion, with baptists, communion in the Lord's supper with their own sect only.

Close election, an election in which the votes for different candidates are nearly equal.

CO-ADJU'TORSHIP, *n.* State of a coadjutor; joint assistance. *Pope.*

COG. To the etymology add, after *wheel;* Sw. *kugge.*

COHESIBIL'ITY, *n.* The tendency which one part of matter evinces to unite with another part of matter, so as to form, out of different bodies, one common mass. It is opposed to *divisibility*. *Good.*

COHE'SIBLE, *a.* Capable of cohesion.

CONCENTRATE.
2. To increase the specific gravity of a body.

CONDUCTION.
2. Transmission through or by means of a conductor. *Henry's Chim.*

CRANIOG'NOMY, *n.* [Gr. κρανιον, L. *cranium*, the skull, and Gr. γνωμων, index.] The doctrine or science of determining the properties or characteristics of the mind by the conformation of the skull. *Good.*

DAC'TYLAR, *a.* Pertaining to a dactyl; reducing from three to two syllables. *Scott.*

DEN'ARCOTIZE, *v. t.* [*de* and *narcotic.*] To deprive of the narcotic principle or quality; as, to *denarcotize* opium. *Journ. of Science.*

DEPOSITARY.
2. In *law*, one to whom goods are bailed to be kept for the bailor without a recompense. *Kent.*

DIGESTIBIL'ITY, *n.* The quality of being digestible.

DIMIN'ISHABLE, *a.* Capable of being reduced in size or quantity.

DISHONOR, *v. t.*
4. To refuse or decline to accept or pay; as, to *dishonor* a bill of exchange.

DISOBLI'GEMENT, *n.* The act of disobliging. *Milton.*

DISSOCIABLE.
2. Incongruous; not reconcilable with. *Warburton.*

Dormant partner, in commerce and manufactories, a partner who takes no share in the active business of a company or partnership, but is entitled to a share of the profits and subject to a share in losses. He is called also *sleeping partner.*

DUF'FEL, *n.* [D.] A kind of coarse woolen cloth, having a thick nap or frieze.

DYNAM'ICS, *n.* [Gr. δυναμις, power.] That branch of mechanical philosophy which treats of the force of moving bodies; the science of moving powers, and the effect of moving bodies acting on each other and producing motion.

EM'PHASIZE, *v. t.* To utter or pronounce with a particular or more forcible stress of voice; as, to *emphasize* a word, for the purpose of rendering the sense more distinct or impressive than other words in the sentence.

ENABLE. [Norm. *enhabler.* See *Able.*]

EPISOD'ICALLY, *adv.* By way of episode. *Scott.*

ETHE'RIALIZE, *v. t.* To convert into ether, or into a very subtil fluid. *Good.*

ETHE'RIALIZED, *pp.* Converted into ether or a very subtil fluid; as an *etherialized* and incorporeal substrate. *Good.*

EXTRA-DO'TAL, *a.* Not belonging to dower paraphernal. *Kent.*

EYESTONE, *n.* A small calcarious stone used for taking substances from between the lid and ball of the eye.

FOOT'STALK, *n.* [*foot* and *stalk.*] In *botany*, a petiole; a partial stem supporting the leaf, or connecting it with the stem or branch. Sometimes, but rarely, the same footstalk supports both the leaf and fructification, as in Turnera and Hibiscus. *Martyn.*

GANG, *n.* [Sax. D. Dan. G. *gang;* Sw. *gång*, a going, a pace or gait, a way, a passage, an alley, an avenue, a porch, portico or gallery; G. *erzreicher gang*, and Dan. *mineralisk gang*, a metallic vein, a streak in a mine; Goth. *gagg*, a way or street; *gaggan*, to go, to walk.]

3. In *mining*, literally a course or vein, but appropriately the earthy, stony, saline or combustible substance which contains the ore of metals, or is only mingled with it, without being chimically combined. This is called the *gang* or matrix of the ore. It differs from a mineralizer, in not being combined with the metal. *Cleaveland.*

[This word, in the latter sense, is most unwarrantably and erroneously written *gangue*.]

GEODIF'EROUS, *a.* [*geode* and L. *fero.*] Producing geodes.

GEOGON'IC, *a.* Pertaining to geogony, or the formation of the earth. *Humboldt.*

GRAVE.

5. Important; momentous; having a serious and interesting import. *Lord Eldon. Kent.*

HEXADAC'TYLOUS, *a.* [Gr. εξ and δακτυλος.] Having six toes.

IM'POTENCE. [L. *impotentia; in* and *potentia*, from *potens*, from the root of L. *possum, posse*, which consists of the elements *Pd* or *Pt*. See *Power*.]

INTEND'EDLY, *adv.* With intention or purpose; by design. *Milton.*

Joint stock, the capital or fund of a company or partnership in business.

LIFE.

26. The state of being in force, or the term for which an instrument has legal operation; as the *life* of an execution.

MAGNIF'ICALLY, *adv.* In a magnificent manner.

MAN'DATARY.

3. In *law*, one who undertakes, without a recompense, to do some act for another in respect to the thing bailed to him. *Kent.*

MONARCHIZE.

2. To convert to a monarchy. *Milton.*

MONITO'RIAL, *a.* Relating to a monitor.

2. Performed by monitors or a monitor; as *monitorial* instruction.

3. Conducted by or under the instruction of monitors, or subordinate teachers; as *monitorial* schools.

MONODAC'TYLOUS, *a.* [Gr. μονος and δακτυλος.] Having one toe only, as an animal.

MON'ODIST, *n.* One who writes a monody. *Scott.*

NITRIFICA'TION, *n.* The process of forming niter.

NI'TRIFY, *v. t.* [*niter* and L. *facio.*] To form into niter.

NU'MEROUSLY, *adv.* In great numbers.

OBJECT.

3. To offer; to exhibit. [*Little used.*] *Warburton.*

OBNOXIOUS.

6. Hurtful; noxious. *Milton.*

PARAPHER'NAL, *a.* Pertaining to or consisting in parapherna; as *paraphernal* property. *Kent.*

PAL'SY, *v. t. s* as *z.* To paralyze; to deprive of the power of motion; to destroy energy. *Dwight.*

POSTNUP'TIAL, *a.* [*post* and *nuptial.*] Being or happening after marriage; as a *postnuptial* settlement on a wife. *Kent.*

PRA'IRY, *n.* [Fr. *prairie.*] An extensive tract of land, mostly level, destitute of trees, and covered with tall coarse grass. These *prairies* are numerous in the United States, west of the Alleghany mountains, especially between the Ohio, Mississippi and the great lakes.

PRIZE, *v. t.* To raise with a lever. [See *Pry.*]

PRÖVEN, a word used by Scottish writers for *proved.*

PYR'RHIN, *n.* [Gr. πυρινος.] A vegeto-animal substance, detected in rain water by M. Brandes. *Journ. of Science.*

RACK'ET, *n.* A snow shoe.

RE-IMPRIS'ON, *v. t.* [See *Prison.*] To imprison a second time, or for the same cause, or after release from imprisonment. *Kent.*

RE-IMPRIS'ONED, *pp.* Imprisoned a second time for the same cause.

RE-IMPRIS'ONING, *ppr.* Imprisoning again for the same cause.

RE-IMPRIS'ONMENT, *n.* The act of confining in prison a second time for the same cause, after a release from prison. *Kent.*

SALU'TATORY, *a.* Greeting; an epithet applied to the oration which introduces the exercises of commencement in American colleges.

SE'A-WORTHINESS, *n.* The state of being able to resist the ordinary violence of wind and weather; as that of a ship. *Kent.*

SID'EROSCOPE, *n.* [Gr. σιδηρος, iron, and σκοπεω, to view or explore.]

An instrument lately invented in France, for detecting small quantities of iron in any substance, mineral, vegetable or animal. *Ferrusac's Bul.* 1827.

SKIM'INGTON, SKIM'ITRY, a vulgar word from the Danish *skiemt*, a jest or sport; *skiemter*, to jest, joke, sport; used in the phrase, *to ride skimington* or *skimitry.*

STOCK'HOLDER, *n.* [*stock* and *hold.*] One who is a proprietor of stock in the public funds, or in the funds of a bank or other company.

SYNERGET'IC, *a.* [Gr. συνεργητικος.] Co-operating. *Dean Tucker.*

TEGUMENT'ARY, *a.* Pertaining to teguments, or consisting of teguments.

UNSE'AWORTHINESS, *n.* The state of being unable to sustain the ordinary violence of the sea in a tempest. *Kent.*

CORRECTIONS.

READ—AC'CENT or ACCENT', *v. t.*; ACQUA'INTANCE; ADMIS'SION; ADUNC'OUS: AL'ARMWATCH; AWFUL; AWHI'LE; AMEN'ITY; AWEATHER; AWL'WORT; AG'ONIZE, *v. i.*; ALTERABIL'ITY; AZO'TE; BA'ILIF; CA'ITIF; CLIF; DANDRUF; MASTIF; CUD'GELER; CRYS'TALITE; CHRYSOLITE, for CRYSOLITE; CALLI'OPE; CHIVALRY; CHIVALROUS; HE'ART, in all its compounds; HYPOGYNOUS, *a.*; MAGNIFICENCE; PROLIX'; SENS'UAL; SENS'UALIST; SHOOD, [after *should*;] UNCLINCH; UNCLINCHED. Dele *Alexiterical* and *Testaceology.*

Under AMAZON, read *Herodotus.*

Under *Compound Blowpipe*, read 1801.

BORON. The undecomposable base of boracic acid. *Parke.*

BROOMCORN is sometimes called Sorghum Saccharatum.

Under FLAKE, read It. *fiocco.* Under FLAME, read It. *fiammo.*

ISOTHERM'AL. Having an equal degree of heat, or a like temperature.

Under METONYMY, read *poems.*

Under MORTGAGE, dele the words, "The term *mortgage* is applicable only to real estate," and add,

2. A pledge of goods or chattels by a debtor to a creditor, as security for the debt.

Under MUSTACHES, dele Whiskers.

Under REDOUTABLE, in *redoubtable*, dele *b.*

Under TALK, dele *B.* before *Trumbull.*

Under *Dispatch*, in the Introduction, add: Dr. Johnson himself wrote *dispatch.* The word thus written occurs twice in his Dictionary under *Send*, and five times under *Speed*. and this orthography has been continued to the present time. It has been transcribed into all the dictionaries made from Johnson's, at least into all which I have examined, even down to Chalmers and Jameson.

When a word of more syllables than one has not the usual mark of accent, the pointed vowel designates the accented syllable; as in REPROACH, REMÖVE.

C before *k*, is mute; as in *brick, sick.*

In the first volume, there are a few mistakes in the orthography of the Arabic words; and probably some inaccuracies have occurred in expressing the Ethiopic vowels. These and other literal errors however cannot be numerous, and to the English reader they are not of importance.

THE END.